The NIV Comprehensive Concordance

The NIV Comprehensive Concordance

NEW INTERNATIONAL VERSION

Hodder & Stoughton
LONDON SYDNEY AUCKLAND

THE NIV COMPREHENSIVE CONCORDANCE

First published in Great Britain 2001

10 9 8 7 6 5 4 3 2 1

British Library Cataloguing in Publication Data: A record for this book is available on application to the British Library

ISBN 0 340 75707 8

Printed and bound in Great Britain by Clays Ltd,
St Ives plc, for
Hodder & Stoughton Ltd
A Division of Hodder Headline Ltd
338 Euston Road
London NWl 3BH

Contributors

Editorial Consultant
Martin H. Manser

Project Manager
Emma Redfern

Biographical and Place-name Entries and Phrases
Gary Benfold
Brian Kelly
Neil Le Tissier
Debra Reid
Robin Routledge
Arthur Rowe
Martin Selman

Secretarial Support and Collating
Jacqueline Angell
Rosalind Desmond
Lynda Drury
Chris Pudsey

Editing and Proofreading
Lynn Elias
Emma Redfern
Rosalind Robertson

Page Design
Kenneth Burnley

Typesetting
Tradespools Ltd, Frome, Great Britain

Contents

Introduction

A concordance is an index that lists alphabetically the words which appear in Bible texts. A concordance may be used in Bible or word studies, and also to find half-remembered passages. For example, you may not be able to remember fully the extract "as Moses lifted up the snake in the desert, so the Son of Man must be lifted up," or you may wish to know in which book of the Bible it is found. By looking in the concordance at the key entry words **Moses**, **lifted**, **snake**, **desert**, or at the phrase **Son of Man** you will find extracts of the verse and its location at John 3:14. This concordance lists every word in the NIV, except for those words listed at the back of the book. It is a complete concordance in that for each entry word or phrase all occurrences are given, including those in the Psalm titles.

Phrases

As an additional feature, occurrences of over 350 phrases such as **Son of God** and **Voice of the LORD** are provided. This makes it much easier to pick out entries for these key phrases rather than reading through the many entries at **Son** or **God**, at **Voice** or **LORD**. The most well-known phrases only appear. These are listed on pp. xxff and range from **Aaron's staff** to **Zeal of the LORD Almighty**. However, variants are not listed. For example, **Face to the ground** is listed but the variant, **Faces to the ground** is not. Note that the entries **Son** and **God** do *not* contain Bible extracts with the phrase **Son of God**; these appear only at the phrase entry **Son of God**. This is the case for all phrases and their principal words. See 4. in 'Notes'.

Biographical and place-name entries

To help you in your Bible study there are about 250 descriptive entries on people such as **Moses**, **Joshua**, **Jesus** and **Paul** and a similar number of geographical entries on places such as **Sinai** and **Babylon**. These appear in addition to the Bible extracts. For example, **Michal** and **Michmash**:

Michal

Daughter of Saul (1Sa 14:49). Became David's wife (1Sa 18:20–29); warned him of Saul's plot (1Sa 19:11–17). Given to Paltiel (1Sa 25:44); returned to David (2Sa 3:13–16). Despised David (2Sa 6:16–23; 1Ch 15:29).

1Sa 14:49 Merab, and that of the younger was **M**.
18:20 Now Saul's daughter **M** was in love
18:27 gave him his daughter **M** in marriage.
18:28 and that his daughter **M** loved David,
19:11 But **M**, David's wife, warned him, "If
19:12 **M** let David down through a window,
19:13 **M** took an idol and laid it on the
19:14 capture David, **M** said: "He is ill."
19:17 Saul said to **M**, "Why did you deceive
19:17 **M** told him, "He said to me, 'Let me
25:44 Saul had given his daughter **M**,
2Sa 3:13 bring **M** daughter of Saul when you
3:14 "Give me my wife **M**, whom I betrothed
6:16 **M** daughter of Saul watched from a
6:20 **M** daughter of Saul came out to meet
6:21 David said to **M**, "It was before the
6:23 **M** daughter of Saul had no children
1Ch 15:29 **M** daughter of Saul watched from a

Michmash

A town of Benjamin north of Jerusalem. Scene of battle between Israel and the Philistines where Jonathan's men won a great victory (1Sa 13:2, 5–7; 14:4–15, 31). The Assyrians stored supplies here (Isa 10:28).

1Sa 13: 2 **M** and in the hill country of Bethel,
13: 5 and camped at **M**, east of Beth Aven.
13:11 Philistines were assembling at **M**,
13:16 while the Philistines camped at **M**.
13:23 had gone out to the pass at **M**.
14: 5 cliff stood to the north towards **M**,
14:31 **M** to Aijalon, they were exhausted.
Ezr 2:27 of **M** 122
Ne 7:31 of **M** 122
11:31 **M**, Aija, Bethel and its settlements,
Isa 10:28 Migron; they store supplies at **M**.

Word differences

In the English language, words with the same spelling sometimes have very different meanings. For example **arm** refers to part of the body and **arm** is also associated with warfare. These are distinguished by a raised number, for example: **arm**[1] and **arm**[2]. For other (mostly function words) only some occurrences are included:

Does is listed only in the sense of female deer not as the verb "And hope does not disappoint us"

Just is listed in the sense of fair, equitable rather than the adverb "just as God commanded"

Might is listed in the sense of strength rather than the auxiliary verb "that I might show you my power"

Mine is listed in the sense of a place for extracting minerals, rather than the possessive "My lover is mine and I am his"

On is listed in the sense of the place, rather than the preposition "every living creature that moves on the ground" and the personal name "On son of Peleth"

Own is listed in the sense to possess rather than the adjective "take the plank out of your own eye"

So is listed as the place name rather than "And it was so"

Till is listed in the sense to cultivate rather than in the preposition "wrestled with him till daybreak"

Well is listed in the sense of a place containing water rather than "He treated Abram well"

Will is listed in the sense of purpose; Exodus 18:15 "the people come to me to seek God's will" rather than the verb "You will hear of wars and rumours of wars" (although the verb meaning to leave in inheritance is included, see Leviticus 25:46)

Notes

1. Main entry words are listed in alphabetical order. This alphabetical order is based on a word-by-word system not letter-by-letter and hyphens are to be ignored. For example:

Ekron
El-Berith
El Bethel
El Paran
Elah
Elation

Words with an apostrophe come immediately after the basic headword, thus,

God
God's
God's wrath
God Almighty
God-breathed
Goddess

2. Under the main entry word, Bible extracts are listed in Bible-book order (a list of Bible book abbreviations is given on p. xxx). The entry word in the Bible extract is reduced to its initial character, which appears in bold.

A capital letter in the extract indicates a capital letter in the Bible text. For example, **Hammer**:

Hammer (Hammered, Hammers)

Ex	25:31	lampstand of pure gold and **h** it out
Nu	16:38	**H** the censers into sheets to overlay
Jdg	4:21	picked up a tent peg and a **h** and
	5:26	her right hand for the workman's **h**.
1Ki	6: 7	and no **h**, chisel or any other iron
Isa	41: 7	he who smooths with the **h** spurs on
Jer	10: 4	they fasten it with **h** and nails so
	23:29	a **h** that breaks a rock in pieces?
	50:23	is the **h** of the whole earth!

3. As with most concordances, 'related forms' of a word, such as the plural, appear at the primary entry word. For example, the first entry **Aaron** is followed by (**Aaron's**, **Aaronic**). Each of the words in brackets relates back to the primary entry word, for example, **Aaronic** (**Aaron**). For example, **Melon** and **Melons**:

Melon (Melons)

Jer	10: 5	Like a scarecrow in a **m** patch, their

Melons (Melon)

Nu	11: 5	**m**, leeks, onions and garlic.
Isa	1: 8	field of **m**, like a city under siege.

4. Phrases related to a primary entry word appear in brackets in italic, for example, **Aaron's** (**Aaron**, ***Aaron's staff***) and **Staff** (***Aaron's staff***, **Flagstaff**, **Staffs**).

5. Phrases usually show full Bible extracts but in some cases where the key word is not the first in the phrase or the first word is not listed as an entry word only scripture references will appear. For example **I am with you**:

I am with you

Ge 26:24; 28:15; Jos 3:7; 1Sa 14:7; 2Ki 10:15; Isa 41:10; 43:5; Jer 1:8, 19; 15:20; 30:11; 42:11; 46:28; Hag 1:13; 2:4; Mt 28:20; Jn 7:33; Ac 18:10; 1Co 5:3, 4; Gal 4:18

A list of phrases is provided on p. xxff. Those that include only scripture references are indicated with an asterisk.

6. In the people and place-name entries, a bold numeral indicates a different person or place with the same name. For example, **Levi**:

Levi (Levi's, Levite, Levites, Levitical)
1. Son of Jacob by Leah (Ge 29:34; 35:23); with Simeon killed Shechemites to avenge rape of sister Dinah (Ge 34); blessed by Jacob (Ge 49:5–7). **2.** Tribe descended from Levi. Blessed by Moses (Dt 33:8–11). Numbered separately (Nu 1:47–49; 3:14–39; 26:57–62); responsible for tabernacle (Nu 1:50–53; 3:14–37; 4; 8; 18:2–4); dedicated to God in place of firstborn (Nu 3:11–13,40–41). Given towns (Nu 35; Jos 21) but not land (Nu 18:20–24; 26:62; Dt 10:9; Jos 13:14); allocated land in new division (Eze 48:13–14). **3.** See *Matthew*.

7. It must be noted that, although as lengthy as possible, the extract is just that, part of a greater whole. The reader is therefore urged to read the relevant Bible text (the Anglicised or American NIV) in its fuller context.

8. For use with the American NIV, word differences and spelling differences between the Anglicised and North American editions are provided at the back of the book.

9. Cross references are used when the reader would expect a particular entry which appears elsewhere for example, **Mediterranean Sea** See **Great Sea** and **Another** See **One another**. Cross references are also used to refer the reader to a source of additional information: **Aquila** See **Priscilla**. Some cross references refer the reader to a particular part of additional information, **Judea** See **Judah 3**. where the number three refers to the third definition at the entry **Judah**. For example:

Judea See **Judah 3.**
Mt 2: 1 Jesus was born in Bethlehem in **J**,
2: 5 "In Bethlehem in **J**," they replied,
2:22 reigning in **J** in place of his father
3: 1 came, preaching in the Desert of **J**
3: 5 **J** and the whole region of the Jordan.
4:25 the Decapolis, Jerusalem, **J** and the
19: 1 **J** to the other side of the Jordan.
24:16 let those who are in **J** flee to the

10. As in all NIV Bibles, 'Lord' appears in more than one form. The first entry is **LORD**; the personal name of God, the divine name *Yahweh* (see p.599). The next entry is **Lord** *Adonai* which appears as **Lord**[1] (see p.618). The verb appears as **Lord**[2] (see p.621).

11. Phrases which include **LORD** or **Lord** vary slightly. For example the phrase **Angel of the LORD** appears, as does the separate phrase entry **Angel of the Lord**. But the phrase **Fear of the Lord** lists less than four Bible extracts

so does not appear separately. Rather, it is listed under the phrase **Fear of the LORD/Lord** and appears thus:

Fear of the LORD/Lord

2Ch	17:10	The f fell on all the kingdoms of
	19: 7	Now let the f be upon you. Judge
	19: 9	and wholeheartedly in the f.
Job	28:28	he said to man, 'The f—that is
Ps	19: 9	The f is pure, enduring for ever.
	34:11	to me; I will teach you the f.
	111:10	The f is the beginning of wisdom;
Pr	1: 7	The f is the beginning of knowledge,
	2: 5	you will understand the f and find
	9:10	"The f is the beginning of wisdom,
	10:27	The f adds length to life, but the
	14:27	The f is a fountain of life, turning
	15:16	Better a little with the f than
	15:33	The f teaches a man wisdom, and
	16: 6	through the f a man avoids evil.
	19:23	The f leads to life: Then one rests
	22: 4	Humility and the f bring wealth and
	23:17	but always be zealous for the f.
Isa	11: 2	Spirit of knowledge and of the f—
	11: 3	he will delight in the f. He will
	33: 6	the f is the key to this treasure.
Ac	9:31	it grew in numbers, living in the f.

Explanatory Diagram

B

C

HIGH 441 HIGH PLACES

A → **High (*God Most High, High place, High places, High priest*, Highborn, Higher, Highest, High-grade, *Most high*)**

Ge 6:15 long, 75 feet wide and 45 feet **h**.
7:17 lifted the ark **h** above the earth.
7:19 and all the **h** mountains under the
29: 7 Look," he said, "the sun is still **h**
Ex 25:10 and a cubit and a half **h**.
25:23 cubit wide and a cubit and a half **h**.
27: 1 three cubits **h**; it is to be square,
27:18 cubits **h**, and with bronze bases.
30: 2 a cubit wide, and two cubits **h**
37: 1 and a cubit and a half **h**.
37:10 and a cubit and a half **h**.
37:25 a cubit wide, and two cubits **h**
38: 1 three cubits **h**; it was square,
38:18 of the courtyard, five cubits **h**,
Lev 26:13 you to walk with heads held **h**.
Nu 14:40 went up towards the **h** hill country
14:44 went up towards the **h** hill country
Dt 3: 5 **h** walls and with gates and bars,
12: 2 all the places on the **h** mountains
26:19 fame and honour **h** above all the
28: 1 **h** above all the nations on earth.
28:52 until the **h** fortified walls
Jdg 16:25 While they were in **h** spirits, they
1Sa 2: 1 in the LORD my horn is lifted **h**.
18: 5 Saul gave him a **h** rank in the army.
25:36 He was in **h** spirits and very drunk.
2Sa 13:28 "Listen! When Amnon is in **h** spirits
22:17 "He reached down from on **h** and took
1Ki 6: 2 long, twenty wide and thirty **h**.
6:20 long, twenty wide and twenty **h**.
6:23 of olive wood, each ten cubits **h**.
7: 2 fifty wide and thirty **h**, with four
7: 4 Its windows were placed **h** in sets of
7:15 each eight cubits **h** and twelve
7:16 each capital was five cubits **h**.
7:19 shape of lilies, four cubits **h**.
7:23 from rim to rim and five cubits **h**.
7:27 cubits long, four wide and three **h**.
14:23 Asherah poles on every **h** hill and
2Ki 17:10 Asherah poles on every **h** hill and
25:17 Each pillar was twenty-seven feet **h**
25:17 pillar was four and a half feet **h**
2Ch 3: 4 of the building and twenty cubits **h**
4: 1 twenty cubits wide and ten cubits **h**
4: 2 from rim to rim and five cubits **h**.
6:13 five cubits wide and three cubits **h**
Ezr 6: 3 ninety feet **h** and ninety feet wide
Ne 8: 4 Ezra the scribe stood on a **h** wooden
Est 1:10 when King Xerxes was in **h** spirits
5: 9 that day happy and in **h** spirits.
5:14 gallows built, seventy-five feet **h**
7: 9 A gallows seventy-five feet **h**
10: 3 and held in **h** esteem by his many
Job 5:11 The lowly he sets on **h**, and those
10:16 If I hold my head **h**, you stalk me
16:19 is in heaven; my advocate is on **h**.
31: 2 his heritage from the Almighty on **h**
31:28 have been unfaithful to God on **h**.
35: 5 gaze at the clouds so **h** above you.
39:27 command and build his nest on **h**?
Ps 7: 7 Rule over them from on **h**;
18:16 He reached down from on **h** and took

E

Ecc 10: 6 Fools are put in many **h** positions,
Isa 2:14 mountains and all the **h** hills,
6: 1 saw the Lord seated on a throne, **h**
16: 3 your shadow like night—at **h** noon
25:12 bring down your **h** fortified walls
26: 5 He humbles those who dwell on **h**,
26:11 O LORD, your hand is lifted **h**,
30:13 sin will become for you like a **h** wall
30:25 **h** mountain and every lofty hill.
32:15 Spirit is poured upon us from on **h**,
33: 5 is exalted, for he dwells on **h**;
40: 9 to Zion, go up on a **h** mountain.
57: 7 made your bed on a **h** and lofty hill
57:15 this is what the **h** and lofty One
57:15 "I live in a **h** and holy place, but
58: 4 expect your voice to be heard on **h**.
Jer 2:20 on every **h** hill and under every
3: 6 She has gone up on every **h** hill
16: 6 "Both **h** and low will die in this
17: 2 spreading trees and on the **h** hills.
25:30 'The LORD will roar from on **h**;
39: 3 Nergal-Sharezer a **h** official and all
39:13 Nergal-Sharezer a **h** official and all
49:16 Though you build your nest as **h** as
51: 9 skies, it rises as **h** as the clouds.'
51:58 and her **h** gates set on fire;
52:21 the pillars was eighteen cubits **h**
52:22 of the one pillar was five cubits **h**
Lam 1:13 "From on **h** he sent fire, sent it
Eze 1:18 Their rims were **h** and awesome, and
1:26 and **h** above on the throne was a
6:13 on every **h** hill and on all the
17:22 plant it on a **h** and lofty mountain.
19:11 towered **h** above the thick foliage,
20:28 saw any **h** hill or any leafy tree,
20:40 the **h** mountain of Israel,
23:23 and men of **h** rank, all mounted
24: 9 I, too, will pile the wood **h**.
27: 4 Your domain was on the **h** seas;
27:26 oarsmen take you out to the **h** seas
31: 3 **h**, its top above the thick foliage.
31:10 LORD says: Because it towered on **h**,
31:14 are ever to tower proudly on **h**.
34: 6 the mountains and on every **h** hill.
40: 2 and set me on a very **h** mountain,
40: 5 measuring rod thick and one rod **h**.
40:12 each alcove was a wall one cubit **h**,
40:42 cubit and a half wide and a cubit **h**.
41:22 three cubits **h** and two cubits square
43:14 it is two cubits **h** and a cubit wide
43:14 is four cubits **h** and a cubit wide.
43:15 The altar hearth is four cubits **h**,
Da 2:48 placed Daniel in a **h** position
3: 1 ninety feet **h** and nine feet wide,
5:19 of the **h** position he gave him,
Hab 2: 9 to set his nest on **h**, to escape
3:10 roared and lifted its waves on **h**.
Mt 4: 8 devil took him to a very **h** mountain
17: 1 them up a **h** mountain by themselves.
20:25 and their **h** officials exercise
Mk 6:21 gave a banquet for his **h** officials
9: 2 him and led them up a **h** mountain,
10:42 and their **h** officials exercise
Lk 3: 2 during the **h** priesthood of Annas and
4:38 was suffering from a **h** fever.

High place ← D
1Sa 9:12 people have a sacrifice at the **h**.
9:13 before he goes up to the **h** to eat.
9:14 towards them on his way up to the **h**
9:19 "Go up ahead of me to the **h**,
9:25 After they came down from the **h**
10: 5 coming down from the **h** with lyres,
10:13 prophesying, he went to the **h**.
1Ki 3: 4 for that was the most important **h**,
11: 7 Solomon built a **h** for Chemosh the
2Ki 17:11 At every **h** they burned incense, as
23:15 the **h** made by Jeroboam son of Nebat
23:15 that altar and **h** he demolished.
23:15 He burned the **h** and ground it to
1Ch 16:39 of the LORD at the **h** in Gibeon
21:29 at that time on the **h** at Gibeon.
2Ch 1: 3 assembly went to the **h** at Gibeon,
1:13 to Jerusalem from the **h** at Gibeon
Isa 16:12 Moab appears at her **h**, she only
Eze 20:29 What is this **h** you go to?'"
Mic 1: 5 is Judah's **h**? Is it not Jerusalem?
Lk 4: 5 The devil led him up to a **h** and

High places ← D
Lev 26:30 will destroy your **h**, cut down your
Nu 33:52 idols, and demolish all their **h**.
Dt 33:29 and you will trample down their **h**.
1Ki 3: 2 were still sacrificing at the **h**,
3: 3 and burned incense on the **h**.
12:31 Jeroboam built shrines on **h** and
12:32 priests at the **h** he had made.
13: 2 will sacrifice the priests of the **h**
13:32 against all the shrines on the **h**
13:33 appointed priests for the **h** from
13:33 a priest he consecrated for the **h**.
14:23 They also set up for themselves **h**,
15:14 Although he did not remove the **h**,
22:43 The **h**, however, were not removed,
2Ki 12: 3 The **h**, however, were not removed;
14: 4 The **h**, however, were not removed;
15: 4 The **h**, however, were not removed;
15:35 The **h**, however, were not removed;
16: 4 and burned incense at the **h**,
17: 9 themselves **h** in all their towns.
17:29 people of Samaria had made at the **h**
17:32 as priests in the shrines at the **h**.
18: 4 removed the **h**, smashed the sacred
18:22 whose **h** and altars Hezekiah removed
21: 3 rebuilt the **h** his father Hezekiah
23: 5 on the **h** of the towns of Judah
23: 8 towns of Judah and desecrated the **h**
23: 9 priests of the **h** did not serve
23:13 The king also desecrated the **h** that
23:19 defiled all the shrines at the **h**
23:20 priests of those **h** on the altars
2Ch 11:15 appointed his own priests for the **h**
14: 3 the foreign altars and the **h**,
14: 5 He removed the **h** and incense altars
15:17 Although he did not remove the **h**
17: 6 removed the **h** and the Asherah poles
20:33 The **h**, however, were not removed,
21:11 He had also built **h** on the hills
28: 4 and burned incense at the **h**,
28:25 In every town in Judah he built **h**
31: 1 They destroyed the **h** and the altars

F

Key

A Primary entry word
B Related phrase
C Related word
D Phrase entry
E Entry word/phrase reduced to bold initial character
F Extracts appear in Bible book order

A Brief Introduction to the NIV

The New International Version is a completely new translation of the Holy Bible made by over a hundred scholars working directly from the best available Hebrew, Aramaic and Greek texts. It had its beginning in 1965 when, after several years of exploratory study by committees from the Christian Reformed Church and the National Association of Evangelicals, a group of scholars met at Palos Heights, Illinois, and concurred in the need for a new translation of the Bible in contemporary English. This group, though not made up of official church representatives, was transdenominational. Its conclusion was endorsed by a large number of leaders from many denominations who met in Chicago in 1966.

Responsibility for the new version was delegated by the Palos Heights group to a self-governing body of fifteen, the Committee on Bible Translation, composed for the most part of biblical scholars from colleges, universities and seminaries. In 1967 the New York Bible Society (now the International Bible Society) generously undertook the financial sponsorship of the project – a sponsorship that made it possible to enlist the help of many distinguished scholars. The fact that participants from the United States, Great Britain, Canada, Australia and New Zealand worked together gave the project its international scope. That they were from many denominations – including Anglican, Assemblies of God, Baptist, Brethren, Christian Reformed, Church of Christ, Evangelical Free, Lutheran, Mennonite, Methodist, Nazarene, Presbyterian, Wesleyan and other churches – helped to safeguard the translation from sectarian bias.

How it was made helps to give the New International Version its distinctiveness. The translation of each book was assigned to a team of scholars. Next, one of the Intermediate Editorial Committees revised the initial translation, with constant reference to the Hebrew, Aramaic or Greek. Their work then went to one of the General Editorial Committees, which checked it in

detail and made another thorough revision. This revision in turn was carefully reviewed by the Committee on Bible Translation, which made further changes and then released the final version for publication. In this way the entire Bible underwent three revisions, during each of which the translation was examined for its faithfulness to the original languages and for its English style.

All this involved many thousands of hours of research and discussion regarding the meaning of the texts and the precise way of putting them into English. It may well be that no other translation has been made by a more thorough process of review and revision from committee to committee than this one.

From the beginning of the project, the Committee on Bible Translation held to certain goals for the New International Version: that it would be an accurate translation and one that would have clarity and literary quality and so prove suitable for public and private reading, teaching, preaching, memorising and liturgical use. The Committee also sought to preserve some measure of continuity with the long tradition of translating the Scriptures into English.

In working towards these goals, the translators were united in their commitment to the authority and infallibility of the Bible as God's Word in written form. They believe that it contains the divine answer to the deepest needs of humanity, that it sheds unique light on our path in a dark world, and that it sets forth the way to our eternal well-being.

The first concern of the translators has been the accuracy of the translation and its fidelity to the thought of the biblical writers. They have weighed the significance of the lexical and grammatical details of the Hebrew, Aramaic and Greek texts. At the same time, they have striven for more than a word-for-word translation. Because thought patterns and syntax differ from language to language, faithful communication of the meaning of the writers of the Bible demands frequent modifications in sentence structure and constant regard for the contextual meanings of words.

A sensitive feeling for style does not always accompany scholarship. Accordingly the Committee on Bible Translation submitted the developing version to a number of stylistic consultants. Two of them read every book of both Old and New Testaments twice – once

before and once after the last major revision – and made invaluable suggestions. Samples of the translation were tested for clarity and ease of reading by various kinds of people – young and old, highly educated and less well educated, ministers and laymen.

Concern for clear and natural English – that the New International Version should be idiomatic but not idiosyncratic, contemporary but not dated – motivated the translators and consultants. At the same time, they tried to reflect the differing styles of the biblical writers. In view of the international use of English, the translators sought to avoid obvious Americanisms on the one hand and obvious Anglicisms on the other. A British edition reflects the comparatively few differences of significant idiom and of spelling.

As for the traditional pronouns "thou", "thee" and "thine" in reference to the Deity, the translators judged that to use these archaisms (along with old verb forms such as "doest", "wouldest" and "hadst") would violate accuracy in translation. Neither Hebrew, Aramaic nor Greek uses special pronouns for the persons of the Godhead. A present-day translation is not enhanced by forms that in the time of the King James Version were used in everyday speech, whether referring to God or man.

There is a sense in which the work of translation is never wholly finished. This applies to all great literature and uniquely so to the Bible. In 1973 the New Testament in the New International Version was published. Since then, suggestions for corrections and revisions have been received from various sources. The Committee on Bible Translation carefully considered the suggestions and adopted a number of them. These were incorporated in the first printing of the entire Bible in 1978. Additional revisions were made by the Committee on Bible Translation in 1983 and appear in printings after that date.

In regard to the divine name *YHWH*, commonly referred to as the *Tetragrammaton*, the translators adopted the device used in most English versions of rendering that name as "LORD" in capital letters to distinguish it from *Adonai*, another Hebrew word rendered "Lord", for which small letters are used. Wherever the two names stand together in the Old Testament as a compound name of God, they are rendered "Sovereign LORD".

As for other proper nouns, the familiar spellings of the Authorised Version are generally retained. Names traditionally spelled with "ch", except where it is final, are usually spelled in this translation with "k" or "c", since the biblical languages do not have the sound that "ch" frequently indicates in English – for example, in *chant*. For well-known names such as Zechariah, however, the traditional spelling has been retained. Variation in the spelling of names in the original languages has usually not been indicated. Where a person or place has two or more different names in the Hebrew, Aramaic or Greek texts, the more familiar one has generally been used.

Like all the translations of the Bible, made as they are by imperfect man, this one undoubtedly falls short of its goals. Yet we are grateful to God for the extent to which he has enabled us to realise these goals and for the strength he has given us and our colleagues to complete our task. We offer this version of the Bible to him in whose name and for whose glory it has been made. We pray that it will lead many into a better understanding of the Holy Scriptures and a fuller knowledge of Jesus Christ the incarnate Word, of whom the Scriptures so faithfully testify.

Extract from the Preface to the New International Version,
by The Committee on Bible Translation
June 1978
(Revised August 1983)

Names of the translators and editors may be secured from the International Bible Society 1820 Jet Stream Drive, Colorado Springs, CO 80921-3696, U.S.A.

List of Phrases

List of Phrases
(continued)

List of Phrases
(continued)

List of Biographies

List of Biographies *(continued)*

List of Biographies *(continued)*

List of Place-name Entries

List of Place-name Entries *(continued)*

Abbreviations for Books of the Bible

The Old Testament

Genesis *Ge*
Exodus *Ex*
Leviticus *Lev*
Numbers *Nu*
Deuteronomy *Dt*
Joshua *Jos*
Judges *Jdg*
Ruth *Ru*
1 Samuel *1Sa*
2 Samuel *2Sa*
1 Kings *1Ki*
2 Kings *2Ki*
1 Chronicles *1Ch*
2 Chronicles *2Ch*
Ezra *Ezr*
Nehemiah *Ne*
Esther *Est*
Job *Job*
Psalms *Ps*
Proverbs *Pr*
Ecclesiastes *Ecc*
Song of Songs *SS*
Isaiah *Isa*
Jeremiah *Jer*
Lamentations *La*
Ezekiel *Eze*
Daniel *Da*
Hosea *Hos*
Joel *Joel*
Amos *Am*
Obadiah *Ob*
Jonah *Jnh*
Micah *Mic*
Nahum *Na*
Habakkuk *Hab*
Zephaniah *Zep*
Haggai *Hag*
Zechariah *Zec*
Malachi *Mal*

The New Testament

Matthew *Mt*
Mark *Mk*
Luke *Lk*
John *Jn*
Acts *Ac*
Romans *Ro*
1 Corinthians *1Co*
2 Corinthians *2Co*
Galatians *Gal*
Ephesians *Eph*
Philippians *Php*
Colossians *Col*
1 Thessalonians *1Th*
2 Thessalonians *2Th*
1 Timothy *1Ti*
2 Timothy *2Ti*
Titus *Tit*
Philemon *Phm*
Hebrews *Heb*
James *Jas*
1 Peter *1Pe*
2 Peter *2Pe*
1 John *1Jn*
2 John *2Jn*
3 John *3Jn*
Jude *Jude*
Revelation *Rev*

Aaron (Aaron's, Aaronic)

Brother of Moses; appointed as his spokesman (Ex 4:14–16; 7:1–2). Held up Moses' hands in battle (Ex 17:12). Consecrated as priest (Ex 28:1–4; 29; Lev 8; Heb 5:4). Made golden calf (Ex 32); opposed Moses (Nu 12:1–3). Priesthood challenged (Nu 16); staff budded as confirmation of his call (Nu 17). With Moses, excluded from Canaan (Nu 20:12). Death (Nu 20:22-29).

Ex 4:14 "What about your brother, **A** the
4:27 The LORD said to **A**, "Go into the
4:28 Moses told **A** everything the LORD had
4:29 Moses and **A** brought together all the
4:30 **A** told them everything the LORD had
5: 1 Afterwards Moses and **A** went to
5: 4 the king of Egypt said, "Moses and **A**,
5:20 Moses and **A** waiting to meet them,
6:13 Now the LORD spoke to Moses and **A**
6:20 Jochebed, who bore him **A** and Moses.
6:23 **A** married Elisheba, daughter of
6:25 Eleazar son of **A** married one of the
6:26 was this same **A** and Moses to whom
6:27 It was the same Moses and **A**.
7: 1 your brother **A** will be your prophet.
7: 2 and your brother **A** is to tell
7: 6 Moses and **A** did just as the LORD
7: 7 years old and **A** eighty-three years
7: 8 The LORD said to Moses and **A**,
7: 9 'Perform a miracle,' then say to **A**,
7:10 Moses and **A** went to Pharaoh and did
7:10 **A** threw his staff down in front of
7:19 The LORD said to Moses, "Tell **A**,
7:20 Moses and **A** did just as the LORD had
7:22 and **A**, just as the LORD had said.
8: 5 the LORD said to Moses, "Tell **A**,
8: 6 **A** stretched out his hand over the
8: 8 Pharaoh summoned Moses and **A** and
8:12 After Moses and **A** left Pharaoh,
8:15 and **A**, just as the LORD had said.
8:16 the LORD said to Moses, "Tell **A**,
8:17 They did this, and when **A** stretched
8:25 Pharaoh summoned Moses and **A** and
9: 8 the LORD said to Moses and **A**, "Take
9:12 he would not listen to Moses and **A**,
9:27 Pharaoh summoned Moses and **A**. "This
10: 3 Moses and **A** went to Pharaoh and said
10: 8 Moses and **A** were brought back to
10:11 Then Moses and **A** were driven out of
10:16 Pharaoh quickly summoned Moses and **A**
11:10 Moses and **A** performed all these
12: 1 The LORD said to Moses and **A** in
12:28 what the LORD commanded Moses and **A**.
12:31 summoned Moses and **A** and said,
12:43 The LORD said to Moses and **A**, "These
12:50 the LORD had commanded Moses and **A**.
16: 2 grumbled against Moses and **A**.
16: 6 Moses and **A** said to all the
16: 9 Moses told **A**, "Say to the entire
16:10 While **A** was speaking to the whole
16:33 Moses said to **A**, "Take a jar and put
16:34 the LORD commanded Moses, **A** put the
17:10 and Moses, **A** and Hur went to the top
17:12 **A** and Hur held his hands up—one on
18:12 and **A** came with all the elders of
19:24 "Go down and bring **A** up with you.
24: 1 "Come up to the LORD, you and **A**,
24: 9 Moses and **A**, Nadab and Abihu, and
24:14 **A** and Hur are with you, and anyone
27:21 **A** and his sons are to keep the lamps
28: 1 "Have **A** your brother brought to you
28: 2 **A**, to give him dignity and honour.
28: 3 they are to make garments for **A**,
28: 4 for your brother **A** and his sons,
28:12 **A** is to bear the names on his
28:29 "Whenever **A** enters the Holy Place,
28:30 Thus **A** will always bear the means
28:35 **A** must wear it when he ministers.
28:41 on your brother **A** and his sons,
28:43 **A** and his sons must wear them
28:43 ordinance for **A** and his descendants.
29: 4 bring **A** and his sons to the entrance
29: 5 Take the garments and dress **A** with
29: 9 Then tie sashes on **A** and his sons.
29: 9 way you shall ordain **A** and his sons.
29:10 and **A** and his sons shall lay their

Ex 29:15 "Take one of the rams, and **A** and his
29:19 "Take the other ram, and **A** and his
29:20 of the right ears of **A** and his sons,
29:21 sprinkle it on **A** and his garments
29:24 Put all these in the hands of **A** and
29:27 ram that belong to **A** and his sons:
29:28 the Israelites for **A** and his sons.
29:32 **A** and his sons are to eat the meat
29:35 "Do for **A** and his sons everything I
29:44 the altar and will consecrate **A** and
30: 7 "**A** must burn fragrant incense on the
30:10 Once a year **A** shall make atonement
30:19 **A** and his sons are to wash their
30:21 is to be a lasting ordinance for **A**
30:30 "Anoint **A** and his sons and
31:10 both the sacred garments for **A** the
32: 1 they gathered round **A** and said,
32: 2 **A** answered them, "Take off the gold
32: 3 ear-rings and brought them to **A**.
32: 5 **A** saw this, he built an altar in
32:21 He said to **A**, "What did these people
32:22 "Do not be angry, my lord," **A**
32:25 that **A** had let them get out of
32:35 they did with the calf **A** had made.
34:30 **A** and all the Israelites saw Moses,
34:31 Moses called to them; so **A** and all
35:19 sacred garments for **A** the priest
38:21 of Ithamar son of **A**, the priest.
39: 1 for **A**, as the LORD commanded Moses.
39:27 For **A** and his sons, they made tunics
39:41 both the sacred garments for **A** the
40:12 "Bring **A** and his sons to the
40:13 dress **A** in the sacred garments,
40:31 Moses and **A** and his sons used it to
Lev 1: 7 The sons of **A** the priest are to put
2: 3 offering belongs to **A** and his sons;
2:10 offering belongs to **A** and his sons;
6: 9 "Give **A** and his sons this command:
6:16 **A** and his sons shall eat the rest
6:18 Any male descendant of **A** may eat it.
6:20 "This is the offering **A** and his sons
6:25 "Say to **A** and his sons: 'These are
7:10 equally to all the sons of **A**.
7:31 breast belongs to **A** and his sons.
7:33 The son of **A** who offers the blood
7:34 have given them to **A** the priest and
7:35 LORD by fire that were allotted to **A**
8: 2 "Bring **A** and his sons, their
8: 6 Moses brought **A** and his sons forward
8: 7 He put the tunic on **A**, tied the sash
8:14 and **A** and his sons laid their hands
8:18 and **A** and his sons laid their hands
8:22 the ram for the ordination, and **A**
8:27 He put all these in the hands of **A**
8:30 sprinkled them on **A** and his garments
8:30 So he consecrated **A** and his garments
8:31 Moses then said to **A** and his sons,
8:31 '**A** and his sons are to eat it.'
8:36 **A** and his sons did everything the
9: 1 On the eighth day Moses summoned **A**
9: 2 He said to **A**, "Take a bull calf for
9: 7 Moses said to **A**, "Come to the altar
9: 8 **A** came to the altar and slaughtered
9:15 **A** then brought the offering that was
9:20 then **A** burned the fat on the altar.
9:21 **A** waved the breasts and the right
9:22 **A** lifted his hands towards the
9:23 Moses and **A** then went into the Tent
10: 3 Moses then said to **A**, "This is what
10: 3 **A** remained silent.
10: 6 Moses said to **A** and his sons Eleazar
10: 8 Then the LORD said to **A**,
10:12 Moses said to **A** and his remaining
10:19 **A** replied to Moses, "Today they
11: 1 The LORD said to Moses and **A**,
13: 1 The LORD said to Moses and **A**,
13: 2 he must be brought to **A** the priest
14:33 The LORD said to Moses and **A**,
15: 1 The LORD said to Moses and **A**,
16: 1 after the death of the two sons of **A**
16: 2 "Tell your brother **A** not to come
16: 3 "This is how **A** is to enter the
16: 6 "**A** is to offer the bull for his own
16: 9 **A** shall bring the goat whose lot
16:11 "**A** shall bring the bull for his own
16:17 **A** goes in to make atonement in the

Lev 16:20 "When **A** has finished making
16:23 "Then **A** is to go into the Tent of
17: 2 "Speak to **A** and his sons and to all
21: 1 Speak to the priests, the sons of **A**
21:17 "Say to **A**: 'For the generations to
21:21 No descendant of **A** the priest who
21:24 Moses told this to **A** and his sons
22: 2 "Tell **A** and his sons to treat with
22: 4 "'If a descendant of **A** has an
22:18 "Speak to **A** and his sons and to all
24: 3 **A** is to tend the lamps before the
24: 9 belongs to **A** and his sons, who are
Nu 1: 3 You and **A** are to number by their
1:17 Moses and **A** took these men whose
1:44 **A** and the twelve leaders of Israel,
2: 1 The LORD said to Moses and **A**:
3: 1 is the account of the family of **A**
3: 2 The names of the sons of **A** were
3: 4 the lifetime of their father **A**.
3: 6 them to **A** the priest to assist him.
3: 9 Give the Levites to **A** and his sons;
3:10 Appoint **A** and his sons to serve as
3:32 was Eleazar son of **A**, the priest.
3:38 Moses and **A** and his sons were to
3:39 Moses and **A** according to their clans,
3:48 Israelites to **A** and his sons."
3:51 Moses gave the redemption money to **A**
4: 1 The LORD said to Moses and **A**:
4: 5 the camp is to move, **A** and his sons
4:15 "After **A** and his sons have finished
4:16 "Eleazar son of **A**, the priest, is to
4:17 The LORD said to Moses and **A**,
4:19 **A** and his sons are to go into the
4:27 the direction of **A** and his sons.
4:28 of Ithamar son of **A**, the priest.
4:33 of Ithamar son of **A**, the priest."
4:34 Moses, **A** and the leaders of the
4:37 Moses and **A** counted them according
4:41 Moses and **A** counted them according
4:45 Moses and **A** counted them according
4:46 Moses, **A** and the leaders of Israel
6:23 "Tell **A** and his sons, 'This is how
7: 8 of Ithamar son of **A**, the priest.
8: 2 "Speak to **A** and say to him, 'When
8: 3 **A** did so; he set up the lamps so
8:11 **A** is to present the Levites before
8:13 Make the Levites stand in front of **A**
8:19 given the Levites as gifts to **A**
8:20 Moses, **A** and the whole Israelite
8:21 Then **A** presented them as a wave
8:22 the supervision of **A** and his sons.
9: 6 came to Moses and **A** that same
10: 8 "The sons of **A**, the priests, are to
12: 1 Miriam and **A** began to talk against
12: 4 At once the LORD said to Moses, **A**
12: 5 the Tent and summoned **A** and Miriam.
12:10 **A** turned towards her and saw that
13:26 They came back to Moses and **A** and
14: 2 grumbled against Moses and **A**,
14: 5 Moses and **A** fell face down in front
14:26 The LORD said to Moses and **A**:
15:33 Moses and **A** and the whole assembly,
16: 3 oppose Moses and **A** and said to them,
16:11 Who is **A** that you should grumble
16:16 LORD tomorrow—you and they and **A**.
16:17 **A** are to present your censers also."
16:18 and stood with Moses and **A** at the
16:20 The LORD said to Moses and **A**,
16:22 Moses and **A** fell face down and cried
16:37 "Tell Eleazar son of **A**, the priest,
16:40 no-one except a descendant of **A**
16:41 grumbled against Moses and **A**.
16:42 **A** and turned towards the Tent of
16:43 Moses and **A** went to the front of the
16:46 Moses said to **A**, "Take your censer
16:47 **A** did as Moses said, and ran into
16:47 but **A** offered the incense and made
16:50 **A** returned to Moses at the entrance
18: 1 The LORD said to **A**, "You, your sons
18: 8 the LORD said to **A**, "I myself have
18:20 The LORD said to **A**, "You will have
18:28 the LORD's portion to **A** the priest.
19: 1 The LORD said to Moses and **A**:
20: 2 in opposition to Moses and **A**.
20: 6 Moses and **A** went from the assembly
20: 8 **A** gather the assembly together.

Nu 20:10 He and A gathered the assembly
20:12 the LORD said to Moses and A,
20:23 Edom, the LORD said to Moses and A,
20:24 "A will be gathered to his people.
20:25 Call A and his son Eleazar and take
20:26 for A will be gathered to his people;
20:28 And A died there on top of the
20:29 the whole community learned that A
25: 7 Phinehas son of Eleazar, the son of A
25:11 the son of A, the priest, has turned
26: 1 and Eleazar son of A, the priest,
26: 9 A and were among Korah's followers
26:59 A, Moses and their sister Miriam.
26:60 A was the father of Nadab and Abihu,
26:64 A the priest when they counted the
27:13 your people, as your brother A was,
33: 1 under the leadership of Moses and A.
33:38 At the LORD's command A the priest
33:39 A was a hundred and twenty-three
Dt 9:20 the LORD was angry enough with A to
9:20 but at that time I prayed for A too.
10: 6 There A died and was buried, and
32:50 just as your brother A died on Mount
Jos 21: 4 The Levites who were descendants of A
21:10 assigned to the descendants of A who
21:13 to the descendants of A the priest
21:19 the descendants of A, were thirteen,
24: 5 "'Then I sent Moses and A, and I
24:33 Eleazar son of A died and was buried
Jdg 20:28 the son of A, ministering before it.
1Sa 12: 6 A and brought your forefathers up
12: 8 and the LORD sent Moses and A, who
1Ch 6: 3 The children of Amram: A, Moses and
6: 3 sons of A: Nadab, Abihu, Eleazar and
6:49 A and his descendants were the ones
6:50 These were the descendants of A:
6:54 A who were from the Kohathite clan,
6:57 the descendants of A were given
12:27 of the family of A with 3,700 men,
15: 4 descendants of A and the Levites:
23:13 The sons of Amram: A and Moses. A
23:32 their brothers the descendants of A,
24: 1 sons of A: The sons of A were Nadab,
24:19 for them by their forefather A,
24:31 brothers the descendants of A did,
27:17 son of Kemuel; over A: Zadok;
2Ch 13: 9 the sons of A, and the Levites, and
13:10 of A, and the Levites assist them.
26:18 the descendants of A, who have been
29:21 the descendants of A, to offer these
31:19 for the priests, the descendants of A
35:14 the descendants of A, were
Ezr 7: 5 the son of A the chief priest—
Ne 10:38 A priest descended from A is to
12:47 portion for the descendants of A.
Ps 77:20 a flock by the hand of Moses and A.
99: 6 Moses and A were among his priests,
105:26 He sent Moses his servant, and A,
106:16 A, who was consecrated to the LORD.
115:10 O house of A, trust in the LORD—he
115:12 Israel, he will bless the house of A,
118: 3 Let the house of A say: "His love
135:19 LORD; O house of A, praise the LORD;
Mic 6: 4 Moses to lead you, also A and Miriam.
Lk 1: 5 Elizabeth was also a descendant of A.
Ac 7:40 They told A, 'Make us gods who will
Heb 5: 4 be called by God, just as A was.
7:11 Melchizedek, not in the order of A?

Aaron's (Aaron, *Aaron's staff*)

Ex 15:20 Miriam the prophetess, A sister,
28:30 so they may be over A heart whenever
28:38 will be on A forehead, and he will
28:38 It will be on A forehead continually
28:40 sashes and headbands for A sons, to
29:26 breast of the ram for A ordination,
29:29 "A sacred garments will belong to
Lev 1: 5 and then A sons the priests shall
1: 8 A sons the priests shall arrange the
1:11 and A sons the priests shall
2: 2 take it to A sons the priests. The
3: 2 Then A sons the priests shall
3: 5 A sons are to burn it on the altar
3: 8 Then A sons shall sprinkle its blood
3:13 Then A sons shall sprinkle its blood
6:14 A sons are to bring it before the
Lev 8: 9 he placed the turban on A head and
8:12 some of the anointing oil on A head
8:13 he brought A sons forward, put
8:23 put it on the lobe of A right ear,
8:24 Moses also brought A sons forward
10: 1 A sons Nadab and Abihu took their
10: 4 sons of A uncle Uzziel, and said to
10:16 Ithamar, A remaining sons, and asked,
Nu 3: 3 Those were the names of A sons, the
17: 3 On the staff of Levi write A name,
17:10 The LORD said to Moses, "Put back A
20:26 Remove A garments and put them on
20:28 Moses removed A garments and put
1Ch 23:28 The duty of the Levites was to help A
Ps 133: 2 running down on A beard, down upon

Aaron's staff

Ex 7:12 But A swallowed up their staff. Yet
Nu 17: 6 tribes, and A was among them.
17: 8 A, which represented the house of Levi
Heb 9: 4 A that had budded, and the stone

Aaronic (Aaron)

2Ch 35:14 themselves and for the A priests.

Abaddon

Rev 9:11 Hebrew is A, and in Greek, Apollyon.

Abagtha

Est 1:10 Bigtha, A, Zethar and Carcas—

Abana

2Ki 5:12 Are not A and Pharpar, the rivers of

Abandon (Abandoned, Abandons)

Dt 4:31 he will not a or destroy you or
Jos 10: 6 at Gilgal: "Do not a your servants.
1Ki 6:13 and will not a my people Israel."
2Ch 12: 5 therefore I now a you to Shishak.'"
Ne 9:19 you did not a them in the desert.
9:31 not put an end to them or a them,
Ps 16:10 you will not a me to the grave, nor
138: 8 do not a the works of your hands.
Jer 12: 7 "I will forsake my house, a my
48:28 A your towns and dwell among the
Eze 27:29 All who handle the oars will a their
Ac 2:27 you will not a me to the grave, nor
1Ti 4: 1 later times some will a the faith

Abandoned (Abandon)

Ge 24:27 who has not a his kindness and
Dt 29:25 "It is because this people a the
32:15 He a the God who made him and
Jdg 4:15 a his chariot and fled on foot.
5: 6 the days of Jael, the roads were a
6:13 Egypt?' But now the LORD has a us
1Sa 30:13 My master a me when I became ill
31: 7 died, they a their towns and fled.
2Sa 5:21 The Philistines a their idols there,
1Ki 18:18 You have a the LORD's commands and
2Ki 7: 7 fled in the dusk and a their tents
1Ch 10: 7 died, they a their towns and fled.
14:12 The Philistines had a their gods
2Ch 11:14 The Levites even a their
12: 1 with him a the law of the LORD.
12: 5 'You have a me; therefore I now
16: 5 building Ramah and a his work.
24:18 They a the temple of the LORD, the
Ne 9:28 Then you a them to the hand of their
Job 18: 4 is the earth to be a for your sake?
Ps 78:60 He a the tabernacle of Shiloh, the
Isa 2: 6 You have a your people, the house of
10:14 the nations; as men gather a eggs,
17: 9 a to thickets and undergrowth.
27:10 an a settlement, forsaken like the
32:14 The fortress will be a, the noisy
54: 7 "For a brief moment I a you, but
Jer 7:29 for the LORD has rejected and a this
49:25 Why has the city of renown not been a
Lam 2: 7 The Lord has rejected his altar and a
Mic 5: 3 Therefore Israel will be a until the
Zep 2: 4 Gaza will be a and Ashkelon left in
Ac 2:31 that he was not a to the grave, nor
Ro 1:27 In the same way the men also a
2Co 4: 9 persecuted, but not a; struck down,
Jude : 6 of authority but a their own home—

Abandons (Abandon)

Jn 10:12 he a the sheep and runs away.

Abarim, Mountains of

Mountain range east of the Jordan and Dead Sea. Includes Mount Nebo at its northern point. From here Moses viewed the promised land (Nu 27:12; Dt 32:49) and the death of Jehoiakim was proclaimed (Jer 22:20).

Nu 27:12 "Go up this mountain in the A Range
33:47 in the mountains of A, near Nebo.
33:48 They left the mountains of A and
Dt 32:49 "Go up into the A Range to Mount
Jer 22:20 A, for all your allies are crushed.

Abashed

Isa 24:23 The moon will be a, the sun ashamed;

Abba

Mk 14:36 "A, Father," he said, "everything
Ro 8:15 And by him we cry, "A, Father."
Gal 4: 6 Spirit who calls out, "A, Father.

Abda

1Ki 4: 6 Adoniram son of A—in charge of
Ne 11:17 and A son of Shammua, the son of

Abdeel

Jer 36:26 Shelemiah son of A to arrest Baruch

Abdi

1Ch 6:44 Ethan son of Kishi, the son of A,
2Ch 29:12 Kish son of A and Azariah son of
Ezr 10:26 Jehiel, A, Jeremoth and Elijah.

Abdiel

1Ch 5:15 Ahi son of A, the son of Guni, was

Abdomen

Nu 5:21 to waste away and your a to swell.
5:22 a swells and your thigh wastes away.
5:27 her a will swell and her thigh waste

Abdon

Jos 19:28 went to A, Rehob, Hammon and Kanah,
21:30 from the tribe of Asher, Mishal, A,
Jdg 12:13 After him, A son of Hillel, from
12:15 A son of Hillel died, and was buried
1Ch 6:74 of Asher they received Mashal, A,
8:23 A, Zicri, Hanan,
8:30 his firstborn son was A, followed by
9:36 his firstborn son was A, followed by
2Ch 34:20 Ahikam son of Shaphan, A son of

Abednego

Formerly Azariah; member of Jewish nobility taken to Babylon with Daniel, Meshach and Shadrach (Da 1:3–7). Refused unclean food (Da 1:8–16); appointed as administrator (Da 2:49). Refused to worship golden image; kept safe in fiery furnace (Da 3).

Da 1: 7 Mishael, Meshach; and to Azariah, A.
2:49 Meshach and A administrators over
3:12 Meshach and A—who pay no attention
3:13 summoned Shadrach, Meshach and A.
3:14 "Is it true, Shadrach, Meshach and A,
3:16 Shadrach, Meshach and A replied to
3:19 Meshach and A, and his attitude
3:20 Meshach and A and throw them into
3:22 who took up Shadrach, Meshach and A,
3:26 "Shadrach, Meshach and A, servants
3:26 Meshach and A came out of the fire,
3:28 Meshach and A, who has sent his
3:29 Meshach and A be cut into pieces and
3:30 and A in the province of Babylon.

Abel

Second son of Adam. Shepherd (Ge 4:2); offered sacrifice acceptable to God (Ge 4:4; Heb 11:4); killed by his brother Cain (Ge 4:8).

Ge 4: 2 she gave birth to his brother A
4: 2 Now A kept flocks, and Cain worked

Ge 4: 4 A brought fat portions from some of
4: 4 with favour on A and his offering,
4: 8 Cain said to his brother A, "Let's
4: 8 his brother A and killed him.
4: 9 to Cain, "Where is your brother A?"
4:25 place of A, since Cain killed him."
2Sa 20:18 answer at A,' and that settled it.
Mt 23:35 from the blood of righteous A to the
Lk 11:51 from the blood of A to the blood of
Heb 11: 4 By faith A offered God a better
12:24 a better word than the blood of A.

Abel Beth Maacah

2Sa 20:14 all the tribes of Israel to A
20:15 Joab came and besieged Sheba in A.
1Ki 15:20 He conquered Ijon, Dan, A and all
2Ki 15:29 Ijon, A, Janoah, Kedesh and Hazor.

Abel Keramim

Jdg 11:33 vicinity of Minnith, as far as A.

Abel Maim

2Ch 16: 4 They conquered Ijon, Dan, A and all

Abel Meholah

Jdg 7:22 far as the border of A near Tabbath.
1Ki 4:12 Beth Shan to A across to Jokmeam;
19:16 from A to succeed you as prophet.

Abel Mizraim

Ge 50:11 place near the Jordan is called A.

Abel Shittim

Nu 33:49 the Jordan from Beth Jeshimoth to A.

Abhor (Abhorred, Abhorrent, Abhors)

Lev 26:11 among you, and I will not a you.
26:15 if you reject my decrees and a my
26:30 of your idols, and I will a you.
26:44 I will not reject them or a them so
Dt 7:26 Utterly a and detest it, for it is
23: 7 Do not a an Edomite, for he is your
23: 7 Do not a an Egyptian, because you
Ps 26: 5 I a the assembly of evildoers and
119:163 I hate and a falsehood but I love
139:21 and a those who rise up against you?
Am 6: 8 "I a the pride of Jacob and detest
Ro 2:22 You who a idols, do you rob temples?

Abhorred (Abhor)

Lev 20:23 they did all these things, I a them.
26:43 rejected my laws and a my decrees.
Ps 106:40 his people and a his inheritance.
Isa 49: 7 was despised and a by the nation,

Abhorrent (Abhor)

Jer 15: 4 I will make them a to all the
24: 9 I will make them a and an offence to
29:18 plague and will make them a to all
34:17 a to all the kingdoms of the earth.

Abhors (Abhor)

Ps 5: 6 and deceitful men the LORD a.
Pr 11: 1 The LORD a dishonest scales, but

Abi-Albon

2Sa 23:31 A the Arbathite, Azmaveth the

Abiasaph

Ex 6:24 of Korah were Assir, Elkanah and A.

Abiathar

Son of Ahimelech; priest in time of Saul and David. Escaped Saul's massacre of priests who helped David (1Sa 22:20–23). Faithful to David (1Sa 23:6; 2Sa 15:24–29;). Supported Adonijah (1Ki 1:7); deposed by Solomon (1Ki 2:26).

1Sa 22:20 A, son of Ahimelech son of Ahitub,
22:22 David said to A: "That day, when
23: 6 (Now A son of Ahimelech had brought
23: 9 to A the priest, "Bring the ephod.
30: 7 David said to A the priest, the son
1Sa 30: 7 me the ephod." A brought it to him,
2Sa 8:17 and Ahimelech son of A were priests;
15:24 They set down the ark of God, and A
15:27 son Ahimaaz and Jonathan son of A.
15:27 and A take your two sons with you.
15:29 Zadok and A took the ark of God back
15:35 Won't the priests Zadok and A be
15:36 son of A, are there with them.
17:15 Hushai told Zadok and A, the priests,
19:11 sent this message to Zadok and A,
20:25 Sheva was secretary; Zadok and A
1Ki 1: 7 of Zeruiah and with A the priest,
1:19 A the priest and Joab the commander
1:25 of the army and A the priest.
1:42 Jonathan son of A the priest arrived.
2:22 for him and for A the priest and
2:26 To A the priest the king said, "Go
2:27 Solomon removed A from the
2:35 replaced A with Zadok the priest.
4: 4 Zadok and A—priests;
1Ch 15:11 David summoned Zadok and A the
18:16 and Ahimelech son of A were priests;
24: 6 Ahimelech son of A and the heads of
27:34 by Jehoiada son of Benaiah and by A.
Mk 2:26 In the days of A the high priest, he

Abib

Ex 13: 4 Today, in the month of A, you are
23:15 appointed time in the month of A,
34:18 appointed time in the month of A,
Dt 16: 1 Observe the month of A and celebrate
16: 1 because in the month of A he brought

Abida

Ge 25: 4 Ephah, Epher, Hanoch, A and Eldaah.
1Ch 1:33 Ephah, Epher, Hanoch, A and Eldaah.

Abidan

Nu 1:11 from Benjamin, A son of Gideoni;
2:22 of Benjamin is A son of Gideoni.
7:60 On the ninth day A son of Gideoni,
7:65 the offering of A son of Gideoni.
10:24 A son of Gideoni was over the

Abiel

1Sa 9: 1 whose name was Kish son of A, the
14:51 Abner's father Ner were sons of A.
1Ch 11:32 Hurai from the ravines of Gaash, A

Abiezer (Abiezrite, Abiezrites)

Jos 17: 2 people of Manasseh—the clans of A,
Jdg 8: 2 than the full grape harvest of A?
2Sa 23:27 A from Anathoth, Mebunnai the
1Ch 7:18 gave birth to Ishhod, A and Mahlah.
11:28 Ikkesh from Tekoa, A from Anathoth,
27:12 The ninth, for the ninth month, was A

Abiezrite (Abiezer)

Jdg 6:11 Ophrah that belonged to Joash the A,

Abiezrites (Abiezer)

Jdg 6:24 day it stands in Ophrah of the A.
6:34 summoning the A to follow him.
8:32 his father Joash in Ophrah of the A.

Abigail

1. David's sister (1Ch 2:16-17). **2.** Wife of Nabal (1Sa 25:3); entreated David to spare his life (1Sa 25:14–35). Married David after Nabal's death (1Sa 25:40–43); mother of Kiliab (Daniel) (2Sa 3:3; 1Ch 3:1).

1Sa 25: 3 was Nabal and his wife's name was A.
25:14 of the servants told Nabal's wife A:
25:18 A lost no time. She took two hundred
25:23 A saw David, she quickly got off her
25:32 David said to A, "Praise be to the
25:36 A went to Nabal, he was in the house
25:39 to A, asking her to become his wife.
25:40 went to Carmel and said to A,
25:42 A quickly got on a donkey and,
27: 3 and A of Carmel, the widow of Nabal.
30: 5 and A, the widow of Nabal of Carmel.
2Sa 2: 2 and A, the widow of Nabal of Carmel.
3: 3 his second, Kileab the son of A the
2Sa 17:25 an Israelite who had married A, the
1Ch 2:16 Their sisters were Zeruiah and A.
2:17 A was the mother of Amasa, whose
3: 1 Daniel the son of A of Carmel;

Abihail

Nu 3:35 Merarite clans was Zuriel son of A;
1Ch 2:29 Abishur's wife was named A, who bore
5:14 These were the sons of A son of Huri,
2Ch 11:18 A, the daughter of Jesse's son Eliab.
Est 2:15 the daughter of his uncle A) to go
9:29 Queen Esther, daughter of A, along

Abihu

Ex 6:23 Nadab and A, Eleazar and Ithamar.
24: 1 you and Aaron, Nadab and A, and
24: 9 Moses and Aaron, Nadab and A, and
28: 1 with his sons Nadab and A, Eleazar
Lev 10: 1 Aaron's sons Nadab and A took their
Nu 3: 2 and A, Eleazar and Ithamar.
3: 4 Nadab and A, however, fell dead
26:60 Aaron was the father of Nadab and A,
26:61 Nadab and A died when they made an
1Ch 6: 3 The sons of Aaron: Nadab, A, Eleazar
24: 1 were Nadab, A, Eleazar and Ithamar.
24: 2 Nadab and A died before their father

Abihud

1Ch 8: 3 The sons of Bela were: Addar, Gera, A

Abijah (Abijah's)

1Sa 8: 2 the name of his second was A, and
1Ki 14: 1 At that time A son of Jeroboam
14:31 And A his son succeeded him as king.
15: 1 of Nebat, A became king of Judah,
15: 7 There was war between A and Jeroboam.
15: 8 A rested with his fathers and was
2Ki 18: 2 His mother's name was A daughter of
1Ch 2:24 A the wife of Hezron bore him Ashhur
3:10 Solomon's son was Rehoboam, A his
6:28 the firstborn and A the second son.
7: 8 Jeremoth, A, Anathoth and Alemeth.
24:10 seventh to Hakkoz, the eighth to A,
2Ch 11:20 who bore him A, Attai, Ziza and
11:22 Rehoboam appointed A son of Maacah
12:16 And A his son succeeded him as king.
13: 1 of Jeroboam, A became king of Judah,
13: 2 There was war between A and Jeroboam.
13: 3 A went into battle with a force of
13: 4 A stood on Mount Zemaraim, in the
13:15 and all Israel before A and Judah.
13:17 A and his men inflicted heavy losses
13:19 A pursued Jeroboam and took from him
13:20 regain power during the time of A.
13:21 A grew in strength. He married
14: 1 A rested with his fathers and was
29: 1 His mother's name was A daughter of
Ne 10: 7 Meshullam, A, Mijamin,
12: 4 Iddo, Ginnethon, A,
Mt 1: 7 father of A, A the father of Asa,
Lk 1: 5 to the priestly division of A;

Abijah's (Abijah)

1Ki 15: 6 Jeroboam throughout ⌊A⌋ lifetime
15: 7 for the other events of A reign, and
2Ch 13:22 The other events of A reign, what he
Ne 12:17 of A, Zicri; of Miniamin's and of

Abilene

Lk 3: 1 and Lysanias tetrarch of A—

Ability (Able)

Ge 47: 6 of any among them with special a,
Ex 31: 3 with skill, a and knowledge in all
35:31 with skill, a and knowledge in all
35:34 tribe of Dan, the a to teach others.
36: 1 a to know how to carry out all the
36: 2 person to whom the LORD had given a
Dt 8:18 for it is he who gives you the a to
Ezr 2:69 According to their a they gave to
Da 5:12 and also the a to interpret dreams,
Mt 25:15 one talent, each according to his a.
Ac 8:19 said, "Give me also this a so that
11:29 each according to his a, decided to

2Co 1: 8 far beyond our **a** to endure, so that
8: 3 were able, and even beyond their **a**.

Abimael

Ge 10:28 Obal, **A**, Sheba,
1Ch 1:22 Obal, **A**, Sheba,

Abimelech (Abimelech's)

1. King of Gerar in time of Abraham. Took Sarah, Abraham's wife, thinking she was his sister (Ge 20). Made covenant with Abraham (Ge 21:22–34). **2.** King of Gerar in time of Isaac. Rebuked Isaac for deceit (Ge 26:8–10); later made covenant with him (Ge 26:26–31). **3.** Son of Gideon (Jdg 8:31). Murdered brothers (Jdg 9:5); crowned king at Shechem (Jdg 9:6). Death (Jdg 9:54).

Ge 20: 2 Then **A** king of Gerar sent for Sarah
20: 3 God came to **A** in a dream one night
20: 4 Now **A** had not gone near her, so he
20: 8 Early the next morning **A** summoned
20: 9 **A** called Abraham in and said, "What
20:10 **A** asked Abraham, "What was your
20:14 **A** brought sheep and cattle and male
20:15 **A** said, "My land is before you; live
20:17 and God healed **A**, his wife and his
21:22 At that time **A** and Phicol the
21:25 Abraham complained to **A** about a well
21:26 **A** said, "I don't know who has done
21:27 to **A**, and the two men made a treaty.
21:29 **A** asked Abraham, "What is the
21:32 **A** and Phicol the commander of his
26: 1 **A** king of the Philistines in Gerar.
26: 8 **A** king of the Philistines looked
26: 9 **A** summoned Isaac and said, "She is
26:10 **A** said, "What is this you have done
26:11 **A** gave orders to all the people:
26:16 **A** said to Isaac, "Move away from us;
26:26 Meanwhile, **A** had come to him from
Jdg 8:31 bore him a son, whom he named **A**.
9: 1 **A** son of Jerub-Baal went to his
9: 3 **A**, for they said, "He is our brother.
9: 4 and **A** used it to hire reckless
9: 6 pillar in Shechem to crown **A** king.
9:16 in good faith when you made **A** king,
9:18 and made **A**, the son of his slave
9:19 may **A** be your joy, and may you be
9:20 let fire come out from **A** and consume
9:20 and Beth Millo, and consume **A**!"
9:21 he was afraid of his brother **A**.
9:22 After **A** had governed Israel for
9:23 God sent an evil spirit between **A**
9:23 who acted treacherously against **A**.
9:24 might be avenged on their brother **A**
9:25 by, and this was reported to **A**.
9:27 eating and drinking, they cursed **A**.
9:28 Gaal son of Ebed said, "Who is **A**,
9:28 father! Why should we serve **A**?
9:29 to **A**, 'Call out your whole army!'"
9:31 Under cover he sent messengers to **A**,
9:34 **A** and all his troops set out by
9:35 entrance to the city gate just as **A**
9:38 'Who is **A** that we should be subject
9:39 citizens of Shechem and fought **A**.
9:40 **A** chased him, and many fell wounded
9:41 **A** stayed in Arumah, and Zebul drove
9:42 fields, and this was reported to **A**.
9:44 **A** and the companies with him rushed
9:45 All that day **A** pressed his attack
9:47 **A** heard that they had assembled
9:49 the men cut branches and followed **A**.
9:50 Next **A** went to Thebez and besieged
9:52 **A** went to the tower and stormed it.
9:55 the Israelites saw that **A** was dead,
9:56 Thus God repaid the wickedness that **A**
10: 1 After the time of **A** a man of
2Sa 11:21 Who killed **A** son of Jerub-Besheth?
Ps 34: T pretended to be insane before **A**,

Abimelech's (Abimelech)

Ge 20:18 closed up every womb in **A** household
21:25 of water that **A** servants had seized.

Abinadab (Abinadab's)

1Sa 16: 8 Jesse called **A** and made him pass in
17:13 second, **A**; and the third, Shammah.
31: 2 his sons Jonathan, **A** and Malki-Shua.
2Sa 6: 3 house of **A**, which was on the hill.
6: 3 sons of **A**, were guiding the new
1Ch 2:13 second son was **A**, the third Shimea,
8:33 Jonathan, Malki-Shua, **A** and Esh-Baal.
9:39 Jonathan, Malki-Shua, **A** and Esh-Baal.
10: 2 his sons Jonathan, **A** and Malki-Shua.

Abinadab's (Abinadab)

1Sa 7: 1 They took it to **A** house on the hill
1Ch 13: 7 They moved the ark of God from **A**

Abinoam

Jdg 4: 6 She sent for Barak son of **A** from
4:12 they told Sisera that Barak son of **A**
5: 1 and Barak son of **A** sang this song:
5:12 captive your captives, O son of **A**.'

Abiram

Nu 16: 1 certain Reubenites—Dathan and **A**,
16:12 Moses summoned Dathan and **A**, the
16:24 the tents of Korah, Dathan and **A**.'"
16:25 Moses got up and went to Dathan and **A**
16:27 the tents of Korah, Dathan and **A**.
16:27 Dathan and **A** had come out and were
26: 9 of Eliab were Nemuel, Dathan and **A**.
26: 9 The same Dathan and **A** were the
Dt 11: 6 what he did to Dathan and **A**, sons of
1Ki 16:34 at the cost of his firstborn son **A**,
Ps 106:17 Dathan; it buried the company of **A**.

Abishag

1Ki 1: 3 for a beautiful girl and found **A**,
1:15 **A** the Shunammite was attending him.
2:17 me **A** the Shunammite as my wife."
2:21 she said, "Let **A** the Shunammite be
2:22 "Why do you request **A** the Shunammite

Abishai

Son of David's sister, Zeruiah; brother of Joab (1Sa 26:6; 1Ch 2:16). One of David's leading warriors (1Ch 11:15–21; 18:12; 2Sa 18:2; 20:6). Wanted to kill Saul (1Sa 26:7–8), Shimei (2Sa 16:9; 19:21).

1Sa 26: 6 the Hittite and **A** son of Zeruiah,
26: 6 "I'll go with you," said **A**.
26: 7 David and **A** went to the army by
26: 8 **A** said to David, "Today God has
26: 9 David said to **A**, "Don't destroy him!
2Sa 2:18 were there: Joab, **A** and Asahel.
2:24 Joab and **A** pursued Abner, and as the
3:30 (Joab and his brother **A** murdered
10:10 under the command of **A** his brother
10:14 before **A** and went inside the city.
16: 9 **A** son of Zeruiah said to the king,
16:11 David then said to **A** and all his
18: 2 a third under Joab's brother **A** son
18: 5 The king commanded Joab, **A** and Ittai,
18:12 king commanded you and **A** and Ittai,
19:21 **A** son of Zeruiah said, "Shouldn't
20: 6 David said to **A**, "Now Sheba son of
20: 7 went out under the command of **A**.
20:10 **A** pursued Sheba son of Bicri.
21:17 **A** son of Zeruiah came to David's
23:18 **A** the brother of Joab son of Zeruiah
1Ch 2:16 three sons were **A**, Joab and Asahel.
11:20 **A** the brother of Joab was chief of
18:12 **A** son of Zeruiah struck down
19:11 under the command of **A** his brother,
19:15 brother **A** and went inside the city.

Abishalom

1Ki 15: 2 name was Maacah daughter of **A**.
15:10 name was Maacah daughter of **A**.

Abishua

1Ch 6: 4 Phinehas, Phinehas the father of **A**,
6: 5 **A** the father of Bukki, Bukki the
6:50 son, Phinehas his son, **A** his son,
8: 4 **A**, Naaman, Ahoah,
Ezr 7: 5 the son of **A**, the son of Phinehas,

Abishur (Abishur's)

1Ch 2:28 The sons of Shammai: Nadab and **A**.

Abishur's (Abishur)

1Ch 2:29 **A** wife was named Abihail, who bore

Abital

2Sa 3: 4 the fifth, Shephatiah the son of **A**;
1Ch 3: 3 the fifth, Shephatiah the son of **A**;

Abitub

1Ch 8:11 By Hushim he had **A** and Elpaal.

Abiud

Mt 1:13 Zerubbabel the father of **A**, **A** the

Ablaze

Dt 5:23 while the mountain was **a** with fire,
9:15 mountain while it was **a** with fire.
Job 41:21 His breath sets coals **a**, and flames
Ps 83:14 or a flame sets the mountains **a**,
Isa 9:18 it sets the forest thickets **a**, so
30:33 of burning sulphur, sets it **a**.
33:12 cut thornbushes they will be set **a**."
43: 2 the flames will not set you **a**.
50:11 and of the torches you have set **a**.
64: 2 fire sets twigs **a** and causes water
Da 7: 9 fire, and its wheels were all **a**.
Rev 8: 8 all **a**, was thrown into the sea.

Able (Ability)

Ge 13: 6 they were not **a** to stay together.
14:23 be **a** to say, 'I made Abram rich.'
45: 3 brothers were not **a** to answer him,
Ex 7:18 will not be **a** to drink its water.'"
18:23 you will be **a** to stand the strain,
Lev 26:26 ten women will be **a** to bake your
26:37 be **a** to stand before your enemies.
Nu 1: 3 more who are **a** to serve in the army.
1:20 who were **a** to serve in the army were
1:22 **a** to serve in the army were counted
1:24 who were **a** to serve in the army were
1:26 who were **a** to serve in the army were
1:28 who were **a** to serve in the army were
1:30 who were **a** to serve in the army were
1:32 who were **a** to serve in the army were
1:34 who were **a** to serve in the army were
1:36 who were **a** to serve in the army were
1:38 who were **a** to serve in the army were
1:40 who were **a** to serve in the army were
1:42 who were **a** to serve in the army were
1:45 were **a** to serve in Israel's army
5:28 and will be **a** to have children.
14:16 'The LORD was not **a** to bring these
22: 6 Perhaps then I will be **a** to defeat
22:11 Perhaps then I will be **a** to fight
22:37 me? Am I really not **a** to reward you?"
26: 2 **a** to serve in the army of Israel."
Dt 7:24 No-one will be **a** to stand up against
9:28 'Because the LORD was not **a** to take
11:25 No man will be **a** to stand against
31: 2 and I am no longer **a** to lead you.
Jos 1: 5 No-one will be **a** to stand up against
10: 8 of them will be **a** to withstand you."
17:12 Yet the Manassites were not **a** to
22:27 will not be **a** to say to ours,
23: 9 no-one has been **a** to withstand you.
24:19 "You are not **a** to serve the LORD.
Jdg 2:14 they were no longer **a** to resist.
8: 3 What was I **a** to do compared to you?"
1Sa 17: 9 If he is **a** to fight and kill me, we
17:33 Saul replied, "You are not **a** to go
1Ki 3: 9 For who is **a** to govern this great
2Ki 2:16 "we your servants have fifty **a** men.
9:37 be **a** to say, 'This is Jezebel.'"
18:35 has been **a** to save his land from me?
1Ch 9:13 They were **a** men, responsible for
12: 2 they were armed with bows and were **a**
12: 8 **a** to handle the shield and spear.
26: 7 Elihu and Semakiah were also **a** men.
26: 9 who were **a** men—18 in all.
26:30 his relatives—seventeen hundred **a**
26:32 who were **a** men and heads of families,
29:14 that we should be **a** to give as
2Ch 1:10 for who is **a** to govern this great
2: 6 who is **a** to build a temple for him,
13: 3 hundred thousand **a** fighting men,

2Ch 13: 3 eight hundred thousand **a** troops.
13:17 casualties among Israel's **a** men.
20:37 and were not **a** to set sail to trade.
25: 5 **a** to handle the spear and shield.
30: 3 They had not been **a** to celebrate it
32:13 **a** to deliver their land from my hand?
32:14 been **a** to save his people from me?
32:15 has been **a** to deliver his people from
Ne 8: 2 and all who were **a** to understand.
10:28 daughters who are **a** to understand—
11: 6 in Jerusalem totalled 468 **a** men.
11:14 his associates, who were **a** men—128
Job 41:10 Who then is **a** to stand against me?
Ps 36:12 fallen—thrown down, not **a** to rise!
Isa 36:20 has been **a** to save his land from me?
Eze 7:19 Their silver and gold will not be **a**
Da 2:26 "Are you **a** to tell me what I saw in
2:47 you were **a** to reveal this mystery."
3:15 be **a** to rescue you from my hand?"
3:17 the God we serve is **a** to save us
4:37 who walk in pride he is **a** to humble.
5:16 Now I have heard that you are **a** to
6:20 **a** to rescue you from the lions?"
11:16 will be **a** to stand against him.
11:25 but he will not be **a** to stand
Hos 5:13 But he is not **a** to cure you, not **a**
Zep 1:18 their silver nor their gold will be **a**
Mt 9:28 "Do you believe that I am **a** to do
18:25 Since he was not **a** to pay, the
26:61 am **a** to destroy the temple of God
Mk 3:20 disciples were not even **a** to eat.
6:19 to kill him. But she was not **a** to,
Lk 1:20 you will be silent and not **a** to speak
8:19 but they were not **a** to get near him
13:24 try to enter and will not be **a** to.
14:29 and is not **a** to finish it,
14:30 to build and was not **a** to finish.'
14:31 consider whether he is **a** with ten
14:32 If he is not **a**, he will send a
21:15 will be **a** to resist or contradict.
21:36 and pray that you may be **a** to escape
21:36 **a** to stand before the Son of Man."
Jn 18:28 wanted to be **a** to eat the Passover.
Ac 5:39 if it is from God, you will not be **a**
15:10 nor our fathers have been **a** to bear?
19:40 In that case we would not be **a** to
22:13 that very moment I was **a** to see him.
24: 8 you will be **a** to learn the truth
27:16 **a** to make the lifeboat secure.
Ro 8:39 will be **a** to separate us from the
11:23 for God is **a** to graft them in again.
12: 2 Then you will be **a** to test and
14: 4 for the Lord is **a** to make him stand.
16:25 Now to him who is **a** to establish you
1Co 12:28 those **a** to help others, those with
2Co 8: 3 gave as much **a** they were **a**, and even
9: 8 God is **a** to make all grace abound to
Eph 3: 4 In reading this, then, you will be **a**
3:20 Now to him who is **a** to do
6:13 you may be **a** to stand your ground,
Php 1:10 that you may be **a** to discern what is
1Ti 3: 2 respectable, hospitable, **a** to teach,
2Ti 1:12 am convinced that he is **a** to guard
2:24 everyone, **a** to teach, not resentful.
3: 7 always learning but never **a** to
3:15 which are **a** to make you wise for
Heb 2:18 he is **a** to help those who are being
3:19 we see that they were not **a** to enter,
5: 2 He is **a** to deal gently with those
7:25 Therefore he is **a** to save completely
9: 9 sacrifices being offered were not **a**
Jas 3: 2 **a** to keep his whole body in check.
4:12 one who is **a** to save and destroy.
2Pe 1:15 be **a** to remember these things.
Jude :24 To him who is **a** to keep you from
Rev 5: 5 He is **a** to open the scroll and its

Able-bodied

Dt 3:18 But all your **a** men, armed for battle,
2Sa 24: 9 **a** men who could handle a sword,
1Ch 5:18 **a** men who could handle shield and

Abner (Abner's)

Saul's cousin and commander of his army (1Sa 14:50; 17:55). Made Ishbosheth king after Saul's death (2Sa 2:8-9). Killed Asahel, Joab's brother (2Sa 2:18-25). Defected to David (2Sa 3:6-21). Murdered by Joab and Abishai to avenge Asahel's death (2Sa 3:26-30).

1Sa 14:50 of Saul's army was **A** son of Ner,
17:55 he said to **A**, commander of the army,
17:55 "**A**, whose son is that young man?" **A**
17:57 **A** took him and brought him before
20:25 **A** sat next to Saul, but David's place
26: 5 He saw where Saul and **A** son of Ner,
26: 7 **A** and the soldiers were lying round
26:14 He called out to the army and to **A**
26:14 "Aren't you going to answer me, **A**?" **A**
2Sa 2: 8 Meanwhile, **A** son of Ner, the
2:12 **A** son of Ner, together with the men
2:14 **A** said to Joab, "Let's have some of
2:17 and **A** and the men of Israel were
2:19 He chased **A**, turning neither to the
2:20 **A** looked behind him and asked, "Is
2:21 **A** said to him, "Turn aside to the
2:22 Again **A** warned Asahel, "Stop chasing
2:23 so **A** thrust the butt of his spear
2:24 Joab and Abishai pursued **A**, and as
2:25 the men of Benjamin rallied behind **A**.
2:26 **A** called out to Joab, "Must the
2:29 All that night **A** and his men marched
2:30 Joab returned from pursuing **A** and
2:31 360 Benjamites who were with **A**.
3: 6 **A** had been strengthening his own
3: 7 And Ish-Bosheth said to **A**, "Why did
3: 8 **A** was very angry because of what
3: 9 May God deal with **A**, be it ever so
3:11 to **A**, because he was afraid of him.
3:12 **A** sent messengers on his behalf to
3:16 Then **A** said to him, "Go back home!"
3:17 **A** conferred with the elders of
3:19 **A** also spoke to the Benjamites in
3:20 **A**, who had twenty men with him, came
3:21 **A** said to David, "Let me go at once
3:21 sent **A** away, and he went in peace.
3:22 But **A** was no longer with David in
3:23 he was told that **A** son of Ner had
3:24 have you done? Look, **A** came to you.
3:25 You know **A** son of Ner; he came to
3:26 David and sent messengers after **A**,
3:27 Now when **A** returned to Hebron, Joab
3:28 the blood of **A** son of Ner.
3:30 his brother Abishai murdered **A**
3:31 and walk in mourning in front of **A**.
3:32 They buried **A** in Hebron, and the
3:33 The king sang this lament for **A**:
3:33 **A** have died as the lawless die?
3:37 part in the murder of **A** son of Ner.
4: 1 Ish-Bosheth son of Saul heard that **A**
1Ki 2: 5 **A** son of Ner and Amasa son of Jether.
2:32 Both of them—**A** son of Ner,
1Ch 26:28 **A** son of Ner and Joab son of Zeruiah,
27:21 over Benjamin: Jaasiel son of **A**;

Abner's (Abner)

1Sa 14:51 Saul's father Kish and **A** father Ner
2Sa 3:32 and the king wept aloud at **A** tomb.
4:12 and buried it in **A** tomb at Hebron.

Abnormally

1Co 15: 8 to me also, as to one **a** born.

Aboard (Board)

Eze 27: 8 men, O Tyre, were **a** as your seamen.
Jnh 1: 3 After paying the fare, he went **a** and
Jn 21:11 Simon Peter climbed **a** and dragged
Ac 20:13 where we were going to take Paul **a**.
20:14 he met us at Assos, we took him **a**
21: 6 **a** the ship, and they returned home.
27:17 the men had hoisted it **a**, they

Abode

Job 38:19 "What is the way to the **a** of light?
Isa 33:20 a peaceful **a**, a tent that will not

Abolish (Abolished, Abolishing)

Da 11:31 and will **a** the daily sacrifice.
Hos 2:18 Bow and sword and battle I will **a**
Mt 5:17 "Do not think that I have come to **a**
5:17 come to **a** them but to fulfil them.

Abolished (Abolish)

Da 12:11 time that the daily sacrifice is **a**
Gal 5:11 the offence of the cross has been **a**.

Abolishing (Abolish)

Eph 2:15 by **a** in his flesh the law with its

Abominable

Isa 66:17 rats and other **a** things—they will
Jer 32:34 They set up their **a** idols in the
Rev 17: 4 filled with **a** things and the filth

Abomination that causes desolation

Da 9:27; 11:31; 12:11; Mt 24:15; Mk 13:14

Abominations (Abominable, *Abomination that causes desolation*)

Pr 26:25 him, for seven **a** fill his heart.
Isa 66: 3 and their souls delight in their **a**;
Rev 17: 5 AND OF THE **A** OF THE EARTH.

Abound (Abounding, Abounds)

2Ki 9:22 of your mother Jezebel **a**?"
Ps 4: 7 when their grain and new wine **a**.
72: 7 will **a** till the moon is no more.
72:16 Let corn **a** throughout the land; on
2Co 9: 8 God is able to make all grace **a** to
9: 8 need, you will **a** in every good work.
Php 1: 9 that your love may **a** more and more

Abounding (Abound)

Ex 34: 6 anger, **a** in love and faithfulness,
Nu 14:18 'The LORD is slow to anger, **a** in
Dt 33:23 "Naphtali is **a** with the favour of
Ne 9:17 slow to anger and **a** in love.
Ps 86: 5 **a** in love to all who call to you.
86:15 anger, **a** in love and faithfulness.
103: 8 gracious, slow to anger, **a** in love.
Pr 8:24 there were no springs **a** with water;
Joel 2:13 slow to anger and **a** in love, and he
Jnh 4: 2 slow to anger and **a** in love, a God

Abounds (Abound)

Hab 1: 3 me; there is strife, and conflict **a**.

Abraham (Abraham's, Abram, Abram's, *Father Abraham, God of Abraham*)

Formerly Abram ("exalted father"). Descendant of Shem and son of Terah (Ge 11:10–27); married to Sarah (Ge 11:29). With Terah, travelled from Ur to Haran. Obeyed God's call to continue journey to Canaan (Ge 12:1–5). In Egypt (Ge 12:10), passed Sarah off as his sister (Ge 12: 11–20). Divided the land with his nephew, Lot (Ge 13:5–17); settled at Hebron (Ge 13:18). Rescued Lot (Ge 14:1–16); blessed by Melchizedek (Ge 14:18–20). Name changed to Abraham ("father of many") (Ge 17:5; Ne 9:7). Father of Ishmael by Hagar (Ge 16). Entertained angelic visitors (Ge 18:1–8); promised a son by Sarah (Ge 18:9–15; 17:16). Pleaded for Sodom (Ge 18:22–32). In Gerar (Ge 20:1), passed Sarah off as his sister (Ge 20:2–18). Father of Isaac (Ge 21:1–7); dismissed Hagar and Ishmael (Ge 21:8–14). Made treaty with Abimelech (Ge 21:22–34). Tested by God's command to sacrifice Isaac (Ge 22). Secured wife for Isaac (Ge 24). Death (Ge 25:7–11). God's covenant with (Ge 12:1–3; 15; 17; 22:15–18; Ex 2:24; Lk 1:72–73; Heb 6:13–15). Example of faith (Heb 11:8–12); faith credited as righteousness (Ge 15:6; Ro 4:3; Gal 3:6–9). Described as father of God's people (Isa 51:2; Ac 13:26; Gal 3:26–29); God's servant (Ge 26:24); God's friend (2Ch 20:7; Isa 41:8; Jas 2:23).

Ge 17: 5 called Abram; your name will be **A**,
17: 9 God said to **A**, "As for you, you must
17:15 God also said to **A**, "As for Sarai
17:17 **A** fell face down; he laughed and
17:18 **A** said to God, "If only Ishmael
17:22 he had finished speaking with **A**, God
17:23 On that very day **A** took his son
17:24 **A** was ninety-nine years old when he
17:26 **A** and his son Ishmael were both
18: 1 The LORD appeared to **A** near the
18: 2 **A** looked up and saw three men
18: 6 **A** hurried into the tent to Sarah.

Ge 18:11 A and Sarah were already old and
18:13 the LORD said to A, "Why did Sarah
18:16 and A walked along with them to see
18:17 the LORD said, "Shall I hide from A
18:18 A will surely become a great and
18:19 for A what he has promised him."
18:22 A remained standing before the LORD.
18:23 A approached him and said: "Will you
18:27 A spoke up again: "Now that I have
18:31 A said, "Now that I have been so
18:33 the LORD had finished speaking with A
18:33 he left, and A returned home.
19:27 Early the next morning A got up and
19:29 he remembered A, and he brought Lot
20: 1 Now A moved on from there into the
20: 2 there A said of his wife Sarah, "She
20: 9 Abimelech called A in and said,
20:10 Abimelech asked A, "What was your
20:11 A replied, "I said to myself, 'There
20:14 female slaves and gave them to A,
20:17 A prayed to God, and God healed
21: 2 and bore a son to A in his old age,
21: 3 A gave the name Isaac to the son
21: 4 his son Isaac was eight days old, A
21: 5 A was a hundred years old when his
21: 7 she added, "Who would have said to A
21: 8 was weaned A held a great feast.
21: 9 Egyptian had borne to A was mocking,
21:10 she said to A, "Get rid of that
21:11 The matter distressed A greatly
21:14 Early the next morning A took some
21:22 commander of his forces said to A,
21:24 A said, "I swear it."
21:25 A complained to Abimelech about a
21:27 A brought sheep and cattle and gave
21:28 A set apart seven ewe lambs from the
21:29 Abimelech asked A, "What is the
21:33 A planted a tamarisk tree in
21:34 A stayed in the land of the
22: 1 Some time later God tested A. He
22: 1 He said to him, "A!" "Here I am," he
22: 3 Early the next morning A got up and
22: 4 On the third day A looked up and saw
22: 6 A took the wood for the burnt
22: 7 "Father?" "Yes, my son?" A replied.
22: 8 A answered, "God himself will
22: 9 A built an altar there and arranged
22:11 "A! A!" "Here I am," he replied.
22:13 A looked up and there in a thicket
22:14 A called that place The LORD Will
22:15 The angel of the LORD called to A
22:19 A returned to his servants, and they
22:19 And A stayed in Beersheba.
22:20 Some time later A was told, "Milcah
23: 2 and A went to mourn for Sarah and to
23: 3 A rose from beside his dead wife and
23: 5 The Hittites replied to A,
23: 7 A rose and bowed down before the
23:10 he replied to A in the hearing of
23:12 Again A bowed down before the people
23:14 Ephron answered A,
23:16 A agreed to Ephron's terms and
23:18 to A as his property in the presence
23:19 Afterwards A buried his wife Sarah
23:20 A by the Hittites as a burial site.
24: 1 A was now old and well advanced in
24: 6 not take my son back there," A said.
24: 9 under the thigh of his master A
24:12 "O LORD, God of my master A, give
24:12 and show kindness to my master A.
24:27 the God of my master A, who has not
24:42 'O LORD, God of my master A, if you
24:48 the God of my master A, who had led
25: 1 A took another wife, whose name was
25: 5 A left everything he owned to Isaac.
25: 7 Altogether, A lived a hundred and
25: 8 A breathed his last and died at a
25:10 the field A had bought from the
25:10 A was buried with his wife Sarah.
25:12 Hagar the Egyptian, bore to A.
25:19 A became the father of Isaac,
26: 5 A obeyed me and kept my requirements,
26:18 had stopped up after A died,
26:24 for the sake of my servant A."
28: 4 descendants the blessing given to A,
28: 4 an alien, the land God gave to A."

Ge 28: 9 and daughter of Ishmael son of A,
35:12 The land I gave to A and Isaac I
35:27 where A and Isaac had stayed.
48:15 whom my fathers A and Isaac walked,
48:16 the names of my fathers A and Isaac,
49:30 near Mamre in Canaan, which A bought
49:31 There A and his wife Sarah were
50:13 near Mamre, which A had bought as a
50:24 on oath to A, Isaac and Jacob."
Ex 2:24 with A, with Isaac and with Jacob.
6: 3 I appeared to A, to Isaac and to
6: 8 to give to A, to Isaac and to Jacob.
32:13 Remember your servants A, Isaac and
33: 1 to the land I promised on oath to A,
Lev 26:42 A, and I will remember the land.
Nu 32:11 on oath to A, Isaac and Jacob—
Dt 1: 8 he would give to your fathers—to A,
6:10 to A, Isaac and Jacob, to give
9: 5 your fathers, to A, Isaac and Jacob.
9:27 Remember your servants A, Isaac and
29:13 to your fathers, A, Isaac and Jacob.
30:20 to your fathers, A, Isaac and Jacob.
34: 4 is the land I promised on oath to A,
Jos 24: 2 including Terah the father of A and
2Ki 13:23 covenant with A, Isaac and Jacob.
1Ch 1:27 Abram (that is, A).
1:28 The sons of A: Isaac and Ishmael.
1:34 A was the father of Isaac. The sons
16:16 the covenant he made with A, the
29:18 O LORD, God of our fathers A, Isaac
2Ch 20: 7 to the descendants of A your friend?
Ne 9: 7 Ur of the Chaldeans and named him A.
Ps 105: 6 O descendants of A his servant,
105: 9 the covenant he made with A, the
105:42 holy promise given to his servant A.
Isa 29:22 who redeemed A, says to the house of
41: 8 you descendants of A my friend,
51: 2 look to A, your father, and to Sarah,
63:16 you are our Father, though A does
Jer 33:26 descendants of A, Isaac and Jacob.
Eze 33:24 'A was only one man, yet he
Mic 7:20 and show mercy to A, as you pledged
Mt 1: 1 the son of David, the son of A:
1: 2 A was the father of Isaac, Isaac the
1:17 generations in all from A to David,
3: 9 'We have A as our father.
3: 9 God can raise up children for A.
8:11 their places at the feast with A,
Lk 1:55 to A and his descendants for ever,
3: 8 'We have A as our father.
3: 8 God can raise up children for A.
3:34 the son of Isaac, the son of A, the
13:16 a daughter of A, whom Satan has kept
13:28 when you see A, Isaac and Jacob and
16:23 A far away, with Lazarus by his side.
16:25 "But A replied, 'Son, remember that
16:29 "A replied, 'They have Moses and the
19: 9 this man, too, is a son of A.
Jn 8:39 "A is our father," they answered.
8:39 "then you would do the things A did.
8:40 A did not do such things.
8:52 A died and so did the prophets,
8:57 said to him, "and you have seen A!"
8:58 "before A was born, I am!
Ac 3:25 He said to A, 'Through your
7: 5 though at that time A had no child.
7: 8 he gave A the covenant of
7: 8 And A became the father of Isaac and
7:16 placed in the tomb that A had bought
7:17 for God to fulfil his promise to A,
13:26 "Brothers, children of A, and you
Ro 4: 1 What then shall we say that A, our
4: 2 If, in fact, A was justified by
4: 3 "A believed God, and it was credited
4:13 was not through law that A and his
4:16 to those who are of the faith of A.
4:18 Against all hope, A in hope believed
11: 1 of A, from the tribe of Benjamin.
Gal 3: 6 Consider A: "He believed God, and it
3: 7 those who believe are children of A.
3: 8 the gospel in advance to A: "All
3: 9 along with A, the man of faith.
3:14 blessing given to A might come to the
3:16 The promises were spoken to A and to
3:18 gave it to A through a promise.
4:22 For it is written that A had two

Heb 6:13 God made his promise to A, since
6:15 after waiting patiently, A received
7: 1 He met A returning from the defeat
7: 2 A gave him a tenth of everything.
7: 4 A gave him a tenth of the plunder!
7: 5 their brothers are descended from A.
7: 6 yet he collected a tenth from A and
7: 9 the tenth, paid the tenth through A,
7:10 when Melchizedek met A, Levi was
11: 8 By faith A, when called to go to a
11:11 By faith A, even though he was past
11:17 By faith A, when God tested him,
11:19 A reasoned that God could raise the
Jas 2:21 Was not our ancestor A considered
2:23 "A believed God, and it was credited
1Pe 3: 6 like Sarah, who obeyed A and called

Abraham's (Abraham)

Ge 17:27 every male in A household, including
20:18 household because of A wife Sarah.
22:23 these eight sons to A brother Nahor.
24:15 who was the wife of A brother Nahor.
24:34 he said, "I am A servant.
24:52 A servant heard what they said, he
24:59 her nurse and A servant and his men.
25:11 After A death, God blessed his son
25:12 This is the account of A son Ishmael,
25:19 This is the account of A son Isaac.
26: 1 besides the earlier famine of A time
1Ch 1:32 The sons born to Keturah, A
Lk 16:22 the angels carried him to A side.
Jn 8:33 They answered him, "We are A
8:37 I know you are A descendants. Yet
8:39 "If you were A children," said Jesus,
Ro 4: 9 We have been saying that A faith was
4:16 may be guaranteed to all A offspring
9: 7 descendants are they all A children.
9: 8 who are regarded as A offspring.
2Co 11:22 Are they A descendants? So am I.
Gal 3:29 then you are A seed, and heirs
Heb 2:16 angels he helps, but A descendants.

Abram (Abraham)

Ge 11:26 the father of A, Nahor and Haran.
11:27 Terah became the father of A, Nahor
11:29 A and Nahor both married. The name
11:31 Terah took his son A, his grandson
11:31 the wife of his son A, and together
12: 1 The LORD had said to A, "Leave your
12: 4 A left, as the LORD had told him;
12: 4 A was seventy-five years old when he
12: 6 A travelled through the land as far
12: 7 The LORD appeared to A and said, "To
12: 9 A set out and continued towards the
12:10 and A went down to Egypt to live
12:14 A came to Egypt, the Egyptians saw
12:16 He treated A well for her sake, and A
12:18 Pharaoh summoned A. "What have you
12:20 Pharaoh gave orders about A to his
13: 1 A went up from Egypt to the Negev,
13: 2 A had become very wealthy in
13: 4 A called on the name of the LORD.
13: 5 Now Lot, who was moving about with A,
13: 8 A said to Lot, "Let's not have any
13:12 A lived in the land of Canaan, while
13:14 The LORD said to A after Lot had
13:18 A moved his tents and went to live
14:13 and reported this to A the Hebrew.
14:13 Now A was living near the great
14:13 Aner, all of whom were allied with A.
14:14 A heard that his relative had been
14:15 During the night A divided his men
14:17 After A returned from defeating
14:19 he blessed A, saying, "Blessed be A
14:20 A gave him a tenth of everything.
14:21 The king of Sodom said to A, "Give
14:22 A said to the king of Sodom, "I have
14:23 be able to say, 'I made A rich.'
15: 1 A in a vision: "Do not be afraid, A.
15: 2 A said, "O Sovereign LORD, what can
15: 3 A said, "You have given me no
15: 6 A believed the LORD, and he credited
15: 8 A said, "O Sovereign LORD, how can I
15:10 A brought all these to him, cut them
15:11 carcasses, but A drove them away.

Ge 15:12 the sun was setting, **A** fell into a
15:18 LORD made a covenant with **A** and said,
16: 2 she said to **A**, "The LORD has kept me
16: 2 **A** agreed to what Sarai said.
16: 3 after **A** had been living in Canaan
16: 5 Sarai said to **A**, "You are
16: 6 "Your servant is in your hands," **A**
16:15 Hagar bore **A** a son, and **A** gave the
16:16 **A** was eighty-six years old when
17: 1 **A** was ninety-nine years old, the
17: 3 **A** fell face down, and God said to
17: 5 No longer will you be called **A**; your
1Ch 1:27 **A** (that is, Abraham).
Ne 9: 7 "You are the LORD God, who chose **A**

Abram's (Abraham)

Ge 11:29 The name of **A** wife was Sarai, and
12:17 household because of **A** wife Sarai.
13: 7 quarrelling arose between **A** herdsmen
14:12 They also carried off **A** nephew Lot
16: 1 Now Sarai, **A** wife, had borne him no

Abroad

Ps 41: 6 then he goes out and spreads it **a**.
112: 9 He has scattered **a** his gifts to the
SS 4:16 that its fragrance may spread **a**.
2Co 9: 9 is written: "He has scattered **a** his

Abronah

Nu 33:34 They left Jotbathah and camped at **A**.
33:35 They left **A** and camped at Ezion

Absalom (Absalom's)

Son of David (2Sa 3:3). Had Amnon killed for raping his sister, Tamar (2Sa 13:23–29); fled from David (2Sa 13:37–38). Returned (2Sa 14:21–23); reconciled to David (2Sa 14:33). Conspired against David (2Sa 15:1–12); proclaimed king (2Sa 16:15–22). Defeated, killed by Joab (2Sa 18:6–10); mourned by David (2Sa 18:33).

2Sa 3: 3 **A** the son of Maacah daughter of
13: 1 beautiful sister of **A** son of David.
13:20 Her brother **A** said to her, "Has that
13:22 **A** never said a word to Amnon, either
13:24 **A** went to the king and said, "Your
13:25 Although **A** urged him, he still
13:26 **A** said, "If not, please let my
13:27 **A** urged him, so he sent with him
13:28 **A** ordered his men, "Listen! When
13:29 Absalom's men did to Amnon what **A**
13:30 "**A** has struck down all the king's
13:34 Meanwhile, **A** had fled. Now the man
13:37 **A** fled and went to Talmai son of
13:38 After **A** fled and went to Geshur, he
13:39 of the king longed to go to **A**,
14: 1 that the king's heart longed for **A**.
14:21 Go, bring back the young man **A**."
14:23 Joab went to Geshur and brought **A**
14:24 So **A** went to his own house and did
14:25 for his handsome appearance as **A**.
14:27 sons and a daughter were born to **A**.
14:28 **A** lived for two years in Jerusalem
14:29 **A** sent for Joab in order to send him
14:32 **A** said to Joab, "Look, I sent word
14:33 Then the king summoned **A**, and he
14:33 And the king kissed **A**.
15: 1 In the course of time, **A** provided
15: 2 **A** would call out to him, "What town
15: 3 **A** would say to him, "Look, your
15: 4 **A** would add, "If only I were
15: 5 **A** would reach out his hand, take
15: 6 **A** behaved in this way towards all
15: 7 At the end of four years, **A** said to
15:10 **A** sent secret messengers throughout
15:10 then say, '**A** is king in Hebron.'"
15:11 from Jerusalem had accompanied **A**.
15:12 While **A** was offering sacrifices, he
15:13 of the men of Israel are with **A**."
15:14 or none of us will escape from **A**.
15:19 us? Go back and stay with King **A**.
15:31 is among the conspirators with **A**.
15:34 you return to the city and say to **A**,
15:37 Jerusalem as **A** was entering the city.
16: 8 the kingdom over to your son **A**.
16:15 Meanwhile, **A** and all the men of
16:16 David's friend, went to **A** and said
16:17 **A** asked Hushai, "Is this the love
2Sa 16:18 Hushai said to **A**, "No, the one
16:20 **A** said to Ahithophel, "Give us your
16:22 they pitched a tent for **A** on the
16:23 That was how both David and **A**
17: 1 Ahithophel said to **A**, "I would
17: 4 This plan seemed good to **A** and to
17: 5 **A** said, "Summon also Hushai the
17: 6 Hushai came to him, **A** said,
17: 7 Hushai replied to **A**, "The advice
17: 9 among the troops who follow **A**.'
17:14 **A** and all the men of Israel said,
17:14 in order to bring disaster on **A**.
17:15 "Ahithophel has advised **A** and the
17:18 a young man saw them and told **A**. So
17:24 David went to Mahanaim, and **A**
17:25 **A** had appointed Amasa over the army
17:26 The Israelites and **A** camped in the
18: 5 with the young man **A** for my sake.
18: 5 **A** to each of the commanders.
18: 9 Now **A** happened to meet David's men.
18:10 just seen **A** hanging in an oak tree."
18:12 Protect the young man **A** for my sake.'
18:14 **A** was still alive in the oak tree.
18:15 **A**, struck him and killed him.
18:17 They took **A**, threw him into a big
18:18 During his life-time **A** had taken a
18:29 The king asked, "Is the young man **A**
18:32 "Is the young man **A** safe?" The
18:33 "O my son **A**! My son, my son **A**! If
18:33 instead of you—**A**, my son!"
19: 1 king is weeping and mourning for **A**."
19: 4 "O my son **A**! O **A**, my son, my son!
19: 6 I see that you would be pleased if **A**
19: 9 has fled the country because of **A**;
19:10 **A**, whom we anointed to rule over us,
20: 6 will do us more harm than **A** did.
1Ki 1: 6 handsome and was born next after **A**.)
2: 7 me when I fled from your brother **A**.
2:28 with Adonijah though not with **A**,
1Ch 3: 2 the third, **A** the son of Maacah
2Ch 11:20 he married Maacah daughter of **A**, who
11:21 Rehoboam loved Maacah daughter of **A**
Ps 3: T When he fled from his son **A**.

Absalom's (Absalom)

2Sa 13: 4 with Tamar, my brother **A** sister."
13:20 brother **A** house, a desolate woman.
13:23 Two years later, when **A**
13:29 **A** men did to Amnon what Absalom had
13:32 This has been **A** expressed intention
14:30 So **A** servants set the field on fire.
14:31 Joab did go to **A** house and he said
15:12 and **A** following kept on increasing.
17:20 **A** men came to the woman at the house,
18: 9 oak, **A** head got caught in the tree.
18:14 plunged them into **A** heart while
18:18 it is called **A** Monument to this day.

Absence (Absent)

Ac 24:17 "After an **a** of several years, I came
Php 1:27 you or only hear about you in my **a**,
2:12 but now much more in my **a**—continue

Absent (Absence)

Pr 10:19 words are many, sin is not **a**, but he
2Co 10:11 we are in our letters when we are **a**,
13: 2 I now repeat it while **a**: On my
13:10 I write these things when I am **a**,
Col 2: 5 For though I am **a** from you in body,

Absolute

1Ti 5: 2 women as sisters, with **a** purity.

Abstain (Abstained, Abstains)

Ex 19:15 **A** from sexual relations."
Nu 6: 3 he must **a** from wine and other
Ac 15:20 telling them to **a** from food polluted
15:29 You are to **a** from food sacrificed to
21:25 **a** from food sacrificed to idols,
1Ti 4: 3 order them to **a** from certain foods,
1Pe 2:11 to **a** from sinful desires, which war

Abstained (Abstain)

Ex 31:17 day he **a** from work and rested.'"

Abstains (Abstain)

Ro 14: 6 gives thanks to God; and he who **a**,

Abundance (Abundant)

Ge 27:28 an **a** of grain and new wine.
41:29 Seven years of great **a** are coming
41:30 Then all the **a** in Egypt will be
41:31 The **a** in the land will not be
41:34 Egypt during the seven years of **a**.
41:47 During the seven years of **a** the land
41:48 in those seven years of **a** in Egypt
41:53 The seven years of **a** in Egypt came
Dt 33:19 will feast on the **a** of the seas,
1Ch 29:16 O LORD our God, as for all this **a**
29:21 sacrifices in **a** for all Israel.
2Ch 29:35 There were burnt offerings in **a**,
Ne 9:25 olive groves and fruit trees in **a**.
Job 36:31 the nations and provides food in **a**.
Ps 36: 8 They feast in the **a** of your house;
65:11 and your carts overflow with **a**.
66:12 but you brought us to a place of **a**.
73:10 to them and drink up waters in **a**.
Pr 20:15 Gold there is, and rubies in **a**, but
Ecc 5:12 **a** of a rich man permits him no sleep.
Isa 7:22 of the **a** of the milk they give, he
30:33 with an **a** of fire and wood; the
33:23 Then an **a** of spoils will be divided
66:11 and delight in her overflowing **a**."
Jer 2:22 with soda and use an **a** of soap,
31:14 I will satisfy the priests with **a**,
40:12 an **a** of wine and summer fruit.
Mt 13:12 given more, and he will have an **a**.
25:29 given more, and he will have an **a**.
Lk 12:15 in the **a** of his possessions."
1Pe 1: 2 Grace and peace be yours in **a**.
2Pe 1: 2 Grace and peace be yours in **a**
Jude : 2 Mercy, peace and love be yours in **a**.

Abundant (Abundance, Abundantly)

Nu 24: 7 their seed will have **a** water.
Dt 28:11 The LORD will grant you **a** prosperity
32: 2 grass, like **a** rain on tender plants.
2Ch 11:23 He gave them **a** provisions and took
Ne 5:18 an **a** supply of wine of all kinds.
9:37 of our sins, its **a** harvest goes to
Est 1: 7 and the royal wine was **a**, in keeping
Job 36:28 and **a** showers fall on mankind.
Ps 68: 9 You gave **a** showers, O God; you
78:15 gave them water as **a** as the seas;
132:15 I will bless her with **a** provisions;
145: 7 They will celebrate your **a** goodness
Pr 12:11 He who works his land will have **a**
13:23 A poor man's field may produce **a**
14: 4 of an ox comes an **a** harvest.
28:19 He who works his land will have **a**
Isa 23:18 LORD, for **a** food and fine clothes.
Jer 33: 6 let them enjoy **a** peace and security.
33: 9 will tremble at the **a** prosperity and
Eze 17: 5 planted it like a willow by **a** water,
17: 8 had been planted in good soil by **a**
19:10 full of branches because of **a** water.
31: 5 long, spreading because of **a** waters.
31: 7 for its roots went down to **a** waters.
31: 9 I made it beautiful with **a** branches,
31:15 and its **a** waters were restrained.
32:13 **a** waters no longer to be stirred by
Da 4:12 fruit **a**, and on it was food for all.
4:21 with beautiful leaves and **a** fruit,
Joel 2:23 He sends you **a** showers, both autumn
Ro 5:17 receive God's **a** provision of grace

Abundantly (Abundant)

Ge 24:35 The LORD has blessed my master **a**,
Jos 17:14 and the LORD has blessed us **a**."
Ps 65: 9 land and water it; you enrich it **a**.
78:20 gushed out, and streams flowed **a**.
1Ti 1:14 of our Lord was poured out on me **a**,

Abuse (Abused, Abusive, Abusively)

1Sa 31: 4 come and run me through and **a** me.
1Ch 10: 4 fellows will come and **a** me.
Ps 55:10 walls; malice and **a** are within it.
Pr 9: 7 rebukes a wicked man incurs **a**.
1Pe 4: 4 dissipation, and they heap **a** on you.

Abused (Abuse)
Jdg 19:25 and they raped her and a her

Abusive (Abuse)
Ac 18: 6 the Jews opposed Paul and became a,
2Ti 3: 2 lovers of money, boastful, proud, a,

Abusively (Abuse)
Ac 13:45 a against what Paul was saying.
Jude :10 Yet these men speak a against

Abutted
Eze 40:18 a the sides of the gateways and was

Abyss
Lk 8:31 not to order them to go into the A.
Rev 9: 1 given the key to the shaft of the A.
9: 2 he opened the A, smoke rose from it
9: 2 darkened by the smoke from the A.
9:11 king over them the angel of the A,
11: 7 the beast that comes up from the A
17: 8 of the A and go to his destruction.
20: 1 having the key to the A and holding
20: 3 He threw him into the A, and locked

Acacia (Acacias)
Ex 25: 5 red and hides of sea cows; a wood;
25:10 "Have them make a chest of a wood
25:13 make poles of a wood and overlay
25:23 "Make a table of a wood—two cubits
25:28 Make the poles of a wood, overlay
26:15 "Make upright frames of a wood for
26:26 "Also make crossbars of a wood: five
26:32 posts of a wood overlaid with gold
26:37 posts of a wood overlaid with gold.
27: 1 "Build an altar of a wood, three
27: 6 Make poles of a wood for the altar
30: 1 "Make an altar of a wood for burning
30: 5 Make the poles of a wood and overlay
35: 7 red and hides of sea cows; a wood;
35:24 and everyone who had a wood for any
36:20 They made upright frames of a wood
36:31 They also made crossbars of a wood:
36:36 They made four posts of a wood for
37: 1 Bezalel made the ark of a wood—two
37: 4 he made poles of a wood and overlaid
37:10 They made the table of a wood—two
37:15 a wood and were overlaid with gold.
37:25 the altar of incense out of a wood.
37:28 They made the poles of a wood and
38: 1 altar of burnt offering of a wood,
38: 6 They made the poles of a wood and
Dt 10: 3 I made the ark out of a wood and
Isa 41:19 and the a, the myrtle and the olive.

Acacias (Acacia)
Joel 3:18 and will water the valley of a.

Acbor
Ge 36:38 Shaul died, Baal-Hanan son of A
36:39 Baal-Hanan son of A died, Hadad
2Ki 22:12 son of Shaphan, A son of Micaiah,
22:14 Hilkiah the priest, Ahikam, A,
1Ch 1:49 Shaul died, Baal-Hanan son of A
Jer 26:22 however, sent Elnathan son of A to
36:12 Elnathan son of A, Gemariah son of

Accent
Mt 26:73 of them, for your a gives you away."

Accept (Acceptable, Acceptance, Accepted, Accepting, Accepts)
Ge 14:23 that I will a nothing belonging to
14:24 I will a nothing but what my men
21:30 He replied, "A these seven lambs
23:13 I will pay the price of the field. A
33:10 in your eyes, a this gift from me.
33:11 Please a the present that was
Ex 22:11 The owner is to a this, and no
23: 8 "Do not a a bribe, for a bribe
Lev 22:25 you must not a such animals from the
26:23 you do not a my correction but
Nu 7: 5 "A these from them, that they may be
16:15 the LORD, "Do not a their offering.
32:30 they must a their possession with
35:31 "'Do not a a ransom for the life of
35:32 "'Do not a a ransom for anyone who
Dt 16:19 Do not a a bribe, for a bribe blinds
20:11 If they a and open their gates, all
21: 8 A this atonement for your people
1Sa 2:15 a boiled meat from you, but only raw.
10: 4 bread, which you will a from them.
26:19 me, then may he a an offering.
2Sa 24:23 him, "May the LORD your God a you.
2Ki 5:15 a now a gift from your servant."
5:16 whom I serve, I will not a a thing.
5:23 He urged Gehazi to a them, and then
5:26 or to a clothes, olive groves,
Est 4: 4 sackcloth, but he would not a them.
Job 2:10 Shall we a good from God, and not
22:22 A instruction from his mouth and lay
42: 8 and I will a his prayer and not deal
Ps 15: 5 not a a bribe against the innocent.
20: 3 and a your burnt offerings.
119:108 A, O LORD, the willing praise of my
Pr 1:25 my advice and would not a my rebuke,
1:30 since they would not a my advice and
2: 1 My son, if you a my words and store
4:10 Listen, my son, a what I say, and
6:35 He will not a any compensation; he
10: 8 The wise in heart a commands, but a
19:20 Listen to advice and a instruction,
Ecc 5:19 a his lot and be happy in his work
Isa 29:24 who complain will a instruction."
Jer 14:10 So the LORD does not a them; he will
14:12 grain offerings, I will not a them.
Eze 20:40 serve me, and there I will a them.
20:41 I will a you as fragrant incense
22:12 In you men a bribes to shed blood;
43:27 a you, declares the Sovereign LORD."
Da 4:27 Therefore, O king, be pleased to a
Am 5:22 grain offerings, I will not a them.
Zep 3: 7 'Surely you will fear me and a
Mal 1: 8 he a you?" says the LORD Almighty.
1: 9 he a you?"—says the LORD Almighty.
1:10 I will a no offering from your hands.
1:13 should I a them from your hands?"
Mt 11:14 if you are willing to a it, he is
19:11 Jesus replied, "Not everyone can a
19:12 The one who can a this should a it."
Mk 4:20 hear the word, a it, and produce a
Jn 3:11 you people do not a our testimony.
5:34 Not that I a human testimony; but I
5:41 "I do not a praise from men,
5:43 and you do not a me; but if someone
5:43 in his own name, you will a him.
5:44 How can you believe if you a praise
6:60 is a hard teaching. Who can a it?"
12:48 rejects me and does not a my words;
14:17 The world cannot a him, because it
Ac 16:21 for us Romans to a or practise."
22:18 will not a your testimony about me.'
Ro 14: 1 A him whose faith is weak, without
15: 7 A one another, then, just as Christ
1Co 2:14 The man without the Spirit does not a
16:11 No-one, then, should refuse to a him.
Jas 1:21 and humbly a the word planted in you,
1Jn 5: 9 We a man's testimony, but God's

Acceptable (Accept)
Ex 28:38 so that they will be a to the LORD.
Lev 1: 3 so that it will be a to the LORD.
22:21 without defect or blemish to be a.
22:27 From the eighth day on, it will be a
27: 9 is a as an offering to the LORD,
27:11 one that is not a as an offering to
Jdg 14: 3 "Isn't there an a woman among your
Pr 21: 3 more a to the LORD than sacrifice.
Isa 58: 5 call a fast, a day a to the LORD?
Jer 6:20 Your burnt offerings are not a; your
Mal 1:14 "Cursed is the cheat who has an a
3: 4 and Jerusalem will be a to the LORD,
Ro 15:16 might become an offering a to God,
15:31 may be a to the saints there,
2Co 8:12 the gift is a according to what one
Php 4:18 an a sacrifice, pleasing to God.
1Pe 2: 5 a to God through Jesus Christ.

Acceptance (Accept)
Ro 11:15 their a be but life from the dead?
1Ti 1:15 saying that deserves full a:
4: 9 saying that deserves full a

Accepted (Accept)
Ge 4: 7 will you not be a? But if you do not
33:11 because Jacob insisted, Esau a it.
Lev 1: 4 and it will be a on his behalf to
7:18 on the third day, it will not be a.
19: 5 that it will be a on your behalf.
19: 7 day, it is impure and will not be a.
22:19 that it may be a on your behalf.
22:20 it will not be a on your behalf.
22:23 not be a in fulfilment of a vow.
22:25 They will not be a on your behalf,
22:29 that it will be a on your behalf.
23:11 LORD so it will be a on your behalf;
Nu 31:51 Moses and Eleazar the priest a from
31:54 Moses and Eleazar the priest a the
Jdg 13:23 he would not have a a burnt offering
1Sa 8: 3 and a bribes and perverted justice.
12: 3 From whose hand have I a a bribe to
25:35 David a from her hand what she had
Job 42: 9 them; and the LORD a Job's prayer.
Isa 56: 7 sacrifices will be a on my altar;
60: 7 will be a as offerings on my altar,
Lk 4:24 "no prophet is a in his home town.
Jn 3:33 The man who has a it has certified
17: 8 words you gave me and they a them.
Ac 2:41 Those who a his message were
8:14 that Samaria had a the word of God,
15: 8 showed that he a them by giving the
Ro 10:16 not all the Israelites a the good
14: 3 the man who does, for God has a him.
15: 7 then, just as Christ a you, in order
2Co 11: 4 different gospel from the one you a,
Gal 1: 9 a gospel other than what you a, let
1Th 2:13 which you heard from us, you a it
Heb 10:34 a the confiscation of your property,

Accepting (Accept)
2Ki 5:20 by not a from him what he brought.
Isa 33:15 and keeps his hand from a bribes,

Accepts (Accept)
Dt 10:17 shows no partiality and a no bribes.
27:25 "Cursed is the man who a a bribe to
Ps 6: 9 cry for mercy; the LORD a my prayer.
Pr 17:23 A wicked man a a bribe in secret to
Mic 7: 3 the judge a bribes, the powerful
Zep 3: 2 She obeys no-one, she a no
Mal 2:13 a them with pleasure from your hands.
Jn 3:32 heard, but no-one a his testimony.
13:20 I tell you the truth, whoever a
13:20 whoever a anyone I send a me; and
13:20 whoever a me a the one who sent me."
Ac 10:35 a men from every nation who fear him
Heb 12: 6 he punishes everyone he a as a son."
Jas 1:27 Religion that God our Father a as

Access
Est 1:14 Media who had special a to the king
Ro 5: 2 through whom we have gained a by
Eph 2:18 For through him we both have a to

Accessories
Ex 25:39 for the lampstand and all these a.
30:27 the lampstand and its a, the altar of
31: 8 pure gold lampstand and all its a,
35:14 its a, lamps and oil for the light;
37:24 They made the lampstand and all its a
39:37 its row of lamps and all its a, and
Nu 4:10 they are to wrap it and all its a in

Accidentally
Nu 35:11 who has killed someone a may flee.
35:15 has killed another a can flee there.
Jos 20: 3 that anyone who kills a person a and
20: 9 killed someone a could flee to these

Acclaim (Acclamation)
Ps 89:15 are those who have learned to a you,
Isa 24:14 the west they a the LORD's majesty.

Acclamation (Acclaim)
2Ch 15:14 an oath to the LORD with loud a,

Acco
Jdg 1:31 drive out those living in A or Sidon or

Accompanied (Accompany)
Ge 50: 7 All Pharaoh's officials a him—the
Ru 1:22 Naomi returned from Moab a by Ruth
1Sa 10:26 a by valiant men whose hearts God
2Sa 15:11 Two hundred men from Jerusalem had a
15:18 six hundred Gittites who had a him
1Ki 20: 1 A by thirty-two kings with their
1Ch 15:16 a by musical instruments: lyres,
25: 1 a by harps, lyres and cymbals.
2Ch 5:12 a by 120 priests sounding trumpets.
5:13 A by trumpets, cymbals and other
29:27 singing to the LORD began also, a by
29:35 that a the burnt offerings.
30:21 a by the LORD's instruments of
Jer 17:25 a by the men of Judah and those
22: 4 riding in chariots and on horses, a
Mk 6: 1 his home town, a by his disciples.
16:20 his word by the signs that a it.
Jn 19:39 He was a by Nicodemus, the man who
Ac 18:18 Syria, a by Priscilla and Aquila.
20: 4 He was a by Sopater son of Pyrrhus
20:38 Then they a him to the ship.
21: 5 and children a us out of the city,
21:16 Some of the disciples from Caesarea a
1Co 10: 4 drank from the spiritual rock that a
Jas 2:17 if it is not a by action, is dead.

Accompanies (Accompany)
Isa 40:10 with him, and his recompense a him.
62:11 him, and his recompense a him."
2Co 9:13 obedience that a your confession of

Accompany (Accompanied, Accompanies, Accompanying)
Ge 33:12 "Let us be on our way; I'll a you.
Dt 28: 2 a you if you obey the LORD your God:
1Sa 28: 1 and your men will a me in the army."
Ne 10:38 A priest descended from Aaron is to a
Est 5:12 a the king to the banquet she gave.
Ecc 8:15 Then joy will a him in his work all
Mk 16:17 these signs will a those who believe:
1Co 16: 4 for me to go also, they will a me.
2Co 8:19 he was chosen by the churches to a
Heb 6: 9 your case—things that a salvation.

Accompanying (Accompany)
Nu 28: 7 The a drink offering is to be a

Accomplice
Pr 29:24 The a of a thief is his own enemy;

Accomplish (Accomplished, Accomplishes, Accomplishing)
Ge 50:20 but God intended it for good to a
Dt 9: 5 to a what he swore to your fathers,
2Ki 8:13 servant, a mere dog, a such a feat?"
19:31 of the LORD Almighty will a this.
Ecc 2: 2 And what does pleasure a?"
Isa 9: 7 of the LORD Almighty will a this.
37:32 of the LORD Almighty will a this.
44:28 'He is my shepherd and will a all
55:11 but will a what I desire and achieve
Jer 48:30 the LORD, "and her boasts a nothing.
Rev 17:17 has put it into their hearts to a his

Accomplished (Accomplish)
Jdg 8: 2 he answered them, "What have I a
Isa 26:12 that we have a you have done for us.
Mt 5:18 from the Law until everything is a.
Lk 1:45 the Lord has said to her will be a!"
Ro 15:18 what Christ has a through me in
Eph 3:11 which he a in Christ Jesus our Lord.
Rev 10: 7 the mystery of God will be a, just

Accomplishes (Accomplish)
Jer 23:20 fully a the purposes of his heart.
30:24 fully a the purposes of his heart.

Accomplishing (Accomplish)
2Ki 10:30 "Because you have done well in a
Jn 11:47 "What are we a?" they asked. "Here

Accord (Accordance, Accorded)
Nu 24:13 I could not do anything of my own a,
2Ki 10:15 "Are you in a with me, as I am with
Jer 5: 5 But with one a they too had broken
Jn 10:18 me, but I lay it down of my own a.
12:49 For I did not speak of my own a, but
Tit 2: 1 You must teach what is in a with

Accordance (Accord)
Ex 12: 4 in a with what each person will eat.
24: 8 with you in a with all these words."
34:27 "Write down these words, for in a
Nu 6:21 the LORD in a with his separation,
9: 3 a with all its rules and regulations.
9:14 in a with its rules and regulations.
9:23 in a with his command through Moses.
14:19 In a with your great love, forgive
Dt 2:37 in a with the command of the LORD
Jos 6:22 to her, in a with your oath to her."
15:13 In a with the LORD's command to him,
22: 9 which they had acquired in a with
1Ki 16:12 in a with the word of the LORD
16:34 in a with the word of the LORD
2Ki 9:26 in a with the word of the LORD."
14: 6 in a with what is written in the
14:25 in a with the word of the LORD, the
16:11 Uriah the priest built an altar in a
17:13 in a with the entire Law that I
17:33 in a with the customs of the nations
22:13 they have not acted in a with all
23:16 in a with the word of the LORD
23:25 in a with all the Law of Moses.
24: 2 He sent them to destroy Judah, in a
1Ch 5: 1 record in a with his birthright,
6:49 making atonement for Israel, in a
15:15 in a with the word of the LORD.
16:40 morning and evening, in a with
2Ch 25: 4 but acted in a with what is written
34:21 they have not acted in a with all
34:32 this in a with the covenant of God,
Ezr 3: 2 in a with what is written in the Law
3: 4 in a with what is written, they
7:18 in a with the will of your God.
7:25 you, Ezra, in a with the wisdom of
10: 3 in a with the counsel of my lord and
10: 8 in a with the decision of the
Ne 8:18 and on the eighth day, in a with the
Ps 109:26 Help me, O LORD my God; save me in a
119:149 Hear my voice in a with your love;
Jer 42: 5 if we do not act in a with everything
Eze 7: 9 I will repay you in a with your
25:14 and they will deal with Edom in a
35:11 I will treat you in a with the anger
Da 1:13 servants in a with what you see."
6: 8 in a with the laws of the Medes and
6:12 "The decree stands—in a with the
Mt 2:16 in a with the time he had learned
22:16 the way of God in a with the truth.
Mk 12:14 the way of God in a with the truth.
Lk 20:21 the way of God in a with the truth.
Jn 19:40 was in a with Jewish burial customs.
Ro 8: 5 but those who live in a with the
8:27 for the saints in a with God's will.
12: 3 in a with the measure of faith God
Eph 1: 5 in a with his pleasure and will—
1: 7 in a with the riches of God's grace
4:21 in a with the truth that is in Jesus
2Th 2: 9 in a with the work of Satan displayed

Accorded (Accord)
Ge 45:13 Tell my father about all the honour a

Account (Accountable, Accounted, Accounting, Accounts)
Ge 2: 4 This is the a of the heavens and the
5: 1 This is the written a of Adam's line.
6: 9 This is the a of Noah. Noah was a
10: 1 This is the a of Shem, Ham and
11:10 This is the a of Shem. Two years
11:27 This is the a of Terah. Terah became
25:12 the a of Abraham's son Ishmael, whom
25:19 This is the a of Abraham's son Isaac.
26: 7 place might kill me on a of Rebekah,
26: 9 I might lose my life on a of her."
36: 1 This is the a of Esau (that is, Edom)
36: 9 This is the a of Esau the father of
37: 2 This is the a of Jacob. Joseph, a
Ex 12: 4 a the number of people there are.
Nu 3: 1 This is the a of the family of Aaron
6: 7 ceremonially unclean on a of them,
9: 6 unclean on a of a dead body.
13:27 They gave Moses this a: "We went
Dt 9: 4 No, it is on a of the wickedness of
9: 5 a of the wickedness of these nations,
18:19 name, I myself will call him to a.
Jos 22:23 may the LORD himself call us to a.
1Sa 17:32 "Let no-one lose heart on a of this
20:16 the LORD call David's enemies to a."
23:10 and destroy the town on a of me.
2Sa 11:18 Joab sent David a full a of the
11:19 the king this a of the battle,
13: 2 of illness on a of his sister Tamar,
21: 1 The LORD said, "It is on a of Saul
1Ki 9:15 Here is the a of the forced labour
11:27 Here is the a of how he rebelled
2Ki 22: 7 they need not a for the money
1Ch 27:24 Wrath came on Israel on a of this
2Ch 24:22 LORD see this and call you to a."
24:27 The a of his sons, the many
Est 10: 2 together with a full a of the
Job 31:14 What will I answer when called to a?
31:37 I would give him an a of my every
Ps 10:13 "He won't call me to a"?
10:15 call him to a for his wickedness
56: 7 On no a let them escape; in your
Ecc 3:15 and God will call the past to a.
Isa 2:22 Of what a is he?
23:13 this people that is now of no a! The
Eze 16:14 the nations on a of your beauty,
28:17 Your heart became proud on a of your
Mt 10:18 On my a you will be brought before
11: 6 who does not fall away on a of me."
12:36 men will have to give a on the day of
26:31 you will all fall away on a of me,
26:33 away on a of you, I never will."
Mk 12:26 in the a of the bush, how God said
13: 9 On a of me you will stand before
Lk 1: 1 Many have undertaken to draw up an a
1: 3 a for you, most excellent Theophilus,
7:23 who does not fall away on a of me."
16: 2 you? Give an a of your management,
20:37 in the a of the bush, even Moses
21:12 governors, and all on a of my name.
Jn 12:11 for on a of him many of the Jews
Ac 4: 9 If we are being called to a today
19:40 not be able to a for this commotion,
Ro 5:13 taken into a when there is no law.
11:28 they are enemies on your a; but as
11:28 are loved on a of the patriarchs,
14:12 then, each of us will give an a of
1Co 6: 4 even men of little a in the church!
2Co 7:12 it was not on a of the one who did
Php 1:26 Jesus will overflow on a of me.
4:17 for what may be credited to your a.
Heb 4:13 eyes of him to whom we must give a.
13:17 over you as men who must give an a.
1Pe 4: 5 they will have to give a to him who
1Jn 2:12 have been forgiven on a of his name.
Rev 16:21 And they cursed God on a of the

Accountable (Account)
Eze 3:18 and I will hold you a for his blood.
3:20 and I will hold you a for his blood.
33: 6 hold the watchman a for his blood.'
33: 8 and I will hold you a for his blood.
34:10 and will hold them a for my flock.
Da 6: 2 The satraps were made a to them so
Jnh 1:14 Do not hold us a for killing an
Ro 3:19 and the whole world held a to God.

Accounted (Account)
Ezr 8:34 Everything was a for by number and

Accounting (Account)
Ge 9: 5 lifeblood I will surely demand an a.
9: 5 I will demand an a from every animal.

Ge 9: 5 an a for the life of his fellow man.
42:22 Now we must give an a for his blood."
2Ki 12:15 They did not require an a from those

Accounts (Account)
Job 21:29 Have you paid no regard to their a—
Mt 18:23 to settle a with his servants.
25:19 returned and settled a with them.

Accredited (Credit)
Ac 2:22 a man a by God to you by miracles,

Accumulate (Accumulated)
Dt 17:17 a large amounts of silver and gold.

Accumulated (Accumulate)
Ge 12: 5 all the possessions they had a and
31:18 along with all the goods he had a in
1Ki 10:26 Solomon a chariots and horses; he
2Ch 1:14 Solomon a chariots and horses; he

Accurate (Accurately)
Dt 25:15 You must have a and honest weights
Pr 11: 1 but a weights are his delight.
Eze 45:10 You are to use a scales, an a ephah
45:10 a scales, an a ephah and an a bath.
Ac 23:15 more a information about his case.
23:20 more a information about him.

Accurately (Accurate)
Ac 18:25 fervour and taught about Jesus a,

Accursed (Curse)
Nu 5:27 she will become a among her people.
2Ki 22:19 that they would become a and laid
Isa 65:20 a hundred will be considered a.
Mic 6:10 and the short ephah, which is a?
2Pe 2:14 are experts in greed—an a brood!

Accusation (Accuse)
Ezr 4: 6 they lodged an a against the people
Mic 6: 2 Hear, O mountains, the LORD's a;
Ac 23:29 I found that the a had to do with
24: 9 The Jews joined in the a, asserting
Col 1:22 without blemish and free from a—
1Ti 5:19 Do not entertain an a against an
Jude : 9 to bring a slanderous a against him,

Accusations (Accuse)
Ps 35:20 but devise false a against those who
Ac 26: 2 against all the a of the Jews,
2Pe 2:11 do not bring slanderous a against

Accuse (Accusation, Accusations, Accused, Accuser, Accusers, Accuses, Accusing)
Dt 19:16 the stand to a a man of a crime,
1Sa 22:15 Of course not! Let not the king a
2Sa 3: 8 Yet now you a me of an offence
Ps 50:21 rebuke you and a you to your face.
103: 9 He will not always a, nor will he
109: 4 In return for my friendship they a
Pr 3:30 Do not a a man for no reason—when
Isa 57:16 I will not a for ever, nor will I
Hos 4: 4 let no man a another, for your
Zec 3: 1 standing at his right side to a him.
Mt 12:10 Looking for a reason to a Jesus,
Mk 3: 2 looking for a reason to a Jesus,
Lk 3:14 "Don't extort money and don't a
6: 7 looking for a reason to a Jesus,
23: 2 they began to a him, saying, "We
Jn 5:45 "But do not think I will a you
10:36 a me of blasphemy because I said,
1Pe 2:12 though they a you of doing wrong,

Accused (Accuse)
Nu 35:12 so that a person a of murder may not
35:25 The assembly must protect the one a
35:26 "But if the a ever goes outside the
35:27 a without being guilty of murder.
35:28 The a must stay in his city of
Dt 19:15 not enough to convict a man a of any
Jos 20: 5 they must not surrender the one a,
21:13 refuge for one a of murder), Libnah,
21:21 for one a of murder) and Gezer,
21:27 one a of murder) and Be Eshtarah,
21:32 city of refuge for one a of murder),
21:38 for one a of murder), Mahanaim,
Ne 5: 7 I pondered them in my mind and then a
Da 6:24 the men who had falsely a Daniel
Mt 27:12 he was a by the chief priests and
Mk 15: 3 The chief priests a him of many
Lk 16: 1 was a of wasting his possessions.
Ac 22:30 why Paul was being a by the Jews,

Accuser (Accuse)
Job 31:35 my a put his indictment in writing.
Ps 109: 6 let an a stand at his right hand.
Isa 50: 8 Who is my a? Let him confront me!
Jn 5:45 Your a is Moses, on whom your hopes
Rev 12:10 For the a of our brothers, who

Accusers (Accuse)
Ps 71:13 May my a perish in shame; may those
109:20 my a, to those who speak evil of me.
109:25 I am an object of scorn to my a;
109:29 My a will be clothed with disgrace
Jer 18:19 Listen to me, O LORD; hear what my a
Ac 23:30 I also ordered his a to present to
23:35 hear your case when your a get here.
24:12 My a did not find me arguing with
25:16 any man before he has faced his a
25:18 his a got up to speak, they did not

Accuses (Accuse)
Job 40: 2 him? Let him who a God answer him!"
Isa 54:17 will refute every tongue that a you.
Rev 12:10 who a them before our God day and

Accusing (Accuse)
Ps 31:20 you keep them safe from a tongues.
Mk 15: 4 how many things they are a you of."
Lk 23:10 standing there, vehemently a him.
Jn 8: 6 in order to have a basis for a him.
Ac 23:28 I wanted to know why they were a him,
26: 7 of this hope that the Jews are a me.
Ro 2:15 now a, now even defending them.)

Accustomed (Custom)
Jer 2:24 a wild donkey a to the desert,
13:23 you do good who are a to doing evil.
1Co 8: 7 Some people are still so a to idols

Achaia
Roman province, with capital Corinth (2Co 1:1); governed by a pro-consul (Ac 18:12). Linked with Macedonia to denote the whole of Greece (Ac 19:21; Ro 15:26; 1Th 1:7–8); may refer specifically to Corinth. Christians from here contributed to Paul's collection for the poor in Jerusalem (Ro 15:26–27). Visited by Paul (Ac 18:1–18) and Apollos (Ac 18:27). The household of Stephanas were the first converts here (1Co 16:15).

Ac 18:12 While Gallio was proconsul of A, the
18:27 Apollos wanted to go to A, the
19:21 passing through Macedonia and A.
Ro 15:26 For Macedonia and A were pleased to
1Co 16:15 were the first converts in A,
2Co 1: 1 with all the saints throughout A:
9: 2 year you in A were ready to give;
11:10 A will stop this boasting of mine.
1Th 1: 7 the believers in Macedonia and A.
1: 8 from you not only in Macedonia and A

Achaicus
1Co 16:17 Fortunatus and A arrived, because

Achan
Sinned by keeping spoils after conquest of Jericho thus causing Israel's defeat at Ai; stoned as punishment (Jos 7).

Jos 7: 1 the devoted things; A son of Carmi,
7:18 and A son of Carmi, the son of Zimri,
7:19 Joshua said to A, "My son, give
7:20 A replied, "It is true! I have
7:24 together with all Israel, took A son
7:26 Over A they heaped up a large pile
22:20 A son of Zerah acted unfaithfully

Achar
1Ch 2: 7 The son of Carmi: A, who brought

Ache
Pr 14:13 Even in laughter the heart may a,

Achieve (Achieved, Achievement, Achievements, Achieving)
Job 5:12 so that their hands a no success.
Ecc 2:11 had done and what I had toiled to a,
Isa 55:11 a the purpose for which I sent it.
Da 11:24 he will invade them and will a what

Achieved (Achieve)
1Ki 9: 1 and had a all he had desired to do,
16:27 what he did and the things he a, are
22:45 the things he a and his military

Achievement (Achieve)
Ecc 4: 4 I saw that all labour and all a

Achievements (Achieve)
1Ki 10: 6 your a and your wisdom is true.
15:23 all his a, all he did and the cities
16: 5 what he did and his a, are they not
2Ki 10:34 all he did, and all his a, are they
13: 8 all he did and his a, are they not
13:12 all he did and his a, including his
14:15 what he did and his a, including his
14:28 all he did, and his military a,
20:20 all his a and how he made the pool
2Ch 9: 5 your a and your wisdom is true.

Achieving (Achieve)
2Co 4:17 momentary troubles are a for us an

Achish
King of Gath, with whom David sought refuge and feigned insanity (1Sa 21:10–15), and later feigned loyal service (1Sa 27:2–12).

1Sa 21:10 Saul and went to A king of Gath.
21:11 the servants of A said to him,
21:12 very much afraid of A king of Gath.
21:14 A said to his servants, "Look at the
27: 2 over to A son of Maoch king of Gath.
27: 3 and his men settled in Gath with A.
27: 5 David said to A, "If I have found
27: 6 on that day A gave him Ziklag, and
27: 9 Then he returned to A.
27:10 A asked, "Where did you go raiding
27:12 A trusted David and said to himself,
28: 1 A said to David, "You must
28: 2 A replied, "Very well, I will make
29: 2 were marching at the rear with A.
29: 3 A replied, "Is this not David, also
29: 6 A called David and said to him, "As
29: 9 A answered, "I know that you have
1Ki 2:39 two of Shimei's slaves ran off to A
2:40 A at Gath in search of his slaves.

Achor, Valley of
Not far from Jericho at the entrance to the promised land. Name, meaning "trouble", given because Achan and family were killed here for hoarding spoil from Jericho (Jos 7:24–26). Becomes a symbol of hope for God's restored people (Hos 2:15; Isa 65:10).

Jos 7:24 all that he had, to the Valley of A.
7:26 called the Valley of A ever since.
15: 7 of A and turned north to Gilgal,
Isa 65:10 and the Valley of A a resting place
Hos 2:15 make the Valley of A a door of hope.

Acknowledge (Acknowledged, Acknowledges, Acknowledgment)
Dt 4:39 A and take to heart this day that
21:17 He must a the son of his unloved
33: 9 his brothers or a his own children,
1Ch 28: 9 "And you, my son Solomon, a the God
Ps 79: 6 on the nations that do not a you,
87: 4 among those who a me—Philistia too,
Pr 3: 6 in all your ways a him, and he will
Isa 19:21 in that day they will a the LORD.

Isa 29:23 they will a the holiness of the Holy
33:13 done; you who are near, a my power!
45: 4 of honour, though you do not a me.
59:12 with us, and we a our iniquities:
61: 9 All who see them will a that they
63:16 not know us or Israel a us; you,
Jer 3:13 Only a your guilt—you have
9: 3 do not a me," declares the LORD.
9: 6 refuse to a me," declares the LORD.
10:25 on the nations that do not a you,
14:20 O LORD, we a our wickedness and the
Eze 12:16 a all their detestable practices.
Da 4:25 until you a that the Most High is
4:26 to you when you a that Heaven rules.
4:32 until you a that the Most High is
11:39 will greatly honour those who a him.
Hos 2:20 and you will a the LORD.
5: 4 their heart; they do not a the LORD.
6: 3 Let us a the LORD; let us press on
6: 3 a the LORD; let us press on to a him.
8: 2 out to me, 'O our God, we a you!'
13: 4 shall a no God but me, no Saviour
Mt 10:32 a him before my Father in heaven.
Lk 12: 8 also a him before the angels of God.
Ac 23: 8 but the Pharisees a them all.)
24: 3 we a this with profound gratitude.
1Co 14:37 let him a that what I am writing to
2Ti 3: 7 always learning but never able to a
1Jn 4: 3 every spirit that does not a Jesus
2Jn : 7 Many deceivers, who do not a Jesus
Rev 3: 5 but will a his name before my Father
3: 9 feet and a that I have loved you.

Acknowledged (Acknowledge)

Lev 22:32 I must be a as holy by the
1Ch 29:22 Then they a Solomon son of David as
Ps 32: 5 I a my sin to you and did not cover
Isa 45: 5 you, though you have not a me,
Da 5:21 until he a that the Most High God is
Hos 2: 8 She has not a that I was the one who
Lk 7:29 when they heard Jesus' words, a that
Jn 9:22 anyone who a that Jesus was the

Acknowledges (Acknowledge)

Ps 91:14 I will protect him, for he a my name.
Mt 10:32 "Whoever a me before men, I will
Lk 12: 8 "I tell you, whoever a me before men,
1Jn 2:23 a the Son has the Father also.
4: 2 Every spirit that a that Jesus
4:15 If anyone a that Jesus is the Son of

Acknowledgment (Acknowledge)

Hos 4: 1 no love, no a of God in the land.
6: 6 a of God rather than burnt offerings.

Acquaintance (Acquaintances, Acquainted)

Php 4:15 in the early days of your a with the

Acquaintances (Acquaintance)

Job 19:13 a are completely estranged from me.

Acquainted (Acquaintance)

Ac 24:22 Felix, who was well a with the Way,
26: 3 especially so because you are well a
Gal 1:18 I went up to Jerusalem to get a with
Heb 5:13 being still an infant, is not a with

Acquire (Acquired, Acquires, Acquiring)

Ge 34:10 trade in it, and a property in it."
Lev 25:28 if he does not a the means to repay
Dt 17:16 The king, moreover, must not a great
Ru 4: 5 you a the dead man's widow, in order
Ne 5:16 for the work; we did not a any land.

Acquired (Acquire)

Ge 12: 5 and the people they had a in Haran,
12:16 and Abram a sheep and cattle, male
36: 6 all the goods he had a in Canaan,
46: 6 possessions they had a in Canaan,
47:27 They a property there and were
Nu 31:50 gold articles each of us a—armlets,
Jos 22: 9 their own land, which they had a in
Ru 4:10 I have also a Ruth the Moabitess,
2Ch 32:29 He built villages and a great
Ecc 2: 8 I a men and women singers, and a
Isa 15: 7 the wealth they have a and stored up
Jer 48:36 The wealth they a is gone.
Rev 3:17 You say, 'I am rich; I have a wealth

Acquires (Acquire)

Lev 25:26 and a sufficient means to redeem it,
Pr 18:15 The heart of the discerning a

Acquiring (Acquire)

Pr 1: 3 for a a disciplined and prudent life,

Acquit (Acquitted, Acquitting)

Ex 23: 7 death, for I will not a the guilty.
Isa 5:23 who a the guilty for a bribe, but
Mic 6:11 Shall I a a man with dishonest

Acquitted (Acquit)

Mt 12:37 For by your words you will be a, and

Acquitting (Acquit)

Dt 25: 1 a the innocent and condemning the
Pr 17:15 A the guilty and condemning the

Acre

1Sa 14:14 men in an area of about half an a.

Acsah

Jos 15:16 "I will give my daughter A in
15:17 his daughter A to him in marriage.
Jdg 1:12 "I will give my daughter A in
1:13 his daughter A to him in marriage.
1Ch 2:49 Caleb's daughter was A.

Acshaph

Jos 11: 1 Madon, to the kings of Shimron and A,
12:20 the king of A one
19:25 included: Helkath, Hali, Beten, A,

Act (Acted, Acting, Action, Actions, Active, Activity, Acts)

Ex 8:29 Only be sure that Pharaoh does not a
Lev 20:21 it is an a of impurity; he has
Nu 5:13 she has not been caught in the a),
23:19 Does he speak and then not a? Does
Dt 17:10 You must a according to the
17:11 A according to the law they teach
24:13 a in the sight of the LORD your God.
Jdg 20: 6 lewd and disgraceful a in Israel.
1Sa 14: 6 Perhaps the LORD will a on our
2Sa 6: 7 Uzzah because of his irreverent a;
14: 2 A like a woman who has spent many
1Ki 8:32 hear from heaven and a. Judge
8:39 Forgive and a; deal with each man
21: 7 "Is this how you a as king over
2Ch 6:23 hear from heaven and a. Judge
19:11 A with courage, and may the LORD be
24: 5 But the Levites did not a at once.
Ezr 10:14 Let our officials a for the whole
Ne 5:15 for God I did not a like that.
Ps 119:126 is time for you to a, O LORD; your
Pr 3:27 it, when it is in your power to a.
Isa 43:13 When I a, who can reverse it?"
52:13 See, my servant will a wisely; he
Jer 6:28 and iron; they all a corruptly.
42: 5 if we do not a in accordance with
Eze 24:14 The time has come for me to a. I
Da 9:19 forgive! O Lord, hear and a! For
11:23 he will a deceitfully, and with only
Mic 6: 8 To a justly and to love mercy and to
Zep 3: 7 to a corruptly in all they did.
Jn 8: 4 was caught in the a of adultery.
Ac 4: 9 an a of kindness shown to a cripple
Ro 5:18 so also the result of one a of
12: 1 is your spiritual a of worship.
2Co 8: 6 this a of grace on your part.
10: 6 we will be ready to punish every a
12:18 did he? Did we not a in the same
Php 2:13 to a according to his good purpose.
Col 4: 5 Be wise in the way you a towards
2Th 1:11 and every a prompted by your faith.
Jas 2:12 Speak and a as those who are going

Acted (Act)

Dt 32: 5 They have a corruptly towards him;
Jos 7: 1 the Israelites a unfaithfully in
22:20 Achan son of Zerah a unfaithfully
22:31 because you have not a unfaithfully
Jdg 9:16 "Now if you have a honourably and in
9:19 if then you have a honourably and in
9:23 a treacherously against Abimelech.
15: 7 Samson said to them, "Since you've a
1Sa 13:13 "You a foolishly," Samuel said. "You
21:13 in their hands he a like a madman,
26:21 Surely I have a like a fool and have
1Ki 8:47 done wrong, we have a wickedly';
20:25 agreed with them and a accordingly.
2Ki 12:15 they a with complete honesty.
22:13 they have not a in accordance with
2Ch 6:37 we have done wrong and a wickedly';
11:23 He a wisely, dispersing some of his
25: 4 but a in accordance with what is
34:21 they have not a in accordance with
Ne 1: 7 We have a very wickedly towards you.
9:33 a faithfully, while we did wrong.
Ps 106: 6 we have done wrong and a wickedly.
Isa 48: 3 suddenly I a, and they came to pass.
Jer 38: 9 "My lord the king, these men have a
Eze 25:15 'Because the Philistines a in
Lk 16: 8 manager because he had a shrewdly.
24:28 Jesus a as if he were going further.
Ac 3:17 "Now, brothers, I know that you a in
1Ti 1:13 I a in ignorance and unbelief.

Acting (Act)

2Sa 12:21 "Why are you a in this way? While
2Ki 10:19 But Jehu was a deceptively in order
22: 7 because they are a faithfully."
Eze 16:30 things, a like a brazen prostitute!
Mal 2:14 "Why?" It is because the LORD is a
Ro 14:15 eat, you are no longer a in love.
1Co 3: 3 Are you not a like mere men?
7:36 If anyone thinks he is a improperly
Gal 2:14 I saw that they were not a in line

Action (Act)

Jer 32:39 give them singleness of heart and a,
Da 11:28 He will take a against it and then
Lk 23:51 consented to their decision and a.
Ac 7:22 and was powerful in speech and a.
2Co 9: 2 has stirred most of them to a.
Jas 2:17 it is not accompanied by a, is dead.
1Pe 1:13 Therefore, prepare your minds for a;

Actions (Act)

Pr 20:11 Even a child is known by his a, by
Isa 66:18 "And I, because of their a and their
Jer 4:18 "Your own conduct and a have brought
7: 3 says: Reform your ways and your a,
7: 5 really change your ways and your a
18:11 and reform your ways and your a.'
26:13 Now reform your ways and your a and
35:15 your wicked ways and reform your a;
44:22 could no longer endure your wicked a
44:25 and your wives have shown by your a
Eze 14:22 you see their conduct and their a,
14:23 you see their conduct and their a,
20:43 all the a by which you have defiled
24:14 according to your conduct and your a
36:17 it by their conduct and their a.
36:19 to their conduct and their a.
Mt 11:19 But wisdom is proved right by her a."
2Co 10:11 be in our a when we are present.
11:15 end will be what their a deserve.
Gal 6: 4 Each one should test his own a. Then
Tit 1:16 God, but by their a they deny him.
Jas 2:22 You see that his faith and his a
1Jn 3:12 Because his own a were evil and his
3:18 or tongue but with a and in truth.

Active (Act)

Phm : 6 I pray that you may be a in sharing
Heb 4:12 For the word of God is living and a.

Activity (Act)
Ne 11:23 which regulated their daily a.
Ecc 3: 1 a season for every a under heaven:
3:17 a time for every a, a time for every
Ac 5:38 a is of human origin, it will fail.
2Co 10:15 of a among you will greatly expand,

Acts (Act)
Ex 6: 6 arm and with mighty a of judgment.
7: 4 with mighty a of judgment I will
Jdg 5:11 They recite the righteous a of the
5:11 a of his warriors in Israel.
1Sa 12: 7 a performed by the LORD for you
1Ch 16: 9 to him; tell of all his wonderful a.
2Ch 32:32 his a of devotion are written in the
35:26 Josiah's reign and his a of devotion,
Est 10: 2 all his a of power and might,
Ps 71:16 come and proclaim your mighty a,
71:24 of your righteous a all day long,
105: 2 to him; tell of all his wonderful a.
106: 2 Who can proclaim the mighty a of the
145: 4 they will tell of your mighty a.
145:12 all men may know of your mighty a
150: 2 Praise him for his a of power;
Pr 12:10 kindest a of the wicked are cruel.
13:16 Every prudent man a out of knowledge,
Isa 59: 6 a of violence are in their hands.
64: 4 who a on behalf of those who wait
64: 6 and all our righteous a are like
Jer 13:27 a on the hills and in the fields.
29:26 you should put any madman who a like
Eze 22: 9 mountain shrines and commit lewd a.
Da 9:16 keeping with all your righteous a,
Mic 6: 5 know the righteous a of the LORD
Mt 6: 1 "Be careful not to do your 'a of
Jn 7: 4 become a public figure a in secret.
Ro 1:27 Men committed indecent a with other
Gal 5:19 The a of the sinful nature are
Heb 6: 1 from a that lead to death,
9:14 cleanse our consciences from a that
10:17 he adds: "Their sins and lawless a I
Jude :15 a they have done in the ungodly way,
Rev 15: 4 righteous a have been revealed."
19: 8 for the righteous a of the saints.

Aczib
Jos 15:44 Keilah, A and Mareshah—nine towns
19:29 out at the sea in the region of A,
Jdg 1:31 or A or Helbah or Aphek or Rehob,
Mic 1:14 The town of A will prove deceptive

Adadah
Jos 15:22 Kinah, Dimonah, A,

Adah
Ge 4:19 Lamech married two women, one named A
4:20 A gave birth to Jabal; he was the
4:23 Lamech said to his wives, "A and
36: 2 A daughter of Elon the Hittite,
36: 4 A bore Eliphaz to Esau, Basemath
36:10 the son of Esau's wife A, and Reuel,
36:12 were grandsons of Esau's wife A.
36:16 in Edom; they were grandsons of A.

Adaiah
2Ki 22: 1 daughter of A; she was from Bozkath.
1Ch 6:41 the son of Zerah, the son of A,
8:21 A, Beraiah and Shimrath were the
9:12 A son of Jeroham, the son of Pashhur,
2Ch 23: 1 Maaseiah son of A, and Elishaphat son
Ezr 10:29 A, Jashub, Sheal and Jeremoth.
10:39 Shelemiah, Nathan, A,
Ne 11: 5 the son of Hazaiah, the son of A,
11:12 A son of Jeroham, the son of Pelaliah

Adalia
Est 9: 8 Poratha, A, Aridatha,

Adam (Adam's)
First man. Created by God (Ge 1:27); placed in Eden (Ge 2:15); given Eve as helper (Ge 2:19–24). Disobeyed God (Ge 3; Ro 5:14) and so brought sin into world (Ro 5:12, 15-19). Jesus is described as "the last Adam" (1Co 15:45).

Ge 2:20 for A no suitable helper was found.
3:17 To A he said, "Because you listened
3:20 A named his wife Eve, because she
3:21 for A and his wife and clothed them.
4: 1 A lay with his wife Eve, and she
4:25 A lay with his wife again, and she
5: 3 A had lived 130 years, he had a son
5: 4 After Seth was born, A lived 800
5: 5 Altogether, A lived 930 years, and
Jos 3:16 at a town called A in the vicinity
1Ch 1: 1 A, Seth, Enosh,
Hos 6: 7 Like A, they have broken the
Lk 3:38 Seth, the son of A, the son of God.
Ro 5:14 death reigned from the time of A to
5:14 as did A, who was a pattern of the
1Co 15:22 For as in A all die, so in Christ
15:45 is written: "The first man A became
15:45 the last A, a life-giving spirit.
1Ti 2:13 For A was formed first, then Eve.
2:14 A was not the one deceived; it was
Jude :14 Enoch, the seventh from A,

Adam's (Adam)
Ge 5: 1 This is the written account of A

Adamah
Jos 19:36 A, Ramah, Hazor,

Adami Nekeb
Jos 19:33 passing A and Jabneel to Lakkum and

Adar
Ezr 6:15 on the third day of the month A,
Est 3: 7 the twelfth month, the month of A.
3:13 the twelfth month, the month of A,
8:12 the twelfth month, the month of A.
9: 1 the month of A, the edict commanded
9:15 fourteenth day of the month of A,
9:17 thirteenth day of the month of A,
9:19 of A as a day of joy and feasting,
9:21 and fifteenth days of the month of A

Adbeel
Ge 25:13 of Ishmael, Kedar, A, Mibsam,
1Ch 1:29 of Ishmael, Kedar, A, Mibsam,

Add (Added, Adding, Addition, Additional, Adds)
Ge 30:24 "May the LORD a to me another son.
Lev 2:13 a salt to all your offerings.
5:16 a a fifth of the value to that and
6: 5 He must make restitution in full, a
6:12 Every morning the priest is to a
22:14 and a a fifth of the value to it.
27:13 he must a a fifth to its value.
27:15 he must a a fifth to its value, and
27:19 he must a a fifth to its value, and
27:31 must a a fifth of the value to it.
Nu 5: 7 a one fifth to it and give it all to
Dt 4: 2 Do not a to what I command you and
12:32 do not a to it or take away from it.
20: 8 the officers shall a, "Is any man
2Sa 15: 4 Absalom would a, "If only I were
2Ki 20: 6 I will a fifteen years to your life.
1Ch 22:14 And you may a to them.
2Ch 28:13 Do you intend to a to our sin and
Pr 1: 5 let the wise listen and a to their
9: 9 man and he will a to his learning.
30: 6 Do not a to his words, or he will
Isa 5: 8 Woe to you who a house to house and
29: 1 the city where David settled! A year
38: 5 I will a fifteen years to your life.
Jer 7:21 says: Go ahead, a your burnt
30:19 I will a to their numbers, and they
Eze 16:43 Did you not a lewdness to all your
Mt 6:27 Who of you by worrying can a a single
Lk 12:25 Who of you by worrying can a a single
Gal 3:15 Just as no-one can set aside or a to
2Pe 1: 5 make every effort to a to your faith
Rev 22:18 God will a to him the plagues

Addar
Jos 15: 3 up to A and curved around to Karka.
1Ch 8: 3 The sons of Bela were: A, Gera,

Added (Add)
Ge 16:10 The angel a, "I will so increase
21: 7 she a, "Who would have said to
24:25 she a, "We have plenty of straw and
30:28 He a, "Name your wages, and I will
38:25 And she a, "See if you recognise
Ex 12:34 their dough before the yeast was a,
Lev 10: 1 put fire in them and a incense; and
Nu 36: 3 a to that of the tribe they marry
36: 4 their inheritance will be a to that
Dt 5:22 darkness; and he a nothing more.
Jdg 19:13 He a, "Come, let's try to reach
Ru 2:20 She a, "That man is our close
3:17 a, "He gave me these six measures of
1Sa 12:19 for we have a to all our other sins
26:18 he a, "Why is my lord pursuing his
2Sa 19:35 be an a burden to my lord the king?
1Ki 2:14 he a, "I have something to say to
22:28 Then he a, "Mark my words, all you
2Ch 2:12 Hiram a: "Praise be to the LORD, the
18:27 Then he a, "Mark my words, all you
Est 5:12 "And that's not all," Haman a. "I'm
Pr 9:11 and years will be a to your life.
Ecc 3:14 a to it and nothing taken from it.
Jer 36:32 many similar words were a to them.
40: 5 Nebuzaradan a, "Go back to Gedaliah
44:19 The women a, "When we burned incense
45: 3 You said, 'Woe to me! The LORD has a
Zec 1:15 angry, but they a to the calamity.'
5: 6 And he a, "This is the iniquity of
Lk 3:20 Herod a this to them all: He locked
Jn 1:51 He then a, "I tell you the truth,
Ac 1:26 so he was a to the eleven apostles.
2:41 were a to their number that day.
2:47 And the Lord a to their number daily
5:14 the Lord and were a to their number.
Ro 5:20 The law was a so that the trespass
Gal 2: 6 those men a nothing to my message.
3:19 It was a because of transgressions
Rev 19: 9 a, "These are the true words of God.

Adder (Adders)
Job 20:16 the fangs of an a will kill him.
Isa 59: 5 when one is broken, an a is hatched.

Adders (Adder)
Isa 30: 6 of lions and lionesses, of a and

Addi
Lk 3:28 the son of Melki, the son of A, the

Addicted
Tit 2: 3 not to be slanderers or a to much

Adding (Add)
Lev 27:27 value, a a fifth of the value to it.
2Sa 14:11 of blood from a to the destruction,
1Ki 11:25 a to the trouble caused by Hadad.
Ezr 10:10 foreign women, a to Israel's guilt.
Ecc 7:27 "this is what I have discovered: "A

Addition (Add)
Ge 28: 9 in a to the wives he already had.
Lev 9:17 a to the morning's burnt offering.
23:38 These offerings are in a to those
23:38 in a to your gifts and whatever you
Nu 6:21 in a to whatever else he can afford.
16:49 in a to those who had died because
28:10 in a to the regular burnt offering
28:23 Prepare these in a to the regular
28:24 it is to be prepared in a to the
28:31 in a to the regular burnt offering
29: 6 These are in a to the monthly and
29:11 in a to the sin offering for
29:16 in a to the regular burnt offering
29:19 in a to the regular burnt offering
29:22 in a to the regular burnt offering
29:25 in a to the regular burnt offering
29:28 in a to the regular burnt offering
29:31 in a to the regular burnt offering
29:34 in a to the regular burnt offering
29:38 in a to the regular burnt offering
29:39 "In a to what you vow and your
35: 6 In a, give them forty-two other towns

Dt 29: 1 in **a** to the covenant he had made
Jos 13:22 In **a** to those slain in battle, the
Jdg 20:15 in **a** to seven hundred chosen men
1Ki 5:11 in **a** to twenty thousand baths, of
15:20 and all Kinnereth in **a** to Naphtali.
2Ch 31:16 In **a**, they distributed to the males
Ezr 1: 6 in **a** to all the freewill offerings.
Ne 5:15 from them in **a** to food and wine.
Ecc 12:12 Be warned, my son, of anything in **a**
Eze 16:23 In **a** to all your other wickedness,
39:14 in **a** to them, others will bury those
44: 7 In **a** to all your other detestable
Lk 24:22 In **a**, some of our women amazed us.
2Co 7:13 By all this we are encouraged. In **a**
8:22 In **a**, we are sending with them our
Eph 6:16 In **a** to all this, take up the shield

Additional (Add)
Ge 43:22 We have also brought **a** silver with
Ex 26:12 for the **a** length of the tent
Nu 3:48 the redemption of the **a** Israelites

Addon
Ezr 2:59 Tel Harsha, Kerub, **A** and Immer, but
Ne 7:61 Tel Harsha, Kerub, **A** and Immer, but

Address (Addressed, Addresses)
Dt 20: 2 shall come forward and **a** the army.
Ac 12:21 delivered a public **a** to the people.
1Co 3: 1 Brothers, I could not **a** you as

Addressed (Address)
Ac 2:14 raised his voice and **a** the crowd:
5:35 he **a** them: "Men of Israel, consider
15: 7 Peter got up and **a** them: "Brothers,

Addresses (Address)
Heb 12: 5 that **a** you as sons: "My son,

Adds (Add)
Job 34:37 To his sin he **a** rebellion;
Pr 10:22 wealth, and he **a** no trouble to it.
10:27 The fear of the LORD **a** length to
Heb 10:17 he **a**: "Their sins and lawless acts I
Rev 22:18 anyone **a** anything to them, God will

Adequately
Ac 18:26 to him the way of God more **a**.

Adhere
2Ki 17:34 They neither worship the LORD nor **a**

Adiel
1Ch 4:36 Asaiah, **A**, Jesimiel, Benaiah,
9:12 of Malkijah; and Maasai son of **A**,
27:25 Azmaveth son of **A** was in charge of

Adin
Ezr 2:15 of **A** 454
8: 6 of the descendants of **A**, Ebed son of
Ne 7:20 of **A** 655
10:16 Adonijah, Bigvai, **A**,

Adina
1Ch 11:42 **A** son of Shiza the Reubenite, who

Adithaim
Jos 15:36 Shaaraim, **A** and Gederah (or

Adjourned
Ac 24:22 with the Way, **a** the proceedings.

Adlai
1Ch 27:29 Shaphat son of **A** was in charge of

Admah
Ge 10:19 **A** and Zeboiim, as far as Lasha.
14: 2 Shinab king of **A**, Shemeber king of
14: 8 the king of Gomorrah, the king of **A**,
Dt 29:23 **A** and Zeboiim, which the LORD
Hos 11: 8 Israel? How can I treat you like **A**?

Admatha
Est 1:14 Shethar, **A**, Tarshish, Meres, Marsena

Administer (Administered, Administering, Administration, Administrator, Administrators)
1Ki 3:28 he had wisdom from God to **a** justice.
2Ch 19: 8 heads of Israelite families to **a** the
Ezr 7:25 appoint magistrates and judges to **a**
Jer 21:12 "'**A** justice every morning; rescue
Zec 7: 9 '**A** true justice; show mercy and
2Co 8:19 which we **a** in order to honour the
8:20 of the way we **a** this liberal gift.

Administered (Administer)
Heb 11:33 **a** justice, and gained what was

Administering (Administer)
1Ki 3:11 but for discernment in **a** justice,
1Pe 4:10 **a** God's grace in its various forms.

Administration (Administer)
1Co 12:28 those with gifts of **a**, and those
Eph 3: 2 Surely you have heard about the **a** of
3: 9 to make plain to everyone the **a** of

Administrator (Administer)
2Ki 10: 5 the palace **a**, the city governor, the
18:18 Eliakim son of Hilkiah the palace **a**,
18:37 Eliakim son of Hilkiah the palace **a**,
19: 2 He sent Eliakim the palace **a**, Shebna
Isa 36: 3 Eliakim son of Hilkiah the palace **a**,
36:22 Eliakim son of Hilkiah the palace **a**,
37: 2 He sent Eliakim the palace **a**, Shebna

Administrators (Administer)
2Ch 35: 8 Hilkiah, Zechariah and Jehiel, the **a**
Est 9: 3 the governors and the king's **a**
Da 2:49 Meshach and Abednego **a** over the
6: 2 with three **a** over them, one of whom
6: 3 distinguished himself among the **a**
6: 4 At this, the **a** and the satraps tried
6: 6 the **a** and the satraps went as a
6: 7 The royal **a**, prefects, satraps,

Admirable
Php 4: 8 whatever is lovely, whatever is **a**

Admit (Admitted)
Jos 20: 4 Then they are to **a** him into their
Job 27: 5 I will never **a** you are in the right;
40:14 I myself will **a** to you that your own
Isa 48: 6 Will you not **a** them? "From now on I
Hos 5:15 my place until they **a** their guilt.
Ac 24:14 However, I **a** that I worship the God
2Co 11:21 To my shame I **a** that we were too

Admitted (Admit)
Ne 13: 1 ever be **a** into the assembly of God,
Heb 11:13 And they **a** that they were aliens and

Admonish (Admonished, Admonishing, Admonition)
Col 3:16 and **a** one another with all wisdom,
1Th 5:12 over you in the Lord and who **a** you.

Admonished (Admonish)
Ne 9:26 They killed your prophets, who had **a**
9:30 By your Spirit you **a** them through

Admonishing (Admonish)
Col 1:28 We proclaim him, **a** and teaching

Admonition (Admonish)
Mal 2: 1 "And now this **a** is for you,
2: 4 have sent you this **a** so that my

Adna
Ezr 10:30 the descendants of Pahath-Moab: **A**,
Ne 12:15 of Harim's, **A**; of Meremoth's, Helkai;

Adnah
1Ch 12:20 of Manasseh who defected to him: **A**,
2Ch 17:14 commanders of units of 1,000: **A** the

Adoni-Bezek
Jdg 1: 5 was there that they found **A** and
1: 6 **A** fled, but they chased him and
1: 7 **A** said, "Seventy kings with their

Adonijah (Adonijah's)
1. Son of David, by Haggith (2Sa 3:4; 1Ch 3:2). Attempted to succeed David as king (1Ki 1); killed by Solomon's order after he requested Abishag for his wife (1Ki 2). **2.** Levite and teacher of the Law (2Ch 17:8–9).

2Sa 3: 4 the fourth, **A** the son of Haggith;
1Ki 1: 5 Now **A**, whose mother was Haggith, put
1: 7 **A** conferred with Joab son of Zeruiah
1: 8 David's special guard did not join **A**.
1: 9 **A** then sacrificed sheep, cattle and
1:11 "Have you not heard that **A**, the son
1:13 Why then has **A** become king?'
1:18 now **A** has become king, and you, my
1:24 my lord the king, declared that **A**
1:25 him and saying, 'Long live King **A**!'
1:41 **A** and all the guests who were with
1:42 **A** said, "Come in. A worthy man like
1:50 **A**, in fear of Solomon, went and took
1:51 Solomon was told, "**A** is afraid of
1:53 And **A** came and bowed down to King
2:13 Now **A**, the son of Haggith, went to
2:19 King Solomon to speak to him for **A**,
2:21 in marriage to your brother **A**."
2:22 Abishag the Shunammite for **A**?
2:23 be it ever so severely, if **A** does
2:24 **A** shall be put to death today!"
2:25 and he struck down **A** and he died.
2:28 who had conspired with **A** though not
1Ch 3: 2 the fourth, **A** the son of Haggith;
2Ch 17: 8 Asahel, Shemiramoth, Jehonathan, **A**,
Ne 10:16 **A**, Bigvai, Adin,

Adonijah's (Adonijah)
1Ki 1:49 At this, all **A** guests rose in alarm

Adonikam
Ezr 2:13 of **A** 666
8:13 of the descendants of **A**, the last
Ne 7:18 of **A** 667

Adoniram
2Sa 20:24 **A** was in charge of forced labour;
1Ki 4: 6 **A** son of Abdon—in charge of forced
5:14 **A** was in charge of the forced labour.
12:18 King Rehoboam sent out **A**, who was in
2Ch 10:18 King Rehoboam sent out **A**, who was in

Adoni-Zedek
Jos 10: 1 Now **A** king of Jerusalem heard that
10: 3 **A** king of Jerusalem appealed to

Adopt (Adopted, Adoption)
Job 15: 5 Your sin prompts your mouth; you **a**

Adopted (Adopt)
Est 2:15 for Esther (the girl Mordecai had **a**,
Ps 106:35 they mingled with the nations and **a**
Eph 1: 5 he predestined us to be **a** as his

Adoption (Adopt)
Ro 8:23 we wait eagerly for our **a** as sons,
9: 4 the people of Israel. Theirs is the **a**

Adoraim
2Ch 11: 9 **A**, Lachish, Azekah,

Adore
SS 1: 4 How right they are to **a** you!

Adorn (Adorned, Adornment, Adorns)
Job 40:10 **a** yourself with glory and splendour,
Ps 144:12 like pillars carved to **a** a palace.

Pr 1: 9 head and a chain to a your neck.
Isa 60: 7 and I will a my glorious temple.
60:13 to a the place of my sanctuary; and
Jer 4:30 with paint? You a yourself in vain.
10: 4 They a it with silver and gold; they

Adorned (Adorn)

2Sa 1:24 who a your garments with ornaments
2Ch 3: 6 He a the temple with precious stones.
Ps 45: 8 from palaces a with ivory the music
Eze 16:11 I a you with jewellery: I put
16:13 you were a with gold and silver;
28:13 every precious stone a you: ruby,
Hos 10: 1 prospered, he a his sacred stones.
Am 3:15 the houses a with ivory will be
Lk 21: 5 temple was a with beautiful stones

Adornment (Adorn)

1Pe 3: 3 should not come from outward a,

Adorns (Adorn)

Ps 93: 5 Your statutes stand firm; holiness a
Isa 61:10 as a bridegroom a his head like a
61:10 a bride a herself with her jewels.

Adrammelech

2Ki 17:31 as sacrifices to A and Anammelech,
19:37 his sons A and Sharezer cut him down
Isa 37:38 his sons A and Sharezer cut him down

Adramyttium

Ac 27: 2 We boarded a ship from A about to

Adriatic

Ac 27:27 still being driven across the A Sea,

Adriel

1Sa 18:19 given in marriage to A of Meholah.
2Sa 21: 8 A son of Barzillai the Meholathite.

Adullam (Adullamite)

Canaanite city whose king was defeated by Joshua (Jos 12:15). Allotted to the tribe of Judah (Jos 15:35), it was fortified by Rehoboam as part of his southern defences (2Ch 11:7). David and his men hid from Saul in Adullam's caves (1Sa 22:1; 2Sa 23:13; 1Ch 11:15).

Ge 38: 1 to stay with a man of A named Hirah.
Jos 12:15 the king of Libnah one the king of A
15:35 Jarmuth, A, Socoh, Azekah,
1Sa 22: 1 Gath and escaped to the cave of A.
2Sa 23:13 came down to David at the cave of A,
1Ch 11:15 David to the rock at the cave of A,
2Ch 11: 7 Beth Zur, Soco, A,
Ne 11:30 Zanoah, A and their villages, in
Mic 1:15 the glory of Israel will come to A.

Adullamite (Adullam)

Ge 38:12 friend Hirah the A went with him.
38:20 the young goat by his friend the A

Adulterer (Adultery)

Lev 20:10 both the a and the adulteress must
Job 24:15 The eye of the a watches for dusk;
Heb 13: 4 the a and all the sexually immoral.

Adulterers (Adultery)

Ps 50:18 him; you throw in your lot with a.
Isa 57: 3 you offspring of a and prostitutes!
Jer 9: 2 all a, a crowd of unfaithful people.
23:10 The land is full of a; because of
Hos 7: 4 They are all a, burning like an oven
Mal 3: 5 a and perjurers, against those who
Lk 18:11 robbers, evildoers, a—or even like
1Co 6: 9 sexually immoral nor idolaters nor a
1Ti 1:10 for a and perverts, for slave

Adulteress (Adultery)

Lev 20:10 and the a must be put to death.
Pr 2:16 will save you also from the a, from
5: 3 For the lips of an a drip honey, and
5:20 Why be captivated, my son, by an a?
6:26 and the a preys upon your very life.
Pr 7: 5 they will keep you from the a, from
22:14 The mouth of an a is a deep pit;
30:20 "This is the way of an a: She eats
Hos 3: 1 she is loved by another and is an a.
Mt 5:32 causes her to become an a, and
Ro 7: 3 is still alive, she is called an a.
7: 3 from that law and is not an a,

Adulteries (Adultery)

Jer 3: 8 sent her away because of all her a.
13:27 your a and lustful neighings, your
Rev 14: 8 drink the maddening wine of her a."
17: 2 intoxicated with the wine of her a."
17: 4 things and the filth of her a.
18: 3 drunk the maddening wine of her a.
19: 2 who corrupted the earth by her a.

Adulterous (Adultery)

Eze 6: 9 have been grieved by their a hearts,
16:32 "'You a wife! You prefer strangers
23:45 are a and blood is on their hands.
Hos 1: 2 "Go, take to yourself an a wife and
2: 2 Let her remove the a look from her
Mt 12:39 He answered, "A wicked and a
16: 4 A wicked and a generation looks for
Mk 8:38 in this a and sinful generation,
Jas 4: 4 You a people, don't you know that

Adultery (Adulterer, Adulterers, Adulteress, Adulteries, Adulterous)

Ex 20:14 "You shall not commit a.
Lev 20:10 "'If a man commits a with another
Dt 5:18 "You shall not commit a.
Ps 51: T David had committed a with Bathsheba.
Pr 6:32 a man who commits a lacks judgment;
Jer 3: 6 tree and has committed a there.
3: 8 she also went out and committed a.
3: 9 and committed a with stone and wood.
5: 7 yet they committed a and thronged to
7: 9 "'Will you steal and murder, commit a
23:14 They commit a and live a lie.
29:23 committed a with their neighbours'
Eze 16:38 who commit a and who shed blood;
23:37 for they have committed a and blood
23:37 They committed a with their idols;
23:43 I said about the one worn out by a,
23:45 women who commit a and shed blood,
Hos 1: 2 a in departing from the LORD."
2: 4 because they are the children of a.
4: 2 lying and murder, stealing and a;
4:13 and your daughters-in-law to a.
4:14 daughters-in-law when they commit a,
4:15 "Though you commit a, O Israel, let
Mt 5:27 that it was said, 'Do not commit a.'
5:28 committed a with her in his heart.
5:32 marries the divorced woman commits a
15:19 murder, a, sexual immorality, theft,
19: 9 marries another woman commits a."
19:18 "'Do not murder, do not commit a, do
Mk 7:21 sexual immorality, theft, murder, a,
10:11 another woman commits a against her.
10:12 marries another man, she commits a."
10:19 'Do not murder, do not commit a, do
Lk 16:18 and marries another woman commits a,
16:18 marries a divorced woman commits a.
18:20 'Do not commit a, do not murder, do
Jn 8: 3 brought in a woman caught in a.
8: 4 woman was caught in the act of a.
Ro 2:22 say that people should not commit a,
2:22 do you commit a? You who abhor idols,
13: 9 The commandments, "Do not commit a,"
Jas 2:11 For he who said, "Do not commit a,"
2:11 If you do not commit a but do
2Pe 2:14 With eyes full of a, they never stop
Rev 2:22 and I will make those who commit a
17: 2 the kings of the earth committed a
18: 3 The kings of the earth committed a
18: 9 the earth who committed a with her

Adults

1Co 14:20 infants, but in your thinking be a.

Adummim

Jos 15: 7 the Pass of A south of the gorge.
18:17 which faces the Pass of A, and ran

Advance (Advanced, Advances, Advancing)

Dt 1: 7 Break camp and a into the hill
Jos 6: 7 he ordered the people, "A! March
8: 5 I and all those with me will a on
Jdg 4:15 At Barak's a, the LORD routed Sisera
9:33 In the morning at sunrise, a against
2Sa 22:30 With your help I can a against a
Job 19:12 His troops a in force; they build a
30:14 They a as through a gaping breach;
Ps 18:29 With your help I can a against a
27: 2 evil men a against me to devour my
Pr 30:27 locusts have no king, yet they a
Eze 38:16 You will a against my people Israel
Da 11:13 a with a huge army fully equipped.
Joel 3:12 a into the Valley of Jehoshaphat,
Hab 1: 9 Their hordes a like a desert wind
Ro 9:23 whom he prepared in a for glory—
2Co 9: 5 urge the brothers to visit you in a
Gal 3: 8 and announced the gospel in a to
Eph 2:10 God prepared in a for us to do.
Php 1:12 has really served to a the gospel.

Advanced (Advance)

Ge 18:11 already old and well a in years,
24: 1 Abraham was now old and well a in
Jos 13: 1 Joshua was old and well a in years,
23: 1 by then old and well a in years,
23: 2 them: "I am old and well a in years.
Jdg 1:10 They a against the Canaanites living
1:11 From there they a against the people
11:29 there he a against the Ammonites.
1Sa 17:12 time he was old and well a in years.
2Sa 10:13 Joab and the troops with him a to
1Ki 1: 1 King David was old and well a in
20:21 The king of Israel a and overpowered
2Ki 24:10 a on Jerusalem and laid siege to it,
1Ch 19:14 Joab and the troops with him a to
19:17 he a against them and formed his
Job 32: 7 'Age should speak; a years should
Ps 18:12 brightness of his presence clouds a,
48: 4 the kings joined forces, when they a

Advances (Advance)

Jer 4:13 Look! He a like the clouds, his
46:22 serpent as the enemy a in force;
Na 2: 1 An attacker a against you, Nineveh.

Advancing (Advance)

1Ki 20:17 reported, "Men are a from Samaria.
Eze 38: 9 a like a storm; you will be like a
Mt 11:12 a, and forceful men lay hold of it.
Gal 1:14 I was a in Judaism beyond many Jews

Advantage

Ex 22:22 "Do not take a of a widow or an
Lev 25:14 him, do not take a of each other.
25:17 Do not take a of each other, but
Dt 24:14 Do not take a of a hired man who is
Ecc 3:19 man has no a over the animal.
6: 8 What a has a wise man over a fool?
7:12 but the a of knowledge is this: that
Isa 30: 5 nor a, but only shame and disgrace."
Ro 3: 1 What a, then, is there in being a
2Co 11:20 or exploits you or takes a of you or
1Th 4: 6 wrong his brother or take a of him.
Heb 13:17 for that would be of no a to you.
Jude :16 and flatter others for their own a.

Adventurers

Jdg 9: 4 a, who became his followers.
11: 3 where a group of a gathered around

Adversaries (Adversary)

Dt 32:41 on my a and repay those who hate me.
2Sa 19:22 This day you have become my a!
22:40 you made my a bow at my feet.
Job 27: 7 the wicked, my a like the unjust!
Ps 18:39 you made my a bow at my feet.
44: 7 our enemies, you put our a to shame.
44:10 enemy, and our a have plundered us.
74:23 Do not ignore the clamour of your a,
89:23 before him and strike down his a.
92:11 My eyes have seen the defeat of my a;

Ps 106:11 The waters covered their **a**; not one
139:20 intent; your **a** misuse your name.
Da 4:19 enemies and its meaning to your **a**!
Lk 21:15 wisdom that none of your **a** will be

Adversary (Adversaries, Adversity)
Dt 32:27 lest the **a** misunderstand and say,
1Ki 5: 4 side, and there is no **a** or disaster.
11:14 LORD raised up against Solomon an **a**,
11:23 raised up against Solomon another **a**,
11:25 Rezon was Israel's **a** as long as
Est 7: 6 Esther said, "The **a** and enemy is
Mt 5:25 "Settle matters quickly with your **a**
Lk 12:58 you are going with your **a** to the
18: 3 'Grant me justice against my **a**.'

Adversity (Adversary)
Pr 17:17 times, and a brother is born for **a**.
Isa 30:20 of **a** and the water of affliction,

Advice (Advise)
Ex 18:19 you some **a**, and may God be with you.
Nu 31:16 the ones who followed Balaam's **a**.
2Sa 15:34 me by frustrating Ahithophel's **a**.
16:20 said to Ahithophel, "Give us your **a**.
16:23 Now in those days the **a** Ahithophel
16:23 regarded all of Ahithophel's **a**.
17: 6 said, "Ahithophel has given this **a**.
17: 7 Hushai replied to Absalom, "The **a**
17:14 "The **a** of Hushai the Arkite is
17:14 frustrate the good **a** of Ahithophel
17:23 Ahithophel saw that his **a** had not
20:22 to all the people with her wise **a**,
1Ki 12: 8 Rehoboam rejected the **a** the elders
12: 9 He asked them, "What is your **a**? How
12:13 the **a** given him by the elders,
12:14 he followed the **a** of the young men
12:28 After seeking **a**, the king made two
2Ch 10: 8 Rehoboam rejected the **a** the elders
10: 9 He asked them, "What is your **a**? How
10:13 Rejecting the **a** of the elders,
10:14 he followed the **a** of the young men
Est 1:21 his nobles were pleased with this **a**,
2: 4 This **a** appealed to the king, and he
Job 26: 3 What **a** you have offered to one
Pr 1:25 since you ignored all my **a** and would
1:30 since they would not accept my **a** and
12: 5 the **a** of the wicked is deceitful.
12:15 to him, but a wise man listens to **a**.
13:10 wisdom is found in those who take **a**.
19:20 Listen to **a** and accept instruction,
20:18 Make plans by seeking **a**; if you wage
Isa 19:11 of Pharaoh give senseless **a**.
Eze 11: 2 and giving wicked **a** in this city.
Da 4:27 O king, be pleased to accept my **a**:
Ac 27:11 followed the **a** of the pilot and of
27:21 "Men, you should have taken my **a** not
2Co 8:10 here is my **a** about what is best for

Advisable (Advise)
1Co 16: 4 If it seems **a** for me to go also,

Advise (Advice, Advisable, Advised, Adviser, Advisers)
2Sa 17:11 "So I **a** you: Let all Israel, from
1Ki 1:12 Now then, let me **a** you how you can
12: 6 "How would you **a** me to answer these
2Ch 10: 6 "How would you **a** me to answer these
Ac 5:38 Therefore, in the present case I **a**

Advised (Advise)
2Sa 17:15 "Ahithophel has **a** Absalom and the
17:15 but I have **a** them to do so and so.
17:21 has **a** such and such against you."
1Ki 20:23 the officials of the king of Aram **a**
Jn 18:14 Caiaphas was the one who had **a** the

Adviser (Advise)
Ge 26:26 with Ahuzzath his personal **a** and
1Ki 4: 5 priest and personal **a** to the king;
2Ch 25:16 "Have we appointed you an **a** to the

Advisers (Advise)
2Sa 8:18 and David's sons were royal **a**.
2Ki 25:19 the fighting men and five royal **a**.
2Ch 22: 4 they became his **a**, to his undoing.
25:17 king of Judah consulted his **a**,
Ezr 7:14 his seven **a** to enquire about Judah
7:15 gold that the king and his **a** have
7:28 his **a** and all the king's powerful
8:25 his **a**, his officials and all Israel
Est 6:13 His **a** and his wife Zeresh said to
Job 12:20 He silences the lips of trusted **a**
Pr 11:14 falls, but many **a** make victory sure.
15:22 but with many **a** they succeed.
24: 6 guidance, and for victory many **a**.
Jer 52:25 the fighting men, and seven royal **a**.
Da 3: 2 prefects, governors, **a**, treasurers,
3: 3 the satraps, prefects, governors, **a**,
3:24 feet in amazement and asked his **a**,
3:27 and royal **a** crowded around them.
4:36 My **a** and nobles sought me out, and I
6: 7 prefects, satraps, **a** and governors

Advocate (Advocating)
Job 16:19 is in heaven; my **a** is on high.

Advocating (Advocate)
Ac 16:21 by **a** customs unlawful for us Romans
17:18 "He seems to be **a** foreign gods.

Aeneas
Ac 9:33 There he found a man named **A**, a
9:34 "**A**," Peter said to him, "Jesus
9:34 up your mat. Immediately **A** got up.

Aenon
Jn 3:23 Now John also was baptising at **A**

Affair (Affairs)
Nu 25:18 **a** of Peor and their sister Cozbi,
1Sa 22:15 nothing at all about this whole **a**."

Affairs (Affair)
1Ch 26:32 to God and for the **a** of the king.
Ne 11:24 in all **a** relating to the people.
Ps 112: 5 who conducts his **a** with justice.
Pr 31:27 She watches over the **a** of her
Da 3:12 the **a** of the province of Babylon—
6: 4 Daniel in his conduct of government **a**
1Co 7:32 Lord's **a**—how he can please the Lord.
7:33 concerned about the **a** of this world
7:34 is concerned about the Lord's **a**:
7:34 concerned about the **a** of this world
1Ti 5:17 The elders who direct the **a** of the
2Ti 2: 4 soldier gets involved in civilian **a**

Affect (Affected, Affects)
Job 35: 6 If you sin, how does that **a** him? If

Affected (Affect)
Lev 13:50 the **a** article for seven days.
13:55 After the **a** article has been washed,
13:55 mildew has **a** one side or the other.

Affection
Dt 7: 7 The LORD did not set his **a** on you
10:15 Yet the LORD set his **a** on your
Eze 24:21 of your eyes, the object of your **a**.
2Co 6:12 We are not withholding our **a** from
7:15 his **a** for you is all the greater
Php 1: 8 of you with the **a** of Christ Jesus.

Affects (Affect)
Job 35: 8 Your wickedness **a** only a man like

Affirm (Reaffirm)
1Ti 1: 7 about or what they so confidently **a**.

Affixing (Fix)
Ne 9:38 priests are **a** their seals to it."

Afflict (Afflicted, Afflicting, Affliction, Afflictions)
Lev 26:24 **a** you for your sins seven times over.
Dt 28:27 The LORD will **a** you with the boils
28:28 The LORD will **a** you with madness,
28:35 The LORD will **a** your knees and legs
Ps 55:19 will hear them and **a** them—Selah
Na 1:12 ⌊O Judah⌋ I will **a** you no more.

Afflicted (Afflict)
Dt 29:22 diseases with which the LORD has **a** it
Jos 24: 5 and I **a** the Egyptians by what I did
Jdg 2:18 those who oppressed and **a** them.
Ru 1:21 Why call me Naomi? The LORD has **a** me;
1Sa 5: 6 upon them and **a** them with tumours.
5: 9 He **a** the people of the city, both
5:12 Those who did not die were **a** with
1Ki 8:35 their sin because you have **a** them,
2Ki 15: 5 The LORD **a** the king with leprosy
17:20 he **a** them and gave them into the
2Ch 6:26 their sin because you have **a** them,
16:12 Asa was **a** with a disease in his feet.
21:18 After all this, the LORD **a** Jehoram
26:20 leave, because the LORD had **a** him.
Job 2: 7 **a** Job with painful sores from the
30:11 God has unstrung my bow and **a** me,
36: 6 alive but gives the **a** their rights.
Ps 9:12 he does not ignore the cry of the **a**.
9:18 nor the hope of the **a** ever perish.
10:17 O LORD, the desire of the **a**; you
22:24 the suffering of the **a** one;
25:16 to me, for I am lonely and **a**.
34: 2 LORD; let the **a** hear and rejoice.
72: 2 your **a** ones with justice.
72: 4 He will defend the **a** among the
72:12 out, the **a** who have no-one to help.
74:19 the lives of your **a** people for ever.
76: 9 to save all the **a** of the land.
88:15 From my youth I have been **a** and
90:15 for as many days as you have **a** us,
102: T A prayer of an **a** man. When he is
116:10 therefore I said, "I am greatly **a**.
119:67 Before I was **a** I went astray, but
119:71 was good for me to be **a** so that I
119:75 and in faithfulness you have **a** me.
Isa 1: 5 head is injured, your whole heart **a**.
14:32 in her his **a** people will find refuge
49:13 will have compassion on his **a** ones.
51:21 Therefore hear this, you **a** one, made
53: 4 by God, smitten by him, and **a**.
53: 7 He was oppressed and **a**, yet he did
54:11 "O **a** city, lashed by storms and not
Jer 14:19 Do you despise Zion? Why have you **a**
Na 1:12 Although I have **a** you, O Judah, I
Zec 11:11 and so the **a** of the flock who were

Afflicting (Afflict)
2Sa 24:16 to the angel who was **a** the people,

Affliction (Afflict)
Dt 16: 3 eat unleavened bread, the bread of **a**,
Job 10:15 full of shame and drowned in my **a**.
36: 8 in chains, held fast by cords of **a**,
36:15 he speaks to them in their **a**.
36:21 evil, which you seem to prefer to **a**.
Ps 25:18 Look upon my **a** and my distress and
31: 7 you saw my **a** and knew the anguish of
31:10 my strength fails because of my **a**,
107:17 **a** because of their iniquities.
107:41 he lifted the needy out of their **a**
119:92 I would have perished in my **a**.
Ecc 5:17 with great frustration, **a** and anger.
Isa 30:20 of adversity and the water of **a**,
48:10 have tested you in the furnace of **a**.
Lam 1: 3 After **a** and harsh labour, Judah has
1: 7 In the days of her **a** and wandering
1: 9 "Look, O LORD, on my **a**, for the
3: 1 I am the man who has seen **a** by the
3:19 I remember my **a** and my wandering,
3:33 For he does not willingly bring **a** or
Ro 12:12 Be joyful in hope, patient in **a**,

Afflictions (Afflict)
Lev 26:21 I will multiply your **a** seven times
1Ki 8:38 one aware of the **a** of his own heart,
2Ch 6:29 one aware of his **a** and pains,
Col 1:24 lacking in regard to Christ's **a**,
Rev 2: 9 I know your **a** and your poverty—yet

Afford (Afforded)
Lev 5: 7 "If he cannot a a lamb, he is to
5:11 "If, however, he cannot a two doves
12: 8 If she cannot a a lamb, she is to
14:21 "If, however, he is poor and cannot a
14:22 which he can a, one for a sin
14:30 pigeons, which the person can a,
14:32 who cannot a the regular offerings
27: 8 what the man making the vow can a.
Nu 6:21 addition to whatever else he can a.

Afforded (Afford)
Ro 7: 8 sin, seizing the opportunity a by
7:11 For sin, seizing the opportunity a

Aflame (Flame)
Isa 13: 8 aghast at each other, their faces a.

Afoot (Foot)
Ac 14: 5 There was a plot a among the

Afraid (*Do not be afraid*, Fear)
Ge 3:10 a because I was naked; so I hid."
18:15 Sarah was a, so she lied and said,
19:30 for he was a to stay in Zoar.
20: 8 had happened, they were very much a.
26: 7 he was a to say, "She is my wife.
28:17 He was a and said, "How awesome is
31:31 Jacob answered Laban, "I was a,
32:11 for I am a he will come and attack
35:17 be a, for you have another son."
42: 4 was a that harm might come to him.
43:23 "Don't be a. Your God, the God of
50:19 Joseph said to them, "Don't be a. Am
50:21 then, don't be a. I will provide for
Ex 2:14 Then Moses was a and thought,
3: 6 because he was a to look at God.
34:30 and they were a to come near him.
Lev 26: 6 lie down and no-one will make you a.
Nu 12: 8 a to speak against my servant Moses?"
21:34 The LORD said to Moses, "Do not be a
Dt 2: 4 be a of you, but be very careful.
5: 5 because you were a of the fire and
13:11 all Israel will hear and be a, and
17:13 All the people will hear and be a,
19:20 people will hear of this and be a,
20: 3 Do not be faint-hearted or a; do not
20: 8 the officers shall add, "Is any man a
21:21 All Israel will hear of it and be a.
Jdg 6:27 But because he was a of his family
7:10 If you are a to attack, go down to
8:20 because he was only a boy and was a.
9:21 he was a of his brother Abimelech.
Ru 3:11 now, my daughter, don't be a. I will
1Sa 3:15 He was a to tell Eli the vision,
4: 7 the Philistines were a. "A god has
7: 7 were a because of the Philistines.
15:24 I was a of the people and so I gave
18:12 Saul was a of David, because the
18:15 successful he was, he was a of him.
18:29 Saul became still more a of him, and
21:12 very much a of Achish king of Gath.
22:23 Stay with me; don't be a; the man
23: 3 to him, "Here in Judah we are a.
23:17 "Don't be a," he said. "My father
28: 5 he was a; terror filled his heart.
28:13 The king said to her, "Don't be a.
2Sa 1:14 David asked him, "Why were you not a
3:11 to Abner, because he was a of him.
6: 9 David was a of the LORD that day and
9: 7 "Don't be a," David said to him,
10:19 a to help the Ammonites any more.
12:18 David's servants were a to tell him
13:28 Don't be a. Have not I given you
14:15 because the people have made me a.
1Ki 1:51 Solomon was told, "Adonijah is a of
17:13 Elijah said to her, "Don't be a. Go
19: 3 Elijah was a and ran for his life.
2Ki 6:16 "Don't be a," the prophet answered.
1Ch 13:12 David was a of God that day and
21:30 because he was a of the sword of the
2Ch 32:18 them a in order to capture the city.
Ezr 4: 4 and make them a to go on building.
Ne 2: 2 I was very much a,
4:14 of the people, "Don't be a of them.
6:16 all the surrounding nations were a
Est 9: 2 other nationalities were a of them.
Job 6:21 see something dreadful and are a.
11:19 lie down, with no-one to make you a,
39:22 He laughs at fear, a of nothing; he
Ps 27: 1 of my life—of whom shall I be a?
56: 3 I am a, I will trust in you.
56: 4 in God I trust; I will not be a.
56:11 in God I trust; I will not be a.
118: 6 The LORD is with me; I will not be a.
Pr 3:24 you lie down, you will not be a;
Ecc 9: 2 with those who are a to take them.
12: 5 men are a of heights and of dangers
Isa 7: 4 Be careful, keep calm and don't be a.
12: 2 I will trust and not be a.
17: 2 down, with no-one to make them a.
20: 5 in Egypt will be a and put to shame.
40: 9 lift it up, do not be a; say to the
Jer 23: 4 and they will no longer be a or
30:10 and no-one will make him a.
38:19 "I am a of the Jews who have gone
41:18 They were a of them because Ishmael
46:27 and no-one will make him a.
51:46 Do not lose heart or be a when
Eze 2: 6 you, son of man, do not be a of them
34:28 safety, and no-one will make them a.
39:26 land with no-one to make them a.
Da 1:10 the official told Daniel, "I am a of
4: 5 I had a dream that made me a. As I
Joel 2:21 Be not a, O land; be glad and
2:22 Be not a, O wild animals, for the
Jnh 1: 5 All the sailors were a and each
Mic 4: 4 and no-one will make them a,
7:17 LORD our God and will be a of you.
Zep 3:13 down and no-one will make them a."
Mt 2:22 father Herod, he was a to go there.
8:26 of little faith, why are you so a?"
10:26 "So do not be a of them. There is
10:28 Rather, be a of the One who can
10:31 don't be a; you are worth more than
14: 5 but he was a of the people, because
14:30 when he saw the wind, he was a and,
17: 7 "Get up," he said. "Don't be a."
21:26 if we say, 'From men'—we are a of
21:46 but they were a of the crowd because
25:25 I was a and went out and hid your
28: 4 The guards were so a of him that
28: 8 a yet filled with joy, and ran to
Mk 4:40 so a? Do you still have no faith?"
5:15 in his right mind; and they were a.
5:36 ruler, "Don't be a; just believe.
6:50 Take courage! It is I. Don't be a.
9:32 and were a to ask him about it.
10:32 while those who followed were a.
12:12 But they were a of the crowd; so
16: 8 to anyone, because they were a.
Lk 5:10 a; from now on you will catch men."
8:35 in his right mind; and they were a.
8:50 "Don't be a; just believe, and she
9:34 were a as they entered the cloud.
9:45 and they were a to ask him about it.
12: 7 Don't be a; you are worth more than
19:21 I was a of you, because you are a
20:19 But they were a of the people.
22: 2 Jesus, for they were a of the people.
Jn 6:20 he said to them, "It is I; don't be a
9:22 because they were a of the Jews,
19: 8 Pilate heard this, he was even more a
Ac 9:26 but they were all a of him, not
23:10 commander was a Paul would be torn
24:25 Felix was a and said, "That's enough
Ro 11:20 Do not be arrogant, but be a.
13: 4 But if you do wrong, be a, for he
2Co 11: 3 I am a that just as Eve was deceived
12:20 For I am a that when I come I may
12:21 I am a that when I come again my God
Gal 2:12 he was a of those who belonged to the
1Th 3: 5 I was a that in some way the tempter
Heb 11:23 they were not a of the king's edict.
13: 6 Lord is my helper; I will not be a.
2Pe 2:10 not a to slander celestial beings;

Afterbirth (Bear[1])
Dt 28:57 the a from her womb and the children

Afternoon
Jdg 19: 8 Wait till a!" So the two of them ate
Lk 9:12 Late in the a the Twelve came to him
Ac 3: 1 time of prayer—at three in the a.
10: 3 One day at about three in the a he
10:30 at this hour, at three in the a.

Agabus
Ac 11:28 One of them, named A, stood up and
21:10 named A came down from Judea.

Agag (Agagite)
Nu 24: 7 "Their king will be great than A;
1Sa 15: 8 He took A king of the Amalekites
15: 9 Saul and the army spared A and the
15:20 and brought back A their king.
15:32 Samuel said, "Bring me A king of the
15:32 A came to him confidently, thinking,
15:33 Samuel put A to death before the LORD

Agagite (Agag)
Est 3: 1 the A, elevating him and giving him
3:10 the A, the enemy of the Jews.
8: 3 end to the evil plan of Haman the A,
8: 5 the A, devised and wrote to destroy
9:24 For Haman son of Hammedatha, the A,

Agate
Ex 28:19 in the third row a jacinth, an a and
39:12 in the third row a jacinth, an a and

Age (*Age to come*, Aged, Ageing, Age-old, Ages, *End of the age*, *Old age*)
Ge 17:17 bear a child at the a of ninety?"
18:11 Sarah was past the a of childbearing.
50:26 Joseph died at the a of a hundred
Nu 4: 3 men from thirty to fifty years of a
4:23 men from thirty to fifty years of a
4:30 men from thirty to fifty years of a
4:35 men from thirty to fifty years of a
4:39 men from thirty to fifty years of a
4:43 men from thirty to fifty years of a
4:47 men from thirty to fifty years of a
8:25 at the a of fifty, they must retire
Jos 5: 4 all the men of military a—died in
5: 6 a when they left Egypt had died,
24:29 died at the a of a hundred and ten.
Jdg 2: 8 died at the a of a hundred and ten.
2Sa 19:32 a very old man, eighty years of a.
1Ki 14: 4 his sight was gone because of his a.
2Ch 24:15 at the a of a hundred and thirty.
Ezr 3: 8 Levites twenty years of a
Job 32: 7 I thought, 'A should speak; advanced
Da 1:10 than the other young men of your a?
5:31 the kingdom, at the a of sixty-two.
Zec 8: 4 with cane in hand because of his a.
Mt 12:32 not be forgiven either in this a or
Mk 10:30 as much in this present a (homes,
Lk 18:30 many times as much in this a and,
18:30 in the a to come, eternal life."
20:34 Jesus replied, "The people of this a
20:35 worthy of taking part in that a
Jn 9:21 is of a; he will speak for himself."
9:23 parents said, "He is of a; ask him.
1Co 1:20 Where is the philosopher of this a?
2: 6 but not the wisdom of this a or of
2: 6 this a, who are coming to nothing.
2: 8 None of the rulers of this a
3:18 of this a, he should become a "fool"
2Co 4: 4 The god of this a has blinded the
Gal 1: 4 rescue us from the present evil a,
1:14 Judaism beyond many Jews of my own a
Eph 1:21 a but also in the one to come.
1Ti 6:19 a firm foundation for the coming a,
Tit 2:12 and godly lives in this present a,
Heb 6: 5 God and the powers of the coming a,
11:11 even though he was past a—and Sarah

Age to come
Mt 12:32 either in this age or in the a.
Mk 10:30 and in the a, eternal life.
Lk 18:30 age and, in the a, eternal life."

Aged (Age)
Ge 43:27 "How is your a father you told me
44:20 we answered, 'We have an a father,
Lev 19:32 "Rise in the presence of the a,
1Ki 1:15 Bathsheba went to see the a king in
2Ch 36:17 man nor young woman, old man or a.
Job 12:12 Is not wisdom found among the a?
15:10 The grey-haired and the a are on our
32: 9 the a who understand what is right.
Pr 17: 6 children are a crown to the a,
Isa 25: 6 a banquet of a wine—the best of
47: 6 on the a you laid a very heavy yoke.

Agee
2Sa 23:11 Next to him was Shammah son of A the

Ageing (Age)
Heb 8:13 obsolete and a will soon disappear.

Agent
Ne 11:24 was the king's a in all affairs
Ro 13: 4 He is God's servant, an a of wrath

Age-old (Age)
Ge 49:26 than the bounty of the a hills.
Jdg 5:21 away, the a river, the river Kishon.
Isa 58:12 and will raise up the a foundations;
Hab 3: 6 crumbled and the a hills collapsed.

Ages (Age)
Ge 43:33 before him in the order of their a,
Lev 27: 3 set the value of a male between the a
27: 5 If it is a person between the a of
Isa 45:17 or disgraced, to a everlasting.
Joel 2: 2 old nor ever will be in a to come.
Ac 15:18 that have been known for a.
Ro 16:25 the mystery hidden for long a past,
1Co 10:11 the fulfilment of the a has come.
Eph 2: 7 in order that in the coming a he
3: 9 which for a past was kept hidden in
Col 1:26 kept hidden for a and generations,
Heb 9:26 the end of the a to do away with sin
Jude :25 all a, now and for evermore! Amen.
Rev 15: 3 true are your ways, King of the a.

Aggression (Aggressive, Aggressor)
Isa 14: 6 subdued nations with relentless a.

Aggressive (Aggression)
Isa 18: 2 an a nation of strange speech, whose
18: 7 an a nation of strange speech, whose

Aggressor (Aggression)
Isa 16: 4 the a will vanish from the land.

Aghast
Job 26:11 The pillars of the heavens quake, a
Isa 13: 8 a at each other, their faces aflame.

Agitating (Agitators)
Ac 17:13 a the crowds and stirring them up.

Agitators (Agitating)
Gal 5:12 for those a, I wish they would go

Agony
Ps 6: 2 LORD, heal me, for my bones are in a.
42:10 My bones suffer mortal a as my foes
Jer 4:19 Oh, the a of my heart! My heart
Eze 30:16 to Egypt; Pelusium will writhe in a.
Mic 4:10 Writhe in a, O Daughter of Zion,
Zec 9: 5 it and fear; Gaza will writhe in a,
Lk 16:24 because I am in a in this fire.'
16:25 is comforted here and you are in a.
Ac 2:24 freeing him from the a of death,
Rev 9: 5 And the a they suffered was like
16:10 Men gnawed their tongues in a

Agree (Agreed, Agreeing, Agreement, Agreements, Agrees)
Ge 34:17 if you will not a to be circumcised,
2Sa 14:16 Perhaps the king will a to deliver
1Ki 20: 8 listen to him or a to his demands."
22:13 a with theirs, and speak favourably."
2Ch 18:12 a with theirs, and speak favourably."
Mt 18:19 earth a about anything you ask for,
20:13 Didn't you a to work for a denarius?
Mk 14:56 him, but their statements did not a.
14:59 even then their testimony did not a.
Ac 5: 9 Peter said to her, "How could you a
Ro 7:16 if I do what I do not want to do, I a
1Co 1:10 that all of you a with one another
Php 4: 2 to a with each other in the Lord.
1Ti 6: 3 does not a to the sound instruction

Agreed (Agree)
Ge 16: 2 Abram a to what Sarai said.
23:16 Abraham a to Ephron's terms and
30:34 "A," said Laban. "Let it be as you
34:24 a with Hamor and his son Shechem,
37:27 His brothers a.
Ex 2:21 Moses a to stay with the man, who
Jos 2:21 "A," she replied. "Let it be as you
Jdg 15:13 "A," they answered. "We will only
17:11 the Levite a to live with him, and
1Ki 15:20 Ben-Hadad a with King Asa and sent
20:25 He a with them and acted accordingly.
2Ki 12: 8 The priests a that they would not
1Ch 13: 4 The whole assembly a to do this,
2Ch 16: 4 Ben-Hadad a with King Asa and sent
20:36 He a with him to construct a fleet
30:23 The whole assembly then a to
Est 9:23 the Jews a to continue the
Jer 34:10 a that they would free their male
34:10 They a, and set them free.
Da 1:14 he a to this and tested them for ten
6: 7 advisers and governors have all a
Am 3: 3 unless they have a to do so?
Mt 20: 2 He a to pay them a denarius for the
Lk 22: 5 They were delighted and a to give
Ac 15:25 we all a to choose some men and send
23:20 He said: "The Jews have a to ask you
Gal 2: 9 They a that we should go to the

Agreeing (Agree)
Rev 17:17 accomplish his purpose by a to give

Agreement (Agree)
Ge 26:28 a between us'—between us and you.
2Sa 3:12 "Whose land is it? Make an a with me,
3:13 "Good," said David. "I will make an a
Ne 9:38 we are making a binding a, putting
Job 2:11 met together by a to go and
41: 4 Will he make an a with you for you
Isa 28:15 with the grave we have made an a.
28:18 a with the grave will not stand.
Da 11:23 After coming to an a with him, he
Ac 15:15 The words of the prophets are in a
2Co 6:16 What a is there between the temple
1Jn 5: 8 the blood; and the three are in a.

Agreements (Agree)
Hos 10: 4 take false oaths and make a;

Agrees (Agree)
Ac 7:42 This a with what is written in the
24:14 I believe everything that a with the
1Co 4:17 which a with what I teach everywhere

Agrippa
1. Herod Agrippa I, grandson of Herod the Great. Jewish king, killed apostle James and imprisoned Peter (Ac 12:1–4); sudden death (Ac 12:20–23). **2.** Herod Agrippa II, son of Herod Agrippa I, before whom Paul appeared at Caesarea (Ac 25:13–26:32).

Ac 25:13 A few days later King A and Bernice
25:22 A said to Festus, "I would like to
25:23 The next day A and Bernice came with
25:24 Festus said: "King A, and all who
25:26 and especially before you, King A,
26: 1 A said to Paul, "You have permission
26: 2 "King A, I consider myself fortunate
26:19 "So then, King A, I was not
26:27 King A, do you believe the prophets?
26:28 A said to Paul, "Do you think that
26:32 A said to Festus, "This man could

Aground (Ground)
Ac 27:17 Fearing that they would run a on the
27:26 Nevertheless, we must run a on some
27:39 to run the ship a if they could.
27:41 the ship struck a sand-bar and ran a.

Agur
Pr 30: 1 The sayings of A son of Jakeh—an

Ahab (Ahab's)
1. Son of Omri; evil king of Israel (1Ki 16:29–30). Married Jezebel; encouraged worship of Baal (1Ki 16:31–33). Opposed by Elijah (1Ki 17:1; 18:17–20). Defeated Arameans (1Ki 20); condemned for sparing Ben-Hadad (1Ki 20:42). Murdered Naboth and stole his vineyard (1Ki 21). Opposed by Micaiah (1Ki 22:1–28); killed (1Ki 22:34–38). **2.** False prophet (Jer 29:21–22).

1Ki 16:28 And A his son succeeded him as king.
16:29 A son of Omri became king of Israel,
16:30 A son of Omri did more evil in the
16:33 A also made an Asherah pole and did
17: 1 from Tishbe in Gilead, said to A,
18: 1 present yourself to A, and I will
18: 2 Elijah went to present himself to A.
18: 3 A had summoned Obadiah, who was in
18: 5 A had said to Obadiah, "Go through
18: 6 A going in one direction and Obadiah
18: 9 over to A to be put to death?
18:12 If I go and tell A and he doesn't
18:15 surely present myself to A today."
18:16 Obadiah went to meet A and told him,
18:16 told him, and A went to meet Elijah.
18:20 A sent word throughout all Israel
18:41 Elijah said to A, "Go, eat and drink,
18:42 A went off to eat and drink, but
18:44 So Elijah said, "Go and tell A,
18:45 came on and A rode off to Jezreel.
18:46 ahead of A all the way to Jezreel.
19: 1 Now A told Jezebel everything Elijah
20: 2 He sent messengers into the city to A
20:10 Ben-Hadad sent another message to A:
20:13 Meanwhile a prophet came to A king
20:14 "But who will do this?" asked A. The
20:15 A summoned the young officers of the
20:33 A had him come up into his chariot.
20:34 ⌞A said,⌟ "On the basis of a treaty
21: 1 to the palace of A king of Samaria.
21: 2 A said to Naboth, "Let me have your
21: 4 A went home, sullen and angry
21:15 she said to A, "Get up and take
21:16 A heard that Naboth was dead, he got
21:18 "Go down to meet A king of Israel,
21:20 A said to Elijah, "So you have found
21:21 cut off from A every last male in
21:24 "Dogs will eat those belonging to A
21:25 (There was never a man like A, who
21:27 A heard these words, he tore his
21:29 "Have you noticed how A has humbled
22:20 the LORD said, 'Who will entice A
22:40 A rested with his fathers. And
22:41 the fourth year of A king of Israel.
22:49 At that time Ahaziah son of A said
22:51 Ahaziah son of A became king of
2Ki 3: 1 Joram son of A became king of Israel
3: 5 after A died, the king of Moab
8:16 In the fifth year of Joram son of A
8:18 as the house of A had done, for he
8:18 for he married a daughter of A.
8:25 In the twelfth year of Joram son of A
8:27 in the ways of the house of A
8:27 as the house of A had done, for he
8:28 Ahaziah went with Joram son of A to
8:29 of A, because he had been wounded.
9: 7 You are to destroy the house of A
9: 8 The whole house of A will perish. I
9: 8 I will cut off from A every last
9: 9 I will make the house of A like the
9:25 riding together in chariots behind A
9:29 the eleventh year of Joram, son of A,
10: 1 seventy sons of the house of A.
10:10 against the house of A will fail.
10:11 who remained of the house of A,
10:18 "A served Baal a little; Jehu will
10:30 house of A all I had in mind to do,

2Ki 21: 3 pole, as **A** king of Israel had done.
21:13 used against the house of **A**.
2Ch 18: 1 allied himself with **A** by marriage.
18: 2 he went down to visit **A** in Samaria.
18: 2 **A** slaughtered many sheep and cattle
18: 3 **A** king of Israel asked Jehoshaphat
18:19 the LORD said, 'Who will entice **A**
21: 6 as the house of **A** had done, for he
21: 6 for he married a daughter of **A**.
21:13 just as the house of **A** did.
22: 3 in the ways of the house of **A**,
22: 4 as the house of **A** had done, for
22: 5 Joram son of **A** king of Israel to war
22: 6 of **A** because he had been wounded.
22: 7 anointed to destroy the house of **A**.
22: 8 judgment on the house of **A**,
Jer 29:21 the God of Israel, says about **A** son
29:22 LORD treat you like Zedekiah and **A**,

Ahab's (Ahab)

1Ki 16:34 In **A** time, Hiel of Bethel rebuilt
21: 8 she wrote letters in **A** name, placed
22:39 for the other events of **A** reign,
2Ki 1: 1 After **A** death, Moab rebelled against
8:27 was related by marriage to **A** family.
10: 1 and to the guardians of **A** children.
10:17 of **A** family; he destroyed them,
Mic 6:16 and all the practices of **A** house,

Aharah

1Ch 8: 1 Ashbel the second son, **A** the third,

Aharhel

1Ch 4: 8 and of the clans of **A** son of Harum.

Ahasbai

2Sa 23:34 Eliphelet son of **A** the Maacathite,

Ahava

Ezr 8:15 **A**, and we camped there three days.
8:21 There, by the **A** Canal, I proclaimed
8:31 from the **A** Canal to go to Jerusalem.

Ahaz

Son of Jotham; king of Judah (2Ki 16). Worshipped foreign gods (2Ki 16:3–4,10–18; 2Ch 28:2–4, 22–25). Attacked by Aram and Israel (2Ki 16:5–6; 2Ch 28:5–8). Turned for help to Assyria rather than God (2Ki 16:7–9; 2Ch 28:16; Isa 7:3–17).

2Ki 15:38 And **A** his son succeeded him as king.
16: 1 **A** son of Jotham king of Judah began
16: 2 **A** was twenty years old when he
16: 5 **A**, but they could not overpower him.
16: 7 **A** sent messengers to say to
16: 8 **A** took the silver and gold found in
16:10 King **A** went to Damascus to meet
16:11 that King **A** had sent from Damascus
16:11 finished it before King **A** returned.
16:15 King **A** then gave these orders to
16:16 Uriah the priest did just as King **A**
16:17 King **A** took away the side panels and
16:19 the other events of the reign of **A**,
16:20 **A** rested with his fathers and was
17: 1 In the twelfth year of **A** king of
18: 1 of **A** king of Judah began to reign.
20:11 had gone down on the stairway of **A**.
23:12 the roof near the upper room of **A**,
1Ch 3:13 **A** his son, Hezekiah his son,
8:35 Micah: Pithon, Melech, Tarea and **A**.
8:36 **A** was the father of Jehoaddah,
9:41 Micah: Pithon, Melech, Tahrea and **A**.
9:42 **A** was the father of Jadah, Jadah was
2Ch 27: 9 And **A** his son succeeded him as king.
28: 1 **A** was twenty years old when he
28:16 At that time King **A** sent to the king
28:19 Judah because of **A** king of Israel,
28:21 **A** took some of the things from the
28:22 In his time of trouble King **A** became
28:24 **A** gathered together the furnishings
28:27 **A** rested with his fathers and was
29:19 King **A** removed in his unfaithfulness
Isa 1: 1 **A** and Hezekiah, kings of Judah.
7: 1 **A** son of Jotham, the son of Uzziah,
7: 2 of **A** and his people were shaken,
7: 3 to meet **A** at the end of the aqueduct
Isa 7:10 Again the LORD spoke to **A**,
7:12 **A** said, "I will not ask; I will not
14:28 This oracle came in the year King **A**
38: 8 has gone down on the stairway of **A**.
Hos 1: 1 Jotham, **A** and Hezekiah, kings of
Mic 1: 1 **A** and Hezekiah, kings of Judah—the
Mt 1: 9 of **A**, **A** the father of Hezekiah,

Ahaziah (Ahaziah's)

1Ki 22:40 Ahab rested with his fathers. And **A**
22:49 At that time **A** son of Ahab said to
22:51 **A** son of Ahab became king of Israel
2Ki 1: 2 Now **A** had fallen through the lattice
1:17 Because **A** had no son, Joram
8:24 And **A** his son succeeded him as king.
8:25 **A** son of Jehoram king of Judah began
8:26 **A** was twenty-two years old when he
8:28 **A** went with Joram son of Ahab to war
8:29 Then **A** son of Jehoram king of Judah
9:16 **A** king of Judah had gone down to see
9:21 Joram king of Israel and **A** king of
9:23 calling out to **A**, "Treachery, **A**!"
9:27 **A** king of Judah saw what had
9:29 Ahab, **A** had become king of Judah.)
10:13 he met some relatives of **A** king of
10:13 "We are relatives of **A**, and we have
11: 1 Athaliah the mother of **A** saw that
11: 2 of King Jehoram and sister of **A**,
11: 2 took Joash son of **A** and stole him
12:18 Jehoram and **A**, the kings of
13: 1 of Joash son of **A** king of Judah,
14:13 Joash, the son of **A**, at Beth Shemesh.
1Ch 3:11 Jehoram his son, **A** his son, Joash
2Ch 20:35 an alliance with **A** king of Israel,
20:37 you have made an alliance with **A**,
21:17 left to him except **A**, the youngest.
22: 1 The people of Jerusalem made **A**,
22: 1 So **A** son of Jehoram king of Judah
22: 2 **A** was twenty-two years old when he
22: 6 Then **A** son of Jehoram king of Judah
22: 7 When **A** arrived, he went out with
22: 8 attending **A**, and he killed them.
22: 9 He then went in search of **A**, and his
22: 9 was no-one in the house of **A** powerful
22:10 Athaliah the mother of **A** saw that
22:11 took Joash son of **A** and stole him
25:23 Joash, the son of **A**, at Beth Shemesh.

Ahaziah's (Ahaziah)

2Ki 1:18 for all the other events of **A** reign,
2Ch 22: 7 Through **A** visit to Joram, God
22: 7 Joram, God brought about **A** downfall.
22: 8 Judah and the sons of **A** relatives,
22:11 was **A** sister, she hid the child from

Ahban

1Ch 2:29 Abihail, who bore him **A** and Molid.

Aher

1Ch 7:12 the Hushites the descendants of **A**.

Ahi

1Ch 5:15 **A** son of Abdiel, the son of Guni,
7:34 The sons of Shomer: **A**, Rohgah,

Ahiah

Ne 10:26 **A**, Hanan, Anan,

Ahiam

2Sa 23:33 son of Shammah the Hararite, **A** son
1Ch 11:35 **A** son of Sacar the Hararite, Eliphal

Ahian

1Ch 7:19 The sons of Shemida were: **A**, Shechem,

Ahiezer

Nu 1:12 from Dan, **A** son of Ammishaddai;
2:25 of Dan is **A** son of Ammishaddai.
7:66 On the tenth day **A** son of
7:71 offering of **A** son of Ammishaddai.
Nu 10:25 **A** son of Ammishaddai was in command.
1Ch 12: 3 **A** their chief and Joash the sons of

Ahihud

Nu 34:27 **A** son of Shelomi, the leader from
1Ch 8: 7 who was the father of Uzza and **A**.

Ahijah (Ahijah's)

1Sa 14: 3 among whom was **A**, who was wearing an
14:18 Saul said to **A**, "Bring the ark of
1Ki 4: 3 Elihoreph and **A**, sons of
11:29 and **A** the prophet of Shiloh met him
11:30 **A** took hold of the new cloak he was
12:15 of Nebat through **A** the Shilonite.
14: 2 Then go to Shiloh. **A** the prophet is
14: 4 Now **A** could not see; his sight was
14: 5 the LORD had told **A**, "Jeroboam's
14: 6 when **A** heard the sound of her
14:18 through his servant the prophet **A**.
15:27 Baasha son of **A** of the house of
15:29 his servant **A** the Shilonite—
15:33 Baasha son of **A** became king of all
21:22 Nebat and that of Baasha son of **A**,
2Ki 9: 9 like the house of Baasha son of **A**.
1Ch 2:25 firstborn, Bunah, Oren, Ozem and **A**.
8: 7 Naaman, **A** and Gera, who deported
11:36 Hepher the Mekerathite, **A** the
2Ch 9:29 in the prophecy of **A** the Shilonite
10:15 of Nebat through **A** the Shilonite.

Ahijah's (Ahijah)

1Ki 14: 4 said and went to **A** house in Shiloh.

Ahikam

2Ki 22:12 **A** son of Shaphan, Acbor son of
22:14 Hilkiah the priest, **A**, Acbor,
25:22 Babylon appointed Gedaliah son of **A**,
2Ch 34:20 He gave these orders to Hilkiah, **A**
Jer 26:24 Furthermore, **A** son of Shaphan
39:14 him over to Gedaliah son of **A**,
40: 5 "Go back to Gedaliah son of **A**, the
40: 6 Jeremiah went to Gedaliah son of **A**
40: 7 son of **A** as governor over the land
40: 9 Gedaliah son of **A**, the son of
40:11 and had appointed Gedaliah son of **A**,
40:14 son of **A** did not believe them.
40:16 Gedaliah son of **A** said to Johanan
41: 1 men to Gedaliah son of **A** at Mizpah.
41: 2 and struck down Gedaliah son of **A**,
41: 6 he said, "Come to Gedaliah son of **A**.
41:10 had appointed Gedaliah son of **A**.
41:16 Gedaliah son of **A**: the soldiers,
41:18 had killed Gedaliah son of **A**,
43: 6 had left with Gedaliah son of **A**,

Ahilud

2Sa 8:16 Jehoshaphat son of **A** was recorder;
20:24 Jehoshaphat son of **A** was recorder;
1Ki 4: 3 Jehoshaphat son of **A**—recorder;
4:12 Baana son of **A**—in Taanach and
1Ch 18:15 Jehoshaphat son of **A** was recorder;

Ahimaaz

1Sa 14:50 name was Ahinoam daughter of **A**.
2Sa 15:27 son **A** and Jonathan son of Abiathar.
15:36 Their two sons, **A** son of Zadok and
17:17 Jonathan and **A** were staying at En
17:20 "Where are **A** and Jonathan?" The
18:19 Now **A** son of Zadok said, "Let me run
18:22 **A** son of Zadok again said to Joab,
18:23 So Joab said, "Run!" Then **A** ran by
18:27 first one runs like **A** son of Zadok.
18:28 **A** called out to the king, "All is
18:29 "Is the young man Absalom safe?" **A**
1Ki 4:15 **A**—in Naphtali (he had married
1Ch 6: 8 of Zadok, Zadok the father of **A**,
6: 9 **A** the father of Azariah, Azariah the
6:53 Zadok his son and **A** his son.

Ahiman

Nu 13:22 where **A**, Sheshai and Talmai, the
Jos 15:14 **A** and Talmai—descendants of Anak.
Jdg 1:10 and defeated Sheshai, **A** and Talmai.
1Ch 9:17 Akkub, Talmon, **A** and their brothers,

Ahimelech
1. Priest at Nob who helped David (1Sa 21:1–9); killed by Saul (1Sa 22:9–19). **2.** One of David's soldiers (1Sa 26:6).

1Sa 21: 1 David went to Nob, to **A** the priest. **A**
21: 2 David answered **A** the priest, "The
21: 8 David asked **A**, "Don't you have a
22: 9 Jesse come to **A** son of Ahitub at Nob.
22:10 **A** enquired of the LORD for him; he
22:11 the king sent for the priest **A** son
22:14 **A** answered the king, "Who of all
22:16 "You shall surely die, **A**, you and
22:20 Abiathar, son of **A** son of Ahitub,
23: 6 (Now Abiathar son of **A** had brought
26: 6 David then asked **A** the Hittite and
30: 7 the son of **A**, "Bring me the ephod.
2Sa 8:17 Zadok son of Ahitub and **A** son of
1Ch 18:16 Zadok son of Ahitub and **A** son of
24: 3 and **A** a descendant of Ithamar,
24: 6 **A** son of Abiathar and the heads of
24:31 **A**, and the heads of families of the
Ps 52: T "David has gone to the house of **A**.

Ahimoth
1Ch 6:25 The descendants of Elkanah: Amasai, **A**

Ahinadab
1Ki 4:14 **A** son of Iddo—in Mahanaim;

Ahinoam
1Sa 14:50 His wife's name was **A** daughter of
25:43 David had also married **A** of Jezreel,
27: 3 and David had his two wives: **A** of
30: 5 captured—**A** of Jezreel and Abigail,
2Sa 2: 2 **A** of Jezreel and Abigail, the widow
3: 2 was Amnon the son of **A** of Jezreel;
1Ch 3: 1 the son of **A** of Jezreel; the second,

Ahio
2Sa 6: 3 Uzzah and **A**, sons of Abinadab, were
6: 4 with the ark of God on it, and **A** was
1Ch 8:14 **A**, Shashak, Jeremoth,
8:31 Gedor, **A**, Zeker
9:37 Gedor, **A**, Zechariah and Mikloth.
13: 7 cart, with Uzzah and **A** guiding it.

Ahira
Nu 1:15 from Naphtali, **A** son of Enan."
2:29 people of Naphtali is **A** son of Enan.
7:78 On the twelfth day **A** son of Enan,
7:83 was the offering of **A** son of Enan.
10:27 **A** son of Enan was over the division

Ahiram (Ahiramite)
Nu 26:38 clan; through **A**, the Ahiramite clan;

Ahiramite (Ahiram)
Nu 26:38 clan; through Ahiram, the **A** clan;

Ahisamach
Ex 31: 6 **A**, of the tribe of Dan, to help him.
35:34 given both him and Oholiab son of **A**,
38:23 with him was Oholiab son of **A**, of

Ahishahar
1Ch 7:10 Kenaanah, Zethan, Tarshish and **A**.

Ahishar
1Ki 4: 6 **A**—in charge of the palace; Adoniram

Ahithophel (Ahithophel's)
David's counsellor; gave support to Absalom (2Sa 15:12; 16:21–23). Hanged himself when his advice was ignored (2Sa 17).

2Sa 15:12 he also sent for **A** the Gilonite,
15:31 Now David had been told, "**A** is among
16:15 to Jerusalem, and **A** was with him.
16:20 Absalom said to **A**, "Give us your
16:21 **A** answered, "Lie with your father's
16:23 Now in those days the advice **A** gave
17: 1 **A** said to Absalom, "I would choose
17: 6 Hushai came to him, Absalom said, "**A**
17: 7 **A** has given is not good this time.
17:14 the Arkite is better than that of **A**.
17:14 to frustrate the good advice of **A**
17:15 "**A** has advised Absalom and the
17:21 **A** has advised such and such against
17:23 **A** saw that his advice had not been
23:34 Eliam son of **A** the Gilonite,
1Ch 27:33 **A** was the king's counsellor. Hushai
27:34 **A** was succeeded by Jehoiada son of

Ahithophel's (Ahithophel)
2Sa 15:31 turn **A** counsel into foolishness."
15:34 can help me by frustrating **A** advice.
16:23 Absalom regarded all of **A** advice.

Ahitub
1Sa 14: 3 He was a son of Ichabod's brother **A**
22: 9 come to Ahimelech son of **A** at Nob.
22:11 of **A** and his father's whole family,
22:12 Saul said, "Listen now, son of **A**."
22:20 Abiathar, son of Ahimelech son of **A**,
2Sa 8:17 Zadok son of **A** and Ahimelech son of
1Ch 6: 7 of Amariah, Amariah the father of **A**,
6: 8 **A** the father of Zadok, Zadok the
6:11 of Amariah, Amariah the father of **A**,
6:12 **A** the father of Zadok, Zadok the
6:52 Meraioth his son, Amariah his son, **A**
9:11 the son of Meraioth, the son of **A**,
18:16 Zadok son of **A** and Ahimelech son of
Ezr 7: 2 the son of Zadok, the son of **A**,
Ne 11:11 **A**, supervisor in the house of God,

Ahlab
Jdg 1:31 living in Acco or Sidon or **A** or Aczib

Ahlai
1Ch 2:31 Sheshan was the father of **A**.
11:41 Uriah the Hittite, Zabad son of **A**,

Ahoah
1Ch 8: 4 Abishua, Naaman, **A**,

Ahohite
2Sa 23: 9 him was Eleazar son of Dodai the **A**.
23:28 Zalmon the **A**, Maharai the
1Ch 11:12 the **A**, one of the three mighty men.
11:29 Sibbecai the Hushathite, Ilai the **A**,
27: 4 the second month was Dodai the **A**;

Ahumai
1Ch 4: 2 Jahath the father of **A** and Lahad.

Ahuzzam
1Ch 4: 6 Naarah bore him **A**, Hepher, Temeni

Ahuzzath
Ge 26:26 with **A** his personal adviser and

Ahzai
Ne 11:13 the son of **A**, the son of

Ai
1. Canaanite town east of Bethel, near to Abram's camp and altar (Ge 12:8; 13:3–4). Attacked and finally defeated by Joshua (Jos 8) although Achan's sin led to earlier failure (Jos 7:4–5). Also called Aiath (Isa 10:28) and possibly Aija (Ne 11:31). See *Achor*.
2. Ammonite city east of the Jordan in Moab (Jer 49:3). Exact location unknown.

Ge 12: 8 Bethel on the west and **A** on the east.
13: 3 **A** where his tent had been earlier
Jos 7: 2 Now Joshua sent men from Jericho to **A**
7: 2 So the men went up and spied out **A**.
7: 3 peole will have to go up against **A**
7: 4 they were routed by the men of **A**,
8: 1 with you, and go up and attack **A**
8: 1 into your hands the king of **A**, his
8: 2 You shall do to **A** and its king as
8: 3 whole army moved out to attack **A**.
8: 9 Bethel and **A**, to the west of **A**
8:10 of Israel marched before them to **A**.
8:11 They set up camp north of **A**, with
8:12 and **A**, to the west of the city.
8:14 the king of **A** saw this, he and all
8:16 All the men of **A** were called to
8:17 Not a man remained in **A** or Bethel
8:18 "Hold out towards **A** the javelin
8:18 held out his javelin towards **A**.
8:20 The men of **A** looked back and saw the
8:21 round and attacked the men of **A**.
8:23 they took the king of **A** alive and
8:24 all the men of **A** in the fields
8:24 **A** and killed those who were in it.
8:25 fell that day—all the people of **A**.
8:26 he had destroyed all who lived in **A**.
8:28 Joshua burned **A** and made it a
8:29 He hung the king of **A** on a tree and
9: 3 Joshua had done to Jericho and **A**,
10: 1 taken **A** and totally destroyed it,
10: 1 doing to **A** and its king as he had
10: 2 royal cities; it was larger than **A**,
12: 9 the king of Jericho one the king of **A**
Ezr 2:28 of Bethel and **A** 223
Ne 7:32 of Bethel and **A** 123
Jer 49: 3 Wail, O Heshbon, for **A** is destroyed!

Aiah (Aiah's)
Ge 36:24 The sons of Zibeon: **A** and Anah. This
2Sa 3: 7 named Rizpah daughter of **A**.
21:10 Rizpah daughter of **A** took sackcloth
1Ch 1:40 The sons of Zibeon: **A** and Anah.

Aiah's (Aiah)
2Sa 21: 8 the two sons of **A** daughter Rizpah,
21:11 David was told what **A** daughter

Aiath
Isa 10:28 They enter **A**; they pass through

Aid
Ge 50:24 But God will surely come to your **a**
50:25 "God will surely come to your **a**, and
Ex 13:19 "God will surely come to your **a**, and
Ru 1: 6 the LORD had come to the **a** of his
Ps 35: 2 and buckler; arise and come to my **a**.
60:11 Give us **a** against the enemy, for the
106: 4 come to my **a** when you save them,
108:12 Give us **a** against the enemy, for the
Isa 38:14 I am troubled; O Lord, come to my **a**!"
Php 4:16 **a** again and again when I was in need.

Aija
Ne 11:31 **A**, Bethel and its settlements,

Aijalon
Jos 10:12 O moon, over the Valley of **A**."
19:42 Shaalabbin, **A**, Ithlah,
21:24 **A** and Gath Rimmon, together with
Jdg 1:35 **A** and Shaalbim, but when the power
12:12 Elon died, and was buried in **A** in
1Sa 14:31 Michmash to **A**, they were exhausted.
1Ch 6:69 **A** and Gath Rimmon, together with
8:13 of families of those living in **A**
2Ch 11:10 Zorah, **A** and Hebron. These were
28:18 **A** and Gederoth, as well as Soco,

Ails
Job 16: 3 What **a** you that you keep on arguing?

Aim (Aimlessly)
Ps 21:12 when you **a** at them with drawn bow.
64: 3 **a** their words like deadly arrows.
1Co 7:34 Her **a** is to be devoted to the Lord
2Co 13:11 Finally, brothers, good-bye. **A** for

Aimlessly (Aim)
1Co 9:26 I do not run like a man running **a**;

Ain
Nu 34:11 to Riblah on the east side of **A**
Jos 15:32 Lebaoth, Shilhim, **A** and Rimmon
19: 7 **A**, Rimmon, Ether and Ashan—four
21:16 **A**, Juttah and Beth Shemesh,
1Ch 4:32 **A**, Rimmon, Token and Ashan—five

Air (Airing, Mid-air)
Ge 1:26 of the sea and the birds of the a,
1:28 the birds of the a and over every
1:30 all the birds of the a and all the
2:19 field and all the birds of the a.
2:20 birds of the a and all the beasts of
6: 7 and birds of the a—for I am grieved
7:23 of the a were wiped from the earth.
9: 2 earth and all the birds of the a,
Ex 9: 8 the a in the presence of Pharaoh.
9:10 Moses tossed it into the a, and
Dt 4:17 or any bird that flies in the a,
28:26 birds of the a and the beasts of
1Sa 17:44 birds of the a and the beasts of
17:46 birds of the a and the beasts of
2Sa 21:10 she did not let the birds of the a
1Ki 14:11 and the birds of the a will feed on
16: 4 and the birds of the a will feed on
21:24 and the birds of the a will feed on
Job 12: 7 birds of the a, and they will tell
28:21 even from the birds of the a.
35:11 us wiser than the birds of the a?'
41:16 the next that no a can pass between.
Ps 8: 8 the birds of the a, and the fish of
79: 2 as food to the birds of the a,
104:12 The birds of the a nest by the
Ecc 10:20 because a bird of the a may carry
Jer 7:33 birds of the a and the beasts of
9:10 birds of the a have fled and the
15: 3 the birds of the a and the beasts of
16: 4 birds of the a and the beasts of
19: 7 birds of the a and the beasts of
34:20 birds of the a and the beasts of
Eze 29: 5 of the earth and the birds of the a.
31: 6 All the birds of the a nested in its
31:13 All the birds of the a settled on
32: 4 I will let all the birds of the a
38:20 the birds of the a, the beasts of
Da 2:38 of the field and the birds of the a.
4:12 and the birds of the a lived in its
4:21 branches for the birds of the a—
Hos 2:18 the birds of the a and the creatures
4: 3 birds of the a and the fish of the
7:12 pull them down like birds of the a.
Zep 1: 3 birds of the a and the fish of
Mt 6:26 Look at the birds of the a; they do
8:20 "Foxes have holes and birds of the a
13:32 birds of the a come and perch in
Mk 4:32 birds of the a can perch in its
Lk 8: 5 and the birds of the a ate it up.
9:58 "Foxes have holes and birds of the a
13:19 of the a perched in its branches."
Ac 10:12 of the earth and birds of the a.
11: 6 reptiles, and birds of the a.
22:23 cloaks and flinging dust into the a,
1Co 9:26 not fight like a man beating the a.
14: 9 You will just be speaking into the a.
Eph 2: 2 the ruler of the kingdom of the a,
1Th 4:17 clouds to meet the Lord in the a.
Rev 16:17 poured out his bowl into the a,

Airing (Air)
Pr 18: 2 but delights in a his own opinions.

Akan
Ge 36:27 sons of Ezer: Bilhan, Zaavan and A.
1Ch 1:42 sons of Ezer: Bilhan, Zaavan and A.

Akeldama
Ac 1:19 A, that is, Field of Blood.)

Akim
Mt 1:14 father of A, A the father of Eliud,

Akkad
Ge 10:10 Erech, A and Calneh, in Shinar.

Akkub
1Ch 3:24 Eliashib, Pelaiah, A, Johanan,
9:17 The gatekeepers: Shallum, A, Talmon,
Ezr 2:42 Talmon, A, Hatita and Shobai 139
2:45 Lebanah, Hagabah, A,
Ne 7:45 Talmon, A, Hatita and Shobai 138
8: 7 Bani, Sherebiah, Jamin, A,
Ne 11:19 The gatekeepers: A, Talmon and their
12:25 Obadiah, Meshullam, Talmon and A

Alabaster
Mt 26: 7 a woman came to him with an a jar of
Mk 14: 3 a woman came with an a jar of very
Lk 7:37 she brought an a jar of perfume,

Alamoth
1Ch 15:20 to play the lyres according to a,
Ps 46: T According to a. A song.

Alarm (Alarmed)
1Ki 1:49 guests rose in a and dispersed.
Job 33: 7 No fear of me should a you, nor
Ps 31:22 In my a I said, "I am cut off from
Da 4:19 let the dream or its meaning a you.
11:44 the east and the north will a him,
Joel 2: 1 Blow the trumpet in Zion; sound the a
2Co 7:11 what indignation, what a, what

Alarmed (Alarm)
Jos 10: 2 He and his people were very much a
2Sa 4: 1 courage, and all Israel became a.
2Ch 20: 3 A, Jehoshaphat resolved to enquire
Job 40:23 the river rages, he is not a; he is
Da 5:10 "Don't be a! Don't look so pale!
Mt 24: 6 but see to it that you are not a.
Mk 13: 7 and rumours of wars, do not be a.
16: 5 on the right side, and they were a.
16: 6 "Don't be a," he said. "You are
Ac 16:38 were Roman citizens, they were a.
20:10 "Don't be a," he said. "He's alive!"
22:29 The commander himself was a when he
2Th 2: 2 not to become easily unsettled or a

Alas
Jer 4:31 "A! I am fainting; my life is given
6: 4 let us attack at noon! But, a, the
15:10 A, my mother, that you gave me birth,
22:18 'A, my brother! A, my sister!' They
22:18 'A, my master! A, his splendour!'
34: 5 "A, O master!" I myself make this
Eze 6:11 "A!" because of all the wicked and
30: 2 "'Wail and say, "A for that day!
Joel 1:15 A for that day! For the day of the

Alcove (Alcoves)
Eze 40:12 In front of each a was a wall one
40:13 a to the top of the opposite one;

Alcoves (Alcove)
Eze 40: 7 The a for the guards were one rod
40: 7 the a were five cubits thick.
40:10 Inside the east gate were three a on
40:12 and the a were six cubits square.
40:16 The a and the projecting walls
40:21 Its a—three on each side—its
40:29 Its a, its projecting walls and its
40:33 Its a, its projecting walls and its
40:36 did its a, its projecting walls and

Alemeth
1Ch 6:60 Geba, A and Anathoth, together with
7: 8 Jeremoth, Abijah, Anathoth and A.
8:36 Jehoaddah was the father of A,
9:42 Jadah was the father of A, Azmaveth

Alert
Jos 8: 4 All of you be on the a.
Ps 17:11 eyes a, to throw me to the ground.
Isa 21: 7 on camels, let him be a, fully a."
Mk 13:33 Be on guard! Be a! You do not know
Eph 6:18 With this in mind, be a and always
1Th 5: 6 but let us be a and self-controlled.
1Pe 5: 8 Be self-controlled and a. Your enemy

Alexander
Mk 15:21 Simon, the father of A and Rufus,
Ac 4: 6 and so were Caiaphas, John, A and
19:33 The Jews pushed A to the front, and
1Ti 1:20 Among them are Hymenaeus and A, whom
2Ti 4:14 A the metalworker did me a great

Alexandria (Alexandrian)
Port on west of Nile delta on Mediterranean coast. Capital city of Egypt in Greco–Roman period; second city of Roman Empire with large Jewish community. Jews who argued with Stephen came from here (Ac 6:9) as did Apollos (Ac 18:24).

Ac 6: 9 A as well as the provinces of
18:24 a native of A, came to Ephesus.

Alexandrian (Alexandria)
Ac 27: 6 There the centurion found an A ship
28:11 It was an A ship with the figurehead

Algum (Algum-wood, Almug-wood)
2Ch 2: 8 "Send me also cedar, pine and a logs

Algum-wood (Algum)
2Ch 9:10 also brought a and precious stones.
9:11 The king used the a to make steps

Alien (Alien's, Alienate, Alienated, Aliens)
Ge 17: 8 where you are now an a, I will give
19: 9 "This fellow came here as an a, and
21:23 country where you are living as an a
23: 4 "I am an a and a stranger among you.
28: 4 an a, the land God gave to Abraham."
Ex 2:22 have become an a in a foreign land."
12:19 whether he is an a or native-born.
12:48 "An a living among you who wants to
12:49 and to the a living among you."
18: 3 have become an a in a foreign land";
20:10 nor the a within your gates.
22:21 "Do not ill-treat an a or oppress
23: 9 "Do not oppress an a; you yourselves
23:12 and the a as well, may be refreshed.
Lev 16:29 or an a living among you—
17: 8 "Say to them: 'Any Israelite or any a
17:10 "'Any Israelite or any a living
17:12 an a living among you eat blood."
17:13 "'Any Israelite or any a living
17:15 "'Anyone, whether native-born or a,
19:10 Leave them for the poor and the a. I
19:33 "'When an a lives with you in your
19:34 The a living with you must be
20: 2 'Any Israelite or any a living in
22:18 either an Israelite or an a living
23:22 Leave them for the poor and the a. I
24:16 Whether an a or native-born, when he
24:22 law for the a and the native-born.
25:35 help him as you would an a or a
25:47 "'If an a or a temporary resident
25:47 sells himself to the a living among
Nu 9:14 "'An a living among you who wants to
9:14 for the a and the native-born.'"
15:14 whenever an a or anyone else living
15:15 you and for the a living among you;
15:15 a shall be the same before the LORD:
15:16 you and to the a living among you.'"
15:29 is a native-born Israelite or an a.
15:30 whether native-born or a, blasphemes
Dt 1:16 or between one of them and an a.
5:14 nor the a within your gates, so that
10:18 the a, giving him food and clothing.
14:21 You may give it to an a living in
23: 7 you lived as an a in his country.
24:14 or an a living in one of your towns.
24:17 Do not deprive the a or the
24:19 Leave it for the a, the fatherless
24:20 the a, the fatherless and the widow.
24:21 the a, the fatherless and the widow.
26:12 the a, the fatherless and the widow,
26:13 the a, the fatherless and the widow,
27:19 the a, the fatherless or the widow.
28:43 The a who lives among you will rise
Jos 20: 9 Any of the Israelites or any a
Jdg 19:12 We won't go into an a city, whose
2Sa 1:13 I am the son of an a, an Amalekite,"
Job 15:19 given when no a passed among them):
19:15 stranger; they look upon me as an a.
Ps 39:12 For I dwell with you as an a, a
69: 8 I am a stranger to my brothers, an a
81: 9 you shall not bow down to an a god.
94: 6 They slay the widow and the a; they

Ps 105:23 lived as an a in the land of Ham.
146: 9 The LORD watches over the a and
Isa 28:21 and perform his task, his a task.
Jer 7: 6 if you do not oppress the a, the
22: 3 Do no wrong or violence to the a,
Eze 14: 7 "'When any Israelite or any a living
22: 7 in you they have oppressed the a and
22:29 the a, denying them justice.
47:23 In whatever tribe the a settles,
Hos 8:12 they regarded them as something a.
Zec 7:10 the fatherless, the a or the poor.

Alien's (Alien)
Lev 25:47 you or to a member of the a clan,

Alienate (Alien)
Gal 4:17 What they want is to a you from us,

Alienated (Alien)
Job 19:13 "He has a my brothers from me; my
Gal 5: 4 by law have been a from Christ;
Col 1:21 Once you were a from God and were

Aliens (Alien)
Ex 6: 4 of Canaan, where they lived as a.
22:21 him, for you were a in Egypt.
23: 9 be a, because you were a in Egypt.
Lev 18:26 The native-born and the a living
19:34 Love him as yourself, for you were a
25:23 and you are but a and my tenants.
Nu 15:26 a living among them will be forgiven,
19:10 and for the a living among them.
35:15 a and any other people living among
Dt 10:19 you are to love those who are a, for
10:19 for you yourselves were a in Egypt.
14:29 inheritance of their own) and the a,
16:11 and the a, the fatherless and the
16:14 and the Levites, the a, the
26:11 you and the Levites and the a among
29:11 and the a living in your camps who
31:12 women and children, and the a living
Jos 8:33 All Israel, a and citizens alike,
8:35 and the a who lived among them.
2Sa 4: 3 have lived there as a to this day.
1Ch 22: 2 David gave orders to assemble the a
29:15 We are a and strangers in your sight,
2Ch 2:17 Solomon took a census of all the a
30:25 including the a who had come from
Isa 14: 1 A will join them and unite with the
61: 5 A will shepherd your flocks;
Lam 5: 2 over to a, our homes to foreigners.
Eze 47:22 for the a who have settled among you
Mal 3: 5 a of justice, but do not fear me,"
Eph 2:19 you are no longer foreigners and a,
Heb 11:13 they were a and strangers on earth.
1Pe 2:11 Dear friends, I urge you, as a and

Alive (Life)
Ge 6:19 and female, to keep them a with you.
6:20 will come to you to be kept a.
7: 3 kinds a throughout the earth.
11:28 While his father Terah was still a,
43:28 our father is still a and well.
45:26 They told him, "Joseph is still a!
45:28 convinced! My son Joseph is still a.
46:30 for myself that you are still a."
Ex 4:18 to see if any of them are still a.
22: 4 "If the stolen animal is found a in
Lev 16:10 the scapegoat shall be presented a
Nu 16:30 and they go down a into the grave,
16:33 They went down a into the grave,
Dt 4: 4 the LORD your God are still a today.
5: 3 with all of us who are a here today.
6:24 and be kept a, as is the case today.
20:16 not leave a anything that breathes.
31:27 LORD while I am still a and with you,
Jos 8:23 they took the king of Ai a and
14:10 he has kept me a for forty-five
1Sa 2: 6 "The LORD brings death and makes a;
14:36 and let us not leave one of them a.
15: 8 He took Agag king of the Amalekites a
25:22 a one male of all who belong to him!"
25:34 would have been left a by daybreak."
27: 9 he did not leave a man or woman a,
27:11 He did not leave a man or woman a to
2Sa 1: 9 throes of death, but I'm still a.'
12:21 While the child was a, you fasted
12:22 was still a, I fasted and wept.
17:12 nor any of his men will be left a.
18:14 Absalom was still a in the oak tree.
19: 6 a today and all of us were dead.
1Ki 3:23 'My son is a and your son is dead,'
3:23 No! Your son is dead and mine is a.'"
3:26 The woman whose son was a was filled
17:23 and said "Look, your son is a!"
18: 5 mules a so we will not have to kill
20:18 take them a; if they have come out
20:18 have come out for war, take them a."
20:32 " The king answered, "Is he still a?
21:15 He is no longer a, but dead."
2Ki 7:12 take them a and get into the city.'"
10:14 "Take them a!" he ordered. So they
10:14 So they took them a and slaughtered
2Ch 25:12 also captured ten thousand men a,
Ne 5: 2 eat and stay a, we must get grain."
Job 36: 6 He does not keep the wicked a but
Ps 22:29 those who cannot keep themselves a.
33:19 death and keep them a in famine.
55:15 let them go down a to the grave,
124: 3 us, they would have swallowed us a;
Pr 1:12 let's swallow them a, like the grave,
Ecc 4: 2 than the living, who are still a.
Isa 7:21 In that day, a man will keep a a
Lam 1:11 for food to keep themselves a.
1:19 for food to keep themselves a.
Mt 27:63 he was still a that deceiver said,
Mk 16:11 they heard that Jesus was a and that
Lk 15:24 a again; he was lost and is found.
15:32 a again; he was lost and is found.'"
20:38 the living, for to him all are a."
24:23 vision of angels, who said he was a.
Jn 21:22 "If I want him to remain a until I
21:23 "If I want him to remain a until I
Ac 1: 3 convincing proofs that he was a.
9:41 widows and presented her to them a.
20:10 "Don't be alarmed," he said. "He's a!
20:12 The people took the young man home a
25:19 named Jesus whom Paul claimed was a.
Ro 6:11 to sin but a to God in Christ Jesus.
7: 2 to her husband as long as he is a,
7: 3 a, she is called an adulteress.
7: 9 Once I was a apart from law; but
8:10 is a because of righteousness.
1Co 15:22 so in Christ all will be made a.
2Co 4:11 For we who are a are always being
Eph 2: 5 made us a with Christ even when we
Col 2:13 nature, God made you a with Christ.
1Th 4:15 we tell you that we who are still a,
4:17 After that, we who are still a and
1Pe 3:18 the body but made a by the Spirit,
Rev 1:18 and behold I am a for ever and ever!
3: 1 of being a, but you are dead.
19:20 The two of them were thrown a into

All generations
Ge 9:12; Ex 40:15; Ps 33:11; 45:17; 72:5; 85:5; 89:1, 4; 90:1; 100:5; 102:12, 24; 119:90; 135:13; 145:13; 146:10; Pr 27:24; Isa 13:20; 51:8; 60:15; Joel 3:20; Lk 1:48; Eph 3:21

All Israel
Ex 18:25; Dt 1:1; 5:1; 11:6; 13:11; 21:21; 27:9; 31:1, 7, 11; 32:45; 34:12; Jos 3:7, 17; 4:14; 7:24, 25; 8:15, 21, 33; 10:15, 29, 31, 34, 36, 38, 43; 23:2; Jdg 8:27; 1Sa 2:22; 3:20; 4:1, 5; 7:5; 11:2; 12:1; 13:4, 20; 18:16; 19:5; 24:2; 25:1; 28:3; 2Sa 2:9; 3:12, 21, 37; 4:1; 5:5; 8:15; 10:17; 12:12; 14:25; 16:21, 22; 17:10, 11, 13; 1Ki 1:20; 2:15; 3:28; 4:1, 7; 5:13; 8:62, 65; 11:42; 12:16, 18, 20; 14:13, 18; 15:27, 33; 18:20; 22:17; 2Ki 3:6; 9:14; 1Ch 9:1; 11:1, 10; 12:38; 14:8; 15:3, 28; 18:14; 19:17; 21:5; 28: 4, 8; 29:21, 23, 25, 26; 2Ch 1:2; 7:8; 9:30; 10:3, 16; 12:1; 13:4, 15; 18:16; 24:5; 28:23; 29:24; 30:1; 35:3; Ezr 6:17; 8:25, 35; 10:5; Ne 12:47; 13:26; Da 9:7, 11; Mal 4:4; Ac 2:36; Ro 11:26

All nations
Ge 18:18; 22:18; 26:4; Ex 19:5; Dt 28:64; 1Ki 4:34; Ps 67:2; 72:11, 17; 148:11; Isa 2:2; 14:26; 25:7; 34:2; 56:7; 61:11; 66:18; Jer 3:17; 27:7; 33:9; Eze 32:12; Joel 3:2; Ob 15; Hag 2:7; Mt 24:9, 14; 28:19; Mk 11:17; 13:10; Lk 24:47; Ac 14:16; Ro 16:26; Gal 3:8; Rev 15:4

All people
Ge 6:13; Jer 17:20; 45:5; Eze 21:5; Joel 2:28; Lk 2:31; Jn 17:2; Ac 2:17; 17:30; Gal 6:10; Rev 19:18

All peoples
Ge 12:3; 28:14; Dt 7:7; 1Ki 9:7; 1Ch 16:24; 2Ch 7:20; Ps 96:3; Isa 25:6, 7; Da 7:14; Ac 3:25

All the firstborn
Ex 11:5; 12:29; 13:12; 34:19; Nu 3:13, 40, 41, 42, 45; 8:17, 18; Ps 78:51; 105:36

All the Israelites
Ex 10:23; 12:42, 50; 16:6; 34:30, 32; Lev 17:2; 21:24; 22:18; Nu 1:45; 8:19; 14:2, 10, 39; 16:34; 17:9; Dt 29:2; Jos 3:1; 7:23; 8:24; Jdg 2:4; 10:8; 20:1; 1Sa 2:14; 11:15; 14:22, 40; 15:6; 17:11; 28:4; 2Sa 7:7; 15:6; 18:17; 1Ki 8:63; 11:16; 12:1, 20; 16:17; 2Ki 7:13; 1Ch 10:7; 11:4; 13:5, 6, 8; 17:6; 2Ch 7:3, 6; 10:1, 16; 11:3; Ro 10:16

All the people
Ge 6:12; 26:11; 29:22; 35:6; Ex 11:8; 12:6; 18:21; 19:11; 32:3; 33:8; Lev 9:23, 24; 10:3; 16:33; Nu 13:32; 14:1; 15:26; 31:26; Dt 13:9; 17:7, 13; 20:11; 27:14, 15, 16, 17, 18, 19, 20, 21, 22, 23, 24, 25, 26; Jos 2:24; 5:5; 6:5; 7:3; 8:25; 11:14; 24:2, 27; Jdg 9:49, 51; 16:30; 20:2, 8, 26; Ru 4:9; 1Sa 2:23; 7:2; 10:24; 11:15; 12:18; 18:5; 2Sa 3:31, 32, 34, 36, 37; 6:19; 15:17, 23, 24, 30; 16:14; 17:2, 3, 16, 22; 19:39; 20:22; 1Ki 1:39, 40; 9:20; 12:12; 18:24, 30, 39; 2Ki 10:9, 18; 11:14, 18, 19, 20; 14:21; 16:15; 17:20; 23:2, 3, 21; 25:26; 1Ch 13:4; 16:36, 43; 28:21; 2Ch 7:4, 5; 8:7; 10:12; 20:18; 23:13, 17, 20, 21; 24:10; 26:1; 29:36; 32:9; 34:9, 30; 35:13; Ezr 3:11; 7:25; 10:9; Ne 4:16 ; 8:1, 3, 5, 6, 9, 11, 12; 9:10; Est 1:5; Job 1:3; Ps 33:8; 106:48; Ecc 4:16; Isa 9:9; Jer 19:14; 25:1, 2; 26:2, 7, 8, 9, 11, 12, 16, 18; 28:1, 5, 7, 11; 29:16, 25; 34:8, 19; 36:6, 9, 10; 38:1, 4; 41:13, 14; 42:1, 8; 43:4; 44:15, 20, 24; Eze 38:20; 39:13, 25; 45:16, 22; Da 9:6; Am 9:1; Zec 7:5; Mal 2:9; Mt 12:23; 13:2; 22:10; 27:25; Mk 1:5; 4:1; 5:20; 6:39; 9:15; Lk 2:10; 3:21; 4:28, 36; 7:29; 8:37, 47, 52; 18:43; 19:7, 48; 20:6, 45; 21:38; 23:48; 24:19; Jn 8:2; Ac 2:47; 3:9, 11; 4:10, 21; 5:34; 8:9, 10; 10:41; 13:24; Heb 9:19

All the peoples
Dt 7:6, 16, 19; 14:2; 28:10; Jos 4:24; 1Ki 8:43, 60; 2Ch 6:33; 32:13; Ps 67:3, 5; 97:6; Jer 1:15; 25:9; Da 3:7; 4:35; 5:19; 6:25; Hab 2:5; Zep 3:20; Rev 1:7

Allammelech
Jos 19:26 A, Amad and Mishal. On the west the

Allegiance (Ally)
1Ki 12:27 they will again give their a to
Isa 19:18 and swear a to the LORD Almighty.
Eze 21:23 to those who have sworn a to him,

Allegory
Eze 17: 2 "Son of man, set forth an a and tell

Alleys
Lk 14:21 a of the town and bring in the poor,

Alliance (Ally)
1Ki 3: 1 Solomon made an a with Pharaoh king
2Ch 20:35 Jehoshaphat king of Judah made an a
20:37 "Because you have made an a with
Ps 83: 5 they form an a against you—
Isa 30: 1 forming an a, but not by my Spirit,
Jer 50: 9 bring against Babylon an a of great
Da 11: 6 the king of the North to make an a,
11:17 an a with the king of the South.

Allied (Ally)
Ge 14: 5 Kedorlaomer and the kings a with him
14:13 Aner, all of whom were a with Abram.

Ge 14:17 Kedorlaomer and the kings a with him,
Jos 13:21 Hur and Reba—princes a with Sihon
1Ki 20:16 the 32 kings a with him were in
2Ch 18: 1 he a himself with Ahab by marriage.
Ps 94:20 Can a corrupt throne be a with you—
Isa 7: 2 "Aram has a itself with Ephraim"; so

Allies (Ally)

1Ch 5:20 and all their a over to them,
Jer 13:21 you cultivated as your special a?
22:20 Abarim, for all your a are crushed.
22:22 away, and your a will go into exile.
30:14 All your a have forgotten you; they
Lam 1:19 "I called to my a but they betrayed
Eze 30: 6 "This is what the LORD says: "The a
31:17 Those who lived in its shade, its a
32:21 leaders will say of Egypt and her a,
Da 11: 6 After some years, they will become a.
Ob : 7 All your a will force you to the
Na 1:12 "Although they have a and are
3: 9 Put and Libya were among her a.

All-night (Night)

Jos 10: 9 After an a march from Gilgal, Joshua

Allocate

Jos 13: 6 Be sure to a this land to Israel for

Allon

1Ch 4:37 Ziza son of Shiphi, the son of A,

Allon Bacuth

Ge 35: 8 So it was named A.

Allot (Allotment, Allots, Allotted, Allotting)

Eze 45: 1 "When you a the land as an
47:22 You are to a it as an inheritance
48:29 "This is the land you are to a as an

Allotment (Allot)

Ge 47:22 because they received a regular a
47:22 enough from the a Pharaoh gave them.
Dt 12:12 no a or inheritance of their own.
14:27 no a or inheritance of their own.
14:29 that the Levites (who have no a or
18: 1 no a or inheritance with Israel.
Jos 15: 1 The a for the tribe of Judah, clan
16: 1 The a for Joseph began at the Jordan
17: 1 This was the a for the tribe of
17: 2 this a was for the rest of the
17:14 "Why have you given us only one a
17:17 You will have not only one a
Eze 48:13 the Levites will have an a 25,000

Allots (Allot)

Job 20:29 Such is the fate God a the wicked,
21:17 them, the fate God a in his anger?
27:13 "Here is the fate God a to the
Isa 34:17 He a their portions; his hand

Allotted (Allot)

Lev 7:35 LORD by fire that were a to Aaron
Nu 26:53 "The land is to be a to them as an
34: 2 the land that will be a to you as an
36: 3 a to us will be taken away.
Dt 32: 9 his people, Jacob his a inheritance.
Jos 14: 1 tribal clans of Israel a to them.
18:11 Their a territory lay between the
19:49 the land into its a portions,
21: 4 a thirteen towns from the tribes of
21: 5 Kohath's descendants were a ten towns
21: 6 The descendants of Gershon were a
21: 8 the Israelites a to the Levites
21: 9 they a the following towns by
21:20 a towns from the tribe of Ephraim:
21:40 All the towns a to the Merarite
23: 4 Remember how I have a as an
24:33 which had been a to his son Phinehas
Jdg 1: 3 with us into the territory a to us,
1Sa 18:26 So before the a time elapsed,
1Ch 6:54 locations of their settlements a as
6:61 Kohath's descendants were a ten towns
1Ch 6:62 clan by clan, were a thirteen towns
6:63 clan by clan, were a twelve towns
6:65 they a the previously named towns.
Ne 5:14 ate the food a to the governor.
5:18 I never demanded the food a to the
Job 7: 3 I have been a months of futility,
21:21 when his a months come to an end?
Ps 78:55 a their lands to them as an
125: 3 over the land a to the righteous,
Eze 47:22 along with you they are to be a an
Da 12:13 rise to receive your a inheritance."

Allotting (Allot)

Ne 9:22 a to them even the remotest

Allow (Allowance, Allowed, Allowing, Allows)

Ex 10:25 Moses said, "You must a us to have
22:18 "Do not a a sorceress to live.
Nu 33:55 those you a to remain will become
35:32 so a him to go back and live on his
Jdg 6:39 Let me make just one more request. A
1Sa 16:22 Saul sent word to Jesse, saying, "A
24: 7 and did not a them to attack Saul.
2Ch 20:10 whose territory you would not a
Job 11:14 and a no evil to dwell in your tent,
Ps 132: 4 I will a no sleep to my eyes, no
Pr 6: 4 A no sleep to your eyes, no slumber
Jer 13:14 I will a no pity or mercy or
Eze 45: 8 will a the house of Israel to possess
Mk 5:12 the pigs; a us to go into them."
11:16 would not a anyone to carry
Lk 4:41 them and would not a them to speak,
Ac 16: 7 Spirit of Jesus would not a them to.
27: 7 When the wind did not a us to hold
Ro 14:16 Do not a what you consider good to

Allowance (Allow)

2Ki 25:30 a regular a as long as he lived.
Jer 52:34 a regular a as long as he lived,
Lk 12:42 their food a at the proper time?

Allowed (Allow)

Ge 3:22 He must not be a to reach out his
31: 7 God has not a him to harm me.
46:34 Then you will be a to settle in the
48:11 has a me to see your children too."
Lev 11:39 "If an animal that you are a to eat
Nu 31:15 "Have you a all the women to live?"
Dt 7:22 You will not be a to eliminate them
24: 4 who divorced her, is not a to marry
Jdg 2:23 The LORD had a those nations to
3:28 Moab, they a no-one to cross over.
2Sa 8: 2 and the third length was a to live.
1Ki 1:48 the God of Israel, who has a my eyes
1Ch 16:21 He a no man to oppress them; for
2Ch 25:13 had not a to take part in the war
34:11 of Judah had a to fall into ruin.
Est 1: 8 guest was a to drink in his own way,
4: 2 in sackcloth was a to enter it.
Job 31:30 I have not a my mouth to sin by
Ps 105:14 He a no-one to oppress them; for
Eze 33:12 if he sins, will not be a to live
Da 7:12 a to live for a period of time.)
Ac 27: 3 in kindness to Paul, a him to go to
28: 4 sea, Justice has not a him to live."
28:16 we got to Rome, Paul was a to live
1Co 14:34 They are not a to speak, but must be

Allowing (Allow)

Lev 22:16 by a them to eat the sacred
Jdg 1:34 a them to come down into the plain.

Allows (Allow)

Ex 21:22 husband demands and the court a.
Ro 14: 2 One man's faith a him to eat

All-surpassing (Surpass)

2Co 4: 7 a power is from God and not from us.

Allure (Alluring)

Hos 2:14 "Therefore I am now going to a her;

Alluring (Allure)

Na 3: 4 a, the mistress of sorceries, who

Ally (Allegiance, Alliance, Allied, Allies)

Jos 23:12 "But if you turn away and a
Isa 48:14 The LORD's chosen a will carry out

Almighty (*God Almighty, LORD Almighty, Lord Almighty, LORD God Almighty, Lord God Almighty*, Might)

Ge 49:25 who helps you, because of the A, who
Nu 24: 4 who sees a vision from the A, who
24:16 who sees a vision from the A, who
Ru 1:20 the A has made my life very bitter.
1:21 A has brought misfortune upon me."
Job 5:17 not despise the discipline of the A.
6: 4 The arrows of the A are in me, my
6:14 he forsakes the fear of the A.
8: 3 Does God pervert justice? Does the A
8: 5 look to God and plead with the A,
11: 7 Can you probe the limits of the A?
13: 3 I desire to speak to the A and to
15:25 God and vaunts himself against the A,
21:15 Who is the A, that we should serve
21:20 let him drink of the wrath of the A.
22: 3 What pleasure would it give the A if
22:17 us alone! What can the A do to us?'
22:23 If you return to the A, you will be
22:25 the A will be your gold, the
22:26 then you will find delight in the A
23:16 the A has terrified me.
24: 1 "Why does the A not set times for
27: 2 who has denied me justice, the A,
27:10 Will he find delight in the A? Will
27:11 ways of the A I will not conceal.
27:13 a ruthless man receives from the A:
29: 5 the A was still with me and my
31: 2 his heritage from the A on high?
31:35 now my defence—let the A answer me;
32: 8 the A, that gives him understanding.
33: 4 the breath of the A gives me life.
34:10 to do evil, from the A to do wrong.
34:12 that the A would pervert justice.
35:13 empty plea; the A pays no attention
37:23 The A is beyond our reach and
40: 2 "Will the one who contends with the A
Ps 68:14 the A scattered the kings in the
91: 1 will rest in the shadow of the A.
Isa 13: 6 come like destruction from the A.
Eze 1:24 waters, like the voice of the A,
Joel 1:15 come like destruction from the A.
Rev 1: 8 who was, and who is to come, the A."
4: 8 A, who was, and is, and is to come.

Almodad

Ge 10:26 Joktan was the father of A, Sheleph,
1Ch 1:20 Joktan was the father of A, Sheleph,

Almon

Jos 21:18 Anathoth and A, together with their

Almon Diblathaim

Nu 33:46 They left Dibon Gad and camped at A.
33:47 They left A and camped in the

Almond (Almonds)

Ge 30:37 a and plane trees and made white
Ex 25:33 Three cups shaped like a flowers
25:34 a flowers with buds and blossoms.
37:19 Three cups shaped like a flowers
37:20 a flowers with buds and blossoms.
Ecc 12: 5 when the a tree blossoms and the
Jer 1:11 the branch of an a tree," I replied.

Almonds (Almond)

Ge 43:11 myrrh, some pistachio nuts and a.
Nu 17: 8 budded, blossomed and produced a.

Almug-wood (Algum)

1Ki 10:11 cargoes of a and precious stones.
10:12 The king used the a to make supports
10:12 So much a has never been imported or

Aloes

Nu 24: 6 a river, like a planted by the LORD
Ps 45: 8 with myrrh and a and cassia;
Pr 7:17 I have perfumed my bed with myrrh, a
SS 4:14 and a and all the finest spices.
Jn 19:39 and a, about seventy-five pounds.

Alone (Lonely)

Ge 2:18 "It is not good for the man to be a.
32:24 Jacob was left a, and a man wrestled
Ex 4:26 the LORD let him a. (At that time
14:12 'Leave us a; let us serve the
18:14 Why do you a sit as judge, while all
18:18 for you; you cannot handle it a.
21: 3 If he comes a, he is to go free a;
24: 2 Moses a is to approach the LORD; the
32:10 Now leave me a so that my anger may
Lev 13:46 must live a; he must live outside
Nu 11:17 you will not have to carry it a.
18: 1 and you and your sons a are to bear
Dt 1: 9 heavy a burden for me to carry a.
8: 3 man does not live on bread a but on
9:14 Let me a, so that I may destroy them
16:20 Follow justice and justice a, so
32:12 The LORD a led him; no foreign god
33:28 Israel will live in safety a;
Jdg 3:20 was sitting a in the upper room of
1Sa 21: 1 are you a? Why is no-one with you?"
25:24 "My lord, let the blame be on me a.
2Sa 16:11 then, this Benjamite! Leave him a;
18:24 looked out, he saw a man running a.
18:25 The king said, "If he is a, he must
18:26 "Look, another man running a!" The
1Ki 3:18 We were a; there was no-one in the
8:39 you a know the hearts of all men),
11:29 of them were a out in the country,
2Ki 4:27 "Leave her a! She is in bitter
19:15 you a are God over all the kingdoms
19:19 know that you a, O LORD, are God."
23:18 "Leave it a," he said. "Don't let
2Ch 6:30 (for you a know the hearts of men),
Ezr 4: 3 We a will build it for the LORD, the
Ne 9: 6 You a are the LORD. You made the
Est 4:13 you a of all the Jews will escape.
Job 7:16 Let me a; my days have no meaning.
7:19 me, or let me a even for an instant?
9: 8 He a stretches out the heavens and
14: 6 look away from him and let him a,
15:19 (to whom a the land was given when
19: 4 my error remains my concern a.
21:14 Yet they say to God, 'Leave us a! We
22:17 They said to God, 'Leave us a! What
23:13 "But he stands a, and who can oppose
28:23 it and he a knows where it dwells,
Ps 4: 8 a, O LORD, make me dwell in safety.
62: 1 My soul finds rest in God a; my
62: 2 He a is my rock and my salvation; he
62: 5 Find rest, O my soul, in God a; my
62: 6 He a is my rock and my salvation; he
71:16 your righteousness, yours a.
72:18 Israel, who a does marvellous deeds.
76: 7 You a are to be feared. Who can
83:18 you a are the Most High over all
86:10 do marvellous deeds; you a are God.
102: 7 have become like a bird a on a roof.
136: 4 to him who a does great wonders,
148:13 for his name a is exalted; his
Pr 5:17 Let them be yours a, never to be
9:12 are a mocker, you a will suffer."
Ecc 4: 8 There was a man all a; he had
4:11 But how can one keep warm a?
SS 4: 2 has its twin; not one of them is a.
6: 6 has its twin; not one of them is a.
Isa 2:11 LORD a will be exalted in that day.
2:17 LORD a will be exalted in that day,
5: 8 is left and you live a in the land.
26:13 us, but your name a do we honour.
37:16 you a are God over all the kingdoms
37:20 know that you a, O LORD, are God."
44:24 who has made all things, who a
45:24 They will say of me, 'In the LORD a
49:21 brought these up? I was left all a,
63: 3 "I have trodden the winepress a;
Jer 15:17 never made merry with them; I sat a
41: 8 So he let them a and did not kill
Jer 49:31 gates nor bars; its people live a.
Lam 3:28 Let him sit a in silence, for the
Eze 9: 8 they were killing and I was left a,
14:16 They a would be saved, but the land
14:18 They a would be saved.
37: 3 said, "O Sovereign LORD, you a know.
44:16 They a are to enter my sanctuary;
44:16 they a are to come near my table to
Da 10: 8 I was left a, gazing at this great
11: 8 will leave the king of the North a.
Hos 4:17 is joined to idols; leave him a!
8: 9 like a wild donkey wandering a.
Mt 4: 4 'Man does not live on bread a, but
14:23 When evening came, he was there a,
27:49 The rest said, "Now leave him a.
Mk 2: 7 Who can forgive sins but God a?"
4:10 he was a, the Twelve and the others
4:34 But when he was a with his own
6:47 of the lake, and he was a on land.
9: 2 mountain, where they were all a.
10:18 "No-one is good—except God a.
14: 6 "Leave her a," said Jesus. "Why are
15:36 "Now leave him a. Let's see if
Lk 4: 4 'Man does not live on bread a.'"
5:21 Who can forgive sins but God a?"
9:36 spoken, they found that Jesus was a.
13: 8 "'Sir,' the man replied, 'leave it a
18:19 "No-one is good—except God a.
Jn 6:22 but that they had gone away a.
8:16 are right, because I am not a.
8:29 he has not left me a, for I always
12: 7 "Leave her a," Jesus replied. "It
16:32 You will leave me all a. Yet I am
16:32 I am not a, for my Father is with me.
17:20 "My prayer is not for them a. I pray
Ac 5:38 Leave these men a! Let them go! For
Ro 4:23 to him" were written not for him a,
14: 7 For none of us lives to himself a
14: 7 and none of us dies to himself a.
1Co 7: 4 to her a but also to her husband.
7: 4 to him a but also to his wife.
1Ti 5: 5 left all a puts her hope in God and
6:16 who a is immortal and who lives in
Jas 2:24 by what he does and not by faith a.
Rev 15: 4 to your name? For you a are holy.

Aloof

Job 21:16 a from the counsel of the wicked.
22:18 a from the counsel of the wicked.
Ob :11 On the day you stood a while

Aloth

1Ki 4:16 son of Hushai—in Asher and in A;

Aloud (Loud)

Ge 27:38 too, my father!" Then Esau wept a.
29:11 kissed Rachel and began to weep a.
Nu 14: 1 raised their voices and wept a.
Jdg 2: 4 the Israelites, the people wept a,
Ru 1: 9 Then she kissed them and they wept a
1Sa 11: 4 to the people, they all wept a.
24:16 voice, David my son?" And he wept a.
30: 4 David and his men wept a until they
2Sa 3:32 and the king wept a at Abner's tomb.
13:19 went away, weeping a as she went.
15:23 The whole countryside wept a as all
19: 4 The king covered his face and cried a
Ezr 3:12 wept a when they saw the foundation
Ne 8: 3 He read it a from daybreak till noon
13: 1 read a in the hearing of the people
Job 2:12 recognise him; they began to weep a,
Ps 3: 4 To the LORD I cry a, and he answers
26: 7 proclaiming a your praise and
81: 1 shout a to the God of Jacob!
95: 1 a to the Rock of our salvation.
142: 1 I cry a to the LORD; I lift up my
Pr 1:20 Wisdom calls a in the street, she
2: 3 if you call out for insight and cry a
8: 3 city, at the entrances, she cries a:
Isa 12: 6 Shout a and sing for joy, people of
33: 7 Look, their brave men cry a in the
44:23 done this; shout a, O earth beneath.
58: 1 "Shout it a, do not hold back. Raise
Jer 4: 5 throughout the land!' Cry a and say:
51:61 see that you read all these words a.
Mic 4: 9 Why do you now cry a—have you no
Zep 3:14 Sing, O Daughter of Zion; shout a,
Gal 4:27 break forth and cry a, you who have

Alpha

Rev 1: 8 "I am the A and the Omega," says the
21: 6 I am the A and the Omega, the
22:13 I am the A and the Omega, the First

Alphaeus

Mt 10: 3 James son of A, and Thaddaeus;
Mk 2:14 he walked along, he saw Levi son of A
3:18 James son of A, Thaddaeus, Simon the
Lk 6:15 Matthew, Thomas, James son of A,
Ac 1:13 James son of A and Simon the Zealot,

Altar (*Altar of burnt offering, Altar of incense, Altars, Horns of the altar*)

Ge 8:20 Noah built an a to the LORD and,
12: 7 So he built an a there to the LORD,
12: 8 There he built an a to the LORD and
13: 4 where he had first built an a. There
13:18 where he built an a to the LORD.
22: 9 Abraham built an a there and arranged
22: 9 him on the a, on top of the wood.
26:25 Isaac built an a there and called on
33:20 There he set up an a and called it
35: 1 and build an a there to God, who
35: 3 where I will build an a to God, who
35: 7 There he built an a, and he called
Ex 17:15 Moses built an a and called it The
20:24 "'Make an a of earth for me and
20:25 If you make an a of stones for me,
20:26 do not go up to my a on steps, lest
21:14 away from my a and put him to death.
24: 4 built an a at the foot of the
24: 6 other half he sprinkled on the a.
27: 1 "Build an a of acacia wood, three
27: 2 so that the horns and the a are of
27: 2 and overlay the a with bronze.
27: 5 Put it under the ledge of the a so
27: 5 so that it is halfway up the a.
27: 6 Make poles of acacia wood for the a
27: 7 sides of the a when it is carried.
27: 8 Make the a hollow, out of boards. It
28:43 approach the a to minister in the
29:12 the rest of it at the base of the a.
29:13 fat on them, and burn them on the a.
29:16 it against the a on all sides.
29:18 burn the entire ram on the a. It is
29:20 blood against the a on all sides.
29:21 take some of the blood on the a and
29:25 burn them on the a along with the
29:36 Purify the a by making atonement for
29:37 for the a and consecrate it.
29:37 Then the a will be most holy, and
29:38 offer on the a regularly each day:
29:44 the a and will consecrate Aaron and
30: 1 "Make an a of acacia wood for
30: 4 Make two gold rings for the a below
30: 6 Put the a in front of the curtain
30: 7 fragrant incense on the a every
30: 9 Do not offer on this a any other
30:18 and the a, and put water in it.
30:20 Also, when they approach the a to
32: 5 Aaron saw this, he built an a in
38: 2 so that the horns and the a were of
38: 2 and they overlaid the a with bronze.
38: 4 They made a grating for the a, a
38: 4 under its ledge, halfway up the a.
38: 7 the sides of the a for carrying it.
38:30 the bronze a with its bronze grating
39:38 the gold a, the anointing oil, the
39:39 the bronze a with its bronze grating,
40: 7 and the a and put water in it.
40:10 consecrate the a, and it will be most
40:26 Moses placed the gold a in the Tent
40:29 He set the a of burnt offering near
40:30 a and put water in it for washing,
40:32 the a, as the LORD commanded Moses.
40:33 around the tabernacle and a and put
Lev 1: 5 sprinkle it against the a on all
1: 7 fire on the a and arrange wood on
1: 8 the burning wood that is on the a.
1: 9 is to burn all of it on the a.

Lev 1:11 north side of the **a** before the LORD,
1:11 blood against the **a** on all sides.
1:12 the burning wood that is on the **a**.
1:13 all of it and burn it on the **a**.
1:15 The priest shall bring it to the **a**,
1:15 off the head and burn it on the **a**;
1:15 be drained out on the side of the **a**.
1:16 side of the **a**, where the ashes are.
1:17 wood that is on the fire on the **a**.
2: 2 this as a memorial portion on the **a**,
2: 8 priest, who shall take it to the **a**.
2: 9 the **a** as an offering made by fire,
2:12 on the **a** as a pleasing aroma.
3: 2 blood against the **a** on all sides.
3: 5 Aaron's sons are to burn it on the **a**
3: 8 blood against the **a** on all sides.
3:11 The priest shall burn them on the **a**
3:13 blood against the **a** on all sides.
3:16 The priest shall burn them on the **a**
4:19 fat from it and burn it on the **a**,
4:25 of the blood at the base of the **a**.
4:26 He shall burn all the fat on the **a**
4:30 of the blood at the base of the **a**.
4:31 on the **a** as an aroma pleasing to
4:34 of the blood at the base of the **a**.
4:35 the priest shall burn it on the **a** on
5: 9 offering against the side of the **a**;
5: 9 be drained out at the base of the **a**.
5:12 burn it on the **a** on top of the
6: 9 the **a** hearth throughout the night,
6: 9 fire must be kept burning on the **a**.
6:10 the **a** and place them beside the **a**.
6:12 The fire on the **a** must be kept
6:13 **a** continuously; it must not go out.
6:14 before the LORD, in front of the **a**.
6:15 on the **a** as an aroma pleasing to
7: 2 against the **a** on all sides.
7: 5 The priest shall burn them on the **a**
7:31 priest shall burn the fat on the **a**,
8:11 He sprinkled some of the oil on the **a**
8:11 anointing the **a** and all its utensils
8:15 of the blood at the base of the **a**.
8:16 their fat, and burned it on the **a**.
8:19 blood against the **a** on all sides.
8:21 ram on the **a** as a burnt offering,
8:24 blood against the **a** on all sides.
8:28 burned them on the **a** on top of the
8:30 some of the blood from the **a** and
9: 7 Moses said to Aaron, "Come to the **a**
9: 8 Aaron came to the **a** and slaughtered
9: 9 he poured out at the base of the **a**.
9:10 On the **a** he burned the fat, the
9:12 it against the **a** on all sides.
9:13 head, and he burned them on the **a**.
9:14 top of the burnt offering on the **a**.
9:17 burned it on the **a** in addition to
9:18 it against the **a** on all sides.
9:20 then Aaron burned the fat on the **a**.
9:24 and the fat portions on the **a**.
10:12 beside the **a**, for it is most holy.
14:20 offer it on the **a**, together with the
16:12 coals from the **a** before the LORD
16:18 "Then he shall come out to the **a**
16:20 the Tent of Meeting and the **a**, he
16:25 fat of the sin offering on the **a**.
16:33 for the Tent of Meeting and the **a**,
17: 6 sprinkle the blood against the **a** of
17:11 atonement for yourselves on the **a**;
21:23 **a**, and so desecrate my sanctuary.
22:22 Do not place any of these on the **a**
Nu 3:26 surrounding the tabernacle and **a**,
4:11 "Over the gold **a** they are to spread
4:13 **a** and spread a purple cloth over it.
4:14 used for ministering at the **a**,
4:26 surrounding the tabernacle and **a**,
5:25 the LORD and bring it to the **a**.
5:26 and burn it on the **a**; after that,
7: 1 the **a** and all its utensils.
7:10 the **a** was anointed, the leaders
7:10 and presented them before the **a**.
7:11 for the dedication of the **a**."
7:84 of the **a** when it was anointed:
7:88 of the **a** after it was anointed.
16:38 into sheets to overlay the **a**,
16:39 them hammered out to overlay the **a**,
16:46 along with fire from the **a**, and
Nu 18: 3 **a**, or both they and you will die.
18: 5 the care of the sanctuary and the **a**,
18: 7 at the **a** and inside the curtain.
18:17 Sprinkle their blood on the **a** and
23: 2 offered a bull and a ram on each **a**.
23: 4 on each **a** I have offered a bull and
23:14 offered a bull and a ram on each **a**.
23:30 offered a bull and a ram on each **a**.
Dt 12:27 Present your burnt offerings on the **a**
12:27 beside the **a** of the LORD your God,
16:21 **a** you build to the LORD your God,
26: 4 front of the **a** of the LORD your God.
27: 5 Build there an **a** to the LORD your
27: 5 the LORD your God, an **a** of stones.
27: 6 Build the **a** of the LORD your God
33:10 and whole burnt offerings on your **a**.
Jos 8:30 Joshua built on Mount Ebal an **a** to
8:31 Law of Moses—an **a** of uncut stones,
9:27 for the **a** of the LORD at the place
22:10 an imposing **a** there by the Jordan.
22:11 built the **a** on the border of Canaan
22:16 an **a** in rebellion against him now?
22:19 us by building an **a** for yourselves,
22:19 than the **a** of the LORD our God.
22:23 If we have built our own **a** to turn
22:26 'Let us get ready and build an **a**
22:28 Look at the replica of the LORD's **a**,
22:29 building an **a** for burnt offerings,
22:29 other than the **a** of the LORD our God
22:34 the Gadites gave the **a** this name:
Jdg 6:24 Gideon built an **a** to the LORD there
6:25 Tear down your father's **a** to Baal
6:26 build a proper kind of **a** to the LORD
6:28 there was Baal's **a**, demolished, with
6:28 sacrificed on the newly-built **a**!
6:30 because he has broken down Baal's **a**
6:31 when someone breaks down his **a**."
6:32 because he broke down Baal's **a**.
13:20 the flame blazed up from the **a**
21: 4 the next day the people built an **a**
1Sa 2:28 to go up to my **a**, to burn incense,
2:33 I do not cut off from my **a** will be
7:17 And he built an **a** there to the LORD.
14:35 Saul built an **a** to the LORD; it was
2Sa 24:18 "Go up and build an **a** to the LORD on
24:21 "so that I can build an **a** to the
24:25 David built an **a** to the LORD there
1Ki 1:53 they brought him down from the **a**.
2:29 of the LORD and was beside the **a**.
3: 4 thousand burnt offerings on that **a**.
6:20 and he also overlaid the **a** of cedar.
6:22 He also overlaid with gold the **a**
7:48 the golden **a**; the golden table on
8:22 Solomon stood before the **a** of the
8:31 oath before your **a** in this temple,
8:54 he rose from before the **a** of the
8:64 because the bronze **a** before the LORD
9:25 on the **a** he had built for the LORD,
12:32 and offered sacrifices on the **a**.
12:33 on the **a** he had built at Bethel.
12:33 went up to the **a** to make offerings.
13: 1 by the **a** to make an offering.
13: 2 He cried out against the **a** by the
13: 2 "O **a**, **a**! This is what the LORD says:
13: 3 The **a** will be split apart and the
13: 4 cried out against the **a** at Bethel,
13: 4 from the **a** and said, "Seize him!"
13: 5 Also, the **a** was split apart and its
13:32 of the LORD against the **a** in Bethel
16:32 He set up an **a** for Baal in the
18:26 danced around the **a** they had made.
18:30 repaired the **a** of the LORD, which was
18:32 With the stones he built an **a** in the
18:35 The water ran down around the **a** and
2Ki 11:11 round the king—near the **a** and the
12: 9 He placed it beside the **a**, on the
16:10 He saw an **a** in Damascus and sent to
16:10 Uriah the priest a sketch of the **a**,
16:11 Uriah the priest built an **a** in
16:12 back from Damascus and saw the **a**,
16:13 his fellowship offerings on the **a**.
16:14 The bronze **a** that stood before the
16:14 the temple—from between the new **a**
16:14 it on the north side of the new **a**.
16:15 "On the large new **a**, offer the
16:15 Sprinkle on the **a** all the blood of
2Ki 16:15 the bronze **a** for seeking guidance."
18:22 worship before this **a** in Jerusalem"?
23: 9 at the **a** of the LORD in Jerusalem,
23:15 Even the **a** at Bethel, the high place
23:15 that **a** and high place he demolished.
23:16 and burned on the **a** to defile it,
23:17 pronounced against the **a** of Bethel
1Ch 21:18 build an **a** to the LORD on the
21:22 that I can build an **a** to the LORD,
21:26 David built an **a** to the LORD there
2Ch 1: 5 the bronze **a** that Bezalel son of Uri,
1: 6 Solomon went up to the bronze **a**
4: 1 He made a bronze **a** twenty cubits
4:19 the golden **a**; the tables on which
5:12 stood on the east side of the **a**,
6:12 Solomon stood before the **a** of the
6:22 oath before your **a** in this temple,
7: 7 because the bronze **a** he had made
7: 9 dedication of the **a** for seven days
8:12 On the **a** of the LORD that he had
15: 8 He repaired the **a** of the LORD that
23:10 round the king—near the **a** and the
26:19 the incense **a** in the LORD's temple,
29:19 are now in front of the LORD's **a**."
29:21 to offer these on the **a** of the LORD.
29:22 the blood and sprinkled it on the **a**;
29:22 and sprinkled their blood on the **a**;
29:22 and sprinkled their blood on the **a**.
29:24 presented their blood on the **a** for a
29:27 the burnt offering on the **a**.
32:12 one **a** and burn sacrifices on it'?
33:16 he restored the **a** of the LORD and
35:16 offerings on the **a** of the LORD,
Ezr 3: 2 his associates began to build the **a**
3: 3 they built the **a** on its foundation
7:17 and sacrifice them on the **a** of the
Ne 10:34 burn on the **a** of the LORD our God,
Ps 26: 6 and go about your **a**, O LORD,
43: 4 Then will I go to the **a** of God, to
51:19 bulls will be offered on your **a**.
84: 3 place near your **a**, O LORD Almighty,
Isa 6: 6 he had taken with tongs from the **a**.
19:19 In that day there will be an **a** to
27: 9 When he makes all the **a** stones to be
29: 2 she will be to me like an **a** hearth.
36: 7 "You must worship before this **a**"
40:16 Lebanon is not sufficient for **a**
56: 7 sacrifices will be accepted on my **a**;
60: 7 be accepted as offerings on my **a**,
Lam 2: 7 The Lord has rejected his **a** and
Eze 8: 5 the **a** I saw this idol of jealousy.
8:16 the **a**, were about twenty-five men.
9: 2 in and stood beside the bronze **a**.
40:46 priests who have charge of the **a**.
40:47 And the **a** was in front of the temple.
41:22 There was a wooden **a** three cubits
43:13 "These are the measurements of the **a**
43:13 And this is the height of the **a**:
43:15 The **a** hearth is four cubits high,
43:16 The **a** hearth is square, twelve
43:17 The steps of the **a** face east."
43:18 blood upon the **a** when it is built:
43:20 the **a** and make atonement for it.
43:22 and the **a** is to be purified as it
43:26 atonement for the **a** and cleanse it;
43:27 and fellowship offerings on the **a**.
45:19 corners of the upper ledge of the **a**
47: 1 side of the temple, south of the **a**.
Joel 1:13 wail, you who minister before the **a**.
2:17 between the temple porch and the **a**.
Am 2: 8 They lie down beside every **a** on
3:14 the horns of the **a** will be cut off
9: 1 I saw the Lord standing by the **a**,
Zec 9:15 for sprinkling the corners of the **a**.
14:20 the sacred bowls in front of the **a**.
Mal 1: 7 "You place defiled food on my **a**.
1:10 not light useless fires on my **a**!
2:13 You flood the LORD's **a** with tears.
Mt 5:23 you are offering your gift at the **a**
5:24 your gift there in front of the **a**.
23:18 'If anyone swears by the **a**, it means
23:19 or the **a** that makes the gift sacred?
23:20 Therefore, he who swears by the **a**
23:35 between the temple and the **a**.
Lk 11:51 between the **a** and the sanctuary.
Ac 17:23 I even found an **a** with this

1Co 9:13 a share in what is offered on the a?
10:18 the sacrifices participate in the a?
Heb 7:13 that tribe has ever served at the a.
13:10 We have an a from which those who
Jas 2:21 he offered his son Isaac on the a?
Rev 6: 9 I saw under the a the souls of those
8: 3 censer, came and stood at the a.
8: 3 on the golden a before the throne.
8: 5 filled it with fire from the a, and
9:13 of the golden a that is before God.
11: 1 a, and count the worshippers there.
14:18 came from the a and called in a loud
16: 7 I heard the a respond: "Yes, Lord

Altar of burnt offering

Ex 30:28 the a and all its utensils, and the
31: 9 the a and all its utensils, the
35:16 the a with its bronze grating, its
38: 1 They built the a of acacia wood,
40: 6 "Place the a in front of the
40:10 anoint the a and all its utensils;
40:29 He set the a near the entrance to
Lev 4: 7 shall pour out at the base of the a
4:10 the priest shall burn them on the a.
4:18 shall pour out at the base of the a
4:25 put it on the horns of the a and
4:30 put it on the horns of the a and
4:34 put it on the horns of the a and
1Ch 6:49 who presented offerings on the a
16:40 to the LORD on the a regularly,
21:26 him with fire from heaven on the a.
21:29 and the a were at that time on the
22: 1 be here, and also the a for Israel."
2Ch 29:18 the a with all its utensils, and the

Altar of incense

Ex 30:27 and its accessories, the a,
31: 8 and all its accessories, the a,
35:15 the a with its poles, the anointing
37:25 They made the a out of acacia wood.
40: 5 Place the gold a in front of the ark
1Ch 6:49 on the a in connection with all that
28:18 of the refined gold for the a.
2Ch 26:16 the LORD to burn incense on the a.
Lk 1:11 standing at the right side of the a.
Heb 9: 4 which had the golden a and the

Altars (Altar)

Ex 34:13 Break down their a, smash their
Lev 26:30 cut down your incense a and pile
Nu 3:31 the table, the lampstand, the a, the
23: 1 Balaam said, "Build me seven a here,
23: 4 "I have prepared seven a, and on
23:14 and there he built seven a and
23:29 Balaam said, "Build me seven a here,
Dt 7: 5 Break down their a, smash their
12: 3 Break down their a, smash their
Jdg 2: 2 but you shall break down their a.
1Ki 19:10 broken down your a, and put your
19:14 broken down your a, and put your
2Ki 11:18 They smashed the a and idols to
11:18 priest of Baal in front of the a.
18:22 high places and a Hezekiah removed,
21: 3 a to Baal and made an Asherah pole,
21: 4 He built a in the temple of the LORD,
21: 5 he built a to all the starry hosts.
23:12 He pulled down the a the kings of
23:12 and the a Manasseh had built in the
23:20 a and burned human bones on them.
2Ch 14: 3 He removed the foreign a and the
14: 5 incense a in every town in Judah,
23:17 They smashed the a and idols and
23:17 priest of Baal in front of the a.
28:24 set up a at every street corner in
30:14 They removed the a in Jerusalem and
30:14 cleared away the incense a and threw
31: 1 the a throughout Judah and Benjamin
32:12 remove this god's high places and a,
33: 3 he also erected a to the Baals and
33: 4 He built a in the temple of the LORD,
33: 5 he built a to all the starry hosts.
33:15 as well as all the a he had built on
34: 4 Under his direction the a of the
34: 4 the incense a that were above them,
34: 5 the bones of the priests on their a,
2Ch 34: 7 he tore down the a and the Asherah
34: 7 all the incense a throughout Israel.
Isa 17: 8 They will not look to the a, the
17: 8 incense a their fingers have made.
27: 9 or incense a will be left standing.
36: 7 high places and a Hezekiah removed,
65: 3 and burning incense on a of brick;
Jer 11:13 O Judah; and the a you have set up
17: 1 hearts and on the horns of their a.
17: 2 Even their children remember their a
Eze 6: 4 Your a will be demolished and your
6: 4 and your incense a will be smashed;
6: 5 scatter your bones around your a.
6: 6 so that your a will be laid waste
6: 6 your incense a broken down, and what
6:13 among their idols around their a,
Hos 8:11 "Though Ephraim built many a for sin
8:11 these have become a for sinning.
10: 1 his fruit increased he built more a
10: 2 demolish their a and destroy their
10: 8 will grow up and cover their a.
12:11 Their a will be like piles of stones
Am 3:14 I will destroy the a of Bethel; the
Ro 11: 3 your prophets and torn down your a

Alter (Altered)

Ps 89:34 I will not violate my covenant or a

Altered (Alter)

Da 6: 8 in writing so that it cannot be a

Alternate (Alternated)

Ex 28:34 are to a around the hem of the robe.

Alternated (Alternate)

Ex 39:26 The bells and pomegranates a around
Eze 41:18 Palm trees a with cherubim. Each

Alush

Nu 33:13 They left Dophkah and camped at A.
33:14 They left A and camped at Rephidim,

Alvah

Ge 36:40 and regions: Timna, A, Jetheth,
1Ch 1:51 of Edom were: Timna, A, Jetheth,

Alvan

Ge 36:23 The sons of Shobal: A, Manahath,
1Ch 1:40 The sons of Shobal: A, Manahath,

Always

Ge 26:29 just as we did not molest you but a
Ex 19: 9 and will a put their trust in you.
28:30 Thus Aaron will a bear the means of
29:28 This is a to be the regular share
Lev 25:32 "'The Levites a have the right to
Nu 22:30 which you have a ridden, to this day?
Dt 5:29 fear me and keep all my commands a,
6:24 so that we might a prosper and be
11: 1 decrees, his laws and his commands a.
12:28 so that it may a go well with you
14:23 learn to revere the LORD your God a.
15:11 There will a be poor people in the
18: 5 and minister in the LORD's name a.
19: 9 your God and to walk a in his ways
28:13 a be at the top, never at the bottom.
Jos 4:24 you might a fear the LORD your God."
1Sa 1:22 the LORD, and he will live there a."
2:35 minister before my anointed one a.
7:17 he a went back to Ramah, where his
2Sa 9: 7 and you will a eat at my table."
9:10 your master, will a eat at my table.
9:13 because he a ate at the king's table,
1Ki 5: 1 a been on friendly terms with David.
9: 3 My eyes and my heart will a be there.
11:36 a have a lamp before me in Jerusalem,
12: 7 they will a be your servants."
22: 8 anything good about me, but a bad.
2Ki 17:37 You must a be careful to keep the
1Ch 16:11 and his strength; seek his face a.
2Ch 7:16 My eyes and my heart will a be there.
10: 7 they will a be your servants."
18: 7 anything good about me, but a bad.
Job 31:32 door was a open to the traveller—
Ps 9:18 the needy will not a be forgotten,
10: 5 His ways are a prosperous; he is
10: 6 a be happy and never have trouble."
16: 8 I have set the LORD a before me.
34: 1 his praise will a be on my lips.
35:27 joy and gladness; may they a say,
37:26 They are a generous and lend freely;
40:11 love and your truth a protect me.
40:16 those who love your salvation a say,
51: 3 and my sin is a before me.
56: 5 they are a plotting to harm me.
70: 4 those who love your salvation a say,
71: 3 rock of refuge to which I can a go
71:14 as for me, I shall a have hope;
73:12 This is what the wicked are like—a
73:23 Yet I am a with you; you hold me by
103: 9 He will not a accuse, nor will he
105: 4 and his strength; seek his face a.
109:15 May their sins a remain before the
119:44 I will a obey your law, for ever and
119:117 a have regard for your decrees.
119:132 a do to those who love your name.
Pr 5:19 may her breasts satisfy you a,
6:14 heart—he a stirs up dissension.
8:30 day, rejoicing a in his presence,
23: 7 for he is the kind of man who is a
23:17 but a be zealous for the fear of the
28:14 Blessed is the man who a fears the
29:14 his throne will a be secure.
Ecc 9: 8 A be clothed in white, and a anoint
Isa 57:16 nor will I a be angry, for then the
58:11 The LORD will guide you a; he will
60:11 Your gates will a stand open, they
Jer 3: 5 will you a be angry? Will your wrath
8: 5 Why does Jerusalem a turn away? They
12: 1 You are a righteous, O LORD, when I
12: 2 You are a on their lips but far from
17: 8 heat comes; its leaves are a green.
32:39 so that they will a fear me for
35: 7 things, but must a live in tents.
Lam 5:20 Why do you a forget us? Why do you
Hos 7: 2 engulf them; they are a before me.
12: 6 justice, and wait for your God a.
Mal 1: 4 a under the wrath of the LORD.
Mt 18:10 their angels in heaven a see the face
26:11 The poor you will a have with you,
26:11 you, but you will not a have me.
28:20 you a, to the very end of the age."
Mk 14: 7 The poor you will a have with you,
14: 7 But you will not a have me.
Lk 15:31 'you are a with me, and everything I
18: 1 they should a pray and not give up.
21:36 Be a on the watch, and pray that you
Jn 5:17 Jesus said to them, "My Father is a
8:29 alone, for I a do what pleases him."
11:42 I knew that you a hear me, but I
12: 8 You will a have the poor among you,
12: 8 you, but you will not a have me."
18:20 "I a taught in synagogues or at the
Ac 2:25 him: "'I saw the Lord a before me.
7:51 You a resist the Holy Spirit!
9:36 a doing good and helping the poor.
24:16 I strive a to keep my conscience
Ro 15:20 has a been my ambition to preach the
1Co 1: 4 I a thank God for you because of his
13: 7 a protects, a trusts, a hopes, a
15:58 Let nothing move you. A give
2Co 1:19 "No", but in him it has a been "Yes.
2:14 thanks be to God, who a leads us in
4:10 We a carry around in our body the
4:11 For we who are alive are a being
5: 6 Therefore we are a confident and
6:10 sorrowful, yet a rejoicing; poor,
Gal 4:18 a and not just when I am with you.
Eph 5:20 a giving thanks to God the Father
6:18 a keep on praying for all the saints.
Php 1: 4 In all my prayers for all of you, I a
1:20 a Christ will be exalted in my body,
2:12 my dear friends, as you have a
4: 4 Rejoice in the Lord a. I will say it
Col 1: 3 We a thank God, the Father of our
4: 6 Let your conversation be a full of
4:12 He is a wrestling in prayer for you,
1Th 1: 2 We a thank God for all of you,
2:16 In this way they a heap up their

1Th 3: 6 He has told us that you **a** have
5:15 but **a** try to be kind to each other
5:16 Be joyful **a**; pray continually;
2Th 1: 3 We ought **a** to thank God for you,
2:13 we ought **a** to thank God for you,
2Ti 3: 7 **a** learning but never able to
Tit 1:12 **a** liars, evil brutes, lazy gluttons."
Phm : 4 I **a** thank my God as I remember you
Heb 3:10 'Their hearts are **a** going astray,
7:25 he **a** lives to intercede for them.
1Pe 3:15 **A** be prepared to give an answer to
2Pe 1:12 I will **a** remind you of these things,
1:15 **a** be able to remember these things.

Amad
Jos 19:26 Allammelech, **A** and Mishal. On the

Amal
1Ch 7:35 Helem: Zophah, Imna, Shelesh and **A**.

Amalek (Amalekite, Amalekites)
Ge 36:12 named Timna, who bore him **A**.
36:16 Korah, Gatam and **A**. These were the
Ex 17:14 the memory of **A** from under heaven."
Nu 24:20 Balaam saw **A** and uttered his oracle:
24:20 "**A** was first among the nations, but
Dt 25:19 the memory of **A** from under heaven.
Jdg 5:14 from Ephraim, whose roots were in **A**
1Sa 15: 5 Saul went to the city of **A** and set
2Sa 8:12 Ammonites and the Philistines, and **A**.
1Ch 1:36 Zepho, Gatam and Kenaz; by Timna: **A**.
18:11 Ammonites and the Philistines, and **A**.
Ps 83: 7 Gebal, Ammon and **A**, Philistia, with

Amalekite (Amalek)
Ex 17:13 Joshua overcame the **A** army with the
1Sa 30:13 am an Egyptian, the slave of an **A**.
2Sa 1: 8 "He asked me, 'Who are you?' "'An **A**,'
1:13 son of an alien, an **A**," he answered.

Amalekites (Amalek)
Ge 14: 7 the whole territory of the **A**,
Ex 17: 8 The **A** came and attacked the
17: 9 our men and go out to fight the **A**.
17:10 Joshua fought the **A** as Moses had
17:11 his hands, the **A** were winning.
17:16 **A** from generation to generation."
Nu 13:29 The **A** live in the Negev; the
14:25 Since the **A** and Canaanites are
14:43 for the **A** and Canaanites will face
14:45 the **A** and Canaanites who lived in
Dt 25:17 Remember what the **A** did to you along
Jdg 3:13 Getting the Ammonites and **A** to join
6: 3 the Midianites, **A** and other eastern
6:33 Now all the Midianites, **A** and other
7:12 The Midianites, the **A** and all the
10:12 the Sidonians, the **A** and the
12:15 in the hill country of the **A**.
1Sa 14:48 fought valiantly and defeated the **A**,
15: 2 'I will punish the **A** for what they
15: 3 Now go, attack the **A** and totally
15: 6 "Go away, leave the **A** so that I do
15: 6 So the Kenites moved away from the **A**.
15: 7 Saul attacked the **A** all the way from
15: 8 He took Agag king of the **A** alive,
15:15 The soldiers brought them from the **A**;
15:18 destroy those wicked people, the **A**
15:20 **A** and brought back Agag their king.
15:32 said, "Bring me Agag king of the **A**.
27: 8 Geshurites, the Girzites and the **A**.
28:18 out his fierce wrath against the **A**,
30: 1 Now the **A** had raided the Negev and
30:18 David recovered everything the **A** had
2Sa 1: 1 the **A** and stayed in Ziklag two days.
1Ch 4:43 They killed the remaining **A** who had

Amam
Jos 15:26 **A**, Shema, Moladah,

Amana
SS 4: 8 Descend from the crest of **A**, from

Amariah (Amariah's)
1Ch 6: 7 Meraioth the father of **A**, **A** the
6:11 Azariah the father of **A**, **A** the
6:52 Meraioth his son, **A** his son, Ahitub
23:19 **A** the second, Jahaziel the third and
24:23 **A** the second, Jahaziel the third and
2Ch 19:11 "**A** the chief priest will be over you
31:15 Eden, Miniamin, Jeshua, Shemaiah, **A**
Ezr 7: 3 the son of **A**, the son of Azariah,
10:42 Shallum, **A** and Joseph.
Ne 10: 3 Pashhur, **A**, Malkijah,
11: 4 the son of Zechariah, the son of **A**,
12: 2 **A**, Malluch, Hattush,
Zep 1: 1 the son of Gedaliah, the son of **A**,

Amariah's (Amariah)
Ne 12:13 of Ezra's, Meshullam; of **A**,

Amasa
David's nephew (1Ch 2:17). In charge of Absalom's army (2Sa 17:24–25); made commander of David's army (2Sa 19:13); treacherously killed by Joab his cousin (2Sa 20:9–10; 1Ki 2:5).

2Sa 17:25 Absalom had appointed **A** over the
17:25 **A** was the son of a man named Jether,
19:13 say to **A**, 'Are you not my own flesh
20: 4 the king said to **A**, "Summon the men
20: 5 when **A** went to summon Judah, he took
20: 8 rock in Gibeon, **A** came to meet them.
20: 9 Joab said to **A**, "How are you, my
20: 9 Then Joab took **A** by the beard with his
20:10 **A** was not on his guard against the
20:10 Without being stabbed again, **A** died.
20:11 One of Joab's men stood beside **A** and
20:12 **A** lay wallowing in his blood in the
20:12 everyone who came up to **A** stopped,
20:13 After **A** had been removed from the
1Ki 2: 5 Abner son of Ner and **A** son of Jether.
2:32 **A** son of Jether, commander of Judah's
1Ch 2:17 Abigail was the mother of **A**, whose
2Ch 28:12 Jehizkiah son of Shallum, and **A** son

Amasai
1Ch 6:25 The descendants of Elkanah: **A**,
6:35 the son of Mahath, the son of **A**,
12:18 the Spirit came upon **A**, chief of the
15:24 Shebaniah, Joshaphat, Nethanel, **A**,
2Ch 29:12 Mahath son of **A** and Joel son of

Amashsai
Ne 11:13 **A** son of Azarel, the son of Ahzai

Amasiah
2Ch 17:16 next, **A** son of Zicri, who

Amassed (Amasses)
Ecc 2: 8 I **a** silver and gold for myself, and
Eze 28: 4 **a** gold and silver in your treasuries.

Amasses (Amassed)
Pr 28: 8 interest **a** it for another, who

Amazed (Amazement)
Isa 29: 9 Be stunned and **a**, blind yourselves
Hab 1: 5 and watch—and be utterly **a**.
Mt 7:28 the crowds were **a** at his teaching,
8:27 The men were **a** and asked, "What kind
9:33 The crowd was **a** and said, "Nothing
13:54 in their synagogue, and they were **a**.
15:31 The people were **a** when they saw the
21:20 the disciples saw this, they were **a**.
22:22 they heard this, they were **a**. So
Mk 1:22 The people were **a** at his teaching,
1:27 The people were all so **a** that they
2:12 This **a** everyone and they praised God,
5:20 And all the people were **a**.
6: 2 and many who heard him were **a**.
6: 6 he was **a** at their lack of faith.
6:51 died down. They were completely **a**,
10:24 The disciples were **a** at his words.
10:26 The disciples were even more **a**, and
11:18 whole crowd was **a** at his teaching.
12:17 And they were **a** at him.
15: 5 made no reply, and Pilate was **a**.
Lk 2:18 all who heard it were **a** at what the
2:47 Everyone who heard him was **a** at his
4:22 All spoke well of him and were **a** at
4:32 They were **a** at his teaching, because
4:36 All the people were **a** and said to
5:26 Everyone was **a** and gave praise to
7: 9 Jesus heard this, he was **a** at him,
9:43 they were all **a** at the greatness of
11:14 mute spoke, and the crowd was **a**.
24:22 In addition, some of our women **a** us.
Jn 5:28 "Do not be **a** at this, for a time is
7:15 The Jews were **a** and asked, "How did
Ac 2: 7 Utterly **a**, they asked: "Are not all
2:12 **A** and perplexed, they asked one
7:31 he saw this, he was **a** at the sight.
8: 9 and **a** all the people of Samaria.
8:11 They followed him because he had **a**
13:12 **a** at the teaching about the Lord.

Amazement (Amazed, Amazing)
Da 3:24 feet in **a** and asked his advisers,
Mt 27:14 the great **a** of the governor.
Mk 7:37 People were overwhelmed with **a**. "He
Lk 8:25 In fear and **a** they asked one another,
24:41 not believe it because of joy and **a**,
Jn 5:20 Yes, to your **a** he will show him even
Ac 3:10 and **a** at what had happened to him.

Amaziah (Amaziah's)
2Ki 12:21 And **A** his son succeeded him as king.
13:12 including his war against **A** king of
14: 1 **A** son of Joash king of Judah began
14: 8 **A** sent messengers to Jehoash son of
14: 9 Jehoash king of Israel replied to **A**
14:11 **A**, however, would not listen, so
14:11 He and **A** king of Judah faced each
14:13 Jehoash king of Israel captured **A**
14:15 including his war against **A** king of
14:17 **A** son of Joash king of Judah lived
14:21 him king in place of his father **A**.
14:22 after **A** rested with his fathers.
14:23 In the fifteenth year of **A** son of
15: 1 of **A** king of Judah began to reign.
15: 3 LORD, just as his father **A** had done.
1Ch 3:12 **A** his son, Azariah his son, Jotham
4:34 Meshobab, Jamlech, Joshah son of **A**,
6:45 the son of Hashabiah, the son of **A**,
2Ch 24:27 And **A** his son succeeded him as king.
25: 1 **A** was twenty-five years old when he
25: 5 **A** called the people of Judah
25: 9 **A** asked the man of God, "But what
25:10 **A** dismissed the troops who had come
25:11 **A** then marshalled his strength and
25:13 Meanwhile the troops that **A** had sent
25:14 **A** returned from slaughtering the
25:15 anger of the LORD burned against **A**,
25:17 After **A** king of Judah consulted his
25:18 Jehoash king of Israel replied to **A**
25:20 **A**, however, would not listen, for
25:21 He and **A** king of Judah faced each
25:23 Jehoash king of Israel captured **A**
25:25 **A** son of Joash king of Judah lived
25:27 From the time that **A** turned away
26: 1 him king in place of his father **A**.
26: 2 after **A** rested with his fathers.
26: 4 LORD, just as his father **A** had done.
Am 7:10 **A** the priest of Bethel sent a
7:12 **A** said to Amos, "Get out, you seer!
7:14 Amos answered **A**, "I was neither a

Amaziah's (Amaziah)
2Ki 14:18 for the other events of **A** reign, are
2Ch 25:26 for the other events of **A** reign,

Amazing (Amazement)
Jos 3: 5 LORD will do **a** things among you."
Jdg 13:19 And the LORD did an **a** thing while
Pr 30:18 three things that are too **a** for me,

Ambassador (Ambassadors)
Eph 6:20 for which I am an **a** in chains. Pray

Ambassadors (Ambassador)
Isa 57: 9 You sent your **a** far away; you
2Co 5:20 We are therefore Christ's **a**, as

Ambition

Ro 15:20 has always been my **a** to preach the
Gal 5:20 selfish **a**, dissensions, factions
Php 1:17 preach Christ out of selfish **a**,
2: 3 Do nothing out of selfish **a** or vain
1Th 4:11 Make it your **a** to lead a quiet life,
Jas 3:14 envy and selfish **a** in your hearts,
3:16 For where you have envy and selfish **a**

Ambush (Ambushes)

Jos 8: 2 Set an **a** behind the city."
8: 4 You are to set an **a** behind the city.
8: 7 you are to rise up from **a** and take
8: 9 and they went to the place of **a** and
8:12 set them in **a** between Bethel and Ai,
8:13 city and the **a** to the west of it.
8:14 But he did not know that an **a** had
8:19 soon as he did this, the men in the **a**
8:21 all Israel saw that the **a** had taken
8:22 The men of the **a** also came out of
Jdg 9:25 to **a** and rob everyone who passed by,
9:43 and set an **a** in the fields.
20:29 Israel set an **a** around Gibeah.
20:33 and the Israelite **a** charged out of
20:36 on the **a** they had set near Gibeah.
20:37 The men who had been in **a** made a
20:38 had arranged with the **a** that they
1Sa 15: 5 Amalek and set an **a** in the ravine.
2Ch 13:13 of Judah the **a** was behind them.
Ps 10: 8 from **a** he murders the innocent,
64: 4 They shoot from **a** at the innocent
Jer 51:12 station the watchmen, prepare an **a**!
Hos 6: 9 marauders lie in **a** for a man, so do
Ac 23:21 of them are waiting in **a** for him.
25: 3 an **a** to kill him along the way.

Ambushes (Ambush)

2Ch 20:22 the LORD set **a** against the men of

Amen

Nu 5:22 "'Then the woman is to say, "**A**. So
Dt 27:15 Then all the people shall say, "**A**!
27:16 Then all the people shall say, "**A**!
27:17 Then all the people shall say, "**A**!
27:18 Then all the people shall say, "**A**!
27:19 Then all the people shall say, "**A**!
27:20 Then all the people shall say, "**A**!
27:21 Then all the people shall say, "**A**!
27:22 Then all the people shall say, "**A**!
27:23 Then all the people shall say, "**A**!
27:24 Then all the people shall say, "**A**!
27:25 Then all the people shall say, "**A**!
27:26 Then all the people shall say, "**A**!
1Ki 1:36 "**A**! May the LORD, the God of my lord
1Ch 16:36 Then all the people said "**A**" and
Ne 5:13 said, "**A**," and praised the LORD.
8: 6 "**A**! **A**!" Then they bowed down and
Ps 41:13 **A** and **A**.
72:19 **A** and **A**.
89:52 Praise be to the LORD for ever! **A**
89:52 be to the LORD for ever! **A** and **A**.
106:48 Let all the people say, "**A**!" Praise
Jer 11: 5 I answered, "**A**, LORD."
28: 6 He said, "**A**! May the LORD do so! May
Ro 1:25 Creator—who is for ever praised. **A**.
9: 5 God over all, for ever praised! **A**.
11:36 To him be the glory for ever! **A**.
15:33 The God of peace be with you all. **A**.
16:27 for ever through Jesus Christ! **A**.
1Co 14:16 "**A**" to your thanksgiving, since he
16:24 to all of you in Christ Jesus. **A**.
2Co 1:20 And so through him the "**A**" is spoken
Gal 1: 5 to whom be glory for ever and ever. **A**
6:18 be with your spirit, brothers. **A**.
Eph 3:21 generations, for ever and ever! **A**.
Php 4:20 be glory for ever and ever. **A**.
4:23 Jesus Christ be with your spirit. **A**
1Ti 1:17 and glory for ever and ever. **A**.
6:16 be honour and might for ever. **A**.
2Ti 4:18 To him be glory for ever and ever. **A**.
Heb 13:21 whom be glory for ever and ever. **A**.
1Pe 4:11 and the power for ever and ever. **A**.
5:11 be the power for ever and ever. **A**.
2Pe 3:18 be glory both now and for ever! **A**.
Jude :25 all ages, now and for evermore! **A**.
Rev 1: 6 and power for ever and ever! **A**.
1: 7 So shall it be! **A**.
3:14 write: These are the words of the **A**,
5:14 The four living creatures said, "**A**",
7:12 saying: "**A**! Praise and glory and
7:12 be to our God for ever and ever. **A**
19: 4 And they cried: "**A**, Hallelujah!"
22:20 **A**. Come, Lord Jesus.
22:21 Lord Jesus be with God's people. **A**.

Amends

2Sa 21: 3 How shall I make **a** so that you will
Job 20:10 His children must make **a** to the poor;
Pr 14: 9 Fools mock at making **a** for sin, but

Amethyst

Ex 28:19 row a jacinth, an agate and an **a**;
39:12 row a jacinth, an agate and an **a**;
Rev 21:20 eleventh jacinth, and the twelfth **a**.

Ami

Ezr 2:57 Hattil, Pokereth-Hazzebaim and **A**

Amittai

2Ki 14:25 Jonah son of **A**, the prophet from
Jnh 1: 1 of the LORD came to Jonah son of **A**:

Ammah

2Sa 2:24 they came to the hill of **A**, near

Ammiel

Nu 13:12 the tribe of Dan, **A** son of Gemalli;
2Sa 9: 4 of Makir son of **A** in Lo Debar."
9: 5 from the house of Makir son of **A**.
17:27 and Makir son of **A** from Lo Debar,
1Ch 3: 5 were by Bathsheba daughter of **A**.
26: 5 **A** the sixth, Issachar the seventh

Ammihud

Nu 1:10 from Ephraim, Elishama son of **A**;
2:18 of Ephraim is Elishama son of **A**.
7:48 On the seventh day Elishama son of **A**,
7:53 the offering of Elishama son of **A**.
10:22 Elishama son of **A** was in command.
34:20 Shemuel son of **A**, from the tribe of
34:28 Pedahel son of **A**, the leader from
2Sa 13:37 Talmai son of **A**, the king of Geshur.
1Ch 7:26 Ladan his son, **A** his son, Elishama
9: 4 Uthai son of **A**, the son of Omri, the

Amminadab

Ex 6:23 Aaron married Elisheba, daughter of **A**
Nu 1: 7 from Judah, Nahshon son of **A**;
2: 3 people of Judah is Nahshon son of **A**.
7:12 son of **A** of the tribe of Judah.
7:17 the offering of Nahshon son of **A**.
10:14 Nahshon son of **A** was in command.
Ru 4:19 father of Ram, Ram the father of **A**,
4:20 **A** the father of Nahshon, Nahshon the
1Ch 2:10 Ram was the father of **A**, and **A** the
6:22 The descendants of Kohath: **A** his son,
15:10 from the descendants of Uzziel, **A**
15:11 Shemaiah, Eliel and **A** the Levites.
Mt 1: 4 Ram the father of **A**, **A** the father of
Lk 3:33 the son of **A**, the son of Ram, the

Ammishaddai

Nu 1:12 from Dan, Ahiezer son of **A**;
2:25 people of Dan is Ahiezer son of **A**.
7:66 On the tenth day Ahiezer son of **A**,
7:71 the offering of Ahiezer son of **A**.
10:25 Ahiezer son of **A** was in command.

Ammizabad

1Ch 27: 6 son **A** was in charge of his division.

Ammon (Ammonite, Ammonites)

Territory inhabited by Ammonites east of the Jordan between Arnon and Jabbok rivers; with capital Rabbah. Western part captured by the Amorites, later occupied by Israel (Dt 2:21–23; Jdg 11:13–23). Its inhabitants frequently warred against the Israelites (1Sa 11:1; 2Sa 10:6–14; 12:26–28; 2Ch 27:5) and its destruction is prophesied (Jer 49:1–6; Eze 21:28–32; Am 1:13–15; Zep 2:8–11).

Jdg 11:28 The king of **A**, however, paid no
11:33 Thus Israel subdued **A**.
2Ki 23:13 detestable god of the people of **A**.
2Ch 20:10 "But now here are men from **A**, Moab
20:22 set ambushes against the men of **A**
20:23 The men of **A** and Moab rose up
Ne 13:23 women from Ashdod, **A** and Moab.
Ps 83: 7 Gebal, **A** and Amalek, Philistia, with
Jer 9:26 Egypt, Judah, Edom, **A**, Moab and all
25:21 Edom, Moab and **A**;
27: 3 Moab, **A**, Tyre and Sidon through the
40:11 all the Jews in Moab, **A**, Edom and
Eze 25: 5 **A** into a resting place for sheep.
Da 11:41 **A** will be delivered from his hand.
Am 1:13 "For three sins of **A**, even for four,

Ammonite (Ammon)

Dt 23: 3 No **A** or Moabite or any of his
Jos 13:25 half the **A** country as far as Aroer,
Jdg 11:12 Jephthah sent messengers to the **A**
11:14 sent back messengers to the **A** king,
1Sa 11: 1 Nahash the **A** went up and besieged
11: 2 Nahash the **A** replied, "I will make a
2Sa 10: 3 the **A** nobles said to Hanun their
12:31 He did this to all the **A** towns. Then
23:37 Zelek the **A**, Naharai the Beerothite,
1Ki 14:21 name was Naamah; she was an **A**.
14:31 name was Naamah; she was an **A**.
2Ki 24: 2 Moabite and **A** raiders against him.
1Ch 11:39 Zelek the **A**, Naharai the Berothite,
19: 3 the **A** nobles said to Hanun, "Do you
20: 3 David did this to all the **A** towns.
2Ch 12:13 name was Naamah; she was an **A**.
24:26 son of Shimeath an **A** woman, and
Ne 2:10 the **A** official heard about this,
2:19 Tobiah the **A** official and Geshem the
4: 3 Tobiah the **A**, who was at his side,
13: 1 there it was found written that no **A**

Ammonites (Ammon)

Ge 19:38 he is the father of the **A** of today.
Nu 21:24 but only as far as the **A**, because
Dt 2:19 you come to the **A**, do not harass
2:19 of any land belonging to the **A**.
2:20 but the **A** called them Zamzummites.
2:21 destroyed them from before the **A**,
2:37 on any of the land of the **A**,
3:11 It is still in Rabbah of the **A**.)
3:16 River, which is the border of the **A**.
Jos 12: 2 River, which is the border of the **A**.
13:10 Heshbon, out to the border of the **A**.
Jdg 3:13 Getting the **A** and Amalekites to join
10: 6 **A** and the gods of the Philistines.
10: 7 hands of the Philistines and the **A**,
10: 9 The **A** also crossed the Jordan to
10:11 Amorites, the **A**, the Philistines,
10:17 the **A** were called to arms and camped
10:18 attack against the **A** will be the head
11: 4 Some time later, when the **A** made war
11: 6 commander, so we can fight the **A**."
11: 8 now; come with us to fight the **A**,
11: 9 you take me back to fight the **A**
11:13 The king of the **A** answered
11:15 land of Moab or the land of the **A**.
11:27 between the Israelites and the **A**."
11:29 there he advanced against the **A**.
11:30 "If you give the **A** into my
11:31 from the **A** will be the LORD's,
11:32 Jephthah went over to fight the **A**,
11:36 avenged you of your enemies, the **A**.
12: 1 "Why did you go to fight the **A**
12: 2 in a great struggle with the **A**,
12: 3 and crossed over to fight the **A**,
1Sa 11:10 They said to the **A**, "Tomorrow we
11:11 they broke into the camp of the **A**
12:12 of the **A** was moving against you,
14:47 the **A**, Edom, the kings of Zobah, and
2Sa 8:12 Edom and Moab, the **A** and the
10: 1 the king of the **A** died, and his son
10: 2 men came to the land of the **A**,
10: 6 the **A** realised that they had become

2Sa 10: 8 The A came out and drew up in battle
10:10 and deployed them against the A.
10:11 but if the A are too strong for you,
10:14 the A saw that the Arameans were
10:14 the A and came to Jerusalem.
10:19 were afraid to help the A any more.
11: 1 They destroyed the A and besieged
12: 9 killed him with the sword of the A.
12:26 Joab fought against Rabbah of the A
17:27 son of Nahash from Rabbah of the A,
1Ki 11: 1 A, Edomites, Sidonians and Hittites.
11: 5 Molech the detestable god of the A.
11: 7 Molech the detestable god of the A.
11:33 and Molech the god of the A, and
1Ch 18:11 A and the Philistines, and Amalek.
19: 1 Nahash king of the A died, and his
19: 2 of the A to express sympathy to him,
19: 6 the A realised that they had become
19: 6 Hanun and the A sent a thousand
19: 7 while the A were mustered from their
19: 9 The A came out and drew up in battle
19:11 they were deployed against the A.
19:12 but if the A are too strong for you,
19:15 the A saw that the Arameans were
19:19 not willing to help the A any more.
20: 1 He laid waste the land of the A and
2Ch 20: 1 After this, the Moabites and A with
26: 8 The A brought tribute to Uzziah, and
27: 5 Jotham made war on the king of the A
27: 5 That year the A paid him a hundred
27: 5 The A brought him the same amount
Ezr 9: 1 A, Moabites, Egyptians and Amorites.
Ne 4: 7 Tobiah, the Arabs, the A and the men
Isa 11:14 and the A will be subject to them.
Jer 40:14 Baalis king of the A has sent Ishmael
41:10 and set out to cross over to the A.
41:15 from Johanan and fled to the A.
49: 1 Concerning the A: This is what the
49: 2 battle cry against Rabbah of the A
49: 6 I will restore the fortunes of the A
Eze 21:20 to come against Rabbah of the A
21:28 LORD says about the A and their
25: 2 the A and prophesy against them.
25:10 I will give Moab along with the A to
25:10 so that the A will not be remembered
Zep 2: 8 of Moab and the taunts of the A,
2: 9 the A like Gomorrah—a place of

Amnon (Amnon's)

David's firstborn son (2Sa 3:2). Raped Absalom's sister, Tamar (2Sa 13:1–22); killed by Absalom's men (2Sa 13:23–29).

2Sa 3: 2 was A the son of Ahinoam of Jezreel;
13: 1 In the course of time, A son of
13: 2 A became frustrated to the point of
13: 3 Now A had a friend named Jonadab son
13: 4 He asked A, "Why do you, the king's
13: 4 Won't you tell me?" A said to him,
13: 6 A lay down and pretended to be ill.
13: 6 When the king came to see him, A
13: 7 A and prepare some food for him."
13: 8 her brother A, who was lying down.
13: 9 "Send everyone out of here," A said.
13:10 A said to Tamar, "Bring the food
13:10 it to her brother A in his bedroom.
13:15 A hated her with intense hatred. In
13:15 A said to her, "Get up and get out!"
13:20 "Has that A, your brother, been with
13:22 Absalom never said a word to A,
13:22 he hated A because he had disgraced
13:26 let my brother A come with us.
13:27 A and the rest of the king's sons.
13:28 "Listen! When A is in high spirits
13:28 you, 'Strike A down,' then kill him.
13:29 Absalom's men did to A what Absalom
13:32 all the princes; only A is dead.
13:32 day that A raped his sister Tamar.
13:33 Only A is dead."
1Ch 3: 1 The firstborn was A the son of
4:20 The sons of Shimon: A, Rinnah,

Amnon's (Amnon)

2Sa 13:39 he was consoled concerning A death.

Amok (Amok's)

Ne 12: 7 Sallu, A, Hilkiah and Jedaiah. These

Amok's (Amok)

Ne 12:20 of Sallu's, Kallai; of A, Eber;

Amon (Amon's)

1Ki 22:26 "Take Micaiah and send him back to A
2Ki 21:18 And A his son succeeded him as king.
21:19 A was twenty-two years old when he
21:24 all who had plotted against King A,
1Ch 3:14 A his son, Josiah his son.
2Ch 18:25 "Take Micaiah and send him back to A
33:20 And A his son succeeded him as king.
33:21 A was twenty-two years old when he
33:22 A worshipped and offered sacrifices
33:23 the LORD; A increased his guilt.
33:25 all who had plotted against King A,
Ne 7:59 Hattil, Pokereth-Hazzebaim and A
Jer 1: 2 of Josiah son of A king of Judah,
25: 3 A king of Judah until this very day
46:25 I am about to bring punishment on A
Zep 1: 1 of Josiah son of A king of Judah:
Mt 1:10 father of A, A the father of Josiah,

Amon's (Amon)

2Ki 21:23 A officials conspired against him
21:25 for the other events of A reign, and
2Ch 33:24 A officials conspired against him

Amorite (Amorites)

Ge 14:13 near the great trees of Mamre the A,
Nu 21:13 desert extending into A territory.
Dt 2:24 Sihon the A, king of Heshbon, and
4:47 the two A kings east of the Jordan.
Jos 5: 1 Now when all the A kings west of the
10: 6 because all the A kings from the
24:12 before you—also the two A kings.
Eze 16: 3 was an A and your mother a Hittite.
16:45 was a Hittite and your father an A.
Am 2: 9 "I destroyed the A before them,

Amorites (Amorite)

Ge 10:16 Jebusites, A, Girgashites,
14: 7 A who were living in Hazezon Tamar.
15:16 for the sin of the A has not yet
15:21 A, Canaanites, Girgashites and
48:22 I took from the A with my sword and
Ex 3: 8 A, Perizzites, Hivites and Jebusites.
3:17 Hittites, A, Perizzites, Hivites and
13: 5 Hittites, A, Hivites and
23:23 bring you into the land of the A,
33: 2 A, Hittites, Perizzites, Hivites and
34:11 I will drive out before you the A,
Nu 13:29 Jebusites and A live in the hill
21:13 of Moab, between Moab and the A.
21:21 to say to Sihon king of the A:
21:25 cities of the A and occupied them,
21:26 was the city of Sihon king of the A,
21:29 as captives to Sihon king of the A.
21:31 Israel settled in the land of the A.
21:32 and drove out the A who were there.
21:34 of the A, who reigned in Heshbon."
22: 2 all that Israel had done to the A,
32:33 the kingdom of Sihon king of the A
32:39 and drove out the A who were there.
Dt 1: 4 he had defeated Sihon king of the A,
1: 7 into the hill country of the A;
1:19 of the A through all that vast
1:20 reached the hill country of the A,
1:27 the hands of the A to destroy us.
1:44 The A who lived in those hills came
3: 2 of the A, who reigned in Heshbon."
3: 8 A the territory east of the Jordan,
3: 9 the Sidonians; the A call it Senir.)
4:46 in the land of Sihon king of the A,
7: 1 Girgashites, A, Canaanites,
20:17 A, Canaanites, Perizzites, Hivites
31: 4 the kings of the A, whom he
Jos 2:10 the two kings of the A east of the
3:10 Girgashites, A and Jebusites.
7: 7 the hands of the A to destroy us?
9: 1 A, Canaanites, Perizzites, Hivites
9:10 kings of the A east of the Jordan
10: 5 the five kings of the A—the kings
10:12 On the day the LORD gave the A over
11: 3 in the east and west; to the A,
12: 2 Sihon king of the A, who reigned in
Jos 12: 8 A, Canaanites, Perizzites, Hivites
13: 4 far as Aphek, the region of the A,
13:10 all the towns of Sihon king of the A,
13:21 king of the A, who ruled at Heshbon.
24: 8 "'I brought you to the land of the A
24:11 as did also the A, Perizzites,
24:15 the A, in whose land you are living.
24:18 the A, who lived in the land.
Jdg 1:34 The A confined the Danites to the
1:35 the A were determined also to hold
1:36 The boundary of the A was from
3: 5 A, Perizzites, Hivites and Jebusites.
6:10 of the A, in whose land you live.
10: 8 Jordan in Gilead, the land of the A.
10:11 A, the Ammonites, the Philistines,
11:19 messengers to Sihon king of the A,
11:21 of the A who lived in that country,
11:23 the God of Israel, has driven the A
1Sa 7:14 was peace between Israel and the A.
2Sa 21: 2 Israel but were survivors of the A;
1Ki 4:19 (the country of Sihon king of the A
9:20 All the people left from the A,
21:26 like the A the LORD drove out before
2Ki 21:11 He has done more evil than the A who
1Ch 1:14 Jebusites, A, Girgashites,
2Ch 8: 7 A, Perizzites, Hivites and Jebusites
Ezr 9: 1 Ammonites, Moabites, Egyptians and A.
Ne 9: 8 Hittites, A, Perizzites, Jebusites
Ps 135:11 Sihon king of the A, Og king of
136:19 Sihon king of the A His love
Am 2:10 to give you the land of the A.

Amos

1. Prophet from Tekoa (Am 1:1); spoke against Israel (Am 7:10–17). **2.** Ancestor of Jesus. (Lk 3:25).

Am 1: 1 The words of A, one of the shepherds
7: 8 asked me, "What do you see, A?"
7:10 "A is raising a conspiracy against
7:11 For this is what A is saying:
7:12 Amaziah said to A, "Get out, you
7:14 A answered Amaziah, "I was neither a
8: 2 "What do you see, A?" he asked. "A
Lk 3:25 the son of Mattathias, the son of A,

Amount (Amounted, Amounts)

Ge 43:12 Take double the a of silver with you,
43:15 the a of silver, and Benjamin also.
Ex 12: 4 You are to determine the a of lamb
38:24 The total a of the gold from the
Lev 25: 8 a to a period of forty-nine years.
27: 8 is too poor to pay the specified a,
27:16 to the a of seed required for it
1Sa 30:16 revelling because of the great a of
2Ki 12:10 was a large a of money in the chest,
12:11 the a had been determined, they gave
1Ch 22: 3 He provided a large a of iron to
2Ch 14:13 carried off a large a of plunder.
20:25 and they found among them a great a
24:11 that there was a large a of money,
24:11 and collected a great a of money.
27: 5 Ammonites brought him the same a
31: 5 a great a, a tithe of everything.
31:10 and this great a is left over."
Est 4: 7 including the exact a of money Haman
Isa 41:29 they are all false! Their deeds a to
Da 1: 5 The king assigned them a daily a of
Mt 13:33 mixed into a large a of flour until
Lk 13:21 mixed into a large a of flour until
19: 8 I will pay back four times the a."

Amounted (Amount)

Ru 2:17 and it a to about an ephah.
2Ch 4:18 All these things that Solomon made a
29:33 sacrifices a to six hundred bulls

Amounts (Amount)

Ex 30:34 pure frankincense, all in equal a,
38:21 These are the a of the materials
Dt 17:17 large a of silver and gold.
Mk 12:41 Many rich people threw in large a.
2Co 10:10 and his speaking a to nothing."

Amoz

2Ki 19: 2 to the prophet Isaiah son of A.
19:20 Isaiah son of A sent a message to

2Ki 20: 1 The prophet Isaiah son of **A** went to
2Ch 26:22 by the prophet Isaiah son of **A**.
32:20 the prophet Isaiah son of **A** cried
32:32 of the prophet Isaiah son of **A**
Isa 1: 1 Isaiah son of **A** saw during the
2: 1 This is what Isaiah son of **A** saw
13: 1 Babylon that Isaiah son of **A** saw:
20: 2 LORD spoke through Isaiah son of **A**.
37: 2 to the prophet Isaiah son of **A**.
37:21 Isaiah son of **A** sent a message to
38: 1 The prophet Isaiah son of **A** went to

Amphipolis
Ac 17: 1 they had passed through **A** and

Ampliatus
Ro 16: 8 Greet **A**, whom I love in the Lord.

Amram (Amram's, Amramites)
Ex 6:18 The sons of Kohath were **A**, Izhar,
6:20 **A** married his father's sister
6:20 **A** lived 137 years.
Nu 3:19 The Kohathite clans: **A**, Izhar,
26:58 (Kohath was the forefather of **A**;
26:59 To **A** she bore Aaron, Moses and their
1Ch 6: 2 The sons of Kohath: **A**, Izhar, Hebron
6: 3 The children of **A**: Aaron, Moses and
6:18 The sons of Kohath: **A**, Izhar, Hebron
23:12 The sons of Kohath: **A**, Izhar, Hebron
23:13 The sons of **A**: Aaron and Moses.
24:20 from the sons of **A**: Shubael; from
Ezr 10:34 descendants of Bani: Maadai, **A**, Uel,

Amram's (Amram)
Nu 26:59 the name of **A** wife was Jochebed, a

Amramites (Amram)
Nu 3:27 To Kohath belonged the clans of the **A**
1Ch 26:23 From the **A**, the Izharites, the

Amraphel
Ge 14: 1 At this time **A** king of Shinar,
14: 9 Tidal king of Goiim, **A** king of

Amzi
1Ch 6:46 the son of **A**, the son of Bani, the
Ne 11:12 the son of Pelaliah, the son of **A**,

Anab
Jos 11:21 Debir and **A**, from all the hill
15:50 **A**, Eshtemoh, Anim,

Anah
Ge 36: 2 and Oholibamah daughter of **A** and
36:14 daughter of **A** and granddaughter
36:18 Esau's wife Oholibamah daughter of **A**.
36:20 region: Lotan, Shobal, Zibeon, **A**,
36:24 The sons of Zibeon: Aiah and **A**. This
36:24 This is the **A** who discovered the hot
36:25 The children of **A**: Dishon and
36:25 Dishon and Oholibamah daughter of **A**.
36:29 chiefs: Lotan, Shobal, Zibeon, **A**,
1Ch 1:38 Zibeon, **A**, Dishon, Ezer and Dishan.
1:40 The sons of Zibeon: Aiah and **A**
1:41 The son of **A**: Dishon. The sons of

Anaharath
Jos 19:19 Hapharaim, Shion, **A**,

Anaiah
Ne 8: 4 Shema, **A**, Uriah, Hilkiah and
10:22 Pelatiah, Hanan, **A**,

Anak (Anakites)
Nu 13:22 Talmai, the descendants of **A**, lived.
13:28 We even saw descendants of **A** there.
13:33 of **A** come from the Nephilim).
Jos 15:13 (Arba was the forefather of **A**.)
15:14 Ahiman and Talmai—descendants of **A**.
21:11 (Arba was the forefather of **A**.)
Jdg 1:20 drove from it the three sons of **A**.

Anakites (Anak)
Dt 1:28 We even saw the **A** there.'"
2:10 and numerous, and as tall as the **A**.
2:11 Like the **A**, they too were considered
2:21 and numerous, and as tall as the **A**.
9: 2 The people are strong and tall—**A**!
9: 2 "Who can stand up against the **A**?
Jos 11:21 **A** from the hill country: from Hebron,
11:22 No **A** were left in Israelite
14:12 You yourself heard then that the **A**
14:15 was the greatest man among the **A**.
15:14 Caleb drove out the three **A**—Sheshai,

Anamites
Ge 10:13 Ludites, **A**, Lehabites, Naphtuhites,
1Ch 1:11 Ludites, **A**, Lehabites, Naphtuhites,

Anammelech
2Ki 17:31 and **A**, the gods of Sepharvaim.

Anan
Ne 10:26 Ahiah, Hanan, Anan,

Anani
1Ch 3:24 Johanan, Delaiah and **A**—seven in all.

Ananiah
Ne 3:23 of **A**, made repairs beside his house.
11:32 in Anathoth, Nob and **A**,

Ananias
1. With wife Sapphira, died for lying to God (Ac 5:1–11). **2.** Disciple, sent to heal and baptise Saul (Paul) in Damascus (Ac 9:10–19). **3.** High priest before whom Paul appeared (Ac 22:30–23:5; 24:1).

Ac 5: 1 Now a man named **A**, together with his
5: 3 Peter said, "**A**, how is it that Satan
5: 5 **A** heard this, he fell down and died.
5: 8 price you and **A** got for the land?"
9:10 there was a disciple named **A**.
9:10 "**A**!" "Yes, Lord," he answered.
9:12 In a vision he has seen a man named **A**
9:13 "Lord," **A** answered, "I have heard
9:15 the Lord said to **A**, "Go! This man is
9:17 **A** went to the house and entered it.
22:12 "**A** man named **A** came to see me. He
23: 2 At this the high priest **A** ordered
24: 1 Five days later the high priest **A**

Anath
Jdg 3:31 After Ehud came Shamgar son of **A**,
5: 6 "In the days of Shamgar son of **A**, in

Anathoth (Anathothite)
Levite village north-east of Jerusalem, in Benjamin territory (Jos 21:18). Home of Abiezer (2Sa 23:27), Jehu (1Ch 12:3), Abiathar (1Ki 2:26) and Jeremiah (Jer 1:1; 29:27). Its inhabitants threatened Jeremiah and so faced God's punishment (Jer 11:21–23). During Babylonian siege of Jerusalem, God instructed Jeremiah to purchase a field here as an assurance of eventual redemption (Jer 32:1–15). The Assyrian army passed through here en route to Jerusalem (Isa 10:30).

Jos 21:18 **A** and Almon, together with their
2Sa 23:27 Abiezer from **A**, Mebunnai the
1Ki 2:26 said, "Go back to your fields in **A**.
1Ch 6:60 **A**, together with their pasture-lands.
7: 8 Jeremoth, Abijah, **A** and Alemeth.
11:28 Ikkesh from Tekoa, Abiezer from **A**,
Ezr 2:23 of **A** 128
Ne 7:27 of **A** 128
10:19 Hariph, **A**, Nebai,
11:32 in **A**, Nob and Ananiah,
Isa 10:30 Gallim! Listen, O Laishah! Poor **A**!
Jer 1: 1 at **A** in the territory of Benjamin.
11:21 men of **A** who are seeking your life
11:23 **A** in the year of their punishment.'"
29:27 **A**, who poses as a prophet among you?
32: 7 'Buy my field at **A**, because as
32: 8 at **A** in the territory of Benjamin.
32: 9 I bought the field at **A** from my

Anathothite (Anathoth)
1Ch 12: 3 of Azmaveth; Beracah, Jehu the **A**,
27:12 was Abiezer the **A**, a Benjamite.

Ancestor (Ancestors, Ancestral, Ancestry)
Ge 10:21 was the **a** of all the sons of Eber.
Jos 17: 1 Makir was the **a** of the Gileadites,
Heb 7:10 Levi was still in the body of his **a**.
Jas 2:21 Was not our **a** Abraham considered

Ancestors (Ancestor)
Lev 26:45 remember the covenant with their **a**
1Ki 19: 4 my life; I am no better than my **a**."
Am 2: 4 gods, the gods their **a** followed
Ac 28:17 or against the customs of our **a**,

Ancestral (Ancestor)
Nu 1:16 the leaders of their **a** tribes.
13: 2 **a** tribe send one of its leaders."
17: 2 leader of each of their **a** tribes.
17: 3 staff for the head of each **a** tribe.
17: 6 leader of each of their **a** tribes,
18: 2 Bring your fellow Levites from your **a**
26:55 to the names for its **a** tribe.
33:54 it according to your **a** tribes.
36: 3 be taken from our **a** inheritance
Ne 11:20 of Judah, each on his **a** property.

Ancestry (Ancestor)
Nu 1:18 The people indicated their **a** by
Eze 16: 3 Your **a** and birth were in the land of
21:30 land of your **a**, I will judge you.
29:14 to Upper Egypt, the land of their **a**.
Ro 9: 5 and from them is traced the human **a**
Heb 7:16 basis of a regulation as to his **a**

Anchor (Anchored, Anchors)
Ac 27:13 so they weighed **a** and sailed along
27:17 **a** and let the ship be driven along.
Heb 6:19 We have this hope as an **a** for the

Anchored (Anchor)
Mk 6:53 landed at Gennesaret and **a** there.

Anchors (Anchor)
Ac 27:29 they dropped four **a** from the stern
27:30 going to lower some **a** from the bow.
27:40 Cutting loose the **a**, they left them

Ancient (*Ancient of days*, Ancients)
Ge 49:26 the blessings of the **a** mountains,
Dt 33:15 with the choicest gifts of the **a**
1Sa 27: 8 (From **a** times these peoples had
1Ch 4:22 (These records are from **a** times.)
Ezr 4:15 a place of rebellion from **a** times.
Ps 24: 7 O you gates; be lifted up, you **a**
24: 9 O you gates; lift them up, you **a**
68:33 to him who rides the **a** skies above,
119:52 I remember your **a** laws, O LORD, and
Pr 22:28 Do not move an **a** boundary stone set
23:10 Do not move an **a** boundary stone or
Isa 19:11 men, a disciple of the **a** kings"?
43:13 Yes, and from **a** days I am he. No-one
44: 7 since I established my **a** people,
46:10 from **a** times, what is still to come.
58:12 Your people will rebuild the **a** ruins
61: 4 They will rebuild the **a** ruins and
64: 4 Since **a** times no-one has heard, no
Jer 5:15 an **a** and enduring nation, a people
6:16 ask for the **a** paths, ask where the
18:15 in their ways and in the **a** paths.
Eze 25:15 **a** hostility sought to destroy Judah,
26:20 as in **a** ruins, with those who go
35: 5 "'Because you harboured an **a**
36: 2 **a** heights have become our possession.
Mic 5: 2 are from of old, from **a** times."
Hab 3: 6 The **a** mountains crumbled and the
2Pe 2: 5 if he did not spare the **a** world when
Rev 12: 9 **a** serpent called the devil,
20: 2 He seized the dragon, that **a** serpent,

Ancient of days
Da 7: 9 in place, and the **A** took his seat.
7:13 the **A** and was led into his presence.
7:22 until the **A** came and pronounced

Ancients (Ancient)
Heb 11: 2 This is what the **a** were commended

Andrew
Apostle; brother of Simon Peter (Mt 4:18–20; 10:2; Mk 1:16–18,29); introduced boy with loaves and fish to Jesus (Jn 6:8–9); brought Greeks to Jesus (Jn 12:22). Former disciple of John the Baptist (Jn 1:35–40); brought Simon to Jesus (Jn 1:41).

Mt 4:18 Simon called Peter and his brother **A**.
10: 2 called Peter) and his brother **A**;
Mk 1:16 he saw Simon and his brother **A**
1:29 and John to the home of Simon and **A**.
3:18 **A**, Philip, Bartholomew, Matthew,
13: 3 John and **A** asked him privately,
Lk 6:14 **A**, James, John, Philip, Bartholomew,
Jn 1:40 **A**, Simon Peter's brother, was one of
1:41 The first thing **A** did was to find
1:44 Philip, like **A** and Peter, was from
6: 8 Another of his disciples, **A**, Simon
12:22 Philip went to tell **A**; **A** and Philip
Ac 1:13 John, James and **A**; Philip and Thomas,

Andronicus
Ro 16: 7 Greet **A** and Junias, my relatives who

Anem
1Ch 6:73 Ramoth and **A**, together with their

Aner
Ge 14:13 a brother of Eshcol and **A**, all of
14:24 with me—to **A**, Eshcol and Mamre.
1Ch 6:70 the Israelites gave **A** and Bileam,

Anew (New)
Mt 26:29 drink it **a** with you in my Father's
Mk 14:25 I drink it **a** in the kingdom of God."

Angel (*Angel of God, Angel of the Lord, Angel of the Lord*, Angel's, Angels, Archangel)
Ge 16:10 The **a** added, "I will so increase
24: 7 he will send his **a** before you so
24:40 will send his **a** with you and make
48:16 the **A** who has delivered me from all
Ex 23:20 "See, I am sending an **a** ahead of you
23:23 My **a** will go ahead of you and bring
32:34 of, and my **a** will go before you.
33: 2 I will send an **a** before you and
Nu 20:16 an **a** and brought us out of Egypt.
Jdg 5:23 'Curse Meroz,' said the **a** of the
2Sa 24:16 the **a** stretched out his hand to
24:16 the **a** who was afflicting the people,
24:17 David saw the **a** who was striking
1Ki 13:18 And an **a** said to me by the word of
19: 5 All at once an **a** touched him and
1Ch 21:15 God sent an **a** to destroy Jerusalem.
21:15 But as the **a** was doing so, the Lord
21:15 the **a** who was destroying the people,
21:20 he turned and saw the **a**; his four
21:27 the Lord spoke to the **a**, and he put
2Ch 32:21 the Lord sent an **a**, who annihilated
Job 33:23 "Yet if there is an **a** on his side as
Isa 63: 9 the **a** of his presence saved them.
Da 3:28 who has sent his **a** and rescued his
6:22 My God sent his **a**, and he shut the
Hos 12: 4 He struggled with the **a** and overcame
Zec 1: 9 "What are these, my lord?" The **a** who
1:13 words to the **a** who talked with me.
1:14 the **a** who was speaking to me said,
1:19 I asked the **a** who was speaking to me,
2: 3 the **a** who was speaking to me left,
2: 3 left, and another **a** came to meet
3: 3 clothes as he stood before the **a**.
3: 4 The **a** said to those who were
4: 1 the **a** who talked with me returned
4: 4 I asked the **a** who talked with me,
4:11 I asked the **a**, "What are these two
5: 5 the **a** who was speaking to me came
5:10 I asked the **a** who was speaking to me.
6: 4 I asked the **a** who was speaking to me,
6: 5 The **a** answered me, "These are the
Mt 28: 5 The **a** said to the women, "Do not be
Lk 1:13 the **a** said to him: "Do not be afraid,
Lk 1:18 Zechariah asked the **a**, "How can I be
1:19 The **a** answered, "I am Gabriel. I
1:26 In the sixth month, God sent the **a**
1:28 The **a** went to her and said,
1:30 the **a** said to her, "Do not be afraid,
1:34 "How will this be," Mary asked the **a**,
1:35 The **a** answered, "The Holy Spirit
1:38 Then the **a** left her.
2:10 the **a** said to them, "Do not be
2:13 with the **a**, praising God and saying,
2:21 he was named Jesus, the name the **a**
22:43 An **a** from heaven appeared to him and
Jn 12:29 others said an **a** had spoken to him.
Ac 6:15 his face was like the face of an **a**.
7:30 "After forty years had passed, an **a**
7:35 **a** who appeared to him in the bush.
7:38 with the **a** who spoke to him on Mount
10: 4 "What is it, Lord?" he asked. The **a**
10: 7 the **a** who spoke to him had gone,
10:22 A holy **a** told him to have you come
11:13 He told us how he had seen an **a**
12: 8 the **a** said to him, "Put on your
12: 8 you and follow me," the **a** told him.
12: 9 he had no idea that what the **a** was
12:10 one street, suddenly the **a** left him.
12:11 the Lord sent his **a** and rescued
12:15 so, they said, "It must be his **a**.
23: 9 a spirit or an **a** has spoken to him?"
27:23 Last night an **a** of the God whose I
1Co 10:10 were killed by the destroying **a**.
2Co 11:14 masquerades as an **a** of light.
Gal 1: 8 even if we or an **a** from heaven
Rev 1: 1 sending his **a** to his servant John,
2: 1 "To the **a** of the church in Ephesus
2: 8 "To the **a** of the church in Smyrna
2:12 "To the **a** of the church in Pergamum
2:18 "To the **a** of the church in Thyatira
3: 1 "To the **a** of the church in Sardis
3: 7 "To the **a** of the church in
3:14 "To the **a** of the church in Laodicea
5: 2 I saw a mighty **a** proclaiming in a
7: 2 I saw another **a** coming up from the
8: 3 Another **a**, who had a golden censer,
8: 5 the **a** took the censer, filled it
8: 7 The first **a** sounded his trumpet, and
8: 8 The second **a** sounded his trumpet,
8:10 The third **a** sounded his trumpet, and
8:12 The fourth **a** sounded his trumpet,
9: 1 The fifth **a** sounded his trumpet, and
9:11 They had as king over them the **a** of
9:13 The sixth **a** sounded his trumpet, and
9:14 said to the sixth **a** who had the
10: 1 I saw another mighty **a** coming down
10: 5 the **a** I had seen standing on the sea
10: 7 in the days when the seventh **a** is
10: 8 of the **a** who is standing on the sea
10: 9 I went to the **a** and asked him to
11:15 The seventh **a** sounded his trumpet,
14: 6 I saw another **a** flying in mid-air,
14: 8 A second **a** followed and said,
14: 9 A third **a** followed them and said in
14:15 another **a** came out of the temple and
14:17 Another **a** came out of the temple in
14:18 Still another **a**, who had charge of
14:19 The **a** swung his sickle on the earth,
16: 2 The first **a** went and poured out his
16: 3 The second **a** poured out his bowl on
16: 4 The third **a** poured out his bowl on
16: 5 I heard the **a** in charge of the
16: 8 The fourth **a** poured out his bowl on
16:10 The fifth **a** poured out his bowl on
16:12 The sixth **a** poured out his bowl on
16:17 The seventh **a** poured out his bowl
17: 3 the **a** carried me away in the Spirit
17: 7 the **a** said to me: "Why are you
17:15 the **a** said to me, "The waters you
18: 1 After this I saw another **a** coming
18:21 a mighty **a** picked up a boulder the
19: 9 the **a** said to me, "Write: 'Blessed
19:17 I saw an **a** standing in the sun, who
20: 1 I saw an **a** coming down out of heaven,
21:15 The **a** who talked with me had a
21:17 measurement, which the **a** was using.
22: 1 the **a** showed me the river of the
22: 6 The **a** said to me, "These words are
22: 6 sent his **a** to show his servants the
Rev 22: 8 **a** who had been showing them to me.
22:16 "I, Jesus, have sent my **a** to give

Angel of God
Ge 21:17 God heard the boy crying, and the **a**
31:11 The **a** said to me in the dream,
Ex 14:19 the **a**, who had been travelling in
Jdg 6:20 The **a** said to him, "Take the meat
13: 6 He looked like an **a**, very awesome. I
13: 9 God heard Manoah, and the **a** came
1Sa 29: 9 in my eyes as an **a**; nevertheless,
2Sa 14:17 an **a** in discerning good and evil.
14:20 My lord has wisdom like that of an **a**
19:27 My lord the king is like an **a**; so do
Ac 10: 3 He distinctly saw an **a**, who came to
Gal 4:14 were an **a**, as if I were Christ Jesus

Angel of the Lord
Ge 16: 7 The **a** found Hagar near a spring in
16: 9 the **a** told her, "Go back to your
16:11 The **a** also said to her: "You are now
22:11 the **a** called out to him from heaven,
22:15 The **a** called to Abraham from heaven
Ex 3: 2 **a** appeared to him in flames of fire
Nu 22:22 **a** stood in the road to oppose him.
22:23 the donkey saw the **a** standing in the
22:24 the **a** stood in a narrow path between
22:25 the donkey saw the **a**, she pressed
22:26 the **a** moved on ahead and stood in a
22:27 the donkey saw the **a**, she lay down
22:31 and he saw the **a** standing in the
22:32 The **a** asked him, "Why have you
22:34 Balaam said to the **a**, "I have sinned.
22:35 The **a** said to Balaam, "Go with the
Jdg 2: 1 The **a** went up from Gilgal to Bokim
2: 4 the **a** had spoken these things to all
5:23 'Curse Meroz,' said the **a**. 'Curse
6:11 The **a** came and sat down under the
6:12 the **a** appeared to Gideon, he said,
6:21 the **a** touched the meat and the
6:21 And the **a** disappeared.
6:22 Gideon realised that it was the **a**,
6:22 I have seen the **a** face to face!"
13: 3 The **a** appeared to her and said, "You
13:13 The **a** answered, "Your wife must do
13:15 Manoah said to the **a**, "We would like
13:16 The **a** replied, "Even though you
13:16 did not realise that it was the **a**.)
13:17 Manoah enquired of the **a**, "What is
13:20 heaven, the **a** ascended in the flame.
13:21 the **a** did not show himself again to
13:21 Manoah realised that it was the **a**.
2Sa 24:16 **a** was then at the threshing-floor
1Ki 19: 7 The **a** came back a second time and
2Ki 1: 3 the **a** said to Elijah the Tishbite,
1:15 The **a** said to Elijah, "Go down with
19:35 That night the **a** went out and put to
1Ch 21:12 the **a** ravaging every part of Israel.
21:15 The **a** was then standing at the
21:16 David looked up and saw the **a**
21:18 the **a** ordered Gad to tell David to
21:30 he was afraid of the sword of the **a**.
Ps 34: 7 The **a** encamps around those who fear
35: 5 wind, with the **a** driving them away;
35: 6 slippery, with the **a** pursuing them.
Isa 37:36 the **a** went out and put to death a
Zec 1:11 they reported to the **a**, who was
1:12 the **a** said, "Lord Almighty, how long
3: 1 high priest standing before the **a**,
3: 5 clothed him, while the **a** stood by.
3: 6 The **a** gave this charge to Joshua:
12: 8 God, like the **A** going before them.

Angel of the Lord
Mt 1:20 after he had considered this, an **a**
1:24 Joseph woke up, he did what the **a**
2:13 they had gone, an **a** appeared to
2:19 After Herod died, an **a** appeared in a
28: 2 for an **a** came down from heaven and,
Lk 1:11 an **a** appeared to him, standing at
2: 9 An **a** appeared to them, and the glory
Ac 5:19 during the night an **a** opened the
8:26 Now an **a** said to Philip, "Go south
12: 7 Suddenly an **a** appeared and a light
12:23 an **a** struck him down, and he was

Angel's (Angel)

Rev 8: 4 went up before God from the **a** hand.
10:10 I took the little scroll from the **a**

Angels (Angel)

Ge 19: 1 The two **a** arrived at Sodom in the
19:15 With the coming of dawn, the **a** urged
28:12 and the **a** of God were ascending and
32: 1 Jacob also went on his way, and the **a**
Job 1: 6 One day the **a** came to present
2: 1 On another day the **a** came to present
4:18 if he charges his **a** with error,
38: 7 and all the **a** shouted for joy?
Ps 78:25 Men ate the bread of **a**; he sent them
78:49 hostility—a band of destroying **a**.
91:11 For he will command his **a** concerning
103:20 Praise the LORD, you his **a**, you
148: 2 Praise him, all his **a**, praise him,
Mt 4: 6 "He will command his **a** concerning
4:11 the devil left him, and **a** came and
13:39 the age, and the harvesters are **a**.
13:41 The Son of Man will send out his **a**,
13:49 The **a** will come and separate the
16:27 in his Father's glory with his **a**,
18:10 For I tell you that their **a** in
22:30 they will be like the **a** in heaven.
24:31 he will send his **a** with a loud
24:36 not even the **a** in heaven, nor the
25:31 and all the **a** with him, he will sit
25:41 prepared for the devil and his **a**.
26:53 more than twelve legions of **a**?
Mk 1:13 wild animals, and **a** attended him.
8:38 his Father's glory with the holy **a**."
12:25 they will be like the **a** in heaven.
13:27 he will send his **a** and gather his
13:32 not even the **a** in heaven, nor the
Lk 2:15 the **a** had left them and gone into
4:10 "He will command his **a** concerning
9:26 of the Father and of the holy **a**.
12: 8 acknowledge him before the **a** of God.
12: 9 be disowned before the **a** of God.
15:10 **a** of God over one sinner who repents.
16:22 the **a** carried him to Abraham's side.
20:36 longer die; for they are like the **a**.
24:23 vision of **a**, who said he was alive.
Jn 1:51 and the **a** of God ascending and
20:12 saw two **a** in white, seated where
Ac 7:53 through **a** but have not obeyed it."
23: 8 and that there are neither **a** nor
Ro 8:38 neither **a** nor demons, neither the
1Co 4: 9 universe, to **a** as well as to men.
6: 3 Do you not know that we will judge **a**?
11:10 For this reason, and because of the **a**
13: 1 in the tongues of men and of **a**,
Gal 3:19 into effect through **a** by a mediator.
Col 2:18 of **a** disqualify you for the prize.
2Th 1: 7 in blazing fire with his powerful **a**.
1Ti 3:16 was seen by **a**, was preached among
5:21 God and Christ Jesus and the elect **a**,
Heb 1: 4 he became as much superior to the **a**
1: 5 For to which of the **a** did God ever
1: 6 says, "Let all God's **a** worship him.
1: 7 In speaking of the **a** he says, "He
1: 7 He makes his **a** winds, his servants
1:13 To which of the **a** did God ever say,
1:14 Are not all **a** ministering spirits
2: 2 For if the message spoken by **a** was
2: 5 is not to **a** that he has subjected
2: 7 made him a little lower than the **a**;
2: 9 was made a little lower than the **a**,
2:16 For surely it is not **a** he helps, but
12:22 thousands of **a** in joyful assembly,
13: 2 entertained **a** without knowing it.
1Pe 1:12 **a** long to look into these things.
3:22 and is at God's right hand—with **a**,
2Pe 2: 4 For if God did not spare **a** when they
2:11 yet even **a**, although they are
Jude : 6 the **a** who did not keep their
Rev 1:20 are the **a** of the seven churches,
3: 5 his name before my Father and his **a**.
5:11 and heard the voice of many **a**,
7: 1 After this I saw four **a** standing at
7: 2 to the four **a** who had been given
7:11 All the **a** were standing round the
8: 2 I saw the seven **a** who stand before
Rev 8: 6 the seven **a** who had the seven
8:13 to be sounded by the other three **a**!"
9:14 "Release the four **a** who are bound at
9:15 the four **a** who had been kept ready
12: 7 Michael and his **a** fought against the
12: 7 the dragon and his **a** fought back.
12: 9 to the earth, and his **a** with him.
14:10 of the holy **a** and of the Lamb.
15: 1 seven **a** with the seven last plagues
15: 6 Out of the temple came the seven **a**
15: 7 gave to the seven **a** seven golden
15: 8 of the seven **a** were completed.
16: 1 the temple saying to the seven **a**,
17: 1 One of the seven **a** who had the seven
21: 9 One of the seven **a** who had the seven
21:12 and with twelve **a** at the gates.

Anger (*Anger of the LORD*, Angered, Angers, Angry, *Slow to anger*)

Ge 39:19 slave treated me," he burned with **a**.
49: 6 killed men in their **a** and hamstrung
49: 7 Cursed be their **a**, so fierce, and
Ex 4:14 the LORD's **a** burned against Moses
11: 8 Then Moses, hot with **a**, left Pharaoh.
15: 7 **a**; it consumed them like stubble.
22:24 My **a** will be aroused, and I will
32:10 Now leave me alone so that my **a** may
32:11 "why should your **a** burn against your
32:12 Turn from your fierce **a**; relent and
32:19 **a** burned and he threw the tablets
Lev 26:28 in my **a** I will be hostile towards
Nu 11: 1 he heard them his **a** was aroused.
14:18 'The LORD is slow to **a**, abounding in
24:10 Balak's **a** burned against Balaam. He
25: 3 And the LORD's **a** burned against them.
25: 4 fierce **a** may turn away from Israel."
25:11 the priest, has turned my **a** away
32:10 The LORD's **a** was aroused that day
32:13 The LORD's **a** burned against Israel
Dt 4:25 LORD your God and provoking him to **a**,
6:15 is a jealous God and his **a** will burn
7: 4 and the LORD's **a** will burn against
9: 7 LORD your God to **a** in the desert.
9:18 sight and so provoking him to **a**.
9:19 I feared the **a** and wrath of the LORD,
11:17 the LORD's **a** will burn against you,
13:17 the LORD will turn from his fierce **a**
29:23 the LORD overthrew in fierce **a**.
29:24 land? Why this fierce, burning **a**?"
29:27 Therefore the LORD's **a** burned
29:28 In furious **a** and in great wrath the
31:29 to **a** by what your hands have made."
Jos 7: 1 the LORD's **a** burned against Israel.
7:26 the LORD turned from his fierce **a**.
23:16 the LORD's **a** will burn against you,
Jdg 2:12 They provoked the LORD to **a**
2:14 In his **a** against Israel the LORD
14:19 **a**, he went up to his father's house.
1Sa 11: 6 him in power, and he burned with **a**.
17:28 he burned with **a** at him and asked,
20:30 Saul's **a** flared up at Jonathan and
20:34 got up from the table in fierce **a**;
2Sa 6: 7 The LORD's **a** burned against Uzzah
11:20 the king's **a** may flare up, and he
12: 5 David burned with **a** against the man
1Ki 14: 9 to **a** and thrust me behind your back.
14:15 LORD to **a** by making Asherah poles.
14:22 **a** more than their fathers had done.
15:30 the LORD, the God of Israel, to **a**.
16: 2 to provoke me to **a** by their sins.
16: 7 provoking him to **a** by the things he
16:13 to **a** by their worthless idols.
16:26 to **a** by their worthless idols.
16:33 the God of Israel, to **a** than did all
21:22 to **a** and have caused Israel to sin.'
22:53 to **a**, just as his father had done.
2Ki 13: 3 the LORD's **a** burned against Israel,
17:11 things that provoked the LORD to **a**.
17:17 of the LORD, provoking him to **a**.
21: 6 of the LORD, provoking him to **a**.
21:15 have provoked me to **a** from the day
22:13 Great is the LORD's **a** that burns
22:17 provoked me to **a** by all the idols
22:17 my **a** will burn against this place
23:19 that had provoked the LORD to **a**.
2Ki 23:26 away from the heat of his fierce **a**,
23:26 had done to provoke him to **a**.
24:20 was because of the LORD's **a** that all
1Ch 13:10 The LORD's **a** burned against Uzzah,
15:13 our God broke out in **a** against us.
2Ch 12:12 the LORD's **a** turned from him, and he
24:18 **a** came upon Judah and Jerusalem.
25:15 The **a** of the LORD burned against
28:11 the LORD's fierce **a** rests on you."
28:13 and his fierce **a** rests on Israel."
28:25 LORD, the God of his fathers, to **a**.
29:10 his fierce **a** will turn away from us.
30: 8 fierce **a** will turn away from you.
33: 6 of the LORD, provoking him to **a**.
34:21 Great is the LORD's **a** that is poured
34:25 **a** by all that their hands have made,
34:25 my **a** will be poured out on this
Ezr 8:22 **a** is against all who forsake him."
10:14 until the fierce **a** of our God in
Est 1:12 became furious and burned with **a**.
2: 1 Later when the **a** of King Xerxes had
Job 4: 9 at the blast of his **a** they perish.
9: 5 it and overturns them in his **a**.
9:13 God does not restrain his **a**; even
10:17 me and increase your **a** towards me;
14:13 conceal me till your **a** has passed!
16: 9 God assails me and tears me in his **a**
18: 4 tear yourself to pieces in your **a**,
19:11 His **a** burns against me; he counts me
20:23 God will vent his burning **a** against
21:17 them, the fate God allots in his **a**?
32: 5 more to say, his **a** was aroused.
35:15 further, that his **a** never punishes
Ps 2: 5 he rebukes them in his **a** and
4: 4 In your **a** do not sin; when you are
6: 1 O LORD, do not rebuke me in your **a**
7: 6 Arise, O LORD, in your **a**; rise up
27: 9 do not turn your servant away in **a**
30: 5 For his **a** lasts only a moment, but
37: 8 Refrain from **a** and turn from wrath;
38: 1 O LORD, do not rebuke me in your **a**
55: 3 upon me and revile me in their **a**.
56: 7 **a**, O God, bring down the nations.
69:24 let your fierce **a** overtake them.
74: 1 O God? Why does your **a** smoulder
77: 9 Has he in **a** withheld his compassion?"
78:31 God's **a** rose against them; he put to
78:38 **a** and did not stir up his full wrath.
78:49 He unleashed against them his hot **a**,
78:50 He prepared a path for his **a**; he did
80: 4 how long will your **a** smoulder
85: 3 wrath and turned from your fierce **a**.
85: 5 your **a** through all generations?
90: 7 We are consumed by your **a** and
90:11 Who knows the power of your **a**? For
95:11 I declared on oath in my **a**, "They
103: 9 nor will he harbour his **a** for ever;
106:29 they provoked the LORD to **a** by their
124: 3 their **a** flared against us, they
138: 7 your hand against the **a** of my foes,
Pr 15: 1 wrath, but a harsh word stirs up **a**.
21:14 A gift given in secret soothes **a**,
27: 4 **A** is cruel and fury overwhelming,
29: 8 up a city, but wise men turn away **a**.
29:11 A fool gives full vent to his **a**, but
30:33 so stirring up **a** produces strife."
Ecc 5:17 great frustration, affliction and **a**.
7: 9 for **a** resides in the lap of fools.
10: 4 If a ruler's **a** rises against you, do
Isa 5:25 Therefore the LORD's **a** burns against
5:25 Yet for all this, his **a** is not
7: 4 of the fierce **a** of Rezin
9:12 Yet for all this, his **a** is not
9:17 Yet for all this, his **a** is not
9:21 Yet for all this, his **a** is not
10: 4 Yet for all this, his **a** is not
10: 5 "Woe to the Assyrian, the rod of my **a**
10: 6 him against a people who **a** me,
10:25 Very soon my **a** against you will end
12: 1 your **a** has turned away and you have
13: 9 cruel day, with wrath and fierce **a**
13:13 in the day of his burning **a**.
14: 6 which in **a** struck down peoples with
30:27 with burning **a** and dense clouds of
30:30 with raging **a** and consuming fire,
42:25 he poured out on them his burning **a**,

Isa 54: 8 In a surge of a I hid my face from
57:17 punished him, and hid my face in a
60:10 Though in a I struck you, in favour
63: 3 I trampled them in my a and trod
63: 6 I trampled the nations in my a; in
66:15 he will bring down his a with fury,
Jer 4: 8 lament and wail, for the fierce a of
4:26 the LORD, before his fierce a.
7:18 to other gods to provoke me to a.
7:20 My a and my wrath will be poured out
8:19 "Why have they provoked me to a with
10:24 a, lest you reduce me to nothing.
11:17 me to a by burning incense to Baal.
12:13 because of the LORD's fierce a."
15:14 for my a will kindle a fire that
17: 4 my a, and it will burn for ever."
18:23 with them in the time of your a.
21: 5 arm in a and fury and great wrath.
25: 6 to a with what your hands have made.
25:38 and because of the LORD's fierce a.
32:29 people provoked me to a by burning
32:31 this city has so aroused my a and
32:37 in my furious a and great wrath;
33: 5 men I will slay in my a and wrath.
36: 7 for the a and wrath pronounced
42:18 'As my a and wrath have been poured
44: 3 They provoked me to a by burning
44: 6 Therefore, my fierce a was poured
44: 8 Why provoke me to a with what your
49:37 my fierce a," declares the LORD.
50:13 of the LORD's a she will not be
52: 3 was because of the LORD's a that all
Lam 1:12 on me in the day of his fierce a?
2: 1 of Zion with the cloud of his a!
2: 1 his footstool in the day of his a.
2: 3 In fierce a he has cut off every
2: 6 in his fierce a he has spurned both
2:21 slain them in the day of your a;
2:22 In the day of the LORD's a no-one
3:43 "You have covered yourself with a
3:66 Pursue them in a and destroy them
4:11 he has poured out his fierce a.
Eze 3:14 and in the a of my spirit,
5:13 "Then my a will cease and my wrath
5:15 I inflict punishment on you in a
7: 3 and I will unleash my a against you.
7: 8 on you and spend my a against you;
8:17 and continually provoke me to a?
8:18 Therefore I will deal with them in a;
13:13 and in my a hailstones and torrents
16:26 a with your increasing promiscuity.
16:38 vengeance of my wrath and jealous a.
16:42 jealous a will turn away from you;
20: 8 spend my a against them in Egypt.
20:21 my a against them in the desert.
20:28 offerings that provoked me to a,
21:31 breathe out my fiery a against you;
22:20 so will I gather you in my a and my
22:31 and consume them with my fiery a,
23:25 I will direct my jealous a against
25:14 accordance with my a and my wrath;
35:11 treat you in accordance with the a
38:18 my hot a will be aroused, declares
43: 8 So I destroyed them in my a.
Da 9:16 turn away your a and your wrath from
11:20 yet not in a or in battle.
Hos 8: 5 O Samaria! My a burns against them.
11: 9 I will not carry out my fierce a,
12:14 has bitterly provoked him to a;
13:11 in my a I gave you a king, and in my
14: 4 for my a has turned away from them.
Am 1:11 his a raged continually and his fury
Jnh 3: 9 turn from his fierce a so that we
Mic 5:15 I will take vengeance in a and wrath
Na 1: 6 Who can endure his fierce a? His
Hab 3:12 and in a you threshed the nations.
Zep 2: 2 before the fierce a of the LORD
2: 3 on the day of the LORD's a.
3: 8 my wrath on them—all my fierce a.
3: 8 by the fire of my jealous a.
Zec 10: 3 "My a burns against the shepherds,
Mt 18:34 In a his master turned him over to
Mk 3: 5 He looked round at them in a and,
Ro 2: 8 evil, there will be wrath and a.
2Co 12:20 jealousy, outbursts of a, factions,
Eph 4:26 "In your a do not sin": Do not let
4:31 Get rid of all bitterness, rage and a
Col 3: 8 of all such things as these: a,
1Ti 2: 8 in prayer, without a or disputing.
Heb 3:11 I declared on oath in my a, 'They
4: 3 "So I declared on oath in my a,
11:27 not fearing the king's a; he
Jas 1:20 for man's a does not bring about the

Anger of the LORD

Nu 11:33 the a burned against the people
12: 9 The a burned against them, and he
Jdg 3: 8 The a burned against Israel so
2Sa 24: 1 Again the a burned against Israel
2Ch 25:15 The a burned against Amaziah, and
29: 8 a has fallen on Judah and Jerusalem
Jer 4: 8 fierce a has not turned away from
23:20 a will not turn back until he fully
25:37 laid waste because of the fierce a
30:24 fierce a will not turn back until
51:45 your lives! Run from the fierce a
Zep 2: 2 before the fierce a comes upon you

Angered (Anger)

Dt 32:16 a him with their detestable idols.
32:19 he was a by his sons and daughters.
32:21 and a me with their worthless idols.
Ezr 5:12 our fathers a the God of heaven, he
Ps 78:58 They a him with their high places;
106:32 By the waters of Meribah they a the
Pr 22:24 do not associate with one easily a,
Zec 8:14 no pity when your fathers a me,"
1Co 13: 5 not easily a, it keeps no record

Angers (Anger)

Pr 20: 2 he who a him forfeits his life.

Angle

2Ch 26: 9 a of the wall, and he fortified them.
Ne 3:19 to the armoury as far as the a.
3:20 from the a to the entrance of the
3:24 house to the a and the corner,
3:25 son of Uzai worked opposite the a

Angry (Anger)

Ge 4: 5 very a, and his face was downcast.
4: 6 the LORD said to Cain, "Why are you a
18:30 he said, "May the Lord not be a, but
18:32 he said, "May the Lord not be a, but
27:45 your brother is no longer a with you
30: 2 Jacob became a with her and said,
31:35 "Don't be a, my lord, that I cannot
31:36 Jacob was a and took Laban to task.
40: 2 Pharaoh was a with his two officials,
41:10 Pharaoh was once a with his servants,
44:18 Do not be a with your servant,
45: 5 do not be a with yourselves for
Ex 16:20 So Moses was a with them.
32:22 "Do not be a, my lord," Aaron
Lev 10: 6 will be a with the whole community.
10:16 he was a with Eleazar and Ithamar,
Nu 11:10 a, and Moses was troubled.
16:15 Moses became very a and said to the
16:22 will you be a with the entire
22:22 God was very a when he went, and the
22:27 was a and beat her with his staff.
31:14 Moses was a with the officers of the
32:14 the LORD even more a with Israel.
Dt 1:34 said, he was a and solemnly swore:
1:37 of you the LORD became a with me
3:26 of you the LORD was a with me and
4:21 The LORD was a with me because of
9: 8 that he was a enough to destroy you.
9:19 a enough with you to destroy you.
9:20 the LORD was a enough with Aaron to
9:22 You also made the LORD a at Taberah,
31:17 On that day I will become a with
32:21 I will make them a by a nation that
Jos 22:18 a with the whole community of Israel.
Jdg 2:20 Therefore the LORD was very a with
6:39 Gideon said to God, "Do not be a
9:30 Gaal son of Ebed said, he was very a
10: 7 he became a with them. He sold them
1Sa 18: 8 Saul was very a; this refrain galled
29: 4 the Philistine commanders were a
2Sa 3: 8 Abner was very a because of what
6: 8 David was a because the LORD's wrath
19:42 Why are you a about it? Have we
22: 8 they trembled because he was a.
1Ki 8:46 and you become a with them and give
11: 9 The LORD became a with Solomon
20:43 Sullen and a, the king of Israel
21: 4 Ahab went home, sullen and a because
2Ki 5:11 Naaman went away a and said, "I
13:19 The man of God was a with him and
17:18 the LORD was very a with Israel and
1Ch 13:11 David was a because the LORD's wrath
2Ch 6:36 and you become a with them and give
16:10 Asa was a with the seer because of
26:19 ready to burn incense, became a.
28: 9 the God of your fathers, was a with
Ezr 9:14 be a enough with us to destroy us,
Ne 4: 1 became a and was greatly incensed.
4: 7 were being closed, they were very a.
5: 6 and these charges, I was very a.
Est 2:21 became a and conspired to
Job 32: 2 of the family of Ram, became very a
32: 3 He was also a with the three friends,
42: 7 "I am a with you and your two
Ps 2:12 Kiss the Son, lest he be a and you
18: 7 they trembled because he was a.
60: 1 you have been a—now restore us!
76: 7 can stand before you when you are a?
78:21 the LORD heard them, he was very a;
78:59 God heard them, he was very a; he
78:62 he was very a with his inheritance.
79: 5 How long, O LORD? Will you be a for
85: 5 Will you be a with us for ever? Will
89:38 been very a with your anointed one.
95:10 For forty years I was a with that
106:40 Therefore the LORD was a with his
Pr 25:23 so a sly tongue brings a looks.
29:22 An a man stirs up dissension, and a
Ecc 5: 6 Why should God be a at what you say
SS 1: 6 My mother's sons were a with me and
Isa 12: 1 Although you were a with me, your
27: 4 I am not a. If only there were
34: 2 The LORD is a with all nations; his
47: 6 I was a with my people and
54: 9 So now I have sworn not to be a with
57:16 nor will I always be a, for then the
64: 5 to sin against them, you were a.
64: 9 Do not be a beyond measure, O LORD;
Jer 2:35 you say, 'I am innocent; he is not a
3: 5 will you always be a? Will your
3:12 the LORD, 'I will not be a for ever.
10:10 When he is a, the earth trembles;
37:15 They were a with Jeremiah and had
Lam 5:22 us and are a with us beyond measure.
Eze 16:42 you; I will be calm and no longer a.
Da 2:12 This made the king so a and furious
Jnh 4: 1 was greatly displeased and became a.
4: 4 "Have you any right to be a?
4: 9 have a right to be a about the vine?"
4: 9 "I am a enough to die."
Mic 2: 7 "Is the Spirit of the LORD a? Does
7:18 a for ever but delight to show mercy.
Hab 3: 8 Were you a with the rivers, O LORD?
Zec 1: 2 "The LORD was very a with your
1:12 been a with these seventy years?"
1:15 I am very a with the nations that
1:15 I was only a little a, but they added
7:12 So the LORD Almighty was very a.
Mt 5:22 I tell you that anyone who is a with
Lk 14:21 Then the owner of the house became a
15:28 "The older brother became a and
Jn 7:23 why are you a with me for healing
Ro 10:19 I will make you a by a nation that
Eph 4:26 sun go down while you are still a,
Heb 3:10 That is why I was a with that
3:17 with whom was he a for forty years?
Jas 1:19 slow to speak and slow to become a,
Rev 11:18 The nations were a; and your wrath

Anguish (Anguished)

Ex 15:14 a will grip the people of Philistia
Dt 2:25 tremble and be in a because of you."
1Sa 1:16 here out of my great a and grief."
Job 6: 2 "If only my a could be weighed and
7:11 speak out in the a of my spirit,

Job 15:24 Distress and **a** fill him with terror;
26: 5 "The dead are in deep **a**, those
Ps 6: 3 My soul is in **a**. How long, O LORD,
25:17 have multiplied; free me from my **a**.
31: 7 and knew the **a** of my soul.
31:10 My life is consumed by **a** and my
38: 8 crushed; I groan in **a** of heart.
39: 2 anything good, my **a** increased.
55: 4 My heart is in **a** within me; the
116: 3 the **a** of the grave came upon me; I
118: 5 In my **a** I cried to the LORD, and he
Pr 31: 6 wine to those who are in **a**;
Isa 13: 8 Terror will seize them, pain and **a**
23: 5 be in **a** at the report from Tyre.
38:15 years because of this **a** of my soul.
38:17 my benefit that I suffered such **a**.
65:14 but you will cry out from **a** of heart
Jer 4:19 Oh, my **a**, my **a**! I writhe in pain. Oh,
6:24 **A** has gripped us, pain like that of
15: 8 bring down on them **a** and terror.
49:24 her; **a** and pain have seized her,
50:43 **A** has gripped him, pain like that of
Lam 1: 4 grieve, and she is in bitter **a**.
Eze 27:31 will weep over you with **a** of soul
30: 4 Egypt, and **a** will come upon Cush.
30: 9 **A** will take hold of them on the day
Da 10:16 "I am overcome with **a** because of the
Joel 2: 6 nations are in **a**; every face turns
Am 5:16 cries of **a** in every public square.
Hab 3: 7 the dwellings of Midian in **a**.
Zep 1:15 a day of distress and **a**, a day of
Lk 21:25 On the earth, nations will be in **a**
22:44 being in **a**, he prayed more earnestly,
Jn 16:21 her baby is born she forgets the **a**
Ro 9: 2 I have great sorrow and unceasing **a**
2Co 2: 4 and **a** of heart and with many tears,

Anguished (Anguish)

Jer 48: 5 on the road down to Horonaim **a** cries
Da 6:20 he called to Daniel in an **a** voice,

Aniam

1Ch 7:19 were: Ahian, Shechem, Likhi and **A**.

Anim

Jos 15:50 Anab, Eshtemoh, **A**,

Animal (Animals)

Ge 6:20 of every kind of **a** and of every kind
7: 2 you seven of every kind of clean **a**,
7: 2 of unclean **a**, a male and its mate,
7:14 They had with them every wild **a**
9: 5 demand an accounting from every **a**.
37:20 say that a ferocious **a** devoured him.
37:33 Some ferocious **a** has devoured him.
43:16 slaughter an **a** and prepare dinner;
Ex 9: 4 so that no **a** belonging to the
9: 6 **a** belonging to the Israelites died.
9:19 **a** that has not been brought in and
11: 7 not a dog will bark at any man or **a**.
13: 2 belongs to me, whether man or **a**."
13:15 firstborn in Egypt, both man and **a**.
19:13 Whether man or **a**, he shall not be
21:34 owner, and the dead **a** will be his.
21:35 the money and the dead **a** equally.
21:36 **a** for **a**, and the dead **a** will be his.
22: 4 "If the stolen **a** is found alive in
22:10 an ox, a sheep or any other **a** to his
22:12 if the **a** was stolen from the
22:13 If it was torn to pieces by a wild **a**,
22:13 be required to pay for the torn **a**.
22:14 "If a man borrows an **a** from his
22:15 if the owner is with the **a**, the
22:15 If the **a** was hired, the money paid
22:19 with an **a** must be put to death.
22:31 So do not eat the meat of an **a** torn
Lev 1: 2 **a** from either the herd or the flock.
3: 1 and he offers an **a** from the herd,
3: 1 before the LORD an **a** without defect.
3: 6 "If he offers an **a** from the flock
7:21 or an unclean **a** or any unclean,
7:24 The fat of an **a** found dead or torn
7:25 Anyone who eats the fat of an **a** from
7:26 not eat the blood of any bird or **a**.
11: 3 You may eat any **a** that has a split
Lev 11:26 "Every **a** that has a split hoof not
11:39 "If an **a** that you are allowed to
17:13 living among you who hunts any **a**
18:23 an **a** and defile yourself with it.
18:23 **a** to have sexual relations with it;
20:15 man has sexual relations with an **a**,
20:15 to death, and you must kill the **a**.
20:16 "If a woman approaches an **a** to have
20:16 it, kill both the woman and the **a**.
20:25 Do not defile yourselves by any **a** or
22:24 You must not offer to the LORD an **a**
24:18 someone's **a** must make restitution
24:21 Whoever kills an **a** must make
27: 9 "If what he vowed is an **a** that is
27: 9 an **a** given to the LORD becomes holy.
27:10 should substitute one **a** for another,
27:11 vowed is a ceremonially unclean **a**
27:11 **a** must be presented to the priest,
27:13 If the owner wishes to redeem the **a**,
27:26 may dedicate the firstborn of an **a**,
27:28 whether man or **a** or family land—may
27:32 every tenth **a** that passes under the
27:33 both the **a** and its substitute become
Nu 3:13 in Israel, whether man or **a**.
8:17 Israel, whether man or **a**, is mine.
18:15 both man and **a**, that is offered to
Dt 4:17 or like any **a** on earth or any bird
14: 6 You may eat any **a** that has a split
15:21 If an **a** has a defect, is lame or
16: 2 to the LORD your God an **a** from
27:21 who has sexual relations with any **a**.
Job 39:15 that some wild **a** may trample them.
Ps 50:10 for every **a** of the forest is mine,
Pr 12:10 man cares for the needs of his **a**,
Ecc 3:19 man has no advantage over the **a**.
3:21 of the **a** goes down into the earth?"
Jer 51:62 so that neither man nor **a** will live
Eze 29:11 No foot of man or **a** will pass
44:31 bird or **a**, found dead or torn by
Da 4:16 let him be given the mind of an **a**
5:21 people and given the mind of an **a**;
8: 4 No **a** could stand against him, and
Hos 13: 8 them; a wild **a** will tear them apart.
Mal 1:14 a blemished **a** to the Lord.
Heb 12:20 "If even an **a** touches the mountain,
Jas 3: 3 obey us, we can turn the whole **a**.

Animals (Animal)

Ge 1:24 wild **a**, each according to its kind.
1:25 God made the wild **a** according to
3: 1 of the wild **a** the LORD God had made.
3:14 the livestock and all the wild **a**!
6: 7 the face of the earth—men and **a**,
7: 8 Pairs of clean and unclean **a**, of
7:16 The **a** going in were male and female
7:21 livestock, wild **a**, all the creatures
7:23 men and **a** and the creatures that
8: 1 all the wild **a** and the livestock
8:17 the **a**, and all the creatures that
8:19 All the **a** and all the creatures that
8:20 taking some of all the clean **a** and
9:10 the livestock and all the wild **a**,
30:40 **a** that belonged to Laban.
30:40 and did not put them with Laban's **a**.
30:41 in the troughs in front of the **a**
30:42 if the **a** were weak, he would not
30:42 So the weak **a** went to Laban and the
31:39 I did not bring you **a** torn by wild
32:17 owns all these **a** in front of you?'
33:13 just one day, all the **a** will die.
34:23 and all their other **a** become ours?
36: 6 all his other **a** and all the goods he
45:17 Load your **a** and return to the land
Ex 8:17 ground, gnats came upon men and **a**.
8:18 And the gnats were on men and **a**.
9: 7 of the **a** of the Israelites had died.
9: 9 on men and **a** throughout the land."
9:10 boils broke out on men and **a**.
9:22 **a** and on everything growing in the
9:25 in the fields—both men and **a**;
12: 5 The **a** you choose must be year-old
12:12 every firstborn—both men and **a**
12:21 "Go at once and select the **a** for
20:10 not your **a**, nor the alien within
23:11 the wild **a** may eat what they leave.
23:29 and the wild **a** too numerous for you.
Lev 5: 2 carcasses of unclean wild **a** or of
7:24 **a** may be used for any other purpose,
11: 2 "Say to the Israelites: 'Of all the **a**
11:27 Of all the **a** that walk on all fours,
11:29 "'Of the **a** that move about on the
11:46 are the regulations concerning **a**,
17:15 by wild **a** must wash his clothes
19:19 "'Do not mate different kinds of **a**.
20:25 unclean **a** and between unclean and
22: 8 found dead or torn by wild **a**
22:25 you must not accept such **a** from the
25: 7 and the wild **a** in your land.
26:22 I will send wild **a** against you, and
27:27 If it is one of the unclean **a**, he
Nu 7:87 The total number of **a** for the burnt
7:88 The total number of **a** for the
18:15 every firstborn male of unclean **a**.
28:31 Be sure the **a** are without defect.
31:11 spoils, including the people and **a**,
31:26 the people and **a** that were captured.
31:30 donkeys, sheep, goats or other **a**.
31:47 out of every fifty persons and **a**,
Dt 5:14 your donkey or any of your **a**, nor
7:22 the wild **a** will multiply around you.
12:15 you may slaughter your **a** in any of
12:21 you may slaughter **a** from the herds
14: 4 These are the **a** you may eat: the ox,
Jdg 20:48 including the **a** and everything else
2Sa 21:10 them by day or the wild **a** by night.
1Ki 4:33 **a** and birds, reptiles and fish.
18: 5 will not have to kill any of our **a**."
2Ki 3: 9 themselves or for the **a** with them.
3:17 cattle and your other **a** will drink.
2Ch 29:33 The **a** consecrated as sacrifices
35:11 while the Levites skinned the **a**.
35:13 They roasted the Passover **a** over the
Job 5:23 wild **a** will be at peace with you.
12: 7 "But ask the **a**, and they will teach
37: 8 The **a** take cover; they remain in
40:20 and all the wild **a** play nearby.
Ps 66:15 I will sacrifice fat **a** to you and an
135: 8 Egypt, the firstborn of men and **a**.
148:10 wild **a** and all cattle, small
Ecc 3:18 may see that they are like the **a**.
3:19 Man's fate is like that of the **a**;
Isa 1:11 of rams and the fat of fattened **a**; I
18: 6 birds of prey and to the wild **a**;
18: 6 all summer, the wild **a** all winter.
30: 6 An oracle concerning the **a** of the
40:16 its **a** enough for burnt offerings.
43:20 The wild **a** honour me, the jackals
Jer 9:10 air have fled and the **a** are gone.
12: 4 the **a** and birds have perished.
21: 6 men and **a**—and they will die of a
27: 5 its people and the **a** that are on it,
27: 6 make even the wild **a** subject to him.
28:14 give him control over the wild **a**.'"
31:27 with the offspring of men and of **a**.
32:43 without men or **a**, for it has been
33:10 a desolate waste, without men or **a**.
33:10 inhabited by neither men nor **a**
33:12 desolate and without men or **a**—in
36:29 and cut off both men and **a** from it?"
50: 3 it; both men and **a** will flee away.
Eze 4:14 found dead or torn by wild **a**.
8:10 detestable **a** and all the idols of
14:13 it and kill its men and their **a**,
14:17 and I kill its men and their **a**,
14:19 killing its men and their **a**,
14:21 plague—to kill its men and their **a**!
25:13 Edom and kill its men and their **a**.
29: 8 you and kill your men and their **a**.
33:27 give to the wild **a** to be devoured,
34: 3 the wool and slaughter the choice **a**,
34: 5 they became food for all the wild **a**.
34: 8 has become food for all the wild **a**,
34:28 nor will wild **a** devour them.
36:11 the number of men and **a** upon you,
39: 4 of carrion birds and to the wild **a**.
39:17 kind of bird and all the wild **a**:
39:18 of them fattened **a** from Bashan.
44:31 found dead or torn by wild **a**.
Da 4:14 Let the **a** flee from under it and the
4:15 the **a** among the plants of the earth.
4:23 live like the wild **a**, until seven times
4:25 and will live with the wild **a**;

Da 4:32 and you will live with the wild a;
Hos 2:12 and wild a will devour them.
Joel 1:20 Even the wild a pant for you; the
2:22 Be not afraid, O wild a, for the
Hab 2:17 destruction of a will terrify you.
Zep 1: 3 "I will sweep away both men and a;
Zec 14:15 and all the a in those camps.
Mal 1: 8 you bring blind a for sacrifice, is
1: 8 sacrifice crippled or diseased a,
1:13 crippled or diseased a and offer
Mk 1:13 the wild a, and angels attended him.
Ac 10:12 contained all kinds of four-footed a,
11: 6 and saw four-footed a of the earth,
15:20 meat of strangled a and from blood.
15:29 a and from sexual immorality.
21:25 a and from sexual immorality."
Ro 1:23 man and birds and a and reptiles.
1Co 15:39 a have another, birds another and
Heb 13:11 blood of a into the Most Holy Place
Jas 3: 7 All kinds of a, birds, reptiles and
Jude :10 like unreasoning a—these are the

Ankle (Ankle-deep, Ankles)
Isa 3:20 the head-dresses and a chains and

Ankle-deep (Ankle, Deep)
Eze 47: 3 led me through water that was a.

Ankles (Ankle)
2Sa 22:37 me, so that my a do not turn over.
Ps 18:36 me, so that my a do not turn over.
Isa 3:16 with ornaments jingling on their a.
Ac 3: 7 the man's feet and a became strong.

Anna
Widow; prophetess of the tribe of Asher; recognised the baby Jesus as the Messiah when he was brought into the temple (Lk 2:36-38).
Lk 2:36 There was also a prophetess, A, the

Annals
1Ki 11:41 in the book of the a of Solomon?
14:19 of the a of the kings of Israel.
14:29 book of the a of the kings of Judah?
15: 7 book of the a of the kings of Judah?
15:23 book of the a of the kings of Judah?
15:31 of the a of the kings of Israel?
16: 5 of the a of the kings of Israel?
16:14 of the a of the kings of Israel?
16:20 of the a of the kings of Israel?
16:27 of the a of the kings of Israel?
22:39 of the a of the kings of Israel?
22:45 book of the a of the kings of Judah?
2Ki 1:18 of the a of the kings of Israel?
8:23 book of the a of the kings of Judah?
10:34 of the a of the kings of Israel?
12:19 book of the a of the kings of Judah?
13: 8 of the a of the kings of Israel?
13:12 of the a of the kings of Israel?
14:15 of the a of the kings of Israel?
14:18 book of the a of the kings of Judah?
14:28 of the a of the kings of Israel?
15: 6 book of the a of the kings of Judah?
15:11 of the a of the kings of Israel.
15:15 of the a of the kings of Israel.
15:21 of the a of the kings of Israel?
15:26 of the a of the kings of Israel.
15:31 of the a of the kings of Israel?
15:36 book of the a of the kings of Judah?
16:19 book of the a of the kings of Judah?
20:20 book of the a of the kings of Judah?
21:17 book of the a of the kings of Judah?
21:25 book of the a of the kings of Judah?
23:28 book of the a of the kings of Judah?
24: 5 book of the a of the kings of Judah?
1Ch 27:24 in the book of the a of King David.
2Ch 20:34 are written in the a of Jehu son of
33:18 in the a of the kings of Israel.
Ne 12:23 were recorded in the book of the a.
Est 2:23 the a in the presence of the king.
10: 2 a of the kings of Media and Persia?

Annas
High priest (Lk 3:2). Questioned Jesus (Jn 18:13,19–24); questioned Peter and John (Ac 4:5–7).
Lk 3: 2 during the high priesthood of A and
Jn 18:13 brought him first to A, who was the
18:24 A sent him, still bound, to Caiaphas
Ac 4: 6 A the high priest was there, and so

Annihilate (Annihilated, Annihilation)
Dt 9: 3 you will drive them out and a them
2Sa 21: 2 Israel and Judah had tried to a them
2Ch 20:23 Mount Seir to destroy and a them.
Est 3:13 kill and a all the Jews—young and
8:11 kill and a any armed force of any
Da 11:44 a great rage to destroy and a many.

Annihilated (Annihilate)
2Ch 32:21 the LORD sent an angel, who a all

Annihilation (Annihilate)
Est 4: 8 the text of the edict for their a,
7: 4 for destruction and slaughter and a.

Anniversary
Dt 16: 6 the a of your departure from Egypt.

Annotations (Note)
2Ch 13:22 in the a of the prophet Iddo.
24:27 in the a on the book of the kings.

Announce (Announced, Announcement, Announces, Announcing)
Jdg 7: 3 a now to the people, 'Anyone who
Isa 42: 9 spring into being I a them to you."
48:20 A this with shouts of joy and
Jer 4: 5 "A in Judah and proclaim in
5:20 "A this to the house of Jacob and
18: 7 If at any time I a that a nation or
18: 9 if at another time I a that a nation
46:14 "A this in Egypt, and proclaim it in
48:20 Wail and cry out! A by the Arnon
50: 2 "A and proclaim among the nations,
51:31 messenger follows messenger to a to
Zec 9:12 O prisoners of hope; even now I a
Mt 6: 2 do not a it with trumpets, as the

Announced (Announce)
Ex 32: 5 a, "Tomorrow there will be a
Lev 23:44 Moses a to the Israelites the
Ru 4: 9 Boaz a to the elders and all the
1Ki 20:13 came to Ahab king of Israel and a,
Ps 68:11 The Lord a the word, and great was
Isa 48: 3 my mouth a them and I made them
48: 5 before they happened I a them to you
Lam 1:21 May you bring the day you have a
Da 4:17 "The decision is a by messengers,
Lk 23: 4 Pilate a to the chief priests and
Gal 3: 8 and a the gospel in advance to
Heb 2: 3 which was first a by the Lord, was
Rev 10: 7 he a to his servants the prophets."

Announcement (Announce)
Isa 48:16 "From the first a I have not spoken

Announces (Announce)
Dt 13: 1 a to you a miraculous sign or wonder,
Job 36:33 His thunder a the coming storm; even

Announcing (Announce)
Jer 4:15 A voice is a from Dan, proclaiming

Annoyance
Pr 12:16 A fool shows his a at once, but a

Annual (Annually)
Ex 30:10 This a atonement must be made with
Jdg 21:19 look, there is the a festival of the
1Sa 1:21 offer the a sacrifice to the LORD
2:19 husband to offer the a sacrifice.
20: 6 his home town, because an a
2Ch 8:13 New Moons and the three a
Heb 10: 3 those sacrifices are an a reminder

Annually (Annual)
2Ch 24: 5 the money due a from all Israel,
Est 9:21 to have them celebrate a the

Annulled (Nullify)
Isa 28:18 Your covenant with death will be a;

Anoint (Anointed, Anointing)
Ex 28:41 and his sons, a and ordain them.
29: 7 Take the anointing oil and a him by
29:36 for it, and a it to consecrate it.
30:26 use it to a the Tent of Meeting, the
30:30 "A Aaron and his sons and consecrate
40: 9 "Take the anointing oil and a the
40:10 a the altar of burnt offering and
40:11 A the basin and its stand and
40:13 a him and consecrate him so that he
40:15 A them just as you anointed their
Jdg 9: 8 One day the trees went out to a a
9:15 'If you really want to a me king
1Sa 9:16 A him leader over my people Israel;
15: 1 "I am the one the LORD sent to a you
16: 3 are to a for me the one I indicate."
16:12 Then the LORD said, "Rise and a him;
1Ki 1:34 the prophet a him king over Israel.
19:15 get there, a Hazael king over Aram.
19:16 Also, a Jehu son of Nimshi king over
19:16 and a Elisha son of Shaphat from
2Ki 9: 3 LORD says: I a you king over Israel.
9: 6 'I a you king over the LORD's people
9:12 says: I a you king over Israel.'"
Ps 23: 5 a my head with oil; my cup overflows.
Ecc 9: 8 and always a your head with oil.
Da 9:24 and prophecy and to a the most holy.
Mk 16: 1 that they might go to a Jesus' body.
Jas 5:14 a him with oil in the name of the

Anointed (Anoint, *Anointed One*, *LORD's anointed*)
Ge 31:13 I am the God of Bethel, where you a
Ex 29:29 they can be a and ordained in them.
40:15 Anoint them just as you a their
Lev 4: 3 "'If the a priest sins, bringing
4: 5 the a priest shall take some of the
4:16 the a priest is to take some of the
6:20 to the LORD on the day he is a:
6:22 The son who is to succeed him as a
7:36 On the day they were a, the LORD
8:10 Moses took the anointing oil and a
8:12 head and a him to consecrate him.
16:32 The priest who is a and ordained to
Nu 3: 3 the a priests, who were ordained to
7: 1 he a it and consecrated it and all
7: 1 He also a and consecrated the altar
7:10 the altar was a, the leaders brought
7:84 dedication of the altar when it was a
7:88 of the altar after it was a.
35:25 priest, who was a with holy oil.
1Sa 2:10 king and exalt the horn of his a."
10: 1 a you leader over his inheritance?
12: 3 the presence of the LORD and his a.
12: 5 and also his a is witness this day,
15:17 The LORD a you king over Israel.
16: 6 a stands here before the LORD."
16:13 Samuel took the horn of oil and a
24: 6 him; for he is the a of the LORD."
26: 9 on the LORD's a and be guiltless?
2Sa 2: 4 a David king over the house of Judah.
2: 7 of Judah has a me king over them."
3:39 today, though I am the a king, I am
5: 3 and they a David king over Israel.
5:17 David had been a king over Israel,
12: 7 'I a you king over Israel, and I
19:10 Absalom, whom we a to rule over us,
22:51 shows unfailing kindness to his a,
23: 1 the man a by the God of Jacob,
1Ki 1:39 from the sacred tent and a Solomon.
1:45 prophet have a him king at Gihon.
5: 1 a king to succeed his father David,
2Ki 11:12 They a him, and the people clapped
23:30 a him and made him king in place of
1Ch 11: 3 and they a David king over Israel,
14: 8 had been a king over all Israel,
16:22 "Do not touch my a ones; do my
2Ch 22: 7 had a to destroy the house of Ahab.
23:11 They a him and shouted, "Long live
Ps 18:50 shows unfailing kindness to his a,
20: 6 Now I know that the LORD saves his a;
45: 2 your lips have been a with grace,

Ps 89:20 with my sacred oil I have **a** him.
105:15 "Do not touch my **a** ones; do my
Isa 45: 1 "This is what the LORD says to his **a**,
61: 1 **a** me to preach good news to the poor.
Eze 28:14 You were **a** as a guardian cherub, for
Zec 4:14 he said, "These are the two who are **a**
Mk 6:13 They drove out many demons and **a**
Lk 4:18 **a** me to preach good news to the poor.
Ac 4:27 your holy servant Jesus, whom you **a**.
10:38 how God **a** Jesus of Nazareth with the
2Co 1:21 He **a** us,

Anointed one

1Sa 2:35 he will minister before my **a** always.
2Ch 6:42 O LORD God, do not reject your **a**.
Ps 2: 2 against the LORD and against his **A**.
28: 8 a fortress of salvation for his **a**.
84: 9 O God; look with favour on your **a**.
89:38 have been very angry with your **a**.
89:51 have mocked every step of your **a**.
132:10 your servant, do not reject your **a**.
132:17 David and set up a lamp for my **a**.
Da 9:25 and rebuild Jerusalem until the **A**,
9:26 After the sixty-two 'sevens', the **A**
Hab 3:13 deliver your people, to save your **a**.
Ac 4:26 the Lord and against his **A**.',

Anointing (Anoint, *Anointing oil*)

Ex 40:15 Their **a** will be to a priesthood that
Lev 8:11 **a** the altar and all its utensils and
1Ch 29:22 **a** him before the LORD to be ruler
Ps 45: 7 by **a** you with the oil of joy.
Heb 1: 9 by **a** you with the oil of joy."
1Jn 2:20 you have an **a** from the Holy One, and
2:27 the **a** you received from him remains
2:27 But as his **a** teaches you about all
2:27 as that **a** is real, not counterfeit

Anointing oil

Ex 25: 6 spices for the **a** and for the fragrant
29: 7 Take the **a** and anoint him by pouring
29:21 some of the **a** and sprinkle it on
30:25 Make these into a sacred **a**, a
30:25 It will be the sacred **a**.
30:31 **a** for the generations to come.
31:11 the **a** and fragrant incense for the
35: 8 spices for the **a** and for the fragrant
35:15 the **a** and the fragrant incense; the
35:28 the **a** and for the fragrant incense.
37:29 They also made the sacred **a** and the
39:38 the gold altar, the **a**, the fragrant
40: 9 "Take the **a** and anoint the
Lev 8: 2 their garments, the **a**, the bull for
8:10 Moses took the **a** and anointed the
8:12 He poured some of the **a** on Aaron's
8:30 Moses took some of the **a** and some of
10: 7 die, because the LORD's **a** is on you.
21:10 has had the **a** poured on his head
21:12 been dedicated by the **a** of his God.
Nu 4:16 regular grain offering and the **a**.

Another See One another

Answerable

Mt 5:22 'Raca,' is **a** to the Sanhedrin.

Ant (Ants)

Pr 6: 6 Go to the **a**, you sluggard; consider

Antelope

Dt 14: 5 ibex, the **a** and the mountain sheep.
Isa 51:20 street, like **a** caught in a net.

Anthothijah

1Ch 8:24 Hananiah, Elam, **A**,

Antichrist (Antichrists)

1Jn 2:18 you have heard that the **a** is coming,
2:22 **a**—he denies the Father and the Son.
4: 3 This is the spirit of the **a**, which
2Jn : 7 person is the deceiver and the **a**.

Antichrists (Antichrist)

1Jn 2:18 coming, even now many **a** have come.

Anticipating

Ac 12:11 the Jewish people were **a**."

Antioch

1. Cosmopolitan capital city of Roman province of Syria, on bank of River Orontes, about 15 miles inland from Mediterranean port of Seleucia. Home of Nicolas, one of the first "deacons" (Ac 6:5). Persecuted believers arrived from Jerusalem to evangelise Jews (Ac 11:19), and Greeks (Ac 11:20–21). Barnabas and Paul also came here (Ac 11:22–26). Term "Christian" first used here (Ac 11:26). Became the base for Paul's 3 missionary journeys (Ac 13:1–3; 15:35–41; 18:23). Dispute arose here about circumcision (Ac 15:1–2), which was later decided at the council of Jerusalem. **2.** City in province of either Pisidia or Phrygia (disputed) in southern Asia Minor. On first missionary journey, Paul preached in its synagogue, and though many Gentiles were converted, he experienced Jewish opposition and was expelled (Ac 13:14–51). Paul returned on his way home (Ac 14:21), and possibly again on his second journey (Ac 16:6). He refers to his persecution here in a letter to Timothy (2Ti 3:11).

Ac 6: 5 Nicolas from **A**, a convert to Judaism.
11:19 **A**, telling the message only to Jews.
11:20 went to **A** and began to speak to
11:22 and they sent Barnabas to **A**.
11:26 he found him, he brought him to **A**.
11:26 were called Christians first at **A**.
11:27 came down from Jerusalem to **A**.
13: 1 In the church at **A** there were
13:14 From Perga they went on to Pisidian **A**
14:19 some Jews came from **A** and Iconium
14:21 returned to Lystra, Iconium and **A**,
14:26 From Attalia they sailed back to **A**,
15: 1 Some men came down from Judea to **A**
15:22 them to **A** with Paul and Barnabas.
15:23 in **A**, Syria and Cilicia: Greetings.
15:30 were sent off and went down to **A**,
15:35 Paul and Barnabas remained in **A**,
18:22 the church and then went down to **A**.
18:23 After spending some time in **A**, Paul
Gal 2:11 Peter came to **A**, I opposed him to
2Ti 3:11 kinds of things happened to me in **A**,

Antipas

Rev 2:13 even in the days of **A**, my faithful

Antipatris See Aphek 1.

Ac 23:31 night and brought him as far as **A**.

Ants (Ant)

Pr 30:25 **A** are creatures of little strength,

Anub

1Ch 4: 8 Koz, who was the father of **A** and

Anvil

Isa 41: 7 spurs on him who strikes the **a**.

Anxieties (Anxious)

Lk 21:34 drunkenness and the **a** of life, and

Anxiety (Anxious)

Ps 94:19 **a** was great within me, your
Ecc 11:10 then, banish **a** from your heart and
Eze 4:16 people will eat rationed food in **a**
12:19 eat their food in **a** and drink their
Php 2:28 may be glad and I may have less **a**.
1Pe 5: 7 Cast all your **a** on him because he

Anxious (Anxieties, Anxiety, Anxiously)

Dt 28:65 There the LORD will give you an **a**
Ps 139:23 test me and know my **a** thoughts.
Pr 12:25 An **a** heart weighs a man down, but a
Ecc 2:22 **a** striving with which he labours
Php 4: 6 Do not be **a** about anything, but in

Anxiously (Anxious)

Lk 2:48 I have been **a** searching for you."

Apartment

Jer 36:22 king was sitting in the winter **a**,

Apelles

Ro 16:10 Greet **A**, tested and approved in

Apes

1Ki 10:22 silver and ivory, and **a** and baboons.
2Ch 9:21 silver and ivory, and **a** and baboons.

Aphek

1. City on coastal Plain of Sharon whose king was defeated by Joshua (Jos 12:18). Used as a Philistine encampment (1Sa 4:1; 29:1). Later rebuilt as Roman city Antipatris, where Paul was taken on his way to Caesarea (Ac 23:31). **2.** Town east of Galilee, where Ahab overcame the Aramean army (1Ki 20:26–30). Elisha predicted another Aramean defeat at Aphek (2Ki 13:17). **3.** Canaanite city (also known as Aphik) in Asher's territory (Jos 19:30–31; Jdg 1:31–32).

Jos 12:18 the king of **A** one
13: 4 Arah of the Sidonians as far as **A**
19:30 Ummah, **A** and Rehob. There were
Jdg 1:31 or Aczib or Helbah or **A** or Rehob,
1Sa 4: 1 Ebenezer, and the Philistines at **A**.
29: 1 gathered all their forces at **A**,
1Ki 20:26 up to **A** to fight against Israel.
20:30 of them escaped to the city of **A**,
2Ki 13:17 destroy the Arameans at **A**."

Aphekah

Jos 15:53 Janim, Beth Tappuah, **A**,

Aphiah

1Sa 9: 1 Becorath, the son of **A** of Benjamin.

Apollonia

Ac 17: 1 had passed through Amphipolis and **A**,

Apollos

Disciple from Alexandria, well versed in the Scriptures (Ac 18:24–25); instructed by Priscilla and Aquila in Ephesus (Ac 18:26). Ministered in Corinth (Ac 18:27–19:1; 1Co 1:12; 3:5–9) and on Crete (Tit 3:13).

Ac 18:24 Meanwhile a Jew named **A**, a native of
18:27 **A** wanted to go to Achaia, the
19: 1 While **A** was at Corinth, Paul took
1Co 1:12 "I follow **A**"; another, "I follow
3: 4 "I follow **A**," are you not mere
3: 5 What, after all, is **A**? And what is
3: 6 I planted the seed, **A** watered it,
3:22 whether Paul or **A** or Cephas or the
4: 6 to myself and **A** for your benefit,
16:12 Now about our brother **A**: I strongly
Tit 3:13 **A** on their way and see that they

Apollyon

Rev 9:11 Hebrew is Abaddon, and in Greek, **A**.

Apostle (Apostles, Apostles', Apostleship, Apostolic, Super-apostles)

Ro 1: 1 called to be an **a** and set apart for
11:13 Inasmuch as I am the **a** to the
1Co 1: 1 Paul, called to be an **a** of Christ
9: 1 Am I not free? Am I not an **a**? Have I
9: 2 Even though I may not be an **a** to
15: 9 not even deserve to be called an **a**,
2Co 1: 1 Paul, an **a** of Christ Jesus by the
12:12 The things that mark an **a**—signs,
Gal 1: 1 Paul, an **a**—sent not from men nor by
2: 8 of Peter as an **a** to the Jews,
2: 8 my ministry as an **a** to the Gentiles.
Eph 1: 1 Paul, an **a** of Christ Jesus by the
Col 1: 1 Paul, an **a** of Christ Jesus by the
1Ti 1: 1 Paul, an **a** of Christ Jesus by the
2: 7 I was appointed a herald and an **a**
2Ti 1: 1 Paul, an **a** of Christ Jesus by the
1:11 a herald and an **a** and a teacher.
Tit 1: 1 Paul, a servant of God and an **a** of
Heb 3: 1 **a** and high priest whom we confess.
1Pe 1: 1 Peter, an **a** of Jesus Christ, To
2Pe 1: 1 Simon Peter, a servant and **a** of

Apostles (Apostle)

Mt 10: 2 These are the names of the twelve **a**:
Mk 3:14 appointed twelve—designating them **a**

Mk 6:30 The a gathered round Jesus and
Lk 6:13 of them, whom he also designated a:
9:10 the a returned, they reported to
11:49 'I will send them prophets and a,
17: 5 The a said to the Lord, "Increase
22:14 the hour came, Jesus and his a
24:10 with them who told this to the a.
Ac 1: 2 Holy Spirit to the a he had chosen.
1:26 so he was added to the eleven a.
2:37 and said to Peter and the other a,
2:43 miraculous signs were done by the a.
4: 2 the a were teaching the people
4:33 With great power the a continued to
4:36 a Levite from Cyprus, whom the a
5:12 The a performed many miraculous
5:18 They arrested the a and put them in
5:21 sent to the jail for the a.
5:26 with his officers and brought the a.
5:27 Having brought the a, they made them
5:29 Peter and the other a replied: "We
5:40 They called the a in and had them
5:41 The a left the Sanhedrin, rejoicing
6: 6 They presented these men to the a,
8: 1 and all except the a were scattered
8:14 the a in Jerusalem heard that
9:27 took him and brought him to the a.
11: 1 The a and the brothers throughout
14: 4 with the Jews, others with the a.
14:14 when the a Barnabas and Paul heard
15: 2 a and elders about this question.
15: 4 by the church and the a and elders,
15: 6 The a and elders met to consider
15:22 the a and elders, with the whole
15:23 letter: The a and elders, your
16: 4 the decisions reached by the a
Ro 16: 7 They are outstanding among the a,
1Co 4: 9 God has put us a on display at
9: 5 as do the other a and the LORD's
12:28 God has appointed first of all a,
12:29 Are all a? Are all prophets? Are all
15: 7 to James, then to all the a,
15: 9 For I am the least of the a and do
2Co 11:13 For such men are false a, deceitful
11:13 masquerading as a of Christ.
Gal 1:17 see those who were a before I was,
1:19 I saw none of the other a—only
Eph 2:20 built on the foundation of the a and
3: 5 Spirit to God's holy a and prophets.
4:11 was he who gave some to be a, some
1Th 2: 6 As a of Christ we could have been a
2Pe 3: 2 our Lord and Saviour through your a.
Jude :17 a of our Lord Jesus Christ foretold.
Rev 2: 2 those who claim to be a but are not,
18:20 O heaven! Rejoice, saints and a and
21:14 names of the twelve a of the Lamb.

Apostles' (Apostle)
Ac 2:42 They devoted themselves to the a
4:35 put it at the a feet, and it was
4:37 the money and put it at the a feet.
5: 2 the rest and put it at the a feet.
8:18 the a hands, he offered them

Apostleship (Apostle)
Ro 1: 5 we received grace and a to call
1Co 9: 2 are the seal of my a in the Lord.

Apostolic (Apostle)
Ac 1:25 to take over this a ministry, which

Appaim
1Ch 2:30 The sons of Nadab: Seled and A.
2:31 The son of A: Ishi, who was the

Appalled
Lev 26:32 enemies who live there will be a.
1Ki 9: 8 all who pass by will be a and will
2Ch 7:21 all who pass by will be a and say,
Ezr 9: 3 my head and beard and sat down a.
9: 4 I sat there a until the evening
Job 17: 8 Upright men are a at this; the
18:20 Men of the west are a at his fate;
Ps 40:15 "Aha! Aha!" be a at their own shame.
Isa 52:14 Just as there were many who were a
59:16 he was a that there was no-one to
Isa 63: 5 I was a that no-one gave support; so
Jer 2:12 Be a at this, O heavens, and
4: 9 and the prophets will be a."
18:16 be a and will shake their heads.
19: 8 all who pass by will be a and will
49:17 all who pass by will be a and will
Eze 4:17 They will be a at the sight of each
26:16 trembling every moment, a at you.
27:35 All who live in the coastlands are a
28:19 All the nations who knew you are a
32:10 I will cause many peoples to be a at
Da 8:27 I was a by the vision; it was beyond

Appeal (Appealed, Appealing, Appeals)
Dt 15: 9 He may then a to the LORD against
Job 5: 8 "But if it were I, I would a to God;
Ps 77:10 I thought, "To this I will a: the
Ac 25:11 I a to Caesar!"
25:21 Paul made his a to be held over for
25:25 but because he made his a to the
28:19 I was compelled to a to Caesar—not
1Co 1:10 I a to you, brothers, in the name of
2Co 5:20 God were making his a through us.
8:17 For Titus not only welcomed our a,
10: 1 I a to you—I, Paul, who am "timid"
13:11 Aim for perfection, listen to my a,
1Th 2: 3 For the a we make does not spring
Phm :9 yet I a to you on the basis of love.
:10 I a to you for my son Onesimus, who
1Pe 5: 1 To the elders among you, I a as a

Appealed (Appeal)
Ex 5:15 the Israelite foremen went and a to
Jos 10: 3 Adoni-Zedek king of Jerusalem a to
Est 2: 4 a to the king, and he followed it.
Lk 23:20 Wanting to release Jesus, Pilate a
Ac 25:12 he declared: "You have a to Caesar.
26:32 set free if he had not a to Caesar."
Ro 11: 2 he a to God against Israel: "Lord,

Appealing (Appeal)
2Pe 2:18 by a to the lustful desires of sinful

Appeals (Appeal)
2Sa 19:28 to make any more a to the king?"

Appear (Appearance, Appearances, Appeared, Appearing, Appears, Reappears)
Ge 1: 9 to one place, and let dry ground a.
27:12 I would a to be tricking him and
Ex 4: 1 say, 'The LORD did not a to you'?"
10:28 Make sure you do not a before me
10:29 "I will never a before you again.
22: 8 the owner of the house must a before
23:15 is to a before me empty-handed.
23:17 are to a before the Sovereign LORD.
34:20 is to a before me empty-handed.
34:23 are to a before the Sovereign LORD,
34:24 year to a before the LORD your God.
Lev 9: 4 For today the LORD will a to you.'"
9: 6 the glory of the LORD may a to you."
13: 4 not a to be more than skin deep
13: 7 he must a before the priest again.
13:32 not a to be more than skin deep,
14:37 or reddish depressions that a to be
16: 2 or else he will die, because I a in
Nu 16:16 "You and all your followers are to a
Dt 16:16 all your men must a before the LORD
16:16 No man should a before the LORD
31:11 all Israel comes to a before the
1Sa 3:21 The LORD continued to a at Shiloh,
2Sa 9: 2 They called him to a before David,
Ezr 10: 8 Anyone who failed to a within three
Job 19:18 me; when I a, they ridicule me.
Ps 102:16 For the LORD will rebuild Zion and a
SS 2:12 Flowers a on the earth; the season
Isa 1:12 you come to a before me, who has
58: 8 and your healing will quickly a;
Eze 16:52 they a more righteous than you.
16:52 have made your sisters a righteous.
Da 7:23 fourth kingdom that will a on earth.
11: 2 Three more kings will a in Persia,
Da 11: 3 a mighty king will a, who will rule
Hos 6: 3 he will a; he will come to us like
Zec 9:14 the LORD will a over them; his arrow
Mt 23:28 In the same way, on the outside you a
24:11 many false prophets will a and
24:24 false prophets will a and perform
24:30 of the Son of Man will a in the sky,
Mk 13:22 false prophets will a and perform
Lk 19:11 of God was going to a at once.
Ac 5:27 they made them a before the
11:13 He told us how he had seen an angel a
19:30 Paul wanted to a before the crowd,
2Co 5:10 For we must all a before the
Col 3: 4 you also will a with him in glory.
Heb 9:24 now to a for us in God's presence.
9:28 and he will a a second time, not to

Appearance (Appear)
Lev 13:55 if the mildew has not changed its a,
1Sa 16: 7 "Do not consider his a or his height,
16: 7 a, but the LORD looks at the heart."
16:12 He was ruddy, with a fine a and
2Sa 14:25 for his handsome a as Absalom.
Ecc 8: 1 a man's face and changes its hard a.
SS 5:15 His a is like Lebanon, choice as its
Isa 52:14 his a was so disfigured beyond that
53: 2 in his a that we should desire him.
Lam 4: 7 than rubies, their a like sapphires.
Eze 1: 5 In a their form was that of a man,
1:13 The a of the living creatures was
1:16 This was the a and structure of the
1:28 Like the a of a rainbow in the
1:28 This was the a of the likeness of
8: 2 a was as bright as glowing metal.
10:10 for their a, the four of them looked
10:22 Their faces had the same a as those
40: 3 and I saw a man whose a was like
Da 1:13 compare our a with that of the young
2:31 dazzling statue, awesome in a.
Joel 2: 4 They have the a of horses; they
Mt 16: 3 You know how to interpret the a of
28: 3 His a was like lightning, and his
Lk 9:29 he was praying, the a of his face
12:56 the a of the earth and the sky.
Gal 2: 6 God does not judge by external
Php 2: 8 being found in a as a man, he
Col 2:23 Such regulations indeed have an a of
Rev 4: 3 the one who sat there had the a of

Appearances (Appear)
Jn 7:24 Stop judging by mere a, and make a

Appeared (Appear)
Ge 2: 5 no shrub of the field had yet a on
12: 7 The LORD a to Abram and said, "To
12: 7 there to the LORD, who had a to him.
15:17 a and passed between the pieces.
17: 1 the LORD a to him and said, "I am
18: 1 The LORD a to Abraham near the great
26: 2 The LORD a to Isaac and said, "Do
26:24 That night the LORD a to him and
35: 1 who a to you when you were fleeing
35: 9 God a to him again and blessed him.
46:29 As soon as Joseph a before him, he
48: 3 Jacob said to Joseph, "God Almighty a
Ex 3: 2 There the angel of the LORD a to him
3:16 Isaac and Jacob—a to me and said: I
4: 5 and the God of Jacob—has a to you."
6: 3 I a to Abraham, to Isaac and to
16:14 on the ground a on the desert floor.
Lev 9:23 of the LORD a to all the people.
Nu 14:10 Then the glory of the LORD a at the
16:19 the LORD a to the entire assembly.
16:42 it and the glory of the LORD a.
20: 6 and the glory of the LORD a to them.
Dt 31:15 the LORD a at the Tent in a pillar
32:17 gods that recently a, gods your
Jdg 6:12 the angel of the LORD a to Gideon,
13: 3 The angel of the LORD a to her and
13:10 The man who a to me the other day!"
14:11 he a, he was given thirty companions.
1Ki 3: 5 At Gibeon the LORD a to Solomon
9: 2 the LORD a to him a second time, as
9: 2 time, as he had a to him at Gibeon.
11: 9 of Israel, who had a to him twice.

2Ki 2:11 **a** and separated the two of them,
2Ch 1: 7 That night God **a** to Solomon and said
3: 1 the LORD had **a** to his father David.
7:12 the LORD **a** to him at night and said:
Jer 31: 3 The LORD **a** to us in the past, saying:
Eze 1:16 Each **a** to be made like a wheel
1:27 I saw that from what **a** to be his
8: 2 From what **a** to be his waist down he
37: 8 I looked, and tendons and flesh **a** on
Da 5: 5 the fingers of a human hand **a**
8: 1 the one that had already **a** to me.
11: 4 After he has **a**, his empire will be
Mt 1:20 an angel of the Lord **a** to him in a
2: 7 them the exact time the star had **a**.
2:13 they had gone, an angel of the Lord **a**
2:19 Lord **a** in a dream to Joseph in
13:26 formed ears, then the weeds also **a**.
17: 3 Just then there **a** before them Moses
27:53 into the holy city and **a** to many
Mk 9: 4 there **a** before them Elijah and Moses,
9: 7 a cloud **a** and enveloped them, and a
14:43 Judas, one of the Twelve, **a**.
16: 9 he **a** first to Mary Magdalene, out of
16:12 Afterwards Jesus **a** in a different
16:14 Later Jesus **a** to the Eleven as they
Lk 1:11 an angel of the Lord **a** to him,
1:80 until he **a** publicly to Israel.
2: 9 An angel of the Lord **a** to them, and
2:13 the heavenly host **a** with the angel,
7:16 "A great prophet has **a** among us,"
9: 8 others that Elijah had **a**, and still
9:31 **a** in glorious splendour, talking
9:34 While he was speaking, a cloud **a** and
22:43 An angel from heaven **a** to him and
24:34 Lord has risen and has **a** to Simon."
Jn 8: 2 At dawn he **a** again in the temple
21: 1 Afterwards Jesus **a** again to his
21:14 This was now the third time Jesus **a**
Ac 1: 3 He **a** to them over a period of forty
5:36 Some time ago Theudas **a**, claiming to
5:37 After him, Judas the Galilean **a** in
7: 2 listen to me! The God of glory **a** to
7:30 an angel **a** to Moses in the flames of
7:35 the angel who **a** to him in the bush.
8:40 Philip, however, **a** at Azotus and
9:17 Jesus, who **a** to you on the road as you
12: 7 Suddenly an angel of the Lord **a** and
25: 2 Jewish leaders **a** before him and
25: 7 Paul **a**, the Jews who had come down
26:16 I have **a** to you to appoint you as a
27:20 neither sun nor stars **a** for many
1Co 15: 5 that he **a** to Peter, and then to the
15: 6 After that, he **a** to more than five
15: 7 he **a** to James, then to all the
15: 8 last of all he **a** to me also, as to
1Ti 3:16 He **a** in a body, was vindicated by the
Tit 2:11 brings salvation has **a** to all men.
3: 4 and love of God our Saviour **a**,
Heb 9:26 But now he has **a** once for all at the
1Jn 1: 2 The life **a**; we have seen it and
1: 2 was with the Father and has **a** to us.
3: 5 you know that he **a** so that he might
3: 8 **a** was to destroy the devil's work.
Rev 12: 1 A great and wondrous sign **a** in
12: 3 another sign **a** in heaven: an

Appearing (Appear)

Ex 16:10 glory of the LORD **a** in the cloud.
Ps 21: 9 At the time of your **a** you will make
Zec 5: 5 up and see what this is that is **a**."
Jn 8:13 "Here you are, **a** as your own witness;
1Ti 6:14 the **a** of our Lord Jesus Christ,
2Ti 1:10 has now been revealed through the **a**
4: 1 and in view of his **a** and his kingdom,
4: 8 to all who have longed for his **a**.
Tit 2:13 **a** of our great God and Saviour,

Appears (Appear)

Ge 9:14 and the rainbow **a** in the clouds,
9:16 Whenever the rainbow **a** in the clouds,
Lev 13: 3 sore **a** to be more than skin deep,
13:14 whenever raw flesh **a** on him, he will
13:19 swelling or reddish-white spot **a**,
13:20 and if it **a** to be more than skin
13:24 spot **a** in the raw flesh of the burn,
Lev 13:25 and it **a** to be more than skin deep,
13:30 and if it **a** to be more than skin
13:34 and **a** to be no more than skin deep,
Dt 13: 1 or one who foretells by dreams, **a**
Ps 84: 7 till each **a** before God in Zion.
Pr 27:25 the hay is removed and new growth **a**
SS 6:10 Who is this that **a** like the dawn,
Isa 16:12 Moab **a** at her high place, she only
60: 2 upon you and his glory **a** over you.
Na 3:17 but when the sun **a** they fly away,
Mal 3: 2 Who can stand when he **a**? For he will
Col 3: 4 Christ, who is your life, **a**, then
Heb 7:15 another priest like Melchizedek **a**,
Jas 4:14 You are a mist that **a** for a little
1Pe 5: 4 the Chief Shepherd **a**, you will
1Jn 2:28 continue in him, so that when he **a**
3: 2 But we know that when he **a**, we shall

Appease

Pr 16:14 of death, but a wise man will **a** it.
Ac 16:39 They came to **a** them and escorted

Appetite (Appetites)

Nu 11: 6 now we have lost our **a**; we never see
Pr 16:26 The labourer's **a** works for him; his
Ecc 6: 7 mouth, yet his **a** is never satisfied.
6: 9 eye sees than the roving of the **a**.
Isa 5:14 Therefore the grave enlarges its **a**
Jer 50:19 his **a** will be satisfied on the hills

Appetites (Appetite)

Isa 56:11 They are dogs with mighty **a**; they
Ro 16:18 our Lord Christ, but their own **a**.

Apphia

Phm : 2 to **A** our sister, to Archippus our

Appius

Ac 28:15 **A** and the Three Taverns to meet us.

Apple (Apples)

Dt 32:10 he guarded him as the **a** of his eye,
Ps 17: 8 Keep me as the **a** of your eye; hide
Pr 7: 2 my teachings as the **a** of your eye.
SS 2: 3 Like an **a** tree among the trees of
8: 5 Under the **a** tree I roused you;
Joel 1:12 the palm and the **a** tree—all the
Zec 2: 8 you touches the **a** of his eye—

Apples (Apple)

Pr 25:11 A word aptly spoken is like **a** of
SS 2: 5 me with **a**, for I am faint with love.
7: 8 the fragrance of your breath like **a**,

Applied (Apply)

2Ki 20: 7 **a** it to the boil, and he recovered.
Pr 24:32 I **a** my heart to what I observed and
Ecc 1:17 I **a** myself to the understanding of
8: 9 All this I saw, as I **a** my mind to
8:16 I **a** my mind to know wisdom and to
Da 4:19 "My lord, if only the dream **a** to
1Co 4: 6 Now, brothers, I have **a** these things

Applies (Apply)

Ex 12:49 The same law **a** to the native-born
21:31 This law also **a** if the bull gores a
Lev 7: 7 "The same law **a** to both the sin
Nu 8:24 "This **a** to the Levites: Men
15:29 One and the same law **a** to everyone
19:14 "This is the law that **a** when a

Apply (Applied, Applies, Applying)

Nu 5:30 and is to **a** this entire law to her.
15:16 The same laws and regulations will **a**
Job 5:27 So hear it and **a** it to yourself."
Pr 22:17 wise; **a** your heart to what I teach,
23:12 **A** your heart to instruction and your
Isa 38:21 "Prepare a poultice of figs and **a** it

Applying (Apply)

Pr 2: 2 turning your ear to wisdom and **a**
Heb 9:10 **a** until the time of the new order.

Appoint (Appointed, Appointing, Appointment, Appoints)

Ge 41:34 Let Pharaoh **a** commissioners over the
Ex 18:21 **a** them as officials over thousands,
Nu 1:50 Instead, **a** the Levites to be in
3:10 **A** Aaron and his sons to serve as
27:16 mankind, **a** a man over this
34:18 **a** one leader from each tribe to help
Dt 16:18 **A** judges and officials for each of
17:15 be sure to **a** over you the king the
20: 9 they shall **a** commanders over it.
Jos 18: 4 **A** three men from each tribe. I will
1Sa 2:36 "**A** me to some priestly office so
8: 5 now **a** a king to lead us, such as all
2Ki 10: 5 We will not **a** anyone as king; you do
1Ch 15:16 told the leaders of the Levites to **a**
Ezr 7:25 **a** magistrates and judges to
Ne 7: 3 Also **a** residents of Jerusalem as
Est 2: 3 Let the king **a** commissioners in
Ps 61: 7 **a** your love and faithfulness to
89:27 I will also **a** him my firstborn, the
109: 6 **A** an evil man to oppose him; let an
Jer 1:10 See, today I **a** you over nations and
23:32 lies, yet I did not send or **a** them.
49:19 Who is the chosen one I will **a** for
50:44 Who is the chosen one I will **a** for
51:27 **A** a commander against her; send up
Da 6: 1 pleased Darius to **a** 120 satraps to
Hos 1:11 and they will **a** one leader and will
Ac 26:16 I have appeared to you to **a** you as a
1Co 6: 4 **a** as judges even men of little
1Th 5: 9 For God did not **a** us to suffer wrath
Tit 1: 5 and **a** elders in every town,

Appointed (Appoint)

Ge 18:14 I will return to you at the **a** time
Ex 5:14 The Israelite foremen **a** by Pharaoh's
13:10 You must keep this ordinance at the **a**
23:15 Do this at the **a** time in the month
31: 6 Moreover, I have **a** Oholiab son of
34:18 Do this at the **a** time in the month
Lev 16:21 in the care of a man **a** for the task.
23: 2 'These are my **a** feasts, the **a** feasts
23: 4 "'These are the LORD's **a** feasts, the
23: 4 are to proclaim at their **a** times:
23:37 ("'These are the LORD's **a** feasts,
23:44 to the Israelites the **a** feasts of
Nu 1:16 These were the men **a** from the
3:32 He was **a** over those who were
3:36 The Merarites were **a** to take care of
9: 2 the Passover at the **a** time.
9: 3 Celebrate it at the **a** time, at
9: 7 the other Israelites at the **a** time?"
9:13 the LORD's offering at the **a** time.
10:10 your **a** feasts and New Moon festivals
16: 2 had been **a** members of the council.
28: 2 'See that you present to me at the **a**
29:39 these for the LORD at your **a** feasts:
Dt 1:15 wise and respected men, and **a** them
Jos 4: 4 men he had **a** from the Israelites,
1Sa 8: 1 Samuel grew old, he **a** his sons as
12: 6 "It is the LORD who **a** Moses and
13:14 and **a** him leader of his people,
25:30 and has **a** him leader over Israel,
2Sa 6:21 he **a** me ruler over the LORD's people
7:11 ever since the time I **a** leaders over
15: 4 Absalom would add, "If only I were **a**
17:25 Absalom had **a** Amasa over the army in
18: 1 **a** over them commanders of thousands
1Ki 1:35 **a** him ruler over Israel and Judah."
12:31 **a** priests from all sorts of people,
13:33 but once more **a** priests for the high
2Ki 12:11 they gave the money to the men **a** to
17:32 but they also **a** all sorts of their
22: 5 Make them entrust it to the men **a** to
23: 5 He did away with the pagan priests **a**
25:22 Nebuchadnezzar king of Babylon **a**
25:23 Babylon had **a** Gedaliah as governor,
1Ch 15:17 the Levites **a** Heman son of Joel;
16: 4 He **a** some of the Levites to minister
17:10 ever since the time I **a** leaders over
22: 2 he **a** stonecutters to prepare dressed
23:31 New Moon festivals and at **a** feasts.
24: 3 for their **a** order of ministering.
24:19 This was their **a** order of

1Ch 26:10 his father had a him the first),
2Ch 2: 4 at the a feasts of the LORD our God.
8:14 he a the divisions of the priests
8:14 He also a the gatekeepers by
11:15 he a his own priests for the high
11:22 Rehoboam a Abijah son of Maacah to
19: 5 He a judges in the land, in each of
19: 8 In Jerusalem also, Jehoshaphat a
20:21 Jehoshaphat a men to sing to the
25:16 "Have we a you an adviser to the
31: 3 New Moons and a feasts as written in
32: 6 He a military officers over the
34:10 they entrusted it to the men a to
35: 2 He a the priests to their duties and
36:23 he has a me to build a temple for
Ezr 1: 2 he has a me to build a temple for
3: 5 all the a sacred feasts of the LORD,
5:14 Sheshbazzar, whom he had a governor,
Ne 5:14 when I was a to be their governor in
6: 7 have even a prophets to make this
7: 1 the singers and the Levites were a.
9:17 in their rebellion a a leader in
10:33 New Moon festivals and a feasts; for
12:44 At that time men were a to be in
Est 8: 2 And Esther a him over Haman's estate.
8:12 The day a for the Jews to do this in
9:27 way prescribed and at the time a.
Job 20:29 the heritage a for them by God."
30:23 to the place a for all the living.
34:13 Who a him over the earth? Who put
Ps 75: 2 You say, "I choose the a time; it is
102:13 favour to her; the a time has come.
Pr 8:23 I was a from eternity, from the
Isa 1:14 Your New Moon festivals and your a
Jer 1: 5 I a you as a prophet to the nations."
6:17 I a watchmen over you and said,
8: 7 Even the stork in the sky knows her a
14:14 I have not sent them or a them or
29:26 'The LORD has a you priest in place
33:20 no longer come at their a time,
40: 5 whom the king of Babylon has a over
40: 7 the king of Babylon had a Gedaliah
40:11 and had a Gedaliah son of Ahikam,
41: 2 had a as governor over the land.
41:10 guard had a Gedaliah son of Ahikam.
41:18 had a as governor over the land.
Lam 1: 4 for no-one comes to her a feasts.
2: 6 The LORD has made Zion forget her a
2: 7 LORD as on the day of an a feast.
Eze 21:11 "'The sword is a to be polished, to
36:38 at Jerusalem during her a feasts.
44:24 and my decrees for all my a feasts,
45:17 the a feasts of the house of Israel.
46: 9 before the LORD at the a feasts,
46:11 "'At the festivals and the a feasts,
Da 1:11 chief official had a over Daniel,
2:24 whom the king had a to execute the
2:49 at Daniel's request the king a
5:11 a him chief of the magicians,
8:19 concerns the a time of the end.
11:27 end will still come at the a time.
11:29 "At the a time he will invade the
11:35 it will still come at the a time.
Hos 2:11 her Sabbath days—all her a feasts.
6:11 "Also for you, Judah, a harvest is a.
9: 5 What will you do on the day of your a
12: 9 as in the days of your a feasts.
Mic 6: 9 "Heed the rod and the One who a it.
Hab 1:12 O LORD, you have a them to execute
2: 3 For the revelation awaits an a time;
Zep 2: 2 before the a time arrives and that
3:18 "The sorrows for the a feasts I will
Mt 8:29 to torture us before the a time?"
26:18 Teacher says: My a time is near.
Mk 3:14 He a twelve—designating them
3:16 These are the twelve he a: Simon (to
Lk 10: 1 After this the Lord a seventy-two
12:14 Jesus replied, "Man, who a me a
19:12 himself a king and then to return.
Jn 15:16 but I chose you and a you to go and
Ac 3:20 who has been a for you—even Jesus.
10:42 whom God a as judge of the living
12:21 On the a day Herod, wearing his
13:48 were a for eternal life believed.
14:23 Paul and Barnabas a elders for them
15: 2 So Paul and Barnabas were a, along
Ac 17:31 with justice by the man he has a.
Ro 9: 9 "At the a time I will return, and
1Co 4: 5 judge nothing before the a time; wait
12:28 in the church God has a first of all
Eph 1:22 a him to be head over everything for
1Ti 2: 7 for this purpose I was a a herald
2Ti 1:11 of this gospel I was a a herald and
Tit 1: 3 at his a season he brought his word
Heb 1: 2 whom he a heir of all things, and
3: 2 He was faithful to the one who a him,
5: 1 is a to represent them in matters
7:28 which came after the law, a the Son,
8: 3 Every high priest is a to offer both

Appointing (Appoint)

Ezr 3: 8 a Levites twenty years of age and
1Ti 1:12 me faithful, a me to his service.

Appointment (Appoint)

2Ch 31:13 by a of King Hezekiah and Azariah

Appoints (Appoint)

Jer 31:35 This is what the LORD says, he who a
Heb 7:28 For the law a as high priests men

Apportioned (Portion)

Dt 4:19 a to all the nations under heaven.
Eph 4: 7 grace has been given as Christ a it.

Appraised

Job 28:27 he looked at wisdom and a it; he

Apprehensive

Lk 21:26 Men will faint from terror, a of

Approach (Approached, Approaches, Approaching)

Ex 19:22 Even the priests, who a the LORD,
24: 2 Moses alone is to a the LORD; the
28:43 a the altar to minister in the Holy
30:20 Also, when they a the altar to
Lev 10: 3 "'Among those who a me I will show
18: 6 "'No-one is to a any close relative
18:19 "'Do not a a woman to have sexual
21:23 go near the curtain or a the altar,
1Sa 10: 5 As you a the town, you will meet a
Job 31:37 step; like a prince I would a him.
36:33 even the cattle make known its a.
40:19 his Maker can a him with his sword.
41:13 coat? Who would a him with a bridle?
Ecc 12: 1 and the years a when you will say,
Isa 5:19 Let it a, let the plan of the Holy
41: 5 They a and come forward;
Lam 2: 3 right hand at the a of the enemy.
Eze 42:13 where the priests who a the LORD
Hos 7: 6 they a him with intrigue. Their
Eph 3:12 a God with freedom and confidence.
Heb 4:16 Let us then a the throne of grace

Approached (Approach)

Ge 18:23 Abraham a him and said: "Will you
33: 3 seven times as he a his brother.
33: 6 the maidservants and their children a
Ex 14:10 Pharaoh a, the Israelites looked up,
20:21 a the thick darkness where God was.
32:19 Moses a the camp and saw the calf
40:32 the Tent of Meeting or a the altar,
Lev 16: 1 Aaron who died when they a the LORD.
Nu 3:38 Anyone else who a the sanctuary was
27: 1 Hoglah, Milcah and Tirzah. They a
Dt 22:14 "I married this woman, but when I a
Jos 8:11 a the city and arrived in front of
14: 6 Now the men of Judah a Joshua at
21: 1 Now the family heads of the Levites a
Jdg 3:20 Ehud then a him while he was sitting
9:52 But as he a the entrance to the
14: 5 As they a the vineyards of Timnah,
15:14 he a Lehi, the Philistines came
Ru 3: 7 Ruth a quietly, uncovered his feet
1Sa 9:18 Saul a Samuel in the gateway and
17:40 sling in his hand, a the Philistine.
30:21 David and his men a, he greeted them.
2Sa 15: 5 Also, whenever anyone a him to bow
2Sa 16: 5 King David a Bahurim, a man from the
2Ki 16:12 a it and presented offerings on it.
1Ch 21:21 David a, and when Araunah looked and
Est 5: 2 a and touched the tip of the sceptre.
Jer 42: 1 from the least to the greatest a
Da 3:26 Nebuchadnezzar then a the opening of
7:13 He a the Ancient of Days and was led
7:16 I a one of those standing there and
Mt 14:15 evening a, the disciples came to him
17:14 they came to the crowd, a man a
21: 1 they a Jerusalem and came to
21:34 the harvest time a, he sent his
27:57 evening a, there came a rich man
Mk 11: 1 they a Jerusalem and came to
15:42 So as evening a,
Lk 7:12 he a the town gate, a dead person
9:51 the time a for him to be taken up to
18:35 Jesus a Jericho, a blind man was
19:29 he a Bethphage and Bethany at the
19:41 he a Jerusalem and saw the city, he
22:47 He a Jesus to kiss him,
24:28 they a the village to which they

Approaches (Approach)

Lev 20:16 "'If a woman a an animal to have
Nu 3:10 a the sanctuary must be put to death.
Dt 23:11 as evening a he is to wash himself,
2Ki 11: 8 Anyone who a your ranks must be put
Est 4:11 any man or woman who a the king in

Approaching (Approach)

Ge 24:63 as he looked up, he saw camels a.
Lev 18:14 a his wife to have sexual relations;
2Ki 9:17 in Jezreel saw Jehu's troops a,
Lk 22: 1 Bread, called the Passover, was a,
Jn 1:47 Jesus saw Nathanael a, he said of
6:19 they saw Jesus a the boat, walking
Ac 10: 9 on their journey and a the city,
27:27 the sailors sensed they were a land.
Heb 10:25 all the more as you see the Day a.
1Jn :14 is the confidence we have in a God:

Appropriate

Ge 49:28 giving each the blessing a to him.
1Ti 2:10 a for women who profess to worship

Approval (Approve)

Jdg 18: 6 Your journey has the LORD's a."
Est 2:17 a more than any of the other virgins.
Hos 8: 4 they choose princes without my a.
Jn 6:27 Father has placed his seal of a."
Ac 8: 1 Saul was there, giving a to his
22:20 I stood there giving my a and
1Co 11:19 to show which of you have God's a.
Gal 1:10 Am I now trying to win the a of men,

Approve (Approval, Approved, Approves)

1Sa 29: 6 you, but the rulers don't a of you.
Ps 49:13 followers, who a their sayings.
Lk 11:48 you testify that you a of what your
Ro 1:32 also a of those who practise them.
2:18 if you know his will and a of what
12: 2 Then you will be able to test and a
1Co 16: 3 of introduction to the men you a

Approved (Approve)

Ro 14:18 way is pleasing to God and a by men.
16:10 Greet Apelles, tested and a in
2Co 10:18 one who commends himself who is a,
1Th 2: 4 On the contrary, we speak as men a
2Ti 2:15 to present yourself to God as one a,

Approves (Approve)

Ro 14:22 not condemn himself by what he a.

Aprons

Ac 19:12 handkerchiefs and a that had touched

Apt (Aptitude, Aptly)

Pr 15:23 A man finds joy in giving an a reply

Aptitude (Apt)

Da 1: 4 showing a for every kind of learning

Aptly (Apt)
Pr 25:11 A word a spoken is like apples of

Aqueduct
2Ki 18:17 stopped at the a of the Upper Pool,
Isa 7: 3 to meet Ahaz at the end of the a of
36: 2 When the commander stopped at the a

Aquila See Priscilla
Ac 18: 2 There he met a Jew named A, a native
18:18 accompanied by Priscilla and A.
18:19 where Paul left Priscilla and A.
18:26 When Priscilla and A heard him, they
Ro 16: 3 Greet Priscilla and A, my
1Co 16:19 A and Priscilla greet you warmly in
2Ti 4:19 Greet Priscilla and A and the

Ar
Nu 21:15 A and lie along the border of Moab."
21:28 It consumed A of Moab, the citizens
Dt 2: 9 I have given A to the descendants of
2:18 to pass by the region of Moab at A.
2:29 and the Moabites, who live in A, did
Isa 15: 1 A in Moab is ruined, destroyed in a

Ara
1Ch 7:38 of Jether: Jephunneh, Pispah and A.

Arab (Arabia, Arabian, Arabs)
Jos 15:52 A, Dumah, Eshan,
Ne 2:19 and Geshem the A heard about it,
6: 1 Tobiah, Geshem the A and the rest of
Isa 13:20 no A will pitch his tent there,

Arabah (Beth Arabah)
Valley stretching from Mount Hermon in the north to the Gulf of Aqaba in the south, including the Sea of Galilee, River Jordan and Dead Sea. On their journey to the promised land, the Israelites travelled and camped in this region (Dt 2:8). Sea of Arabah (Dt 3:17, etc) = Dead Sea.

Dt 1: 1 in the A—opposite Suph, between
1: 7 the neighbouring peoples in the A,
2: 8 We turned from the A road, which
3:17 border was the Jordan in the A,
3:17 from Kinnereth to the Sea of the A
4:49 included all the A east of the
4:49 the A, below the slopes of Pisgah.
11:30 in the A in the vicinity of Gilgal.
Jos 3:16 flowing down to the Sea of the A
8:14 a certain place overlooking the A.
11: 2 in the A south of Kinnereth, in the
11:16 the western foothills, the A and the
12: 1 all the eastern side of the A:
12: 3 He also ruled over the eastern A
12: 3 to the Sea of the A (the Salt Sea),
12: 8 the western foothills, the A, the
1Sa 23:24 of Maon, in the A south of Jeshimon.
2Sa 2:29 and his men marched through the A.
4: 7 travelled all night by way of the A.
2Ki 14:25 Lebo Hamath to the Sea of the A,
25: 4 They fled towards the A,
Isa 33: 9 Sharon is like the A, and Bashan and
Jer 39: 4 two walls, and headed towards the A.
52: 7 They fled towards the A,
Eze 47: 8 into the A, where it enters the Sea.
Am 6:14 Lebo Hamath to the valley of the A."
Zec 14:10 Jerusalem, will become like the A.

Arabia (Arab)
2Ch 9:14 Also all the kings of A and the
Isa 21:13 An oracle concerning A: You caravans
21:13 who camp in the thickets of A,
Jer 25:24 all the kings of A and all the kings
Eze 27:21 "'A and all the princes of Kedar
30: 5 Cush and Put, Lydia and all A, Libya
Gal 1:17 A and later returned to Damascus.
4:25 Now Hagar stands for Mount Sinai in A

Arabian (Arab)
1Ki 10:15 traders and from all the A kings and

Arabs (Arab)
2Ch 17:11 and the A brought him flocks: seven
21:16 the A who lived near the Cushites.
22: 1 who came with the A into the camp,
26: 7 against the A who lived in Gur Baal
Ne 4: 7 when Sanballat, Tobiah, the A, the
Ac 2:11 Cretans and A—we hear them

Arad
Nu 21: 1 the Canaanite king of A, who lived
33:40 The Canaanite king of A, who lived
Jos 12:14 the king of Hormah one the king of A
Jdg 1:16 Desert of Judah in the Negev near A.
1Ch 8:15 Zebadiah, A, Eder,

Arah
Jos 13: 4 from A of the Sidonians as far as
1Ch 7:39 The sons of Ulla: A, Hanniel and
Ezr 2: 5 of A 775
Ne 6:18 son-in-law to Shecaniah son of A,
7:10 of A 652

Aram (Aramaic, Aramean, Arameans)
Region north of Palestine, from Lebanon to beyond the River Euphrates. Known also as Paddan Aram and Aram Naharaim and by its Greek name Syria. Named after son of Shem (Ge 10:22), whose descendants spread rapidly around this area. Rebekah, Leah, Rachel and Jacob lived here (Ge 25:20; 27:43–44; 28:2; 29:16–28). Balaam came from here (Nu 23:7; Dt 23:4). The Israelites often served its gods (Jdg 10:6; 2Ch 28:23), and suffered at the hand of its army (1Ki 11:25; 2Ki 6:8; 13:4). At one stage Judah and Syria teamed up against Israel (1Ki 15:18–20) but at other times Israel and Syria joined together against Judah (2Ki 16:5). Its downfall was prophesied (Isa 7:1–8; Am 1:5). Roman province in NT times (Mt 4:24) of which Quirinius was governor (Lk 2:2). Paul travelled through here (Ac 15:41; 18:18; 21:3).

Ge 10:22 Elam, Asshur, Arphaxad, Lud and A.
10:23 The sons of A: Uz, Hul, Gether and
22:21 brother, Kemuel (the father of A),
Nu 23: 7 "Balak brought me from A, the king
Jdg 3:10 king of A into the hands of Othniel,
10: 6 and the gods of A, the gods of Sidon,
2Sa 15: 8 servant was living at Geshur in A,
1Ki 11:25 in A and was hostile towards Israel.
15:18 of A, who was ruling in Damascus.
19:15 there, anoint Hazael king over A.
20: 1 Now Ben-Hadad king of A mustered his
20:20 But Ben-Hadad king of A escaped on
20:22 king of A will attack you again."
20:23 the officials of the king of A
22: 1 was no war between A and Israel.
22: 3 to retake it from the king of A?"
22:31 Now the king of A had ordered his
2Ki 5: 1 of the army of the king of A.
5: 1 him the LORD had given victory to A.
5: 2 Now bands from A had gone out and
5: 5 "By all means, go," the king of A
6: 8 Now the king of A was at war with
6:11 This enraged the king of A. He
6:23 A stopped raiding Israel's territory.
6:24 Some time later, Ben-Hadad king of A
8: 7 and Ben-Hadad king of A was ill.
8: 9 "Your son Ben-Hadad king of A has
8:13 become king of A," answered Elisha.
8:28 Hazael king of A at Ramoth Gilead.
8:29 in his battle with Hazael king of A.
9:14 Gilead against Hazael king of A,
9:15 in the battle with Hazael king of A.
12:17 About this time Hazael king of A
12:18 A, who then withdrew from Jerusalem.
13: 3 king of A and Ben-Hadad his son.
13: 4 the king of A was oppressing Israel.
13: 5 they escaped from the power of A.
13: 7 for the king of A had destroyed the
13:17 of victory over A!" Elisha declared.
13:19 A and completely destroyed it.
13:22 Hazael king of A oppressed Israel
13:24 Hazael king of A died, and Ben-Hadad
15:37 LORD began to send Rezin king of A
16: 5 Rezin king of A and Pekah son of
2Ki 16: 6 At that time, Rezin king of A
16: 6 A by driving out the men of Judah.
16: 7 me out of the hand of the king of A
1Ch 1:17 Elam, Asshur, Arphaxad, Lud and A.
1:17 of A: Uz, Hul, Gether and Meshech.
2:23 (But Geshur and A captured Havvoth
7:34 Shomer: Ahi, Rohgah, Hubbah and A.
2Ch 16: 2 of A, who was ruling in Damascus.
16: 7 "Because you relied on the king of A
16: 7 of A has escaped from your hand.
18:30 Now the king of A had ordered his
22: 5 Hazael king of A at Ramoth Gilead.
22: 6 in his battle with Hazael king of A.
24:23 the army of A marched against Joash;
28: 5 God handed him over to the king of A.
28:23 "Since the gods of the kings of A
Isa 7: 1 was king of Judah, King Rezin of A
7: 2 Now the house of David was told, "A
7: 4 and A and of the son of Remaliah.
7: 5 A, Ephraim and Remaliah's son have
7: 8 for the head of A is Damascus, and
17: 3 the remnant of A will be like the
Eze 27:16 "'A did business with you because of
Hos 12:12 Jacob fled to the country of A;
Am 1: 5 The people of A will go into exile

Aram Maacah
1Ch 19: 6 from Aram Naharaim, A and Zobah.

Aram Naharaim See Aram; Mesopotamia
Ge 24:10 He set out for A and made his way to
Dt 23: 4 in A to pronounce a curse on you.
Jdg 3: 8 of Cushan-Rishathaim king of A,
1Ch 19: 6 from A, Aram Maacah and Zobah.
Ps 60: T For teaching. When he fought A and

Aram Zobah
Ps 60: T When he fought Aram Naharaim and A,

Aramaic (Aram)
2Ki 18:26 in A, since we understand it.
Ezr 4: 7 in A script and in the A language.
Isa 36:11 in A, since we understand it.
Da 2: 4 astrologers answered the king in A,
Jn 5: 2 which in A is called Bethesda and
19:13 Pavement (which in A is Gabbatha).
19:17 (which in A is called Golgotha).
19:20 was written in A, Latin and Greek.
20:16 A, "Rabboni!" (which means Teacher).
Ac 21:40 all silent, he said to them in A:
22: 2 they heard him speak to them in A,
26:14 I heard a voice saying to me in A,

Aramean (Aram)
Ge 25:20 of Bethuel the A from Paddan Aram
25:20 Aram and sister of Laban the A.
28: 5 to Laban son of Bethuel the A, the
31:20 Moreover, Jacob deceived Laban the A
31:24 God came to Laban the A in a dream
Dt 26: 5 "My father was a wandering A, and he
2Sa 8: 6 He put garrisons in the A kingdom of
10: 6 they hired twenty thousand A foot
1Ki 20:29 on the A foot soldiers in one day.
2Ki 5:20 master was too easy on Naaman, this A
7:10 "We went into the A camp and not a
7:14 the king sent them after the A army.
24: 2 The LORD sent Babylonian, A, Moabite
1Ch 7:14 descendant through his A concubine.
18: 6 He put garrisons in the A kingdom of
2Ch 24:24 Although the A army had come with
Jer 35:11 escape the Babylonian and A armies.

Arameans (Aram)
2Sa 8: 5 the A of Damascus came to help
8: 6 and the A became subject to him and
10: 8 while the A of Zobah and Rehob and
10: 9 and deployed them against the A.
10:11 Joab said, "If the A are too strong
10:13 the A, and they fled before him.
10:14 the Ammonites saw that the A were
10:15 After the A saw that they had been
10:16 Hadadezer had A brought from beyond
10:17 The A formed their battle lines to

2Sa 10:19 So the A were afraid to help the
1Ki 10:29 kings of the Hittites and of the A.
20:20 At that, the A fled, with the
20:21 and inflicted heavy losses on the A.
20:26 spring Ben-Hadad mustered the A
20:27 while the A covered the countryside.
20:28 'Because the A think the LORD is a
22:11 the A until they are destroyed.'"
22:35 up in his chariot facing the A.
2Ki 6: 9 because the A are going down there."
7: 4 to the camp of the A and surrender.
7: 5 up and went to the camp of the A.
7: 6 for the Lord had caused the A to
7:12 tell you what the A have done to us.
7:15 equipment the A had thrown away in
7:16 out and plundered the camp of the A.
8:28 The A wounded Joram;
8:29 to recover from the wounds the A had
9:15 to recover from the wounds the A had
13:17 completely destroy the A at Aphek."
1Ch 18: 5 the A of Damascus came to help
18: 6 and the A became subject to him and
19:10 and deployed them against the A.
19:12 Joab said, "If the A are too strong
19:14 the A, and they fled before him.
19:15 the Ammonites saw that the A were
19:16 After the A saw that they had been
19:16 they sent messengers and had A
19:17 David formed his lines to meet the A
19:19 So the A were not willing to help
2Ch 1:17 kings of the Hittites and of the A.
18:10 the A until they are destroyed.'"
18:34 chariot facing the A until evening.
22: 5 The A wounded Joram;
24:25 the A withdrew, they left Joash
28: 5 The A defeated him and took many of
Isa 9:12 A from the east and Philistines from
Am 9: 7 from Caphtor and the A from Kir?

Aran
Ge 36:28 The sons of Dishan: Uz and A.
1Ch 1:42 The sons of Dishan: Uz and A.

Ararat, Mountains of
Range between Black Sea and Caspian Sea, from which streams converged to form Rivers Tigris and Euphrates. Traditionally the resting place of Noah's ark (Ge 8:4). Sennacherib's two sons fled here after murdering him (2Ki 19:37; Isa 37:38). One of the kingdoms God would use to punish Babylon (Jer 51:24–27).

Ge 8: 4 came to rest on the mountains of A.
2Ki 19:37 and they escaped to the land of A.
Isa 37:38 and they escaped to the land of A.
Jer 51:27 kingdoms: A, Minni and Ashkenaz.

Araunah
2Sa 24:16 threshing-floor of A the Jebusite.
24:18 threshing-floor of A the Jebusite."
24:20 A looked and saw the king and his
24:21 A said, "Why has my lord the king
24:22 A said to David, "Let my lord the
24:23 O king, A gives all this to the king.
24:23 A also said to him, "May the LORD
24:24 the king replied to A, "No, I insist
1Ch 21:15 threshing-floor of A the Jebusite.
21:18 threshing-floor of A the Jebusite.
21:20 While A was threshing wheat, he
21:21 David approached, and when A looked
21:23 A said to David, "Take it! Let my
21:24 King David replied to A, "No, I
21:25 David paid A six hundred shekels of
21:28 threshing-floor of A the Jebusite,
2Ch 3: 1 It was on the threshing-floor of A

Arba
Jos 14:15 to be called Kiriath Arba after A,
15:13 (A was the forefather of Anak.)
21:11 (A was the forefather of Anak.)

Arbathite
2Sa 23:31 Abi-Albon the A, Azmaveth the
1Ch 11:32 the ravines of Gaash, Abiel the A,

Arbite
2Sa 23:35 Hezro the Carmelite, Paarai the A,

Arbiter (Arbitrate)
Lk 12:14 me a judge or an a between you?"

Arbitrate (Arbiter)
Job 9:33 If only there were someone to a

Archangel (Angel)
1Th 4:16 with the voice of the a and with the
Jude : 9 even the a Michael, when he was

Archelaus
Mt 2:22 when he heard that A was reigning in

Archer (Archers)
Ge 21:20 lived in the desert and became an a.
Pr 26:10 Like an a who wounds at random is he
Jer 51: 3 Let not the a string his bow, nor
Am 2:15 The a will not stand his ground, the

Archers (Archer)
Ge 49:23 With bitterness a attacked him; they
1Sa 31: 3 and when the a overtook him, they
2Sa 11:24 the a shot arrows at your servants
1Ch 10: 3 a overtook him, they wounded him.
2Ch 35:23 A shot King Josiah, and he told his
Job 16:13 his a surround me. Without pity, he
Isa 66:19 Libyans and Lydians (famous as a),
Jer 4:29 At the sound of horsemen and a every
50:29 "Summon a against Babylon, all those

Archippus
Col 4:17 Tell A: "See to it that you complete
Phm : 2 to Apphia our sister, to A our

Architect
Heb 11:10 whose a and builder is God.

Archives
Ezr 4:15 that a search may be made in the a
5:17 let a search be made in the royal a
6: 1 a stored in the treasury at Babylon.

Ard (Ardite)
Ge 46:21 Ehi, Rosh, Muppim, Huppim and A.
Nu 26:40 The descendants of Bela through A
26:40 A and Naaman were: through A,

Ardent
2Co 7: 7 your deep sorrow, your a concern for

Ardite (Ard)
Nu 26:40 through Ard, the A clan; through

Ardon
1Ch 2:18 were her sons: Jesher, Shobab and A.

Area (Areas)
Ge 25:18 His descendants settled in the a
34: 2 the ruler of that a, saw her, he
Ex 10:14 a of the country in great numbers.
Lev 10:17 in the sanctuary a? It is most holy;
10:18 in the sanctuary a, as I commanded."
13:33 be shaved except for the diseased a,
16: 3 Aaron is to enter the sanctuary a:
Nu 8: 2 the a in front of the lampstand.'"
35: 5 have this a as pasture-land for the
Jos 13: 5 the a of the Gebalites; and all
19:46 Me Jarkon and Rakkon, with the a
Jdg 19: 1 Now a Levite who lived in a remote a
19:18 to a remote a in the hill country of
1Sa 9: 4 and through the a around Shalisha,
14:14 men in an a of about half an acre.
23:23 will go with you; if he is in the a,
27: 9 Whenever David attacked an a, he did
2Sa 5: 9 He built up the a around it, from
1Ch 5: 8 a from Aroer to Nebo and Baal Meon.
Ne 12:29 from Beth Gilgal, and from the a of
Eze 40: 5 completely surrounding the temple a.
41: 9 The open a between the side rooms of
Eze 41:11 to the side rooms from the open a,
41:11 a was five cubits wide all round.
41:20 From the floor to the a above the
42:15 what was inside the temple a,
42:15 gate and measured the a all around:
42:20 he measured the a on all four sides.
43:12 All the surrounding a on top of the
43:21 the temple a outside the sanctuary.
45: 1 wide; the entire a will be holy.
45: 5 An a 25,000 cubits long and 10,000
45: 6 the city as its property an a 5,
45: 7 the a formed by the sacred district
48:15 "The remaining a, 5,000 cubits wide
48:18 What remains of the a, bordering on
48:21 "What remains on both sides of the a
48:22 of the a that belongs to the prince.
48:22 The a belonging to the prince will
Mt 4:13 in the a of Zebulun and Naphtali—
21:12 Jesus entered the temple a and drove
21:15 shouting in the temple a, "Hosanna
Mk 5:10 again not to send them out of the a.
11:15 Jesus entered the temple a and began
Lk 4:37 spread throughout the surrounding a.
19:45 he entered the temple a and began
Jn 2:15 and drove all from the temple a,
8:20 while teaching in the temple a
10:23 Jesus was in the temple a walking in
11:56 and as they stood in the temple a
Ac 16: 3 of the Jews who lived in that a,
20: 2 He travelled through that a,
21:28 a and defiled this holy place."
21:29 had brought him into the temple a.)
2Co 10:15 our a of activity among you will

Areas (Area)
Jos 13: 1 large a of land to be taken over.
14: 1 Now these are the a the Israelites
Jdg 19:29 sent them into all the a of Israel.
1Ki 20:34 "You may set up your own market a in
2Ch 27: 4 forts and towers in the wooded a.
Eze 48:21 Both these a running the length of

Areli (Arelite)
Ge 46:16 Shuni, Ezbon, Eri, Arodi and A.
Nu 26:17 clan; through A, the Arelite clan.

Arelite (Areli)
Nu 26:17 clan; through Areli, the A clan.

Arena
1Co 4: 9 like men condemned to die in the a.

Areopagus
Ac 17:19 brought him to a meeting of the A,
17:22 up in the meeting of the A and said:
17:34 a member of the A, also a woman

Aretas
2Co 11:32 In Damascus the governor under King A

Argob
Dt 3: 4 region of A, Og's kingdom in Bashan.
3:13 (The whole region of A in Bashan
3:14 took the whole region of A as far as
1Ki 4:13 as well as the district of A in
2Ki 15:25 along with A and Arieh, in the

Argue (Argued, Arguing, Argument, Arguments)
Jdg 18:25 The Danites answered, "Don't a with
Job 9:14 How can I find words to a with him?
13: 3 Almighty and to a my case with God.
13: 8 Will you a the case for God?
15: 3 Would he a with useless words, with
Pr 25: 9 If you a your case with a neighbour,
Isa 43:26 Review the past for me, let us a the
Jn 6:52 the Jews began to a sharply among
Ac 6: 9 These men began to a with Stephen,
Ro 3: 7 Someone might a, "If my falsehood

Argued (Argue)
1Ki 3:22 And so they a before the king.
Mk 9:34 had a about who was the greatest.
Ac 23: 9 Pharisees stood up and a vigorously.

Arguing (Argue)
2Sa 19: 9 the people were all **a** with each
Job 16: 3 What ails you that you keep on **a**?
Mk 9:14 the teachers of the law **a** with them.
9:16 "What are you **a** with them about?" he
9:33 "What were you **a** about on the road?
Ac 19: 8 **a** persuasively about the kingdom of
24:12 My accusers did not find me **a** with
Php 2:14 everything without complaining or **a**,

Argument (Argue)
Job 13: 6 Hear now my **a**; listen to the plea of
Lk 9:46 An **a** started among the disciples as
Jn 3:25 An **a** developed between some of
Ro 3: 5 wrath on us? (I am using a human **a**.)
Heb 6:16 is said and puts an end to all **a**.

Arguments (Argue)
Job 6:25 words! But what do your **a** prove?
23: 4 before him and fill my mouth with **a**.
32:12 none of you has answered his **a**.
32:14 I will not answer him with your **a**.
Isa 41:21 "Set forth your **a**," says Jacob's
59: 4 They rely on empty **a** and speak lies;
2Co 10: 5 We demolish **a** and every pretension
Col 2: 4 may deceive you by fine-sounding **a**.
2Ti 2:23 to do with foolish and stupid **a**,
Tit 3: 9 and **a** and quarrels about the law,

Arid
Mt 12:43 it goes through **a** places seeking
Lk 11:24 it goes through **a** places seeking

Aridai
Est 9: 9 Parmashta, Arisai, **A** and Vaizatha,

Aridatha
Est 9: 8 Poratha, Adalia, **A**,

Arieh
2Ki 15:25 along with Argob and **A**, in the

Ariel
Ezr 8:16 I summoned Eliezer, **A**, Shemaiah,
Isa 29: 1 Woe to you, **A**, **A**, the city where
29: 2 Yet I will besiege **A**; she will mourn
29: 7 the nations that fight against **A**,

Aright (Right)
Ps 90:12 Teach us to number our days **a**, that

Arimathea
Mt 27:57 there came a rich man from **A**, named
Mk 15:43 Joseph of **A**, a prominent member of
Lk 23:51 He came from the Judean town of **A**
Jn 19:38 Later, Joseph of **A** asked Pilate for

Arioch
Ge 14: 1 **A** king of Ellasar, Kedorlaomer king
14: 9 Amraphel king of Shinar and **A** king
Da 2:14 **A**, the commander of the king's guard,
2:15 **A** then explained the matter to Daniel.
2:24 Daniel went to **A**, whom the king had
2:25 **A** took Daniel to the king at once

Arisai
Est 9: 9 Parmashta, **A**, Aridai and Vaizatha,

Arise (Rise)
Nu 23:18 he uttered his oracle: "**A**, Balak,
Jdg 5:12 **A**, O Barak! Take captive your
2Ch 6:41 "Now **a**, O LORD God, and come to
Est 4:14 the Jews will **a** from another place,
Ps 3: 7 **A**, O LORD! Deliver me, O my God!
7: 6 **A**, O LORD, in your anger; rise up
9:19 **A**, O LORD, let not man triumph; let
10:12 **A**, LORD! Lift up your hand, O God.
12: 5 needy, I will now **a**," says the LORD.
35: 2 Take up shield and buckler; **a** and
59: 4 **A** to help me; look on my plight!
68: 1 May God **a**, may his enemies be
73:20 so when you **a**, O Lord, you will
102:13 You will **a** and have compassion on
Ps 132: 8 **a**, O LORD, and come to your resting
Pr 31:28 Her children **a** and call her blessed;
SS 2:10 My lover spoke and said to me, "**A**,
2:13 **A**, come, my darling; my beautiful
Isa 33:10 "Now will I **a**," says the LORD. "Now
60: 1 "**A**, shine, for your light has come,
Jer 6: 4 "Prepare for battle against her! **A**,
6: 5 **a**, let us attack at night and
30:21 their ruler will **a** from among them.
49:28 "**A**, and attack Kedar and destroy the
49:31 "**A** and attack a nation at ease,
Lam 2:19 **A**, cry out in the night, as the
Da 7:24 After them another king will **a**,
8:23 king, a master of intrigue, will **a**.
11: 7 "One from her family line will **a** to
12: 1 who protects your people, will **a**.
Hab 2: 7 Will not your debtors suddenly **a**?
Ac 20:30 Even from your own number men will **a**
Ro 15:12 one who will **a** to rule over the

Arisen (Rise)
Dt 13:13 that wicked men have **a** among you and

Arises (Rise)
Ecc 10: 5 sort of error that **a** from a ruler:

Aristarchus
Ac 19:29 The people seized Gaius and **A**,
20: 4 **A** and Secundus from Thessalonica,
27: 2 **A**, a Macedonian from Thessalonica,
Col 4:10 My fellow-prisoner **A** sends you his
Phm :24 do Mark, **A**, Demas and Luke, my

Aristobulus
Ro 16:10 who belong to the household of **A**.

Ark[1]
Ge 6:14 make yourself an **a** of cypress wood;
6:15 it: The **a** is to be 450 feet long,
6:16 Make a roof for it and finish the **a**
6:16 Put a door in the side of the **a** and
6:18 and you will enter the **a**—you and
6:19 You are to bring into the **a** two of
7: 1 "Go into the **a**, you and your whole
7: 7 **a** to escape the waters of the flood.
7: 9 the **a**, as God had commanded Noah.
7:13 of his three sons, entered the **a**.
7:15 them came to Noah and entered the **a**.
7:17 lifted the **a** high above the earth.
7:18 and the **a** floated on the surface of
7:23 left, and those with him in the **a**.
8: 1 that were with him in the **a**,
8: 4 the **a** came to rest on the mountains
8: 6 the window he had made in the **a**
8: 9 so it returned to Noah in the **a**.
8: 9 brought it back to himself in the **a**.
8:10 again sent out the dove from the **a**.
8:13 removed the covering from the **a**
8:16 "Come out of the **a**, you and your
8:19 of the **a**, one kind after another.
9:10 all those that came out of the **a**
9:18 of the **a** were Shem, Ham and Japheth.
Mt 24:38 up to the day Noah entered the **a**;
Lk 17:27 up to the day Noah entered the **a**.
Heb 11: 7 fear built an **a** to save his family.
1Pe 3:20 of Noah while the **a** was being built.

Ark[2] (*Ark of God, Ark of the covenant, Ark of the Lord, Ark of the Testimony*)
Ex 25:15 to remain in the rings of this **a**;
25:16 put in the **a** the Testimony, which I
25:21 Place the cover on top of the **a** and
25:21 **a** and put in the **a** the Testimony,
35:12 the **a** with its poles and the
37: 1 Bezalel made the **a** of acacia
37: 5 on the sides of the **a** to carry it.
40: 3 and shield the **a** with the curtain.
40:20 Testimony and placed it in the **a**,
40:20 attached the poles to the **a** and put
40:21 he brought the **a** into the tabernacle
Lev 16: 2 of the atonement cover on the **a**,
Nu 3:31 responsible for the care of the **a**,
10:35 Whenever the **a** set out, Moses said,
Nu 14:44 though neither Moses nor the **a** of
Dt 10: 3 I made the **a** out of acacia wood and
10: 5 put the tablets in the **a** I had made,
Jos 3: 4 you and the **a**; do not go near it."
3:15 carried the **a** reached the Jordan
4:10 Now the priests who carried the **a**
6: 4 of rams' horns in front of the **a**.
6: 8 blowing their trumpets, and the **a** of
6: 9 and the rear guard followed the **a**.
6:11 he had the **a** of the LORD carried
1Sa 4: 3 **a** of the LORD's covenant from Shiloh,
4: 5 the **a** of the LORD's covenant came
5: 2 they carried the **a** into Dagon's
5: 7 "The **a** of the god of Israel must not
5: 8 "What shall we do with the **a** of the
5: 8 **a** of the god of Israel moved to Gath.
5: 8 moved the **a** of the God of Israel.
5:10 "They have brought the **a** of the god
5:11 "Send the **a** of the god of Israel
6: 3 They answered, "If you return the **a**
6:13 the **a**, they rejoiced at the sight.
6:20 To whom will the **a** go up from here?"
7: 2 twenty years in all, that the **a**
2Sa 6: 2 the cherubim that are on the **a**.
11:11 Uriah said to David, "The **a** and
1Ki 2:26 because you carried the **a** of the
3:15 stood before the **a** of the Lord's
8: 1 to bring up the **a** of the LORD's
8: 3 arrived, the priests took up the **a**,
8: 5 about him were before the **a**,
8: 6 The priests then brought the **a** of
8: 7 their wings over the place of the **a**
8: 7 the **a** and its carrying poles.
8: 9 There was nothing in the **a** except
8:21 provided a place there for the **a**,
1Ch 6:31 LORD after the **a** came to rest there.
13: 3 Let us bring the **a** of our God back
13: 6 **a** that is called by the Name.
13: 9 the **a**, because the oxen stumbled.
13:10 he had put his hand on the **a**.
13:13 He did not take the **a** to be with him
15:23 were to be doorkeepers for the **a**.
15:24 also to be doorkeepers for the **a**.
15:27 the Levites who were carrying the **a**,
2Ch 5: 2 to bring up the **a** of the LORD's
5: 4 arrived, the Levites took up the **a**,
5: 5 they brought up the **a** and the Tent
5: 6 about him were before the **a**,
5: 7 The priests then brought the **a** of
5: 8 their wings over the place of the **a**
5: 8 the **a** and its carrying poles.
5: 9 extending from the **a**, could be seen
5:10 There was nothing in the **a** except
6:11 There I have placed the **a**, in which
6:41 place, you and the **a** of your might.
35: 3 "Put the sacred **a** in the temple that
Ps 78:61 He sent the ark of his might into
132: 8 place, you and the **a** of your might.
Heb 9: 4 This **a** contained the gold jar of
9: 5 Above the **a** were the cherubim of the
Rev 11:19 was seen the **a** of his covenant.

Ark of God
1Sa 3: 3 temple of the LORD, where the **a** was.
4:11 The **a** was captured, and Eli's two
4:13 because his heart feared for the **a**.
4:17 dead, and the **a** has been captured."
4:18 he mentioned the **a**, Eli fell
4:19 When she heard the news that the **a**
4:21 of the capture of the **a**
4:22 Israel, for the **a** has been captured
5: 1 the Philistines had captured the **a**,
5:10 they sent the **a** to Ekron. As the **a**
14:18 Saul said to Ahijah, "Bring the **a**."
2Sa 6: 2 Judah to bring up from there the **a**,
6: 3 They set the **a** on a new cart and
6: 4 with the **a** on it, and Ahio was
6: 6 of the **a**, because the oxen stumbled.
6: 7 down and he died there beside the **a**.
6:12 everything he has, because of the **a**.
6:12 brought up the **a** from the house of
7: 2 while the **a** remains in a tent."
15:24 They set down the **a**, and Abiathar
15:25 the king said to Zadok, "Take the **a**
2Sa 15:29 Zadok and Abiathar took the **a** back

1Ch 13: 5 to bring the a from Kiriath Jearim.
13: 6 bring up from there the a the LORD,
13: 7 They moved the a from Abinadab's
13:12 "How can I ever bring the a to me?
13:14 The a remained with the family of
15: 1 prepared a place for the a and
15: 2 but the Levites may carry the a,
15:15 the Levites carried the a with the
15:24 were to blow trumpets before the a.
16: 1 They brought the a and set it inside
2Ch 1: 4 Now David had brought up the a from

Ark of the covenant

Nu 10:33 The a of the LORD went before them
Dt 10: 8 of Levi to carry the a of the LORD,
31: 9 the sons of Levi, who carried the a
31:25 who carried the a of the LORD:
31:26 beside the a of the LORD your God.
Jos 3: 3 "When you see the a of the LORD your
3: 6 Take up the a and pass on ahead of
3: 8 Tell the priests who carry the a:
3:11 See, the a of the Lord of all the
3:14 the priests carrying the a went ahead
3:17 The priests who carried the a of the
4: 7 cut off before the a of the LORD.
4: 9 priests who carried the a had stood.
4:18 river carrying the a of the LORD.
6: 6 "Take up the a of the LORD and make
8:33 on both sides of the a of the LORD,
Jdg 20:27 In those days the a of God was there,
1Sa 4: 4 and they brought back the a of the
4: 4 were there with the a of God.
2Sa 15:24 with him were carrying the a of God.
1Ki 6:19 to set the a of the LORD there.
1Ch 15:25 went to bring up the a of the LORD
15:26 who were carrying the a of the LORD,
15:28 all Israel brought up the a of the
15:29 the a of the LORD was entering the
16: 6 regularly before the a of God.
16:37 his associates before the a of the
17: 1 the a of the LORD is under a tent."
22:19 so that you may bring the a of the
28: 2 place of rest for the a of the LORD,
28:18 wings and shelter the a of the LORD.
Jer 3:16 no longer say, 'The a of the LORD.
Heb 9: 4 of incense and the gold-covered a.

Ark of the LORD

Jos 3:13 soon as the priests who carry the a
4: 5 said to them, "Go over before the a
4:11 the a and the priests came to the
6: 7 armed guard going ahead of the a."
6:11 had the a carried around the city,
6:12 and the priests took up the a.
6:13 the a and blowing the trumpets.
6:13 followed the a, while the trumpets
7: 6 face down to the ground before the a
1Sa 4: 6 that the a had come into the camp,
5: 3 his face on the ground before the a!
5: 4 his face on the ground before the a!
6: 1 a had been in Philistine territory
6: 2 "What shall we do with the a? Tell
6: 8 Take the a and put it on the cart,
6:11 They placed the a on the cart and
6:15 The Levites took down the a,
6:18 rock on which they set the a, is a
6:19 because they had looked into the a.
6:21 Philistines have returned the a.
7: 1 Jearim came and took up the a.
7: 1 Eleazar his son to guard the a.
2Sa 6: 9 "How can the a ever come to me?
6:10 He was not willing to take the a to
6:11 The a remained in the house of
6:13 those who were carrying the a had
6:15 Israel brought up the a with shouts
6:16 the a was entering the City of David,
6:17 They brought the a and set it in its
1Ki 8: 4 they brought up the a and the Tent
1Ch 15: 2 the LORD chose them to carry the a
15: 3 to bring up the a to the place he
15:12 yourselves and bring up the a,
15:14 bring up the a, the God of Israel.
16: 4 Levites to minister before the a,
2Ch 8:11 places the a has entered are holy."

Ark of the Testimony

Ex 25:22 two cherubim that are over the a,
26:33 and place the a behind the curtain.
26:34 Put the atonement cover on the a in
30: 6 of the curtain that is before the a
30:26 anoint the Tent of Meeting, the a,
31: 7 the Tent of Meeting, the a with the
39:35 the a with its poles and the
40: 3 Place the a in it and shield the ark
40: 5 altar of incense in front of the a
40:21 the a, as the LORD commanded him.
Nu 4: 5 curtain and cover the a with it.
7:89 above the atonement cover on the a.
Jos 4:16 "Command the priests carrying the a

Arkite (Arkites)

2Sa 15:32 Hushai the A was there to meet him,
16:16 Hushai the A, David's friend, went
17: 5 "Summon also Hushai the A, so that
17:14 advice of Hushai the A is better
1Ch 27:33 Hushai the A was the king's friend.

Arkites (Arkite)

Ge 10:17 Hivites, A, Sinites,
Jos 16: 2 the territory of the A in Ataroth,
1Ch 1:15 Hivites, A, Sinites,

Arm[1] (*Arm of the LORD*, Armrests, Arms, *Outstretched arm*)

Ex 15:16 By the power of your a they will be
Nu 11:23 "Is the LORD's a too short? You will
20:11 Moses raised his a and struck the
Dt 33:20 like a lion, tearing at a or head.
2Sa 1:10 the band on his a and have brought
2Ki 5:18 he is leaning on my a and I bow
7: 2 The officer on whose a the king was
7:17 the officer on whose a he leaned
2Ch 32: 8 With him is only the a of flesh, but
Job 26: 2 you have saved the a that is feeble!
31:22 let my a fall from the shoulder, let
35: 9 relief from the a of the powerful.
38:15 and their upraised a is broken.
40: 9 Do you have an a like God's, and can
Ps 10:15 Break the a of the wicked and evil
44: 3 nor did their a bring them victory;
44: 3 your a, and the light of your face,
77:15 With your mighty a you redeemed your
79:11 a preserve those condemned to die.
89:10 strong a you scattered your enemies.
89:13 Your a is endued with power; your
89:21 My hand will sustain him; surely my a
98: 1 his holy a have worked salvation
SS 2: 6 His left a is under my head, and his
2: 6 head, and his right a embraces me.
8: 3 His left a is under my head and his
8: 3 my head and his right a embraces me.
8: 6 like a seal on your a; for love is
Isa 17: 5 harvests the corn with his a—as
30:30 will make them see his a coming down
30:32 in battle with the blows of his a.
40:10 with power, and his a rules for him.
44:12 forges it with the might of his a.
48:14 his a will be against the Babylonians
50: 2 Was my a too short to ransom you? Do
51: 5 a will bring justice to the nations.
51: 5 to me and wait in hope for my a.
52:10 The LORD will lay bare his holy a
59:16 his own a worked salvation for him,
60: 4 your daughters are carried on the a
62: 8 his right hand and by his mighty a
63: 5 my own a worked salvation for me,
63:12 who sent his glorious a of power to
66:12 on her a and dandled on her knees.
Jer 21: 5 and a mighty a in anger and fury
48:25 Moab's horn is cut off; her a is
Eze 4: 7 with bared a prophesy against her.
17: 9 It will not take a strong a or many
30:21 "Son of man, I have broken the a of
30:22 the good a as well as the broken one,
Zec 11:17 May the sword strike his a and his
11:17 May his a be completely withered,
Lk 1:51 performed mighty deeds with his a;

Arm[2] (Armed, Armies, Armlets, Armour, Armour-bearer, Armour-bearers, Armoury, Arms, Army)

Nu 31: 3 Moses said to the people, "A some of
32:17 we are ready to a ourselves and go
32:20 "If you will do this—if you will a
1Pe 4: 1 a yourselves also with the same

Arm of the LORD/Lord

Isa 51: 9 O a; awake, as in days gone by, as
53: 1 and to whom has the a been revealed?
59: 1 Surely the a is not too short to
Jn 12:38 to whom has the a been revealed?"

Armageddon

Rev 16:16 place that in Hebrew is called A.

Armed (Arm[2])

Ex 13:18 went up out of Egypt a for battle.
Nu 31: 5 twelve thousand men a for battle, a
32:21 if all of you will go a over the
32:27 your servants, every man a for
32:29 every man a for battle, cross over
32:30 if they do not cross over with you a,
32:32 over before the LORD into Canaan a,
Dt 3:18 But all your able-bodied men, a for
Jos 1:14 but all your fighting men, fully a,
4:12 a, in front of the Israelites, as
4:13 About forty thousand a for battle
6: 3 the city once with all the a men.
6: 7 with the a guard going ahead of the
6: 9 The a guard marched ahead of the
6:13 The a men went ahead of them and the
Jdg 18:11 a for battle, set out from Zorah and
18:16 The six hundred Danites, a for
18:17 the six hundred a men stood at the
20: 2 thousand soldiers a with swords.
20:25 all of them a with swords.
20:35 Benjamites, all a with swords.
1Sa 2: 4 who stumbled are a with strength.
2Sa 21:16 and who was a with a new sword,
22:40 You a me with strength for battle;
2Ki 3:25 but men a with slings surrounded it
1Ch 12: 2 they were a with bows and were able
12:23 These are the numbers of the men a
12:24 6,800 a for battle;
12:37 a with every type of weapon—120,000.
20: 1 to war, Joab led out the a forces.
2Ch 14: 8 a with small shields and with bows.
17:17 200,000 men a with bows and shields;
17:18 next, Jehozabad, with 180,000 men a
Est 8:11 kill and annihilate any a force of
Ps 18:39 You a me with strength for battle;
65: 6 having a yourself with strength,
78: 9 The men of Ephraim, though a with
93: 1 in majesty and is a with strength.
Pr 6:11 a bandit and scarcity like an a man.
24:34 a bandit and scarcity like an a man.
Isa 15: 4 Therefore the a men of Moab cry out,
Jer 6:23 They are a with bow and spear; they
50:42 They are a with bows and spears;
Eze 38: 4 your horsemen fully a, and a great
Da 11:31 "His a forces will rise up to
Mt 26:47 With him was a large crowd a with
Mk 14:43 With him was a crowd a with swords
Lk 11:21 "When a strong man, fully a, guards

Armies (Arm[2])

Ex 14:20 coming between the a of Egypt and
Jdg 8:10 all that were left of the a of the
1Sa 17:26 defy the a of the living God?"
17:36 has defied the a of the living God.
17:45 a of Israel, whom you have defied.
1Ki 2: 5 to the two commanders of Israel's a,
Ps 44: 9 us; you no longer go out with our a.
60:10 us and no longer go out with our a?
68:12 "Kings and a flee in haste; in the
108:11 us and no longer go out with our a?
Isa 34: 2 his wrath is upon all their a.
Jer 35:11 escape the Babylonian and Aramean a.
Lk 21:20 see Jerusalem being surrounded by a,
Heb 11:34 in battle and routed foreign a.
Rev 19:14 The a of heaven were following him,
19:19 the kings of the earth and their a

Armlets (Arm[2])
Nu 31:50 **a**, bracelets, signet rings,

Armoni
2Sa 21: 8 the king took A and Mephibosheth,

Armour (Arm[2], Armour-bearer, Armour-bearers)
1Sa 14: 1 said to the young man bearing his **a**,
17: 5 wore a coat of scale **a** of bronze
17:38 He put a coat of **a** on him and a
31: 9 off his head and stripped off his **a**,
31:10 They put his **a** in the temple of the
1Ki 20:11 'One who puts on his **a** should not
22:34 Israel between the sections of his **a**.
1Ch 10: 9 him and took his head and his **a**,
10:10 They put his **a** in the temple of
2Ch 18:33 Israel between the sections of his **a**.
26:14 spears, helmets, coats of **a**, bows
Ne 4:16 with spears, shields, bows and **a**.
Isa 45: 1 him and to strip kings of their **a**,
Jer 46: 4 Polish your spears, put on your **a**!
51: 3 his bow, nor let him put on his **a**.
Lk 11:22 he takes away the **a** in which the man
Ro 13:12 darkness and put on the **a** of light.
Eph 6:11 Put on the full **a** of God so that you
6:13 Therefore put on the full **a** of God,

Armour-bearer (Arm[2], Armour)
Jdg 9:54 Hurriedly he called to his **a**, "Draw
1Sa 14: 6 Jonathan said to his young **a**, "Come,
14: 7 "Do all that you have in mind," his **a**
14:12 shouted to Jonathan and his **a**,
14:12 So Jonathan said to his **a**, "Climb
14:13 feet, with his **a** right behind him.
14:13 **a** followed and killed behind him.
14:14 his **a** killed some twenty men in an
14:17 and his **a** who were not there.
31: 4 Saul said to his **a**, "Draw your sword
31: 4 But the **a** was terrified and would
31: 5 the **a** saw that Saul was dead, he too
31: 6 Saul and his three sons and his **a**
2Sa 23:37 the **a** of Joab son of Zeruiah,
1Ch 10: 4 Saul said to his **a**, "Draw your sword
10: 4 But his **a** was terrified and would
10: 5 the **a** saw that Saul was dead, he too
11:39 the **a** of Joab son of Zeruiah,

Armour-bearers (Arm[2], Armour)
1Sa 16:21 much, and David became one of his **a**.
2Sa 18:15 ten of Joab's **a** surrounded Absalom,

Armoury (Arm[2])
2Ki 20:13 **a** and everything found among his
Ne 3:19 ascent to the **a** as far as the angle.
Isa 39: 2 the fine oil, his entire **a** and

Armrests (Arm[1])
1Ki 10:19 On both sides of the seat were **a**,
2Ch 9:18 On both sides of the seat were **a**,

Arms[1] (Arm[1])
Ge 16: 5 I put my servant in your **a**, and now
24:30 and the bracelets on his sister's **a**,
24:47 her nose and the bracelets on her **a**,
33: 4 **a** around his neck and kissed him.
45:14 he threw his **a** around his brother
46:29 he threw his **a** around his father and
48:14 and crossing his **a**, he put his left
49:24 his bow remained steady, his strong **a**
Nu 11:12 you tell me to carry them in my **a**,
Dt 33:27 underneath are the everlasting **a**.
Jdg 15:14 The ropes on his **a** became like
16:12 off his **a** as if they were threads.
2Sa 12: 3 his cup and even slept in his **a**.
12: 8 and your master's wives into your **a**.
22:35 my **a** can bend a bow of bronze
1Ki 17:19 He took him from her **a**, carried him
2Ki 4:16 "you will hold a son in your **a**.
Ps 18:34 my **a** can bend a bow of bronze
129: 7 nor the one who gathers fill his **a**.
Pr 31:17 her **a** are strong for her tasks.
31:20 She opens her **a** to the poor and
SS 5:14 His **a** are rods of gold set with
Isa 40:11 He gathers the lambs in his **a** and
49:22 will bring your sons in their **a**
Jer 38:12 under your **a** to pad the ropes.
Lam 2:12 lives ebb away in their mothers' **a**.
Eze 13:20 and I will tear them from your **a**;
16:11 jewellery: I put bracelets on your **a**
23:42 and they put bracelets on the **a** of
30:22 I will break both his **a**, the good
30:24 I will strengthen the **a** of the king
30:24 but I will break the **a** of Pharaoh,
30:25 I will strengthen the **a** of the king
30:25 but the **a** of Pharaoh will fall limp.
Da 2:32 its chest and **a** of silver, its belly
10: 6 his **a** and legs like the gleam of
Hos 11: 3 taking them by the **a**; but they did
Mk 9:36 Taking him in his **a**, he said to them,
10:16 he took the children in his **a**, put
Lk 2:28 Simeon took him in his **a** and praised
15:20 his **a** around him and kissed him.
Ac 20:10 young man and put his **a** around him.
Heb 12:12 Therefore, strengthen your feeble **a**

Arms[2] (Arm[2])
Jdg 6:35 calling them to **a**, and also into
10:17 the Ammonites were called to **a** and
2Sa 22:33 is God who **a** me with strength and
2Ki 3:21 young and old, who could bear **a** was
Ps 18:32 is God who **a** me with strength and
Eze 38: 8 many days you will be called to **a**.

Army (Arm[2])
Ex 14: 4 through Pharaoh and all his **a**,
14: 6 made ready and took his **a** with him.
14:17 glory through Pharaoh and all his **a**,
14:19 travelling in front of Israel's **a**
14:24 **a** and threw it into confusion.
14:28 the entire **a** of Pharaoh that had
15: 4 Pharaoh's chariots and his **a** he has
17:13 Joshua overcame the Amalekite **a** with
Nu 1: 3 more who are able to serve in the **a**.
1:20 serve in the **a** were listed by name,
1:22 **a** were counted and listed by name,
1:24 serve in the **a** were listed by name,
1:26 serve in the **a** were listed by name,
1:28 serve in the **a** were listed by name,
1:30 serve in the **a** were listed by name,
1:32 serve in the **a** were listed by name,
1:34 serve in the **a** were listed by name,
1:36 serve in the **a** were listed by name,
1:38 serve in the **a** were listed by name,
1:40 serve in the **a** were listed by name,
1:42 serve in the **a** were listed by name,
1:45 were able to serve in Israel's **a**
20:20 them with a large and powerful **a**.
21:23 He mustered his entire **a** and marched
21:33 Og king of Bashan and his whole **a**
21:34 you, with his whole **a** and his land.
21:35 whole **a**, leaving them no survivors.
26: 2 able to serve in the **a** of Israel."
31:14 angry with the officers of the **a**
31:48 who were over the units of the **a**
Dt 2:32 Sihon and all his **a** came out to meet
2:33 with his sons and his whole **a**.
3: 1 Og king of Bashan with his whole **a**
3: 2 you with his whole **a** and his land.
3: 3 Og king of Bashan and all his **a**.
11: 4 what he did to the Egyptian **a**, to
20: 1 and an **a** greater than yours,
20: 2 come forward and address the **a**.
20: 5 The officers shall say to the **a**:
20: 9 have finished speaking to the **a**,
Jos 5:14 the **a** of the LORD I have now come.
5:15 The commander of the LORD's **a**
8: 1 Take the whole **a** with you, and go up
8: 3 Joshua and the whole **a** moved out to
10: 7 up from Gilgal with his entire **a**,
10:21 The whole **a** then returned safely to
10:24 said to the **a** commanders who had
10:33 Joshua defeated him and his **a**
11: 4 a huge **a**, as numerous as the sand
11: 7 Joshua and his whole **a** came against
Jdg 4: 2 The commander of his **a** was Sisera,
4: 7 the commander of Jabin's **a**, with his
4:15 all his chariots and **a** by the sword,
4:16 Barak pursued the chariots and **a** as
Jdg 7:22 The **a** fled to Beth Shittah towards
8:11 and fell upon the unsuspecting **a**.
8:12 them, routing their entire **a**.
9:29 Abimelech, 'Call out your whole **a**!'"
20:10 to get provisions for the **a**.
20:10 Then, when the **a** arrives at Gibeah
1Sa 4:17 and the **a** has suffered heavy losses.
12: 9 the commander of the **a** of Hazor, and
13: 6 and that their **a** was hard pressed,
14:15 panic struck the whole **a**—those in
14:16 saw the **a** melting away in all
14:25 The entire **a** entered the woods, and
14:28 "Your father bound the **a** under a
14:38 all you who are leaders of the **a**,
14:50 of Saul's **a** was Abner son of Ner,
15: 9 Saul and the **a** spared Agag and the
17:20 He reached the camp as the **a** was
17:46 Philistine **a** to the birds of the air
17:55 commander of the **a**, "Abner, whose
18: 5 Saul gave him a high rank in the **a**.
26: 5 commander of the **a**, had lain down.
26: 5 with the **a** encamped around him.
26: 7 David and Abishai went to the **a** by
26:14 He called out to the **a** and to Abner
28: 1 men will accompany me in the **a**."
28: 5 Saul saw the Philistine **a**, he was
28:19 The LORD will also hand over the **a**
29: 6 to have you serve with me in the **a**.
31: 7 saw that the Israelite **a** had fled
2Sa 1:12 and for the **a** of the LORD and the
2: 8 the commander of Saul's **a**, had taken
5:24 of you to strike the Philistine **a**."
8: 9 defeated the entire **a** of Hadadezer,
8:16 Joab son of Zeruiah was over the **a**;
10: 7 with the entire **a** of fighting men.
10:16 of Hadadezer's **a** leading them.
10:18 Shobach the commander of their **a**,
11: 1 men and the whole Israelite **a**.
11:17 some of the men in David's **a** fell;
12:29 David mustered the entire **a** and went
12:31 his entire **a** returned to Jerusalem.
17:25 Amasa over the **a** in place of Joab.
18: 6 The **a** marched into the field to
18: 7 There the **a** of Israel was defeated
19: 2 for the whole **a** the victory that day
19:13 of my **a** in place of Joab.'"
20:23 Joab was over Israel's entire **a**;
24: 2 the king said to Joab and the **a**
24: 4 however, overruled Joab and the **a**
1Ki 1:19 and Joab the commander of the **a**,
1:25 commanders of the **a** and Abiathar
2:32 commander of Israel's **a**, and Amasa
2:32 commander of Judah's **a**—were better
2:35 Benaiah son of Jehoiada over the **a**
11:15 Joab the commander of the **a**, who had
11:21 commander of the **a** was also dead.
16:15 The **a** was encamped near Gibbethon,
16:16 Omri, the commander of the **a**, king
20: 1 king of Aram mustered his entire **a**.
20:13 'Do you see this vast **a**? I will give
20:19 of the city with the **a** behind
20:25 You must also raise an **a** like the
20:28 I will deliver this vast **a** into your
22:36 a cry spread through the **a**: "Every
2Ki 3: 9 the **a** had no more water for
4:13 king or the commander of the **a**?'"
5: 1 Now Naaman was commander of the **a**
6:15 an **a** with horses and chariots had
6:24 king of Aram mobilised his entire **a**
7: 6 chariots and horses and a great **a**,
7:14 king sent them after the Aramean **a**.
8:21 his **a**, however, fled back home.
9: 5 he arrived, he found the **a** officers
13: 7 Nothing had been left of the **a** of
18:17 his field commander with a large **a**,
25: 1 against Jerusalem with his whole **a**.
25: 4 and the whole **a** fled at night
25: 5 the Babylonian **a** pursued the king
25:10 The whole Babylonian **a**, under the
25:23 all the **a** officers and their men
25:26 together with the **a** officers, fled
1Ch 10: 7 the valley saw that the **a** had fled
12:14 These Gadites were **a** commanders;
12:21 and they were commanders in his **a**.
12:22 he had a great **a**, like the **a** of God.
14:15 of you to strike the Philistine **a**."

1Ch 14:16 they struck down the Philistine **a**
18: 9 defeated the entire **a** of Hadadezer
18:15 Joab son of Zeruiah was over the **a**;
19: 8 with the entire **a** of fighting men.
19:16 of Hadadezer's **a** leading them.
19:18 Shophach the commander of their **a**.
20: 3 his entire **a** returned to Jerusalem.
25: 1 with the commanders of the **a**,
26:26 and by the other **a** commanders.
27: 1 all that concerned the **a** divisions
27: 3 chief of all the **a** officers for the
27: 5 The third **a** commander, for the third
27:34 was the commander of the royal **a**.
2Ch 13: 8 You are indeed a vast **a** and have
14: 8 Asa had an **a** of three hundred
14: 9 a vast **a** and three hundred chariots,
14:11 we have come against this vast **a**.
14:13 Asa and his **a** pursued them as far as
16: 7 the **a** of the king of Aram has
16: 8 Libyans a mighty **a** with great
20: 2 "A vast **a** is coming against you from
20:12 this vast **a** that is attacking us.
20:15 discouraged because of this vast **a**.
20:21 they went out at the head of the **a**,
20:24 and looked towards the vast **a**,
24:23 At the turn of the year, the **a** of
24:24 Although the Aramean **a** had come with
24:24 into their hands a much larger **a**.
25:11 and led his **a** to the Valley of Salt,
25:12 The **a** of Judah also captured ten
26:11 Uzziah had a well-trained **a**, ready
26:13 Under their command was an **a** of
26:14 and slingstones for the entire **a**.
28: 9 he went out to meet the **a** when it
32: 7 of Assyria and the vast **a** with him,
33:11 the LORD brought against them the **a**
Ne 2: 9 sent **a** officers and cavalry with me.
4: 2 his associates and the **a** of Samaria,
Ps 27: 3 Though an **a** besiege me, my heart
33:16 No king is saved by the size of his **a**
136:15 swept Pharaoh and his **a** into the Red
Pr 30:31 and a king with his **a** around him.
Isa 13: 4 Almighty is mustering an **a** for war.
36: 2 his field commander with a large **a**
43:17 the **a** and reinforcements together,
Jer 4:16 'A besieging **a** is coming from a
6:22 "Look, an **a** is coming from the land
32: 2 The **a** of the king of Babylon was
34: 1 all his **a** and all the kingdoms and
34: 7 while the **a** of the king of Babylon
34:21 to the **a** of the king of Babylon,
37: 5 Pharaoh's **a** had marched out of Egypt,
37: 7 'Pharaoh's **a**, which has marched out
37:10 Babylonian **a** that is attacking you
37:11 After the Babylonian **a** had withdrawn
37:11 Jerusalem because of Pharaoh's **a**,
38: 3 to the **a** of the king of Babylon,
39: 1 his whole **a** and laid siege to it.
39: 5 the Babylonian **a** pursued them and
40: 7 all the **a** officers and their men who
40:13 Johanan son of Kareah and all the **a**
41:11 Johanan son of Kareah and all the **a**
41:13 the **a** officers who were with him,
41:16 Johanan son of Kareah and all the **a**
42: 1 all the **a** officers, including
42: 8 all the **a** officers who were with him
43: 4 Johanan son of Kareah and all the **a**
43: 5 Johanan son of Kareah and all the **a**
46: 2 the **a** of Pharaoh Neco king of Egypt,
50:41 "Look! An **a** is coming from the north;
51: 3 young men; completely destroy her **a**.
52: 4 against Jerusalem with his whole **a**.
52: 7 through, and the whole **a** fled.
52: 8 the Babylonian **a** pursued King
52:14 The whole Babylonian **a** under the
Lam 1:15 **a** against me to crush my young men.
Eze 1:24 Almighty, like the tumult of an **a**.
17:15 Egypt to get horses and a large **a**.
17:17 Pharaoh with his mighty **a** and great
26: 7 with horsemen and a great **a**.
27:10 served as soldiers in your **a**.
29:18 **a** in a hard campaign against Tyre;
29:18 Yet he and his **a** got no reward from
29:19 plunder the land as pay for his **a**.
29:20 because he and his **a** did it for me,
30:11 He and his **a**—the most ruthless of
Eze 32:22 "Assyria is there with her whole **a**;
32:23 pit and her **a** lies around her grave.
32:31 "Pharaoh—he and all his **a**—will see
37:10 stood up on their feet—a vast **a**.
38: 4 out with your whole **a**—your horses,
38:15 horses, a great horde, a mighty **a**.
Da 3:20 in his **a** to tie up Shadrach,
11:10 for war and assemble a great **a**,
11:11 a large **a**, but it will be defeated.
11:12 the **a** is carried off, the king of
11:13 of the North will muster another **a**,
11:13 with a huge **a** fully equipped.
11:22 an overwhelming **a** will be swept away
11:25 "With a large **a** he will stir up his
11:25 with a large and very powerful **a**,
11:26 his **a** will be swept away, and many
Joel 2: 2 a large and mighty **a** comes,
2: 5 like a mighty **a** drawn up for battle.
2:11 LORD thunders at the head of his **a**
2:20 "I will drive the northern **a** far
2:25 my great **a** that I sent among you.
Mt 22: 7 The king was enraged. He sent his **a**
Rev 19:19 the rider on the horse and his **a**.

Arnan

1Ch 3:21 of **A**, of Obadiah and of Shecaniah.

Arnon (Arnon's)

Swift river stream running from the mountains of Gilead into the Dead Sea. It separated Moab from the Amorite kingdom (Nu 21:13; 22:36; Jdg 11:18), and later Moab and Israel (Nu 21:25–26; Dt 2:24; 3:8,16; Jos 12:1–2; Jdg 11:21–22). After Moab's destruction fugitives fled here (Isa 16:2–4).

Nu 21:13 there and camped alongside the **A**,
21:13 The **A** is the border of Moab, between
21:14 in Suphah and the ravines, the **A**
21:24 his land from the **A** to the Jabbok,
21:26 him all his land as far as the **A**.
22:36 at the Moabite town on the **A** border,
Dt 2:24 "Set out now and cross the **A** Gorge.
2:36 From Aroer on the rim of the **A** Gorge,
3: 8 the **A** Gorge as far as Mount Hermon.
3:12 north of Aroer by the **A** Gorge,
3:16 from Gilead down to the **A** Gorge
4:48 the **A** Gorge to Mount Siyon (that
Jos 12: 1 from the **A** Gorge to Mount Hermon,
12: 2 Aroer on the rim of the **A** Gorge
13: 9 Aroer on the rim of the **A** Gorge,
13:16 Aroer on the rim of the **A** Gorge,
Jdg 11:13 took away my land from the **A** to
11:18 camped on the other side of the **A**.
11:18 of Moab, for the **A** was its border.
11:22 capturing all of it from the **A** to
11:26 and all the towns along the **A**.
2Ki 10:33 **A** Gorge through Gilead to Bashan.
Isa 16: 2 women of Moab at the fords of the **A**.
Jer 48:20 by the **A** that Moab is destroyed.

Arnon's (Arnon)

Nu 21:28 of Moab, the citizens of **A** heights.

Arodi (Arodite)

Ge 46:16 Shuni, Ezbon, Eri, **A** and Areli.
Nu 26:17 through **A**, the Arodite clan; through

Arodite (Arodi)

Nu 26:17 through Arodi, the **A** clan; through

Aroer (Aroerite)

1. Amorite city on northern bank of Arnon Gorge (Dt 2:36; 4:48; Jos 12:2). Captured by Israel and given to Reuben and Gad (Dt 3:12). Taken during Jehu's reign by King Hazael of Syria (2Ki 10:32–33). **2.** Town in Gilead, facing Rabbah, on the boundary between Gad and the Ammonites (Jos 13:25). Restored and enlarged by descendants of Gad (Nu 32:34). 20 towns between Aroer and Minnith destroyed by Jephthah (Jdg 11:32–33). Exact location unknown. **3.** Town in southern Judah (1Sa 30:28). Possibly the same place as Adadah (Jos 15:22) or modern Ararah (12 miles south-east of Beersheba).

Nu 32:34 Gadites built up Dibon, Ataroth, **A**,
Dt 2:36 From **A** on the rim of the Arnon Gorge,
3:12 north of **A** by the Arnon Gorge,
4:48 This land extended from **A** on the rim
Jos 12: 2 He ruled from **A** on the rim of the
13: 9 extended from **A** on the rim of the
13:16 The territory from **A** on the rim of
13:25 country as far as **A**, near Rabbah;
Jdg 11:26 **A**, the surrounding settlements and
11:33 He devastated twenty towns from **A** to
1Sa 30:28 to those in **A**, Siphmoth,
2Sa 24: 5 they camped near **A**, south of the
2Ki 10:33 Reuben and Manasseh), from **A** by the
1Ch 5: 8 area from **A** to Nebo and Baal Meon.
Isa 17: 2 The cities of **A** will be deserted and
Jer 48:19 road and watch, you who live in **A**.

Aroerite (Aroer)

1Ch 11:44 and Jeiel the sons of Hotham the **A**,

Aroma (Aromatic)

Ge 8:21 The LORD smelled the pleasing **a** and
Ex 29:18 a pleasing **a**, an offering made to
29:25 for a pleasing **a** to the LORD,
29:41 a pleasing **a**, an offering made to
Lev 1: 9 by fire, an **a** pleasing to the LORD.
1:13 by fire, an **a** pleasing to the LORD.
1:17 by fire, an **a** pleasing to the LORD.
2: 2 by fire, an **a** pleasing to the LORD.
2: 9 by fire, an **a** pleasing to the LORD.
2:12 on the altar as a pleasing **a**.
3: 5 by fire, an **a** pleasing to the LORD.
3:16 offering made by fire, a pleasing **a**.
4:31 altar as an **a** pleasing to the LORD.
6:15 altar as an **a** pleasing to the LORD.
6:21 pieces as an **a** pleasing to the LORD.
8:21 a pleasing **a**, an offering made to
8:28 a pleasing **a**, an offering made to
17: 6 fat as an **a** pleasing to the LORD.
23:13 to the LORD by fire, a pleasing **a**
23:18 by fire, an **a** pleasing to the LORD.
26:31 in the pleasing **a** of your offerings.
Nu 15: 3 from the herd or the flock, as an **a**
15: 7 it as an **a** pleasing to the LORD.
15:10 by fire, an **a** pleasing to the LORD.
15:13 fire as an **a** pleasing to the LORD.
15:14 fire as an **a** pleasing to the LORD,
15:24 as an **a** pleasing to the LORD,
18:17 by fire, an **a** pleasing to the LORD.
28: 2 by fire, as an **a** pleasing to me.'
28: 6 at Mount Sinai as a pleasing **a**,
28: 8 by fire, an **a** pleasing to the LORD.
28:13 a pleasing **a**, an offering made to
28:24 days as an **a** pleasing to the LORD;
28:27 old as an **a** pleasing to the LORD.
29: 2 an **a** pleasing to the LORD, prepare a
29: 6 to the LORD by fire—a pleasing **a**.
29: 8 Present as an **a** pleasing to the LORD
29:13 fire as an **a** pleasing to the LORD,
29:36 fire as an **a** pleasing to the LORD,
Jer 48:11 as she did, and her **a** is unchanged.
2Co 2:15 For we are to God the **a** of Christ

Aromatic (Aroma)

Ge 2:12 a resin and onyx are also there.)

Arose (Rise)

Ge 13: 7 quarrelling **a** between Abram's
Jdg 5: 7 I, Deborah, **a**, **a** a mother in Israel.
1Sa 1:19 Early the next morning they **a** and
Est 8: 4 and she **a** and stood before him.
SS 5: 5 I **a** to open for my lover, and my
Jnh 1: 4 and such a violent storm **a** that the
Lk 22:24 Also a dispute **a** among them as to
Ac 6: 9 Opposition **a**, however, from members
19:23 About that time there **a** a great
Gal 2: 4 This matter **a** because some false

Arouse (Rouse)

SS 2: 7 **a** or awaken love until it so desires.
3: 5 **a** or awaken love until it so desires.
8: 4 **a** or awaken love until it so desires.
Ro 11:14 in the hope that I may somehow **a** my
1Co 10:22 Are we trying to **a** the Lord's

Aroused (Rouse)
Ex 22:24 My anger will be **a**, and I will kill
Nu 11: 1 when he heard them his anger was **a**.
32:10 The LORD's anger was **a** that day and
Dt 9: 8 At Horeb you **a** the LORD's wrath so
2Ch 21:16 The LORD **a** against Jehoram the
36:16 the LORD was **a** against his people
Job 17: 8 innocent are **a** against the ungodly.
32: 5 more to say, his anger was **a**.
Ps 78:58 **a** his jealousy with their idols.
Jer 32:31 this city has so **a** my anger and
51:39 while they are **a**, I will set out a
Eze 38:18 be **a**, declares the Sovereign LORD.
Hos 11: 8 within me; all my compassion is **a**.
Ac 21:30 The whole city was **a**, and the people
Ro 7: 5 the sinful passions **a** by the law

Arouses (Rouse)
Pr 6:34 for jealousy **a** a husband's fury, and

Arpad
2Ki 18:34 Where are the gods of Hamath and **A**?
19:13 the king of **A**, the king of the city
Isa 10: 9 like **A**, and Samaria like Damascus?
36:19 Where are the gods of Hamath and **A**?
37:13 the king of **A**, the king of the city
Jer 49:23 Concerning Damascus: "Hamath and **A**

Arphaxad
Ge 10:22 The sons of Shem: Elam, Asshur, **A**,
10:24 **A** was the father of Shelah, and
11:10 old, he became the father of **A**.
11:11 after he became the father of **A**,
11:12 **A** had lived 35 years, he became the
11:13 **A** lived 403 years and had other sons
1Ch 1:17 The sons of Shem: Elam, Asshur, **A**,
1:18 **A** was the father of Shelah, and
1:24 Shem, **A**, Shelah,
Lk 3:36 the son of Cainan, the son of **A**, the

Arrange (Arranged, Arrangement, Arrangements)
Lev 1: 7 on the altar and **a** wood on the fire.
1: 8 Aaron's sons the priests shall **a** the
1:12 and the priest shall **a** them,
6:12 **a** the burnt offering on the fire and

Arranged (Arrange)
Ge 15:10 cut them in two and **a** the halves
22: 9 an altar there and **a** the wood on it.
Jdg 20:38 The men of Israel had **a** with the
2Sa 23: 5 covenant, **a** and secured in every
1Ki 18:33 He **a** the wood, cut the bull into
2Ki 9:30 she painted her eyes, **a** her hair and
2Ch 35:10 The service was **a** and the priests
Mt 26:48 Now the betrayer had **a** a signal with
Mk 14:44 Now the betrayer had **a** a signal with
Ac 28:23 They **a** to meet Paul on a certain day,
1Co 12:18 in fact God has **a** the parts in the
Heb 9: 6 everything had been **a** like this, the

Arrangement (Arrange)
Eze 43:11 the design of the temple—its **a**,
Ac 20:13 **a** because he was going there on foot.

Arrangements (Arrange)
2Co 9: 5 finish the **a** for the generous gift

Array (Arrayed)
Ge 2: 1 were completed in all their vast **a**.
Dt 4:19 the stars—all the heavenly **a**—do

Arrayed (Array)
Ps 110: 3 **A** in holy majesty, from the womb of
Isa 61:10 and **a** me in a robe of righteousness,

Arrest (Arrested, Arresting)
Jer 36:26 Shelemiah son of Abdeel to **a** Baruch
Mt 10:19 when they **a** you, do not worry about
21:46 They looked for a way to **a** him, but
26: 4 they plotted to **a** Jesus in some sly
26:48 "The one I kiss is the man; **a** him.
26:55 teaching, and you did not **a** me.
Mk 12:12 they looked for a way to **a** him
14: 1 sly way to **a** Jesus and kill him.
14:44 **a** him and lead him away under guard."
14:49 temple courts, and you did not **a** me.
Lk 20:19 for a way to **a** him immediately,
Jn 7:32 sent temple guards to **a** him.
11:57 report it so that they might **a** him.
18:36 fight to prevent my **a** by the Jews.
Ac 9:14 to **a** all who call on your name."
2Co 11:32 Damascenes guarded in order to **a** me.

Arrested (Arrest)
Jer 37:13 the son of Hananiah, **a** him and said,
37:14 he **a** Jeremiah and brought him to the
Mt 14: 3 Now Herod had **a** John and bound him
26:50 forward, seized Jesus and **a** him.
26:57 Those who had **a** Jesus took him to
Mk 6:17 had given orders to have John **a**,
13:11 Whenever you are **a** and brought to
14:46 The men seized Jesus and **a** him.
Jn 18:12 and the Jewish officials **a** Jesus.
Ac 1:16 as guide for those who **a** Jesus
5:18 They **a** the apostles and put them in
12: 1 about this time that King Herod **a**
21:33 The commander came up and **a** him and
28:17 I was **a** in Jerusalem and handed over

Arresting (Arrest)
Ac 12: 4 After **a** him, he put him in prison,
22: 4 **a** both men and women and throwing

Arrival (Arrive)
Ge 43:25 their gifts for Joseph's **a** at noon,
Ezr 3: 8 **a** at the house of God in Jerusalem,
Jn 11:17 On his **a**, Jesus found that Lazarus

Arrive (Arrival, Arrived, Arrives, Arriving)
Ex 1:19 give birth before the midwives **a**."
Ne 2: 7 me safe-conduct until I **a** in Judah?
Job 6:20 **a** there, only to be disappointed.
1Co 16: 3 Then, when I **a**, I will give letters

Arrived (Arrive)
Ge 12: 5 land of Canaan, and they **a** there.
19: 1 The two angels **a** at Sodom in the
33:18 he **a** safely at the city of Shechem
37:14 When Joseph **a** at Shechem,
42: 6 So when Joseph's brothers **a**, they
46:28 When they **a** in the region of Goshen,
Nu 10:21 was to be set up before they **a**.
20: 1 community **a** at the Desert of Zin,
Dt 9: 7 day you left Egypt until you **a** here,
11: 5 desert until you **a** at this place,
Jos 8:11 the city and **a** in front of it.
Jdg 3:27 he **a** there, he blew a trumpet in the
7:13 Gideon **a** just as a man was telling a
Ru 1:19 When they **a** in Bethlehem, the whole
2: 4 Just then Boaz **a** from Bethlehem and
1Sa 4:13 he **a**, there was Eli sitting on his
10:10 they **a** at Gibeah, a procession of
13:10 **a**, and Saul went out to greet him.
16: 4 When he **a** at Bethlehem, the elders
16: 6 they **a**, Samuel saw Eliab and thought,
25: 9 David's men **a**, they gave Nabal this
25:12 they **a**, they reported every word.
26: 4 learned that Saul had definitely **a**.
30:26 David **a** in Ziklag, he sent some of
2Sa 1: 2 On the third day a man **a** from Saul's
2:32 night and **a** at Hebron by daybreak.
3:23 Joab and all the soldiers with him **a**,
4: 5 and they **a** there in the heat of the
11:22 The messenger set out, and when he **a**
15:32 David **a** at the summit, where people
15:37 David's friend Hushai **a** at Jerusalem
16:14 **a** at their destination exhausted.
18:31 the Cushite **a** and said, "My lord the
19:30 my lord the king has **a** home safely."
1Ki 1:22 with the king, Nathan the prophet **a**.
1:42 son of Abiathar the priest **a**.
8: 3 all the elders of Israel had **a**, the
12:21 Rehoboam **a** in Jerusalem, he mustered
22:15 he **a**, the king asked him, "Micaiah,
2Ki 6:32 but before he **a**, Elisha said to the
9: 5 he **a**, he found the army officers
10: 7 the letter **a**, these men took the
10: 8 the messenger **a**, he told Jehu, "They
2Ch 5: 4 all the elders of Israel had **a**, the
11: 1 Rehoboam **a** in Jerusalem, he mustered
18:14 he **a**, the king asked him, "Micaiah,
22: 7 When Ahaziah **a**, he went out with
Ezr 2:68 they **a** at the house of the LORD in
7: 8 Ezra **a** in Jerusalem in the fifth
7: 9 and he **a** in Jerusalem on the first
8:32 we **a** in Jerusalem, where we rested
Est 6:14 the king's eunuchs **a** and hurried
Isa 30: 4 and their envoys have **a** in Hanes,
Eze 7:12 The time has come, the day has **a**.
23:40 and when they **a** you bathed yourself
33:22 Now the evening before the man **a**,
47: 7 I **a** there, I saw a great number of
Zec 6:10 Jedaiah, who have **a** from Babylon.
Mt 8:28 he **a** at the other side in the region
17:24 After Jesus and his disciples **a** in
25:10 to buy the oil, the bridegroom **a**.
26:47 Judas, one of the Twelve, **a**.
Mk 3:31 Jesus' mother and brothers **a**.
11:27 They **a** again in Jerusalem, and while
14:17 evening came, Jesus **a** with the
Lk 8:51 he **a** at the house of Jairus, he did
Jn 4:45 he **a** in Galilee, the Galileans
4:47 this man heard that Jesus had **a** in
12: 1 Six days before the Passover, Jesus **a**
20: 6 Simon Peter, who was behind him, **a**
Ac 1:13 they **a**, they went upstairs to the
5:21 high priest and his associates **a**,
8:15 they **a**, they prayed for them that
9:39 Peter went with them, and when he **a**
10:24 The following day he **a** in Caesarea.
11:23 he **a** and saw the evidence of the
13: 5 they **a** at Salamis, they proclaimed
18:19 They **a** at Ephesus, where Paul left
19: 1 the interior and **a** at Ephesus.
20: 2 the people, and finally **a** in Greece,
20:15 set sail from there and **a** off Kios.
20:15 on the following day **a** at Miletus.
20:18 they **a**, he said to them: "You know
21:17 we **a** at Jerusalem, the brothers
23:33 the cavalry **a** in Caesarea, they
25:13 Bernice **a** at Caesarea to pay their
28:13 From there we set sail and **a** at
1Co 16:17 Fortunatus and Achaicus **a**, because
Gal 2:12 But when they **a**, he began to draw

Arrives (Arrive)
Jdg 20:10 Then, when the army **a** at Gibeah in
1Sa 16:11 we will not sit down until he **a**."
1Ki 14: 5 When she **a**, she will pretend to be
Hos 13:13 without wisdom; when the time **a**,
Zep 2: 2 before the appointed time **a** and that
Mt 12:44 When it **a**, it finds the house
Lk 11:25 **a**, it finds the house swept clean
Heb 13:23 If he **a** soon, I will come with him

Arriving (Arrive)
Ru 1:22 her daughter-in-law, **a** in Bethlehem
1Ki 10: 2 **A** at Jerusalem with a very great
2Ch 9: 1 **A** with a very great caravan—with
28:12 those who were **a** from the war.
Ac 5:22 on **a** at the jail, the officers did
14:27 On **a** there, they gathered the church
17:10 On **a** there, they went to the Jewish
18:27 On **a**, he was a great help to those
25: 1 Three days after **a** in the province,
27: 7 and had difficulty **a** off Cnidus.

Arrogance (Arrogant)
Dt 1:43 in your **a** you marched up into the
1Sa 2: 3 or let your mouth speak such **a**,
15:23 and **a** like the evil of idolatry.
Job 35:12 out because of the **a** of the wicked.
Ps 10: 2 In his **a** the wicked man hunts down
17:10 and their mouths speak with **a**.
73: 8 in their **a** they threaten oppression.
Pr 8:13 I hate pride and **a**, evil behaviour
Isa 2:17 The **a** of man will be brought low and
9: 9 who say with pride and **a** of heart,
13:11 I will put an end to the **a** of the
Jer 48:29 **a** and the haughtiness of her heart.

Eze 7:10 the rod has budded, a has blossomed!
Hos 5: 5 Israel's a testifies against them;
7:10 Israel's a testifies against him,
Mk 7:22 envy, slander, a and folly.
2Co 12:20 slander, gossip, a and disorder.

Arrogant (Arrogance, Arrogantly)

2Ki 14:10 defeated Edom and now you are a.
2Ch 25:19 Edom, and now you are a and proud.
Ne 9:16 they, our forefathers, became a
9:29 a and disobeyed your commands.
Ps 5: 5 The a cannot stand in your presence;
73: 3 For I envied the a when I saw the
75: 4 To the a I say, 'Boast no more,'
86:14 The a are attacking me, O God; a
94: 4 They pour out a words; all the
119:21 You rebuke the a, who are cursed
119:51 The a mock me without restraint,
119:69 Though the a have smeared me with
119:78 May the a be put to shame for
119:85 The a dig pitfalls for me, contrary
119:122 let not the a oppress me.
123: 4 the proud, much contempt from the a.
Pr 17: 7 A lips are unsuited to a fool
21:24 The proud and a man—"Mocker" is his
Isa 2:11 The eyes of the a man will be
5:15 humbled, the eyes of the a humbled.
33:19 You will see those a people no more,
Jer 13:15 Hear and pay attention, do not be a,
43: 2 and all the a men said to Jeremiah,
50:31 "See, I am against you, O a one,"
50:32 The a one will stumble and fall and
Eze 16:49 Sodom: She and her daughters were a,
Da 5:20 when his heart became a and hardened
Hab 2: 5 indeed, wine betrays him; he is a
Zep 3: 4 Her prophets are a; they are
Mal 3:15 now we call the a blessed. Certainly
4: 1 All the a and every evildoer will be
Ro 1:30 slanderers, God-haters, insolent, a
11:20 Do not be a, but be afraid.
1Co 4:18 Some of you have become a, as if I
4:19 only how these a people are talking,
1Ti 6:17 a nor to put their hope in wealth,
2Pe 2:10 Bold and a, these men are not afraid

Arrogantly (Arrogant)

Ex 18:11 to those who had treated Israel a
Ne 9:10 how a the Egyptians treated them.
Job 36: 9 have done—that they have sinned a.
Ps 31:18 they speak a against the righteous.

Arrow (Arrows)

1Sa 20:36 boy ran, he shot an a beyond him.
20:37 place where Jonathan's a had fallen,
20:37 "Isn't the a beyond you?
20:38 up the a and returned to his master.
2Ki 9:24 The a pierced his heart and he
13:17 "The LORD's a of victory, the a of
19:32 enter this city or shoot an a here.
Job 20:24 a bronze-tipped a pierces him.
34: 6 his a inflicts an incurable wound.'
Ps 91: 5 night, nor the a that flies by day,
Pr 7:23 till an a pierces his liver, like a
25:18 Like a club or a sword or a sharp a
Isa 7:24 Men will go there with bow and a,
37:33 enter this city or shoot an a here.
49: 2 a and concealed me in his quiver.
Jer 9: 8 Their tongue is a deadly a; it
Zec 9:14 the LORD will appear over them; his a

Arrows (Arrow)

Ex 19:13 surely be stoned or shot with a
Nu 24: 8 with their a they pierce them.
Dt 32:23 them and expend my a against them.
32:42 I will make my a drunk with blood,
1Sa 20:20 I will shoot three a to the side of
20:21 send a boy and say, 'Go, find the a.
20:21 If I say to him, 'Look, the a are
20:22 if I say to the boy, 'Look, the a
20:36 boy, "Run and find the a I shoot.
2Sa 11:20 they would shoot a from the wall?
11:24 the archers shot a at your servants
22:15 He shot a and scattered the enemies,
2Ki 13:15 Elisha said, "Get a bow and some a,"
13:18 he said, "Take the a," and the king
1Ch 12: 2 were able to shoot a or to sling
2Ch 26:15 to shoot a and hurl large stones.
Job 6: 4 The a of the Almighty are in me, my
41:28 A do not make him flee; slingstones
Ps 7:13 he makes ready his flaming a.
11: 2 they set their a against the strings
18:14 He shot his a and scattered the
38: 2 For your a have pierced me, and your
45: 5 Let your sharp a pierce the hearts
57: 4 men whose teeth are spears and a
58: 7 the bow, let their a be blunted.
64: 3 and aim their words like deadly a.
64: 7 God will shoot them with a; suddenly
76: 3 There he broke the flashing a, the
77:17 your a flashed back and forth.
120: 4 punish you with a warrior's sharp a,
127: 4 Like a in the hands of a warrior are
144: 6 shoot you're a and rout them.
Pr 26:18 shooting firebrands or deadly a
Isa 5:28 Their a are sharp, all their bows
Jer 50: 9 Their a will be like skilled
50:14 Shoot at her! Spare no a, for she
51:11 "Sharpen the a, take up the shields!
Lam 3:12 and made me the target for his a.
3:13 He pierced my heart with a from his
Eze 5:16 deadly and destructive a of famine,
21:21 an omen: He will cast lots with a,
39: 3 your a drop from your right hand.
39: 9 and a, the war clubs and spears.
Hab 3: 9 your bow, you called for many a.
3:11 at the glint of your flying a,
Eph 6:16 all the flaming a of the evil one.

Arsenal

Jer 50:25 The LORD has opened his a and

Art (Artisans, Artistic, Arts)

2Ch 2: 7 and experienced in the a of

Artaxerxes

King of Persia. Stopped work on walls of Jerusalem (Ezr 4:17–23). Provided resources for Temple worship under Ezra (Ezr 7); reversed earlier decision to allow rebuilding of walls under Nehemiah (Ne 2:1–10).

Ezr 4: 7 in the days of A king of Persia,
4: 7 his associates wrote a letter to A.
4: 8 Jerusalem to A the king as follows:
4:11 To King A, From your servants, the
4:23 letter of King A was read to Rehum
6:14 Cyrus, Darius and A, kings of Persia.
7: 1 during the reign of A king of Persia,
7: 7 in the seventh year of King A.
7:11 This is a copy of the letter King A
7:12 A, king of kings, To Ezra the priest,
7:21 Now I, King A, order all the
8: 1 Babylon during the reign of King A:
Ne 2: 1 in the twentieth year of King A,
5:14 from the twentieth year of King A,
13: 6 for in the thirty-second year of A

Artemas

Tit 3:12 soon as I send A or Tychicus to you,

Artemis

Ac 19:24 who made silver shrines of A,
19:27 great goddess A will be discredited,
19:28 "Great is A of the Ephesians!
19:34 "Great is A of the Ephesians!
19:35 of the great A and of her image,

Artificial

Ne 3:16 a pool and the House of the Heroes.

Artisans (Art)

2Ki 24:14 men, and all the craftsmen and a
24:16 war, and a thousand craftsmen and a.
Jer 24: 1 the craftsmen and the a of Judah
29: 2 a had gone into exile from Jerusalem.

Artistic (Art)

Ex 31: 4 to make a designs for work in gold,
35:32 to make a designs for work in gold,
35:33 in all kinds of a craftsmanship.

Arts (Art)

Ex 7:11 the same things by their secret a:
7:22 the same things by their secret a,
8: 7 the same things by their secret a;
8:18 by their secret a, they could not.
Rev 9:21 their magic a, their sexual
21: 8 those who practise magic a, the
22:15 those who practise magic a, the

Arubboth

1Ki 4:10 Ben-Hesed—in A (Socoh and all the

Arumah

Jdg 9:41 Abimelech stayed in A, and Zebul

Arvad (Arvadites)

Eze 27: 8 Men of Sidon and A were your oarsmen;
27:11 Men of A and Helech manned your

Arvadites (Arvad)

Ge 10:18 A, Zemarites and Hamathites. Later
1Ch 1:16 A, Zemarites and Hamathites.

Arza

1Ki 16: 9 getting drunk in the home of A, the

As surely as the LORD lives

Jdg 8:19; Ru 3:13; 1Sa 14:45; 19:6; 20:3, 21; 25:26; 26:10, 16; 28:10; 29:6; 2Sa 4:9; 12:5; 14:11; 15:21; 1Ki 1:29; 2:24; 22:14; 2Ki 2:2, 4, 6; 4:30; 5:16, 20; 2Ch 18:13; Jer 4:2; 5:2; 12:16; 16:14, 15; 23:7, 23:8; 38:16; Hos 4:15

As the LORD/Lord commanded

Ex 7:6, 10; 16:34; 17:1; 39:1, 5, 21, 26, 29, 31, 32; 40:16, 19, 21, 23, 25, 27, 29, 32; Lev 8:4, 9, 13, 17, 21, 29; 9:10; 16:34; 24:23; Nu 1:19, 54; 2:33; 3:42; 4:49; 8:3, 20, 22; 9:5; 15:36; 17:11; 20:27; 26:4; 27:11, 22; 31:7, 31, 41, 47; 36:10; Dt 10:5; Jos 11:15; 2Sa 5:25; Mt 27:10

Asa (Asa's)

King of Judah (1Ki 15:9–10). Removed idols and reformed worship (1Ki 15:11–15; 2Ch 14:2–5; 15). Rebuilt Judah's cities (2Ch 14:6–7). Relied on God against the Cushites (2Ch 14:9–15); relied on Aram, instead of God, against Israel, rebuked by Hanani the seer (1Ki 15:15–22; 2Ch 16). Death (2Ch 16:12–14).

1Ki 15: 8 And A his son succeeded him as king.
15: 9 of Israel, A became king of Judah,
15:11 A did what was right in the eyes of
15:13 A cut the pole down and burned it in
15:16 There was war between A and Baasha
15:17 the territory of A king of Judah.
15:18 A then took all the silver and gold
15:20 Ben-Hadad agreed with King A and
15:22 King A issued an order to all Judah
15:22 With them King A built up Geba in
15:24 A rested with his fathers and was
15:25 the second year of A king of Judah,
15:28 the third year of A king of Judah
15:32 There was war between A and Baasha
15:33 In the third year of A king of Judah,
16: 8 In the twenty-sixth year of A king
16:10 year of A king of Judah.
16:15 In the twenty-seventh year of A king
16:23 In the thirty-first year of A king
16:29 In the thirty-eighth year of A king
22:41 Jehoshaphat son of A became king of
22:43 walked in the ways of his father A
22:46 after the reign of his father A.
1Ch 3:10 son, A his son, Jehoshaphat his son,
9:16 of Jeduthun; and Berekiah son of A,
2Ch 14: 1 A his son succeeded him as king, and
14: 2 A did what was good and right in the
14: 8 A had an army of three hundred
14:10 A went out to meet him, and they
14:11 A called to the LORD his God and
14:12 the Cushites before A and Judah.
14:13 A and his army pursued them as far
15: 2 He went out to meet A and said to
15: 2 to me, A and all Judah and Benjamin.
15: 8 A heard these words and the prophecy

2Ch 15:16 King A also deposed his grandmother
15:16 A cut the pole down, broke it up and
16: 1 the territory of A king of Judah.
16: 2 A then took the silver and gold out
16: 4 Ben-Hadad agreed with King A and
16: 6 King A brought all the men of Judah,
16: 7 to A king of Judah and said to him:
16:10 A was angry with the seer because of
16:10 At the same time A brutally
16:12 A was afflicted with a disease in his
16:13 A died and rested with his fathers.
17: 2 that his father A had captured.
20:32 He walked in the ways of his father A
21:12 Jehoshaphat or of A king of Judah.
Jer 41: 9 A had made as part of his defence
Mt 1: 7 of Abijah, Abijah the father of A,
1: 8 A the father of Jehoshaphat,

Asa's (Asa)

1Ki 15:14 A heart was fully committed to the
15:23 for all the other events of A reign,
2Ch 15:10 of the fifteenth year of A reign.
15:17 A heart was fully committed to the
15:19 the thirty-fifth year of A reign.
16: 1 In the thirty-sixth year of A reign
16:11 The events of A reign, from

Asahel (Asahel's)

David's nephew; brother of Joab and Abishai (1Ch 2:16). One of David's leading warriors (2Sa 23:24; 1Ch 11:26; 27:7). Killed by Abner after a rash pursuit (2Sa 2:18–23); avenged by Joab (2Sa 3:26–27).

2Sa 2:18 were there: Joab, Abishai and A.
2:18 Now A was as fleet-footed as a wild
2:20 that you, A?" "It is," he answered.
2:21 But A would not stop chasing him.
2:22 Again Abner warned A, "Stop chasing
2:23 A refused to give up the pursuit; so
2:23 butt of his spear into A's stomach,
2:30 Besides A, nineteen of David's men
2:32 They took A and buried him in his
3:27 avenge the blood of his brother A,
3:30 brother A in the battle of Gibeon.)
23:24 Among the Thirty were: A the brother
1Ch 2:16 three sons were Abishai, Joab and A.
11:26 The mighty men were: A the brother
27: 7 for the fourth month, was A the
2Ch 17: 8 Nethaniah, Zebadiah, A, Shemiramoth,
31:13 Jehiel, Azaziah, Nahath, A, Jerimoth,
Ezr 10:15 Only Jonathan son of A and Jahzeiah

Asahel's (Asahel)

2Sa 2:23 butt of his spear into A stomach,

Asaiah

2Ki 22:12 and A the king's attendant:
22:14 Ahikam, Acbor, Shaphan and A went to
1Ch 4:36 A, Adiel, Jesimiel, Benaiah,
6:30 Shimea his son, Haggiah his son and A
9: 5 Of the Shilonites: A the firstborn
15: 6 from the descendants of Merari, A
15:11 and Uriel, A, Joel, Shemaiah, Eliel
2Ch 34:20 and A the king's attendant:

Asaph (Asaph's)

1. Levite, in charge of music in the tabernacle and temple (1Ch 6:39; 15:17–19; 16:4–7,37; 1Ch 25:6; Ne 12:46). Composed several psalms (2Ch 29:30; Ps 50; 73–83). His sons set apart for musical and prophetic ministry (1Ch 25; 2Ch 20:14; 35:15; Ezr 2:41; 3:10; Ne 11:17). **2.** Keeper of the king's forest (Ne 2:8). **3.** Hezekiah's recorder (2Ki 18:18, 37; Isa 36:3, 22).

2Ki 18:18 Joah son of A the recorder went out
18:37 of A the recorder went to Hezekiah,
1Ch 6:39 Heman's associate A, who served at
6:39 A son of Berekiah, the son of Shimea,
9:15 Mica, the son of Zicri, the son of A;
15:17 A son of Berekiah; and from their
15:19 The musicians Heman, A and Ethan
16: 5 A was the chief, Zechariah second,
16: 5 harps, A was to sound the cymbals,
16: 7 That day David first committed to A
16:37 David left A and his associates
25: 1 set apart some of the sons of A,
1Ch 25: 2 From the sons of A: Zaccur, Joseph,
25: 2 The sons of A were under the
25: 2 A were under the supervision of A,
25: 6 A, Jeduthun and Heman were under the
25: 9 The first lot, which was for A, fell
26: 1 son of Kore, one of the sons of A.
2Ch 5:12 All the Levites who were musicians—A
20:14 of A, as he stood in the assembly.
29:13 from the descendants of A, Zechariah
29:30 words of David and of A the seer.
35:15 The musicians, the descendants of A,
35:15 A, Heman and Jeduthun the king's
Ezr 2:41 The singers: the descendants of A 128
3:10 and the Levites (the sons of A) with
Ne 2: 8 may I have a letter to A, keeper of
7:44 The singers: the descendants of A 148
11:17 the son of Zabdi, the son of A, the
12:35 the son of Zaccur, the son of A,
12:46 in the days of David and A, there
Ps 50: T A psalm of A.
73: T A psalm of A.
74: T A maskil of A.
75: T For the director of music. To the
76: T A psalm of A. A song.
77: T For Jeduthun. Of A. A psalm.
78: T A maskil of A.
79: T A psalm of A.
80: T Of A. A psalm.
81: T According to gittith. Of A.
82: T A psalm of A.
83: T A song. A psalm of A.
Isa 36: 3 of A the recorder went out to him.
36:22 and Joah son of A the recorder went

Asaph's (Asaph)

Ne 11:22 Uzzi was one of A descendants, who

Asarel

1Ch 4:16 Ziph, Ziphah, Tiria and A.

Asarelah

1Ch 25: 2 Zaccur, Joseph, Nethaniah and A.

Ascend (Ascended, Ascending, Ascent, Ascents)

Dt 30:12 "Who will a into heaven to get it
Ps 24: 3 Who may a the hill of the LORD? Who
Isa 14:13 You said in your heart, "I will a to
14:14 I will a above the tops of the
Jn 6:62 What if you see the Son of Man a to
Ac 2:34 For David did not a to heaven, and
Ro 10: 6 'Who will a into heaven?'" (that is,

Ascended (Ascend)

Jdg 13:20 angel of the LORD a in the flame.
2Ki 19:23 "With my many chariots I have a the
Ps 47: 5 God has a amid shouts of joy, the
68:18 you a on high, you led captives in
Isa 37:24 'With my many chariots I have a the
Eph 4: 8 This is why it says: "When he a on
4: 9 (What does "he a" mean except that
4:10 who a higher than all the heavens,

Ascending (Ascend)

Ge 28:12 of God were a and descending on it.
Eze 41: 7 the temple was built in a stages,
Jn 1:51 a and descending on the Son of Man."

Ascent (Ascend)

Ne 3:19 a to the armoury as far as the angle.
12:37 City of David on the a to the wall

Ascents

Ps 120: T A song of a.
121: T A song of a.
122: T A song of a. Of David.
123: T A song of a.
124: T A song of a. Of David.
125: T A song of a.
126: T A song of a.
127: T A song of a. Of Solomon.
128: T A song of a.
129: T A song of a.
Ps 130: T A song of a.
131: T A song of a. Of David.
132: T A song of a.
133: T A song of a. Of David.
134: T A song of a.

Ascribe

1Ch 16:28 A to the LORD, O families of
16:28 a to the LORD glory and strength,
16:29 a to the LORD the glory due to his
Job 36: 3 afar; I will a justice to my Maker.
Ps 29: 1 A to the LORD, O mighty ones, a to
29: 2 A to the LORD the glory due to his
96: 7 A to the LORD, O families of
96: 7 a to the LORD glory and strength.
96: 8 A to the LORD the glory due to his

Asenath

Ge 41:45 gave him A daughter of Potiphera,
41:50 two sons were born to Joseph by A
46:20 Joseph by A daughter of Potiphera,

Ash (Ashes)

Lev 4:12 it in a wood fire on the a heap.
1Sa 2: 8 and lifts the needy from the a heap;
Ps 113: 7 and lifts the needy from the a heap;
Lam 4: 5 in purple now lie on a heaps.

Ashamed (Shame)

2Sa 19: 3 are a when they flee from battle.
2Ki 2:17 they persisted until he was too a to
8:11 a fixed gaze until Hazael felt a.
2Ch 30:15 The priests and the Levites were a
Ezr 8:22 I was a to ask the king for soldiers
9: 6 prayed: "O my God, I am too a and
Ps 6:10 All my enemies will be a and
83:17 May they ever be a and dismayed; may
Isa 1:29 "You will be a because of the sacred
23: 4 Be a, O Sidon, and you, O fortress
24:23 The moon will be abashed, the sun a;
29:22 "No longer will Jacob be a; no
33: 9 Lebanon is a and withers; Sharon is
41:11 you will surely be a and disgraced;
Jer 6:15 Are they a of their loathsome
8:12 Are they a of their loathsome
22:22 Then you will be a and disgraced
31:19 I was a and humiliated because I
48:13 Moab will be a of Chemosh, as the
48:13 was a when they trusted in Bethel.
50:12 your mother will be greatly a; she
Eze 16:52 So then, be a and bear your disgrace,
16:54 be a of all you have done in giving
16:61 you will remember your ways and be a
16:63 you will remember and be a and never
36:32 Be a and disgraced for your conduct,
43:10 that they may be a of their sins.
43:11 if they are a of all they have done,
Hos 10: 6 Israel will be a of its wooden idols.
Mic 3: 7 The seers will be a and the diviners
7:16 Nations will see and be a, deprived
Zec 13: 4 "On that day every prophet will be a
Mk 8:38 If anyone is a of me and my words in
8:38 the Son of Man will be a of him when
Lk 9:26 If anyone is a of me and my words,
9:26 the Son of Man will be a of him when
16: 3 enough to dig, and I'm a to beg
Ro 1:16 I am not a of the gospel, because
6:21 a of? Those things result in death!
2Co 9: 4 be a of having been so confident.
10: 8 you down, I will not be a of it.
Php 1:20 and hope that I will in no way be a,
2Th 3:14 him, in order that he may feel a.
2Ti 1: 8 do not be a to testify about our
1: 8 our Lord, or a of me his prisoner.
1:12 Yet I am not a, because I know whom
1:16 me and was not a of my chains.
2:15 a workman who does not need to be a
Tit 2: 8 that those who oppose you may be a
Heb 2:11 Jesus is not a to call them brothers.
11:16 Therefore God is not a to be called
1Pe 3:16 in Christ may be a of their slander.
4:16 do not be a, but praise God that you

Ashan

Jos 15:42 Libnah, Ether, **A**,
19: 7 Rimmon, Ether and **A**—four towns
1Ch 4:32 Rimmon, Token and **A**—five towns—
6:59 **A**, Juttah and Beth Shemesh, together

Ashbel (Ashbelite)

Ge 46:21 sons of Benjamin: Bela, Beker, **A**,
Nu 26:38 the Belaite clan; through **A**, the
1Ch 8: 1 **A** the second son, Aharah the third,

Ashbelite (Ashbel)

Nu 26:38 the **A** clan; through Ahiram, the

Ashdod

Probably the capital of the 5 Philistine cities, 3 miles from the Mediterranean coast and 20 miles north of Gaza. Its inhabitants survived Joshua's advances against them (Jos 11:22). Its people suffered punishment when the captured ark of the covenant was placed in Dagon's temple here (1Sa 5:1–7). Captured by King Uzziah of Judah (2Ch 26:6), but generally remained independent. Amos prophesied against it (Am 1:8), and Sargon of Assyria attacked and captured it (Isa 20:1). Later prophets also predicted its fall (Jer 25:20; Zep 2:4; Zec 9:6). Its inhabitants opposed the rebuilding of Jerusalem (Ne 4:7–8), and Israelites were rebuked for intermarrying with them (Ne 13:23–25). Later known as Azotus, and evangelised by the deacon Philip (Ac 8:40).

Jos 11:22 in Gaza, Gath and **A** did any survive.
13: 3 in Gaza, **A**, Ashkelon, Gath and Ekron
15:46 of **A**, together with their villages;
15:47 **A**, its surrounding settlements and
1Sa 5: 1 God, they took it from Ebenezer to **A**.
5: 3 the people of **A** rose early the next
5: 5 temple at **A** step on the threshold.
5: 6 the people of **A** and its vicinity;
5: 7 the men of **A** saw what was happening,
6:17 **A**, Gaza, Ashkelon, Gath and Ekron.
2Ch 26: 6 the walls of Gath, Jabneh and **A**.
26: 6 He then rebuilt towns near **A** and
Ne 4: 7 the Ammonites and the men of **A** heard
13:23 women from **A**, Ammon and Moab.
13:24 children spoke the language of **A** or
Isa 20: 1 to **A** and attacked and captured it
Jer 25:20 Ekron, and the people left at **A**);
Am 1: 8 I will destroy the king of **A** and the
3: 9 Proclaim to the fortresses of **A** and
Zep 2: 4 **A** will be emptied and Ekron uprooted.
Zec 9: 6 Foreigners will occupy **A**, and I will

Asher (Asher's)

1. Son of Jacob by Zilpah (Ge 30:12–13; 35:26; Ex 1:4; 1Ch 2:2); blessed by Jacob (Ge 49:20). **2.** Tribe descended from Asher. Blessed by Moses (Dt 33:24–25). Included in census (Nu 1:40–41; 26:44–47); apportioned land (Jos 19:24–31; Eze 48:2). Supported Gideon (Jdg 6:35; 7:23) and David (1Ch 12:36) but not Deborah (Jdg 5:17). **3.** Territory along Mediterranean coast of Palestine, between Tyre and Mount Carmel. Its boundaries and towns were clearly listed (Jos 19:24–31). Allotted to descendants of Jacob's eighth son, who failed to drive out all the Canaanites (Jdg 1:31–32). **4.** Town east of Shechem and west of River Jordan, in territory of Manasseh (Jos 17:7).

Ge 30:13 So she named him **A**.
35:26 Leah's maidservant Zilpah: Gad and **A**.
46:17 The sons of **A**: Imnah, Ishvah, Ishvi
Ex 1: 4 Dan and Naphtali; Gad and **A**.
Nu 1:13 from **A**, Pagiel son of Ocran;
1:40 From the descendants of **A**: All the
1:41 The number from the tribe of **A** was
2:27 The tribe of **A** will camp next to
2:27 people of **A** is Pagiel son of Ocran.
7:72 people of **A**, brought his offering.
10:26 over the division of the tribe of **A**,
13:13 from the tribe of **A**, Sethur son of
26:44 The descendants of **A** by their clans
26:46 (**A** had a daughter named Serah.)
26:47 These were the clans of **A**; those
34:27 the leader from the tribe of **A**;
Dt 27:13 Gad, **A**, Zebulun, Dan and Naphtali.
33:24 About **A** he said: "Most blessed of
33:24 "Most blessed of sons is **A**; let him
Jos 17: 7 **A** to Micmethath east of Shechem.
17:10 bordered **A** on the north and Issachar
17:11 Within Issachar and **A**, Manasseh also
19:24 for the tribe of **A**, clan by clan.
19:31 of the tribe of **A**, clan by clan.
19:34 It touched Zebulun on the south, **A**
21: 6 **A**, Naphtali and the half-tribe of
21:30 from the tribe of **A**, Mishal, Abdon,
Jdg 1:31 Nor did **A** drive out those living in
1:32 of this the people of **A** lived among
5:17 **A** remained on the coast and stayed
6:35 and also into **A**, Zebulun and
7:23 Israelites from Naphtali, **A** and all
1Ki 4:16 Baana son of Hushai—in **A** and in
1Ch 2: 2 Benjamin, Naphtali, Gad and **A**.
6:62 **A** and Naphtali, and from the part of
6:74 from the tribe of **A** they received
7:30 The sons of **A**: Imnah, Ishvah, Ishvi
7:40 All these were descendants of **A**
12:36 men of **A**, experienced soldiers
2Ch 30:11 Nevertheless, some men of **A**,
Eze 48: 2 "**A** will have one portion; it will
48: 3 territory of **A** from east to west.
48:34 the gate of Gad, the gate of **A** and
Lk 2:36 of Phanuel, of the tribe of **A**.
Rev 7: 6 from the tribe of **A** 12,000, from the

Asher's (Asher)

Ge 49:20 "**A** food will be rich; he will

Asherah (Asherahs)

Ex 34:13 stones and cut down their **A** poles.
Dt 7: 5 cut down their **A** poles and burn
12: 3 and burn their **A** poles in the fire;
16:21 Do not set up any wooden **A** pole
Jdg 6:25 and cut down the **A** pole beside it.
6:26 Using the wood of the **A** pole that
6:28 demolished, with the **A** pole beside
6:30 and cut down the **A** pole beside it."
1Ki 14:15 the LORD to anger by making **A** poles.
14:23 sacred stones and **A** poles on every
15:13 she had made a repulsive **A** pole.
16:33 Ahab also made an **A** pole and did
18:19 prophets of **A**, who eat at Jezebel's
2Ki 13: 6 **A** pole remained standing in Samaria.
17:10 They set up sacred stones and **A**
17:16 the shape of calves, and an **A** pole.
18: 4 stones and cut down the **A** poles.
21: 3 altars to Baal and made an **A** pole,
21: 7 He took the carved **A** pole he had
23: 4 Baal and **A** and all the starry hosts.
23: 6 He took the **A** pole from the temple
23: 7 and where women did weaving for **A**.
23:14 cut down the **A** poles and covered
23:15 powder, and burned the **A** pole also.
2Ch 14: 3 stones and cut down the **A** poles.
15:16 she had made a repulsive **A** pole.
17: 6 places and the **A** poles from Judah.
19: 3 for you have rid the land of the **A**
24:18 and worshipped **A** poles and idols.
31: 1 stones and cut down the **A** poles.
33: 3 to the Baals and made **A** poles.
33:19 set up **A** poles and idols before
34: 3 **A** poles, carved idols and cast
34: 4 **A** poles, the idols and the images.
34: 7 he tore down the altars and the **A**
Isa 17: 8 they will have no regard for the **A**
27: 9 no **A** poles or incense altars will
Jer 17: 2 **A** poles beside the spreading trees
Mic 5:14 I will uproot from among you your **A**

Asherahs (Asherah)

Jdg 3: 7 God and served the Baals and the **A**.

Ashes (Ash, *Dust and ashes, Sackcloth and ashes*)

Ex 27: 3 of bronze—its pots to remove the **a**,
Lev 1:16 side of the altar, where the **a** are.
4:12 where the **a** are thrown, and burn it
6:10 and shall remove the **a** of the burnt
6:11 and carry the **a** outside the camp to
Nu 4:13 "They are to remove the **a** from the
19: 9 shall gather up the **a** of the heifer
19:10 The man who gathers up the **a** of the
19:17 "For the unclean person, put some **a**
2Sa 13:19 Tamar put **a** on her head and tore the
1Ki 13: 3 and the **a** on it will be poured out."
13: 5 the altar was split apart and its **a**
2Ki 23: 4 Valley and took the **a** to Bethel.
Job 2: 8 with it as he sat among the **a**.
13:12 Your maxims are proverbs of **a**; your
Ps 102: 9 For I eat **a** as my food and mingle my
147:16 wool and scatters the frost like **a**.
Isa 44:20 He feeds on **a**, a deluded heart
61: 3 them a crown of beauty instead of **a**,
Jer 6:26 put on sackcloth and roll in **a**;
31:40 where dead bodies and **a** are thrown,
Eze 27:30 dust on their heads and roll in **a**.
28:18 and I reduced you to **a** on the ground
Mal 4: 3 they will be **a** under the soles of
Heb 9:13 bulls and the **a** of a heifer
2Pe 2: 6 and Gomorrah by burning them to **a**,

Ashhur

1Ch 2:24 bore him **A** the father of Tekoa.
4: 5 **A** the father of Tekoa had two wives,

Ashima

2Ki 17:30 and the men from Hamath made **A**;

Ashkelon

One of the five Philistine cities, on the Mediterranean coast about 12 miles north of Gaza. It posed a regular threat to the judges of Israel, though the men of Judah captured it for a while (Jdg 1:18). Samson later killed 30 of its men (Jdg 14:19). Named in David's lament about Saul and Jonathan's deaths (2Sa 1:20). Amos prophesied its destruction (Am 1:8), which saw fulfilment when Sargon of Assyria attacked and captured it (Isa 20:1).

Jos 13: 3 Ashdod, **A**, Gath and Ekron—that of
Jdg 1:18 The men of Judah also took Gaza, **A**
14:19 He went down to **A**, struck down
1Sa 6:17 for Ashdod, Gaza, **A**, Gath and Ekron.
2Sa 1:20 proclaim it not in the streets of **A**,
Jer 25:20 of the Philistines (those of **A**,
47: 5 in mourning; **A** will be silenced.
47: 7 it to attack **A** and the coast?"
Am 1: 8 the one who holds the sceptre in **A**.
Zep 2: 4 Gaza will be abandoned and **A** left in
2: 7 will lie down in the houses of **A**.
Zec 9: 5 **A** will see it and fear; Gaza will
9: 5 her king and **A** will be deserted.

Ashkenaz

Ge 10: 3 The sons of Gomer: **A**, Riphath and
1Ch 1: 6 The sons of Gomer: **A**, Riphath and
Jer 51:27 these kingdoms: Ararat, Minni and **A**.

Ashnah

Jos 15:33 foothills: Eshtaol, Zorah, **A**,
15:43 Iphtah, **A**, Nezib,

Ashore (Shore)

Lk 8:27 Jesus stepped **a**, he was met by a
Jn 21:11 aboard and dragged the net **a**.

Ashpenaz

Da 1: 3 the king ordered **A**, chief of his

Ashtaroth

Dt 1: 4 Og king of Bashan, who reigned in **A**.
Jos 9:10 Og king of Bashan, who reigned in **A**.
12: 4 who reigned in **A** and Edrei.
13:12 who had reigned in **A** and Edrei and
13:31 half of Gilead, and **A** and Edrei (the
1Ch 6:71 **A**, together with their pasture-lands;

Ashterathite

1Ch 11:44 Uzzia the **A**, Shama and Jeiel the

Ashteroth Karnaim

Ge 14: 5 out and defeated the Rephaites in **A**,

Ashtoreth (Ashtoreths)
1Ki 11: 5 He followed **A** the goddess of the
11:33 **A** the goddess of the Sidonians,
2Ki 23:13 **A** the vile goddess of the Sidonians,

Ashtoreths (Ashtoreth)
Jdg 2:13 him and served Baal and the **A**.
10: 6 They served the Baals and the **A**, and
1Sa 7: 3 the **A** and commit yourselves to the
7: 4 and **A**, and served the LORD only.
12:10 LORD and served the Baals and the **A**.
31:10 his armour in the temple of the **A**

Ashurbanipal
Ezr 4:10 honourable **A** deported and settled in

Ashuri
2Sa 2: 9 He made him king over Gilead, **A** and

Ashvath
1Ch 7:33 of Japhlet: Pasach, Bimhal and **A**.

Asia
Ac 2: 9 Judea and Cappadocia, Pontus and **A**,
6: 9 as the provinces of Cilicia and **A**.
16: 6 the word in the province of **A**.
19:10 of **A** heard the word of the Lord.
19:22 the province of **A** a little longer.
19:26 practically the whole province of **A**.
19:27 the province of **A** and the world,
20: 4 Trophimus from the province of **A**.
20:16 spending time in the province of **A**,
20:18 day I came into the province of **A**.
21:27 Jews from the province of **A** saw Paul
24:19 some Jews from the province of **A**,
27: 2 of **A**, and we put out to sea.
Ro 16: 5 to Christ in the province of **A**.
1Co 16:19 The churches in the province of **A**
2Co 1: 8 we suffered in the province of **A**.
2Ti 1:15 the province of **A** has deserted me,
1Pe 1: 1 Galatia, Cappadocia, **A** and Bithynia,
Rev 1: 4 seven churches in the province of **A**:

Asiel
1Ch 4:35 the son of Seraiah, the son of **A**,

Asleep (Sleep)
Ge 41: 5 He fell **a** again and had a second
Jdg 4:21 him while he lay fast **a**, exhausted.
1Sa 26: 7 and there was Saul, lying **a** inside
1Ki 3:20 my side while I your servant was **a**.
19: 5 lay down under the tree and fell **a**
Job 3:13 in peace; I would be **a** and at rest
Mt 9:24 The girl is not dead but **a**." But
25: 5 they all became drowsy and fell **a**.
28:13 and stole him away while we were **a**.'
Mk 5:39 The child is not dead but **a**."
14:37 "are you **a**? Could you not keep watch
Lk 8:23 they sailed, he fell **a**. A squall
8:52 "She is not dead but **a**."
22:45 found them **a**, exhausted from sorrow.
Jn 11:11 "Our friend Lazarus has fallen **a**;
Ac 7:60 When he had said this, he fell **a**.
13:36 he fell **a**; he was buried with his
20: 9 When he was sound **a**, he fell to
1Co 11:30 and a number of you have fallen **a**.
15: 6 living, though some have fallen **a**.
15:18 those also who have fallen **a** in
15:20 of those who have fallen **a**.
1Th 4:13 be ignorant about those who fall **a**,
4:14 those who have fallen **a** in him.
4:15 not precede those who have fallen **a**.
5: 6 let us not be like others, who are **a**,
5:10 whether we are awake or **a**, we may

Asnah
Ezr 2:50 **A**, Meunim, Nephussim,

Aspatha
Est 9: 7 killed Parshandatha, Dalphon, **A**,

Asriel (Asrielite)
Nu 26:31 through **A**, the Asrielite clan;
Jos 17: 2 **A**, Shechem, Hepher and Shemida.
1Ch 7:14 The descendants of Manasseh: **A** was

Asrielite (Asriel)
Nu 26:31 through Asriel, the **A** clan; through

Assail (Assailant, Assails)
Ps 17: 9 from the wicked who **a** me, from my
55: 4 me; the terrors of death **a** me.

Assailant (Assail)
Dt 25:11 to rescue her husband from his **a**,

Assails (Assail)
Job 16: 9 God **a** me and tears me in his anger

Assassinate (Assassinated, Assassination, Assassins)
Est 2:21 and conspired to **a** King Xerxes.
6: 2 who had conspired to **a** King Xerxes.

Assassinated (Assassinate)
2Ki 12:20 against him and **a** him at Beth Millo,
15:10 **a** him and succeeded him as king.
15:14 **a** him and succeeded him as king.
15:25 he **a** Pekahiah, along with Argob and
15:30 He attacked and **a** him, and then
21:23 him and **a** the king in his palace.
25:25 came with ten men and **a** Gedaliah and
2Ch 33:24 against him and **a** him in his palace.
Jer 41:16 he had **a** Gedaliah son of Ahikam:

Assassination (Assassinate)
Jer 41: 4 The day after Gedaliah's **a**, before

Assassins (Assassinate)
2Ki 14: 6 Yet he did not put the sons of the **a**

Assault (Assaults)
Dt 21: 5 decide all cases of dispute and **a**.
Ps 62: 3 How long will you **a** a man? Would all

Assaults (Assault)
Dt 17: 8 lawsuits or **a**—take them to the
19:11 **a** and kills him, and then flees to
Job 28: 9 Man's hand **a** the flinty rock and

Assemble (Assembled, Assemblies, Assembling, Assembly)
Ge 49: 2 "**A** and listen, sons of Jacob; listen
Ex 3:16 "Go, **a** the elders of Israel and say
Nu 8: 9 and **a** the whole Israelite community.
10: 3 the whole community is to **a** before
10: 4 of Israel—are to **a** before you.
Dt 4:10 "**A** the people before me to hear my
31:12 **A** the people—men, women and
31:28 **A** before me all the elders of your
Jdg 21: 5 Israel has failed to **a** before the
21: 5 anyone who failed to **a** before the
21: 8 to **a** before the LORD at Mizpah?"
1Sa 7: 5 Samuel said, "**A** all Israel at Mizpah
2Sa 3:21 "Let me go at once and **a** all Israel
1Ch 22: 2 David gave orders to **a** the aliens
28: 1 of Israel to **a** at Jerusalem:
Ezr 10: 7 all the exiles to **a** in Jerusalem.
Ne 7: 5 my God put it into my heart to **a** the
Est 8:11 the right to **a** and protect themselves
Ps 47: 9 The nobles of the nations **a** as the
102:22 the peoples and the kingdoms **a** to
Isa 4: 5 over those who **a** there a cloud of
11:12 he will **a** the scattered people of
43: 9 gather together and the peoples **a**.
45:20 "Gather together and come; **a**, you
60: 4 All **a** and come to you; your sons
Jer 49:14 "**A** yourselves to attack it! Rise up
Eze 39:17 '**A** and come together from all around
Da 11:10 His sons will prepare for war and **a**
Joel 3:11 from every side, and **a** there.
Am 3: 9 "**A** yourselves on the mountains of
Mic 4: 6 "I will gather the lame; I will **a**
Zep 3: 8 I have decided to **a** the nations, to
Ac 22:30 priests and all the Sanhedrin to **a**.

Assembled (Assemble)
Ex 35: 1 Moses **a** the whole Israelite
Dt 33: 5 when the leaders of the people **a**,
33:21 When the heads of the people **a**, he
Jos 24: 1 Joshua **a** all the tribes of Israel at
Jdg 9:47 Abimelech heard that they had **a**
10:17 Israelites **a** and camped at Mizpah.
16:23 Now the rulers of the Philistines **a**
20: 1 man and **a** before the LORD in Mizpah.
1Sa 7: 6 they had **a** at Mizpah, they drew
7: 7 heard that Israel had **a** at Mizpah,
13: 5 The Philistines **a** to fight Israel,
14:20 Saul and all his men **a** and went to
17: 1 for war and **a** at Socoh in Judah.
17: 2 Saul and the Israelites **a** and camped
25: 1 Now Samuel died, and all Israel **a**
28: 4 The Philistines **a** and came and set
2Sa 2:30 pursuing Abner and **a** all his men.
1Ki 18:20 and **a** the prophets on Mount Carmel.
20:15 Then he **a** the rest of the Israelites,
1Ch 13: 5 David **a** all the Israelites, from the
15: 3 David **a** all Israel in Jerusalem to
2Ch 12: 5 **a** in Jerusalem for fear of Shishak,
15: 9 he **a** all Judah and Benjamin and the
15:10 They **a** at Jerusalem in the third
20:26 On the fourth day they **a** in the
29: 4 **a** them in the square on the east
29:15 they had **a** their brothers and
30: 3 the people had not **a** in Jerusalem.
30:13 A very large crowd of people **a** in
30:25 and all who had **a** from Israel,
32: 4 A large force of men **a**, and they
32: 6 **a** them before him in the square at
Ezr 3: 1 people **a** as one man in Jerusalem.
8:15 I **a** them at the canal that flows
Ne 5:16 All my men were **a** there for the work;
8: 1 all the people **a** as one man in the
Est 2:19 the virgins were **a** a second time,
9: 2 The Jews **a** in their cities in all
9:16 also **a** to protect themselves
9:18 The Jews in Susa, however, had **a** on
Ps 7: 7 Let the **a** peoples gather round you.
Da 3: 3 all the other provincial officials **a**
Mt 26: 3 **a** in the palace of the high priest,
26:57 of the law and the elders had **a**.
Lk 1:10 **a** worshippers were praying outside.
24:33 and those with them, **a** together
Ac 28:17 When they had **a**, Paul said to them:
1Co 5: 4 you are **a** in the name of our Lord

Assemblies (Assemble)
Lev 23: 2 you are to proclaim as sacred **a**.
23: 4 the sacred **a** you are to proclaim at
23:37 sacred **a** for bringing offerings made
Isa 1:13 I cannot bear your evil **a**.
Am 5:21 feasts; I cannot stand your **a**.

Assembling (Assemble)
1Sa 13:11 the Philistines were **a** at Michmash,

Assembly (Assemble)
Ge 49: 6 let me not join their **a**, for they
Ex 12:16 On the first day hold a sacred **a**,
16: 3 to starve this entire **a** to death."
Lev 4:14 the **a** must bring a young bull as a
8: 3 gather the entire **a** at the entrance
8: 4 and the **a** gathered at the entrance
8: 5 Moses said to the **a**, "This is what
9: 5 and the entire **a** came near and stood
19: 2 "Speak to the entire **a** of Israel and
23: 3 Sabbath of rest, a day of sacred **a**.
23: 7 On the first day hold a sacred **a** and
23: 8 a sacred **a** and do no regular work.'"
23:21 a sacred **a** and do no regular work.
23:24 a commemorated with trumpet blasts.
23:27 Hold a sacred **a** and deny yourselves,
23:35 The first day is a sacred **a**; do no
23:36 on the eighth day hold a sacred **a**
23:36 It is the closing **a**; do no regular
24:14 and the entire **a** is to stone him.
24:16 The entire **a** must stone him. Whether

Nu 10: 7 To gather the **a**, blow the trumpets,
13:26 to the whole **a** and showed them the
14: 2 and the whole **a** said to them, "If
14: 5 whole Israelite **a** gathered there.
14: 7 said to the entire Israelite **a**, "The
14:10 the whole **a** talked about stoning
15:33 to Moses and Aaron and the whole **a**,
15:35 **a** must stone him outside the camp."
15:36 the **a** took him outside the camp and
16: 3 set yourselves above the LORD's **a**?"
16:19 the LORD appeared to the entire **a**.
16:21 "Separate yourselves from this **a** so
16:22 entire **a** when only one man sins?"
16:24 "Say to the **a**, 'Move away from the
16:26 He warned the **a**, "Move back from the
16:42 when the **a** gathered in opposition to
16:45 "Get away from this **a** so that I can
16:46 to the **a** to make atonement for them.
16:47 and ran into the midst of the **a**.
20: 6 Moses and Aaron went from the **a** to
20: 8 brother Aaron gather the **a** together.
20:10 He and Aaron gathered the **a** together
25: 6 the whole **a** of Israel while they
25: 7 left the **a**, took a spear in his
27: 2 leaders and the whole **a**, and said,
27:19 the entire **a** and commission him in
27:22 Eleazar the priest and the whole **a**.
28:18 On the first day hold a sacred **a** and
28:25 On the seventh day hold a sacred **a**
28:26 a sacred **a** and do no regular work.
29: 1 a sacred **a** and do no regular work.
29: 7 this seventh month hold a sacred **a**.
29:12 a sacred **a** and do no regular work.
29:35 "'On the eighth day hold an **a** and do
31:12 the Israelite **a** at their camp on the
35:12 before he stands trial before the **a**.
35:24 the **a** must judge between him and the
35:25 The **a** must protect the one accused
Dt 5:22 your whole **a** there on the mountain
9:10 of the fire, on the day of the **a**.
10: 4 of the fire, on the day of the **a**.
16: 8 on the seventh day hold an **a** to the
18:16 on the day of the **a** when you said,
23: 1 cutting may enter the **a** of the LORD.
23: 2 may enter the **a** of the LORD,
23: 3 may enter the **a** of the LORD,
23: 8 to them may enter the **a** of the LORD.
31:30 hearing of the whole **a** of Israel:
33: 4 the possession of the **a** of Jacob.
Jos 8:35 not read to the whole **a** of Israel,
9:15 of the **a** ratified it by oath.
9:18 because the leaders of the **a** had
9:18 **a** grumbled against the leaders,
18: 1 The whole **a** of the Israelites
20: 6 he has stood trial before the **a**
20: 9 to standing trial before the **a**.
22:12 the whole **a** of Israel gathered at
22:16 "The whole **a** of the LORD says: 'How
Jdg 20: 2 in the **a** of the people of God,
21: 8 had come to the camp for the **a**.
21:10 the **a** sent twelve thousand fighting
21:13 the whole **a** sent an offer of peace
21:16 the elders of the **a** said, "With the
1Ki 8: 5 King Solomon and the entire **a** of
8:14 While the whole **a** of Israel was
8:22 in front of the whole **a** of Israel,
8:55 He stood and blessed the whole **a** of
8:65 and all Israel with him—a vast **a**,
12: 3 and he and the whole **a** of Israel
12:20 called him to the **a** and made him
2Ki 10:20 Jehu said, "Call an **a** in honour of
1Ch 13: 2 He then said to the whole **a** of
13: 4 The whole **a** agreed to do this,
28: 8 all Israel and of the **a** of the LORD,
29: 1 King David said to the whole **a**: "My
29:10 LORD in the presence of the whole **a**,
29:20 David said to the whole **a**, "Praise
2Ch 1: 3 Solomon and the whole **a** went to the
1: 5 and the **a** enquired of him there.
5: 6 King Solomon and the entire **a** of
6: 3 While the whole **a** of Israel was
6:12 in front of the whole **a** of Israel
6:13 then knelt down before the whole **a**
7: 8 and all Israel with him—a vast **a**,
7: 9 On the eighth day they held an **a**,
20: 5 Jehoshaphat stood up in the **a** of
2Ch 20:14 of Asaph, as he stood in the **a**.
23: 3 the whole **a** made a covenant with the
24: 6 by the **a** of Israel for the Tent of
28:14 of the officials and all the **a**.
29:23 brought before the king and the **a**
29:28 The whole **a** bowed in worship, while
29:31 So the **a** brought sacrifices and
29:32 The number of burnt offerings the **a**
30: 2 his officials and the whole **a** in
30: 4 both to the king and to the whole **a**.
30:23 The whole **a** then agreed to celebrate
30:24 thousand sheep and goats for the **a**,
30:25 The entire **a** of Judah rejoiced,
Ezr 10: 8 expelled from the **a** of the exiles.
10:12 The whole **a** responded with a loud
10:14 Let our officials act for the whole **a**
Ne 5:13 **a** said, "Amen," and praised the LORD.
8: 2 priest brought the Law before the **a**,
8:18 with the regulation, there was an **a**.
13: 1 ever be admitted into the **a** of God,
Job 30:28 I stand up in the **a** and cry for help.
Ps 1: 5 sinners in the **a** of the righteous.
22:25 theme of my praise in the great **a**;
26: 5 I abhor the **a** of evildoers and
26:12 the great **a** I will praise the LORD.
35:18 I will give you thanks in the great **a**
40: 9 proclaim righteousness in the great **a**
40:10 and your truth from the great **a**.
68:26 praise the LORD in the **a** of Israel.
82: 1 God presides in the great **a**; he
89: 5 too, in the **a** of the holy ones.
107:32 Let them exalt him in the **a** of the
111: 1 council of the upright and in the **a**.
149: 1 his praise in the **a** of the saints.
Pr 5:14 ruin in the midst of the whole **a**."
24: 7 **a** at the gate he has nothing to say.
26:26 wickedness will be exposed in the **a**.
Isa 14:13 sit enthroned on the mount of **a**,
Jer 26:17 and said to the entire **a** of people,
44:15 women who were present—a large **a**
Lam 1:10 you had forbidden to enter your **a**.
Joel 1:14 Declare a holy fast; call a sacred **a**.
2:15 a holy fast, call a sacred **a**.
2:16 Gather the people, consecrate the **a**;
Mic 2: 5 will have no-one in the **a** of the
Lk 23: 1 the whole **a** rose and led him off to
Ac 5:21 full **a** of the elders of Israel
7:38 was in the **a** in the desert, with
15:12 The whole **a** became silent as they
19:32 The **a** was in confusion: Some were
19:39 up, it must be settled in a legal **a**.
19:41 had said this, he dismissed the **a**.
23: 7 Sadducees, and the **a** was divided.
Heb 12:22 thousands of angels in joyful **a**,

Asserted (Asserting)

Lk 22:59 About an hour later another **a**,

Asserting (Asserted)

Ac 24: 9 The Jews joined in the accusation, **a**

Assessments

2Ki 23:35 of the land according to their **a**.

Asshur (Asshurites, Assyria)

Ge 2:14 it runs along the east side of **A**.
10:22 The sons of Shem: Elam, **A**, Arphaxad,
25:18 of Egypt, as you go towards **A**.
Nu 24:22 destroyed when **A** takes you captive."
24:24 Kittim; they will subdue **A** and Eber,
1Ch 1:17 The sons of Shem: Elam, **A**, Arphaxad,
Eze 27:23 Sheba, **A** and Kilmad traded with you.

Asshurites (Asshur)

Ge 25: 3 **A**, the Letushites and the Leummites.

Assign (Assigned, Assignment, Assignments, Assigns, Reassign)

Nu 4:19 **a** to each man his work and what he
4:27 You shall **a** to them as their
4:32 **A** to each man the specific things he
8:26 This, then, is how you are to **a** the
34:13 Moses commanded the Israelites: "**A**
34:17 **a** the land for you as an inheritance:
Nu 34:18 from each tribe to help **a** the land.
34:29 the men the LORD commanded to **a** the
1Sa 8:12 Some he will **a** to be commanders of
Job 22:24 **a** your nuggets to the dust, your
Mt 24:51 He will cut him to pieces and **a** him
Lk 12:46 **a** him a place with the unbelievers.

Assigned (Assign)

Ge 40: 4 The captain of the guard **a** them to
Nu 2: 9 All the men **a** to the camp of Judah,
2:16 All the men **a** to the camp of Reuben,
2:24 All the men **a** to the camp of Ephraim,
2:31 All the men **a** to the camp of Dan
4:49 **a** his work and told what to carry.
Jos 13: 8 of the LORD, had **a** it to them.
14: 2 Their inheritances were **a** by lot to
19:51 the tribal clans of Israel **a** by lot
21:10 (these towns were **a** to the
24: 4 I **a** the hill country of Seir to Esau,
1Sa 15:20 "I went on the mission the LORD **a** me.
27: 5 let a place be **a** to me in one of the
29: 4 may return to the place you **a** him.
1Ki 7:14 and did all the work **a** to him.
14:27 **a** these to the commanders of the
2Ki 8: 6 Then he **a** an official to her case
1Ch 6:48 Their fellow Levites were **a** to all
6:54 (they were **a** to the descendants of
9:22 The gatekeepers had been **a** to their
9:29 Others were **a** to take care of the
26:29 were **a** duties away from the temple,
2Ch 2:18 He **a** 70,000 of them to be carriers
12:10 **a** these to the commanders of the
23: 6 guard what the LORD has **a** to them.
25: 5 **a** them according to their families
30:22 For the seven days they ate their **a**
31: 2 Hezekiah **a** the priests and Levites
33: 8 the land I **a** to your forefathers,
Ne 12:31 I also **a** two large choirs to give
13:10 I also learned that the portions **a**
13:30 **a** them duties, each to his own task.
Est 2: 9 He **a** to her seven maids selected
4: 5 one of the king's eunuchs **a** to
Job 7: 3 nights of misery have been **a** to me.
Ps 16: 5 LORD, you have **a** me my portion and
104: 8 to the place you **a** for them.
Isa 53: 9 He was **a** a grave with the wicked,
Eze 4: 5 I have **a** you the same number of days
4: 6 **a** you 40 days, a day for each year.
Da 1: 5 The king **a** them a daily amount of
1:10 king, who has **a** your food and drink.
Mk 13:34 each with his **a** task, and tells the
Ac 22:10 all that you have been **a** to do.'
1Co 3: 5 the Lord has **a** to each his task.
7:17 in life that the Lord **a** to him
2Co 10:13 to the field God has **a** to us,

Assignment (Assign)

1Ch 23:11 counted as one family with one **a**.

Assignments (Assign)

2Ch 23:18 to whom David had made **a** in the

Assigns (Assign)

Mic 2: 4 me! He **a** our fields to traitors.'"

Assir

Ex 6:24 The sons of Korah were **A**, Elkanah
1Ch 6:22 his son, Korah his son, **A** his son,
6:23 Elkanah his son, Ebiasaph his son, **A**
6:37 the son of Tahath, the son of **A**, the

Assist (Assistance, Assistant, Assistants, Assisted)

Nu 1: 5 names of the men who are to **a** you:
3: 6 them to Aaron the priest to **a** him.
8:26 They may **a** their brothers in
18: 2 to join you and **a** you when you and
2Ch 8:14 to **a** the priests according to each
13:10 of Aaron, and the Levites **a** them.
Ezr 8:20 had established to **a** the Levites.
Job 29:12 fatherless who had none to **a** him.
Ro 15:24 have you **a** me on my journey there,

Assistance (Assist)
Ezr 8:36 who then gave **a** to the people

Assistant (Assist)
Ex 24:13 Moses set out with Joshua his **a**, and
33:11 but his young **a** Joshua son of Nun
Nu 11:28 who had been Moses' **a** since youth,
Dt 1:38 your **a**, Joshua son of Nun, will
Jos 1: 1 said to Joshua son of Nun, Moses' **a**:
Ne 6: 5 Sanballat sent his **a** to me with the
13:13 the son of Mattaniah, their **a**,

Assistants (Assist)
Ne 5:15 Their **a** also lorded it over the

Assisted (Assist)
2Ch 31:15 Shemaiah, Amariah and Shecaniah **a**
Ezr 1: 6 All their neighbours **a** them with
6:22 so that he **a** them in the work on the

Associate (Associated, Associates)
Jos 23: 7 Do not **a** with these nations that
23:12 with them and **a** with them,
1Ch 6:39 Heman's **a** Asaph, who served at his
Pr 22:24 do not **a** with one easily angered,
Jn 4: 9 (For Jews do not **a** with Samaritans.)
Ac 10:28 Jew to **a** with a Gentile or visit him.
Ro 12:16 not be proud, but be willing to **a**
1Co 5: 9 to **a** with sexually immoral people
5:11 you must not **a** with anyone who calls
2Th 3:14 Do not **a** with him, in order that he

Associated (Associate)
Ne 13: 4 He was closely **a** with Tobiah,
Eze 37:16 Judah and the Israelites **a** with him.
37:16 all the house of Israel **a** with him.'
37:19 of the Israelite tribes **a** with him,

Associates (Associate)
1Ch 6:44 from their **a**, the Merarites, at his
16: 7 first committed to Asaph and his **a**
16:37 David left Asaph and his **a** before
16:38 sixty-eight **a** to minister with them.
Ezr 3: 2 his **a** began to build the altar of
4: 7 his **a** wrote a letter to Artaxerxes.
4: 9 together with the rest of their
4:17 the rest of their **a** living in
4:23 Shimshai the secretary and their **a**,
5: 3 and Shethar-Bozenai and their **a** went
5: 6 and Shethar-Bozenai and their **a**, the
6:13 **a** carried it out with diligence.
Ne 4: 2 in the presence of his **a** and the
10:10 their **a**: Shebaniah, Hodiah, Kelita,
11:12 their **a**, who carried on work for the
11:13 his **a**, who were heads of families
11:14 his **a**, who were able men—128 men.
11:17 Bakbukiah second among his **a**;
11:19 Talmon and their **a**, who kept watch
12: 7 leaders of the priests and their **a**
12: 8 who, together with his **a**, was in
12: 9 Bakbukiah and Unni, their **a**, stood
12:24 Jeshua son of Kadmiel, and their **a**,
12:36 his **a**—Shemaiah, Azarel, Milalai,
Job 34: 8 He keeps company with evildoers; he **a**
Zec 3: 8 O high priest Joshua and your **a**
Ac 5:17 the high priest and all his **a**, who
5:21 When the high priest and his **a**

Assos
Ac 20:13 ahead to the ship and sailed for **A**,
20:14 he met us at **A**, we took him aboard

Assume (Assumed)
Ne 10:32 "We **a** the responsibility for
10:35 "We also **a** responsibility for

Assumed (Assume)
1Sa 14:47 After Saul had **a** rule over Israel,
Ac 21:29 **a** that Paul had brought him into the

Assurance (Assure)
1Sa 17:18 and bring back some **a** from them.
Est 9:30 of Xerxes—words of goodwill and **a**—
Job 24:22 established, they have no **a** of life.
1Ti 3:13 **a** in their faith in Christ Jesus.
Heb 10:22 a sincere heart in full **a** of faith,

Assure (Assurance, Assured, Assures, Reassure)
Lk 4:25 I **a** you that there were many widows
Gal 1:20 I **a** you before God that what I am

Assured (Assure)
Dt 9: 3 be **a** today that the LORD your God is
Jos 2:14 "Our lives for your lives!" the men **a**
1Sa 10:16 Saul replied, "He **a** us that the
Job 36: 4 Be **a** that my words are not false;
Jer 26:15 Be **a**, however, that if you put me to
Ac 2:36 "Therefore let all Israel be **a** of
Col 4:12 the will of God, mature and fully **a**.

Assures (Assure)
Jer 5:24 **a** us of the regular weeks of harvest.

Assyria (Assyria's, Assyrian, Assyrians)
Originally a city on the west bank of River Tigris, also known as Asshur (Ge 2:14), probably named after a son of Shem (Ge 10:22). It grew into a powerful empire with capital city Nineveh. Its king, Tiglath-Pileser III invaded Israel (2Ki 15:19), and deported Israelites (2Ki 15:29), and this continued under Sargon (2Ki 17:6, 23). Then Sennacherib invaded Judah (2Ki 18:13), but this ultimately failed (2Ki 19:35–36; Isa 37:36–37). The prophets predicted its fall (Isa 10:12; 30:31; Mic 5:4–6; Zep 2:13).

Ge 10:11 From that land he went to **A**, where
2Ki 15:19 Pul king of **A** invaded the land, and
15:20 silver to be given to the king of **A**.
15:20 So the king of **A** withdrew and stayed
15:29 Tiglath-Pileser king of **A** came and
15:29 and deported the people to **A**.
16: 7 king of **A**, "I am your servant and
16: 8 sent it as a gift to the king of **A**.
16: 9 The king of **A** complied by attacking
16:10 to meet Tiglath-Pileser king of **A**.
16:18 LORD, in deference to the king of **A**.
17: 3 Shalmaneser king of **A** came up to
17: 4 the king of **A** discovered that Hoshea
17: 4 paid tribute to the king of **A**
17: 5 The king of **A** invaded the entire
17: 6 the king of **A** captured Samaria and
17: 6 and deported the Israelites to **A**.
17:23 in **A**, and they are still there.
17:24 The king of **A** brought people from
17:26 was reported to the king of **A**: "The
17:27 the king of **A** gave this order: "Make
18: 7 He rebelled against the king of **A**
18: 9 Shalmaneser king of **A** marched
18:11 The king of **A** deported Israel to **A**
18:13 Sennacherib king of **A** attacked all
18:14 of **A** at Lachish: "I have done wrong.
18:14 The king of **A** exacted from Hezekiah
18:16 LORD, and gave it to the king of **A**.
18:17 The king of **A** sent his supreme
18:19 the king of **A**, says: On what are you
18:23 bargain with my master, the king of **A**
18:28 of the great king, the king of **A**!
18:30 into the hand of the king of **A**.'
18:31 This is what the king of **A** says:
18:33 land from the hand of the king of **A**?
19: 4 whom his master, the king of **A**, has
19: 6 of the king of **A** have blasphemed me.
19: 8 that the king of **A** had left Lachish,
19:10 be handed over to the king of **A**.'
19:11 of **A** have done to all the countries,
19:20 concerning Sennacherib king of **A**.
19:32 LORD says concerning the king of **A**:
19:36 Sennacherib king of **A** broke camp and
20: 6 city from the hand of the king of **A**.
23:29 River to help the king of **A**.
1Ch 5: 6 king of **A** took into exile.
5:26 spirit of Pul king of **A** (that is,
5:26 Tiglath-Pileser king of **A**), who took
2Ch 28:16 Ahaz sent to the king of **A** for help.
28:20 Tiglath-Pileser king of **A** came to
28:21 of **A**, but that did not help him.
2Ch 30: 6 from the hand of the kings of **A**.
32: 1 king of **A** came and invaded Judah.
32: 4 "Why should the kings of **A** come and
32: 7 of **A** and the vast army with him,
32: 9 Later, when Sennacherib king of **A**
32:10 "This is what Sennacherib king of **A**
32:11 us from the hand of the king of **A**
32:22 **A** and from the hand of all others.
33:11 army commanders of the king of **A**,
Ezr 4: 2 king of **A**, who brought us here."
6:22 the attitude of the king of **A**,
Ne 9:32 days of the kings of **A** until today.
Ps 83: 8 Even **A** has joined them to lend
Isa 7:17 Judah—he will bring the king of **A**
7:18 and for bees from the land of **A**.
7:20 beyond the River—the king of **A**
8: 4 be carried off by the king of **A**."
8: 7 the king of **A** with all his pomp.
10:12 "I will punish the king of **A** for the
11:11 that is left of his people from **A**,
11:16 of his people that is left from **A**,
19:23 will be a highway from Egypt to **A**.
19:23 and the Egyptians to **A**.
19:24 Egypt and **A**, a blessing on the earth.
19:25 "Blessed be Egypt my people, **A** my
20: 1 sent by Sargon king of **A**, came to
20: 4 the king of **A** will lead away
20: 6 deliverance from the king of **A**!
27:13 Those who were perishing in **A** and
30:31 The voice of the LORD will shatter **A**;
31: 8 "**A** will fall by a sword that is not
36: 1 Sennacherib king of **A** attacked all
36: 2 the king of **A** sent his field
36: 4 the king of **A**, says: On what are you
36: 8 the king of **A**: I will give you two
36:13 of the great king, the king of **A**!
36:15 into the hand of the king of **A**.'
36:16 This is what the king of **A** says:
36:18 land from the hand of the king of **A**?
37: 4 whom his master, the king of **A**, has
37: 6 of the king of **A** have blasphemed me.
37: 8 that the king of **A** had left Lachish,
37:10 be handed over to the king of **A**.'
37:11 of **A** have done to all the countries,
37:21 me concerning Sennacherib king of **A**,
37:33 LORD says concerning the king of **A**:
37:37 Sennacherib king of **A** broke camp and
38: 6 city from the hand of the king of **A**.
52: 4 live; lately, **A** has oppressed them.
Jer 2:18 to **A** to drink water from the River?
2:36 by Egypt as you were by **A**.
50:17 to devour him was the king of **A**;
50:18 land as I punished the king of **A**.
Lam 5: 6 We submitted to Egypt and **A** to get
Eze 31: 3 Consider **A**, once a cedar in Lebanon,
32:22 "**A** is there with her whole army; she
Hos 5:13 then Ephraim turned to **A**, and sent
7:11 calling to Egypt, now turning to **A**.
8: 9 For they have gone up to **A** like a
9: 3 to Egypt and eat unclean food in **A**.
10: 6 It will be carried to **A** as tribute
11: 5 will not **A** rule over them because
11:11 birds from Egypt, like doves from **A**.
12: 1 treaty with **A** and sends olive oil
14: 3 **A** cannot save us; we will not mount
Mic 5: 6 They will rule the land of **A** with
7:12 you from **A** and the cities of Egypt,
Na 3:18 O king of **A**, your shepherds slumber;
Zep 2:13 against the north and destroy **A**,
Zec 10:10 from Egypt and gather them from **A**.

Assyria's (Assyria)
Zec 10:11 **A** pride will be brought down and

Assyrian (Assyria)
2Ki 19:17 "It is true, O LORD, that the **A**
19:35 thousand men in the **A** camp.
2Ch 32:21 officers in the camp of the **A** king.
Isa 10: 5 "Woe to the **A**, the rod of my anger,
14:25 I will crush the **A** in my land; on my
37:18 "It is true, O LORD, that the **A**
37:36 thousand men in the **A** camp.
Mic 5: 5 When the **A** invade our land and
5: 6 He will deliver us from the **A** when

Assyrians (Assyria)
2Ki 18:10 At the end of three years the **A** took
Isa 10:24 do not be afraid of the **A**, who beat
19:23 The **A** will go to Egypt and the
19:23 and **A** will worship together.
23:13 The **A** have made it a place for
Eze 16:28 in prostitution with the **A** too,
23: 5 she lusted after her lovers, the **A**
23: 7 to all the elite of the **A**
23: 9 lovers, the **A**, for whom she lusted.
23:12 She too lusted after the **A**—governors
23:23 and all the **A** with them, handsome

Astir (Stir)
Ps 83: 2 See how your enemies are **a**, how your
Isa 14: 9 The grave below is all **a** to meet you

Astonished (Astonishment)
Job 21: 5 Look at me and be **a**; clap your hand
Mt 8:10 Jesus heard this, he was **a** and said
12:23 All the people were **a** and said,
19:25 they were greatly **a** and asked, "Who
22:33 the crowds heard this, they were **a**
Mk 5:42 At this they were completely **a**.
10:32 and the disciples were **a**, while
Lk 2:48 his parents saw him, they were **a**.
5: 9 For he and all his companions were **a**
8:56 Her parents were **a**, but he ordered
20:26 **a** by his answer, they became silent.
Jn 7:21 I did one miracle, and you are all **a**.
Ac 3:11 all the people were **a** and came
4:13 ordinary men, they were **a** and they
8:13 And he followed Philip everywhere, **a**
9:21 All those who heard him were **a** and
10:45 **a** that the gift of the Holy Spirit
12:16 the door and saw him, they were **a**.
Gal 1: 6 I am **a** that you are so quickly
Rev 13: 3 world was **a** and followed the beast.
17: 6 When I saw her, I was greatly **a**.
17: 7 the angel said to me: "Why are you **a**?
17: 8 will be **a** when they see the beast,

Astonishing (Astonishment)
Da 12: 6 these **a** things are fulfilled?"

Astonishment (Astonished, Astonishing)
Ge 43:33 and they looked at each other in **a**.
Lk 1:63 **a** he wrote, "His name is John.

Astound (Astounded, Astounding)
Isa 29:14 Therefore once more I will **a** these

Astounded (Astound)
Ps 48: 5 they saw ⌞her⌟ and were **a**;

Astounding (Astound)
Lam 1: 9 Her fall was **a**; there was none to
Da 8:24 He will cause **a** devastation and will

Astray (Stray)
Nu 5:12 wife goes **a** and is unfaithful to
5:19 you have not gone **a** and become
5:20 if you have gone **a** while married to
5:29 law of jealousy when a woman goes **a**
Dt 13:13 have led the people of their town **a**
17:17 wives, or his heart will be led **a**.
27:18 who leads the blind **a** on the road.
1Ki 11: 3 concubines, and his wives led him **a**.
2Ki 21: 9 Manasseh led them **a**, so that they
2Ch 21:11 themselves and had led Judah **a**.
33: 9 Judah and the people of Jerusalem **a**,
Job 19: 4 If it is true that I have gone **a**, my
Ps 58: 3 Even from birth the wicked go **a**;
95:10 are a people whose hearts go **a**,
119:67 Before I was afflicted I went **a**, but
Pr 5:23 led **a** by his own great folly.
7:21 With persuasive words she led him **a**;
10:17 ignores correction leads others **a**.
12:26 the way of the wicked leads them **a**.
14:22 Do not those who plot evil go **a**? But
20: 1 is led **a** by them is not wise.
Isa 3:12 O my people, your guides lead you **a**
Isa 9:16 and those who are guided are led **a**.
19:13 of her peoples have led Egypt **a**.
30:28 the peoples a bit that leads them **a**.
53: 6 We all, like sheep, have gone **a**,
Jer 4: 1 out of my sight and no longer go **a**,
23:13 by Baal and led my people Israel **a**.
23:32 "They tell them and lead my people **a**
50: 6 their shepherds have led them **a** and
Eze 13:10 "'Because they lead my people **a**,
44:10 went far from me when Israel went **a**
44:15 when the Israelites went **a** from me,
48:11 did not go **a** as the Levites did when
48:11 did when the Israelites went **a**.
Hos 4:12 spirit of prostitution leads them **a**
Am 2: 4 they hve been led **a** by false gods,
Mic 3: 5 the prophets who lead my people **a**,
Jn 16: 1 told you so that you will not go **a**.
Ac 19:26 led **a** large numbers of people here
1Co 12: 2 influenced and led **a** to mute idols.
2Co 11: 3 your minds may somehow be led **a** from
Gal 2:13 hypocrisy even Barnabas was led **a**.
Heb 3:10 Their hearts are always going **a**,
5: 2 who are ignorant and are going **a**,
1Pe 2:25 For you were like sheep going **a**, but
1Jn 2:26 those who are trying to lead you **a**.
3: 7 do not let anyone lead you **a**.
Rev 12: 9 Satan, who leads the whole world **a**.
18:23 spell all the nations were led **a**.

Astrologer (Astrologers)
Da 2:10 of any magician or enchanter or **a**.

Astrologers (Astrologer)
Isa 47:13 Let your **a** come forward, those
Da 2: 2 **a** to tell him what he had dreamed.
2: 4 the **a** answered the king in Aramaic,
2: 5 The king replied to the **a**, "This is
2:10 The **a** answered the king, "There is
3: 8 At this time some **a** came forward and
4: 7 the magicians, enchanters, **a** and
5: 7 **a** and diviners to be brought and
5:11 enchanters, **a** and diviners.

Asunder
Ps 136:13 to him who divided the Red Sea **a**
Isa 24:19 **a**, the earth is thoroughly shaken.

Aswan
Isa 49:12 west, some from the region of **A**."
Eze 29:10 to **A**, as far as the border of Cush.
30: 6 From Migdol to **A** they will fall by

Asyncritus
Ro 16:14 Greet **A**, Phlegon, Hermes, Patrobas,

Atad
Ge 50:10 they reached the threshing-floor of **A**
50:11 at the threshing-floor of **A**,

Atarah
1Ch 2:26 was **A**; she was the mother of Onam.

Ataroth
Nu 32: 3 "**A**, Dibon, Jazer, Nimrah, Heshbon,
32:34 The Gadites built up Dibon, **A**, Aroer,
Jos 16: 2 the territory of the Arkites in **A**,
16: 7 went down from Janoah to **A** and

Ataroth Addar
Jos 16: 5 their inheritance went from **A** in the
18:13 Bethel) and went down to **A** on the

Ate (Eat)
Ge 3: 6 wisdom, she took some and **a** it.
3: 6 who was with her, and he **a** it.
3:12 fruit from the tree, and I **a** it."
3:13 "The serpent deceived me, and I **a**.
3:17 **a** from the tree about which I
18: 8 While they **a**, he stood near them
19: 3 bread without yeast, and they **a**.
24:54 he and the men who were with him **a**
25:34 He **a** and drank, and then got up and
26:30 for them, and they **a** and drank.
Ge 27:25 Jacob brought it to him and he **a**;
27:33 I **a** it just before you came and I
31:46 heap, and they **a** there by the heap.
39: 6 with anything except the food he **a**.
41: 4 the cows that were ugly and gaunt **a**
41:20 The lean, ugly cows **a** up the seven
41:21 even after they **a** them, no-one could
43:32 and the Egyptians who **a** with him by
Ex 16: 3 meat and **a** all the food we wanted,
16:35 The Israelites **a** manna for forty
16:35 they **a** manna until they reached the
24:11 they saw God, and they **a** and drank.
Nu 11: 5 We remember the fish we **a** in Egypt
25: 2 **a** and bowed down before these gods.
Dt 9: 9 I **a** no bread and drank no water.
9:18 I **a** no bread and drank no water,
29: 6 You **a** no bread and drank no wine or
32:38 the gods who **a** the fat of their
Jos 5:11 that very day, they **a** some of the
5:12 they **a** this food from the land;
5:12 they **a** of the produce of Canaan.
Jdg 14: 9 his hands and **a** as he went along.
14: 9 gave them some, and they too **a** it.
19: 8 So the two of them **a** together.
Ru 2:14 She **a** all she wanted and had some
1Sa 1:18 Then she went her way and **a**
14:32 and **a** them, together with the blood.
28:25 before Saul and his men, and they **a**.
30:12 He **a** and was revived, for he had not
2Sa 9:11 So Mephibosheth **a** at David's table
9:13 because he always **a** at the king's
11:13 At David's invitation, he **a** and
12:20 they served him food, and he **a**.
1Ki 4:20 **a**, they drank and they were happy.
13:19 him and **a** and drank in his house.
13:22 You came back and **a** bread and drank
19: 6 **a** and drank and then lay down again.
19: 8 he got up and **a** and drank.
19:21 gave it to the people, and they **a**.
2Ki 4:44 he set it before them, and they **a**
6:29 we cooked my son and **a** him. The next
7: 8 They **a** and drank, and carried away
9:34 Jehu went in and **a** and drank. "Take
23: 9 they **a** unleavened bread with their
25:29 **a** regularly at the king's table.
1Ch 29:22 They **a** and drank with great joy in
2Ch 30:18 yet they **a** the Passover, contrary to
30:22 For the seven days they **a** their
Ezr 6:21 had returned from the exile **a** it,
10: 6 While he was there, he **a** no food and
Ne 5:14 **a** the food allotted to the governor.
5:17 Jews and officials **a** at my table,
9:25 They **a** to the full and were
Job 42:11 came and **a** with him in his house.
Ps 78:25 Men **a** the bread of angels; he sent
78:29 They **a** till they had more than
105:35 they **a** up every green thing in their
105:35 **a** up the produce of their soil.
106:28 **a** sacrifices offered to lifeless
Isa 44:19 its coals, I roasted meat and I **a**.
Jer 15:16 your words came, I **a** them; they were
52:33 **a** regularly at the king's table.
Lam 4: 5 Those who once **a** delicacies are
Eze 3: 3 So I **a** it, and it tasted as sweet
Da 1:15 the young men who **a** the royal food.
4:33 He was driven away from people and **a**
5:21 donkeys and **a** grass like cattle;
10: 3 I **a** no choice food; no meat or wine
Mt 9:10 and **a** with him and his disciples.
12: 4 and he and his companions **a** the
13: 4 and the birds came and **a** it up.
14:20 They all **a** and were satisfied, and
14:21 The number of those who **a** was about
15:37 They all **a** and were satisfied.
15:38 The number of those who **a** was four
Mk 1: 6 and he **a** locusts and wild honey.
2:26 he entered the house of God and **a**
4: 4 and the birds came and **a** it up.
6:42 They all **a** and were satisfied,
8: 8 The people **a** and were satisfied.
Lk 4: 2 He **a** nothing during those days, and
6: 4 he **a** what is lawful only for priests
8: 5 and the birds of the air **a** it up.
9:17 They all **a** and were satisfied, and
13:26 "Then you will say, 'We **a** and drank
24:43 he took it and **a** it in their

Jn 6:26 you a the loaves and had your fill.
6:31 Our forefathers a the manna in the
6:49 Your forefathers a the manna in the
6:58 Your forefathers a manna and died,
Ac 2:46 a together with glad and sincere
10:41 us who a and drank with him after
11: 3 uncircumcised men and a with them."
20:11 again and broke bread and a.
27:36 They were all encouraged and a some
1Co 10: 3 They all a the same spiritual
Rev 10:10 from the angel's hand and a it.

Ater

Ezr 2:16 of **A** (through Hezekiah) 98
2:42 **A**, Talmon, Akkub, Hatita and Shobai
Ne 7:21 of **A** (through Hezekiah) 98
7:45 **A**, Talmon, Akkub, Hatita and Shobai
10:17 **A**, Hezekiah, Azzur,

Athach

1Sa 30:30 to those in Hormah, Bor Ashan, **A**

Athaiah

Ne 11: 4 of Judah: **A** son of Uzziah,

Athaliah

Daughter of Ahab; wife of Jehoram, king of Judah; mother of Ahaziah (2Ki 8:18,26; 2Ch 22:2). Encouraged idolatry (2Ki 8:18,27). After Ahaziah's death, killed royal family (except Joash) and reigned for six years (2Ki 11:1–3; 2Ch 22:10–12). Killed by order of Jehoida, who made Joash king (2Ki 11:4–16; 2Ch 23:1–15).

2Ki 8:26 His mother's name was **A**, a
11: 1 **A** the mother of Ahaziah saw that her
11: 2 him from **A**; so he was not killed.
11: 3 six years while **A** ruled the land.
11:13 **A** heard the noise made by the guards
11:14 Then **A** tore her robes and called out,
11:20 And the city was quiet, because **A**
1Ch 8:26 Shamsherai, Shehariah, **A**,
2Ch 22: 2 name was **A**, a granddaughter of Omri.
22:10 **A** the mother of Ahaziah saw that her
22:11 she hid the child from **A** so that she
22:12 six years while **A** ruled the land.
23:12 **A** heard the noise of the people
23:13 Then **A** tore her robes and shouted,
23:21 **A** had been slain with the sword.
24: 7 Now the sons of that wicked woman **A**
Ezr 8: 7 son of **A**, and with him 70 men;

Atharim

Nu 21: 1 was coming along the road to **A**,

Athenians (Athens)

Ac 17:21 (All the **A** and the foreigners who

Athens (Athenians)

Political and cultural centre of Greek state of Attica visited by Paul. Paul argued with the Athenians about their idolatry (Ac 17:16–32).

Ac 17:15 who escorted Paul brought him to **A**
17:16 While Paul was waiting for them in **A**,
17:22 "Men of **A**! I see that in every way
18: 1 After this, Paul left **A** and went to
1Th 3: 1 best to be left by ourselves in **A**.

Athlai

Ezr 10:28 Jehohanan, Hananiah, Zabbai and **A**.

Athlete

2Ti 2: 5 Similarly, if anyone competes as an a

Atone (Atonement)

Ex 30:15 to the LORD to a for your lives.
2Ch 29:24 a sin offering to a for all Israel,
Da 9:24 to put an end to sin, to a for

Atoned (Atonement)

Dt 21: 8 And the bloodshed will be a for.
1Sa 3:14 be a for by sacrifice or offering.'"
Pr 16: 6 love and faithfulness sin is a for;
Isa 6: 7 is taken away and your sin a for."
Isa 22:14 day this sin will not be a for,"
27: 9 then, will Jacob's guilt be a for,

Atonement (Atone, Atoned, Atoning, *Day of Atonement*)

Ex 25:17 "Make an a cover of pure gold—two
26:34 Put the a cover on the ark of the
29:33 a was made for their ordination
29:36 day as a sin offering to make a.
29:36 Purify the altar by making a for it,
29:37 For seven days make a for the altar
30: 6 before the a cover that is over the
30:10 Once a year Aaron shall make a on
30:10 This annual a must be made with the
30:16 Receive the a money from the
30:16 the LORD, making a for your lives."
31: 7 the ark of the Testimony with the a
32:30 perhaps I can make a for your sin."
35:12 the ark with its poles and the a
37: 6 He made the a cover of pure
39:35 with its poles and the a cover;
40:20 the ark and put the a cover over it.
Lev 1: 4 on his behalf to make a for him.
4:20 In this way the priest will make a
4:26 In this way the priest will make a
4:31 a for him, and he will be forgiven.
4:35 In this way the priest will make a
5: 6 shall make a for him for his sin.
5:10 make a for him for the sin he has
5:13 In this way the priest will make a
5:16 who will make a for him with the ram
5:18 In this way the priest will make a
6: 7 In this way the priest will make a
6:30 to make a in the Holy Place must not
7: 7 to the priest who makes a with them.
8:15 he consecrated it to make a for it.
8:34 by the LORD to make a for you.
9: 7 make a for yourself and the people;
9: 7 for the people and make a for them,
10:17 making a for them before the LORD.
12: 7 before the LORD to make a for her,
12: 8 the priest will make a for her, and
14:18 and make a for him before the LORD.
14:19 make a for the one to be cleansed
14:20 a for him, and he will be clean.
14:21 to be waved to make a for him,
14:29 to make a for him before the LORD.
14:31 In this way the priest will make a
14:53 In this way he will make a for the
15:15 In this way he will make a before
15:30 In this way he will make a for her
16: 2 in front of the a cover on the ark,
16: 2 in the cloud over the a cover.
16: 6 a for himself and his household.
16:10 to be used for making a by sending
16:11 a for himself and his household,
16:13 the a cover above the Testimony,
16:14 it on the front of the a cover;
16:14 seven times before the a cover.
16:15 on the a cover and in front of it.
16:16 In this way he will make a for the
16:17 to make a in the Most Holy Place
16:17 having made a for himself, his
16:18 before the LORD and make a for it.
16:20 "When Aaron has finished making a
16:24 a for himself and for the people.
16:27 into the Most Holy Place to make a,
16:30 on this day a will be made for you,
16:32 father as high priest is to make a.
16:33 make a for the Most Holy Place, for
16:34 **A** is to be made once a year for all
17:11 make a for yourselves on the altar;
17:11 blood that makes a for one's life.
19:22 the priest is to make a for him
Nu 5: 8 ram with which a is made for him.
6:11 to make a for him because he sinned
7:89 a cover on the ark of the Testimony.
8:12 offering, to make a for the Levites.
8:19 to make a for them so that no plague
8:21 and made a for them to purify them.
15:25 The priest is to make a for the
15:28 The priest is to make a before the
15:28 and when a has been made for him, he
16:46 to the assembly to make a for them.
16:47 the incense and made a for them.
Nu 25:13 God and made a for the Israelites."
28:22 as a sin offering to make a for you.
28:30 Include one male goat to make a for
29: 5 as a sin offering to make a for you.
29:11 addition to the sin offering for a
31:50 a for ourselves before the LORD."
35:33 Bloodshed pollutes the land, and a
Dt 21: 8 Accept this a for your people Israel,
32:43 and make a for his land and people.
1Ch 6:49 making a for Israel, in accordance
28:11 its inner rooms and the place of a.
Ne 10:33 for sin offerings to make a for
Eze 16:63 Then, when I make a for you for all
43:20 purify the altar and make a for it.
43:26 For seven days they are to make a
45:15 offerings to make a for the people,
45:17 to make a for the house of Israel.
45:20 so you are to make a for the temple.
Ro 3:25 God presented him as a sacrifice of a
Heb 2:17 make a for the sins of the people.
9: 5 Glory, overshadowing the a cover.

Atoning (Atonement)

Ex 30:10 the blood of the a sin offering
1Jn 2: 2 He is the a sacrifice for our sins,
4:10 Son as an a sacrifice for our sins.

Atroth Beth Joab

1Ch 2:54 the Netophathites, **A**, half the

Atroth Shophan

Nu 32:35 **A**, Jazer, Jogbehah,

Attach (Attached, Attaching)

Ex 28:14 and a the chains to the settings.
28:26 Make two gold rings and a them to
28:27 Make two more gold rings and a them
28:37 Fasten a blue cord to it to a it to
29: 6 Put the turban on his head and a the
39:31 they fastened a blue cord to it to a
Eze 37: 6 I will a tendons to you and make

Attached (Attach)

Ge 29:34 last my husband will become a to me,
32:32 tendon a to the socket of the hip,
Ex 28: 7 is to have two shoulder pieces a to
39: 4 which were a to two of its corners,
39:19 They made two gold rings and a them
39:20 made two more gold rings and a them
39:25 made bells of pure gold and a them
40:20 a the poles to the ark and put the
1Ki 6:10 a to the temple by beams of cedar.
7:28 They had side panels a to uprights.
7:32 of the wheels were a to the stand.
7:35 were a to the top of the stand.
2Ch 3:16 and a them to the chains.
9:18 and a footstool of gold was a to it.
Eze 40:43 long, were a to the wall all around.

Attaching (Attach)

Ex 28:25 a them to the shoulder pieces of the
39:18 a them to the shoulder pieces of the

Attack (Attacked, Attacker, Attackers, Attacking, Attacks)

Ge 14:15 men to a them and he routed them,
32:11 for I am afraid he will come and a
34:30 join forces against me and a me,
43:18 He wants to a us and overpower us
49:19 but he will a them at their heels.
Nu 13:31 "We can't a those people; they are
20:18 march out and a you with the sword."
Dt 20:10 you march up to a a city, make its
Jos 8: 1 army with you, and go up and a Ai.
8: 3 the whole army moved out to a Ai.
9:18 the Israelites did not a them,
10: 4 "Come up and help me a Gibeon," he
10:19 Pursue your enemies, a them from
Jdg 7:10 If you are afraid to a, go down to
7:11 will be encouraged to a the camp.
9:43 out of the city, he rose to a them.
9:45 All that day Abimelech pressed his a
10:18 "Whoever will launch the a against
18: 9 They answered, "Come on, let's a

Jdg 18:25 or some hot-tempered men will a you,
20:34 men made a frontal a on Gibeah.
1Sa 7: 7 the Philistines came up to a them.
14:14 In that first a Jonathan and his
15: 3 Now go, a the Amalekites and totally
17:48 the Philistine moved closer to a him,
23: 2 "Shall I go and a these Philistines?"
23: 2 a the Philistines and save Keilah."
24: 7 and did not allow them to a Saul.
2Sa 5: 6 to a the Jebusites, who lived there.
5:19 "Shall I go and a the Philistines?
5:23 a them in front of the balsam trees.
11:25 Press the a against the city and
17: 2 I would a him while he is weary and
17: 9 If he should a your troops first,
17:12 we will a him wherever he may be
1Ki 20:12 he ordered his men: "Prepare to a.
20:12 So they prepared to a the city.
20:22 the king of Aram will a you again."
22:12 "A Ramoth Gilead and be victorious,"
22:15 "A and be victorious," he answered,
22:32 So they turned to a him, but when
2Ki 3: 8 "By what route shall we a?" he asked.
7: 6 Hittite and Egyptian kings to a us!"
12:17 Then he turned to a Jerusalem.
17: 3 king of Assyria came up to a Hoshea,
18:25 Furthermore, have I come to a and
1Ch 11: 6 David had said, "Whoever leads the a
14:10 "Shall I go and a the Philistines?
14:14 a them in front of the balsam trees.
2Ch 18: 2 and urged him to a Ramoth Gilead.
18:11 "A Ramoth Gilead and be victorious,"
18:14 "A and be victorious," he answered,
18:31 So they turned to a him, but
Ne 4:12 "Wherever you turn, they will a us.
Est 8:11 a them and their women and children;
9: 2 a those seeking their destruction.
Job 15:21 all seems well, marauders a him.
15:24 him, like a king poised to a,
19: 3 reproached me; shamelessly you a me.
30:21 the might of your hand you a me.
Ps 27: 2 a me, they will stumble and fall.
56: 1 me; all day long they press their a.
59: 4 wrong, yet they are ready to a me.
109: 3 me; they a me without cause.
109:28 they a they will be put to shame
Isa 21: 2 Elam, a! Media, lay siege! I will
29: 7 that a her and her fortress and
36:10 Furthermore, have I come to a and
54:15 If anyone does a you, it will not be
Jer 5: 6 a lion from the forest will a them,
6: 4 Arise, let us a at noon! But, alas,
6: 5 arise, let us a at night and destroy
6:23 to a you, O Daughter of Zion."
12: 9 other birds of prey surround and a?
18:18 So come, let's a him with our
37: 8 the Babylonians will return and a
37:19 Babylon will not a you or this land'?
43:11 He will come and a Egypt, bringing
46:13 king of Babylon to a Egypt:
47: 7 when he has ordered it to a Ashkelon
49: 4 riches and say, 'Who will a me?'
49:14 Assemble yourselves to a it! Rise up
49:28 "Arise, and a Kedar and destroy the
49:31 "Arise and a a nation at ease, which
50: 3 A nation from the north will a her
50:21 "A the land of Merathaim and those
50:42 to a you, O Daughter of Babylon.
51:48 destroyers will a her," declares the
Eze 38:11 I will a a peaceful and unsuspecting
Da 8: 7 I saw him a the ram furiously,
11: 7 He will a the forces of the king of
11:39 He will a the mightiest fortresses
Hos 13: 8 I will a them and rip them open.
Joel 3: 9 the fighting men draw near and a.
Zec 12: 9 all the nations that a Jerusalem.
14:13 another, and they will a each other.
Ac 16:22 The crowd joined in the a against
18:10 and no-one is going to a and harm
18:12 the Jews made a united a on Paul
2Ti 4:18 will rescue me from every evil a
Rev 11: 7 a them, and overpower and kill them.

Attacked (Attack)

Ge 4: 8 a his brother Abel and killed him.
34:25 took their swords and a the
49:19 "Gad will be a by a band of raiders,
49:23 With bitterness archers a him; they
Ex 17: 8 The Amalekites came and a the
Nu 14:45 a them and beat them down all the
21: 1 he a the Israelites and captured
Jos 8:21 turned round and a the men of Ai.
10: 5 positions against Gibeon and a it.
10:29 on from Makkedah to Libnah and a it.
10:31 up positions against it and a it.
10:34 up positions against it and a it.
10:36 up from Eglon to Hebron and a it.
10:38 with him turned round and a Debir.
11: 7 at the Waters of Merom and a them,
19:47 so they went up and a Leshem, took
Jdg 1: 4 Judah a, the LORD gave the
1: 8 The men of Judah a Jerusalem also
1:17 a the Canaanites living in Zephath,
1:22 Now the house of Joseph a Bethel,
3:13 Eglon came and a Israel, and they
11:12 us that you have a our country?"
15: 8 He a them viciously and slaughtered
18:27 They a them with the sword and
1Sa 13: 3 Jonathan a the Philistine outpost at
13: 4 "Saul has a the Philistine outpost,
15: 7 Saul a the Amalekites all the way
27: 9 Whenever David a an area, he did not
30: 1 They had a Ziklag and burned it,
2Sa 12:29 to Rabbah, and a and captured it.
1Ki 2:32 of my father David he a two men
9:16 (Pharaoh king of Egypt had a and
14:25 Shishak king of Egypt a Jerusalem.
20: 1 up and besieged Samaria and a it.
2Ki 3:25 surrounded it and a it as well.
12:17 went up and a Gath and captured it.
14:11 listen, so Jehoash king of Israel a.
15:10 He a him in front of the people,
15:14 He a Shallum son of Jabesh in
15:16 starting out from Tirzah, a Tiphsah
15:30 He a and assassinated him, and then
18:13 Sennacherib king of Assyria a all
1Ch 4:41 They a the Hamites in their
20: 1 Joab a Rabbah and left it in ruins.
2Ch 12: 2 Shishak king of Egypt a Jerusalem in
12: 9 Shishak king of Egypt a Jerusalem,
13:14 were being a at both front and rear.
14:15 They also a the camps of the
21:17 They a Judah, invaded it and carried
25:21 Jehoash king of Israel a. He and
28:17 The Edomites had again come and a
36: 6 Nebuchadnezzar king of Babylon a him
Est 8: 7 "Because Haman a the Jews, I have
Job 1:15 the Sabeans a and carried them off.
Ps 53: 5 scattered the bones of those who a
124: 2 not been on our side when men a us,
Isa 20: 1 to Ashdod and a and captured it—
36: 1 Sennacherib king of Assyria a all
Jer 47: 1 Philistines before Pharaoh a Gaza:
49:28 Nebuchadnezzar king of Babylon a:
Zec 14:16 the nations that have a Jerusalem

Attacker (Attack)

Na 2: 1 An a advances against you, Nineveh.

Attackers (Attack)

Ps 35:15 a gathered against me when I was

Attacking (Attack)

1Ki 22:20 'Who will entice Ahab into a Ramoth
2Ki 16: 7 of the king of Israel who are a me."
16: 9 The king of Assyria complied by a
2Ch 18:19 king of Israel into a Ramoth Gilead
20:12 to face this vast army that is a us.
35:21 It is not you I am a at this time,
Ps 54: 3 Strangers are a me; ruthless men
56: 2 long; many are a me in their pride.
86:14 The arrogant are a me, O God; a
Jer 21: 2 king of Babylon is a us.
32:24 to the Babylonians who are a it.
32:29 The Babylonians who are a this city
37:10 Babylonian army that is a you

Attacks (Attack)

Ge 32: 8 He thought, "If Esau comes and a one
Ex 21:15 "Anyone who a his father or his
Dt 22:26 who a and murders his neighbour,
Jos 15:16 who a and captures Kiriath Sepher."
Jdg 1:12 who a and captures Kiriath Sepher."
2Sa 22:44 "You have delivered me from the a of
Job 30:12 On my right the tribe a; they lay
Ps 18:43 You have delivered me from the a of
55:20 My companion a his friends; he
Pr 21:22 A wise man a the city of the mighty
Isa 54:15 whoever a you will surrender to you.
Eze 38:18 When Gog a the land of Israel,
Lk 11:22 someone stronger a and overpowers
Jn 10:12 wolf a the flock and scatters it.

Attai

1Ch 2:35 servant Jarha, and she bore him A.
2:36 A was the father of Nathan, Nathan
12:11 A the sixth, Eliel the seventh,
2Ch 11:20 him Abijah, A, Ziza and Shelomith.

Attain (Attained, Attaining, Attains)

Ps 139: 6 for me, too lofty for me to a.
Pr 2:19 None who go to her return or a the
Gal 3: 3 to a your goal by human effort?
Php 3:11 to a to the resurrection from the

Attained (Attain)

Pr 16:31 it is a by a righteous life.
Ro 9:31 law of righteousness, has not a it.
Php 3:16 live up to what we have already a.
Heb 7:11 If perfection could have been a

Attaining (Attain)

Pr 1: 2 for a wisdom and discipline;
Eph 4:13 a to the whole measure of the

Attains (Attain)

Pr 11:19 The truly righteous man a life,

Attalia

Ac 14:25 word in Perga, they went down to A.
14:26 From A they sailed back to Antioch,

Attempt

Ac 27:30 In an a to escape from the ship,

Attend (Attendance, Attendant, Attendants, Attended, Attending, Attends)

Ge 39:11 day he went into the house to a
1Ki 1: 2 to a the king and take care of him.
Est 4: 5 king's eunuchs assigned to a her,

Attendance (Attend)

SS 8:13 in the gardens with friends in a,

Attendant (Attend)

Ge 39: 4 favour in his eyes and became his a.
1Ki 19:21 to follow Elijah and became his a.
2Ki 22:12 secretary and Asaiah the king's a:
2Ch 34:20 secretary and Asaiah the king's a:
Lk 4:20 gave it back to the a and sat down.
Ac 13: 7 who was an a of the proconsul,

Attendants (Attend)

Ge 45: 1 control himself before all his a,
Ex 2: 5 a were walking along the river bank.
Jdg 3:19 "Quiet!" And all his a left him.
1Sa 8:14 olive groves and give them to his a.
8:15 and give it to his officials and a.
16:15 Saul's a said to him, "See, an evil
16:17 Saul said to his a, "Find someone
18:22 Saul ordered his a: "Speak to David
18:22 and his a all like you; now become
18:26 the a told David these things, he
19: 1 Jonathan and all the a to kill David.
28: 7 Saul then said to his a, "Find me a
2Ki 5:15 Naaman and all his a went back to
24:12 his mother, his a, his nobles and
Ezr 8:17 bring a to us for the house of
Est 1:12 when the a delivered the king's
2: 2 the king's personal a proposed, "Let
6: 3 been done for him," his a answered.

Est 6: 5 His a answered, "Haman is standing
Jer 25:19 Pharaoh king of Egypt, his a, his
36:24 The king and all his a who heard all
36:31 and his a for their wickedness;
37: 2 Neither he nor his a nor the people
Mt 14: 2 he said to his a, "This is John the
22:13 "Then the king told the a, 'Tie him
Ac 10: 7 devout soldier who was one of his a.

Attended (Attend)
Ge 40: 4 them to Joseph, and he a them.
Jdg 14:20 friend who had a him at his wedding.
1Sa 25:42 a by her five maids, went with
Da 7:10 Thousands upon thousands a him; ten
Mt 4:11 left him, and angels came and a him.
Mk 1:13 the wild animals, and angels a him.

Attending (Attend)
1Sa 4:20 she was dying, the women a her said,
1Ki 1:15 Abishag the Shunammite was a him.
10: 5 the a servants in their robes,
2Ch 9: 4 the a servants in their robes,
22: 8 been a Ahaziah, and he killed them.
Est 7: 9 Harbona, one of the eunuchs a the

Attends (Attend)
Jn 3:29 The friend who a the bridegroom

Attention (Attentive, Attentively)
Ge 39:23 The warder paid no a to anything
Ex 4: 8 "If they do not believe you or pay a
5: 9 keep working and pay no a to lies."
15:26 if you pay a to his commands and
16:20 However, some of them paid no a to
23:21 Pay a to him and listen to what he
Nu 5:15 offering to draw a to guilt.
Dt 1:45 but he paid no a to your weeping and
7:12 If you pay a to these laws and are
17: 4 this has been brought to your a,
28:13 If you pay a to the commands of the
Jdg 11:28 The king of Ammon, however, paid no a
Ru 4: 4 I should bring the matter to your a
1Sa 4:20 But she did not respond or pay any a.
25:25 May my lord pay no a to that wicked
1Ki 8:28 Yet give a to your servant's prayer
18:29 no-one answered, no-one paid a.
2Ch 6:19 Yet give a to your servant's prayer
33:10 and his people, but they paid no a.
Ne 8:13 to give a to the words of the Law.
9:30 Yet they paid no a, so you handed
9:34 they did not pay a to your commands
Est 9:25 when the plot came to the king's a,
Job 7:17 of him, that you give him so much a,
32:12 I gave you my full a. But not one of
33: 1 my words; pay a to everything I say.
33:31 "Pay a, Job, and listen to me; be
35:13 plea; the Almighty pays no a to it.
Pr 4: 1 pay a and gain understanding.
4:20 My son, pay a to what I say; listen
5: 1 My son, pay a to my wisdom, listen
7:24 listen to me; pay a to what I say.
17: 4 a liar pays a to a malicious tongue.
22:17 Pay a and listen to the sayings of
27:23 give careful a to your herds;
Ecc 7:21 Do not pay a to every word people
Isa 28:23 Listen and hear my voice; pay a and
34: 1 and listen; pay a, you peoples!
42:20 many things, but have paid no a
42:23 this or pay close a in time to come?
48:18 If only you had paid a to my
Jer 7:24 they did not listen or pay a;
7:26 they did not listen to me or pay a.
11: 8 they did not listen or pay a;
13:15 Hear and pay a, do not be arrogant,
17:23 Yet they did not listen or pay a;
18:18 and pay no a to anything he says."
25: 4 you have not listened or paid any a.
34:14 did not listen to me or pay a to me.
35:15 have not paid a or listened to me.
37: 2 paid any a to the words the LORD had
44: 5 they did not listen or pay a; they
Eze 40: 4 hear with your ears and pay a to
44: 5 listen closely and give a to
44: 5 Give a to the entrance of the temple
Da 3:12 pay no a to you, O king.
6:13 pays no a to you, O king, or to the
9:13 our sins and giving a to your truth.
11:18 he will turn his a to the coastlands
Hos 5: 1 "Hear this, you priests! Pay a, you
Zec 1: 4 or pay a to me, declares the LORD.
7:11 "But they refused to pay a;
Mal 2:13 wail because he no longer pays a to
Mt 7: 3 no a to the plank in your own eye?
22: 5 "But they paid no a and went
22:16 you pay no a to who they are.
24: 1 him to call his a to its buildings.
Mk 12:14 because you pay no a to who they are;
Lk 6:41 no a to the plank in your own eye?
Ac 3: 5 the man gave them his a, expecting
6: 4 will give our a to prayer and the
8: 6 all paid close a to what he said.
8:10 both high and low, gave him their a
Tit 1:14 will pay no a to Jewish myths or to
Heb 2: 1 We must pay more careful a,
Jas 2: 3 If you show special a to the man
2Pe 1:19 and you will do well to pay a to it,
3Jn :10 if I come, I will call a to what he

Attentive (Attention)
2Ch 6:40 your ears a to the prayers offered
7:15 my ears a to the prayers offered in
Ne 1: 6 let your ear be a and your eyes open
1:11 O Lord, let your ear be a to the
Ps 34:15 and his ears are a to their cry;
130: 2 your ears be a to my cry for mercy.
1Pe 3:12 and his ears are a to their prayer,

Attentively (Attention)
Ne 8: 3 listened a to the Book of the Law.
Jer 8: 6 I have listened a, but they do not

Attested
1Sa 3:20 was a as a prophet of the LORD.

Attitude (Attitudes)
Ge 31: 2 Jacob noticed that Laban's a towards
31: 5 "I see that your father's a towards
1Ki 11:11 "Since this is your a and you have
Ezr 6:22 the a of the king of Assyria,
Da 3:19 and his a towards them changed.
Eph 4:23 to be made new in the a of your
Php 2: 5 Your a should be the same as that of
1Pe 4: 1 arm yourselves also with the same a,

Attitudes (Attitude)
Heb 4:12 the thoughts and a of the heart.

Attract (Attracted, Attractive)
Isa 53: 2 He had no beauty or majesty to a us

Attracted (Attract)
Dt 21:11 a beautiful woman and are a to her,
Est 2:17 Now the king was a to Esther more

Attractive (Attract)
Jdg 15: 2 sister more a? Take her instead."
Zec 9:17 How a and beautiful they will be!
Tit 2:10 teaching about God our Saviour a.

Audience
1Ki 10:24 The whole world sought a with
2Ch 9:23 All the kings of the earth sought a
Pr 29:26 Many seek an a with a ruler, but it
Ac 12:20 together and sought an a with him.
25:23 entered the a room with the high

Augustus
Lk 2: 1 In those days Caesar A issued a

Aunt
Lev 18:14 sexual relations; she is your a.
20:20 "If a man sleeps with his a, he has

Author
Ac 3:15 You killed the a of life, but God
Heb 2:10 should make the a of their salvation
12: 2 Let us fix our eyes on Jesus, the a

Authorisation (Authority)
Ac 15:24 us without our a and disturbed you,

Authorised (Authority)
Ezr 3: 7 Joppa, as a by Cyrus king of Persia.
5: 3 "Who a you to rebuild this temple
5: 9 "Who a you to rebuild this temple

Authorities (Authority)
Lk 12:11 rulers and a, do not worry about how
Jn 7:26 Have the a really concluded that he
Ac 16:19 into the market-place to face the a.
Ro 13: 1 submit himself to the governing a,
13: 1 The a that exist have been
13: 5 it is necessary to submit to the a,
13: 6 for the a are God's servants, who
Eph 3:10 rulers and a in the heavenly realms,
6:12 against the a, against the powers of
Col 1:16 thrones or powers or rulers or a;
2:15 having disarmed the powers and a, he
Tit 3: 1 to be subject to rulers and a,
1Pe 3:22 a and powers in submission to him.

Authority (Authorities, Authorisation, Authorised)
Ge 41:35 up the grain under the a of Pharaoh,
Nu 27:20 Give him some of your a so that the
Dt 1:15 and appointed them to have a over
Ezr 7:24 that you have no a to impose taxes,
Ne 3: 7 a of the governor of Trans-Euphrates.
Est 9:29 wrote with full a to confirm this
Isa 22:21 him and hand your a over to him.
Jer 5:31 the priests rule by their own a,
Da 4:31 Your royal a has been taken from you.
7: 6 heads, and it was given a to rule.
7:12 beasts had been stripped of their a,
7:14 He was given a, glory and sovereign
Mt 7:29 he taught as one who had a, and not
8: 9 For I myself am a man under a, with
9: 6 Man has a on earth to forgive sins.
9: 8 God, who had given such a to men.
10: 1 gave them a to drive out evil
20:25 high officials exercise a over them.
21:23 "By what a are you doing these
21:23 "And who gave you this a?"
21:24 by what a I am doing these things.
21:27 by what a I am doing these things.
28:18 Jesus came to them and said, "All a
Mk 1:22 a, not as the teachers of the law.
1:27 A new teaching—and with a! He even
2:10 Man has a on earth to forgive sins .
3:15 to have a to drive out demons.
6: 7 and gave them a over evil spirits.
10:42 high officials exercise a over them.
11:28 "By what a are you doing these
11:28 "And who gave you a to do this?"
11:29 by what a I am doing these things.
11:33 by what a I am doing these things."
Lk 4: 6 "I will give you all their a and
4:32 teaching, because his message had a.
4:36 "What is this teaching? With a and
5:24 Man has a on earth to forgive sins.
7: 8 For I myself am a man under a, with
9: 1 he gave them power and a to drive
10:19 I have given you a to trample on
20: 2 "Tell us by what a you are doing
20: 2 "Who gave you this a?"
20: 8 by what a I am doing these things."
20:20 to the power and a of the governor.
22:25 and those who exercise a over them
Jn 2:18 us to prove your a to do all this?"
5:27 he has given him a to judge because
10:18 I have a to lay it down and a to
17: 2 For you granted him a over all
Ac 1: 7 the Father has set by his own a.
9:14 he has come here with a from the
26:10 On the a of the chief priests I put
26:12 I was going to Damascus with the a
Ro 7: 1 that the law has a over a man only
13: 1 for there is no a except that which
13: 2 he who rebels against the a is
13: 3 be free from fear of the one in a?
1Co 11:10 to have a sign of a on her head.
15:24 destroyed all dominion, a and power.
2Co 10: 8 about the a the Lord gave us for

2Co 13:10 not have to be harsh in my use of a
13:10 the a the Lord gave me for building
Eph 1:21 far above all rule and a, power and
Col 2:10 is the Head over every power and a.
1Th 4: 2 gave you by the a of the Lord Jesus.
1Ti 2: 2 for kings and all those in a, that
2:12 a over a man; she must be silent.
Tit 2:15 Encourage and rebuke with all a.
Heb 13:17 your leaders and submit to their a.
1Pe 2:13 to every a instituted among men:
2:13 to the king, as the supreme a,
2Pe 2:10 of the sinful nature and despise a.
Jude : 6 did not keep their position of a
: 8 a and slander celestial beings.
:25 majesty, power and a, through Jesus
Rev 2:26 I will give a over the nations—
2:27 as I have received a from my Father.
12:10 of our God, and the a of his Christ.
13: 2 power and his throne and great a.
13: 4 because he had given a to the beast,
13: 5 exercise his a for forty-two months.
13: 7 And he was given a over every tribe,
13:12 He exercised all the a of the first
17:12 a as kings along with the beast.
17:13 give their power and a to the beast.
18: 1 He had great a, and the earth was
20: 4 those who had been given a to judge.

Autumn
Dt 11:14 both a and spring rains, so that
Ps 84: 6 a rains also cover it with pools.
Jer 5:24 who gives a and spring rains in
Joel 2:23 you the a rains in righteousness.
2:23 both a and spring rains, as before.
Jas 5: 7 he is for the a and spring rains.
Jude :12 a trees, without fruit and uprooted

Avail (Available)
Isa 16:12 her shrine to pray, it is to no a.
Da 11:27 and lie to each other, but to no a,

Available (Avail)
1Ki 7:36 a space, with wreaths all around.

Aven
Am 1: 5 the king who is in the Valley of A

Avenge (Vengeance)
Lev 26:25 will bring the sword upon you to a
Dt 32:35 It is mine to a; I will repay. In
32:43 he will a the blood of his servants
1Sa 24:12 And may the LORD a the wrongs you
2Sa 3:27 to a the blood of his brother Asahel
2Ki 9: 7 and I will a the blood of my
Est 8:13 to a themselves on their enemies.
Ps 79:10 you a the outpoured blood of your
Isa 1:24 my foes and a myself on my enemies.
Jer 5: 9 a myself on such a nation as this?
5:29 a myself on such a nation as this?
9: 9 a myself on such a nation as this?"
15:15 A me on my persecutors. You are
51:36 I will defend your cause and a
Ro 12:19 to a; I will repay," says the Lord.
Heb 10:30 "It is mine to a; I will repay,"
Rev 6:10 of the earth and a our blood?"

Avenged (Vengeance)
Ge 4:24 If Cain is a seven times, then
Jos 10:13 till the nation a itself on its
Jdg 9:24 might be a on their brother
11:36 a you of your enemies, the Ammonites.
1Sa 14:24 I have a myself on my enemies!"
25:31 bloodshed or of having a himself.
2Sa 4: 8 This day the LORD has a my lord the
Ps 58:10 will be glad when they are a,
Eze 5:13 them will subside, and I will be a.
Ac 7:24 and a him by killing the Egyptian.
Rev 19: 2 a on her the blood of his servants."

Avenger (*Avenger of blood*, Vengeance)
Nu 35:12 will be places of refuge from the a,
Ps 8: 2 to silence the foe and the a.

Avenger of blood
Nu 35:19 The a shall put the murderer to
35:21 The a shall put the murderer to
35:24 a according to these regulations.
35:25 one accused of murder from the a
35:27 the a finds him outside the city,
35:27 the a may kill the accused without
Dt 19: 6 Otherwise, the a might pursue him in
19:12 and hand him over to the a to die.
Jos 20: 3 and find protection from the a.
20: 5 If the a pursues him, they must not
20: 9 not be killed by the a prior to
2Sa 14:11 a from adding to the destruction,

Avenges (Vengeance)
2Sa 22:48 He is the God who a me, who puts the
Ps 9:12 For he who a blood remembers; he
18:47 He is the God who a me, who subdues
94: 1 O LORD, the God who a, O God who a,

Avenging (Vengeance)
1Sa 25:26 from bloodshed and from a yourself
25:33 and from a myself with my own hands.
Na 1: 2 The LORD is a jealous and a God; the

Avert
Jer 11:15 Can consecrated meat a your

Avith
Ge 36:35 His city was named A.
1Ch 1:46 His city was named A.

Avoid (Avoids)
Ne 5: 9 a the reproach of our Gentile
Ps 38:11 My friends and companions a me
Pr 4:15 A it, do not travel on it; turn from
19: 7 how much more do his friends a him!
20: 3 is to a man's honour to a strife,
20:19 so a a man who talks too much.
Ecc 7:18 who fears God will a all extremes.
Eze 46:20 to a bringing them into the outer
Zep 1: 9 On that day I will punish all who a
Jn 18:28 and to a ceremonial uncleanness the
Ac 15:29 You will do well to a these things.
20:16 to a spending time in the province
2Co 8:20 We want to a any criticism of the
Gal 6:12 The only reason they do this is to a
1Th 4: 3 that you should a sexual immorality;
5:22 A every kind of evil.
2Ti 2:16 A godless chatter, because those who
Tit 3: 9 a foolish controversies and

Avoids (Avoid)
Pr 16: 6 the fear of the LORD a man a evil.
16:17 The highway of the upright a evil;

Avva
2Ki 17:24 Cuthah, A, Hamath and Sepharvaim and

Avvim
Jos 18:23 A, Parah, Ophrah,

Avvites
Dt 2:23 for the A who lived in villages as
Jos 13: 3 Gath and Ekron—that of the A);
2Ki 17:31 the A made Nibhaz and Tartak, and

Await (Wait)
Isa 24:17 Terror and pit and snare a you,
Jer 48:43 Terror and pit and snare a you,
Hos 9: 8 yet snares a him on all his paths,
Gal 5: 5 by faith we eagerly a through the
Php 3:20 And we eagerly a a Saviour from

Awaits (Wait)
Job 17: 1 days are cut short, the grave a me.
Ps 65: 1 Praise a you, O God, in Zion; to you
Pr 15:10 Stern discipline a him who leaves
28:22 and is unaware that poverty a him.
Ecc 3:19 same fate a them both: As one dies,
9: 1 knows whether love or hate a him.
Ob : 5 what a disaster a you—would they
Hab 2: 3 For the revelation a an appointed

Awake (Wake)
Job 14:12 not a or be roused from their sleep.
Ps 7: 6 A, my God; decree justice.
17:15 when I a, I shall be satisfied with
35:23 A, and rise to my defence! Contend
44:23 A, O Lord! Why do you sleep? Rouse
57: 8 A, my soul! A, harp and lyre! I will
102: 7 I lie a; I have become like a bird
108: 2 A, harp and lyre! I will awaken the
139:18 When I a, I am still with you.
Pr 6:22 when you a, they will speak to you.
20:13 a and you will have food to spare.
SS 4:16 A, north wind, and come, south wind!
5: 2 I slept but my heart was a. Listen!
Isa 51: 9 A, a! Clothe yourself with strength,
51: 9 a, as in days gone by, as in
51:17 A, a! Rise up, O Jerusalem, you who
52: 1 A, a, O Zion, clothe yourself with
Jer 51:39 then sleep for ever and not a,"
51:57 will sleep for ever and not a,"
Da 12: 2 will a: some to everlasting life,
Zec 13: 7 "A, O sword, against my shepherd,
Lk 9:32 but when they became fully a, they
1Th 5:10 whether we are a or asleep, we may
Rev 16:15 a and keeps his clothes with him,

Awaken (Wake)
Ps 57: 8 harp and lyre! I will a the dawn.
80: 2 A your might; come and save us.
108: 2 Awake, harp and lyre! I will a the
SS 2: 7 or a love until it so desires.
3: 5 or a love until it so desires.
8: 4 or a love until it so desires.

Awakened (Wake)
1Ki 18:27 Maybe he is sleeping and must be a."
2Ki 4:31 and told him, "The boy has not a.

Awakens (Wake)
Isa 29: 8 but he a, and his hunger remains; as
29: 8 a faint, with his thirst unquenched.

Awakes (Wake)
Ps 73:20 a dream when one a, so when you

Award
2Ti 4: 8 the righteous Judge, will a to me on

Aware
Ge 19:33 He was not a of it when she lay down
19:35 Again he was not a of it when she
28:16 this place, and I was not a of it."
Ex 34:29 he was not a that his face was
Lev 4:14 they become a of the sin they
4:23 he is made a of the sin he committed,
4:28 he is made a of the sin he committed,
Nu 15:24 without the community being a of it,
1Sa 14: 3 No-one was a that Jonathan had left.
1Ki 8:38 each one a of the afflictions of his
2Ch 6:29 one a of his afflictions and pains,
Ne 4:15 our enemies heard that we were a of
Mt 12:15 A of this, Jesus withdrew from that
16: 8 A of their discussion, Jesus asked,
24:50 him and at an hour he is not a of.
26:10 A of this, Jesus said to them, "Why
Mk 8:17 A of their discussion, Jesus asked
Lk 12:46 him and at an hour he is not a of.
Jn 6:61 A that his disciples were grumbling
Ac 10:28 He said to them: "You are well a
Gal 4:21 are you not a of what the law says?

Awe (Awesome, Overawed)
1Sa 12:18 in a of the LORD and of Samuel.
1Ki 3:28 they held the king in a, because
Job 25: 2 "Dominion and a belong to God; he
Ps 119:120 of you; I stand in a of your laws.
Ecc 5: 7 Therefore stand in a of God.
Isa 29:23 stand in a of the God of Israel.
Jer 2:19 LORD your God and have no a of me,"
33: 9 and they will be in a and will
Hab 3: 2 I stand in a of your deeds, O LORD.
Mal 2: 5 me and stood in a of my name.
Mt 9: 8 they were filled with a; and they
Lk 1:65 The neighbours were all filled with a

Lk 5:26 They were filled with **a** and said,
7:16 They were all filled with **a** and
Ac 2:43 Everyone was filled with **a**, and many
Heb 12:28 God acceptably with reverence and **a**,

Awesome (Awe)

Ge 28:17 He was afraid and said, "How **a** is
Ex 15:11 **a** in glory, working wonders?
34:10 will see how **a** is the work that I,
Dt 4:34 or by great and **a** deeds, like all
7:21 is among you, is a great and **a** God.
10:17 the great God, mighty and **a**, who
10:21 **a** wonders you saw with your own eyes.
28:58 and **a** name—the LORD your God—
34:12 performed the **a** deeds that Moses did
Jdg 13: 6 looked like an angel of God, very **a**.
2Sa 7:23 and to perform great and **a** wonders
1Ch 17:21 and to perform great and **a** wonders
Ne 1: 5 God of heaven, the great and **a** God,
4:14 who is great and **a**, and fight for
9:32 O our God, the great, mighty and **a**
Job 10:16 display your **a** power against me.
37:22 splendour; God comes in **a** majesty.
Ps 45: 4 let your right hand display **a** deeds.
47: 2 How **a** is the LORD Most High, the
65: 5 You answer us with **a** deeds of
66: 3 Say to God, "How **a** are your deeds!
66: 5 Come and see what God has done, how **a**
68:35 You are **a**, O God, in your sanctuary;
89: 7 is more **a** than all who surround him.
99: 3 Let them praise your great and **a**
106:22 miracles in the land of Ham and **a**
111: 9 for ever—holy and **a** is his name.
145: 6 tell of the power of your **a** works,
Isa 64: 3 For when you did **a** things that we
Eze 1:18 Their rims were high and **a**, and all
1:22 expanse, sparkling like ice, and **a**.
Da 2:31 dazzling statue, **a** in appearance.
9: 4 "O Lord, the great and **a** God, who
Zep 2:11 The LORD will be **a** to them when he

Awful

Jdg 20: 3 "Tell us how this **a** thing happened.
20:12 **a** crime that was committed among you?
Ne 9:18 when they committed **a** blasphemies.
9:26 you; they committed **a** blasphemies.
Jer 30: 7 How **a** that day will be! None will be

Awl

Ex 21: 6 and pierce his ear with an **a**.
Dt 15:17 take an **a** and push it through his

Awnings

Eze 27: 7 your **a** were of blue and purple from

Awoke (Wake)

Ge 9:24 Noah **a** from his wine and found out
28:16 Jacob **a** from his sleep, he thought,
Jdg 16:14 the Philistines are upon you!" He **a**
16:20 the Philistines are upon you!" He **a**
1Ki 3:15 Solomon **a**—and he realised it had
Ps 78:65 the Lord **a** as from sleep, as a man
Jer 31:26 At this I **a** and looked around. My

Axe (Axe-head, Axes)

Dt 19: 5 and as he swings his **a** to fell a
20:19 its trees by putting an **a** to them,
Jdg 9:48 He took an **a** and cut off some
Ecc 10:10 If the **a** is dull and its edge
Isa 10:15 Does the **a** raise itself above him
10:34 down the forest thickets with an **a**;
Mt 3:10 The **a** is already at the root of the
Lk 3: 9 The **a** is already at the root of the

Axe-head (Axe)

2Ki 6: 5 the iron **a** fell into the water.

Axes (Axe)

1Sa 13:20 mattocks, **a** and sickles sharpened.
13:21 and **a** and for repointing goads.
2Sa 12:31 with saws and with iron picks and **a**,
1Ch 20: 3 with saws and with iron picks and **a**.
Ps 74: 5 They behaved like men wielding **a** to
Ps 74: 6 panelling with their **a** and hatchets.
Jer 46:22 with **a**, like men who cut down trees.

Axles

1Ki 7:30 four bronze wheels with bronze **a**,
7:32 and the **a** of the wheels were
7:33 the **a**, rims, spokes and hubs were

Ayyah

1Ch 7:28 all the way to **A** and its villages.

Azaliah

2Ki 22: 3 Shaphan son of **A**, the son of
2Ch 34: 8 he sent Shaphan son of **A** and

Azaniah

Ne 10: 9 The Levites: Jeshua son of **A**, Binnui

Azarel

1Ch 12: 6 Elkanah, Isshiah, **A**, Joezer and
25:18 the eleventh to **A**, his sons and
27:22 over Dan: **A** son of Jeroham. These
Ezr 10:41 **A**, Shelemiah, Shemariah,
Ne 11:13 men; Amashsai son of **A**,
12:36 his associates—Shemaiah, **A**, Milalai,

Azariah (Azariah's, Uzziah)

1Ki 4: 2 these were his chief officials: **A**
4: 5 **A** son of Nathan—in charge of the
2Ki 14:21 all the people of Judah took **A**, who
15: 1 **A** son of Amaziah king of Judah began
15: 7 **A** rested with his fathers and was
15: 8 In the thirty-eighth year of **A** king
15:17 In the thirty-ninth year of **A** king
15:23 In the fiftieth year of **A** king of
15:27 In the fifty-second year of **A** king
1Ch 2: 8 The son of Ethan: **A**.
2:38 of Jehu, Jehu the father of **A**,
2:39 **A** the father of Helez, Helez the
3:12 Amaziah his son, **A** his son, Jotham
6: 9 Ahimaaz the father of **A**, **A** the
6:10 Johanan the father of **A** (it was he
6:11 **A** the father of Amariah, Amariah the
6:13 of Hilkiah, Hilkiah the father of **A**,
6:14 **A** the father of Seraiah, and Seraiah
6:36 the son of **A**, the son of Zephaniah,
9:11 **A** son of Hilkiah, the son of
2Ch 15: 1 The Spirit of God came upon **A** son of
15: 8 of **A** son of Oded the prophet,
21: 2 the sons of Jehoshaphat, were **A**,
23: 1 of a hundred: **A** son of Jeroham,
23: 1 Ishmael son of Jehohanan, **A** son of
26:17 **A** the priest with eighty other
26:20 **A** the chief priest and all the other
28:12 some of the leaders in Ephraim—**A**
29:12 Joel son of **A**; from the Merarites,
29:12 Kish son of Abdi and **A** son of
31:10 **A** the chief priest, from the family
31:13 **A** the official in charge of the
Ezr 7: 1 the son of **A**, the son of Hilkiah,
7: 3 the son of Amariah, the son of **A**,
Ne 3:23 **A** son of Maaseiah, the son of
7: 7 Jeshua, Nehemiah, **A**, Raamiah,
8: 7 Hodiah, Maaseiah, Kelita, **A**, Jozabad,
10: 2 Seraiah, **A**, Jeremiah,
12:33 along with **A**, Ezra, Meshullam,
Jer 43: 2 **A** son of Hoshaiah and Johanan son of
Da 1: 6 Daniel, Hananiah, Mishael and **A**.
1: 7 Mishael, Meshach; and to **A**, Abednego.
1:11 Daniel, Hananiah, Mishael and **A**,
1:19 Hananiah, Mishael and **A**; so they
2:17 his friends Hananiah, Mishael and **A**.

Azariah's (Azariah)

2Ki 15: 6 for the other events of **A** reign, and
Ne 3:24 **A** house to the angle and the corner,

Azariahu

2Ch 21: 2 Zechariah, **A**, Michael and Shephatiah.

Azaz

1Ch 5: 8 Bela son of **A**, the son of Shema, the

Azaziah

1Ch 15:21 Mikneiah, Obed-Edom, Jeiel and **A**
27:20 over the Ephraimites: Hoshea son of **A**
2Ch 31:13 Jehiel, **A**, Nahath, Asahel, Jerimoth,

Azbuk

Ne 3:16 Beyond him, Nehemiah son of **A**, ruler

Azekah

Jos 10:10 down all the way to **A** and Makkedah.
10:11 the road down from Beth Horon to **A**,
15:35 Jarmuth, Adullam, Socoh, **A**,
1Sa 17: 1 Ephes Dammim, between Socoh and **A**.
2Ch 11: 9 Adoraim, Lachish, **A**,
Ne 11:30 and in **A** and its settlements.
Jer 34: 7 still holding out—Lachish and **A**.

Azel

1Ch 8:37 son, Eleasah his son and **A** his son.
8:38 **A** had six sons, and these were their
8:38 All these were the sons of **A**.
9:43 son, Eleasah his son and **A** his son.
9:44 **A** had six sons, and these were their
9:44 These were the sons of **A**.
Zec 14: 5 valley, for it will extend to **A**.

Azgad

Ezr 2:12 of **A** 1,222
8:12 of the descendants of **A**, Johanan son
Ne 7:17 of **A** 2,322
10:15 Bunni, **A**, Bebai,

Aziel

1Ch 15:20 Zechariah, **A**, Shemiramoth, Jehiel,

Aziza

Ezr 10:27 Mattaniah, Jeremoth, Zabad and **A**.

Azmaveth

2Sa 23:31 Abi-Albon the Arbathite, **A** the
1Ch 8:36 **A** and Zimri, and Zimri was the
9:42 Jadah was the father of Alemeth, **A**
11:33 **A** the Baharumite, Eliahba the
12: 3 Jeziel and Pelet the sons of **A**;
27:25 **A** son of Adiel was in charge of the
Ezr 2:24 of **A** 42
Ne 12:29 and from the area of Geba and **A**,

Azmon

Nu 34: 4 go to Hazar Addar and over to **A**,
Jos 15: 4 then passed along to **A** and joined

Aznoth Tabor

Jos 19:34 The boundary ran west through **A** and

Azor

Mt 1:13 of Eliakim, Eliakim the father of **A**,
1:14 **A** the father of Zadok, Zadok the

Azotus

Ac 8:40 Philip, however, appeared at **A** and

Azriel

1Ch 5:24 **A**, Jeremiah, Hodaviah and Jahdiel.
27:19 over Naphtali: Jerimoth son of **A**;
Jer 36:26 a son of the king, Seraiah son of **A**

Azrikam

1Ch 3:23 Hizkiah and **A**—three in all.
8:38 and these were their names: **A**,
9:14 **A**, the son of Hashabiah, a Merarite;
9:44 and these were their names: **A**,
2Ch 28: 7 **A** the officer in charge of the
Ne 11:15 the son of **A**, the son of Hashabiah,

Azubah

1Ki 22:42 name was **A** daughter of Shilhi.
1Ch 2:18 by his wife **A** (and by Jerioth).
2:19 **A** died, Caleb married Ephrath, who
2Ch 20:31 name was **A** daughter of Shilhi.

Azzan

Nu 34:26 Paltiel son of **A**, the leader from

Azzur

Ne 10:17 Ater, Hezekiah, **A**,
Jer 28: 1 the prophet Hananiah son of **A**, who
Eze 11: 1 of **A** and Pelatiah son of Benaiah,

Baal (Baal's, Baals)
Nu 25: 3 Israel joined in worshipping the **B**
25: 5 in worshipping the **B** of Peor."
Dt 4: 3 everyone who followed the **B** of Peor,
Jdg 2:13 they forsook him and served **B** and
6:25 Tear down your father's altar to **B**
6:31 If **B** really is a god, he can defend
6:32 "Jerub-Baal," saying, "Let **B** contend
1Ki 16:31 began to serve Baal and worship him
16:32 He set up an altar for **B** in the
16:32 temple of **B** that he built in Samaria
18:19 fifty prophets of **B** and the four
18:21 but if **B** is God, follow him.
18:22 **B** has four hundred and fifty prophets
18:25 Elijah said to the prophets of **B**,
18:26 Then they called on the name of **B**
18:26 "O **B**, answer us!" they shouted.
18:40 them, "Seize the prophets of **B**.
19:18 knees have not bowed down to **B**
22:53 He served and worshipped **B** and
2Ki 3: 2 stone of **B** that his father had made.
10:18 Ahab served **B** a little; Jehu will
10:19 Now summon all the prophets of **B**,
10:19 to hold a great sacrifice for **B**.
10:19 order to destroy the ministers of **B**.
10:20 "Call an assembly in honour of **B**.
10:21 all the ministers of **B** came;
10:21 They crowded into the temple of **B**
10:22 robes for all the ministers of **B**.
10:23 of Recab went into the temple of **B**.
10:23 Jehu said to the ministers of **B**,
10:23 here with you—only ministers of **B**."
10:25 the inner shrine of the temple of **B**.
10:26 of the temple of **B** and burned it.
10:27 They demolished the sacred stone of **B**
10:27 and tore down the temple of **B**,
10:28 Jehu destroyed **B** worship in Israel.
11:18 to the temple of **B** and tore it down.
11:18 killed Mattan the priest of **B**
17:16 starry hosts, and they worshipped **B**.
21: 3 to **B** and made an Asherah pole,
23: 4 LORD all the articles made for **B**
23: 5 those who burned incense to **B**,
1Ch 5: 5 Micah his son, Reaiah his son, **B** his
8:30 by Zur, Kish, **B**, Ner, Nadab,
9:36 by Zur, Kish, **B**, Ner, Nadab,
2Ch 23:17 to the temple of **B** and tore it down.
23:17 priest of **B** in front of the altars.
26: 7 in Gur **B** and against the Meunites.
Ps 106:28 yoked themselves to the **B** of Peor
Jer 2: 8 The prophets prophesied by **B**,
7: 9 burn incense to **B** and follow other
11:13 burn incense to that shameful god **B**
11:17 me to anger by burning incense to **B**.
12:16 once taught my people to swear by **B**
19: 5 They have built the high places of **B**
19: 5 sons in the fire as offerings to **B**
23:13 They prophesied by **B** and led my
23:27 forgot my name through **B** worship.
32:29 burning incense on the roofs to **B**
32:35 They built high places for **B** in the
Hos 2: 8 and gold—which they used for **B**.
13: 1 became guilty of **B** worship and died.
Zep 1: 4 from this place every remnant of **B**,
Ro 11: 4 who have not bowed the knee to **B**."

Baal's (Baal)
Jdg 6:28 there was **B** altar, demolished, with
6:30 because he has broken down **B** altar
6:31 "Are you going to plead **B** cause?
6:32 him," because he broke down **B** altar.

Baal Gad
Jos 11:17 which rises towards Seir, to **B** in
12: 7 from **B** in the Valley of Lebanon to
13: 5 **B** below Mount Hermon to Lebo Hamath.

Baal Hamon
SS 8:11 Solomon had a vineyard in **B**; he let

Baal Hazor
2Sa 13:23 at **B** near the border of Ephraim,

Baal Hermon
Jdg 3: 3 from Mount **B** to Lebo Hamath.
1Ch 5:23 **B**, that is, to Senir (Mount Hermon).

Baal Meon
Nu 32:38 as well as Nebo and **B** (these names
1Ch 5: 8 the area from Aroer to Nebo and **B**.
Eze 25: 9 **B** and Kiriathaim—the glory of that

Baal Peor
Dt 4: 3 own eyes what the LORD did at **B**.
Hos 9:10 But when they came to **B**, they

Baal Perazim
2Sa 5:20 David went to **B**, and there he
5:20 So that place was called **B**.
1Ch 14:11 David and his men went up to **B**, and
14:11 So that place was called **B**.

Baal Shalishah
2Ki 4:42 A man came from **B**, bringing the man

Baal Tamar
Jdg 20:33 places and took up positions at **B**,

Baal Zephon
Ex 14: 2 by the sea, directly opposite **B**.
14: 9 sea near Pi Hahiroth, opposite **B**.
Nu 33: 7 east of **B**, and camped near Migdol.

Baalah
Jos 15: 9 towards **B** (that is, Kiriath Jearim).
15:10 curved westward from **B** to Mount Seir,
15:11 to Mount **B** and reached Jabneel.
15:29 **B**, Iim, Ezem,
2Sa 6: 2 He and all his men set out from **B** of
1Ch 13: 6 the Israelites with him went to **B**

Baalath
Jos 19:44 Eltekeh, Gibbethon, **B**,
1Ki 9:18 **B**, and Tadmor in the desert, within
1Ch 4:33 around these towns as far as **B**.
2Ch 8: 6 well as **B** and all his store cities,

Baalath Beer
Jos 19: 8 as far as **B** (Ramah in the Negev).

Baal-Berith
Jdg 8:33 They set up **B** as their god
9: 4 of silver from the temple of **B**,

Baal-Hanan
Ge 36:38 Shaul died, **B** son of Acbor succeeded
36:39 **B** son of Acbor died, Hadad succeeded
1Ch 1:49 Shaul died, **B** son of Acbor succeeded
1:50 **B** died, Hadad succeeded him as king.
27:28 **B** the Gederite was in charge of the

Baalis
Jer 40:14 said to him, "Don't you know that **B**

Baals (Baal)
Jdg 2:11 eyes of the LORD and served the **B**.
3: 7 and served the **B** and the Asherahs.
8:33 prostituted themselves to the **B**.
10: 6 They served the **B** and the Ashtoreths
10:10 forsaking our God and serving the **B**
1Sa 7: 4 the Israelites put away their **B** and
12:10 and served the **B** and the Ashtoreths.
1Ki 18:18 commands and have followed the **B**.
2Ch 17: 3 He did not consult the **B**
24: 7 even its sacred objects for the **B**.
28: 2 cast idols for worshipping the **B**.
33: 3 to the **B** and made Asherah poles.
34: 4 the altars of the **B** were torn down;
Jer 2:23 I have not run after the **B**'? See how
9:14 they have followed the **B**,
Hos 2:13 days she burned incense to the **B**;
2:17 I will remove the names of the **B**
11: 2 They sacrificed to the **B** and they

Baal-Zebub (Beelzebub)
2Ki 1: 2 "Go and consult **B**, the god of Ekron,
1: 3 off to consult **B**, the god of Ekron?'
1: 6 you are sending men to consult **B**,
1:16 have sent messengers to consult **B**,

Baana
1Ki 4:12 **B** son of Ahilud—in Taanach and
4:16 **B** son of Hushai—in Asher and in
Ne 3: 4 Zadok son of **B** also made repairs.

Baanah
2Sa 4: 2 One was named **B** and the other Recab;
4: 5 Now Recab and **B**, the sons of Rimmon
4: 6 Recab and his brother **B** slipped away.
4: 9 answered Recab and his brother **B**,
23:29 Heled son of **B** the Netophathite,
1Ch 11:30 Heled son of **B** the Netophathite,
Ezr 2: 2 Mispar, Bigvai, Rehum and **B**): The
Ne 7: 7 Mispereth, Bigvai, Nehum and **B**):
10:27 Malluch, Harim and **B**

Baara
1Ch 8: 8 had divorced his wives Hushim and **B**.

Baaseiah
1Ch 6:40 the son of Michael, the son of **B**,

Baasha (Baasha's)
1Ki 15:16 There was war between Asa and **B** king
15:17 **B** king of Israel went up against
15:19 Now break your treaty with **B** king of
15:21 **B** heard this, he stopped building
15:22 and timber **B** had been using there.
15:27 **B** son of Ahijah of the house of
15:28 **B** killed Nadab in the third year of
15:32 There was war between Asa and **B** king
15:33 **B** son of Ahijah became king of all
16: 1 to Jehu son of Hanani against **B**:
16: 3 am about to consume **B** and his house
16: 4 Dogs will eat those belonging to **B**
16: 6 **B** rested with his fathers and was
16: 7 son of Hanani to **B** and his house,
16: 8 Elah son of **B** became king of Israel,
16:12 Zimri destroyed the whole family of **B**
16:12 against **B** through the prophet Jehu—
16:13 of all the sins **B** and his son Elah
21:22 Nebat and that of **B** son of Ahijah,
2Ki 9: 9 like the house of **B** son of Ahijah.
2Ch 16: 1 **B** king of Israel went up against
16: 3 Now break your treaty with **B** king
16: 5 **B** heard this, he stopped building
16: 6 stones and timber **B** had been using.
Jer 41: 9 defence against **B** king of Israel.

Baasha's (Baasha)
1Ki 16: 5 for the other events of **B** reign,
16:11 he killed off **B** whole family.

Babbler (Babbling)
Ac 17:18 "What is this **b** trying to say?"

Babbling (Babbler)
Mt 6: 7 do not keep on **b** like pagans

Babel (Babylon)
Ge 11: 9 That is why it was called **B**—because

Babies (Baby)
Ge 25:22 The **b** jostled each other within her,
Ex 2: 6 "This is one of the Hebrew **b**," she
Lk 18:15 People were also bringing **b** to Jesus
Ac 7:19 newborn **b** so that they would die.
1Pe 2: 2 Like newborn **b**, crave pure spiritual

Baboons
1Ki 10:22 silver and ivory, and apes and **b**.
2Ch 9:21 silver and ivory, and apes and **b**.

Baby (Baby's, Babies)
Ex 2: 6 She opened it and saw the **b**. He was
2: 7 Hebrew women to nurse the **b** for you?"
2: 9 "Take this **b** and nurse him for me,
2: 9 the woman took the **b** and nursed him.
1Ki 3:17 had a **b** while she was there with me.
3:18 was born, this woman also had a **b**.
3:26 her the living **b**! Don't kill him!"
3:27 Give the living **b** to the first woman.
Isa 49:15 "Can a mother forget the **b** at her

Lk 1:41 the **b** leaped in her womb, and
1:44 the **b** in my womb leaped for joy.
1:57 was time for Elizabeth to have her **b**,
2: 6 the time came for the **b** to be born,
2:12 You will find a **b** wrapped in cloths
2:16 the **b**, who was lying in the manger.
Jn 16:21 but when her **b** is born she forgets

Baby's (Baby)

Ex 2: 8 the girl went and got the **b** mother.

Babylon (Babylon's, Babel, Babylonia, Babylonian, Babylonians, Babylonians')

1. City on the Euphrates in the Land of Shinar, founded by Nimrod (Ge 10:10). Became capital city of Babylonian Empire; known for its great splendour (Da 4:30). Its destruction was prophesied (Isa 47; Jer 50). The city was taken by the Persians. **2.** Name used generally for Babylonia. **3.** Used figuratively for Rome to emphasise its opposition to God (Rev 14:8; 16:19).

Ge 10:10 first centres of his kingdom were **B**,
2Ki 17:24 of Assyria brought people from **B**,
17:30 The men from **B** made Succoth Benoth,
20:12 **B** sent Hezekiah letters and a gift,
20:14 "They came from **B**."
20:17 this day, will be carried off to **B**.
20:18 in the palace of the king of **B**."
24: 1 Nebuchadnezzar king of **B** invaded the
24: 7 because the king of **B** had taken all
24:10 king of **B** advanced on Jerusalem
24:12 the reign of the king of **B**,
24:15 took Jehoiachin captive to **B**.
24:15 He also took from Jerusalem to **B** the
24:16 The king of **B** also deported to **B** the
24:20 rebelled against the king of **B**.
25: 1 Nebuchadnezzar king of **B** marched
25: 6 He was taken to the king of **B** at
25: 7 bronze shackles and took him to **B**.
25: 8 year of Nebuchadnezzar king of **B**,
25: 8 of the king of **B**, came to Jerusalem.
25:11 who had gone over to the king of **B**.
25:13 and they carried the bronze to **B**.
25:20 them to the king of **B** at Riblah.
25:22 Nebuchadnezzar king of **B** appointed
25:23 **B** had appointed Gedaliah as governor,
25:24 serve the king of **B**, and it will go
25:27 year Evil-Merodach became king of **B**,
25:28 other kings who were with him in **B**.
1Ch 9: 1 taken captive to **B** because of their
2Ch 32:31 envoys were sent by the rulers of **B**
33:11 bronze shackles and took him to **B**.
36: 6 Nebuchadnezzar king of **B** attacked
36: 6 bronze shackles to take him to **B**.
36: 7 Nebuchadnezzar also took to **B**
36:10 sent for him and brought him to **B**,
36:18 He carried to **B** all the articles
36:20 He carried into exile to **B** the
Ezr 1:11 exiles came up from **B** to Jerusalem.
2: 1 whom Nebuchadnezzar king of **B** had
2: 1 to **B** (they returned to Jerusalem
4: 9 Erech and **B**, the Elamites of Susa,
5:12 king of **B**, who destroyed this temple
5:12 temple and deported the people to **B**.
5:13 the first year of Cyrus king of **B**,
5:14 He even removed from the temple of **B**
5:14 and brought to the temple in **B**.
5:17 in the royal archives of **B**
6: 1 stored in the treasury at **B**.
6: 5 in Jerusalem and brought to **B**,
7: 6 this Ezra came up from **B**. He was a
7: 9 He had begun his journey from **B** on
7:16 may obtain from the province of **B**,
8: 1 who came up with me from **B** during
Ne 7: 6 exiles whom Nebuchadnezzar king of **B**
13: 6 of **B** I had returned to the king.
Est 2: 6 by Nebuchadnezzar king of **B**,
Ps 87: 4 "I will record Rahab and **B** among
137: 1 By the rivers of **B** we sat and wept
137: 8 O Daughter of **B**, doomed to
Isa 13: 1 An oracle concerning **B** that Isaiah
13:19 **B**, the jewel of kingdoms, the glory
14: 4 up this taunt against the king of **B**:
14:22 "I will cut off from **B** her name and
Isa 21: 9 '**B** has fallen, has fallen!
39: 1 King of **B** sent Hezekiah letters and
39: 3 "They came to me from **B**."
39: 6 this day, will be carried off to **B**.
39: 7 in the palace of the king of **B**."
43:14 "For your sake I will send to **B** and
47: 1 Virgin Daughter of **B**; sit on the
48:14 will carry out his purpose against **B**
48:20 Leave **B**, flee from the Babylonians!
Jer 20: 4 all Judah over to the king of **B**,
20: 4 away to **B** or put them to the sword.
20: 5 as plunder and carry it off to **B**.
20: 6 your house will go into exile to **B**.
21: 2 king of **B** is attacking us.
21: 4 are using to fight the king of **B**
21: 7 to Nebuchadnezzar king of **B** and to
21:10 into the hands of the king of **B**
22:25 king of **B** and to the Babylonians.
24: 1 to **B** by Nebuchadnezzar king of **B**,
25: 1 year of Nebuchadnezzar king of **B**.
25: 9 servant Nebuchadnezzar king of **B**,"
25:11 the king of **B** for seventy years.
25:12 I will punish the king of **B** and his
27: 6 my servant Nebuchadnezzar king of **B**;
27: 8 of **B** or bow its neck under his yoke,
27: 9 'You will not serve the king of **B**.'
27:11 yoke of the king of **B** and serve him,
27:12 king of **B**; serve him and his people,
27:13 that will not serve the king of **B**?
27:14 'You will not serve the king of **B**,'
27:16 house will be brought back from **B**.
27:17 Serve the king of **B**, and you will
27:18 and in Jerusalem not be taken to **B**.
27:20 which Nebuchadnezzar king of **B** did
27:20 Judah into exile from Jerusalem to **B**,
27:22 'They will be taken to **B** and there
28: 2 break the yoke of the king of **B**.
28: 3 **B** removed from here and took to **B**.
28: 4 her exiles from Judah who went to **B**,'
28: 4 break the yoke of the king of **B**.'"
28: 6 exiles back to this place from **B**.
28:11 yoke of Nebuchadnezzar king of **B**
28:14 king of **B**, and they will serve him.
29: 1 into exile from Jerusalem to **B**.
29: 3 sent to King Nebuchadnezzar in **B**.
29: 4 into exile from Jerusalem to **B**:
29:10 seventy years are completed for **B**,
29:15 has raised up prophets for us in **B**,"
29:20 I have sent away from Jerusalem to **B**.
29:21 over to Nebuchadnezzar king of **B**,
29:22 who are in **B** will use this curse:
29:22 the king of **B** burned in the fire.'
29:28 He has sent this message to us in **B**:
32: 2 The army of the king of **B** was then
32: 3 king of **B**, and he will capture it.
32: 4 be handed over to the king of **B**,
32: 5 He will take Zedekiah to **B**, where
32:28 king of **B**, who will capture it.
32:36 be handed over to the king of **B**';
34: 1 While Nebuchadnezzar king of **B** and
34: 2 king of **B**, and he will burn it down.
34: 3 You will see the king of **B** with your
34: 3 And you will go to **B**.
34: 7 while the army of the king of **B** was
34:21 of **B**, which has withdrawn from you.
35:11 when Nebuchadnezzar king of **B**
36:29 the king of **B** would certainly come
37: 1 Judah by Nebuchadnezzar king of **B**;
37:17 be handed over to the king of **B**."
37:19 **B** will not attack you or this land'?
38: 3 king of **B**, who will capture it.'"
38:17 to the officers of the king of **B**,
38:18 to the officers of the king of **B**,
38:22 to the officials of the king of **B**.
38:23 will be captured by the king of **B**
39: 1 Nebuchadnezzar king of **B** marched
39: 3 all the officials of the king of **B**
39: 3 other officials of the king of **B**.
39: 5 **B** at Riblah in the land of Hamath,
39: 6 There at Riblah the king of **B**
39: 7 bronze shackles to take him to **B**.
39: 9 carried into exile to **B** the people
39:11 Now Nebuchadnezzar king of **B** had
39:13 the other officers of the king of **B**
40: 1 were being carried into exile to **B**.
40: 4 Come with me to **B**, if you like, and
Jer 40: 5 whom the king of **B** has appointed
40: 7 the king of **B** had appointed Gedaliah
40: 7 not been carried into exile to **B**,
40: 9 serve the king of **B**, and it will go
40:11 king of **B** had left a remnant in Judah
41: 2 killing the one whom the king of **B**
41:18 whom the king of **B** had appointed as
42:11 Do not be afraid of the king of **B**,
43: 3 us or carry us into exile to **B**."
43:10 my servant Nebuchadnezzar king of **B**,
44:30 over to Nebuchadnezzar king of **B**,
46: 2 by Nebuchadnezzar king of **B**
46:13 king of **B** to attack Egypt:
46:26 king of **B** and his officers.
49:28 which Nebuchadnezzar king of **B**
49:30 "Nebuchadnezzar king of **B** has
50: 1 **B** and the land of the Babylonians:
50: 2 '**B** will be captured; Bel will be put
50: 8 "Flee out of **B**; leave the land of
50: 9 bring against **B** an alliance of great
50:13 All who pass **B** will be horrified and
50:14 "Take up your positions round **B**,
50:16 Cut off from **B** the sower, and the
50:17 bones was Nebuchadnezzar king of **B**."
50:18 "I will punish the king of **B** and his
50:23 How desolate is **B** among the nations!
50:24 I set a trap for you, O **B**, and you
50:28 refugees from **B** declaring in Zion
50:29 "Summon archers against **B**, all those
50:34 but unrest to those who live in **B**.
50:35 "against those who live in **B** and
50:42 to attack you, O Daughter of **B**.
50:43 The king of **B** has heard reports
50:44 chase **B** from its land in an instant.
50:45 what the LORD has planned against **B**,
51: 1 **B** and the people of Leb Kamai.
51: 2 I will send foreigners to **B** to
51: 4 They will fall down slain in **B**,
51: 6 "Flee from **B**! Run for your lives! Do
51: 7 **B** was a gold cup in the LORD's hand;
51: 8 **B** will suddenly fall and be broken.
51: 9 "'We would have healed **B**, but she
51:11 because his purpose is to destroy **B**.
51:12 a banner against the walls of **B**!
51:12 his decree against the people of **B**.
51:24 "Before your eyes I will repay **B** and
51:29 for the LORD's purposes against **B**
51:29 lay waste the land of **B** so that
51:31 announce to the king of **B** that his
51:33 "The Daughter of **B** is like a
51:34 "Nebuchadnezzar king of **B** has
51:35 violence done to our flesh be upon **B**
51:37 **B** will be a heap of ruins, a haunt
51:41 What a horror **B** will be among the
51:42 The sea will rise over **B**; its
51:44 I will punish Bel in **B** and make him
51:44 And the wall of **B** will fall.
51:47 when I will punish the idols of **B**;
51:48 in them will shout for joy over **B**,
51:49 "**B** must fall because of Israel's
51:49 the earth have fallen because of **B**.
51:53 Even if **B** reaches the sky and
51:54 "The sound of a cry comes from **B**,
51:55 The LORD will destroy **B**; he will
51:56 A destroyer will come against **B**;
51:59 when he went to **B** with Zedekiah king
51:60 disasters that would come upon **B**
51:60 that had been recorded concerning **B**.
51:61 "When you get to **B**, see that you
51:64 say, 'So will **B** sink to rise no more
52: 3 rebelled against the king of **B**.
52: 4 Nebuchadnezzar king of **B** marched
52: 9 He was taken to the king of **B** at
52:10 There at Riblah the king of **B**
52:11 bronze shackles and took him to **B**,
52:12 year of Nebuchadnezzar king of **B**,
52:12 who served the king of **B**, came to
52:15 who had gone over to the king of **B**.
52:17 they carried all the bronze to **B**.
52:26 them to the king of **B** at Riblah.
52:31 year Evil-Merodach became king of **B**,
52:32 other kings who were with him in **B**.
52:34 Day by day the king of **B** gave
Eze 17:12 'The king of **B** went to Jerusalem and
17:12 bringing them back with him to **B**.
17:16 he shall die in **B**, in the land of

Eze 17:20 I will bring him to **B** and execute
19: 9 and brought him to the king of **B**.
21:19 the sword of the king of **B** to take,
21:21 For the king of **B** will stop at the
24: 2 because the king of **B** has laid siege
26: 7 Tyre Nebuchadnezzar king of **B**,
29:18 "Son of man, Nebuchadnezzar king of **B**
29:19 king of **B**, and he will carry off its
30:10 hand of Nebuchadnezzar king of **B**.
30:24 strengthen the arms of the king of **B**
30:25 the arms of the king of **B**,
30:25 sword into the hand of the king of **B**
32:11 the king of **B** will come against you.
Da 1: 1 king of **B** came to Jerusalem and
2:12 execution of all the wise men of **B**.
2:14 to put to death the wise men of **B**,
2:18 with the rest of the wise men of **B**.
2:24 to execute the wise men of **B**,
2:24 "Do not execute the wise men of **B**.
2:48 ruler over the entire province of **B**
2:49 over the province of **B**,
3: 1 plain of Dura in the province of **B**.
3:12 of the province of **B**—Shadrach,
3:30 and Abednego in the province of **B**.
4: 6 all the wise men of **B** be brought
4:29 the roof of the royal palace of **B**,
4:30 he said, "Is not this the great **B** I
5: 7 and said to these wise men of **B**,
7: 1 first year of Belshazzar king of **B**,
Mic 4:10 You will go to **B**; there you will be
Zec 2: 7 you who live in the Daughter of **B**!"
6:10 who have arrived from **B**
Mt 1:11 at the time of the exile to **B**.
1:12 After the exile to **B**: Jeconiah was
1:17 from David to the exile to **B**,
Ac 7:43 I will send you into exile' beyond **B**.
1Pe 5:13 She who is in **B**, chosen together
Rev 14: 8 "Fallen! Fallen is **B** the Great,
16:19 God remembered **B** the Great and gave
17: 5 **B** THE GREAT THE MOTHER OF PROSTITUTES
18: 2 "Fallen! Fallen is **B** the Great! She
18:10 "'Woe! Woe, O great city, O **B**, city
18:21 great city of **B** will be thrown down,

Babylon's (Babylon)

Jer 50:46 At the sound of **B** capture the earth
51:30 **B** warriors have stopped fighting;
51:58 "**B** thick wall will be levelled and

Babylonia (Babylon)

Located on the plain between the Euphrates and Tigris Rivers. Also called "land of Shinar" (Ge 10:10) and "land of the Chaldeans" (Jer 24:5). Following the fall of Jerusalem, the people of Judah were exiled here (2Ki 25:21; 2Ch 36:20) just as Isaiah had prophesied (2Ki 20:16–18; Isa 39:5–7). They left here 50 years later (Ezra 1).

Jos 7:21 the plunder a beautiful robe from **B**,
Isa 11:11 from Cush, from Elam, from **B**, from
Jer 50:10 **B** will be plundered; all who plunder
51:24 all who live in **B** for all the wrong
51:35 who live in **B**," says Jerusalem.
Eze 11:24 brought me to the exiles in **B** in the
12:13 in my snare; I will bring him to **B**,
16:29 your promiscuity to include **B**,
Da 1: 2 off to the temple of his god in **B**
Zec 5:11 He replied, "To the country of **B** to

Babylonian (Babylon)

2Ki 24: 2 The LORD sent **B**, Aramean, Moabite
25: 5 the **B** army pursued the king and
25:10 The whole **B** army, under the
25:24 "Do not be afraid of the **B** officials,
Jer 35:11 to escape the **B** and Aramean armies.
37:10 entire **B** army that is attacking you
37:11 After the **B** army had withdrawn from
39: 5 the **B** army pursued them and overtook
41: 3 as the **B** soldiers who were there.
52: 8 the **B** army pursued King Zedekiah and
52:14 The whole **B** army under the commander
Eze 23:15 them looked like **B** chariot officers,
Da 9: 1 was made ruler over the **B** kingdom—

Babylonians (Babylon)

2Ki 25: 4 the **B** were surrounding the city.
25:13 The **B** broke up the bronze pillars,
25:25 the **B** who were with him at Mizpah.
25:26 fled to Egypt for fear of the **B**.
2Ch 36:17 up against them the king of the **B**,
Isa 23:13 Look at the land of the **B**, this
43:14 bring down as fugitives all the **B**,
47: 1 without a throne, Daughter of the **B**.
47: 5 go into darkness, Daughter of the **B**;
48:14 his arm will be against the **B**.
48:20 Leave Babylon, flee from the **B**!
Jer 21: 4 the **B** who are outside the wall
21: 9 goes out and surrenders to the **B**
22:25 king of Babylon and to the **B**.
24: 5 this place to the land of the **B**.
25:12 the land of the **B**, for their guilt,"
32: 4 not escape out of the hands of the **B**
32: 5 If you fight against the **B**,
32:24 over to the **B** who are attacking it.
32:25 city will be handed over to the **B**,
32:28 to hand this city over to the **B**
32:29 The **B** who are attacking this city
32:43 it has been handed over to the **B**.'
33: 5 in the fight with the **B**: 'They will
37: 5 and when the **B** who were besieging
37: 8 the **B** will return and attack this
37: 9 'The **B** will surely leave us.
37:13 "You are deserting to the **B**!
37:14 "I am not deserting to the **B**."
38: 2 goes over to the **B** will live.
38:18 to the **B** and they will burn it down;
38:19 Jews who have gone over to the **B**,
38:19 for the **B** may hand me over to them
38:23 will be brought out to the **B**.
39: 8 The **B** set fire to the royal palace
40: 9 "Do not be afraid to serve the **B**,"
40:10 to represent you before the **B** who
41:18 to escape the **B**. They were afraid of
43: 3 against us to hand us over to the **B**,
50: 1 Babylon and the land of the **B**:
50: 8 of Babylon; leave the land of the **B**,
50:25 has work to do in the land of the **B**.
50:35 "A sword against the **B**!" declares
50:45 purposed against the land of the **B**:
51:54 destruction from the land of the **B**.
52: 7 the **B** were surrounding the city.
52:17 The **B** broke up the bronze pillars,
Eze 1: 3 Kebar River in the land of the **B**.
23:17 the **B** came to her, to the bed of
23:23 the **B** and all the Chaldeans, the men
Da 1: 4 language and literature of the **B**.
5:30 Belshazzar, king of the **B**, was slain,
Hab 1: 6 I am raising up the **B**, that ruthless

Babylonians' (Babylon)

Isa 13:19 the glory of the **B** pride, will be

Baca

Ps 84: 6 they pass through the Valley of **B**,

Backbone (Bone)

Lev 3: 9 fat tail cut off close to the **b**,

Background

Est 2:10 her nationality and family **b**,
2:20 Esther had kept secret her family **b**

Backsliding (Backslidings)

Jer 2:19 punish you; your **b** will rebuke you.
3:22 people; I will cure you of **b**.
14: 7 For our **b** is great; we have sinned
15: 6 "You keep on **b**. So I will lay hands
Eze 37:23 save them from all their sinful **b**,

Backslidings (Backsliding)

Jer 5: 6 rebellion is great and their **b** many.

Bad (Badly, Worse, Worst)

Ge 18:21 **b** as the outcry that has reached me.
31:24 to Jacob, either good or **b**."
31:29 to Jacob, either good or **b**.'
37: 2 their father a **b** report about them.
Ex 7:21 and the river smelled so **b** that the
Lev 27:10 substitute a good one for a **b** one,
27:10 or a **b** one for a good one; if he
27:12 will judge its quality as good or **b**.
27:14 will judge its quality as good or **b**.
27:33 not pick out the good from the **b**
Nu 13:19 Is it good or **b**? What kind of towns
13:32 among the Israelites a **b** report
14:36 by spreading a **b** report about it—
14:37 the **b** report about the land
24:13 good or **b**, to go beyond the command
Dt 1:39 who do not yet know good from **b**
22:14 slanders her and gives her a **b** name,
22:19 given an Israelite virgin a **b** name.
2Sa 13:22 either good or **b**; he hated Amnon
1Ki 14: 6 I have been sent to you with **b** news.
22: 8 good about me, but always **b**.
22:18 anything good about me, but only **b**?"
2Ki 2:19 the water is **b** and the land is
2Ch 18: 7 good about me, but always **b**.
18:17 anything good about me, but only **b**?"
Ne 6:13 give me a **b** name to discredit me.
Ps 112: 7 He will have no fear of **b** news;
Pr 25:10 will never lose your **b** reputation.
25:19 Like a **b** tooth or a lame foot is
Ecc 7:14 be happy; but when times are **b**,
8: 3 Do not stand up for a **b** cause, for
9: 2 the good and the **b**, the clean and
10: 1 dead flies give perfume a **b** smell,
Isa 5: 2 grapes, but it yielded only **b** fruit.
5: 4 grapes, why did it yield only **b**?
41:23 Do something, whether good or **b**, so
Jer 24: 2 so **b** that they could not be eaten.
24: 3 are so **b** that they cannot be eaten."
24: 8 are so **b** that they cannot be eaten,'
29:17 that are so **b** they cannot be eaten.
49:23 for they have heard **b** news.
Zep 1:12 will do nothing, either good or **b**.'
Mt 6:23 if your eyes are **b**, your whole body
7:17 fruit, but a **b** tree bears **b** fruit.
7:18 A good tree cannot bear **b** fruit, and
7:18 and a **b** tree cannot bear good fruit.
12:33 or make a tree **b** and its fruit will
12:33 a tree **b** and its fruit will be **b**,
13:48 in baskets, but threw the **b** away.
22:10 could find, both good and **b**,
Mk 9:39 next moment say anything **b** about me,
Lk 6:43 "No good tree bears **b** fruit, nor
6:43 nor does a **b** tree bear good fruit.
11:34 But when they are **b**, your body also
16:25 while Lazarus received **b** things, but
Jn 11:39 "by this time there is a **b** odour,
Ac 17: 5 **b** characters from the market-place,
28:21 or said anything **b** about you.
Ro 9:11 or had done anything good or **b**
1Co 15:33 Do not be misled: "**B** company corrupts
2Co 5:10 in the body, whether good or **b**.
6: 8 **b** report and good report;
2Ti 3:13 impostors will go from **b** to worse,
Tit 2: 8 they have nothing **b** to say about us.

Badly (Bad)

Ge 50:17 they committed in treating you so **b**.
1Sa 24:17 me well, but I have treated you **b**.
2Ch 35:23 "Take me away; I am **b** wounded.
Mk 12:27 You are **b** mistaken!"

Baffled

Da 5: 9 His nobles were **b**.
Ac 9:22 **b** the Jews living in Damascus

Bag (Baggage, Bags)

Dt 25:13 two differing weights in your **b**
1Sa 17:40 in the pouch of his shepherd's **b**
17:49 Reaching into his **b** and taking out a
Job 14:17 My offences will be sealed up in a **b**;
Pr 16:11 weights in the **b** are of his making.
Mic 6:11 scales, with a **b** of false weights?
Mt 10:10 take no **b** for the journey, or extra
Mk 6: 8 bread, no **b**, no money in your belts.
Lk 9: 3 no **b**, no bread, no money, no extra
10: 4 Do not take a purse or **b** or sandals;
22:35 "When I sent you without purse, **b** or
22:36 take it, and also a **b**; and if you
Jn 12: 6 a thief; as keeper of the money **b**,

Baggage (Bag)
1Sa 10:22 he has hidden himself among the **b**."

Bags (Bag)
Ge 42:25 Joseph gave orders to fill their **b**
43:11 best products of the land in your **b**
2Ki 5:23 the two talents of silver in two **b**,
12:10 of the LORD and put it into **b**.
Isa 46: 6 Some pour out gold from their **b** and

Baharumite
1Ch 11:33 Azmaveth the **B**, Eliahba the

Bahurim
2Sa 3:16 weeping behind her all the way to **B**.
16: 5 King David approached **B**, a man from
17:18 and went to the house of a man in **B**.
19:16 the Benjamite from **B**, hurried down
1Ki 2: 8 the Benjamite from **B**, who called

Bail
Ac 17: 9 they put Jason and the others on **b**

Bakbakkar
1Ch 9:15 **B**, Heresh, Galal and Mattaniah son

Bakbuk
Ezr 2:51 **B**, Hakupha, Harhur,
Ne 7:53 **B**, Hakupha, Harhur,

Bakbukiah
Ne 11:17 **B**, second among his associates;
12: 9 **B** and Unni, their associates, stood
12:25 Mattaniah, **B**, Obadiah, Meshullam,

Bake (Baked, Baker, Bakers, Bakes, Baking)
Ge 11: 3 make bricks and **b** them thoroughly.
18: 6 and knead it and **b** some bread."
Ex 16:23 So **b** what you want to **b** and boil
Lev 24: 5 "Take fine flour and **b** twelve loaves
26:26 ten women will be able to **b** your
Eze 4:12 **b** it in the sight of the people,
4:15 "I will let you **b** your bread over
46:20 offering and **b** the grain offering,

Baked (Bake)
Ge 40:17 all kinds of **b** goods for Pharaoh,
Ex 12:39 they **b** cakes of unleavened bread.
Lev 2: 4 "If you bring a grain offering **b**
6:17 It must not be **b** with yeast;
7: 9 Every grain offering **b** in an oven
23:17 **b** with yeast, as a wave offering
1Sa 28:24 it and **b** bread without yeast.
2Sa 13: 8 the bread in his sight and **b** it.
1Ki 19: 6 a cake of bread **b** over hot coals,
2Ki 4:42 bread **b** from the first ripe corn,
Isa 44:19 I even **b** bread over its coals,
Da 2:33 partly of iron and partly of **b** clay.
2:41 partly of **b** clay and partly of iron,
2:43 you saw the iron mixed with **b** clay,

Baker (Bake)
Ge 40: 1 the cupbearer and the **b** of the king
40: 2 the chief cupbearer and the chief **b**,
40: 5 and the **b** of the king of Egypt,
40:16 the chief **b** saw that Joseph had
40:20 chief cupbearer and the chief **b**
40:22 he hanged the chief **b**, just as
41:10 he imprisoned me and the chief **b** in
Hos 7: 4 oven whose fire the **b** need not stir

Bakers (Bake)
1Sa 8:13 to be perfumers and cooks and **b**.
Jer 37:21 given bread from the street of the **b**

Bakes (Bake)
Isa 44:15 he kindles a fire and **b** bread.

Baking (Bake)
Ge 19: 3 **b** bread without yeast, and they ate.
1Ch 9:31 for **b** the offering bread.
23:29 the unleavened wafers, the **b** and the

Balaam (Balaam's)
Prophet, requested by Balak to curse Israel (Nu 22:4–11; 2Pe 2:15); forbidden by God (Nu 22:12); rebuked by his donkey (Nu 22:21–34). Curse turned to blessing (Nu 23–24; Dt 23:4–5; Jos 24:9–10). Advice led to Israel's seduction (Nu 31:15–16). Killed in Israel's defeat of Midianites (Nu 31:8; Jos 13:22).

Nu 22: 5 sent messengers to summon **B** son of
22: 7 When they came to **B**, they told him
22: 8 "Spend the night here," **B** said
22: 9 God came to **B** and asked, "Who are
22:10 **B** said to God, "Balak son of Zippor,
22:12 God said to **B**, "Do not go with them.
22:13 The next morning **B** got up and said
22:14 said, "**B** refused to come with us.
22:16 They came to **B** and said: "This is
22:18 **B** answered them, "Even if Balak gave
22:20 That night God came to **B** and said,
22:21 **B** got up in the morning, saddled his
22:22 **B** was riding on his donkey, and his
22:23 **B** beat her to get her back on the
22:27 she lay down under **B**, and he was
22:28 and she said to **B**, "What have I done
22:29 **B** answered the donkey, "You have
22:30 The donkey said to **B**, "Am I not your
22:34 **B** said to the angel of the LORD, "I
22:35 The angel of the LORD said to **B**, "Go
22:35 So **B** went with the princes of Balak.
22:36 Balak heard that **B** was coming, he
22:37 Balak said to **B**, "Did I not send you
22:38 I have come to you now," **B** replied.
22:39 **B** went with Balak to Kiriath Huzoth.
22:40 gave some to **B** and the princes
22:41 The next morning Balak took **B** up to
23: 1 **B** said, "Build me seven altars here,
23: 2 Balak did as **B** said, and the two of
23: 3 **B** said to Balak, "Stay here beside
23: 4 God met with him, and **B** said, "I
23: 7 **B** uttered his oracle: "Balak brought
23:11 Balak said to **B**, "What have you done
23:15 **B** said to Balak, "Stay here beside
23:16 The LORD met with **B** and put a
23:25 Balak said to **B**, "Neither curse them
23:26 **B** answered, "Did I not tell you I
23:27 Balak said to **B**, "Come, let me take
23:28 Balak took **B** to the top of Peor,
23:29 **B** said, "Build me seven altars here,
23:30 Balak did as **B** had said, and offered
24: 1 Now when **B** saw that it pleased the
24: 2 **B** looked out and saw Israel encamped
24: 3 "The oracle of **B** son of Beor, the
24:10 Balak's anger burned against **B**.
24:12 **B** answered Balak, "Did I not tell
24:15 "The oracle of **B** son of Beor, the
24:20 **B** saw Amalek and uttered his oracle:
24:25 **B** got up and returned home and Balak
31: 8 killed **B** son of Beor with the sword.
Dt 23: 4 and they hired **B** son of Beor from
23: 5 LORD your God would not listen to **B**
Jos 13:22 had put to the sword **B** son of Beor,
24: 9 he sent for **B** son of Beor
24:10 I would not listen to **B**, so he
Ne 13: 2 had hired **B** to call a curse down
Mic 6: 5 and what **B** son of Beor answered.
2Pe 2:15 to follow the way of **B** son of Beor,
Rev 2:14 there who hold to the teaching of **B**,

Balaam's (Balaam)
Nu 22:25 wall, crushing **B** foot against it.
22:31 the LORD opened **B** eyes, and he saw
23: 5 The LORD put a message in **B** mouth
31:16 the ones who followed **B** advice
Jude :11 rushed for profit into **B** error;

Baladan
2Ki 20:12 Merodach-Baladan son of **B** king of
Isa 39: 1 Merodach-Baladan son of **B** king of

Balah
Jos 19: 3 Hazar Shual, **B**, Ezem,

Balak (Balak's)
Nu 22: 2 Now **B** son of Zippor saw all that
22: 4 So **B** son of Zippor, who was king of
22: 5 **B** said: "A people has come out of
22: 7 they told him what **B** had said.
22:10 "**B** son of Zippor, king of Moab,
22:14 the Moabite princes returned to **B**
22:15 **B** sent other princes, more numerous
22:16 "This is what **B** son of Zippor says:
22:18 "Even if **B** gave me his palace
22:35 So Balaam went with the princes of **B**.
22:36 When **B** heard that Balaam was coming,
22:37 **B** said to Balaam, "Did I not send
22:39 Balaam went with **B** to Kiriath Huzoth.
22:40 **B** sacrificed cattle and sheep,
22:41 The next morning **B** took Balaam up to
23: 2 **B** did as Balaam said, and the two of
23: 3 Balaam said to **B**, "Stay here beside
23: 5 to **B** and give him this message."
23: 7 "**B** brought me from Aram,
23:11 **B** said to Balaam, "What have you
23:13 **B** said to him, "Come with me to
23:15 Balaam said to **B**, "Stay here beside
23:16 to **B** and give him this message."
23:17 **B** asked him, "What did the LORD say?"
23:18 he uttered his oracle: "Arise, **B**,
23:25 **B** said to Balaam, "Neither curse
23:27 **B** said to Balaam, "Come, let me take
23:28 **B** took Balaam to the top of Peor,
23:30 **B** did as Balaam had said, and
24:12 Balaam answered **B**, "Did I not tell
24:13 'Even if **B** gave me his palace filled
24:25 and **B** went his own way.
Jos 24: 9 **B** son of Zippor, the king of Moab,
Jdg 11:25 Are you better than **B** son of Zippor,
Mic 6: 5 My people, remember what **B** king of
Rev 2:14 who taught **B** to entice the

Balak's (Balak)
Nu 22:13 Balaam got up and said to **B** princes,
24:10 **B** anger burned against Balaam.

Balance (Balances)
Lev 25:27 the **b** to the man to whom he sold it;
Ps 62: 9 if weighed on a **b**, they are nothing
Isa 40:12 on the scales and the hills in a **b**?

Balances (Balance)
Pr 16:11 Honest scales and **b** are from the

Bald (Baldhead, Baldness)
Lev 13:40 lost his hair and is **b**, he is clean.
13:41 and has a **b** forehead, he is clean.
13:42 sore on his **b** head or forehead,
Isa 3:17 the LORD will make their scalps **b**."
Mic 1:16 make yourselves as **b** as the vulture,

Baldhead (Bald)
2Ki 2:23 "Go on up, you **b**!" they said.
2:23 "Go on up, you **b**!"

Baldness (Bald)
Isa 3:24 instead of well-dressed hair, **b**;

Ball
Isa 22:18 He will roll you up tightly like a **b**

Balm
Ge 37:25 loaded with spices, **b** and myrrh,
43:11 a little **b** and a little honey,
2Ch 28:15 food and drink, and healing **b**.
Jer 8:22 Is there no **b** in Gilead? Is there no
46:11 "Go up to Gilead and get **b**, O Virgin
51: 8 Wail over her! Get **b** for her pain;
Eze 27:17 honey, oil and **b** for your wares.

Balsam
2Sa 5:23 attack them in front of the **b** trees.
5:24 marching in the tops of the **b** trees,
1Ch 14:14 attack them in front of the **b** trees.
14:15 marching in the tops of the **b** trees,

Bamah
Eze 20:29 (It is called **B** to this day.)

Bamoth
Nu 21:19 to Nahaliel, from Nahaliel to **B**,
21:20 from **B** to the valley in Moab where

Bamoth Baal
Nu 22:41 Balak took Balaam up to **B**,
Jos 13:17 including Dibon, **B**, Beth Baal Meon,

Ban
1Ch 2: 7 the **b** on taking devoted things.

Band (Banded, Bands)
Ge 49:19 "Gad will be attacked by a **b** of
Ex 39:23 and a **b** around this opening, so that
2Sa 1:10 the **b** on his arm and have brought
23:13 a **b** of Philistines was encamped
1Ki 7:35 was a circular **b** half a cubit deep.
11:24 became the leader of a **b** of rebels
2Ki 13:21 suddenly they saw a **b** of raiders;
19:31 out of Mount Zion a **b** of survivors.
1Ch 11:15 a **b** of Philistines was encamped
Ps 22:16 a **b** of evil men has encircled me,
78:49 a **b** of destroying angels.
86:14 a **b** of ruthless men seeks my life
94:21 **b** together against the righteous
Isa 31: 4 though a whole **b** of shepherds is
37:32 out of Mount Zion a **b** of survivors.
Ac 5:37 and led a **b** of people in revolt.

Bandaged
Isa 1: 6 cleansed or **b** or soothed with oil.
Lk 10:34 He went to him and **b** his wounds,

Banded (Band)
Nu 14:35 which has **b** together against me.
16:11 all your followers have **b** together.
27: 3 who **b** together against the LORD, but
2Sa 23:11 When the Philistines **b** together at a

Bandit (Bandits)
Pr 6:11 poverty will come on you like a **b**
23:28 Like a **b** she lies in wait, and
24:34 poverty will come on you like a **b**

Bandits (Bandit)
Ezr 8:31 us from enemies and **b** along the way.
Hos 7: 1 into houses, **b** rob in the streets;
2Co 11:26 in danger from **b**, in danger from my

Bands (Band)
Ex 27:10 silver hooks and **b** on the posts.
27:11 silver hooks and **b** on the posts.
27:17 are to have silver **b** and hooks,
36:38 the posts and their **b** with gold
38:10 silver hooks and **b** on the posts.
38:11 silver hooks and **b** on the posts.
38:12 silver hooks and **b** on the posts.
38:17 The hooks and **b** on the posts were
38:17 posts of the courtyard had silver **b**.
38:19 Their hooks and **b** were silver, and
38:28 and to make their **b**.
2Sa 4: 2 men who were leaders of raiding **b**.
2Ki 5: 2 Now **b** from Aram had gone out and had
6:23 So the **b** from Aram stopped raiding
1Ch 12:18 made them leaders of his raiding **b**.
12:21 They helped David against raiding **b**,
Hos 6: 9 so do **b** of priests; they murder on

Bangles
Isa 3:18 the **b** and headbands and crescent

Bani
1Ch 6:46 the son of Amzi, the son of **B**,
9: 4 the son of Imri, the son of **B**,
Ezr 2:10 of **B** 642
8:10 of the descendants of **B**, Shelomith
10:29 From the descendants of **B**: Meshullam,
10:34 From the descendants of **B**: Maadai,
Ne 3:17 by the Levites under Rehum son of **B**.
8: 7 The Levites—Jeshua, **B**, Sherebiah,
9: 4 the Levites—Jeshua, **B**, Kadmiel,
9: 5 the Levites—Jeshua, Kadmiel, **B**,
10:13 Hodiah, **B** and Beninu.
Ne 10:14 Parosh, Pahath-Moab, Elam, Zattu, **B**,
11:22 in Jerusalem was Uzzi son of **B**,

Banish (Banished, Banishment)
2Ki 13:23 unwilling to destroy them or **b** them
Ps 5:10 **B** them for their many sins, for they
125: 5 the LORD will **b** with the evildoers.
Ecc 11:10 So then, **b** anxiety from your heart
Jer 8: 3 Wherever I **b** them, all the survivors
24: 9 and cursing, wherever I **b** them.
25:10 I will **b** from them the sounds of joy
27:10 I will **b** you and you will perish.
27:15 Therefore, I will **b** you and you will
32:37 where I **b** them in my furious anger
Zec 13: 2 I will **b** the names of the idols

Banished (Banish)
Ge 3:23 the LORD God **b** him from the Garden
Dt 30: 4 Even if you have been **b** to the most
2Sa 14:13 king has not brought back his **b** son?
14:14 he devises ways so that a **b** person
1Ch 12: 1 he was **b** from the presence of Saul
Job 18:18 darkness and is **b** from the world.
20: 8 **b** like a vision of the night.
30: 5 They were **b** from their fellow-men,
Isa 24:11 all gaiety is **b** from the earth.
Jer 16:15 the countries where he had **b** them.
23: 8 the countries where he had **b** them.
23:12 they will be **b** to darkness and there
29:14 and places where I have **b** you,"
Jnh 2: 4 'I have been **b** from your sight;
Zec 5: 3 every thief will be **b**, and according
5: 3 who swears falsely will be **b**.

Banishment (Banish)
Ezr 7:26 **b**, confiscation of property, or

Bank (Banks, Embankment, Riverbank)
Ge 41:17 I was standing on the **b** of the Nile,
Ex 2: 3 the reeds along the **b** of the Nile.
2: 5 were walking along the river **b**.
7:15 Wait on the **b** of the Nile to meet
Jos 13:23 Reubenites was the **b** of the Jordan.
2Ki 2:13 and stood on the **b** of the Jordan.
Eze 47: 6 led me back to the **b** of the river.
Da 10: 4 **b** of the great river, the Tigris,
12: 5 one on this **b** of the river and one
12: 5 the river and one on the opposite **b**.
Mt 8:32 down the steep **b** into the lake
Mk 5:13 rushed down the steep **b**
Lk 8:33 down the steep **b** into the lake

Bankers
Mt 25:27 put my money on deposit with the **b**,

Banks (Bank)
1Ch 12:15 when it was overflowing all its **b**,
Isa 8: 7 all its channels, run over all its **b**
Eze 47:12 will grow on both **b** of the river.

Banner (Banners)
Ex 17:15 and called it The LORD is my **B**.
Ps 60: 4 a **b** to be unfurled against the bow.
SS 2: 4 and his **b** over me is love.
Isa 5:26 He lifts up a **b** for the distant
11:10 will stand as a **b** for the peoples;
11:12 He will raise a **b** for the nations
13: 2 Raise a **b** on a bare hilltop, shout
18: 3 when a **b** is raised on the mountains,
30:17 a mountaintop, like a **b** on a hill."
49:22 I will lift up my **b** to the peoples;
62:10 Raise a **b** for the nations.
Jer 50: 2 lift up a **b** and proclaim it;
51:12 Lift up a **b** against the walls of
51:27 "Lift up a **b** in the land! Blow the
Eze 27: 7 was your sail and served as your **b**;

Banners (Banner)
Nu 2: 2 standard with the **b** of his family."
Ps 20: 5 and will lift up our **b**
SS 6: 4 Jerusalem, majestic as troops with **b**.

Banquet (Banquets)
1Sa 25:36 holding a **b** like that of a king.
Est 1: 3 he gave a **b** for all his nobles
1: 5 the king gave a **b**, lasting seven
1: 9 Queen Vashti also gave a **b** for the
2:18 the king gave a great **b**, Esther's **b**,
5: 4 to a **b** I have prepared for him."
5: 5 went to the **b** Esther had prepared.
5: 8 to the **b** I will prepare for them.
5:12 the king to the **b** she gave.
6:14 away to the **b** Esther had prepared.
7: 8 the palace garden to the **b** hall,
SS 2: 4 He has taken me to the **b** hall, and
Isa 25: 6 a **b** of aged wine—the best of meats
Da 5: 1 King Belshazzar gave a great **b** for a
5:10 his nobles, came into the **b** hall.
Mt 22: 2 prepared a wedding **b** for his son.
22: 3 to the **b** to tell them to come,
22: 4 Come to the wedding **b**.'
22: 8 'The wedding **b** is ready, but those I
22: 9 invite to the **b** anyone you find.'
25:10 went in with him to the wedding **b**.
Mk 6:21 On his birthday Herod gave a **b** for
Lk 5:29 Levi held a great **b** for Jesus at his
12:36 master to return from a wedding **b**,
14:13 when you give a **b**, invite the poor,
14:16 a great **b** and invited many guests.
14:17 At the time of the **b** he sent his
14:24 invited will get a taste of my **b**.'"
Jn 2: 8 and take it to the master of the **b**.
2: 9 the master of the **b** tasted the water

Banquets (Banquet)
Isa 5:12 They have harps and lyres at their **b**,
Mt 23: 6 they love the place of honour at **b**
Mk 12:39 and the places of honour at **b**.
Lk 20:46 and the places of honour at **b**.

Baptise (Baptised, Baptising, Baptism, Baptisms, Baptist)
Mt 3:11 "I **b** you with water for repentance.
3:11 He will **b** you with the Holy Spirit
Mk 1: 8 I **b** you with water, but he will **b**
Lk 3:16 John answered them all, "I **b** you
3:16 He will **b** you with the Holy Spirit
Jn 1:25 questioned him, "Why then do you **b**
1:26 "I **b** with water," John replied, "but
1:33 the one who sent me to **b** with water
1:33 he who will **b** with the Holy Spirit.'
1Co 1:14 I am thankful that I did not **b** any
1:17 For Christ did not send me to **b**, but

Baptised (Baptise)
Mt 3: 6 Confessing their sins, they were **b**
3:13 to the Jordan to be **b** by John.
3:14 be **b** by you, and do you come to me?"
3:16 As soon as Jesus was **b**, he went up
Mk 1: 5 were **b** by him in the Jordan River.
1: 9 and was **b** by John in the Jordan.
10:38 be **b** with the baptism I am **b** with?"
10:39 be **b** with the baptism I am **b** with,
16:16 Whoever believes and is **b** will be
Lk 3: 7 crowds coming out to be **b** by him,
3:12 Tax collectors also came to be **b**.
3:21 all the people were being **b**, Jesus
3:21 were being **b**, Jesus was **b** too.
7:29 because they had been **b** by John.
7:30 they had not been **b** by John.)
Jn 3:22 he spent some time with them, and **b**.
3:23 were constantly coming to be **b**.
4: 2 not Jesus who **b**, but his disciples.
Ac 1: 5 For John **b** with water, but in a few
1: 5 you will be **b** with the Holy Spirit."
2:38 Peter replied, "Repent and be **b**,
2:41 Those who accepted his message were **b**
8:12 they were **b**, both men and women.
8:13 Simon himself believed and was **b**.
8:16 **b** into the name of the Lord Jesus.
8:36 Why shouldn't I be **b**?"
8:38 into the water and Philip **b** him.
9:18 He got up and was **b**,
10:47 people from being **b** with water?
10:48 he ordered that they be **b** in the
11:16 'John **b** with water, but you will be **b**
16:15 the members of her household were **b**,

Ac 16:33 he and all his family were **b**.
18: 8 who heard him believed and were **b**.
19: 5 On hearing this, they were **b** into
22:16 be **b** and wash your sins away,
Ro 6: 3 who were **b** into Christ Jesus
6: 3 Christ Jesus were **b** into his death?
1Co 1:13 Were you **b** into the name of Paul?
1:15 no-one can say that you were **b** into
1:16 Yes, I also **b** the household of
1:16 I don't remember if I **b** anyone else.)
10: 2 They were all **b** into Moses in the
12:13 For we were all **b** by one Spirit into
15:29 what will those do who are **b** for the
15:29 why are people **b** for them?
Gal 3:27 for all of you who were **b** into

Baptising (Baptise)

Mt 3: 7 Sadducees coming to where he was **b**,
28:19 **b** them in the name of the Father and
Mk 1: 4 John came, **b** in the desert region
Jn 1:28 of the Jordan, where John was **b**.
1:31 but the reason I came **b** with water
3:23 Now John also was **b** at Aenon near
3:26 well, he is **b**, and everyone is going
4: 1 and **b** more disciples than John,
10:40 John had been **b** in the early days.

Baptism (Baptise, *Baptism of repentance*)

Mt 21:25 John's **b**—where did it come from?
Mk 10:38 with the **b** I am baptised with?"
10:39 with the **b** I am baptised with,
11:30 John's **b**—was it from heaven,
Lk 12:50 I have a **b** to undergo, and how
20: 4 John's **b**—was it from heaven,
Ac 1:22 beginning from John's **b** to the time
10:37 after the **b** that John preached—
13:24 John preached repentance and **b**
18:25 though he knew only the **b** of John.
19: 3 "Then what **b** did you receive?"
19: 3 "John's **b**," they replied.
19: 4 Paul said, "John's **b** was a **b** of
Ro 6: 4 through **b** into death in order that,
Eph 4: 5 one Lord, one faith, one **b**;
Col 2:12 having been buried with him in **b** and
1Pe 3:21 this water symbolises **b** that now

Baptism of repentance

Mk 1: 4 a **b** for the forgiveness of sins.
Lk 3: 3 a **b** for the forgiveness of sins.
Ac 19: 4 Paul said, "John's baptism was a **b**.

Baptisms (Baptise)

Heb 6: 2 instruction about **b**, the laying on

Baptist (Baptise)

Mt 3: 1 In those days John the **B** came,
11:11 anyone greater than John the **B**;
11:12 From the days of John the **B** until
14: 2 "This is John the **B**; he has risen
14: 8 a platter the head of John the **B**."
16:14 They replied, "Some say John the **B**;
17:13 talking to them about John the **B**.
Mk 6:14 "John the **B** has been raised
6:24 "The head of John the **B**,"
6:25 head of John the **B** on a platter."
8:28 They replied, "Some say John the **B**;
Lk 7:20 "John the **B** sent us to you to ask,
7:33 For John the **B** came neither eating
9:19 They replied, "Some say John the **B**;

Bar (Barred, Bars)

Jdg 16: 3 and tore them loose, **b** and all.
Ne 7: 3 make them shut the doors and **b** them.
Isa 9: 4 the **b** across their shoulders,

Barabbas

Criminal, released by Pilate instead of Jesus (Mt 27:15–26; Mk 15:6–15; Lk 23:18–25; Jn 18:40).

Mt 27:16 had a notorious prisoner, called **B**.
27:17 **B**, or Jesus who is called Christ?"
27:20 persuaded the crowd to ask for **B**
27:21 "**B**," they answered.
Mt 27:26 Then he released **B** to them.
Mk 15: 7 A man called **B** was in prison with
15:11 to have Pilate release **B** instead.
15:15 Pilate released **B** to them.
Lk 23:18 with this man! Release **B** to us!"
23:19 **B** had been thrown into prison for an
Jn 18:40 "No, not him! Give us **B**!" Now **B** had

Barak (Barak's)

Summoned by Deborah to lead Israel against Canaanites (Jdg 4–5; 1Sa 12:11; Heb 11:32).

Jdg 4: 6 She sent for **B** son of Abinoam from
4: 8 **B** said to her, "If you go with me,
4: 9 So Deborah went with **B** to Kedesh,
4:12 that **B** son of Abinoam had gone up
4:14 Deborah said to **B**, "Go! This is the
4:14 So **B** went down Mount Tabor,
4:16 **B** pursued the chariots and army
4:22 **B** came by in pursuit of Sisera,
5: 1 On that day Deborah and **B** son of
5:12 break out in song! Arise, O **B**! Take
5:15 yes, Issachar was with **B**,
1Sa 12:11 Then the LORD sent Jerub-Baal, **B**,
Heb 11:32 **B**, Samson, Jephthah, David, Samuel

Barak's (Barak)

Jdg 4:15 At **B** advance, the LORD routed Sisera

Barakel

Job 32: 2 Elihu son of **B** the Buzite,
32: 6 Elihu son of **B** the Buzite said:

Barbarian

Col 3:11 circumcised or uncircumcised, **b**,

Barber's

Eze 5: 1 use it as a **b** razor to shave

Barbs

Nu 33:55 will become **b** in your eyes

Bare (Bared, Barefoot)

Jdg 14: 6 tore the lion apart with his **b** hands
2Sa 22:16 laid **b** at the rebuke of the LORD,
2Ki 9:13 them under him on the **b** steps.
Job 28: 9 lays **b** the roots of the mountains.
Ps 18:15 of the earth laid **b** at your rebuke,
29: 9 and strips the forests **b**.
Isa 13: 2 Raise a banner on a **b** hilltop, shout
23:13 the stripped its fortress **b**
27:10 they strip its branches **b**.
47: 2 Lift up your skirts, **b** your legs,
52:10 The LORD will lay **b** his holy arm in
Jer 2:25 Do not run until your feet are **b** and
49:10 I will strip Esau **b**; I will uncover
Eze 13:14 that its foundation will be laid **b**.
16: 7 you who were naked and **b**.
16:22 when you were naked and **b**,
16:39 and leave you naked and **b**.
23:29 They will leave you naked and **b**,
24: 7 She poured it on the **b** rock;
24: 8 I put her blood on the **b** rock,
26: 4 her rubble and make her a **b** rock.
26:14 I will make you a **b** rock, and you
29:18 every head was rubbed **b**
Hos 2: 3 as **b** as on the day she was born;
Mic 1: 6 and lay **b** her foundations.
1Co 14:25 secrets of his heart will be laid **b**.
Heb 4:13 Everything is uncovered and laid **b**
2Pe 3:10 and everything in it will be laid **b**.

Bared (Bare)

Isa 20: 4 with buttocks **b**—to Egypt's shame.
Eze 4: 7 and with **b** arm prophesy against her.

Barefoot (Bare, Foot)

2Sa 15:30 his head was covered and he was **b**.
Isa 20: 2 going around stripped and **b**.
20: 3 gone stripped and **b** for three years,
20: 4 will lead away stripped and **b**
Mic 1: 8 wail; I will go about **b** and naked.

Bargain

2Ki 18:23 "Come now, make a **b** with my master,
Isa 36: 8 "Come now, make a **b** with my master,

Barhumite

2Sa 23:31 the Arbathite, Azmaveth the **B**,

Bariah

1Ch 3:22 **B**, Neariah and Shaphat—six in all.

Bar-Jesus

Ac 13: 6 sorcerer and false prophet named **B**,

Bark[1]

Ge 30:37 stripes on them by peeling the **b**
Joel 1: 7 It has stripped off their **b** and

Bark[2]

Ex 11: 7 among the Israelites not a dog will **b**
Isa 56:10 they cannot **b**; they lie around and

Barkos

Ezr 2:53 **B**, Sisera, Temah,
Ne 7:55 **B**, Sisera, Temah,

Barley

Ex 9:31 (The flax and **b** were destroyed,
9:31 since the **b** was in the ear and the
Lev 27:16 of silver to a homer of **b** seed.
Nu 5:15 an ephah of **b** flour on her behalf.
Dt 8: 8 a land with wheat and **b**, vines and
Jdg 7:13 "A round loaf of **b** bread came
Ru 1:22 as the **b** harvest was beginning.
2:17 Then she threshed the **b** she had
2:23 **b** and wheat harvests were finished.
3: 2 winnowing **b** on the threshing-floor.
3:15 he poured into it six measures of **b**
3:17 "He gave me these six measures of **b**,
2Sa 14:30 is next to mine, and he has **b** there.
17:28 They also brought wheat and **b**, flour
21: 9 just as the **b** harvest was beginning.
1Ki 4:28 **b** and straw for the chariot horses
2Ki 4:42 twenty loaves of **b** bread baked
7: 1 two seahs of **b** for a shekel at the
7:16 and two seahs of **b** sold for a shekel,
7:18 two seahs of **b** for a shekel at the
1Ch 11:13 where there was a field full of **b**,
2Ch 2:10 twenty thousand cors of **b**,
2:15 send his servants the wheat and **b**
27: 5 of wheat and ten thousand cors of **b**.
Job 31:40 of wheat and weeds instead of **b**.
Isa 28:25 **b** in its plot, and spelt in its
Jer 41: 8 **b**, oil and honey, hidden in a field.
Eze 4: 9 "Take wheat and **b**, beans and lentils,
4:12 Eat the food as you would a **b** cake;
13:19 handfuls of **b** and scraps of bread.
45:13 of an ephah from each homer of **b**.
Hos 3: 2 and about a homer and a lethek of **b**.
Joel 1:11 grieve for the wheat and the **b**,
Jn 6: 9 a boy with five small **b** loaves
6:13 pieces of the five **b** loaves left
Rev 6: 6 three quarts of **b** for a day's wages.

Barn (Barns)

Hag 2:19 Is there yet any seed left in the **b**?
Mt 3:12 gathering his wheat into the **b** and
13:30 and bring it into my **b**.'"
Lk 3:17 and to gather the wheat into his **b**,
12:24 they have no storeroom or **b**;

Barnabas

Name (meaning "son of encouragement") given to Joseph, a disciple from Cyprus (Ac 4:36). Apostle (Ac 14:14) and missionary (Gal 2:9). Introduced Paul to Jerusalem apostles (Ac 9:27). Sent to Antioch where he worked with Paul (Ac 11:22–26). With Paul on first missionary journey (Ac 13–14) and at Council of Jerusalem (Ac 15:2–35); parted company over his cousin John Mark (Ac 15:36–40).

Ac 4:36 **B** (which means Son of Encouragement),
9:27 **B** took him and brought him to the
11:22 and they sent **B** to Antioch.
11:25 **B** went to Tarsus to look for Saul,

Ac 11:26 So for a whole year **B** and Saul met
11:30 gift to the elders by **B** and Saul.
12:25 when **B** and Saul had finished
13: 1 there were prophets and teachers: **B**,
13: 2 "Set apart for me **B** and Saul for the
13: 7 sent for **B** and Saul
13:42 Paul and **B** were leaving the
13:43 followed Paul and **B**, who talked
13:46 Paul and **B** answered them boldly:
13:50 persecution against Paul and **B**,
14: 1 At Iconium Paul and **B** went as usual
14: 3 Paul and **B** spent considerable time
14:12 **B** they called Zeus, and Paul they
14:14 when the apostles **B** and Paul heard
14:20 The next day he and **B** left for Derbe.
14:23 Paul and **B** appointed elders for them
15: 2 brought Paul and **B** into sharp dispute
15: 2 So Paul and **B** were appointed, along
15:12 became silent as they listened to **B**
15:22 them to Antioch with Paul and **B**.
15:25 with our dear friends **B** and Paul—
15:35 Paul and **B** remained in Antioch,
15:36 Paul said to **B**, "Let us go back
15:37 **B** wanted to take John, also called
15:39 **B** took Mark and sailed for Cyprus,
1Co 9: 6 Or is it only I and **B** who must work
Gal 2: 1 to Jerusalem, this time with **B**.
2: 9 gave me and **B** the right hand of
2:13 hypocrisy even **B** was led astray.
Col 4:10 as does Mark, the cousin of **B**.

Barns (Barn)
Dt 28: 8 LORD will send a blessing on your **b**
Ps 144:13 Our **b** will be filled with every kind
Pr 3:10 your **b** will be filled to overflowing,
Mt 6:26 not sow or reap or store away in **b**,
Lk 12:18 I will tear down my **b** and build

Barracks
Ac 21:34 that Paul be taken into the **b**.
21:37 were about to take Paul into the **b**,
22:24 ordered Paul to be taken into the **b**.
23:10 by force and bring him into the **b**.
23:16 he went into the **b** and told Paul.
23:32 him, while they returned to the **b**.

Barred (Bar)
Pr 18:19 are like the **b** gates of a citadel.
Isa 24:10 the entrance to every house is **b**.
Lam 3: 9 He has **b** my way with blocks of stone;
Jnh 2: 6 the earth beneath **b** me in for ever.

Barren
Ge 11:30 Now Sarai was **b**; she had no children.
25:21 of his wife, because she was **b**.
Ge 29:31 opened her womb, but Rachel was **b**.
Ex 23:26 none will miscarry or be **b** in your
Nu 23: 3 Then he went off to a **b** height.
Dt 32:10 in a **b** and howling waste.
1Sa 2: 5 She who was **b** has borne seven
Job 3: 7 May that night be **b**; may no shout of
15:34 company of the godless will be **b**,
24:21 They prey on the **b** and childless
Ps 113: 9 He settles the **b** woman in her home
Pr 30:16 the grave, the **b** womb, land, which
Isa 41:18 I will make rivers flow on **b** heights,
49: 9 and find pasture on every **b** hill.
49:21 I was bereaved and **b**;
54: 1 "Sing, O **b** woman, you who never bore
Jer 2: 6 and led us through the **b** wilderness,
3: 2 "Look up to the **b** heights and see.
3:21 A cry is heard on the **b** heights,
4:11 "A scorching wind from the **b** heights
7:29 take up a lament on the **b** heights,
12:12 Over all the **b** heights in the desert
14: 6 Wild donkeys stand on the **b** heights
Joel 2:20 pushing it into a parched and **b** land,
Lk 1: 7 because Elizabeth was **b**; and they
1:36 and she who was said to be **b**
23:29 'Blessed are the **b** women, the wombs
Gal 4:27 "Be glad, O **b** woman,
Heb 11:11 and Sarah herself was **b**—

Barrier
Jer 5:22 an everlasting **b** it cannot cross.
Eph 2:14 and has destroyed the **b**,

Bars (Bar)
Lev 26:13 I broke the **b** of your yoke and
Dt 3: 5 high walls and with gates and **b**,
1Sa 23: 7 entering a town with gates and **b**."
1Ki 4:13 walled cities with bronze gate **b**);
2Ch 8: 5 with walls and with gates and **b**,
14: 7 them, with towers, gates and **b**.
Ne 3: 3 its doors and bolts and **b** in place.
3: 6 its doors and bolts and **b** in place.
3:13 its doors and bolts and **b** in place.
3:14 its doors and bolts and **b** in place.
3:15 its doors and bolts and **b** in place.
Job 38:10 and set its doors and **b** in place,
Ps 68:30 Humbled, may it bring **b** of silver.
107:16 bronze and cuts through **b** of iron.
147:13 he strengthens the **b** of your gates
Isa 45: 2 of bronze and cut through **b** of iron.
Jer 49:31 nation that has neither gates nor **b**;
51:30 the **b** of her gates are broken.
Lam 2: 9 their **b** he has broken and destroyed.
Eze 34:27 when I break the **b** of their yoke and
38:11 walls and without gates and **b**.
Hos 11: 6 will destroy the **b** of their gates
Na 3:13 fire has consumed their **b**.

Barsabbas
Ac 1:23 Joseph called **B** (also known as
15:22 They chose Judas (called **B**) and

Barter
Job 6:27 fatherless and **b** away your friend.
41: 6 Will traders **b** for him?
Lam 1:11 they **b** their treasures for food

Bartholomew
One of the twelve apostles (Mt 10:2–3; Mk 3:16–18; Lk 6:13–14; Ac 1:13). May also have been known as Nathanael.

Mt 10: 3 Philip and **B**; Thomas and Matthew
Mk 3:18 Andrew, Philip, **B**, Matthew, Thomas,
Lk 6:14 Andrew, James, John, Philip, **B**,
Ac 1:13 Philip and Thomas, **B** and Matthew;

Bartimaeus
Blind beggar healed by Jesus (Mk 10:46–52; Lk 19:35–43; Mt 20:29–34).

Mk 10:46 a blind man, **B** (that is, the Son of

Baruch
Secretary and companion of Jeremiah. Wrote down Jeremiah's prophecies and read them to the people (Jer 36). Jeremiah gave him deeds of field in Anathoth (Jer 32:12–16). Accused of influencing Jeremiah; taken with him to Egypt (Jer 43:1–7). God's word to (Jer 45).

Ne 3:20 Next to him, **B** son of Zabbai
10: 6 Daniel, Ginnethon, **B**,
11: 5 Maaseiah son of **B**, the son of
Jer 32:12 I gave this deed to **B** son of Neriah,
32:13 I gave **B** these instructions:
32:16 I gave the deed of purchase to **B**
36: 4 Jeremiah called **B** son of Neriah,
36: 4 to him, **B** wrote them on the scroll.
36: 5 Jeremiah told **B**, "I am restricted; I
36: 8 **B** son of Neriah did everything
36:10 **B** read to all the people
36:13 **B** read to the people from the scroll,
36:14 to say to **B**, "Bring the scroll
36:14 So **B** son of Neriah went to them
36:15 So **B** read it to them.
36:16 and said to **B**, "We must report
36:17 they asked **B**, "Tell us, how did you
36:18 "Yes," **B** replied, "he dictated all
36:19 the officials said to **B**, "You and
36:26 to arrest **B** the scribe
36:27 the words that **B** had written
36:32 it to the scribe **B** son of Neriah,
36:32 and as Jeremiah dictated, **B** wrote on
43: 3 **B** son of Neriah is inciting you
43: 6 the prophet and **B** son of Neriah.
45: 1 what Jeremiah the prophet told **B**
45: 1 after **B** had written on a scroll the
45: 2 the God of Israel, says to you, **B**:

Barzillai
2Sa 17:27 and **B** the Gileadite from
19:31 **B** the Gileadite also came down from
19:32 Now **B** was a very old man, eighty
19:33 The king said to **B**, "Cross over with
19:34 **B** answered the king, "How many more
19:39 The king kissed **B** and gave him his
19:39 and **B** returned to his home.
21: 8 to Adriel son of **B** the Meholathite.
1Ki 2: 7 "But show kindness to the sons of **B**
Ezr 2:61 **B** (a man who had married a daughter
2:61 a daughter of **B** the Gileadite
Ne 7:63 **B** (a man who had married a daughter
7:63 a daughter of **B** the Gileadite

Base (Based, Bases, Basic, Basing, Basis)
Ex 25:31 and hammer it out, **b** and shaft;
29:12 rest of it at the **b** of the altar.
37:17 hammered it out, **b** and shaft;
38:27 100 talents, one talent for each **b**.
Lev 4: 7 shall pour out at the **b** of the altar
4:18 the **b** of the altar of burnt offering
4:25 of the blood at the **b** of the altar.
4:30 of the blood at the **b** of the altar.
4:34 of the blood at the **b** of the altar.
5: 9 drained out at the **b** of the altar.
8:15 of the blood at the **b** of the altar.
9: 9 he poured out at the **b** of the altar.
Nu 8: 4 gold—from its **b** to its blossoms.
2Ki 16:17 and set it on a stone **b**.
Job 30: 8 A **b** and nameless brood, they were
SS 3:10 Its posts he made of silver, its **b**
Isa 3: 5 old, the **b** against the honourable.
Eze 31: 4 streams flowed all around its **b**
41: 8 I saw that the temple had a raised **b**
41:11 and the **b** adjoining the open area
41:22 its **b** and its sides were of wood.

Based (Base)
Lev 25:50 The price for his release is to be **b**
Nu 26:53 **b** on the number of names.
Ro 2: 2 who do such things is **b** on truth.
10: 2 their zeal is not **b** on knowledge.
Gal 3:12 The law is not **b** on faith;
Col 2:22 **b** on human commands and teachings.

Basemath
Ge 26:34 also **B** daughter of Elon the Hittite.
36: 3 also **B** daughter of Ishmael and
36: 4 bore Eliphaz to Esau, **B** bore Reuel,
36:10 and Reuel, the son of Esau's wife **B**.
36:13 were grandsons of Esau's wife **B**.
36:17 were grandsons of Esau's wife **B**.
1Ki 4:15 had married **B** daughter of Solomon);

Bases (Base)
Ex 26:19 make forty silver **b** to go under them
26:19 go under them—two **b** for each frame,
26:21 forty silver **b**—two under each frame.
26:25 and sixteen silver **b**—two under
26:32 gold and standing on four silver **b**.
26:37 And cast five bronze **b** for them.
27:10 with twenty posts and twenty bronze **b**
27:11 with twenty posts and twenty bronze **b**
27:12 curtains, with ten posts and ten **b**.
27:14 with three posts and three **b**,
27:15 side, with three posts and three **b**.
27:16 four posts and four **b**.
27:17 bands and hooks, and bronze **b**.
27:18 five cubits high, and with bronze **b**.
35:11 frames, crossbars, posts and **b**;
35:17 the courtyard with its posts and **b**,
36:24 made forty silver **b** to go under them
36:24 go under them—two **b** for each frame,
36:26 forty silver **b**—two under each frame.
36:30 sixteen silver **b**—two under
36:36 them and cast their four silver **b**.
36:38 and made their five **b** of bronze.
38:10 with twenty posts and twenty bronze **b**
38:11 twenty posts and twenty bronze **b**,
38:12 with ten posts and ten **b**, with
38:14 with three posts and three **b**,
38:15 with three posts and three **b**.

Ex 38:17 The **b** for the posts were bronze.
38:19 with four posts and four bronze **b**.
38:27 to cast the **b** for the sanctuary
38:27 100 **b** from the 100 talents,
38:30 They used it to make the **b** for the
38:31 the **b** for the surrounding courtyard
39:33 frames, crossbars, posts and **b**;
39:40 the courtyard with its posts and **b**,
40:18 he put the **b** in place, erected the
Nu 3:36 its crossbars, posts, **b**, all its
3:37 with their **b**, tent pegs and ropes.
4:31 its crossbars, posts and **b**,
4:32 surrounding courtyard with their **b**,
SS 5:15 of marble set on **b** of pure gold.

Basework

1Ki 7:31 **b** it measured a cubit and a half.

Bashan

Nu 21:33 went up along the road towards **B**,
21:33 and Og king of **B** and his whole army
32:33 the kingdom of Og king of **B**—the
Dt 1: 4 king of **B**, who reigned in Ashtaroth.
3: 1 went up along the road towards **B**,
3: 1 and Og king of **B** with his whole army
3: 3 hands Og king of **B** and all his army.
3: 4 region of Argob, Og's kingdom in **B**.
3:10 all **B** as far as Salecah and Edrei,
3:10 Edrei, towns of Og's kingdom in **B**.
3:11 (Only Og king of **B** was left of the
3:13 The rest of Gilead and also all of **B**,
3:13 (The whole region of Argob in **B** used
3:14 this day **B** is called Havvoth Jair.)
4:43 and Golan in **B**, for the Manassites.
4:47 land and the land of Og king of **B**,
29: 7 Og king of **B** came out to fight
32:14 with choice rams of **B** and the finest
33:22 a lion's cub, springing out of **B**."
Jos 9:10 king of **B**, who reigned in Ashtaroth.
12: 4 the territory of Og king of **B**,
12: 5 Salecah, all of **B** to the border of
13:11 Hermon and all **B** as far as Salecah—
13:12 that is, the whole kingdom of Og in **B**
13:30 Mahanaim and including all of **B**,
13:30 the entire realm of Og king of **B**
13:30 all the settlements of Jair in **B**,
13:31 Edrei (the royal cities of Og in **B**).
17: 1 who had received Gilead and **B**
17: 5 Gilead and **B** east of the Jordan,
20: 8 Golan in **B** in the tribe of Manasseh.
21: 6 and the half-tribe of Manasseh in **B**.
21:27 Golan in **B** (a city of refuge for one
22: 7 Manasseh Moses had given land in **B**,
1Ki 4:13 well as the district of Argob in **B**
4:19 and the country of Og king of **B**).
2Ki 10:33 the Arnon Gorge through Gilead to **B**.
1Ch 5:11 The Gadites lived next to them in **B**,
5:12 then Janai and Shaphat, in **B**.
5:16 The Gadites lived in Gilead, in **B**
5:23 in the land from **B** to Baal Hermon,
6:62 the tribe of Manasseh that is in **B**.
6:71 Golan in **B** and also Ashtaroth,
Ne 9:22 and the country of Og king of **B**.
Ps 22:12 strong bulls of **B** encircle me.
68:15 The mountains of **B** are majestic
68:15 rugged are the mountains of **B**.
68:22 "I will bring them from **B**; I will
135:11 Og king of **B** and all the kings
136:20 and Og king of **B**—
Isa 2:13 and lofty, and all the oaks of **B**,
33: 9 and **B** and Carmel drop their leaves.
Jer 22:20 let your voice be heard in **B**, cry
50:19 and he will graze on Carmel and **B**;
Eze 27: 6 Of oaks from **B** they made your oars;
39:18 fattened animals from **B**.
Am 4: 1 Hear this word, you cows of **B**
Mic 7:14 in **B** and Gilead as in days long ago.
Na 1: 4 **B** and Carmel wither and the blossoms
Zec 11: 2 wail, oaks of **B**;

Basic (Base)

Gal 4: 3 under the **b** principles of the world.
Col 2: 8 the **b** principles of this world
2:20 the **b** principles of this world,

Basin (Basins, Washbasin)

Ex 12:22 dip it into the blood in the **b** and
30:18 "Make a bronze **b**, with its bronze
30:28 utensils, and the **b** with its stand.
31: 9 its utensils, the **b** with its stand—
35:16 the bronze **b** with its stand;
38: 8 They made the bronze **b** and its
39:39 its utensils; the **b** with its stand;
40: 7 place the **b** between the Tent of
40:11 Anoint the **b** and its stand and
40:30 He placed the **b** between the Tent of
Lev 8:11 and the **b** with its stand,
1Ki 7:30 a **b** resting on four supports
7:38 **b** to go on each of the ten stands.
Jn 13: 5 After that, he poured water into a **b**

Basing (Base)

2Ki 18:19 On what are you **b** this confidence
2Ch 32:10 On what are you **b** your confidence,
Isa 36: 4 On what are you **b** this confidence

Basins (Basin)

1Ki 7:38 He then made ten bronze **b**, each
7:40 He also made the **b** and shovels and
7:43 the ten stands with their ten **b**;
2Ki 12:13 was not spent for making silver **b**,
16:17 the **b** from the movable stands.
2Ch 4: 6 He then made ten **b** for washing and
4:14 the stands with their **b**;
Jer 52:19 the imperial guard took away the **b**,

Basis (Base)

Lev 25:15 on the **b** of the number of years
25:15 And he is to sell to you on the **b** of
1Ki 20:34 "On the **b** of a treaty
Eze 16:61 on the **b** of my covenant with you.
Da 6: 5 "We will never find any **b** for
Lk 23: 4 no **b** for a charge against this man."
23:14 no **b** for your charges against him.
Jn 8: 6 order to have a **b** for accusing him.
18:38 I find no **b** for a charge against him.
19: 4 find no **b** for a charge against him."
19: 6 find no **b** for a charge against him."
Phm : 9 yet I appeal to you on the **b** of love.
Heb 7:11 (for on the **b** of it the law was given
7:16 not on the **b** of a regulation as to
7:16 but on the **b** of the power of an

Basket (Basketfuls, Baskets)

Ge 40:17 In the top **b** were all kinds of baked
40:17 birds were eating them out of the **b**
Ex 2: 3 she got a papyrus **b** for him and
2: 5 She saw the **b** among the reeds and
29: 3 Put them in a **b** and present them in
29:23 the **b** of bread made without yeast
29:32 ram and the bread that is in the **b**.
Lev 8: 2 and the **b** containing bread
8:26 from the **b** of bread made without
8:31 from the **b** of ordination offerings,
Nu 6:15 and a **b** of bread made without yeast—
6:17 present the **b** of unleavened bread
6:19 a cake and a wafer from the **b**,
Dt 23:24 want, but do not put any in your **b**.
26: 2 is giving you and put them in a **b**.
26: 4 The priest shall take the **b** from
26:10 Place the **b** before the LORD your
28: 5 Your **b** and your kneading trough will
28:17 Your **b** and your kneading trough will
Jdg 6:19 Putting the meat in a **b** and its
Ps 81: 6 hands were set free from the **b**.
Isa 40:12 held the dust of the earth in a **b**,
Jer 24: 2 One **b** had very good figs, like those
24: 2 the other **b** had very poor figs,
Am 8: 1 LORD showed me: a **b** of ripe fruit.
8: 2 "A **b** of ripe fruit," I answered.
Zec 5: 6 He replied, "It is a measuring **b**.
5: 7 and there in the **b** sat a woman!
5: 8 he pushed her back into the **b** and
5: 9 they lifted up the **b** between
5:10 "Where are they taking the **b**?"
5:11 **b** will be set there in its place."
Ac 9:25 lowered him in a **b** through an
2Co 11:33 I was lowered in a **b** from a window

Basketfuls (Basket)

Mt 14:20 the disciples picked up twelve **b** of
15:37 the disciples picked up seven **b** of
16: 9 and how many **b** you gathered?
16:10 and how many **b** you gathered?
6:43 the disciples picked up twelve **b** of
8: 8 the disciples picked up seven **b** of
8:19 how many **b** of pieces did you pick up?
8:20 how many **b** of pieces did you pick up?
Lk 9:17 the disciples picked up twelve **b** of

Baskets (Basket)

Ge 40:16 On my head were three **b** of bread.
40:18 "The three **b** are three days.
2Ki 10: 7 They put their heads in **b**
Jer 24: 1 the LORD showed me two **b** of figs
Mt 13:48 and collected the good fish in **b**,
Jn 6:13 filled twelve **b** with the pieces of

Bat (Bats)

Lev 11:19 kind of heron, the hoopoe and the **b**.
Dt 14:18 kind of heron, the hoopoe and the **b**.

Batch

Ro 11:16 then the whole **b** is holy; if the
1Co 5: 6 works through the whole **b** of dough?
5: 7 **b** without yeast—as you really are.
Gal 5: 9 works through the whole **b** of dough."

Bath (Bathe)

Isa 5:10 will produce only a **b** of wine,
Eze 45:10 an accurate ephah and an accurate **b**.
45:11 The ephah and the **b** are to be the
45:11 the **b** containing a tenth of a homer
45:14 measured by the **b**, is a tenth of a **b**
Jn 13:10 "A person who has had a **b** needs only

Bath Rabbim

SS 7: 4 pools of Heshbon by the gate of **B**.

Bathe (Bath, Bathed, Bathing, Baths)

Ex 2: 5 daughter went down to the Nile to **b**,
Lev 14: 8 shave off all his hair and **b** with
14: 9 He must wash his clothes and **b**
15: 5 wash his clothes and **b** with water,
15: 6 wash his clothes and **b** with water,
15: 7 wash his clothes and **b** with water,
15: 8 wash his clothes and **b** with water,
15:10 wash his clothes and **b** with water,
15:11 wash his clothes and **b** with water,
15:13 and **b** himself with fresh water,
15:16 he must **b** his whole body with water,
15:18 both must **b** with water, and they
15:21 wash his clothes and **b** with water,
15:22 wash his clothes and **b** with water,
15:27 wash his clothes and **b** with water,
16: 4 so he must **b** himself with water
16:24 He shall **b** himself with water in a
16:26 clothes and **b** himself with water;
16:28 clothes and **b** himself with water;
17:15 wash his clothes and **b** with water,
17:16 if he does not wash his clothes and **b**
Nu 19: 7 clothes and **b** himself with water.
19: 8 wash his clothes and **b** with water,
19:19 wash his clothes and **b** with water,
Dt 33:24 and let him **b** his feet in oil.
Ps 58:10 when they **b** their feet in the blood

Bathed (Bathe)

Lev 22: 6 unless he has **b** himself with water.
1Ki 22:38 Samaria (where the prostitutes **b**),
Isa 34: 6 The sword of the LORD is **b** in blood,
Eze 16: 9 "'I **b** you with water and washed the
23:40 and when they arrived you **b** yourself

Bathing (Bathe)

2Sa 11: 2 From the roof he saw a woman **b**.
Job 36:30 about him, **b** the depths of the sea.

Baths (Bathe)

1Ki 5:11 in addition to twenty thousand **b**,
7:26 It held two thousand **b**.
7:38 bronze basins each holding forty **b**

2Ch 2:10 twenty thousand **b** of wine and twenty
2:10 and twenty thousand **b** of olive oil."
4: 5 It held three thousand **b**.
Ezr 7:22 a hundred **b** of wine, a hundred **b** of
Eze 45:14 consists of ten **b** or one homer,
45:14 ten **b** are equivalent to a homer).

Bathsheba
Wife of Uriah; committed adultery with David and became his wife (2Sa 11). Secured succession for her son, Solomon (1Ki 1:11–40). Included in Jesus' genealogy (Mt 1:6).

2Sa 11: 3 "Isn't this **B**, the daughter of Eliam
12:24 David comforted his wife **B**, and he
1Ki 1:11 Nathan asked **B**, Solomon's mother,
1:15 **B** went to see the aged king in his
1:16 **B** bowed low and knelt before the
1:28 King David said, "Call in **B**." So she
1:31 **B** bowed low with her face to the
2:13 Haggith, went to **B**, Solomon's mother.
2:13 **B** asked him, "Do you come peacefully?
2:18 "Very well," **B** replied, "I will
2:19 **B** went to King Solomon to speak to
1Ch 3: 5 four were by **B** daughter of Ammiel.
Ps 51: T David had committed adultery with **B**.

Bats (Bat)
Isa 2:20 throw away to the rodents and **b**

Battered (Battering)
Isa 24:12 in ruins, its gate is **b** to pieces.

Battering (Battered, Battering-rams)
2Sa 20:15 were **b** the wall to bring it down,
Isa 22: 5 a day of **b** down walls and of crying
Ac 27:18 We took such a violent **b** from the

Battering-rams (Battering)
Eze 4: 2 against it and put **b** around it.
21:22 Jerusalem, where he is to set up **b**,
21:22 to set **b** against the gates
26: 9 He will direct the blows of his **b**

Battle (Battlements, Battle-bow, Battles)
Ge 14: 8 **b** lines in the Valley of
Ex 13:18 went up out of Egypt armed for **b**.
Nu 10: 9 you go into **b** in your own land
21:33 out to meet them in **b** at Edrei.
31: 4 Send into **b** a thousand men from each
31: 5 twelve thousand men armed for **b**, a
31: 6 Moses sent them into **b**, a thousand
31:14 hundreds—who returned from the **b**.
31:21 to the soldiers who had gone into **b**,
31:27 the soldiers who took part in the **b**
31:28 From the soldiers who fought in the **b**
31:36 of those who fought in the **b**
32:20 yourselves before the LORD for **b**,
32:27 your servants, every man armed for **b**,
32:29 every man armed for **b**, cross over
Dt 2:24 of it and engage him in **b**.
2:32 came out to meet us in **b** at Jahaz,
3: 1 out to meet us in **b** at Edrei.
3:18 armed for **b**, must cross over ahead
20: 2 When you are about to go into **b**,
20: 3 going into **b** against your enemies.
20: 5 or he may die in **b** and someone else
20: 6 die in **b** and someone else enjoy it.
20: 7 or he may die in **b** and someone else
20:12 and they engage you in **b**, lay siege
Jos 4:13 About forty thousand armed for **b**
8:14 meet Israel in **b** at a certain place
11:19 Israelites, who took them all in **b**.
13:22 In addition to those slain in **b**,
14:11 to go out to **b** now as I was then.
Jdg 3: 2 had not had previous **b** experience):
8:13 from the **b** by the Pass of Heres.
18:11 clan of the Danites, armed for **b**,
18:16 six hundred Danites, armed for **b**,
20:20 took up **b** positions against them
20:23 "Shall we go up again to **b** against
Jdg 20:28 "Shall we go up again to **b** with
20:39 men of Israel would turn in the **b**
20:39 defeating them as in the first **b**."
20:42 but they could not escape the **b**.
1Sa 4: 2 and as the **b** spread, Israel was
4:12 a Benjamite ran from the **b** line
4:16 "I have just come from the **b** line;
7:10 drew near to engage Israel in **b**.
13:22 on the day of the **b** not a soldier
14:20 his men assembled and went to the **b**.
14:22 they joined the **b** in hot pursuit.
14:23 and the **b** moved on beyond Beth Aven.
17: 2 **b** line to meet the Philistines.
17: 8 do you come out and line up for **b**?
17:20 going out to its **b** positions,
17:22 **b** lines and greeted his brothers.
17:28 you came down only to watch the **b**."
17:47 LORD saves; for the **b** is the LORD's,
17:48 towards the **b** line to meet him.
18:30 commanders continued to go out to **b**,
23: 8 Saul called up all his forces for **b**,
26:10 or he will go into **b** and perish.
29: 4 He must not go with us into **b**, or he
29: 9 'He must not go up with us into **b**.'
30:24 that of him who went down to the **b**.
2Sa 1: 4 He said, "The men fled from the **b**.
1:25 "How the mighty have fallen in **b**!
2:17 The **b** that day was very fierce, and
3:30 brother Asahel in the **b** of Gibeon.)
8:10 on his victory in **b** over Hadadezer,
10: 8 drew up in **b** formation at the
10: 9 Joab saw that there were **b** lines in
10:17 The Arameans formed their **b** lines to
11:18 sent David a full account of the **b**.
11:19 the king this account of the **b**,
17:11 you yourself leading them into **b**.
18: 6 and the **b** took place in the forest
18: 8 The **b** spread out over the whole
19: 3 are ashamed when they flee from **b**.
19:10 to rule over us, has died in **b**.
21:15 Once again there was a **b** between the
21:17 again will you go out with us to **b**,
21:18 **b** with the Philistines, at Gob.
21:19 In another **b** with the Philistines at
21:20 In still another **b**, which took place
22:35 He trains my hands for **b**; my arms
22:40 You armed me with strength for **b**;
23: 9 gathered at Pas Dammin for **b**
1Ki 2: 5 their blood in peacetime as if in **b**,
20:14 And who will start the **b**?" he asked.
20:29 on the seventh day the **b** was joined.
20:39 went into the thick of the **b**,
22:30 "I will enter the **b** in disguise, but
22:30 disguised himself and went into **b**.
22:35 All day long the **b** raged, and the
2Ki 3:26 the king of Moab saw that the **b** had
8:29 in his **b** with Hazael king of Aram.
9:15 in the **b** with Hazael king of Aram.
13:25 taken in **b** from his father Jehoahaz.
14: 7 of Salt and captured Sela in **b**,
23:29 Josiah marched out to meet him in **b**,
1Ch 5:18 a bow, and who were trained for **b**.
5:20 they cried out to him during the **b**.
5:22 fell slain, because the **b** was God's
7: 4 they had 36,000 men ready for **b**, for
7:40 The number of men ready for **b**, as
11:13 Philistines gathered there for **b**.
12: 1 the warriors who helped him in **b**;
12: 8 ready for **b** and able to handle the
12:23 the numbers of the men armed for **b**
12:24 6,800 armed for **b**;
12:25 men of Simeon, warriors ready for **b**
12:33 experienced soldiers prepared for **b**
12:35 men of Dan, ready for **b**—28,600;
12:36 soldiers prepared for **b**—40,000;
14:15 move out to **b**, because that will
18:10 on his victory in **b** over Hadadezer,
19: 7 their towns and moved out for **b**.
19: 9 drew up in **b** formation at the
19:10 Joab saw that there were **b** lines in
19:17 formed his **b** lines opposite them.
19:17 To meet the Arameans in **b**,
20: 5 In another **b** with the Philistines,
20: 6 In still another **b**, which took place
26:27 Some of the plunder taken in **b** they
2Ch 13: 3 Abijah went into **b** with a force of
2Ch 13: 3 and Jeroboam drew up a **b** line
13:12 will sound the **b** cry against you.
13:15 the men of Judah raised the **b** cry.
13:15 At the sound of their **b** cry, God
14:10 and they took up **b** positions in the
17:18 with 180,000 men armed for **b**.
18:29 "I will enter the **b** in disguise, but
18:29 disguised himself and went into **b**.
18:34 All day long the **b** raged, and the
20:15 For the **b** is not yours, but God's.
20:17 You will not have to fight this **b**.
22: 6 in his **b** with Hazael king of Aram.
25: 8 you go and fight courageously in **b**,
35:20 Josiah marched out to meet him in **b**.
35:22 himself to engage him in **b**.
Job 5:20 in **b** from the stroke of the sword.
38:23 of trouble, for days of war and **b**?
39:25 He catches the scent of **b** from afar,
39:25 shout of commanders and the **b** cry.
Ps 18:34 He trains my hands for **b**;
18:39 You armed me with strength for **b**;
24: 8 and mighty, the LORD mighty in **b**.
55:18 He ransoms me unharmed from the **b**
78: 9 bows, turned back on the day of **b**;
89:43 and have not supported him in **b**.
110: 3 will be willing on your day of **b**.
140: 7 shields my head in the day of **b**—
144: 1 my hands for war, my fingers for **b**.
Pr 21:31 horse is made ready for the day of **b**
Ecc 9:11 to the swift or the **b** to the strong,
SS 3: 8 all experienced in **b**, each with his
Isa 3:25 by the sword, your warriors in **b**.
8: 9 Prepare for **b**, and be shattered!
8: 9 Prepare for **b**, and be shattered!
9: 5 Every warrior's boot used in **b** and
21:15 the bent bow and from the heat of **b**.
22: 2 by the sword, nor did they die in **b**.
27: 4 I would march against them in **b**;
28: 6 who turn back the **b** at the gate.
30:32 them in **b** with the blows of his arm.
31: 4 **b** on Mount Zion and on its heights.
31: 9 at sight of the **b** standard their
42:13 with a shout he will raise the **b** cry
Jer 4:19 the trumpet; I have heard the **b** cry.
4:21 How long must I see the **b** standard
6: 4 "Prepare for **b** against her! Arise,
6:23 men in **b** formation to attack you,
8: 6 course like a horse charging into **b**.
18:21 young men slain by the sword in **b**.
20:16 in the morning, a **b** cry at noon.
46: 3 and small, and march out for **b**!
48:14 are warriors, men in valiant **b**'?
49: 2 "when I will sound the **b** cry against
49:14 to attack it! Rise up for **b**!"
50:22 The noise of **b** is in the land, the
50:42 men in **b** formation to attack you,
51:20 "You are my war club, my weapon for **b**
51:27 Prepare the nations for **b** against
51:28 Prepare the nations for **b** against
Eze 7:14 no-one will go into **b**, for my wrath
13: 5 in the **b** on the day of the LORD.
21:22 to sound the **b** cry, to set battering-
Da 11:10 carry the **b** as far as his fortress.
11:20 destroyed, yet not in anger or in **b**.
11:26 swept away, and many will fall in **b**.
11:40 of the South will engage him in **b**,
Hos 1: 7 sword or **b**, or by horses and
2:18 Bow and sword and **b** I will abolish
5: 8 Raise the **b** cry in Beth Aven; lead
10:14 the roar of **b** will rise against your
10:14 Beth Arbel on the day of **b**,
Joel 2: 5 like a mighty army drawn up for **b**.
Am 1:14 amid war cries on the day of **b**,
Ob : 1 and let us go against her for **b**"—
Mic 2: 8 a care, like men returning from **b**.
Zep 1:16 a day of trumpet and **b** cry against
Zec 10: 3 make them like a proud horse in **b**.
10: 5 trampling the muddy streets in **b**.
14: 3 as he fights in the day of **b**.
1Co 14: 8 call, who will get ready for **b**?
Heb 11:34 who became powerful in **b** and
Jas 4: 1 from your desires that **b** within you?
Rev 9: 7 looked like horses prepared for **b**.
9: 9 horses and chariots rushing into **b**.
16:14 **b** on the great day of God Almighty.
20: 8 and Magog—to gather them for **b**.

Battle-bow (Battle, Bow[1])
Zec 9:10 Jerusalem, and the **b** will be broken.
10: 4 him the **b**, from him every ruler.

Battlefield (Field)
Jdg 20:21 Israelites on the **b** that day.
1Sa 4: 2 four thousand of them on the **b**.

Battlements (Battle)
Isa 54:12 I will make your **b** of rubies, your

Battles (Battle)
1Sa 8:20 go out before us and fight our **b**."
18:17 bravely and fight the **b** of the LORD.
25:28 because he fights the LORD's **b**.
2Ch 32: 8 God to help us and to fight our **b**.

Bay
Jos 15: 2 southern boundary started from the **b**
15: 5 started from the **b** of the sea at
18:19 at the northern **b** of the Salt Sea,
Ac 27:39 but they saw a **b** with a sandy beach,

Bazluth
Ezr 2:52 **B**, Mehida, Harsha,
Ne 7:54 **B**, Mehida, Harsha,

Be Eshtarah
Jos 21:27 **B**, together with their pasture-lands

Beach
Ac 21: 5 and there on the **b** we knelt to pray.
27:39 but they saw a bay with a sandy **b**,
27:40 to the wind and made for the **b**.

Beak
Ge 8:11 there in its **b** was a freshly plucked

Bealiah
1Ch 12: 5 Eluzai, Jerimoth, **B**, Shemariah and

Bealoth
Jos 15:24 Ziph, Telem, **B**,

Beam (Beams)
Ezr 6:11 a **b** is to be pulled from his house

Beams (Beam)
1Ki 6: 9 roofing it with **b** and cedar planks.
6:10 to the temple by **b** of cedar.
6:36 and one course of trimmed cedar **b**.
7: 2 columns supporting trimmed cedar **b**.
7: 3 was roofed with cedar above the **b**
7: 3 forty-five **b**, fifteen to a row.
7:11 stones, cut to size, and cedar **b**.
7:12 and one course of trimmed cedar **b**,
2Ch 3: 7 He overlaid the ceiling **b**,
34:11 and timber for joists and **b** for the
Ne 2: 8 so he will give me timber to make **b**
3: 3 They laid its **b** and put its doors
3: 6 They laid its **b** and put its doors
Ps 104: 3 lays the **b** of his upper chambers on
SS 1:17 The **b** of our house are cedars; our
Jer 22: 7 they will cut up your fine cedar **b**
Hab 2:11 the **b** of the woodwork will echo it.
Zep 2:14 the **b** of cedar will be exposed.

Beans
2Sa 17:28 and roasted grain, **b** and lentils,
Eze 4: 9 "Take wheat and barley, **b** and

Bear[1] (Afterbirth, Bearable, Bearing, Bears, Birth, Birthday, Birth-pains, Birthright, Bore, Born, Borne, Childbearing, Childbirth, Firstborn, Highborn, Lowborn, Native-born, Newborn, Rebirth, Stillborn, Unborn)
Ge 1:11 land that **b** fruit with seed in it,
4:13 "My punishment is more than I can **b**.
17:17 **b** a child at the age of ninety?"
17:19 your wife Sarah will **b** you a son,
17:21 whom Sarah will **b** to you
Ge 30: 3 so that she can **b** children
43: 9 **b** the blame before you all my life.
44:32 I will **b** the blame before you, my
Ex 16:29 **B** in mind that the LORD has given
28:12 Aaron is to **b** the names on his
28:29 he will **b** the names of the sons of
28:30 Thus Aaron will always **b** the means
28:38 and he will **b** the guilt involved in
Lev 19:18 "Do not seek revenge or **b** a grudge
Nu 5:31 **b** the consequences of her sin.'"
9:13 will **b** the consequences of his sin.
18: 1 to **b** the responsibility for offences
18: 1 to **b** the responsibility for offences
18:22 or they will **b** the consequences of
18:23 **b** the responsibility for offences
Dt 1:12 how can I **b** your problems and your
21:15 and both **b** him sons but the
Jdg 5:14 those who **b** a commander's staff.
10:16 could **b** Israel's misery no longer.
2Ki 3:21 young and old, who could **b** arms was
19:30 take root below and **b** fruit above.
Est 8: 6 For how can I **b** to see disaster fall
8: 6 How can I **b** to see the destruction
Job 20:13 though he cannot **b** to let it go and
21: 3 **B** with me while I speak, and after I
36: 2 "**B** with me a little longer and I
39: 2 Do you count the months till they **b**?
Ps 38: 4 me like a burden too heavy to **b**.
89:50 how I **b** in my heart the taunts of
92:14 They will still **b** fruit in old age,
Pr 18:14 but a crushed spirit who can **b**?
30:21 trembles, under four it cannot **b** up:
Isa 1:13 I cannot **b** your evil assemblies.
11: 1 his roots a Branch will **b** fruit.
24: 6 its people must **b** their guilt.
37:31 take root below and **b** fruit above.
53:11 and he will **b** their iniquities.
65:23 They will not toil in vain or **b**
Jer 12: 2 taken root; they grow and **b** fruit.
12:13 So **b** the shame of your harvest
14: 9 we **b** your name; do not forsake us!
15:16 I **b** your name, O LORD God Almighty.
17: 8 drought and never fails to **b** fruit."
30: 6 Ask and see: Can a man **b** children?
Lam 3:27 is good for a man to **b** the yoke
5: 7 no more, and we **b** their punishment.
Eze 4: 4 You are to **b** their sin for the
4: 5 **b** the sin of the house of Israel.
4: 6 and **b** the sin of the house of Judah.
14:10 They will **b** their guilt—the prophet
16:52 **B** your disgrace, for you have
16:52 be ashamed and **b** your disgrace
16:54 that you may **b** your disgrace and be
16:58 You will **b** the consequences of your
17: 8 **b** fruit and become a splendid vine.'
17:23 **b** fruit and become a splendid cedar.
23:35 you must **b** the consequences of your
23:49 **b** the consequences of your sins of
32:24 They **b** their shame with those who go
32:25 they **b** their shame with those who go
32:30 **b** their shame with those who go down
34:29 land or **b** the scorn of the nations.
44:10 **b** the consequences of their sin.
44:12 **b** the consequences of their sin,
44:13 they must **b** the shame of their
47:12 Every month they will **b**, because the
Da 9:19 city and your people **b** your Name."
Hos 9:16 Even if they **b** children, I will slay
10: 2 and now they must **b** their guilt.
13:16 The people of Samaria must **b** their
Am 7:10 The land cannot **b** all his words.
9:12 and all the nations that **b** my name,"
Mic 6:16 will **b** the scorn of the nations."
7: 9 I will **b** the LORD's wrath,
Na 1:14 have no descendants to **b** your name.
Mt 7:18 A good tree cannot **b** bad fruit, and
7:18 and a bad tree cannot **b** good fruit.
7:19 Every tree that does not **b** good
21:19 "May you never **b** fruit again!"
Mk 4: 7 so that they did not **b** grain.
Lk 1:13 Your wife Elizabeth will **b** you a son,
1:42 and blessed is the child you will **b**!
6:43 nor does a bad tree **b** good fruit.
Jn 15: 2 while every branch that does **b** fruit
15: 4 No branch can **b** fruit by itself;
15: 4 Neither can you **b** fruit unless you
Jn 15: 5 he will **b** much fruit; apart from me
15: 8 that you **b** much fruit, showing
15:16 and **b** fruit—fruit that will last.
16:12 say to you, more than you can now **b**.
Ac 15:10 nor our fathers have been able to **b**?
15:17 and all the Gentiles who **b** my name,
Ro 7: 4 order that we might **b** fruit to God.
13: 4 he does not **b** the sword for nothing.
15: 1 We who are strong ought to **b** with
1Co 10:13 be tempted beyond what you can **b**.
15:49 so shall we **b** the likeness of the
Gal 6:17 I **b** on my body the marks of Jesus.
Col 3:13 **B** with each other and forgive
Heb 9:28 not to **b** sin, but to bring salvation
12:20 they could not **b** what was commanded:
Heb 13:22 I urge you to **b** with my word
Jas 3:12 My brothers, can a fig-tree **b** olives,
3:12 or a grapevine **b** figs? Neither can a
1Pe 4:16 but praise God that you **b** that name.
2Pe 3:15 **B** in mind that our Lord's patience

Bear[2] (Bears[2])
1Sa 17:34 When a lion or a **b** came and carried
17:36 has killed both the lion and the **b**;
17:37 the paw of the **b** will deliver me
2Sa 17: 8 as a wild **b** robbed of her cubs.
Job 9: 9 He is the Maker of the **B** and Orion,
38:32 or lead out the **B** with its cubs?
Pr 17:12 Better to meet a **b** robbed of her
28:15 Like a roaring lion or a charging **b**
Isa 11: 7 The cow will feed with the **b**, their
Lam 3:10 Like a **b** lying in wait, like a lion
Da 7: 5 second beast, which looked like a **b**.
Hos 13: 8 Like a **b** robbed of her cubs, I will
Am 5:19 fled from a lion only to meet a **b**,
Rev 13: 2 but had feet like those of a **b**

Bearable (Bear[1])
Mt 10:15 be more **b** for Sodom and Gomorrah
11:22 will be more **b** for Tyre and Sidon
11:24 I tell you that it will be more **b**
Lk 10:12 it will be more **b** on that day
10:14 will be more **b** for Tyre and Sidon at

Beard (Beards)
Lev 14: 9 he must shave his head, his **b**,
19:27 or clip off the edges of your **b**.
1Sa 21:13 and letting saliva run down his **b**.
2Sa 10: 4 shaved off half of each man's **b**,
20: 9 Then Joab took Amasa by the **b**
Ezr 9: 3 pulled hair from my head and **b**
Ps 133: 2 running down on the **b**, running
133: 2 running down on Aaron's **b**, down
Isa 15: 2 head is shaved and every **b** cut off.
50: 6 cheeks to those who pulled out my **b**;
Jer 48:37 Every head is shaved and every **b** cut
Eze 5: 1 razor to shave your head and your **b**.

Beards (Beard)
Lev 21: 5 or shave off the edges of their **b**
2Sa 10: 5 at Jericho till your **b** have grown,
1Ch 19: 5 at Jericho till you **b** have grown,
Isa 7:20 legs, and to take off your **b** also.
Jer 41: 5 eighty men who had shaved off their **b**

Bearing (Bear[1])
Ge 1:12 plants **b** seed according to their
1:12 trees **b** fruit with seed in it
30: 1 Rachel saw that she was not **b** Jacob
Nu 13:23 branch **b** a single cluster of grapes.
Jdg 8:18 "each one with the **b** of a prince.
1Sa 14: 1 said to the young man **b** his armour,
2Ch 12:11 guards went with him, **b** the shields
Pr 30:29 four that move with stately **b**:
Isa 1:14 burden to me; I am weary of **b** them.
60: 6 And all from Sheba will come, **b** gold
Jer 4:31 a groan as of one **b** her first child—
Joel 2:22 The trees are **b** their fruit;
Ro 2:15 their consciences also **b** witness,
Eph 4: 2 **b** with one another in love.
Col 1: 6 this gospel is **b** fruit and growing,
1:10 **b** fruit in every good work,
Heb 13:13 the camp, **b** the disgrace he bore.
Rev 22: 2 **b** twelve crops of fruit, yielding

Bears[1] (Bear[1])
Ge 49:21 "Naphtali is a doe set free that **b**
Ex 21: 4 and she **b** him sons or daughters,
Dt 25: 6 The first son she **b** shall carry on
28:57 her womb and the children she **b**.
1Ki 8:43 this house I have built **b** your Name.
2Ch 6:33 house that I have built **b** your Name.
20: 9 before this temple that **b** your Name
Job 39: 1 Do you watch when the doe **b** her fawn?
Ps 68:19 Saviour, who daily **b** our burdens.
Jer 7:10 in this house which **b** my Name,
7:11 Has this house, which **b** my Name,
7:14 now do to the house that **b** my Name,
7:30 idols in the house that **b** my Name
25:29 disaster on the city that **b** my Name,
32:34 idols in the house that **b** my Name
34:15 me in the house that **b** my Name.
Da 9:18 of the city that **b** your Name.
Mt 7:17 every good tree **b** good fruit,
7:17 fruit, but a bad tree **b** bad fruit.
Lk 6:43 "No good tree **b** bad fruit, nor does
13: 9 If it **b** fruit next year, fine! If
Jn 15: 2 He cuts off every branch in me that **b**
Gal 4:24 and **b** children who are to be slaves:
4:27 O barren woman, who **b** no children;
1Pe 2:19 For it is commendable if a man **b** up

Bears[2] (Bear[2])
2Ki 2:24 Then two **b** came out of the woods and
Isa 59:11 We all growl like **b**; we moan

Beast (Beasts)
2Ki 14: 9 Then a wild **b** in Lebanon came along
2Ch 25:18 Then a wild **b** in Lebanon came along
Ps 36: 6 O Lord, you preserve both man and **b**.
68:30 Rebuke the **b** among the reeds, the
73:22 I was a brute **b** before you.
Isa 35: 9 nor will any ferocious **b** get up on
Jer 7:20 on man and **b**, on the trees of the
Da 7: 5 "And there before me was a second **b**,
7: 6 there before me was another **b**,
7: 6 This **b** had four heads, and it was
7: 7 there before me was a fourth **b**
7:11 I kept looking until the **b** was slain
7:19 the true meaning of the fourth **b**,
7:19 the **b** that crushed and devoured
7:23 'The fourth **b** is a fourth kingdom
Jnh 3: 7 his nobles: Do not let any man or **b**,
3: 8 let man and **b** be covered with
Zec 8:10 there were no wages for man or **b**.
2Pe 2:16 a donkey—a **b** without speech
Rev 11: 7 the **b** that comes up from the Abyss
13: 1 And I saw a **b** coming out of the sea.
13: 2 The **b** I saw resembled a leopard, but
13: 2 The dragon gave the **b** his power and
13: 3 One of the heads of the **b** seemed to
13: 3 was astonished and followed the **b**.
13: 4 he had given authority to the **b**,
13: 4 and they also worshipped the **b** and
13: 4 "Who is like the **b**? Who can make
13: 5 The **b** was given a mouth to utter
13: 8 of the earth will worship the **b**
13:11 I saw another **b**, coming out of the
13:12 of the first **b** on his behalf,
13:12 its inhabitants worship the first **b**
13:14 to do on behalf of the first **b**,
13:14 the **b** who was wounded by the sword
13:15 breath to the image of the first **b**,
13:17 which is the name of the **b**
13:18 calculate the number of the **b**,
14: 9 "If anyone worships the **b** and his
14:11 who worship the **b** and his image,
15: 2 who had been victorious over the **b**
16: 2 who had the mark of the **b**
16:10 out his bowl on the throne of the **b**,
16:13 out of the mouth of the **b** and out of
17: 3 saw a woman sitting on a scarlet **b**
17: 7 of the woman and of the **b** she rides,
17: 8 The **b**, which you saw, once was, now
17: 8 be astonished when they see the **b**,
17:11 The **b** who once was, and now is not,
17:12 authority as kings along with the **b**.
17:13 their power and authority to the **b**.
17:16 The **b** and the ten horns you saw will
17:17 to give the **b** their power to rule,
Rev 19:19 I saw the **b** and the kings of the
19:20 the **b** was captured, and with him the
19:20 who had received the mark of the **b**
20: 4 They had not worshipped the **b** or his
20:10 where the **b** and the false prophet

Beasts (Beast)
Ge 1:30 to all the **b** of the earth and all
2:19 the ground all the **b** of the field
2:20 the air and all the **b** of the field.
9: 2 fall upon all the **b** of the earth
31:39 animals torn by wild **b**;
Ex 22:31 meant of an animal torn by wild **b**;
Lev 26: 6 I will remove savage **b** from the land,
Dt 28:26 of the air and the **b** of the earth,
32:24 against them the fangs of wild **b**,
1Sa 17:44 of the air and the **b** of the field!"
17:46 of the air and the **b** of the earth,
Job 5:22 need not fear the **b** of the earth.
28: 8 Proud **b** do not set foot on it, and
35:11 who teaches more to us than to the **b**
Ps 8: 7 and the **b** of the field,
49:12 he is like the **b** that perish.
49:20 is like the **b** that perish.
57: 4 I lie among ravenous **b**—
74:19 the life of your dove to wild **b**;
79: 2 your saints to the **b** of the earth.
104:11 They give water to all the **b** of the
104:20 and all the **b** of the forest prowl.
Pr 30:30 a lion, mighty among **b**, who retreats
Isa 46: 1 idols are borne by **b** of burden.
56: 9 Come, all you **b** of the field, come
56: 9 and devour, all you **b** of the forest!
Jer 7:33 of the air and the **b** of the earth,
12: 9 Go and gather all the wild **b**;
15: 3 **b** of the earth to devour and destroy.
16: 4 of the air and the **b** of the earth."
19: 7 of the air and the **b** of the earth.
34:20 of the air and the **b** of the earth.
Eze 5:17 I will send famine and wild **b**
14:15 "Or if I send wild **b** through that
14:15 pass through it because of the **b**,
14:21 famine and wild **b** and plague—to
29: 5 I will give you as food to the **b** of
31: 6 all the **b** of the field gave birth
31:13 and all the **b** of the field were
32: 4 all the **b** of the earth gorge
34:25 rid the land of wild **b** so that they
38:20 birds of the air, the **b** of the field
Da 2:38 the **b** of the field and the birds of
4:12 Under it the **b** of the field found
4:21 giving shelter to the **b** of the field,
7: 3 Four great **b**, each different from
7: 7 different from all the former **b**,
7:12 (The other **b** had been stripped of
7:17 'The four great **b** are four kingdoms
Hos 2:18 for them with the **b** of the field
4: 3 the **b** of the field and the birds of
Mic 5: 8 like a lion among the **b** of the
Zep 2:15 a lair for wild **b**! All who pass by
Ac 11: 6 **b**, reptiles, and birds of the air.
1Co 15:32 If I fought wild **b** in Ephesus for
2Pe 2:12 They are like brute **b**, creatures of
2:12 and like **b** they too will perish.
Rev 6: 8 and by the wild **b** of the earth.

Beat (Beaten, Beating, Beatings, Beats)
Ex 9:25 it **b** down everything growing in the
Nu 14:45 **b** them down all the way to Hormah.
22:23 **b** her to get her back on the road.
22:25 So he **b** her again.
22:27 was angry and **b** her with his staff.
22:28 to make you **b** me these three times?"
Dt 1:44 **b** you down from Seir all the way to
24:20 you **b** the olives from your trees, do
2Sa 22:43 I **b** them as fine as the dust of the
Ne 13:25 I **b** some of the men and pulled out
Ps 18:42 I **b** them as fine as dust borne on
78:66 He **b** back his enemies; he put them
Pr 23:35 They **b** me, but I don't feel it!
SS 5: 7 They **b** me, they bruised me; they
Isa 2: 4 They will **b** their swords into
10:24 who **b** you with a rod and lift up a
32:12 **B** your breasts for the pleasant
Isa 49:10 desert heat or the sun **b** upon them.
50: 6 I offered my back to those who **b** me,
Jer 31:19 I came to understand, I **b** my breast.
Eze 21:12 Therefore **b** your breast.
Joel 3:10 **B** your ploughshares into swords and
Mic 4: 3 They will **b** their swords into
Na 2: 7 and **b** upon their breasts.
Mt 7:25 and the winds blew and **b** against
7:27 and the winds blew and **b** against
21:35 they **b** one, killed another,
24:49 begins to **b** his fellow-servants
Mk 12: 3 they seized him, **b** him and sent him
12: 5 some of them they **b**, others they
14:65 And the guards took him and **b** him.
Lk 10:30 **b** him and went away,
12:45 he then begins to **b** the menservants
18:13 but **b** his breast and said, 'God,
20:10 **b** him and sent him away empty-handed.
20:11 but that one also they **b** and treated
23:48 they **b** their breasts and went away.
Ac 16:37 "They **b** us publicly without a trial,
18:17 and **b** him in front of the court.
22:19 and **b** those who believe in you.
1Co 9:27 No, I **b** my body and make it my slave
Rev 7:16 The sun will not **b** upon them,

Beaten (Beat)
Ex 5:14 slave drivers were **b** and were asked,
5:16 bricks!' Your servants are being **b**,
Nu 22:32 "Why have you **b** your donkey these
Dt 25: 2 If the guilty man deserves to be **b**,
Jdg 20:36 the Benjamites saw that they were **b**.
1Ki 6:32 cherubim and palm trees with **b** gold.
Isa 1: 5 Why should you be **b** any more? Why do
17: 6 as when an olive tree is **b**, leaving
24:13 as when an olive tree is **b**, or as
28:18 sweeps by, you will be **b** down by it.
28:27 cummin; caraway is **b** out with a rod,
Jer 20: 2 he had Jeremiah the prophet **b** and
37:15 had him **b** and imprisoned in the
Lk 12:47 wants will be **b** with many blows.
12:48 punishment will be **b** with few blows.
Ac 16:22 ordered them to be stripped and **b**.
2Co 6: 9 we live on; **b**, and yet not killed;
11:25 Three times I was **b** with rods, once

Beating (Beat)
Ex 2:11 He saw an Egyptian **b** a Hebrew,
Pr 18: 6 strife, and his mouth invites a **b**.
Lk 22:63 Jesus began mocking and **b** him.
Ac 19:16 He gave them such a **b** that they ran
21:32 his soldiers, they stopped **b** Paul.
1Co 9:26 I do not fight like a man **b** the air.
1Pe 2:20 receive a **b** for doing wrong

Beatings (Beat)
Pr 19:29 and **b** for the backs of fools.
20:30 evil, and **b** purge the inmost being.
2Co 6: 5 in **b**, imprisonments and riots; in

Beats (Beat)
Ex 21:20 "If a man **b** his male or female slave

Beautiful (Beauty)
Ge 6: 2 that the daughters of men were **b**,
12:11 "I know what a **b** woman you are.
12:14 saw that she was a very **b** woman.
24:16 The girl was very **b**, a virgin;
26: 7 of Rebekah, because she is **b**."
29:17 Rachel was lovely in form, and **b**.
49:21 a doe set free that bears **b** fawns.
Nu 24: 5 "How **b** are your tents, O Jacob,
Dt 21:11 notice among the captives a **b** woman
Jos 7:21 I saw in the plunder a **b** robe from
1Sa 25: 3 She was an intelligent and **b** woman,
2Sa 11: 2 The woman was very **b**,
13: 1 **b** sister of Absalom son of David.
14:27 was Tamar, and she became a **b** woman.
1Ki 1: 3 for a **b** girl and found Abishag,
1: 4 The girl was very **b**; she took care
Est 2: 2 for **b** young virgins for the king.
2: 3 to bring all these **b** girls into the
Job 38:31 "Can you bind the **b** Pleiades?
42:15 found women as **b** as Job's daughters,

Ps 48: 2 It is **b** in its loftiness,
Pr 11:22 a **b** woman who shows no discretion.
24: 4 filled with rare and **b** treasures.
Ecc 3:11 He has made everything **b** in its time.
SS 1: 8 If you do not know, most **b** of women,
1:10 Your cheeks are **b** with ear-rings,
1:15 How **b** you are, my darling! Oh, how **b**!
2:10 my **b** one, and come with me.
2:13 my **b** one, come with me."
4: 1 How **b** you are, my darling! Oh, how **b**!
4: 7 All **b** you are, my darling;
5: 9 most **b** of women?
6: 1 most **b** of women?
6: 4 You are **b**, my darling, as Tirzah,
7: 1 How **b** your sandalled feet,
7: 6 How **b** you are and how pleasing,
Isa 4: 2 of the LORD will be **b** and glorious,
28: 5 a **b** wreath for the remnant of his
52: 7 How **b** on the mountains are the feet
Jer 3:19 most **b** inheritance of any nation.
6: 2 Daughter of Zion, so **b** and delicate.
11:16 olive tree with fruit **b** in form.
46:20 "Egypt is a **b** heifer, but a gadfly
Eze 7:20 They were proud of their **b** jewellery
16: 7 and became the most **b** of jewels.
16:12 ears and a **b** crown on your head.
16:13 You became very **b** and rose to be
20: 6 and honey, the most **b** of all lands.
20:15 and honey, most **b** of all lands—
23:42 sister and **b** crowns on their heads.
27:24 they traded with you **b** garments,
31: 3 cedar in Lebanon, with **b** branches
31: 9 I made it **b** with abundant branches,
33:32 who sings love songs with a **b** voice
Da 4:12 Its leaves were **b**, its fruit
4:21 with **b** leaves and abundant fruit,
8: 9 to the east and towards the **B** Land.
11:16 establish himself in the **B** Land
11:41 He will also invade the **B** Land.
11:45 the seas at the **b** holy mountain.
Zec 9:17 How attractive and **b** they will be!
Mt 23:27 which look **b** on the outside but
26:10 She has done a **b** thing to me.
Mk 14: 6 She has done a **b** thing to me.
Lk 21: 5 temple was adorned with **b** stones
Ac 3: 2 carried to the temple gate called **B**,
3:10 begging at the temple gate called **B**,
Ro 10:15 "How **b** are the feet of those who
1Pe 3: 5 in God used to make themselves **b**.

Beautifully (Beauty)
Rev 21: 2 a bride **b** dressed for her husband.

Beauty (Beautiful, Beautifully)
Est 1:11 in order to display her **b** to the
2: 3 let **b** treatments be given to them.
2: 9 her **b** treatments and special food.
2:12 twelve months of **b** treatments
Ps 27: 4 to gaze upon the **b** of the LORD and
37:20 will be like the **b** of the fields,
45:11 The king is enthralled by your **b**;
50: 2 From Zion, perfect in **b**, God shines
Pr 6:25 not lust in your heart after her **b**
31:30 and **b** is fleeting;
Isa 3:24 sackcloth; instead of **b**, branding.
28: 1 to the fading flower, his glorious **b**
28: 4 That fading flower, his glorious **b**,
33:17 Your eyes will see the king in his **b**
53: 2 He had no **b** or majesty to attract us
61: 3 them a crown of **b** instead of ashes,
Lam 2:15 the perfection of **b**, the joy of the
Eze 16:14 the nations on account of your **b**,
16:14 I had given you made your **b** perfect,
16:15 "'But you trusted in your **b** and used
16:15 who passed by and your **b** became his.
16:25 lofty shrines and degraded your **b**,
27: 3 say, O Tyre, "I am perfect in **b**.
27: 4 brought your **b** to perfection.
27:11 they brought your **b** to perfection.
28: 7 draw their swords against your **b**
28:12 full of wisdom and perfect in **b**.
28:17 became proud on account of your **b**,
31: 7 It was majestic in **b**, with its
Eze 31: 8 the garden of God could match its **b**.
Jas 1:11 falls and its **b** is destroyed.
1Pe 3: 3 Your **b** should not come from outward
3: 4 **b** of a gentle and quiet spirit,

Bebai
Ezr 2:11 of **B** 623
8:11 of the descendants of **B**, Zechariah
8:11 Zechariah son of **B**,
10:28 From the descendants of **B**: Jehohanan,
Ne 7:16 of **B** 628
10:15 Bunni, Azgad, **B**,

Beckon
Isa 13: 2 shout to them; **b** to them to enter
49:22 "See, I will **b** to the Gentiles,

Becorath
1Sa 9: 1 the son of **B**, the son of Aphiah of

Bed (Bedding, Bedridden, Bedroom, Bedrooms, Beds, Sickbed)
Ge 19: 4 Before they had gone to **b**, all the
39: 7 "Come to **b** with me!
39:10 he refused to go to **b** with her
39:12 "Come to **b** with me!" But he left his
48: 2 his strength and sat up on the **b**.
49: 4 for you went up onto your father's **b**
49:33 he drew his feet up into the **b**,
Ex 8: 3 and your bedroom and onto your **b**,
21:18 does not die but is confined to **b**,
Lev 15: 4 "'Any **b** the man with a discharge
15: 5 Anyone who touches his **b** must wash
15:21 Whoever touches her **b** must wash his
15:23 Whether it is the **b** or anything she
15:24 any **b** he lies on will be unclean.
15:26 Any **b** she lies on while her
15:26 as is her **b** during her monthly
Dt 3:11 His **b** was made of iron and was more
22:30 must not dishonour his father's **b**.
27:20 for he dishonours his father's **b**.
1Sa 19:13 took an idol and laid it on the **b**,
19:15 "Bring him up to me in his **b**
19:16 there was the idol in the **b**,
2Sa 4: 7 was lying on the **b** in his bedroom.
4:11 in his own house and on his own **b**
11: 2 One evening David got up from his **b**
13: 5 "Go to **b** and pretend to be ill,"
13:11 said, "Come to **b** with me, my sister.
1Ki 1:47 the king bowed in worship on his **b**
17:19 was staying, and laid him on his **b**.
21: 4 on his **b** sulking and refused to eat.
2Ki 1: 4 not leave the **b** you are lying on.
1: 6 not leave the **b** you are lying on.
1:16 never leave the **b** you are lying on.
4:10 roof and put in it a **b** and a table,
4:21 She went up and laid him on the **b** of
4:34 he got on the **b** and lay upon the boy,
4:35 then got onto the **b** and stretched
1Ch 5: 1 he defiled his father's marriage **b**,
2Ch 24:25 and they killed him in his **b**.
Job 7:13 I think my **b** will comfort me and my
14:11 a river **b** becomes parched and dry,
17:13 if I spread out my **b** in darkness,
33:19 may be chastened on a **b** of pain
Ps 6: 6 I flood my **b** with weeping
36: 4 Even on his **b** he plots evil;
41: 3 restore him from his **b** of illness.
63: 6 On my **b** I remember you; I think of
132: 3 not enter my house or go to my **b**—
139: 8 if I make my **b** in the depths,
Pr 7:16 I have covered my **b** with coloured
7:17 I have perfumed my **b** with myrrh,
22:27 your very **b** will be snatched
26:14 so a sluggard turns on his **b**.
31:22 She makes coverings for her **b**; she
SS 1:16 And our **b** is verdant.
3: 1 All night long on my **b** I looked for
Isa 19: 5 the river **b** will be parched and dry.
28:20 The **b** is too short to stretch out on,
57: 7 You have made your **b** on a high and
57: 8 Forsaking me, you uncovered your **b**,
Eze 22:10 who dishonour their fathers' **b**;
23:17 to the **b** of love,
32:25 A **b** is made for her among the slain,
Da 2:28 mind as you lay on your **b** are these:
Da 4: 5 As I was lying in my **b**, the images
4:10 I saw while lying in my **b**: I looked,
4:13 visions I saw while lying in my **b**,
7: 1 his mind as he was lying on his **b**.
Mt 8:14 lying in **b** with a fever.
Mk 1:30 Simon's mother-in-law was in **b** with
4:21 put it under a bowl or a **b**? Instead,
7:30 found her child lying on the **b**,
Lk 8:16 it in a jar or puts it under a **b**.
11: 7 and my children are with me in **b**.
17:34 night two people will be in one **b**;
Ac 28: 8 His father was sick in **b**, suffering
Heb 13: 4 and the marriage **b** kept pure, for
Rev 2:22 I will cast her on a **b** of suffering,

Bedad
Ge 36:35 Husham died, Hadad son of **B**, who
1Ch 1:46 Husham died, Hadad son of **B**, who

Bedan
1Ch 7:17 The son of Ulam: **B**. These were the

Bedding (Bed)
2Sa 17:28 brought **b** and bowls and articles of

Bedeiah
Ezr 10:35 Benaiah, **B**, Keluhi,

Bedridden (Bed)
Ac 9:33 who had been **b** for eight years.

Bedroom (Bed, Room)
Ex 8: 3 come up into your palace and your **b**
2Sa 4: 7 he was lying on the bed in his **b**.
13:10 "Bring the food here into my **b**
13:10 it to her brother Amnon in his **b**.
2Ki 6:12 the very words you speak in your **b**."
11: 2 She put him and his nurse in a **b** to
2Ch 22:11 and put him and his nurse in a **b**.
Ecc 10:20 or curse the rich in your **b**, because

Bedrooms (Bed, Room)
Ps 105:30 went up into the **b** of their rulers.

Beds (Bed)
Job 30: 6 forced to live in the dry stream **b**,
33:15 on men as they slumber in their **b**,
Ps 4: 4 when you are on your **b**, search
149: 5 honour and sing for joy on their **b**.
SS 5:13 His cheeks are like **b** of spice
6: 2 to the **b** of spices, to browse in the
Isa 57: 8 a pact with those whose **b** you love,
Hos 7:14 their hearts but wail upon their **b**.
Am 3:12 on the edge of their **b**
6: 4 You lie on **b** inlaid with ivory and
Mic 2: 1 to those who plot evil on their **b**!
Ac 5:15 laid them on **b** and mats so that at

Beeliada
1Ch 14: 7 Elishama, **B** and Eliphelet.

Beelzebub (Baal-Zebub)
Mt 10:25 head of the house has been called **B**,
12:24 by **B**, the prince of demons,
12:27 if I drive out demons by **B**, by whom
Mk 3:22 "He is possessed by **B**! By the prince
Lk 11:15 "By **B**, the prince of demons,
11:18 claim that I drive out demons by **B**.
11:19 Now if I drive out demons by **B**, by

Beer[1]
Nu 21:16 From there they continued on to **B**,
Jdg 9:21 Jotham fled, escaping to **B**, and he

Beer[2]
1Sa 1:15 I have not been drinking wine or **b**;
Pr 20: 1 Wine is a mocker and **b** a brawler;
31: 4 not for rulers to crave **b**,
31: 6 Give **b** to those who are perishing,
Isa 24: 9 the **b** is bitter to its drinkers.
28: 7 stagger from wine and reel from **b**:
28: 7 Priests and prophets stagger from **b**

Isa 28: 7 with wine; they reel from **b**,
29: 9 from wine, stagger, but not from **b**.
56:12 Let us drink our fill of **b**!
Mic 2:11 plenty of wine and **b**,'

Beer Elim
Isa 15: 8 their lamentation as far as **B**.

Beer Lahai Roi
Ge 16:14 That is why the well was called **B**;
24:62 Now Isaac had come from **B**, for he
25:11 son Isaac, who then lived near **B**.

Beera
1Ch 7:37 Hod, Shamma, Shilshah, Ithran and **B**.

Beerah
1Ch 5: 6 **B** his son, whom Tiglath-Pileser king
5: 6 **B** was a leader of the Reubenites.

Beeri
Ge 26:34 he married Judith daughter of **B** the
Hos 1: 1 Hosea son of **B** during the reigns of

Beeroth (Beerothite)
Jos 9:17 Kephirah, **B** and Kiriath Jearim.
18:25 Gibeon, Ramah, **B**,
2Sa 4: 2 **B** is considered part of Benjamin,
4: 3 the people of **B** fled to Gittaim and
Ezr 2:25 of Kiriath Jearim, Kephirah and **B** 743
Ne 7:29 of Kiriath Jearim, Kephirah and **B** 743

Beerothite (Beeroth)
2Sa 4: 2 they were sons of Rimmon the **B** from
4: 5 the sons of Rimmon the **B**, set out
4: 9 the sons of Rimmon the **B**, "As surely
23:37 Zelek the Ammonite, Naharai the **B**,

Beersheba
Chief city of the Negev, in territory of Simeon (Jos 19:1–2). Site of well where Abimelech made an oath with Abraham (Ge 21:31), and Isaac (Ge 26:32–33). Hagar (Ge 21:17–19), Abraham (Ge 21:33), Isaac (Ge 26:23–24) and Jacob (Ge 46:1–4) encountered God here. It became a focus for pilgrimage (Am 5:5), rivalling Bethel and Gilgal. Samuel's sons were judges here (1Sa 8:1–2); Elijah passed through as he fled from Jezebel (1Ki 19:3).

Ge 21:14 way and wandered in the desert of **B**.
21:31 that place was called **B**, because the
21:32 After the treaty had been made at **B**,
21:33 Abraham planted a tamarisk tree in **B**,
22:19 and they set off together for **B**.
22:19 And Abraham stayed in **B**.
26:23 From there he went up to **B**.
26:33 day the name of the town has been **B**.
28:10 Jacob left **B** and set out for Haran.
46: 1 and when he reached **B**, he offered
46: 5 Jacob left **B**, and Israel's sons took
Jos 15:28 Hazar Shual, **B**, Biziothiah,
19: 2 included: **B** (or Sheba), Moladah,
Jdg 20: 1 all the Israelites from Dan to **B**
1Sa 3:20 all Israel from Dan to **B** recognised
8: 2 was Abijah, and they served at **B**.
2Sa 3:10 Israel and Judah from Dan to **B**."
17:11 Let all Israel, from Dan to **B**
24: 2 the tribes of Israel from Dan to **B**
24: 7 went on to **B** in the Negev of Judah.
24:15 of the people from Dan to **B** died.
1Ki 4:25 Judah and Israel, from Dan to **B**,
19: 3 When he came to **B** in Judah, he left
2Ki 12: 1 name was Zibiah; she was from **B**.
23: 8 the high places from Geba to **B**,
1Ch 4:28 They lived in **B**, Moladah, Hazar
21: 2 count the Israelites from **B** to Dan.
2Ch 19: 4 **B** to the hill country of Ephraim
24: 1 name was Zibiah; she was from **B**.
30: 5 throughout Israel from **B** to Dan,
Ne 11:27 in **B** and its settlements,
11:30 way from **B** to the Valley of Hinnom.
Am 5: 5 go to Gilgal, do not journey to **B**.
8:14 'As surely as the god of **B** lives'—

Bees
Dt 1:44 they chased you like a swarm of **b**
Jdg 14: 8 it was a swarm of **b** and some honey,
Ps 118:12 They swarmed around me like **b**, but
Isa 7:18 and for **b** from the land of Assyria.

Befall (Befalls)
Job 5:19 you; in seven no harm will **b** you.
Ps 91:10 no harm will **b** you, no disaster will

Befalls (Befall)
Pr 12:21 No harm **b** the righteous, but the

Before God
Ge 21:23; Ex 18:19; Jos 24:1; Jdg 21:2; 1Sa 30:15; 1Ch 13:8, 10; 16:1; 2Ch 34:27; Job 9:2; 25:4; 26:6; 33:6; Ps 56:13; 68:2, 3, 8; 84:7; Pr 2:17; Ecc 5:2; 8:2, 12; Lk 1:8; 18:14; 24:19; Ac 8:21; 10:4; 24:16; Ro 4:2; 2Co 2:17; 3:4; 7:12; Gal 1:20; 3:11; 2Ti 2:14; 1Pe 2:20; 1Jn 3:21; Rev 8:2, 4; 9:13; 11:16

Before the LORD
Ge 10:9, 10; 13:10; 18:22; 19:27; 24:52; Ex 16:9, 33; 22:11; 27:21; 28:12, 29, 30, 35; 29:23, 24, 26, 42; 30:8, 16; 34:24; 40:23, 25; Lev 1:5, 11; 3:1, 7, 12; 4:4, 6, 7, 15, 17, 18, 24; 6:7, 14, 25; 7:30; 8:26, 27, 29; 9:2, 4, 5, 21; 10:1, 2, 15, 17, 19; 12:7; 14:11, 12, 16, 18, 23, 24, 27, 29, 31; 15:14, 15, 30; 16:7, 10, 12, 13, 18, 30; 19:22; 23:11, 20, 28, 40; 24:3, 4, 6, 8; Nu 3:4; 5:16, 18, 25, 30; 6:16, 20; 7:3; 8:10, 11, 21; 14:37; 15:15, 28; 16:7, 16, 17, 38, 40; 17:7; 18:19; 20:3; 25:4; 26:61; 27:5, 21; 31:50, 54; 32:20, 21, 22, 27, 29, 32; Dt 1:45; 4:10; 6:25; 9:18, 25; 10:8; 12:12, 18; 16:11, 16; 18:13; 26:5,10; 31:11; Jos 4:13; 6:8, 26; 7:23; Jdg 5:5; 11:11; 20:1, 23, 26; 21:8; 1Sa 1:19, 22; 2:11, 18; 3:1; 7:6; 8:21; 10:19, 25; 11:15; 12:7; 15:33; 16:6; 20:8; 21:6; 21:7; 23:18; 26:19; 2Sa 3:28; 5:3; 6:5, 14, 16, 17, 21; 7:18; 21:6, 7, 9; 23:16; 1Ki 2:45; 8:59, 62, 64, 65; 9:25; 19:11; 22:21; 2Ki 16:14; 19:14; 22:19; 1Ch 11:3, 18; 16:33; 17:16; 23:13, 31; 29:20, 22; 2Ch 1:6; 7:4; 14:13; 18:20; 20:13, 18; 27:6; 28:13; 31:20; 33:23; Job 1:6; 2:1; Ps 37:7; 95:6; 96:13; 98:6, 9; 109:14, 15; 116:9; Pr 15:11; Isa 23:18; 37:14; Jer 4:26; 36:7, 9; Eze 41:22; 43:24; 45:4; 46:9; Joel 1:9; 2:17; Mic 6:6; Zec 2:13; Mal 3:14;

Before the Lord
Jdg 21:5; Ps 97:5; Lk 1:17, 76; 1Th 5:27; Jas 4:10; Rev 11:4

Befuddled
Isa 28: 7 **b** with wine; they reel from beer,

Beg (Beggar, Beggars, Begged, Begging)
Jdg 13: 8 "O LORD, I **b** you, let the man of God
1Sa 15:25 Now I **b** you, forgive my sin and come
2Sa 24:10 Now, O LORD, I **b** you, take away the
2Ki 8: 3 king to **b** for her house and land.
8: 5 **b** the king for her house and land.
1Ch 21: 8 Now, I **b** you, take away the guilt of
Est 4: 8 the king's presence to **b** for mercy
7: 7 to **b** Queen Esther for his life.
Job 19:16 though I **b** him with my own mouth.
Lam 4: 4 its mouth; the children **b** for bread,
Am 7: 5 "Sovereign LORD, I **b** you, stop!
Lk 8:28 High God? I **b** you, don't torture me!"
9:38 "Teacher, I **b** you to look at my son,
16: 3 to dig, and I'm ashamed to **b**—
16:27 "He answered, 'Then I **b** you, father,
Jn 9: 8 the same man who used to sit and **b**?"
Ac 3: 2 where he was put every day to **b** from
26: 3 I **b** you to listen to me patiently.
2Co 10: 2 I **b** you that when I come I may not

Beggar (Beg)
Lk 16:20 At his gate was laid a **b** named
16:22 "The time came when the **b** died and
Ac 3:11 While the **b** held on to Peter and

Beggars (Beg)
Ps 109:10 May his children be wandering **b**; may

Begged (Beg)
2Ki 1:13 "Man of God," he **b**, "please have
Est 8: 3 She **b** him to put an end to the evil
Hos 12: 4 he wept and **b** for his favour.
Mt 8:31 The demons **b** Jesus, "If you drive us
14:36 **b** him to let the sick just touch the
18:26 'Be patient with me,' he **b**,
18:29 fell to his knees and **b** him,
18:32 debt of yours because you **b** me to.
Mk 1:40 A man with leprosy came to him and **b**
5:10 he **b** Jesus again and again not to
5:12 The demons **b** Jesus, "Send us among
5:18 demon-possessed **b** to go with him.
6:56 They **b** him to let them touch even
7:26 She **b** Jesus to drive the demon out
7:32 **b** him to place his hand on the man.
8:22 blind man and **b** Jesus to touch him.
Lk 5:12 his face to the ground and **b** him,
8:31 they **b** him repeatedly not to order
8:32 The demons **b** Jesus to let them go
8:38 had gone out **b** to go with him,
9:40 I **b** your disciples to drive it out,
Jn 4:47 he went to him and **b** him to come and
Heb 12:19 those who heard it **b**

Begging (Beg)
Job 41: 3 Will he keep **b** you for mercy?
Ps 37:25 forsaken or their children **b** bread.
Mk 10:46 was sitting by the roadside **b**.
Lk 18:35 man was sitting by the roadside **b**.
Jn 9: 8 who had formerly seen him **b** asked,
Ac 3:10 the same man who used to sit **b**
16: 9 man of Macedonia standing and **b** him,
19:31 sent him a message **b** him not to

Beginning (Beginnings)
Ge 1: 1 In the **b** God created the heavens and
44:12 to search, **b** with the oldest
Lev 23:39 "'So **b** with the fifteenth day of the
Dt 11:12 from the **b** of the year to its end.
31:24 the words of this law from **b** to end,
31:30 the words of this song from **b** to end
Jdg 7:19 camp at the **b** of the middle watch,
Ru 1:22 as the barley harvest was **b**.
1Sa 3:12 against his family—from **b** to end.
2Sa 7:10 them any more, as they did at the **b**
21: 9 just as the barley harvest was **b**.
21:10 From the **b** of the harvest till the
1Ch 17: 9 them any more, as they did at the **b**
29:29 from **b** to end, they are written in
2Ch 9:29 from **b** to end, are they not written
12:15 from **b** to end, are they not written
16:11 The events of Asa's reign, from **b** to
20:34 from **b** to end, are written in the
25:26 from **b** to end, are they not written
26:22 from **b** to end, are recorded by the
28:26 from **b** to end, are written in the
35:27 all the events, from **b** to end, are
Ezr 4: 6 At the **b** of the reign of Xerxes,
Ps 102:25 In the **b** you laid the foundations of
111:10 The fear of the LORD is the **b** of
Pr 1: 7 The fear of the LORD is the **b** of
8:23 from the **b**, before the world began.
9:10 "The fear of the LORD is the **b** of
20:21 quickly gained at the **b** will not
Ecc 3:11 what God has done from **b** to end.
7: 8 end of a matter is better than its **b**
10:13 At the **b** his words are folly; at the
Isa 1:26 old, your counsellors as at the **b**.
40:21 Has it not been told you from the **b**?
41: 4 forth the generations from the **b**? I,
41:26 Who told of this from the **b**, so that
46:10 I make known the end from the **b**,
Jer 17:12 A glorious throne, exalted from the **b**
25:29 See, I am **b** to bring disaster on the
Eze 25: 9 **b** at its frontier towns—
40: 1 at the **b** of the year, on the tenth
42:12 There was a doorway at the **b** of the
48:30 of the city: **B** on the north side,
Da 12: 1 from the **b** of nations until then.
Mic 1:13 You were the **b** of sin to the
Mt 14:30 he was afraid and, **b** to sink, cried
19: 4 "that at the **b** the Creator 'made
19: 8 But it was not this way from the **b**.
20: 8 **b** with the last ones hired and going

Mt 24: 8 All these are the **b** of birth-pains.
24:21 unequalled from the **b** of the world
Mk 1: 1 The **b** of the gospel about Jesus
10: 6 "But at the **b** of creation God 'made
13: 8 These are the **b** of birth-pains.
13:19 of distress unequalled from the **b**,
Lk 1: 3 investigated everything from the **b**,
11:50 been shed since the **b** of the world,
24:27 **b** with Moses and all the Prophets,
24:47 name to all nations, **b** at Jerusalem.
Jn 1: 1 In the **b** was the Word, and the Word
1: 2 He was with God in the **b**.
6:64 For Jesus had known from the **b**
8:44 He was a murderer from the **b**, not
15:27 you have been with me from the **b**.
Ac 1:22 **b** from John's baptism to the time
10:37 **b** in Galilee after the baptism that
11:15 them as he had come on us at the **b**.
26: 4 from the **b** of my life in my own
2Co 3: 1 Are we **b** to commend ourselves again?
8: 6 since he had earlier made a **b**, to
Gal 3: 3 After **b** with the Spirit,
Col 1:18 he is the **b** and the firstborn
2Th 2:13 because from the **b** God chose you to
2Ti 1: 9 Christ Jesus before the **b** of time,
Tit 1: 2 lie, promised before the **b** of time,
Heb 1:10 He also says, "In the **b**, O Lord, you
7: 3 without genealogy, without **b** of days
2Pe 2:20 at the end than they were at the **b**.
3: 4 as it has since the **b** of creation."
1Jn 1: 1 That which was from the **b**, which we
2: 7 one, which you have had since the **b**.
2:13 have known him who is from the **b**.
2:14 have known him who is from the **b**.
2:24 heard from the **b** remains in you.
3: 8 devil has been sinning from the **b**.
3:11 the message you heard from the **b**:
2Jn : 5 but one we have had from the **b**.
: 6 As you have heard from the **b**, his
Rev 21: 6 the Omega, the **B** and the End.
22:13 and the Last, the **B** and the End.

Beginnings (Beginning)
Job 8: 7 Your **b** will seem humble, so

Begotten
Isa 45:10 'What have you **b**?' or to his mother,

Begrudge
Dt 28:56 foot—will **b** the husband she loves

Behalf
Ge 23: 8 with Ephron son of Zohar on my **b**
25:21 Isaac prayed to the LORD on **b** of his
Lev 1: 4 on his **b** to make atonement for him.
14:31 LORD on **b** of the one to be cleansed."
19: 5 that it will be accepted on your **b**.
22:19 that it may be accepted on your **b**.
22:20 it will not be accepted on your **b**.
22:25 They will not be accepted on your **b**,
22:29 that it will be accepted on your **b**.
23:11 so it will be accepted on your **b**;
24: 8 on **b** of the Israelites,
Nu 3:38 sanctuary on **b** of the Israelites.
5:15 an ephah of barley flour on her **b**.
8:19 of Meeting on **b** of the Israelites
1Sa 7: 9 cried out to the LORD on Israel's **b**
14: 6 Perhaps the LORD will act on our **b**.
2Sa 3:12 Abner sent messengers on his **b** to
14: 8 I will issue an order on your **b**."
21:14 God answered prayer on **b** of the land.
24:25 Then the LORD answered prayer on **b**
2Ki 4:13 Can we speak on your **b** to the king
Est 8: 8 on **b** of the Jews as seems best
Job 6:22 'Give something on my **b**, pay a
8: 6 now he will rouse himself on your **b**
13: 7 Will you speak wickedly on God's **b**?
16:21 on **b** of a man he pleads with God as
36: 2 there is more to be said on God's **b**.
Ps 45: 4 forth victoriously on **b** of truth,
66: 5 how awesome his works on man's **b**!
Isa 8:19 consult the dead on **b** of the living?
58:10 spend yourselves on **b** of the hungry
64: 4 acts on **b** of those who wait for him.
65: 8 so will I do on **b** of my servants;
Jer 18:20 spoke on their **b** to turn your wrath
Eze 22:30 stand before me in the gap on **b** of
Jn 8:14 "Even if I testify on my own **b**, my
16:26 I will ask the Father on your **b**.
Ro 15: 8 of the Jews on **b** of God's truth,
2Co 1:11 Then many will give thanks on our **b**
5:20 We implore you on Christ's **b**:
Php 1:29 granted to you on **b** of Christ
Col 1: 7 minister of Christ on our **b**,
Heb 6:20 before us, has entered on our **b**.
Rev 13:12 of the first beast on his **b**,
13:14 power to do on **b** of the first beast,
19:20 the miraculous signs on his **b**.

Behave (Behaved, Behaves, Behaviour)
1Ki 1: 6 "Why do you **b** as you do?"
Ro 13:13 Let us **b** decently, as in the daytime,

Behaved (Behave)
2Sa 15: 6 Absalom **b** in this way towards all
1Ki 21:26 He **b** in the vilest manner by going
Ps 74: 5 They **b** like men wielding axes to cut
Jer 2:23 Baals'? See how you **b** in the valley;
16:12 you have **b** more wickedly than your

Behaves (Behave)
Pr 21:24 name; he **b** with overweening pride.

Behaviour (Behave)
Est 3: 4 Mordecai's **b** would be tolerated,
Pr 8:13 evil **b** and perverse speech.
Col 1:21 your minds because of your evil **b**.
1Pe 3: 1 words by the **b** of their wives,
3:16 speak maliciously against your good **b**

Beheaded
Mt 14:10 had John **b** in the prison.
Mk 6:16 "John, the man I **b**, has been raised
6:27 The man went, **b** John in the prison,
Lk 9: 9 Herod said, "I **b** John. Who, then, is
Rev 20: 4 the souls of those who had been **b**

Beheld (Behold)
Ps 63: 2 and **b** your power and your glory.

Behemoth
Job 40:15 "Look at the **b**, which I made along

Behold (Beheld)
Nu 24:17 I **b** him, but not near.
Isa 65:17 "**B**, I will create new heavens and a
Rev 1:18 and **b** I am alive for ever and ever!
16:15 "**B**, I come like a thief! Blessed is
22: 7 "**B**, I am coming soon! Blessed is he
22:12 "**B**, I am coming soon! My reward is

Beka (Bekas)
Ge 24:22 out a gold nose ring weighing a **b**
Ex 38:26 one **b** per person, that is, half a

Bekas (Beka)
1Ki 10:16 **b** of gold went into each shield.
2Ch 9:15 six hundred **b** of hammered gold went
9:16 hundred **b** of gold in each shield.

Beker (Bekerite)
Ge 46:21 The sons of Benjamin: Bela, **B**,
Nu 26:35 through **B**, the Bekerite clan;
1Ch 7: 6 Three sons of Benjamin: Bela, **B** and
7: 8 The sons of **B**: Zemirah, Joash,
7: 8 All these were the sons of **B**.

Bekerite (Beker)
Nu 26:35 the **B** clan; through Tahan, the

Bel
Isa 46: 1 **B** bows down, Nebo stoops low; their
Jer 50: 2 'Babylon will be captured; **B** will be
51:44 I will punish **B** in Babylon and make

Bela (Belaite)
Ge 14: 2 and the king of **B** (that is, Zoar).
14: 8 Zeboiim and the king of **B** (that is,
36:32 **B** son of Beor became king of Edom.
36:33 **B** died, Jobab son of Zerah from
46:21 The sons of Benjamin: **B**, Beker,
Nu 26:38 through **B**, the Belaite clan;
26:40 The descendants of **B** through Ard and
1Ch 1:43 king reigned: **B** son of Beor,
1:44 when **B** died, Jobab son of Zerah
5: 8 **B** son of Azaz, the son of Shema, the
7: 6 Three sons of Benjamin: **B**, Beker and
7: 7 The sons of **B**: Ezbon, Uzzi, Uzziel,
8: 1 Benjamin was the father of **B** his
8: 3 The sons of **B** were: Addar, Gera,

Belaite (Bela)
Nu 26:38 the **B** clan; through Ashbel, the

Belial
2Co 6:15 is there between Christ and **B**?

Belief (Believe)
2Th 2:13 and through **b** in the truth.

Beliefs (Believe)
Job 11: 4 You say to God, 'My **b** are flawless

Believe (Belief, Beliefs, Believed, Believer, Believers, Believes, Believing, Repent and believe)
Ge 45:26 Jacob was stunned; he did not **b** them.
Ex 4: 1 "What if they do not **b** me or listen
4: 5 "is so that they may **b** that the LORD,
4: 8 the LORD said, "If they do not **b** you
4: 8 sign, they may **b** the second.
4: 9 if they do not **b** these two signs or
Nu 14:11 How long will they refuse to **b** in me,
1Ki 10: 7 I did not **b** these things until I
2Ch 9: 6 I did not **b** what they said until I
32:15 Do not **b** him, for no god of any
Job 9:16 do not **b** he would give me a hearing.
Ps 78:22 for they did not **b** in God or trust
78:32 of his wonders, they did not **b**.
106:24 land; they did not **b** his promise.
119:66 judgment, for I **b** in your commands.
Pr 26:25 do not **b** him, for seven abominations
Isa 43:10 so that you may know and **b** me
Jer 29:31 him, and has led you to **b** a lie,
40:14 son of Ahikam did not **b** them.
Lam 4:12 The kings of the earth did not **b**,
Hab 1: 5 would not **b**, even if you were told.
Mt 9:28 "Do you **b** that I am able to do this?"
18: 6 little ones who **b** in me to sin,
21:22 If you **b**, you will receive whatever
21:25 ask, 'Then why didn't you **b** him?'
21:32 and you did not **b** him, but the tax
24:23 or, 'There he is!' do not **b** it.
24:26 in the inner rooms,' do not **b** it.
27:42 the cross, and we will **b** in him.
Mk 5:36 ruler, "Don't be afraid; just **b**.
9:24 I do **b**; help me overcome my
9:42 little ones who **b** in me to sin,
11:24 **b** that you have received it
11:31 ask, 'Then why didn't you **b** him?'
13:21 'Look, there he is!' do not **b** it.
15:32 the cross, that we may see and **b**.
16:11 she had seen him, they did not **b** it.
16:13 but they did not **b** them either.
16:14 their stubborn refusal to **b** those
16:16 does not **b** will be condemned.
16:17 signs will accompany those who **b**:
Lk 1:20 because you did not **b** my words,
8:12 so that they may not **b** and be saved.
8:13 They **b** for a while, but in the time

Lk 8:50 just **b**, and she will be healed."
20: 5 he will ask, 'Why didn't you **b** him?'
22:67 "If I tell you, you will not **b**
24:11 they did not **b** the women, because
24:25 **b** all that the prophets have spoken!
24:41 while they still did not **b** it
Jn 1: 7 so that through him all men might **b**.
1:50 Jesus said, "You **b** because I told
3:12 of earthly things and you do not **b**;
3:12 you **b** if I speak of heavenly things?
3:18 but whoever does not **b** stands
4:21 Jesus declared, "**B** me, woman, a time
4:42 "We no longer **b** just because of what
4:48 Jesus told him, "you will never **b**.
5:38 for you do not **b** the one he sent.
5:44 How can you **b** if you accept praise
5:46 If you believed Moses, you would **b**
5:47 since you do not **b** what he wrote,
5:47 how are you going to **b** what I say?"
6:29 this: to **b** in the one he has sent."
6:30 that we may see it and **b** you?
6:36 have seen me and still you do not **b**.
6:64 there are some of you who do not **b**.
6:64 did not **b** and who would betray him.
6:69 We **b** and know that you are the Holy
7: 5 For even his own brothers did not **b**
8:24 **b** that I am the one I claim to be,
8:45 I tell the truth, you do not **b** me!
8:46 the truth, why don't you **b** me?
9:18 The Jews still did not **b** that he had
9:35 "Do you **b** in the Son of Man?
9:36 "Tell me so that I may **b** in him."
9:38 the man said, "Lord, I **b**," and he
10:25 "I did tell you, but you do not **b**.
10:26 you do not **b** because you are not my
10:37 Do not **b** me unless I do what my
10:38 if I do it, even though you do not **b**
10:38 even though you do not **b** me, **b** the
11:15 I was not there, so that you may **b**.
11:26 Do you **b** this?"
11:27 "I **b** that you are the Christ,
11:42 that they may **b** that you sent me."
11:48 everyone will **b** in him, and then the
12:37 they still would not **b** in him.
12:39 For this reason they could not **b**,
12:44 he does not **b** in me only, but in the
13:19 does happen you will **b** that I am He.
14:10 Don't you **b** that I am in the Father,
14:11 **B** me when I say that I am in the
14:11 or at least **b** on the evidence of the
14:29 that when it does happen you will **b**.
16: 9 to sin, because men do not **b** in me;
16:30 makes us **b** that you came from God."
16:31 "You **b** at last!" Jesus answered.
17:20 will **b** in me through their message,
17:21 world may **b** that you have sent me.
19:35 he testifies so that you also may **b**.
20:25 into his side, I will not **b** it."
20:27 Stop doubting and **b**."
20:31 these are written that you may **b**
Ac 13:41 never **b**, even if someone told you.'"
14: 2 the Jews who refused to **b** stirred up
15: 7 the message of the gospel and **b**.
15:11 No! We **b** it is through the grace of
16:31 They replied, "**B** in the Lord Jesus,
16:34 **b** in God—he and his whole family.
19: 4 He told the people to **b** in the one
19: 9 they refused to **b** and publicly
22:19 and beat those who **b** in you.
24:14 I **b** everything that agrees with the
26:27 King Agrippa, do you **b** the prophets?
28:24 he said, but others would not **b**.
Ro 3:22 faith in Jesus Christ to all who **b**.
4:11 he is the father of all who **b** but
4:24 for us who **b** in him who raised Jesus
6: 8 we **b** that we will also live with him
10: 9 "Jesus is Lord," and **b** in your heart
10:10 For it is with your heart that you **b**
10:14 And how can they **b** in the one of
Ro 14:22 whatever you **b** about these things
16:26 all nations might **b** and obey him—
1Co 1:21 was preached to save those who **b**.
3: 5 through whom you came to **b**—as the
11:18 you, and to some extent I **b** it.
2Co 4:13 faith we also **b** and therefore speak,
Gal 3: 5 or because you **b** what you heard?
Gal 3: 7 Understand, then, that those who **b**
3:22 might be given to those who **b**.
Eph 1:19 great power for us who **b**.
Php 1:29 **b** on him, but also to suffer for him,
1Th 2:13 God, which is at work in you who **b**.
4:14 We **b** that Jesus died and rose again
4:14 rose again and so we **b** that God will
2Th 2:11 so that they will **b** the lie
1Ti 1:16 **b** on him and receive eternal life.
4: 3 those who **b** and who know the truth.
4:10 men, and especially of those who **b**.
Tit 1: 6 a man whose children **b** and are not
1:15 those who are corrupted and do not **b**
Heb 10:39 but of those who **b** and are saved.
11: 6 comes to him must **b** that he exists
Jas 1: 6 he must **b** and not doubt,
2:19 You **b** that there is one God. Good!
2:19 Even the demons **b** that—and shudder.
1Pe 1: 8 you **b** in him and are filled with an
1:21 Through him you **b** in God, who raised
2: 7 Now to you who **b**, this stone is
2: 7 But to those who do not **b**,
3: 1 if any of them do not **b** the word,
1Jn 3:23 to **b** in the name of his Son,
4: 1 Dear friends, do not **b** every spirit,
5:10 Anyone who does not **b** God has made
5:13 I write these things to you who **b**
Jude : 5 later destroyed those who did not **b**.

Believed (Believe)

Ge 15: 6 Abram **b** the LORD, and he credited it
Ex 4:31 they **b**. And when they heard that the
Job 29:24 I smiled at them, they scarcely **b** it;
Ps 106:12 they **b** his promises and sang his
116:10 I **b**; therefore I said, "I am greatly
Isa 53: 1 Who has **b** our message and to whom
Jnh 3: 5 The Ninevites **b** God. They declared a
Mt 8:13 will be done just as you **b** it would.
Lk 1:45 Blessed is she who has **b** that what
Jn 1:12 to those who **b** in his name, he gave
2:22 Then they **b** the Scripture and the
2:23 he was doing and **b** in his name.
3:18 has not **b** in the name of God's one
4:39 Samaritans from that town **b** in him
4:53 So he and all his household **b**.
5:46 If you **b** Moses, you would believe me,
7:39 who **b** in him were later to receive.
7:48 rulers or of the Pharisees **b** in him?
8:31 To the Jews who had **b** him, Jesus
10:42 in that place many **b** in Jesus.
11:40 if you **b**, you would see the glory
12:38 "Lord, who has **b** our message and to
12:42 even among the leaders **b** in him.
16:27 and have **b** that I came from God.
17: 8 and they **b** that you sent me.
20: 8 He saw and **b**.
20:29 you have **b**; blessed are those who
20:29 who have not seen and yet have **b**."
Ac 4: 4 many who heard the message **b**, and
5:14 more and more men and women **b** in the
8:12 when they **b** Philip as he preached
8:13 Simon himself **b** and was baptised.
9:42 and many people **b** in the Lord.
11:17 who **b** in the Lord Jesus Christ, who
11:21 people **b** and turned to the Lord.
13:12 he **b**, for he was amazed at the
13:48 were appointed for eternal life **b**.
14: 1 great number of Jews and Gentiles **b**.
17:12 Many of the Jews **b**, as did also a
17:34 men became followers of Paul and **b**.
18: 8 and his entire household **b** in the
18: 8 who heard him **b** and were baptised.
18:27 help to those who by grace had **b**.
19: 2 receive the Holy Spirit when you **b**?"
19:18 Many of those who **b** now came and
21:20 how many thousands of Jews have **b**,
Ro 4: 3 "Abraham **b** God, and it was credited
4:17 in whom he **b**—the God who gives life
Ro 4:18 Against all hope, Abraham in hope **b**
10:14 call on the one they have not **b** in?
10:16 For Isaiah says, "Lord, who has **b**
13:11 is nearer now than when we first **b**.
1Co 15: 2 Otherwise, you have **b** in vain.
15:11 we preach, and this is what you **b**.
2Co 4:13 "I **b**; therefore I have spoken."
Gal 3: 6 Consider Abraham: "He **b** God, and it
Eph 1:13 Having **b**, you were marked in him
1Th 2:10 blameless we were among you who **b**.
2Th 1:10 at among all those who have **b**.
1:10 because you **b** our testimony to you.
2:12 condemned who have not **b** the truth
1Ti 3:16 was **b** on in the world, was taken up
2Ti 1:12 because I know whom I have **b**, and am
Heb 4: 3 Now we who have **b** enter that rest,
Jas 2:23 "Abraham **b** God, and it was credited
1Jn 5:10 because he has not **b** the testimony

Believer (Believe)

1Ki 18: 3 (Obadiah was a devout **b** in the LORD.
Ac 16: 1 whose mother was a Jewess and a **b**,
16:15 "If you consider me a **b** in the Lord,"
1Co 7:12 brother has a wife who is not a **b**
7:13 a woman has a husband who is not a **b**
2Co 6:15 **b** have in common with an unbeliever?
1Ti 5:16 If any woman who is a **b** has widows

Believers (Believe)

Jn 4:41 of his words many more became **b**.
Ac 1:15 Peter stood up among the **b**
2:44 All the **b** were together and had
4:32 All the **b** were one in heart and mind.
5:12 And all the **b** used to meet together
9:41 Then he called the **b** and the widows
10:45 The circumcised **b** who had come with
11: 2 the circumcised **b** criticised
15: 2 along with some other **b**, to go up to
15: 5 some of the **b** who belonged to the
15:23 To the Gentile **b** in Antioch, Syria
21:25 for the Gentile **b**, we have written
1Co 6: 5 enough to judge a dispute between **b**?
14:22 Tongues, then, are a sign, not for **b**
Gal 6:10 those who belong to the family of **b**.
1Th 1: 7 you became a model to all the **b** in
1Ti 4:12 but set an example for the **b** in
6: 2 who benefit from their service are **b**
Jas 2: 1 My brothers, as **b** in our glorious
1Pe 2:17 Love the brotherhood of **b**, fear God

Believes (Believe)

Pr 14:15 A simple man **b** anything, but a
Mk 9:23 is possible for him who **b**."
11:23 but **b** that what he says will happen,
16:16 Whoever **b** and is baptised will be
Jn 3:15 that everyone who **b** in him may have
3:16 that whoever **b** in him shall not
3:18 Whoever **b** in him is not condemned,
3:36 Whoever **b** in the Son has eternal
5:24 whoever hears my word and **b** him who
6:35 who **b** in me will never be thirsty.
6:40 **b** in him shall have eternal life,
6:47 he who **b** has everlasting life.
7:38 Whoever **b** in me, as the Scripture
11:25 He who **b** in me will live, even
11:26 whoever lives and **b** in me will never
12:44 Jesus cried out, "When a man **b** in me,
12:46 so that no-one who **b** in me should
Ac 10:43 everyone who **b** in him receives
13:39 Through him everyone who **b** is
Ro 1:16 for the salvation of everyone who **b**:
10: 4 be righteousness for everyone who **b**.
1Jn 5: 1 Everyone who **b** that Jesus is the
5: 5 who **b** that Jesus is the Son of God.
5:10 Anyone who **b** in the Son of God has

Believing (Believe)

Jn 20:31 by **b** you may have life in his name.
Ac 9:26 not **b** that he really was a disciple.
1Co 7:14 sanctified through her **b** husband.
1Co 7:15 A **b** man or woman is not bound in
9: 5 the right to take a **b** wife along
Gal 3: 2 the law, or by **b** what you heard?
1Ti 6: 2 Those who have **b** masters are not to

Bellow (Bellows)

Job 6: 5 or an ox **b** when it has fodder?

Bellows (Bellow)

Jer 6:29 The **b** blow fiercely to burn away the

Bells

Ex 28:33 the robe, with gold **b** between them.
28:34 The gold **b** and the pomegranates are
28:35 The sound of the **b** will be heard
39:25 they made **b** of pure gold and
39:26 The **b** and pomegranates alternated
Zec 14:20 be inscribed on the **b** of the horses,

Belly

Ge 3:14 You will crawl on your **b** and you
Lev 11:42 whether it moves on its **b** or walks
Jdg 3:21 and plunged it into the king's **b**.
2Sa 20:10 and Joab plunged it into his **b**, and
Job 15: 2 fill his **b** with the hot east wind?
20:23 he has filled his **b**, God will vent
40:16 what power in the muscles of his **b**!
Da 2:32 silver, its **b** and thighs of bronze,
Mt 12:40 nights in the **b** of a huge fish,

Belong (Belonged, Belonging, Belongings, Belongs)

Ge 32:17 'To whom do you **b**, and where are you
32:18 'They **b** to your servant Jacob.
40: 8 "Do not interpretations **b** to God?
45:11 who **b** to you will become destitute.'
Ex 13:12 of your livestock **b** to the LORD.
21: 4 the woman and her children shall **b**
29:27 ram that **b** to Aaron and his sons:
29:29 "Aaron's sacred garments will **b** to
Lev 5:13 The rest of the offering will **b** to
7: 7 They **b** to the priest who makes
25:30 shall **b** permanently to the buyer
25:55 for the Israelites **b** to me as
Nu 5: 9 bring to a priest will **b** to him.
5:10 the priest will **b** to the priest.'"
6:20 they are holy and **b** to the priest,
Dt 10:14 To the LORD your God **b** the heavens,
20:15 and do not **b** to the nations nearby.
29:29 The secret things **b** to the LORD our
29:29 but the things revealed **b** to us and
33: 8 and Urim **b** to the man you favoured.
Jos 2:13 and all who **b** to them, and that you
6:22 bring her out and all who **b** to her,
1Sa 25:22 alive one male of all who **b** to him!"
30:13 David asked him, "To whom do you **b**,
1Ki 8:41 "As for the foreigner who does not **b**
2Ch 6:32 "As for the foreigner who does not **b**
Ne 5: 5 and our vineyards **b** to others."
Job 12:13 "To God **b** wisdom and power; counsel
12:16 To him **b** strength and victory;
25: 2 "Dominion and awe **b** to God; he
Ps 47: 9 for the kings of the earth **b** to God;
95: 4 and the mountain peaks **b** to him.
104:18 high mountains **b** to the wild goats;
115:16 The highest heavens **b** to the LORD,
Pr 16: 1 To man **b** the plans of the heart,
SS 7:10 I **b** to my lover, and his desire is
Isa 44: 5 One will say, 'I **b** to the LORD';
Jer 5:10 these people do not **b** to the LORD.
Eze 13: 9 They will not **b** to the council of my
18: 4 well as the son—both alike **b** to me.
44:29 devoted to the LORD will **b** to them.
44:30 special gifts will **b** to the priests.
45: 5 cubits wide will **b** to the Levites,
45: 6 **b** to the whole house of Israel.
46:16 it will also **b** to his descendants;
48:21 city property will **b** to the prince.
48:21 portions will **b** to the prince,
Zep 2: 7 will **b** to the remnant of the house
Zec 9: 7 Those who are left will **b** to our God
Mt 20:23 These places **b** to those for whom
Mk 9:41 in my name because you **b** to Christ
10:40 These places **b** to those for whom
13:14 standing where it does not **b**
Jn 8:44 You **b** to your father, the devil, and
8:47 hear is that you do not **b** to God."
14:24 they **b** to the Father who sent me.
15:19 As it is, you do not **b** to the world,
Ac 5: 4 Didn't it **b** to you before it was
Ro 1: 6 who are called to **b** to Jesus Christ.
7: 4 that you might **b** to another, to him
8: 9 of Christ, he does not **b** to Christ.
14: 8 we live or die, we **b** to the Lord.
16:10 **b** to the household of Aristobulus.
1Co 7: 4 The wife's body does not **b** to her
7: 4 husband's body does not **b** to him
7:39 wishes, but he must **b** to the LORD.
9:19 Though I am free and **b** to no man,
12:15 Because I am not a hand, I do not **b**
12:16 Because I am not an eye, I do not **b**
15:23 when he comes, those who **b** to him.
2Co 10: 7 we **b** to Christ just as much as he.
Gal 3:29 If you **b** to Christ, then you are
5:24 Those who **b** to Christ Jesus have
6:10 who **b** to the family of believers.
Php 4:22 those who **b** to Caesar's household.
1Th 5: 5 **b** to the night or to the darkness.
5: 8 since we **b** to the day, let us be
Jas 2: 7 the noble name of him to whom you **b**?
1Jn 2:19 us, but they did not really **b** to us.
3:19 This then is how we know that we **b**
Rev 19: 1 and glory and power **b** to our God,

Belonged (Belong)

Ge 30:40 animals that **b** to Laban.
31: 1 wealth from what **b** to our father."
Nu 3:21 To Gershon **b** the clans of the
3:27 To Kohath **b** the clans of the
3:33 To Merari **b** the clans of the
27: 1 **b** to the clans of Manasseh
Dt 11: 6 every living thing that **b** to them.
30: 5 to the land that **b** to your fathers,
Jos 6:23 and brothers and all who **b** to her.
6:25 with her family and all who **b** to her,
14:14 Hebron has **b** to Caleb son of
17: 6 The land of Gilead **b** to the rest
17: 8 of Manasseh, **b** to the Ephraimites.)
17:10 On the south the land **b** to Ephraim,
Jdg 6:11 Ophrah that **b** to Joash the Abiezrite,
Ru 4: 3 that **b** to our brother Elimelech.
1Sa 27: 6 **b** to the kings of Judah ever since.
2Sa 8: 7 gold shields that **b** to the officers
8: 8 towns that **b** to Hadadezer,
9: 7 that **b** to your grandfather Saul,
9: 9 that **b** to Saul and his family.
12: 4 the ewe lamb that **b** to the poor man
16: 4 "All that **b** to Mephibosheth is now
1Ki 6:22 altar that **b** to the inner sanctuary.
2Ki 8: 6 "Give back everything that **b** to her,
9:21 that had **b** to Naboth the Jezreelite.
9:25 that **b** to Naboth the Jezreelite.
11:10 shields that had **b** to King David and
12:16 of the LORD; it **b** to the priests.
14:28 Hamath, which had **b** to Yaudi,
1Ch 5: 2 rights of the firstborn **b** to Joseph)
18: 8 towns that **b** to Hadadezer,
2Ch 23: 9 shields that had **b** to King David
26:23 for burial that **b** to the kings,
Eze 23:41 the incense and oil that **b** to me.
46:19 which **b** to the priests, and showed
Lk 1: 5 who **b** to the priestly division of
2: 4 he **b** to the house and line of David.
5:30 the teachers of the law who **b** to
Jn 15:19 If you **b** to the world, it would love
Ac 9: 2 found any there who **b** to the Way
12: 1 arrested some who **b** to the church,
15: 5 the believers who **b** to the party
27: 1 who **b** to the Imperial Regiment.
28: 7 an estate near by that **b** to Publius
Gal 2:12 who **b** to the circumcision group.
Col 2:20 as though you still **b** to it,
Heb 7:13 He of whom these things are said **b**
1Jn 2:19 For if they had **b** to us, they would
1Jn 2:19 showed that none of them **b** to us.
3:12 like Cain, who **b** to the evil one

Belonging (Belong)

Ge 14:23 that I will accept nothing **b** to you,
50: 8 those **b** to his father's household.
Ex 9: 4 no animal **b** to the Israelites
9: 6 one animal **b** to the Israelites died.
Lev 7:20 fellowship offering **b** to the LORD,
7:21 fellowship offering **b** to the LORD,
25:34 the pasture-land **b** to their towns
Nu 1:50 furnishings and everything **b** to it.
16:26 Do not touch anything **b** to them,
17: 5 The staff **b** to the man I choose will
31:42 The half **b** to the Israelites, which
Dt 2:19 of any land **b** to the Ammonites.
Jos 17: 9 There were towns **b** to Ephraim lying
Ru 2: 3 working in a field **b** to Boaz,
1Sa 6:18 towns **b** to the five rulers—
9: 3 Now the donkeys **b** to Saul's father
25:34 not one male **b** to Nabal would have
30:14 **b** to Judah and the Negev of Caleb.
1Ki 14:11 Dogs will eat those **b** to Jeroboam
14:13 He is the only one **b** to Jeroboam who
16: 4 Dogs will eat those **b** to Baasha who
21: 1 vineyard **b** to Naboth the Jezreelite.
21:24 "Dogs will eat those **b** to Ahab who
1Ch 7: 5 **b** to all the clans of Issachar,
9:18 **b** to the camp of the Levites.
22:19 the sacred articles **b** to God into
23: 7 **B** to the Gershonites: Ladan and
26:21 families **b** to Ladan the Gershonite,
28: 1 **b** to the king and his sons,
2Ch 34:33 the territory **b** to the Israelites,
Ezr 1: 7 **b** to the temple of the LORD,
Eze 37:16 '**B** to Judah and the Israelites
37:16 'Ephraim's stick, **b** to Joseph and
48:22 The area **b** to the prince will lie
Lk 5: 3 the one **b** to Simon, and asked him to
1Pe 2: 9 a holy nation, a people **b** to God,
Rev 13: 8 the book of life **b** to the Lamb

Belongings (Belong)

Ge 45:20 Never mind about your **b**, because the
Jdg 14:19 stripped them of their **b** and gave
Jer 10:17 Gather up your **b** to leave the land,
46:19 Pack your **b** for exile, you who live
Eze 12: 3 "Therefore, son of man, pack your **b**
12: 4 bring out your **b** packed for exile.
12: 5 wall and take your **b** out through it.
12: 7 I took my **b** out at dusk, carrying

Belongs (Belong)

Ge 14:24 the share that **b** to the men who went
19:12 anyone else in the city who **b** to you?
23: 9 cave of Machpelah, which **b** to him
31:16 our father **b** to us and our children.
31:37 what have you found that **b** to your
47:18 is gone and our livestock **b** to you,
47:26 a fifth of the produce **b** to Pharaoh.
49:10 until he comes to whom it **b** and the
Ex 13: 2 **b** to me, whether man or animal."
20:17 anything that **b** to your neighbour."
34:19 "The first offspring of every womb **b**
40: 4 Bring in the table and set out what **b**
Lev 2: 3 The rest of the grain offering **b** to
2:10 The rest of the grain offering **b** to
7: 9 **b** to the priest who offers it,
7:10 **b** equally to all the sons of Aaron.
7:14 it **b** to the priest who sprinkles
7:31 the breast **b** to Aaron and his sons.
14:13 the guilt offering **b** to the priest
24: 9 It **b** to Aaron and his sons,
27:26 since the firstborn already **b** to the
27:30 **b** to the LORD; it is holy to the
Nu 5: 8 the restitution **b** to the LORD and
16: 5 show who **b** to him and who is holy,
16:30 with everything that **b** to them, and
18: 9 that part **b** to you and your sons.
Dt 1:17 of any man, for judgment **b** to God.
5:21 anything that **b** to your neighbour."
21:17 The right of the firstborn **b** to him.
Jos 7:15 fire, along with all that **b** to him.
1Sa 15: 3 destroy everything that **b** to them.
1Ki 22: 3 "Don't you know that Ramoth Gilead **b**
1Ch 29:16 your hand, and all of it **b** to you.
Job 41:11 Everything under heaven **b** to me.
Ps 22:28 for dominion **b** to the LORD and he
89:18 Indeed, our shield **b** to the LORD,
111:10 To him **b** eternal praise.
Jer 46:10 that day **b** to the LORD, the LORD
Eze 18: 4 For every living soul **b** to me, the

Eze 21:27 he comes to whom it rightfully **b**;
46:17 **b** to his sons only; it is theirs.
48:22 of the area that **b** to the prince.
Mt 19:14 of heaven **b** to such as these."
25:25 See, here is what **b** to you.'
Mk 10:14 kingdom of God **b** to such as these.
Lk 6:30 **b** to you, do not demand it back.
18:16 kingdom of God **b** to such as these.
Jn 3:29 The bride **b** to the bridegroom.
3:31 is from the earth **b** to the earth,
8:35 but a son **b** to it for ever.
8:47 He who **b** to God hears what God says.
16:15 All that **b** to the Father is mine.
Ac 1:25 which Judas left to go where he **b**."
Ro 12: 5 and each member **b** to all the others.
2Co 10: 7 If anyone is confident that he **b** to
Col 3: 5 Put to death, therefore, whatever **b**
Rev 7:10 "Salvation **b** to our God, who sits on
17:11 He **b** to the seven and is going to

Beloved (Love)
Dt 33:12 "Let the **b** of the LORD rest secure
SS 5: 9 How is your **b** better than others,
5: 9 How is your **b** better than others,
Jer 11:15 "What is my **b** doing in my temple

Belshazzar (Belshazzar's)
King of Babylon at time of its overthrow by Darius. Downfall announced by Daniel, who interpreted writing on the wall (Da 5).

Da 5: 1 King **B** gave a great banquet for a
5: 2 While **B** was drinking his wine, he
5: 9 King **B** became even more terrified
5:22 "But you his son, O **B**, have not
5:30 **B**, king of the Babylonians, was slain
7: 1 first year of **B** king of Babylon

Belshazzar's (Belshazzar)
Da 5:29 at **B** command, Daniel was clothed in
8: 1 In the third year of King **B** reign,

Belt (Belts)
Ex 12:11 with your cloak tucked into your **b**,
1Sa 18: 4 even his sword, his bow and his **b**.
2Sa 18:11 of silver and a warrior's **b**."
20: 8 was a **b** with a dagger in its sheath.
1Ki 2: 5 and with that blood stained the **b**
18:46 tucking his cloak into his **b**, he ran
2Ki 1: 8 with a leather **b** round his waist.
4:29 "Tuck your cloak into your **b**, take
9: 1 "Tuck your cloak into your **b**, take
Ps 109:19 like a **b** tied for ever round him.
Isa 5:27 not a **b** is loosened at the waist,
11: 5 Righteousness will be his **b** and
Jer 13: 1 "Go and buy a linen **b** and put it
13: 2 I bought a **b**, as the LORD directed,
13: 4 "Take the **b** you bought and are
13: 6 get the **b** I told you to hide there."
13: 7 I went to Perath and dug up the **b**
13:10 be like this **b**—completely useless!
13:11 as a **b** is bound round a man's waist,
Da 10: 5 **b** of the finest gold round his waist.
Mt 3: 4 he had a leather **b** round his waist.
Mk 1: 6 with a leather **b** round his waist,
Ac 21:11 Coming over to us, he took Paul's **b**,
21:11 will bind the owner of this **b**
Eph 6:14 Stand firm then, with the **b** of truth

Belteshazzar
Name given to Daniel in Babylon (Da 1:7).

Da 1: 7 to Daniel, the name **B**;
2:26 The king asked Daniel (also called **B**)
4: 8 (He is called **B**, after the name of
4: 9 I said, "**B**, chief of the magicians,
4:18 Now, **B**, tell me what it means,
4:19 Daniel (also called **B**) was greatly
4:19 "**B**, do not let the dream
4:19 **B** answered, "My lord, if only the
5:12 Daniel whom the king called **B**,
10: 1 given to Daniel (who was called **B**).

Belts (Belt)
Eze 23:15 with **b** round their waists and
Mt 10: 9 gold or silver or copper in your **b**;
Mk 6: 8 bread, no bag, no money in your **b**.

Ben Hinnom
Jos 15: 8 ran up the Valley of **B** along the
18:16 the hill facing the Valley of **B**,
2Ki 23:10 which was in the Valley of **B**,
2Ch 28: 3 sacrifices in the Valley of **B**
33: 6 sons in the fire in the Valley of **B**,
Jer 7:31 of Topheth in the Valley of **B**
7:32 call it Topheth or the Valley of **B**,
19: 2 go out to the Valley of **B**, near the
19: 6 Topheth or the Valley of **B**,
32:35 Valley of **B** to sacrifice their sons

Ben-Abinadab
1Ki 4:11 **B**—in Naphoth Dor (he was married to

Benaiah
2Sa 8:18 **B** son of Jehoiada was over the
20:23 **B** son of Jehoiada was over the
23:20 **B** son of Jehoiada was a valiant
23:21 **B** went against him with a club.
23:22 Such were the exploits of **B** son of
23:30 **B** the Pirathonite, Hiddai from the
1Ki 1: 8 Zadok the priest, **B** son of Jehoiada,
1:10 not invite Nathan the prophet or **B**
1:26 and **B** son of Jehoiada,
1:32 the prophet and **B** son of Jehoiada.
1:36 **B** son of Jehoiada answered the king,
1:38 **B** son of Jehoiada,
1:44 **B** son of Jehoiada,
2:25 King Solomon gave orders to **B** son of
2:29 Solomon ordered **B** son of Jehoiada,
2:30 **B** entered the tent of the LORD and
2:30 **B** reported to the king, "This is
2:31 the king commanded **B**, "Do as he says.
2:34 **B** son of Jehoiada went up and struck
2:35 The king put **B** son of Jehoiada over
2:46 the king gave the order to **B** son of
4: 4 **B** son of Jehoiada
1Ch 4:36 Asaiah, Adiel, Jesimiel, **B**,
11:22 **B** son of Jehoiada was a valiant
11:23 **B** went against him with a club.
11:24 Such were the exploits of **B** son of
11:31 in Benjamin, **B** the Pirathonite,
15:18 Shemiramoth, Jehiel, Unni, Eliab, **B**,
15:20 Jehiel, Unni, Eliab, Maaseiah and **B**
15:24 Amasai, Zechariah, **B** and Eliezer
16: 5 Eliab, **B**, Obed-Edom and Jeiel.
16: 6 **B** and Jahaziel the priests were to
18:17 **B** son of Jehoiada was over the
27: 5 was **B** son of Jehoiada the priest.
27: 6 This was the **B** who was a mighty man
27:14 **B** the Pirathonite, an Ephraimite.
27:34 Jehoiada son of **B** and by Abiathar.
2Ch 20:14 the son of **B**, the son of Jeiel,
31:13 Eliel, Ismakiah, Mahath and **B** were
Ezr 10:25 Mijamin, Eleazar, Malkijah and **B**.
10:30 Kelal, **B**, Maaseiah, Mattaniah,
10:35 **B**, Bedeiah, Keluhi,
10:43 Zabad, Zebina, Jaddai, Joel and **B**.
Eze 11: 1 and Pelatiah son of **B**, leaders of
11:13 prophesying, Pelatiah son of **B** died.

Ben-Ammi
Ge 19:38 and she named him **B**; he is the

Benches
Mt 21:12 and the **b** of those selling doves.
Mk 11:15 and the **b** of those selling doves,

Bend (Bending, Bent)
Ge 49:15 he will **b** his shoulder to the burden
2Sa 22:35 my arms can **b** a bow of bronze.
Ps 7:12 he will **b** and string his bow.
11: 2 For look, the wicked **b** their bows;
18:34 my arms can **b** a bow of bronze.
37:14 The wicked draw the sword and **b** the
Isa 65:12 and you will all **b** down for the
Zec 9:13 I will **b** Judah as I **b** my bow and

Ben-Deker
1Ki 4: 9 **B**—in Makaz, Shaalbim, Beth Shemesh

Bending (Bend)
Lk 24:12 **B** over, he saw the strips of linen

Bene Berak
Jos 19:45 Jehud, **B**, Gath Rimmon,

Bene Jaakan
Nu 33:31 They left Moseroth and camped at **B**.
33:32 They left **B** and camped at Hor

Benefactors
Lk 22:25 over them call themselves **B**.

Beneficial (Benefit)
1Co 6:12 for me"—but not everything is **b**.
10:23 not everything is **b**.

Benefit (Beneficial, Benefited, Benefits)
Job 22: 2 "Can a man be of **b** to God? Can even
22: 2 Can even a wise man **b** him?
Ecc 5:11 And what **b** are they to the owner
Isa 38:17 Surely it was for my **b** that I
57:12 your works, and they will not **b** you.
Jer 23:32 They do not **b** these people in the
Jn 11:42 but I said this for the **b** of the
12:30 voice was for your **b**, not mine.
Ro 6:21 What **b** did you reap at that time
6:22 the **b** you reap leads to holiness,
1Co 4: 6 to myself and Apollos for your **b**,
2Co 1:15 you first so that you might **b** twice.
4:15 All this is for your **b**, so that the
Eph 4:29 that it may **b** those who listen.
1Ti 6: 2 because those who **b** from their
Phm :20 that I may have some **b** from you

Benefited (Benefit)
1Sa 19: 4 what he has done has **b** you greatly.

Benefits (Benefit)
Dt 18: 8 He is to share equally in their **b**
Ps 103: 2 O my soul, and forget not all his **b**
Pr 11:17 A kind man **b** himself, but a cruel
Ecc 7:11 thing and **b** those who see the sun.
Jn 4:38 have reaped the **b** of their labour."

Ben-Geber
1Ki 4:13 **B**—in Ramoth Gilead (the settlements

Ben-Hadad (Ben-Hadad's)
1Ki 15:18 and sent them to **B** son of Tabrimmon,
15:20 **B** agreed with King Asa and sent the
20: 1 Now **B** king of Aram mustered his
20: 2 "This is what **B** says: "Your silver
20: 5 "This is what **B** says: 'I sent to
20: 9 left and took the answer back to **B**.
20:10 **B** sent another message to Ahab:
20:12 **B** heard this message while he and
20:16 while **B** and the 32 kings
20:17 Now **B** had dispatched scouts, who
20:20 But **B** king of Aram escaped on
20:26 next spring **B** mustered the Arameans
20:30 And **B** fled to the city and hid in an
20:32 servant **B** says: 'Please let me live.
20:33 "Yes, your brother **B**!" they said.
20:33 When **B** came out, Ahab had him come
20:34 took from your father," **B** offered.
2Ki 6:24 Some time later, **B** king of Aram
8: 7 and **B** king of Aram was ill.
8: 9 "Your son **B** king of Aram has sent me
8:14 When **B** asked, "What did Elisha say
13: 3 Hazael king of Aram and **B** his son.
13:24 and **B** his son succeeded him as king.
13:25 recaptured from **B** son of Hazael
2Ch 16: 2 and sent it to **B** king of Aram,

2Ch 16: 4 **B** agreed with King Asa and sent the
Jer 49:27 will consume the fortresses of **B**."
Am 1: 4 will consume the fortresses of **B**.

Ben-Hadad's (Ben-Hadad)

1Ki 20: 9 he replied to **B** messengers, "Tell my

Ben-Hail

2Ch 17: 7 he sent his officials **B**, Obadiah,

Ben-Hanan

1Ch 4:20 The sons of Shimon: Amnon, Rinnah, **B**

Ben-Hesed

1Ki 4:10 **B**—in Arubboth (Socoh and all the

Ben-Hur (Hur)

1Ki 4: 8 **B**—in the hill country of Ephraim;

Beninu

Ne 10:13 Hodiah, Bani and **B**.

Benjamin (Benjamin's, Benjamite, Benjamites)

1. Jacob's youngest son; second by Rachel, who died in childbirth (Ge 35:16–18, 24; 46:19). Jacob's favourite after loss of Joseph. Father reluctant to allow him to go to Egypt (Ge 42:38; 43); brothers' concern about him led Joseph to make himself known (Ge 44–45). Blessed by Jacob (Ge 49:27). **2.** Tribe descended from Benjamin. Blessed by Moses (Dt 33:12). Included in census (Nu 1:36–37; 26:38–41). Apportioned land (Jos 18:11–28; Eze 48:23); did not take full possession (Jdg 1:21). Almost destroyed by other tribes (Jdg 20–21). Tribe of Saul (1Sa 9:1); followed Ishbosheth (2Sa 2:8–9); later gave support to David (1Ch 12:29; 1Ki 12:21). Tribe of Esther (Est 2:5) and Paul (Php 3:5). **3.** Hilly territory west of River Jordan, with Ephraim to the north, Judah to the south, and Dan to the west. Its boundaries and towns were clearly listed (Jos 18:11–28). Allotted to descendants of Jacob's youngest son, who failed to drive out the Jebusites from Jerusalem (Jdg 1:21). Its people were almost destroyed by the other tribes of Israel because of their sin at Gibeah (Jdg 19–21).

Ge 35:18 But his father named him **B**.
35:24 The sons of Rachel: Joseph and **B**.
42: 4 Jacob did not send **B**, Joseph's
42:36 no more, and now you want to take **B**.
43:14 brother and **B** come back with you.
43:15 the amount of silver, and **B** also.
43:16 Joseph saw **B** with them, he said to
43:29 he looked about and saw his brother **B**
45:12 and so can my brother **B**, that it is
45:14 arms around his brother **B** and wept,
45:14 and **B** embraced him, weeping.
45:22 to **B** he gave three hundred shekels
46:19 Jacob's wife Rachel: Joseph and **B**.
46:21 The sons of **B**: Bela, Beker, Ashbel,
49:27 "**B** is a ravenous wolf;
Ex 1: 3 Issachar, Zebulun and **B**;
Nu 1:11 from **B**, Abidan son of Gideoni;
1:36 From the descendants of **B**: All the
1:37 from the tribe of **B** was 35,400
2:22 The tribe of **B** will be next.
2:22 leader of the people of **B** is Abidan
7:60 the leader of the people of **B**,
10:24 over the division of the tribe of **B**.
13: 9 from the tribe of **B**, Palti son of
26:38 The descendants of **B** by their clans
26:41 These were the clans of **B**;
34:21 son of Kislon, from the tribe of **B**;
Dt 27:12 Levi, Judah, Issachar, Joseph and **B**.
33:12 About **B** he said: "Let the beloved of
Jos 18:11 The lot came up for the tribe of **B**,
18:20 of the clans of **B** on all sides.
18:21 The tribe of **B**, clan by clan, had
18:28 the inheritance of **B** for its clans.
21: 4 the tribes of Judah, Simeon and **B**.
21:17 from the tribe of **B** they gave them
Jdg 5:14 **B** was with the people who followed
10: 9 **B** and the house of Ephraim;
Jdg 19:14 sun set as they neared Gibeah in **B**.
20: 4 to Gibeah in **B** to spend the night.
20:10 the army arrives at Gibeah in **B**,
20:12 sent men throughout the tribe of **B**,
20:17 Israel, apart from **B**, mustered
20:24 the Israelites drew near to **B** the
20:28 battle with **B** our brother, or not?"
20:35 The LORD defeated **B** before Israel,
20:36 of Israel had given way before **B**,
20:41 and the men of **B** were terrified,
20:48 The men of Israel went back to **B** and
21:15 The people grieved for **B**, because
21:16 "With the women of **B** destroyed, how
21:21 of Shiloh and go to the land of **B**.
1Sa 9: 1 of Becorath, the son of Aphiah of **B**.
9: 4 passed through the territory of **B**,
9:16 send you a man from the land of **B**.
9:21 of all the clans of the tribe of **B**?
10: 2 tomb, at Zelzah on the border of **B**.
10:20 the tribe of **B** was chosen.
10:21 he brought forward the tribe of **B**,
13: 2 were with Jonathan at Gibeah in **B**.
13:15 and went up to Gibeah in **B**,
13:16 were staying in Gibeah of **B**,
14:16 Saul's lookouts at Gibeah in **B** saw
22: 7 Saul said to them, "Listen, men of **B**!
2Sa 2: 9 also over Ephraim, **B** and all Israel.
2:15 for **B** and Ish-Bosheth son of Saul,
2:25 the men of **B** rallied behind Abner.
3:19 the whole house of **B** wanted to do.
4: 2 from the tribe of **B**—
21:14 at Zela in **B**, and did everything the
23:29 Ithai son of Ribai from Gibeah in **B**,
1Ki 4:18 Shimei son of Ela—in **B**;
12:21 house of Judah and the tribe of **B**
12:23 to the whole house of Judah and **B**,
15:22 built up Geba in **B**, and also Mizpah.
1Ch 2: 2 Dan, Joseph, **B**, Naphtali, Gad and
6:60 from the tribe of **B** they were given
6:65 Simeon and **B** they allotted the
7: 6 Three sons of **B**: Bela, Beker and
7:10 The sons of Bilhan: Jeush, **B**, Ehud,
8: 1 **B** was the father of Bela his
8:40 All these were the descendants of **B**.
9: 3 Those from Judah, from **B**, and from
9: 9 The people from **B**, as listed in
11:31 Ithai son of Ribai from Gibeah in **B**,
12: 2 of Saul from the tribe of **B**):
12:29 men of **B**, Saul's kinsmen—3,000,
21: 6 Joab did not include Levi and **B** in
27:21 over **B**: Jaasiel son of Abner;
2Ch 11: 1 mustered the house of Judah and **B**
11: 3 all the Israelites in Judah and **B**,
11:10 fortified cities in Judah and **B**.
11:12 So Judah and **B** were his.
11:23 the districts of Judah and **B**,
14: 8 hundred and eighty thousand from **B**,
15: 2 to me, Asa and all Judah and **B**.
15: 8 from the whole land of Judah and **B**
15: 9 he assembled all Judah and **B** and
17:17 From **B**: Eliada, a valiant soldier,
25: 5 of hundreds for all Judah and **B**.
31: 1 the altars throughout Judah and **B**
34: 9 **B** and the inhabitants of Jerusalem.
34:32 he made everyone in Jerusalem and **B**
Ezr 1: 5 the family heads of Judah and **B**, and
4: 1 the enemies of Judah and **B** heard
10: 9 and **B** had gathered in Jerusalem.
10:32 **B**, Malluch and Shemariah.
Ne 3:23 Beyond them, **B** and Hasshub made
11: 4 Judah and **B** lived in Jerusalem):
11: 7 From the descendants of **B**: Sallu son
11:36 the Levites of Judah settled in **B**.
12:34 Judah, **B**, Shemaiah, Jeremiah,
Est 2: 5 of Susa a Jew of the tribe of **B**,
Ps 68:27 There is the little tribe of **B**,
80: 2 before Ephraim, **B** and Manasseh.
Jer 1: 1 at Anathoth in the territory of **B**.
6: 1 "Flee for safety, people of **B**! Flee
17:26 from the territory of **B** and the
20: 2 Upper Gate of **B** at the LORD's temple.
32: 8 at Anathoth in the territory of **B**.
32:44 and witnessed in the territory of **B**,
33:13 in the territory of **B**, in the
37:12 to go to the territory of **B** to get
37:13 when he reached the **B** Gate, the
Jer 38: 7 the king was sitting in the **B** Gate,
Eze 48:22 border of Judah and the border of **B**.
48:23 **B** will have one more portion;
48:24 territory of **B** from east to west.
48:32 the gate of **B** and the gate of Dan.
Hos 5: 8 cry in Beth Aven; lead on, O **B**.
Ob :19 and **B** will possess Gilead.
Zec 14:10 from the **B** Gate to the site of the
Ac 13:21 Saul son of Kish, of the tribe of **B**
Ro 11: 1 of Abraham, from the tribe of **B**.
Php 3: 5 of the tribe of **B**, a Hebrew of
Rev 7: 8 from the tribe of **B** 12,000.

Benjamin's (Benjamin)

Ge 43:34 **B** portion was five times as much as
44:12 And the cup was found in **B** sack.

Benjamite (Benjamin)

Jdg 3:15 the son of Gera the **B**.
20:46 twenty-five thousand **B** swordsmen
21: 1 his daughter in marriage to a **B**."
21:17 The **B** survivors must have heirs,"
21:18 be anyone who gives a wife to a **B**.'
1Sa 4:12 a **B** ran from the battle line
9: 1 There was a **B**, a man of standing,
9:21 Saul answered, "But am I not a **B**,
2Sa 16:11 How much more, then, this **B**! Leave
19:16 Shimei son of Gera, the **B** from
20: 1 Sheba son of Bicri, a **B**,
1Ki 2: 8 Shimei son of Gera, the **B**
1Ch 27:12 was Abiezer the Anathothite, a **B**.
Ps 7: T to the LORD concerning Cush, a **B**.

Benjamites (Benjamin)

Jdg 1:21 The **B**, however, failed to dislodge
1:21 the Jebusites live there with the **B**.
19:16 Gibeah (the men of the place were **B**
20: 3 (The **B** heard that the Israelites had
20:13 But the **B** would not listen to their
20:15 the **B** mobilised twenty-six thousand
20:18 go first to fight against the **B**?"
20:20 of Israel went out to fight the **B**
20:21 The **B** came out of Gibeah and cut
20:23 go up again to battle against the **B**
20:25 when the **B** came out from Gibeah
20:30 They went up against the **B** on the
20:31 The **B** came out to meet them and were
20:32 While the **B** were saying, "We are
20:34 The fighting was so heavy that the **B**
20:35 25,100 **B**, all armed with swords.
20:36 the **B** saw that they were beaten.
20:39 The **B** had begun to inflict
20:40 the **B** turned and saw the smoke of
20:43 They surrounded the **B**, chased them
20:44 Eighteen thousand **B** fell, all of
20:45 They kept pressing after the **B**
21: 6 grieved for their brothers, the **B**.
21:13 sent an offer of peace to the **B**
21:14 the **B** returned at that time and
21:20 they instructed the **B**, saying, "Go
21:23 So that is what the **B** did.
2Sa 2:31 David's men had killed 360 **B** who
3:19 Abner also spoke to the **B** in person.
19:17 With him were a thousand **B**, along
1Ch 9: 7 Of the **B**: Sallu son of Meshullam,
12:16 Other **B** and some men from Judah also
Ne 11:31 The descendants of the **B** from Geba

Beno

1Ch 24:26 The son of Jaaziah: **B**.
24:27 The sons of Merari: from Jaaziah: **B**,

Ben-Oni

Ge 35:18 she was dying—she named her son **B**.

Bent (Bend)

Ex 10:10 Clearly you are **b** on evil.
1Sa 24: 9 'David is **b** on harming you'?
1Ki 18:42 **b** down to the ground and put his
Ps 44:16 of the enemy, who is **b** on revenge.
69:23 and their backs be **b** for ever.
106:43 but they were **b** on rebellion and
Pr 16:30 he who purses his lips is **b** on evil.
17:11 An evil man is **b** only on rebellion;

Isa 21:15 from the **b** bow and from the heat
51:13 who is **b** on destruction? For where
Eze 22: 9 slanderous men **b** on shedding blood
Da 11:27 kings, with their hearts **b** on evil
Hos 11: 4 their neck and **b** down to feed them.
Hab 1: 9 they all come **b** on violence.
Lk 4:39 **b** over her and rebuked the fever,
13:11 She was **b** over and could not
Jn 8: 6 But Jesus **b** down and started to
20: 5 He **b** over and looked in at the
20:11 she **b** over to look into the
Ro 11:10 and their backs be **b** for ever."
Rev 6: 2 as a conqueror **b** on conquest.

Ben-Zoheth
1Ch 4:20 descendants of Ishi: Zoheth and **B**.

Beon
Nu 32: 3 Heshbon, Elealeh, Sebam, Nebo and **B**—

Beor
Ge 36:32 Bela son of **B** became king of Edom.
Nu 22: 5 to summon Balaam son of **B**,
24: 3 "The oracle of Balaam son of **B**,
24:15 "The oracle of Balaam son of **B**,
31: 8 Balaam son of **B** with the sword.
Dt 23: 4 and they hired Balaam son of **B** from
Jos 13:22 put to the sword Balaam son of **B**,
24: 9 son of **B** to put a curse on you.
1Ch 1:43 Bela son of **B**, whose city was
Mic 6: 5 and what Balaam son of **B** answered.
2Pe 2:15 follow the way of Balaam son of **B**,

Bera
Ge 14: 2 went to war against **B** king of Sodom,

Beracah
1Ch 12: 3 Azmaveth; **B**, Jehu the Anathothite,
2Ch 20:26 they assembled in the Valley of **B**,
20:26 called the Valley of **B** to this day.

Beraiah
1Ch 8:21 Adaiah, **B** and Shimrath were the sons

Berea (Bereans)
City in Macedonia, about 50 miles south-west of Thessalonica. Paul fled here with Silas after trouble in Thessalonica (Ac 17:10). Its people were receptive to the gospel and searched the scriptures daily (Ac 17:11). Jews from Thessalonica followed Paul here, forcing Paul to leave; Silas and Timothy continued the work (Ac 17:13–14). Home of Paul's helper Sopater (Ac 20:4).

Ac 17:10 sent Paul and Silas away to **B**.
17:13 was preaching the word of God at **B**,
17:14 but Silas and Timothy stayed at **B**.
20: 4 by Sopater son of Pyrrhus from **B**,

Bereans (Berea)
Ac 17:11 the **B** were of more noble character

Bereave (Bereaved, Bereavement, Bereaves)
Hos 9:12 I will **b** them of every one.

Bereaved (Bereave)
Ge 43:14 As for me, if I am **b**, I am **b**."
Isa 49:21 I was **b** and barren;

Bereavement (Bereave)
Isa 49:20 The children born during your **b** will
Jer 15: 7 I will bring **b** and destruction on my

Bereaves (Bereave)
Lam 1:20 Outside the sword **b**; inside, there

Bered
Ge 16:14 still there, between Kadesh and **B**.
1Ch 7:20 **B** his son, Tahath his son, Eleadah

Berekiah
1Ch 3:20 Ohel, **B**, Hasadiah and Jushab-Hesed.
6:39 Asaph son of **B**, the son of Shimea,
9:16 and **B** son of Asa,
15:17 from his brothers, Asaph son of **B**;
15:23 **B** and Elkanah were to be doorkeepers
2Ch 28:12 **B** son of Meshillemoth, Jehizkiah son
Ne 3: 4 Next to him Meshullam son of **B**, the
3:30 Next to them, Meshullam son of **B**
6:18 the daughter of Meshullam son of **B**.
Zec 1: 1 Zechariah son of **B**, the son of Iddo:
1: 7 Zechariah son of **B**, the son of Iddo.

Beri (Berites)
1Ch 7:36 Suah, Harnepher, Shual, **B**, Imrah,

Beriah (Berite)
Ge 46:17 Imnah, Ishvah, Ishvi and **B**.
46:17 The sons of **B**: Heber and Malkiel.
Nu 26:44 through **B**, the Beriite clan;
26:45 through the descendants of **B**:
1Ch 7:23 He named him **B**, because there had
7:30 Imnah, Ishvah, Ishvi and **B**.
7:31 The sons of **B**: Heber and Malkiel,
8:13 **B** and Shema, who were heads of
8:16 Ishpah and Joha were the sons of **B**.
23:10 Jahath, Ziza, Jeush and **B**.
23:11 but Jeush and **B** did not have many

Beriite (Beriah)
Nu 26:44 through Beriah, the **B** clan;

Berites (Beri)
2Sa 20:14 through the entire region of the **B**,

Bernice
Ac 25:13 A few days later King Agrippa and **B**
25:23 The next day Agrippa and **B** came with
26:30 and **B** and those sitting with them.

Berothah
Eze 47:16 **B** and Sibraim (which lies on the

Berothai (Berothite)
2Sa 8: 8 From Tebah and **B**, towns that

Berothite (Berothai)
1Ch 11:39 Zelek the Ammonite, Naharai the **B**,

Beryl
Ex 28:17 shall be a ruby, a topaz and a **b**;
39:10 there was a ruby, a topaz and a **b**;
Eze 28:13 jasper, sapphire, turquoise and **b**.
Rev 21:20 the eighth **b**, the ninth topaz, the

Besai
Ezr 2:49 Uzza, Paseah, **B**,
Ne 7:52 **B**, Meunim, Nephussim,

Beset
Ps 41: 8 "A vile disease has **b** him;
55: 5 Fear and trembling have **b** me;

Besiege (Siege)
Dt 20:19 people, that you should **b** them?
28:52 They will **b** all the cities
1Sa 23: 8 to Keilah to **b** David and his men.
2Sa 12:28 and **b** the city and capture it.
2Ch 6:28 or when enemies **b** them in any of
Ps 27: 3 Though an army **b** me, my heart will
Isa 29: 2 Yet I will **b** Ariel; she will mourn
29: 7 her and her fortress and **b** her,
Eze 4: 3 be under siege, and you shall **b** it.
Lk 11:53 and to **b** him with questions,

Besieged (Siege)
Jdg 9:50 Abimelech went to Thebez and **b** it
1Sa 11: 1 Nahash the Ammonite went up and **b**
2Sa 11: 1 They destroyed the Ammonites and **b**
20:15 All the troops with Joab came and **b**
1Ki 20: 1 and **b** Samaria and attacked it.
2Ki 16: 5 fight against Jerusalem and **b** Ahaz,
1Ch 20: 1 and went to Rabbah and **b** it,
Ps 31:21 love to me when I was in a **b** city.
Lam 3: 5 He has **b** me and surrounded me with
Da 1: 1 Babylon came to Jerusalem and **b** it.
Zec 12: 2 Judah will be **b** as well as Jerusalem.

Besieges (Siege)
1Ki 8:37 or when an enemy **b** them in any of

Besieging (Siege)
1Ki 15:27 Nadab and all Israel were **b** it.
2Ki 24:11 while his officers were **b** it.
Jer 4:16 'A **b** army is coming from a distant
21: 4 who are outside the wall **b** you.
21: 9 Babylonians who are **b** you will live;
32: 2 of Babylon was then **b** Jerusalem,
37: 5 Babylonians who were **b** Jerusalem

Besodeiah
Ne 3: 6 of Paseah and Meshullam son of **B**.

Besor
1Sa 30: 9 **B** Ravine, where some stayed behind,
30:21 were left behind at the **B** Ravine.

Best (Good)
Ge 16: 6 "Do with her whatever you think **b**."
27:15 Rebekah took the **b** clothes of Esau
43:11 Put some of the **b** products
45:18 I will give you the **b** of the land
45:20 the **b** of all Egypt will be yours.'"
45:23 loaded with the **b** things of Egypt,
47: 6 brothers in the **b** part of the land.
47:11 property in the **b** part of the land,
Ex 14: 7 He took six hundred of the **b**
15: 4 The **b** of Pharaoh's officers are
22: 5 the **b** of his own field or vineyard.
23:19 "Bring the **b** of the firstfruits
34:26 "Bring the **b** of the firstfruits
Nu 13:20 Do your **b** to bring back some of
18:29 the **b** and holiest part of everything
18:30 'When you present the **b** part,
18:32 By presenting the **b** part of it
Dt 33:14 with the **b** the sun brings forth
33:16 with the **b** gifts of the earth and
33:21 He chose the **b** land for himself; the
Jos 8: 3 He chose thirty thousand of his **b**
10: 7 including all the **b** fighting men.
Jdg 10:15 Do with us whatever you think **b**,
Ru 3: 3 yourself, and put on your **b** clothes.
1Sa 1:23 "Do what seems **b** to you," Elkanah
8:14 He will take the **b** of your fields
8:16 the **b** of your cattle and donkeys
14:36 "Do whatever seems **b** to you,"
14:40 "Do what seems **b** to you,"
15: 9 and the **b** of the sheep and cattle,
15:15 they spared the **b** of the sheep and
15:21 the **b** of what was devoted to God,
27: 1 The **b** thing I can do is to escape to
2Sa 10: 9 so he selected some of the **b** troops
18: 4 "I will do whatever seems **b** to you.
23:20 He struck down two of Moab's **b** men.
1Ki 20: 3 and the **b** of your wives and children
2Ki 10: 3 choose the **b** and most worthy of your
10: 5 you do whatever you think **b**."
1Ch 11:22 He struck down two of Moab's **b** men.
19:10 so he selected some of the **b** troops
Ezr 7:18 do whatever seems **b** with the rest
Est 2: 9 maids into the **b** place in the harem.
3: 8 king's **b** interest to tolerate them.
8: 8 of the Jews as seems **b** to you,
Pr 5: 9 lest you give your **b** strength to
SS 7: 9 and your mouth like the **b** wine.
Isa 1:19 you will eat the **b** from the land;
25: 6 **b** of meats and the finest of wines.
48:17 who teaches you what is **b** for you,
Jer 18: 4 pot, shaping it as seemed **b** to him.
Eze 24: 4 Fill it with the **b** of these bones;
31:16 the choicest and **b** of Lebanon, all
44:30 The **b** of all the firstfruits and of
48:14 This is the **b** of the land and must
Da 11:15 even their **b** troops will not have
Jnh 1:13 the men did their **b** to row back

Mic 7: 4 The **b** of them is like a brier,
Zec 11:12 I told them, "If you think it **b**,
Lk 15:22 Bring the **b** robe and put it on him.
Jn 2:10 but you have saved the **b** till now."
2Co 8:10 here is my advice about what is **b**
Php 1:10 may be able to discern what is **b**
1Th 3: 1 **b** to be left by ourselves in Athens.
2Ti 2:15 Do your **b** to present yourself to God
4: 9 Do your **b** to come to me quickly,
4:21 Do your **b** to get here before winter.
Tit 3:12 do your **b** to come to me at Nicopolis,
Heb 12:10 a little while as they thought **b**;

Bestow (Bestowed, Bestower, Bestowing, Bestows)

Ps 3: 3 **b** glory on me and lift up my head.
31:19 which you **b** in the sight of men
Isa 45: 4 and **b** on you a title of honour,
61: 3 to **b** on them a crown of beauty
62: 2 that the mouth of the LORD will **b**.
Jer 23: 2 I will **b** punishment on you for the

Bestowed (Bestow)

1Ch 29:25 **b** on him royal splendour such as
Ps 21: 5 have **b** on him splendour and majesty.
89:19 "I have **b** strength on a warrior;
Jer 23: 2 away and have not **b** care on them,

Bestower (Bestow)

Isa 23: 8 Tyre, the **b** of crowns,

Bestowing (Bestow)

Pr 8:21 **b** wealth on those who love me

Bestows (Bestow)

Job 5:10 He **b** rain on the earth;
Ps 84:11 the LORD **b** favour and honour;
133: 3 For there the LORD **b** his blessing,

Beten

Jos 19:25 Helkath, Hali, **B**, Acshaph,

Beth Anath

Jos 19:38 Iron, Migdal El, Horem, **B**
Jdg 1:33 those living in Beth Shemesh or **B**;
1:33 **B** became forced labourers for them.

Beth Anoth

Jos 15:59 Maarath, **B** and Eltekon—six towns

Beth Arabah

Jos 15: 6 and continued north of **B** to
15:61 In the desert: **B**, Middin, Secacah,
18:18 continued to the northern slope of **B**
18:22 **B**, Zemaraim, Bethel,

Beth Arbel

Hos 10:14 devastated **B** on the day of battle,

Beth Ashbea

1Ch 4:21 the clans of the linen workers at **B**,

Beth Aven

Jos 7: 2 which is near **B** to the east of
18:12 coming out at the desert of **B**.
1Sa 13: 5 and camped at Michmash, east of **B**.
14:23 and the battle moved on beyond **B**.
Hos 4:15 not go to Gilgal; do not go up to **B**.
5: 8 Raise the battle cry in **B**;
10: 5 Samaria fear for the calf-idol of **B**.

Beth Azmaveth

Ne 7:28 of **B** 42

Beth Baal Meon

Jos 13:17 including Dibon, Bamoth Baal, **B**,

Beth Barah

Jdg 7:24 Jordan ahead of them as far as **B**.
7:24 waters of the Jordan as far as **B**.

Beth Biri

1Ch 4:31 Beth Marcaboth, Hazar Susim, **B** and

Beth Car

1Sa 7:11 along the way to a point below **B**.

Beth Dagon

Jos 15:41 Gederoth, **B**, Naamah and Makkedah
19:27 It then turned east towards **B**,

Beth Diblathaim

Jer 48:22 to Dibon, Nebo and **B**,

Beth Eden

Am 1: 5 the one who holds the sceptre in **B**.

Beth Eked

2Ki 10:12 At **B** of the Shepherds,
10:14 by the well of **B**—forty-two men.

Beth Emek

Jos 19:27 and went north to **B** and Neiel,

Beth Ezel

Mic 1:11 **B** is in mourning; its protection is

Beth Gader

1Ch 2:51 and Hareph the father of **B**.

Beth Gamul

Jer 48:23 to Kiriathaim, **B** and Beth Meon,

Beth Gilgal

Ne 12:29 from **B**, and from the area of Geba

Beth Haggan

2Ki 9:27 he fled up the road to **B**.

Beth Hakkerem

Ne 3:14 Recab, ruler of the district of **B**.
Jer 6: 1 Raise the signal over **B**! For

Beth Haram

Jos 13:27 in the valley, **B**, Beth Nimrah,

Beth Haran

Nu 32:36 Beth Nimrah and **B** as fortified

Beth Hoglah

Jos 15: 6 went up to **B** and continued north of
18:19 then went to the northern slope of **B**
18:21 cities: Jericho, **B**, Emek Keziz,

Beth Horon

Jos 10:10 them along the road going up to **B**
10:11 on the road down from **B** to Azekah,
16: 3 as far as the region of Lower **B**
16: 5 Ataroth Addar in the east to Upper **B**
18:13 Addar on the hill south of Lower **B**.
18:14 From the hill facing **B** on the south
21:22 Kibzaim and **B**, together with their
1Sa 13:18 another towards **B**, and the third
1Ki 9:17 He built up Lower **B**,
1Ch 6:68 Jokmeam, **B**,
7:24 Upper **B** as well as Uzzen Sheerah.
2Ch 8: 5 He rebuilt Upper **B** and Lower **B** as
25:13 Judean towns from Samaria to **B**.

Beth Jeshimoth

Nu 33:49 the Jordan from **B** to Abel Shittim.
Jos 12: 3 to **B**, and then southward below the
13:20 the slopes of Pisgah, and **B**
Eze 25: 9 beginning at its frontier towns—**B**,

Beth Lebaoth

Jos 19: 6 **B** and Sharuhen—thirteen towns and

Beth Marcaboth

Jos 19: 5 Ziklag, **B**, Hazar Susah,
1Ch 4:31 **B**, Hazar Susim, Beth Biri and

Beth Meon

Jer 48:23 to Kiriathaim, Beth Gamul and **B**,

Beth Millo

Jdg 9: 6 all the citizens of Shechem and **B**
9:20 citizens of Shechem and **B**, and let
9:20 citizens of Shechem and **B**,
2Ki 12:20 and assassinated him at **B**,

Beth Nimrah

Nu 32:36 **B** and Beth Haran as fortified cities,
Jos 13:27 in the valley, Beth Haram, **B**,

Beth Ophrah

Mic 1:10 In **B** roll in the dust.

Beth Pazzez

Jos 19:21 Remeth, En Gannim, En Haddah and **B**.

Beth Pelet

Jos 15:27 Hazar Gaddah, Heshmon, **B**,
Ne 11:26 in Jeshua, in Moladah, in **B**,

Beth Peor

Dt 3:29 we stayed in the valley near **B**.
4:46 were in the valley near **B** east of
34: 6 in Moab, in the valley opposite **B**,
Jos 13:20 **B**, the slopes of Pisgah,

Beth Rapha

1Ch 4:12 Eshton was the father of **B**,

Beth Rehob

Jdg 18:28 The city was in a valley near **B**.
2Sa 10: 6 foot soldiers from **B** and Zobah,

Beth Shan

Jos 17:11 Manasseh also had **B**, Ibleam and the
17:16 both those in **B** and its settlements
Jdg 1:27 did not drive out the people of **B**
1Sa 31:10 fastened his body to the wall of **B**.
31:12 journeyed through the night to **B**.
31:12 Saul and his sons from the wall of **B**
2Sa 21:12 from the public square at **B**,
1Ki 4:12 and in all of **B** next to Zarethan
4:12 **B** to Abel Meholah across to Jokmeam;
1Ch 7:29 Along the borders of Manasseh were **B**,

Beth Shemesh

1. Town in Valley of Sorek, about 15 miles south-west of Jerusalem, on the border of Judah (Jos 15:10). Probably also called Ir Shemesh (Jos 19:41). Allotted to tribe of Dan and assigned to the Levites (Jos 21:16; 1Ch 6:59). The stolen ark of the covenant, was sent here by the Philistines where it remained until it was taken to Kiriath Jearim (1Sa 6:10–7:2). Located in one of Solomon's 12 districts (1Ki 4:9), it was the scene of battle between Jehoash and Amaziah (2Ki 14:11–14; 2Ch 25:21–23). Captured by the Philistines in the time of Ahaz (2Ch 28:18). **2.** Town between Mount Tabor and River Jordan, on the border between the territories of Issachar and Naphtali (Jos 19:22). **3.** Fortified town in Naphtali (Jos 19:35, 38), from which Canaanites were not driven out (Jdg 1:33).

Jos 15:10 down to **B** and crossed to Timnah.
19:22 touched Tabor, Shahazumah and **B**,
19:38 Migdal El, Horem, Beth Anath and **B**.
21:16 Ain, Juttah and **B**, together with
Jdg 1:33 drive out those living in **B**
1:33 and those living in **B** and Beth Anath
1Sa 6: 9 up to its own territory, towards **B**,
6:12 the cows went straight up towards **B**,
6:12 them as far as the border of **B**.
6:13 Now the people of **B** were harvesting
6:14 came to the field of Joshua of **B**,
6:15 On that day the people of **B** offered
6:18 day in the field of Joshua of **B**.
6:19 God struck down some of the men of **B**,
6:20 the men of **B** asked, "Who can stand
1Ki 4: 9 Ben-Deker—in Makaz, Shaalbim, **B** and
2Ki 14:11 Judah faced each other at **B** in Judah.
14:13 of Joash, the son of Ahaziah, at **B**.

1Ch 6:59 Ashan, Juttah and **B**, together with
2Ch 25:21 Judah faced each other at **B** in Judah.
25:23 of Joash, the son of Ahaziah, at **B**.
28:18 They captured and occupied **B**,

Beth Shittah

Jdg 7:22 The army fled to **B** towards Zererah

Beth Tappuah

Jos 15:53 Janim, **B**, Aphekah,

Beth Togarmah

Eze 27:14 "Men of **B** exchanged work horses,
38: 6 and **B** from the north

Beth Zur

Jos 15:58 Halhul, **B**, Gedor,
1Ch 2:45 and Maon was the father of **B**.
2Ch 11: 7 **B**, Soco, Adullam,
Ne 3:16 ruler of a half-district of **B**, made

Bethany

1. Village on eastern slope of Mount of Olives, about 2 miles east of Jerusalem (Jn 11:18). Home of Mary, Martha and Lazarus (Jn 11:1). Jesus was anointed here in the home of Simon the Leper (Mt 26:6–7, Mk 14:3). Near to the site of Jesus' ascension (Lk 24:50–51). **2.** Town on eastern side of the River Jordan where John was baptising (Jn 1:28). Exact location uncertain.

Mt 21:17 to **B**, where he spent the night.
26: 6 While Jesus was in **B** in the home of
Mk 11: 1 and **B** at the Mount of Olives,
11:11 he went out to **B** with the Twelve.
11:12 The next day as they were leaving **B**,
14: 3 While he was in **B**, reclining at the
Lk 19:29 he approached Bethphage and **B** at the
24:50 led them out to the vicinity of **B**,
Jn 1:28 This all happened at **B** on the other
11: 1 He was from **B**, the village of Mary
11:18 **B** was less than two miles from
12: 1 Jesus arrived at **B**, where Lazarus

Bethel

1. Town about 12 miles north of Jerusalem, originally known as Luz. Abraham built an altar close by (Ge 12:8; 13:3–4). Jacob renamed the city after his vision (Ge 28:19) and later settled here (Ge 35:1). Conquered by Joshua (Jos 8:17); allotted to Benjamin (Jos 18:22) but taken by the house of Joseph (Jdg 1:22–26). Because the ark of the covenant was kept here (Jdg 20:27), it became a place of divine enquiry (Jdg 20:18; 21:2–3). Centre of worship for northern kingdom, and site for one of Jeroboam's golden calves (1Ki 12:27–29). Denounced for its idolatry (Hos 10:15; Am 5:5–6); Josiah broke down its altar (2Ki 23:15). **2.** City in the territory of Simeon near Ziklag (1Sa 30:26–31). Bethul (Jos 19:4) and Bethuel (1Ch 4:30) are probably variants. Exact location unknown.

Ge 12: 8 went on towards the hills east of **B**
12: 8 **B** on the west and Ai on the east.
13: 3 place to place until he came to **B**,
13: 3 to the place between **B** and Ai where
28:19 He called that place **B**, though the
31:13 I am the God of **B**, where you
35: 1 God said to Jacob, "Go up to **B**
35: 3 come, let us go up to **B**, where I
35: 6 (that is, **B**) in the land of Canaan.
35: 8 was buried under the oak below **B**.
35:15 where God had talked with him **B**.
35:16 they moved on from **B**. While they
Jos 7: 2 is near Beth Aven to the east of **B**,
8: 9 and lay in wait between **B** and Ai,
8:12 set them in ambush between **B** and Ai
8:17 Not a man remained in Ai or **B** who
12: 9 the king of Ai (near **B**)
12:16 the king of **B** one
16: 1 desert into the hill country of **B**.
16: 2 went on from **B** (that is, Luz),
18:13 the south slope of Luz (that is **B**)
18:22 Beth Arabah, Zemaraim, **B**,
Jdg 1:22 Now the house of Joseph attacked **B**,
1:23 When they sent men to spy out **B**
Jdg 4: 5 **B** in the hill country of Ephraim,
20:18 The Israelites went up to **B**
20:26 all the people, went up to **B**,
20:31 the one leading to **B** and the other
21: 2 The people went to **B**, where they sat
21:19 to the north of **B**, and east of the
21:19 road that goes from **B** to Shechem,
1Sa 7:16 circuit from **B** to Gilgal to Mizpah,
10: 3 Three men going up to God at **B** will
13: 2 and in the hill country of **B**,
30:27 He sent it to those who were in **B**,
1Ki 12:29 One he set up in **B**, and the other in
12:32 This he did in **B**, sacrificing to the
12:32 And at **B** he also installed priests
12:33 on the altar he had built at **B**.
13: 1 a man of God came from Judah to **B**,
13: 4 God cried out against the altar at **B**,
13:10 return by the way he had come to **B**.
13:11 a certain old prophet living in **B**,
13:32 of the LORD against the altar in **B**
16:34 Hiel of **B** rebuilt Jericho.
2Ki 2: 2 Stay here; the LORD has sent me to **B**.
2: 2 So they went down to **B**.
2: 3 The company of the prophets at **B**
2:23 From there Elisha went up to **B**.
10:29 of the golden calves at **B** and Dan.
17:28 from Samaria came to live in **B**
23: 4 Valley and took the ashes to **B**.
23:15 Even the altar at **B**, the high place
23:17 pronounced against the altar of **B**
23:19 Just as he had done at **B**, Josiah
1Ch 7:28 **B** and its surrounding villages,
2Ch 13:19 and took from him the towns of **B**,
Ezr 2:28 of **B** and Ai 223
Ne 7:32 of **B** and Ai 123
11:31 Aija, **B** and its settlements,
Jer 48:13 was ashamed when they trusted in **B**.
Hos 10:15 Thus will it happen to you, O **B**,
12: 4 He found him at **B** and talked
Am 3:14 I will destroy the altars of **B**;
4: 4 "Go to **B** and sin; go to Gilgal and
5: 5 do not seek **B**, do not go to Gilgal,
5: 5 and **B** will be reduced to nothing."
5: 6 **B** will have no-one to quench it.
7:10 Amaziah the priest of **B** sent a
7:13 Don't prophesy any more at **B**,
Zec 7: 2 The people of **B** had sent Sharezer

Bethesda

Jn 5: 2 pool, which in Aramaic is called **B**

Bethlehem (Bethlehemite)

1. Town in Judah about 5 miles south of Jerusalem. Also known as Ephrath (Ge 35:16,19; 48:7), Ephrathah (Ru 4:11; 1Ch 4:4; Ps 132:6) and Bethlehem Ephrathah (Mic 5:2). Rachel buried near here (Ge 35:19; 48:7); book of Ruth set here. David's birthplace where he was anointed (1Sa 16:1–13). Micah predicted Messiah's birth here (Mic 5:2; Mt 2:6), fulfilled by Christ's birth in the "town of David" (Lk 2:11). **2.** Town in territory of Zebulun, about 7 miles north-west of Nazareth (Jos 19:15). Probably the home of Ibzan (Jdg 12:8).

Ge 35:19 on the way to Ephrath (that is, **B**).
48: 7 the road to Ephrath" (that is, **B**).
Jos 19:15 Nahalal, Shimron, Idalah and **B**.
Jdg 12: 8 After him, Ibzan of **B** led Israel.
12:10 Ibzan died, and was buried in **B**.
17: 7 A young Levite from **B** in Judah, who
17: 9 "I'm a Levite from **B** in Judah," he
19: 1 took a concubine from **B** in Judah.
19: 2 to her father's house in **B**, Judah.
19:18 "We are on our way from **B** in Judah
19:18 I have been to **B** in Judah and now I
Ru 1: 1 and a man from **B** in Judah, together
1: 2 They were Ephrathites from **B**, Judah.
1:19 women went on until they came to **B**.
1:19 When they arrived in **B**, the whole
1:22 her daughter-in-law, arriving in **B**
2: 4 Just then Boaz arrived from **B** and
4:11 in Ephrathah and be famous in **B**.
1Sa 16: 1 I am sending you to Jesse of **B**.
16: 4 When he arrived at **B**, the elders
16:18 I have seen a son of Jesse of **B**
17:12 Jesse, who was from **B** in Judah.
1Sa 17:15 Saul to tend his father's sheep at **B**.
17:58 the son of your servant Jesse of **B**."
20: 6 asked my permission to hurry to **B**,
20:28 asked me for permission to go to **B**.
2Sa 2:32 him in his father's tomb at **B**.
23:14 the Philistine garrison was at **B**.
23:15 from the well near the gate of **B**!"
23:16 from the well near the gate of **B**
23:24 of Joab, Elhanan son of Dodo from **B**,
1Ch 2:51 Salma the father of **B**, and Hareph
2:54 The descendants of Salma: **B**,
4: 4 of Ephrathah and father of **B**.
11:16 the Philistine garrison was at **B**.
11:17 from the well near the gate of **B**!"
11:18 from the well near the gate of **B**
11:26 of Joab, Elhanan son of Dodo from **B**,
2Ch 11: 6 **B**, Etam, Tekoa,
Ezr 2:21 the men of **B** 123
Ne 7:26 the men of **B** and Netophah 188
Jer 41:17 near **B** on their way to Egypt
Mic 5: 2 "But you, **B** Ephrathah, though you
Mt 2: 1 After Jesus was born in **B** in Judea,
2: 5 "In **B** in Judea," they replied, "for
2: 6 "'But you, **B**, in the land of Judah,
2: 8 He sent them to **B** and said, "Go and
2:16 orders to kill all the boys in **B**
Lk 2: 4 to **B** the town of David, because he
2:15 "Let's go to **B** and see this thing
Jn 7:42 from **B**, the town where David lived?"

Bethlehemite (Bethlehem)

2Sa 21:19 Elhanan son of Jaare-Oregim the **B**

Bethphage

Town near Bethany, on slopes of Mount of Olives, near the road from Jerusalem to Jericho. Here the disciples found colt for Jesus to ride into Jerusalem (Mt 21:1; Mk 11:1; Lk 19:29).

Mt 21: 1 came to **B** on the Mount of Olives,
Mk 11: 1 **B** and Bethany at the Mount of Olives,
Lk 19:29 As he approached **B** and Bethany

Bethsaida

1. City north of Sea of Galilee, east of River Jordan. Originally a small town, but Philip the Tetrarch raised its status to a city and called it Julias. Home of Peter, Andrew and Philip (Jn 1:44), and possibly James and John (Lk 5:10). **2.** City east of the Jordan, about 2 miles north of Sea of Galilee. Site associated with the feeding of the 5000 (Lk 9:10–17), and healing a blind man (Mk 8:22–26).
(Possibly these two descriptions relate to the same place.)

Mt 11:21 "Woe to you, Korazin! Woe to you, **B**!
Mk 6:45 go on ahead of him to **B**,
8:22 They came to **B**, and some people
Lk 9:10 by themselves to a town called **B**,
10:13 "Woe to you, Korazin! Woe to you, **B**!
Jn 1:44 and Peter, was from the town of **B**.
12:21 They came to Philip, who was from **B**

Bethuel

Ge 22:22 Kesed, Hazo, Pildash, Jidlaph and **B**."
22:23 **B** became the father of Rebekah.
24:15 the daughter of **B** son of Milcah,
24:24 **B**, the son that Milcah bore to Nahor.
24:47 'The daughter of **B** son of Nahor,
24:50 Laban and **B** answered, "This is from
25:20 of **B** the Aramean from Paddan Aram
28: 2 the house of your mother's father **B**.
28: 5 to Laban son of **B** the Aramean,
1Ch 4:30 **B**, Hormah, Ziklag,

Bethul

Jos 19: 4 Eltolad, **B**, Hormah,

Betonim

Jos 13:26 from Heshbon to Ramath Mizpah and **B**,

Betray (Betrayed, Betrayer, Betraying, Betrays)

1Ch 12:17 But if you have come to **b** me to my
Ps 89:33 nor will I ever **b** my faithfulness.

Pr 16:10 and his mouth should not **b** justice.
25: 9 do not **b** another man's confidence,
Isa 16: 3 do not **b** the refugees.
24:16 Woe to me! The treacherous **b**!
24:16 With treachery the treacherous **b**!"
Mt 10:21 "Brother will **b** brother to death,
24:10 and will **b** and hate each other,
26:21 the truth, one of you will **b** me."
26:23 into the bowl with me will **b** me.
26:25 Judas, the one who would **b** him, said,
Mk 13:12 "Brother will **b** brother to death,
14:10 went to the chief priests to **b** Jesus
14:18 the truth, one of you will **b** me—
Lk 22: 4 with them how he might **b** Jesus.
22:21 the hand of him who is going to **b** me
Jn 6:64 did not believe and who would **b** him.
6:71 of the Twelve, was later to **b** him.)
12: 4 who was later to **b** him, objected,
13: 2 Iscariot, son of Simon, to **b** Jesus.
13:11 For he knew who was going to **b** him,
13:21 truth, one of you is going to **b** me."
21:20 "Lord, who is going to **b** you?"

Betrayed (Betray)

2Sa 19:26 But Ziba my servant **b** me.
Ps 73:15 I would have **b** your children.
Isa 33: 1 O traitor, you who have not been **b**!
33: 1 you stop betraying, you will be **b**.
Jer 12: 6 even they have **b** you;
Lam 1: 2 All her friends have **b** her;
1:19 "I called to my allies but they **b** me.
Mt 10: 4 Zealot and Judas Iscariot, who **b** him.
17:22 going to be **b** into the hands of men.
20:18 and the Son of Man will be **b** to the
26:45 Man is **b** into the hands of sinners.
27: 3 Judas, who had **b** him, saw that Jesus
27: 4 said, "for I have **b** innocent blood.
Mk 3:19 Judas Iscariot, who **b** him.
9:31 going to be **b** into the hands of men.
10:33 "and the Son of Man will be **b** to the
14:41 Man is **b** into the hands of sinners.
Lk 9:44 to be **b** into the hands of men."
21:16 You will be **b** even by parents,
Jn 18: 2 Now Judas, who **b** him, knew the place,
Ac 7:52 And now you have **b** and murdered him
1Co 11:23 on the night he was **b**, took bread,

Betrayer (Betray)

Mt 26:46 Rise, let us go! Here comes my **b**!"
26:48 Now the **b** had arranged a signal with
Mk 14:42 Rise! Let us go! Here comes my **b**!"
14:44 Now the **b** had arranged a signal with

Betraying (Betray)

Isa 33: 1 you stop **b**, you will be betrayed.
Lk 22:48 Jesus asked him, "Judas, are you **b**

Betrays (Betray)

Pr 11:13 A gossip **b** a confidence, but a
20:19 A gossip **b** a confidence; so avoid a
Isa 21: 2 The traitor **b**, the looter takes loot.
Hab 2: 5 indeed, wine **b** him; he is arrogant
Mt 26:24 woe to that man who **b** the Son of Man
Mk 14:21 woe to that man who **b** the Son of Man
Lk 22:22 but woe to that man who **b** him."

Betroth (Betrothed)

Hos 2:19 I will **b** you to me for ever;
2:19 I will **b** you in righteousness
2:20 I will **b** you in faithfulness, and

Betrothed (Betroth)

Dt 22:27 and though the **b** girl screamed,
2Sa 3:14 "Give me my wife Michal, whom I **b** to

Better (Good)

Ge 29:19 Laban said, "It's **b** that I give her
Ex 14:12 It would have been **b** for us to serve
Nu 11:18 to eat! We were **b** off in Egypt!"
14: 3 it be **b** for us to go back to Egypt?"
Dt 17:20 not consider himself **b** than his
Jdg 8: 2 **b** than the full grape harvest
9: 2 'Which is **b** for you: to have all
11:25 Are you **b** than Balak son of Zippor,
Jdg 18:19 Isn't it **b** that you serve a tribe
Ru 4:15 who loves you and who is **b** to you
1Sa 14:30 How much **b** it would have been if the
15:22 LORD? To obey is **b** than sacrifice,
15:22 to heed is **b** than the fat of rams.
15:28 your neighbours—to one **b** than you.
16:16 upon you, and you will feel **b**."
16:23 he would feel **b**, and the evil spirit
29: 4 How **b** could he regain his master's
2Sa 14:32 be **b** for me if I were still there!"'
17:14 Arkite is **b** than that of Ahithophel.
18: 3 It would be **b** now for you to give
1Ki 2:32 **b** men and more upright than he.
19: 4 I am no **b** than my ancestors."
21: 2 I will give you a **b** vineyard
2Ki 5:12 **b** than any of the waters of Israel?
2Ch 21:13 house, men who were **b** than you.
Est 1:19 to someone else who is **b** than she.
Ps 37:16 **B** the little that the righteous have
63: 3 Because your love is **b** than life,
84:10 **B** is one day in your courts than
118: 8 It is **b** to take refuge in the LORD
118: 9 It is **b** to take refuge in the LORD
Pr 3:14 and yields **b** returns than gold.
8:19 My fruit is **b** than fine gold;
12: 9 **B** to be a nobody and yet have a
15:16 **B** a little with the fear of the LORD
15:17 **B** a meal of vegetables where there
16: 8 **B** a little with righteousness than
16:16 How much **b** to get wisdom than gold,
16:19 **B** to be lowly in spirit and among
16:32 **B** a patient man than a warrior,
17: 1 **B** a dry crust with peace and quiet
17:12 **B** to meet a bear robbed of her cubs
19: 1 **B** a poor man whose walk is blameless
19:22 **b** to be poor than a liar.
21: 9 **B** to live on a corner of the roof
21:19 **B** to live in a desert than with a
22: 1 to be esteemed is **b** than silver or
25: 7 is **b** for him to say to you,
25:24 **B** to live on a corner of the roof
27: 5 **B** is open rebuke than hidden love.
27:10 **b** a neighbour nearby than a brother
28: 6 **B** a poor man whose walk is blameless
Ecc 2:13 I saw that wisdom is **b** than folly,
2:13 just as light is **b** than darkness.
2:24 A man can do nothing **b** than to eat
3:12 I know that there is nothing **b** for
3:22 I saw that there is nothing **b** for a
4: 3 **b** than both is he who has not yet
4: 6 **B** one handful with tranquillity than
4: 9 Two are **b** than one, because they
4:13 **B** a poor but wise youth than an old
5: 5 It is **b** not to vow than to make
6: 3 a stillborn child is **b** off than he.
6: 9 **B** what the eye sees than the roving
7: 1 A good name is **b** than fine perfume,
7: 1 the day of death **b** than the day of
7: 2 is **b** to go to a house of mourning
7: 3 Sorrow is **b** than laughter,
7: 5 is **b** to heed a wise man's rebuke
7: 8 The end of a matter is **b** than its
7: 8 and patience is **b** than pride.
7:10 Do not say, "Why were the old days **b**
8:12 I know that it will go **b** with
8:15 because nothing is **b** for a man under
9: 4 a live dog is **b** off than a dead lion
9:16 I said, "Wisdom is **b** than strength."
9:18 Wisdom is **b** than weapons of war,
SS 5: 9 How is your beloved **b** than others,
5: 9 How is your beloved **b** than others,
Isa 56: 5 a name **b** than sons and daughters;
56:12 will be like today, or even far **b**.
Lam 4: 9 Those killed by the sword are **b** off
Eze 15: 2 how is the wood of a vine **b** than
Da 1:15 **b** nourished than any of the young
1:20 he found them ten times **b** than all
Hos 2: 7 for then I was **b** off than now.'
Am 6: 2 Are they **b** off than your two
Jnh 4: 3 it is **b** for me to die than to live."
4: 8 be **b** for me to die than to live."
Na 3: 8 Are you **b** than Thebes, situated on
Mt 5:29 It is **b** for you to lose one part of
5:30 It is **b** for you to lose one part of
18: 6 it would be **b** for him to have a
18: 8 It is **b** for you to enter life maimed
Mt 18: 9 It is **b** for you to enter life with
19:10 it is **b** not to marry."
26:24 **b** for him if he had not been born."
Mk 5:26 instead of getting **b** she grew worse.
9:42 it would be **b** for him to be thrown
9:43 It is **b** for you to enter life maimed
9:45 **b** for you to enter life crippled
9:47 It is **b** for you to enter the kingdom
14:21 **b** for him if he had not been born."
Lk 5:39 new, for he says, 'The old is **b**.'"
10:42 Mary has chosen what is **b**, and it
14:10 'Friend, move up to a **b** place.'
17: 2 **b** for him to be thrown into the sea
Jn 4:52 as to the time when his son got **b**,
11:12 "LORD, if he sleeps, he will get **b**."
11:50 You do not realise that it is **b** for
Ro 3: 9 Are we any **b**? Not at all! We have
14:21 is **b** not to eat meat or drink wine
1Co 7: 9 **b** to marry than to burn with passion.
7:38 who does not marry her does even **b**.
8: 8 if we do not eat, and no **b** if we do.
Eph 1:17 so that you may know him **b**.
Php 1:23 be with Christ, which is **b** by far;
2: 3 consider others **b** than yourselves.
1Ti 6: 2 they are to serve them even **b**,
Phm :16 **b** than a slave, as a dear brother
Heb 6: 9 we are confident of **b** things
7:19 and a **b** hope is introduced, by which
7:22 the guarantee of a **b** covenant.
8: 6 and it is founded on **b** promises.
9:23 with **b** sacrifices than these.
10:34 had **b** and lasting possessions.
11: 4 Abel offered God a **b** sacrifice
11:16 they were longing for a **b** country
11:35 they might gain a **b** resurrection.
11:40 God had planned something **b** for us
12:24 a **b** word than the blood of Abel.
1Pe 3:17 is **b**, if it is God's will, to suffer
2Pe 2:21 would have been **b** for them not to

Beulah

Isa 62: 4 called Hephzibah, and your land **B**;

Beware

2Ki 6: 9 "**B** of passing that place, because
Job 36:21 **B** of turning to evil, which you seem
Isa 22:17 "**B**, the LORD is about to take firm
Jer 7:32 **b**, the days are coming, declares the
9: 4 "**B** of your friends; do not trust
19: 6 **b**, the days are coming, declares the
Lk 20:46 "**B** of the teachers of the law. They

Bewildered (Bewilderment)

Est 3:15 but the city of Susa was **b**.
Isa 21: 3 I am **b** by what I see.
Mk 16: 8 Trembling and **b**, the women went out

Bewilderment (Bewildered)

Ac 2: 6 a crowd came together in **b**, because

Bewitched (Witchcraft)

Gal 3: 1 You foolish Galatians! Who has **b** you?

Bezai

Ezr 2:17 of **B** 323
Ne 7:23 of **B** 324
10:18 Hodiah, Hashum, **B**,

Bezalel

Craftsman of the tribe of Judah (1Ch 2:20; 2Ch1:5) chosen, with Oholiab, to organise building of the tabernacle (Ex 31:1–6; 35:30–36:7). Credited with making the ark (Ex 37:1–9).

Ex 31: 2 "See I have chosen **B** son of Uri,
35:30 the LORD has chosen **B** son of Uri
36: 1 **B**, Oholiab and every skilled person
36: 2 Moses summoned **B** and Oholiab and
37: 1 **B** made the ark of acacia wood—
38:22 (**B** son of Uri, the son of Hur,
1Ch 2:20 of Uri, and Uri the father of **B**.
2Ch 1: 5 the bronze altar that **B** son of Uri,
Ezr 10:30 Mattaniah, **B**, Binnui and Manasseh.

Bezek

Jdg 1: 4 struck down ten thousand men at **B**.
1Sa 11: 8 Saul mustered them at **B**, the men of

Bezer
Dt 4:43 **B** in the desert plateau,
Jos 20: 8 they designated **B** in the desert
21:36 from the tribe of Reuben, **B**, Jahaz,
1Ch 6:78 They received **B** in the desert,
7:37 **B**, Hod, Shamma, Shilshah, Ithran

Bicri
2Sa 20: 1 **B**, a Benjamite, happened to be there.
20: 2 David to follow Sheba son of **B**.
20: 6 "Now Sheba son of **B** will do us more
20: 7 Jerusalem to pursue Sheba son of **B**.
20:10 Abishai pursued Sheba son of **B**.
20:13 with Joab to pursue Sheba son of **B**.
20:21 A man named Sheba son of **B**, from the
20:22 cut off the head of Sheba son of **B**

Bidding
Ps 103:20 who do his **b**, who obey his word.
148: 8 clouds, stormy winds that do his **b**,

Bidkar
2Ki 9:25 Jehu said to **B**, his chariot officer,

Bier
2Sa 3:31 David himself walked behind the **b**.
2Ch 16:14 They laid him on a **b** covered with

Big (Bigger)
Ex 29:20 on the **b** toes of their right feet.
Lev 8:23 and on the **b** toe of his right foot.
8:24 on the **b** toes of their right feet.
14:14 and on the **b** toe of his right foot.
14:17 and on the **b** toe of his right foot,
14:25 and on the **b** toe of his right foot.
14:28 and on the **b** toe of his right foot.
Jdg 1: 6 and cut off his thumbs and **b** toes.
1: 7 their thumbs and **b** toes cut off
9:38 "Where is your **b** talk now,
2Sa 18:17 threw him into a **b** pit in the forest
Mt 27:60 He rolled a **b** stone in front of the
Mk 4:32 with such **b** branches that the birds
Ac 22:28 "I had to pay a **b** price for my

Bigger (Big)
Lk 7:43 one who had the **b** debt cancelled.
12:18 tear down my barns and build **b** ones,

Bigtha
Est 1:10 **B**, Abagtha, Zethar and Carcas—

Bigthana
Est 2:21 **B** and Teresh, two of the king's
6: 2 Mordecai had exposed **B** and Teresh,

Bigvai
Ezr 2: 2 Mordecai, Bilshan, Mispar, **B**, Rehum
2:14 of **B** 2,056
8:14 of the descendants of **B**, Uthai and
Ne 7: 7 Mordecai, Bilshan, Mispereth, **B**,
7:19 of **B** 2,067
10:16 Adonijah, **B**, Adin,

Bildad See **Job[1] 2.**
Job 2:11 Eliphaz the Temanite, **B** the Shuhite
8: 1 **B** the Shuhite
18: 1 **B** the Shuhite
25: 1 **B** the Shuhite
42: 9 Eliphaz the Temanite, **B** the Shuhite

Bileam
1Ch 6:70 the Israelites gave Aner and **B**,

Bilgah (Bilgah's)
1Ch 24:14 the fifteenth to **B**, the sixteenth to
Ne 12: 5 Mijamin, Moadiah, **B**,

Bilgah's (Bilgah)
Ne 12:18 of **B**, Shammua; of Shemaiah's,

Bilgai
Ne 10: 8 Maaziah, **B** and Shemaiah. These were

Bilhah
Ge 29:29 Laban gave his servant girl **B** to his
30: 3 she said, "Here is **B**, my maidservant.
30: 4 she gave him her servant **B** as a wife.
30: 7 Rachel's servant **B** conceived again
35:22 slept with his father's concubine **B**
35:25 The sons of Rachel's maidservant **B**:
37: 2 the sons of **B** and the sons of Zilpah,
46:25 were the sons born to Jacob by **B**,
1Ch 4:29 **B**, Ezem, Tolad,
7:13 and Shillem—the descendants of **B**.

Bilhan
Ge 36:27 The sons of Ezer: **B**, Zaavan and Akan.
1Ch 1:42 The sons of Ezer: **B**, Zaavan and Akan.
7:10 The son of Jediael: **B**. The sons of **B**:

Bill
Lk 16: 6 "The manager told him,'Take your **b**,
16: 7 "He told him,'Take your **b** and make

Billowed (Billows)
Ex 19:18 The smoke **b** up from it like smoke

Billows (Billowed)
Joel 2:30 blood and fire and **b** of smoke.
Ac 2:19 blood and fire and **b** of smoke.

Bilshan
Ezr 2: 2 Seraiah, Reelaiah, Mordecai, **B**,
Ne 7: 7 Raamiah, Nahamani, Mordecai, **B**,

Bimhal
1Ch 7:33 Pasach, **B** and Ashvath.

Bind (Binding, Bindings, Binds, Bound)
Nu 30: 2 an oath to **b** himself by a pledge,
Dt 6: 8 hands and **b** them on your foreheads.
11:18 hands and **b** them on your foreheads.
Ne 10:29 and **b** themselves with a curse and an
Job 38:31 "Can you **b** the beautiful Pleiades?
Ps 119:61 Though the wicked **b** me with ropes,
149: 8 to **b** their kings with fetters,
Pr 3: 3 **b** them around your neck,
6:21 **B** them upon your heart for ever;
7: 3 **B** them on your fingers; write them
Isa 8:16 **B** up the testimony and seal up the
56: 6 foreigners who **b** themselves to the
61: 1 He has sent me to **b** up the
Jer 50: 5 They will come and **b** themselves to
Eze 34:16 I will **b** up the injured and
Hos 6: 1 but he will **b** up our wounds.
Mt 16:19 whatever you **b** on earth will be bound
18:18 whatever you **b** on earth will be bound
Mk 5: 3 and no-one could **b** him any more, not
Ac 21:11 will **b** the owner of this belt

Binding (Bind)
Ge 37: 7 We were **b** sheaves of corn out in the
Nu 30: 9 or divorced woman will be **b** on her.
30:14 her vows or the pledges **b** on her.
Jos 2:17 will not be **b** on us unless,
Jdg 16:21 **B** him with bronze shackles, they set
Ne 9:38 we are making a **b** agreement, putting
Heb 2: 2 the message spoken by angels was **b**,

Bindings (Bind)
Jdg 15:14 and the **b** dropped from his hands.

Binds (Bind)
Nu 30: 3 or **b** herself by a pledge
30: 6 rash promise by which she **b** herself
30: 8 he nullifies the vow that **b** her or
30: 8 rash promise by which she **b** herself,
30:10 or **b** herself by a pledge under oath
Job 5:18 For he wounds, but he also **b** up;
30:18 he **b** me like the neck of my garment
147: 3 and **b** up their wounds.

Isa 30:26 when the Lord **b** up the bruises of
Col 3:14 **b** them all together in perfect unity.

Binea
1Ch 8:37 Moza was the father of **B**;
9:43 Moza was the father of **B**;

Binnui
Ezr 8:33 son of Jeshua and Noadiah son of **B**.
10:30 Mattaniah, Bezalel, **B** and Manasseh.
10:38 From the descendants of **B**: Shimei,
Ne 3:18 countrymen under **B** son of Henadad,
3:24 Next to him, **B** son of Henadad
7:15 of **B** 648
10: 9 The Levites: Jeshua son of Azaniah, **B**
12: 8 The Levites were Jeshua, **B**, Kadmiel,

Bird (Bird's, Birds)
Ge 1:21 winged **b** according to its kind.
6:20 Two of every kind of **b**,
7: 3 also seven of every kind of **b**,
7:14 and every **b** according to its kind,
Lev 7:26 eat the blood of any **b** or animal.
14: 6 He is then to take the live **b** and
14: 6 into the blood of the **b** that was
14: 7 the live **b** in the open fields.
14:51 the scarlet yarn and the live **b**,
14:51 dip them into the blood of the dead **b**
14:52 the fresh water, the live **b**, the
14:53 he is to release the live **b** in the
17:13 who hunts any animal or **b** that may
20:25 defile yourselves by any animal or **b**
Dt 4:17 or like any animal on earth or any **b**
14:11 You may eat any clean **b**.
Job 28: 7 No **b** of prey knows that hidden path,
41: 5 Can you make a pet of him like a **b**
Ps 11: 1 "Flee like a **b** to your mountain.
50:11 I know every **b** in the mountains, and
102: 7 become like a **b** alone on a roof.
124: 7 We have escaped like a **b** out of the
Pr 6: 5 a **b** from the snare of the fowler.
7:23 like a **b** darting into a snare,
27: 8 Like a **b** that strays from its nest
Ecc 10:20 because a **b** of the air may carry
10:20 and a **b** on the wing may report what
Isa 46:11 From the east I summon a **b** of prey;
Jer 4:25 every **b** in the sky had flown away.
12: 9 like a speckled **b** of prey that
Lam 3:52 without cause hunted me like a **b**.
Eze 39:17 Call out to every kind of **b** and all
44:31 must not eat anything, **b** or animal,
Da 4:33 and his nails like the claws of a **b**.
7: 6 it had four wings like those of a **b**.
Hos 9:11 glory will fly away like a **b**—
Am 3: 5 Does a **b** fall into a trap on the
Rev 18: 2 for every unclean and detestable **b**.

Bird's (Bird)
Lev 14:52 purify the house with the **b** blood
Dt 22: 6 If you come across a **b** nest beside

Birds (Bird)
Ge 1:20 and let **b** fly above the earth across
1:22 let the **b** increase on the earth."
1:26 of the sea and the **b** of the air,
1:28 the **b** of the air and over every
1:30 all the **b** of the air and all the
2:19 the field and all the **b** of the air.
2:20 the **b** of the air and all the beasts
6: 7 and **b** of the air—for I am grieved
7: 8 of **b** and of all creatures that move
7:21 **b**, livestock, wild animals,
7:23 the **b** of the air were wiped from the
8:17 the **b**, the animals, and all the
8:19 all the **b**—everything that moves on
8:20 all the clean animals and clean **b**,
9: 2 the earth and all the **b** of the air,
9:10 **b**, the livestock and all the wild
15:10 **b**, however, he did not cut in half.
15:11 **b** of prey came down on the carcasses,
40:17 but the **b** were eating them out of
40:19 And the **b** will eat away your flesh."
Lev 1:14 is a burnt offering of **b**,
11:13 "'These are the **b** you are to detest

Lev 11:46 animals, **b**, every living thing
14: 4 live clean **b** and some cedar wood,
14: 5 order that one of the **b** be killed
14:49 to take two **b** and some cedar wood,
14:50 He shall kill one of the **b** over
20:25 and between unclean and clean **b**.
Dt 28:26 be food for all the **b** of the air
1Sa 17:44 "and I'll give your flesh to the **b**
17:46 Philistine army to the **b** of the air
2Sa 21:10 she did not let the **b** of the air
1Ki 4:33 animals and **b**, reptiles and fish.
14:11 and the **b** of the air will feed on
16: 4 and the **b** of the air will feed on
21:24 and the **b** of the air will feed on
Job 12: 7 or the **b** of the air, and they will
28:21 even from the **b** of the air.
35:11 us wiser than the **b** of the air?'
Ps 8: 8 the **b** of the air, and the fish of
78:27 flying **b** like sand on the seashore.
79: 2 as food to the **b** of the air,
104:12 The **b** of the air nest by the waters;
104:17 There the **b** make their nests; the
148:10 small creatures and flying **b**,
Pr 1:17 a net in full view of all the **b**!
Ecc 9:12 or **b** are taken in a snare, so men
12: 4 men rise up at the sound of **b**,
Isa 16: 2 Like fluttering **b** pushed from the
18: 6 be left to the mountain **b** of prey
18: 6 the **b** will feed on them all summer,
31: 5 Like **b** hovering overhead, the LORD
Jer 5:26 lie in wait like men who snare **b**
5:27 Like cages full of **b**, their houses
7:33 become food for the **b** of the air
9:10 The **b** of the air have fled and the
12: 4 the animals and **b** have perished.
12: 9 other **b** of prey surround and attack?
15: 3 the **b** of the air and the beasts
16: 4 become food for the **b** of the air
19: 7 as food to the **b** of the air
34:20 become food for the **b** of the air
Eze 13:20 which you ensnare people like **b**
13:20 the people that you ensnare like **b**.
17:23 **B** of every kind will nest in it;
29: 5 of the earth and the **b** of the air.
31: 6 All the **b** of the air nested in its
31:13 All the **b** of the air settled on the
32: 4 I will let all the **b** of the air
38:20 fish of the sea, the **b** of the air
39: 4 as food to all kinds of carrion **b**
Da 2:38 of the field and the **b** of the air.
4:12 and the **b** of the air lived in its
4:14 and the **b** from its branches.
4:21 its branches for the **b** of the air—
Hos 2:18 the **b** of the air and the creatures
4: 3 the beasts of the field and the **b** of
7:12 pull them down like **b** of the air.
11:11 They will come trembling like **b** from
Zep 1: 3 **b** of the air and the fish of the sea.
Mt 6:26 Look at the **b** of the air; they do
8:20 and **b** of the air have nests,
13: 4 and the **b** came and ate it up.
13:32 the **b** of the air come and perch
Mk 4: 4 and the **b** came and ate it up.
4:32 **b** of the air can perch in its shade."
Lk 8: 5 and the **b** of the air ate it up.
9:58 and **b** of the air have nests
12:24 much more valuable you are than **b**!
13:19 and the **b** of the air perched in
Ac 10:12 of the earth and **b** of the air.
11: 6 beasts, reptiles, and **b** of the air.
Ro 1:23 man and **b** and animals and reptiles.
1Co 15:39 **b** another and fish another.
Jas 3: 7 All kinds of animals, **b**, reptiles
Rev 19:17 to all the **b** flying in mid-air,
19:21 **b** gorged themselves on their flesh.

Birsha
Ge 14: 2 **B** king of Gomorrah, Shinab king of

Birth (Bear[1])
Ge 3:16 you will give **b** to children.
4: 1 became pregnant and gave **b** to Cain.
4: 2 Later she gave **b** to his brother Abel.
4:17 became pregnant and gave **b** to Enoch.
4:20 Adah gave **b** to Jabal; he was the
4:25 she gave **b** to a son and named him
11:28 the Chaldeans, in the land of his **b**.
25:13 listed in the order of their **b**:
25:24 the time came for her to give **b**,
25:26 old when Rebekah gave **b** to them.
29:32 Leah became pregnant and gave **b** to a
29:33 and when she gave **b** to a son she
29:34 and when she gave **b** to a son she
29:35 and when she gave **b** to a son she
30:21 Some time later she gave **b** to a
30:23 She became pregnant and gave **b** to a
30:25 After Rachel gave **b** to Joseph, Jacob
31: 8 the flocks gave **b** to speckled young;
35:16 Rachel began to give **b** and had great
38: 3 she became pregnant and gave **b** to a
38: 4 She conceived again and gave **b** to a
38: 5 She gave **b** to still another son and
38: 5 was at Kezib that she gave **b** to him.
38:27 the time came for her to give **b**,
38:28 she was giving **b**, one of them put
50:23 were placed at **b** on Joseph's knees.
Ex 1:19 give **b** before the midwives arrive."
2: 2 she became pregnant and gave **b** to a
2:22 Zipporah gave **b** to a son, and Moses
21:22 she gives **b** prematurely but there is
28:10 in the order of their **b**—six names
Lev 12: 2 pregnant and gives **b** to a son
12: 5 If she gives **b** to a daughter, for
12: 7 who gives **b** to a boy or a girl.
Nu 11:12 Did I give them **b**? Why do you tell
Dt 32:18 you forgot the God who gave you **b**.
Jdg 13: 5 because you will conceive and give **b**
13: 5 a Nazirite, set apart to God from **b**,
13: 7 will conceive and give **b** to a son.
13: 7 from **b** until the day of his death.'"
13:24 The woman gave **b** to a boy and named
16:17 a Nazirite set apart to God since **b**.
Ru 1:12 tonight and then gave **b** to sons—
4:13 and she gave **b** to a son.
4:15 than seven sons, has given him **b**."
1Sa 1:20 Hannah conceived and gave **b** to a son.
2:21 **b** to three sons and two daughters.
4:19 she went into labour and gave **b**, but
4:20 you have given **b** to a son.
2Sa 12:24 She gave **b** to a son, and they named
1Ki 11: 3 He had seven hundred wives of royal **b**
2Ki 4:17 that same time she gave **b** to a son,
19: 3 children come to the point of **b**
1Ch 2:49 She also gave **b** to Shaaph the father
4: 9 saying, "I gave **b** to him in pain.
4:17 One of Mered's wives gave **b** to
4:18 (His Judean wife gave **b** to Jered
7:14 She gave **b** to Makir the father
7:16 Makir's wife Maacah gave **b** to a son
7:18 His sister Hammoleketh gave **b** to
7:23 became pregnant and gave **b** to a son.
Job 3: 1 mouth and cursed the day of his **b**.
3: 3 "May the day of my **b** perish,
3:11 "Why did I not perish at **b**, and die
15:35 They conceive trouble and give **b** to
31:18 and from my **b** I guided the widow—
38:29 gives **b** to the frost from the
39: 1 know when the mountain goats give **b**?
39: 2 Do you know the time they give **b**?
Ps 7:14 trouble gives **b** to disillusionment.
22:10 From **b** I was cast upon you;
51: 5 Surely I was sinful at **b**, sinful
58: 3 Even from **b** the wicked go astray;
71: 6 From my **b** I have relied on you;
Pr 8:24 there were no oceans, I was given **b**,
8:25 before the hills, I was given **b**,
23:25 may she who gave you **b** rejoice!
Ecc 7: 1 of death better than the day of **b**.
10:17 O land whose king is of noble **b**
SS 8: 5 she who was in labour gave you **b**.
Isa 7:14 with child and will give **b** to a son,
8: 3 she conceived and gave **b** to a son.
23: 4 neither been in labour nor given **b**;
26:17 woman with child and about to give **b**
26:18 in pain, but we gave **b** to wind.
26:18 not given **b** to people of the world.
26:19 the earth will give **b** to her dead.
33:11 conceive chaff, you give **b** to straw
37: 3 children come to the point of **b**
45:10 'What have you brought to **b**?'
46: 3 and have carried since your **b**.
Isa 48: 8 you were called a rebel from **b**.
49: 1 from my **b** he has made mention of
51: 2 and to Sarah, who gave you **b**.
59: 4 conceive trouble and give **b** to evil.
66: 7 she goes into labour, she gives **b**;
66: 8 than she gives **b** to her children.
66: 9 Do I bring to the moment of **b** and
Jer 2:14 Is Israel a servant, a slave by **b**?
2:27 and to stone, 'You gave me **b**.
15:10 Alas, my mother, that you gave me **b**,
22:26 who gave you **b** into another country,
50:12 who gave you **b** will be disgraced.
Eze 16: 3 Your ancestry and **b** were in the land
23: 4 They were mine and gave **b** to sons
31: 6 all the beasts of the field gave **b**
Hos 1: 6 Gomer conceived again and gave **b** to
5: 7 give **b** to illegitimate children.
9:11 no **b**, no pregnancy, no conception.
Mic 5: 3 when she who is in labour gives **b**
Mt 1:18 This is how the **b** of Jesus Christ
1:21 She will give **b** to a son, and you
1:23 with child and will give **b** to a son,
1:25 with her until she gave **b** to a son.
Lk 1:14 many will rejoice because of his **b**,
1:15 with the Holy Spirit even from **b**.
1:31 You will be with child and give **b** to
1:57 have her baby, she gave **b** to a son.
2: 7 she gave **b** to her firstborn, a son.
11:27 who gave you **b** and nursed you."
19:12 He said: "A man of noble **b** went to a
Jn 3: 6 Flesh gives **b** to flesh, but the
3: 6 but the Spirit gives **b** to spirit.
9: 1 he saw a man blind from **b**.
9:34 "You were steeped in sin at **b**; how
16:21 A woman giving **b** to a child has pain
Ac 3: 2 Now a man crippled from **b** was being
7: 8 him eight days after his **b**.
14: 8 lame from **b** and had never walked.
1Co 1:26 not many were of noble **b**.
Gal 1:15 when God, who set me apart from **b**
2:15 "We who are Jews by **b** and not
Eph 2:11 you who are Gentiles by **b** and called
Jas 1:15 it gives **b** to sin; and sin, when it
1:15 it is full-grown, gives **b** to death.
1:18 He chose to give us **b** through the
1Pe 1: 3 given us new **b** into a living hope
Rev 12: 2 in pain as she was about to give **b**.
12: 4 the woman who was about to give **b**,
12: 5 She gave **b** to a son, a male child,
12:13 who had given **b** to the male child.

Birthday (Bear[1])
Ge 40:20 Now the third day was Pharaoh's **b**,
Mt 14: 6 On Herod's **b** the daughter of
Mk 6:21 On his **b** Herod gave a banquet for

Birth-pains (Bear[1], Pains)
Mt 24: 8 All these are the beginning of **b**.
Mk 13: 8 These are the beginning of **b**.

Birthright (Bear[1])
Ge 25:31 Jacob replied, "First sell me your **b**.
25:32 "What good is the **b** to me?"
25:33 oath to him, selling his **b** to Jacob.
25:34 So Esau despised his **b**.
27:36 He took my **b**, and now he's taken
1Ch 5: 1 record in accordance with his **b**,

Birzaith
1Ch 7:31 Malkiel, who was the father of **B**.

Bishlam
Ezr 4: 7 **B**, Mithredath, Tabeel and the rest

Bit[1] (Bite, Bits[1])
Nu 21: 6 they **b** the people and many

Bit[2] (Bits[2])
2Ki 19:28 in your nose and my **b** in your mouth,
Ps 32: 9 but must be controlled by **b**
Isa 30:28 a **b** that leads them astray.
37:29 in your nose and my **b** in your mouth,

Bite (Bit, Bites, Biting, Bitten)
Jer 8:17 and they will **b** you,"
Am 5:19 the wall only to have a snake **b** him.
9: 3 I will command the serpent to **b** them.
Jn 6: 7 bread for each one to have a **b**!"

Bites (Bite)
Ge 49:17 that **b** the horse's head
Pr 23:32 In the end it **b** like a snake and
Ecc 10:11 If a snake **b** before it is charmed,

Bithiah
1Ch 4:18 daughter **B**, whom Mered had married.

Bithron
2Sa 2:29 continued through the whole **B**

Bithynia
Ac 16: 7 they tried to enter **B**, but the
1Pe 1: 1 Galatia, Cappadocia, Asia and **B**,

Biting (Bite)
Gal 5:15 If you keep on **b** and devouring each

Bits[1] (Bit[1])
Am 6:11 pieces and the small house into **b**.

Bits[2] (Bit[2])
Jas 3: 3 we put **b** into the mouths of horses

Bitten (Bite)
Nu 21: 8 who is **b** can look at it and live."
21: 9 Then when anyone was **b** by a snake
Ecc 10: 8 through a wall may be **b** by a snake.

Bitter (Bitterly, Bitterness)
Ge 27:34 he burst out with a loud and **b** cry
Ex 1:14 They made their lives **b** with hard
12: 8 along with **b** herbs, and bread
15:23 drink its water because it was **b**.
Nu 5:18 the **b** water that brings a curse.
5:19 may this **b** water that brings a curse
5:23 then wash them off into the **b** water.
5:24 make the woman drink the **b** water
5:24 enter her and cause **b** suffering.
5:27 go into her and cause **b** suffering
9:11 with unleavened bread and **b** herbs.
Dt 29:18 you that produces such **b** poison.
Ru 1:13 It is more **b** for me than for you,
1:20 Almighty has made my life very **b**.
1Sa 14:52 All the days of Saul there was **b** war
30: 6 each one was **b** in spirit because of
1Ki 2: 8 who called down **b** curses on me
2Ki 4:27 She is in **b** distress, but the LORD
Job 3:20 misery, and life to the **b** of soul,
13:26 For you write down **b** things against
23: 2 "Even today my complaint is **b**;
Ps 71:20 made me see troubles, many and **b**,
107:12 he subjected them to **b** labour;
Pr 5: 4 in the end she is **b** as gall,
27: 7 even what is **b** tastes sweet.
Ecc 7:26 I find more **b** than death the woman
Isa 5:20 who put **b** for sweet and sweet for **b**.
24: 9 the beer is **b** to its drinkers.
Jer 2:19 realise how evil and **b** it is for you
4:18 This is your punishment. How **b** it is!
6:26 with **b** wailing as for an only son,
9:15 eat **b** food and drink poisoned water.
23:15 "I will make them eat **b** food and
Lam 1: 4 grieve, and she is in **b** anguish.
3:15 He has filled me with **b** herbs and
Eze 21: 6 them with broken heart and **b** grief.
27:31 anguish of soul and with **b** mourning.
Am 8:10 and the end of it like a **b** day.
Zep 1:14 on the day of the LORD will be **b**,
Heb 12:15 that no **b** root grows up to cause
Jas 3:14 if you harbour **b** envy and selfish
Rev 8:11 A third of the waters turned **b**, and
8:11 from the waters that had become **b**.

Bitterly (Bitter)
Ge 50:10 they lamented loudly and **b**;
Nu 14:39 all the Israelites, they mourned **b**.
Jdg 5:23 'Curse its people **b**, because they
21: 2 raising their voices and weeping **b**.
2Sa 13:36 and all his servants wept very **b**.
2Ki 14:26 The LORD had seen how **b** everyone
20: 3 And Hezekiah wept **b**.
Ezr 10: 1 They too wept **b**.
Est 4: 1 into the city, wailing loudly and **b**.
Isa 22: 4 "Turn away from me; let me weep **b**.
33: 7 streets; the envoys of peace weep **b**.
38: 3 And Hezekiah wept **b**.
Jer 13:17 of your pride; my eyes will weep **b**,
22:10 rather, weep **b** for him who is exiled,
48: 5 to Luhith, weeping **b** as they go;
Lam 1: 2 **B** she weeps at night, tears are upon
Eze 27:30 They will raise their voice and cry **b**
Hos 12:14 Ephraim has **b** provoked him to anger;
Zec 12:10 and grieve **b** for him as one grieves
Mt 26:75 And he went outside and wept **b**.
Lk 22:62 he went outside and wept **b**.

Bitterness (Bitter)
Ge 49:23 With **b** archers attacked him;
Dt 32:32 poison, and their clusters with **b**.
1Sa 1:10 In **b** of soul Hannah wept much
15:32 "Surely the **b** of death is past.
2Sa 2:26 you realise that this will end in **b**?
Job 7:11 I will complain in the **b** of my soul.
10: 1 and speak out in the **b** of my soul.
21:25 Another man dies in **b** of soul,
27: 2 who has made me taste **b** of soul,
Pr 14:10 Each heart knows its own **b**,
17:25 and **b** to the one who bore him.
Lam 3: 5 surrounded me with **b** and hardship.
3:19 my wandering, the **b** and the gall.
Eze 3:14 in **b** and in the anger of my spirit,
Am 5: 7 You who turn justice into **b** and cast
6:12 the fruit of righteousness into **b**—
Ac 8:23 For I see that you are full of **b**
Ro 3:14 mouths are full of cursing and **b**."
Eph 4:31 Get rid of all **b**, rage and anger,

Bitumen
Ge 11: 3 instead of stone, and **b** for mortar.

Biziothiah
Jos 15:28 Hazar Shual, Beersheba, **B**,

Biztha
Est 1:10 **B**, Harbona, Bigtha, Abagtha, Zethar

Black (Blackened, Blacker, Blackest, Blackness)
Ex 10:15 all the ground until it was **b**.
Lev 11:13 eagle, the vulture, the **b** vulture,
11:14 the red kite, any kind of **b** kite,
13:31 and there is no **b** hair in it,
13:37 and **b** hair has grown in it,
Dt 4:11 with **b** clouds and deep darkness.
14:12 eagle, the vulture, the **b** vulture,
14:13 the red kite, the **b** kite, any kind
1Ki 18:45 the sky grew **b** with clouds,
Job 30:30 My skin grows **b** and peels;
SS 5:11 his hair is wavy and **b** as a raven.
Zec 6: 2 had red horses, the second **b**,
6: 6 The one with the **b** horses is going
Mt 5:36 make even one hair white or **b**.
Rev 6: 5 and there before me was a **b** horse!
6:12 The sun turned **b** like sackcloth made

Blackened (Black)
Job 30:28 I go about **b**, but not by the sun;

Blacker (Black)
Lam 4: 8 now they are **b** than soot;

Blackest (Black)
Job 28: 3 recesses for ore in the **b** darkness.
2Pe 2:17 **B** darkness is reserved for them.
Jude :13 for whom **b** darkness has been

Blackness (Black)
Job 3: 5 may **b** overwhelm its light.
Joel 2: 2 and gloom, a day of clouds and **b**.
Am 5: 8 who turns **b** into dawn and darkens
Zep 1:15 and gloom, a day of clouds and **b**,

Blacksmith
1Sa 13:19 Not a **b** could be found in the whole
Isa 44:12 **b** takes a tool and works with it
54:16 "See, it is I who created the **b**

Blade
Jdg 3:22 Even the handle sank in after the **b**,
Eze 21:16 wherever your **b** is turned.

Blame
Ge 43: 9 bear the **b** before you all my life.
44:10 rest of you will be free from **b**."
44:32 I will bear the **b** before you, my
1Sa 25:24 "My lord, let the **b** be on me alone.
2Sa 14: 9 "My lord the king, let the **b** rest on
Ro 9:19 "Then why does God still **b** us?
1Ti 5: 7 so that no-one may be open to **b**.
6:14 keep this command without spot or **b**

Blameless (Blamelessly)
Ge 6: 9 **b** among the people of his time,
17: 1 Almighty; walk before me and be **b**.
Dt 18:13 You must be **b** before the LORD your
2Sa 22:24 I have been **b** before him and have
22:26 to the **b** you show yourself **b**,
Job 1: 1 This man was **b** and upright;
1: 8 he is **b** and upright, a man who fears
2: 3 he is **b** and upright, a man who fears
4: 6 and your **b** ways your hope?
8:20 "Surely God does not reject a **b** man
9:20 if I were **b**, it would pronounce me
9:21 "Although I am **b**, I have no concern
9:22 destroys both the **b** and the wicked.'
12: 4 though righteous and **b**!
22: 3 would he gain if your ways were **b**?
31: 6 and he will know that I am **b**—
Ps 15: 2 He whose walk is **b** and who does what
18:23 I have been **b** before him and have
18:25 to the **b** you show yourself **b**,
19:13 Then will I be **b**, innocent of great
26: 1 for I have led a **b** life;
26:11 I lead a **b** life; redeem me and be
37:18 The days of the **b** are known to the
37:37 Consider the **b**, observe the upright;
84:11 withhold from those whose walk is **b**.
101: 2 I will be careful to lead a **b** life—
101: 2 I will walk in my house with **b** heart.
101: 6 he whose walk is **b** will minister
119: 1 Blessed are they whose ways are **b**,
119:80 May my heart be **b** towards your
Pr 2: 7 a shield to those whose walk is **b**,
2:21 and the **b** will remain in it;
11: 5 The righteousness of the **b** makes a
11:20 delights in those whose ways are **b**.
19: 1 Better a poor man whose walk is **b**
20: 7 The righteous man leads a **b** life;
28: 6 Better a poor man whose walk is **b**
28:10 **b** will receive a good inheritance.
28:18 He whose walk is **b** is kept safe,
Eze 28:15 You were **b** in your ways from the day
1Co 1: 8 so that you will be **b** on the day of
Eph 1: 4 world to be holy and **b** in his sight.
5:27 any other blemish, but holy and **b**.
Php 1:10 pure and **b** until the day of Christ,
2:15 that you may become **b** and pure,
1Th 2:10 **b** we were among you who believed.
3:13 so that you will be **b** and holy
5:23 soul and body be kept **b** at the
Tit 1: 6 An elder must be **b**, the husband of
1: 7 he must be **b**—not overbearing, not
Heb 7:26 **b**, pure, set apart from sinners,
2Pe 3:14 spotless, **b** and at peace with him.
Rev 14: 5 found in their mouths; they are **b**.

Blamelessly (Blameless)
Lk 1: 6 commandments and regulations **b**.

Blanket (Blankets)
Isa 28:20 the **b** too narrow to wrap around you.

Blankets (Blanket)
Jdg 5:10 sitting on your saddle **b**, and you
Eze 27:20 "Dedan traded in saddle **b** with you.

Blaspheme (Blasphemed, Blasphemer, Blasphemes, Blasphemies, Blaspheming, Blasphemous, Blasphemy)
Ex 22:28 "Do not **b** God or curse the ruler of
Ac 26:11 and I tried to force them to **b**.
1Ti 1:20 over to Satan to be taught not to **b**.
2Pe 2:12 these men **b** in matters they do not
Rev 13: 6 He opened his mouth to **b** God, and to

Blasphemed (Blaspheme)
Lev 24:11 The son of the Israelite woman **b** the
2Ki 19: 6 of the king of Assyria have **b** me.
19:22 Who is it you have insulted and **b**?
Isa 37: 6 of the king of Assyria have **b** me.
37:23 Who is it you have insulted and **b**?
52: 5 day long my name is constantly **b**.
Eze 20:27 your fathers **b** me by forsaking me:
Ac 19:37 robbed temples nor **b** our goddess.
Ro 2:24 "God's name is **b** among the Gentiles

Blasphemer (Blaspheme)
Lev 24:14 "Take the **b** outside the camp.
24:23 they took the **b** outside the camp
1Ti 1:13 Even though I was once a **b** and a

Blasphemes (Blaspheme)
Lev 24:16 anyone who **b** the name of the LORD
24:16 **b** the Name, he must be put to death.
Nu 15:30 native-born or alien, **b** the LORD
Mk 3:29 whoever **b** against the Holy Spirit
Lk 12:10 anyone who **b** against the Holy Spirit

Blasphemies (Blaspheme)
Ne 9:18 or when they committed awful **b**.
9:26 they committed awful **b**.
Mk 3:28 and **b** of men will be forgiven them.
Rev 13: 5 a mouth to utter proud words and **b**

Blaspheming (Blaspheme)
Mt 9: 3 "This fellow is **b**!
Mk 2: 7 He's **b**! Who can forgive sins but God

Blasphemous (Blaspheme)
Rev 13: 1 and on each head a **b** name.
17: 3 beast that was covered with **b** names

Blasphemy (Blaspheme)
Mt 12:31 I tell you, every sin and **b** will be
12:31 but the **b** against the Spirit will
26:65 "He has spoken **b**! Why do we need any
26:65 Look, now you have heard the **b**.
Mk 14:64 "You have heard the **b**. What do you
Lk 5:21 "Who is this fellow who speaks **b**?
Jn 10:33 "but for **b**, because you, a mere man,
10:36 **b** because I said, 'I am God's Son'?
Ac 6:11 of **b** against Moses and against God."

Blast (Blasts)
Ex 15: 8 By the **b** of your nostrils the waters
19:13 when the ram's horn sounds a long **b**
19:16 mountain, and a very loud trumpet **b**.
Nu 10: 5 a trumpet **b** is sounded, the tribes
10: 6 At the sounding of a second **b**, the
10: 6 **b** will be the signal for setting out.
10: 9 sound a **b** on the trumpets.
Jos 6: 5 you hear them sound a long **b** on the
6:16 the priests sounded the trumpet **b**,
2Sa 22:16 the **b** of breath from his nostrils.
Job 4: 9 at the **b** of his anger they perish.
39:25 At the **b** of the trumpet he snorts,
Ps 18:15 the **b** of breath from your nostrils.
98: 6 trumpets and the **b** of the ram's horn
147:17 Who can withstand his icy **b**?
Isa 27: 8 with his fierce **b** he drives her out,
Eze 22:20 a furnace to melt it with a fiery **b**,
Am 2: 2 war cries and the **b** of the trumpet.
Heb 12:19 to a trumpet **b** or to such a voice

Blasts (Blast)
Lev 23:24 commemorated with trumpet **b**.
Rev 8:13 because of the trumpet **b** about to be

Blastus
Ac 12:20 Having secured the support of **B**, a

Blaze (Blazed, Blazes, Blazing)
Nu 21:28 a **b** from the city of Sihon.
Jer 48:45 a **b** from the midst of Sihon;

Blazed (Blaze)
Dt 4:11 it **b** with fire to the very heavens,
Jdg 13:20 the flame **b** up from the altar
2Sa 22: 9 burning coals **b** out of it.
22:13 bolts of lightning **b** forth.
Ps 18: 8 burning coals **b** out of it.
106:18 Fire **b** among their followers;
Jnh 4: 8 and the sun **b** on Jonah's head

Blazes (Blaze)
Hos 7: 6 morning it **b** like a flaming fire.
Joel 2: 3 fire devours, behind them a flame **b**.

Blazing (Blaze)
Ge 15:17 a smoking brazier with a **b** torch
SS 8: 6 like **b** fire, like a mighty flame.
Isa 10:16 fire will be kindled like a **b** flame.
34: 9 her land will become **b** pitch!
62: 1 her salvation like a **b** torch.
Eze 20:47 The **b** flame will not be quenched,
Da 3: 6 be thrown into a **b** furnace."
3:11 will be thrown into a **b** furnace.
3:15 thrown immediately into a **b** furnace.
3:17 If we are thrown into the **b** furnace,
3:20 and throw them into the **b** furnace.
3:21 bound and thrown into the **b** furnace.
3:23 tied, fell into the **b** furnace.
3:26 the opening of the **b** furnace
7:11 and thrown into the **b** fire.
Ac 26:13 sun, **b** around me and my companions.
2Th 1: 7 in **b** fire with his powerful angels.
Rev 1:14 and his eyes were like **b** fire.
2:18 whose eyes are like **b** fire and whose
4: 5 the throne, seven lamps were **b**.
8:10 and a great star, **b** like a torch,
19:12 His eyes are like **b** fire, and on his

Bleach
Mk 9: 3 anyone in the world could **b** them.

Bleat (Bleating)
Isa 34:14 and wild goats will **b** to each other;

Bleating (Bleat)
1Sa 15:14 Samuel said, "What then is this **b** of

Bleeding (Blood)
Lev 12: 4 days to be purified from her **b**.
12: 5 days to be purified from her **b**.
Mt 9:20 a woman who had been subject to **b**
Mk 5:25 been subject to **b** for twelve years.
5:29 Immediately her **b** stopped and she
Lk 8:43 been subject to **b** for twelve years,
8:44 and immediately her **b** stopped.
Ac 19:16 ran out of the house naked and **b**.

Blemish (Blemished, Blemishes)
Lev 22:21 it must be without defect or **b**
Nu 19: 2 a red heifer without defect or **b**
2Sa 14:25 of his foot there was no **b** in him.
Eph 5:27 stain or wrinkle or any other **b**,
Col 1:22 without **b** and free from accusation—
1Pe 1:19 Christ, a lamb without **b** or defect.

Blemished (Blemish)
Mal 1:14 sacrifices a **b** animal to the LORD.

Blemishes (Blemish)
2Pe 2:13 They are blots and **b**, revelling in
Jude :12 These men are **b** at your love feasts,

Blend (Blended)
Ex 30:25 fragrant **b**, the work of a perfumer.
30:35 make a fragrant **b** of incense,

Blended (Blend)
2Ch 16:14 with spices and various **b** perfumes,
SS 7: 2 goblet that never lacks **b** wine.

Bless (Blessed, Blessedness, Blesses, Blessing, Blessings)
Ge 12: 2 into a great nation and I will **b** you
12: 3 I will **b** those who **b** you, and
17:16 I will **b** her and will surely give
17:16 I will **b** her so that she will be the
17:20 I have heard you: I will surely **b**
22:17 I will surely **b** you and make your
26: 3 I will be with you and will **b** you.
26:24 I will **b** you and will increase
27:29 and those who **b** you be blessed."
27:34 "**B** me—me too, my father!
27:38 "**B** me too, my father!"
28: 3 May God Almighty **b** you and make you
32:26 not let you go unless you **b** me."
48: 9 them to me so that I may **b** them."
48:16 from all harm—may he **b** these boys.
Ex 12:32 And also **b** me."
20:24 I will come to you and **b** you.
Nu 6:23 is how you are to **b** the Israelites.
6:24 "'"The LORD **b** you and keep you;
6:27 the Israelites, and I will **b** them."
22: 6 For I know that those you **b** are
23:11 you have done nothing but **b** them!"
23:20 I have received a command to **b**;
23:25 them at all nor **b** them at all !"
24: 1 it pleased the LORD to **b** Israel,
24: 9 "May those who **b** you be blessed and
Dt 1:11 times and **b** you as he has promised!
7:13 He will love you and **b** you and
7:13 He will **b** the fruit of your womb,
14:29 **b** you in all the work of your hands.
15: 4 inheritance, he will richly **b** you,
15: 6 For the LORD your God will **b** you as
15:10 God will **b** you in all your work
15:18 God will **b** you in everything you do.
16:15 For the LORD your God will **b** you in
23:20 so that the LORD your God may **b** you
24:19 **b** you in all the work of your hands.
26:15 and **b** your people Israel
27:12 on Mount Gerizim to **b** the people:
28: 8 **b** you in the land he is giving you.
28:12 and to **b** all the work of your hands.
30:16 and the LORD your God will **b** you in
33:11 **B** all his skills, O LORD, and be
33:13 "May the LORD **b** his land
Jos 8:33 to **b** the people of Israel.
Jdg 17: 2 "The LORD **b** you, my son!"
Ru 2: 4 "The LORD **b** you!" they called back.
2:20 "The LORD **b** him!" Naomi said to her
3:10 "The LORD **b** you, my daughter," he
1Sa 2:20 Eli would **b** Elkanah and his wife,
9:13 because he must **b** the sacrifice;
15:13 "The LORD **b** you! I have carried out
23:21 "The LORD **b** you for your concern
2Sa 2: 5 "The LORD **b** you for showing this
6:20 David returned home to **b** his
7:29 Now be pleased to **b** the house of
21: 3 you will **b** the LORD's inheritance?"
1Ch 4:10 "Oh, that you would **b** me and enlarge
16:43 David returned home to **b** his family.
17:27 Now you have been pleased to **b** the
2Ch 30:27 the Levites stood to **b** the people,
Job 31:20 his heart did not **b** me for warming
Ps 5:12 For surely, O LORD, you **b** the
28: 9 and **b** your inheritance
41: 2 he will **b** him in the land
62: 4 With their mouths they **b**,
65:10 it with showers and **b** its crops.
67: 1 May God be gracious to us and **b** us
67: 6 and God, our God, will **b** us.
67: 7 God will **b** us, and all the ends of
72:15 pray for him and **b** him all day long.
109:28 They may curse, but you will **b**;
115:12 The LORD remembers us and will **b** us:
115:12 He will **b** the house of Israel,
115:12 he will **b** the house of Aaron,

Ps 115:13 he will **b** those who fear the LORD
118:26 Blessed is he who comes in the name
128: 5 May the LORD **b** you from Zion
129: 8 we **b** you in the name of the LORD."
132:15 will **b** her with abundant provisions
134: 3 heaven and earth, **b** you from Zion.
Pr 30:11 and do not **b** their mothers;
Isa 19:25 The LORD Almighty will **b** them,
Jer 31:23 'The LORD **b** you, O righteous
Eze 34:26 I will **b** them and the places
Hag 2:19 "'From this day on I will **b** you.'"
Zec 4: 7 to shouts of 'God **b** it! God **b** it!'"
Lk 6:28 **b** those who curse you, pray for
Ac 3:26 he sent him first to you to **b** you by
Ro 12:14 **B** those who persecute you; **b** and do
1Co 4:12 When we are cursed, we **b**; when we
Heb 6:14 "I will surely **b** you and give you

Blessed (Bless, *God blessed*)

Ge 5: 2 He created them male and female and **b**
9:26 He also said, "**B** be the LORD, the
12: 3 on earth will be **b** through you."
14:19 he **b** Abram, saying, "**B** be Abram by
14:20 **b** be God Most High, who delivered
18:18 on earth will be **b** through him.
22:18 all nations on earth will be **b**,
24: 1 and the LORD had **b** him in every way.
24:31 "Come, you who are **b** by the LORD,"
24:35 The LORD has **b** my master abundantly,
24:60 they **b** Rebekah and said to her, "Our
26: 4 all nations on earth will be **b**,
26:12 hundredfold, because the LORD **b** him.
26:29 And now you are **b** by the LORD."
27:23 of his brother Esau; so he **b** him.
27:27 he **b** him and said, "Ah, the smell of
27:27 of a field that the LORD has **b**.
27:29 and those who bless you be **b**."
27:33 I **b** him—and indeed he will be **b**!"
28: 1 Isaac called for Jacob and **b** him
28: 6 Esau learned that Isaac had **b** Jacob
28: 6 and that when he **b** him he commanded
28:14 All peoples on earth will be **b**
30:27 the LORD has **b** me because of you."
30:30 LORD has **b** you wherever I have been.
31:55 and his daughters and **b** them.
32:29 ask my name?" Then he **b** him there.
35: 9 God appeared to him again and **b** him.
39: 5 the LORD **b** the household of the
47: 7 After Jacob **b** Pharaoh,
47:10 Jacob **b** Pharaoh and went out from
48: 3 land of Canaan, and there he **b** me
48:15 he **b** Joseph and said, "May the God
48:20 He **b** them that day and said, "In
49:28 father said to them when he **b** them,
Ex 20:11 **b** the Sabbath day and made it holy.
32:29 and he has **b** you this day."
39:43 So Moses **b** them.
Lev 9:22 hands towards the people and **b** them.
9:23 When they came out, they **b** the
Nu 22: 6 I know that those you bless are **b**,
22:12 those people, because they are **b**."
23:20 he has **b**, and I cannot change it.
24: 9 "May those who bless you be **b**
24:10 you have **b** them these three times.
Dt 2: 7 The LORD your God has **b** you in all
7:14 You will be **b** more than any other
12: 7 because the LORD your God has **b** you.
14:24 you have been **b** by the LORD your God
15:14 him as the LORD your God has **b** you.
16:17 the way the LORD your God has **b** you.
28: 3 You will be **b** in the city and **b** in
28: 4 The fruit of your womb will be **b**,
28: 5 and your kneading trough will be **b**.
28: 6 You will be **b** when you come in and **b**
33:20 "**B** is he who enlarges Gad's domain!
33:24 "Most **b** of sons is Asher;
33:29 **B** are you, O Israel! Who is like you,
Jos 14:13 Joshua **b** Caleb son of Jephunneh and
17:14 and the LORD has **b** us abundantly."
22: 6 Joshua **b** them and sent them away,
22: 7 Joshua sent them home, he **b** them,
24:10 so he **b** you again and again,
Jdg 5:24 "Most **b** of women be Jael, the wife
5:24 most **b** of tent-dwelling women.
13:24 He grew and the LORD **b** him,
Ru 2:19 **B** be the man who took notice of you!"
1Sa 25:33 May you be **b** for your good judgment
26:25 Saul said to David, "May you be **b**,
2Sa 6:11 LORD **b** him and his entire household.
6:12 "The LORD has **b** the household of
6:18 he **b** the people in the name of the
7:29 of your servant will be **b** for ever."
14:22 pay him honour, and he **b** the king.
1Ki 2:45 King Solomon will be **b**, and David's
8:14 the king turned round and **b** them.
8:55 He stood and **b** the whole assembly of
8:66 They **b** the king and then went home,
1Ch 13:14 and the LORD **b** his household and
16: 2 **b** the people in the name of the LORD.
17:27 **b** it, and it will be **b** for ever."
26: 5 (For God had **b** Obed-Edom.)
2Ch 6: 3 the king turned round and **b** them.
31: 8 the LORD and **b** his people Israel.
31:10 because the LORD has **b** his people,
Ne 9: 5 "**B** be your glorious name, and may
Job 1:10 You have **b** the work of his hands,
5:17 "**B** is the man whom God corrects;
29: 4 God's intimate friendship **b** my house,
29:13 The man who was dying **b** me;
42:12 The LORD **b** the latter part of Job's
Ps 1: 1 **B** is the man who does not walk in
2:12 **B** are all who take refuge in him.
32: 1 **B** is he whose transgressions are
32: 2 **B** is the man whose sin the LORD does
33:12 **B** is the nation whose God is the
34: 8 **b** is the man who takes refuge in him.
37:26 their children will be **b**.
40: 4 **B** is the man who makes the LORD his
41: 1 **B** is he who has regard for the weak;
45: 2 since God has **b** you for ever.
49:18 while he lived he counted himself **b**
65: 4 **B** are those you choose and bring
72:17 All nations will be **b** through him,
72:17 and they will call him **b**.
84: 4 **B** are those who dwell in your house;
84: 5 **B** are those whose strength is in you,
84:12 **b** is the man who trusts in you.
89:15 **B** are those who have learned to
94:12 **B** is the man you discipline, O LORD,
106: 3 **B** are they who maintain justice,
107:38 he **b** them, and their numbers greatly
112: 1 **B** is the man who fears the LORD,
112: 2 generation of the upright will be **b**.
115:15 May you be **b** by the LORD, the Maker
118:26 **B** is he who comes in the name of the
119: 1 **B** are they whose ways are blameless,
119: 2 **B** are they who keep his statutes
127: 5 **B** is the man whose quiver is full of
128: 1 **B** are all who fear the LORD,
128: 4 Thus is the man **b** who fears the LORD.
144:15 **B** are the people of whom this is
144:15 **B** are the people whose God is the
146: 5 **B** is he whose help is the God of
Pr 3:13 **B** is the man who finds wisdom,
3:18 those who lay hold of her will be **b**.
5:18 May your fountain be **b**,
8:32 **b** are those who keep my ways.
8:34 **B** is the man who listens to me,
14:21 **b** is he who is kind to the needy.
16:20 and **b** is he who trusts in the LORD.
20: 7 **b** are his children after him.
20:21 will not be **b** at the end.
22: 9 A generous man will himself be **b**,
28:14 **B** is the man who always fears the
28:20 A faithful man will be richly **b**,
29:18 but **b** is he who keeps the law.
31:28 Her children arise and call her **b**;
Ecc 10:17 **B** are you, O land whose king is of
SS 6: 9 The maidens saw her and called her **b**;
Isa 19:25 "**B** be Egypt my people, Assyria my
30:18 **B** are all who wait for him!
32:20 how **b** you will be, sowing your seed
51: 2 and I **b** him and made him many.
56: 2 **B** is the man who does this, the man
61: 9 they are a people the LORD has **b**."
65:23 they will be a people **b** by the LORD,
Jer 4: 2 then the nations will be **b** by him
17: 7 "But **b** is the man who trusts in the
20:14 the day my mother bore me not be **b**!
Da 12:12 **B** is the one who waits for and
Mal 3:12 "Then all the nations will call you **b**
Mal 3:15 now we call the arrogant **b**.
Mt 5: 3 "**B** are the poor in spirit,
5: 4 **B** are those who mourn, for they will
5: 5 **B** are the meek, for they will
5: 6 **B** are those who hunger and thirst
5: 7 **B** are the merciful, for they will
5: 8 **B** are the pure in heart,
5: 9 **B** are the peacemakers, for they will
5:10 **B** are those who are persecuted
5:11 "**B** are you when people insult you,
11: 6 **B** is the man who does not fall away
13:16 **b** are your eyes because they see,
16:17 Jesus replied, "**B** are you, Simon
21: 9 "**B** is he who comes in the name
23:39 '**B** is he who comes in the name of
25:34 'Come, you who are **b** by my Father;
Mk 10:16 put his hands on them and **b** them.
11: 9 "**B** is he who comes in the name
11:10 "**B** is the coming kingdom of our
14:61 the Christ, the Son of the **B** One?"
Lk 1:42 "**B** are you among women,
1:42 and **b** is the child you will bear!
1:45 **B** is she who has believed that what
1:48 all generations will call me **b**,
2:34 Simeon **b** them and said to Mary, his
6:20 "**B** are you who are poor,
6:21 **B** are you who hunger now, for you
6:21 **B** are you who weep now, for you will
6:22 **B** are you when men hate you, when
7:23 **B** is the man who does not fall away
10:23 **B** are the eyes that see what you see.
11:27 "**B** is the mother who gave you birth
11:28 "**B** rather are those who hear
13:35 '**B** is he who comes in the name of
14:14 you will be **b**. Although they cannot
14:15 "**B** is the man who will eat at the
19:38 "**B** is the king who comes in the name
23:29 '**B** are the barren women, the wombs
24:50 he lifted up his hands and **b** them.
Jn 12:13 "**B** is he who comes in the name
12:13 "**B** is the King of Israel!
13:17 you will be **b** if you do them.
20:29 **b** are those who have not seen
Ac 3:25 all peoples on earth will be **b**.'
20:35 is more **b** to give than to receive.'"
Ro 4: 7 "**B** are they whose transgressions are
4: 8 **B** is the man whose sin the Lord will
14:22 **B** is the man who does not condemn
Gal 3: 8 "All nations will be **b** through you."
3: 9 those who have faith are **b**
Eph 1: 3 who has **b** us in the heavenly realms
1Ti 1:11 to the glorious gospel of the **b** God
6:15 God, the **b** and only Ruler, the King
Tit 2:13 while we wait for the **b** hope—the
Heb 7: 1 the defeat of the kings and **b** him,
7: 6 and **b** him who had the promises.
7: 7 without doubt the lesser person is **b**
11:20 By faith Isaac **b** Jacob and Esau in
11:21 By faith Jacob, when he was dying, **b**
Jas 1:12 **B** is the man who perseveres under
1:25 it—he will be **b** in what he does.
5:11 As you know, we consider **b** those
1Pe 3:14 suffer for what is right, you are **b**.
4:14 you are **b**, for the Spirit of glory
Rev 1: 3 **B** is the one who reads the words of
1: 3 and **b** are those who hear it and take
14:13 **B** are the dead who die in the Lord
16:15 **B** is he who stays awake
19: 9 '**B** are those who are invited
20: 6 **B** and holy are those who have part
22: 7 **B** is he who keeps the words
22:14 "**B** are those who wash their robes,

Blessedness (Bless)

Ro 4: 6 when he speaks of the **b** of the man
4: 9 Is this **b** only for the circumcised,

Blesses (Bless)

Ge 49:25 because of the Almighty, who **b** you
Ps 10: 3 **b** the greedy and reviles the LORD.
29:11 the LORD **b** his people with peace.
37:22 those the LORD **b** will inherit
147:13 and **b** your people within you.
Pr 3:33 but he **b** the home of the righteous.
27:14 If a man loudly **b** his neighbour
Ro 10:12 and richly **b** all who call on him,

Blessing (Bless)

Ge 12: 2 name great, and you will be a **b**.
17:18 Ishmael might live under your **b**!"
27: 4 I may give you my **b** before I die."
27: 7 so that I may give you my **b** in the
27:10 may give you his **b** before he dies."
27:12 a curse on myself rather than a **b**."
27:19 so that you may give me your **b**."
27:25 to eat, so that I may give you my **b**.
27:30 After Isaac finished **b** him and Jacob
27:31 so that you may give me your **b**."
27:35 came deceitfully and took your **b**."
27:36 and now he's taken my **b**!"
27:36 "Haven't you reserved any **b** for me?
27:38 "Do you have only one **b**, my father?
27:41 of the **b** his father had given him.
28: 4 descendants the **b** given to Abraham,
39: 5 The **b** of the LORD was on everything
48:20 name will Israel pronounce this **b**:
49:28 each the **b** appropriate to him.
Ex 23:25 and his **b** will be on your food
Lev 25:21 I will send you such a **b** in the
Dt 11:26 before you today a **b** and a curse—
11:27 the **b** if you obey the commands of
12:15 the **b** the LORD your God gives you.
23: 5 turned the curse into a **b** for you,
28: 8 The LORD will send a **b** on your barns
29:19 he invokes a **b** on himself and
33: 1 This is the **b** that Moses the man of
33:23 of the LORD and is full of his **b**;
2Sa 7:29 your **b** the house of your servant
13:25 refused to go, but gave him his **b**.
19:39 kissed Barzillai and gave him his **b**,
Ne 9: 5 be exalted above all **b** and praise.
13: 2 however, turned the curse into a **b**.)
Ps 3: 8 May your **b** be on your people.
24: 5 He will receive **b** from the LORD
109:17 he found no pleasure in **b**—
129: 8 "The **b** of the LORD be upon you;
133: 3 For there the LORD bestows his **b**,
Pr 10: 7 memory of the righteous will be a **b**,
10:22 The **b** of the LORD brings wealth,
11:11 Through the **b** of the upright a city
11:26 **b** crowns him who is willing to sell.
24:25 and rich **b** will come upon them.
Isa 19:24 Egypt and Assyria, a **b** on the earth.
44: 3 and my **b** on your descendants.
65:16 Whoever invokes a **b** in the land will
Jer 16: 5 because I have withdrawn my **b**, my
Eze 34:26 season; there will be showers of **b**.
44:30 that a **b** may rest on your household.
Joel 2:14 have pity and leave behind a **b**—
Mic 2: 9 You take away my **b** from their
Zec 8:13 I save you, and you will be a **b**.
Mal 3:10 pour out so much **b** that you will not
Lk 24:51 While he was **b** them, he left them
Jn 1:16 all received one **b** after another.
Ac 15:33 with the **b** of peace to return
Ro 15:29 the full measure of the **b** of Christ.
Gal 3:14 in order that the **b** given to Abraham
Eph 1: 3 with every spiritual **b** in Christ.
Heb 6: 7 it is farmed receives the **b** of God.
12:17 when he wanted to inherit this **b**,
12:17 though he sought the **b** with tears.
1Pe 3: 9 but with **b**, because to this you were
3: 9 called so that you may inherit a **b**.

Blessings (Bless)

Ge 49:25 you with **b** of the heavens above
49:25 **b** of the deep that lies below,
49:25 **b** of the breast and womb.
49:26 Your father's **b** are greater than the
49:26 than the **b** of the ancient mountains,
Dt 10: 8 and to pronounce **b** in his name,
11:29 to proclaim on Mount Gerizim the **b**,
16:10 **b** the LORD your God has given you.
21: 5 pronounce **b** in the name of the LORD
28: 2 All these **b** will come upon you and
30: 1 all these **b** and curses I have set
30:19 you life and death, **b** and curses.
Jos 8:34 the law—the **b** and the curses
1Ch 23:13 to pronounce **b** in his name for ever.
Ps 21: 3 You welcomed him with rich **b**
21: 6 Surely you have granted him eternal **b**
Ps 128: 2 **b** and prosperity will be yours.
Pr 10: 6 **B** crown the head of the righteous,
Hos 3: 5 LORD and to his **b** in the last days.
Mal 2: 2 upon you, and I will curse your **b**.
Ac 13:34 holy and sure **b** promised to David.'
Ro 15:27 shared in the Jews' spiritual **b**,
15:27 to share with them their material **b**.
1Co 9:23 gospel, that I may share in its **b**.

Blew (Blow[1])

Ex 15:10 you **b** with your breath, and the sea
Jos 6: 9 of the priests who **b** the trumpets,
Jdg 3:27 he **b** a trumpet in the hill country
6:34 and he **b** a trumpet, summoning the
7:19 They **b** their trumpets and broke the
7:20 The three companies **b** the trumpets
2Sa 2:28 Joab **b** the trumpet, and all the men
2Ki 9:13 Then they **b** the trumpet and shouted,
2Ch 7: 6 the priests **b** their trumpets
13:14 The priests **b** their trumpets
Hag 1: 9 What you brought home, I **b** away. Why?
Mt 7:25 the streams rose, and the winds **b**
7:27 the streams rose, and the winds **b**

Blight (Blighted)

Dt 28:22 with **b** and mildew, which will plague
1Ki 8:37 or **b** or mildew, locusts or
2Ch 6:28 or **b** or mildew, locusts or
Am 4: 9 I struck them with **b** and mildew.
Hag 2:17 all the work of your hands with **b**,

Blighted (Blight)

Ps 102: 4 My heart is **b** and withered like
Hos 9:16 Ephraim is **b**, their root is withered,

Blind (Blinded, Blindfolds, Blindness, Blinds)

Ex 4:11 Who gives him sight or makes him **b**?
Lev 19:14 a stumbling-block in front of the **b**
21:18 **b** or lame, disfigured or deformed;
22:22 Do not offer to the LORD the **b**,
Dt 15:21 is lame or **b**, or has any serious
27:18 "Cursed is the man who leads the **b**
28:29 about like a **b** man in the dark.
1Sa 2:33 only to **b** your eyes with tears
2Sa 5: 6 **b** and the lame can ward you off.
5: 8 "The '**b** and lame' will not enter
Job 29:15 I was eyes to the **b** and feet to the
Ps 146: 8 the LORD gives sight to the **b**,
Isa 29: 9 Be stunned and amazed, **b** yourselves
29:18 darkness the eyes of the **b** will see.
35: 5 will the eyes of the **b** be opened and
42: 7 to open eyes that are **b**, to free
42:16 I will lead the **b** by ways they have
42:18 "Hear, you deaf; look, you **b**, and
42:19 Who is **b** but my servant, and deaf
42:19 is **b** like the one committed to me,
42:19 **b** like the servant of the LORD?
43: 8 those who have eyes but are **b**,
44: 9 who would speak up for them are **b**;
56:10 Israel's watchmen are **b**, they all
59:10 Like the **b** we grope along the wall,
Jer 31: 8 Among them will be the **b** and the
Lam 4:14 the streets like men who are **b**.
Zep 1:17 and they will walk like **b** men,
Zec 12: 4 **b** all the horses of the nations.
Mal 1: 8 you bring **b** animals for sacrifice,
Mt 9:27 two **b** men followed him, calling out,
9:28 the **b** men came to him, and he asked
11: 5 The **b** receive sight, the lame walk,
12:22 man who was **b** and mute,
15:14 Leave them; they are **b** guides.
15:14 a **b** man, both will fall into a pit."
15:30 bringing the lame, the **b**, the
15:31 the lame walking and the **b** seeing.
20:30 Two **b** men were sitting by the
21:14 The **b** and the lame came to him at
23:16 "Woe to you, **b** guides! You say,
23:17 You **b** fools! Which is greater:
23:19 You **b** men! Which is greater:
23:24 You **b** guides! You strain out a gnat
23:26 **B** Pharisee! First clean the inside
Mk 8:22 and some people brought a **b** man
8:23 He took the **b** man by the hand and
10:46 a **b** man, Bartimaeus
10:49 So they called to the **b** man,
10:51 The **b** man said, "Rabbi, I want to
Lk 4:18 and recovery of sight for the **b**,
6:39 "Can a **b** man lead a **b** man? Will they
7:21 and gave sight to many who were **b**.
7:22 The **b** receive sight, the lame walk,
14:13 poor, the crippled, the lame, the **b**,
14:21 the crippled, the **b** and the lame.'
18:35 a **b** man was sitting by the roadside
Jn 5: 3 lie—the **b**, the lame, the paralysed.
9: 1 he saw a man **b** from birth.
9: 2 or his parents, that he was born **b**?"
9:13 Pharisees the man who had been **b**.
9:17 they turned again to the **b** man,
9:18 did not believe that he had been **b**
9:19 Is this the one you say was born **b**?
9:20 "and we know he was born **b**.
9:24 summoned the man who had been **b**.
9:25 I do know. I was **b** but now I see!"
9:32 of opening the eyes of a man born **b**.
9:39 so that the **b** will see and those who
9:39 and those who see will become **b**."
9:40 "What? Are we **b** too?
9:41 Jesus said, "If you were **b**, you
10:21 Can a demon open the eyes of the **b**?"
11:37 he who opened the eyes of the **b** man
Ac 9: 9 For three days he was **b**, and did not
13:11 You are going to be **b**, and for a
Ro 2:19 that you are a guide for the **b**,
2Pe 1: 9 he is short-sighted and **b**, and has
Rev 3:17 pitiful, poor, **b** and naked.

Blinded (Blind)

Zec 11:17 withered, his right eye totally **b**!"
Jn 12:40 "He has **b** their eyes and deadened
Ac 22:11 brilliance of the light had **b** me.
2Co 4: 4 The god of this age has **b** the minds
1Jn 2:11 because the darkness has **b** him.

Blindfolded

Mk 14:65 they **b** him, struck him
Lk 22:64 They **b** him and demanded, "Prophesy!

Blindfolds (Blind)

Job 9:24 of the wicked, he **b** its judges.

Blindness (Blind)

Ge 19:11 with **b** so that they could not find
Dt 28:28 madness, **b** and confusion of mind.
2Ki 6:18 LORD, "Strike these people with **b**.
6:18 So he struck them with **b**,

Blinds (Blind)

Ex 23: 8 for a bribe **b** those who see
Dt 16:19 for a bribe **b** the eyes of the wise

Block (Blocked, Blocking, Blocks)

Isa 44:19 Shall I bow down to a **b** of wood?"
Eze 39:11 It will **b** the way of travellers,
Hos 2: 6 Therefore I will **b** her path with

Blocked (Block)

Lev 15: 3 flowing from his body or is **b**,
2Ch 32: 4 and they **b** all the springs and the
32:30 was Hezekiah who **b** the upper outlet
Job 19: 8 He has **b** my way so that I cannot
Pr 15:19 The way of the sluggard is **b** with

Blocking (Block)

2Ch 32: 3 military staff about **b** off the water

Blocks (Block)

1Ki 5:17 large **b** of quality stone to provide
6: 7 only **b** dressed at the quarry
7: 9 were made of **b** of high-grade stone
Lam 3: 9 He has barred my way with **b** of stone;

Blood (*Avenger of blood*, Bleeding, *Blood of Christ*, *Blood of the covenant*, Bloodshed, Bloodshot, Blood-stained, Bloodstains, Bloodthirsty, *Flesh and blood*, Lifeblood)

Ge 4:10 Your brother's **b** cries out to me
4:11 your brother's **b** from your hand.
9: 6 "Whoever sheds the **b** of man, by man
9: 6 by man shall his **b** be shed; for in
37:22 "Don't shed any **b**. Throw him into
37:26 kill our brother and cover up his **b**?
37:31 a goat and dipped the robe in the **b**.
42:22 must give an accounting for his **b**."
49:11 his robes in the **b** of grapes.
Ex 4: 9 river will become **b** on the ground."
4:25 "Surely you are a bridegroom of **b**
4:26 bridegroom of **b**", referring to
7:17 Nile, and it will be changed into **b**.
7:19 they will turn to **b**.
7:19 **B** will be everywhere in Egypt, even
7:20 all the water was changed into **b**.
7:21 **B** was everywhere in Egypt.
12: 7 they are to take some of the **b** and
12:13 The **b** will be a sign for you on the
12:13 I see the **b**, I will pass over you.
12:22 dip it into the **b** in the basin and
12:22 put some of the **b** on the top and on
12:23 he will see the **b** on the top and
23:18 "Do not offer the **b** of a sacrifice
24: 6 Moses took half of the **b** and put it
24: 8 Moses then took the **b**, sprinkled it
29:12 Take some of the bull's **b** and put it
29:16 Slaughter it and take the **b** and
29:20 Slaughter it, take some of its **b** and
29:20 Then sprinkle **b** against the altar
29:21 take some of the **b** on the altar and
30:10 the **b** of the atoning sin offering
34:25 "Do not offer the **b** of a sacrifice
Lev 1: 5 the priests shall bring the **b**
1:11 **b** against the altar on all sides.
1:15 its **b** shall be drained out on the
3: 2 **b** against the altar on all sides.
3: 8 **b** against the altar on all sides.
3:13 **b** against the altar on all sides.
3:17 You must not eat any fat or any **b**.'"
4: 5 shall take some of the bull's **b**
4: 6 He is to dip his finger into the **b**
4: 7 put some of the **b** on the horns
4: 7 The rest of the bull's **b** he shall
4:16 bull's **b** into the Tent of Meeting.
4:17 He shall dip his finger into the **b**
4:18 He is to put some of the **b** on the
4:18 The rest of the **b** he shall pour out
4:25 the priest shall take some of the **b**
4:25 of the **b** at the base of the altar.
4:30 the priest is to take some of the **b**
4:30 of the **b** at the base of the altar.
4:34 the priest shall take some of the **b**
4:34 of the **b** at the base of the altar.
5: 9 is to sprinkle some of the **b** of the
5: 9 the rest of the **b** must be drained
6:27 and if any of the **b** is spattered on
6:30 any sin offering whose **b** is brought
7: 2 and its **b** is to be sprinkled against
7:14 the **b** of the fellowship offerings.
7:26 not eat the **b** of any bird or animal.
7:27 If anyone eats **b**, that person must
7:33 The son of Aaron who offers the **b**
8:15 the bull and took some of the **b**,
8:15 He poured out the rest of the **b** at
8:19 **b** against the altar on all sides.
8:23 took some of its **b** and put it on the
8:24 **b** on the lobes of their right ears,
8:24 **b** against the altar on all sides.
8:30 some of the **b** from the altar and
9: 9 His sons brought the **b** to him,
9: 9 and he dipped his finger into the **b**
9: 9 the rest of the **b** he poured out
9:12 His sons handed him the **b**, and he
9:18 His sons handed him the **b**, and he
10:18 Since its **b** was not taken into the
12: 7 clean from her flow of **b**.
14: 6 into the **b** of the bird that was
14:14 The priest is to take some of the **b**
Lev 14:17 top of the **b** of the guilt offering.
14:25 take some of its **b** and put it on the
14:28 he put the **b** of the guilt offering
14:51 dip them into the **b** of the dead bird
14:52 purify the house with the bird's **b**,
15:19 a woman has her regular flow of **b**,
15:25 "'When a woman has a discharge of **b**
16:14 He is to take some of the bull's **b**
16:15 take its **b** behind the curtain and do
16:15 with it as he did with the bull's **b**:
16:18 He shall take some of the bull's **b**
16:18 some of the goat's **b** and put it on
16:19 He shall sprinkle some of the **b** on
16:27 whose **b** was brought into the Most
17: 4 he has shed **b** and must be cut off
17: 6 The priest is to sprinkle the **b**
17:10 living among them who eats any **b**
17:10 against that person who eats **b**
17:11 the life of a creature is in the **b**,
17:11 it is the **b** that makes atonement for
17:12 "None of you may eat **b**, nor may an
17:12 an alien living among you eat **b**."
17:13 drain out the **b** and cover it with
17:14 the life of every creature is its **b**.
17:14 "You must not eat the **b** of any
17:14 the life of every creature is its **b**;
19:26 "'Do not eat any meat with the **b**
20: 9 and his **b** will be on his own head.
20:11 their **b** will be on their own heads.
20:12 their **b** will be on their own heads.
20:13 their **b** will be on their own heads.
20:16 their **b** will be on their own heads.
20:27 **b** will be on their own heads.'"
Nu 18:17 Sprinkle their **b** on the altar and
19: 4 to take some of its **b** on his finger
19: 5 hide, flesh, **b** and offal.
23:24 and drinks the **b** of his victims."
35:33 the land on which **b** has been shed,
35:33 by the **b** of the one who shed it.
Dt 12:16 must not eat the **b**; pour it out
12:23 be sure you do not eat the **b**,
12:23 because the **b** is the life, and you
12:24 must not eat the **b**; pour it out
12:27 your God, both the meat and the **b**.
12:27 The **b** of your sacrifices must be
15:23 you must not eat the **b**; pour it out
19:10 Do this so that innocent **b** will not
19:13 the guilt of shedding innocent **b**,
21: 7 "Our hands did not shed this **b**,
21: 8 guilty of the **b** of an innocent man.
21: 9 the guilt of shedding innocent **b**,
32:14 You drank the foaming **b** of the grape.
32:42 I will make my arrows drunk with **b**,
32:42 **b** of the slain and the captives,
32:43 for he will avenge the **b** of his
Jos 2:19 his **b** will be on his own head;
2:19 his **b** will be on our head if a hand
Jdg 9:24 the shedding of their **b**, might be
1Sa 14:32 and ate them, together with the **b**.
14:33 by eating meat that has **b** in it.
14:34 by eating meat with **b** still in it.
26:20 Now do not let my **b** fall to the
2Sa 1:16 "Your **b** be on your own head.
1:22 From the **b** of the slain, from the
3:27 And there, to avenge the **b** of his
3:28 the **b** of Abner son of Ner.
3:29 May his **b** fall upon the head of Joab
4:11 not now demand his **b** from your hand
16: 7 out, you man of **b**, you scoundrel!
16: 8 The LORD has repaid you for all the **b**
16: 8 to ruin because you are a man of **b**!"
20:12 Amasa lay wallowing in his **b** in the
23:17 "Is it not the **b** of men who went at
1Ki 2: 5 He killed them, shedding their **b** in
2: 5 and with that **b** stained the belt
2: 9 grey head down to the grave in **b**."
2:31 of the innocent **b** that Joab shed.
2:32 The LORD will repay him for the **b** he
2:33 May the guilt of their **b** rest on the
2:37 your **b** will be on your own head."
18:28 their custom, until their **b** flowed.
21:19 where dogs licked up Naboth's **b**,
21:19 will lick up your **b**—yes, yours!'"
22:35 The **b** from his wound ran onto the
22:38 and the dogs licked up his **b**, as the
2Ki 3:22 the water looked red—like **b**.
2Ki 3:23 "That's **b**!" they said. "Those kings
9: 7 and I will avenge the **b** of my
9: 7 the **b** of all the LORD's servants
9:26 'Yesterday I saw the **b** of Naboth and
9:26 **b** of Naboth and the **b** of his sons,
9:33 and some of her **b** spattered the wall
16:13 and sprinkled the **b** of his
16:15 Sprinkle on the altar all the **b** of
21:16 Manasseh also shed so much innocent **b**
24: 4 including the shedding of innocent **b**.
24: 4 filled Jerusalem with innocent **b**,
25:25 who was of royal **b**, came with ten
1Ch 11:19 "Should I drink the **b** of these men
22: 8 'You have shed much **b** and have
22: 8 much **b** on the earth in my sight.
28: 3 you are a warrior and have shed **b**.'
2Ch 29:22 and the priests took the **b** and
29:22 and sprinkled their **b** on the altar;
29:22 and sprinkled their **b** on the altar.
29:24 presented their **b** on the altar for a
30:16 the **b** handed to them by the Levites.
35:11 and the priests sprinkled the **b**
Ne 5: 5 same flesh and **b** as our countrymen
Job 16:18 "O earth, do not cover my **b**;
39:30 His young ones feast on **b**, and
Ps 9:12 For he who avenges **b** remembers;
16: 4 not pour out their libations of **b**
50:13 of bulls or drink the **b** of goats?
58:10 their feet in the **b** of the wicked.
68:23 your feet in the **b** of your foes,
72:14 precious is their **b** in his sight.
78:44 He turned their rivers to **b**;
79: 3 They have poured out **b** like water
79:10 the outpoured **b** of your servants.
105:29 He turned their waters into **b**,
106:38 They shed innocent **b**, the **b** of their
106:38 the land was desecrated by their **b**.
Pr 1:11 let's lie in wait for someone's **b**,
1:16 into sin, they are swift to shed **b**.
1:18 These men lie in wait for their own **b**
6:17 tongue, hands that shed innocent **b**,
12: 6 of the wicked lie in wait for **b**,
30:33 and as twisting the nose produces **b**,
Isa 1:11 the **b** of bulls and lambs and goats.
1:15 Your hands are full of **b**;
9: 5 every garment rolled in **b** will be
15: 9 Dimon's waters are full of **b**, but I
26:21 The earth will disclose the **b** shed
34: 3 will be soaked with their **b**.
34: 6 The sword of the LORD is bathed in **b**,
34: 6 the **b** of lambs and goats,
34: 7 Their land will be drenched with **b**,
49:26 drunk on their own **b**, as with wine.
59: 3 For your hands are stained with **b**,
59: 7 they are swift to shed innocent **b**.
63: 3 their **b** spattered my garments,
63: 6 and poured their **b** on the ground."
66: 3 is like one who presents pig's **b**,
Jer 7: 6 not shed innocent **b** in this place,
19: 4 place with the **b** of the innocent.
22: 3 not shed innocent **b** in this place.
22:17 on shedding innocent **b** and on
26:15 guilt of innocent **b** on yourselves
41: 1 who was of royal **b** and had been one
46:10 it has quenched its thirst with **b**.
51:35 "May our **b** be on those who live in
Lam 4:13 within her the **b** of the righteous.
4:14 They are so defiled with **b** that
Eze 3:18 will hold you accountable for his **b**.
3:20 will hold you accountable for his **b**.
16: 6 and saw you kicking about in your **b**,
16: 6 and as you lay there in your **b** I
16: 9 and washed the **b** from you and put
16:22 and bare, kicking about in your **b**.
16:36 you gave them your children's **b**,
16:38 who commit adultery and who shed **b**;
16:38 I will bring upon you the **b**
18:10 a violent son, who sheds **b** or does
18:13 and his **b** will be on his own head.
21:32 your **b** will be shed in your land,
22: 3 doom by shedding **b** in her midst
22: 4 because of the **b** you have shed
22: 6 are in you uses his power to shed **b**.
22: 9 slanderous men bent on shedding **b**;
22:12 In you men accept bribes to shed **b**;
22:13 the **b** you have shed in your midst.

Eze 22:27 they shed **b** and kill people to make
23:37 adultery and **b** is on their hands.
23:45 who commit adultery and shed **b**,
23:45 adulterous and **b** is on their hands.
24: 7 "For the **b** she shed is in her midst:
24: 8 I put her **b** on the bare rock,
28:23 her and make **b** flow in her streets.
32: 6 drench the land with your flowing **b**
33: 4 his **b** will be on his own head.
33: 5 his **b** will be on his own head.
33: 6 the watchman accountable for his **b**.'
33: 8 will hold you accountable for his **b**.
33:25 Since you eat meat with the **b** still
33:25 look to your idols and shed **b**,
36:18 because they had shed **b** in the land
39:17 There you will eat flesh and drink **b**.
39:18 drink the **b** of the princes of the
39:19 and drink **b** till you are drunk.
43:18 **b** upon the altar when it is built:
43:20 You are to take some of its **b** and
44: 7 you offered me food, fat and **b**,
44:15 to offer sacrifices of fat and **b**,
45:19 The priest is to take some of the **b**
Hos 6: 8 stained with footprints of **b**.
Joel 2:30 **b** and fire and billows of smoke.
2:31 the moon to **b** before the coming of
3:19 in whose land they shed innocent **b**.
Mic 7: 2 All men lie in wait to shed **b**;
Na 3: 1 Woe to the city of **b**, full of lies,
Hab 2: 8 For you have shed man's **b**;
2:17 For you have shed man's **b**;
Zep 1:17 Their **b** will be poured out like dust
Zec 9: 7 I will take the **b** from their mouths,
9:11 because of the **b** of my covenant
Mt 23:30 in shedding the **b** of the prophets.'
23:35 **b** that has been shed on earth,
23:35 from the **b** of righteous Abel to the **b**
27: 4 "for I have betrayed innocent **b**.
27: 6 the treasury, since it is **b** money."
27: 8 called the Field of **B** to this day.
27:24 "I am innocent of this man's **b**,"
27:25 "Let his **b** be on us and on
Lk 11:50 for the **b** of all the prophets
11:51 from the **b** of Abel to the **b** of
13: 1 Galileans whose **b** Pilate had mixed
22:20 my **b**, which is poured out for you.
22:44 drops of **b** falling to the ground.
Jn 6:53 his **b**, you have no life in you.
6:54 Whoever eats my flesh and drinks my **b**
6:55 real food and my **b** is real drink.
6:56 Whoever eats my flesh and drinks my **b**
19:34 a sudden flow of **b** and water.
Ac 1:19 Akeldama, that is, Field of **B**.)
2:19 **b** and fire and billows of smoke.
2:20 the moon to **b** before the coming of
5:28 to make us guilty of this man's **b**."
15:20 of strangled animals and from **b**.
15:29 from **b**, from the meat of strangled
18: 6 "Your **b** be on your own heads!
20:26 I am innocent of the **b** of all men.
20:28 which he bought with his own **b**.
21:25 from **b**, from the meat of strangled
22:20 the **b** of your martyr Stephen was
Ro 3:15 " Their feet are swift to shed **b**;
3:25 atonement, through faith in his **b**.
5: 9 we have now been justified by his **b**,
1Co 11:25 the new covenant in my **b**; do this,
11:27 against the body and **b** of the Lord.
Eph 1: 7 we have redemption through his **b**,
Col 1:20 through his **b**, shed on the cross.
Heb 9: 7 and never without **b**, which he
9:12 He did not enter by means of the **b**
9:12 Holy Place once for all by his own **b**,
9:13 The **b** of goats and bulls and the
9:18 was not put into effect without **b**.
9:19 he took the **b** of calves, together
9:21 he sprinkled with the **b** both the
9:22 everything be cleansed with **b**,
9:22 and without the shedding of **b**
9:25 year with **b** that is not his own.
10: 4 it is impossible for the **b** of bulls
10:19 Most Holy Place by the **b** of Jesus,
11:28 Passover and the sprinkling of **b**,
12: 4 to the point of shedding your **b**.
12:24 and to the sprinkled **b** that speaks a
12:24 a better word than the **b** of Abel.
Heb 13:11 The high priest carries the **b** of
13:12 the people holy through his own **b**.
13:20 who through the **b** of the eternal
1Pe 1: 2 Jesus Christ and sprinkling by his **b**:
1Jn 1: 7 and the **b** of Jesus, his Son,
5: 6 came by water and **b**—Jesus Christ.
5: 6 by water only, but by water and **b**.
5: 8 the Spirit, the water and the **b**;
Rev 1: 5 has freed us from our sins by his **b**,
5: 9 and with your **b** you purchased men
6:10 of the earth and avenge our **b**?"
6:12 the whole moon turned **b** red,
7:14 them white in the **b** of the Lamb.
8: 7 came hail and fire mixed with **b**,
8: 8 A third of the sea turned into **b**,
11: 6 power to turn the waters into **b**
12:11 They overcame him by the **b** of the
14:20 and **b** flowed out of the press,
16: 3 and it turned into **b** like that of a
16: 4 springs of water, and they became **b**.
16: 6 for they have shed the **b** of your
16: 6 them **b** to drink as they deserve."
17: 6 was drunk with the **b** of the saints,
17: 6 the **b** of those who bore testimony to
18:24 In her was found the **b** of prophets
19: 2 on her the **b** of his servants."
19:13 He is dressed in a robe dipped in **b**,

Blood of Christ
1Co 10:16 thanks a participation in the **b**?
Eph 2:13 been brought near through the **b**.
Heb 9:14 How much more, then, will the **b**, who
1Pe 1:19 with the precious **b**, a lamb without

Blood of the covenant
Ex 24: 8 "This is the **b** that the LORD has
Mt 26:28 This is my **b**, which is poured out
Mk 14:24 "This is my **b**, which is poured out
Heb 9:20 He said, "This is the **b**, which God
10:29 the **b** that sanctified him,

Bloodguilt (Guilt)
Ps 51:14 Save me from **b**, O God, the God who
Joel 3:21 Their **b**, which I have not pardoned,

Blood-relative (Blood-relatives, Relative)
Lev 25:49 An uncle or a cousin or any **b** in his

Blood-relatives (Blood-relative, Relative)
Eze 11:15 your brothers who are your **b**

Bloodshed (Blood)
Ex 22: 2 the defender is not guilty of **b**;
22: 3 after sunrise, he is guilty of **b**.
Lev 17: 4 man shall be considered guilty of **b**;
Nu 35:33 **B** pollutes the land, and atonement
Dt 17: 8 whether **b**, lawsuits or assaults
19:10 so that you will not be guilty of **b**.
21: 8 And the **b** will be atoned for.
22: 8 bring the guilt of **b** on your house
1Sa 25:26 from **b** and from avenging yourself.
25:31 the staggering burden of needless **b**
25:33 for keeping me from **b** this day and
2Ch 19:10 **b** or other concerns of the law,
Isa 5: 7 And he looked for justice, but saw **b**;
Jer 48:10 on him who keeps his sword from **b**!
Eze 5:17 Plague and **b** will sweep through you,
7:23 because the land is full of **b**
9: 9 the land is full of **b** and the city
14:19 pour out my wrath upon it through **b**
22: 2 Will you judge this city of **b**?
24: 6 "Woe to the city of **b**, to the pot
24: 9 "Woe to the city of **b**!
35: 6 I will give you over to **b**
35: 6 did not hate **b**, **b** will pursue you.
38:22 judgment upon him with plague and **b**
Hos 4: 2 break all bounds, and **b** follows **b**.
12:14 leave upon him the guilt of his **b**
Mic 3:10 who build Zion with **b**, and Jerusalem
Hab 2:12 "Woe to him who builds a city with **b**

Bloodshot (Blood)
Pr 23:29 needless bruises? Who has **b** eyes?

Blood-stained (Blood)
2Sa 21: 1 on account of Saul and his **b** house

Bloodstains (Blood)
Isa 4: 4 he will cleanse the **b** from Jerusalem

Bloodthirsty (Blood)
Ps 5: 6 **b** and deceitful men the LORD abhors
26: 9 with sinners, my life with **b** men,
55:23 **b** and deceitful men will not live
59: 2 evildoers and save me from **b** men.
139:19 O God! Away from me, you **b** men!
Pr 29:10 **B** men hate a man of integrity

Bloom
Ex 9:31 in the ear and the flax was in **b**.
SS 2:15 our vineyards that are in **b**.
6:11 or the pomegranates were in **b**.
7:12 and if the pomegranates are in **b**
Isa 35: 2 will burst into **b**; it will rejoice

Blossom (Blossomed, Blossoming, Blossoms)
1Ki 7:26 the rim of a cup, like a lily **b**.
2Ch 4: 5 the rim of a cup, like a lily **b**.
Isa 18: 5 For, before the harvest, when the **b**
27: 6 Israel will bud and **b** and fill all
35: 1 the wilderness will rejoice and **b**.
Hos 14: 5 he will **b** like a lily.
14: 7 He will **b** like a vine, and his fame
Jas 1:11 **b** falls and its beauty is destroyed.

Blossomed (Blossom)
Ge 40:10 As soon as it budded, it **b**, and its
Nu 17: 8 had budded, **b** and produced almonds.
Eze 7:10 the rod has budded, arrogance has **b**!

Blossoming (Blossom)
SS 2:13 the **b** vines spread their fragrance.

Blossoms (Blossom)
Ex 25:31 and **b** shall be of one piece with it.
25:33 buds and **b** are to be on one branch,
25:34 like almond flowers with buds and **b**.
37:17 and **b** were of one piece with it.
37:19 with buds and **b** were on one branch,
37:20 like almond flowers with buds and **b**.
Nu 8: 4 gold—from its base to its **b**.
Job 15:33 like an olive tree shedding its **b**.
Ecc 12: 5 when the almond tree **b** and the
SS 1:14 lover is to me a cluster of henna **b**
7:12 if their **b** have opened, and if the
Na 1: 4 wither and the **b** of Lebanon fade.

Blot (Blots, Blotted)
Ex 17:14 because I will completely **b** out the
32:32 then **b** me out of the book you have
32:33 against me I will **b** out of my book.
Dt 9:14 **b** out their name from under heaven.
25:19 you shall **b** out the memory of Amalek
29:20 **b** out his name from under heaven.
32:26 and **b** out their memory from mankind,
2Ki 14:27 he would **b** out the name of Israel
Ne 4: 5 or **b** out their sins from your sight
13:14 and do not **b** out what I have
Ps 51: 1 compassion **b** out my transgressions.
51: 9 and **b** out all my iniquity
Jer 18:23 Do not forgive their crimes or **b** out
Rev 3: 5 I will never **b** out his name from the

Blots (Blot)
Isa 43:25 "I, even I, am he who **b** out your
2Pe 2:13 They are **b** and blemishes, revelling

Blotted (Blot)
Dt 25: 6 name will not be **b** out from Israel.
Ps 9: 5 **b** out their name for ever and ever.
69:28 May they be **b** out of the book of
109:13 **b** out from the next generation.
109:14 sin of his mother never be **b** out.

Blow[1] (Blew, Blowing, Blown, Blows[1], Wind-blown)

Ex 10:13 and the LORD made an east wind **b**
Nu 10: 7 gather the assembly, **b** the trumpets
10: 8 the priests, are to **b** the trumpets.
Jdg 7:18 I and all who are with me **b** our
7:18 then from all around the camp **b**
7:20 hands the trumpets they were to **b**,
1Ki 1:34 **B** the trumpet and shout, 'Long live
1Ch 15:24 to **b** trumpets before the ark of God.
16: 6 the priests were to **b** the trumpets
Ps 68: 2 may you **b** them away; as wax melts
SS 4:16 come, south wind! **B** on my garden,
Isa 5:24 and their flowers **b** away like dust;
19: 7 parched, will **b** away and be no more.
41:16 and a gale will **b** them away.
57:13 a mere breath will **b** them away.
Jer 6:29 The bellows **b** fiercely to burn away
51:27 **B** the trumpet among the nations!
Eze 7:14 Though they **b** the trumpet and get
22:21 I will **b** on you with my fiery wrath
33: 6 does not **b** the trumpet to warn the
Joel 2: 1 **B** the trumpet in Zion; sound the
2:15 **B** the trumpet in Zion, declare a
Ac 27:13 a gentle south wind began to **b**, they

Blow[2] (Blows[2])

Ex 21:19 the one who struck the **b** will not be
Jdg 16:28 and let me with one **b** get revenge on
1Sa 6:19 the heavy **b** the LORD had dealt them,
2Ch 21:14 that is yours, with a heavy **b**.
Ps 39:10 I am overcome by the **b** of your hand.
Jer 14:17 a grievous wound, a crushing **b**.
Eze 7: 9 it is I the LORD who strikes the **b**.
24:16 "Son of man, with one **b** I am about

Blowing (Blow[1])

Jos 6: 4 with the priests **b** the trumpets.
6: 8 **b** their trumpets, and the ark of the
6:13 ark of the LORD and **b** the trumpets.
2Ki 11:14 land were rejoicing and **b** trumpets.
2Ch 23:13 land were rejoicing and **b** trumpets,
Hos 13:15 **b** in from the desert; his spring
Jn 6:18 A strong wind was **b** and the waters
Ac 2: 2 Suddenly a sound like the **b** of a
Rev 7: 1 to prevent any wind from **b**, on

Blown (Blow[1])

1Sa 13: 3 Then Saul had the trumpet **b**
Ps 68: 2 As smoke is **b** away by the wind,
Isa 29: 5 the ruthless hordes like **b** chaff.
Eph 4:14 and **b** here and there by every wind
Jas 1: 6 the sea, **b** and tossed by the wind.
Jude :12 clouds without rain, **b** along by

Blows[1] (Blow[1])

Ps 1: 4 are like chaff that the wind **b** away.
103:16 the wind **b** over it and it is gone,
Ecc 1: 6 The wind **b** to the south and turns to
Isa 27: 8 as on a day the east wind **b**.
40: 7 the breath of the LORD **b** on them.
40:24 than he **b** on them and they wither,
Jer 4:11 in the desert **b** towards my people,
Eze 33: 3 **b** the trumpet to warn the people,
Lk 12:55 the south wind **b**, you say, 'It's
Jn 3: 8 The wind **b** wherever it pleases.

Blows[2] (Blow[2])

Job 20:23 him and rain down his **b** upon him.
Pr 6:33 **B** and disgrace are his lot, and his
20:30 **B** and wounds cleanse away evil, and
Isa 14: 6 struck down peoples with unceasing **b**,
30:32 in battle with the **b** of his arm.
Eze 26: 9 He will direct the **b** of his
Lk 12:47 wants will be beaten with many **b**.
12:48 will be beaten with few **b**.

Blue

Ex 25: 4 **b**, purple and scarlet yarn and fine
26: 1 of finely twisted linen and **b**,
26: 4 Make loops of **b** material along the
26:31 "Make a curtain of **b**, purple and
26:36 to the tent make a curtain of **b**,
27:16 of **b**, purple and scarlet yarn and
28: 5 Make them use gold, and **b**, purple
28: 6 "Make the ephod of gold, and of **b**,
28: 8 and with **b**, purple and scarlet yarn,
28:15 and of **b**, purple and scarlet yarn,
28:28 the rings of the ephod with **b** cord,
28:31 of the ephod entirely of **b** cloth,
28:33 Make pomegranates of **b**, purple and
28:37 Fasten a **b** cord to it to attach it
35: 6 **b**, purple and scarlet yarn and fine
35:23 Everyone who had **b**, purple or
35:25 **b**, purple or scarlet yarn or fine
35:35 designers, embroiderers in **b**, purple
36: 8 and **b**, purple and scarlet yarn,
36:11 they made loops of **b** material along
36:35 They made the curtain of **b**, purple
36:37 the tent they made a curtain of **b**,
38:18 entrance to the courtyard was of **b**,
38:23 and an embroiderer in **b**, purple and
39: 1 From the **b**, purple and scarlet yarn
39: 2 They made the ephod of gold, and of **b**
39: 3 cut strands to be worked into the **b**,
39: 5 and with **b**, purple and scarlet yarn,
39: 8 and of **b**, purple and scarlet yarn,
39:21 the rings of the ephod with **b** cord,
39:22 of **b** cloth—the work of a weaver—
39:24 They made pomegranates of **b**, purple
39:29 and **b**, purple and scarlet yarn,
39:31 they fastened a **b** cord to it to
Nu 4: 6 spread a cloth of solid **b** over that
4: 7 a **b** cloth and put on it the plates,
4: 9 " They are to take a **b** cloth and
4:11 altar they are to spread a **b** cloth
4:12 wrap them in a **b** cloth, cover that
15:38 with a **b** cord on each tassel.
2Ch 2: 7 and in purple, crimson and **b** yarn,
2:14 **b** and crimson yarn and fine linen.
3:14 He made the curtain of **b**, purple and
Est 1: 6 had hangings of white and **b** linen,
8:15 royal garments of **b** and white,
Jer 10: 9 have made is then dressed in **b**
Eze 23: 6 clothed in **b**, governors and
27: 7 your awnings were of **b** and purple
27:24 **b** fabric, embroidered work and
Rev 9:17 red, dark **b**, and yellow as sulphur.

Blunted

Ps 58: 7 draw the bow, let their arrows be **b**.

Blurts

Pr 12:23 but the heart of fools **b** out folly.

Blush

Jer 3: 3 you refuse to **b** with shame.
6:15 they do not even know how to **b**.
8:12 they do not even know how to **b**.

Blustering

Job 8: 2 Your words are a **b** wind.

Boanerges

Mk 3:17 **B**, which means Sons of Thunder);

Board (Aboard, Boarded, Boards)

Eze 27: 9 Veteran craftsmen of Gebal were on **b**
27:27 and everyone else on **b** will sink
Ac 21: 2 Phoenicia, went on **b** and set sail.
27: 6 sailing for Italy and put us on **b**.
27:37 Altogether there were 276 of us on **b**.

Boarded (Board)

Ac 27: 2 We **b** a ship from Adramyttium about

Boards (Board)

Ex 27: 8 Make the altar hollow, out of **b**.
38: 7 They made it hollow, out of **b**.
1Ki 6:15 its interior walls with cedar **b**,
6:16 with cedar **b** from floor to ceiling

Boars

Ps 80:13 **B** from the forest ravage it

Boast (Boasted, Boasters, Boastful, Boastfully, Boasting, Boasts)

Jdg 7: 2 In order that Israel may not **b**
1Ki 20:11 not **b** like one who takes it off.' "
Ps 34: 2 My soul will **b** in the LORD;
44: 8 In God we make our **b** all day long,
49: 6 and **b** of their great riches?
52: 1 Why do you **b** of evil, you mighty man?
52: 1 Why do you **b** all day long,
75: 4 To the arrogant I say, '**B** no more,'
97: 7 those who **b** in idols—worship him,
Pr 27: 1 Do not **b** about tomorrow, for you do
Isa 10:15 or the saw **b** against him who uses it?
28:15 You **b**, "We have entered into a
61: 6 and in their riches you will **b**.
Jer 9:23 "Let not the wise man **b** of his
9:23 or the strong man **b** of his strength
9:23 or the rich man **b** of his riches,
9:24 let him who boasts **b** about this:
49: 4 Why do you **b** of your valleys, **b** of
51:41 the **b** of the whole earth seized!
Am 4: 5 **b** about them, you Israelites,
Ob :12 nor **b** so much in the day of their
Ro 4: 2 he had something to **b** about—but not
11:18 do not **b** over those branches. If you
1Co 1:29 that no-one may **b** before him.
1:31 "Let him who boasts **b** in the Lord.
4: 7 why do you **b** as though you did not?
9:15 have anyone deprive me of this **b**.
9:16 I cannot **b**, for I am compelled to
13: 4 it does not **b**, it is not proud.
2Co 1:12 Now this is our **b**: Our conscience
1:14 can **b** of us just as we will **b** of you
10: 8 For even if I **b** somewhat freely
10:13 We, however, will not **b** beyond
10:16 For we do not want to **b** about work
10:17 "Let him who boasts **b** in the Lord.
11:12 with us in the things they **b** about.
11:18 way the world does, I too will **b**.
11:21 What anyone else dares to **b** about
11:21 as a fool—I also dare to **b** about.
11:30 If I must **b**, I will **b** of the things
12: 5 I will **b** about a man like that,
12: 5 but I will not **b** about myself,
12: 6 Even if I should choose to **b**,
12: 9 Therefore I will **b** all the more
Gal 6:13 that they may **b** about your flesh.
6:14 May I never **b** except in the cross
Eph 2: 9 not by works, so that no-one can **b**.
Php 2:16 in order that I may **b** on the day of
2Th 1: 4 Therefore, among God's churches we **b**
Heb 3: 6 courage and the hope of which we **b**.
Jas 3:14 do not **b** about it or deny the truth.
4:16 As it is, you **b** and brag. All such
Jude :16 they **b** about themselves and flatter

Boasted (Boast)

Ex 15: 9 "The enemy **b**, 'I will pursue, I will
Est 5:11 Haman **b** to them about his vast
Isa 20: 5 Those who trusted in Cush and **b** in
Jer 13:20 to you, the sheep of which you **b**?
Eze 35:13 You **b** against me and spoke against
Ac 8: 9 He **b** that he was someone great,
2Co 7:14 I had **b** to him about you,

Boasters (Boast)

Jer 48:45 of Moab, the skulls of the noisy **b**.

Boastful (Boast)

Ps 12: 3 flattering lips and every **b** tongue
Da 7:11 the **b** words the horn was speaking.
Ro 1:30 God-haters, insolent, arrogant and **b**;
2Ti 3: 2 lovers of money, **b**, proud, abusive,
2Pe 2:18 For they mouth empty, **b** words and,

Boastfully (Boast)

Da 7: 8 of a man and a mouth that spoke **b**.
7:20 had eyes and a mouth that spoke **b**.

Boasting (Boast)

Ps 94: 4 all the evildoers are full of **b**.
Ro 3:27 Where, then, is **b**? It is excluded.
1Co 3:21 So then, no more **b** about men!
5: 6 Your **b** is not good. Don't you know

2Co 7:14 so our **b** about you to Titus has
9: 2 and I have been **b** about it to the
9: 3 our **b** about you in this matter should
10:13 but will confine our **b** to the field
10:14 We are not going too far in our **b**,
10:15 limits by **b** of work done by others.
11:10 of Achaia will stop this **b** of mine.
11:16 a fool, so that I may do a little **b**.
11:17 In this self-confident **b** I am not
11:18 Since many are **b** in the way the
12: 1 I must go on **b**. Although there is
Jas 4:16 boast and brag. All such **b** is evil.
1Jn 2:16 the **b** of what he has and does

Boasts (Boast)

1Sa 2: 1 My mouth **b** over my enemies, for I
Ps 10: 3 He **b** of the cravings of his heart;
Pr 20:14 he goes and **b** about his purchase.
25:14 man who **b** of gifts he does not give.
Isa 16: 6 her insolence—but her **b** are empty.
Jer 9:24 let him who **b** boast about this :
48:30 "and her **b** accomplish nothing.
Hos 12: 8 Ephraim **b**, "I am very rich; I have
1Co 1:31 "Let him who **b** boast in the Lord.
2Co 10:17 "Let him who **b** boast in the Lord.
Jas 3: 5 of the body, but it makes great **b**.
Rev 18: 7 In her heart she **b**,'I sit as queen;

Boat (Boats, Lifeboat)

Mt 4:21 They were in a **b** with their father
4:22 immediately they left the **b** and
8:23 he got into the **b** and his disciples
8:24 so that the waves swept over the **b**.
9: 1 Jesus stepped into a **b**, crossed over
13: 2 that he got into a **b** and sat in it,
14:13 by **b** privately to a solitary place.
14:22 made the disciples get into the **b**
14:24 the **b** was already a considerable
14:29 Then Peter got down out of the **b**,
14:32 they climbed into the **b**, the wind
14:33 those who were in the **b** worshipped
15:39 he got into the **b** and went to the
Mk 1:19 John in a **b**, preparing their nets.
1:20 Zebedee in the **b** with the hired men
3: 9 to have a small **b** ready for him,
4: 1 a **b** and sat in it out on the lake,
4:36 him along, just as he was, in the **b**.
4:37 the waves broke over the **b**,
5: 2 Jesus got out of the **b**, a man with
5:18 Jesus was getting into the **b**,
5:21 Jesus had again crossed over by **b** to
6:32 they went away by themselves in a **b**
6:45 made his disciples get into the **b**
6:47 the **b** was in the middle of the lake
6:51 he climbed into the **b** with them, and
6:54 soon as they got out of the **b**,
8:10 he got into the **b** with his disciples
8:13 he left them, got back into the **b**
8:14 loaf they had with them in the **b**.
Lk 5: 3 and taught the people from the **b**.
5: 7 the other **b** to come and help them,
8:22 So they got into a **b** and set out.
8:23 so that the **b** was being swamped,
8:37 So he got into the **b** and left.
Jn 6:17 where they got into a **b** and set off
6:19 they saw Jesus approaching the **b**,
6:21 were willing to take him into the **b**,
6:21 immediately the **b** reached the shore
6:22 that only one **b** had been there,
21: 3 So they went out and got into the **b**,
21: 6 your net on the right side of the **b**
21: 8 The other disciples followed in the **b**

Boats (Boat)

Job 9:26 They skim past like **b** of papyrus,
Isa 18: 2 by sea in papyrus **b** over the water.
Mk 4:36 There were also other **b** with him.
Lk 5: 2 he saw at the water's edge two **b**,
5: 3 He got into one of the **b**, the one
5: 7 **b** so full that they began to sink.
5:11 they pulled their **b** up on shore,
Jn 6:23 some **b** from Tiberias landed near the
6:24 they got into the **b** and went to

Boaz

Wealthy and benevolent landowner from Bethlehem; married Ruth, the widow of a relative, fulfilling the responsibility of kinsman-redeemer (Ru 2–4). Ancestor of David (Ru 4:17–22; 1Ch 2:5–15) and of Jesus (Mt 1:5).

Ru 2: 1 a man of standing, whose name was **B**.
2: 3 working in a field belonging to **B**,
2: 4 Just then **B** arrived from Bethlehem
2: 5 **B** asked the foreman of his
2: 8 **B** said to Ruth, "My daughter, listen
2:11 **B** replied, "I've been told all about
2:14 At mealtime **B** said to her, "Come
2:15 she got up to glean, **B** gave orders
2:19 the man I worked with today is **B**,"
2:23 close to the servant girls of **B**
3: 2 Is not **B**, with whose servant girls
3: 7 **B** had finished eating and drinking
3:16 told her everything **B** had done for
4: 1 Meanwhile **B** went up to the town gate
4: 1 **B** said, "Come over here, my friend,
4: 2 **B** took ten of the elders of the town
4: 5 **B** said, "On the day you buy the land
4: 8 the kinsman-redeemer said to **B**, "Buy
4: 9 **B** announced to the elders and all
4:13 **B** took Ruth and she became his wife.
4:21 Salmon the father of **B**, **B** the father
1Ki 7:21 Jakin and the one to the north **B**.
1Ch 2:11 of Salmon, Salmon the father of **B**,
2:12 **B** the father of Obed and Obed the
2Ch 3:17 Jakin and the one to the north **B**.
Mt 1: 5 Salmon the father of **B**, whose mother
1: 5 **B** the father of Obed, whose mother
Lk 3:32 the son of Obed, the son of **B**,

Bodies (Body)

Ge 34:27 sons of Jacob came upon the dead **b**
47:18 our lord except our **b** and our land.
Ex 30:32 Do not pour it on men's **b** and do
Lev 19:28 "'Do not cut your **b** for the dead
21: 5 of their beards or cut their **b**.
26:30 pile your dead **b** on the lifeless
Nu 8: 7 then make them shave their whole **b**
14:29 In this desert your **b** will fall
14:32 your **b** will fall in this desert.
14:33 last of your **b** lies in the desert.
1Sa 31:12 They took down the **b** of Saul and his
2Sa 4:12 hung the **b** by the pool in Hebron.
21:10 down from the heavens on the **b**,
2Ki 10:25 The guards and officers threw the **b**
19:35 morning—there were all the dead **b**!
1Ch 10:12 took the **b** of Saul and his sons and
2Ch 20:24 they saw only dead **b** lying on the
Ne 9:37 They rule over our **b** and our cattle
Ps 44:25 the dust ; our **b** cling to the ground.
73: 4 their **b** are healthy and strong.
79: 2 They have given the dead **b** of your
Isa 5:25 and the dead **b** are like refuse
26:19 dead will live; their **b** will rise
34: 3 their dead **b** will send up a stench;
37:36 morning—there were all the dead **b**!
66:24 **b** of those who rebelled against me;
Jer 9:22 "'The dead **b** of men will lie like
16: 4 and their dead **b** will become food
31:40 where dead **b** and ashes are thrown,
33: 5 ' They will be filled with the dead **b**
34:20 Their dead **b** will become food for
41: 9 the **b** of the men he had killed
Lam 4: 7 their **b** more ruddy than rubies,
Eze 6: 5 I will lay the dead **b** of the
10:12 Their entire **b**, including their
11: 7 The **b** you have thrown there are the
Da 3:27 the fire had not harmed their **b**,
Am 6:10 if a relative who is to burn the **b**
8: 3 many **b**—flung everywhere! Silence!"
Na 2:10 **b** tremble, every face grows pale.
3: 3 piles of dead, **b** without number,
Hab 2:15 that he can gaze on their naked **b**.
Mt 24:29 and the heavenly **b** will be shaken.'
27:52 and the **b** of many holy people
Mk 13:25 and the heavenly **b** will be shaken.'
Lk 21:26 for the heavenly **b** will be shaken.
Jn 19:31 Because the Jews did not want the **b**
19:31 legs broken and the **b** taken down.
Ac 7:16 Their **b** were brought back to Shechem
7:42 to the worship of the heavenly **b**.
Ro 1:24 of their **b** with one another.
7: 5 at work in our **b**, so that we bore
8:11 to your mortal **b** through his Spirit,
8:23 as sons, the redemption of our **b**.
12: 1 to offer your **b** as living sacrifices,
1Co 6:15 Do you not know that your **b** are
10: 5 **b** were scattered over the desert.
15:40 heavenly **b** and there are earthly **b**;
15:40 the splendour of the heavenly **b**
15:40 the splendour of the earthly **b**
Eph 5:28 to love their wives as their own **b**.
Php 3:21 will transform our lowly **b** so that
Heb 3:17 sinned, whose **b** fell in the desert?
10:22 having our **b** washed with pure water.
13:11 the **b** are burned outside the camp.
Jude : 8 these dreamers pollute their own **b**,
Rev 11: 8 Their **b** will lie in the street of
11: 9 on their **b** and refuse them burial.
18:13 carriages; and **b** and souls of men.

Bodily (Body)

Lev 15: 2 'When any man has a **b** discharge,
22: 4 skin disease or a **b** discharge,
Lk 3:22 descended on him in **b** form
Col 2: 9 of the Deity lives in **b** form,

Body (Bodies, Bodily, *Body of Christ*, Embodiment, *One body*, *Whole body*)

Ge 15: 4 from your own **b** will be your heir."
35:11 and kings will come from your **b**.
Ex 22:27 the only covering he has for his **b**.
28:42 as a covering for the **b**,
Lev 6:10 linen undergarments next to his **b**,
15: 3 flowing from his **b** or is blocked,
16: 4 linen undergarments next to his **b**;
21:11 a place where there is a dead **b**.
Nu 5: 2 unclean because of a dead **b**.
5:22 enter your **b** so that your abdomen
6: 6 LORD he must not go near a dead **b**.
6:11 being in the presence of the dead **b**.
9: 6 unclean on account of a dead **b**.
9: 7 become unclean because of a dead **b**,
9:10 are unclean because of a dead **b**
19:11 "Whoever touches the dead **b** of
19:13 Whoever touches the dead **b** of anyone
25: 8 Israelite and into the woman's **b**.
Dt 4: 8 laws as this **b** of laws I am setting
21: 2 and measure the distance from the **b**
21: 3 the elders of the town nearest the **b**
21: 6 the elders of the town nearest the **b**
21:22 death and his **b** is hung on a tree,
21:23 you must not leave his **b** on the tree
Jos 8:29 Joshua ordered them to take his **b**
1Sa 5: 4 the threshold; only his **b** remained.
31:10 his **b** to the wall of Beth Shan.
2Sa 7:12 who will come from your own **b**,
1Ki 13:22 Therefore your **b** will not be buried
13:24 and his **b** was thrown down on the
13:25 Some people who passed by saw the **b**
13:25 with the lion standing beside the **b**,
13:28 he went out and found the **b** thrown
13:28 eaten the **b** nor mauled the donkey.
13:29 the prophet picked up the **b** of the
13:30 he laid the **b** in his own tomb, and
2Ki 4:34 out upon him, the boy's **b** grew warm.
6:30 he had sackcloth on his **b**.
9:37 Jezebel's **b** will be like refuse on
13:21 the man's **b** into Elisha's tomb.
13:21 When the **b** touched Elisha's bones,
23:30 Josiah's servants brought his **b** in a
Ezr 8:20 the temple servants—a **b** that David
Job 4:15 and the hair on my **b** stood on end.
7: 5 My **b** is clothed with worms and scabs,
7:15 death, rather than this **b** of mine.
14:22 He feels but the pain of his own **b**
21: 6 am terrified; trembling seizes my **b**.
21:24 his **b** well nourished, his bones rich
30:30 my **b** burns with fever.
Ps 16: 9 my **b** also will rest secure,
31: 9 my soul and my **b** with grief.
38: 3 wrath there is no health in my **b**;
38: 7 there is no health in my **b**.
63: 1 my **b** longs for you, in a dry and

Ps 109:18 it entered into his **b** like water,
109:24 my **b** is thin and gaunt.
139:16 your eyes saw my unformed **b**.
Pr 3: 8 This will bring health to your **b**
5:11 when your flesh and **b** are spent.
14:30 A heart at peace gives life to the **b**,
Ecc 11: 5 or how the **b** is formed in a mother's
11:10 and cast off the troubles of your **b**,
12:12 and much study wearies the **b**.
SS 5:14 His **b** is like polished ivory
Isa 17: 4 the fat of his **b** will waste away.
20: 2 Take off the sackcloth from your **b**
21: 3 At this my **b** is racked with pain,
Jer 13:22 torn off and your **b** ill-treated.
26:23 his **b** thrown into the burial place
36:30 his **b** will be thrown out and exposed
Eze 1:11 and two wings covering its **b**.
1:23 each had two wings covering its **b**.
16:25 offering your **b** with increasing
Da 4:33 His **b** was drenched with the dew of
5:21 and his **b** was drenched with the dew
7:11 its **b** destroyed and thrown into the
10: 6 His **b** was like chrysolite, his face
Mic 6: 7 the fruit of my **b** for the sin of my
Hag 2:13 dead **b** touches one of these things,
Zec 13: 6 'What are these wounds on your **b**?'
Mt 5:29 for you to lose one part of your **b**
5:30 for you to lose one part of your **b**
6:22 " The eye is the lamp of the **b**. If
6:25 or about your **b**, what you will wear.
6:25 the **b** more important than clothes?
10:28 kill the **b** but cannot kill the soul.
10:28 can destroy both soul and **b** in hell.
14:12 John's disciples came and took his **b**
15:17 the stomach and then out of the **b**?
26:12 she poured this perfume on my **b**,
26:26 saying, "Take and eat; this is my **b**.
26:41 is willing, but the **b** is weak."
27:58 he asked for Jesus' **b**, and Pilate
27:59 Joseph took the **b**, wrapped it in a
27:64 steal the **b** and tell the people that
Mk 5:29 she felt in her **b** that she was freed
6:29 took his **b** and laid it in a tomb.
7:19 his stomach, and then out of his **b**.
14: 8 She poured perfume on my **b**
14:22 saying, "Take it; this is my **b**.
14:38 is willing, but the **b** is weak."
15:43 to Pilate and asked for Jesus' **b**.
15:45 it was so, he gave the **b** to Joseph.
15:46 took down the **b**, wrapped it in the
16: 1 they might go to anoint Jesus' **b**.
Lk 11:34 Your eye is the lamp of your **b**.
11:34 your **b** also is full of darkness.
12: 4 afraid of those who kill the **b**
12: 5 after the killing of the **b**, has power
12:22 or about your **b**, what you will wear.
12:23 and the **b** more than clothes
17:37 """Where there is a dead **b**, there the
22:19 "This is my **b** given for you; do this
23:52 to Pilate, he asked for Jesus' **b**.
23:55 tomb and how his **b** was laid in it.
24: 3 not find the **b** of the Lord Jesus.
24:23 didn't find his **b**. They came and
Jn 2:21 the temple he had spoken of was his **b**
19:38 asked Pilate for the **b** of Jesus.
19:38 he came and took the **b** away.
19:40 Taking Jesus' **b**, the two of them
20:12 seated where Jesus' **b** had been,
Ac 1:18 his **b** burst open and all his
2:26 my **b** also will live in hope,
2:31 the grave, nor did his **b** see decay.
5: 6 wrapped up his **b**, and carried him
9:37 and her **b** was washed and placed in
13:36 with his fathers and his **b** decayed.
Ro 4:19 fact that his **b** was as good as dead
6: 6 **b** of sin might be done away with,
6:12 not let sin reign in your mortal **b**
6:13 Do not offer the parts of your **b** to
6:13 and offer the parts of your **b** to him
6:19 the parts of your **b** in slavery
7:23 law at work in the members of my **b**,
7:24 will rescue me from this **b** of death?
8:10 if Christ is in you, your **b** is dead
8:13 misdeeds of the **b**, you will live,
1Co 6:13 The **b** is not meant for sexual
6:13 the Lord, and the Lord for the **b**.
1Co 6:16 one with her in **b**? For it is said,
6:18 a man commits are outside his **b**,
6:18 sexually sins against his own **b**.
6:19 Do you not know that your **b** is a
6:20 Therefore honour God with your **b**.
7: 4 The wife's **b** does not belong to her
7: 4 In the same way, the husband's **b**
7:34 to the Lord in both **b** and spirit.
9:27 No, I beat my **b** and make it my slave
11:24 "This is my **b**, which is for you; do
11:27 against the **b** and blood of the Lord.
11:29 drinks without recognising the **b** of
12:12 The **b** is a unit, though it is made
12:14 Now the **b** is not made up of one part
12:15 a hand, I do not belong to the **b**,"
12:15 reason cease to be part of the **b**.
12:16 an eye, I do not belong to the **b**,"
12:16 reason cease to be part of the **b**.
12:18 God has arranged the parts in the **b**,
12:19 all one part, where would the **b** be?
12:22 On the contrary, those parts of the **b**
12:24 has combined the members of the **b**
12:25 should be no division in the **b**,
13: 3 and surrender my **b** to the flames,
15:35 With what kind of **b** will they come?"
15:37 you do not plant the **b** that will be
15:38 God gives it a **b** as he has
15:38 kind of seed he gives its own **b**.
15:42 The **b** that is sown is perishable,
15:44 is sown a natural **b**, it is raised
15:44 it is raised a spiritual **b**.
15:44 If there is a natural **b**,
15:44 there is also a spiritual **b**.
2Co 4:10 We always carry around in our **b** the
4:10 Jesus may also be revealed in our **b**.
4:11 may be revealed in our mortal **b**.
5: 6 we are at home in the **b**
5: 8 away from the **b** and at home with
5: 9 whether we are at home in the **b**
5:10 the things done while in the **b**,
7: 1 that contaminates **b** and spirit,
7: 5 this **b** of ours had no rest, but we
12: 2 it was in the **b** or out of the **b**
12: 3 in the **b** or apart from the **b**
Gal 2:20 The life I live in the **b**, I live by
6:17 I bear on my **b** the marks of Jesus.
Eph 1:23 which is his **b**, the fulness of him
2:11 done in the **b** by the hands of men)—
5:23 his **b**, of which he is the Saviour.
5:29 no-one ever hated his own **b**, but he
5:30 for we are members of his **b**.
Php 1:20 Christ will be exalted in my **b**,
1:22 If I am to go on living in the **b**,
1:24 for you that I remain in the **b**.
3:21 they will be like his glorious **b**.
Col 1:18 he is the head of the **b**, the church;
1:22 reconciled you by Christ's physical **b**
1:24 sake of his **b**, which is the church.
2: 5 For though I am absent from you in **b**,
2:23 and their harsh treatment of the **b**,
1Th 4: 4 his own **b** in a way that is holy
5:23 May your whole spirit, soul and **b** be
1Ti 3:16 He appeared in a **b**, was vindicated
4:14 **b** of elders laid their hands on you.
Heb 7:10 was still in the **b** of his ancestor.
10: 5 but a **b** you prepared for me;
10:10 the **b** of Jesus Christ once for all.
10:20 through the curtain, that is, his **b**,
Jas 2:26 the **b** without the spirit is dead, so
3: 5 the tongue is a small part of the **b**
3: 6 of evil among the parts of the **b**.
1Pe 2:24 He himself bore our sins in his **b** on
3:18 He was put to death in the **b** but made
3:21 not the removal of dirt from the **b**
4: 1 since Christ suffered in his **b**,
4: 1 suffered in his **b** is done with sin.
4: 6 according to men in regard to the **b**,
2Pe 1:13 as I live in the tent of this **b**,
Jude : 9 with the devil about the **b** of Moses,

Body of Christ

Ro 7: 4 also died to the law through the **b**,
1Co 10:16 we break a participation in the **b**?
12:27 Now you are the **b**, and each one of
Eph 4:12 so that the **b** may be built

Bodyguard (Guard)

1Sa 22:14 captain of your **b** and highly
28: 2 I will make you my **b** for life."
2Sa 23:23 And David put him in charge of his **b**.
1Ch 11:25 And David put him in charge of his **b**.

Bohan

Jos 15: 6 to the Stone of **B** son of Reuben.
18:17 to the Stone of **B** son of Reuben.

Boil[1] (Boiled, Boiling)

Ex 16:23 and **b** what you want to **b**.
Isa 64: 2 twigs ablaze and causes water to **b**,
Eze 24: 5 bring it to the **b** and cook the bones

Boil[2] (Boils)

Lev 13:18 "When someone has a **b** on his skin
13:19 in the place where the **b** was,
13:20 that has broken out where the **b** was.
13:23 it is only a scar from the **b**, and
2Ki 20: 7 and applied it to the **b**,
Isa 38:21 and apply it to the **b**, and he will

Boiled (Boil[1])

Nu 6:19 his hands a **b** shoulder of the ram,
1Sa 2:13 and while the meat was being **b**,
2:15 he won't accept **b** meat from you,
2Ch 35:13 and **b** the holy offerings in pots,

Boiling (Boil[1])

Job 41:20 from a **b** pot over a fire of reeds.
41:31 the depths churn like a **b** cauldron
Jer 1:13 "What do you see?" "I see a **b** pot,

Boils (Boil[2])

Ex 9: 9 and festering **b** will break out on
9:10 **b** broke out on men and animals.
9:11 because of the **b** that were on them
Dt 28:27 The LORD will afflict you with the **b**
28:35 with painful **b** that cannot be cured,

Bokeru

1Ch 8:38 **B**, Ishmael, Sheariah, Obadiah and
9:44 **B**, Ishmael, Sheariah, Obadiah and

Bokim

Jdg 2: 1 went up from Gilgal to **B** and said,
2: 5 they called that place **B**. There they

Bold (Boldly, Boldness)

Ge 18:27 "Now that I have been so **b** as to
18:31 "Now that I have been so **b** as to
Ps 138: 3 you made me **b** and stout-hearted.
Pr 21:29 A wicked man puts up a **b** front,
28: 1 the righteous are as **b** as a lion.
2Co 3:12 we have such a hope, we are very **b**.
10: 1 but "**b**" when away!
10: 2 may not have to be as **b** as I expect
Phm : 8 although in Christ I could be **b** and
2Pe 2:10 **B** and arrogant, these men are not

Boldly (Bold)

Ex 14: 8 Israelites, who were marching out **b**.
Nu 33: 3 **b** in full view of all the Egyptians,
Mk 15:43 went **b** to Pilate and asked for Jesus'
Ac 4:31 Spirit and spoke the word of God **b**.
9:28 speaking **b** in the name of the Lord.
13:46 Paul and Barnabas answered them **b**:
14: 3 speaking **b** for the Lord, who
18:26 He began to speak **b** in the synagogue.
19: 8 and spoke **b** there for three months,
28:31 **B** and without hindrance he preached
Ro 10:20 Isaiah **b** says, "I was found by those
15:15 I have written to you quite **b** on

Boldness (Bold)

Lk 11: 8 yet because of the man's **b** he will
Ac 4:29 to speak your word with great **b**.

Bolt (Bolted, Bolts)

2Sa 13:17 of here and **b** the door after her."

Bolted (Bolt)
2Sa 13:18 his servant put her out and **b** the

Bolts (Bolt)
Dt 33:25 The **b** of your gates will be iron and
2Sa 22:13 **b** of lightning blazed forth.
22:15 **b** of lightning and routed them.
Ne 3: 3 its doors and **b** and bars in place.
3: 6 its doors and **b** and bars in place.
3:13 its doors and **b** and bars in place.
3:14 its doors and **b** and bars in place.
3:15 its doors and **b** and bars in place.
Job 38:35 Do you send the lightning **b** on their
Ps 18:12 with hailstones and **b** of lightning.
18:14 great **b** of lightning and routed them.
78:48 their livestock to **b** of lightning.

Bond (Bondage, Bonds)
Eze 20:37 you into the **b** of the covenant.
Eph 4: 3 the Spirit through the **b** of peace.

Bondage (Bond)
Ge 47:19 our land will be in **b** to Pharaoh.
47:25 we will be in **b** to Pharaoh."
Ex 6: 9 of their discouragement and cruel **b**.
Ezr 9: 8 eyes and a little relief in our **b**.
9: 9 God has not deserted us in our **b**.
Isa 14: 3 suffering and turmoil and cruel **b**,
Jer 34: 9 was to hold a fellow Jew in **b**.
34:10 slaves and no longer hold them in **b**.
Ro 8:21 be liberated from its **b** to decay

Bonds (Bond)
Jer 2:20 off your yoke and tore off your **b**;
5: 5 off the yoke and torn off the **b**.
30: 8 necks and will tear off their **b**;
Hos 10:10 put them in **b** for their double sin.

Bone (Backbone, Bones)
Ge 2:23 "This is now **b** of my bones
Nu 19:16 or anyone who touches a human **b** or a
19:18 anyone who has touched a human **b**
Pr 25:15 and a gentle tongue can break a **b**.
Eze 37: 7 and the bones came together, **b** to **b**.
39:15 land and one of them sees a human **b**,

Bones (Bone)
Ge 2:23 "This is now bone of my **b** and flesh
50:25 must carry my **b** up from this place."
Ex 12:46 Do not break any of the **b**.
13:19 Moses took the **b** of Joseph with him
13:19 my **b** up with you from this place."
Nu 9:12 till morning or break any of its **b**.
24: 8 nations and break their **b** in pieces;
Jos 24:32 Joseph's **b**, which the Israelites had
1Sa 31:13 they took their **b** and buried them
2Sa 21:12 he went and took the **b** of Saul and
21:13 David brought the **b** of Saul and his
21:13 the **b** of those who had been killed
21:14 They buried the **b** of Saul and his
1Ki 13: 2 and human **b** will be burned on you.'"
13:31 lay my **b** beside his **b**.
2Ki 13:21 When the body touched Elisha's **b**,
23:14 and covered the sites with human **b**.
23:16 he had the **b** removed from them and
23:18 "Don't let anyone disturb his **b**."
23:18 So they spared his **b** and those of
23:20 altars and burned human **b** on them.
1Ch 10:12 Then they buried their **b** under the
2Ch 34: 5 He burned the **b** of the priests on
Job 2: 5 hand and strike his flesh and **b**,
4:14 seized me and made all my **b** shake.
10:11 knit me together with **b** and sinews?
19:20 I am nothing but skin and **b**;
20:11 The youthful vigour that fills his **b**
21:24 his **b** rich with marrow.
30:17 Night pierces my **b**; my gnawing pains
33:19 with constant distress in his **b**,
33:21 his **b**, once hidden, now stick out.
40:18 His **b** are tubes of bronze, his limbs
Ps 6: 2 LORD, heal me, for my **b** are in agony.
22:14 and all my **b** are out of joint.
22:17 I can count all my **b**; people stare
31:10 my affliction, and my **b** grow weak.
Ps 32: 3 I kept silent, my **b** wasted away
34:20 he protects all his **b**, not one of
38: 3 my **b** have no soundness because of my
42:10 My **b** suffer mortal agony as my foes
51: 8 let the **b** you have crushed rejoice.
53: 5 God scattered the **b** of those who
102: 3 my **b** burn like glowing embers.
102: 5 groaning I am reduced to skin and **b**.
109:18 like water, into his **b** like oil.
141: 7 so our **b** have been scattered
Pr 3: 8 your body and nourishment to your **b**.
12: 4 wife is like decay in his **b**.
14:30 to the body, but envy rots the **b**.
15:30 and good news gives health to the **b**.
16:24 to the soul and healing to the **b**.
17:22 but a crushed spirit dries up the **b**.
Isa 38:13 but like a lion he broke all my **b**;
Jer 8: 1 the **b** of the kings and officials
8: 1 the **b** of the priests and prophets,
8: 1 and the **b** of the people of Jerusalem
20: 9 like a fire, a fire shut up in my **b**.
23: 9 broken within me; all my **b** tremble.
50:17 the last to crush his **b**
Lam 1:13 sent fire, sent it down into my **b**.
3: 4 flesh grow old and has broken my **b**.
4: 8 Their skin has shrivelled on their **b**
Eze 6: 5 scatter your **b** around your altars.
24: 4 Fill it with the best of these **b**;
24: 5 Pile wood beneath it for the **b**;
24: 5 it to the boil and cook the **b** in it.
24:10 and let the **b** be charred.
32:27 for their sins rested on their **b**,
37: 1 of a valley; it was full of **b**.
37: 2 and I saw a great many **b** on the
37: 2 of the valley, **b** that were very dry.
37: 3 "Son of man, can these **b** live?"
37: 4 "Prophesy to these **b** and say
37: 4 'Dry **b**, hear the word of the LORD!
37: 5 the Sovereign LORD says to these **b**:
37: 7 the **b** came together, bone to bone.
37:11 these **b** are the whole house of Israel
37:11 They say, 'Our **b** are dried up and
Da 6:24 them and crushed all their **b**.
Am 2: 1 the **b** of Edom's king,
3:12 only two leg **b** or a piece of an ear,
Mic 3: 2 people and the flesh from their **b**;
3: 3 skin and break their **b** in pieces;
Hab 3:16 decay crept into my **b**, and my legs
Mt 23:27 dead men's **b** and everything unclean.
Lk 24:39 flesh and **b**, as you see I have."
Jn 19:36 "Not one of his **b** will be broken,
Heb 11:22 and gave instructions about his **b**.

Book (*Book of life, Book of the covenant, Book of the kings, Book of the Law,* Books)
Ex 32:32 me out of the **b** you have written."
32:33 against me I will blot out of my **b**.
Nu 21:14 the **B** of the Wars of the LORD says:
Dt 28:58 which are written in this **b**, and do
29:20 All the curses written in this **b**
29:27 all the curses written in this **b**.
31:24 After Moses finished writing in a **b**
Jos 10:13 as it is written in the **B** of Jashar.
2Sa 1:18 (it is written in the **B** of Jashar):
1Ki 11:41 in the **b** of the annals of Solomon?
14:19 the **b** of the annals of the kings
14:29 the **b** of the annals of the kings
15: 7 the **b** of the annals of the kings
15:23 the **b** of the annals of the kings
15:31 the **b** of the annals of the kings
16: 5 the **b** of the annals of the kings
16:14 the **b** of the annals of the kings
16:20 the **b** of the annals of the kings
16:27 the **b** of the annals of the kings
22:39 the **b** of the annals of the kings
22:45 the **b** of the annals of the kings
2Ki 1:18 the **b** of the annals of the kings
8:23 the **b** of the annals of the kings
10:34 the **b** of the annals of the kings
12:19 the **b** of the annals of the kings
13: 8 the **b** of the annals of the kings
13:12 the **b** of the annals of the kings
14:15 the **b** of the annals of the kings
14:18 the **b** of the annals of the kings
2Ki 14:28 the **b** of the annals of the kings
15: 6 the **b** of the annals of the kings
15:11 the **b** of the annals of the kings
15:15 the **b** of the annals of the kings
15:21 the **b** of the annals of the kings
15:26 the **b** of the annals of the kings
15:31 the **b** of the annals of the kings
15:36 the **b** of the annals of the kings
16:19 the **b** of the annals of the kings
20:20 the **b** of the annals of the kings
21:17 the **b** of the annals of the kings
21:25 the **b** of the annals of the kings
22:10 the priest has given me a **b**.
22:13 in this **b** that has been found.
22:13 have not obeyed the words of this **b**;
22:16 in the **b** the king of Judah has read.
23: 3 of the covenant written in this **b**.
23:24 the law written in the **b** that Hilkiah
23:28 the **b** of the annals of the kings
24: 5 the **b** of the annals of the kings
1Ch 27:24 the **b** of the annals of King David.
2Ch 25: 4 in the **B** of Moses, where the LORD
34:16 Shaphan took the **b** to the king and
34:18 the priest has given me a **b**.
34:21 in this **b** that has been found.
34:21 with all that is written in this **b**."
34:24 all the curses written in the **b** that
34:31 of the covenant written in this **b**.
35:12 as is written in the **B** of Moses.
Ezr 6:18 what is written in the **B** of Moses.
Ne 8: 5 Ezra opened the **b**. All the people
12:23 recorded in the **b** of the annals.
13: 1 On that day the **B** of Moses was read
Est 2:23 was recorded in the **b** of the annals
6: 1 he ordered the **b** of the chronicles,
10: 2 the **b** of the annals of the kings
Ps 139:16 were written in your **b** before one
Jer 25:13 all that are written in this **b** and
30: 2 'Write in a **b** all the words I have
Da 10:21 what is written in the **B** of Truth.
12: 1 written in the **b**—will be delivered.
Na 1: 1 The **b** of the vision of Nahum
Mk 12:26 you not read in the **b** of Moses,
Lk 3: 4 in the **b** of the words of Isaiah
20:42 declares in the **B** of Psalms
Jn 20:30 which are not recorded in this **b**.
Ac 1: 1 In my former **b**, Theophilus, I wrote
1:20 "it is written in the **B** of Psalms, "'
7:42 is written in the **b** of the prophets:
8:28 reading the **b** of Isaiah the prophet.
Rev 22: 7 words of the prophecy in this **b**."
22: 9 of all who keep the words of this **b**.
22:10 words of the prophecy of this **b**,
22:18 words of the prophecy of this **b**:
22:18 the plagues described in this **b**.
22:19 words away from this **b** of prophecy,
22:19 which are described in this **b**.

Book of life
Ps 69:28 May they be blotted out of the **b** and
Php 4: 3 whose names are in the **b**.
Rev 3: 5 never blot out his name from the **b**,
13: 8 in the **b** belonging to the Lamb
17: 8 names have not been written in the **b**
20:12 book was opened, which is the **b**.
20:15 name was not found written in the **b**,
21:27 names are written in the Lamb's **b**.

Book of the covenant
Ex 24: 7 he took the **B** and read it to the
2Ki 23: 2 hearing all the words of the **B**,
23:21 as it is written in this **B**."
2Ch 34:30 hearing all the words of the **B**,

Book of the kings
1Ch 9: 1 the genealogies in the **b** of Israel.
2Ch 16:11 in the **b** of Judah and Israel.
20:34 are recorded in the **b** of Israel.
24:27 written in the annotations on the **b**.
25:26 in the **b** of Judah and Israel?
27: 7 in the **b** of Israel and Judah.
28:26 in the **b** of Judah and Israel.
32:32 Amoz in the **b** of Judah and Israel.
35:27 in the **b** of Israel and Judah.
36: 8 in the **b** of Israel and Judah.

Book of the Law
Dt 28:61 disaster not recorded in this **B**,
29:21 of the covenant written in this **B**.
30:10 decrees that are written in this **B**
31:26 "Take this **B** and place it beside the
Jos 1: 8 Do not let this **B** depart from your
8:31 what is written in the **B** of Moses
8:34 as it is written in the **B**.
23: 6 that is written in the **B** of Moses,
24:26 Joshua recorded these things in the **B**
2Ki 14: 6 **B** of Moses where the LORD commanded:
22: 8 the **B** in the temple of the LORD.
22:11 the king heard the words of the **B**,
2Ch 17: 9 taking with them the **B** of the LORD;
34:14 Hilkiah the priest found the **B** of
34:15 the **B** in the temple of the LORD.
Ne 8: 1 scribe to bring out the **B** of Moses,
8: 3 listened attentively to the **B**.
8: 8 They read from the **B** of God, making
8:18 Ezra read from the **B** of God.
9: 3 read from the **B** of the LORD their
Gal 3:10 to do everything written in the **B**."

Books (Book)
Ecc 12:12 Of making many **b** there is no end,
Da 7:10 was seated, and the **b** were opened.
Jn 21:25 for the **b** that would be written.
Rev 20:12 the throne, and **b** were opened.
20:12 they had done as recorded in the **b**.

Boosting
Am 8: 5 **b** the price and cheating with

Boot
Isa 9: 5 Every warrior's **b** used in battle

Booth (Booths)
Mt 9: 9 sitting at the tax collector's **b**.
Mk 2:14 sitting at the tax collector's **b**.
Lk 5:27 name of Levi sitting at his tax **b**.

Booths (Booth)
Lev 23:42 Live in **b** for seven days:
23:42 Israelites are to live in **b**
23:43 I made the Israelites live in **b**
Ne 8:14 were to live in **b** during the feast
8:15 palms and shades trees, to make **b**"
8:16 themselves **b** on their own roofs,
8:17 exile built **b** and lived in them.

Booty
2Ch 14:14 since there was much **b** there.
Jer 49:32 and their large herds will be **b**.

Bor Ashan
1Sa 30:30 to those in Hormah, **B**,

Border (Bordered, Bordering, Borders)
Ge 25:18 **b** of Egypt, as you go towards Asshur.
49:13 his **b** will extend towards Sidon.
Ex 16:35 until they reached the **b** of Canaan.
Nu 20:23 At Mount Hor, near the **b** of Edom,
21:13 The Arnon is the **b** of Moab, between
21:15 of Ar and lie along the **b** of Moab."
21:24 because their **b** was fortified.
22:36 the Moabite town on the Arnon **b**,
33:37 at Mount Hor, on the **b** of Edom.
33:44 at Iye Abarim, on the **b** of Moab.
34: 3 Desert of Zin along the **b** of Edom.
Dt 3:14 as far as the **b** of the Geshurites
3:16 middle of the gorge being the **b**)
3:16 which is the **b** of the Ammonites.
3:17 Its western **b** was the Jordan in the
Jos 4:19 Gilgal on the eastern **b** of Jericho.
12: 2 which is the **b** of the Ammonites.
12: 5 Salecah, all of Bashan to the **b** of
12: 5 to the **b** of Sihon king of Heshbon.
13:10 out to the **b** of the Ammonites.
16: 8 From Tappuah the **b** went west to the
22:11 built the altar on the **b** of Canaan
Jdg 7:22 the **b** of Abel Meholah near Tabbath.
11:18 of Moab, for the Arnon was its **b**.
1Sa 6:12 as far as the **b** of Beth Shemesh.
10: 2 at Zelzah on the **b** of Benjamin.
2Sa 13:23 at Baal Hazor near the **b** of Ephraim,
1Ki 4:21 as far as the **b** of Egypt.
2Ki 3:21 called up and stationed on the **b**.
2Ch 9:26 as far as the **b** of Egypt.
26: 8 and his fame spread as far as the **b**
Ps 78:54 Thus he brought them to the **b** of his
Isa 15: 8 outcry echoes along the **b** of Moab;
19:19 and a monument to the LORD at its **b**.
Eze 29:10 to Aswan, as far as the **b** of Cush.
45: 7 from the western to the eastern **b**
47:16 the **b** between Damascus and Hamath),
47:16 which is on the **b** of Hauran.
47:17 along the northern **b** of Damascus,
47:17 with the **b** of Hamath to the north.
48: 1 and the northern **b** of Damascus
48: 1 its **b** from the east side to the west
48: 2 it will **b** the territory of Dan
48: 3 it will **b** the territory of Asher
48: 4 it will **b** the territory of Naphtali
48: 5 it will **b** the territory of Manasseh
48: 6 it will **b** the territory of Ephraim
48: 7 it will **b** the territory of Reuben
48:21 the sacred portion to the eastern **b**,
48:21 the 25,000 cubits to the western **b**.
48:22 **b** of Judah and the **b** of Benjamin.
48:24 it will **b** the territory of Benjamin
48:25 it will **b** the territory of Simeon
48:26 it will **b** the territory of Issachar
48:27 it will **b** the territory of Zebulun
Ob : 7 your allies will force you to the **b**;
Lk 17:11 the **b** between Samaria and Galilee.
Ac 16: 7 they came to the **b** of Mysia,

Bordered (Border)
Jos 17:10 **b** Asher on the north and Issachar on

Bordering (Border)
Eze 45: 7 "'The prince will have the land **b**
48: 8 "**B** the territory of Judah from east
48:12 **b** the territory of the Levites.
48:18 the area, **b** on the sacred portion

Borderland (Land)
1Sa 13:18 and the third towards the **b**

Borders (Border)
Ge 10:19 the **b** of Canaan reached from Sidon
23:17 the trees within the **b** of the field
Ex 13: 7 be seen anywhere within your **b**.
23:31 "I will establish your **b** from the
1Ch 7:29 Along the **b** of Manasseh were
Ps 147:14 He grants peace to your **b** and
Isa 26:15 have extended all the **b** of the land.
60:18 ruin or destruction within your **b**,
Eze 11:10 judgment on you at the **b** of Israel.
11:11 judgment on you at the **b** of Israel.
Am 1:13 in order to extend his **b**
Mic 5: 6 our land and marches into our **b**.
Zec 9: 2 upon Hamath too, which **b** on it,
Mal 1: 5 even beyond the **b** of Israel!'

Bore (Bear[1])
Ge 16:15 Hagar **b** Abram a son, and Abram gave
16:16 years old when Hagar **b** him Ishmael.
21: 2 Sarah became pregnant and **b** a son to
21: 3 name Isaac to the son Sarah **b** him.
22:23 Milcah **b** these eight sons to Abraham'
24:24 the son that Milcah **b** to Nahor."
24:47 son of Nahor, whom Milcah **b** to him.
25: 2 She **b** him Zimran, Jokshan, Medan,
25:12 Hagar the Egyptian, **b** to Abraham.
30: 5 she became pregnant and **b** him a son.
30: 7 again and **b** Jacob a second son.
30:10 Leah's servant Zilpah **b** Jacob a son.
30:12 Leah's servant Zilpah **b** Jacob a
30:17 pregnant and **b** Jacob a fifth son.
30:19 Leah conceived again and **b** Jacob a
30:39 And they **b** young that were streaked
31: 8 all the flocks **b** streaked young.
31:39 I **b** the loss myself.
36: 4 Adah **b** Eliphaz to Esau, Basemath **b**
36: 5 Oholibamah **b** Jeush, Jalam and Korah.
Ge 36:12 named Timna, who **b** him Amalek.
36:14 **b** to Esau: Jeush, Jalam and Korah.
44:27 know that my wife **b** me two sons.
46:15 These were the sons Leah **b** to Jacob
Ex 6:20 Jochebed, who **b** him Aaron and Moses.
6:23 and she **b** him Nadab and Abihu,
6:25 and she **b** him Phinehas.
Nu 26:59 To Amram she **b** Aaron, Moses and
Jdg 8:31 **b** him a son, whom he named Abimelech.
11: 2 Gilead's wife also **b** him sons,
Ru 4:12 of Perez, whom Tamar **b** to Judah."
1Sa 20:30 the shame of the mother who **b** you?
2Sa 11:27 she became his wife and **b** him a son.
1Ki 11:20 The sister of Tahpenes **b** him a son
14:28 the guards **b** the shields,
1Ch 2: 4 Tamar, Judah's daughter-in-law, **b**
2:19 Caleb married Ephrath, who **b** him Hur.
2:21 and she **b** him Segub.
2:24 **b** him Ashhur the father of Tekoa.
2:29 Abihail, who **b** him Ahban and Molid.
2:35 servant Jarha, and she **b** him Attai.
4: 6 Naarah **b** him Ahuzzam, Hepher, Temeni
2Ch 11:19 She **b** him sons: Jeush, Shemariah and
11:20 who **b** him Abijah, Attai, Ziza and
Pr 17:25 and bitterness to the one who **b** him.
SS 6: 9 the favourite of the one who **b** her.
Isa 49:21 'Who **b** me these?
51:18 Of all the sons she **b** there was none
53:12 For he **b** the sin of many, and made
54: 1 you who never **b** a child;
Jer 20:14 day my mother **b** me not be blessed!
31:19 I **b** the disgrace of my youth.'
Eze 16:20 daughters whom you **b** to me and
23:37 their children, whom they **b** to me,
Hos 1: 3 and she conceived and **b** him a son.
Lk 23:29 the wombs that never **b**'
Ro 7: 5 so that we **b** fruit for death.
9:22 **b** with great patience the objects of
Heb 13:13 bearing the disgrace he **b**.
1Pe 2:24 He himself **b** our sins in his body on
Rev 17: 6 of those who **b** testimony to Jesus.

Bored
2Ki 12: 9 a chest and **b** a hole in its lid.

Born (Bear[1], *Born again*)
Ge 4:18 To Enoch was **b** Irad, and Irad was
5: 4 After Seth was **b**, Adam lived 800
5:30 After Noah was **b**, Lamech lived 595
6: 1 and daughters were **b** to them,
10:21 Sons were also **b** to Shem, whose
10:25 Two sons were **b** to Eber: One was
14:14 318 trained men **b** in his household
17:12 including those **b** in your household
17:13 Whether **b** in your household or
17:17 "Will a son be **b** to a man a hundred
17:23 all those **b** in his household or
17:27 including those **b** in his household
21: 5 old when his son Isaac was **b** to him.
35:26 who were **b** to him in Paddan Aram.
36: 5 who were **b** to him in Canaan.
37: 3 because he had been **b** to him in his
41:50 two sons were **b** to Joseph by Asenath
44:20 a young son **b** to him in his old age.
46:18 These were the children **b** to Jacob
46:20 In Egypt, Manasseh and Ephraim were **b**
46:22 who were **b** to Jacob—fourteen in all.
46:25 These were the sons **b** to Jacob by
46:27 With the two sons who had been **b** to
48: 5 your two sons **b** to you in Egypt
48: 6 Any children **b** to you after them
Ex 1:22 "Every boy that is **b** you must throw
12:48 take part like one **b** in the land.
23:12 and the slave **b** in your household,
Lev 18: 9 was **b** in the same home or elsewhere.
18:11 **b** to your father; she is your sister.
22:11 or if a slave is **b** in his household,
22:27 "When a calf, a lamb or a goat is **b**,
25:45 of their clans **b** in your country,
Nu 26:59 who was **b** to the Levites in Egypt.
Dt 23: 2 No-one **b** of a forbidden marriage nor
23: 8 The third generation of children **b**
Jos 5: 5 but all the people **b** in the desert
Jdg 13: 8 to bring up the boy who is to be **b**."
18:29 forefather Dan, who was **b** to Israel

2Sa 3: 2 Sons were **b** to David in Hebron:
3: 5 These were **b** to David in Hebron.
5:13 sons and daughters were **b** to him.
5:14 the names of the children **b** to him
12:14 the son **b** to you will die."
14:27 Three sons and a daughter were **b** to
1Ki 1: 6 and was **b** next after Absalom.)
3:18 The third day after my child was **b**,
13: 2 will be **b** to the house of David.
2Ki 20:18 that will be **b** to you, will be taken
1Ch 1:19 Two sons were **b** to Eber: One was
1:32 The sons **b** to Keturah, Abraham's
2: 3 These three were **b** to him by a
2: 9 The sons **b** to Hezron were: Jerahmeel,
3: 1 sons of David **b** to him in Hebron:
3: 4 These six were **b** to David in Hebron,
3: 5 these were the children **b** to him
8: 8 Sons were **b** to Shaharaim in Moab
14: 4 the names of the children **b** to him
Job 3: 3 the night it was said, 'A boy is **b**!'
5: 7 Yet man is **b** to trouble as surely as
8: 9 for we were **b** only yesterday
11:12 a wild donkey's colt can be **b** a man.
14: 1 "Man **b** of woman is of few days
15: 7 "Are you the first man ever **b**?
15:14 or one **b** of woman, that could be
25: 4 How can one **b** of woman be pure?
38:21 you know, for you were already **b**!
Ps 78: 6 even the children yet to be **b**,
87: 4 will say, 'This one was **b** in Zion.'"
87: 5 "This one and that one were **b** in her,
87: 6 "This one was **b** in Zion.
90: 2 Before the mountains were **b** or you
127: 4 a warrior are sons **b** in one's youth.
Pr 17:17 and a brother is **b** for adversity.
Ecc 2: 7 other slaves who were **b** in my house.
3: 2 a time to be **b** and a time to die,
4:14 **b** in poverty within his kingdom.
Isa 9: 6 For to us a child is **b**, to us a son
39: 7 and blood who will be **b** to you,
49: 1 Before I was **b** the LORD called me;
49:20 The children **b** during your
66: 8 Can a country be **b** in a day
Jer 1: 5 before you were **b** I set you apart;
16: 3 sons and daughters **b** in this land
20:14 Cursed be the day I was **b**! May the
20:15 "A child is **b** to you—a son!
22:26 where neither of you was **b**,
Eze 16: 4 On the day you were **b** your cord was
16: 5 day you were **b** you were despised.
Hos 2: 3 as bare as on the day she was **b**;
Zec 13: 3 to whom he was **b**, will say to him,
Mt 1:16 was **b** Jesus, who is called Christ.
2: 1 After Jesus was **b** in Bethlehem
2: 2 who has been **b** king of the Jews?
2: 4 them where the Christ was to be **b**.
11:11 Among those **b** of women
19:12 because they were **b** that way;
26:24 for him if he had not been **b**."
Mk 7:26 The woman was a Greek, **b** in Syrian
14:21 for him if he had not been **b**."
Lk 1:35 holy one to be **b** will be called
2: 6 the time came for the baby to be **b**,
2:11 a Saviour has been **b** to you;
7:28 I tell you, among those **b** of women
Jn 1:13 children **b** not of natural descent,
1:13 or a husband's will, but **b** of God.
3: 4 "How can a man be **b** when he is old?"
3: 4 into his mother's womb to be **b**!"
3: 5 he is **b** of water and the Spirit.
3: 8 is with everyone **b** of the Spirit."
8:58 "before Abraham was **b**, I am!
9: 2 his parents, that he was **b** blind?"
9:19 "Is this the one you say was **b** blind?
9:20 "and we know he was **b** blind.
9:32 opening the eyes of a man **b** blind.
16:21 but when her baby is **b** she forgets
16:21 that a child is **b** into the world.
18:37 In fact, for this reason I was **b**,
Ac 7:20 "At that time Moses was **b**,
22: 3 "I am a Jew, **b** in Tarsus of Cilicia,
22:28 "But I was **b** a citizen,"
Ro 9:11 Yet, before the twins were **b** or had
1Co 11:12 so also man is **b** of woman.
15: 8 to me also, as to one abnormally **b**.
Gal 4: 4 his Son, **b** of a woman, **b** under law,
Gal 4:23 His son by the slave woman was **b** in
4:23 was **b** as the result of a promise.
4:29 the son **b** in the ordinary way
4:29 son **b** by the power of the Spirit.
Heb 11:23 for three months after he was **b**,
2Pe 2:12 **b** only to be caught and destroyed
1Jn 2:29 what is right has been **b** of him.
3: 9 No-one who is **b** of God will continue
3: 9 because he has been **b** of God.
4: 7 has been **b** of God and knows God.
5: 1 Jesus is the Christ is **b** of God,
5: 4 for everyone **b** of God overcomes the
5:18 We know that anyone **b** of God does
5:18 one who was **b** of God keeps him safe,
Rev 12: 4 her child the moment it was **b**.

Born again

Jn 3: 3 the kingdom of God unless he is **b**."
3: 7 at my saying, 'You must be **b**.'
1Pe 1:23 For you have been **b**, not of

Borne (Bear[1])

Ge 16: 1 Now Sarai, Abram's wife, had **b** him
16:15 name Ishmael to the son she had **b**.
21: 7 I have **b** him a son in his old age."
21: 9 had **b** to Abraham was mocking,
22:20 has **b** sons to your brother Nahor:
24:36 My master's wife Sarah has **b** him a
29:34 because I have **b** him three sons.
30:20 because I have **b** him six sons.
31:43 or about the children they have **b**?
34: 1 Now Dinah, the daughter Leah had **b**
1Sa 2: 5 She who was barren has **b** seven
2Sa 12:15 that Uriah's wife had **b** to David,
21: 8 whom she had **b** to Saul, together
21: 8 whom she had **b** to Adriel son of
1Ki 3:21 saw that it wasn't the son I had **b**."
Ps 18:42 I beat them as fine as dust **b** on the
Isa 46: 1 idols are **b** by beasts of burden.
49:15 no compassion on the child she has **b**
Hag 2:19 and the olive tree have not **b** fruit.
Mt 20:12 who have **b** the burden of the work
1Co 15:49 just as we have **b** the likeness of

Borrow (Borrowed, Borrower, Borrows)

Dt 15: 6 many nations but will **b** from none.
28:12 many nations but will **b** from none.
Ne 5: 4 "We have had to **b** money to pay
Ps 37:21 The wicked **b** and do not repay,
Mt 5:42 the one who wants to **b** from you.

Borrowed (Borrow)

2Ki 6: 5 "it was **b**!
Jer 15:10 I have neither lent nor **b**,

Borrower (Borrow)

Ex 22:15 the **b** will not have to pay.
Pr 22: 7 and the **b** is servant to the lender.
Isa 24: 2 for **b** as for lender,

Borrows (Borrow)

Ex 22:14 "If a man **b** an animal from his

Bosom (Bosoms)

Pr 5:20 embrace the **b** of another man's wife?
Eze 23: 8 caressed her virgin **b** and poured
23:21 when in Egypt your **b** was caressed

Bosoms (Bosom)

Eze 23: 3 fondled and their virgin **b** caressed.

Bother (Bothering)

2Sa 14:10 and he will not **b** you again."
Mk 5:35 "Why **b** the teacher any more?"
Lk 8:49 "Don't **b** the teacher any more."
11: 7 the one inside answers, 'Don't **b** me.

Bothering (Bother)

Mt 26:10 "Why are you **b** this woman? She has
Mk 14: 6 "Why are you **b** her? She has done a
Lk 18: 5 yet because this widow keeps **b** me,

Bottled-up

Job 32:19 inside I am like **b** wine, like new

Bottles

Isa 3:20 sashes, the perfume **b** and charms,

Boughs

Ps 80:11 sent out its **b** to the Sea, its
118:27 With **b** in hand, join in the festal
Isa 10:33 will lop off the **b** with great power.
17: 6 four or five on the fruitful **b**,"
Eze 17: 6 branches and put out leafy **b**.
31: 5 its **b** increased and its branches
31: 6 birds of the air nested in its **b**,
31: 7 with its spreading **b**, for its roots
31: 8 could the pine trees equal its **b**,
31:12 Its **b** fell on the mountains and in

Bought (Buy)

Ge 17:12 or **b** with money from a foreigner
17:13 Whether born in your household or **b**
17:23 his household or **b** with his money,
17:27 his household or **b** from a foreigner,
25:10 the field Abraham had **b** from the
33:19 For a hundred pieces of silver, he **b**
39: 1 **b** him from the Ishmaelites
47:20 Joseph **b** all the land in Egypt for
47:23 "Now that I have **b** you and your land
49:30 which Abraham **b** as a burial place
49:32 The field and the cave in it were **b**
50:13 Abraham had **b** as a burial place
Ex 12:44 Any slave you have **b** may eat of it
15:16 until the people you **b** pass by.
Lev 27:22 to the LORD a field he has **b**,
27:24 to the person from whom he **b** it,
Jos 24:32 in the tract of land that Jacob **b**
Ru 4: 9 that I have **b** from Naomi all the
2Sa 12: 3 one little ewe lamb that he had **b**.
24:24 So David **b** the threshing-floor and
1Ki 16:24 **b** the hill of Samaria from Shemer
Ne 5: 8 we have **b** back our Jewish brothers
Job 28:15 cannot be **b** with the finest gold,
28:16 cannot be **b** with the gold of Ophir,
28:19 it cannot be **b** with pure gold.
Ecc 2: 7 I **b** male and female slaves and had
Isa 43:24 You have not **b** any fragrant calamus
Jer 13: 2 I **b** a belt, as the LORD directed,
13: 4 "Take the belt you **b** and are wearing
32: 9 I **b** the field at Anathoth from my
32:15 will again be **b** in this land.'
32:43 Once more fields will be **b** in this
32:44 Fields will be **b** for silver,
Eze 27:19 "'Danites and Greeks from Uzal **b**
Hos 3: 2 I **b** her for fifteen shekels of
Mt 13:44 sold all he had and **b** that field.
13:46 and sold everything he had and **b** it.
Mk 15:46 Joseph **b** some linen cloth,
16: 1 and Salome **b** spices so that they
Lk 14:18 I have just **b** a field, and I must go
14:19 'I have just **b** five yoke of oxen
Ac 1:18 Judas **b** a field; there he fell
7:16 in the tomb that Abraham had **b**
20:28 which he **b** with his own blood.
1Co 6:20 you were **b** at a price. Therefore
7:23 You were **b** at a price; do not become
2Pe 2: 1 the sovereign Lord who **b** them

Boulder

Rev 18:21 a mighty angel picked up a **b** the

Bound (Bind)

Ge 22: 9 He **b** his son Isaac and laid him on
42:24 from them and **b** before their eyes.
44:30 is closely **b** up with the boy's life,
Nu 30: 4 by which she **b** herself will stand.
30: 5 by which she **b** herself will stand;
30: 7 by which she **b** herself will stand.
30:11 by which she **b** herself will stand.
Jdg 15:13 So they **b** him with two new ropes
1Sa 14:24 because Saul had **b** the people under
14:27 had **b** the people with the oath,
14:28 "Your father **b** the army under a
25:29 the life of my master will be **b**
2Sa 3:34 Your hands were not **b**, your feet

2Ki 25: 7 Then they put out his eyes, **b** him
2Ch 33:11 **b** him with bronze shackles
36: 6 **b** him with bronze shackles to take
Job 16: 8 You have **b** me—and it has become a
36: 8 if men are **b** in chains, held fast by
Pr 22:15 Folly is **b** up in the heart of a
Isa 16:14 as a servant **b** by contract would
21:16 "Within one year, as a servant **b** by
24:22 like prisoners **b** in a dungeon;
56: 3 Let no foreigner who has **b** himself
Jer 13:11 as a belt is **b** round a man's waist
13:11 so I **b** the whole house of Israel and
39: 7 he put out Zedekiah's eyes and **b** him
40: 1 He had found Jeremiah **b** in chains
52:11 he put out Zedekiah's eyes, **b** him
Lam 1:14 "My sins have been **b** into a yoke;
Eze 3:25 you will be **b** so that you cannot go
30:21 It has not been **b** up for healing or
34: 4 healed the sick or **b** up the injured.
Da 3:21 turbans and other clothes, were **b**
4:15 its roots, **b** with iron and bronze,
4:23 the stump, **b** with iron and bronze,
Jnh 1: 3 he found a ship **b** for that port.
Mt 14: 3 Herod had arrested John and **b** him
16:19 bind on earth will be **b** in heaven,
18:18 bind on earth will be **b** in heaven,
23:16 of the temple, he is **b** by his oath.'
23:18 gift on it, he is **b** by his oath.'
27: 2 They **b** him, led him away and handed
Mk 6:17 and he had him **b** and put in prison.
15: 1 They **b** Jesus, led him away and
Lk 13:16 kept **b** for eighteen long years,
13:16 on the Sabbath day from what **b** her?"
17: 1 cause people to sin are **b** to come,
Jn 18:12 officials arrested Jesus. They **b** him
18:24 Annas sent him, still **b**, to Caiaphas
Ac 12: 6 **b** with two chains, and sentries
21:13 I am ready not only to be **b**,
21:33 ordered him to be **b** with two chains.
23:12 **b** themselves with an oath not to eat
28:20 Israel that I am **b** with this chain."
Ro 1:14 I am **b** both to Greeks and non-Greeks,
7: 2 by law a married woman is **b** to her
7: 6 now, by dying to what once **b** us, we
11:32 For God has **b** all men over to
1Co 7:15 A believing man or woman is not **b** in
7:39 A woman is **b** to her husband as long
Jude : 6 **b** with everlasting chains for
Rev 9:14 are **b** at the great river Euphrates."
20: 2 and **b** him for a thousand years.

Boundaries (Boundary)

Nu 34: 2 as an inheritance will have these **b**:
34:12 land, with its **b** on every side.'"
Dt 32: 8 he set up **b** for the peoples
Jos 15:12 These are the **b** around the people of
18:20 These were the **b** that marked out the
2Ki 14:25 He was the one who restored the **b** of
Ps 74:17 was you who set all the **b** of the
Pr 15:25 but he keeps the widow's **b** intact.
Isa 10:13 I removed the **b** of nations,
Eze 47:13 "These are the **b** by which you are to
Mic 7:11 come, the day for extending your **b**.

Boundary (Boundaries, Boundless, Bounds)

Nu 34: 3 On the east, your southern **b** will
34: 6 "Your western **b** will be the coast
34: 6 This will be your **b** on the west.
34: 7 "For your northern **b**, run a line
34: 8 Then the **b** will go to Zedad,
34: 9 This will be your **b** on the north.
34:10 "For your eastern **b**, run a line
34:11 The **b** will go down from Shepham to
34:12 the **b** will go down along the Jordan
Dt 19:14 Do not move your neighbour's **b** stone
27:17 who moves his neighbour's **b** stone.
Jos 13:23 The **b** of the Reubenites was the bank
15: 2 Their southern **b** started from the
15: 4 This is their southern **b**.
15: 5 The eastern **b** is the Salt Sea as far
15: 5 The northern **b** started from the bay
15: 7 The **b** then went up to Debir from the
15: 9 From the hilltop the **b** headed
15:11 The **b** ended at the sea.
Jos 15:12 The western **b** is the coastline of
15:21 **b** of Edom were: Kabzeel, Eder, Jagur,
16: 5 The **b** of their inheritance
17: 7 The **b** ran southward from there to
17: 8 Tappuah itself, on the **b** of Manasseh
17: 9 the **b** continued south to the Kanah
17: 9 but the **b** of Manasseh was the
18:12 On the north side their **b** began at
18:14 **b** turned south along the western side
18:15 and the **b** came out at the spring of
18:16 The **b** went down to the foot of the
18:19 This was the southern **b**.
18:20 The Jordan formed the **b** on the
19:10 The **b** of their inheritance went
19:14 There the **b** went round on the north
19:22 The **b** touched Tabor, Shahazumah and
19:26 **b** touched Carmel and Shihor Libnath.
19:29 The **b** then turned back towards Ramah
19:33 Their **b** went from Heleph and the
19:34 The **b** ran west through Aznoth Tabor
22:25 The LORD has made the Jordan a **b**
Jdg 1:36 The **b** of the Amorites was from
Job 24: 2 Men move **b** stones; they pasture
26:10 for a **b** between light and darkness.
Ps 16: 6 The **b** lines have fallen for me in
104: 9 You set a **b** they cannot cross;
Pr 8:29 he gave the sea its **b** so that the
22:28 Do not move an ancient **b** stone set
23:10 Do not move an ancient **b** stone or
Jer 5:22 I made the sand a **b** for the sea,
Eze 47:15 "This is to be the **b** of the land:
47:17 The **b** will extend from the sea to
47:17 This will be the north **b**.
47:18 "On the east side the **b** will run
47:18 This will be the east **b**.
47:19 This will be the south **b**.
47:20 the Great Sea will be the **b**
47:20 This will be the west **b**.
48:28 "The southern **b** of Gad will run
Hos 5:10 are like those who move **b** stones.

Bounding

SS 2: 8 the mountains, **b** over the hills.

Boundless (Boundary)

Ps 119:96 but your commands are **b**.
Na 3: 9 Cush and Egypt were her **b** strength;

Bounds (Boundary)

Hos 4: 2 they break all **b**, and bloodshed
2Co 7: 4 all our troubles my joy knows no **b**.

Bounty

Ge 49:26 than the **b** of the age-old hills.
Dt 28:12 the storehouse of his **b**, to send
1Ki 10:13 he had given her out of his royal **b**.
Ps 65:11 You crown the year with your **b**,
68:10 from your **b**, O God, you provided
Jer 31:12 will rejoice in the **b** of the LORD
31:14 my people will be filled with my **b**

Bow[1] (Battle-bow, Bowmen, Bows, Bow-shot)

Ge 27: 3 get your weapons—your quiver and **b**
48:22 Amorites with my sword and my **b**."
49:24 his **b** remained steady, his strong
Jos 24:12 not do it with your own sword and **b**.
1Sa 18: 4 even his sword, his **b** and his belt.
2Sa 1:18 Judah be taught this lament of the **b**
1:22 the **b** of Jonathan did not turn back
22:35 my arms can bend a **b** of bronze.
1Ki 22:34 someone drew his **b** at random and hit
2Ki 6:22 captured with your own sword or **b**?
9:24 Jehu drew his **b** and shot Joram
13:15 "Get a **b** and some arrows,"
13:16 "Take the **b** in your hands," he said
1Ch 5:18 who could use a **b**, and who were
8:40 warriors who could handle the **b**.
2Ch 18:33 someone drew his **b** at random and hit
Job 29:20 in me, the **b** ever new in my hand.'
30:11 Now that God has unstrung my **b** and
Ps 7:12 he will bend and string his **b**.
18:34 my arms can bend a **b** of bronze.
Ps 21:12 when you aim at them with drawn **b**.
37:14 bend the **b** to bring down the poor
44: 6 I do not trust in my **b**, my sword
46: 9 breaks the **b** and shatters the spear,
58: 7 they draw the **b**, let their arrows
60: 4 banner to be unfurled against the **b**.
78:57 as unreliable as a faulty **b**.
Isa 7:24 Men will go there with **b** and arrow,
21:15 from the bent **b** and from the heat
22: 3 been captured without using the **b**.
41: 2 to wind-blown chaff with his **b**.
Jer 6:23 They are armed with **b** and spear;
9: 3 make ready their tongue like a **b**,
46: 9 men of Lydia who draw the **b**.
49:35 "See, I will break the **b** of Elam,
50:14 Babylon, all you who draw the **b**.
50:29 Babylon, all those who draw the **b**.
51: 3 Let not the archer string his **b**,
Lam 2: 4 Like an enemy he has strung his **b**;
3:12 He drew his **b** and made me the target
Eze 39: 3 I will strike your **b** from your left
Hos 1: 5 In that day I will break Israel's **b**
1: 7 and I will save them—not by **b**,
2:18 **B** and sword and battle I will
7:16 Most High; they are like a faulty **b**.
Hab 3: 9 You uncovered your **b**, you called for
Zec 9:13 I will bend Judah as I bend my **b** and
Ac 27:30 to lower some anchors from the **b**.
27:41 The **b** stuck fast and would not move,
Rev 6: 2 a white horse! Its rider held a **b**,

Bow[2] (Bowed, Bowing, Bows)

Ge 27:29 and peoples **b** down to you.
27:29 sons of your mother **b** down to you.
37:10 **b** down to the ground before you?"
49: 8 father's sons will **b** down to you.
Ex 20: 5 You shall not **b** down to them or
23:24 Do not **b** down before their gods or
Lev 26: 1 in your land to **b** down before it.
Dt 5: 9 You shall not **b** down to them or
8:19 gods and worship and **b** down to them,
11:16 other gods and **b** down to them.
26:10 LORD your God and **b** down before him.
30:17 and if you are drawn away to **b** down
33: 3 At your feet they all **b** down,
Jos 23: 7 not serve them or **b** down to them.
23:16 serve other gods and **b** down to them
1Sa 2:36 will come and **b** down before him
2Sa 15: 5 approached him to **b** down before him
16: 4 "I humbly **b**," Ziba said. "May I
22:40 made my adversaries **b** at my feet.
2Ki 5:18 the temple of Rimmon to **b** down
5:18 he is leaning on my arm and I **b**
5:18 I **b** down in the temple of Rimmon,
17:35 other gods or **b** down to them
17:36 **b** down and to him offer sacrifices.
Ps 5: 7 I **b** down towards your holy temple.
18:39 made my adversaries **b** at my feet.
22:27 the nations will **b** down before him,
72: 9 The desert tribes will **b** before him
72:11 All kings will **b** down to him and all
81: 9 shall not **b** down to an alien god.
95: 6 Come, let us **b** down in worship,
138: 2 I will **b** down towards your holy
Pr 14:19 Evil men will **b** down in the presence
Isa 2: 8 **b** down to the work of their hands,
44:19 Shall I **b** down to a block of wood?"
45:14 They will **b** down before you and
45:23 Before me every knee will **b**;
46: 2 They stoop and **b** down together;
46: 6 and they **b** down and worship it.
49: 7 princes will see and **b** down,
49:23 They will **b** down before you
60:14 all who despise you will **b** down at
66:23 **b** down before me," says the LORD.
Jer 27: 8 Babylon or **b** its neck under his yoke,
27:11 if any nation will **b** its neck under
27:12 I said, "**B** your neck under the yoke
Mic 5:13 **b** down to the work of your hands.
6: 6 and **b** down before the exalted God?
Zep 1: 5 those who **b** down on the roofs to
1: 5 those who **b** down and swear by the
Mt 4: 9 "if you will **b** down and worship me.
Ro 14:11 'Every knee will **b** before me;
Php 2:10 name of Jesus every knee should **b**,

Bowed (Bow[2])

Ge 18: 2 meet them and **b** low to the ground.
19: 1 **b** down with his face to the ground.
23: 7 Abraham rose and **b** down before the
23:12 Again Abraham **b** down before the
24:26 the man **b** down and worshipped the
24:48 I **b** down and worshipped the LORD. I
24:52 **b** down to the ground before the LORD.
33: 3 He himself went on ahead and **b** down
33: 6 children approached and **b** down.
33: 7 and her children came and **b** down.
33: 7 and Rachel, and they too **b** down.
37: 7 round mine and **b** down to it."
42: 6 they **b** down to him with their faces
43:26 **b** down before him to the ground.
43:28 And they **b** low to pay him honour.
48:12 **b** down with his face to the ground.
Ex 4:31 they **b** down and worshipped.
12:27 the people **b** down and worshipped.
18: 7 and **b** down and kissed him.
32: 8 They have **b** down to it and
34: 8 Moses **b** to the ground at once and
Nu 22:31 So he **b** low and fell face down.
25: 2 ate and **b** down before these gods.
Dt 29:26 other gods and **b** down to them,
Ru 2:10 At this, she **b** down with her face
1Sa 20:41 bowed down before Jonathan
24: 8 David **b** down and prostrated himself
25:23 **b** down before David with her face
25:41 She **b** down with her face to the
28:14 and he **b** down and prostrated himself
2Sa 9: 6 he **b** down to pay him honour.
9: 8 Mephibosheth **b** down and said, "What
14:33 and he came in and **b** down with his
18:21 **b** down before Joab and ran off.
18:28 He **b** down before the king
24:20 went out and **b** down before the king
1Ki 1:16 Bathsheba **b** low and knelt before the
1:23 and **b** with his face to the ground.
1:31 Bathsheba **b** low with her face to the
1:47 And the king **b** in worship on his
1:53 And Adonijah came and **b** down to
2:19 **b** down to her and sat down
18: 7 Obadiah recognised him, **b** down to
19:18 whose knees have not **b** down to Baal
2Ki 2:15 and **b** to the ground before him.
4:37 She came in, fell at his feet and **b**
17:16 They **b** down to all the starry hosts,
21: 3 He **b** down to all the starry hosts
21:21 had worshipped, and **b** down to them.
1Ch 21:21 **b** down before David with his face
29:20 they **b** low and fell prostrate
2Ch 20:18 Jehoshaphat **b** with his face to the
25:14 **b** down to them and burned sacrifices
29:28 The whole assembly **b** in worship,
29:30 and **b** their heads and worshipped.
33: 3 He **b** down to all the starry hosts
Ne 8: 6 Then they **b** down and worshipped
Ps 35:14 I **b** my head in grief as though
38: 6 I am **b** down and brought very low;
57: 6 I was **b** down in distress.
145:14 and lifts up all who are **b** down.
146: 8 LORD lifts up those who are **b** down,
Lam 2:10 have **b** their heads to the ground.
Da 10:15 While he was saying this to me, I **b**
Mt 2:11 and they **b** down and worshipped him.
Lk 24: 5 In their fright the women **b** down
Jn 19:30 **b** his head and gave up his spirit.
Ro 11: 4 who have not **b** the knee to Baal."

Bowels

2Ch 21:15 with a lingering disease of the **b**,
21:15 disease causes your **b** to come out.'"
21:18 with an incurable disease of the **b**.
21:19 his **b** came out because of the

Bowing (Bow[2])

Ge 37: 9 and eleven stars were **b** down to me."
Ex 11: 8 **b** down before me and saying, 'Go,
Dt 4:19 not be enticed into **b** down to them
17: 3 **b** down to them or to the sun or the
Isa 58: 5 Is it only for **b** one's head like a
60:14 oppressors will come **b** before you;
Eze 8:16 were **b** down to the sun in the east.

Bowl (Bowlful, Bowls, Bowl-shaped)

Nu 7:13 and one silver sprinkling **b** weighing
7:19 and one silver sprinkling **b** weighing
7:25 and one silver sprinkling **b** weighing
7:31 and one silver sprinkling **b** weighing
7:37 and one silver sprinkling **b** weighing
7:43 and one silver sprinkling **b** weighing
7:49 and one silver sprinkling **b** weighing
7:55 and one silver sprinkling **b** weighing
7:61 and one silver sprinkling **b** weighing
7:67 and one silver sprinkling **b** weighing
7:73 and one silver sprinkling **b** weighing
7:79 and one silver sprinkling **b** weighing
7:85 each sprinkling **b** seventy shekels.
Jdg 5:25 in a **b** fit for nobles she brought
2Ki 2:20 "Bring me a new **b**," he said,
Ecc 12: 6 or the golden **b** is broken;
Zec 4: 2 gold lampstand with a **b** at the top
4: 3 one on the right of the **b**
9:15 they will be full like a **b** used for
Mt 5:15 light a lamp and put it under a **b**.
26:23 into the **b** with me will betray me.
Mk 4:21 lamp to put it under a **b** or a bed?
14:20 who dips bread into the **b** with me.
Lk 11:33 it will be hidden, or under a **b**.
Rev 16: 2 and poured out his **b** on the land,
16: 3 The second angel poured out his **b** on
16: 4 The third angel poured out his **b** on
16: 8 The fourth angel poured out his **b** on
16:10 The fifth angel poured out his **b** on
16:12 The sixth angel poured out his **b** on
16:17 The seventh angel poured out his **b**

Bowlful (Bowl)

Jdg 6:38 and wrung out the dew—a **b** of water.
Ps 80: 5 have made them drink tears by the **b**.
Am 6: 6 You drink wine by the **b** and use the

Bowls (Bowl)

Ex 24: 6 half of the blood and put it in **b**,
25:29 **b** for the pouring out of offerings.
27: 3 **b**, meat forks and firepans.
37:16 dishes and **b** and its pitchers for
38: 3 **b**, meat forks and firepans.
Nu 4: 7 dishes and **b**, and the jars for drink
4:14 forks, shovels and sprinkling **b**.
7:84 sprinkling **b** and twelve gold dishes.
2Sa 17:28 brought bedding and **b** and articles
1Ki 7:40 basins and shovels and sprinkling **b**.
7:45 the pots, shovels and sprinkling **b**.
7:50 wick trimmers, sprinkling **b**, dishes
2Ki 12:13 wick trimmers, sprinkling **b**,
25:15 sprinkling **b**—all that were made of
1Ch 28:17 forks, sprinkling **b** and pitchers;
2Ch 4: 8 made a hundred gold sprinkling **b**.
4:11 pots and shovels and sprinkling **b**.
4:22 sprinkling **b**, dishes and censers;
Ezr 1:10 gold **b** 30 matching silver **b** 410
8:27 20 **b** of gold valued at 1,000 darics,
Ne 7:70 50 **b** and 530 garments for priests.
Pr 23:30 who go to sample **b** of mixed wine.
Isa 22:24 vessels, from the **b** to all the jars.
65:11 fill **b** of mixed wine for Destiny,
Jer 35: 5 I set **b** full of wine and some cups
52:18 wick trimmers, sprinkling **b**, dishes
52:19 censers, sprinkling **b**, pots,
52:19 pots, lampstands, dishes and **b** used
Zec 14:20 the sacred **b** in front of the altar.
Rev 5: 8 holding golden **b** full of incense,
15: 7 **b** filled with the wrath of God,
16: 1 **b** of God's wrath on the earth."
17: 1 had the seven **b** came and said to me,
21: 9 seven **b** full of the seven last

Bowl-shaped (Bowl)

1Ki 7:20 above the **b** part next to the network,
7:41 two **b** capitals on top of the pillars
7:41 **b** capitals on top of the pillars;
7:42 **b** capitals on top of the pillars);
2Ch 4:12 two **b** capitals on top of the pillars
4:12 **b** capitals on top of the pillars;
4:13 **b** capitals on top of the pillars);

Bowmen (Bow[1])

Isa 21:17 The survivors of the **b**, the warriors

Bows[1] (Bow[1])

1Sa 2: 4 "The **b** of the warriors are broken,
1Ch 12: 2 they were armed with **b** and were able
2Ch 14: 8 armed with small shields and with **b**.
17:17 men armed with **b** and shields;
26:14 spears, helmets, coats of armour, **b**
Ne 4:13 with their swords, spears and **b**.
4:16 with spears, shields, **b** and armour.
Ps 11: 2 For look, the wicked bend their **b**;
37:15 hearts, and their **b** will be broken.
78: 9 men of Ephraim, though armed with **b**
Isa 5:28 all their **b** are strung;
13:18 Their **b** will strike down the young
Jer 50:42 They are armed with **b** and spears;
51:56 and their **b** will be broken.
Eze 39: 9 the **b** and arrows, the war clubs and

Bows[2] (Bow[2])

Ps 66: 4 All the earth **b** down to you;
Isa 44:15 he makes an idol and **b** down to it.
44:17 he **b** down to it and worships.
46: 1 Bel **b** down, Nebo stoops low;

Bow-shot (Bow[1])

Ge 21:16 sat down nearby about a **b** away,

Boy (Boy's, Boyhood, Boys)

Ge 21:12 about the **b** and your maidservant.
21:14 and then sent her off with the **b**.
21:15 put the **b** under one of the bushes.
21:16 thought, "I cannot watch the **b** die.
21:17 God heard the **b** crying, and the
21:17 heard the **b** crying as he lies there.
21:18 Lift the **b** up and take him by the
21:19 with water and gave the **b** a drink.
21:20 God was with the **b** as he grew up.
22: 5 while I and the **b** go over there.
22:12 "Do not lay a hand on the **b**,"
37:30 The **b** isn't there! Where can I turn
42:22 I tell you not to sin against the **b**?
43: 8 "Send the **b** along with me and we
44:22 'The **b** cannot leave his father;
44:30 "So now, if the **b** is not with us
44:31 sees that the **b** isn't there, he will
44:33 my lord's slave in place of the **b**,
44:33 let the **b** return with his brothers.
44:34 my father if the **b** is not with me?
Ex 1:16 if it is a **b**, kill him; but if it is
1:22 "Every **b** that is born you must throw
Lev 12: 3 On the eighth day the **b** is to be
12: 7 who gives birth to a **b** or a girl.
Jdg 8:20 he was only a **b** and was afraid.
13: 5 because the **b** is to be a Nazirite,
13: 7 because the **b** will be a Nazirite
13: 8 bring up the **b** who is to be born."
13:24 The woman gave birth to a **b** and
1Sa 1:22 "After the **b** is weaned, I will take
1:24 After he was weaned, she took the **b**
1:25 they brought the **b** to Eli,
2:11 the **b** ministered before the LORD
2:18 —a **b** wearing a linen ephod.
2:21 Meanwhile, the **b** Samuel grew up in
2:26 the **b** Samuel continued to grow in
3: 1 The **b** Samuel ministered before the
3: 8 that the LORD was calling the **b**.
4:21 She named the **b** Ichabod, saying,
17:33 you are only a **b**, and he has been
17:42 over and saw that he was only a **b**,
20:21 I will send a **b** and say, 'Go, find
20:22 if I say to the **b**, 'Look, the arrows
20:35 He had a small **b** with him,
20:36 he said to the **b**, "Run and find the
20:36 As the **b** ran, he shot an arrow
20:37 the **b** came to the place where
20:38 The **b** picked up the arrow
20:39 (The **b** knew nothing of all this;
20:40 Jonathan gave his weapons to the **b**
20:41 After the **b** had gone, David got up
30:19 young or old, **b** or girl,
1Ki 11:17 Hadad, still only a **b**, fled to Egypt
14: 3 tell you what will happen to the **b**
14:12 foot in your city, the **b** will die.
14:17 threshold of the house, the **b** died.
17:21 he stretched himself out on the **b**

2Ki 4:20 the **b** sat on her lap until noon,
4:31 told him, "The **b** has not awakened.
4:32 was the **b** lying dead on his couch.
4:34 he got on the bed and lay upon the **b**,
4:35 The **b** sneezed seven times and opened
5:14 became clean like that of a young **b**.
Job 3: 3 night it was said,'A **b** is born!'
Pr 4: 3 I was a **b** in my father's house,
Isa 7:16 before the **b** knows enough to reject
8: 4 Before the **b** knows how to say
Mt 17:17 Bring the **b** here to me."
17:18 and it came out of the **b**, and he was
Mk 9:19 put up with you? Bring the **b** to me."
9:20 threw the **b** into a convulsion.
9:26 The **b** looked so much like a corpse
10:20 these I have kept since I was a **b**."
Lk 2:43 the **b** Jesus stayed behind in
9:42 Even while the **b** was coming, the
9:42 healed the **b** and gave him back to
18:21 these I have kept since I was a **b**,"
Jn 4:51 with the news that his **b** was living.
6: 9 "Here is a **b** with five small barley

Boy's (Boy)
Ge 44:30 is closely bound up with the **b** life,
44:32 Your servant guaranteed the **b** safety
Jdg 13:12 the rule for the **b** life and work?"
1Ki 17:21 God, let this **b** life return to him!"
17:22 **b** life returned to him, and he lived.
2Ki 4:29 Lay my staff on the **b** face."
4:31 and laid the staff on the **b** face,
4:34 out upon him, the **b** body grew warm.
Mk 9:21 Jesus asked the **b** father, "How long
9:24 Immediately the **b** father exclaimed,

Boyhood (Boy)
Ge 46:34 have tended livestock from our **b** on

Boys (Boy)
Ge 25:24 there were twin **b** in her womb.
25:27 The **b** grew up, and Esau became a
38:27 there were twin **b** in her womb.
48:16 all harm—may he bless these **b**.
Ex 1:17 them to do; they let the **b** live.
1:18 Why have you let the **b** live?"
Nu 31:17 Now kill all the **b**. And kill every
2Ki 4: 1 to take my two **b** as his slaves."
Job 19:18 Even the little **b** scorn me; when I
Isa 3: 4 I will make **b** their officials;
Lam 5:13 **b** stagger under loads of wood.
Joel 3: 3 people and traded **b** for prostitutes;
Zec 8: 5 with **b** and girls playing there."
Mt 2:16 he gave orders to kill all the **b** in

Bozez
1Sa 14: 4 was called **B**, and the other Seneh.

Bozkath
Jos 15:39 Lachish, **B**, Eglon,
2Ki 22: 1 daughter of Adaiah; she was from **B**.

Bozrah
Ge 36:33 Jobab son of Zerah from **B** succeeded
1Ch 1:44 Jobab son of Zerah from **B** succeeded
Isa 34: 6 the LORD has a sacrifice in **B**
63: 1 Who is this coming from Edom, from **B**,
Jer 48:24 to Kerioth and **B**—to all the towns
49:13 "that **B** will become a ruin and an
49:22 down, spreading its wings over **B**.
Am 1:12 will consume the fortresses of **B**."

Brace (Bracing)
Job 38: 3 **B** yourself like a man;
40: 7 "**B** yourself like a man;
Na 2: 1 watch the road, **b** yourselves,

Bracelets
Ge 24:22 and two gold **b** weighing ten shekels.
24:30 and the **b** on his sister's arms,
24:47 in her nose and the **b** on her arms,
Nu 31:50 **b**, signet rings, ear-rings and
Isa 3:19 the ear-rings and **b** and veils,
Eze 16:11 I put **b** on your arms
23:42 they put **b** on the arms of the woman

Bracing (Brace)
Jdg 16:29 **B** himself against them, his right

Brag
Am 4: 5 **b** about your freewill offerings—
Ro 2:17 **b** about your relationship to God;
2:23 You who **b** about the law, do you
Jas 4:16 As it is, you boast and **b**.

Braided (Braids)
Ex 28:14 two **b** chains of pure gold, like a
28:22 "For the breastpiece make **b** chains
39:15 For the breastpiece they made **b**
1Ti 2: 9 not with **b** hair or gold or pearls
1Pe 3: 3 such as **b** hair and the wearing of

Braids (Braided)
Jdg 16:13 "If you weave the seven **b** of my head
16:13 Delilah took the seven **b** of his head,
16:19 shave off the seven **b** of his hair,

Brambles
Isa 34:13 nettles and **b** her strongholds.

Branch (Branches)
Ge 49:11 his colt to the choicest **b**;
Ex 25:33 and blossoms are to be on one **b**,
25:33 three on the next **b**, and the same
37:19 buds and blossoms were on one **b**,
37:19 three on the next **b** and the same for
Nu 4: 2 "Take a census of the Kohathite **b** of
13:23 **b** bearing a single cluster of grapes.
Isa 4: 2 In that day the **B** of the LORD will
9:14 palm **b** and reed in a single day;
11: 1 from his roots a **B** will bear fruit.
14:19 out of your tomb like a rejected **b**;
19:15 do—head or tail, palm **b** or reed.
Jer 1:11 the **b** of an almond tree," I replied.
23: 5 raise up to David a righteous **B**,
33:15 will make a righteous **B** sprout from
Eze 8:17 at them putting the **b** to their nose!
15: 2 **b** on any of the trees in the forest?
19:14 No strong **b** is left on it fit for a
Zec 3: 8 am going to bring my servant, the **B**.
6:12 'Here is the man whose name is the **B**,
6:12 and he will **b** out from his place and
Mal 4: 1 a root or a **b** will be left to them.
Jn 15: 2 He cuts off every **b** in me that bears
15: 2 while every **b** that does bear fruit
15: 4 No **b** can bear fruit by itself;
15: 6 he is like a **b** that is thrown away

Branches (Branch)
Ge 30:37 Jacob, however, took fresh-cut **b**
30:37 the white inner wood of the **b**.
30:38 he placed the peeled **b** in all the
30:39 they mated in front of the **b**.
30:41 Jacob would place the **b** in the
30:41 so that they would mate near the **b**,
40:10 on the vine were three **b**.
40:12 "The three **b** are three days.
49:22 a spring, whose **b** climb over a wall.
Ex 25:32 Six **b** are to extend from the sides
25:33 six **b** extending from the lampstand.
25:35 of **b** extending from the lampstand,
25:35 under the third pair—six **b** in all.
25:36 The buds and **b** shall all be of one
37:18 Six **b** extended from the sides of the
37:19 six **b** extending from the lampstand.
37:21 One bud was under the first pair of **b**
37:21 under the third pair—six **b** in all.
37:22 The buds and the **b** were all of one
Lev 23:40 and palm fronds, leafy **b** and poplars,
Dt 24:20 do not go over the **b** a second time.
Jdg 9:48 He took an axe and cut off some **b**,
9:49 all the men cut **b** and followed
2Sa 18: 9 under the thick **b** of a large oak,
Ne 8:15 **b** from olive and wild olive trees,
8:16 brought back **b** and built themselves
Job 15:32 and his **b** will not flourish.
18:16 and his **b** wither above.
29:19 the dew will lie all night on my **b**.
Ps 80:10 shade, the mighty cedars with its **b**.
104:12 the waters; they sing among the **b**.
Isa 17: 6 or three olives on the topmost **b**,
18: 5 down and take away the spreading **b**.
27:10 lie down; they strip its **b** bare.
Jer 5:10 Strip off her **b**, for these people do
6: 9 pass your hand over the **b** again,
11:16 on fire, and its **b** will be broken.
48:32 Your **b** spread as far as the sea;
Eze 17: 6 Its **b** turned towards him, but its
17: 6 produced **b** and put out leafy boughs.
17: 7 stretched out its **b** to him for water
17: 8 water so that it would produce **b**,
17:23 it will produce **b** and bear fruit
17:23 find shelter in the shade of its **b**.
19:10 full of **b** because of abundant water.
19:11 Its **b** were strong, fit for a ruler's
19:11 for its height and for its many **b**.
19:12 **b** withered and fire consumed them.
19:14 Fire spread from one of its main **b**
21:19 where the road **b** off to the city.
31: 3 with beautiful **b** overshadowing the
31: 5 increased and its **b** grew long,
31: 6 of the field gave birth under its **b**;
31: 8 the plane trees compare with its **b**
31: 9 I made it beautiful with abundant **b**,
31:12 its **b** lay broken in all the ravines
31:13 of the field were among its **b**.
36: 8 will produce **b** and fruit for my
Da 4:12 birds of the air lived in its **b**;
4:14 Cut down the tree and trim off its **b**;
4:14 under it and the birds from its **b**.
4:21 nesting places in its **b** for the birds
Joel 1: 7 it away, leaving their **b** white.
Zec 4:12 "What are these two olive **b** beside
Mt 13:32 of the air come and perch in its **b**."
21: 8 while others cut **b** from the trees
Mk 4:32 with such big **b** that the birds of
11: 8 spread **b** they had cut in the fields.
Lk 13:19 birds of the air perched in its **b**."
Jn 12:13 They took palm **b** and went out to
15: 5 "I am the vine; you are the **b**.
15: 6 such **b** are picked up, thrown into
Ro 11:16 if the root is holy, so are the **b**.
11:17 If some of the **b** have been broken
11:18 do not boast over those **b**. If you do,
11:19 You will say then, "**B** were broken
11:21 God did not spare the natural **b**,
11:24 natural **b**, be grafted into their
Heb 9:19 scarlet wool and **b** of hyssop,
Rev 7: 9 were holding palm **b** in their hands.

Branding
Isa 3:24 sackcloth; instead of beauty, **b**.

Brandish (Brandished, Brandishes, Brandishing)
Ps 35: 3 **B** spear and javelin against those
Isa 10:15 up, or a club **b** him who is not wood!
Eze 32:10 you when I **b** my sword before them.

Brandished (Brandish)
Na 2: 3 ready; the spears of pine are **b**.

Brandishes (Brandish)
Eze 30:25 Babylon and he **b** it against Egypt.

Brandishing (Brandish)
Eze 38: 4 shields, all of them **b** their swords.

Brave (Bravely, Bravest)
1Sa 14:52 whenever Saul saw a mighty or **b** man,
16:18 He is a **b** man and a warrior.
2Sa 2: 7 Now then, be strong and **b**, for Saul
13:28 you this order? Be strong and **b**."
17:10 and that those with him are **b**.
1Ch 5:24 They were **b** warriors, famous men,
7:40 **b** warriors and outstanding leaders.
8:40 The sons of Ulam were **b** warriors who
12: 8 They were **b** warriors, ready for
12:21 for all of them were **b** warriors, and
12:28 Zadok, a **b** young warrior, with 22
12:30 men of Ephraim, **b** warriors, famous
28: 1 mighty men and all the **b** warriors.
2Ch 14: 8 All these were **b** fighting men.
Isa 33: 7 Look, their **b** men cry aloud in the

Bravely (Brave)
1Sa 18:17 only serve me **b** and fight the battles
2Sa 10:12 Be strong and let us fight **b** for our
1Ch 19:13 Be strong and let us fight **b** for our

Bravest (Brave)
2Sa 17:10 even the **b** soldier, whose heart is
Am 2:16 Even the **b** warriors will flee naked

Brawler (Brawlers, Brawling)
Pr 20: 1 Wine is a mocker and beer a **b**;

Brawlers (Brawler)
Isa 5:14 with all their **b** and revellers.

Brawling (Brawler)
Eph 4:31 rage and anger, **b** and slander, along

Bray (Brayed)
Job 6: 5 Does a wild donkey **b** when it has

Brayed (Bray)
Job 30: 7 They **b** among the bushes and huddled

Brazen
Pr 7:13 and with a **b** face she said:
Jer 3: 3 Yet you have the **b** look of a
Eze 16:30 things, acting like a **b** prostitute!

Brazier
Ge 15:17 a smoking **b** with a blazing torch
Jer 36:22 burning in the **b** in front of him.
36:23 knife and threw them into the **b**,
Zec 12: 6 of Judah like a **b** in a woodpile,

Breach (Breaches, Breaching)
Job 30:14 They advance as through a gaping **b**;
Ps 106:23 stood in the **b** before him

Breaches (Breach)
Isa 22: 9 of David had many **b** in its defences;

Breaching (Breach)
Ps 144:14 There will be no **b** of walls,
Pr 17:14 Starting a quarrel is like **b** a dam;

Bread (*Bread of life, Bread of the Presence, Feast of Unleavened Bread, Unleavened bread*)
Ge 14:18 of Salem brought out **b** and wine.
18: 6 flour and knead it and bake some **b**."
19: 3 baking **b** without yeast, and they ate
25:34 Jacob gave Esau some **b** and some
27:17 tasty food and the **b** she had made.
40:16 On my head were three baskets of **b**.
45:23 **b** and other provisions for his
Ex 12: 8 herbs, and **b** made without yeast.
12:15 For seven days you are to eat **b** made
12:18 In the first month you are to eat **b**
13: 6 For seven days eat **b** made without
16: 4 rain down **b** from heaven for you.
16: 8 all the **b** you want in the morning,
16:12 morning you will be filled with **b**.
16:15 the **b** the LORD has given you to eat.
16:29 day he gives you **b** for two days.
16:31 The people of Israel called the **b**
16:32 so they can see the **b** I gave you to
18:12 elders of Israel to eat **b** with Moses'
23:15 seven days eat **b** made without yeast,
29: 2 make **b**, and cakes mixed with oil,
29:23 the basket of **b** made without yeast
29:32 and the **b** that is in the basket.
29:34 or any **b** is left over till morning,
34:18 For seven days eat **b** made without
34:28 without eating **b** or drinking water.
40:23 set out the **b** on it before the LORD,
Lev 7:12 offer cakes of **b** made without yeast
7:13 with cakes of **b** made with yeast.
8: 2 containing **b** made without yeast,
8:26 the basket of **b** made without yeast,
8:26 he took a cake of **b**, and one made
8:31 eat it there with the **b** from the
Lev 8:32 the rest of the meat and the **b**.
23: 6 you must eat **b** made without yeast.
23:14 You must not eat any **b**, or roasted
23:18 Present with this **b** seven male lambs,
23:20 with the **b** of the firstfruits.
24: 5 flour and bake twelve loaves of **b**,
24: 7 memorial portion to represent the **b**
24: 8 This **b** is to be set out before the
26:26 I cut off your supply of **b**,
26:26 be able to bake your **b** in one oven,
26:26 they will dole out the **b** by weight.
Nu 4: 7 the **b** that is continually there is
6:15 a basket of **b** made without yeast
21: 5 There is no **b**! There is no water!
28:17 seven days eat **b** made without yeast.
Dt 8: 3 man does not live on **b** alone
8: 9 a land where **b** will not be scarce
9: 9 I ate no **b** and drank no water.
9:18 I ate no **b** and drank no water,
16: 3 Do not eat it with **b** made with yeast,
16: 3 but for seven days eat unleavened **b**,
16: 3 the **b** of affliction, because you
23: 4 did not come to meet you with **b**
29: 6 You ate no **b** and drank no wine
Jos 9: 5 All the **b** of their food supply was
9:12 This **b** of ours was warm when we
Jdg 6:19 of flour he made **b** without yeast.
6:21 consuming the meat and the **b**.
7:13 "A round loaf of barley **b** came
8: 5 "Give my troops some **b**; they are
8: 6 Why should we give **b** to your troops?"
8:15 we give **b** to your exhausted men?'"
19:19 and **b** and wine for ourselves
Ru 2:14 Have some **b** and dip it in the wine
1Sa 2:36 silver and a crust of **b** and plead,
10: 3 another three loaves of **b**,
10: 4 and offer you two loaves of **b**,
16:20 Jesse took a donkey loaded with **b**,
17:17 these ten loaves of **b** for your
21: 3 give me five loaves of **b**,
21: 4 "I don't have any ordinary **b** to hand;
21: 4 there is some consecrated **b**
21: 6 the priest gave him the consecrated **b**
21: 6 since there was no **b** there except
21: 6 and replaced by hot **b** on the day
22:13 giving him **b** and a sword and
25:11 Why should I take my **b** and water,
25:18 She took two hundred loaves of **b**,
28:24 and baked **b** without yeast.
2Sa 3:35 if I taste **b** or anything else before
6:19 he gave a loaf of **b**, a cake of dates
13: 6 and make some special **b** in my sight,
13: 8 the **b** in his sight and baked it.
13: 9 she took the pan and served him the **b**
13:10 And Tamar took the **b** she had
16: 1 loaded with two hundred loaves of **b**,
16: 2 the **b** and fruit are for the men to
1Ki 13: 8 would I eat **b** or drink water here.
13: 9 'You must not eat **b** or drink water
13:16 nor can I eat **b** or drink water with
13:17 'You must not eat **b** or drink water
13:18 that he may eat **b** and drink water.
13:22 You came back and ate **b** and drank
14: 3 Take ten loaves of **b** with you,
17: 6 The ravens brought him **b** and meat
17: 6 and **b** and meat in the evening,
17:11 "And bring me, please, a piece of **b**.
17:12 "I don't have any **b**—only a handful
17:13 But first make a small cake of **b** for
19: 6 a cake of **b** baked over hot coals,
22:27 give him nothing but **b** and water
2Ki 4:42 **b** baked from the first ripe corn,
18:32 a land of **b** and vineyards, a land of
23: 9 **b** with their fellow priests.
1Ch 9:31 for baking the offering **b**.
9:32 Sabbath the **b** set out on the table.
16: 3 he gave a loaf of **b**, a cake of dates
23:29 They were in charge of the **b** set out
28:16 for each table for consecrated **b**;
2Ch 2: 4 for setting out the consecrated **b**
13:11 They set out the **b** on the
18:26 give him nothing but **b** and water
29:18 for setting out the consecrated **b**,
Ne 9:15 In their hunger you gave them **b**
10:33 for the **b** set out on the table;
Job 23:12 of his mouth more than my daily **b**.
Job 31:17 if I have kept my **b** to myself,
Ps 14: 4 who devour my people as men eat **b**
37:25 or their children begging **b**.
41: 9 he who shared my **b**, has lifted up
53: 4 who devour my people as men eat **b**
78:25 Men ate the **b** of angels; he sent
80: 5 You have fed them with the **b** of
104:15 and **b** that sustains his heart.
105:40 satisfied them with the **b** of heaven.
Pr 4:17 They eat the **b** of wickedness and
6:26 reduces you to a loaf of **b**,
28:21 man will do wrong for a piece of **b**.
30: 8 but give me only my daily **b**.
31:27 and does not eat the **b** of idleness.
Ecc 11: 1 Cast your **b** upon the waters, for
Isa 28:28 Grain must be ground to make **b**;
30:20 LORD gives you the **b** of adversity
33:16 His **b** will be supplied, and water
36:17 new wine, a land of **b** and vineyards.
44:15 he kindles a fire and bakes **b**.
44:19 I even baked **b** over its coals,
51:14 their dungeon, nor will they lack **b**.
55: 2 Why spend money on what is not **b**,
55:10 for the sower and **b** for the eater,
Jer 7:18 cakes of **b** for the Queen of Heaven.
37:21 given **b** from the street of the
37:21 all the **b** in the city was gone.
38: 9 is no longer any **b** in the city."
42:14 the trumpet or be hungry for **b**,'
Lam 1:11 people groan as they search for **b**;
2:12 "Where is **b** and wine?" as they faint
4: 4 the children beg for **b**, but no-one
5: 6 Egypt and Assyria to get enough **b**.
5: 9 We get our **b** at the risk of our
Eze 4: 9 and use them to make **b** for yourself.
4:15 "I will let you bake your **b** over cow
13:19 handfuls of barley and scraps of **b**.
45:21 you shall eat **b** made without yeast.
Hos 9: 4 be to them like the **b** of mourners;
Am 4: 5 Burn leavened **b** as a thank-offering
4: 6 city and lack of **b** in every town,
7:12 Earn your **b** there and do your
Ob : 7 those who eat your **b** will set a trap
Hag 2:12 and that fold touches some **b** or stew,
Mt 4: 3 God, tell these stones to become **b**."
4: 4 'Man does not live on **b** alone,
6:11 Give us today our daily **b**.
7: 9 "Which of you, if his son asks for **b**,
12: 4 his companions ate the consecrated **b**
14:17 "We have here only five loaves of **b**
15:26 not right to take the children's **b**
15:33 "Where could we get enough **b** in this
16: 5 the disciples forgot to take **b**.
16: 7 It is because we didn't bring any **b**."
16: 8 among yourselves about having no **b**?
16:11 I was not talking to you about **b**?
16:12 guard against the yeast used in **b**,
26:26 While they were eating, Jesus took **b**,
Mk 2:26 of God and ate the consecrated **b**,
6: 8 no **b**, no bag, no money in your
6:37 on **b** and give it to them to eat?"
6:43 of broken pieces of **b** and fish.
7:27 not right to take the children's **b**
8: 4 anyone get enough **b** to feed them?"
8:14 disciples had forgotten to bring **b**,
8:16 "It is because we have no **b**.
8:17 are you talking about having no **b**?
14:20 who dips **b** into the bowl with me.
14:22 While they were eating, Jesus took **b**,
Lk 4: 3 God, tell this stone to become **b**."
4: 4 'Man does not live on **b** alone.'"
6: 4 and taking the consecrated **b**, he ate
7:33 neither eating **b** nor drinking wine,
9: 3 no **b**, no money, no extra tunic.
9:13 "We have only five loaves of **b** and
11: 3 Give us each day our daily **b**.
11: 5 'Friend, lend me three loaves of **b**,
11: 8 him the **b** because he is his friend,
22:19 he took **b**, gave thanks and broke it,
24:30 he took **b**, gave thanks, broke it and
24:35 by them when he broke the **b**.
Jn 6: 5 we buy **b** for these people to eat?"
6: 7 **b** for each one to have a bite!"
6:23 where the people had eaten the **b**
6:31 gave them **b** from heaven to eat.'"
6:32 who has given you the **b** from heaven,

Jn 6:32 gives you the true **b** from heaven.
6:33 For the **b** of God is he who comes
6:34 "from now on give us this **b**.
6:41 the **b** that came down from heaven."
6:50 here is the **b** that comes down from
6:51 I am the living **b** that came down
6:51 If anyone eats of this **b**, he will
6:51 This **b** is my flesh, which I will
6:58 This is the **b** that came down from
6:58 feeds on this **b** will live for ever."
13:18 He who share my **b** has lifted up his
13:26 to whom I will give this piece of **b**
13:26 Then, dipping the piece of **b**, he
13:27 soon as Judas took the **b**, Satan
13:30 soon as Judas had taken the **b**, he
21: 9 there with fish on it, and some **b**.
21:13 Jesus came, took the **b** and gave it
Ac 2:42 to the breaking of **b** and to prayer.
2:46 They broke **b** in their homes and ate
20: 7 week we came together to break **b**.
20:11 he went upstairs again and broke **b**
27:35 After he said this, he took some **b**
1Co 5: 8 but with **b** without yeast, the **b** of
10:16 And is not the **b** that we break a
11:23 the night he was betrayed, took **b**,
11:26 For whenever you eat this **b** and
11:27 Therefore, whoever eats the **b** or
11:28 eats of the **b** and drinks of the cup.
2Co 9:10 **b** for food will also supply and
2Th 3:12 settle down and earn the **b** they eat.
Heb 9: 2 the table and the consecrated **b**;

Bread of life
Jn 6:35 Jesus declared, "I am the **b**. He who
6:48 I am the **b**.

Bread of the Presence
Ex 25:30 Put the **b** on this table to be before
35:13 and all its articles and the **b**;
39:36 with all its articles and the **b**;
1Sa 21: 6 was no bread there except the **b**
1Ki 7:48 the golden table on which was the **b**;
2Ch 4:19 the tables on which was the **b**;

Breadth
Ge 13:17 Go, walk through the length and **b** of
1Ki 4:29 and a **b** of understanding as
Isa 8: 8 the **b** of your land, O Immanuel!"
40:12 or with the **b** of his hand marked off
Rev 20: 9 They marched across the **b** of the

Breakers
Ps 42: 7 your waves and **b** have swept over me.
93: 4 mightier than the **b** of the sea—
Jnh 2: 3 all your waves and **b** swept over me.

Breakfast
Jn 21:12 Jesus said to them, "Come and have **b**.

Breast (Breastpiece, Breastplate, Breastplates, Breasts)
Ge 49:25 blessings of the **b** and womb.
Ex 29:26 After you take the **b** of the ram for
29:27 the **b** that was waved and the thigh
Lev 7:30 together with the **b**, and wave the **b**
7:31 the **b** belongs to Aaron and his sons.
7:34 I have taken the **b** that is waved and
8:29 He also took the **b**—Moses' share of
10:14 your daughters may eat the **b** that
10:15 the **b** that was waved must be brought
Nu 6:20 together with the **b** that was waved
18:18 just as the **b** of the wave offering
1Ki 3:20 her **b** and put her dead son by my **b**.
Job 24: 9 child is snatched from the **b**;
Ps 22: 9 trust in you even at my mother's **b**.
Isa 28: 9 to those just taken from the **b**?
49:15 a mother forget the baby at her **b**
Jer 31:19 I came to understand, I beat my **b**.
Eze 21:12 Therefore beat your **b**.
Joel 2:16 children, those nursing at the **b**.
Lk 18:13 but beat his **b** and said, 'God, have

Breastpiece (Breast)
Ex 25: 7 to be mounted on the ephod and **b**.
28: 4 the garments they are to make: a **b**,
28:15 "Fashion a **b** for making decisions
28:22 "For the **b** make braided chains of
28:23 fasten them to two corners of the **b**.
28:24 the rings at the corners of the **b**,
28:26 to the other two corners of the **b**
28:28 The rings of the **b** are to be tied to
28:28 **b** will not swing out from the ephod.
28:29 over his heart on the **b** of decision
28:30 the Urim and the Thummim in the **b**,
29: 5 ephod, the ephod itself and the **b**.
35: 9 to be mounted on the ephod and **b**.
35:27 to be mounted on the ephod and **b**.
39: 8 They fashioned the **b**—the work of a
39:15 For the **b** they made braided chains
39:16 to two of the corners of the **b**.
39:17 the rings at the corners of the **b**,
39:19 to the other two corners of the **b**
39:21 They tied the rings of the **b** to the
39:21 **b** would not swing out from the ephod
Lev 8: 8 He placed the **b** on him and put the
8: 8 put the Urim and Thummim in the **b**.

Breastplate (Breast)
Isa 59:17 He put on righteousness as his **b**,
Eph 6:14 the **b** of righteousness in place,
1Th 5: 8 putting on faith and love as a **b**

Breastplates (Breast)
Rev 9: 9 They had **b** like **b** of iron,
9:17 Their **b** were fiery red, dark blue,

Breasts (Breast)
Lev 9:20 these they laid on the **b**, and then
9:21 Aaron waved the **b** and the right
Job 3:12 and **b** that I might be nursed?
Pr 5:19 may her **b** satisfy you always,
SS 1:13 of myrrh resting between my **b**.
4: 5 Your two **b** are like two fawns,
7: 3 Your **b** are like two fawns, twins
7: 7 and your **b** like clusters of fruit.
7: 8 May your **b** be like the clusters of
8: 1 who was nursed at my mother's **b**!
8: 8 and her **b** are not yet grown.
8:10 and my **b** are like towers.
Isa 32:12 Beat your **b** for the pleasant fields,
60:16 of nations and be nursed at royal **b**.
66:11 be satisfied at her comforting **b**;
Lam 4: 3 Even jackals offer their **b** to nurse
Eze 16: 7 Your **b** were formed and your hair
23: 3 In that land their **b** were fondled
23:21 caressed and your young **b** fondled.
23:34 dash it to pieces and tear your **b**.
Hos 2: 2 unfaithfulness from between her **b**.
9:14 that miscarry and **b** that are dry.
Na 2: 7 and beat upon their **b**.
Lk 23:29 bore and the **b** that never nursed!'
23:48 they beat their **b** and went away.

Breath (*Breath of life*, Breathe, Breathed, Breathes, Breathing, God-breathed)
Ex 15:10 you blew with your **b**, and the sea
2Sa 22:16 at the blast of **b** from his nostrils.
Job 4: 9 At the **b** of God they are destroyed;
7: 7 O God, that my life is but a **b**;
9:18 He would not let me regain my **b** but
12:10 creature and the **b** of all mankind.
15:30 **b** of God's mouth will carry him away.
19:17 My **b** is offensive to my wife;
26:13 By his **b** the skies became fair;
27: 3 the **b** of God in my nostrils,
32: 8 the **b** of the Almighty, that gives
33: 4 the **b** of the Almighty gives me life
34:14 and he withdrew his spirit and **b**,
37:10 The **b** of God produces ice, and the
41:21 His **b** sets coals ablaze, and flames
Ps 18:15 the blast of **b** from your nostrils.
33: 6 starry host by the **b** of his mouth.
39: 5 Each man's life is but a **b**.
39:11 like a moth—each man is but a **b**.
62: 9 Lowborn men are but a **b**, the
Ps 62: 9 together they are only a **b**.
104:29 when you take away their **b**,
135:17 nor is there **b** in their mouths.
144: 4 Man is like a **b**; his days are like a
150: 6 Let everything that has **b** praise the
Ecc 3:19 All have the same **b**; man has no
SS 7: 8 the fragrance of your **b** like apples,
Isa 2:22 who has but a **b** in his nostrils.
11: 4 with the **b** of his lips he will slay
25: 4 For the **b** of the ruthless is like a
30:28 His **b** is like a rushing torrent,
30:33 the **b** of the LORD, like a stream of
33:11 your **b** is a fire that consumes you.
40: 7 the **b** of the LORD blows on them.
42: 5 who gives **b** to its people, and life
57:13 a mere **b** will blow them away.
57:16 the **b** of man that I have created.
59:19 that the **b** of the LORD drives along.
Jer 4:31 the Daughter of Zion gasping for **b**,
10:14 are a fraud; they have no **b** in them.
38:16 who has given us **b**, I will neither
51:17 are a fraud; they have no **b** in them.
Lam 4:20 The LORD's anointed, our very life **b**,
Eze 37: 5 bones: I will make **b** enter you,
37: 6 I will put **b** in you, and you will
37: 8 but there was no **b** in them.
37: 9 he said to me, "Prophesy to the **b**;
37: 9 O **b**, and breathe into these slain,
37:10 and **b** entered them; they came to
Hab 2:19 and silver; there is no **b** in it.
Ac 17:25 life and **b** and everything else.
2Co 1:17 that in the same **b** I say, "Yes, yes"
2Th 2: 8 overthrow with the **b** of his mouth
Rev 11:11 a **b** of life from God entered them,
13:15 He was given power to give **b** to the

Breath of life
Ge 1:30 everything that has the **b** in it
2: 7 breathed into his nostrils the **b**,
6:17 every creature that has the **b** in it.
7:15 all creatures that have the **b**
7:22 Everything on dry land that had the **b**
Rev 11:11 a **b** from God entered them,

Breathe (Breath)
Jer 15: 9 will grow faint and **b** her last.
Eze 21:31 **b** out my fiery anger against you;
37: 9 O breath, and **b** into these slain,
Da 10:17 is gone and I can hardly **b**."

Breathed (Breath)
Ge 2: 7 **b** into his nostrils the breath of
25: 8 Abraham **b** his last and died at a
25:17 He **b** his last and died, and he was
35:18 she **b** her last—for she was dying
35:29 he **b** his last and died and was
49:33 **b** his last and was gathered to his
Jos 10:40 He totally destroyed all who **b**, just
11:11 not sparing anything that **b**,
11:14 not sparing anyone that **b**.
1Ki 15:29 not leave Jeroboam anyone that **b**,
Mk 15:37 With a loud cry, Jesus **b** his last.
Lk 23:46 When he had said this, he **b** his last.
Jn 20:22 with that he **b** on them and said,

Breathes (Breath)
Dt 20:16 do not leave alive anything that **b**.
Job 14:10 he **b** his last and is no more.

Breathing (Breath)
1Ki 17:17 and worse, and finally stopped **b**.
Ps 27:12 rise up against me, **b** out violence.
Ac 9: 1 Meanwhile, Saul was still **b** out

Bred (Breed)
Est 8:10 horses especially **b** for the king.

Breed (Bred, Breeding, Breeds)
Job 21:10 Their bulls never fail to **b**;

Breeding (Breed)
Ge 31:10 "In the **b** season I once had a dream

Breeds (Breed)
Pr 13:10 Pride only **b** quarrels, but wisdom is

Breeze (Breezes)
Ps 78:39 a passing **b** that does not return.

Breezes (Breeze)
Ps 147:18 stirs up his **b**, and the waters flow.

Bribe (Bribery, Bribes, Bribing)
Ex 23: 8 "Do not accept a **b**, for a **b** blinds
Dt 16:19 Do not accept a **b**, for a **b** blinds
27:25 "Cursed is the man who accepts a **b**
1Sa 12: 3 From whose hand have I accepted a **b**
Job 36:18 do not let a large **b** turn you aside.
Ps 15: 5 not accept a **b** against the innocent.
Pr 6:35 refuse the **b**, however great it is.
17: 8 A **b** is a charm to the one who gives
17:23 A wicked man accepts a **b** in secret
21:14 and a **b** concealed in the cloak
Ecc 7: 7 a fool, and a **b** corrupts the heart.
Isa 5:23 who acquit the guilty for a **b**,
Mic 3:11 Her leaders judge for a **b**,
Ac 24:26 that Paul would offer him a **b**,

Bribery (Bribe)
2Ch 19: 7 is no injustice or partiality or **b**."

Bribes (Bribe)
Dt 10:17 no partiality and accepts no **b**.
1Sa 8: 3 accepted **b** and perverted justice.
Job 15:34 the tents of those who love **b**.
Ps 26:10 whose right hands are full of **b**.
Pr 15:27 but he who hates **b** will live.
29: 4 who is greedy for **b** tears it down.
Isa 1:23 all love **b** and chase after gifts.
33:15 and keeps his hand from accepting **b**,
Eze 22:12 In you men accept **b** to shed blood;
Am 5:12 You oppress the righteous and take **b**
Mic 7: 3 the judge accepts **b**, the powerful

Bribing (Bribe)
Eze 16:33 **b** them to come to you from

Brick (Brickmaking, Bricks, Brickwork)
Ge 11: 3 They used **b** instead of stone, and
Ex 1:14 with hard labour in **b** and mortar
Isa 65: 3 and burning incense on altars of **b**;
Jer 43: 9 bury them in clay in the **b** pavement

Brickmaking (Brick)
2Sa 12:31 and he made them work at **b**.

Bricks (Brick)
Ge 11: 3 make **b** and bake them thoroughly.
Ex 5: 7 the people with straw for making **b**;
5: 8 the same number **b** as before;
5:14 meet your quote of **b** yesterday or
5:16 'Make **b**!' Your servants are being
5:18 must produce your full quota of **b**."
5:19 of **b** required of you for each day."
Isa 9:10 "The **b** have fallen down, but we will

Brickwork (Brick)
Na 3:14 tread the mortar, repair the **b**!

Bridal (Bride)
Ge 29:27 Finish this daughter's **b** week;

Bride (Bridal, Bride-price)
Ge 34:12 Make the price for the **b** and the
1Sa 18:25 king wants no other price for the **b**
Ps 45: 9 is the royal **b** in gold of Ophir.
SS 4: 8 Come with me from Lebanon, my **b**,
SS 4: 9 my sister, my **b**; you have stolen my
4:10 my sister, my **b**! How much more
4:11 sweetness as the honeycomb, my **b**;
4:12 my sister, my **b**; you are a spring
5: 1 my sister, my **b**; I have gathered my
Isa 49:18 you will put them on, like a **b**.
61:10 a **b** adorns herself with her jewels.
62: 5 a bridegroom rejoices over his **b**,
Jer 2: 2 how as a **b** you loved me and followed
2:32 a **b** her wedding ornaments? Yet my
7:34 to the voices of **b** and bridegroom
16: 9 of **b** and bridegroom in this place.
25:10 the voices of **b** and bridegroom,
33:11 the voices of **b** and bridegroom,
Joel 2:16 his room and the **b** her chamber.
Jn 3:29 The **b** belongs to the bridegroom.
Rev 18:23 The voice of bridegroom and **b** will
19: 7 and his **b** has made herself ready.
21: 2 prepared as a **b** beautifully dressed
21: 9 you the **b**, the wife of the Lamb."
22:17 The Spirit and the **b** say, "Come!"

Bridegroom (Bridegroom's, Bridegrooms)
Ex 4:25 "Surely you are a **b** of blood to me,
4:26 (At that time she said "**b** of blood",
Ps 19: 5 which is like a **b** coming forth from
Isa 61:10 as a **b** adorns his head like a priest,
62: 5 as a **b** rejoices over his bride,
Jer 7:34 to the voices of bride and **b** in the
16: 9 voices of bride and **b** in this place.
25:10 the voices of bride and **b**, the sound
33:11 the voices of bride and **b**, and the
Joel 2:16 Let the **b** leave his room and the
Mt 9:15 "How can the guests of the **b** mourn
9:15 when the **b** will be taken from them;
25: 1 lamps and went out to meet the **b**.
25: 5 The **b** was a long time in coming,
25: 6 Here's the **b**! Come out to meet him!'
25:10 way to buy the oil, the **b** arrived.
Mk 2:19 "How can the guests of the **b** fast
2:20 the time will come when the **b** will
Lk 5:34 make the guests of the **b** fast
5:35 when the **b** will be taken from them;
Jn 2: 9 Then he called the **b** aside
3:29 The bride belongs to the **b**.
3:29 The friend who attends the **b** waits
Rev 18:23 The voice of **b** and bride will never

Bridegroom's (Bridegroom)
Jn 3:29 of joy when he hears the **b** voice.

Bridegrooms (Bridegroom)
Jdg 14:10 feast there, as was customary for **b**.

Bride-price (Bride, Price)
Ex 22:16 he must pay the **b**, and she shall
22:17 he must still pay the **b** for virgins.

Bridle (Bridles)
Job 41:13 Who would approach him with a **b**?
Ps 32: 9 must be controlled by bit and **b**

Bridles (Bridle)
Rev 14:20 rising as high as the horses' **b**

Brief (Briefly)
Ezr 9: 8 "But now, for a **b** moment, the LORD
Job 20: 5 that the mirth of the wicked is **b**,
Isa 54: 7 "For a **b** moment I abandoned you,

Briefly (Brief)
Ac 24: 4 you be kind enough to hear us **b**.
Eph 3: 3 as I have already written **b**.
1Pe 5:12 I have written to you **b**, encouraging

Brier (Briers)
Mic 7: 4 The best of them is like a **b**,

Briers (Brier)
Jdg 8: 7 flesh with desert thorns and **b**."
8:16 them with desert thorns and **b**.
Job 31:40 let **b** come up instead of wheat and
Isa 5: 6 and **b** and thorns will grow there.
7:23 there will be only **b** and thorns.
7:24 will be covered with **b** and thorns.
7:25 there for fear of the **b** and thorns;
9:18 a fire; it consumes **b** and thorns,
10:17 and consume his thorns and his **b**.
27: 4 If only there were **b** and thorns
32:13 a land overgrown with thorns and **b**
55:13 instead of **b** the myrtle will grow.
Eze 2: 6 Do not be afraid, though **b** and
28:24 who are painful **b** and sharp thorns.
Hos 9: 6 of silver will be taken over by **b**,
Lk 6:44 from thorn-bushes, or grapes from **b**.

Bright (Brightened, Brightens, Brighter, Brightness)
Lev 13: 2 a rash or a **b** spot on his skin
14:56 for a swelling, a rash or a **b** spot,
Job 25: 5 If even the moon is not **b** and the
37:21 at the sun, **b** as it is in the skies
SS 6:10 fair as the moon, **b** as the sun,
Eze 1:13 it was **b**, and lightning flashed out
8: 2 was as **b** as glowing metal.
Mt 17: 5 a **b** cloud enveloped them,
Lk 9:29 became as **b** as a flash of lightning.
Ac 22: 6 suddenly a **b** light from heaven
Rev 19: 8 Fine linen, **b** and clean, was given
22:16 of David, and the **b** Morning Star."

Brightened (Bright)
1Sa 14:27 hand to his mouth, and his eyes **b**.
14:29 See how my eyes **b** when I tasted a

Brightens (Bright)
Pr 16:15 when a king's face **b**, it means life
Ecc 8: 1 Wisdom **b** a man's face and changes

Brighter (Bright)
Job 11:17 Life will be **b** than noonday, and
Pr 4:18 ever **b** till the full light of day.
Isa 30:26 the sunlight will be seven times **b**,
Lam 4: 7 Their princes were **b** than snow and
Ac 26:13 I saw a light from heaven, **b** than

Brightness (Bright)
2Sa 22:13 Out of the **b** of his presence bolts
23: 4 like the **b** after rain that brings
Ps 18:12 Out of the **b** of his presence clouds
Isa 59: 9 for **b**, but we walk in deep shadows.
60: 3 and kings to the **b** of your dawn.
60:19 nor will the **b** of the moon shine on
Da 12: 3 shine like the **b** of the heavens,
Am 5:20 pitch-dark, without a ray of **b**?

Brilliance (Brilliant)
Ac 22:11 the **b** of the light had blinded me.
Rev 1:16 like the sun shining in all its **b**.
21:11 and its **b** was like that of a very

Brilliant (Brilliance)
Ecc 9:11 or wealth to the **b** or favour to the
Eze 1: 4 lightning and surrounded by **b** light.
1:27 fire; and **b** light surrounded him.

Brim
Pr 3:10 your vats will **b** over with new wine.
Jn 2: 7 so they filled them to the **b**.

Brink
Pr 5:14 I have come to the **b** of utter ruin

Brittle
Da 2:42 will be partly strong and partly **b**.

Broad (Broaden)
Nu 25: 4 and expose them in **b** daylight
2Sa 12:11 lie with your wives in **b** daylight.
12:12 in **b** daylight before all Israel.'"
Ne 3: 8 Jerusalem as far as the **B** Wall.
12:38 Tower of the Ovens to the **B** Wall,
Job 37:10 ice, and the **b** waters become frozen.
Isa 30:23 your cattle will graze in **b** meadows.
33:21 It will be like a place of **b** rivers

Am 8: 9 and darken the earth in **b** daylight.
Mt 7:13 wide is the gate and **b** is the road
2Pe 2:13 is to carouse in **b** daylight.

Broaden (Broad)

2Sa 22:37 You **b** the path beneath me, so that
Ps 18:36 You **b** the path beneath me, so that

Broiled

Lk 24:42 They gave him a piece of **b** fish,

Broken-hearted (Heart)

Ps 34:18 The LORD is close to the **b** and saves
109:16 the poor and the needy and the **b**.
147: 3 He heals the **b** and binds up their
Isa 61: 1 He has sent me to bind up the **b**,

Brokenness

Isa 65:14 of heart and wail in **b** of spirit.

Bronze (Bronze-tipped)

Ge 4:22 kinds of tools out of **b** and iron.
Ex 25: 3 from them: gold, silver and **b**;
26:11 make fifty **b** clasps and put them in
26:37 And cast five **b** bases for them.
27: 2 piece, and overlay the altar with **b**.
27: 3 Make all its utensils of **b**—its pots
27: 4 a **b** network, and make a **b** ring at
27: 6 the altar and overlay them with **b**.
27:10 with twenty posts and twenty **b** bases
27:11 with twenty posts and twenty **b** bases
27:17 silver bands and hooks, and **b** bases.
27:18 five cubits high, and with **b** bases.
27:19 for the courtyard, are to be of **b**.
30:18 "Make a **b** basin, with its **b** stand,
31: 4 for work in gold, silver and **b**,
35: 5 an offering of gold, silver and **b**;
35:16 burnt offering with its **b** grating,
35:16 the **b** basin with its stand;
35:24 an offering of silver or **b** brought
35:32 for work in gold, silver and **b**,
36:18 They made fifty **b** clasps to fasten
36:38 gold and made their five bases of **b**.
38: 2 and they overlaid the altar with **b**.
38: 3 They made all its utensils of **b**
38: 4 a **b** network, to be under its ledge,
38: 5 They cast **b** rings to hold the poles
38: 5 the four corners of the **b** grating.
38: 6 wood and overlaid them with **b**.
38: 8 made the **b** basin and its **b** stand
38:10 with twenty posts and twenty **b** bases,
38:11 had twenty posts and twenty **b** bases,
38:17 The bases for the posts were **b**.
38:19 with four posts and four **b** bases.
38:20 of the surrounding courtyard were **b**.
38:29 The **b** from the wave offering was 70
38:30 the **b** altar with its **b** grating and
39:39 the **b** altar with its **b** grating,
Lev 6:28 but if it is cooked in a **b** pot,
26:19 and the ground beneath you like **b**.
Nu 4:13 remove the ashes from the **b** altar
16:39 Eleazar the priest collected the **b**
21: 9 Moses made a **b** snake and put it up
21: 9 and looked at the **b** snake, he lived.
31:22 Gold, silver, **b**, iron, tin,
Dt 28:23 The sky over your head will be **b**,
33:25 of your gates will be iron and **b**,
Jos 6:19 gold and the articles of **b** and iron
6:24 gold and the articles of **b** and iron
22: 8 with silver, gold, **b** and iron,
Jdg 16:21 Binding him with **b** shackles, they
1Sa 17: 5 He had a **b** helmet on his head and
17: 5 of **b** weighing five thousand shekels;
17: 6 on his legs he wore **b** greaves,
17: 6 a **b** javelin was slung on his back.
17:38 on him and a **b** helmet on his head.
2Sa 8: 8 David took a great quantity of **b**.
8:10 articles of silver and gold and **b**.
21:16 whose **b** spearhead weighed three
22:35 my arms can bend a bow of **b**.
1Ki 4:13 walled cities with **b** gate bars);
7:14 a man of Tyre and a craftsman in **b**.
7:14 experienced in all kinds of **b** work.
7:15 He cast two **b** pillars, each eighteen
1Ki 7:16 He also made two capitals of cast **b**
7:27 He also made ten movable stands of **b**;
7:30 stand had four **b** wheels with **b** axles
7:38 He then made ten **b** basins, each
7:45 of the LORD were of burnished **b**.
7:47 weight of the **b** was not determined.
8:64 because the **b** altar before the LORD
14:27 King Rehoboam made **b** shields to
2Ki 16:14 The **b** altar that stood before the
16:15 the **b** altar for seeking guidance."
16:17 He removed the Sea from the **b** bulls
18: 4 He broke into pieces the **b** snake
25: 7 bound him with **b** shackles and took
25:13 The Babylonians broke up the **b**
25:13 the movable stands and the **b** Sea
25:13 and they carried the **b** to Babylon.
25:14 wick trimmers, dishes and all the **b**
25:16 The **b** from the two pillars, the Sea
25:17 The **b** capital on top of one pillar
25:17 and pomegranates of **b** all around.
1Ch 15:19 Ethan were to sound the **b** cymbals;
18: 8 David took a great quantity of **b**,
18: 8 which Solomon used to make the **b** Sea,
18: 8 the pillars and various **b** articles.
18:10 articles of gold and silver and **b**.
22: 3 and more **b** than could be weighed.
22:14 quantities of **b** and iron too great
22:16 in gold and silver, **b** and iron
29: 2 silver for the silver, **b** for the **b**,
29: 7 eighteen thousand talents of **b** and a
2Ch 1: 5 the **b** altar that Bezalel son of Uri,
1: 6 Solomon went up to the **b** altar
2: 7 work in gold and silver, **b** and iron,
2:14 **b** and iron, stone and wood, and with
4: 1 He made a **b** altar twenty cubits long,
4: 9 and overlaid the doors with **b**.
4:16 of the LORD were of polished **b**.
4:18 weight of the **b** was not determined.
6:13 Now he had made a **b** platform,
7: 7 because the **b** altar he had made
12:10 King Rehoboam made **b** shields to
24:12 in iron and **b** to repair the temple.
33:11 bound him with **b** shackles and took
36: 6 bound him with **b** shackles to take
Ezr 8:27 of polished **b**, as precious as gold.
Job 6:12 strength of stone? Is my flesh **b**?
37:18 skies, hard as a mirror of cast **b**?
40:18 His bones are tubes of **b**, his limbs
41:27 Iron he treats like straw and **b** like
Ps 18:34 my arms can bend a bow of **b**.
107:16 for he breaks down gates of **b** and
Isa 45: 2 I will break down gates of **b**
48: 4 neck were iron, your forehead was **b**.
60:17 Instead of **b** I will bring you gold,
60:17 Instead of wood I will bring you **b**,
Jer 1:18 an iron pillar and a **b** wall to stand
6:28 They are **b** and iron; they all act
15:12 iron—iron from the north—or **b**?
15:20 a fortified wall of **b**; they will
39: 7 and bound him with **b** shackles
52:11 bound him with **b** shackles and took
52:17 The Babylonians broke up the **b**
52:17 the movable stands and the **b** Sea
52:17 they carried all the **b** to Babylon.
52:18 dishes and all the **b** articles used
52:20 The **b** from the two pillars, the Sea
52:20 the Sea and the twelve **b** bulls under
52:22 The **b** capital on the top of the one
52:22 and pomegranates of **b** all around.
Eze 1: 7 a calf and gleamed like burnished **b**.
9: 2 in and stood beside the **b** altar.
27:13 and articles of **b** for your wares.
40: 3 a man whose appearance was like **b**;
Da 2:32 silver, its belly and thighs of **b**,
2:35 the iron, the clay, the **b**, the
2:39 a third kingdom, one of **b**,
2:45 the **b**, the clay, the silver and the
4:15 its roots, bound with iron and **b**,
4:23 the stump, bound with iron and **b**,
5: 4 silver, of **b**, iron, wood and stone.
5:23 of **b**, iron, wood and stone, which
7:19 with its iron teeth and **b** claws—
10: 6 legs like the gleam of burnished **b**,
Mic 4:13 I will give you hoofs of **b** and you
Zec 6: 1 two mountains—mountains of **b**!
Rev 1:15 His feet were like **b** glowing in a
Rev 2:18 and whose feet are like burnished **b**.
9:20 and idols of gold, silver, **b**, stone
18:12 costly wood, **b**, iron and marble;

Bronze-tipped (Bronze)

Job 20:24 iron weapon, a **b** arrow pierces him.

Brooches

Ex 35:22 **b**, ear-rings, rings and ornaments.

Brood

Nu 32:14 "And here you are, a **b** of sinners,
Job 30: 8 A base and nameless **b**, they were
Isa 1: 4 a **b** of evildoers, children given to
57: 4 Are you not a **b** of rebels,
Mt 3: 7 "You **b** of vipers! Who warned you to
12:34 You **b** of vipers, how can you who are
23:33 "You snakes! You **b** of vipers!
Lk 3: 7 "You **b** of vipers! Who warned you to
2Pe 2:14 are experts in greed—an accursed **b**!

Brook

2Sa 17:20 "They crossed over the **b**.
1Ki 17: 4 You will drink from the **b**, and I
17: 6 evening, and he drank from the **b**.
17: 7 Some time later the **b** dried up
Ps 110: 7 He will drink from a **b** beside the
Pr 18: 4 fountain of wisdom is a bubbling **b**.
Jer 15:18 will you be to me like a deceptive **b**

Broom

1Ki 19: 4 He came to a **b** tree, sat down under
Job 30: 4 food was the root of the **b** tree.
Ps 120: 4 with burning coals of the **b** tree.
Isa 14:23 her with the **b** of destruction,"

Broth

Jdg 6:19 meat in a basket and its **b** in a pot,
6:20 on this rock, and pour out the **b**.
Isa 65: 4 whose pots hold **b** of unclean meat;

Brother (Brother's, Brotherhood, Brother-in-law, Brotherly, Brothers)

Ge 4: 2 Later she gave birth to his **b** Abel.
4: 8 Now Cain said to his **b** Abel, "Let's
4: 8 attacked his **b** Abel and killed him.
4: 9 "Where is your **b** Abel?"
10:21 Shem, whose older **b** was Japheth;
10:25 was divided; his **b** was named Joktan.
14:13 a **b** of Eshcol and Aner, all of whom
20:13 we go, say of me, "He is my **b**.
20:16 To Sarah he said, "I am giving your **b**
22:20 she has borne sons to your **b** Nahor:
22:21 Uz the firstborn, Buz his **b**, Kemuel
22:23 eight sons to Abraham's **b** Nahor.
24:15 was the wife of Abraham's **b** Nahor.
24:29 Now Rebekah had a **b** named Laban,
24:48 of my master's **b** for his son.
24:53 gifts to her **b** and to her mother.
24:55 her **b** and her mother replied,
25:26 After this, his **b** came out, with his
27: 6 your father say to your **b** Esau,
27:11 "But my **b** Esau is a hairy man,
27:23 were hairy like those of his **b** Esau
27:30 his **b** Esau came in from hunting.
27:35 he said, "Your **b** came deceitfully
27:40 the sword and you will serve your **b**.
27:41 then I will kill my **b** Jacob."
27:42 "Your **b** Esau is consoling himself
27:43 Flee at once to my **b** Laban in Haran.
27:45 your **b** is no longer angry with you
28: 2 daughters of Laban, your mother's **b**.
28: 5 the **b** of Rebekah, who was the mother
29:10 his mother's **b**, and Laban's sheep,
32: 3 to his **b** Esau in the land of Seir,
32: 6 "We went to your **b** Esau, and now he
32:11 I pray, from the hand of my **b** Esau,
32:13 he selected a gift for his **b** Esau:
32:17 "When my **b** Esau meets you and asks,
33: 3 seven times as he approached his **b**.
33: 9 said, "I already have plenty, my **b**.
35: 1 you were fleeing from your **b** Esau."
35: 7 him when he was fleeing from his **b**.
36: 6 land some distance from his **b** Jacob.

Ge 37:26 kill our **b** and cover up his blood?
37:27 is our **b**, our own flesh and blood.
38: 8 to produce offspring for your **b**."
38: 9 from producing offspring for his **b**.
38:29 drew back his hand, his **b** came out,
38:30 his **b**, who had the scarlet thread on
42: 4 did not send Benjamin, Joseph's **b**,
42:15 unless your youngest **b** comes here.
42:16 Send one of your number to get your **b**
42:20 you must bring your youngest **b** to me,
42:21 are being punished because of our **b**.
42:34 bring your youngest **b** to me so I
42:34 Then I will give your **b** back to you,
42:38 his **b** is dead and he is the only one
43: 3 again unless your **b** is with you.'
43: 4 If you will send our **b** along with us,
43: 5 again unless your **b** is with you.'"
43: 6 telling the man you had another **b**?"
43: 7 'Do you have another **b**?' We simply
43: 7 say, 'Bring your **b** down here'?"
43:13 Take your **b** also and go back to the
43:14 let your other **b** and Benjamin come
43:29 he looked about and saw his **b**
43:29 "Is this your youngest **b**, the one
43:30 Deeply moved at the sight of his **b**,
44:19 'Do you have a father or a **b**?'
44:20 His **b** is dead, and he is the only
44:23 'Unless your youngest **b** comes down
44:26 Only if our youngest **b** is with us
44:26 unless our youngest **b** is with us.'
45: 4 "I am your **b** Joseph, the one you
45:12 and so can my **b** Benjamin, that it is
45:14 he threw his arms around his **b**
48:19 Nevertheless, his younger **b** will be
Ex 4:14 "What about your **b**, Aaron the Levite?
7: 1 your **b** Aaron will be your prophet.
7: 2 and your **b** Aaron is to tell Pharaoh
28: 1 "Have Aaron your **b** brought to you
28: 2 Make sacred garments for your **b**
28: 4 for your **b** Aaron and his sons,
28:41 After you put these clothes on your **b**
32:27 his **b** and friend and neighbour.'"
Lev 16: 2 The LORD said to Moses: "Tell your **b**
18:14 "'Do not dishonour your father's **b**
18:16 that would dishonour your **b**.
19:17 "'Do not hate your **b** in your heart.
20:21 he has dishonoured his **b**.
21: 2 father, his son or daughter, his **b**,
Nu 6: 7 Even if his own father or mother or **b**
20: 8 "Take the staff, and you and your **b**
20:14 "This is what your **b** Israel says:
27:13 to your people, as your **b** Aaron was,
36: 2 our **b** Zelophehad to his daughters.
Dt 1:16 the case is between **b** Israelites
3:18 over ahead of your **b** Israelites.
13: 6 If your very own **b**, or your son or
15: 2 from his fellow Israelite or **b**,
15: 3 cancel any debt your **b** owes you.
15: 7 or tight-fisted towards your poor **b**.
15: 9 your needy **b** and give him nothing.
17:15 one who is not a **b** Israelite.
19:18 false testimony against his **b**,
19:19 him as he intended to do to his **b**.
22: 2 If the **b** does not live near you or
23: 7 abhor an Edomite, for he is your **b**.
23:19 Do not charge your **b** interest,
23:20 but not a **b** Israelite, so that the
24: 7 kidnapping one of his **b** Israelites
24:14 whether he is a **b** Israelite or an
25: 3 **b** will be degraded in your eyes.
25: 5 Her husband's **b** shall take her and
25: 6 carry on the name of the dead **b**
25: 7 "My husband's **b** refuses to carry on
28:54 have no compassion on his own **b**
32:50 as your **b** Aaron died on Mount Hor
Jos 15:17 Othniel son of Kenaz, Caleb's **b**,
Jdg 1:13 Caleb's younger **b**, took it; so Caleb
3: 9 Caleb's younger **b**, who saved them.
9: 3 for they said, "He is our **b**.
9:18 of Shechem because he is your **b**)—
9:21 he was afraid of his **b** Abimelech.
9:24 might be avenged on their **b**
20:28 battle with Benjamin our **b**, or not?"
Ru 4: 3 that belonged to our **b** Elimelech.
1Sa 14: 3 He was a son of Ichabod's **b** Ahitub
17:28 Eliab, David's oldest **b**, heard him

1Sa 20:29 and my **b** has ordered me to be there.
26: 6 Abishai son of Zeruiah, Joab's **b**,
2Sa 1:26 I grieve for you, Jonathan my **b**;
2:22 I look your **b** Joab in the face?"
3:27 to avenge the blood of his **b** Asahel,
3:30 (Joab and his **b** Abishai murdered
3:30 he had killed their **b** Asahel
4: 6 Recab and his **b** Baanah slipped away.
4: 9 David answered Recab and his **b**
10:10 under the command of Abishai his **b**
13: 3 Jonadab son of Shimeah, David's **b**.
13: 4 with Tamar, my **b** Absalom's sister."
13: 7 "Go to the house of your **b** Amnon and
13: 8 Tamar went to the house of her **b**
13:10 it to her **b** Amnon in his bedroom.
13:12 "Don't, my **b**!" she said to him.
13:20 Her **b** Absalom said to her,
13:20 "Has that Amnon, your **b**, been with
13:20 quiet now, my sister; he is your **b**.
13:20 Tamar lived in **b** Absalom's house,
13:26 please let my **b** Amnon come with us.
13:32 Jonadab son of Shimeah, David's **b**,
14: 7 'Hand over the one who struck his **b**
14: 7 the life of his **b** whom he killed;
18: 2 a third under Joab's **b** Abishai
20: 9 "How are you, my **b**?" Then Joab took
20:10 **b** Abishai pursued Sheba son of Bicri.
21:21 of Shimeah, David's **b**, killed him.
23:18 Abishai the **b** of Joab son of Zeruiah
23:24 were: Asahel the **b** of Joab,
1Ki 1:10 the special guard or his **b** Solomon.
2: 7 me when I fled from your **b** Absalom.
2:15 and the kingdom has gone to my **b**;
2:21 in marriage to your **b** Adonijah."
2:22 after all, he is my older **b**—
9:13 are these you have given me, my **b**?"
13:30 mourned over him and said "Oh, my **b**!
20:32 "Is he still alive? He is my **b**.
20:33 "Yes, your **b** Ben-Hadad!" they said.
1Ch 1:19 was divided; his **b** was named Joktan.
2:32 The sons of Jada, Shammai's **b**:
2:42 The sons of Caleb the **b** of Jerahmeel:
4:11 Kelub, Shuhah's **b**, was the father of
7:15 His **b** was named Sheresh, and his
7:35 The sons of his **b** Helem: Zophah,
8:39 The sons of his **b** Eshek: Ulam his
11:20 Abishai the **b** of Joab was chief of
11:26 The mighty men were: Asahel the **b** of
11:38 Joel the **b** of Nathan, Mibhar son of
11:45 Jediael son of Shimri, his **b** Joha
19:11 under the command of Abishai his **b**,
19:15 they too fled before his **b** Abishai
20: 5 Lahmi the **b** of Goliath the Gittite,
20: 7 Jonathan son of Shimea, David's **b**,
24:25 The **b** of Micah: Isshiah;
24:31 The families of the oldest **b** were
26:22 the sons of Jehieli, Zetham and his **b**
27: 7 was Asahel the **b** of Joab; his son
27:18 over Judah: Elihu, a **b** of David;
2Ch 31:12 and his **b** Shimei was next in rank.
31:13 under Conaniah and Shimei his **b**,
36: 4 made Eliakim, a **b** of Jehoahaz, king
36: 4 But Neco took Eliakim's **b** Jehoahaz
Ezr 7:18 You and your **b** Jews may then do
Ne 7: 2 I put in charge of Jerusalem my **b**
Job 30:29 I have become a **b** of jackals,
Ps 35:14 as though for my friend or **b**.
50:20 You speak continually against your **b**
Pr 17:17 and a **b** is born for adversity.
18: 9 is **b** to one who destroys.
18:19 An offended **b** is more unyielding
18:24 a friend who sticks closer than a **b**.
27:10 neighbour nearby than a **b** far away.
Ecc 4: 8 all alone; he had neither son nor **b**.
SS 8: 1 If only you were to me like a **b**, who
Isa 9:19 the fire; no-one will spare his **b**.
19: 2 **b** will fight against **b**,
41: 6 helps the other and says to his **b**,
Jer 9: 4 For every **b** is a deceiver, and every
22:18 'Alas, my **b**! Alas, my sister!'
31:34 a man his **b**, saying, 'Know the LORD,'
Eze 18:18 robbed his **b** and did what was wrong
38:21 man's sword will be against his **b**.
44:25 son or daughter, **b** or unmarried
Am 1:11 Because he pursued his **b**
Ob :10 of the violence against your **b** Jacob,

Ob :12 You should not look down on your **b**
Mic 7: 2 each hunts his **b** with a net.
Hag 2:22 fall, each by the sword of his **b**.
Mal 1: 2 "Was not Esau Jacob's **b**?" the LORD
Mt 4:18 Simon called Peter and his **b** Andrew.
4:21 James son of Zebedee and his **b** John.
5:22 his **b** will be subject to judgment.
5:22 Again, anyone who says to his **b**,
5:23 your **b** has something against you,
5:24 First go and be reconciled to your **b**
7: 4 How can you say to your **b**, 'Let me
10: 2 his **b** Andrew; James son of Zebedee,
10: 2 James son of Zebedee, and his **b** John;
10:21 "**B** will betray **b** to death, and a
12:50 is my **b** and sister and mother."
14: 3 of Herodias, his **b** Philip's wife,
17: 1 James and John the **b** of James, and
18:15 "If your **b** sins against you, go and
18:15 to you, you have won your **b** over.
18:21 how many times shall I forgive my **b**
18:35 you forgive your **b** from your heart."
22:24 his **b** must marry the widow and have
22:25 children, he left his wife to his **b**.
22:26 happened to the second and third **b**,
Mk 1:16 he saw Simon and his **b** Andrew
1:19 of Zebedee and his **b** John in a boat,
3:17 James son of Zebedee and his **b** John
3:35 Whoever does God's will is my **b** and
5:37 Peter, James and John the **b** of James.
6: 3 this Mary's son and the **b** of James,
6:17 **b** Philip's wife, whom he had married.
12:19 if a man's **b** dies and leaves a wife
12:19 widow and have children for his **b**.
13:12 "**B** will betray **b** to death, and a
Lk 3: 1 his **b** Philip Tetrarch of Iturea
6:14 his **b** Andrew, James, John,
6:42 How can you say to your **b**, '**B**, let
12:13 tell my **b** to divide the inheritance
15:27 'Your **b** has come,' he replied,
15:28 "The older **b** became angry and
15:32 because this **b** of yours was dead and
17: 3 "If your **b** sins, rebuke him,
20:28 if a man's **b** dies and leaves a wife
20:28 widow and have children for his **b**.
Jn 1:40 Andrew, Simon Peter's **b**, was one of
1:41 to find his **b** Simon and tell him,
6: 8 Andrew, Simon Peter's **b**, spoke up,
11: 2 This Mary, whose **b** Lazarus now lay
11:19 comfort them in the loss of their **b**.
11:21 been here, my **b** would not have died.
11:23 Jesus said to her, "Your **b** will rise
11:32 here, my **b** would not have died."
Ac 9:17 "**B** Saul, the Lord—Jesus, who
12: 2 He had James, the **b** of John, put to
21:20 Then they said to Paul: "You see, **b**,
22:13 He stood beside me and said, '**B** Saul,
Ro 14:10 You, then, why do you judge your **b**?
14:10 Or why do you look down on your **b**?
14:15 If your **b** is distressed because of
14:15 destroy your **b** for whom Christ died.
14:21 else that will cause your **b** to fall.
16:23 **b** Quartus send you their greetings.
1Co 1: 1 will of God, and our **b** Sosthenes,
5:11 anyone who calls himself a **b**
6: 6 one **b** goes to law against another
7:12 If any **b** has a wife who is not
8:11 this weak **b**, for whom Christ died,
8:13 I eat causes my **b** to fall into sin,
16:12 Now about our **b** Apollos: I strongly
2Co 1: 1 the will of God, and Timothy our **b**,
2:13 I did not find my **b** Titus there.
8:18 we are sending along with him the **b**
8:22 we are sending with them our **b** who
12:18 go to you and I sent our **b** with him.
Gal 1:19 apostles—only James, the Lord's **b**.
Eph 6:21 Tychicus, the dear **b** and faithful
Php 2:25 Epaphroditus my **b**, fellow-worker
Col 1: 1 the will of God, and Timothy our **b**,
4: 7 He is a dear **b**, a faithful minister
4: 9 and dear **b**, who is one of you.
1Th 3: 2 We sent Timothy, who is our **b** and
4: 6 no-one should wrong his **b**
2Th 3: 6 keep away from every **b** who is idle
3:15 as an enemy, but warn him as a **b**.
Phm :1 of Christ Jesus, and Timothy our **b**,
:7 because you, **b**, have refreshed the

Phm :16 better than a slave, as a dear **b**.
:16 as a man and as a **b** in the Lord.
:20 I do wish, **b**, that I may have some
Heb 8:11 a man his **b**, saying,'Know the Lord,'
13:23 I want you to know that our **b**
Jas 1: 9 The **b** in humble circumstances ought
2:15 Suppose a **b** or sister is without
4:11 Anyone who speaks against his **b**
1Pe 5:12 whom I regard as a faithful **b**,
2Pe 3:15 just as our dear **b** Paul also wrote
1Jn 2: 9 his **b** is still in the darkness.
2:10 Whoever loves his **b** lives in the
2:11 whoever hates his **b** is in the
3:10 is anyone who does not love his **b**.
3:12 to the evil one and murdered his **b**.
3:15 Anyone who hates his **b** is a murderer,
3:17 sees his **b** in need but has no pity
4:20 yet hates his **b**, he is a liar.
4:20 For anyone who does not love his **b**,
4:21 loves God must also love his **b**.
5:16 If anyone sees his **b** commit a sin
Jude : 1 a servant of Jesus Christ and a **b** of
Rev 1: 9 I, John, your **b** and companion in the

Brother's (Brother)

Ge 4: 9 "Am I my **b** keeper?"
4:10 Listen! Your **b** blood cries out to me
4:11 receive your **b** blood from your hand.
4:21 His **b** name was Jubal; he was the
27:44 a while until your **b** fury subsides.
38: 8 "Lie with your **b** wife and fulfil
38: 9 so whenever he lay with his **b** wife,
Lev 18:16 sexual relations with your **b** wife;
20:21 "If a man marries his **b** wife, it is
Dt 22: 1 If you see your **b** ox or sheep
22: 3 the same if you find your **b** donkey
22: 4 If you see your **b** donkey or his ox
25: 7 does not want to marry his **b** wife,
25: 7 to carry on his **b** name in Israel.
25: 9 his **b** widow shall go up to him in
25: 9 not build up his **b** family line."
Job 1:13 drinking wine at the oldest **b** house,
1:18 drinking wine at the oldest **b** house,
Pr 27:10 and do not go to your **b** house when
Hos 12: 3 In the womb he grasped his **b** heel;
Mt 7: 3 the speck of sawdust in your **b** eye
7: 5 to remove the speck from your **b** eye.
Mk 6:18 lawful for you to have your **b** wife."
Lk 3:19 because of Herodias, his **b** wife,
6:41 the speck of sawdust in your **b** eye
6:42 to remove the speck from your **b** eye.
Ro 14:13 or obstacle in your **b** way.
1Jn 3:12 were evil and his **b** were righteous.

Brotherhood (Brother)

Am 1: 9 disregarding a treaty of **b**,
Zec 11:14 the **b** between Judah and Israel.
1Pe 2:17 everyone: Love the **b** of believers,

Brother-in-law (Brother)

Ge 38: 8 fulfil your duty to her as a **b** to
Dt 25: 5 and fulfil the duty of a **b** to her.
25: 7 not fulfil the duty of a **b** to me."
Jdg 4:11 the descendants of Hobab, Moses' **b**,

Brotherly (Brother)

Ro 12:10 Be devoted to one another in **b** love.
1Th 4: 9 Now about **b** love we do not need to
2Pe 1: 7 **b** kindness; and to **b** kindness, love.

Brothers (Brother)

Ge 9:22 and told his two **b** outside.
9:25 of slaves will he be to his **b**."
13: 8 herdsmen and mine, for we are **b**.
16:12 in hostility towards all his **b**."
25:18 in hostility towards all their **b**.
27:29 Be lord over your **b**, and may the
29: 4 Jacob asked the shepherds, "My **b**,
34:11 Shechem said to Dinah's father and **b**,
34:25 Simeon and Levi, Dinah's **b**, took
37: 2 was tending the flocks with his **b**,
37: 4 his **b** saw that their father loved
37: 5 and when he told it to his **b**,
37: 8 His **b** said to him, "Do you intend to
Ge 37: 9 dream, and he told it to his **b**.
37:10 he told his father as well as his **b**,
37:10 Will your mother and I and your **b**
37:11 His **b** were jealous of him, but his
37:12 Now his **b** had gone to graze their
37:13 "As you know, your **b** are grazing the
37:14 with your **b** and with the flocks,
37:16 He replied, "I'm looking for my **b**.
37:17 So Joseph went after his **b**
37:23 when Joseph came to his **b**, they
37:26 Judah said to his **b**, "What will we
37:27 own flesh and blood." His **b** agreed.
37:28 his **b** pulled Joseph up out of the
37:30 He went back to his **b** and said,
38: 1 At that time, Judah left his **b** and
38:11 "He may die too, just like his **b**.
42: 3 ten of Joseph's **b** went down to buy
42: 6 So when Joseph's **b** arrived, they
42: 7 soon as Joseph saw his **b**, he
42: 8 Although Joseph recognised his **b**,
42:13 "Your servants were twelve **b**, the
42:19 let one of your **b** stay here in
42:28 been returned," he said to his **b**.
42:32 We were twelve **b**, sons of one father.
42:33 Leave one of your **b** here with me,
43:32 him by himself, the **b** by themselves,
44:14 house when Judah and his **b** came in,
44:33 and let the boy return with his **b**.
45: 1 when he made himself known to his **b**.
45: 3 Joseph said to his **b**, "I am Joseph!
45: 3 his **b** were not able to answer him,
45: 4 Joseph said to his **b**, "Come close to
45:15 he kissed all his **b** and wept over
45:15 Afterwards his **b** talked with him.
45:16 palace that Joseph's **b** had come,
45:17 Pharaoh said to Joseph, "Tell your **b**,
45:24 he sent his **b** away, and as they were
46:31 Joseph said to his **b** and to his
46:31 'My **b** and my father's household, who
47: 1 "My father and **b**, with their flocks
47: 2 He chose five of his **b** and presented
47: 3 Pharaoh asked the **b**, "What is your
47: 5 father and your **b** have come to you,
47: 6 settle your father and your **b**
47:11 Joseph settled his father and his **b**
47:12 his **b** and all his father's household
48: 6 reckoned under the names of their **b**.
48:22 to you, as one who is over your **b**,
49: 5 "Simeon and Levi are **b**—their
49: 8 "Judah, your **b** will praise you;
49:26 the brow of the prince among his **b**.
50: 8 his **b** and those belonging to his
50:14 together with his **b** and all the
50:15 Joseph's **b** saw that their father was
50:17 I ask you to forgive your **b** the sins
50:18 His **b** then came and threw themselves
50:24 Joseph said to his **b**, "I am about to
Ex 1: 6 Now Joseph and all his **b** and all
32:29 you were against your own sons and **b**
Lev 21:10 the one among his **b** who has had the
Nu 8:26 They may assist their **b** in
20: 3 our **b** fell dead before the LORD!
27: 9 give his inheritance to his **b**.
27:10 If he has no **b**, give his inheritance
27:10 his inheritance to his father's **b**.
27:11 If his father had no **b**, give his
Dt 1:16 between your **b** and judge fairly,
1:28 Our **b** have made us lose heart.
2: 4 of your **b** the descendants of Esau,
2: 8 we went on past our **b** the
3:20 until the LORD gives rest to your **b**
10: 9 share or inheritance among their **b**;
15: 7 If there is a poor man among your **b**
15:11 to be open-handed towards your **b**
17:15 He must be from among your own **b**.
17:20 consider himself better than his **b**
18: 2 have no inheritance among their **b**;
18:15 like me from among your own **b**.
18:18 prophet like you from among their **b**;
20: 8 **b** will not become disheartened too."
25: 5 If **b** are living together and one of
33: 9 He did not recognise his **b** or
33:16 the brow of the prince among his **b**.
33:24 let him be favoured by his **b**,
Jos 1:14 must cross over ahead of your **b**.
1:14 You are to help your **b**
Jos 2:13 my **b** and sisters, and all who belong
2:18 your **b** and all your family into your
6:23 and **b** and all who belonged to her.
14: 8 my **b** who went up with me made the
17: 4 give us an inheritance among our **b**.
17: 4 along with the **b** of their father,
22: 3 you have not deserted your **b** but
22: 4 given your **b** rest as he promised,
22: 7 side of the Jordan with their **b**.
22: 8 and divide with your **b** the plunder
Jdg 1: 3 Judah said to the Simeonites their **b**,
1:17 went with the Simeonites their **b**
8:19 Gideon replied, "Those were my **b**,
9: 1 went to his mother's **b** in Shechem
9: 3 the **b** repeated all this to the
9: 5 seventy **b**, the sons of Jerub-Baal.
9:24 who had helped him murder his **b**.
9:26 Now Gaal son of Ebed moved with his **b**
9:31 "Gaal son of Ebed and his **b** have
9:41 drove Gaal and his **b** out of Shechem.
9:56 father by murdering his seventy **b**.
11: 3 Jephthah fled from his **b** and settled
16:31 his **b** and his father's whole family
18: 8 their **b** asked them, "How did you
18:14 the land of Laish said to their **b**,
20:23 against the Benjamites, our **b**?"
21: 6 grieved for their **b**, the Benjamites.
21:22 their fathers or **b** complain to us,
1Sa 16:13 him in the presence of his **b**,
17:17 ten loaves of bread for your **b**
17:18 See how your **b** are and bring back
17:22 the battle lines and greeted his **b**.
20:29 in your eyes, let me go to see my **b**.
22: 1 When his **b** and his father's
30:23 David replied, "No, my **b**, you must
2Sa 2:26 your men to stop pursuing their **b**?"
2:27 pursuit of their **b** until morning."
19:12 You are my **b**, my own flesh and blood.
19:41 "Why did our **b**, the men of Judah,
1Ki 1: 9 He invited all his **b**, the king's
12:24 against your **b**, the Israelites.
1Ch 4: 9 Jabez was more honourable than his **b**.
4:27 but his **b** did not have many children;
5: 2 Judah was the strongest of his **b**
9:17 and their **b**, Shallum their chief
9:25 Their **b** in their villages had to
9:32 Some of their Kohathite **b** were in
13: 2 far and wide to the rest of our **b**
15:16 to appoint their **b** as singers
15:17 from his **b**, Asaph, son of Berekiah;
15:17 and from their **b** the Merarites,
15:18 with them their **b** next in rank:
23:32 under their **b** the descendants of
24:31 They also cast lots, just as their **b**
28: 2 "Listen to me, my **b** and my people.
2Ch 11: 4 Do not go up to fight against your **b**.
11:22 to be the chief prince among his **b**,
19:10 wrath will come on you and your **b**.
21: 2 Jehoram's **b**, the sons of Jehoshaphat,
21: 4 he put all his **b** to the sword along
21:13 You have also murdered your own **b**,
29:15 they had assembled their **b** and
30: 7 Do not be like your fathers and **b**,
30: 9 then your **b** and your children will
35: 9 with Shemaiah and Nethanel, his **b**,
Ezr 3: 8 the rest of their **b** (the priests and
3: 9 Jeshua and his sons and **b** and
3: 9 their sons and **b**—all Levites
6:20 for their **b** the priests and for
8:18 and Sherebiah's sons and **b**, 18 men;
8:19 and his **b** and nephews, 20 men.
8:24 Hashabiah and ten of their **b**,
10:18 and his **b**: Maaseiah, Eliezer, Jarib
Ne 1: 2 Hanani, one of my **b**, came from Judah
4:14 and fight for your **b**, your sons and
4:23 Neither I nor my **b** nor my men nor
5: 1 great outcry against their Jewish **b**.
5: 8 **b** who were sold to the Gentiles.
5: 8 Now you are selling your **b**, only for
5:10 I and my **b** and my men are also
5:14 neither I nor my **b** ate the food
10:29 these now join their **b** the nobles
13:13 distributing the supplies to their **b**
Job 6:15 my **b** are as undependable as
19:13 "He has alienated my **b** from me;
19:17 my wife; I am loathsome to my own **b**.

Job 22: 6 You demanded security from your **b**
42:11 All his **b** and sisters and everyone
42:15 an inheritance along with their **b**.
Ps 22:22 I will declare your name to my **b**;
69: 8 I am a stranger to my **b**, an alien
122: 8 For the sake of my **b** and friends,
133: 1 How good and pleasant it is when **b**
Pr 6:19 man who stirs up dissension among **b**.
17: 2 the inheritance as one of the **b**.
Isa 3: 6 A man will seize one of his **b** at his
66: 5 "Your **b** who hate you, and exclude
66:20 they will bring all your **b**, from all
Jer 7:15 all your **b**, the people of Ephraim.'
9: 4 your friends; do not trust your **b**.
12: 6 Your **b**, your own family—even they
35: 3 and his **b** and all his sons—
Eze 11:15 "Son of man, your **b**—your **b** who are
Hos 2: 1 "Say of your **b**,'My people', and of
13:15 even though he thrives among his **b**.
Mic 5: 3 his **b** return to join the Israelites.
Mt 1: 2 Jacob the father of Judah and his **b**,
1:11 his **b** at the time of the exile
4:18 he saw two **b**, Simon called Peter and
4:21 he saw two other **b**, James son of
5:47 if you greet only your **b**, what are
12:46 his mother and **b** stood outside,
12:47 "Your mother and **b** are standing
12:48 "Who is my mother, and who are my **b**?
12:49 "Here are my mother and my **b**.
13:55 aren't his **b** James, Joseph, Simon
19:29 everyone who has left houses or **b** or
20:24 they were indignant with the two **b**.
22:25 Now there were seven **b** among us.
23: 8 only one Master and you are all **b**.
25:40 one of the least of these **b** of mine,
28:10 Go and tell my **b** to go to Galilee;
Mk 3:31 Jesus' mother and **b** arrived.
3:32 and **b** are outside looking for you."
3:33 "Who are my mother and my **b**?"
3:34 "Here are my mother and my **b**
10:29 "no-one who has left home or **b** or
10:30 **b**, sisters, mothers, children and
12:20 Now there were seven **b**. The first
Lk 8:19 Jesus' mother and **b** came to see him
8:20 Someone told him, "Your mother and **b**
8:21 "My mother and **b** are those who hear
14:12 do not invite your friends, your **b**
14:26 his wife and children, his **b** and
16:28 I have five **b**. Let him warn them,
18:29 who has left home or wife or **b**
20:29 Now there were seven **b**. The first
21:16 parents, **b**, relatives and friends,
22:32 turned back, strengthen your **b**."
Jn 2:12 his mother and **b** and his disciples.
7: 3 Jesus' **b** said to him, "You ought to
7: 5 For even his own **b** did not believe
7:10 However, after his **b** had left for
20:17 Go instead to my **b** and tell them,
21:23 the rumour spread among the **b**
Ac 1:14 the mother of Jesus, and with his **b**.
1:16 said, "**B**, the Scripture had to be
2:29 "**B**, I can tell you confidently that
2:37 "**B**, what shall we do?
3:17 "Now, **b**, I know that you acted in
6: 3 **B**, choose seven men from among you
7: 2 "**B** and fathers, listen to me!
7:13 Joseph told his **b** who he was, and
7:26 'Men, you are **b**; why do you want to
9:30 the **b** learned of this, they took him
10:23 some of the **b** from Joppa went along.
11: 1 The apostles and the **b** throughout
11:12 These six **b** also went with me, and
11:29 help for the **b** living in Judea.
12:17 "Tell James and the **b** about this,"
13:15 "**B**, if you have a message of
13:26 "**B**, children of Abraham, and you
13:38 "Therefore, my **b**, I want you to know
14: 2 poisoned their minds against the **b**.
15: 1 to Antioch and were teaching the **b**:
15: 3 This news made all the **b** very glad.
15: 7 "**B**, you know that some time ago God
15:13 James spoke up: "**B**, listen to me.
15:22 men who were leaders among the **b**.
15:23 The apostles and elders, your **b**,
15:32 to encourage and strengthen the **b**.
15:33 they were sent off by the **b** with the
Ac 15:36 "Let us go back and visit the **b** in
15:40 by the **b** to the grace of the Lord.
16: 2 The **b** at Lystra and Iconium spoke
16:40 met with the **b** and encouraged them.
17: 6 they dragged Jason and some other **b**
17:10 soon as it was night, the **b** sent
17:14 The **b** immediately sent Paul to the
18:18 Then he left the **b** and sailed for
18:27 the **b** encouraged him and wrote to
21: 7 greeted the **b** and stayed with them
21:17 the **b** received us warmly.
22: 1 "**B** and fathers, listen now to my
22: 5 from them to their **b** in Damascus,
23: 1 "My **b**, I have fulfilled my duty to
23: 5 Paul replied, "**B**, I did not realise
23: 6 "My **b**, I am a Pharisee, the son of a
28:14 There we found some **b** who invited us
28:15 The **b** there had heard that we were
28:17 "My **b**, although I have done nothing
28:21 and none of the **b** who have come from
Ro 1:13 I do not want you to be unaware, **b**,
7: 1 you not know, **b**—for I am speaking
7: 4 So, my **b**, you also died to the law
8:12 Therefore, **b**, we have an obligation—
8:29 might be the firstborn among many **b**.
9: 3 sake of my **b**, those of my own race,
10: 1 **B**, my heart's desire and prayer to
11:25 to be ignorant of this mystery, **b**,
12: 1 Therefore, I urge you, **b**, in view of
15:14 I myself am convinced, my **b**, that
15:30 I urge you, **b**, by our Lord Jesus
16:14 Patrobas, Hermas and the **b** with them.
16:17 I urge you, **b**, to watch out for
1Co 1:10 I appeal to you, **b**, in the name of
1:11 My **b**, some from Chloe's household
1:26 **B**, think of what you were when you
2: 1 I came to you, **b**, I did not come
3: 1 **B**, I could not address you as
4: 6 Now, **b**, I have applied these things
6: 8 do wrong, and you do this to your **b**.
7:24 **B**, each man, as responsible to God,
7:29 What I mean, **b**, is that the time is
8:12 you sin against your **b** in this way
9: 5 and the Lord's **b** and Cephas?
10: 1 to be ignorant of the fact, **b**,
11:33 then, my **b**, when you come together
12: 1 Now about spiritual gifts, **b**, I do
14: 6 Now, **b**, if I come to you and speak
14:20 **B**, stop thinking like children.
14:26 What then shall we say, **b**? When you
14:39 Therefore, my **b**, be eager to
15: 1 Now, **b**, I want to remind you of the
15: 6 hundred of the **b** at the same time,
15:31 I die every day—I mean that, **b**
15:50 I declare to you, **b**, that flesh and
15:58 Therefore, my dear **b**, stand firm.
16:11 I am expecting him along with the **b**.
16:12 urged him to go to you with the **b**.
16:15 I urge you, **b**,
16:20 All the **b** here send you greetings.
2Co 1: 8 do not want you to be uninformed, **b**
8: 1 now, **b**, we want you to know about
8:23 among you; as for our **b**, they are
9: 3 I am sending the **b** in order that our
9: 5 I thought it necessary to urge the **b**
11: 9 for the **b** who came from Macedonia
11:26 at sea; and in danger from false **b**.
13:11 Finally, **b**, good-bye. Aim for
Gal 1: 2 all the **b** with me, To the churches
1:11 I want you to know, **b**, that the
2: 4 some false **b** had infiltrated our
3:15 **B**, let me take an example from
4:12 I plead with you, **b**, become like me,
4:28 Now you, **b**, like Isaac, are children
4:31 Therefore, **b**, we are not children of
5:11 **B**, if I am still preaching
5:13 You, my **b**, were called to be free.
6: 1 **B**, if someone is caught in a sin,
6:18 Jesus Christ be with your spirit, **b**.
Eph 6:23 Peace to the **b**, and love with faith
Php 1:12 Now I want you to know, **b**, that what
1:14 most of the **b** in the Lord have
3: 1 Finally, my **b**, rejoice in the Lord!
3:13 **B**, I do not consider myself yet to
3:17 following my example, **b**, and take
4: 1 Therefore, my **b**, you whom I love and
Php 4: 8 Finally, **b**, whatever is true,
4:21 The **b** who are with me send greetings.
Col 1: 2 To the holy and faithful **b** in Christ
4:15 Give my greetings to the **b** at
1Th 1: 4 For we know, **b** loved by God, that he
2: 1 You know, **b**, that our visit to you
2: 9 Surely you remember, **b**, our toil and
2:14 For you, **b**, became imitators of
2:17 But, **b**, when we were torn away from
3: 7 Therefore, **b**, in all our distress
4: 1 Finally, **b**, we instructed you how to
4:10 in fact, you do love all the **b**
4:10 urge you, **b**, to do so more and more.
4:13 **B**, we do not want you to be ignorant
5: 1 Now, **b**, about times and dates we do
5: 4 you, **b**, are not in darkness so that
5:12 Now we ask you, **b**, to respect those
5:14 we urge you, **b**, warn those who are
5:25 **B**, pray for us.
5:26 Greet all the **b** with a holy kiss.
5:27 have this letter read to all the **b**.
2Th 1: 3 always to thank God for you, **b**,
2: 1 gathered to him, we ask you, **b**,
2:13 **b** loved by the Lord, because from
2:15 then, **b**, stand firm and hold to the
3: 1 Finally, **b**, pray for us that the
3: 6 we command you, **b**, to keep away from
3:13 for you, **b**, never tire of doing what
1Ti 4: 6 you point these things out to the **b**,
5: 1 Treat younger men as **b**,
6: 2 respect for them because they are **b**.
2Ti 4:21 Pudens, Linus, Claudia and all the **b**.
Heb 2:11 Jesus is not ashamed to call them **b**.
2:12 "I will declare your name to my **b**;
2:17 to be made like his **b** in every way,
3: 1 Therefore, holy **b**, who share in the
3:12 See to it, **b**, that none of you has a
7: 5 their **b**—even though their **b** are
10:19 Therefore, **b**, since we have
13: 1 Keep on loving each other as **b**.
13:22 **B**, I urge you to bear with my word
Jas 1: 2 Consider it pure joy, my **b**, whenever
1:16 Don't be deceived, my dear **b**.
1:19 My dear **b**, take note of this:
2: 1 My **b**, as believers in our glorious
2: 5 Listen, my dear **b**: Has not God
2:14 What good is it, my **b**, if a man
3: 1 should presume to be teachers, my **b**
3:10 My **b**, this should not be.
3:12 My **b**, can a fig-tree bear olives, or
4:11 **B**, do not slander one another.
5: 7 Be patient, then, **b**, until the
5: 9 Don't grumble against each other, **b**,
5:10 **B**, as an example of patience in the
5:12 Above all, my **b**, do not swear—
5:19 My **b**, if one of you should wander
1Pe 1:22 you have sincere love for your **b**,
3: 8 as **b**, be compassionate and humble.
5: 9 because you know that your **b**
2Pe 1:10 Therefore, my **b**, be all the more
1Jn 3:13 Do not be surprised, my **b**, if the
3:14 to life, because we love our **b**.
3:16 to lay down our lives for our **b**.
3Jn : 3 gave me great joy to have some **b**
: 5 in what you are doing for the **b**,
:10 he refuses to welcome the **b**.
Rev 6:11 **b** who were to be killed as they had
12:10 For the accuser of our **b**, who
19:10 **b** who hold to the testimony of Jesus.
22: 9 with your **b** the prophets and of all

Brow

Ge 3:19 By the sweat of your **b** you will eat
49:26 **b** of the prince among his brothers.
Dt 33:16 **b** of the prince among his brothers.
Job 16:15 my skin and buried my **b** in the dust.
Lk 4:29 and took him to the **b** of the hill on

Brown

Zec 1: 8 him were red, **b** and white horses.

Browse (Browses)

SS 4: 5 a gazelle that **b** among the lilies.
6: 2 to **b** in the gardens and to gather

Browses (Browse)
SS 2:16 he **b** among the lilies.
6: 3 is mine; he **b** among the lilies.

Bruise (Bruised, Bruises)
Ex 21:25 wound for wound, **b** for **b**.

Bruised (Bruise)
Lev 22:24 are **b**, crushed, torn or cut.
Ps 105:18 They **b** his feet with shackles, his
SS 5: 7 They beat me, they **b** me; they took
Isa 42: 3 A **b** reed he will not break, and a
Mt 12:20 A **b** reed he will not break, and a

Bruises (Bruise)
Pr 23:29 has needless **b**? Who has bloodshot
Isa 1: 6 only wounds and **b** and open sores,
30:26 when the LORD binds up the **b** of his

Brush (Brushwood)
Job 30: 4 In the **b** they gathered salt herbs,

Brushing
Eze 3:13 creatures **b** against each other

Brushwood (Brush, Wood)
Ac 28: 3 Paul gathered a pile of **b** and, as he

Brutal (Brute)
Eze 21:31 **b** men, men skilled in destruction.
2Ti 3: 3 **b**, not lovers of the good,

Brutally (Brute)
2Ch 16:10 Asa **b** oppressed some of the people.
Eze 34: 4 You have ruled them harshly and **b**.
1Co 4:11 we are **b** treated, we are homeless.

Brute (Brutal, Brutally, Brutes)
Ps 73:22 I was a **b** beast before you.
2Pe 2:12 They are like **b** beasts, creatures of

Brutes (Brute)
Tit 1:12 liars, evil **b**, lazy gluttons."

Bubastis
Eze 30:17 The young men of Heliopolis and **B**

Bubbling
Pr 18: 4 the fountain of wisdom is a **b** brook.
Isa 35: 7 pool, the thirsty ground **b** springs.

Bucket (Buckets)
Isa 40:15 the nations are like a drop in a **b**;

Buckets (Bucket)
Ex 7:19 in the wooden **b** and stone jars."
Nu 24: 7 Water will flow from their **b**;

Buckled (Buckler)
Eph 6:14 with the belt of truth **b** round your

Buckler (Buckled)
Ps 35: 2 Take up shield and **b**; arise and come

Bud (Budded, Buds)
Ex 25:35 One **b** shall be under the first pair
25:35 a second **b** under the second pair,
25:35 and a third **b** under the third
37:21 One **b** was under the first pair of
37:21 a second **b** under the second pair,
37:21 and a third **b** under the third
Job 14: 9 yet at the scent of water it will **b**
Isa 17:11 you bring them to **b**, yet the harvest
27: 6 Israel will **b** and blossom and fill
55:10 earth and making it **b** and flourish,
Hab 3:17 Though the fig-tree does not **b** and

Budded (Bud)
Ge 40:10 As soon as it **b**, it blossomed, and
Nu 17: 8 **b**, blossomed and produced almonds.

SS 6:11 to see if the vines had **b**
7:12 to see if the vines have **b**,
Eze 7:10 rod has **b**, arrogance has blossomed!
Heb 9: 4 Aaron's staff that had **b**, and the

Buds (Bud)
Ex 25:31 **b** and blossoms shall be of one piece
25:33 shaped like almond flowers with **b**
25:34 almond flowers with **b** and blossoms.
25:36 The **b** and branches shall all be of
37:17 **b** and blossoms were of one piece
37:19 **b** and blossoms were on one branch,
37:20 almond flowers with **b** and blossoms.
37:22 The **b** and the branches were all of

Buffeted
Mt 14:24 **b** by the waves because the wind was

Build (Builder, Builders, Building, Buildings, Builds, Built, Rebuild, Well-built)
Ge 6:15 This is how you are to **b** it: The ark
11: 4 "Come, let us **b** ourselves a city,
16: 2 I can **b** a family through her.
30: 3 through her I too can **b** a family."
35: 1 and **b** an altar there to God, who
35: 3 where I will **b** an altar to God,
Ex 20:25 do not **b** it with dressed stones,
27: 1 "**B** an altar of acacia wood,
Nu 23: 1 Balaam said, "**B** me seven altars
23:29 Balaam said, "**B** me seven altars,
32:16 "We would like to **b** pens here for
32:24 **B** cities for your women and children,
Dt 6:10 flourishing cities you did not **b**,
8:12 you **b** fine houses and settle down,
16:21 altar you **b** to the LORD your God,
19: 3 **B** roads to them and divide into
20:20 use them to **b** siege works until the
22: 8 you **b** a new house, make a parapet
25: 9 not **b** up his brother's family line."
27: 5 **B** there an altar to the LORD your
27: 6 **B** the altar of the LORD your God
28:30 You will **b** a house, but you will
Jos 22:16 **b** yourselves an altar in rebellion
22:26 'Let us get ready and **b** an altar
24:13 not toil and cities you did not **b**;
Jdg 6:26 **b** a proper kind of altar to the LORD
2Sa 7: 5 the one to **b** me a house to dwell in?
7:13 He is the one who will **b** a house
7:27 saying,'I will **b** a house for you.
24:18 "Go up and **b** an altar to the LORD
24:21 "so that I can **b** an altar to the
1Ki 2:36 "**B** yourself a house in Jerusalem
5: 3 could not **b** a temple for the Name
5: 5 I intend, therefore, to **b** a temple
5: 5 will **b** the temple for my Name.'
6: 1 began to **b** the temple of the LORD.
8:17 **b** a temple for the Name of the LORD,
8:18 'Because it was in your heart to **b**
8:19 you are not the one to **b** the temple,
8:19 who will **b** the temple for my Name.'
9:15 conscripted to **b** the LORD's temple,
9:19 he desired to **b** in Jerusalem,
11:38 I will **b** you a dynasty as enduring
2Ki 6: 2 **b** a place there for us to live.
19:32 or **b** a siege ramp against it.
1Ch 14: 1 carpenters to **b** a palace for him.
17: 4 the one to **b** me a house to dwell in.
17:10 the LORD will **b** a house for you:
17:12 He is the one who will **b** a house
17:25 that you will **b** a house for him.
21:18 **b** an altar to the LORD on the
21:22 that I can **b** an altar to the LORD,
22: 6 him to **b** a house for the LORD,
22: 7 I had it in my heart to **b** a house
22: 8 are not to **b** a house for my Name,
22:10 He is the one who will **b** a house
22:11 and may you have success and **b** the
22:19 Begin to **b** the sanctuary of the LORD
28: 2 I had it in my heart to **b** a house as
28: 2 our God, and I made plans to **b** it.
28: 3 God said to me,'You are not to **b** a
28: 6 who will **b** my house and my courts,
28:10 you to **b** a temple as a sanctuary.
29:19 decrees and to do everything to **b**

2Ch 2: 1 Solomon gave orders to **b** a temple
2: 3 him cedar to **b** a palace to live in.
2: 4 Now I am about to **b** a temple for the
2: 5 "The temple I am going to **b** will be
2: 6 who is able to **b** a temple for him,
2: 6 Who then am I to **b** a temple for him,
2: 9 the temple I **b** must be large and
2:12 who will **b** a temple for the LORD and
3: 1 Solomon began to **b** the temple of the
6: 7 **b** a temple for the Name of the LORD,
6: 8 'Because it was in your heart to **b** a
6: 9 you are not the one to **b** the temple,
6: 9 who will **b** the temple for my Name.'
8: 6 he desired to **b** in Jerusalem,
14: 7 "Let us **b** up these towns," he said
36:23 he has appointed me to **b** a temple
Ezr 1: 2 he has appointed me to **b** a temple
1: 3 Judah and **b** the temple of the LORD,
1: 5 **b** the house of the LORD in Jerusalem.
3: 2 his associates began to **b** the altar
4: 2 "Let us help you **b** because, like you,
4: 3 We alone will **b** it for the LORD,
6:14 the elders of the Jews continued to **b**
Job 19:12 they **b** a siege ramp against me
20:19 he has seized houses he did not **b**.
30:12 they **b** their siege ramps against me.
39:27 your command and **b** his nest on high?
Ps 28: 5 them down and never **b** them up again.
51:18 **b** up the walls of Jerusalem.
Pr 24:27 after that, **b** your house.
Ecc 3: 3 a time to tear down and a time to **b**,
SS 8: 9 If she is a wall, we will **b** towers
Isa 37:33 shield or **b** a siege ramp against it.
54:11 I will **b** you with stones of turquoise
57:14 "**B** up, **b** up, prepare the road!
62:10 **B** up, **b** up the highway! Remove the
65:21 They will **b** houses and dwell in them;
65:22 No longer will they **b** houses and
66: 1 Where is the house you will **b** for me?
Jer 1:10 and overthrow, to **b** and to plant."
6: 6 and **b** siege ramps against Jerusalem.
22:14 'I will **b** myself a great palace
24: 6 I will **b** them up and not tear them
29: 5 "**B** houses and settle down; plant
29:28 Therefore **b** houses and settle down;
31: 4 I will **b** you up again and you will
31:28 watch over them to **b** and to plant,
35: 7 Also you must never **b** houses, sow
42:10 'If you stay in this land, I will **b**
49:16 Though you **b** your nest as high as
Eze 4: 2 **b** a ramp up to it, set up camps
11: 3 'Will it not soon be time to **b**
21:22 **b** a ramp and to erect siege works.
22:30 among them who would **b** up the wall
26: 8 **b** a ramp up to your walls and raise
28:26 will **b** houses and plant vineyards;
Da 11:15 the king of the North will come and **b**
Am 9:11 ruins, and **b** it as it used to be,
Mic 3:10 who **b** Zion with bloodshed, and
Hab 1:10 **b** earthen ramps and capture them.
Zep 1:13 They will **b** houses but not live in
Hag 1: 8 bring down timber and **b** the house,
Zec 5:11 of Babylonia to **b** a house for it.
6:12 place and **b** the temple of the LORD.
6:13 is he who will **b** the temple of the
6:15 help to **b** the temple of the LORD,
Mal 1: 4 "They may **b**, but I will demolish.
Mt 16:18 and on this rock I will **b** my church,
23:29 You **b** tombs for the prophets and
27:40 the temple and **b** it in three days,
Mk 14:58 will **b** another, not made by man.'"
15:29 the temple and **b** it in three days,
Lk 11:47 "Woe to you, because you **b** tombs for
11:48 the prophets, and you **b** their tombs.
12:18 I will tear down my barns and **b**
14:28 "Suppose one of you wants to **b** a
14:30 'This fellow began to **b** and was
19:43 will **b** an embankment against you
Jn 2:20 "It has taken forty-six years to **b**
Ac 7:49 What kind of house will you **b** for me?
20:32 which can **b** you up and give you an
Ro 15: 2 neighbour for his good, to **b** him up.
1Co 14:12 excel in gifts that **b** up the church.
1Th 5:11 Therefore encourage one another and **b**
Heb 8: 5 he was about to **b** the tabernacle:
Jude :20 you, dear friends, **b** yourselves up

Builder (Build)

1Co 3:10 I laid a foundation as an expert **b**,
Heb 3: 3 just as the **b** of a house has greater
3: 4 but God is the **b** of everything.
11:10 whose architect and **b** is God.

Builders (Build)

2Ki 12:11 of the LORD—the carpenters and **b**,
22: 6 the carpenters, the **b** and the masons.
2Ch 34:11 and **b** to purchase dressed stone,
Ezr 3:10 the **b** laid the foundation of the
Ne 4: 5 thrown insults in the face of the **b**.
4:18 each of the **b** wore his sword at his
Ps 118:22 The stone the **b** rejected has become
127: 1 the house, its **b** labour in vain.
Eze 27: 4 **b** brought your beauty to perfection.
Mt 21:42 "'The stone the **b** rejected has
Mk 12:10 "'The stone the **b** rejected has
Lk 20:17 "'The stone the **b** rejected has
Ac 4:11 He is "'the stone you **b** rejected,
1Pe 2: 7 "The stone the **b** rejected has

Building (Build)

Ge 4:17 Cain was then **b** a city, and he named
11: 5 and the tower that the men were **b**.
11: 8 earth, and they stopped **b** the city.
Jos 22:19 us by **b** an altar for yourselves,
22:29 by **b** an altar for burnt offerings,
1Ki 3: 1 David until he finished **b** his palace
5:18 and stone for the **b** of the temple.
6: 5 he built a structure around the **b**,
6: 7 In **b** the temple, only blocks dressed
6:12 "As for this temple you are **b**, if
6:38 He had spent seven years **b** it.
9: 1 Solomon had finished **b** the temple of
15:21 Baasha heard this, he stopped **b**
2Ki 25: 9 Every important **b** he burned down.
1Ch 22: 2 stone for **b** the house of God.
29:16 **b** you a temple for your Holy Name,
2Ch 3: 2 He began **b** on the second day of the
3: 3 The foundation Solomon laid for **b**
3: 4 across the width of the **b** and twenty
16: 5 Baasha heard this, he stopped **b**
32: 5 of the wall and **b** towers on it.
Ezr 3: 8 the **b** of the house of the LORD.
4: 1 exiles were **b** a temple for the LORD,
4: 3 with us in **b** a temple to our God.
4: 4 and make them afraid to go on **b**.
5: 4 of the men constructing this **b**?"
5: 8 The people are **b** it with large
6:14 They finished **b** the temple according
Ne 3: 1 **b** as far as the Tower of the Hundred,
4: 3 "What they are **b**—if even a fox
4:17 who were **b** the wall. Those who
6: 6 and therefore you are **b** the wall.
Jer 52:13 Every important **b** he burned down.
Eze 41:12 The **b** facing the temple courtyard on
41:12 The wall of the **b** was five cubits
41:13 and the temple courtyard and the **b**
41:15 he measured the length of the **b**
42: 2 The **b** whose door faced north was a
42: 5 lower and middle floors of the **b**.
Mic 7:11 The day for **b** your walls will come,
Lk 6:48 He is like a man **b** a house, who dug
17:28 buying and selling, planting and **b**.
Ro 15:20 be **b** on someone else's foundation.
1Co 3: 9 you are God's field, God's **b**.
3:10 and someone else is **b** on it.
2Co 5: 1 we have a **b** from God, an eternal
10: 8 authority the Lord gave us for **b**
13:10 **b** you up, not for tearing you down.
Eph 2:21 In him the whole **b** is joined
4:29 but only what is helpful for **b**

Buildings (Build)

1Ki 9:10 Solomon built these two **b**—the
1Ch 15: 1 After David had constructed **b** for
28:11 its **b**, its storerooms, its upper
29: 4 overlaying of the walls of the **b**,
2Ch 32:28 He also made **b** to store the harvest
34:11 beams for the **b** that the kings of
Isa 22:10 You counted the **b** in Jerusalem and
Jer 22:23 who are nestled in cedar **b**, how you
Eze 40: 2 were some **b** that looked like a city.
Mt 24: 1 him to call his attention to its **b**.
Mk 13: 1 massive stones! What magnificent **b**!"
13: 2 "Do you see all these great **b**?"

Builds (Build)

Job 27:18 The house he **b** is like a moth's
Ps 127: 1 Unless the LORD **b** the house, its
147: 2 The LORD **b** up Jerusalem; he gathers
Pr 14: 1 The wise woman **b** her house, but with
17:19 he who **b** a high gate invites
Jer 22:13 "Woe to him who **b** his palace by
Am 9: 6 he who **b** his lofty palace in the
Hab 2: 9 "Woe to him who **b** his realm by
2:12 "Woe to him who **b** a city with
1Co 3:10 each one should be careful how he **b**.
3:12 If any man **b** on this foundation
8: 1 Knowledge puffs up, but love **b** up.
Eph 4:16 grows and **b** itself up in love, as

Built (Build)

Ge 8:20 Noah **b** an altar to the LORD and,
10:11 he **b** Nineveh, Rehoboth Ir,
12: 7 So he **b** an altar there to the LORD,
12: 8 There he **b** an altar to the LORD and
13: 4 where he had first **b** an altar.
13:18 where he **b** an altar to the LORD.
22: 9 Abraham **b** an altar there and
26:25 Isaac **b** an altar there and called
33:17 where he **b** a place for himself
35: 7 There he **b** an altar, and he called
Ex 1:11 and they **b** Pithom and Rameses as
17:15 Moses **b** an altar and called it The
24: 4 **b** an altar at the foot of the
32: 5 he **b** an altar in front of the calf
38: 1 They **b** the altar of burnt offering
Nu 13:22 Hebron had been **b** seven years before
23:14 and there he **b** seven altars and
32:34 The Gadites **b** up Dibon, Ataroth,
32:36 cities, and **b** pens for their flocks.
Dt 20: 5 "Has anyone **b** a new house and not
Jos 8:30 Joshua **b** on Mount Ebal an altar to
8:31 He **b** it according to what is written
11:13 any of the cities **b** on their mounds
19:50 he **b** up the town and settled there.
22:10 the half-tribe of Manasseh **b** an
22:11 the Israelites heard that they had **b**
22:23 If we have **b** our own altar to turn
22:28 LORD's altar, which our fathers **b**,
Jdg 1:26 where he **b** a city and called it Luz,
6:24 Gideon **b** an altar to the LORD there
21: 4 the next day the people **b** an altar
Ru 4:11 together **b** up the house of Israel.
1Sa 7:17 And he **b** an altar there to the LORD.
14:35 Saul **b** an altar to the LORD; it was
2Sa 5: 9 He **b** up the area around it, from the
5:11 and they **b** a palace for David.
7: 7 you not **b** me a house of cedar?"'
20:15 They **b** a siege ramp up to the city,
24:25 David **b** an altar to the LORD there
1Ki 3: 2 yet been **b** for the Name of the LORD.
6: 2 The temple that King Solomon **b** for
6: 5 **b** a structure around the building,
6: 7 temple site while it was being **b**.
6: 9 he **b** the temple and completed it,
6:10 he **b** the side rooms all along the
6:14 Solomon **b** the temple and completed
6:36 he **b** the inner courtyard of three
7: 2 He **b** the Palace of the Forest of
7: 7 He **b** the throne hall, the Hall of
8:13 I have indeed **b** a magnificent temple
8:16 a temple **b** for my Name to be there,
8:20 and I have **b** the temple for the Name
8:27 How much less this temple I have **b**!
8:43 this house I have **b** bears your Name.
8:44 the temple I have **b** for your Name,
8:48 the temple I have **b** for your Name;
9: 3 this temple, which you have **b**,
9:10 Solomon **b** these two buildings
9:17 He **b** up Lower Beth Horon,
9:24 to the palace Solomon had **b** for her,
9:25 on the altar he had **b** for the LORD,
9:26 King Solomon also **b** ships at Ezion
10: 4 of Solomon and the palace he had **b**,
11: 7 Solomon **b** a high place for Chemosh
11:27 Solomon had **b** the supporting
11:38 enduring as the one I **b** for David
1Ki 12:25 there he went out and **b** up Peniel.
12:31 Jeroboam **b** shrines on high places
12:33 on the altar he had **b** at Bethel.
15:22 With them King Asa **b** up Geba in
15:23 all he did and the cities he **b**, are
16:24 of silver and **b** a city on the hill,
16:32 temple of Baal that he **b** in Samaria.
18:32 With the stones he **b** an altar in the
22:39 the palace he **b** and inlaid with
22:48 Now Jehoshaphat **b** a fleet of trading
2Ki 16:11 Uriah the priest **b** an altar in
16:18 that had been **b** at the temple
17: 9 they **b** themselves high places in all
21: 4 He **b** altars in the temple of the
21: 5 he **b** altars to all the starry hosts.
23:12 and the altars Manasseh had **b** in the
23:13 ones Solomon king of Israel had **b**
23:19 that the kings of Israel had **b**
25: 1 and **b** siege works all around it.
1Ch 6:10 the temple Solomon **b** in Jerusalem),
6:32 Solomon **b** the temple of the LORD
7:24 His daughter was Sheerah, who **b**
8:12 Misham, Shemed (who **b** Ono and Lod
11: 8 He **b** up the city around it, from the
17: 6 you not **b** me a house of cedar?"'
21:26 David **b** an altar to the LORD there
22: 5 and the house to be **b** for the LORD
22:19 will be **b** for the Name of the LORD."
2Ch 3: 8 He **b** the Most Holy Place, its length
6: 2 I have **b** a magnificent temple for
6: 5 a temple **b** for my Name to be there,
6:10 and I have **b** the temple for the Name
6:18 much less this temple that I have **b**!
6:33 house that I have **b** bears your Name.
6:34 the temple I have **b** for your Name,
6:38 temple that I have **b** for your Name;
8: 1 Solomon **b** the temple of the LORD
8: 4 He also **b** up Tadmor in the desert
8: 4 the store cities he had **b** in Hamath.
8:11 David to the palace he had **b** for her,
8:12 he had **b** in front of the portico,
9: 3 as well as the palace he had **b**,
11: 5 Rehoboam lived in Jerusalem and **b** up
14: 6 He **b** up the fortified cities of
14: 7 So they **b** and prospered.
16: 6 With them he **b** up Geba and Mizpah.
17:12 he **b** forts and store cities in
20: 8 and have **b** in it a sanctuary for
20:36 After these were **b** at Ezion Geber,
21:11 He had also **b** high places on the
26: 9 Uzziah **b** towers in Jerusalem at the
26:10 He also **b** towers in the desert and
27: 4 He **b** towns in the Judean hills and
28:25 In every town in Judah he **b** high
32: 5 He **b** another wall outside that one
32:29 He **b** villages and acquired great
33: 4 He **b** altars in the temple of the
33: 5 he **b** altars to all the starry hosts.
33:15 as well as all the altars he had **b**
33:19 and the sites where he **b** high places
35: 3 son of David king of Israel **b**.
Ezr 3: 3 they **b** the altar on its foundation
4:13 if this city is **b** and its walls
4:16 if this city is **b** and its walls
5:11 temple that was **b** many years ago,
5:11 great king of Israel **b** and finished.
Ne 3: 2 The men of Jericho **b** the adjoining
3: 2 Zaccur son of Imri **b** next to them.
8: 4 wooden platform **b** for the occasion.
8:16 **b** themselves booths on their own
8:17 exile **b** booths and lived in them.
12:29 for the singers had **b** villages for
Est 5:14 "Have a gallows **b**, seventy-five feet
5:14 Haman, and he had the gallows **b**.
Job 3:14 who **b** for themselves places now
Ps 78:69 He **b** his sanctuary like the heights,
122: 3 Jerusalem is **b** like a city that is
Pr 9: 1 Wisdom has **b** her house; she has hewn
24: 3 By wisdom a house is **b**, and through
Ecc 2: 4 I **b** houses for myself and planted
9:14 and **b** huge siegeworks against it.
SS 4: 4 tower of David, **b** with elegance;
Isa 5: 2 He **b** a watchtower in it and cut out
22:11 You **b** a reservoir between the two
44:26 'They shall be **b**,' and of their
Jer 7:31 They have **b** the high places of

Jer 18: 9 kingdom is to be **b** up and planted,
18:15 in bypaths and on roads not **b** up.
19: 5 They have **b** the high places of Baal
32:24 "See how the siege ramps are **b** up to
32:31 From the day it was **b** until now,
32:35 They **b** high places for Baal in the
35: 9 or **b** houses to live in or had
45: 4 I will overthrow what I have **b**
52: 4 and **b** siege works all around it.
Eze 13:10 when a flimsy wall is **b**, they cover
16:24 you **b** a mound for yourself and made
16:25 **b** your lofty shrines and degraded
16:31 you **b** your mounds at the head of
17:17 when ramps are **b** and siege works
41: 7 temple was **b** in ascending stages,
43:18 blood upon the altar when it is **b**:
46:23 fire **b** all round under the ledge.
Da 4:30 I have **b** as the royal residence,
Hos 8:11 "Though Ephraim **b** many altars for
8:14 forgotten his Maker and **b** palaces;
10: 1 As his fruit increased, he **b** more
Am 5:11 though you have **b** stone mansions,
7: 7 wall that had been **b** true to plumb,
Hag 1: 2 come for the LORD's house to be **b**.'"
Zec 8: 9 strong so that the temple may be **b**.
9: 3 Tyre has **b** herself a stronghold;
Mt 7:24 man who **b** his house on the rock.
7:26 foolish man who **b** his house on sand.
21:33 winepress in it and **b** a watchtower.
Mk 12: 1 the winepress and **b** a watchtower.
Lk 4:29 of the hill on which the town was **b**,
6:48 not shake it, because it was well **b**.
6:49 a man who **b** a house on the ground
7: 5 our nation and has **b** our synagogue
Ac 7:47 was Solomon who **b** the house for him.
17:24 does not live in temples **b** by hands.
28: 2 They **b** a fire and welcomed us all
1Co 3:14 If what he has **b** survives, he will
2Co 5: 1 in heaven, not **b** by human hands.
Eph 2:20 **b** on the foundation of the apostles
2:22 in him you too are being **b** together
4:12 that the body of Christ may be **b**
Col 2: 7 rooted and **b** up in him, strengthened
Heb 3: 4 For every house is **b** by someone, but
11: 7 **b** an ark to save his family.
1Pe 2: 5 are being **b** into a spiritual house
3:20 of Noah while the ark was being **b**.

Bukki
Nu 34:22 **B** son of Jogli, the leader from the
1Ch 6: 5 Abishua the father of **B**, **B** the
6:51 **B** his son, Uzzi his son, Zerahiah
Ezr 7: 4 the son of Uzzi, the son of **B**,

Bukkiah
1Ch 25: 4 for Heman, from his sons: **B**,
25:13 the sixth to **B**, his sons and

Bul
1Ki 6:38 the eleventh year in the month of **B**,

Bulges (Bulging)
Job 15:27 with fat and his waist **b** with flesh,

Bulging (Bulges)
Isa 30:13 like a high wall, cracked and **b**,

Bull (Bull's, Bulls)
Ex 21:28 "If a **b** gores a man or a woman to
21:28 the **b** must be stoned to death, and
21:28 the **b** will not be held responsible.
21:29 If, however, the **b** has had the habit
21:29 the **b** must be stoned and the owner
21:31 This law also applies if the **b** gores
21:32 If the **b** gores a male or female
21:32 the slave, and the **b** must be stoned.
21:35 "If a man's **b** injures the **b** of
21:36 that the **b** had the habit of goring,
29: 1 young **b** and two rams without defect.
29: 3 with the **b** and the two rams.
29:10 "Bring the **b** to the front of the
29:36 Sacrifice a **b** each day as a sin
Lev 1: 5 He is to slaughter the young **b**
4: 3 he must bring to the LORD a young **b**
Lev 4: 4 He is to present the **b** at the
4: 8 fat from the **b** of the sin offering
4:11 the hide of the **b** and all its flesh,
4:12 that is, all the rest of the **b**—
4:14 the assembly must bring a young **b** as
4:15 and the **b** shall be slaughtered
4:20 do with this **b** just as he did with
4:20 did with the **b** for the sin offering.
4:21 he shall take the **b** outside the camp
4:21 burn it as he burned the first **b**.
8: 2 the **b** for the sin offering.
8:14 presented the **b** for the sin offering
8:15 Moses slaughtered the **b** and took
8:17 the **b** with its hide and its flesh
9: 2 He said to Aaron, "Take a **b** calf for
16: 3 with a young **b** for a sin offering
16: 6 "Aaron is to offer the **b** for his own
16:11 "Aaron shall bring the **b** for his own
16:11 the **b** for his own sin offering.
16:27 The **b** and the goat for the sin
23:18 defect, one young **b** and two rams.
Nu 7:15 one young **b**, one ram and one male
7:21 one young **b**, one ram and one male
7:27 one young **b**, one ram and one male
7:33 one young **b**, one ram and one male
7:39 one young **b**, one ram and one male
7:45 one young **b**, one ram and one male
7:51 one young **b**, one ram and one male
7:57 one young **b**, one ram and one male
7:63 one young **b**, one ram and one male
7:69 one young **b**, one ram and one male
7:75 one young **b**, one ram and one male
7:81 one young **b**, one ram and one male
8: 8 Make them take a young **b** with its
8: 8 a second young **b** for a sin offering.
15: 8 "When you prepare a young **b** as a
15: 9 bring with the **b** a grain offering of
15:11 Each **b** or ram, each lamb or young
15:24 offer a young **b** for a burnt offering
23: 2 offered a **b** and a ram on each altar.
23: 4 altar I have offered a **b** and a ram."
23:14 offered a **b** and a ram on each altar.
23:30 offered a **b** and a ram on each altar.
28:12 With each **b** there is to be a grain
28:14 With each **b** there is to be a drink
28:20 With each **b** prepare a grain offering
28:28 With each **b** there is to be a grain
29: 2 a burnt offering of one young **b**,
29: 3 With the **b** prepare a grain offering
29: 8 LORD a burnt offering of one young **b**,
29: 9 With the **b** prepare a grain offering
29:36 a burnt offering of one **b**, one ram
29:37 With the **b**, the ram and the lambs,
Dt 18: 3 people who sacrifice a **b** or a sheep
33:17 In majesty he is like a firstborn **b**;
Jdg 6:25 "Take the second **b** from your
6:26 the second **b** as a burnt offering."
6:28 the second **b** sacrificed on the
1Sa 1:24 along with a three-year-old **b**,
1:25 they had slaughtered the **b**, they
2Sa 6:13 sacrificed a **b** and a fattened calf.
1Ki 18:23 I will prepare the other **b** and put
18:26 they took the **b** given them and
18:33 cut the **b** into pieces and laid it
2Ch 13: 9 consecrate himself with a young **b**
Ps 50: 9 I have no need of a **b** from your
69:31 than a **b** with its horns and hoofs.
106:20 an image of a **b**, which eats grass.
Isa 34: 7 the **b** calves and the great bulls.
66: 3 whoever sacrifices a **b** is like one
Eze 43:19 give a young **b** as a sin offering
43:21 take the **b** for the sin offering
43:22 as it was purified with the **b**.
43:23 you are to offer a young **b** and a ram
43:25 a young **b** and a ram from the flock,
45:18 to take a young **b** without defect
45:22 a **b** as a sin offering for himself
45:24 an ephah for each **b** and an ephah
46: 6 New Moon he is to offer a young **b**,
46: 7 grain offering one ephah with the **b**,
46:11 offering is to be an ephah with a **b**,

Bull's (Bull)
Ex 29:12 Take some of the **b** blood and put it
29:14 burn the **b** flesh and its hide and
Lev 4: 5 shall take some of the **b** blood
Lev 4: 7 The rest of the **b** blood he shall
4:15 hands on the **b** head before the LORD,
4:16 take some of the **b** blood into the
16:14 He is to take some of the **b** blood
16:15 with it as he did with the **b** blood:
16:18 He shall take some of the **b** blood

Bulls (Bull)
Ge 32:15 forty cows and ten **b**, and twenty
Ex 24: 5 sacrificed young **b** as fellowship
Nu 7:87 offering came to twelve young **b**,
8:12 their hands on the heads of the **b**,
23: 1 seven **b** and seven rams for me."
23:29 seven **b** and seven rams for me."
28:11 a burnt offering of two young **b**,
28:19 a burnt offering of two young **b**,
28:27 a burnt offering of two young **b**,
29:13 burnt offering of thirteen young **b**,
29:14 With each of the thirteen **b** prepare
29:17 second day prepare twelve young **b**,
29:18 With the **b**, rams and lambs, prepare
29:20 "'On the third day prepare eleven **b**,
29:21 With the **b**, rams and lambs, prepare
29:23 "'On the fourth day prepare ten **b**,
29:24 With the **b**, rams and lambs, prepare
29:26 "'On the fifth day prepare nine **b**,
29:27 With the **b**, rams and lambs, prepare
29:29 "'On the sixth day prepare eight **b**,
29:30 With the **b**, rams and lambs, prepare
29:32 "'On the seventh day prepare seven **b**,
29:33 With the **b**, rams and lambs, prepare
1Ki 7:25 The Sea stood on twelve **b**, three
7:29 were lions, **b** and cherubim—
7:29 Above and below the lions and **b** were
7:44 the Sea and the twelve **b** under it;
18:23 Get two **b** for us. Let them choose
18:25 "Choose one of the **b** and prepare it
2Ki 16:17 He removed the Sea from the bronze **b**
1Ch 15:26 sseven **b** and seven rams were
29:21 offerings to him: a thousand **b**,
2Ch 4: 3 Below the rim, figures of **b**
4: 3 The **b** were cast in two rows in one
4: 4 The Sea stood on twelve **b**,
4:15 the Sea and the twelve **b** under it;
29:21 They brought seven **b**, seven rams,
29:22 they slaughtered the **b**, and the
29:32 the assembly brought was seventy **b**,
29:33 amounted to six hundred **b** and
30:24 king of Judah provided a thousand **b**
30:24 provided them with a thousand **b**
Ezr 6: 9 Whatever is needed—young **b**, rams,
6:17 of God they offered a hundred **b**,
7:17 With this money be sure to buy **b**,
8:35 of Israel: twelve **b** for all Israel,
Job 21:10 Their **b** never fail to breed;
42: 8 now take seven **b** and seven rams and
Ps 22:12 Many **b** surround me; strong **b** of
50:13 Do I eat the flesh of **b** or drink the
51:19 **b** will be offered on your altar.
66:15 I will offer **b** and goats.
68:30 the herd of **b** among the calves of
Isa 1:11 the blood of **b** and lambs and goats.
34: 7 the bull calves and the great **b**.
Jer 50:27 Kill all her young **b**; let them go
52:20 the Sea and the twelve bronze **b**
Eze 39:18 goats and **b**—all of them fattened
45:23 the Feast he is to provide seven **b**
Hos 12:11 Do they sacrifice **b** in Gilgal?
Ac 14:13 brought **b** and wreaths to the city
Heb 9:13 The blood of goats and **b** and the
10: 4 it is impossible for the blood of **b**

Bunah
1Ch 2:25 firstborn, **B**, Oren, Ozem and Ahijah.

Bunch
Ex 12:22 Take a **b** of hyssop, dip it into the

Bundle (Bundles)
1Sa 25:29 securely in the **b** of the living

Bundles (Bundle)
Ru 2:16 some stalks for her from the **b** and
Mt 13:30 and tie them in **b** to be burned;

Bunni

Ne 9: 4 Bani, Kadmiel, Shebaniah, **B**,
10:15 **B**, Azgad, Bebai,
11:15 the son of Hashabiah, the son of **B**;

Burden (Burdened, Burdens, Burdensome)

Ge 49:15 he will bend his shoulder to the **b**
Nu 11:11 put the **b** of all these people on me?
11:14 the **b** is too heavy for me.
11:17 They will help you carry the **b** of
Dt 1: 9 too heavy a **b** for me to carry alone.
1Sa 25:31 staggering **b** of needless bloodshed
2Sa 13:25 we would only be a **b** to you.
15:33 go with me, you will be a **b** to me.
19:35 be an added **b** to my lord the king?
Ne 5:15 placed a heavy **b** on the people
Job 7:20 Have I become a **b** to you?
Ps 38: 4 My guilt has overwhelmed me like a **b**
81: 6 He says, "I removed the **b** from their
Pr 27: 3 Stone is heavy and sand a **b**, but
Ecc 1:13 What a heavy **b** God has laid on men!
3:10 I have seen the **b** God has laid on
Isa 1:14 They have become a **b** to me; I am
10:27 In that day their **b** will be lifted
14:25 his **b** removed from their shoulders."
46: 1 idols are borne by beasts of **b**.
46: 1 are burdensome, a **b** for the weary.
46: 2 unable to rescue the **b**, they
Zep 3:18 they are a **b** and a reproach to you.
Mal 1:13 you say, 'What a **b**!' and you sniff
Mt 11:30 my yoke is easy and my **b** is light
20:12 us who have borne the **b** of the work
Ac 15:28 to us not to **b** you with anything
2Co 11: 9 I was not a **b** to anyone, for the
11: 9 I have kept myself from being a **b** to
12:13 a **b** to you? Forgive me this wrong!
12:14 and I will not be a **b** to you,
12:16 I have not been a **b** to you.
1Th 2: 6 we could have been a **b** to you,
2: 9 day in order not to be a **b** to anyone
2Th 3: 8 we would not be a **b** to any of you.
Heb 13:17 work will be a joy, not a **b**,
Rev 2:24 will not impose any other **b** on you):

Burdened (Burden)

Isa 43:23 I have not **b** you with grain
43:24 But you have **b** me with your sins and
Mic 6: 3 How have I **b** you? Answer me.
Mt 11:28 all you who are weary and **b**,
2Co 5: 4 we groan and are **b**, because we do
Gal 5: 1 be **b** again by a yoke of slavery.
1Ti 5:16 not let the church be **b** with them,

Burdens (Burden)

Nu 4:24 clans as they work and carry **b**:
Dt 1:12 **b** and your disputes all by myself?
Ps 66:11 into prison and laid **b** on our banks
68:19 our Saviour, who daily bears our **b**.
73: 5 They are free from the **b** common to
Isa 9: 4 you have shattered the yoke that **b**
Lk 11:46 because you load people down with **b**
Gal 6: 2 Carry each other's **b**, and in this

Burdensome (Burden)

Isa 46: 1 images that are carried about are **b**
1Jn 5: 3 And his commands are not **b**,

Burial (Bury)

Ge 23: 4 Sell me some property for a **b** site
23: 9 full price as a **b** site among you."
23:20 Abraham by the Hittites as a **b** site.
49:30 which Abraham bought as a **b** place
50:13 Abraham had bought as a **b** place
2Ch 26:23 in a field for **b** that belonged to
Ecc 6: 3 and does not receive proper **b**,
Isa 14:20 you will not join them in **b**, for you
Jer 22:19 He will have the **b** of a donkey—
26:23 the **b** place of the common people.)
Eze 39:11 "On that day I will give Gog a **b**
Mt 26:12 she did it to prepare me for **b**.
27: 7 field as a **b** place for foreigners.
Mk 14: 8 body beforehand to prepare for my **b**.
Jn 12: 7 for the day of my **b**.
Jn 19:40 in accordance with Jewish **b** customs.
20: 7 well as the **b** cloth that had been
Rev 11: 9 on their bodies and refuse them **b**.

Buried (Bury)

Ge 15:15 in peace and be **b** at a good old age.
23:19 Afterwards Abraham **b** his wife Sarah
25: 9 His sons Isaac and Ishmael **b** him in
25:10 Abraham was **b** with his wife Sarah.
35: 4 **b** them under the oak at Shechem.
35: 8 was **b** under the oak below Bethel.
35:19 Rachel died and was **b** on the way to
35:29 And his sons Esau and Jacob **b** him.
47:30 Egypt and bury me where they are **b**.
48: 7 So I **b** her there beside the road to
49:31 Abraham and his wife Sarah were **b**,
49:31 Rebekah were **b**, and there I **b** Leah.
50:13 **b** him in the cave in the field of
Nu 11:34 because there they **b** the people who
20: 1 There Miriam died and was **b**.
Dt 10: 6 There Aaron died and was **b**, and
34: 6 He **b** him in Moab, in the valley
Jos 24:30 they **b** him in the land of his
24:32 were **b** at Shechem in the tract of
24:33 Eleazar son of Aaron died and was **b**
Jdg 2: 9 they **b** him in the land of his
8:32 was **b** in the tomb of his father
10: 2 then he died, and was **b** in Shamir.
10: 5 Jair died, he was **b** in Kamon.
12: 7 died, and was **b** in a town in Gilead.
12:10 Ibzan died, and was **b** in Bethlehem.
12:12 Elon died, and was **b** in Aijalon in
12:15 Abdon son of Hillel died, and was **b**
16:31 They brought him back and **b** him
Ru 1:17 I will die, and there I will be **b**.
1Sa 25: 1 and they **b** him at his home in Ramah.
28: 3 and **b** him in his own town of Ramah.
31:13 they took their bones and **b** them
2Sa 2: 4 men of Jabesh Gilead who had **b** Saul,
2:32 They took Asahel and **b** him in his
3:32 They **b** Abner in Hebron, and the king
4:12 and **b** it in Abner's tomb at Hebron.
17:23 died and was **b** in his father's tomb.
21:14 They **b** the bones of Saul and his son
1Ki 2:10 and was **b** in the City of David.
2:34 was **b** on his own land in the desert.
11:43 he rested with his fathers and was **b**
13:22 be **b** in the tomb of your fathers.'"
13:31 grave where the man of God is **b**;
14:13 belonging to Jeroboam who will be **b**,
14:18 They **b** him, and all Israel mourned
14:31 **b** with them in the City of David.
15: 8 and was **b** in the City of David.
15:24 rested with his fathers and was **b**
16: 6 his fathers and was **b** in Tirzah.
16:28 his fathers and was **b** in Samaria.
22:37 to Samaria, and they **b** him there.
22:50 was **b** with them in the city of David
2Ki 8:24 **b** with them in the City of David.
9:28 **b** him with his fathers in his tomb
10:35 his fathers and was **b** in Samaria.
12:21 He died and was **b** with his fathers
13: 9 his fathers and was **b** in Samaria.
13:13 Jehoash was **b** in Samaria with the
13:20 Elisha died and was **b**. Now Moabite
14:16 was **b** in Samaria with the kings of
14:20 was **b** in Jerusalem with his fathers,
15: 7 **b** near them in the City of David.
15:38 **b** with them in the City of David,
16:20 **b** with them in the City of David.
21:18 and was **b** in his palace garden,
21:26 He was **b** in his grave in the garden
22:20 fathers, and you will be **b** in peace.
23:30 Jerusalem and **b** him in his own tomb.
1Ch 10:12 Then they **b** their bones under the
2Ch 9:31 rested with his fathers and was **b**
12:16 and was **b** in the City of David.
14: 1 and was **b** in the City of David.
16:14 They **b** him in the tomb that he had
21: 1 **b** with them in the City of David.
21:20 and was **b** in the City of David,
22: 9 They **b** him, for they said, "He was
24:16 He was **b** with the kings in the City
24:25 So he died and was **b** in the City of
25:28 was **b** with his fathers in the City
26:23 was **b** near them in a field for
2Ch 27: 9 and was **b** in the City of David.
28:27 and was **b** in the city of Jerusalem,
32:33 was **b** on the hill where the tombs
33:20 his fathers and was **b** in his palace.
34:28 fathers, and you will be **b** in peace.
35:24 He was **b** in the tombs of his fathers,
Ne 2: 3 my fathers are **b** lies in ruins,
2: 5 are **b** so that I can rebuild it."
Job 16:15 my skin and **b** my brow in the dust.
Ps 106:17 it **b** the company of Abiram.
Ecc 8:10 Then too, I saw the wicked **b**—
Jer 8: 2 They will not be gathered up or **b**,
16: 4 They will not be mourned or **b** but
16: 6 They will not be **b** or mourned, and
20: 6 There you will die and be **b**, you
25:33 not be mourned or gathered up or **b**,
43:10 over these stones I have **b** here;
Eze 39:11 and all his hordes will be **b** there.
39:15 **b** it in the Valley of Hamon Gog.
Mt 14:12 came and took his body and **b** it.
Lk 16:22 The rich man also died and was **b**.
Ac 2:29 the patriarch David died and was **b**
5: 6 and carried him out and **b** him.
5: 9 feet of the men who **b** your husband
5:10 out and **b** her beside her husband.
8: 2 Godly men **b** Stephen and mourned
13:36 he was **b** with his fathers
Ro 6: 4 We were therefore **b** with him through
1Co 15: 4 that he was **b**, that he was raised on
Col 2:12 having been **b** with him in baptism

Buries (Bury)

Pr 19:24 The sluggard **b** his hand in the dish;
26:15 The sluggard **b** his hand in the dish;

Burn (*Altar of burnt offering*, Burned, Burning, Burns, Burnt, *Burnt offering*, *Burnt offerings*, Burnt-out)

Ex 3: 2 bush was on fire it did not **b** up.
3: 3 —why the bush does not **b** up."
12:10 left till morning, you must **b** it.
21:25 **b** for **b**, wound for wound, bruise for
29:13 on them, and **b** them on the altar.
29:14 **b** the bull's flesh and its hide and
29:18 **b** the entire ram on the altar.
29:25 and **b** them on the altar along with
29:34 is left over till morning, **b** it up.
30: 7 "Aaron must **b** fragrant incense on
30: 8 He must **b** incense again when he
30: 8 so that incense will **b** regularly
32:10 that my anger may **b** against them
32:11 "why should your anger **b** against
Lev 1: 9 is to **b** all of it on the altar.
1:13 all of it and **b** it on the altar.
1:15 wring off the head and **b** it on the
1:17 the priest shall **b** it on the wood
2: 2 and **b** this as a memorial portion on
2: 9 **b** it on the altar as an offering
2:11 for you are not to **b** any yeast or
2:16 The priest shall **b** the memorial
3: 5 Aaron's sons are to **b** it on the
3:11 The priest shall **b** them on the altar
3:16 The priest shall **b** them on the altar
4:10 Then the priest shall **b** them on the
4:12 **b** it in a wood fire on the ash heap.
4:19 fat from it and **b** it on the altar,
4:21 **b** it as he burned the first bull.
4:26 He shall **b** all the fat on the altar
4:31 the priest shall **b** it on the altar
4:35 the priest shall **b** it on the altar
5:12 **b** it on the altar on top of the
6:12 **b** the fat of the fellowship
6:15 and **b** the memorial portion on the
7: 5 The priest shall **b** them on the altar
7:31 The priest shall **b** the fat on the
8:32 **b** up the rest of the meat and the
13:24 "When someone has a **b** on his skin
13:24 appears in the raw flesh of the **b**,
13:25 that has broken out in the **b**.
13:28 it is a swelling from the **b**, and the
13:28 it is only a scar from the **b**.
13:52 He must **b** up the clothing, or the
13:55 **B** it with fire, whether the mildew
16:25 He shall also **b** the fat of the sin

Lev 17: 6 **b** the fat as an aroma pleasing to
Nu 5:26 and **b** it on the altar; after that,
16:40 come to **b** incense before the LORD,
18:17 **b** their fat as an offering made by
Dt 6:15 God and his anger will **b** against you,
7: 4 the LORD's anger will **b** against you
7: 5 poles and **b** their idols in the fire.
7:25 The images of their gods you are to **b**
11:17 the LORD's anger will **b** against you,
12: 3 smash their sacred stones and **b**
12:31 They even **b** their sons and daughters
13:16 completely **b** the town and all its
29:20 and zeal will **b** against that man.
Jos 11: 6 their horses and **b** their chariots."
11:13 Yet Israel did not **b** any of the
23:16 the LORD's anger will **b** against you,
Jdg 12: 1 **b** down your house over your head."
14:15 or we will **b** you and your father's
1Sa 2:28 to go up to my altar, to **b** incense,
1Ki 14:10 I will **b** up the house of Jeroboam
22:43 offer sacrifices and **b** incense
2Ki 12: 3 offer sacrifices and **b** incense
14: 4 offer sacrifices and **b** incense
15: 4 offer sacrifices and **b** incense
15:35 offer sacrifices and **b** incense
22:17 my anger will **b** against this place
23: 5 to **b** incense on the high places
1Ch 14:12 gave orders to **b** them in the fire.
2Ch 2: 6 a place to **b** sacrifices before him?
4:20 to **b** in front of the inner sanctuary
26:16 **b** incense on the altar of incense.
26:18 Uzziah, to **b** incense to the LORD.
26:18 have been consecrated to **b** incense.
26:19 in his hand ready to **b** incense,
28:25 to **b** sacrifices to other gods
29: 7 They did not **b** incense or present
29:11 before him and to **b** incense."
32:12 one altar and **b** sacrifices on it'?
Ne 10:34 **b** on the altar of the LORD our God,
Ps 79: 5 long will your jealousy **b** like fire?
89:46 How long will your wrath **b** like fire?
102: 3 my bones **b** like glowing embers.
Isa 1:31 both will **b** together, with no-one
10:17 in a single day it will **b** and
47:14 the fire will **b** them up.
57: 5 You **b** with lust among the oaks and
Jer 4: 4 or my wrath will break out and **b**
4: 4 **b** with no-one to quench it.
6:29 The bellows blow fiercely to **b** away
7: 9 **b** incense to Baal and follow other
7:20 and it will **b** and not be quenched.
7:31 to **b** their sons and daughters in the
11:12 to the gods to whom they **b** incense,
11:13 **b** incense to that shameful god Baal
15:14 a fire that will **b** against you."
17: 4 my anger, and it will **b** for ever."
18:15 they **b** incense to worthless idols,
19: 5 **b** their sons in the fire as offerings
21:12 or my wrath will break out and **b**
21:12 **b** with no-one to quench it.
32:29 they will **b** it down, along with the
33:18 to **b** grain offerings and to present
34: 2 of Babylon, and he will **b** it down.
34:22 against it, take it and **b** it down.
36:25 urged the king not to **b** the scroll,
37: 8 they will capture it and **b** it down.'
37:10 come out and **b** this city down."
38:18 Babylonians and they will **b** it down;
43:12 he will **b** their temples and take
43:13 will **b** down the temples of the gods
44:17 **b** incense to the Queen of Heaven
44:25 out the vows we made to **b** incense
48:35 places and **b** incense to their gods
Eze 5: 2 **b** a third of the hair with fire
5: 4 them into the fire and **b** them up.
16:41 They will **b** down your houses and
23:47 daughters and **b** down their houses.
39: 9 use the weapons for fuel and **b** them
43:21 **b** it in the designated part of the
Hos 4:13 and **b** offerings on the hills,
Am 4: 5 **B** leavened bread as a thank-offering
6:10 if a relative who is to **b** the bodies
Na 2:13 "I will **b** up your chariots in smoke,
Mal 4: 1 it will **b** like a furnace.
Lk 1: 9 temple of the Lord and **b** incense.
3:17 but he will **b** up the chaff with
1Co 7: 9 to marry than to **b** with passion.
2Co 11:29 into sin, and I do not inwardly **b**?
Rev 17:16 eat her flesh and **b** her with fire.

Burned (Burn)

Ge 38:24 her out and have her **b** to death!"
39:19 slave treated me," he **b** with anger.
Ex 4:14 the LORD's anger **b** against Moses and
32:19 his anger **b** and he threw the tablets
32:20 he took the calf they had made and **b**
40:27 **b** fragrant incense on it, as the
Lev 4:21 and burn it as he **b** the first bull.
4:26 **b** the fat of the fellowship offering.
6:22 share and is to be **b** completely.
6:23 **b** completely; it must not be eaten."
6:30 must not be eaten; it must be **b**.
7:17 till the third day must be **b** up.
7:19 must not be eaten; it must be **b** up.
8:16 their fat, and **b** it on the altar.
8:17 its offal he **b** up outside the camp,
8:20 He cut the ram into pieces and **b** the
8:21 and **b** the whole ram on the altar
8:28 **b** them on the altar on top of the
9:10 On the altar he **b** the fat, the
9:11 the flesh and the hide he **b** up
9:13 head, and he **b** them on the altar.
9:14 the legs and **b** them on top of the
9:17 took a handful of it and **b** it on the
9:20 then Aaron **b** the fat on the altar.
10:16 and found that it had been **b** up,
13:52 the article must be **b** up.
13:57 has the mildew must be **b** with fire.
16:27 flesh and offal are to be **b** up.
19: 6 until the third day must be **b** up.
20:14 Both he and they must be **b** in the
21: 9 she must be **b** in the fire.
Nu 11: 1 Then fire from the LORD **b** among them
11: 3 fire from the LORD had **b** among them.
11:33 the anger of the LORD **b** against the
12: 9 The anger of the LORD **b** against them,
16:39 brought by those who had been **b** up,
19: 5 the heifer is to be **b**—its hide, flesh,
19:17 put some ashes from the **b**
24:10 Balak's anger **b** against Balaam.
25: 3 And the LORD's anger **b** against them.
31:10 They **b** all the towns where the
32:13 The LORD's anger **b** against Israel
Dt 9:21 you had made, and **b** it in the fire.
29:27 Therefore the LORD's anger **b** against
Jos 6:24 they **b** the whole city and everything
7: 1 So the LORD's anger **b** against Israel.
7:25 had stoned the rest, they **b** them.
8:28 Joshua **b** Ai and made it a permanent
11: 9 their horses and **b** their chariots.
11:11 breathed, and he **b** up Hazor itself.
11:13 except Hazor, which Joshua **b**.
Jdg 3: 8 The anger of the LORD **b** against
15: 5 He **b** up the shocks and standing corn,
15: 6 and **b** her and her father to death.
18:27 the sword and **b** down their city.
1Sa 2:15 even before the fat was **b**, the
2:16 "Let the fat be **b** up first, and then
11: 6 him in power, and he **b** with anger.
17:28 he **b** with anger at him and asked,
30: 1 They had attacked Ziklag and **b** it,
30:14 And we **b** Ziklag."
31:12 went to Jabesh, where they **b** them.
2Sa 6: 7 The LORD's anger **b** against Uzzah
12: 5 David **b** with anger against the man
23: 7 they are **b** up where they lie."
24: 1 Again the anger of the LORD **b**
1Ki 3: 3 and **b** incense on the high places.
11: 8 who **b** incense and offered sacrifices
13: 2 and human bones will be **b** on you.'"
15:13 down and **b** it in the Kidron Valley.
18:38 the fire of the LORD fell and **b** up
19:21 He **b** the ploughing equipment to cook
2Ki 10:26 out of the temple of Baal and **b** it.
13: 3 the LORD's anger **b** against Israel,
16: 4 He offered sacrifices and **b** incense
17:11 At every high place they **b** incense,
17:31 and the Sepharvites **b** their children
22:17 they have forsaken me and **b** incense
23: 4 He **b** them outside Jerusalem in the
23: 5 those who **b** incense to Baal, to the
23: 6 outside Jerusalem and **b** it there.
2Ki 23: 8 where the priests had **b** incense.
23:11 **b** the chariots dedicated to the sun.
23:15 He **b** the high place and ground it to
23:15 and **b** the Asherah pole also.
23:16 and **b** on the altar to defile it,
23:20 altars and **b** human bones on them.
23:26 which **b** against Judah because of all
25: 9 Every important building he **b** down.
1Ch 13:10 The LORD's anger **b** against Uzzah,
2Ch 15:16 it up and **b** it in the Kidron Valley.
25:14 to them and **b** sacrifices to them.
25:15 The anger of the LORD **b** against
28: 3 He **b** sacrifices in the Valley of Ben
28: 4 He offered sacrifices and **b** incense
34: 5 He **b** the bones of the priests on
34:25 they have forsaken me and **b** incense
36:19 they **b** all the palaces and destroyed
Ne 1: 3 its gates have been **b** with fire."
2:17 and its gates have been **b** with fire.
4: 2 heaps of rubble—**b** as they are?"
Est 1:12 became furious and **b** with anger.
Job 1:16 and **b** up the sheep and the servants,
Ps 39: 3 as I meditated, the fire **b**;
74: 7 They **b** your sanctuary to the ground;
74: 8 They **b** every place where God was
80:16 Your vine is cut down, it is **b** with
Pr 6:27 his lap without his clothes being **b**?
Isa 1: 7 your cities **b** with fire; your fields
24: 6 earth's inhabitants are **b** up,
33:12 The peoples will be **b** as if to lime;
43: 2 you will not be **b**; the flames will
64:11 has been **b** with fire, and all that
65: 7 "Because they **b** sacrifices on the
Jer 2:15 his towns are **b** and deserted.
19: 4 they have **b** sacrifices in it to gods
19:13 all the houses where they **b** incense
29:22 the king of Babylon **b** in the fire.'
36:23 the entire scroll was **b** in the fire.
36:27 After the king **b** the scroll
36:28 which Jehoiakim king of Judah **b** up.
36:29 You **b** that scroll and said,
36:32 king of Judah had **b** in the fire.
38:17 and this city will not be **b** down;
38:23 and this city will be **b** down."
44:19 The women added, "When we **b** incense
44:21 think about the incense **b** in the
44:23 you have **b** incense and have sinned
52:13 Every important building he **b** down.
Lam 2: 3 He has **b** in Jacob like a flaming
Eze 15: 5 the fire has **b** it and it is charred?
24:11 be melted and its deposit **b** away.
Da 11:33 or be **b** or captured or plundered.
Hos 2:13 I will punish her for the days she **b**
11: 2 Baals and they **b** incense to images.
Joel 1:19 **b** up all the trees of the field.
Am 2: 1 Because he **b**, as if to lime,
Mic 1: 7 all her temple gifts will be **b** with
Mt 13:30 and tie them in bundles to be **b**;
13:40 "As the weeds are pulled up and **b** in
22: 7 those murderers and **b** their city.
Jn 5:35 John was a lamp that **b** and gave
15: 6 thrown into the fire and **b**.
Ac 19:19 together and **b** them publicly.
1Co 3:15 If it is **b** up, he will suffer loss;
Heb 6: 8 In the end it will be **b**.
13:11 the bodies are **b** outside the camp.
Rev 8: 7 A third of the earth was **b** up,
8: 7 a third of the trees were **b** up,
8: 7 and all the green grass was **b** up.

Burning (Burn)

Ge 19:24 the LORD rained down **b** sulphur on
Ex 15: 7 You unleashed your **b** anger;
27:20 so that the lamps may be kept **b**.
27:21 his sons are to keep the lamps **b**
30: 1 "Make an altar of acacia wood for **b**
Lev 1: 8 on the **b** wood that is on the altar.
1:12 on the **b** wood that is on the altar.
3: 5 offering that is on the **b** wood,
6: 9 fire must be kept **b** on the altar.
6:12 The fire on the altar must be kept **b**;
6:13 The fire must be kept **b** on the altar
16:12 take a censer full of **b** coals
24: 2 the lamps may be kept **b** continually.
Nu 19: 6 and throw them onto the **b** heifer.
Dt 29:23 The whole land will be a **b** waste of

Dt 29:24 Why this fierce, **b** anger?"
33:16 of him who dwelt in the **b** bush.
Jdg 14:19 **B** with anger, he went up to his
2Sa 14: 7 They would put out the only **b** coal
22: 9 his mouth, **b** coals blazed out of it.
1Ki 9:25 **b** incense before the LORD along with
2Ki 18: 4 Israelites had been **b** incense to it.
2Ch 2: 4 for **b** fragrant incense before him,
Job 18: 5 the flame of his fire stops **b**.
18:15 **b** sulphur is scattered over his
20:23 God will vent his **b** anger against
Ps 11: 6 will rain fiery coals and **b** sulphur;
18: 8 his mouth, **b** coals blazed out of it.
18:28 You, O LORD, keep my lamp **b**; my God
118:12 died out as quickly as **b** thorns;
120: 4 with **b** coals of the broom tree.
140:10 Let **b** coals fall upon them; may they
Pr 25:22 In doing this, you will heap **b** coals
Isa 9: 5 will be destined for **b**, will be fuel
13:13 Almighty, in the day of his **b** anger.
30:27 with **b** anger and dense clouds of
30:33 stream of **b** sulphur, sets it ablaze.
33:14 of us can dwell with everlasting **b**?"
34: 9 her dust into **b** sulphur; her land
35: 7 The **b** sand will become a pool, the
42:25 he poured out on them his **b** anger,
44:15 is man's fuel for **b**; some of it he
65: 3 and **b** incense on altars of brick;
65: 5 a fire that keeps **b** all day.
Jer 1:16 in **b** incense to other gods and in
11:17 me to anger by **b** incense to Baal.
32:29 by **b** incense on the roofs to Baal
36:22 **b** in the brazier in front of him.
44: 3 They provoked me to anger by **b**
44: 5 or stop **b** incense to other gods.
44: 8 **b** incense to other gods in Egypt,
44:15 wives were **b** incense to other gods,
44:18 ever since we stopped **b** incense to
Eze 1:13 **b** coals of fire or like torches.
10: 2 Fill your hands with **b** coals from
36: 5 In my **b** zeal I have spoken against
38:22 hailstones and **b** sulphur on him and
Hos 7: 4 **b** like an oven whose fire the baker
13: 5 the desert, in the land of **b** heat.
Am 4:11 You were like a **b** stick snatched
Zec 3: 2 a **b** stick snatched from the fire?"
8: 2 Zion; I am **b** with jealousy for her."
Mt 3:12 **b** up the chaff with unquenchable
Lk 1:10 the time for the **b** of incense came,
12:35 for service and keep your lamps **b**,
24:32 "Were not our hearts **b** within us
Jn 21: 9 they saw a fire of **b** coals there
Ac 7:30 to Moses in the flames of a **b** bush
Ro 12:20 you will heap **b** coals on his head."
Heb 12:18 be touched and that is **b** with fire;
2Pe 2: 6 and Gomorrah by **b** them to ashes,
Rev 14:10 He will be tormented with **b** sulphur
18: 9 see the smoke of **b**, they will weep
18:18 they see the smoke of her **b**, they
19:20 into the fiery lake of **b** sulphur.
20:10 thrown into the lake of **b** sulphur.
21: 8 be in the fiery lake of **b** sulphur.

Burnished
1Ki 7:45 temple of the LORD were of **b** bronze.
Eze 1: 7 of a calf and gleamed like **b** bronze.
Da 10: 6 and legs like the gleam of **b** bronze,
Rev 2:18 and whose feet are like **b** bronze.

Burns (Burn)
Ex 22: 6 **b** shocks of grain or standing corn
Lev 16:28 The man who **b** them must wash his
Nu 19: 8 The man who **b** it must also wash his
Dt 32:22 that **b** to the realm of death below.
1Ki 14:10 as one **b** dung, until it is all gone.
2Ki 22:13 Great is the LORD's anger that **b**
Job 19:11 His anger **b** against me; he counts me
30:30 and peels; my body **b** with fever.
31:12 It is a fire that **b** to Destruction;
Ps 46: 9 spear, he **b** the shields with fire.
SS 8: 6 It **b** like blazing fire, like a
Isa 5:25 Therefore the LORD's anger **b** against
9:18 Surely wickedness **b** like a fire;
44:16 Half of the wood he **b** in the fire;
66: 3 and whoever **b** memorial incense, like
Jer 48:45 it **b** the foreheads of Moab,
Eze 15: 4 **b** both ends and chars the middle,
Hos 8: 5 O Samaria! My anger **b** against them.
Hab 1:16 net and **b** incense to his drag-net,
Zec 10: 3 "My anger **b** against the shepherds,

Burnt offering
Ge 22:2, 3, 6, 7, 8, 13; Ex 18:12; 29:18, 25, 42; 30:9, 28; 31:9; 35:16; 38:1; 40:6, 10, 29; Lev 1:3, 4, 6, 9, 10, 13, 14, 17, 3:5; 4:7, 10, 18, 24, 25, 29, 30, 33, 34; 5:7, 10; 6:9, 10, 12, 25; 7:2, 8, 37; 8:18, 21, 28; 9:2, 3, 7, 12, 13, 14, 16, 17, 22, 24; 10:19; 12:6, 8; 14:13, 19, 22, 31; 15:15, 30; 16:3, 5, 24; 17:8; 22:18; 23:12, 18; Nu 6:11, 14, 16; 7:15, 21, 27, 33, 39, 45, 51, 57, 63, 69, 75, 81, 87; 8:12; 15:5, 8, 24; 28:3, 6, 10, 11, 13, 14, 15, 19, 23, 24, 27, 31; 29:2, 8, 11, 13, 16, 19, 22, 25, 28, 31, 34, 36, 38; Dt 13:16; Jdg 6:26, 11:31; 13:16, 23; 1Sa 6:14; 7:9, 10; 13:9, 12; 2Sa 24:22; 2Ki 10:25; 16:13, 15; 1Ch 6:49; 16:40; 21:24, 26, 29; 22:1; 2Ch 7:1; 29:18, 24, 27, 28; Ezr 8:35; Job 1:5; 42:8; Eze 43:24; 45:23; 46:2, 4, 12, 13, 15

Burnt offerings
Ge 8:20; Ex10:25; 20:24; 24:5; 32:6; 40:29; Lev 23:37; Nu 10:10; 15:3; 29:6, 39; Dt 12:6, 11, 13, 27; 27:6; 33:10; Jos 8:31; 22:23, 26, 27, 28, 29; Jdg 20:26; 21:4; 1Sa 6:15; 10:8; 15:22; 2Sa 6:17, 18; 24:24, 25; 1Ki 3:4, 15; 8:64; 9:25; 10:5; 2Ki 5:17; 10:24; 16:15; 1Ch 16:1, 2, 40; 21:23, 26; 23:31; 29:21; 2Ch1:6; 2:4; 4:6; 7:7; 8:12; 9:4; 13:11; 23:18; 24:14; 29:7, 31, 32, 34, 35; 30:15; 31:2, 3; 35:12, 14, 16; Ezr 3:2, 3, 4, 5, 6; 6:9; 8:35; Ne 10:33; Ps 20:3; 40:6; 50:8; 51:16, 19; 66:13; Isa 1:11; 40:16; 43:23; 56:7; Jer 6 :20; 7:21, 22; 14:12; 17:26; 33:18; Eze 40:38, 39, 42; 43:18, 27; 44:11; 45:15, 17, 25; Hos 6:6; Am 5:22; Mic 6:6; Mk 12:33; Heb 10:6, 8

Burnt-out (Burn)
Jer 51:25 cliffs, and make you a **b** mountain.

Burst (Bursts)
Ge 7:11 springs of the great deep **b** forth,
27:34 he **b** out with a loud and bitter cry
Job 26: 8 clouds do not **b** under their weight.
32:19 wine, like new wineskins ready to **b**.
38: 8 doors when it **b** forth from the womb,
Ps 60: 1 and **b** forth upon us;
98: 4 **b** into jubilant song with music;
Isa 35: 2 will **b** into bloom; it will rejoice
44:23 **B** into song, you mountains, you
49:13 **b** into song, O mountains!
52: 9 **B** into songs of joy together, you
54: 1 **b** into song, shout for joy,
55:12 hills will **b** into song before you,
Jer 23:19 See, the storm of the LORD will **b**
30:23 See, the storm of the LORD will **b**
Eze 7:10 It has come! Doom has **b** forth,
13:11 and violent winds will **b** forth.
Mt 9:17 If they do, the skins will **b**, the
Mk 2:22 the wine will **b** the skins,
Lk 5:37 the new wine will **b** the skins,
Ac 1:18 his body **b** open and all his

Bursts (Burst)
Job 16:14 Again and again he **b** upon me;

Bury (Burial, Buried, Buries, Burying)
Ge 23: 4 site here so that I can **b** my dead."
23: 6 **B** your dead in the choicest of the
23: 8 "If you are willing to let me **b** my
23:11 **B** your dead."
23:13 me so that I can **b** my dead there."
23:15 between me and you? **B** your dead."
47:29 Do not **b** me in Egypt,
47:30 Egypt and **b** me where they are buried.
49:29 **B** me with my fathers in the cave in
50: 5 "I am about to die; **b** me in the tomb
50: 5 **b** my father; then I will return.'"
50: 6 Pharaoh said, "Go up and **b** your
50: 7 Joseph went up to **b** his father.
50:14 had gone with him to **b** his father.
Dt 21:23 Be sure to **b** him that same day,
1Ki 2:31 Strike him down and **b** him, and so
11:15 who had gone up to **b** the dead, had
13:29 own city to mourn for him and **b** him.
13:31 "When I die, **b** me in the grave where
14:13 Israel will mourn for him and **b** him
2Ki 9:10 at Jezreel, and no-one will **b** her.
9:34 **b** her, for she was a king's daughter.
9:35 when they went out to **b** her, they
Job 27:15 The plague will **b** those who survive
40:13 **B** them all in the dust together;
Ps 79: 3 and there is no-one to **b** the dead.
Jer 7:32 for they will **b** the dead in Topheth
14:16 There will be no-one to **b** them or
19:11 They will **b** the dead in Topheth
43: 9 **b** them in clay in the brick pavement
Lam 3:29 Let him **b** his face in the dust—
Eze 39:13 the people of the land will **b** them
39:14 **b** those that remain on the ground.
Hos 9: 6 them, and Memphis will **b** them.
Mt 8:21 first let me go and **b** my father."
8:22 and let the dead **b** their own dead."
Lk 9:59 first let me go and **b** my father."
9:60 "Let the dead **b** their own dead,

Burying (Bury)
Ge 23: 6 you his tomb for **b** your dead."
50:14 After **b** his father, Joseph returned
Nu 33: 4 who were **b** all their firstborn, whom
2Sa 2: 5 to Saul your master by **b** him.
1Ki 13:31 After **b** him, he said to his sons,
2Ki 13:21 while some Israelites were **b** a man,
Eze 39:12 **b** them in order to cleanse the land.

Bush (Bushes)
Ex 3: 2 in flames of fire from within a **b**.
3: 2 **b** was on fire it did not burn up.
3: 3 sight—why the **b** does not burn up."
3: 4 God called to him from within the **b**,
Dt 33:16 of him who dwelt in the burning **b**.
Jer 17: 6 He will be like a **b** in the
48: 6 become like a **b** in the desert.
Mk 12:26 in the account of the **b**, how God
Lk 20:37 in the account of the **b**, even Moses
Ac 7:30 **b** in the desert near Mount Sinai.
7:35 angel who appeared to him in the **b**.

Bushels
Lk 16: 7 thousand **b** of wheat,' he replied.

Bushes (Bush)
Ge 21:15 she put the boy under one of the **b**.
Job 30: 7 They brayed among the **b** and huddled

Business
1Sa 21: 8 because the king's **b** was urgent."
Est 3: 9 for the men who carry out this **b**."
Ecc 4: 8 too is meaningless—a miserable **b**!
Eze 27:12 "'Tarshish did **b** with you because of
27:16 "'Aram did **b** with you because of
27:18 did **b** with you in wine from Helbon
27:21 **b** with you in lambs, rams and goats.
Da 8:27 I got up and went about the king's **b**.
Zec 8:10 No-one could go about his **b** safely
Mt 22: 5 to his field, another to his **b**.
Jn 15:15 does not know his master's **b**.
Ac 19:24 in no little **b** for the craftsmen.
19:25 receive a good income from this **b**.
1Co 5:12 What **b** is it of mine to judge those
1Th 4:11 to mind your own **b** and to work with
Jas 1:11 away even while he goes about his **b**.
4:13 there, carry on **b** and make money."

Bustles
Ps 39: 6 He **b** about, but only in vain;

Busy
1Ki 18:27 in thought, or **b**, or travelling.
20:40 While your servant was **b** here and
Isa 32: 6 his mind is **b** with evil:
Hag 1: 9 each of you is **b** with his own house.
2Th 3:11 They are not **b**; they are busybodies.
Tit 2: 5 to be **b** at home, to be kind, and to

Busybodies
2Th 3:11 They are not busy; they are **b**.
1Ti 5:13 **b**, saying things they ought not to.

Butchered
1Sa 14:32 they **b** them on the ground and ate
Jer 12: 3 Drag them off like sheep to be **b**!

Butt (Butting)
2Sa 2:23 **b** of his spear into Asahel's stomach,

Butter
Ps 55:21 His speech is smooth as **b**, yet war
Pr 30:33 For as churning the milk produces **b**,

Butting (Butt)
Eze 34:21 **b** all the weak sheep with your horns

Buttocks
2Sa 10: 4 garments in the middle at the **b**,
1Ch 19: 4 garments in the middle at the **b**,
Isa 20: 4 exiles, young and old, with **b** bared

Buy (Bought, Buyer, Buyers, Buying, Buys)
Ge 41:57 the countries came to Egypt to **b**
42: 2 Go down there and **b** some for us, so
42: 3 went down to **b** grain from Egypt.
42: 5 among those who went to **b** grain,
42: 7 Canaan," they replied, "to **b** food.
42:10 "Your servants have come to **b** food.
43: 2 Go back and **b** us a little more food."
43: 4 we will go down and **b** food for you.
43:20 down here the first time to **b** food.
43:22 additional silver with us to **b** food.
44:25 'Go back and **b** a little more food.'
47:19 **B** us and our land in exchange for
47:22 However, he did not **b** the land of
Ex 21: 2 "If you **b** a Hebrew servant, he is to
Lev 25:14 your countrymen or **b** any from him,
25:15 You are to **b** from your countryman on
25:44 from them you may **b** slaves.
25:45 You may also **b** some of the temporary
27:27 he may **b** it back at its set value,
Dt 14:26 Use the silver to **b** whatever you
28:68 slaves, but no-one will **b** you.
Ru 4: 4 suggest that you **b** it in the
4: 5 Boaz said, "On the day you **b** the
4: 8 "**B** it yourself." And he removed his
2Sa 24:21 "To **b** your threshing-floor," David
Ezr 7:17 With this money be sure to **b** bulls,
Ne 10:31 we will not **b** from them on the
Pr 23:23 **B** the truth and do not sell it;
Isa 55: 1 come, **b** and eat! Come, **b** wine and
Jer 13: 1 "Go and **b** a linen belt and put it
19: 1 "Go and **b** a clay jar from a potter.
32: 7 '**B** my field at Anathoth, because as
32: 7 it is your right and duty to **b** it.'
32: 8 '**B** my field at Anathoth in the
32: 8 and possess it, **b** it for yourself.
32:25 '**B** the field with silver and have
Lam 5: 4 We must **b** the water we drink;
Mt 14:15 and **b** themselves some food."
25: 9 sell oil and **b** some for yourselves.'
25:10 were on their way to **b** the oil,
27: 7 they decided to use the money to **b**
27:10 used them to **b** the potter's field
Mk 6:36 and **b** themselves something to eat."
Lk 9:13 go and **b** food for all this crowd."
22:36 a sword, sell your cloak and **b** one.
Jn 4: 8 had gone into the town to **b** food.)
6: 5 we **b** bread for these people to eat?"
6: 7 "Eight months' wages would not **b**
13:29 to **b** what was needed for the Feast,
Ac 8:20 could **b** the gift of God with money!
1Co 7:30 those who **b** something, as if it were
Rev 3:18 I counsel you to **b** from me gold
13:17 that no-one could **b** or sell unless

Buyer (Buy)
Lev 25:28 remain in the possession of the **b**
25:30 to the **b** and his descendants.
25:50 He and his **b** are to count the time
Pr 20:14 no good, it's no good!" says the **b**;
Isa 24: 2 for seller as for **b**, for borrower as
Eze 7:12 Let not the **b** rejoice nor the seller

Buyers (Buy)
Zec 11: 5 Their **b** slaughter them and go

Buying (Buy)
Ge 47:14 payment for the grain they were **b**,
Am 8: 6 **b** the poor with silver and the needy
Mt 21:12 all who were **b** and selling there.
Mk 11:15 those who were **b** and selling there.
Lk 17:28 **b** and selling, planting and building.

Buys (Buy)
Lev 22:11 if a priest **b** a slave with money,
Pr 31:16 She considers a field and **b** it;
Rev 18:11 no-one **b** their cargoes any more—

Buz (Buzite)
Ge 22:21 Uz the firstborn, **B** his brother,
1Ch 5:14 the son of Jahdo, the son of **B**.
Jer 25:23 Dedan, Tema, **B** and all who are in

Buzi
Eze 1: 3 Ezekiel the priest, the son of **B**,

Buzite (Buz)
Job 32: 2 Elihu son of Barakel the **B**, of
32: 6 Elihu son of Barakel the **B** said:

By faith
Ac 3:16; 15:9; 26:18; Ro 1:17; 3:28, 30; 4:11, 13, 16; 5:2; 9:30, 32; 10:6; 11:20; 2Co 1:24; 5:7; Gal 2:16, 20; 3:8, 11, 14, 24; 5:5; Php 3:9; 1Th 1:3; 1Ti 1:4; Heb 10:38; 11:3, 4, 5, 7, 8, 9, 11, 13, 17, 20, 21, 22, 23, 24, 27, 28, 29, 30, 31; Jas 2:24

Bypaths (Path)
Jer 18:15 walk in **b** and on roads not built up.

Byword (Word)
1Ki 9: 7 Israel will then become a **b** and an
2Ch 7:20 I will make it a **b** and an object of
Job 17: 6 "God has made me a **b** to everyone, a
30: 9 I have become a **b** among them.
Ps 44:14 You have made us a **b** among the
Jer 24: 9 a reproach and a **b**, an object of
Eze 14: 8 man and make him an example and a **b**.
23:10 She became a **b** among women, and
Joel 2:17 of scorn, a **b** among the nations.

Cab
2Ki 6:25 a **c** of seed pods for five shekels.

Cabbon
Jos 55:40 **C**, Lahmas, Kitlish,

Cabul
Jos 19:27 and Neiel, passing **C** on the left.
1Ki 9:13 And he called them the Land of **C**,

Caesar (Caesar's)
Mt 22:17 it right to pay taxes to **C** or not?"
22:21 Then he said to them, "Give to **C**
Mk 12:14 Is it right to pay taxes to **C** or not?
12:17 Jesus said to them, "Give to **C** what
Lk 2: 1 In those days **C** Augustus issued a
3: 1 year of the reign of Tiberius **C**—
20:22 Is it right for us to pay taxes to **C**
20:25 He said to them, "Then give to **C**
23: 2 He opposes payment of taxes to **C**
Jn 19:12 this man go, you are no friend of **C**.
19:12 who claims to be a king opposes **C**."
19:15 "We have no king but **C**," the chief
Ac 25: 8 or against the temple or against **C**."
25:11 I appeal to **C**!"
25:12 declared: "You have appealed to **C**.
25:12 To **C** you will go!"
25:21 held until I could send him to **C**."
26:32 free if he had not appealed to **C**."
27:24 You must stand trial before **C**;
28:19 I was compelled to appeal to **C**—

Caesar's (Caesar)
Mt 22:21 "**C**," they replied. Then he said to
22:21 Give to Caesar what is **C**, and to God
Mk 12:16 "**C**," they replied.
12:17 Give to Caesar what is **C** and to God
Lk 20:25 "**C**," they replied. He said to them,
20:25 "Then give to Caesar what is **C**,
Ac 17: 7 They are all defying **C** decrees,
25:10 **C** court, where I ought to be tried.
Php 4:22 those who belong to **C** household.

Caesarea
Mediterranean port about 30 miles north of Joppa and capital of Judea. Herod Agrippa I died here (Ac 12:19–23); Agrippa II visited with Bernice (Ac 25:13). Home of Cornelius, to whom Peter ministered (Ac 10:1, 24), and Philip the Evangelist (Ac 6:5). Paul passed through on his journeys (Ac 9:30; 18:22; 21:8) and was imprisoned here for 2 years before being sent to Rome (Ac 23:23, 33; 25:4; 27:1).

Ac 8:40 in all the towns until he reached **C**.
9:30 they took him down to **C** and sent him
10: 1 At **C** there was a man named Cornelius,
10:24 The following day he arrived in **C**.
11:11 men who had been sent to me from **C**
12:19 Judea to **C** and stayed there a while.
18:22 When he landed at **C**, he went up and
21: 8 Leaving the next day, we reached **C**
21:16 Some of the disciples from **C**
23:23 spearmen to go to **C** at nine tonight.
23:33 When the cavalry arrived in **C**, they
24: 1 down to **C** with some of the elders
25: 1 Festus went up from **C** to Jerusalem,
25: 4 "Paul is being held at **C**, and I
25: 6 he went down to **C**, and the next day
25:13 King Agrippa and Bernice arrived at **C**
25:24 him in Jerusalem and here in **C**,

Caesarea Philippi
City north of Sea of Galilee, on south-west slope of Mount Hermon. Known as Paneas (after the god Pan) until Philip the Tetrarch renamed it. Northernmost limit of Jesus' ministry, where Simon Peter proclaimed him "the Christ" (Mt 16:13–16; Mk 8:27–29).

Mt 16:13 Jesus came to the region of **C**, he
Mk 8:27 went on to the villages around **C**.

Cage (Cages)
Eze 19: 9 With hooks they pulled him into a **c**

Cages (Cage)
Jer 5:27 Like **c** full of birds, their houses

Caiaphas
High priest at time of Jesus' arrest (Mt 26:57–68; Jn 18:13,24). Unknowingly foretold the significance of Jesus' death (Jn 11:49–52; 18:14). Questioned Peter and John (Ac 4:5–7).

Mt 26: 3 the high priest, whose name was **C**,
26:57 had arrested Jesus took him to **C**,
Lk 3: 2 the high priesthood of Annas and **C**,
Jn 11:49 one of them, named **C**, who was high
18:13 of **C**, the high priest that year.
18:14 **C** was the one who had advised the
18:24 Annas sent him, still bound, to **C**
18:28 the Jews led Jesus from **C** to the
Ac 4: 6 and so were **C**, John, Alexander and

Cain
Eldest son of Adam and Eve (Ge 4:1). Farmer (Ge 4:2; murdered his brother, Abel, when sacrifice not accepted by God (Ge 4:3–8; 1Jn 3:12). Given mark of protection to limit punishment (Ge 4:9-16).

Ge 4: 1 became pregnant and gave birth to **C**.
4: 2 kept flocks, and **C** worked the soil.
4: 3 In the course of time **C** brought some
4: 5 but on **C** and his offering he did not
4: 5 So **C** was very angry, and his face
4: 6 the LORD said to **C**, "Why are you
4: 8 Now **C** said to his brother Abel,
4: 8 **C** attacked his brother Abel
4: 9 the LORD said to **C**, "Where is your
4:13 **C** said to the LORD, "My punishment
4:15 if anyone kills **C**, he will suffer
4:15 Then the LORD put a mark on **C** so
4:16 **C** went out from the LORD's presence

Ge 4:17 C lay with his wife, and she became
4:17 C was then building a city, and he
4:24 If C is avenged seven times, then
4:25 place of Abel, since C killed him."
Heb 11: 4 God a better sacrifice than C did.
1Jn 3:12 Do not be like C, who belonged to
Jude :11 They have taken the way of C;

Cainan

Lk 3:36 the son of C, the son of Arphaxad,

Cake (Cakes)

Ex 29:23 and a c made with oil, and a wafer.
Lev 8:26 he took a c of bread, and one made
Nu 6:19 and a c and a wafer from the basket,
15:20 Present a c from the first of your
1Sa 30:12 part of a c of pressed figs and two
2Sa 6:19 a c of dates and a c of raisins to
1Ki 17:13 But first make a small c of bread
19: 6 there by his head was a c of bread
1Ch 16: 3 a c of dates and a c of raisins to
Eze 4:12 Eat the food as you would a barley c;
Hos 7: 8 Ephraim is a flat c not turned over.

Cakes (Cake)

Ex 12:39 they baked c of unleavened bread.
29: 2 make bread, and c mixed with oil
Lev 2: 4 c made without yeast
7:12 offer c of bread made without yeast
7:12 and c of fine flour well-kneaded and
7:13 with c of bread made with yeast.
Nu 6:15 c made of fine flour mixed with oil,
11: 8 it in a pot or made it into c.
1Sa 25:18 roasted grain, a hundred c of raisins
25:18 and two hundred c of pressed figs,
30:12 pressed figs and two c of raisins.
2Sa 16: 1 a hundred c of raisins, a hundred c
1Ki 14: 3 c and a jar of honey, and go to him.
1Ch 12:40 fig c, raisin c, wine, oil, cattle
Jer 7:18 c of bread for the Queen of Heaven.
44:19 we were making c like her image
Hos 3: 1 gods and love the sacred raisin c."

Calah

Ge 10:11 he built Nineveh, Rehoboth Ir, C
10:12 Resen, which is between Nineveh and C

Calamities (Calamity)

Dt 29:22 the c that have fallen on the land
32:23 "I will heap c upon them and expend
1Sa 10:19 out of all your c and distresses.
2Sa 19: 7 will be worse for you than all the c
Job 5:19 From six c he will rescue you;
Pr 24:22 and who knows what c they can bring?
Isa 51:19 These double c have come upon you—
Lam 3:38 that both c and good things come?

Calamity (Calamities)

2Sa 12:11 I am going to bring c upon you.
24:16 Lord was grieved because of the c
1Ch 21:15 and was grieved because of the c
2Ch 20: 9 'If c comes upon us, whether the
Ne 13:18 so that our God brought all this c
Job 18:12 C is hungry for him; disaster is
21:17 How often does c come upon them,
21:30 man is spared from the day of c,
Ps 107:39 humbled by oppression, c and sorrow;
Pr 1:26 I will mock when c overtakes you—
1:27 when c overtakes you like a storm,
14:32 When c comes, the wicked are brought
21:23 and his tongue keeps himself from c.
24:16 the wicked are brought down by c.
Isa 47:11 A c will fall upon you that you
Jer 14:16 pour out on them the c they deserve.
32:42 all this great c on this people,
48:16 her c will come quickly.
Eze 6:10 in vain to bring this c on them.
7:26 C upon c will come, and rumour upon
35: 5 to the sword at the time of their c,
Joel 2:13 love, and he relents from sending c.
Ob :13 nor look down on them in their c in
Jnh 1: 7 out who is responsible for this c.
4: 2 a God who relents from sending c.
Mic 2: 3 proudly, for it will be a time of c.
Hab 3:16 c to come on the nation invading us.
Zec 1:15 angry, but they added to the c.'

Calamus

SS 4:14 nard and saffron, c and cinnamon,
Isa 43:24 You have not bought any fragrant c
Jer 6:20 Sheba or sweet c from a distant land?
Eze 27:19 iron, cassia and c for your wares.

Calcol

1Ki 4:31 C and Darda, the sons of Mahol.
1Ch 2: 6 Heman, C and Darda—five in all.

Calculate (Calculated)

Rev 13:18 let him c the number of the beast,

Calculated (Calculate)

Ac 19:19 When they c the value of the scrolls,

Caleb (Caleb's, Calebite)

One of spies sent to explore Canaan (Nu 13:6); with Joshua encouraged the people to go in (Nu 13:30; 14:6–9). Allowed to enter land because of his faith (Nu 26:65; 32:12; Dt 1:36). Given possession of Hebron (Jos 14:6–15; 15:13–19).

Nu 13: 6 from the tribe of Judah, C son of
13:30 C silenced the people before Moses
14: 6 and C son of Jephunneh,
14:24 my servant C has a different spirit
14:30 except C son of Jephunneh and Joshua
14:38 and C son of Jephunneh survived.
26:65 not one of them was left except C
32:12 not one except C son of Jephunneh
34:19 These are their names: C son of
Dt 1:36 except C son of Jephunneh. He will
Jos 14: 6 and C son of Jephunneh the Kenizzite
14:13 Joshua blessed C son of Jephunneh
14:14 Hebron has belonged to C son of
15:13 Joshua gave to C son of Jephunneh a
15:14 From Hebron C drove out the three
15:16 C said, "I will give my daughter
15:17 C gave his daughter Acsah to him
15:18 When she got off her donkey, C asked
15:19 So C gave her the upper and lower
21:12 C son of Jephunneh as his possession.
Jdg 1:12 C said, "I will give my daughter
1:13 so C gave his daughter Acsah to him
1:14 When she got off her donkey, C asked
1:15 Then C gave her the upper and lower
1:20 Hebron was given to C, who drove
1Sa 30:14 to Judah and the Negev of C.
1Ch 2: 9 Hezron were: Jerahmeel, Ram and C.
2:18 C son of Hezron had children by his
2:19 Azubah died, C married Ephrath, who
2:42 The sons of C the brother of
2:50 These were the descendants of C.
4:15 The sons of C son of Jephunneh: Iru,
6:56 were given to C son of Jephunneh.

Caleb's (Caleb)

Jos 15:17 Othniel son of Kenaz, C brother,
Jdg 1:13 Othniel son of Kenaz, C younger
3: 9 C younger brother, who saved them.
1Ch 2:46 C concubine Ephah was the mother of
2:48 C concubine Maacah was the mother of
2:49 C daughter was Acsah.

Caleb Ephrathah

1Ch 2:24 After Hezron died in C, Abijah the

Calebite (Caleb)

1Sa 25: 3 but her husband, a C, was surly and

Calf (Calf-idol, Calf-idols, Calve, Calved, Calves)

Ge 18: 7 and selected a choice, tender c
18: 8 and the c that had been prepared,
Ex 32: 4 an idol cast in the shape of a c,
32: 5 he built an altar in front of the c
32: 8 an idol cast in the shape of a c.
32:19 camp and saw the c and the dancing,
32:20 he took the c they had made and
32:24 into the fire, and out came this c!"
32:35 they did with the c Aaron had made.
Lev 9: 2 "Take a bull c for your sin offering
9: 3 a c and a lamb—both a year old and
9: 8 the c as a sin offering for himself.
22:27 "When a c, a lamb or a goat is born,
Dt 9:16 an idol cast in the shape of a c.
9:21 the c you had made, and burned it in
1Sa 28:24 The woman had a fattened c at the
2Sa 6:13 sacrificed a bull and a fattened c.
2Ch 11:15 the goat and c idols he had made.
Ne 9:18 themselves an image of a c and said,
Ps 29: 6 He makes Lebanon skip like a c,
106:19 At Horeb they made a c and
Pr 15:17 than a fattened c with hatred.
Isa 11: 6 the c and the lion and the yearling
Jer 31:18 'You disciplined me like an unruly c,
34:18 I will treat like the c they cut in
34:19 walked between the pieces of the c,
Eze 1: 7 their feet were like those of a c
Hos 8: 6 This c—a craftsman has made it;
8: 6 broken in pieces, that c of Samaria.
Lk 15:23 Bring the fattened c and kill it.
15:27 father has killed the fattened c
15:30 you kill the fattened c for him!'
Ac 7:41 made an idol in the form of a c.

Calf-idol (Calf, Idol)

Hos 8: 5 Throw out your c, O Samaria! My
10: 5 Samaria fear for the c of Beth Aven.

Calf-idols (Calf, Idol)

Hos 13: 2 human sacrifice and kiss the c."

Call (Called, Calling, Calls, So-called)

Ge 4:26 began to c on the name of the Lord.
17:15 c her Sarai; her name will be Sarah.
17:19 you a son, and you will c him Isaac.
24:57 they said, "Let's c the girl and ask
30:13 I am! The women will c me happy.
Nu 20:25 C Aaron and his son Eleazar and take
Dt 3: 9 Sidonians; the Amorites c it Senir.)
4:26 I c heaven and earth as witnesses
18:19 I myself will c him to account.
30:19 This day I c heaven and earth as
31:14 C Joshua and present yourselves at
31:28 c heaven and earth to testify
Jos 22:23 the Lord himself c us to account.
Jdg 8: 1 c us when you went to fight Midian?"
9:29 Abimelech, 'C out your whole army!'"
Ru 1:20 "Don't c me Naomi," she told them.
1:20 "C me Mara, because the Almighty
1:21 Why c me Naomi? The Lord has
1Sa 3: 5 But Eli said, "I did not c; go back
3: 6 "My son," Eli said, "I did not c;
12:17 I will c upon the Lord to send
20:16 Lord c David's enemies to account."
23:28 they c this place Sela Hammahlekoth.
2Sa 15: 2 Absalom would c out to him, "What
22: 4 I c to the Lord, who is worthy of
1Ki 1:28 King David said, "C in Bathsheba."
1:32 King David said, "C in Zadok the
18:24 you c on the name of your god, and I
18:24 I will c on the name of the Lord.
18:25 C on the name of your god, but do
2Ki 4:12 "C the Shunammite." So he called
4:15 Elisha said, "C her." So he called
4:36 "C the Shunammite." And he did.
5:11 c on the name of the Lord his God,
10:20 Jehu said, "C an assembly in honour
1Ch 16: 8 Give thanks to the Lord, c on his
2Ch 24:22 Lord see this and c you to account."
Ne 13: 2 Balaam to c a curse down on them.
Job 5: 1 "C if you will, but who will answer
14:15 You will c and I will answer you;
19: 7 I c for help, there is no justice.
27:10 Will he c upon God at all times?
Ps 4: 1 Answer me when I c to you, O my
4: 3 the Lord will hear when I c to him.
10:13 "He won't c me to account"
10:15 c him to account for his wickedness
14: 4 bread and who do not c on the Lord?
17: 6 I c on you, O God, for you will

Ps 18: 3 I **c** to the LORD, who is worthy of
20: 9 save the king! Answer us when we **c**!
27: 7 Hear my voice when I **c**, O LORD; be
28: 1 To you I **c**, O LORD my Rock; do not
28: 2 Hear my cry for mercy as I **c** to you
50:15 **c** upon me in the day of trouble;
53: 4 eat bread and who do not **c** on God?
55:16 I **c** to God, and the LORD saves me.
56: 9 my enemies will turn back when I **c**
61: 2 From the ends of the earth I **c** to
61: 2 I **c** as my heart grows faint; lead me
65: 8 fades you **c** forth songs of joy.
72:17 him, and they will **c** him blessed.
79: 6 kingdoms that do not **c** on your name;
80:18 us, and we will **c** on your name.
86: 3 for I **c** to you all day long.
86: 5 in love to all who **c** to you.
86: 7 In the day of my trouble I will **c** to
88: 9 I **c** to you, O LORD, every day;
89:26 He will **c** out to me, 'You are my
91:15 He will **c** upon me, and I will answer
102: 2 to me; when I **c**, answer me quickly.
105: 1 Give thanks to the LORD, **c** on his
116: 2 I will **c** on him as long as I live.
116:13 and **c** on the name of the LORD.
116:17 you and **c** on the name of the LORD.
119:145 I **c** with all my heart; answer me, O
119:146 I **c** out to you; save me and I will
120: 1 I **c** on the LORD in my distress, and
141: 1 O LORD, I **c** to you; come quickly to
141: 1 Hear my voice when I **c** to you.
145:18 The LORD is near to all who **c** on him,
145:18 him, to all who **c** on him in truth.
147: 9 for the young ravens when they **c**.
Pr 1:28 "Then they will **c** to me but I will
2: 3 if you **c** out for insight and cry
7: 4 and **c** understanding your kinsman;
8: 1 Does not wisdom **c** out? Does not
8: 4 "To you, O men, I **c** out; I raise my
31:28 Her children arise and **c** her blessed;
Ecc 3:15 and God will **c** the past to account.
Isa 5:20 Woe to those who **c** evil good and
7:14 to a son, and will **c** him Immanuel.
8: 2 I will **c** in Uriah the priest and
8:12 "Do not **c** conspiracy everything that
8:12 that these people **c** conspiracy;
12: 4 "Give thanks to the LORD, **c** on his
30: 7 I **c** her Rahab the Do-Nothing.
44: 5 another will **c** himself by the name
48: 2 you who **c** yourselves citizens of the
54: 6 The LORD will **c** you back as if you
55: 6 be found; **c** on him while he is near.
58: 5 ashes? Is that what you **c** a fast,
58: 9 you will **c**, and the LORD will answer;
58:13 if you **c** the Sabbath a delight and
60:14 and will **c** you the City of the LORD,
60:18 but you will **c** your walls Salvation
62: 4 No longer will they **c** you Deserted,
62: 6 You who **c** on the LORD, give
65: 1 To a nation that did not **c** on my
65:24 Before they **c** I will answer; while
Jer 3:17 At that time they will **c** Jerusalem
3:19 I thought you would **c** me 'Father'
7:27 you **c** to them, they will not answer.
7:32 when people will no longer **c** it
9:17 "Consider now! **C** for the wailing
10:25 peoples who do not **c** on your name.
11:14 I will not listen when they **c** to me
19: 6 when people will no longer **c** this
29:12 you will **c** upon me and come and pray
33: 3 '**C** to me and I will answer you and
Lam 3: 8 Even when I **c** out or cry for help,
3:21 Yet this I **c** to mind and therefore I
Eze 9: 1 I heard him **c** out in a loud voice,
36:29 I will **c** for the corn and make it
39:17 **C** out to every kind of bird and all
Da 5:12 **C** for Daniel, and he will tell you
Hos 1: 4 the LORD said to Hosea, "**C** him
1: 6 Then the LORD said to Hosea, "**C** her
1: 9 the LORD said, "**C** him Lo-Ammi, for
2:16 "you will **c** me 'my husband'; you
2:16 you will no longer **c** me 'my master'.
11: 7 Even if they **c** to the Most High, he
Joel 1:14 Declare a holy fast; **c** a sacred
1:19 To you, O LORD, I **c**, for fire has
2:15 a holy fast, **c** a sacred assembly.
Jnh 1: 6 "How can you sleep? Get up and **c** on
3: 8 Let everyone **c** urgently on God. Let
Hab 1: 2 How long, O LORD, must I **c** for help,
Zep 3: 9 that all of them may **c** on the name
Zec 13: 9 They will **c** on my name and I will
Mal 3:12 "Then all the nations will **c** you
3:15 now we **c** the arrogant blessed.
Mt 1:23 and they will **c** him Immanuel"—which
9:13 to **c** the righteous, but sinners."
20: 8 '**C** the workers and pay them their
23: 7 and to have men **c** them 'Rabbi'.
23: 9 do not **c** anyone on earth 'father',
24: 1 to **c** his attention to its buildings.
24:31 his angels with a loud trumpet **c**,
26:53 Do you think I cannot **c** on my Father,
26:74 he began to **c** down curses on himself
Mk 2:17 to **c** the righteous, but sinners."
3:31 they sent someone in to **c** him.
10:18 "Why do you **c** me good?" Jesus
10:49 Jesus stopped and said, "**C** him." So
14:71 He began to **c** down curses on himself,
15:12 the one you **c** the king of the Jews?"
15:18 they began to **c** out to him, "Hail,
Lk 1:48 all generations will **c** me blessed,
5:32 I have not come to **c** the righteous,
6:46 "Why do you **c** me, 'Lord, Lord,' and
9:54 "Lord, do you want us to **c** fire down
18:19 "Why do you **c** me good?" Jesus
22:25 over them **c** themselves Benefactors.
Jn 4:16 He told her, "Go, **c** your husband and
9:11 He replied, "The man they **c** Jesus
13:13 "You **c** me 'Teacher' and 'Lord', and
15:15 I no longer **c** you servants, because
Ac 2:39 all whom the Lord our God will **c**."
9:14 to arrest all who **c** on your name."
9:21 among those who **c** on this name?
10:15 "Do not **c** anything impure that God
10:28 not **c** any man impure or unclean.
11: 9 'Do not **c** anything impure that God
24:14 of the Way, which they **c** a sect.
Ro 1: 5 apostleship to **c** people from among
2:17 Now you, if you **c** yourself a Jew; if
9:25 he says in Hosea: "I will **c** them 'my
9:25 and I will **c** her 'my loved one'
10:12 and richly blesses all who **c** on him,
10:14 How, then, can they **c** on the one
11:29 for God's gifts and his **c** are
1Co 1: 2 those everywhere who **c** on the name of
14: 8 the trumpet does not sound a clear **c**,
2Co 1:23 I **c** God as my witness that it was in
Eph 2:11 "uncircumcised" by those who **c**
1Th 4: 7 For God did not **c** us to be impure,
4:16 and with the trumpet **c** of God,
2Ti 2:22 **c** on the Lord out of a pure heart.
Heb 2:11 is not ashamed to **c** them brothers.
Jas 5:14 He should **c** the elders of the church
1Pe 1:17 Since you **c** on a Father who judges
3Jn :10 if I come, I will **c** attention to
Rev 8:13 in mid-air **c** out in a loud voice:

Called (Call)

Ge 1: 5 God **c** the light "day", and the
1: 5 and the darkness he **c** "night".
1: 8 God **c** the expanse "sky". And there
1:10 God **c** the dry ground "land", and the
1:10 and the gathered waters he **c** "seas".
2:19 the man **c** each living creature,
2:23 of my flesh; she shall be **c** 'woman',
3: 9 the LORD God **c** to the man, "Where
5: 2 And when they were created, he **c**
11: 9 That is why it was **c** Babel—because
12: 8 LORD and **c** on the name of the LORD.
13: 4 Abram **c** on the name of the LORD.
14:14 he **c** out the 318 trained men born in
16:14 That is why the well was **c** Beer
17: 5 No longer will you be **c** Abram; your
19: 5 They **c** to Lot, "Where are the men
19:22 (That is why the town was **c** Zoar.)
20: 9 Abimelech **c** Abraham in and said,
21:17 and the angel of God **c** to Hagar from
21:31 that place was **c** Beersheba, because
21:33 and there he **c** upon the name of the
22:11 the angel of the LORD **c** out to him
22:14 Abraham **c** that place The LORD Will
22:15 The angel of the LORD **c** to Abraham
Ge 24:58 they **c** Rebekah and asked her, "Will
25:30 (That is why he was also **c** Edom.
26:25 Isaac built an altar there and **c** on
26:33 He **c** it Shibah, and to this day the
27: 1 he **c** for Esau his older son and said
28: 1 Isaac **c** for Jacob and blessed him
28:19 He **c** that place Bethel, though the
28:19 though the city used to be **c** Luz.
31:47 Laban **c** it Jegar Sahadutha, and
31:47 Sahadutha, and Jacob **c** it Galeed.
31:48 That is why it was **c** Galeed.
31:49 was also **c** Mizpah, because he said,
32:30 Jacob **c** the place Peniel, saying,
33:17 That is why the place is **c** Succoth.
33:20 altar and **c** it El Elohe Israel.
35: 7 and he **c** the place El Bethel,
35:10 you will no longer be **c** Jacob;
35:15 Jacob **c** the place where God had
39:14 she **c** her household servants. "Look,"
47:29 he **c** for his son Joseph and said to
48:16 May they be **c** by my name and the
49: 1 Jacob **c** for his sons and said:
50:11 near the Jordan is **c** Abel Mizraim.
Ex 3: 4 God **c** to him from within the bush,
15:23 (That is why the place is **c** Marah.)
16:31 The people of Israel **c** the bread
17: 7 he **c** the place Massah and Meribah
17:15 and **c** it The LORD is my Banner.
19: 3 Moses went up to God, and the LORD **c**
19:20 **c** Moses to the top of the mountain.
24:16 **c** to Moses from within the cloud.
34:31 Moses **c** to them; so Aaron and all
Lev 1: 1 The LORD **c** to Moses and spoke to him
Nu 1:18 they **c** the whole community together
11: 3 that place was **c** Taberah, because
13:24 That place was **c** the Valley of
32:41 settlements and **c** them Havvoth Jair.
32:42 and **c** it Nobah after himself.
Dt 2:11 but the Moabites **c** them Emites.
2:20 the Ammonites **c** them Zamzummites.
3: 9 (Hermon is **c** Sirion by the Sidonians;
3:14 this day Bashan is **c** Havvoth Jair.)
28:10 you are **c** by the name of the LORD,
Jos 3:16 at a town **c** Adam in the vicinity of
4: 4 Joshua **c** together the twelve men he
5: 9 place has been **c** Gilgal to this day.
6: 6 Joshua son of Nun **c** the priests and
7:26 **c** the Valley of Achor ever since.
8:16 All the men of Ai were **c** to pursue
14:15 (Hebron used to be **c** Kiriath Arba
15:15 Debir (formerly **c** Kiriath Sepher).
Jdg 1:10 Hebron (formerly **c** Kiriath Arba)
1:11 Debir (formerly **c** Kiriath Sepher).
1:17 Therefore it was **c** Hormah.
1:23 to spy out Bethel (formerly **c** Luz),
1:26 where he built a city and **c** it Luz,
2: 5 they **c** that place Bokim. There they
6:24 there and **c** it The LORD is Peace.
6:32 that day they **c** Gideon "Jerub-Baal,"
7:15 to the camp of Israel and **c** out,
7:23 Asher and all Manasseh were **c** out,
7:24 So all the men of Ephraim were **c**
9:54 Hurriedly he **c** to his armour-bearer,
10: 4 to this day are **c** Havvoth Jair.
10:17 the Ammonites were **c** to arms and
12: 1 The men of Ephraim **c** out their
12: 2 and although I **c**, you didn't save me
12: 4 Jephthah then **c** together the men of
15:17 and the place was **c** Ramath Lehi.
15:19 So the spring was **c** En Hakkore, and
16: 9 With men hidden in the room, she **c**
16:12 with men hidden in the room, she **c**
16:14 Again she **c** to him, "Samson, the
16:19 she **c** a man to shave off the seven
16:20 she **c**, "Samson, the Philistines are
16:25 So they **c** Samson out of the prison,
18:12 Jearim is **c** Mahaneh Dan to this day.
18:22 **c** together and overtook the Danites.
18:23 that you **c** out your men to fight?"
18:29 the city used to be **c** Laish.
Ru 2: 4 "The LORD bless you!" they **c** back.
1Sa 1: 2 He had two wives; one was **c** Hannah
3: 4 the LORD **c** Samuel. Samuel answered,
3: 5 Eli and said, "Here I am; you **c** me.
3: 6 Again the LORD **c**, "Samuel!" And
3: 6 Eli and said, "Here I am; you **c** me.

1Sa 3: 8 The LORD **c** Samuel a third time, and
3: 8 Eli and said, "Here I am; you **c** me.
3:16 Eli **c** him and said, "Samuel, my son."
5: 8 they **c** together all the rulers of
5:11 they **c** together all the rulers of
6: 2 the Philistines **c** for the priests
9: 9 of today used to be **c** a seer.)
9:26 and Samuel **c** to Saul on the roof,
12:18 Samuel **c** upon the LORD, and that
14: 4 was **c** Bozez, and the other Seneh.
16: 8 Jesse **c** Abinadab and made him pass
19: 7 Jonathan **c** David and told him the
20:37 Jonathan **c** out after him, "Isn't the
23: 8 Saul **c** up all his forces for battle,
24: 8 David went out of the cave and **c** out
26:14 He **c** out to the army and to Abner
28:15 **c** on you to tell me what to do."
29: 6 Achish **c** David and said to him, "As
2Sa 1: 7 he turned round and saw me, he **c** out
1:15 David **c** one of his men and said, "Go,
2:16 in Gibeon was **c** Helkath Hazzurim.
2:26 Abner **c** out to Joab, "Must the sword
5: 9 fortress and **c** it the City of David.
5:20 So that place was **c** Baal Perazim.
6: 2 which is **c** by the Name, the name of
6: 8 day that place is **c** Perez Uzzah.
9: 2 They **c** him to appear before David,
13:17 He **c** his personal servant and said,
18:18 is **c** Absalom's Monument to this day.
18:25 The watchman **c** out to the king and
18:26 and he **c** down to the gatekeeper,
18:28 Ahimaaz **c** out to the king, "All is
20:16 a wise woman **c** from the city,
22: 7 In my distress I **c** to the LORD; I **c**
1Ki 2: 8 the Benjamite from Bahurim, who **c**
9:13 And he **c** them the Land of Cabul, a
12:20 they sent and **c** him to the assembly
17:10 He **c** to her and asked, "Would you
17:11 she was going to get it, he **c**, "And
18:26 Then they **c** on the name of Baal from
20:39 the king passed by, the prophet **c**
22: 9 the king of Israel **c** one of his
2Ki 2:24 He turned round, looked at them and **c**
3:10 "Has the LORD **c** us three kings
3:13 "because it was the LORD who **c** us
3:21 **c** up and stationed on the border.
4:12 he **c** her, and she stood before him.
4:15 Elisha said, "Call her." So he **c** her,
4:22 She **c** her husband and said, "Please
7:10 they went and **c** out to the city
9:17 he **c** out, "I see some troops coming.
9:32 He looked up at the window and **c** out,
11:14 tore her robes and **c** out, "Treason!
18: 4 (It was **c** Nehushtan.)
18:18 They **c** for the king; and Eliakim son
18:28 the commander stood and **c** out in
20:11 the prophet Isaiah **c** upon the LORD,
23: 1 the king **c** together all the elders
1Ch 4:14 It was **c** this because its people
9:23 of the LORD—the house **c** the Tent.
11: 7 and so it was **c** the City of David.
13: 6 ark that is **c** by the Name.
13:11 day that place is **c** Perez Uzzah.
14:11 So that place was **c** Baal Perazim.
15: 4 He **c** together the descendants of
21:26 He **c** on the LORD, and the LORD
22: 6 he **c** for his son Solomon and charged
2Ch 7:14 if my people, who are **c** by my name,
14:11 Asa **c** to the LORD his God and said,
18: 8 the king of Israel **c** one of his
20:26 **c** the Valley of Beracah to this day.
24: 5 He **c** together the priests and
25: 5 Amaziah **c** the people of Judah
32:18 they **c** out in Hebrew to the people
34:29 the king **c** together all the elders
Ezr 2:61 Gileadite and was **c** by that name).
Ne 5: 7 So I **c** together a large meeting to
7:63 Gileadite and was **c** by that name).
9: 4 Sherebiah, Bani and Kenani—who **c**
13:11 neglected?" Then I **c** them together
13:25 I rebuked them and **c** curses down on
Est 4:11 since I was **c** to go to the king."
9:26 (Therefore these days were **c** Purim,
Job 12: 4 though I **c** upon God and he answered—
31:14 What will I answer when **c** to account?
Ps 18: 6 In my distress I **c** to the LORD; I
Ps 30: 2 O LORD my God, I **c** to you for help
30: 8 To you, O LORD, I **c**; to the Lord I
31:22 for mercy when I **c** to you for help.
34: 6 This poor man **c**, and the LORD heard
81: 7 In your distress you **c** and I rescued
99: 6 Samuel was among those who **c** on his
99: 6 **c** on the LORD and he answered them.
105:16 He **c** down famine on the land and
116: 4 I **c** on the name of the LORD:
138: 3 I **c**, you answered me; you made me
Pr 1:24 since you rejected me when I **c** and
16:21 The wise in heart are **c** discerning,
SS 5: 6 I **c** him but he did not answer.
6: 9 The maidens saw her and **c** her
Isa 1:26 Afterwards you will be **c** the City of
4: 1 only let us be **c** by your name.
4: 3 who remain in Jerusalem, will be **c**
9: 6 And he will be **c** Wonderful
19:18 will be **c** the City of Destruction.
22:12 The Lord, the LORD Almighty, **c** you
31: 4 shepherds is **c** together against him,
32: 5 No longer will the fool be **c** noble
34:12 nothing there to be **c** a kingdom,
35: 8 it will be **c** the Way of Holiness.
36:13 the commander stood and **c** out in
41: 9 from its farthest corners I **c** you.
42: 6 "I, the LORD, have **c** you in
43: 7 everyone who is **c** by my name, whom I
43:22 "Yet you have not **c** upon me,
47: 1 will you be **c** tender or delicate.
47: 5 will you be **c** queen of kingdoms.
48: 1 you who are **c** by the name of Israel
48: 8 are; you were **c** a rebel from birth.
48:12 O Jacob, Israel, whom I have **c**: I am
48:15 I, have spoken; yes, I have **c** him.
49: 1 Before I was born the LORD **c** me;
50: 2 When I **c**, why was there no-one to
51: 2 When I **c** him he was but one, and I
54: 5 he is **c** the God of all the earth.
56: 7 **c** a house of prayer for all nations."
58:12 will be **c** Repairer of Broken Walls,
61: 3 They will be **c** oaks of righteousness,
61: 6 you will be **c** priests of the LORD,
62: 2 you will be **c** by a new name that the
62: 4 But you will be **c** Hephzibah, and
62:12 They will be **c** the Holy People, the
62:12 LORD; and you will be **c** Sought After,
63:19 they have not been **c** by your name.
65:12 for I **c** but you did not answer,
66: 4 For when I **c**, no-one answered, when
Jer 3: 4 Have you not just **c** to me: 'My
6:30 They are **c** rejected silver, because
7:13 I **c** you, but you did not answer.
11:16 The LORD **c** you a thriving olive tree
23: 6 be **c**: The LORD Our Righteousness.
30:17 'because you are **c** an outcast, Zion
33:16 be **c**: The LORD Our Righteousness.'
35:17 **c** to them, but they did not answer.'"
36: 4 Jeremiah **c** Baruch son of Neriah, and
42: 8 he **c** together Johanan son of Kareah
Lam 1:19 "I **c** to my allies but they betrayed
2:15 "Is this the city that was **c** the
3:55 I **c** on your name, O LORD, from the
3:57 You came near when I **c** you, and you
Eze 9: 3 Then the LORD **c** to the man clothed
10:13 I heard the wheels being **c** "the
20:29 go to?'" (It is **c** Bamah to this day.
38: 8 After many days you will be **c** to
39:11 will be **c** the Valley of Hamon Gog.
39:16 (Also a town **c** Hamonah will be there.
Da 2:26 asked Daniel (also **c** Belteshazzar),
4: 8 (He is **c** Belteshazzar, after the
4:14 He **c** in a loud voice: 'Cut down the
4:19 Daniel (also **c** Belteshazzar) was
5: 7 The king **c** out for the enchanters,
5:12 This man Daniel, whom the king **c**
6:20 he came near the den, he **c** to Daniel
10: 1 to Daniel (who was **c** Belteshazzar).
Hos 1:10 will be **c** 'sons of the living God'.
2:23 to the one I **c** 'Not my loved one'.
2:23 I will say to those **c** 'Not my people'
11: 1 him, and out of Egypt I **c** my son.
11: 2 the more I **c** Israel, the further
Jnh 2: 2 He said: "In my distress I **c** to the
2: 2 From the depths of the grave I **c** for
Hab 3: 9 your bow, you **c** for many arrows.
Hag 1:11 I **c** for a drought on the fields and
Zec 6: 8 he **c** to me, "Look, those going
7:13 "'When I **c**, they did not listen; so
7:13 so when they **c**, I would not listen,'
8: 3 Jerusalem will be **c** the City of Truth
8: 3 will be **c** the Holy Mountain."
11: 7 Then I took two staffs and **c** one
11:10 I took my staff **c** Favour and broke
11:14 I broke my second staff **c** Union,
Mal 1: 4 They will be **c** the Wicked Land, a
2: 5 this **c** for reverence and he revered
Mt 1:16 was born Jesus, who is **c** Christ.
2: 4 he had **c** together all the people's
2: 7 Herod **c** the Magi secretly and found
2:15 prophet: "Out of Egypt I **c** my son.
2:23 went and lived in a town **c** Nazareth
2:23 prophets: "He will be **c** a Nazarene.
4:18 Simon **c** Peter and his brother Andrew.
4:21 their nets. Jesus **c** them,
5: 9 for they will be **c** sons of God.
5:19 be **c** least in the kingdom of heaven,
5:19 be **c** great in the kingdom of heaven.
10: 1 He **c** his twelve disciples to him and
10: 2 Simon (who is **c** Peter) and his
10:25 If the head of the house has been **c**
15:10 Jesus **c** the crowd to him and said,
15:32 Jesus **c** his disciples to him and
18: 2 He **c** a little child and had him
18:32 "Then the master **c** the servant in.
20:25 Jesus **c** them together and said, "You
20:32 Jesus stopped and **c** them. "What do
21:13 "'My house will be **c** a house of
23: 8 "But you are not to be **c** 'Rabbi',
23:10 Nor are you to be **c** 'teacher', for
25:14 who **c** his servants and entrusted his
26:14 one of the Twelve—the one **c** Judas
26:36 disciples to a place **c** Gethsemane,
27: 8 That is why it has been **c** the Field
27:16 a notorious prisoner, **c** Barabbas.
27:17 Barabbas, or Jesus who is **c** Christ?"
27:22 Jesus who is **c** Christ?" Pilate asked.
27:33 They came to a place **c** Golgotha
Mk 1:20 Without delay he **c** them, and they
3:13 Jesus went up on a mountainside and **c**
3:23 Jesus **c** them and spoke to them in
7:14 Again Jesus **c** the crowd to him and
8: 1 **c** his disciples to him and said,
8:34 he **c** the crowd to him along with his
9:35 Sitting down, Jesus **c** the Twelve and
10:42 Jesus **c** them together and said, "You
10:49 So they **c** to the blind man, "Cheer
11:17 "'My house will be **c** a house of
14:32 They went to a place **c** Gethsemane,
15: 7 A man **c** Barabbas was in prison with
15:16 and **c** together the whole company of
15:22 Jesus to the place **c** Golgotha
Lk 1:32 He will be great and will be **c** the
1:35 to be born will be **c** the Son of God.
1:60 and said, "No! He is to be **c** John.
1:76 you, my child, will be **c** a prophet
2:25 was a man in Jerusalem **c** Simeon
6:13 morning came, he **c** his disciples to
6:15 Alphaeus, Simon who was **c** the Zealot,
7:11 Jesus went to a town **c** Nain, and his
8: 2 Mary (**c** Magdalene) from whom seven
8: 8 When he said this, he **c** out, "He
9: 1 Jesus had **c** the Twelve together, he
9:10 by themselves to a town **c** Bethsaida,
9:38 A man in the crowd **c** out, "Teacher,
10:39 She had a sister **c** Mary, who sat at
11:27 a woman in the crowd **c** out, "Blessed
13:12 Jesus saw her, he **c** her forward and
15:19 no longer worthy to be **c** your son;
15:21 no longer worthy to be **c** your son.'
15:26 he **c** one of the servants and asked
16: 2 he **c** him in and asked him, 'What is
16: 5 "So he **c** in each one of his master's
16:24 he **c** to him, 'Father Abraham, have
17:13 **c** out in a loud voice, "Jesus,
18:16 Jesus **c** the children to him and said,
18:38 He **c** out, "Jesus, Son of David, have
19:13 he **c** ten of his servants and gave
19:29 at the hill **c** the Mount of Olives,
21:37 on the hill **c** the Mount of Olives,
22: 1 of Unleavened Bread, **c** the Passover
22: 3 Satan entered Judas, **c** Iscariot, one

Lk 22:47 and the man who was **c** Judas, one of
23:13 Pilate **c** together the chief priests,
23:33 they came to the place **c** the Skull,
23:46 Jesus **c** out with a loud voice,
24:13 were going to a village **c** Emmaus,
Jn 1:42 You will be **c** Cephas" (which, when
1:48 the fig-tree before Philip **c** you."
2: 9 Then he **c** the bridegroom aside
4: 5 came to a town in Samaria **c** Sychar,
4:25 that Messiah" (**c** Christ) "is coming.
5: 2 which in Aramaic is **c** Bethesda and
10:35 If he **c** them 'gods', to whom the
11:16 Thomas (**c** Didymus) said to the rest
11:28 back and **c** her sister Mary aside.
11:43 Jesus **c** in a loud voice, "Lazarus,
11:47 the chief priests and the Pharisees **c**
11:54 to a village **c** Ephraim, where he
12:17 him when he **c** Lazarus from the tomb
15:15 Instead, I have **c** you friends, for
19:17 (which in Aramaic is **c** Golgotha).
20:24 Now Thomas (**c** Didymus), one of the
21: 2 Simon Peter, Thomas (**c** Didymus),
21: 5 He **c** out to them, "Friends, haven't
Ac 1:12 from the hill **c** the Mount of Olives,
1:19 so they **c** that field in their
1:23 Joseph **c** Barsabbas, (also known as
3: 2 to the temple gate **c** Beautiful,
3:10 at the temple gate **c** Beautiful,
3:11 in the place **c** Solomon's Colonnade.
4: 9 If we are being **c** to account today
4:18 they **c** them in again and commanded
4:36 whom the apostles **c** Barnabas (which
5:21 they **c** together the Sanhedrin—the
5:40 They **c** the apostles in and had them
6: 9 of the Freedmen (as it was **c**)
9:10 The Lord **c** to him in a vision,
9:41 Then he **c** the believers and the
10: 5 a man named Simon who is **c** Peter.
10: 7 Cornelius **c** two of his servants and
10:18 They **c** out, asking if Simon who was
10:24 had **c** together his relatives and
10:32 to Joppa for Simon who is **c** Peter.
11:13 to Joppa for Simon who is **c** Peter.
11:26 were **c** Christians first at Antioch.
12:12 John, also **c** Mark, where many people
12:25 taking with them John, also **c** Mark.
13: 1 Simeon **c** Niger, Lucius of Cyrene,
13: 2 the work to which I have **c** them."
13: 9 Saul, who was also **c** Paul, filled
14:10 and **c** out, "Stand up on your feet!"
14:12 Barnabas they **c** Zeus, and Paul they **c**
15:22 They chose Judas (**c** Barsabbas) and
15:37 Barnabas wanted to take John, also **c**
16:10 **c** us to preach the gospel to them.
16:29 The jailer **c** for lights, rushed in
17: 7 there is another king, one **c** Jesus."
19:25 He **c** them together, along with the
23: 6 **c** out in the Sanhedrin, "My brothers,
23:17 Paul **c** one of the centurions and
23:23 he **c** two of his centurions and
24: 2 Paul was **c** in, Tertullus presented
27: 8 and came to a place **c** Fair Havens,
27:14 a wind of hurricane force, **c** the
27:16 the lee of a small island **c** Cauda,
28: 1 out that the island was **c** Malta.
28:17 Three days later he **c** together the
Ro 1: 1 Paul, a servant of Christ Jesus, **c**
1: 6 you also are among those who are **c**
1: 7 are loved by God and **c** to be saints:
7: 3 still alive, she is **c** an adulteress.
8:28 been **c** according to his purpose.
8:30 those he predestined, he also **c**;
8:30 those he **c**, he also justified;
9:24 even us, whom he also **c**, not only
9:26 will be **c** 'sons of the living God'."
1Co 1: 1 Paul, **c** to be an apostle of Christ
1: 2 in Christ Jesus and **c** to be holy,
1: 9 God, who has **c** you into fellowship
1:24 to those whom God has **c**, both Jews
1:26 of what you were when you were **c**.
7:15 God has **c** us to live in peace.
7:17 to him and to which God has **c** him.
7:18 already circumcised when he was **c**?
7:18 a man uncircumcised when he was **c**?
7:20 which he was in when God **c** him.
7:21 Were you a slave when you were **c**?
1Co 7:22 For he who was a slave when he was **c**
7:22 man when he was **c** is Christ's slave.
7:24 in the situation God **c** him to.
15: 9 not even deserve to be **c** an apostle,
Gal 1: 6 who **c** you by the grace of Christ
1:15 and **c** me by his grace, was pleased
5:13 You, my brothers, were **c** to be free.
Eph 1:18 know the hope to which he has **c** you,
2:11 by birth and **c** "uncircumcised"
4: 4 were **c** to one hope when you were **c**—
Php 3:14 **c** me heavenwards in Christ Jesus.
Col 3:15 of one body you were **c** to peace.
4:11 Jesus, who is **c** Justus, also sends
2Th 2: 4 that is **c** God or is worshipped,
2:14 He **c** you to this through our gospel,
1Ti 6:12 the eternal life to which you were **c**
6:20 of what is falsely **c** knowledge,
2Ti 1: 9 who has saved us and **c** us to a holy
Heb 3:13 as long as it is **c** Today, so that
5: 4 must be **c** by God, just as Aaron was.
9: 2 bread; this was **c** the Holy Place.
9: 3 was a room **c** the Most Holy Place,
9:15 that those who are **c** may receive the
11: 8 By faith Abraham, when **c** to go to a
11:16 Therefore God is not ashamed to be **c**
Jas 2:23 and he was **c** God's friend.
1Pe 1:15 just as he who **c** you is holy, so be
2: 9 declare the praises of him who **c** you
2:21 To this you were **c**, because Christ
3: 6 like Sarah, who obeyed Abraham and **c**
3: 9 **c** so that you may inherit a blessing.
5:10 the God of all grace, who **c** you to
2Pe 1: 3 **c** us by his own glory and goodness.
1Jn 3: 1 that we should be **c** children of God!
Jude : 1 To those who have been **c**, who are
Rev 6:10 They **c** out in a loud voice, "How
6:16 They **c** to the mountains and the
7: 2 He **c** out in a loud voice to the four
11: 8 which is figuratively **c** Sodom and
12: 9 ancient serpent **c** the devil,
14:15 **c** in a loud voice to him who was
14:18 came from the altar and **c** in a loud
16:16 that in Hebrew is **c** Armageddon.
17:14 **c**, chosen and faithful followers."
19:11 whose rider is **c** Faithful and True.

Calling (Call)

Ex 33: 7 away, **c** it the "tent of meeting".
Nu 10: 2 and use them for **c** the community
Jdg 6:35 **c** them to arms, and also into Asher,
12: 1 without **c** us to go with you?
1Sa 3: 8 that the LORD was **c** the boy.
3:10 **c** as at the other times, "Samuel!
1Ki 16:24 **c** it Samaria, after Shemer, the name
2Ki 9:23 Joram turned about and fled, **c** out
14: 7 **c** it Joktheel, the name it has to
2Ch 30: 5 from Beersheba to Dan, **c** the people
Est 5:10 **C** together his friends and Zeresh,
Ps 69: 3 I am worn out **c** for help; my throat
Pr 9:15 **c** out to those who pass by, who go
Isa 6: 3 they were **c** to one another: "Holy,
40: 3 A voice of one **c**: "In the desert
41: 2 **c** him in righteousness to his
41: 4 **c** forth the generations from the
Jer 25:29 for I am **c** down a sword upon all who
Da 8:16 I heard a man's voice from the Ulai **c**
Hos 7:11 **c** to Egypt, now turning to Assyria.
Am 7: 4 The Sovereign LORD was **c** for
Mic 6: 9 Listen! The LORD is **c** to the city—
Mt 3: 3 "A voice of one **c** in the desert,
9:27 two blind men followed him, **c** out,
11:16 market-places and **c** out to others:
27:47 this, they said, "He's **c** Elijah.
Mk 1: 3 "a voice of one **c** in the desert,
6: 7 **C** the Twelve to him, he sent them
10:49 "Cheer up! On your feet! He's **c** you.
12:43 **C** his disciples to him, Jesus said,
15:35 they said, "Listen, he's **c** Elijah.
Lk 3: 4 "A voice of one **c** in the desert,
7:18 all these things. **C** two of them,
7:32 and **c** out to each other:
Jn 1:23 "I am the voice of one **c** in the
5:18 but he was even **c** God his own Father,
Ac 22:16 wash your sins away, **c** on his name.'
Eph 4: 1 worthy of the **c** you have received.
2Th 1:11 God may count you worthy of his **c**,
Heb 3: 1 who share in the heavenly **c**, fix
4: 7 **c** it Today, when a long time later
8:13 By **c** this covenant "new", he has
2Pe 1:10 to make your **c** and election sure.

Callous (Calloused)

Ps 17:10 They close up their **c** hearts, and
73: 7 From their **c** hearts comes iniquity;
119:70 Their hearts are **c** and unfeeling,

Calloused (Callous)

Isa 6:10 Make the heart of this people **c**;
Mt 13:15 For this people's heart has become **c**;
Ac 28:27 For this people's heart has become **c**;

Calls (Call)

Ge 46:33 Pharaoh **c** you in and asks, 'What is
1Sa 3: 9 "Go and lie down, and if he **c** you,
26:14 "Who are you who **c** to the king?
Ps 42: 7 Deep **c** to deep in the roar of your
147: 4 the stars and **c** them each by name.
Pr 1:20 Wisdom **c** aloud in the street, she
9: 3 She has sent out her maids, and she **c**
Isa 21:11 Someone **c** to me from Seir,
40:26 one by one, and **c** them each by name.
41:25 the rising sun who **c** on my name.
59: 4 No-one **c** for justice; no-one pleads
64: 7 No-one **c** on your name or strives to
Hos 7: 7 fall, and none of them **c** on me.
Joel 2:32 everyone who **c** on the name of the
2:32 among the survivors whom the LORD **c**.
Am 5: 8 who **c** for the waters of the sea and
9: 6 who **c** for the waters of the sea and
Zep 2:14 Their **c** will echo through the
Mt 22:43 Spirit, **c** him 'Lord'? For he says,
22:45 If then David **c** him 'Lord', how can
Mk 12:37 David himself **c** him 'Lord'. How then
Lk 15: 6 goes home. Then he **c** his friends and
15: 9 she finds it, she **c** her friends and
20:37 for he **c** the Lord 'the God of
20:44 David **c** him 'Lord'. How then can he
Jn 10: 3 He **c** his own sheep by name and leads
Ac 2:21 everyone who **c** on the name of the
Ro 4:17 **c** things that are not as though they
9:12 not by works but by him who **c**—she
10:13 for, "Everyone who **c** on the name of
1Co 5:11 associate with anyone who **c** himself
Gal 4: 6 Spirit who **c** out, "Abba, Father.
5: 8 not come from the one who **c** you.
1Th 2:12 **c** you into his kingdom and glory.
5:24 The one who **c** you is faithful and he
Rev 2:20 Jezebel, who **c** herself a prophetess.
13:10 This **c** for patient endurance and
13:18 This **c** for wisdom. If anyone has
14:12 This **c** for patient endurance on the
17: 9 "This **c** for a mind with wisdom. The

Calm (Calmed, Calmness, Calms)

Ps 107:30 They were glad when it grew **c**, and
Isa 7: 4 Say to him, 'Be careful, keep **c** and
Eze 16:42 I will be **c** and no longer angry.
Jnh 1:11 you to make the sea **c** down for us?"
1:12 he replied, "and it will become **c**.
1:15 and the raging sea grew **c**.
Mt 8:26 the waves, and it was completely **c**.
Mk 4:39 died down and it was completely **c**.
Lk 8:24 the storm subsided, and all was **c**.

Calmed (Calm)

Ne 8:11 The Levites **c** all the people, saying,

Calmness (Calm)

Ecc 10: 4 **c** can lay great errors to rest.

Calms (Calm)

Pr 15:18 but a patient man **c** a quarrel.

Calneh

Ge 10:10 Erech, Akkad and **C**, in Shinar.
Am 6: 2 Go to **C** and look at it; go from

Calno

Isa 10: 9 'Has not **C** fared like Carchemish?

Calve (Calf)
Job 21:10 their cows **c** and do not miscarry.

Calved (Calf)
1Sa 6: 7 have **c** and have never been yoked.

Calves (Calf)
Dt 7:13 the **c** of your herds and the lambs of
28: 4 the young of your livestock—the **c**
28:18 and the **c** of your herds and the
28:51 new wine or oil, nor any **c** of your
1Sa 6: 7 take their **c** away and pen them up.
6:10 to the cart and penned up their **c**.
14:32 taking sheep, cattle and **c**, they
15: 9 the fat **c** and lambs—everything that
1Ki 1: 9 cattle and fattened **c** at the Stone
1:19 fattened **c**, and sheep, and has
1:25 of cattle, fattened **c**, and sheep.
12:28 advice, the king made two golden **c**.
12:32 sacrificing to the **c** he had made.
2Ki 10:29 of the golden **c** at Bethel and Dan.
17:16 two idols cast in the shape of **c**,
2Ch 13: 8 **c** that Jeroboam made to be your gods.
Ps 68:30 of bulls among the **c** of the nations.
Isa 27:10 like the desert; there the **c** graze,
34: 7 the bull **c** and the great bulls.
Jer 46:21 in her ranks are like fattened **c**.
Am 6: 4 dine on choice lambs and fattened **c**.
Mic 6: 6 burnt offerings, with **c** a year old?
Mal 4: 2 leap like **c** released from the stall.
Heb 9:12 means of the blood of goats and **c**;
9:19 he took the blood of **c**, together

Camel (Camel's, Camel-loads, Camels, Camels', She-camel)
Ge 24:64 saw Isaac. She got down from her **c**
Lev 11: 4 The **c**, though it chews the cud, does
Dt 14: 7 eat the **c**, the rabbit or the coney.
Mt 19:24 it is easier for a **c** to go through
23:24 strain out a gnat but swallow a **c**.
Mk 10:25 is easier for a **c** to go through the
Lk 18:25 Indeed, it is easier for a **c** to go

Camel's (Camel)
Ge 31:34 **c** saddle and was sitting on them.
Mt 3: 4 John's clothes were made of **c** hair,
Mk 1: 6 John wore clothing made of **c** hair,

Camel-loads (Camel, Load)
2Ki 8: 9 taking with him as a gift forty **c** of

Camels (Camel)
Ge 12:16 menservants and maidservants, and **c**.
24:10 took ten of his master's **c** and left,
24:11 He made the **c** kneel down near the
24:14 'Drink, and I'll water your **c**
24:19 "I'll draw water for your **c** too,
24:20 and drew enough for all his **c**.
24:22 the **c** had finished drinking, the man
24:30 standing by the **c** near the spring.
24:31 the house and a place for the **c**."
24:32 the house, and the **c** were unloaded.
24:32 and fodder were brought for the **c**,
24:35 and maidservants, and **c** and donkeys.
24:44 and I'll draw water for your **c** too,"
24:46 'Drink, and I'll water your **c** too.
24:46 I drank, and she watered the **c** also.
24:61 mounted their **c** and went back with
24:63 he looked up, he saw **c** approaching.
30:43 and menservants, and **c** and donkeys.
31:17 put his children and his wives on **c**,
32: 7 the flocks and herds and **c** as well.
32:15 thirty female **c** with their young,
37:25 Their **c** were loaded with spices,
Ex 9: 3 donkeys and **c** and on your cattle and
Jdg 6: 5 to count the men and their **c**;
7:12 Their **c** could no more be counted
1Sa 15: 3 cattle and sheep, **c** and donkeys.'"
27: 9 cattle, donkeys and **c**, and clothes.
30:17 men who rode off on **c** and fled.
1Ki 10: 2 caravan—with **c** carrying spices,
1Ch 5:21 of the Hagrites—fifty thousand **c**,
12:40 food on donkeys, **c**, mules and oxen.
27:30 Ishmaelite was in charge of the **c**.
2Ch 9: 1 caravan—with **c** carrying spices,
14:15 off droves of sheep and goats and **c**.
Ezr 2:67 435 **c** and 6,720 donkeys.
Ne 7:69 435 **c** and 6,720 donkeys.
Job 1: 3 three thousand **c**, five hundred yoke
1:17 down on your **c** and carried them off.
42:12 six thousand **c**, a thousand yoke of
Isa 21: 7 riders on donkeys or riders on **c**,
30: 6 their treasures on the humps of **c**,
60: 6 Herds of **c** will cover your land,
60: 6 land, young **c** of Midian and Ephah.
66:20 and on mules and **c**," says the LORD.
Jer 49:29 off with all their goods and **c**.
49:32 Their **c** will become plunder, and
Eze 25: 5 turn Rabbah into a pasture for **c**
Zec 14:15 the **c** and donkeys, and all the

Camels' (Camel)
Jdg 8:21 the ornaments off their **c** necks.
8:26 chains that were on their **c** necks.

Camp (Camped, Campfires, Camping, Camps, Encamp, Encamped, Encamps)
Ge 32: 2 "This is the **c** of God!" So he named
32:21 he himself spent the night in the **c**.
Ex 14: 2 to turn back and **c** near Pi Hahiroth,
14: 2 They are to **c** by the sea, directly
16:13 quail came and covered the **c**, and in
16:13 was a layer of dew around the **c**.
19:16 Everyone in the **c** trembled.
19:17 Moses led the people out of the **c** to
29:14 hide and its offal outside the **c**.
32:17 "There is the sound of war in the **c**.
32:19 Moses approached the **c** and saw the
32:26 he stood at the entrance to the **c**
32:27 Go back and forth through the **c** from
33: 7 it outside the **c** some distance away,
33: 7 the tent of meeting outside the **c**.
33:11 Then Moses would return to the **c**,
36: 6 sent this word throughout the **c**:
Lev 4:12 the **c** to a place ceremonially clean,
4:21 he shall take the bull outside the **c**
6:11 and carry the ashes outside the **c** to
8:17 its offal he burned up outside the **c**,
9:11 the hide he burned up outside the **c**.
10: 4 carry your cousins outside the **c**,
10: 5 outside the **c**, as Moses ordered.
13:46 alone; he must live outside the **c**.
14: 3 The priest is to go outside the **c**
14: 8 After this he may come into the **c**,
16:26 afterwards he may come into the **c**.
16:27 must be taken outside the **c**; their
16:28 afterwards he may come into the **c**.
17: 3 or a goat in the **c** or outside of
24:10 the **c** between him and an Israelite.
24:14 "Take the blasphemer outside the **c**.
24:23 outside the **c** and stoned him.
Nu 1:52 in his own **c** under his own standard.
2: 2 "The Israelites are to **c** round the
2: 3 the divisions of the **c** of Judah are
2: 5 The tribe of Issachar will **c** next to
2: 9 All the men assigned to the **c** of
2:10 **c** of Reuben under their standard.
2:12 The tribe of Simeon will **c** next to
2:16 All the men assigned to the **c** of
2:17 the Tent of Meeting and the **c** of the
2:18 **c** of Ephraim under their standard.
2:24 All the men assigned to the **c** of
2:25 the **c** of Dan, under their standard.
2:27 The tribe of Asher will **c** next to
2:31 All the men assigned to the **c** of Dan
3:23 The Gershonite clans were to **c** on
3:29 The Kohathite clans were to **c** on the
3:35 they were to **c** on the north side of
3:38 to **c** to the east of the tabernacle,
4: 5 the **c** is to move, Aaron and his sons
4:15 and when the **c** is ready to move, the
5: 2 send away from the **c** anyone who has
5: 3 send them outside the **c** so that they
5: 3 their **c**, where I dwell among them."
5: 4 this; they sent them outside the **c**.
9:18 the tabernacle, they remained in **c**.
9:22 the Israelites would remain in **c** and
10:14 The divisions of the **c** of Judah went
Nu 10:18 The divisions of the **c** of Reuben
10:22 The divisions of the **c** of Ephraim
10:25 the divisions of the **c** of Dan set
10:31 You know where we should **c** in the
10:34 by day when they set out from the **c**.
11: 1 some of the outskirts of the **c**.
11: 9 the dew settled on the **c** at night,
11:26 and Medad, had remained in the **c**.
11:26 them, and they prophesied in the **c**.
11:27 and Medad are prophesying in the **c**."
11:30 elders of Israel returned to the **c**.
11:31 It brought them down all around the **c**
11:32 spread them out all around the **c**.
12:14 her outside the **c** for seven days;
12:15 Miriam was confined outside the **c**
14:44 LORD's covenant moved from the **c**.
15:35 must stone him outside the **c**."
15:36 the assembly took him outside the **c**
19: 3 it is to be taken outside the **c** and
19: 7 He may then come into the **c**, but he
19: 9 clean place outside the **c**. They shall
31:12 at their **c** on the plains of Moab,
31:13 went to meet them outside the **c**.
31:19 must stay outside the **c** seven days.
31:24 Then you may come into the **c**."
Dt 1: 7 Break **c** and advance into the hill
1:33 to search out places for you to **c**
2:14 fighting men had perished from the **c**,
2:15 eliminated them from the **c**.
23:10 to go outside the **c** and stay there.
23:11 at sunset he may return to the **c**.
23:12 Designate a place outside the **c**
23:14 about in your **c** to protect you
23:14 Your **c** must be holy, so that he will
Jos 1:11 "Go through the **c** and tell the
3: 2 the officers went throughout the **c**,
3:14 when the people broke **c** to cross the
4: 8 their **c**, where they put them down.
5: 8 were in **c** until they were healed.
6:11 to **c** and spent the night there.
6:14 the city once and returned to the **c**.
6:18 Otherwise you will make the **c** of
6:23 in a place outside the **c** of Israel.
8:11 They set up **c** north of Ai, with the
8:13 in the **c** to the north of the city
9: 6 they went to Joshua in the **c** at
10: 6 word to Joshua in the **c** at Gilgal:
10:15 with all Israel to the **c** at Gilgal.
10:21 to Joshua in the **c** at Makkedah,
10:43 with all Israel to the **c** at Gilgal.
11: 5 **c** together at the Waters of Merom,
18: 9 to Joshua in the **c** at Shiloh.
Jdg 7: 1 The **c** of Midian was north of them in
7: 8 Now the **c** of Midian lay below him in
7: 9 "Get up, go down against the **c**,
7:10 to the **c** with your servant Purah
7:11 will be encouraged to attack the **c**.
7:11 went down to the outposts of the **c**.
7:13 came tumbling into the Midianite **c**.
7:14 and the whole **c** into his hands."
7:15 He returned to the **c** of Israel and
7:15 the Midianite **c** into your hands."
7:17 edge of the **c**, do exactly as I do.
7:18 then from all around the **c** blow
7:19 reached the edge of the **c** at the
7:21 man held his position around the **c**,
7:22 LORD caused the men throughout the **c**
18:12 On their way they set up **c** near
20:19 got up and pitched **c** near Gibeah.
21: 8 had come to the **c** for the assembly.
21:12 them to the **c** at Shiloh in Canaan.
1Sa 4: 3 the soldiers returned to **c**, the
4: 5 the LORD's covenant came into the **c**,
4: 6 all this shouting in the Hebrew **c**?"
4: 6 ark of the LORD had come into the **c**,
4: 7 "A god has come into the **c**," they
11:11 broke into the **c** of the Ammonites
13:17 Philistine **c** in three detachments.
14:15 army—those in the **c** and field,
14:19 Philistine **c** increased more and more.
14:21 had gone up with them to their **c**
17: 1 They pitched **c** at Ephes Dammim,
17: 4 Gath, came out of the Philistine **c**.
17:17 your brothers and hurry to their **c**.
17:20 He reached the **c** as the army was
17:53 Philistines, they plundered their **c**.

1Sa 26: 3 Saul made his **c** beside the road on
26: 5 Saul was lying inside the **c**,
26: 6 "Who will go down into the **c** with me
26: 7 lying asleep inside the **c** with his
28: 4 and came and set up **c** at Shunem,
28: 4 Israelites and set up **c** at Gilboa.
2Sa 1: 2 day a man arrived from Saul's **c**,
1: 3 I have escaped from the Israelite **c**."
1Ki 16:16 the Israelites in the **c** heard that
16:16 Israel that very day there in the **c**.
2Ki 3:24 the Moabites came to the **c** of Israel
6: 8 "I will set up my **c** in such and such
7: 4 So let's go over to the **c** of the
7: 5 At dusk they got up and went to the **c**
7: 5 edge of the **c**, not a man was there,
7: 7 They left the **c** as it was and ran
7: 8 the **c** and entered one of the tents.
7:10 "We went into the Aramean **c** and not
7:12 the **c** to hide in the countryside,
7:16 and plundered the **c** of the Arameans.
19:35 thousand men in the Assyrian **c**.
19:36 Sennacherib king of Assyria broke **c**
1Ch 9:18 belonging to the **c** of the Levites.
2Ch 22: 1 who came with the Arabs into the **c**,
32:21 in the **c** of the Assyrian king.
Ps 78:28 He made them come down inside their **c**
106:16 In the **c** they grew envious of Moses
Isa 10:29 say, "We will **c** overnight at Geba.
21:13 who **c** in the thickets of Arabia,
37:36 thousand men in the Assyrian **c**.
37:37 Sennacherib king of Assyria broke **c**
Mic 4:10 the city to **c** in the open field.
Heb 13:11 the bodies are burned outside the **c**.
13:13 Let us, then, go to him outside the **c**
Rev 20: 9 **c** of God's people, the city he loves.

Campaign (Campaigns)

Jos 10:42 lands Joshua conquered in one **c**,
Eze 29:18 his army in a hard **c** against Tyre;
29:18 from the **c** he led against Tyre.

Campaigns (Campaign)

1Sa 18:13 and David led the troops in their **c**.
18:16 because he led them in their **c**.
2Sa 5: 2 who led Israel on their military **c**.
1Ch 11: 2 who led Israel on their military **c**.

Camped (Camp)

Ge 31:25 Laban and his relatives **c** there too.
33:18 and **c** within sight of the city.
Ex 13:20 After leaving Succoth they **c** at
14: 9 they **c** by the sea near Pi Hahiroth,
15:27 and they **c** there near the water.
17: 1 They **c** at Rephidim, but there was no
18: 5 he was **c** near the mountain of God.
19: 2 and Israel **c** there in the desert in
Nu 21:10 The Israelites moved on and **c** at
21:11 they set out from Oboth and **c** in Iye
21:12 From there they moved on and **c** in
21:13 They set out from there and **c**
22: 1 **c** along the Jordan across from
33: 5 The Israelites left Rameses and **c** at
33: 6 They left Succoth and **c** at Etham, on
33: 7 of Baal Zephon, and **c** near Migdol.
33: 8 Desert of Etham, they **c** at Marah.
33: 9 palm trees, and they **c** there.
33:10 They left Elim and **c** by the Red Sea.
33:11 They left the Red Sea and **c** in the
33:12 They left the Desert of Sin and **c** at
33:13 They left Dophkah and **c** at Alush.
33:14 They left Alush and **c** at Rephidim,
33:15 They left Rephidim and **c** in the
33:16 They left the Desert of Sinai and **c**
33:17 They left Kibroth Hattaavah and **c** at
33:18 They left Hazeroth and **c** at Rithmah.
33:19 left Rithmah and **c** at Rimmon Perez.
33:20 left Rimmon Perez and **c** at Libnah.
33:21 They left Libnah and **c** at Rissah.
33:22 They left Rissah and **c** at Kehelathah.
33:23 They left Kehelathah and **c** at Mount
33:24 left Mount Shepher and **c** at Haradah.
33:25 They left Haradah and **c** at Makheloth.
33:26 They left Makheloth and **c** at Tahath.
33:27 They left Tahath and **c** at Terah.
33:28 They left Terah and **c** at Mithcah.
Nu 33:29 They left Mithcah and **c** at Hashmonah.
33:30 They left Hashmonah and **c** at Moseroth
33:31 left Moseroth and **c** at Bene Jaakan
33:32 They left Bene Jaakan and **c** at Hor
33:33 They left Hor Haggidgad and **c** at
33:34 They left Jotbathah and **c** at Abronah.
33:35 left Abronah and **c** at Ezion Geber.
33:36 They left Ezion Geber and **c** at Kadesh
33:37 They left Kadesh and **c** at Mount Hor,
33:41 They left Mount Hor and **c** at Zalmonah
33:42 They left Zalmonah and **c** at Punon.
33:43 They left Punon and **c** at Oboth.
33:44 They left Oboth and **c** at Iye Abarim,
33:45 They left Iyim and **c** at Dibon Gad.
33:46 They left Dibon Gad and **c** at Almon
33:47 They left Almon Diblathaim and **c** in
33:48 **c** on the plains of Moab by the
33:49 There on the plains of Moab they **c**
Jos 3: 1 where they **c** before crossing over.
4:19 **c** at Gilgal on the eastern border of
5:10 while **c** at Gilgal on the plains of
Jdg 6: 4 They **c** on the land and ruined the
6:33 and **c** in the Valley of Jezreel.
7: 1 his men **c** at the spring of Harod.
10:17 were called to arms and **c** in Gilead,
10:17 Israelites assembled and **c** at Mizpah.
11:18 **c** on the other side of the Arnon.
15: 9 The Philistines went up and **c** in
1Sa 4: 1 The Israelites **c** at Ebenezer, and
13: 5 **c** at Michmash, east of Beth Aven.
13:16 while the Philistines **c** at Michmash.
17: 2 the Israelites assembled and **c** in
26: 5 went to the place where Saul had **c**.
29: 1 Israel **c** by the spring in Jezreel.
2Sa 11:11 lord's men are **c** in the open fields.
17:26 The Israelites and Absalom **c** in the
24: 5 After crossing the Jordan, they **c**
1Ki 20:27 The Israelites **c** opposite them like
20:29 For seven days they **c** opposite each
1Ch 19: 7 who came and **c** near Medeba, while
Ezr 8:15 Ahava, and we **c** there three days.
Jer 52: 4 They **c** outside the city and built

Campfires (Camp, Fire)

Jdg 5:16 Why did you stay among the **c** to hear
Ps 68:13 Even while you sleep among the **c**,

Camping (Camp)

Nu 10: 5 tribes **c** on the east are to set out.

Camps (Camp)

Ge 25:16 to their settlements and **c**.
Nu 2:17 will set out in the middle of the **c**.
2:32 All those in the **c**, by their
10: 2 and for having the **c** set out.
10: 6 the **c** on the south are to set out.
31:10 had settled, as well as all their **c**.
Dt 29:11 and the aliens living in your **c** who
2Ch 14:15 They also attacked the **c** of the
Ps 68:12 in the **c** men divide the plunder.
Eze 4: 2 build a ramp up to it, set up **c**
25: 4 They will set up their **c** and pitch
Am 4:10 nostrils with the stench of your **c**,
Zec 14:15 and all the animals in those **c**.

Cana

A Galilean village where Jesus changed water into wine (Jn 2:1–11) and healed the son of a royal official (Jn 4:46–54). Home of Nathanael (Jn 21:2).

Jn 2: 1 wedding took place at **C** in Galilee.
2:11 Jesus performed at **C** in Galilee.
4:46 Once more he visited **C** in Galilee,
21: 2 Nathanael from **C** in Galilee, the

Canaan (Canaanite, Canaanites, *Land of Canaan*)

Region between River Jordan and Mediterranean Sea, originally occupied by descendants of Ham's youngest son (Ge 9:18). God promised to give it to Abram and his descendants (Ge 12:1–7), so they settled here (Ge 13:12; 31:18; 33:18). It was a fruitful land in Moses' time (Nu 13:27–29) but God promised it to the Israelites who captured it under Joshua (Jos 1:1–3), and it became the land of Israel.

Ge 9:18 (Ham was the father of **C**.)
9:22 Ham, the father of **C**, saw his father'
9:25 he said, "Cursed be **C**! The lowest of
9:26 of Shem! May **C** be the slave of Shem.
9:27 of Shem, and may **C** be his slave."
10: 6 of Ham: Cush, Mizraim, Put and **C**.
10:15 **C** was the father of Sidon his
10:19 the borders of **C** reached from Sidon
11:31 from Ur of the Chaldeans to go to **C**.
16: 3 after Abram had been living in **C** ten
33:18 safely at the city of Shechem in **C**
36: 2 took his wives from the women of **C**:
36: 5 of Esau, who were born to him in **C**.
36: 6 all the goods he had acquired in **C**,
42:32 is now with our father in **C**.'
46: 6 possessions they had acquired in **C**,
47: 4 because the famine is severe in **C**
47:13 **C** wasted away because of the famine.
47:14 that was to be found in Egypt and **C**
47:15 the people of Egypt and **C** was gone,
49:30 near Mamre in **C**, which Abraham
Ex 15:15 the people of **C** will melt away;
16:35 until they reached the border of **C**.
Nu 13:17 Moses sent them to explore **C**, he
26:19 sons of Judah, but they died in **C**.
32:30 their possession with you in **C**."
32:32 over before the LORD into **C** armed,
33:40 who lived in the Negev of **C**, heard
33:51 'When you cross the Jordan into **C**,
34: 2 'When you enter **C**, the land that
35:10 'When you cross the Jordan into **C**,
35:14 and three in **C** as cities of refuge.
Dt 32:49 across from Jericho, and view **C**, the
Jos 5:12 year they ate of the produce of **C**.
21: 2 at Shiloh in **C** and said to them,
22: 9 at Shiloh in **C** to return to Gilead,
22:11 built the altar on the border of **C**
22:32 and the leaders returned to **C** from
24: 3 and led him throughout **C** and gave him
Jdg 3: 1 not experienced any of the wars in **C**
4: 2 a king of **C**, who reigned in Hazor.
5:19 the kings of **C** fought at Taanach
21:12 them to the camp at Shiloh in **C**.
1Ch 1: 8 of Ham: Cush, Mizraim, Put and **C**.
1:13 **C** was the father of Sidon his
Ps 106:38 they sacrificed to the idols of **C**,
135:11 of Bashan and all the kings of **C**—
Isa 19:18 Egypt will speak the language of **C**
Ob :20 Israelite exiles who are in **C** will
Zep 2: 5 you, O **C**, land of the Philistines.
Ac 7:11 "Then a famine struck all Egypt and **C**
13:19 he overthrew seven nations in **C** and

Canaanite (Canaan)

Ge 10:18 Later the **C** clans scattered
28: 1 him: "Do not marry a **C** woman.
28: 6 "Do not marry a **C** woman,"
28: 8 how displeasing the **C** women were to
38: 2 There Judah met the daughter of a **C**
46:10 Zohar and Shaul the son of a **C** woman.
Ex 6:15 Zohar and Shaul the son of a **C** woman.
Nu 21: 1 the **C** king of Arad, who lived in the
33:40 The **C** king of Arad, who lived in the
Jos 5: 1 all the **C** kings along the coast
13: 3 all of it counted as **C** (the territory
Jdg 1:32 among the **C** inhabitants of the land.
1:33 among the **C** inhabitants of the land,
4:23 On that day God subdued Jabin, the **C**
4:24 Jabin, **C** king, until they destroyed
1Ki 9:16 He killed its **C** inhabitants and then
1Ch 2: 3 These three were born to him by a **C**
Zec 14:21 **C** in the house of the LORD Almighty.
Mt 15:22 A **C** woman from that vicinity came to

Canaanites (Canaan)

Ge 12: 6 At that time the **C** were in the land.
13: 7 The **C** and Perizzites were also
15:21 Amorites, **C**, Girgashites and
24: 3 of the **C**, among whom I am living,
24:37 of the **C**, in whose land I live,
34:30 me a stench to the **C** and Perizzites,
50:11 the **C** who lived there saw the
Ex 3: 8 milk and honey—the home of the **C**,
3:17 in Egypt into the land of the **C**,
13: 5 brings you into the land of the **C**,
13:11 land of the **C** and gives it to you,

Ex 23:23 Hittites, Perizzites, C, Hivites and
23:28 C and Hittites out of your way.
33: 2 before you and drive out the C,
34:11 C, Hittites, Perizzites, Hivites and
Nu 13:29 and the C live near the sea and
14:25 Since the Amalekites and C are
14:43 for the Amalekites and C will face
14:45 the Amalekites and C who lived in
21: 3 plea and gave the C over to them.
Dt 1: 7 to the land of the C and to Lebanon,
7: 1 Girgashites, Amorites, C, Perizzites,
11:30 in the territory of those C living
20:17 Amorites, C, Perizzites, Hivites and
Jos 3:10 drive out before you the C, Hittites,
7: 9 The C and the other people of the
9: 1 Amorites, C, Perizzites, Hivites and
11: 3 to the C in the east and west; to
12: 8 Amorites, C, Perizzites, Hivites and
13: 4 from the south, all the land of the C
16:10 They did not dislodge the C living
16:10 to this day the C live among the
17:12 for the C were determined to live in
17:13 they subjected the C to forced labour
17:16 and all the C who live in the plain
17:18 though the C have iron chariots and
24:11 Perizzites, C, Hittites, Girgashites,
Jdg 1: 1 up and fight for us against the C?"
1: 3 to us, to fight against the C.
1: 4 the LORD gave the C and Perizzites
1: 5 to rout the C and Perizzites.
1: 9 the C living in the hill country,
1:10 They advanced against the C living
1:17 attacked the C living in Zephath,
1:27 for the C were determined to live in
1:28 they pressed the C into forced
1:29 Nor did Ephraim drive out the C
1:29 C continued to live there among them.
1:30 Neither did Zebulun drive out the C
3: 3 all the C, the Sidonians, and the
3: 5 The Israelites lived among the C,
2Sa 24: 7 all the towns of the Hivites and C.
Ezr 9: 1 like those of the C, Hittites,
Ne 9: 8 his descendants the land of the C,
9:24 You subdued before them the C, who
9:24 land; you handed the C over to them,
Eze 16: 3 and birth were in the land of the C;

Canal (Canals)
Ezr 8:15 I assembled them at the **c** that flows
8:21 There, by the Ahava C, I proclaimed
8:31 from the Ahava C to go to Jerusalem.
Da 8: 2 the vision I was beside the Ulai C.
8: 3 two horns, standing beside the **c**,
8: 6 ram I had seen standing beside the **c**

Canals (Canal)
Ex 7:19 of Egypt—over the streams and **c**,
8: 5 over the streams and **c** and ponds,
Isa 19: 6 The **c** will stink; the streams of

Cancel (Cancelled, Cancelling)
Dt 15: 1 every seven years you must **c** debts.
15: 2 Every creditor shall **c** the loan he
15: 3 **c** any debt your brother owes you.
Ne 10:31 the land and will **c** all debts.

Cancelled (Cancel)
Mt 18:27 on him, **c** the debt and let him go.
18:32 'I **c** all that debt of yours because
Lk 7:42 him back, so he **c** the debts of both.
7:43 the one who had the bigger debt **c**.
Col 2:14 having **c** the written code, with its

Cancelling (Cancel)
Dt 15: 2 time for **c** debts has been proclaimed.
15: 9 the year for **c** debts, is near,"
31:10 in the year for **c** debts, during the

Candace
Ac 8:27 of C, queen of the Ethiopians.

Cane
Ex 30:23 cinnamon, 250 shekels of fragrant **c**,
Zec 8: 4 with **c** in hand because of his age.

Canneh
Eze 27:23 "Haran, C and Eden and merchants of

Canopy
2Sa 22:12 He made darkness his **c** around him—
2Ki 16:18 He took away the Sabbath **c** that had
Ps 18:11 He made darkness his covering, his **c**
Isa 4: 5 over all the glory will be a **c**.
40:22 stretches out the heavens like a **c**,
Jer 43:10 will spread his royal **c** above them.

Capable
Ex 18:21 select **c** men from all the people
18:25 He chose **c** men from all Israel and
1Ch 26: 6 family because they were very **c** men.
26: 8 their relatives were **c** men with the
26:31 and **c** men among the Hebronites were
Ezr 8:18 they brought us Sherebiah, a **c** man,

Capernaum
City on northern shore of Sea of Galilee, where Jesus resided after leaving Nazareth (Mt 4:13; 9:1). Jesus taught in its synagogue (Mk 1:21; Lk 4:31; Jn 6:59), and performed significant miracles here (Mk 1:34), e.g., healing centurion's son (Mt 8:5–13; Lk 7:1–10), Peter's mother-in-law (Mk 1:30–31; Lk 4:38–39), a paralytic (Mt 9:1–8; Mk 2:3–12; Lk 5:18–26), and a man possessed by an evil spirit (Mk 1:21–26; Lk 4:31–35). Though a base for Jesus' ministry, he cursed it for its unbelief (Mt 11:23–24; Lk 10:15).

Mt 4:13 he went and lived in C, which was by
8: 5 When Jesus had entered C, a centurion
11:23 you, C, will you be lifted up to the
17:24 Jesus and his disciples arrived in C,
Mk 1:21 They went to C, and when the Sabbath
2: 1 when Jesus again entered C, the
9:33 They came to C. When he was in the
Lk 4:23 we have heard that you did in C.'"
4:31 he went down to C, a town in Galilee,
7: 1 hearing of the people, he entered C.
10:15 you, C, will you be lifted up to the
Jn 2:12 After this he went down to C with
4:46 official whose son lay sick at C.
6:17 and set off across the lake for C.
6:24 and went to C in search of Jesus.
6:59 teaching in the synagogue in C.

Capes
Isa 3:22 the fine robes and the **c** and cloaks,

Caphtor (Caphtorites)
Dt 2:23 the Caphtorites coming out from C
Jer 47: 4 the remnant from the coasts of C.
Am 9: 7 the Philistines from C and the

Caphtorites (Caphtor)
Ge 10:14 whom the Philistines came) and C.
Dt 2:23 the C coming out from Caphtor
1Ch 1:12 whom the Philistines came) and C.

Capital (Capitals)
Dt 21:22 If a man guilty of a **c** offence is
1Ki 7:16 each **c** was five cubits high.
7:17 of the pillars, seven for each **c**.
7:18 He did the same for each **c**.
2Ki 25:17 The bronze **c** on top of one pillar
2Ch 3:15 each with a **c** on top measuring
Jer 52:22 The bronze **c** on the top of the one

Capitals (Capital)
1Ki 7:16 He also made two **c** of cast bronze to
7:17 the **c** on top of the pillars, seven
7:18 decorate the **c** on top of the pillars.
7:19 The **c** on top of the pillars in the
7:20 On the **c** of both pillars, above the
7:22 The **c** on top were in the shape of
7:41 the two bowl-shaped **c** on top of the
7:41 bowl-shaped **c** on top of the pillars;
7:42 bowl-shaped **c** on top of the pillars);
2Ch 4:12 the two bowl-shaped **c** on top of the
4:12 bowl-shaped **c** on top of the pillars;
4:13 bowl-shaped **c** on top of the pillars);

Cappadocia
Ac 2: 9 Judea and C, Pontus and Asia,
1Pe 1: 1 Galatia, C, Asia and Bithynia,

Capstone (Stone)
Ps 118:22 builders rejected has become the **c**;
Zec 4: 7 Then he will bring out the **c** to
Mt 21:42 builders rejected has become the **c**;
Mk 12:10 builders rejected has become the **c**;
Ac 4:11 rejected, which has become the **c**.',
1Pe 2: 7 builders rejected has become the **c**,"

Captain (Captains)
Ge 37:36 officials, the **c** of the guard.
39: 1 the **c** of the guard, bought him from
40: 3 in the house of the **c** of the guard,
40: 4 The **c** of the guard assigned them to
41:10 in the house of the **c** of the guard.
41:12 us, a servant of the **c** of the guard.
1Sa 22:14 the king's son-in-law, **c** of your
2Ki 1: 9 he sent to Elijah a **c** with his
1: 9 The **c** went up to Elijah, who was
1:10 Elijah answered the **c**, "If I am a
1:10 and consumed the **c** and his men.
1:11 Elijah another **c** with his fifty men.
1:11 The **c** said to him, "Man of God, this
1:13 the king sent a third **c** with his
1:13 This third **c** went up and fell on his
Isa 3: 3 the **c** of fifty and man of rank, the
Jer 37:13 the **c** of the guard, whose name was
Jnh 1: 6 The **c** went to him and said, "How can
Ac 4: 1 The priests and the **c** of the temple
5:24 On hearing this report, the **c** of the
5:26 At that, the **c** went with his officers
Rev 18:17 "Every sea **c**, and all who travel by

Captains (Captain)
Jdg 5:14 From Makir **c** came down, from Zebulun
1Ki 9:22 his officers, his **c**, and the
2Ki 1:14 the first two **c** and all their men.
2Ch 8: 9 commanders of his **c**, and commanders

Captivate (Capture)
Pr 6:25 or let her **c** you with her eyes,

Captivated (Capture)
Pr 5:19 may you ever be **c** by her love.
5:20 Why be **c**, my son, by an adulteress?

Captive (Capture)
Ge 14:14 that his relative had been taken **c**,
Nu 24:22 destroyed when Asshur takes you **c**."
Dt 1:39 ones that you said would be taken **c**,
Jdg 5:12 **c** your captives, O son of Abinoam.'
1Sa 30: 2 had taken **c** the women and all who
30: 3 and sons and daughters taken **c**.
1Ki 8:46 **c** to his own land, far away or near;
8:47 in the land where they are held **c**,
8:48 of their enemies who took them **c**,
20:39 with a **c** and said, 'Guard this man.
2Ki 5: 2 taken **c** a young girl from Israel,
17:27 "Make one of the priests you took **c**
24:15 Nebuchadnezzar took Jehoiachin **c** to
1Ch 3:17 The descendants of Jehoiachin the **c**:
5:21 took one hundred thousand people **c**,
9: 1 The people of Judah were taken **c** to
2Ch 6:36 them **c** to a land far away or near;
6:37 in the land where they are held **c**,
28: 8 The Israelites took **c** from their
Ezr 2: 1 king of Babylon had taken **c** to
Ne 7: 6 king of Babylon had taken **c**
Est 2: 6 **c** with Jehoiachin king of Judah.
Ps 69:33 and does not despise his **c** people.
106:46 to be pitied by all who held them **c**.
SS 7: 5 the king is held **c** by its tresses.
Isa 52: 2 on your neck, O **c** Daughter of Zion.
Jer 13:17 the LORD's flock will be taken **c**.
22:12 the place where they have led him **c**;
41:10 Ishmael son of Nethaniah took them **c**
41:14 All the people Ishmael had taken **c**
43:12 their temples and take their gods **c**.
48: 7 you too will be taken **c**, and Chemosh
Lam 1: 5 gone into exile, **c** before the foe.
Eze 6: 9 where they have been carried **c**,

Eze 21:23 them of their guilt and take them **c**.
21:24 have done this, you will be taken **c**.
Am 1: 6 Because she took **c** whole communities
Na 3:10 Yet she was taken **c** and went into
Hab 2: 5 nations and takes **c** all the peoples.
Ac 8:23 full of bitterness and **c** to sin."
2Co 10: 5 and we take **c** every thought to make
Col 2: 8 See to it that no-one takes you **c**
2Ti 2:26 who has taken them **c** to do his will.

Captives (Capture)
Ge 31:26 off my daughters like **c** in war.
Nu 21:29 as **c** to Sihon king of the Amorites.
31:12 brought the **c**, spoils and plunder to
31:19 must purify yourselves and your **c**.
Dt 21:10 them into your hands and you take **c**,
21:11 if you notice among the **c** a beautiful
32:42 the blood of the slain and the **c**,
Jdg 5:12 captive your **c**, O son of Abinoam.'
Job 3:18 **C** also enjoy their ease; they no
Ps 68:18 on high, you led **c** in your train;
126: 1 the LORD brought back the **c** to Zion,
Isa 10: 4 will remain but to cringe among the **c**
14: 2 They will make **c** of their captors
14:17 and would not let his **c** go home?"
20: 4 the Egyptian **c** and Cushite exiles,
42: 7 to free **c** from prison and to release
49: 9 to say to the **c**, 'Come out,' and to
49:24 or **c** rescued from the fierce?
49:25 "Yes, **c** will be taken from warriors,
61: 1 to proclaim freedom for the **c** and
Jer 40: 1 among all the **c** from Jerusalem
41:10 Ishmael made **c** of all the rest of
Eze 12:11 They will go into exile as **c**.
Am 1: 9 she sold whole communities of **c**
Eph 4: 8 he led **c** in his train and gave gifts

Captivity (Capture)
Dt 28:41 them, because they will go into **c**.
Jdg 18:30 until the time of the **c** of the land.
2Ki 25:21 went into **c**, away from her land.
2Ch 6:37 you in the land of their **c** and say,
6:38 of their **c** where they were taken,
29: 9 daughters and our wives are in **c**.
Ezr 2: 1 came up from the **c** of the exiles,
3: 8 returned from the **c** to Jerusalem)
8:35 the exiles who had returned from **c**
9: 7 been subjected to the sword and **c**,
Ne 4: 4 them over as plunder in a land of **c**.
7: 6 who came up from the **c** of the exiles
Ps 78:61 He sent the ark of his might into **c**
144:14 no going into **c**, no cry of distress
Isa 46: 2 they themselves go off into **c**.
Jer 15: 2 to starvation; those for **c**, to **c**.'
29:14 "and will bring you back from **c**.
30: 3 Judah back from **c** and restore them
31:23 "When I bring them back from **c**, the
33: 7 Israel back from **c** and will rebuild
43:11 **c** to those destined for **c**, and the
48:46 exile and your daughters into **c**.
52:27 went into **c**, away from her land.
Lam 2:14 expose your sin to ward off your **c**.
Eze 29:14 I will bring them back from **c** and
30:17 cities themselves will go into **c**.
30:18 and her villages will go into **c**.
39:25 I will now bring Jacob back from **c**
Rev 13:10 If anyone is to go into **c**, into **c** he

Captors (Capture)
2Ch 30: 9 will be shown compassion by their **c**
Ps 137: 3 for there our **c** asked us for songs,
Isa 14: 2 They will make captives of their **c**
Jer 50:33 All their **c** hold them fast, refusing

Capture (Captivate, Captivated, Captive, Captives, Captivity, Captors, Captured, Captures, Capturing, Recapture)
Dt 20:19 fighting against it to **c** it, do not
1Sa 4:21 because of the **c** of the ark of God
19:14 Saul sent the men to **c** David, Michal
19:20 he sent men to **c** him. But when they
23:26 in on David and his men to **c** them,
2Sa 12:28 and besiege the city and **c** it.
2Ki 6:13 "so that I can send men and **c** him.
2Ch 32:18 them afraid in order to **c** the city.
Job 40:24 Can anyone **c** him by the eyes, or
Jer 18:22 for they have dug a pit to **c** me and
32: 3 king of Babylon, and he will **c** it.
32:28 king of Babylon, who will **c** it.
37: 8 they will **c** it and burn it down.'
38: 3 king of Babylon, who will **c** it.'"
50:46 At the sound of Babylon's **c** the
Da 11:15 ramps and will **c** a fortified city.
Hab 1:10 they build earthen ramps and **c** them.
Mt 26:55 out with swords and clubs to **c** me?
Mk 14:48 out with swords and clubs to **c** me?

Captured (Capture)
Nu 21: 1 the Israelites and **c** some of them.
21:25 Israel **c** all the cities of the
21:32 the Israelites **c** its surrounding
31: 9 The Israelites **c** the Midianite women
31:26 the people and animals that were **c**.
32:39 **c** it and drove out the Amorites who
32:41 Jair, a descendant of Manasseh, **c**
32:42 Nobah **c** Kenath and its surrounding
Dt 2:35 the plunder from the towns we had **c**
21:13 the clothes she was wearing when **c**.
Jos 8:19 and **c** it and quickly set it on fire.
10:35 They **c** it that same day and put it
11:10 Joshua turned back and **c** Hazor
11:17 He **c** all their kings and struck them
Jdg 7:25 They also **c** two of the Midianite
8:12 but he pursued them and **c** them,
9:45 he had **c** it and killed its people.
9:50 to Thebez and besieged it and **c** it.
12: 5 The Gileadites **c** the fords of the
1Sa 4:11 The ark of God was **c**, and Eli's two
4:17 and the ark of God has been **c**."
4:19 news that the ark of God had been **c**
4:22 for the ark of God has been **c**."
5: 1 After the Philistines had **c** the ark
7:14 **c** from Israel were restored to her,
30: 5 David's two wives had been **c**—
2Sa 5: 7 Nevertheless, David **c** the fortress
8: 4 David **c** a thousand of his chariots,
12:26 Ammonites and **c** the royal citadel.
12:29 to Rabbah, and attacked and **c** it.
1Ki 9:16 of Egypt had attacked and **c** Gezer.
2Ki 6:22 "Would you kill men you have **c** with
12:17 went up and attacked Gath and **c** it.
14: 7 Valley of Salt and **c** Sela in battle,
14:13 Jehoash king of Israel **c** Amaziah
17: 6 the king of Assyria **c** Samaria and
18:10 So Samaria was **c** in Hezekiah's sixth
18:13 fortified cities of Judah and **c** them.
25: 6 he was **c**. He was taken to the king
1Ch 2:23 (But Geshur and Aram **c** Havvoth Jair,
11: 5 Nevertheless, David **c** the fortress
18: 4 David **c** a thousand of his chariots,
2Ch 8: 3 then went to Hamath Zobah and **c** it.
12: 4 he **c** the fortified cities of Judah
15: 8 he had **c** in the hills of Ephraim.
17: 2 Ephraim that his father Asa had **c**.
22: 9 **c** him while he was hiding in Samaria.
25:12 The army of Judah also **c** ten
25:23 Jehoash king of Israel **c** Amaziah
28:18 They **c** and occupied Beth Shemesh,
Ne 9:25 They **c** fortified cities and fertile
Isa 8:15 broken, they will be snared and **c**."
13:15 Whoever is **c** will be thrust through;
20: 1 to Ashdod and attacked and **c** it—
22: 3 have been **c** without using the bow.
28:13 be injured and snared and **c**.
36: 1 fortified cities of Judah and **c** them.
Jer 10:18 on them so that they may be **c**."
34: 3 surely be **c** and handed over to him.
38:23 will be **c** by the king of Babylon;
38:28 guard until the day Jerusalem was **c**.
39: 5 They **c** him and took him to
48: 1 Kiriathaim will be disgraced and **c**;
48:41 Kerioth will be **c** and the strongholds
50: 2 'Babylon will be **c**; Bel will be put
50: 9 and from the north she will be **c**.
50:24 and **c** because you opposed the LORD.
51:31 Babylon that his entire city is **c**,
51:41 "How Sheshach will be **c**, the boast
51:56 her warriors will be **c**, and their
52: 9 he was **c**. He was taken to the king
Da 11:33 or be burned or **c** or plundered.
Am 4:10 the sword, along with your **c** horses.
Zec 14: 2 the city will be **c**, the houses
Rev 19:20 But the beast was **c**, and with him

Captures (Capture)
Jos 15:16 who attacks and **c** Kiriath Sepher."
Jdg 1:12 who attacks and **c** Kiriath Sepher."

Capturing (Capture)
Jdg 11:22 **c** all of it from the Arnon to the
2Ki 16: 9 by attacking Damascus and **c** it.

Caravan (Caravans)
Ge 37:25 **c** of Ishmaelites coming from Gilead.
1Ki 10: 2 at Jerusalem with a very great **c**
2Ch 9: 1 Arriving with a very great **c**—with

Caravans (Caravan)
Job 6:18 **C** turn aside from their routes; they
6:19 The **c** of Tema look for water, the
Isa 21:13 You **c** of Dedanites, who camp in the

Caraway
Isa 28:25 does he not sow **c** and scatter cummin?
28:27 **C** is not threshed with a sledge, nor
28:27 **c** is beaten out with a rod, and

Carcas
Est 1:10 Bigtha, Abagtha, Zethar and **C**—

Carcass (Carcasses)
Lev 11:26 **c** of any of them will be unclean.
11:37 If a **c** falls on any seeds that are
11:38 **c** falls on it, it is unclean for you.
11:39 the **c** will be unclean till evening.
11:40 Anyone who eats some of the **c** must
11:40 Anyone who picks up the **c** must wash
Jdg 14: 8 aside to look at the lion's **c**.
14: 9 taken the honey from the lion's **c**.
Mt 24:28 Wherever there is a **c**, there the

Carcasses (Carcass)
Ge 15:11 birds of prey came down on the **c**,
Lev 5: 2 the **c** of unclean wild animals
11: 8 not eat their meat or touch their **c**;
11:11 meat and you must detest their **c**.
11:24 **c** will be unclean till evening.
11:25 Whoever picks up one of their **c** must
11:27 **c** will be unclean till evening.
11:28 Anyone who picks up their **c** must
11:35 Anything that one of their **c** falls
11:36 touches one of these **c** is unclean.
Dt 14: 8 to eat their meat or touch their **c**.
28:26 Your **c** will be food for all the
1Sa 17:46 Today I will give the **c** of the
Jer 7:33 the **c** of this people will become
19: 7 and I will give their **c** as food to

Carchemish
2Ch 35:20 up to fight at **C** on the Euphrates,
Isa 10: 9 'Has not Calno fared like **C**? Is not
Jer 46: 2 which was defeated at **C** on the

Care (Cared, Careful, Carefully, Cares, Caring)
Ge 2:15 of Eden to work it and take **c** of it.
30:29 your livestock has fared under my **c**.
30:35 he placed them in the **c** of his sons.
32:16 He put them in the **c** of his servants,
33:13 that I must **c** for the ewes and cows
39: 4 to his **c** everything he owned.
39: 6 he left in Joseph's **c** everything he
39: 8 he owns he has entrusted to my **c**.
39:23 to anything under Joseph's **c**,
42:37 Entrust him to my **c**, and I will bring
Ex 12: 6 Take **c** of them until the fourteenth
Lev 6: 2 or left in his **c** or stolen, or if he
16:21 **c** of a man appointed for the task.
Nu 1:50 to take **c** of it and encamp round it.
1:53 **c** of the tabernacle of the Testimony.

Nu 3: 8 They are to take **c** of all the
3:25 the **c** of the tabernacle and tent,
3:28 for the **c** of the sanctuary.
3:31 They were responsible for the **c** of
3:32 for the **c** of the sanctuary.
3:36 **c** of the frames of the tabernacle,
3:38 They were responsible for the **c** of
4: 4 the **c** of the most holy things.
18: 4 be responsible for the **c** of the Tent
18: 5 for the **c** of the sanctuary
31:30 for the **c** of the LORD's tabernacle."
31:47 for the **c** of the LORD's tabernacle.
Dt 7:11 Therefore, take **c** to follow the
2Sa 15:16 concubines to take **c** of the palace.
16:21 he left to take **c** of the palace.
18: 3 to flee, they won't **c** about us.
18: 3 Even if half of us die, they won't **c**;
19:24 He had not taken **c** of his feet or
20: 3 he had left to take **c** of the palace
1Ki 1: 2 attend the king and take **c** of him.
1: 4 she took **c** of the king and waited on
2Ki 9:34 "Take **c** of that cursed woman," he
1Ch 9:29 Others were assigned to take **c** of
9:30 some of the priests took **c** of mixing
26:28 were in the **c** of Shelomith and his
27:32 Hacmoni took **c** of the king's sons.
2Ch 25:24 that had been in the **c** of Obed-Edom,
32:22 He took **c** of them on every side.
Ezr 10:13 this matter cannot be taken **c** of in
Est 2: 3 Let them be placed under the **c** of
2: 8 Susa and put under the **c** of Hegai.
2:14 of the harem to the **c** of Shaashgaz,
Job 3: 4 may God above not **c** about it; may no
21:21 For what does he **c** about the family
Ps 8: 4 the son of man that you **c** for him?
65: 9 You **c** for the land and water it; you
88: 5 more, who are cut off from your **c**.
95: 7 his pasture, the flock under his **c**.
144: 3 O LORD, what is man that you **c** for
Pr 29: 7 The righteous **c** about justice for
SS 1: 6 and made me take **c** of the vineyards;
Isa 13:17 who do not **c** for silver and have no
34:15 she will hatch them, and **c** for her
Jer 6:20 What do I **c** about incense from Sheba
15:15 O LORD; remember me and **c** for me.
23: 2 and have not bestowed **c** on them,
30:14 you; they **c** nothing for you.
Eze 34: 2 Israel who only take **c** of themselves!
34: 2 not shepherds take **c** of the flock?
34: 3 but you do not take **c** of the flock.
Hos 14: 8 I will answer him and **c** for him.
Am 7:14 I also took **c** of sycamore-fig trees.
Mic 2: 8 from those who pass by without a **c**,
Zep 2: 7 The LORD their God will **c** for them;
Zec 10: 3 LORD Almighty will **c** for his flock,
11:16 land who will not **c** for the lost,
Mt 27:55 from Galilee to **c** for his needs.
Mk 4:38 "Teacher, don't you **c** if we drown?
5:26 deal under the **c** of many doctors
Lk 10:34 him to an inn and took **c** of him.
10:40 "Lord, don't you **c** that my sister
13: 7 he said to the man who took **c** of the
18: 4 I don't fear God or **c** about men,
Jn 21:16 Jesus said, "Take **c** of my sheep."
Ac 13:40 Take **c** that what the prophets have
24:23 his friends to take **c** of his needs.
1Co 4: 3 I **c** very little if I am judged by
Php 2:25 whom you sent to take **c** of my needs.
1Ti 3: 5 how can he take **c** of God's church?)
6:20 what has been entrusted to your **c**.
Heb 2: 6 the son of man that you **c** for him?
1Pe 1:10 intently and with the greatest **c**,
5: 2 of God's flock that is under your **c**,
Rev 12: 6 might be taken **c** of for 1,260 days.
12:14 where she would be taken **c** of for a

Cared (Care)
Dt 32:10 He shielded him and **c** for him; he
Ru 4:16 laid him in her lap and **c** for him.
Lam 2:20 the children they have **c** for? Should
2:22 those I **c** for and reared, my enemy
Eze 34: 8 **c** for themselves rather than for my
Hos 12:13 Egypt, by a prophet he **c** for him.
13: 5 I **c** for you in the desert, in the
Mk 15:41 followed him and **c** for his needs.
Lk 18: 2 neither feared God nor **c** about men.

Jn 12: 6 He did not say this because he **c**
Ac 7:20 he was **c** for in his father's house.

Carefree (Care)
Ps 73:12 always **c**, they increase in wealth.
Eze 23:42 "The noise of a **c** crowd was around
Zep 2:15 This is the **c** city that lived in

Careful (Care)
Ge 31:24 "Be **c** not to say anything to Jacob,
31:29 'Be **c** not to say anything to Jacob,
Ex 19:12 'Be **c** that you do not go up the
23:13 "Be **c** to do everything I have said
34:12 Be **c** not to make a treaty with those
34:15 "Be **c** not to make a treaty with
Lev 18: 4 You must obey my laws and be **c** to
25:18 "'Follow my decrees and be **c** to obey
26: 3 "'If you follow my decrees and are **c**
Dt 2: 4 be afraid of you, but be very **c**.
4: 9 Only be **c**, and watch yourselves
4:23 Be **c** not to forget the covenant of
5:32 be **c** to do what the LORD your God
6: 3 Hear, O Israel, and be **c** to obey so
6:12 be **c** that you do not forget the LORD,
6:25 if we are **c** to obey all this law
7:12 these laws and are **c** to follow them,
8: 1 Be **c** to follow every command I am
8:11 Be **c** that you do not forget the LORD
11:16 Be **c**, or you will be enticed to turn
12: 1 laws you must be **c** to follow in the
12:13 Be **c** not to sacrifice your burnt
12:19 Be **c** not to neglect the Levites as
12:28 Be **c** to obey all these regulations I
12:30 be **c** not to be ensnared by enquiring
15: 5 are **c** to follow all these commands I
15: 9 Be **c** not to harbour this wicked
17:10 Be **c** to do everything they direct
24: 8 very **c** to do exactly as the priests,
Jos 1: 7 Be **c** to obey all the law my servant
1: 8 be **c** to do everything written in it.
22: 5 be very **c** to keep the commandment
23: 6 be **c** to obey all that is written in
23:11 be very **c** to love the LORD your God.
1Ki 8:25 if only your sons are **c** in all they
2Ki 10:31 Yet Jehu was not **c** to keep the law
17:37 You must always be **c** to keep the
21: 8 if only they will be **c** to do
1Ch 22:13 you will have success if you are **c**
28: 8 Be **c** to follow all the commands of
2Ch 6:16 if only your sons are **c** in all they
33: 8 if only they will be **c** to do
Ezr 4:22 Be **c** not to neglect this matter.
Job 36:18 Be **c** that no-one entices you by
Ps 101: 2 I will be **c** to lead a blameless life
Pr 13:24 loves him is **c** to discipline him.
27:23 give **c** attention to your herds;
Isa 7: 4 Say to him, 'Be **c**, keep calm and
Jer 17:21 Be **c** not to carry a load on the
17:24 if you are **c** to obey me, declares
22: 4 For if you are **c** to carry out these
Eze 11:20 they will follow my decrees and be **c**
18:19 has been **c** to keep all my decrees,
20:19 my decrees and be **c** to keep my laws.
20:21 they were not **c** to keep my laws—
36:27 my decrees and be **c** to keep my laws.
37:24 my laws and be **c** to keep my decrees.
Mic 7: 5 in your embrace be **c** of your words.
Hag 1: 5 says: "Give **c** thought to your ways.
1: 7 says: "Give **c** thought to your ways.
2:15 "'Now give **c** thought to this from
2:18 give **c** thought to the day when the
2:18 temple was laid. Give **c** thought:
Mt 2: 8 Go and make a **c** search for the child.
6: 1 "Be **c** not to do your 'acts of
16: 6 "Be **c**," Jesus said to them. "Be on
Mk 8:15 "Be **c**," Jesus warned them. "Watch
Lk 17:20 not come with your **c** observation,
21:34 "Be **c**, or your hearts will be
Ro 12:17 Be **c** to do what is right in the eyes
1Co 3:10 each one should be **c** how he builds.
8: 9 Be **c**, however, that the exercise of
10:12 firm, be **c** that you don't fall!
Eph 5:15 Be very **c**, then, how you live—not
2Ti 4: 2 great patience and **c** instruction.
Tit 3: 8 be **c** to devote themselves to

Heb 2: 1 We must pay more **c** attention,
4: 1 let us be **c** that none of you be

Carefully (Care)
Ge 27: 8 Now, my son, listen **c** and do what I
Ex 15:26 He said, "If you listen **c** to the
23:22 If you listen **c** to what he says and
Dt 4: 6 Observe them **c**, for this will show
4:15 Therefore watch yourselves very **c**,
11:22 If you **c** observe all these commands
16:12 Egypt, and follow **c** these decrees.
17:19 follow **c** all the words of this law
19: 9 you **c** follow all these laws I
24: 8 follow **c** what I have commanded them.
26:16 **c** observe them with all your heart
28: 1 **c** follow all his commands that I
28:13 give you this day and **c** follow them,
28:15 do not **c** follow all his commands and
28:58 If you do not **c** follow all the words
29: 9 **C** follow the terms of this covenant,
31:12 follow **c** all the words of this law.
32:46 to obey **c** all the words of this law.
Jos 8: 4 "Listen **c**. You are to set an ambush
Jdg 6:29 When they **c** investigated, they were
2Ch 19: 6 He told them, "Consider **c** what you
19: 7 Judge **c**, for with the LORD our God
Ezr 8:29 Guard them **c** until you weigh them
Ne 10:29 God and to obey **c** all the commands,
Job 13:17 Listen **c** to my words; let your ears
21: 2 "Listen **c** to my words; let this be
Eze 3:10 he said to me, "Son of man, listen **c**
44: 5 "Son of man, look **c**, listen closely
Da 10:11 consider **c** the words I am about to
Mk 4:24 "Consider **c** what you hear," he
Lk 1: 3 since I myself have **c** investigated
4:10 concerning you to guard you **c**;
8:18 Therefore consider **c** how you listen.
9:44 "Listen **c** to what I am about to tell
14: 1 Pharisee, he was being **c** watched.
15: 8 and search **c** until she finds it?
Ac 2:14 this to you; listen **c** to what I say.
5:35 consider **c** what you intend to do to
16:23 was commanded to guard them **c**.
17:23 For as I walked around and looked **c**
1Co 14:29 others should weigh **c** what is said.

Careless (Carelessly)
Mt 12:36 for every **c** word they have spoken.

Carelessly (Careless)
Lev 5: 4 in any matter one might **c** swear

Cares (Care)
Dt 11:12 is a land the LORD your God **c** for;
Job 39:16 **c** not that her labour was in vain,
Ps 55:22 Cast your **c** on the LORD and he will
142: 4 no refuge; no-one **c** for my life.
Pr 12:10 A righteous man **c** for the needs of
Ecc 5: 3 a dream comes when there are many **c**,
Jer 12:11 waste because there is no-one who **c**.
30:17 an outcast, Zion for whom no-one **c**.'
Na 1: 7 He **c** for those who trust in him,
Jn 10:13 hand and **c** nothing for the sheep.
Eph 5:29 but he feeds and **c** for it, just as
1Pe 5: 7 anxiety on him because he **c** for you.

Caressed (Caressing)
Eze 23: 3 fondled and their virgin bosoms **c**.
23: 8 **c** her virgin bosom and poured out
23:21 when in Egypt your bosom was **c**

Caressing (Caressed)
Ge 26: 8 and saw Isaac **c** his wife Rebekah.

Cargo (Cargoes)
Eze 27:25 heavy **c** in the heart of the sea.
Jnh 1: 5 And they threw the **c** into the sea to
Ac 21: 3 where our ship was to unload its **c**.
27:10 and bring great loss to ship and **c**,
27:18 they began to throw the **c** overboard.

Cargoes (Cargo)
1Ki 10:11 c of almug-wood and precious stones.
Rev 18:11 no-one buys their c any more—
18:12 c of gold, silver, precious stones
18:13 c of cinnamon and spice, of incense,

Caring (Care)
1Th 2: 7 a mother c for her little children.
1Ti 5: 4 practice by c for their own family

Carites
2Ki 11: 4 the C and the guards and had them
11:19 the C, the guards and all the people

Carmel (Carmelite)
1. Wooded mountain range overlooking Mediterranean coast, west of Sea of Galilee. Site of contest between Elijah and prophets of Baal (1Ki 18:19–39). The Shunammite woman found Elisha here (2Ki 4:25). Used figuratively on account of its fruitfulness (SS 7:6; Isa 33:9; 35:2; Jer 46:18; 50:19; Am 1:2; 9:3; Na 1:4).
2. Town in hill country of Judah, about 8 miles south of Hebron. Site of Saul's monument to himself (1Sa 15:12). Home of Nabal's widow Abigail (who David married, 1Sa 25), and one of David's mighty men (2Sa 23:35; 1Ch 11:37).

Jos 12:22 one the king of Jokneam in C
15:55 Maon, C, Ziph, Juttah,
19:26 touched C and Shihor Libnath.
1Sa 15:12 he was told, "Saul has gone to C.
25: 2 who had property there at C, was
25: 2 sheep, which he was shearing in C.
25: 5 "Go up to Nabal at C and greet him
25: 7 at C nothing of theirs was missing.
25:40 His servants went to C and said to
27: 3 Abigail of C, the widow of Nabal.
30: 5 Abigail, the widow of Nabal of C.
2Sa 2: 2 Abigail, the widow of Nabal of C.
3: 3 Abigail the widow of Nabal of C;
1Ki 18:19 over Israel to meet me on Mount C.
18:20 assembled the prophets on Mount C.
18:42 but Elijah climbed to the top of C,
2Ki 2:25 he went on to Mount C and from there
4:25 came to the man of God at Mount C.
1Ch 3: 1 Daniel the son of Abigail of C;
SS 7: 5 Your head crowns you like Mount C.
Isa 33: 9 and Bashan and C drop their leaves.
35: 2 the splendour of C and Sharon; they
Jer 46:18 the mountains, like C by the sea.
50:19 and he will graze on C and Bashan;
Am 1: 2 dry up, and the top of C withers."
9: 3 hide themselves on the top of C,
Na 1: 4 Bashan and C wither and the blossoms

Carmelite (Carmel)
2Sa 23:35 Hezro the C, Paarai the Arbite,
1Ch 11:37 Hezro the C, Naarai son of Ezbai,

Carmi (Carmite)
Ge 46: 9 Reuben: Hanoch, Pallu, Hezron and C.
Ex 6:14 were Hanoch and Pallu, Hezron and C.
Nu 26: 6 clan; through C, the Carmite clan.
Jos 7: 1 Achan son of C, the son of Zimri
7:18 and Achan son of C, the son of Zimri,
1Ch 2: 7 The son of C: Achar, who brought
4: 1 Perez, Hezron, C, Hur and Shobal.
5: 3 Israel: Hanoch, Pallu, Hezron and C.

Carmite (Carmi)
Nu 26: 6 clan; through Carmi, the C clan.

Carnelian
Rev 4: 3 had the appearance of jasper and c.
21:20 the fifth sardonyx, the sixth c, the

Carouse (Carousing)
2Pe 2:13 Their idea of pleasure is to c in

Carousing (Carouse)
1Pe 4: 3 orgies, c and detestable idolatry.

Carpenter (Carpenter's, Carpenters)
Isa 44:13 The c measures with a line and makes
Mk 6: 3 Isn't this the c? Isn't this Mary's

Carpenter's (Carpenter)
Mt 13:55 "Isn't this the c son? Isn't his

Carpenters (Carpenter)
2Sa 5:11 along with cedar logs and c and
2Ki 12:11 of the LORD—the c and builders,
22: 6 the c, the builders and the masons.
1Ch 14: 1 and c to build a palace for him.
22:15 masons and c, as well as men skilled
2Ch 24:12 They hired masons and c to restore
34:11 They also gave money to the c and
Ezr 3: 7 they gave money to the masons and c,

Carpus
2Ti 4:13 bring the cloak that I left with C

Carriage (Carriages)
SS 3: 7 Look! It is Solomon's c, escorted by
3: 9 King Solomon made for himself the c;

Carriages (Carriage)
Rev 18:13 horses and c; and bodies and souls

Carried (Carry)
Ge 14:12 They also c off Abram's nephew Lot
22: 6 he himself c the fire and the knife.
31:26 and you've c off my daughters like
34:29 They c off all their wealth and all
40:15 For I was forcibly c off from the
50:13 They c him to the land of Canaan and
Ex 10:19 locusts and c them into the Red Sea.
12:34 and c it on their shoulders in
19: 4 and how I c you on eagles' wings
27: 7 two sides of the altar when it is c.
34: 4 c the two stone tablets in his hands.
Lev 10: 5 they came and c them, still in their
Nu 10:17 and Merarites, who c it, set out.
13:23 Two of them c it on a pole between
Dt 1:31 you saw how the LORD your God c you,
2:35 had captured we c off for ourselves.
3: 7 their cities we c off for ourselves.
31: 9 the sons of Levi, who c the ark of
31:25 the Levites who c the ark of the
33:21 he c out the LORD's righteous will,
Jos 3:15 Yet as soon as the priests who c the
3:17 The priests who c the ark of the
4: 8 c them over with them to their camp,
4: 9 the priests who c the ark of the
4:10 Now the priests who c the ark
6:11 he had the ark of the LORD c around
8:33 facing those who c it—the priests,
11:14 The Israelites c off for themselves
22: 3 c out the mission the LORD your God
Jdg 3:18 on their way the men who had c it.
5:19 they c off no silver, no plunder.
16: 3 c them to the top of the hill that
21:23 one and c her off to be his wife.
Ru 2:18 She c it back to town, and her
1Sa 5: 2 they c the ark into Dagon's temple
15:11 and has not c out my instructions.
15:13 have c out the LORD's instructions."
17:34 and c off a sheep from the flock,
23: 5 and c off their livestock.
30: 2 c them off as they went on their way.
2Sa 5:21 and David and his men c them off.
23:16 of Bethlehem and c it back to David.
1Ki 2:26 because you c the ark of the
8: 4 The priests and Levites c them up,
14:26 He c off the treasures of the temple
15:22 they c away from Ramah the stones
16:20 and the rebellion he c out, are they
17:19 c him to the upper room where he was
17:23 Elijah picked up the child and c him
2Ki 4:20 him up and c him to his mother,
5:23 and they c them ahead of Gehazi.
7: 8 and c away silver, gold and clothes,
18:12 to the commands nor c them out.
20:17 this day, will be c off to Babylon.
23:34 But he took Jehoahaz and c him off
24:14 He c into exile all Jerusalem: all
25:11 commander of the guard c into exile
25:13 and they c the bronze to Babylon.
1Ch 11:18 of Bethlehem and c it back to David.
15:15 the Levites c the ark of God with
18: 7 David took the gold shields c by the
23:32 And so the Levites c out their
2Ch 5: 5 priests, who were Levites, c them up;
8:16 All Solomon's work was c out, from
12: 9 he c off the treasures of the temple
14:13 c off a large amount of plunder.
14:15 c off droves of sheep and goats and
16: 6 and they c away from Ramah the
21:17 and c off all the goods found in the
24:12 the men who c out the work required
25:13 c off great quantities of plunder.
28: 8 which they c back to Samaria.
28:17 attacked Judah and c away prisoners,
29:16 and c it out to the Kidron Valley.
35: 3 It is not to be c about on your
35:16 was c out for the celebration of the
36: 4 Jehoahaz and c him off to Egypt.
36:18 He c to Babylon all the articles
36:20 He c into exile to Babylon the
Ezr 1: 7 which Nebuchadnezzar had c away from
5: 8 The work is being c on with
6:12 Let it be c out with diligence.
6:13 associates c it out with diligence.
Ne 3:17 c out repairs for his district.
4:17 Those who c materials did their work
11:12 their associates, who c on work for
Est 2: 6 who had been c into exile from
4:17 Mordecai went away and c out all of
9: 1 by the king was to be c out.
Job 1:15 the Sabeans attacked and c them off.
1:17 down on your camels and c them off.
10:19 or had been c straight from the womb
15:12 Why has your heart c you away, and
21:32 He is c to the grave, and watch is
22:16 They were c off before their time,
Ecc 8:11 for a crime is not quickly c out,
Isa 8: 4 be c off by the king of Assyria."
39: 6 this day, will be c off to Babylon.
41: 4 Who has done this and c it through,
46: 1 The images that are c about are
46: 3 and have c since your birth.
53: 4 our infirmities and c our sorrows,
60: 4 and your daughters are c on the arm.
63: 9 and c them all the days of old.
66:12 you will nurse and be c on her arm
Jer 10: 5 must be c because they cannot walk.
13:19 be c into exile, c completely away.
24: the artisans of Judah were c into
27:20 when he c Jehoiachin son of Jehoiakim
29: 1 Nebuchadnezzar had c into exile from
29: 4 says to all those I c into exile
29: 7 to which I have c you into exile.
29:14 from which I c you into exile."
35:16 c out the command their forefather
39: 9 c into exile to Babylon the people
40: 1 were being c into exile to Babylon.
40: 7 not been c into exile to Babylon,
49:29 their shelters will be c off with
52:15 c into exile some of the poorest
52:17 they c all the bronze to Babylon.
52:28 people Nebuchadnezzar c into exile:
Eze 6: 9 in the nations where they have been c
16:16 where you c on your prostitution.
17: 4 and c it away to a land of merchants,
17:12 and c off her king and her nobles,
17:13 c away the leading men of the land,
23:14 "But she c her prostitution still
23:18 she c on her prostitution openly and
30: 4 her wealth will be c away and her
44:15 who faithfully c out the duties of
Da 1: 2 These he c off to the temple of his
11:12 When the army is c off, the king of
Hos 10: 6 will be c to Assyria as tribute for
Joel 3: 5 my gold and c off my finest treasures
Ob :11 while strangers c off his wealth
Na 2: 7 the city be exiled and c away
Mal 2: 3 and you will be c off with it.
Mt 8:17 our infirmities and c our diseases."
14:11 to the girl, who c it to her mother.
Mk 2: 3 him a paralytic, c by four of them.
6:55 c the sick on mats to wherever they
Lk 7:12 a dead person was being c out—the
16:22 the angels c him to Abraham's side.
Jn 20:15 "Sir, if you have c him away, tell
Ac 3: 2 c to the temple gate called Beautiful
5: 6 body, and c him out and buried him.

Ac 5:10 finding her dead, c her out and
13:29 they had c out all that was written
21:35 he had to be c by the soldiers.
23:30 I was informed of a plot to be c out
Heb 13: 9 Do not be c away by all kinds of
2Pe 1:21 were c along by the Holy Spirit.
3:17 c away by the error of lawless men
Rev 17: 3 the angel c me away in the Spirit
21:10 he c me away in the Spirit to a

Carriers (Carry)

1Ki 5:15 Solomon had seventy thousand c and
2Ch 2: 2 seventy thousand men as c and
2:18 He assigned 70,000 of them to be c
Eze 27:25 "The ships of Tarshish serve as c

Carries (Carry)

Nu 11:12 as a nurse c an infant, to the land
Dt 1:31 as a father c his son, all the way
32:11 them and c them on its pinions.
Job 23:14 He c out his decree against me, and
27:21 The east wind c him off, and he is
Isa 40:11 arms and c them close to his heart;
44:26 who c out the words of his servants
Hag 2:12 If a person c consecrated meat in
Heb 13:11 The high priest c the blood of

Carrion

Eze 39: 4 you as food to all kinds of c birds

Carry (Carried, Carriers, Carries, Carrying)

Ge 44: 1 with as much food as they can c,
45:27 carts Joseph had sent to c him back,
47:30 c me out of Egypt and bury me where
50:25 must c my bones up from this place."
Ex 13:19 and then you must c my bones up with
25:14 on the sides of the chest to c it.
25:28 with gold and c the table with them.
30: 4 hold the poles used to c it.
36: 1 ability to know how to c out all the
36: 3 to c out the work of constructing the
37: 5 on the sides of the ark to c it.
37:27 hold the poles used to c it.
Lev 4: 5 and c it into the Tent of Meeting.
6:11 and c the ashes outside the camp to
10: 4 "Come here; c your cousins outside
16:22 The goat will c on itself all their
26:14 to me and c out all these commands,
26:15 and fail to c out all my commands
Nu 1:50 They are to c the tabernacle and all
4:15 The Kohathites are to c those things
4:19 man his work and what he is to c.
4:24 clans as they work and c burdens:
4:25 They are to c the curtains of the
4:27 responsibility all they are to c.
4:31 to c the frames of the tabernacle,
4:32 man the specific things he is to c.
4:49 his work and told what to c.
7: 9 because they were to c on their
11:12 do you tell me to c them in my arms,
11:14 I cannot c all these people by
11:17 They will help you c the burden of
11:17 you will not have to c it alone.
31: 3 c out the LORD's vengeance on them.
Dt 1: 9 heavy a burden for me to c alone.
10: 8 Levi to c the ark of the covenant
14:24 cannot c your tithe (because the
25: 6 The first son she bears shall c on
25: 7 c on his brother's name in Israel.
29:11 who chop your wood and c your water.
Jos 3: 8 Tell the priests who c the ark of
3:13 soon as the priests who c the ark of
4: 3 to c them over with you and put them
6: 4 Make seven priests c trumpets of
6: 6 priests c trumpets in front of it."
8: 2 except that you may c off their
8:27 Israel did c off for themselves the
1Sa 3:12 At that time I will c out against
20:40 and said, "Go, c them back to town."
21:15 to c on like this in front of me?
28:18 you did not obey the LORD or c out
2Sa 18:18 son to c on the memory of my name.
24:12 them for me to c out against you.'"
1Ki 1:30 I will surely c out today what I
3: 7 do not know how to c out my duties.
6:12 c out my regulations and keep all my
18:12 the LORD may c you when I leave you.
20: 6 you value and c it away.'"
2Ki 4:19 a servant, "C him to his mother."
5:17 much earth as a pair of mules can c,
1Ch 15: 2 "No-one but the Levites may c the
15: 2 the LORD chose them to c the ark
21:10 them for me to c out against you.'"
23:26 the Levites no longer need to c the
2Ch 20:25 Jehoshaphat and his men went to c
24:11 chest and c it back to its place.
30:12 of mind to c out what the king
Est 3: 9 the men who c out this business."
9:13 c out this day's edict tomorrow also,
Job 12: 6 who c their god in their hands.
15:30 of God's mouth will c him away.
20:28 A flood will c off his house,
24:10 c the sheaves, but still go hungry.
Ps 28: 9 their shepherd and c them for ever.
37: 7 they c out their wicked schemes.
149: 9 to c out the sentence written
Ecc 5:15 labour that he can c in his hand.
10:20 a bird of the air may c your words,
Isa 5:29 and c it off with no-one to rescue.
10:23 The Lord, the LORD Almighty, will c
13: 3 I have summoned my warriors to c out
15: 7 they c away over the Ravine of the
28:19 often as it comes it will c you away;
30: 1 "to those who c out plans that are
30: 6 c their riches on donkeys' backs,
33:23 even the lame will c off plunder.
45:20 Ignorant are those who c about idols
46: 4 I have made you and I will c you;
46: 7 They lift it to their shoulders and c
48:14 will c out his purpose against
49:22 c your daughters on their shoulders.
52:11 you who c the vessels of the LORD.
57:13 The wind will c all of them off,
Jer 17:21 Be careful not to c a load on the
20: 4 who will c them away to Babylon or
20: 5 as plunder and c it off to Babylon.
22: 4 For if you are careful to c out
43: 3 us or c us into exile to Babylon."
44:25 'We will certainly c out the vows we
46: 9 men of Cush and Put who c shields,
51:12 The LORD will c carry out his purpose
Eze 12: 6 are watching and c them out at dusk.
25:17 I will c out great vengeance on them
29:19 and he will c off its wealth.
38:13 to c off silver and gold, to take
Da 11: 8 and gold and c them off to Egypt.
11:10 c the battle as far as his fortress.
Hos 5:14 and go away; I will c them off,
11: 9 I will not c out my fierce anger,
Am 6:10 comes to c them out of the house
Mic 2: 1 At morning's light they c it out
Mt 3:11 I, whose sandals I am not fit to c.
12:29 c off his possessions unless he
27:32 and they forced him to c the cross.
Mk 3:27 c off his possessions unless he
11:16 not allow anyone to c merchandise
15:21 and they forced him to c the cross.
Lk 11:46 down with burdens they can hardly c,
14:27 anyone who does not c his cross and
23:26 him and made him c it behind Jesus.
Jn 5:10 the law forbids you to c your mat."
8:44 want to c out your father's desire.
Ac 5: 9 door, and they will c you out also."
9:15 to c my name before the Gentiles
Ro 7:18 what is good, but I cannot c it out.
9:28 For the Lord will c out his sentence
2Co 4:10 We always c around in our body the
8:19 accompany us as we c the offering,
Gal 6: 2 C each other's burdens, and in this
6: 5 for each one should c his own load.
Php 1: 6 will c it on to completion until the
Heb 9: 6 outer room to c on their ministry.
Jas 4:13 c on business and make money."

Carrying (Carry)

Ex 25:28 hold the poles used in c the table.
37:14 hold the poles used in c the table.
37:15 The poles for c the table were made
38: 7 on the sides of the altar for c it.
Nu 4:10 of sea cows and put it on a c frame.
4:12 sea cows and put them on a c frame.
4:15 Kohathites are to come to do the c.
4:27 All their service, whether c or
4:47 serving and c the Tent of Meeting
10:21 the Kohathites set out, c the holy
Dt 27:26 the words of this law by c them out.
Jos 3: 3 the priests, who are Levites, c it,
3:14 the priests c the ark of the
4:16 "Command the priests c the ark of
4:18 c the ark of the covenant of the LORD
6: 8 seven priests c the seven trumpets
6:13 seven priests c the seven trumpets
1Sa 10: 3 One will be c three young goats,
2Sa 6:13 those who were c the ark of the LORD
15:24 c the ark of the covenant of God.
1Ki 8: 7 the ark and its c poles.
10: 2 great caravan—with camels c spices,
10:22 Once every three years it returned c
1Ch 12:24 men of Judah, c shield and spear
12:34 37,000 men c shields and spears;
15:26 God had helped the Levites who were c
15:27 as were all the Levites who were c
28: 7 in c out my commands and laws,
2Ch 5: 8 and covered the ark and its c poles.
7:11 and had succeeded in c out all he
9: 1 great caravan—with camels c spices,
9:21 c gold, silver and ivory, and apes
Ne 6: 3 "I am c on a great project and
10:32 "We assume the responsibility for c
Ps 126: 6 who goes out weeping, c seed to sow,
126: 6 songs of joy, c sheaves with him.
Jer 17:27 by not c any load as you come through
Eze 12: 7 c them on my shoulders while they
44: 8 Instead of c out your duty in regard
Mal 3:14 What did we gain by c out his
Mk 14:13 man c a jar of water will meet you.
Lk 5:18 Some men came c a paralytic on a mat
7:14 coffin, and those c it stood still.
22:10 man c a jar of water will meet you.
Jn 18: 3 c torches, lanterns and weapons.
19:17 C his own cross, he went out to the
Ac 23:31 the soldiers, c out their orders,
27:43 and kept them from c out their plan.
1Co 16:10 for he is c on the work of the Lord,
1Jn 5: 2 loving God and c out his commands.

Carshena

Est 1:14 were closest to the king—C, Shethar,

Cart (Carts, Cartwheel, Threshing-cart)

Nu 7: 3 each leader and a c from every two.
1Sa 6: 7 "Now then, get a new c ready, with
6: 7 Hitch the cows to the c, but take
6: 8 ark of the LORD and put it on the c,
6:10 cows and hitched them to the c
6:11 placed the ark of the LORD on the c
6:14 The c came to the field of Joshua of
6:14 people chopped up the wood of the c
2Sa 6: 3 They set the ark of God on a new c
6: 3 of Abinadab, were guiding the new c
1Ch 13: 7 on a new c, with Uzzah and Ahio
Isa 5:18 and wickedness as with c ropes,
Am 2:13 "Now then, I will crush you as a c.

Carts (Cart)

Ge 45:19 'Do this: Take some c from Egypt for
45:21 Joseph gave them c, as Pharaoh had
45:27 and when he saw the c Joseph had
46: 5 their wives in the c that Pharaoh
Nu 7: 3 gifts before the LORD six covered c
7: 6 Moses took the c and oxen and gave
7: 7 He gave two c and four oxen to the
7: 8 he gave four c and eight oxen to the
Ps 65:11 and your c overflow with abundance.

Cartwheel (Cart)

Isa 28:27 nor is a c rolled over cummin;.

Carved (Carves, Carvings)

Lev 26: 1 and do not place a c stone in your
Nu 33:52 Destroy all their c images and their

Jdg 17: 3 to make a c image and a cast idol.
18:14 other household gods, a c image and
18:17 went inside and took the c image,
18:18 Micah's house and took the c image,
18:20 household gods and the c image
1Ki 6:18 c with gourds and open flowers.
6:29 he c cherubim, palm trees and open
6:32 on the two olive wood doors he c
6:35 He c cherubim, palm trees and open
2Ki 21: 7 He took the c Asherah pole he had
2Ch 3: 7 and he c cherubim on the walls.
33: 7 He took the c image he had made and
34: 3 poles, c idols and cast images.
Ps 74: 6 They smashed all the c panelling
144:12 be like pillars c to adorn a palace.
Eze 41:18 were c cherubim and palm trees.
41:19 were c all round the whole temple.
41:20 c on the wall of the outer sanctuary.
41:25 the outer sanctuary were c cherubim
41:25 trees like those c on the walls,
41:26 with palm trees c on each side.
Mic 5:13 I will destroy your c images and
Na 1:14 I will destroy the c images and
Hab 2:18 is an idol, since a man has c it?

Carves (Carved)

Dt 27:15 "Cursed is the man who c an image or

Carvings (Carved)

1Ki 6:35 gold hammered evenly over the c.

Case (Cases)

Ex 18:22 them bring every difficult c to you;
Lev 5: 4 in any c when he learns of it he
5:13 as in the c of the grain offering.'"
Nu 27: 5 Moses brought their c before the
Dt 1:16 whether the c is between brother
1:17 Bring me any c too hard for you, and
6:24 be kept alive, as is the c today.
22:26 This c is like that of someone who
25: 1 and the judges will decide the c,
Jos 20: 4 c before the elders of that city.
2Sa 15: 4 a complaint or c could come to me
20:21 That is not the c. A man named Sheba
1Ki 15: 5 in the c of Uriah the Hittite.
2Ki 8: 6 official to her c and said to him,
2Ch 19:10 In every c that comes before you
Job 13: 3 Almighty and to argue my c with God.
13: 8 Will you argue the c for God?
13:18 Now that I have prepared my c, I
23: 4 I would state my c before him and
23: 7 man could present his c before him,
29:16 I took up the c of the stranger.
35:14 that your c is before him and you
37:19 up our c because of our darkness.
Pr 18:17 The first to present his c seems
22:23 for the LORD will take up their c
23:11 he will take up their c against you.
25: 9 If you argue your c with a neighbour,
Isa 1:17 plead the c of the widow.
1:23 widow's c does not come before them.
41:21 "Present your c," says the LORD.
43:26 state the c for your innocence.
59: 4 no-one pleads his c with integrity.
Jer 5:28 the c of the fatherless to win it,
12: 1 O LORD, when I bring a c before you.
Lam 3:58 O Lord, you took up my c; you
Mic 6: 1 "Stand up, plead your c before the
6: 2 For the LORD has a c against his
7: 9 until he pleads my c and establishes
Lk 13:33 In any c, I must keep going today
Ac 5:38 Therefore, in the present c I advise
19:40 In that c we would not be able to
23:15 accurate information about his c.
23:30 present to you their c against him.
23:35 he said, "I will hear your c when
24: 2 Tertullus presented his c before
24:22 he said, "I will decide your c.
25:14 discussed Paul's c with the king.
25:17 I did not delay the c, but convened
1Co 5:10 In that c you would have to leave
14: 7 Even in the c of lifeless things
2Co 10:14 as would be the c if we had not come
Gal 3:15 established, so it is in this c.
5:11 In that c the offence of the cross
2Ti 3: 9 as in the c of those men, their
Heb 6: 9 confident of better things in your c
7: 8 In the one c, the tenth is collected
7: 8 but in the other c, by him who is
9:16 In the c of a will, it is necessary

Cases (Case)

Ex 18:22 simple c they can decide themselves.
18:26 The difficult c they brought to
22: 9 In all c of illegal possession of an
22: 9 to bring their c before the judges.
Dt 17: 8 If c come before your courts that
21: 5 decide all c of dispute and assault.
24: 8 In c of leprous diseases be very
Ezr 10:16 they sat down to investigate the c,
1Co 6: 2 not competent to judge trivial c?

Casiphia

Ezr 8:17 I sent them to Iddo, the leader in C.
8:17 the temple servants in C, so that

Casluhites

Ge 10:14 C (from whom the Philistines came)
1Ch 1:12 C (from whom the Philistines came)

Cassia

Ex 30:24 500 shekels of c—all according to
Ps 45: 8 fragrant with myrrh and aloes and c;
Eze 27:19 iron, c and calamus for your wares..

Cast (Casting, Casts, Downcast, Outcast)

Ex 25:12 C four gold rings for it and fasten
26:37 And c five bronze bases for them.
32: 4 an idol c in the shape of a calf,
32: 8 an idol c in the shape of a calf.
34:17 "Do not make c idols.
36:36 them and c their four silver bases.
37: 3 He c four gold rings for it and
37:13 They c four gold rings for the table
38: 5 They c bronze rings to hold the
38:27 to c the bases for the sanctuary
Lev 16: 8 He is to c lots for the two
19: 4 make gods of c metal for yourselves.
Nu 33:52 carved images and their c idols,
Dt 9:12 have made a c idol for themselves."
9:16 an idol c in the shape of a calf.
Jos 18: 6 here to me and I will c lots for you
18: 8 Then return to me, and I will c lots
18:10 Joshua then c lots for them in
Jdg 17: 3 to make a carved image and a c idol.
18:14 a carved image and a c idol?
18:17 other household gods and the c idol
18:18 other household gods and the c idol
1Sa 14:42 Saul said, "C the lot between me and
2Sa 23: 6 evil men are all to be c aside like
1Ki 7:15 He c two bronze pillars, each
7:16 He also made two capitals of c bronze
7:23 He made the Sea of c metal, circular
7:24 The gourds were c in two rows in one
7:30 c with wreaths on each side.
7:33 spokes and hubs were all of c metal.
7:37 They were all c in the same moulds
7:46 The king had them c in clay moulds
2Ki 17:16 two idols c in the shape of calves,
1Ch 24:31 They also c lots, just as their
25: 8 as student, c lots for their duties.
26:13 Lots were c for each gate, according
26:14 Then lots were c for his son
2Ch 4: 2 He made the Sea of c metal, circular
4: 3 The bulls were c in two rows in one
4:17 The king had them c in clay moulds
28: 2 c idols for worshipping the Baals.
34: 3 poles, carved idols and c images.
Ne 9:18 even when they c for themselves an
10:34 have c lots to determine when each
11: 1 and the rest of the people c lots to
Est 3: 7 they c the *pur* (that is, the lot)
9:24 had c the *pur* (that is, the lot)
Job 6:27 You would even c lots for the
37:18 skies, hard as a mirror of c bronze?
Ps 22:10 From birth I was c upon you; from my
22:18 them and c lots for my clothing.
50:17 and c my words behind you.
Ps 51:11 Do not c me from your presence or
55:22 C your cares on the LORD and he will
71: 9 Do not c me away when I am old;
73:18 ground; you c them down to ruin.
89:44 and c his throne to the ground.
106:19 and worshipped an idol c from metal.
Pr 16:33 The lot is c into the lap, but its
23: 5 C but a glance at riches, and they
29:18 the people c off restraint; but
Ecc 11: 1 C your bread upon the waters, for
11:10 and c off the troubles of your body,
Isa 14:12 You have been c down to the earth,
14:19 you are c out of your tomb like a
19: 8 all who c hooks into the Nile;
38: 8 I will make the shadow c by the sun
57:20 rest, whose waves c up mire and mud.
Jer 22:28 out, c into a land they do not know?
23:39 and c you out of my presence
Lam 3:31 For men are not c off by the Lord
Eze 21:21 He will c lots with arrows, he will
31:11 to its wickedness. I c it aside,
32: 3 of people I will c my net over you,
Joel 3: 3 They c lots for my people and traded
Am 4: 3 you will be c out towards Harmon,"
5: 7 and c righteousness to the ground
Ob :11 his gates and c lots for Jerusalem,
Jnh 1: 7 "Come, let us c lots to find out who
1: 7 c lots and the lot fell on Jonah.
Mic 5:12 and you will no longer c spells.
Na 1:14 destroy the carved images and c idols
3:10 Lots were c for her nobles, and all
Mal 3:11 your fields will not c their fruit,"
Mk 15:24 c lots to see what each would get.
Jn 19:24 them and c lots for my clothing.
Ac 1:26 they c lots, and the lot fell to
26:10 to death, I c my vote against them.
1Pe 5: 7 C all your anxiety on him because he
Rev 2:22 I will c her on a bed of suffering..

Casting (Cast)

Pr 18:18 C the lot settles disputes and keeps
Eze 24: 6 by piece without c lots for them.
26: 3 you, like the sea c up its waves.
Mt 4:18 They were c a net into the lake, for
27:35 divided up his clothes by c lots.
Mk 1:16 Andrew c a net into the lake,
Lk 23:34 divided up his clothes by c lots.

Castor

Ac 28:11 of the twin gods C and Pollux.

Casts (Cast)

Dt 18:11 or c spells, or who is a medium or
27:15 who carves an image or c an idol
Ps 15: 3 and c no slur on his fellow-man,
147: 6 but c the wicked to the ground
Isa 26: 5 ground and c it down to the dust.
40:19 As for an idol, a craftsman c it,
44:10 Who shapes a god and c an idol,

Casualties

Jdg 20:31 They began to inflict c on the
20:39 to inflict c on the men of Israel
2Sa 18: 7 and the c that day were great
1Ki 20:29 inflicted a hundred thousand c
2Ch 13:17 there were five hundred thousand c
28: 5 Israel, who inflicted heavy c on him.
Na 3: 3 Many c, piles of dead,

Catastrophe

Ge 19:29 and he brought Lot out of the c that
Isa 47:11 a c you cannot foresee will suddenly

Catch (Catches, Caught)

Ge 44: 4 and when you c up with them, say to
Dt 32:11 that spreads its wings to c them and
Jos 2: 5 Go after them quickly. You may c up
Job 23: 9 to the south, I c no glimpse of him.
Ps 10: 9 he lies in wait to c the helpless;
SS 2:15 C for us the foxes, the little foxes
Jer 2:34 you did not c them breaking in.
5:26 like those who set traps to c men.
16:16 the LORD, "and they will c them.
Hos 2: 7 after her lovers but not c them;

Hos 7:12 flocking together, I will **c** them.
Am 3: 5 earth when there is nothing to **c**?
Mt 17:27 Take the first fish you **c**; open its
Mk 12:13 to Jesus to **c** him in his words.
Lk 5: 4 and let down the nets for a **c**."
5: 9 at the **c** of fish they had taken,
5:10 afraid; from now on you will **c** men."
11:54 waiting to **c** him in something he
20:20 They hoped to **c** Jesus in something

Catches (Catch)

Job 5:13 He **c** the wise in their craftiness,
39:25 He **c** the scent of battle from afar,
Ps 10: 9 he **c** the helpless and drags them off
Hab 1:15 he **c** them in his net, he gathers
1Co 3:19 "He **c** the wise in their craftiness"

Cattle

Ge 12:16 and Abram acquired sheep and **c**, male
20:14 Abimelech brought sheep and **c** and
21:27 Abraham brought sheep and **c** and gave
24:35 He has given him sheep and **c**, silver
32: 5 I have **c** and donkeys, sheep and
47:17 and goats, their **c** and donkeys.
Ex 9: 3 and on your **c** and sheep and goats.
11: 5 all the firstborn of the **c** as well.
20:24 your sheep and goats and your **c**.
22: 1 he must pay back five head of **c** for
22:30 Do the same with your **c** and your
Lev 7:23 any of the fat of **c**, sheep or goats.
22:19 a male without defect from the **c**,
26:22 destroy your **c** and make you so few
Nu 22:40 Balak sacrificed **c** and sheep, and
31:28 persons, **c**, donkeys, sheep or goats.
31:30 whether persons, **c**, donkeys, sheep,
31:33 72,000 **c**,
31:38 36,000 **c**, of which the tribute for
31:44 36,000 **c**,
35: 3 in and pasture-lands for their **c**,
Dt 11:15 grass in the fields for your **c**,
14:26 silver to buy whatever you like: **c**,
Jos 6:21 young and old, **c**, sheep and donkeys.
7:24 his sons and daughters, his **c**,
Jdg 6: 4 neither sheep nor **c** nor donkeys.
1Sa 8:16 maidservants and the best of your **c**
14:32 taking sheep, **c** and calves, they
14:34 'Each of you bring me your **c** and
15: 3 **c** and sheep, camels and donkeys.'"
15: 9 Agag and the best of the sheep and **c**,
15:14 is this lowing of **c** that I hear?"
15:15 **c** to sacrifice to the LORD your God,
15:21 The soldiers took sheep and **c** from
22:19 and its **c**, donkeys and sheep.
27: 9 **c**, donkeys and camels, and clothes.
2Sa 12: 2 a very large number of sheep and **c**,
12: 4 from taking one of his own sheep or **c**
1Ki 1: 9 Adonijah then sacrificed sheep, **c**
1:19 He has sacrificed great numbers of **c**,
1:25 of **c**, fattened calves, and sheep.
4:23 ten head of stall-fed **c**,
4:23 twenty of pasture-fed **c** and a
8: 5 sacrificing so many sheep and **c** that
8:63 twenty-two thousand **c** and a hundred
2Ki 3:17 **c** and your other animals will drink.
1Ch 12:40 raisin cakes, wine, oil, **c** and sheep,
2Ch 5: 6 sacrificing so many sheep and **c** that
7: 5 of twenty-two thousand head of **c**
15:11 to the LORD seven hundred head of **c**
18: 2 Ahab slaughtered many sheep and **c**
32:28 made stalls for various kinds of **c**,
35: 7 and also three thousand **c**—all from
35: 8 offerings and three hundred **c**.
35: 9 hundred head of **c** for the Levites.
35:12 They did the same with the **c**.
Ne 9:37 They rule over our bodies and our **c**
10:36 firstborn of our sons and of our **c**,
Job 18: 3 Why are we regarded as **c** and
36:33 even the **c** make known its approach.
Ps 50:10 and the **c** on a thousand hills.
78:48 He gave over their **c** to the hail,
104:14 He makes grass grow for the **c**,
147: 9 He provides food for the **c** and for
148:10 wild animals and all **c**, small
Isa 7:25 they will become places where **c** are
22:13 slaughtering of **c** and killing of
30:23 your **c** will graze in broad meadows.
32:20 your **c** and donkeys range free.
63:14 like **c** that go down to the plain,
Jer 9:10 and the lowing of **c** is not heard.
Eze 32:13 I will destroy all her **c** from beside
32:13 of man or muddied by the hoofs of **c**.
Da 4:25 you will eat grass like **c** and be
4:32 animals; you will eat grass like **c**.
4:33 from people and ate grass like **c**.
5:21 wild donkeys and ate grass like **c**;
Joel 1:18 How the **c** moan! The herds mill about
Jnh 4:11 from their left, and many **c** as well.
Hab 3:17 in the pen and no **c** in the stalls,
Hag 1:11 on men and **c**, and on the labour of
Mt 22: 4 fattened **c** have been slaughtered,
Jn 2:14 courts he found men selling **c**,
2:15 the temple area, both sheep and **c**;
Rev 18:13 of fine flour and wheat; **c** and sheep;

Cauda

Ac 27:16 the lee of a small island called **C**,

Caught (Catch)

Ge 22:13 thicket he saw a ram **c** by its horns.
27:27 When Isaac **c** the smell of his
31:23 **c** up with him in the hill country of
39:12 She **c** him by his cloak and said,
44: 6 When he **c** up with them, he repeated
Ex 10:19 which **c** up the locusts and carried
21:16 when he is **c** must be put to death.
22: 2 "If a thief is **c** breaking in and is
22: 7 if he is **c**, must pay back double.
Nu 5:13 and she has not been **c** in the act),
11:22 fish in the sea were **c** for them?"
Dt 24: 7 If a man is **c** kidnapping one of his
Jos 7:15 He who is **c** with the devoted things
8:22 so that they were **c** in the middle,
Jdg 1: 6 but they chased him and **c** him, and
8:14 He **c** a young man of Succoth and
15: 4 went out and **c** three hundred foxes
21:23 each man **c** one and carried her off
1Sa 9:17 When Samuel **c** sight of Saul,
15:27 Saul **c** hold of the hem of his robe,
2Sa 18: 9 Absalom's head got **c** in the tree.
Job 4:12 to me, my ears **c** a whisper of it.
Ps 9:15 are **c** in the net they have hidden.
10: 2 who are **c** in the schemes he devises.
59:12 lips, let them be **c** in their pride.
Pr 6:31 Yet if he is **c**, he must pay
30:28 a lizard can be **c** with the hand,
Ecc 9:12 As fish are **c** in a cruel net,
Isa 13:15 who are **c** will fall by the sword.
22: 3 All you who were **c** were taken
24:18 out of the pit will be **c** in a snare.
51:20 street, like antelope **c** in a net.
Jer 2:26 "As a thief is disgraced when he is **c**
6:11 husband and wife will be **c** in it,
41:12 They **c** up with him near the great
48:27 Was she **c** among thieves, that you
48:44 out of the pit will be **c** in a snare;
50:24 and you were **c** before you knew it;
Lam 4:20 life breath, was **c** in their traps.
Eze 12:13 and he will be **c** in my snare; I will
17:20 him, and he will be **c** in my snare.
Am 3: 4 in his den when he has **c** nothing?
Mt 13:47 the lake and **c** all kinds of fish.
14:31 Jesus reached out his hand and **c** him.
Lk 5: 5 all night and haven't **c** anything.
5: 6 they **c** such a large number of fish
Jn 8: 3 brought in a woman **c** in adultery.
8: 4 woman was **c** in the act of adultery.
21: 3 boat, but that night they **c** nothing.
21:10 some of the fish you have just **c**."
Ac 27:15 The ship was **c** by the storm and
2Co 12: 2 ago was **c** up to the third heaven.
12: 4 was **c** up to paradise. He heard
12:16 that I am, I **c** you by trickery!
Gal 6: 1 Brothers, if someone is **c** in a sin,
1Th 4:17 will be **c** up together with them
2Pe 2:12 born only to be **c** and destroyed, and.

Cauldron (Cauldrons)

1Sa 2:14 into the pan or kettle or **c** or pot,
Job 41:31 the depths churn like a boiling **c**.

Cauldrons (Cauldron)

2Ch 35:13 the holy offerings in pots, **c** and

Caulk

Eze 27: 9 as shipwrights to **c** your seams.

Cause (Caused, Causes, Causing)

Ex 20:24 Wherever I **c** my name to be honoured,
23:33 or they will **c** you to sin against me,
33:19 "I will **c** all my goodness to pass
Nu 5:21 "may the LORD **c** your people to curse
5:24 enter her and **c** bitter suffering.
5:27 it will go into her and **c** bitter
16: 5 chooses he will **c** to come near him.
32:15 will be the **c** of their destruction."
Dt 3:28 will **c** them to inherit the land that
10:18 He defends the **c** of the fatherless
28:25 The LORD will **c** you to be defeated
33: 7 With his own hands he defends his **c**.
Jos 22:25 **c** ours to stop fearing the LORD.
Jdg 6:31 "Are you going to plead Baal's **c**?
1Sa 24:15 May he consider my **c** and uphold it;
25:39 who has upheld my **c** against Nabal
1Ki 8:45 and their plea, and uphold their **c**.
8:49 and their plea, and uphold their **c**.
8:50 and **c** their conquerors to show them
8:59 may uphold the **c** of his servant
8:59 the **c** of his people Israel according
2Ki 2:21 Never again will it **c** death or make
14:10 Why ask for trouble and **c** your own
2Ch 6:35 and their plea, and uphold their **c**.
6:39 and their pleas, and uphold their **c**.
20:27 **c** to rejoice over their enemies.
25:19 Why ask for trouble and **c** your own
Job 5: 8 to God; I would lay my **c** before him.
Ps 7: 4 or without **c** have robbed my foe—
9: 4 For you have upheld my right and my **c**
35: 7 they hid their net for me without **c**
35: 7 and without **c** dug a pit for me,
35:19 me who are my enemies without **c**;
37: 6 the justice of your **c** like the
43: 1 Vindicate me, O God, and plead my **c**
69: 4 many are my enemies without **c**,
74:22 Rise up, O God, and defend your **c**;
82: 3 Defend the **c** of the weak and
109: 3 they attack me without **c**.
119:78 to shame for wronging me without **c**;
119:86 me, for men persecute me without **c**.
119:154 Defend my **c** and redeem me; preserve
119:161 Rulers persecute me without **c**, but
140:12 and upholds the **c** of the needy.
146: 7 He upholds the **c** of the oppressed
Pr 24:28 against your neighbour without **c**,
Ecc 8: 3 Do not stand up for a bad **c**, for he
Isa 1:17 Defend the **c** of the fatherless,
1:23 They do not defend the **c** of the
16: 5 and speeds the **c** of righteousness.
30:30 The LORD will **c** men to hear his
34: 8 of retribution, to uphold Zion's **c**.
40:27 my **c** is disregarded by my God"?
47:12 succeed, perhaps you will **c** terror.
53:10 to crush him and **c** him to suffer,
58:14 and I will **c** you to ride on the
64: 2 **c** the nations to quake before you!
Jer 11:20 for to you I have committed my **c**.
20:12 for to you I have committed my **c**.
22:16 He defended the **c** of the poor and
30:13 There is no-one to plead your **c**, no
40:15 take your life and **c** all the Jews
50:34 He will vigorously defend their **c** so
51:36 "See, I will defend your **c** and
Lam 3:52 Those who were my enemies without **c**
3:59 Uphold my **c**!
Eze 14:23 I have done nothing in it without **c**,
32:10 I will **c** many peoples to be appalled
32:12 I will **c** your hordes to fall by the
33:12 **c** him to fall when he turns from it.
36:12 I will **c** people, my people Israel,
36:15 peoples or **c** your nation to fall,
Da 8:24 He will **c** astounding devastation and
8:25 He will **c** deceit to prosper, and he
Mt 18: 7 of the things that **c** people to sin!
Lk 2:34 "This child is destined to **c** the
17: 1 "Things that **c** people to sin are
17: 2 **c** one of these little ones to sin.

Ro 14:21 that will **c** your brother to fall.
16:17 watch out for those who **c** divisions
1Co 8:13 so that I will not **c** him to fall.
10:32 Do not **c** anyone to stumble, whether
2Co 4:15 more people may **c** thanksgiving to
Gal 6:17 Finally, let no-one **c** me trouble,
Php 4: 3 at my side in the **c** of the gospel,
Heb 12:15 no bitter root grows up to **c** trouble
Rev 13:15 and **c** all who refused to worship the

Caused (Cause)

Ge 2:21 the LORD God **c** the man to fall into
5:29 **c** by the ground the LORD has cursed."
20:13 God **c** me to wander from my father's
Jdg 7:22 the LORD **c** the men throughout the
1Ki 11:25 adding to the trouble **c** by Hadad.
14:16 and has **c** Israel to commit."
15:26 which he had **c** Israel to commit.
15:30 and had **c** Israel to commit,
15:34 which he had **c** Israel to commit.
16: 2 **c** my people Israel to sin and to
16:13 and had **c** Israel to commit,
16:19 and had **c** Israel to commit.
16:26 which he had **c** Israel to commit, so
21:22 to anger and have **c** Israel to sin.'
22:52 son of Nebat, who **c** Israel to sin.
2Ki 3: 3 which he had **c** Israel to commit;
7: 6 for the Lord had **c** the Arameans to
10:29 which he had **c** Israel to commit
10:31 which he had **c** Israel to commit.
13: 2 which he had **c** Israel to commit,
13: 6 which he had **c** Israel to commit;
13:11 which he had **c** Israel to commit;
14:24 which he had **c** Israel to commit.
15: 9 which he had **c** Israel to commit.
15:18 which he had **c** Israel to commit.
15:24 which he had **c** Israel to commit.
15:28 which he had **c** Israel to commit.
17:21 and **c** them to commit a great sin.
21:16 sin that he had **c** Judah to commit,
23:15 who had **c** Israel to sin—even that
2Ch 21:11 had **c** the people of Jerusalem to
Ezr 6:12 May God, who has **c** his Name to dwell
Job 34:28 They **c** the cry of the poor to come
Ps 106:46 He **c** them to be pitied by all who
111: 4 He has **c** his wonders to be
140: 9 with the trouble their lips have **c**.
Isa 21: 2 to an end all the groaning she **c**.
Jer 50: 6 and **c** them to roam on the mountains.
Eze 32:30 despite the terror **c** by their power.
Da 1: 9 Now God had **c** the official to show
Am 3: 6 to a city, has not the LORD **c** it?
Mal 2: 8 teaching have **c** many to stumble;
2: 9 "So I have **c** you to be despised and
Ac 9:21 "Isn't he the man who **c** havoc in
10:40 the third day and **c** him to be seen.
17: 6 "These men who have **c** trouble all
2Co 2: 5 If anyone has **c** grief, he has not so
7: 8 Even if I **c** you sorrow by my letter,
Jas 4: 5 that the spirit he **c** to live in us
2Pe 1: 4 in the world **c** by evil desires.

Causes (Cause)

Nu 5:21 denounce you when he **c** your thigh to
2Ch 21:15 disease **c** your bowels to come out.'"
Ps 7:16 The trouble he **c** recoils on himself;
Pr 10:10 He who winks maliciously **c** grief,
Isa 8:14 be a stone that **c** men to stumble
61:11 up and a garden **c** seeds to grow,
64: 2 twigs ablaze and **c** water to boil,
Da 8:13 the rebellion that **c** desolation, and
9:27 up an abomination that **c** desolation,
11:31 the abomination that **c** desolation.
12:11 the abomination that **c** desolation
Mt 5:29 If your right eye **c** you to sin,
5:30 if your right hand **c** you to sin, cut
5:32 **c** her to become an adulteress, and
5:45 He **c** his sun to rise on the evil and
13:41 that **c** sin and all who do evil.
18: 6 if anyone **c** one of these little ones
18: 8 If your hand or your foot **c** you to
18: 9 if your eye **c** you to sin, gouge it
24:15 'the abomination that **c** desolation',
Mk 9:42 "And if anyone **c** one of these little
9:43 If your hand **c** you to sin, cut it
Mk 9:45 if your foot **c** you to sin, cut it
9:47 if your eye **c** you to sin, pluck it
13:14 'the abomination that **c** desolation'
Ro 9:33 a stone that **c** men to stumble
14:20 that **c** someone else to stumble.
1Co 8:13 if what I eat **c** my brother to fall
Col 2:19 sinews, grows as God **c** it to grow.
Jas 4: 1 What **c** fights and quarrels among you?
1Pe 2: 8 "A stone that **c** men to stumble.

Causing (Cause)

Dt 8: 3 He humbled you, **c** you to hunger and
1Ki 17:20 staying with, by **c** her son to die?"
Ps 105:29 into blood, **c** their fish to die.
Rev 13:13 even **c** fire to come down from heaven

Cautioned (Cautious)

Ac 23:22 dismissed the young man and **c** him,

Cautious (Cautioned)

Pr 12:26 A righteous man is **c** in friendship,

Cavalry

Ne 2: 9 sent army officers and **c** with me.
Da 11:40 and **c** and a great fleet of ships.
Joel 2: 4 of horses; they gallop along like **c**.
Na 3: 3 Charging **c**, flashing swords and
Hab 1: 8 Their **c** gallops headlong; their
Ac 23:32 The next day they let the **c** go on
23:33 the **c** arrived in Caesarea, they

Cave (Caves)

Ge 19:30 and his two daughters lived in a **c**.
23: 9 he will sell me the **c** of Machpelah,
23:11 and I give you the **c** that is in it.
23:17 the field and the **c** in it,
23:19 buried his wife Sarah in the **c** in the
23:20 the field and the **c** in it were
25: 9 in the **c** of Machpelah near Mamre,
49:29 **c** in the field of Ephron the Hittite,
49:30 the **c** in the field of Machpelah,
49:32 The field and the **c** in it were
50:13 in the **c** in the field of Machpelah,
Jos 10:16 and hidden in the **c** at Makkedah.
10:17 found hiding in the **c** at Makkedah,
10:18 rocks up to the mouth of the **c**,
10:22 Joshua said, "Open the mouth of the **c**
10:23 brought the five kings out of the **c**
10:27 the **c** where they had been hiding.
10:27 At the mouth of the **c** they placed
Jdg 15: 8 stayed in a **c** in the rock of Etam.
15:11 down to the **c** in the rock of Etam
1Sa 22: 1 David left Gath and escaped to the **c**
24: 3 a **c** was there, and Saul went in to
24: 3 and his men were far back in the **c**.
24: 7 And Saul left the **c** and went his way.
24: 8 David went out of the **c** and called
24:10 LORD gave you into my hands in the **c**.
2Sa 17: 9 Even now, he is hidden in a **c** or
23:13 down to David at the **c** of Adullam,
1Ki 19: 9 There he went into a **c** and spent the
19:13 out and stood at the mouth of the **c**.
1Ch 11:15 to the rock at the **c** of Adullam,
Ps 57: T he had fled from Saul into the **c**.
142: T When he was in the **c**. A prayer.
Jer 48:28 makes its nest at the mouth of a **c**.
Jn 11:38 It was a **c** with a stone laid across

Caverns

Isa 2:21 They will flee to **c** in the rocks and

Caves (Cave)

Jdg 6: 2 mountain clefts, **c** and strongholds.
1Sa 13: 6 they hid in **c** and thickets, among
1Ki 18: 4 prophets and hidden them in two **c**,
18:13 of the LORD's prophets in two **c**,
Isa 2:19 Men will flee to **c** in the rocks and
Jer 49: 8 Turn and flee, hide in deep **c**, you
49:30 "Flee quickly away! Stay in deep **c**,
Eze 33:27 those in strongholds and **c** will die
Heb 11:38 and in **c** and holes in the ground.
Rev 6:15 every free man hid in **c** and among

Cease (Ceased, Ceasing)

Ge 8:22 winter, day and night will never **c**."
Jos 9:23 You will never **c** to serve as
2Ki 18: 6 LORD and did not **c** to follow him;
Ne 9:19 pillar of cloud did not **c** to guide
Est 9:28 **c** to be celebrated by the Jews,
Job 3:17 There the wicked **c** from turmoil, and
6:17 that **c** to flow in the dry season,
Ps 46: 9 He makes wars **c** to the ends of the
Ecc 12: 3 when the grinders **c** because they are
Isa 16: 4 to an end, and destruction will **c**;
Jer 18:14 from distant sources ever **c** to flow?
31:36 ever **c** to be a nation before me."
47: 6 to your scabbard; **c** and be still.'
Eze 5:13 "Then my anger will **c** and my wrath
1Co 12:15 reason **c** to be part of the body.
12:16 reason **c** to be part of the body.
13: 8 there are prophecies, they will **c**;

Ceased (Cease)

Jdg 5: 7 Village life in Israel **c**, **c** until I,
Ps 36: 3 he has **c** to be wise and to do good.

Ceasing (Cease)

Ps 35:15 They slandered me without **c**.
Jer 14:17 with tears night and day without **c**;

Cedar (Cedars)

Lev 14: 4 live clean birds and some **c** wood,
14: 6 together with the **c** wood, the
14:49 **c** wood, scarlet yarn and hyssop.
14:51 he is to take the **c** wood, the hyssop,
14:52 the live bird, the **c** wood, the
Nu 19: 6 The priest is to take some **c** wood,
2Sa 5:11 along with **c** logs and carpenters and
7: 2 "Here I am, living in a palace of **c**,
7: 7 you not built me a house of **c**?"'
1Ki 4:33 from the **c** of Lebanon to the hyssop
5: 8 in providing the **c** and pine logs.
5:10 all the **c** and pine logs he wanted,
6: 9 roofing it with beams and **c** planks.
6:10 to the temple by beams of **c**.
6:15 He lined its interior walls with **c**
6:16 with **c** boards from floor to ceiling
6:18 The inside of the temple was **c**,
6:18 Everything was **c**; no stone was to be
6:20 and he also overlaid the altar of **c**.
6:36 and one course of trimmed **c** beams.
7: 2 **c** columns supporting trimmed **c** beams.
7: 3 was roofed with **c** above the beams
7: 7 it with **c** from floor to ceiling.
7:11 stones, cut to size, and **c** beams.
7:12 and one course of trimmed **c** beams,
9:11 the **c** and pine and gold he wanted.
10:27 and **c** as plentiful as sycamore-fig
2Ki 14: 9 sent a message to a **c** in Lebanon,
1Ch 14: 1 along with **c** logs, stonemasons and
17: 1 "Here I am, living in a palace of **c**,
17: 6 you not built me a house of **c**?"'
22: 4 He also provided more **c** logs than
2Ch 1:15 and **c** as plentiful as sycamore-fig
2: 3 "Send me **c** logs as you did for my
2: 3 him **c** to build a palace to live in.
2: 8 "Send me also **c**, pine and algum logs
9:27 and **c** as plentiful as sycamore-fig
25:18 sent a message to a **c** in Lebanon,
Ezr 3: 7 so that they would bring **c** logs by
Job 40:17 His tail sways like a **c**; the sinews
Ps 92:12 they will grow like a **c** of Lebanon;
SS 8: 9 will enclose her with panels of **c**.
Isa 41:19 I will put in the desert the **c** and
Jer 22: 7 They will cut up your fine **c** beams
22:14 panels it with **c** and decorates it
22:15 you a king to have more and more **c**?
22:23 who are nestled in **c** buildings
Eze 17: 3 Taking hold of the top of a **c**,
17:22 the very top of a **c** and plant it;
17:23 bear fruit and become a splendid **c**.
27: 5 they took a **c** from Lebanon to make a
31: 3 Consider Assyria, once a **c** in
Hos 14: 5 Like a **c** of Lebanon he will send
14: 6 his fragrance like a **c** of Lebanon.
Zep 2:14 the beams of **c** will be exposed.
Zec 11: 2 Wail, O pine tree, for the **c** has

Cedars (Cedar)
Nu 24: 6 the LORD, like c beside the waters.
Jdg 9:15 and consume the c of Lebanon!'
1Ki 5: 6 "So give orders that c of Lebanon be
2Ki 19:23 I have cut down its tallest c, the
Ps 29: 5 The voice of the LORD breaks the c;
29: 5 breaks in pieces the c of Lebanon.
80:10 the mighty c with its branches.
104:16 the c of Lebanon that he planted.
148: 9 all hills, fruit trees and all c,
SS 1:17 The beams of our house are c; our
5:15 is like Lebanon, choice as its c.
Isa 2:13 for all the c of Lebanon, tall and
9:10 but we will replace them with c."
14: 8 Even the pine trees and the c of
37:24 I have cut down its tallest c, the
44:14 He cut down c, or perhaps took a
Eze 31: 8 The c in the garden of God could not
Am 2: 9 though he was tall as the c and
Zec 11: 1 so that fire may devour your c!

Ceiling
1Ki 6:15 the floor of the temple to the c,
6:16 with cedar boards from floor to c
7: 7 it with cedar from floor to c.
2Ch 3: 7 He overlaid the c beams, door-frames,

Celebrate (Celebrated, Celebrating, Celebration, Celebrations)
Ex 10: 9 we are to c a festival to the LORD."
12:14 c it as a festival to the LORD
12:17 "C the Feast of Unleavened Bread,
12:17 C this day as a lasting ordinance
12:47 The whole community of Israel must c
12:48 who wants to c the LORD's Passover
23:14 "Three times a year you are to c a
23:15 "C the Feast of Unleavened Bread;
23:16 "C the Feast of Harvest with the
23:16 "C the Feast of Ingathering at the
34:18 "C the Feast of Unleavened Bread.
34:22 "C the Feast of Weeks with the
Lev 23:39 c the festival to the LORD for seven
23:41 C this as a festival to the LORD for
23:41 to come; c it in the seventh month.
Nu 9: 2 "Make the Israelites c the Passover
9: 3 C it at the appointed time, at
9: 4 Moses told the Israelites to c the
9: 6 some of them could not c the
9:10 may still c the LORD's Passover.
9:11 They are to c it on the fourteenth
9:12 When they c the Passover, they must
9:13 a journey fails to c the Passover,
9:14 who wants to c the LORD's Passover
29:12 C a festival to the LORD for seven
Dt 16: 1 and c the Passover of the LORD
16:10 c the Feast of Weeks to the LORD
16:13 C the Feast of Tabernacles for seven
16:15 For seven days c the Feast to the
Jdg 16:23 to Dagon their god and to c,
2Sa 6:21 Israel—I will c before the LORD.
2Ki 23:21 "C the Passover to the LORD your God,
2Ch 30: 1 and c the Passover to the LORD,
30: 2 c the Passover in the second month.
30: 3 They had not been able to c it at
30: 5 and c the Passover to the LORD,
30:13 c the Feast of Unleavened Bread
30:23 The whole assembly then agreed to c
Ne 8:12 to send portions of food and to c
12:27 were brought to Jerusalem to c
Est 9:21 to have them c annually the
Ps 145: 7 They will c your abundant goodness
Isa 30:29 on the night you c a holy festival;
Na 1:15 C your festivals, O Judah,
Zec 14:16 and to c the Feast of Tabernacles.
14:18 go up to c the Feast of Tabernacles.
14:19 go up to c the Feast of Tabernacles.
Mt 26:18 I am going to c the Passover with my
Lk 15:23 Let's have a feast and c.
15:24 and is found.' So they began to c.
15:29 goat so I could c with my friends.
15:32 we had to c and be glad, because
Rev 11:10 will c by sending each other gifts,

Celebrated (Celebrate)
Jos 5:10 the Israelites c the Passover.
1Ki 8:65 They c it before the LORD our God
2Ki 23:23 was c to the LORD in Jerusalem.
2Ch 7: 9 for they had c the dedication of the
30: 5 It had not been c in large numbers
30:21 c the Feast of Unleavened Bread for
30:23 another seven days they c joyfully.
35: 1 Josiah c the Passover to the LORD in
35:17 The Israelites who were present c
35:18 c such a Passover as did Josiah,
35:19 This Passover was c in the
Ezr 3: 4 they c the Feast of Tabernacles with
6:16 c the dedication of the house of God
6:19 month, the exiles c the Passover.
6:22 For seven days they c with joy the
Ne 8:17 Israelites had not c it like this.
8:18 They c the feast for seven days, and
Est 9:28 never cease to be c by the Jews,

Celebrating (Celebrate)
Ex 31:16 c it for the generations to come as
2Sa 6: 5 the whole house of Israel were c
1Ch 13: 8 David and all the Israelites were c
15:29 she saw King David dancing and c,
Est 8:17 among the Jews, with feasting and c.

Celebration (Celebrate)
1Sa 11:15 all the Israelites held a great c.
2Ch 35:16 out for the c of the Passover
Est 8:15 And the city of Susa held a joyous c.
9:22 and their mourning into a day of c.
9:23 the Jews agreed to continue the c
Ac 7:41 held a c in honour of what their
Col 2:16 a New Moon c or a Sabbath day.

Celebrations (Celebrate)
Hos 2:11 I will stop all her c: her yearly

Celestial
2Pe 2:10 are not afraid to slander c beings;
Jude : 8 authority and slander c beings.

Cell
Jer 37:16 Jeremiah was put into a vaulted c in
Ac 12: 7 appeared and a light shone in the c.
16:24 he put them in the inner c and

Cenchrea
Eastern port of Corinth. Paul cut his hair off before sailing from here (Ac 18:18). Phoebe served the church based here (Ro 16:1).

Ac 18:18 he had his hair cut off at C
Ro 16: 1 Phoebe, a servant of the church in C.

Censer (Censers)
Lev 16:12 He is to take a c full of burning
Nu 16:17 Each man is to take his c and put
16:18 each man took his c, put fire and
16:46 Moses said to Aaron, "Take your c
2Ch 26:19 Uzziah, who had a c in his hand
Eze 8:11 Each had a c in his hand, and a
Rev 8: 3 Another angel, who had a golden c,
8: 5 the angel took the c, filled it with

Censers (Censer)
Lev 10: 1 sons Nadab and Abihu took their c,
Nu 16: 6 followers are to do this: Take c
16:17 put incense in it—250 c in all—and
16:17 You and Aaron are to present your c
16:37 to take the c out of the smouldering
16:37 distance away, for the c are holy—
16:38 the c of the men who sinned at the
16:38 Hammer the c into sheets to overlay
16:39 the priest collected the bronze c
1Ki 7:50 sprinkling bowls, dishes and c;
2Ki 25:15 the imperial guard took away the c
2Ch 4:22 sprinkling bowls, dishes and c;
Jer 52:19 the basins, c, sprinkling bowls, pots,

Census
Ex 30:12 "When you take a c of the Israelites
38:25 in the c was 100 talents and 1,775
Nu 1: 2 "Take a c of the whole Israelite
1:49 in the c of the other Israelites.
4: 2 "Take a c of the Kohathite branch of
4:22 "Take a c also of the Gershonites by
14:29 who was counted in the c and who has
26: 2 "Take a c of the whole Israelite
26: 4 "Take a c of men twenty years old or
2Sa 24: 1 Go and take a c of Israel and Judah."
2Ki 12: 4 the money collected in the c,
1Ch 21: 1 incited David to take a c of Israel.
2Ch 2:17 Solomon took a c of all the aliens
2:17 after the c his father David had
Lk 2: 1 a decree that a c should be taken of
2: 2 This was the first c that took place
Ac 5:37 appeared in the days of the c

Central (Centre)
Jdg 16:29 Samson reached towards the two c

Centrally (Centre)
Dt 19: 2 three cities c located in the land

Centre (Central, Centrally, Centres)
Ex 26:28 The c crossbar is to extend from end
28:32 with an opening for the head in its c
36:33 They made the c crossbar so that it
39:23 with an opening in the c of the robe
Nu 35: 5 the north, with the town in the c.
Jdg 9:37 people are coming down from the c of
1Ki 7:25 hindquarters were towards the c.
2Ch 4: 4 hindquarters were towards the c.
6:13 it in the c of the outer court.
Eze 1: 4 The c of the fire looked like
5: 5 I have set in the c of the nations,
38:12 goods, living at the c of the land."
48: 8 sanctuary will be in the c of it.
48:10 In the c of it will be the sanctuary
48:15 The city will be in the c of it
48:21 sanctuary will be in the c of them.
48:22 will lie in the c of the area
Rev 4: 6 In the c, around the throne, were
5: 6 standing in the c of the throne,
7:17 For the Lamb at the c of the throne

Centres (Centre)
Ge 10:10 The first c of his kingdom were

Centurion (Centurion's, Centurions)
Mt 8: 5 a c came to him asking for help.
8: 8 The c replied, "Lord, I do not
8:13 Jesus said to the c, "Go! It will be
27:54 the c and those with him who were
Mk 15:39 the c, who stood there in front of
15:44 Summoning the c, he asked him if
15:45 he learned from the c that it was so,
Lk 7: 3 The c heard of Jesus and sent some
7: 6 the c sent friends to say to him:
23:47 The c, seeing what had happened,
Ac 10: 1 there was a man named Cornelius, a c
10:22 "We have come from Cornelius the c.
22:25 Paul said to the c standing there,
22:26 the c heard this, he went to the
23:18 The c said, "Paul, the prisoner
24:23 He ordered the c to keep Paul under
27: 1 handed over to a c named Julius,
27: 6 There the c found an Alexandrian
27:11 the c, instead of listening to what
27:31 Paul said to the c and the soldiers,
27:43 the c wanted to spare Paul's life

Centurion's (Centurion)
Lk 7: 2 There a c servant, whom his master

Centurions (Centurion)
Ac 23:17 Paul called one of the c and said,
23:23 he called two of his c and ordered

Cephas (Peter)
Jn 1:42 You will be called C" (which, when
1Co 1:12 another, "I follow C"; still another,
3:22 whether Paul or Apollos or C or the
9: 5 and the Lord's brothers and C?

Ceremonial (Ceremony)
Lev 14: 2 at the time of his c cleansing,
15:13 off seven days for his c cleansing;
Mk 7: 3 they give their hands a c washing,
Jn 2: 6 used by the Jews for c washing,
3:25 Jew over the matter of c washing.
11:55 c cleansing before the Passover.
18:28 and to avoid c uncleanness the Jews
Heb 9:10 food and drink and various c washings
13: 9 not by c foods, which are of no

Ceremonially (Ceremony)
Lev 4:12 outside the camp to a place c clean,
5: 2 a person touches anything c unclean
6:11 the camp to a place that is c clean.
7:19 that touches anything c unclean
7:19 meat, anyone c clean may eat it.
10:14 Eat them in a c clean place; they
11: 4 split hoof; it is c unclean for you.
12: 2 will be c unclean for seven days,
12: 7 be c clean from her flow of blood.
13: 3 he shall pronounce him c unclean.
14: 8 with water; then he will be c clean.
15:28 and after that she will be c clean.
15:33 lies with a woman who is c unclean.
17:15 and he will be c unclean till
21: 1 must not make himself c unclean
22: 3 any of your descendants is c unclean
27:11 If what he vowed is a c unclean
Nu 5: 2 is c unclean because of a dead body.
6: 7 he must not make himself c unclean
8: 6 Israelites and make them c clean.
9: 6 c unclean on account of a dead body.
9:13 if a man who is c clean and not on a
18:11 household who is c clean may eat it.
18:13 household who is c clean may eat it.
19: 7 he will be c unclean till evening.
19: 9 in a c clean place outside the camp.
19:18 a man who is c clean is to take some
Dt 12:15 the c unclean and the clean may eat
12:22 the c unclean and the clean may eat.
14: 7 hoof; they are c unclean for you.
15:22 Both the c unclean and the clean may
1Sa 20:26 c unclean—surely he is unclean."
2Ch 13:11 the bread on the c clean table
30:17 for all those who were not c clean
Ezr 6:20 themselves and were all c clean.
Ne 12:30 Levites had purified themselves c,
Isa 66:20 of the LORD in c clean vessels.
Eze 22:10 period, when they are c unclean.
Ac 24:18 I was c clean when they found me in
Heb 9:13 sprinkled on those who are c unclean

Ceremonies (Ceremony)
Heb 9:21 and everything used in its c.

Ceremony (Ceremonial, Ceremonially, Ceremonies)
Ge 50:11 are holding a solemn c of mourning.
Ex 12:25 you as he promised, observe this c.
12:26 you, 'What does this c mean to you?'
13: 5 are to observe this c in this month:

Certain (Certainly, Certainty)
Ge 15:13 the LORD said to him, "Know for c
28:11 he reached a c place, he stopped for
Nu 16: 1 the son of Levi, and c Reubenites
Jos 8:14 at a c place overlooking the Arabah.
Jdg 13: 2 A c man of Zorah, named Manoah, from
1Sa 1: 1 There was a c man from Ramathaim, a
21: 2 "The king charged me with a c matter
21: 2 told them to meet me at a c place.
25: 2 A c man in Maon, who had property
2Sa 12: 1 "There were two men in a c town,
1Ki 13:11 Now there was a c old prophet living
2Ki 19: 7 him that when he hears a c report,
2Ch 17: 8 With them were c Levites—Shemaiah,
Ne 7:73 along with c of the people and the
Est 3: 8 "There is a c people dispersed and
Isa 37: 7 so that when he hears a c report,
Da 2: 8 the king answered, "I am c that you
Hos 5: 9 of Israel I proclaim what is c.
Mt 26:18 "Go into the city to a c man and
Mk 15:21 A c man from Cyrene, Simon, the
Lk 7:41 "Two men owed money to a c
11: 1 Jesus was praying in a c place.
12:16 a c rich man produced a good crop.
14:16 Jesus replied: "A c man was
18: 2 He said: "In a c town there was a
18:18 A c ruler asked him, "Good teacher,
Jn 3:25 and a c Jew over the matter of
4:46 And there was a c royal official
Ac 7:16 at Shechem for a c sum of money.
28:23 arranged to meet Paul on a c day,
Gal 2:12 Before c men came from James, he
1Ti 1: 3 so that you may command c men
4: 3 order them to abstain from c foods,
Heb 4: 7 Therefore God again set a c day,
11: 1 for and c of what we do not see.
2Pe 1:19 word of the prophets made more c,
Jude : 4 For c men whose condemnation was

Certainly (Certain)
Ex 22: 3 "A thief must c make restitution,
22:23 out to me, I will c hear their cry.
23:33 gods will c be a snare to you."
Nu 13:30 of the land, for we can c do it."
22:33 I would c have killed you by now,
27: 7 You must c give them property as an
Dt 4:26 there long but will c be destroyed.
13: 9 You must c put him to death. Your
13:15 you must c put to the sword all who
23:21 for the LORD your God will c demand
30:18 day that you will c be destroyed.
31:18 I will c hide my face on that day
Jos 3:10 that he will c drive out before you
Jdg 11:10 witness; we will c do as you say."
21: 5 at Mizpah should c be put to death.
1Sa 25:28 for the LORD will c make a lasting
30: 8 "You will c overtake them and
1Ki 11:11 I will most c tear the kingdom away
13:32 towns of Samaria will c come true."
2Ki 1: 4 You will c die!'" So Elijah went.
1: 6 you are lying on. You will c die!'"'
1:16 you are lying on. You will c die!"
8:10 'You will c recover'; but the LORD
8:14 He told me that you would c recover."
Jer 32: 4 will c be handed over to the king of
36:29 the king of Babylon would c come
38: 3 'This city will c be handed over to
42: 4 "I will c pray to the LORD your God
44:17 We will c do everything we said we
44:25 'We will c carry out the vows we
Da 3:24 the fire?" They replied, "C, O king.
Am 7:17 And Israel will c go into exile,
Hab 2: 3 it will c come and will not delay.
Mal 3:15 C the evildoers prosper, and even
Mt 5:20 c not enter the kingdom of heaven.
10:42 he will c not lose his reward."
24:34 this generation will c not pass away
Mk 9:41 Christ will c not lose his reward.
13:30 this generation will c not pass away
Lk 21:32 this generation will c not pass away
22:59 "C this fellow was with him, for he
Ac 21:22 What shall we do? They will c hear
Ro 3: 6 C not! If that were so, how could
6: 5 we will c also be united with him in
7: 7 then? Is the law sin? C not! Indeed
1Co 11:22 Shall I praise you for this? C not!
Gal 3:21 would c have come by the law.
1Th 2:18 to come to you—c I, Paul, did
4:15 will c not precede those who have

Certainty (Certain)
Lk 1: 4 that you may know the c of the
Jn 17: 8 They knew with c that I came from

Certificate (Certified)
Dt 24: 1 and he writes her a c of divorce,
24: 3 her and writes her a c of divorce,
Isa 50: 1 "Where is your mother's c of divorce
Jer 3: 8 I gave faithless Israel her c of
Mt 5:31 wife must give her a c of divorce.'
19: 7 a c of divorce and send her away?"
Mk 10: 4 a c of divorce and send her away."

Certified (Certificate)
Jn 3:33 has c that God is truthful.

Chaff
Job 13:25 leaf? Will you chase after dry c?
21:18 wind, like c swept away by a gale?
41:28 flee; slingstones are like c to him.
Ps 1: 4 Not so the wicked! They are like c
35: 5 May they be like c before the wind,
83:13 O my God, like c before the wind.
Isa 17:13 driven before the wind like c on the
29: 5 the ruthless hordes like blown c.
33:11 You conceive c, you give birth to
40:24 a whirlwind sweeps them away like c.
41: 2 sword, to wind-blown c with his bow.
41:15 them, and reduce the hills to c.
Jer 13:24 "I will scatter you like c driven by
Da 2:35 c on a threshing-floor in the summer.
Hos 13: 3 like c swirling from a
Zep 2: 2 and that day sweeps on like c,
Mt 3:12 up the c with unquenchable fire."
Lk 3:17 up the c with unquenchable fire."

Chain (Chained, Chains)
Ge 41:42 and put a gold c around his neck.
2Ch 3: 5 it with palm tree and c designs.
Pr 1: 9 head and a c to adorn your neck.
Da 5: 7 a gold c placed around his neck,
5:16 a gold c placed around your neck,
5:29 a gold c was placed around his neck,
Mk 5: 3 him any more, not even with a c.
Ac 28:20 Israel that I am bound with this c."
Rev 20: 1 and holding in his hand a great c.

Chained (Chain)
Mk 5: 4 For he had often been c hand and
Lk 8:29 and though he was c hand and foot
2Ti 2: 9 point of being c like a criminal.
2: 9 But God's word is not c.
Heb 11:36 others were c and put in prison.

Chains (Chain)
Ex 28:14 two braided c of pure gold, like a
28:14 and attach the c to the settings.
28:22 "For the breastpiece make braided c
28:24 Fasten the two gold c to the rings
28:25 the other ends of the c to the two
39:15 braided c of pure gold, like a rope.
39:17 They fastened the two gold c to the
39:18 the other ends of the c to the two
Jdg 8:26 c that were on their camels' necks.
1Ki 6:21 and he extended gold c across the
7:17 A network of interwoven c festooned
2Ki 23:33 Pharaoh Neco put him in c at Riblah
2Ch 3:16 He made interwoven c and put them on
3:16 and attached them to the c.
Job 36: 8 if men are bound in c, held fast by
Ps 2: 3 "Let us break their c," they say,
107:10 prisoners suffering in iron c,
107:14 gloom and broke away their c.
116:16 you have freed me from my c.
Ecc 7:26 is a trap and whose hands are c.
Isa 3:20 the head-dresses and ankle c and
28:22 or your c will become heavier;
40:19 gold and fashions silver c for it.
45:14 behind you, coming over to you in c.
52: 2 Free yourself from the c on your
58: 6 to loose the c of injustice and
Jer 40: 1 He had found Jeremiah bound in c
40: 4 today I am freeing you from the c on
Lam 3: 7 he has weighed me down with c.
Eze 7:23 "Prepare c, because the land is full
Na 3:10 and all her great men were put in c.
Mk 5: 4 but he tore the c apart and broke
Lk 8:29 he had broken his c and had been
Ac 12: 6 bound with two c, and sentries stood
12: 7 and the c fell off Peter's wrists.
16:26 open, and everybody's c came loose.
21:33 ordered him to be bound with two c.
22:29 had put Paul, a Roman citizen, in c.
26:29 what I am, except for these c."
Eph 6:20 for which I am an ambassador in c.
Php 1: 7 for whether I am in c or defending
1:13 else that I am in c for Christ.
1:14 of my c, most of the brothers in the
1:17 up trouble for me while I am in c.
Col 4: 3 of Christ, for which I am in c.

Col 4:18 Remember my **c**. Grace be with you.
2Ti 1:16 me and was not ashamed of my **c**.
Phm :10 who became my son while I was in **c**.
:13 me while I am in **c** for the gospel.
Jude : 6 **c** for judgment on the great Day.

Chair
1Sa 1: 9 Now Eli the priest was sitting on a **c**
4:13 there was Eli sitting on his **c** by
4:18 off his **c** by the side of the gate.
2Ki 4:10 and a table, a **c** and a lamp for him.

Chalcedony
Rev 21:19 the third **c**, the fourth emerald,

Chaldea (Chaldean, Chaldeans)
Eze 23:15 chariot officers, natives of **C**.
23:16 and sent messengers to them in **C**.

Chaldean (Chaldea)
Ezr 5:12 them over to Nebuchadnezzar the **C**,

Chaldeans (Chaldea)
Ge 11:28 Haran died in Ur of the **C**, in the
11:31 from Ur of the **C** to go to Canaan.
15: 7 who brought you out of Ur of the **C**
Ne 9: 7 Ur of the **C** and named him Abraham.
Job 1:17 "The **C** formed three raiding parties
Eze 12:13 the land of the **C**, but he will not
23:14 wall, figures of **C** portrayed in red,
23:23 the Babylonians and all the **C**, the
Ac 7: 4 "So he left the land of the **C** and

Chalk
Isa 27: 9 be like **c** stones crushed to pieces,

Challenge (Challenged)
2Ki 14: 8 the **c**: "Come, meet me face to face.
2Ch 25:17 he sent this **c** to Jehoash son of
Jer 49:19 Who is like me and who can **c** me? And
50:44 Who is like me and who can **c** me? And
Mal 3:15 and even those who **c** God escape.'"

Challenged (Challenge)
Jn 8:13 The Pharisees **c** him, "Here you are,
18:26 **c** him, "Didn't I see you with him in

Chamber (Chambers)
Job 37: 9 The tempest comes out from its **c**,
Ps 45:13 glorious is the princess within her **c**
Joel 2:16 leave his room and the bride her **c**.

Chambers (Chamber)
Ezr 8:29 the **c** of the house of the LORD
Ps 104: 3 lays the beams of his upper **c** on
104:13 the mountains from his upper **c**;
Pr 7:27 leading down to the **c** of death.
SS 1: 4 Let the king bring me into his **c**.

Chameleon
Lev 11:30 wall lizard, the skink and the **c**.

Champion (Champions)
1Sa 17: 4 A **c** named Goliath, who was from Gath,
17:23 Goliath, the Philistine **c** from Gath,
Ps 19: 5 a **c** rejoicing to run his course.

Champions (Champion)
Isa 5:22 drinking wine and **c** at mixing drinks,

Chance
Jos 8:20 but they had no **c** to escape in any
1Sa 6: 9 us and that it happened to us by **c**."
19: 2 Saul is looking for a **c** to kill you.
Ecc 9:11 but time and **c** happen to them all.
Mk 6:31 they did not even have a **c** to eat,

Change (Changed, Changers, Changes, Changing, Money-changers)
Ge 35: 2 yourselves and **c** your clothes.
Ex 13:17 **c** their minds and return to Egypt."
Lev 13:16 Should the raw flesh **c** and turn
Nu 23:19 of man, that he should **c** his mind.
23:20 he has blessed, and I cannot **c** it.
1Sa 15:29 does not lie or **c** his mind;
15:29 a man, that he should **c** his mind."
2Sa 14:20 Your servant Joab did this to **c** the
1Ki 8:47 if they have a **c** of heart in the
13:33 Jeroboam did not **c** his evil ways,
2Ch 6:37 if they have a **c** of heart in the
Ezr 6:12 who lifts a hand to **c** this decree
Job 9:27 I will **c** my expression, and smile,'
14:20 **c** his countenance and send him away.
Ps 55:19 **c** their ways and have no fear of God.
102:26 Like clothing you will **c** them and
110: 4 The LORD has sworn and will not **c**
Jer 7: 5 If you really **c** your ways and your
13:16 darkness and **c** it to deep gloom.
13:23 Can the Ethiopian **c** his skin or the
Da 2: 9 things, hoping the situation will **c**.
7:25 try to **c** the set times and the laws.
Mal 3: 6 "I the LORD do not **c**. So you, O
Mt 18: 3 "I tell you the truth, unless you **c**
Ac 6:14 **c** the customs Moses handed down to
Gal 4:20 could be with you now and **c** my tone,
Heb 7:12 For when there is a **c** of the
7:12 there must also be a **c** of the law.
7:21 "The Lord has sworn and will not **c**
12:17 He could bring about no **c** of mind,
Jas 1:17 does not **c** like shifting shadows.
4: 9 **C** your laughter to mourning
Jude : 4 who **c** the grace of our God into

Changed (Change)
Ge 31:41 and you **c** my wages ten times.
41:14 When he had shaved and **c** his clothes,
Ex 7:15 the staff that was **c** into a snake.
7:17 Nile, and it will be **c** into blood.
7:20 and all the water was **c** into blood.
10:19 the LORD **c** the wind to a very strong
14: 5 Pharaoh and his officials **c** their
Lev 13:55 and if the mildew has not **c** its
Nu 32:38 Baal Meon (these names were **c**) and
Jdg 7:19 just after they had **c** the guard.
1Sa 10: 6 will be **c** into a different person.
10: 9 God **c** Saul's heart, and all these
2Sa 12:20 put on lotions and **c** his clothes, he
1Ki 2:15 But things **c**, and the kingdom has
2Ki 23:34 and **c** Eliakim's name to Jehoiakim.
24: 1 But then he **c** his mind and rebelled
24:17 place and **c** his name to Zedekiah.
2Ch 36: 4 and **c** Eliakim's name to Jehoiakim.
Jer 2:11 Has a nation ever **c** its gods? (Yet
15: 7 for they have not **c** their ways.
34:11 afterwards they **c** their minds and
Da 3:19 and his attitude towards them **c**.
4:16 Let his mind be **c** from that of a man
6:15 that the king issues can be **c**."
6:17 Daniel's situation might not be **c**.
Hos 11: 8 Zeboiim? My heart is **c** within me;
Mt 21:29 but later he **c** his mind and went.
Lk 9:29 the appearance of his face **c**, and
Ac 28: 6 **c** their minds and said he was a god.
1Co 15:51 all sleep, but we will all be **c**—
15:52 imperishable, and we will be **c**.
Heb 1:12 robe; like a garment they will be **c**.

Changes (Change)
Ezr 6:11 I decree that if anyone **c** this edict,
Ecc 8: 1 face and **c** its hard appearance.
Da 2:21 He **c** times and seasons; he sets up

Changing (Change)
Ge 31: 7 yet your father has cheated me by **c**
Ezr 6:22 **c** the attitude of the king of Assyria
Jer 2:36 do you go about so much, **c** your ways?

Channel (Channelled, Channels)
Job 38:25 Who cuts a **c** for the torrents of

Channelled (Channel)
2Ch 32:30 **c** the water down to the west side of

Channels (Channel)
Job 6:17 and in the heat vanish from their **c**.
Isa 8: 7 It will overflow all its **c**, run over
Eze 31: 4 and sent their **c** to all the trees of
Zec 4: 2 on it, with seven **c** to the lights.

Chant
Eze 32:16 "This is the lament they will **c** for
32:16 The daughters of the nations will **c**
32:16 and all her hordes they will **c** it,

Chaos
Isa 34:11 the measuring line of **c**

Character (Characters)
Ru 3:11 that you are a woman of noble **c**.
Pr 12: 4 A wife of noble **c** is her husband's
31:10 A wife of noble **c** who can find? She
Ac 17:11 Now the Bereans were of more noble **c**
Ro 5: 4 perseverance, **c**; and **c**, hope.
1Co 15:33 "Bad company corrupts good **c**.

Characters (Character)
Ac 17: 5 up some bad **c** from the market-place,

Charcoal
Pr 26:21 **c** to embers and as wood to fire, so

Charge (Charged, Charges, Charging)
Ge 24: 2 the one in **c** of all that he had,
39: 4 Potiphar put him in **c** of his
39: 5 From the time he put him in **c** of his
39: 6 everything he had; with Joseph in **c**,
39: 8 he refused. "With me in **c**," he told
39:22 the warder put Joseph in **c** of all
41:33 put him in **c** of the land of Egypt.
41:40 You shall be in **c** of my palace, and
41:41 in **c** of the whole land of Egypt."
41:43 him in **c** of the whole land of Egypt.
47: 6 put them in **c** of my own livestock."
Ex 5: 6 and foremen in **c** of the people:
22:25 a money-lender; **c** him no interest.
23: 7 Have nothing to do with a false **c**
Lev 5: 1 when he hears a public **c** to testify
Nu 1:50 appoint the Levites to be in **c** of
4:16 the priest, is to have **c** of the oil
4:16 He is to be in **c** of the entire
7: 2 in **c** of those who were counted,
18: 8 "I myself have put you in **c** of the
Dt 22:20 If, however, the **c** is true and no
23:19 Do not **c** your brother interest,
23:20 You may **c** a foreigner interest, but
2Sa 20:24 Adoniram was in **c** of forced labour;
23:23 David put him in **c** of his bodyguard.
1Ki 2: 1 die, he gave a **c** to Solomon his son.
4: 5 in **c** of the district officers;
4: 6 Ahishar—in **c** of the palace;
4: 6 son of Abda—in **c** of forced labour.
5:14 was in **c** of the forced labour.
9:23 officials in **c** of Solomon's projects
11:28 he put him in **c** of the whole labour
12:18 who was in **c** of forced labour, but
16: 9 man in **c** of the palace at Tirzah.
18: 3 Obadiah, who was in **c** of his palace.
2Ki 7:17 arm he leaned in **c** of the gate,
11:15 who were in **c** of the troops: "Bring
15: 5 Jotham the king's son had **c** of the
25:19 he took the officer in **c** of the
25:19 chief officer in **c** of conscripting
1Ch 6:31 These are the men David put in **c** of
9:11 official in **c** of the house of God;
9:20 Eleazar was in **c** of the gatekeepers,
9:23 They and their descendants were in **c**
9:27 and they had **c** of the key for
9:28 Some of them were in **c** of the
9:32 brothers were in **c** of preparing for
11:25 David put him in **c** of his bodyguard.
15:22 Kenaniah the head Levite was in **c** of
15:27 in **c** of the singing of the choirs.
23:28 LORD: to be in **c** of the courtyards,
23:29 They were in **c** of the bread set out
26:20 Their fellow Levites were in **c** of
26:22 They were in **c** of the treasuries of
26:24 the officer in **c** of the treasuries.
26:26 Shelomith and his relatives were in **c**
26:32 and King David put them in **c** of the

1Ch 27: 2 In c of the first division, for the
27: 4 In c of the division for the second
27: 6 Ammizabad was in c of his division.
27:25 Azmaveth son of Adiel was in c of
27:25 Jonathan son of Uzziah was in c of
27:26 Ezri son of Kelub was in c of the
27:27 Shimei the Ramathite was in c of the
27:27 Zabdi the Shiphmite was in c of the
27:28 Baal-Hanan the Gederite was in c of
27:28 in c of the supplies of olive oil.
27:29 Shitrai the Sharonite was in c of
27:29 in c of the herds in the valleys.
27:30 Obil the Ishmaelite was in c of the
27:30 Meronothite was in c of the donkeys.
27:31 Jaziz the Hagrite was in c of the
27:31 in c of King David's property.
28: 1 and the officials in c of all the
28: 8 "So now I c you in the sight of all
29: 6 officials in c of the king's work
2Ch 10:18 who was in c of forced labour, but
23:14 who were in c of the troops, and
24:13 The men in c of the work were
26:21 Jotham his son had c of the palace
28: 7 Azrikam the officer in c of the
31:12 Conaniah, a Levite, was in c of
31:13 official in c of the temple of God.
31:14 keeper of the East Gate, was in c of
34:13 had c of the labourers and
Ne 7: 2 I put in c of Jerusalem my brother
11:16 who had c of the outside work of the
11:21 Ziha and Gishpa were in c of them.
12: 8 in c of the songs of thanksgiving.
12:44 men were appointed to be in c of the
13: 4 Eliashib the priest had been put in c
13:13 and a Levite named Pedaiah in c of
Est 2: 3 the king's eunuch, who is in c of
2: 8 to Hegai, who had c of the harem.
2:14 who was in c of the concubines.
2:15 was in c of the harem, suggested.
Job 34:13 Who put him in c of the whole world?
Ps 69:27 C them with crime upon crime; do not
SS 2: 7 Daughters of Jerusalem, I c you by
3: 5 Daughters of Jerusalem, I c you by
5: 8 O daughters of Jerusalem, I c you—
5: 9 than others, that you c us so?
8: 4 Daughters of Jerusalem, I c you: Do
Isa 3: 6 take c of this heap of ruins!"
22:15 Shebna, who is in c of the palace:
33:18 is the officer in c of the towers?"
Jer 15:13 I will give as plunder, without c,
29:26 to be in c of the house of the LORD;
40: 7 and had put him in c of the men,
46: 9 C, O horses! Drive furiously,
52:25 he took the officer in c of the
52:25 chief officer in c of conscripting
Eze 40:45 priests who have c of the temple,
40:46 the priests who have c of the altar.
44: 8 you put others in c of my sanctuary.
44:11 having c of the gates of the temple
44:14 Yet I will put them in c of the
Da 2:48 placed him in c of all its wise men.
Hos 4: 1 because the LORD has a c to bring
4: 4 "But let no man bring a c, let no
12: 2 The LORD has a c to bring against
Joel 2: 7 They c like warriors; they scale
Mic 6: 2 he is lodging a c against Israel.
Zec 3: 6 The angel of the LORD gave this c to
3: 7 my house and have c of my courts,
Mt 24:45 whom the master has put in c of the
24:47 put him in c of all his possessions.
25:21 I will put you in c of many things.
25:23 I will put you in c of many things.
26:63 "I c you under oath by the living God
27:14 no reply, not even to a single c—
27:37 the written c against him:
Mk 3:21 they went to take c of him, for they
13:34 house and puts his servants in c,
15:26 The written notice of the c against
Lk 12:42 whom the master puts in c of his
12:44 put him in c of all his possessions.
19:17 small matter, take c of ten cities.'
19:19 "His master answered, 'You take c of
23: 4 no basis for a c against this man."
Jn 13:29 Since Judas had c of the money, some
18:38 find no basis for a c against him.
19: 4 I find no basis for a c against him."
Jn 19: 6 I find no basis for a c against him."
19:16 So the soldiers took c of Jesus.
Ac 8:27 an important official in c of all
23:29 but there was no c against him that
25:18 they did not c him with any of the
28:19 c to bring against my own people.
Ro 3: 9 We have already made the c that Jews
8:33 Who will bring any c against those
1Co 9:18 the gospel I may offer it free of c,
2Co 11: 7 the gospel of God to you free of c?
Gal 3:24 the law was put in c to lead us to
1Th 5:27 I c you before the Lord to have this
1Ti 5:21 I c you, in the sight of God and
6:13 made the good confession, I c you
2Ti 4: 1 and his kingdom, I give you this c:
Tit 1: 6 the c of being wild and disobedient.
Phm :18 or owes you anything, c it to me.
Rev 14:18 Still another angel, who had c of
16: 5 I heard the angel in c of the waters

Charged (Charge)

Dt 1:16 I c your judges at that time: Hear
Jos 6:20 so every man c straight in, and they
Jdg 20:33 and the Israelite ambush c out of
1Sa 21: 2 "The king c me with a certain matter
1Ch 22: 6 and c him to build a house for the
Eze 18:20 of the wicked will be c against him.
Da 8: 4 I watched the ram as he c towards
8: 6 canal and c at him in great rage.
Ac 18:13 "This man," they c, "is persuading
19:40 in danger of being c with rioting

Charges (Charge)

1Ki 21:13 c against Naboth before the people,
Ne 5: 6 I heard their outcry and these c, I
Job 4:18 if he c his angels with error,
10: 2 tell me what c you have against me.
13:19 Can anyone bring c against me? If so,
22: 4 rebukes you and brings c against you?
23: 6 No, he would not press c against me.
24:12 But God c no-one with wrongdoing.
39:21 his strength, and c into the fray.
Isa 50: 8 Who then will bring c against me?
Jer 2: 9 "Therefore I bring c against you
2: 9 c against your children's children.
2:29 "Why do you bring c against me? You
25:31 for the LORD will bring c against
Da 6: 4 find grounds for c against Daniel
6: 5 "We will never find any basis for c
Hos 4: 4 those who bring c against a priest.
Lk 23:14 no basis for your c against him.
Jn 18:29 c are you bringing against this man?"
Ac 7: 1 priest asked him, "Are these c true?"
19:38 are proconsuls. They can press c.
24: 1 c against Paul before the governor.
24: 8 c we are bringing against him."
24:13 they cannot prove to you the c they
24:19 to be here before you and bring c
25: 2 and presented the c against Paul.
25: 5 and press c against the man there,
25: 7 bringing many serious c against him,
25: 9 trial before me there on these c?"
25:11 But if the c brought against me by
25:15 elders of the Jews brought c against
25:16 to defend himself against their c.
25:20 and stand trial there on these c.
25:27 specifying the c against him."

Charging (Charge)

Ne 5:11 and also the usury you are c
Job 1:22 In all this, Job did not sin by c
15:26 defiantly c against him with a thick,
Pr 28:15 Like a roaring lion or a c bear is a
Jer 8: 6 course like a horse c into battle.
Na 3: 3 C cavalry, flashing swords and

Chariot (Charioteers, Chariots)

Ge 41:43 He had him ride in a c as his second
46:29 Joseph had his c made ready and went
Ex 14: 6 he had his c made ready and took his
Jdg 4:15 abandoned his c and fled on foot.
5:28 'Why is his c so long in coming? Why
2Sa 8: 4 all but a hundred of the c horses.
15: 1 Absalom provided himself with a c
1Ki 4:26 c horses, and twelve thousand horses.
4:28 the c horses and the other horses.
7:33 The wheels were made like c wheels;
10:26 which he kept in the c cities and
10:29 They imported a c from Egypt for six
12:18 into his c and escape to Jerusalem.
18:44 'Hitch up your c and go down before
20:25 horse for horse and c for c
20:33 Ahab had him come up into his c.
22:31 ordered his thirty-two c commanders,
22:32 the c commanders saw Jehoshaphat,
22:33 the c commanders saw that he was not
22:34 The king told his c driver, "Wheel
22:35 and the king was propped up in his c
22:35 ran onto the floor of the c,
22:38 They washed the c at a pool in
2Ki 2:11 suddenly a c of fire and horses of
5:21 he got down from the c to meet him.
5:26 man got down from his c to meet you?
8:21 surrounded him and his c commanders,
9:16 he got into his c and rode to
9:21 "Hitch up my c," Joram ordered. And
9:21 each in his own c, to meet Jehu.
9:24 heart and he slumped down in his c.
9:25 Jehu said to Bidkar, his c officer,
9:27 They wounded him in his c
9:28 His servants took him by c to
10:15 and Jehu helped him up into the c.
10:16 Then he made him ride in his c.
23:30 in a c from Megiddo to Jerusalem
1Ch 18: 4 all but a hundred of the c horses.
28:18 He also gave him the plan for the c,
2Ch 1:14 which he kept in the c cities and
1:17 They imported a c from Egypt for six
9:25 which he kept in the c cities and
10:18 into his c and escape to Jerusalem.
18:30 Aram had ordered his c commanders,
18:31 the c commanders saw Jehoshaphat,
18:32 for when the c commanders saw that
18:33 The king told the c driver, "Wheel
18:34 propped himself up in his c facing
21: 9 surrounded him and his c commanders,
35:24 they took him out of his c, put him
35:24 put him in the other c he had and
Ps 76: 6 Jacob, both horse and c lie still.
104: 3 He makes the clouds his c
Isa 5:28 their c wheels like a whirlwind.
21: 9 Look, here comes a man in a c with a
Jer 51:21 with you I shatter c and driver,
Eze 23:15 c officers, natives of Chaldea.
23:23 c officers and men of high rank, all
Mic 1:13 Lachish, harness the team to the c.
Zec 6: 2 The first c had red horses, the
Ac 8:28 on his way home was sitting in his c
8:29 The Spirit told Philip, "Go to that c
8:30 Philip ran up to the c and heard the
8:38 he gave orders to stop the c. Then

Charioteers (Chariot)

1Sa 13: 5 six thousand c, and soldiers as
2Sa 8: 4 c and twenty thousand foot soldiers.
10:18 killed seven hundred of their c
1Ki 9:22 commanders of his chariots and c.
1Ch 18: 4 c and twenty thousand foot soldiers.
19: 6 chariots and c from Aram Naharaim,
19: 7 thirty-two thousand chariots and c,
19:18 killed seven thousand of their c
2Ch 8: 9 commanders of his chariots and c.
Isa 22: 6 up the quiver, with her c and horses;
Jer 46: 9 O horses! Drive furiously, O c!

Chariots (Chariot)

Ge 50: 9 C and horsemen also went up with him.
Ex 14: 7 He took six hundred of the best c,
14: 7 along with all the other c of Egypt,
14: 9 Pharaoh's horses and c, horsemen and
14:17 through his c and his horsemen.
14:18 Pharaoh, his c and his horsemen."
14:23 and all Pharaoh's horses and c and
14:25 He made the wheels of their c come
14:26 Egyptians and their c and horsemen."
14:28 covered the c and horsemen—the
15: 4 Pharaoh's c and his army he has
15:19 Pharaoh's horses, c and horsemen
Dt 11: 4 to its horses and c, how he

Dt 20: 1 **c** and an army greater than yours,
Jos 11: 4 number of horses and **c**—a huge army,
11: 6 their horses and burn their **c**."
11: 9 their horses and burned their **c**.
17:16 who live in the plain have iron **c**,
17:18 iron **c** and though they are strong,
24: 6 **c** and horsemen as far as the Red Sea.
Jdg 1:19 the plains, because they had iron **c**.
4: 3 he had nine hundred iron **c** and had
4: 7 with his **c** and his troops to the
4:13 iron **c** and all the men with him,
4:15 and all his **c** and army by the sword,
4:16 Barak pursued the **c** and army as far
5:28 Why is the clatter of his **c** delayed?'
1Sa 8:11 them serve with his **c** and horses,
8:11 and they will run in front of his **c**.
8:12 of war and equipment for his **c**.
13: 5 with three thousand **c**, six thousand
2Sa 1: 6 the **c** and riders almost upon him.
8: 4 David captured a thousand of his **c**,
1Ki 1: 5 So he got **c** and horses ready, with
9:19 the towns for his **c** and for his
9:22 commanders of his **c** and charioteers.
10:26 Solomon accumulated **c** and horses; he
10:26 he had fourteen hundred **c** and
16: 9 who had command of half his **c**,
20: 1 kings with their horses and **c**,
20:21 overpowered the horses and **c** and
2Ki 2:12 The **c** and horsemen of Israel!"
5: 9 Naaman went with his horses and **c**
6:14 he sent horses and **c** and a strong
6:15 and **c** had surrounded the city.
6:17 and **c** of fire all round Elisha.
7: 6 of **c** and horses and a great army,
7:14 they selected two **c** with their
8:21 Jehoram went to Zair with all his **c**.
9:25 I were riding together in **c** behind
10: 2 with you and you have **c** and horses,
13: 7 ten **c** and ten thousand foot soldiers,
13:14 "The **c** and horsemen of Israel!"
18:24 on Egypt for **c** and horsemen?
19:23 And you have said, "With my many **c**
23:11 burned the **c** dedicated to the sun.
1Ch 18: 4 David captured a thousand of his **c**,
19: 6 **c** and charioteers from Aram Naharaim,
19: 7 They hired thirty-two thousand **c** and
2Ch 1:14 Solomon accumulated **c** and horses;
1:14 he had fourteen hundred **c** and
8: 6 and all the cities for his **c** and for
8: 9 commanders of his **c** and charioteers.
9:25 four thousand stalls for horses and **c**
12: 3 With twelve hundred **c** and sixty
14: 9 with a vast army and three hundred **c**,
16: 8 great numbers of **c** and horsemen?
21: 9 with his officers and all his **c**.
Ps 20: 7 Some trust in **c** and some in horses,
68:17 The **c** of God are tens of thousands
SS 1: 9 to one of the **c** of Pharaoh.
6:12 me among the royal **c** of my people.
Isa 2: 7 of horses; there is no end to the **c**.
21: 7 he sees **c** with teams of horses,
22: 7 Your choicest valleys are full of **c**,
22:18 there your splendid **c** will remain—
31: 1 trust in the multitude of their **c**
36: 9 on Egypt for **c** and horsemen?
37:24 And you have said, 'With my many **c**
43:17 who drew out the **c** and horses, the
66:15 and his **c** are like a whirlwind; he
66:20 in **c** and wagons, and on mules and
Jer 4:13 his **c** come like a whirlwind, his
17:25 will come riding in **c** and on horses,
22: 4 palace, riding in **c** and on horses,
47: 3 at the noise of enemy **c** and the
50:37 A sword against her horses and **c** and
Eze 23:24 **c** and wagons and with a throng of
26: 7 with horses and **c**, with horsemen
26:10 wagons and **c** when he enters your
Da 11:40 will storm out against him with **c**
Joel 2: 5 With a noise like that of **c** they
Mic 5:10 from among you and demolish your **c**.
Na 2: 3 The metal on the **c** flashes on the
2: 4 The **c** storm through the streets,
2:13 "I will burn up your **c** in smoke, and
3: 2 galloping horses and jolting **c**!
Hab 3: 8 your horses and your victorious **c**?
Hag 2:22 I will overthrow **c** and their drivers;
Zec 6: 1 there before me were four **c** coming
9:10 I will take away the **c** from Ephraim
Rev 9: 9 horses and **c** rushing into battle.

Charm (Charmed, Charmer, Charming, Charms)
Pr 17: 8 A bribe is a **c** to the one who gives
31:30 **C** is deceptive, and beauty is

Charmed (Charm)
Ecc 10:11 If a snake bites before it is **c**,
Jer 8:17 vipers that cannot be **c**, and they

Charmer (Charm)
Ps 58: 5 that will not heed the tune of the **c**,
Ecc 10:11 there is no profit for the **c**.

Charming (Charm)
Pr 26:25 Though his speech is **c**, do not
SS 1:16 Oh, how **c**! And our bed is verdant.

Charms (Charm)
Isa 3:20 sashes, the perfume bottles and **c**,
Eze 13:18 Woe to the women who sew magic **c** on
13:20 I am against your magic **c** with which

Charred (Chars)
Jdg 15:14 ropes on his arms became like **c** flax,
Eze 15: 5 the fire has burned it and it is **c**?
24:10 the spices; and let the bones be **c**.

Chars (Charred)
Eze 15: 4 burns both ends and **c** the middle,

Chase (Chased, Chases, Chasing)
Lev 26: 8 Five of you will **c** a hundred, and a
26: 8 and a hundred of you will **c** ten
Dt 32:30 How could one man **c** a thousand, or
Job 13:25 leaf? Will you **c** after dry chaff?
Isa 1:23 all love bribes and **c** after gifts.
Jer 49:19 **c** Edom from its land in an instant.
50:44 I will **c** Babylon from its land in an
Hos 2: 7 She will **c** after her lovers but not

Chased (Chase)
Dt 1:44 they **c** you like a swarm of bees and
Jos 7: 5 They **c** the Israelites from the city
8:24 in the desert where they had **c** them,
Jdg 1: 6 Adoni-Bezek fled, but they **c** him and
9:40 Abimelech **c** him, and many fell
20:43 **c** them and easily overran them in the
2Sa 2:19 He **c** Abner, turning neither to the
2Ki 9:27 Jehu **c** him, shouting, "Kill him too!"
Jer 50:17 flock that lions have **c** away.
Lam 4:19 they **c** us over the mountains and lay

Chases (Chase)
Pr 12:11 he who **c** fantasies lacks judgment.
28:19 but the one who **c** fantasies will

Chasing (Chase, *Chasing after the wind*)
1Sa 17:53 the Israelites returned from **c** the
2Sa 2:21 But Asahel would not stop **c** him.
2:22 Abner warned Asahel, "Stop **c** me!

Chasing after the wind
Ecc 1:14 all of them are meaningless, a **c**.
1:17 I learned that this, too, is a **c**.
2:11 everything was meaningless, a **c**;
2:17 All of it is meaningless, a **c**.
2:26 This too is meaningless, a **c**.
4: 4 This too is meaningless, a **c**.
4: 6 than two handfuls with toil and **c**.
4:16 This too is meaningless, a **c**.
6: 9 This too is meaningless, a **c**.

Chasm
Lk 16:26 between us and you a great **c** has

Chastened
Job 33:19 Or a man may be **c** on a bed of pain
Ps 118:18 The LORD has **c** me severely, but he

Chatter (Chattering)
1Ti 6:20 Turn away from godless **c** and the
2Ti 2:16 Avoid godless **c**, because those who

Chattering (Chatter)
Pr 10: 8 but a **c** fool comes to ruin.
10:10 grief, and a **c** fool comes to ruin.

Cheaper
Jn 2:10 then the **c** wine after the guests

Cheat (Cheated, Cheating, Cheats)
Mal 1:14 "Cursed is the **c** who has an
1Co 6: 8 Instead, you yourselves **c** and do

Cheated (Cheat)
Ge 31: 7 yet your father has **c** me by changing
1Sa 12: 3 Whom have I **c**? Whom have I oppressed?
12: 4 "You have not **c** or oppressed us,"
Lk 19: 8 and if I have **c** anybody out of
1Co 6: 7 be wronged? Why not rather be **c**?

Cheating (Cheat)
Am 8: 5 price and **c** with dishonest scales,

Cheats (Cheat)
Lev 6: 2 his care or stolen, or if he **c** him,

Check (Checked)
Ge 30:33 you **c** on the wages you have paid me.
Jas 3: 2 able to keep his whole body in **c**.

Checked (Check)
2Ki 6:10 the king of Israel **c** on the place
Ezr 8:15 When I **c** among the people and the
Ps 106:30 intervened, and the plague was **c**.

Cheek (Cheeks)
Job 16:10 they strike my **c** in scorn and unite
Lam 3:30 Let him offer his **c** to one who would
Mic 5: 1 Israel's ruler on the **c** with a rod.
Mt 5:39 someone strikes you on the right **c**,
Lk 6:29 If someone strikes you on one **c**,

Cheeks (Cheek)
SS 1:10 Your **c** are beautiful with ear-rings,
5:13 His **c** are like beds of spice
Isa 50: 6 my **c** to those who pulled out my beard
Lam 1: 2 at night, tears are upon her **c**.

Cheer (Cheered, Cheerful, Cheerfully, Cheering, Cheers)
1Ki 21: 7 over Israel? Get up and eat! **C** up.
Mk 10:49 "**C** up! On your feet! He's calling

Cheered (Cheer)
Php 2:19 be **c** when I receive news about you.

Cheerful (Cheer)
Pr 15:13 A happy heart makes the face **c**, but
15:15 the **c** heart has a continual feast.
15:30 A **c** look brings joy to the heart,
17:22 A **c** heart is good medicine, but a
2Co 9: 7 compulsion, for God loves a **c** giver.

Cheerfully (Cheer)
Ro 12: 8 is showing mercy, let him do it **c**.

Cheering (Cheer)
1Ki 1:45 From there they have gone up **c**, and
2Ch 23:12 the people running and **c** the king,
Ecc 2: 3 I tried **c** myself with wine, and

Cheers (Cheer)
Jdg 9:13 'Should I give up my wine, which **c**
Pr 12:25 man down, but a kind word **c** him up.

Cheese (Cheeses)
2Sa 17:29 and c from cows' milk for David
Job 10:10 out like milk and curdle me like c,

Cheeses (Cheese)
1Sa 17:18 Take along these ten c to the

Chemosh
Nu 21:29 O people of C! He has given up his
Jdg 11:24 Will you not take what your god C
1Ki 11: 7 Solomon built a high place for C the
11:33 C the god of the Moabites, and
2Ki 23:13 for C the vile god of Moab, and for
Jer 48: 7 and C will go into exile, together
48:13 Moab will be ashamed of C, as the
48:46 The people of C are destroyed;

Cherish (Cherished, Cherishes)
Ps 17:14 You still the hunger of those you c;
83: 3 they plot against those you c.

Cherished (Cherish)
Ps 66:18 If I had c sin in my heart, the Lord
Hos 9:16 I will slay their c offspring."

Cherishes (Cherish)
Pr 19: 8 he who c understanding prospers.

Cherub (Cherubim)
Ex 25:19 Make one c on one end and the second
25:19 end and the second c on the other;
37: 8 He made one c on one end and the
37: 8 end and the second c on the other;
1Ki 6:24 One wing of the first c was five
6:25 The second c also measured ten
6:26 The height of each c was ten cubits.
6:27 The wing of one c touched one wall,
2Ch 3:11 One wing of the first c was five
3:11 touched the wing of the other c.
3:12 Similarly one wing of the second c
3:12 touched the wing of the first c.
Eze 10:14 faces: One face was that of a c,
28:14 You were anointed as a guardian c,
28:16 and I expelled you, O guardian c,
41:18 Each c had two faces:

Cherubim (Cherub)
Ge 3:24 c and a flaming sword flashing back
Ex 25:18 make two c out of hammered gold at
25:19 the c of one piece with the cover,
25:20 The c are to have their wings spread
25:20 The c are to face each other,
25:22 above the cover between the two c
26: 1 purple and scarlet yarn, with c
26:31 with c worked into it by a skilled
36: 8 purple and scarlet yarn, with c
36:35 with c worked into it by a skilled
37: 7 he made two c out of hammered gold
37: 9 The c had their wings spread upwards,
37: 9 The c faced each other, looking
Nu 7:89 the two c above the atonement cover
1Sa 4: 4 who is enthroned between the c.
2Sa 6: 2 between the c that are on the ark.
22:11 He mounted the c and flew; he soared
1Ki 6:23 he made a pair of c of olive wood,
6:25 c were identical in size and shape.
6:27 He placed the c inside the innermost
6:28 He overlaid the c with gold.
6:29 c, palm trees and open flowers.
6:32 two olive wood doors he carved c,
6:32 c and palm trees with beaten gold.
6:35 He carved c, palm trees and open
7:29 uprights were lions, bulls and c—
7:36 He engraved c, lions and palm trees
8: 6 put it beneath the wings of the c.
8: 7 The c spread their wings over the
2Ki 19:15 enthroned between the c, you alone
1Ch 13: 6 who is enthroned between the c—the
28:18 the c of gold that spread their wings
2Ch 3: 7 gold, and he carved c on the walls.
3:10 c and overlaid them with gold.
3:11 The total wing-span of the c was
3:13 The wings of these c extended twenty
3:14 fine linen, with c worked into it.
5: 7 put it beneath the wings of the c.
5: 8 The c spread their wings over the
Ps 18:10 He mounted the c and flew; he soared
80: 1 you who sit enthroned between the c,
99: 1 he sits enthroned between the c,
Isa 37:16 enthroned between the c, you alone
Eze 9: 3 of Israel went up from above the c,
10: 1 that was over the heads of the c.
10: 2 Go in among the wheels beneath the c.
10: 2 with burning coals from among the c
10: 3 Now the c were standing on the south
10: 4 of the LORD rose from above the c
10: 5 The sound of the wings of the c
10: 6 among the wheels, from among the c,"
10: 7 one of the c reached out his hand to
10: 8 (Under the wings of the c could be
10: 9 I looked, and I saw beside the c
10: 9 one beside each of the c; the wheels
10:11 of the four directions the c faced;
10:11 did not turn about as the c went.
10:11 The c went in whatever direction the
10:14 Each of the c had four faces: One
10:15 the c rose upwards. These were the
10:16 the c moved, the wheels beside them
10:16 and when the c spread their wings to
10:17 the c stood still, they also stood
10:17 and when the c rose, they rose with
10:18 the temple and stopped above the c.
10:19 While I watched, the c spread their
10:20 and I realised that they were c.
11:22 the c, with the wheels beside them,
41:18 were carved c and palm trees. Palm
41:18 Palm trees alternated with c. Each
41:20 c and palm trees were carved on the
41:25 the outer sanctuary were carved c
Heb 9: 5 Above the ark were the c of the

Chest (Chests)
Ex 25:10 "Have them make a c of acacia
25:14 on the sides of the c to carry it.
Dt 10: 1 the mountain. Also make a wooden c.
10: 2 Then you are to put them in the c."
1Sa 6: 8 and in a c beside it put the gold
6:11 along with it the c containing the
6:15 together with the c containing the
2Ki 12: 9 Jehoiada the priest took a c and
12: 9 put into the c all the money that was
12:10 a large amount of money in the c,
2Ch 24: 8 At the king's command, a c was made
24:10 them into the c until it was full.
24:11 Whenever the c was brought in by the
24:11 empty the c and carry it back to its
Job 41:24 His c is hard as rock, hard as a
Da 2:32 its c and arms of silver, its belly
Rev 1:13 and with a golden sash round his c.

Chests Chest)
Rev 15: 6 wore golden sashes round their c.

Chew (Chewed, Chews)
Lev 11: 4 "'There are some that only c the cud
11: 7 does not c the cud; it is unclean
11:26 not c the cud is unclean for you;
Dt 14: 7 However, of those that c the cud or
14: 7 Although they c the cud, they do not
14: 8 a split hoof, it does not c the cud.

Chewed (Chew)
Jnh 4: 7 c the vine so that it withered.

Chews (Chew)
Lev 11: 3 divided and that c the cud.
11: 4 The camel, though it c the cud, does
11: 5 The coney, though it c the cud, does
11: 6 The rabbit, though it c the cud,
Dt 14: 6 divided in two and that c the cud.

Chicks
Mt 23:37 as a hen gathers her c under her
Lk 13:34 as a hen gathers her c under her

Chief (*Chief priests*, Chiefs)
Ge 24: 2 He said to the c servant in his
40: 2 the c cupbearer and the c baker,
40: 9 the c cupbearer told Joseph his
40:16 the c baker saw that Joseph had
40:20 the c cupbearer and the c baker
40:21 He restored the c cupbearer to his
40:22 he hanged the c baker, just as
40:23 The c cupbearer, however, did not
41: 9 the c cupbearer said to Pharaoh,
41:10 and he imprisoned me and the c baker
Nu 3:32 The c leader of the Levites was
25:15 a tribal c of a Midianite family.
Dt 29:10 your God—your leaders and c men,
Jos 22:14 With him they sent ten of the c men,
2Sa 23: 8 a Tahkemonite, was c of the Three;
23:13 three of the thirty c men came down
23:18 son of Zeruiah was c of the Three.
1Ki 4: 2 these were his c officials: Azariah
9:23 They were also the c officials in
2Ki 10:11 as well as all his c men, his close
15:25 One of his c officers, Pekah son of
18:17 his c officer and his field
25:18 as prisoners Seraiah the c priest,
25:19 took the secretary who was c officer
1Ch 5: 7 Jeiel the c, Zechariah,
5:12 Joel was the c, Shapham the second,
9:17 and their brothers, Shallum their c
11:11 a Hacmonite, was c of the officers;
11:20 Abishai the brother of Joab was c of
11:42 who was c of the Reubenites, and the
12: 3 Ahiezer their c and Joash the sons
12: 9 Ezer was the c, Obadiah the second
12:18 the Spirit came upon Amasai, c of
16: 5 Asaph was the c, Zechariah second,
18:17 were c officials at the king's side.
26:12 through their c men, had duties for
26:31 Jeriah was their c according to the
27: 3 and c of all the army officers
27: 5 He was c and there were 24,000 men
2Ch 8:10 were also King Solomon's c officials
11:22 be the c prince among his brothers,
19:11 "Amariah the c priest will be over
24: 6 the c priest and said to him,
24:11 the officer of the c priest would
26:20 Azariah the c priest and all the
31:10 Azariah the c priest, from the
Ezr 7: 5 the son of Aaron the c priest—
Ne 11: 9 Joel son of Zicri was their c
11:14 Their c officer was Zabdiel son of
11:22 The c officer of the Levites in
Job 29: 9 the c men refrained from speaking
29:25 the way for them and sat as their c;
Isa 2: 2 established as c among the mountains;
33:18 "Where is that c officer? Where is
Jer 20: 1 the c officer in the temple of the
39: 3 Nebo-Sarsekim a c officer,
39:13 Nebushazban a c officer,
52:24 as prisoners Seraiah the c priest,
52:25 took the secretary who was c officer
Eze 38: 2 the c prince of Meshech and Tubal;
38: 3 O Gog, c prince of Meshech and Tubal.
39: 1 O Gog, c prince of Meshech and Tubal.
Da 1: 3 the king ordered Ashpenaz, c of his
1: 7 The c official gave them new names:
1: 8 and he asked the c official for
1:11 c official had appointed over Daniel,
1:18 the c official presented them to
4: 9 "Belteshazzar, c of the magicians,
5:11 appointed him c of the magicians,
10:13 Then Michael, one of the c princes,
Mic 4: 1 as c among the mountains;
Lk 19: 2 a c tax collector and was wealthy.
Ac 14:12 Hermes because he was the c speaker.
19:14 Seven sons of Sceva, a Jewish c
28: 7 the c official of the island.
Eph 2:20 Jesus himself as the c cornerstone.
1Pe 5: 4 the C Shepherd appears, you will

Chief priests
Mt 2: 4 people's c and teachers of the law,
16:21 c and teachers of the law, and that
20:18 the c and the teachers of the law.
21:15 when the c and the teachers of the
21:23 the c and the elders of the people
21:45 the c and the Pharisees heard Jesus'
26: 3 the c and the elders of the people
26:14 called Judas Iscariot—went to the c

Mt 26:47 the **c** and the elders of the people.
26:59 The **c** and the whole Sanhedrin were
27: 1 Early in the morning, all the **c** and
27: 3 coins to the **c** and the elders.
27: 6 The **c** picked up the coins and said,
27:12 he was accused by the **c** and the
27:20 the **c** and the elders persuaded the
27:41 In the same way the **c**, the teachers
27:62 **c** and the Pharisees went to Pilate.
28:11 reported to the **c** everything that had
28:12 the **c** had met with the elders and
Mk 8:31 elders, **c** and teachers of the law,
10:33 to the **c** and teachers of the law.
11:18 The **c** and the teachers of the law
11:27 the **c**, the teachers of the law and
14: 1 and the **c** and the teachers of the
14:10 to the **c** to betray Jesus to them.
14:43 sent from the **c**, the teachers of the
14:53 and all the **c**, elders and teachers
14:55 The **c** and the whole Sanhedrin were
15: 1 Very early in the morning, the **c**,
15: 3 The **c** accused him of many things.
15:10 knowing it was out of envy that the **c**
15:11 the **c** stirred up the crowd to have
15:31 In the same way the **c** and the
Lk 9:22 **c** and teachers of the law, and he
19:47 But the **c**, the teachers of the law
20: 1 the **c** and the teachers of the law,
20:19 The teachers of the law and the **c**
22: 2 the **c** and the teachers of the law
22: 4 Judas went to the **c** and the officers
22:52 Jesus said to the **c**, the officers of
22:66 both the **c** and teachers of the law,
23: 4 Pilate announced to the **c** and the
23:10 The **c** and the teachers of the law
23:13 Pilate called together the **c**, the
24:20 The **c** and our rulers handed him over
Jn 7:32 Then the **c** and the Pharisees sent
7:45 went back to the **c** and Pharisees,
11:47 the **c** and the Pharisees called a
11:57 the **c** and Pharisees had given orders
12:10 the **c** made plans to kill Lazarus as
18: 3 officials from the **c** and Pharisees.
18:35 "It was your people and your **c** who
19: 6 soon as the **c** and their officials
19:15 no king but Caesar," the **c** answered.
19:21 The **c** of the Jews protested to
Ac 4:23 the **c** and elders had said to them.
5:24 temple guard and the **c** were puzzled,
9:14 with authority from the **c** to arrest
9:21 to take them as prisoners to the **c**?"
22:30 **c** and all the Sanhedrin to assemble.
23:14 They went to the **c** and elders and
25: 2 where the **c** and Jewish leaders
25:15 I went to Jerusalem, the **c** and
26:10 On the authority of the **c** I put many
26:12 authority and commission of the **c**.

Chiefs (Chief)

Ge 36:15 These were the **c** among Esau's
36:15 Esau: **C** Teman, Omar, Zepho, Kenaz,
36:16 These were the **c** descended from
36:17 **C** Nahath, Zerah, Shammah and Mizzah.
36:17 These were the **c** descended from
36:18 **C** Jeush, Jalam and Korah.
36:18 These were the **c** descended from
36:19 is, Edom), and these were their **c**.
36:21 sons of Seir in Edom were Horite **c**.
36:29 These were the Horite **c**: Lotan,
36:30 These were the Horite **c**, according
36:40 These were the **c** descended from Esau,
36:43 These were the **c** of Edom, according
Ex 15:15 The **c** of Edom will be terrified, the
Jos 13:21 defeated him and the Midianite **c**,
1Ki 8: 1 and the **c** of the Israelite families,
1Ch 1:51 Hadad also died. The **c** of Edom were:
1:54 and Iram. These were the **c** of Edom.
7: 3 All five of them were **c**.
8:28 **c** as listed in their genealogy,
9:34 **c** as listed in their genealogy, and
11:10 These were the **c** of David's mighty
11:15 Three of the thirty **c** came down to
12:32 200 **c**, with all their relatives
2Ch 5: 2 and the **c** of the Israelite families,

Child (Child's, Childhood, Childish, Childless, Children, Children's, Grandchildren)

Ge 4:25 "God has granted me another **c** in
16:11 now with **c** and you will have a son.
17:17 Sarah bear a **c** at the age of ninety?"
18:13 really have a **c**, now that I am old?'
21: 8 The **c** grew and was weaned, and on
Ex 2: 2 When she saw that he was a fine **c**,
2: 3 Then she placed the **c** in it and put
2:10 the **c** grew older, she took him to
Jdg 11:34 of tambourines! She was an only **c**.
Ru 4:16 Naomi took the **c**, laid him in her
1Sa 1:27 I prayed for this **c**, and the LORD
2Sa 12:15 the LORD struck the **c** that Uriah's
12:16 David pleaded with God for the **c**.
12:18 On the seventh day the **c** died.
12:18 to tell him that the **c** was dead,
12:18 "While the **c** was still living, we
12:18 How can we tell him the **c** is dead?
12:19 and he realised that the **c** was dead.
12:19 "Is the **c** dead?" he asked. "Yes,"
12:21 While the **c** was alive, you fasted
12:21 the **c** is dead, you get up and eat!"
12:22 He answered, "While the **c** was still
12:22 gracious to me and let the **c** live.'
1Ki 3: 7 But I am only a little **c** and do not
3:18 The third day after my **c** was born,
3:25 "Cut the living **c** in two and give
17:23 Elijah picked up the **c** and carried
2Ki 4:18 The **c** grew, and one day he went out
4:26 all right? Is your **c** all right?'"
2Ch 22:11 was Ahaziah's sister, she hid the **c**
Job 3:16 in the ground like a stillborn **c**,
24: 9 The fatherless **c** is snatched from
Ps 58: 8 like a stillborn **c**, may they not see
131: 2 like a weaned **c** with its mother,
131: 2 a weaned **c** is my soul within me.
Pr 4: 3 tender, and an only **c** of my mother,
20:11 Even a **c** is known by his actions, by
22: 6 Train a **c** in the way he should go,
22:15 Folly is bound up in the heart of a **c**
23:13 Do not withhold discipline from a **c**;
29:15 but a **c** left to himself disgraces
Ecc 6: 3 a stillborn **c** is better off than he.
Isa 7:14 with **c** and will give birth to a son,
9: 6 For to us a **c** is born, to us a son
10:19 few that a **c** could write them down.
11: 6 and a little **c** will lead them.
11: 8 **c** put his hand into the viper's nest.
26:17 a woman with **c** and about to give
26:18 We were with **c**, we writhed in pain,
49:15 compassion on the **c** she has borne?
54: 1 woman, you who never bore a **c**;
66:13 a mother comforts her **c**, so will I
Jer 1: 6 know how to speak; I am only a **c**."
1: 7 to me, "Do not say, 'I am only a **c**.
4:31 groan as of one bearing her first **c**
20:15 "A **c** is born to you—a son!
31:20 my dear son, the **c** in whom I delight?
Hos 11: 1 "When Israel was a **c**, I loved him,
13:13 but he is a **c** without wisdom;
Zec 12:10 for him as one mourns for an only **c**,
Mt 1:18 be with **c** through the Holy Spirit.
1:23 "The virgin will be with **c** and will
2: 8 and make a careful search for the **c**.
2: 9 over the place where the **c** was.
2:11 they saw the **c** with his mother Mary,
2:13 "Get up," he said, "take the **c** and
2:13 to search for the **c** to kill him."
2:14 he got up, took the **c** and his mother
2:20 said, "Get up, take the **c** and his
2:21 he got up, took the **c** and his mother
10:21 and a father his **c**; children will
18: 2 He called a little **c** and had him
18: 4 whoever humbles himself like this **c**
18: 5 "And whoever welcomes a little **c**
Mk 5:39 The **c** is not dead but asleep."
5:40 him, and went in where the **c** was.
7:30 She went home and found her **c** lying
9:36 He took a little **c** and had him stand
10:15 a little **c** will never enter it."
12:21 but he also died, leaving no **c**.
13:12 brother to death, and a father his **c**.
Lk 1:31 You will be with **c** and give birth to
Lk 1:36 is going to have a **c** in her old age,
1:42 and blessed is the **c** you will bear!
1:59 day they came to circumcise the **c**,
1:62 what he would like to name the **c**.
1:66 "What then is this **c** going to be?"
1:76 you, my **c**, will be called a prophet
1:80 the **c** grew and became strong in
2: 5 to him and was expecting a **c**.
2:17 had been told them about this **c**,
2:27 When the parents brought in the **c**
2:34 "This **c** is destined to cause the
2:38 spoke about the **c** to all who were
2:40 the **c** grew and became strong; he was
8:54 by the hand and said, "My **c**, get up!"
9:38 look at my son, for he is my only **c**.
9:47 took a little **c** and made him stand
9:48 "Whoever welcomes this little **c** in
18:17 a little **c** will never enter it."
Jn 4:49 "Sir, come down before my **c** dies.
7:22 you circumcise a **c** on the Sabbath.
7:23 Now if a **c** can be circumcised on the
16:21 A woman giving birth to a **c** has pain
16:21 joy that a **c** is born into the world.
Ac 7: 5 at that time Abraham had no **c**.
7:20 was born, and he was no ordinary **c**.
13:10 "You are a **c** of the devil and an
26: 4 I have lived ever since I was a **c**,
1Co 13:11 I was a **c**, I talked like a **c**,
13:11 like a **c**, I reasoned like a **c**.
Gal 4: 1 is that as long as the heir is a **c**,
Heb 11:23 they saw he was no ordinary **c**,
1Jn 3:10 do what is right is not a **c** of God;
5: 1 the father loves his **c** as well.
Rev 12: 4 devour her **c** the moment it was born.
12: 5 She gave birth to a son, a male **c**,
12: 5 And her **c** was snatched up to God and
12:13 who had given birth to the male **c**.

Child's (Child)

2Ki 4:30 the **c** mother said, "As surely as the
Job 33:25 his flesh is renewed like a **c**; it is
Mt 2:20 trying to take the **c** life are dead."
Mk 5:40 he took the **c** father and mother and
Lk 2:33 The **c** father and mother marvelled at
8:51 James, and the **c** father and mother.

Childbearing (Bear[1])

Ge 3:16 greatly increase your pains in **c**;
18:11 and Sarah was past the age of **c**.
1Ti 2:15 women will be saved through **c**—if

Childbirth (Bear[1])

Ge 35:17 she was having great difficulty in **c**,
Ex 1:16 "When you help the Hebrew women in **c**
Isa 42:14 in **c**, I cry out, I gasp and pant.
Hos 13:13 Pains as of a woman in **c** come to him,
Ro 8:22 been groaning as in the pains of **c**
Gal 4:19 I am again in the pains of **c**

Childhood (Child)

Ge 8:21 of his heart is evil from **c**.
Isa 47:12 which you have laboured at since **c**.
47:15 with and trafficked with since **c**.
Mk 9:21 like this?" "From **c**," he answered.

Childish (Child)

1Co 13:11 a man, I put **c** ways behind me.

Childless (Child)

Ge 15: 2 can you give me since I remain **c**
Lev 20:20 held responsible; they will die **c**.
20:21 his brother. They will be **c**.
Dt 7:14 none of your men or women will be **c**,
32:25 street the sword will make them **c**;
Jdg 13: 2 wife who was sterile and remained **c**.
13: 3 "You are sterile and **c**, but you are
1Sa 15:33 "As your sword has made women **c**, so
15:33 will your mother be **c** among women.
Job 24:21 They prey on the barren and **c** woman,
Jer 18:21 Let their wives be made **c** and widows;
22:30 "Record this man as if **c**, a man who
Eze 5:17 you, and they will leave you **c**.
14:15 they leave it **c** and it becomes
36:14 or make your nation **c**, declares the
Lk 20:29 one married a woman and died **c**.

Children (Child, *Children of God*)

Ge 3:16 with pain you will give birth to **c**.
6: 4 daughters of men and had **c** by them.
11:30 Now Sarai was barren; she had no **c**.
15: 3 Abram said, "You have given me no **c**;
16: 1 Abram's wife, had borne him no **c**.
16: 2 "The LORD has kept me from having **c**.
18:19 so that he will direct his **c** and his
20:17 girls so they could have **c** again,
21: 7 to Abraham that Sarah would nurse **c**?
21:23 with me or my **c** or my descendants.
29:35 Then she stopped having **c**.
30: 1 she was not bearing Jacob any **c**,
30: 1 So she said to Jacob, "Give me **c**, or
30: 2 God, who has kept you from having **c**?"
30: 3 her so that she can bear **c** for me
30: 9 saw that she had stopped having **c**,
30:26 Give me my wives and **c**, for whom I
31:16 our father belongs to us and our **c**.
31:17 Jacob put his **c** and his wives on
31:43 the **c** are my **c**, and the flocks
31:43 or about the **c** they have borne?
32:11 and also the mothers with their **c**.
33: 1 men; so he divided the **c** among Leah,
33: 2 He put the maidservants and their **c**
33: 2 Leah and her **c** next, and Rachel and
33: 5 looked up and saw the women and **c**.
33: 5 Jacob answered, "They are the **c** God
33: 6 maidservants and their **c** approached
33: 7 Next, Leah and her **c** came and bowed
33:13 "My lord knows that the **c** are tender
33:14 and that of the **c**, until I come to my
34:29 wealth and all their women and **c**,
36:25 The **c** of Anah: Dishon and Oholibamah
42:36 them, "You have deprived me of my **c**.
43: 8 you and our **c** may live and not die.
45:10 your **c** and grandchildren, your
45:19 Egypt for your **c** and your wives,
46: 5 their **c** and their wives in the carts
46:18 These were the **c** born to Jacob by
47:12 according to the number of their **c**.
47:24 and your households and your **c**."
48: 6 Any **c** born to you after them will be
48:11 has allowed me to see your **c** too."
50: 8 Only their **c** and their flocks and
50:21 I will provide for you and your **c**."
50:23 the third generation of Ephraim's **c**.
50:23 Also the **c** of Makir son of Manasseh
Ex 10: 2 that you may tell your **c** and
10:10 you go, along with your women and **c**!
10:24 Even your women and **c** may go with
12:26 your **c** ask you, 'What does this
12:37 men on foot, besides women and **c**.
17: 3 our **c** and livestock die of thirst?"
20: 5 am a jealous God, punishing the **c**
21: 4 the woman and her **c** shall belong to
21: 5 and **c** and do not want to go free,'
22:24 become widows and your **c** fatherless.
34: 7 he punishes the **c** and their **c** for
Lev 10:14 given to you and your **c** as your share
10:15 regular share for you and your **c**,
18:21 "Do not give any of your **c** to be
20: 2 who give any of his **c** to Molech
20: 3 for by giving his **c** to Molech,
20: 4 man gives one of his **c** to Molech
22:13 yet has no **c**, and she returns to
25:41 he and his **c** are to be released, and
25:46 You can will them to your **c** as
25:54 he and his **c** are to be released in
26:22 and they will rob you of your **c**,
Nu 5:28 of guilt and will be able to have **c**.
14: 3 and **c** will be taken as plunder.
14:18 he punishes the **c** for the sin of the
14:31 for your **c** that you said would be
14:33 Your **c** will be shepherds here for
16:27 **c** and little ones at the entrances
31: 9 captured the Midianite women and **c**
32:16 and cities for our women and **c**.
32:17 Meanwhile our women and **c** will live
32:24 Build cities for your women and **c**,
32:26 Our **c** and wives, our flocks and
Dt 1:39 your **c** who do not yet know good from
2:34 destroyed them—men, women and **c**.
3: 6 every city—men, women and **c**.
3:19 However, your wives, your **c** and your
Dt 4: 9 to your **c** and to their **c** after them.
4:10 land and may teach them to their **c**."
4:25 have had **c** and grandchildren and
4:40 go well with you and your **c** after you
5: 9 am a jealous God, punishing the **c**
5:29 well with them and their **c** for ever!
6: 2 that you, your **c** and their **c** after
6: 7 Impress them on your **c**. Talk about
11: 2 Remember today that your **c** were not
11: 5 was not your **c** who saw what he did
11:19 Teach them to your **c**, talking about
11:21 that your days and the days of your **c**
12:25 well with you and your **c** after you,
12:28 well with you and your **c** after you,
14: 1 You are the **c** of the LORD your God.
20:14 for the women, the **c**, the livestock
23: 8 The third generation of **c** born to
24:16 not be put to death for their **c**,
24:16 nor **c** put to death for their fathers;
28:54 wife he loves or his surviving **c**,
28:55 flesh of his **c** that he is eating.
28:57 from her womb and the **c** she bears.
29:11 together with your **c** and your wives,
29:22 Your **c** who follow you in later
29:29 belong to us and to our **c** for ever,
30: 2 you and your **c** return to the LORD
30:19 so that you and your **c** may
31:12 Assemble the people—men, women and **c**
31:13 Their **c**, who do not know this law,
32: 5 shame they are no longer his **c**,
32:20 generation, **c** who are unfaithful.
32:46 so that you may command your **c** to
33: 9 brothers or acknowledge his own **c**,
Jos 1:14 Your wives, your **c** and your
4: 6 In the future, when your **c** ask you, '
8:35 including the women and **c**, and the
14: 9 and that of your **c** for ever,
Jdg 18:21 Putting their little **c**, their
21:10 there, including the women and **c**.
1Sa 1: 2 Peninnah had **c**, but Hannah had none.
2: 5 She who was barren has borne seven **c**,
2:20 "May the LORD give you **c** by this
15: 3 **c** and infants, cattle and sheep,
22:19 with its men and women, its **c** and
30:22 man may take his wife and **c** and go."
2Sa 5:14 These are the names of the **c** born to
6:23 Michal daughter of Saul had no **c** to
12: 3 and it grew up with him and his **c**.
1Ki 11:20 Genubath lived with Pharaoh's own **c**.
20: 3 best of your wives and **c** are mine.'"
20: 5 and gold, your wives and your **c**.
20: 7 When he sent for my wives and my **c**,
2Ki 8:12 dash their little **c** to the ground,
10: 1 and to the guardians of Ahab's **c**.
14: 6 not be put to death for their **c**,
14: 6 nor **c** put to death for their fathers;
17:31 and the Sepharvites burned their **c**
17:41 their **c** and grandchildren continue
19: 3 as when **c** come to the point of birth
1Ch 2:18 Caleb son of Hezron had **c** by his
2:30 and Appaim. Seled died without **c**.
2:32 and Jonathan. Jether died without **c**.
3: 5 these were the **c** born to him there:
4:18 These were the **c** of Pharaoh's
4:27 his brothers did not have many **c**;
6: 3 The **c** of Amram: Aaron, Moses and
7: 4 for they had many wives and **c**.
14: 4 These are the names of the **c** born to
2Ch 20:13 with their wives and **c** and little
25: 4 not be put to death for their **c**,
25: 4 nor **c** put to death for their fathers;
30: 9 then your brothers and your **c** will
Ezr 8:21 and our **c**, with all our possessions.
9:12 **c** as an everlasting inheritance.'
10: 1 women and **c**—gathered round him.
10: 3 away all these women and their **c**,
10:44 some of them had **c** by these wives.
Ne 12:43 The women and **c** also rejoiced. The
13:24 Half of their **c** spoke the language
Est 3:13 young and old, women and little **c**
8:11 attack them and their women and **c**;
Job 1: 5 "Perhaps my **c** have sinned and cursed
5: 4 His **c** are far from safety, crushed
5:25 You will know that your **c** will be
8: 4 your **c** sinned against him, he gave
17: 5 reward, the eyes of his **c** will fail.
Job 20:10 His **c** must make amends to the poor;
21: 8 They see their **c** established around
21:11 They send forth their **c** as a flock;
24: 5 wasteland provides food for their **c**.
27:14 However many his **c**, their fate is
29: 5 with me and my **c** were around me,
42:16 he saw his **c** and their **c** to the
Ps 8: 2 From the lips of **c** and infants you
17:14 they store up wealth for their **c**.
34:11 Come, my **c**, listen to me; I will
37:25 forsaken or their **c** begging bread.
37:26 freely; their **c** will be blessed.
69:36 the **c** of his servants will inherit
72: 4 people and save the **c** of the needy;
73:15 thus," I would have betrayed your **c**.
78: 4 We will not hide them from their **c**;
78: 5 our forefathers to teach their **c**,
78: 6 even the **c** yet to be born, and they
78: 6 and they in turn would tell their **c**.
90:16 servants, your splendour to their **c**.
102:28 The **c** of your servants will live in
103:13 a father has compassion on his **c**, so
103:17 righteousness with their children's **c**
109: 9 May his **c** be fatherless and his wife
109:10 May his **c** be wandering beggars; may
109:12 or take pity on his fatherless **c**.
112: 2 His **c** will be mighty in the land;
113: 9 in her home as a happy mother of **c**.
115:14 you increase, both you and your **c**.
127: 3 from the LORD, **c** a reward from him.
128: 6 may you live to see your children's **c**
148:12 young men and maidens, old men and **c**.
Pr 13:22 an inheritance for his children's **c**,
14:26 and for his **c** it will be a refuge.
17: 6 parents are the pride of their **c**.
17: 6 Children's children are a crown to
20: 7 life; blessed are his **c** after him.
31:28 Her **c** arise and call her blessed;
Ecc 6: 3 A man may have a hundred **c** and live
Isa 1: 2 "I reared **c** and brought them up, but
1: 4 of evildoers, **c** given to corruption!
3: 4 officials; mere **c** will govern them.
8:18 and the **c** the LORD has given me.
13:18 will they look with compassion on **c**.
28: 9 To **c** weaned from their milk,
29:23 they see among them their **c**, the
30: 1 "Woe to the obstinate **c**," declares
30: 9 deceitful **c**, **c** unwilling to listen
37: 3 as when **c** come to the point of birth
38:19 their **c** about your faithfulness.
43: 5 I will bring your **c** from the east
45:11 do you question me about my **c**, or
47: 8 be a widow or suffer the loss of **c**.'
47: 9 single day: loss of **c** and widowhood.
48:19 your **c** like its numberless grains;
49:20 The **c** born during your bereavement
49:25 with you, and your **c** I will save.
54: 1 because more are the **c** of the
57: 5 you sacrifice your **c** in the ravines
59:21 or from the mouths of your **c**, or
65:23 They will not toil in vain or bear **c**
66: 8 than she gives birth to her **c**.
Jer 2: 9 charges against your children's **c**.
4:22 They are senseless **c**; they have no
5: 7 Your **c** have forsaken me and sworn by
6:11 "Pour it out on the **c** in the street
7:18 The **c** gather wood, the fathers light
9:21 it has cut off the **c** from the
17: 2 Even their **c** remember their altars
18:21 give their **c** over to famine; hand
22:28 Why will he and his **c** be hurled out,
30: 6 Ask and see: Can a man bear **c**? Then
30:20 Their **c** will be as in days of old,
31:15 Rachel weeping for her **c** and
31:15 because her **c** are no more."
31:17 Your **c** will return to their own land.
32:18 into the laps of their **c** after them.
32:39 and the good of their **c** after them.
36:31 I will punish him and his **c** and his
38:23 "All your wives and **c** will be
40: 7 women and **c** who were the poorest in
41:16 women, **c** and court officials he had
43: 6 women and **c** and the king's daughters
44: 7 the **c** and infants, and so leave
47: 3 will not turn to help their **c**;
49:10 His **c**, relatives and neighbours will

Lam 1: 5 Her **c** have gone into exile, captive
1:16 My **c** are destitute because the enemy
2:11 because **c** and infants faint in the
2:19 to him for the lives of your **c**,
2:20 the **c** they have cared for? Should
3:33 affliction or grief to the **c** of men.
4: 4 the **c** beg for bread, but no-one gives
4:10 women have cooked their own **c**,
Eze 5:10 your midst fathers will eat their **c**,
5:10 and **c** will eat their fathers.
9: 6 young men and maidens, women and **c**,
16:21 You slaughtered my **c** and sacrificed
16:45 who despised her husband and her **c**;
16:45 despised their husbands and their **c**.
20:18 I said to their **c** in the desert, "Do
20:21 " 'But the **c** rebelled against me:
23:37 they even sacrificed their **c**, whom
23:39 sacrificed their **c** to their idols,
36:12 never again deprive them of their **c**.
36:13 and deprive your nation of its **c**,"
37:25 and their **c** and their children's **c**
47:22 settled among you and who have **c**.
Da 6:24 den, along with their wives and **c**.
Hos 1: 2 wife and **c** of unfaithfulness,
2: 4 I will not show my love to her **c**,
2: 4 because they are the **c** of adultery.
4: 6 your God, I also will ignore your **c**.
5: 7 they give birth to illegitimate **c**.
9:12 Even if they bring up **c**, I will
9:13 bring out their **c** to the slayer."
9:16 Even if they bear **c**, I will slay
10:14 dashed to the ground with their **c**.
11:10 **c** will come trembling from the west.
Joel 1: 3 Tell it to your **c**, and let your
1: 3 and let your **c** tell it to their **c**,
1: 3 and their **c** to the next generation.
2:16 gather the **c**, those nursing at the
Mic 1:16 for the **c** in whom you delight;
2: 9 my blessing from their **c** for ever.
Zec 10: 7 Their **c** will see it and be joyful;
10: 9 **c** will survive, and they will return.
Mal 4: 6 hearts of the fathers to their **c**,
4: 6 and the hearts of the **c** to their
Mt 2:18 Rachel weeping for her **c** and
3: 9 God can raise up **c** for Abraham.
7:11 how to give good gifts to your **c**,
10:21 **c** will rebel against their parents
11:16 They are like **c** sitting in the
11:25 and revealed them to little **c**.
14:21 thousand men, besides women and **c**.
15:38 four thousand, besides women and **c**.
18: 3 you change and become like little **c**,
18:25 his wife and his **c** and all that he
19:13 little **c** were brought to Jesus for
19:14 Jesus said, "Let the little **c** come
19:29 or sisters or father or mother or **c**
21:15 the **c** shouting in the temple area,
21:16 "Do you hear what these **c** are saying?
21:16 " 'From the lips of **c** and infants you
22:24 that if a man dies without having **c**,
22:24 marry the widow and have **c** for him.
22:25 and since he had no **c**, he left his
23:37 longed to gather your **c** together,
27:25 Let his blood be on us and on our **c**!"
Mk 7:27 "First let the **c** eat all they want,"
9:37 little **c** in my name welcomes me;
10:13 People were bringing little **c** to
10:14 "Let the little **c** come to me, and do
10:16 he took the **c** in his arms, put his
10:24 "**C**, how hard it is to enter the
10:29 or **c** or fields for me and the
10:30 brothers, sisters, mothers, **c** and
12:19 dies and leaves a wife but no **c**,
12:19 widow and have **c** for his brother.
12:20 and died without leaving any **c**.
12:22 In fact, none of the seven left any **c**
13:12 **C** will rebel against their parents
Lk 1: 7 they had no **c**, because Elizabeth was
1:17 hearts of the fathers to their **c**
3: 8 God can raise up **c** for Abraham.
7:32 They are like **c** sitting in the
7:35 wisdom is proved right by all her **c**."
10:21 and revealed them to little **c**.
11: 7 locked, and my **c** are with me in bed.
11:13 how to give good gifts to your **c**,
13:34 longed to gather your **c** together,
Lk 14:26 his wife and **c**, his brothers and
18:16 Jesus called the **c** to him and said,
18:16 "Let the little **c** come to me, and do
18:29 or wife or brothers or parents or **c**
19:44 you and the **c** within your walls.
20:28 dies and leaves a wife but no **c**,
20:28 widow and have **c** for his brother.
20:31 way the seven died, leaving no **c**.
20:36 They are God's **c**, since they are **c**
23:28 weep for yourselves and for your **c**.
Jn 1:13 **c** born not of natural descent, nor
8:39 "If you were Abraham's **c**," said
8:41 "We are not illegitimate **c**," they
13:33 "My **c**, I will be with you only a
Ac 2:39 The promise is for you and your **c**
13:26 "Brothers, **c** of Abraham, and you
13:33 he has fulfilled for us, their **c**, by
21: 5 **c** accompanied us out of the city,
21:21 them not to circumcise their **c**
Ro 8:16 with our spirit that we are God's **c**.
8:17 Now if we are **c**, then we are
9: 7 are they all Abraham's **c**. On the
9: 8 it is not the natural **c** who are
9: 8 not the natural **c** who are God's **c**,
9:10 but Rebekah's **c** had one and the same
1Co 4:14 you, but to warn you, as my dear **c**.
7:14 Otherwise your **c** would be unclean,
14:20 Brothers, stop thinking like **c**. In
2Co 6:13 a fair exchange—I speak as to my **c**—
12:14 After all, **c** should not have to save
12:14 parents, but parents for their **c**.
Gal 3: 7 those who believe are **c** of Abraham.
4: 3 also, when we were **c**, we were in
4:19 My dear **c**, for whom I am again in
4:24 and bears **c** who are to be slaves:
4:25 she is in slavery with her **c**.
4:27 O barren woman, who bears no **c**;
4:27 because more are the **c** of the
4:28 Now you, brothers, like Isaac, are **c**
4:31 Therefore, brothers, we are not **c** of
Eph 5: 1 of God, therefore, as dearly loved **c**
5: 8 light in the Lord. Live as **c** of light
6: 1 **C**, obey your parents in the Lord,
6: 4 Fathers, do not exasperate your **c**;
Col 3:20 **C**, obey your parents in everything,
3:21 Fathers, do not embitter your **c**, or
1Th 2: 7 a mother caring for her little **c**.
2:11 as a father deals with his own **c**,
1Ti 3: 4 his **c** obey him with proper respect.
3:12 manage his **c** and his household well.
5: 4 if a widow has **c** or grandchildren,
5:10 such as bringing up **c**, showing
5:14 to have **c**, to manage their homes and
Tit 1: 6 a man whose **c** believe and are not
2: 4 women to love their husbands and **c**,
Heb 2:13 am I, and the **c** God has given me."
2:14 Since the **c** have flesh and blood, he
12: 8 illegitimate **c** and not true sons.
1Pe 1:14 obedient **c**, do not conform to the
1Jn 2: 1 My dear **c**, I write this to you so
2:12 I write to you, dear **c**, because your
2:13 I write to you dear **c**, because you
2:18 Dear **c**, this is the last hour; and
2:28 now, dear **c**, continue in him, so
3: 7 Dear **c**, do not let anyone lead you
3:10 and who the **c** of the devil are:
3:18 Dear **c**, let us not love with words
4: 4 You, dear **c**, are from God and have
5:21 Dear **c**, keep yourselves from idols.
2Jn : 1 To the chosen lady and her **c**, whom I
: 4 some of your **c** walking in the truth,
:13 The **c** of your chosen sister send
3Jn : 4 that my **c** are walking in the truth.
Rev 2:23 I will strike her **c** dead. Then all

Children of God

Jn 1:12 he gave the right to become **c**—
11:52 nation but also for the scattered **c**,
Ro 8:21 into the glorious freedom of the **c**.
Php 2:15 **c** without fault in a crooked and
1Jn 3: 1 that we should be called **c**! And that
3: 2 Dear friends, now we are **c**, and what
3:10 This is how we know who the **c** are
5: 2 is how we know that we love the **c**:
5:19 We know that we are **c**, and that the

Children's (Child)

Ps 103:17 with their **c** children—
128: 6 may you live to see your **c** children.
Pr 13:22 an inheritance for his **c** children,
17: 6 **C** children are a crown to the aged,
Isa 54:13 LORD, and great will be your **c** peace.
Jer 2: 9 charges against your **c** children.
31:29 and the **c** teeth are set on edge.'
Eze 16:36 because you gave them your **c** blood,
18: 2 and the **c** teeth are set on edge'?
37:25 their children and their **c** children
Mt 15:26 "It is not right to take the **c** bread
Mk 7:27 it is not right to take the **c** bread
7:28 under the table eat the **c** crumbs."

Chin

Lev 13:29 has a sore on the head or on the **c**,
13:30 infectious disease of the head or **c**.

Chirp

Isa 10:14 a wing, or opened its mouth to **c**.' "

Chisel (Chiselled, Chiselling, Chisels)

Ex 34: 1 "**C** out two stone tablets like the
Dt 10: 1 "**C** out two stone tablets like the
1Ki 6: 7 and no hammer, **c** or any other iron
Jer 10: 3 a craftsman shapes it with his **c**.

Chiselled (Chisel)

Ex 34: 4 Moses **c** out two stone tablets like
Dt 10: 3 **c** out two stone tablets like the

Chiselling (Chisel)

Isa 22:16 **c** your resting place in the rock?

Chisels (Chisel)

Isa 44:13 he roughs it out with **c** and marks it

Chloe's

1Co 1:11 My brothers, some from **C** household

Choice (Choose)

Ge 18: 7 he ran to the herd and selected a **c**,
27: 9 and bring me two **c** young goats,
Lev 23:40 are to take **c** fruit from the trees,
Dt 12:11 and all the **c** possessions you have
32:14 with **c** rams of Bashan and the finest
1Sa 2:29 fattening yourselves on the **c** parts
1Ki 4:23 deer, gazelles, roebucks and **c** fowl.
1Ch 7:40 families, **c** men, brave warriors and
21:11 is what the LORD says: 'Take your **c**:
Ne 5:18 Each day one ox, six **c** sheep and
8:10 Nehemiah said, "Go and enjoy **c** food
Job 36:16 of your table laden with **c** food.
Pr 8:10 knowledge rather than **c** gold,
8:19 what I yield surpasses **c** silver.
10:20 tongue of the righteous is **c** silver,
18: 8 words of a gossip are like **c** morsels;
21:20 wise are stores of **c** food and oil,
26:22 words of a gossip are like **c** morsels;
SS 4:13 with **c** fruits, with henna and nard,
4:16 his garden and taste its **c** fruits.
5:15 is like Lebanon, **c** as its cedars.
Isa 1:22 your **c** wine is diluted with water.
Jer 2:21 I had planted you like a **c** vine of
Eze 20:40 your offerings and your **c** gifts,
24: 4 **c** pieces—the leg and the shoulder.
34: 3 wool and slaughter the **c** animals,
Da 1:16 the guard took away their **c** food and
10: 3 I ate no **c** food; no meat or wine
Am 5:22 Though you bring **c** fellowship
6: 4 dine on **c** lambs and fattened calves.
Zec 11:16 but will eat the meat of the **c** sheep,
Jn 2:10 "Everyone brings out the **c** wine
Ac 15: 7 some time ago God made a **c** among you
Ro 8:20 not by its own **c**, but by the will of

Choicest (Choose)

Ge 23: 6 Bury your dead in the **c** of our tombs.
49:11 his colt to the **c** branch; he will
Dt 33:15 with the **c** gifts of the ancient
2Ki 19:23 tallest cedars, the **c** of its pines.

Job 22:25 be your gold, the **c** silver for you.
33:20 and his soul loathes the **c** meal.
Isa 5: 2 and planted it with the **c** vines.
16: 8 have trampled down the **c** vines,
22: 7 Your **c** valleys are full of chariots,
37:24 tallest cedars, the **c** of its pines.
Eze 31:16 of Eden, the **c** and best of Lebanon,
Hab 1:16 in luxury and enjoys the **c** food.

Choir (Choirs)
Ne 12:38 The second **c** proceeded in the

Choirs (Choir)
1Ch 15:27 in charge of the singing of the **c**.
Ne 12:31 I also assigned two large **c** to give
12:40 The two **c** that gave thanks then took
12:42 The **c** sang under the direction of

Choke (Choked)
Mt 13:22 the deceitfulness of wealth **c** it,
18:28 He grabbed him and began to **c** him.
Mk 4:19 other things come in and **c** the word,

Choked (Choke)
Mt 13: 7 which grew up and **c** the plants.
Mk 4: 7 which grew up and **c** the plants, so
Lk 8: 7 grew up with it and **c** the plants.
8:14 way they are **c** by life's worries,

Choose (Choice, Choicest, Chooses, Choosing, Chose, Chosen)
Ex 12: 5 The animals you **c** must be year-old
17: 9 "**C** some of our men and go to
34:16 you **c** some of their daughters as
Nu 14: 4 they said to each other, "We should **c**
17: 5 The staff belonging to the man I **c**
Dt 1:13 **C** some wise, understanding and
7: 7 **c** you because you were more numerous
12: 5 the place the LORD your God will **c**
12:11 to the place the LORD your God will **c**
12:14 LORD will **c** in one of your tribes,
12:18 the place the LORD your God will **c**
12:26 and go to the place the LORD will **c**.
14:23 will **c** as a dwelling for his Name,
14:24 the LORD will **c** to put his Name
14:25 the place the LORD your God will **c**.
15:20 LORD your God at the place he will **c**.
16: 2 will **c** as a dwelling for his Name.
16: 6 except in the place he will **c** as a
16: 7 the place the LORD your God will **c**.
16:11 **c** as a dwelling for his Name—you,
16:15 God at the place the LORD will **c**.
16:16 LORD your God at the place he will **c**:
17: 8 the place the LORD your God will **c**.
17:10 you at the place the LORD will **c**.
18: 6 to the place the LORD will **c**,
26: 2 God will **c** as a dwelling for his
30:19 Now **c** life, so that you and your
31:11 LORD your God at the place he will **c**,
Jos 3:12 Now then, **c** twelve men from the
4: 2 "**C** twelve men from among the people,
9:27 LORD at the place the LORD would **c**.
24:15 then **c** for yourselves this day whom
1Sa 17: 8 **C** a man and have him come down to me.
2Sa 17: 1 "I would **c** twelve thousand men and
24:12 **C** one of them for me to carry out
1Ki 18:23 Get two bulls for us. Let them **c** one
18:25 "**C** one of the bulls and prepare it
2Ki 10: 3 **c** the best and most worthy of your
18:32 **C** life and not death! "Do not listen
1Ch 21:10 **C** one of them for me to carry out
Ps 65: 4 Blessed are those you **c** and bring
75: 2 You say, "I **c** the appointed time; it
78:67 he did not **c** the tribe of Ephraim;
Pr 1:29 and did not **c** to fear the LORD,
3:31 a violent man or **c** any of his ways,
8:10 **C** my instruction instead of silver,
16:16 **c** understanding rather than silver!
Isa 7:15 to reject the wrong and **c** the right.
7:16 to reject the wrong and **c** the right,
14: 1 once again he will **c** Israel and will
56: 4 who **c** what pleases me and hold fast
66: 4 I also will **c** harsh treatment for
Jer 3:14 I will **c** you—one from a town and
33:26 and will not **c** one of his sons to
Eze 33: 2 and the people of the land **c** one of
Hos 8: 4 they **c** princes without my approval.
Zec 1:17 comfort Zion and **c** Jerusalem.'"
2:12 land and will again **c** Jerusalem.
Jn 15:16 You did not **c** me, but I chose you
Ac 1:21 Therefore it is necessary to **c** one
6: 3 Brothers, **c** seven men from among you
15:22 decided to **c** some of their own men
15:25 we all agreed to **c** some men and send
2Co 12: 6 Even if I should **c** to boast, I would
Php 1:22 Yet what shall I **c**? I do not know!
1Pe 4: 3 pagans **c** to do—living in debauchery,

Chooses (Choose)
Lev 16: 2 Aaron not to come whenever he **c**
Nu 16: 5 The man he **c** he will cause to come
16: 7 The man the LORD **c** will be the one
Dt 12:21 the LORD your God **c** to put his Name
17:15 you the king the LORD your God **c**.
23:16 he likes and in whatever town he **c**.
2Sa 15:15 to do whatever our lord the king **c**."
Ps 68:16 at the mountain where God **c** to reign,
Isa 41:24 he who **c** you is detestable.
Mt 11:27 to whom the Son **c** to reveal him.
Lk 10:22 to whom the Son **c** to reveal him."
Jn 7:17 If anyone **c** to do God's will, he
Jas 4: 4 Anyone who **c** to be a friend of the

Choosing (Choose)
1Ki 12:33 a month of his own **c**, he offered
Ro 9:22 What if God, **c** to show his wrath and

Chop (Chopped)
Dt 29:11 **c** your wood and carry your water.
Jer 46:23 They will **c** down her forest,"
Mic 3: 3 who **c** them up like meat for the pan,

Chopped (Chop)
1Sa 6:14 The people **c** up the wood of the cart

Chose (Choose)
Ge 6: 2 and they married any of them they **c**.
13:11 Lot **c** for himself the whole plain of
47: 2 He **c** five of his brothers and
Ex 18:25 He **c** capable men from all Israel and
Dt 4:37 and **c** their descendants after them,
10:15 and he **c** you, their descendants,
33:21 He **c** the best land for himself; the
Jos 8: 3 He **c** thirty thousand of his best
Jdg 5: 8 they **c** new gods, war came to the
1Sa 2:28 I **c** your father out of all the
13: 2 Saul **c** three thousand men from
17:40 **c** five smooth stones from the stream,
2Sa 6:21 "It was before the LORD, who **c** me
1Ki 11:34 whom I **c** and who observed my
11:36 the city where I **c** to put my Name.
2Ki 23:27 the city I **c**, and this temple, about
1Ch 15: 2 because the LORD **c** them to carry the
28: 4 **c** me from my whole family to be king
28: 4 He **c** Judah as leader, and from the
28: 4 house of Judah he **c** my family,
2Ch 24: 3 Jehoiada **c** two wives for him, and he
Ne 9: 7 "You are the LORD God, who **c** Abram
Job 29:25 I **c** the way for them and sat as
Ps 33:12 the people he **c** for his inheritance.
47: 4 He **c** our inheritance for us, the
78:68 he **c** the tribe of Judah, Mount Zion,
78:70 He **c** David his servant and took him
Isa 65:12 my sight and **c** what displeases me."
66: 4 my sight and **c** what displeases me."
Eze 20: 5 LORD says: On the day I **c** Israel,
Lk 6:13 to him and **c** twelve of them,
Jn 5:35 you **c** for a time to enjoy his light.
15:16 You did not choose me, but I **c** you
Ac 6: 5 They **c** Stephen, a man full of faith
13:17 The God of the people of Israel **c**
15:22 They **c** Judas (called Barsabbas) and
15:40 Paul **c** Silas and left, commended by
1Co 1:27 God **c** the foolish things of the
1:27 God **c** the weak things of the world
1:28 He **c** the lowly things of this world
Eph 1: 4 For he **c** us in him before the
2Th 2:13 because from the beginning God **c** you
Heb 11:25 He **c** to be ill-treated along with
Jas 1:18 He **c** to give us birth through the

Chosen (Choose)
Ge 18:19 For I have **c** him, so that he will
24:14 you have **c** for your servant Isaac.
24:44 the LORD has **c** for my master's son.'
Ex 31: 2 "See I have **c** Bezalel son of Uri,
35:30 "See, the LORD has **c** Bezalel son of
Lev 16:10 the goat **c** by lot as the scapegoat
Dt 7: 6 The LORD your God has **c** you out of
14: 2 **c** you to be his treasured possession.
18: 5 for the LORD your God has **c** them and
21: 5 for the LORD your God has **c** them to
Jos 24:22 that you have **c** to serve the LORD.
Jdg 10:14 Go and cry out to the gods you have **c**
20:15 **c** men from those living in Gibeah.
20:16 hundred **c** men who were left-handed,
1Sa 8:18 for relief from the king you have **c**,
10:20 near, the tribe of Benjamin was **c**.
10:21 by clan, and Matri's clan was **c**.
10:21 Finally Saul son of Kish was **c**. But
10:24 "Do you see the man the LORD has **c**?
12:13 Now here is the king you have **c**, the
16: 1 I have **c** one of his sons to be king."
16: 8 "The LORD has not **c** this one either."
16: 9 said, "Nor has the LORD **c** this one.
16:10 to him, "The LORD has not **c** these.
24: 2 Saul took three thousand **c** men from
26: 2 with his three thousand **c** men of
2Sa 6: 1 Israel **c** men, thirty thousand in all.
16:18 "No, the one **c** by the LORD, by these
21: 6 at Gibeah of Saul—the LORD's **c** one.
1Ki 3: 8 is here among the people you have **c**,
8:16 I have not **c** a city in any tribe of
8:16 **c** David to rule my people Israel.'
8:44 LORD towards the city you have **c**
8:48 towards the city you have **c** and the
11:13 sake of Jerusalem, which I have **c**."
11:32 which I have **c** out of all the tribes
14:21 the city the LORD had **c** out of all
2Ki 21: 7 which I have **c** out of all the tribes
1Ch 9:22 Altogether, those **c** to be gatekeepers
16:13 O sons of Jacob, his **c** ones.
16:41 Jeduthun and the rest of those **c** and
28: 5 he has **c** my son Solomon to sit on the
28: 6 for I have **c** him to be my son, and I
28:10 Consider now, for the LORD has **c** you
29: 1 Solomon, the one whom God has **c**,
2Ch 6: 5 I have not **c** a city in any tribe of
6: 5 nor have I **c** anyone to be the leader
6: 6 now I have **c** Jerusalem for my Name
6: 6 **c** David to rule my people Israel.'
6:34 to you towards this city you have **c**
6:38 towards the city you have **c** and
7:12 and have **c** this place for myself as
7:16 I have **c** and consecrated this temple
12:13 the city the LORD had **c** out of all
29:11 for the LORD has **c** you to stand
33: 7 which I have **c** out of all the tribes
Ne 1: 9 I have **c** as a dwelling for my Name.'
Ps 25:12 instruct him in the way **c** for him.
89: 3 "I have made a covenant with my **c**
105: 6 O sons of Jacob, his **c** ones.
105:26 servant, and Aaron, whom he had **c**.
105:43 his **c** ones with shouts of joy;
106: 5 enjoy the prosperity of your **c** ones,
106:23 had not Moses, his **c** one, stood in
119:30 I have **c** the way of truth; I have
119:173 help me, for I have **c** your precepts.
132:13 For the LORD has **c** Zion, he has
135: 4 For the LORD has **c** Jacob to be his
Isa 1:29 of the gardens that you have **c**.
41: 8 my servant, Jacob, whom I have **c**,
41: 9 **c** you and have not rejected you.
42: 1 whom I uphold, my **c** one in whom I
43:10 "and my servant whom I have **c**, so
43:20 to give drink to my people, my **c**,
44: 1 my servant, Israel, whom I have **c**.
44: 2 my servant, Jeshurun, whom I have **c**.
45: 4 of Israel my **c**, I summon you by name
48:14 The LORD's **c** ally will carry out his
49: 7 Holy One of Israel, who has **c** you."
58: 5 Is this the kind of fast I have **c**,
58: 6 this the kind of fasting I have **c**:

Isa 65: 9 my **c** people will inherit them,
65:15 You will leave your name to my **c**
65:22 my **c** ones will long enjoy the works
66: 3 They have **c** their own ways, and
Jer 49:19 Who is the **c** one I will appoint for
50:44 Who is the **c** one I will appoint for
Am 3: 2 "You only have I **c** of all the
Hag 2:23 for I have **c** you,' declares the LORD
Zec 3: 2 Satan! The LORD, who has **c** Jerusalem,
Mt 12:18 "Here is my servant whom I have **c**,
22:14 "For many are invited, but few are **c**.
27:15 release a prisoner **c** by the crowd.
Mk 13:20 the sake of the elect, whom he has **c**,
Lk 1: 9 he was **c** by lot, according to the
9:35 "This is my Son, whom I have **c**;
10:42 Mary has **c** what is better, and it
18: 7 bring about justice for his **c** ones,
23:35 he is the Christ of God, the **C** One."
Jn 6:70 Jesus replied, "Have I not **c** you,
13:18 all of you; I know those I have **c**.
15:19 but I have **c** you out of the world.
Ac 1: 2 Holy Spirit to the apostles he had **c**.
1:24 Show us which of these two you have **c**
9:15 "Go! This man is my **c** instrument to
10:41 by witnesses whom God had already **c**
22:14 'The God of our fathers has **c** you to
Ro 8:33 charge against those whom God has **c**?
11: 5 time there is a remnant **c** by grace.
16:13 Greet Rufus, **c** in the Lord, and his
2Co 8:19 What is more, he was **c** by the
Eph 1:11 In him we were also **c**, having been
Col 1:27 To them God has **c** to make known
3:12 Therefore, as God's **c** people, holy
1Th 1: 4 loved by God, that he has **c** you,
Jas 2: 5 Has not God **c** those who are poor in
1Pe 1: 2 who have been **c** according to the
1:20 He was **c** before the creation of the
2: 4 but **c** by God and precious to him—
2: 6 a **c** and precious cornerstone,
2: 9 you are a **c** people, a royal
5:13 She who is in Babylon, **c** together
2Jn : 1 To the **c** lady and her children,
:13 The children of your **c** sister send
Rev 17:14 called, **c** and faithful followers."

Christ (*Blood of Christ, Body of Christ, Christ Jesus*, Christ's, Christian, Christians, Christs, *Cross of Christ, In Christ, Jesus Christ*, Lord Jesus Christ, Messiah)

Mt 1:16 was born Jesus, who is called **C**.
1:17 fourteen from the exile to the **C**.
2: 4 them where the **C** was to be born.
11: 2 John heard in prison what **C** was
16:16 Simon Peter answered, "You are the **C**,
16:20 to tell anyone that he was the **C**.
22:42 "What do you think about the **C**?
23:10 for you have one Teacher, the **C**.
24: 5 'I am the **C**,' and will deceive many.
24:23 'Look, here is the **C**!' or, 'There he
26:63 if you are the **C**, the Son of God."
26:68 said, "Prophesy to us, **C**. Who hit
27:17 Barabbas, or Jesus who is called **C**?"
27:22 Jesus who is called **C**?" Pilate asked.
Mk 8:29 am?" Peter answered, "You are the **C**.
9:41 **C** will certainly not lose his reward.
12:35 say that the **C** is the son of David?
13:21 'Look, here is the **C**!' or, 'Look,
14:61 the **C**, the Son of the Blessed One?"
15:32 Let this **C**, this King of Israel,
Lk 2:11 been born to you; he is **C** the Lord.
2:26 die before he had seen the Lord's **C**.
3:15 if John might possibly be the **C**.
4:41 because they knew he was the **C**.
9:20 I am?" Peter answered, "The **C** of God.
20:41 they say the **C** is the Son of David?
22:67 "If you are the **C**," they said, "tell
23: 2 Caesar and claims to be **C**, a king."
23:35 he is the **C** of God, the Chosen One."
23:39 "Aren't you the **C**? Save yourself and
24:26 Did not the **C** have to suffer these
24:46 The **C** will suffer and rise from the
Jn 1:20 confessed freely, "I am not the **C**.
1:25 the **C**, nor Elijah, nor the Prophet?"
1:41 found the Messiah" (that is, the **C**).
Jn 3:28 not the **C** but am sent ahead of him.'
4:25 that Messiah" (called **C**) "is coming.
4:29 I ever did. Could this be the **C**?"
7:26 really concluded that he is the **C**?
7:27 when the **C** comes, no-one will know
7:31 They said, "When the **C** comes, will
7:41 Others said, "He is the **C**." Still
7:41 Still others asked, "How can the **C**
7:42 Does not the Scripture say that the **C**
9:22 acknowledged that Jesus was the **C**
10:24 If you are the **C**, tell us plainly."
11:27 "I believe that you are the **C**, the
12:34 Law that the **C** will remain for ever,
20:31 you may believe that Jesus is the **C**,
Ac 2:31 spoke of the resurrection of the **C**,
2:36 you crucified, both Lord and **C**."
3:18 saying that his **C** would suffer.
3:20 that he may send the **C**, who has been
5:42 the good news that Jesus is the **C**.
8: 5 Samaria and proclaimed the **C** there.
9:22 by proving that Jesus is the **C**.
17: 3 explaining and proving that the **C**
17: 3 I am proclaiming to you is the **C**,"
18: 5 to the Jews that Jesus was the **C**.
18:28 the Scriptures that Jesus was the **C**.
26:23 that the **C** would suffer and, as the
Ro 5: 6 powerless, **C** died for the ungodly.
5: 8 were still sinners, **C** died for us.
6: 4 just as **C** was raised from the dead
6: 8 Now if we died with **C**, we believe
6: 9 For we know that since **C** was raised
8: 9 Spirit of **C**, he does not belong to **C**.
8:10 if **C** is in you, your body is dead
8:11 he who raised **C** from the dead will
8:17 heirs—of God and co-heirs with **C**,
8:35 separate us from the love of **C**?
9: 3 cut off from **C** for the sake of my
9: 5 is traced the human ancestry of **C**,
10: 4 **C** is the end of the law so that
10: 6 (that is, to bring **C** down)
10: 7 is, to bring **C** up from the dead).
10:17 is heard through the word of **C**.
14: 9 For this very reason, **C** died and
14:15 your brother for whom **C** died.
14:18 anyone who serves **C** in this way is
15: 3 For even **C** did not please himself
15: 7 then, just as **C** accepted you,
15: 8 For I tell you that **C** has become a
15:18 what **C** has accomplished through me
15:19 fully proclaimed the gospel of **C**.
15:20 the gospel where **C** was not known,
15:29 full measure of the blessing of **C**.
16: 5 convert to **C** in the province of Asia.
16:16 All the churches of **C** send greetings.
16:18 not serving our Lord **C**, but their own
1Co 1: 1 Paul, called to be an apostle of **C**
1: 6 our testimony about **C** was confirmed
1:12 Cephas"; still another, "I follow **C**.
1:13 Is **C** divided? Was Paul crucified for
1:17 For **C** did not send me to baptise,
1:23 we preach **C** crucified: a
1:24 **C** the power of God and the wisdom of
2:16 him?" But we have the mind of **C**.
3:23 you are of **C**, and **C** is of God.
4: 1 ought to regard us as servants of **C**
4:10 We are fools for **C**, but you are so
5: 7 For **C**, our Passover lamb, has been
6:15 bodies are members of **C** himself?
6:15 Shall I then take the members of **C**
8:11 this weak brother, for whom **C** died,
8:12 weak conscience, you sin against **C**.
9:12 rather than hinder the gospel of **C**.
10: 4 them, and that rock was **C**.
11: 1 as I follow the example of **C**.
11: 3 that the head of every man is **C**,
11: 3 is man, and the head of **C** is God.
12:12 they form one body. So it is with **C**.
15: 3 that **C** died for our sins according
15:12 if it is preached that **C** has been
15:13 then not even **C** has been raised.
15:14 if **C** has not been raised, our
15:15 God that he raised **C** from the dead.
15:16 then **C** has not been raised either.
15:17 if **C** has not been raised, your faith
15:20 **C** has indeed been raised from the
15:23 in his own turn: **C**, the first fruits;
1Co 15:27 himself, who put everything under **C**.
2Co 1: 5 For just as the sufferings of **C** flow
1: 5 through **C** our comfort overflows.
2:10 in the sight of **C** for your sake,
2:12 to Troas to preach the gospel of **C**
2:15 For we are to God the aroma of **C**
3: 3 You show that you are a letter from **C**
3: 4 this is ours through **C** before God.
4: 4 glory of **C**, who is the image of God.
4: 6 the glory of God in the face of **C**.
5:10 before the judgment seat of **C**,
5:16 we once regarded **C** in this way, we do
5:18 reconciled us to himself through **C**
6:15 What harmony is there between **C** and
8:23 of the churches and an honour to **C**.
9:13 your confession of the gospel of **C**,
10: 1 By the meekness and gentleness of **C**,
10: 5 thought to make it obedient to **C**.
10: 7 is confident that he belongs to **C**,
10: 7 we belong to **C** just as much as he.
10:14 as far as you with the gospel of **C**.
11: 2 I promised you to one husband, to **C**,
11: 3 your sincere and pure devotion to **C**.
11:10 surely as the truth of **C** is in me,
11:13 masquerading as apostles of **C**.
11:23 Are they servants of **C**? (I am out of
13: 3 since you are demanding proof that **C**
Gal 1: 6 who called you by the grace of **C**
1: 7 trying to pervert the gospel of **C**.
1:10 men, I would not be a servant of **C**.
2:17 that **C** promotes sin? Absolutely not!
2:20 I have been crucified with **C** and I
2:20 I no longer live, but **C** lives in me.
2:21 the law, **C** died for nothing!"
3:13 **C** redeemed us from the curse of the
3:16 seed", meaning one person, who is **C**.
3:24 to lead us to **C** that we might be
3:27 all of you who were baptised into **C**
3:27 have clothed yourselves with **C**
3:29 If you belong to **C**, then you are
4:19 childbirth until **C** is formed in you,
5: 1 for freedom that **C** has set us free.
5: 2 **C** will be of no value to you at all.
5: 4 by law have been alienated from **C**;
6: 2 way you will fulfil the law of **C**.
Eph 1:10 together under one head, even **C**.
2: 5 made us alive with **C** even when we
2: 6 God raised us up with **C** and seated
2:12 that time you were separate from **C**,
3: 4 my insight into the mystery of **C**,
3: 8 the unsearchable riches of **C**,
3:17 that **C** may dwell in your hearts
3:18 and high and deep is the love of **C**,
4: 7 has been given as **C** apportioned it.
4:13 whole measure of the fulness of **C**.
4:15 him who is the Head, that is, **C**.
4:20 You, however, did not come to know **C**
5: 2 just as **C** loved us and gave himself
5: 5 in the kingdom of **C** and of God.
5:14 the dead, and **C** will shine on you."
5:21 one another out of reverence for **C**.
5:23 wife as **C** is the head of the church,
5:24 Now as the church submits to **C**, so
5:25 just as **C** loved the church and gave
5:29 for it, just as **C** does the church—
5:32 I am talking about **C** and the church.
6: 5 of heart, just as you would obey **C**.
6: 6 but like slaves of **C**, doing the will
Php 1: 1 Paul and Timothy, servants of **C**
1:10 and blameless until the day of **C**,
1:13 else that I am in chains for **C**.
1:15 is true that some preach **C** out of
1:17 The former preach **C** out of selfish
1:18 motives or true, **C** is preached.
1:20 always **C** will be exalted in my body,
1:21 For to me, to live is **C** and to die
1:23 be with **C**, which is better by far;
1:27 a manner worthy of the gospel of **C**.
1:29 been granted to you on behalf of **C**
2: 1 from being united with **C**, if any
2:16 that I may boast on the day of **C**
2:30 he almost died for the work of **C**,
3: 7 now consider loss for the sake of **C**.
3: 8 them rubbish, that I may gain **C**
3:10 I want to know **C** and the power of
Col 1: 7 minister of **C** on our behalf,

Col 1:27 this mystery, which is **C** in you,
2: 2 know the mystery of God, namely, **C**,
2: 8 of this world rather than on **C**.
2:11 but with the circumcision done by **C**,
2:13 nature, God made you alive with **C**.
2:20 Since you died with **C** to the basic
3: 1 then, you have been raised with **C**,
3: 1 **C** is seated at the right hand of God.
3: 3 life is now hidden with **C** in God.
3: 4 **C**, who is your life, appears, then
3:11 free, but **C** is all, and is in all.
3:15 Let the peace of **C** rule in your
3:16 Let the word of **C** dwell in you
3:24 It is the Lord **C** you are serving.
4: 3 proclaim the mystery of **C**, for which
1Th 2: 6 As apostles of **C** we could have been
3: 2 in spreading the gospel of **C**,
1Ti 5:11 overcome their dedication to **C**,
Heb 3: 6 **C** is faithful as a son over God's
5: 5 **C** also did not take upon himself the
6: 1 about **C** and go on to maturity,
9:11 **C** came as high priest of the good
9:15 For this reason **C** is the mediator of
9:24 For **C** did not enter a man-made
9:26 **C** would have had to suffer many
9:28 **C** was sacrificed once to take away
10: 5 Therefore, when **C** came into the
11:26 regarded disgrace for the sake of **C**
1Pe 1:11 to which the Spirit of **C** in them was
1:11 the sufferings of **C** and the glories
2:21 because **C** suffered for you, leaving
3:15 in your hearts set apart **C** as Lord.
3:18 For **C** died for sins once for all,
4: 1 Therefore, since **C** suffered in his
4:13 participate in the sufferings of **C**,
4:14 insulted because of the name of **C**,
1Jn 2:22 man who denies that Jesus is the **C**.
5: 1 that Jesus is the **C** is born of God,
2Jn : 9 the teaching of **C** does not have God;
Rev 11:15 kingdom of our Lord and of his **C**,
12:10 our God, and the authority of his **C**.
20: 4 reigned with **C** for a thousand years.
20: 6 will be priests of God and of **C** and

Christ Jesus
Ac 24:24 to him as he spoke about faith in **C**.
Ro 1: 1 Paul, a servant of **C**, called to be
3:24 the redemption that came by **C**.
6: 3 into **C** were baptised into his death?
6:11 dead to sin but alive to God in **C**.
6:23 God is eternal life in **C** our Lord.
8: 1 condemnation for those who are in **C**,
8: 2 through **C** the law of the Spirit of
8:34 Who is he that condemns? **C**, who died
8:39 love of God that is in **C** our Lord.
15: 5 among yourselves as you follow **C**,
15:16 to be a minister of **C** to the
15:17 Therefore I glory in **C** in my service
16: 3 and Aquila, my fellow-workers in **C**.
1Co 1: 1 Paul, called to be an apostle of **C**
1: 2 to those sanctified in **C** and called
1: 4 because of his grace given you in **C**.
1:30 is because of him that you are in **C**,
4:15 for in **C** I became your father
4:17 remind you of my way of life in **C**,
15:31 as I glory over you in **C** our Lord.
16:24 My love to all of you in **C**. Amen.
2Co 1: 1 Paul, an apostle of **C** by the will of
13: 5 Do you not realise that **C** is in you—
Gal 2: 4 to spy on the freedom we have in **C**
2:16 So we, too, have put our faith in **C**
3:14 come to the Gentiles through **C**,
3:26 all sons of God through faith in **C**,
3:28 female, for you are all one in **C**.
4:14 of God, as if I were **C** himself.
5: 6 For in **C** neither circumcision nor
5:24 Those who belong to **C** have crucified
Eph 1: 1 Paul, an apostle of **C** by the will of
1: 1 in Ephesus, the faithful in **C**:
2: 6 him in the heavenly realms in **C**,
2: 7 in his kindness to us in **C**.
2:10 created in **C** to do good works, which
2:13 now in **C** you who once were far away
2:20 **C** himself as the chief cornerstone.
3: 1 I, Paul, the prisoner of **C** for the sake
Eph 3: 6 together in the promise in **C**.
3:11 which he accomplished in **C** our Lord.
3:21 and in **C** throughout all generations,
Php 1: 1 Paul and Timothy, servants of **C**,
1: 1 To all the saints in **C** at Philippi,
1: 6 on to completion until the day of **C**.
1: 8 all of you with the affection of **C**.
1:26 your joy in **C** will overflow on
2: 5 should be the same as that of **C**:
3: 3 who glory in **C**, and who put no
3: 8 greatness of knowing **C** my Lord,
3:12 of that for which **C** took hold of me.
3:14 God has called me heavenwards in **C**.
4: 7 your hearts and your minds in **C**.
4:19 to his glorious riches in **C**.
4:21 Greet all the saints in **C**. The
Col 1: 1 Paul, an apostle of **C** by the will of
1: 4 we have heard of your faith in **C** and
2: 6 then, just as you received **C** as Lord,
4:12 and a servant of **C**, sends greetings.
1Th 2:14 churches in Judea, which are in **C**:
5:18 for this is God's will for you in **C**.
1Ti 1: 1 Paul, an apostle of **C** by the command
1: 1 God our Saviour and of **C** our hope,
1: 2 from God the Father and **C** our Lord.
1:12 I thank **C** our Lord, who has given me
1:14 the faith and love that are in **C**.
1:15 **C** came into the world to save
1:16 **C** might display his unlimited
2: 5 between God and men, the man **C**,
3:13 great assurance in their faith in **C**.
4: 6 you will be a good minister of **C**,
5:21 in the sight of God and **C** and the
6:13 and of **C**, who while testifying
2Ti 1: 1 Paul, an apostle of **C** by the will of
1: 1 to the promise of life that is in **C**,
1: 2 from God the Father and **C** our Lord.
1: 9 in **C** before the beginning of time,
1:10 **C**, who has destroyed death and has
1:13 teaching, with faith and love in **C**.
2: 1 be strong in the grace that is in **C**.
2: 3 with us like a good soldier of **C**.
2:10 that is in **C**, with eternal glory.
3:12 godly life in **C** will be persecuted,
3:15 for salvation through faith in **C**.
4: 1 In the presence of God and of **C**, who
Tit 1: 4 God the Father and **C** our Saviour.
Phm : 1 Paul, a prisoner of **C**, and Timothy
: 9 man and now also a prisoner of **C**—
:23 Epaphras, my fellow-prisoner in **C**,

Christ's (Christ)
1Co 7:22 man when he was called is **C** slave.
9:21 from God's law but am under **C** law),
2Co 5:14 For **C** love compels us, because we
5:20 We are therefore **C** ambassadors, as
5:20 We implore you on **C** behalf:
12: 9 so that **C** power may rest on me.
12:10 That is why, for **C** sake, I delight
Col 1:22 reconciled you by **C** physical body
1:24 lacking in regard to **C** afflictions,
2Th 3: 5 into God's love and **C** perseverance.
1Pe 5: 1 a witness of **C** sufferings and one

Christian (Christ)
Ac 26:28 time you can persuade me to be a **C**?"
1Pe 4:16 However, if you suffer as a **C**, do

Christians (Christ)
Ac 11:26 were called **C** first at Antioch.

Christs (Christ)
Mt 24:24 For false **C** and false prophets will
Mk 13:22 For false **C** and false prophets will

Chronic
Lev 13:11 is a **c** skin disease and the priest

Chronicles
Est 6: 1 so he ordered the book of the **c**,

Chrysolite
Ex 28:20 in the fourth row a **c**, an onyx and a
39:13 in the fourth row a **c**, an onyx and a
SS 5:14 His arms are rods of gold set with **c**.
Eze 1:16 They sparkled like **c**, and all four
10: 9 the wheels sparkled like **c**.
28:13 topaz and emerald, **c**, onyx and
Da 10: 6 His body was like **c**, his face like
Rev 21:20 the sixth carnelian, the seventh **c**,

Chrysoprase
Rev 21:20 the ninth topaz, the tenth **c**, the

Church (Churches)
Mt 16:18 and on this rock I will build my **c**,
18:17 to listen to them, tell it to the **c**;
18:17 he refuses to listen even to the **c**,
Ac 5:11 Great fear seized the whole **c** and
8: 1 out against the **c** at Jerusalem,
8: 3 Saul began to destroy the **c**. Going
9:31 the **c** throughout Judea, Galilee and
11:22 the ears of the **c** at Jerusalem,
11:26 Barnabas and Saul met with the **c**
12: 1 arrested some who belonged to the the **c**,
12: 5 Peter was kept in prison, but the **c**
13: 1 In the **c** at Antioch there were
14:23 elders for them in each **c** and,
14:27 they gathered the **c** together and
15: 3 The **c** sent them on their way, and as
15: 4 they were welcomed by the **c** and the
15:22 with the whole **c**, decided to choose
15:30 they gathered the **c** together and
18:22 greeted the **c** and then went down to
20:17 to Ephesus for the elders of the **c**.
20:28 Be shepherds of the **c** of God, which
Ro 16: 1 a servant of the **c** in Cenchrea.
16: 5 Greet also the **c** that meets at their
16:23 whose hospitality I and the whole **c**
1Co 1: 2 To the **c** of God in Corinth, to those
4:17 what I teach everywhere in every **c**.
5:12 mine to judge those outside the **c**?
6: 4 even men of little account in the **c**!
10:32 Jews, Greeks or the **c** of God—
11:18 that when you come together as a **c**,
11:22 Or do you despise the **c** of God and
12:28 in the **c** God has appointed first of
14: 4 but he who prophesies edifies the **c**.
14: 5 so that the **c** may be edified.
14:12 excel in gifts that build up the **c**.
14:19 in the **c** I would rather speak five
14:23 if the whole **c** comes together and
14:26 done for the strengthening of the **c**.
14:28 speaker should keep quiet in the **c**
14:35 for a woman to speak in the **c**.
15: 9 because I persecuted the **c** of God.
16:19 the **c** that meets at their house.
2Co 1: 1 To the **c** of God in Corinth, together
Gal 1:13 **c** of God and tried to destroy it.
Eph 1:22 be head over everything for the **c**,
3:10 through the **c**, the manifold wisdom
3:21 to him be glory in the **c** and in
5:23 wife as Christ is the head of the **c**,
5:24 Now as the **c** submits to Christ, so
5:25 just as Christ loved the **c** and gave
5:27 her to himself as a radiant **c**,
5:29 for it, just as Christ does the **c**—
5:32 I am talking about Christ and the **c**.
Php 3: 6 for zeal, persecuting the **c**; as for
4:15 not one **c** shared with me in the
Col 1:18 he is the head of the body, the **c**;
1:24 sake of his body, which is the **c**.
4:15 to Nympha and the **c** in her house.
4:16 see that it is also read in the **c** of
1Th 1: 1 To the **c** of the Thessalonians in God
2Th 1: 1 To the **c** of the Thessalonians in God
1Ti 3: 5 how can he take care of God's **c**?)
3:15 which is the **c** of the living God,
5:16 not let the **c** be burdened with them,
5:16 so that the **c** can help those widows
5:17 who direct the affairs of the **c** well
Phm : 2 and to the **c** that meets in your home:
Heb 12:23 to the **c** of the firstborn, whose
Jas 5:14 He should call the elders of the **c**
3Jn : 6 They have told the **c** about your love.
: 9 I wrote to the **c**, but Diotrephes,
:10 to do so and puts them out of the **c**.
Rev 2: 1 "To the angel of the **c** in Ephesus
2: 8 "To the angel of the **c** in Smyrna
2:12 "To the angel of the **c** in Pergamum

Rev 2:18 "To the angel of the c in Thyatira
3: 1 "To the angel of the c in Sardis
3: 7 "To the angel of the c in
3:14 "To the angel of the c in Laodicea

Churches (Church)
Ac 15:41 and Cilicia, strengthening the c.
16: 5 the c were strengthened in the faith
Ro 16: 4 Not only I but all the c of the
16:16 All the c of Christ send greetings.
1Co 7:17 is the rule I lay down in all the c.
11:16 other practice—nor do the c of God.
14:34 women should remain silent in the c.
16: 1 Do what I told the Galatian c to do.
16:19 The c in the province of Asia send
2Co 8: 1 that God has given the Macedonian c.
8:18 praised by all the c for his service
8:19 What is more, he was chosen by the c
8:23 they are representatives of the c
8:24 in you, so that the c can see it.
11: 8 I robbed other c by receiving
11:28 of my concern for all the c.
12:13 How were you inferior to the other c,
Gal 1: 2 To the c in Galatia:
1:22 I was personally unknown to the c of
1Th 2:14 became imitators of God's c in Judea,
2:14 those c suffered from the Jews,
2Th 1: 4 Therefore, among God's c we boast
Rev 1: 4 John, To the seven c in the province
1:11 send it to the seven c: to Ephesus,
1:20 stars are the angels of the seven c,
1:20 seven lampstands are the seven c.
2: 7 hear what the Spirit says to the c.
2:11 hear what the Spirit says to the c.
2:17 hear what the Spirit says to the c.
2:23 Then all the c will know that I am
2:29 hear what the Spirit says to the c.
3: 6 hear what the Spirit says to the c.
3:13 hear what the Spirit says to the c.
3:22 hear what the Spirit says to the c."
22:16 give you this testimony for the c.

Churn (Churned, Churning, Churns)
Job 41:31 He makes the depths c like a boiling

Churned (Churn)
Job 26:12 By his power he c up the sea; by his

Churning (Churn)
Job 30:27 The c inside me never stops; days of
Pr 30:33 For as c the milk produces butter,
Eze 32: 2 c the water with your feet and
Da 7: 2 winds of heaven c up the great sea.
Hab 3:15 your horses, c the great waters.

Churns (Churn)
Isa 51:15 who c up the sea so that its waves

Chuza
Lk 8: 3 Joanna the wife of C, the manager of

Cilicia
Region along southern coast of Asia Minor; capital Tarsus was the birthplace of Paul (Ac 21:39; 22:3). Cilician Jews argued with Stephen in Jerusalem (Ac 6:9). Paul came here soon after his conversion (Gal 1:21), and again on his second missionary journey (Ac 15:41).

Ac 6: 9 well as the provinces of C and Asia.
15:23 in Antioch, Syria and C: Greetings.
15:41 He went through Syria and C,
21:39 "I am a Jew, from Tarsus in C,
22: 3 "I am a Jew, born in Tarsus of C,
23:34 Learning that he was from C,
27: 5 off the coast of C and Pamphylia,
Gal 1:21 Later I went to Syria and C.

Cinnamon
Ex 30:23 250 shekels) of fragrant c,
Pr 7:17 my bed with myrrh, aloes and c.
SS 4:14 nard and saffron, calamus and c,
Rev 18:13 cargoes of c and spice, of incense,

Circle (Circled, Circling, Circuit, Circular, Circumference, Encircle)
2Sa 5:23 "Do not go straight up, but c round
1Ch 14:14 "Do not go straight up, but c round
Isa 40:22 He sits enthroned above the c of the
Mk 3:34 he looked at those seated in a c

Circled (Circle)
Jos 6:15 day they c the city seven times.

Circling (Circle)
Jos 6:11 carried around the city, c it once.

Circuit (Circle)
1Sa 7:16 From year to year he went on a c
Ps 19: 6 and makes its c to the other;

Circular (Circle)
1Ki 7:23 the Sea of cast metal, c in shape,
7:31 that had a c frame one cubit deep.
7:35 top of the stand there was a c band
2Ch 4: 2 the Sea of cast metal, c in shape,

Circulated
Mt 28:15 c among the Jews to this very day.

Circumcise (Circumcised, Circumcising, Circumcision)
Dt 10:16 C your hearts, therefore, and do not
30: 6 The LORD your God will c your hearts
Jos 5: 2 knives and c the Israelites again."
Jer 4: 4 C yourselves to the LORD, c your
Lk 1:59 eighth day they came to c the child,
2:21 when it was time to c him, he was
Jn 7:22 you c a child on the Sabbath.
Ac 21:21 telling them not to c their children

Circumcised (Circumcise)
Ge 17:10 Every male among you shall be c.
17:12 you who is eight days old must be c,
17:13 with your money, they must be c.
17:14 who has not been c in the flesh,
17:23 and c them, as God told him.
17:24 ninety-nine years old when he was c,
17:26 Ishmael were both c on that same day.
17:27 from a foreigner, was c with him.
21: 4 Abraham c him, as God commanded him.
34:14 our sister to a man who is not c.
34:17 if you will not agree to be c, we'll
34:22 our males be c, as they themselves
34:24 and every male in the city was c.
Ex 12:44 may eat of it after you have c him,
12:48 all the males in his household c;
Lev 12: 3 On the eighth day the boy is to be c.
Jos 5: 3 flint knives and c the Israelites
5: 5 the people that came out had been c,
5: 7 and these were the ones Joshua c.
5: 7 they had not been c on the way.
5: 8 after the whole nation had been c,
Jer 9:25 all who are c only in the flesh—
Jn 7:23 Now if a child can be c on the
Ac 7: 8 c him eight days after his birth.
10:45 The c believers who had come with
11: 2 the c believers criticised
15: 1 "Unless you are c, according to the
15: 5 "The Gentiles must be c and required
16: 3 so he c him because of the Jews who
Ro 2:25 become as though you had not been c.
2:26 If those who are not c keep the
2:26 be regarded as though they were c?
2:27 The one who is not c physically and
3:30 who will justify the c by faith and
4: 9 Is this blessedness only for the c,
4:10 it credited? Was it after he was c,
4:11 all who believe but have not been c,
4:12 he is also the father of the c who
4:12 not only are c but who also walk
4:12 father Abraham had before he was c.
1Co 7:18 Was a man already c when he was
Gal 2: 3 to be c, even though he was a Greek.
5: 2 you that if you let yourselves be c,
5: 3 every man who lets himself be c that
Gal 6:12 are trying to compel you to be c.
6:13 Not even those who are c obey the
6:13 yet they want you to be c that they
Php 3: 5 c on the eighth day, of the people
Col 2:11 In him you were also c, in the
3:11 Here there is no Greek or Jew, c or

Circumcising (Circumcise)
Ge 34:15 become like us by c all your males.

Circumcision (Circumcise)
Ge 17:11 You are to undergo c, and it will be
Ex 4:26 "bridegroom of blood", referring to c
Jn 7:22 Yet, because Moses gave you c
Ac 7: 8 he gave Abraham the covenant of c.
Ro 2:25 C has value if you observe the law,
2:27 you have the written code and c,
2:28 is c merely outward and physical.
2:29 inwardly; and c is c of the heart,
3: 1 a Jew, or what value is there in c?
4:11 he received the sign of c, a seal of
1Co 7:19 C is nothing and uncircumcision is
Gal 2:12 those who belonged to the c group.
5: 6 For in Christ Jesus neither c nor
5:11 Brothers, if I am still preaching c,
6:15 Neither c nor uncircumcision means
Eph 2:11 "the c" (that done in the body by
Php 3: 3 For it is we who are the c, we who
Col 2:11 not with a c done by the hands of
2:11 men but with the c done by Christ,
Tit 1:10 especially those of the c group.

Circumference (Circle)
Jer 52:21 high and twelve cubits in c;

Circumstances
1Ch 29:30 and the c that surrounded him and
Ro 4:10 Under what c was it credited? Was it
1Co 7:15 man or woman is not bound in such c;
Php 4:11 to be content whatever the c.
Col 4: 8 that you may know about our c
1Th 5:18 give thanks in all c, for this is
Jas 1: 9 The brother in humble c ought to
1Pe 1:11 trying to find out the time and c to

Cistern (Cisterns)
Ge 37:22 Throw him into this c here in the
37:24 took him and threw him into the c.
37:24 Now the c was empty; there was no
37:28 pulled Joseph up out of the c
37:29 Reuben returned to the c and saw
Lev 11:36 A spring, however, or a c for
1Sa 19:22 and went to the great c at Secu.
2Ki 18:31 and drink water from his own c,
Pr 5:15 Drink water from your own c, running
Isa 30:14 or scooping water out of a c."
36:16 and drink water from his own c,
Jer 38: 6 and put him into the c of Malkijah,
38: 6 Jeremiah by ropes into the c;
38: 7 they had put Jeremiah into the c.
38: 9 They have thrown him into a c, where
38:10 out of the c before he dies."
38:11 with ropes to Jeremiah in the c.
38:13 ropes and lifted him out of the c.
41: 7 them and threw them into a c.
41: 9 Now the c where he threw all the

Cisterns (Cistern)
Ge 37:20 throw him into one of these c and
1Sa 13: 6 among the rocks, and in pits and c.
2Ch 26:10 towers in the desert and dug many c,
Jer 2:13 c, broken c that cannot hold water.
14: 3 they go to the c but find no water.

Citadel (Citadels)
2Sa 12:26 Ammonites and captured the royal c.
1Ki 16:18 he went into the c of the royal
2Ki 15:25 c of the royal palace at Samaria.
Ezr 6: 2 A scroll was found in the c of
Ne 1: 1 year, while I was in the c of Susa,
2: 8 the gates of the c by the temple
7: 2 Hananiah the commander of the c,
Est 1: 2 his royal throne in the c of Susa,
1: 5 greatest, who were in the c of Susa.

Est 2: 3 into the harem at the **c** of Susa.
2: 5 Now there was in the **c** of Susa a Jew
2: 8 many girls were brought to the **c** of
3:15 edict was issued in the **c** of Susa.
8:14 was also issued in the **c** of Susa.
9: 6 In the **c** of Susa, the Jews killed
9:11 The number of those slain in the **c**
9:12 ten sons of Haman in the **c** of Susa.
Pr 18:19 are like the barred gates of a **c**.
Isa 32:14 **c** and watchtower will become a
Da 8: 2 In my vision I saw myself in the **c**

Citadels (Citadel)

Ps 48: 3 God is in her **c**; he has shown
48:13 view her **c**, that you may tell of
122: 7 walls and security within your **c**."
Isa 34:13 Thorns will overrun her **c**, nettles

Cities (*Cities of refuge*, City)

Ge 13:12 Lot lived among the **c** of the plain
19:25 Thus he overthrew those **c** and the
19:25 including all those living in the **c**—
19:29 God destroyed the **c** of the plain
19:29 overthrew the **c** where Lot had lived.
22:17 of the **c** of their enemies,
41:35 to be kept in the **c** for food.
41:48 in Egypt and stored it in the **c**.
Ex 1:11 and Rameses as store **c** for Pharaoh.
Lev 26:25 When you withdraw into your **c**, I
26:31 I will turn your **c** into ruins and
26:33 waste, and your **c** will lie in ruins.
Nu 13:28 the **c** are fortified and very large.
21: 2 we will totally destroy their **c**."
21:25 Israel captured all the **c** of the
32:16 and **c** for our women and children.
32:17 children will live in fortified **c**,
32:24 Build **c** for your women and children,
32:26 will remain here in the **c** of Gilead.
32:33 its **c** and the territory around them.
32:36 as fortified **c**, and built pens for
32:38 gave names to the **c** they rebuilt.
Dt 1:28 the **c** are large, with walls up to the
3: 4 At that time we took all his **c**.
3: 4 There was not one of the sixty **c**
3: 5 All these **c** were fortified with high
3: 7 **c** we carried off for ourselves.
4:41 Moses set aside three **c** east of the
4:42 one of these **c** and save his life.
4:43 The **c** were these: Bezer in the
6:10 flourishing **c** you did not build,
9: 1 **c** that have walls up to the sky.
19: 2 set aside for yourselves three **c**
19: 5 to one of these **c** and save his life.
19: 7 to set aside for yourselves three **c**.
19: 9 you are to set aside three more **c**.
19:11 and then flees to one of these **c**,
20:15 **c** that are at a distance from you
20:16 However, in the **c** of the nations the
28:52 They will lay siege to all the **c**
28:52 They will besiege all the **c**
28:55 you during the siege of all your **c**.
28:57 enemy will inflict on you in your **c**.
Jos 9:17 on the third day came to their **c**:
10: 2 like one of the royal **c**; it was
10:19 and don't let them reach their **c**,
10:20 were left reached their fortified **c**.
11:12 Joshua took all these royal **c** and
11:13 Yet Israel did not burn any of the **c**
11:14 plunder and livestock of these **c**,
13:31 Edrei (the royal **c** of Og in Bashan).
14:12 their **c** were large and fortified,
18:21 clan by clan, had the following **c**:
19:35 The fortified **c** were Ziddim, Zer,
20: 4 "When he flees to one of these **c**, he
20: 9 could flee to these designated **c**
24:13 not toil and **c** you did not build;
2Sa 10:12 for our people and the **c** of our God.
20: 6 fortified **c** and escape from us."
1Ki 4:13 walled **c** with bronze gate bars);
8:37 besieges them in any of their **c**,
9:19 well as all his store **c** and the
10:26 which he kept in the chariot **c**
15:23 all he did and the **c** he built, are
20:34 "I will return the **c** my father took
22:39 and the **c** he fortified, are they not
2Ki 18:13 **c** of Judah and captured them.
19:25 fortified **c** into piles of stone.
1Ch 19:13 for our people and the **c** of our God.
2Ch 1:14 which he kept in the chariot **c**
6:28 besiege them in any of their **c**,
8: 4 the store **c** he had built in Hamath.
8: 5 and Lower Beth Horon as fortified **c**,
8: 6 well as Baalath and all his store **c**,
8: 6 and all the **c** for his chariots and
9:25 which he kept in the chariot **c**
11:10 fortified **c** in Judah and Benjamin.
11:12 put shields and spears in all the **c**,
11:23 Benjamin, and to all the fortified **c**.
12: 4 he captured the fortified **c** of Judah
14: 6 He built up the fortified **c** of Judah,
16: 4 Maim and all the store **c** of Naphtali.
17: 2 in all the fortified **c** of Judah
17:12 he built forts and store **c** in
17:19 in the fortified **c** throughout Judah.
19: 5 in each of the fortified **c** of Judah.
19:10 fellow countrymen who live in the **c**
21: 3 as well as fortified **c** in Judah, but
32: 1 He laid siege to the fortified **c**,
33:14 in all the fortified **c** in Judah.
Ne 9:25 They captured fortified **c** and
Est 9: 2 The Jews assembled in their **c** in all
Ps 9: 6 you have uprooted their **c**; even the
69:35 Zion and rebuild the **c** of Judah.
Isa 1: 7 is desolate, your **c** burned with fire;
6:11 "Until the **c** lie ruined and without
14:17 who overthrew its **c** and would not
14:21 and cover the earth with their **c**.
17: 2 The **c** of Aroer will be deserted and
17: 9 In that day their strong **c**, which
19:18 In that day five **c** in Egypt will
25: 3 **c** of ruthless nations will revere
36: 1 **c** of Judah and captured them.
37:26 fortified **c** into piles of stone.
54: 3 and settle in their desolate **c**.
61: 4 they will renew the ruined **c** that
64:10 Your sacred **c** have become a desert;
Jer 4: 5 Let us flee to the fortified **c**!'
4:16 a war cry against the **c** of Judah.
5:17 the fortified **c** in which you trust.
8:14 Let us flee to the fortified **c** and
13:19 The **c** in the Negev will be shut up,
14: 2 "Judah mourns, her **c** languish; they
34: 7 the other **c** of Judah that were still
34: 7 the only fortified **c** left in Judah.
46: 8 I will destroy **c** and their people.'
48:18 you and ruin your fortified **c**.
Eze 26:19 like **c** no longer inhabited, and when
29:12 and her **c** will lie desolate for
29:12 for forty years among ruined **c**.
30: 7 and their **c** will lie among ruined **c**.
30:17 **c** themselves will go into captivity.
36:35 Eden; the **c** that were lying in ruins,
36:38 So will the ruined **c** be filled with
Hos 8:14 But I will send fire upon their **c**
11: 6 Swords will flash in their **c**, will
Am 9:14 the ruined **c** and live in them.
Mic 5:11 I will destroy the **c** of your land
5:14 Asherah poles and demolish your **c**.
7:12 you from Assyria and the **c** of Egypt,
Hab 1:10 They laugh at all fortified **c**; they
2: 8 lands and **c** and everyone in them.
2:17 lands and **c** and everyone in them.
Zep 1:16 battle cry against the fortified **c**
3: 6 Their **c** are destroyed; no-one will
Zec 8:20 inhabitants of many **c** will yet come,
Mt 10:23 finish going through the **c** of Israel
11:20 Jesus began to denounce the **c** in
Lk 19:17 small matter, take charge of ten **c**.'
19:19 'You take charge of five **c**.'
Ac 14: 6 fled to the Lycaonian **c** of Lystra
26:11 went to foreign **c** to persecute them.
2Pe 2: 6 if he condemned the **c** of Sodom and
Rev 16:19 and the **c** of the nations collapsed.

Cities of refuge

Nu 35: 6 you give the Levites will be **c**,
35:11 select some towns to be your **c**, to
35:13 six towns you give will be your **c**.
35:14 the Jordan and three in Canaan as **c**.
Jos 20: 2 the Israelites to designate the **c**,

Citizen (Citizens, Citizenship, Fellow-citizens)

Lk 15:15 he went and hired himself out to a **c**
Ac 21:39 in Cilicia, a **c** of no ordinary city.
22:25 **c** who hasn't even been found guilty?"
22:26 "This man is a Roman **c**."
22:27 "Tell me, are you a Roman **c**?"
22:28 "But I was born a **c**," Paul replied.
22:29 had put Paul, a Roman **c**, in chains.
23:27 I had learned that he is a Roman **c**.

Citizens (Citizen)

Nu 21:28 Ar of Moab, the **c** of Arnon's heights.
Jos 8:33 All Israel, aliens and **c** alike, with
24:11 The **c** of Jericho fought against you,
Jdg 9: 2 "Ask all the **c** of Shechem, 'Which is
9: 3 all this to the **c** of Shechem,
9: 6 all the **c** of Shechem and Beth Millo
9: 7 "Listen to me, **c** of Shechem, so that
9:18 king over the **c** of Shechem because
9:20 **c** of Shechem and Beth Millo, and let
9:20 from you, **c** of Shechem and Beth Millo
9:23 Abimelech and the **c** of Shechem,
9:24 Abimelech and on the **c** of Shechem,
9:25 In opposition to him these **c** of
9:26 its **c** put their confidence in him.
9:39 Gaal led out the **c** of Shechem and
9:46 On hearing this, the **c** in the tower
1Sa 23:11 Will the **c** of Keilah surrender me to
23:12 "Will the **c** of Keilah surrender me
2Sa 21:12 Jonathan from the **c** of Jabesh Gilead.
Isa 48: 2 you who call yourselves **c** of the
Eze 26:17 a power on the seas, you and your **c**;
Ac 16:37 even though we are Roman **c**, and threw
16:38 that Paul and Silas were Roman **c**,

Citizenship (Citizen)

Ac 22:28 "I had to pay a big price for my **c**.
Eph 2:12 excluded from **c** in Israel and
Php 3:20 our **c** is in heaven. And we eagerly

Citron

Rev 18:12 scarlet cloth; every sort of **c** wood,

City (Cities, *City of David*, *City of God*, City's, *Holy City*)

Ge 4:17 Cain was then building a **c**, and he
10:12 and Calah; that is the great **c**.
11: 4 "Come, let us build ourselves a **c**,
11: 5 the LORD came down to see the **c** and
11: 8 and they stopped building the **c**.
18:24 are fifty righteous people in the **c**?
18:26 righteous people in the **c** of Sodom,
18:28 the whole **c** because of five people?"
19: 1 was sitting in the gateway of the **c**.
19: 4 part of the **c** of Sodom—both young
19:12 or anyone else in the **c** who belongs
19:14 the LORD is about to destroy the **c**!"
19:15 swept away when the **c** is punished."
19:16 and led them safely out of the **c**,
23:10 who had come to the gate of his **c**.
23:18 who had come to the gate of the **c**.
28:19 though the **c** used to be called Luz.
33:18 arrived safely at the **c** of Shechem
33:18 and camped within sight of the **c**.
34:20 went to the gate of their **c** to speak
34:24 All the men who went out of the **c**
34:24 every male in the **c** was circumcised.
34:25 and attacked the unsuspecting **c**,
34:27 looted the **c** where their sister had
34:28 in the **c** and out in the fields.
36:32 His **c** was named Dinhabah.
36:35 His **c** was named Avith.
36:39 His **c** was named Pau, and his wife's
41:48 In each **c** he put the food grown in
44: 4 They had not gone far from the **c**
44:13 their donkeys and returned to the **c**.
Ex 9:29 "When I have gone out of the **c**, I
9:33 left Pharaoh and went out of the **c**.
Lev 25:29 If a man sells a house in a walled **c**,
25:30 the house in the walled **c** shall
Nu 21:26 Heshbon was the **c** of Sihon king of
21:27 rebuilt; let Sihon's **c** be restored.
21:28 Heshbon, a blaze from the **c** of Sihon.

Nu 24:19 and destroy the survivors of the **c**."
35:25 to the **c** of refuge to which he fled.
35:26 the **c** of refuge to which he has
35:27 of blood finds him outside the **c**,
35:28 The accused must stay in his **c** of
35:32 who has fled to a **c** of refuge
Dt 3: 6 destroying every **c**—men, women and
17: 5 done this evil deed to your **c** gate
19:12 bring him back from the **c**, and hand
20:10 you march up to attack a **c**, make its
20:12 you in battle, lay siege to that **c**.
20:14 and everything else in the **c**,
20:19 you lay siege to a **c** for a long time,
20:20 until the **c** at war with you falls.
28: 3 You will be blessed in the **c** and
28:16 You will be cursed in the **c** and
34: 3 the **C** of Palms, as far as Zoar.
Jos 2: 5 to close the **c** gate, the men left.
2:15 she lived in was part of the **c** wall.
6: 3 March around the **c** once with all the
6: 4 march around the **c** seven times, with
6: 5 then the wall of the **c** will collapse
6: 7 "Advance! March around the **c**, with
6:11 around the **c**, circling it once.
6:14 they marched around the **c** once and
6:15 marched around the **c** seven times in
6:15 day they circled the **c** seven times.
6:16 For the LORD has given you the **c**!
6:17 The **c** and all that is in it are to
6:20 straight in, and they took the **c**.
6:21 They devoted the **c** to the LORD and
6:24 they burned the whole **c** and
6:26 who undertakes to rebuild this **c**,
7: 5 **c** gate as far as the stone quarries
8: 1 Ai, his people, his **c** and his land.
8: 2 Set an ambush behind the **c**."
8: 4 are to set an ambush behind the **c**.
8: 5 those with me will advance on the **c**,
8: 6 we have lured them away from the **c**,
8: 7 rise up from ambush and take the **c**.
8: 8 you have taken the **c**, set it on fire.
8:11 approached the **c** and arrived in front
8:11 the valley between them and the **c**.
8:12 Bethel and Ai, to the west of the **c**.
8:13 in the camp to the north of the **c**
8:14 he and all the men of the **c** hurried
8:14 been set against him behind the **c**.
8:16 and were lured away from the **c**.
8:17 They left the **c** open and went in
8:18 into your hand I will deliver the **c**.
8:19 They entered the **c** and captured it
8:20 of the **c** rising against the sky,
8:21 saw that the ambush had taken the **c**
8:21 that smoke was going up from the **c**,
8:22 also came out of the **c** against them,
8:27 the livestock and plunder of this **c**,
8:29 down at the entrance of the **c** gate.
10: 2 because Gibeon was an important **c**,
10:28 He put the **c** and its king to the
10:30 The LORD also gave that **c** and its
10:30 The **c** and everyone in it Joshua put
10:32 The **c** and everyone in it he put to
10:37 They took the **c** and put it to the
10:39 They took the **c**, its king and its
11:19 not one **c** made a treaty of peace
15: 8 the Jebusite **c** (that is, Jerusalem).
15:62 Nibshan, the **C** of Salt and En Gedi
18:16 the Jebusite **c** and so to En Rogel.
18:28 Zelah, Haeleph, the Jebusite **c** (that
19:29 and went to the fortified **c** of Tyre,
20: 4 stand in the entrance of the **c** gate
20: 4 case before the elders of that **c**.
20: 4 they are to admit him into their **c**
20: 6 He is to stay in that **c** until he has
21:12 the fields and villages around the **c**
21:13 they gave Hebron (a **c** of refuge
21:21 were given Shechem (a **c** of refuge
21:27 Golan in Bashan (a **c** of refuge for
21:32 Kedesh in Galilee (a **c** of refuge for
21:38 Ramoth in Gilead (a **c** of refuge for
Jdg 1: 8 **c** to the sword and set it on fire.
1:16 went up from the **C** of Palms with
1:17 and they totally destroyed the **c**.
1:18 Ekron—each **c** with its territory.
1:24 out of the **c** and they said to him,
1:24 "Show us how to get into the **c** and

Jdg 1:25 and they put the **c** to the sword but
1:26 where he built a **c** and called it Luz,
3:13 took possession of the **C** of Palms.
5: 8 war came to the **c** gates, and not a
5:11 the LORD went down to the **c** gates.
9:30 Zebul the governor of the **c** heard
9:31 are stirring up the **c** against you.
9:33 at sunrise, advance against the **c**.
9:35 to the **c** gate just as Abimelech
9:43 saw the people coming out of the **c**,
9:44 at the entrance to the **c** gate.
9:45 pressed his attack against the **c**
9:45 Then he destroyed the **c** and scattered
9:51 Inside the **c**, however, was a strong
9:51 the people of the **c**—fled.
16: 2 for him all night at the **c** gate.
16: 3 hold of the doors of the **c** gate,
18:27 the sword and burned down their **c**.
18:28 **c** was in a valley near Beth Rehob.
18:28 rebuilt the **c** and settled there.
18:29 the **c** used to be called Laish.
19:11 "Come, let's stop at this **c** of the
19:12 We won't go into an alien **c**, whose
19:15 They went and sat in the **c** square,
19:17 saw the traveller in the **c** square,
19:22 men of the **c** surrounded the house.
20:11 and united as one man against the **c**.
20:31 them and were drawn away from the **c**.
20:32 them away from the **c** to the roads."
20:37 and put the whole **c** to the sword.
20:38 a great cloud of smoke from the **c**,
20:40 of smoke began to rise from the **c**,
20:40 the whole **c** going up into the sky.
1Sa 5: 9 the LORD's hand was against that **c**,
5: 9 He afflicted the people of the **c**,
5:11 For death had filled the **c** with
5:12 outcry of the **c** went up to heaven.
15: 5 Saul went to the **c** of Amalek and set
27: 5 live in the royal **c** with you?"
2Sa 10: 3 to explore the **c** and spy it out and
10: 8 at the entrance to their **c** gate,
10:14 Abishai and went inside the **c**.
11:16 while Joab had the **c** under siege, he
11:17 the men of the **c** came out and fought
11:20 'Why did you get so close to the **c**
11:23 back to the entrance to the **c** gate.
11:25 Press the attack against the **c** and
12:28 and besiege the **c** and capture it.
12:28 Otherwise I shall take the **c**,
12:30 great quantity of plunder from the **c**
15: 2 of the road leading to the **c** gate.
15:14 upon us and put the **c** to the sword."
15:24 people had finished leaving the **c**.
15:25 the ark of God back into the **c**.
15:27 "Aren't you a seer? Go back to the **c**
15:34 if you return to the **c** and say to
15:37 as Absalom was entering the **c**.
17:13 If he withdraws into a **c**, then all
17:13 Israel will bring ropes to that **c**,
17:17 not risk being seen entering the **c**.
18: 3 you to give us support from the **c**."
19: 3 The men stole into the **c** that day as
20:15 They built a siege ramp up to the **c**,
20:16 a wise woman called from the **c**,
20:19 You are trying to destroy a **c** that
20:21 man, and I'll withdraw from the **c**.
20:22 his men dispersed from the **c**, each
1Ki 1:41 meaning of all the noise in the **c**?"
1:45 and the **c** resounds with it.
8:16 I have not chosen a **c** in any tribe
8:44 LORD towards the **c** you have chosen
8:48 towards the **c** you have chosen and
11:32 David and the **c** of Jerusalem,
11:36 the **c** where I chose to put my Name.
13:25 the **c** where the old prophet lived.
13:29 own **c** to mourn for him and bury him.
14:11 to Jeroboam who die in the **c**, and the
14:12 set foot in your **c**, the boy will die.
14:21 the **c** the LORD had chosen out of all
15:24 them in the **c** of his father David.
16: 4 to Baasha who die in the **c**, and the
16:18 Zimri saw that the **c** was taken, he
16:24 of silver and built a **c** on the hill,
20: 2 He sent messengers into the **c** to
20:12 So they prepared to attack the **c**.
20:19 marched out of the **c** with the army

1Ki 20:30 The rest of them escaped to the **c** of
20:30 to the **c** and hid in an inner room.
21: 8 who lived in Naboth's **c** with him.
21:11 nobles who lived in Naboth's **c** did
21:13 So they took him outside the **c** and
21:24 belonging to Ahab who die in the **c**,
22:26 to Amon the ruler of the **c** and to
2Ki 2:19 The men of the **c** said to Elisha,
3:19 You will overthrow every fortified **c**
3:27 him as a sacrifice on the **c** wall.
6:14 went by night and surrounded the **c**.
6:15 and chariots had surrounded the **c**.
6:19 not the road and this is not the **c**.
6:20 After they entered the **c**, Elisha
6:25 There was a great famine in the **c**;
7: 3 at the entrance of the **c** gate.
7: 4 If we say, 'We'll go into the **c**'
7:10 they went and called out to the **c**
7:12 them alive and get into the **c**.'"
7:13 the horses that are left in the **c**.
9:15 don't let anyone slip out of the **c**
10: 2 horses, a fortified **c** and weapons,
10: 5 the **c** governor, the elders and the
10: 6 with the leading men of the **c**, who
10: 8 of the **c** gate until morning."
11:20 And the **c** was quiet, because
15:16 everyone in the **c** and its vicinity,
17: 9 From watchtower to fortified **c** they
18: 8 From watchtower to fortified **c**, he
18:30 this **c** will not be given into the
19:13 the king of the **c** of Sepharvaim, or
19:32 enter this **c** or shoot an arrow here.
19:33 he will not enter this **c**, declares
19:34 I will defend this **c** and save it,
20: 6 And I will deliver you and this **c**
20: 6 I will defend this **c** for my sake and
20:20 which he brought water into the **c**,
23: 8 the Gate of Joshua, the **c** governor,
23: 8 which is on the left of the **c** gate.
23:17 The men of the **c** said, "It marks the
23:27 will reject Jerusalem, the **c** I chose,
24:11 came up to the **c** while his officers
25: 1 He encamped outside the **c** and built
25: 2 The **c** was kept under siege until the
25: 3 famine in the **c** had become so severe
25: 4 the **c** wall was broken through, and
25: 4 Babylonians were surrounding the **c**.
25:11 the people who remained in the **c**,
25:19 Of those still in the **c**, he took the
25:19 of his men who were found in the **c**.
1Ch 1:43 of Beor, whose **c** was named Dinhabah.
1:46 him as king. His **c** was named Avith.
1:50 His **c** was named Pau, and his wife's
6:56 the fields and villages around the **c**
6:57 were given Hebron (a **c** of refuge),
6:67 Shechem (a **c** of refuge), and Gezer,
11: 8 He built up the **c** around it, from
11: 8 Joab restored the rest of the **c**.
19: 9 at the entrance to their **c**, while the
19:15 Abishai and went inside the **c**.
20: 2 great quantity of plunder from the **c**
2Ch 6: 5 I have not chosen a **c** in any tribe
6:34 when they pray to you towards this **c**
6:38 towards the **c** you have chosen and
12:13 the **c** the LORD had chosen out of all
15: 6 by another and one **c** by another,
18:25 to Amon the ruler of the **c** and to
23:21 And the **c** was quiet, because
25:28 with his fathers in the **C** of Judah.
28:15 at Jericho, the **C** of Palms, and
28:27 was buried in the **c** of Jerusalem,
29:20 gathered the **c** officials together
32: 3 water from the springs outside the **c**,
32: 6 him in the square at the **c** gate
32:18 afraid in order to capture the **c**.
33:15 and he threw them out of the **c**.
34: 8 and Maaseiah the ruler of the **c**,
Ezr 4:10 settled in the **c** of Samaria and
4:12 that rebellious and wicked **c**.
4:13 the king should know that if this **c**
4:15 find that this **c** is a rebellious **c**,
4:15 That is why this **c** was destroyed.
4:16 We inform the king that if this **c** is
4:19 and it was found that this **c** has a
4:21 so that this **c** will not be rebuilt
Ne 2: 3 the **c** where my fathers are buried

Ne 2: 5 let him send me to the c in Judah
2: 8 for the c wall and for the residence
7: 4 Now the c was large and spacious,
11: 9 over the Second District of the c.
13:18 calamity upon us and upon this c?
Est 3:15 but the c of Susa was bewildered.
4: 1 went out into the c, wailing loudly
4: 6 in the open square of the c in front
6: 9 on the horse through the c streets,
6:11 on horseback through the c streets,
8:11 in every c the right to assemble
8:15 c of Susa held a joyous celebration.
8:17 In every province and in every c,
9:28 in every province and in every c,
Job 24:12 groans of the dying rise from the c,
29: 7 "When I went to the gate of the c
Ps 31:21 to me when I was in a besieged c.
48: 1 the c of our God, his holy mountain.
48: 2 Mount Zion, the c of the Great King.
48: 8 so have we seen in the c of the LORD
48: 8 in the c of our God: God makes her
55: 9 I see violence and strife in the c.
55:11 forces are at work in the c;
59: 6 like dogs, and prowl about the c.
59:14 like dogs, and prowl about the c.
60: 9 Who will bring me to the fortified c?
101: 8 evildoer from the c of the LORD.
107: 4 way to a c where they could settle.
107: 7 way to a c where they could settle.
107:36 founded a c where they could settle.
108:10 Who will bring me to the fortified c?
122: 3 Jerusalem is built like a c that is
127: 1 Unless the LORD watches over the c,
Pr 1:21 in the gateways of the c she makes
8: 3 beside the gates leading into the c,
9: 3 from the highest point of the c.
9:14 seat at the highest point of the c,
10:15 of the rich is their fortified c,
11:10 righteous prosper, the c rejoices;
11:11 of the upright a c is exalted,
16:32 his temper than one who takes a c.
18:11 of the rich is their fortified c;
18:19 more unyielding than a fortified c,
21:22 A wise man attacks the c of the
25:28 Like a c whose walls are broken down
29: 8 Mockers stir up a c, but wise men
31:23 Her husband is respected at the c
31:31 bring her praise at the c gate.
Ecc 7:19 powerful than ten rulers in a c.
8:10 praise in the c where they did this.
9:14 There was once a small c with only a
9:15 Now there lived in that c a man poor
9:15 and he saved the c by his wisdom.
SS 3: 2 I will get up now and go about the c,
3: 3 as they made their rounds in the c.
5: 7 as they made their rounds in the c.
Isa 1: 8 of melons, like a c under siege.
1:21 See how the faithful c has become a
1:26 C of Righteousness, the Faithful C."
14:31 Wail, O gate! Howl, O c! Melt away,
17: 1 a c but will become a heap of ruins.
17: 3 The fortified c will disappear from
19: 2 c against c, kingdom against kingdom.
19:18 will be called the C of Destruction.
22: 2 commotion, O c of tumult and revelry?
22: 7 horsemen are posted at the c gates;
23: 7 Is this your c of revelry, the old,
23: 7 the old, old c, whose feet have
23:16 "Take up a harp, walk through the c,
24:10 The ruined c lies desolate; the
24:12 The c is left in ruins, its gate is
25: 2 You have made the c a heap of rubble,
25: 2 foreigners' stronghold a c no more;
26: 1 We have a strong c; God makes
26: 5 he lays the lofty c low; he levels
27:10 The fortified c stands desolate, an
28: 1 to that c, the pride of those laid
29: 1 Ariel, the c where David settled!
32:13 merriment and for this c of revelry.
32:14 the noisy c deserted; citadel and
32:19 and the c is levelled completely,
33:20 Look upon Zion, the c of our
36:15 this c will not be given into the
37:13 the king of the c of Sepharvaim, or
37:33 enter this c or shoot an arrow here.
37:34 he will not enter this c," declares
Isa 37:35 "I will defend this c and save it,
38: 6 I will deliver you and this c from
38: 6 king of Assyria. I will defend this c
45:13 He will rebuild my c and set my
54:11 "O afflicted c, lashed by storms and
60:14 and will call you the C of the LORD,
62:12 After, the C No Longer Deserted.
66: 6 Hear that uproar from the c, hear
Jer 1:18 Today I have made you a fortified c,
5: 1 the truth, I will forgive this c.
6: 6 This c must be punished; it is
8:16 it, the c and all who live there."
14:18 if I go into the c, I see the ravages
15: 7 fork at the c gates of the land.
17:24 the gates of this c on the Sabbath,
17:25 of this c with their officials.
17:25 this c will be inhabited for ever.
19: 8 I will devastate this c and make it
19:11 I will smash this nation and this c
19:12 I will make this c like Topheth.
19:15 I am going to bring on this c and
20: 5 wealth of this c—all its products,
21: 4 And I will gather them inside this c.
21: 6 those who live in this c—both men
21: 7 in this c who survive the plague,
21: 9 Whoever stays in this c will die by
21:10 I have determined to do this c harm
22: 8 by this c and will ask one another,
22: 8 done such a thing to this great c?'
23:39 c I gave to you and your fathers.
25:29 on the c that bears my Name,
26: 6 this c an object of cursing among
26: 9 c will be desolate and deserted?"
26:11 he has prophesied against this c.
26:12 against this house and this c
26:15 this c and on those who live in it,
26:20 things against this c and this land
27:17 Why should this c become a ruin?
27:19 furnishings that are left in this c,
29: 7 prosperity of the c to which I have
29:16 all the people who remain in this c,
30:18 the c will be rebuilt on her ruins,
31:38 "when this c will be rebuilt for me
31:40 The c will never again be uprooted
32: 3 this c over to the king of Babylon,
32:24 ramps are built up to take the c.
32:24 the c will be handed over to the
32:25 though the c will be handed over to
32:28 I am about to hand this c over to
32:29 Babylonians who are attacking this c
32:31 this c has so aroused my anger and
32:36 "You are saying about this c, 'By
33: 4 says about the houses in this c and
33: 5 I will hide my face from this c
33: 9 this c will bring me renown, joy,
34: 2 this c over to the king of Babylon,
34:22 I will bring them back to this c.
37: 8 will return and attack this c;
37:10 come out and burn this c down."
37:12 Jeremiah started to leave the c to
37:21 all the bread in the c was gone.
38: 2 'Whoever stays in this c will die by
38: 3 'This c will certainly be handed over
38: 4 the soldiers who are left in this c,
38: 9 is no longer any bread in the c."
38:17 and this c will not be burned down;
38:18 this c will be handed over to the
38:23 and this c will be burned down."
39: 2 year, the c wall was broken through.
39: 4 they fled; they left the c at night
39: 9 the people who remained in the c,
39:16 against this c through disaster, not
41: 7 they went into the c, Ishmael son of
49:25 Why has the c of renown not been
51:31 that his entire c is captured,
52: 4 They camped outside the c and built
52: 5 The c was kept under siege until the
52: 6 famine in the c had become so severe
52: 7 the c wall was broken through, and
52: 7 They left the c at night through the
52: 7 Babylonians were surrounding the c.
52:15 and those who remained in the c,
52:25 Of those still in the c, he took the
52:25 of his men who were found in the c.
Lam 1: 1 How deserted lies the c, once so
1:19 my elders perished in the c while
Lam 2:11 faint in the streets of the c.
2:12 wounded men in the streets of the c,
2:15 "Is this the c that was called the
3:51 because of all the women of my c.
5:14 The elders are gone from the c gate;
Eze 4: 1 and draw the c of Jerusalem on it.
4: 3 an iron wall between and the c
5: 2 of the hair with fire inside the c.
5: 2 it with the sword all around the c.
7:15 and those in the c will be devoured
7:23 and the c is full of violence.
9: 1 "Bring the guards of the c here,
9: 4 "Go throughout the c of Jerusalem
9: 5 "Follow him through the c and kill,
9: 7 and began killing throughout the c.
9: 9 and the c is full of injustice.
10: 2 and scatter them over the c." And as
11: 2 and giving wicked advice in this c.
11: 3 houses? This c is a cooking pot,
11: 6 You have killed many people in this c
11: 7 are the meat and this c is the pot,
11: 9 I will drive you out of the c and
11:11 This c will not be a pot for you,
11:23 the LORD went up from within the c
17: 4 he planted it in a c of traders.
21:19 the road branches off to the c.
22: 2 Will you judge this c of bloodshed?
22: 3 O c that brings on herself doom by
22: 5 you, O infamous c, full of turmoil.
22:20 put you inside the c and melt you.
24: 6 "'Woe to the c of bloodshed, to the
24: 9 "'Woe to the c of bloodshed! I, too,
26:10 as men enter a c whose walls have
26:17 "'How you are destroyed, O c of
26:19 says: When I make you a desolate c,
33:21 me and said, "The c has fallen!"
40: 1 year after the fall of the c—
40: 2 some buildings that looked like a c.
43: 3 seen when he came to destroy the c
45: 6 "'You are to give the c as its
45: 7 district and the property of the c.
48:15 for the common use of the c,
48:15 The c will be in the centre of
48:17 The pasture-land for the c will be
48:18 food for the workers of the c.
48:19 The workers from the c who farm it
48:20 along with the property of the c.
48:21 c property will belong to the prince.
48:22 the property of the c will lie in
48:30 "These will be the exits of the c:
48:31 the gates of the c will be named
48:35 "And the name of the c from that
Da 9:16 Jerusalem, your c, your holy hill.
9:18 of the c that bears your Name.
9:19 c and your people bear your Name."
9:26 destroy the c and the sanctuary.
11:15 and will capture a fortified c.
Hos 6: 8 Gilead is a c of wicked men, stained
Joel 2: 9 They rush upon the c; they run along
Am 3: 6 a trumpet sounds in a c, do not the
3: 6 When disaster comes to a c, has not
4: 6 "I gave you empty stomachs in every c
5: 3 "The c that marches out a thousand
5: 9 and brings the fortified c to ruin),
6: 8 up the c and everything in it."
7:17 will become a prostitute in the c,
Jnh 1: 2 "Go to the great c of Nineveh and
3: 2 "Go to the great c of Nineveh and
3: 3 Now Nineveh was a very important c
3: 4 first day, Jonah started into the c.
4: 5 sat down at a place east of the c.
4: 5 to see what would happen to the c.
4:11 be concerned about that great c?"
Mic 4:10 for now you must leave the c to camp
5: 1 Marshal your troops, O c of troops,
6: 9 Listen! The LORD is calling to the c
Na 2: 5 They dash to the c wall; the
2: 7 is decreed that the c be exiled
3: 1 Woe to the c of blood, full of lies,
Hab 2:12 "Woe to him who builds a c with
Zep 2:15 This is the carefree c that lived in
3: 1 Woe to the c of oppressors,
3: 7 I said to the c, 'Surely you will
3:11 because I will remove from this c
Zec 2: 4 'Jerusalem will be a c without walls
8: 3 will be called the C of Truth,

Zec 8: 5 The c streets will be filled with
8:21 the inhabitants of one c will go to
14: 2 against it; the c will be captured,
14: 2 Half of the c will go into exile,
14: 2 people will not be taken from the c.
Mt 5:14 A c on a hill cannot be hidden.
5:35 for it is the c of the Great King.
12:25 and every c or household divided
21:10 the whole c was stirred and asked
21:17 he left them and went out of the c
21:18 as he was on his way back to the c,
22: 7 those murderers and burned their c.
26:18 He replied, "Go into the c to a
28:11 some of the guards went into the c
Mk 10:46 were leaving the c, a blind man,
11:19 evening came, they went out of the c.
14:13 "Go into the c, and a man carrying a
14:16 The disciples left, went into the c
Lk 19:41 he approached Jerusalem and saw the c
21:21 let those in the c get out, and let
21:21 in the country not enter the c.
22:10 He replied, "As you enter the c, a
23:19 for an insurrection in the c, and for
24:49 but stay in the c until you have
Jn 19:20 Jesus was crucified was near the c,
Ac 1:12 a Sabbath day's walk from the c.
4:27 the people of Israel in this c to
7:58 dragged him out of the c and began
8: 5 Philip went down to a c in Samaria
8: 8 there was great joy in that c.
8: 9 Simon had practised sorcery in the c
9: 6 "Now get up and go into the c, and
9:24 on the c gates in order to kill him.
10: 9 approaching the c, Peter went up on
11: 5 "I was in the c of Joppa praying,
12:10 to the iron gate leading to the c.
13:44 almost the whole c gathered to hear
13:50 and the leading men of the c.
14: 4 The people of the c were divided;
14:13 whose temple was just outside the c,
14:13 brought bulls and wreaths to the c
14:19 outside the c, thinking he was dead.
14:20 he got up and went back into the c.
14:21 They preached the good news in that c
15:21 in every c from the earliest times
16:12 c of that district of Macedonia.
16:13 On the Sabbath we went outside the c
16:14 a dealer in purple cloth from the c
16:20 are throwing our c into an uproar
16:39 requesting them to leave the c.
17: 5 a mob and started a riot in the c.
17: 6 brothers before the c officials,
17: 8 the crowd and the c officials were
17:16 to see that the c was full of idols.
18:10 I have many people in this c."
19:29 Soon the whole c was in an uproar.
19:35 The c clerk quietened the crowd and
19:35 the c of Ephesus is the guardian of
20:23 in every c the Holy Spirit warns me
21: 5 accompanied us out of the c,
21:29 the Ephesian in the c with Paul
21:30 The whole c was aroused, and the
21:31 c of Jerusalem was in an uproar.
21:39 Cilicia, a citizen of no ordinary c.
22: 3 Cilicia, but brought up in this c.
24:12 synagogues or anywhere else in the c.
25:23 and the leading men of the c.
2Co 11:26 from Gentiles; in danger in the c,
11:32 had the c of the Damascenes guarded
Gal 4:25 to the present c of Jerusalem,
Heb 11:10 For he was looking forward to the c
11:16 for he has prepared a c for them.
12:22 Jerusalem, the c of the living God.
13:12 Jesus also suffered outside the c
13:14 For here we do not have an enduring c
13:14 looking for the c that is to come.
Jas 4:13 we will go to this or that c,
Rev 2:13 death in your c—where Satan lives.
3:12 God and the name of the c of my God,
11: 8 lie in the street of the great c,
11:13 and a tenth of the c collapsed.
14:20 in the winepress outside the c,
16:19 The great c split into three parts,
17:18 The woman you saw is the great c
18:10 O great c, O Babylon, c of power!
18:16 cry out: "'Woe! Woe, O great c,
Rev 18:18 there ever a c like this great c?'
18:19 "'Woe! Woe, O great c, where all who
18:21 "With such violence the great c of
20: 9 of God's people, the c he loves.
21:14 The wall of the c had twelve
21:15 the c, its gates and its walls.
21:16 The c was laid out like a square, as
21:16 He measured the c with the rod and
21:18 c of pure gold, as pure as glass.
21:19 The foundations of the c walls were
21:21 The great street of the c was of
21:22 I did not see a temple in the c,
21:23 The c does not need the sun or the
22: 2 middle of the great street of the c.
22: 3 God and of the Lamb will be in the c,
22:14 may go through the gates into the c.

City of David

2Sa 5: 7 the fortress of Zion, the C.
5: 9 in the fortress and called it the C.
6:10 of the LORD to be with him in the C.
6:12 Obed-Edom to the C with rejoicing.
6:16 ark of the LORD was entering the C,
1Ki 2:10 his fathers and was buried in the C.
3: 1 He brought her to the C until he
8: 1 LORD's covenant from Zion, the C.
9:24 from the C to the palace Solomon had
11:27 gap in the wall of the c his father.
11:43 and was buried in the c his father.
14:31 and was buried with them in the C.
15: 8 his fathers and was buried in the C.
22:50 with them in the c his father.
2Ki 8:24 and was buried with them in the C.
9:28 his fathers in his tomb in the C.
1Ki 12:21 buried with his fathers in the C.
14:20 Jerusalem with his fathers, in the C.
15: 7 and was buried near them in the C.
15:38 in the C, the city of his father.
16:20 and was buried with them in the C.
1Ch 11: 5 the fortress of Zion, the C.
11: 7 and so it was called the C.
13:13 the ark to be with him in the C.
15: 1 buildings for himself in the C,
15:29 of the LORD was entering the C,
2Ch 5: 2 LORD's covenant from Zion, the C.
8:11 from the C to the palace he had built
9:31 and was buried in the c his father.
12:16 his fathers and was buried in the C.
14: 1 his fathers and was buried in the C.
16:14 he had cut out for himself in the C.
21: 1 and was buried with them in the C.
21:20 was buried in the C, but not in the
24:16 He was buried with the kings in the C
24:25 So he died and was buried in the C,
27: 9 his fathers and was buried in the C.
32: 5 the supporting terraces of the C.
32:30 down to the west side of the C.
33:14 he rebuilt the outer wall of the C,
Ne 3:15 as the steps going down from the C.
12:37 of the C on the ascent to the wall
Isa 22: 9 you saw that the C had many breaches

City of God

Ps 46: 4 river whose streams make glad the c,
87: 3 Glorious things are said of you, O c:

City's (City)

Ro 16:23 Erastus, who is the c director of

Civilian

2Ti 2: 4 soldier gets involved in c affairs

Clad

Na 2: 3 red; the warriors are c in scarlet.
Zep 1: 8 and all those c in foreign clothes.

Claim (Claimed, Claiming, Claims, Reclaim)

2Sa 19:43 a greater c on David than you have.
Ne 2:20 or any c or historic right to it."
Job 3: 5 May darkness and deep shadow c it
41:11 Who has a c against me that I must
Ps 73: 9 Their mouths lay c to heaven, and
Pr 25: 6 do not c a place among great men;
Jer 23:38 Although you c, 'This is the oracle
23:38 you must not c, 'This is the oracle
Lk 11:18 I say this because you c that I
Jn 4:20 but you Jews c that the place where
8:24 believe that I am the one I c to be,
8:28 know that I am the one I c to be,
8:54 My Father, whom you c as your God,
9:41 c you can see, your guilt remains.
10:33 you, a mere man, c to be God."
Ro 3: 8 as some c that we say—"Let us do
2Co 3: 5 to c anything for ourselves,
Tit 1:16 They c to know God, but by their
1Jn 1: 6 If we c to have fellowship with him
1: 8 If we c to be without sin, we
1:10 If we c we have not sinned, we make
Rev 2: 2 that you have tested those who c to
3: 9 who c to be Jews though they are not,

Claimed (Claim)

2Sa 18: 8 c more lives that day than the sword.
1Ki 18:10 And whenever a nation or kingdom c
Mk 6:15 And still others c, "He is a prophet,
Jn 9: 9 Some c that he was. Others said, "No,
19: 7 because he c to be the Son of God."
19:21 this man c to be king of the Jews."
Ac 4:32 No-one c that any of his possessions
25:19 named Jesus whom Paul c was alive.
Ro 1:22 Although they c to be wise, they

Claiming (Claim)

Mt 24: 5 in my name, c, 'I am the Christ,'
Mk 13: 6 will come in my name, c, 'I am he,'
Lk 21: 8 will come in my name, c, 'I am he,'
Jn 8:25 "Just what I have been c all along,"
Ac 5:36 Theudas appeared, c to be somebody,

Claims (Claim)

2Sa 15: 3 "Look, your c are valid and proper,
Pr 20: 6 Many a man c to have unfailing love,
Ecc 8:17 Even if a wise man c he knows, he
Jer 23:34 c, 'This is the oracle of the LORD,'
Lk 23: 2 Caesar and c to be Christ, a king."
Jn 19:12 who c to be a king opposes Caesar."
Jas 2:14 my brothers, if a man c to have
1Jn 2: 6 Whoever c to live in him must walk
2: 9 Anyone who c to be in the light but

Clamour

Ps 74:23 Do not ignore the c of your
Isa 31: 4 shouts or disturbed by their c

Clan (Clans)

Ge 24:38 my father's family and to my own c,
24:40 a wife for my son from my own c and
24:41 Then, when you go to my c, you will
Ex 6:25 of the Levite families, c by c.
Lev 25:10 property and each to his own c.
25:41 and he will go back to his own c and
25:47 you or to a member of the alien's c,
25:49 in his c may redeem him. Or if he
Nu 2:34 set out, each with his c and family.
26: 5 through Hanoch, the Hanochite c;
26: 5 through Pallu, the Palluite c;
26: 6 through Hezron, the Hezronite c;
26: 6 through Carmi, the Carmite c.
26:12 through Nemuel, the Nemuelite c;
26:12 through Jamin, the Jaminite c
26:12 through Jakin, the Jakinite c;
26:13 through Zerah, the Zerahite c;
26:13 through Shaul, the Shaulite c.
26:15 through Zephon, the Zephonite c;
26:15 through Haggi, the Haggite c;
26:15 through Shuni, the Shunite c;
26:16 through Ozni, the Oznite c;
26:16 through Eri, the Erite c;
26:17 through Arodi, the Arodite c;
26:17 through Areli, the Arelite c.
26:20 through Shelah, the Shelanite c;
26:20 through Perez, the Perezite c;
26:20 through Zerah, the Zerahite c.
26:21 through Hezron, the Hezronite c;
26:21 through Hamul, the Hamulite c.

Nu 26:23 Tolaite **c**; through Puah, the Puite **c**;
26:24 through Jashub, the Jashubite **c**;
26:24 through Shimron, the Shimronite **c**.
26:26 through Sered, the Seredite **c**;
26:26 through Elon, the Elonite **c**;
26:26 through Jahleel, the Jahleelite **c**.
26:29 the Makirite **c** (Makir was the father
26:29 through Gilead, the Gileadite **c**.
26:30 through Iezer, the Iezerite **c**;
26:30 through Helek, the Helekite **c**;
26:31 through Asriel, the Asrielite **c**;
26:31 through Shechem, the Shechemite **c**;
26:32 through Shemida, the Shemidaite **c**;
26:32 through Hepher, the Hepherite **c**.
26:35 through Shuthelah, the Shuthelahite **c**;
26:35 through Beker, the Bekerite **c**;
26:35 through Tahan, the Tahanite **c**.
26:36 through Eran, the Eranite **c**.
26:38 through Bela, the Belaite **c**;
26:38 through Ashbel, the Ashbelite **c**;
26:38 through Ahiram, the Ahiramite **c**;
26:39 through Shupham, the Shuphamite **c**;
26:39 through Hupham, the Huphamite **c**.
26:40 through Ard, the Ardite **c**;
26:40 through Naaman, the Naamite **c**.
26:42 through Shuham, the Shuhamite **c**.
26:44 through Imnah, the Imnite **c**;
26:24 through Ishvi, the Ishvite **c**;
26:44 through Beriah, the Beriite **c**;
26:45 through Heber, the Heberite **c**;
26:45 through Malkiel, the Malkielite **c**.
26:48 through Jahzeel, the Jahzeelite **c**;
26:48 through Guni, the Gunite **c**;
26:49 through Jezer, the Jezerite **c**;
26:49 through Shillem, the Shillemite **c**.
26:57 through Gershon, the Gershonite **c**;
26:57 through Kohath, the Kohathite **c**;
26:57 through Merari, the Merarite **c**.
26:58 were Levite clans: the Libnite **c**,
26:58 the Hebronite **c**, the Mahlite **c**, the
26:58 the Mushite **c**, the Korahite **c**.
27: 4 from his **c** because he had no son?
27:11 in his **c**, that he may possess it.
36: 1 The family heads of the **c** of Gilead
36: 6 within the tribal **c** of their father.
36: 8 someone in her father's tribal **c**,
36:12 in their father's **c** and tribe.
Dt 29:18 no man or woman, **c** or tribe among
Jos 7:14 LORD takes shall come forward **c** by **c**;
7:14 the **c** that the LORD takes shall come
7:17 He had the **c** of the Zerahites come
13:15 to the tribe of Reuben, **c** by **c**:
13:23 of the Reubenites, **c** by **c**.
13:24 given to the tribe of Gad, **c** by **c**:
13:28 inheritance of the Gadites, **c** by **c**.
13:29 the descendants of Manasseh, **c** by **c**:
13:31 half of the sons of Makir, **c** by **c**.
15: 1 **c** by **c**, extended down to the
15:20 of the tribe of Judah, **c** by **c**:
16: 5 the territory of Ephraim, **c** by **c**;
16: 8 tribe of the Ephraimites, **c** by **c**.
18:11 for the tribe of Benjamin, **c** by **c**.
18:21 The tribe of Benjamin, **c** by **c**, had
19: 1 out for the tribe of Simeon, **c** by **c**.
19: 8 the tribe of the Simeonites, **c** by **c**.
19:10 lot came up for Zebulun, **c** by **c**:
19:16 the inheritance of Zebulun, **c** by **c**.
19:17 lot came out for Issachar, **c** by **c**.
19:23 of the tribe of Issachar, **c** by **c**.
19:24 out for the tribe of Asher, **c** by **c**.
19:31 of the tribe of Asher, **c** by **c**.
19:32 lot came out for Naphtali, **c** by **c**:
19:39 of the tribe of Naphtali, **c** by **c**.
19:40 out for the tribe of Dan, **c** by **c**.
19:48 of the tribe of Dan, **c** by **c**.
21: 4 came out for the Kohathites, **c** by **c**.
21: 7 The descendants of Merari, **c** by **c**,
Jdg 4:17 Hazor and the **c** of Heber the Kenite.
6:15 My **c** is the weakest in Manasseh,
9: 1 to them and to all his mother's **c**,
12: 9 in marriage to those outside his **c**,
12: 9 women as wives from outside his **c**.
13: 2 Manoah, from the **c** of the Danites,
17: 7 been living within the **c** of Judah,
18:11 six hundred men from the **c** of the
18:19 serve a tribe and **c** in Israel as
Ru 2: 1 from the **c** of Elimelech, a man of
2: 3 who was from the **c** of Elimelech.
1Sa 9:21 and is not my **c** the least of all the
10:21 **c** by **c**, and Matri's **c** was chosen.
18:18 family or my father's **c** in Israel,
20: 6 being made there for his whole **c**.'
2Sa 14: 7 Now the whole **c** has risen up against
16: 5 a man from the same **c** as Saul's
1Ch 4:27 so their entire **c** did not become as
6:54 Aaron who were from the Kohathite **c**,
6:62 The descendants of Gershon, **c** by **c**,
6:63 The descendants of Merari, **c** by **c**,
6:71 From the **c** of the half-tribe of
Jer 3:14 two from a **c**—and bring you to Zion.
Zec 12:12 The land will mourn, each **c** by
12:12 the **c** of the house of David and
12:12 the **c** of the house of Nathan and
12:13 the **c** of the house of Levi and their
12:13 the **c** of Shimei and their wives,

Clanging

1Co 13: 1 a resounding gong or a **c** cymbal.

Clans (Clan)

Ge 10: 5 by their **c** within their nations,
10:18 Later the Canaanite **c** scattered
10:20 These are the sons of Ham by their **c**
10:31 These are the sons of Shem by their **c**
10:32 These are the **c** of Noah's sons,
36:40 according to their **c** and regions:
Ex 6:14 These were the **c** of Reuben.
6:15 These were the **c** of Simeon.
6:17 The sons of Gershon, by **c**, were
6:19 **c** of Levi according to their records.
6:24 These were the Korahite **c**.
Lev 25:45 of their **c** born in your country,
Nu 1: 2 community by their **c** and families,
1:16 were the heads of the **c** of Israel.
1:18 ancestry by their **c** and families,
1:20 the records of their **c** and families.
1:22 the records of their **c** and families.
1:24 the records of their **c** and families.
1:26 the records of their **c** and families.
1:28 the records of their **c** and families.
1:30 the records of their **c** and families.
1:32 the records of their **c** and families.
1:34 the records of their **c** and families.
1:36 the records of their **c** and families.
1:38 the records of their **c** and families.
1:40 the records of their **c** and families.
1:42 the records of their **c** and families.
3:15 the Levites by their families and **c**.
3:18 the Gershonite **c**: Libni and Shimei.
3:19 The Kohathite **c**: Amram, Izhar,
3:20 The Merarite **c**: Mahli and Mushi.
3:20 These were the Levite **c**, according to
3:21 To Gershon belonged the **c** of the
3:21 these were the Gershonite **c**.
3:23 The Gershonite **c** were to camp on the
3:27 To Kohath belonged the **c** of the
3:27 these were the Kohathite **c**.
3:29 The Kohathite **c** were to camp on the
3:30 of the families of the Kohathite **c**
3:33 To Merari belonged the **c** of the
3:33 Mushites; these were the Merarite **c**.
3:35 Merarite **c** was Zuriel son of Abihail;
3:39 Moses and Aaron according to their **c**,
4: 2 the Levites by their **c** and families.
4:18 "See that the Kohathite tribal **c** are
4:22 Gershonites by their families and **c**.
4:24 Gershonite **c** as they work and carry
4:28 Gershonite **c** at the Tent of Meeting.
4:29 "Count the Merarites by their **c** and
4:33 This is the service of the Merarite **c**
4:34 Kohathites by their **c** and families.
4:36 counted by **c**, were 2,750.
4:37 **c** who served in the Tent of Meeting.
4:38 counted by their **c** and families.
4:40 counted by their **c** and families,
4:41 **c** who served at the Tent of Meeting.
4:42 The Merarites were counted by their **c**
4:44 counted by their **c**, were 3,200.
4:45 total of those in the Merarite **c**.
4:46 the Levites by their **c** and families.
Nu 10: 4 —the heads of the **c** of Israel
26: 7 These were the **c** of Reuben; those
26:12 The descendants of Simeon by their **c**
26:14 These were the **c** of Simeon; there
26:15 The descendants of Gad by their **c**
26:18 These were the **c** of Gad; those
26:20 The descendants of Judah by their **c**
26:22 These were the **c** of Judah; those
26:23 descendants of Issachar by their **c**
26:25 These were the **c** of Issachar; those
26:26 The descendants of Zebulun by their **c**
26:27 These were the **c** of Zebulun; those
26:28 The descendants of Joseph by their **c**
26:34 These were the **c** of Manasseh; those
26:35 descendants of Ephraim by their **c**:
26:37 These were the **c** of Ephraim; those
26:37 descendants of Joseph by their **c**.
26:38 descendants of Benjamin by their **c** were:
26:41 These were the **c** of Benjamin; those
26:42 the descendants of Dan by their **c**:
26:42 These were the **c** of Dan:
26:43 All of them were Shuhamite **c**; and
26:44 The descendants of Asher by their **c**
26:47 These were the **c** of Asher; those
26:48 descendants of Naphtali by their **c**
26:50 These were the **c** of Naphtali; those
26:57 Levites who were counted by their **c**:
26:58 These also were Levite **c**: the
27: 1 to the **c** of Manasseh son of Joseph.
31: 5 were supplied from the **c** of Israel.
33:54 land by lot, according to your **c**.
36: 1 who were from the **c** of the
36:12 They married within the **c** of the
Jos 7:17 The **c** of Judah came forward, and he
14: 1 tribal **c** of Israel allotted to them.
15:12 the people of Judah by their **c**.
17: 2 of Manasseh—the **c** of Abiezer,
17: 2 Manasseh son of Joseph by their **c**.
18:20 of the **c** of Benjamin on all sides.
18:28 inheritance of Benjamin for its **c**.
19:51 the heads of the tribal **c** of Israel
21: 5 from the **c** of the tribes of Ephraim,
21: 6 the **c** of the tribes of Issachar,
21:10 from the Kohathite **c** of the Levites,
21:20 The rest of the Kohathite **c** of the
21:26 to the rest of the Kohathite **c**.
21:27 The Levite **c** of the Gershonites were
21:33 All the towns of the Gershonite **c**
21:34 The Merarite **c** (the rest of the
21:40 towns allotted to the Merarite **c**,
22:14 division among the Israelite **c**.
22:21 to the heads of the **c** of Israel:
22:30 the heads of the **c** of the Israelites
Jdg 18: 2 These men represented all their **c**.
21:24 went home to their tribes and **c**,
1Sa 9:21 all the **c** of the tribe of Benjamin?
10:19 the LORD by your tribes and **c**."
23:23 him down among all the **c** of Judah."
1Ch 2:53 the **c** of Kiriath Jearim: the
2:55 the **c** of scribes who lived at Jabez:
4: 2 These were the **c** of the Zorathites.
4: 8 of the **c** of Aharhel son of Harum.
4:21 the **c** of the linen workers at
4:38 by name were leaders of their **c**.
5: 7 Their relatives by **c**, listed
6:19 These are the **c** of the Levites
6:60 Kohathite **c**, were thirteen in all.
6:61 the **c** of half the tribe of Manasseh.
6:66 Some of the Kohathite **c** were given
6:70 to the rest of the Kohathite **c**.
7: 5 belonging to all the **c** of Issachar,
12:30 brave warriors, famous in their own **c**
Job 31:34 so dreaded the contempt of the **c**
Jer 2: 4 all you **c** of the house of Israel.
31: 1 "I will be the God of all the **c** of
Mic 5: 2 though you are small among the **c** of
Zec 12:14 all the rest of the **c** and their

Clap (Clapped, Claps)

Job 21: 5 **c** your hand over your mouth.
Ps 47: 1 **C** your hands, all you nations; shout
98: 8 Let the rivers **c** their hands, let
Pr 30:32 evil, **c** your hand over your mouth!
Isa 55:12 of the field will **c** their hands.
Lam 2:15 All who pass your way **c** their hands

Clapped (Clap)
2Ki 11:12 They anointed him, and the people c
Eze 25: 6 c your hands and stamped your feet,

Claps (Clap)
Job 27:23 c its hands in derision and hisses
34:37 scornfully he c his hands among us
Na 3:19 about you c his hands at your fall,

Clash
Ps 150: 5 praise him with the c of cymbals,

Clasp (Clasped, Clasps)
Isa 2: 6 Philistines and c hands with pagans.

Clasped (Clasp)
Mt 28: 9 him, c his feet and worshipped him.

Clasps (Clasp)
Ex 26: 6 make fifty gold c and use them to
26:11 make fifty bronze c and put them in
26:33 Hang the curtain from the c and
35:11 c, frames, crossbars, posts and
36:13 they made fifty gold c and used them
36:18 They made fifty bronze c to fasten
39:33 its c, frames, crossbars, posts and

Classify
2Co 10:12 We do not dare to c or compare

Clatter
Jdg 5:28 is the c of his chariots delayed?'
Na 3: 2 The crack of whips, the c of wheels,

Claudia
2Ti 4:21 Linus, C and all the brothers.

Claudius
Ac 11:28 This happened during the reign of C.)
18: 2 because C had ordered all the Jews
23:26 C Lysias, To His Excellency,

Claws
Da 4:33 and his nails like the c of a bird.
7:19 with its iron teeth and bronze c—

Clay
Lev 6:28 The c pot that the meat is cooked in
11:33 If one of them falls into a c pot,
14: 5 killed over fresh water in a c pot.
14:42 take new c and plaster the house.
14:50 birds over fresh water in a c pot.
15:12 "'A c pot that the man touches must
Nu 5:17 shall take some holy water in a c jar
1Ki 7:46 The king had them cast in c moulds
2Ch 4:17 The king had them cast in c moulds
Job 4:19 more those who live in houses of c,
10: 9 Remember that you moulded me like c.
13:12 your defences are defences of c.
27:16 dust and clothes like piles of c,
33: 6 God; I too have been taken from c.
38:14 The earth takes shape like c under a
Ps 12: 6 furnace of c, purified seven times.
Isa 29:16 were thought to be like the c!
41:25 if he were a potter treading the c.
45: 9 Does the c say to the potter, 'What
64: 8 We are the c, you are the potter; we
Jer 18: 4 the pot he was shaping from the c
18: 6 "Like c in the hand of the potter,
19: 1 "Go and buy a c jar from a potter.
32:14 and put them in a c jar so that they
43: 9 bury them in c in the brick pavement
Lam 4: 2 are now considered as pots of c,
Eze 4: 1 "Now, son of man, take a c tablet,
Da 2:33 of iron and partly of baked c.
2:34 feet of iron and c and smashed them.
2:35 the iron, the c, the bronze, the
2:41 of baked c and partly of iron,
2:41 even as you saw iron mixed with c.
2:42 toes were partly iron and partly c,
2:43 you saw the iron mixed with baked c,
2:43 any more than iron mixes with c.
2:45 broke the iron, the bronze, the c,
Na 3:14 Work the c, tread the mortar, repair
Ro 9:21 to make out of the same lump of c
2Co 4: 7 we have this treasure in jars of c
2Ti 2:20 but also of wood and c; some are for

Clean (Cleanness, Cleanse, Cleansed, Cleanses, Cleansing)
Ge 7: 2 you seven of every kind of c animal,
7: 8 Pairs of c and unclean animals, of
8:20 taking some of all the c animals and
8:20 of all the c animals and c birds,
20: 5 a clear conscience and c hands."
Lev 4:12 the camp to a place ceremonially c,
6:11 to a place that is ceremonially c.
7:19 anyone ceremonially c may eat it.
10:10 between the unclean and the c,
10:14 Eat them in a ceremonially c place;
11:32 till evening, and then it will be c.
11:36 for collecting water remains c,
11:37 are to be planted, they remain c.
11:47 between the unclean and the c,
12: 7 c from her flow of blood.
12: 8 for her, and she will be c.'"
13: 6 pronounce him c; it is only a rash.
13: 6 wash his clothes, and he will be c.
13: 7 to the priest to be pronounced c,
13:13 he shall pronounce that person c.
13:13 it has all turned white, he is c.
13:17 person c; then he will be c.
13:23 the priest shall pronounce him c.
13:28 the priest shall pronounce him c;
13:34 the priest shall pronounce him c.
13:34 wash his clothes, and he will be c.
13:35 the skin after he is pronounced c,
13:37 He is c, and the priest shall
13:37 the priest shall pronounce him c.
13:39 out on the skin; that person is c.
13:40 lost his hair and is bald, he is c.
13:41 and has a bald forehead, he is c.
13:58 be washed again, and it will be c."
13:59 for pronouncing them c or unclean.
14: 4 live c birds and some cedar wood,
14: 7 disease and pronounce him c.
14: 8 then he will be ceremonially c.
14: 9 with water, and he will be c.
14:11 The priest who pronounces him c
14:20 atonement for him, and he will be c.
14:48 house c, because the mildew is gone.
14:53 for the house, and it will be c."
14:57 to determine when something is c or
15: 8 discharge spits on someone who is c,
15:13 with fresh water, and he will be c.
15:28 that she will be ceremonially c.
16:30 you will be c from all your sins.
17:15 till evening; then he will be c.
20:25 make a distinction between c and
20:25 and between unclean and c birds.
22: 7 the sun goes down, he will be c, and
Nu 8: 6 and make them ceremonially c.
9:13 if a man who is ceremonially c and
18:11 who is ceremonially c may eat it.
18:13 who is ceremonially c may eat it.
19: 9 "A man who is c shall gather up the
19: 9 ceremonially c place outside the camp
19:12 the seventh day; then he will be c.
19:12 and seventh days, he will not be c.
19:18 a man who is ceremonially c is to
19:19 The man who is c is to sprinkle the
19:19 and that evening he will be c.
31:23 the fire, and then it will be c.
31:24 wash your clothes and you will be c.
Dt 12:15 unclean and the c may eat it.
12:22 unclean and the c may eat.
14:11 You may eat any c bird.
14:20 any winged creature that is c you
15:22 unclean and the c may eat it,
2Ki 5:14 became c like that of a young boy.
2Ch 13:11 bread on the ceremonially c table
30:17 those who were not ceremonially c
30:19 even if he is not c according to the
Ezr 6:20 and were all ceremonially c.
Job 17: 9 with c hands will grow stronger.
33: 9 I am c and free from guilt.
37:21 after the wind has swept them c.
Ps 24: 4 He who has c hands and a pure heart,
51: 7 me with hyssop, and I shall be c;
Pr 20: 9 heart pure; I am c and without sin"?
Ecc 9: 2 and the bad, the c and the unclean,
Isa 1:16 wash and make yourselves c. Take
66:20 the LORD in ceremonially c vessels.
Eze 16: 4 you washed with water to make you c,
22:26 between the unclean and the c;
24:13 you will not be c again until my
36:25 I will sprinkle c water on you, and
36:25 and you will be c; I will cleanse
44:23 between the unclean and the c.
Am 7: 2 they had stripped the land c, I
Zec 3: 5 I said, "Put a c turban on his head."
3: 5 So they put a c turban on his head
Mt 8: 2 you are willing, you can make me c."
8: 3 "I am willing," he said. "Be c!"
12:44 unoccupied, swept c and put in order.
23:25 you hypocrites! You c the outside of
23:26 Blind Pharisee! First c the inside
23:26 and then the outside also will be c.
27:59 body, wrapped it in a c linen cloth,
Mk 1:40 you are willing, you can make me c."
1:41 "I am willing," he said. "Be c!"
7:19 this, Jesus declared all foods "c".
Lk 5:12 you are willing, you can make me c."
5:13 "I am willing," he said. "Be c!" And
11:25 arrives, it finds the house swept c
11:39 "Now then, you Pharisees c the
11:41 and everything will be c for you.
Jn 13:10 wash his feet; his whole body is c.
13:10 you are c, though not every one of
13:11 was why he said not every one was c.
15: 3 You are already c because of the
Ac 10:15 anything impure that God has made c."
11: 9 anything impure that God has made c.'
24:18 I was ceremonially c when they found
Ro 14:20 All food is c, but it is wrong for a
Heb 9:13 them so that they are outwardly c.
Rev 15: 6 They were dressed in c, shining
19: 8 Fine linen, bright and c, was given
19:14 dressed in fine linen, white and c.

Cleanness (Clean)
2Sa 22:21 according to the c of my hands he has
22:25 according to my c in his sight.
Job 22:30 through the c of your hands."
Ps 18:20 according to the c of my hands he has
18:24 to the c of my hands in his sight.

Cleanse (Clean)
Lev 16:19 with his finger seven times to c it
16:30 will be made for you, to c you.
Ps 51: 2 Wash away all my iniquity and c me
51: 7 C me with hyssop, and I shall be
Pr 20:30 Blows and wounds c away evil, and
Isa 4: 4 he will c the bloodstains from
Jer 4:11 my people, but not to winnow or c;
33: 8 I will c them from all the sin they
Eze 24:13 Because I tried to c you but you
36:25 and you will be clean; I will c you
36:33 the day I c you from all your sins,
37:23 backsliding, and I will c them.
39:12 burying them in order to c the land.
39:14 "'Men will be regularly employed to c
39:16 And so they will c the land.'
43:26 atonement for the altar and c it;
Zec 13: 1 to c them from sin and impurity.
Mt 10: 8 c those who have leprosy,
Heb 9:14 c our consciences from acts that
10:22 having our hearts sprinkled to c us

Cleansed (Clean)
Lev 14: 4 be brought for the one to be c.
14: 7 to be c of the infectious disease
14: 8 "The person to be c must wash his
14:11 shall present both the one to be c
14:14 of the right ear of the one to be c,
14:17 of the right ear of the one to be c,
14:18 put on the head of the one to be c
14:19 one to be c from his uncleanness.
14:25 of the right ear of the one to be c,
14:28 of the right ear of the one to be c,
14:29 put on the head of the one to be c,
14:31 LORD on behalf of the one to be c."

Lev 15:13 "When a man is **c** from his discharge,
15:28 "When she is **c** from her discharge,
22: 4 the sacred offerings until he is **c**.
Nu 19:19 The person being **c** must wash his
Jos 22:17 have not **c** ourselves from that sin,
2Ki 5:10 will be restored and you will be **c**."
5:12 Couldn't I wash in them and be **c**?"
Pr 30:12 and yet are not **c** of their filth;
Isa 1: 6 **c** or bandaged or soothed with oil.
Eze 24:13 would not be **c** from your impurity,
44:26 After he is **c**, he must wait seven
Lk 4:27 not one of them was **c**—only Naaman
17:14 And as they went, they were **c**.
17:17 Jesus asked, "Were not all ten **c**?
Heb 9:22 nearly everything be **c** with blood,
10: 2 would have been **c** once for all,
2Pe 1: 9 he has been **c** from his past sins.

Cleanses (Clean)

2Ti 2:21 If a man **c** himself from the latter,

Cleansing (Clean)

Lev 14: 2 at the time of his ceremonial **c**, when
14:23 he must bring them for his **c** to the
14:32 the regular offerings for his **c**.
15:13 off seven days for his ceremonial **c**;
Nu 6: 9 the day of his **c**—the seventh day.
8: 7 Sprinkle the water of **c** on them;
19: 9 for use in the water of **c**; it is for
19:13 Because the water of **c** has not been
19:20 The water of **c** has not been
19:21 who sprinkles the water of **c** must
19:21 who touches the water of **c** will
31:23 be purified with the water of **c**.
Mk 1:44 that Moses commanded for your **c**,
Lk 5:14 that Moses commanded for your **c**,
Jn 11:55 ceremonial **c** before the Passover.
Eph 5:26 **c** her by the washing with water

Clear (Cleared, Clearly)

Ge 20: 5 a **c** conscience and clean hands."
20: 6 you did this with a **c** conscience
Ex 24:10 of sapphire, **c** as the sky itself.
27:20 to bring you **c** oil of pressed olives
Lev 24: 2 to bring you **c** oil of pressed olives
24:12 the LORD should be made **c** to them.
Nu 15:34 not **c** what should be done to him.
Jos 17:15 go up into the forest and **c** land for
17:18 **C** it, and its farthest limits will be
2Sa 19: 6 You have made it **c** today that the
1Ki 2:31 and so **c** me and my father's house of
Ne 8: 8 making it **c** and giving the meaning
Isa 32: 4 tongue will be fluent and **c**.
Eze 34:18 not enough for you to drink **c** water?
Mt 3:12 and he will **c** his threshing-floor,
Lk 3:17 his hand to **c** his threshing-floor
Jn 8:43 Why is my language not **c** to you?
Ac 18: 6 heads! I am **c** of my responsibility.
24:16 my conscience **c** before God and man.
1Co 4: 4 My conscience is **c**, but that does
14: 8 trumpet does not sound a **c** call,
15:27 it is **c** that this does not include
2Co 7:11 what eagerness to **c** yourselves, what
11: 6 perfectly **c** to you in every way.
Php 1:13 a result, it has become **c** throughout
3:15 that too God will make **c** to you.
1Th 3:11 **c** the way for us to come to you.
1Ti 3: 9 of the faith with a **c** conscience.
2Ti 1: 3 forefathers did, with a **c** conscience
3: 9 their folly will be **c** to everyone.
Heb 6:17 **c** to the heirs of what was promised,
7:14 For it is **c** that our Lord descended
7:15 what we have said is even more **c** if
9: 9 **c** the conscience of the worshipper.
13:18 are sure that we have a **c** conscience
1Pe 3:16 keeping a **c** conscience, so that
4: 7 Therefore be **c** minded and
2Pe 1:14 Lord Jesus Christ has made **c** to me.
Rev 4: 6 like a sea of glass, **c** as crystal.
21:11 jewel, like a jasper, **c** as crystal.
22: 1 as **c** as crystal, flowing from the

Cleared (Clear)

Nu 5:28 she will be **c** of guilt and will be
1Sa 14:41 taken by lot, and the men were **c**.
2Ch 30:14 **c** away the incense altars and threw
Job 33:32 speak up, for I want you to be **c**.
35: 2 You say, 'I shall be **c** by God.'
Ps 80: 9 You **c** the ground for it, and it took
Isa 5: 2 He dug it up and **c** it of stones and

Clearly (Clear)

Ge 26:28 They answered, "We saw **c** that the
Ex 10:10 children! **C** you are bent on evil.
Nu 12: 8 With him I speak face to face, **c** and
24: 3 the oracle of one whose eye sees **c**,
24:15 the oracle of one whose eye sees **c**,
Dt 27: 8 you shall write very **c** all the words
Jos 9:24 "Your servants were **c** told how the
1Sa 2:27 'Did I not **c** reveal myself to your
Jer 23:20 to come you will understand it **c**.
Mt 7: 5 and then you will see **c** to remove
Mk 8:25 restored, and he saw everything **c**.
Lk 6:42 and then you will see **c** to remove
Jn 16:29 **c** and without figures of speech.
Ro 1:20 and divine nature—have been **c** seen,
3: 5 out God's righteousness more **c**,
Gal 2:11 face, because he was **c** in the wrong.
3: 1 Christ was **c** portrayed as crucified.
3:11 **C** no-one is justified before God by
Col 4: 4 Pray that I may proclaim it **c**, as I
1Ti 4: 1 The Spirit **c** says that in later

Cleft (Clefts)

Ex 33:22 I will put you in a **c** in the rock

Clefts (Cleft)

Jdg 6: 2 mountain **c**, caves and strongholds.
SS 2:14 My dove in the **c** of the rock, in the
Jer 49:16 you who live in the **c** of the rocks,
Ob : 3 you who live in the **c** of the rocks

Clement

Php 4: 3 along with **C** and the rest of my

Cleopas

Lk 24:18 One of them, named **C**, asked him,

Clerestory

1Ki 6: 4 He made narrow **c** windows in the

Clerk

Ac 19:35 The city **c** quietened the crowd and

Clever (Cleverly, Cleverness)

Isa 3: 3 skilled craftsman and **c** enchanter.
5:21 own eyes and **c** in their own sight.

Cleverly (Clever)

Hos 13: 2 **c** fashioned images, all of them the
2Pe 1:16 We did not follow **c** invented stories

Cleverness (Clever)

Isa 25:11 pride despite the **c** of their hands.

Cliff (Cliffs)

1Sa 14: 4 reach the Philistine outpost was a **c**;
14: 5 One **c** stood to the north towards
2Ch 25:12 took them to the top of a **c** and
Job 39:28 He dwells on a **c** and stays there at
Lk 4:29 in order to throw him down the **c**.

Cliffs (Cliff)

Ps 141: 6 will be thrown down from the **c**,
Jer 51:25 roll you off the **c**, and make you a
Eze 38:20 the **c** will crumble and every wall

Climax

Eze 21:25 of punishment has reached its **c**,
21:29 of punishment has reached its **c**.
35: 5 time their punishment reached its **c**,

Climb (Climbed, Climbing, Climbs)

Ge 49:22 whose branches **c** over a wall.
1Sa 14:10 'Come up to us,' we will **c** up,
14:12 "**C** up after me; the LORD has given
SS 7: 8 I said, "I will **c** the palm tree; I
Jer 4:29 thickets; some **c** up among the rocks.
Joel 2: 9 They **c** into the houses; like thieves
Am 9: 2 Though they **c** up to the heavens,

Climbed (Climb)

Dt 32:50 There on the mountain that you have **c**
34: 1 Moses **c** Mount Nebo from the plains
Jos 15: 8 From there it **c** to the top of the
Jdg 9: 7 he **c** up on the top of Mount Gerizim
9:51 in and **c** up on the tower roof.
1Sa 14:13 Jonathan **c** up, using his hands and
2Sa 17:18 courtyard, and they **c** down into it.
17:21 had gone, the two **c** out of the well
1Ki 18:42 but Elijah **c** to the top of Carmel,
Ne 4: 3 building—if even a fox **c** up on it,
Isa 57: 8 you **c** into it and opened it wide;
Jer 9:21 Death has **c** in through our windows
Eze 40: 6 He **c** its steps and measured the
Mt 14:32 they **c** into the boat, the wind died
Mk 6:51 he **c** into the boat with them, and
Lk 19: 4 he ran ahead and **c** a sycamore-fig
Jn 21:11 Simon Peter **c** aboard and dragged the

Climbing (Climb)

2Ch 20:16 They will be **c** up by the Pass of Ziz,

Climbs (Climb)

Isa 24:18 whoever **c** out of the pit will be
Jer 48:44 whoever **c** out of the pit will be
Jn 10: 1 but **c** in by some other way, is a

Cling (Clinging, Clings, Clung)

Dt 28:60 you dreaded, and they will **c** to you.
2Ki 5:27 Naaman's leprosy will **c** to you and
Job 41:17 **c** together and cannot be parted.
Ps 31: 6 I hate those who **c** to worthless idols
44:25 dust; our bodies **c** to the ground.
101: 3 men I hate; they shall not **c** to me.
137: 6 May my tongue **c** to the roof of my
Jer 8: 5 **c** to deceit; they refuse to return.
Jnh 2: 8 "Those who **c** to worthless idols
Ro 12: 9 Hate what is evil; **c** to what is good.

Clinging (Cling)

1Ki 1:51 and is **c** to the horns of the altar.

Clings (Cling)

Job 8:15 he **c** to it, but it does not hold.
Ps 63: 8 My soul **c** to you; your right hand

Clip

Lev 19:27 or **c** off the edges of your beard.

Cloak (Cloaks)

Ge 39:12 She caught him by his **c** and said,
39:12 me!" But he left his **c** in her hand
39:13 she saw that he had left his **c** in
39:15 he left his **c** beside me and ran out
39:16 She kept his **c** beside her until his
39:18 he left his **c** beside me and ran out
Ex 4: 6 said, "Put your hand inside your **c**.
4: 6 So Moses put his hand into his **c**,
4: 7 "Now put it back into your **c**," he
4: 7 Moses put his hand back into his **c**,
12:11 with your **c** tucked into your belt,
22:26 If you take your neighbour's **c** as a
22:27 his **c** is the only covering he has
Dt 22: 3 or his **c** or anything he loses.
22:12 the four corners of the **c** you wear.
24:13 Return his **c** to him by sunset so
24:17 take the **c** of the widow as a pledge.
1Ki 11:29 met him on the way, wearing a new **c**.
11:30 Ahijah took hold of the new **c** he was
18:46 tucking his **c** into his belt, he ran
19:13 he pulled his **c** over his face and went
19:19 to him and threw his **c** around him.
2Ki 2: 8 Elijah took his **c**, rolled it up and
2:13 He picked up the **c** that had fallen
2:14 he took the **c** that had fallen from
4:29 "Tuck your **c** into your belt, take my
4:39 gourds and filled the fold of his **c**.
9: 1 "Tuck your **c** into your belt, take

Ezr 9: 3 I heard this, I tore my tunic and c,
9: 5 with my tunic and c torn, and fell
Ps 109:19 May it be like a c wrapped about him,
109:29 and wrapped in shame as in a c.
Pr 21:14 and a bribe concealed in the c
30: 4 has wrapped up the waters in his c?
SS 5: 7 they took away my c, those watchmen
Isa 3: 6 "You have a c, you be our leader;
59:17 wrapped himself in zeal as in a c.
Mt 5:40 tunic, let him have your c as well.
9:20 him and touched the edge of his c.
9:21 only touch his c, I will be healed."
14:36 sick just touch the edge of his c,
24:18 in the field go back to get his c.
Mk 5:27 him in the crowd and touched his c,
6:56 them touch even the edge of his c,
10:50 Throwing his c aside, he jumped to
13:16 in the field go back to get his c.
Lk 6:29 If someone takes your c, do not stop
8:44 him and touched the edge of his c,
22:36 a sword, sell your c and buy one.
Ac 12: 8 "Wrap your c around you and follow me
2Ti 4:13 you come, bring the c that I left

Cloaks (Cloak)
2Ki 9:13 They hurried and took their c and
Isa 3:22 the fine robes and the capes and c,
Mt 21: 7 placed their c on them, and Jesus sat
21: 8 A very large crowd spread their c on
Mk 11: 7 threw their c over it, he sat on it.
11: 8 Many people spread their c on the
Lk 19:35 c on the colt and put Jesus on it.
19:36 people spread their c on the road.
Ac 22:23 throwing off their c and flinging

Clods
Job 38:38 and the c of earth stick together?
Joel 1:17 seeds are shrivelled beneath the c.

Clopas
Jn 19:25 mother's sister, Mary the wife of C,

Close[1] (Closed, Closes, Closing, Enclose, Enclosed)
Ge 46: 4 Joseph's own hand will c your eyes."
Lev 14:38 house and c it up for seven days.
20: 4 people of the community c their eyes
Jos 2: 5 when it was time to c the city gate,
Ne 6:10 and let us c the temple doors,
Ps 17:10 They c up their callous hearts, and
69:15 up or the pit c its mouth over me.
Isa 6:10 their ears dull and c their eyes.
66: 9 "Do I c up the womb when I bring to
Lam 3:56 "Do not c your ears to my cry for
Eze 22: 4 You have brought your days to a c,
Da 12: 4 you, Daniel, c up and seal the words
Mt 6: 6 go into your room, c the door and
Lk 21:34 c on you unexpectedly like a trap.

Close[2] (Close-knit, Closely, Closer, Closest)
Ge 27:22 Jacob went c to his father Isaac,
45: 4 Joseph said to his brothers, "Come c
48:10 So Joseph brought his sons c to him,
48:13 hand, and brought them c to him.
Ex 25:27 The rings are to be c to the rim to
28:27 c to the seam just above the
37:14 The rings were put c to the rim to
39:20 c to the seam just above the
Lev 3: 9 the entire fat tail cut off c to the
18: 6 No-one is to approach any c relative
18:12 she is your father's c relative.
18:13 she is your mother's c relative.
18:17 daughter; they are her c relatives.
20:19 for that would dishonour a c relative
21: 2 except for a c relative, such as his
Nu 5: 8 if that person has no c relative to
22:25 she pressed c to the wall, crushing
Jdg 16: 9 snaps when it comes c to a flame.
Ru 2:20 "That man is our c relative; he is
2:23 Ruth stayed c to the servant girls
2Sa 11:20 'Why did you get so c to the city to
11:21 Why did you get so c to the wall?'
12:11 give them to one who is c to you,
1Ki 21: 1 The vineyard was in Jezreel, c to
21: 2 garden, since it is c to my palace.
2Ki 10:11 all his chief men, his c friends and
11: 8 Stay c to the king wherever he goes."
2Ch 23: 7 Stay c to the king wherever he goes."
Job 13:27 you keep c watch on all my paths by
33:11 he keeps c watch on all my paths.'
41:16 each is so c to the next that no air
Ps 34:18 The LORD is c to the broken-hearted
41: 9 Even my c friend, whom I trusted, he
55:13 myself, my companion, my c friend,
88:15 I have been afflicted and c to death;
148:14 Israel, the people c to his heart.
Pr 16:28 and a gossip separates c friends.
17: 9 the matter separates c friends.
Isa 40:11 and carries them c to his heart;
42:23 or pay c attention in time to come?
56: 1 for my salvation is c at hand and my
Jer 30:21 him near and he will come c to me,
30:21 will devote himself to be c to me?'
Joel 2: 1 the LORD is coming. It is c at hand—
Zec 13: 7 against the man who is c to me!"
Lk 20:20 Keeping a c watch on him, they sent
Jn 4:47 heal his son, who was c to death.
Ac 8: 6 paid c attention to what he said.
9:24 Day and night they kept c watch on
10:24 his relatives and c friends.
Rev 6: 8 Hades was following c behind him.

Closed (Close[1])
Ge 2:21 ribs and c up the place with flesh.
8: 2 floodgates of the heavens had been c,
20:18 for the LORD had c up every womb in
Lev 14:46 goes into the house while it is c up
Nu 16:33 they owned; the earth c over them,
Jdg 3:22 sword out, and the fat c in over it.
1Sa 1: 5 her, and the LORD had c her womb.
1: 6 the LORD had c her womb, her rival
Ne 4: 7 the gaps were being c, they were very
Job 17: 4 You have c their minds to
Ecc 12: 4 the doors to the street are c and
Isa 32: 3 those who see will no longer be c,
44:18 c so that they cannot understand.
Jer 6:10 ears are c so that they cannot hear.
Lam 3:54 the waters c over my head, and I
Da 12: 9 Daniel, because the words are c up
Mt 13:15 ears, and they have c their eyes.
Ac 28:27 ears, and they have c their eyes.

Close-knit (Close[2], Knit)
Job 40:17 the sinews of his thighs are c.

Closely (Close[2])
Ge 24:21 the man watched her c to learn
43: 7 us c about ourselves and our family.
44:30 is c bound up with the boy's life,
Dt 4: 9 and watch yourselves c so that you
2Sa 19:42 because the king is c related to us.
1Ki 3:21 at him c in the morning light,
Ne 13: 4 He was c associated with Tobiah,
Job 23:11 My feet have c followed his steps; I
Ps 122: 3 a city that is c compacted together.
Pr 4:20 to what I say; listen c to my words.
Jer 2:10 send to Kedar and observe c; see if
Eze 44: 5 look carefully, listen c and give
Mk 3: 2 so they watched him c to see if he
14:67 himself, she looked c at him.
Lk 6: 7 so they watched him c to see if he
22:56 She looked c at him and said, "This
Ac 7:31 As he went over to look more c,
1Ti 4:16 Watch your life and doctrine c.

Closer (Close[2])
Ex 3: 5 "Do not come any c," God said. "Take
1Sa 17:41 of him, kept coming c to David.
17:48 the Philistine moved c to attack him,
2Sa 18:25 And the man came c and c.
Pr 18:24 friend who sticks c than a brother.

Closes (Close[1])
Pr 28:27 but he who c his eyes to them
Lk 13:25 of the house gets up and c the door,

Closest (Close[2])
Dt 13: 6 or your c friend secretly entices you
Est 1:14 were c to the king—Carshena,
Ps 88: 8 You have taken from me my c friends
88:18 me; the darkness is my c friend.

Closing (Close[1])
Lev 23:36 the c assembly; do no regular work.
1Sa 23:26 As Saul and his forces were c in on
Ps 77: 4 You kept my eyes from c; I was too
Eze 21:14 c in on them from every side.

Cloth (Cloths)
Ex 28:31 of the ephod entirely of blue c,
39:22 of blue c—the work of a weaver—
Lev 11:32 made of wood, c, hide or sackcloth.
Nu 4: 6 spread a c of solid blue over that
4: 7 a blue c and put on it the plates,
4: 8 they are to spread a scarlet c,
4: 9 "They are to take a blue c and cover
4:11 altar they are to spread a blue c
4:12 wrap them in a blue c, cover that
4:13 altar and spread a purple c over it.
Dt 22:17 the c before the elders of the town,
1Sa 21: 9 is wrapped in a c behind the ephod.
2Ki 8:15 the next day he took a thick c,
Isa 19:10 The workers in c will be dejected,
30:22 like a menstrual c and say to them,
Eze 16:13 and costly fabric and embroidered c.
Mt 9:16 "No-one sews a patch of unshrunk c
27:59 body, wrapped it in a clean linen c,
Mk 2:21 "No-one sews a patch of unshrunk c
15:46 Joseph bought some linen c, took
Lk 19:20 kept it laid away in a piece of c.
23:53 wrapped it in linen c and placed it
Jn 11:44 of linen, and a c around his face.
Jn 20: 7 well as the burial c that had been
20: 7 The c was folded up by itself,
Ac 16:14 a dealer in purple c from the city
Rev 18:12 purple, silk and scarlet c; every

Clothe (Clothed, Clothes, Clothing)
Job 10:11 c me with skin and flesh and knit me
39:19 or c his neck with a flowing mane?
40:10 c yourself in honour and majesty.
Ps 45: 3 c yourself with splendour and majesty
73: 6 they c themselves with violence.
132:16 I will c her priests with salvation,
132:18 I will c his enemies with shame, but
Isa 22:21 I will c him with your robe and
50: 3 I c the sky with darkness and make
51: 9 Awake, awake! C yourself with
52: 1 Awake, awake, O Zion, c yourself
58: 7 to c him, and not to turn away from
Eze 34: 3 You eat the curds, c yourselves with
Mt 6:30 will he not much more c you,
25:38 in, or needing clothes and c you?
25:43 I needed clothes and you did not c me
Lk 12:28 will he c you, O you of little faith!
Ro 13:14 Rather, c yourselves with the Lord
1Co 15:53 For the perishable must c itself
Col 3:12 c yourselves with compassion,
1Pe 5: 5 c yourselves with humility towards

Clothed (Clothe)
Ge 3:21 for Adam and his wife and c them.
Lev 8: 7 c him with the robe and put the ephod
2Sa 1:24 weep for Saul, who c you in scarlet
1Ch 15:27 Now David was c in a robe of fine
21:16 c in sackcloth, fell face down.
2Ch 6:41 O LORD God, be c with salvation,
28:15 plunder they c all who were naked.
Est 4: 2 because no-one c in sackcloth was
Job 7: 5 My body is c with worms and scabs,
8:22 Your enemies will be c in shame, and
Ps 30:11 my sackcloth and c me with joy,
35:26 me be c with shame and disgrace.
65:12 the hills are c with gladness.
104: 1 are c with splendour and majesty.
109:29 My accusers will be c with disgrace
132: 9 May your priests be c with
Pr 31:21 for all of them are c in scarlet.
31:22 she is c in fine linen and purple.
31:25 She is c with strength and dignity;
Ecc 9: 8 Always be c in white, and always

Isa 61:10 For he has c me with garments of
Eze 7:18 They will put on sackcloth and be c
7:27 the prince will be c with despair,
9: 2 With them was a man c in linen who
9: 3 LORD called to the man c in linen
10: 2 The LORD said to the man c in linen,
16:10 I c you with an embroidered dress
23: 6 c in blue, governors and commanders,
26:16 C with terror, they will sit on the
31:15 Because of it I c Lebanon with gloom,
Da 5: 7 will be c in purple and have a gold
5:16 you will be c in purple and have a
5:29 Daniel was c in purple, a gold
12: 6 said to the man c in linen, who was
12: 7 The man c in linen, who was above
Zec 3: 5 clean turban on his head and c him,
6:13 and he will be c with majesty and
Mt 25:36 I needed clothes and you c me, I was
Lk 24:49 been c with power from on high."
Jn 19: 2 They c him in a purple robe
1Co 15:54 the perishable has been c with the
2Co 5: 2 Meanwhile we groan, longing to be c
5: 3 when we are c, we will not be found
5: 4 to be c with our heavenly dwelling,
Gal 3:27 Christ have c yourselves with Christ.
Rev 11: 3 for 1,260 days, c in sackcloth."
12: 1 in heaven: a woman c with the sun,

Clothes (Clothe)

Ge 27:15 Rebekah took the best c of Esau her
27:27 When Isaac caught the smell of his c,
28:20 give me food to eat and c to wear
35: 2 purify yourselves and change your c.
37:29 Joseph was not there, he tore his c.
37:34 Jacob tore his c, put on sackcloth
38:14 she took off her widow's c, covered
38:19 veil and put on her widow's c again.
41:14 When he had shaved and changed his c,
44:13 At this, they tore their c. Then
45:22 of silver and five sets of c.
Ex 19:10 and tomorrow. Make them wash their c
19:14 them, and they washed their c.
28:41 After you put these c on your
Lev 6:10 shall then put on his linen c,
6:11 he is to take off these c and put on
10: 6 and do not tear your c, or you will
11:25 of their carcasses must wash his c,
11:28 up their carcasses must wash his c,
11:40 some of the carcass must wash his c,
11:40 picks up the carcass must wash his c,
13: 6 wash his c, and he will be clean.
13:34 wash his c, and he will be clean.
13:45 infectious disease must wear torn c,
14: 8 to be cleansed must wash his c,
14: 9 He must wash his c and bathe himself
14:47 eats in the house must wash his c.
15: 5 wash his c and bathe with water,
15: 6 wash his c and bathe with water,
15: 7 wash his c and bathe with water,
15: 8 that person must wash his c and
15:10 wash his c and bathe with water,
15:11 wash his c and bathe with water,
15:13 he must was his c and bathe himself
15:21 wash his c and bathe with water,
15:22 wash his c and bathe with water,
15:27 wash his c and bathe with water,
16:26 must wash his c and bathe himself
16:28 must wash his c and bathe himself
17:15 wash his c and bathe with water,
17:16 if he does not wash his c and bathe
21:10 hair become unkempt or tear his c.
Nu 8: 7 and wash their c, and so purify
8:21 themselves and washed their c.
14: 6 had explored the land, tore their c
19: 7 must wash his c and bathe himself
19: 8 wash his c and bathe with water,
19:10 of the heifer must also wash his c,
19:19 wash his c and bathe with water,
19:21 of cleansing must also wash his c,
31:24 On the seventh day wash your c and
Dt 8: 4 Your c did not wear out and your
21:13 put aside the c she was wearing when
22:11 Do not wear c of wool and linen
29: 5 your c did not wear out, nor did the
Jos 7: 6 Joshua tore his c and fell face down
Jos 9: 5 on their feet and wore old c.
9:13 And our c and sandals are worn out
Jdg 11:35 he saw her, he tore his c and cried,
14:12 linen garments and thirty sets of c.
14:13 linen garments and thirty sets of c.
14:19 gave their c to those who had
17:10 a year, your c and your food."
Ru 3: 3 yourself, and put on your best c.
1Sa 4:12 his c torn and dust on his head.
27: 9 cattle, donkeys and camels, and c.
28: 8 putting on other c, and at night he
2Sa 1: 2 c torn and with dust on his head.
1:11 took hold of their c and tore them.
3:31 "Tear your c and put on sackcloth
12:20 put on lotions and changed his c, he
13:31 The king stood up, tore his c and
13:31 servants stood by with their c torn.
14: 2 Dress in mourning c, and don't use
19:24 trimmed his moustache or washed his c
1Ki 21:27 Ahab heard these words, he tore his c
2Ki 2:12 of his own c and tore them apart.
5:26 or to accept c, olive groves,
7: 8 carried away silver, gold and c, and
18:37 with their c torn, and told him what
19: 1 he tore his c and put on sackcloth
25:29 Jehoiachin put aside his prison c
2Ch 28:15 They provided them with c and
Ne 4:23 took off our c; each had his weapon,
9:21 their c did not wear out nor did
Est 4: 1 he tore his c, put on sackcloth and
4: 4 She sent c for him to put on instead
Job 9:31 so that even my c would detest me.
24: 7 Lacking c, they spend the night
24:10 Lacking c, they go about naked; they
27:16 like dust and c like piles of clay,
37:17 You who swelter in your c when the
Pr 6:27 his lap without his c being burned?
23:21 poor, and drowsiness c them in rags.
Isa 4: 1 our own food and provide our own c;
23:18 LORD, for abundant food and fine c.
32:11 Strip off your c, put sackcloth round
36:22 with their c torn, and told him what
37: 1 he tore his c and put on sackcloth
Jer 2:34 On your c men find the lifeblood of
36:24 no fear, nor did they tear their c.
38:11 He took some old rags and worn-out c
38:12 c under your arms to pad the ropes.
41: 5 torn their c and cut themselves came
52:33 Jehoiachin put aside his prison c
Eze 16:13 your c were of fine linen and costly
16:18 you took your embroidered c to put
16:39 They will strip you of your c and
23:26 They will also strip you of your c
42:14 They are to put on other c before
44:17 they are to wear linen c; they must
44:19 they are to take off the c they have
44:19 and put on other c, so that they do
Da 3:21 trousers, turbans and other c, were
Zep 1: 8 and all those clad in foreign c.
Hag 1: 6 You put on c, but are not warm. You
Zec 3: 3 Now Joshua was dressed in filthy c
3: 4 before him, "Take off his filthy c.
Mt 3: 4 John's c were made of camel's hair,
6:25 and the body more important than c?
6:28 "And why do you worry about c? See
6:30 If that is how God c the grass of
11: 8 to see? A man dressed in fine c? No,
11: 8 wear fine c are in kings' palaces.
17: 2 his c became as white as the light.
22:11 there who was not wearing wedding c.
22:12 get in here without wedding c?'
25:36 I needed c and you clothed me, I was
25:38 you in, or needing c and clothe you?
25:43 I needed c and you did not clothe me,
25:44 or needing c or sick or in prison,
26:65 the high priest tore his c and said,
27:31 the robe and put his own c on him.
27:35 divided up his c by casting lots.
28: 3 and his c were white as snow.
Mk 5:28 she thought, "If I just touch his c,
5:30 crowd and asked "Who touched my c?"
9: 3 His c became dazzling white, whiter
14:63 The high priest tore his c. "Why do
15:20 robe and put his own c on him.
15:24 they crucified him. Dividing up his c
Lk 7:25 to see? A man dressed in fine c? No,
Lk 7:25 those who wear expensive c and
8:27 had not worn c or lived in a house,
9:29 and his c became as bright as a
10:30 They stripped him of his c, beat him
12:23 than food, and the body more than c.
12:28 If that is how God c the grass of
23:34 divided up his c by casting lots.
24: 4 suddenly two men in c that gleamed
Jn 11:44 Take off the grave c and let him go."
13:12 he put on his c and returned to his
19:23 they took his c, dividing them into
Ac 7:58 the witnesses laid their c at the
10:30 a man in shining c stood before
12: 8 the angel said to him, "Put on your c
14:14 they tore their c and rushed out
18: 6 he shook out his c in protest and
22:20 c of those who were killing him.'
1Ti 2: 9 or gold or pearls or expensive c,
Jas 2: 2 wearing a gold ring and fine c,
2: 2 poor man in shabby c also comes in.
2: 3 to the man wearing fine c and say,
2:15 sister is without c and daily food.
5: 2 rotted, and moths have eaten your c.
1Pe 3: 3 of gold jewellery and fine c.
Rev 3: 4 Sardis who have not soiled their c.
3:18 become rich; and white c to wear,
16:15 awake and keeps his c with him,

Clothing (Clothe)

Ge 24:53 and articles of c and gave them to
45:22 To each of them he gave new c, but
Ex 3:22 of silver and gold and for c,
12:34 in kneading troughs wrapped in c.
12:35 of silver and gold and for c.
21:10 of her food, c and marital rights.
Lev 13:47 "If any c is contaminated with
13:47 with mildew—any woollen or linen c,
13:49 if the contamination in the c, or
13:51 if the mildew has spread in the c,
13:52 He must burn up the c, or the woven
13:53 the mildew has not spread in the c,
13:56 the contaminated part out of the c,
13:57 if it reappears in the c, or in the
13:58 The c, or the woven or knitted
13:59 by mildew in woollen or linen c,
14:55 for mildew in c or in a house,
15:17 Any c or leather that has semen on
19:19 c woven of two kinds of material.
Dt 10:18 the alien, giving him food and c.
22: 5 A woman must not wear men's c, nor a
22: 5 nor a man wear women's c, for the
Jos 22: 8 and a great quantity of c—and
Jdg 3:16 to his right thigh under his c.
2Ki 5: 5 shekels of gold and ten sets of c.
5:22 of silver and two sets of c.'"
5:23 in two bags, with two sets of c.
7:15 the whole road strewn with the c
2Ch 20:25 c and also articles of value—more
Job 22: 6 men of their c, leaving them naked.
29:14 I put on righteousness as my c;
30:18 great power God becomes like c to me;
31:19 seen anyone perishing for lack of c,
Ps 22:18 among them and cast lots for my c.
102:26 Like c you will change them and they
Pr 27:26 the lambs will provide you with c,
Isa 3: 7 I have no food or c in my house; do
3:24 instead of fine c, sackcloth;
59: 6 Their cobwebs are useless for c;
63: 3 my garments, and I stained all my c.
Eze 18: 7 hungry and provides c for the naked.
18:16 hungry and provides c for the naked.
Da 7: 9 His c was as white as snow; the hair
Zec 14:14 quantities of gold and silver and c.
Mt 7:15 They come to you in sheep's c, but
Mk 1: 6 John wore c made of camel's hair,
Jn 13: 4 took off his outer c, and wrapped a
19:24 among them and cast lots for my c.
Ac 9:39 showing him the robes and other c
20:33 anyone's silver or gold or c.
1Ti 6: 8 if we have food and c, we will be
Jude :23 the c stained by corrupted flesh.

Cloths (Cloth)

Eze 16: 4 rubbed with salt or wrapped in c.
Lk 2: 7 She wrapped him in c and placed him
2:12 wrapped in c and lying in a manger."

Cloud (Cloudburst, Clouds, *Pillar of cloud*, Thundercloud)

Ex 14:20 Throughout the night the **c** brought
14:24 down from the pillar of fire and **c**
16:10 of the LORD appearing in the **c**.
19: 9 going to come to you in a dense **c**,
19:16 with a thick **c** over the mountain,
24:15 up on the mountain, the **c** covered it,
24:16 For six days the **c** covered the
24:16 called to Moses from within the **c**.
24:18 Moses entered the **c** as he went on up
34: 5 the LORD came down in the **c** and
40:34 the **c** covered the Tent of Meeting,
40:35 because the **c** had settled upon it,
40:36 whenever the **c** lifted from above the
40:37 if the **c** did not lift, they did not
40:38 the **c** of the LORD was over the
40:38 and fire was in the **c** by night, in
Lev 16: 2 in the **c** over the atonement cover.
Nu 9:15 was set up, the **c** covered it.
9:15 the **c** above the tabernacle looked like
9:16 the **c** covered it, and at night it
9:17 Whenever the **c** lifted from above the
9:17 wherever the **c** settled, the
9:18 As long as the **c** stayed over the
9:19 the **c** remained over the tabernacle a
9:20 Sometimes the **c** was over the
9:21 Sometimes the **c** stayed only from
9:21 whenever the **c** lifted, they set out.
9:22 Whether the **c** stayed over the
10:11 the **c** lifted from above the
10:12 until the **c** came to rest in the
10:34 The **c** of the LORD was over them by
11:25 the LORD came down in the **c** and
12:10 the **c** lifted from above the Tent,
14:14 that your **c** stays over them, and
16:42 suddenly the **c** covered it and the
Dt 1:33 in fire by night and in a **c** by day,
5:22 the **c** and the deep darkness; and he
31:15 and the **c** stood over the entrance to
Jdg 20:38 up a great **c** of smoke from the city,
1Ki 8:10 the **c** filled the temple of the LORD.
8:11 their service because of the **c**,
8:12 that he would dwell in a dark **c**;
18:44 "A **c** as small as a man's hand is
2Ch 5:13 of the LORD was filled with a **c**,
5:14 their service because of the **c**,
6: 1 that he would dwell in a dark **c**;
Job 3: 5 may a **c** settle over it; may blackness
7: 9 a **c** vanishes and is gone, so he who
30:15 wind, my safety vanishes like a **c**.
Ps 78:14 He guided them with the **c** by day and
105:39 He spread out a **c** as a covering, and
Pr 16:15 favour is like a rain **c** in spring.
Isa 4: 5 a **c** of smoke by day and a glow of
14:31 all you Philistines! A **c** of smoke
18: 4 a **c** of dew in the heat of harvest."
19: 1 on a swift **c** and is coming to Egypt.
25: 5 is reduced by the shadow of a **c**,
44:22 swept away your offences like a **c**,
Lam 2: 1 of Zion with the **c** of his anger!
3:44 You have covered yourself with a **c**
Eze 1: 4 immense **c** with flashing lightning
8:11 a fragrant **c** of incense was rising.
10: 3 in, and a **c** filled the inner court.
10: 4 The **c** filled the temple, and the
32: 7 I will cover the sun with a **c**,
38: 9 will be like a **c** covering the land.
38:16 Israel like a **c** that covers the land.
Mt 17: 5 a bright **c** enveloped them, and a
17: 5 and a voice from the **c** said, "This
Mk 9: 7 a **c** appeared and enveloped them, and
9: 7 a voice came from the **c**: "This is my
Lk 9:34 While he was speaking, a **c** appeared
9:34 were afraid as they entered the **c**.
9:35 A voice came from the **c**, saying,
12:54 "When you see a **c** rising in the west,
21:27 the Son of Man coming in a **c** with
Ac 1: 9 and a **c** hid him from their sight.
1Co 10: 1 forefathers were all under the **c**
10: 2 into Moses in the **c** and in the sea.
Heb 12: 1 by such a great **c** of witnesses,
Rev 10: 1 He was robed in a **c**, with a rainbow
11:12 And they went up to heaven in a **c**,
14:14 and there before me was a white **c**,
14:14 on the **c** was one "like a son of man"
14:15 to him who was sitting on the **c**,
14:16 he who was seated on the **c** swung his

Cloudburst (Cloud)

Isa 30:30 fire, with **c**, thunderstorm and hail.

Cloudless

2Sa 23: 4 morning at sunrise on a **c** morning,

Clouds (Cloud)

Ge 9:13 I have set my rainbow in the **c**, and
9:14 Whenever I bring **c** over the earth
9:14 and the rainbow appears in the **c**,
9:16 Whenever the rainbow appears in the **c**
Dt 4:11 with black **c** and deep darkness.
33:26 you and on the **c** in his majesty.
Jdg 5: 4 poured, the **c** poured down water.
2Sa 22:10 down; dark **c** were under his feet.
22:12 him—the dark rain **c** of the sky.
1Ki 18:45 Meanwhile, the sky grew black with **c**,
Job 20: 6 heavens and his head touches the **c**,
22:14 Thick **c** veil him, so he does not see
26: 8 He wraps up the waters in his **c**, yet
26: 8 **c** do not burst under their weight.
26: 9 full moon, spreading his **c** over it.
35: 5 gaze at the **c** so high above you.
36:28 the **c** pour down their moisture and
36:29 understand how he spreads out the **c**,
37:11 He loads the **c** with moisture; he
37:13 He brings the **c** to punish men, or to
37:15 Do you know how God controls the **c**
37:16 Do you know how the **c** hang poised,
38: 9 I made the **c** its garment and wrapped
38:34 "Can you raise your voice to the **c**
38:37 Who has the wisdom to count the **c**?
Ps 18: 9 down; dark **c** were under his feet.
18:11 him—the dark rain **c** of the sky.
18:12 brightness of his presence **c** advanced
68: 4 extol him who rides on the **c**—his
77:17 The **c** poured down water, the skies
97: 2 **C** and thick darkness surround him;
104: 3 He makes the **c** his chariot and rides
135: 7 He makes **c** rise from the ends of the
147: 8 He covers the sky with **c**; he supplies
148: 8 lightning and hail, snow and **c**,
Pr 3:20 divided, and the **c** let drop the dew.
8:28 he established the **c** above and fixed
25:14 Like **c** and wind without rain is a
Ecc 11: 3 If **c** are full of water, they pour
11: 4 looks at the **c** will not reap.
12: 2 and the **c** return after the rain;
Isa 5: 6 command the **c** not to rain on it."
5:30 the light will be darkened by the **c**.
14:14 I will ascend above the tops of the **c**
30:27 with burning anger and dense **c** of
45: 8 let the **c** shower it down.
60: 8 "Who are these that fly along like **c**,
Jer 4:13 Look! He advances like the **c**, his
10:13 **c** rise from the ends of the earth.
51: 9 skies, it rises as high as the **c**.'
51:16 **c** rise from the ends of the earth.
Eze 1:28 a rainbow in the **c** on a rainy day,
30: 3 a day of **c**, a time of doom for the
30:18 She will be covered with **c**, and her
34:12 on a day of **c** and darkness.
Da 7:13 of man, coming with the **c** of heaven.
Joel 2: 2 and gloom, a day of **c** and blackness.
Na 1: 3 and **c** are the dust of his feet.
Zep 1:15 and gloom, a day of **c** and blackness,
Zec 10: 1 is the LORD who makes the storm **c**.
Mt 24:30 the Son of Man coming on the **c** of
26:64 One and coming on the **c** of heaven."
Mk 13:26 in **c** with great power and glory.
14:62 One and coming on the **c** of heaven."
1Th 4:17 the **c** to meet the Lord in the air.
Jude :12 They are **c** without rain, blown along
Rev 1: 7 Look, he is coming with the **c**, and

Club (Clubs)

2Sa 23:21 Benaiah went against him with a **c**.
1Ch 11:23 Benaiah went against him with a **c**.
Job 41:29 A **c** seems to him but a piece of
Pr 25:18 Like a **c** or a sword or a sharp arrow
Isa 10: 5 in whose hand is the **c** of my wrath!
10:15 or a **c** brandish him who is not wood!
10:24 and lift up a **c** against you, as Egypt
Jer 51:20 "You are my war **c**, my weapon for

Clubs (Club)

Eze 39: 9 and arrows, the war **c** and spears.
Mt 26:47 large crowd armed with swords and **c**,
26:55 out with swords and **c** to capture me?
Mk 14:43 was a crowd armed with swords and **c**,
14:48 out with swords and **c** to capture me?
Lk 22:52 you have come with swords and **c**?

Clung (Cling)

Ru 1:14 good-bye, but Ruth **c** to her.
2Ki 3: 3 Nevertheless he **c** to the sins of
Lam 1: 9 Her filthiness **c** to her skirts; she

Cluster (Clusters)

Nu 13:23 branch bearing a single **c** of grapes.
13:24 the **c** of grapes the Israelites cut
SS 1:14 My lover is to me a **c** of henna
Isa 65: 8 juice is still found in a **c** of grapes
Mic 7: 1 there is no **c** of grapes to eat,

Clusters (Cluster)

Ge 40:10 and its **c** ripened into grapes.
Dt 32:32 poison, and their **c** with bitterness.
SS 7: 7 and your breasts like **c** of fruit.
7: 8 breasts be like the **c** of the vine,
Rev 14:18 **c** of grapes from the earth's vine,

Clutches

Job 5:15 them from the **c** of the powerful.
6:23 me from the **c** of the ruthless'?
16:11 thrown me into the **c** of the wicked.
Hab 2: 9 on high, to escape the **c** of ruin!
Ac 12:11 rescued me from Herod's **c** and from

Cnidus

Ac 27: 7 and had difficulty arriving off **C**.

Coal (Coals)

2Sa 14: 7 out the only burning **c** I have left,
Isa 6: 6 to me with a live **c** in his hand,

Coals (Coal)

Lev 16:12 **c** from the altar before the LORD
Nu 16:37 scatter the **c** some distance away,
2Sa 22: 9 mouth, burning **c** blazed out of it.
1Ki 19: 6 a cake of bread baked over hot **c**,
Job 41:21 His breath sets **c** ablaze, and flames
Ps 11: 6 On the wicked he will rain fiery **c**
18: 8 mouth, burning **c** blazed out of it.
120: 4 with burning **c** of the broom tree.
140:10 Let burning **c** fall upon them; may
Pr 6:28 Can a man walk on hot **c** without his
25:22 you will heap burning **c** on his head,
Isa 30:14 found for taking **c** from a hearth
44:12 and works with it in the **c**;
44:19 I even baked bread over its **c**,
47:14 Here are no **c** to warm anyone; here
54:16 blacksmith who fans the **c** into flame
Eze 1:13 burning **c** of fire or like torches.
10: 2 Fill your hands with burning **c** from
24:11 set the empty pot on the **c** till it
Jn 21: 9 they saw a fire of burning **c** there
Ro 12:20 will heap burning **c** on his head."

Coarse

Eph 5: 4 foolish talk or **c** joking, which are

Coast (Coastlands, Coastline, Coasts)

Nu 34: 6 "Your western boundary will be the **c**
Dt 1: 7 in the Negev and along the **c**, to the
Jos 5: 1 all the Canaanite kings along the **c**
9: 1 along the entire **c** of the Great Sea
Jdg 5:17 on the **c** and stayed in his coves.
2Ch 8:17 Geber and Elath on the **c** of Edom.
Isa 20: 6 people who live on this **c** will say,
Jer 47: 7 it to attack Ashkelon and the **c**?"
Eze 25:16 destroy those remaining along the **c**.
26:16 all the princes of the **c** will step

Lk 6:17 and from the c of Tyre and Sidon,
Ac 17:14 immediately sent Paul to the c,
27: 2 along the c of the province of Asia,
27: 5 off the c of Cilicia and Pamphylia,
27: 8 We moved along the c with difficulty

Coastlands (Coast)
Jer 25:22 the kings of the c across the sea;
31:10 O nations; proclaim it in distant c:
Eze 26:15 c tremble at the sound of your fall,
26:18 Now the c tremble on the day of your
27:15 and many c were your customers; they
27:35 All who live in the c are appalled
39: 6 those who live in safety in the c,
Da 11:18 he will turn his attention to the c
11:30 Ships of the western c will oppose

Coastline (Coast)
Jos 15:12 The western boundary is the c of the
15:47 of Egypt and the c of the Great Sea.

Coasts (Coast)
Jer 2:10 Cross over to the c of Kittim and
47: 4 the remnant from the c of Caphtor.
Eze 27: 3 merchant of peoples on many c, 'This
27: 6 of cypress wood from the c of Cyprus
27: 7 and purple from the c of Elishah.

Coat (Coated, Coating, Coats)
Ge 6:14 and c it with pitch inside and out.
Dt 27: 2 stones and c them with plaster.
27: 4 you today, and c them with plaster.
1Sa 17: 5 wore a c of scale armour of bronze
17:38 He put a c of armour on him and a
Job 41:13 Who can strip off his outer c? Who

Coated (Coat)
Ex 2: 3 for him and c it with tar and pitch.

Coating (Coat)
Pr 26:23 Like a c of glaze over earthenware

Coats (Coat)
2Ch 26:14 spears, helmets, c of armour, bows

Coax
Jdg 14:15 "C your husband into explaining the

Cobra (Cobras)
Ps 58: 4 of a c that has stopped its ears,
91:13 will tread upon the lion and the c;
Isa 11: 8 will play near the hole of the c,

Cobras (Cobra)
Dt 32:33 of serpents, the deadly poison of c.

Cobwebs (Web)
Isa 59: 6 Their c are useless for clothing;

Cock
Pr 30:31 a strutting c, a he-goat, and a king
Mt 26:34 "this very night, before the c crows,
26:74 the man!" Immediately a c crowed.
26:75 "Before the c crows, you will disown
Mk 13:35 or when the c crows, or at dawn.
14:30 tonight—before the c crows twice
14:72 the c crowed the second time
14:72 "Before the c crows twice you will
Lk 22:34 Peter, before the c crows today,
22:60 as he was speaking, the c crowed.
22:61 "Before the c crows today, you will
Jn 13:38 before the c crows, you will disown
18:27 at that moment a c began to crow.

Cocoon
Job 27:18 house he builds is like a moth's c,

Code
Ro 2:27 even though you have the written c
2:29 by the Spirit, not by the written c.
7: 6 not in the old way of the written c.
Col 2:14 having cancelled the written c, with

Coffin
Ge 50:26 him, he was placed in a c in Egypt.
Lk 7:14 he went up and touched the c, and

Co-heirs (Inherit)
Ro 8:17 heirs of God and c with Christ, if

Cohorts
Job 9:13 the c of Rahab cowered at his feet.

Coiled (Coiling)
2Sa 22: 6 The cords of the grave c around me;
Ps 18: 5 The cords of the grave c around me;

Coiling (Coiled)
Isa 27: 1 Leviathan the c serpent; he will

Coin (Coins)
Mt 17:27 and you will find a four-drachma c.
22:19 Show me the c used for paying the
Mk 12:16 They brought the c, and he asked
Lk 15: 9 with me; I have found my lost c.'

Coins (Coin)
Mt 26:15 counted out for him thirty silver c.
27: 3 returned the thirty silver c to the
27: 6 The chief priests picked up the c
27: 9 "They took the thirty silver c, the
Mk 12:42 put in two very small copper c,
Lk 10:35 The next day he took out two silver c
15: 8 "Or suppose a woman has ten silver c
21: 2 put in two very small copper c.
Jn 2:15 and cattle; he scattered the c of the

Cold
Ge 8:22 seedtime and harvest, c and heat,
31:40 in the daytime and the c at night,
Job 24: 7 to cover themselves in the c.
37: 9 the c from the driving winds.
Pr 25:20 who takes away a garment on a c day,
25:25 Like c water to a weary soul is good
Na 3:17 that settle in the walls on a c day
Zec 14: 6 will be no light, no c or frost.
Mt 10:42 if anyone gives even a cup of c water
24:12 the love of most will grow c,
Jn 18:18 was c, and the servants and officials
Ac 28: 2 us all because it was raining and c.
2Co 11:27 food; I have been c and naked.
Rev 3:15 that you are neither c nor hot.
3:16 neither hot nor c—I am about to

Col-Hozeh
Ne 3:15 C, ruler of the district of Mizpah.
11: 5 Maaseiah son of Baruch, the son of C,

Collapse (Collapsed, Collapses)
Jos 6: 5 will c and the people will go up,
Ps 10:10 His victims are crushed, they c;
Eze 26:18 in the sea are terrified at your c.'
Mt 15:32 hungry, or they may c on the way."
Mk 8: 3 they will c on the way, because some

Collapsed (Collapse)
Jos 6:20 the wall c; so every man charged
Jdg 7:13 that the tent overturned and c."
1Ki 20:30 c on twenty-seven thousand of them.
Job 1:19 It c on them and they are dead, and
Hab 3: 6 crumbled and the age-old hills c.
Lk 6:49 c and its destruction was complete."
Rev 11:13 earthquake and a tenth of the city c.
16:19 and the cities of the nations c.

Collapses (Collapse)
Isa 30:13 that c suddenly, in an instant.
Eze 13:12 the wall c, will people not ask you,
Na 2: 6 are thrown open and the palace c.

Collar
Ex 28:32 There shall be a woven edge like a c
39:23 of the robe like the opening of a c,
Ps 133: 2 beard, down upon the c of his robes.

Collect (Collected, Collecting, Collection, Collections, Collector, Collector's, Collectors, Collects)
Ge 41:35 They should c all the food of these
Nu 3:47 c five shekels for each one,
2Ki 12: 4 "C all the money that is brought as
12: 8 c any more money from the people
2Ch 20:25 that it took three days to c it.
24: 5 and c the money due annually from all
Ne 10:37 it is the Levites who c the tithes
Mt 13:30 First c the weeds and tie them in
17:25 do the kings of the earth c duty
21:34 to the tenants to c his fruit.
Mk 12: 2 to c from them some of the fruit of
Lk 3:13 "Don't c any more than you are
Heb 7: 5 c a tenth from the people—that is,

Collected (Collect)
Ge 41:48 Joseph c all the food produced in
47:14 Joseph c all the money that was to
Nu 3:49 Moses c the redemption money from
3:50 Israelites he c silver weighing
16:39 Eleazar the priest c the bronze
2Ki 12: 4 the LORD—the money c in the census,
22: 4 doorkeepers have c from the people.
2Ch 24:11 and c a great amount of money.
34: 9 had c from the people of Manasseh,
Ecc 12:11 their c sayings like firmly embedded
Zec 14:14 will be c—great quantities of gold
Mt 13:48 they sat down and c the good fish
Lk 19:23 I could have c it with interest?'
Heb 7: 6 yet he c a tenth from Abraham and
7: 8 In the one case, the tenth is c by

Collecting (Collect)
Lev 11:36 however, or a cistern for c water

Collection (Collect)
Isa 57:13 let your c of idols save you!
1Co 16: 1 Now about the c for God's people: Do

Collections (Collect)
1Co 16: 2 I come no c will have to be made.

Collector (Collect)
Da 11:20 "His successor will send out a tax c
Mt 10: 3 Thomas and Matthew the tax c;
18:17 him as you would a pagan or a tax c.
Lk 5:27 Jesus went out and saw a tax c by
18:10 a Pharisee and the other a tax c.
18:11 adulterers—or even like this tax c.
18:13 "But the tax c stood at a distance.
19: 2 was a chief tax c and was wealthy.

Collector's (Collect)
Mt 9: 9 Matthew sitting at the tax c booth.
Mk 2:14 Alphaeus sitting at the tax c booth.

Collectors (Collect)
Mt 5:46 Are not even the tax c doing that?
9:10 house, many tax c and "sinners"
9:11 eat with tax c and 'sinners'?"
11:19 a friend of tax c and "sinners".
17:24 the c of the two-drachma tax came to
21:31 the tax c and prostitutes are
21:32 the tax c and the prostitutes did.
Mk 2:15 many tax c and "sinners" were eating
2:16 eating with the "sinners" and tax c,
2:16 he eat with tax c and 'sinners'?"
Lk 3:12 Tax c also came to be baptised.
5:29 tax c and others were eating with
5:30 and drink with tax c and 'sinners'?"
7:29 All the people, even the tax c, when
7:34 a friend of tax c and "sinners".
15: 1 Now the tax c and "sinners" were all

Collects (Collect)
Heb 7: 9 Levi, who c the tenth, paid the tenth

Colonnade (Column)
1Ki 7: 6 He made a c fifty cubits long and
Jn 10:23 temple area walking in Solomon's C.

Ac 3:11 in the place called Solomon's **C**.
5:12 to meet together in Solomon's **C**.

Colonnades (Column)
Jn 5: 2 is surrounded by five covered **c**.

Colony
Ac 16:12 a Roman **c** and the leading city of

Colosse
City in Phrygia, in Lycus Valley, about 12 miles east of Laodicea. Paul wrote to the church here (Col 1:2), possibly established by Epaphras (Col 1:7; 4:12), and led by Archippus (Col 4:17; Phm 2). Home of Onesimus (Col 4:9).

Col 1: 2 faithful brothers in Christ at **C**:

Coloured (Colourful, Colours, Dark-coloured, Multicoloured)
Pr 7:16 I have covered my bed with **c** linens

Colourful (Coloured)
Jdg 5:30 **c** garments as plunder for Sisera,
5:30 **c** garments embroidered, highly

Colours (Coloured)
1Ch 29: 2 turquoise, stones of various **c**, and
Eze 17: 3 plumage of varied **c** came to Lebanon.

Colt
Ge 49:11 his **c** to the choicest branch; he
Job 11:12 a wild donkey's **c** can be born a man.
Zec 9: 9 on a **c**, the foal of a donkey.
Mt 21: 2 tied there, with her **c** by her.
21: 5 on a **c**, the foal of a donkey.'"
21: 7 They brought the donkey and the **c**,
Mk 11: 2 you will find a **c** tied there, which
11: 4 They went and found a **c** outside in
11: 5 "What are you doing, untying that **c**?
11: 7 they brought the **c** to Jesus and
Lk 19:30 you will find a **c** tied there, which
19:33 they were untying the **c**, its owners
19:33 "Why are you untying the **c**?
19:35 cloaks on the **c** and put Jesus on it.
Jn 12:15 is coming, seated on a donkey's **c**."

Column (Colonnade, Colonnades, Columns)
Jdg 20:40 when the **c** of smoke began to rise
SS 3: 6 from the desert like a **c** of smoke,
Isa 9:18 it rolls upward in a **c** of smoke.

Columns (Column)
1Ki 7: 2 **c** supporting trimmed cedar beams.
7: 3 rested on the **c**—forty-five beams,
Jer 36:23 read three or four **c** of the scroll,
Joel 2:20 with its front **c** going into the
Zep 2:14 the screech owl will roost on her **c**.

Comb (Combed)
Ps 19:10 than honey, than honey from the **c**.
Pr 24:13 honey from the **c** is sweet to your

Combed (Comb)
Isa 19: 9 Those who work with **c** flax will

Combine (Combined)
Heb 4: 2 who heard did not **c** it with faith.

Combined (Combine)
1Co 12:24 But God has **c** the members of the

Comfort (Comforted, Comforter, Comforters, Comforting, Comforts)
Ge 5:29 "He will **c** us in the labour and
37:35 All his sons and daughters came to **c**
Ru 2:13 "You have given me **c** and have spoken
1Ch 7:22 and his relatives came to **c** him.
Job 2:11 and sympathise with him and **c** him.
7:13 I think my bed will **c** me and my
16: 5 **c** from my lips would bring you relief
36:16 to the **c** of your table laden with
Ps 23: 4 your rod and your staff, they **c** me.
71:21 You will increase my honour and **c** me
119:50 My **c** in my suffering is this: Your
119:52 laws, O LORD, and I find **c** in them.
119:76 May your unfailing love be my **c**,
119:82 I say, "When will you **c** me?"
Isa 40: 1 **C**, **c** my people, says your God.
51: 3 The LORD will surely **c** Zion and will
51:19 have come upon you—who can **c** you?
57:18 will guide him and restore **c** to him,
61: 2 of our God, to **c** all who mourn,
66:13 so will I **c** you; and you will be
Jer 16: 7 No-one will offer food to **c** those
31:13 them **c** and joy instead of sorrow.
Lam 1: 2 her lovers there is none to **c** her.
1: 9 astounding; there was none to **c** her.
1:16 No-one is near to **c** me, no-one to
1:17 hands, but there is no-one to **c** her.
1:21 but there is no-one to **c** me.
2:13 that I may **c** you, O Virgin Daughter
Eze 16:54 all you have done in giving them **c**.
Na 3: 7 Where can I find anyone to **c** you?"
Zec 1:17 again **c** Zion and choose Jerusalem.'"
10: 2 that are false, they give **c** in vain.
Lk 6:24 you have already received your **c**.
Jn 11:19 **c** them in the loss of their brother.
1Co 14: 3 strengthening, encouragement and **c**.
2Co 1: 3 of compassion and the God of all **c**,
1: 4 so that we can **c** those in any
1: 4 **c** we ourselves have received from God
1: 5 also through Christ our **c** overflows.
1: 6 it is for your **c** and salvation; if
1: 6 it is for your **c**, which produces in
1: 7 so also you share in our **c**.
2: 7 you ought to forgive and **c** him, so
7: 7 but also by the **c** you had given him.
Php 2: 1 if any **c** from his love, if any
Col 4:11 God, and they have proved a **c** to me.

Comforted (Comfort)
Ge 24:67 Isaac was **c** after his mother's death.
37:35 comfort him, but he refused to be **c**.
2Sa 12:24 David **c** his wife Bathsheba, and he
Job 42:11 They **c** and consoled him over all the
Ps 77: 2 hands and my soul refused to be **c**.
86:17 O LORD, have helped me and **c** me.
Isa 12: 1 has turned away and you have **c** me.
52: 9 for the LORD has **c** his people, he
54:11 lashed by storms and not **c**, I will
66:13 and you will be **c** over Jerusalem."
Jer 31:15 and refusing to be **c**, because her
Mt 2:18 and refusing to be **c**, because they
5: 4 those who mourn, for they will be **c**.
Lk 16:25 he is **c** here and you are in agony.
Ac 20:12 man home alive and were greatly **c**.
2Co 1: 6 if we are **c**, it is for your comfort
7: 6 God, who comforts the downcast, **c** us

Comforter (Comfort)
Ecc 4: 1 the oppressed—and they have no **c**;
4: 1 oppressors—and they have no **c**.
Jer 8:18 O my **C** in sorrow, my heart is faint

Comforters (Comfort)
Job 16: 2 like these; miserable **c** are you all!
Ps 69:20 was none, for **c**, but I found none.

Comforting (Comfort)
Isa 66:11 and be satisfied at her **c** breasts;
Zec 1:13 the LORD spoke kind and **c** words to
Jn 11:31 been with Mary in the house, **c** her,
1Th 2:12 encouraging, **c** and urging you to

Comforts (Comfort)
Job 29:25 I was like one who **c** mourners.
Isa 49:13 For the LORD **c** his people and will
51:12 "I, even I, am he who **c** you. Who are
66:13 a mother **c** her child, so will I
2Co 1: 4 who **c** us in all our troubles, so
7: 6 God, who **c** the downcast, comforted

Command (Commanded, Commander, Commander's, Commander-in-chief, Commanders, Commanding, Commandment, Commandments, Commands, Second-in-command)
Ex 7: 2 You are to say everything I **c** you,
27:20 "**C** the Israelites to bring you clear
34:11 Obey what I **c** you today. I will
38:21 which were recorded at Moses' **c** by
Lev 6: 9 "Give Aaron and his sons this **c**:
10: 1 before the LORD, contrary to his **c**.
24: 2 "**C** the Israelites to bring you clear
Nu 3:39 counted at the LORD's **c** by Moses
4:37 to the LORD's **c** through Moses.
4:41 them according to the LORD's **c**.
4:45 to the LORD's **c** through Moses.
4:49 At the LORD's **c** through Moses, each
5: 2 "**C** the Israelites to send away from
9:18 At the LORD's **c** the Israelites set
9:18 set out, and at his **c** they encamped.
9:20 at the LORD's **c** they would encamp,
9:20 then at his **c** they would set out.
9:23 At the LORD's **c** they encamped, and
9:23 and at the LORD's **c** they set out.
9:23 accordance with his **c** through Moses.
10:13 time, at the LORD's **c** through Moses.
10:14 Nahshon son of Amminadab was in **c**.
10:18 Elizur son of Shedeur was in **c**.
10:22 Elishama son of Ammihud was in **c**.
10:25 Ahiezer son of Ammishaddai was in **c**.
13: 3 at the LORD's **c** Moses sent them out
14:41 "Why are you disobeying the LORD's **c**?
20:24 my **c** at the waters of Meribah.
22:18 go beyond the **c** of the LORD my God.
23:20 I have received a **c** to bless; he has
24:13 to go beyond the **c** of the LORD
27:14 both of you disobeyed my **c** to honour
27:21 At his **c** he and the entire community
27:21 and at his **c** they will come in."
28: 2 "Give this **c** to the Israelites and
31:49 counted the soldiers under our **c**,
33: 2 At the LORD's **c** Moses recorded the
33:38 At the LORD's **c** Aaron the priest
34: 2 "**C** the Israelites and say to them:
35: 2 "**C** the Israelites to give the
36: 5 at the LORD's **c** Moses gave this
Dt 1:26 against the **c** of the LORD your God.
1:43 You rebelled against the LORD's **c**
2:37 in accordance with the **c** of the LORD
4: 2 Do not add to what I **c** you and do
8: 1 Be careful to follow every **c** I am
9:23 But you rebelled against the **c** of
11:28 turn from the way that I **c** you today
12:11 you are to bring everything I **c** you:
12:14 there observe everything I **c** you.
12:32 See that you do all I **c** you; do not
15:11 Therefore I **c** you to be open-handed
15:15 That is why I give you this **c** today.
17: 3 contrary to my **c** has worshipped
18:18 will tell them everything I **c** him.
19: 7 This is why I **c** you to set aside for
19: 9 follow all these laws I **c** you today
24:18 That is why I **c** you to do this.
24:22 That is why I **c** you to do this.
27: 4 as I **c** you today, and coat them with
30: 2 to everything I **c** you today,
30:16 For I **c** you today to love the LORD
31:23 The LORD gave this **c** to Joshua son
31:25 he gave this **c** to the Levites who
32:46 so that you may **c** your children to
Jos 1:13 "Remember the **c** that Moses the
1:18 whatever you may **c** them, will be put
4:16 "**C** the priests carrying the ark of
15:13 In accordance with the LORD's **c** to
17: 4 father, according to the LORD's **c**.
22: 9 the **c** of the LORD through Moses.
Jdg 9:29 If only this people were under my **c**!
1Sa 13:13 "You have not kept the **c** the LORD
13:14 you have not kept the LORD's **c**."
15:24 I violated the LORD's **c** and your

1Sa 16:16 Let our lord c his servants here to
18:13 and gave him c over a thousand men,
2Sa 10:10 under the c of Abishai his brother
18: 2 out—a third under the c of Joab,
20: 7 went out under the c of Abishai.
1Ki 2:43 the LORD and obey the c I gave you?"
5:17 At the king's c they removed from
9: 4 I c and observe my decrees and laws,
11:10 Solomon did not keep the LORD's c.
11:38 If you do whatever I c you and walk
13:21 the c the LORD your God gave you.
16: 9 who had c of half his chariots,
18:36 done all these things at your c.
2Ki 24: 3 to Judah according to the LORD's c,
1Ch 11: 6 up first, and so he received the c.
12: 9 Obadiah the second in c, Eliab the
12:32 all their relatives under their c;
19:11 under the c of Abishai his brother,
21: 6 the king's c was repulsive to him.
21: 7 This c was also evil in the sight of
22:12 when he puts you in c over Israel,
28:21 the people will obey your every c."
2Ch 7:13 or c locusts to devour the land or
7:17 I c, and observe my decrees and laws,
24: 8 At the king's c, a chest was made
26:13 Under their c was an army of 307,500
30: 6 At the king's c, couriers went
35:22 to what Neco had said at God's c
Ezr 6:14 to the c of the God of Israel
Est 1: 8 By the king's c each guest was
1:12 attendants delivered the king's c,
1:15 not obeyed the c of King Xerxes
3: 3 "Why do you disobey the king's c?
3:15 Spurred on by the king's c, the
8:14 out, spurred on by the king's c.
Job 39:27 Does the eagle soar at your c and
Ps 71: 3 always go; give the c to save me,
78:23 Yet he gave a c to the skies above
91:11 For he will c his angels concerning
147:15 He sends his c to the earth; his
Pr 8:29 the waters would not overstep his c,
Pr 13:13 but he who respects a c is rewarded.
Ecc 8: 2 Obey the king's c, I say, because
8: 5 Whoever obeys his c will come to no
Isa 5: 6 c the clouds not to rain on it."
Jer 1: 7 you to and say whatever I c you.
1:17 up and say to them whatever I c you.
7:23 I gave them this c: Obey me, and I
7:23 Walk in all the ways I c you, that it
7:31 something I did not c, nor did it
11: 4 'Obey me and do everything I c you,
19: 5 something I did not c or mention,
26: 2 Tell them everything I c you; do not
35: 6 Jonadab son of Recab gave us this c:
35:14 drink wine and this c has been kept.
35:14 they obey their forefather's c.
35:16 the c their forefather gave them,
35:18 'You have obeyed the c of your
43: 4 c to stay in the land of Judah.
Lam 1:18 yet I rebelled against his c.
Eze 21:22 to give the c to slaughter, to sound
38: 7 about you, and take c of them.
Da 3:22 The king's c was so urgent and the
3:28 defied the king's c and were willing
4:26 The c to leave the stump of the tree
5:29 at Belshazzar's c, Daniel was
6:24 At the king's c, the men who had
Joel 2:11 and mighty are those who obey his c.
Am 6:11 For the LORD has given the c, and he
9: 3 I will c the serpent to bite them.
9: 4 I will c the sword to slay them.
9: 9 "For I will give the c, and I will
Na 1:14 The LORD has given a c concerning
Mt 4: 6 "He will c his angels concerning you,
15: 3 "And why do you break the c of God
19: 7 "Why then," they asked, "did Moses c
Mk 9:25 "I c you, come out of him and never
10: 3 "What did Moses c you?" he replied.
Lk 4:10 "He will c his angels concerning you
Jn 10:18 This c I received from my Father."
12:50 I know that his c leads to eternal
13:34 "A new c I give you: Love one another
14:15 you love me, you will obey what I c.
15:12 My c is this: Love each other as I
15:14 You are my friends if you do what I c
Jn 15:17 This is my c: Love each other.
Ac 1: 4 he gave them this c: "Do not leave
16:18 "In the name of Jesus Christ I c you
19:13 Paul preaches, I c you to come out."
25:23 At the c of Festus, Paul was brought
Ro 5:14 who did not sin by breaking a c,
16:26 by the c of the eternal God,
1Co 7: 6 this as a concession, not as a c.
7:10 To the married I give this c (not I,
7:25 I have no c from the Lord, but I give
14:37 I am writing to you is the Lord's c.
Gal 5:14 law is summed up in a single c:
1Th 4:16 with a loud c, with the voice of the
2Th 3: 4 will continue to do the things we c.
3: 6 we c you, brothers, to keep away
3:12 Such people we c and urge in the
1Ti 1: 1 an apostle of Christ Jesus by the c
1: 3 so that you may c certain men not to
1: 5 The goal of this c is love, which
4:11 C and teach these things.
6:14 to keep this c without spot or blame
6:17 C those who are rich in this present
6:18 C them to do good, to be rich in
Tit 1: 3 to me by the c of God our Saviour,
Heb 11: 3 the universe was formed at God's c,
2Pe 2:21 sacred c that was passed on to them.
3: 2 the c given by our Lord and Saviour
1Jn 2: 7 I am not writing you a new c but an
2: 7 old c is the message you have heard.
2: 8 Yet I am writing you a new c; its
3:23 this is his c: to believe in the
4:21 he has given us this c: Whoever
2Jn : 5 I am not writing you a new c but one
: 6 his c is that you walk in love.
Rev 3:10 Since you have kept my c to endure

Commanded (Command, *As the LORD commanded*)

Ge 2:16 the LORD God c the man, "You are
3:11 tree from which I c you not to eat?"
3:17 from the tree about which I c you,
6:22 Noah did everything just as God c
7: 5 Noah did all that the LORD c him.
7: 9 entered the ark, as God had c Noah.
7:16 living thing, as God had c Noah.
21: 4 circumcised him, as God c him.
28: 1 for Jacob and blessed him and c him:
28: 6 that when he blessed him he c him,
45:21 as Pharaoh had c, and he also gave
50:12 Jacob's sons did as he had c them:
Ex 4:28 signs he had c him to perform.
6:13 and he c them to bring the Israelites
7:20 Aaron did just as the LORD had c.
12:28 what the LORD c Moses and Aaron.
12:50 what the LORD had c Moses and Aaron.
16:16 This is what the LORD has c: 'Each
16:23 "This is what the LORD c: 'Tomorrow
16:24 as Moses c, and it did not stink or
16:32 "This is what the LORD has c: 'Take
16:34 the LORD c Moses, Aaron put the
19: 7 words the LORD had c him to speak.
23:15 made without yeast, as I c you.
29:35 his sons everything I have c you,
31: 6 to make everything I have c you:
31:11 are to make them just as I c you."
32: 8 to turn away from what I c them
32:28 The Levites did as Moses c, and that
34: 4 as the LORD had c him; and he carried
34:18 made without yeast, as I c you.
34:34 the Israelites what he had been c,
35: 1 the things the LORD has c you to do:
35: 4 "This is what the LORD has c
35:10 and make everything the LORD has c:
35:29 LORD through Moses had c them to do.
36: 1 do the work just as the LORD has c."
36: 5 the work the LORD c to be done."
38:22 made everything the LORD c Moses;
39:42 work just as the LORD had c Moses.
39:43 had done it just as the LORD had c.
Lev 7:36 the LORD c that the Israelites give
7:38 on the day he c the Israelites
8: 5 is what the LORD has c to be done."
8:31 as I c, saying, 'Aaron and his sons
Lev 8:34 What has been done today was c by
8:35 for that is what I have been c."
8:36 everything the LORD c through Moses.
9: 5 They took the things Moses c to the
9: 6 "This is what the LORD has c you to
9: 7 for them, as the LORD has c."
9:21 LORD as a wave offering, as Moses c.
10:13 LORD by fire; for so I have been c.
10:15 your children, as the LORD has c."
10:18 goat in the sanctuary area, as I c."
17: 2 them: 'This is what the LORD has c:
Nu 2:34 did everything the LORD c Moses;
3:16 Moses counted them, as he was c by
3:51 as he was c by the word of the LORD.
19: 2 of the law that the LORD has c:
20: 9 LORD's presence, just as he c him.
29:40 Israelites all that the LORD c him.
34:13 Moses c the Israelites: "Assign this
34:29 These are the men the LORD c to
36: 2 They said, "When the LORD c my lord
Dt 1: 3 the LORD had c him concerning them.
1:19 Then, as the LORD our God c us, we
1:41 and fight, as the LORD our God c us.
3:18 I c you at that time: "The LORD your
3:21 At that time I c Joshua: "You have
4: 5 and laws as the LORD my God c me,
4:13 the Ten Commandments, which he c you
5:12 as the LORD your God has c you.
5:15 c you to observe the Sabbath day.
5:16 as the LORD your God has c you, so
5:32 do what the LORD your God has c you;
5:33 that the LORD your God has c you,
6:20 laws the LORD our God has c you?"
6:24 The LORD c us to obey all these
6:25 as he has c us, that will be our
9:12 away quickly from what I c them
9:16 the way that the LORD had c you.
12:21 as I have c you, and in your own
13: 5 the LORD your God c you to follow.
18:20 anything I have not c him to say,
20:17 the LORD your God has c you.
24: 8 follow carefully what I have c them.
26:13 the widow, according to all you c.
26:14 God; I have done everything you c me.
27: 1 Moses and the elders of Israel c the
27:11 On the same day Moses c the people:
29: 1 covenant the LORD c Moses to make
31: 5 do to them all that I have c you.
31:10 Moses c them: "At the end of every
31:29 to turn from the way I have c you.
34: 9 and did what the LORD had c Moses.
Jos 1: 9 Have I not c you? Be strong and
1:16 "Whatever you have c us we will do,
4: 8 the Israelites did as Joshua c them.
4:10 had c Joshua was done by the people,
4:17 Joshua c the priests, "Come up out
6:10 Joshua had c the people, "Do not
6:16 Joshua c the people, "Shout! For the
7:11 my covenant, which I c them to keep.
8: 8 Do what the LORD has c. See to it;
8:31 Moses the servant of the LORD had c
8:33 had formerly c when he gave
8:35 not a word of all that Moses had c
9:24 LORD your God had c his servant Moses
10:40 the LORD, the God of Israel, had c.
11:12 Moses the servant of the LORD had c.
11:15 so Moses c Joshua, and Joshua did it;
11:15 undone of all that the LORD c Moses.
11:20 mercy, as the LORD had c Moses.
14: 2 as the LORD had c through Moses.
14: 5 land, just as the LORD had c Moses.
17: 4 "The LORD c Moses to give us an
19:50 the LORD had c. They gave him the
21: 2 "The LORD c through Moses that you
21: 3 So, as the LORD had c, the Israelites
21: 8 as the LORD had c through Moses.
22: 2 Moses the servant of the LORD c,
22: 2 have obeyed me in everything I c.
23:16 which he c you, and go and serve
Jdg 13:14 She must do everything I have c her."
2Sa 7: 7 I c to shepherd my people Israel,
18: 5 The king c Joab, Abishai and Ittai,
18:12 In our hearing the king c you and
21:14 and did everything the king c.
24:19 David went up, as the LORD had c

1Ki 2:31 the king c Benaiah, "Do as he says.
11:11 which I c you, I will most certainly
13: 9 For I was c by the word of the LORD:
17: 9 I have c a widow in that place to
18:40 Elijah c them, "Seize the prophets
2Ki 7:14 He c the drivers, "Go and find out
11: 5 He c them, saying, "This is what you
14: 6 the Law of Moses where the LORD c:
17:13 Law that I c your fathers to obey
17:35 he c them: "Do not worship any other
18:12 Moses the servant of the LORD c.
18:36 the king had c, "Do not answer him.
21: 8 careful to do everything I c them
1Ch 6:49 that Moses the servant of God had c.
14:16 David did as God c him, and they
15:15 as Moses had c in accordance with
16:15 the word he c, for a thousand
17: 6 whom I c to shepherd my people,
24:19 LORD, the God of Israel, had c him.
2Ch 8:13 offerings c by Moses for Sabbaths,
8:18 Hiram sent him ships c by his own
14: 4 He c Judah to seek the LORD, the God
25: 4 where the LORD c: "Fathers shall not
29:21 The king c the priests, the
29:25 c by the LORD through his prophets.
33: 8 I c them concerning all the laws,
35: 6 doing what the LORD c through Moses."
Ezr 4: 3 Cyrus, the king of Persia, c us."
Ne 8: 1 which the LORD had c for Israel.
8:14 which the LORD had c through Moses,
13:22 I c the Levites to purify themselves
Est 1:10 he c the seven eunuchs who served
1:17 'King Xerxes c Queen Vashti to be
3: 2 the king had c this concerning him.
6:10 "Go at once," the king c Haman. "Get
9: 1 c by the king was to be carried out.
9:14 the king c that this be done. An
Ps 33: 9 came to be; he c, and it stood firm
78: 5 which he c our forefathers to teach
105: 8 the word he c, for a thousand
106:34 the peoples as the LORD had c them,
148: 5 LORD, for he c and they were created.
Isa 13: 3 I have c my holy ones; I have
36:21 the king had c, "Do not answer him.
Jer 11: 4 the terms I c your forefathers when
11: 8 the covenant I had c them to follow
17:22 day holy, as I c your forefathers.
26: 8 everything the LORD had c him to say,
32:23 did not do what you c them to do.
32:35 though I never c, nor did it enter
35: 8 Jonadab son of Recab c us.
35:10 our forefather Jonadab c us.
36:26 Instead, the king c Jerahmeel, a son
38:10 the king c Ebed-Melech the Cushite,
47: 7 how can it rest when the LORD has c
50:21 "Do everything I have c you.
Eze 9:11 word, saying, "I have done as you c.
10: 6 the LORD c the man in linen, "Take
12: 7 I did as I was c. During the day I
24:18 next morning I did as I had been c.
37: 7 I prophesied as I was c. And as I
37:10 I prophesied as he c me, and breath
Da 3: 4 "This is what you are c to do, O
3:20 c some of the strongest soldiers in
4: 6 I c that all the wise men of Babylon
Am 2:12 and c the prophets not to prophesy.
Jnh 2:10 the LORD c the fish, and it vomited
Zec 1: 6 which I c my servants the prophets,
Mt 1:24 c him and took Mary home as his wife.
8: 4 Moses c, as a testimony to them."
28:20 to obey everything I have c you.
Mk 1:44 that Moses c for your cleansing,
7:36 Jesus c them not to tell anyone. But
Lk 5:14 that Moses c for your cleansing,
8:29 For Jesus had c the evil spirit to
Jn 8: 5 In the Law Moses c us to stone such
12:49 c me what to say and how to say it.
14:31 I do exactly what my Father has c me.
18:11 Jesus c Peter, "Put your sword away!
Ac 4:18 they called them in again and c them
10:33 the Lord has c you to tell us."
10:42 He c us to preach to the people and
13:47 For this is what the Lord has c us:
16:23 was c to guard them carefully.
1Co 9:14 In the same way, the Lord has c that
Heb 9:20 which God has c you to keep."
Heb 12:20 they could not bear what was c: "If
1Jn 3:23 and to love one another as he c us.
2Jn : 4 the truth, just as the Father c us.

Commander (Command)

Ge 21:22 the c of his forces said to Abraham,
21:32 and Phicol the c of his forces
26:26 and Phicol the c of his forces.
Jos 5:14 "but as c of the army of the LORD
5:15 The c of the LORD's army replied,
Jdg 4: 2 The c of his army was Sisera, who
4: 7 lure Sisera, the c of Jabin's army
11: 6 "Come," they said, "be our c, so we
11:11 made him head and c over them.
1Sa 12: 9 the c of the army of Hazor, and into
14:50 The name of the c of Saul's army was
17:18 Take along these ten cheeses to the c
17:55 he said to Abner, c of the army,
26: 5 the c of the army, had lain down.
2Sa 2: 8 Meanwhile, Abner son of Ner, the c
10:16 c of Hadadezer's army leading them.
10:18 c of their army, and he died there.
19:13 the c of my army in place of Joab.'"
23:19 He became their c, even though he was
1Ki 1:19 Abiathar the priest and Joab the c
2:32 Abner son of Ner, c of Israel's army,
2:32 Amasa son of Jether, c of Judah's
11:15 Joab the c of the army, who had gone
11:21 Joab the c of the army was also dead.
16:16 proclaimed Omri, the c of the army
2Ki 4:13 to the king or the c of the army?'"
5: 1 Now Naaman was c of the army of the
9: 5 "I have a message for you, c," he
9: 5 "For you, c," he replied.
18:17 king of Assyria sent his supreme c,
18:17 his chief officer and his field c
18:19 The field c said to them, "Tell
18:26 Shebna and Joah said to the field c,
18:27 the c replied, "Was it only to your
18:28 the c stood and called out in Hebrew:
18:37 told him what the field c had said.
19: 4 hear all the words of the field c,
19: 8 the field c heard that the king of
25: 8 Nebuzaradan c of the imperial guard,
25:10 under the c of the imperial guard,
25:11 Nebuzaradan the c of the guard
25:12 the c left behind some of the
25:15 The c of the imperial guard took
25:18 The c of the guard took as prisoners
25:20 Nebuzaradan the c took them all and
1Ch 11:21 above the Three and became their c,
19:16 c of Hadadezer's army leading them.
19:18 killed Shophach the c of their army.
27: 5 The third army c, for the third
27: 8 was the c Shamhuth the Izrahite.
27:34 Joab was the c of the royal army.
2Ch 17:14 Adnah the c, with 300,000 fighting
17:15 next, Jehohanan the c, with 280,000;
Ne 7: 2 with Hananiah the c of the citadel,
Pr 6: 7 has no c, no overseer or ruler,
Isa 20: 1 In the year that the supreme c, sent
36: 2 the king of Assyria sent his field c
36: 2 When the c stopped at the aqueduct
36: 4 The field c said to them, "Tell
36:11 Shebna and Joah said to the field c,
36:12 the c replied, "Was it only to your
36:13 the c stood and called out in Hebrew,
36:22 told him what the field c had said.
37: 4 will hear the words of the field c,
37: 8 the field c heard that the king of
55: 4 a leader and c of the peoples.
Jer 39: 9 Nebuzaradan c of the imperial guard
39:10 Nebuzaradan the c of the guard left
39:11 Nebuzaradan c of the imperial guard:
39:13 Nebuzaradan the c of the guard,
40: 1 Nebuzaradan c of the imperial guard
40: 2 the c of the guard found Jeremiah,
40: 5 Then the c gave him provisions and
41:10 Nebuzaradan c of the imperial guard
43: 6 Nebuzaradan c of the imperial guard
51:27 Appoint a c against her; send up
52:12 Nebuzaradan c of the imperial guard,
52:14 The whole Babylonian army under the c
52:15 Nebuzaradan the c of the guard
52:19 The c of the imperial guard took
52:24 The c of the guard took as prisoners
Jer 52:26 Nebuzaradan the c took them all and
52:30 the c of the imperial guard.
Da 2:14 Arioch, the c of the king's guard,
11:18 but a c will put an end to his
Jn 18:12 the detachment of soldiers with its c
Ac 21:31 news reached the c of the Roman
21:32 When the rioters saw the c and his
21:33 The c came up and arrested him and
21:34 and since the c could not get at the
21:37 he asked the c, "May I say something
22:24 the c ordered Paul to be taken into
22:26 he went to the c and reported it.
22:27 The c went to Paul and asked, "Tell
22:28 the c said, "I had to pay a big
22:29 The c himself was alarmed when he
22:30 The next day, since the c wanted to
23:10 the c was afraid Paul would be torn
23:15 the Sanhedrin petition the c to
23:17 "Take this young man to the c; he has
23:18 he took him to the c. The centurion
23:19 The c took the young man by the hand,
23:22 The c dismissed the young man and
24:22 "When Lysias the c comes," he said,

Commander's (Command)

Jdg 5:14 Zebulun those who bear a c staff.
Ac 21:40 Having received the c permission,

Commander-in-chief (Command)

1Ki 4: 4 Benaiah son of Jehoiada—c; Zadok
1Ch 11: 6 on the Jebusites will become c.

Commanders (Command)

Nu 31:14 the c of thousands and c of hundreds
31:48 the c of thousands and c of hundreds
31:52 c of thousands and c of hundreds
31:54 c of thousands and c of hundreds
Dt 1:15 over you—as c of thousands,
20: 9 army, they shall appoint c over it.
Jos 10:24 to the army c who had come with him,
1Sa 8:12 be c of thousands and c of fifties,
18:30 The Philistine c continued to go out
22: 7 c of thousands and c of hundreds?
29: 3 The c of the Philistines asked,
29: 4 the Philistine c were angry with him
29: 9 the Philistine c have said, 'He must
2Sa 18: 1 c of thousands and c of hundreds.
18: 5 concerning Absalom to each of the c.
19: 6 c and their men mean nothing to you.
24: 2 the king said to Joab and the army c
24: 4 overruled Joab and the army c; so
1Ki 1:25 the c of the army and Abiathar the
2: 5 did to the two c of Israel's armies,
9:22 c of his chariots and charioteers.
14:27 assigned these to the c of the guard
15:20 sent the c of his forces against the
20:14 officers of the provincial c will do
20:15 officers of the provincial c, 232 men
20:17 officers of the provincial c went out
20:19 officers of the provincial c marched
22:31 ordered his thirty-two chariot c,
22:32 the chariot c saw Jehoshaphat, they
22:33 the chariot c saw that he was not
2Ki 8:21 surrounded him and his chariot c,
11: 4 for the c of units of a hundred,
11: 9 The c of units of a hundred did just
11:10 he gave the c the spears and shields
11:15 Jehoiada the priest ordered the c of
11:19 He took with him the c of hundreds,
1Ch 12:14 These Gadites were army c; the least
12:21 and they were c in his army.
13: 1 c of thousands and c of hundreds.
15:25 elders of Israel and the c of units
21: 2 said to Joab and the c of the army,
25: 1 together with the c of the army,
26:26 c of thousands and c of hundreds,
26:26 hundreds, and by the other army c.
27: 1 c of thousands and c of hundreds,
28: 1 the c of the divisions in the
28: 1 the c of thousands and c of hundreds,
29: 6 the c of thousands and c of hundreds,

2Ch 1: 2 c of thousands and c of hundreds,
8: 9 c of his captains, and c of his
11:11 their defences and put c in them,
12:10 assigned these to the c of the guard
16: 4 sent the c of his forces against the
17:14 from Judah, c of units of 1,000:
18:30 of Aram had ordered his chariot c,
18:31 the chariot c saw Jehoshaphat, they
18:32 for when the chariot c saw that he
21: 9 surrounded him and his chariot c,
23: 1 He made a covenant with the c of
23: 9 he gave the c of units of a hundred
23:14 Jehoiada the priest sent out the c
23:20 He took with him the c of hundreds,
25: 5 to c of thousands and c of hundreds
33:11 the army c of the king of Assyria,
33:14 He stationed military c in all the
Job 39:25 the shout of c and the battle cry.
Isa 10: 8 'Are not my c all kings?' he says.
31: 9 battle standard their c will panic,"
Eze 23: 6 clothed in blue, governors and c,
23:12 the Assyrians—governors and c,
23:23 all of them governors and c, chariot
Da 11: 5 but one of his c will become even
Mk 6:21 for his high officials and military c

Commanding (Command)

Dt 30:11 Now what I am c you today is not too
Ezr 4: 8 Rehum the c officer and Shimshai the
4: 9 Rehum the c officer and Shimshai the
4:17 this reply: To Rehum the c officer,
Ac 23: 3 the law by c that I be struck!"
2Co 8: 8 I am not c you, but I want to test
2Ti 2: 4 wants to please his c officer.

Commandment (Command)

Jos 22: 5 be very careful to keep the c and
Mt 22:36 "Teacher, which is the greatest c in
22:38 This is the first and greatest c.
Mk 12:31 There is no c greater than these."
Lk 23:56 the Sabbath in obedience to the c.
Ro 7: 8 the opportunity afforded by the c,
7: 9 when the c came, sin sprang to life
7:10 I found that the very c that was
7:11 the opportunity afforded by the c,
7:11 and through the c put me to death.
7:12 then, the law is holy, and the c is
7:13 so that through the c sin might
13: 9 and whatever other c there may be,
Eph 6: 2 is the first c with a promise—
Heb 9:19 Moses had proclaimed every c of the

Commandments (Command)

Ex 20: 6 of those who love me and keep my c.
34:28 words of the covenant—the Ten C.
Dt 4:13 the Ten C, which he commanded you to
5:10 of those who love me and keep my c.
5:22 These are the c the LORD proclaimed
6: 6 These c that I give you today are to
9:10 were all the c the LORD proclaimed
10: 4 the Ten C he had proclaimed to you
Ecc 12:13 Fear God and keep his c,
Mt 5:19 breaks one of the least of these c
19:17 you want to enter life, obey the c."
22:40 the Prophets hang on these two c."
Mk 10:19 You know the c: 'Do not murder, do
12:28 "of all the c, which is the most
Lk 1: 6 Lord's c and regulations blamelessly.
18:20 You know the c: 'Do not commit
Ro 13: 9 The c, "Do not commit adultery," "Do
Eph 2:15 the law with its c and regulations.
Rev 12:17 those who obey God's c and hold to
14:12 saints who obey God's c and remain

Commands (Command)

Ge 26: 5 my c, my decrees and my laws."
Ex 8:27 to the LORD our God, as he c us."
15:26 if you pay attention to his c and
16:28 to keep my c and my instructions?
18:23 If you do this and God so c, you
24:12 with the law and c I have written
25:22 you all my c for the Israelites.
34:32 and he gave them all the c the LORD
Lev 4: 2 forbidden in any of the LORD's c—
4:13 is forbidden in any of the LORD's c,
4:22 in any of the c of the LORD his God,
4:27 any of the LORD's c, he is guilty.
5:17 is forbidden in any of the LORD's c,
22:31 "Keep my c and follow them. I am the
26: 3 and are careful to obey my c,
26:14 to me and carry out all these c,
26:15 fail to carry out all my c and so
27:34 These are the c the LORD gave Moses
Nu 9: 8 out what the LORD c concerning you."
15:22 any of these c the LORD gave Moses—
15:23 any of the LORD's c to you through
15:31 the LORD's word and broken his c,
15:39 will remember all the c of the LORD,
15:40 you will remember to obey all my c
30: 1 of Israel: "This is what the LORD c:
32:25 your servants will do as our lord c.
36: 6 This is what the LORD c for
36:13 These are the c and regulations the
Dt 4: 2 but keep the c of the LORD your God
4:40 Keep his decrees and c, which I am
5:29 to fear me and keep all my c always,
5:31 me so that I may give you all the c,
6: 1 These are the c, decrees and laws
6: 2 his decrees and c that I give you,
6:17 Be sure to keep the c of the LORD
7: 9 those who love him and keep his c.
7:11 Therefore, take care to follow the c,
8: 2 whether or not you would keep his c.
8: 6 Observe the c of the LORD your God,
8:11 failing to observe his c, his laws
10:13 to observe the LORD's c and decrees
11: 1 decrees, his laws and his c always.
11: 8 Observe therefore all the c I am
11:13 if you faithfully obey the c I am
11:22 If you carefully observe all these c
11:27 if you obey the c of the LORD
11:28 if you disobey the c of the LORD
13: 4 Keep his c and obey him; serve him
13:18 keeping all his c that I am giving
15: 5 all these c I am giving you today.
26:13 have not turned aside from your c
26:16 The LORD your God c you this day to
26:17 will keep his decrees, c and laws,
26:18 and that you are to keep all his c.
27: 1 all these c that I give you today.
27:10 c and decrees that I give you today."
28: 1 all his c that I give you today,
28: 9 if you keep the c of the LORD your
28:13 If you pay attention to the c of the
28:14 Do not turn aside from any of the c
28:15 c and decrees I am giving you today,
28:45 the c and decrees he gave you.
30: 8 all his c I am giving you today.
30:10 keep his c and decrees that are
30:16 and to keep his c, decrees and laws;
Jos 22: 5 to obey his c, to hold fast to him
Jdg 2:17 way of obedience to the LORD's c.
3: 4 they would obey the LORD's c,
4: 6 "The LORD, the God of Israel, c you:
1Sa 12:14 him and do not rebel against his c,
12:15 and if you rebel against his c, his
2Sa 9:11 lord the king c his servant to do.
1Ki 2: 3 and keep his decrees and c, his laws
3:14 obey my statutes and c as David your
6:12 and keep all my c and obey them,
8:58 in all his ways and to keep the c,
8:61 and obey his c, as at this time."
9: 6 do not observe the c and decrees I
11:34 and who observed my c and statutes.
11:38 eyes by keeping my statutes and c,
14: 8 who kept my c and followed me with
15: 5 keep any of the LORD's c all the days
18:18 You have abandoned the LORD's c and
20:24 Remove all the kings from their c
2Ki 17:13 Observe my c and decrees, in
17:16 They forsook all the c of the LORD
17:19 even Judah did not keep the c of the
17:34 the laws and c that the LORD gave
17:37 the laws and c he wrote for you.
18: 6 kept the c the LORD had given Moses.
18:12 They neither listened to the c nor
23: 3 follow the LORD and keep his c,
1Ch 28: 7 in carrying out my c and laws,
28: 8 all the c of the LORD your God,
1Ch 29:19 devotion to keep your c,
2Ch 7:19 forsake the decrees and c I have
8:15 did not deviate from the king's c to
14: 4 fathers, and to obey his laws and c.
17: 4 followed his c rather than the
19:10 c, decrees or ordinances—you are to
24:20 'Why do you disobey the LORD's c?
31:21 in obedience to the law and the c,
34:31 follow the LORD and keep his c,
Ezr 7:11 c and decrees of the LORD for Israel:
9:10 this? For we have disregarded the c
9:14 Shall we again break your c and
10: 3 of those who fear the c of our God.
Ne 1: 5 those who love him and obey his c,
1: 7 We have not obeyed the c, decrees
1: 9 if you return to me and obey my c,
9:13 and decrees and c that are good.
9:14 your holy Sabbath and gave them c,
9:16 and did not obey your c.
9:29 arrogant and disobeyed your c.
9:34 they did not pay attention to your c
10:29 God and to obey carefully all the c,
10:32 responsibility for carrying out the c
12:45 the c of David and his son Solomon.
Job 23:12 I have not departed from the c of
36:10 and c them to repent of their evil.
36:32 and c it to strike its mark.
37:12 earth to do whatever he c them.
Ps 19: 8 The c of the LORD are radiant,
78: 7 his deeds but would keep his c.
89:31 my decrees and fail to keep my c,
112: 1 who finds great delight in his c.
119: 6 to shame when I consider all your c.
119:10 do not let me stray from your c.
119:19 earth; do not hide your c from me.
119:21 cursed and who stray from your c.
119:32 I run in the path of your c, for you
119:35 Direct me in the path of your c, for
119:47 for I delight in your c because I
119:48 I lift up my hands to your c, which
119:60 hasten and not delay to obey your c.
119:66 judgment, for I believe in your c.
119:73 me understanding to learn your c.
119:86 All your c are trustworthy; help me,
119:96 a limit; but your c are boundless.
119:98 Your c make me wiser than my enemies,
119:115 that I may keep the c of my God!
119:127 I love your c more than gold, more
119:131 mouth and pant, longing for your c.
119:143 upon me, but your c are my delight.
119:151 O LORD, and all your c are true.
119:166 O LORD, and I follow your c.
119:172 word, for all your c are righteous.
119:176 for I have not forgotten your c.
Pr 2: 1 words and store up my c within you,
3: 1 but keep my c in your heart,
4: 4 heart; keep my c and you will live.
6:20 My son, keep your father's c and do
6:23 For these c are a lamp, this
7: 1 words and store up my c within you.
7: 2 Keep my c and you will live; guard
10: 8 The wise in heart accept c, but a
Isa 48:18 only you had paid attention to my c,
58: 2 has not forsaken the c of its God.
Jer 7:22 I did not just give them c about
22: 4 are careful to carry out these c,
22: 5 if you do not obey these c, declares
Da 9: 4 all who love him and obey his c,
9: 5 turned away from your c and laws.
Zep 2: 3 of the land, you who do what he c.
Mt 5:19 teaches these c will be called great
Mk 7: 8 You have let go of the c of God and
7: 9 setting aside the c of God in order
Lk 8:25 "Who is this? He c even the winds
Jn 14:21 Whoever has my c and obeys them, he
15:10 If you obey my c, you will remain in
15:10 just as I have obeyed my Father's c
Ac 17:30 c all people everywhere to repent.
1Co 7:19 Keeping God's c is what counts.
Col 2:22 are based on human c and teachings.
Tit 1:14 the c of those who reject the truth.
1Jn 2: 3 come to know him if we obey his c.
2: 4 but does not do what he c is a liar,
3:22 obey his c and do what pleases him.
3:24 Those who obey his c live in him,
5: 2 loving God and carrying out his c.

1Jn 5: 3 This is love for God: to obey his **c**.
5: 3 And his **c** are not burdensome,
2Jn : 6 that we walk in obedience to his **c**.

Commemorate (Commemorated)

Ex 12:14 "This is a day you are to **c**; for the
13: 3 "**C** this day, the day you came out of
Jdg 11:40 to **c** the daughter of Jephthah
2Ch 35:25 singers **c** Josiah in the laments.

Commemorated (Commemorate)

Lev 23:24 assembly **c** with trumpet blasts.

Commend (Commendable, Commended, Commends)

Ps 145: 4 One generation will **c** your works to
Ecc 8:15 I **c** the enjoyment of life, because
Ro 13: 3 do what is right and he will **c** you.
16: 1 I **c** to you our sister Phoebe, a
2Co 3: 1 Are we beginning to **c** ourselves
4: 2 **c** ourselves to every man's conscience
5:12 We are not trying to **c** ourselves to
6: 4 as servants of God we **c** ourselves
10:12 with some who **c** themselves.
1Pe 2:14 wrong and to **c** those who do right.

Commendable (Commend)

1Pe 2:19 For it is **c** if a man bears up under
2:20 you endure it, this is **c** before God.

Commended (Commend)

Ne 11: 2 The people **c** all the men who
Job 29:11 of me, and those who saw me **c** me,
Lk 16: 8 "The master **c** the dishonest manager
Ac 15:40 **c** by the brothers to the grace of the
2Co 12:11 I ought to have been **c** by you, for I
Heb 11: 2 This is what the ancients were **c** for.
11: 4 By faith he was **c** as a righteous man,
11: 5 he was **c** as one who pleased God.
11:39 These were all **c** for their faith,

Commends (Commend)

Pr 15: 2 The tongue of the wise **c** knowledge,
2Co 10:18 For it is not the one who **c** himself
10:18 but the one whom the Lord **c**.

Commission (Commissioned, Commissioners)

Nu 27:19 and **c** him in their presence.
Dt 3:28 **c** Joshua, and encourage and
31:14 Tent of Meeting, where I will **c** him.
Ac 26:12 and **c** of the chief priests.
Col 1:25 the **c** God gave me to present to you

Commissioned (Commission)

Nu 27:23 he laid his hands on him and **c** him,

Commissioners (Commission)

Ge 41:34 Let Pharaoh appoint **c** over the land
Est 2: 3 Let the king appoint **c** in every

Commit (Commits, Committed, Committing)

Ex 20:14 "You shall not **c** adultery.
Dt 5:18 "You shall not **c** adultery.
1Sa 7: 3 and **c** yourselves to the LORD and
1Ki 14:16 and has caused Israel to **c**."
15:26 which he had caused Israel to **c**.
15:30 and had caused Israel to **c**,
15:34 which he had caused Israel to **c**.
16:13 and had caused Israel to **c**,
16:19 and had caused Israel to **c**.
16:26 which he had caused Israel to **c**, so
16:31 **c** the sins of Jeroboam son of Nebat,
2Ki 3: 3 which he had caused Israel to **c**;
10:29 which he had caused Israel to **c**
10:31 which he had caused Israel to **c**.
13: 2 which he had caused Israel to **c**,
13: 6 which he had caused Israel to **c**;
13:11 which he had caused Israel to **c**;
14:24 which he had caused Israel to **c**.
15: 9 which he had caused Israel to **c**.
15:18 which he had caused Israel to **c**.
15:24 which he had caused Israel to **c**.
15:28 which he had caused Israel to **c**.
17:21 and caused them to **c** a great sin.
21:16 sin that he had caused Judah to **c**,
Ezr 9:14 who **c** such detestable practices?
Ne 6:13 that I would **c** a sin by doing this,
Ps 31: 5 Into your hands I **c** my spirit;
37: 5 **C** your way to the LORD; trust in him
Pr 16: 3 **C** to the LORD whatever you do, and
Jer 7: 9 and murder, **c** adultery and perjury,
23:14 They **c** adultery and live a lie.
Eze 16:38 who **c** adultery and who shed blood;
16:51 Samaria did not **c** half the sins you
18: 7 He does not **c** robbery, but gives his
18:16 He does not **c** robbery, but gives his
22: 9 mountain shrines and **c** lewd acts.
22:29 practise extortion and **c** robbery;
23:45 women who **c** adultery and shed blood,
Hos 4:14 when they **c** adultery, because the men
4:15 "Though you **c** adultery, O Israel,
Mt 5:27 it was said, 'Do not **c** adultery.'
19:18 "Do not murder, do not **c** adultery,
Mk 10:19 'Do not murder, do not **c** adultery,
Lk 18:20 'Do not **c** adultery, do not murder,
23:46 into your hands I **c** my spirit.
Ac 20:32 "Now I **c** you to God and to the word
Ro 2:22 that people should not **c** adultery,
2:22 do you **c** adultery? You who abhor
13: 9 The commandments, "Do not **c** adultery,
1Co 10: 8 We should not **c** sexual immorality,
Jas 2:11 For he who said, "Do not **c** adultery,"
2:11 you do not **c** adultery but do **c** murder
1Pe 4:19 should **c** themselves to their faithful
1Jn 5:16 If anyone sees his brother **c** a sin
Rev 2:22 and I will make those who **c** adultery

Commits (Commit)

Lev 5:15 "When a person **c** a violation and
6: 3 **c** any such sin that people may do—
20:10 "If a man **c** adultery with another
Ps 10:14 The victim **c** himself to you; you are
36: 4 he **c** himself to a sinful course
Pr 6:32 a man who **c** adultery lacks judgment;
29:22 and a hot-tempered one **c** many sins.
Ecc 8:12 Although a wicked man **c** a hundred
Eze 18:12 He **c** robbery. He does not return what
18:14 who sees all the sins his father **c**,
18:24 **c** sin and does the same detestable
18:26 from his righteousness and **c** sin,
22:11 In you one man **c** a detestable
Mt 5:32 the divorced woman **c** adultery.
19: 9 marries another woman **c** adultery."
Mk 10:11 woman **c** adultery against her.
10:12 another man, she **c** adultery."
Lk 16:18 marries another woman **c** adultery,
16:18 marries a divorced woman **c** adultery.
1Co 6:18 All other sins a man **c** are outside

Committed (Commit)

Ge 31:36 sin have I **c** that you hunt me down?
50:17 they **c** in treating you so badly.
Ex 32:30 the people, "You have **c** a great sin.
32:31 a great sin these people have **c**!
Lev 4: 3 a sin offering for the sin he has **c**.
4:14 they become aware of the sin they **c**,
4:23 he is made aware of the sin he **c**, he
4:28 he is made aware of the sin he **c**, he
4:28 he **c** a female goat without defect.
4:35 for him for the sin he has **c**,
5: 6 as a penalty for the sin he has **c**,
5:10 for him for the sin he has **c**,
5:13 for any of these sins he has **c**,
5:18 the wrong he has **c** unintentionally,
19:22 before the LORD for the sin he has **c**,
Nu 5: 7 must confess the sin he has **c**. He
12:11 us the sin we have so foolishly **c**.
Dt 9:18 because of all the sin you had **c**,
19:15 any crime or offence he may have **c**.
22:26 she has **c** no sin deserving death.
Jdg 20: 6 because they **c** this lewd and
20:12 awful crime that was **c** among you?
1Sa 14:38 find out what sin has been **c** today.
1Ki 8:50 offences they have **c** against you,
8:61 your hearts must be fully **c** to the
14:16 sins Jeroboam has **c** and has caused
14:22 By the sins they **c** they stirred up
15: 3 He **c** all the sins his father had
15:14 fully **c** to the LORD all his life.
15:30 of the sins Jeroboam had **c** and had
16:13 **c** and had caused Israel to commit,
16:19 of the sins he had **c**, doing evil in
16:19 the sin he had **c** and had caused
2Ki 21:11 "Manasseh king of Judah has **c** these
21:17 including the sin he **c**, are they not
1Ch 16: 7 That day David first **c** to Asaph and
2Ch 15:17 fully **c** to the LORD all his life.
16: 9 whose hearts are fully **c** to him.
34:16 everything that has been **c** to them.
Ne 1: 6 father's house, have **c** against you.
9:18 or when they **c** awful blasphemies.
9:26 to you; they **c** awful blasphemies.
Job 13:23 How many wrongs and sins have I **c**?
Ps 51: T David had **c** adultery with Bathsheba.
Isa 42:19 Who is blind like the one **c** to me,
Jer 2:13 "My people have **c** two sins: They
3: 6 tree and has **c** adultery there.
3: 8 she also went out and **c** adultery.
3: 9 and **c** adultery with stone and wood.
5: 7 yet they **c** adultery and thronged to
11:20 them, for to you I have **c** my cause.
16:10 have we **c** against the LORD our God?'
20:12 them, for to you I have **c** my cause.
29:23 **c** adultery with their neighbours'
33: 8 all the sin they have **c** against me
37:18 "What crime have I **c** against you or
41:11 Ishmael son of Nethaniah had **c**,
44: 9 Have you forgotten the wickedness **c**
44: 9 queens of Judah and the wickedness **c**
Eze 18:21 away from all the sins he has **c**
18:22 None of the offences he has **c** will
18:24 of the sins he has **c**, he will die.
18:26 of the sin he has **c** he will die.
18:27 away from the wickedness he has **c**
18:28 considers all the offences he has **c**
18:31 of all the offences you have **c**,
23:37 for they have **c** adultery and blood
23:37 They **c** adultery with their idols;
33:16 None of the sins he has **c** will be
Mal 2:11 A detestable thing has been **c** in
Mt 5:28 **c** adultery with her in his heart.
11:27 "All things have been **c** to me by my
27:23 "Why? What crime has he **c**?" asked
Mk 15: 7 who had **c** murder in the uprising.
15:14 "Why? What crime has he **c**?" asked
Lk 10:22 "All things have been **c** to me by my
23:22 "Why? What crime has this man **c**? I
Ac 14:23 with prayer and fasting, **c** them to
14:26 where they had been **c** to the grace
Ro 1:27 Men **c** indecent acts with other men,
3:25 the sins **c** beforehand unpunished
1Co 9:17 discharging the trust **c** to me.
2Co 5:19 And he has **c** to us the message of
Heb 9: 7 sins the people had **c** in ignorance.
9:15 the sins **c** under the first covenant.
1Pe 2:22 "He **c** no sin, and no deceit was
Rev 17: 2 the kings of the earth **c** adultery
18: 3 The kings of the earth **c** adultery
18: 9 kings of the earth who **c** adultery

Committing (Commit)

Hos 6: 9 road to Shechem, **c** shameful crimes.
Rev 2:14 to idols and by **c** sexual immorality.

Common

Ge 11: 1 had one language and a **c** speech.
Lev 10:10 between the holy and the **c**,
2Sa 16:10 "What do you and I have in **c**, you
19:22 "What do you and I have in **c**, you
1Ki 10:27 The king made silver as **c** in
2Ki 23: 6 over the graves of the **c** people.
2Ch 1:15 The king made silver and gold as **c**
9:27 The king made silver as **c** in
Ne 7: 5 the officials and the **c** people for
Ps 73: 5 They are free from the burdens **c** to
Pr 1:14 us, and we will share a **c** purse"—
22: 2 Rich and poor have this in **c**: The
29:13 and the oppressor have this in **c**:
Ecc 9: 2 All share a **c** destiny—the righteous
Jer 26:23 the burial place of the **c** people.)

Eze 22:26 between the holy and the **c**;
42:20 to separate the holy from the **c**.
44:23 between the holy and the **c** and show
48:15 for the **c** use of the city,
Ac 2:44 together and had everything in **c**.
Ro 9:21 noble purposes and some for **c** use?
1Co 10:13 seized you except what is **c** to man.
12: 7 the Spirit is given for the **c** good.
2Co 6:14 and wickedness have in **c**?
6:15 have in **c** with an unbeliever?
Tit 1: 4 To Titus, my true son in our **c** faith:

Commotion
Job 39: 7 He laughs at the **c** in the town; he
Isa 22: 2 O town full of **c**, O city of tumult
Jer 3:23 Surely the idolatrous **c** on the hills
10:22 The report is coming—a great **c**
Mk 5:38 Jesus saw a **c**, with people crying
5:39 "Why all this **c** and wailing? The
Ac 12:18 In the morning, there was no small **c**
19:40 not able to account for this **c**,

Communities (Community)
Am 1: 6 Because she took captive whole **c**
1: 9 Because she sold whole **c** of captives

Community (Community's, Communities)
Ge 28: 3 until you become a **c** of peoples.
35:11 A nation and a **c** of nations will
48: 4 I will make you a **c** of peoples, and
Ex 12: 3 Tell the whole **c** of Israel that on
12: 6 when all the people of the **c** of
12:19 be cut off from the **c** of Israel,
12:47 The whole **c** of Israel must celebrate
16: 1 The whole Israelite **c** set out from
16: 2 In the desert the whole **c** grumbled
16: 9 "Say to the entire Israelite **c**,
16:10 speaking to the whole Israelite **c**,
16:22 **c** came and reported this to Moses.
17: 1 The whole Israelite **c** set out from
34:31 leaders of the **c** came back to him,
35: 1 Moses assembled the whole Israelite **c**
35: 4 Moses said to the whole Israelite **c**,
35:20 the whole Israelite **c** withdrew from
38:25 from those of the **c** who were counted
Lev 4:13 "If the whole Israelite **c** sins
4:13 even though the **c** is unaware of the
4:15 The elders of the **c** are to lay their
4:21 This is the sin offering for the **c**.
4:27 "If a member of the **c** sins
10: 6 LORD will be angry with the whole **c**.
10:17 to take away the guilt of the **c**
16: 5 From the Israelite **c** he is to take
16:17 household and the whole **c** of Israel.
16:33 priests and all the people of the **c**.
20: 2 The people of the **c** are to stone him.
20: 4 If the people of the **c** close their
Nu 1: 2 census of the whole Israelite **c** by
1:16 were the men appointed from the **c**,
1:18 they called the whole **c** together on
1:53 will not fall on the Israelite **c**.
3: 7 for the whole **c** at the Tent of
4:34 Moses, Aaron and the leaders of the **c**
8: 9 and assemble the whole Israelite **c**.
8:20 Aaron and the whole Israelite **c** did
10: 2 and use them for calling the **c**
10: 3 the whole **c** is to assemble before you
13:26 **c** at Kadesh in the Desert of Paran.
14: 1 That night all the people of the **c**
14:27 "How long will this wicked **c** grumble
14:35 these things to this whole wicked **c**,
14:36 and made the whole **c** grumble against
15:15 The **c** is to have the same rules for
15:24 without the **c** being aware of it,
15:24 then the whole **c** is to offer a young
15:25 atonement for the whole Israelite **c**,
15:26 The whole Israelite **c** and the aliens
16: 2 well-known **c** leaders who had been
16: 3 The whole **c** is holy, every one of
16: 9 from the rest of the Israelite **c**
16: 9 before the **c** and minister to them?
16:33 perished and were gone from the **c**.
16:41 The next day the whole Israelite **c**
Nu 19: 9 shall be kept by the Israelite **c**
19:20 he must be cut off from the **c**,
20: 1 **c** arrived at the Desert of Zin,
20: 2 Now there was no water for the **c**,
20: 4 Why did you bring the LORD's **c** into
20: 8 of the rock for the **c** so that they
20:11 and the **c** and their livestock drank.
20:12 this **c** into the land I give them."
20:22 The whole Israelite **c** set out from
20:27 in the sight of the whole **c**.
20:29 the whole **c** learned that Aaron had
26: 2 the whole Israelite **c** by families
26: 9 the **c** officials who rebelled against
27:14 for when the **c** rebelled at the
27:16 mankind, appoint a man over this **c**
27:20 the whole Israelite **c** will obey him.
27:21 At his command he and the entire **c**
31:13 **c** went to meet them outside the camp.
31:26 the family heads of the **c** are to
31:27 in the battle and the rest of the **c**.
32: 2 to the leaders of the **c**, and said,
Jos 9:21 and water-carriers for the entire **c**.
9:27 water-carriers for the **c** and for the
22:17 a plague fell on the **c** of the LORD!
22:18 be angry with the whole **c** of Israel.
22:20 did not wrath come upon the whole **c**
22:30 the leaders of the **c**—the heads of
2Ch 31:18 daughters of the whole **c** listed in
Jer 30:20 and their **c** will be established
Ac 25:24 The whole Jewish **c** has petitioned me

Community's (Community)
Nu 31:43 the **c** half—was 337,500 sheep,

Compact (Compacted)
2Sa 3:21 so that they may make a **c** with you,
5: 3 the king made a **c** with them at
1Ch 11: 3 he made a **c** with them at Hebron

Compacted (Compact)
Ps 122: 3 a city that is closely **c** together.

Companies (Company)
Jdg 7:16 the three hundred men into three **c**,
7:20 The three **c** blew the trumpets and
9:34 positions near Shechem in four **c**.
9:43 divided them into three **c** and set an
9:44 Abimelech and the **c** with him rushed
9:44 Then two **c** rushed upon those in the
2Ki 11: 5 You who are in the three **c** that are
11: 7 you who are in the other two **c** that

Companion (Companions)
1Ki 20:35 said to his **c**, "Strike me with your
Job 30:29 a brother of jackals, a **c** of owls.
Ps 55:13 is you, a man like myself, my **c**, my
55:20 My **c** attacks his friends; he
Pr 13:20 wise, but a **c** of fools suffers harm.
28: 7 **c** of gluttons disgraces his father.
29: 3 but a **c** of prostitutes squanders his
Rev 1: 9 I, John, your brother and **c** in the

Companions (Companion)
Jdg 14:11 he appeared, he was given thirty **c**.
2Ki 9: 2 get him away from his **c** and take him
Ps 38:11 My friends and **c** avoid me because of
45: 7 your God, has set you above your **c**
45:14 her virgin **c** follow her and are
88:18 You have taken my **c** and loved ones
Pr 18:24 A man of many **c** may come to ruin,
Isa 1:23 Your rulers are rebels, **c** of thieves;
Mt 12: 3 did when he and his **c** were hungry?
12: 4 and he and his **c** ate the consecrated
26:51 With that, one of Jesus' **c** reached
Mk 1:36 Simon and his **c** went to look for him,
2:25 and his **c** were hungry and in need?
2:26 And he also gave some to his **c**."
Lk 5: 9 For he and all his **c** were astonished
6: 3 did when he and his **c** were hungry?
6: 4 And he also gave some to his **c**."
9:32 Peter and his **c** were very sleepy,
24:24 some of our **c** went to the tomb and
Ac 13:13 From Paphos, Paul and his **c** sailed
16: 6 Paul and his **c** travelled throughout
19:29 Paul's travelling **c** from Macedonia,
20:34 my own needs and the needs of my **c**.
22: 9 My **c** saw the light, but they did not
22:11 My **c** led me by the hand into
26:13 the sun, blazing around me and my **c**.
Heb 1: 9 your God, has set you above your **c**

Company (Companies)
Ge 13: 9 whole land before you? Let's part **c**.
13:11 the east. The two men parted **c**:
50: 9 It was a very large **c**.
Jdg 9:37 and a **c** is coming from the direction
2Ki 1: 9 a captain with his **c** of fifty men.
2: 3 The **c** of the prophets at Bethel came
2: 5 The **c** of the prophets at Jericho
2: 7 Fifty men of the **c** of the prophets
2:15 The **c** of the prophets from Jericho,
4: 1 The wife of a man from the **c** of the
4:38 While the **c** of the prophets was
5:22 'Two young men from the **c** of the
6: 1 The **c** of the prophets said to Elisha,
9: 1 **c** of the prophets and said to him,
Ezr 2: 2 in **c** with Zerubbabel, Jeshua,
2:64 The whole **c** numbered 42,360,
Ne 7: 7 in **c** with Zerubbabel, Jeshua,
7:66 The whole **c** numbered 42,360,
8:17 The whole **c** that had returned from
Job 15:34 For the **c** of the godless will be
34: 8 He keeps **c** with evildoers; he
Ps 14: 5 present in the **c** of the righteous.
68:11 the **c** of those who proclaimed it:
106:17 Dathan; it buried the **c** of Abiram.
Pr 21:16 comes to rest in the **c** of the dead.
24: 1 wicked men, do not desire their **c**;
Jer 15:17 I never sat in the **c** of revellers,
Eze 27:34 all your **c** have gone down with you.
Ob :20 This **c** of Israelite exiles who are
Mt 27:27 the whole **c** of soldiers round him.
Mk 15:16 together the whole **c** of soldiers.
Lk 2:13 Suddenly a great **c** of the heavenly
2:44 Thinking he was in their **c**, they
Ac 15:39 disagreement that they parted **c**.
Ro 15:24 I have enjoyed your **c** for a while.
1Co 15:33 Do not be misled: "Bad **c** corrupts

Compare (Compared, Comparing, Comparison)
Job 28:17 Neither gold nor crystal can **c** with
28:19 The topaz of Cush cannot **c** with it;
39:13 but they cannot **c** with the pinions
Ps 86: 8 O Lord; no deeds can **c** with yours.
89: 6 For who in the skies above can **c**
Pr 3:15 nothing you desire can **c** with her.
8:11 nothing you desire can **c** with her.
Isa 40:18 To whom, then, will you **c** God? What
40:18 What image will you **c** him to?
40:25 "To whom will you **c** me? Or who is my
46: 5 "To whom will you **c** me or count me
Lam 2:13 I say for you? With what can I **c** you,
Eze 31: 8 nor could the plane trees **c** with its
Da 1:13 **c** our appearance with that of the
Mt 11:16 "To what can I **c** this generation?
Lk 7:31 "To what, then, can I **c** the people
13:18 of God like? What shall I **c** it to?
13:20 "What shall I **c** the kingdom of God to
2Co 10:12 We do not dare to classify or **c**
10:12 and **c** themselves with themselves,

Compared (Compare)
Jdg 8: 2 "What have I accomplished **c** to you?
8: 3 What was I able to do **c** to you?" At
Isa 46: 5 will you liken me that we may be **c**?
Eze 31: 2 "'Who can be **c** with you in
31:18 "'Which of the trees of Eden can be **c**
Php 3: 8 I consider everything a loss **c** to

Comparing (Compare)
Ro 8:18 not worth **c** with the glory that will
2Co 8: 8 **c** it with the earnestness of others.
Gal 6: 4 without **c** himself to somebody else,

Comparison (Compare)
2Co 3:10 now in **c** with the surpassing glory.

Compasses
Isa 44:13 with chisels and marks it with c.

Compassion (Compassionate, Compassions)
Ex 33:19 I will have c on whom I will have c.
Dt 13:17 have c on you, and increase your
28:54 have no c on his own brother or the
30: 3 have c on you and gather you again
32:36 have c on his servants when he sees
Jdg 2:18 for the LORD had c on them as they
1Ki 3:26 c for her son and said to the king,
2Ki 13:23 had c and showed concern for them
2Ch 30: 9 your children will be shown c by
Ne 9:19 "Because of your great c you did not
9:27 and in your great c you gave them
9:28 and in your c you delivered them
Ps 51: 1 according to your great c blot out my
77: 9 Has he in anger withheld his c?
90:13 will it be? Have c on your servants.
102:13 You will arise and have c on Zion,
103: 4 pit and crowns you with love and c,
103:13 a father has c on his children, so
103:13 LORD has c on those who fear him;
116: 5 and righteous; our God is full of c.
119:77 Let your c come to me that I may
119:156 Your c is great, O LORD; preserve
135:14 people and have c on his servants.
145: 9 he has c on all he has made
Isa 13:18 will they look with c on children.
14: 1 The LORD will have c on Jacob; once
27:11 so their Maker has no c on them,
30:18 to you; he rises to show you c.
49:10 He who has c on them will guide them
49:13 will have c on his afflicted ones.
49:15 no c on the child she has borne?
51: 3 will look with c on all her ruins;
54: 7 with deep c I will bring you back.
54: 8 kindness I will have c on you,"
54:10 says the LORD, who has c on you.
60:10 you, in favour I will show you c.
63: 7 to his c and many kindnesses.
63:15 and c are withheld from us.
Jer 12:15 I will again have c and will bring
13:14 I will allow no pity or mercy or c
15: 6 destroy you; I can no longer show c.
21: 7 show them no mercy or pity or c.'
30:18 tents and have c on his dwellings;
31:20 I have great c for him,"
33:26 their fortunes and have c on them.'"
42:12 show you c so that he will have c
Lam 3:32 he will show c, so great is his
Eze 9: 5 and kill, without showing pity or c.
16: 5 had c enough to do any of these
39:25 have c on all the people of Israel,
Hos 2:19 and justice, in love and c.
11: 8 within me; all my c is aroused.
13:14 "I will have no c,
14: 3 for in you the fatherless find c."
Am 1:11 brother with a sword, stifling all c,
Jnh 3: 9 God may yet relent and with c turn
3:10 he had c and did not bring upon them
Mic 7:19 You will again have c on us; you
Zec 7: 9 show mercy and c to one another.
10: 6 I will restore them because I have c
Mal 3:17 just as in c a man spares his son
Mt 9:36 he saw the crowds, he had c on them,
14:14 had c on them and healed their sick.
15:32 "I have c for these people; they
20:34 Jesus had c on them and touched
Mk 1:41 Filled with c, Jesus reached out his
6:34 he had c on them, because they were
8: 2 "I have c for these people; they
Lk 15:20 him and was filled with c for him;
Ro 9:15 and I will have c on whom I have c."
2Co 1: 3 the Father of c and the God of all
Php 2: 1 the Spirit, if any tenderness and c,
Col 3:12 clothe yourselves with c, kindness,
Jas 5:11 The Lord is full of c and mercy.

Compassionate (Compassion)
Ex 22:27 out to me, I will hear, for I am c.
34: 6 the LORD, the c and gracious God,
2Ch 30: 9 the LORD your God is gracious and c.
Ne 9:17 gracious and c, slow to anger and
Ps 86:15 you, O Lord, are a c and gracious
103: 8 The LORD is c and gracious, slow to
111: 4 the LORD is gracious and c.
112: 4 gracious and c and righteous man.
145: 8 The LORD is gracious and c, slow to
Lam 4:10 With their own hands c women have
Joel 2:13 for he is gracious and c, slow to
Jnh 4: 2 that you are a gracious and c God,
Eph 4:32 Be kind and c to one another,
1Pe 3: 8 love as brothers, be c and humble.

Compassions (Compassion)
Lam 3:22 not consumed, for his c never fail.

Compel (Compelled, Compels, Compulsion)
Gal 6:12 trying to c you to be circumcised.

Compelled (Compel)
1Sa 13:12 felt c to offer the burnt offering."
Ezr 4:23 and c them by force to stop.
Ac 20:22 "And now, c by the Spirit, I am
28:19 I was c to appeal to Caesar—
1Co 9:16 I cannot boast, for I am c to preach.
Gal 2: 3 was with me, was c to be circumcised,

Compels (Compel)
Ex 3:19 you go unless a mighty hand c him.
Job 32:18 and the spirit within me c me;
2Co 5:14 For Christ's love c us, because we

Compensate (Compensation)
Ex 21:26 servant go free to c for the eye.
21:27 servant go free to c for the tooth.

Compensation (Compensate)
Pr 6:35 He will not accept any c; he will

Compete (Competes)
Jer 12: 5 how can you c with horses? If you

Competence (Competent)
2Co 3: 5 ourselves, but our c comes from God.

Competent (Competence)
Ro 15:14 and c to instruct one another.
1Co 6: 2 you not c to judge trivial cases?
2Co 3: 5 Not that we are c in ourselves to
3: 6 He has made us c as ministers of a

Competes (Compete)
1Co 9:25 Everyone who c in the games goes
2Ti 2: 5 Similarly, if anyone c as an athlete,
2: 5 unless he c according to the rules.

Complacency (Complacent)
Pr 1:32 the c of fools will destroy them;
Eze 30: 9 ships to frighten Cush out of her c.

Complacent (Complacency)
Isa 32: 9 You women who are so c, rise up and
32:11 Tremble, you c women; shudder, you
Am 6: 1 Woe to you who are c in Zion, and to
Zep 1:12 lamps and punish those who are c,

Complain (Complained, Complaining, Complaint, Complaints)
Jdg 21:22 their fathers or brothers c to us,
Job 7:11 will c in the bitterness of my soul.
33:13 Why do you c to him that he answers
Isa 29:24 who c will accept instruction."
40:27 Why do you say, O Jacob, and c, O
56: 3 And let not any eunuch c, "I am
Lam 3:39 Why should any living man c when

Complained (Complain)
Ge 21:25 Abraham c to Abimelech about a well
Nu 11: 1 Now the people c about their
Lk 5:30 to their sect c to his disciples,
Ac 6: 1 the Grecian Jews among them c

Complaining (Complain)
Php 2:14 Do everything without c or arguing,

Complaint (Complain)
2Sa 15: 2 Whenever anyone came with a c to be
15: 4 Then everyone who has a c or case
Job 7:13 me and my couch will ease my c,
9:27 If I say, 'I will forget my c, I
10: 1 I will give free rein to my c
21: 4 "Is my c directed to man? Why should
23: 2 "Even today my c is bitter; his hand
Ps 64: 1 Hear me, O God, as I voice my c;
142: 2 I pour out my c before him; before
Hab 2: 1 what answer I am to give to this c.
Ac 18:14 "If you Jews were making a c about

Complaints (Complain)
Nu 14:27 the c of these grumbling Israelites.
Pr 23:29 Who has strife? Who has c? Who has

Complete (Completed, Completing, Completion)
Ex 5:13 "C the work required of you for each
Dt 16:15 your hands, and your joy will be c.
1Ki 7: 1 to c the construction of his palace.
2Ki 12:15 because they acted with c honesty.
Est 2:12 she had to c twelve months of beauty
Zec 4: 9 temple; his hands will also c it.
Lk 6:49 and its destruction was c."
14:28 see if he has enough money to c it?
Jn 3:29 That joy is mine, and it is now c.
15:11 in you and that your joy may be c.
16:24 receive, and your joy will be c.
17:23 May they be brought to c unity to
Ac 3:16 c healing to him, as you can all see.
20:24 c the task the Lord Jesus has given
Ro 15:14 c in knowledge and competent to
2Co 7:16 I am glad I can have c confidence in
8: 7 in knowledge, in c earnestness and
10: 6 once your obedience is c.
Php 2: 2 make my joy c by being like-minded,
Col 2: 2 the full riches of c understanding,
4:17 "See to it that you c the work you
Jas 1: 4 mature and c, not lacking anything.
2:22 his faith was made c by what he did.
1Jn 1: 4 We write this to make our joy c.
2: 5 God's love is truly made c in him.
4:12 in us and his love is made c in us.
4:17 In this way, love is made c among us
2Jn :12 to face, so that our joy may be c.
Rev 3: 2 your deeds c in the sight of my God.

Completed (Complete)
Ge 2: 1 Thus the heavens and the earth were c
29:21 My time is c, and I want to lie with
Ex 39:32 the Tent of Meeting, was c.
Lev 8:33 the days of your ordination are c,
Jos 3:17 had c the crossing on dry ground.
1Ki 6: 9 he built the temple and c it,
6:14 Solomon built the temple and c it.
7:22 And so the work on the pillars was c.
2Ch 29:28 of the burnt offering was c.
36:21 until the seventy years were c in
Ezr 6:15 The temple was c on the third day of
Ne 6: 9 for the work, and it will not be c.
6:15 the wall was c on the twenty-fifth
Isa 40: 2 that her hard service has been c,
Jer 29:10 "When seventy years are c for
Da 11:36 until the time of wrath is c,
12: 7 broken, all these things will be c."
Lk 1:23 his time of service was c, he
2:22 to the Law of Moses had been c,
12:50 how distressed I am until it is c!
Jn 19:28 Later, knowing that all was now c,
Ac 14:26 of God for the work they had now c.
Ro 15:28 after I have c this task and have
Rev 6:11 to be killed as they had been was c.
15: 1 because with them God's wrath is c.
15: 8 plagues of the seven angels were c.

Completing (Complete)
Jn 17: 4 by c the work you gave me to do.
Ac 13:25 John was c his work, he said: 'Who

Completion (Complete)
2Ch 8:16 of the LORD was laid until its c.
2Co 8: 6 bring also to c this act of grace

2Co 8:11 may be matched by your c of it,
Php 1: 6 to c until the day of Christ Jesus.

Complied (Comply)
2Ki 16: 9 The king of Assyria c by attacking

Compliments
Pr 23: 8 eaten and will have wasted your c.

Comply (Complied)
Est 3: 4 spoke to him but he refused to c.

Composed
2Ch 35:25 Jeremiah c laments for Josiah, and

Comprehend (Comprehended)
Job 28:13 Man does not c its worth; it cannot
Ecc 8:17 No-one can c what goes on under the
8:17 he knows, he cannot really c it.

Comprehended (Comprehend)
Job 38:18 Have you c the vast expanses of the

Compulsion (Compel)
1Co 7:37 who is under no c but has control
2Co 9: 7 not reluctantly or under c, for God

Compute
Lev 25:52 he is to c that and pay for his

Conaniah
2Ch 31:12 C, a Levite, was in charge of these
31:13 under C and Shimei his brother,
35: 9 Also C along with Shemaiah and

Conceal (Concealed, Conceals)
Lev 16:13 and the smoke of the incense will c
Job 14:13 and c me till your anger has passed!
27:11 ways of the Almighty I will not c.
40:22 The lotuses c him in their shadow;
Ps 40:10 I do not c your love and your truth
Pr 25: 2 is the glory of God to c a matter;
Isa 26:21 her; she will c her slain no longer.
Jer 49:10 so that he cannot c himself.

Concealed (Conceal)
Jdg 9:34 took up c positions near Shechem in
Job 10:13 "But this is what you c in your
24:15 see me,' and he keeps his face c.
28:21 c even from the birds of the air.
31:33 if I have c my sin as men do, by
Pr 21:14 c in the cloak pacifies great wrath.
26:26 His malice may be c by deception,
Isa 49: 2 arrow and c me in his quiver.
Jer 16:17 me, nor is their sin c from my eyes.
Mt 10:26 There is nothing c that will not be
Mk 4:22 and whatever is c is meant to be
Lk 8:17 and nothing c that will not be known
12: 2 There is nothing c that will not be

Conceals (Conceal)
Pr 10:18 He who c his hatred has lying lips,
28:13 He who c his sins does not prosper,

Concede (Concession)
Dt 32:31 our Rock, as even our enemies c.

Conceit (Conceited, Conceits)
Isa 16: 6 pride—her overweening pride and c,
Jer 48:29 pride—her overweening pride and c,
Php 2: 3 out of selfish ambition or vain c,

Conceited (Conceit)
1Sa 17:28 I know how c you are and how wicked
Ro 11:25 brothers, so that you may not be c:
12:16 people of low position. Do not be c.
2Co 12: 7 To keep me from becoming c because
Gal 5:26 Let us not become c, provoking and
1Ti 3: 6 or he may become c and fall under
6: 4 he is c and understands nothing. He
2Ti 3: 4 treacherous, rash, c, lovers of

Conceits (Conceit)
Ps 73: 7 c of their minds know no limits.

Conceive (Conceived, Conceives, Conception)
Nu 11:12 Did I c all these people? Did I give
Jdg 13: 3 you are going to c and have a son.
13: 5 you will c and give birth to a son.
13: 7 'You will c and give birth to a son.
Ru 4:13 the LORD enabled her to c, and she
Job 15:35 They c trouble and give birth to
Isa 33:11 You c chaff, you give birth to straw;
59: 4 c trouble and give birth to evil.

Conceived Conceive)
Ge 16: 4 He slept with Hagar, and she c. When
29:33 She c again, and when she gave birth
29:34 Again she c, and when she gave birth
29:35 She c again, and when she gave birth
30: 7 Rachel's servant Bilhah c again and
30:19 Leah c again and bore Jacob a sixth
38: 4 She c again and gave birth to a son
1Sa 1:20 in the course of time Hannah c and
2:21 she c and gave birth to three sons
2Sa 11: 5 The woman c and sent word to David,
Ps 51: 5 sinful from the time my mother c me.
SS 3: 4 to the room of the one who c me.
8: 5 roused you; there your mother c you,
Isa 8: 3 I went to the prophetess, and she c
46: 3 whom I have upheld since you were c,
59:13 uttering lies our hearts have c.
Hos 1: 3 and she c and bore him a son.
1: 6 Gomer c again and gave birth to a
2: 5 and has c them in disgrace.
Mt 1:20 is c in her is from the Holy Spirit.
Lk 2:21 had given him before he had been c.
1Co 2: 9 no ear has heard, no mind has c what
Jas 1:15 Then, after desire has c, it gives

Conceives (Conceive)
Ps 7:14 is pregnant with evil and c trouble

Conception (Conceive)
Hos 9:11 bird—no birth, no pregnancy, no c.

Concern (Concerned, Concerns)
Ge 39: 6 he did not c himself with anything
39: 8 "my master does not c himself with
1Sa 23:21 The LORD bless you for your c for me.
2Ki 13:23 had compassion and showed c for them
Job 9:21 "Although I am blameless, I have no c
19: 4 astray, my error remains my c alone.
Ps 131: 1 I do not c myself with great matters
Pr 29: 7 poor, but the wicked have no such c.
Eze 36:21 I had c for my holy name, which the
Ac 15:14 how God at first showed his c by
18:17 But Gallio showed no c whatever.
1Co 7:32 I would like you to be free from c.
12:25 should have equal c for each other.
2Co 7: 7 your deep sorrow, your ardent c for
7:11 what alarm, what longing, what c,
8:16 of Titus the same c I have for you.
11:28 of my c for all the churches.
Php 4:10 last you have renewed your c for me.

Concerned (Concern)
Ge 21:11 Abraham greatly because it c his son.
Ex 2:25 the Israelites and was c about them.
3: 7 and I am c about their suffering.
4:31 that the LORD was c about them
1Sa 22: 8 None of you is c about me or tells
2Sa 13:33 My lord the king should not be c
1Ch 27: 1 king in all that c the army divisions
Ps 142: 4 no-one is c for me. I have no refuge;
Eze 36: 9 I am c for you and will look on you
Da 10: 1 was true and it c a great war.
Jnh 4:10 "You have been c about this vine,
4:11 I not be c about that great city?"
Ro 11:28 far as the gospel is c, they are
11:28 but as far as election is c,
1Co 7:32 man is c about the Lord's affairs—
7:33 a married man is c about the affairs
7:34 An unmarried woman or virgin is c
7:34 But a married woman is c about the
1Co 9: 9 Is it about oxen that God is c?
Php 4:10 Indeed, you have been c, but you had
2Ti 3: 8 far as the faith is c, are rejected.

Concerns (Concern)
2Ch 19:10 bloodshed or other c of the law,
Eze 12:10 This oracle c the prince in
Da 8:17 the vision c the time of the end."
8:19 c the appointed time of the end.
8:26 for it c the distant future."
10:14 the vision c a time yet to come."

Concession (Concede)
1Co 7: 6 I say this as a c, not as a command.

Conclude (Concluded, Concludes, Concluding, Conclusion)
Ro 3: 9 What shall we c then? Are we any

Concluded (Conclude)
Ecc 9: 1 I reflected on all this and c that
Jn 7:26 really c that he is the Christ?

Concludes (Conclude)
Ps 72:20 This c the prayers of David son of

Concluding (Conclude)
Ac 16:10 c that God had called us to preach

Conclusion (Conclude)
Ecc 12:13 Now all has been heard; here is the c

Concubine (Concubines)
Ge 22:24 His c, whose name was Reumah, also
35:22 slept with this father's c Bilhah,
36:12 Esau's son Eliphaz also had a c
Jdg 8:31 His c, who lived in Shechem, also
19: 1 took a c from Bethlehem in Judah.
19: 9 the man, with his c and his servant,
19:10 his two saddled donkeys and his c.
19:24 is my virgin daughter, and his c.
19:25 So the man took his c and sent her
19:27 there lay his c, fallen in the
19:29 he took a knife and cut up his c,
20: 4 "I and my c came to Gibeah in
20: 5 They raped my c, and she died.
20: 6 I took my c, cut her into pieces and
2Sa 3: 7 Now Saul had had a c named Rizpah
3: 7 did you sleep with my father's c?"
21:11 daughter Rizpah, Saul's c, had done,
1Ch 1:32 The sons born to Keturah, Abraham's c
2:46 Caleb's c Ephah was the mother of
2:48 Caleb's c Maacah was the mother of
7:14 descendant through his Aramean c.

Concubines (Concubine)
Ge 25: 6 he gave gifts to the sons of his c
2Sa 5:13 David took more c and wives in
15:16 ten c to take care of the palace.
16:21 "Lie with your father's c whom he
16:22 lay with his father's c in the sight
19: 5 and the lives of your wives and c.
20: 3 he took the ten c he had left to
1Ki 11: 3 and three hundred c, and his wives
1Ch 3: 9 of David, besides his sons by his c.
2Ch 11:21 than any of his other wives and c.
11:21 he had eighteen wives and sixty c,
Est 2:14 eunuch who was in charge of the c.
SS 6: 8 eighty c, and virgins beyond number;
6: 9 the queens and c praised her.
Da 5: 2 and his c might drink from them.
5: 3 his wives and his c drank from them.
5:23 and your c drank wine from them.

Condemn (Condemnation, Condemned, Condemning, Condemns, Self-condemned)
Job 9:20 were innocent, my mouth would c me;
10: 2 I will say to God: Do not c me, but
34:17 Will you c the just and mighty One?
34:29 if he remains silent, who can c him?
40: 8 Would you c me to justify yourself?
Ps 94:21 and c the innocent to death.
109: 7 guilty, and may his prayers c him.

Ps 109:31 save his life from those who c him.
Isa 50: 9 Who is he who will c me? They will
Mt 12:41 with this generation and c it;
12:42 with this generation and c it;
20:18 They will c him to death
Mk 10:33 They will c him to death and will
Lk 6:37 Do not c, and you will not be
11:31 men of this generation and c them;
11:32 with this generation and c it;
Jn 3:17 Son into the world to c the world,
7:51 "Does our law c a man without first
8:11 "Then neither do I c you," Jesus
12:48 I spoke will c him at the last day.
Ro 2:27 yet obeys the law will c you who,
14: 3 must not c the man who does,
14:22 not c himself by what he approves.
2Co 7: 3 I do not say this to c you; I have
1Jn 3:20 whenever our hearts c us. For God is
3:21 Dear friends, if our hearts do not c

Condemnation (Condemn)

Jer 42:18 and horror, of c and reproach;
44:12 and horror, of c and reproach.
Ro 3: 8 may result"? Their c is deserved.
5:16 followed one sin and brought c,
5:18 of one trespass was c for all men,
8: 1 Therefore, there is now no c for
2Pe 2: 3 Their c has long been hanging over
Jude : 4 For certain men whose c was written

Condemned (Condemn)

Dt 13:17 None of those c things shall be
Job 32: 3 to refute Job, and yet had c him.
Ps 34:21 the foes of the righteous will be c.
34:22 will be c who takes refuge in him.
37:33 let them be c when brought to trial.
79:11 of your arm preserve those c to die.
102:20 and release those c to death."
Mt 12: 7 you would not have c the innocent.
12:37 and by your words you will be c."
23:33 How will you escape being c to hell?
27: 3 saw that Jesus was c, he was seized
Mk 14:64 What do you think?" They all c him
16:16 whoever does not believe will be c.
Lk 6:37 not condemn, and you will not be c.
Jn 3:18 Whoever believes in him is not c,
3:18 does not believe stands c already
5:24 has eternal life and will not be c;
5:29 have done evil will rise to be c.
8:10 where are they? Has no-one c you?"
16:11 prince of this world now stands c.
Ac 25:15 against him and asked that he be c.
Ro 3: 7 why am I still c as a sinner?"
8: 3 And so he c sin in sinful man,
14:23 the man who has doubts is c if he
1Co 4: 9 like men c to die in the arena.
11:32 we will not be c with the world.
Gal 1: 8 to you, let him be eternally c!
1: 9 accepted, let him be eternally c!
2Th 2:12 that all will be c who have not
Tit 2: 8 soundness of speech that cannot be c,
Heb 11: 7 By his faith he c the world and
Jas 5: 6 You have c and murdered innocent men,
5:12 and your "No", no, or you will be c.
2Pe 2: 6 if he c the cities of Sodom and
Rev 19: 2 He has c the great prostitute who

Condemning (Condemn)

Dt 25: 1 the innocent and c the guilty.
1Ki 8:32 c the guilty and bringing down on his
Pr 17:15 Acquitting the guilty and c the
Ac 13:27 yet in c him they fulfilled the
Ro 2: 1 you are c yourself, because you who

Condemns (Condemn)

Job 15: 6 Your own mouth c you, not mine; your
Pr 12: 2 LORD, but the LORD c a crafty man.
Ro 8:34 Who is he that c? Christ Jesus, who
2Co 3: 9 If the ministry that c men is

Condition (Conditions)

Ge 34:15 our consent to you on one c only:
34:22 the c that our males be circumcised,
1Sa 11: 2 on the c that I gouge out the right eye
Pr 27:23 Be sure you know the c of your
Mt 12:45 And the final c of that man is worse
Lk 11:26 And the final c of that man is worse
Jn 5: 6 had been in this c for a long time,

Conditions (Condition)

Jer 32:11 copy containing the terms and c,

Conduct (Conducted, Conducts, Safe-conduct)

Est 1:17 For the queen's c will become known
1:18 who have heard about the queen's c
Job 21:31 Who denounces his c to his face? Who
34:11 brings upon him what his c deserves.
Pr 10:23 A fool finds pleasure in evil c, but
20:11 by whether his c is pure and right.
21: 8 the c of the innocent is upright.
Ecc 6: 8 how to c himself before others?
Jer 4:18 "Your own c and actions have brought
6:15 Are they ashamed of their loathsome c
8:12 Are they ashamed of their loathsome c
17:10 to reward a man according to his c,
32:19 reward everyone according to his c
Eze 7: 3 I will judge you according to your c
7: 4 I will surely repay you for your c
7: 8 I will judge you according to your c
7: 9 repay you in accordance with your c
7:27 deal with them according to their c,
14:22 and when you see their c and their
14:23 you see their c and their actions,
16:27 who were shocked by your lewd c.
20:43 There you will remember your c and
24:14 to your c and your actions,
36:17 it by their c and their actions.
36:17 Their c was like a woman's monthly
36:19 to their c and their actions.
36:32 for your c, O house of Israel!
Da 6: 4 in his c of government affairs,
Ac 13:18 he endured their c for about forty
Php 1:27 c yourselves in a manner worthy of
1Ti 3:15 how people ought to c themselves

Conducted (Conduct)

2Co 1:12 we have c ourselves in the world,

Conducts (Conduct)

Ps 112: 5 who c his affairs with justice.

Coney (Conies)

Lev 11: 5 The c, though it chews the cud, does
Dt 14: 7 eat the camel, the rabbit or the c.

Confections

Eze 27:17 exchanged wheat from Minnith and c,

Confer (Conferred, Conferring)

Ne 6: 7 king; so come, let us c together."
Lk 22:29 I c on you a kingdom, just as my

Conferred (Confer)

2Sa 3:17 Abner c with the elders of Israel
1Ki 1: 7 Adonijah c with Joab son of Zeruiah
1Ch 13: 1 David c with each of his officers,
Lk 22:29 just as my Father c one on me,
Ac 4:15 the Sanhedrin and then c together.
25:12 After Festus had c with his council,

Conferring (Confer)

2Ki 6: 8 After c with his officers, he said,

Confess (Confessed, Confesses, Confessing, Confession)

Lev 5: 5 he must c in what way he has
16:21 c over it all the wickedness and
26:40 "'But if they will c their sins and
Nu 5: 7 must c the sin he has committed. He
1Ki 8:33 turn back to you and c your name,
8:35 c your name and turn from their sin
2Ch 6:24 when they turn back and c your name,
6:26 c your name and turn from their sin
Ne 1: 6 of Israel. I c the sins we Israelites,
Ps 32: 5 I said, "I will c my transgressions
38:18 I c my iniquity; I am troubled by my
Jn 1:20 He did not fail to c, but confessed
12:42 would not c their faith for fear
Ro 10: 9 That if you c with your mouth,
10:10 your mouth that you c and are saved.
14:11 me; every tongue will c to God.'"
Php 2:11 every tongue c that Jesus Christ is
Heb 3: 1 apostle and high priest whom we c.
13:15 fruit of lips that c his name.
Jas 5:16 Therefore c your sins to each other
1Jn 1: 9 If we c our sins, he is faithful and

Confessed (Confess)

1Sa 7: 6 they fasted and there they c,
Ne 9: 2 They stood in their places and c
Da 9: 4 I prayed to the LORD my God and c:
Jn 1:20 but c freely, "I am not the Christ."
Ac 19:18 came and openly c their evil deeds.

Confesses (Confess)

Pr 28:13 but whoever c and renounces them
2Ti 2:19 "Everyone who c the name of the Lord

Confessing (Confess)

Ezr 10: 1 While Ezra was praying and c,
Da 9:20 c my sin and the sin of my people
Mt 3: 6 C their sins, they were baptised by
Mk 1: 5 C their sins, they were baptised by

Confession (Confess)

Ezr 10:11 Now make c to the LORD, the God of
Ne 9: 3 and spent another quarter in c and
2Co 9:13 your c of the gospel of Christ,
1Ti 6:12 c in the presence of many witnesses.
6:13 Pilate made the good c, I charge

Confide (Confides, Confiding)

Jdg 16:15 'I love you,' when you won't c in me?

Confidence (Confident, Confidently, Self-confidence, Self-confident)

Jdg 9:26 and its citizens put their c in him.
2Ki 18:19 what are you basing this c of yours?
2Ch 32: 8 And the people gained c from what
32:10 says: On what are you basing your c,
Job 4: 6 Should not your piety be your c and
Ps 71: 5 Sovereign LORD, my c since my youth.
Pr 3:26 for the LORD will be your c and will
3:32 but takes the upright into his c.
11:13 A gossip betrays a c, but a
20:19 A gossip betrays a c; so avoid a man
25: 9 do not betray another man's c,
31:11 Her husband has full c in her and
Isa 32:17 will be quietness and c for ever.
36: 4 what are you basing this c of yours?
Jer 17: 7 in the LORD, whose c is in him.
49:31 a nation at ease, which lives in c,"
Eze 29:16 Egypt will no longer be a source of c
Mic 7: 5 a neighbour; put no c in a friend.
2Co 2: 3 I had c in all of you, that you
3: 4 Such c as this is ours through
7: 4 I have great c in you; I take great
7:16 I am glad I can have complete c in
8:22 so because of his great c in you.
Eph 3:12 may approach God with freedom and c.
Php 3: 3 and who put no c in the flesh—
3: 4 I myself have reasons for such c.
3: 4 to put c in the flesh, I have more:
2Th 3: 4 We have c in the Lord that you are
Heb 3:14 till the end the c we had at first.
4:16 approach the throne of grace with c,
10:19 Therefore, brothers, since we have c
10:35 do not throw away your c; it will be
13: 6 we say with c, "The Lord is my
1Jn 3:21 not condemn us, we have c before
4:17 will have c on the day of judgment,
5:14 This is the c we have in approaching

Confident (Confidence)

Job 6:20 distressed, because they had been c;
Ps 27: 3 against me, even then will I be c.

Ps 27:13 I am still c of this: I will see the
Lk 18: 9 To some who were c of their own
2Co 1:15 I was c of this, I planned to visit
5: 6 Therefore we are always c and know
5: 8 We are c, I say, and would prefer to
9: 4 be ashamed of having been so c.
10: 7 If anyone is c that he belongs to
Gal 5:10 I am c in the Lord that you will
Php 1: 6 being c of this, that he who began a
2:24 I am c in the Lord that I myself
Phm :21 C of your obedience, I write to you,
Heb 6: 9 friends, we are c of better things
1Jn 2:28 so that when he appears we may be c

Confidently (Confidence)
1Sa 15:32 Agag came to him c, thinking,
Ac 2:29 "Brothers, I can tell you c that the
1Ti 1: 7 about or what they so c affirm.

Confides (Confide)
Ps 25:14 The LORD c in those who fear him; he

Confiding (Confide)
1Sa 20: 2 great or small, without c in me.

Confine (Confined, Confinement, Confines)
Nu 12:14 C her outside the camp for seven
2Co 10:13 but will c our boasting to the field

Confined (Confine)
Ge 39:20 where the king's prisoners were c.
40: 3 the same prison where Joseph was c.
Ex 21:18 and he does not die but is c to bed,
Nu 12:15 Miriam was c outside the camp for
Jdg 1:34 The Amorites c the Danites to the
Ps 88: 8 I am c and cannot escape;
Jer 32: 2 and Jeremiah the prophet was c in
33: 1 While Jeremiah was still c in the
39:15 While Jeremiah had been c in the

Confinement (Confine)
2Sa 20: 3 They were kept in c till the day of

Confines (Confine)
Job 11:10 "If he comes along and c you in

Confirm (Confirmed, Confirming, Confirms)
Ge 17: 2 I will c my covenant between me and
26: 3 will c the oath I swore to your
Nu 30:13 Her husband may c or nullify any vow
Dt 29:13 to c you this day as his people,
1Ki 1:14 come in and c what you have said."
Est 9:29 wrote with full authority to c this
Da 9:27 He will c a covenant with many for
Ac 15:27 Silas to c by word of mouth what we
Ro 15: 8 c the promises made to the

Confirmed (Confirm)
Dt 4:31 which he c to them by oath.
1Sa 11:15 all the people went to Gilgal and c
1Ch 16:17 He c it to Jacob as a decree, to
2Ch 1: 9 promise to my father David be c,
Est 9:32 Esther's decree c these regulations
Job 28:27 appraised it; he c it and tested it.
Ps 105:10 He c it to Jacob as a decree, to
119:106 I have taken an oath and c it, that
Mk 16:20 Lord worked with them and c his word
Ac 14: 3 the Lord, who c the message of his
1Co 1: 6 our testimony about Christ was c in
Heb 2: 3 was c to us by those who heard him.
6:17 was promised, he c it with an oath.

Confirming (Confirm)
2Ki 23: 3 thus c the words of the covenant
Php 1: 7 or defending and c the gospel,

Confirms (Confirm)
Nu 30:14 then he c all her vows or the
30:14 He c them by saying nothing to her

Dt 8:18 and so c his covenant, which he
Ro 9: 1 conscience c it in the Holy Spirit—
Heb 6:16 and the oath c what is said and puts

Confiscation
Ezr 7:26 c of property, or imprisonment.
Heb 10:34 accepted the c of your property,

Conflict (Conflicts)
Hab 1: 3 me; there is strife, and c abounds.
Gal 5:17 They are in c with each other, so

Conflicts (Conflict)
2Co 7: 5 c on the outside, fears within.

Conform (Conformed, Conformity, Conforms)
Ro 12: 2 Do not c any longer to the pattern
1Pe 1:14 do not c to the evil desires you

Conformed (Conform)
Eze 5: 7 You have not even c to the standards
11:12 but have c to the standards of the
Ro 8:29 to be c to the likeness of his Son,

Conformity (Conform)
Eph 1:11 in c with the purpose of his will,

Conforms (Conform)
1Ti 1:11 that c to the glorious gospel of the

Confound
Ps 55: 9 the wicked, O Lord, c their speech,

Confront (Confronted, Confronting, Confronts)
Ex 8:20 c Pharoah as he goes to the water
9:13 the morning, c Pharoah and say to him
Jdg 14: 4 an occasion to c the Philistines;
1Sa 12: 7 because I am going to c you with
Job 9:32 that we might c each other in court.
30:27 never stops; days of suffering c me.
33: 5 you can; prepare yourself and c me.
Ps 17:13 Rise up, O LORD, c them, bring them
Isa 50: 8 Who is my accuser? Let him c me!
Eze 16: 2 "Son of man, c Jerusalem with her
20: 4 Then c them with the detestable
22: 2 Then c her with all her detestable
23:36 Then c them with their detestable

Confronted (Confront)
2Sa 22: 6 around me; the snares of death c me.
22:19 They c me in the day of my disaster,
2Ch 26:18 They c him and said, "It is not
28:12 c those who were arriving from the
Ps 18: 5 around me; the snares of death c me.
18:18 They c me in the day of my disaster,

Confronting (Confront)
Isa 27: 4 there were briers and thorns c me!
30:11 c us with the Holy One of Israel!"

Confronts (Confront)
Job 31:14 what will I do when God c me? What

Confuse (Confused, Confusing, Confusion)
Ge 11: 7 let us go down and c their language
Ps 55: 9 C the wicked, O Lord, confound

Confused (Confuse)
Ge 11: 9 c the language of the whole world.

Confusing (Confuse)
Pr 23:33 and your mind imagine c things.

Confusion (Confuse)
Ex 14: 3 wandering around the land in c,
14:24 Egyptian army and threw it into c.
23:27 into c every nation you encounter.

Dt 7:23 great c until they are destroyed.
28:20 The LORD will send on you curses, c
28:28 madness, blindness and c of mind.
Jos 10:10 The LORD threw them into c before
1Sa 14:20 found the Philistines in total c,
2Sa 18:29 "I saw great c just as Joab was
Ps 35:26 my distress be put to shame and c;
40:14 take my life be put to shame and c;
70: 2 seek my life be put to shame and c;
71:24 me have been put to shame and c.
Isa 41:29 their images are but wind and c.
Jer 51:34 he has thrown us into c, he has made
Mic 7: 4 Now is the time of their c.
Ac 19:32 The assembly was in c: Some were
Gal 1: 7 some people are throwing you into c
5:10 The one who is throwing you into c

Congealed
Ex 15: 8 waters c in the heart of the sea.

Congratulate
2Sa 8:10 c him on his victory in battle over
1Ki 1:47 the royal officials have come to c
1Ch 18:10 c him on his victory in battle over

Congregation (Congregations)
Ps 22:22 in the c I will praise you.
68:26 Praise God in the great c; praise
Ac 13:43 the c was dismissed, many of the
Heb 2:12 in the presence of the c I will sing

Congregations (Congregation)
1Co 14:33 As in all the c of the saints,

Conies (Coney)
Ps 104:18 the crags are a refuge for the c.
Pr 30:26 c are creatures of little power, yet

Conjure
Isa 47:11 you will not know how to c it away.

Connected (Connecting, Connection)
Lev 3: 3 the inner parts or is c to them,
3: 9 the inner parts or is c to them,
3:14 the inner parts or is c to them,
4: 8 the inner parts or is c to them,

Connecting (Connected)
Ex 28:28 c it to the waistband, so that the
39:21 c it to the waistband so that the

Connection (Connected)
Nu 18: 7 priests in c with everything at the
1Ch 6:49 on the altar of incense in c with
Ac 11:19 by the persecution in c with Stephen
Col 2:19 He has lost c with the Head, from

Conquer (Conquered, Conqueror, Conquerors, Conquers, Conquest)
Dt 2:31 Now begin to c and possess his land."
2Ch 32: 1 thinking to c them for himself.
Rev 13: 7 against the saints and to c them.

Conquered (Conquer)
Ge 14: 7 and they c the whole territory of the
Nu 24:18 Edom will be c; Seir, his enemy,
24:18 Seir, his enemy, will be c, but
Jos 10:42 lands Joshua c in one campaign,
12: 6 the LORD, and the Israelites c them.
12: 7 c on the west side of the Jordan,
23: 4 nations I c—between the Jordan
1Ki 15:20 He c Ijon, Dan, Abel Beth Maacah and
2Ch 16: 4 They c Ijon, Dan, Abel Maim and all
27: 5 king of the Ammonites and c them.
Heb 11:33 who through faith c kingdoms,

Conqueror (Conquer)
Mic 1:15 I will bring a c against you who
Rev 6: 2 he rode out as a c bent on conquest.

Conquerors (Conquer)
1Ki 8:47 you in the land of their c and say,
8:50 cause their c to show them mercy;
Ro 8:37 more than c through him who loved us.

Conquers (Conquer)
2Sa 5: 8 "Anyone who c the Jebusites will

Conquest (Conquer)
Am 6:13 you who rejoice in the c of Lo Debar
Rev 6: 2 rode out as a conqueror bent on c.

Conscience (Conscience', Consciences, Conscience-stricken, Conscientious)
Ge 20: 5 with a clear c and clean hands."
20: 6 I know you did this with a clear c,
1Sa 25:31 my master will not have on his c the
Job 27: 6 my c will not reproach me as long as
Ac 23: 1 to God in all good c to this day."
24:16 I strive always to keep my c clear
Ro 9: 1 c confirms it in the Holy Spirit—
13: 5 punishment but also because of c.
1Co 4: 4 My c is clear, but that does not
8: 7 their c is weak, it is defiled.
8:10 For if anyone with a weak c sees you
8:12 wound their weak c, you sin against
10:25 without raising questions of c,
10:27 you without raising questions of c.
10:29 the other man's c, I mean, not yours.
10:29 my freedom be judged by another's c?
2Co 1:12 this is our boast: Our c testifies
4: 2 every man's c in the sight of God.
5:11 I hope it is also plain to your c.
1Ti 1: 5 and a good c and a sincere faith.
1:19 holding on to faith and a good c.
3: 9 truths of the faith with a clear c.
2Ti 1: 3 with a clear c, as night and day I
Heb 9: 9 to clear the c of the worshipper.
10:22 to cleanse us from a guilty c
13:18 We are sure that we have a clear c
1Pe 3:16 keeping a clear c, so that those who
3:21 the pledge of a good c towards God.

Conscience' (Conscience)
1Co 10:28 man who told you and for c sake—

Consciences (Conscience)
Ro 2:15 their c also bearing witness, and
1Ti 4: 2 whose c have been seared as with a
Tit 1:15 their minds and c are corrupted.
Heb 9:14 cleanse our c from acts that lead to

Conscience-stricken (Conscience)
1Sa 24: 5 Afterwards, David was c for having
2Sa 24:10 David was c after he had counted the

Conscientious (Conscience)
2Ch 29:34 for the Levites had been more c in

Conscious
Ro 3:20 through the law we become c of sin.
1Pe 2:19 suffering because he is c of God.

Conscripted (Conscripting)
1Ki 5:13 King Solomon c labourers from all
9:15 forced labour Solomon c to build
9:21 Solomon c for his slave labour force,
2Ch 2: 2 He c seventy thousand men as
8: 8 Solomon c for his slave labour force,

Conscripting (Conscripted)
2Ki 25:19 charge of c the people of the land
Jer 52:25 charge of c the people of the land

Consecrate (Consecrated, Consecrating, Consecration, Reconsecrated)
Ex 13: 2 "C to me every firstborn male. The
19:10 and c them today and tomorrow.
19:22 the LORD, must c themselves,
28:38 the sacred gifts the Israelites c,
28:41 C them so they may serve me as
29: 1 what you are to do to c them
29:27 "C those parts of the ordination ram
29:36 for it, and anoint it to c it.
29:37 atonement for the altar and c it.
29:44 "So I will c the Tent of Meeting and
Ex 29:44 the altar and will c Aaron and his
30:29 You shall c them so they will be
30:30 Aaron and his sons and c them.
40: 9 in it; c it and all its furnishings,
40:10 and all its utensils; c the altar,
40:11 the basin and its stand and c them.
40:13 anoint him and c him so that he may
Lev 8:11 the basin with its stand, to c them.
8:12 head and anointed him to c him.
11:44 I am the LORD your God; c yourselves
16:19 c it from the uncleanness of the
20: 7 "'C yourselves and be holy, because
22: 2 offerings the Israelites c to me,
22: 3 that the Israelites c to the LORD,
25:10 C the fiftieth year and proclaim
Nu 6:11 That same day he is to c his head.
11:18 "Tell the people: 'C yourselves in
Jos 3: 5 "C yourselves, for tomorrow the
7:13 "Go, c the people. Tell them,
7:13 'C yourselves in preparation for
Jdg 17: 3 "I solemnly c my silver to the LORD
1Sa 16: 5 C yourselves and come to the
1Ch 15:12 fellow Levites are to c yourselves
23:13 to c the most holy things, to offer
29: 5 Now, who is willing to c himself
2Ch 13: 9 Whoever comes to c himself with a
29: 5 Levites! C yourselves now and c the
30:17 could not c their lambs to the LORD.
35: 6 c yourselves and prepare the lambs
Isa 66:17 "Those who c and purify themselves
Eze 44:19 so that they do not c the people by
Joel 2:16 Gather the people, c the assembly;

Consecrated (Consecrate)
Ex 19:14 he c them, and they washed their
29:21 sons and their garments will be c.
29:43 and the place will be c by my glory.
Lev 8:10 and everything in it, and so c them.
8:15 So he c it to make atonement for it.
8:30 So he c Aaron and his garments and
Nu 6: 8 his separation he is c to the LORD.
7: 1 it and c it and all its furnishings.
7: 1 c the altar and all its utensils.
15:40 commands and will be c to your God.
Dt 12:26 take your c things and whatever you
1Sa 7: 1 c Eleazar his son to guard the ark
16: 5 Then he c Jesse and his sons and
21: 4 there is some c bread here—provided
21: 6 the priest gave him the c bread,
1Ki 8:64 On that same day the king c the
9: 3 before me; I have c this temple,
9: 7 this temple I have c for my Name.
13:33 a priest he c for the high places.
1Ch 15:14 the priests and Levites c themselves
28:16 of gold for each table for c bread;
2Ch 2: 4 for setting out the c bread
5:11 who were there had c themselves
7: 7 Solomon c the middle part of the
7:16 I have chosen and c this temple so
7:20 temple which I have c for my Name.
23: 6 they may enter because they are c,
26:18 who have been c to burn incense.
29:15 their brothers and c themselves,
29:17 eight more days they c the temple
29:18 the c bread, with all its articles.
29:19 We have prepared and c all the
29:33 The animals c as sacrifices amounted
29:34 and until other priests had been c,
30: 3 not enough priests had c themselves
30: 8 sanctuary, which he has c for ever.
30:15 were ashamed and c themselves and
30:17 in the crowd had not c themselves
30:24 number of priests c themselves.
31:14 to the LORD and also the c gifts.
35: 3 and who had been c to the LORD:
36:14 LORD, which he had c in Jerusalem.
Ezr 8:28 as these articles are c to the LORD.
Ps 50: 5 "Gather to me my c ones, who made a
106:16 and of Aaron, who was c to the LORD.
Jer 11:15 Can c meat avert your punishment?
Eze 48:11 This will be for the c priests, the
Hos 9:10 they c themselves to that shameful
Zep 1: 7 he has c those he has invited.
Hag 2:12 If a person carries c meat in the
2:12 other food, does it become c?'"
Mt 12: 4 and his companions ate the c bread
Mk 2:26 house of God and ate the c bread,
Lk 2:23 male is to be c to the Lord"),
6: 4 and taking the c bread, he ate what
1Ti 4: 5 it is c by the word of God and
Heb 9: 2 the table and the c bread; this was

Consecrating (Consecrate)
2Ch 29:34 more conscientious in c themselves
31:18 they were faithful in c themselves.
Eze 46:20 the outer court and c the people."

Consecration (Consecrate)
Ex 28: 3 garments for Aaron, for his c,
29:33 was made for their ordination and c.
2Ch 29:17 They began the c on the first day of

Consent (Consented)
Ge 34:15 We will give our c to you on one
34:22 the men will c to live with us as
34:23 ours? So let us give our c to them,
Job 39: 9 "Will the wild ox c to serve you?
Hos 8: 4 They set up kings without my c; they
Ac 23:21 for your c to their request."
1Co 7: 5 except by mutual c and for a time,
Phm :14 want to do anything without your c,

Consented (Consent)
Mt 3:15 all righteousness." Then John c.
Lk 22: 6 He c, and watched for an opportunity
23:51 who had not c to their decision and

Consequences (Consequently)
Nu 5:31 woman will bear the c of her sin.'"
9:13 That man will bear the c of his sin.
18:22 the c of their sin and will die.
Eze 16:58 You will bear the c of your lewdness
23:35 c of your lewdness and prostitution."
23:49 bear the c of your sins of idolatry.
44:10 idols must bear the c of their sin.
44:12 they must bear the c of their sin,

Consequently (Consequences)
Ro 5:18 C, just as the result of one
10:17 C, faith comes from hearing the
13: 2 C, he who rebels against the
Eph 2:19 C, you are no longer foreigners and

Consider (Considerable, Considerate, Considered, Considers, Reconsider)
Ex 30:32 sacred, and you are to c it sacred.
30:37 yourselves; c it holy to the LORD.
Lev 19:23 c it forbidden; it must not be eaten.
21: 8 C them holy, because I the LORD am
Nu 23: 9 not c themselves one of the nations.
Dt 15:18 Do not c it a hardship to set your
17:20 not c himself better than his
32: 7 c the generations long past.
Jdg 5:10 and you who walk along the road, c
19:30 about it! C it! Tell us what to do!"
1Sa 12:24 c what great things he has done for
16: 7 "Do not c his appearance or his
24:15 May he c my cause and uphold it; may
1Ki 2: 9 now, do not c him innocent. You are
1Ch 28:10 C now, for the LORD has chosen you
2Ch 19: 6 He told them, "C carefully what you
Job 4: 7 "C now: Who, being innocent, has
13:24 Why do you hide your face and c me
23: 5 answer me, and c what he would say.
37:14 "Listen to this, Job; stop and c God'
Ps 5: 1 to my words, O LORD, c my sighing
8: 3 I c your heavens, the work of your
10:14 grief; you c it to take it in hand.
37:37 C the blameless, observe the upright;
45:10 Listen, O daughter, c and give ear:
48:13 c well her ramparts, view her
50:22 "C this, you who forget God, or I
77:12 works and c all your mighty deeds.
107:43 and c the great love of the LORD.
119: 6 to shame when I c all your commands
119:15 on your precepts and c your ways.

Ps 119:128 I c all your precepts right, I hate
137: 6 I do not c Jerusalem my highest joy.
143: 5 and c what your hands have done.
Pr 6: 6 c its ways and be wise!
20:25 rashly and only later to c his vows.
Ecc 2:12 I turned my thoughts to c wisdom,
7:13 C what God has done: Who can
7:14 be happy; but when times are bad, c:
Isa 41:20 see and know, may c and understand
41:22 so that we may c them and know
47: 7 But you did not c these things
Jer 2:19 C then and realise how evil and
2:23 in the valley; c what you have done.
2:31 "You of this generation, c the word
5: 1 and c, search through her squares.
9:17 "C now! Call for the wailing women
Lam 1: 9 skirts; she did not c her future.
1:11 O LORD, and c, for I am despised."
2:20 "Look, O LORD, and c: Whom have you
Eze 31: 3 C Assyria, once a cedar in Lebanon,
43:10 of their sins. Let them c the plan,
47:22 You are to c them as native-born
Da 8:25 and he will c himself superior.
9:23 Therefore, c the message and
10:11 c carefully the words I am about to
Hag 2:15 c how things were before one stone
Mk 4:24 "C carefully what you hear," he
Lk 7: 7 That is why I did not even c myself
8:18 Therefore c carefully how you listen.
12:24 C the ravens: They do not sow or
12:27 "C how the lilies grow. They do not
14:31 Will he not first sit down and c
Ac 4:29 Now, Lord, c their threats and
5:35 "Men of Israel, c carefully what
13:46 and do not c yourselves worthy of
15: 6 The apostles and elders met to c
16:15 "If you c me a believer in the Lord,"
20:24 However, I c my life worth nothing
26: 2 "King Agrippa, I c myself fortunate
26: 8 Why should any of you c it
Ro 8:18 I c that our present sufferings are
11:18 If you do, c this: You do not
11:22 C therefore the kindness and
14:16 Do not allow what you c good to be
1Co 10:18 C the people of Israel: Do not those
2Co 10: 7 he should c again that we belong to
Gal 3: 6 C Abraham: "He believed God, and it
Php 2: 3 c others better than yourselves.
2: 6 did not c equality with God
3: 7 was to my profit I now c loss
3: 8 What is more, I c everything a loss
3: 8 I c them rubbish, that I may gain
3:13 Brothers, I do not c myself yet to
1Ti 6: 1 should c their masters worthy of
Phm :17 if you c me a partner, welcome him
Heb 10:24 let us c how we may spur one another
12: 3 C him who endured such opposition
13: 7 C the outcome of their way of life
Jas 1: 2 C it pure joy, my brothers, whenever
3: 5 C what a great forest is set on fire
5:11 you know, we c blessed those who

Considerable (Consider)

Mt 14:24 the boat was already a c distance
Ac 14: 3 Paul and Barnabas spent c time there,

Considerate (Consider)

Tit 3: 2 to be peaceable and c, and to show
Jas 3:17 c, submissive, full of mercy and
1Pe 2:18 c, but also to those who are harsh.
3: 7 Husbands, in the same way be c as

Considered (Consider)

Ge 30:33 dark-coloured, will be c stolen."
Lev 17: 4 man shall be c guilty of bloodshed;
25:31 them are to be c as open country.
Dt 2:11 they too were c Rephaites, but the
2:20 (That too was c a land of the
1Sa 26:21 Because you c my life precious today,
2Sa 4: 2 Beeroth is c part of Benjamin,
1Ki 10:21 c of little value in Solomon's days.
16:31 He not only c it trivial to commit
2Ch 9:20 c of little value in Solomon's day.
Ne 13:13 these men were c trustworthy.
Job 1: 8 "Have you c my servant Job?
2: 3 "Have you c my servant Job?
18: 3 cattle and c stupid in your sight?
34: 6 Although I am right, I am c a liar;
Ps 44:22 we are c as sheep to be slaughtered.
119:59 I have c my ways and have turned my
Isa 53: 4 yet we c him stricken by God,
65:20 reach a hundred will be c accursed.
Lam 4: 2 are now c as pots of clay, the work
Hos 9: 7 the prophet is c a fool, the
Mt 1:20 after he had c this, an angel of the
14: 5 because they c him a prophet.
Lk 20:35 those who are c worthy of taking
22:24 which of them was c to be greatest.
Ro 8:36 are c as sheep to be slaughtered."
2Co 11:12 an opportunity to be c equal with us
1Ti 1:12 that he c me faithful, appointing me
Heb 11:11 because he c him faithful who had
Jas 2:21 our ancestor Abraham c righteous
2:25 Rahab the prostitute c righteous

Considers (Consider)

Job 33:10 fault with me; he c me his enemy.
Ps 33:15 of all, who c everything they do.
Pr 31:16 She c a field and buys it; out of
Eze 18:28 he c all the offences he has
Ro 14: 5 One man c one day more sacred than
14: 5 another man c every day alike.
Jas 1:26 If anyone c himself religious and

Consign (Consigning)

Isa 43:28 and I will c Jacob to destruction
Eze 32:18 of Egypt and c to the earth below

Consigning (Consign)

2Sa 12:31 c them to labour with saws and with
1Ch 20: 3 c them to labour with saws and with

Consist (Consisted, Consisting, Consists)

Lev 2: 4 it is to c of fine flour: cakes made
Eze 45:12 The shekel is to c of twenty gerahs.
Lk 12:15 a man's life does not c in the

Consisted (Consist)

Jos 17: 5 Manasseh's share c of ten tracts of
1Ch 27: 1 Each division c of 24,000 men.

Consisting (Consist)

Eze 46:14 c of a sixth of an ephah with a

Consists (Consist)

Eze 45:14 (which c of ten baths or one homer,
Eph 5: 9 (for the fruit of the light c in all

Consolation (Console)

Job 6:10 I would still have this c—my joy
21: 2 let this be the c you give me.
Ps 94:19 your c brought joy to my soul.
Lk 2:25 He was waiting for the c of Israel,

Consolations (Console)

Job 15:11 Are God's c not enough for you,

Console (Consolation, Consolations, Consoled, Consoling)

Job 21:34 "So how can you c me with your
Isa 22: 4 Do not try to c me over the
51:19 famine and sword—who can c you?
Jer 16: 7 anyone give them a drink to c them.

Consoled (Console)

2Sa 13:39 he was c concerning Amnon's death.
Job 42:11 They comforted and c him over all
Eze 14:22 you will be c regarding the disaster
14:23 You will be c when you see their
31:16 were c in the earth below.
32:31 he will be c for all his hordes that

Consoling (Console)

Ge 27:42 "Your brother Esau is c himself with

Consort

Ps 26: 4 men, nor do I c with hypocrites;
Hos 4:14 the men themselves c with harlots

Conspicuous

Eze 19:11 c for its height and for its many

Conspiracy (Conspire)

2Sa 15:12 And so the c gained strength, and
2Ki 15:15 and the c he led, are written in the
Ps 64: 2 Hide me from the c of the wicked,
Isa 8:12 "Do not call c everything that
8:12 that these people call c; do not
Jer 11: 9 the LORD said to me, "There is a c
Eze 22:25 There is a c of her princes within
Am 7:10 "Amos is raising a c against you in
Ac 23:12 The next morning the Jews formed a c

Conspirators (Conspire)

2Sa 15:31 "Ahithophel is among the c with

Conspire (Conspiracy, Conspirators, Conspired)

Ps 2: 1 Why do the nations c and the peoples
31:13 they c against me and plot to take
56: 6 They c, they lurk, they watch my
59: 3 Fierce men c against me for no
71:10 who wait to kill me c together.
83: 3 With cunning they c against your
105:25 people, to c against his servants.
Mic 7: 3 they desire—they all c together.
Ac 4:27 c against your holy servant Jesus,

Conspired (Conspire)

1Sa 22: 8 Is that why you have all c against
22:13 "Why have you c against me, you and
1Ki 2:28 Joab, who had c with Adonijah
2Ki 9:14 the son of Nimshi, c against Joram.
10: 9 It was I who c against my master and
12:20 His officials c against him and
14:19 They c against him in Jerusalem, and
15:10 Shallum son of Jabesh c against
15:25 Pekah son of Remaliah, c against him.
15:30 Hoshea son of Elah c against Pekah
21:23 Amon's officials c against him and
2Ch 24:25 His officials c against him for
24:26 Those who c against him were Zabad,
25:27 they c against him in Jerusalem and
33:24 Amon's officials c against him and
Est 2:21 and c to assassinate King Xerxes.
6: 2 had c to assassinate King Xerxes.
Da 2: 9 You have c to tell me misleading and
Ac 9:23 had gone by, the Jews c to kill him,

Constant (Constantly)

Nu 17: 5 will rid myself of this c grumbling
Dt 28:66 You will live in c suspense, filled
Job 33:19 pain with c distress in his bones,
Pr 19:13 wife is like a c dripping.
27:15 like a c dripping on a rainy day;
Isa 51:13 that you live in c terror every day
Eze 30:16 Memphis will be in c distress.
Ac 27:33 "you have been in c suspense and
1Ti 6: 5 c friction between men of corrupt
Heb 5:14 who by c use have trained themselves

Constantly (Constant)

Ps 106: 3 justice, who c do what is right.
119:109 Though I c take my life in my hands,
Isa 52: 5 day long my name is c blasphemed.
Jn 3:23 people were c coming to be baptised.
Ac 1:14 They all joined together c in prayer,
Ro 1: 9 is my witness how c I remember
2Co 11:26 I have been c on the move. I have
2Th 1:11 With this in mind, we c pray for you,
2Ti 1: 3 day I c remember you in my prayers.

Constellations

2Ki 23: 5 the c and to all the starry hosts.
Job 9: 9 the Pleiades and the c of the south.
38:32 Can you bring forth the c in their
Isa 13:10 The stars of heaven and their c will

Construct (Constructed, Constructing, Construction, Constructive)
2Ch 20:36 He agreed with him to **c** a fleet of

Constructed (Construct)
1Ki 9:24 her, he **c** the supporting terraces.
1Ch 15: 1 After David had **c** buildings for
Eze 40:17 that had been **c** all round the court;

Constructing (Construct)
Ex 36: 1 all the work of **c** the sanctuary
36: 3 out the work of **c** the sanctuary.
Ezr 5: 4 names of the men **c** this building?"

Construction (Construct)
1Ki 7: 1 to complete the **c** of his palace.
2Ki 16:10 with detailed plans for its **c**.
Ezr 5:16 under **c** but is not yet finished."
6: 8 Jews in the **c** of this house of God:

Constructive (Construct)
1Co 10:23 —but not everything is **c**.

Consult (Consultation, Consulted, Consulting, Consults)
1Sa 28: 8 "**C** a spirit for me," he said, "and
28:16 Samuel said, "Why do you **c** me, now
2Ki 1: 2 "Go and **c** Baal-Zebub, the god of
1: 3 to **c** Baal-Zebub, the god of Ekron?'
1: 6 you are sending men to **c** Baal-Zebub,
1:16 is no God in Israel for you to **c**
1:16 sent messengers to **c** Baal-Zebub,
8: 8 **C** the LORD through him; ask him,
2Ch 17: 3 He did not **c** the Baals
25:15 "Why do you **c** this people's gods,
Est 1:13 king to **c** experts in matters of law
Pr 15:12 correction; he will not **c** the wise.
Isa 8:19 men tell you to **c** mediums and
8:19 **c** the dead on behalf of the living?
19: 3 they will **c** the idols and the
40:14 Whom did the LORD **c** to enlighten him,
Eze 21:21 he will **c** his idols, he will examine
Hos 4:12 of my people. They **c** a wooden idol
Gal 1:16 the Gentiles, I did not **c** any man,

Consultation (Consult)
1Ch 12:19 after **c**, their rulers sent him away.

Consulted (Consult)
1Ki 12: 6 King Rehoboam **c** the elders who had
12: 8 **c** the young men who had grown up
2Ki 21: 6 and **c** mediums and spiritists.
1Ch 10:13 and even **c** a medium for guidance,
2Ch 10: 6 King Rehoboam **c** the elders who had
10: 8 **c** the young men who had grown up
25:17 king of Judah **c** his advisers,
32: 3 he **c** with his officials and military
33: 6 and **c** mediums and spiritists.
Jer 8: 2 have followed and **c** and worshipped.

Consulting (Consult)
2Ch 20:21 After **c** the people, Jehoshaphat
Isa 30: 2 who go down to Egypt without **c** me;

Consults (Consult)
Dt 18:11 or spiritist or who **c** the dead.
Eze 14:10 be as guilty as the one who **c** him.

Consume (Consumed, Consumes, Consuming)
Dt 5:25 we die? This great fire will **c** us,
Jdg 9:15 and **c** the cedars of Lebanon!'
9:20 come out from Abimelech and **c** you,
9:20 and Beth Millo, and **c** Abimelech!"
1Ki 16: 3 I am about to **c** Baasha and his house,
21:21 I will **c** your descendants and cut
2Ki 1:10 and **c** you and your fifty men!"
1:12 and **c** you and your fifty men!"
Job 5: 5 The hungry **c** his harvest, taking it
15:34 **c** the tents of those who love bribes.
20:26 A fire unfanned will **c** him and
Ps 21: 9 them up, and his fire will **c** them.
39:11 you **c** their wealth like a moth—
59:13 **c** them in wrath, **c** them till they
Ecc 5:11 increase, so do those who **c** them.
Isa 10:17 and **c** his thorns and his briers.
26:11 reserved for your enemies **c** them.
Jer 17:27 that will **c** her fortresses.'"
21:14 that will **c** everything around you.'"
49:27 will **c** the fortresses of Ben-Hadad."
50:32 that will **c** all who are around her."
Eze 15: 7 the fire, the fire will yet **c** them.
20:47 **c** all your trees, both green and dry.
21:28 to **c** and to flash like lightning!
22:31 them and **c** them with my fiery anger,
Hos 8:14 that will **c** their fortresses."
Am 1: 4 will **c** the fortresses of Ben-Hadad.
1: 7 of Gaza that will **c** her fortresses.
1:10 of Tyre that will **c** her fortresses."
1:12 will **c** the fortresses of Bozrah."
1:14 that will **c** her fortresses amid war
2: 2 will **c** the fortresses of Kerioth.
2: 5 will **c** the fortresses of Jerusalem."
Ob :18 they will set it on fire and **c** it.
Na 3:15 down and, like grasshoppers, **c** you.
Zec 12: 6 They will **c** right and left all the
Jn 2:17 "Zeal for your house will **c** me.
Heb 10:27 fire that will **c** the enemies of God.

Consumed (Consume)
Ge 31:40 This was my situation: The heat **c** me
Ex 15: 7 anger; it **c** them like stubble.
Lev 6:10 that the fire has **c** on the altar
9:24 **c** the burnt offering and the fat
10: 2 the presence of the LORD and **c** them,
Nu 11: 1 **c** some of the outskirts of the camp.
11:33 teeth and before it could be **c**,
16:35 and **c** the 250 men who were offering
21:28 It **c** Ar of Moab, the citizens of
2Ki 1:10 and **c** the captain and his men.
1:12 heaven and **c** him and his fifty men.
1:14 and **c** the first two captains and
2Ch 7: 1 and **c** the burnt offering and the
Ps 31:10 My life is **c** by anguish and my years
78:63 Fire **c** their young men, and their
90: 7 We are **c** by your anger and terrified
106:18 followers; a flame **c** the wicked.
119:20 My soul is **c** with longing for your
Ecc 10:12 but a fool is **c** by his own lips.
Isa 42:25 it **c** them, but they did not take
Jer 3:24 **c** the fruits of our fathers' labour
Lam 3:22 of the LORD's great love we are not **c**
4:11 fire in Zion that **c** her foundations.
Eze 19:12 branches withered and fire **c** them.
19:14 its main branches and **c** its fruit.
23:25 you who are left will be **c** by fire.
28:18 and it **c** you, and I reduced you to
Na 1:10 they will be **c** like dry stubble.
3:13 your enemies; fire has **c** their bars.
Zep 1:18 jealousy the whole world will be **c**,
3: 8 **c** by the fire of my jealous anger.
Zec 9: 4 the sea, and she will be **c** by fire.
Rev 18: 8 She will be **c** by fire, for mighty is

Consumes (Consume)
Ps 69: 9 for zeal for your house **c** me, and
83:14 fire **c** the forest or a flame sets
97: 3 Fire goes before him and **c** his foes
Isa 9:18 like a fire; it **c** briers and thorns,
24: 6 Therefore a curse **c** the earth; its
33:11 your breath is a fire that **c** you.
Jer 5:14 fire and these people the wood it **c**.
Lam 2: 3 fire that **c** everything around it.

Consuming (Consume, *Consuming fire*)
Dt 32:24 **c** pestilence and deadly plague;
Jdg 6:21 the rock, **c** the meat and the bread
Joel 2: 5 like a crackling fire **c** stubble,

Consuming fire
Ex 24:17 like a **c** on top of the mountain.
Dt 4:24 For the LORD your God is a **c**, a
2Sa 22: 9 **c** came from his mouth,
Ps 18: 8 **c** came from his mouth,
Isa 30:27 of wrath, and his tongue is a **c**.
30:30 coming down with raging anger and **c**,
33:14 "Who of us can dwell with the **c**? Who
Heb 12:29 for our "God is a **c**."

Contact
Hag 2:13 defiled by **c** with a dead body

Contain (Contained, Container, Containing, Contains)
1Ki 8:27 the highest heaven, cannot **c** you.
2Ch 2: 6 the highest heavens, cannot **c** him?
6:18 the highest heavens, cannot **c** you.
Ecc 8: 8 has power over the wind to **c** it;
2Pe 3:16 His letters **c** some things that are

Contained (Contain)
Ac 10:12 **c** all kinds of four-footed animals,
Heb 9: 4 This ark **c** the gold jar of manna,

Container (Contain)
Nu 19:15 every open **c** without a lid fastened

Containing (Contain)
Ex 13: 3 mighty hand. Eat nothing **c** yeast.
23:18 to me along with anything **c** yeast.
34:25 to me along with anything **c** yeast,
Lev 8: 2 basket **c** bread made without yeast,
1Sa 6:11 along with it the chest **c** the gold
6:15 together with the chest **c** the gold
Jer 32:11 copy **c** the terms and conditions,
36:27 scroll **c** the terms and conditions,
Eze 45:11 the bath **c** a tenth of a homer and

Contains (Contain)
Job 28: 6 and its dust **c** nuggets of gold.
Pr 15: 6 The house of the righteous **c** great

Contaminated (Contaminates, Contamination)
Lev 13:47 "If any clothing is **c** with mildew
13:54 he shall order that the **c** article be
13:56 he is to tear the **c** part out of the
14:40 he is to order that the **c** stones be

Contaminates (Contaminated)
2Co 7: 1 everything that **c** body and spirit,

Contamination (Contaminated)
Lev 13:49 if the **c** in the clothing, or leather,
13:52 article that has the **c** in it,
13:59 regulations concerning **c** by mildew

Contemplating
Isa 33:15 and shuts his eyes against **c** evil—

Contempt (Contemptible, Contemptuous)
Lev 22: 9 and die for treating them with **c**.
Nu 14:11 will these people treat me with **c**?
14:23 treated me with **c** will ever see it.
16:30 men have treated the LORD with **c**."
Dt 17:12 The man who shows **c** for the judge or
1Sa 2:17 treating the LORD's offering with **c**.
25:39 Nabal for treating me with **c**.
2Sa 12:14 enemies of the LORD show utter **c**,
19:43 So why do you treat us with **c**? Were
Job 12: 5 Men at ease have **c** for misfortune as
12:21 He pours **c** on nobles and disarms the
31:34 so dreaded the **c** of the clans that I
Ps 31:11 I am the utter **c** of my neighbours
31:18 for with pride and **c** they speak
107:40 he who pours **c** on nobles made them
119:22 Remove from me scorn and **c**, for I
123: 3 on us, for we have endured much **c**.
123: 4 the proud, much **c** from the arrogant.
Pr 14:31 He who oppresses the poor shows **c**
17: 5 He who mocks the poor shows **c** for
18: 3 wickedness comes, so does **c**, and

Pr 27:11 answer anyone who treats me with **c**.
Eze 22: 7 treated father and mother with **c**;
Da 12: 2 others to shame and everlasting **c**.
Hos 12:14 and will repay him for his **c**.
Na 3: 6 you with **c** and make you a spectacle.
Mal 1: 6 "It is you, O priests, who show **c**
1: 6 'How have we shown **c** for your name?'
Ro 2: 4 Or do you show **c** for the riches of
Gal 4:14 did not treat me with **c** or scorn.
1Th 5:20 do not treat prophecies with **c**.

Contemptible (Contempt)
1Sa 3:13 his sons made themselves **c**, and he
Eze 35:12 have heard all the **c** things you
Da 11:21 "He will be succeeded by a **c** person
Mal 1: 7 By saying that the LORD's table is **c**.
1:12 and of its food, 'It is **c**.'

Contemptuous (Contempt)
Dt 17:13 be afraid, and will not be **c** again.
Pr 19:16 he who is **c** of his ways will die.

Contend (Contended, Contending, Contends, Contention, Contentious)
Ge 6: 3 "My Spirit will not **c** with man for
Jdg 6:32 saying, "Let Baal **c** with him,"
Ps 35: 1 **C**, O LORD, with those who **c** with me;
35:23 **C** for me, my God and Lord.
127: 5 **c** with their enemies in the gate.
Ecc 6:10 **c** with one who is stronger than he.
Isa 27: 8 By warfare and exile you **c** with her—
49:25 I will **c** with those who **c** with you,
Jude : 3 urge you to **c** for the faith that was

Contended (Contend)
Dt 33: 8 **c** with him at the waters of Meribah.
Php 4: 3 help these women who have **c** at my

Contending (Contend)
Php 1:27 **c** as one man for the faith of the

Contends (Contend)
Job 40: 2 "Will the one who **c** with the
Jer 15:10 whom the whole land strives and **c**!

Content (Contented, Contentment, Contents)
Jos 7: 7 If only we had been **c** to stay on the
Pr 13:25 The righteous eat to their hearts' **c**,
19:23 one rests **c**, untouched by trouble.
Ecc 4: 8 his eyes were not **c** with his wealth.
Lk 3:14 people falsely—be **c** with your pay."
Php 4:11 to be **c** whatever the circumstances.
4:12 I have learned the secret of being **c**
1Ti 6: 8 clothing, we will be **c** with that.
Heb 13: 5 money and be **c** with what you have,

Contented (Content)
Da 4: 4 home in my palace, **c** and prosperous.

Contention (Contend)
Ps 80: 6 You have made us a source of **c** to

Contentious (Contend)
1Co 11:16 If anyone wants to be **c** about this,

Contentment (Content)
Job 36:11 in prosperity and their years in **c**.
SS 8:10 in his eyes like one bringing **c**.
1Ti 6: 6 godliness with **c** is great gain.

Contents
Lev 1:16 He is to remove the crop with its **c**

Contest
Heb 10:32 a great **c** in the face of suffering.

Continual (Continue)
1Ki 14:30 There was **c** warfare between Rehoboam
2Ch 12:15 There was **c** warfare between Rehoboam

Pr 15:15 the cheerful heart has a **c** feast.
Eph 4:19 of impurity, with a **c** lust for more.

Continually (Continue)
Ex 28:38 It will be on Aaron's forehead **c** so
Lev 24: 2 the lamps may be kept burning **c**.
24: 3 LORD from evening till morning, **c**.
24: 4 before the LORD must be tended **c**.
Nu 4: 7 that is **c** there is to remain on it.
Dt 11:12 eyes of the LORD your God are **c** on
1Ki 10: 8 who **c** stand before you and hear your
2Ch 9: 7 who **c** stand before you and hear your
24:14 were presented **c** in the temple
Ps 26: 3 me, and I walk **c** in your truth.
50:20 You speak **c** against your brother and
74:23 of your enemies, which rises **c**.
Isa 27: 3 LORD, watch over it; I water it **c**.
28:24 does he plough **c**? Does he keep on
65: 3 a people who **c** provoke me to my very
Jer 33:18 me **c** to offer burnt offerings,
Eze 8:17 violence and **c** provoke me to anger?
Da 6:16 God, whom you serve **c**, rescue you!"
6:20 has your God, whom you serve **c**, been
Am 1:11 because his anger raged **c** and his
Ob :16 so all the nations will drink **c**;
Lk 24:53 they stayed **c** at the temple,
1Th 1: 3 We **c** remember before our God and
2:13 we also thank God **c** because, when
5:17 pray **c**;
Heb 13:15 therefore, let us **c** offer to God

Continue (Continual, Continually, Continued, Continues, Continuing, Continuously)
Ex 9: 2 them go and **c** to hold them back,
33:13 you and **c** to find favour with you.
40:15 will **c** for all generations to come."
Lev 25:22 will **c** to eat from it until the
25:35 so that he can **c** to live among you.
25:36 countryman may **c** to live among you.
26: 5 Your threshing will **c** until grape
26: 5 grape harvest will **c** until planting,
26:23 but **c** to be hostile towards me,
Nu 26:27 me but **c** to be hostile towards me,
34: 4 cross south of Scorpion Pass, **c** on
34: 9 **c** to Ziphron and end at Hazar Enan.
34:11 **c** along the slopes east of the Sea
Dt 22:19 She shall **c** to be his wife; he must
Jos 13:13 they **c** to live among the Israelites
Jdg 19:27 and stepped out to **c** on his way,
Ru 2:13 "May I **c** to find favour in your eyes,
2Sa 7:29 that it may **c** for ever in your sight;
1Ki 8:23 who **c** wholeheartedly in your way.
2Ki 17:41 **c** to do as their fathers did.
1Ch 17:27 that it may **c** for ever in your sight;
2Ch 6:14 who **c** wholeheartedly in your way.
Est 9:23 the Jews agreed to **c** the celebration
Ps 36:10 **C** your love to those who know you,
72:17 ever; may it **c** as long as the sun.
89:36 that his line will **c** for ever and
Isa 47: 7 You said, 'I will **c** for ever—the
Jer 3: 5 angry? Will your wrath **c** for ever?'
18:12 We will **c** with our own plans; each
23:26 How long will this **c** in the hearts
Eze 20:31 you **c** to defile yourselves with all
21:13 the sword despises, does not **c**?
Da 4:27 that then your prosperity will **c**."
9:26 a flood: War will **c** until the end,
12:10 but the wicked will **c** to be wicked.
Hos 4:18 they **c** their prostitution; their
Mal 2: 4 that my convenant with Levi may **c**,"
Jn 17:26 and will **c** to make you known in
Ac 13:43 urged them to **c** in the grace of God.
Ro 1:32 they not only **c** to do these very
11:22 provided that you **c** in his kindness.
2Co 1:10 hope that he will **c** to deliver us,
11: 9 you in any way, and will **c** to do so.
Gal 2:10 All they asked was that we should **c**
3:10 "Cursed is everyone who does not **c**
Php 1:18 Yes, and I will **c** to rejoice,
1:25 and I will **c** with all of you for
2:12 **c** to work out your salvation with
Col 1:23 if you **c** in your faith, established
2: 6 Jesus as Lord, **c** to live in him,

2Th 2: 7 will **c** to do so till he is taken
3: 4 will **c** to do the things we command.
1Ti 2:15 if they **c** in faith, love and
2Ti 3:14 as for you, **c** in what you have
Heb 6:10 his people and **c** to help them.
1Pe 4:19 faithful Creator and **c** to do good.
1Jn 2:28 now, dear children, **c** in him, so
3: 9 No-one who is born of God will **c** to
5:18 born of God does not **c** to sin;
2Jn : 9 Anyone who runs ahead and does not **c**
3Jn : 3 and how you **c** to walk in the truth.
Rev 22:11 Let him who does wrong **c** to do wrong;
22:11 let him who is vile **c** to be vile;
22:11 let him who does right **c** to do right;
22:11 let him who is holy **c** to be holy.

Continued (Continue)
Ge 8: 5 The waters **c** to recede until the
12: 9 Abram set out and **c** towards the
26:13 The man became rich, and his wealth **c**
29: 1 Jacob **c** on his journey and came to
30:36 **c** to tend the rest of Laban's flocks.
42: 2 He **c**, "I have heard that there is
Ex 36: 3 And the people **c** to bring freewill
Nu 9:16 That is how it **c** to be; the cloud
21:16 From there they **c** on to Beer, the
Jos 9:21 They **c**, "Let them live, but let them
15: 3 **c** on to Zin and went over to the
15: 6 went up to Beth Hoglah and **c** north
15: 7 **c** along to the waters of En Shemesh
15:10 **c** down to Beth Shemesh and crossed
16: 6 **c** to the sea. From Micmethath on the
17: 9 the boundary **c** south to the Kanah
18:16 It **c** down the Hinnom Valley along
18:17 went to En Shemesh, **c** to Geliloth,
18:18 **c** to the northern slope of Beth
19:13 **c** eastward to Gath Hepher and
Jdg 1:29 **c** to live there among them.
14:17 her, because she **c** to press him.
18:31 They **c** to use the idols Micah had
1Sa 2:26 the boy Samuel **c** to grow in stature
3:21 The LORD **c** to appear at Shiloh, and
7:15 Samuel **c** as judge over Israel all
18:30 The Philistine commanders **c** to go
30:10 and four hundred men **c** the pursuit.
2Sa 2:27 the men would have **c** the pursuit of
2:29 They crossed the Jordan, **c** through
15:30 David **c** up the Mount of Olives,
16:13 David and his men **c** along the road
20:18 She **c**, "Long ago they used to say,
1Ki 2:17 he **c**, "Please ask King Solomon—he
3: 6 You have **c** this great kindness to
5:11 Solomon **c** to do this for Hiram year
18:29 they **c** their frantic prophesying
22:19 Micaiah **c**, "Therefore hear the word
22:43 and the people **c** to offer sacrifices
2Ki 12: 3 the people **c** to offer sacrifices
13: 6 Israel to commit; they **c** in them.
13:11 Israel to commit; he **c** in them.
14: 4 the people **c** to offer sacrifices
15: 4 the people **c** to offer sacrifices
15:35 the people **c** to offer sacrifices
2Ch 12:13 firmly in Jerusalem and **c** as king.
18:18 Micaiah **c**, "Therefore hear the word
27: 2 however, **c** their corrupt practices.
29:28 All this **c** until the sacrifice of
33:17 The people, however, **c** to sacrifice
Ezr 6:14 the elders of the Jews **c** to build
10: 6 because he **c** to mourn over the
Ne 4:21 we **c** the work with half the men
5: 9 I **c**, "What you are doing is not
12:37 At the Fountain Gate they **c** directly
Est 2:20 for she **c** to follow Mordecai's
Job 27: 1 Job **c** his discourse:
29: 1 Job **c** his discourse:
36: 1 Elihu **c**:
Ps 78:17 they **c** to sin against him, rebelling
Isa 64: 5 But when we **c** to sin against them,
Jer 32:20 Egypt and have **c** them to this day,
Da 7:11 "Then I **c** to watch because of the
10:12 he **c**, "Do not be afraid, Daniel.
Mk 4:24 carefully what you hear," he **c**.
Lk 4:24 "I tell you the truth," he **c**, "no
15:11 Jesus **c**: "There was a man who had
Jn 8:23 he **c**, "You are from below; I am from

Jn 12:17 from the dead **c** to spread the word.
Ac 2:46 Every day they **c** to meet together in
4:33 With great power the apostles **c** to
12:24 the word of God **c** to increase and
14: 7 where they **c** to preach the good news.
15:38 and had not **c** with them in the work.
21: 5 was up, we left and **c** on our way.
21: 7 We **c** our voyage from Tyre and landed
27:20 many days and the storm **c** raging,

Continues (Continue)

Lev 15: 3 Whether it **c** flowing from his body
15:25 discharge that **c** beyond her period,
15:26 her discharge **c** will be unclean,
Ps 100: 5 **c** through all generations.
119:90 Your faithfulness **c** through all
2Co 10:15 Our hope is that, as your faith **c** to
1Ti 5: 5 **c** night and day to pray and to ask
Jas 1:25 and **c** to do this, not forgetting
1Jn 3: 6 No-one who **c** to sin has either seen
2Jn : 9 whoever **c** in the teaching has both

Continuing (Continue)

Ex 28:29 as a **c** memorial before the LORD.
Nu 15:23 **c** through the generations to come—
Ro 13: 8 the **c** debt to love one another
Heb 7:23 prevented them from **c** in office;
2Pe 2: 9 judgment, while **c** their punishment.

Continuously (Continue)

Lev 6:13 be kept burning on the altar **c**;

Contract

Isa 16:14 as a servant bound by **c** would count
21:16 as a servant bound by **c** would count

Contradict

Lk 21:15 will be able to resist or **c**.

Contrary

Lev 10: 1 before the LORD, **c** to his command.
Dt 17: 3 **c** to my command has worshipped other
Jos 22:27 On the **c**, it is to be a witness
2Ch 30:18 the Passover, **c** to what was written.
Ps 119:85 dig pitfalls for me, **c** to your law.
Ac 18:13 worship God in ways **c** to the law."
Ro 9: 7 On the **c**, "It is through Isaac that
11:24 and **c** to nature were grafted into a
12:20 On the **c**: "If your enemy is hungry,
16:17 **c** to the teaching you have learned.
1Co 9:12 On the **c**, we put up with anything
12:22 On the **c**, those parts of the body
2Co 2:17 On the **c**, in Christ we speak before
4: 2 On the **c**, by setting forth the truth
10: 4 On the **c**, they have divine power to
Gal 2: 7 On the **c**, they saw that I had been
3:12 law is not based on faith; on the **c**,
5:17 desires what is **c** to the Spirit,
5:17 what is **c** to the sinful nature.
1Th 2: 4 On the **c**, we speak as men approved
2Th 3: 8 On the **c**, we worked night and day,
1Ti 1:10 else is **c** to the sound doctrine
2Ti 1:17 On the **c**, when he was in Rome, he

Contribute (Contributed, Contributing, Contribution, Contributions)

2Ki 15:20 Every wealthy man had to **c** fifty

Contributed (Contribute)

2Ch 31: 3 The king **c** from his own possessions
35: 8 His officials also **c** voluntarily to
Ne 7:70 Some of the heads of the families **c**
12:47 all Israel **c** the daily portions for

Contributing (Contribute)

Ro 12: 8 if it is **c** to the needs of others,

Contribution (Contribute)

Ex 29:28 It is the **c** the Israelites are to
Lev 7:14 a **c** to the LORD; it belongs to the
7:32 offerings to the priest as a **c**.
Ne 10:34 a **c** of wood to burn on the altar of
Ro 15:26 Achaia were pleased to make a **c** for

Contributions (Contribute)

Lev 22:12 she may not eat any of the sacred **c**.
Nu 5: 9 All the sacred **c** the Israelites
2Ch 24:10 the people brought their **c** gladly,
31:10 their **c** to the temple of the LORD,
31:12 they faithfully brought in the **c**,
31:14 distributing the **c** made to the LORD
Ne 10:39 are to bring their **c** of grain, new
12:44 for the **c**, firstfruits and tithes.
13: 5 as well as the **c** for the priests.
13:31 I also made provision for **c** of wood

Contrite

Ps 51:17 a broken and **c** heart, O God, you
Isa 57:15 but also with him who is **c** and lowly
57:15 and to revive the heart of the **c**.
66: 2 **c** in spirit, and trembles at my word.

Control (Controlled, Controlling, Controls, Self-control, Self-controlled)

Ge 45: 1 Joseph could no longer **c** himself
Ex 32:25 that Aaron had let them get out of **c**
Jos 18: 1 country was brought under their **c**,
2Sa 8: 1 Ammah from the **c** of the Philistines.
8: 3 his **c** along the Euphrates River.
1Ki 11:24 where they settled and took **c**.
1Ch 18: 1 from the **c** of the Philistines.
18: 3 his **c** along the Euphrates River.
2Ch 17: 5 established the kingdom under his **c**;
25: 3 After the kingdom was firmly in his **c**
Pr 29:11 a wise man keeps himself under **c**.
Ecc 2:19 Yet he will have **c** over all the work
Jer 28:14 give him **c** over the wild animals.'"
Da 11:43 He will gain **c** of the treasures of
Ro 6:20 free from the **c** of righteousness.
1Co 7: 9 if they cannot **c** themselves, they
7:37 but has **c** over his own will,
14:32 are subject to the **c** of prophets.
Php 3:21 him to bring everything under his **c**,
1Th 4: 4 should learn to **c** his own body
2Ti 3: 6 and gain **c** over weak-willed women,
1Jn 5:19 is under the **c** of the evil one.
Rev 16: 9 who had **c** over these plagues, but

Controlled (Control)

Jdg 10: 4 They **c** thirty towns in Gilead, which
1Ch 2:22 who **c** twenty-three towns in Gilead.
Ps 32: 9 but must be **c** by bit and bridle
Ro 7: 5 For when we were **c** by the sinful
8: 6 **c** by the Spirit is life and peace;
8: 8 Those **c** by the sinful nature cannot
8: 9 You, however, are **c** not by the

Controlling (Control)

Ge 43:31 **c** himself, said, "Serve the food."

Controls (Control)

Job 37:15 Do you know how God **c** the clouds and
Pr 16:32 a man who **c** his temper than one who

Controversies

Ac 26: 3 with all the Jewish customs and **c**.
1Ti 1: 4 These promote **c** rather than God's
6: 4 He has an unhealthy interest in **c**
Tit 3: 9 avoid foolish **c** and genealogies and

Convened (Convenes)

Ac 25: 6 and the next day he **c** the court and
25:17 I did not delay the case, but **c** the

Convenes (Convened)

Job 11:10 and **c** a court, who can oppose him?

Convenient

Ac 24:25 I find it **c**, I will send for you."

Conversation

1Sa 19: 7 David and told him the whole **c**.
Jer 38:24 know about this **c**, or you may die.
38:27 had heard his **c** with the king.
Col 4: 6 Let your **c** be always full of grace,

Convert (Converted, Converts)

Mt 23:15 over land and sea to win a single **c**,
Ac 6: 5 Nicolas from Antioch, a **c** to Judaism.
Ro 16: 5 **c** to Christ in the province of Asia.
1Ti 3: 6 He must not be a recent **c**, or he may

Converted (Convert)

Ac 15: 3 told how the Gentiles had been **c**.

Converts (Convert)

Ac 2:11 (both Jews and **c** to Judaism);
13:43 the Jews and devout **c** to Judaism
1Co 16:15 Stephanas were the first **c** in Achaia,

Convict (Convicted, Conviction, Convictions)

Dt 19:15 One witness is not enough to **c** a man
2Sa 14:13 does he not **c** himself, for the king
Pr 24:25 will go well with those who **c** the
Jn 16: 8 he will **c** the world of guilt
Jude :15 and to **c** all the ungodly of all

Convicted (Convict)

Jas 2: 9 are **c** by the law as law-breakers.

Conviction (Convict)

1Th 1: 5 the Holy Spirit and with deep **c**.

Convictions (Convict)

Jos 14: 7 him back a report according to my **c**,

Convince (Convinced, Convincing)

Ac 28:23 tried to **c** them about Jesus from the

Convinced (Convince)

Ge 45:28 Israel said, "I'm **c**! My son Joseph
Lk 16:31 they will not be **c** even if someone
Ac 19:26 hear how this fellow Paul has **c** and
Ac 26: 9 "I too was **c** that I ought to do all
26:26 I am **c** that none of this has escaped
28:24 Some were **c** by what he said, but
Ro 2:19 if you are **c** that you are a guide
8:38 For I am **c** that neither death nor
14: 5 should be fully **c** in his own mind.
14:14 **c** that no food is unclean in itself.
15:14 I myself am **c**, my brothers, that you
1Co 14:24 he will be **c** by all that he is a
2Co 5:14 because we are **c** that one died for
Php 1:25 **C** of this, I know that I will remain,
2Ti 1:12 and am **c** that he is able to guard
3:14 have learned and have become **c** of,

Convincing (Convince)

Ac 1: 3 many **c** proofs that he was alive.

Convocations

Isa 1:13 New Moons, Sabbaths and **c**—I cannot

Convulsed (Convulsion)

Ps 77:16 and writhed; the very depths were **c**.
Mk 9:26 The spirit shrieked, **c** him violently

Convulsion (Convulsed, Convulsions)

Mk 9:20 immediately threw the boy into a **c**.
Lk 9:42 threw him to the ground in a **c**.

Convulsions (Convulsion)

Lk 9:39 **c** so that he foams at the mouth.

Cooing

SS 2:12 the **c** of doves is heard in our land.

Cook (Cooked, Cooking, Cooks)
Ex 23:19 c a young goat in its mother's milk.
29:31 and c the meat in a sacred place.
34:26 c a young goat in its mother's milk."
Lev 8:31 "C the meat at the entrance to the
Dt 14:21 c a young goat in its mother's milk.
1Sa 9:23 Samuel said to the c, "Bring the
9:24 the c took up the leg with what was
1Ki 19:21 c the meat and gave it to the people,
2Ki 4:38 pot and c some stew for these men."
Eze 24: 5 to the boil and c the bones in it.
24:10 C the meat well, mixing in the
46:20 priests will c the guilt offering
46:24 c the sacrifices of the people."
Zec 14:21 take some of the pots and c in them.

Cooked (Cook)
Ex 12: 9 Do not eat the meat raw or c in
Lev 2: 7 If your grain offering is c in a pan,
6:28 The clay pot that the meat is c in
6:28 but if it is c in a bronze pot,
7: 9 or c in a pan or on a griddle
Nu 11: 8 They c it in a pot or made it into
2Ki 6:29 we c my son and ate him. The next
Lam 4:10 women have c their own children,

Cooking (Cook)
Ge 25:29 Once when Jacob was c some stew,
Lev 11:35 an oven or c pot must be broken up.
Eze 11: 3 This city is a c pot, and we are the
24: 3 "Put on the c pot; put it on and
Zec 14:20 and the c pots in the LORD's house

Cooks (Cook)
1Sa 8:13 to be perfumers and c and bakers.

Cool (Coolness)
Ge 3: 8 in the garden in the c of the day,
Jer 18:14 Do its c waters from distant sources
Lk 16:24 his finger in water and c my tongue,

Coolness (Cool)
Pr 25:13 Like the c of snow at harvest time

Copied (Copy)
Jos 8:32 Joshua c on stones the law of Moses,
Pr 25: 1 c by the men of Hezekiah king of
Eze 16:47 and c their detestable practices,

Copies (Copy)
Jer 32:14 both the sealed and unsealed c of
Heb 9:23 was necessary, then, for the c of

Copper
Dt 8: 9 and you can dig c out of the hills.
Job 28: 2 earth, and c is smelted from ore
Eze 22:18 all of them are the c, tin, iron and
22:20 men gather silver, c, iron, lead and
24:11 its c glows so its impurities may be
Mt 10: 9 gold or silver or c in your belts;
Mk 12:42 and put in two very small c coins,
Lk 21: 2 widow put in two very small c coins.

Copy (Copied, Copies)
Dt 17:18 himself on a scroll a c of this law,
2Ki 11:12 he presented him with a c of the
2Ch 23:11 they presented him with a c of the
Ezr 4:11 (This is a c of the letter they sent
4:23 c of the letter of King Artaxerxes
5: 6 This is a c of the letter that
7:11 c of the letter King Artaxerxes
Est 3:14 A c of the text of the edict was to
4: 8 He also gave him a c of the text of
8:13 A c of the text of the edict was to
Jer 32:11 sealed c containing the terms
32:11 as well as the unsealed c—
Heb 8: 5 They serve at a sanctuary that is a c
9:24 that was only a c of the true one;

Cor (Cors)
Eze 45:14 is a tenth of a bath from each c

Coral
Job 28:18 C and jasper are not worthy of
Eze 27:16 c and rubies for your merchandise.

Corban
Mk 7:11 from me is C' (that is, a gift

Cord (Cords)
Ge 38:18 "Your seal and its c, and the staff
38:25 seal and c and staff these are."
Ex 28:28 the rings of the ephod with blue c,
28:37 Fasten a blue c to it to attach it
39:21 the rings of the ephod with blue c,
39:31 they fastened a blue c to it to
Nu 15:38 with a blue c on each tassel.
Jos 2:18 you have tied this scarlet c in the
2:21 tied the scarlet c in the window.
2Sa 8: 2 them off with a length of c.
Job 41: 2 Can you put a c through his nose or
Ecc 4:12 A c of three strands is not quickly
12: 6 Remember him—before the silver c is
Eze 16: 4 On the day you were born your c was
40: 3 in the gateway with a linen c

Cordial (Cordially)
Ezr 5: 7 To King Darius: C greetings.

Cordially (Cordial)
Ps 28: 3 who speak c with their neighbours
Jer 9: 8 With his mouth each speaks c to his

Cords (Cord)
2Sa 22: 6 The c of the grave coiled around me;
Est 1: 6 fastened with c of white linen and
Job 4:21 Are not the c of their tent pulled
36: 8 held fast by c of affliction,
38:31 Can you loose the c of Orion?
Ps 18: 4 The c of death entangled me; the
18: 5 The c of the grave coiled around me;
116: 3 The c of death entangled me, the
129: 4 me free from the c of the wicked.
140: 5 they have spread out the c of their
Pr 5:22 him; the c of his sin hold him fast.
Isa 5:18 who draw sin along with c of deceit,
54: 2 lengthen your c, strengthen your
58: 6 and untie the c of the yoke,
Eze 27:24 with c twisted and tightly knotted.
Hos 11: 4 I led them with c of human kindness,
Jn 2:15 he made a whip out of c, and drove

Coriander
Ex 16:31 It was white like c seed and tasted
Nu 11: 7 The manna was like c seed and looked

Corinth (Corinthians)
Capital of Achaia, an important trading port between Rome and the East. Paul worked with Aquila and Priscilla here (Ac 18:1–2) and appeared before Proconsul Gallio (Ac 18:12–17). Paul left for Syria (Ac 18:18), and Apollos came to preach (Ac 18:27–19:1). Paul wrote to the church (1Co 1:2; 2Co 1:1), and returned at least twice (2Co 12:14; 13:1–3).

Ac 18: 1 Paul left Athens and went to C.
18:18 Paul stayed on in C for some time.
19: 1 While Apollos was at C, Paul took
1Co 1: 2 To the church of God in C, to those
2Co 1: 1 To the church of God in C, together
1:23 you that I did not return to C.
2Ti 4:20 Erastus stayed in C, and I left

Corinthians (Corinth)
Ac 18: 8 and many of the C who heard him
2Co 6:11 We have spoken freely to you, C, and

Cormorant
Lev 11:17 the little owl, the c, the great owl,
Dt 14:17 the desert owl, the osprey, the c,

Corn
Ge 37: 7 We were binding sheaves of c out in
41: 5 Seven ears of c, healthy and good,
41: 6 After them, seven other ears of c
41: 7 The thin ears of c swallowed up the
41:22 dreams I also saw seven ears of c,
41:24 The thin ears of c swallowed up the
41:26 and the seven good ears of c are
41:27 ears of c scorched by the east wind:
Ex 22: 6 or standing c or the whole field,
Dt 16: 9 to put the sickle to the standing c.
23:25 not put a sickle to his standing c.
Jdg 15: 5 the standing c of the Philistines.
15: 5 burned up the shocks and standing c,
2Ki 4:42 c, along with some ears of new c.
Job 24:24 they are cut off like ears of c.
Ps 65: 9 to provide the people with c,
65:13 and the valleys are mantled with c;
72:16 Let c abound throughout the land;
Isa 17: 5 a reaper gathers the standing c
17: 5 harvests the c with his arm—as
17: 5 ears of c in the Valley of Rephaim.
36:17 your own—a land of c and new wine,
Jer 9:22 like cut c behind the reaper, with
50:11 frolic like a heifer threshing c
Eze 36:29 I will call for the c and make it
Hos 14: 7 He will flourish like the c. He will
Mt 12: 1 to pick some ears of c and eat them.
Mk 2:23 they began to pick some ears of c.
4:28 All by itself the soil produces c
Lk 6: 1 began to pick some ears of c,

Cornelius
God-fearing Roman centurion stationed at Caesarea (Ac 10:1–2). Sent for Peter (Ac 10:1–8,19–33); heard gospel, received Holy Spirit, baptised (Ac 10:34–48); first Gentile convert.

Ac 10: 1 At Caesarea there was a man named C,
10: 3 who came to him and said, "C!"
10: 4 C stared at him in fear. "What is it,
10: 7 C called two of his servants and a
10:17 the men sent by C found out where
10:22 The men replied, "We have come from C
10:24 C was expecting them and had called
10:25 Peter entered the house, C met him
10:30 C answered: "Four days ago I was in
10:31 said, 'C, God has heard your prayer

Corner (Corners, Cornerstone, Cornerstones)
Ru 3: 9 "Spread the c of your garment over
1Sa 24: 4 and cut off a c of Saul's robe.
24: 5 for having cut off a c of his robe.
24:11 c of your robe but did not kill you.
1Ki 7:34 each c, projecting from the stand.
7:39 at the south-east c of the temple.
2Ki 14:13 from the Ephraim Gate to the C Gate
2Ch 4:10 the south side, at the south-east c.
25:23 from the Ephraim Gate to the C Gate
26: 9 towers in Jerusalem at the C Gate,
26:15 on the c defences to shoot arrows
28:24 at every street c in Jerusalem.
Ne 3:24 house to the angle and the c,
3:31 and as far as the room above the c;
3:32 between the room above the c and the
Pr 7: 8 going down the street near her c,
7:12 the squares, at every c she lurks.)
21: 9 Better to live on a c of the roof
25:24 Better to live on a c of the roof
Jer 31:38 the Tower of Hananel to the C Gate.
31:40 as far as the c of the Horse Gate,
Eze 16: 8 I spread the c of my garment over
46:21 and I saw in each c another court.
Zep 1:16 cities and against the c towers.
Zec 14:10 to the C Gate, and from the Tower of
Ac 26:26 because it was not done in a c.

Corners (Corner)
Ex 25:26 the four c, where the four legs are.
26:23 make two frames for the c at the far
26:24 At these two c they must be double
27: 2 Make a horn at each of the four c,
27: 4 each of the four c of the network.
28: 7 pieces attached to two of its c,
28:23 them to two c of the breastpiece.
28:24 rings at the c of the breastpiece,
28:26 attach them to the other two c of
36:28 two frames were made for the c of
36:29 At these two c the frames were

Ex 37:13 four c, where the four legs were.
38: 2 made a horn at each of the four c,
38: 5 the four c of the bronze grating.
39: 4 were attached to two of its c,
39:16 to two of the c of the breastpiece.
39:17 rings at the c of the breastpiece,
39:19 attached them to the other two c of
Nu 15:38 tassels on the c of your garments,
Dt 22:12 Make tassels on the four c of the
Job 1:19 and struck the four c of the house.
Isa 41: 9 from its farthest c I called you.
Eze 7: 2 come upon the four c of the land.
41:22 its c, its base and its sides were
43:20 on the four c of the upper ledge and
45:19 on the four c of the upper ledge of
46:21 and led me round to its four c,
46:22 In the four c of the outer court
46:22 in the four c was the same size.
Zec 9:15 for sprinkling the c of the altar.
Mt 6: 5 on the street c to be seen by men.
22: 9 Go to the street c and invite to the
Ac 10:11 let down to earth by its four c.
11: 5 let down from heaven by its four c,
Rev 7: 1 standing at the four c of the earth,
20: 8 nations in the four c of the earth

Cornerstone (Corner, Stone)
Job 38: 6 footings set, or who laid its c—
Isa 28:16 a precious c for a sure foundation;
Jer 51:26 rock will be taken from you for a c,
Zec 10: 4 From Judah will come the c, from him
Eph 2:20 Christ Jesus himself as the chief c.
1Pe 2: 6 a chosen and precious c, and the one

Cornerstones (Corner, Stone)
Isa 19:13 the c of her peoples have led Egypt

Cornfield (Field)
Dt 23:25 If you enter your neighbour's c, you

Cornfields (Field)
Mt 12: 1 At that time Jesus went through the c
Mk 2:23 Jesus was going through the c,
Lk 6: 1 Jesus was going through the c,

Corpse (Corpses)
Lev 22: 4 he touches something defiled by a c
Isa 14:19 Like a c trampled underfoot,
Mk 9:26 The boy looked so much like a c that

Corpses (Corpse)
Na 3: 3 people stumbling over the c—

Correct (Corrected, Correcting, Correction, Corrections, Correctly, Corrects)
Job 6:26 Do you mean to c what I say, and
40: 2 contends with the Almighty c him?
Jer 10:24 C me, LORD, but only with justice—
2Ti 4: 2 c, rebuke and encourage—

Corrected (Correct)
Pr 29:19 A servant cannot be c by mere words;

Correcting (Correct)
2Ti 3:16 c and training in righteousness,

Correction (Correct)
Lev 26:23 you do not accept my c but continue
Job 36:10 He makes them listen to c and
Pr 5:12 discipline! How my heart spurned c!
10:17 ignores c leads others astray.
12: 1 but he who hates c is stupid.
13:18 but whoever heeds c is honoured.
15: 5 but whoever heeds c shows prudence.
15:10 the path; he who hates c will die.
15:12 A mocker resents c; he will not
15:32 whoever heeds c gains understanding.
29:15 The rod of c imparts wisdom, but a
Jer 2:30 people; they did not respond to c.
5: 3 you crushed them but they refused c.
7:28 the LORD its God or responded to c.

Zep 3: 2 She obeys no-one, she accepts no c.
3: 7 you will fear me and accept c!'

Corrections (Correct)
Pr 6:23 c of discipline are the way to life,

Correctly (Correct)
Jdg 12: 6 he could not pronounce the word c,
Jer 1:12 The LORD said to me, "You have seen c
Lk 7:43 "You have judged c," Jesus said.
10:28 "You have answered c," Jesus replied.
2Ti 2:15 and who c handles the word of truth.

Corrects (Correct)
Job 5:17 "Blessed is the man whom God c; so
Pr 9: 7 "Whoever c a mocker invites insult;

Corresponding (Corresponds)
1Ch 23: 6 c to the sons of Levi: Gershon,
2Ch 3: 8 its length c to the width of the
Eze 42:12 to the c wall extending eastward,

Corresponds (Corresponding)
Gal 4:25 c to the present city of Jerusalem,

Corroded (Corrosion)
Jas 5: 3 Your gold and silver are c. Their

Corrosion (Corroded)
Jas 5: 3 Their c will testify against you and

Corrupt (Corrupted, Corruption, Corruptly, Corrupts)
Ge 6:11 Now the earth was c in God's sight
6:12 God saw how c the earth had become,
Ex 32: 7 up out of Egypt, have become c.
Dt 4:16 that you do not become c and make
4:25 become c and make any kind of idol,
9:12 brought out of Egypt have become c.
31:29 you are sure to become utterly c
Jdg 2:19 more c than those of their fathers,
2Ch 27: 2 continued their c practices.
Job 15:16 how much less man, who is vile and c,
Ps 14: 1 They are c, their deeds are vile;
14: 3 they have together become c; there
53: 1 They are c, and their ways are vile;
53: 3 they have together become c; there
94:20 Can a c throne be allied with you—
Pr 4:24 keep c talk far from your lips.
6:12 who goes about with a c mouth,
Pr 19:28 A c witness mocks at justice, and
Jer 2:21 turn against me into a c, wild vine?
Eze 20:44 your evil ways and your c practices,
Da 6: 4 and neither c nor negligent.
11:32 With flattery he will c those who
Hos 5: 3 turned to prostitution; Israel is c.
Ac 2:40 yourselves from this c generation."
1Ti 6: 5 friction between men of c mind,
2Pe 2:10 the c desire of the sinful nature

Corrupted (Corrupt)
Ge 6:12 people on earth had c their ways.
Eze 28:17 and you c your wisdom because of
2Co 7: 2 we have c no-one, we have exploited
Eph 4:22 is being c by its deceitful desires;
Tit 1:15 but to those who are c and do not
1:15 their minds and consciences are c.
Jude :23 the clothing stained by c flesh.
Rev 19: 2 who c the earth by her adulteries.

Corruption (Corrupt)
2Ki 23:13 on the south of the Hill of C—
Ezr 9:11 polluted by the c of its peoples.
Job 17:14 if I say to c, 'You are my father,'
Ps 55:23 down the wicked into the pit of c;
Isa 1: 4 of evildoers, children given to c!
Da 6: 4 They could find no c in him, because
Hos 9: 9 They have sunk deep into c, as in
2Pe 1: 4 escape the c in the world caused by
2:20 If they have escaped the c of the

Corruptly (Corrupt)
Dt 32: 5 They have acted c towards him; to
Jer 6:28 are bronze and iron; they all act c.
Zep 3: 7 eager to act c in all they did.

Corrupts (Corrupt)
Ecc 7: 7 a fool, and a bribe c the heart.
1Co 15:33 Do not be misled: "Bad company c
Jas 3: 6 It c the whole person, sets the

Cors (Cor)
1Ki 4:22 c of fine flour and sixty c of meal,
5:11 Solomon gave Hiram twenty thousand c
2Ch 2:10 twenty thousand c of ground wheat,
2:10 twenty thousand c of barley, twenty
27: 5 of silver, ten thousand c of wheat
27: 5 and ten thousand c of barley.
Ezr 7:22 a hundred c of wheat, a hundred

Cos
Ac 21: 1 out to sea and sailed straight to C.

Cosam
Lk 3:28 C, the son of Elmadam, the son of Er,

Cosmetic (Cosmetics)
2Sa 14: 2 and don't use any c lotions.

Cosmetics (Cosmetic)
Est 2:12 myrrh and six with perfumes and c.

Cost (Costly, Costs)
Nu 11: 5 the fish we ate in Egypt at no c—
16:38 who sinned at the c of their lives.
Jos 6:26 "At the c of his firstborn son will
6:26 at the c of his youngest will he set
2Sa 24:24 burnt offerings that c me nothing.
1Ki 16:34 He laid its foundations at the c of
16:34 and he set up its gates at the c of
1Ch 12:19 They said, "It will c us our heads
Pr 4: 7 c all you have, get understanding.
7:23 knowing it will c him his life.
23: 7 who is always thinking about the c.
Isa 55: 1 milk without money and without c.
Lk 14:28 estimate the c to see if he has
Rev 21: 6 I will give to drink without c from

Costly (Cost)
Ge 24:53 he also gave c gifts to her brother
Est 1: 6 mother-of-pearl and other c stones.
Ps 49: 8 the ransom for a life is c, no
Eze 16:10 and covered you with c garments.
16:13 and c fabric and embroidered cloth.
Da 11:38 with precious stones and c gifts.
1Co 3:12 c stones, wood, hay or straw,
Rev 18:12 c wood, bronze, iron and marble;

Costs (Cost)
1Ch 21:24 a burnt offering that c me nothing."
Ezr 6: 4 The c are to be paid by the royal
Pr 6:31 c him all the wealth of his house.

Couch (Couches)
Ge 49: 4 bed, onto my c and defiled it.
1Sa 28:23 up from the ground and sat on the c.
2Ki 4:32 was the boy lying dead on his c.
Est 7: 8 on the c where Esther was reclining.
Job 7:13 me and my c will ease my complaint,
Ps 6: 6 weeping and drench my c with tears.
Eze 23:41 You sat on an elegant c, with a

Couches (Couch)
Est 1: 6 There were c of gold and silver on a
Am 3:12 beds and in Damascus on their c."
6: 4 with ivory and lounge on your c.

Council (Councils)
Ge 49: 6 Let me not enter their c, let me not
Nu 16: 2 had been appointed members of the c.
Job 15: 8 Do you listen in on God's c? Do you
Ps 89: 7 In the c of the holy ones God is
107:32 praise him in the c of the elders.
111: 1 c of the upright and in the assembly.

Jer 23:18 them has stood in the c of the LORD
23:22 if they had stood in my c, they
Eze 13: 9 not belong to the c of my people
Mk 15:43 a prominent member of the C, who was
Lk 22:66 At daybreak the c of the elders of
23:50 Joseph, a member of the C, a good
Jn 3: 1 a member of the Jewish ruling c.
Ac 17:33 At that, Paul left the C.
22: 5 also the high priest and all the C
25:12 After Festus had conferred with his c

Councils (Council)
Mt 10:17 will hand you over to the local c
Mk 13: 9 will be handed over to the local c

Counsel (Counselled, Counsellor, Counsellors, Counsels)
2Sa 15:31 Ahithophel's c into foolishness."
1Ki 22: 5 "First seek the c of the LORD.
2Ch 18: 4 "First seek the c of the LORD.
22: 5 He also followed their c when he
25:16 this and have not listened to my c."
Ezr 10: 3 in accordance with the c of my lord
Job 12:13 c and understanding are his.
21:16 aloof from the c of the wicked.
22:18 aloof from the c of the wicked.
29:21 waiting in silence for my c.
38: 2 "Who is this that darkens my c with
42: 3 'Who is this that obscures my c
Ps 1: 1 not walk in the c of the wicked
32: 8 go; I will c you and watch over you.
73:24 You guide me with your c, and
106:13 had done and did not wait for his c.
107:11 and despised the c of the Most High.
Pr 8:14 C and sound judgment are mine; I
15:22 Plans fail for lack of c, but with
22:20 for you, sayings of c and knowledge,
27: 9 friend springs from his earnest c.
Isa 11: 2 the Spirit of c and of power, the
16: 3 "Give us c, render a decision. Make
28:29 wonderful in c and magnificent in
41:28 no-one among them to give c,
45:21 it—let them take c together.
47:13 All the c you have received has only
Jer 18:18 nor will c from the wise, nor the
38:15 Even if I did give you c, you would
49: 7 Has c perished from the prudent? Has
Eze 7:26 lost, as will the c of the elders.
1Ti 5:14 I c younger widows to marry, to have
Rev 3:18 I c you to buy from me gold refined

Counselled (Counsel)
Mic 6: 5 remember what Balak king of Moab c

Counsellor (Counsel)
2Sa 15:12 David's c, to come from Giloh, his
1Ch 26:14 his son Zechariah, a wise c, and
27:32 Jonathan, David's uncle, was a c, a
27:33 Ahithophel was the king's c. Hushai
Isa 3: 3 the c, skilled craftsman and clever
9: 6 And he will be called Wonderful C,
40:13 LORD, or instructed him as his c?
Mic 4: 9 you no king? Has your c perished,
Jn 14:16 another C to be with you for ever—
14:26 the C, the Holy Spirit, whom the
15:26 "When the C comes, whom I will send
16: 7 Unless I go away, the C will not
Ro 11:34 of the Lord? Or who has been his c?"

Counsellors (Counsel)
Ezr 4: 5 They hired c to work against them
Job 3:14 with kings and c of the earth, who
12:17 He leads c away stripped and makes
Ps 119:24 are my delight; they are my c.
Isa 1:26 of old, your c as at the beginning.
19:11 c of Pharaoh give senseless advice.

Counsels (Counsel)
Ps 16: 7 I will praise the LORD, who c me;
Na 1:11 against the LORD and c wickedness.

Count (Counted, Counting, Counts)
Ge 13:16 so that if anyone could c the dust,
15: 5 up at the heavens and c the stars
Ge 15: 5 the stars—if indeed you can c them.
16:10 they will be too numerous to c."
Ex 30:12 census of the Israelites to c them,
Lev 15:13 he is to c off seven days for his
15:28 she must c off seven days, and after
23:15 offering, c off seven full weeks.
23:16 C off fifty days up to the day after
25: 8 "'C off seven sabbaths of years—
25:50 He and his buyer are to c the time
Nu 1:49 "You must not c the tribe of Levi or
3:15 "C the Levites by their families and
3:15 C every male a month old or more."
3:40 said to Moses, "C all the firstborn
4: 3 C all the men from thirty to fifty
4:23 C all the men from thirty to fifty
4:29 "C the Merarites by their clans and
4:30 C all the men from thirty to fifty
6:12 The previous days do not c, because
23:10 Who can c the dust of Jacob or
31:26 community are to c all the people
Dt 16: 9 C off seven weeks from the time you
Jdg 6: 5 It was impossible to c the men and
1Ki 3: 8 people, too numerous to c or number.
1Ch 21: 2 "Go and c the Israelites from
27:24 Joab son of Zeruiah began to c the
Job 14:16 Surely then you will c my steps but
19:15 and my maidservants c me a stranger;
31: 4 see my ways and c my every step?
38:37 Who has the wisdom to c the clouds?
39: 2 Do you c the months till they bear?
Ps 22:17 I can c all my bones; people stare
32: 2 sin the LORD does not c against him
48:12 Zion, go round her, c her towers,
139:18 Were I to c them, they would
139:22 for them; I c them my enemies.
Isa 16:14 bound by contract would c them,
21:16 bound by contract would c it,
46: 5 "To whom will you compare me or c me
Ro 4: 8 the Lord will never c against him."
6:11 In the same way, c yourselves dead
2Th 1:11 that our God may c you worthy of his
Rev 7: 9 great multitude that no-one could c,
11: 1 altar, and c the worshippers there.

Counted (Count)
Ge 13:16 then your offspring could be c.
32:12 of the sea, which cannot be c.'"
Ex 30:12 for his life at the time he is c.
30:13 crosses over to those already c is
38:25 c in the census was 100 talents
38:26 who had crossed over to those c,
Nu 1:19 he c them in the Desert of Sinai:
1:22 the army were c and listed by name,
1:44 These were the men c by Moses and
1:45 were c according to their families.
1:47 were not c along with the others.
2:32 c according to their families.
2:33 The Levites, however, were not c
3:16 Moses c them, as he was commanded by
3:22 old or more who were c was 7,500.
3:34 old or more who were c was 6,200.
3:39 The total number of Levites c at the
3:42 Moses c all the firstborn of the
4:34 the leaders of the community c the
4:36 c by clans, were 2,750.
4:37 Moses and Aaron c them according to
4:38 The Gershonites were c by their
4:40 c by their clans and families, were
4:41 Moses and Aaron c them according to
4:42 The Merarites were c by their clans
4:44 c by their clans, were 3,200.
4:45 Moses and Aaron c them according to
4:46 c all the Levites by their clans
4:49 were c, as the LORD commanded Moses.
7: 2 in charge of those who were c, made
14:29 old or more who was c in the census
26:57 These were the Levites who were c by
26:62 They were not c along with the other
26:63 These are the ones c by Moses and
26:63 when they c the Israelites on the
26:64 Not one of them was among those c by
26:64 when they c the Israelites in the
31:49 "Your servants have c the soldiers
Jos 13: 3 all of it c as Canaanite (the
Jdg 7:12 no more be c than the sand on the
Jdg 21: 9 For when they c the people, they
1Sa 13:15 Saul c the men who were with him.
2Sa 2:15 they stood up and were c off—twelve
24:10 after he had c the fighting men,
1Ki 8: 5 they could not be recorded or c.
2Ki 12:10 c the money that had been brought
1Ch 9:28 they c them when they were brought
21:17 ordered the fighting men to be c?
22: 4 more cedar logs than could be c,
23: 3 thirty years old or more were c,
23:11 c as one family with one assignment.
23:14 were c as part of the tribe of Levi.
23:24 their names and c individually,
23:27 the Levites were c from those twenty
2Ch 5: 6 they could not be recorded or c.
Ezr 1: 8 who c them out to Sheshbazzar the
Job 5: 9 fathomed, miracles that cannot be c.
9:10 fathomed, miracles that cannot be c.
Ps 49:18 Though while he lived he c himself
88: 4 I am c among those who go down to
Ecc 1:15 what is lacking cannot be c.
Isa 22:10 You c the buildings in Jerusalem and
Jer 46:23 than locusts, they cannot be c.
Hos 1:10 which cannot be measured or c.
Mt 26:15 c out for him thirty silver coins.
Ac 5:41 had been c worthy of suffering
2Th 1: 5 and as a result you will be c worthy

Countenance
Job 14:20 you change his c and send him away.

Counterfeit
2Th 2: 9 of c miracles, signs and wonders,
1Jn 2:27 that anointing is real, not c—

Counting (Count)
Ge 46:26 descendants, not c his sons' wives
Dt 24:15 because he is poor and is c on it.
Jdg 8:26 not c the ornaments, the pendants
2Co 5:19 not c men's sins against them.

Countless
Nu 10:36 to the c thousands of Israel."
Job 21:33 him, and a c throng goes before him.
Jer 33:22 me as c as the stars of the sky
Heb 11:12 as c as the sand on the seashore.

Countries (Country)
Ge 41:57 all the c came to Egypt to buy grain
Dt 29:16 through the c on the way here.
1Ki 4:21 These c brought tribute and were
2Ki 18:35 Who of all the gods of these c has
19:11 done to all the c, destroying them
2Ch 9:28 from Egypt and from all other c.
20:29 came upon all the kingdoms of the c
Isa 10:14 so I gathered all the c; not one
Isa 36:20 Who of all the gods of these c has
37:11 done to all the c, destroying them
Jer 16:15 the c where he had banished them.
23: 3 all the c where I have driven them
23: 8 the c where he had banished them.
27: 6 Now I will hand all your c over to
28: 8 against many c and great kingdoms.
Jer 40:11 Ammon, Edom and all the other c
40:12 the c where they had been scattered.
51:28 officials, and all the c they rule.
Eze 5: 5 the nations, with c all around her.
5: 6 than the nations and c around her.
11:16 and scattered them among the c,
11:16 them in the c where they have gone.'
11:17 the c where you have been scattered,
12:15 and scatter them through the c.
20:23 and scatter them through the c,
20:34 gather you from the c where you have
20:41 the c where you have been scattered,
22: 4 and a laughing-stock to all the c.
22:15 and scatter you through the c;
25: 7 and exterminate you from the c.
29:12 and scatter them through the c.
30:23 and scatter them through the c.
30:26 and scatter them through the c.
34:13 nations and gather them from the c,
35:10 "These two nations and c will be
36:19 they were scattered through the c;
36:24 I will gather you from all the c and
39:27 them from the c of their enemies,

Da 9: 7 both near and far, in all the **c**
11:40 He will invade many **c** and sweep
11:41 Many **c** will fall, but Edom, Moab and
11:42 He will extend his power over many **c**;
Zec 8: 7 from the **c** of the east and the west.

Country (Countries, Countryside, Countryman, Countrymen)

Ge 10:30 Sephar, in the eastern hill **c**.
12: 1 "Leave your **c**, your people and your
14: 6 the Horites in the hill **c** of Seir,
15:13 be strangers in a **c** not their own,
21:23 Show to me and the **c** where you are
24: 4 will go to my **c** and my own relatives
24: 5 son back to the **c** you came from?"
25:27 a man of the open **c**, while Jacob was
25:29 came in from the open **c**, famished.
27: 3 go out to the open **c** to hunt some
27: 5 Esau left for the open **c** to hunt
31:21 he headed for the hill **c** of Gilead.
31:23 up with him in the hill **c** of Gilead.
31:25 in the hill **c** of Gilead when Laban
31:54 a sacrifice there in the hill **c**
32: 3 in the land of Seir, the **c** of Edom.
32: 9 'Go back to your **c** and your
36: 8 Edom) settled in the hill **c** of Seir.
36: 9 the Edomites in the hill **c** of Seir.
36:35 defeated Midian in the **c** of Moab,
41:36 should be held in reserve for the **c**,
41:36 **c** may not be ruined by the famine."
41:56 famine had spread over the whole **c**,
Ex 1:10 fight against us and leave the **c**."
6: 1 he will drive them out of his **c**."
6:11 let the Israelites go out of his **c**."
7: 2 let the Israelites go out of his **c**.
8: 2 will plague your whole **c** with frogs.
10: 4 bring locusts into your **c** tomorrow.
10:14 area of the **c** in great numbers.
11:10 let the Israelites go out of his **c**.
12:33 the people to hurry and leave the **c**.
13:17 through the Philistine **c**, though
18:27 and Jethro returned to his own **c**.
Lev 25:24 Throughout the **c** that you hold as a
25:31 them are to be considered as open **c**.
25:45 of their clans born in your **c**,
26: 6 sword will not pass through your **c**.
26:34 you are in the **c** of your enemies;
Nu 13:17 the Negev and on into the hill **c**.
13:29 and Amorites live in the hill **c**;
14:40 went up towards the high hill **c**.
14:44 went up towards the high hill **c**,
14:45 Canaanites who lived in that hill **c**
20:17 Please let us pass through your **c**.
21:22 "Let us pass through your **c**. We will
22: 6 them and drive them out of the **c**.
22:13 "Go back to your own **c**, for the LORD
Dt 1: 7 into the hill **c** of the Amorites;
1:19 went towards the hill **c** of the
1:20 "You have reached the hill **c** of the
1:24 They left and went up into the hill **c**
1:41 it easy to go up into the hill **c**.
1:43 you marched up into the hill **c**.
2: 1 our way around the hill **c** of Seir.
2: 3 made your way around this hill **c**
2: 5 Esau the hill **c** of Seir as his own.
2:24 Amorite, king of Heshbon, and his **c**.
2:27 "Let us pass through your **c**. We will
2:31 deliver Sihon and his **c** over to you.
3:12 half of the hill **c** of Gilead, together
3:25 —that fine hill **c** and Lebanon."
9:28 the **c** from which you brought us
11: 3 king of Egypt and to his whole **c**;
22:25 if out in the **c** a man happens to
22:27 the man found the girl out in the **c**,
23: 7 you lived as an alien in his **c**.
28: 3 in the city and blessed in the **c**.
28:16 in the city and cursed in the **c**.
28:24 The LORD will turn the rain of your **c**
28:40 have olive trees throughout your **c**
Jos 1: 4 all the Hittite **c**—to the Great Sea
2: 9 all who live in this **c** are melting
7: 9 the other people of the **c** will hear
9: 1 these things—those in the hill **c**,
9: 6 "We have come from a distant **c**;
9: 9 have come from a very distant **c**
9:11 those living in our **c** said to us,
Jos 10: 6 the Amorite kings from the hill **c**
10:40 including the hill **c**, the Negev, the
11: 3 and Jebusites in the hill **c**;
11:16 took this entire land: the hill **c**,
11:21 the Anakites from the hill **c**:
11:21 from all the hill **c** of Judah,
11:21 and from all the hill **c** of Israel.
12: 8 the hill **c**, the western foothills,
13:21 with Sihon—who lived in that **c**.
13:25 half the Ammonite **c** as far as Aroer
14:12 Now give me this hill **c** that the
15:48 In the hill **c**: Shamir, Jattir, Socoh,
16: 1 desert into the hill **c** of Bethel.
17:15 "and if the hill **c** of Ephraim is too
17:16 "The hill **c** is not enough for us,
17:18 the forested hill **c** as well. Clear
18: 1 **c** was brought under their control,
18:12 and headed west into the hill **c**,
19:50 Serah in the hill **c** of Ephraim.
20: 7 Galilee in the hill **c** of Naphtali,
20: 7 Shechem in the hill **c** of Ephraim,
20: 7 is, Hebron) in the hill **c** of Judah.
21:11 in the hill **c** of Judah. (Arba was
21:21 In the hill **c** of Ephraim they were
22:33 the **c** where the Reubenites and the
24: 4 I assigned the hill **c** of Seir to
24:30 in the hill **c** of Ephraim, north of
24:33 Phinehas in the hill **c** of Ephraim.
Jdg 1: 9 the Canaanites living in the hill **c**,
1:19 They took possession of the hill **c**,
1:34 confined the Danites to the hill **c**,
2: 9 in the hill **c** of Ephraim, north of
3:27 he blew a trumpet in the hill **c** of
4: 5 and Bethel in the hill **c** of Ephraim,
6: 3 other eastern peoples invaded the **c**.
7:24 throughout the hill **c** of Ephraim,
10: 1 in Shamir, in the hill **c** of Ephraim.
11:12 us that you have attacked our **c**?"
11:17 us permission to go through your **c**,'
11:18 the eastern side of the **c** of Moab,
11:19 through your **c** to our own place.'
11:21 of the Amorites who lived in that **c**,
12:15 in the hill **c** of the Amalekites.
17: 1 Now a man named Micah from the hill **c**
17: 8 house in the hill **c** of Ephraim.
18: 2 The men entered the hill **c** of
18:13 From there they went on to the hill **c**
19: 1 area in the hill **c** of Ephraim
19:16 old man from the hill **c** of Ephraim,
19:18 the hill **c** of Ephraim where I live.
Ru 1: 1 live for a while in the **c** of Moab.
1Sa 1: 1 a Zuphite from the hill **c** of Ephraim,
6: 5 rats that are destroying the **c**,
6:18 towns with their **c** villages.
9: 4 he passed through the hill **c** of
13: 2 Michmash and in the hill **c** of Bethel,
14:22 had hidden in the hill **c** of Ephraim
14:29 My father has made trouble for the **c**.
27: 5 the **c** towns, that I may live there.
2Sa 10: 8 were by themselves in the open **c**.
19: 9 has fled the **c** because of Absalom;
20:21 from the hill **c** of Ephraim, has
1Ki 4: 8 Ben-Hur—in the hill **c** of Ephraim;
4:19 **c** of Sihon king of the Amorites
4:19 and the **c** of Og king of Bashan).
10: 6 "The report I heard in my own **c**
10:13 with her retinue to her own **c**.
11:21 so that I may return to my own **c**."
11:22 back to your own **c**?" Pharaoh asked.
11:29 two of them were alone out in the **c**,
12:25 hill **c** of Ephraim and lived there.
14:11 will feed on those who die in the **c**.
16: 4 feed on those who die in the **c**."
21:24 feed on those who die in the **c**."
2Ki 5:22 to me from the hill **c** of Ephraim.
8: 6 the day she left the **c** until now."
13:20 used to enter the **c** every spring.
17:26 what the god of that **c** requires.
18:25 against this **c** and destroy it.'"
19: 7 he will return to his own **c**, and
24: 7 not march out from his own **c** again,
1Ch 1:46 defeated Midian in the **c** of Moab,
4:42 of Ishi, invaded the hill **c** of Seir.
6:67 In the hill **c** of Ephraim they were
19: 3 and spy out the **c** and overthrow it?"
19: 9 were by themselves in the open **c**.
2Ch 9: 5 "The report I heard in my own **c**
9:12 with her retinue to her own **c**.
13: 4 in the hill **c** of Ephraim, and said,
14: 1 the **c** was at peace for ten years.
19: 4 Beersheba to the hill **c** of Ephraim
Ne 8:15 "Go out into the hill **c** and bring
9:22 They took over the **c** of Sihon king
9:22 and the **c** of Og king of Bashan.
Ps 78:54 the hill **c** his right hand had taken.
105:31 flies, and gnats throughout their **c**.
105:33 and shattered the trees of their **c**.
Pr 28: 2 a **c** is rebellious, it has many
29: 4 justice a king gives a **c** stability
Isa 1: 7 Your **c** is desolate, your cities
13: 5 his wrath—to destroy the whole **c**.
22:18 a ball and throw you into a large **c**.
36:10 against this **c** and destroy it.'"
37: 7 he will return to his own **c**, and
63:13 in open **c**, they did not stumble;
66: 8 Can a **c** be born in a day or a nation
Jer 12: 5 horses? If you stumble in safe **c**,
12:15 his own inheritance and his own **c**.
14:18 If I go into the **c**, I see those
15:13 of all your sins throughout your **c**.
17: 3 because of sin throughout your **c**.
17:26 from the hill **c** and the Negev,
22:26 who gave you birth into another **c**,
25:11 This whole **c** will become a desolate
32:44 Judah and in the towns of the hill **c**,
33:13 In the towns of the hill **c**, of the
40: 4 Look, the whole **c** lies before you;
40: 7 men who were still in the open **c**
40:13 army officers still in the open **c**
Eze 7:15 in the **c** will die by the sword,
14:13 "Son of man, if a **c** sins against me
14:15 I send wild beasts through that **c**
14:17 "Or if I bring a sword against that **c**
21:19 take, both starting from the same **c**.
33:27 those out in the **c** I will give to
Da 11: 9 South but will retreat to his own **c**.
11:19 his own **c** but will stumble and fall,
11:28 to his own **c** with great wealth,
11:28 it and then return to his own **c**.
Hos 12:12 Jacob fled to the **c** of Aram; Israel
Am 7:17 you yourself will die in a pagan **c**.
Jnh 1: 8 What is your **c**? From what people
Zec 5:11 He replied, "To the **c** of Babylonia
6: 6 horses is going towards the north **c**,
6: 8 those going towards the north **c** have
Mt 2:12 to their **c** by another route.
14:35 sent word to all the surrounding **c**.
Mk 15:21 passing by on his way in from the **c**,
16:12 while they were walking in the **c**.
Lk 1:39 to a town in the hill **c** of Judea,
1:65 and throughout the hill **c** of Judea
3: 3 He went into all the **c** around the
7:17 Judea and the surrounding **c**.
14:23 'Go out to the roads and **c** lanes and
15: 4 leave the ninety-nine in the open **c**
15:13 set off for a distant **c** and there
15:14 a severe famine in that whole **c**,
15:15 himself out to a citizen of that **c**,
19:12 of noble birth went to a distant **c**
21:21 those in the **c** not enter the city.
23:26 who was on his way in from the **c**,
Jn 4:44 prophet has no honour in his own **c**.)
11:55 many went up from the **c** to Jerusalem
Ac 7: 3 'Leave your **c** and your people,' God
7: 6 be strangers in a **c** not their own,
7: 7 come out of that **c** and worship me
9:32 Peter travelled about the **c**, he went
10:39 the **c** of the Jews and in Jerusalem.
12:20 the king's **c** for their food supply.
13:17 power he led them out of that **c**,
14: 6 and Derbe and to the surrounding **c**,
26: 4 in my own **c**, and also in Jerusalem.
2Co 11:26 in danger in the **c**, in danger at sea;
Heb 11: 9 like a stranger in a foreign **c**;
11:14 are looking for a **c** of their own.
11:15 If they had been thinking of the **c**
11:16 for a better **c**—a heavenly one.

Countryman (Country, Man)

Lev 25:15 You are to buy from your **c** on the
25:25 come and redeem what his **c** has sold.
25:36 **c** may continue to live among you.

Countrymen (Country, Men)
Lev 25:14 "If you sell land to one of your **c**
25:25 "If one of your **c** becomes poor and
25:35 "If one of your **c** becomes poor and
25:39 "If one of your **c** becomes poor
25:47 one of your **c** becomes poor and sells
Nu 32: 6 your **c** go to war while you sit here?
2Sa 15:20 I am going? Go back, and take your **c**.
2Ch 19:10 fellow **c** who live in the cities—
28:11 **c** that you have taken as prisoners,
28:15 back to their fellow **c** at Jericho,
35: 5 of your fellow **c**, the lay people.
35: 6 the lambs for your fellow **c**,
Ne 3:18 the repairs were made by their **c**
5: 5 the same flesh and blood as our **c**
5: 7 are exacting usury from your own **c**!"
Jer 22:13 making his **c** work for nothing, not
29:16 your **c** who did not go with you into
34:15 of you proclaimed freedom to his **c**.
34:17 freedom for your fellow **c**. So I now
Eze 3:11 Go now to your **c** in exile and speak
33: 2 "Son of man, speak to your **c** and say
33:12 "Therefore, son of man, say to your **c**
33:17 "Yet your **c** say, 'The way of the
33:30 your **c** are talking together about
37:18 "When your **c** ask you, 'Won't you
2Co 11:26 in danger from my own **c**, in danger
1Th 2:14 You suffered from your own **c** the

Countryside (Country)
1Sa 30:16 scattered over the **c**, eating,
2Sa 15:23 The whole **c** wept aloud as all the
18: 8 battle spread out over the whole **c**,
1Ki 20:27 while the Arameans covered the **c**.
2Ki 7:12 have left the camp to hide in the **c**,
Job 5:10 earth; he sends water upon the **c**.
SS 7:11 Come, my lover, let us go to the **c**,
Mk 1: 5 The whole Judean **c** and all the
5:14 and reported this in the town and **c**,
6:36 they can go to the surrounding **c**
6:56 into villages, towns or **c**—they
Lk 4:14 him spread through the whole **c**.
8:34 and reported this in the town and **c**,
9:12 to the surrounding villages and **c**
Jn 3:22 went out into the Judean **c**,

Counts (Count)
Job 19:11 he **c** me among his enemies.
Jer 33:13 the one who **c** them,' says the LORD.
Jn 6:63 life; the flesh **c** for nothing.
1Co 7:19 Keeping God's commands is what **c**.
Gal 5: 6 The only thing that **c** is faith
6:15 anything; what **c** is a new creation.

Courage (Courageous, Courageously)
Jos 2:11 everyone's **c** failed because of you,
5: 1 had the **c** to face the Israelites.
2Sa 4: 1 he lost **c**, and all Israel became
7:27 found **c** to offer you this prayer.
1Ch 17:25 servant has found **c** to pray to you.
2Ch 15: 8 son of Oded the prophet, he took **c**.
19:11 Act with **c**, and may the LORD be with
Ezr 7:28 I took **c** and gathered leading men
10: 4 support you, so take **c** and do it."
Ps 107:26 in their peril their **c** melted away.
Eze 22:14 Will your **c** endure or your hands be
Da 11:25 and **c** against the king of the South.
Mt 14:27 said to them: "Take **c**! It is I.
Mk 6:50 to them and said, "Take **c**! It is I.
Ac 4:13 they saw the **c** of Peter and John and
23:11 "Take **c**! As you have testified about
27:22 now I urge you to keep up your **c**,
27:25 keep up your **c**, men, for I have
1Co 16:13 the faith; be men of **c**; be strong.
Php 1:20 but will have sufficient **c** so that
Heb 3: 6 if we hold on to our **c** and the hope

Courageous (Courage, *Strong and courageous*)
Jos 1: 7 Be strong and very **c**. Be careful to
2Ch 26:17 with eighty other **c** priests of the

Courageously (Courage)
2Ch 25: 8 Even if you go and fight **c** in battle,
Php 1:14 word of God more **c** and fearlessly.

Courier (Couriers)
Jer 51:31 One **c** follows another and messenger

Couriers (Courier)
2Ch 30: 6 At the king's command, **c** went
30:10 The **c** went from town to town in
Est 3:13 Dispatches were sent by **c** to all the
3:15 the **c** went out, and the edict was
8:10 and sent them by mounted **c**, who rode
8:14 The **c**, riding the royal horses,

Course (Courses)
Ge 4: 3 In the **c** of time Cain brought some
Dt 2:37 the land along the **c** of the Jabbok
1Sa 1:20 in the **c** of time Hannah conceived
22:15 Of **c** not! Let not the king accuse
2Sa 2: 1 In the **c** of time, David enquired of
8: 1 In the **c** of time, David defeated the
10: 1 In the **c** of time, the king of the
13: 1 In the **c** of time, Amnon son of David
15: 1 In the **c** of time, Absalom provided
21:18 In the **c** of time, there was another
1Ki 6:36 and one **c** of trimmed cedar beams.
7:12 and one **c** of trimmed cedar beams,
1Ch 18: 1 In the **c** of time, David defeated the
19: 1 In the **c** of time, Nahash king of the
20: 4 In the **c** of time, war broke out with
2Ch 21:19 In the **c** of time, at the end of the
Job 1: 5 a period of feasting had run its **c**,
Ps 19: 5 a champion rejoicing to run his **c**.
36: 4 he commits himself to a sinful **c**
102:23 In the **c** of my life he broke my
Pr 2: 8 for he guards the **c** of the just and
15:21 of understanding keeps a straight **c**.
16: 9 In his heart a man plans his **c**, but
17:23 secret to pervert the **c** of justice.
Ecc 1: 6 it goes, ever returning on its **c**.
Jer 8: 6 Each pursues his own **c** like a horse
23:10 The prophets follow an evil **c**
Joel 2: 7 in line, not swerving from their **c**.
Ac 27: 7 wind did not allow us to hold our **c**,
Ro 10:18 Did they not hear? Of **c** they did:
2Co 12:18 same spirit and follow the same **c**?
13: 5 —unless, of **c**, you fail the test?
Jas 3: 6 sets the whole **c** of his life on fire,

Courses (Course)
Jdg 5:20 from their **c** they fought against
1Ki 6:36 of three **c** of dressed stone and one
7:12 a wall of three **c** of dressed stone
Ezr 6: 4 with three **c** of large stones and one

Court (Courts, Courtyard, Courtyards)
Ge 50: 4 Joseph said to Pharaoh's **c**, "If I
50: 7 the dignitaries of his **c** and all
Ex 21:22 husband demands and the **c** allows.
Dt 25: 1 they are to take it to **c** and the
Jdg 4: 5 She held **c** under the Palm of Deborah
1Ki 3:15 Then he gave a feast for all his **c**.
2Ki 20: 4 Before Isaiah had left the middle **c**,
23:11 They were in the **c** near the room of
1Ch 26:18 for the **c** to the west, there were
26:18 at the road and two at the **c** itself.
2Ch 4: 9 and the large **c** and the doors for
4: 9 the large **c** and the doors for the **c**,
6:13 it in the centre of the outer **c**.
Ne 3:25 palace near the **c** of the guard.
Est 4:11 approaches the king in the inner **c**
5: 1 stood in the inner **c** of the palace,
5: 2 he saw Queen Esther standing in the **c**
6: 4 The king said, "Who is in the **c**?"
6: 4 Haman had just entered the outer **c**
6: 5 "Haman is standing in the **c**.
Job 5: 4 crushed in **c** without a defender.
9:32 we might confront each other in **c**.
11:10 convenes a **c**, who can oppose him?
11:19 afraid, and many will **c** your favour.
31:21 knowing that I had influence in **c**,
Pr 22:22 and do not crush the needy in **c**,
25: 8 do not bring hastily to **c**, for what
29: 9 If a wise man goes to **c** with a fool,
Isa 3:13 The LORD takes his place in **c**; he
29:21 who ensnare the defender in **c** and
Jer 19:14 and stood in the **c** of the LORD's
29: 2 the **c** officials and the leaders of
34:19 the **c** officials, the priests and all
41:16 women, children and **c** officials he
Eze 8: 3 to the north gate of the inner **c**,
8: 7 brought me to the entrance to the **c**.
8:16 He then brought me into the inner **c**
10: 3 in, and a cloud filled the inner **c**.
10: 4 and the **c** was full of the radiance
10: 5 be heard as far away as the outer **c**,
40:17 he brought me into the outer **c**.
40:17 been constructed all round the **c**;
40:19 to the outside of the inner **c**;
40:20 north, leading into the outer **c**.
40:23 There was a gate to the inner **c**
40:27 The inner **c** also had a gate facing
40:28 he brought me into the inner **c**
40:30 the gateways around the inner **c**
40:31 Its portico faced the outer **c**; palm
40:32 he brought me to the inner **c** on the
40:34 Its portico faced the outer **c**; palm
40:37 Its portico faced the outer **c**; palm
40:44 within the inner **c**, were two rooms,
40:47 he measured the **c**: It was square—a
41:15 and the portico facing the **c**,
42: 1 led me northward into the outer **c**
42: 3 twenty cubits from the inner **c**
42: 3 the pavement of the outer **c**,
42: 7 to the rooms and the outer **c**;
42: 8 the outer **c** was fifty cubits long,
42: 9 as one enters them from the outer **c**.
42:10 length of the wall of the outer **c**,
42:14 they are not to go into the outer **c**
43: 5 up and brought me into the inner **c**,
44:17 they enter the gates of the inner **c**,
44:17 of the inner **c** or inside the temple.
44:19 they go out into the outer **c** where
44:21 wine when he enters the inner **c**.
44:27 On the day he goes into the inner **c**
45:19 and on the gateposts of the inner **c**.
46: 1 The gate of the inner **c** facing east
46:20 bringing them into the outer **c** and
46:21 He then brought me to the outer **c**
46:21 and I saw in each corner another **c**.
46:22 In the four corners of the outer **c**
Da 1: 3 chief of his **c** officials, to bring
2:49 himself remained at the royal **c**.
7:10 The **c** was seated, and the books were
7:26 "'But the **c** will sit, and his power
Am 5:10 you hate the one who reproves in **c**
Mt 5:25 adversary who is taking you to **c**.
Ac 18:12 on Paul and brought him into **c**.
18:16 he had them ejected from the **c**.
18:17 and beat him in front of the **c**.
25: 6 and the next day he convened the **c**
25:10 now standing before Caesar's **c**,
25:17 but convened the **c** the next day and
1Co 4: 3 by you or by any human **c**; indeed,
Jas 2: 6 ones who are dragging you into **c**?
Rev 11: 2 exclude the outer **c**; do not measure

Courts (Court)
Dt 17: 8 If cases come before your **c** that are
2Ki 21: 5 In both **c** of the temple of the LORD,
23:12 the two **c** of the temple of the LORD.
1Ch 28: 6 who will build my house and my **c**,
28:12 for the **c** of the temple of the LORD
2Ch 33: 5 In both **c** of the temple of the LORD,
Ne 8:16 in the **c** of the house of God
13: 7 a room in the **c** of the house of God.
Ps 65: 4 and bring near to live in your **c**!
84: 2 even faints, for the **c** of the LORD;
84:10 Better is one day in your **c** than a
92:13 will flourish in the **c** of our God.
96: 8 an offering and come into his **c**.
100: 4 thanksgiving and his **c** with praise;
116:19 in the **c** of the house of the LORD—
135: 2 in the **c** of the house of our God.
Isa 1:12 this of you, this trampling of my **c**?
62: 9 drink it in the **c** of my sanctuary."
Eze 9: 7 and fill the **c** with the slain.

Eze 42: 6 had no pillars, as the c had;
46:22 of the outer court were enclosed c,
46:22 each of the c in the four corners
46:23 of the four c was a ledge of stone,
Am 5:12 the poor of justice in the c.
5:15 good; maintain justice in the c.
Zec 3: 7 my house and have charge of my c,
8:16 true and sound judgment in your c;
Mt 21:23 Jesus entered the temple c, and,
26:55 day I sat in the temple c teaching,
Mk 11:16 merchandise through the temple c.
11:27 Jesus was walking in the temple c,
12:35 Jesus was teaching in the temple c,
14:49 teaching in the temple c, and you
Lk 2:27 Spirit, he went into the temple c.
2:46 days they found him in the temple c,
20: 1 teaching the people in the temple c
22:53 I was with you in the temple c, and
Jn 2:14 In the temple c he found men selling
7:14 to the temple c and begin to teach.
7:28 Jesus, still teaching in the temple c
8: 2 he appeared again in the temple c,
Ac 2:46 to meet together in the temple c.
3: 2 from those going into the temple c.
3: 8 he went with them into the temple c,
5:20 "Go, stand in the temple c," he said,
5:21 At daybreak they entered the temple c
5:25 the temple c teaching the people."
5:42 Day after day, in the temple c and
19:38 c are open and there are proconsuls.
24:18 found me in the temple c doing this.
26:21 the Jews seized me in the temple c

Courtyard (Court)

Ex 27: 9 "Make a c for the tabernacle. The
27:12 "The west end of the c shall be
27:13 c shall also be fifty cubits wide.
27:16 "For the entrance to the c, provide
27:17 All the posts around the c are to
27:18 The c shall be a hundred cubits long
27:19 for the c, are to be of bronze.
35:17 the curtains of the c with its posts
35:17 curtain for the entrance to the c;
35:18 and for the c, and their ropes;
38: 9 Next they made the c. The south side
38:15 entrance to the c, with three posts
38:16 All the curtains around the c were
38:17 the posts of the c had silver bands.
38:18 The curtain for the entrance to the c
38:18 curtains of the c, five cubits high,
38:20 of the surrounding c were bronze.
38:31 the bases for the surrounding c and
38:31 and those for the surrounding c.
39:40 the curtains of the c with its posts
39:40 curtain for the entrance to the c;
39:40 the ropes and tent pegs for the c;
40: 8 Set up the c around it and put the
40: 8 curtain at the entrance to the c.
40:33 Moses set up the c around the
40:33 curtain at the entrance to the c.
Lev 6:16 it in the c of the Tent of Meeting.
6:26 in the c of the Tent of Meeting.
Nu 3:26 the curtains of the c, the curtain
3:26 to the c surrounding the tabernacle
3:37 the surrounding c with their bases,
4:26 the curtains of the c surrounding
4:32 the surrounding c with their bases,
2Sa 17:18 He had a well in his c, and they
1Ki 6:36 built the inner c of three courses
7: 9 from the outside to the great c and
7:12 The great c was surrounded by a wall
7:12 as was the inner c of the temple of
8:64 c in front of the temple of the LORD,
2Ch 4: 9 He made the c of the priests, and
7: 7 c in front of the temple of the LORD,
20: 5 the LORD in the front of the new c
24:21 death in the c of the LORD's temple.
29:16 They brought out to the c of the
Est 2:11 to and fro near the c of the harem
Jer 26: 2 Stand in the c of the LORD's house
32: 2 was confined in the c of the guard
32: 8 came to me in the c of the guard
32:12 Jews sitting in the c of the guard.
33: 1 confined in the c of the guard,
36:10 which was in the upper c at the
Jer 36:20 they went to the king in the c
37:21 to be placed in the c of the guard
37:21 remained in the c of the guard.
38: 6 which was in the c of the guard.
38:13 remained in the c of the guard.
38:28 Jeremiah remained in the c of the
39:14 taken out of the c of the guard.
39:15 been confined in the c of the guard,
Eze 40:14 was up to the portico facing the c.
41:12 The building facing the temple c on
41:13 and the temple c and the building
41:14 The width of the temple c on the
41:15 the c at the rear of the temple,
42: 1 to the rooms opposite the temple c
42:10 adjoining the temple c and opposite
42:13 facing the temple c are the priests'
Mt 26:58 up to the c of the high priest.
26:69 Now Peter was sitting out in the c,
Mk 14:54 right into the c of the high priest.
14:66 While Peter was below in the c, one
Lk 22:55 a fire in the middle of the c and
Jn 18:15 with Jesus into the high priest's c,

Courtyards (Court)

Ex 8:13 houses, in the c and in the fields.
1Ch 23:28 the LORD: to be in charge of the c,
2Ch 23: 5 in the c of the temple of the LORD.
Ne 8:16 in their c, in the courts of the

Cousin (Cousins)

Lev 25:49 An uncle or a c or any
Est 2: 7 Mordecai had a c named Hadassah,
Jer 32: 8 my c Hanamel came to me in the
32: 9 field at Anathoth from my c Hanamel
32:12 in the presence of my c Hanamel and
Col 4:10 as does Mark, the c of Barnabas.

Cousins (Cousin)

Lev 10: 4 carry your c outside the camp, away
Nu 36:11 their c on their father's side.
1Ch 23:22 Their c, the sons of Kish, married

Covenant (*Ark of the covenant, Blood of the covenant, Book of the covenant, Covenant of the LORD, Covenanted, Covenants, Everlasting covenant, My covenant, New covenant*)

Ge 9:12 God said, "This is the sign of the c
9:12 a c for all generations to come:
9:13 of the c between me and the earth.
9:17 "This is the sign of the c I have
15:18 On that day the LORD made a c with
17:10 the c you are to keep: Every male
17:11 sign of the c between me and you.
31:44 Come now, let's make a c, you and I,
Ex 2:24 he remembered his c with Abraham,
23:32 Do not make a c with them or with
31:16 generations to come as a lasting c.
34:10 "I am making a c with you.
34:27 made a c with you and with Israel."
Ex 34:28 on the tablets the words of the c
Lev 2:13 Do not leave the salt of the c of
24: 8 of the Israelites, as a lasting c.
26:25 you to avenge the breaking of the c.
26:45 for their sake I will remember the c
Nu 14:44 nor the ark of the LORD's c moved
25:13 He and his descendants will have a c
Dt 4:13 He declared to you his c, the Ten
4:31 forget the c with your forefathers,
5: 2 The LORD our God made a c with us at
5: 3 fathers that the LORD made this c,
7: 9 keeping his c of love to a thousand
7:12 God will keep his c of love with you,
8:18 and so confirms his c, which he
9: 9 the tablets of the c that the LORD
9:11 stone tablets, the tablets of the c.
9:15 tablets of the c were in my hands.
17: 2 LORD your God in violation of his c,
29: 1 These are the terms of the c the
29: 1 c he had made with them at Horeb.
29: 9 Carefully follow the terms of this c,
29:12 into a c with the LORD your God,
29:12 a c the LORD is making with you this
29:14 I am making this c, with its oath,
Dt 29:21 c written in this Book of the Law.
29:25 the c he made with them when he
31:16 me and break the c I made with them.
33: 9 over your word and guarded your c.
Jos 6: 8 ark of the LORD's c followed them.
24:25 Joshua made a c for the people, and
Jdg 2: 2 you shall not make a c with the
2:20 this nation has violated the c
1Sa 4: 3 the ark of the LORD's c from Shiloh,
4: 5 the ark of the LORD's c came into
18: 3 Jonathan made a c with David because
20: 8 into a c with you before the LORD.
20:16 Jonathan made a c with the house of
22: 8 son makes a c with the son of Jesse.
23:18 The two of them made a c before the
1Ki 3:15 before the ark of the Lord's c
8: 1 bring up the ark of the LORD's c
8: 6 brought the ark of the LORD's c
8: 9 where the LORD made a c with the
8:23 you who keep your c of love with
19:10 The Israelites have rejected your c,
19:14 The Israelites have rejected your c,
2Ki 11: 4 He made a c with them and put them
11:12 presented him with a copy of the c
11:17 Jehoiada then made a c between the
11:17 a c between the king and the people.
13:23 his c with Abraham, Isaac and Jacob.
17:15 They rejected his decrees and the c
17:35 LORD made a c with the Israelites,
17:38 Do not forget the c I have made with
18:12 but had violated his c—all that
23: 3 renewed the c in the presence of the
23: 3 words of the c written in this book.
23: 3 people pledged themselves to the c.
1Ch 16:15 He remembers his c for ever, the
16:16 the c he made with Abraham, the oath
2Ch 5: 2 bring up the ark of the LORD's c
5: 7 brought the ark of the LORD's c to
5:10 where the LORD made a c with the
6:14 you who keep your c of love with
13: 5 descendants for ever by a c of salt?
15:12 They entered into a c to seek the
21: 7 Nevertheless, because of the c the
23: 1 He made a c with the commanders of
23: 3 the whole assembly made a c with the
23:11 presented him with a copy of the c
23:16 Jehoiada then made a c that he and
29:10 Now I intend to make a c with the
34:31 renewed the c in the presence of the
34:31 words of the c written in this book.
34:32 c of God, the God of their fathers.
Ezr 10: 3 Now let us make a c before our God
Ne 1: 5 who keeps his c of love with those
9: 8 and you made a c with him to give to
9:32 who keeps his c of love, do not let
13:29 the c of the priesthood and of the
Job 5:23 For you will have a c with the
31: 1 "I made a c with my eyes not to look
Ps 25:10 those who keep the demands of his c.
25:14 him; he makes his c known to them.
44:17 you or been false to your c.
50: 5 who made a c with me by sacrifice."
55:20 his friends; he violates his c.
60: T To the tune of "The Lily of the C".
74:20 Have regard for your c, because
78:10 they did not keep God's c and
78:37 they were not faithful to his c.
80: T the tune of "The Lilies of the c".
89: 3 You said, "I have made a c with my
89:39 You have renounced the c with your
103:18 with those who keep his c and
105: 8 He remembers his c for ever, the
105: 9 the c he made with Abraham, the oath
106:45 for their sake he remembered his c
111: 5 him; he remembers his c for ever.
111: 9 he ordained his c for ever—
Pr 2:17 ignored the c she made before God.
Isa 28:15 You boast, "We have entered into a c
28:18 Your c with death will be annulled;
42: 6 make you to be a c for the people
49: 8 make you to be a c for the people,
Jer 11: 2 "Listen to the terms of this c and
11: 3 does not obey the terms of this c—
11: 6 the terms of this c and follow them.
11: 8 on them all the curses of the c
11:10 the c I made with their forefathers.

Jer 14:21 your **c** with us and do not break it.
31:32 will not be like the **c** I made with
31:33 "This is the **c** that I will make with
34: 8 King Zedekiah had made a **c** with all
34:10 people who entered into this **c**
34:13 I made a **c** with your forefathers
34:15 You even made a **c** before me in the
34:18 terms of the **c** they made before me,
50: 5 **c** that will not be forgotten.
Eze 16: 8 oath and entered into a **c** with you,
16:59 despised my oath by breaking the **c**.
16:60 Yet I will remember the **c** I made
17:18 despised the oath by breaking the **c**.
20:37 bring you into the bond of the **c**.
30: 5 Libya and the people of the **c** land
34:25 "I will make a **c** of peace with them
37:26 I will make a **c** of peace with them;
Da 9: 4 who keeps his **c** of love with all who
9:27 He will confirm a **c** with many for
11:22 a prince of the **c** will be destroyed.
11:28 will be set against the holy **c**.
11:30 vent his fury against the holy **c**.
11:30 to those who forsake the holy **c**.
11:32 those who have violated the **c**,
Hos 2:18 In that day I will make a **c** for them
6: 7 Like Adam, they have broken the **c**—
Zec 11:10 **c** I had made with all the nations.
Mal 2: 5 a **c** of life and peace, and I gave
2: 8 you have violated the **c** with Levi,"
2:10 Why do we profane the **c** of our
2:14 the wife of your marriage **c**.
3: 1 the messenger of the **c**, whom you
Lk 1:72 fathers and to remember his holy **c**,
Ac 3:25 of the **c** God made with your fathers.
7: 8 gave Abraham the **c** of circumcision
2Co 3:14 veil remains when the old **c** is read.
Gal 3:15 **c** that has been duly established,
3:17 does not set aside the **c** previously
4:24 One **c** is from Mount Sinai and bears
Heb 7:22 become the guarantee of a better **c**.
8: 6 as the **c** of which he is mediator is
8: 7 nothing wrong with that first **c**,
8: 9 will not be like the **c** I made with
8:10 This is the **c** I will make with the
8:13 By calling this **c** "new", he has made
9: 1 Now the first **c** had regulations for
9: 4 and the stone tablets of the **c**.
9:15 sins committed under the first **c**.
9:18 This is why even the first **c** was not
10:16 "This is the **c** I will make with them
13:20 through the blood of the eternal **c**
Rev 11:19 temple was seen the ark of his **c**.

Covenant of the LORD/Lord

Nu 10:33 The ark of the **c** went before them
Dt 4:23 Be careful not to forget the **c** your
10: 8 of Levi to carry the ark of the **c**,
29:25 because this people abandoned the **c**,
31: 9 of Levi, who carried the ark of the **c**
31:25 Levites who carried the ark of the **c**:
31:26 it beside the ark of the **c** your God.
Jos 3: 3 "When you see the ark of the **c** your
3:11 See, the ark of the **c** of all the
3:17 priests who carried the ark of the **c**
4: 7 was cut off before the ark of the **c**.
4:18 the river carrying the ark of the **c**.
6: 6 "Take up the ark of the **c** and make
7:15 He has violated the **c** and has done a
8:33 on both sides of the ark of the **c**,
23:16 If you violate the **c** your God, which
1Sa 4: 4 back the ark of the **c** Almighty,
1Ki 6:19 to set the ark of the **c** there.
8:21 in which is the **c** that he made with
1Ch 15:25 to bring the **c** from the house of
15:26 who were carrying the ark of the **c**,
15:28 up the ark of the **c** with shouts,
15:29 the ark of the **c** was entering the
16:37 before the ark of the **c** to minister
17: 1 the ark of the **c** is under a tent."
22:19 that you may bring the ark of the **c**
28: 2 place of rest for the ark of the **c**,
28:18 wings and shelter the ark of the **c**.
2Ch 6:11 in which is the **c** that he made with
Jer 3:16 no longer say, 'The ark of the **c**.
22: 9 'Because they have forsaken the **c**

Covenanted (Covenant)

2Ch 7:18 as I **c** with David your father when I
Hag 2: 5 'This is what I **c** with you when you

Covenants (Covenant)

Ro 9: 4 the **c**, the receiving of the law, the
Gal 4:24 for the women represent two **c**.
Eph 2:12 foreigners to the **c** of the promise,

Cover (Covered, Covering, Coverings, Covers, Cover-up, Gold-covered)

Ge 20:16 This is to **c** the offence against you
37:26 kill our brother and **c** up his blood?
Ex 10: 5 They will **c** the face of the ground
21:33 or digs one and fails to **c** it and
25:17 "Make an atonement **c** of pure gold
25:18 hammered gold at the ends of the **c**.
25:19 of one piece with the **c**, at the two
25:20 overshadowing the **c** with them.
25:20 each other, looking towards the **c**.
25:21 Place the **c** on top of the ark and
25:22 There, above the **c** between the two
26:13 of the tabernacle so as to **c** it.
26:34 Put the atonement **c** on the ark of
30: 6 before the atonement **c** that is over
31: 7 Testimony with the atonement **c** on it,
33:22 **c** you with my hand until I have
35:12 with its poles and the atonement **c**
37: 6 He made the atonement **c** of pure gold
37: 7 hammered gold at the ends of the **c**.
37: 8 made them of one piece with the **c**.
37: 9 overshadowing the **c** with them.
37: 9 each other, looking towards the **c**.
39:35 with its poles and the atonement **c**;
40:20 ark and put the atonement **c** over it.
Lev 13:45 **c** the lower part of his face and
16: 2 front of the atonement **c** on the ark,
16: 2 in the cloud over the atonement **c**.
16:13 the atonement **c** above the Testimony,
16:14 it on the front of the atonement **c**;
16:14 seven times before the atonement **c**.
16:15 sprinkle it on the atonement **c** and
17:13 out the blood and **c** it with earth,
Nu 4: 5 **c** the ark of the Testimony with it.
4: 6 to **c** this with hides of sea cows
4: 8 **c** that with hides of sea cows and
4: 9 a blue cloth and **c** the lampstand
4:11 **c** that with hides of sea cows and
4:12 **c** that with hides of sea cows
7:89 **c** on the ark of the Testimony.
22: 5 they **c** the face of the land and have
Dt 23:13 dig a hole and **c** up your excrement.
Jdg 9:31 Under **c** he sent messengers to
1Ki 18: 6 they divided the land they were to **c**,
Ne 4: 5 Do not **c** up their guilt or blot out
Job 14:17 up in a bag; you will **c** over my sin.
16:18 "O earth, do not **c** my blood; may my
21:26 in the dust, and worms **c** them both.
24: 7 nothing to **c** themselves in the cold.
37: 8 The animals take **c**; they remain in
38:34 **c** yourself with a flood of water?
Ps 10: 9 He lies in wait like a lion in **c**;
17:12 like a great lion crouching in **c**.
32: 5 to you and did not **c** up my iniquity.
83:16 **C** their faces with shame so that men
84: 6 autumn rains also **c** it with pools.
91: 4 He will **c** you with his feathers, and
104: 9 never again will they **c** the earth.
Isa 8: 8 Its outspread wings will **c** the
10:31 flight; the people of Gebim take **c**.
11: 9 of the LORD as the waters **c** the sea.
14:11 out beneath you and worms **c** you.
14:21 and **c** the earth with their cities.
54: 9 Noah would never again **c** the earth.
59: 6 **c** themselves with what they make.
60: 6 Herds of camels will **c** your land,
Jer 3:25 shame, and let our disgrace **c** us.
14: 3 and despairing, they **c** their heads.
14: 4 are dismayed and **c** their heads.
46: 8 'I will rise and **c** the earth;
51:42 its roaring waves will **c** her.
Eze 12: 6 **C** your face so that you cannot see
12:12 He will **c** his face so that he cannot
13:10 is built, they **c** it with whitewash,
13:11 therefore tell those who **c** it with
Eze 24: 7 ground, where the dust would **c** it.
24:17 do not **c** the lower part of your face
24:22 You will not **c** the lower part of
26:10 many that they will **c** you with dust.
26:19 over you and its vast waters **c** you,
32: 7 I will **c** the the heavens and darken
32: 7 I will **c** the sun with a cloud,
37: 6 come upon you and **c** you with skin;
Hos 2: 9 linen, intended to **c** her nakedness.
10: 8 will grow up and **c** their altars.
10: 8 "**C** us!" and to the hills, "Fall on
Mic 3: 7 They will all **c** their faces because
Hab 2:14 the LORD, as the waters **c** the sea.
2:16 you, and disgrace will **c** your glory.
Zec 5: 7 the **c** of lead was raised, and there
5: 8 the lead **c** down over its mouth.
Lk 23:30 "Fall on us!" and to the hills "**C** us!
1Co 11: 6 If a woman does not **c** her head, she
11: 6 shaved off, she should **c** her head.
11: 7 A man ought not to **c** his head, since
1Th 2: 5 we put on a mask to **c** up greed—
Heb 9: 5 Glory, overshadowing the atonement **c**.
Jas 5:20 and **c** over a multitude of sins.
Rev 3:18 so that you can **c** your shameful

Covered (Cover)

Ge 7:19 under the entire heavens were **c**.
7:20 The waters rose and **c** the mountains
9:23 and **c** their father's nakedness.
24:65 So she took her veil and **c** herself.
27:16 She also **c** his hands and the smooth
38:14 **c** herself with a veil to disguise
38:15 prostitute, for she had **c** her face.
Ex 8: 6 the frogs came up and **c** the land.
10:15 They **c** all the ground until it was
10:22 darkness **c** all Egypt for three days.
14:28 and **c** the chariots and horsemen
15: 5 The deep waters have **c** them; they
15:10 your breath, and the sea **c** them.
16:13 evening quail came and **c** the camp,
19:18 Mount Sinai was **c** with smoke,
24:15 up on the mountain, the cloud **c** it,
24:16 six days the cloud **c** the mountain,
40:34 the cloud **c** the Tent of Meeting, and
Lev 13:13 the disease has **c** his whole body,
Nu 7: 3 gifts before the LORD six **c** carts
9:15 was set up, the cloud **c** it.
9:16 the cloud **c** it, and at night it
16:42 suddenly the cloud **c** it and the
Jos 24: 7 the sea over them and **c** them.
Jdg 4:19 gave him a drink, and **c** him up.
6:39 dry and the ground **c** with dew."
6:40 dry; all the ground was **c** with dew.
2Sa 15:30 his head was **c** and he was barefoot.
15:30 the people with him **c** their heads
19: 4 The king **c** his face and cried aloud,
1Ki 6:15 and **c** the floor of the temple with
6:21 Solomon **c** the inside of the temple
6:30 He also **c** the floors of both the
7: 7 he **c** it with cedar from floor to
20:27 the Arameans **c** the countryside.
2Ki 3:25 on every good field until it was **c**.
18:16 gold with which he had **c** the doors
23:14 and **c** the sites with human bones.
2Ch 3: 5 **c** it with fine gold and decorated it
5: 8 **c** the ark and its carrying poles.
16:14 laid him on a bier **c** with spices
Est 6:12 home, with his head **c**, in grief,
7: 8 king's mouth, they **c** Haman's face.
Job 15:27 "Though his face is **c** with fat and
29: 9 and **c** their mouths with their hands;
Ps 32: 1 are forgiven, whose sins are **c**.
34: 5 their faces are never **c** with shame.
44:15 long, and my face is **c** with shame
44:19 and **c** us over with deep darkness.
65:13 The meadows are **c** with flocks and
71:13 me be **c** with scorn and disgrace.
80:10 The mountains were **c** with its shade,
85: 2 of your people and **c** all their sins.
89:45 have **c** him with a mantle of shame.
104: 6 You **c** it with the deep as with a
106:11 The waters **c** their adversaries; not
140: 9 be **c** with the trouble their lips
Pr 7:16 I have **c** my bed with coloured linens
24:31 the ground was **c** with weeds, and the
Isa 6: 2 With two wings they **c** their faces,

Isa 6: 2 with two they **c** their feet, and with
7:24 will be **c** with briers and thorns.
14:19 branch; you are **c** with the slain,
28: 8 All the tables are **c** with vomit and
29:10 he has **c** your heads (the seers).
30:22 silver and your images **c** with gold;
34: 6 it is **c** with fat—the blood of
51:16 **c** you with the shadow of my hand—
Jer 48:37 and every waist is **c** with sackcloth.
Lam 2: 1 the Lord has **c** the Daughter of Zion
3:43 "You have **c** yourself with anger and
3:44 You have **c** yourself with a cloud so
Eze 7:18 Their faces will be **c** with shame and
13:12 is the whitewash you **c** it with?"
13:14 I will tear down the wall you have **c**
13:15 those who **c** it with whitewash.
16: 8 over you and **c** your nakedness.
16:10 and **c** you with costly garments.
24: 8 rock, so that it would not be **c**.
30:18 She will be **c** with clouds, and her
31:15 I **c** the deep springs with mourning
37: 8 appeared on them and skin **c** them,
41:16 the threshold was **c** with wood.
41:16 the windows, and the windows were **c**.
Da 9: 7 but this day we are **c** with shame—
9: 8 and our fathers are **c** with shame
Ob :10 you will be **c** with shame; you will
Jnh 3: 6 took off his royal robes, **c** himself
3: 8 man and beast be **c** with sackcloth
Mic 7:10 see it and will be **c** with shame,
Hab 2:19 It is **c** with gold and silver;
3: 3 His glory **c** the heavens and his
Lk 5:12 came along who was **c** with leprosy.
16:20 beggar named Lazarus, **c** with sores
Jn 5: 2 is surrounded by five **c** colonnades.
Ac 7:57 At this they **c** their ears and,
Ro 4: 7 are forgiven, whose sins are **c**.
1Co 11: 4 with his head **c** dishonours his head.
Rev 4: 6 **c** with eyes, in front and behind.
4: 8 and was **c** with eyes all around,
17: 3 that was **c** with blasphemous names

Covering (Cover)
Ge 8:13 Noah then removed the **c** from the ark
Ex 22:27 his cloak is the only **c** he has for
26:14 Make for the tent a **c** of ram skins
26:14 over that a **c** of hides of sea cows.
28:42 undergarments as a **c** for the body
29:13 the **c** of the liver, and both kidneys
29:22 the **c** of the liver, both kidneys
35:11 tabernacle with its tent and its **c**,
36:19 made for the tent a **c** of ram skins
36:19 over that a **c** of hides of sea cows.
39:34 the **c** of ram skins dyed red,
39:34 the **c** of hides of sea cows and the
40:19 and put the **c** over the tent,
Lev 3: 4 and the **c** of the liver, which he
3:10 and the **c** of the liver, which he
3:15 and the **c** of the liver, which he
4: 9 and the **c** of the liver, which he
7: 4 and the **c** of the liver, which is to
8:16 the **c** of the liver, and both kidneys
8:25 the **c** of the liver, both kidneys and
9:10 the kidneys and the **c** of the liver
9:19 the kidneys and the **c** of the liver—
Nu 4:10 all its accessories in a **c** of hides
4:14 to spread a **c** of hides of sea cows
4:15 finished **c** the holy furnishings
4:25 the Tent of Meeting, its **c** and the
4:25 its **c** and the outer **c** of hides of
Jdg 4:18 her tent, and she put a **c** over him.
1Sa 19:13 **c** it with a garment and putting some
2Sa 17:19 His wife took a **c** and spread it out
Ps 18:11 He made darkness his **c**, his canopy
105:39 He spread out a cloud as a **c**, and a
Isa 50: 3 darkness and make sackcloth its **c**."
Eze 1:11 side, and two wings **c** its body.
1:23 and each had two wings **c** its body.
38: 9 you will be like a cloud **c** the land.
Mal 2:16 "and I hate a man's **c** himself with
1Co 11:15 For long hair is given to her as a **c**.

Coverings (Cover)
Ge 3: 7 together and made **c** for themselves.
Nu 3:25 its **c**, the curtain at the entrance
Pr 31:22 She makes **c** for her bed; she is

Covers (Cover)
Ex 22:15 money paid for the hire **c** the loss.
Lev 3: 3 all the fat that **c** the inner parts
3: 9 all the fat that **c** the inner parts
3:14 all the fat that **c** the inner parts
4: 8 the fat that **c** the inner parts or is
7: 3 and the fat that **c** the inner parts,
13:12 it **c** all the skin of the infected
Nu 22:11 out of Egypt **c** the face of the land.
1Ki 1: 1 warm even when they put **c** over him.
Job 22:11 see, and why a flood of water **c** you.
23:17 the thick darkness that **c** my face.
26: 9 He **c** the face of the full moon,
Ps 10:11 he **c** his face and never sees."
69: 7 for your sake, and shame **c** my face.
147: 8 He **c** the sky with clouds; he
Pr 10:12 but love **c** over all wrongs.
17: 9 He who **c** over an offence promotes
Isa 25: 7 the sheet that **c** all nations;
60: 2 See, darkness **c** the earth and thick
Jer 51:51 been insulted and shame **c** our faces,
Eze 38:16 Israel like a cloud that **c** the land.
2Co 3:15 Moses is read, a veil **c** their hearts.
1Pe 4: 8 love **c** over a multitude of sins.

Cover-up (Cover)
1Pe 2:16 use your freedom as a **c** for evil;

Coves
Jdg 5:17 on the coast and stayed in his **c**.

Covet (Coveted, Coveting, Covetous)
Ex 20:17 shall not **c** your neighbour's house.
20:17 shall not **c** your neighbour's wife
34:24 and no-one will **c** your land when you
Dt 5:21 shall not **c** your neighbour's wife.
7:25 Do not **c** the silver and gold on them,
Mic 2: 2 They **c** fields and seize them, and
Ro 7: 7 if the law had not said, "Do not **c**.
13: 9 "Do not steal," "Do not **c**," and
Jas 4: 2 You kill and **c**, but you cannot have

Coveted (Covet)
Jos 7:21 shekels, I **c** them and took them.
Ac 20:33 I have not **c** anyone's silver or gold

Coveting (Covet)
Ro 7: 7 not have known what **c** really was

Covetous (Covet)
Ro 7: 8 in me every kind of **c** desire.

Cow (Cows, Cows')
Lev 22:28 Do not slaughter a **c** or a sheep and
Isa 7:21 keep alive a young **c** and two goats.
11: 7 The **c** will feed with the bear, their
Eze 4:15 **c** manure instead of human excrement."

Cowardly (Cower)
Rev 21: 8 the **c**, the unbelieving, the vile,

Cower (Cowardly, Cowered, Cowering)
Dt 33:29 Your enemies will **c** before you, and

Cowered (Cower)
Job 9:13 the cohorts of Rahab **c** at his feet.

Cowering (Cower)
Isa 51:14 The **c** prisoners will soon be set

Cows (Cow)
Ge 32:15 forty **c** and ten bulls, and twenty
33:13 and **c** that are nursing their young.
41: 2 of the river there came up seven **c**,
41: 3 After them, seven other **c**, ugly and
41: 4 the **c** that were ugly and gaunt ate
41: 4 gaunt ate up the seven sleek, fat **c**.
41:18 of the river there came up seven **c**,
41:19 After them, seven other **c** came
41:19 ugly **c** in all the land of Egypt.
41:20 The lean, ugly **c** ate up the seven
Ge 41:20 the seven fat **c** that came up first.
41:26 The seven good **c** are seven years,
41:27 The seven lean, ugly **c** that came up
Ex 25: 5 ram skins dyed red and hides of sea **c**
26:14 that a covering of hides of sea **c**.
35: 7 ram skins dyed red and hides of sea **c**
35:23 red or hides of sea **c** brought them.
36:19 that a covering of hides of sea **c**.
39:34 of sea **c** and the shielding curtain;
Nu 4: 6 to cover this with hides of sea **c**,
4: 8 of sea **c** and put its poles in place.
4:10 **c** and put it on a carrying frame.
4:11 of sea **c** and put its poles in place.
4:12 **c** and put them on a carrying frame.
4:14 of sea **c** and put its poles in place.
4:25 outer covering of hides of sea **c**,
1Sa 6: 7 get a new cart ready, with two **c**
6: 7 Hitch the **c** to the cart, but take
6:10 they did this. They took two such **c**
6:12 the **c** went straight up towards
6:14 **c** as a burnt offering to the LORD.
Job 21:10 their **c** calve and do not miscarry.
Am 4: 1 Hear this word, you **c** of Bashan on

Cows' (Cow)
2Sa 17:29 sheep, and cheese from **c** milk for

Cozbi
Nu 25:15 put to death was **C** daughter of Zur,
25:18 affair of Peor and their sister **C**,

Cozeba
1Ch 4:22 Jokim, the men of **C**, and Joash and

Crack (Cracked)
Na 3: 2 The **c** of whips, the clatter of

Cracked (Crack)
Jos 9: 4 and old wineskins, **c** and mended.
9:13 were new, but see how **c** they are.
Jdg 9:53 on his head and **c** his skull.
Isa 30:13 like a high wall, **c** and bulging,
Jer 14: 4 The ground is **c** because there is no

Crackling
Ecc 7: 6 Like the **c** of thorns under the pot,
Joel 2: 5 like a **c** fire consuming stubble,

Craft (Craftiness, Crafts, Craftsman, Craftsman's, Craftsmanship, Craftsmen, Crafty, Handcrafted)
1Ch 28:21 any **c** will help you in all the work.

Craftiness (Craft)
Job 5:13 He catches the wise in their **c**, and
1Co 3:19 "He catches the wise in their **c**"
Eph 4:14 **c** of men in their deceitful scheming.

Crafts (Craft)
Ex 31: 3 and knowledge in all kinds of **c**—
35:31 and knowledge in all kinds of **c**—

Craftsman (Craft)
Ex 26: 1 worked into them by a skilled **c**.
26:31 worked into it by a skilled **c**.
28: 6 linen—the work of a skilled **c**.
28:15 decisions—the work of a skilled **c**.
36: 8 worked into them by a skilled **c**.
36:35 worked into it by a skilled **c**.
38:23 the tribe of Dan—a **c** and designer
39: 3 fine linen—the work of a skilled **c**.
39: 8 —the work of a skilled **c**.
1Ki 7:14 was a man of Tyre and a **c** in bronze.
Pr 8:30 I was the **c** at his side. I was
Isa 3: 3 skilled **c** and clever enchanter.
40:19 for an idol, a **c** casts it, and a
40:20 He looks for a skilled **c** to set up
41: 7 The **c** encourages the goldsmith, and
Jer 10: 3 and a **c** shapes it with his chisel.
10: 9 What the **c** and goldsmith have made
Hos 8: 6 This calf—a **c** has made it; it is

Craftsman's (Craft)
Dt 27:15 the work of the **c** hands—and sets
SS 7: 1 like jewels, the work of a **c** hands.

Craftsmanship (Craft)
Ex 31: 5 and to engage in all kinds of **c**.
35:33 engage in all kinds of artistic **c**.

Craftsmen (Craft)
Ex 31: 6 Also I have given skill to all the **c**
35:35 skill to do all kinds of work as **c**,
35:35 of them master **c** and designers.
36: 4 all the skilled **c** who were doing all
1Ki 5:18 The **c** of Solomon and Hiram and the
2Ki 24:14 and all the **c** and artisans—a total
24:16 war, and a thousand **c** and artisans.
1Ch 4:14 this because its people were **c**.
22:16 bronze and iron—**c** beyond number.
29: 5 all the work to be done by the **c**.
2Ch 2: 7 **c**, whom my father David provided.
2:14 He will work with your **c** and with
Ne 11:35 and Ono, and in the Valley of the **C**.
Isa 44:11 put to shame; **c** are nothing but men.
Jer 24: 1 the **c** and the artisans of Judah were
29: 2 the **c** and the artisans had gone into
52:15 along with the rest of the **c** and
Eze 27: 9 Veteran **c** of Gebal were on board as
Hos 13: 2 images, all of them the work of **c**.
Zec 1:20 the LORD showed me four **c**.
1:21 but the **c** have come to terrify them
Ac 19:24 in no little business for the **c**.
19:38 If, then, Demetrius and his fellow **c**

Crafty (Craft)
Ge 3: 1 Now the serpent was more **c** than any
1Sa 23:22 They tell me he is very **c**.
Job 5:12 He thwarts the plans of the **c**, so
15: 5 you adopt the tongue of the **c**.
Pr 7:10 like a prostitute and with **c** intent.
12: 2 LORD, but the LORD condemns a **c** man.
14:17 things, and a **c** man is hated.
2Co 12:16 Yet, **c** fellow that I am, I caught

Crag (Crags)
Dt 32:13 and with oil from the flinty **c**,
Job 39:28 night; a rocky **c** is his stronghold.
Ps 78:16 he brought streams out of a rocky **c**

Crags (Crag)
1Sa 24: 2 men near the **C** of the Wild Goats.
Ps 104:18 the **c** are a refuge for the conies.
Pr 30:26 yet they make their home in the **c**;
Isa 2:21 to the overhanging **c** from dread of
57: 5 ravines and under the overhanging **c**.
Am 6:12 Do horses run on the rocky **c**? Does

Crash
Zep 1:10 Quarter, and a loud **c** from the hills.
Mt 7:27 house, and it fell with a great **c**."

Crave (Craved, Craves, Craving, Cravings)
Nu 11: 4 with them began to **c** other food
Dt 12:20 and you **c** meat and say, "I would
Pr 23: 3 Do not **c** his delicacies, for that
23: 6 stingy man, do not **c** his delicacies;
31: 4 wine, not for rulers to **c** beer,
Mic 7: 1 none of the early figs that I **c**.
1Pe 2: 2 **c** pure spiritual milk, so that by

Craved (Crave)
Nu 11:34 the people who had **c** other food.
Ps 78:18 test by demanding the food they **c**.
78:29 for he had given them what they **c**.
78:30 they turned from the food they **c**,

Craves (Crave)
Pr 13: 4 The sluggard **c** and gets nothing, but
21:10 The wicked man **c** evil; his neighbour
21:26 All day long he **c** for more, but the

Craving (Crave)
Job 20:20 he will have no respite from his **c**;
Ps 106:14 In the desert they gave in to their **c**
Pr 10: 3 but he thwarts the **c** of the wicked.
13: 2 unfaithful have a **c** for violence.
21:25 The sluggard's **c** will be the death
Jer 2:24 sniffing the wind in her **c**—in her

Cravings (Crave)
Ps 10: 3 He boasts of the **c** of his heart; he
Eph 2: 3 gratifying the **c** of our sinful
1Jn 2:16 —the **c** of sinful man, the lust of

Crawl (Crawling)
Ge 3:14 You will **c** on your belly and you
Mic 7:17 like creatures that **c** on the ground.

Crawling (Crawl)
Lev 22: 5 or if he touches any **c** thing that
1Sa 14:11 "The Hebrews are **c** out of the holes
Eze 8:10 the walls all kinds of **c** things

Cream
Job 20:17 the rivers flowing with honey and **c**.
29: 6 my path was drenched with **c** and the

Create (Created, Creates, Creating, Creation, Creator)
Ps 51:10 **C** in me a pure heart, O God, and
Isa 4: 5 LORD will **c** over all of Mount Zion
45: 7 I form the light and **c** darkness, I
45: 7 I bring prosperity and **c** disaster; I,
45:18 he did not **c** it to be empty, but
65:17 "Behold, I will **c** new heavens and a
65:18 rejoice for ever in what I will **c**,
65:18 for I will **c** Jerusalem to be a
Jer 31:22 The LORD will **c** a new thing on earth
Mal 2:10 Did not one God **c** us? Why do we
Eph 2:15 His purpose was to **c** in himself one

Created (Create)
Ge 1: 1 In the beginning God **c** the heavens
1:21 God **c** the great creatures of the sea
1:27 God **c** man in his own image, in the
1:27 he **c** him; male and female he **c** them.
2: 4 and the earth when they were **c**.
5: 1 When God **c** man, he made him in the
5: 2 He **c** them male and female and
5: 2 And when they were **c**, he called them
6: 7 "I will wipe mankind, whom I have **c**,
Dt 4:32 from the day God **c** man on the earth;
Ps 89:12 You **c** the north and the south; Tabor
89:47 For what futility you have **c** all men!
102:18 a people not yet **c** may praise the
104:30 you send your Spirit, they are **c**,
Ps 139:13 For you **c** my inmost being; you knit
148: 5 for he commanded and they were **c**.
Isa 40:26 Who **c** all these? He who brings out
41:20 the Holy One of Israel has **c** it.
42: 5 **c** the heavens and stretched them out,
43: 1 what the LORD says—he who **c** you,
43: 7 whom I **c** for my glory, whom I formed
45: 8 with it; I, the LORD, have **c** it.
45:12 the earth and **c** mankind upon it.
45:18 LORD says—he who **c** the heavens,
48: 7 They are **c** now, and not long ago;
54:16 "See, it is I who **c** the blacksmith
54:16 have **c** the destroyer to work havoc;
57:16 the breath of man that I have **c**.
Eze 21:30 In the place where you were **c**, in
28:13 day you were **c** they were prepared.
28:15 from the day you were **c** till
Mk 13:19 the beginning when God **c** the world,
Ro 1:25 and worshipped and served **c** things
1Co 11: 9 neither was man **c** for woman, but
Eph 2:10 **c** in Christ Jesus to do good works,
3: 9 hidden in God, who **c** all things.
4:24 on the new self, **c** to be like God
Col 1:16 For by him all things were **c**: things
1:16 things were **c** by him and for him.
1Ti 4: 3 which God **c** to be received with
4: 4 For everything God **c** is good, and
Heb 12:27 **c** things—so that what cannot be
Jas 1:18 a kind of firstfruits of all he **c**.
Rev 4:11 for you **c** all things, and by your
4:11 they were **c** and have their being."
10: 6 who **c** the heavens and all that is in

Creates (Create)
Am 4:13 who forms the mountains, **c** the wind,

Creating (Create)
Ge 2: 3 all the work of **c** that he had done.
Isa 57:19 **c** praise on the lips of the mourners

Creation (Create)
Hab 2:18 who makes it trusts in his own **c**;
Mt 13:35 hidden since the **c** of the world."
25:34 for you since the **c** of the world.
Mk 10: 6 "But at the beginning of **c** God 'made
16:15 and preach the good news to all **c**.
Jn 17:24 loved me before the **c** of the world.
Ro 1:20 For since the **c** of the world God's
8:19 The **c** waits in eager expectation for
8:20 For the **c** was subjected to
8:21 that the **c** itself will be liberated
8:22 We know that the whole **c** has been
8:39 nor anything else in all **c**, will be
2Co 5:17 he is a new **c**; the old has gone, the
Gal 6:15 anything; what counts is a new **c**.
Eph 1: 4 For he chose us in him before the **c**
Col 1:15 God, the firstborn over all **c**.
Heb 4: 3 finished since the **c** of the world.
4:13 Nothing in all **c** is hidden from
9:11 is to say, not a part of this **c**.
9:26 many times since the **c** of the world.
1Pe 1:20 He was chosen before the **c** of the
2Pe 3: 4 as it has since the beginning of **c**."
Rev 3:14 true witness, the ruler of God's **c**.
13: 8 was slain from the **c** of the world.
17: 8 of life from the **c** of the world

Creator (Create)
Ge 14:19 God Most High, **C** of heaven and earth.
14:22 God Most High, **C** of heaven and earth,
Dt 32: 6 your **C**, who made you and formed you?
Ecc 12: 1 Remember your **C** in the days of your
Isa 27:11 and their **C** shows them no favour.
40:28 God, the **C** of the ends of the earth.
43:15 Holy One, Israel's **C**, your King."
Mt 19: 4 the **C** 'made them male and female',
Ro 1:25 than the **C**—who is for ever praised.
Col 3:10 in knowledge in the image of its **C**.
1Pe 4:19 to their faithful **C** and continue to

Creature (Creatures)
Ge 1:28 living **c** that moves on the ground."
2:19 the man called each living **c**,
6:17 **c** that has the breath of life in it.
6:20 of every kind of **c** that moves along
7: 4 earth every living **c** I have made."
7:14 every **c** that moves along the ground
8:17 Bring out every kind of living **c**
9: 2 upon every **c** that moves along the
9:10 with every living **c** that was with
9:10 with you—every living **c** on earth.
9:12 and you and every living **c** with you,
Lev 11:41 "'Every **c** that moves about on the
11:42 You are not to eat any **c** that moves
11:44 **c** that moves about on the ground.
11:46 **c** that moves about on the ground.
17:11 For the life of a **c** is in the blood,
17:14 the life of every **c** is its blood.
17:14 "You must not eat the blood of any **c**,
17:14 the life of every **c** is its blood;
Dt 4:18 or like any **c** that moves along the
14:20 any winged **c** that is clean you may
Job 12:10 In his hand is the life of every **c**
14:15 long for the **c** your hands have made.
41:33 is his equal—a **c** without fear.
Ps 136:25 who gives food to every **c**.
145:21 Let every **c** praise his holy name for
Isa 47: 8 "Now then, listen, you wanton **c**,
Eze 1:11 one touching the wing of another **c**
1:15 beside each **c** with its four faces.
38:20 the beasts of the field, every **c**
Da 4:12 branches; from it every **c** was fed.
Col 1:23 proclaimed to every **c** under heaven,
Rev 4: 7 The first living **c** was like a lion,
5:13 I heard every **c** in heaven and on
6: 3 I heard the second living **c** say,
6: 5 the third living **c** say, "Come!"
6: 7 voice of the fourth living **c** say,

Creatures (Creature, *Living creatures*)
Ge 1:21 God created the great **c** of the sea
1:24 **c** that move along the ground, and
1:25 and all the **c** that move along the
1:26 the **c** that move along the ground."
1:30 the **c** that move on the ground
6: 7 and **c** that move along the ground,
7: 8 of all **c** that move along the ground,
7:15 Pairs of all **c** that have the breath
7:21 all the **c** that swarm over the earth
7:23 men and animals and the **c** that move
8:17 the animals, and all the **c** that move
8:19 the **c** that move along the ground
Lev 5: 2 of unclean **c** that move along the
11: 9 "'Of all the **c** living in the water
11:10 all **c** in the seas or streams that do
11:21 There are, however, some winged **c**
11:23 all other winged **c** that have four
11:43 defile yourselves by any of these **c**.
Dt 14: 9 Of all the **c** living in the water,
Ps 50:11 and the **c** of the field are mine.
74:14 him as food to the **c** of the desert.
80:13 and the **c** of the field feed on it.
104:24 all; the earth is full of your **c**.
104:25 vast and spacious, teeming with **c**
148: 7 great sea **c** and all ocean depths,
148:10 cattle, small **c** and flying birds,
Pr 30:25 Ants are **c** of little strength, yet
30:26 conies are **c** of little power, yet
Isa 13:21 desert **c** will lie there, jackals
23:13 have made it a place for desert **c**;
34:14 Desert **c** will meet with hyenas, and
34:14 there the night **c** will also repose
Jer 50:39 "So desert **c** and hyenas will live
Eze 1:13 moved back and forth among the **c**;
1:14 The **c** sped back and forth like
1:17 of the four directions the **c** faced;
1:17 did not turn about as the **c** went.
1:21 the **c** moved, they also moved; when
1:21 when the **c** stood still, they also
1:21 and when the **c** rose from the ground,
1:24 the **c** moved, I heard the sound of
Hos 2:18 the **c** that move along the ground.
Mic 7:17 like **c** that crawl on the ground.
Hab 1:14 sea, like sea **c** that have no ruler.
Zep 2:14 lie down there, **c** of every kind.
Jas 3: 7 birds, reptiles and **c** of the sea are
2Pe 2:12 like brute beasts, **c** of instinct

Credit (Accredited, Credited, Creditor, Creditors, Credits)
Est 2:22 to the king, giving **c** to Mordecai.
Lk 6:32 what **c** is that to you? Even 'sinners'
6:33 what **c** is that to you? Even 'sinners'
6:34 what **c** is that to you? Even 'sinners'
Ro 4:24 to whom God will **c** righteousness
1Pe 2:20 how is it to your **c** if you receive a

Credited (Credit)
Ge 15: 6 Abram believed the LORD, and he **c** it
Lev 7:18 It will not be **c** to the one who
1Sa 18: 8 "They have **c** David with tens of
Ps 106:31 This was **c** to him as righteousness
Eze 18:20 the righteous man will be **c** to him,
Ro 4: 3 it was **c** to him as righteousness."
4: 4 his wages are not **c** to him as a gift,
4: 5 his faith is **c** as righteousness.
4: 9 faith was **c** to him as righteousness.
4:10 Under what circumstances was it **c**?
4:11 righteousness might be **c** to them.
4:22 This is why "it was **c** to him as
4:23 The words "it was **c** to him" were
Gal 3: 6 it was **c** to him as righteousness."
Php 4:17 for what may be **c** to your account.
Jas 2:23 it was **c** to him as righteousness

Creditor (Credit)
Dt 15: 2 Every **c** shall cancel the loan he
2Ki 4: 1 But now his **c** is coming to take my
Ps 109:11 May a **c** seize all he has; may
Isa 24: 2 as for lender, for debtor as for **c**.

Creditors (Credit)
Isa 50: 1 Or to which of my **c** did I sell you?

Credits (Credit)
Ro 4: 6 God **c** righteousness apart from works:

Crept
1Sa 24: 4 Then David **c** up unnoticed and cut
Hab 3:16 at the sound; decay **c** into my bones,

Crescens
2Ti 4:10 **C** has gone to Galatia, and Titus to

Crescent
Isa 3:18 and headbands and **c** necklaces,

Crest
Est 6: 8 with a royal **c** placed on its head.
SS 4: 8 Descend from the **c** of Amana, from

Cretans (Crete)
Ac 2:11 **C** and Arabs—we hear them declaring
Tit 1:12 "**C** are always liars, evil brutes,

Crete (Cretans)
Large island in Mediterranean Sea, about 60 miles south of Greece, where Paul's ship sheltered from a storm (Ac 27:8). Titus organised the church here (Tit 1:5).

Ac 27: 7 to the lee of **C**, opposite Salmone.
27:12 This was a harbour in **C**, facing both
27:13 and sailed along the shore of **C**.
27:21 taken my advice not to sail from **C**;
Tit 1: 5 The reason I left you in **C** was that

Crevice (Crevices)
Jer 13: 4 hide it there in a **c** in the rocks."

Crevices (Crevice)
Isa 7:19 ravines and in the **c** in the rocks,
Jer 16:16 hill and from the **c** of the rocks.

Cricket
Lev 11:22 locust, katydid, **c** or grasshopper.

Cried (Cry)
Ge 41:55 the people **c** to Pharaoh for food.
45: 1 and he **c** out, "Make everyone leave
Ex 2:23 groaned in their slavery and **c** out,
8:12 Moses **c** out to the LORD about the
14:10 terrified and **c** out to the LORD.
15:25 Moses **c** out to the LORD, and the
17: 4 Moses **c** out to the LORD, "What am I
Nu 11: 2 the people **c** out to Moses, he prayed
12:13 Moses **c** out to the LORD, "O God,
16:22 and Aaron fell face down and **c** out,
20:16 we **c** out to the LORD, he heard our
Dt 26: 7 we **c** out to the LORD, the God of our
Jos 24: 7 they **c** to the LORD for help, and he
Jdg 3: 9 when they **c** out to the LORD, he
3:15 the Israelites **c** out to the LORD
4: 3 years, they **c** to the LORD for help.
5:28 behind the lattice she **c** out,
6: 6 they **c** out to the LORD for help.
6: 7 the Israelites **c** to the LORD because
10:10 the Israelites **c** out to the LORD,
10:12 you and you **c** to me for help,
11:35 he saw her, he tore his clothes and **c**
14:17 She **c** the whole seven days of the
15:18 very thirsty, he **c** out to the LORD,
21: 3 "O LORD, the God of Israel," they **c**,
1Sa 5:10 the people of Ekron **c** out, "They
7: 9 He **c** out to the LORD on Israel's
12: 8 they **c** to the LORD for help, and
12:10 They **c** out to the LORD and said, 'We
15:11 he **c** out to the LORD all that night.
28:12 the woman saw Samuel, she **c** out at
2Sa 19: 4 The king covered his face and **c**
22:42 They **c** for help, but there was
1Ki 13: 2 He **c** out against the altar by the
13: 4 **c** out against the altar at Bethel,
13:21 He **c** out to the man of God who had
17:20 he **c** out to the LORD, "O LORD my
17:21 boy three times and **c** to the LORD,
18:39 they fell prostrate and **c**, "The LORD
22:32 him, but when Jehoshaphat **c** out,
2Ki 2:12 Elisha saw this and **c** out, "My
4: 1 of the prophets **c** out to Elisha,
4:40 but as they began to eat it, they **c**
6: 5 "Oh, my lord," he **c** out, "it was
6:26 a woman **c** to him, "Help me, my lord
13:14 "My father! My father!" he **c**. "The
1Ch 4:10 Jabez **c** out to the God of Israel,
5:20 they **c** out to him during the battle.
2Ch 13:14 Then they **c** out to the LORD. The
18:31 **c** out, and the LORD helped him.
32:20 **c** out in prayer to heaven about this.
Ne 9:27 were oppressed they **c** out to you.
9:28 And when they **c** out to you again,
Job 29:12 I rescued the poor who **c** for help,
Ps 18: 6 to the LORD; I **c** to my God for help.
18:41 They **c** for help, but there was
22: 5 They **c** to you and were saved; in you
30: 8 I called; to the Lord I **c** for mercy:
31:17 O LORD, for I have **c** out to you;
66:17 I **c** out to him with my mouth; his
77: 1 I **c** out to God for help;
77: 1 I **c** out to God to hear me.
107: 6 they **c** out to the LORD in their
107:13 they **c** to the LORD in their trouble,
107:19 they **c** to the LORD in their trouble,
107:28 they **c** out to the LORD in their
118: 5 In my anguish I **c** to the LORD, and
137: 7 "Tear it down," they **c**, "tear it
Isa 6: 5 "Woe to me!" I **c**. "I am ruined! For
38:14 I **c** like a swift or thrush, I moaned
Eze 11:13 Then I fell face down and **c** out in a
Am 7: 2 I **c** out, "Sovereign LORD, forgive!
7: 5 I **c** out, "Sovereign LORD, I beg you,
Jnh 1: 5 and each **c** out to his own god.
1:14 they **c** to the LORD, "O LORD, please
Mt 14:26 "It's a ghost," they said, and **c** out
14:30 beginning to sink, **c** out, "Lord,
27:46 About the ninth hour Jesus **c** out in
27:50 Jesus had **c** out again in a loud
Mk 1:23 possessed by an evil spirit **c** out,
3:11 and **c** out, "You are the Son of God.
6:49 thought he was a ghost. They **c** out,
15:34 at the ninth hour Jesus **c** out in a
Lk 4:33 He **c** out at the top of his voice,
8:28 he saw Jesus, he **c** out and fell at
23:18 With one voice they **c** out, "Away
Jn 7:28 **c** out, "Yes, you know me, and you
12:44 Jesus **c** out, "When a man believes in
20:16 She turned towards him and **c** out in
Ac 7:60 he fell on his knees and **c** out,
Rev 7:10 they **c** out in a loud voice:
12: 2 She was pregnant and **c** out in pain
19: 4 And they **c**: "Amen, Hallelujah!"
19:17 who **c** in a loud voice to all the

Cries (Cry)
Ge 4:10 blood **c** out to me from the ground.
Ex 22:27 When he **c** out to me, I will hear,
Nu 16:34 At their **c**, all the Israelites
Job 30:24 when he **c** for help in his distress.
31:38 "if my land **c** out against me and all
Ps 47: 1 nations; shout to God with **c** of joy.
Pr 1:21 head of the noisy streets she **c** out,
8: 3 city, at the entrances, she **c** aloud:
Isa 5: 7 but heard **c** of distress.
15: 5 My heart **c** out over Moab; her
26:17 birth writhes and **c** out in her pain,
46: 7 Though one **c** out to it, it does not
56:12 "Come," each one **c**, "let me get wine!
Jer 30: 5 "'**C** of fear are heard—terror, not
46:12 shame; your **c** will fill the earth.
48: 3 Listen to the **c** from Horonaim,
48: 3 **c** of great havoc and destruction.
48: 5 **c** over the destruction are heard.
Hos 8: 2 Israel **c** out to me, 'O our God, we
Am 1:14 amid war **c** on the day of battle,
2: 2 war **c** and the blast of the trumpet.
5:16 **c** of anguish in every public square.
Jn 1:15 He **c** out, saying, "This was he
Ro 9:27 Isaiah **c** out concerning Israel:
Heb 5: 7 petitions with loud **c** and tears to
Jas 5: 4 The **c** of the harvesters have reached

Crime (Crimes, Criminal, Criminals)
Ge 31:36 "What is my **c**?" he asked Laban.
Dt 19:15 **c** or offence he may have committed.

Dt 19:16 the stand to accuse a man of a c,
25: 2 the number of lashes his c deserves,
Jdg 9:24 God did this in order that the c
20:12 c that was committed among you?
1Sa 20: 1 "What have I done? What is my c? How
Ezr 6:11 And for this c his house is to be
Ps 69:27 Charge them with c upon c; do not
Ecc 8:11 the sentence for a c is not quickly
Jer 37:18 "What c have I committed against you
Hab 2:12 and establishes a town by c!
Mt 27:23 "Why? What c has he committed?"
Mk 15:14 "Why? What c has he committed?"
Lk 23:22 "Why? What c has this man committed?
Ac 18:14 some misdemeanour or serious c,
24:20 state what c they found in me when
28:18 not guilty of any c deserving death.

Crimes (Crime)
Ecc 8:12 a wicked man commits a hundred c
Jer 18:23 Do not forgive their c or blot out
41:11 all the c Ishmael son of Nethaniah
Hos 6: 9 to Shechem, committing shameful c.
7: 1 and the c of Samaria revealed.
Ac 25:18 with any of the c I had expected.
Rev 18: 5 and God has remembered her c.

Criminal (Crime)
Lk 23:40 the other c rebuked him. "Don't you
Jn 18:30 "If he were not a c," they replied,
2Ti 2: 9 the point of being chained like a c.
1Pe 4:15 or any other kind of c, or even as

Criminals (Crime)
1Ki 1:21 son Solomon will be treated as c."
Lk 23:32 Two other men, both c, were also led
23:33 along with the c—one on his right,
23:39 One of the c who hung there hurled

Crimson
2Ch 2: 7 and in purple, c and blue yarn,
2:14 and blue and c yarn and fine linen.
3:14 purple and c yarn and fine linen,
Isa 1:18 though they are red as c, they
63: 1 with his garments stained c? Who is

Cringe (Cringing)
Ps 18:44 obey me; foreigners c before me.
66: 3 that your enemies c before you.
81:15 Those who hate the LORD would c
Isa 10: 4 Nothing will remain but to c among

Cringing (Cringe)
2Sa 22:45 foreigners come c to me; as soon as

Cripple (Crippled, Cripples)
Ac 4: 9 for an act of kindness shown to a c

Crippled (Cripple)
Lev 21:19 no man with a c foot or hand,
2Sa 4: 4 to leave, he fell and became c.
9: 3 of Jonathan; he is c in both feet."
9:13 table, and he was c in both feet.
Mal 1: 8 you sacrifice c or diseased animals,
1:13 "When you bring injured, c or
Mt 15:30 bringing the lame, the blind, the c,
15:31 the c made well, the lame walking
18: 8 to enter life maimed or c than to
Mk 9:45 It is better for you to enter life c
Lk 13:11 a woman was there who had been c by
14:13 poor, the c, the lame, the blind,
14:21 the c, the blind and the lame.'
Ac 3: 2 Now a man c from birth was being
14: 8 In Lystra there sat a man c in his

Cripples (Cripple)
Ac 8: 7 many paralytics and c were healed.

Crisis
1Co 7:26 Because of the present c, I think

Crispus
Ac 18: 8 C, the synagogue ruler, and his
1Co 1:14 any of you except C and Gaius,

Critical (Criticism)
1Sa 13: 6 saw that their situation was c

Criticised (Criticism)
Jdg 8: 1 Midian?" And they c him sharply.
Ac 11: 2 the circumcised believers c him

Criticism (Critical, Criticised)
2Co 8:20 We want to avoid any c of the way we

Crocus
Isa 35: 1 rejoice and blossom. Like the c,

Crooked
Dt 32: 5 but a warped and c generation.
2Sa 22:27 to the c you show yourself shrewd.
Ps 18:26 to the c you show yourself shrewd.
125: 5 those who turn to c ways the LORD
Pr 2:15 whose paths are c and who are
5: 6 paths are c, but she knows it not.
8: 8 just; none of them is c or perverse.
10: 9 who takes c paths will be found out.
Ecc 7:13 can straighten what he has made c?
Isa 59: 8 They have turned them into c roads;
Lam 3: 9 of stone; he has made my paths c.
Lk 3: 5 The c roads shall become straight,
Php 2:15 in a c and depraved generation,

Crop (Crops)
Ge 47:24 when the c comes in, give a fifth of
Lev 1:16 He is to remove the c with its
25:22 you will eat from the old c and will
Isa 5: 2 Then he looked for a c of good
Am 7: 1 just as the second c was coming up.
Hab 3:17 though the olive c fails and the
Mt 13: 8 good soil, where it produced a c—
13:23 He produces a c, yielding a hundred,
21:41 his share of the c at harvest time."
Mk 4: 8 It came up, grew and produced a c,
4:20 accept it, and produce a c—thirty,
Lk 8: 8 It came up and yielded a c, a
8:15 it, and by persevering produce a c.
12:16 certain rich man produced a good c.
Jn 4:36 even now he harvests the c for
Heb 6: 7 that produces a c useful to those
Jas 5: 7 the land to yield its valuable c

Crops (Crop)
Ge 4:12 will no longer yield its c for you.
26:12 Isaac planted c in that land and the
Ex 23:10 sow your fields and harvest the c,
23:16 of the c you sow in your field.
23:16 you gather in your c from the field.
Lev 23:39 after you have gathered the c of the
25: 3 your vineyards and gather their c.
25:15 of years left for harvesting c.
25:16 selling you is the number of c.
25:20 we do not plant or harvest our c?"
26: 4 and the ground will yield its c and
26:20 your soil will not yield its c,
Dt 7:13 the c of your land—your grain, new
22: 9 not only the c you plant but also
28: 4 and the c of your land and the young
28:11 the c of your ground—in the land he
28:18 and the c of your land, and the
28:42 your trees and the c of your land.
28:51 the c of your land until you are
30: 9 livestock and the c of your land.
Jdg 6: 3 the Israelites planted their c,
6: 4 ruined the c all the way to Gaza and
2Sa 9:10 the land for him and bring in the c,
Ne 10:35 of our c and of every fruit tree.
10:37 we will bring a tithe of our c to
Job 31: 8 have sown, and may my c be uprooted.
Ps 65:10 it with showers and bless its c.
78:46 He gave their c to the grasshopper,
Pr 3: 9 with the firstfruits of all your c;
10: 5 He who gathers c in summer is a wise
28: 3 a driving rain that leaves no c.
Jer 35: 9 in or had vineyards, fields or c.
Eze 34:27 and the ground will yield its c;
34:29 for them a land renowned for its c,
36:30 of the trees and the c of the field,
Hag 1:10 their dew and the earth its c.
Zec 8:12 the ground will produce its c, and
Mal 3:11 prevent pests from devouring your c,
Lk 12:17 I do? I have no place to store my c.'
Ac 14:17 from heaven and c in their seasons;
2Ti 2: 6 first to receive a share of the c.
Jas 5:18 rain, and the earth produced its c.
Rev 22: 2 bearing twelve c of fruit, yielding

Cross (*Cross of Christ*, Crossed, Crosses, Crossing, Crossings)
Ex 30:14 All who c over, those twenty years
Nu 32: 5 Do not make us c the Jordan."
32:27 will c over to fight before the
32:29 c over the Jordan with you before
32:30 if they do not c over with you armed,
32:32 We will c over before the LORD into
33:51 'When you c the Jordan into Canaan,
34: 4 c south of Scorpion Pass, continue
35:10 'When you c the Jordan into Canaan,
Dt 2:13 the LORD said, "Now get up and c the
2:24 "Set out now and c the Arnon Gorge.
2:29 did for us—until we c the Jordan
3:18 armed for battle, must c over ahead
3:27 you are not going to c this Jordan.
4:21 swore that I would not c the Jordan
4:22 this land; I will not c the Jordan;
4:22 but you are about to c over and take
9: 1 You are now about to c the Jordan to
11:31 You are about to c the Jordan to
12:10 you will c the Jordan and settle in
30:13 "Who will c the sea to get it and
31: 2 to me, 'You shall not c the Jordan.'
31: 3 The LORD your God himself will c
31: 3 Joshua also will c over ahead of you,
34: 4 but you will not c over into it."
Jos 1: 2 get ready to c the Jordan River into
1:11 you will c the Jordan here to go in
1:14 must c over ahead of your brothers.
3:14 when the people broke camp to c the
Jdg 3:28 Moab, they allowed no-one to c over.
12: 5 "Let me c over," the men of Gilead
1Sa 14: 4 pass that Jonathan intended to c
14: 8 Jonathan said, "Come, then; we will c
30:10 were too exhausted to c the ravine.
2Sa 17:16 in the desert; c over without fail,
17:21 "Set out and c the river at once;
19:31 to c the Jordan with the king
19:33 "C over with me and stay with me in
19:36 Your servant will c over the Jordan
19:37 Let him c over with my lord the king.
19:38 The king said, "Kimham shall c over
1Ki 2:37 leave and c the Kidron Valley,
Ps 104: 9 You set a boundary they cannot c;
Isa 11:15 so that men can c over in sandals.
23: 6 C over to Tarshish; wail, you people
23:12 "Up, c over to Cyprus; even there
51:10 so that the redeemed might c over?
Jer 2:10 C over to the coasts of Kittim and
5:22 an everlasting barrier it cannot c.
5:22 they may roar, but they cannot c it.
9:12 like a desert that no-one can c?
41:10 set out to c over to the Ammonites.
Eze 33:28 desolate so that no-one will c them.
47: 5 it was a river that I could not c,
47: 5 in—a river that no-one could c.
Mt 8:18 to c to the other side of the lake.
10:38 anyone who does not take his c and
16:24 and take up his c and follow me.
27:32 and they forced him to carry the c.
27:40 Come down from the c, if you are
27:42 Let him come down now from the c,
Mk 8:34 and take up his c and follow me.
15:21 and they forced him to carry the c.
15:30 come down from the c and save
15:32 come down now from the c, that we
Lk 9:23 take up his c daily and follow me.
14:27 anyone who does not carry his c and
16:26 can anyone c over from there to us.'
23:26 and put the c on him and made him
Jn 19:17 Carrying his own c, he went out to
19:19 prepared and fastened to the c.
19:25 Near the c of Jesus stood his mother,
Ac 2:23 to death by nailing him to the c.
1Co 1:18 For the message of the c is
Gal 5:11 offence of the c has been abolished.

Gal 6:14 May I never boast except in the **c** of
Eph 2:16 both of them to God through the **c**,
Php 2: 8 to death—even death on a **c**!
Col 1:20 through his blood, shed on the **c**.
2:14 took it away, nailing it to the **c**.
2:15 them, triumphing over them by the **c**.
Heb 12: 2 joy set before him endured the **c**,

Cross of Christ

1Co 1:17 lest the **c** be emptied of its power.
Gal 6:12 to avoid being persecuted for the **c**.
Php 3:18 many live as enemies of the **c**.

Crossbar (Crossbars)

Ex 26:28 The centre **c** is to extend from end
36:33 They made the centre **c** so that it

Crossbars (Crossbar)

Ex 26:26 "Also make **c** of acacia wood: five
26:29 and make gold rings to hold the **c**.
26:29 Also overlay the **c** with gold.
35:11 clasps, frames, **c**, posts and bases;
36:31 They also made **c** of acacia wood:
36:34 and made gold rings to hold the **c**.
36:34 They also overlaid the **c** with gold.
39:33 clasps, frames, **c**, posts and bases;
40:18 inserted the **c** and set up the posts.
Nu 3:36 its **c**, posts, bases, all its
4:31 tabernacle, its **c**, posts and bases,
Jer 27: 2 "Make a yoke out of straps and **c**

Crossed (Cross)

Ge 32:10 I had only my staff when I **c** this
32:22 sons and **c** the ford of the Jabbok.
Ex 38:26 from everyone who had **c** over to
Dt 2:13 Zered Valley." So we **c** the valley.
2:14 Barnea until we **c** the Zered Valley.
27: 2 you have **c** the Jordan into the land
27: 3 when you have **c** over to enter the
27: 4 you have **c** the Jordan, set up these
27:12 you have **c** the Jordan, these tribes
Jos 3:16 the people **c** over opposite Jericho.
4: 7 When it **c** the Jordan, the waters of
4:11 soon as all of them had **c**, the ark
4:12 the half-tribe of Manasseh **c** over,
4:13 **c** over before the LORD to the
4:22 tell them, 'Israel **c** the Jordan on
4:23 before you until you had **c** over.
4:23 it up before us until we had **c** over.
5: 1 the Israelites until we had **c** over,
15: 3 **c** south of Scorpion Pass, continued
15:10 to Beth Shemesh and **c** to Timnah.
16: 2 **c** over to the territory of the
18:13 From there it **c** to the south slope
24:11 "Then you **c** the Jordan and came to
Jdg 6:33 **c** over the Jordan and camped in the
8: 4 came to the Jordan and **c** it.
10: 9 The Ammonites also **c** the Jordan to
11:29 He **c** Gilead and Manasseh, passed
12: 1 **c** over to Zaphon and said to
12: 3 and **c** over to fight the Ammonites,
1Sa 13: 7 Some Hebrews even **c** the Jordan to
26:13 David **c** over to the other side and
2Sa 2:29 They **c** the Jordan, continued through
10:17 **c** the Jordan and went to Helam.
15:23 The king also **c** the Kidron Valley,
17:20 them, "They **c** over the brook.
17:22 with him set out and **c** the Jordan.
17:22 was left who had not **c** the Jordan.
17:24 and Absalom **c** the Jordan with all
19:18 They **c** at the ford to take the
19:18 When Shimei son of Gera **c** the Jordan,
19:39 all the people **c** the Jordan, and
19:39 Jordan, and then the king **c** over.
19:40 the king **c** over to Gilgal, Kimham **c**
2Ki 2: 8 two of them **c** over on dry ground.
2: 9 they had **c**, Elijah said to Elisha,
2:14 and to the left, and he **c** over.
1Ch 12:15 was they who **c** the Jordan in the
19:17 all Israel and **c** the Jordan
Mt 9: 1 Jesus stepped into a boat, **c** over
14:34 they had **c** over, they landed at
Mk 5:21 Jesus had again **c** over by boat to
6:53 they had **c** over, they landed at
Mk 8:13 the boat and **c** to the other side.
Jn 5:24 he has **c** over from death to life.
6: 1 Some time after this, Jesus **c** to the
18: 1 disciples and **c** the Kidron Valley.
Ac 20:15 The day after that we **c** over to

Crosses (Cross)

Ex 30:13 Each one who **c** over to those already
Jn 19:31 left on the **c** during the Sabbath,

Cross-examined (Examine)

Ac 12:19 he **c** the guards and ordered that

Crossing (Cross)

Ge 31:21 and **c** the River, he headed for the
48:14 **c** his arms, he put his left hand
Dt 4:14 you are **c** the Jordan to possess.
4:26 you are **c** the Jordan to possess.
6: 1 you are **c** the Jordan to possess,
11: 8 you are **c** the Jordan to possess,
11:11 the land you are **c** the Jordan to
30:18 **c** the Jordan to enter and possess.
31:13 you are **c** the Jordan to possess."
32:47 you are **c** the Jordan to possess."
Jos 3: 1 where they camped before **c** over.
3:17 had completed the **c** on dry ground.
4: 1 the whole nation had finished **c** the
2Sa 24: 5 After **c** the Jordan, they camped near
Da 8: 5 **c** the whole earth without touching
Ac 21: 2 We found a ship **c** over to Phoenicia,

Crossings (Cross)

Jer 51:32 the river **c** seized, the marshes set

Crossroads (Road)

Jer 6:16 "Stand at the **c** and look; ask for
Ob :14 You should not wait at the **c** to cut

Crouch (Crouches, Crouching)

Nu 24: 9 Like a lion they **c** and lie down,
Job 38:40 they **c** in their dens or lie in wait
39: 3 They **c** down and bring forth their

Crouches (Crouch)

Ge 49: 9 Like a lion he **c** and lies down, like

Crouching (Crouch)

Ge 4: 7 sin is **c** at your door; it desires to
Ps 17:12 prey, like a great lion **c** in cover.

Crow (Crowed, Crows)

Jn 18:27 at that moment a cock began to **c**.

Crowd (Crowded, Crowding, Crowds)

Ex 23: 2 "Do not follow the **c** in doing wrong.
23: 2 justice by siding with the **c**,
Jdg 6:31 Joash replied to the hostile **c**
2Sa 6:19 **c** of Israelites, both men and women.
2Ch 30:13 A very large **c** of people assembled
30:17 Since many in the **c** had not
Ezr 10: 1 a large **c** of Israelites—men, women
Job 31:34 I so feared the **c** and so dreaded the
Ps 64: 2 from that noisy **c** of evildoers.
Jer 9: 2 a **c** of unfaithful people.
Eze 7:11 none of that **c**—no wealth, nothing
7:12 for wrath is upon the whole **c**.
7:13 the whole **c** will not be reversed.
7:14 for my wrath is upon the whole **c**.
23:42 "The noise of a carefree **c** was
Mt 8:18 Jesus saw the **c** around him, he gave
9: 8 the **c** saw this, they were filled
9:23 the flute players and the noisy **c**,
9:25 After the **c** had been put outside, he
9:33 The **c** was amazed and said, "Nothing
11: 7 Jesus began to speak to the **c** about
12:46 Jesus was still talking to the **c**,
13:34 Jesus spoke all these things to the **c**
13:36 he left the **c** and went into the
14:14 Jesus landed and saw a large **c**, he
14:22 side, while he dismissed the **c**.
15:10 Jesus called the **c** to him and said,
15:33 this remote place to feed such a **c**?"
Mt 15:35 He told the **c** to sit down on the
15:39 After Jesus had sent the **c** away, he
17:14 they came to the **c**, a man approached
20:29 Jericho, a large **c** followed him.
20:31 The **c** rebuked them and told them to
21: 8 A very large **c** spread their cloaks
21:46 but they were afraid of the **c**
26:47 With him was a large **c** armed with
26:55 At that time Jesus said to the **c**,
27:15 release a prisoner chosen by the **c**.
27:17 when the **c** had gathered, Pilate
27:20 the elders persuaded the **c** to ask
27:24 washed his hands in front of the **c**.
Mk 2: 4 get him to Jesus because of the **c**,
2:13 A large **c** came to him, and he began
3: 7 and a large **c** from Galilee followed.
3: 9 of the **c** he told his disciples to
3:20 and again a **c** gathered, so that he
3:32 A **c** was sitting around him, and they
4: 1 The **c** that gathered round him was so
4:36 Leaving the **c** behind, they took him
5:21 a large **c** gathered round him while
5:24 A large **c** followed and pressed
5:27 him in the **c** and touched his cloak,
5:30 He turned around in the **c** and asked,
6:34 Jesus landed and saw a large **c**, he
6:45 Bethsaida, while he dismissed the **c**.
7:14 Again Jesus called the **c** to him and
7:17 After he had left the **c** and entered
7:33 away from the **c**, Jesus put his
8: 1 days another large **c** gathered.
8: 6 He told the **c** to sit down on the
8:34 he called the **c** to him along with
9:14 they saw a large **c** around them and
9:17 A man in the **c** answered, "Teacher,
9:25 Jesus saw that a **c** was running to
10:46 together with a large **c**, were
11:18 whole **c** was amazed at his teaching.
12:12 But they were afraid of the **c**;
12:37 **c** listened to him with delight.
12:41 watched the **c** putting their money
14:43 With him was a **c** armed with swords
15: 8 The **c** came up and asked Pilate to do
15:11 the chief priests stirred up the **c**
15:15 Wanting to satisfy the **c**, Pilate
Lk 3:10 should we do then?" the **c** asked.
4:30 he walked right through the **c** and
5:19 a way to do this because of the **c**,
5:19 of the **c**, right in front of Jesus.
5:29 and a large **c** of tax collectors and
6:17 A large **c** of his disciples was there
7: 9 and turning to the **c** following him,
7:11 and a large **c** went along with him.
7:12 large **c** from the town was with her.
7:24 Jesus began to speak to the **c** about
8: 4 While a large **c** was gathering and
8:19 to get near him because of the **c**.
8:40 a **c** welcomed him, for they were all
9:12 "Send the **c** away so they can go to
9:13 we go and buy food for all this **c**."
9:37 the mountain, a large **c** met him.
9:38 A man in the **c** called out, "Teacher,
11:14 mute spoke, and the **c** was amazed.
11:27 things, a woman in the **c** called out,
12: 1 Meanwhile, when a **c** of many
12:13 Someone in the **c** said to him,
12:54 He said to the **c**: "When you see a
18:36 he heard the **c** going by, he asked
19: 3 man he could not, because of the **c**.
19:37 the whole **c** of disciples began
19:39 Some of the Pharisees in the **c** said
22: 6 over to them when no **c** was present.
22:47 While he was still speaking a **c** came
23: 4 to the chief priests and the **c**,
Jn 5:13 away into the **c** that was there.
6: 2 a great **c** of people followed him
6: 5 Jesus looked up and saw a great **c**
6:22 The next day the **c** that had stayed
6:24 Once the **c** realised that neither
7:20 demon-possessed," the **c** answered.
7:31 Still, many in the **c** put their faith
7:32 The Pharisees heard the **c** whispering
12: 9 Meanwhile a large **c** of Jews found
12:12 The next day the great **c** that had
12:17 Now the **c** that was with him when he
12:29 The **c** that was there and heard it

Jn 12:34 The c spoke up, "We have heard from
Ac 2: 6 they heard this sound, a c came
2:14 his voice and addressed the c:
14:11 the c saw what Paul had done, they
14:13 c wanted to offer sacrifices to them.
14:14 and rushed out into the c, shouting:
14:18 keeping the c from sacrificing to
14:19 and Iconium and won the c over.
16:22 The c joined in the attack against
17: 5 in order to bring them out to the c.
17: 8 the c and the city officials were
19:30 Paul wanted to appear before the c,
19:33 the c shouted instructions to him.
19:35 The city clerk quietened the c and
21:27 up the whole c and seized him,
21:32 and soldiers and ran down to the c.
21:34 Some in the c shouted one thing and
21:36 The c that followed kept shouting,
21:40 on the steps and motioned to the c.
22:22 The c listened to Paul until he said
24:12 or stirring up a c in the synagogues
24:18 There was no c with me, nor was I

Crowded (Crowd)

Jdg 16:27 Now the temple was c with men and
2Ki 10:21 They c into the temple of Baal until
Jer 26: 9 And all the people c around Jeremiah
Da 3:27 and royal advisers c around them.

Crowding (Crowd)

Mk 3: 9 him, to keep the people from c him.
5:31 "You see the people c against you,"
Lk 5: 1 with the people c round him and
8:45 are c and pressing against you."

Crowds (Crowd)

Mt 4:25 Large c from Galilee, the Decapolis,
5: 1 Now when he saw the c, he went up on
7:28 the c were amazed at his teaching,
8: 1 mountainside, large c followed him.
9:36 he saw the c, he had compassion on
13: 2 Such large c gathered round him that
14:13 Hearing of this, the c followed him
14:15 Send the c away, so that they can go
15:30 Great c came to him, bringing the
19: 2 Large c followed him, and he healed
21: 9 The c that went ahead of him and
21:11 The c answered, "This is Jesus, the
22:33 the c heard this, they were
23: 1 Jesus said to the c and to his
Mk 10: 1 Again c of people came to him, and
Lk 3: 7 John said to the c coming out to be
5:15 so that c of people came to hear him
8:42 his way, the c almost crushed him.
9:11 the c learned about it and followed
9:18 "Who do the c say I am?
11:29 the c increased, Jesus said, "This
14:25 Large c were travelling with Jesus,
Jn 7:12 Among the c there was widespread
Ac 5:16 C gathered also from the towns
8: 6 the c heard Philip and saw the
13:45 the Jews saw the c, they were filled
17:13 agitating the c and stirring them

Crowed (Crow)

Mt 26:74 know the man!" Immediately a cock c.
Mk 14:72 Immediately the cock c the second
Lk 22:60 Just as he was speaking, the cock c.

Crown (Crowned, Crowns)

Jdg 9: 6 in Shechem to c Abimelech king.
2Sa 1:10 And I took the c that was on his
12:30 He took the c from the head of their
2Ki 11:12 the king's son and put the c on him;
1Ch 20: 2 David took the c from the head of
2Ch 23:11 the king's son and put the c on him;
Est 1:11 wearing her royal c, in order to
2:17 So he set a royal c on her head and
8:15 a large c of gold and a purple robe
Job 19: 9 and removed the c from my head.
31:36 I would put it on like a c.
Ps 21: 3 placed a c of pure gold on his head.
65:11 You c the year with your bounty, and
89:39 and have defiled his c in the dust.
132:18 c on his head shall be resplendent."
Pr 4: 9 present you with a c of splendour."
10: 6 Blessings c the head of the
12: 4 noble character is her husband's c,
14:24 The wealth of the wise is their c,
16:31 Grey hair is a c of splendour; it is
17: 6 Children's children are a c to the
27:24 c is not secure for all generations.
SS 3:11 look at King Solomon wearing the c,
3:11 the c with which his mother crowned
Isa 28: 5 Lord Almighty will be a glorious c,
35:10 everlasting joy will c their heads.
51:11 everlasting joy will c their heads.
61: 3 them a c of beauty instead of ashes,
62: 3 You will be a c of splendour in the
Jer 2:16 have shaved the c of your head.
Lam 5:16 The c has fallen from our head. Woe
Eze 16:12 ears and a beautiful c on your head.
21:26 Take off the turban, remove the c.
Zec 6:11 Take the silver and gold and make a c
6:14 The c will be given to Heldai,
9:16 in his land like jewels in a c.
Mt 27:29 twisted together a c of thorns and
Mk 15:17 a c of thorns and set it on him.
Jn 19: 2 The soldiers twisted together a c of
19: 5 Jesus came out wearing the c of
1Co 9:25 They do it to get a c that will not
9:25 to get a c that will last for ever.
Php 4: 1 my joy and c, that is how you should
1Th 2:19 or the c in which we will glory
2Ti 2: 5 he does not receive the victor's c
4: 8 Now there is in store for me the c
Jas 1:12 he will receive the c of life that
1Pe 5: 4 c of glory that will never fade away.
Rev 2:10 and I will give you the c of life.
3:11 so that no-one will take your c.
6: 2 and he was given a c, and he rode
12: 1 and a c of twelve stars on her head.
14:14 "like a son of man" with a c of gold

Crowned (Crown)

Ps 8: 5 and c him with glory and honour.
Pr 14:18 the prudent are c with knowledge.
SS 3:11 crown with which his mother c him
Heb 2: 7 you c him with glory and honour
2: 9 now c with glory and honour because

Crowns (Crown)

Ps 68:21 c of those who go on in their sins.
103: 4 and c you with love and compassion,
149: 4 he c the humble with salvation.
Pr 11:26 c him who is willing to sell.
SS 7: 5 Your head c you like Mount Carmel.
Isa 23: 8 the bestower of c, whose merchants
Jer 13:18 c will fall from your heads."
Eze 23:42 and beautiful c on their heads.
Rev 4: 4 and had c of gold on their heads.
4:10 lay their c before the throne and
9: 7 they wore something like c of gold,
12: 3 ten horns and seven c on his heads.
13: 1 with ten c on his horns, and on each
19:12 fire, and on his head are many c.

Crows (Crow)

Mt 26:34 before the cock c, you will disown
26:75 "Before the cock c, you will disown
Mk 13:35 or when the cock c, or at dawn.
14:30 tonight—before the cock c twice you
14:72 "Before the cock c twice you will
Lk 22:34 Peter, before the cock c today, you
22:61 "Before the cock c today, you will
Jn 13:38 before the cock c, you will disown

Crucible

Pr 17: 3 The c for silver and the furnace for
27:21 The c for silver and the furnace for

Crucified (Crucify)

Mt 20:19 to be mocked and flogged and c.
26: 2 of Man will be handed over to be c."
27:26 and handed him over to be c.
27:35 they had c him, they divided up his
27:38 Two robbers were c with him, one on
27:44 way the robbers who were c with him
28: 5 are looking for Jesus, who was c.
Mk 15:15 and handed him over to be c.
15:24 they c him. Dividing up his clothes,
15:25 was the third hour when they c him.
15:27 They c two robbers with him, one on
15:32 Those c with him also heaped
16: 6 for Jesus the Nazarene, who was c.
Lk 23:23 demanded that he be c, and their
23:33 there they c him, along with the
24: 7 be c and on the third day be raised
24:20 sentenced to death, and they c him;
Jn 19:16 handed him over to them to be c.
19:18 Here they c him, and with him two
19:20 for the place where Jesus was c was
19:23 the soldiers c Jesus, they took his
19:32 first man who had been c with Jesus,
19:41 At the place where Jesus was c,
Ac 2:36 whom you c, both Lord and Christ."
4:10 whom you c but whom God raised from
Ro 6: 6 For we know that our old self was c
1Co 1:13 Christ divided? Was Paul c for you
1:23 preach Christ c: a stumbling-block
2: 2 you except Jesus Christ and him c.
2: 8 would not have c the Lord of glory.
2Co 13: 4 For to be sure, he was c in weakness,
Gal 2:20 I have been c with Christ and I no
3: 1 Christ was clearly portrayed as c.
5:24 have c the sinful nature with its
6:14 been c to me, and I to the world.
Rev 11: 8 Egypt, where also their Lord was c.

Crucify (Crucified, Crucifying)

Mt 23:34 Some of them you will kill and c;
27:22 They all answered, "C him!"
27:23 shouted all the louder, "C him!"
27:31 Then they led him away to c him.
Mk 15:13 "C him!" they shouted.
15:14 shouted all the louder, "C him!"
15:20 Then they led him out to c him.
Lk 23:21 they kept shouting, "C him! C him!"
Jn 19: 6 "C! C!" But Pilate answered, "You
19: 6 answered, "You take him and c him.
19:10 either to free you or to c you?"
19:15 "Take him away! Take him away! C him!
19:15 "Shall I c your king?" Pilate asked.

Crucifying (Crucify)

Heb 6: 6 they are c the Son of God all over

Cruel (Cruelly, Cruelty)

Ge 49: 7 so fierce, and their fury, so c!
Ex 6: 9 their discouragement and c bondage.
Dt 28:33 but c oppression all your days.
Ps 71: 4 from the grasp of evil and c men.
Pr 5: 9 and your years to one who is c,
11:17 but a c man brings trouble on
12:10 kindest acts of the wicked are c.
27: 4 Anger is c and fury overwhelming,
Ecc 9:12 come: As fish are caught in a c net,
Isa 13: 9 —a c day, with wrath and fierce
14: 3 suffering and turmoil and c bondage,
19: 4 over to the power of a c master,
Jer 6:23 spear; they are c and show no mercy.
15:21 redeem you from the grasp of the c."
30:14 and punished you as would the c,
50:42 they are c and without mercy.

Cruelly (Cruel)

Jdg 4: 3 had c oppressed the Israelites for

Cruelty (Cruel)

Na 3:19 for who has not felt your endless c?

Crumble (Crumbled, Crumbles, Crumbling)

Lev 2: 6 C it and pour oil on it; it is a
Eze 38:20 the cliffs will c and every wall

Crumbled (Crumble)

Hab 3: 6 The ancient mountains c and the

Crumbles (Crumble)

Job 14:18 "But as a mountain erodes and c and

Crumbling (Crumble)
Job 15:28 no-one lives, houses **c** to rubble.

Crumbs
Mt 15:27 "but even the dogs eat the **c** that
Mk 7:28 the table eat the children's **c**."

Crush (Crushed, Crushes, Crushing)
Ge 3:15 and hers; he will **c** your head,
Nu 24:17 He will **c** the foreheads of Moab, the
Job 6: 9 that God would be willing to **c** me,
9:17 He would **c** me with a storm and
19: 2 you torment me and **c** me with words?
24:11 They **c** olives among the terraces;
39:15 unmindful that a foot may **c** them,
40:12 him, **c** the wicked where they stand.
Ps 68:21 Surely God will **c** the heads of his
72: 4 the needy; he will **c** the oppressor.
74: 8 "We will **c** them completely!"
89:23 I will **c** his foes before him and
94: 5 They **c** your people, O LORD; they
110: 5 **c** kings on the day of his wrath.
Pr 22:22 and do not **c** the needy in court,
Isa 14:25 I will **c** the Assyrian in my land; on
41:15 thresh the mountains and **c** them,
53:10 Yet it was the LORD's will to **c** him
Jer 50:17 the last to **c** his bones was
Lam 1:15 army against me to **c** my young men.
3:34 To **c** underfoot all prisoners in the
Da 2:40 it will **c** and break all the others.
2:44 It will **c** all those kingdoms and
Am 2:13 "Now then, I will **c** you as a cart
4: 1 **c** the needy and say to your husbands,
Mic 6:15 **c** grapes but not drink the wine.
Ro 16:20 The God of peace will soon **c** Satan

Crushed (Crush)
Lev 2:14 offer **c** heads of new grain roasted
2:16 portion of the **c** grain and the oil,
22:24 are bruised, **c**, torn or cut.
Nu 11: 8 in a hand mill or **c** it in a mortar.
Dt 9:21 Then I **c** it and ground it to powder
Jdg 5:26 She struck Sisera, she **c** his head,
10: 8 who that year shattered and **c** them.
2Sa 22:38 "I pursued my enemies and **c** them;
22:39 I **c** them completely, and they could
2Ch 14:13 **c** before the LORD and his forces.
15: 6 One nation was being **c** by another
34: 7 poles and **c** the idols to powder
Job 4:19 who are **c** more readily than a moth!
5: 4 **c** in court without a defender.
16:12 he seized me by the neck and **c** me.
34:25 them in the night and they are **c**.
Ps 10:10 His victims are **c**, they collapse;
18:38 I **c** them so that they could not rise;
34:18 and saves those who are **c** in spirit.
38: 8 I am feeble and utterly **c**; I groan
44: 2 you **c** the peoples and made our
44:19 you **c** us and made us a haunt for
51: 8 let the bones you have **c** rejoice.
74:14 was you who **c** the heads of Leviathan
89:10 You **c** Rahab like one of the slain;
Pr 17:22 but a **c** spirit dries up the bones.
18:14 but a **c** spirit who can bear?
Isa 21:10 people, **c** on the threshing-floor,
23:12 O Virgin Daughter of Sidon, now **c**!
27: 9 to be like chalk stones **c** to pieces,
53: 5 he was **c** for our iniquities; the
Jer 5: 3 **c** them but they refused correction.
8:21 Since my people are **c**, I am **c**;
22:20 Abarim, for all your allies are **c**.
Eze 30: 8 to Egypt and all her helpers are **c**.
Da 6:24 them and **c** all their bones.
7: 7 it **c** and devoured its victims and
7:19 the beast that **c** and devoured its
Hab 3:13 You **c** the leader of the land of
Mal 1: 4 Edom may say, "Though we have been **c**,
Mt 21:44 but he on whom it falls will be **c**."
Lk 8:42 on his way, the crowds almost **c** him.
20:18 but he on whom it falls will be **c**."
2Co 4: 8 pressed on every side, but not **c**;

Crushes (Crush)
Ps 143: 3 pursues me, he **c** me to the ground;
Pr 15: 4 but a deceitful tongue **c** the spirit.
Pr 15:13 but heartache **c** the spirit.
Am 2:13 as a cart **c** when loaded with grain.

Crushing (Crush)
Nu 22:25 wall, **c** Balaam's foot against it.
Dt 23: 1 No-one who has been emasculated by **c**
Ps 110: 6 and **c** the rulers of the whole earth.
Isa 3:15 What do you mean by **c** my people and
Jer 14:17 suffered a grievous wound, a **c** blow.
Da 7:23 earth, trampling it down and **c** it.

Crust (Encrusted)
1Sa 2:36 silver and a **c** of bread and plead,
Pr 17: 1 Better a dry **c** with peace and quiet

Crutch
2Sa 3:29 or who leans on a **c** or who falls

Cry (Cried, Cries, Crying)
Ge 27:34 with a loud and bitter **c** and said
Ex 2:23 and their **c** for help because of
3: 9 now the **c** of the Israelites has
22:23 If you do and they **c** out to me, I
22:23 me, I will certainly hear their **c**.
Lev 13:45 face and **c** out, 'Unclean! Unclean!'
Nu 20:16 he heard our **c** and sent an angel and
Dt 24:15 Otherwise he may **c** to the LORD
33: 7 "Hear, O LORD, the **c** of Judah;
Jos 6:10 "Do not give a war **c**, do not raise
Jdg 10:14 Go and **c** out to the gods you have
1Sa 4:13 the whole town sent up a **c**.
8:18 that day comes, you will **c** out for
9:16 people, for their **c** has reached me."
17:20 positions, shouting the war **c**.
2Sa 22: 7 my voice; my **c** came to his ears.
1Ki 8:28 Hear the **c** and the prayer that your
8:52 to them whenever they **c** out to you.
17:22 The LORD heard Elijah's **c**, and the
22:36 a **c** spread through the army:
1Ch 16:35 **C** out, "Save us, O God our Saviour;
2Ch 6:19 Hear the **c** and the prayer that your
13:12 will sound the battle **c** against you.
13:15 the men of Judah raised the battle **c**.
13:15 At the sound of their battle **c**, God
20: 9 will **c** out to you in our distress,
Ne 9: 9 you heard their **c** at the Red Sea.
Job 16:18 may my **c** never be laid to rest!
19: 7 "Though I **c**, 'I've been wronged!'
24:12 souls of the wounded **c** out for help.
27: 9 Does God listen to his **c** when
30:20 "I **c** out to you, O God, but you do
30:28 up in the assembly and **c** for help.
34:28 They caused the **c** of the poor to
34:28 so that he heard the **c** of the needy.
35: 9 "Men **c** out under a load of
35:12 He does not answer when men **c** out
36:13 them, they do not **c** for help.
38:41 raven when its young **c** out to God
39:25 of commanders and the battle **c**.
Ps 3: 4 To the LORD I **c** aloud, and he
5: 2 Listen to my **c** for help, my King and
6: 9 The LORD has heard my **c** for mercy;
9:12 not ignore the **c** of the afflicted.
10:17 them, and you listen to their **c**,
17: 1 my righteous plea; listen to my **c**.
18: 6 my **c** came before him, into his ears.
22: 2 O my God, I **c** out by day, but you do
22:24 but has listened to his **c** for help.
28: 2 Hear my **c** for mercy as I call to you
28: 6 for he has heard my **c** for mercy.
29: 9 And in his temple all **c**, "Glory!"
31:22 Yet you heard my **c** for mercy when
34:15 his ears are attentive to their **c**;
34:17 The righteous **c** out, and the LORD
39:12 O LORD, listen to my **c** for help; be
40: 1 LORD; he turned to me and heard my **c**.
55:17 Evening, morning and noon I **c** out in
57: 2 I **c** out to God Most High, to God,
61: 1 Hear my **c**, O God; listen to my
72:12 For he will deliver the needy who **c**
84: 2 my flesh **c** out for the living God.
86: 6 O LORD; listen to my **c** for mercy.
88: 1 day and night I **c** out before you.
88: 2 before you; turn your ear to my **c**.
Ps 88:13 I **c** to you for help, O LORD; in the
102: 1 let my **c** for help come to you.
106:44 distress when he heard their **c**;
116: 1 my voice; he heard my **c** for mercy.
119:147 I rise before dawn and **c** for help;
119:169 May my **c** come before you, O LORD;
130: 1 Out of the depths I **c** to you,
130: 2 ears be attentive to my **c** for mercy.
140: 6 Hear, O LORD, my **c** for mercy.
142: 1 I **c** aloud to the LORD; I lift up my
142: 5 I **c** to you, O LORD; I say, "You are
142: 6 Listen to my **c**, for I am in
143: 1 prayer, listen to my **c** for mercy;
144:14 no **c** of distress in our streets.
145:19 he hears their **c** and saves them.
Pr 2: 3 and **c** aloud for understanding
21:13 shuts his ears to the **c** of the poor
21:13 too will **c** out and not be answered.
30:15 'Give! Give!' they **c**. "There are
Isa 3: 7 in that day he will **c** out, "I have
8: 9 Raise the war **c**, you nations, and be
10:30 **C** out, O Daughter of Gallim! Listen,
15: 4 Heshbon and Elealeh **c** out, their
15: 4 the armed men of Moab **c** out, and
19:20 When they **c** out to the LORD because
24:11 In the streets they **c** out for wine;
30:19 How gracious he will be when you **c**
33: 7 Look, their brave men **c** aloud in the
40: 6 A voice says, "**C** out." And I said,
40: 6 And I said, "What shall I **c**?" "All
42: 2 He will not shout or **c** out, or raise
42:13 a shout he will raise the battle **c**
42:14 I **c** out, I gasp and pant.
57:13 you **c** out for help, let your
58: 9 you will **c** for help, and he will
65:14 but you will **c** out from anguish of
Jer 3:21 A **c** is heard on the barren heights,
4: 5 the land!' **C** aloud and say:
4:16 a war **c** against the cities of Judah.
4:19 trumpet; I have heard the battle **c**.
4:31 I hear a **c** as of a woman in labour,
4:31 the **c** of the Daughter of Zion
8:19 Listen to the **c** of my people from a
11:11 Although they **c** out to me, I will
11:12 **c** out to the gods to whom they burn
12: 6 have raised a loud **c** against you.
14: 2 and a **c** goes up from Jerusalem.
14:12 I will not listen to their **c**; though
18:22 Let a **c** be heard from their houses
20: 8 Whenever I speak, I **c** out
20:16 in the morning, a battle **c** at noon.
22:20 "Go up to Lebanon and **c** out, let
22:20 **c** out from Abarim, for all your
25:36 Hear the **c** of the shepherds, the
30:15 Why do you **c** out over your wound,
31: 6 There will be a day when watchmen **c**
47: 2 The people will **c** out; all who dwell
47: 6 "'Ah, sword of the LORD,' you **c**,
48: 4 broken; her little ones will **c** out.
48:20 Wail and **c** out! Announce by the
48:31 for all Moab I **c** out, I moan for the
48:34 "The sound of their **c** rises from
49: 2 "when I will sound the battle **c**
49: 3 **C** out, O inhabitants of Rabbah!
49:21 their **c** will resound to the Red Sea.
50:46 **c** will resound among the nations.
51:54 "The sound of a **c** comes from Babylon,
Lam 2:18 The hearts of the people **c** out to
2:19 Arise, **c** out in the night, as the
3: 8 Even when I call out or **c** for help,
3:56 close your ears to my **c** for relief."
4:15 You are unclean!" men **c** to them.
Eze 6:11 stamp your feet and **c** out "Alas!"
21:12 **C** out and wail, son of man, for it
21:22 to sound the battle **c**, to set
27:28 will quake when your seamen **c** out.
27:30 They will raise their voice and **c**
Hos 5: 8 Raise the battle **c** in Beth Aven;
7:14 They do not **c** out to me from their
Joel 1:14 LORD your God, and **c** out to the LORD.
Jnh 2: 2 for help, and you listened to my **c**.
Mic 3: 4 they will **c** out to the LORD, but he
4: 9 Why do you now **c** aloud—have you no
Na 2: 8 "Stop! Stop!" they **c**, but no-one
Hab 1: 2 listen? Or **c** out to you, "Violence!"
2:11 The stones of the wall will **c** out,

Zep 1:10 "a **c** will go up from the Fish Gate,
1:14 Listen! The **c** on the day of the LORD
1:16 a day of trumpet and battle **c**
Mt 12:19 He will not quarrel or **c** out; no-one
25: 6 "At midnight the **c** rang out: 'Here's
Mk 5: 5 **c** out and cut himself with stones.
15:37 With a loud **c**, Jesus breathed his
15:39 heard his **c** and saw how he died, he
Lk 7:13 out to her and he said, "Don't **c**.
7:32 we sang a dirge, and you did not **c**.'
18: 7 who **c** out to him day and night? Will
19:40 keep quiet, the stones will **c** out."
Ro 8:15 And by him we **c**, "Abba, Father."
Gal 4:27 break forth and **c** aloud, you who
Rev 18:10 they will stand far off and **c**: "'Woe!
18:16 **c** out: "'Woe! Woe, O great city,
18:19 and with weeping and mourning **c** out:

Crying (Cry)

Ge 21:17 God heard the boy **c**, and the angel
21:17 heard the boy **c** as he lies there.
Ex 2: 6 He was **c**, and she felt sorry for him.
3: 7 I have heard them **c** out because of
5: 8 lazy; that is why they are **c** out,
14:15 "Why are you **c** out to me? Tell the
Jdg 7:21 Midianites ran, **c** out as they fled.
1Sa 7: 8 "Do not stop **c** out to the LORD our
Isa 22: 5 walls and of **c** out to the mountains.
65:19 the sound of weeping and of **c** will
Eze 9: 8 I fell face down, **c** out, "Ah,
Mt 15:22 **c** out, "Lord, Son of David, have
15:23 away, for she keeps **c** out after us."
Mk 5:38 with people **c** and wailing loudly.
Jn 20:11 Mary stood outside the tomb **c**. As
20:13 They asked her, "Woman, why are you **c**
20:15 "Woman," he said, "why are you **c**?
Ac 9:39 All the widows stood around him, **c**
Jas 5: 4 your fields are **c** out against you.
Rev 21: 4 more death or mourning or **c** or pain,

Crystal

Job 28:17 Neither gold nor **c** can compare with
Rev 4: 6 like a sea of glass, clear as **c**.
Rev 21:11 jewel, like a jasper, clear as **c**.
22: 1 as clear as **c**, flowing from the

Cub (Cubs)

Ge 49: 9 You are a lion's **c**, O Judah; you
Dt 33:22 About Dan he said: "Dan is a lion's **c**

Cubit (Cubits)

Ex 25:10 a **c** and a half wide, and a **c** and a
25:17 cubits long and a **c** and a half wide.
25:23 a **c** wide and a **c** and a half high.
26:13 The tent curtains will be a **c** longer
26:16 cubits long and a **c** and a half wide,
30: 2 be square, a **c** long and a **c** wide,
36:21 cubits long and a **c** and a half wide,
37: 1 a **c** and a half wide, and a **c** and a
37: 6 cubits long and a **c** and a half wide.
37:10 a **c** wide, and a **c** and a half high.
37:25 It was square, a **c** long and a **c** wide,
1Ki 7:24 gourds encircled it—ten to a **c**.
7:31 had a circular frame one **c** deep.
7:31 basework it measured a **c** and a half.
7:32 of each wheel was a **c** and a half.
7:35 was a circular band half a **c** deep.
2Ch 3: 3 (using the **c** of the old standard).
4: 3 of bulls encircled it—ten to a **c**.
Eze 40: 5 of which was a **c** and a handbreadth.
40:12 each alcove was a wall one **c** high,
40:42 each a **c** and a half long, a **c** and a
40:42 a **c** and a half wide and a **c** high.
43:13 that **c** being a **c** and a handbreadth:
43:13 Its gutter is a **c** deep and a **c** wide,
43:14 it is two cubits high and a **c** wide,
43:14 it is four cubits high and a **c** wide.
43:17 rim of half a **c** and a gutter of a **c**

Cubits (Cubit)

Ex 25:10 acacia wood—two and a half **c** long,
25:17 Two and a half **c** long and a cubit
25:23 table of acacia wood—two **c** long
26: 2 twenty-eight **c** long and four **c** wide
26: 8 size—thirty **c** long and four **c** wide.
Ex 26:16 Each frame is to be ten **c** long and a
27: 1 altar of acacia wood, three **c** high;
27: 1 square, five **c** long and five **c** wide.
27: 9 The south side shall be a hundred **c**
27:11 shall also be a hundred **c** long and
27:12 be fifty **c** wide and have curtains,
27:13 shall also be fifty **c** wide.
27:14 Curtains fifteen **c** long are to be on
27:15 curtains fifteen **c** long are to be on
27:16 provide a curtain twenty **c** long, of
27:18 The courtyard shall be a hundred **c**
27:18 a hundred **c** long and fifty **c** wide,
30: 2 and two **c** high—its horns of one
36: 9 twenty-eight **c** long and four **c** wide
36:15 size—thirty **c** long and four **c** wide.
36:21 Each frame was ten **c** long and a
37: 1 acacia wood—two and a half **c** long,
37: 6 two and a half **c** long and a cubit
37:10 table of acacia wood—two **c** long,
37:25 and two **c** high—its horns of one
38: 1 of acacia wood three **c** high; it was
38: 1 square, five **c** long and five **c** wide.
38: 9 The south side was a hundred **c** long
38:11 The north side was also a hundred **c**
38:12 The west end was fifty **c** wide and
38:13 the sunrise, was also fifty **c** wide.
38:14 Curtains fifteen **c** long were on one
38:15 curtains fifteen **c** long were on the
38:18 It was twenty **c** long and, like the
38:18 of the courtyard, five **c** high,
1Ki 6: 2 was sixty **c** long, twenty wide and
6: 3 that is twenty **c**, and projected ten **c**
6: 6 The lowest floor was five **c** wide,
6: 6 the middle floor six **c** and the
6:10 The height of each was five **c**, and
6:16 He partitioned off twenty **c** at the
6:17 front of this room was forty **c** long.
6:20 The inner sanctuary was twenty **c**
6:23 of olive wood, each ten **c** high.
6:24 of the first cherub was five **c** long,
6:24 the other wing five **c**—ten **c** from
6:25 The second cherub also measured ten **c**
6:26 The height of each cherub was ten **c**.
7: 2 Forest of Lebanon a hundred **c** long,
7: 6 He made a colonnade fifty **c** long and
7:10 some measuring ten **c** and some eight.
7:15 eighteen **c** high and twelve **c** round,
7:16 each capital was five **c** high.
7:19 in the shape of lilies, four **c** high.
7:23 ten **c** from rim to rim and five **c**
7:23 a line of thirty **c** to measure round
7:27 each was four **c** long, four wide and
7:38 baths and measuring four **c** across,
2Ch 3: 3 the temple of God was sixty **c** long
3: 3 twenty **c** wide (using the cubit of
3: 4 was twenty **c** long across the width
3: 4 of the building and twenty **c** high.
3: 8 twenty **c** long and twenty **c** wide.
3:11 of the cherubim was twenty **c**.
3:11 of the first cherub was five **c** long
3:11 while its other wing, also five **c**
3:12 the second cherub was five **c** long
3:12 and its other wing, also five **c** long,
3:13 of these cherubim extended twenty **c**.
3:15 a capital on top measuring five **c**.
3:15 were thirty-five **c** long, each with
4: 1 He made a bronze altar twenty **c** long,
4: 1 twenty **c** wide and ten **c** high.
4: 2 ten **c** from rim to rim and five **c**
4: 2 took a line of thirty **c** to measure
6:13 five **c** long, five **c** wide and three **c**
Jer 52:21 Each of the pillars was eighteen **c**
52:21 eighteen **c** high and twelve **c** in
52:22 of the one pillar was five **c** high
Eze 40: 5 in the man's hand was six long **c**,
40: 7 the alcoves were five **c** thick.
40: 9 was eight **c** deep and its jambs were
40: 9 jambs were two **c** thick. The portico
40:11 ten **c** and its length was thirteen **c**.
40:12 and the alcoves were six **c** square.
40:13 the distance was twenty-five **c** from
40:14 the inside of the gateway—sixty **c**.
40:15 far end of its portico was fifty **c**.
40:19 it was a hundred **c** on the east side
40:21 fifty **c** long and twenty-five **c** wide.
40:23 opposite one; it was a hundred **c**.
Eze 40:25 fifty **c** long and twenty-five **c** wide.
40:27 the south side; it was a hundred **c**.
40:29 fifty **c** long and twenty-five **c** wide.
40:30 twenty-five **c** wide and five **c** deep.)
40:33 fifty **c** long and twenty-five **c** wide.
40:36 fifty **c** long and twenty-five **c** wide.
40:47 hundred **c** long and a hundred **c** wide.
40:48 were five **c** wide on either side.
40:48 of the entrance was fourteen **c**
40:48 were three **c** wide on either side.
40:49 The portico was twenty **c** wide, and
40:49 and twelve **c** from front to back.
41: 1 of the jambs was six **c** on each side.
41: 2 The entrance was ten **c** wide, and the
41: 2 on each side of it were five **c** wide.
41: 2 was forty **c** long and twenty **c** wide.
41: 3 the entrance; each was two **c** wide.
41: 3 The entrance was six **c** wide, and the
41: 3 each side of it were seven **c** wide.
41: 4 inner sanctuary; it was twenty **c**,
41: 4 and its width was twenty **c** across
41: 5 of the temple; it was six **c** thick,
41: 5 round the temple was four **c** wide.
41: 8 the length of the rod, six long **c**.
41: 9 of the side rooms was five **c** thick.
41:10 the priests' rooms was twenty **c**
41:11 open area was five **c** wide all round.
41:12 on the west side was seventy **c** wide.
41:12 The wall of the building was five **c**
41:12 round, and its length was ninety **c**.
41:13 the temple; it was a hundred **c** long,
41:13 walls were also a hundred **c** long.
41:14 of the temple, was a hundred **c**.
41:15 on each side; it was a hundred **c**.
41:22 There was a wooden altar three **c**
41:22 three **c** high and two **c** square;
42: 2 a hundred **c** long and fifty **c** wide.
42: 3 Both in the section twenty **c** from
42: 4 ten **c** wide and a hundred **c** long.
42: 7 in front of the rooms for fifty **c**.
42: 8 to the outer court was fifty **c** long,
42: 8 the sanctuary was a hundred **c** long.
42:16 rod; it was five hundred **c**.
42:17 five hundred **c** by the measuring rod.
42:18 five hundred **c** by the measuring rod.
42:19 five hundred **c** by the measuring rod.
42:20 wall round it, five hundred **c** long
42:20 five hundred **c** wide, to separate
43:13 measurements of the altar in long **c**,
43:14 it is two **c** high and a cubit wide,
43:14 it is four **c** high and a cubit wide.
43:15 The altar hearth is four **c** high, and
43:16 twelve **c** long and twelve **c** wide.
43:17 fourteen **c** long and fourteen **c** wide,
45: 1 25,000 **c** long and 20,000 **c** wide; the
45: 2 Of this, a section 500 **c** square is
45: 2 with 50 **c** around it for open land.
45: 3 25,000 **c** long and 10,000 **c** wide.
45: 5 An area 25,000 **c** long and 10,000 **c**
45: 6 area 5,000 **c** wide and 25,000 **c** long,
46:22 forty **c** long and thirty **c** wide; each
47: 3 he measured off a thousand **c** and
47: 4 He measured off another thousand **c**
48: 8 It will be 25,000 **c** wide, and its
48: 9 be 25,000 **c** long and 10,000 **c** wide.
48:10 It will be 25,000 **c** long on the
48:10 10,000 **c** wide on the west side,
48:10 10,000 **c** wide on the east side and
48:10 and 25,000 **c** long on the south side.
48:13 25,000 **c** long and 10,000 **c** wide.
48:13 be 25,000 **c** and its width 10,000 **c**.
48:15 5,000 **c** wide and 25,000 **c** long,
48:16 the north side 4,500 **c**,
48:16 the south side 4,500 **c**,
48:16 the east side 4,500 **c**,
48:16 and the west side 4,500 **c**.
48:17 the city will be 250 **c** on the north,
48:17 250 **c** on the south, 250 **c** on the
48:17 and 250 **c** on the west.
48:18 will be 10,000 **c** on the east side
48:18 and 10,000 **c** on the west side.
48:20 be a square, 25,000 **c** on each side.
48:21 the 25,000 **c** of the sacred portion
48:21 the 25,000 **c** to the western border.
48:30 north side, which is 4,500 **c** long,
48:32 "On the east side, which is 4,500 **c**

Eze 48:33 south side, which measures 4,500 **c**,
48:34 "On the west side, which is 4,500 **c**
48:35 all around will be 18,000 **c**.
Rev 21:17 He measured its wall and it was 144 **c**

Cubs (Cub)
2Sa 17: 8 as a wild bear robbed of her **c**.
Job 4:11 the **c** of the lioness are scattered.
38:32 or lead out the Bear with its **c**?
Pr 17:12 Better to meet a bear robbed of her **c**
Jer 51:38 young lions, they growl like lion **c**.
Eze 19: 2 the young lions and reared her **c**.
19: 3 She brought up one of her **c**, and he
19: 5 of her **c** and made him a strong lion.
Hos 13: 8 Like a bear robbed of her **c**, I will
Na 2:11 and the **c**, with nothing to fear?
2:12 The lion killed enough for his **c** and

Cucumbers
Nu 11: 5 **c**, melons, leeks, onions and garlic.

Cud
Lev 11: 3 divided and that chews the **c**.
11: 4 "'There are some that only chew the **c**
11: 4 The camel, though it chews the **c**,
11: 5 The coney, though it chews the **c**,
11: 6 The rabbit, though it chews the **c**,
11: 7 does not chew the **c**; it is unclean
11:26 does not chew the **c** is unclean
Dt 14: 6 divided in two and that chews the **c**.
14: 7 However, of those that chew the **c** or
14: 7 Although they chew the **c**, they do
14: 8 split hoof, it does not chew the **c**.

Cultivate (Cultivated)
Dt 28:39 You will plant vineyards and **c** them
Ps 104:14 and plants for man to **c**—bringing

Cultivated (Cultivate)
Isa 5: 6 neither pruned nor **c**, and briers and
7:25 for all the hills once **c** by the hoe,
Jer 13:21 those you **c** as your special allies?
Eze 36:34 The desolate land will be **c** instead
Ro 11:24 were grafted into a **c** olive tree,

Cummin
Isa 28:25 he not sow caraway and scatter **c**?
28:27 nor is a cartwheel rolled over **c**;
28:27 out with a rod, and **c** with a stick.
Mt 23:23 of your spices—mint, dill and **c**.

Cun
1Ch 18: 8 From Tebah and **C**, towns that

Cunning
Ps 64: 6 the mind and heart of man are **c**.
83: 3 With **c** they conspire against your
2Co 11: 3 Eve was deceived by the serpent's **c**,
Eph 4:14 by the **c** and craftiness of men in

Cup (Cups)
Ge 40:11 Pharaoh's **c** was in my hand, and I
40:11 squeezed them into Pharaoh's **c**
40:11 and put the **c** in his hand."
40:13 and you will put Pharaoh's **c** in his
40:21 again put the **c** into Pharaoh's hand,
44: 2 put my **c**, the silver one, in the
44: 5 Isn't this the **c** my master drinks
44:12 the **c** was found in Benjamin's sack.
44:16 one who was found to have the **c**."
44:17 to have the **c** will become my slave.
2Sa 12: 3 It shared his food, drank from his **c**
1Ki 7:26 the rim of a **c**, like a lily blossom.
2Ch 4: 5 the rim of a **c**, like a lily blossom.
Ps 16: 5 assigned me my portion and my **c**;
23: 5 my head with oil; my **c** overflows.
75: 8 In the hand of the LORD is a **c** full
116:13 I will lift up the **c** of salvation
Pr 23:31 when it sparkles in the **c**, when it
Isa 51:17 hand of the LORD the **c** of his wrath,
51:22 I have taken out of your hand the **c**
Isa 51:22 **c** that made you stagger; from that **c**,
Jer 25:15 "Take from my hand this **c** filled
25:17 I took the **c** from the LORD's hand
25:28 if they refuse to take the **c** from
49:12 to drink the **c** must drink it,
51: 7 Babylon was a gold **c** in the LORD's
Lam 4:21 But to you also the **c** will be passed;
Eze 23:31 so I will put her **c** into your hand.
23:32 drink your sister's **c**, a **c** large
23:33 the **c** of ruin and desolation,
23:33 the **c** of your sister Samaria
Hab 2:16 The **c** from the LORD's right hand
Zec 12: 2 "I am going to make Jerusalem a **c**
Mt 10:42 gives even a **c** of cold water
20:22 "Can you drink the **c** I am going to
20:23 "You will indeed drink from my **c**,
23:25 clean the outside of the **c** and dish,
23:26 clean the inside of the **c** and dish,
26:27 he took the **c**, gave thanks and
26:39 may this **c** be taken from me.
26:42 if it is not possible for this **c** to
Mk 9:41 anyone who gives you a **c** of water in
10:38 "Can you drink the **c** I drink or be
10:39 "You will drink the **c** I drink and be
14:23 he took the **c**, gave thanks and
14:36 Take this **c** from me. Yet not what I
Lk 11:39 clean the outside of the **c** and dish,
22:17 After taking the **c**, he gave thanks
22:20 after the supper he took the **c**,
22:20 "This **c** is the new covenant in my
22:42 are willing, take this **c** from me;
Jn 18:11 the **c** the Father has given me?"
1Co 10:16 Is not the **c** of thanksgiving for
10:21 You cannot drink the **c** of the Lord
10:21 of the Lord and the **c** of demons too;
11:25 after supper he took the **c**, saying,
11:25 "This **c** is the new covenant in my
11:26 you eat this bread and drink this **c**,
11:27 eats the bread or drinks the **c** of
11:28 of the bread and drinks of the **c**.
Rev 14:10 strength into the **c** of his wrath.
16:19 gave her the **c** filled with the wine
17: 4 She held a golden **c** in her hand,
18: 6 her a double portion from her own **c**.

Cupbearer (Cupbearers)
Ge 40: 1 Some time later, the **c** and the baker
40: 2 the chief **c** and the chief baker,
40: 5 each of the two men—the **c** and the
40: 9 the chief **c** told Joseph his dream.
40:13 you used to do when you were his **c**.
40:20 the chief **c** and the chief baker in
40:21 He restored the chief **c** to his
40:23 The chief **c**, however, did not
41: 9 the chief **c** said to Pharaoh, "Today
Ne 1:11 I was **c** to the king.

Cupbearers (Cupbearer)
1Ki 10: 5 his **c**, and the burnt offerings he
2Ch 9: 4 the **c** in their robes and the burnt

Cups (Cup)
Ex 25:31 its flowerlike **c**, buds and blossoms
25:33 Three **c** shaped like almond flowers
25:34 four **c** shaped like almond flowers
37:17 its flowerlike **c**, buds and blossoms
37:19 Three **c** shaped like almond flowers
37:20 on the lampstand were four **c** shaped
Jer 35: 5 I set bowls full of wine and some **c**
Mk 7: 4 washing of **c**, pitchers and kettles.)

Curdle (Curds)
Job 10:10 out like milk and **c** me like cheese,

Curdled (Curds)
Jdg 5:25 for nobles she brought him **c** milk.

Curds (Curdle, Curdled)
Ge 18: 8 He then brought some **c** and milk and
Dt 32:14 with **c** and milk from herd and flock
2Sa 17:29 honey and **c**, sheep, and cheese from
Isa 7:15 He will eat **c** and honey when he
7:22 they give, he will have **c** to eat.
7:22 in the land will eat **c** and honey.
Eze 34: 3 You eat the **c**, clothe yourselves

Cure (Cured)
2Ki 5: 3 He would **c** him of his leprosy."
5: 6 that you may **c** him of his leprosy."
5:11 the spot and **c** me of my leprosy.
Jer 3:22 I will **c** you of backsliding."
17: 9 above all things and beyond **c**.
30:15 your pain that has no **c**? Because of
Hos 5:13 But he is not able to **c** you,
Lk 9: 1 out all demons and to **c** diseases,

Cured (Cure)
Dt 28:27 itch, from which you cannot be **c**.
28:35 with painful boils that cannot be **c**,
2Ki 5: 7 to me to be **c** of his leprosy?
Mt 8: 3 Immediately he was **c** of his leprosy.
11: 5 those who have leprosy are **c**, the
Mk 1:42 the leprosy left him and he was **c**.
Lk 6:18 troubled by evil spirits were **c**,
7:21 At that very time Jesus **c** many who
7:22 those who have leprosy are **c**, the
8: 2 also some women who had been **c** of
8:36 the demon-possessed man had been **c**.
Jn 5: 9 At once the man was **c**; he picked up
Ac 19:12 their illnesses were **c** and the evil
28: 9 sick on the island came and were **c**.

Current (Currents)
Ge 23:16 to the weight **c** among the merchants.

Currents (Current)
Jnh 2: 3 and the **c** swirled about me; all your

Curry
Pr 19: 6 Many **c** favour with a ruler, and

Curse (Accursed, Cursed, Curses, Cursing)
Ge 4:11 Now you are under a **c** and driven
8:21 "Never again will I **c** the ground
12: 3 and whoever curses you I will **c**; and
27:12 **c** on myself rather than a blessing."
27:13 him, "My son, let the **c** fall on me.
27:29 May those who **c** you be cursed and
Ex 22:28 "Do not blaspheme God or **c** the ruler
Lev 19:14 "'Do not **c** the deaf or put a
24:11 blasphemed the Name with a **c**;
Nu 5:18 the bitter water that brings a **c**.
5:19 water that brings a **c** not harm you.
5:21 put the woman under this **c** of the
5:21 the LORD cause your people to **c**
5:22 May this water that brings a **c** enter
5:24 the bitter water that brings a **c**,
5:27 to drink the water that brings a **c**,
22: 6 Now come and put a **c** on these people,
22: 6 and those you **c** are cursed."
22:11 Now come and put a **c** on them for me.
22:12 You must not put a **c** on those people,
22:17 and put a **c** on these people for me."
23: 7 'Come,' he said, '**c** Jacob for me;
23: 8 How can I **c** those whom God has not
23:11 me? I brought you to **c** my enemies,
23:13 And from there, **c** them for me."
23:25 "Neither **c** them at all nor bless
23:27 let you **c** them for me from there."
24: 9 and those who **c** you be cursed!"
24:10 "I summoned you to **c** my enemies, but
Dt 11:26 before you today a blessing and a **c**
11:28 the **c** if you disobey the commands of
21:23 is hung on a tree is under God's **c**.
23: 4 Naharaim to pronounce a **c** on you.
23: 5 turned the **c** into a blessing for you
Jos 9:23 You are now under a **c**: You will
24: 9 Balaam son of Beor to put a **c** on you.
Jdg 5:23 '**C** Meroz,' said the angel of the
5:23 '**C** its people bitterly, because they
9:57 The **c** of Jotham son of Jerub-Baal
17: 2 About which I heard you utter a **c**—
2Sa 16: 9 "Why should this dead dog **c** my lord
16:10 '**C** David,' who can ask, 'Why do you
16:11 let him **c**, for the LORD has told him
2Ki 2:24 a **c** on them in the name of the LORD.
Ne 10:29 and bind themselves with a **c** and an
13: 2 Balaam to call a **c** down on them.

Ne 13: 2 turned the **c** into a blessing.)
Job 1:11 he will surely **c** you to your face."
2: 5 he will surely **c** you to your face."
2: 9 to your integrity? **C** God and die!"
3: 8 May those who **c** days **c** that day,
31:30 by invoking a **c** against his life—
Ps 62: 4 bless, but in their hearts they **c**.
102: 8 rail against me use my name as a **c**.
109:17 He loved to pronounce a **c**—may it
109:28 They may **c**, but you will bless; when
Pr 3:33 The LORD's **c** is on the house of the
11:26 People **c** the man who hoards grain,
24:24 will **c** him and nations denounce him.
26: 2 undeserved **c** does not come to rest.
27:14 morning, it will be taken as a **c**.
30:10 will **c** you, and you will pay for it.
30:11 "There are those who **c** their fathers
Ecc 10:20 or **c** the rich in your bedroom,
Isa 8:21 will **c** their king and their God.
24: 6 Therefore a **c** consumes the earth;
65:15 your name to my chosen ones as a **c**;
Jer 23:10 because of the **c** the land lies
29:22 who are in Babylon will use this **c**:
48:10 "A **c** on him who is lax in doing the
48:10 A **c** on him who keeps his sword from
Lam 3:65 hearts, and may your **c** be on them!
Zec 5: 3 "This is the **c** that is going out
Mal 2: 2 "I will send a **c** upon you, and I
2: 2 you, and I will **c** your blessings.
3: 9 You are under a **c**—the whole nation
4: 6 come and strike the land with a **c**."
Lk 6:28 bless those who **c** you, pray for
Jn 7:49 of the law—there is a **c** on them."
Ro 12:14 persecute you; bless and do not **c**.
1Co 16:22 not love the Lord—a **c** be on him.
Gal 3:10 on observing the law are under a **c**,
3:13 Christ redeemed us from the **c** of the
3:13 by becoming a **c** for us, for it is
Jas 3: 9 and with it we **c** men, who have been
Rev 22: 3 No longer will there be any **c**. The

Cursed (Curse)

Ge 3:14 "**C** are you above all the livestock
3:17 "**C** is the ground because of you;
5:29 by the ground the LORD has **c**."
9:25 "**C** be Canaan! The lowest of slaves
27:29 May those who curse you be **c** and
49: 7 **C** be their anger, so fierce, and
Lev 20: 9 He has **c** his father or his mother,
Nu 22: 6 blessed, and those you curse are **c**."
23: 8 I curse those whom God has not **c**?
24: 9 and those who curse you be **c**!"
Dt 27:15 "**C** is the man who carves an image or
27:16 "**C** is the man who dishonours his
27:17 "**C** is the man who moves his
27:18 "**C** is the man who leads the blind
27:19 "**C** is the man who withholds justice
27:20 "**C** is the man who sleeps with his
27:21 "**C** is the man who has sexual
27:22 "**C** is the man who sleeps with his
27:23 "**C** is the man who sleeps with his
27:24 "**C** is the man who kills his
27:25 "**C** is the man who accepts a bribe to
27:26 "**C** is the man who does not uphold
28:16 You will be **c** in the city and **c** in
28:17 and your kneading trough will be **c**.
28:18 The fruit of your womb will be **c**,
28:19 **c** when you come in and **c** when you go
Jos 6:26 "**C** before the LORD is the man who
Jdg 9:27 and drinking, they **c** Abimelech.
21:18 '**C** be anyone who gives a wife to a
1Sa 14:24 "**C** be any man who eats food before
14:28 '**C** be any man who eats food today!'
17:43 the Philistine **c** David by his gods.
26:19 may they be **c** before the LORD!
2Sa 16: 5 of Gera, and he **c** as he came out.
16: 7 he **c**, Shimei said, "Get out, get out,
19:21 for this? He **c** the LORD's anointed."
1Ki 21:10 that he has **c** both God and the king.
21:13 "Naboth has **c** both God and the king.
2Ki 9:34 "Take care of that **c** woman," he said,
Job 1: 5 sinned and **c** God in their hearts.
3: 1 mouth and **c** the day of his birth.
5: 3 root, but suddenly his house was **c**.
24:18 their portion of the land is **c**,
Ps 119:21 You rebuke the arrogant, who are **c**
Ecc 7:22 times you yourself have **c** others.
Jer 11: 3 '**C** is the man who does not obey the
17: 5 "**C** is the one who trusts in man,
20:14 **C** be the day I was born! May the day
20:15 **C** be the man who brought my father
Mal 1:14 "**C** is the cheat who has an
2: 2 Yes, I have already **c** them, because
Mt 25:41 'Depart from me, you who are **c**, into
Mk 11:21 The fig-tree you **c** has withered!"
Ro 9: 3 For I could wish that I myself were **c**
1Co 4:12 When we are **c**, we bless; when we are
12: 3 "Jesus be **c**," and no-one can say,
Gal 3:10 "**C** is everyone who does not continue
3:13 **C** is everyone who is hung on a tree."
Heb 6: 8 and is in danger of being **c**.
Rev 16: 9 heat and they **c** the name of God,
16:11 **c** the God of heaven because of their
16:21 And they **c** God on account of the

Curses (Curse)

Ge 12: 3 and whoever **c** you I will curse; and
Ex 21:17 "Anyone who **c** his father or mother
Lev 20: 9 "'If anyone **c** his father or mother,
24:15 Say to the Israelites: 'If anyone **c**
Nu 5:23 "'The priest is to write these **c** on
Dt 11:29 blessings, and on Mount Ebal the **c**.
27:13 Mount Ebal to pronounce **c**: Reuben,
28:15 all these **c** will come upon you and
28:20 The LORD will send on you **c**,
28:45 All these **c** will come upon you. They
29:20 All the **c** written in this book will
29:21 according to all the **c** of the
29:27 it all the **c** written in this book.
30: 1 all these blessings and **c** I have set
30: 7 these **c** on your enemies who hate
30:19 you life and death, blessings and **c**.
Jos 8:34 the blessings and the **c**—just as it
1Ki 2: 8 called down bitter **c** on me the day
2Ch 34:24 all the **c** written in the book that
Ne 13:25 I rebuked them and called **c** down on
Ps 10: 7 His mouth is full of **c** and lies and
37:22 but those he **c** will be cut off.
59:12 For the **c** and lies they utter,
Pr 20:20 If a man **c** his father or mother, his
28:27 his eyes to them receives many **c**.
Jer 11: 8 So I brought on them all the **c** of
15:10 nor borrowed, yet everyone **c** me.
Da 9:11 "Therefore the **c** and sworn judgments
Mt 15: 4 'Anyone who **c** his father or mother
26:74 he began to call down **c** on himself
Mk 7:10 'Anyone who **c** his father or mother
14:71 He began to call down **c** on himself,

Cursing (Curse)

2Sa 16:10 If he is **c** because the LORD said to
16:12 for the **c** I am receiving today."
16:13 **c** as he went and throwing stones at
Ps 109:18 He wore **c** as his garment; it entered
Ecc 7:21 or you may hear your servant **c** you—
Jer 24: 9 and **c**, wherever I banish them.
25:18 and scorn and **c**, as they are today;
26: 6 **c** among all the nations of the earth.
29:18 earth and an object of **c** and horror,
42:18 will be an object of **c** and horror,
44: 8 make yourselves an object of **c** and
44:12 They will become an object of **c** and
44:22 your land became an object of **c** and
49:13 of horror, of reproach and of **c**;
Hos 4: 2 There is only **c**, lying and murder,
Zec 8:13 you have been an object of **c** among
Ro 3:14 "Their mouths are full of **c** and
Jas 3:10 of the same mouth come praise and **c**.

Curtain (*Curtain of the temple, Curtains*)

Ex 26: 4 the edge of the end **c** in one set,
26: 4 with the end **c** in the other set.
26: 5 Make fifty loops on one **c** and fifty
26: 5 loops on the end **c** of the other set,
26: 9 Fold the sixth **c** double at the
26:10 the edge of the end **c** in one set
26:10 edge of the end **c** in the other set.
26:12 the half **c** that is left over is to
26:31 "Make a **c** of blue, purple and
26:33 Hang the **c** from the clasps and place
26:33 ark of the Testimony behind the **c**.
26:33 The **c** will separate the Holy Place
26:35 Place the table outside the **c** on the
26:36 make a **c** of blue, purple and
26:37 Make gold hooks for this **c** and five
27:16 provide a **c** twenty cubits long, of
27:21 In the Tent of Meeting, outside the **c**
30: 6 Put the altar in front of the **c** that
35:12 cover and the **c** that shields it;
35:15 the **c** for the doorway at the
35:17 **c** for the entrance to the courtyard;
36:11 the edge of the end **c** in one set,
36:11 with the end **c** in the other set.
36:12 They also made fifty loops on one **c**
36:12 loops on the end **c** of the other set,
36:17 the edge of the end **c** in one set
36:17 edge of the end **c** in the other set.
36:35 They made the **c** of blue, purple and
36:37 they made a **c** of blue, purple and
38:18 The **c** for the entrance to the
38:27 for the sanctuary and for the **c**
39:34 of sea cows and the shielding **c**;
39:38 the **c** for the entrance to the tent;
39:40 and the **c** for the entrance to the
40: 3 in it and shield the ark with the **c**.
40: 5 **c** at the entrance to the tabernacle.
40: 8 **c** at the entrance to the courtyard.
40:21 hung the shielding **c** and shielded
40:22 side of the tabernacle outside the **c**
40:26 Tent of Meeting in front of the **c**
40:28 he put up the **c** at the entrance to
40:33 **c** at the entrance to the courtyard.
Lev 4: 6 in front of the **c** of the sanctuary.
4:17 LORD seven times in front of the **c**.
16: 2 the Most Holy Place behind the **c**
16:12 incense and take them behind the **c**.
16:15 take its blood behind the **c** and do
21:23 he must not go near the **c** or
24: 3 Outside the **c** of the Testimony in
Nu 3:25 its coverings, the **c** at the entrance
3:26 the **c** at the entrance to the
3:31 the **c**, and everything related to
4: 5 take down the shielding **c** and cover
4:26 the **c** for the entrance, the ropes
18: 7 at the altar and inside the **c**.
2Ch 3:14 He made the **c** of blue, purple and
Heb 6:19 the inner sanctuary behind the **c**,
9: 3 Behind the second **c** was a room
10:20 us through the **c**, that is, his body,

Curtain of the temple

Mt 27:51 At that moment the **c** was torn in two
Mk 15:38 The **c** was torn in two from top to
Lk 23:45 And the **c** was torn in two.

Curtains (Curtain)

Ex 26: 1 "Make the tabernacle with ten **c** of
26: 2 All the **c** are to be the same
26: 3 Join five of the **c** together, and do
26: 6 use them to fasten the **c** together so
26: 7 "Make **c** of goat hair for the tent
26: 8 All eleven **c** are to be the same size
26: 9 Join five of the **c** together into one
26:12 the additional length of the tent **c**,
26:13 The tent **c** will be a cubit longer on
27: 9 to have **c** of finely twisted linen,
27:11 cubits long and is to have **c**,
27:12 have **c**, with ten posts and ten bases.
27:14 **C** fifteen cubits long are to be on
27:15 **c** fifteen cubits long are to be on
27:18 with **c** of finely twisted linen five
35:17 the **c** of the courtyard with its
36: 8 **c** of finely twisted linen and blue,
36: 9 All the **c** were the same size—
36:10 They joined five of the **c** together
36:13 fasten the two sets of **c** together
36:14 They made **c** of goat hair for the
36:15 All eleven **c** were the same
36:16 They joined five of the **c** into one
38: 9 and had **c** of finely twisted linen,
38:12 end was fifty cubits wide and had **c**,
38:14 **C** fifteen cubits long were on one
38:15 **c** fifteen cubits long were on the
38:16 All the **c** around the courtyard were

Ex 38:18 **c** of the courtyard, five cubits high,
39:40 the **c** of the courtyard with its
Nu 3:26 the **c** of the courtyard, the curtain
4:25 They are to carry the **c** of the
4:25 the **c** for the entrance to the Tent
4:26 the **c** of the courtyard surrounding
SS 1: 5 Kedar, like the tent **c** of Solomon.
Isa 54: 2 stretch your tent **c** wide, do not

Curved

Jos 15: 3 up to Addar and **c** around to Karka.
15:10 **c** westward from Baalah to Mount Seir,
16: 6 it **c** eastward to Taanath Shiloh,
18:17 then **c** north, went to En Shemesh,

Cush (Cushite, Cushites)

1. Country south of Egypt. Land of precious stones (Job 28:19) and tall smooth-skinned people (Isa 18:2, 7). Linked with Egypt in war, sometimes against Israel (2Ki 19:9; 2Ch 12:3; Jer 46:9; Eze 38:5). Prophets proclaimed judgment upon Cush (Isa 18:1; Zep 2:12), but some of its inhabitants would join the people of God (Ps 68:31; Isa 11:11; 18:7). **2.** Land bordering the Gihon River that flowed from Eden (Ge 2:10–14). Exact location unknown.

Ge 2:13 winds through the entire land of **C**.
10: 6 The sons of Ham: **C**, Mizraim, Put and
10: 7 The sons of **C**: Seba, Havilah, Sabtah,
10: 8 **C** was the father of Nimrod, who grew
1Ch 1: 8 The sons of Ham: **C**, Mizraim, Put and
1: 9 The sons of **C**: Seba, Havilah, Sabta,
1:10 **C** was the father of Nimrod, who grew
Est 1: 1 stretching from India to **C**:
8: 9 stretching from India to **C**.
Job 28:19 The topaz of **C** cannot compare with
Ps 7: T the LORD concerning **C**, a Benjamite.
68:31 **C** will submit herself to God.
87: 4 and Tyre, along with **C**—and will
Isa 11:11 from Upper Egypt, from **C**, from Elam,
18: 1 wings along the rivers of **C**,
20: 3 and portent against Egypt and **C**,
20: 5 Those who trusted in **C** and boasted
43: 3 ransom, **C** and Seba in your stead.
45:14 of Egypt and the merchandise of **C**,
Jer 46: 9 O warriors—men of **C** and Put who
Eze 29:10 to Aswan, as far as the border of **C**.
30: 4 Egypt, and anguish will come upon **C**.
30: 5 **C** and Put, Lydia and all Arabia,
30: 9 frighten **C** out of her complacency.
38: 5 Persia, **C** and Put will be with them,
Na 3: 9 **C** and Egypt were her boundless
Zep 3:10 From beyond the rivers of **C** my

Cushan

Hab 3: 7 I saw the tents of **C** in distress,

Cushan-Rishathaim

Jdg 3: 8 hands of **C** king of Aram Naharaim,
3:10 The LORD gave **C** king of Aram into

Cushi

Jer 36:14 the son of Shelemiah, the son of **C**,
Zep 1: 1 LORD that came to Zephaniah son of **C**,

Cushion

Mk 4:38 was in the stern, sleeping on a **c**.

Cushite (Cush)

Nu 12: 1 his **C** wife, for he had married a **C**.
2Sa 18:21 Joab said to a **C**, "Go, tell the king
18:21 **C** bowed down before Joab and ran off.
18:22 may, please let me run behind the **C**.
18:23 way of the plain and outran the **C**.
18:31 the **C** arrived and said, "My lord the
18:32 The king asked the **C**, "Is the young
18:32 The **C** replied, "May the enemies of
2Ki 19: 9 the **C** king of Egypt, was marching
2Ch 14: 9 Zerah the **C** marched out against them
Isa 20: 4 the Egyptian captives and **C** exiles,
37: 9 Tirhakah, the **C** king of Egypt,
Jer 38: 7 Ebed-Melech, a **C**, an official in the
38:10 the king commanded Ebed-Melech the **C**,
38:12 Ebed-Melech the **C** said to Jeremiah,
39:16 "Go and tell Ebed-Melech the **C**,

Cushites (Cush)

2Ch 12: 3 and **C** that came with him from Egypt,
14:12 The LORD struck down the **C** before
14:12 before Asa and Judah. The **C** fled,
14:13 Such a great number of **C** fell that
16: 8 Were not the **C** and Libyans a mighty
21:16 of the Arabs who lived near the **C**.
Am 9: 7 the same to me as the **C**?"
Zep 2:12 "You too, O **C**, will be slain by my

Custody

Ge 40: 3 put them in **c** in the house of the
40: 4 they had been in **c** for some time,
40: 7 in **c** with him in his master's house,
42:17 he put them all in **c** for three days.
Lev 24:12 They put him in **c** until the will of
Nu 15:34 they kept him in **c**, because it was
1Ch 29: 8 in the **c** of Jehiel the Gershonite.

Custom (Accustomed, Customary, Customs)

Ge 19:31 us, as is the **c** all over the earth.
29:26 Laban replied, "It is not our **c** here
Jdg 8:24 (It was the **c** of the Ishmaelites to
11:39 From this comes the Israelite **c**
1Ki 18:28 swords and spears, as was their **c**,
2Ki 11:14 by the pillar, as the **c** was.
Est 9:27 to establish the **c** that they
Job 1: 5 This was Job's regular **c**.
Mt 27:15 Now it was the governor's **c** at the
Mk 10: 1 and as was his **c**, he taught them.
15: 6 Now it was the **c** at the Feast to
Lk 1: 9 according to the **c** of the priesthood,
2:27 him what the **c** of the Law required,
2:42 up to the Feast, according to the **c**.
4:16 into the synagogue, as was his **c**.
Jn 18:39 is your **c** for me to release to you
Ac 15: 1 according to the **c** taught by Moses,
17: 2 his **c** was, Paul went into the
25:16 it is not the Roman **c** to hand over

Customary (Custom)

Jdg 14:10 there, as was **c** for bridegrooms.
1Sa 20:25 He sat in his **c** place by the wall,
Est 1:13 Since it was **c** for the king to
Eze 24:17 face or eat the **c** food of mourners."
24:22 face or eat the **c** food of mourners.
Mk 14:12 when it was **c** to sacrifice the

Customers

Eze 27:15 and many coastlands were your **c**;
27:21 the princes of Kedar were your **c**;

Customs (Custom)

Lev 18:30 not follow any of the detestable **c**
20:23 You must not live according to the **c**
2Ki 17:33 in accordance with the **c** of the
Est 3: 8 kingdom whose **c** are different
Ps 106:35 the nations and adopted their **c**.
Jer 10: 3 For the **c** of the peoples are
Jn 19:40 in accordance with Jewish burial **c**.
Ac 6:14 the **c** Moses handed down to us."
16:21 by advocating **c** unlawful for us
21:21 children or live according to our **c**.
26: 3 all the Jewish **c** and controversies.
28:17 or against the **c** of our ancestors,
Gal 2:14 force Gentiles to follow Jewish **c**?

Cut (Cuts, Cutter, Cutting, Fresh-cut)

Ge 9:11 Never again will all life be **c** off
15:10 **c** them in two and arranged the
15:10 however, he did not **c** in half.
17:14 will be **c** off from his people; he
22: 3 When he had **c** enough wood for the
Ex 4:25 **c** off her son's foreskin and
12:15 seventh must be **c** off from Israel.
12:19 **c** off from the community of Israel,
29:17 **C** the ram into pieces and wash the
30:33 must be **c** off from his people.'"
30:38 must be **c** off from his people."
31: 5 to **c** and set stones, to work in wood,
31:14 day must be **c** off from his people.
34:13 and **c** down their Asherah poles.
35:33 to **c** and set stones, to work in wood
39: 3 **c** strands to be worked into the blue,
Lev 1: 6 burnt offering and **c** it into pieces.
1:12 He is to **c** it into pieces, and the
3: 9 the entire fat tail **c** off close to
7:20 must be **c** off from his people.
7:21 must be **c** off from his people.'"
7:25 LORD must be **c** off from his people.
7:27 must be **c** off from his people.'"
8:20 He **c** the ram into pieces and burned
17: 4 and must be **c** off from his people.
17: 9 man must be **c** off from his people.
17:10 and will **c** him off from his people.
17:14 anyone who eats it must be **c** off."
18:29 must be **c** off from their people.
19: 8 must be **c** off from his people.
19:27 "Do not **c** the hair at the sides of
19:28 "Do not **c** your bodies for the dead
20: 3 I will **c** him off from his people;
20: 5 his family and will **c** off from their
20: 6 I will **c** him off from his people.
20:17 They must be **c** off before the eyes
20:18 must be **c** off from their people.
21: 5 of their beards or **c** their bodies.
22: 3 must be **c** off from my presence.
22:24 are bruised, crushed, torn or **c**.
23:29 day must be **c** off from his people.
26:26 I **c** off your supply of bread, ten
26:30 **c** down your incense altars and pile
Nu 4:18 are not **c** off from the Levites.
9:13 that person must be **c** off from his
13:23 they **c** off a branch bearing a single
13:24 grapes the Israelites **c** off there.
15:30 must be **c** off from his people.
15:31 that person must surely be **c** off;
19:13 That person must be **c** off from
19:20 he must be **c** off from the community,
Dt 7: 5 **c** down their Asherah poles and burn
12: 3 **c** down the idols of their gods and
12:29 The LORD your God will **c** off before
14: 1 Do not **c** yourselves or shave the
19: 5 forest with his neighbour to **c** wood,
20:19 Do not **c** them down. Are the trees of
20:20 However, you may **c** down trees that
25:12 you shall **c** off her hand. Show her
25:18 and **c** off all who were lagging
Jos 3:13 flowing downstream will be **c** off
3:16 (the Salt Sea) was completely **c** off.
4: 7 the flow of the Jordan was **c** off
4: 7 the waters of the Jordan were **c** off.
8:22 Israel **c** them down, leaving them
10:10 **c** them down all the way to Azekah
Jdg 1: 6 and **c** off his thumbs and big toes.
1: 7 their thumbs and big toes **c** off
6:25 **c** down the Asherah pole beside it.
6:26 of the Asherah pole that you **c** down,
6:28 the Asherah pole beside it **c** down
6:30 **c** down the Asherah pole beside it."
9:48 He took an axe and **c** off some
9:49 all the men **c** branches and followed
19:29 he took a knife and **c** up his
20: 6 I took my concubine, **c** her into
20:21 **c** down twenty-two thousand
20:25 they **c** down another eighteen
20:42 out of the towns **c** them down there.
20:45 the Israelites **c** down five thousand
21: 6 "Today one tribe is **c** off from
1Sa 2:31 when I will **c** short your strength
2:33 Every one of you that I do not **c** off
11: 7 a pair of oxen, **c** them into pieces
17:46 strike you down and **c** off your head.
17:51 he killed him, he **c** off his head
20:15 do not ever **c** off your kindness from
20:15 not even when the LORD has **c** off
24: 4 and **c** off a corner of Saul's robe.
24: 5 having **c** off a corner of his robe.
24:11 I **c** off the corner of your robe but
24:21 you will not **c** off my descendants
28: 9 He has **c** off the mediums and
31: 9 They **c** off his head and stripped off
2Sa 4: 7 and killed him, they **c** off his head.
4:12 They **c** off their hands and feet and

2Sa 7: 9 and I have **c** off all your enemies
10: 4 **c** off their garments in the middle
14:16 trying to **c** off both me and my son
14:26 Whenever he **c** the hair of his
14:26 he used to **c** his hair from time to
16: 9 Let me go over and **c** off his head."
20:22 and they **c** off the head of Sheba son
1Ki 3:25 "**C** the living child in two and give
3:26 you shall have him. **C** him in two!"
5: 6 that cedars of Lebanon be **c** for me.
5:18 **c** and prepared the timber and stone
7: 9 of high-grade stone **c** to size
7:11 were high-grade stones, **c** to size
9: 7 I will **c** off Israel from the land I
14:10 I will **c** off from Jeroboam every
14:14 will **c** off the family of Jeroboam.
15:13 Asa **c** the pole down and burned it in
18:23 and let them **c** it into pieces and
18:33 **c** the bull into pieces and laid it
21:21 **c** off from Ahab every last male in
2Ki 3:19 You will **c** down every good tree,
3:25 springs and **c** down every good tree.
4:39 When he returned, he **c** them up into
6: 4 Jordan and began to **c** down trees.
6: 6 Elisha **c** a stick and threw it there,
6:32 someone to **c** off my head? Look,
9: 8 I will **c** off from Ahab every last
10:25 So they **c** them down with the sword.
18: 4 stones and **c** down the Asherah poles.
19: 7 have him **c** down with the sword.'"
19:23 I have **c** down its tallest cedars,
19:37 Adrammelech and Sharezer **c** him down
23:14 **c** down the Asherah poles and covered
1Ch 17: 8 and I have **c** off all your enemies
19: 4 shaved them, **c** off their garments in
2Ch 2:10 the woodsmen who **c** the timber,
2:16 we will **c** all the logs from Lebanon
14: 3 stones and **c** down the Asherah poles.
15:16 Asa **c** the pole down, broke it up and
16:14 in the tomb that he had **c** out for
31: 1 stones and **c** down the Asherah poles.
32:21 his sons **c** him down with the sword.
34: 4 he **c** to pieces the incense altars
34: 7 **c** to pieces all the incense altars
Job 6: 9 to let loose his hand and **c** me off!
14: 7 If it is **c** down, it will sprout
17: 1 is broken, my days are **c** short,
24:24 they are **c** off like ears of corn.
26:12 by his wisdom he **c** Rahab to pieces.
27: 8 has the godless when he is **c** off,
Ps 12: 3 May the LORD **c** off all flattering
31:22 "I am **c** off from your sight!"
34:16 to **c** off the memory of them from the
37: 9 For evil men will be **c** off, but
37:22 but those he curses will be **c** off.
37:28 of the wicked will be **c** off;
37:34 wicked are **c** off, you will see it.
37:38 future of the wicked will be **c** off.
74: 5 to **c** through a thicket of trees.
75:10 I will **c** off the horns of all the
80:16 Your vine is **c** down, it is burned
88: 5 more, who are **c** off from your care.
89:45 You have **c** short the days of his
101: 8 I will **c** off every evildoer from the
102:23 my strength; he **c** short my days.
109:13 May his descendants be **c** off, their
109:15 that he may **c** off the memory of them
118:10 the name of the LORD I **c** them off.
118:11 the name of the LORD I **c** them off.
118:12 the name of the LORD I **c** them off.
129: 4 he has **c** me free from the cords
Pr 2:22 the wicked will be **c** off from the
10:27 the years of the wicked are **c** short.
10:31 but a perverse tongue will be **c** out.
23:18 and your hope will not be **c** off.
24:14 and your hope will not be **c** off.
Isa 5: 2 and **c** out a winepress as well.
6:13 leave stumps when they are **c** down,
9:14 the LORD will **c** off from Israel both
10:34 He will **c** down the forest thickets
11:13 and Judah's enemies will be **c** off;
14: 8 no woodsman comes to **c** us down."
14:22 "I will **c** off from Babylon her name
15: 2 is shaved and every beard **c** off.
18: 5 he will **c** off the shoots with
18: 5 and **c** down and take away the
Isa 22:16 to **c** out a grave for yourself here,
22:25 load hanging on it will be **c** down.
29:20 an eye for evil will be **c** down—
33:12 like **c** thornbushes they will be set
37: 7 have him **c** down with the sword.'"
37:24 I have **c** down its tallest cedars,
37:38 **c** him down with the sword, and they
38:12 and he has **c** me off from the loom;
44:14 He **c** down cedars, or perhaps took a
45: 2 bronze and **c** through bars of iron.
48: 9 from you, so as not to **c** you off.
48:19 **c** off nor destroyed from before me."
51: 1 to the rock from which you were **c**
51: 9 Was it not you who **c** Rahab to pieces,
53: 8 **c** off from the land of the living;
56: 5 name that will not be **c** off.
Jer 6: 6 "**C** down the trees and build siege
7:29 **C** off your hair and throw it away;
9:21 it has **c** off the children from the
9:22 like **c** corn behind the reaper, with
10: 3 they **c** a tree out of the forest,
11:19 let us **c** him off from the land of
16: 6 **c** himself or shave his head for them.
22: 7 and they will **c** up your fine cedar
34:18 treat like the calf they **c** in two
36:23 the king **c** them off with a scribe's
36:29 **c** off both men and animals from it?"
41: 5 torn their clothes and **c** themselves
46:22 axes, like men who **c** down trees.
47: 4 to **c** off all survivors who could
47: 5 how long will you **c** yourselves?
48:25 Moab's horn is **c** off; her arm is
48:37 is shaved and every beard **c** off;
50:16 **C** off from Babylon the sower, and
51:13 come, the time for you to be **c** off.
Lam 2: 3 In fierce anger he has **c** off every
3:54 I thought I was about to be **c** off.
Eze 4:16 "Son of man, I will **c** off the supply
5:16 you and **c** off your supply of food.
14: 8 I will **c** him off from my people.
14:13 against it to **c** off its food supply
16: 4 you were born your cord was not **c**,
21: 3 **c** off from you both the righteous
21: 4 I am going to **c** off the righteous
23:25 They will **c** off your noses and your
23:47 The mob will stone them and **c** them
25: 7 I will **c** you off from the nations
25:16 and I will **c** off the Kerethites and
30:15 and **c** off the hordes of Thebes.
31:12 nations **c** it down and left it.
35: 7 **c** off from it all who come and go.
37:11 and our hope is gone; we are **c** off.'
39:10 the fields or **c** it from the forests,
Da 2: 5 I will have you **c** into pieces and
2:34 you were watching, a rock was **c** out,
2:45 of the rock **c** out of a mountain,
3:29 Meshach and Abednego be **c** into
4:14 '**C** down the tree and trim off its
4:23 '**C** down the tree and destroy it, but
9:26 will be **c** off and will have nothing.
Hos 6: 5 Therefore I **c** you in pieces with my
Joel 1: 9 **c** off from the house of the LORD.
1:16 Has not the food been **c** off before
Am 3:14 be **c** off and fall to the ground.
Ob : 9 will be **c** down in the slaughter.
:14 to **c** down their fugitives,
Na 1:12 they will be **c** off and pass away.
3:15 you; the sword will **c** you down and,
Zep 1: 3 **c** off man from the face of the earth,
1: 4 I will **c** off from this place every
3: 6 "I have **c** off nations; their
3: 7 Then her dwelling would not be **c** off,
Zec 9: 6 **c** off the pride of the Philistines.
11: 2 the dense forest has been **c** down!
Mal 2:12 may the LORD **c** him off from the
Mt 3:10 be **c** down and thrown into the fire.
5:30 to sin, **c** it off and throw it away.
7:19 is **c** down and thrown into the fire.
18: 8 to sin, **c** it off and throw it away.
21: 8 while others **c** branches from the
24:22 If those days had not been **c** short,
24:51 He will **c** him to pieces and assign
27:60 tomb that he had **c** out of the rock.
Mk 5: 5 cry out and **c** himself with stones.
9:43 hand causes you to sin, **c** it off.
9:45 foot causes you to sin, **c** it off.
Mk 11: 8 branches they had **c** in the fields.
13:20 If the Lord had not **c** short those
15:46 placed it in a tomb **c** out of rock.
Lk 3: 9 be **c** down and thrown into the fire."
12:46 He will **c** him to pieces and assign
13: 7 **C** it down! Why should it use up the
13: 9 fine! If not, then **c** it down.'"
23:53 placed it in a tomb **c** in the rock,
Jn 18:26 the man whose ear Peter had **c** off,
Ac 2:37 they were **c** to the heart and said
3:23 **c** off from among his people.'
18:18 Before he sailed, he had his hair **c**
27:32 the soldiers **c** the ropes that held
Ro 9: 3 **c** off from Christ for the sake of my
11:22 Otherwise, you also will be **c** off.
11:24 if you were **c** out of an olive tree
1Co 11: 6 she should have her hair **c** off; and
11: 6 to have her hair **c** or shaved off,
2Co 11:12 to **c** the ground from under those
Gal 5: 7 Who **c** in on you and kept you from

Cuthah

2Ki 17:24 **C**, Avva, Hamath and Sepharvaim and
17:30 the men from **C** made Nergal, and the

Cuts (Cut)

Job 28: 4 where people dwell he **c** a shaft,
38:25 Who **c** a channel for the torrents of
Ps 107:16 bronze and **c** through bars of iron.
Jn 15: 2 He **c** off every branch in me that

Cutter (Cut)

Ex 28:11 the way a gem **c** engraves a seal.

Cutting (Cut)

Dt 23: 1 emasculated by crushing or **c**
2Ki 6: 5 one of them was **c** down a tree, the
2Ch 2: 8 men are skilled in **c** timber there.
Ps 78:31 **c** down the young men of Israel.
Pr 26: 6 Like **c** off one's feet or drinking
Jer 44: 7 **c** off from Judah the men and women,
Mt 26:51 of the high priest, **c** off his ear.
Mk 14:47 of the high priest, **c** off his ear.
Lk 22:50 high priest, **c** off his right ear.
Jn 18:10 servant, **c** off his right ear.
Ac 27:40 **C** loose the anchors, they left them

Cycle

Isa 29: 1 and let your **c** of festivals go on.

Cymbal (Cymbals)

1Co 13: 1 a resounding gong or a clanging **c**.

Cymbals (Cymbal)

2Sa 6: 5 lyres, tambourines, sistrums and **c**.
1Ch 13: 8 lyres, tambourines, **c** and trumpets.
15:16 instruments: lyres, harps and **c**.
15:19 Ethan were to sound the bronze **c**;
15:28 and of **c**, and the playing of lyres
16: 5 and harps, Asaph was to sound the **c**,
16:42 the sounding of the trumpets and **c**
25: 1 accompanied by harps, lyres and **c**.
25: 6 with **c**, lyres and harps, for the
2Ch 5:12 and playing **c**, harps and lyres.
5:13 Accompanied by trumpets, **c** and other
29:25 in the temple of the LORD with **c**,
Ezr 3:10 Levites (the sons of Asaph) with **c**,
Ne 12:27 the music of **c**, harps and lyres.
Ps 150: 5 praise him with the clash of **c**,
150: 5 praise him with resounding **c**.

Cypress

Ge 6:14 make yourself an ark of **c** wood; make
Isa 41:19 the fir and the **c** together,
44:14 cedars, or perhaps took a **c** or oak.
60:13 the pine, the fir and the **c** together,
Eze 27: 6 of **c** wood from the coasts of Cyprus

Cyprus

Large island in Mediterranean Sea, about 60 miles west of Syria. Mentioned by Isaiah and Ezekiel (Isa 23:1, 12; Eze 27:6). Home of Barnabas (Ac 4:36); refuge for

believers (Ac 11:19). Barnabas came here with Paul (Ac 13:4), and then Mark (Ac 15:39). Home of Mnason (Ac 21:16).

Isa 23: 1 From the land of **C** word has come to
23:12 "Up, cross over to **C**; even there
Eze 27: 6 the coasts of **C** they made your deck,
Ac 4:36 Joseph, a Levite from **C**, whom the
11:19 as far as Phoenicia **C** and Antioch,
11:20 Some of them, however, men from **C**
13: 4 Seleucia and sailed from there to **C**.
15:39 Barnabas took Mark and sailed for **C**,
21: 3 After sighting **C** and passing to the
21:16 He was a man from **C** and one of the
27: 4 passed to the lee of **C** because the

Cyrene

Mt 27:32 they met a man from **C**, named Simon,
Mk 15:21 A certain man from **C**, Simon, the
Lk 23:26 they seized Simon from **C**, who was on
Ac 2:10 and the parts of Libya near **C**;
6: 9 Jews of **C** and Alexandria as well as
11:20 however, men from Cyprus and **C**, went
13: 1 Simeon called Niger, Lucius of **C**,

Cyrus

King of Persia. Issued edict to allow exiles to return to rebuild Jerusalem temple (2Ch 36:22–23; Ezr 1:1–4; 5:13; 6:3); gave back articles taken from temple (Ezr 1:7–11; :14–15; 6:5) and provided funds for building work (Ezr 3:7; 6:4). Place in God's purpose foretold by Isaiah (Isa 44:28–45:7,13).

2Ch 36:22 In the first year of **C** king of
36:22 the LORD moved the heart of **C** king
36:23 "This is what **C** king of Persia says:
Ezr 1: 1 the first year of **C** king of Persia,
1: 1 the LORD moved the heart of **C** king
1: 2 "This is what **C** king of Persia says:
1: 7 Moreover, King **C** brought out the
1: 8 **C** king of Persia had them brought by
3: 7 as authorised by **C** king of Persia.
4: 3 **C**, the king of Persia, commanded us."
4: 5 entire reign of **C** king of Persia
5:13 "However, in the first year of **C**
5:13 King **C** issued a decree to rebuild
5:14 "Then King **C** gave them to a man
5:17 to see if King **C** did in fact issue
6: 3 In the first year of King **C**, the
6:14 God of Israel and the decrees of **C**,
Isa 44:28 who says of **C**, 'He is my shepherd
45: 1 to **C**, whose right hand I take hold
45:13 raise up **C** in my righteousness
Da 1:21 until the first year of King **C**.
6:28 and the reign of **C** the Persian.
10: 1 third year of **C** king of Persia,

Dabbesheth

Jos 19:11 touched **D**, and extended to the

Daberath

Jos 19:12 and went on to **D** and up to Japhia.
21:28 the tribe of Issachar, Kishion, **D**,
1Ch 6:72 of Issachar they received Kedesh, **D**,

Dagger

2Sa 2:16 his **d** into his opponent's side,
20: 8 was a belt with a **d** in its sheath.
20:10 guard against the **d** in Joab's hand,

Dagon (Dagon's)

Jdg 16:23 a great sacrifice to **D** their god
1Sa 5: 2 Dagon's temple and set it beside **D**.
5: 3 there was **D**, fallen on his face on
5: 3 They took **D** and put him back in his
5: 4 there was **D**, fallen on his face on
5: 5 neither the priests of **D** nor any
5: 7 heavy upon us and upon **D** our god."
1Ch 10:10 hung up his head in the temple of **D**.

Dagon's (Dagon)

1Sa 5: 2 they carried the ark into **D** temple
5: 5 others who enter **D** temple at Ashdod

Daily (Day)

Nu 29: 6 **d** burnt offerings with their grain
1Ki 4:22 Solomon's **d** provisions were thirty
2Ch 8:13 according to the **d** requirement for
31:16 the **d** duties of their various tasks,
Ezr 6: 9 be given them **d** without fail,
Ne 11:23 which regulated their **d** activity.
12:47 Israel contributed the **d** portions
Job 23:12 of his mouth more than my **d** bread.
Ps 68:19 Saviour, who **d** bears our burdens.
Pr 8:34 watching **d** at my doors, waiting at
30: 8 riches, but give me only my **d** bread.
Eze 43:25 a male goat **d** for a sin offering;
Da 1: 5 The king assigned them a **d** amount of
8:11 took away the **d** sacrifice from him,
8:12 and the **d** sacrifice were given over
8:13 vision concerning the **d** sacrifice,
11:31 and will abolish the **d** sacrifice.
12:11 "From the time that the **d** sacrifice
Mt 6:11 Give us today our **d** bread.
Lk 9:23 take up his cross **d** and follow me.
11: 3 Give us each day our **d** bread.
Ac 2:47 number **d** those who were being saved.
6: 1 in the **d** distribution of food.
16: 5 in the faith and grew **d** in numbers.
19: 9 **d** in the lecture hall of Tyrannus.
2Co 11:28 I face **d** the pressure of my concern
1Th 4:12 that your **d** life may win the respect
Tit 3:14 they may provide for **d** necessities
Heb 3:13 encourage one another **d**, as long as
Jas 2:15 is without clothes and **d** food.

Dalmanutha

Mk 8:10 and went to the region of **D**.

Dalmatia

2Ti 4:10 has gone to Galatia, and Titus to **D**.

Dalphon

Est 9: 7 They also killed Parshandatha, **D**,

Dam

Pr 17:14 a quarrel is like breaching a **d**;

Damage (Damaged)

2Ki 12: 5 whatever **d** is found in the temple."
12: 7 "Why aren't you repairing the **d** done
Ac 27:21 spared yourselves this **d** and loss.
Rev 6: 6 and do not **d** the oil and the wine!"

Damaged (Damage)

Lev 21:20 or running sores or **d** testicles.

Damaris

Ac 17:34 also a woman named **D**, and a number

Damascenes (Damascus)

2Co 11:32 had the city of the **D** guarded in

Damascus (Damascenes)

Capital city of Syria (Aram) (Isa 7:8), at foot of Mount Hermon, north-east of Sea of Galilee. Home of Abram's servant Eliezer (Ge 15:2). Base for attacks on Israel; captured by David (2Sa 8:5–6; 1Ch 18:5–6), but later rebelled (1Ki 11:23). Recaptured by Jeroboam II (2Ki 14:28), but became Rezin's base for attack on Jerusalem (2Ki 16:5). Prosperous (Eze 27:18), due to rivers Abana and Pharpar (2Ki 5:12). Final destruction prophesied (Isa 17:1; Am1:5), and fulfilled through Assyria. Became part of kingdom of Aretas (2Co 11:32). Saul converted on road to Damascus (Ac 9:1–8), and met Ananias here (Ac 9:10–22). Jewish inhabitants were angered by Paul's preaching (Ac 9:25; 2Co 11:32–33). Paul returned later (Gal 1:17).

Ge 14:15 them as far as Hobah, north of **D**.
15: 2 inherit my estate is Eliezer of **D**?"
2Sa 8: 5 the Arameans of **D** came to help
8: 6 in the Aramean kingdom of **D**,
1Ki 11:24 the rebels went to D, where they
15:18 king of Aram, who was ruling in **D**.
19:15 you came, and go to the Desert of **D**.
20:34 set up your own market areas in **D**,
2Ki 5:12 the rivers of **D**, better than any of
8: 7 Elisha went to **D**, and Ben-Hadad king
8: 9 of all the finest wares of **D**.
14:28 for Israel both **D** and Hamath, which
16: 9 by attacking **D** and capturing it.
16:10 King Ahaz went to **D** to meet
16:10 He saw an altar in **D** and sent to
16:11 that King Ahaz had sent from **D**
16:12 the king came back from **D** and saw
1Ch 18: 5 the Arameans of **D** came to help
18: 6 in the Aramean kingdom of **D**,
2Ch 16: 2 king of Aram, who was ruling in **D**.
24:23 all the plunder to their king in **D**.
28: 5 as prisoners and brought them to **D**.
28:23 offered sacrifices to the gods of **D**,
SS 7: 4 tower of Lebanon looking towards **D**.
Isa 7: 8 for the head of Aram is **D**, and the
7: 8 and the head of **D** is only Rezin.
8: 4 'My mother', the wealth of **D** and the
10: 9 like Arpad, and Samaria like **D**?
17: 1 An oracle concerning **D**: "See, **D** will
17: 3 and royal power from **D**; the remnant
Jer 49:23 Concerning **D**: "Hamath and Arpad are
49:24 **D** has become feeble, she has turned
49:27 "I will set fire to the walls of **D**;
Eze 27:18 "'**D**, because of your many products
47:16 on the border between **D** and Hamath),
47:17 along the northern border of **D**, with
47:18 will run between Hauran and **D**,
48: 1 the northern border of **D** next to
Am 1: 3 "For three sins of **D**, even for four,
1: 5 I will break down the gate of **D**;
3:12 beds and in **D** on their couches."
5:27 I will send you into exile beyond **D**,"
Zec 9: 1 will rest upon **D**—for the eyes of
Ac 9: 2 for letters to the synagogues in **D**,
9: 3 he neared **D** on his journey, suddenly
9: 8 So they led him by the hand into **D**.
9:10 In **D** there was a disciple named
9:19 days with the disciples in **D**.
9:22 baffled the Jews living in **D** by
9:27 in **D** he had preached fearlessly
22: 5 from them to their brothers in **D**,
22: 6 "About noon as I came near **D**,
22:10 up,' the Lord said,'and go into **D**.
22:11 led me by the hand into **D**, because
26:12 I was going to **D** with the authority
26:20 First to those in **D**, then to those
2Co 11:32 In **D** the governor under King Aretas
Gal 1:17 into Arabia and later returned to **D**.

Dampness

SS 5: 2 my hair with the **d** of the night."

Dan (Danite, Danites)

1. Son of Jacob by Bilhah (Ge 30:4–6; 35:25); blessed by Jacob (Ge 49:16–17). **2.** Tribe descended from Dan. Blessed by Moses (Dt 33:22). Included in census (Nu 1:38–39; 26:42–43). Apportioned land (Jos 19:40–48; Eze 48:1); unable to take full possession (Jdg 1:34), most of tribe migrated northwards to Laish (Jdg 18). Tribe of Samson (Jdg 13). **3.** Territory given to tribe of Dan on Mediterranean coast (hence shipping trade, Jdg 5:17). Smallest portion of land allotted to a tribe (Jos 19:40–48). Due to Amorite activity, some Danites forced to migrate north (Jdg 1:34). **4.** City near the sources of River Jordan. As the city at Israel's most northern point it appears to describe the extent of the land (Jdg 20:1; 1Sa 3:20; 2Sa 3:10; 17:11; 24:2, 15; 1Ki 4:25; 1Ch 21:2; 30:5). Known originally as Leshem (Jos 19:47), or Laish (Jdg 18:7). Jeroboam set up a golden calf here (1Ki 12:28–30). Conquered by Ben-Hadad of Aram (1Ki 15:20, 2Ch 16:4).

Ge 14:14 and went in pursuit as far as **D**.
30: 6 Because of this she named him **D**.
35:25 maidservant Bilhah: **D** and Naphtali.
46:23 The son of **D**: Hushim.
49:16 "**D** will provide justice for his
49:17 **D** will be a serpent by the roadside,
Ex 1: 4 **D** and Naphtali; Gad and Asher.
31: 6 of the tribe of **D**, to help him.
35:34 of the tribe of **D**, the ability to
38:23 of the tribe of **D**—a craftsman and
Nu 1:12 from **D**, Ahiezer son of Ammishaddai;

Nu 1:38 From the descendants of Dan: All the
1:39 The number from the tribe of D was
2:25 the camp of D, under their standard.
2:25 The leader of the people of D is
2:31 All the men assigned to the camp of D
7:66 the leader of the people of D,
10:25 divisions of the camp of D set out,
13:12 from the tribe of D, Ammiel son of
26:42 These were the clans of D:
26:42 These were the descendants of Dan by
34:22 the leader from the tribe of D;
Dt 27:13 Gad, Asher, Zebulun, D and Naphtali.
33:22 About D he said: "D is a lion's cub,
34: 1 the whole land—from Gilead to D,
Jos 19:40 for the tribe of D, clan by clan.
19:47 named it D after their forefather.)
19:48 of the tribe of D, clan by clan.
21: 5 of Ephraim, D and half of Manasseh.
21:23 Also from the tribe of D they
Jdg 5:17 And D, why did he linger by the
13:25 Mahaneh D, between Zorah and Eshtaol.
18:12 is called Mahaneh D to this day.
18:29 They named it D after their
18:29 named it D after their forefather D,
18:30 were priests for the tribe of D
20: 1 the Israelites from D to Beersheba
1Sa 3:20 all Israel from D to Beersheba
2Sa 3:10 and Judah from D to Beersheba."
17:11 from D to Beersheba—as numerous as
24: 2 of Israel from D to Beersheba
24:15 the people from D to Beersheba died.
1Ki 4:25 from D to Beersheba, lived in safety,
12:29 up in Bethel, and the other in D.
12:30 went even as far as D to worship
15:20 He conquered Ijon, D, Abel Beth
2Ki 10:29 the golden calves at Bethel and D.
1Ch 2: 2 D, Joseph, Benjamin, Naphtali, Gad
12:35 men of D, ready for battle—28,600;
21: 2 the Israelites from Beersheba to D.
27:22 over D: Azarel son of Jeroham.
2Ch 2:14 whose mother was from D and whose
16: 4 They conquered Ijon, D, Abel Maim
30: 5 from Beersheba to D, calling the
Jer 4:15 A voice is announcing from D,
8:16 the enemy's horses is heard from D;
Eze 48: 1 D will have one portion; it will
48: 2 territory of D from east to west.
48:32 gate of Benjamin and the gate of D.

Dan Jaan

2Sa 24: 6 on to D and around towards Sidon.

Dance (Danced, Dances, Dancing)

Job 21:11 a flock; their little ones d about.
Ecc 3: 4 a time to mourn and a time to d,
SS 6:13 Shulammite as on the d of Mahanaim?
Jer 31: 4 and go out to d with the joyful.
31:13 maidens will d and be glad, young
Mt 11:17 flute for you, and you did not d;
Lk 7:32 flute for you, and you did not d;

Danced (Dance)

1Sa 18: 7 they d, they sang: "Saul has slain
2Sa 6:14 David, wearing a linen ephod, d
1Ki 18:26 d around the altar they had made.
Mt 14: 6 d for them and pleased Herod so
Mk 6:22 daughter of Herodias came in and d,

Dances (Dance)

1Sa 21:11 the one they sing about in their d:
29: 5 Daviod they sang about in their d:

Dancing (Dance)

Ex 15:20 her, with tambourines and d.
32:19 the camp and saw the calf and the d,
Jdg 11:34 d to the sound of tambourines! She
21:21 of Shiloh come out to join in the d,
21:23 While the girls were d, each man
1Sa 18: 6 meet King Saul with singing and d,
2Sa 6:16 David leaping and d before the LORD,
1Ch 15:29 And when she saw King David d and
Ps 30:11 You turned my wailing into d; you
149: 3 Let them praise his name with d and
150: 4 praise him with tambourine and d,
Lam 5:15 our d has turned to mourning.
Lk 15:25 the house, he heard music and d.

Dandled

Isa 66:12 on her arm and d on her knees.

Danger (Dangerous, Dangers, Endanger)

1Sa 20:21 lives, you are safe; there is no d.
Pr 22: 3 A prudent man sees d and takes
27:12 The prudent see d and take refuge,
Mt 5:22 will be in d of the fire of hell.
Lk 8:23 swamped, and they were in great d.
Ac 19:27 There is d not only that our trade
19:40 is, we are in d of being charged
Ro 8:35 famine or nakedness or d or sword?
2Co 11:26 I have been in d from rivers,
11:26 in d from bandits, in d from my own
11:26 in d from Gentiles; in d in the city,
11:26 in d in the country, in d at sea;
Heb 6: 8 and is in d of being cursed.

Dangerous (Danger)

Ac 27: 9 and sailing had already become d

Dangers (Danger)

Ecc 12: 5 men are afraid of heights and of d

Dangles

Job 28: 4 of man; far from men he d and sways.

Daniel (Daniel's)

1. Son of David and Abigail (1Ch 3:1). **2.** Ancient figure regarded as an outstanding example of righteousness and wisdom (Eze 14:14,20; 28:3). **3.** Hebrew of noble descent among those taken as captives to Babylon to be trained in the king's service (Da 1:3–6); renamed Belteshazzar (Da 1:7); refused to eat unclean food (Da 1:8–16). Possessed great understanding (Da 1:17,20); interpreted Nebuchadnezzar's dreams (Da 2:24–45; 4:19–27), writing on wall (Da 5:13–29). Held government posts under Nebuchadnezzar (Da 2:48), Belshazzar (Da 5:29), Darius (Da 6:1–2). Refused to obey king's decree; thrown into lions' den (Da 6). Visions predicting coming of Messianic kingdom (Da 7–12).

1Ch 3: 1 D the son of Abigail of Carmel;
Ezr 8: 2 the descendants of Ithamar, D;
Ne 10: 6 D, Ginnethon, Baruch,
Eze 14:14 if these three men—Noah, D and Job
14:20 even if Noah, D and Job were in it,
28: 3 Are you wiser than D? Is no secret
Da 1: 6 Among these were some from Judah: D,
1: 7 names: to D, the name Belteshazzar;
1: 8 D resolved not to defile himself
1: 9 to show favour and sympathy to D,
1:10 the official told D, "I am afraid of
1:11 D then said to the guard whom the
1:11 D, Hananiah, Mishael and Azariah,
1:17 And D could understand visions and
1:19 and he found none equal to D,
1:21 D remained there until the first
2:13 and men were sent to look for D and
2:14 D spoke to him with wisdom and tact.
2:15 then explained the matter to D.
2:16 At this, D went in to the king and
2:17 D returned to his house and
2:19 was revealed to D in a vision.
2:19 Then D praised the God of heaven
2:24 D went to Arioch, whom the king had
2:25 Arioch took D to the king at once
2:26 The king asked D (also called
2:27 D replied, "No wise man, enchanter,
2:46 fell prostrate before D and paid
2:47 The king said to D, "Surely your God
2:48 the king placed D in a high position
2:49 while D himself remained at the
4: 8 Finally, D came into my presence and
4:19 D (also called Belteshazzar) was
5:12 This man D, whom the king called
5:12 Call for D, and he will tell you
5:13 D was brought before the king, and
Da 5:13 "Are you D, one of the exiles my
5:17 D answered the king, "You may keep
5:29 D was clothed in purple, a gold
6: 2 over them, one of whom was D.
6: 3 Now D so distinguished himself among
6: 4 find grounds for charges against D
6: 5 for charges against this man D
6:10 Now when D learned that the decree
6:11 these men went as a group and found D
6:13 "D, who is one of the exiles from
6:14 he was determined to rescue D and
6:16 they brought D and threw him into
6:16 The king said to D, "May your God,
6:20 he came near the den, he called to D
6:20 "D, servant of the living God, has
6:21 D answered, "O king, live for ever!
6:23 orders to lift D out of the den.
6:23 And when D was lifted from the den,
6:24 the men who had falsely accused D
6:26 fear and reverence the God of D.
6:27 He has rescued D from the power of
6:28 D prospered during the reign of
7: 1 D had a dream, and visions passed
7: 2 D said: "In my vision at night I
7:15 "I, D, was troubled in spirit, and
7:28 I, D, was deeply troubled by my
8: 1 I, D, had a vision, after the one
8:15 While I, D, was watching the vision
8:27 I, D, was exhausted and lay ill for
9: 2 reign, I, D, understood from the
9:22 and said to me, "D, I have now come
10: 1 to D (who was called Belteshazzar).
10: 2 At that time I, D, mourned for three
10: 7 I, D, was the only one who saw the
10:11 He said, "D, you who are highly
10:12 he continued, "Do not be afraid, D.
12: 4 you, D, close up and seal the words
12: 5 I, D, looked, and there before me
12: 9 He replied, "Go your way, D, because
Mt 24:15 spoken of through the prophet D

Daniel's (Daniel)

Da 2:49 Moreover, at D request the king
6:17 D situation might not be changed.

Danite (Dan)

Lev 24:11 the daughter of Dibri the D.)

Danites (Dan)

Jos 19:47 (But the D had difficulty taking
Jdg 1:34 The Amorites confined the D to the
13: 2 from the clan of the D, had a wife
18: 1 And in those days the tribe of the D
18: 2 the D sent five warriors from Zorah
18:11 hundred men from the clan of the D,
18:16 The six hundred D, armed for battle,
18:22 called together and overtook the D.
18:23 the D turned and said to Micah,
18:25 The D answered, "Don't argue with us,
Jdg 18:26 the D went their way, and Micah,
18:28 D rebuilt the city and settled there.
18:30 There the D set up for themselves
Eze 27:19 "D and Greeks from Uzal bought your

Dannah

Jos 15:49 D, Kiriath Sannah (that is, Debir),

Dappled

Zec 6: 3 the third white, and the fourth d
6: 6 the d horses towards the south."

Darda

1Ki 4:31 Calcol and D, the sons of Mahol.
1Ch 2: 6 Heman, Calcol and D–five in all.

Dare (Dared, Dares, Daring)

2Sa 3:11 Ish-Bosheth did not d to say another
Job 13:16 godless man would d come before him!
Pr 29:24 is put under oath and d not testify.
Jn 2:16 How d you turn my Father's house
9:34 sin at birth; how d you lecture us!"
Ac 7:32 with fear and did not d to look.
23: 4 "You d to insult God's high priest?
Ro 5: 7 man someone might possibly d to die.

1Co 6: 1 **d** he take it before the ungodly for
2Co 10:12 We do not **d** to classify or compare
11:21 as a fool—I also **d** to boast about.
Jude : 9 did not **d** to bring a slanderous

Dared (Dare)

Est 7: 5 man who has **d** to do such a thing?"
Mt 22:46 **d** to ask him any more questions.
Mk 12:34 no-one **d** ask him any more questions.
Lk 20:40 no-one **d** to ask him any more
Jn 21:12 None of the disciples **d** ask him,
Ac 5:13 No-one else **d** join them, even though
1Th 2: 2 we **d** to tell you his gospel in

Dares (Dare)

Ge 49: 9 like a lioness—who **d** to rouse him?
Nu 24: 9 like a lioness—who **d** to rouse them?
Job 41:14 Who **d** open the doors of his mouth,
Lam 4:14 no-one **d** to touch their garments.
2Co 11:21 What anyone else **d** to boast about—I

Darics

1Ch 29: 7 talents and ten thousand **d** of gold,
Ezr 8:27 20 bowls of gold valued at 1,000 **d**,

Daring (Dare)

Job 32: 6 not **d** to tell you what I know.

Darius

1. Mede, who became ruler of Babylon (Da 5:31; 9:1). Appointed Daniel as leading official (Da 6:2,28). Possibly to be identified with Cyrus. **2.** Darius the Great, king of Persia (Hag 1:1; Zec 1:1); revived Cyrus' edict allowing work on rebuilding temple to continue (Ezr 4:24–6:15). **3.** Darius II, king of Persia (Ne 12:22).

Ezr 4: 5 to the reign of **D** king of Persia.
4:24 of the reign of **D** king of Persia.
5: 5 until a report could go to **D** and
5: 6 of Trans-Euphrates, sent to King **D**.
5: 7 To King **D**: Cordial greetings.
6: 1 King **D** then issued an order, and
6:12 I **D** have decreed it. Let it be
6:13 because of the decree King **D** had
6:14 **D** and Artaxerxes, kings of Persia.
6:15 sixth year of the reign of King **D**.
Ne 12:22 in the reign of **D** the Persian.
Da 5:31 **D** the Mede took over the kingdom, at
6: 1 pleased **D** to appoint 120 satraps to
6: 6 and said: "O King **D**, live for ever!
6: 9 King **D** put the decree in writing.
6:25 King **D** wrote to all the peoples,
6:28 prospered during the reign of **D** and
9: 1 In the first year of **D** son of Xerxes
11: 1 in the first year of **D** the Mede, I
Hag 1: 1 In the second year of King **D**, on the
1:15 month in the second year of King **D**.
Hag 2:10 in the second year of **D**, the word of
Zec 1: 1 month of the second year of **D**,
1: 7 in the second year of **D**, the word of
7: 1 In the fourth year of King **D**, the

Dark (Dark-coloured, Darken, Darkened, Darkening, Darkens, Darker, Darkest, Darkness, Pitch-dark)

Dt 28:29 about like a blind man in the **d**.
2Sa 22:10 **d** clouds were under his feet.
22:12 him—the **d** rain clouds of the sky.
1Ki 8:12 that he would dwell in a **d** cloud;
2Ch 6: 1 that he would dwell in a **d** cloud;
Job 3: 9 May its morning stars become **d**; may
18: 6 The light in his tent becomes **d**; the
22:11 why it is so **d** that you cannot see,
24:16 In the **d**, men break into houses, but
34:22 There is no **d** place, no deep shadow,
Ps 18: 9 **d** clouds were under his feet.
18:11 him—the **d** rain clouds of the sky.
35: 6 may their path be **d** and slippery,
74:20 fill the **d** places of the land.
105:28 He sent darkness and made the land **d**
139:12 even the darkness will not be **d** to
Pr 2:13 straight paths to walk in **d** ways,
7: 9 fading, as the **d** of night set in.
31:15 She gets up while it is still **d**; she
Ecc 12: 2 and the moon and the stars grow **d**,
SS 1: 5 **D** am I, yet lovely, O daughters of
1: 5 **d** like the tents of Kedar, like the
1: 6 Do not stare at me because I am **d**,
Isa 50:10 Let him who walks in the **d**, who
Jer 4:28 mourn and the heavens above grow **d**,
Eze 30:18 **D** will be the day at Tahpanhes when
Mic 3: 6 and the day will go **d** for them.
Mt 10:27 What I tell you in the **d**, speak in
Mk 1:35 while it was still **d**, Jesus got up,
Lk 11:36 and no part of it **d**, it will be
12: 3 What you have said in the **d** will be
Jn 6:17 By now it was **d**, and Jesus had not
12:35 The man who walks in the **d** does not
20: 1 while it was still **d**, Mary Magdalene
Ro 2:19 a light for those who are in the **d**,
Eph 6:12 against the powers of this **d** world
2Pe 1:19 as to a light shining in a **d** place,
Rev 8:12 so that a third of them turned **d**.
9:17 red, **d** blue, and yellow as sulphur.

Dark-coloured (Coloured, Dark)

Ge 30:32 every **d** lamb and every spotted or
30:33 any lamb that is not **d**, will be
30:35 white on them) and all the **d** lambs,
30:40 **d** animals that belonged to Laban.

Darken (Dark)

Eze 32: 7 cover the heavens and **d** their stars;
32: 8 in the heavens I will **d** over you;
Am 8: 9 and **d** the earth in broad daylight.

Darkened (Dark)

Job 6:16 **d** by thawing ice and swollen with
Ps 69:23 May their eyes be **d** so that they
SS 1: 6 I am dark, because I am **d** by the sun.
Isa 5:30 the light will be **d** by the clouds.
13:10 The rising sun will be **d** and the
Joel 2:10 the sun and moon are **d**, and the
3:15 The sun and moon will be **d**, and the
Mt 24:29 "'the sun will be **d**, and the moon
Mk 13:24 "'the sun will be **d**, and the moon
Ro 1:21 and their foolish hearts were **d**.
11:10 May their eyes be **d** so they cannot
Eph 4:18 They are **d** in their understanding
Rev 9: 2 were **d** by the smoke from the Abyss.

Darkening (Dark)

Jer 13:16 your feet stumble on the **d** hills.

Darkens (Dark)

Job 38: 2 "Who is this that **d** my counsel with
Am 5: 8 into dawn and **d** day into night,

Darker (Dark)

Ge 49:12 His eyes will be **d** than wine, his

Darkest (Dark)

Ps 88: 6 in the lowest pit, in the **d** depths.

Darkness (Dark)

Ge 1: 2 **d** was over the surface of the deep,
1: 4 he separated the light from the **d**.
1: 5 "day", and the **d** he called "night".
1:18 night, and to separate light from **d**.
15:12 thick and dreadful **d** came over him.
15:17 the sun had set and **d** had fallen, a
Ex 10:21 so that **d** will spread over Egypt
10:21 over Egypt—**d** that can be felt."
10:22 **d** covered all Egypt for three days.
14:20 the cloud brought **d** to the one side
20:21 the thick **d** where God was.
Dt 4:11 with black clouds and deep **d**.
5:22 the fire, the cloud and the deep **d**;
5:23 you heard the voice out of the **d**,
Jos 24: 7 and he put **d** between you and the
1Sa 2: 9 the wicked will be silenced in **d**.
2Sa 22:12 He made **d** his canopy around him—
22:29 the LORD turns my **d** into light.
Job 3: 4 That day—may it turn to **d**; may God
Job 3: 5 May **d** and deep shadow claim it once
3: 6 That night—may thick **d** seize it;
5:14 **D** comes upon them in the daytime; at
10:22 where even the light is like **d**."
11:17 and **d** will become like morning.
12:22 He reveals the deep things of **d** and
12:25 They grope in **d** with no light; he
15:22 He despairs of escaping the **d**; he is
15:23 he knows the day of **d** is at hand.
15:30 He will not escape the **d**; a flame
17:12 in the face of **d** they say, 'Light is
17:13 grave, if I spread out my bed in **d**,
18:18 He is driven from light into **d** and
19: 8 he has shrouded my paths in **d**.
20:26 total **d** lies in wait for his
22:13 Does he judge through such **d**?
23:17 Yet I am not silenced by the **d**, by
23:17 by the thick **d** that covers my face.
24:17 of them, deep **d** is their morning;
24:17 make friends with the terrors of **d**.
26:10 for a boundary between light and **d**.
28: 3 Man puts an end to the **d**; he
28: 3 recesses for ore in the blackest **d**.
29: 3 and by his light I walked through **d**!
30:26 I looked for light, then came **d**.
37:19 draw up our case because of our **d**.
38: 9 garment and wrapped it in thick **d**,
38:19 of light? And where does **d** reside?
Ps 18:11 He made **d** his covering, his canopy
18:28 my God turns my **d** into light.
44:19 and covered us over with deep **d**.
82: 5 They walk about in **d**; all the
88:12 wonders known in the place of **d**,
88:18 from me; the **d** is my closest friend.
91: 6 the pestilence that stalks in the **d**,
97: 2 Clouds and thick **d** surround him;
104:20 You bring **d**, it becomes night, and
105:28 He sent **d** and made the land dark—
107:10 Some sat in **d** and the deepest gloom,
107:14 He brought them out of **d** and the
112: 4 Even in **d** light dawns for the
139:11 If I say, "Surely the **d** will hide me
139:12 even the **d** will not be dark to you;
139:12 the day, for **d** is as light to you.
143: 3 me dwell in **d** like those long dead.
Pr 4:19 the way of the wicked is like deep **d**;
20:20 lamp will be snuffed out in pitch **d**.
Ecc 2:13 just as light is better than **d**.
2:14 while the fool walks in the **d**; but I
5:17 All his days he eats in **d**, with
6: 4 departs in **d**, and in **d** its name is
11: 8 But let him remember the days of **d**,
Isa 5:20 who put **d** for light and light for **d**,
5:30 he will see **d** and distress; even the
8:22 distress and **d** and fearful gloom,
8:22 they will be thrust into utter **d**.
9: 2 The people walking in **d** have seen a
29:15 who do their work in **d** and think,
29:18 out of gloom and **d** the eyes of the
42: 7 from the dungeon those who sit in **d**.
42:16 I will turn the **d** into light before
45: 3 I will give you the treasures of **d**,
45: 7 I form the light and create **d**, I
45:19 from somewhere in a land of **d**; I
47: 5 "Sit in silence, go into **d**, Daughter
49: 9 and to those in **d**, 'Be free!'
50: 3 I clothe the sky with **d** and make
58:10 then your light will rise in the **d**,
59: 9 We look for light, but all is **d**; for
60: 2 See, **d** covers the earth and thick **d**
61: 1 release from **d** for the prisoners,
Jer 2: 6 a land of drought and **d**, a land
2:31 to Israel or a land of great **d**?
13:16 LORD your God before he brings the **d**,
13:16 he will turn it to thick **d** and
23:12 they will be banished to **d** and
Lam 3: 2 made me walk in **d** rather than light;
3: 6 He has made me dwell in **d** like those
Eze 8:12 house of Israel are doing in the **d**,
32: 8 I will bring **d** over your land,
34:12 scattered on a day of clouds and **d**.
Da 2:22 he knows what lies in **d**, and light
Joel 2: 2 a day of **d** and gloom, a day of
2:31 The sun will be turned to **d** and the
Am 4:13 he who turns dawn to **d**, and treads
5:18 LORD? That day will be **d**, not light.

Am 5:20 Will not the day of the LORD be **d**,
Mic 3: 6 visions, and **d**, without divination.
7: 8 Thought I sit in **d**, the LORD will be
Na 1: 8 he will pursue his foes into **d**.
Zep 1:15 a day of **d** and gloom, a day of
Mt 4:16 the people living in **d** have seen a
6:23 your whole body will be full of **d**.
6:23 you is **d**, how great is that **d**!
8:12 into the **d**, where there will be
22:13 and throw him outside, into the **d**,
25:30 into the **d**, where there will be
27:45 ninth hour **d** came over all the land.
Mk 15:33 At the sixth hour **d** came over the
Lk 1:79 to shine on those living in **d** and in
11:34 bad, your body also is full of **d**.
11:35 that the light within you is not **d**.
22:53 this is your hour—when **d** reigns."
23:44 and **d** came over the whole land
Jn 1: 5 The light shines in the **d**, but the **d**
3:19 but men loved **d** instead of light
8:12 will never walk in **d**, but will have
12:35 the light, before **d** overtakes you.
12:46 who believes in me should stay in **d**.
Ac 2:20 The sun will be turned to **d** and the
13:11 Immediately mist and **d** came over
26:18 eyes and turn them from **d** to light,
Ro 13:12 put aside the deeds of **d** and put on
1Co 4: 5 bring to light what is hidden in **d**
2Co 4: 6 "Let light shine out of **d**," made his
6:14 fellowship can light have with **d**?
Eph 5: 8 For you were once **d**, but now you are
5:11 with the fruitless deeds of **d**, but
Col 1:13 rescued us from the dominion of **d**
1Th 5: 4 you, brothers, are not in **d** so that
5: 5 not belong to the night or to the **d**.
Heb 12:18 with fire; to **d**, gloom and storm;
1Pe 2: 9 out of **d** into his wonderful light.
2Pe 2:17 Blackest **d** is reserved for them.
1Jn 1: 5 in him there is no **d** at all.
1: 6 with him yet walk in the **d**, we lie
2: 8 because the **d** is passing and the
2: 9 hates his brother is still in the **d**.
2:11 whoever hates his brother is in the **d**
2:11 and walks around in the **d**; he does
Jude : 6 own home—these he has kept in **d**,
:13 **d** has been reserved for ever.
Rev 16:10 and his kingdom was plunged into **d**.

Darkon
Ezr 2:56 Jaala, **D**, Giddel,
Ne 7:58 Jaala, **D**, Giddel,

Darling
SS 1: 9 I liken you, my **d**, to a mare
1:15 How beautiful you are, my **d**! Oh, how
2: 2 Like a lily among thorns is my **d**
2:10 "Arise, my **d**, my beautiful one, and
2:13 Arise, come, my **d**; my beautiful one
4: 1 How beautiful you are, my **d**! Oh, how
4: 7 All beautiful you are, my **d**; there
5: 2 my **d**, my dove, my flawless one.
6: 4 You are beautiful, my **d**, as Tirzah,

Dart (Darting)
Job 41:21 ablaze, and flames **d** from his mouth.
41:26 the spear or the **d** or the javelin.
Na 2: 4 they **d** about like lightning.

Darting (Dart)
Pr 7:23 like a bird **d** into a snare, little
26: 2 fluttering sparrow or a **d** swallow,
Isa 14:29 fruit will be a **d**, venomous serpent.
30: 6 of adders and **d** snakes, the envoys

Dash (Dashed, Dashes)
Jdg 20:37 ambush made a sudden **d** into Gibeah,
2Ki 8:12 **d** their little children to the
Ps 2: 9 will **d** them to pieces like pottery."
Eze 23:34 **d** it to pieces and tear your breasts.
Na 2: 5 They **d** to the city wall; the
Lk 19:44 They will **d** you to the ground, you
Rev 2:27 he will **d** them to pieces like

Dashed (Dash)
2Ch 25:12 down so that all were **d** to pieces.
Ps 119:116 live; do not let my hopes be **d**.
Isa 13:16 Their infants will be **d** to pieces
Hos 10:14 **d** to the ground with their children.
13:16 little ones will be **d** to the ground,
Na 3:10 Her infants were **d** to pieces at the
Ac 27:29 Fearing that we would be **d** against

Dashes (Dash)
Ps 137: 9 and **d** them against the rocks.

Date (Dates[1])
Eze 24: 2 "Son of man, record this **d**, this
24: 2 record this **d**, this very **d**, because
Ac 21:26 to give notice of the **d** when the

Dates[1] (Date)
Ac 1: 7 the times or **d** the Father has set
1Th 5: 1 Now, brothers, about times and **d** we

Dates[2]
2Sa 6:19 he gave a loaf of bread, a cake of **d**
1Ch 16: 3 he gave a loaf of bread, a cake of **d**

Dathan
Nu 16: 1 and certain Reubenites—**D** and Abiram,
16:12 Moses summoned **D** and Abiram, the
16:24 the tents of Korah, **D** and Abiram.'"
16:25 Moses got up and went to **D** and
16:27 the tents of Korah, **D** and Abiram.
16:27 **D** and Abiram had come out and were
26: 9 the sons of Eliab were Nemuel, **D** and
26: 9 The same **D** and Abiram were the
Dt 11: 6 what he did to **D** and Abiram, sons of
Ps 106:17 The earth opened up and swallowed **D**;

Daughter (*Daughter of Zion*, Daughter's, Daughter-in-law, Daughters, Daughters-in-law, Granddaughter, Granddaughters)
Ge 11:29 was Milcah; she was the **d** of Haran,
19:31 One day the older **d** said to the
19:33 older **d** went in and lay with him.
19:34 The next day the older **d** said to the
19:35 the younger **d** went and lay with him.
19:37 The older **d** had a son, and she named
19:38 The younger **d** also had a son, and
20:12 is my sister, the **d** of my father
24:15 She was the **d** of Bethuel son of
24:23 he asked, "Whose **d** are you? Please
24:24 "I am the **d** of Bethuel, the son
24:47 "I asked her, 'Whose **d** are you?'
24:47 'The **d** of Bethuel son of Nahor,
25:20 he married Rebekah **d** of Bethuel the
26:34 he married Judith **d** of Beeri the
26:34 also Basemath **d** of Elon the Hittite.
28: 9 sister of Nebaioth and **d** of Ishmael
29: 6 comes his **d** Rachel with the sheep."
29:10 Jacob saw Rachel **d** of Laban, his
29:18 return for your younger **d** Rachel."
29:23 he took his **d** Leah and gave her to
29:24 Zilpah to his **d** as her maidservant.
29:26 to give the younger **d** in marriage
29:28 him his **d** Rachel to be his wife.
29:29 to his **d** Rachel as her maidservant.
30:21 Some time later she gave birth to a **d**
34: 1 Now Dinah, the **d** Leah had borne to
34: 3 was drawn to Dinah **d** of Jacob,
34: 5 Jacob heard that his **d** Dinah had
34: 7 lying with Jacob's **d**—a thing that
34: 8 Shechem has his heart set on your **d**.
34:19 he was delighted with Jacob's **d**.
36: 2 Canaan: Adah **d** of Elon the Hittite,
36: 2 and Oholibamah **d** of Anah and
36: 3 also Basemath **d** of Ishmael and
36:14 of Esau's wife Oholibamah **d** of Anah
36:18 Esau's wife Oholibamah **d** of Anah.
36:25 Dishon and Oholibamah **d** of Anah.
36:39 **d** of Matred, the **d** of Me-Zahab.
38: 2 There Judah met the **d** of a Canaanite
38:12 Judah's wife, the **d** of Shua, died.
41:45 and gave him Asenath **d** of Potiphera,
41:50 Asenath **d** of Potiphera, priest of On.
Ge 46:15 in Paddan Aram, besides his **d** Dinah.
46:18 given to his **d** Leah—sixteen in all.
46:20 Asenath **d** of Potiphera, priest of On.
46:25 given to his **d** Rachel—seven in all.
Ex 2: 5 Pharaoh's **d** went down to the Nile to
2: 7 his sister asked Pharaoh's **d**, "Shall
2: 9 Pharaoh's **d** said to her, "Take this
2:10 she took him to Pharaoh's **d** and he
2:21 his **d** Zipporah to Moses in marriage.
6:23 married Elisheba, **d** of Amminadab
20:10 neither you, nor your son or **d**, nor
21: 7 "If a man sells his **d** as a servant,
21: 9 he must grant her the rights of a **d**.
21:31 if the bull gores a son or a **d**.
Lev 12: 5 If she gives birth to a **d**, for two
12: 6 purification for a son or **d** are
18: 9 your father's **d** or your mother's **d**,
18:10 your son's **d** or your daughter's **d**
18:11 with the **d** of your father's wife,
18:17 with both a woman and her **d**.
18:17 her son's **d** or her daughter's **d**
19:29 "'Do not degrade your **d** by making
20:17 the **d** of either his father or his
21: 2 father, his son or **d**, his brother,
21: 9 "'If a priest's **d** defiles herself by
22:12 If a priest's **d** marries anyone other
22:13 if a priest's **d** becomes a widow or
24:11 the **d** of Dibri the Danite.)
Nu 25:15 was put to death was Cozbi **d** of Zur,
25:18 the **d** of a Midianite leader, the
26:46 (Asher had a **d** named Serah.)
27: 8 give his inheritance over to his **d**.
27: 9 If he has no **d**, give his inheritance
30:16 young **d** still living in his house.
36: 8 Every **d** who inherits land in any
Dt 5:14 neither you, nor your son or **d**, nor
13: 6 or your son or **d**, or the wife you
18:10 sacrifices his son or **d** in the fire,
22:16 "I gave my **d** in marriage to this man,
22:17 I did not find your **d** to be a virgin.
27:22 the **d** of his father or the **d** of his
28:56 she loves and her own son or **d**
Jos 15:16 Caleb said, "I will give my **d** Acsah
15:17 gave his **d** Acsah to him in marriage.
Jdg 1:12 Caleb said, "I will give my **d** Acsah
1:13 gave his **d** Acsah to him in marriage.
11:34 come out to meet him but his **d**,
11:34 for her he had neither son nor **d**.
11:35 "Oh! My **d**! You have made me
11:40 the **d** of Jephthah the Gileadite.
19:24 Look, here is my virgin **d**, and his
21: 1 his **d** in marriage to a Benjamite."
Ru 2: 2 Naomi said to her, "Go ahead, my **d**."
2: 8 Boaz said to Ruth, "My **d**, listen to
2:22 "It will be good for you, my **d**, to
3: 1 "My **d**, should I not try to find a
3:10 "The LORD bless you, my **d**," he
3:11 now, my **d**, don't be afraid. I will
3:16 "How did it go, my **d**?" Then she told
3:18 Naomi said, "Wait, my **d**, until you
1Sa 14:49 The name of his older **d** was Merab,
14:50 His wife's name was Ahinoam **d** of
17:25 He will also give him his **d** in
18:17 to David, "Here is my older **d** Merab.
18:19 Saul's **d**, to be given to David, she
18:20 Now Saul's **d** Michal was in love with
18:27 gave him his **d** Michal in marriage.
18:28 and that his **d** Michal loved David,
25:44 Saul had given his **d** Michal, David's
2Sa 3: 3 Maacah **d** of Talmai king of Geshur;
3: 7 a concubine named Rizpah **d** of Aiah.
3:13 bring Michal **d** of Saul when you
6:16 Michal **d** of Saul watched from a
6:20 Michal **d** of Saul came out to meet
6:23 Michal **d** of Saul had no children to
11: 3 Bathsheba, the **d** of Eliam and
12: 3 his arms. It was like a **d** to him.
14:27 Three sons and a **d** were born to
17:25 the **d** of Nahash and sister of
21: 8 the two sons of Aiah's **d** Rizpah,
21: 8 the five sons of Saul's **d** Merab,
21:10 Rizpah **d** of Aiah took sackcloth and
21:11 David was told what Aiah's **d** Rizpah,
1Ki 3: 1 king of Egypt and married his **d**.
4:11 married to Taphath **d** of Solomon);
4:15 had married Basemath **d** of Solomon);

1Ki 7: 8 Pharaoh's **d**, whom he had married.
9:16 gift to his **d**, Solomon's wife.
9:24 After Pharaoh's **d** had come up from
11: 1 women besides Pharaoh's **d**—Moabites,
15: 2 name was Maacah **d** of Abishalom.
15:10 name was Maacah **d** of Abishalom.
16:31 also married Jezebel **d** of Ethbaal
22:42 name was Azubah **d** of Shilhi.
2Ki 8:18 done, for he married a **d** of Ahab.
9:34 bury her, for she was a king's **d**."
11: 2 Jehosheba, the **d** of King Jehoram and
14: 9 'Give your **d** to my son in marriage.
15:33 name was Jerusha **d** of Zadok.
18: 2 name was Abijah **d** of Zechariah.
19:21 The **D** of Jerusalem tosses her head
21:19 name was Meshullemeth **d** of Haruz;
22: 1 Jedidah **d** of Adaiah; she was from
23:10 his son or **d** in the fire to Molech.
23:31 Hamutal **d** of Jeremiah; she was
23:36 Zebidah **d** of Pedaiah; she was from
24: 8 His mother's name was Nehushta **d** of
24:18 Hamutal **d** of Jeremiah; she was
1Ch 1:50 **d** of Matred, the **d** of Me-Zahab.
2: 3 by a Canaanite woman, the **d** of Shua.
2:21 Hezron lay with the **d** of Makir
2:35 Sheshan gave his **d** in marriage to
2:49 Caleb's **d** was Acsah.
3: 2 Absalom the son of Maacah **d** of
3: 5 four were by Bathsheba **d** of Ammiel.
4:18 **d** Bithiah, whom Mered had married.
7:24 His **d** was Sheerah, who built Lower
15:29 **d** of Saul watched from a window.
2Ch 8:11 Solomon brought Pharaoh's **d** up from
11:18 who was the **d** of David's son
11:18 Abihail, the **d** of Jesse's son Eliab.
11:20 he married Maacah **d** of Absalom, who
11:21 Rehoboam loved Maacah **d** of Absalom
13: 2 Maacah, a **d** of Uriel of Gibeah.
20:31 name was Azubah **d** of Shilhi.
21: 6 done, for he married a **d** of Ahab.
22:11 Jehosheba, the **d** of King Jehoram,
22:11 Jehosheba, the **d** of King Jehoram
25:18 'Give your **d** to my son in marriage.
27: 1 name was Jerusha **d** of Zadok.
29: 1 name was Abijah **d** of Zechariah.
Ezr 2:61 who had married a **d** of Barzillai
Ne 6:18 the **d** of Meshullam son of Berekiah.
7:63 who had married a **d** of Barzillai
Est 2: 7 taken her as his own **d** when her
2:15 the **d** of his uncle Abihail) to go to
9:29 Queen Esther, **d** of Abihail, along
Job 42:14 The first **d** he named Jemimah, the
Ps 45:10 Listen, O **d**, consider and give ear:
45:12 The **D** of Tyre will come with a gift,
137: 8 **D** of Babylon, doomed to destruction
SS 6: 9 is unique, the only **d** of her mother,
7: 1 O prince's **d**! Your graceful legs are
Isa 10:30 Cry out, O **D** of Gallim! Listen, O
23:10 as along the Nile, O **D** of Tarshish,
23:12 O Virgin **D** of Sidon, now crushed!
37:22 **D** of Zion despises and mocks you.
47: 1 in the dust, Virgin **D** of Babylon;
47: 1 a throne, **D** of the Babylonians.
47: 5 darkness, **D** of the Babylonians;
Jer 14:17 for my virgin **d**—my people—has
31:22 will you wander, O unfaithful **d**?
46:11 and get balm, O Virgin **D** of Egypt.
46:24 The **D** of Egypt will be put to shame,
48:18 O inhabitants of the **D** of Dibon, for
49: 4 O unfaithful **d**, you trust in your
50:42 to attack you, O **D** of Babylon.
51:33 "The **D** of Babylon is like a
52: 1 name was Hamutal **d** of Jeremiah;
Lam 1:15 has trampled the Virgin **D** of Judah.
2: 2 the strongholds of the **D** of Judah.
2: 5 and lamentation for the **D** of Judah.
2:13 I compare you, O **D** of Jerusalem?
2:15 their heads at the **D** of Jerusalem:
4:21 Rejoice and be glad, O **D** of Edom,
4:22 But, O **D** of Edom, he will punish
Eze 14:20 they could save neither son nor **d**.
16:44 about you: "Like mother, like **d**.
16:45 You are a true **d** of your mother, who
22:11 his sister, his own father's **d**.
44:25 son or **d**, brother or unmarried
Da 11: 6 The **d** of the king of the South will
11:17 And he will give him a **d** in marriage
Hos 1: 3 he married Gomer **d** of Diblaim, and
1: 6 again and gave birth to a **d**.
Mic 4: 8 will come to the **D** of Jerusalem."
7: 6 a **d** rises up against her mother,
Zep 3:14 all your heart, O **D** of Jerusalem!
Zec 2: 7 you who live in the **D** of Babylon!"
9: 9 Shout, **D** of Jerusalem! See, your
Mal 2:11 by marrying the **d** of a foreign god.
Mt 9:18 him and said, "My **d** has just died.
9:22 "Take heart, **d**," he said, "your
10:35 his father, a **d** against her mother,
10:37 loves his son or **d** more than me is
14: 6 the **d** of Herodias danced for them
15:22 have mercy on me! My **d** is suffering
15:28 **d** was healed from that very hour.
Mk 5:23 with him, "My little **d** is dying.
5:34 "**D**, your faith has healed you.
5:35 "Your **d** is dead," they said. "Why
6:22 the **d** of Herodias came in and danced,
7:25 a woman whose little **d** was possessed
7:26 to drive the demon out of her **d**.
7:29 may go; the demon has left your **d**."
Lk 2:36 **d** of Phanuel, of the tribe of Asher.
8:42 his only **d**, a girl of about twelve,
8:48 "**D**, your faith has healed you.
8:49 "Your **d** is dead," he said. "Don't
12:53 mother against **d** and **d** against
13:16 this woman, a **d** of Abraham,
Ac 7:21 Pharaoh's **d** took him and brought
Heb 11:24 be known as the son of Pharaoh's **d**.

Daughter of Zion

2Ki 19:21 Virgin **D** despises you and mocks you.
Ps 9:14 your praises in the gates of the **D**
Isa 1: 8 The **D** is left like a shelter in a
10:32 at the mount of the **D**, at the hill
16: 1 the desert, to the mount of the **D**.
37:22 Virgin **D** despises and mocks you.
52: 2 chains on your neck, O captive **D**.
62:11 "Say to the **D**, 'See, your Saviour
Jer 4:31 the cry of the **D** gasping for breath,
6: 2 I will destroy the **D**, so beautiful
6:23 formation to attack you, O **D**."
Lam 1: 6 splendour has departed from the **D**.
2: 1 How the Lord has covered the **D** with
2: 4 like fire on the tent of the **D**.
2: 8 to tear down the wall around the **D**.
2:10 The elders of the **D** sit on the
2:13 that I may comfort you, O Virgin **D**?
2:18 O wall of the **D**, let your tears flow
4:22 O **D**, your punishment will end; he
Mic 1:13 were the beginning of sin to the **D**,
4: 8 O stronghold of the **D**, the former
4:10 Writhe in agony, O **D**, like a woman
4:13 "Rise and thresh, O **D**, for I will
Zep 3:14 Sing, O **D**; shout aloud, O Israel! Be
Zec 2:10 "Shout and be glad, O **D**. For I am
9: 9 Rejoice greatly, O **D**! Shout,
Mt 21: 5 "Say to the **D**, 'See, your king comes
Jn 12:15 "Do not be afraid, O **D**; see, your

Daughter's (Daughter)

Ge 29:27 Finish this **d** bridal week; then we
Lev 18:10 son's daughter or your **d** daughter;
18:17 son's daughter or her **d** daughter;
Dt 22:17 is the proof of my **d** virginity."
2Sa 14:27 The **d** name was Tamar, and she became

Daughter-in-law (Daughter)

Ge 11:31 and his **d** Sarai, the wife of his son
38:11 Judah then said to his **d** Tamar,
38:16 Not realising that she was his **d**, he
38:24 "Your **d** Tamar is guilty of
Lev 18:15 have sexual relations with your **d**.
20:12 "If a man sleeps with his **d**, both
Ru 1:22 Ruth the Moabitess, her **d**, arriving
2:20 LORD bless him!" Naomi said to her **d**.
2:22 Naomi said to Ruth her **d**, "It will
4:15 For your **d**, who loves you and who is
1Sa 4:19 His **d**, the wife of Phinehas, was
1Ch 2: 4 Tamar, Judah's **d**, bore him Perez and
Eze 22:11 another shamefully defiles his **d**,
Mic 7: 6 a **d** against her mother-in-law—
Mt 10:35 a **d** against her mother-in-law—
Lk 12:53 mother-in-law against **d** and
12:53 and **d** against mother-in-law."

Daughters (Daughter)

Ge 5: 4 800 years and had other sons and **d**.
5: 7 807 years and had other sons and **d**.
5:10 815 years and had other sons and **d**.
5:13 840 years and had other sons and **d**.
5:16 830 years and had other sons and **d**.
5:19 800 years and had other sons and **d**.
5:22 300 years and had other sons and **d**.
5:26 782 years and had other sons and **d**.
5:30 595 years and had other sons and **d**.
6: 1 the earth and **d** were born to them,
6: 2 that the **d** of men were beautiful,
6: 4 the the **d** of men and had children
11:11 500 years and had other sons and **d**.
11:13 403 years and had other sons and **d**.
11:15 403 years and had other sons and **d**.
11:17 430 years and had other sons and **d**.
11:19 209 years and had other sons and **d**.
11:21 207 years and had other sons and **d**.
11:23 200 years and had other sons and **d**.
11:25 119 years and had other sons and **d**.
19: 8 Look, I have two **d** who have never
19:12 sons or **d**, or anyone else in the
19:14 who were pledged to marry his **d**.
19:15 wife and your two **d** who are here,
19:16 of his two **d** and led them safely out
19:30 Lot and his two **d** left Zoar and
19:30 He and his two **d** lived in a cave.
19:36 both of Lot's **d** became pregnant by
24: 3 my son from the **d** of the Canaanites,
24:13 and the **d** of the townspeople are
24:37 my son from the **d** of the Canaanites,
28: 2 **d** of Laban, your mother's brother.
29:16 Now Laban had two **d**; the name of the
31:26 off my **d** like captives in war.
31:28 my grandchildren and my **d** good-bye.
31:31 take your **d** away from me by force.
31:41 two **d** and six years for your flocks,
31:43 "The women are my **d**, the children
31:43 I do today about these **d** of mine,
31:50 If you ill-treat my **d** or if you take
31:50 if you take any wives besides my **d**,
31:55 and his **d** and blessed them. Then he
34: 9 Intermarry with us; give us your **d**
34: 9 and take our **d** for yourselves.
34:16 give you our **d** and take your **d**
34:21 marry their **d** and they can marry
36: 6 Esau took his wives and sons and **d**
37:35 All his sons and **d** came to comfort
46: 7 and his **d** and granddaughters—
46:15 **d** of his were thirty-three in all.
Ex 2:16 Now a priest of Midian had seven **d**,
2:20 "And where is he?" he asked his **d**.
3:22 you will put on your sons and **d**.
6:25 Aaron married one of the **d** of Putiel,
10: 9 with our sons and **d**, and with our
21: 4 a wife and she bears him sons or **d**,
32: 2 **d** are wearing, and bring them to me."
34:16 you choose some of their **d** as wives
34:16 those **d** prostitute themselves to
Lev 10:14 you and your sons and your **d** may eat
26:29 your sons and the flesh of your **d**.
Nu 18:11 sons and **d** as your regular share.
18:19 sons and **d** as your regular share.
21:29 his **d** as captives to Sihon king of
26:33 he had only **d**, whose names were
27: 1 The **d** of Zelophehad son of Hepher,
27: 1 The names of the **d** were Mahlah, Noah,
27: 7 "What Zelophehad's **d** are saying is
36: 2 of our brother Zelophehad to his **d**.
36: 6 LORD commands for Zelophehad's **d**:
36:10 Zelophehad's **d** did as the LORD
36:11 Zelophehad's **d**—Mahlah, Tirzah,
Dt 7: 3 Do not give your **d** to their sons or
7: 3 or take their **d** for your sons,
12:12 your sons and **d**, your menservants
12:18 your sons and **d**, your menservants
12:31 They even burn their sons and **d** in
16:11 your sons and **d**, your menservants
16:14 your sons and **d**, your menservants
28:32 Your sons and **d** will be given to
28:41 You will have sons and **d** but you

Dt 28:53 **d** the LORD your God has given you.
32:19 he was angered by his sons and **d**.
Jos 7:24 the gold wedge, his sons and **d**, his
17: 3 had no sons but only **d**, whose names
17: 6 the **d** of the tribe of Manasseh
Jdg 3: 6 They took their **d** in marriage and
3: 6 and gave their own **d** to their sons,
12: 9 He had thirty sons and thirty **d**.
12: 9 He gave his **d** away in marriage to
21: 7 give them any of our **d** in marriage?"
21:18 We can't give them our **d** as wives,
21:22 you did not give your **d** to them.'"
Ru 1:11 Naomi said, "Return home, my **d**. Why
1:12 Return home, my **d**; I am too old to
1:13 remain unmarried for them? No, my **d**.
1Sa 1: 4 Peninnah and to all her sons and **d**.
2:21 gave birth to three sons and two **d**.
8:13 He will take your **d** to be perfumers
30: 3 wives and sons and **d** taken captive.
30: 6 in spirit because of his sons and **d**.
2Sa 1:20 lest the **d** of the Philistines be
1:20 the **d** of the uncircumcised rejoice.
1:24 "O **d** of Israel, weep for Saul, who
5:13 more sons and **d** were born to him.
13:18 the virgin **d** of the king wore.
19: 5 the lives of your sons and **d** and the
2Ki 17:17 They sacrificed their sons and **d** in
1Ch 2:34 Sheshan had no sons—only **d**. He had
4:27 Shimei had sixteen sons and six **d**,
7:15 named Zelophehad, who had only **d**.
14: 3 the father of more sons and **d**.
23:22 without having sons: he had only **d**.
25: 5 Heman fourteen sons and three **d**.
2Ch 11:21 twenty-eight sons and sixty **d**.
13:21 had twenty-two sons and sixteen **d**.
24: 3 for him, and he had sons and **d**.
28: 8 hundred thousand wives, sons and **d**.
29: 9 **d** and our wives are in captivity.
31:18 the wives, and the sons and **d** of the
Ezr 9: 2 They have taken some of their **d** as
9:12 Therefore, do not give your **d** in
9:12 sons or take their **d** for your sons.
Ne 3:12 next section with the help of his **d**.
4:14 your **d**, your wives and your homes."
5: 2 "We and our sons and **d** are numerous;
5: 5 subject our sons and **d** to slavery.
5: 5 Some of our **d** have already been
10:28 and **d** who are able to understand—
10:30 "We promise not to give our **d** in
10:30 us or take their **d** for our sons.
13:25 not to give your **d** in marriage
13:25 nor are you to take their **d** in
Job 1: 2 He had seven sons and three **d**,
1:13 Job's sons and **d** were feasting
1:18 "Your sons and **d** were feasting and
42:13 he also had seven sons and three **d**.
42:15 found women as beautiful as Job's **d**,
Ps 45: 9 **D** of kings are among your honoured
106:37 their sons and their **d** to demons.
106:38 the blood of their sons and **d**, whom
144:12 and our **d** will be like pillars
Pr 30:15 "The leech has two **d**. 'Give! Give!'
SS 1: 5 yet lovely, O **d** of Jerusalem,
2: 7 **D** of Jerusalem, I charge you by the
3: 5 **D** of Jerusalem, I charge you by the
3:10 inlaid by the **d** of Jerusalem.
3:11 Come out, you **d** of Zion, and look at
5: 8 O **d** of Jerusalem, I charge you—if
5:16 this my friend, O **d** of Jerusalem.
8: 4 **D** of Jerusalem, I charge you: Do not
Isa 23: 4 reared sons nor brought up **d**."
32: 9 you **d** who feel secure, hear what I
32:11 you **d** who feel secure! Strip off
43: 6 my **d** from the ends of the earth—
49:22 and carry your **d** on their shoulders.
56: 5 and a name better than sons and **d**;
60: 4 and your **d** are carried on the arm.
Jer 3:24 flocks and herds, their sons and **d**.
5:17 devour your sons and **d**; they will
7:31 burn their sons and **d** in the fire
9:20 Teach your **d** how to wail; teach one
11:22 sword, their sons and **d** by famine.
14:16 their wives, their sons or their **d**.
16: 2 and have sons or **d** in this place."
16: 3 sons and **d** born in this land and
19: 9 eat the flesh of their sons and **d**,
Jer 29: 6 Marry and have sons and **d**; find
29: 6 sons and give your **d** in marriage,
29: 6 that they too may have sons and **d**.
32:35 their sons and **d** to Molech,
35: 8 our sons and **d** have ever drunk
41:10 the king's **d** along with all the
43: 6 women and children and the king's **d**
48:46 exile and your **d** into captivity.
Eze 13:17 set your face against the **d** of your
14:16 could not save their own sons or **d**.
14:18 could not save their own sons or **d**.
14:22 and **d** who will be brought out of it.
16:20 "'And you took your sons and **d** whom
16:27 the **d** of the Philistines, who were
16:46 to the north of you with her **d**;
16:46 south of you with her **d**, was Sodom.
16:48 your sister Sodom and her **d** never
16:48 did what you and your **d** have done.
16:49 Sodom: She and her **d** were arrogant,
16:53 the fortunes of Sodom and her **d**
16:53 and of Samaria and her **d**, and your
16:55 your sisters, Sodom with her **d** and
16:55 Samaria with her **d**, will return
16:57 you are now scorned by the **d** of Edom
16:57 and the **d** of the Philistines—all
16:61 I will give them to you as **d**, but
23: 2 two women, **d** of the same mother.
23: 4 mine and gave birth to sons and **d**.
23:10 took away her sons and **d** and killed
23:25 They will take away your sons and **d**,
23:47 they will kill their sons and **d** and
24:21 The sons and **d** you left behind will
24:25 and their sons and **d** as well—
32:16 The **d** of the nations will chant it;
32:18 her and the **d** of mighty nations,
Hos 4:13 your **d** turn to prostitution
4:14 "I will not punish your **d** when they
Joel 2:28 Your sons and **d** will prophesy, your
3: 8 I will sell your sons and **d** to the
Am 7:17 sons and **d** will fall by the sword.
Lk 23:28 "**D** of Jerusalem, do not weep for
Ac 2:17 Your sons and **d** will prophesy, your
21: 9 He had four unmarried **d** who
2Co 6:18 and you will be my sons and **d**,
1Pe 3: 6 You are her **d** if you do what is

Daughters-in-law (Daughter)

Ru 1: 6 her **d** prepared to return home from
1: 7 With her two **d** she left the place
1: 8 Naomi said to her two **d**, "Go back,
Hos 4:13 prostitution and your **d** to adultery.
4:14 nor your **d** when they commit adultery,

David (*City of David*, *David's*, *Father David*, *House of David*, *Servant David*, *Son of David*)

Israel's second and greatest king; ancestor of Jesus (Mt 1:1; Ro 1:3; Rev 22:16); type of promised Messiah (Isa 11:1; Eze 34:23–24; 37:24–25).
Singer of psalms and songs (2Sa 23:1; Am 6:5). Son of Jesse of Bethlehem (Ru 4:17; 1Sa 17:12). Anointed king by Samuel (1Sa 16:1–13). Entered Saul's service as musician (1Sa 16:14–23). Killed Goliath (1Sa 17:32–54). Friendship with Jonathan (1Sa 18:1–4; 19:1–7; 20; 23:16–18; 2Sa 1:25–26). Fled because of Saul's hostility (1Sa 19; 21–23). Spared Saul's life (1Sa 24; 26). Among the Philistines (1Sa 21:10–15; 27–29). Lament for Saul and Jonathan (2Sa 1).
Anointed king of Judah at Hebron (2Sa 2:1–7). War with Saul's family (2Sa 2–4). United northern and southern tribes as king over all Israel (2Sa 5:1–4; 1Ch 11:1–3; 12:38–40). Captured Jerusalem from Jebusites (2Sa 5:6–10; 1Ch 11:4–9); installed ark there (2Sa 6; 1Ch 15–16). Promised lasting dynasty by God (2Sa 7; 1Ch 17; Ps 89; 132). Established empire: defeated Philistines (2Sa 5:17–25; 1Ch 14:8–17; 2Sa 21:15–22; 1Ch 20:4–8), Moabites, Arameans, Edomites (2Sa 8:1–14; 1Ch 18:1–13), Ammonites (2Sa 10; 1Ch 19). Committed adultery with Bathsheba; murdered Uriah (2Sa 11); rebuked by Nathan (2Sa 12:1–14); repented (Ps 51). Married Bathsheba and other wives (1Sa 18:27; 25:39–43; 2Sa 5:13; 11:27); father of Solomon, Absalom, Adonijah, etc. (2Sa 3:2–5; 1Ch 3:1–9). Absalom's revolt (2Sa 15–18). Preparations for temple (1Ch 22; 28–29). Appointment of Solomon as successor (1Ki 1:28–48). Death (1Ki 2:10–12; 1Ch 29:26–28).

Ru 4:17 father of Jesse, the father of **D**.
4:22 of Jesse, and Jesse the father of **D**.
1Sa 16:13 of the LORD came upon **D** in power.
16:19 your son **D**, who is with the sheep."
16:20 sent them with his son **D** to Saul.
16:21 **D** came to Saul and entered his
16:21 **D** became one of his armour-bearers.
16:22 "Allow **D** to remain in my service,
16:23 Saul, **D** would take his harp and play.
17:12 Now **D** was the son of an Ephrathite
17:14 **D** was the youngest. The three oldest
17:15 **D** went back and forth from Saul to
17:17 Now Jesse said to his son **D**, "Take
17:20 Early in the morning **D** left the
17:22 **D** left his things with the keeper of
17:23 his usual defiance, and **D** heard it.
17:26 **D** asked the men standing near him,
17:29 "Now what have I done?" said **D**.
17:31 What **D** said was overheard and
17:32 **D** said to Saul, "Let no-one lose
17:34 **D** said to Saul, "Your servant has
17:37 Saul said to **D**, "Go, and the LORD
17:38 Saul dressed **D** in his own tunic. He
17:39 **D** fastened on his sword over the
17:41 of him, kept coming closer to **D**.
17:42 He looked **D** over and saw that he was
17:43 He said to **D**, "Am I a dog, that you
17:43 the Philistine cursed **D** by his gods.
17:45 **D** said to the Philistine, "You come
17:48 **D** ran quickly towards the battle
17:50 **D** triumphed over the Philistine with
17:51 **D** ran and stood over him. He took
17:54 **D** took the Philistine's head and
17:55 Saul watched **D** going out to meet the
17:57 soon as **D** returned from killing the
17:57 **D** still holding the Philistine's
17:58 **D** said, "I am the son of your
18: 1 After **D** had finished talking with
18: 1 became one in spirit with **D**, and he
18: 2 From that day Saul kept **D** with him
18: 3 Jonathan made a covenant with **D**
18: 4 he was wearing and gave it to **D**,
18: 5 Whatever Saul sent him to do, **D** did
18: 6 returning home after **D** had killed
18: 7 and **D** his tens of thousands."
18: 8 "They have credited **D** with tens of
18: 9 on Saul kept a jealous eye on **D**.
18:10 while **D** was playing the harp, as he
18:11 to himself, "I'll pin **D** to the wall.
18:11 But **D** eluded him twice.
18:12 Saul was afraid of **D**, because the
18:12 LORD was with **D** but had left Saul.
18:13 he sent **D** away from him and gave him
18:13 **D** led the troops in their campaigns.
18:16 all Israel and Judah loved **D**,
18:17 Saul said to **D**, "Here is my older
18:18 **D** said to Saul, "Who am I, and what
18:19 Saul's daughter, to be given to **D**,
18:20 daughter Michal was in love with **D**,
18:21 So Saul said to **D**, "Now you have a
18:22 "Speak to **D** privately and say, 'Look,
18:23 repeated these words to **D**. But **D** said
18:24 Saul's servants told him what **D** had
18:25 Saul replied, "Say to **D**, 'The king
18:25 Saul's plan was to have **D** fall by
18:26 the attendants told **D** these things,
18:27 **D** and his men went out and killed
18:28 realised that the LORD was with **D**
18:28 that his daughter Michal loved **D**,
18:30 they did, **D** met with more success
19: 1 and all the attendants to kill **D**.
19: 1 But Jonathan was very fond of **D**
19: 4 Jonathan spoke well of **D** to Saul his
19: 5 an innocent man like **D** by killing
19: 6 lives, **D** will not be put to death."
19: 7 Jonathan called **D** and told him the
19: 7 Saul, and **D** was with Saul as before.
19: 8 Once more war broke out, and **D** went
19: 9 While **D** was playing the harp,
19:10 but **D** eluded him as Saul drove the
19:10 That night **D** made good his escape.
19:12 Michal let **D** down through a window,
19:14 Saul sent the men to capture **D**,

1Sa 19:15 Saul sent the men back to see **D** and
19:18 **D** had fled and made his escape, he
19:19 Word came to Saul: "**D** is in Naioth
19:22 "Where are Samuel and **D**?" "Over in
20: 1 **D** fled from Naioth at Ramah and went
20: 3 **D** took an oath and said, "Your
20: 4 Jonathan said to **D**, "Whatever you
20: 5 **D** said, "Look, tomorrow is the New
20: 6 '**D** earnestly asked my permission to
20:10 **D** asked, "Who will tell me if your
20:12 Jonathan said to **D**: "By the LORD,
20:17 Jonathan made **D** reaffirm his oath
20:18 Jonathan said to **D**: "Tomorrow is the
20:24 **D** hid in the field, and when the New
20:26 "Something must have happened to **D**
20:28 answered, "**D** earnestly asked me for
20:33 that his father intended to kill **D**.
20:34 father's shameful treatment of **D**.
20:35 to the field for his meeting with **D**.
20:39 all this; only Jonathan and **D** knew.)
20:41 After the boy had gone, **D** got up
20:41 wept together—but **D** wept the most.
20:42 Jonathan said to **D**, "Go in peace,
20:42 Then **D** left, and Jonathan went
21: 1 **D** went to Nob, to Ahimelech the
21: 2 **D** answered Ahimelech the priest,
21: 4 the priest answered **D**, "I don't have
21: 5 **D** replied, "Indeed women have been
21: 8 **D** asked Ahimelech, "Don't you have a
21: 9 **D** said, "There is none like it;
21:10 That day **D** fled from Saul and went
21:11 "Isn't this **D**, the king of the land?
21:11 and **D** his tens of thousands'?"
21:12 **D** took these words to heart and was
22: 1 **D** left Gath and escaped to the cave
22: 3 From there **D** went to Mizpah in Moab
22: 4 as long as **D** was in the stronghold.
22: 5 the prophet Gad said to **D**, "Do not
22: 5 So **D** left and went to the forest
22: 6 Now Saul heard that **D** and his men
22:14 all your servants is as loyal as **D**,
22:17 because they too have sided with **D**.
22:20 Ahitub, escaped and fled to join **D**.
22:21 He told **D** that Saul had killed the
22:22 **D** said to Abiathar: "That day, when
23: 1 **D** was told, "Look, the Philistines
23: 4 Once again **D** enquired of the LORD,
23: 5 **D** and his men went to Keilah, fought
23: 6 him when he fled to **D** at Keilah.)
23: 7 Saul was told that **D** had gone to
23: 7 for **D** has imprisoned himself by
23: 8 to Keilah to besiege **D** and his men.
23: 9 **D** learned that Saul was plotting
23:10 **D** said, "O LORD, God of Israel,
23:12 Again **D** asked, "Will the citizens of
23:13 **D** and his men, about six hundred in
23:13 that **D** had escaped from Keilah,
23:14 **D** stayed in the desert strongholds
23:14 God did not give **D** into his hands.
23:15 While **D** was at Horesh in the Desert
23:16 Saul's son Jonathan went to **D** at
23:18 went home, but **D** remained at Horesh.
23:19 "Is not **D** hiding among us in the
23:22 Find out where **D** usually goes and
23:24 Now **D** and his men were in the Desert
23:25 and when **D** was told about it, he
23:25 the Desert of Maon in pursuit of **D**.
23:26 and **D** and his men were on the other
23:26 in on **D** and his men to capture them,
23:28 Saul broke off his pursuit of **D** and
23:29 **D** went up from there and lived in
24: 1 "**D** is in the Desert of En Gedi.
24: 2 set out to look for **D** and his men
24: 3 **D** and his men were far back in the
24: 4 Then **D** crept up unnoticed and cut
24: 5 **D** was conscience-stricken
24: 7 With these words **D** rebuked his men
24: 8 **D** went out of the cave and called
24: 8 **D** bowed down and prostrated himself
24: 9 men say, '**D** is bent on harming you'?
24:16 **D** finished saying this, Saul asked,
24:16 "Is that your voice, **D** my son?"
24:22 **D** gave his oath to Saul. Then Saul
24:22 but **D** and his men went up to the
25: 1 **D** moved down into the Desert of Maon.
25: 4 While **D** was in the desert, he heard

1Sa 25: 8 **D** whatever you can find for them.'"
25:10 "Who is this **D**? Who is this son of
25:13 **D** said to his men, "Put on your
25:13 on their swords, and **D** put on his.
25:13 four hundred men went up with **D**,
25:14 "**D** sent messengers from the desert
25:20 there were **D** and his men descending
25:21 **D** had just said, "It's been useless—
25:22 May God deal with **D**, be it ever so
25:23 Abigail saw **D**, she quickly got off
25:23 bowed down before **D** with her face
25:32 **D** said to Abigail, "Praise be to the
25:35 **D** accepted from her hand what she
25:39 **D** heard that Nabal was dead, he said,
25:39 Then **D** sent word to Abigail, asking
25:40 "**D** has sent us to you to take you to
25:43 **D** had also married Ahinoam of
26: 1 "Is not **D** hiding on the hill of
26: 2 of Israel, to search there for **D**.
26: 3 Jeshimon, but **D** stayed in the desert.
26: 5 **D** set out and went to the place
26: 6 **D** then asked Ahimelech the Hittite
26: 7 **D** and Abishai went to the army by
26: 8 Abishai said to **D**, "Today God has
26: 9 **D** said to Abishai, "Don't destroy
26:12 **D** took the spear and water jug near
26:13 **D** crossed over to the other side and
26:15 **D** said, "You're a man, aren't you?
26:17 "Is that your voice, **D** my son?"
26:17 **D** replied, "Yes it is, my lord the
26:21 Come back, **D** my son. Because you
26:22 is the king's spear," **D** answered.
26:25 Saul said to **D**, "May you be blessed,
26:25 "May you be blessed, my son **D**; you
26:25 So **D** went on his way, and Saul
27: 1 **D** thought to himself, "One of these
27: 2 **D** and the six hundred men with him
27: 3 **D** and his men settled in Gath with
27: 3 and **D** had his two wives: Ahinoam of
27: 4 Saul was told that **D** had fled to
27: 5 **D** said to Achish, "If I have found
27: 7 **D** lived in Philistine territory for
27: 8 Now **D** and his men went up and raided
27: 9 Whenever **D** attacked an area, he did
27:10 **D** would say, "Against the Negev of
27:11 on us and say, 'This is what **D** did.
27:12 Achish trusted **D** and said to himself,
28: 1 Achish said to **D**, "You must
28: 2 **D** said, "Then you will see for
28:17 it to one of your neighbours—to **D**.
29: 2 **D** and his men were marching at the
29: 3 "Is this not **D**, who was an officer
29: 5 Isn't this the **D** they sang about in
29: 5 and **D** his tens of thousands'?"
29: 6 Achish called **D** and said to him, "As
29: 8 "But what have I done?" asked **D**.
29:11 **D** and his men got up early in the
30: 1 **D** and his men reached Ziklag on the
30: 3 **D** and his men came to Ziklag, they
30: 4 **D** and his men wept aloud until they
30: 6 **D** was greatly distressed because the
30: 6 **D** found strength in the LORD his God.
30: 7 **D** said to Abiathar the priest, the
30: 8 **D** enquired of the LORD, "Shall I
30: 9 **D** and the six hundred men with him
30:10 But **D** and four hundred men continued
30:11 in a field and brought him to **D**.
30:13 **D** asked him, "To whom do you belong,
30:15 **D** asked him, "Can you lead me down
30:16 He led **D** down, and there they were,
30:17 **D** fought them from dusk until the
30:18 **D** recovered everything the
30:19 **D** brought everything back.
30:21 **D** came to the two hundred men who
30:21 They came out to meet **D** and the
30:21 As **D** and his men approached, he
30:23 **D** replied, "No, my brothers, you
30:25 **D** made this a statute and ordinance
30:26 **D** arrived in Ziklag, he sent some of
30:31 where **D** and his men had roamed.
2Sa 1: 1 After the death of Saul, **D** returned
1: 2 When he came to **D**, he fell to the
1: 3 "Where have you come from?" **D** asked
1: 4 "What happened?" **D** asked. "Tell me."
1: 5 **D** said to the young man who brought
1:11 **D** and all the men with him took hold

2Sa 1:13 **D** said to the young man who brought
1:14 **D** asked him, "Why were you not
1:15 **D** called one of his men and said,
1:16 For **D** had said to him, "Your blood
1:17 **D** took up this lament concerning
2: 1 In the course of time, **D** enquired of
2: 1 **D** asked, "Where shall I go?"
2: 2 **D** went up there with his two wives,
2: 3 **D** also took the men who were with
2: 4 anointed **D** king over the house of
2: 4 When **D** was told that it was the men
2:10 house of Judah, however, followed **D**.
2:11 The length of time **D** was king in
2:15 son of Saul, and twelve for **D**.
3: 1 **D** grew stronger and stronger, while
3: 2 Sons were born to **D** in Hebron: His
3: 5 These were born to **D** in Hebron.
3: 8 I haven't handed you over to **D**. Yet
3: 9 do for **D** what the LORD promised him
3:12 on his behalf to say to **D**, "Whose
3:13 "Good," said **D**. "I will make an
3:14 **D** sent messengers to Ish-Bosheth son
3:17 you have wanted to make **D** your king.
3:18 Now do it! For the LORD promised **D**,
3:19 Then he went to Hebron to tell **D**
3:20 came to **D** at Hebron, **D** prepared a
3:21 Abner said to **D**, "Let me go at once
3:21 So **D** sent Abner away, and he went
3:22 But Abner was no longer with **D** in
3:22 because **D** had sent him away, and he
3:26 Joab then left **D** and sent messengers
3:26 well of Sirah. But **D** did not know it.
3:28 Later, when **D** heard about this, he
3:31 **D** said to Joab and all the people
3:31 **D** himself walked behind the bier.
3:35 they all came and urged **D** to eat
3:35 but **D** took an oath, saying,
4: 8 to **D** at Hebron and said to the king,
4: 9 **D** answered Recab and his brother
4:12 **D** gave an order to his men, and they
5: 1 All the tribes of Israel came to **D**
5: 3 Israel had come to King **D** at Hebron,
5: 3 they anointed **D** king over Israel.
5: 4 **D** was thirty years old when he
5: 6 The Jebusites said to **D**, "You will
5: 6 They thought, "**D** cannot get in here.
5: 7 **D** captured the fortress of Zion,
5: 8 On that day, **D** said, "Anyone who
5: 9 **D** then took up residence in the
5:11 king of Tyre sent messengers to **D**,
5:11 and they built a palace for **D**.
5:12 **D** knew that the LORD had established
5:13 **D** took more concubines and wives
5:17 the Philistines heard that **D** had
5:17 but **D** heard about it and went down
5:19 **D** enquired of the LORD, "Shall I go
5:20 **D** went to Baal Perazim, and there he
5:21 and **D** and his men carried them off.
5:23 **D** enquired of the LORD, and he
5:25 **D** did as the LORD commanded him, and
6: 1 **D** again brought together out of
6: 5 **D** and the whole house of Israel were
6: 8 **D** was angry because the LORD's wrath
6: 9 **D** was afraid of the LORD that day
6:12 Now King **D** was told, "The LORD has
6:12 So **D** went down and brought up the
6:14 **D**, wearing a linen ephod, danced
6:16 And when she saw King **D** leaping and
6:17 the tent that **D** had pitched for it,
6:17 and **D** sacrificed burnt offerings and
6:20 **D** returned home to bless his
6:21 **D** said to Michal, "It was before the
7:17 Nathan reported to **D** all the words
7:18 King **D** went in and sat before the
7:20 "What more can **D** say to you? For you
8: 1 In the course of time, **D** defeated
8: 2 **D** also defeated the Moabites. He
8: 2 subject to **D** and brought tribute.
8: 3 Moreover, **D** fought Hadadezer son of
8: 4 **D** captured a thousand of his
8: 5 **D** struck down twenty-two thousand of
8: 6 LORD gave **D** victory wherever he went.
8: 7 **D** took the gold shields that
8: 8 **D** took a great quantity of bronze.
8: 9 Tou king of Hamath heard that **D** had
8:10 he sent his son Joram to King **D** to

2Sa 8:11 King **D** dedicated these articles to
8:13 **D** became famous after he returned
8:14 the Edomites became subject to **D**.
8:14 LORD gave **D** victory wherever he went.
8:15 **D** reigned over all Israel, doing
9: 1 **D** asked, "Is there anyone still left
9: 2 They called him to appear before **D**,
9: 5 King **D** had him brought from Lo Debar,
9: 6 came to **D**, he bowed down to pay him
9: 6 **D** said, "Mephibosheth!" "Your
9: 7 "Don't be afraid," **D** said to him,
10: 2 **D** thought, "I will show kindness to
10: 2 So **D** sent a delegation to express
10: 3 "Do you think **D** is honouring your
10: 3 Hasn't **D** sent them to you to explore
10: 5 **D** was told about this, he sent
10: 7 On hearing this, **D** sent Joab out
10:17 **D** was told of this, he gathered all
10:17 to meet **D** and fought against him.
10:18 and **D** killed seven hundred of their
11: 1 **D** sent Joab out with the king's men
11: 1 But **D** remained in Jerusalem.
11: 2 One evening **D** got up from his bed
11: 3 **D** sent someone to find out about her.
11: 4 **D** sent messengers to get her. She
11: 5 word to **D**, saying, "I am pregnant.
11: 6 **D** sent this word to Joab: "Send me
11: 6 the Hittite." And Joab sent him to **D**.
11: 7 **D** asked him how Joab was, how the
11: 8 **D** said to Uriah, "Go down to your
11:10 **D** was told, "Uriah did not go home,"
11:11 Uriah said to **D**, "The ark and Israel
11:12 **D** said to him, "Stay here one more
11:13 with him, and **D** made him drunk.
11:14 In the morning **D** wrote a letter to
11:18 Joab sent **D** a full account of the
11:22 and when he arrived he told **D**
11:23 The messenger said to **D**, "The men
11:25 **D** told the messenger, "Say this to
11:27 **D** had her brought to his house, and
11:27 But the thing **D** had done displeased
12: 1 The LORD sent Nathan to **D**. When he
12: 5 **D** burned with anger against the man
12: 7 Nathan said to **D**, "You are the man!
12:13 **D** said to Nathan, "I have sinned
12:15 that Uriah's wife had borne to **D**,
12:16 **D** pleaded with God for the child. He
12:18 we spoke to **D** but he would not
12:19 **D** noticed that his servants were
12:20 **D** got up from the ground. After he
12:24 **D** comforted his wife Bathsheba, and
12:27 Joab then sent messengers to **D**,
12:29 **D** mustered the entire army and went
12:31 Then **D** and his entire army returned
13: 1 In the course of time, Amnon son of **D**
13: 1 sister of Absalom son of **D**.
13: 7 **D** sent word to Tamar at the palace:
13:21 King **D** heard all this, he was
13:30 the report came to **D**: "Absalom has
13:37 King **D** mourned for his son every day.
15:13 A messenger came and told **D**, "The
15:14 **D** said to all his officials who were
15:22 **D** said to Ittai, "Go ahead, march on.
15:30 **D** continued up the Mount of Olives,
15:31 Now **D** had been told, "Ahithophel is
15:31 So **D** prayed, "O LORD, turn
15:32 **D** arrived at the summit, where
15:33 **D** said to him, "If you go with me,
16: 1 **D** had gone a short distance beyond
16: 5 King **D** approached Bahurim, a man
16: 6 He pelted **D** and all the king's
16:10 'Curse **D**,' who can ask, 'Why do you
16:11 **D** then said to Abishai and all his
16:13 **D** and his men continued along the
16:23 That was how both **D** and Absalom
17: 1 and set out tonight in pursuit of **D**.
17:16 a message immediately and tell **D**,
17:17 and they were to go and tell King **D**,
17:21 the well and went to inform King **D**.
17:22 **D** and all the people with him set
17:24 **D** went to Mahanaim, and Absalom
17:27 **D** came to Mahanaim, Shobi son of
17:29 milk for **D** and his people to eat.
18: 1 **D** mustered the men who were with him
18: 2 **D** sent the troops out–a third under
18:24 While **D** was sitting between the
2Sa 19:11 King **D** sent this message to Zadok
19:16 the men of Judah to meet King **D**.
19:22 **D** replied, "What do you and I have
19:43 a greater claim on **D** than you have.
20: 1 "We have no share in **D**, no part in
20: 2 all the men of Israel deserted **D** to
20: 3 **D** returned to his palace in
20: 6 **D** said to Abishai, "Now Sheba son of
20:11 whoever is for **D**, let him follow
20:21 hand against the king, against **D**.
21: 1 During the reign of **D**, there was a
21: 1 so **D** sought the face of the LORD.
21: 3 **D** asked the Gibeonites, "What shall
21: 4 you want me to do for you?" **D** asked.
21: 7 between **D** and Jonathan son of Saul.
21:11 **D** was told what Aiah's daughter
21:13 **D** brought the bones of Saul and his
21:15 **D** went down with his men to fight
21:16 a new sword, said he would kill **D**.
21:22 fell at the hands of **D** and his men.
22: 1 **D** sang to the LORD the words of this
22:51 to **D** and his descendants for ever."
23: 1 These are the last words of **D**:
23: 1 "The oracle of **D** son of Jesse, the
23: 9 he was with **D** when they taunted the
23:13 down to **D** at the cave of Adullam,
23:14 At that time **D** was in the stronghold,
23:15 **D** longed for water and said, "Oh,
23:16 Bethlehem and carried it back to **D**.
23:17 lives?" And **D** would not drink it.
23:23 **D** put him in charge of his bodyguard.
24: 1 and he incited **D** against them,
24:10 **D** was conscience-stricken after he
24:11 Before **D** got up the next morning,
24:12 "Go and tell **D**, 'This is what the
24:13 Gad went to **D** and said to him,
24:14 **D** said to Gad, "I am in deep
24:17 **D** saw the angel who was striking
24:18 On that day Gad went to **D** and said
24:19 **D** went up, as the LORD had commanded
24:21 your threshing-floor," **D** answered,
24:22 Araunah said to **D**, "Let my lord the
24:24 So **D** bought the threshing-floor and
24:25 **D** built an altar to the LORD there
1Ki 1: 1 King **D** was old and well advanced in
1:13 Go in to King **D** and say to him, 'My
1:28 King **D** said, "Call in Bathsheba." So
1:31 "May my lord King **D** live for ever!
1:32 King **D** said, "Call in Zadok the
1:37 than the throne of my lord King **D**!"
1:43 lord King **D** has made Solomon king.
1:47 to congratulate our lord King **D**,
2: 1 the time drew near for **D** to die, he
2:10 **D** rested with his fathers and was
2:33 But on **D** and his descendants, his
3:14 and commands as **D** your father did,
5: 1 been on friendly terms with **D**.
5: 7 for he has given **D** a wise son to
6:12 the promise I gave to **D** your father.
8:16 chosen **D** to rule my people Israel.'
8:20 I have succeeded **D** my father and now
9: 4 as **D** your father did, and do all I
9: 5 as I promised **D** your father when I
11: 4 the heart of **D** his father had been.
11: 6 as **D** his father had done.
11:12 for the sake of **D** your father,
11:13 tribe for the sake of **D** my servant
11:15 Earlier when **D** was fighting with
11:21 Hadad heard that **D** rested with his
11:24 **D** destroyed the forces of Zobah;
11:33 laws as **D**, Solomon's father, did.
11:34 life for the sake of **D** my servant,
11:36 so that **D** my servant may always
11:38 and commands, as **D** my servant did,
11:38 enduring as the one I built for **D**
12:16 "What share do we have in **D**, what
12:16 Look after your own house, O **D**!"
15: 3 heart of **D** his forefather had been.
15: 5 For **D** had done what was right in the
2Ki 8:19 for **D** and his descendants for ever.
11:10 shields that had belonged to King **D**
16: 2 Unlike **D** his father, he did not do
19:34 and for the sake of **D** my servant."
21: 7 of which the LORD had said to **D** and
1Ch 2:15 the sixth Ozem and the seventh **D**.
3: 1 These were the sons of **D** born to him
1Ch 3: 4 These six were born to **D** in Hebron,
3: 4 **D** reigned in Jerusalem for
3: 9 All these were the sons of **D**,
4:31 their towns until the reign of **D**.
6:31 These are the men **D** put in charge of
7: 2 During the reign of **D**, the
9:22 of trust by **D** and Samuel the seer.
10:14 the kingdom over to **D** son of Jesse.
11: 1 All Israel came together to **D** at
11: 3 Israel had come to King **D** at Hebron,
11: 3 and they anointed **D** king over Israel,
11: 4 **D** and all the Israelites marched to
11: 5 said to **D**, "You will not get in here.
11: 5 **D** captured the fortress of Zion,
11: 6 **D** had said, "Whoever leads the
11: 7 **D** then took up residence in the
11: 9 **D** became more and more powerful,
11:13 He was with **D** at Pas Dammim when the
11:15 came to **D** to the rock at the cave
11:16 At that time **D** was in the stronghold,
11:17 **D** longed for water and said, "Oh,
11:18 Bethlehem and carried it back to **D**.
11:19 bring it back, **D** would not drink it.
11:25 **D** put him in charge of his bodyguard.
12: 1 These were the men who came to **D** at
12: 8 Some Gadites defected to **D** at his
12:16 also came to **D** in his stronghold.
12:17 **D** went out to meet them and said to
12:18 "We are yours, O **D**! We are with you,
12:18 So **D** received them and made them
12:19 the men of Manasseh defected to **D**
12:20 **D** went to Ziklag, these were the men
12:21 They helped **D** against raiding bands,
12:22 Day after day men came to help **D**,
12:23 men armed for battle who came to **D**
12:31 by name to come and make **D** king
12:33 to help **D** with undivided loyalty
12:38 to make **D** king over all Israel.
12:38 also of one mind to make **D** king.
12:39 The men spent three days there with **D**
13: 1 **D** conferred with each of his
13: 5 **D** assembled all the Israelites, from
13: 6 **D** and all the Israelites with him
13: 8 **D** and all the Israelites were
13:11 **D** was angry because the LORD's wrath
13:12 **D** was afraid of God that day and
14: 1 king of Tyre sent messengers to **D**,
14: 2 **D** knew that the LORD had established
14: 3 In Jerusalem **D** took more wives and
14: 8 the Philistines heard that **D** had
14: 8 but **D** heard about it and went out to
14:10 **D** enquired of God: "Shall I go and
14:11 **D** and his men went up to
14:12 and **D** gave orders to burn them in
14:14 **D** enquired of God again, and God
14:16 **D** did as God commanded him, and they
15: 1 After **D** had constructed buildings
15: 2 **D** said, "No-one but the Levites may
15: 3 **D** assembled all Israel in Jerusalem
15:11 **D** summoned Zadok and Abiathar the
15:16 **D** told the leaders of the Levites to
15:25 **D** and the elders of Israel and the
15:27 Now **D** was clothed in a robe of fine
15:27 **D** also wore a linen ephod.
15:29 And when she saw King **D** dancing and
16: 1 the tent that **D** had pitched for it,
16: 2 After **D** had finished sacrificing the
16: 7 That day **D** first committed to Asaph
16:37 **D** left Asaph and his associates
16:39 **D** left Zadok the priest and his
16:43 **D** returned home to bless his family.
17: 1 After **D** was settled in his palace,
17: 2 Nathan replied to **D**, "Whatever you
17:15 Nathan reported to **D** all the words
17:16 King **D** went in and sat before the
17:18 "What more can **D** say to you for
18: 1 **D** defeated the Philistines and
18: 2 **D** also defeated the Moabites, and
18: 3 **D** fought Hadadezer king of Zobah,
18: 4 **D** captured a thousand of his
18: 5 **D** struck down twenty-two thousand of
18: 6 gave **D** victory everywhere he went.
18: 7 **D** took the gold shields carried by
18: 8 **D** took a great quantity of bronze
18: 9 Tou king of Hamath heard that **D** had
18:10 he sent his son Hadoram to King **D** to

1Ch 18:11 King **D** dedicated these articles to
18:13 the Edomites became subject to **D**.
18:13 gave **D** victory everywhere he went.
18:14 **D** reigned over all Israel, doing
19: 2 **D** thought, "I will show kindness to
19: 2 So **D** sent a delegation to express
19: 3 "Do you think **D** is honouring your
19: 5 someone came and told **D** about the
19: 8 On hearing this, **D** sent Joab out
19:17 **D** was told of this, he gathered all
19:17 **D** formed his lines to meet the
19:18 and **D** killed seven thousand of
19:19 made peace with **D** and became
20: 1 it, but **D** remained in Jerusalem.
20: 2 **D** took the crown from the head of
20: 3 **D** did this to all the Ammonite towns.
20: 3 Then **D** and his entire army returned
20: 8 fell at the hands of **D** and his men.
21: 1 **D** to take a census of Israel.
21: 2 **D** said to Joab and the commanders of
21: 5 the number of the fighting men to **D**:
21: 8 **D** said to God, "I have sinned
21:10 "Go and tell **D**, 'This is what the
21:11 Gad went to **D** and said to him, "This
21:13 **D** said to Gad, "I am in deep
21:16 **D** looked up and saw the angel of the
21:16 Then **D** and the elders, clothed in
21:17 **D** said to God, "Was it not I who
21:18 LORD ordered Gad to tell **D** to go up
21:19 **D** went up in obedience to the word
21:21 **D** approached, and when Araunah
21:21 bowed down before **D** with his face
21:22 **D** said to him, "Let me have the site
21:23 Araunah said to **D**, "Take it! Let my
21:24 King **D** replied to Araunah, "No, I
21:25 **D** paid Araunah six hundred shekels
21:26 **D** built an altar to the LORD there
21:28 when **D** saw that the LORD had
21:30 **D** could not go before it to enquire
22: 1 **D** said, "The house of the LORD God
22: 2 **D** gave orders to assemble the aliens
22: 4 brought large numbers of them to **D**.
22: 5 **D** said, "My son Solomon is young and
22: 5 So **D** made extensive preparations
22: 7 **D** said to Solomon: "My son, I had it
22:17 **D** ordered all the leaders of Israel
23: 1 **D** was old and full of years, he made
23: 4 **D** said, "Of these, twenty-four
23: 6 **D** divided the Levites into groups
23:25 For **D** had said, "Since the LORD, the
23:27 to the last instructions of **D**,
24: 3 **D** separated them into divisions for
24:31 in the presence of King **D** and of
25: 1 **D**, together with the commanders of
26:26 for the things dedicated by King **D**,
26:32 and King **D** put them in charge of the
27:18 over Judah: Elihu, a brother of **D**;
27:23 **D** did not take the number of the men
27:24 in the book of the annals of King **D**.
28: 1 **D** summoned all the officials of
28: 2 King **D** rose to his feet and said:
28:11 **D** gave his son Solomon the plans for
28:19 "All this," **D** said, "I have in
28:20 **D** also said to Solomon his son, "Be
29: 1 King **D** said to the whole assembly:
29: 9 **D** the king also rejoiced greatly.
29:10 **D** praised the LORD in the presence
29:20 **D** said to the whole assembly,
29:26 **D** son of Jesse was king over all
2Ch 1: 4 Now **D** had brought up the ark of God
1: 8 "You have shown great kindness to **D**
2:12 He has given King **D** a wise son,
2:14 those of my lord, **D** your father.
3: 1 Jebusite, the place provided by **D**.
6: 6 chosen **D** to rule my people Israel.'
6:10 I have succeeded **D** my father and now
6:42 love promised to **D** your servant."
7: 6 which King **D** had made for praising
7:10 good things the LORD had done for **D**
7:17 if you walk before me as **D** your
7:18 as I covenanted with **D** your father
8:11 in the palace of **D** king of Israel,
8:14 what **D** the man of God had ordered.
10:16 "What share do we have in **D**, what
10:16 Look after your own house, O **D**!"
11:17 walking in the ways of **D** and
2Ch 13: 5 given the kingship of Israel to **D**
21: 7 covenant the LORD had made with **D**,
23: 3 concerning the descendants of **D**.
23: 9 shields that had belonged to King **D**
23:18 to whom **D** had made assignments in
23:18 and singing, as **D** had ordered.
28: 1 Unlike **D** his father, he did not do
29:25 lyres in the way prescribed by **D** and
29:27 the instruments of **D** king of Israel.
29:30 words of **D** and of Asaph the seer.
33: 7 of which God had said to **D** and to
35: 4 written by **D** king of Israel
35:15 were in the places prescribed by **D**,
Ezr 3:10 as prescribed by **D** king of Israel.
8: 2 of the descendants of **D**, Hattush
8:20 a body that **D** and the officials had
Ne 3:16 to a point opposite the tombs of **D**,
12:24 as prescribed by **D** the man of God.
12:36 prescribed by **D** the man of God.
12:45 commands of **D** and his son Solomon.
12:46 in the days of **D** and Asaph,
Ps 3: T A psalm of **D**. When he fled from his
4: T stringed instruments. A psalm of **D**.
5: T For flutes. A psalm of **D**.
6: T to sheminith. A psalm of **D**.
7: T A shiggaion of **D**, which he sang to
8: T According to gittith. A psalm of **D**.
9: T Death of the Son". A psalm of **D**.
11: T For the director of music. Of **D**.
12: T to sheminith. A psalm of **D**.
13: T director of music. A psalm of **D**.
14: T For the director of music. Of **D**.
15: T A psalm of **D**.
16: T A miktam of **D**.
17: T A prayer of **D**.
18: T Of **D** the servant of the LORD.
18:50 to **D** and his descendants for ever.
19: T director of music. A psalm of **D**.
20: T director of music. A psalm of **D**.
21: T director of music. A psalm of **D**.
22: T Doe of the morning". A psalm of **D**.
23: T A psalm of **D**.
24: T Of **D**. A psalm.
25: T Of **D**.
26: T Of **D**.
27: T Of **D**.
28: T Of **D**.
29: T A psalm of **D**.
30: T the dedication of the temple. Of **D**.
31: T director of music. A psalm of **D**.
32: T Of **D**. A maskil.
34: T Of **D**. When he pretended to be insane
35: T Of **D**.
36: T Of **D** the servant of the LORD.
37: T Of **D**.
38: T A psalm of **D**. A petition.
39: T For Jeduthun. A psalm of **D**.
40: T For the director of music. Of **D**.
41: T director of music. A psalm of **D**.
51: T A psalm of **D**. When the prophet
51: T after **D** had committed adultery with
52: T A maskil of **D**. When Doeg the
52: T "**D** has gone to the house of
53: T to mahalath. A maskil of **D**.
54: T A maskil of **D**. When the Ziphites
54: T "Is not **D** hiding among us?"
55: T instruments. A maskil of **D**.
56: T Of **D**. A miktam. When the
57: T Of **D**. A miktam. When he had
58: T Of **D**. A miktam.
59: T Of **D**. A miktam. When Saul had
60: T A miktam of **D**. For teaching.
61: T With stringed instruments. Of **D**.
62: T For Jeduthun. A psalm of **D**.
63: T A psalm of **D**. When he was in the
64: T director of music. A psalm of **D**.
65: T A psalm of **D**. A song.
68: T Of **D**. A psalm. A song.
69: T To ⌊the tune of⌋ "Lilies". Of **D**.
70: T For the director of music. Of **D**.
72:20 the prayers of **D** son of Jesse.
78:70 He chose **D** his servant and took him
78:72 **D** shepherded them with integrity of
86: T A prayer of **D**.
89: 3 one, I have sworn to **D** my servant,
89:20 I have found **D** my servant; with my
Ps 89:35 holiness—and I will not lie to **D**—
89:49 in your faithfulness you swore to **D**?
101: T Of **D**. A psalm.
103: T Of **D**.
108: T A song. A psalm of **D**.
109: T For the director of music. Of **D**.
110: T Of **D**. A psalm.
122: T A song of ascents. Of **D**.
124: T A song of ascents. Of **D**.
131: T A song of ascents. Of **D**.
132: 1 O LORD, remember **D** and all the
132:10 For the sake of **D** your servant, do
132:11 The LORD swore an oath to **D**, a sure
132:17 "Here I will make a horn grow for **D**
133: T A song of ascents. Of **D**.
138: T Of **D**.
139: T For the director of music. Of **D**.
140: T director of music. A psalm of **D**.
141: T A psalm of **D**.
142: T A maskil of **D**. When he was in the
143: T A psalm of **D**.
144: T Of **D**.
145: T A psalm of praise. Of **D**.
SS 4: 4 Your neck is like the tower of **D**,
Isa 29: 1 Ariel, the city where **D** settled!
37:35 and for the sake of **D** my servant!"
55: 3 you, my faithful love promised to **D**.
Jer 22:30 none will sit on the throne of **D**
23: 5 "when I will raise up to **D** a
30: 9 the LORD their God and **D** their king,
33:17 '**D** will never fail to have a man to
33:21 my covenant with **D** my servant—and
33:21 **D** will no longer have a descendant
33:22 I will make the descendants of **D** my
33:26 of Jacob and **D** my servant and will
36:30 no-one to sit on the throne of **D**;
Eze 37:25 and **D** my servant will be their
Hos 3: 5 the LORD their God and **D** their king.
Am 6: 5 You strum away on your harps like **D**
Zec 12: 8 feeblest among them will be like **D**,
Mt 1: 6 Jesse the father of King **D**.
1: 6 **D** was the father of Solomon whose
1:17 in all from Abraham to **D**,
1:17 fourteen from **D** to the exile to
12: 3 "Haven't you read what **D** did when
22:43 "How is it then that **D**, speaking by
22:45 If then **D** calls him 'Lord', how can
Mk 2:25 "Have you never read what **D** did when
12:36 **D** himself, speaking by the Holy
12:37 **D** himself calls him 'Lord'. How then
Lk 1:27 man named Joseph, a descendant of **D**.
2: 4 to Bethlehem the town of **D**, because
2: 4 belonged to the house and line of **D**.
2:11 Today in the town of **D** a Saviour has
6: 3 "Have you never read what **D** did when
20:42 **D** himself declares in the Book of
20:44 **D** calls him 'Lord'. How then can he
Jn 7:42 Bethlehem, the town where **D** lived?"
Ac 1:16 the mouth of **D** concerning Judas,
2:25 **D** said about him: "I saw the Lord
2:29 the patriarch **D** died and was buried,
2:34 For **D** did not ascend to heaven, and
7:45 in the land until the time of **D**,
13:22 removing Saul, he made **D** their king.
13:22 'I have found **D** son of Jesse a man
13:34 and sure blessings promised to **D**.'
13:36 "For when **D** had served God's purpose
Ro 1: 3 human nature was a descendant of **D**,
4: 6 **D** says the same thing when he speaks
11: 9 **D** says: "May their table become a
2Ti 2: 8 from the dead, descended from **D**.
Heb 4: 7 long time later he spoke through **D**,
11:32 Jephthah, **D**, Samuel and the prophets,
Rev 3: 7 and true, who holds the key of **D**.
5: 5 Judah, the Root of **D**, has triumphed.
22:16 am the Root and the Offspring of **D**,

David's (David)

1Sa 17:28 Eliab, **D** oldest brother, heard him
19:11 Saul sent men to **D** house to watch it
19:11 But Michal, **D** wife, warned him, "If
20:15 cut off every one of **D** enemies from
20:16 the LORD call **D** enemies to account."
20:25 next to Saul, but **D** place was empty.
20:27 the month, **D** place was empty again.
23: 3 **D** men said to him, "Here in Judah we

1Sa 25: 9 **D** men arrived, they gave Nabal this
25: 9 gave Nabal this message in **D** name.
25:10 Nabal answered **D** servants, "Who is
25:12 **D** men turned round and went back.
25:42 went with **D** messengers and became
25:44 had given his daughter Michal, **D** wife
26:17 Saul recognised **D** voice and said,
30: 5 **D** two wives had been captured
30:20 saying, "This is **D** plunder.
30:22 among **D** followers said, "Because
2Sa 2:13 Joab son of Zeruiah and **D** men went
2:17 of Israel were defeated by **D** men.
2:30 of **D** men were found missing.
2:31 **D** men had killed 360 Benjamites who
3: 5 the sixth, Ithream the son of **D** wife
3:10 establish **D** throne over Israel and
3:22 Just then **D** men and Joab returned
5: 8 'lame and blind' who are **D** enemies.
8:18 and **D** sons were royal advisers.
9:11 ate at **D** table like one of the
10: 2 When **D** men came to the land of the
10: 4 Hanun seized **D** men, shaved off half
10: 6 had become an offence to **D** nostrils,
11:13 At **D** invitation, he ate and drank
11:17 some of the men in **D** army fell;
12:18 **D** servants were afraid to tell him
12:30 stones—and it was placed on **D** head.
13: 3 Jonadab son of Shimeah, **D** brother.
13:32 Jonadab son of Shimeah, **D** brother,
15:12 **D** counsellor, to come from Giloh,
15:37 **D** friend Hushai arrived at Jerusalem
16: 6 guard were on **D** right and left.
16:16 Hushai the Arkite, **D** friend, went to
18: 7 of Israel was defeated by **D** men,
18: 9 Now Absalom happened to meet **D** men.
20:26 Ira the Jairite was **D** priest.
21:17 son of Zeruiah came to **D** rescue;
21:17 Then **D** men swore to him, saying,
21:21 of Shimeah, **D** brother, killed him.
23: 8 These are the names of **D** mighty men:
24:11 had come to Gad the prophet, **D** seer:
1Ki 1: 8 Shimei and Rei and **D** special guard
1:11 king without our lord **D** knowing it?
1:38 put Solomon on King **D** mule and
2:45 and **D** throne will remain secure
11:39 I will humble **D** descendants because
15: 4 Nevertheless, for **D** sake the LORD
1Ch 11:10 were the chiefs of **D** mighty men
11:11 this is the list of **D** mighty men:
14:17 **D** fame spread throughout every land,
18:17 and **D** sons were chief officials at
19: 2 When **D** men came to Hanun in the land
19: 4 Hanun seized **D** men, shaved them, cut
19: 6 had become an offence to **D** nostrils,
20: 2 stones—and it was placed on **D** head.
20: 7 of Shimea, **D** brother, killed him.
21: 9 The LORD said to Gad, **D** seer,
26:31 In the fortieth year of **D** reign a
27:31 in charge of King **D** property.
27:32 Jonathan, **D** uncle, was a counsellor,
29:24 as well as all of King **D** sons,
29:29 for the events of King **D** reign, from
2Ch 11:18 who was the daughter of **D** son
13: 8 is in the hands of **D** descendants.
29:26 stood ready with **D** instruments
32:33 the tombs of **D** descendants are.
Ps 59: T sent men to watch **D** house in order
Isa 9: 7 He will reign on **D** throne and over
Jer 13:13 the kings who sit on **D** throne
17:25 kings who sit on **D** throne will come
22: 2 of Judah, you who sit on **D** throne
22: 4 then kings who sit on **D** throne will
29:16 about the king who sits on **D** throne
33:15 righteous Branch sprout from **D** line;
Am 9:11 day I will restore **D** fallen tent.
Jn 7:42 from **D** family and from Bethlehem,
Ac 15:16 return and rebuild **D** fallen tent.

Dawn (Dawned, Dawns)

Ge 19:15 With the coming of **d**, the angels
Jdg 16: 2 night, saying, "At **d** we'll kill him.
19:25 the night, and at **d** they let her go.
1Sa 14:36 by night and plunder them till **d**,
Ne 4:21 light of **d** till the stars came out.
Job 3: 9 and not see the first rays of **d**,
Job 4:20 Between **d** and dusk they are broken
7: 4 night drags on, and I toss till **d**.
38:12 morning, or shown the **d** its place,
41:18 his eyes are like the rays of **d**.
Ps 37: 6 your righteousness shine like the **d**,
57: 8 harp and lyre! I will awaken the **d**.
108: 2 harp and lyre! I will awaken the **d**.
110: 3 from the womb of the **d** you will
119:147 I rise before **d** and cry for help;
139: 9 If I rise on the wings of the **d**, if
Pr 4:18 is like the first gleam of **d**,
SS 6:10 Who is this that appears like the **d**,
Isa 8:20 this word, they have no light of **d**.
14:12 O morning star, son of the **d**! You
38:13 I waited patiently till **d**, but like
58: 8 light will break forth like the **d**,
60: 3 kings to the brightness of your **d**.
62: 1 righteousness shines out like the **d**,
Da 6:19 At the first light of **d**, the king
Joel 2: 2 Like **d** spreading across the
Am 4:13 he who turns **d** to darkness, and
5: 8 who turns blackness into **d** and
Jnh 4: 7 at **d** the next day God provided a
Mt 28: 1 at **d** on the first day of the week,
Mk 13:35 or when the cock crows, or at **d**.
Jn 8: 2 At **d** he appeared again in the temple
Ac 27:33 Just before **d** Paul urged them all to

Dawned (Dawn)

Ge 44: 3 morning **d**, the men were sent on
Dt 33: 2 Sinai and **d** over them from Seir;
Isa 9: 2 the shadow of death a light has **d**.
Mt 4:16 the shadow of death a light has **d**."
Ac 12:12 this had **d** on him, he went to the

Dawns (Dawn)

Ps 65: 8 where morning **d** and evening fades
112: 4 Even in darkness light **d** for the
Hos 10:15 When that day **d**, the king of Israel
2Pe 1:19 until the day **d** and the morning star

Day (Daily, *Day of Atonement, Day of judgment, Day of the Lord, Day of the Lord, Day of wrath*, Day's, Daybreak, Daylight, Days, Daytime, *Last day, Seventh day*, Midday, Seven-day, *Third day*, Three-day)

Ge 1: 5 God called the light "**d**", and the
1: 5 and there was morning—the first **d**.
1: 8 and there was morning—the second **d**.
1:14 to separate the **d** from the night,
1:16 greater light to govern the **d**
1:18 to govern the **d** and the night, and
1:19 and there was morning—the fourth **d**.
1:23 and there was morning—the fifth **d**.
1:31 and there was morning—the sixth **d**.
3: 8 in the garden in the cool of the **d**,
7:11 on the seventeenth **d** of the second
7:11 on that **d** all the springs of the
7:13 On that very **d** Noah and his sons,
8: 4 on the seventeenth **d** of the seventh
8: 5 and on the first **d** of the tenth
8:13 By the first **d** of the first month of
8:14 By the twenty-seventh **d** of the
8:22 **d** and night will never cease."
15:18 On that **d** the LORD made a covenant
17:23 On that very **d** Abraham took his son
17:26 both circumcised on that same **d**.
18: 1 to his tent in the heat of the **d**.
19:31 One **d** the older daughter said to the
19:34 The next **d** the older daughter said
21: 8 and on the **d** Isaac was weaned
22:14 And to this **d** it is said, "On the
26:32 That **d** Isaac's servants came and
26:33 and to this **d** the name of the town
27: 2 and don't know the **d** of my death.
27:45 should I lose both of you in one **d**?"
30:35 That same **d** he removed all the male
31:39 whatever was stolen by **d** or night.
32:32 Therefore to this **d** the Israelites
33:13 driven hard just one **d**, all the
33:16 that **d** Esau started on his way back
35: 3 answered me in the **d** of my distress
35:20 and to this **d** that pillar marks
Ge 39:10 though she spoke to Joseph **d** after **d**,
39:11 One **d** he went into the house to
48:15 my shepherd all my life to this **d**,
48:20 He blessed them that **d** and said, "In
Ex 2:11 One **d**, after Moses had grown up, he
2:13 The next **d** he went out and saw two
5: 6 That same **d** Pharaoh gave this order
5:13 work required of you for each **d**,
5:19 bricks required of you for each **d**."
8:22 "'But on that **d** I will deal
9: 6 the next **d** the LORD did it: All the
9:18 from the **d** it was founded till now.
10: 6 **d** they settled in this land till now.
10:13 land all that **d** and all that night.
10:28 The **d** you see my face you will die."
12: 3 on the tenth **d** of this month each
12: 6 until the fourteenth **d** of the month,
12:14 "This is a **d** you are to commemorate;
12:15 On the first **d** remove the yeast from
12:15 from the first **d** until the seventh
12:16 On the first **d** hold a sacred
12:17 because it was on this very **d** that I
12:17 Celebrate this **d** as a lasting
12:18 the evening of the fourteenth **d**
12:18 the evening of the twenty-first **d**.
12:41 to the very **d**, all the LORD's
12:51 on that very **d** the LORD brought the
13: 3 "Commemorate this **d**, the **d** you came
13: 8 On that **d** tell your son, 'I do this
13:21 By **d** the LORD went ahead of them in
13:21 they could travel by **d** or night.
13:22 Neither the pillar of cloud by **d** nor
14:30 That **d** the LORD saved Israel from
16: 1 on the fifteenth **d** of the second
16: 4 each **d** and gather enough for that **d**.
16: 5 On the sixth **d** they are to prepare
16:22 On the sixth **d**, they gathered twice
16:23 'Tomorrow is to be a **d** of rest, a
16:29 on the sixth **d** he gives you bread
16:30 the people rested on the seventh **d**.
18:13 The next **d** Moses took his seat to
19: 1 on the very **d**—they came to the
19:11 because on that **d** the LORD will come
20: 8 "Remember the Sabbath **d** by keeping
20:11 the LORD blessed the Sabbath **d** and
21:21 the slave gets up after a **d** or two,
22:30 but give them to me on the eighth **d**.
29:36 Sacrifice a bull each **d** as a sin
29:38 on the altar regularly each **d**:
31:14 whoever does any work on that **d**
31:15 does any work on the Sabbath **d**
32: 6 the next **d** the people rose early and
32:28 and that **d** about three thousand of
32:29 and he has blessed you this **d**."
32:30 The next **d** Moses said to the people,
35: 2 your holy **d**, a Sabbath of rest to
35: 3 of your dwellings on the Sabbath **d**."
40: 2 on the first **d** of the first month.
40:17 on the first **d** of the first month
40:37 not set out—until the **d** it lifted.
40:38 LORD was over the tabernacle by **d**,
Lev 6: 5 to the owner on the **d** he presents
6:20 to the LORD on the **d** he is anointed:
7:15 be eaten on the **d** it is offered;
7:16 be eaten on the **d** he offers it,
7:16 over may be eaten on the next **d**.
7:35 his sons on the **d** they were
7:36 On the **d** they were anointed, the
7:38 on the **d** he commanded the Israelites
8:35 the Tent of Meeting **d** and night for
9: 1 On the eighth **d** Moses summoned Aaron
12: 3 On the eighth **d** the boy is to be
14:10 "On the eighth **d** he must bring two
14:23 "On the eighth **d** he must bring them
15:14 On the eighth **d** he must take two
15:29 On the eighth **d** she must take two
16:29 On the tenth **d** of the seventh month
16:30 on this **d** atonement will be made for
19: 6 **d** you sacrifice it or on the next **d**;
22:27 From the eighth **d** on, it will be
22:28 a sheep and its young on the same **d**.
22:30 must be eaten that same **d**; leave
23: 3 of rest, a **d** of sacred assembly.
23: 5 the fourteenth **d** of the first month.
23: 6 On the fifteenth **d** of that month the
23: 7 On the first **d** hold a sacred

Lev 23:11 wave it on the **d** after the Sabbath.
23:12 On the **d** you wave the sheaf, you
23:14 until the very **d** you bring this
23:15 "From the **d** after the Sabbath,
23:15 the **d** you brought the sheaf of the
23:16 the **d** after the seventh Sabbath
23:21 On that same **d** you are to proclaim a
23:24 'On the first **d** of the seventh month
23:24 month you are to have a **d** of rest,
23:27 "The tenth **d** of this seventh month
23:28 Do no work on that **d**, because it is
23:29 on that **d** must be cut off from his
23:30 anyone who does any work on that **d**.
23:32 From the evening of the ninth **d** of
23:34 'On the fifteenth **d** of the seventh
23:35 The first **d** is a sacred assembly; do
23:36 and on the eighth **d** hold a sacred
23:37 drink offerings required for each **d**.
23:39 "'So beginning with the fifteenth **d**
23:39 the first **d** is a **d** of rest, and the
23:39 the eighth **d** also is a day of rest.
23:40 On the first **d** you are to take
25: 9 on the tenth **d** of the seventh month;
27:23 must pay its value on that **d** as
Nu 1: 1 on the first **d** of the second month
1:18 on the first **d** of the second month.
6: 9 his head on the **d** of his cleansing
6:10 on the eighth **d** he must bring two
6:11 same **d** he is to consecrate his head.
7:11 "Each **d** one leader is to bring his
7:12 brought his offering on the first **d**
7:18 On the second **d** Nethanel son of Zuar,
7:30 On the fourth **d** Elizur son of
7:36 On the fifth **d** Shelumiel son of
7:42 On the sixth **d** Eliasaph son of Deuel,
7:54 On the eighth **d** Gamaliel son of
7:60 On the ninth **d** Abidan son of Gideoni,
7:66 On the tenth **d** Ahiezer son of
7:72 On the eleventh **d** Pagiel son of
7:78 On the twelfth **d** Ahira son of Enan,
9: 3 at twilight on the fourteenth **d** of
9: 5 the fourteenth **d** of the first month.
9: 6 celebrate the Passover on that **d**
9: 6 came to Moses and Aaron that same **d**
9:11 fourteenth **d** of the second month at
9:15 On the **d** the tabernacle, the Tent of
9:21 Whether by **d** or by night, whenever
10:11 On the twentieth **d** of the second
10:34 over them by **d** when they set out
11:19 You will not eat it for just one **d**,
11:32 All that **d** and night and all the
11:32 the next **d** the people went out and
14:14 a pillar of cloud by **d** and a pillar
15:23 from the **d** the LORD gave them and
15:32 gathering wood on the Sabbath **d**.
16:41 The next **d** the whole Israelite
17: 8 The next **d** Moses entered the Tent of
22:30 you have always ridden, to this **d**?
28: 3 as a regular burnt offering each **d**.
28: 9 "'On the Sabbath **d**, make an offering
28:16 "'On the fourteenth **d** of the first
28:17 On the fifteenth **d** of this month
28:18 On the first **d** hold a sacred
28:24 every **d** for seven days as an aroma
28:26 "'On the **d** of firstfruits, when you
29: 1 "'On the first **d** of the seventh
29: 1 a **d** for you to sound the trumpets.
29: 7 "'On the tenth **d** of this seventh
29:12 "'On the fifteenth **d** of the seventh
29:17 "'On the second **d** prepare twelve
29:23 "'On the fourth **d** prepare ten bulls,
29:26 "'On the fifth **d** prepare nine bulls,
29:29 "'On the sixth **d** prepare eight bulls,
29:35 "'On the eighth **d** hold an assembly
30:14 nothing to her about it from **d** to **d**,
32:10 The LORD's anger was aroused that **d**
33: 3 the fifteenth **d** of the first month,
33: 3 month, the **d** after the Passover.
33:38 where he died on the first **d** of the
Dt 1: 3 In the fortieth year, on the first **d**
1:33 fire by night and in a cloud by **d**,
2:22 have lived in their place to this **d**.
2:25 This very **d** I will begin to put the
3:14 so that to this **d** Bashan is called
4:10 Remember the **d** you stood before the
4:15 the **d** the LORD spoke to you at
Dt 4:26 as witnesses against you this **d**
4:32 from the **d** God created man on the
4:39 Acknowledge and take to heart this **d**
5:12 "Observe the Sabbath **d** by keeping it
5:15 you to observe the Sabbath **d**.
8:11 decrees that I am giving you this **d**.
9: 7 From the **d** you left Egypt until you
9:10 the fire, on the **d** of the assembly.
10: 4 the fire, on the **d** of the assembly.
16: 4 of the first **d** remain until morning.
18:16 the **d** of the assembly when you said,
21:23 Be sure to bury him that same **d**,
24:15 Pay him his wages each **d** before
26:16 The LORD your God commands you this **d**
26:17 You have declared this **d** that the
26:18 the LORD has declared this **d** that
27:11 On the same **d** Moses commanded the
28:13 I give you this **d** and carefully
28:29 **d** after **d** you will be oppressed and
28:32 eyes watching for them **d** after **d**,
28:66 filled with dread both night and **d**,
29: 4 to this **d** the LORD has not given you
29:12 the LORD is making with you this **d**
29:13 to confirm you this **d** as his people,
30:18 I declare to you this **d** that you
30:19 This **d** I call heaven and earth as
31:14 "Now the **d** of your death is near.
31:17 On that **d** I will become angry with
31:17 and on that **d** they will ask, 'Have
31:18 certainly hide my face on that **d**
31:22 Moses wrote down this song that **d**
32:35 their **d** of disaster is near and
32:46 solemnly declared to you this **d**,
32:48 On that same **d** the LORD told Moses,
33:12 for he shields him all **d** long, and
34: 6 to this **d** no-one knows where his
Jos 1: 8 mouth; meditate on it **d** and night,
4: 9 And they are there to this **d**.
4:14 That **d** the LORD exalted Joshua in
4:19 On the tenth **d** of the first month
5: 9 has been called Gilgal to this **d**.
5:10 On the evening of the fourteenth **d**
5:11 The **d** after the Passover, that very **d**
5:12 The manna stopped the **d** after they
6:10 until the **d** I tell you to shout.
6:14 on the second **d** they marched around
6:25 among the Israelites to this **d**.
7:26 of rocks, which remains to this **d**.
8:25 fell that **d**—all the people of Ai.
8:28 ruins, a desolate place to this **d**.
8:29 over it, which remains to this **d**.
9:12 on the **d** we left to come to you.
9:27 That **d** he made the Gibeonites
9:27 And that is what they are to this **d**.
10:12 On the **d** the LORD gave the Amorites
10:13 delayed going down about a full **d**.
10:14 There has never been a **d** like it
10:14 a **d** when the LORD listened to a man.
10:27 rocks, which are there to this **d**.
10:28 That **d** Joshua took Makkedah. He put
10:32 and Joshua took it on the second **d**.
10:35 They captured it that same **d** and put
13:13 live among the Israelites to this **d**.
14: 9 on that **d** Moses swore to me, 'The
14:11 today as the **d** Moses sent me out;
14:12 that the LORD promised me that **d**.
15:18 One **d** when she came to Othniel, she
15:63 to this **d** the Jebusites live there
16:10 to this **d** the Canaanites live among
22: 3 For a long time now–to this very **d**–
22:17 Up to this very **d** we have not
22:22 to the LORD, do not spare us this **d**.
22:24 that some **d** your descendants might
23: 9 to this **d** no-one has been able to
24:15 then choose for yourselves this **d**
24:25 On that **d** Joshua made a covenant for
Jdg 1:14 One **d** when she came to Othniel, she
1:21 to this **d** the Jebusites live there
1:26 it Luz, which is its name to this **d**.
3:30 That **d** Moab was made subject to
4:14 "Go! This is the **d** the LORD has
4:23 On that **d** God subdued Jabin, the
5: 1 On that **d** Deborah and Barak son of
6:24 To this **d** it stands in Ophrah of the
6:32 that **d** they called Gideon
6:38 Gideon rose early the next **d**; he
Jdg 9: 8 One **d** the trees went out to anoint a
9:42 The next **d** the people of Shechem
9:45 All that **d** Abimelech pressed his
10: 4 to this **d** are called Havvoth Jair.
11:27 decide the dispute this **d** between
13: 7 birth until the **d** of his death.'"
13:10 man who appeared to me the other **d**!"
14:15 On the fourth **d**, they said to Samson'
16: 1 One **d** Samson went to Gaza, where he
16:16 she prodded him **d** after **d** until he
18:12 is called Mahaneh Dan to this **d**.
19: 5 On the fourth **d** they got up early
19: 8 On the morning of the fifth **d**, when
19: 9 night here; the **d** is nearly over.
19:11 Jebus and the **d** was almost gone,
19:30 not since the **d** the Israelites came
20:21 Israelites on the battlefield that **d**.
20:22 stationed themselves the first **d**.
20:24 drew near to Benjamin the second **d**.
20:26 They fasted that **d** until evening and
20:35 and on that **d** the Israelites struck
20:46 On that **d** twenty-five thousand
21: 4 Early the next **d** the people built an
Ru 3: 1 One **d** Naomi her mother-in-law said
4: 5 Boaz said, "On the **d** you buy the
4:14 "Praise be to the LORD, who this **d**
1Sa 1: 4 Whenever the **d** came for Elkanah to
2:34 will both die on the same **d**.
4:12 That same **d** a Benjamite ran from the
4:16 line; I fled from it this very **d**.
5: 3 of Ashdod rose early the next **d**,
5: 5 That is why to this **d** neither the
6:15 On that **d** the people of Beth Shemesh
6:16 then returned that same **d** to Ekron.
6:18 is a witness to this **d** in the field
7: 6 On that **d** they fasted and there they
7:10 But that **d** the LORD thundered with
8: 8 the **d** I brought them up out of
8: 8 Egypt until this **d**, forsaking me
8:18 that **d** comes, you will cry out for
8:18 LORD will not answer you in that **d**."
9:15 Now the **d** before Saul came, the LORD
9:24 " And Saul dined with Samuel that **d**.
10: 9 these signs were fulfilled that **d**.
11:11 The next **d** Saul separated his men
11:11 them until the heat of the **d**.
11:13 this **d** the LORD has rescued Israel."
12: 2 leader from my youth until this **d**.
12: 5 also his anointed is witness this **d**,
12:18 **d** the LORD sent thunder and rain.
13:22 on the **d** of the battle not a soldier
14: 1 One **d** Jonathan son of Saul said to
14:23 the LORD rescued Israel that **d**, and
14:24 of Israel were in distress that **d**,
14:31 That **d**, after the Israelites had
14:37 But God did not answer him that **d**.
15:35 Until the **d** Samuel died, he did not
16:13 and from that **d** on the Spirit of the
17:10 the Philistine said, "This **d** I defy
17:46 This **d** the LORD will hand you over
18: 2 From that **d** Saul kept David with him
18:10 The next **d** an evil spirit from God
19:24 He lay that way all that **d** and night.
20: 5 the evening of the **d** after tomorrow.
20:12 by this time the **d** after tomorrow!
20:19 The **d** after tomorrow, towards
20:26 Saul said nothing that **d**, for he
20:27 the next **d**, the second **d** of the
20:34 second **d** of the month he did not
21: 6 bread on the **d** it was taken away.
21: 7 of Saul's servants was there that **d**,
21:10 That **d** David fled from Saul and went
22:15 Was that **d** the first time I enquired
22:18 That **d** he killed eighty-five men who
22:22 "That **d**, when Doeg the Edomite was
23:14 **D** after **d** Saul searched for him, but
24: 4 "This is the **d** the LORD spoke of
24:10 This **d** you have seen with your own
25:16 Night and **d** they were a wall around
25:33 for keeping me from bloodshed this **d**
27: 6 on that **d** Achish gave him Ziklag,
28:20 eaten nothing all that **d** and night.
29: 3 and from the **d** he left Saul until
29: 6 From the **d** you came to me until now,
29: 8 from the **d** I came to you until now?
30:17 until the evening of the next **d**,

1Sa 30:25 for Israel from that **d** to this.
31: 6 his men died together that same **d**.
31: 8 The next **d**, when the Philistines
2Sa 2:17 The battle that **d** was very fierce,
3: 8 This very **d** I am loyal to the house
3:35 eat something while it was still **d**;
3:37 on that **d** all the people and all
3:38 man has fallen in Israel this **d**?
4: 3 lived there as aliens to this **d**.
4: 5 arrived there in the heat of the **d**
4: 8 This **d** the LORD has avenged my lord
5: 8 On that **d**, David said, "Anyone who
6: 8 and to this **d** that place is called
6: 9 David was afraid of the LORD that **d**
6:23 no children to the **d** of her death.
7: 6 from the **d** I brought the Israelites
7: 6 Israelites up out of Egypt to this **d**.
11:12 "Stay here one more **d**, and tomorrow
11:12 in Jerusalem that **d** and the next.
13:32 **d** that Amnon raped his sister Tamar.
13:37 David mourned for his son every **d**.
18: 7 the casualties that **d** were great
18: 8 more lives that **d** than the sword.
18:18 called Absalom's Monument to this **d**.
19: 2 the victory that **d** was turned into
19: 2 because on that **d** the troops heard
19: 3 The men stole into the city that **d**
19:19 **d** my lord the king left Jerusalem.
19:22 This **d** you have become my
19:24 the **d** the king left until the **d** he
20: 3 till the **d** of their death, living
21:10 birds of the air touch them by **d**
22:19 They confronted me in the **d** of my
23:10 about a great victory that **d**.
23:20 pit on a snowy **d** and killed a lion.
24:18 On that **d** Gad went to David and said
1Ki 2: 8 on me the **d** I went to Mahanaim.
2:37 The **d** you leave and cross the Kidron
2:42 'On the **d** you leave to go anywhere
3: 6 to sit on his throne this very **d**.
8:16 'Since the **d** I brought my people
8:28 is praying in your presence this **d**.
8:29 towards this temple night and **d**,
8:59 to the LORD our God **d** and night,
8:64 On that same **d** the king consecrated
8:66 On the following **d** he sent the
9:13 Cabul, a name they have to this **d**.
9:21 labour force, as it is to this **d**.
10:12 been imported or seen since that **d**.)
12:19 the house of David to this **d**.
12:32 the fifteenth **d** of the eighth month,
12:33 On the fifteenth **d** of the eighth
13: 3 That same **d** the man of God gave a
13:11 man of God had done there that **d**.
14:14 This is the **d**! What? Yes, even now.
16:16 Israel that very **d** there in the camp.
17:14 **d** the LORD gives rain on the land.'"
17:15 So there was food every **d** for Elijah
20:29 the Aramean foot soldiers in one **d**.
21: 9 "Proclaim a **d** of fasting and seat
21:29 not bring this disaster in his **d**,
22:25 **d** you go to hide in an inner room."
22:35 All **d** long the battle raged, and the
2Ki 2:22 has remained wholesome to this **d**,
4: 8 One **d** Elisha went to Shunem. And a
4:11 One **d** when Elisha came, he went up
4:18 The child grew, and one **d** he went
6:29 The next **d** I said to her, 'Give up
7: 9 This is a **d** of good news and we are
8: 6 from the **d** she left the country
8:15 the next **d** he took a thick cloth,
8:22 To this **d** Edom has been in rebellion
10:27 used it for a latrine to this **d**.
13:23 To this **d** he has been unwilling to
14: 7 Joktheel, the name it has to this **d**.
15: 5 with leprosy until the **d** he died,
16: 6 Elath and have lived there to this **d**.
17:34 To this **d** they persist in their
17:41 To this **d** their children and
19: 3 This **d** is a **d** of distress and rebuke
19:37 One **d**, while he was worshipping in
20:17 have stored up until this **d**,
21:15 from the **d** their forefathers came
21:15 came out of Egypt until this **d**."
25: 1 on the tenth **d** of the tenth month,
25: 3 By the ninth **d** of the fourth month
2Ki 25:27 prison on the twenty-seventh **d** of
25:30 **D** by **d** the king gave Jehoiachin a
1Ch 4:41 them, as is evident to this **d**.
4:43 and they have lived there to this **d**.
5:26 of Gozan, where they are to this **d**.
9:33 for the work **d** and night.
10: 8 The next **d**, when the Philistines
11:22 pit on a snowy **d** and killed a lion.
12:22 **D** after **d** men came to help David,
13:11 to this **d** that place is called
13:12 David was afraid of God that **d** and
16: 7 That **d** David first committed to
16:23 proclaim his salvation **d** after **d**.
17: 5 in a house from the **d** I brought
17: 5 Israel up out of Egypt to this **d**.
26:17 There were six Levites a **d** on the
26:17 four a **d** on the north, four a **d** on
29:21 The next **d** they made sacrifices to
29:22 in the presence of the LORD that **d**.
2Ch 3: 2 He began building on the second **d** of
6: 5 'Since the **d** I brought my people out
6:20 towards this temple **d** and night,
7: 9 On the eighth **d** they held an
7:10 On the twenty-third **d** of the seventh
8: 8 labour force, as it is to this **d**.
8:16 from the **d** the foundation of the
9:20 of little value in Solomon's **d**.
10:19 the house of David to this **d**.
18:24 **d** you go to hide in an inner room."
18:34 All **d** long the battle raged, and the
20:26 On the fourth **d** they assembled in
20:26 the Valley of Beracah to this **d**.
21:10 To this **d** Edom has been in rebellion
26:21 had leprosy until the **d** he died.
28: 6 In one **d** Pekah son of Remaliah
29:17 on the first **d** of the first month,
29:17 and by the eighth **d** of the month
29:17 finishing in the sixteenth **d** of the
30:15 fourteenth **d** of the second month.
30:21 priests sang to the LORD every **d**,
35: 1 the fourteenth **d** of the first month.
35:25 and to this **d** all the men and women
Ezr 3: 4 offerings prescribed for each **d**.
3: 6 On the first **d** of the seventh month
5:16 From that **d** to the present it has
6:19 On the fourteenth **d** of the first
7: 9 on the first **d** of the first month,
7: 9 on the first **d** of the fifth month,
8:31 On the twelfth **d** of the first month
8:33 On the fourth **d**, in the house of our
9:15 We are left this **d** as a remnant.
10: 9 And on the twentieth **d** of the ninth
10:13 be taken care of in a **d** or two,
10:16 On the first **d** of the tenth month
10:17 by the first **d** of the first month
Ne 1: 6 is praying before you **d** and night
4: 2 Will they finish in a **d**? Can they
4: 9 posted a guard **d** and night to meet
4:16 From that **d** on, half of my men did
4:22 guards by night and workmen by **d**."
5:18 Each **d** one ox, six choice sheep and
6:10 One **d** I went to the house of
8: 2 on the first **d** of the seventh month,
8: 9 **d** is sacred to the LORD your God.
8:10 This **d** is sacred to our Lord. Do not
8:11 "Be still, for this is a sacred **d**.
8:13 On the second **d** of the month, the
8:17 of Joshua son of Nun until that **d**,
8:18 **D** after **d**, from the first **d** to the
8:18 on the eighth **d**, in accordance with
9: 1 On the twenty-fourth **d** of the same
9: 3 their God for a quarter of the **d**,
9:10 yourself, which remains to this **d**.
9:12 By **d** you led them with a pillar of
9:19 By **d** the pillar of cloud did not
10:31 on the Sabbath or on any holy **d**.
12:43 on that **d** they offered great
13: 1 On that **d** the Book of Moses was read
13:15 them against selling food on that **d**.
13:17 doing—desecrating the Sabbath **d**?
13:19 be brought in on the Sabbath **d**.
13:22 in order to keep the Sabbath **d** holy.
Est 1:18 This very **d** the Persian and Median
2:11 Every **d** he walked to and fro near
3: 4 **D** after **d** they spoke to him but he
3: 7 of Haman to select a **d** and month.
Est 3:12 on the thirteenth **d** of the first
3:13 on a single **d**, the thirteenth **d** of
3:14 that they would be ready for that **d**.
4:16 or drink for three days, night or **d**.
5: 1 On the third **d** Esther put on her
5: 9 Haman went out that **d** happy and in
7: 2 were drinking wine on that second **d**,
8: 1 That same **d** King Xerxes gave Queen
8: 9 twenty-third **d** of the third month,
8:12 The **d** appointed for the Jews to do
8:12 thirteenth **d** of the twelfth month,
8:13 the Jews would be ready on that **d**
9: 1 On the thirteenth **d** of the twelfth
9: 1 On this **d** the enemies of the Jews
9:11 reported to the king that same **d**.
9:15 fourteenth **d** of the month of Adar,
9:17 This happened on the thirteenth **d** of
9:17 and made it a **d** of feasting and joy.
9:18 and made it a **d** of feasting and joy.
9:19 of Adar as a **d** of joy and feasting,
9:19 **d** for giving presents to each other.
9:22 mourning into a **d** of celebration.
Job 1: 6 One **d** the angels came to present
1:13 One **d** when Job's sons and daughters
2: 1 On another **d** the angels came to
3: 1 mouth and cursed the **d** of his birth.
3: 3 "May the **d** of my birth perish, and
3: 4 That **d**—may it turn to darkness; may
3: 8 May those who curse days curse that **d**
3:16 infant who never saw the light of **d**?
15:23 knows the **d** of darkness is at hand.
17:12 These men turn night into **d**; in the
20:28 waters on the **d** of God's wrath.
21:30 is spared from the **d** of calamity,
24:16 men break into houses, but by **d** they
Ps 1: 2 on his law he meditates **d** and night.
7:11 God who expresses his wrath every **d**.
13: 2 and every **d** have sorrow in my heart?
18:18 They confronted me in the **d** of my
19: 2 **D** after **d** they pour forth speech;
22: 2 O my God, I cry out by **d**, but you do
25: 5 and my hope is in you all **d** long.
27: 5 For in the **d** of trouble he will keep
32: 3 away through my groaning all **d** long.
32: 4 For **d** and night your hand was heavy
35:28 and of your praises all **d** long.
37:13 for he knows their **d** is coming.
38: 6 all **d** long I go about mourning.
38:12 all **d** long they plot deception.
42: 3 My tears have been my food **d** and
42: 3 while men say to me all **d** long,
42: 8 By **d** the LORD directs his love, at
42:10 saying to me all **d** long, "Where is
44: 8 In God we make our boast all **d** long,
44:15 My disgrace is before me all **d** long,
44:22 Yet for your sake we face death all **d**
46: 5 God will help her at break of **d**.
50:15 call upon me in the **d** of trouble;
52: 1 Why do you boast all **d** long, you
55:10 **D** and night they prowl about on its
56: 1 all **d** long they press their attack.
56: 2 My slanderers pursue me all **d** long;
56: 5 All **d** long they twist my words; they
61: 8 name and fulfil my vows **d** after **d**.
71: 8 declaring your splendour all **d** long.
71:15 of your salvation all **d** long, though
71:17 **d** I declare your marvellous deeds.
71:24 of your righteous acts all **d** long,
72:15 for him and bless him all **d** long.
73:14 All **d** long I have been plagued; I
74:16 The **d** is yours, and yours also the
74:22 how fools mock you all **d** long.
78: 9 turned back on the **d** of battle;
78:14 He guided them with the cloud by **d**
78:42 the **d** he redeemed them from the
78:43 the **d** he displayed his miraculous
81: 3 moon is full, on the **d** of our Feast;
84:10 Better is one **d** in your courts than
86: 3 for I call to you all **d** long.
86: 7 In the **d** of my trouble I will call
88: 1 **d** and night I cry out before you.
88: 9 I call to you, O LORD, every **d**;
88:17 All **d** long they surround me like a
89:16 They rejoice in your name all **d** long;
90: 4 are like a **d** that has just gone by,
91: 5 nor the arrow that flies by **d**,

Ps 92: T A psalm. A song. For the Sabbath **d**.
95: 8 did that **d** at Massah in the desert,
96: 2 proclaim his salvation **d** after **d**.
102: 8 All **d** long my enemies taunt me;
110: 3 will be willing on your **d** of battle.
110: 5 crush kings on the **d** of his wrath.
118:24 This is the **d** the LORD has made; let
119:91 Your laws endure to this **d**, for all
119:97 law! I meditate on it all **d** long.
119:164 Seven times a **d** I praise you for
121: 6 the sun will not harm you by **d**, nor
136: 8 the sun to govern the **d**,
137: 7 Edomites did on the **d** Jerusalem fell.
139:12 the night will shine like the **d**,
140: 2 hearts and stir up war every **d**.
140: 7 shields my head in the **d** of battle—
145: 2 Every **d** I will praise you and extol
146: 4 very **d** their plans come to nothing.
Pr 4:18 brighter till the full light of **d**.
7: 9 at twilight, as the **d** was fading, as
8:30 I was filled with delight **d** after **d**,
16: 4 even the wicked for a **d** of disaster.
21:26 All **d** long he craves for more, but
21:31 is made ready for the **d** of battle,
25:20 takes away a garment on a cold **d**,
27: 1 not know what a **d** may bring forth.
27:15 a constant dripping on a rainy **d**;
Ecc 7: 1 **d** of death better than the **d** of
8: 8 has power over the **d** of his death.
8:16 eyes not seeing sleep **d** or night—
SS 2:17 Until the **d** breaks and the shadows
3:11 crowned him on the **d** of his wedding,
3:11 wedding, the **d** his heart rejoiced.
4: 6 Until the **d** breaks and the shadows
8: 8 sister for the **d** she is spoken for?
Isa 2:11 LORD alone will be exalted in that **d**.
2:12 The LORD Almighty has a **d** in store
2:17 LORD alone will be exalted in that **d**,
2:20 In that **d** men will throw away to the
3: 7 in that **d** he will cry out, "I have
3:18 In that **d** the Lord will snatch away
4: 1 In that **d** seven women will take hold
4: 2 In that **d** the Branch of the LORD
4: 5 there a cloud of smoke by **d** and a
4: 6 and shade from the heat of the **d**,
5:30 In that **d** they will roar over it
7:18 In that **d** the LORD will whistle for
7:20 In that **d** the Lord will use a razor
7:21 In that **d**, a man will keep alive a
7:23 In that **d**, in every place where
9: 4 For as in the **d** of Midian's defeat,
9:14 palm branch and reed in a single **d**;
10: 3 will you do on the **d** of reckoning,
10:17 in a single **d** it will burn and
10:20 In that **d** the remnant of Israel, the
10:27 In that **d** their burden will be
10:32 This **d** they will halt at Nob; they
11:10 In that **d** the Root of Jesse will
11:11 In that **d** the Lord will reach out
12: 1 In that **d** you will say: "I will
12: 4 In that **d** you will say: "Give thanks
13: 9 a cruel **d**, with wrath and fierce
13:13 in the **d** of his burning anger.
14: 3 On the **d** the LORD gives you relief
17: 4 "In that **d** the glory of Jacob will
17: 7 In that **d** men will look to their
17: 9 In that **d** their strong cities, which
17:11 though on the **d** you set them out,
17:11 the **d** of disease and incurable pain.
19:16 In that **d** the Egyptians will be like
19:18 In that **d** five cities in Egypt will
19:19 In that **d** there will be an altar to
19:21 **d** they will acknowledge the LORD.
19:23 In that **d** there will be a highway
19:24 In that **d** Israel will be the third,
20: 6 In that **d** the people who live on
21: 8 "**D** after **d**, my lord, I stand on the
22: 5 The Lord, the LORD Almighty, has a **d**
22: 5 a **d** of battering down walls and of
22: 8 And you looked in that **d** to the
22:12 called you on that **d** to weep and to
22:14 "Till your dying **d** this sin will not
22:20 "In that **d** I will summon my servant,
22:25 "In that **d**," declares the LORD
24:21 In that **d** the LORD will punish the
25: 9 In that **d** they will say, "Surely
Isa 26: 1 In that **d** this song will be sung in
27: 1 In that **d**, the LORD will punish
27: 2 In that **d**—" Sing about a fruitful
27: 3 I guard it **d** and night so that
27: 8 out, as on a **d** the east wind blows.
27:12 In that **d** the LORD will thresh from
27:13 in that **d** a great trumpet will sound.
28: 5 In that **d** the LORD Almighty will be
28:19 by **d** and by night, it will sweep
29:18 In that **d** the deaf will hear the
30:23 In that **d** your cattle will graze in
30:25 In the **d** of great slaughter, when
31: 7 For in that **d** every one of you will
34: 8 For the LORD has a **d** of vengeance, a
34:10 will not be quenched night and **d**;
37: 3 This **d** is a **d** of distress and rebuke
37:38 One **d**, while he was worshipping in
38:12 **d** and night you made an end of me.
38:13 **d** and night you made an end of me.
39: 6 have stored up until this **d**,
47: 9 in a moment, on a single **d**: loss of
49: 8 and in the **d** of salvation I will
51:13 you live in constant terror every **d**
52: 5 "And all **d** long my name is
52: 6 therefore in that **d** they will know
58: 2 For **d** after **d** they seek me out; they
58: 3 "Yet on the **d** of your fasting, you
58: 5 only a **d** for a man to humble himself?
58: 5 a fast, a **d** acceptable to the LORD?
58:13 doing as you please on my holy **d**,
58:13 and the LORD's holy **d** honourable,
60:11 they will never be shut, **d** or night,
60:19 sun will no more be your light by **d**,
61: 2 and the **d** of vengeance of our God,
62: 6 will never be silent **d** or night.
63: 4 For the **d** of vengeance was in my
65: 2 All **d** long I have held out my hands
65: 5 a fire that keeps burning all **d**.
66: 8 Can a country be born in a **d** or a
Jer 3:25 from our youth till this **d** we have
4: 9 "In that **d**," declares the LORD, "the
7:25 **d** after **d**, again and again I sent
9: 1 I would weep **d** and night for the
12: 3 them apart for the **d** of slaughter!
14:17 tears night and **d** without ceasing;
15: 9 Her sun will set while it is still **d**;
16:13 will serve other gods **d** and night,
17:16 I have not desired the **d** of despair.
17:17 are my refuge in the **d** of disaster.
17:18 Bring on them the **d** of disaster;
17:21 to carry a load on the Sabbath **d**
17:22 but keep the Sabbath **d** holy, as I
17:24 but keep the Sabbath **d** holy by not
17:27 to keep the Sabbath **d** holy by not
17:27 gates of Jerusalem on the Sabbath **d**,
18:17 my face in the **d** of their disaster."
20: 3 The next **d**, when Pashhur released
20: 7 I am ridiculed all **d** long; everyone
20: 8 me insult and reproach all **d** long.
20:14 Cursed be the **d** I was born!
20:14 May the **d** my mother bore me not be
25: 3 Amon king of Judah until this very **d**
27:22 remain until the **d** I come for them,'
30: 7 How awful that **d** will be! None will
30: 8 "'In that **d**,' declares the LORD
31: 6 There will be a **d** when watchmen cry
31:35 who appoints the sun to shine by **d**,
32:20 and have continued them to this **d**,
32:31 From the **d** it was built until now,
33:20 break my covenant with the **d** and my
33:20 so that **d** and night no longer come
33:25 not established my covenant with **d**
35:14 To this **d** they do not drink wine,
36: 6 house of the LORD on a **d** of fasting
36:30 heat by **d** and the frost by night.
37:21 the street of the bakers each **d**
38:28 until the **d** Jerusalem was captured.
39: 2 on the ninth **d** of the fourth month
39:17 I will rescue you on that **d**,
41: 4 The **d** after Gedaliah's assassination,
44:10 To this **d** they have not humbled
46:10 that **d** belongs to the Lord, the LORD
46:10 the LORD Almighty—a **d** of vengeance,
46:21 for the **d** of disaster is coming upon
47: 4 For the **d** has come to destroy all
48:41 In that **d** the hearts of Moab's
Jer 49:22 In that **d** the hearts of Edom's
49:26 will be silenced in that **d**,"
50:27 Woe to them! For their **d** has come,
50:30 will be silenced in that **d**,"
50:31 "for your **d** has come, the time for
51: 2 every side in the **d** of her disaster.
52: 4 on the tenth **d** of the tenth month,
52: 6 By the ninth **d** of the fourth month
52:11 in prison till the **d** of his death.
52:12 On the tenth **d** of the fifth month,
52:31 twenty-fifth **d** of the twelfth month.
52:34 **D** by **d** the king of Babylon gave
52:34 he lived, till the **d** of his death.
Lam 1:12 on me in the **d** of his fierce anger?
1:13 me desolate, faint all the **d** long.
1:21 May you bring the **d** you have
2: 1 his footstool in the **d** of his anger.
2: 7 as on the **d** of an appointed feast.
2:16 This is the **d** we have waited for; we
2:18 flow like a river **d** and night;
2:21 slain them in the **d** of your anger;
2:22 "As you summon to a feast **d**, so you
2:22 In the **d** of the LORD's anger no-one
3: 3 me again and again, all **d** long.
3:14 they mock me in song all **d** long.
3:62 and mutter against me all **d** long.
Eze 1: 1 in the fourth month on the fifth **d**,
1:28 rainbow in the clouds on a rainy **d**,
2: 3 in revolt against me to this very **d**.
4: 6 you 40 days, a **d** for each year.
4:10 food to eat each **d** and eat it at
7: 7 The time has come, the **d** is near;
7:10 "The **d** is here! It has come! Doom
7:12 The time has come, the **d** has arrived.
7:19 them in the **d** of the LORD's wrath.
8: 1 in the sixth month on the fifth **d**,
12: 7 During the **d** I brought out my things
16: 4 On the **d** you were born your cord was
16: 5 **d** you were born you were despised.
16:56 sister Sodom in the **d** of your pride,
20: 1 in the fifth month on the tenth **d**,
20: 5 LORD says: On the **d** I chose Israel,
20: 6 On that **d** I swore to them that I
20:29 (It is called Bamah to this **d**.)
20:31 with all your idols to this **d**.
21:25 whose **d** has come, whose time of
21:29 whose **d** has come, whose time of
22:14 be strong in the **d** I deal with you?
23:39 On the very **d** they sacrificed their
24: 1 on the tenth month on the tenth **d**,
24: 2 laid siege to Jerusalem this very **d**.
24:25 the **d** I take away their stronghold,
24:26 on that **d** a fugitive will come to
26: 1 In the eleventh year, on the first **d**
26:18 tremble on the **d** of your fall;
27:27 the sea on the **d** of your shipwreck.
28:13 on the **d** you were created they were
28:15 from the **d** you were created till
29: 1 the tenth month on the twelfth **d**,
29:17 the first month on the first **d**,
29:21 "On that **d** I will make a horn grow
30: 2 "'Wail and say, "Alas for that **d**!
30: 3 For the **d** is near, the **d** of the
30: 3 a **d** of clouds, a time of doom for
30: 9 "'On that **d** messengers will go out
30: 9 of them on the **d** of Egypt's doom,
30:18 Dark will be the **d** at Tahpanhes when
31: 1 in the third month on the first **d**,
31:15 On the **d** it was brought down to the
32: 1 the twelfth month on the first **d**,
32:10 On the **d** of your downfall each of
32:17 on the fifteenth **d** of the month, the
33:21 in the tenth month on the fifth **d**, a
34:12 on a **d** of clouds and darkness.
36:33 On that **d** I cleanse you from all
38:10 On that **d** thoughts will come into
38:14 the Sovereign LORD says: In that **d**,
38:18 This is what will happen in that **d**:
39: 8 This is the **d** I have spoken of.
39:11 "'On that **d** I will give Gog a burial
39:13 and the **d** I am glorified will be a
39:13 will be a memorable **d** for them,
39:22 From that **d** forward the house of
40: 1 **d** the hand of the LORD was upon me
43:22 "On the second **d** you are to offer a
43:27 from the eighth **d** on, the priests

Eze 44:27 On the **d** he goes into the inner
45:18 In the first month on the first **d**
45:21 on the fourteenth **d** you are to
45:22 On that **d** the prince is to provide a
45:23 Every **d** during the seven days of the
45:25 seventh month on the fifteenth **d**,
46: 1 but on the Sabbath **d** and on the **d** of
46: 4 brings to the LORD on the Sabbath **d**
46: 6 On the **d** of the New Moon he is to
46:12 as he does on the Sabbath **d**.
46:13 "Every **d** you are to provide a
Da 6:10 Three times a **d** he got down on his
6:13 He still prays three times a **d**."
9: 7 but this **d** we are covered with
9:15 a name that endures to this **d**,
10: 4 On the twenty-fourth **d** of the first
10:12 Since the first **d** that you set your
Hos 1: 5 In that **d** I will break Israel's bow
1:11 for great will be the **d** of Jezreel.
2: 3 as bare as on the **d** she was born;
2:15 in the **d** she came up out of Egypt.
2:16 "In that **d**," declares the LORD, "you
2:18 In that **d** I will make a covenant for
2:21 "In that **d** I will respond," declares
4: 5 You stumble **d** and night, and the
5: 9 laid waste on the **d** of reckoning.
6: 2 on the third **d** he will restore us,
7: 5 On the **d** of the festival of our king
9: 5 on the **d** of your appointed feasts,
10:14 Beth Arbel on the **d** of battle,
10:15 When that **d** dawns, the king of
12: 1 he pursues the east wind all **d**
Joel 1:15 Alas for that **d**! For the **d** of the
2: 2 a **d** of darkness and gloom, a **d** of
3:18 "In that **d** the mountains will drip
Am 1:14 amid war cries on the **d** of battle,
1:14 amid violent winds on a stormy **d**.
2:16 will flee naked on that **d**,"
3:14 "On the **d** I punish Israel for her
5: 8 into dawn and darkens **d** into night,
5:18 That **d** will be darkness, not light.
6: 3 You put off the evil **d** and bring
8: 3 "In that **d**," declares the Sovereign
8: 9 "In that **d**," declares the Sovereign
8:10 and the end of it like a bitter **d**.
8:13 "In that **d** "the lovely young women
9:11 "In that **d** I will restore David's
Ob : 8 "In that **d**," declares the LORD,
:11 On the **d** you stood aloof while
:12 brother in the **d** of his misfortune,
:12 Judah in the **d** of their destruction,
:12 so much in the **d** of their trouble.
:13 people in the **d** of their disaster,
:13 calamity in the **d** of their disaster,
:13 wealth in the **d** of their disaster.
:14 survivors in the **d** of their trouble.
Jnh 3: 4 On the first **d**, Jonah started into
4: 7 at dawn the next **d** God provided a
Mic 2: 4 In that **d** men will ridicule you;
3: 6 and the **d** will go dark for them.
4: 6 "In that **d**," declares the LORD, "I
4: 7 Mount Zion from that **d** and for ever.
5:10 "In that **d**," declares the LORD, "I
7: 4 The **d** of your watchmen has come,
7: 4 the **d** God visits you. Now is the
7:11 The **d** for building your walls will
7:11 the **d** for extending your boundaries.
7:12 In that **d** people will come to you
Na 2: 3 on the **d** they are made ready;
3:17 settle in the walls on a cold **d**
Hab 3: 2 Renew them in our **d**, in our time
3:16 Yet I will wait patiently for the **d**
Zep 1: 8 On the **d** of the LORD's sacrifice I
1: 9 On that **d** I will punish all who
1:10 "On that **d**," declares the LORD, "a
1:15 That **d** will be a **d** of wrath,
1:15 a **d** of distress and anguish,
1:15 a **d** of trouble and ruin,
1:15 a **d** of darkness and gloom
1:15 a **d** of clouds and blackness,
1:16 a **d** of trumpet and battle cry
1:18 them on the **d** of the LORD's wrath.
2: 2 and that **d** sweeps on like chaff,
2: 2 **d** of the LORD's wrath comes upon you.
2: 3 on the **d** of the LORD's anger.
3: 5 and every new **d** he does not fail,
Zep 3: 8 the **d** I will stand up to testify.
3:11 On that **d** you will not be put to
3:16 On that **d** they will say to Jerusalem,
Hag 1: 1 on the first **d** of the sixth month,
1:15 on the twenty-fourth **d** of the sixth
2: 1 On the twenty-first **d** of the seventh
2:10 On the twenty-fourth **d** of the ninth
2:15 thought to this from this **d** on
2:18 'From this **d** on, from this
2:18 twenty-fourth **d** of the ninth month,
2:18 give careful thought to the **d** when
2:19 "'From this **d** on I will bless you.'"
2:20 on the twenty-fourth **d** of the month:
2:23 "'On that **d**,' declares the LORD
Zec 1: 7 On the twenty-fourth **d** of the
2:11 joined with the LORD in that **d** and
3: 9 the sin of this land in a single **d**.
3:10 "'In that **d** each of you will invite
4:10 "Who despises the **d** of small things?
6:10 Go the same **d** to the house of
7: 1 on the fourth **d** of the ninth month,
9:16 their God will save them on that **d**
11:11 was revoked on that **d**, and so the
12: 3 On that **d**, when all the nations of
12: 4 On that **d** I will strike every horse
12: 6 "On that **d** I will make the leaders
12: 8 On that **d** the LORD will shield those
12: 9 On that **d** I will set out to destroy
12:11 On that **d** the weeping in Jerusalem
13: 1 "On that **d** a fountain will be opened
13: 2 "On that **d**, I will banish the names
13: 4 "On that **d** every prophet will be
14: 3 as he fights in the **d** of battle.
14: 4 On that **d** his feet will stand on the
14: 6 On that **d** there will be no light, no
14: 7 will be a unique **d**, without daytime
14: 8 On that **d** living water will flow out
14: 9 On that **d** there will be one LORD,
14:13 On that **d** men will be stricken by
14:20 On that **d** HOLY TO THE LORD
14:21 And on that **d** there will no longer
Mal 3: 2 who can endure the **d** of his coming?
3:17 "in the **d** when I make up my
4: 1 "Surely the **d** is coming; it will
4: 1 and that **d** that is coming will set
4: 3 on the **d** when I do these things,"
Mt 6:34 Each **d** has enough trouble of its own.
7:22 Many will say to me on that **d**, 'Lord,
11:23 it would have remained to this **d**.
12: 5 in the temple desecrate the **d**
13: 1 That same **d** Jesus went out of the
20: 2 to pay them a denarius for the **d**
20: 6 here all **d** long doing nothing?'
20:12 of the work and the heat of the **d**.'
22:23 That same **d** the Sadducees, who say
22:46 and from that **d** on no-one dared to
24:36 "No-one knows about that **d** or hour,
24:38 up to the **d** Noah entered the ark;
24:42 know on what **d** your Lord will come.
24:50 on a **d** when he does not expect him
25:13 you do not know the **d** or the hour.
26:17 On the first **d** of the Feast of
26:29 until that **d** when I drink it anew
26:55 Every **d** I sat in the temple courts
27: 8 called the Field of Blood to this **d**.
27:62 The next **d**, the one after
27:62 the one after Preparation **D**, the
Mt 28: 1 at dawn on the first **d** of the week,
28:15 among the Jews to this very **d**.
Mk 2:20 them, and on that **d** they will fast.
4:27 Night and **d**, whether he sleeps or
4:35 That **d** when evening came, he said to
5: 5 Night and **d** among the tombs and in
6:35 By this time it was late in the **d**,
11:12 The next **d** as they were leaving
13:32 "No-one knows about that **d** or hour,
14:12 On the first **d** of the Feast of
14:25 until that **d** when I drink it anew
14:49 Every **d** I was with you, teaching in
15:42 Preparation **D** (that is, the **d** before
16: 2 Very early on the first **d** of the
16: 9 Jesus rose early on the first **d** of
Lk 1:20 to speak until the **d** this happens,
1:59 On the eighth **d** they came to
2:21 On the eighth **d**, when it was time to
2:37 night and **d**, fasting and praying.
Lk 2:44 company, they travelled on for a **d**.
4:16 and on the Sabbath **d** he went into
5: 1 One **d** as Jesus was standing by the
5:17 One **d** as he was teaching, Pharisees
6:23 "Rejoice in that **d** and leap for joy,
8:22 One **d** Jesus said to his disciples,
9:37 The next **d**, when they came down from
10:12 more bearable on that **d** for Sodom
10:35 The next **d** he took out two silver
11: 1 One **d** Jesus was praying in a certain
11: 3 Give us each **d** our daily bread.
12:46 on a **d** when he does not expect him
13:16 the Sabbath **d** from what bound her?"
13:33 tomorrow and the next **d**—for surely
14: 5 falls into a well on the Sabbath **d**,
16:19 linen and lived in luxury every **d**.
17: 4 sins against you seven times in a **d**,
17:24 For the Son of Man in his **d** will be
17:27 up to the **d** Noah entered the ark.
17:29 the **d** Lot left Sodom, fire and
17:30 "It will be just like this on the **d**
17:31 On that **d** no-one who is on the roof
18: 7 who cry out to him **d** and night? Will
19:42 even you, had only known on this **d**
19:47 Every **d** he was teaching at the
20: 1 One **d** as he was teaching the people
21:34 and that **d** will close on you
21:37 Each **d** Jesus was teaching at the
22: 7 came the **d** of Unleavened Bread on
22:53 Every **d** I was with you in the temple
23:12 That **d** Herod and Pilate became
23:54 was Preparation **D**, and the Sabbath
24: 1 On the first **d** of the week, very
24:13 Now that same **d** two of them were
24:29 evening; the **d** is almost over.
Jn 1:29 The next **d** John saw Jesus coming
1:35 The next **d** John was there again with
1:39 staying, and spent that **d** with him.
1:43 The next **d** Jesus decided to leave
5: 9 The **d** on which this took place was a
5:17 at his work to this very **d**, and I,
6:22 The next **d** the crowd that had stayed
7:37 On the last and greatest **d** of the
8:56 at the thought of seeing my **d**;
9: 4 long as it is **d**, we must do the work
9:14 Now the **d** on which Jesus had made
11: 9 man who walks by **d** will not stumble,
11:53 from that **d** on they plotted to take
12: 7 perfume for the **d** of my burial.
12:12 The next **d** the great crowd that had
14:20 On that **d** you will realise that I am
16:23 In that **d** you will no longer ask me
16:26 In that **d** you will ask in my name.
19:14 was the **d** of Preparation of Passover
19:31 Now it was the **d** of Preparation, and
19:31 next **d** was to be a special Sabbath.
19:42 it was the Jewish **d** of Preparation
20: 1 Early on the first **d** of the week,
20:19 On the evening of that first **d** of
Ac 1: 2 until the **d** he was taken up to
2: 1 the **d** of Pentecost came, they were
2:29 and his tomb is here to this **d**.
2:41 were added to their number that **d**.
2:46 Every **d** they continued to meet
3: 1 One **d** Peter and John were going up
3: 2 where he was put every **d** to beg from
4: 3 put them in jail until the next **d**.
4: 5 The next **d** the rulers, elders and
5:42 **D** after **d**, in the temple courts and
7:26 The next **d** Moses came upon two
8: 1 On that **d** a great persecution
9:24 **D** and night they kept close watch
10: 3 One **d** at about three in the
10: 9 About noon the following **d** as they
10:23 The next **d** Peter started out with
10:24 The following **d** he arrived in
12:21 On the appointed **d** Herod, wearing
14:20 The next **d** he and Barnabas left for
16:11 and the next **d** on to Neapolis.
17:11 examined the Scriptures every **d** to
17:17 as well as in the market-place **d** by **d**
17:31 For he has set a **d** when he will
19:15 One **d** the evil spirit answered
20: 7 On the first **d** of the week we came
20: 7 he intended to leave the next **d**,
20:15 The next **d** we set sail from there

Ac 20:15 The **d** after that we crossed over to
20:15 the following **d** arrived at Miletus.
20:16 if possible, by the **d** of Pentecost.
20:18 from the first **d** I came into the
20:31 each of you night and **d** with tears.
21: 1 The next **d** we went to Rhodes and
21: 7 and stayed with them for a **d**.
21: 8 Leaving the next **d**, we reached
21:18 The next **d** Paul and the rest of us
21:26 The next **d** Paul took the men and
22:30 The next **d**, since the commander
23: 1 in all good conscience to this **d**."
23:32 The next **d** they let the cavalry go
25: 6 and the next **d** he convened the court
25:17 but convened the court the next **d**
25:23 The next **d** Agrippa and Bernice came
26: 7 earnestly serve God **d** and night.
26:22 I have had God's help to this very **d**,
27: 3 The next **d** we landed at Sidon; and
27:18 the next **d** they began to throw the
28:13 The next **d** the south wind came up,
28:13 the following **d** we reached Puteoli.
28:23 to meet Paul on a certain **d**,
Ro 2: 5 yourself for the **d** of God's wrath,
2:16 This will take place on the **d** when
8:36 "For your sake we face death all **d**
10:21 "All **d** long I have held out my
11: 8 could not hear, to this very **d**."
13:12 nearly over; the **d** is almost here.
14: 5 One man considers one **d** more sacred
14: 5 another man considers every **d** alike.
14: 6 He who regards one **d** as special,
1Co 1: 8 on the **d** of our Lord Jesus Christ.
3:13 the **D** will bring it to light.
10: 8 in one **d** twenty-three thousand of
15:31 I die every **d**—I mean that, brothers
16: 2 On the first **d** of every week, each
2Co 3:14 for to this **d** the same veil remains
3:15 Even to this **d** when Moses is read, a
4:16 we are being renewed **d** by **d**.
6: 2 in the **d** of salvation I helped you.
6: 2 favour, now is the **d** of salvation.
11:25 a night and a **d** in the open sea,
Eph 4:30 were sealed for the **d** of redemption.
6:13 so that when the **d** of evil comes,
Php 1: 5 gospel from the first **d** until now,
1: 6 until the **d** of Christ Jesus.
1:10 and blameless until the **d** of Christ,
2:16 that I may boast on the **d** of Christ
3: 5 circumcised on the eighth **d**, of the
Col 1: 6 among you since the **d** you heard it
1: 9 since the **d** we heard about you, we
2:16 New Moon celebration or a Sabbath **d**.
1Th 2: 9 we worked night and **d** in order not
3:10 Night and **d** we pray most earnestly
5: 4 **d** should surprise you like a thief.
5: 5 sons of the light and sons of the **d**.
5: 8 since we belong to the **d**, let us be
2Th 1:10 on the **d** he comes to be glorified in
2: 3 for ⌊that **d** will not come⌋ until the
3: 8 we worked night and **d**, labouring and
1Ti 5: 5 continues night and **d** to pray and
2Ti 1: 3 as night and **d** I constantly remember
1:12 I have entrusted to him for that **d**.
1:18 find mercy from the LORD on that **d**!
4: 8 will award to me on that **d**—and not
Heb 4: 7 Therefore God again set a certain **d**,
4: 8 have spoken later about another **d**.
7:27 need to offer sacrifices **d** after **d**,
10:11 **D** after **d** every priest stands and
10:25 more as you see the **D** approaching.
Jas 5: 5 yourselves in the **d** of slaughter.
1Pe 2:12 glorify God on the **d** he visits us.
2Pe 1:19 until the **d** dawns and the morning
2: 8 living among them **d** after **d**, was
3: 8 dear friends: With the Lord a **d** is
3: 8 and a thousand years are like a **d**.
3:12 you look forward to the **d** of God and
3:12 That **d** will bring about the
Jude : 6 chains for judgment on the great **D**.
Rev 1:10 On the Lord's **D** I was in the Spirit,
4: 8 **D** and night they never stop saying:
6:17 For the great **d** of their wrath has
7:15 serve him **d** and night in his temple;
8:12 A third of the **d** was without light,
9:15 **d** and month and year were released
Rev 12:10 them before our God **d** and night,
14:11 There is no rest **d** or night for
16:14 on the great **d** of God Almighty.
18: 8 Therefore in one **d** her plagues will
20:10 **d** and night for ever and ever.
21:25 On no **d** will its gates ever be shut,

Day of Atonement
Lev 23:27 day of this seventh month is the **D**.
23:28 because it is the **D**, when atonement
25: 9 on the **D** sound the trumpet

Day of judgment
Mt 10:15 for Sodom and Gomorrah on the **d**
11:22 Tyre and Sidon on the **d** than for you.
11:24 for Sodom on the **d** than for you."
12:36 will have to give account on the **d**
2Pe 2: 9 to hold the unrighteous for the **d**,
3: 7 kept for the **d** and destruction of
1Jn 4:17 we will have confidence on the **d**,

Day of the LORD
Isa 13: 6 Wail, for the **d** is near; it will
13: 9 See, the **d** is coming—a cruel day,
Eze 13: 5 stand firm in the battle on the **d**.
30: 3 For the day is near, the **d** is near—
Joel 1:15 Alas for that day! For the **d** is near;
2: 1 land tremble, for the **d** is coming.
2:11 The **d** is great; it is dreadful. Who
2:31 coming of the great and dreadful **d**.
3:14 **d** is near in the valley of decision.
Am 5:18 Woe to you who long for the **d**! Why
5:18 Why do you long for the **d**? That day
5:20 Will not the **d** be darkness, not
Ob :15 "The **d** is near for all nations. As
Zep 1: 7 Sovereign LORD, for the **d** is near.
1:14 "The great **d** is near—near and
1:14 Listen! The cry on the **d** will be
Zec 14: 1 A **d** is coming when your plunder will
Mal 4: 5 that great and dreadful **d** comes.

Day of the Lord
Ac 2:20 coming of the great and glorious **d**.
1Co 5: 5 and his spirit saved on the **d**.
2Co 1:14 we will boast of you in the **d** Jesus.
1Th 5: 2 for you know very well that the **d**
2Th 2: 2 saying that the **d** has already come.
2Pe 3:10 the **d** will come like a thief. The

Day of wrath
Job 21:30 that he is delivered from the **d**?
Pr 11: 4 Wealth is worthless in the **d**, but
Eze 22:24 had no rain or showers in the **d**.'
Zep 1:15 That day will be a **d**, a day of

Day's (Day)
Nu 11:31 as far as a **d** walk in any direction.
1Ki 8:59 Israel according to each **d** need,
19: 4 while he himself went a **d** journey
1Ch 16:37 according to each **d** requirements.
2Ch 8:14 according to each **d** requirement.
Est 9:13 carry out this **d** edict tomorrow
Ac 1:12 a Sabbath **d** walk from the city.
Rev 6: 6 "A quart of wheat for a **d** wages, and
6: 6 three quarts of barley for a **d** wages

Daybreak (Day)
Ge 32:24 and a man wrestled with him till **d**.
32:26 the man said, "Let me go, for it is **d**
Ex 14:27 at **d** the sea went back to its place.
Jos 6:15 On the seventh day, they got up at **d**
Jdg 19:26 At **d** the woman went back to the
1Sa 9:26 They rose about **d** and Samuel called
25:34 would have been left alive by **d**."
25:36 So she told him nothing until **d**.
2Sa 2:32 night and arrived at Hebron by **d**.
17:22 By **d**, no-one was left who had not
Ne 8: 3 He read it aloud from **d** till noon as
Lk 4:42 At **d** Jesus went out to a solitary
22:66 At **d** the council of the elders of
Ac 5:21 At **d** they entered the temple courts,

Daylight (Day, Light[1])
Nu 25: 4 them in broad **d** before the LORD,
Jdg 19:26 at the door and lay there until **d**.
2Sa 12:11 will lie with your wives in broad **d**.
12:12 in broad **d** before all Israel.'"
2Ki 7: 9 If we wait until **d**, punishment will
Job 3: 9 may it wait for **d** in vain and not
24:14 **d** is gone, the murderer rises up and
Jer 6: 4 alas, the **d** is fading, and the
Am 8: 9 and darken the earth in broad **d**.
Mt 10:27 you in the dark, speak in the **d**;
Lk 12: 3 in the dark will be heard in the **d**,
Jn 11: 9 "Are there not twelve hours of **d**?
Ac 16:35 when it was **d**, the magistrates sent
20:11 After talking until **d**, he left.
27:29 from the stern and prayed for **d**.
27:39 **d** came, they did not recognise the
2Pe 2:13 pleasure is to carouse in broad **d**.

Days (*Ancient of Days*, Day, *Days are coming*, *Days to come*, *Forty Days*, *Last days*, *Seven days*, Seven-day, *Seventh day*, *Six days*, *Three days*)
Ge 1:14 to mark seasons and **d** and years,
3:14 eat dust all the **d** of your life.
3:17 eat of it all the **d** of your life.
6: 3 **d** will be a hundred and twenty years.
6: 4 were on the earth in those **d**—
7:24 the earth for a hundred and fifty **d**.
8: 3 the end of the hundred and fifty **d**
8:10 He waited seven more **d** and again
8:12 He waited seven more **d** and sent the
17:12 is eight **d** old must be circumcised,
21: 4 his son Isaac was eight **d** old,
24:55 girl remain with us ten **d** or so;
27:41 "The **d** of mourning for my father
29:20 seemed like only a few **d** to him
37:34 and mourned for his son many **d**.
50: 3 Egyptians mourned for him seventy **d**.
50: 4 the **d** of mourning had passed, Joseph
Ex 12:16 Do no work at all on these **d**, except
16: 5 much as they gather on the other **d**."
16:29 day he gives you bread for two **d**.
Lev 8:33 until the **d** of your ordination are
12: 4 the woman must wait thirty-three **d**
12: 4 the **d** of her purification are over.
12: 5 wait sixty-six **d** to be purified
12: 6 "'When the **d** of her purification for
15:25 discharge of blood for many **d** at a
15:25 just as in the **d** of her period.
23:16 Count off fifty **d** up to the day
Nu 6:12 The previous **d** do not count, because
9:20 over the tabernacle only a few **d**;
9:22 for two **d** or a month or a year,
11:19 or two **d**, or five, ten or twenty **d**,
19:12 on the third and seventh **d**, he will
19:19 person on the third and seventh **d**,
20:29 of Israel mourned for him thirty **d**.
31:19 On the third and seventh **d** you must
Dt 1: 2 (It takes eleven **d** to go from Horeb
1:46 you stayed in Kadesh many **d**—all the
4:30 then in later **d** you will return to
4:32 Ask now about the former **d**, long
5:33 prolong your **d** in the land that you
11:21 that your **d** and the **d** of your
11:21 as many as the **d** that the heavens
16: 3 so that all the **d** of your life you
17:19 to read it all the **d** of his life
28:33 but cruel oppression all your **d**.
32: 7 Remember the **d** of old; consider the
33:25 and your strength will equal your **d**.
34: 8 Moses in the plains of Moab thirty **d**,
Jos 1: 5 against you all the **d** of your life.
4:14 revered him all the **d** of his life,
Jdg 5: 6 "In the **d** of Shamgar son of Anath,
5: 6 in the **d** of Jael, the roads were
11:40 go out for four **d** to commemorate
15:20 years in the **d** of the Philistines.
17: 6 In those **d** Israel had no king;
18: 1 In those **d** Israel had no king. And
18: 1 And in those **d** the tribe of the
19: 1 In those **d** Israel had no king. Now a
20:27 (In those **d** the ark of the covenant
21:25 In those **d** Israel had no king;
Ru 1: 1 In the **d** when the judges ruled,
1Sa 1:11 the LORD for all the **d** of his life,
3: 1 In those **d** the word of the LORD was
7:15 over Israel all the **d** of his life.

1Sa 14:52 All the **d** of Saul there was bitter
18:29 his enemy for the rest of his **d**.
25:10 away from their masters these **d**.
25:38 About ten **d** later, the LORD struck
27: 1 "One of these **d** I shall be destroyed
28: 1 In those **d** the Philistines gathered
2Sa 1: 1 and stayed in Ziklag two **d**.
7:12 your **d** are over and you rest with
14: 2 spent many **d** grieving for the dead.
16:23 Now in those **d** the advice Ahithophel
21: 9 death during the first **d** of harvest,
24: 8 the end of nine months and twenty **d**.
1Ki 8:65 and seven **d** more, fourteen **d** in all.
10:21 of little value in Solomon's **d**.
11:34 him ruler all the **d** of his life
15: 5 commands all the **d** of his life—
21:29 on his house in the **d** of his son."
2Ki 10:32 In those **d** the LORD began to reduce
15:37 (In those **d** the LORD began to send
19:25 In **d** of old I planned it; now I have
20: 1 In those **d** Hezekiah became ill and
23:22 Not since the **d** of the judges who
23:22 nor throughout the **d** of the kings of
1Ch 4:41 in the **d** of Hezekiah king of Judah.
7:22 Ephraim mourned for them many **d**,
17:11 your **d** are over and you go to be
21:12 **d** of plague in the land, with the
29:15 Our **d** on earth are like a shadow,
2Ch 14: 1 and in his **d** the country was at
15: 5 In those **d** it was not safe to travel
26: 5 during the **d** of Zechariah,
29:17 For eight more **d** they consecrated
30:23 celebrate the festival seven more **d**;
30:26 for since the **d** of Solomon son of
32:24 In those **d** Hezekiah became ill and
32:26 upon them during the **d** of Hezekiah.
35:18 since the **d** of the prophet Samuel;
36: 9 Jerusalem for three months and ten **d**.
Ezr 4: 7 the **d** of Artaxerxes king of Persia,
9: 7 From the **d** of our forefathers until
Ne 1: 4 For some **d** I mourned and fasted and
5:18 and every ten **d** an abundant supply
6:15 of Elul, in fifty-two **d**.
6:17 Also, in those **d** the nobles of Judah
8:17 From the **d** of Joshua son of Nun
9:32 from the **d** of the kings of Assyria
12: 7 their associates in the **d** of Jeshua.
12:12 In the **d** of Joiakim, these were the
12:22 of the Levites in the **d** of Eliashib,
12:26 They served in the **d** of Joiakim son
12:26 and in the **d** of Nehemiah the
12:46 For long ago, in the **d** of David and
12:47 in the **d** of Zerubbabel and of
13:15 In those **d** I saw men in Judah
13:23 Moreover, in those **d** I saw men of
Est 1: 4 For a full 180 **d** he displayed the
1: 5 these **d** were over, the king gave a
4:11 But thirty **d** have passed since I was
9:21 fourteenth and fifteenth **d** of the
9:22 to observe the **d** as **d** of feasting
9:26 (Therefore these **d** were called Purim,
9:27 fail observe these two **d** every year,
9:28 These **d** should be remembered and
9:28 And these **d** of Purim should never
9:31 to establish these **d** of Purim at
Job 3: 6 be included among the **d** of the year
3: 8 May those who curse **d** curse that day,
7: 1 not his **d** like those of a hired man?
7: 6 "My **d** are swifter than a weaver's
7:16 Let me alone; my **d** have no meaning.
8: 9 and our **d** on earth are but a shadow.
9:25 "My **d** are swifter than a runner;
10: 5 Are your **d** like those of a mortal or
10:20 Are not my few **d** almost over? Turn
14: 1 "Man born of woman is of few **d** and
14: 5 Man's **d** are determined; you have
14:14 All the **d** of my hard service I will
15:20 All his **d** the wicked man suffers
17: 1 is broken, my **d** are cut short,
17:11 My **d** have passed, my plans are
24: 1 know him look in vain for such **d**?
29: 2 for the **d** when God watched over me,
29: 4 Oh, for the **d** when I was in my prime,
29:18 **d** as numerous as the grains of sand.
30:16 ebbs away; **d** of suffering grip me.
30:27 **d** of suffering confront me.
Job 33:25 restored as in the **d** of his youth.
36:11 they will spend the rest of their **d**
38:23 of trouble, for **d** of war and battle?
Ps 21: 4 length of **d**, for ever and ever.
23: 6 will follow me all the **d** of my life,
25:13 He will spend his **d** in prosperity,
27: 4 of the LORD all the **d** of my life,
34:12 life and desires to see many good **d**,
37:18 The **d** of the blameless are known to
37:19 **d** of famine they will enjoy plenty.
39: 4 life's end and the number of my **d**;
39: 5 You have made my **d** a mere
44: 1 you did in their **d**, in **d** long ago.
49: 5 Why should I fear when evil **d** come,
55:23 men will not live out half their **d**.
61: 6 Increase the **d** of the king's life,
72: 7 In his **d** the righteous will flourish;
77: 5 I thought about the former **d**, the
78:33 he ended their **d** in futility and
89:45 You have cut short the **d** of his
90: 9 All our **d** pass away under your wrath;
90:10 The length of our **d** is seventy years
90:12 Teach us to number our **d** aright,
90:14 sing for joy and be glad all our **d**.
90:15 Make us glad for as many **d** as you
93: 5 your house for endless **d**, O LORD.
94:13 grant him relief from **d** of trouble,
102: 3 For my **d** vanish like smoke; my bones
102:11 My **d** are like the evening shadow;
102:23 my strength; he cut short my **d**.
102:24 O my God, in the midst of my **d**;
103:15 for man, his **d** are like grass, he
109: 8 May his **d** be few; may another take
128: 5 from Zion all the **d** of your life;
139:16 All the **d** ordained for me were
143: 5 I remember the **d** of long ago;
144: 4 his **d** are like a fleeting shadow.
Pr 9:11 For through me your **d** will be many,
15:15 All the **d** of the oppressed are
31:12 not harm, all the **d** of her life.
Ecc 2: 3 during the few **d** of their lives.
2:23 All his **d** his work is pain and grief;
5:17 All his **d** he eats in darkness, with
5:18 the few **d** of life God has given him
5:20 seldom reflects on the **d** of his life
6:12 during the few and meaningless **d** he
7:10 Do not say, "Why were the old **d**
8:13 **d** will not lengthen like a shadow.
8:15 all the **d** of the life God has given
9: 9 whom you love, all the **d** of this
9: 9 the sun—all your meaningless **d**.
11: 1 after many **d** you will find it again.
11: 8 him remember the **d** of darkness,
11: 9 give you joy in the **d** of your youth.
12: 1 your Creator in the **d** of your youth
12: 1 before the **d** of trouble come and the
Isa 1:26 restore your judges as in **d** of old,
2: 2 In the last **d** the mountain of the
13:22 and her **d** will not be prolonged.
24:22 prison and be punished after many **d**.
30:26 like the light of seven full **d**, when
37:26 In **d** of old I planned it; now I have
38: 1 In those **d** Hezekiah became ill and
38:20 instruments all the **d** of our lives
43:13 Yes, and from ancient **d** I am he.
51: 9 awake, as in **d** gone by, as in
53:10 see his offspring and prolong his **d**,
54: 9 "To me this is like the **d** of Noah,
60:20 and your **d** of sorrow will end.
63: 9 and carried them all the **d** of old.
63:11 his people recalled the **d** of old,
63:11 the **d** of Moses and his people—
65:20 it an infant who lives but a few **d**,
65:22 For as the **d** of a tree, so will be
65:22 so will be the **d** of my people; my
Jer 2:32 have forgotten me, **d** without number.
3:16 In those **d**, when your numbers have
3:18 In those **d** the house of Judah will
5:18 "Yet even in those **d**," declares the
13: 6 Many **d** later the LORD said to me,
16: 9 Before your eyes and in your **d** I
20:18 and sorrow and to end my **d** in shame?
23: 6 In his **d** Judah will be saved and
26:18 in the **d** of Hezekiah king of Judah.
30:20 children will be as in **d** of old,
31:29 "In those **d** people will no longer
Jer 33:15 "'In those **d** and at that time I will
33:16 In those **d** Judah will be saved and
42: 7 Ten **d** later the word of the LORD
50: 4 "In those **d**, at that time," declares
50:20 In those **d**, at that time," declares
Lam 1: 7 In the **d** of her affliction and
1: 7 that were hers in **d** of old.
4:18 end was near, our **d** were numbered,
5:21 may return; renew our **d** as of old
Eze 4: 4 number of **d** you lie on your side.
4: 5 same number of **d** as the years of
4: 5 So for 390 **d** you will bear the sin
4: 6 I have assigned you 40 **d**, a day for
4: 8 have finished the **d** of your siege.
4: 9 the 390 **d** you lie on your side.
5: 2 the **d** of your siege come to an end,
12:22 'The **d** go by and every vision comes
12:23 Say to them, 'The **d** are near when
12:25 For in your **d**, you rebellious house,
16:22 not remember the **d** of your youth,
16:43 not remember the **d** of your youth
16:60 with you in the **d** of your youth,
22: 4 You have brought your **d** to a close,
23:19 as she recalled the **d** of her youth,
38: 8 After many **d** you will be called to
38:17 not the one I spoke of in former **d**
43:27 At the end of these **d**, from the
46: 1 is to be shut on the six working **d**,
Da 1:12 "Please test your servants for ten **d**:
1:14 to this and tested them for ten **d**.
1:15 At the end of the ten **d** they looked
5:26 God has numbered the **d** of your reign
6: 7 god or man during the next thirty **d**,
6:12 during the next thirty **d** anyone who
8:27 exhausted and lay ill for several **d**.
10:13 kingdom resisted me twenty-one **d**.
11: 6 In those **d** she will be handed over,
12:11 is set up, there will be 1,290 **d**.
12:12 and reaches the end of the 1,335 **d**.
12:13 and then at the end of the **d** you
Hos 2:11 Sabbath **d**—all her appointed feasts.
2:13 I will punish her for the **d** she
2:15 will sing as in the **d** of her youth,
3: 3 "You are to live with me for many **d**;
3: 4 for many **d** without king or prince,
6: 2 After two **d** he will revive us; on
9: 5 on the festival **d** of the LORD?
9: 7 The **d** of punishment are coming,
9: 7 the **d** of reckoning are at hand.
9: 9 corruption, as in the **d** of Gibeah.
10: 9 "Since the **d** of Gibeah, you have
12: 9 in the **d** of your appointed feasts.
Joel 1: 2 like this ever happened in your **d**
1: 2 or in the **d** of your forefathers?
2:29 I will pour out my Spirit in those **d**.
3: 1 "In those **d** and at that time, when I
Jnh 3: 4 "Forty more **d** and Nineveh will be
Mic 7:14 Bashan and Gilead as in **d** long ago.
7:15 "As in the **d** when you came out of
7:20 oath to our fathers in **d** long ago.
Hab 1: 5 am going to do something in your **d**
Zec 8:23 "In those **d** ten men from all
14: 5 in the **d** of Uzziah king of Judah.
Mal 3: 4 as in **d** gone by, as in former years.
Mt 3: 1 In those **d** John the Baptist came,
11:12 From the **d** of John the Baptist until
23:30 'If we had lived in the **d** of our
24:19 How dreadful it will be in those **d**
24:22 If those **d** had not been cut short,
24:22 the elect those **d** will be shortened.
24:29 after the distress of those **d**
24:37 As it was in the **d** of Noah, so it
24:38 For in the **d** before the flood,
26: 2 "As you know, the Passover is two **d**
Mk 2: 1 A few **d** later, when Jesus again
2:26 In the **d** of Abiathar the high priest,
8: 1 During those **d** another large crowd
13:17 How dreadful it will be in those **d**
13:19 those will be **d** of distress
13:20 If the Lord had not cut short those **d**
13:24 "But in those **d**, following that
14: 1 were only two **d** away, and the chief
Lk 1:25 "In these **d** he has shown his favour
1:75 righteousness before him all our **d**.
2: 1 In those **d** Caesar Augustus issued a
4: 2 He ate nothing during those **d**, and

Lk 5:35 them; in those **d** they will fast."
6:12 One of those **d** Jesus went out to a
9:28 About eight **d** after Jesus said this,
13:14 on those **d**, not on the Sabbath."
17:22 see one of the **d** of the Son of Man,
17:26 "Just as it was in the **d** of Noah, so
17:26 it be in the **d** of the Son of Man.
17:28 "It was the same in the **d** of Lot.
19:43 The **d** will come upon you when your
21:23 How dreadful it will be in those **d**
24:18 have happened there in these **d**?"
Jn 2:12 There they stayed for a few **d**.
4:40 stay with them, and he stayed two **d**.
4:43 After the two **d** he left for Galilee.
10:40 had been baptising in the early **d**.
11: 6 he stayed where he was two more **d**.
11:17 already been in the tomb for four **d**.
11:39 for he has been there four **d**."
Ac 1: 5 but in a few **d** you will be baptised
1:15 In those **d** Peter stood up among the
2:18 will pour out my Spirit in those **d**,
3:24 have spoken, have foretold these **d**.
5:37 appeared in the **d** of the census
6: 1 In those **d** when the number of
7: 8 him eight **d** after his birth.
9:19 Saul spent several **d** with the
9:23 After many **d** had gone by, the Jews
10:30 Cornelius answered: "Four **d** ago I
10:48 Peter to stay with them for a few **d**.
13:31 for many **d** he was seen by those who
13:41 am going to do something in your **d**
16:12 And we stayed there several **d**.
16:18 She kept this up for many **d**. Finally
17: 2 and on three Sabbath **d** he reasoned
20: 6 and five **d** later joined the others
21:10 After we had been there a number of **d**
21:26 the **d** of purification would end
24: 1 Five **d** later the high priest Ananias
24:11 no more than twelve **d** ago I went up
24:24 Several **d** later Felix came with his
25: 6 After spending eight or ten **d** with
25:13 A few **d** later King Agrippa and
25:14 Since they were spending many **d**
27: 7 We made slow headway for many **d** and
27:20 appeared for many **d** and the storm
27:33 "For the last fourteen **d**," he said,
Gal 1:18 Peter and stayed with him fifteen **d**.
4:10 You are observing special **d** and
Eph 5:16 opportunity, because the **d** are evil.
Php 4:15 in the early **d** of your acquaintance
Heb 5: 7 During the **d** of Jesus' life on earth,
7: 3 without beginning of **d** or end of
10:32 Remember those earlier **d** after you
1Pe 3:10 would love life and see good **d**
3:20 waited patiently in the **d** of Noah
Rev 2:10 will suffer persecution for ten **d**.
2:13 even in the **d** of Antipas, my
9: 6 During those **d** men will seek death,
10: 7 in the **d** when the seventh angel is
11: 3 they will prophesy for 1,260 **d**,
11: 9 For three and a half **d** men from
11:11 after the three and a half **d** a
12: 6 might be taken care of for 1,260 **d**.

Days are coming

Jer 7:32 beware, the **d**, declares the LORD,
9:25 "The **d**," declares the LORD, "when I
Jer 16:14 "However, the **d**," declares the LORD,
19: 6 beware, the **d**, declares the LORD,
23: 5 "The **d**," declares the LORD, "when I
23: 7 "So then, the **d**," declares the LORD,
30: 3 The **d**,' declares the LORD, 'when I
31:27 "The **d**," declares the LORD, "when I
31:38 "The **d**," declares the LORD, "when
33:14 "The **d**,' declares the LORD, 'when I
48:12 **d**," declares the LORD, "when I will
49: 2 the **d**," declares the LORD, "when I
51:52 "But **d**," declares the LORD, "when I
Am 8:11 "The **d**," declares the Sovereign LORD,
9:13 "The **d**," declares the LORD, "when

Days to come

Ge 49: 1 you what will happen to you in **d**.
Ex 13:14 "In **d** when your son asks you, 'What
Nu 24:14 people will do to your people in **d**."
Dt 31:29 In **d**, disaster will fall upon you
Pr 31:25 and dignity; she can laugh at the **d**.
Ecc 2:16 in **d** both will be forgotten.
Isa 27: 6 In **d** Jacob will take root, Israel
30: 8 that for the **d** it may be an
Jer 23:20 In **d** you will understand it clearly.
30:24 In **d** you will understand this.
48:47 restore the fortunes of Moab in **d**,"
49:39 restore the fortunes of Elam in **d**,"
Eze 38:16 In **d**, O Gog, I will bring you
Da 2:28 Nebuchadnezzar what will happen in **d**.

Daytime (Day)

Ge 31:40 The heat consumed me in the **d** and
Jdg 6:27 it at night rather than in the **d**.
Job 5:14 Darkness comes upon them in the **d**;
Eze 12: 3 belongings for exile and in the **d**,
12: 4 During the **d**, while they watch,
Zec 14: 7 a unique day, without **d** or night-time
Ro 13:13 Let us behave decently, as in the **d**,

Dazzling

Da 2:31 an enormous **d** statue, awesome in
Mk 9: 3 His clothes became **d** white, whiter

Deacon (Deacons)

1Ti 3:12 A **d** must be the husband of but one

Deacons (Deacon)

Php 1: 1 together with the overseers and **d**:
1Ti 3: 8 **D**, likewise, are to be men worthy of
3:10 against them, let them serve as **d**.

Dead (Die, Half-dead, *Raised from the dead*, *Resurrection from the dead*, *Resurrection of the dead*)

Ge 20: 3 "You are as good as **d** because of the
23: 3 Abraham rose from beside his **d** wife
23: 4 site here so that I can bury my **d**."
23: 6 Bury your **d** in the choicest of our
23: 6 you his tomb for burying your **d**."
23: 8 you are willing to let me bury my **d**,
23:11 Bury your **d**."
23:13 me so that I can bury my **d** there."
23:15 between me and you? Bury your **d**."
34:27 The sons of Jacob came upon the **d**
42:38 his brother is **d** and he is the only
44:20 His brother is **d**, and he is the only
50:15 saw that their father was **d**,
Ex 4:19 men who wanted to kill you are **d**."
12:30 was not a house without someone **d**.
14:30 the Egyptians lying **d** on the shore.
21:34 owner, and the **d** animal will be his.
21:35 the money and the **d** animal equally.
21:36 and the **d** animal will be his.
Lev 7:24 The fat of an animal found **d** or torn
11:31 touches them when they are **d** will
14:51 them into the blood of the **d** bird
17:15 who eats anything found **d** or torn by
19:28 "'Do not cut your bodies for the **d**
21:11 a place where there is a **d** body.
22: 8 He must not eat anything found **d** or
26:30 pile your **d** bodies on the lifeless
Nu 3: 4 Nadab and Abihu, however, fell **d**
5: 2 unclean because of a **d** body.
6: 6 LORD he must not go near a **d** body.
6:11 being in the presence of the **d** body.
9: 6 unclean on account of a **d** body.
9: 7 become unclean because of a **d** body,
9:10 unclean because of a **d** body or are
16:48 He stood between the living and the **d**
19:11 "Whoever touches the **d** body of
19:13 Whoever touches the **d** body of anyone
20: 3 our brothers fell **d** before the LORD!
Dt 14: 1 the front of your heads for the **d**,
14:21 not eat anything you find already **d**.
18:11 or spiritist or who consults the **d**.
25: 6 carry on the name of the **d** brother
26:14 have I offered any of it to the **d**.
Jos 1: 2 "Moses my servant is **d**. Now then,
Jdg 3:25 their lord fallen to the floor, **d**.
4:22 the tent peg through his temple—**d**.
5:27 where he sank, there he fell—**d**.
9:55 Abimelech was **d**, they went home.
Ru 1: 8 you have shown to your **d** and to me.
2:20 kindness to the living and the **d**.
4: 5 you acquire the **d** man's widow, in
4: 5 name of the **d** with his property."
4:10 the name of the **d** with his property,
1Sa 4:17 Hophni and Phinehas, are **d**, and the
4:19 and her husband were **d**, she went into
17:51 saw that their hero was **d**, they
17:52 Their **d** were strewn along the
24:14 are you pursuing? A **d** dog? A flea?
25:39 David heard that Nabal was **d**, he
28: 3 Now Samuel was **d**, and all Israel had
31: 5 the armour-bearer saw that Saul was **d**
31: 8 the Philistines came to strip the **d**,
2Sa 1: 4 And Saul and his son Jonathan are **d**."
1: 5 Saul and his son Jonathan are **d**?"
2: 7 for Saul your master is **d**, and the
4:10 a man told me, 'Saul is **d**,' and
9: 8 you should notice a **d** dog like me?"
11:21 servant Uriah the Hittite is **d**.'"
11:24 servant Uriah the Hittite is **d**."
11:26 heard that her husband was **d**, she
12:18 to tell him that the child was **d**,
12:18 How can we tell him the child is **d**?
12:19 he realised that the child was **d**.
12:19 "Is the child **d**?" he asked. "Yes,"
12:19 "Yes," they replied, "he is **d**."
12:21 the child is **d**, you get up and eat!"
12:23 now that he is **d**, why should I fast?
13:32 all the princes; only Amnon is **d**.
13:33 that all the king's sons are **d**.
13:33 Only Amnon is **d**."
14: 2 spent many days grieving for the **d**.
14: 5 I am indeed a widow; my husband is **d**.
16: 9 "Why should this **d** dog curse my lord
18:20 today, because the king's son is **d**."
19: 6 alive today and all of us were **d**.
23:10 to Eleazar, but only to strip the **d**.
1Ki 3:20 and put her **d** son by my breast.
3:21 up to nurse my son—and he was **d**!
3:22 one is my son; the **d** one is yours.
3:22 "No! The **d** one is yours; the living
3:23 'My son is alive and your son is **d**,'
3:23 Your son is **d** and mine is alive.'"
11:15 who had gone up to bury the **d**, had
11:21 commander of the army was also **d**.
21:14 "Naboth has been stoned and is **d**.
21:15 He is no longer alive, but **d**."
21:16 Ahab heard that Naboth was **d**, he got
2Ki 4: 1 "Your servant my husband is **d**, and
4:32 was the boy lying **d** on his couch.
8: 5 Elisha had restored the **d** to life,
11: 1 of Ahaziah saw that her son was **d**,
19:35 there were all the **d** bodies!
1Ch 10: 5 the armour-bearer saw that Saul was **d**
10: 8 the Philistines came to strip the **d**,
21:14 thousand men of Israel fell **d**.
2Ch 20:24 they saw only **d** bodies lying on the
22:10 of Ahaziah saw that her son was **d**,
Job 1:19 It collapsed on them and they are **d**,
26: 5 "The **d** are in deep anguish, those
Ps 6: 5 No-one remembers you when he is **d**.
31:12 by them as though I were **d**;
79: 2 They have given the **d** bodies of your
79: 3 and there is no-one to bury the **d**.
88: 5 I am set apart with the **d**, like the
88:10 Do you show your wonders to the **d**?
88:10 Do those who are **d** rise up and
110: 6 heaping up the **d** and crushing the
115:17 is not the **d** who praise the LORD,
143: 3 dwell in darkness like those long **d**.
Pr 2:18 her paths to the spirits of the **d**.
9:18 little do they know that the **d** are
21:16 to rest in the company of the **d**.
Ecc 4: 2 I declared that the **d**, who had
9: 3 and afterwards they join the **d**.
9: 4 dog is better off than a **d** lion!
9: 5 but the **d** know nothing; they have no
10: 1 **d** flies give perfume a bad smell, so
Isa 5:25 and the **d** bodies are like refuse
8:19 why consult the **d** on behalf of the
19: 3 the idols and the spirits of the **d**,
26:14 They are now **d**, they live no more;
26:19 your **d** will live; their bodies will
26:19 the earth will give birth to her **d**.
34: 3 their **d** bodies will send up a stench;

Isa 37:36 there were all the **d** bodies!
59:10 among the strong, we are like the **d**.
66:24 look upon the **d** bodies of those who
Jer 7:32 for they will bury the **d** in Topheth
9:22 "'The **d** bodies of men will lie like
16: 4 and their **d** bodies will become food
16: 7 comfort those who mourn for the **d**
19:11 They will bury the **d** in Topheth
22:10 Do not weep for the **d** king or mourn
31:40 The whole valley where **d** bodies and
33: 5 'They will be filled with the **d**
34:20 Their **d** bodies will become food for
41: 9 of Nethaniah filled it with the **d**.
Lam 3: 6 dwell in darkness like those long **d**.
Eze 4:14 found **d** or torn by wild animals.
6: 5 I will lay the **d** bodies of the
11: 6 and filled its streets with the **d**.
24:17 Groan quietly; do not mourn for the **d**
44:25 by going near a **d** person; however,
44:25 if the **d** person was his father or
44:31 found **d** or torn by wild animals.
Am 1: 8 the last of the Philistines is **d**,"
Na 3: 3 piles of **d**, bodies without number,
Hag 2:13 **d** body touches one of these things,
Mt 2:20 to take the child's life are **d**."
8:22 me, and let the **d** bury their own **d**."
9:24 The girl is not **d** but asleep."
10: 8 Heal the sick, raise the **d**, cleanse
11: 5 the deaf hear, the **d** are raised, and
14: 2 he has risen from the **d**! That is why
22:32 the God of the **d** but of the living."
23:27 **d** men's bones and everything unclean.
28: 4 they shook and became like **d** men.
28: 7 'He has risen from the **d** and is
Mk 5:35 "Your daughter is **d**," they said.
5:39 The child is not **d** but asleep."
9: 9 the Son of Man had risen from the **d**.
9:10 what "rising from the **d**" meant.
9:26 a corpse that many said, "He's **d**.
12:25 the **d** rise, they will neither marry
12:26 Now about the **d** rising—have you not
12:27 He is not the God of the **d**, but of
15:44 to hear that he was already **d**.
Lk 7:12 a **d** person was being carried out
7:15 The **d** man sat up and began to talk,
7:22 the deaf hear, the **d** are raised, and
8:49 "Your daughter is **d**," he said.
8:52 "She is not **d** but asleep."
8:53 at him, knowing that she was **d**.
9:60 "Let the **d** bury their own **d**, but you
15:24 For this son of mine was **d** and is
15:32 because this brother of yours was **d**
16:30 if someone from the **d** goes to them,
16:31 even if someone rises from the **d**.'"
17:37 He replied, "Where there is a **d** body,
20:37 even Moses showed that the **d** rise,
20:38 He is not the God of the **d**, but of
24: 5 you look for the living among the **d**?
24:46 rise from the **d** on the third day,
Jn 5:21 For just as the Father raises the **d**
5:25 has now come when the **d** will hear
11:14 told them plainly, "Lazarus is **d**,
11:39 Martha, the sister of the **d** man,
11:44 The **d** man came out, his hands and
12:17 the tomb and raised him from the **d**
19:33 found that he was already **d**, they
20: 9 that Jesus had to rise from the **d**.)
Ac 2:24 God raised him from the **d**, freeing
3:15 life, but God raised him from the **d**.
5:10 finding her **d**, carried her out and
5:30 our fathers raised Jesus from the **d**
9:40 Turning towards the **d** woman, he said,
10:40 God raised him from the **d** on the
10:41 with him after he rose from the **d**.
10:42 as judge of the living and the **d**.
13:30 God raised him from the **d**,
13:34 fact that God raised him from the **d**,
14:19 outside the city, thinking he was **d**.
17: 3 had to suffer and rise from the **d**.
17:31 all men by raising him from the **d**."
20: 9 third storey and was picked up **d**.
25:19 about a **d** man named Jesus whom Paul
26: 8 it incredible that God raises the **d**?
26:23 as the first to rise from the **d**,
28: 6 him to swell up or suddenly fall **d**,
Ro 4:17 God who gives life to the **d**
Ro 4:19 fact that his body was as good as **d**
4:19 that Sarah's womb was also **d**.
4:24 raised Jesus our Lord from the **d**.
6:11 In the same way, count yourselves **d**
7: 8 For apart from law, sin is **d**.
8:10 if Christ is in you, your body is **d**
8:11 him who raised Jesus from the **d** is
8:11 he who raised Christ from the **d** will
10: 7 is, to bring Christ up from the **d**).
10: 9 God raised him from the **d**, you will
11:15 acceptance be but life from the **d**?
14: 9 Lord of both the **d** and the living.
1Co 6:14 God raised the Lord from the **d**, and
15:15 God that he raised Christ from the **d**.
15:15 him if in fact the **d** are not raised.
15:16 For if the **d** are not raised, then
15:29 who are baptised for the **d**? If the
15:29 If the **d** are not raised at all,
15:32 I gained? If the **d** are not raised,
15:35 may ask, "How are the **d** raised?
15:52 the **d** will be raised imperishable
2Co 1: 9 but on God, who raises the **d**.
4:14 raised the Lord Jesus from the **d**
Gal 1: 1 Father, who raised him from the **d**—
Eph 1:20 Christ when he raised him from the **d**
2: 1 you were **d** in your transgressions
2: 5 when we were **d** in transgressions
5:14 Wake up, O sleeper, rise from the **d**,
Col 1:18 and the firstborn from among the **d**,
2:12 of God, who raised him from the **d**.
2:13 you were **d** in your sins and in the
1Th 4:16 and the **d** in Christ will rise first.
1Ti 5: 6 the widow who lives for pleasure is **d**
2Ti 4: 1 who will judge the living and the **d**,
Heb 11: 4 still speaks, even though he is **d**.
11:12 this one man, and he as good as **d**,
11:19 reasoned that God could raise the **d**,
11:35 Women received back their **d**, raised
13:20 back from the **d** our Lord Jesus,
Jas 2:17 is not accompanied by action, is **d**.
2:26 the body without the spirit is **d**,
2:26 so faith without deeds is **d**.
1Pe 1: 3 of Jesus Christ from the **d**,
1:21 who raised him from the **d** and
4: 5 ready to judge the living and the **d**.
4: 6 even to those who are now **d**,
Jude :12 without fruit and uprooted—twice **d**.
Rev 1: 5 the firstborn from the **d**, and the
1:17 him, I fell at his feet as though **d**.
1:18 I was **d**, and behold I am alive for
2:23 I will strike her children **d**. Then
3: 1 of being alive, but you are **d**.
11:18 The time has come for judging the **d**,
14:13 Blessed are the **d** who die in the
16: 3 into blood like that of a **d** man,
20: 5 (The rest of the **d** did not come to
20:12 I saw the **d**, great and small,
20:12 The **d** were judged according to what
20:13 The sea gave up the **d** that were in
20:13 and death and Hades gave up the **d**

Dead Sea

At southern end of Jordan Valley, about 50 miles long and averaging about 10 miles wide. Up to 1,300 feet below sea level with salt and potash deposits more concentrated than in any other lake or sea in the world. Known as Salt Sea, Eastern Sea and Sea of Arabah. Mostly mentioned as a boundary – to the land of Israel (Nu 34:3, 12; 2Ki 14:25; Eze 47:18), tribal territory (Dt 3:17; Jos 15:2, 5; 18:19), neighbouring kingdoms (Dt 4:49; Jos 12:3). Its source was cut off when Israelites crossed into promised land (Jos 3:16). Israel's enemies will be driven into it (Joel 2:20), and living water will flow into it from Jerusalem (Zec 14:8).

Deadened (Die)

Jn 12:40 their eyes and **d** their hearts,

Deadly (Die)

Ex 10:17 to take this **d** plague away from me."
Dt 32:24 consuming pestilence and **d** plague;
32:33 of serpents, the **d** poison of cobras.
Ps 7:13 He has prepared his **d** weapons; he
64: 3 and aim their words like **d** arrows.
Ps 91: 3 snare and from the **d** pestilence.
144:10 his servant David from the **d** sword.
Pr 21: 6 is a fleeting vapour and a **d** snare.
26:18 shooting firebrands or **d** arrows
Jer 9: 8 Their tongue is a **d** arrow; it speaks
16: 4 "They will die of **d** diseases. They
Eze 5:16 with my **d** and destructive arrows of
9: 2 each with a **d** weapon in his hand.
Mk 16:18 when they drink **d** poison, it will
2Co 1:10 delivered us from such a **d** peril,
Jas 3: 8 a restless evil, full of **d** poison.

Deaf

Ex 4:11 Who makes him **d** or mute? Who gives
Lev 19:14 "'Do not curse the **d** or put a
Dt 1:45 weeping and turned a **d** ear to you.
Ps 28: 1 my Rock; do not turn a **d** ear to me.
38:13 I am like a **d** man, who cannot hear,
39:12 for help; be not **d** to my weeping.
Pr 28: 9 If anyone turns a **d** ear to the law,
Isa 29:18 In that day the **d** will hear the
35: 5 and the ears of the **d** unstopped.
42:18 "Hear, you **d**; look, you blind, and
42:19 and **d** like the messenger I send?
43: 8 are blind, who have ears but are **d**.
Mic 7:16 mouths and their ears will become **d**.
Mt 11: 5 the **d** hear, the dead are raised, and
Mk 7:32 man who was **d** and could hardly talk,
7:37 the **d** hear and the mute speak."
9:25 "You **d** and mute spirit," he said, "I
Lk 7:22 the **d** hear, the dead are raised, and

Deal (Dealer, Dealing, Dealings, Deals, Dealt)

Ge 21:23 that you will not **d** falsely with me
Ex 1:10 Come, we must **d** shrewdly with them
8:22 on that day I will **d** differently
Ru 1:17 May the LORD **d** with me, be it ever
1Sa 3:17 May God **d** with you, be it ever
14:44 Saul said, "May God **d** with me, be it
20:13 may the LORD **d** with me, be it ever
24: 4 hands for you to **d** with as you wish.
25:22 May God **d** with David, be it ever so
2Sa 3: 9 May God **d** with Abner, be it ever so
3:22 with them a great **d** of plunder.
3:35 "May God **d** with me, be it ever so
19:13 May God **d** with me, be it ever so
1Ki 2: 6 **D** with him according to your wisdom,
2:23 "May God **d** with me, be it ever so
8:39 Forgive and act; **d** with each man
19: 2 "May the gods **d** with me, be it ever
20:10 "May the gods **d** with me, be it ever
2Ki 6:31 He said, "May God **d** with me, be it
2Ch 6:30 Forgive, and **d** with each man
12:15 the seer that **d** with genealogies?
28: 8 They also took a great **d** of plunder,
Ne 5: 7 a large meeting to **d** with them
9:24 to **d** with them as they pleased.
Job 42: 8 **d** with you according to your folly.
Ps 109:21 **d** well with me for your name's sake
119:124 **D** with your servant according to
Isa 10:11 shall I not **d** with Jerusalem and her
23:17 years, the LORD will **d** with Tyre.
Jer 2: 8 Those who **d** with the law did not
7: 5 and **d** with each other justly,
18:23 **d** with them in the time of your
24: 8 'so will I **d** with Zedekiah king of
32: 5 he will remain until I **d** with him,
Lam 1:22 **d** with them as you have dealt with
Eze 7:27 I will **d** with them according to
8:18 Therefore I will **d** with them in
16:59 I will **d** with you as you deserve,
20:44 when I **d** with you for my name's sake
22:14 be strong in the day I **d** with you?
23:25 and they will **d** with you in fury.
23:29 They will **d** with you in hatred and
25:14 and they will **d** with Edom in
31:11 for him to **d** with according to its
Zep 3:19 At that time I will **d** with all who
Zec 8:11 now I will not **d** with the remnant of
Mt 27:19 suffered a great **d** today in a dream
Mk 5:26 She had suffered a great **d** under the
Ac 16:16 She earned a great **d** of money for
2Ti 4:14 did me a great **d** of harm.
Heb 5: 2 He is able to **d** gently with those

Dealer (Deal)

Ac 16:14 a **d** in purple cloth from the city of

Dealing (Deal)

2Sa 7:19 this your usual way of **d** with man,
Ezr 10:17 they finished **d** with all the men
Lk 16: 8 more shrewd in **d** with their own
2Co 13: 3 He is not weak in **d** with you, but is

Dealings (Deal)

1Sa 25: 3 was surly and mean in his **d**.

Deals (Deal)

Dt 25:16 things, anyone who **d** dishonestly.
Jer 5: 1 one person who **d** honestly and seeks
1Th 2:11 as a father **d** with his own children,

Dealt (Deal)

Ex 10: 2 how I **d** harshly with the Egyptians
1Sa 6:19 the heavy blow the LORD had **d** them,
2Sa 22:21 "The LORD has **d** with me according to
Ps 18:20 The LORD has **d** with me according to
Isa 10:11 as I **d** with Samaria and her idols?'"
Lam 1:22 **d** with me because of all my sins.
Eze 39:24 I **d** with them according to their
Ac 7:19 He **d** treacherously with our people
1Th 2:11 For you know that we **d** with each of

Dear (Dearer, Dearly)

2Sa 1:26 my brother; you were very **d** to me.
Ps 102:14 For her stones are **d** to your
Jer 31:20 Is not Ephraim my **d** son, the child
Jn 2: 4 "**D** woman, why do you involve me?"
19:26 "**D** woman, here is your son,
Ac 15:25 our **d** friends Barnabas and Paul—
Ro 16: 5 Greet my **d** friend Epenetus, who was
16: 9 in Christ, and my **d** friend Stachys.
16:12 Greet my **d** friend Persis, another
1Co 4:14 but to warn you, as my **d** children.
10:14 Therefore, my **d** friends, flee from
15:58 Therefore, my **d** brothers, stand firm.
2Co 7: 1 we have these promises, **d** friends,
12:19 everything we do, **d** friends, is for
Gal 4:19 My **d** children, for whom I am again
Eph 6:21 Tychicus, the **d** brother and faithful
Php 2:12 Therefore, my **d** friends, as you have
4: 1 stand firm in the Lord, **d** friends!
Col 1: 7 Epaphras, our **d** fellow-servant,
4: 7 He is a **d** brother, a faithful
4: 9 our faithful and **d** brother, who is
4:14 Our **d** friend Luke, the doctor, and
1Th 2: 8 because you had become so **d** to us.
1Ti 6: 2 are believers, and **d** to them.
2Ti 1: 2 To Timothy, my **d** son: Grace, mercy
Phm : 1 our **d** friend and fellow-worker,
:16 better than a slave, as a **d** brother.
:16 He is very **d** to me but even dearer
Heb 6: 9 we speak like this, **d** friends,
Jas 1:16 Don't be deceived, my **d** brothers.
1:19 My **d** brothers, take note of this:
2: 5 Listen, my **d** brothers: Has not God
1Pe 2:11 **D** friends, I urge you, as aliens and
4:12 **D** friends, do not be surprised at
2Pe 3: 1 **D** friends, this is now my second
3: 8 forget this one thing, **d** friends:
3:14 then, **d** friends, since you are
3:15 just as our **d** brother Paul also
3:17 Therefore, **d** friends, since you
1Jn 2: 1 My **d** children, I write this to you
2: 7 **D** friends, I am not writing you a
2:12 I write to you, **d** children, because
2:13 I write to you, **d** children, because
2:18 **D** children, this is the last hour;
2:28 now, **d** children, continue in him, so
3: 2 **D** friends, now we are children of
3: 7 **D** children, do not let anyone lead
3:18 **D** children, let us not love with
3:21 **D** friends, if our hearts do not
4: 1 **D** friends, do not believe every
4: 4 You, **d** children, are from God and
4: 7 **D** friends, let us love one another,
4:11 **D** friends, since God so loved us, we
5:21 **D** children, keep yourselves from
2Jn : 5 now, **d** lady, I am not writing you a
3Jn : 1 The elder, To my **d** friend Gaius,
: 2 **D** friend, I pray that you may enjoy
: 5 **D** friend, you are faithful in what
:11 **D** friend, do not imitate what is
Jude : 3 **D** friends, although I was very eager
:17 But, **d** friends, remember what the
:20 you, **d** friends, build yourselves up

Dearer (Dear)

Phm :16 very dear to me but even **d** to you,

Dearly (Dear)

Hos 4:18 their rulers **d** love shameful ways.
Eph 5: 1 God, therefore, as **d** loved children
Col 3:12 chosen people, holy and **d** loved,

Death (Die, *Life and death, Shadow of death*)

Ge 24:67 was comforted after his mother's **d**.
25:11 After Abraham's **d**, God blessed his
26:11 his wife shall surely be put to **d**."
27: 2 man and don't know the day of my **d**.
38: 7 sight; so the LORD put him to **d**.
38:10 sight; so he put him to **d** also.
38:24 her out and have her burned to **d**!"
42:37 put both of my sons to **d** if I do
Ex 16: 3 starve this entire assembly to **d**."
19:12 mountain shall surely be put to **d**.
21:12 kills him shall surely be put to **d**.
21:14 away from my altar and put him to **d**.
21:15 or his mother must be put to **d**.
21:16 when he is caught must be put to **d**.
21:17 father or mother must be put to **d**.
21:28 a bull gores a man or a woman to **d**,
21:28 the bull must be stoned to **d**, and
21:29 and the owner also must be put to **d**.
22:19 with an animal must be put to **d**.
23: 7 an innocent or honest person to **d**,
31:14 who desecrates it must be put to **d**;
31:15 on the Sabbath day must be put to **d**.
35: 2 any work on it must be put to **d**.
Lev 16: 1 Moses after the **d** of the two sons
19:20 they are not to be put to **d**,
20: 2 children to Molech must be put to **d**.
20: 4 Molech and they fail to put him to **d**,
20: 9 or mother, he must be put to **d**.
20:10 and the adulteress must be put to **d**.
20:11 man and the woman must be put to **d**;
20:12 both of them must be put to **d**.
20:13 They must be put to **d**; their blood
20:15 he must be put to **d**, and you must
20:16 They must be put to **d**; their blood
20:27 among you must be put to **d**.
24:16 name of the LORD must be put to **d**.
24:16 the Name, he must be put to **d**.
24:17 a human being, he must be put to **d**.
24:21 kills a man must be put to **d**.
27:29 be ransomed; he must be put to **d**.
Nu 1:51 who goes near it shall be put to **d**.
3:10 the sanctuary must be put to **d**."
3:38 the sanctuary was to be put to **d**.
11:15 put me to **d** right now—if I have
14:15 If you put these people to **d** all at
15:36 the camp and stoned him to **d**,
16:29 If these men die a natural **d** and
18: 7 the sanctuary must be put to **d**."
19:16 or someone who has died a natural **d**,
19:18 or someone who has died a natural **d**.
23:10 Let me die the **d** of the righteous,
25: 5 "Each of you must put to **d** those of
25:15 put to **d** was Cozbi daughter of Zur,
35:16 the murderer shall be put to **d**.
35:17 the murderer shall be put to **d**.
35:18 the murderer shall be put to **d**.
35:19 blood shall put the murderer to **d**;
35:19 he meets him, he shall put him to **d**.
35:21 shall be put to **d**; he is a murderer.
35:21 the murderer to **d** when he meets him.
35:25 He must stay there until the **d** of
35:28 until the **d** of the high priest;
35:28 only after the **d** of the high priest
35:30 put to **d** as a murderer only on the
35:30 But no-one is to be put to **d** on the
35:31 He must surely be put to **d**.
35:32 before the **d** of the high priest.
Dt 9:28 out to put them to **d** in the desert.'
13: 5 prophet or dreamer must be put to **d**,
13: 9 You must certainly put him to **d**.
13: 9 be the first in putting him to **d**,
13:10 Stone him to **d**, because he tried to
17: 5 gate and stone that person to **d**.
17: 6 witnesses a man shall be put to **d**,
17: 6 but no-one shall be put to **d** on the
17: 7 be the first in putting him to **d**,
17:12 the LORD your God must be put to **d**.
18:20 of other gods, must be put to **d**."
19: 6 though he is not deserving of **d**,
21:21 of his town shall stone him to **d**.
21:22 put to **d** and his body is hung on a
22:21 of her town shall stone her to **d**.
22:24 stone them to **d**–the girl because
22:26 has committed no sin deserving **d**.
24:16 Fathers shall not be put to **d** for
24:16 nor children put to **d** for their
30:15 and prosperity, **d** and destruction.
31:14 "Now the day of your **d** is near.
31:29 For I know that after my **d** you are
32:22 that burns to the realm of **d** below.
32:39 I put to **d** and I bring to life, I
33: 1 on the Israelites before his **d**.
Jos 1: 1 After the **d** of Moses the servant of
1:18 may command them, will be put to **d**.
2:13 and that you will save us from **d**."
11:17 struck them down, putting them to **d**.
20: 6 until the **d** of the high priest who
Jdg 1: 1 After the **d** of Joshua, the
6:31 him shall be put to **d** by morning!
13: 7 from birth until the day of his **d**.'"
14:15 and your father's household to **d**.
15: 6 and burned her and her father to **d**.
16:16 after day until he was tired to **d**.
20:13 so that we may put them to **d** and
21: 5 Mizpah should certainly be put to **d**.
Ru 1:17 but **d** separates you and me."
2:11 since the **d** of your husband—
1Sa 2: 6 "The LORD brings **d** and makes alive;
2:25 the LORD's will to put them to **d**.
5:11 For **d** had filled the city with
6:19 putting seventy of them to **d** because
11:12 to us and we will put them to **d**."
11:13 Saul said, "No-one shall be put to **d**
14:45 Jonathan, and he was not put to **d**.
15: 3 put to **d** men and women, children
15:32 "Surely the bitterness of **d** is past.
15:33 put Agag to **d** before the LORD at
19: 6 lives, David will not be put to **d**."
20: 3 is only a step between me and **d**."
20:32 "Why should he be put to **d**? What has
22:22 the **d** of your father's whole family.
28: 9 for my life to bring about my **d**?"
2Sa 1: 1 After the **d** of Saul, David returned
1: 9 throes of **d**, but I'm still alive.'
1:23 and in **d** they were not parted.
4:10 him and put him to **d** in Ziklag.
6:23 had no children to the day of her **d**.
8: 2 two lengths of them were put to **d**,
13:39 was consoled concerning Amnon's **d**.
14: 7 so that we may put him to **d** for the
14:32 of anything, let him put me to **d**."
15:21 whether it means life or **d**, there
17: 3 The **d** of the man you seek will mean
19:21 "Shouldn't Shimei be put to **d** for
19:22 anyone be put to **d** in Israel today?
19:28 nothing but **d** from my lord the king,
20: 3 confinement till the day of their **d**
21: 1 because he put the Gibeonites to **d**."
21: 4 right to put anyone in Israel to **d**.
21: 9 put to **d** during the first days of
22: 5 "The waves of **d** swirled about me;
22: 6 me; the snares of **d** confronted me.
1Ki 1:51 his servant to **d** with the sword.'"
2: 8 will not put you to **d** by the sword.'
2:24 Adonijah shall be put to **d** today!"
2:26 but I will not put you to **d** now,
3:11 nor have asked for the **d** of your
11:40 and stayed there until Solomon's **d**.
12:18 but all Israel stoned him to **d**.
18: 9 servant over to Ahab to be put to **d**?
19:10 your prophets to **d** with the sword.
19:14 your prophets to **d** with the sword.
19:17 Jehu will put to **d** any who escape

1Ki 19:17 Elisha will put to **d** any who escape
21:10 take him out and stone him to **d**."
21:13 the city and stoned him to **d**.
21:15 that Naboth had been stoned to **d**,
22:20 and going to his **d** there?'
2Ki 1: 1 After Ahab's **d**, Moab rebelled
2:21 Never again will it cause **d** or make
4:40 "O man of God, there is **d** in the pot!
11: 8 your ranks must be put to **d**.
11:15 put to **d** in the temple of the LORD."
11:16 grounds, and there she was put to **d**.
14: 6 put the sons of the assassins to **d**,
14: 6 "Fathers shall not be put to **d** for
14: 6 nor children put to **d** for their
14:17 for fifteen years after the **d** of
16: 9 to Kir and put Rezin to **d**.
18:32 Choose life and not **d**! "Do not
19:35 put to **d** a hundred and eighty-five
20: 1 ill and was at the point of **d**.
1Ch 2: 3 so the LORD put him to **d**.
10:14 So the LORD put him to **d** and turned
22: 5 extensive preparations before his **d**.
2Ch 1:11 nor for the **d** of your enemies,
10:18 but the Israelites stoned him to **d**.
15:13 were to be put to **d**, whether small
18:19 and going to his **d** there?'
22: 4 for after his father's **d** they became
22: 9 He was brought to Jehu and put to **d**.
23: 7 enters the temple must be put to **d**.
23:14 her to **d** at the temple of the LORD."
23:15 and there they put her to **d**.
24:17 After the **d** of Jehoiada, the
24:21 stoned him to **d** in the courtyard
25: 4 Yet he did not put their sons to **d**,
25: 4 "Fathers shall not be put to **d** for
25: 4 nor children put to **d** for their
25:25 for fifteen years after the **d** of
32:24 ill and was at the point of **d**.
Ezr 7:26 king must surely be punished by **d**,
Est 4:11 but one law: that he be put to **d**.
9:15 and they put to **d** in Susa three
Job 3:21 to those who long for **d** that does
5:20 In famine he will ransom you from **d**,
7:15 that I prefer strangling and **d**,
9:23 a scourge brings sudden **d**, he mocks
17:16 Will it go down to the gates of **d**?
26: 6 **D** is naked before God; Destruction
28:22 Destruction and **D** say, 'Only a
30:23 I know you will bring me down to **d**,
33:22 and his life to the messengers of **d**.
38:17 Have the gates of **d** been shown to
Ps 9: T ⌊the tune of⌋ "The **D** of the Son".
9:13 and lift me up from the gates of **d**,
13: 3 to my eyes, or I will sleep in **d**;
18: 4 The cords of **d** entangled me; the
18: 5 the snares of **d** confronted me.
22:15 mouth; you lay me in the dust of **d**.
33:19 to deliver them from **d** and keep them
44:22 Yet for your sake we face **d** all day
49:14 the grave, and **d** will feed on them.
55: 4 the terrors of **d** assail me.
55:15 Let **d** take my enemies by surprise;
56:13 For you have delivered me from **d** and
68:20 Sovereign LORD comes escape from **d**.
72:13 the needy and save the needy from **d**.
78:31 put to **d** the sturdiest among them,
78:50 he did not spare them from **d**
88:15 I have been afflicted and close to **d**;
89:48 What man can live and not see **d**, or
90: 5 You sweep men away in the sleep of **d**;
94:17 soon have dwelt in the silence of **d**.
94:21 and condemn the innocent to **d**.
102:20 and release those condemned to **d**."
107:18 food and drew near the gates of **d**.
109:16 but hounded to **d** the poor and the
116: 3 The cords of **d** entangled me, the
116: 8 have delivered my soul from **d**, my
116:15 of the LORD is the **d** of his saints.
118:18 but he has not given me over to **d**.
141: 8 refuge—do not give me over to **d**.
Pr 2:18 For her house leads down to **d** and
5: 5 Her feet go down to **d**; her steps
7:27 leading down to the chambers of **d**.
8:36 himself; all who hate me love **d**."
10: 2 but righteousness delivers from **d**.
11: 4 but righteousness delivers from **d**.
Pr 11:19 he who pursues evil goes to his **d**.
13:14 turning a man from the snares of **d**.
14:12 a man, but in the end it leads to **d**.
14:27 turning a man from the snares of **d**.
14:32 in **d** the righteous have a refuge.
15:11 **D** and Destruction lie open before
16:14 A king's wrath is a messenger of **d**,
16:25 a man, but in the end it leads to **d**.
19:18 do not be a willing party to his **d**.
21:25 sluggard's craving will be the **d** of
23:14 the rod and save his soul from **d**.
24:11 Rescue those being led away to **d**;
27:20 **D** and Destruction are never
28:17 will be a fugitive till **d**; let
Ecc 7: 1 the day of **d** better than the day
7: 2 for **d** is the destiny of every man;
7:26 I find more bitter than **d** the woman
8: 8 has power over the day of his **d**.
SS 8: 6 arm; for love is as strong as **d**,
Isa 25: 8 he will swallow up **d** for ever. The
28:15 have entered into a covenant with **d**,
28:18 Your covenant with **d** will be
37:36 put to **d** a hundred and eighty-five
38: 1 ill and was at the point of **d**.
38:10 must I go through the gates of **d**
38:18 **d** cannot sing your praise;
53: 9 and with the rich in his **d**, though
53:12 he poured out his life unto **d**,
57: 2 they find rest as they lie in **d**.
65:15 Sovereign LORD will put you to **d**,
Jer 8: 3 evil nation will prefer **d** to life,
9:21 **D** has climbed in through our windows
15: 2 "'Those destined for **d**, to **d**; those
18:21 let their men be put to **d**, their
21: 8 the way of life and the way of **d**.
26:11 "This man should be sentenced to **d**
26:15 however, that if you put me to **d**,
26:16 man should not be sentenced to **d**!
26:19 anyone else in Judah put him to **d**?
26:21 the king sought to put him to **d**.
26:24 over to the people to be put to **d**.
29:21 put them to **d** before your very eyes.
38: 4 king, "This man should be put to **d**.
38: 9 where he will starve to **d** when there
43:11 bringing **d** to those destined for **d**,
52:11 him in prison till the day of his **d**.
52:34 as he lived, till the day of his **d**.
Lam 1:20 bereaves; inside, there is only **d**.
Eze 18:13 he will surely be put to **d** and his
18:23 Do I take any pleasure in the **d** of
18:32 For I take no pleasure in the **d** of
28: 8 violent **d** in the heart of the seas.
28:10 will die the **d** of the uncircumcised
31:14 height; they are all destined for **d**,
33:11 I take no pleasure in the **d** of the
Da 2:13 was issued to put the wise men to **d**,
2:13 and his friends to put them to **d**.
2:14 had gone out to put to **d** the wise
5:19 Those the king wanted to put to **d**,
5:19 he put to **d**; those he wanted to
Hos 13:14 grave; I will redeem them from **d**.
13:14 Where, O **d**, are your plagues? Where,
Hab 2: 5 grave and like **d** is never satisfied,
Mt 2:15 where he stayed until the **d** of Herod.
10:21 "Brother will betray brother to **d**,
10:21 parents and have them put to **d**.
15: 4 father or mother must be put to **d**.'
16:28 will not taste **d** before they see
20:18 They will condemn him to **d**
24: 9 over to be persecuted and put to **d**,
26:38 with sorrow to the point of **d**.
26:59 so that they could put him to **d**.
26:66 "He is worthy of **d**," they answered.
27: 1 to the decision to put Jesus to **d**.
Mk 7:10 father or mother must be put to **d**.'
9: 1 will not taste **d** before they see
10:33 They will condemn him to **d** and will
13:12 "Brother will betray brother to **d**,
13:12 parents and have them put to **d**.
14:34 with sorrow to the point of **d**,"
14:55 so that they could put him to **d**,
14:64 all condemned him as worthy of **d**.
Lk 9:27 will not taste **d** before they see
15:17 spare, and here I am starving to **d**!
21:16 and they will put some of you to **d**.
22:33 to go with you to prison and to **d**."
Lk 23:15 he has done nothing to deserve **d**.
23:22 in him no grounds for the **d** penalty.
24:20 to be sentenced to **d**, and they
Jn 4:47 heal his son, who was close to **d**.
5:24 he has crossed over from **d** to life.
8:51 keeps my word, he will never see **d**."
8:52 your word, he will never taste **d**.
11: 4 "This sickness will not end in **d**.
11:13 Jesus had been speaking of his **d**,
12:33 He said this to show the kind of **d**
18:32 indicating the kind of **d** he was
21:19 **d** by which Peter would glorify God.
Ac 2:23 to **d** by nailing him to the cross.
2:24 freeing him from the agony of **d**,
2:24 for **d** to keep its hold on him.
5:33 furious and wanted to put them to **d**.
7: 4 After the **d** of his father, God sent
8: 1 was there, giving approval to his **d**.
12: 2 of John, put to **d** with the sword.
13:28 no proper ground for a **d** sentence,
22: 4 followers of this Way to their **d**,
23:29 him that deserved **d** or imprisonment.
25:11 of doing anything deserving **d**, I do
25:25 he had done nothing deserving of **d**,
26:10 when they were put to **d**, I cast my
26:31 that deserves **d** or imprisonment."
28:18 not guilty of any crime deserving **d**.
Ro 1:32 those who do such things deserve **d**,
4:25 He was delivered over to **d** for our
5:10 to him through the **d** of his Son,
5:12 through one man, and **d** through sin,
5:12 and in this way **d** came to all men
5:14 Nevertheless, **d** reigned from the
5:17 **d** reigned through that one man
5:21 that, just as sin reigned in **d**, so
6: 3 Jesus were baptised into his **d**?
6: 4 baptism into **d** in order that,
6: 5 united with him like this in his **d**,
6: 9 **d** no longer has mastery over him.
6:10 The **d** he died, he died to sin once
6:13 have been brought from **d** to life;
6:16 which leads to **d**, or to obedience,
6:21 Those things result in **d**!
6:23 For the wages of sin is **d**, but the
7: 5 bodies, so that we bore fruit for **d**.
7:10 to bring life actually brought **d**.
7:11 through the commandment put me to **d**.
7:13 then, become **d** to me? By no means!
7:13 it produced **d** in me through what was
7:24 will rescue me from this body of **d**?
8: 2 me free from the law of sin and **d**.
8: 6 The mind of sinful man is **d**, but the
8:13 put to **d** the misdeeds of the body,
8:36 is written: "For your sake we face **d**
8:38 For I am convinced that neither **d**
1Co 3:22 or **d** or the present or the future
11:26 the Lord's **d** until he comes.
15:21 For since **d** came through a man, the
15:26 The last enemy to be destroyed is **d**.
15:54 "**D** has been swallowed up in victory.
15:55 "Where, O **d**, is your victory? Where,
15:55 Where, O **d**, is your sting?"
15:56 The sting of **d** is sin, and the power
2Co 1: 9 hearts we felt the sentence of **d**.
2:16 To the one we are the smell of **d**; to
3: 7 Now if the ministry that brought **d**,
4:10 around in our body the **d** of Jesus,
4:11 given over to **d** for Jesus' sake,
4:12 then, **d** is at work in us, but life
7:10 regret, but worldly sorrow brings **d**.
11:23 been exposed to **d** again and again.
Eph 2:16 which he put to **d** their hostility.
Php 1:20 in my body, whether by life or by **d**.
2: 8 obedient to **d**—even **d** on a cross!
3:10 becoming like him in his **d**,
Col 1:22 through **d** to present you holy in
3: 5 Put to **d**, therefore, whatever
2Ti 1:10 Christ Jesus, who has destroyed **d**
Heb 2: 9 and honour because he suffered **d**,
2: 9 God he might taste **d** for everyone.
2:14 by his **d** he might destroy him who
2:14 the power of **d**—that is, the devil—
2:15 held in slavery by their fear of **d**.
5: 7 the one who could save him from **d**,
6: 1 that lead to **d**, and of faith in God,
7:23 since **d** prevented them from

Heb 9:14 from acts that lead to **d**, so that
9:16 prove the **d** of the one who made it,
11: 5 so that he did not experience **d**; he
11:19 he did receive Isaac back from **d**.
11:37 they were put to **d** by the sword.
Jas 1:15 it is full-grown, gives birth to **d**.
5:20 will save him from **d** and cover over
1Pe 3:18 He was put to **d** in the body but made
1Jn 3:14 We know that we have passed from **d**
3:14 who does not love remains in **d**.
5:16 a sin that does not lead to **d**,
5:16 those whose sin does not lead to **d**.
5:16 There is a sin that leads to **d**. I am
5:17 is sin that does not lead to **d**.
Rev 1:18 And I hold the keys of **d** and Hades.
2:10 Be faithful, even to the point of **d**,
2:11 not be hurt at all by the second **d**.
2:13 **d** in your city—where Satan lives.
6: 8 a pale horse! Its rider was named **D**,
9: 6 During those days men will seek **d**,
9: 6 long to die, but **d** will elude them.
12:11 lives so much as to shrink from **d**.
18: 8 her: **d**, mourning and famine.
20: 6 The second **d** has no power over them,
20:13 and **d** and Hades gave up the dead
20:14 **d** and Hades were thrown into the
20:14 The lake of fire is the second **d**.
21: 4 There will be no more **d** or mourning
21: 8 This is the second **d**."

Death's (Die)
Job 18:13 **d** firstborn devours his limbs.

Deathly (Die)
Jer 30: 6 in labour, every face turned **d** pale?
Da 10: 8 turned **d** pale and I was helpless.

Deaths (Die)
1Sa 4:21 the **d** of her father-in-law and her

Debate (Debated, Debating)
Ac 15: 2 into sharp dispute and **d** with them.
18:28 refuted the Jews in public **d**,

Debated (Debate)
Ac 9:29 He talked and **d** with the Grecian

Debating (Debate)
Mk 12:28 of the law came and heard them **d**.

Debauchery
Ro 13:13 not in sexual immorality and **d**,
2Co 12:21 and **d** in which they have indulged.
Gal 5:19 sexual immorality, impurity and **d**;
Eph 5:18 get drunk on wine, which leads to **d**.
1Pe 4: 3 pagans choose to do—living in **d**,

Debir
Jos 10: 3 king of Lachish and **D** king of Eglon.
10:38 him turned round and attacked **D**.
10:39 They did to **D** and its king as they
11:21 from Hebron, **D** and Anab, from all
12:13 the king of **D** one the king of Geder
13:26 from Mahanaim to the territory of **D**;
15: 7 The boundary then went up to **D** from
Jos 15:15 **D** (formerly called Kiriath Sepher).
15:49 Dannah, Kiriath Sannah (that is, **D**),
21:15 Holon, **D**,
Jdg 1:11 **D** (formerly called Kiriath Sepher).
1Ch 6:58 Hilen, **D**,

Deborah
1. Prophetess, one of Israel's judges. Appointed Barak to lead Israel against Canaanites (Jdg 4–5).
2. Rebekah's nurse (Ge 35:8).

Ge 35: 8 Now **D**, Rebekah's nurse, died and was
Jdg 4: 4 **D**, a prophetess, the wife of
4: 5 She held court under the Palm of **D**
4: 9 "Very well," **D** said, "I will go with
4: 9 So **D** went with Barak to Kedesh,
4:10 him, and **D** also went with him.
4:14 **D** said to Barak, "Go! This is the
5: 1 On that day **D** and Barak son of
Jdg 5: 7 ceased until I, **D**, arose, arose a
5:12 'Wake up, wake up, **D**! Wake up, wake
5:15 The princes of Issachar were with **D**;

Debt (Debtor, Debtors, Debts)
Dt 15: 3 cancel any **d** your brother owes you.
24: 6 the upper one—as security for a **d**,
1Sa 22: 2 in distress or in **d** or discontented
Job 24: 9 of the poor is seized for a **d**.
Mt 18:25 that he had be sold to repay the **d**.
18:27 him, cancelled the **d** and let him go.
18:30 prison until he could pay the **d**.
18:32 'I cancelled all that **d** of yours
Lk 7:43 one who had the bigger **d** cancelled.
Ro 13: 8 Let no **d** remain outstanding, except
13: 8 continuing **d** to love one another,

Debtor (Debt)
Isa 24: 2 for lender, for **d** as for creditor.

Debtors (Debt)
Hab 2: 7 Will not your **d** suddenly arise? Will
Mt 6:12 as we also have forgiven our **d**.
Lk 16: 5 in each one of his master's **d**.

Debts (Debt)
Dt 15: 1 every seven years you must cancel **d**.
15: 2 cancelling **d** has been proclaimed.
15: 9 the year for cancelling **d**, is near,"
31:10 in the year for cancelling **d**,
2Ki 4: 7 "Go, sell the oil and pay your **d**.
Ne 10:31 the land and will cancel all **d**.
Pr 22:26 in pledge or puts up security for **d**;
Mt 6:12 Forgive us our **d**, as we also have
Lk 7:42 back, so he cancelled the **d** of both.

Decapolis
Mt 4:25 Large crowds from Galilee, the **D**,
Mk 5:20 began to tell in the **D** how much
7:31 Galilee and into the region of the **D**.

Decay (Decayed)
Ps 16:10 will you let your Holy One see **d**.
49: 9 live on for ever and not see **d**.
49:14 their forms will **d** in the grave,
Pr 12: 4 wife is like **d** in his bones.
Isa 5:24 so their roots will **d** and their
Hab 3:16 **d** crept into my bones, and my legs
Ac 2:27 will you let your Holy One see **d**.
2:31 the grave, nor did his body see **d**.
13:34 him from the dead, never to **d**,
13:35 will not let your Holy One see **d**.'
13:37 raised from the dead did not see **d**.
Ro 8:21 be liberated from its bondage to **d**

Decayed (Decay)
Jer 49: 7 the prudent? Has their wisdom **d**?
Ac 13:36 with his fathers and his body **d**.

Deceit (Deceive)
Job 15:35 to evil; their womb fashions **d**."
27: 4 and my tongue will utter no **d**.
31: 5 or my foot has hurried after **d**—
Ps 5: 9 with their tongue they speak **d**.
32: 2 him and in whose spirit is no **d**.
50:19 evil and harness your tongue to **d**.
52: 2 sharpened razor, you who practise **d**.
101: 7 No-one who practises **d** will dwell in
Pr 6:14 who plots evil with **d** in his heart—
12:20 There is **d** in the hearts of those
26:24 but in his heart he harbours **d**.
Isa 5:18 who draw sin along with cords of **d**,
30:12 on oppression and depended on **d**,
53: 9 nor was any **d** in his mouth.
Jer 5:27 their houses are full of **d**; they
6:13 and priests alike, all practise **d**.
8: 5 cling to **d**; they refuse to return.
8:10 and priests alike, all practise **d**.
9: 6 in their **d** they refuse to
9: 8 is a deadly arrow; it speaks with **d**.
Da 8:25 He will cause **d** to prosper, and he
Hos 7: 1 They practise **d**, thieves break into
11:12 lies, the house of Israel with **d**.
Zep 1: 9 of their gods with violence and **d**.
3:13 nor will **d** be found in their mouths.
Zec 10: 2 The idols speak **d**, diviners see
Mk 7:22 greed, malice, **d**, lewdness, envy,
Ac 13:10 full of all kinds of **d** and trickery.
Ro 1:29 envy, murder, strife, **d** and malice.
3:13 their tongues practise **d**.
1Pe 2: 1 yourselves of all malice and all **d**,
2:22 and no **d** was found in his mouth."

Deceitful (Deceive)
Job 11:11 Surely he recognises **d** men; and when
Ps 5: 6 and **d** men the LORD abhors.
17: 1 it does not rise from **d** lips.
26: 4 I do not sit with **d** men, nor do I
36: 3 words of his mouth are wicked and **d**;
43: 1 rescue me from **d** and wicked men.
52: 4 every harmful word, O you **d** tongue!
55:23 bloodthirsty and **d** men will not live
109: 2 for wicked and **d** men have opened
119:29 Keep me from **d** ways; be gracious to
120: 2 from lying lips and from **d** tongues.
120: 3 and what more besides, O **d** tongue?
144: 8 of lies, whose right hands are **d**.
144:11 of lies, whose right hands are **d**.
Pr 12: 5 but the advice of the wicked is **d**.
14:25 lives, but a false witness is **d**.
15: 4 but a **d** tongue crushes the spirit.
17:20 tongue is **d** falls into trouble.
Isa 30: 9 These are rebellious people, **d**
Jer 17: 9 The heart is **d** above all things and
Hos 10: 2 Their heart is **d**, and now they must
2Co 11:13 men are false apostles, **d** workmen,
Eph 4:14 of men in their **d** scheming.
4:22 is being corrupted by its **d** desires;
1Pe 3:10 evil and his lips from **d** speech.
Rev 21:27 who does what is shameful or **d**,

Deceitfully (Deceive)
Ge 27:35 he said, "Your brother came **d** and
34:13 Jacob's sons replied **d** as they spoke
Ex 8:29 that Pharaoh does not act **d** again
Job 13: 7 Will you speak **d** for him?
Da 11:23 he will act **d**, and with only a few
Mic 6:12 are liars and their tongues speak **d**.

Deceitfulness (Deceive)
Ps 119:118 decrees, for their **d** is in vain.
Mt 13:22 life and the **d** of wealth choke it,
Mk 4:19 worries of this life, the **d** of wealth
Heb 3:13 of you may be hardened by sin's **d**.

Deceive (Deceit, Deceitful, Deceitfully, Deceitfulness, Deceived, Deceiver, Deceivers, Deceives, Deceiving, Deception, Deceptive)
Ge 31:27 did you run off secretly and **d** me?
Lev 19:11 "'Do not lie. "'Do not **d** one another.
Jos 9:22 "Why did you **d** us by saying, 'We
1Sa 19:17 "Why did you **d** me like this and
2Sa 3:25 he came to **d** you and observe your
2Ki 18:29 says: Do not let Hezekiah **d** you.
19:10 you depend on **d** you when he says,
2Ch 32:15 Now do not let Hezekiah **d** you and
Job 13: 9 Could you **d** him as you might **d** men?
15:31 Let him not **d** himself by trusting
Pr 14: 5 A truthful witness does not **d**, but a
24:28 cause, or use your lips to **d**.
Isa 36:14 says: Do not let Hezekiah **d** you.
37:10 not let the god you depend on **d** you
Jer 29: 8 and diviners among you **d** you.
37: 9 the LORD says: Do not **d** yourselves,
Ob : 7 your friends will **d** and overpower
Zec 13: 4 garment of hair in order to **d**.
Mt 24: 5 'I am the Christ,' and will **d** many.
24:11 false prophets will appear and **d** many
24:24 miracles to **d** even the elect—if
Mk 13: 6 'I am he,' and will **d** many.
13:22 **d** the elect—if that were possible.
Ro 16:18 they **d** the minds of naive people.
1Co 3:18 Do not **d** yourselves. If any one of
Eph 5: 6 Let no-one **d** you with empty words,
Col 2: 4 you this so that no-one may **d** you
2Th 2: 3 Don't let anyone **d** you in any way,

Jas 1:22 to the word, and so **d** yourselves.
1Jn 1: 8 without sin, we **d** ourselves and the
Rev 20: 8 will go out to **d** the nations in the

Deceived (Deceive)

Ge 3:13 said, "The serpent **d** me, and I ate.
27:36 He has **d** me these two times:
29:25 Rachel, didn't I? Why have you **d** me?"
31:20 Moreover, Jacob **d** Laban the Aramean
31:26 "What have you done? You've **d** me,
Nu 25:18 they **d** you in the affair of Peor
1Sa 28:12 "Why have you **d** me? You are Saul!
Job 12:16 both **d** and deceiver are his.
Isa 19:13 the leaders of Memphis are **d**; the
Jer 4:10 how completely you have **d** this
20: 7 O LORD, you **d** me, and I was **d**; you
20:10 "Perhaps he will be **d**; then we will
49:16 the pride of your heart have **d** you,
Hos 7:11 "Ephraim is like a dove, easily **d**
Ob : 3 The pride of your heart has **d** you,
Lk 21: 8 "Watch out that you are not **d**.
Jn 7:47 "You mean he has **d** you also?" the
Ro 7:11 **d** me, and through the commandment
1Co 6: 9 the kingdom of God? Do not be **d**:
2Co 11: 3 I am afraid that just as Eve was **d**
Gal 6: 7 Do not be **d**: God cannot be mocked.
1Ti 2:14 Adam was not the one **d**; it was the
2:14 woman who was **d** and became a sinner.
2Ti 3:13 bad to worse, deceiving and being **d**.
Tit 3: 3 disobedient, **d** and enslaved by all
Jas 1:16 Don't be **d**, my dear brothers.
Rev 13:14 he **d** the inhabitants of the earth.
20:10 the devil, who **d** them, was thrown

Deceiver (Deceive)

Job 12:16 both deceived and **d** are his.
Jer 9: 4 For every brother is a **d**, and every
Mic 2:11 If a liar and **d** comes and says,'I
Mt 27:63 he was still alive that **d** said,
2Jn : 7 person is the **d** and the antichrist.

Deceivers (Deceive)

Ps 49: 5 come, when wicked **d** surround me—
Tit 1:10 mere talkers and **d**, especially those
2Jn : 7 Many **d**, who do not acknowledge Jesus

Deceives (Deceive)

Pr 26:19 is a man who **d** his neighbour and
Jer 9: 5 Friend **d** friend, and no-one speaks
Mt 24: 4 "Watch out that no-one **d** you.
Mk 13: 5 them: "Watch out that no-one **d** you.
Jn 7:12 replied, "No, he **d** the people."
Gal 6: 3 when he is nothing, he **d** himself.
2Th 2:10 in every sort of evil that **d** those
Jas 1:26 he **d** himself and his religion is

Deceiving (Deceive)

Lev 6: 2 by **d** his neighbour about something
1Ti 4: 1 follow **d** spirits and things taught
2Ti 3:13 bad to worse, **d** and being deceived.
Rev 20: 3 to keep him from **d** the nations any

Decency (Decently)

1Ti 2: 9 with **d** and propriety, not with

Decently (Decency)

Ro 13:13 Let us behave **d**, as in the daytime,

Deception (Deceive)

Ps 12: 2 their flattering lips speak with **d**.
38:12 my ruin; all day long they plot **d**.
Pr 14: 8 ways, but the folly of fools is **d**.
26:26 His malice may be concealed by **d**,
Jer 3:23 on the hills and mountains is a **d**;
9: 6 You live in the midst of **d**; in their
Hos 10:13 evil, you have eaten the fruit of **d**.
Mt 27:64 This last **d** will be worse than the
2Co 4: 2 we do not use **d**, nor do we distort

Deceptive (Deceive)

Pr 11:18 The wicked man earns **d** wages, but he
23: 3 his delicacies, for that food is **d**.
31:30 Charm is **d**, and beauty is fleeting;
Jer 7: 4 Do not trust in **d** words and say,
7: 8 look, you are trusting in **d** words
15:18 Will you be to me like a **d** brook,
Mic 1:14 will prove **d** to the kings of Israel.
Col 2: 8 through hollow and **d** philosophy,

Decide (Decided, Decision, Decisions)

Ex 18:16 and I **d** between the parties and
18:22 simple cases they can **d** themselves.
33: 5 and I will **d** what to do with you.'"
Dt 21: 5 **d** all cases of dispute and assault.
25: 1 and the judges will **d** the case,
Jdg 11:27 Let the LORD, the Judge, **d** the
1Sa 24:15 May the LORD be our judge and **d**
2Sa 24:13 think it over and **d** how I should
1Ch 21:12 Now then, **d** how I should answer the
Job 22:28 What you **d** on will be done, and
34:33 You must **d**, not I; so tell me what
Isa 11: 3 or **d** by what he hears with his ears;
Eze 44:24 and **d** it according to my ordinances.
Jn 19:24 "Let's **d** by lot who will get it."
Ac 4:21 They could not **d** how to punish them,
24:22 he said, "I will **d** your case."

Decided (Decide)

Ge 41:32 matter has been firmly **d** by God,
Ex 18:26 the simple ones they **d** themselves.
Jdg 4: 5 to her to have their disputes **d**.
2Ch 24: 4 Some time later Joash **d** to restore
30: 2 the whole assembly in Jerusalem **d** to
30: 5 They **d** to send a proclamation
Est 7: 7 the king had already **d** his fate,
Jer 4:28 I have **d** and will not turn back."
Da 2: 5 "This is what I have firmly **d**: If
2: 8 that this is what I have firmly **d**:
Zep 3: 8 I have **d** to assemble the nations, to
Mt 27: 7 they **d** to use the money to buy the
Lk 23:24 Pilate **d** to grant their demand.
Jn 1:43 The next day Jesus **d** to leave for
9:22 for already the Jews had **d** that
Ac 3:13 though he had **d** to let him go.
4:28 will had **d** beforehand should happen.
7:23 he **d** to visit his fellow Israelites
11:29 **d** to provide help for the brothers
15:22 with the whole church, **d** to choose
19:21 Paul **d** to go to Jerusalem, passing
20: 3 he **d** to go back through Macedonia.
20:16 Paul had **d** to sail past Ephesus to
25:25 the Emperor I **d** to send him to Rome.
27: 1 was **d** that we would sail for Italy,
27:12 the majority **d** that we should sail
27:39 where they **d** to run the ship aground
2Co 9: 7 Each man should give what he has **d**
Tit 3:12 because I have **d** to winter there.

Decimated

2Sa 21: 5 against us so that we have been **d**

Decision (Decide)

Ex 28:29 heart on the breastpiece of **d**
2Sa 15: 2 be placed before the king for a **d**,
Ezr 5:17 king send us his **d** in this matter.
10: 8 in accordance with the **d** of the
Pr 16:33 but its every **d** is from the LORD.
Isa 16: 3 "Give us counsel, render a **d**. Make
Da 4:17 "'The **d** is announced by messengers,
Joel 3:14 multitudes in the valley of **d**! For
3:14 the LORD is near in the valley of **d**.
Mt 27: 1 came to the **d** to put Jesus to death.
Mk 15: 1 the whole Sanhedrin, reached a **d**.
Lk 23:51 who had not consented to their **d** and
Jn 1:13 nor of human **d** or a husband's will,
Ac 21:25 we have written to them our **d** that
25:21 to be held over for the Emperor's **d**,

Decisions (Decide)

Ex 28:15 "Fashion a breastpiece for making **d**—
28:30 always bear the means of making **d**
Nu 27:21 who will obtain **d** for him by
Dt 17:10 You must act according to the **d** they
17:11 teach you and the **d** they give you.
Isa 11: 4 give **d** for the poor of the earth.
28: 7 they stumble when rendering **d**.
58: 2 They ask me for just **d** and seem
Jn 8:16 if I do judge, my **d** are right,
Ac 16: 4 they delivered the **d** reached by the

Deck (Decked, Decks)

Eze 27: 6 they made your **d**, inlaid with ivory.
Jnh 1: 5 But Jonah had gone below **d**, where he

Decked (Deck)

Hos 2:13 **d** herself with rings and jewellery,

Decks (Deck)

Ge 6:16 and make lower, middle and upper **d**.

Declare (Declared, Declares, Declaring)

Ex 22: 9 The one whom the judges **d** guilty
Dt 5: 1 the laws I **d** in your hearing today.
5: 5 to **d** to you the word of the LORD,
21: 7 they shall **d**: "Our hands did not
26: 3 "I **d** today to the LORD your God that
26: 5 you shall **d** before the LORD your God:
30:18 I **d** to you this day that you will
32:40 I lift my hand to heaven and **d**: As
1Ki 1:36 God of my lord the king, so **d** it.
8:32 **D** the innocent not guilty, and so
2Ki 9: 3 and pour the oil on his head and **d**,
1Ch 16:24 **D** his glory among the nations, his
17:10 "'I **d** to you that the LORD will
2Ch 6:23 **D** the innocent not guilty and so
Job 34:34 "Men of understanding **d**, wise men
Ps 5:10 **D** them guilty, O God! Let their
9:14 that I may **d** your praises in the
19: 1 The heavens **d** the glory of God; the
22:22 I will **d** your name to my brothers;
40: 5 them, they would be too many to **d**.
51:15 and my mouth will **d** your praise.
71:17 this day I **d** your marvellous deeds.
71:18 till I **d** your power to the next
75: 9 for me, I will **d** this for ever; I
89: 2 I will **d** that your love stands firm
96: 3 **D** his glory among the nations, his
106: 2 of the LORD or fully **d** his praise?
Isa 41:22 Or **d** to us the things to come,
42: 9 and new things I **d**; before they
44: 7 Let him **d** and lay out before me what
45:19 speak the truth; I **d** what is right.
45:21 **D** what is to be, present it—let
58: 1 **D** to my people their rebellion
Jer 23:31 and yet **d**,'The LORD declares.'
Eze 38:19 In my zeal and fiery wrath I **d** that
Da 4:17 the holy ones **d** the verdict, so that
Joel 1:14 **D** a holy fast; call a sacred
2:15 trumpet in Zion, **d** a holy fast,
Mic 3: 8 to **d** to Jacob his transgression,
Ac 20:26 Therefore, I **d** to you today that I
1Co 15:50 I **d** to you, brothers, that flesh and
Gal 5: 3 Again I **d** to every man who lets
Eph 6:20 I may **d** it fearlessly, as I should.
Heb 2:12 He says, "I will **d** your name to my
1Pe 2: 9 that you may **d** the praises of him
1Jn 1: 5 we have heard from him and **d** to you:

Declared (Declare)

Nu 14:17 be displayed, just as you have **d**:
Dt 4:13 He **d** to you his covenant, the Ten
26:17 You have **d** this day that the LORD is
26:18 the LORD has **d** this day that you are
26:19 He has **d** that he will set you in
32:46 I have solemnly **d** to you this day,
1Ki 1:24 "Have you, my lord the king, **d** that
8:53 just as you **d** through your servant
13: 3 "This is the sign the LORD has **d**:
13:32 For the message he **d** by the word of
22:11 had made iron horns and he **d**,
22:28 Micaiah **d**, "If you ever return
22:38 as the word of the LORD had **d**.
2Ki 9: 6 poured the oil on Jehu's head and **d**,
13:17 of victory over Aram!" Elisha **d**.
24:13 the LORD had **d**, Nebuchadnezzar
2Ch 18:10 and he **d**, "This is what the LORD
18:27 Micaiah **d**, "If you ever return
Job 15:18 what wise men have **d**, hiding nothing

Ps 88:11 Is your love **d** in the grave, your
95:11 I **d** on oath in my anger, "They shall
102:21 the name of the LORD will be **d** in
Pr 30: 1 This man **d** to Ithiel, to Ithiel and
Ecc 4: 2 I **d** that the dead, who had already
Isa 5: 9 The LORD Almighty has **d** in my
45:21 Who foretold this long ago, who **d** it
Jnh 3: 5 They **d** a fast, and all of them, from
Mt 26:35 Peter **d**, "Even if I have to die with
26:61 **d**, "This fellow said,'I am able to
Mk 7:19 Jesus **d** all foods "clean".)
10:20 "Teacher," he **d**, "all these I have
12:36 speaking by the Holy Spirit, **d**:
14:29 Peter **d**, "Even if all fall away, I
Jn 1:49 Nathanael **d**, "Rabbi, you are the Son
3: 3 In reply Jesus **d**, "I tell you the
4:21 Jesus **d**, "Believe me, woman, a time
4:26 Jesus **d**, "I who speak to you am he."
6:35 Jesus **d**, "I am the bread of life. He
7:46 way this man does," the guards **d**.
8:11 neither do I condemn you," Jesus **d**.
Ac 20:21 I have **d** to both Jews and Greeks
25:12 he **d**: "You have appealed to Caesar.
28:23 **d** to them the kingdom of God and
Ro 1: 4 **d** with power to be the Son of God,
2:13 the law who will be **d** righteous.
3:20 Therefore no-one will be **d** righteous
Heb 3:11 I **d** on oath in my anger,'They shall
4: 3 "So I **d** on oath in my anger,'They
7: 8 case, by him who is **d** to be living.
7:17 For it is **d**: "You are a priest for

Declares (Declare, *Declares the LORD, Declares the Lord*)

Ex 21: 5 "But if the servant **d**,'I love my
1Sa 2:30 the God of Israel, **d**:'I promised
2:30 But now the LORD **d**:'Far be it from
2Sa 7:11 "'The LORD **d** to you that the LORD
Isa 1:24 the Mighty One of Israel, **d**: "Ah, I
56: 8 The Sovereign LORD **d**—he who
Jer 9:22 Say, "This is what the LORD **d**: "'The
23:31 and yet declare,'The LORD **d**.'
46:18 "As surely as I live," **d** the King,
48:15 down in the slaughter," **d** the King,
51:57 for ever and not awake," **d** the King,
Eze 5:11 as I live, **d** the Sovereign LORD,
11: 8 against you, **d** the Sovereign LORD.
11:21 have done, **d** the Sovereign LORD."
12:25 I say, **d** the Sovereign LORD.'"
12:28 fulfilled, **d** the Sovereign LORD.'"
13: 6 They say, "The LORD **d**", when the
13: 7 "The LORD **d**", though I have not
13: 8 against you, **d** the Sovereign LORD.
13:16 no peace, **d** the Sovereign LORD."'
14:11 their God, **d** the Sovereign LORD.'"
14:14 righteousness, **d** the Sovereign LORD.
14:16 as I live, **d** the Sovereign LORD,
14:18 as I live, **d** the Sovereign LORD,
14:20 as I live, **d** the Sovereign LORD,
14:23 cause, **d** the Sovereign LORD."
15: 8 unfaithful, **d** the Sovereign LORD."
16: 8 **d** the Sovereign LORD, and you became
16:14 perfect, **d** the Sovereign LORD.
16:19 what happened, **d** the Sovereign LORD.
16:23 Woe to you, **d** the Sovereign LORD.
16:30 "'How weak-willed you are, **d** the
16:43 you have done, **d** the Sovereign LORD.
16:48 as I live, **d** the Sovereign LORD,
16:63 humiliation, **d** the Sovereign LORD.'"
17:16 "'As surely as I live, **d** the
18: 3 "As surely as I live, **d** the
18: 9 surely live, **d** the Sovereign LORD.
18:23 of the wicked? **d** the Sovereign LORD.
18:30 to his ways, **d** the Sovereign LORD.
18:32 of anyone, **d** the Sovereign LORD.
20: 3 of me, **d** the Sovereign LORD.'
20:31 **d** the Sovereign LORD, I will not let
20:33 as I live, **d** the Sovereign LORD,
20:36 judge you, **d** the Sovereign LORD.
20:40 the high mountain of Israel, **d** the
20:44 of Israel, **d** the Sovereign LORD.'"
21: 7 take place, **d** the Sovereign LORD."
21:13 not continue? **d** the Sovereign LORD.'
22:12 forgotten me, **d** the Sovereign LORD.
22:31 have done, **d** the Sovereign LORD."
23:34 I have spoken, **d** the Sovereign LORD.
Eze 24:14 actions, **d** the Sovereign LORD.'"
25:14 vengeance, **d** the Sovereign LORD.'"
26: 5 I have spoken, **d** the Sovereign LORD.
26:14 have spoken, **d** the Sovereign LORD.
26:21 be found, **d** the Sovereign LORD."
28:10 have spoken, **d** the Sovereign LORD.'"
29:20 did it for me, **d** the Sovereign LORD.
30: 6 within her, **d** the Sovereign LORD.
31:18 his hordes, **d** the Sovereign LORD.'"
32: 8 your land, **d** the Sovereign LORD.
32:14 like oil, **d** the Sovereign LORD.
32:16 chant it, **d** the Sovereign LORD."
32:31 by the sword, **d** the Sovereign LORD.
32:32 by the sword, **d** the Sovereign LORD."
33:11 as I live, **d** the Sovereign LORD,
34: 8 as I live, **d** the Sovereign LORD,
34:15 them lie down, **d** the Sovereign LORD.
34:30 are my people, **d** the Sovereign LORD.
34:31 am your God, **d** the Sovereign LORD.'"
35: 6 as I live, **d** the Sovereign LORD,
35:11 as I live, **d** the Sovereign LORD,
36:14 childless, **d** the Sovereign LORD.
36:15 to fall, **d** the Sovereign LORD.'"
36:23 am the LORD, **d** the Sovereign LORD,
36:32 for your sake, **d** the Sovereign LORD.
38:18 be aroused, **d** the Sovereign LORD.
38:21 my mountains, **d** the Sovereign LORD.
39: 5 I have spoken, **d** the Sovereign LORD.
39: 8 take place, **d** the Sovereign LORD.
39:10 looted them, **d** the Sovereign LORD.
39:13 day for them, **d** the Sovereign LORD.
39:20 every kind,' **d** the Sovereign LORD.
39:29 of Israel, **d** the Sovereign LORD."
43:19 before me, **d** the Sovereign LORD.
43:27 accept you, **d** the Sovereign LORD."
44:12 of their sin, **d** the Sovereign LORD.
44:15 fat and blood, **d** the Sovereign LORD.
44:27 for himself, **d** the Sovereign LORD.
45: 9 my people, **d** the Sovereign LORD.
45:15 the people, **d** the Sovereign LORD.
47:23 inheritance," **d** the Sovereign LORD.
48:29 portions," **d** the Sovereign LORD.
Am 4: 5 love to do," **d** the Sovereign LORD.
6: 8 by himself—the LORD God Almighty **d**:
6:14 For the LORD God Almighty **d**, "I will
8: 3 "In that day," **d** the Sovereign LORD,
8: 9 "In that day," **d** the Sovereign LORD,
8:11 "The days are coming," **d** the
Zec 5: 4 The LORD Almighty **d**,'I will send it
12: 1 the spirit of man within him, **d**:
Lk 20:42 David himself **d** in the Book of
Ro 2:16 Jesus Christ, as my gospel **d**.
Gal 3:22 the Scripture **d** that the whole world

Declares the LORD

Ge 22:16 said, "I swear by myself, **d**, that
Nu 14:28 tell them,'As surely as I live, **d**,
2Ki 9:26 Naboth and the blood of his sons **d**,
9:26 for it on this plot of ground, **d**.
19:33 he will not enter this city, **d**.
22:19 in my presence, I have heard you, **d**.
2Ch 34:27 in my presence, I have heard you, **d**.
Isa 14:22 "I will rise up against them," **d**
14:22 her offspring and descendants," **d**.
14:23 broom of destruction," **d** Almighty.
17: 3 of the Israelites," **d** Almighty.
17: 6 boughs," **d**, the God of Israel.
19: 4 over them," **d**, the LORD Almighty.
22:25 "In that day," **d** Almighty, "the peg
Isa 30: 1 "Woe to the obstinate children," **d**,
31: 9 their commanders will panic," **d**,
37:34 he will not enter this city," **d**.
41:14 for I myself will help you," **d**, your
43:10 "You are my witnesses," **d**, "and my
43:12 You are my witnesses," **d**, "that I am
49:18 As surely as I live," **d**, "you will
52: 5 "And now what do I have here?" **d**.
52: 5 and those who rule them mock," **d**.
54:17 is their vindication from me," **d**.
55: 8 neither are your ways my ways," **d**.
59:20 Jacob who repent of their sins," **d**.
66: 2 and so they came into being?" **d**.
66:17 will meet their end together," **d**.
66:22 I make will endure before me," **d**,
Jer 1: 8 am with you and will rescue you," **d**.
1:15 of the northern kingdoms," **d**.
Jer 1:19 am with you and will rescue you," **d**.
2: 3 and disaster overtook them,'" **d**.
2: 9 bring charges against you again," **d**.
2:12 and shudder with great horror," **d**.
2:29 You have all rebelled against me," **d**.
3: 1 would you now return to me?" **d**.
3:10 her heart, but only in pretence," **d**.
3:12 "'Return, faithless Israel,' **d**,'I
3:12 for I am merciful,' **d**,'I will not be
3:13 tree, and have not obeyed me,'" **d**.
3:14 "Return, faithless people," **d**, "for
3:16 increased greatly in the land," **d**,
3:20 to me, O house of Israel," **d**.
4: 1 return, O Israel, return to me," **d**.
4: 9 "In that day," **d**, "the king and the
4:17 she has rebelled against me,'" **d**.
5: 9 Should I not punish them for this?" **d**
5:11 been utterly unfaithful to me," **d**.
5:15 O house of Israel," **d**, "I am
5:18 "Yet even in those days," **d**, "I will
5:22 Should you not fear me?" **d**. "Should
5:29 Should I not punish them for this?" **d**
6:12 those who live in the land," **d**.
7:11 to you? But I have been watching! **d**.
7:13 you were doing all these things, **d**,
7:19 am I the one they are provoking? **d**.
7:30 Judah have done evil in my eyes, **d**.
7:32 beware, the days are coming, **d**, when
8: 1 "'At that time, **d**, the bones of the
8: 3 prefer death to life, **d** Almighty.'
8:13 "'I will take away their harvest, **d**.
8:17 charmed, and they will bite you," **d**.
9: 3 they do not acknowledge me," **d**.
9: 6 they refuse to acknowledge me," **d**.
9: 9 Should I not punish them for this?" **d**
9:24 earth, for in these I delight," **d**.
9:25 "The days are coming," **d**, "when I
12:17 uproot and destroy it," **d**.
13:11 the whole house of Judah to me,' **d**,
13:14 other, fathers and sons alike, **d**.
13:25 portion I have decreed for you," **d**,
15: 3 of destroyers against them," **d**,
15: 6 You have rejected me," **d**. "You keep
15: 9 the sword before their enemies," **d**.
15:20 with you to rescue and save you," **d**.
16: 5 and my pity from this people," **d**.
16:11 because your fathers forsook me,' **d**,
16:14 "However, the days are coming," **d**,
16:16 I will send for many fishermen," **d**,
17:24 if you are careful to obey me, **d**,
18: 6 do with you as this potter does?" **d**.
19: 6 beware, the days are coming, **d**, when
19:12 place and to those who live here, **d**.
21: 7 After that, **d**, I will hand over
21:10 do this city harm and not good, **d**.
21:13 this valley on the rocky plateau, **d**
21:14 punish you as your deeds deserve, **d**.
22: 5 if you do not obey these commands, **d**,
22:16 not what it means to know me?" **d**.
22:24 "As surely as I live," **d**, "even if
23: 1 the sheep of my pasture!" **d**.
23: 2 you for the evil you have done," **d**.
23: 4 nor will any be missing," **d**.
23: 5 "The days are coming," **d**, "when I
23: 7 "So then, the days are coming," **d**,
23:11 temple I find their wickedness," **d**.
23:12 in the year they are punished," **d**.
23:23 "Am I only a God nearby," **d**, "and not
23:24 places so that I cannot see him?" **d**.
23:24 "Do not I fill heaven and earth?" **d**.
23:28 what has straw to do with grain?" **d**.
23:29 "Is not my word like fire," **d**, "and
23:30 "Therefore," **d**, "I am against the
23:31 Yes," **d**, "I am against the prophets
23:32 those who prophesy false dreams," **d**.
23:32 these people in the least," **d**.
23:33 oracle? I will forsake you, **d**.'
25: 7 "But you did not listen to me," **d**,
25: 9 Nebuchadnezzar king of Babylon," **d**,
25:12 for their guilt," **d**, "and will make
25:29 who live on the earth, **d** Almighty.'
25:31 put the wicked to the sword,'" **d**.
27: 8 the sword, famine and plague, **d**
27:11 to till it and to live there, **d**.
27:15 'I have not sent them,' **d**.'They are
27:22 until the day I come for them,' **d**.

Jer 28: 4 from Judah who went to Babylon,' **d**,
29: 9 I have not sent them," **d**.
29:11 I know the plans I have for you," **d**,
29:14 I will be found by you," **d**, "and
29:14 where I have banished you," **d**,
29:19 have not listened to my words," **d**,
29:19 exiles have not listened either," **d**.
29:23 I know it and am a witness to it," **d**.
29:32 **d**, because he has preached rebellion
30: 3 The days are coming,' **d**,'when I
30: 8 "'In that day,' **d** Almighty,'I will
30:10 do not be dismayed, O Israel,' **d**.
30:11 I am with you and will save you,' **d**.
30:17 to health and heal your wounds,' **d**,
30:21 himself to be close to me?' **d**.
31: 1 "At that time," **d**, "I will be the
31:14 will be filled with my bounty," **d**.
31:16 for your work will be rewarded," **d**.
31:17 there is hope for your future," **d**.
31:20 I have great compassion for him," **d**.
31:27 "The days are coming," **d**, "when I
31:28 over them to build and to plant," **d**.
31:31 "The time is coming," **d**, "when I
31:32 though I was a husband to them," **d**.
31:33 house of Israel after that time," **d**.
31:34 least of them to the greatest," **d**.
31:36 decrees vanish from my sight," **d**,
31:37 because of all they have done," **d**.
31:38 "The days are coming," **d**, "when this
32: 5 remain until I deal with him, **d**.
32:30 with what their hands have made, **d**.
32:44 I will restore their fortunes, **d**."
33:14 "'The days are coming,' **d**,'when I
34: 5 I myself make this promise, **d**.
34:17 'freedom' for you, **d**—'freedom' to
34:22 I am going to give the order, **d**, and
35:13 a lesson and obey my words?' **d**.
39:17 I will rescue you on that day, **d**;
39:18 life, because you trust in me, **d**.'"
42:11 Do not be afraid of him, **d**, for I am
44:29 I will punish you in this place,' **d**,
45: 5 will bring disaster on all people, **d**
46: 5 there is terror on every side," **d**.
46:23 They will chop down her forest," **d**,
46:26 be inhabited as in times past," **d**.
46:28 my servant, for I am with you," **d**.
48:12 days are coming," **d**, "when I will
48:25 is cut off; her arm is broken," **d**.
48:30 her insolence but it is futile," **d**,
48:35 and burn incense to their gods," **d**.
48:38 like a jar that no-one wants," **d**.
48:43 await you, O people of Moab," **d**.
48:44 Moab the year of her punishment," **d**.
48:47 of Moab in days to come," **d**.
49: 2 the days are coming," **d**, "when I
49: 6 the fortunes of the Ammonites," **d**.
49:13 I swear by myself," **d**, "that Bozrah
49:16 there I will bring you down," **d**.
49:26 silenced in that day," **d** Almighty.
49:30 caves, you who live in Hazor," **d**.
49:31 which lives in confidence," **d**, "a
49:32 on them from every side," **d**.
49:37 upon them, even my fierce anger," **d**.
49:38 destroy her king and officials," **d**.
49:39 of Elam in days to come," **d**.
50: 4 "In those days, at that time," **d**,
50:10 her will have their fill," **d**.
50:20 In those days, at that time," **d**,
50:21 and completely destroy them," **d**.
50:30 will be silenced in that day," **d**.
50:35 "A sword against the Babylonians!" **d**
50:40 with their neighbouring towns," **d**,
51:24 wrong they have done in Zion," **d**.
51:25 you who destroy the whole earth," **d**.
51:26 you will be desolate for ever," **d**.
51:39 sleep for ever and not awake," **d**.
51:48 destroyers will attack her," **d**.
51:52 "But days are coming," **d**, "when I
51:53 send destroyers against her," **d**.
Eze 16:58 and your detestable practices, **d**.
37:14 spoken, and I have done it, **d**.'"
Hos 2:13 her lovers, but me she forgot," **d**.
2:16 "In that day," **d**, "you will call me
2:21 "In that day I will respond," **d**—
11:11 will settle them in their homes," **d**.
Joel 2:12 "Even now," **d**, "return to me with
Am 2:11 this not true, people of Israel?" **d**.
2:16 will flee naked on that day," **d**.
3:10 "They do not know how to do right," **d**
3:15 the mansions will be demolished," **d**.
4: 3 will be cast out towards Harmon," **d**.
4: 6 yet you have not returned to me," **d**.
4: 8 yet you have not returned to me," **d**.
4: 9 yet you have not returned to me," **d**.
4:10 yet you have not returned to me," **d**.
4:11 yet you have not returned to me," **d**.
9: 7 the same to me as the Cushites?" **d**.
9: 8 destroy the house of Jacob," **d**.
9:12 name," **d**, who will do these things.
9:13 "The days are coming," **d**, "when the
Ob : 4 there I will bring you down," **d**.
: 8 "In that day," **d**, "will I not
Mic 4: 6 "In that day," **d**, "I will gather the
5:10 "In that day," **d**, "I will destroy
Na 2:13 "I am against you," **d** Almighty. "I
3: 5 "I am against you," **d** Almighty. "I
Zep 1: 2 from the face of the earth," **d**.
1: 3 man from the face of the earth," **d**.
1:10 "On that day," **d**, "a cry will go up
2: 9 Therefore, as surely as I live," **d**
3: 8 Therefore wait for me," **d**, "for the
Hag 1: 9 Why?" **d** Almighty. "Because of my
1:13 to the people: "I am with you," **d**.
2: 4 now be strong, O Zerubbabel,' **d**.'Be
2: 4 people of the land,' **d**,'and work.
2: 4 For I am with you,' **d** Almighty.
2: 8 and the gold is mine,' **d** Almighty.
2: 9 I will grant peace,' **d** Almighty."
2:14 and this nation in my sight,' **d**.
2:17 yet you did not turn to me,' **d**.
2:23 "'On that day,' **d** Almighty,'I will
2:23 Zerubbabel son of Shealtiel,' **d**,
2:23 for I have chosen you,' **d** Almighty."
Zec 1: 3 'Return to me,' **d** Almighty,'and I
1: 4 listen or pay attention to me, **d**.
1:16 out over Jerusalem,' **d** Almighty.
2: 5 be a wall of fire around it,' **d**
2: 6 Flee from the land of the north," **d**,
2: 6 you to the four winds of heaven," **d**.
2:10 and I will live among you," **d**.
3:10 his vine and fig-tree,' **d** Almighty."
8: 6 seem marvellous to me?" **d** Almighty.
8:11 as I did in the past," **d** Almighty.
8:17 I hate all this," **d**.
10:12 and in his name they will walk," **d**.
11: 6 pity on the people of the land," **d**.
12: 4 and its rider with madness," **d**.
13: 2 be remembered no more," **d** Almighty.
13: 7 man who is close to me!" **d** Almighty.
13: 8 In the whole land," **d**, "two-thirds

Declares the Lord

Isa 3:15 of the poor?" **d**, the LORD Almighty.
19: 4 fierce king will rule over them, **d**
Jer 2:19 no awe of me," **d**, the LORD Almighty.
49: 5 on you from all those around you," **d**
50:31 O arrogant one," **d**, the LORD
Am 3:13 of Jacob," **d**, the LORD God Almighty.
Heb 8: 8 "The time is coming, **d**, when I will
8: 9 and I turned away from them, **d**.
8:10 house of Israel after that time, **d**.

Declaring (Declare)

Ps 71: 8 **d** your splendour all day long.
Jer 50:28 refugees from Babylon **d** in Zion how
Ac 2:11 we hear them **d** the wonders of God

Declined

Ac 18:20 to spend more time with them, he **d**.

Decorate (Decorated, Decorates, Decorating, Decorations)

1Ki 7:18 **d** the capitals on top of the pillars.
Mt 23:29 and **d** the graves of the righteous.

Decorated (Decorate)

2Ki 25:17 **d** with a network and pomegranates
2Ch 3: 5 covered it with fine gold and **d** it
SS 5:14 polished ivory **d** with sapphires.
Jer 52:22 **d** with a network and pomegranates
Eze 40:16 walls were **d** with palm trees.
40:31 outer court; palm trees **d** its jambs,
40:34 palm trees **d** the jambs on either
40:37 palm trees **d** the jambs on either
Rev 21:19 **d** with every kind of precious stone.

Decorates (Decorate)

Jer 22:14 it with cedar and **d** it in red.

Decorating (Decorate)

1Ki 7:41 the two sets of network **d** the two
7:42 **d** the bowl-shaped capitals on top of
2Ch 4:12 the two sets of network **d** the two
4:13 **d** the bowl-shaped capitals on top of

Decorations (Decorate)

Eze 40:22 its portico and its palm tree **d** had
40:26 it had palm tree **d** on the faces of

Decrease (Decreased)

Lev 25:16 you are to **d** the price, because what
Jer 29: 6 Increase in number there; do not **d**.

Decreased (Decrease)

Ps 107:39 their numbers **d**, and they were
Jer 30:19 and they will not be **d**; I will bring

Decree (Decreed, Decrees)

Ex 15:25 There the LORD made a **d** and a law
1Ch 16:17 He confirmed it to Jacob as a **d**, to
Ezr 5:13 a **d** to rebuild this house of God.
5:17 issue a **d** to rebuild this house of
6: 3 the king issued a **d** concerning the
6: 8 Moreover, I hereby **d** what you are to
6:11 Furthermore, I **d** that if anyone
6:12 who lifts a hand to change this **d**
6:13 Then, because of the **d** King Darius
7:13 Now I **d** that any of the Israelites
Est 1:19 let him issue a royal **d** and let it
3: 9 let a **d** be issued to destroy them,
8: 8 Now write another **d** in the king's
9:32 Esther's **d** confirmed these
Job 23:14 He carries out his **d** against me, and
28:26 he made a **d** for the rain and a path
Ps 2: 7 I will proclaim the **d** of the LORD:
7: 6 Awake, my God; **d** justice.
81: 4 this is a **d** for Israel, an ordinance
105:10 He confirmed it to Jacob as a **d**, to
148: 6 gave a **d** that will never pass away.
Jer 51:12 his **d** against the people of Babylon.
Da 2:13 the **d** was issued to put the wise men
2:15 did the king issue such a harsh **d**?"
3:10 You have issued a **d**, O king, that
3:29 Therefore I **d** that the people of any
4:24 is the **d** the Most High has issued
6: 7 enforce the **d** that anyone who prays
6: 8 Now, O king, issue the **d** and put it
6: 9 King Darius put the **d** in writing.
6:10 Now when Daniel learned that the **d**
6:12 and spoke to him about his royal **d**:
6:12 "Did you not publish a **d** that during
6:12 "The **d** stands—in accordance with
6:13 or to the **d** you put in writing.
6:15 no **d** or edict that the king issues
6:26 "I issue a **d** that in every part of
9:25 From the issuing of the **d** to restore
Jnh 3: 7 "By the **d** of the king and his nobles:
Lk 2: 1 Caesar Augustus issued a **d** that a
Ro 1:32 Although they know God's righteous **d**

Decreed (Decree)

1Ki 22:23 The LORD has **d** disaster for you."
2Ki 8: 1 because the LORD has **d** a famine in
2Ch 18:22 The LORD has **d** disaster for you."
Ezr 6:12 I Darius have **d** it. Let it be
Est 2: 1 done and what he had **d** about her.
9:31 Jew and Queen Esther had **d** for them,
Job 14: 5 you have **d** the number of his months
Ps 78: 5 He **d** statutes for Jacob and
Isa 10:22 Destruction has been **d**,
10:23 destruction **d** upon the whole land.
28:22 the destruction **d** against the whole
Jer 11:17 has **d** disaster for you, because
13:25 lot, the portion I have **d** for you,"

Jer 16:10 'Why has the LORD **d** such a great
40: 2 God **d** this disaster for this place.
Lam 1:17 The LORD has **d** for Jacob that his
2:17 his word, which he **d** long ago.
3:37 it happen if the Lord has not **d** it?
Da 4:31 "This is what is **d** for you, King
9:24 "Seventy'sevens' are **d** for your
9:26 end, and desolations have been **d**.
9:27 end that is **d** is poured out on him."
Na 2: 7 is **d** that the city be exiled and
Lk 22:22 Son of Man will go as it has been **d**,

Decrees (Decree)
Ge 26: 5 my commands, my **d** and my laws."
Ex 15:26 to his commands and keep all his **d**,
18:16 inform them of God's **d** and laws."
18:20 Teach them the **d** and laws, and show
Lev 10:11 all the **d** the LORD has given them
18: 4 laws and be careful to follow my **d**.
18: 5 Keep my **d** and laws, for the man who
18:26 you must keep my **d** and my laws. The
19:19 "Keep my **d**.
19:37 "Keep all my **d** and all my laws and
20: 8 Keep my **d** and follow them. I am the
20:22 "Keep all my **d** and laws and follow
25:18 "Follow my **d** and be careful to obey
26: 3 "If you follow my **d** and are careful
26:15 if you reject my **d** and abhor my laws
26:43 rejected my laws and abhorred my **d**.
26:46 These are the **d**, the laws and the
Dt 4: 1 Hear now, O Israel, the **d** and laws I
4: 5 See, I have taught you **d** and laws as
4: 6 who will hear about all these **d** and
4: 8 great as to have such righteous **d**
4:14 me at that time to teach you the **d**
4:40 Keep his **d** and commands, which I am
4:45 These are the stipulations, **d** and
5: 1 O Israel, the **d** and the laws I
5:31 **d** and laws that you are to teach
6: 1 These are the commands, **d** and laws
6: 2 his **d** and commands that I give you,
6:17 stipulations and **d** he has given you.
6:20 **d** and laws the LORD our God has
6:24 to obey all these **d** and to fear the
7:11 **d** and laws I give you today.
8:11 his **d** that I am giving you this day.
10:13 to observe the LORD's commands and **d**
11: 1 **d**, his laws and his commands always.
11:32 be sure that you obey all the **d** and
12: 1 These are the **d** and laws you must be
16:12 Egypt, and follow carefully these **d**.
17:19 the words of this law and these **d**
26:16 this day to follow these **d** and laws;
26:17 that you will keep his **d**, commands
27:10 and **d** that I give you today."
28:15 and **d** I am giving you today,
28:45 the commands and **d** he gave you.
30:10 keep his commands and **d** that are
30:16 and to keep his commands, **d** and laws;
Jos 24:25 he drew up for them **d** and laws.
2Sa 22:23 I have not turned away from his **d**.
1Ki 2: 3 and keep his **d** and commands, his
6:12 if you follow my **d**, carry out my
8:58 **d** and regulations he gave our
8:61 to live by his **d** and obey his
9: 4 I command and observe my **d** and laws,
9: 6 do not observe the commands and **d** I
11:11 have not kept my covenant and my **d**,
2Ki 17:13 Observe my commands and **d**, in
17:15 They rejected his **d** and the covenant
17:34 nor adhere to the **d** and ordinances,
2Ki 17:37 to keep the **d** and ordinances,
23: 3 regulations and **d** with all his heart
1Ch 22:13 if you are careful to observe the **d**
29:19 your commands, requirements and **d**
2Ch 7:17 I command, and observe my **d** and laws,
7:19 forsake the **d** and commands I have
19:10 commands, **d** or ordinances—you are
33: 8 **d** and ordinances given through Moses.
34:31 regulations and **d** with all his heart
Ezr 6:14 and the **d** of Cyrus, Darius and
7:10 teaching its **d** and laws in Israel.
7:11 and **d** of the LORD for Israel:
Ne 1: 7 We have not obeyed the commands, **d**
9:13 and **d** and commands that are good.
Ne 9:14 **d** and laws through your servant
10:29 and **d** of the LORD our Lord.
Ps 18:22 I have not turned away from his **d**.
44: 4 my God, who **d** victories for Jacob.
89:31 if they violate my **d** and fail to
94:20 one that brings on misery by its **d**?
99: 7 his statutes and the **d** he gave them.
119: 5 were steadfast in obeying your **d**!
119: 8 I will obey your **d**; do not utterly
119:12 be to you, O LORD; teach me your **d**.
119:16 I delight in your **d**; I will not
119:23 servant will meditate on your **d**.
119:26 you answered me; teach me your **d**.
119:33 Teach me, O LORD, to follow your **d**;
119:48 I love, and I meditate on your **d**.
119:54 Your **d** are the theme of my song
119:64 your love, O LORD; teach me your **d**.
119:68 you do is good; teach me your **d**.
119:71 so that I might learn your **d**.
119:80 heart be blameless towards your **d**,
119:83 the smoke, I do not forget your **d**.
119:112 My heart is set on keeping your **d** to
119:117 shall always have regard for your **d**.
119:118 You reject all who stray from your **d**,
119:124 to your love and teach me your **d**.
119:135 your servant and teach me your **d**.
119:145 me, O LORD, and I will obey your **d**.
119:155 for they do not seek out your **d**.
119:171 praise, for you teach me your **d**.
147:19 to Jacob, his laws and **d** to Israel.
Pr 31: 5 drink and forget what the law **d**,
Isa 10: 1 to those who issue oppressive **d**,
Jer 31:35 who **d** the moon and stars to shine by
31:36 "Only if these **d** vanish from my
44:10 **d** I set before you and your fathers.
44:23 law or his **d** or his stipulations,
Eze 5: 6 has rebelled against my laws and **d**
5: 6 my laws and has not followed my **d**.
5: 7 not followed my **d** or kept my laws.
11:12 for you have not followed my **d** or
11:20 they will follow my **d** and be careful
18: 9 He follows my **d** and faithfully keeps
18:17 He keeps my laws and follows my **d**.
18:19 has been careful to keep all my **d**,
18:21 keeps all my **d** and does what is
20:11 I gave them my **d** and made known to
20:13 They did not follow my **d** but
20:16 did not follow my **d** and desecrated
20:19 I am the LORD your God; follow my **d**
20:21 They did not follow my **d**, they were
20:24 rejected my **d** and desecrated my
33:15 follows the **d** that give life, and
36:27 follow my **d** and be careful to keep
37:24 my laws and be careful to keep my **d**.
44:24 They are to keep my laws and my **d**
Am 2: 4 and have not kept his **d**, because
Zec 1: 6 did not my words and my **d**, which I
Mal 3: 7 you have turned away from my **d** and
4: 4 the **d** and laws I gave him at Horeb
Ac 17: 7 They are all defying Caesar's **d**,

Dedan (Dedanites)
Ge 10: 7 The sons of Raamah: Sheba and **D**.
25: 3 Jokshan was the father of Sheba and **D**
25: 3 the descendants of **D** were the
1Ch 1: 9 The sons of Raamah: Sheba and **D**.
1:32 The sons of Jokshan: Sheba and **D**.
Jer 25:23 **D**, Tema, Buz and all who are in
49: 8 in deep caves, you who live in **D**,
Eze 25:13 from Teman to **D** they will fall by
27:20 "**D** traded in saddle blankets with
38:13 Sheba and **D** and the merchants of

Dedanites (Dedan)
Isa 21:13 You caravans of **D**, who camp in the

Dedicate (Dedicated, Dedicates, Dedication)
Lev 27: 2 'If anyone makes a special vow to **d**
27:26 "No-one, however, may **d** the
Nu 6:12 He must **d** himself to the LORD for
Dt 20: 5 in battle and someone else may **d** it.
2Ch 2: 4 to **d** it to him for burning fragrant
Pr 20:25 is a trap for a man to **d** something
Eze 43:26 and cleanse it; thus they will **d** it.

Dedicated (Dedicate)
Lev 21:12 **d** by the anointing oil of his God.
Nu 6: 9 thus defiling the hair he has **d**, he
6:18 must shave off the hair that he **d**.
18: 6 **d** to the LORD to do the work at the
Dt 20: 5 built a new house and not **d** it?
2Sa 8:11 King David **d** these articles to the
8:12 He also **d** the plunder taken from
1Ki 7:51 the things his father David had **d**
8:63 Israelites **d** the temple of the LORD.
15:15 that he and his father had **d**.
2Ki 12:18 the sacred objects **d** by his fathers
12:18 the gifts he himself had **d**
23:11 the kings of Judah had **d** to the sun.
23:11 burned the chariots **d** to the sun.
1Ch 18:11 King David **d** these articles to the
26:20 and the treasuries for the **d** things.
26:26 for the things **d** by King David,
26:27 they **d** for the repair of the temple
26:28 everything **d** by Samuel the seer and
26:28 and all the other **d** things were in
28:12 for the treasuries for the **d** things.
2Ch 5: 1 the things his father David had **d**
7: 5 all the people **d** the temple of God.
15:18 that he and his father had **d**.
29:31 "You have now **d** yourselves to the
31: 6 holy things **d** to the LORD their God,
31:12 contributions, tithes and **d** gifts.
Ne 3: 1 They **d** it and set its doors in place,
3: 1 Tower of the Hundred which they **d**,
Lk 21: 5 stones and with gifts **d** to God.

Dedicates (Dedicate)
Lev 27:14 "'If a man **d** his house as something
27:15 If the man who **d** his house redeems
27:16 "'If a man **d** to the LORD part of his
27:17 If he **d** his field during the Year of
27:18 if he **d** his field after the Jubilee,
27:19 If the man who **d** the field wishes to
27:22 "'If a man **d** to the LORD a field he

Dedication (Dedicate, *Feast of Dedication*)
Nu 6:19 has shaved off the hair of his **d**,
7:10 brought their offerings for its **d**
7:11 offering for the **d** of the altar."
7:84 **d** of the altar when it was anointed:
7:88 **d** of the altar after it was anointed.
2Ch 7: 9 for they had celebrated the **d** of the
Ezr 6:16 the **d** of the house of God with joy.
6:17 For the **d** of this house of God they
Ne 12:27 At the **d** of the wall of Jerusalem,
12:27 celebrate joyfully the **d** with songs
Ps 30: T A song. For the **d** of the temple.
Da 3: 2 to the **d** of the image he had set up.
3: 3 assembled for the **d** of the image
1Ti 5:11 desires overcome their **d** to Christ,

Deed (Deeds)
Dt 17: 5 or woman who has done this evil **d**
Ecc 3:17 every activity, a time for every **d**."
12:14 For God will bring every **d** into
Jer 32:10 I signed and sealed the **d**, had it
32:11 I took the **d** of purchase—the sealed
32:12 I gave this **d** to Baruch son of
32:12 the witnesses who had signed the **d**
32:14 copies of the **d** of purchase,
32:16 "After I had given the **d** of purchase
Lk 24:19 powerful in word and **d** before God
Col 3:17 whatever you do, whether in word or **d**
2Th 2:17 strengthen you in every good **d** and

Deeds (Deed, *Evil deeds, Good deeds*)
Dt 3:24 do the **d** and mighty works you do?
4:34 or by great and awesome **d**, like all
34:12 the awesome **d** that Moses did in the
1Sa 2: 3 who knows, and by him **d** are weighed.
2:23 about these wicked **d** of yours.
1Ch 16:24 his marvellous **d** among all peoples.

Job 34:25 he takes note of their **d**, he
Ps 14: 1 They are corrupt, their **d** are vile;
17: 4 for the **d** of men—by the word of
26: 7 and telling of all your wonderful **d**.
28: 4 Repay them for their **d** and for their
45: 4 your right hand display awesome **d**.
65: 5 You answer us with awesome **d** of
66: 3 Say to God, "How awesome are your **d**!
71:17 day I declare your marvellous **d**.
72:18 Israel, who alone does marvellous **d**.
73:28 I will tell of all your **d**.
75: 1 men tell of your wonderful **d**.
77:11 I will remember the **d** of the LORD;
77:12 and consider all your mighty **d**.
78: 4 the praiseworthy **d** of the LORD,
78: 7 and would not forget his **d** but
86: 8 O Lord; no **d** can compare with yours.
86:10 For you are great and do marvellous **d**
88:12 righteous **d** in the land of oblivion?
90:16 May your **d** be shown to your servants,
92: 4 For you make me glad by your **d**,
96: 3 his marvellous **d** among all peoples.
101: 3 The **d** of faithless men I hate; they
03: 7 Moses, his **d** to the people of Israel:
106:22 of Ham and awesome **d** by the Red Sea.
106:29 LORD to anger by their wicked **d**,
106:39 their **d** they prostituted themselves.
107: 8 love and his wonderful **d** for men,
107:15 love and his wonderful **d** for men,
107:21 love and his wonderful **d** for men.
107:24 LORD, his wonderful **d** in the deep.
107:31 love and his wonderful **d** for men.
111: 3 Glorious and majestic are his **d**, and
141: 4 to take part in wicked **d** with men
141: 5 is ever against the **d** of evildoers;
145: 6 and I will proclaim your great **d**.
Pr 8:22 of his works, before his **d** of old;
Isa 3: 8 their words and **d** are against the
3:10 will enjoy the fruit of their **d**.
5:12 but they have no regard for the **d** of
32: 8 plans, and by noble **d** he stands.
41:29 Their **d** amount to nothing; their
59: 6 Their **d** are evil **d**, and acts of
63: 7 the **d** for which he is to be praised,
65: 7 full payment for their former **d**."
Jer 17:10 according to what his **d** deserve."
21:14 I will punish you as your **d** deserve,
25:14 according to their **d** and the work
32:19 your purposes and mighty are your **d**.
32:19 to his conduct and as his **d** deserve.
32:44 and **d** will be signed, sealed and
48: 7 Since you trust in your **d** and riches,
50:29 Repay her for her **d**; do to her as
Eze 22:28 Her prophets whitewash these **d** for
36:31 your evil ways and wicked **d**,
Hos 4: 9 ways and repay them for their **d**.
5: 4 "Their **d** do not permit them to
9:15 Because of their sinful **d**, I will
12: 2 and repay him according to his **d**.
Ob :15 **d** will return upon your own head.
Mic 7:13 as the result of their **d**.
Hab 3: 2 I stand in awe of your **d**, O LORD.
Lk 1:51 He has performed mighty **d** with his
23:41 we are getting what our **d** deserve.
Jn 3:19 of light because their **d** were evil.
3:20 for fear that his **d** will be exposed.
Ac 26:20 prove their repentance by their **d**.
Ro 13:12 So let us put aside the **d** of
Eph 5:11 do with the fruitless **d** of darkness,
Jas 2:14 claims to have faith but has no **d**?
2:18 will say, "You have faith; I have **d**.
2:18 Show me your faith without **d**, and I
2:20 that faith without **d** is useless?
2:26 is dead, so faith without **d** is dead.
3:13 by **d** done in the humility that comes
2Pe 2: 8 by the lawless **d** he saw and heard)—
Rev 2: 2 I know your **d**, your hard work and
2:19 I know your **d**, your love and faith,
2:23 each of you according to your **d**.
3: 1 I know your **d**; you have a reputation
3: 2 I have not found your **d** complete in
3: 8 I know your **d**. See, I have placed
3:15 I know your **d**, that you are neither
14:13 for their **d** will follow them."
15: 3 "Great and marvellous are your **d**,

Deep (Ankle-deep, Deeper, Deepest, Deeply, Deeps, Depth, Depths)

Ge 1: 2 was over the surface of the **d**,
2:21 the man to fall into a **d** sleep;
7:11 springs of the great **d** burst forth,
8: 2 Now the springs of the **d** and the
15:12 Abram fell into a **d** sleep, and a
49:25 blessings of the **d** that lies below,
Ex 15: 5 The **d** waters have covered them; they
15: 8 the **d** waters congealed in the heart
Lev 13: 3 appears to be more than skin **d**,
13: 4 not appear to be more than skin **d**
13:20 if it appears to be more than skin **d**
13:21 not more than skin **d** and has faded,
13:25 it appears to be more than skin **d**,
13:26 not more than skin **d** and has faded,
13:30 if it appears to be more than skin **d**
13:31 not seem to be more than skin **d**
13:32 not appear to be more than skin **d**,
13:34 appears to be no more than skin **d**,
Dt 4:11 with black clouds and **d** darkness.
5:22 the cloud and the **d** darkness; and he
33:13 with the **d** waters that lie below;
1Sa 26:12 LORD had put them into a **d** sleep.
2Sa 22:17 he drew me out of **d** waters.
24:14 "I am in **d** distress. Let us fall
1Ki 7:31 had a circular frame one cubit **d**.
7:35 was a circular band half a cubit **d**.
18:27 Perhaps he is **d** in thought, or busy
1Ch 21:13 "I am in **d** distress. Let me fall
Job 3: 5 May darkness and **d** shadow claim it
4:13 night, when **d** sleep falls on men,
7:12 the sea, or the monster of the **d**,
10:21 to the land of gloom and **d** shadow,
10:22 night, of **d** shadow and disorder,
12:22 He reveals the **d** things of darkness
12:22 and brings **d** shadows into the light.
16:16 weeping, **d** shadows ring my eyes;
24:17 them, **d** darkness is their morning
26: 5 "The dead are in **d** anguish, those
28:14 The **d** says, 'It is not in me'; the
33:15 when **d** sleep falls on men as they
34:22 There is no dark place, no **d** shadow,
38:16 or walked in the recesses of the **d**?
38:30 when the surface of the **d** is frozen?
41:32 would think the **d** had white hair.
Ps 18:16 he drew me out of **d** waters.
33: 7 he puts the **d** into storehouses.
36: 6 your justice like the great **d**.
42: 7 **D** calls to **d** in the roar of your
44:19 and covered us over with **d** darkness.
69: 2 I have come into the **d** waters;
69:14 who hate me, from the **d** waters.
104: 6 You covered it with the **d** as with a
107:24 LORD, his wonderful deeds in the **d**.
Pr 4:19 of the wicked is like **d** darkness;
7:18 Come, let's drink **d** of love till
8:27 the horizon on the face of the **d**,
8:28 securely the fountains of the **d**,
18: 4 words of a man's mouth are **d** waters
19:15 Laziness brings on **d** sleep, and the
20: 5 of a man's heart are **d** waters,
22:14 mouth of an adulteress is a **d** pit;
23:27 for a prostitute is a **d** pit and a
25: 3 heavens are high and the earth is **d**,
Isa 29:10 LORD has brought over you a **d** sleep
30:33 Its fire pit has been made **d** and
44:27 who says to the watery **d**, 'Be dry,
51:10 the waters of the great **d**, who made
54: 7 **d** compassion I will bring you back.
59: 9 but we walk in **d** shadows.
Jer 13:16 darkness and change it to **d** gloom.
49: 8 Turn and flee, hide in **d** caves, you
49:30 "Flee quickly away! Stay in **d** caves,
Lam 2:13 Your wound is as **d** as the sea.
Eze 23:32 a cup large and **d**; it will bring
31: 4 **d** springs made it grow tall;
31:15 covered the **d** springs with mourning
40: 6 of the gate; it was one rod **d**.
40: 7 facing the temple was one rod **d**.
40: 9 was eight cubits **d** and its jambs
40:30 cubits wide and five cubits **d**.)
43:13 is a cubit **d** and a cubit wide,
47: 5 was **d** enough to swim in—a river
Da 2:22 He reveals **d** and hidden things; he
8:18 **d** sleep, with my face to the ground.
10: 9 a **d** sleep, my face to the ground.
Hos 5: 2 The rebels are **d** in slaughter.
9: 9 They have sunk **d** into corruption, as
Am 7: 4 dried up the great **d** and devoured
Jnh 1: 5 he lay down and fell into a **d** sleep.
2: 3 You hurled me into the **d**, into the
2: 5 the **d** surrounded me; seaweed was
Hab 3:10 the **d** roared and lifted its waves
Mk 7:34 and with a **d** sigh said to him,
Lk 5: 4 "Put out into **d** water, and let down
6:48 dug down **d** and laid the foundation
Jn 4:11 to draw with and the well is **d**.
Ac 20: 9 into a **d** sleep as Paul talked on
27:28 was one hundred and twenty feet **d**.
27:28 and found it was ninety feet **d**.
Ro 10: 7 "or 'Who will descend into the **d**?'"
1Co 2:10 things, even the **d** things of God.
2Co 7: 7 your **d** sorrow, your ardent concern
Eph 3:18 high and **d** is the love of Christ,
1Th 1: 5 Holy Spirit and with **d** conviction.
1Ti 3: 9 They must keep hold of the **d** truths
Rev 2:24 learned Satan's so-called **d** secrets

Deeper (Deep)

Lev 14:37 be **d** than the surface of the wall,
Job 11: 8 They are **d** than the depths of the

Deepest (Deep)

Job 10:22 to the land of **d** night, of deep
Ps 107:10 Some sat in darkness and the **d** gloom,
107:14 out of darkness and the **d** gloom and
Isa 7:11 **d** depths or in the highest heights."

Deeply (Deep)

Ge 43:30 **D** moved at the sight of his brother,
1Sa 1:15 "I am a woman who is **d** troubled.
Isa 66:11 you will drink **d** and delight in her
Da 7:28 I, Daniel, was **d** troubled by my
Mk 3: 5 **d** distressed at their stubborn
8:12 He sighed **d** and said, "Why does this
14:33 to be **d** distressed and troubled.
Jn 11:33 was **d** moved in spirit and troubled.
11:38 Jesus, once more **d** moved, came to
Ac 8: 2 Stephen and mourned **d** for him.
1Pe 1:22 love one another **d**, from the heart.
4: 8 Above all, love each other **d**,

Deeps (Deep)

Pr 3:20 by his knowledge the **d** were divided,

Deer

Dt 12:15 as if it were gazelle or **d**,
12:22 Eat them as you would gazelle or **d**.
14: 5 the **d**, the gazelle, the roe **d**, the
15:22 eat it, as if it were gazelle or **d**.
2Sa 22:34 He makes my feet like the feet of a **d**
1Ki 4:23 as well as **d**, gazelles, roebucks and
Ps 18:33 He makes my feet like the feet of a **d**
42: 1 the **d** pants for streams of water, so
Pr 5:19 A loving doe, a graceful **d**—may her
7:22 like a **d** stepping into a noose
Isa 35: 6 will the lame leap like a **d**, and the
Lam 1: 6 Her princes are like **d** that find no
Hab 3:19 makes my feet like the feet of a **d**,

Defamed

Isa 48:11 How can I let myself be **d**? I will

Defeat (Defeated, Defeating)

Ex 32:18 it is not the sound of **d**; it is the
Nu 22: 6 I will be able to **d** them and
Jdg 2:15 **d** them, just as he had sworn to them.
1Sa 4: 3 "Why did the LORD bring **d** upon us
2Ki 13:19 now you will **d** it only three times."
Ps 92:11 My eyes have seen the **d** of my
Isa 9: 4 For as in the day of Midian's **d**, you
Jer 37:10 Even if you were to **d** the entire
Heb 7: 1 the **d** of the kings and blessed him,

Defeated (Defeat)

Ge 14: 5 **d** the Rephaites in Ashteroth Karnaim,
36:35 Hadad son of Bedad, who **d** Midian in

Lev 26:17 that you will be **d** by your enemies;
Nu 14:42 You will be **d** by your enemies,
Dt 1: 4 This was after he had **d** Sihon king
1: 4 and at Edrei had **d** Og king of Bashan,
1:42 You will be **d** by your enemies.'"
4:46 who reigned in Heshbon and was **d** by
7: 2 over to you and you have **d** them,
28: 7 up against you will be **d** before you.
28:25 The LORD will cause you to be **d**
29: 7 to fight against us, but we **d** them.
Jos 10:10 **d** them in a great victory at Gibeon.
10:33 but Joshua **d** him and his army—until
11: 8 They **d** them and pursued them all the
12: 1 the land whom the Israelites had **d**
13:12 **d** them and taken over their land.
13:21 Moses had **d** him and the Midianite
Jdg 1:10 and **d** Sheshai, Ahiman and Talmai.
11:21 Israel's hands, and they **d** them.
20:35 The LORD **d** Benjamin before Israel,
1Sa 4: 2 Israel was **d** by the Philistines, who
4:10 the Israelites were **d** and every man
14:48 He fought valiantly and **d** the
2Sa 2:17 men of Israel were **d** by David's men.
5:20 Baal Perazim, and there he **d** them.
8: 1 David **d** the Philistines and subdued
8: 2 David also **d** the Moabites. He made
8: 9 had **d** the entire army of Hadadezer,
10:19 saw that they had been **d** by Israel,
18: 7 There the army of Israel was **d** by
1Ki 8:33 "When your people Israel have been **d**
2Ki 13:19 **d** Aram and completely destroyed it.
13:25 Three times Jehoash **d** him, and so he
14: 7 He was the one who **d** ten thousand
14:10 You have indeed **d** Edom and now you
18: 8 he **d** the Philistines, as far as Gaza
1Ch 1:46 Hadad son of Bedad, who **d** Midian in
5:10 who were **d** at their hands; they
14:11 Baal Perazim, and there he **d** them.
18: 1 In the course of time, David **d** the
18: 2 David also **d** the Moabites, and they
18: 9 that David had **d** the entire army
19:19 saw that they had been **d** by Israel,
2Ch 6:24 "When your people Israel have been **d**
20:22 invading Judah, and they were **d**.
25:19 to yourself that you have **d** Edom
28: 5 The Arameans **d** him and took many of
28:23 gods of Damascus, who had **d** him;
Jer 46: 2 which was **d** at Carchemish on the
46: 5 retreating, their warriors are **d**.
Da 11:11 a large army, but it will be **d**.
1Co 6: 7 you have been completely **d** already.

Defeating (Defeat)
Ge 14:17 Abram returned from **d** Kedorlaomer
Jdg 20:32 "We are **d** them as before," the
20:39 are **d** them as in the first battle."
2Sa 1: 1 David returned from **d** the Amalekites
Da 7:21 war against the saints and **d** them,

Defect (Defected, Defects)
Ex 12: 5 must be year-old males without **d**,
29: 1 a young bull and two rams without **d**.
Lev 1: 3 he is to offer a male without **d**.
1:10 he is to offer a male without **d**.
3: 1 before the LORD an animal without **d**.
3: 6 to offer a male or female without **d**.
4: 3 a young bull without **d** as a sin
4:23 his offering a male goat without **d**.
4:28 committed a female goat without **d**.
4:32 he is to bring a female without **d**.
5:15 without **d** and of the proper value
5:18 without **d** and of the proper value.
6: 6 without **d** and of the proper value.
9: 2 both without **d**, and present them
9: 3 both a year old and without **d**—for
14:10 each without **d**, along with
21:17 who has a **d** may come near to offer
21:18 No man who has any **d** may come near:
21:20 or who has any eye **d**, or who has
21:21 who has any **d** is to come near to
21:21 He has a **d**; he must not come near to
21:23 yet because of his **d**, he must not go
22:19 you must present a male without **d**
22:20 Do not bring anything with a **d**,
22:21 it must be without **d** or blemish to
Lev 23:12 LORD a lamb a year old without **d**,
23:18 each a year old and without **d**,
Nu 6:14 lamb without **d** for a burnt offering,
6:14 a year-old ewe lamb without **d** for a
6:14 a year-old male lamb without **d** for
19: 2 a red heifer without **d** or blemish
28: 3 LORD: two lambs a year old without **d**,
28: 9 of two lambs a year old without **d**,
28:11 lambs a year old, all without **d**.
28:19 lambs a year old, all without **d**.
28:31 Be sure the animals are without **d**.
29: 2 lambs a year old, all without **d**.
29: 8 lambs a year old, all without **d**.
29:13 lambs a year old, all without **d**.
29:17 lambs a year old, all without **d**.
29:20 lambs a year old, all without **d**.
29:23 lambs a year old, all without **d**.
29:26 lambs a year old, all without **d**.
29:29 lambs a year old, all without **d**.
29:32 lambs a year old, all without **d**.
29:36 lambs a year old, all without **d**.
Dt 15:21 If an animal has a **d**, is lame or
17: 1 sheep that has any **d** or flaw in it,
Eze 43:22 goat without **d** for a sin offering,
43:23 ram from the flock, both without **d**.
43:25 ram from the flock, both without **d**.
45:18 take a young bull without **d** and
45:23 without **d** as a burnt offering to
46: 4 male lambs and a ram, all without **d**.
46: 6 six lambs and a ram, all without **d**.
46:13 without **d** for a burnt offering to
Da 1: 4 young men without any physical **d**,
1Pe 1:19 Christ, a lamb without blemish or **d**.

Defected (Defect)
1Ch 12: 8 Some Gadites **d** to David at his
12:19 Some of the men of Manasseh **d** to
12:20 men of Manasseh who **d** to him: Adnah,

Defects (Defect)
Lev 22:25 they are deformed and have **d**.'"

Defence (Defend)
2Ch 11: 5 and built up towns for **d** in Judah:
Job 31:35 I sign now my **d**—let the Almighty
Ps 35:23 Awake, and rise to my **d**! Contend for
Jer 41: 9 his **d** against Baasha king of Israel.
Na 3: 8 The river was her **d**, the waters her
Ac 7:24 so he went to his **d** and avenged him
19:33 order to make a **d** before the people.
22: 1 and fathers, listen now to my **d**."
24:10 this nation; so I gladly make my **d**.
25: 8 Paul made his **d**: "I have done
26: 1 with his hand and began his **d**:
26: 2 as I make my **d** against all the
26:24 point Festus interrupted Paul's **d**.
1Co 9: 3 This is my **d** to those who sit in
Php 1:16 am put here for the **d** of the gospel.
2Ti 4:16 At my first **d**, no-one came to my
1Jn 2: 1 who speaks to the Father in our **d**

Defences (Defend)
2Ch 11:11 He strengthened their **d** and put
26:15 on the corner **d** to shoot arrows and
Job 13:12 of ashes; your **d** are **d** of clay.
Isa 22: 8 the **d** of Judah are stripped away.
22: 9 of David had many breaches in its **d**;
Joel 2: 8 through **d** without breaking ranks.
Na 3:14 strengthen your **d**! Work the clay,

Defend (Defence, Defences, Defended, Defender, Defenders, Defending, Defends)
Jdg 6:31 he can **d** himself when someone breaks
2Ki 19:34 I will **d** this city and save it, for
20: 6 I will **d** this city for my sake and
Job 13:15 I will surely **d** my ways to his face.
Ps 72: 4 He will **d** the afflicted among the
74:22 Rise up, O God, and **d** your cause;
82: 2 "How long will you **d** the unjust and
82: 3 **D** the cause of the weak and
119:154 **D** my cause and redeem me; preserve
Pr 31: 9 **d** the rights of the poor and needy.
Ecc 4:12 overpowered, two can **d** themselves.
Isa 1:17 **D** the cause of the fatherless, plead
Isa 1:23 They do not **d** the cause of the
37:35 "I will **d** this city and save it, for
38: 6 of Assyria. I will **d** this city.
Jer 5:28 do not **d** the rights of the poor.
50:34 He will vigorously **d** their cause so
51:36 "See, I will **d** your cause and avenge
Da 3:16 we do not need to **d** ourselves before
Zec 9: 8 I will **d** my house against marauding
Lk 12:11 about how you will **d** yourselves or
21:14 how you will **d** yourselves.
Ac 25:16 to **d** himself against their charges.

Defended (Defend)
2Sa 23:12 He **d** it and struck the Philistines
1Ch 11:14 They **d** it and struck the Philistines
Jer 22:16 He **d** the cause of the poor and needy,

Defender (Defend)
Ex 22: 2 the **d** is not guilty of bloodshed;
Job 5: 4 crushed in court without a **d**.
Ps 68: 5 to the fatherless, a **d** of widows,
Pr 23:11 for their **D** is strong; he will take
Isa 19:20 he will send them a saviour and **d**,
29:21 who ensnare the **d** in court and with

Defenders (Defend)
2Sa 11:16 where he knew the strongest **d** were.

Defending (Defend)
2Ki 9:14 all Israel had been **d** Ramoth Gilead
Ps 10:18 **d** the fatherless and the oppressed,
Ro 2:15 now accusing, now even **d** them.)
2Co 12:19 we have been **d** ourselves to you?
Php 1: 7 or **d** and confirming the gospel,

Defends (Defend)
Dt 10:18 He **d** the cause of the fatherless and
33: 7 With his own hands he **d** his cause.
Isa 51:22 your God, who **d** his people: "See, I

Deference (Deferred)
2Ki 16:18 LORD, in **d** to the king of Assyria.

Deferred (Deference)
Pr 13:12 Hope **d** makes the heart sick, but a

Defiance (Defy)
1Sa 17:23 and shouted his usual **d**, and David

Defiant (Defy)
Pr 7:11 (She is loud and **d**, her feet never

Defiantly (Defy)
Nu 15:30 "'But anyone who sins **d**, whether
Job 15:26 **d** charging against him with a thick,

Defied (Defy)
1Sa 17:36 has **d** the armies of the living God.
17:45 armies of Israel, whom you have **d**.
1Ki 13:21 'You have **d** the word of the LORD and
13:26 of God who **d** the word of the LORD.
Isa 65: 7 the mountains and **d** me on the hills,
Jer 48:26 her drunk, for she has **d** the LORD.
48:42 as a nation because she **d** the LORD.
50:29 **d** the LORD, the Holy One of Israel.
Da 3:28 in him and **d** the king's command

Defies (Defy)
Pr 18: 1 he **d** all sound judgment.

Defile (Defiled, Defilement, Defiles, Defiling)
Ex 20:25 will **d** it if you use a tool on it.
Lev 11:43 Do not **d** yourselves by any of these
18:20 wife and **d** yourself with her.
18:23 an animal and **d** yourself with it.
18:24 "'Do not **d** yourselves in any of
18:28 if you **d** the land, it will vomit you
18:30 and do not **d** yourselves with them.

Lev 20:25 Do not **d** yourselves by any animal or
21: 4 him by marriage, and so **d** himself.
21:15 that he will not **d** his offspring
Nu 5: 3 so that they will not **d** their camp,
18:32 you will not **d** the holy offerings
35:34 Do not **d** the land where you live and
2Ki 23:16 and burned on the altar to **d** it,
Isa 30:22 you will **d** your idols overlaid with
Eze 7:21 of the earth, and they will **d** it.
9: 7 "**D** the temple and fill the courts
14:11 nor will they **d** themselves any more
18: 6 He does not **d** his neighbour's wife
18:15 He does not **d** his neighbour's wife.
20: 7 **d** yourselves with the idols of Egypt.
20:18 or **d** yourselves with their idols.
20:30 Will you **d** yourselves the way your
20:31 you continue to **d** yourselves with
37:23 They will no longer **d** themselves
43: 7 will never again **d** my holy name—
44:25 "'A priest must not **d** himself by
44:25 sister, then he may **d** himself.
Da 1: 8 Daniel resolved not to **d** himself
1: 8 not to **d** himself in this way.
Heb 12:15 up to cause trouble and **d** many.
Rev 14: 4 did not **d** themselves with women,

Defiled (Defile)

Ge 34: 5 that his daughter Dinah had been **d**,
34:13 their sister Dinah had been **d**,
34:27 city where their sister had been **d**.
49: 4 bed, onto my couch and **d** it.
Lev 18:24 to drive out before you became **d**.
18:25 Even the land was **d**; so I punished
18:27 before you, and the land became **d**.
19:31 for you will be **d** by them.
20: 3 he has **d** my sanctuary and profaned
21: 7 not marry women **d** by prostitution
21:14 or a woman **d** by prostitution, but
22: 4 he touches something **d** by a corpse
Nu 5:20 you have **d** yourself by sleeping with
5:27 If she has **d** herself and been
5:28 the woman has not **d** herself and is
6:12 he became **d** during his separation.
19:20 he has **d** the sanctuary of the LORD.
Dt 22: 9 the fruit of the vineyard will be **d**.
24: 4 her again after she has been **d**.
Jos 22:19 If the land you possess is **d**, come
2Sa 1:21 the shield of the mighty was **d**,
2Ki 23:19 Josiah removed and **d** all the shrines
1Ch 5: 1 but when he **d** his father's marriage
Ne 13:29 because they **d** the priestly office
Job 31: 7 my eyes, or if my hands have been **d**,
Ps 74: 7 **d** the dwelling-place of your Name.
79: 1 they have **d** your holy temple,
89:39 and have **d** his crown in the dust.
106:39 They **d** themselves by what they did;
Isa 24: 5 The earth is **d** by its people; they
52: 1 and **d** will not enter you again.
Jer 2: 7 But you came and **d** my land and made
2:23 "How can you say,'I am not **d**;
3: 1 Would not the land be completely **d**?
3: 2 You have **d** the land with your
3: 9 she **d** the land and committed
7:30 that bears my Name and have **d** it.
16:18 because they have **d** my land with the
19:13 of Judah will be **d** like this place,
32:34 house that bears my Name and **d** it.
Lam 4:14 They are so **d** with blood that no-one
Eze 4:13 people of Israel will eat **d** food
4:14 I have never **d** myself.
5:11 because you have **d** my sanctuary with
20:26 I let them become **d** through their
20:43 by which you have **d** yourselves,
22: 4 become **d** by the idols you have made.
22:16 you have been **d** in the eyes of the
23: 7 **d** herself with all the idols of
23:13 I saw that she too **d** herself; both
23:17 love, and in their lust they **d** her.
23:17 After she had been **d** by them, she
23:30 and **d** yourself with their idols.
23:38 they **d** my sanctuary and desecrated
36:17 they **d** it by their conduct and their
36:18 they had **d** it with their idols.
43: 8 they **d** my holy name by their
Hos 6:10 to prostitution and Israel is **d**.
Mic 2:10 it is **d**, it is ruined, beyond all
4:11 They say, "Let her be **d**, let our
Zep 3: 1 of oppressors, rebellious and **d**!
Hag 2:13 Haggai said, "If a person **d** by
2:13 of these things, does it become **d**?"
2:13 the priests replied, "it becomes **d**.
2:14 and whatever they offer there is **d**.
Mal 1: 7 "You place **d** food on my altar.
1: 7 "But you ask,'How have we **d** you?'
Ac 21:28 temple area and **d** this holy place."
1Co 8: 7 their conscience is weak, it is **d**.

Defilement (Defile)

2Ch 29: 5 Remove all **d** from the sanctuary.

Defiles (Defile)

Lev 21: 9 "'If a priest's daughter **d** herself
Nu 5:29 **d** herself while married to her
19:13 himself **d** the LORD's tabernacle.
Eze 18:11 He **d** his neighbour's wife.
22: 3 midst and **d** herself by making idols,
22:11 shamefully **d** his daughter-in-law,
33:26 each of you **d** his neighbour's wife.

Defiling (Defile)

Lev 15:31 uncleanness for **d** my dwelling-place,
Nu 6: 9 thus **d** the hair he has dedicated, he
2Ch 36:14 and **d** the temple of the LORD, which

Definite

1Sa 23:23 come back to me with **d** information.
Ac 25:26 I have nothing **d** to write to His

Deformed (Form)

Lev 21:18 is blind or lame, disfigured or **d**;
22:23 ox or a sheep that is **d** or stunted,
22:25 they are **d** and have defects.'"

Defraud (Fraud)

Lev 19:13 "'Do not **d** your neighbour or rob him.
Hos 12: 7 dishonest scales; he loves to **d**.
Mic 2: 2 They **d** a man of his home, a
Mal 3: 5 against those who **d** labourers of
Mk 10:19 do not **d**, honour your father and

Defy (Defiance, Defiant, Defiantly, Defied, Defies, Defying)

1Sa 17:10 "This day I **d** the ranks of Israel!
17:25 out? He comes out to **d** Israel.
17:26 **d** the armies of the living God?"

Defying (Defy)

Isa 3: 8 the LORD, **d** his glorious presence.
Ac 17: 7 They are all **d** Caesar's decrees,

Degrade (Degraded, Degrading)

Lev 19:29 "'Do not **d** your daughter by making

Degraded (Degrade)

Dt 25: 3 your brother will be **d** in your eyes.
Eze 16:25 lofty shrines and **d** your beauty,

Degrading (Degrade)

Ro 1:24 **d** of their bodies with one another.

Deity

Col 2: 9 all the fulness of the **D** lives in

Dejected

Ge 40: 6 morning, he saw that they were **d**.
Isa 19:10 The workers in cloth will be **d**, and

Delaiah

1Ch 3:24 Johanan, **D** and Anani—seven in all.
24:18 the twenty-third to **D** and the
Ezr 2:60 The descendants of **D**, Tobiah and
Ne 6:10 to the house of Shemaiah son of **D**,
7:62 the descendants of **D**, Tobiah and
Jer 36:12 **D** son of Shemaiah, Elnathan son of
36:25 Even though Elnathan, **D** and Gemariah

Delay (Delayed)

Ge 45: 9 Come down to me; don't **d**.
2Ki 9: 3 Then open the door and run; don't **d**!"
Ps 40:17 my deliverer; O my God, do not **d**.
70: 5 and my deliverer; O LORD, do not **d**.
119:60 I will hasten and not **d** to obey your
Ecc 5: 4 to God, do not **d** in fulfilling it.
Isa 48: 9 For my own name's sake I **d** my wrath;
Jer 4: 6 Flee for safety without **d**! For I am
Eze 12:25 and it shall be fulfilled without **d**.
Da 9:19 O my God, do not **d**, because your
Hab 2: 3 will certainly come and will not **d**.
Mk 1:20 Without **d** he called them, and they
Ac 25:17 they came here with me, I did not **d**
Heb 10:37 is coming will come and will not **d**.
Rev 10: 6 and said, "There will be no more **d**!

Delayed (Delay)

Ge 43:10 if we had not **d**, we could have
Jos 10:13 and **d** going down about a full day.
Jdg 5:28 is the clatter of his chariots **d**?'
Isa 46:13 and my salvation will not be **d**.
Eze 12:28 None of my words will be **d** any
1Ti 3:15 if I am **d**, you will know how people

Delegation

Jos 9: 4 They went as a **d** whose donkeys were
2Sa 10: 2 So David sent a **d** to express his
1Ch 19: 2 So David sent a **d** to express his
Lk 14:32 If he is not able, he will send a **d**
19:14 him and sent a **d** after him to say,

Deliberately

Ex 21:14 man schemes and kills another man **d**,
Heb 10:26 If we **d** keep on sinning after we
2Pe 3: 5 they **d** forget that long ago by God's

Delicacies (Delicate)

Ge 49:20 he will provide **d** fit for a king.
Ps 141: 4 let me not eat of their **d**.
Pr 23: 3 Do not crave his **d**, for that food is
23: 6 of a stingy man, do not crave his **d**;
Jer 51:34 and filled his stomach with our **d**,
Lam 4: 5 Those who once ate **d** are destitute

Delicacy (Delicate)

SS 7:13 and at our door is every **d**, both new

Delicate (Delicacies, Delicacy)

Isa 47: 1 more will you be called tender or **d**.
Jer 6: 2 Daughter of Zion, so beautiful and **d**.

Delicious

Pr 9:17 food eaten in secret is **d**!"

Delight (Delighted, Delightful, Delighting, Delights)

Lev 26:31 and I will take no **d** in the pleasing
Dt 30: 9 The LORD will again **d** in you and
1Sa 2: 1 for I **d** in your deliverance.
15:22 Samuel replied: "Does the LORD **d** in
Ne 1:11 who **d** in revering your name.
Job 22:26 Surely then you will find **d** in the
27:10 Will he find **d** in the Almighty? Will
Ps 1: 2 his **d** is in the law of the LORD, and
16: 3 glorious ones in whom is all my **d**.
35: 9 in the LORD and **d** in his salvation.
35:27 May those who **d** in my vindication
37: 4 **D** yourself in the LORD and he will
43: 4 of God, to God, my joy and my **d**.
51:16 You do not **d** in sacrifice, or I
51:19 whole burnt offerings to **d** you; then
62: 4 lofty place; they take **d** in lies.
68:30 Scatter the nations who **d** in war.
111: 2 are pondered by all who **d** in them.
112: 1 who finds great **d** in his commands.
119:16 I **d** in your decrees; I will not
119:24 Your statutes are my **d**; they are my
119:35 your commands, for there I find **d**.
119:47 for I **d** in your commands because I

Ps 119:70 and unfeeling, but I **d** in your law.
119:77 I may live, for your law is my **d**.
119:92 If your law had not been my **d**, I
119:143 upon me, but your commands are my **d**.
119:174 O LORD, and your law is my **d**.
147:10 nor his **d** in the legs of a man;
149: 4 For the LORD takes **d** in his people;
Pr 1:22 How long will mockers **d** in mockery
2:14 who **d** in doing wrong and rejoice in
8:30 I was filled with **d** day after day,
11: 1 but accurate weights are his **d**.
29:17 he will bring **d** to your soul.
Ecc 2:10 My heart took **d** in all my work, and
SS 1: 4 We rejoice and **d** in you; we will
2: 3 I **d** to sit in his shade, and his
Isa 5: 7 of Judah are the garden of his **d**.
11: 3 he will **d** in the fear of the LORD.
13:17 for silver and have no **d** in gold.
32:14 **d** of donkeys, a pasture for flocks,
42: 1 my chosen one in whom I **d**; I will
55: 2 soul will **d** in the richest of fare.
58:13 if you call the Sabbath a **d** and the
61:10 I **d** greatly in the LORD; my soul
62: 4 for the LORD will take **d** in you,
65:18 to be a **d** and its people a joy.
65:19 Jerusalem and take **d** in my people;
66: 3 their souls **d** in their abominations;
66:11 and **d** in her overflowing abundance."
Jer 9:24 in these I **d**," declares the LORD.
15:16 they were my joy and my heart's **d**,
31:20 my dear son, the child in whom I **d**?
49:25 abandoned, the town in which I **d**?
Eze 24:16 away from you the **d** of your eyes.
24:21 the **d** of your eyes, the object of
24:25 joy and glory, the **d** of their eyes,
Hos 7: 3 "They **d** the king with their
Mic 1:16 for the children in whom you **d**;
7:18 angry for ever but **d** to show mercy.
Zep 3:17 He will take great **d** in you, he will
Mt 12:18 the one I love, in whom I **d**; I will
Mk 12:37 large crowd listened to him with **d**.
Lk 1:14 He will be a joy and **d** to you, and
Ro 7:22 in my inner being I **d** in God's law
1Co 13: 6 Love does not **d** in evil but rejoices
2Co 12:10 I **d** in weaknesses, in insults, in
Col 2: 5 **d** to see how orderly you are and how

Delighted (Delight)

Ge 34:19 he was **d** with Jacob's daughter.
Ex 18: 9 Jethro was **d** to hear about all the
Dt 30: 9 just as he **d** in your fathers,
2Sa 22:20 he rescued me because he **d** in me.
1Ki 10: 9 who has **d** in you and placed you on
2Ch 9: 8 who has **d** in you and placed you on
Est 5:14 This suggestion **d** Haman, and he had
Ps 18:19 he rescued me because he **d** in me.
Isa 1:29 the sacred oaks in which you have **d**;
Mk 14:11 They were **d** to hear this and
Lk 13:17 but the people were **d** with all the
22: 5 They were **d** and agreed to give him
2Co 7:13 we were especially **d** to see how
1Th 2: 8 we were **d** to share with you
2Th 2:12 the truth but have **d** in wickedness.

Delightful (Delight)

Ps 16: 6 surely I have a **d** inheritance.
SS 1: 2 for your love is more **d** than wine.
4:10 How **d** is your love, my sister, my
Mal 3:12 a **d** land," says the LORD Almighty.

Delighting (Delight)

Pr 8:31 his whole world and **d** in mankind.

Delights (Delight)

Est 6: 6 for the man the king **d** to honour?"
6: 7 "For the man the king **d** to honour,
6: 9 robe the man the king **d** to honour
6: 9 for the man the king **d** to honour!'"
6:11 for the man the king **d** to honour!"
Ps 22: 8 him deliver him, since he **d** in him."
35:27 **d** in the well-being of his servant."
36: 8 them drink from your river of **d**.
37:23 If the LORD **d** in a man's way, he
147:11 the LORD **d** in those who fear him,
Pr 3:12 loves, as a father the son he **d** in.
10:23 a man of understanding **d** in wisdom.
11:20 **d** in those whose ways are blameless.
12:22 but he **d** in men who are truthful.
14:35 A king **d** in a wise servant, but a
15:21 Folly **d** a man who lacks judgment,
18: 2 but **d** in airing his own opinions.
23:24 he who has a wise son **d** in him.
Ecc 2: 8 as well—the **d** of the heart of man.
SS 7: 6 how pleasing, O love, with your **d**!
Col 2:18 let anyone who **d** in false humility

Delilah

Betrayed Samson (Jdg 16:4–22).

Jdg 16: 4 Valley of Sorek whose name was **D**.
16: 6 **D** said to Samson, "Tell me the
16:10 **D** said to Samson, "You have made a
16:12 **D** took new ropes and tied him with
16:13 **D** then said to Samson, "Until now,
16:13 **D** took the seven braids of his head
16:18 **D** saw that he had told her

Deliver (Deliverance, Delivered, Deliverer, Deliverers, Delivering, Delivers, Delivery)

Nu 21: 2 "If you will **d** these people into our
Dt 1:27 he brought us out of Egypt to **d** us
2:31 **d** Sihon and his country over to you.
7:23 the LORD your God will **d** them over
23:14 you and to **d** your enemies to you.
31: 5 The LORD will **d** them to you, and you
32:39 and no-one can **d** out of my hand.
Jos 7: 7 to **d** us into the hands of the
8:18 into your hand I will **d** the city.
Jdg 7: 2 for me to **d** Midian into their hands.
1Sa 4: 8 Woe to us! Who will **d** us from the
7: 3 and he will **d** you out of the hand of
9:16 he will **d** my people from the hand of
12:10 But now **d** us from the hands of our
17:37 the paw of the bear will **d** me from
26:24 my life and **d** me from all trouble."
2Sa 14:16 king will agree to **d** his servant
1Ki 20:28 I will **d** this vast army into your
2Ki 17:39 it is he who will **d** you from the
18:29 He cannot **d** you from my hand.
18:30 'The LORD will surely **d** us; this
18:32 when he says, 'The LORD will **d** us.'
18:35 the LORD **d** Jerusalem from my hand?"
19: 3 and there is no strength to **d** them.
19:12 destroyed by my forefathers **d** them:
19:19 Now, O LORD our God, **d** us from his
20: 6 And I will **d** you and this city from
1Ch 16:35 gather us and **d** us from the nations
2Ch 32:13 able to **d** their land from my hand?
32:14 can your god **d** you from my hand?
32:15 able to **d** his people from my hand
32:15 will your god **d** you from my hand!"
Ezr 7:19 **D** to the God of Jerusalem all the
Job 6:23 **d** me from the hand of the enemy,
22:30 He will **d** even one who is not
Ps 3: 2 saying of me, "God will not **d** him.
3: 7 Arise, O LORD! **D** me, O my God!
6: 4 Turn, O LORD, and **d** me; save me
7: 1 and **d** me from all who pursue me,
22: 8 **d** him, since he delights in him."
22:20 **D** my life from the sword, my
31: 1 shame; **d** me in your righteousness.
31:15 **d** me from my enemies and from those
33:19 to **d** them from death and keep them
50:15 will **d** you, and you will honour me."
59: 1 **D** me from my enemies, O God;
59: 2 **D** me from evildoers and save me from
69:14 **d** me from those who hate me, from
71: 2 Rescue me and **d** me in your
71: 4 **D** me, O my God, from the hand of the
72:12 For he will **d** the needy who cry out,
79: 9 **d** us and forgive our sins for your
82: 4 **d** them from the hand of the wicked.
91:15 I will **d** him and honour him.
109:21 of the goodness of your love, **d** me.
119:153 Look upon my suffering and **d** me, for
119:170 **d** me according to your promise.
144: 7 **d** me and rescue me from the mighty
144:11 **D** me and rescue me from the hands of
Pr 20:22 Wait for the LORD, and he will **d** you.
Isa 31: 5 he will shield it and **d** it, he will
36:14 deceive you. He cannot **d** you!
36:15 'The LORD will surely **d** us; this
36:18 when he says, 'The LORD will **d** us.
36:20 the LORD **d** Jerusalem from my hand?"
37: 3 and there is no strength to **d** them.
37:12 destroyed by my forefathers **d** them
37:20 Now, O LORD our God, **d** us from his
38: 6 I will **d** you and this city from the
43:13 No-one can **d** out of my hand. When I
Jer 15:11 The LORD said, "Surely I will **d** you
42:11 save you and **d** you from his hands.
Am 6: 8 **d** up the city and everything in it."
Mic 5: 6 He will **d** us from the Assyrian when
Hab 3:13 You came out to **d** your people, to
Mt 6:13 but **d** us from the evil one.'
Lk 21:12 They will **d** you to synagogues and
2Co 1:10 a deadly peril, and he will **d** us.
1:10 hope that he will continue to **d** us,

Deliverance (Deliver)

Ge 45: 7 and to save your lives by a great **d**.
49:18 "I look for your **d**, O LORD.
Ex 14:13 Stand firm and you will see the **d**
Jdg 13: 5 and he will begin the **d** of Israel
1Sa 2: 1 my enemies, for I delight in your **d**.
14:45 about this great **d** in Israel?
2Ch 12: 7 them but will soon give them **d**.
20:17 see the **d** the LORD will give you,
Est 4:14 relief and **d** for the Jews will arise
Job 13:16 Indeed, this will turn out for my **d**,
Ps 3: 8 From the LORD comes **d**. May your
32: 7 and surround me with songs of **d**.
33:17 A horse is a vain hope for **d**;
78:22 believe in God or trust in his **d**.
Isa 20: 6 those we fled to for help and **d** from
59:11 for **d**, but it is far away.
Joel 2:32 and in Jerusalem there will be **d**,
Ob :17 on Mount Zion will be **d**; it will be
Php 1:19 to me will turn out for my **d**.

Delivered (Deliver)

Ge 14:20 who **d** your enemies into your hand."
48:16 the Angel who has **d** me from all harm
Dt 2:33 the LORD our God **d** him over to us
7: 2 the LORD your God has **d** them over to
Jos 6: 2 "See, I have **d** Jericho into your
8: 1 For I have **d** into your hands the
24:10 again, and I **d** you out of his hand.
Jdg 13: 1 so the LORD **d** them into the hands of
16:23 **d** Samson, our enemy, into our hands."
16:24 "Our god has **d** our enemy into our
1Sa 7:14 and Israel **d** the neighbouring
10:18 and I **d** you from the power of Egypt
11: 9 sun is hot tomorrow, you will be **d**.
12:11 and he **d** you from the hands of your
17:37 The LORD who **d** me from the paw of
2Sa 4: 9 who has **d** me out of all trouble,
12: 7 and I **d** you from the hand of Saul.
18:19 **d** him from the hand of his enemies."
18:28 He has **d** up the men who lifted their
18:31 good news! The LORD has **d** you today
19: 9 "The king **d** us from the hand of our
22: 1 the LORD **d** him from the hand of all
22:44 "You have **d** me from the attacks of
1Ki 1:29 who has **d** me out of every trouble,
9:28 gold, which they **d** to King Solomon.
2Ki 17:13 that I **d** to you through my servants
18:33 Has the god of any nation ever **d** his
19:11 them completely. And will you be **d**?
2Ch 8:18 gold, which they **d** to King Solomon.
13:16 and God **d** them into their hands.
16: 8 the LORD, he **d** them into your hand.
24:24 the LORD **d** into their hands a much
Ezr 8:36 They also **d** the king's orders to the
Ne 9:28 you **d** them time after time.
Est 1:12 attendants **d** the king's command,
Job 21:30 that he is **d** from the day of wrath?
22:30 who will be **d** through the cleanness
23: 7 I would be **d** for ever from my judge.
Ps 18: T the LORD **d** him from the hand of all
18:43 You have **d** me from the attacks of
22: 4 they trusted and you **d** them.
34: 4 he **d** me from all my fears.

Ps 54: 7 For he has **d** me from all my troubles,
56:13 For you have **d** me from death and my
60: 5 hand, that those you love may be **d**.
86:13 **d** me from the depths of the grave.
106:43 Many times he **d** them, but they were
107: 6 and he **d** them from their distress.
108: 6 hand, that those you love may be **d**.
116: 8 For you, O LORD, have **d** my soul
119:117 Uphold me, and I shall be **d**; I shall
Isa 36:18 Has the god of any nation ever **d**
37:11 them completely. And will you be **d**?
Eze 35: 5 **d** the Israelites over to the sword
Da 1: 2 the Lord **d** Jehoiakim king of Judah
11:41 of Ammon will be **d** from his hand.
12: 1 written in the book—will be **d**.
Lk 24: 7 'The Son of Man must be **d** into the
Ac 12:21 **d** a public address to the people.
15:30 church together and **d** the letter.
16: 4 they **d** the decisions reached by the
23:33 they **d** the letter to the governor
Ro 4:25 He was **d** over to death for our sins
2Co 1:10 He has **d** us from such a deadly peril,
2Th 3: 2 pray that we may be **d** from wicked
2Ti 4:17 And I was **d** from the lion's mouth.
Jude : 5 the Lord **d** his people out of Egypt,

Deliverer (Deliver)

Jdg 3: 9 he raised up for them a **d**, Othniel
3:15 and he gave them a **d**—Ehud, a
2Sa 22: 2 is my rock, my fortress and my **d**;
2Ki 13: 5 The LORD provided a **d** for Israel,
Ps 18: 2 is my rock, my fortress and my **d**;
40:17 You are my help and my **d**; O my God,
70: 5 You are my help and my **d**; O LORD,
140: 7 O Sovereign LORD, my strong **d**, who
144: 2 my stronghold and my **d**, my shield,
Ac 7:35 be their ruler and **d** by God himself,
Ro 11:26 "The **d** will come from Zion; he will

Deliverers (Deliver)

Ne 9:27 great compassion you gave them **d**,
Ob :21 **D** will go up on Mount Zion to govern

Delivering (Deliver)

1Sa 14:48 **d** Israel from the hands of those who
24:15 me by **d** me from your hand."

Delivers (Deliver)

Dt 20:13 the LORD your God **d** it into your
21:10 the LORD your God **d** them into your
Job 36:15 those who suffer he **d** in their
Ps 34: 7 those who fear him, and he **d** them.
34:17 he **d** them from all their troubles.
34:19 but the LORD **d** him from them all;
37:40 The LORD helps them and **d** them;
37:40 he **d** them from the wicked and saves
41: 1 the LORD **d** him in times of trouble.
97:10 **d** them from the hand of the wicked.
144:10 who **d** his servant David from the
Pr 10: 2 but righteousness **d** from death.
11: 4 but righteousness **d** from death.
11: 6 The righteousness of the upright **d**
Isa 66: 7 pains come upon her, she **d** a son.

Delivery (Deliver)

Ex 1:16 and observe them on the **d** stool,
1Sa 4:19 was pregnant and near the time of **d**.
Isa 66: 9 and not give **d**?" says the LORD.
66: 9 when I bring to **d**?" says your God.

Deluded (Delusion)

Isa 44:20 on ashes, a **d** heart misleads him;
Rev 19:20 With these signs he had **d** those who

Deluged

2Pe 3: 6 of that time was **d** and destroyed.

Delusion (Deluded, Delusions)

2Th 2:11 God sends them a powerful **d** so that

Delusions (Delusion)

Ps 4: 2 How long wil you love **d** and seek
Jer 14:14 and the **d** of their own minds.
23:26 prophesy the **d** of their own minds?

Demand (Demanded, Demanding, Demands)

Ge 9: 5 for your lifeblood I will surely **d**
9: 5 I will **d** an accounting from every
9: 5 And from each man, too, I will **d** an
Dt 23:21 your God will certainly **d** it of you
2Sa 3:13 But I **d** one thing of you: Do not
4:11 bed—should I not now **d** his blood
21: 4 "We have no right to **d** silver or
1Ki 20: 5 'I sent to **d** your silver and gold,
20: 9 time, but this **d** I cannot meet.
2Ki 18:14 and I will pay whatever you **d** of me.
Ne 5:12 "And we will not **d** anything more
Job 17: 3 "Give me, O God, the pledge you **d**.
Lk 6:30 belongs to you, do not **d** it back.
23:24 Pilate decided to grant their **d**.
1Co 1:22 Jews **d** miraculous signs and Greeks

Demanded (Demand)

Ge 31:39 And you **d** payment from me for
Ex 21:30 However, if payment is **d** of him, he
21:30 his life by paying whatever is **d**.
Jdg 6:30 The men of the town **d** of Joash,
1Ki 20: 9 'Your servant will do all you **d** the
2Ki 6:11 He summoned his officers and **d** of
23:35 Neco the silver and gold he **d**.
Ne 5:18 In spite of all this, I never **d** the
Job 22: 6 You **d** security from your brothers
Ps 137: 3 our tormentors **d** songs of joy;
Mt 18:28 'Pay back what you owe me!' he **d**.
Lk 12:20 night your life will be **d** from you.
12:48 been given much, much will be **d**;
22:64 They blindfolded him and **d**,
23:23 with loud shouts they insistently **d**
Jn 2:18 the Jews **d** of him, "What miraculous
9:10 then were your eyes opened?" they **d**.
18:22 you answer the high priest?" he **d**.

Demanding (Demand)

2Sa 3:14 **d**, "Give me my wife Michal, whom I
Ps 78:18 the test by **d** the food they craved.
2Co 13: 3 since you are **d** proof that Christ is

Demands (Demand)

Ex 21:22 husband **d** and the court allows.
1Ki 20: 8 listen to him or agree to his **d**."
Ne 5:18 the **d** were heavy on these people.
Ps 25:10 who keep the **d** of his covenant.
Isa 43:23 nor wearied you with **d** for incense.
Mic 7: 3 the ruler **d** gifts, the judge

Demas

Fellow-worker with Paul (Col 4:14; Phm 24), who later deserted him (2Ti 4:10).

Col 4:14 the doctor, and **D** send greetings.
2Ti 4:10 for **D**, because he loved this world,
Phm :24 do Mark, Aristarchus, **D** and Luke, my

Demetrius

1. Christian commended by John (3Jn 12).
2. Silversmith who stirred up a riot against Paul in Ephesus (Ac 19:23-41).

Ac 19:24 A silversmith named **D**, who made
19:38 If, then, **D** and his fellow craftsmen
3Jn :12 **D** is well spoken of by everyone–and

Demolish (Demolished)

Ex 23:24 You must **d** them and break their
Nu 33:52 idols, and **d** all their high places.
Jer 43:13 Egypt he will **d** the sacred pillars
Eze 26: 9 and **d** your towers with his weapons.
26:12 **d** your fine houses and throw your
Hos 10: 2 The LORD will **d** their altars and
Mic 5:10 from among you and **d** your chariots.
5:14 Asherah poles and **d** your cities.
Mal 1: 4 says: "They may build, but I will **d**.
2Co 10: 4 have divine power to **d** strongholds.
10: 5 We **d** arguments and every pretension

Demolished (Demolish)

Nu 21:30 We have **d** them as far as Nophah,
Jdg 6:28 there was Baal's altar, **d**, with the
2Ki 10:27 They **d** the sacred stone of Baal and
23:15 that altar and high place he **d**.
2Ch 33: 3 places his father Hezekiah had **d**;
Jer 31:40 will never again be uprooted or **d**."
Eze 6: 4 Your altars will be **d** and your
6: 6 be laid waste and the high places **d**,
Am 3:15 and the mansions will be **d**,"
Zep 1:13 will be plundered, their houses **d**.
3: 6 their strongholds are **d**.

Demon (Demon-possessed, Demon-possession, Demons)

Mt 9:33 the **d** was driven out, the man who
11:18 and they say,'He has a **d**.'
17:18 Jesus rebuked the **d**, and it came out
Mk 7:26 to drive the **d** out of her daughter.
7:29 the **d** has left your daughter."
7:30 lying on the bed, and the **d** gone.
Lk 4:33 possessed by a **d**, an evil spirit.
4:35 Then the **d** threw the man down
7:33 wine, and you say,'He has a **d**.'
8:29 by the **d** into solitary places.
9:42 the **d** threw him to the ground in a
11:14 Jesus was driving out a **d** that was
11:14 When the **d** left, the man who had
Jn 8:49 "I am not possessed by a **d**," said
10:21 sayings of a man possessed by a **d**.
10:21 Can a **d** open the eyes of the blind?"

Demon-possessed (Demon, Possess)

Mt 4:24 those suffering severe pain, the **d**,
8:16 evening came, many who were **d** were
8:28 **d** men coming from the tombs met him.
8:33 what had happened to the **d** men.
9:32 a man who was **d** and could not talk
12:22 they brought him a **d** man who was
Mk 1:32 brought to Jesus all the sick and **d**.
5:16 what had happened to the **d** man—
5:18 had been **d** begged to go with him.
Lk 8:27 he was met by a **d** man from the town.
8:36 people how the **d** man had been cured.
Jn 7:20 "You are **d**," the crowd answered.
8:48 that you are a Samaritan and **d**?"
8:52 "Now we know that you are **d**!
10:20 Many of them said, "He is **d** and
Ac 19:13 Lord Jesus over those who were **d**.

Demon-possession (Demon, Possess)

Mt 15:22 is suffering terribly from **d**."

Demons (Demon)

Dt 32:17 They sacrificed to **d**, which are not
Ps 106:37 their sons and their daughters to **d**.
Mt 7:22 and in your name drive out **d**
8:31 The **d** begged Jesus, "If you drive us
9:34 prince of **d** that he drives out **d**."
10: 8 those who have leprosy, drive out **d**.
12:24 only by Beelzebub, the prince of **d**,
12:24 that this fellow drives out **d**."
12:27 if I drive out **d** by Beelzebub, by
12:28 if I drive out **d** by the Spirit of
Mk 1:34 He also drove out many **d**, but he
1:34 **d** speak because they knew who he was.
1:39 their synagogues and driving out **d**.
3:15 to have authority to drive out **d**.
3:22 prince of **d** he is driving out **d**."
5:12 The **d** begged Jesus, "Send us among
5:15 been possessed by the legion of **d**,
6:13 They drove out many **d** and anointed
9:38 "we saw a man driving out **d** in your
16: 9 out of whom he had driven seven **d**.
16:17 In my name they will drive out **d**;
Lk 4:41 Moreover, **d** came out of many people,
8: 2 from whom seven **d** had come out;
8:30 because many **d** had gone into him.
8:32 The **d** begged Jesus to let them go
8:33 the **d** came out of the man, they went
8:35 man from whom the **d** had gone out,
8:38 The man from whom the **d** had gone out
9: 1 out all **d** and to cure diseases,
9:49 "we saw a man driving out **d** in your
10:17 the **d** submit to us in your name."
11:15 prince of **d**, he is driving out **d**."
11:18 that I drive out **d** by Beelzebub.

Lk 11:19 Now if I drive out **d** by Beelzebub,
11:20 if I drive out **d** by the finger of
13:32 'I will drive out **d** and heal people
Ro 8:38 neither angels nor **d**, neither the
1Co 10:20 of pagans are offered to **d**,
10:20 want you to be participants with **d**.
10:21 of the Lord and the cup of **d** too;
10:21 the Lord's table and the table of **d**.
1Ti 4: 1 spirits and things taught by **d**.
Jas 2:19 Even the **d** believe that—and shudder.
Rev 9:20 they did not stop worshipping **d**,
16:14 They are spirits of **d** performing
18: 2 She has become a home for **d** and a

Demonstrate (Demonstrates, Demonstration)
Ro 3:25 He did this to **d** his justice,
3:26 —he did it to **d** his justice at the

Demonstrates (Demonstrate)
Ro 5: 8 God **d** his own love for us in this:

Demonstration (Demonstrate)
1Co 2: 4 but with a **d** of the Spirit's power,

Den (Dens)
Jer 7:11 Name, become a **d** of robbers to you?
Da 6: 7 shall be thrown into the lions' **d**.
6:12 would be thrown into the lions' **d**?"
6:16 and threw him into the lions' **d**.
6:17 and placed over the mouth of the **d**,
6:19 got up and hurried to the lions' **d**.
6:20 he came near the **d**, he called to
6:23 orders to lift Daniel out of the **d**.
6:23 when Daniel was lifted from the **d**,
6:24 in and thrown into the lions' **d**,
6:24 they reached the floor of the **d**,
Am 3: 4 in his **d** when he has caught nothing?
Na 2:11 Where now is the lions' **d**, the place
Mt 21:13 you are making it 'a **d** of robbers'."
Mk 11:17 you have made it 'a **d** of robbers'."
Lk 19:46 you have made it 'a **d** of robbers'."

Denarii (Denarius)
Mt 18:28 who owed him a hundred **d**.
Lk 7:41 One owed him five hundred **d**, and

Denarius (Denarii)
Mt 20: 2 He agreed to pay them a **d** for the
20: 9 hour came and each received a **d**.
20:10 each one of them also received a **d**.
20:13 Didn't you agree to work for a **d**?
22:19 They brought him a **d**,
Mk 12:15 "Bring me a **d** and let me look at it."
Lk 20:24 "Show me a **d**. Whose portrait and

Denied (Deny)
Job 6:10 had not **d** the words of the Holy One.
27: 2 as God lives, who has **d** me justice,
31:13 "If I have **d** justice to my
31:16 "If I have **d** the desires of the poor
38:15 The wicked are **d** their light, and
Ecc 2:10 I **d** myself nothing my eyes desired;
5: 8 and justice and rights **d**, do not be
Mt 26:70 he **d** it before them all. "I don't
26:72 He **d** it again, with an oath: "I
Mk 14:68 he **d** it. "I don't know or understand
14:70 Again he **d** it. After a little while,
Lk 8:45 When they all **d** it, Peter said,
22:57 he **d** it. "Woman, I don't know him,"
Jn 18:25 He **d** it, saying, "I am not."
18:27 Again Peter **d** it, and at that moment
1Ti 5: 8 he has **d** the faith and is worse than
Rev 3: 8 kept my word and have not **d** my name.

Denies (Deny)
Job 34: 5 am innocent, but God **d** me justice.
1Jn 2:22 It is the man who **d** that Jesus is
2:22 he **d** the Father and the Son.
2:23 No-one who **d** the Son has the Father;

Denounce (Denounced, Denounces)
Nu 5:21 **d** you when he causes your thigh to
23: 7 Jacob for me; come, **d** Israel.'
23: 8 How can I **d** those whom the LORD has
Pr 24:24 will curse him and nations **d** him.
Mt 11:20 Jesus began to **d** the cities in which

Denounced (Denounce)
Nu 23: 8 those whom the LORD has not **d**?
Da 3: 8 came forward and **d** the Jews.
1Co 10:30 why am I **d** because of something I

Denounces (Denounce)
Job 17: 5 If a man **d** his friends for reward,
21:31 Who **d** his conduct to his face?

Dens (Den)
Job 37: 8 take cover; they remain in their **d**.
38:40 they crouch in their **d** or lie in
Ps 104:22 they return and lie down in their **d**.
SS 4: 8 from the lions' **d** and the mountain
Mic 7:17 will come trembling out of their **d**;
Na 2:12 the kill and his **d** with the prey.

Dense
Ge 19:28 and he saw **d** smoke rising from the
Ex 8:24 **D** swarms of flies poured into
19: 9 going to come to you in a **d** cloud,
Isa 30:27 with burning anger and **d** clouds of
Jer 46:23 declares the LORD, "**d** though it be.
Zec 11: 2 the **d** forest has been cut down!

Deny (Denied, Denies, Denying)
Ex 23: 6 "Do not **d** justice to your poor
Lev 16:29 seventh month you must **d** yourselves
16:31 of rest, and you must **d** yourselves;
23:27 a sacred assembly and **d** yourselves,
23:29 Anyone who does not **d** himself on
23:32 for you, and you must **d** yourselves.
Nu 29: 7 You must **d** yourselves and do no work.
30:13 or any sworn pledge to **d** herself.
Job 27: 5 I die, I will not **d** my integrity.
Isa 5:23 but **d** justice to the innocent.
Lam 3:35 to **d** a man his rights before the
Am 2: 7 and **d** justice to the oppressed.
Mt 16:24 he must **d** himself and take up his
Mk 8:34 he must **d** himself and take up his
Lk 9:23 he must **d** himself and take up his
22:34 **d** three times that you know me."
Ac 4:16 miracle, and we cannot **d** it.
Tit 1:16 God, but by their actions they **d** him.
Jas 3:14 not boast about it or **d** the truth.
Jude : 4 **d** Jesus Christ our only Sovereign

Denying (Deny)
Eze 22:29 ill-treat the alien, **d** them justice.
2Ti 3: 5 a form of godliness but **d** its power.
2Pe 2: 1 even **d** the sovereign Lord who bought

Depart (Departed, Departing, Departs, Departure)
Ge 49:10 The sceptre will not **d** from Judah,
Jos 1: 8 Do not let this Book of the Law **d**
2Sa 12:10 therefore, the sword shall never **d**
Job 1:21 mother's womb, and naked I shall **d**.
Ps 39:13 again before I **d** and am no more."
Isa 49:17 those who laid you waste **d** from you.
52:11 **D**, **d**, go out from there! Touch no
59:21 mouth will not **d** from your mouth,
Jer 43:12 himself and **d** from there unscathed.
Mt 25:41 '**D** from me, you who are cursed, into
Php 1:23 I desire to **d** and be with Christ,

Departed (Depart)
Jos 2:21 So she sent them away and they **d**.
1Sa 4:21 "The glory has **d** from Israel"—
4:22 "The glory has **d** from Israel,
16:14 Now the Spirit of the LORD had **d**
Job 23:12 I have not **d** from the commands of
Ps 119:102 I have not **d** from your laws, for you
Isa 14: 9 it rouses the spirits of the **d** to
26:14 those **d** spirits do not rise.
Lam 1: 6 All the splendour has **d** from the
Eze 10:18 the glory of the LORD **d** from over
Jn 4:50 The man took Jesus at his word and **d**.

Departing (Depart)
Hos 1: 2 vilest adultery in **d** from the LORD."

Departs (Depart)
Ps 146: 4 their spirit **d**, they return to the
Ecc 5:15 womb, and as he comes, so he **d**.
5:16 As a man comes, so he **d**,
6: 4 without meaning, it **d** in darkness,

Departure (Depart)
Dt 16: 3 the time of your **d** from Egypt.
16: 6 anniversary of your **d** from Egypt.
SS 5: 6 My heart sank at his **d**. I looked for
Lk 9:31 They spoke about his **d**, which he was
2Ti 4: 6 and the time has come for my **d**.
2Pe 1:15 after my **d** you will always be able.

Depend (Depended, Dependent, Depending, Depends)
2Ki 18:21 king of Egypt to all who **d** on him.
19:10 Do not let the god you **d** on deceive
Ps 62: 7 My salvation and my honour **d** on God;
Isa 36: 6 king of Egypt to all who **d** on him.
37:10 Do not let the god you **d** on deceive
Ro 9:16 does not, therefore, **d** on man's

Depended (Depend)
Isa 30:12 on oppression and **d** on deceit,
Hos 10:13 Because you have **d** on your own
Ac 12:20 because they **d** on the king's country

Dependent (Depend)
Lev 21: 3 or an unmarried sister who is **d** on
1Th 4:12 that you will not be **d** on anybody.

Depending (Depend)
2Ki 18:20 On whom are you **d**, that you rebel
18:21 Look now, you are **d** on Egypt, that
18:22 if you say to me, "We are **d** on the
18:24 **d** on Egypt for chariots and horsemen?
Isa 36: 5 On whom are you **d**, that you rebel
36: 6 Look now, you are **d** on Egypt, that
36: 7 if you say to me, "We are **d** on the
36: 9 **d** on Egypt for chariots and horsemen?

Depends (Depend)
Jer 17: 5 who **d** on flesh for his strength and
Ro 12:18 is possible, as far as it **d** on you,
Gal 3:18 For if the inheritance **d** on the law,
3:18 then it no longer **d** on a promise;
Col 2: 8 which **d** on human tradition and the

Deployed
1Sa 4: 2 The Philistines **d** their forces to
2Sa 10: 9 and **d** them against the Arameans.
10:10 and **d** them against the Ammonites.
1Ch 19:10 and **d** them against the Arameans.
19:11 they were **d** against the Ammonites.

Deported
2Ki 15:29 and **d** the people to Assyria.
16: 9 He **d** its inhabitants to Kir and put
17: 6 and **d** the Israelites to Assyria.
17:26 "The people you **d** and resettled in
18:11 The king of Assyria **d** Israel to
24:16 The king of Babylon also **d** to
1Ch 6:15 Jehozadak was **d** when the LORD sent
8: 6 in Geba and were **d** to Manahath:
8: 7 Naaman, Ahijah and Gera, who **d** them
Ezr 4:10 honourable Ashurbanipal **d** and
5:12 temple and **d** the people to Babylon.

Depose (Deposed, Deposes)
Isa 22:19 I will **d** you from your office, and

Deposed (Depose)
1Ki 15:13 He even **d** his grandmother Maacah
2Ch 15:16 King Asa also **d** his grandmother
Da 5:20 he was **d** from his royal throne and

Deposes (Depose)
Da 2:21 he sets up kings and **d** them.

Deposit (Deposited)
Ezr 5:15 **d** them in the temple in Jerusalem.
Eze 24: 6 whose **d** will not go away!
24:11 may be melted and its **d** burned away.
24:12 its heavy **d** has not been removed,
Mt 25:27 you should have put my money on **d**
Lk 19:23 Why then didn't you put my money on **d**
2Co 1:22 a **d**, guaranteeing what is to come.
5: 5 a **d**, guaranteeing what is to come.
Eph 1:14 who is a **d** guaranteeing our
2Ti 1:14 Guard the good **d** that was entrusted

Deposited (Deposit)
1Sa 10:25 a scroll and **d** it before the LORD.
Ezr 6: 5 are to be **d** in the house of God.

Depraved (Depravity)
Eze 16:47 you soon became more **d** than they.
23:11 she was more **d** than her sister.
Ro 1:28 he gave them over to a **d** mind, to do
Php 2:15 fault in a crooked and **d** generation,
2Ti 3: 8 oppose the truth—men of **d** minds,

Depravity (Depraved)
Ro 1:29 of wickedness, evil, greed and **d**.
2Pe 2:19 they themselves are slaves of **d**

Depressions
Lev 14:37 and if it has greenish or reddish **d**

Deprive (Deprived, Deprives, Depriving)
Ex 21:10 he must not **d** the first one of her
Dt 24:17 Do not **d** the alien or the fatherless
Pr 18: 5 or to **d** the innocent of justice.
31: 5 **d** all the oppressed of their rights.
Isa 10: 2 to **d** the poor of their rights and
29:21 testimony **d** the innocent of justice.
Lam 3:36 to **d** a man of justice—would not
Eze 36:12 again **d** them of their children.
36:13 and **d** your nation of its children,"
Am 5:12 **d** the poor of justice in the courts.
Mal 3: 5 and **d** aliens of justice, but do not
1Co 7: 5 Do not **d** each other except by mutual
9:15 than have anyone **d** me of this boast.

Deprived (Deprive)
Ge 42:36 them, "You have **d** me of my children.
Jer 5:25 your sins have **d** you of good.
Lam 3:17 I have been **d** of peace; I have
Mic 7:16 be ashamed, **d** of all their power.
Ac 8:33 humiliation he was **d** of justice.

Deprives (Deprive)
Job 12:24 He **d** the leaders of the earth of

Depriving (Deprive)
Ecc 4: 8 "and why am I **d** myself of enjoyment?"

Depth (Deep)
Ge 7:20 to a **d** of more than twenty feet.
Lam 3:60 You have seen the **d** of their
Ro 8:39 neither height nor **d**, nor anything
11:33 Oh, the **d** of the riches of the
2Co 2: 4 you know the **d** of my love for you.
Php 1: 9 more in knowledge and **d** of insight,

Depths (Deep)
Ex 15: 5 they sank to the **d** like a stone.
Ne 9:11 hurled their pursuers into the **d**,
Job 11: 8 are deeper than the **d** of the grave
36:30 about him, bathing the **d** of the sea.
41:31 He makes the **d** churn like a boiling
Ps 30: 1 for you lifted me out of the **d** and
63: 9 will go down to the **d** of the earth.
68:22 bring them from the **d** of the sea,
69: 2 I sink in the miry **d**, where there is
69:15 the **d** swallow me up or the pit
71:20 from the **d** of the earth you will
Ps 77:16 the very **d** were convulsed.
86:13 me from the **d** of the grave.
88: 6 in the lowest pit, in the darkest **d**.
95: 4 In his hand are the **d** of the earth,
106: 9 through the **d** as through a desert.
107:26 the heavens and went down to the **d**;
130: 1 Out of the **d** I cry to you, O LORD;
135: 6 earth, in the seas and all their **d**.
139: 8 make my bed in the **d**, you are there.
139:15 together in the **d** of the earth,
148: 7 great sea creatures and all ocean **d**,
Pr 9:18 guests are in the **d** of the grave.
Isa 7:11 whether in the deepest **d** or in the
14:15 to the grave, to the **d** of the pit.
29:15 Woe to those who go to great **d** to
51:10 who made a road in the **d** of the sea
63:13 who led them through the **d**? Like a
Lam 3:55 O LORD, from the **d** of the pit.
Eze 26:19 and when I bring the ocean **d** over
27:34 by the sea in the **d** of the waters;
32:23 Their graves are in the **d** of the pit
Am 9: 2 Though they dig down to the **d** of the
Jnh 2: 2 From the **d** of the grave I called for
Mic 7:19 iniquities into the **d** of the sea.
Zec 10:11 all the **d** of the Nile will dry up.
Mt 11:23 No, you will go down to the **d**.
18: 6 to be drowned in the **d** of the sea.
Lk 10:15 No, you will go down to the **d**.

Deputy
Jdg 9:28 and isn't Zebul his **d**? Serve the men
1Ki 22:47 then no king in Edom; a **d** ruled.

Derbe
Town in Asia Minor, about 16 miles east of Lystra. Paul and Barnabas fled here from trouble in Iconium (Ac 14:6), and gained converts (Ac 14:20–21). Paul visited on second missionary journey (Ac 16:1). Home of Gaius (Ac 20:4).

Ac 14: 6 Lycaonian cities of Lystra and **D**
14:20 next day he and Barnabas left for **D**.
16: 1 He came to **D** and then to Lystra,
20: 4 Gaius from **D**, Timothy also, and

Deride (Derides, Derision)
Hab 1:10 They **d** kings and scoff at rulers.

Derides (Deride)
Pr 11:12 who lacks judgment **d** his neighbour,

Derision (Deride)
Job 27:23 claps its hands in **d** and hisses him
Ps 44:13 the scorn and **d** of those around us.
79: 4 of scorn and **d** to those around us.
Eze 23:32 it will bring scorn and **d**, for it
Mic 6:16 over to ruin and your people to **d**;

Derives
Eph 3:15 in heaven and on earth **d** its name.

Descend (Descendant, Descendants, Descended, Descending, Descends, Descent)
Dt 32: 2 like rain and my words **d** like dew,
Job 17:16 Will we **d** together into the dust?"
Ps 49:17 his splendour will not **d** with him.
SS 4: 8 **D** from the crest of Amana, from the
Isa 5:14 into it will **d** their nobles and
14:19 who **d** to the stones of the pit.
Ro 10: 7 "or 'Who will **d** into the deep?'"

Descendant (Descend)
Lev 6:18 Any male **d** of Aaron may eat it.
21:21 No **d** of Aaron the priest who has any
22: 4 "If a **d** of Aaron has an infectious
Nu 16:40 no-one except a **d** of Aaron should
26:59 a **d** of Levi, who was born to the
32:41 Jair, a **d** of Manasseh, captured
Dt 3:14 Jair, a **d** of Manasseh, took the
2Sa 14: 7 neither name nor **d** on the face of
1Ch 7:14 his **d** through his Aramean concubine.
7:15 Another **d** was named Zelophehad, who
1Ch 9: 4 of Bani, a **d** of Perez son of Judah.
24: 3 the help of Zadok a **d** of Eleazar
24: 3 Eleazar and Ahimelech a **d** of Ithamar,
26:24 Shubael, a **d** of Gershom son of Moses,
27: 3 He was a **d** of Perez and chief of all
2Ch 20:14 a Levite and **d** of Asaph, as he stood
Ezr 5: 1 Zechariah the prophet, a **d** of Iddo,
6:14 prophet and Zechariah, a **d** of Iddo.
Ne 11: 4 the son of Mahalalel, a **d** of Perez;
11: 5 the son of Zechariah, a **d** of Shelah.
Jer 33:21 have a **d** to reign on his throne.
Lk 1: 5 Elizabeth was also a **d** of Aaron.
1:27 to a man named Joseph, a **d** of David.
Ro 1: 3 his human nature was a **d** of David,
11: 1 a **d** of Abraham, from the tribe of

Descendants (Descend)
Ge 9: 9 with you and with your **d** after
15:13 "Know for certain that your **d** will
15:16 In the fourth generation your **d** will
15:18 "To your **d** I give this land, from
16:10 "I will so increase your **d** that they
17: 7 you and your **d** after you for the
17: 7 God and the God of your **d** after you.
17: 8 to you and your **d** after you;
17: 9 you and your **d** after you for the
17:10 with you and your **d** after you,
17:19 covenant for his **d** after him.
21:23 with me or my children or my **d**.
22:17 make your **d** as numerous as the stars
22:17 Your **d** will take possession of the
25: 3 the **d** of Dedan were the Asshurites,
25: 4 All these were **d** of Keturah.
25:18 His **d** settled in the area from
26: 3 For to you and your **d** I will give
26: 4 I will make your **d** as numerous as
26:24 will increase the number of your **d**
28: 4 May he give you and your **d** the
28:13 I will give you and your **d** the land
28:14 Your **d** will be like the dust of the
32:12 your **d** like the sand of the sea,
35:12 give this land to your **d** after you."
36:15 These were the chiefs among Esau's **d**:
46: 8 (Jacob and his **d**) who went to Egypt:
46:26 his direct **d**, not counting his sons'
48: 4 possession to your **d** after you.'
48:19 **d** will become a group of nations."
Ex 1: 5 The **d** of Jacob numbered seventy in
12:24 ordinance for you and your **d**.
28:43 ordinance for Aaron and his **d**.
29:29 garments will belong to his **d**
30:21 his **d** for the generations to come."
32:13 'I will make your **d** as numerous as
32:13 I will give your **d** all this land I
33: 1 saying, 'I will give it to your **d**.'
Lev 21:17 none of your **d** who has a defect may
22: 3 if any of your **d** is ceremonially
23:43 that your **d** will know that I made
25:30 permanently to the buyer and his **d**.
Nu 1:20 From the **d** of Reuben the firstborn
1:22 From the **d** of Simeon: All the men
1:24 From the **d** of Gad: All the men
1:26 From the **d** of Judah: All the men
1:28 From the **d** of Issachar: All the men
1:30 From the **d** of Zebulun: All the men
1:32 From the **d** of Ephraim: All the men
1:34 From the **d** of Manasseh: All the men
1:36 From the **d** of Benjamin: All the men
1:38 From the **d** of Dan: All the men
1:40 From the **d** of Asher: All the men
1:42 From the **d** of Naphtali: All the men
9:10 'When any of you or your **d** are
13:22 and Talmai, the **d** of Anak, lived.
13:28 We even saw **d** of Anak there.
13:33 (the **d** of Anak come from the
14:24 went to, and his **d** will inherit it.
25:13 He and his **d** will have a covenant of
26: 5 The **d** of Reuben, the firstborn son
26:12 The **d** of Simeon by their clans were:
26:15 The **d** of Gad by their clans were:
26:20 The **d** of Judah by their clans were:
26:21 The **d** of Perez were: through Hezron,
26:23 The **d** of Issachar by their clans
26:26 The **d** of Zebulun by their clans were:
26:28 The **d** of Joseph by their clans

Nu 26:29 The **d** of Manasseh: through Makir,
26:30 These were the **d** of Gilead: through
26:35 These were the **d** of Ephraim by their
26:36 These were the **d** of Shuthelah:
26:37 were the **d** of Joseph by their clans.
26:38 The **d** of Benjamin by their clans
26:40 The **d** of Bela through Ard and Naaman
26:42 These were the **d** of Dan by their
26:44 The **d** of Asher by their clans were:
26:45 through the **d** of Beriah: through
26:48 The **d** of Naphtali by their clans
32:39 The **d** of Makir son of Manasseh went
32:40 the Makirites, the **d** of Manasseh,
36: 1 from the clans of the **d** of Joseph,
36: 5 the tribe of the **d** of Joseph is
36:12 of the **d** of Manasseh son of Joseph,
Dt 1: 8 Jacob—and to their **d** after them."
1:36 and I will give him and his **d** the
2: 4 the **d** of Esau, who live in Seir.
2: 8 on past our brothers the **d** of Esau,
2: 9 Ar to the **d** of Lot as a possession."
2:12 but the **d** of Esau drove them out.
2:19 it as a possession to the **d** of Lot."
2:22 had done the same for the **d** of Esau,
2:29 the **d** of Esau, who live in Seir, and
4:37 and chose their **d** after them,
10:15 and he chose you, their **d**, above all
11: 9 to give to them and their **d**,
17:20 Then he and his **d** will reign a long
18: 5 their **d** out of all your tribes to
23: 2 **d** may enter the assembly of the LORD,
23: 3 **d** may enter the assembly of the LORD,
28:46 a wonder to you and your **d** for ever.
28:59 fearful plagues on you and your **d**,
30: 6 hearts and the hearts of your **d**,
31:21 it will not be forgotten by their **d**.
34: 4 I said,'I will give it to your **d**.
Jos 4:21 "In the future when your **d** ask their
13:29 of the **d** of Manasseh, clan by clan:
13:31 This was for the **d** of Makir son of
15:14 Ahiman and Talmai—**d** of Anak.
16: 4 Manasseh and Ephraim, the **d** of
17: 2 are the other male **d** of Manasseh
17: 6 to the rest of the **d** of Manasseh.
21: 4 The Levites who were **d** of Aaron the
21: 5 The rest of Kohath's **d** were allotted
21: 6 The **d** of Gershon were allotted
21: 7 The **d** of Merari, clan by clan,
21:10 were assigned to the **d** of Aaron
21:13 to the **d** of Aaron the priest they
21:19 for the priests, the **d** of Aaron,
22:24 some day your **d** might say to ours,
22:25 So your **d** might cause ours to stop
22:27 Then in the future your **d** will not
22:28 or to our **d**, we will answer: Look at
24: 3 Canaan and gave him many **d**.
24:32 the inheritance of Joseph's **d**.
Jdg 1:16 The **d** of Moses' father-in-law, the
3: 2 teach warfare to the **d** of the
4:11 other Kenites, the **d** of Hobab, Moses'
1Sa 2:33 **d** will die in the prime of life.
20:42 between your **d** and my **d** for ever.
24:21 will not cut off my **d** or wipe out
2Sa 19:28 All my grandfather's **d** deserved
21: 6 let seven of his male **d** be given to
21:16 Ishbi-Benob, one of the **d** of Rapha,
21:18 killed Saph, one of the **d** of Rapha.
21:22 These four were **d** of Rapha in Gath,
22:51 to David and his **d** for ever."
1Ki 2: 4 'If your **d** watch how they live, and
2:33 the head of Joab and his **d** for ever.
2:33 But on David and his **d**, his house
9:21 that is, their **d** remaining in the
11:39 I will humble David's **d** because of
21:21 I will consume your **d** and cut off
2Ki 5:27 cling to you and to your **d** for ever.
8:19 a lamp for David and his **d** for ever.
10:30 your **d** will sit on the throne of
15:12 "Your **d** will sit on the throne of
17:34 **d** of Jacob, whom he named Israel.
20:18 some of your **d**, your own flesh and
1Ch 1:29 These were their **d**: Nebaioth the
1:33 All these were **d** of Keturah.
2:23 **d** of Makir the father of Gilead.
2:33 These were the **d** of Jerahmeel.
2:50 These were the **d** of Caleb. The sons

1Ch 2:52 The **d** of Shobal the father of
2:54 The **d** of Salma: Bethlehem, the
3:17 The **d** of Jehoiachin the captive:
3:21 The **d** of Hananiah: Pelatiah and
3:22 The **d** of Shecaniah: Shemaiah and his
4: 1 The **d** of Judah: Perez, Hezron, Carmi,
4: 4 These were the **d** of Hur, the
4: 6 These were the **d** of Naarah.
4:20 The **d** of Ishi: Zoheth and Ben-Zoheth.
4:24 The **d** of Simeon: Nemuel, Jamin,
4:26 The **d** of Mishma: Hammuel his son,
5: 4 The **d** of Joel: Shemaiah his son, Gog
6:22 The **d** of Kohath: Amminadab his son,
6:25 The **d** of Elkanah: Amasai, Ahimoth,
6:29 The **d** of Merari: Mahli, Libni his
6:49 Aaron and his **d** were the ones who
6:50 These were the **d** of Aaron: Eleazar
6:54 they were assigned to the **d** of Aaron
6:57 the **d** of Aaron were given Hebron (a
6:61 The rest of Kohath's **d** were allotted
6:62 The **d** of Gershon, clan by clan, were
6:63 The **d** of Merari, clan by clan, were
7: 2 **d** of Tola listed as fighting men
7:12 and Huppites were the **d** of Ir,
7:12 Ir, and the Hushites the **d** of Aher.
7:13 Jezer and Shillem—the **d** of Bilhah.
7:14 The **d** of Manasseh: Asriel was his
7:20 The **d** of Ephraim: Shuthelah, Bered
7:29 The **d** of Joseph son of Israel lived
7:40 All these were **d** of Asher—heads of
8: 6 These were the **d** of Ehud, who were
8:40 All these were the **d** of Benjamin.
9:23 They and their **d** were in charge of
15: 4 He called together the **d** of Aaron
15: 5 From the **d** of Kohath, Uriel the
15: 6 from the **d** of Merari, Asaiah the
15: 7 from the **d** of Gershon, Joel the
15: 8 from the **d** of Elizaphan, Shemaiah
15: 9 from the **d** of Hebron, Eliel the
15:10 from the **d** of Uzziel, Amminadab the
16:13 O **d** of Israel his servant, O sons of
20: 4 one of the **d** of the Rephaites, and
20: 8 These were **d** of Rapha in Gath, and
23:13 Aaron was set apart, he and his **d**
23:16 The **d** of Gershom: Shubael was the
23:17 The **d** of Eliezer: Rehabiah was the
23:24 These were the **d** of Levi by their
23:28 help Aaron's **d** in the service of
23:32 under their brothers the **d** of Aaron,
24: 4 Eleazar's **d** than among Ithamar's,
24: 4 heads of families from Eleazar's **d**
24: 4 heads of families from Ithamar's **d**.
24: 5 the **d** of both Eleazar and Ithamar.
24:20 for the rest of the **d** of Levi: from
24:31 as their brothers the **d** of Aaron
26: 8 All these were **d** of Obed-Edom;
26: 8 the work—**d** of Obed-Edom, 62 in all.
26:19 who were **d** of Korah and Merari.
26:21 The **d** of Ladan, who were Gershonites
28: 8 an inheritance to your **d** for ever.
2Ch 8: 8 that is, their **d** remaining in the
13: 5 **d** for ever by a covenant of salt?
13: 8 which is in the hands of David's **d**.
20: 7 to the **d** of Abraham your friend?
21: 7 a lamp for him and his **d** for ever.
23: 3 promised concerning the **d** of David.
26:18 for the priests, the **d** of Aaron,
29:13 from the **d** of Elizaphan, Shimri and
29:13 **d** of Asaph, Zechariah and Mattaniah;
29:14 from the **d** of Heman, Jehiel and
29:14 **d** of Jeduthun, Shemaiah and Uzziel.
29:21 the **d** of Aaron, to offer these on
31:19 for the priests, the **d** of Aaron, who
32:33 where the tombs of David's **d** are.
35:14 because the priests, the **d** of Aaron,
35:15 The musicians, the **d** of Asaph, were
Ezr 2: 3 the **d** of Parosh 2,172
2:36 The priests: the **d** of Jedaiah
2:40 The Levites: the **d** of Jeshua and
2:41 The singers: the **d** of Asaph 128
2:42 the **d** of Shallum, Ater, Talmon,
2:43 The temple servants: the **d** of Ziha,
2:55 The **d** of the servants of Solomon:
2:55 **d** of Sotai, Hassophereth, Peruda,
2:58 The temple servants and the **d** of the
2:60 The **d** of Delaiah, Tobiah and Nekoda

Ezr 2:61 The **d** of Hobaiah, Hakkoz and
3: 9 Kadmiel and his sons (**d** of Hodaviah
8: 2 of the **d** of Phinehas, Gershom;
8: 2 Gershom; of the **d** of Ithamar, Daniel;
8: 2 of the **d** of David, Hattush
8: 3 of the **d** of Shecaniah;
8: 3 of the **d** of Parosh, Zechariah, and
8: 4 of the **d** of Pahath-Moab, Eliehoenai
8: 5 of the **d** of Zattu, Shecaniah son of
8: 6 of the **d** of Adin, Ebed son of
8: 7 of the **d** of Elam, Jeshaiah son of
8: 8 of the **d** of Shephatiah, Zebadiah son
8: 9 of the **d** of Joab, Obadiah son of
8:10 of the **d** of Bani, Shelomith son of
8:11 of the **d** of Bebai, Zechariah son of
8:12 of the **d** of Azgad, Johanan son of
8:13 of the **d** of Adonikam, the last ones,
8:14 of the **d** of Bigvai, Uthai and Zaccur,
8:18 a capable man, from the **d** of Mahli
8:19 with Jeshaiah from the **d** of Merari,
10: 2 Shecaniah son of Jehiel, one of the **d**
10:18 Among the **d** of the priests, the
10:18 From the **d** of Jeshua son of Jozadak,
10:20 From the **d** of Immer: Hanani and
10:21 From the **d** of Harim: Maaseiah,
10:22 From the **d** of Pashhur: Elioenai,
10:25 From the **d** of Parosh: Ramiah,
10:26 From the **d** of Elam: Mattaniah,
10:27 From the **d** of Zattu: Elioenai,
10:28 From the **d** of Bebai: Jehohanan,
10:29 From the **d** of Bani: Meshullam,
10:30 From the **d** of Pahath-Moab: Adna,
10:31 From the **d** of Harim: Eliezer,
10:33 From the **d** of Hashum: Mattenai,
10:34 From the **d** of Bani: Maadai, Amram,
10:38 From the **d** of Binnui: Shimei,
10:43 From the **d** of Nebo: Jeiel,
Ne 7: 8 the **d** of Parosh 2,172
7:39 The priests: the **d** of Jedaiah
7:43 The Levites: the **d** of Jeshua
7:44 The singers: the **d** of Asaph 148
7:45 The gatekeepers: the **d** of Shallum,
7:46 The temple servants: the **d** of Ziha,
7:57 The **d** of the servants of Solomon:
7:57 the **d** of Sotai, Sophereth, Perida,
7:60 the **d** of the servants of Solomon
7:62 the **d** of Delaiah, Tobiah and Nekoda
7:63 the **d** of Habaiah, Hakkoz and
9: 8 to his **d** the land of the Canaanites,
11: 3 Levites, temple servants and **d** of
11: 4 **d** of Judah: Athaiah son of Uzziah,
11: 6 The **d** of Perez who lived in
11: 7 From the **d** of Benjamin: Sallu son of
11:22 Uzzi was one of Asaph's **d**, who were
11:24 one of the **d** of Zerah son of Judah,
11:31 The **d** of the Benjamites from Geba
12:23 The family heads among the **d** of Levi
12:47 the portion for the **d** of Aaron.
Est 9:27 their **d** and all who join them should
9:28 of them die out among their **d**.
9:31 their **d** in regard to their times of
Job 5:25 your **d** like the grass of the earth.
18:19 He has no offspring or **d** among his
Ps 18:50 to David and his **d** for ever.
21:10 You will destroy their **d** from the
22:23 All you **d** of Jacob, honour him!
22:23 Revere him, all you **d** of Israel!
25:13 and his **d** will inherit the land.
77:15 people, the **d** of Jacob and Joseph.
83: 8 to lend strength to the **d** of Lot.
102:28 **d** will be established before you."
105: 6 O **d** of Abraham his servant, O sons
106:27 make their **d** fall among the nations
109:13 May his **d** be cut off, their names
132:11 own **d** I will place on your throne—
Isa 14:22 and survivors, her offspring and **d**,
39: 7 some of your **d**, your own flesh and
41: 8 chosen, you **d** of Abraham my friend,
44: 3 and my blessing on your **d**.
45:19 said to Jacob's **d**,'Seek me in vain.
45:25 in the LORD all the **d** of Israel will
48:19 Your **d** would have been like the sand,
53: 8 And who can speak of his **d**? For he
54: 3 your **d** will dispossess nations and
59:21 from the mouths of their **d** from
61: 9 Their **d** will be known among the

Isa 65: 9 I will bring forth **d** from Jacob, and
65:23 LORD, they and their **d** with them.
66:22 "so will your name and **d** endure.
Jer 23: 8 who brought the **d** of Israel up out
29:32 Shemaiah the Nehelamite and his **d**.
30:10 your **d** from the land of their exile.
31:36 "will the **d** of Israel ever cease to
31:37 reject all the **d** of Israel because
33:22 I will make the **d** of David my
33:26 I will reject the **d** of Jacob and
33:26 the **d** of Abraham, Isaac and Jacob.
35: 6 you nor your **d** must ever drink wine.
35:16 The **d** of Jonadab son of Recab have
46:27 your **d** from the land of their exile.
Eze 20: 5 I swore with uplifted hand to the **d**
44:15 who are Levites and **d** of Zadok and
46:16 it will also belong to his **d**; it is
Da 11: 4 It will not go to his **d**, nor will it
Na 1:14 "You will have no **d** to bear your
Mal 2: 3 "Because of you I will rebuke your **d**;
3: 6 O **d** of Jacob, are not destroyed.
Mt 23:31 **d** of those who murdered the prophets.
Lk 1:55 to Abraham and his **d** for ever, even
Jn 8:33 "We are Abraham's **d** and have never
8:37 I know you are Abraham's **d**. Yet you
Ac 2:30 place one of his **d** on his throne.
7: 5 **d** after him would possess the land,
7: 6 'Your **d** will be strangers in a
8:33 Who can speak of his **d**? For his life
13:23 "From this man's **d** God has brought
Ro 9: 7 Nor because they are his **d** are they
9:29 the Lord Almighty had left us **d**,
2Co 11:22 Are they Abraham's **d**? So am I.
Heb 2:16 angels he helps, but Abraham's **d**.
6:14 bless you and give you many **d**."
7: 5 Now the law requires the **d** of Levi
11:12 came **d** as numerous as the stars in

Descended (Descend)

Ge 36:16 These were the chiefs **d** from Eliphaz
36:17 These were the chiefs **d** from Reuel
36:18 These were the chiefs **d** from Esau's
36:40 These were the chiefs **d** from Esau,
Ex 19:18 because the LORD **d** on it in fire.
19:20 The LORD **d** to the top of Mount Sinai
Jos 16: 3 **d** westward to the territory of the
2Sa 21:20 He also was **d** from Rapha.
1Ki 18:31 one for each of the tribes **d** from
1Ch 2:53 From these **d** the Zorathites and
20: 6 He also was **d** from Rapha.
2Ch 34:12 Levites **d** from Merari, and Zechariah
34:12 and Meshullam, **d** from Kohath.
Ezr 2:59 their families were **d** from Israel:
Ne 7:61 their families were **d** from Israel:
10:38 A priest **d** from Aaron is to
Isa 57: 9 far away; you **d** to the grave itself!
Lk 3:22 the Holy Spirit **d** on him in bodily
Ro 9: 6 who are **d** from Israel are Israel.
Eph 4: 9 **d** to the lower, earthly regions?
4:10 He who **d** is the very one who
2Ti 2: 8 raised from the dead, **d** from David.
Heb 7: 5 their brothers are **d** from Abraham.
7:14 For it is clear that our Lord **d** from

Descending (Descend)

Ge 28:12 of God were ascending and **d** on it.
1Sa 25:20 David and his men **d** towards her,
SS 4: 1 flock of goats **d** from Mount Gilead.
6: 5 like a flock of goats **d** from Gilead.
Mt 3:16 **d** like a dove and lighting on him.
Mk 1:10 and the Spirit **d** on him like a dove.
Jn 1:51 ascending and **d** on the Son of Man."

Descends (Descend)

Isa 34: 5 see, it **d** in judgment on Edom, the

Descent (Descend)

Ge 10:32 lines of **d**, within their nations.
Ne 9: 2 Those of Israelite **d** had separated
13: 3 Israel all who were of foreign **d**.
Eze 44:22 of Israelite **d** or widows of priests.
Da 9: 1 Darius son of Xerxes (a Mede by **d**),
Jn 1:13 children born not of natural **d**, nor
Heb 7: 6 however, did not trace his **d** from

Describe (Described, Describes, Description, Descriptions)

Eze 43:10 "Son of man, **d** the temple to the
Mk 4:30 what parable shall we use to **d** it?

Described (Describe)

1Ki 4:33 He **d** plant life, from the cedar of
Ac 12:17 **d** how the Lord had brought him out
15:14 Simon has **d** to us how God at first
Rev 22:18 to him the plagues **d** in this book.
22:19 holy city, which are **d** in this book.

Describes (Describe)

Ro 10: 5 Moses **d** in this way the

Description (Describe)

Jos 18: 4 of the land and to write a **d** of it,
18: 8 of the land and write a **d** of it.
18: 9 They wrote its **d** on a scroll, town

Descriptions (Describe)

Jos 18: 6 After you have written **d** of the

Desecrate (Desecrated, Desecrates, Desecrating)

Lev 21:12 the sanctuary of his God or **d** it,
21:23 the altar, and so **d** my sanctuary.
22:15 The priests must not **d** the sacred
Dt 21:23 You must not **d** the land the LORD
Eze 7:22 and they will **d** my treasured place;
7:22 robbers will enter it and **d** it.
24:21 I am about to **d** my sanctuary—the
Da 11:31 rise up to **d** the temple fortress
Mt 12: 5 **d** the day and yet are innocent?
Ac 24: 6 even tried to **d** the temple; so we

Desecrated (Desecrate)

Lev 19: 8 he has **d** what is holy to the LORD;
2Ki 23: 8 of Judah and **d** the high places,
23:10 He **d** Topheth, which was in the
23:13 The king also **d** the high places that
Ps 106:38 and the land was **d** by their blood.
Isa 47: 6 my people and **d** my inheritance;
Eze 7:24 and their sanctuaries will be **d**.
20:13 they utterly **d** my Sabbaths.
20:16 follow my decrees and **d** my Sabbaths.
20:21 by them—and they **d** my Sabbaths.
20:24 my decrees and **d** my Sabbaths,
22: 8 my holy things and **d** my Sabbaths.
23:38 my sanctuary and **d** my Sabbaths.
23:39 they entered my sanctuary and **d** it.
25: 3 over my sanctuary when it was **d**
28:18 trade you have **d** your sanctuaries.
Mal 2:11 has **d** the sanctuary the LORD loves,

Desecrates (Desecrate)

Ex 31:14 Anyone who **d** it must be put to death;

Desecrating (Desecrate)

Ne 13:17 you are doing—**d** the Sabbath day?
13:18 against Israel by **d** the Sabbath."
Isa 56: 2 who keeps the Sabbath without **d** it,
56: 6 who keep the Sabbath without **d** it
Eze 44: 7 **d** my temple while you offered me

Desert[1] (Deserts[1])

Ge 14: 6 Seir, as far as El Paran near the **d**.
16: 7 found Hagar near a spring in the **d**;
21:14 and wandered in the **d** of Beersheba.
21:20 lived in the **d** and became an archer.
21:21 he was living in the **D** of Paran,
36:24 discovered the hot springs in the **d**
37:22 into this cistern here in the **d**,
Ex 3: 1 far side of the **d** and came to Horeb,
3:18 take a three-day journey into the **d**
4:27 Aaron, "Go into the **d** to meet Moses.
5: 1 hold a festival to me in the **d**.'"
5: 3 take a three-day journey into the **d**
7:16 that they may worship me in the **d**.
8:27 take a three-day journey into the **d**
8:28 to the LORD your God in the **d**,
13:18 God led the people around by the **d**
13:20 at Etham on the edge of the **d**.
14: 3 in confusion, hemmed in by the **d**.'
14:11 that you brought us to the **d** to die?
14:12 the Egyptians than to die in the **d**!"
15:22 Sea and they went into the **D** of Shur.
15:22 in the **d** without finding water.
16: 1 from Elim and came to the **D** of Sin,
16: 2 In the **d** the whole community
16: 3 you have brought us out into this **d**
16:10 they looked towards the **d**, and there
16:14 the ground appeared on the **d** floor.
16:32 bread I gave you to eat in the **d**
17: 1 community set out from the **D** of Sin,
18: 5 came to him in the **d**, where he was
19: 1 day—they came to the **D** of Sinai.
19: 2 they entered the **D** of Sinai, and
19: 2 in the **d** in front of the mountain.
23:31 and from the **d** to the River.
Lev 7:38 to the LORD, in the **D** of Sinai.
11:18 the white owl, the **d** owl, the osprey,
16:10 it into the **d** as a scapegoat.
16:21 shall send the goat away into the **d**
16:22 the man shall release it in the **d**.
Nu 1: 1 Tent of Meeting in the **D** of Sinai
1:19 he counted them in the **D** of Sinai:
3: 4 fire before him in the **D** of Sinai.
3:14 said to Moses in the **D** of Sinai,
9: 1 spoke to Moses in the **D** of Sinai
9: 5 they did so in the **D** of Sinai at
10:12 set out from the **D** of Sinai
10:12 came to rest in the **D** of Paran.
10:31 know where we should camp in the **d**,
12:16 and encamped in the **D** of Paran.
13: 3 sent them out from the **D** of Paran.
13:21 from the **D** of Zin as far as Rehob,
13:26 at Kadesh in the **D** of Paran.
14: 2 we had died in Egypt! Or in this **d**!
14:16 so he slaughtered them in the **d**.'
14:22 in the **d** but who disobeyed me and
14:25 **d** along the route to the Red Sea."
14:29 In this **d** your bodies will
14:32 you—your bodies will fall in this **d**.
14:33 last of your bodies lies in the **d**.
14:35 They will meet their end in this **d**;
15:32 While the Israelites were in the **d**,
16:13 milk and honey to kill us in the **d**?
20: 1 community arrived at the **D** of Zin,
20: 4 the LORD's community into this **d**,
21: 5 us up out of Egypt to die in the **d**?
21:11 in the **d** that faces Moab towards the
21:13 **d** extending into Amorite territory.
21:18 they went from the **d** to Mattanah,
21:23 out into the **d** against Israel.
24: 1 but turned his face towards the **d**.
26:64 the Israelites in the **D** of Sinai.
26:65 they would surely die in the **d**,
27: 3 "Our father died in the **d**. He was
27:14 at the waters in the **D** of Zin,
27:14 of Meribah Kadesh, in the **D** of Zin.)
32:13 wander in the **d** for forty years,
32:15 leave all this people in the **d**,
33: 6 at Etham, on the edge of the **d**.
33: 8 passed through the sea into the **d**,
33: 8 for three days in the **D** of Etham,
33:11 Red Sea and camped in the **D** of Sin.
33:12 They left the **D** of Sin and camped at
33:15 and camped in the **D** of Sinai.
33:16 They left the **D** of Sinai and camped
33:36 camped at Kadesh, in the **D** of Zin.
34: 3 **D** of Zin along the border of Edom.
Dt 1: 1 the **d** east of the Jordan—that is,
1:19 and dreadful **d** that you have seen,
1:31 in the **d**. There you saw how the LORD
1:40 **d** along the route to the Red Sea."
2: 1 **d** along the route to the Red Sea,
2: 7 your journey through this vast **d**.
2: 8 travelled along the **d** road of Moab.
2:26 From the **d** of Kedemoth I sent
4:43 The cities were these: Bezer in the **d**
8: 2 the way in the **d** these forty years,
8:15 you through the vast and dreadful **d**,
8:16 He gave you manna to eat in the **d**,
9: 7 the LORD your God to anger in the **d**.
9:28 out to put them to death in the **d**.'
11: 5 what he did for you in the **d** until
11:24 will extend from the **d** to Lebanon,
14:17 the **d** owl, the osprey, the cormorant,

Dt 29: 5 years that I led you through the **d**,
32:10 In a **d** land he found him, in a
32:51 of Meribah Kadesh in the **D** of Zin
Jos 1: 4 Your territory will extend from the **d**
5: 4 died in the **d** on the way after
5: 5 but all the people born in the **d**
5: 6 moved about in the **d** forty years.
8:15 them, and they fled towards the **d**.
8:20 who had been fleeing towards the **d**
8:24 in the **d** where they had chased them,
12: 8 the mountain slopes, the **d** and the
14:10 while Israel moved about in the **d**.
15: 1 the **D** of Zin in the extreme south.
15:61 In the **d**: Beth Arabah, Middin,
16: 1 **d** into the hill country of Bethel.
18:12 coming out at the **d** of Beth Aven.
20: 8 Bezer in the **d** on the plateau in
24: 7 you lived in the **d** for a long time.
Jdg 1:16 **D** of Judah in the Negev near Arad.
8: 7 flesh with **d** thorns and briers."
8:16 them with **d** thorns and briers.
11:16 **d** to the Red Sea and on to Kadesh.
11:18 "Next they travelled through the **d**,
11:22 Jabbok and from the **d** to the Jordan.
20:42 Israelites in the direction of the **d**,
20:45 they turned and fled towards the **d**
20:47 into the **d** to the rock of Rimmon,
1Sa 4: 8 with all kinds of plagues in the **d**.
13:18 the Valley of Zeboim facing the **d**.
17:28 you leave those few sheep in the **d**?
23:14 David stayed in the **d** strongholds
23:14 and in the hills of the **D** of Ziph.
23:15 was at Horesh in the **D** of Ziph,
23:24 and his men were in the **D** of Maon,
23:25 rock and stayed in the **D** of Maon.
23:25 the **D** of Maon in pursuit of David.
24: 1 told, "David is in the **D** of En Gedi.
25: 1 David moved down into the **D** of Maon.
25: 4 While David was in the **d**, he heard
25:14 "David sent messengers from the **d** to
25:21 in the **d** so that nothing of his was
26: 2 Saul went down to the **D** of Ziph,
26: 3 Jeshimon, but David stayed in the **d**.
2Sa 15:23 the people moved on towards the **d**.
15:28 I will wait at the fords in the **d**
16: 2 who become exhausted in the **d**."
17:16 the night at the fords in the **d**;
17:29 and tired and thirsty in the **d**."
1Ki 2:34 was buried on his own land in the **d**.
9:18 Baalath, and Tadmor in the **d**, within
19: 4 went a day's journey into the **d**.
19:15 came, and go to the **D** of Damascus.
2Ki 3: 8 "Through the **D** of Edom," he answered.
1Ch 5: 9 the land up to the edge of the **d**.
6:78 received Bezer in the **d**, Jahzah,
12: 8 to David at his stronghold in the **d**.
21:29 which Moses had made in the **d**, and
2Ch 1: 3 LORD's servant had made in the **d**.
8: 4 He also built up Tadmor in the **d** and
20:16 end of the gorge in the **D** of Jeruel.
20:20 they left for the **D** of Tekoa.
20:24 to the place that overlooks the **d**
24: 9 God had required of Israel in the **d**.
26:10 He also built towers in the **d** and
Ne 9:19 you did not abandon them in the **d**.
9:21 years you sustained them in the **d**;
Job 1:19 a mighty wind swept in from the **d**
24: 5 Like wild donkeys in the **d**, the poor
38:26 no man lives, a **d** with no-one in it,
Ps 29: 8 The voice of the LORD shakes the **d**;
29: 8 the LORD shakes the **D** of Kadesh.
55: 7 flee far away and stay in the **d**;
63: T When he was in the **D** of Judah.
65:12 The grasslands of the **d** overflow;
72: 9 The **d** tribes will bow before him and
74:14 as food to the creatures of the **d**.
75: 6 west or from the **d** can exalt a man.
78:15 He split the rocks in the **d** and gave
78:17 in the **d** against the Most High.
78:19 "Can God spread a table in the **d**
78:40 they rebelled against him in the **d**
78:52 led them like sheep through the **d**.
95: 8 you did that day at Massah in the **d**,
102: 6 I am like a **d** owl, like an owl among
105:41 like a river it flowed in the **d**.
106: 9 through the depths as through a **d**.
Ps 106:14 In the **d** they gave in to their
106:26 he would make them fall in the **d**,
107: 4 Some wandered in **d** wastelands,
107:33 He turned rivers into a **d**, flowing
107:35 He turned the **d** into pools of water
136:16 who led his people through the **d**,
Pr 21:19 Better to live in a **d** than with a
SS 3: 6 Who is this coming up from the **d**
8: 5 Who is this coming up from the **d**
Isa 13:21 **d** creatures will lie there, jackals
14:17 the man who made the world a **d**, who
16: 1 from Sela, across the **d**, to the
16: 8 Jazer and spread towards the **d**.
21: 1 oracle concerning the **D** by the Sea
21: 1 from the **d**, from a land of terror.
23:13 made it a place for **d** creatures;
25: 5 like the heat of the **d**. You silence
27:10 forsaken like the **d**; there the
32: 2 like streams of water in the **d** and
32:15 and the **d** becomes a fertile field,
32:16 Justice will dwell in the **d** and
34:11 The **d** owl and screech owl will
34:14 **D** creatures will meet with hyenas,
35: 1 The **d** and the parched land will be
35: 6 the wilderness and streams in the **d**.
40: 3 "In the **d** prepare the way for the
41:18 I will turn the **d** into pools of
41:19 I will put in the **d** the cedar and
42:11 Let the **d** and its towns raise their
43:19 the **d** and streams in the wasteland.
43:20 because I provide water in the **d** and
49:10 **d** heat or the sun beat upon them.
50: 2 I turn rivers into a **d**; their fish
64:10 Your sacred cities have become a **d**;
64:10 Zion is a **d**, Jerusalem a desolation.
Jer 2: 2 and followed me through the **d**,
2:24 a wild donkey accustomed to the **d**,
2:31 "Have I been a **d** to Israel or a land
3: 2 lovers, sat like a nomad in the **d**.
4:11 in the **d** blows towards my people,
4:26 and the fruitful land was a **d**;
5: 6 a wolf from the **d** will ravage them,
9: 2 Oh, that I had in the **d** a lodging
9:10 a lament concerning the **d** pastures.
9:12 like a **d** that no-one can cross?
9:26 who live in the **d** in distant places.
12:12 Over all the barren heights in the **d**
13:24 you like chaff driven by the **d** wind.
17: 6 in the parched places of the **d**,
22: 6 like a **d**, like towns not inhabited.
23:10 the pastures in the **d** are withered.
25:24 foreign people who live in the **d**;
31: 2 the sword will find favour in the **d**;
48: 6 become like a bush in the **d**.
50:12 a wilderness, a dry land, a **d**.
50:39 "So **d** creatures and hyenas will live
51:43 a dry and **d** land, a land where
Lam 4: 3 heartless like ostriches in the **d**.
4:19 and lay in wait for us in the **d**.
5: 9 lives because of the sword in the **d**.
Eze 6:14 desolate waste from the **d** to Diblah
19:13 Now it is planted in the **d**, in a dry
20:10 Egypt and brought them into the **d**.
20:13 Israel rebelled against me in the **d**.
20:13 on them and destroy them in the **d**.
20:15 I swore to them in the **d** that I
20:17 them or put an end to them in the **d**.
20:18 I said to their children in the **d**,
20:21 my anger against them in the **d**.
20:23 I swore to them in the **d** that I
20:35 I will bring you into the **d** of the
20:36 I judged your fathers in the **d** of
23:42 Sabeans were brought from the **d**
29: 5 I will leave you in the **d**, you and
34:25 so that they may live in the **d** and
Hos 2: 3 was born; I will make her like a **d**,
2:14 I will lead here into the **d** and
9:10 it was like finding grapes in the **d**;
13: 5 I cared for you in the **d**, in the
13:15 blowing in from the **d**; his spring
Joel 2: 3 a **d** waste—nothing escapes them.
3:19 Egypt will be desolate, Edom a **d**
Am 2:10 I led you for forty years in the **d**
5:25 for forty years in the **d**, O house
Hab 1: 9 Their hordes advance like a **d** wind
Zep 2:13 utterly desolate and dry as the **d**.
Zep 2:14 The **d** owl and the screech owl will
Mal 1: 3 his inheritance to the **d** jackals."
Mt 3: 1 came, preaching in the **D** of Judea
3: 3 "A voice of one calling in the **d**,
4: 1 led by the Spirit into the **d** to be
11: 7 did you go out into the **d** to see?
24:26 'There he is, out in the **d**,' do not
Mk 1: 3 "a voice of one calling in the **d**,
1: 4 John came, baptising in the **d** region
1:12 the Spirit sent him out into the **d**,
1:13 he was in the **d** for forty days,
Lk 1:80 and he lived in the **d** until he
3: 2 to John son of Zechariah in the **d**.
3: 4 "A voice of one calling in the **d**,
4: 1 and was led by the Spirit in the **d**,
7:24 did you go out into the **d** to see?
Jn 1:23 the voice of one calling in the **d**,
3:14 Moses lifted up the snake in the **d**,
6:31 forefathers ate the manna in the **d**;
6:49 the manna in the **d**, yet they died.
11:54 he withdrew to a region near the **d**,
Ac 7:30 bush in the **d** near Mount Sinai.
7:36 Red Sea and for forty years in the **d**.
7:38 He was in the assembly in the **d**,
7:42 years in the **d**, O house of Israel?
7:44 of the Testimony with them in the **d**.
8:26 "Go south to the road—the **d** road
13:18 for about forty years in the **d**,
21:38 out into the **d** some time ago?"
1Co 10: 5 bodies were scattered over the **d**.
Heb 3: 8 during the time of testing in the **d**,
3:17 sinned, whose bodies fell in the **d**?
Rev 12: 6 The woman fled into the **d** to a place
12:14 the place prepared for her in the **d**,
17: 3 me away in the Spirit into a **d**.

Desert[2] (Deserted, Deserting, Deserts[2])

Ne 9:17 Therefore you did not **d** them,
Jer 17:11 they will **d** him, and in the end he

Deserted (Desert[2])

Lev 26:22 in number that your roads will be **d**.
26:43 For the land will be **d** by them and
Dt 32:18 You **d** the Rock, who fathered you;
Jos 22: 3 you have not **d** your brothers but
2Sa 20: 2 all the men of Israel **d** David to
Ezr 9: 9 our God has not **d** us in our bondage.
Ps 69:25 May their place be **d**; let there be
Isa 6:11 until the houses are left **d** and the
17: 2 The cities of Aroer will be **d** and
32:14 be abandoned, the noisy city **d**;
33: 8 The highways are **d**, no travellers
54: 6 you back as if you were a wife **d**
62: 4 No longer will they call you **D**, or
62:12 Sought After, the City No Longer **D**.
Jer 2:15 his towns are burned and **d**.
4:29 towns are **d**; no-one lives in them.
26: 9 this city will be desolate and **d**?"
33:10 the streets of Jerusalem that are **d**,
38:22 the mud; your friends have **d** you.'
44: 2 Today they lie **d** and in ruins
Lam 1: 1 How **d** lies the city, once so full of
Eze 14: 5 who have all **d** me for their idols.'
36: 4 desolate ruins and the **d** towns
Hos 4:10 because they have **d** the LORD
Am 5: 2 **d** in her own land with no-one to
Zep 3: 6 I have left their streets **d**, with
Zec 9: 5 her king and Ashkelon will be **d**.
Mt 26:56 all the disciples **d** him and fled.
Mk 14:50 everyone **d** him and fled.
Ac 1:20 "'May his place be **d**; let there be
15:38 because he had **d** them in Pamphylia
2Ti 1:15 in the province of Asia has **d** me,
4:10 **d** me and has gone to Thessalonica.
4:16 to my support, but everyone **d** me.

Deserting (Desert[2])

Jer 37:13 "You are **d** to the Babylonians!
37:14 "I am not **d** to the Babylonians."
Gal 1: 6 **d** the one who called you by the

Deserts[1] (Desert[1])

Isa 48:21 when he led them through the **d**;
51: 3 he will make her **d** like Eden,

Jer 2: 6 through a land of **d** and rifts, a
Heb 11:38 They wandered in **d** and mountains,

Deserts[2] (Desert[2])

1Ch 12:19 heads if he **d** to his master Saul.")
Pr 19: 4 but a poor man's friend **d** him.
Jer 14: 5 doe in the field **d** her newborn fawn
Zec 11:17 worthless shepherd, who **d** the flock
Heb 11:38 They wandered in **d** and mountains,

Deserve (Deserved, Deserves, Deserving)

Ge 40:15 to **d** being put in a dungeon."
Lev 26:21 seven times over, as your sins **d**.
Jdg 20:10 it can give them what they **d** for all
1Sa 26:16 you and your men **d** to die, because
1Ki 2:26 You **d** to die, but I will not put you
Ps 28: 4 bring back upon them what they **d**.
94: 2 pay back to the proud what they **d**.
103:10 he does not treat us as our sins **d**
Pr 3:27 withhold good from those who **d** it
Ecc 8:14 men who get what the wicked **d**,
8:14 men who get what the righteous **d**.
Isa 66: 6 LORD repaying his enemies all they **d**.
Jer 14:16 out on them the calamity they **d**.
17:10 according to what his deeds **d**."
21:14 I will punish you as your deeds **d**,
32:19 to his conduct and as his deeds **d**.
49:12 "If those who do not **d** to drink the
Lam 3:64 Pay them back what they **d**, O LORD,
Eze 16:59 says: I will deal with you as you **d**,
Zec 1: 6 us what our ways and practices **d**,
Mt 8: 8 **d** to have you come under my roof.
22: 8 those I invited did not **d** to come.
Lk 7: 6 **d** to have you come under my roof.
23:15 see, he has done nothing to **d** death.
23:41 for we are getting what our deeds **d**.
Ro 1:32 those who do such things **d** death,
1Co 15: 9 not even **d** to be called an apostle,
16:18 Such men **d** recognition.
2Co 11:15 end will be what their actions **d**.
Rev 16: 6 them blood to drink as they **d**."

Deserved (Deserve)

2Sa 19:28 grandfather's descendants **d** nothing
Ezr 9:13 us less than our sins have **d**
Job 33:27 right, but I did not get what I **d**.
Ac 23:29 him that **d** death or imprisonment.
Ro 3: 8 result"? Their condemnation is **d**.

Deserves (Deserve)

Nu 35:31 life of a murderer, who **d** to die.
Dt 25: 2 If the guilty man **d** to be beaten,
25: 2 the number of lashes his crime **d**,
Jdg 9:16 if you have treated him as he **d**—
2Sa 12: 5 the man who did this **d** to die!
Job 34:11 brings upon him what his conduct **d**.
Jer 51: 6 he will pay her what she **d**.
Lk 7: 4 "This man **d** to have you do
10: 7 you, for the worker **d** his wages.
Ac 26:31 that **d** death or imprisonment."
1Ti 1:15 saying that **d** full acceptance:
4: 9 saying that **d** full acceptance
5:18 grain," and "The worker **d** his wages.
Heb 10:29 a man **d** to be punished who has

Deserving (Deserve)

Dt 19: 6 even though he is not **d** of death,
22:26 she has committed no sin **d** death.
Mt 10:13 If the home is **d**, let your peace
Lk 12:48 does things **d** punishment will be
Ac 25:11 guilty of doing anything **d** death,
25:25 he had done nothing **d** of death,
28:18 was not guilty of any crime **d** death.

Design (Designed, Designer, Designers, Designs)

1Ki 7: 8 set farther back, was similar in **d**.
2Ch 2:14 and can execute any **d** given to him.
24:13 to its original **d** and reinforced it.
Eze 43:11 make known to them the **d** of the
43:11 its whole **d** and all its regulations
43:11 faithful to its **d** and follow all
Ac 17:29 image made by man's **d** and skill.

Designate (Designated, Designating)

Ex 21:13 he is to flee to a place I will **d**.
Dt 23:12 **D** a place outside the camp where you
Jos 20: 2 "Tell the Israelites to **d** the cities

Designated (Designate)

Jos 20: 8 they **d** Bezer in the desert on the
20: 9 could flee to these **d** cities
2Sa 24:15 morning until the end of the time **d**,
1Ch 12:31 **d** by name to come and make David
16:41 **d** by name to give thanks to the LORD,
28:14 He **d** the weight of gold for all the
2Ch 28:15 The men **d** by name took the prisoners,
31:19 men were **d** by name to distribute
Ezr 10:16 division, and all of them **d** by name.
Ne 13:31 at **d** times, and for the firstfruits.
Est 9:31 days of Purim at their **d** times,
Eze 43:21 burn it in the **d** part of the temple
Lk 6:13 of them, whom he also **d** apostles:
Heb 5:10 was **d** by God to be high priest in

Designating (Designate)

Mk 3:14 He appointed twelve—**d** them apostles

Designed (Design)

2Ch 26:15 he made machines **d** by skilful men

Designer (Design)

Ex 38:23 the tribe of Dan—a craftsman and **d**,

Designers (Design)

Ex 35:35 **d**, embroiderers in blue, purple and
35:35 of them master craftsmen and **d**.

Designs (Design)

Ex 31: 4 to make artistic **d** for work in gold,
35:32 to make artistic **d** for work in gold,
2Ch 3: 5 it with palm tree and chain **d**.

Desirable (Desire)

Ge 3: 6 and also **d** for gaining wisdom, she
Pr 22: 1 A good name is more **d** than great
Jer 3:19 you like sons and give you a **d** land,

Desire (Desirable, Desired, Desires)

Ge 3:16 Your **d** will be for your husband, and
Dt 5:21 You shall not set your **d** on your
1Sa 9:20 And to whom is all the **d** of Israel
2Sa 19:38 you **d** from me I will do for you."
23: 5 salvation and grant me my every **d**?
1Ch 29:18 keep this **d** in the hearts of your
2Ch 1:11 "Since this is your heart's **d** and
9: 8 and his **d** to uphold them for ever,
Job 13: 3 I **d** to speak to the Almighty and to
21:14 We have no **d** to know your ways.
Ps 10:17 You hear, O LORD, the **d** of the
20: 4 May he give you the **d** of your heart
21: 2 You have granted him the **d** of his
27:12 Do not hand me over to the **d** of my
40: 6 Sacrifice and offering you did not **d**,
40: 8 I **d** to do your will, O my God;
40:14 may all who **d** my ruin be turned
41: 2 surrender him to the **d** of his foes.
51: 6 Surely you **d** truth in the inner
70: 2 may all who **d** my ruin be turned
73:25 earth has nothing I **d** besides you.
Pr 3:15 nothing you **d** can compare with her.
8:11 nothing you **d** can compare with her.
10:24 the righteous **d** will be granted.
11:23 The **d** of the righteous ends only in
12:12 The wicked **d** the plunder of evil men,
17:16 since he has no **d** to get wisdom?
24: 1 wicked men, do not **d** their company;
Ecc 12: 5 along and **d** no longer is stirred.
SS 6:12 my **d** set me among the royal
7:10 I belong to my lover, and his **d** is
Isa 26: 8 and renown are the **d** of our hearts.
53: 2 his appearance that we should **d** him.
55:11 but will accomplish what I **d** and
Eze 24:25 their heart's **d**, and their sons and
Hos 6: 6 For I **d** mercy, not sacrifice, and
Mic 7: 3 the powerful dictate what they **d**
Mal 3: 1 covenant, whom you **d**, will come,"
Mt 9:13 'I **d** mercy, not sacrifice.'
12: 7 'I **d** mercy, not sacrifice,' you
Jn 8:44 want to carry out your father's **d**.
Ro 7: 8 in me every kind of covetous **d**.
7:18 For I have the **d** to do what is good,
9:16 depend on man's **d** or effort, but on
10: 1 Brothers, my heart's **d** and prayer to
1Co 12:31 eagerly **d** the greater gifts. And now
14: 1 love and eagerly **d** spiritual gifts,
2Co 8:10 but also to have the **d** to do so.
8:13 Our **d** is not that others might be
Php 1:23 I **d** to depart and be with Christ,
Heb 10: 5 and offering you did not **d**,
10: 8 you did not **d**, nor were you pleased
13:18 **d** to live honourably in every way.
Jas 1:14 by his own evil **d**, he is dragged
1:15 Then, after **d** has conceived, it
2Pe 2:10 the corrupt **d** of the sinful nature

Desired (Desire)

1Ki 9: 1 and had achieved all he had **d** to do,
9:19 he **d** to build in Jerusalem,
10:13 of Sheba all she **d** and asked for,
2Ch 8: 6 he **d** to build in Jerusalem,
9:12 of Sheba all she **d** and asked for;
Ps 107:30 and he guided them to their **d** haven.
132:13 Zion, he has **d** it for his dwelling:
132:14 sit enthroned, for I have **d** it—
Ecc 2:10 I denied myself nothing my eyes **d**;
Jer 17:16 I have not **d** the day of despair.
Da 11:37 fathers or for the one **d** by women,
Hag 2: 7 and the **d** of all nations will come
Lk 22:15 "I have eagerly **d** to eat this

Desires (Desire)

Ge 4: 7 it **d** to have you, but you must
41:16 will give Pharaoh the answer he **d**."
2Sa 3:21 may rule over all that your heart **d**.
1Ki 11:37 rule over all that your heart **d**;
Job 17:11 and so are the **d** of my heart.
31:16 "If I have denied the **d** of the poor
Ps 34:12 and **d** to see many good days,
37: 4 will give you the **d** of your heart.
103: 5 who satisfies your **d** with good
140: 8 do not grant the wicked their **d**,
145:16 satisfy the **d** of every living thing
145:19 He fulfils the **d** of those who fear
Pr 11: 6 unfaithful are trapped by evil **d**.
13: 4 but the **d** of the diligent are fully
19:22 What a man **d** is unfailing love;
Ecc 6: 2 that he lacks nothing his heart **d**,
SS 2: 7 arouse or awaken love until it so **d**.
3: 5 arouse or awaken love until it so **d**.
8: 4 arouse or awaken love until it so **d**.
Hab 2: 4 "See, he is puffed up; his **d** are not
Mk 4:19 the **d** for other things come in and
Ro 1:24 in the sinful **d** of their hearts to
6:12 body so that you obey its evil **d**.
8: 5 minds set on what that nature **d**;
8: 5 minds set on what the Spirit **d**.
13:14 gratify the **d** of the sinful nature.
Gal 5:16 gratify the **d** of the sinful nature.
5:17 For the sinful nature **d** what is
5:24 nature with its passions and **d**.
Eph 2: 3 and following its **d** and thoughts.
4:22 being corrupted by its deceitful **d**;
Col 3: 5 evil **d** and greed, which is idolatry.
1Ti 3: 1 an overseer, he **d** a noble task.
5:11 For when their sensual **d** overcome
6: 9 into many foolish and harmful **d** that
2Ti 2:22 Flee the evil **d** of youth, and pursue
3: 6 are swayed by all kinds of evil **d**,
4: 3 Instead, to suit their own **d**, they
Jas 1:20 about the righteous life that God **d**.
4: 1 from your **d** that battle within you?
1Pe 1:14 do not conform to the evil **d** you had
2:11 abstain from sinful **d**, which war
4: 2 for evil human **d**, but rather for
2Pe 1: 4 in the world caused by evil **d**.
2:18 by appealing to the lustful **d** of
3: 3 and following their own evil **d**.

1Jn 2:17 The world and its **d** pass away, but
Jude :16 they follow their own evil **d**;
:18 will follow their own ungodly **d**."

Desolate (Desolation, Desolations)

Ge 47:19 and that the land may not become **d**."
Ex 23:29 because the land would become **d** and
Lev 26:34 years all the time that it lies **d**
26:35 All the time that it lies **d**, the
26:43 while it lies **d** without them.
Jos 8:28 of ruins, a **d** place to this day.
2Sa 13:20 brother Absalom's house, a **d** woman.
Job 30: 3 land in **d** wastelands at night.
38:27 to satisfy a **d** wasteland and make it
Isa 1: 7 Your country is **d**, your cities
5: 9 the great houses will become **d**,
13: 9 to make the land **d** and destroy the
24:10 The ruined city lies **d**; the entrance
27:10 The fortified city stands **d**, an
34:10 to generation it will lie **d**;
49: 8 and to reassign its **d** inheritances,
49:19 "Though you were ruined and made **d**
54: 1 are the children of the **d** woman
54: 3 and settle in their **d** cities.
62: 4 you Deserted, or name your land **D**.
Jer 6: 8 **d** so that no-one can live in it."
7:34 for the land will become **d**.
9:10 They are **d** and untravelled, and the
10:22 It will make the towns of Judah **d**,
12:10 pleasant field into a **d** wasteland.
12:11 parched and **d** before me; the whole
25:11 country will become a **d** wasteland,
25:12 LORD, "and will make it **d** for ever.
25:38 and their land will become **d** because
26: 9 this city will be **d** and deserted?"
32:43 'It is a **d** waste, without men or
33:10 a **d** waste, without men or animals.
33:12 'In this place, **d** and without men or
44: 6 them the **d** ruins they are today.
44:22 and a **d** waste without inhabitants,
48: 9 **d**, with no-one to live in them.
49:33 of jackals, a **d** place for ever.
50:13 inhabited but will be completely **d**.
50:23 How **d** is Babylon among the nations!
51:26 for you will be **d** for ever,"
51:43 Her towns will be **d**, a dry and
51:62 live in it; it will be **d** for ever.'
Lam 1: 4 All her gateways are **d**, her priests
1:13 He made me **d**, faint all the day long.
5:18 for Mount Zion, which lies **d**, with
Eze 6:14 make the land a **d** waste from the
12:20 laid waste and the land will be **d**.
14:15 it becomes **d** so that no-one can pass
14:16 be saved, but the land would be **d**.
15: 8 I will make the land **d** because they
26:19 LORD says: When I make you a **d** city,
29: 9 Egypt will become a **d** wasteland.
29:10 and a **d** waste from Migdol to Aswan,
29:12 I will make the land of Egypt **d**
29:12 cities will lie **d** for forty years
30: 7 "'They will be **d** among **d** lands, and
32:15 I make Egypt **d** and strip the land of
33:28 I will make the land a **d** waste, and
33:28 **d** so that no-one will cross them.
33:29 when I have made the land a **d** waste
35: 3 against you and make you a **d** waste.
35: 4 towns into ruins and you will be **d**.
35: 7 I will make Mount Seir a **d** waste and
35: 9 I will make you **d** for ever;
35:14 earth rejoices, I will make you **d**.
35:15 of the house of Israel became **d**,
35:15 You will be **d**, O Mount Seir, you and
36: 4 to the **d** ruins and the deserted
36:34 The **d** land will be cultivated
36:34 lying **d** in the sight of all who
36:35 **d** and destroyed, are now fortified
36:36 and have replanted what was **d**.
38: 8 of Israel, which had long been **d**.
Da 9:17 with favour on your **d** sanctuary.
Joel 3:19 Egypt will be **d**, Edom a desert waste,
Mic 7:13 The earth will become **d** because of
Zep 2:13 utterly **d** and dry as the desert.
Zec 7:14 The land was left so **d** behind them
7:14 how they made the pleasant land **d**.'"
Mt 23:38 Look, your house is left to you **d**.
Lk 13:35 Look, your house is left to you **d**.
Gal 4:27 are the children of the **d** woman

Desolation (*Abomination that causes desolation*, Desolate)

2Ch 36:21 all the time of its **d** it rested,
Isa 17: 9 And all will be **d**.
34:11 of chaos and the plumb-line of **d**.
64:10 Zion is a desert, Jerusalem a **d**.
Eze 23:33 the cup of ruin and **d**, the cup of
Da 8:13 the rebellion that causes **d**, and the
9: 2 that the **d** of Jerusalem would last
9:18 **d** of the city that bears your Name.
Lk 21:20 you will know that its **d** is near.

Desolations (Desolate)

Ps 46: 8 the **d** he has brought on the earth.
Da 9:26 the end, and **d** have been decreed.

Despair (Despaired, Despairing, Despairs)

1Sa 4:20 Don't **d**; you have given birth to a
Job 9:23 he mocks the **d** of the innocent.
Ps 88:15 suffered your terrors and am in **d**.
Ecc 2:20 my heart began to **d** over all my
Isa 19: 9 who work with combed flax will **d**,
61: 3 of praise instead of a spirit of **d**.
Jer 17:16 I have not desired the day of **d**.
Eze 4:16 and drink rationed water in **d**,
7:27 the prince will be clothed with **d**,
12:19 anxiety and drink their water in **d**,
Joel 1:11 **D**, you farmers, wail, you vine
2Co 4: 8 perplexed, but not in **d**;

Despaired (Despair)

2Co 1: 8 endure, so that we **d** even of life.

Despairing (Despair)

Dt 28:65 weary with longing, and a **d** heart.
Job 6:14 "A **d** man should have the devotion of
6:26 treat the words of a **d** man as wind?
Jer 14: 3 and **d**, they cover their heads.

Despairs (Despair)

Job 15:22 He **d** of escaping the darkness; he is

Desperate

2Sa 12:18 is dead? He may do something **d**."
Ps 60: 3 You have shown your people **d** times;
79: 8 to meet us, for we are in **d** need.
142: 6 Listen to my cry, for I am in **d** need;

Despise (Despised, Despises)

Ge 16: 4 she began to **d** her mistress.
1Sa 2:30 those who **d** me will be disdained.
2Sa 12: 9 Why did you **d** the word of the LORD
Est 1:17 and so they will **d** their husbands
Job 5:17 **d** the discipline of the Almighty.
7:16 I **d** my life; I would not live for
9:21 concern for myself; I **d** my own life.
36: 5 "God is mighty, but does not **d** men;
42: 6 Therefore I **d** myself and repent in
Ps 51:17 heart, O God, you will not **d**.
69:33 and does not **d** his captive people.
73:20 you will **d** them as fantasies.
102:17 destitute; he will not **d** their plea.
Pr 1: 7 but fools **d** wisdom and discipline.
3:11 do not **d** the LORD's discipline
6:30 Men do not **d** a thief if he steals to
23:22 not **d** your mother when she is old.
SS 8: 1 kiss you, and no-one would **d** me.
Isa 60:14 all who **d** you will bow down at your
Jer 4:30 lovers **d** you; they seek your life.
14:19 Do you **d** Zion? Why have you
14:21 For the sake of your name do not **d**
23:17 They keep saying to those who **d** me,'
33:24 So they **d** my people and no longer
Lam 1: 8 All who honoured her **d** her, for they
Eze 16:57 those around you who **d** you.
Am 5:10 court and **d** him who tells the truth.
5:21 "I hate, I **d** your religious feasts;
Mic 3: 9 who **d** justice and distort all that
Mt 6:24 devoted to the one and **d** the other.
Lk 16:13 devoted to the one and **d** the other.
1Co 11:22 Or do you **d** the church of God and
Tit 2:15 Do not let anyone **d** you.
2Pe 2:10 the sinful nature and **d** authority.

Despised (Despise)

Ge 25:34 So Esau **d** his birthright.
Nu 15:31 he has **d** the LORD's word and broken
1Sa 10:27 They **d** him and brought him no gifts.
15: 9 **d** and weak they totally destroyed.
17:42 ruddy and handsome, and he **d** him.
2Sa 6:16 the LORD, she **d** him in her heart.
12:10 because you **d** me and took the wife
1Ch 15:29 celebrating, she **d** him in her heart.
2Ch 36:16 God's messengers, **d** his words
Ne 4: 4 Hear us, O our God, for we are **d**.
Ps 22: 6 scorned by men and **d** by the people.
22:24 For he has not **d** or disdained the
53: 5 put them to shame, for God **d** them.
106:24 they **d** the pleasant land; they did
107:11 and **d** the counsel of the Most High.
119:141 Though I am lowly and **d**, I do not
Pr 12: 8 but men with warped minds are **d**.
Ecc 9:16 But the poor man's wisdom is **d**, and
Isa 16:14 and all her many people will be **d**,
33: 8 its witnesses are **d**, no-one is
49: 7 was **d** and abhorred by the nation,
53: 3 He was **d** and rejected by men, a man
53: 3 he was **d**, and we esteemed him not.
Jer 22:28 Is this man Jehoiachin a **d**, broken
49:15 among the nations, **d** among men.
Lam 1:11 O LORD, and consider, for I am **d**."
Eze 16: 5 on the day you were born you were **d**.
16:45 who **d** her husband and her children;
16:45 **d** their husbands and their children.
16:59 **d** my oath by breaking the covenant.
17:16 oath he **d** and whose treaty he broke.
17:18 He **d** the oath by breaking the
17:19 my oath that he **d** and my covenant
22: 8 You have **d** my holy things and
Ob : 2 the nations; you will be utterly **d**.
Mal 2: 9 "So I have caused you to be **d** and
1Co 1:28 the **d** things—and the things that

Despises (Despise)

Ge 16: 5 she knows she is pregnant, she **d** me.
2Ki 19:21 Daughter of Zion **d** you and mocks you.
Ps 15: 4 who **d** a vile man but honours those
Pr 14: 2 but he whose ways are devious **d** him.
14:21 He who **d** his neighbour sins, but
15:20 but a foolish man **d** his mother.
15:32 He who ignores discipline **d** himself,
Isa 37:22 Daughter of Zion **d** and mocks you.
Eze 21:10 The sword **d** every such stick.
21:13 which the sword **d**, does not
Zec 4:10 "Who **d** the day of small things? Men

Despoil (Spoil)

Jer 30:16 all who make spoil of you I will **d**.

Destination

2Sa 16:14 him arrived at their **d** exhausted.

Destine (Destined, Destiny, Predestined)

Isa 65:12 I will **d** you for the sword, and you

Destined (Destine)

Ps 49:14 Like sheep they are **d** for the grave,
Isa 9: 5 in blood will be **d** for burning,
Jer 15: 2 "'Those **d** for death, to death;
43:11 bringing death to those **d** for death,
43:11 captivity to those **d** for captivity,
43:11 the sword to those **d** for the sword.
Eze 31:14 a height; they are all **d** for death,
Lk 2:34 "This child is **d** to cause the
1Co 2: 7 **d** for our glory before time began.
Col 2:22 These are all **d** to perish with use,
1Th 3: 3 quite well that we were **d** for them.
Heb 9:27 Just as man is **d** to die once, and
1Pe 2: 8 is also what they were **d** for.

Destiny (Destine)

Job 8:13 Such is the **d** of all who forget God;
Ps 73:17 then I understood their final **d**.

Ecc 7: 2 for death is the **d** of every man;
9: 2 All share a common **d**—the righteous
9: 3 the sun: The same **d** overtakes all.
Isa 65:11 and fill bowls of mixed wine for **D**,
Php 3:19 Their **d** is destruction, their god is

Destitute

Ge 45:11 who belong to you will become **d**.'
Job 20:19 oppressed the poor and left them **d**;
Ps 102:17 will respond to the prayer of the **d**
Pr 31: 8 for the rights of all who are **d**.
Isa 3:26 **d**, she will sit on the ground.
Lam 1:16 **d** because the enemy has prevailed."
4: 5 Those who once ate delicacies are **d**
Heb 11:37 **d**, persecuted and ill-treated—

Destroy (Destroyed, Destroyer, Destroyers, Destroying, Destroys, Destruction, Destructive)

Ge 6:13 going to **d** both them and the earth.
6:17 to **d** all life under the heavens,
8:21 And never again will I **d** all living
9:11 there be a flood to **d** the earth."
9:15 waters become a flood to **d** all life.
18:28 Will you **d** the whole city because of
18:28 there," he said, "I will not **d** it.
18:31 sake of twenty, I will not **d** it."
18:32 the sake of ten, I will not **d** it."
19:13 we are going to **d** this place.
19:13 great that he has sent us to **d** it."
19:14 the LORD is about to **d** the city!"
20: 4 "Lord, will you **d** an innocent
Ex 15: 9 my sword and my hand will **d** them.'
32:10 against them and that I may **d** them.
33: 3 and I might **d** you on the way."
33: 5 even for a moment, I might **d** you.
Lev 23:30 I will **d** from among his people
26:16 fever that will **d** your sight and
26:22 **d** your cattle and make you so few in
26:30 I will **d** your high places, cut down
26:44 them so as to **d** them completely,
Nu 14:12 them down with a plague and **d** them,
21: 2 we will totally **d** their cities."
24:19 and **d** the survivors of the city."
33:52 **D** all their carved images and their
Dt 1:27 the hands of the Amorites to **d** us.
4:31 he will not abandon or **d** you or
6:15 **d** you from the face of the land.
7: 2 them, then you must **d** them totally.
7: 4 against you and will quickly **d** you.
7:16 You must **d** all the peoples the LORD
7:24 up against you; you will **d** them.
9: 3 He will **d** them; he will subdue them
9: 8 that he was angry enough to **d** you.
9:14 Let me alone, so that I may **d** them
9:19 was angry enough with you to **d** you.
9:20 angry enough with Aaron to **d** him,
9:25 the LORD had said he would **d** you.
9:26 do not **d** your people, your
10:10 It was not his will to **d** you.
12: 2 **D** completely all the places on the
13:15 **D** it completely, both its people and
20:17 Completely **d** them—the Hittites,
20:19 do not **d** its trees by putting an axe
28:63 will please him to ruin and **d** you.
31: 3 He will **d** these nations before you,
33:27 enemy before you, saying, '**D** him!'
Jos 7: 7 the hands of the Amorites to **d** us?
7:12 unless you **d** whatever among you is
11:20 so that he might **d** them totally,
1Sa 15: 3 **d** everything that belongs to them.
15: 6 that I do not **d** you along with them;
15: 9 These they were unwilling to **d**
15:18 'Go and completely **d** those wicked
23:10 and **d** the town on account of me.
26: 9 David said to Abishai, "Don't **d** him!
26:15 Someone came to **d** your lord the king.
2Sa 1:14 your hand to **d** the LORD's anointed?"
11:25 attack against the city and **d** it.
20:19 You are trying to **d** a city that is a
20:20 Far be it from me to swallow up or **d**!
24:16 the angel stretched out his hand to **d**
2Ki 8:19 the LORD was not willing to **d** Judah.
9: 7 You are to **d** the house of Ahab your
10:19 in order to **d** the ministers of Baal.
2Ki 11: 1 to **d** the whole royal family.
13:17 completely **d** the Arameans at Aphek."
13:23 unwilling to **d** them or banish them
18:25 have I come to attack and **d** this
18:25 against this country and **d** it.'"
24: 2 He sent them to **d** Judah, in
1Ch 21:15 God sent an angel to **d** Jerusalem.
2Ch 12: 7 I will not **d** them but will soon give
20:10 away from them and did not **d** them.
20:23 Mount Seir to **d** and annihilate them.
20:23 they helped to **d** one another.
20:37 the LORD will **d** what you have made.
21: 7 not willing to **d** the house of David.
22: 7 had anointed to **d** the house of Ahab.
22:10 she proceeded to **d** the whole royal
25:16 that God has determined to **d** you,
35:21 who is with me, or he will **d** you."
Ezr 6:12 or to **d** this temple in Jerusalem.
9:14 not be angry enough with us to **d** us,
Est 3: 6 Instead Haman looked for a way to **d**
3: 9 let a decree be issued to **d** them,
3:13 provinces with the order to **d**,
8: 5 devised and wrote to **d** the Jews
8:11 to **d**, kill and annihilate any armed
9:24 had plotted against the Jews to **d**
Job 10: 8 Will you now turn and **d** me?
14:19 away the soil, so you **d** man's hope.
Ps 5: 6 You **d** those who tell lies;
21:10 You will **d** their descendants from
54: 5 in your faithfulness **d** them.
57: T ⌊To the tune of⌋ "Do not **D**".
58: T ⌊To the tune of⌋ "Do not **D**".
59: T ⌊To the tune of⌋ "Do not **D**".
69: 4 cause, those who seek to **d** me.
73:27 you **d** all who are unfaithful to you.
74:11 folds of your garment and **d** them!
75: T ⌊To the tune of⌋ "Do not **D**".
78:38 their iniquities and did not **d** them.
83: 4 "Come," they say, "let us **d** them as
94:23 and **d** them for their wickedness;
94:23 the LORD our God will **d** them.
106:23 he said he would **d** them—had not
106:34 They did not **d** the peoples as the
119:95 The wicked are waiting to **d** me, but
143:12 **d** all my foes, for I am your servant.
145:20 him, but all the wicked he will **d**.
Pr 1:32 complacency of fools will **d** them;
Ecc 5: 6 and **d** the work of your hands?
7:16 be overwise—why **d** yourself?
Isa 10: 7 his purpose is to **d**, to put an end
10:18 it will completely **d**, as when a
11: 9 They will neither harm nor **d** on all
13: 5 his wrath—to **d** the whole country.
13: 9 and **d** the sinners within it.
14:30 But your root I will **d** by famine;
25: 7 On this mountain he will **d** the
32: 7 he makes up evil schemes to **d** the
34: 2 He will totally **d** them, he will give
36:10 have I come to attack and **d** this
36:10 against this country and **d** it.'"
65: 8 'Don't **d** it, there is yet some good
65: 8 my servants; I will not **d** them all.
65:25 They will neither harm nor **d** on all
Jer 1:10 to **d** and overthrow, to build and to
4:27 though I will not **d** it completely.
5:10 them, but do not **d** them completely.
5:17 With the sword they will **d** the
5:18 LORD, "I will not **d** you completely.
6: 2 I will **d** the Daughter of Zion, so
6: 5 arise, let us attack at night and **d**
11:19 "Let us **d** the tree and its fruit;
12:17 uproot and **d** it," declares the LORD.
14:12 Instead, I will **d** them with the
15: 3 beasts of the earth to devour and **d**.
15: 6 So I will lay hands on you and **d** you;
17:18 **d** them with double destruction.
21:10 Babylon, and he will **d** it with fire.'
25: 9 I will completely **d** them and make
27: 8 the LORD, until I **d** it by his hand.
30:11 'Though I completely **d** all the
30:11 you, I will not completely **d** you.
31:28 and to overthrow, **d** and bring
36:29 **d** this land and cut off both men and
44: 8 You will **d** yourselves and make
44:11 disaster on you and to **d** all Judah.
46: 8 I will **d** cities and their people.'
Jer 46:28 "Though I completely **d** all the
46:28 you, I will not completely **d** you.
47: 4 For the day has come to **d** all the
47: 4 LORD is about to **d** the Philistines
49:20 **d** their pasture because of them.
49:28 Kedar and **d** the people of the East.
49:38 and **d** her king and officials,"
50:21 Pursue, kill and completely **d** them,"
50:26 **d** her and leave her no remnant.
50:45 **d** their pasture because of them.
51: 3 young men; completely **d** her army.
51:11 because his purpose is to **d** Babylon.
51:20 nations, with you I **d** kingdoms,
51:25 you who **d** the whole earth,"
51:55 The LORD will **d** Babylon; he will
51:62 have said you will **d** this place,
Lam 3:66 Pursue them in anger and **d** them from
Eze 5:16 of famine, I will shoot to **d** you.
6: 3 you, and I will **d** your high places.
9: 8 Are you going to **d** the entire
11:13 completely **d** the remnant of Israel?"
14: 9 **d** him from among my people Israel.
16:39 mounds and **d** your lofty shrines.
17:17 siege works erected to **d** many lives.
20:13 on them and **d** them in the desert.
20:17 did not **d** them or put an end to them
22:30 not have to **d** it, but I found none.
25: 7 I will **d** you, and you will know that
25:15 ancient hostility sought to **d** Judah,
25:16 **d** those remaining along the coast.
26: 4 They will **d** the walls of Tyre and
30:11 will be brought in to **d** the land.
30:13 "'I will **d** the idols and put an end
32:13 I will **d** all her cattle from beside
34:16 the sleek and the strong I will **d**.
43: 3 had seen when he came to **d** the city
Da 4:23 'Cut down the tree and **d** it, but
8:24 **d** the mighty men and the holy people.
8:25 When they feel secure, he will **d**
9:26 will **d** the city and the sanctuary.
11:16 and will have the power to **d** it.
11:26 will try to **d** him; his army will be
11:44 great rage to **d** and annihilate many.
Hos 4: 5 So I will **d** your mother—
10: 2 altars and **d** their sacred stones.
11: 6 will **d** the bars of their gates and
Am 1: 5 I will **d** the king who is in the
1: 8 I will **d** the king of Ashdod and the
2: 3 I will **d** her ruler and kill all her
3:14 I will **d** the altars of Bethel;
9: 8 I will **d** it from the face of the
9: 8 not totally **d** the house of Jacob,"
Ob : 8 "will I not **d** the wise men of Edom,
Mic 1: 7 with fire; I will **d** all her images.
5:10 "I will **d** your horses from among you
5:11 I will **d** the cities of your land and
5:12 I will **d** your witchcraft and you
5:13 I will **d** your carved images and your
6:13 Therefore, I have begun to **d** you, to
Na 1:14 I will **d** the carved images and
Zep 2: 5 I will **d** you, and none will be left."
2:13 against the north and **d** Assyria,
Zec 5: 4 It will remain in his house and **d** it,
9: 4 and **d** her power on the sea,
9:15 They will **d** and overcome with
12: 9 On that day I will set out to **d** all
Mt 6:19 where moth and rust **d**, and where
6:20 where moth and rust do not **d**, and
10:28 can **d** both soul and body in hell.
26:61 'I am able to **d** the temple of God
27:40 "You who are going to **d** the temple
Mk 1:24 Have you come to **d** us? I know who
14:58 "We heard him say, 'I will **d** this
15:29 You who are going to **d** the temple
Lk 4:34 Have you come to **d** us? I know who
6: 9 do evil, to save life or to **d** it?"
9:54 fire down from heaven to **d** them?"
Jn 2:19 Jesus answered them, "**D** this temple,
10:10 comes only to steal and kill and **d**;
Ac 6:14 Jesus of Nazareth will **d** this place
8: 3 Saul began to **d** the church.
Ro 14:15 **d** your brother for whom Christ died.
14:20 Do not **d** the work of God for the
1Co 1:19 For it is written: "I will **d** the
3:17 God will **d** him; for God's temple is
6:13 for food"—but God will **d** them both.

Gal 1:13 the church of God and tried to **d** it.
1:23 the faith he once tried to **d**."
2Th 2: 8 **d** by the splendour of his coming.
2Ti 2:18 place, and they **d** the faith of some.
Heb 2:14 **d** him who holds the power of death
Jas 4:12 the one who is able to save and **d**.
1Jn 3: 8 appeared was to **d** the devil's work.
Jude :10 are the very things that **d** them.
Rev 11:18 destroying those who **d** the earth."

Destroyed (Destroy)

Ge 13:10 the LORD **d** Sodom and Gomorrah.)
19:29 when God **d** the cities of the plain,
34:30 me, I and my household will be **d**."
Ex 9:31 (The flax and barley were **d**, since
9:32 not **d**, because they ripen later.)
22:20 god other than the LORD must be **d**.
Lev 10: 6 for those the LORD has **d** by fire.
Nu 21: 3 They completely **d** them and their
21:29 Woe to you, O Moab! You are **d**,
21:30 Heshbon is **d** all the way to Dibon.
24:22 yet you Kenites will be **d** when
Dt 2:12 They **d** the Horites from before them
2:21 The LORD **d** them from before the
2:22 he **d** the Horites from before them.
2:23 **d** them and settled in their place.)
2:34 **d** them—men, women and children.
3: 6 We completely **d** them, as we had done
4: 3 The LORD your God **d** from among you
4:26 there long but will certainly be **d**.
7:23 great confusion until they are **d**.
8:19 you today that you will surely be **d**.
8:20 Like the nations the LORD **d** before
8:20 **d** for not obeying the LORD your God.
12:30 after they have been **d** before you,
19: 1 the LORD your God has **d** the nations
28:20 until you are **d** and come to sudden
28:21 until he has **d** you from the land
28:24 down from the skies until you are **d**.
28:45 and overtake you until you are **d**,
28:48 on your neck until he has **d** you.
28:51 crops of your land until you are **d**.
28:61 Book of the Law, until you are **d**.
30:18 day that you will certainly be **d**.
31: 4 whom he **d** along with their land.
31:17 face from them, and they will be **d**.
Jos 2:10 the Jordan, whom you completely **d**.
6:21 **d** with the sword every living thing
7:15 devoted things shall be **d** by fire,
8:26 until he had **d** all who lived in Ai.
10: 1 Joshua had taken Ai and totally **d** it,
10:20 Joshua and the Israelites **d** them
10:28 sword and totally **d** everyone in it.
10:35 sword and totally **d** everyone in it,
10:37 totally **d** it and everyone in it.
10:39 Everyone in it they totally **d**.
10:40 He totally **d** all who breathed,
11:11 They totally **d** them, not sparing
11:12 He totally **d** them, as Moses the
11:14 sword until they completely **d** them,
11:21 At that time Joshua went and **d** the
11:21 totally **d** them and their towns.
23:15 until he has **d** you from this good
24: 8 I **d** them from before you, and you
Jdg 1:17 Zephath, and they totally **d** the city.
4:24 Canaanite king, until they **d** him.
9:45 Then he **d** the city and scattered
21:16 "With the women of Benjamin **d**, how
1Sa 15: 8 people he totally **d** with the sword.
15: 9 despised and weak they totally **d**.
15:15 God, but we totally **d** the rest."
15:20 I completely **d** the Amalekites and
27: 1 I shall be **d** by the hand of Saul.
30: 3 they found it **d** by fire and their
2Sa 11: 1 They **d** the Ammonites and besieged
14:11 so that my son shall not be **d**.
21: 5 "As for the man who **d** us and plotted
22:38 I did not turn back till they were **d**.
22:41 backs in flight, and I **d** my foes.
1Ki 11:16 they had **d** all the men in Edom.
11:24 when David **d** the forces of Zobah;
15:29 but **d** them all, according to the
16: 7 Jeroboam—and also because he **d** it.
16:12 Zimri **d** the whole family of Baasha,
22:11 the Arameans until they are **d**.'"
2Ki 3:25 They **d** the towns, and each man threw
10:17 he **d** them, according to the word
10:28 Jehu **d** Baal worship in Israel.
13: 7 for the king of Aram had **d** the rest
13:19 defeated Aram and completely **d** it.
19:12 **d** by my forefathers deliver them:
19:18 their gods into the fire and **d** them,
21: 3 places his father Hezekiah had **d**;
21: 9 LORD had **d** before the Israelites.
1Ch 4:41 **d** them, as is evident to this day.
5:25 land, whom God had **d** before them.
2Ch 8: 8 whom the Israelites had not **d**—these
12:12 from him, and he was not totally **d**.
14:14 They **d** all the villages around Gerar,
18:10 the Arameans until they are **d**.'"
31: 1 They **d** the high places and the
31: 1 After they had **d** all of them, the
32:14 of these nations that my fathers **d**
33: 9 LORD had **d** before the Israelites.
36:19 and **d** everything of value there.
Ezr 4:15 That is why this city was **d**.
5:12 king of Babylon, who **d** this temple
Ne 2: 3 and its gates have been **d** by fire?"
2:13 its gates, which had been **d** by fire.
Est 9: 6 Jews killed and **d** five hundred men.
9:12 have killed and **d** five hundred men
Job 4: 7 Where were the upright ever **d**?
4: 9 At the breath of God they are **d**;
19:26 after my skin has been **d**, yet in my
22:20 'Surely our foes are **d**, and fire
Ps 2:12 lest he be angry and you be **d** in
9: 5 the nations and **d** the wicked;
11: 3 the foundations are being **d**, what
18:37 I did not turn back till they were **d**.
18:40 backs in flight, and I **d** my foes.
37:38 all sinners will be **d**; the future of
48: 7 You **d** them like ships of Tarshish
63: 9 They who seek my life will be **d**;
73:19 How suddenly are they **d**, completely
78:47 He **d** their vines with hail and their
79: 7 devoured Jacob and **d** his homeland.
88:16 over me; your terrors have **d** me.
92: 7 flourish, they will be for ever **d**.
105:16 and **d** all their supplies of food;
Pr 6:15 will suddenly be **d**—without remedy.
11: 3 unfaithful are **d** by their duplicity.
11:11 by the mouth of the wicked it is **d**.
14:11 The house of the wicked will be **d**,
21:28 listens to him will be **d** for ever.
22: 8 and the rod of his fury will be **d**.
29: 1 will suddenly be **d**—without remedy.
Isa 5: 5 away its hedge, and it will be **d**;
14:20 **d** your land and killed your people.
15: 1 Ar in Moab is ruined, **d** in a night!
15: 1 Kir in Moab is ruined, **d** in a night!
23: 1 **d** and left without house or harbour.
23:11 Phoenicia that her fortresses be **d**.
23:14 of Tarshish; your fortress is **d**!
33: 1 you who have not been **d**! Woe to you,
33: 1 stop destroying, you will be **d**;
34: 5 Edom, the people I have totally **d**.
37:12 that were **d** by my forefathers
37:19 their gods into the fire and **d** them,
48:19 be cut off nor **d** from before me."
55:13 sign, which will not be **d**."
Jer 4:20 tents are **d**, my shelter in a moment.
9:16 with the sword until I have **d** them."
10:20 My tent is **d**; all its ropes are
10:25 him completely and **d** his homeland.
18: 7 is to be uprooted, torn down and **d**,
24:10 plague against them until they are **d**
44:27 and famine until they are all **d**.
48: 8 will be ruined and the plateau **d**,
48:15 Moab will be **d** and her towns invaded;
48:20 Announce by the Arnon that Moab is **d**.
48:42 Moab will be **d** as a nation because
48:46 O Moab! The people of Chemosh are **d**;
49: 3 "Wail, O Heshbon, for Ai is **d**!
51: 6 Do not be **d** because of her sins.
Lam 2: 5 her palaces and **d** her strongholds.
2: 6 he has **d** his place of meeting.
2: 9 their bars he has broken and **d**.
2:11 the ground because my people are **d**,
2:22 for and reared, my enemy has **d**.
3:48 my eyes because my people are **d**.
4:10 their food when my people were **d**.
Eze 13:14 When it falls, you will be **d** in it;
26:17 "'How you are **d**, O city of renown,
36:35 lying in ruins, desolate and **d**,
36:36 I the LORD have rebuilt what was **d**
43: 8 So I **d** them in my anger.
Da 2:44 up a kingdom that will never be **d**,
6:26 his kingdom will not be **d**, his
7:11 **d** and thrown into the blazing fire.
7:14 kingdom is one that will never be **d**.
7:26 away and completely **d** for ever.
8:25 will be **d**, but not by human power.
11:20 he will be **d**, yet not in anger or
11:22 a prince of the covenant will be **d**.
Hos 4: 6 my people are **d** from lack of
10: 8 high places of wickedness will be **d**
10:15 king of Israel will be completely **d**.
13: 9 "You are **d**, O Israel, because you
Joel 1:10 ground is dried up; the grain is **d**,
1:11 the harvest of the field is **d**.
Am 2: 9 "I **d** the Amorite before them, though
2: 9 I **d** his fruit above and his roots
3:15 houses adorned with ivory will be **d**
7: 9 "The high places of Isaac will be **d**
Ob :10 with shame; you will be **d** for ever.
Mic 5: 9 and all your foes will be **d**.
Na 1:15 they will be completely **d**.
Hab 2: 8 you have **d** lands and cities and
2:17 you have **d** lands and cities and
Zep 3: 6 Their cities are **d**; no-one will be
Zec 11: 3 their rich pastures are **d**! Listen to
14:11 inhabited; never again will it be **d**.
Mal 3: 6 O descendants of Jacob, are not **d**.
Mt 22: 7 He sent his army and **d** those
Lk 17:27 Then the flood came and **d** them all.
17:29 down from heaven and **d** them all.
Ac 27:22 be lost; only the ship will be **d**.
1Co 5: 5 so that the sinful nature may be **d**
8:11 Christ died, is **d** by your knowledge.
15:24 **d** all dominion, authority and power.
15:26 The last enemy to be **d** is death.
2Co 4: 9 abandoned; struck down, but not **d**.
5: 1 if the earthly tent we live in is **d**,
Gal 2:18 If I rebuild what I **d**, I prove that
5:15 out or you will be **d** by each other.
Eph 2:14 and has **d** the barrier, the dividing
Php 1:28 a sign to them that they will be **d**,
2Ti 1:10 Christ Jesus, who has **d** death and
Heb 10:39 of those who shrink back and are **d**,
Jas 1:11 blossom falls and its beauty is **d**.
2Pe 2:12 born only to be caught and **d**, and
3: 6 of that time was deluged and **d**.
3:10 the elements will be **d** by fire,
3:11 Since everything will be **d** in this
Jude : 5 later **d** those who did not believe.
:11 have been **d** in Korah's rebellion.
Rev 8: 9 and a third of the ships were **d**.

Destroyer (Destroy)

Ex 12:23 and he will not permit the **d** to
Isa 16: 4 be their shelter from the **d**.
33: 1 Woe to you, O **d**, you who have not
54:16 have created the **d** to work havoc;
Jer 4: 7 a **d** of nations has set out.
6:26 suddenly the **d** will come upon us.
15: 8 At midday I will bring a **d** against
48: 8 The **d** will come against every town,
48:32 The **d** has fallen on your ripened
51: 1 I will stir up the spirit of a **d**
51:56 A **d** will come against Babylon;
Heb 11:28 so that the **d** of the firstborn would

Destroyers (Destroy)

Jer 12:12 heights in the desert **d** will swarm,
15: 3 "I will send four kinds of **d** against
22: 7 I will send **d** against you, each man
51:48 out of the north **d** will attack her,"
51:53 I will send **d** against her,"
Na 2: 2 though **d** have laid them waste and

Destroying (Destroy)

Dt 3: 6 **d** every city—men, women and
1Sa 6: 5 of the rats that are **d** the country,
2Ki 19:11 the countries, **d** them completely.
1Ch 21:15 to the angel who was **d** the people,
Est 9: 5 killing and **d** them, and they did

Job 30:13 they succeeded in **d** me—without
Ps 52: 7 wealth and grew strong by **d** others!"
78:49 and hostility—a band of **d** angels.
106:23 him to keep his wrath from **d** them.
Isa 33: 1 When you stop **d**, you will be
37:11 the countries, **d** them completely.
Jer 13:14 compassion to keep me from **d** them.'"
23: 1 "Woe to the shepherds who are **d** and
25:36 for the LORD is **d** their pasture.
51:25 "I am against you, O **d** mountain,
Lam 2: 8 did not withhold his hand from **d**.
Hab 1:17 his net, **d** nations without mercy?
Lk 9:39 ever leaves him and is **d** him.
1Co 10:10 did—and were killed by the **d** angel.
Rev 11:18 for **d** those who destroy the earth."

Destroys (Destroy)

Ex 21:26 or maidservant in the eye and **d** it,
Job 9:22 **d** both the blameless and the wicked.'
12:23 He makes nations great, and **d** them;
Ps 91: 6 nor the plague that **d** at midday.
Pr 6:32 judgment; whoever does so **d** himself.
11: 9 With his mouth the godless **d** his
18: 9 in his work is brother to one who **d**.
28:24 wrong"—he is partner to him who **d**.
Ecc 9:18 of war, but one sinner **d** much good.
Jer 48:18 for he who **d** Moab will come up
Zep 2:11 when he **d** all the gods of the land.
Lk 12:33 no thief comes near and no moth **d**.
1Co 3:17 If anyone **d** God's temple, God will

Destruction (Destroy)

Lev 27:29 "No person devoted to **d** may be
Nu 32:15 you will be the cause of their **d**."
Dt 7:10 he will repay to their face by **d**;
7:26 like it, will be set apart for **d**.
7:26 it, for it is set apart for **d**.
29:23 like the **d** of Sodom and Gomorrah
30:15 life and prosperity, death and **d**.
Jos 6:18 your own **d** by taking any of them.
6:18 liable to **d** and bring trouble on it.
7:12 they have been made liable to **d**.
7:12 whatever among you is devoted to **d**.
2Sa 14:11 of blood from adding to the **d**,
22: 5 the torrents of **d** overwhelmed me.
1Ki 13:34 to its **d** from the face of the earth.
Est 4: 7 treasury for the **d** of the Jews.
7: 4 **d** and slaughter and annihilation.
8: 6 I bear to see the **d** of my family?"
9: 2 to attack those seeking their **d**.
9:24 is, the lot) for their ruin and **d**.
Job 5:21 and need not fear when **d** comes.
5:22 You will laugh at **d** and famine, and
21:20 Let his own eyes see his **d**; let him
26: 6 naked before God; **D** lies uncovered.
28:22 **D** and Death say, 'Only a rumour of
31:12 is a fire that burns to **D**; it would
31:23 For I dreaded **d** from God, and for
Ps 5: 9 their heart is filled with **d**.
18: 4 the torrents of **d** overwhelmed me.
30: 9 "What gain is there in my **d**, in my
52: 2 Your tongue plots **d**; it is like a
74: 3 all this **d** the enemy has brought on
88:11 the grave, your faithfulness in **D**?
137: 8 O Daughter of Babylon, doomed to **d**,
Pr 15:11 Death and **D** lie open before the LORD
16:18 Pride goes before **d**, a haughty
17:19 he who builds a high gate invites **d**.
24:22 for those two will send sudden **d**
27:20 Death and **D** are never satisfied, and
Isa 10:22 **D** has been decreed, overwhelming and
10:23 the **d** decreed upon the whole land.
10:25 wrath will be directed to their **d**."
13: 6 will come like **d** from the Almighty.
14:23 will sweep her with the broom of **d**,"
15: 5 to Horonaim they lament their **d**.
16: 4 come to an end, and **d** will cease;
19:18 them will be called the City of **D**.
22: 4 console me over the **d** of my people."
28:22 **d** decreed against the whole land.
30:28 the nations in the sieve of **d**;
38:17 love you kept me from the pit of **d**;
43:28 Jacob to **d** and Israel to scorn.
51:13 of the oppressor, who is bent on **d**?
51:19 who can comfort you?—ruin and **d**,
Isa 59: 7 ruin and **d** mark their ways.
60:18 nor ruin or **d** within your borders,
Jer 4: 6 from the north, even terrible **d**."
6: 1 out of the north, even terrible **d**.
6: 7 Violence and **d** resound in her;
15: 7 I will bring bereavement and **d** on my
17:18 destroy them with double **d**.
20: 8 I cry out proclaiming violence and **d**.
48: 3 Horonaim, cries of great havoc and **d**.
48: 5 cries over the **d** are heard.
50:22 in the land, the noise of great **d**!
51:54 **d** from the land of the Babylonians.
Lam 1: 7 looked at her and laughed at her **d**.
3:47 terror and pitfalls, ruin and **d**."
Eze 21:31 to brutal men, men skilled in **d**.
32: 9 about your **d** among the nations,
Hos 7:13 **D** to them, because they have
8: 4 idols for themselves to their own **d**.
9: 6 Even if they escape from **d**, Egypt
13:14 Where, O grave, is your **d**?
Joel 1:15 will come like **d** from the Almighty.
Am 5: 9 he flashes **d** on the stronghold and
Ob :12 of Judah in the day of their **d**,
Jnh 3:10 upon them the **d** he had threatened.
Hab 1: 3 **D** and violence are before me;
2:17 your **d** of animals will terrify you.
Mt 7:13 broad is the road that leads to **d**,
Lk 6:49 collapsed and its **d** was complete."
Jn 17:12 lost except the one doomed to **d**
Ro 9:22 of his wrath—prepared for **d**?
Gal 6: 8 from that nature will reap **d**;
Php 3:19 Their destiny is **d**, their god is
1Th 5: 3 **d** will come on them suddenly,
2Th 1: 9 will be punished with everlasting **d**
2: 3 is revealed, the man doomed to **d**.
1Ti 6: 9 that plunge men into ruin and **d**.
2Pe 2: 1 bringing swift **d** on themselves.
2: 3 and their **d** has not been sleeping.
3: 7 of judgment and **d** of ungodly men.
3:12 That day will bring about the **d** of
3:16 other Scriptures, to their own **d**.
Rev 17: 8 up out of the Abyss and go to his **d**.
17:11 to the seven and is going to his **d**.

Destructive (Destroy)

Ex 12:13 No **d** plague will touch you when I
Lev 13:51 a **d** mildew; the article is unclean.
13:52 because the mildew is **d**;
14:44 is a **d** mildew; the house is unclean.
Ps 55:11 **D** forces are at work in the city;
Isa 28: 2 Like a hailstorm and a **d** wind, like
Eze 5:16 my deadly and **d** arrows of famine,
13:13 of rain will fall with **d** fury.
2Pe 2: 1 will secretly introduce **d** heresies

Detachment (Detachments)

1Sa 13:23 Now a **d** of Philistines had gone out
Jn 18: 3 Judas came to the grove, guiding a **d**
18:12 the **d** of soldiers with its commander
Ac 23:23 "Get ready a **d** of two hundred

Detachments (Detachment)

1Sa 13:17 from the Philistine camp in three **d**.

Detail (Detailed, Details)

Ac 21:19 Paul greeted them and reported in **d**
Col 2:18 Such a person goes into great **d**
Heb 9: 5 discuss these things in **d** now.

Detailed (Detail)

2Ki 16:10 with **d** plans for its construction.

Details (Detail)

1Ki 6:38 **d** according to its specifications.
1Ch 28:19 in all the **d** of the plan."
29:30 together with the **d** of his reign and

Detain (Detained)

Ge 24:56 he said to them, "Do not **d** me, now
Jdg 13:16 "Even though you **d** me, I will not

Detained (Detain)

1Sa 21: 7 **d** before the LORD; he was Doeg the
Da 10:13 was **d** there with the king of Persia.

Detect

Job 39:29 his food; his eyes **d** it from afar.
Ps 36: 2 too much to **d** or hate his sin.
Ob : 7 trap for you, but you will not **d** it.

Deter (Detriment)

Mt 3:14 John tried to **d** him, saying, "I need

Determine (Determined, Determines)

Ex 12: 4 You are to **d** the amount of lamb
22: 8 **d** whether he has laid his hands on
Lev 14:57 to **d** when something is clean or
25:27 he is to **d** the value for the years
27:18 the priest will **d** the value
27:23 the priest will **d** its value up to
Ne 10:34 the people—have cast lots to **d** when
Da 11:17 He will **d** to come with the might of

Determined (Determine)

Jos 17:12 were **d** to live in that region.
Jdg 1:27 were **d** to live in that land.
1:35 the Amorites were **d** also to hold out
Ru 1:18 Naomi realised that Ruth was **d** to go
1Sa 20: 7 can be sure that he is **d** to harm me.
20: 9 **d** to harm you, wouldn't I tell you?"
2Sa 17:14 For the LORD had **d** to frustrate the
1Ki 7:47 the weight of the bronze was not **d**.
20:42 set free a man I had **d** should die.
2Ki 12:11 the amount had been **d**, they gave the
1Ch 12:38 They came to Hebron fully **d** to make
2Ch 4:18 the weight of the bronze was not **d**.
25:16 "I know that God has **d** to destroy
Job 14: 5 Man's days are **d**; you have decreed
Ecc 7:23 "I am **d** to be wise"—but this was
Isa 14:26 This is the plan **d** for the whole
Jer 21:10 I have **d** to do this city harm and
42:15 'If you are **d** to go to Egypt and you
42:17 Indeed, all who are **d** to go to Egypt
44:11 I am **d** to bring disaster on you and
44:12 **d** to go to Egypt to settle there.
Lam 2: 8 The LORD **d** to tear down the wall
Da 6:14 he was **d** to rescue Daniel and made
11:36 for what has been **d** must take place.
Hos 11: 7 My people are **d** to turn from me.
Hab 2:13 Has not the LORD Almighty **d** that the
Zec 1: 6 deserve, just as he **d** to do."
8:14 "Just as I had **d** to bring disaster
8:15 "so now I have **d** to do good again to
Jn 8:40 is, you are **d** to kill me, a man who
Ac 5:28 are **d** to make us guilty of this
17:26 and he **d** the times set for them and
1Co 15:38 God gives it a body as he has **d**, and

Determines (Determine)

Ps 147: 4 He **d** the number of the stars and
Pr 16: 9 course, but the LORD **d** his steps.
1Co 12:11 them to each one, just as he **d**.

Detest (Detestable, Detested, Detests)

Lev 11:10 in the water—you are to **d**.
11:11 since you are to **d** them, you must
11:11 meat and you must **d** their carcasses.
11:13 "'These are the birds you are to **d**
11:23 that have four legs you are to **d**.
Nu 21: 5 And we **d** this miserable food!"
Dt 7:26 Utterly abhor and **d** it, for it is
Job 9:31 so that even my clothes would **d** me.
19:19 All my intimate friends **d** me;
30:10 They **d** me and keep their distance;
Pr 8: 7 is true, for my lips **d** wickedness.
13:19 soul, but fools **d** turning from evil.
16:12 Kings **d** wrongdoing, for a throne is
24: 9 folly are sin, and men **d** a mocker.
29:27 The righteous **d** the dishonest;
29:27 the wicked **d** the upright.
Am 6: 8 of Jacob and **d** his fortresses;

Detestable (Detest)

Ge 43:32 Hebrews, for that is **d** to Egyptians.
46:34 shepherds are **d** to the Egyptians."
Ex 8:26 our God would be **d** to the Egyptians.
8:26 sacrifices that are **d** in their eyes,

Lev 7:21 any unclean, **d** thing—and then eats
11:12 fins and scales is to be **d** to you.
11:13 eat because they are **d**: the eagle,
11:20 on all fours are to be **d** to you.
11:41 moves about on the ground is **d**;
11:42 all fours or on many feet; it is **d**.
18:22 as one lies with a woman; that is **d**.
18:26 must not do any of these **d** things,
18:29 who does any of these **d** things
18:30 do not follow any of the **d** customs
20:13 both of them have done what is **d**.
Dt 7:25 for it is **d** to the LORD your God.
7:26 Do not bring a **d** thing into your
12:31 kinds of **d** things the LORD hates.
13:14 **d** thing has been done among you,
14: 3 Do not eat any **d** thing.
17: 1 in it, for that would be **d** to him.
17: 4 **d** thing has been done in Israel,
18: 9 the **d** ways of the nations there.
18:12 Anyone who does these things is **d** to
18:12 and because of these **d** practices the
20:18 follow all the **d** things they do in
24: 4 That would be **d** in the eyes of the
27:15 an idol—a thing **d** to the LORD,
29:17 You saw among them their **d** images
32:16 and angered him with their **d** idols.
1Ki 11: 5 Molech the **d** god of the Ammonites.
11: 7 place for Chemosh the **d** god of Moab,
11: 7 Molech the **d** god of the Ammonites.
14:24 engaged in all the **d** practices
2Ki 16: 3 following the **d** ways of the nations
21: 2 following the **d** practices of the
21:11 of Judah has committed these **d** sins.
23:13 the **d** god of the people of Ammon.
23:24 **d** things seen in Judah and Jerusalem.
2Ch 15: 8 He removed the **d** idols from the
28: 3 following the **d** ways of the nations
33: 2 following the **d** practices of the
34:33 Josiah removed all the **d** idols from
36: 8 the **d** things he did and all that was
36:14 following all the **d** practices of the
Ezr 9: 1 peoples with their **d** practices,
9:11 By their **d** practices they have
9:14 peoples who commit such **d** practices?
Pr 6:16 LORD hates, seven that are **d** to him:
21:27 The sacrifice of the wicked is **d**—
28: 9 to the law, even his prayers are **d**.
Isa 1:13 Your incense is **d** to me.
41:24 worthless; he who chooses you is **d**.
44:19 Shall I make a **d** thing from what is
Jer 2: 7 my land and made my inheritance **d**.
4: 1 "If you put your **d** idols out of my
7:10 to do all these **d** things?
7:30 They have set up their **d** idols in
13:27 I have seen your **d** acts on the hills
16:18 my inheritance with their **d** idols."
32:35 a **d** thing and so make Judah sin.
44: 4 not do this **d** thing that I hate!'
44:22 actions and the **d** things you did,
Eze 5: 9 of all your **d** idols, I will do to
5:11 your vile images and **d** practices,
6: 9 done and for all their **d** practices.
6:11 **d** practices of the house of Israel,
7: 3 repay you for all your **d** practices.
7: 4 and the **d** practices among you.
7: 8 repay you for all your **d** practices.
7: 9 and the **d** practices among you.
7:20 make their **d** idols and vile images.
8: 6 the utterly **d** things the house of
8: 6 see things that are even more **d**."
8: 9 and **d** things they are doing here."
8:10 **d** animals and all the idols of the
8:13 doing things that are even more **d**."
8:15 that are even more **d** than this."
8:17 do the **d** things they are doing here?
9: 4 the **d** things that are done in it."
11:18 all its vile images and **d** idols.
11:21 to their vile images and **d** idols,
12:16 acknowledge all their **d** practices.
14: 6 and renounce all your **d** practices!
16: 2 Jerusalem with her **d** practices
16:22 In all your **d** practices and your
16:36 and because of all your **d** idols, and
16:43 to all your other **d** practices?
16:47 ways and copied their **d** practices,
16:50 They were haughty and did **d** things
Eze 16:51 You have done more **d** things than
16:58 your **d** practices, declares the LORD.
18:12 to the idols. He does **d** things.
18:13 he has done all these **d** things,
18:24 same **d** things the wicked man does,
20: 4 the **d** practices of their
22: 2 her with all her **d** practices
22:11 In you one man commits a **d** offence
23:36 them with their **d** practices,
33:26 rely on your sword, you do **d** things
33:29 of all the **d** things they have done.'
36:31 for your sins and **d** practices.
43: 8 my holy name by their **d** practices.
44: 6 your **d** practices, O house of Israel!
44: 7 to all your other **d** practices,
44:13 bear the shame of their **d** practices.
Mal 2:11 A **d** thing has been committed in
Lk 16:15 among men is **d** in God's sight.
Tit 1:16 They are **d**, disobedient and unfit
1Pe 4: 3 orgies, carousing and **d** idolatry.
Rev 18: 2 haunt for every unclean and **d** bird.

Detested (Detest)

Zec 11: 8 flock **d** me, and I grew weary of

Detests (Detest)

Dt 22: 5 LORD your God **d** anyone who does this.
23:18 the LORD your God **d** them both.
25:16 For the LORD your God **d** anyone who
Pr 3:32 for the LORD **d** a perverse man but
11:20 The LORD **d** men of perverse heart but
12:22 The LORD **d** lying lips, but he
15: 8 The LORD **d** the sacrifice of the
15: 9 The LORD **d** the way of the wicked but
15:26 The LORD **d** the thoughts of the
16: 5 The LORD **d** all the proud of heart.
17:15 the innocent—the LORD **d** them both.
20:10 measures—the LORD **d** them both.
20:23 The LORD **d** differing weights, and

Dethroned

2Ch 36: 3 The king of Egypt **d** him in Jerusalem

Detriment (Deter)

Ezr 4:22 to the **d** of the royal interests?

Deuel

Nu 1:14 from Gad, Eliasaph son of **D**;
2:14 people of Gad is Eliasaph son of **D**.
7:42 On the sixth day Eliasaph son of **D**,
7:47 the offering of Eliasaph son of **D**.
10:20 Eliasaph son of **D** was over the

Devastate (Devastated, Devastation)

Jos 22:33 **d** the country where the Reubenites
Job 12:15 he lets them loose, they **d** the land.
Isa 24: 1 to lay waste the earth and **d** it;
Jer 19: 8 I will **d** this city and make it an
51: 2 to winnow her and to **d** her land;
Hos 11: 9 nor will I turn and **d** Ephraim.

Devastated (Devastate)

Jdg 11:33 He **d** twenty towns from Aroer to the
Job 16: 7 you have **d** my entire household.
Ps 78:45 them, and frogs that **d** them.
Isa 61: 4 ruins and restore the places long **d**;
61: 4 that have been **d** for generations.
Jer 4:30 What are you doing, O **d** one?
Eze 6: 6 altars will be laid waste and **d**,
19: 7 strongholds and **d** their towns.
29:12 of Egypt desolate among **d** lands,
Hos 10:14 that all your fortresses will be **d**
10:14 **d** Beth Arbel on the day of battle,

Devastation (Devastate)

1Sa 5: 6 he brought **d** upon them and afflicted
Da 8:24 He will cause astounding **d** and will

Developed (Develops)

Eze 16: 7 You grew up and **d** and became the
Jn 3:25 An argument **d** between some of John's

Develops (Developed)

Jas 1: 3 of your faith **d** perseverance.

Deviate

2Ch 8:15 They did not **d** from the king's

Devices (Devise)

Ps 81:12 hearts to follow their own **d**.

Devil (Devil's)

Mt 4: 1 the desert to be tempted by the **d**.
4: 5 the **d** took him to the holy city and
4: 8 Again, the **d** took him to a very high
4:11 the **d** left him, and angels came and
13:39 the enemy who sows them is the **d**.
25:41 prepared for the **d** and his angels.
Lk 4: 2 forty days he was tempted by the **d**.
4: 3 The **d** said to him, "If you are the
4: 5 The **d** led him up to a high place and
4: 9 The **d** led him to Jerusalem and had
4:13 the **d** had finished all this tempting,
8:12 and then the **d** comes and takes away
Jn 6:70 the Twelve? Yet one of you is a **d**!"
8:44 You belong to your father, the **d**,
13: 2 and the **d** had already prompted Judas
Ac 10:38 who were under the power of the **d**,
13:10 "You are a child of the **d** and an
Eph 4:27 do not give the **d** a foothold.
1Ti 3: 6 under the same judgment as the **d**.
2Ti 2:26 and escape from the trap of the **d**,
Heb 2:14 the power of death—that is, the **d**—
Jas 3:15 is earthly, unspiritual, of the **d**.
4: 7 Resist the **d**, and he will flee from
1Pe 5: 8 Your enemy the **d** prowls around like
1Jn 3: 8 who does what is sinful is of the **d**,
3: 8 because the **d** has been sinning from
3:10 and who the children of the **d** are:
Jude : 9 when he was disputing with the **d**
Rev 2:10 I tell you, the **d** will put some of
12: 9 ancient serpent called the **d**,
12:12 because the **d** has gone down to you!
20: 2 that ancient serpent, who is the **d**,
20:10 the **d**, who deceived them, was thrown

Devil's (Devil)

Eph 6:11 your stand against the **d** schemes.
1Ti 3: 7 into disgrace and into the **d** trap.
1Jn 3: 8 appeared was to destroy the **d** work.

Devious

Pr 2:15 whose paths are crooked and who are **d**
14: 2 he whose ways are **d** despises him.
21: 8 The way of the guilty is **d**, but the

Devise (Devices, Devised, Devises, Devising)

Ps 21:11 against you and **d** wicked schemes,
35:20 but **d** false accusations against
58: 2 No, in your heart you **d** injustice,
119:150 Those who **d** wicked schemes are near,
140: 2 who **d** evil plans in their hearts and
Isa 8:10 **D** your strategy, but it will be
Eze 38:10 mind and you will **d** an evil scheme.

Devised (Devise)

2Sa 14:13 "Why then have you **d** a thing like
Est 8: 3 which he had **d** against the Jews.
8: 5 **d** and wrote to destroy the Jews
9:25 evil scheme Haman had **d** against the
Ps 64: 6 "We have **d** a perfect plan!" Surely
Jer 49:30 he has **d** a plan against you.
Da 11:25 because of the plots **d** against him.
Mt 28:12 met with the elders and **d** a plan,

Devises (Devise)

2Sa 14:14 he **d** ways so that a banished person
Ps 10: 2 who are caught in the schemes he **d**.
Pr 6:18 a heart that **d** wicked schemes, feet

Devising (Devise)

Jer 18:11 for you and **d** a plan against you.

Devote (Devoted, Devotes, Devoting, Devotion, Devout)

1Ch 22:19 Now **d** your heart and soul to seeking
2Ch 31: 4 **d** themselves to the Law of the LORD.
Job 11:13 "Yet if you **d** your heart to him and
Jer 30:21 will **d** himself to be close to me?'
Mic 4:13 You will **d** their ill-gotten gains
1Co 7: 5 that you may **d** yourselves to prayer.
Col 4: 2 **D** yourselves to prayer, being
1Ti 1: 4 nor to **d** themselves to myths and
4:13 Until I come, **d** yourself to the
Tit 3: 8 **d** themselves to doing what is good.
3:14 must learn to **d** themselves to doing

Devoted (Devote)

Lev 27:21 holy, like a field **d** to the LORD;
27:28 everything so **d** is most holy to the
27:29 "No person **d** to destruction may be
Nu 18:14 "Everything in Israel that is **d** to
Jos 6:17 is in it are to be **d** to the LORD.
6:18 keep away from the **d** things, so that
6:21 They **d** the city to the LORD and
7: 1 in regard to the **d** things;
7:11 They have taken some of the **d** things;
7:12 among you is **d** to destruction.
7:13 which is **d** is among you, O Israel.
7:15 He who is caught with the **d** things
22:20 unfaithfully regarding the **d** things,
1Sa 15:21 the best of what was **d** to God, in
1Ki 11: 4 and his heart was not fully **d** to the
15: 3 was not fully **d** to the LORD his God,
1Ch 2: 7 the ban on taking **d** things.
2Ch 17: 6 His heart was **d** to the ways of the
Ezr 7:10 For Ezra had **d** himself to the study
Ne 5:16 Instead, I **d** myself to the work on
Ps 86: 2 Guard my life, for I am **d** to you.
Ecc 1:13 I **d** myself to study and to explore
Eze 11:21 as for those whose hearts are **d** to
20:16 their hearts were **d** to their idols.
44:29 **d** to the LORD will belong to them.
Mt 6:24 **d** to the one and despise the other.
15: 5 from me is a gift **d** to God,'
Mk 7:11 Corban' (that is, a gift **d** to God),
Lk 16:13 **d** to the one and despise the other.
Ac 2:42 They **d** themselves to the apostles'
18: 5 Paul **d** himself exclusively to
Ro 12:10 Be **d** to one another in brotherly
1Co 7:34 Her aim is to be **d** to the Lord in
16:15 and they have **d** themselves to the
2Co 7:12 for yourselves how **d** to us you are.

Devotes (Devote)

Lev 27:28 "But nothing that a man owns and **d**

Devoting (Devote)

1Ti 5:10 **d** herself to all kinds of good deeds.

Devotion (Devote)

2Ki 20: 3 with wholehearted **d** and have done
1Ch 28: 9 and serve him with wholehearted **d**
29: 3 Besides, in my **d** to the temple of my
29:19 **d** to keep your commands,
2Ch 32:32 his acts of **d** are written in the
35:26 of Josiah's reign and his acts of **d**,
Job 6:14 should have the **d** of his friends,
15: 4 you even undermine piety and hinder **d**
Isa 38: 3 with wholehearted **d** and have done
Jer 2: 2 "I remember the **d** of your youth,
Eze 33:31 With their mouths they express **d**,
1Co 7:35 way in undivided **d** to the Lord.
2Co 11: 3 your sincere and pure **d** to Christ.

Devour (Devoured, Devouring, Devours)

Ex 10: 5 They will **d** what little you have
10:12 **d** everything growing in the fields,
Lev 26:38 the land of your enemies will **d** you.
Nu 24: 8 They **d** hostile nations and break
Dt 28:38 little, because locusts will **d** it.
28:51 They will **d** the young of your
32:22 It will **d** the earth and its harvests
2Sa 2:26 "Must the sword **d** for ever? Don't
1Ki 21:23 **d** Jezebel by the wall of Jezreel.'
2Ki 9:10 for Jezebel, dogs will **d** her on the
9:36 Jezreel dogs will **d** Jezebel's flesh.
2Ch 7:13 or command locusts to **d** the land or
Job 20:21 Nothing is left for him to **d**; his
20:26 him and **d** what is left in his tent.
Ps 14: 4 who **d** my people as men eat bread
27: 2 advance against me to **d** my flesh,
53: 4 who **d** my people as men eat bread
Pr 30:14 knives to **d** the poor from the earth,
Isa 9:20 On the right they will **d**, but still
31: 8 sword, not of mortals, will **d** them.
51: 8 the worm will **d** them like wool.
56: 9 come and **d**, all you beasts of the
Jer 5:17 They will **d** your harvests and food,
5:17 **d** your sons and daughters;
5:17 they will **d** your flocks and herds,
5:17 **d** your vines and fig-trees.
8:16 They have come to **d** the land and
12: 9 the wild beasts; bring them to **d**.
12:12 for the sword of the LORD will **d**
15: 3 of the earth to **d** and destroy.
30:16 "But all who **d** you will be devoured;
46:10 The sword will **d** till it is
50:17 The first to **d** him was the king of
Eze 22:25 they **d** people, take treasures and
34:28 nor will wild animals **d** them.
35:12 have been given over to us to **d**."
36:13 "You **d** men and deprive your nation
36:14 therefore you will no longer **d** men
Da 7:23 kingdoms and will **d** the whole earth,
Hos 2:12 and wild animals will **d** them.
5: 7 will **d** them and their fields.
7: 7 hot as an oven; they **d** their rulers.
13: 8 Like a lion I will **d** them; a wild
Am 5: 6 it will **d**, and Bethel will have
Na 2:13 the sword will **d** your young lions.
3:15 There the fire will **d** you; the sword
Hab 1: 8 fly like a vulture swooping to **d**;
3:14 **d** the wretched who were in hiding.
Zec 11: 1 so that fire may **d** your cedars!
Mk 12:40 They **d** widows' houses and for a show
Lk 20:47 They **d** widows' houses and for a show
1Pe 5: 8 lion looking for someone to **d**.
Rev 12: 4 **d** her child the moment it was born.

Devoured (Devour)

Ge 37:20 say that a ferocious animal **d** him.
37:33 Some ferocious animal has **d** him.
Ex 10:15 They **d** all that was left after the
Nu 26:10 died when the fire **d** the 250 men.
Job 31:39 if I have **d** its yield without
Ps 44:11 You gave us up to be **d** like sheep
78:45 He sent swarms of flies that **d** them,
79: 7 for they have **d** Jacob and destroyed
Isa 1:20 rebel, you will be **d** by the sword.
9:12 west have **d** Israel with open mouth.
49:19 those who **d** you will be far away.
Jer 2: 3 all who **d** her were held guilty,
2:30 **d** your prophets like a ravening lion.
10:25 they have **d** Jacob; they have **d** him
30:16 "But all who devour you will be **d**;
50: 7 Whoever found them **d** them; their
51:34 "Nebuchadnezzar king of Babylon has **d**
Eze 7:15 city will be **d** by famine and plague.
19: 3 to tear the prey and he **d** men.
19: 6 to tear the prey and he **d** men.
33:27 give to the wild animals to be **d**,
Da 7: 7 it crushed and **d** its victims and
7:19 **d** its victims and trampled underfoot
Joel 1:19 O LORD, I call, for fire has **d** the
1:20 up and fire has **d** the open pastures.
Am 4: 9 Locusts **d** your fig and olive trees,
7: 4 up the great deep and **d** the land.
Rev 20: 9 came down from heaven and **d** them.

Devouring (Devour)

Dt 9: 3 across ahead of you like a **d** fire.
Isa 29: 6 and tempest and flames of a **d** fire.
Mal 3:11 I will prevent pests from **d** your
Gal 5:15 If you keep on biting and **d** each

Devours (Devour)

Ge 49:27 in the morning he **d** the prey,
Nu 13:32 "The land we explored **d** those
23:24 does not rest till he **d** his prey
Dt 32:42 while my sword **d** flesh: the blood of
2Sa 11:25 the sword **d** one as well as another.
Job 18:13 death's firstborn **d** his limbs.
22:20 destroyed, and fire **d** their wealth.'
Ps 50: 3 not be silent; a fire **d** before him,
Pr 21:20 oil, but a foolish man **d** all he has.
Jer 46:14 for the sword **d** those around you.'
Joel 2: 3 Before them fire **d**, behind them a
Rev 11: 5 their mouths and **d** their enemies.

Devout (Devote)

1Ki 18: 3 Obadiah was a **d** believer in the LORD.
Isa 57: 1 **d** men are taken away, and no-one
Lk 2:25 Simeon, who was righteous and **d**.
Ac 10: 2 He and all his family were **d** and
10: 7 a **d** soldier who was one of his
13:43 many of the Jews and **d** converts to
22:12 He was a **d** observer of the law and

Dew

Ge 27:28 May God give you of heaven's **d** and
27:39 away from the **d** of heaven above.
Ex 16:13 was a layer of **d** around the camp.
16:14 the **d** was gone, thin flakes like
Nu 11: 9 the **d** settled on the camp at night,
Dt 32: 2 rain and my words descend like **d**,
33:13 the precious **d** from heaven above
33:28 new wine, where the heavens drop **d**.
Jdg 6:37 If there is **d** only on the fleece and
6:38 wrung out the **d**—a bowlful of water.
6:39 dry and the ground covered with **d**."
6:40 all the ground was covered with **d**.
2Sa 1:21 may you have neither **d** nor rain, nor
17:12 on him as **d** settles on the ground.
1Ki 17: 1 there will be neither **d** nor rain in
Job 29:19 **d** will lie all night on my branches.
38:28 Who fathers the drops of **d**?
Ps 110: 3 will receive the **d** of your youth.
133: 3 is as if the **d** of Hermon were
Pr 3:20 and the clouds let drop the **d**.
19:12 his favour is like **d** on the grass.
SS 5: 2 My head is drenched with **d**, my hair
Isa 18: 4 cloud of **d** in the heat of harvest."
26:19 Your **d** is like the **d** of the morning;
Da 4:15 be drenched with the **d** of heaven,
4:23 be drenched with the **d** of heaven;
4:25 be drenched with the **d** of heaven.
4:33 was drenched with the **d** of heaven
5:21 was drenched with the **d** of heaven,
Hos 6: 4 like the early **d** that disappears.
13: 3 like the early **d** that disappears,
14: 5 I will be like the **d** to Israel;
Mic 5: 7 many peoples like **d** from the LORD,
Hag 1:10 their **d** and the earth its crops.
Zec 8:12 and the heavens will drop their **d**.

Diadem

Ex 29: 6 attach the sacred **d** to the turban.
39:30 They made the plate, the sacred **d**,
Lev 8: 9 the sacred **d**, on the front of it, as
Isa 62: 3 a royal **d** in the hand of your God.

Diameter

1Ki 7:32 The **d** of each wheel was a cubit and

Diblah

Eze 6:14 the desert to **D**—wherever they live.

Diblaim

Hos 1: 3 he married Gomer daughter of **D**, and

Dibon

Nu 21:30 is destroyed all the way to **D**.
32: 3 "Ataroth, **D**, Jazer, Nimrah, Heshbon,
32:34 The Gadites built up **D**, Ataroth,
Jos 13: 9 whole plateau of Medeba as far as **D**,
13:17 **D**, Bamoth Baal, Beth Baal Meon,
Ne 11:25 in **D** and its settlements, in
Isa 15: 2 **D** goes up to its temple, to its high
Jer 48:18 O inhabitants of the Daughter of **D**,
48:22 to **D**, Nebo and Beth Diblathaim,

Dibon Gad

Nu 33:45 They left Iyim and camped at **D**.
33:46 They left **D** and camped at Almon

Dibri

Lev 24:11 the daughter of **D** the Danite.)

Dictate (Dictated, Dictating, Dictation, Edict)

Jer 36:17 write all this? Did Jeremiah **d** it?"
Mic 7: 3 the powerful **d** what they desire—

Dictated (Dictate)

Jer 36: 4 and while Jeremiah **d** all the words
36: 6 of the LORD that you wrote as I **d**.
36:18 "he **d** all these words to me, and I
36:32 and as Jeremiah **d**, Baruch wrote on

Dictating (Dictate)

Jer 45: 1 the words Jeremiah was then **d**:

Dictation (Dictate)

Jer 36:27 Baruch had written at Jeremiah's **d**,

Didymus

Jn 11:16 Thomas (called **D**) said to the rest
20:24 Now Thomas (called **D**), one of the
21: 2 Simon Peter, Thomas (called **D**),

Die (Dead, Deadened, Deadly, Death, Death's, Deathly, Deaths, Died, Dies, Dying)

Ge 2:17 you eat of it you will surely **d**."
3: 3 must not touch it, or you will **d**.'"
3: 4 "You will not surely **d**," the serpent
19:19 will overtake me, and I'll **d**.
20: 7 sure that you and all yours will **d**."
21:16 thought, "I cannot watch the boy **d**.
25:32 "Look, I am about to **d**," Esau said.
27: 4 give you my blessing before I **d**."
27: 7 presence of the LORD before I **d**.'
30: 1 "Give me children, or I'll **d**!
33:13 one day, all the animals will **d**.
38:11 For he thought, "He may **d** too, just
42: 2 us, so that we may live and not **d**."
42:20 be verified and that you may not **d**.
43: 8 and our children may live and not **d**.
44: 9 is found to have it, he will **d**;
44:22 he leaves him, his father will **d**.'
44:31 that the boy isn't there, he will **d**.
45:28 I will go and see him before I **d**."
46:30 "Now I am ready to **d**, since I have
47:15 Why should we **d** before your eyes?
47:19 seed so that we may live and not **d**,
47:29 the time drew near for Israel to **d**,
48:21 "I am about to **d**, but God will be
50: 5 "I am about to **d**; bury me in the
50:24 to his brothers, "I am about to **d**.
Ex 7:18 The fish in the Nile will **d**, and the
9: 4 to the Israelites will **d**.'"
9:19 out in the field, and they will **d**.'"
10:28 The day you see my face you will **d**."
11: 5 Every firstborn son in Egypt will **d**,
12:33 they said, "we will all **d**!"
14:11 you brought us to the desert to **d**?
14:12 Egyptians than to **d** in the desert!"
17: 3 children and livestock **d** of thirst?"
20:19 have God speak to us or we will **d**."
21:18 does not **d** but is confined to bed,
28:35 he comes out, so that he will not **d**.
28:43 they will not incur guilt and **d**.
30:20 with water so that they will not **d**.
30:21 and feet so that they will not **d**.
Lev 8:35 so that you will not **d**; for that is
10: 6 or you will **d** and the LORD will be
10: 7 the Tent of Meeting or you will **d**,
10: 9 the Tent of Meeting, or you will **d**.
15:31 so they will not **d** in their
16: 2 or else he will **d**, because I appear
16:13 Testimony, so that he will not **d**.
20:20 responsible; they will **d** childless.
21: 1 unclean for any of his people who **d**,
22: 9 become guilty and **d** for treating
Nu 4:15 the holy things or they will **d**.
4:19 that they may live and not **d** when
4:20 even for a moment, or they will **d**."
14:35 in this desert; here they will **d**."
15:35 LORD said to Moses, "The man must **d**.
Nu 16:29 If these men **d** a natural death and
17:10 me, so that they will not **d**."
17:12 "We shall **d**! We are lost, we are
17:13 the tabernacle of the LORD will **d**.
17:13 Are we all going to **d**?"
18: 3 altar, or both they and you will **d**.
18:22 of their sin and will **d**.
18:32 Israelites, and you will not **d**.'"
20: 4 we and our livestock should **d** here?
20:26 to his people; he will **d** there."
21: 5 up out of Egypt to **d** in the desert?
23:10 Let me **d** the death of the righteous,
26:11 The line of Korah, however, did not **d**
26:65 they would surely **d** in the desert,
35:12 may not **d** before he stands trial
35:31 of a murderer, who deserves to **d**.
Dt 4:22 I will **d** in this land; I will not
5:25 now, why should we **d**? This great
5:25 and we will **d** if we hear the voice
18:16 great fire any more, or we will **d**."
19:12 over to the avenger of blood to **d**.
20: 5 or he may **d** in battle and someone
20: 6 or he may **d** in battle and someone
20: 7 or he may **d** in battle and someone
22:22 slept with her and the woman must **d**.
22:25 the man who has done this shall **d**.
24: 7 or sells him, the kidnapper must **d**.
24:16 each is to **d** for his own sin.
31:27 much more will you rebel after I **d**!
32:50 **d** and be gathered to your people,
33: 6 "Let Reuben live and not **d**, nor his
Jdg 6:23 You are not going to **d**."
6:30 He must **d**, because he has broken
13:22 "We are doomed to **d**!" he said to his
15:18 Must I now **d** of thirst and fall into
16:30 "Let me **d** with the Philistines!"
Ru 1:17 Where you **d** I will **d**, and there I
1Sa 2:33 will **d** in the prime of life.
2:34 will both **d** on the same day.
5:12 Those who did not **d** were afflicted
12:19 your servants so that we will not **d**,
14:39 with my son Jonathan, he must **d**.
14:43 And now must I **d**?"
14:44 if you do not **d**, Jonathan."
14:45 "Should Jonathan **d**—he who has
20: 2 "You are not going to **d**! Look, my
20:31 and bring him to me, for he must **d**!"
22:16 the king said, "You shall surely **d**,
26:10 his time will come and he will **d**,
26:16 you and your men deserve to **d**,
2Sa 3:33 Abner have died as the lawless **d**?
11:15 that he will be struck down and **d**."
12: 5 the man who did this deserves to **d**!
12:13 You are not going to **d**.
12:14 the son born to you will **d**."
14:14 cannot be recovered, so we must **d**.
18: 3 Even if half of us **d**, they won't
19:23 said to Shimei, "You shall not **d**.
19:37 that I may **d** in my own town near
1Ki 1:52 if evil is found in him, he will **d**."
2: 1 the time drew near for David to **d**,
2:26 You deserve to **d**, but I will not put
2:30 But he answered, "No, I will **d** here.
2:37 you can be sure you will **d**; your
13:31 "When I **d**, bury me in the grave
14:11 to Jeroboam who **d** in the city,
14:11 feed on those who **d** in the country.
14:12 foot in your city, the boy will **d**.
16: 4 to Baasha who **d** in the city,
16: 4 feed on those who **d** in the country."
17:12 my son, that we may eat it—and **d**."
17:20 with, by causing her son to **d**?"
19: 4 under it and prayed that he might **d**.
20:42 a man I had determined should **d**.
21:24 belonging to Ahab who **d** in the city,
21:24 feed on those who **d** in the country."
2Ki 1: 4 You will certainly **d**!'" So Elijah
1: 6 You will certainly **d**!"'"
1:16 You will certainly **d**!"
7: 3 "Why stay here until we **d**?
7: 4 famine is there, and we will **d**.
7: 4 And if we stay here, we will **d**.
7: 4 if they kill us, then we **d**."
8:10 to me that he will in fact **d**."
14: 6 each is to **d** for his own sins."
20: 1 order, because you are going to **d**;
2Ch 25: 4 each is to **d** for his own sins."
32:11 to let you **d** of hunger and thirst.
Est 9:28 them **d** out among their descendants.
Job 2: 9 to your integrity? Curse God and **d**!"
3:11 "Why did I not perish at birth, and **d**
4:21 up, so that they **d** without wisdom?'
12: 2 people, and wisdom will **d** with you!
13:19 If so, I will be silent and **d**.
14: 8 ground and its stump **d** in the soil,
27: 5 till I **d**, I will not deny my
29:18 'I shall **d** in my own house,
34:20 They **d** in an instant, in the middle
36:12 the sword and **d** without knowledge.
36:14 They **d** in their youth, among male
Ps 37: 2 green plants they will soon **d** away.
41: 5 "When will he **d** and his name perish?
49:10 For all can see that wise men **d**; the
79:11 arm preserve those condemned to **d**.
82: 7 you will **d** like mere men; you will
104:29 they **d** and return to the dust.
105:29 into blood, causing their fish to **d**.
118:17 I will not **d** but live, and will
Pr 5:23 He will **d** for lack of discipline,
10:21 but fools **d** for lack of judgment.
15:10 he who hates correction will **d**.
19:16 is contemptuous of his ways will **d**.
23:13 him with the rod, he will not **d**.
30: 7 O LORD; do not refuse me before I **d**:
Ecc 2:16 the fool, the wise man too must **d**!
3: 2 a time to be born and a time to **d**,
7:17 be a fool—why **d** before your time?
9: 5 For the living know that they will **d**,
Isa 5:13 their men of rank will **d** of hunger
22: 2 the sword, nor did they **d** in battle.
22:13 drink," you say, "for tomorrow we **d**!
22:18 There you will **d** and there your
38: 1 going to **d**; you will not recover."
50: 2 for lack of water and **d** of thirst.
51: 6 and its inhabitants **d** like flies.
51:14 they will not **d** in their dungeon,
59: 5 Whoever eats their eggs will **d**, and
66:24 against me; their worm will not **d**,
Jer 11:21 LORD or you will **d** by our hands'—
11:22 Their young men will **d** by the sword,
16: 4 "They will **d** of deadly diseases.
16: 6 "Both high and low will **d** in this
20: 6 There you will **d** and be buried, you
21: 6 they will **d** of a terrible plague.
21: 9 Whoever stays in this city will **d** by
22:12 He will **d** in the place where they
22:26 was born, and there you both will **d**.
26: 8 seized him and said, "You must **d**!
27:13 Why will you and your people **d** by
28:16 This very year you are going to **d**,
31:30 Instead, everyone will **d** for his own
34: 4 You will not **d** by the sword;
34: 5 you will **d** peacefully. As people
37:20 the secretary, or I shall **d** there."
38: 2 'Whoever stays in this city will **d**
38:24 this conversation, or you may **d**.
38:26 to Jonathan's house to **d** there.'"
42:16 into Egypt, and there you will **d**.
42:17 to settle there will **d** by the sword,
42:22 You will **d** by the sword, famine
44:12 fall by the sword or **d** from famine.
44:12 they will **d** by sword or famine.
Lam 4: 9 who **d** of famine; racked with hunger,
Eze 3:18 'You will surely **d**,' and you do not
3:18 that wicked man will **d** for his sin,
3:19 he will **d** for his sin; but you will
3:20 before him, he will **d**. Since you
3:20 not warn him, he will **d** for his sin.
5:12 A third of your people will **d** of the
6:12 He that is far away will **d** of the
6:12 and is spared will **d** of famine.
7:15 in the country will **d** by the sword,
12:13 not see it, and there he will **d**.
17:16 he shall **d** in Babylon, in the land
18: 4 soul who sins is the one who will **d**.
18:17 He will not **d** for his father's sin;
18:18 his father will **d** for his own sin,
18:20 soul who sins is the one who will **d**.
18:21 he will surely live; he will not **d**.
18:24 sins he has committed, he will **d**.
18:26 and commits sin, he will **d** for it;
18:26 the sin he has committed he will **d**.

Eze 18:28 he will surely live; he will not **d.**
18:31 Why will you **d,** O house of Israel?
28: 8 and you will **d** a violent death in
28:10 You will **d** the death of the
33: 8 'O wicked man, you will surely **d,**'
33: 8 that wicked man will **d** for his sin,
33: 9 he will **d** for his sin, but you will
33:11 Why will you **d,** O house of Israel?'
33:13 he will **d** for the evil he has done.
33:14 'You will surely **d,**' but he then
33:15 he will surely live; he will not **d.**
33:18 and does evil, he will **d** for it.
33:27 and caves will **d** of a plague.
Am 6: 9 left in one house, they too will **d.**
7:11 "'Jeroboam will **d** by the sword, and
7:17 yourself will **d** in a pagan country.
9:10 among my people will **d** by the sword,
Jnh 1:14 let us **d** for taking this man's life.
4: 3 is better for me to **d** than to live."
4: 8 He wanted to **d,** and said, "It would
4: 8 be better for me to **d** than to live."
4: 9 "I am angry enough to **d.**"
Hab 1:12 My God, my Holy One, we will not **d.**
Zec 11: 9 Let the dying **d,** and the perishing
13: 3 'You must **d,** because you have told
Mt 26:35 Peter declared, "Even if I have to **d**
26:52 draw the sword will **d** by the sword.
Mk 9:48 where "'their worm does not **d,** and
14:31 "Even if I have to **d** with you,
Lk 2:26 he would not **d** before he had seen
7: 2 highly, was sick and about to **d.**
13:33 no prophet can **d** outside Jerusalem!
20:36 they can no longer **d;** for they are
Jn 6:50 which a man may eat and not **d.**
8:21 for me, and you will **d** in your sin.
8:24 I told you that you would **d** in your
8:24 be, you will indeed **d** in your sins."
11:16 us also go, that we may **d** with him."
11:26 and believes in me will never **d.**
11:50 better for you that one man **d** for
11:51 Jesus would **d** for the Jewish nation,
12:33 the kind of death he was going to **d.**
18:32 was going to **d** would be fulfilled.
19: 7 and according to that law he must **d,**
21:23 that this disciple would not **d.**
21:23 that he would not **d;** he only said,
Ac 7:19 newborn babies so that they would **d.**
21:13 but also to **d** in Jerusalem for the
25:11 death, I do not refuse to **d.**
Ro 5: 7 Very rarely will anyone **d** for a
5: 7 someone might possibly dare to **d.**
6: 9 he cannot **d** again; death no longer
8:13 to the sinful nature, you will **d;**
14: 8 and if we **d,** we **d** to the Lord.
14: 8 we live or **d,** we belong to the Lord.
1Co 4: 9 men condemned to **d** in the arena.
9:15 I would rather **d** than have anyone
15:22 For as in Adam all **d,** so in Christ
15:31 I **d** every day—I mean that, brothers
15:32 eat and drink, for tomorrow we **d.**"
2Co 7: 3 that we would live or **d** with you.
Php 1:21 to live is Christ and to **d** is gain.
Heb 7: 8 the tenth is collected by men who **d;**
9:27 Just as man is destined to **d** once,
1Pe 2:24 so that we might **d** to sins and live
Rev 3: 2 what remains and is about to **d,**
9: 6 they will long to **d,** but death will
11: 5 who wants to harm them must **d.**
14:13 dead who **d** in the Lord from now on.

Died (Die)

Ge 5: 5 Adam lived 930 years, and then he **d.**
5: 8 Seth lived 912 years, and then he **d.**
5:11 Enosh lived 905 years, and then he **d.**
5:14 Kenan lived 910 years, and then he **d.**
5:17 lived 895 years, and then he **d.**
5:20 Jared lived 962 years, and then he **d.**
5:27 lived 969 years, and then he **d.**
5:31 lived 777 years, and then he **d.**
7:22 breath of life in its nostrils **d.**
9:29 Noah lived 950 years, and then he **d.**
11:28 Haran **d** in Ur of the Chaldeans, in
11:32 Terah lived 205 years, and he **d** in
23: 2 She **d** at Kiriath Arba (that is,
25: 8 Abraham breathed his last and **d** at a
25:17 He breathed his last and **d,** and he
26:18 had stopped up after Abraham **d,**
35: 8 Now Deborah, Rebekah's nurse, **d** and
35:19 Rachel **d** and was buried on the way
35:29 he breathed his last and **d** and was
36:33 Bela **d,** Jobab son of Zerah from
36:34 Jobab **d,** Husham from the land of the
36:35 Husham **d,** Hadad son of Bedad, who
36:36 Hadad **d,** Samlah from Masrekah
36:37 Samlah **d,** Shaul from Rehoboth on the
36:38 Shaul **d,** Baal-Hanan son of Acbor
36:39 Baal-Hanan son of Acbor **d,** Hadad
38:12 wife, the daughter of Shua, **d.**
46:12 Onan had **d** in the land of Canaan).
48: 7 to my sorrow Rachel **d** in the land of
50:16 left these instructions before he **d:**
50:26 Joseph **d** at the age of a hundred and
Ex 1: 6 brothers and all that generation **d,**
2:23 long period, the king of Egypt **d.**
7:21 The fish in the Nile **d,** and the
8:13 The frogs **d** in the houses, in the
9: 6 All the livestock of the Egyptians **d,**
9: 6 belonging to the Israelites **d.**
9: 7 the animals of the Israelites had **d.**
16: 3 "If only we had **d** by the LORD's hand
32:28 three thousand of the people **d.**
Lev 10: 2 them, and they **d** before the LORD.
16: 1 who **d** when they approached the LORD.
Nu 11: 2 to the LORD and the fire **d** down.
14: 2 "If only we had **d** in Egypt!
14:37 and **d** of a plague before the LORD.
16:49 14,700 people **d** from the plague, in
16:49 to those who had **d** because of Korah.
19:16 someone who has **d** a natural death,
19:18 someone who has **d** a natural death.
20: 1 There Miriam **d** and was buried.
20: 3 "If only we had **d** when our brothers
20:28 And Aaron **d** there on top of the
20:29 community learned that Aaron had **d,**
21: 6 the people and many Israelites **d.**
25: 9 those who **d** in the plague numbered
26:10 **d** when the fire devoured the 250 men.
26:19 sons of Judah, but they **d** in Canaan.
26:61 Nadab and Abihu **d** when they made an
27: 3 "Our father **d** in the desert. He was
27: 3 **d** for his own sin and left no sons.
33:38 where he **d** on the first day of the
33:39 years old when he **d** on Mount Hor.
Dt 2:16 fighting men among the people had **d,**
10: 6 There Aaron **d** and was buried, and
32:50 just as your brother Aaron **d** on
34: 5 Moses the servant of the LORD **d**
34: 7 and twenty years old when he **d,**
Jos 5: 4 **d** in the desert on the way after
5: 6 age when they left Egypt had **d,**
10:11 and more of them **d** from the
22:20 the only one who **d** for his sin.'"
24:29 **d** at the age of a hundred and ten.
24:33 Eleazar son of Aaron **d** and was
Jdg 1: 7 him to Jerusalem, and he **d** there.
2: 8 **d** at the age of a hundred and ten.
2:19 when the judge **d,** the people
2:21 the nations Joshua left when he **d.**
3:11 years, until Othniel son of Kenaz **d.**
4: 1 After Ehud **d,** the Israelites once
4:21 temple into the ground, and he **d.**
8:32 Gideon son of Joash **d** at a good old
8:33 No sooner had Gideon **d** than the
9:49 a thousand men and women, also **d.**
9:54 servant ran him through, and he **d.**
10: 2 then he **d,** and was buried in Shamir.
10: 5 Jair **d,** he was buried in Kamon.
12: 7 Then Jephthah the Gileadite **d,** and
12:10 Ibzan **d,** and was buried in Bethlehem.
12:12 Elon **d,** and was buried in Aijalon in
12:15 Abdon son of Hillel **d,** and was
16:30 more when he **d** than while he lived.
20: 5 They raped my concubine, and she **d.**
Ru 1: 3 Now Elimelech, Naomi's husband, **d,**
1: 5 both Mahlon and Kilion also **d,** and
1Sa 4:11 two sons, Hophni and Phinehas, **d.**
4:18 His neck was broken and he **d,** for he
15:35 Until the day Samuel **d,** he did not
25: 1 Now Samuel **d,** and all Israel
25:38 the LORD struck Nabal and he **d.**
31: 5 fell on his sword and **d** with him.
1Sa 31: 6 his men **d** together that same day.
31: 7 and that Saul and his sons had **d,**
2Sa 1: 4 Many of them fell and **d.** And Saul
1:15 So he struck him down, and he **d.**
2:23 He fell there and **d** on the spot.
2:23 place where Asahel had fallen and **d.**
3:27 him in the stomach, and he **d.**
3:33 Abner have **d** as the lawless die?
4: 1 heard that Abner had **d** in Hebron,
6: 7 he **d** there beside the ark of God.
10: 1 the king of the Ammonites **d,** and his
10:18 of their army, and he **d** there.
11:17 moreover, Uriah the Hittite **d.**
11:21 so that he **d** in Thebez? Why did you
11:24 wall, and some of the king's men **d.**
12:18 On the seventh day the child **d.**
17:23 So he **d** and was buried in his
18:33 If only I had **d** instead of you—
19:10 to rule over us, has **d** in battle.
20:10 Without being stabbed again, Amasa **d.**
24:15 the people from Dan to Beersheba **d.**
1Ki 2:25 he struck down Adonijah and he **d.**
3:19 "During the night this woman's son **d**
14:17 threshold of the house, the boy **d.**
16:18 palace on fire around him. So he **d,**
16:22 So Tibni **d** and Omri became king.
22:35 the chariot, and that evening he **d.**
22:37 the king **d** and was brought to
2Ki 1:17 he **d,** according to the word of the
3: 5 after Ahab **d,** the king of Moab
4:20 her lap until noon, and then he **d.**
7:17 and he **d,** just as the man of God had
7:20 him in the gateway, and he **d.**
8:15 over the king's face, so that he **d.**
9:27 he escaped to Megiddo and **d** there.
12:21 He **d** and was buried with his fathers
13:14 from the illness from which he **d.**
13:20 Elisha **d** and was buried. Now Moabite
13:24 Hazael king of Aram **d,** and Ben-Hadad
15: 5 with leprosy until the day he **d,**
23:34 him off to Egypt, and there he **d.**
1Ch 1:44 Bela **d,** Jobab son of Zerah from
1:45 Jobab **d,** Husham from the land of the
1:46 Husham **d,** Hadad son of Bedad, who
1:47 Hadad **d,** Samlah from Masrekah
1:48 Samlah **d,** Shaul from Rehoboth on the
1:49 Shaul **d,** Baal-Hanan son of Acbor
1:50 Baal-Hanan **d,** Hadad succeeded him as
1:51 Hadad also **d.** The chiefs of Edom
2:19 Azubah **d,** Caleb married Ephrath, who
2:24 After Hezron **d** in Caleb Ephrathah,
2:30 Seled **d** without children.
2:32 Jether **d** without children.
10: 5 he too fell on his sword and **d.**
10: 6 Saul and his three sons **d,** and all
10: 6 and all his house **d** together.
10: 7 and that Saul and his sons had **d,**
10:13 Saul **d** because he was unfaithful to
13:10 So he **d** there before God.
19: 1 Nahash king of the Ammonites **d,**
23:22 Eleazar **d** without having sons: he
24: 2 Nadab and Abihu **d** before their
29:28 He **d** at a good old age, having
2Ch 13:20 the LORD struck him down and he **d.**
16:13 Asa **d** and rested with his fathers.
18:34 Then at sunset he **d.**
21:19 the disease, and he **d** in great pain.
24:15 **d** at the age of a hundred and thirty.
24:25 So he **d** and was buried in the City
26:21 had leprosy until the day he **d.**
32:33 of Jerusalem honoured him when he **d.**
35:24 him to Jerusalem, where he **d.**
Est 2: 7 when her father and mother **d.**
Job 10:18 I wish I had **d** before any eye saw me.
42:17 he **d,** old and full of years.
Ps 118:12 but they **d** out as quickly as burning
Ecc 4: 2 who had already **d,** are happier than
Isa 6: 1 In the year that King Uzziah **d,** I
14:28 oracle came in the year King Ahaz **d:**
Jer 28:17 same year, Hananiah the prophet **d.**
Eze 11:13 Pelatiah son of Benaiah **d.**
13:19 killed those who should not have **d**
24:18 and in the evening my wife **d.**
Hos 13: 1 became guilty of Baal worship and **d.**
Jnh 4:10 sprang up overnight and **d** overnight.
Mt 2:19 After Herod **d,** an angel of the Lord

Mt 8:32 into the lake and **d** in the water.
9:18 and said, "My daughter has just **d**.
14:32 into the boat, the wind **d** down.
22:25 The first one married and **d**, and
22:27 Finally, the woman **d**.
27:52 who had **d** were raised to life.
Mk 4:39 Then the wind **d** down and it was
6:51 boat with them, and the wind **d** down.
12:20 and **d** without leaving any children.
12:21 but he also **d**, leaving no child.
12:22 Last of all, the woman **d** too.
15:39 heard his cry and saw how he **d**, he
15:44 he asked him if Jesus had already **d**.
Lk 13: 4 Or those eighteen who **d** when the
16:22 "The time came when the beggar **d** and
16:22 The rich man also **d** and was buried.
20:29 one married a woman and **d** childless.
20:31 the seven **d**, leaving no children.
20:32 Finally, the woman **d** too.
Jn 6:49 the manna in the desert, yet they **d**.
6:58 Your forefathers ate manna and **d**,
8:52 Abraham **d** and so did the prophets,
8:53 He **d**, and so did the prophets.
11:21 here, my brother would not have **d**.
11:32 here, my brother would not have **d**."
18:14 be good if one man **d** for the people.
Ac 2:29 patriarch David **d** and was buried,
5: 5 heard this, he fell down and **d**.
5:10 she fell down at his feet and **d**.
7:15 Egypt, where he and our fathers **d**.
9:37 About that time she became sick and **d**
12:23 and he was eaten by worms and **d**.
Ro 5: 6 powerless, Christ **d** for the ungodly.
5: 8 were still sinners, Christ **d** for us.
5:15 For if the many **d** by the trespass of
6: 2 By no means! We **d** to sin; how can we
6: 7 anyone who has **d** has been freed from
6: 8 Now if we **d** with Christ, we believe
6:10 The death he **d**, he **d** to sin once for
7: 4 So, my brothers, you also **d** to the
7: 9 came, sin sprang to life and I **d**.
8:34 Christ Jesus, who **d**—more than that
14: 9 For this very reason, Christ **d** and
14:15 your brother for whom Christ **d**.
1Co 8:11 this weak brother, for whom Christ **d**,
10: 8 day twenty-three thousand of them **d**.
15: 3 that Christ **d** for our sins according
2Co 5:14 one **d** for all, and therefore all **d**.
5:15 he **d** for all, that those who live
5:15 who **d** for them and was raised again.
Gal 2:19 For through the law I **d** to the law
2:21 the law, Christ **d** for nothing!"
Php 2:27 Indeed he was ill, and almost **d**. But
2:30 he almost **d** for the work of Christ,
Col 2:20 Since you **d** with Christ to the basic
3: 3 For you **d**, and your life is now
1Th 4:14 We believe that Jesus **d** and rose
5:10 He **d** for us so that, whether we are
2Ti 2:11 If we **d** with him, we will also live
Heb 9:15 now that he has **d** as a ransom to set
9:17 in force only when somebody has **d**;
10:28 **d** without mercy on the testimony of
11:13 still living by faith when they **d**.
1Pe 3:18 For Christ **d** for sins once for all,
2Pe 3: 4 Ever since our fathers **d**, everything
Rev 2: 8 Last, who **d** and came to life again.
8: 9 the living creatures in the sea **d**,
8:11 and many people **d** from the waters
16: 3 and every living thing in the sea **d**.

Dies (Die)

Ge 27:10 give you his blessing before he **d**."
Ex 21:20 and the slave **d** as a direct result,
21:35 the bull of another and it **d**,
22: 2 in and is struck so that he **d**,
22:10 it **d** or is injured or is taken away
22:14 or **d** while the owner is not present,
Lev 11:32 one of them **d** and falls on something,
11:39 that you are allowed to eat **d**,
Nu 6: 7 or mother or brother or sister **d**,
6: 9 "'If someone **d** suddenly in his
19:14 applies when a person **d** in a tent:
27: 8 "Say to the Israelites, 'If a man **d**
35:16 with an iron object so that he **d**,
35:17 and he strikes someone so that he **d**,
Nu 35:18 and he hits someone so that he **d**, he
35:20 at him intentionally so that he **d**
35:21 hits him with his fist so that he **d**,
35:23 and he **d**, then since he was not his
Dt 24: 3 her from his house, or if he **d**,
25: 5 and one of them **d** without a son,
Job 14:10 man **d** and is laid low; he breathes
14:14 If a man **d**, will he live again? All
21:23 One man **d** in full vigour, completely
21:25 Another man **d** in bitterness of soul,
Ps 49:17 take nothing with him when he **d**,
Pr 11: 7 a wicked man **d**, his hope perishes;
26:20 without gossip a quarrel **d** down.
Ecc 3:19 them both: As one **d**, so **d** the other.
Isa 65:20 he who **d** at a hundred will be
Jer 38:10 out of the cistern before he **d**."
Mt 22:24 "Moses told us that if a man **d**
Mk 12:19 **d** and leaves a wife but no children,
Lk 20:28 **d** and leaves a wife but no children,
Jn 4:49 "Sir, come down before my child **d**.
11:25 in me will live, even though he **d**;
12:24 wheat falls to the ground and **d**,
12:24 But if it **d**, it produces many seeds.
Ro 7: 2 but if her husband **d**, she is
7: 3 But if her husband **d**, she is
14: 7 and none of us **d** to himself alone.
1Co 7:39 But if her husband **d**, she is free to
15:36 does not come to life unless it **d**.

Difference (Different)

2Sa 19:35 Can I tell the **d** between what is
2Ch 12: 8 so that they may learn the **d** between
Eze 22:26 they teach that there is no **d**
44:23 They are to teach my people the **d**
Ro 3:22 to all who believe. There is no **d**,
10:12 For there is no **d** between Jew and
Gal 2: 6 they were makes no **d** to me;

Differences (Different)

1Co 11:19 No doubt there have to be **d** among

Different (Difference, Differences, Differently, Differing, Differs)

Lev 19:19 "'Do not mate **d** kinds of animals.
Nu 14:24 my servant Caleb has a **d** spirit and
1Sa 10: 6 you will be changed into a **d** person.
Est 1: 7 each one **d** from the other, and the
3: 8 **d** from those of all other people
Da 7: 3 Four great beasts, each **d** from the
7: 7 It was **d** from all the former beasts,
7:19 which was **d** from all the others and
7:23 It will be **d** from all the other
7:24 **d** from the earlier ones; he will
11:29 will be **d** from what it was before.
Mk 16:12 Jesus appeared in a **d** form to two
Ro 12: 6 We have **d** gifts, according to the
1Co 4: 7 For who makes you **d** from anyone else?
12: 4 There are **d** kinds of gifts, but the
12: 5 There are **d** kinds of service, but
12: 6 There are **d** kinds of working, but
12:10 to another speaking in **d** kinds of
12:28 speaking in **d** kinds of tongues.
2Co 11: *4 or if you receive a **d** spirit from
11: 4 or a **d** gospel from the one you
Gal 1: 6 and are turning to a **d** gospel—
4: 1 he is no **d** from a slave, although he
Heb 7:13 are said belonged to a **d** tribe,
Jas 2:25 and sent them off in a **d** direction?

Differently (Different)

Ex 8:22 "'But on that day I will deal **d** with
Php 3:15 And if on some point you think **d**,

Differing (Different)

Dt 25:13 Do not have two **d** weights in your
25:14 Do not have two **d** measures in your
Pr 20:10 **D** weights and **d** measures—the LORD
20:23 The LORD detests **d** weights, and

Differs (Different)

1Co 15:41 and star **d** from star in splendour.

Difficult (Difficulties, Difficulty)

Ge 47: 9 My years have been few and **d**, and
Ex 18:22 but have them bring every **d** case to
18:26 The **d** cases they brought to Moses,
Dt 17: 8 that are too **d** for you to judge
30:11 too **d** for you or beyond your reach.
2Ki 2:10 "You have asked a **d** thing," Elijah
Eze 3: 5 of obscure speech and **d** language,
3: 6 of obscure speech and **d** language,
Da 2:11 What the king asks is too **d**. No-one
4: 9 and no mystery is too **d** for you.
5:12 riddles and solve **d** problems.
5:16 and to solve **d** problems. If you can
Ac 15:19 that we should not make it **d** for the

Difficulties (Difficult)

Dt 31:17 Many disasters and **d** will come upon
31:21 many disasters and **d** come upon them,
2Co 12:10 in hardships, in persecutions, in **d**.

Difficulty (Difficult)

Ge 35:16 began to give birth and had great **d**.
35:17 she was having great **d** in childbirth,
Ex 14:25 come off so that they had **d** driving.
Jos 19:47 (But the Danites had **d** taking
Ac 14:18 Even with these words, they had **d**
27: 7 days and had **d** arriving off Cnidus.
27: 8 We moved along the coast with **d** and

Dig (Digging, Digs, Dug, Gravediggers)

Dt 6:11 wells you did not **d**, and vineyards
8: 9 you can **d** copper out of the hills.
23:13 equipment have something to **d** with,
23:13 **d** a hole and cover up your excrement.
Ps 119:85 The arrogant **d** pitfalls for me,
Eze 8: 8 "Son of man, now **d** into the wall."
12: 5 While they watch, **d** through the wall
Am 9: 2 Though they **d** down to the depths of
Lk 13: 8 I'll **d** round it and fertilise it.
16: 3 I'm not strong enough to **d**, and I'm

Digging (Dig)

Mk 2: 4 after **d** through it, lowered the mat

Dignitaries (Dignity)

Ge 50: 7 accompanied him—the **d** of his court
50: 7 his court and all the **d** of Egypt—
Isa 43:28 I will disgrace the **d** of your temple,

Dignity (Dignitaries)

Ex 28: 2 Aaron, to give him **d** and honour.
28:40 sons, to give them **d** and honour.
Job 30:15 my **d** is driven away as by the wind,
Pr 31:25 She is clothed with strength and **d**;

Digs (Dig)

Ex 21:33 "If a man uncovers a pit or **d** one
Ps 7:15 He who **d** a hole and scoops it out
Pr 26:27 If a man **d** a pit, he will fall into
Ecc 10: 8 Whoever **d** a pit may fall into it;

Diklah

Ge 10:27 Hadoram, Uzal, **D**,
1Ch 1:21 Hadoram, Uzal, **D**,

Dilean

Jos 15:38 **D**, Mizpah, Joktheel,

Diligence (Diligent)

Ezr 5: 8 The work is being carried on with **d**
6:12 Let it be carried out with **d**.
6:13 associates carried it out with **d**.
7:21 with **d** whatever Ezra the priest,
7:23 let it be done with **d** for the temple
Heb 6:11 to show this same **d** to the very end,

Diligent (Diligence, Diligently)

2Ch 24:13 The men in charge of the work were **d**,
Pr 10: 4 but **d** hands bring wealth
12:24 **D** hands will rule, but laziness ends
12:27 the **d** man prizes his possessions.

Pr 13: 4 of the **d** are fully satisfied.
21: 5 The plans of the **d** lead to profit as
1Ti 4:15 Be **d** in these matters; give yourself

Diligently (Diligent)
Zec 6:15 if you **d** obey the LORD your God."
Jn 5:39 You **d** study the Scriptures because
Ro 12: 8 let him govern **d**; if it is showing

Dill
Mt 23:23 of your spices—mint, **d** and cummin.

Diluted
Isa 1:22 your choice wine is **d** with water.

Dim
Job 17: 7 My eyes have grown **d** with grief; my
Ps 88: 9 my eyes are **d** with grief. I call to
Ecc 12: 3 looking through the windows grow **d**;
Lam 5:17 of these things our eyes grow **d**

Dimensions
Job 38: 5 Who marked off its **d**? Surely you
Eze 42:11 and width, with similar exits and **d**.

Diminish
Ps 107:38 and he did not let their herds **d**.

Dimnah
Jos 21:35 **D** and Nahalal, together with their

Dimon (Dimon's)
Isa 15: 9 but I will bring still more upon **D**—

Dimon's (Dimon)
Isa 15: 9 **D** waters are full of blood, but I

Dimonah
Jos 15:22 Kinah, **D**, Adadah,

Din
Jer 51:55 he will silence her noisy **d**.

Dinah (Dinah's)
Daughter of Jacob by Leah (Ge 30:21; 46:15). Raped by Shechem; avenged by Simeon and Levi (Ge 34).

Ge 30:21 birth to a daughter and named her **D**.
34: 1 Now **D**, the daughter Leah had borne
34: 3 His heart was drawn to **D** daughter of
34: 5 Jacob heard that his daughter **D** had
34:13 their sister **D** had been defiled,
34:26 took **D** from Shechem's house and
46:15 Paddan Aram, besides his daughter **D**.

Dinah's (Dinah)
Ge 34:11 Shechem said to **D** father and
34:25 Simeon and Levi, **D** brothers, took

Dine (Dined, Dinner)
1Sa 20: 5 and I am supposed to **d** with the king;
Est 7: 1 the king and Haman went to **d** with
Pr 23: 1 you sit to **d** with a ruler, note well
Am 6: 4 You **d** on choice lambs and fattened

Dined (Dine)
1Sa 9:24 And Saul **d** with Samuel that day.

Dinhabah
Ge 36:32 His city was named **D**.
1Ch 1:43 son of Beor, whose city was named **D**.

Dinner (Dine)
Ge 43:16 slaughter an animal and prepare **d**;
Est 5:14 Then go with the king to the **d** and
Mt 9:10 While Jesus was having **d** at
14: 9 of his oaths and his **d** guests, he
22: 4 invited that I have prepared my **d**:
Mk 2:15 While Jesus was having **d** at Levi's
6:22 she pleased Herod and his **d** guests.
6:26 of his oaths and his **d** guests, he
Lk 7:36 invited Jesus to have **d** with him,
14:12 "When you give a luncheon or **d**, do
Jn 12: 2 Here a **d** was given in Jesus' honour.

Dionysius
Ac 17:34 Among them was **D**, a member of the

Diotrephes
3Jn : 9 I wrote to the church, but **D**, who

Dip (Dipped, Dipping, Dips)
Ex 12:22 Take a bunch of hyssop, **d** it into
Lev 4: 6 He is to **d** his finger into the blood
4:17 He shall **d** his finger into the blood
14: 6 then to take the live bird and **d** it,
14:16 **d** his right forefinger into the oil
14:51 **d** them into the blood of the dead
Nu 19:18 **d** it in the water and sprinkle the
Ru 2:14 Have some bread and **d** it in the wine
Lk 16:24 send Lazarus to **d** the tip of his

Dipped (Dip)
Ge 37:31 a goat and **d** the robe in the blood.
Lev 9: 9 and he **d** his finger into the blood
1Sa 14:27 hand and **d** it into the honeycomb.
2Ki 5:14 he went down and **d** himself in the
Mt 26:23 "The one who has **d** his hand into
Jn 13:26 bread when I have **d** it in the dish.
Rev 19:13 He is dressed in a robe **d** in blood,

Dipping (Dip)
Jn 13:26 Then, **d** the piece of bread, he gave

Dips (Dip)
Mk 14:20 who **d** bread into the bowl with me.

Dire
Dt 28:48 in nakedness and **d** poverty, you will
Isa 21: 2 A **d** vision has been shown to me: The

Direct (Directed, Directing, Direction, Directions, Directives, Directly, Director, Directors, Directs)
Ge 18:19 so that he will **d** his children and
46:26 those who were his **d** descendants,
Ex 21:20 as a **d** result, he must be punished,
Dt 17:10 to do everything they **d** you to do.
2Ch 34:12 Over them to **d** them were Jahath and
Ps 119:35 **D** me in the path of your commands,
119:133 **D** my footsteps according to your
Jer 10:23 it is not for man to **d** his steps.
Eze 23:25 I will **d** my jealous anger against
26: 9 **d** the blows of his battering-rams
2Th 3: 5 May the Lord **d** your hearts into
1Ti 5:17 The elders who **d** the affairs of the

Directed (Direct)
Ge 24:51 master's son, as the LORD has **d**."
45:19 "You are also **d** to tell them, 'Do
47:11 district of Rameses, as Pharaoh **d**.
50: 2 Joseph **d** the physicians in his
Nu 16:40 the LORD **d** him through Moses. This
Dt 2: 1 the Red Sea, as the LORD had **d** me.
4:14 the LORD **d** me at that time to teach
6: 1 laws the LORD your God **d** me to teach
Jos 4:10 people, just as Moses had **d** Joshua.
4:12 the Israelites, as Moses had **d** them.
11: 9 Joshua did to them as the LORD had **d**:
11:23 just as the LORD had **d** Moses, and he
1Sa 17:20 up and set out, as Jesse had **d**.
1Ki 5:16 the project and **d** the workmen.
21:11 as Jezebel **d** in the letters she had
Job 21: 4 "Is my complaint **d** to man? Why
Pr 20:24 A man's steps are **d** by the LORD. How
Isa 10:25 will be **d** to their destruction."
Jer 13: 2 I bought a belt, as the LORD **d**, and
Mt 14:19 he **d** the people to sit down on the
26:19 the disciples did as Jesus had **d**
Mk 6:39 Jesus **d** them to have all the people
Ac 7:44 It had been made as God **d** Moses,
22:24 He **d** that he be flogged and
Tit 1: 5 elders in every town, as I **d** you.

Directing (Direct)
1Ch 15:21 harps, **d** according to sheminith.

Direction (Direct)
Ex 38:21 under the **d** of Ithamar son of Aaron,
Nu 4:27 under the **d** of Aaron and his sons.
4:28 under the **d** of Ithamar son of Aaron,
4:33 under the **d** of Ithamar son of Aaron,
7: 8 They were all under the **d** of Ithamar
11:31 as far as a day's walk in any **d**.
Dt 28: 7 come at you from one **d** but flee
28:25 You will come at them from one **d** but
Jos 8:20 had no chance to escape in any **d**,
Jdg 9:37 the **d** of the soothsayers' tree."
20:42 Israelites in the **d** of the desert,
2Sa 13:34 "I see men in the **d** of Horonaim, on
1Ki 18: 6 in one **d** and Obadiah in another.
2Ki 3:20 flowing from the **d** of Edom!
2Ch 26:11 the officer under the **d** of Hananiah,
34: 4 Under his **d** the altars of the Baals
Ezr 5: 8 making rapid progress under their **d**.
Ne 12:38 choir proceeded in the opposite **d**.
12:42 sang under the **d** of Jezrahiah.
Job 37:12 At his **d** they swirl around over the
Pr 7: 8 walking along in the **d** of her
Eze 9: 2 coming from the **d** of the upper gate
10:11 The cherubim went in whatever **d** the
Jas 2:25 and sent them off in a different **d**?

Directions (Direct)
Ge 46:28 of him to Joseph to get **d** to Goshen.
1Sa 14:16 saw the army melting away in all **d**.
2Ch 35: 4 according to the **d** written by David
Eze 1:17 of the four **d** the creatures faced;
10:11 of the four **d** the cherubim faced;
Ac 21:30 the people came running from all **d**.
1Co 11:34 when I come I will give further **d**.

Directives (Direct)
1Co 11:17 In the following **d** I have no praise

Directly (Direct)
Ge 30:38 so that they would be **d** in front of
Ex 14: 2 by the sea, **d** opposite Baal Zephon.
Lev 25:12 what is taken **d** from the fields.
Ne 12:37 they continued **d** up the steps of
Pr 4:25 ahead, fix your gaze **d** before you.
Lk 20:17 Jesus looked **d** at them and asked,
Ac 14: 9 Paul looked **d** at him, saw that he

Director (Direct)
Ne 11:17 the **d** who led in thanksgiving and
Ps 4: T For the **d** of music. With stringed
5: T For the **d** of music. For flutes.
6: T For the **d** of music. With stringed
8: T For the **d** of music. According to
9: T For the **d** of music. To ⌊the tune of
11: T For the **d** of music. Of David.
12: T For the **d** of music. According to
13: T For the **d** of music. A psalm
14: T For the **d** of music. Of David.
18: T For the **d** of music. Of David the
19: T For the **d** of music. A psalm
20: T For the **d** of music. A psalm
21: T For the **d** of music. A psalm
22: T For the **d** of music. To the tune of
31: T For the **d** of music. A psalm
36: T For the **d** of music. Of David the
39: T For the **d** of music. For Jeduthun.
40: T For the **d** of music. Of David.
41: T For the **d** of music. A psalm
42: T For the **d** of music. A maskil of
44: T For the **d** of music. Of the Sons of
45: T For the **d** of music. To ⌊the tune of
46: T For the **d** of music. Of the Sons of
47: T For the **d** of music. Of the Sons of
49: T For the **d** of music. Of the Sons of
51: T For the **d** of music. A psalm of David.
52: T For the **d** of music. A maskil
53: T For the **d** of music. According to
54: T For the **d** of music. With stringed
55: T For the **d** of music. With stringed
56: T For the **d** of music. To ⌊the tune of
57: T For the **d** of music. ⌊To the tune of

Ps 58: T For the **d** of music. ⌊To the tune of
59: T For the **d** of music. ⌊To the tune of
60: T For the **d** of music. To ⌊the tune of
61: T For the **d** of music. With stringed
62: T For the **d** of music. For Jeduthun.
64: T For the **d** of music. A psalm
65: T For the **d** of music. A psalm
66: T For the **d** of music. A song.
67: T For the **d** of music. With stringed
68: T For the **d** of music. Of David.
69: T For the **d** of music. To ⌊the tune of
70: T For the **d** of music. Of David.
75: T For the **d** of music. ⌊To the tune of
76: T For the **d** of music. With stringed
77: T For the **d** of music. For Jeduthun.
80: T For the **d** of music. To ⌊the tune of
81: T For the **d** of music. According to
84: T For the **d** of music. According to
85: T For the **d** of music. Of the Sons of
88: T For the **d** of music. According to
109: T For the **d** of music. Of David.
139: T For the **d** of music. Of David.
140: T For the **d** of music. A psalm
Hab 3:19 For the **d** of music. On my stringed
Ro 16:23 Erastus, who is the city's **d** of

Directors (Direct)
Ne 12:46 there had been **d** for the singers and

Directs (Direct)
Jdg 20: 9 We'll go up against it as the lot **d**.
Ps 42: 8 By day the LORD **d** his love, at night
Pr 21: 1 he **d** it like a watercourse wherever
Isa 48:17 who **d** you in the way you should go.

Dirge
Mt 11:17 we sang a **d**, and you did not mourn.'
Lk 7:32 we sang a **d**, and you did not cry.'

Dirt
2Sa 16:13 at him and showering him with **d**.
Zec 9: 3 and gold like the **d** of the streets.
1Pe 3:21 not the removal of **d** from the body

Disabled
Jn 5: 3 Here a great number of **d** people used
Heb 12:13 may not be **d**, but rather healed.

Disagreed (Disagreement)
Ac 28:25 They **d** among themselves and began to

Disagreement (Disagree)
Ac 15:39 They had such a sharp **d** that they

Disappear (Disappeared, Disappears)
Nu 27: 4 Why should our father's name **d** from
Ru 4:10 so that his name will not **d** from
Isa 2:18 the idols will totally **d**.
17: 3 The fortified city will **d** from
29:20 the mockers will **d**, and all who have
Mt 5:18 until heaven and earth **d**, not the
5:18 will by any means **d** from the Law
Lk 16:17 is easier for heaven and earth to **d**
Heb 8:13 is obsolete and ageing will soon **d**.
2Pe 3:10 The heavens will **d** with a roar; the

Disappeared (Disappear)
Jdg 6:21 And the angel of the LORD **d**.
1Ki 20:40 was busy here and there, the man **d**.
Lk 24:31 him, and he **d** from their sight.

Disappears (Disappear)
Job 14:11 water **d** from the sea or a river bed
Hos 6: 4 mist, like the early dew that **d**.
13: 3 like the early dew that **d**, like
1Co 13:10 perfection comes, the imperfect **d**.

Disappoint (Disappointed)
Ro 5: 5 hope does not **d** us, because God has

Disappointed (Disappoint)
Job 6:20 they arrive there, only to be **d**.
Ps 22: 5 in you they trusted and were not **d**.
Isa 49:23 those who hope in me will not be **d**."
Jer 2:36 **d** by Egypt as you were by Assyria.

Disapprove
Pr 24:18 or the LORD will see and **d** and turn

Disarmed (Disarms)
Col 2:15 having **d** the powers and authorities,

Disarms (Disarmed)
Job 12:21 contempt on nobles and **d** the mighty

Disaster (Disasters, Disastrous)
Ge 19:19 **d** will overtake me, and I'll die.
Ex 32:12 and do not bring **d** on your people.
32:14 his people the **d** he had threatened.
Dt 28:61 every kind of sickness and **d** not
29:19 This will bring **d** on the watered
29:21 from all the tribes of Israel for **d**,
31:29 In days to come, **d** will fall upon
32:35 their day of **d** is near and their
Jos 24:20 he will turn and bring **d** on you and
Jdg 20:34 did not realise how near **d** was.
20:41 realised that **d** had come upon them.
1Sa 6: 9 LORD has brought this great **d** on us.
25:17 because **d** is hanging over our master
2Sa 17:14 in order to bring **d** on Absalom.
22:19 They confronted me in the day of my **d**
1Ki 5: 4 and there is no adversary or **d**.
8:37 whatever **d** or disease may come,
9: 9 LORD brought all this **d** on them.'"
14:10 to bring **d** on the house of Jeroboam.
21:21 'I am going to bring **d** on you.
21:29 I will not bring this **d** in his day,
22:23 The LORD has decreed **d** for you."
2Ki 6:33 "This **d** is from the LORD. Why should
21:12 going to bring such **d** on Jerusalem
22:16 **d** on this place and its people,
22:20 Your eyes will not see all the **d** I
2Ch 6:28 whatever **d** or disease may come,
7:22 why he brought all this **d** on them.'"
18:22 The LORD has decreed **d** for you."
34:24 I am going to bring **d** on this place
34:28 Your eyes will not see all the **d** I
Est 8: 6 For how can I bear to see **d** fall on
Job 18:12 **d** is ready for him when he falls.
31: 3 **d** for those who do wrong?
Ps 18:18 confronted me in the day of my **d**
37:19 In times of **d** they will not wither;
57: 1 your wings until the **d** has passed.
91:10 no **d** will come near your tent.
140:11 may **d** hunt down men of violence.
Pr 1:26 I in turn will laugh at your **d**;
1:27 when **d** sweeps over you like a
3:25 Have no fear of sudden **d** or of the
6:15 Therefore **d** will overtake him in an
16: 4 even the wicked for a day of **d**.
17: 5 over **d** will not go unpunished.
27:10 brother's house when **d** strikes you
Ecc 11: 2 know what **d** may come upon the land.
Isa 3: 9 They have brought **d** upon themselves.
3:11 Woe to the wicked! **D** is upon them!
10: 3 reckoning, when **d** comes from afar?
31: 2 Yet he too is wise and can bring **d**;
45: 7 I bring prosperity and create **d**;
47:11 **D** will come upon you, and you will
Jer 1:14 "From the north **d** will be poured out
2: 3 held guilty, and **d** overtook them,'"
4: 6 For I am bringing **d** from the north,
4:15 **d** from the hills of Ephraim.
4:20 **D** follows **d**; the whole land lies in
6: 1 For **d** looms out of the north,
6:19 Hear, O earth: I am bringing **d** on
11:11 on them a **d** they cannot escape.
11:12 not help them at all when **d** strikes.
11:17 who planted you, has decreed **d** for
11:23 because I will bring **d** on the men of
15:11 in times of **d** and times of distress.
16:10 decreed such a great **d** against us?
17:17 you are my refuge in the day of **d**.
17:18 Bring on them the day of **d**; destroy
Jer 18: 8 inflict on it the **d** I had planned.
18:11 Look! I am preparing a **d** for you and
18:17 not my face in the day of their **d**."
19: 3 Listen! I am going to bring a **d** on
19:15 every **d** I pronounced against them,
23:12 I will bring **d** on them in the year
25:29 See, I am beginning to bring **d** on
25:32 "Look! **D** is spreading from nation to
26: 3 not bring on them the **d** I was
26:13 the **d** he has pronounced against you.
26:19 so that he did not bring the **d** he
26:19 to bring a terrible **d** on ourselves!"
28: 8 **d** and plague against many countries
31:28 to overthrow, destroy and bring **d**,
32:23 So you brought all this **d** upon them.
35:17 every **d** I pronounced against them.
36: 3 every **d** I plan to inflict on them,
36:31 every **d** I pronounced against them,
39:16 this city through **d**, not prosperity.
40: 2 God decreed this **d** for this place.
42:10 over the **d** I have inflicted on you.
42:17 escape the **d** I will bring on them.'
44: 2 says: You saw the great **d** I brought
44: 7 says: Why bring such great **d** on
44:11 **d** on you and to destroy all Judah.
44:23 **d** has come upon you, as you now see."
45: 5 For I will bring **d** on all people,
46:21 for the day of **d** is coming upon them,
49: 8 **d** on Esau at the time I punish him.
49:32 bring **d** on them from every side,"
49:37 **d** upon them, even my fierce anger,"
51: 2 on every side in the day of her **d**.
51:64 of the **d** I will bring upon her.
Eze 7: 5 says: **D**! An unheard-of **d** is coming.
14:22 the **d** I have brought upon Jerusalem
14:22 every **d** I have brought upon it.
Da 9:12 rulers by bringing upon us great **d**.
9:13 all this **d** has come upon us, yet we
9:14 not hesitate to bring the **d** upon us,
Am 3: 6 When **d** comes to a city, has not the
9:10 '**D** will not overtake or meet us.'
Ob : 5 what a **d** awaits you—would they not
:13 of my people in the day of their **d**,
:13 calamity in the day of their **d**,
:13 their wealth in the day of their **d**.
Mic 1:12 because **d** has come from the LORD
2: 3 "I am planning **d** against this people,
3:11 among us? No **d** will come upon us."
Zec 8:14 "Just as I had determined to bring **d**

Disasters (Disaster)
Dt 28:59 harsh and prolonged **d**, and severe
31:17 Many **d** and difficulties will come
31:17 'Have not these **d** come upon us
31:21 many **d** and difficulties come upon
Jer 51:60 the **d** that would come upon Babylon

Disastrous (Disaster)
Ac 27:10 that our voyage is going to be **d**

Discard (Discarded)
Ps 119:119 All the wicked of the earth you **d**

Discarded (Discard)
Ps 102:26 will change them and they will be **d**.

Discern (Discerned, Discerning, Discernment)
Dt 32:29 this and **d** what their end will be!
Job 6:30 my lips? Can my mouth not **d** malice?
34: 4 Let us **d** for ourselves what is right;
Ps 19:12 Who can **d** his errors? Forgive my
139: 3 You **d** my going out and my lying down;
Php 1:10 that you may be able to **d** what is

Discerned (Discern)
1Co 2:14 because they are spiritually **d**.

Discerning (Discern)
Ge 41:33 let Pharaoh look for a **d** and wise
41:39 is no-one so **d** and wise as you.
2Sa 14:17 an angel of God in **d** good and evil.
1Ki 3: 9 give your servant a **d** heart to
3:12 I will give you a wise and **d** heart,

Pr 1: 5 and let the **d** get guidance—
8: 9 To the **d** all of them are right; they
10:13 Wisdom is found on the lips of the **d**,
14: 6 but knowledge comes easily to the **d**.
14:33 Wisdom reposes in the heart of the **d**
15:14 The **d** heart seeks knowledge, but the
16:21 The wise in heart are called **d**, and
17:24 A **d** man keeps wisdom in view, but a
17:28 and **d** if he holds his tongue.
18:15 heart of the **d** acquires knowledge;
19:25 rebuke a **d** man, and he will gain
28: 7 He who keeps the law is a **d** son, but
Da 2:21 to the wise and knowledge to the **d**.
Hos 14: 9 Who is **d**? He will understand them.

Discernment (Discern)

Dt 32:28 sense, there is no **d** in them.
1Ki 3:11 but for **d** in administering justice,
2Ch 2:12 endowed with intelligence and **d**, who
Job 12:20 and takes away the **d** of elders.
Ps 119:125 I am your servant; give me **d** that I
Pr 3:21 My son, preserve sound judgment and **d**
17:10 A rebuke impresses a man of **d** more
28:11 poor man who has **d** sees through him.

Discharge (Discharged, Discharging)

Lev 15: 2 has a bodily **d**, the **d** is unclean.
15: 3 his **d** will bring about uncleanness:
15: 4 "Any bed the man with a **d** lies on
15: 6 that the man with a **d** sat on must
15: 7 "Whoever touches the man who has a **d**
15: 8 "If the man with the **d** spits on
15:11 "Anyone the man with a **d** touches
15:13 "When a man is cleansed from his **d**,
15:15 LORD for the man because of his **d**.
15:25 "When a woman has a **d** of blood for
15:25 **d** that continues beyond her period,
15:25 unclean as long as she has the **d**,
15:26 she lies on while her **d** continues
15:28 "When she is cleansed from her **d**,
15:30 LORD for the uncleanness of her **d**.
15:32 the regulations for a man with a **d**,
15:33 for a man or a woman with a **d**, and
22: 4 skin disease or a bodily **d**,
Nu 5: 2 skin disease or a **d** of any kind,
2Ti 4: 5 **d** all the duties of your ministry.

Discharged (Discharge)

Ecc 8: 8 As no-one is **d** in time of war, so

Discharging (Discharge)

1Co 9:17 simply **d** the trust committed to me.

Disciple (Disciples, Disciples')

Isa 19:11 wise men, a **d** of the ancient kings"?
Mt 8:21 Another **d** said to him, "Lord, first
10:42 little ones because he is my **d**,
27:57 who had himself become a **d** of Jesus.
Lk 14:26 his own life—he cannot be my **d**.
14:27 cross and follow me cannot be my **d**.
14:33 up everything he has cannot be my **d**.
Jn 9:28 and said "You are this fellow's **d**!
13:23 One of them, the **d** whom Jesus loved,
13:24 Simon Peter motioned to this **d** and
18:15 Simon Peter and another **d** were
18:15 this **d** was known to the high priest,
18:16 The other **d**, who was known to the
19:26 and the **d** whom he loved standing
19:27 to the **d**, "Here is your mother."
19:27 on, this **d** took her into his home.
19:38 Now Joseph was a **d** of Jesus, but
20: 2 to Simon Peter and the other **d**,
20: 3 Peter and the other **d** started for
20: 4 but the other **d** outran Peter and
20: 8 Finally the other **d**, who had reached
21: 7 the **d** whom Jesus loved said to Peter,
21:20 Peter turned and saw that the **d** whom
21:23 brothers that this **d** would not die.
21:24 This is the **d** who testifies to these
Ac 9:10 there was a **d** named Ananias.
9:26 believing that he really was a **d**.
9:36 In Joppa there was a **d** named Tabitha
16: 1 where a **d** named Timothy lived, whose

Disciples (Disciple)

Isa 8:16 and seal up the law among my **d**.
Mt 5: 1 and sat down. His **d** came to him,
8:23 the boat and his **d** followed him.
8:25 The **d** went and woke him, saying,
9:10 came and ate with him and his **d**.
9:11 they asked his **d**, "Why does your
9:14 John's **d** came and asked him, "How is
9:14 fast, but your **d** do not fast?"
9:19 and went with him, and so did his **d**.
9:37 he said to his **d**, "The harvest is
10: 1 He called his twelve **d** to him and
11: 1 finished instructing his twelve **d**,
11: 2 what Christ was doing, he sent his **d**
11: 7 John's **d** were leaving, Jesus began
12: 1 His **d** were hungry and began to pick
12: 2 "Look! Your **d** are doing what is
12:49 Pointing to his **d**, he said, "Here
13:10 The **d** came to him and asked, "Why do
13:36 His **d** came to him and said, "Explain
14:12 John's **d** came and took his body and
14:15 evening approached, the **d** came to
14:19 Then he gave them to the **d**,
14:19 and the **d** gave them to the people.
14:20 the **d** picked up twelve basketfuls
14:22 Immediately Jesus made the **d** get
14:26 the **d** saw him walking on the lake,
15: 2 "Why do your **d** break the tradition
15:12 the **d** came to him and asked, "Do you
15:23 So his **d** came to him and urged him
15:32 Jesus called his **d** to him and said,
15:33 His **d** answered, "Where could we get
15:36 broke them and gave them to the **d**,
15:37 Afterwards the **d** picked up seven
16: 5 the **d** forgot to take bread.
16:13 he asked his **d**, "Who do people say
16:20 he warned his **d** not to tell anyone
16:21 Jesus began to explain to his **d**
16:24 Jesus said to his **d**, "If anyone
17: 6 the **d** heard this, they fell face
17:10 The **d** asked him, "Why then do the
17:13 the **d** understood that he was talking
17:16 I brought him to your **d**, but they
17:19 the **d** came to Jesus in private and
17:23 And the **d** were filled with grief.
17:24 After Jesus and his **d** arrived in
18: 1 At that time the **d** came to Jesus and
19:10 The **d** said to him, "If this is the
19:13 **d** rebuked those who brought them.
19:23 Jesus said to his **d**, "I tell you the
19:25 the **d** heard this, they were greatly
20:17 the twelve **d** aside and said to them,
20:29 Jesus and his **d** were leaving Jericho,
21: 1 Mount of Olives, Jesus sent two **d**,
21: 6 The **d** went and did as Jesus had
21:20 the **d** saw this, they were amazed.
22:16 They sent their **d** to him along with
23: 1 Jesus said to the crowds and to his **d**
24: 1 was walking away when his **d** came up
24: 3 Olives, the **d** came to him privately.
26: 1 all these things, he said to his **d**,
26: 8 the **d** saw this, they were indignant.
26:17 the **d** came to Jesus and asked,
26:18 Passover with my **d** at your house.'"
26:19 the **d** did as Jesus had directed them
26:26 and gave it to his **d**, saying, "Take
26:35 And all the other **d** said the same.
26:36 Jesus went with his **d** to a place
26:40 he returned to his **d** and found them
26:45 he returned to the **d** and said to
26:56 Then all the **d** deserted him and fled.
27:64 Otherwise, his **d** may come and steal
28: 7 go quickly and tell his **d**: 'He has
28: 8 with joy, and ran to tell his **d**.
28:13 'His **d** came during the night and
28:16 the eleven **d** went to Galilee, to the
28:19 Therefore go and make **d** of all
Mk 2:15 were eating with him and his **d**,
2:16 they asked his **d**: "Why does he eat
2:18 Now John's **d** and the Pharisees were
2:18 John's **d** and the **d** of the Pharisees
2:23 and as his **d** walked along, they
3: 7 Jesus withdrew with his **d** to the
3: 9 of the crowd he told his **d** to have a
3:20 and his **d** were not even able to eat.
4:34 his own **d**, he explained everything.
4:35 he said to his **d**, "Let us go over
4:38 The **d** woke him and said to him,
4:40 He said to his **d**, "Why are you so
5:31 against you," his **d** answered,
5:40 mother and the **d** who were with him,
6: 1 his home town, accompanied by his **d**.
6:29 On hearing of this, John's **d** came
6:35 in the day, so his **d** came to him.
6:41 Then he gave them to his **d** to set
6:43 the **d** picked up twelve basketfuls of
6:45 Immediately Jesus made his **d** get
6:48 He saw the **d** straining at the oars,
7: 2 saw some of his **d** eating food with
7: 5 "Why don't your **d** live according to
7:17 his **d** asked him about this parable.
8: 1 Jesus called his **d** to him and said,
8: 4 His **d** answered, "But where in this
8: 6 gave them to his **d** to set before
8: 7 and told the **d** to distribute them.
8: 8 Afterwards the **d** picked up seven
8:10 he got into the boat with his **d** and
8:14 The **d** had forgotten to bring bread,
8:27 Jesus and his **d** went on to the
8:33 when Jesus turned and looked at his **d**
8:34 to him along with his **d** and said:
9:14 they came to the other **d**, they saw a
9:18 I asked your **d** to drive out the
9:28 his **d** asked him privately, "Why
9:31 he was teaching his **d**. He said to
10:10 the **d** asked Jesus about this.
10:13 touch them, but the **d** rebuked them.
10:23 Jesus looked around and said to his **d**
10:24 The **d** were amazed at his words. But
10:26 The **d** were even more amazed, and
10:32 and the **d** were astonished, while
10:46 As Jesus and his **d**, together with a
11: 1 of Olives, Jesus sent two of his **d**,
11:14 And his **d** heard him say it.
12:43 Calling his **d** to him, Jesus said, "I
13: 1 one of his **d** said to him, "Look,
14:12 Jesus' **d** asked him, "Where do you
14:13 he sent two of his **d**, telling them,
14:14 I may eat the Passover with my **d**?'
14:16 The **d** left, went into the city and
14:22 and gave it to his **d**, saying, "Take
14:32 Jesus said to his **d**, "Sit here
14:37 he returned to his **d** and found them
16: 7 go, tell his **d** and Peter, 'He is
16:20 the **d** went out and preached
Lk 5:30 to their sect complained to his **d**,
5:33 They said to him, "John's **d** often
5:33 and so do the **d** of the Pharisees,
6: 1 and his **d** began to pick some ears of
6:13 morning came, he called his **d** to him
6:17 A large crowd of his **d** was there and
6:20 Looking at his **d**, he said: "Blessed
7:11 and his **d** and a large crowd went
7:18 John's **d** told him about all these
8: 9 His **d** asked him what this parable
8:22 One day Jesus said to his **d**, "Let's
8:24 The **d** went and woke him, saying,
8:25 "Where is your faith?" he asked his **d**
9:14 But he said to his **d**, "Make them
9:15 The **d** did so, and everybody sat down.
9:16 Them he gave them to the **d** to set
9:17 the **d** picked up twelve basketfuls
9:18 in private and his **d** were with him,
9:36 The **d** kept this to themselves, and
9:40 I begged your **d** to drive it out, but
9:43 that Jesus did, he said to his **d**,
9:46 An argument started among the **d** as
9:54 the **d** James and John saw this, they
10:23 turned to his **d** and said privately,
10:38 Jesus and his **d** were on their way,
11: 1 When he finished, one of his **d** said
11: 1 to pray, just as John taught his **d**."
12: 1 Jesus began to speak first to his **d**,
12:22 Jesus said to his **d**: "Therefore I
16: 1 Jesus told his **d**: "There was a rich
17: 1 Jesus said to his **d**: "Things that
17:22 he said to his **d**, "The time is
18: 1 Jesus told his **d** a parable to show

Lk 18:15 the **d** saw this, they rebuked them.
18:34 The **d** did not understand any of this.
19:29 sent two of his **d**, saying to them,
19:37 the whole crowd of **d** began joyfully
19:39 "Teacher, rebuke your **d**!
20:45 were listening, Jesus said to his **d**,
21: 5 Some of his **d** were remarking about
22:11 I may eat the Passover with my **d**?'
22:38 The **d** said, "See, Lord, here are two
22:39 of Olives, and his **d** followed him.
22:45 from prayer and went back to the **d**,
Jn 1:35 was there again with two of his **d**.
1:37 the two **d** heard him say this, they
2: 2 Jesus and his **d** had also been
2:11 and his **d** put their faith in him.
2:12 his mother and brothers and his **d**.
2:17 His **d** remembered that it is written:
2:22 his **d** recalled what he had said.
3:22 After this, Jesus and his **d** went out
3:25 developed between some of John's **d**
4: 1 and baptising more **d** than John,
4: 2 not Jesus who baptised, but his **d**.
4: 8 (His **d** had gone into the town to buy
4:27 Just then his **d** returned and were
4:31 Meanwhile his **d** urged him, "Rabbi,
4:33 his **d** said to each other, "Could
6: 3 and sat down with his **d**.
6: 8 Another of his **d**, Andrew, Simon
6:12 he said to his **d**, "Gather the pieces
6:16 evening came, his **d** went down to the
6:22 Jesus had not entered it with his **d**,
6:24 neither Jesus nor his **d** were there,
6:60 On hearing it, many of his **d** said,
6:61 Aware that his **d** were grumbling
6:66 From this time many of his **d** turned
7: 3 your **d** may see the miracles you do.
8:31 to my teaching, you are really my **d**.
9: 2 His **d** asked him, "Rabbi, who sinned,
9:27 Do you want to become his **d**, too?"
9:28 disciple! We are **d** of Moses!
11: 7 he said to his **d**, "Let us go back to
11:12 His **d** replied, "Lord, if he sleeps,
11:13 **d** thought he meant natural sleep.
11:16 Didymus) said to the rest of the **d**,
11:54 Ephraim, where he stayed with his **d**.
12: 4 one of his **d**, Judas Iscariot, who
12:16 At first his **d** did not understand
13:22 His **d** stared at one another, at a
13:35 are my **d**, if you love one another."
15: 8 showing yourselves to be my **d**.
16:17 Some of his **d** said to one another,
16:29 Jesus' **d** said, "Now you are speaking
18: 1 Jesus left with his **d** and crossed
18: 1 and he and his **d** went into it.
18: 2 Jesus had often met there with his **d**.
18:17 "You are not one of his **d**, are you?"
18:19 Jesus about his **d** and his teaching.
18:25 "You are not one of his **d**, are you?"
20:10 the **d** went back to their homes,
20:18 Mary Magdalene went to the **d** with
20:19 when the **d** were together, with the
20:20 The **d** were overjoyed when they saw
20:24 was not with the **d** when Jesus came.
20:25 the other **d** told him, "We have seen
20:26 A week later his **d** were in the house
20:30 signs in the presence of his **d**,
21: 1 Jesus appeared again to his **d**, by
21: 2 and two other **d** were together.
21: 4 **d** did not realise that it was Jesus.
21: 8 The other **d** followed in the boat,
21:12 None of the **d** dared ask him, "Who
21:14 third time Jesus appeared to his **d**
Ac 6: 1 In those days when the number of **d**
6: 2 the Twelve gathered all the **d**
6: 7 The number of **d** in Jerusalem
9: 1 threats against the Lord's **d**.
9:19 several days with the **d** in Damascus.
9:26 he tried to join the **d**, but they
9:38 so when the **d** heard that Peter was
11:26 The **d** were called Christians first
11:29 The **d**, each according to his ability,
13:52 the **d** were filled with joy and with
14:20 after the **d** had gathered round him,
14:21 city and won a large number of **d**.
14:22 strengthening the **d** and encouraging
14:28 stayed there a long time with the **d**.
Ac 15:10 putting on the necks of the **d** a
18:23 Phrygia, strengthening all the **d**.
18:27 wrote to the **d** there to welcome him.
19: 1 at Ephesus. There he found some **d**
19: 9 He took the **d** with him and had
19:30 crowd, but the **d** would not let him.
20: 1 Paul sent for the **d** and, after
20:30 in order to draw away **d** after them.
21: 4 Finding the **d** there, we stayed with
21: 5 All the **d** and their wives and
21:16 Some of the **d** from Caesarea
21:16 from Cyprus and one of the early **d**.

Disciples' (Disciple)

Jn 13: 5 basin and began to wash his **d** feet,

Discipline (Disciplined, Disciplines, Self-discipline)

Dt 4:36 he made you hear his voice to **d** you.
11: 2 **d** of the LORD your God: his majesty,
21:18 not listen to them when they **d** him,
Job 5:17 not despise the **d** of the Almighty.
Ps 6: 1 in your anger or **d** me in your wrath.
38: 1 in your anger or **d** me in your wrath.
39:11 You rebuke and **d** men for their sin;
94:12 Blessed is the man you **d**, O LORD,
Pr 1: 2 for attaining wisdom and **d**; for
1: 7 but fools despise wisdom and **d**.
3:11 My son, do not despise the LORD's **d**
5:12 You will say, "How I hated **d**! How my
5:23 He will die for lack of **d**, led
6:23 corrections of **d** are the way to
10:17 He who heeds **d** shows the way to life,
12: 1 Whoever loves **d** loves knowledge, but
13:18 He who ignores **d** comes to poverty
13:24 who loves him is careful to **d** him.
15: 5 A fool spurns his father's **d**, but
15:10 Stern **d** awaits him who leaves the
15:32 He who ignores **d** despises himself,
19:18 **D** your son, for in that there is
22:15 rod of **d** will drive it far from him.
23:13 Do not withhold **d** from a child; if
23:23 get wisdom, **d** and understanding.
29:17 **D** your son, and he will give you
Jer 17:23 would not listen or respond to **d**.
30:11 I will **d** you but only with justice;
32:33 would not listen or respond to **d**.
46:28 I will **d** you but only with justice;
Hos 5: 2 I will **d** all of them.
Heb 12: 5 do not make light of the Lord's **d**,
12: 7 Endure hardship as **d**; God is
12: 8 (and everyone undergoes **d**), then you
12:11 No **d** seems pleasant at the time, but
Rev 3:19 Those whom I love I rebuke and **d**. So

Disciplined (Discipline)

Pr 1: 3 for acquiring a **d** and prudent life,
Isa 26:16 when you **d** them, they could barely
Jer 31:18 'You **d** me like an unruly calf, and I
31:18 and I have been **d**. Restore me,
1Co 11:32 we are being **d** so that we will not
Tit 1: 8 upright, holy and **d**.
Heb 12: 7 For what son is not **d** by his father?
12: 8 If you are not **d** (and everyone
12: 9 fathers who **d** us and we respected
12:10 Our fathers **d** us for a little while

Disciplines (Discipline)

Dt 8: 5 your heart that as a man **d** his son,
8: 5 his son, so the LORD your God **d** you.
Ps 94:10 Does he who **d** nations not punish?
Pr 3:12 the LORD **d** those he loves, as a
Heb 12: 6 the Lord **d** those he loves, and he
12:10 but God **d** us for our good, that

Disclose (Disclosed)

Job 11: 6 **d** to you the secrets of wisdom, for
Isa 26:21 The earth will **d** the blood shed upon

Disclosed (Disclose)

Mt 10:26 concealed that will not be **d**,
Mk 4:22 whatever is hidden is meant to be **d**,
Lk 8:17 nothing hidden that will not be **d**,
12: 2 concealed that will not be **d**,
Col 1:26 but is now **d** to the saints.
Heb 9: 8 had not yet been **d** as long as the

Discomfort

Jnh 4: 6 shade for his head to ease his **d**,

Discontented

1Sa 22: 2 or in debt or **d** gathered round him,

Discord

Est 1:18 will be no end of disrespect and **d**.
Gal 5:20 hatred, **d**, jealousy, fits of rage,

Discourage (Discouraged, Discouragement, Discouraging)

Nu 32: 7 Why do you **d** the Israelites from
Ezr 4: 4 set out to **d** the people of Judah

Discouraged (Discourage)

Nu 32: 9 they **d** the Israelites from entering
Dt 1:21 Do not be afraid; do not be **d**."
31: 8 Do not be afraid; do not be **d**."
Jos 1: 9 Do not be terrified; do not be **d**,
8: 1 "Do not be afraid; do not be **d**.
10:25 "Do not be afraid; do not be **d**.
1Ch 22:13 Do not be afraid or **d**.
28:20 Do not be afraid or **d**, for the LORD
2Ch 20:15 or **d** because of this vast army.
20:17 Do not be afraid; do not be **d**. Go
32: 7 Do not be afraid or **d** because of the
Job 4: 5 comes to you and you are **d**;
Isa 42: 4 he will not falter or be **d** till he
Eph 3:13 I ask you, therefore, not to be **d**
Col 3:21 children, or they will become **d**.

Discouragement (Discourage)

Ex 6: 9 of their **d** and cruel bondage.

Discouraging (Discourage)

Jer 38: 4 He is **d** the soldiers who are left in

Discourse (Discoursed)

Job 27: 1 Job continued his **d**:
29: 1 Job continued his **d**:

Discoursed (Discourse)

Ac 24:25 Paul **d** on righteousness,

Discover (Discovered)

Ecc 7:14 cannot **d** anything about his future.
7:24 and most profound—who can **d** it?
7:27 another to **d** the scheme of things—
8:17 it out, man cannot **d** its meaning.
2Co 13: 6 I trust that you will **d** that we have

Discovered (Discover)

Ge 26:19 and **d** a well of fresh water there.
36:24 This is the Anah who **d** the hot
Dt 22:28 and rapes her and they are **d**,
Jdg 16: 9 secret of his strength was not **d**.
21: 8 **d** that no-one from Jabesh Gilead
Ru 3: 8 and **d** a woman lying at his feet.
1Sa 22: 6 that David and his men had been **d**.
2Ki 17: 4 the king of Assyria **d** that Hoshea
23:24 had **d** in the temple of the LORD.
Ps 44:21 would not God have **d** it, since he
Ecc 7:27 "this is what I have **d**: "Adding one
Ro 4: 1 our forefather, **d** in this matter?

Discredit (Discredited)

Ne 6:13 would give me a bad name to **d** me.
Job 40: 8 "Would you **d** my justice? Would you

Discredited (Discredit)

Ac 19:27 the great goddess Artemis will be **d**,
2Co 6: 3 so that our ministry will not be **d**.

Discretion

1Ch 22:12 May the LORD give you **d** and
Pr 1: 4 knowledge and **d** to the young—
2:11 **D** will protect you, and

Pr 5: 2 that you may maintain **d** and your
8:12 prudence; I possess knowledge and **d**.
11:22 is a beautiful woman who shows no **d**.

Discriminated
Jas 2: 4 have you not **d** among yourselves and

Discuss (Discussed, Discussing, Discussion, Discussions)
Lk 6:11 and began to **d** with one another
Heb 9: 5 cannot **d** these things in detail now.

Discussed (Discuss)
1Sa 20:23 about the matter you and I **d**—
Mt 16: 7 They **d** this among themselves and
21:25 They **d** it among themselves and said
Mk 8:16 They **d** this with one another and
11:31 They **d** it among themselves and said,
Lk 20: 5 They **d** it among themselves and said,
22: 4 **d** with them how he might betray
24:15 they talked and **d** these things with
Ac 25:14 Festus **d** Paul's case with the king.

Discussing (Discuss)
Mk 9:10 kept the matter to themselves, **d** what
Lk 24:17 He asked them, "What are you **d**

Discussion (Discuss)
Mt 16: 8 Aware of their **d**, Jesus asked, "You
Mk 8:17 Aware of their **d**, Jesus asked them:
Ac 15: 7 After much **d**, Peter got up and

Discussions (Discuss)
Ac 19: 9 had **d** daily in the lecture hall of

Disdained (Disdainful)
1Sa 2:30 but those who despise me will be **d**.
Job 30: 1 have **d** to put with my sheep dogs.
Ps 22:24 For he has not despised or **d** the
Jer 30:19 them honour, and they will not be **d**.

Disdainful (Disdained)
Pr 30:13 so haughty, whose glances are so **d**;

Disease (Diseased, Diseases)
Lev 13: 2 may become an infectious skin **d**,
13: 3 deep, it is an infectious skin **d**.
13: 8 him unclean; it is an infectious **d**.
13: 9 "When anyone has an infectious skin **d**
13:11 is a chronic skin **d** and the priest
13:12 "If the **d** breaks out all over his
13:13 and if the **d** has covered his whole
13:15 is unclean; he has an infectious **d**.
13:20 It is an infectious skin **d** that has
13:25 **d** that has broken out in the burn.
13:25 unclean; it is an infectious skin **d**.
13:27 unclean; it is an infectious skin **d**.
13:30 an infectious **d** of the head or chin.
13:42 it is an infectious **d** breaking out
13:43 like an infectious skin **d**,
13:45 "The person with such an infectious **d**
14: 3 healed of his infectious skin **d**,
14: 7 to be cleansed of the infectious **d**
14:32 anyone who has an infectious skin **d**
14:54 any infectious skin **d**, for an itch,
22: 4 skin **d** or a bodily discharge,
Nu 5: 2 skin **d** or a discharge of any kind,
Dt 7:15 LORD will keep you free from every **d**.
28:22 LORD will strike you with wasting **d**,
1Ki 8:37 whatever disaster or **d** may come,
2Ch 6:28 whatever disaster or **d** may come,
16:12 was afflicted with a **d** in his feet.
16:12 Though his **d** was severe, even in his
21:15 with a lingering **d** of the bowels,
21:15 **d** causes your bowels to come out.'"
21:18 with an incurable **d** of the bowels.
21:19 because of the **d**, and he died in
Ps 41: 8 "A vile **d** has beset him; he will
106:15 for, but sent a wasting **d** upon them.
Isa 10:16 will send a wasting **d** upon his
17:11 in the day of **d** and incurable pain.
Mt 4:23 **d** and sickness among the people.
9:35 and healing every **d** and sickness.
10: 1 and to heal every **d** and sickness.

Diseased (Disease)
Lev 13:33 be shaved except for the **d** area,
13:44 the man is **d** and is unclean. The
14: 2 the regulations for the **d** person
1Ki 15:23 old age, however, his feet became **d**.
Mal 1: 8 you sacrifice crippled or **d** animals,
1:13 crippled or **d** animals and offer them

Diseases (Disease)
Ge 12:17 the LORD inflicted serious **d** on
Ex 15:26 of the **d** I brought on the Egyptians,
Lev 14:57 for infectious skin **d** and mildew.
26:16 wasting **d** and fever that will
Dt 7:15 the horrible **d** you knew in Egypt,
24: 8 In cases of leprous **d** be very
28:21 The LORD will plague you with **d**
28:60 He will bring upon you all the **d** of
29:22 the **d** with which the LORD has
Ps 103: 3 all your sins and heals all your **d**,
Jer 16: 4 "They will die of deadly **d**. They
Mt 4:24 him all who were ill with various **d**,
8:17 our infirmities and carried our **d**."
Mk 1:34 Jesus healed many who had various **d**.
3:10 those with **d** were pushing forward to
Lk 6:18 him and to be healed of their **d**.
7:21 time Jesus cured many who had **d**,
8: 2 been cured of evil spirits and **d**:
9: 1 drive out all demons and to cure **d**,

Disfigure (Disfigured)
Mt 6:16 for they **d** their faces to show men

Disfigured (Disfigure)
Lev 21:18 who is blind or lame, **d** or deformed;
Isa 52:14 was so **d** beyond that of any man

Disgrace (Disgraced, Disgraceful, Disgraces)
Ge 30:23 and said, "God has taken away my **d**.
34:14 That would be a **d** to us.
Lev 20:17 have sexual relations, it is a **d**.
Nu 12:14 would she not have been in **d** for
1Sa 11: 2 you and so bring **d** on all Israel."
17:26 and removes this **d** from Israel?
2Sa 13:13 Where could I get rid of my **d**? And
2Ki 19: 3 a day of distress and rebuke and **d**,
2Ch 32:21 So he withdrew to his own land in **d**.
Ne 1: 3 province are in great trouble and **d**.
2:17 and we will no longer be in **d**."
Ps 6:10 they will turn back in sudden **d**.
35:26 over me be clothed with shame and **d**.
40:14 desire my ruin be turned back in **d**.
44:15 My **d** is before me all day long, and
52: 1 you who are a **d** in the eyes of God?
70: 2 desire my ruin be turned back in **d**.
71:13 harm me be covered with scorn and **d**.
74:21 Do not let the oppressed retreat in **d**
83:17 and dismayed; may they perish in **d**.
109:29 My accusers will be clothed with **d**
119:39 Take away the **d** I dread, for your
Pr 6:33 Blows and **d** are his lot, and his
11: 2 pride comes, then comes **d**, but with
13: 5 but the wicked bring shame and **d**.
14:34 but sin is a **d** to any people.
18: 3 contempt, and with shame comes **d**.
19:26 is a son who brings shame and **d**.
Isa 4: 1 Take away our **d**!"
22:18 you **d** to your master's house!
25: 8 **d** of his people from all the earth.
30: 3 Egypt's shade will bring you **d**.
30: 5 advantage, but only shame and **d**."
37: 3 a day of distress and rebuke and **d**,
43:28 I will **d** the dignitaries of your
45:16 they will go off into **d** together.
54: 4 Do not fear **d**; you will not be
61: 7 and instead of **d** they will rejoice
Jer 3:25 our shame, and let our **d** cover us.
23:40 I will bring upon you everlasting **d**—
31:19 because I bore the **d** of my youth.'
Lam 3:30 him, and let him be filled with **d**.
5: 1 happened to us; look, and see our **d**.
Eze 16:52 Bear your **d**, for you have furnished
16:52 So then, be ashamed and bear your **d**,
16:54 that you may bear your **d** and be
28:16 So I drove you in **d** from the mount
32:30 they went down with the slain in **d**
36:30 so that you will no longer suffer **d**
Hos 2: 5 and has conceived them in **d**.
Mic 2: 6 **d** will not overtake us."
Hab 2:16 to you, and **d** will cover your glory.
Mt 1:19 not want to expose her to public **d**,
Lk 1:25 taken away my **d** among the people."
Ac 5:41 worthy of suffering **d** for the Name.
1Co 11: 6 and if it is a **d** for a woman to have
11:14 man has long hair, it is a **d** to him,
1Ti 3: 7 will not fall into **d** and into the
Heb 6: 6 and subjecting him to public **d**.
11:26 He regarded **d** for the sake of Christ
13:13 the camp, bearing the **d** he bore.

Disgraced (Disgrace)
2Sa 13:22 because he had **d** his sister Tamar.
Ezr 9: 6 "O my God, I am too ashamed and **d** to
Ps 35: 4 May those who seek my life be **d** and
69: 6 May those who hope in you not be **d**
69:19 You know how I am scorned, **d** and
Isa 1:29 you will be **d** because of the gardens
41:11 you will surely be ashamed and **d**;
45:16 of idols will be put to shame and **d**;
45:17 will never be put to shame or **d**,
50: 7 LORD helps me, I will not be **d**.
Jer 2:26 "As a thief is **d** when he is caught,
2:26 so the house of Israel is **d**—they,
15: 9 she will be **d** and humiliated.
20:11 They will fail and be thoroughly **d**;
22:22 **d** because of all your wickedness.
48: 1 Kiriathaim will be **d** and captured;
48: 1 stronghold will be **d** and shattered.
48:20 Moab is **d**, for she is shattered.
50:12 she who gave you birth will be **d**.
51:47 her whole land will be **d** and her
51:51 "We are **d**, for we have been insulted
Eze 36:32 Be ashamed and **d** for your conduct,
Hos 10: 6 Ephraim will be **d**; Israel will be
Mic 3: 7 will be ashamed and the diviners **d**.

Disgraceful (Disgrace)
Ge 34: 7 because Shechem had done a **d** thing
Dt 22:21 She has done a **d** thing in Israel by
Jos 7:15 and has done a **d** thing in Israel!'"
Jdg 19:23 is my guest, don't do this **d** thing.
19:24 this man, don't do such a **d** thing."
20: 6 this lewd and **d** act in Israel.
Pr 10: 5 sleeps during harvest is a **d** son.
12: 4 a **d** wife is like decay in his bones.
17: 2 wise servant will rule over a **d** son
Hos 4: 7 their Glory for something **d**.
1Co 14:35 **d** for a woman to speak in the church.

Disgraces (Disgrace)
Lev 21: 9 she **d** her father; she must be burned
Pr 28: 7 companion of gluttons **d** his father.
29:15 child left to himself **d** his mother.

Disguise (Disguised, Disguises)
Ge 38:14 covered herself with a veil to **d**
1Ki 14: 2 "Go, **d** yourself, so that you won't
22:30 "I will enter the battle in **d**,
2Ch 18:29 "I will enter the battle in **d**,

Disguised (Disguise)
1Sa 28: 8 Saul **d** himself, putting on other
1Ki 20:38 He **d** himself with his headband down
22:30 **d** himself and went into battle.
2Ch 18:29 **d** himself and went into battle.
35:22 **d** himself to engage him in battle.

Disguises (Disguise)
Pr 26:24 A malicious man **d** himself with his

Disgust (Disgusted)
Eze 23:17 she turned away from them in **d**.
23:18 I turned away from her in **d**, just as
23:22 those you turned away from in **d**, and
23:28 to those you turned away from in **d**.

Disgusted (Disgust)
Ge 27:46 Rebekah said to Isaac, "I'm **d** with

Dish (Dishes)
Nu 7:14 one gold **d** weighing ten shekels,
7:20 one gold **d** weighing ten shekels,
7:26 one gold **d** weighing ten shekels,
7:32 one gold **d** weighing ten shekels,
7:38 one gold **d** weighing ten shekels,
7:44 one gold **d** weighing ten shekels,
7:50 one gold **d** weighing ten shekels,
7:56 one gold **d** weighing ten shekels,
7:62 one gold **d** weighing ten shekels,
7:68 one gold **d** weighing ten shekels,
7:74 one gold **d** weighing ten shekels,
7:80 one gold **d** weighing ten shekels,
2Ki 21:13 out Jerusalem as one wipes out a **d**,
1Ch 28:17 the weight of gold for each gold **d**;
28:17 weight of silver for each silver **d**;
Pr 19:24 The sluggard buries his hand in the **d**
26:15 The sluggard buries his hand in the **d**
Mt 23:25 clean the outside of the cup and **d**,
23:26 clean the inside of the cup and **d**,
Lk 11:39 clean the outside of the cup and **d**,
11:41 give what is inside the ⌊**d**⌋ to the
Jn 13:26 when I have dipped it in the **d**.

Dishan
Ge 36:21 Dishon, Ezer and **D**. These sons of
36:28 The sons of **D**: Uz and Aran.
36:30 Dishon, Ezer and **D**. These were the
1Ch 1:38 Zibeon, Anah, Dishon, Ezer and **D**.
1:42 The sons of **D**: Uz and Aran.

Disheartened
Dt 20: 8 his brothers will not become **d** too."
Jer 49:23 They are **d**, troubled like the
Eze 13:22 you **d** the righteous with your lies,

Dishes (Dish)
Ex 25:29 make its plates and **d** of pure gold,
37:16 **d** and bowls and its pitchers for the
Nu 4: 7 **d** and bowls, and the jars for drink
7:84 sprinkling bowls and twelve gold **d**.
7:85 Altogether, the silver **d** weighed
7:86 The twelve gold **d** filled with
7:86 Altogether, the gold **d** weighed a
1Ki 7:50 the pure gold **d**, wick trimmers,
7:50 sprinkling bowls, **d** and censers;
2Ki 25:14 shovels, wick trimmers, **d** and all
2Ch 4:22 sprinkling bowls, **d** and censers; and
24:14 and also **d** and other objects of gold
Ezr 1: 9 gold **d** 30 silver **d** 1,000 silver
Jer 52:18 sprinkling bowls, **d** and all the
52:19 pots, lampstands, **d** and bowls used

Dishon
Ge 36:21 **D**, Ezer and Dishan. These sons of
36:25 The children of Anah: **D** and
36:26 The sons of **D**: Hemdan, Eshban,
36:30 **D**, Ezer and Dishan. These were the
1Ch 1:38 Zibeon, Anah, **D**, Ezer and Dishan.
1:41 The son of Anah: **D**. The sons of **D**:

Dishonest (Dishonestly)
Ex 18:21 trustworthy men who hate **d** gain—and
Lev 19:35 "Do not use **d** standards when
1Sa 8: 3 They turned aside after **d** gain and
Pr 11: 1 The LORD abhors **d** scales, but
13:11 **D** money dwindles away, but he who
20:23 and **d** scales do not please him.
29:27 The righteous detest the **d**; the
Jer 22:17 your heart are set only on **d** gain,
Eze 28:18 By your many sins and **d** trade you
Hos 12: 7 The merchant uses **d** scales; he loves
Am 8: 5 price and cheating with **d** scales,
Mic 6:11 Shall I acquit a man with **d** scales,
Lk 16: 8 "The master commended the **d** manager
16:10 and whoever is **d** with very little
16:10 little will also be **d** with much.
1Ti 3: 8 much wine, and not pursuing **d** gain.
Tit 1: 7 not violent, not pursuing **d** gain.
1:11 that for the sake of **d** gain.

Dishonestly (Dishonest)
Dt 25:16 these things, anyone who deals **d**.

Dishonour (Dishonoured, Dishonours)
Lev 18: 7 "Do not **d** your father by having
18: 8 that would **d** your father.
18:10 daughter; that would **d** you.
18:14 "Do not **d** your father's brother by
18:16 that would **d** your brother.
20:19 for that would **d** a close relative;
Dt 22:30 he must not **d** his father's bed.
Pr 30: 9 steal, and so **d** the name of my God.
Jer 14:21 do not **d** your glorious throne.
20:11 their **d** will never be forgotten.
Lam 2: 2 its princes down to the ground in **d**.
Eze 22:10 are those who **d** their fathers' bed
Jn 8:49 I honour my Father and you **d** me.
Ro 2:23 do you **d** God by breaking the law?
1Co 15:43 is sown in **d**, it is raised in glory;
2Co 6: 8 through glory and **d**, bad report and

Dishonoured (Dishonour)
Lev 20:11 father's wife, he has **d** his father.
20:17 He has **d** his sister and will be held
20:20 with his aunt, he has **d** his uncle.
20:21 of impurity; he has **d** his brother.
Dt 21:14 as a slave, since you have **d** her.
Ezr 4:14 not proper for us to see the king **d**,
1Co 4:10 You are honoured, we are **d**!

Dishonours (Dishonour)
Dt 27:16 "Cursed is the man who **d** his father
27:20 wife, for he **d** his father's bed.
Job 20: 3 I hear a rebuke that **d** me, and my
Mic 7: 6 For a son **d** his father, a daughter
1Co 11: 4 with his head covered **d** his head.
11: 5 with her head uncovered **d** her head

Disillusionment
Ps 7:14 conceives trouble gives birth to **d**.

Dislikes
Dt 22:13 and, after lying with her, **d** her
22:16 marriage to this man, but he **d** her.
24: 3 her second husband **d** her and writes

Dislodge
Jos 15:63 Judah could not **d** the Jebusites, who
16:10 They did not **d** the Canaanites living
Jdg 1:21 failed to **d** the Jebusites, who were

Disloyal
Ps 78:57 Like their fathers they were **d** and

Dismay (Dismayed)
Job 41:22 in his neck; **d** goes before him.
Ps 35: 4 plot my ruin be turned back in **d**.
116:11 in my **d** I said, "All men are liars."

Dismayed (Dismay)
1Sa 17:11 the Israelites were **d** and terrified.
2Ki 19:26 Their people, drained of power, are **d**
Job 4: 5 it strikes you, and you are **d**.
32:15 "They are **d** and have no more to say;
Ps 6:10 All my enemies will be ashamed and **d**;
30: 7 but when you hid your face, I was **d**.
83:17 May they ever be ashamed and **d**; may
143: 4 within me; my heart within me is **d**.
Isa 28:16 the one who trusts will never be **d**.
37:27 Their people, drained of power, are **d**
41:10 do not be **d**, for I am your God.
41:23 we will be **d** and filled with fear.
Jer 8: 9 they will be **d** and trapped.
14: 3 **d** and despairing, they cover their
14: 4 farmers are **d** and cover their heads.
30:10 do not be **d**, O Israel,'
46:27 my servant; do not be **d**, O Israel.
49:23 are **d**, for they have heard bad news.

Dismiss (Dismissed)
Lk 2:29 you now **d** your servant in peace.

Dismissed (Dismiss)
Jdg 2: 6 After Joshua had **d** the Israelites,
1Sa 10:25 **d** the people, each to his own home.
2Ch 25:10 Amaziah **d** the troops who had come to
Mt 14:22 other side, while he **d** the crowd.
14:23 After he had **d** them, he went up on a
Mk 6:45 to Bethsaida, while he **d** the crowd.
Ac 13:43 the congregation was **d**, many of the
19:41 had said this, he **d** the assembly.
23:22 The commander **d** the young man and

Disobedience (Disobey)
Jos 22:22 been in rebellion or **d** to the LORD,
Jer 43: 7 they entered Egypt in **d** to the LORD
Ro 5:19 For just as through the **d** of the one
11:30 mercy as a result of their **d**,
11:32 For God has bound all men over to **d**
2Co 10: 6 be ready to punish every act of **d**,
Heb 2: 2 and **d** received its just punishment,
4: 6 did not go in, because of their **d**.
4:11 by following their example of **d**.

Disobedient (Disobey)
Ne 9:26 "But they were **d** and rebelled
Lk 1:17 the **d** to the wisdom of the righteous
Ac 26:19 "So then, King Agrippa, I was not **d**
Ro 10:21 hands to a **d** and obstinate people."
11:30 Just as you who were at one time **d**
11:31 they too have now become **d** in order
Eph 2: 2 is now at work in those who are **d**.
5: 6 God's wrath comes on those who are **d**.
5:12 to mention what the **d** do in secret.
2Ti 3: 2 proud, abusive, **d** to their parents,
Tit 1: 6 to the charge of being wild and **d**.
1:16 **d** and unfit for doing anything good.
3: 3 At one time we too were foolish, **d**,
Heb 11:31 not killed with those who were **d**.

Disobey (Disobedience, Disobedient, Disobeyed, Disobeying, Disobeys)
Dt 11:28 the curse if you **d** the commands of
2Ch 24:20 'Why do you **d** the LORD's commands?
Est 3: 3 "Why do you **d** the king's command?
Jer 42:13 land,' and so **d** the LORD your God,
Ro 1:30 of doing evil; they **d** their parents;
1Pe 2: 8 stumble because they **d** the message

Disobeyed (Disobey)
Nu 14:22 who **d** me and tested me ten times—
27:14 both of you **d** my command to honour
Jdg 2: 2 Yet you have **d** me. Why have you
Ne 9:29 became arrogant and **d** your commands.
Isa 24: 5 by its people; they have **d** the laws,
Jer 43: 4 all the people **d** the LORD's command
Lk 15:29 for you and never **d** your orders.
Heb 3:18 his rest if not to those who **d**?
1Pe 3:20 who **d** long ago when God waited

Disobeying (Disobey)
Nu 14:41 Moses said, "Why are you **d** the

Disobeys (Disobey)
Eze 33:12 man will not save him when he **d**,

Disorder
Job 10:22 of deep shadow and **d**, where even the
1Co 14:33 For God is not a God of **d** but of
2Co 12:20 slander, gossip, arrogance and **d**.
Jas 3:16 you find **d** and every evil practice.

Disown (Disowned, Disowns)
Pr 30: 9 I may have too much and **d** you
Mt 10:33 **d** him before my Father in heaven.
26:34 crows, you will **d** me three times."
26:35 to die with you, I will never **d** you.
26:75 crows, you will **d** me three times.
Mk 14:30 you yourself will **d** me three times."
14:31 to die with you, I will never **d** you.
14:72 twice you will **d** me three times.
Lk 22:61 today, you will **d** me three times."
Jn 13:38 crows, you will **d** me three times!
2Ti 2:12 If we **d** him, he will also **d** us;
2:13 faithful, for he cannot **d** himself.

Disowned (Disown)
Lk 12: 9 will be **d** before the angels of God.
Ac 3:13 and you **d** him before Pilate, though
3:14 You **d** the Holy and Righteous One

Disowns (Disown)
Job 8:18 its spot, that place **d** it and says,
Mt 10:33 whoever **d** me before men, I will
Lk 12: 9 he who **d** me before men will be

Dispatch (Dispatched, Dispatches)
Isa 10: 6 I **d** him against a people who anger

Dispatched (Dispatch)
1Ki 20:17 Now Ben-Hadad had **d** scouts, who

Dispatches (Dispatch)
Est 1:22 He sent **d** to all parts of the
3:13 **D** were sent by couriers to all the
8: 5 the **d** that Haman son of Hammedatha,
8:10 sealed the **d** with the king's signet

Dispenses
Zep 3: 5 Morning by morning he **d** his justice,

Disperse (Dispersed, Disperses, Dispersing)
Ge 49: 7 them in Jacob and **d** them in Israel.
Eze 12:15 when I **d** them among the nations and
20:23 I would **d** them among the nations
22:15 I will **d** you among the nations and
29:12 And I will **d** the Egyptians among the
30:23 I will **d** the Egyptians among the
30:26 I will **d** the Egyptians among the

Dispersed (Disperse)
2Sa 20:22 and his men **d** from the city, each
1Ki 1:49 guests rose in alarm and **d**.
Est 3: 8 "There is a certain people **d** and
Job 38:24 the place where the lightning is **d**,
Eze 36:19 I **d** them among the nations, and they
Ac 5:36 all his followers were **d**, and it

Disperses (Disperse)
Dt 30: 1 your God **d** you among the nations,
Job 12:23 he enlarges nations, and **d** them.

Dispersing (Disperse)
2Ch 11:23 He acted wisely, **d** some of his sons

Displaces
Pr 30:23 a maidservant who **d** her mistress.

Display (Displayed, Displays)
Dt 22:17 Then her parents shall **d** the cloth
Est 1:11 in order to **d** her beauty to the
Job 10:16 **d** your awesome power against me.
Ps 19: 2 night after night they **d** knowledge.
45: 4 let your right hand **d** awesome deeds.
77:14 you **d** your power among the peoples.
Isa 49: 3 in whom I will **d** my splendour."
60:21 my hands, for the **d** of my splendour.
61: 3 the LORD for the **d** of his splendour.
Eze 39:21 "I will **d** my glory among the nations,
Ro 9:17 that I might **d** my power in you and
1Co 4: 9 on **d** at the end of the procession,
1Ti 1:16 Christ Jesus might **d** his unlimited

Displayed (Display)
Ex 14:31 the LORD **d** against the Egyptians,
Nu 14:17 "Now may the Lord's strength be **d**,
1Ki 11:41 the wisdom he **d**—are they not
Est 1: 4 For a full 180 days he **d** the vast
Job 26: 3 And what great insight you have **d**!
Ps 78:43 the day he **d** his miraculous signs in
Jn 9: 3 work of God might be **d** in his life.
2Th 2: 9 the work of Satan **d** in all kinds

Displays (Display)
Pr 14:29 but a quick-tempered man **d** folly.
Isa 44:23 Jacob, he **d** his glory in Israel.

Displease (Displeased, Displeases, Displeasing, Displeasure)
Nu 11:11 What have I done to **d** you that you
1Sa 29: 7 nothing to **d** the Philistine rulers."
1Th 2:15 They **d** God and are hostile to all

Displeased (Displease)
Ge 48:17 hand on Ephraim's head he was **d**;
Nu 22:34 Now if you are **d**, I will go back."
1Sa 8: 6 **d** Samuel; so he prayed to the LORD.
2Sa 11:27 the thing David had done **d** the LORD.
Ne 13: 8 I was greatly **d** and threw all
Isa 59:15 and was **d** that there was no justice.
Jnh 4: 1 Jonah was greatly **d** and became angry.

Displeases (Displease)
Isa 65:12 in my sight and chose what **d** me."
66: 4 in my sight and chose what **d** me."

Displeasing (Displease)
Ge 28: 8 Esau then realised how **d** the
Dt 24: 1 a woman who becomes **d** to him

Displeasure (Displease)
Ps 85: 4 and put away your **d** towards us.

Disposal (Disposed)
Mt 26:53 at my **d** more than twelve legions
Ac 5: 4 wasn't the money at your **d**? What

Disposed (Disposal)
Ex 3:21 favourably **d** towards this people,
11: 3 favourably **d** towards the people,
12:36 favourably **d** towards the people,
Dt 31:21 I know what they are **d** to do, even
1Sa 20:12 If he is favourably **d** towards you,

Dispossess (Dispossessing)
Dt 9: 1 **d** nations greater and stronger than
11:23 and you will **d** nations larger and
12:29 you are about to invade and **d**.
18:14 The nations you will **d** listen to
Isa 54: 3 your descendants will **d** nations and

Dispossessing (Dispossess)
Dt 12: 2 where the nations you are **d** worship
Eze 45: 9 Stop **d** my people, declares the

Disputable (Dispute)
Ro 14: 1 passing judgment on **d** matters.

Dispute (Disputable, Disputed, Disputes, Disputing)
Ex 18:16 Whenever they have a **d**, it is
24:14 involved in a **d** can go to them."
Dt 19:17 the two men involved in the **d** must
21: 5 decide all cases of **d** and assault.
25: 1 men have a **d**, they are to take it to
Jdg 11:27 the Judge, decide the **d** this day
Job 9: 3 Though one wished to **d** with him, he
9:14 "How then can I **d** with him? How can
Pr 17:14 the matter before a **d** breaks out.
Eze 44:24 "In any **d**, the priests are to serve
Lk 22:24 Also a **d** arose among them as to
Ac 15: 2 into sharp **d** and debate with them.
17:18 philosophers began to **d** with him.
23: 7 he said this, a **d** broke out between
23:10 The **d** became so violent that the
25:19 Instead, they had some points of **d**
1Co 6: 1 If any of you has a **d** with another,
6: 5 to judge a **d** between believers?

Disputed (Dispute)
Ge 26:20 well Esek, because they **d** with him.

Disputes (Dispute)
Ex 18:19 before God and bring their **d** to him.
Dt 1:12 burdens and your **d** all by myself?
1:16 Hear the **d** between your brothers and
Jdg 4: 5 came to her to have their **d** decided.
2Ch 19: 8 the law of the LORD and to settle **d**.
Pr 18:18 Casting the lot settles **d** and keeps
18:19 and **d** are like the barred gates of a
Isa 2: 4 and will settle **d** for many peoples.
Mic 4: 3 will settle **d** for strong nations
1Co 6: 4 Therefore, if you have **d** about such

Disputing (Dispute)
1Ti 2: 8 hands in prayer, without anger or **d**.
Jude : 9 when he was **d** with the devil about

Disqualified (Disqualify)
1Co 9:27 I myself will not be **d** for the prize.

Disqualify (Disqualified)
Col 2:18 of angels **d** you for the prize.

Disquieting
Job 4:13 Amid **d** dreams in the night, when

Disregarded (Disregarding)
Ezr 9:10 For we have **d** the commands
Isa 40:27 my cause is **d** by my God"?

Disregarding (Disregarded)
Am 1: 9 **d** a treaty of brotherhood,

Disrepute
2Pe 2: 2 will bring the way of truth into **d**.

Disrespect
Est 1:18 will be no end of **d** and discord.

Disrobing
2Sa 6:20 **d** in the sight of the slave girls of

Dissension (Dissensions)
Pr 6:14 in his heart—he always stirs up **d**.
6:19 a man who stirs up **d** among brothers.
10:12 Hatred stirs up **d**, but love covers
15:18 A hot-tempered man stirs up **d**, but a
16:28 A perverse man stirs up **d**, and a
28:25 A greedy man stirs up **d**, but he who
29:22 An angry man stirs up **d**, and a
Ro 13:13 debauchery, not in **d** and jealousy.

Dissensions (Dissension)
Gal 5:20 rage, selfish ambition, **d**,

Dissipation
Lk 21:34 hearts will be weighed down with **d**,
1Pe 4: 4 into the same flood of **d**, and they

Dissolved
Isa 34: 4 the stars of the heavens will be **d**

Dissuade (Dissuaded)
Eze 3:18 to **d** him from his evil ways in
33: 8 speak out to **d** him from his ways,

Dissuaded (Dissuade)
Ac 21:14 he would not be **d**, we gave up and

Distaff
Pr 31:19 In her hand she holds the **d** and

Distance (Distant)
Ge 22: 4 up and saw the place in the **d**.
35:16 While they were still some **d** from
36: 6 land some **d** from his brother Jacob.
37:18 they saw him in the **d**, and before he
48: 7 on the way, a little **d** from Ephrath.
Ex 2: 4 His sister stood at a **d** to see what
20:18 with fear. They stayed at a **d**
20:21 The people remained at a **d**, while
24: 1 You are to worship at a **d**,
33: 7 it outside the camp some **d** away,
Nu 2: 2 the Tent of Meeting some **d** from it,
16:37 and scatter the coals some **d** away,
Dt 19: 6 overtake him if the **d** is too great,
20:15 the cities that are at a **d** from you
21: 2 measure the **d** from the body to the
32:52 you will see the land only from a **d**;
Jos 3: 4 But keep a **d** of about a thousand
3:16 It piled up in a heap a great **d** away,
Jdg 18:22 they had gone some **d** from Micah's
1Sa 26:13 on top of the hill some **d** away;
2Sa 11:10 "Haven't you just come from a **d**?
15:17 they halted at a place some **d** away.
16: 1 David had gone a short **d** beyond the
18:13 would have kept your **d** from me."
19:36 Jordan with the king for a short **d**,
2Ki 2: 7 the prophets went and stood at a **d**,
4:25 When he saw her in the **d**, the man of

2Ki 5:19 After Naaman had travelled some **d**,
Job 2:12 they saw him from a **d**, they could
30:10 They detest me and keep their **d**;
Isa 59:14 and righteousness stands at a **d**;
Eze 40:13 the **d** was twenty-five cubits from
40:15 The **d** from the entrance of the
40:19 he measured the **d** from the inside of
48:35 "The **d** all around will be 18,000
Mt 8:30 Some **d** from them a large herd of
14:24 the boat was already a considerable **d**
26:58 Peter followed him at a **d**, right up
27:55 women were there, watching from a **d**.
Mk 5: 6 he saw Jesus from a **d**, he ran and
8: 3 some of them have come a long **d**."
11:13 Seeing in the **d** a fig-tree in leaf,
14:54 Peter followed him at a **d**, right
15:40 Some women were watching from a **d**.
Lk 17:12 leprosy met him. They stood at a **d**
18:13 "But the tax collector stood at a **d**.
22:54 Peter followed at a **d**.
23:49 stood at a **d**, watching these things.
Heb 11:13 saw them and welcomed them from a **d**.
Rev 14:20 bridles for a **d** of 1,600 stadia.

Distant (Distance)

Dt 14:24 if that place is too **d** and you have
29:22 foreigners who come from **d** lands
30: 4 the most **d** land under the heavens,
Jos 9: 6 "We have come from a **d** country;
9: 9 have come from a very **d** country
1Ki 8:41 from a **d** land because of your name—
2Ki 20:14 "From a **d** land," Hezekiah replied.
2Ch 6:32 has come from a **d** land because of
Est 10: 1 the empire, to its **d** shores.
Ps 56: T "A Dove on **D** Oaks".
72:10 kings of Tarshish and of **d** shores
97: 1 be glad; let the **d** shores rejoice.
Pr 25:25 soul is good news from a **d** land.
Isa 5:26 lifts up a banner for the **d** nations
7:18 flies from the **d** streams of Egypt
8: 9 shattered! Listen, all you **d** lands.
39: 3 "From a **d** land," Hezekiah replied.
45:21 who declared it from the **d** past? Was
49: 1 hear this, you **d** nations:
66:19 and Greece, and to the **d** islands
Jer 4:16 army is coming from a **d** land,
5:15 "I am bringing a **d** nation against
6:20 Sheba or sweet calamus from a **d** land?
9:26 who live in the desert in **d** places.
18:14 from **d** sources ever cease to flow?
25:23 Buz and all who are in **d** places;
30:10 surely save you out of a **d** place,
31:10 proclaim it in **d** coastlands:
46:27 surely save you out of a **d** place,
49:32 the winds those who are in **d** places
51:50 Remember the LORD in a **d** land,
Eze 12:27 he prophesies about the **d** future.'
Da 4:22 extends to **d** parts of the earth.
8:26 for it concerns the **d** future."
Zec 10: 9 in **d** lands they will remember me.
Lk 15:13 set off for a **d** country and there
19:12 of noble birth went to a **d** country

Distil

Job 36:27 which **d** as rain to the streams;

Distinction

Ex 8:23 I will make a **d** between my people
9: 4 the LORD will make a **d** between the
11: 7 makes a **d** between Egypt and Israel.
Lev 20:25 "'You must therefore make a **d**
Mal 3:18 you will again see the **d** between the
Ac 15: 9 He made no **d** between us and them,
1Co 14: 7 unless there is a **d** in the notes?

Distinguish (Distinguished, Distinguishing)

Ex 33:16 What else will **d** me and your people
Lev 10:10 You must **d** between the holy and the
11:47 You must **d** between the unclean and
1Ki 3: 9 and to **d** between right and wrong.
Ezr 3:13 No-one could **d** the sound of the
Eze 22:26 they do not **d** between the holy and
44:23 **d** between the unclean and the clean.
Heb 5:14 themselves to **d** good from evil.

Distinguished (Distinguish)

Nu 22:15 numerous and more **d** than the first.
2Sa 6:20 the king of Israel has **d** himself
Da 6: 3 Now Daniel so **d** himself among the
Lk 14: 8 a person more **d** than you may have

Distinguishing (Distinguish)

1Co 12:10 to another **d** between spirits,
2Th 3:17 is the **d** mark in all my letters.

Distort (Distorted)

Jer 23:36 you **d** the words of the living God,
Mic 3: 9 justice and **d** all that is right;
Ac 20:30 **d** the truth in order to draw away
2Co 4: 2 nor do we **d** the word of God.
2Pe 3:16 ignorant and unstable people **d**,

Distorted (Distort)

Eze 27:35 and their faces are **d** with fear.

Distracted

Lk 10:40 Martha was **d** by all the preparations

Distraught

Ps 55: 2 My thoughts trouble me and I am **d**

Distress (Distressed, Distresses, Distressing)

Ge 32: 7 In great fear and **d** Jacob divided
35: 3 who answered me in the day of my **d**
42:21 that's why this **d** has come upon us."
Dt 4:30 you are in **d** and all these things
28:57 in the **d** that your enemy will
Jdg 2:15 They were in great **d**.
10: 9 and Israel was in great **d**.
1Sa 2:32 you will see **d** in my dwelling.
14:24 Now the men of Israel were in **d** that
22: 2 All those who were in **d** or in debt
28:15 "I am in great **d**," Saul said.
2Sa 16:12 may be that the LORD will see my **d**
22: 7 In my **d** I called to the LORD;
24:14 David said to Gad, "I am in deep **d**.
2Ki 4:27 "Leave her alone! She is in bitter **d**,
19: 3 a day of **d** and rebuke and disgrace,
1Ch 21:13 David said to Gad, "I am in deep **d**.
2Ch 15: 4 in their **d** they turned to the LORD,
15: 6 troubling them with every kind of **d**.
20: 9 will cry out to you in our **d**,
33:12 In his **d** he sought the favour of the
Ne 9:37 We are in great **d**.
Est 4: 4 about Mordecai, she was in great **d**.
7: 4 no such **d** would justify disturbing
Job 15:24 **D** and anguish fill him with terror;
20:22 of his plenty, **d** will overtake him;
27: 9 to his cry when **d** comes upon him?
30:24 man when he cries for help in his **d**.
33:19 pain with constant **d** in his bones,
36:16 "He is wooing you from the jaws of **d**
36:19 you so you would not be in **d**?
Ps 4: 1 Give me relief from my **d**;
18: 6 In my **d** I called to the LORD;
20: 1 LORD answer you when you are in **d**;
25:18 Look upon my affliction and my **d** and
31: 9 O LORD, for I am in **d**; my eyes grow
35:26 May all who gloat over my **d** be put
55:17 cry out in **d**, and he hears my voice.
57: 6 for my feet—I was bowed down in **d**.
69:29 I am in pain and **d**; may your
77: 2 I was in **d**, I sought the Lord; at
81: 7 In your **d** you called and I rescued
102: 2 your face from me when I am in **d**.
106:44 he took note of their **d** when he
107: 6 and he delivered them from their **d**.
107:13 and he saved them from their **d**.
107:19 and he saved them from their **d**.
107:28 and he brought them out of their **d**.
119:143 Trouble and **d** have come upon me, but
120: 1 I call on the LORD in my **d**, and he
144:14 no cry of **d** in our streets.
Pr 1:27 when **d** and trouble overwhelm you.
Isa 5: 7 righteousness, but heard cries of **d**.
5:30 he will see darkness and **d**; even the
8:22 **d** and darkness and fearful gloom,
9: 1 more gloom for those who were in **d**.
25: 4 a refuge for the needy in his **d**, a
26:16 LORD, they came to you in their **d**;
30: 6 Through a land of hardship and **d**,
33: 2 morning, our salvation in time of **d**.
37: 3 a day of **d** and rebuke and disgrace,
63: 9 In all their **d** he too was distressed,
Jer 10:18 I will bring **d** on them so that they
11:14 call to me in the time of their **d**.
14: 8 its Saviour in times of **d**, why are
15:11 in times of disaster and times of **d**.
16:19 my refuge in time of **d**, to you the
Lam 1: 3 overtaken her in the midst of her **d**.
1:21 All my enemies have heard of my **d**;
Eze 30:16 Memphis will be in constant **d**.
Da 12: 1 There will be a time of **d** such as
Jnh 2: 2 He said: "In my **d** I called to the
Hab 3: 7 I saw the tents of Cushan in **d**, the
Zep 1:15 a day of **d** and anguish, a day of
1:17 I will bring **d** on the people and
Mt 24:21 For then there will be great **d**,
24:29 "Immediately after the **d** of those
Mk 13:19 those will be days of **d** unequalled
13:24 "But in those days, following that **d**,
Lk 21:23 There will be great **d** in the land
Ro 2: 9 There will be trouble and **d** for
2Co 2: 4 For I wrote to you out of great **d**
1Th 3: 7 Therefore, brothers, in all our **d**
Jas 1:27 widows in their **d** and to keep

Distressed (Distress)

Ge 21:11 The matter **d** Abraham greatly because
21:12 God said to him, "Do not be so **d**
42:21 We saw how **d** he was when he pleaded
45: 5 now, do not be **d** and do not be angry
1Sa 30: 6 David was greatly **d** because the men
Ezr 10: 9 greatly **d** by the occasion and
Job 6:20 They are **d**, because they had been
Isa 8:21 **D** and hungry, they will roam through
54: 6 a wife deserted and **d** in spirit—
63: 9 In all their distress he too was **d**,
Lam 1:20 "See, O LORD, how **d** I am! I am in
Da 6:14 the king heard this, he was greatly **d**
Mt 14: 9 The king was **d**, but because of his
18:31 they were greatly **d** and went and
Mk 3: 5 deeply **d** at their stubborn hearts,
6:26 The king was greatly **d**, but because
14:33 began to be deeply **d** and troubled.
Lk 12:50 how **d** I am until it is completed!
Ac 17:16 he was greatly **d** to see that the
Ro 14:15 If your brother is **d** because of what
2Co 1: 6 If we are **d**, it is for your comfort
2: 3 I should not be **d** by those who
Php 2:26 For he longs for all of you and is **d**
2Pe 2: 7 **d** by the filthy lives of lawless

Distresses (Distress)

1Sa 10:19 out of all your calamities and **d**.
2Co 6: 4 in troubles, hardships and **d**;

Distressing (Distress)

Ex 33: 4 the people heard these **d** words, they

Distribute (Distributed, Distributes, Distributing, Distribution)

Nu 33:54 **D** the land by lot, according to your
33:54 **D** it according to your ancestral
2Ch 31:19 designated by name to **d** portions
Eze 47:21 "You are to **d** this land among
Da 11:24 He will **d** plunder, loot and wealth
11:39 and will **d** the land at a price.
Mk 8: 7 and told the disciples to **d** them.

Distributed (Distribute)

Nu 26:55 Be sure that the land is **d** by lot.
26:56 Each inheritance is to be **d** by lot
Jos 18:10 and there he **d** the land to the
1Ch 6:60 These towns, which were **d** among the
2Ch 31:16 In addition, they **d** to the males
31:17 they **d** to the priests enrolled by
Est 2:18 and **d** gifts with royal liberality.
Jn 6:11 gave thanks, and **d** to those who were
Ac 4:35 it was **d** to anyone as he had need.
Heb 2: 4 Holy Spirit **d** according to his will.

Distributes (Distribute)

Isa 34:17 his hand **d** them by measure.

Distributing (Distribute)
2Ch 31:14 **d** the contributions made to the LORD
31:15 **d** to their fellow priests according
Ne 13:13 **d** the supplies to their brothers.

Distribution (Distribute)
Ac 6: 1 overlooked in the daily **d** of food.

District (Districts)
Ge 47:11 **d** of Rameses, as Pharaoh directed.
1Sa 9: 4 They went on into the **d** of Shaalim,
9: 5 they reached the **d** of Zuph, Saul
1Ki 4: 5 Nathan—in charge of the **d** officers;
4: 7 Solomon also had twelve **d** governors
4:13 as well as the **d** of Argob in Bashan
4:19 He was the only governor over the **d**.
4:27 The **d** officers, each in his month,
2Ki 22:14 lived in Jerusalem, in the Second **D**.
2Ch 34:22 lived in Jerusalem, in the Second **D**.
Ezr 5: 8 know that we went to the **d** of Judah,
Ne 3:14 ruler of the **d** of Beth Hakkerem.
3:15 Col-Hozeh, ruler of the **d** of Mizpah.
3:17 Hashabiah, ruler of half the **d** of
3:17 carried out repairs for his **d**.
11: 9 was over the Second **D** of the city.
Ecc 5: 8 If you see the poor oppressed in a **d**,
Eze 45: 1 a portion of the land as a sacred **d**,
45: 3 In the sacred **d**, measure off a
45: 7 area formed by the sacred **d** and the
Zep 1:11 Wail, you who live in the market **d**;
Mt 2:22 he withdrew to the **d** of Galilee,
Ac 16:12 leading city of that **d** of Macedonia.

Districts (District)
Jdg 5:15 In the **d** of Reuben there was much
5:16 In the **d** of Reuben there was much
1Ch 27:25 the storehouses in the outlying **d**,
2Ch 11:13 **d** throughout Israel sided with him.
11:23 the **d** of Judah and Benjamin,

Disturb (Disturbance, Disturbed, Disturbing)
2Ki 23:18 "Don't let anyone **d** his bones."

Disturbance (Disturb)
Ac 19:23 About that time there arose a great **d**
24:18 me, nor was I involved in any **d**.

Disturbed (Disturb)
1Sa 28:15 "Why have you **d** me by bringing me
2Sa 7:10 of their own and no longer be **d**.
1Ch 17: 9 of their own and no longer be **d**.
Ne 2:10 they were very much **d** that someone
Job 20: 2 me to answer because I am greatly **d**.
Ps 42: 5 O my soul? Why so **d** within me? Put
42:11 O my soul? Why so **d** within me? Put
43: 5 O my soul? Why so **d** within me? Put
Isa 31: 4 their shouts or **d** by their clamour
Lam 1:20 and in my heart I am **d**, for I have
Da 7:15 that passed through my mind **d** me.
Mt 2: 3 King Herod heard this he was **d**, and
Ac 4: 2 They were greatly **d** because the
15:24 without our authorisation and **d** you,

Disturbing (Disturb)
Est 7: 4 distress would justify **d** the king."

Ditches
2Ki 3:16 says: Make this valley full of **d**.

Divide (Divided, Divides, Dividing, Division, Divisions, Divisive, Subdivision, Subdivisions)
Ex 14:16 hand over the sea to **d** the water
15: 9 I will **d** the spoils; I will gorge
21:35 live one and **d** both the money and
Nu 31:27 **D** the spoils between the soldiers
Dt 19: 3 Build roads to them and **d** into three
31: 7 **d** it among them as their inheritance.
Jos 13: 7 **d** it as an inheritance among the
18: 5 You are to **d** the land into seven
22: 8 and **d** with your brothers the
2Sa 19:29 order you and Ziba to **d** the fields."
Job 27:17 and the innocent will **d** his silver.
41: 6 they **d** him up among the merchants?
Ps 22:18 They **d** my garments among them and
68:12 in the camps men **d** the plunder.
Isa 7: 6 it apart and **d** it among ourselves,
53:12 and he will **d** the spoils with the
Eze 5: 1 a set of scales and **d** up the hair.
47:13 by which you are to **d** the land for
47:14 You are to **d** it equally among them.
Mic 2: 5 of the LORD to **d** the land by lot.
Lk 12:13 to **d** the inheritance with me."
22:17 said, "Take this and **d** it among you.
Jude :19 These are the men who **d** you, who

Divided (Divide)
Ge 10:25 because in his time the earth was **d**
14:15 During the night Abram **d** his men to
32: 7 Jacob **d** the people who were with
33: 1 so he **d** the children among Leah,
Ex 14:21 into dry land. The waters were **d**,
Lev 11: 3 completely **d** and that chews the cud.
11: 7 it has a split hoof completely **d**,
11:26 has a split hoof not completely **d**
Dt 14: 6 has a split hoof **d** in two and that
14: 7 have a split hoof completely **d**
32: 8 when he **d** all mankind, he set up
Jos 14: 5 the Israelites **d** the land, just as
Jdg 9:43 he took his men, **d** them into three
1Ki 18: 6 they **d** the land they were to cover,
2Ki 2: 8 The water **d** to the right and to the
2:14 When he struck the water, it **d** to
1Ch 1:19 because in his time the earth was **d**
23: 6 David **d** the Levites into groups
24: 4 and they were **d** accordingly: sixteen
24: 5 They **d** them impartially by drawing
Ne 9:11 You **d** the sea before them, so that
Ps 78:13 He **d** the sea and led them through;
136:13 to him who **d** the Red Sea asunder
Pr 3:20 by his knowledge the deeps were **d**,
Isa 18: 2 speech, whose land is **d** by rivers.
18: 7 whose land is **d** by rivers—the
33:23 an abundance of spoils will be **d**
63:12 who **d** the waters before them, to
Eze 37:22 nations or be **d** into two kingdoms.
Da 2:41 so this will be a **d** kingdom; yet it
5:28 Peres: Your kingdom is **d** and given
Joel 3: 2 among the nations and **d** up my land.
Am 7:17 Your land will be measured and **d** up,
Mic 2: 4 my people's possession is **d** up.
Zec 14: 1 your plunder will be **d** among you.
Mt 12:25 "Every kingdom **d** against itself will
12:25 every city or household **d** against
12:26 If Satan drives out Satan, he is **d**
27:35 they **d** up his clothes by casting
Mk 3:24 If a kingdom is **d** against itself,
3:25 If a house is **d** against itself, that
3:26 if Satan opposes himself and is **d**,
6:41 also **d** the two fish among them all.
Lk 11:17 "Any kingdom **d** against itself will
11:17 a house **d** against itself will fall.
11:18 If Satan is **d** against himself, how
12:52 in one family **d** against each other,
12:53 They will be **d**, father against son
15:12 So he **d** his property between them.
23:34 **d** up his clothes by casting lots.
Jn 7:43 Thus the people were **d** because of
9:16 such miraculous signs?" they were **d**.
10:19 At these words the Jews were again **d**.
19:24 "They **d** my garments among them and
Ac 14: 4 The people of the city were **d**; some
23: 7 Sadducees, and the assembly was **d**.
1Co 1:13 Is Christ **d**? Was Paul crucified for
7:34 his interests are **d**. An unmarried

Divides (Divide)
Ge 49:27 in the evening he **d** the plunder."
Lk 11:22 the man trusted and **d** up the spoils.

Dividing (Divide)
Jos 19:49 they had finished **d** the land into
19:51 And so they finished **d** the land.
Jdg 5:30 'Are they not finding and **d** the
7:16 **D** the three hundred men into three
Isa 9: 3 as men rejoice when **d** the plunder.
Mk 15:24 **D** up his clothes, they cast lots
Jn 19:23 clothes, **d** them into four shares,
Eph 2:14 barrier, the **d** wall of hostility,
Heb 4:12 it penetrates even to **d** soul and

Divination (Divinations, Divine, Diviner, Diviners)
Ge 30:27 I have learned by **d** that the LORD
44: 5 drinks from and also uses for **d**?
44:15 like me can find things out by **d**?"
Lev 19:26 "'Do not practise **d** or sorcery.
Nu 22: 7 taking with them the fee for **d**.
23:23 against Jacob, no **d** against Israel.
Dt 18:10 who practises **d** or sorcery,
18:14 to those who practise sorcery or **d**.
Jos 13:22 Balaam son of Beor, who practised **d**.
1Sa 15:23 For rebellion is like the sin of **d**,
2Ki 17:17 They practised **d** and sorcery and
21: 6 practised sorcery and **d**, and
2Ch 33: 6 practised sorcery, **d** and witchcraft,
Isa 2: 6 they practise **d** like the Philistines
Eze 13:23 see false visions or practise **d**.
Mic 3: 6 visions, and darkness, without **d**.

Divinations (Divination)
Jer 14:14 **d**, idolatries and the delusions of
Eze 12:24 **d** among the people of Israel.
13: 6 visions are false and their **d** a lie
13: 7 and uttered lying **d** when you say,
13: 9 see false visions and utter lying **d**.
21:29 you and lying **d** about you,
22:28 them by false visions and lying **d**.

Divine (Divination)
Isa 35: 4 with **d** retribution he will come to
Ac 8:10 **d** power known as the Great Power."
17:29 we should not think that the **d** being
19:27 will be robbed of her **d** majesty."
Ro 1:20 his eternal power and **d** nature—
9: 4 theirs the **d** glory, the covenants,
2Co 10: 4 **d** power to demolish strongholds.
2Pe 1: 3 His **d** power has given us everything
1: 4 you may participate in the **d** nature

Diviner (Divination)
Da 2:27 enchanter, magician or **d** can explain

Diviners (Divination)
1Sa 6: 2 for the priests and the **d** and said,
Isa 44:25 false prophets and makes fools of **d**,
Jer 27: 9 your **d**, your interpreters of dreams,
29: 8 and **d** among you deceive you.
Da 4: 7 enchanters, astrologers and **d** came,
5: 7 astrologers and **d** to be brought and
5:11 enchanters, astrologers and **d**.
Mic 3: 7 be ashamed and the **d** disgraced.
Zec 10: 2 deceit, **d** see visions that lie;

Division (Divide)
Nu 2: 4 His **d** numbers 74,600.
2: 6 His **d** numbers 54,400.
2: 8 His **d** numbers 57,400.
2:11 His **d** numbers 46,500.
2:13 His **d** numbers 59,300.
2:15 His **d** numbers 45,650.
2:19 His **d** numbers 40,500.
2:21 His **d** numbers 32,200.
2:23 His **d** numbers 35,400.
2:26 His **d** numbers 62,700.
2:28 His **d** numbers 41,500.
2:30 His **d** numbers 53,400.
10:15 over the **d** of the tribe of Issachar
10:16 over the **d** of the tribe of Zebulun.
10:19 over the **d** of the tribe of Simeon,
10:20 over the **d** of the tribe of Gad.
10:23 over the **d** of the tribe of Manasseh,
10:24 over the **d** of the tribe of Benjamin
10:26 over the **d** of the tribe of Asher,
10:27 over the **d** of the tribe of Naphtali
Jos 22:14 family **d** among the Israelite clans.
1Ch 27: 1 Each **d** consisted of 24,000 men.
27: 2 In charge of the first **d**, for the
27: 2 There were 24,000 men in his **d**.
27: 4 In charge of the **d** for the second
27: 4 Mikloth was the leader of his **d**.

1Ch 27: 4 There were 24,000 men in his **d**.
27: 5 and there were 24,000 men in his **d**.
27: 6 Ammizabad was in charge of his **d**.
27: 7 There were 24,000 men in his **d**.
27: 8 There were 24,000 men in his **d**.
27: 9 There were 24,000 men in his **d**.
27:10 There were 24,000 men in his **d**.
27:11 There were 24,000 men in his **d**.
27:12 There were 24,000 men in his **d**.
27:13 There were 24,000 men in his **d**.
27:14 There were 24,000 men in his **d**.
27:15 There were 24,000 men in his **d**.
Ezr 10:16 one from each family **d**, and all of
Lk 1: 5 who belonged to the priestly **d** of
1: 8 Once when Zechariah's **d** was on duty
12:51 on earth? No, I tell you, but **d**.
1Co 12:25 that there should be no **d** in the

Divisions (Divide)

Ge 36:30 to their **d**, in the land of Seir.
Ex 6:26 Israelites out of Egypt by their **d**."
7: 4 I will bring out my **d**, my people
12:17 that I brought your **d** out of Egypt.
12:41 day, all the LORD's **d** left Egypt.
12:51 Israelites out of Egypt by their **d**.
Nu 1: 3 Aaron are to number by their **d** all
1:52 are to set up their tents by **d**,
2: 3 the **d** of the camp of Judah
2: 9 camp of Judah, according to their **d**,
2:10 On the south will be the **d** of the
2:16 of Reuben, according to their **d**,
2:18 On the west will be the **d** of the
2:24 of Ephraim, according to their **d**,
2:25 On the north will be the **d** of the
2:32 camps, by their **d**, number 603,550.
10:14 The **d** of the camp of Judah went
10:18 The **d** of the camp of Reuben went
10:22 The **d** of the camp of Ephraim went
10:25 the **d** of the camp of Dan set out,
10:28 for the Israelite **d** as they set out.
33: 1 by **d** under the leadership of Moses
Jos 11:23 Israel according to their tribal **d**.
12: 7 Israel according to their tribal **d**
18:10 according to their tribal **d**.
1Sa 11:11 Saul separated his men into three **d**;
1Ch 24: 1 These were the **d** of the sons of
24: 3 David separated them into **d** for
26: 1 The **d** of the gatekeepers: From the
26:12 These **d** of the gatekeepers, through
26:19 These were the **d** of the gatekeepers
27: 1 the army **d** that were on duty month
28: 1 the commanders of the **d** in the
28:13 He gave him instructions for the **d**
28:21 The **d** of the priests and Levites are
2Ch 5:11 themselves, regardless of their **d**.
8:14 he appointed the **d** of the priests
8:14 by **d** for the various gates,
23: 8 had not released any of the **d**.
26:11 ready to go out by **d** according to
31: 2 the priests and Levites to **d**—
31:15 to their **d**, old and young alike.
31:16 their responsibilities and their **d**.
31:17 their responsibilities and their **d**.
35: 4 yourselves by families in your **d**,
35:10 in their **d** as the king had ordered.
Ezr 6:18 they installed the priests in their **d**
Ne 11:36 Some of the **d** of the Levites of
Ro 16:17 to watch out for those who cause **d**
1Co 1:10 so that there may be no **d** among you
11:18 there are **d** among you, and to some

Divisive (Divide)

Tit 3:10 Warn a **d** person once, and then warn

Divorce (Divorced, Divorces)

Dt 22:19 must not **d** her as long as he lives.
22:29 can never **d** her as long as he lives.
24: 1 he writes her a certificate of **d**,
24: 3 and writes her a certificate of **d**,
Isa 50: 1 is your mother's certificate of **d**
Jer 3: 8 Israel her certificate of **d**
Mal 2:16 "I hate **d**," says the LORD God of
Mt 1:19 he had in mind to **d** her quietly.
5:31 must give her a certificate of **d**.'
19: 3 **d** his wife for any and every reason?"
Mt 19: 7 certificate of **d** and send her away?"
19: 8 "Moses permitted you to **d** your wives
Mk 10: 2 it lawful for a man to **d** his wife?"
10: 4 certificate of **d** and send her away."
1Co 7:11 And a husband must not **d** his wife.
7:12 to live with him, he must not **d** her.
7:13 live with her, she must not **d** him.
7:27 Are you married? Do not seek a **d**.

Divorced (Divorce)

Lev 21: 7 or **d** from their husbands,
21:14 He must not marry a widow, a **d** woman,
22:13 daughter becomes a widow or is **d**,
Nu 30: 9 or **d** woman will be binding on her.
Dt 24: 4 her first husband, who **d** her, is not
1Ch 8: 8 he had **d** his wives Hushim and Baara.
Eze 44:22 must not marry widows or **d** women;
Mt 5:32 the **d** woman commits adultery.
Lk 16:18 marries a **d** woman commits adultery.

Divorces (Divorce)

Jer 3: 1 "If a man **d** his wife and she leaves
Mt 5:31 "It has been said, 'Anyone who **d** his
5:32 I tell you that anyone who **d** his
19: 9 I tell you that anyone who **d** his
Mk 10:11 He answered, "Anyone who **d** his wife
10:12 if she **d** her husband and marries
Lk 16:18 "Anyone who **d** his wife and marries

Dizahab

Dt 1: 1 and Tophel, Laban, Hazeroth and **D**.

Dizziness

Isa 19:14 has poured into them a spirit of **d**;

Do not be afraid

Ge 15:1; 21:17; 26:24; 46:3; Ex 14:13; 20:20; Nu 14:9; 21:34; Dt 1:17, 21, 29; 3:2, 22; 7:18; 18:22; 20:1; 31:6, 8; Jos 8:1; 10:8, 25; 11:6; Jdg 6:23; 1Sa 12:20; 2Ki 1:15; 19:6; 25:24; 1Ch 22:13; 28:20; 2Ch 20:15, 17; 32:7; Isa 10:24; 37:6; 40:9; 41:14; 43:5; 44:2, 8; 54:4; Jer 1:8; 40:9; 42:11; Eze 2:6; 3:9; Da 10:12, 19; Zec 8:13, 15; Mt 1:20; 10:26, 28; 28:5, 10; Lk 1:13, 30; 2:10; 12:4, 32; Jn 12:15; 14:27; Ac 18:9; 27:24; Rev 1:17; 2:10

Do not fear

Ex 9:30; Ecc 8:13; Isa 8:12; 35:4; 41:10, 13; 51:7; 54:4; 57:11; Jer 10:5; 30:10; 46:27, 28; Lam 3:57; Zep 3:16; Hag 2:5; Mal 3:5; 1Pe 3:14

Doctor (Doctors)

Mt 9:12 healthy who need a **d**, but the sick.
Mk 2:17 healthy who need a **d**, but the sick.
Lk 5:31 healthy who need a **d**, but the sick.
Col 4:14 Our dear friend Luke, the **d**, and

Doctors (Doctor)

Mk 5:26 under the care of many **d** and had

Doctrine (Doctrines)

1Ti 1:10 else is contrary to the sound **d**
4:16 Watch your life and **d** closely.
2Ti 4: 3 men will not put up with sound **d**.
Tit 1: 9 encourage others by sound **d** and
2: 1 what is in accord with sound **d**.

Doctrines (Doctrine)

1Ti 1: 3 not to teach false **d** any longer
6: 3 If anyone teaches false **d** and does

Document (Documents)

Est 8: 8 no **d** written in the king's name

Documents (Document)

Jer 32:14 says: Take these **d**, both the sealed

Dodai

2Sa 23: 9 Next to him was Eleazar son of **D** the
1Ch 11:12 Next to him was Eleazar son of **D** the
27: 4 the second month was **D** the Ahohite;

Dodavahu

2Ch 20:37 Eliezer son of **D** of Mareshah

Dodo

Jdg 10: 1 the son of **D**, rose to save Israel.
2Sa 23:24 Elhanan son of **D** from Bethlehem,
1Ch 11:26 Elhanan son of **D** from Bethlehem,

Doe (Does)

Ge 49:21 "Naphtali is a **d** set free that bears
Job 39: 1 you watch when the **d** bears her fawn?
Ps 22: T "The **D** of the Morning".
Pr 5:19 A loving **d**, a graceful deer—may
Jer 14: 5 Even the **d** in the field deserts her

Doeg

1Sa 21: 7 **D** the Edomite, Saul's head shepherd.
22: 9 **D** the Edomite, who was standing with
22:18 The king then ordered **D**, "You turn
22:18 So **D** the Edomite turned and struck
22:22 "That day, when **D** the Edomite was
Ps 52: T When **D** the Edomite had gone to the

Does (Doe)

SS 2: 7 by the gazelles and by the **d** of the
3:5 by the gazelles and by the **d** of the

Dog (Dog's, Dogs)

Ex 11: 7 among the Israelites not a **d** will
Jdg 7: 5 water with their tongues like a **d**
1Sa 17:43 He said to David, "Am I a **d**, that you
24:14 are you pursuing? A dead **d**? A flea?
2Sa 9: 8 you should notice a dead **d** like me?"
16: 9 "Why should this dead **d** curse my
2Ki 8:13 "How could your servant, a mere **d**,
Job 18:11 on every side and **d** his every step.
Pr 26:11 a **d** returns to its vomit, so a fool
26:17 Like one who seizes a **d** by the ears
Ecc 9: 4 **d** is better off than a dead lion!
2Pe 2:22 "A **d** returns to its vomit,"

Dog's (Dog)

2Sa 3: 8 "Am I a **d** head—on Judah's side?
Isa 66: 3 like one who breaks a **d** neck;

Dogs (Dog)

Ex 22:31 by wild beasts; throw it to the **d**.
1Ki 14:11 **D** will eat those belonging to
16: 4 **D** will eat those belonging to Baasha
21:19 where **d** licked up Naboth's blood,
21:19 **d** will lick up your blood—yes,
21:23 '**D** will devour Jezebel by the wall
21:24 "**D** will eat those belonging to Ahab
22:38 and the **d** licked up his blood, as
2Ki 9:10 for Jezebel, **d** will devour her on
9:36 **d** will devour Jezebel's flesh.
Job 30: 1 disdained to put with my sheep **d**.
Ps 22:16 **D** have surrounded me; a band of evil
22:20 life from the power of the **d**.
59: 6 return at evening, snarling like **d**,
59:14 return at evening, snarling like **d**,
68:23 tongues of your **d** have their share."
Isa 56:10 lack knowledge; they are all mute **d**,
56:11 They are **d** with mighty appetites;
Jer 15: 3 "the sword to kill and the **d** to drag
Mt 7: 6 "Do not give **d** what is sacred; do
15:26 bread and toss it to their **d**."
15:27 "but even the **d** eat the crumbs that
Mk 7:27 bread and toss it to their **d**."
7:28 "but even the **d** under the table eat
Lk 16:21 Even the **d** came and licked his sores.
Php 3: 2 Watch out for those **d**, those men who
Rev 22:15 Outside are the **d**, those who

Dole

Lev 26:26 they will **d** out the bread by weight.

Domain

Dt 33:20 "Blessed is he who enlarges Gad's **d**!
Eze 27: 4 Your **d** was on the high seas; your

Dominion

Job 25: 2 "**D** and awe belong to God; he

Job 38:33 set up ⌊God's⌋ **d** over the earth?
Ps 22:28 for **d** belongs to the LORD and he
103:22 all his works everywhere in his **d**.
114: 2 God's sanctuary, Israel his **d**.
145:13 **d** endures through all generations.
Da 2:37 you **d** and power and might and glory;
4: 3 his **d** endures from generation to
4:22 and your **d** extends to distant parts
4:34 His **d** is an eternal **d**; his kingdom
6:26 be destroyed, his **d** will never end.
7:14 His **d** is an everlasting **d** that will
Mic 4: 8 the former **d** will be restored to you;
1Co 15:24 all **d**, authority and power.
Eph 1:21 power and **d**, and every title that
Col 1:13 For he has rescued us from the **d** of

Donated

Ezr 8:25 had **d** for the house of our God.

Donkey (Donkey's, Donkeys, Donkeys')

Ge 16:12 He will be a wild **d** of a man; his
22: 3 Abraham got up and saddled his **d**.
22: 5 "Stay here with the **d** while I and
42:27 his sack to get feed for his **d**,
49:11 He will tether his **d** to a vine, his
49:14 "Issachar is a scrawny **d** lying down
Ex 4:20 on a **d** and started back to Egypt.
13:13 Redeem with a lamb every firstborn **d**,
20:17 his ox or **d**, or anything that
21:33 it and an ox or a **d** falls into it,
22: 4 whether ox or **d** or sheep—he must
22: 9 a **d**, a sheep, a garment, or any
22:10 "If a man gives a **d**, an ox, a sheep
23: 4 your enemy's ox or **d** wandering off,
23: 5 If you see the **d** of someone who
23:12 so that your ox and your **d** may rest
34:20 Redeem the firstborn **d** with a lamb,
Nu 16:15 I have not taken so much as a **d** from
22:21 saddled his **d** and went with the
22:22 Balaam was riding on his **d**, and his
22:23 the **d** saw the angel of the LORD
22:25 the **d** saw the angel of the LORD, she
22:27 the **d** saw the angel of the LORD, she
22:29 Balaam answered the **d**, "You have
22:30 The **d** said to Balaam, "Am I not
22:30 "Am I not your own **d**, which you
22:32 "Why have you beaten your **d** these
22:33 The **d** saw me and turned away from me
Dt 5:14 nor your ox, your **d** or any of your
5:21 his ox or **d**, or anything that
22: 3 **d** or his cloak or anything he loses.
22: 4 If you see your brother's **d** or his
22:10 Do not plough with an ox and a **d**
28:31 Your **d** will be forcibly taken from
Jos 15:18 When she got off her **d**, Caleb asked
Jdg 1:14 When she got off her **d**, Caleb asked
15:15 Finding a fresh jaw-bone of a **d**, he
19:28 her on his **d** and set out for home.
1Sa 12: 3 have I taken? Whose **d** have I taken?
16:20 Jesse took a **d** loaded with bread, a
25:20 she came riding her **d** into a
25:23 she quickly got off her **d** and bowed
25:42 Abigail quickly got on a **d** and,
2Sa 17:23 he saddled his **d** and set out for his
19:26 'I will have my **d** saddled and will
1Ki 2:40 At this, he saddled his **d** and went
13:13 he said to his sons, "Saddle the **d**
13:13 saddled the **d** for him, he mounted
13:23 him back saddled his **d** for him.
13:24 **d** and the lion standing beside it.
13:27 "Saddle the **d** for me," and they did
13:28 **d** and the lion standing beside it.
13:28 eaten the body nor mauled the **d**.
13:29 laid it on the **d**, and brought it
2Ki 4:22 a **d** so I can go to the man of God
4:24 She saddled the **d** and said to her
Job 6: 5 Does a wild **d** bray when it has grass,
24: 3 They drive away the orphan's **d** and
39: 5 "Who let the wild **d** go free? Who
Pr 26: 3 for the horse, a halter for the **d**,
Isa 1: 3 master, the **d** his owner's manger,
Jer 2:24 a wild **d** accustomed to the desert,
22:19 He will have the burial of a **d**—
Hos 8: 9 like a wild **d** wandering alone.
Zec 9: 9 on a **d**, on a colt, the foal of a **d**.
Mt 21: 2 **d** tied there, with her colt by her.
21: 5 a **d**, on a colt, the foal of a **d**."
21: 7 They brought the **d** and the colt,
Lk 10:34 Then he put the man on his own **d**,
13:15 untie his ox or **d** from the stall
Jn 12:14 Jesus found a young **d** and sat upon
2Pe 2:16 rebuked for his wrongdoing by a **d**

Donkey's (Donkey)

Nu 22:28 the LORD opened the **d** mouth, and she
Jdg 15:16 Samson said, "With a **d** jaw-bone I
15:16 With a **d** jaw-bone I have killed a
2Ki 6:25 a **d** head sold for eighty shekels
Job 11:12 a wild **d** colt can be born a man.
Jn 12:15 king is coming, seated on a **d** colt."

Donkeys (Donkey)

Ge 12:16 male and female **d**, menservants and
24:35 and maidservants, and camels and **d**.
30:43 and menservants, and camels and **d**.
32: 5 I have cattle and **d**, sheep and goats,
32:15 and twenty female **d** and ten male **d**.
34:28 herds and **d** and everything else of
36:24 grazing the **d** of his father Zibeon.
42:26 they loaded their grain on their **d**
43:18 seize us as slaves and take our **d**."
43:24 and provided fodder for their **d**.
44: 3 were sent on their way with their **d**.
44:13 loaded their **d** and returned to the
45:23 ten **d** loaded with the best things of
45:23 and ten female **d** loaded with grain
47:17 sheep and goats, their cattle and **d**.
Ex 9: 3 **d** and camels and on your cattle and
Nu 31:28 persons, cattle, **d**, sheep or goats.
31:30 **d**, sheep, goats or other animals.
31:34 61,000 **d**
31:39 30,500 **d**, of which the tribute for
31:45 30,500 **d**
Jos 6:21 young and old, cattle, sheep and **d**.
7:24 his cattle, **d** and sheep, his tent
9: 4 delegation whose **d** were loaded with
Jdg 5:10 "You who ride on white **d**, sitting on
6: 4 neither sheep nor cattle nor **d**.
10: 4 He had thirty sons, who rode thirty **d**
12:14 grandsons, who rode on seventy **d**.
15:16 jaw-bone I have made **d** of them.
19: 3 had with him his servant and two **d**.
19:10 his two saddled **d** and his concubine.
19:19 fodder for our **d** and bread and wine
19:21 him into his house and fed his **d**.
1Sa 8:16 and **d** he will take for his own use.
9: 3 Now the **d** belonging to Saul's father
9: 3 with you and go and look for the **d**."
9: 4 Shaalim, but the **d** were not there.
9: 5 stop thinking about the **d** and start
9:20 for the **d** you lost three days ago,
10: 2 They will say to you,'The **d** you set
10:14 "Looking for the **d**," he said.
10:16 us that the **d** had been found.
15: 3 cattle and sheep, camels and **d**.'"
22:19 and its cattle, **d** and sheep.
25:18 pressed figs, and loaded them on **d**.
27: 9 cattle, **d** and camels, and clothes.
2Sa 16: 1 He had a string of **d** saddled and
16: 2 "The **d** are for the king's household
2Ki 7: 7 their tents and their horses and **d**.
7:10 anyone—only tethered horses and **d**,
1Ch 5:21 thousand sheep and two thousand **d**.
12:40 food on **d**, camels, mules and oxen.
27:30 Meronothite was in charge of the **d**.
2Ch 28:15 those who were weak they put on **d**.
Ezr 2:67 435 camels and 6,720 **d**.
Ne 7:69 435 camels and 6,720 **d**
13:15 in grain and loading it on **d**,
Job 1: 3 yoke of oxen and five hundred **d**,
1:14 and the **d** were grazing nearby,
24: 5 Like wild **d** in the desert, the poor
42:12 yoke of oxen and a thousand **d**.
Ps 104:11 the wild **d** quench their thirst.
Isa 21: 7 riders on **d** or riders on camels, let
30:24 The oxen and **d** that work the soil
32:14 delight of **d**, a pasture for flocks,
32:20 your cattle and **d** range free.
Jer 14: 6 Wild **d** stand on the barren heights
Eze 23:20 whose genitals were like those of **d**
Da 5:21 he lived with the wild **d** and ate
Zec 14:15 the camels and **d**, and all the

Donkeys' (Donkey)

Isa 30: 6 carry their riches on **d** backs,

Do-Nothing (Nothing)

Isa 30: 7 Therefore I call her Rahab the **D**.

Doom (Doomed)

Dt 32:35 near and their **d** rushes upon them."
Eze 7: 7 **D** has come upon you—you who dwell
7:10 It has come! **D** has burst forth,
22: 3 O city that brings on herself **d** by
30: 3 clouds, a time of **d** for the nations.
30: 9 on the day of Egypt's **d**, for it is
Rev 18:10 In one hour your **d** has come!'

Doomed (Doom)

Jdg 13:22 "We are **d** to die!" he said to his
2Ki 7:13 like all these Israelites who are **d**.
Ps 137: 8 of Babylon, **d** to destruction,
Isa 65:23 or bear children **d** to misfortune;
Jer 8:14 For the LORD our God has **d** us to
Jn 17:12 except the one **d** to destruction
2Th 2: 3 revealed, the man **d** to destruction.

Door (Door-frame, Door-frames, Doorkeeper, Door-keeper, Doorkeepers, Doorpost, Door-post, Doorposts, Doors, Doorway, Doorways)

Ge 4: 7 sin is crouching at your **d**; it
6:16 Put a **d** in the side of the ark and
19: 6 meet them and shut the **d** behind
19: 9 moved forward to break down the **d**.
19:10 back into the house and shut the **d**.
19:11 they struck the men who were at the **d**
19:11 so that they could not find the **d**.
Ex 12:22 of the **d** of his house until morning.
21: 6 He shall take him to the **d** or the
Dt 15:17 it through his ear lobe into the **d**,
22:21 she shall be brought to the **d** of her
Jdg 11:31 whatever comes out of the **d** of my
19:22 Pounding on the **d**, they shouted to
19:26 fell down at the **d** and lay there
19:27 opened the **d** of the house and
2Sa 13:17 of here and bolt the **d** after her."
13:18 her out and bolted the **d** after her.
1Ki 14: 6 the sound of her footsteps at the **d**,
2Ki 4: 4 go inside and shut the **d** behind you
4: 5 shut the **d** behind her and her sons.
4:21 God, then shut the **d** and went out.
4:33 He went in, shut the **d** on the two of
5: 9 stopped at the **d** of Elisha's house.
6:32 shut the **d** and hold it shut against
9: 3 open the **d** and run; don't delay!"
9:10 Then he opened the **d** and ran.
Job 31: 9 I have lurked at my neighbour's **d**,
31:32 **d** was always open to the traveller—
Ps 141: 3 keep watch over the **d** of my lips.
Pr 5: 8 do not go near the **d** of her house,
9:14 She sits at the **d** of her house, on a
26:14 a **d** turns on its hinges, so a
SS 7:13 and at our **d** is every delicacy, both
8: 9 If she is a **d**, we will enclose her
Eze 41:24 Each **d** had two leaves—two hinged
41:24 hinged leaves for each **d**.
42: 2 The building whose **d** faced north was
Hos 2:15 the Valley of Achor a **d** of hope.
Mt 6: 6 go into your room, close the **d** and
7: 7 and the **d** will be opened to you.
7: 8 who knocks, the **d** will be opened.
24:33 that it is near, right at the **d**.
25:10 And the **d** was shut.
25:11 'Sir! Sir!' they said.'Open the **d**
Mk 1:33 The whole town gathered at the **d**,
2: 2 room left, not even outside the **d**,
13:29 that it is near, right at the **d**.
13:34 the one at the **d** to keep watch.
Lk 11: 7 The **d** is already locked, and my
11: 9 and the **d** will be opened to you.
11:10 who knocks, the **d** will be opened.

Lk 12:36 can immediately open the **d** for him.
13:24 to enter through the narrow **d**,
13:25 the house gets up and closes the **d**,
13:25 pleading, 'Sir, open the **d** for us.
Jn 18:16 Peter had to wait outside at the **d**.
18:17 you?" the girl at the **d** asked Peter.
Ac 5: 9 are at the **d**, and they will carry
12:13 named Rhoda came to answer the **d**.
12:14 and exclaimed, "Peter is at the **d**!
12:16 when they opened the **d** and saw him,
14:27 the **d** of faith to the Gentiles.
18: 7 **d** to the house of Titius Justus,
1Co 16: 9 a great **d** for effective work has
2Co 2:12 that the Lord had opened a **d** for me,
Col 4: 3 too, that God may open a **d** for our
Jas 5: 9 The Judge is standing at the **d**!
Rev 3: 8 you an open **d** that no-one can shut.
3:20 I stand at the **d** and knock.
3:20 hears my voice and opens the **d**,
4: 1 me was a **d** standing open in heaven.

Door-frame (Door, Frame)

Ex 12:22 the top and on both sides of the **d**.
12:23 blood on the top and sides of the **d**
Eze 41:21 outer sanctuary had a rectangular **d**,

Door-frames (Door, Frame)

Ex 12: 7 tops of the **d** of the houses where
Dt 6: 9 Write them on the **d** of your houses
11:20 Write them on the **d** of your houses
2Ch 3: 7 He overlaid the ceiling beams, **d**,

Doorkeeper (Door, Keep)

Ps 84:10 I would rather be a **d** in the house

Door-keeper (Door, Keep)

Jer 35: 4 of Maaseiah son of Shallum the **d**.

Doorkeepers (Door, Keep)

2Ki 22: 4 **d** have collected from the people.
23: 4 the priests next in rank and the **d**
25:18 priest next in rank and the three **d**.
1Ch 15:23 Berekiah and Elkanah were to be **d**
15:24 Jehiah were also to be **d** for the ark.
2Ch 23:19 He also stationed **d** at the gates of
34: 9 which the Levites who were the **d** had
34:13 were secretaries, scribes and **d**.
Jer 52:24 priest next in rank and the three **d**.

Doorpost (Door)

1Sa 1: 9 chair by the **d** of the LORD's temple.

Door-post (Door, Post)

Ex 21: 6 take him to the door or the **d** and

Doorposts (Door, Post)

2Ki 18:16 and **d** of the temple of the LORD,
Isa 6: 4 the **d** and thresholds shook and the
57: 8 Behind your doors and your **d** you
Eze 43: 8 threshold and their **d** beside my **d**,
45:19 and put it on the **d** of the temple,

Doors (Door, Post)

Jdg 3:23 he shut the **d** of the upper room
3:24 the **d** of the upper room locked.
3:25 but when he did not open the **d** of
16: 3 took hold of the **d** of the city gate,
1Sa 3:15 the **d** of the house of the LORD.
21:13 making marks on the **d** of the gate
1Ki 6:31 he made **d** of olive wood with
6:32 on the two olive wood **d** he carved
6:34 He also made two pine **d**, each having
7:50 for the **d** of the innermost room,
7:50 **d** of the main hall of the temple.
2Ki 18:16 with which he had covered the **d**
1Ch 22: 3 nails for the **d** of the gateways
2Ch 3: 7 door-frames, walls and **d** of the
4: 9 and the large court and the **d** for
4: 9 and overlaid the **d** with bronze.
4:22 dishes and censers; and the gold **d**
4:22 the inner **d** to the Most Holy Place
4:22 and the **d** of the main hall.
23: 4 Sabbath are to keep watch at the **d**,
2Ch 28:24 He shut the **d** of the LORD's temple
29: 3 he opened the **d** of the temple of the
29: 7 They also shut the **d** of the portico
Ne 3: 1 dedicated it and set its **d** in place
3: 3 its **d** and bolts and bars in place.
3: 6 its **d** and bolts and bars in place.
3:13 They rebuilt it and put its **d** and
3:14 its **d** and bolts and bars in place.
3:15 its **d** and bolts and bars in place.
6: 1 I had not set the **d** in the gates—
6:10 and let us close the temple **d**,
7: 1 and I had set the **d** in place,
7: 3 make them shut the **d** and bar them.
13:19 I ordered the **d** to be shut and not
Job 3:10 for it did not shut the **d** of the
38: 8 "Who shut up the sea behind **d** when
38:10 and set its **d** and bars in place,
41:14 Who dares open the **d** of his mouth,
Ps 24: 7 be lifted up, you ancient **d**,
24: 9 lift them up, you ancient **d**,
78:23 and opened the **d** of the heavens;
Pr 8:34 at my **d**, waiting at my doorway.
Ecc 12: 4 the **d** to the street are closed and
Isa 26:20 enter your rooms and shut the **d**
45: 1 to open **d** before him so that gates
57: 8 Behind your **d** and your doorposts you
Eze 26: 2 and its **d** have swung open to me; now
33:30 walls and at the **d** of the houses,
41:23 the Most Holy Place had double **d**.
41:25 on the **d** of the outer sanctuary were
42: 4 Their **d** were on the north.
Zec 11: 1 Open your **d**, O Lebanon, so that
Mal 1:10 one of you would shut the temple **d**,
Jn 20:19 with the **d** locked for fear of the
20:26 Though the **d** were locked, Jesus came
Ac 5:19 **d** of the jail and brought them out.
5:23 with the guards standing at the **d**;
16:26 At once all the prison **d** flew open,
16:27 and when he saw the prison **d** open,

Doorway (Door, Way)

Ex 12:23 and will pass over that **d**,
35:15 **d** at the entrance to the tabernacle;
Lev 14:38 the priest shall go out of the **d** of
Jdg 4:20 "Stand in the **d** of the tent," he
19:27 fallen in the **d** of the house, with
2Ki 4:15 called her, and she stood in the **d**.
Est 2:21 king's officers who guarded the **d**,
6: 2 king's officers who guarded the **d**,
Pr 8:34 daily at my doors, waiting at my **d**.
Eze 8: 8 dug into the wall and saw a **d** there.
40:38 A room with a **d** was by the portico
42:12 There was a **d** at the beginning of
Mk 11: 4 outside in the street, tied at a **d**.

Doorways (Door, Way)

1Ki 7: 5 All the **d** had rectangular frames;
Eze 42:11 Similar to the **d** on the north
42:12 were the **d** of the rooms on the south.
Zep 2:14 rubble will be in the **d**, the beams

Dophkah

Nu 33:12 the Desert of Sin and camped at **D**.
33:13 They left **D** and camped at Alush.

Dor

Jos 12:23 the king of **D** (in Naphoth **D**) one the
17:11 Ibleam and the people of **D**, Endor,
Jdg 1:27 Taanach or **D** or Ibleam or Megiddo
1Ch 7:29 Taanach, Megiddo and **D**, together

Dorcas (Tabitha)

Also known as Tabitha. Disciple in Joppa, known for her good works (Ac 9:36,39). Died (Ac 9:37); raised to life by Peter (Ac 9:38–42).

Ac 9:36 (which when translated, is **D**), who
9:39 other clothing that **D** had made while

Dothan

Town about 12 miles north of Samaria, on trade route between Syria and Egypt. Joseph betrayed by brothers near here (Ge 37:17). Elisha encountered Aramean soldiers here (2Ki 6:8–19).

Ge 37:17 "I heard them say, 'Let's go to **D**.'"
37:17 his brothers and found them near **D**.
2Ki 6:13 The report came back: "He is in **D**."

Double (Double-edged, Double-minded, Double-pronged)

Ge 43:12 Take **d** the amount of silver with you,
43:15 took the gifts and **d** the amount of
Ex 22: 4 donkey or sheep—he must pay back **d**.
22: 7 if he is caught, must pay back **d**.
22: 9 must pay back **d** to his neighbour.
26: 9 curtain **d** at the front of the tent.
26:24 At these two corners they must be **d**
28:16 long and a span wide—and folded **d**.
36:29 the frames were **d** from the bottom
39: 9 long and a span wide—and folded **d**.
Dt 21:17 giving him a **d** share of all he has.
1Sa 1: 5 to Hannah he gave a **d** portion
2Ki 2: 9 "Let me inherit a **d** portion of your
Isa 40: 2 the LORD's hand **d** for all her sins.
51:19 These **d** calamities have come upon
61: 7 my people will receive a **d** portion,
61: 7 inherit a **d** portion in their land,
Jer 16:18 I will repay them **d** for their
17:18 destroy them with **d** destruction.
Eze 41:23 and the Most Holy Place had **d** doors.
Hos 10:10 put them in bonds for their **d** sin.
1Ti 5:17 church well are worthy of **d** honour,
Rev 18: 6 pay her back **d** for what she has
18: 6 Mix her a **d** portion from her own cup.

Double-edged (Double, Edge)

Jdg 3:16 Now Ehud had made a **d** sword about a
Ps 149: 6 mouths and a **d** sword in their hands,
Pr 5: 4 bitter as gall, sharp as a **d** sword.
Heb 4:12 Sharper than any **d** sword, it
Rev 1:16 of his mouth came a sharp **d** sword.
2:12 of him who has the sharp, **d** sword.

Double-minded (Double, Mind)

Ps 119:113 I hate **d** men, but I love your law.
Jas 1: 8 he is a **d** man, unstable in all he
4: 8 and purify your hearts, you **d**.

Double-pronged (Double)

Eze 40:43 **d** hooks, each a handbreadth long,

Doubt (Doubted, Doubting, Doubts)

Mt 14:31 faith," he said, "why did you **d**?
21:21 if you have faith and do not **d**, not
Mk 11:23 does not **d** in his heart but believes
Ac 12:11 "Now I know without a **d** that the
1Co 11:19 No **d** there have to be differences
Heb 7: 7 without **d** the lesser person is
Jas 1: 6 he must believe and not **d**, because
Jude :22 Be merciful to those who **d**;

Doubted (Doubt)

Mt 28:17 they worshipped him; but some **d**.

Doubting (Doubt)

Jn 20:27 into my side. Stop **d** and believe."

Doubts (Doubt)

Lk 24:38 and why do **d** rise in your minds?
Ro 14:23 the man who has **d** is condemned if he
Jas 1: 6 because he who **d** is like a wave of

Dough

Ex 12:34 the people took their **d** before the
12:39 With the **d** they had brought from
12:39 The **d** was without yeast because they
2Sa 13: 8 She took some **d**, kneaded it, made
Jer 7:18 and the women knead the **d** and make
Hos 7: 4 the kneading of the **d** till it rises.
Mt 13:33 until it worked all through the **d**."
Lk 13:21 until it worked all through the **d**."
Ro 11:16 If the part of the **d** offered as
1Co 5: 6 works through the whole batch of **d**?
Gal 5: 9 works through the whole batch of **d**."

Dove (Doves)

Ge 8: 8 he sent out a **d** to see if the water
8: 9 the **d** could find no place to set its

Ge 8: 9 took the **d** and brought it back to
8:10 again sent out the **d** from the ark.
8:11 the **d** returned to him in the evening,
8:12 more days and sent the **d** out again,
15: 9 along with a **d** and a young pigeon."
Lev 1:14 is to offer a **d** or a young pigeon.
12: 6 pigeon or a **d** for a sin offering.
Ps 55: 6 "Oh, that I had the wings of a **d**!
56: T "A **D** on Distant Oaks".
68:13 the wings of ⌊my⌋ **d** are sheathed
74:19 Do not hand over the life of your **d**
SS 2:14 My **d** in the clefts of the rock, in
5: 2 my darling, my **d**, my flawless one.
6: 9 my **d**, my perfect one, is unique, the
Isa 38:14 thrush, I moaned like a mourning **d**.
Jer 8: 7 and the **d**, the swift and the thrush
48:28 Be like a **d** that makes its nest at
Hos 7:11 "Ephraim is like a **d**, easily
Mt 3:16 like a **d** and lighting on him.
Mk 1:10 Spirit descending on him like a **d**.
Lk 3:22 on him in bodily form like a **d**.
Jn 1:32 heaven as a **d** and remain on him.

Doves (Dove)

Lev 5: 7 he is to bring two **d** or two young
5:11 "'If, however, he cannot afford two **d**
12: 8 she is to bring two **d** or two young
14:22 two **d** or two young pigeons, which he
14:30 he shall sacrifice the **d** or the
15:14 On the eighth day he must take two **d**
15:29 On the eighth day she must take two **d**
Nu 6:10 on the eighth day he must bring two **d**
SS 1:15 Oh, how beautiful! Your eyes are **d**.
2:12 cooing of **d** is heard in our land.
4: 1 Your eyes behind your veil are **d**.
5:12 His eyes are like **d** by the water
Isa 59:11 we moan mournfully like **d**.
60: 8 like clouds, like **d** to their nests?
Eze 7:16 moaning like **d** of the valleys, each
Hos 11:11 from Egypt, like **d** from Assyria.
Na 2: 7 Its slave girls moan like **d**
Mt 10:16 as snakes and as innocent as **d**.
21:12 and the benches of those selling **d**.
Mk 11:15 and the benches of those selling **d**,
Lk 2:24 "a pair of **d** or two young pigeons".
Jn 2:14 sheep and **d**, and others sitting at
2:16 To those who sold **d** he said, "Get

Downcast (Cast)

Ge 4: 5 was very angry, and his face was **d**.
4: 6 are you angry? Why is your face **d**?
1Sa 1:18 and her face was no longer **d**.
Job 22:29 them up!' then he will save the **d**.
Ps 42: 5 Why are you **d**, O my soul? Why so
42: 6 my God. My soul is **d** within me;
42:11 Why are you **d**, O my soul? Why so
43: 5 Why are you **d**, O my soul? Why so
Lam 3:20 them, and my soul is **d** within me.
Lk 24:17 They stood still, their faces **d**.
2Co 7: 6 God, who comforts the **d**, comforted

Downfall (Fall)

1Ki 13:34 house of Jeroboam that led to its **d**
2Ki 14:10 your own **d** and that of Judah also?"
2Ch 22: 7 Joram, God brought about Ahaziah's **d**.
25:19 your own **d** and that of Judah also?"
26:16 powerful, his pride led to his **d**.
28:23 were his **d** and the **d** of all Israel.
Est 6:13 before whom your **d** has started,
Ps 5:10 Let their intrigues be their **d**.
Pr 18:12 Before his **d** a man's heart is proud,
29:16 but the righteous will see their **d**.
Jer 48: 2 Heshbon men will plot her **d**:'Come,
Eze 18:30 then sin will not be your **d**.
32:10 On the day of your **d** each of them
Hos 14: 1 Your sins have been your **d**!
Mic 7:10 your God?" My eyes will see her **d**;

Downhearted (Heart)

1Sa 1: 8 Why don't you eat? Why are you **d**?

Downpour (Pour)

Job 37: 6 to the rain shower,'Be a mighty **d**.'
Isa 28: 2 a driving rain and a flooding **d**,

Downstairs (Stairs)

Ac 10:20 get up and go **d**. Do not hesitate to

Downstream (Stream)

Jos 3:13 its waters flowing **d** will be cut off

Drachmas

Ezr 2:69 for this work 61,000 **d** of gold,
Ne 7:70 To the treasury 1,000 **d** of gold,
7:71 20,000 **d** of gold and 2,200 minas of
7:72 of the people was 20,000 **d** of gold,
Ac 19:19 the total came to fifty thousand **d**.

Drag (Dragged, Dragging, Drags)

2Sa 17:13 and we will **d** it down to the valley
Job 36:20 to **d** people away from their homes.
Ps 28: 3 Do not **d** me away with the wicked,
Pr 21: 7 of the wicked will **d** them away,
Jer 12: 3 **D** them off like sheep to be
15: 3 "the sword to kill and the dogs to **d**
Eze 39: 2 I will turn you around and **d** you
Lk 12:58 or he may **d** you off to the judge,

Dragged (Drag)

2Sa 20:12 he **d** him from the road into a field
Jer 22:19 **d** away and thrown outside the gates
49:20 young of the flock will be **d** away;
50:45 young of the flock will be **d** away;
Lam 3:11 he **d** me from the path and mangled me
Eze 32:20 her be **d** off with all her hordes.
Jn 21:11 climbed aboard and **d** the net ashore
Ac 7:58 **d** him out of the city and began to
8: 3 he **d** off men and women and put them
14:19 They stoned Paul and **d** him outside
16:19 and **d** them into the market-place
17: 6 did not find them, they **d** Jason
21:30 Seizing Paul, they **d** him from the
Jas 1:14 desire, he is **d** away and enticed.

Dragging (Drag)

Jas 2: 6 the ones who are **d** you into court?

Drag-net (Net)

Hab 1:15 he gathers them up in his **d**;
1:16 his net and burns incense to his **d**,

Dragon

Rev 12: 3 an enormous red **d** with seven heads
12: 4 The **d** stood in front of the woman
12: 7 and his angels fought against the **d**,
12: 7 the **d** and his angels fought back.
12: 9 The great **d** was hurled down—that
12:13 the **d** saw that he had been hurled to
12:16 the **d** had spewed out of his mouth.
12:17 the **d** was enraged at the woman and
13: 1 the **d** stood on the shore of the sea.
13: 2 The **d** gave the beast his power and
13: 4 Men worshipped the **d** because he had
13:11 like a lamb, but he spoke like a **d**.
16:13 they came out of the mouth of the **d**,
20: 2 seized the **d**, that ancient serpent,

Drags (Drag)

Job 7: 4 The night **d** on, and I toss till dawn.
24:22 God **d** away the mighty by his power;
Ps 10: 9 helpless and **d** them off in his net.
Ecc 12: 5 the grasshopper **d** himself along and

Drain (Drained, Draining)

Lev 17:13 may be eaten must **d** out the blood
26:16 your sight and **d** away your life.
Eze 23:34 You will drink it and **d** it dry;

Drained (Drain)

Lev 1:15 be **d** out on the side of the altar.
5: 9 be **d** out at the base of the altar.
2Ki 19:26 Their people, **d** of power, are
Isa 37:27 Their people, **d** of power, are
51:17 you who have **d** to its dregs the

Draining (Drain)

Na 2: 8 a pool, and its water is **d** away.

Drank (Drink)

Ge 9:21 he **d** some of its wine, he became
24:46 I **d**, and she watered the camels also.
24:54 ate and **d** and spent the night there.
25:34 He ate and **d**, and then got up and
26:30 feast for them, and they ate and **d**.
27:25 and he brought some wine and he **d**.
43:34 they feasted and **d** freely with him.
Ex 24:11 they saw God, and they ate and **d**.
Nu 20:11 the community and their livestock **d**.
Dt 9: 9 I ate no bread and **d** no water.
9:18 I ate no bread and **d** no water,
29: 6 You ate no bread and **d** no wine or
32:14 You **d** the foaming blood of the grape.
32:38 **d** the wine of their drink offerings?
Jdg 15:19 When Samson **d**, his strength returned
2Sa 11:13 At David's invitation, he ate and **d**
12: 3 It shared his food, **d** from his cup
1Ki 4:20 ate, they **d** and they were happy.
13:19 with him and ate and **d** in his house.
13:22 You came back and ate bread and **d**
17: 6 evening, and he **d** from the brook.
19: 6 He ate and **d** and then lay down again.
19: 8 he got up and ate and **d**.
2Ki 7: 8 They ate and **d**, and carried away
9:34 Jehu went in and ate and **d**. "Take
1Ch 29:22 They ate and **d** with great joy in the
Ezr 10: 6 he ate no food and **d** no water,
Job 29:23 **d** in my words as the spring rain.
Jer 51: 7 The nations **d** her wine; therefore
Da 5: 1 of his nobles and **d** wine with them.
5: 3 and his concubines **d** from them.
5: 4 they **d** the wine, they praised the
5:23 your concubines **d** wine from them.
Ob :16 Just as you **d** on my holy hill, so
Mk 14:23 it to them, and they all **d** from it.
Lk 13:26 "Then you will say,'We ate and **d**
Jn 4:12 who gave us the well and **d** from it
Ac 10:41 **d** with him after he rose from the
1Co 10: 4 **d** the same spiritual drink; for they
10: 4 for they **d** from the spiritual rock

Draw (Drawing, Drawn, Draws, Drew)

Ge 24:11 time the women go out to **d** water.
24:13 are coming out to **d** water.
24:19 "I'll **d** water for your camels too,
24:20 ran back to the well to **d** more water,
24:43 out to **d** water and I say to her,
24:44 "Drink, and I'll **d** water for your
Ex 2:16 and they came to **d** water and fill
15: 9 I will **d** my sword and my hand will
Lev 26:33 will **d** out my sword and pursue you.
Nu 5:15 offering to **d** attention to guilt.
Jos 8:26 For Joshua did not **d** back the hand
Jdg 8:20 But Jether did not **d** his sword,
9:54 "**D** your sword and kill me, so that
20:32 "Let's retreat and **d** them away from
1Sa 9:11 some girls coming out to **d** water,
31: 4 "**D** your sword and run me through,
1Ch 10: 4 "**D** your sword and run me through
Job 37:19 we cannot **d** up our case because of
Ps 37:14 The wicked **d** the sword and bend the
58: 7 flows away; when they **d** the bow,
144:14 our oxen will **d** heavy loads. There
Isa 5:18 Woe to those who **d** sin along with
12: 3 With joy you will **d** water from the
Jer 46: 9 shields, men of Lydia who **d** the bow.
50:14 Babylon, all you who **d** the bow.
50:29 Babylon, all those who **d** the bow.
Eze 4: 1 and **d** the city of Jerusalem on it.
21: 3 I will **d** my sword from its scabbard
28: 7 they will **d** their swords against
30:11 They will **d** their swords against
40:46 the only Levites who may **d** near to
45: 4 **d** near to minister before the LORD.
Joel 3: 9 the fighting men **d** near and attack.
Na 3:14 **D** water for the siege, strengthen
Zep 3: 2 LORD, she does not **d** near to her God.
Hag 2:16 to a wine vat to **d** fifty measures,
Mt 26:52 **d** the sword will die by the sword.
Lk 1: 1 Many have undertaken to **d** up an
Jn 2: 8 he told them, "Now **d** some out and
4: 7 a Samaritan woman came to **d** water,
4:11 to **d** with and the well is deep.

Jn 4:15 to keep coming here to **d** water."
12:32 earth, will **d** all men to myself."
Ac 20:30 to **d** away disciples after them.
Gal 2:12 he began to **d** back and separate
Heb 7:19 by which we **d** near to God.
10: 1 perfect those who **d** near to worship.
10:22 let us **d** near to God with a sincere

Drawing (Draw)

1Sa 17:21 Israel and the Philistines were **d** up
1Ch 24: 5 divided them impartially by **d** lots
Lk 21:28 because your redemption is **d** near."

Drawn (Draw)

Ge 34: 3 His heart was **d** to Dinah daughter of
Nu 22:23 the road with a **d** sword in his hand,
22:31 in the road with his sword **d**.
Dt 30:17 and if you are **d** away to bow down to
Jos 5:13 of him with a **d** sword in his hand.
Jdg 20:31 them and were **d** away from the city.
1Ch 21:16 with a **d** sword in his hand extended
Job 19: 6 wronged me and **d** his net around me.
Ps 3: 6 **d** up against me on every side.
21:12 when you aim at them with **d** bow.
55:21 than oil, yet they are **d** swords.
141: 4 Let not my heart be **d** to what is
Isa 21:15 from the sword, from the **d** sword,
50: 5 been rebellious; I have not **d** back.
Jer 31: 3 I have **d** you with loving-kindness.
Eze 5: 2 For I will pursue them with **d** sword.
5:12 the winds and pursue with **d** sword.
12:14 I will pursue them with **d** sword.
21: 5 have **d** my sword from its scabbard;
21:28 "'A sword, a sword, **d** for the
32:20 The sword is **d**; let her be dragged
Joel 2: 5 like a mighty army **d** up for battle.
Mic 5: 6 the land of Nimrod with **d** sword.
Jn 2: 9 servants who had **d** the water knew.

Draws (Draw)

Job 33:22 His soul **d** near to the pit, and his
36:27 "He **d** up the drops of water, which
Ps 88: 3 and my life **d** near the grave.
Pr 20: 5 a man of understanding **d** them out.
Isa 51: 5 My righteousness **d** near speedily, my
Jn 4:36 Even now the reaper **d** his wages,
6:44 unless the Father who sent me **d** him,

Dread (Dreaded, Dreadful, Dreads)

Ge 9: 2 The fear and **d** of you will fall upon
Ex 1:12 Egyptians came to **d** the Israelites
15:16 terror and **d** will fall upon them.
Nu 22: 3 with **d** because of the Israelites.
Dt 28:66 filled with **d** both night and day,
2Ch 29: 8 an object of **d** and horror and scorn,
Job 9:28 I still **d** all my sufferings, for I
13:11 Would not the **d** of him fall on you?
Ps 14: 5 There they are, overwhelmed with **d**,
31:11 I am a **d** to my friends—those who
53: 5 There they were, overwhelmed with **d**,
53: 5 where there was nothing to **d**.
105:38 **d** of Israel had fallen on them.
119:39 Take away the disgrace I **d**, for your
Isa 2:10 hide in the ground from **d** of the
2:19 to holes in the ground from the **d** of
2:21 to the overhanging crags from **d** of
7:16 two kings you **d** will be laid waste.
8:12 what they fear, and do not **d** it.
8:13 to fear, he is the one you are to **d**,
66: 4 will bring upon them what they **d**.
Jer 42:16 and the famine you **d** will follow you

Dreaded (Dread)

Dt 28:60 the diseases of Egypt that you **d**,
32:27 I **d** the taunt of the enemy, lest the
Job 3:25 what I **d** has happened to me.
31:23 For I **d** destruction from God, and
31:34 and so **d** the contempt of the clans,
Isa 57:11 "Whom have you so **d** and feared that
Da 5:19 of every language **d** and feared him.
Hab 1: 7 They are a feared and **d** people; they

Dreadful (Dread)

Ge 15:12 thick and **d** darkness came over him.
Dt 1:19 and **d** desert that you have seen,
8:15 you through the vast and **d** desert,
Job 6:21 you see something **d** and are afraid.
Eze 14:21 Jerusalem my four **d** judgments—sword
Joel 2:11 day of the LORD is great; it is **d**.
2:31 of the great and **d** day of the LORD.
Mal 4: 5 great and **d** day of the LORD comes.
Mt 24:19 How **d** it will be in those days for
Mk 13:17 How **d** it will be in those days for
Lk 21:23 How **d** it will be in those days for
Heb 10:31 is a **d** thing to fall into the hands

Dreads (Dread)

Pr 10:24 What the wicked **d** will overtake him;

Dream (Dreamed, Dreamer, Dreamers, Dreaming, Dreams)

Ge 20: 3 God came to Abimelech in a **d** one
20: 6 God said to him in the **d**, "Yes, I
28:12 He had a **d** in which he saw a
31:10 I once had a **d** in which I looked up
31:11 The angel of God said to me in the **d**,
31:24 God came to Laban the Aramean in a **d**
37: 5 Joseph had a **d**, and when he told it
37: 6 to them, "Listen to this **d** I had:
37: 8 of his **d** and what he had said.
37: 9 he had another **d**, and he told it to
37: 9 "Listen," he said, "I had another **d**,
37:10 "What is this **d** you had? Will your
40: 5 in prison—had a **d** the same night,
40: 5 and each **d** had a meaning of its own.
40: 9 the chief cupbearer told Joseph his **d**
40: 9 He said to him, "In my **d** I saw a
40:16 "I too had a **d**: On my head were
41: 1 Pharaoh had a **d**: He was standing by
41: 5 had a second **d**: Seven ears of corn,
41: 7 Pharaoh woke up; it had been a **d**.
41:11 Each of us had a **d** the same night,
41:11 and each **d** had a meaning of its own.
41:12 man the interpretation of his **d**.
41:15 Pharaoh said to Joseph, "I had a **d**,
41:15 you hear a **d** you can interpret it."
41:17 Pharaoh said to Joseph, "In my **d** I
41:26 it is one and the same **d**.
41:32 The reason the **d** was given to
Jdg 7:13 as a man was telling a friend his **d**.
7:13 "I had a **d**," he was saying. "A round
7:15 heard the **d** and its interpretation
1Ki 3: 5 to Solomon during the night in a **d**,
3:15 he realised it had been a **d**.
Job 20: 8 Like a **d** he flies away, no more to
33:15 In a **d**, in a vision of the night,
Ps 73:20 a **d** when one awakes, so when you
Ecc 5: 3 a **d** comes when there are many cares,
Isa 29: 7 will be as it is with a **d**,
56:10 around and **d**, they love to sleep.
Jer 23:25 They say, 'I had a **d**! I had a **d**!'
23:28 Let the prophet who has a **d** tell his
23:28 the prophet who has a **d** tell his **d**,
Da 2: 3 he said to them, "I have had a **d**
2: 4 Tell you servants the **d**, and we
2: 5 me what my **d** was and interpret it,
2: 6 if you tell me the **d** and explain it,
2: 6 me the **d** and interpret it for me."
2: 7 the king tell his servants the **d**,
2: 9 If you do not tell me the **d**, there
2: 9 So then, tell me the **d**, and I will
2:16 he might interpret the **d** for him.
2:23 made known to us the **d** of the king."
2:24 and I will interpret his **d** for him."
2:25 can tell the king what his **d** means."
2:26 I saw in my **d** and interpret it?"
2:28 Your **d** and the visions that passed
2:36 "This was the **d**, and now we will
2:45 The **d** is true and the interpretation
4: 5 I had a **d** that made me afraid. As I
4: 6 before me to interpret the **d** for me.
4: 7 I told them the **d**, but they could
4: 8 my presence and I told him the **d**.
4: 9 Here is my **d**; interpret it for me.
4:18 "This is the **d** that I, King
4:19 let the **d** or its meaning alarm you.
4:19 "My lord, if only the **d** applied to
7: 1 Daniel had a **d**, and visions passed
7: 1 He wrote down the substance of his **d**.
Joel 2:28 your old men will **d** dreams, your
Mt 1:20 Lord appeared to him in a **d** and said,
2:12 having been warned in a **d** not to go
2:13 the Lord appeared to Joseph in a **d**.
2:19 appeared in a **d** to Joseph in
2:22 Having been warned in a **d**, he
27:19 deal today in a **d** because of him."
Ac 2:17 visions, your old men will **d** dreams.

Dreamed (Dream)

Ps 126: 1 to Zion, we were like men who **d**.
Da 2: 2 to tell him what he had **d**.

Dreamer (Dream)

Ge 37:19 "Here comes that **d**!" they said to
Dt 13: 3 to the words of that prophet or **d**.
13: 5 That prophet or **d** must be put to

Dreamers (Dream)

Jude : 8 these **d** pollute their own bodies

Dreaming (Dream)

Ecc 5: 7 Much **d** and many words are

Dreams (Dream)

Ge 37:20 Then we'll see what comes of his **d**."
40: 8 "We both had **d**," they answered, "but
40: 8 belong to God? Tell me your **d**."
41: 8 Pharaoh told them his **d**, but no-one
41:12 We told him our **d**, and he
41:22 "In my **d** I also saw seven ears of
41:25 Joseph said to Pharaoh, "The **d** of
42: 9 he remembered his **d** about them and
Nu 12: 6 him in visions, I speak to him in **d**.
Dt 13: 1 or one who foretells by **d**, appears
1Sa 28: 6 answer him by **d** or Urim or prophets.
28:15 me, either by prophets or by **d**.
Job 4:13 Amid disquieting **d** in the night,
7:14 even then you frighten me with **d** and
Isa 29: 8 a hungry man **d** that he is eating,
29: 8 a thirsty man **d** that he is drinking,
Jer 23:27 They think the **d** they tell one
23:32 those who prophesy false **d**,"
27: 9 your interpreters of **d**, your mediums
29: 8 to the **d** you encourage them to have.
Da 1:17 visions and **d** of all kinds.
2: 1 Nebuchadnezzar had **d**; his mind was
5:12 and also the ability to interpret **d**,
Joel 2:28 your old men will dream **d**, your
Zec 10: 2 they tell **d** that are false,
Ac 2:17 visions, your old men will dream **d**.

Dregs

Ps 75: 8 earth drink it down to its very **d**.
Isa 51:17 drained to its **d** the goblet that
Jer 48:11 like wine left on its **d**, not poured
Zep 1:12 who are like wine left on its **d**, who

Drench (Drenched)

Ps 6: 6 weeping and **d** my couch with tears.
65:10 You **d** its furrows and level its
Isa 16: 9 O Heshbon, O Elealeh, I **d** you with
Eze 32: 6 I will **d** the land with your flowing

Drenched (Drench)

Job 24: 8 They are **d** by mountain rains and hug
29: 6 my path was **d** with cream and the
SS 5: 2 My head is **d** with dew, my hair with
Isa 34: 7 Their land will be **d** with blood, and
Da 4:15 "'Let him be **d** with the dew of
4:23 Let him be **d** with the dew of heaven;
4:25 and be **d** with the dew of heaven.
4:33 His body was **d** with the dew of
5:21 body was **d** with the dew of heaven,

Dress (Dressed, Dressing, Well-dressed)

Ex 29: 5 Take the garments and **d** Aaron with
29: 8 Bring his sons and **d** them in
40:13 **d** Aaron in the sacred garments,
40:14 Bring his sons and **d** them in tunics.
2Sa 14: 2 **D** in mourning clothes, and don't use
Jer 4:30 O devastated one? Why **d** yourself in
6:14 They **d** the wound of my people as

Jer 8:11 They **d** the wound of my people as
Eze 16:10 I clothed you with an embroidered **d**
23:12 warriors in full **d**, mounted horsemen,
Lk 12:37 he will **d** himself to serve, will
Jn 21:18 and someone else will **d** you and lead
1Ti 2: 9 I also want women to **d** modestly,

Dressed (Dress)

Ge 41:42 He **d** him in robes of fine linen and
Ex 20:25 do not build it with **d** stones, for
1Sa 17:38 Saul **d** David in his own tunic. He
25:18 two skins of wine, five **d** sheep,
1Ki 5:17 to provide a foundation of **d** stone
6: 7 only blocks **d** at the quarry were
6:36 of three courses of **d** stone
7:12 a wall of three courses of **d** stone
22:10 **D** in their royal robes, the king of
2Ki 12:12 They purchased timber and **d** stone
22: 6 and **d** stone to repair the temple.
1Ch 22: 2 stonecutters to prepare **d** stone
2Ch 5:12 **d** in fine linen and playing cymbals,
18: 9 **D** in their royal robes, the king of
34:11 and builders to purchase **d** stone,
Pr 7:10 **d** like a prostitute and with crafty
Isa 9:10 but we will rebuild with **d** stone;
Jer 10: 9 made is then **d** in blue and purple
Eze 16:10 I **d** you in fine linen and covered
40:42 were also four tables of **d** stone
Da 10: 5 before me was a man **d** in linen,
Zec 3: 3 Now Joshua was **d** in filthy clothes
Mt 6:29 splendour was **d** like one of these.
11: 8 A man **d** in fine clothes? No, those
Mk 5:15 sitting there, **d** and in his right
16: 5 they saw a young man **d** in a white
Lk 7:25 A man **d** in fine clothes? No, those
8:35 sitting at Jesus' feet, **d** and in his
12:27 splendour was **d** like one of these.
12:35 "Be **d** ready for service and keep
16:19 a rich man who was **d** in purple
Jn 21:18 when you were younger you **d** yourself
Ac 1:10 men **d** in white stood beside them.
Rev 1:13 "like a son of man", **d** in a robe
3: 4 me, **d** in white, for they are worthy.
3: 5 will, like them, be **d** in white.
4: 4 They were **d** in white and had crowns
15: 6 They were **d** in clean, shining linen
17: 4 The woman was **d** in purple and
18:16 **d** in fine linen, purple and scarlet
19:13 He is **d** in a robe dipped in blood,
19:14 **d** in fine linen, white and clean.
21: 2 bride beautifully **d** for her husband.

Dressing (Dress)

Lk 23:11 **D** him in an elegant robe, they sent

Drew (Draw)

Ge 14: 8 marched out and **d** up their battle
24:20 and **d** enough for all his camels.
24:45 down to the spring and **d** water,
38:29 when he **d** back his hand, his brother
47:29 the time **d** near for Israel to die,
49:33 he **d** his feet up into the bed,
Ex 2:10 saying, "I **d** him out of the water."
2:19 He even **d** water for us and watered
Jos 24:25 he **d** up for them decrees and laws.
Jdg 3:21 **d** the sword from his right thigh
20:24 the Israelites **d** near to Benjamin
1Sa 7: 6 assembled at Mizpah, they **d** water
7:10 **d** near to engage Israel in battle.
17: 2 and **d** up their battle line to meet
17:51 sword and **d** it from the scabbard.
2Sa 10: 8 The Ammonites came out and **d** up in
22:17 he **d** me out of deep waters.
23:16 **d** water from the well near the gate
1Ki 2: 1 the time **d** near for David to die, he
22:34 someone **d** his bow at random and hit
2Ki 9:24 Jehu **d** his bow and shot Joram
1Ch 11:18 **d** water from the well near the gate
19: 9 The Ammonites came out and **d** up in
2Ch 13: 3 and Jeroboam **d** up a battle line
18:31 God **d** them away from him,
18:33 someone **d** his bow at random and hit
Ps 18:16 he **d** me out of deep waters.
107:18 They loathed all food and **d** near the
Isa 43:17 who **d** out the chariots and horses,
Lam 3:12 He **d** his bow and made me the target
Mt 26:51 **d** it out and struck the servant of
Mk 14:47 one of those standing near **d** his
Jn 18: 6 Jesus said, "I am he," they **d** back
18:10 Simon Peter, who had a sword, **d** it
Ac 7:17 "As the time **d** near for God to
16:27 he **d** his sword and was about to kill
23:19 **d** him aside and asked, "What is it

Dried (Dry)

Ge 8: 7 the water had **d** up from the earth.
8:13 the water had **d** up from the earth.
Jos 2:10 We have heard how the LORD **d** up the
4:23 For the LORD your God **d** up the
4:23 when he **d** it up before us until we
5: 1 how the LORD had **d** up the Jordan
Jdg 16: 7 fresh thongs that have not been **d**,
16: 8 fresh thongs that had not been **d**,
1Ki 17: 7 Some time later the brook **d** up
2Ki 19:24 have **d** up all the streams of Egypt."
Ps 22:15 My strength is **d** up like a potsherd,
74:15 you **d** up the ever-flowing rivers.
106: 9 He rebuked the Red Sea, and it **d** up;
Isa 15: 6 The waters of Nimrim are **d** up and
37:25 have **d** up all the streams of Egypt.'
51:10 Was it not you who **d** up the sea, the
Jer 48:34 even the waters of Nimrim are **d** up.
Eze 37:11 They say, 'Our bones are **d** up and
Joel 1:10 the ground is **d** up; the grain is
1:10 the new wine is **d** up, the oil fails.
1:12 The vine is **d** up and the fig-tree is
1:12 the trees of the field—are **d** up.
1:17 broken down, for the grain has **d** up.
1:20 the streams of water have **d** up and
Am 4: 7 had rain; another had none and **d** up.
7: 4 it **d** up the great deep and devoured
Rev 16:12 and its water was **d** up to prepare

Dries (Dry)

Pr 17:22 but a crushed spirit **d** up the bones.
Isa 24: 4 The earth **d** up and withers, the
24: 7 The new wine **d** up and the vine
Na 1: 4 He rebukes the sea and **d** it up; he

Drift

Heb 2: 1 heard, so that we do not **d** away.

Drink (Drank, *Drink offering*, *Drink offerings*, Drinkers, Drinking, Drinks, Drunk, Drunkard, Drunkard's, Drunkards, Drunken, Drunkenness)

Ge 19:32 Let's get our father to **d** wine and
19:33 they got their father to **d** wine,
19:34 Let's get him to **d** wine again
19:35 they got their father to **d** wine that
21:19 with water and gave the boy a **d**.
24:14 down your jar that I may have a **d**,'
24:14 '**D**, and I'll water your camels too'—
24:18 "**D**, my lord," she said, and quickly
24:18 jar to her hands and gave him a **d**.
24:19 After she had given him a **d**, she
24:43 "Please let me **d** a little water
24:44 if she says to me, "**D**, and I'll draw
24:45 I said to her, 'Please give me a **d**.'
24:46 '**D**, and I'll water your camels too.
30:38 of the flocks when they came to **d**.
30:38 flocks were in heat and came to **d**,
Ex 7:18 will not be able to **d** its water.'"
7:21 the Egyptians could not **d** its water.
7:24 could not **d** the water of the river.
15:23 they came to Marah, they could not **d**
15:24 Moses, saying, "What are we to **d**?"
17: 1 was no water for the people to **d**.
17: 2 Moses and said, "Give us water to **d**.
17: 6 come out of it for the people to **d**.
32: 6 they sat down to eat and **d** and got
32:20 water and made the Israelites **d** it.
Lev 10: 9 not to **d** wine or other fermented **d**
Nu 5:24 He shall make the woman **d** the bitter
5:26 he is to make the woman **d** the water.
5:27 then when she is made to **d** the water
6: 3 fermented **d** and must not **d** vinegar
6: 3 from wine or from other fermented **d**.
6: 3 He must not **d** grape juice or eat
6:20 After that, the Nazirite may **d** wine.
20: 5 And there is no water to **d**!"
20: 8 they and their livestock can **d**."
20:17 vineyard, or **d** water from any well.
20:19 and if we or our livestock **d** any of
21:22 vineyard, or **d** water from any well.
28: 7 a hin of fermented **d** with each lamb.
33:14 was no water for the people to **d**.
Dt 2: 6 food you eat and the water you **d**.'"
2:28 Sell us food to eat and water to **d**
14:26 fermented **d**, or anything you wish.
28:39 not **d** the wine or gather the grapes,
29: 6 drank no wine or other fermented **d**.
Jdg 4:19 gave him a **d**, and covered him up.
7: 5 dog from those who kneel down to **d**."
7: 6 rest got down on their knees to **d**.
13: 4 you **d** no wine or other fermented **d**
13: 7 **d** no wine or other fermented **d** and
13:14 nor **d** any wine or other fermented **d**
19: 6 the two of them sat down to eat and **d**
19:21 they had something to eat and **d**.
Ru 2: 9 go and get a **d** from the water jars
1Sa 30:11 him water to **d** and food to eat—
2Sa 11:11 to eat and **d** and lie with my wife?
23:15 "Oh, that someone would get me a **d**
23:16 But he refused to **d** it; instead, he
23:17 And David would not **d** it.
1Ki 13: 8 would I eat bread or **d** water here.
13: 9 'You must not eat bread or **d** water
13:16 or **d** water with you in this place.
13:17 'You must not eat bread or **d** water
13:18 that he may eat bread and **d** water.
13:22 where he told you not to eat or **d**.
17: 4 You will **d** from the brook, and I
17:10 water in a jar so I may have a **d**?"
18:41 Elijah said to Ahab, "Go, eat and **d**,
18:42 Ahab went off to eat and **d**, but
2Ki 3:17 and your other animals will **d**.
6:22 **d** and then go back to their master."
18:27 own filth and **d** their own urine?"
18:31 and **d** water from his own cistern,
1Ch 11:17 "Oh, that someone would get me a **d**
11:18 But he refused to **d** it; instead, he
11:19 "Should I **d** the blood of these men
11:19 bring it back, David would not **d** it.
2Ch 28:15 food and **d**, and healing balm.
Ezr 3: 7 and gave food and **d** and oil to the
Ne 8:12 all the people went away to eat and **d**
Est 1: 8 was allowed to **d** in his own way,
3:15 The king and Haman sat down to **d**,
4:16 Do not eat or **d** for three days,
Job 1: 4 sisters to eat and **d** with them.
21:20 him **d** of the wrath of the Almighty.
Ps 36: 8 them **d** from your river of delights.
50:13 of bulls or **d** the blood of goats?
73:10 them and **d** up waters in abundance.
75: 8 earth **d** it down to its very dregs.
78:44 they could not **d** from their streams.
80: 5 made them **d** tears by the bowlful.
102: 9 my food and mingle my **d** with tears
110: 7 He will **d** from a brook beside the
Pr 4:17 and **d** the wine of violence.
5:15 **D** water from your own cistern,
7:18 Come, let's **d** deep of love till
9: 5 "Come, eat my food and **d** the wine I
23: 7 "Eat and **d**," he says to you, but his
23:20 Do not join those who **d** too much
23:35 I wake up so I can find another **d**?"
25:21 he is thirsty, give him water to **d**.
31: 4 not for kings to **d** wine, not for
31: 5 lest they **d** and forget what the law
31: 7 let them **d** and forget their poverty
Ecc 2:24 nothing better than to eat and **d**
3:13 That everyone may eat and **d**, and
5:18 and proper for a man to eat and **d**,
8:15 sun than to eat and **d** and be glad.
9: 7 **d** your wine with a joyful heart,
SS 5: 1 Eat, O friends, and **d**;
5: 1 **d** your fill, O lovers.
8: 2 I would give you spiced wine to **d**,
Isa 21: 5 they eat, they **d**! Get up, you
22:13 "Let us eat and **d**," you say, "for
24: 9 No longer do they **d** wine with a song;
36:12 own filth and **d** their own urine?"
36:16 and **d** water from his own cistern,
43:20 to give **d** to my people, my chosen,

Isa 51:22 of my wrath, you will never **d** again.
56:12 "let me get wine! Let us **d** our fill
60:16 You will **d** the milk of nations and
62: 8 will foreigners **d** the new wine
62: 9 **d** it in the courts of my sanctuary."
65:13 will go hungry; my servants will **d**,
66:11 you will **d** deeply and delight in her
Jer 2:18 Now why go to Egypt to **d** water from
2:18 Assyria to **d** water from the River?
8:14 and given us poisoned water to **d**,
9:15 bitter food and **d** poisoned water.
16: 7 give them a **d** to console them.
16: 8 feasting and sit down to eat and **d**.
22:15 not your father have food and **d**?
23:15 bitter food and **d** poisoned water,
25:15 the nations to whom I send you **d** it.
25:16 they **d** it, they will stagger and go
25:17 the nations to whom he sent me **d** it:
25:26 the king of Sheshach will **d** it too.
25:27 **D**, get drunk and vomit, and fall to
25:28 take the cup from your hand and **d**,
25:28 LORD Almighty says: You must **d** it!
35: 2 the LORD and give them wine to **d**."
35: 5 and said to them, "**D** some wine.
35: 6 they replied, "We do not **d** wine,
35: 6 your descendants must ever **d** wine.
35:14 Recab ordered his sons not to **d** wine
35:14 To this day they do not **d** wine,
49:12 not deserve to **d** the cup must **d** it,
49:12 not go unpunished, but must **d** it.
Lam 5: 4 We must buy the water we **d**; our wood
Eze 4:11 hin of water and **d** it at set times.
4:16 and **d** rationed water in despair,
12:18 shudder in fear as you **d** your water.
12:19 and **d** their water in despair,
23:32 "You will **d** your sister's cup, a cup
23:34 You will **d** it and drain it dry; you
25: 4 will eat your fruit and **d** your milk.
34:18 Is it not enough for you to **d** clear
34:19 **d** what you have muddied with your
39:17 There you will eat flesh and **d** blood.
39:18 **d** the blood of the princes of the
39:19 and **d** blood till you are drunk.
44:21 No priest is to **d** wine when he
Da 1:10 who has assigned your food and **d**.
1:12 vegetables to eat and water to **d**.
1:16 food and the wine they were to **d**
5: 2 his concubines might **d** from them.
Hos 2: 5 wool and my linen, my oil and my **d**.'
Joel 3: 3 girls for wine that they might **d**.
Am 2: 8 god they **d** wine taken as fines.
2:12 "But you made the Nazirites **d** wine
4: 8 but did not get enough to **d**,
5:11 you will not **d** their wine.
6: 6 You **d** wine by the bowlful and use
9:14 plant vineyards and **d** their wine;
Ob :16 all the nations will **d** continually;
:16 they will **d** and **d** and be as if they
Jnh 3: 7 anything; do not let them eat or **d**.
Mic 6:15 crush grapes but not **d** the wine.
Hab 2:15 "Woe to him who gives **d** to his
2:16 it is your turn! **D** and be exposed!
Zep 1:13 plant vineyards but not **d** the wine.
Hag 1: 6 You **d**, but never have your fill. You
Zec 9:15 They will **d** and roar as with wine;
Mt 6:25 what you will eat or **d**; or about
6:31 or 'What shall we **d**?' or 'What
20:22 "Can you **d** the cup I am going to **d**?"
20:23 "You will indeed **d** from my cup, but
24:49 and to eat and **d** with drunkards.
25:35 and you gave me something to **d**,
25:37 thirsty and give you something to **d**?
25:42 and you gave me nothing to **d**,
26:27 saying, "**D** from it, all of you.
26:29 I tell you, I will not **d** of this
26:29 until that day when I **d** it anew
26:42 taken away unless I **d** it, may your
27:34 There they offered Jesus wine to **d**,
27:34 tasting it, he refused to **d** it.
27:48 stick, and offered it to Jesus to **d**.
Mk 10:38 "Can you **d** the cup I **d** or be
10:39 "You will **d** the cup I **d** and be
14:25 I will not **d** again of the fruit of
14:25 I **d** it anew in the kingdom of God."
15:36 stick, and offered it to Jesus to **d**.
16:18 and when they **d** deadly poison,
Lk 1:15 to take wine or other fermented **d**,
5:30 **d** with tax collectors and 'sinners'?"
12:19 life easy; eat, **d** and be merry."'
12:29 eat or **d**; do not worry about it.
12:45 and to eat and **d** and get drunk.
17: 8 wait on me while I eat and **d**;
22:18 For I tell you I will not **d** again of
22:30 that you may eat and **d** at my table
Jn 2:10 the guests have had too much to **d**;
4: 7 said to her, "Will you give me a **d**?
4: 9 How can you ask me for a **d**?" (For
4:10 and who it is that asks you for a **d**,
6:53 **d** his blood, you have no life in you.
6:55 is real food and my blood is real **d**.
7:37 thirsty, let him come to me and **d**.
18:11 **d** the cup the Father has given me?"
19:30 he had received the **d**, Jesus said,
Ac 9: 9 and did not eat or **d** anything.
23:12 eat or **d** until they had killed Paul.
23:21 eat or **d** until they have killed him.
Ro 12:20 is thirsty, give him something to **d**.
14:21 is better not to eat meat or **d** wine
1Co 9: 4 Don't we have the right to food and **d**
9: 7 a flock and does not **d** of the milk?
10: 4 drank the same spiritual **d**; for they
10: 7 "The people sat down to eat and **d**
10:21 You cannot **d** the cup of the Lord and
10:31 whether you eat or **d** or whatever you
11:22 Don't you have homes to eat and **d** in?
11:25 you **d** it, in remembrance of me."
11:26 you eat this bread and **d** this cup,
12:13 were all given the one Spirit to **d**.
15:32 us eat and **d**, for tomorrow we die."
Col 2:16 judge you by what you eat or **d**,
Heb 9:10 They are only a matter of food and **d**
Rev 14: 8 the nations **d** the maddening wine
14:10 will **d** of the wine of God's fury,
16: 6 them blood to **d** as they deserve."
21: 6 I will give to **d** without cost from

Drink offering

Ge 35:14 and he poured out a **d** on it;
Ex 29:40 a quarter of a hin of wine as a **d**.
29:41 its **d** as in the morning—a pleasing
30: 9 offering, and do not pour a **d** on it.
Lev 23:13 its **d** of a quarter of a hin of wine.
Nu 6:17 with its grain offering and **d**.
15: 5 a quarter of a hin of wine as a **d**.
15: 7 a third of a hin of wine as a **d**.
15:10 Also bring half a hin of wine as a **d**.
15:24 its prescribed grain offering and **d**,
28: 7 The accompanying **d** is to be a
28: 7 the **d** to the LORD at the sanctuary.
28: 8 **d** that you prepare in the morning.
28: 9 together with its **d** and a grain
28:10 regular burnt offering and its **d**.
28:14 With each bull there is to be a **d** of
28:15 regular burnt offering with its **d**,
28:24 regular burnt offering and its **d**.
29:16 with its grain offering and **d**.
29:22 with its grain offering and **d**.
29:25 with its grain offering and **d**.
29:28 with its grain offering and **d**.
29:31 with its grain offering and **d**.
29:34 with its grain offering and **d**.
29:38 with its grain offering and **d**.
2Ki 16:13 poured out his **d**, and sprinkled the
16:15 their grain offering and their **d**.
Php 2:17 out like a **d** on the sacrifice
2Ti 4: 6 already being poured out like a **d**,

Drink offerings

Ex 37:16 pitchers for the pouring out of **d**.
Lev 23:18 with their grain offerings and **d**
23:37 and **d** required for each day.
Nu 4: 7 and the jars for **d**; the bread that
6:15 with their grain offerings and **d**,
28:31 Prepare these together with their **d**,
29: 6 grain offerings and **d** as specified.
29:11 its grain offering, and their **d**.
29:18 **d** according to the number specified.
29:19 its grain offering, and their **d**.
29:21 **d** according to the number specified.
29:24 **d** according to the number specified.
29:27 **d** according to the number specified.
Nu 29:30 **d** according to the number specified.
29:33 **d** according to the number specified.
29:37 **d** according to the number specified.
29:39 **d** and fellowship offerings.'"
Dt 32:38 and drank the wine of their **d**?
1Ch 29:21 together with their **d**, and other
2Ch 29:35 the **d** that accompanied the burnt
Ezr 7:17 with their grain offerings and **d**,
Isa 57: 6 Yes, to them you have poured out **d**
Jer 7:18 They pour out **d** to other gods to
19:13 and poured out **d** to other gods.'"
32:29 and by pouring out **d** to other gods.
44:17 **d** to her just as we and our fathers,
44:18 of Heaven and pouring out **d** to her,
44:19 of Heaven and poured out **d** to her,
44:19 her image and pouring out **d** to her?"
44:25 pour out **d** to the Queen of Heaven.
52:19 dishes and bowls used for **d**—all
Eze 20:28 incense and poured out their **d**.
45:17 grain offerings and **d** at the
Joel 1: 9 Grain offerings and **d** are cut off
1:13 for the grain offerings and **d** are
2:14 and **d** for the LORD your God.

Drinkers (Drink)

Isa 24: 9 a song; the beer is bitter to its **d**.
Joel 1: 5 and weep! Wail, all you **d** of wine;

Drinking (Drink)

Ge 24:19 too, until they have finished **d**."
24:22 the camels had finished **d**, the man
Ex 7:24 dug along the Nile to get **d** water,
34:28 without eating bread or **d** water.
Jdg 9:27 eating and **d**, they cursed Abimelech.
19: 4 eating and **d**, and sleeping there.
Ru 3: 3 until he has finished eating and **d**.
3: 7 Boaz had finished eating and **d** and
1Sa 1: 9 finished eating and **d** in Shiloh,
1:15 I have not been **d** wine or beer;
30:16 eating, **d** and revelling because of
2Sa 13:28 from **d** wine and I say to you,
1Ki 1:25 eating and **d** with him and saying,
13:23 of God had finished eating and **d**,
20:12 and the kings were **d** in their tents,
2Ki 6:23 they had finished eating and **d**,
1Ch 12:39 eating and **d**, for their families had
Est 5: 6 they were **d** wine, the king again
7: 2 they were **d** wine on that second day,
Job 1:13 **d** wine at the oldest brother's house,
1:18 **d** wine at the oldest brother's house,
Pr 26: 6 off one's feet or **d** violence
Isa 5:22 Woe to those who are heroes at **d**
22:13 eating of meat and **d** of wine!
29: 8 a thirsty man dreams that he is **d**,
Da 5: 2 While Belshazzar was **d** his wine, he
Zec 7: 6 you were eating and **d**, were you not
Mt 11:18 For John came neither eating nor **d**,
11:19 The Son of Man came eating and **d**,
24:38 people were eating and **d**, marrying
Lk 5:33 but yours go on eating and **d**."
5:39 no-one after **d** old wine wants the
7:33 neither eating bread nor **d** wine,
7:34 The Son of Man came eating and **d**,
10: 7 Stay in that house, eating and **d**
17:27 People were eating, **d**, marrying and
17:28 People were eating and **d**, buying and
Ro 14:17 God is not a matter of eating and **d**,
1Ti 5:23 Stop **d** only water, and use a little

Drinks (Drink)

Ge 44: 5 Isn't this the cup my master **d** from
Nu 23:24 and **d** the blood of his victims."
Dt 11:11 and valleys that **d** rain from heaven.
2Sa 19:35 servant taste what he eats and **d**?
Ne 8:10 Go and enjoy choice food and sweet **d**,
Job 6: 4 my spirit **d** in their poison; God's
15:16 corrupt, who **d** up evil like water!
34: 7 What man is like Job, who **d** scorn
Isa 5:11 in the morning to run after their **d**,
5:22 wine and champions at mixing **d**,
44:12 he **d** no water and grows faint.
Hos 4:18 Even when their **d** are gone, they
Am 4: 1 to your husbands, "Bring us some **d**!
Jn 4:13 Jesus answered, "Everyone who **d** this
4:14 whoever **d** the water I give him will

Jn 6:54 Whoever eats my flesh and **d** my blood
6:56 Whoever eats my flesh and **d** my blood
1Co 11:27 whoever eats the bread or **d** the cup
11:28 eats of the bread and **d** of the cup.
11:29 For anyone who eats and **d** without
11:29 Lord eats and **d** judgment on himself.
Heb 6: 7 Land that **d** in the rain often

Drip (Dripped, Dripping)
Pr 5: 3 lips of an adulteress **d** honey,
Joel 3:18 day the mountains will **d** new wine,
Am 9:13 New wine will **d** from the mountains

Dripped (Drip)
SS 5: 5 and my hands **d** with myrrh, my

Dripping (Drip)
Pr 19:13 wife is like a constant **d**.
27:15 is like a constant **d** on a rainy day;
SS 5:13 lips are like lilies **d** with myrrh.

Drive (Driven, Driver, Driver's, Drivers, Drives, Driving, Drove)
Ex 6: 1 he will **d** them out of his country."
11: 1 does, he will **d** you out completely.
23:28 ahead of you to **d** the Hivites,
23:29 I will not **d** them out in a single
23:30 Little by little I will **d** them out
23:31 and you will **d** them out before you.
33: 2 before you and **d** out the Canaanites
34:11 I will **d** out before you the Amorites,
34:24 I will **d** out nations before you and
Lev 18:24 to **d** out before you became defiled.
20:23 I am going to **d** out before you.
Nu 22: 6 them and **d** them out of the country.
22:11 to fight them and **d** them away.'"
33:52 **d** out all the inhabitants of the
33:55 "'But if you do not **d** out the
Dt 4:27 to which the LORD will **d** you.
4:38 to **d** out before you nations greater
7:17 than we are. How can we **d** them out?"
7:22 The LORD your God will **d** out those
9: 3 And you will **d** them out and
9: 4 is going to **d** them out before you.
9: 5 the LORD your God will **d** them out
11:23 the LORD will **d** out all these
18:12 will **d** out those nations before you.
28:34 The sights you see will **d** you mad.
28:36 The LORD will **d** you and the king you
28:37 nations where the LORD will **d** you.
33:27 He will **d** out your enemy before you,
Jos 3:10 **d** out before you the Canaanites,
13: 6 **d** them out before the Israelites.
13:13 the Israelites did not **d** out the
14:12 I will **d** them out just as he said."
17:13 but did not **d** them out completely.
17:18 are strong, you can **d** them out."
23: 5 will **d** them out of your way.
23:13 **d** out these nations before you.
Jdg 1:19 but they were unable to **d** the people
1:27 Manasseh did not **d** out the people of
1:29 Nor did Ephraim **d** out the Canaanites
1:30 Neither did Zebulun **d** out the
1:31 Nor did Asher **d** out those living in
1:33 Neither did Naphtali **d** out those
2: 3 I will not **d** them out before you;
2:21 I will no longer **d** out before them
2:23 he did not **d** them out at once by
11: 7 "Didn't you hate me and **d** me from my
2Ch 13: 9 didn't you **d** out the priests of the
20: 7 did you not **d** out the inhabitants
20:11 by coming to **d** us out of the
Job 24: 3 They **d** away the orphan's donkey and
30:22 You snatch me up and **d** me before the
Ps 36:11 the hand of the wicked **d** me away.
Pr 22:10 **D** out the mocker, and out goes
22:15 discipline will **d** it far from him.
Isa 22:23 I will **d** him like a peg into a firm
Jer 22:22 The wind will **d** all your shepherds
29:18 all the nations where I **d** them.
46: 9 Charge, O horses! **D** furiously,
49: 2 Then Israel will **d** out those who
Eze 4:13 the nations where I will **d** them."
8: 6 things that will **d** me far from my
Eze 11: 7 the pot, but I will **d** you out of it.
11: 9 I will **d** you out of the city and
Hos 9:15 I will **d** them out of my house.
10:11 I will **d** Ephraim, Judah must plough,
Joel 2:20 "I will **d** the northern army far from
Mic 2: 9 You **d** the women of my people from
Mt 7:22 and in your name **d** out demons and
8:31 begged Jesus, "If you **d** us out,
10: 1 gave them authority to **d** out evil
10: 8 who have leprosy, **d** out demons.
12:27 if I **d** out demons by Beelzebub,
12:27 by whom do your people **d** them out?
12:28 if I **d** out demons by the Spirit of
17:19 "Why couldn't we **d** it out?
Mk 3:15 to have authority to **d** out demons.
3:23 "How can Satan **d** out Satan?
7:26 to **d** the demon out of her daughter.
9:18 I asked your disciples to **d** out the
9:28 "Why couldn't we **d** it out?
16:17 In my name they will **d** out demons;
Lk 9: 1 authority to **d** out all demons and to
9:40 I begged your disciples to **d** it out,
11:18 that I **d** out demons by Beelzebub.
11:19 Now if I **d** out demons by Beelzebub,
11:19 by whom do your followers **d** them out?
11:20 if I **d** out demons by the finger of
13:32 'I will **d** out demons and heal people
Jn 6:37 comes to me I will never **d** away.

Driven (Drive)
Ge 4:11 under a curse and **d** from the ground
33:13 If they are **d** hard just one day, all
Ex 10:11 were **d** out of Pharaoh's presence.
12:39 they had been **d** out of Egypt
Nu 32:21 has **d** his enemies out before him—
Dt 9: 4 After the LORD your God has **d** them
12:29 **d** them out and settled in their land,
19: 1 and when you have **d** them out and
Jos 8:15 themselves be **d** back before them,
23: 9 "The LORD has **d** out before you great
Jdg 11:23 has **d** the Amorites out before his
1Sa 26:19 They have now **d** me from my share in
1Ki 14:24 LORD had **d** out before the Israelites.
2Ki 16: 3 LORD had **d** out before the Israelites.
17: 8 the LORD had **d** out before them,
17:11 LORD had **d** out before them had done.
21: 2 LORD had **d** out before the Israelites.
2Ch 28: 3 LORD had **d** out before the Israelites.
33: 2 LORD had **d** out before the Israelites.
Job 6:13 now that success has been **d** from me?
18:18 He is **d** from light into darkness and
30: 8 brood, they were **d** out of the land.
30:15 my dignity is **d** away as by the wind
Ps 109:10 they be **d** from their ruined homes.
Isa 17:13 **d** before the wind like chaff on the
22:25 "the peg **d** into the firm place will
59:14 justice is **d** back, and righteousness
Jer 13:24 "I will scatter you like chaff **d** by
23: 2 **d** them away and have not bestowed
23: 3 the countries where I have **d** them
49: 5 "Every one of you will be **d** away,
Lam 3: 2 He has **d** me away and made me walk in
Eze 34:21 horns until you have **d** them away,
Da 4:25 You will be **d** away from people and
4:32 You will be **d** away from people and
4:33 He was **d** away from people and ate
5:21 He was **d** away from people and given
Am 9: 4 Though they are **d** into exile by
Mic 4: 7 those **d** away a strong nation.
Mt 9:33 the demon was **d** out, the man who had
Mk 16: 9 out of whom he had **d** seven demons.
Lk 8:29 **d** by the demon into solitary places.
Jn 12:31 prince of this world will be **d** out.
Ac 27:15 we gave way to it and were **d** along.
27:17 anchor and let the ship be **d** along.
27:27 being **d** across the Adriatic Sea,
28: 3 a viper, **d** out by the heat, fastened
Jas 3: 4 so large and are **d** by strong winds,
2Pe 2:17 water and mists **d** by a storm.

Driver (Drive)
1Ki 22:34 The king told his chariot **d**, "Wheel
2Ch 18:33 The king told the chariot **d**, "Wheel
Jer 51:21 with you I shatter chariot and **d**,

Driver's (Drive)
Job 3:18 no longer hear the slave **d** shout.
39: 7 town; he does not hear a **d** shout.

Drivers (Drive)
Ex 3: 7 crying out because of their slave **d**,
5: 6 gave this order to the slave **d**
5:10 the slave **d** and the foremen went out
5:13 The slave **d** kept pressing them,
5:14 slave **d** were beaten and were asked,
2Ki 7:14 He commanded the **d**, "Go and find out
Hag 2:22 overthrow chariots and their **d**;

Drives (Drive)
Dt 7: 1 **d** out before you many nations—the
2Ki 9:20 son of Nimshi—he **d** like a madman."
Pr 16:26 works for him; his hunger **d** him on.
19:26 He who robs his father and **d** out his
20:26 he **d** the threshing wheel over them.
Isa 27: 8 with his fierce blast he **d** her out,
28:28 Though he **d** the wheels of his
59:19 that the breath of the LORD **d** along.
Mt 9:34 of demons that he **d** out demons."
12:24 that this fellow **d** out demons."
12:26 If Satan **d** out Satan, he is divided
1Jn 4:18 But perfect love **d** out fear, because

Driving (Drive)
Ge 4:14 Today you are **d** me from the land,
Ex 14:25 off so that they had difficulty **d**.
2Sa 7:23 awesome wonders by **d** out nations and
1Ki 19:19 he himself was **d** the twelfth pair.
2Ki 9:20 The **d** is like that of Jehu son of
16: 6 for Aram by **d** out the men of Judah.
1Ch 17:21 awesome wonders by **d** out nations
Job 37: 9 chamber, the cold from the **d** winds.
Ps 35: 5 the angel of the LORD **d** them away;
Pr 28: 3 like a **d** rain that leaves no crops.
Isa 25: 4 is like a storm **d** against a
28: 2 like a **d** rain and a flooding
Jer 30:23 a **d** wind swirling down on the heads
Eze 46:18 people, **d** them off their property.
Mk 1:39 their synagogues and **d** out demons.
3:22 of demons he is **d** out demons."
9:38 "we saw a man **d** out demons in your
11:15 began **d** out those who were buying
Lk 9:49 "we saw a man **d** out demons in your
11:14 Jesus was **d** out a demon that was
11:15 of demons, he is **d** out demons."
19:45 began **d** out those who were selling.
Ac 19:13 Some Jews who went around **d** out evil
26:24 Your great learning is **d** you insane."

Drop (Dropped, Dropping, Drops)
Dt 28:40 oil, because the olives will **d** off.
33:28 new wine, where the heavens **d** dew.
Pr 3:20 and the clouds let **d** the dew.
17:14 so **d** the matter before a dispute
SS 4:11 Your lips **d** sweetness as the
Isa 33: 9 Bashan and Carmel **d** their leaves.
40:15 nations are like a **d** in a bucket;
Eze 39: 3 your arrows **d** from your right hand.
Zec 8:12 and the heavens will **d** their dew.
Lk 16:17 stroke of a pen to **d** out of the Law.
Rev 6:13 as late figs **d** from a fig-tree when

Dropped (Drop)
Jdg 9:53 a woman **d** an upper millstone on his
15:14 and the bindings **d** from his hands.
2Sa 20: 8 forward, it **d** out of its sheath.
Ac 27:29 they **d** four anchors from the stern

Dropping (Drop)
2Ch 24:10 **d** them into the chest until it was

Drops (Drop)
Nu 35:23 or, without seeing him, **d** a stone on
Job 36:27 "He draws up the **d** of water, which
38:28 a father? Who fathers the **d** of dew?
Lk 22:44 **d** of blood falling to the ground.

Dropsy
Lk 14: 2 of him was a man suffering from **d**.

Dross
Ps 119:119 of the earth you discard like **d**;
Pr 25: 4 Remove the **d** from the silver, and
Isa 1:22 Your silver has become **d**, your
1:25 I will thoroughly purge away your **d**
Eze 22:18 house of Israel has become **d** to me;
22:18 They are but the **d** of silver.
22:19 'Because you have all become **d**,

Drought
Dt 28:22 with scorching heat and **d**, with
Job 12:15 holds back the waters, there is **d**;
24:19 heat and **d** snatch away the melted
Jer 2: 6 a land of **d** and darkness, a land
14: 1 LORD to Jeremiah concerning the **d**:
17: 8 It has no worries in a year of **d**
50:38 A **d** on her waters! They will dry up.
Hag 1:11 I called for a **d** on the fields and

Drove (Drive)
Ge 3:24 After he **d** the man out, he placed on
15:11 carcasses, but Abram **d** them away.
31:18 he **d** all his livestock ahead of him,
Ex 2:17 Some shepherds came along and **d** them
14:21 that night the LORD **d** the sea back
Nu 11:31 LORD and **d** quail in from the sea.
21:32 **d** out the Amorites who were there.
25: 8 He **d** the spear through both of them
32:39 **d** out the Amorites who were there.
Dt 2:12 the descendants of Esau **d** them out.
2:21 who **d** them out and settled in their
2:22 They **d** them out and have lived in
Jos 15:14 From Hebron Caleb **d** out the three
24:12 which **d** them out before you—also
24:18 the LORD **d** out before us all the
Jdg 1:20 **d** from it the three sons of Anak.
1:28 but never **d** them out completely.
4:21 She **d** the peg through his temple
6: 9 I **d** them from before you and gave
9:41 and Zebul **d** Gaal and his brothers
11: 2 were grown up, they **d** Jephthah away.
1Sa 19:10 as Saul **d** the spear into the wall.
30:20 and his men **d** them ahead of the
2Sa 11:23 but we **d** them back to the entrance
1Ki 21:26 the LORD **d** out before Israel.)
1Ch 8:13 who **d** out the inhabitants of Gath.
Ne 13:28 And I **d** him away from me.
Ps 34: T who **d** him away, and he left.
44: 2 With your hand you **d** out the nations
78:55 He **d** out nations before them and
80: 8 **d** out the nations and planted it.
Jer 49: 2 drive out those who **d** her out,"
Eze 28:16 So I **d** you in disgrace from the
29:18 Nebuchadnezzar king of Babylon **d** his
Mt 8:16 and he **d** out the spirits with a word
21:12 and **d** out all who were buying and
Mk 1:34 He also **d** out many demons, but he
6:13 They **d** out many demons and anointed
Lk 4:29 They got up, **d** him out of the town,
Jn 2:15 and **d** all from the temple area,
Ac 7:45 the nations God **d** out before them.
2Co 12:11 fool of myself, but you **d** me to it.
1Th 2:15 and the prophets and also **d** us out.

Droves
Ge 33: 8 "What do you mean by all these **d** I
33:14 at the pace of the **d** before me and
Ex 12:38 as well as large **d** of livestock,
2Ch 14:15 off **d** of sheep and goats and camels.

Drown (Drowned)
Mt 8:25 "Lord, save us! We're going to **d**!
Mk 4:38 "Teacher, don't you care if we **d**?
Lk 8:24 "Master, Master, we're going to **d**!"

Drowned (Drown)
Ex 15: 4 officers are **d** in the Red Sea.
Job 10:15 of shame and **d** in my affliction.
Mt 18: 6 to be **d** in the depths of the sea.
Mk 5:13 steep bank into the lake and were **d**.
Lk 8:33 steep bank into the lake and was **d**.
Heb 11:29 tried to do so, they were **d**.

Drowsiness (Drowsy)
Pr 23:21 poor, and **d** clothes them in rags.

Drowsy (Drowsiness)
Mt 25: 5 they all became **d** and fell asleep.

Drunk (Drink)
Ge 9:21 **d** and lay uncovered inside his tent.
Lev 11:34 that could be **d** from it is unclean.
Dt 32:42 I will make my arrows **d** with blood,
1Sa 1:13 was not heard. Eli thought she was **d**
1:14 long will you keep on getting **d**?
25:36 He was in high spirits and very **d**.
30:12 for he had not eaten any food or **d**
2Sa 11:13 with him, and David made him **d**.
1Ki 16: 9 getting **d** in the home of Arza, the
20:16 him were in their tents getting **d**.
2Ki 19:24 foreign lands and **d** the water there.
SS 5: 1 I have **d** my wine and my milk.
Isa 29: 9 be **d**, but not from wine, stagger,
34: 5 My sword has **d** its fill in the
37:25 foreign lands and **d** the water there.
49:26 **d** on their own blood, as with wine.
51:17 O Jerusalem, you who have **d** from the
51:21 one, made **d**, but not with wine.
63: 6 in my wrath I made them **d** and poured
Jer 25:27 says: Drink, get **d** and vomit, and
35: 8 sons and daughters have ever **d**
48:26 "Make her **d**, for she has defied the
51: 7 she made the whole earth **d**.
51:39 a feast for them and make them **d**,
51:57 make her officials and wise men **d**,
Lam 4:21 you will be **d** and stripped naked.
Eze 39:19 and drink blood till you are **d**.
Na 1:10 among thorns and **d** from their wine;
3:11 You too will become **d**; you will go
Hab 2:15 from the wineskin till they are **d**,
Lk 12:45 and to eat and drink and get **d**.
Ac 2:15 These men are not **d**, as you suppose.
1Co 11:21 One remains hungry, another gets **d**.
Eph 5:18 Do not get **d** on wine, which leads to
1Th 5: 7 and those who get **d**, get **d** at night.
Rev 17: 6 I saw that the woman was **d** with the
18: 3 For all the nations have **d** the

Drunkard (Drink)
Dt 21:20 He is a profligate and a **d**."
Isa 19:14 as a **d** staggers around in his vomit.
24:20 The earth reels like a **d**, it sways
Mt 11:19 'Here is a glutton and a **d**, a friend
Lk 7:34 'Here is a glutton and a **d**, a friend
1Co 5:11 or a slanderer, a **d** or a swindler.

Drunkard's (Drink)
Pr 26: 9 Like a thornbush in a **d** hand is a

Drunkards (Drink)
Job 12:25 he makes them stagger like **d**.
Ps 69:12 mock me, and I am the song of the **d**.
Pr 23:21 for **d** and gluttons become poor, and
Isa 28: 1 the pride of Ephraim's **d**, to the
28: 3 That wreath, the pride of Ephraim's **d**
Joel 1: 5 Wake up, you **d**, and weep! Wail, all
Mt 24:49 and to eat and drink with **d**.
1Co 6:10 nor thieves nor the greedy nor **d** nor

Drunken (Drink)
Ps 107:27 They reeled and staggered like **d** men;
Jer 23: 9 I am like a **d** man, like a man

Drunkenness (Drink)
Ecc 10:17 time—for strength and not for **d**.
Jer 13:13 with **d** all who live in this land,
Eze 23:33 You will be filled with **d** and sorrow,
Lk 21:34 **d** and the anxieties of life, and
Ro 13:13 not in orgies and **d**, not in sexual
Gal 5:21 **d**, orgies, and the like. I warn you
1Ti 3: 3 not given to **d**, not violent but
Tit 1: 7 not quick-tempered, not given to **d**,
1Pe 4: 3 lust, **d**, orgies, carousing and

Drusilla
Ac 24:24 with his wife **D**, who was a Jewess.

Dry (Dried, Dries, Drying)
Ge 1: 9 one place, and let **d** ground appear.
1:10 God called the **d** ground "land", and
7:22 Everything on **d** land that had the
8:13 the surface of the ground was **d**.
8:14 month the earth was completely **d**.
Ex 4: 9 Nile and pour it on the **d** ground.
14:16 can go through the sea on **d** ground.
14:21 east wind and turned it into **d** land.
14:22 went through the sea on **d** ground,
14:29 went through the sea on **d** ground,
15:19 walked through the sea on **d** ground.
Lev 7:10 whether mixed with oil or **d**, belongs
Dt 29:19 the watered land as well as the **d**.
Jos 3:17 **d** ground in the middle of the Jordan,
3:17 completed the crossing on **d** ground.
4:18 they set their feet on the **d** ground
4:22 crossed the Jordan on **d** ground.'
9: 5 their food supply was **d** and mouldy.
9:12 But now see how **d** and mouldy it is.
Jdg 6:37 the fleece and all the ground is **d**,
6:39 This time make the fleece **d**
6:40 Only the fleece was **d**; all the
1Ki 17:14 the jug of oil will not run **d** until
17:16 up and the jug of oil did not run **d**,
2Ki 2: 8 of them crossed over on **d** ground.
Ne 9:11 they passed through it on **d** ground,
Job 6:17 that cease to flow in the **d** season,
13:25 Will you chase after **d** chaff?
14:11 a river bed becomes parched and **d**,
18:16 His roots **d** up below and his
30: 6 to live in the **d** stream beds,
Ps 58: 9 whether they be green or **d**—
63: 1 for you, in a **d** and weary land
66: 6 He turned the sea into **d** land, they
90: 6 by evening it is **d** and withered.
95: 5 it, and his hands formed the **d** land.
Pr 17: 1 Better a **d** crust with peace and
Isa 5:24 as **d** grass sinks down in the flames,
11:15 The LORD will **d** up the gulf of the
19: 5 The waters of the river will **d** up,
19: 5 the river bed will be parched and **d**.
19: 6 of Egypt will dwindle and **d** up.
27:11 its twigs are **d**, they are broken off
42:15 hills and **d** up all their vegetation;
42:15 into islands and **d** up the pools.
44: 3 and streams on the **d** ground; I will
44:27 who says to the watery deep, 'Be **d**,
44:27 and I will **d** up your streams,'
50: 2 By a mere rebuke I **d** up the sea,
53: 2 and like a root out of **d** ground.
56: 3 complain, "I am only a **d** tree.
Jer 2:25 feet are bare and your throat is **d**.
50:12 a wilderness, a **d** land, a desert.
50:38 on her waters! They will **d** up.
51:36 **d** up her sea and make her springs **d**.
51:43 be desolate, a **d** and desert land,
Lam 4: 8 it has become as **d** as a stick.
Eze 17:24 I **d** up the green tree and
17:24 and make the **d** tree flourish.
19:13 the desert, in a **d** and thirsty land.
20:47 all your trees, both green and **d**.
23:34 You will drink it and drain it **d**;
30:12 I will **d** up the streams of the Nile
37: 2 the valley, bones that were very **d**.
37: 4 '**D** bones, hear the word of the LORD!
Hos 9:14 miscarry and breasts that are **d**.
13:15 spring will fail and his well **d** up.
Am 1: 2 the pastures of the shepherds **d** up,
Jnh 2:10 and it vomited Jonah onto **d** land.
Na 1: 4 he makes all the rivers run **d**.
1:10 will be consumed like **d** stubble.
Zep 2:13 desolate and **d** as the desert.
Hag 2: 6 the earth, the sea and the **d** land.
Zec 10:11 the depths of the Nile will **d** up.
Lk 23:31 what will happen when it is **d**?"
Heb 11:29 through the Red Sea as on **d** land;

Drying (Dry)
Jn 13: 5 **d** them with the towel that was

Due
Lev 19:20 freedom, there must be **d** punishment.
Dt 18: 3 This is the share **d** to the priests
32:35 In **d** time their foot will slip;
1Ch 16:29 ascribe to the LORD the glory **d** to
2Ch 24: 5 money **d** annually from all Israel,
31: 4 give the portion **d** to the priests

Job 36:17 now you are laden with the judgment **d**
Ps 29: 2 Ascribe to the LORD the glory **d** to
90:11 great as the fear that is **d** to you.
96: 8 Ascribe to the LORD the glory **d** to
Pr 11:31 If the righteous receive their **d** on
Isa 49: 4 Yet what is **d** to me is in the LORD's
59:18 he will repay the islands their **d**.
Jer 10: 7 King of the nations? This is your **d**.
Mal 1: 6 where is the honour **d** to me? If I am
1: 6 where is the respect **d** to me?" says
Ro 1:27 the **d** penalty for their perversion.
2Co 5:10 that each one may receive what is **d**
Eph 4:18 **d** to the hardening of their hearts.
1Pe 5: 6 that he may lift you up in **d** time.

Dug (Dig)

Ge 21:30 as a witness that I **d** this well."
26:15 **d** in the time of his father Abraham,
26:18 **d** in the time of his father Abraham,
26:19 Isaac's servants **d** in the valley and
26:21 they **d** another well, but they
26:22 He moved on from there and **d** another
26:25 and there his servants **d** a well.
26:32 told him about the well they had **d**.
50: 5 I **d** for myself in the land of Canaan.
Ex 7:24 all the Egyptians **d** along the Nile
Nu 21:18 about the well that the princes **d**,
1Ki 18:32 and he **d** a trench round it large
2Ki 19:24 I have **d** wells in foreign lands and
2Ch 26:10 in the desert and **d** many cisterns,
Ne 9:25 wells already **d**, vineyards, olive
Ps 9:15 fallen into the pit they have **d**;
35: 7 and without cause **d** a pit for me,
57: 6 They **d** a pit in my path—but they
94:13 till a pit is **d** for the wicked.
Isa 5: 2 He **d** it up and cleared it of stones
37:25 I have **d** wells in foreign lands and
Jer 2:13 and have **d** their own cisterns,
13: 7 I went to Perath and **d** up the belt
18:20 Yet they have **d** a pit for me.
18:22 for they have **d** a pit to capture me
Eze 8: 8 So I **d** into the wall and saw a
12: 7 Then in the evening I **d** through the
12:12 **d** in the wall for him to go through.
Mt 21:33 **d** a winepress in it and built a
25:18 **d** a hole in the ground and hid his
Mk 12: 1 He put a wall around it, **d** a pit for
Lk 6:48 who **d** down deep and laid the

Dull

Lev 13:39 and if the spots are **d** white, it is
Ecc 10:10 If the axe is **d** and its edge
Isa 6:10 their ears **d** and close their eyes.
59: 1 to save, nor his ear too **d** to hear.
Lam 4: 1 the fine gold become **d**! The sacred
Mt 15:16 "Are you still so **d**?" Jesus asked
Mk 7:18 "Are you so **d**?" he asked. "Don't you
2Co 3:14 their minds were made **d**, for to this

Dumah

Ge 25:14 Mishma, **D**, Massa,
Jos 15:52 Arab, **D**, Eshan,
1Ch 1:30 Mishma, **D**, Massa, Hadad, Tema,
Isa 21:11 An oracle concerning **D**: Someone

Dumped

Lev 14:41 **d** into an unclean place outside the

Dung

1Ki 14:10 one burns **d**, until it is all gone.
Ne 2:13 the Jackal Well and the **D** Gate,
3:13 of the wall as far as the **D** Gate.
3:14 The **D** Gate was repaired by Malkijah
12:31 to the right, towards the **D** Gate.
Job 20: 7 perish for ever, like his own **d**;

Dungeon (Dungeons)

Ge 40:15 to deserve being put in a **d**."
41:14 he was quickly brought from the **d**.
Ex 12:29 who was in the **d**, and the firstborn
Isa 24:22 like prisoners bound in a **d**;
42: 7 to release from the **d** those who sit
51:14 they will not die in their **d**, nor
Jer 37:16 was put into a vaulted cell in a **d**,

Dungeons (Dungeon)

2Pe 2: 4 gloomy **d** to be held for judgment;

Duplicity

Pr 11: 3 unfaithful are destroyed by their **d**.
Lk 20:23 He saw through their **d** and said to

Dura

Da 3: 1 of **D** in the province of Babylon.

Dusk

Jos 2: 5 At **d**, when it was time to close the
1Sa 30:17 David fought them from **d** until the
2Ki 7: 5 At **d** they got up and went to the
7: 7 they got up and fled in the **d** and
Job 4:20 Between dawn and **d** they are broken
24:15 eye of the adulterer watches for **d**;
Eze 12: 6 watching and carry them out at **d**.
12: 7 I took my belongings out at **d**,
12:12 on his shoulder at **d** and leave,
Hab 1: 8 leopards, fiercer than wolves at **d**.

Dust (*Dust and ashes, Dust of the earth*)

Ge 2: 7 the man from the **d** of the ground
3:14 eat **d** all the days of your life.
3:19 **d** you are and to **d** you will return."
13:16 so that if anyone could count the **d**,
Ex 8:16 and strike the **d** of the ground,'
8:16 of Egypt the **d** will become gnats."
8:17 and struck the **d** of the ground,
8:17 All the **d** throughout the land of
9: 9 will become fine **d** over the whole
Nu 5:17 put some **d** from the tabernacle floor
23:10 Who can count the **d** of Jacob or
Dt 9:21 ground it to powder as fine as **d** and
9:21 threw the **d** into a stream that
28:24 of your country into **d** and powder;
32:24 venom of vipers that glide in the **d**.
Jos 7: 6 and sprinkled **d** on their heads.
1Sa 2: 8 He raises the poor from the **d** and
4:12 his clothes torn and **d** on his head.
2Sa 1: 2 clothes torn and with **d** on his head.
15:32 his robe torn and **d** on his head.
1Ki 16: 2 "I lifted you up from the **d** and made
20:10 if enough **d** remains in Samaria to
2Ki 13: 7 them like the **d** at threshing time.
23: 6 scattered the **d** over the graves of
Ne 9: 1 and having **d** on their heads.
Job 2:12 and sprinkled **d** on their heads.
4:19 whose foundations are in the **d**, who
7:21 For I shall soon lie down in the **d**;
10: 9 Will you now turn me to **d** again?
16:15 my skin and buried my brow in the **d**.
17:16 Will we descend together into the **d**?"
20:11 bones will lie with him in the **d**.
21:26 Side by side they lie in the **d**, and
22:24 assign your nuggets to the **d**, your
27:16 Though he heaps up silver like **d** and
28: 6 and its **d** contains nuggets of gold.
34:15 and man would return to the **d**.
38:38 the **d** becomes hard and the clods of
40:13 Bury them all in the **d** together;
Ps 7: 5 ground and make me sleep in the **d**.
18:42 I beat them as fine as **d** borne on
22:15 you lay me in the **d** of death.
22:29 all who go down to the **d** will kneel
30: 9 Will the **d** praise you? Will it
44:25 We are brought down to the **d**; our
72: 9 him and his enemies will lick the **d**.
78:27 He rained meat down on them like **d**,
89:39 and have defiled his crown in the **d**.
90: 3 You turn men back to **d**, saying,
90: 3 "Return to **d**, O sons of men.
102:14 her very **d** moves them to pity.
103:14 formed, he remembers that we are **d**.
104:29 they die and return to the **d**.
113: 7 He raises the poor from the **d** and
119:25 I am laid low in the **d**; preserve my
Pr 8:26 fields or any of the **d** of the world.
Ecc 3:20 come from **d**, and to **d** all return.
12: 7 the **d** returns to the ground it came
Isa 5:24 and their flowers blow away like **d**;
25:12 down to the ground, to the very **d**.
26: 5 ground and casts it down to the **d**.
26:19 You who dwell in the **d**, wake up and
29: 4 speech will mumble out of the **d**.
29: 4 of the **d** your speech will whisper.
29: 5 enemies will become like fine **d**,
34: 7 and the **d** will be soaked with fat.
34: 9 her **d** into burning sulphur; her land
40:15 they are regarded as **d** on the scales;
40:15 islands as though they were fine **d**.
41: 2 He turns them to **d** with his sword,
47: 1 "Go down, sit in the **d**, Virgin
49:23 they will lick the **d** at your feet.
52: 2 Shake off your **d**; rise up, sit
65:25 but **d** will be the serpent's food.
Jer 17:13 will be written in the **d** because
25:34 in the **d**, you leaders of the flock.
Lam 2:10 they have sprinkled **d** on their heads
2:21 "Young and old lie together in the **d**
3:16 he has trampled me in the **d**.
3:29 Let him bury his face in the **d**—
Eze 24: 7 ground, where the **d** would cover it.
26:10 that they will cover you with **d**.
27:30 **d** on their heads and roll in ashes.
Am 2: 7 poor as upon the **d** of the ground
Jnh 3: 6 sackcloth and sat down in the **d**.
Mic 1:10 In Beth Ophrah roll in the **d**.
7:17 They will lick **d** like a snake, like
Na 1: 3 and clouds are the **d** of his feet.
Zep 1:17 blood will be poured out like **d**
Zec 9: 3 she has heaped up silver like **d**,
Mt 10:14 shake the **d** off your feet when you
Mk 6:11 shake the **d** off your feet when you
Lk 9: 5 shake the **d** off your feet when you
10:11 'Even the **d** of your town that sticks
Ac 13:51 they shook the **d** from their feet in
22:23 cloaks and flinging **d** into the air,
Rev 18:19 They will throw **d** on their heads,

Dust and ashes

Ge 18:27 the Lord, though I am nothing but **d**,
Job 30:19 into the mud, and I am reduced to **d**.
42: 6 I despise myself and repent in **d**.

Dust of the earth

Ge 13:16 will make your offspring like the **d**
28:14 Your descendants will be like the **d**,
2Sa 22:43 I beat them as fine as the **d**;
2Ch 1: 9 people who are as numerous as the **d**.
Isa 40:12 Who has held the **d** in a basket,
Da 12: 2 Multitudes who sleep in the **d** will
1Co 15:47 The first man was of the **d**, the

Duties (Duty)

Ge 39:11 into the house to attend to his **d**,
Ex 18:20 live and the **d** they are to perform.
Nu 3: 7 They are to perform **d** for him and
4:28 Their **d** are to be under the
8:26 their **d** at the Tent of Meeting,
18: 3 to perform all the **d** of the Tent,
1Ki 3: 7 do not know how to carry out my **d**.
1Ch 6:32 They performed their **d** according to
6:48 all the other **d** of the tabernacle,
9:25 share their **d** for seven-day periods.
9:33 were exempt from other **d** because
23:28 of other **d** at the house of God.
25: 8 as student, cast lots for their **d**.
26:12 through their chief men, had **d** for
26:29 assigned **d** away from the temple,
2Ch 8:14 of the priests for their **d**
31: 2 each of them according to their **d** as
31:16 the daily **d** of their various tasks,
35: 2 He appointed the priests to their **d**
Ne 10:33 all the **d** of the house of our God.
13:30 assigned them **d**, each to his own
Eze 44:14 in charge of the **d** of the temple
44:15 who faithfully carried out the **d** of
2Ti 4: 5 all the **d** of your ministry.
Heb 10:11 stands and performs his religious **d**;

Duty (Duties)

Ge 38: 8 your **d** to her as a brother-in-law
Nu 4:31 This is their **d** as they perform
Dt 24: 5 war or have any other **d** laid on him.
25: 5 the **d** of a brother-in-law to her.
25: 7 the **d** of a brother-in-law to me."

1Ki 14:27 commanders of the guard on **d** at the
2Ki 11: 5 that are going on **d** on the Sabbath
11: 7 that normally go off Sabbath **d** are
11: 9 who were going on **d** on the Sabbath
11: 9 and those who were going off **d**—
1Ch 23:28 The **d** of the Levites was to help
27: 1 on **d** month by month throughout the
2Ch 12:10 commanders of the guard on **d** at the
23: 4 Levites who are going on **d** on the
23: 6 except the priests and Levites on **d**;
23: 8 who were going on **d** on the Sabbath
23: 8 those who were going off **d**—for
Ezr 4:13 no more taxes, tribute or **d** will be
4:20 tribute and **d** were paid to them.
7:24 tribute or **d** on any of the priests,
Ne 7: 3 While the gatekeepers are still on **d**,
Ecc 12:13 this is the whole ⌊**d**⌋ of man
Jer 32: 7 it is your right and **d** to buy it.'
Eze 44: 8 Instead of carrying out your **d** in
45:17 will be the **d** of the prince to
Mt 17:25 do the kings of the earth collect **d**
Lk 1: 8 when Zechariah's division was on **d**
17:10 servants; we have only done our **d**.'"
Jn 18:16 on **d** there and brought Peter in.
Ac 23: 1 "My brothers, I have fulfilled my **d**
Ro 15:16 **d** of proclaiming the gospel of God,
1Co 7: 3 fulfil his marital **d** to his wife,

Dwarfed

Lev 21:20 or who is hunchbacked or **d**, or who

Dwell (Dwellers, Dwelling, Dwellings, Dwells, Dwelt, Tent-dwelling)

Ex 25: 8 for me, and I will **d** among them.
29:45 I will **d** among the Israelites and be
29:46 Egypt so that I might **d** among them.
Nu 5: 3 their camp, where I **d** among them."
35:34 land where you live and where I **d**,
35:34 the LORD, **d** among the Israelites.'"
2Sa 7: 5 the one to build me a house to **d** in?
1Ki 8:12 that he would **d** in a dark cloud;
8:13 you, a place for you to **d** for ever."
8:27 "But will God really **d** on earth? The
1Ch 17: 4 the one to build me a house to **d** in.
23:25 has come to **d** in Jerusalem for ever,
2Ch 6: 1 that he would **d** in a dark cloud;
6: 2 you, a place for you to **d** for ever."
6:18 "But will God really **d** on earth with
Ezr 6:12 May God, who has caused his Name to **d**
Job 11:14 and allow no evil to **d** in your tent,
17: 2 my eyes must **d** on their hostility.
28: 4 Far from where people **d** he cuts a
28:12 Where does understanding **d**?
28:20 Where does understanding **d**?
Ps 4: 8 alone, O LORD, make me **d** in safety.
5: 4 with you the wicked cannot **d**.
15: 1 LORD, who may **d** in your sanctuary?
23: 6 **d** in the house of the LORD for ever.
27: 4 I may **d** in the house of the LORD
37: 3 **d** in the land and enjoy safe
37:27 you will **d** in the land for ever.
37:29 the land and **d** in it for ever.
39:12 For I **d** with you as an alien, a
43: 3 mountain, to the place where you **d**.
61: 4 I long to **d** in your tent for ever
68:16 the LORD himself will **d** for ever?
68:18 you, O LORD God, might **d** there.
69:25 there be no-one to **d** in their tents.
69:36 who love his name will **d** there.
84: 4 Blessed are those who **d** in your
84:10 than **d** in the tents of the wicked.
85: 9 that his glory may **d** in our land.
101: 6 that they may **d** with me; he whose
101: 7 practises deceit will **d** in my house
120: 5 Woe to me that I **d** in Meshech, that
143: 3 **d** in darkness like those long dead.
Pr 8:12 I, wisdom, **d** together with prudence
SS 8:13 You who **d** in the gardens with
Isa 1:21 righteousness used to **d** in her—
13:21 her houses; there the owls will **d**,
26: 5 He humbles those who **d** on high, he
26:19 You who **d** in the dust, wake up and
32:16 Justice will **d** in the desert and
33:14 "Who of us can **d** with the consuming
Isa 33:14 us can **d** with everlasting burning?"
33:16 this is the man who will **d** on the
33:24 those who **d** there will be forgiven.
34:17 and **d** there from generation to
38:11 with those who now **d** in this world.
43:18 do not **d** on the past.
44:13 glory, that it may **d** in a shrine.
65:21 They will build houses and **d** in them
Jer 17: 6 He will **d** in the parched places of
47: 2 all who **d** in the land will wail
48:28 Abandon your towns and **d** among the
49:18 live there; no man will **d** in it.
49:33 live there; no man will **d** in it."
50:39 there, and there the owl will **d**.
50:40 live there; no man will **d** in it.
Lam 3: 6 He has made me **d** in darkness like
Eze 7: 7 upon you—you who **d** in the land.
26:20 I will make you **d** in the earth below,
Hos 14: 7 Men will **d** again in his shade. He
Joel 3:17 your God, **d** in Zion, my holy hill.
Zep 2: 6 where the Kerethites **d**, will be a
Zec 8: 3 return to Zion and **d** in Jerusalem.
Jn 5:38 nor does his word **d** in you, for you
Ac 1:20 let there be no-one to **d** in it,'
Eph 3:17 that Christ may **d** in your hearts
Col 1:19 to have all his fulness **d** in him,
3:16 Let the word of Christ **d** in you
Rev 12:12 you heavens and you who **d** in them!

Dwellers (Dwell)

Isa 5: 3 "Now you **d** in Jerusalem and men of

Dwelling (Dwell)

Ge 27:39 "Your **d** will be away from the
Ex 15:13 you will guide them to your holy **d**.
15:17 O LORD, you made for your **d**, the
Dt 12: 5 to put his Name there for his **d**.
12:11 God will choose as a **d** for his Name
14:23 he will choose as a **d** for his Name,
16: 2 LORD will choose as a **d** for his Name
16: 6 he will choose as a **d** for his Name.
16:11 choose as a **d** for his Name—you,
26: 2 God will choose as a **d** for his
1Sa 2:29 offering that I prescribed for my **d**?
2:32 you will see distress in my **d**.
2Sa 7: 6 place to place with a tent as my **d**.
1Ch 9:19 the entrance to the **d** of the LORD.
2Ch 31: 2 at the gates of the LORD's **d**.
Ezr 7:15 of Israel, whose **d** is in Jerusalem,
Ne 1: 9 I have chosen as a **d** for my Name.'
Job 18:15 sulphur is scattered over his **d**.
18:21 Surely such is the **d** of an evil man;
23: 3 if only I could go to his **d**!
Ps 27: 5 he will keep me safe in his **d**;
31:20 in your **d** you keep them safe from
68: 5 of widows, is God in his holy **d**.
91: 9 If you make the Most High your **d**—
132: 5 a **d** for the Mighty One of Jacob."
132:13 Zion, he has desired it for his **d**:
Isa 26:21 See, the LORD is coming out of his **d**
Jer 7:12 where I first made a **d** for my Name,
25:30 he will thunder from his holy **d** and
31:23 O righteous **d**, O sacred mountain.'
Lam 2: 6 He has laid waste his **d** like a
Zep 3: 7 Then her **d** would not be cut off,
Zec 2:13 has roused himself from his holy **d**."
Jn 1:14 flesh and made his **d** among us.
2Co 5: 2 to be clothed with our heavenly **d**,
5: 4 to be clothed with our heavenly **d**,
Eph 2:22 become a **d** in which God lives by his
Rev 21: 3 "Now the **d** of God is with men, and

Dwelling-place (Dwell)

Lev 15:31 my **d**, which is among them.'"
26:11 I will put my **d** among you, and I
Nu 24:21 "Your **d** is secure, your nest is set
Dt 26:15 Look down from heaven, your holy **d**,
2Sa 15:25 and let me see it and his **d** again.
1Ki 8:30 Hear from heaven, your **d**, and when
8:39 hear from heaven, your **d**. Forgive
8:43 hear from heaven, your **d**, and do
8:49 from heaven, your **d**, hear their
1Ch 16:27 strength and joy in his **d**.
17: 5 to another, from one **d** to another.
2Ch 6:21 Hear from heaven, your **d**; and when
2Ch 6:30 hear from heaven, your **d**. Forgive,
6:33 hear from heaven, your **d**, and do
6:39 from heaven, your **d**, hear their
29: 6 away from the LORD's **d** and turned
30:27 prayer reached heaven, his holy **d**.
36:15 had pity on his people and on his **d**.
Ps 33:14 from his **d** he watches all who live
74: 7 they defiled the **d** of your Name.
76: 2 His tent is in Salem, his **d** in Zion.
84: 1 How lovely is your **d**, O LORD
90: 1 Lord, you have been our **d** throughout
132: 7 "Let us go to his **d**; let us worship
Pr 24:15 man's house, do not raid his **d**;
Isa 18: 4 quiet and will look on from my **d**,
Eze 3:12 of the LORD be praised in his **d**!—
37:27 My **d** will be with them; I will be
Mic 1: 3 Look! The LORD is coming from his **d**;
Ac 7:46 provide a **d** for the God of Jacob.
Rev 13: 6 to slander his name and his **d** and

Dwelling-places (Dwell)

Nu 24: 5 tents, O Jacob, your **d**, O Israel!
Isa 32:18 My people will live in peaceful **d**,
Hab 1: 6 earth to seize **d** not their own.

Dwellings (Dwell)

Ex 35: 3 Do not light a fire in any of your **d**
1Ch 4:41 They attacked the Hamites in their **d**
5:10 they occupied the **d** of the Hagrites
Job 38:20 Do you know the paths to their **d**?
Ps 49:11 their **d** for endless generations,
87: 2 Zion more than all the **d** of Jacob.
Isa 58:12 Walls, Restorer of Streets with **D**.
Jer 30:18 tents and have compassion on his **d**;
51:30 Her **d** are set on fire; the bars of
Lam 2: 2 has swallowed up all the **d** of Jacob;
Hab 3: 7 the **d** of Midian in anguish.
Zec 12: 7 "The LORD will save the **d** of Judah
Lk 16: 9 you will be welcomed into eternal **d**.

Dwells (Dwell)

Job 28:23 to it and he alone knows where it **d**,
39:28 He **d** on a cliff and stays there at
Ps 26: 8 the place where your glory **d**.
46: 4 holy place where the Most High **d**.
91: 1 He who **d** in the shelter of the Most
135:21 Zion, to him who **d** in Jerusalem.
Isa 8:18 LORD Almighty, who **d** on Mount Zion.
33: 5 LORD is exalted, for he **d** on high;
Lam 1: 3 She **d** among the nations; she finds
Da 2:22 in darkness, and light **d** with him.
Joel 3:21 The LORD **d** in Zion!
Mt 23:21 by it and by the one who **d** in it.

Dwelt (Dwell)

Dt 33:16 of him who **d** in the burning bush.
2Sa 7: 6 I have not **d** in a house from the
1Ch 17: 5 I have not **d** in a house from the
Job 29:25 I **d** as a king among his troops;
Ps 74: 2 redeemed—Mount Zion, where you **d**.
94:17 soon have **d** in the silence of death

Dwindle (Dwindles)

Isa 19: 6 streams of Egypt will **d** and dry up.

Dwindles (Dwindle)

Pr 13:11 Dishonest money **d** away, but he who

Dyed

Ex 25: 5 skins **d** red and hides of sea cows
26:14 tent a covering of ram skins **d** red,
35: 7 skins **d** red and hides of sea cows
35:23 or goat hair, ram skins **d** red or
36:19 tent a covering of ram skins **d** red,
39:34 the covering of ram skins **d** red, the

Dying (Die)

Ge 35:18 she breathed her last—for she was **d**
1Sa 4:20 she was **d**, the women attending her
2Ch 24:22 who said as he lay **d**, "May the LORD
Job 11:20 their hope will become a **d** gasp."
24:12 The groans of the **d** rise from the
29:13 The man who was **d** blessed me; I made
Isa 22:14 "Till your **d** day this sin will not

Hos 4: 3 air and the fish of the sea are **d**.
Zec 11: 9 Let the **d** die, and the perishing
Mk 5:23 with him, "My little daughter is **d**.
Lk 8:42 a girl of about twelve, was **d**.
Jn 11:37 man have kept this man from **d**?"
Ro 7: 6 now, by **d** to what once bound us, we
2Co 6: 9 **d**, and yet we live on; beaten, and
Heb 11:21 By faith Jacob, when he was **d**,

Dynasty
1Sa 25:28 make a lasting **d** for my master,
1Ki 2:24 has founded a **d** for me as he
11:38 will build you a **d** as enduring as

Dysentery
Ac 28: 8 in bed, suffering from fever and **d**.

Eager (Eagerly, Eagerness)
2Ch 26:20 Indeed, he himself was **e** to leave,
Ps 56: 6 watch my steps, **e** to take my life.
Pr 28:20 **e** to get rich will not go unpunished.
28:22 A stingy man is **e** to get rich and is
31:13 and flax and works with **e** hands.
Isa 58: 2 me out; they seem **e** to know my ways,
58: 2 seem **e** for God to come near them.
Zep 3: 7 **e** to act corruptly in all they did.
Ro 1:15 That is why I am so **e** to preach the
8:19 The creation waits in **e** expectation
1Co 14:12 Since you are **e** to have spiritual
14:39 my brothers, be **e** to prophesy
2Co 8:11 Now finish the work, so that your **e**
Gal 2:10 poor, the very thing I was **e** to do.
Php 2:28 Therefore I am all the more **e** to
1Ti 6:10 Some people, **e** for money, have
Tit 2:14 his very own, **e** to do what is good.
1Pe 3:13 Who is going to harm you if you are **e**
5: 2 not greedy for money, but **e** to serve
2Pe 1:10 my brothers, be all the more **e** to
Jude : 3 although I was very **e** to write to you

Eagerly (Eager)
2Ch 15:15 They sought God **e**, and he was found
Job 7: 2 a hired man waiting **e** for his wages,
Ps 78:34 him; they **e** turned to him again.
Lk 22:15 he said to them, "I have **e** desired
Ro 8:23 groan inwardly as we wait **e** for our
1Co 1: 7 as you **e** wait for our Lord Jesus
12:31 **e** desire the greater gifts. And now
14: 1 Follow the way of love and **e** desire
Gal 5: 5 by faith we **e** await through the
Php 1:20 I **e** expect and hope that I will in
3:20 And we **e** await a Saviour from there,

Eagerness (Eager)
Ac 17:11 received the message with great **e**
2Co 7:11 what **e** to clear yourselves, what
8:19 himself and to show our **e** to help.
9: 2 For I know your **e** to help, and I

Eagle (Eagle's, Eagles, Eagles')
Lev 11:13 they are detestable: the **e**,
Dt 14:12 these you may not eat: the **e**, the
28:49 like an **e** swooping down, a nation
32:11 like an **e** that stirs up its nest
Job 39:27 Does the **e** soar at your command and
Pr 23: 5 and fly off to the sky like an **e**.
30:19 the way of an **e** in the sky, the way
Jer 48:40 "Look! An **e** is swooping down,
49:22 Look! An **e** will soar and swoop down,
Eze 1:10 each also had the face of an **e**.
10:14 and the fourth the face of an **e**.
17: 3 says: A great **e** with powerful wings,
17: 7 "But there was another great **e** with
Da 4:33 hair grew like the feathers of an **e**
7: 4 lion, and it had the wings of an **e**.
Hos 8: 1 An **e** is over the house of the LORD
Ob : 4 Though you soar like the **e** and make
Rev 4: 7 man, the fourth was like a flying **e**.
8:13 I watched, I heard an **e** that was
12:14 given the two wings of a great **e**,

Eagle's (Eagle)
Ps 103: 5 your youth is renewed like the **e**.
Jer 49:16 you build your nest as high as the **e**

Eagles (Eagle)
2Sa 1:23 They were swifter than **e**
Job 9:26 like **e** swooping down on their prey.
Isa 40:31 They will soar on wings like **e**; they
Jer 4:13 his horses are swifter than **e**.
Lam 4:19 Our pursuers were swifter than **e** in

Eagles' (Eagle)
Ex 19: 4 how I carried you on **e** wings

Ear (Ear-ring, Ear-rings, Ears)
Ex 9:31 in the **e** and the flax was in bloom.
21: 6 and pierce his **e** with an awl.
Lev 8:23 it on the lobe of Aaron's right **e**,
14:14 right **e** of the one to be cleansed,
14:17 right **e** of the one to be cleansed,
14:25 right **e** of the one to be cleansed,
14:28 right **e** of the one to be cleansed,
Dt 1:45 weeping and turned a deaf **e** to you.
15:17 take an awl and push it through his **e**
2Ki 19:16 Give **e**, O LORD, and hear; open your
Ne 1: 6 let your **e** be attentive and your
1:11 O Lord, let your **e** be attentive to
Job 12:11 Does not the **e** test words as the
34: 3 For the **e** tests words as the tongue
Ps 5: 1 Give **e** to my words, O LORD,
17: 1 Give **e** to my prayer—it does not
17: 6 me; give **e** to me and hear my prayer.
28: 1 my Rock; do not turn a deaf **e** to me.
31: 2 Turn your **e** to me, come quickly to
45:10 O daughter, consider and give **e**:
49: 4 I will turn my **e** to a proverb; with
71: 2 turn your **e** to me and save me.
88: 2 before you; turn your **e** to my cry.
94: 9 Does he who implanted the **e** not hear?
102: 2 Turn your **e** to me; when I call,
116: 2 he turned his **e** to me, I will call
Pr 2: 2 turning your **e** to wisdom and
25:12 wise man's rebuke to a listening **e**.
28: 9 If anyone turns a deaf **e** to the law,
Ecc 1: 8 nor the **e** its fill of hearing.
Isa 37:17 Give **e**, O LORD, and hear; open your
48: 8 of old your **e** has not been open.
50: 4 **e** to listen like one being taught.
55: 3 Give **e** and come to me; hear me, that
59: 1 to save, nor his **e** too dull to hear.
64: 4 no **e** has perceived, no eye has seen
Da 9:18 Give **e**, O God, and hear; open your
Am 3:12 two leg bones or a piece of an **e**,
Mt 10:27 in your **e**, proclaim from the roofs.
26:51 the high priest, cutting off his **e**.
Mk 4:28 the **e**, then the full grain in the **e**.
14:47 the high priest, cutting off his **e**.
Lk 12: 3 what you have whispered in the **e** in
22:50 priest, cutting off his right **e**.
22:51 touched the man's **e** and healed him.
Jn 18:10 servant, cutting off his right **e**.
18:26 a relative of the man whose **e** Peter
1Co 2: 9 "No eye has seen, no **e** has heard, no
12:16 if the **e** should say, "Because I am
12:17 **e**, where would the sense of smell be?
Rev 2: 7 He who has an **e**, let him hear what
2:11 He who has an **e**, let him hear what
2:17 He who has an **e**, let him hear what
2:29 He who has an **e**, let him hear what
3: 6 He who has an **e**, let him hear what
3:13 He who has an **e**, let him hear what
3:22 He who has an **e**, let him hear what
13: 9 He who has an **e**, let him hear.

Earn (Earned, Earners, Earnings, Earns)
Dt 23:19 anything else that may **e** interest.
Am 7:12 **E** your bread there and do your
Hag 1: 6 You **e** wages, only to put them in a
2Th 3:12 settle down and **e** the bread
Rev 18:17 and all who **e** their living from the sea

Earned (Earn)
Pr 31:31 Give her the reward she has **e**, and
Lk 19:16 'Sir, your mina has **e** ten more.'
19:18 'Sir, your mina has **e** five more.'
Ac 16:16 She **e** a great deal of money for her

Earners (Earn)
Isa 19:10 the wage **e** will be sick at heart.

Earnest (Earnestly, Earnestness)
Pr 27: 9 friend springs from his **e** counsel.
Rev 3:19 So be **e**, and repent.

Earnestly (Earnest)
1Sa 20: 6 'David **e** asked my permission to
20:28 Jonathan answered, "David **e** asked me
Ps 63: 1 O God, you are my God, **e** I seek you;
Hos 5:15 their misery they will **e** seek me."
Mk 5:23 he fell at his feet and pleaded **e**
Lk 7: 4 they came to Jesus, they pleaded **e**
22:44 being in anguish, he prayed more **e**,
Ac 12: 5 church was **e** praying to God for him.
26: 7 as they **e** serve God day and night.
Ro 11: 7 What then? What Israel sought so **e**
1Th 3:10 Night and day we pray most **e** that we
Heb 11: 6 he rewards those who **e** seek him.
Jas 5:17 He prayed **e** that it would not rain,

Earnestness (Earnest)
Dt 18: 6 **e** to the place the LORD will choose,
2Co 7:11 sorrow has produced in you: what **e**,
8: 7 in knowledge, in complete **e** and in
8: 8 comparing it with the **e** of others.

Earnings (Earn)
Dt 23:18 You must not bring the **e** of a female
Pr 31:16 out of her **e** she plants a vineyard.
Isa 23:18 Yet her profit and her **e** will be set

Earns (Earn)
Pr 11:18 The wicked man **e** deceptive wages,

Ear-ring (Ear-rings, Ring)
Jdg 8:24 an **e** from your share of the plunder.
Pr 25:12 Like an **e** of gold or an ornament of

Ear-rings (Ear-ring, Ring)
Ex 32: 2 "Take off the gold **e** that your wives,
32: 3 all the people took off their **e** and
35:22 brooches, **e**, rings and ornaments.
Nu 31:50 bracelets, signet rings, **e** and
Jdg 8:24 of the Ishmaelites to wear gold **e**.)
SS 1:10 Your cheeks are beautiful with **e**,
1:11 We will make you **e** of gold, studded
Isa 3:19 the **e** and bracelets and veils,
Eze 16:12 I put a ring on your nose, **e** on your

Ears (Ear, *Ears to hear*)
Ge 35: 4 they had and the rings in their **e**,
41: 5 had a second dream: Seven **e** of corn,
41: 6 After them, seven other **e** of corn
41: 7 The thin **e** of corn swallowed up the
41: 7 up the seven healthy, full **e**.
41:22 "In my dreams I also saw seven **e** of
41:23 After them, seven other **e**
41:24 The thin **e** of corn swallowed up the
41:24 corn swallowed up the seven good **e**.
41:26 and the seven good **e** of corn are
41:27 so are the seven worthless **e** of corn
Ex 29:20 the right **e** of Aaron and his sons,
Lev 8:24 blood on the lobes of their right **e**,
Dt 23:25 you may pick the **e** with your hands,
29: 4 or eyes that see or **e** that hear.
1Sa 3:11 **e** of everyone who hears of it tingle.
15:14 is this bleating of sheep in my **e**?
2Sa 7:22 as we have heard with our own **e**.
22: 7 my voice; my cry came to his **e**.
2Ki 4:42 corn, along with some **e** of new corn.
19:28 and your insolence has reached my **e**,
21:12 Judah that the **e** of everyone who
1Ch 17:20 as we have heard with our own **e**.
2Ch 6:40 may your eyes be open and your **e**
7:15 Now my eyes will be open and my **e**
Job 4:12 to me, my **e** caught a whisper of it.
13: 1 "My eyes have seen all this, my **e**
13:17 let your **e** take in what I say.
15:21 Terrifying sounds fill his **e**; when

Job 24:24 they are cut off like e of corn.
28:22 a rumour of it has reached our e.'
29:22 my words fell gently on their e.
33:16 he may speak in their e and terrify
42: 5 My e had heard of you but now my
Ps 18: 6 my cry came before him, into his e.
34:15 his e are attentive to their cry;
40: 6 not desire but my e you have pierced
44: 1 We have heard with our e, O God;
58: 4 of a cobra that has stopped its e,
92:11 my e have heard the rout of my
115: 6 they have e, but cannot hear, noses,
130: 2 O Lord, hear my voice. Let your e be
135:17 they have e, but cannot hear, nor is
Pr 18:15 the e of the wise seek it out.
20:12 E that hear and eyes that see—the
21:13 If a man shuts his e to the cry of
23:12 and your e to words of knowledge.
26:17 Like one who seizes a dog by the e
Isa 6:10 their e dull and close their eyes.
6:10 hear with their e, understand with
11: 3 decide by what he hears with his e;
17: 5 e of corn in the Valley of Rephaim.
30:21 your e will hear a voice behind you,
32: 3 the e of those who hear will listen.
33:15 who stops his e against plots of
35: 5 and the e of the deaf unstopped.
37:29 your insolence has reached my e,
42:20 e are open, but you hear nothing."
43: 8 are blind, who have e but are deaf.
50: 5 The Sovereign LORD has opened my e,
Jer 5:21 not see, who have e but do not hear:
6:10 Their e are closed so that they
9:20 open your e to the words of his
19: 3 e of everyone who hears of it tingle.
26:11 You have heard it with your own e!"
Lam 3:56 close your e to my cry for relief."
Eze 8:18 in my e, I will not listen to them."
16:12 e and a beautiful crown on your head.
23:25 will cut off your noses and your e,
40: 4 hear with your e and pay attention
Mic 7:16 mouths and their e will become deaf.
Zec 7:11 their backs and stopped up their e.
Mt 11:15 He who has e, let him hear.
12: 1 to pick some e of corn and eat them.
13: 9 He who has e, let him hear."
13:15 they hardly hear with their e,
13:15 hear with their e, understand with
13:16 see, and your e because they hear.
13:26 the wheat sprouted and formed e,
13:43 He who has e, let him hear.
Mk 2:23 they began to pick some e of corn.
7:33 put his fingers into the man's e.
7:35 At this, the man's e were opened,
8:18 and e but fail to hear? And don't
Lk 1:44 sound of your greeting reached my e,
6: 1 began to pick some e of corn,
Ac 7:51 with uncircumcised hearts and e! You
7:57 At this they covered their e and,
11:22 News of this reached the e of the
17:20 some strange ideas to our e,
28:27 they hardly hear with their e,
28:27 hear with their e, understand with
Ro 11: 8 and e so that they could not hear,
2Ti 4: 3 what their itching e want to hear.
4: 4 They will turn their e away from the
Jas 5: 4 reached the e of the Lord Almighty.
1Pe 3:12 his e are attentive to their prayer,

Ears to hear

Eze 12: 2 do not see and e but do not hear,
Mk 4: 9 Jesus said, "He who has e, let him
4:23 If anyone has e, let him hear."
Lk 8: 8 out, "He who has e, let him hear.
14:35 "He who has e, let him hear."

Earth (*Dust of the earth*, Earth's, Earthen, Earthly, *Ends of the earth, Heaven and earth, Kingdoms of the earth, New earth, Whole earth*)

Ge 1: 1 God created the heavens and the e.
1: 2 Now the e was formless and empty,
1:15 of the sky to give light on the e.
1:17 of the sky to give light on the e,
1:20 let birds fly above the e
1:22 let the birds increase on the e."
1:26 over the livestock, over all the e,
1:28 in number; fill the e and subdue it.
1:30 to all the beasts of the e and all
2: 1 Thus the heavens and the e were
2: 4 and the e when they were created.
2: 4 LORD God made the e and the heavens—
2: 5 the field had yet appeared on the e
2: 5 LORD God had not sent rain on the e
2: 6 streams came up from the e and
4:12 be a restless wanderer on the e."
4:14 be a restless wanderer on the e,
6: 1 on the e and daughters were born
6: 4 The Nephilim were on the e in those
6: 5 man's wickedness on the e had
6: 6 that he had made man on the e,
6: 7 from the face of the e—men and
6:11 Now the e was corrupt in God's sight
6:12 God saw how corrupt the e had become,
6:12 on e had corrupted their ways.
6:13 for the e is filled with violence
6:13 to destroy both them and the e.
6:17 floodwaters on the e to destroy all
6:17 Everything on e will perish.
7: 3 kinds alive throughout the e.
7: 4 I will send rain on the e for forty
7: 4 wipe from the face of the e every
7: 6 when the floodwaters came on the e.
7:10 days the floodwaters came on the e.
7:12 rain fell on the e for forty days
7:17 days the flood kept coming on the e,
7:17 lifted the ark high above the e.
7:18 rose and increased greatly on the e,
7:19 They rose greatly on the e, and all
7:21 that moved on the e perished—birds,
7:21 swarm over the e, and all mankind.
7:23 on the face of the e was wiped out;
7:23 of the air were wiped from the e.
7:24 The waters flooded the e for a
8: 1 over the e, and the waters receded.
8: 3 The water receded steadily from the e
8: 7 the water had dried up from the e.
8: 9 water over all the surface of the e;
8:11 the water had receded from the e.
8:13 the water had dried up from the e.
8:14 month the e was completely dry.
8:17 they can multiply on the e
8:19 moves on the e—came out of the ark,
8:22 "As long as the e endures, seedtime
9: 1 increase in number and fill the e.
9: 2 the e and all the birds of the air,
9: 7 on the e and increase upon it."
9:10 you—every living creature on e.
9:11 there be a flood to destroy the e."
9:13 the covenant between me and the e.
9:14 Whenever I bring clouds over the e
9:16 creatures of every kind on the e."
9:17 between me and all life on the e."
9:19 who were scattered over the e.
10: 8 to be a mighty warrior on the e.
10:25 in his time the e was divided
10:32 out over the e after the flood.
11: 8 them from there over all the e,
12: 3 on e will be blessed through you."
18:18 all nations on e will be blessed
18:25 the Judge of all the e do right?"
19:31 us, as is the custom all over the e.
22:18 all nations on e will be blessed,
24: 3 the God of heaven and the God of e,
26: 4 all nations on e will be blessed,
26:15 stopped up, filling them with e.
28:12 he saw a stairway resting on the e,
28:14 All peoples on e will be blessed
45: 7 to preserve for you a remnant on e
48:16 they increase greatly upon the e."
Ex 9:14 is no-one like me in all the e.
9:15 that would have wiped you off the e.
9:16 might be proclaimed in all the e.
9:29 may know that the e is the LORD's.
15:12 right hand and the e swallowed them.
20: 4 e beneath or in the waters below.
20:11 the LORD made the heavens and the e,
20:24 "'Make an altar of e for me and
31:17 the LORD made the heavens and the e,
32:12 wipe them off the face of the e'?
33:16 other people on the face of the e?"
Lev 17:13 out the blood and cover it with e,
Nu 12: 3 anyone else on the face of the e.
16:30 and the e opens its mouth and
16:32 the e opened its mouth and swallowed
16:33 the e closed over them
16:34 "The e is going to swallow us too!
26:10 The e opened its mouth and swallowed
Dt 3:24 heaven or on e who can do the deeds
4:17 or like any animal on e or any bird
4:32 the day God created man on the e;
4:36 On e he showed you his great fire,
4:39 in heaven above and on the e below.
5: 8 on the e beneath or in the waters
7: 6 the face of the e to be his people,
10:14 heavens, the e and everything in it.
11: 6 when the e opened its mouth right in
11:21 that the heavens are above the e.
14: 2 the peoples on the face of the e,
28: 1 you high above all the nations on e.
28:10 all the peoples on e will see that
28:25 of horror to all the kingdoms on e.
28:26 of the air and the beasts of the e,
28:64 from one end of the e to the other.
32: 1 hear, O e, the words of my mouth.
32:22 It will devour the e and its
33:16 with the best gifts of the e and its
Jos 2:11 in heaven above and on the e below.
3:11 the Lord of all the e will go into
3:13 all the e—set foot in the Jordan,
4:24 all the peoples of the e might know
7: 9 us and wipe out our name from the e.
23:14 am about to go the way of all the e.
Jdg 5: 4 the e shook, the heavens poured, the
1Sa 2: 8 "For the foundations of the e are
17:46 of the air and the beasts of the e,
20:15 enemies from the face of the e."
20:31 as the son of Jesse lives on this e,
2Sa 4:11 your hand and rid the e of you!"
7: 9 names of the greatest men of the e.
7:23 the one nation on e that God went
14: 7 descendant on the face of the e."
22: 8 "The e trembled and quaked, the
22:16 the foundations of the e laid bare
23: 4 that brings the grass from the e.'
1Ki 2: 2 go the way of all the e," he said.
8:23 you in heaven above or on e below
8:27 "But will God really dwell on e? The
8:43 so that all the peoples of the e may
8:60 that all the peoples of the e may
10:23 than all the other kings of the e.
13:34 destruction from the face of the e.
2Ki 5:17 be given as much e as a pair of mules
19:19 so that all kingdoms on e may know
1Ch 1:10 grew to be a mighty warrior on e.
1:19 in his time the e was divided
16:14 God; his judgments are in all the e.
16:23 Sing to the LORD, all the e;
16:30 Tremble before him, all the e! The
16:31 heavens rejoice, let the e be glad;
16:33 LORD, for he comes to judge the e.
17: 8 names of the greatest men of the e.
17:21 the one nation on e whose God went
22: 8 you have shed much blood on the e
29:15 Our days on e are like a shadow,
2Ch 6:14 no God like you in heaven or on e
6:18 "But will God really dwell on e with
6:33 so that all the peoples of the e may
9:22 than all the other kings of the e.
9:23 All the kings of the e sought
16: 9 of the LORD range throughout the e
Ne 9: 6 and all their starry host, the e and
Job 1: 7 roaming through the e and going
1: 8 Job? There is no-one on e like him;
2: 2 roaming through the e and going
2: 3 Job? There is no-one on e like him;
3:14 with kings and counsellors of the e,
5:10 He bestows rain on the e; he sends
5:22 need not fear the beasts of the e.
5:25 descendants like the grass of the e.
7: 1 "Does not man have hard service on e?
8: 9 and our days on e are but a shadow.
9: 6 He shakes the e from its place and
11: 9 Their measure is longer than the e
12: 8 or speak to the e, and it will teach
12:24 He deprives the leaders of the e of
16:18 "O e, do not cover my blood; may my

Job 18: 4 is the e to be abandoned for your
18:17 The memory of him perishes from the e
19:25 in the end he will stand upon the e.
20: 4 ever since man was placed on the e,
20:27 the e will rise up against him.
26: 7 He suspends the e over nothing
28: 2 Iron is taken from the e, and copper
28: 5 The e, from which food comes, is
34:13 Who appointed him over the e? Who
35:11 to us than to the beasts of the e
37: 6 He says to the snow, 'Fall on the e,'
37:13 or to water his e and show his love.
38:13 might take the e by the edges
38:14 The e takes shape like clay under a
38:18 the vast expanses of the e? Tell me,
38:24 east winds are scattered over the e?
38:33 set up ⌊God's⌋ dominion over the e?
38:38 and the clods of e stick together?
41:33 Nothing on e is his equal—a
Ps 2: 2 The kings of the e take their stand
2:10 be warned, you rulers of the e.
8: 1 majestic is your name in all the e!
8: 9 majestic is your name in all the e!
10:18 man, who is of the e, may terrify
18: 7 The e trembled and quaked, and the
18:15 foundations of the e laid bare
19: 4 Their voice goes out into all the e,
21:10 destroy their descendants from the e,
22:29 All the rich of the e will feast and
24: 1 The e is the LORD's, and everything
33: 5 the e is full of his unfailing love.
33: 8 Let all the e fear the LORD; let all
33:14 he watches all who live on e—
34:16 off the memory of them from the e.
46: 2 though the e give way and the
46: 6 he lifts his voice, the e melts.
46: 8 desolations he has brought on the e.
46:10 I will be exalted in the e."
47: 2 High, the great King over all the e!
47: 7 For God is the King of all the e;
47: 9 for the kings of the e belong to God;
50: 1 the LORD, speaks and summons the e
50: 4 the e, that he may judge his people:
57: 5 let your glory be over all the e.
57:11 let your glory be over all the e.
58: 2 hands mete out violence on the e.
58:11 there is a God who judges the e."
63: 9 will go down to the depths of the e.
66: 1 Shout with joy to God, all the e!
66: 4 All the e bows down to you; they
67: 2 that your ways may be known on e,
67: 4 and guide the nations of the e.
68: 8 the e shook, the heavens poured down
71:20 from the depths of the e you will
72: 6 field, like showers watering the e.
73: 9 tongues take possession of the e.
73:25 Whom have I in heaven but you? And e
74:12 old; you bring salvation upon the e.
74:17 who set all the boundaries of the e;
75: 3 When the e and all its people quake,
75: 8 all the wicked of the e drink it
76:12 he is feared by the kings of the e.
77:18 world; the e trembled and quaked.
78:69 the e that he established for ever.
79: 2 your saints to the beasts of the e.
82: 5 the foundations of the e are shaken.
82: 8 Rise up, O God, judge the e, for all
83:18 are the Most High over all the e.
85:11 Faithfulness springs forth from the e
89:11 and yours also the e; you founded
89:27 most exalted of the kings of the e.
90: 2 brought forth the e and the world,
94: 2 Rise up, O Judge of the e; pay back
95: 4 In his hand are the depths of the e,
96: 1 song; sing to the LORD, all the e.
96: 9 tremble before him, all the e.
96:11 Let the heavens rejoice, let the e
96:13 he comes, he comes to judge the e.
97: 1 The LORD reigns, let the e be glad;
97: 4 the world; the e sees and trembles.
97: 5 LORD, before the Lord of all the e.
97: 9 are the Most High over all the e;
98: 4 Shout for joy to the LORD, all the e,
98: 9 LORD, for he comes to judge the e.
99: 1 the cherubim, let the e shake.
100: 1 Shout for joy to the LORD, all the e.
Ps 102:15 of the e will revere your glory.
102:19 high, from heaven he viewed the e,
102:25 you laid the foundations of the e,
103:11 high as the heavens are above the e,
104: 5 He set the e on its foundations; it
104: 9 never again will they cover the e.
104:13 the e is satisfied by the fruit of
104:14 bringing forth food from the e:
104:24 the e is full of your creatures.
104:30 and you renew the face of the e.
104:32 he who looks at the e, and it
104:35 may sinners vanish from the e and
105: 7 God; his judgments are in all the e.
106:17 The e opened up and swallowed Dathan;
108: 5 let your glory be over all the e.
109:15 off the memory of them from the e.
113: 6 to look on the heavens and the e?
114: 7 Tremble, O e, at the presence of the
115:16 LORD, but the e he has given to man.
119:19 I am a stranger on e; do not hide
119:64 The e is filled with your love,
119:87 They almost wiped me from the e, but
119:90 established the e, and it endures.
119:119 All the wicked of the e you discard
135: 6 on the e, in the seas and all their
136: 6 who spread out the e upon the waters,
138: 4 May all the kings of the e praise
139:15 together in the depths of the e,
141: 7 "As one ploughs and breaks up the e,
147: 8 he supplies the e with rain and
147:15 He sends his command to the e; his
148: 7 Praise the LORD from the e, you
148:11 kings of the e and all nations, you
148:11 you princes and all rulers on e,
148:13 is above the e and the heavens.
Pr 8:16 and all nobles who rule on e.
8:26 before he made the e or its fields
8:29 marked out the foundations of the e.
11:31 righteous receive their due on e,
25: 3 the heavens are high and the e is
30:14 devour the poor from the e, the needy
30:21 "Under three things the e trembles,
30:24 "Four things on e are small, yet
Ecc 1: 4 go, but the e remains for ever.
3:21 of the animal goes down into the e?"
5: 2 are on e, so let your words be few.
7:20 There is not a righteous man on e
8:14 else meaningless that occurs on e:
8:16 to observe man's labour on e—his
11: 3 of water, they pour rain upon the e.
SS 2:12 Flowers appear on the e; the season
Isa 1: 2 Hear, O heavens! Listen, O e! For
2:19 when he rises to shake the e.
2:21 when he rises to shake the e.
8:22 they will look towards the e and see
11: 4 decisions for the poor of the e.
11: 4 He will strike the e with the rod of
11: 9 for the e will be full of the
11:12 from the four quarters of the e.
13:13 and the e will shake from its place
14:12 cast down to the e, you who once laid
14:16 the e and made kingdoms tremble,
14:21 and cover the e with their cities.
18: 3 you who live on the e, when a banner
19:24 and Assyria, a blessing on the e.
23: 8 whose traders are renowned in the e?
23: 9 all who are renowned on the e.
23:17 the kingdoms on the face of the e.
24: 1 to lay waste the e and devastate it;
24: 3 The e will be completely laid waste
24: 4 The e dries up and withers, the
24: 4 the exalted of the e languish.
24: 5 The e is defiled by its people; they
24: 6 Therefore a curse consumes the e;
24:11 all gaiety is banished from the e.
24:13 will it be on the e and among the
24:17 snare await you, O people of the e.
24:18 the foundations of the e shake.
24:19 The e is broken up, the e is split
24:19 asunder, the e is thoroughly shaken.
24:20 The e reels like a drunkard, it
24:21 above and the kings on the e below.
25: 8 of his people from all the e.
26: 9 When your judgments come upon the e,
26:18 have not brought salvation to the e;
26:19 the e will give birth to her dead.
Isa 26:21 the people of the e for their sins.
26:21 The e will disclose the blood shed
29: 4 will come ghostlike from the e;
34: 1 you peoples! Let the e hear, and all
37:20 so that all kingdoms on e may know
40:21 understood since the e was founded?
40:22 enthroned above the circle of the e,
42: 4 till he establishes justice on e.
42: 5 who spread out the e and all that
44:23 done this; shout aloud, O e beneath.
44:24 who spread out the e by myself,
45: 8 Let the e open wide, let salvation
45:12 It is I who made the e and created
45:18 God; he who fashioned and made the e,
48:13 hand laid the foundations of the e,
49:13 O heavens; rejoice, O e; burst into
51: 6 look at the e beneath; the heavens
51: 6 the e will wear out like a garment
51:13 and laid the foundations of the e,
51:16 who laid the foundations of the e,
54: 5 he is called the God of all the e.
54: 9 of Noah would never again cover the e
55: 9 "As the heavens are higher than the e
55:10 watering the e and making it bud
60: 2 See, darkness covers the e and thick
62: 7 and makes her the praise of the e.
66: 1 throne, and the e is my footstool.
Jer 4:23 I looked at the e, and it was
4:28 Therefore the e will mourn and the
6:19 Hear, O e: I am bringing disaster on
7:33 of the air and the beasts of the e,
9:24 on e, for in these I delight,"
10:10 When he is angry, the e trembles;
10:11 did not make the heavens and the e,
10:11 will perish from the e and from under
10:12 God made the e by his power; he
15: 3 beasts of the e to devour and
16: 4 of the air and the beasts of the e."
19: 7 of the air and the beasts of the e.
25:26 the kingdoms on the face of the e.
25:29 the e, declares the LORD Almighty.'
25:30 shout against all who live on the e.
25:33 one end of the e to the other.
26: 6 among all the nations of the e.'"
27: 5 outstretched arm I made the e and
28:16 remove you from the face of the e.
31:22 on e—a woman will surround a man."
31:37 the foundations of the e below be
32:17 you have made the heavens and the e
33: 2 he who made the e, the LORD who
33: 9 honour before all nations on e that
34:20 of the air and the beasts of the e.
44: 8 reproach among all the nations on e.
46: 8 'I will rise and cover the e; I will
46:12 shame; your cries will fill the e.
49:21 At the sound of their fall the e
50:46 Babylon's capture the e will tremble;
51:15 " made the e by his power; he
51:49 e have fallen because of Babylon.
Lam 2: 1 of Israel from heaven to e;
4:12 The kings of the e did not believe,
Eze 7:21 of the e, and they will defile it.
8: 3 The Spirit lifted me up between e
26:20 I will make you dwell in the e below,
27:33 you enriched the kings of the e.
28:17 So I threw you to the e; I made a
29: 5 of the e and the birds of the air.
31:12 All the nations of the e came out
31:14 for the e below, among mortal men,
31:16 were consoled in the e below.
31:18 the trees of Eden to the e below;
32: 4 of the e gorge themselves on you.
32:18 consign to the e below both her and
32:24 down uncircumcised to the e below.
38:20 the e will tremble at my presence.
39:18 the blood of the princes of the e
Da 2:10 "There is not a man on e who can do
4:15 animals among the plants of the e.
4:22 extends to distant parts of the e.
4:35 All the peoples of the e are
4:35 of heaven and the peoples of the e.
6:27 wonders in the heavens and on the e.
7:17 kingdoms that will rise from the e.
7:23 kingdom that will appear on e.
8:10 down to the e and trampled on them.
Hos 2:21 and they will respond to the e;

Hos 2:22 the e will respond to the grain, the
6: 3 the spring rains that water the e."
Joel 2:10 Before them the e shakes, the sky
2:30 wonders in the heavens and on the e,
3:16 the e and the sky will tremble.
Am 3: 2 chosen of all the families of the e;
3: 5 Does a trap spring up from the e when
4:13 and treads the high places of the e—
8: 9 and darken the e in broad daylight.
9: 5 he who touches the e and it melts,
9: 6 and sets its foundation on the e,
9: 8 destroy it from the face of the e
Jnh 2: 6 the e beneath barred me in for ever.
Mic 1: 2 O peoples, all of you, listen, O e
1: 3 and treads the high places of the e.
4:13 wealth to the Lord of all the e.
6: 2 everlasting foundations of the e.
7:13 The e will become desolate because
Na 1: 5 The e trembles at his presence, the
2:13 I will leave you no prey on the e.
Hab 2:14 For the e will be filled with the
2:20 let all the e be silent before him."
3: 3 heavens and his praise filled the e.
3: 6 He stood, and shook the e; he looked,
3: 9 You split the e with rivers;
3:12 In wrath you strode through the e
Zep 1: 2 face of the e," declares the LORD.
1: 3 face of the e," declares the LORD.
1:18 end of all who live in the e."
3:20 peoples of the e when I restore your
Hag 1:10 their dew and the e its crops.
2: 6 and the e, the sea and the dry land.
2:21 I will shake the heavens and the e.
Zec 1:10 has sent to go throughout the e."
1:11 "We have gone throughout the e and
4:10 LORD, which range throughout the e.
4:14 to serve the Lord of all the e."
6: 7 straining to go throughout the e.
6: 7 And he said, "Go throughout the e!"
6: 7 So they went throughout the e. Then
12: 1 who lays the foundation of the e,
12: 3 when all the nations of the e are
14:17 If any of the peoples of the e do
Mt 5: 5 meek, for they will inherit the e.
5:13 "You are the salt of the e. But if
5:35 or by the e, for it is his footstool;
6:10 be done on e as it is in heaven.
6:19 up for yourselves treasures on e,
9: 6 has authority on e to forgive sins.
10:34 I have come to bring peace to the e.
12:40 three nights in the heart of the e.
16:19 bind on e will be bound in heaven,
16:19 on e will be loosed in heaven."
17:25 "From whom do the kings of the e
18:18 whatever you bind on e will be bound
18:18 loose on e will be loosed in heaven.
18:19 I tell you that if two of you on e
23: 9 do not call anyone on e'father',
23:35 blood that has been shed on e,
24:30 all the nations of the e will mourn.
27:51 The e shook and the rocks split.
28:18 and on e has been given to me.
Mk 2:10 has authority on e to forgive sins
Lk 2:14 and on e peace to men on whom his
5:24 has authority on e to forgive sins.
12:49 "I have come to bring fire on the e,
12:51 think I came to bring peace on e? No,
12:56 the appearance of the e and the sky.
18: 8 comes, will he find faith on the e?"
21:25 On the e, nations will be in anguish
Jn 3:31 who is from the e belongs to the e,
3:31 the e, and speaks as one from the e.
12:32 I, when I am lifted up from the e,
17: 4 I have brought you glory on e by
Ac 2:19 above and signs on the e below,
3:25 all peoples on e will be blessed.'
4:24 "you made the heaven and the e and
4:26 The kings of the e take their stand
7:49 "Heaven is my throne, and the e is
8:33 For his life was taken from the e."
10:11 let down to e by its four corners.
10:12 of the e and birds of the air.
11: 6 saw four-footed animals of the e,
22:22 the e of him! He's not fit to live!"
Ro 9:17 might be proclaimed in all the e."
9:28 on e with speed and finality."
Ro 10:18 voice has gone out into all the e,
1Co 4:13 of the e, the refuse of the world.
8: 5 gods, whether in heaven or on e
10:26 for, "The e is the Lord's, and
15:48 so are those who are of the e; and
Eph 1:10 and on e together under one head,
3:15 in heaven and on e derives its name.
6: 3 you may enjoy long life on the e."
Php 2:10 in heaven and on e and under the e,
Col 1:16 created: things in heaven and on e,
1:20 whether things on e or things in
Heb 1:10 you laid the foundations of the e,
5: 7 During the days of Jesus' life on e,
8: 4 If he were on e, he would not be a
11:13 they were aliens and strangers on e.
12:25 refused him who warned them on e,
12:26 At that time his voice shook the e,
12:26 only the e but also the heavens."
Jas 5: 5 You have lived on e in luxury and
5:12 heaven or by e or by anything else.
5:18 rain, and the e produced its crops.
2Pe 3: 5 the e was formed out of water and by
3: 7 heavens and e are reserved for fire,
3:10 and the e and everything in it will
Rev 1: 5 and the ruler of the kings of the e.
1: 7 of the e will mourn because of him.
3:10 to test those who live on the e.
5: 3 no-one in heaven or on e or under
5: 3 under the e could open the scroll or
5: 6 of God sent out into all the e.
5:10 God, and they will reign on the e."
5:13 on e and under the e and on the sea,
6: 4 power to take peace from the e and to
6: 8 a fourth of the e to kill by sword,
6: 8 and by the wild beasts of the e.
6:10 of the e and avenge our blood?"
6:13 the stars in the sky fell to e, as
6:15 the kings of the e, the princes, the
7: 1 standing at the four corners of the e
7: 1 holding back the four winds of the e
8: 5 and hurled it on the e; and there
8: 7 and it was hurled down upon the e.
8: 7 A third of the e was burned up, a
8:13 Woe! Woe to the inhabitants of the e,
9: 1 had fallen from the sky to the e.
9: 3 locusts came down upon the e and were
9: 3 like that of scorpions of the e.
9: 4 grass of the e or any plant or tree,
10: 6 the e and all that is in it, and the
11: 4 that stand before the Lord of the e.
11: 6 to strike the e with every kind of
11:10 The inhabitants of the e will gloat
11:10 had tormented those who live on e.
11:18 destroying those who destroy the e."
12: 4 of the sky and flung them to the e.
12: 9 to the e, and his angels with him.
12:12 woe to the e and the sea, because
12:13 that he had been hurled to the e,
12:16 the e helped the woman by opening
13: 8 All inhabitants of the e will
13:11 another beast, coming out of the e.
13:12 and made the e and its inhabitants
13:13 heaven to e in full view of men.
13:14 deceived the inhabitants of the e.
14: 3 who had been redeemed from the e.
14: 6 who live on the e—to every nation,
14: 7 made the heavens, the e, the sea and
14:15 for the harvest of the e is ripe."
14:16 over the e, and the e was harvested.
14:19 The angel swung his sickle on the e,
16: 1 bowls of God's wrath on the e."
16:18 on e, so tremendous was the quake.
17: 2 With her the kings of the e
17: 2 the inhabitants of the e were
17: 5 AND OF THE ABOMINATIONS OF THE E.
17: 8 The inhabitants of the e whose names
17:18 that rules over the kings of the e."
18: 1 e was illuminated by his splendour.
18: 3 The kings of the e committed
18: 3 and the merchants of the e grew rich
18: 9 "When the kings of the e who
18:11 "The merchants of the e will weep
18:24 all who have been killed on the e."
19: 2 corrupted the e by her adulteries.
19:19 the kings of the e and their armies
20: 8 in the four corners of the e—Gog
Rev 20: 9 marched across the breadth of the e
20:11 E and sky fled from his presence,
21: 1 and the first e had passed away,
21:24 kings of the e will bring their

Earth's (Earth)
Ge 27:28 of e richness—an abundance of
27:39 will be away from the e richness,
Job 38: 4 "Where were you when I laid the e
Pr 3:19 By wisdom the LORD laid the e
Isa 24: 6 Therefore e inhabitants are burned
Rev 14:18 e vine, because its grapes are ripe."

Earthen (Earth, Earthenware)
Hab 1:10 they build e ramps and capture them.

Earthenware (Earthen)
Pr 26:23 Like a coating of glaze over e are

Earthly (Earth)
Jn 3:12 I have spoken to you of e things and
1Co 15:40 bodies and there are e bodies;
15:40 of the e bodies is another. The sun
15:48 was the e man, so are those who are
15:49 borne the likeness of the e man,
2Co 5: 1 Now we know that if the e tent we
Eph 4: 9 descended to the lower, e regions?
6: 5 Slaves, obey your e masters with
Php 3:19 Their mind is on e things. But our
Col 3: 2 on things above, not on e things.
3: 5 whatever belongs to your e nature:
3:22 Slaves, obey your e masters in
Heb 9: 1 for worship and also an e sanctuary.
Jas 3:15 but is e, unspiritual, of the devil.
1Pe 4: 2 does not live the rest of his e life

Earthquake (Quake)
1Ki 19:11 an e, but the LORD was not in the e.
19:12 After the e came a fire, but the
Isa 29: 6 with thunder and e and great noise,
Eze 38:19 be a great e in the land of Israel.
Am 1: 1 Israel two years before the e,
Zec 14: 5 You will flee as you fled from the e
Mt 27:54 saw the e and all that had happened,
28: 2 There was a violent e, for an angel
Ac 16:26 Suddenly there was such a violent e
Rev 6:12 There was a great e. The sun turned
8: 5 flashes of lightning and an e.
11:13 e and a tenth of the city collapsed.
11:13 people were killed in the e,
11:19 thunder, an e and a great hailstorm.
16:18 peals of thunder and a severe e.
16:18 No e like it has ever occurred since

Earthquakes (Quake)
Mt 24: 7 be famines and e in various places.
Mk 13: 8 There will be e in various places,
Lk 21:11 There will be great e, famines and

Ease (Easier, Easily, Easy)
Job 3:18 Captives also enjoy their e; they no
7:13 me and my couch will e my complaint,
12: 5 Men at e have contempt for
21:23 vigour, completely secure and at e,
Pr 1:33 and be at e, without fear of harm."
Jer 12: 1 Why do all the faithless live at e?
49:31 "Arise and attack a nation at e,
Lam 1: 5 her masters; her enemies are at e.
Jnh 4: 6 for his head to e his discomfort,

Easier (Ease)
Mt 9: 5 Which is e: to say, 'Your sins are
19:24 Again I tell you, it is e for a
Mk 2: 9 Which is e: to say to the paralytic,
10:25 is e for a camel to go through the
Lk 5:23 Which is e: to say, 'Your sins are
16:17 It is e for heaven and earth to
18:25 Indeed, it is e for a camel to go

Easily (Ease)
Jdg 16: 9 snapped the thongs as e as a piece
20:43 chased them and e overran them in

Pr 14: 6 knowledge comes **e** to the discerning.
22:24 do not associate with one **e** angered,
Hos 7:11 "Ephraim is like a dove, **e** deceived
Ac 24:11 You can **e** verify that no more than
1Co 13: 5 it is not **e** angered, it keeps no
2Co 11: 4 you put up with it **e** enough.
2Th 2: 2 not to become **e** unsettled or alarmed
Heb 12: 1 and the sin that so **e** entangles,

East (Eastern, Eastward, North-easter, South-east)

Ge 2: 8 God had planted a garden in the **e**,
2:14 it runs along the **e** side of Asshur.
3:24 he placed on the **e** side of the
4:16 lived in the land of Nod, **e** of Eden.
12: 8 **e** of Bethel and pitched his tent,
12: 8 Bethel on the west and Ai on the **e**.
13:11 Jordan and set out towards the **e**.
13:14 look north and south, **e** and west.
25: 6 his son Isaac to the land of the **e**.
28:14 to the **e**, to the north and to the
41: 6 and scorched by the **e** wind.
41:23 and thin and scorched by the **e** wind.
41:27 ears of corn scorched by the **e** wind:
Ex 10:13 and the LORD made an **e** wind blow
14:21 **e** wind and turned it into dry land.
27:13 On the **e** end, towards the sunrise,
38:13 The **e** end, towards the sunrise, was
Lev 1:16 throw it to the **e** side of the altar,
Nu 2: 3 On the **e**, towards the sunrise, the
3:38 to camp to the **e** of the tabernacle,
10: 5 camping on the **e** are to set out.
32:19 to us on the **e** side of the Jordan."
33: 7 to the **e** of Baal Zephon, and camped
34: 3 On the **e**, your southern boundary
34:11 to Riblah on the **e** side of Ain
34:11 slopes **e** of the Sea of Kinnereth.
34:15 the **e** side of the Jordan of Jericho,
35: 5 three thousand feet on the **e** side,
Dt 1: 1 the desert **e** of the Jordan—that is,
1: 5 **E** of the Jordan in the territory of
3: 8 the territory **e** of the Jordan,
3:27 look west and north and south and **e**.
4:41 Moses set aside three cities **e** of
4:46 were in the valley near Beth Peor **e**
4:47 two Amorite kings **e** of the Jordan.
4:49 included all the Arabah **e** of the
Jos 1:14 that Moses gave you **e** of the Jordan,
1:15 **e** of the Jordan towards the sunrise."
2:10 the two kings of the Amorites **e** of
7: 2 which is near Beth Aven to the **e** of
9:10 of the Amorites **e** of the Jordan
11: 3 to the Canaanites in the **e** and west;
11: 8 the **e**, until no survivors were left.
12: 1 they took over **e** of the Jordan,
13: 3 from the Shihor River on the **e** of
13: 5 Gebalites; and all Lebanon to the **e**,
13: 8 Moses had given them **e** of the Jordan,
13:27 Heshbon (the **e** side of the Jordan,
13:32 Moab across the Jordan **e** of Jericho.
14: 3 their inheritance **e** of the Jordan
16: 1 **e** of the waters of Jericho, and went
16: 5 Addar in the **e** to Upper Beth
16: 6 passing by it to Janoah on the **e**.
17: 5 Gilead and Bashan **e** of the Jordan,
17: 7 Asher to Micmethath **e** of Shechem.
17:10 on the north and Issachar on the **e**.
18: 7 on the **e** side of the Jordan.
19:12 turned **e** from Sarid towards the
19:27 then turned **e** towards Beth Dagon,
19:34 on the west and the Jordan on the **e**.
20: 8 On the **e** side of the Jordan of
24: 8 Amorites who lived **e** of the Jordan.
Jdg 8:11 the route of the nomads **e** of Nobah
10: 8 the **e** side of the Jordan in Gilead,
20:43 in the vicinity of Gibeah on the **e**.
21:19 to the north of Bethel, and **e** of the
1Sa 13: 5 camped at Michmash, **e** of Beth Aven.
15: 7 Havilah to Shur, to the **e** of Egypt.
1Ki 4:30 the wisdom of all the men of the **E**,
7:25 facing south and three facing **e**.
11: 7 On a hill **e** of Jerusalem, Solomon
17: 3 the Kerith Ravine, **e** of the Jordan.
17: 5 **e** of the Jordan, and stayed there.
2Ki 10:33 **e** of the Jordan in all the land of
13:17 "Open the **e** window," he said, and he
23:13 high places that were **e** of Jerusalem
1Ch 4:39 the outskirts of Gedor to the **e** of
5: 9 To the **e** they occupied the land up
5:10 the entire region **e** of Gilead.
6:78 across the Jordan **e** of Jericho they
7:28 Naaran to the **e**, Gezer and its
9:18 on the **e**, up to the present time.
9:24 sides: **e**, west, north and south.
12:15 valleys, to the **e** and to the west.
12:37 from **e** of the Jordan, men of Reuben,
26:14 The lot for the **E** Gate fell to
26:17 There were six Levites a day on the **e**
2Ch 4: 4 facing south and three facing **e**.
5:12 on the **e** side of the altar,
29: 4 them in the square on the **e** side
31:14 keeper of the **E** Gate, was in charge
Ne 3:26 the **e** and the projecting tower.
3:29 guard at the **E** Gate, made repairs.
12:37 of David to the Water Gate on the **e**.
Job 1: 3 man among all the people of the **E**.
15: 2 fill his belly with the hot **e** wind?
18:20 men of the **e** are seized with horror.
23: 8 "But if I go to the **e**, he is not
27:21 The **e** wind carries him off, and he
38:24 **e** winds are scattered over the earth?
Ps 48: 7 of Tarshish shattered by an **e** wind.
75: 6 No-one from the **e** or the west or
78:26 He let loose the **e** wind from the
103:12 far as the **e** is from the west, so
107: 3 **e** and west, from north and south.
Isa 2: 6 full of superstitions from the **E**;
9:12 Arameans from the **e** and Philistines
11:14 will plunder the people to the **e**.
24:15 Therefore in the **e** give glory to the
27: 8 out, as on a day the **e** wind blows.
41: 2 "Who has stirred up one from the **e**,
43: 5 the **e** and gather you from the west.
46:11 From the **e** I summon a bird of prey;
Jer 18:17 Like a wind from the **e**, I will
31:40 the Kidron Valley on the **e** as far as
49:28 and destroy the people of the **E**.
Eze 8:16 LORD and their faces towards the **e**,
8:16 bowing down to the sun in the **e**.
10:19 to the **e** gate of the LORD's house,
11: 1 the house of the LORD that faces **e**.
11:23 stopped above the mountain **e** of it.
17:10 when the **e** wind strikes it—
19:12 The **e** wind made it shrivel, it was
25: 4 the people of the **E** as a possession.
25:10 the people of the **E** as a possession,
27:26 But the **e** wind will break you to
39:11 those who travel **e** towards the Sea.
40: 6 he went to the gate facing **e**. He
40:10 Inside the **e** gate were three alcoves
40:19 the **e** side as well as on the north.
40:22 as those of the gate facing **e**.
40:23 gate, just as there was on the **e**.
40:32 me to the inner court on the **e** side,
41:14 of the temple courtyard on the **e**,
42: 9 lower rooms had an entrance on the **e**
42:15 he led me out by the **e** gate and
42:16 He measured the **e** side with the
43: 1 man brought me to the gate facing **e**,
43: 2 the God of Israel coming from the **e**.
43: 4 temple through the gate facing **e**.
43:17 The steps of the altar face **e**."
44: 1 the one facing **e**, and it was shut.
45: 7 side and eastward from the **e** side,
46: 1 gate of the inner court facing **e** is
46:12 facing **e** is to be opened for him.
47: 1 the **e** (for the temple faced **e**).
47: 2 outside to the outer gate facing **e**,
47:18 "On the **e** side the boundary will run
47:18 This will be the **e** boundary.
48: 1 from the **e** side to the west side.
48: 2 the territory of Dan from **e** to west.
48: 3 territory of Asher from **e** to west.
48: 4 of Naphtali from **e** to west.
48: 5 of Manasseh from **e** to west.
48: 6 territory of Ephraim from **e** to west.
48: 7 territory of Reuben from **e** to west.
48: 8 territory of Judah from **e** to west
48:48 its length from **e** to west will equal
48: 8 and its length from **e** to west will
48:10 10,000 cubits wide on the **e** side and
Eze 48:16 the **e** side 4,500 cubits, and the west
48:17 the **e**, and 250 cubits on the west.
48:18 will be 10,000 cubits on the **e** side
48:23 from the **e** side to the west side.
48:24 of Benjamin from **e** to west.
48:25 territory of Simeon from **e** to west.
48:26 of Issachar from **e** to west.
48:27 territory of Zebulun from **e** to west.
48:32 the **e** side, which is 4,500 cubits
Da 8: 9 **e** and towards the Beautiful Land.
11:44 reports from the **e** and the north
Hos 12: 1 he pursues the **e** wind all day and
13:15 An **e** wind from the LORD will come,
Am 8:12 to sea and wander from north to **e**,
Jnh 4: 5 sat down at a place **e** of the city.
4: 8 God provided a scorching **e** wind, and
Zec 8: 7 the countries of the **e** and the west.
14: 4 **e** of Jerusalem, and the Mount of
14: 4 will be split in two from **e** to west,
Mt 2: 1 Magi from the **e** came to Jerusalem
2: 2 the **e** and have come to worship him."
2: 9 and the star they had seen in the **e**
8:11 will come from the **e** and the west,
24:27 the **e** is visible even in the west,
Lk 13:29 People will come from **e** and west and
Rev 7: 2 another angel coming up from the **e**,
16:12 the way for the kings from the **E**.
21:13 There were three gates on the **e**,

Eastern (East)

Ge 10:30 Sephar, in the **e** hill country.
29: 1 came to the land of the **e** peoples.
Nu 23: 7 king of Moab from the **e** mountains.
34:10 "For your **e** boundary, run a line
Jos 4:19 Gilgal on the **e** border of Jericho.
12: 1 all the **e** side of the Arabah:
12: 3 He also ruled over the **e** Arabah from
15: 5 The **e** boundary is the Salt Sea as
18:20 formed the boundary on the **e** side.
Jdg 6: 3 other **e** peoples invaded the country.
6:33 Amalekites and other **e** peoples
7:12 the Amalekites and all the other **e**
8:10 left of the armies of the **e** peoples;
11:18 passed along the **e** side of the
Eze 45: 7 from the western to the **e** border
47: 8 "This water flows towards the **e**
47:18 to the **e** sea and as far as Tamar.
48:21 the sacred portion to the **e** border,
Joel 2:20 front columns going into the **e** sea
Zec 14: 8 half to the **e** sea and half to the

Eastward (East)

Ge 11: 2 men moved **e**, they found a plain in
Jos 16: 6 north it curved **e** to Taanath Shiloh,
19:13 continued **e** to Gath Hepher and Eth
1Ki 17: 3 "Leave here, turn **e** and hide in the
Eze 42:12 **e**, by which one enters the rooms.
45: 7 west side and **e** from the east side,
47: 3 the man went **e** with a measuring line
48:21 will extend **e** from the 25,000 cubits

Easy (Ease)

Dt 1:41 it **e** to go up into the hill country.
2Ki 3:18 This is an **e** thing in the eyes of
5:20 "master was too **e** on Naaman, this
Mt 11:30 For my yoke is **e** and my burden is
Lk 12:19 Take life **e**; eat, drink and be merry.

Eat (Ate, Eaten, Eater, Eating, Eats)

Ge 2:16 to **e** from any tree in the garden;
2:17 you must not **e** from the tree of the
2:17 you **e** of it you will surely die."
3: 1 not **e** from any tree in the garden'?"
3: 2 **e** fruit from the trees in the garden,
3: 3 God did say,'You must not **e** fruit
3: 5 "For God knows that when you **e** of it
3:11 which I commanded you not to **e**?"
3:14 **e** dust all the days of your life.
3:17 'You must not **e** of it,' "Cursed is
3:17 **e** of it all the days of your life.
3:18 you will **e** the plants of the field.
3:19 By the sweat of your brow you will **e**
3:22 of life and **e**, and live for ever."
9: 4 "But you must not **e** meat that has

Ge 18: 5 Let me get you something to **e**, so
24:33 "I will not **e** until I have told you
27: 4 food I like and bring it to me to **e**,
27: 7 and prepare me some tasty food to **e**,
27:10 take it to your father to **e**, so that
27:19 Please sit up and **e** some of my game
27:25 bring me some of your game to **e**, so
27:31 "My father, sit up and **e** some of my
28:20 give me food to **e** and clothes to wear
32:32 the Israelites do not **e** the tendon
37:25 they sat down to **e** their meal, they
40:19 the birds will **e** away your flesh."
43:16 they are to **e** with me at noon."
43:25 had heard that they were to **e** there.
43:32 Egyptians could not **e** with Hebrews
Ex 2:20 Invite him to have something to **e**."
12: 4 with what each person will **e**.
12: 7 the houses where they **e** the lambs.
12: 8 That same night they are to **e** the
12: 9 Do not **e** the meat raw or cooked in
12:11 This is how you are to **e** it: with
12:11 **E** it in haste; it is the LORD's
12:15 For seven days you are to **e** bread
12:16 to **e**—that is all you may do.
12:18 In the first month you are to **e**
12:20 **E** nothing made with yeast. Wherever
12:20 live, you must **e** unleavened bread."
12:43 "No foreigner is to **e** of it.
12:44 Any slave you have bought may **e** of
12:45 and a hired worker may not **e** of it.
12:48 No uncircumcised male may **e** of it.
13: 3 **E** nothing containing yeast.
13: 6 For seven days **e** bread made without
13: 7 **E** unleavened bread during those
16: 8 gives you meat to **e** in the evening
16:12 Tell them, 'At twilight you will **e**
16:15 bread the LORD has given you to **e**.
16:25 "**E** it today," Moses said, "because
16:32 bread I gave you to **e** in the desert
18:12 elders of Israel to **e** bread with
22:31 So do not **e** the meat of an animal
23:11 wild animals may **e** what they leave.
23:15 **e** bread made without yeast, as I
29:32 Aaron and his sons are to **e** the meat
29:33 They are to **e** these offerings by
29:33 may **e** them, because they are sacred.
32: 6 Afterwards they sat down to **e** and
34:15 you will **e** their sacrifices. And when
34:18 For seven days **e** bread made without
Lev 3:17 must not **e** any fat or any blood.'"
6:16 Aaron and his sons shall **e** the rest
6:16 they are to **e** it in the courtyard of
6:18 Any male descendant of Aaron may **e**
6:26 The priest who offers it shall **e** it;
6:29 Any male in a priest's family may **e**
7: 6 Any male in a priest's family may **e**
7:19 anyone ceremonially clean may **e** it.
7:23 "Say to the Israelites: 'Do not **e**
7:24 purpose, but you must not **e** it.
7:26 wherever you live, you must not **e**
8:31 **e** it there with the bread from the
8:31 'Aaron and his sons are to **e** it.'
10:12 **e** it prepared without yeast beside
10:13 **E** it in a holy place, because it is
10:14 your sons and your daughters may **e**
10:14 **E** them in a ceremonially clean place;
10:17 "Why didn't you **e** the sin offering
11: 2 land, these are the ones you may **e**:
11: 3 You may **e** any animal that has a
11: 4 split hoof, but you must not **e** them.
11: 8 You must not **e** their meat or touch
11: 9 may **e** any that have fins and scales.
11:11 you must not **e** their meat and you
11:13 not **e** because they are detestable:
11:21 walk on all fours that you may **e**:
11:22 Of these you may **e** any kind of
11:39 that you are allowed to **e** dies,
11:42 You are not to **e** any creature that
17:12 "None of you may **e** blood, nor may an
17:12 an alien living among you **e** blood."
17:14 "You must not **e** the blood of any
19:25 in the fifth year you may **e** its
19:26 "Do not **e** any meat with the blood
21:22 He may **e** the most holy food of his
22: 4 he may not **e** the sacred offerings
22: 6 He must not **e** any of the sacred

Lev 22: 7 and after that he may **e** the sacred
22: 8 He must not **e** anything found dead or
22:10 family may **e** the sacred offering,
22:10 a priest or his hired worker **e** it.
22:11 that slave may **e** his food.
22:12 **e** any of the sacred contributions.
22:13 she may **e** of her father's food.
22:13 person, however, may **e** any of it.
22:16 by allowing them to **e** the sacred
23: 6 you must **e** bread made without yeast.
23:14 You must not **e** any bread, or roasted
24: 9 who are to **e** it in a holy place,
25:12 **e** only what is taken directly from
25:19 **e** your fill and live there in safety.
25:20 You may ask, "What will we **e** in the
25:22 you will **e** from the old crop and
25:22 will continue to **e** from it until the
26: 5 and you will **e** all the food you want
26:16 because your enemies will **e** it.
26:26 **e**, but you will not be satisfied.
26:29 You will **e** the flesh of your sons
Nu 6: 3 grape juice or **e** grapes or raisins.
6: 4 he must not **e** anything that comes
9:11 They are to **e** the lamb, together
11: 4 "If only we had meat to **e**!
11:13 wailing to me, 'Give us meat to **e**!'
11:18 for tomorrow, when you will **e** meat.
11:18 "If only we had meat to **e**! We were
11:19 You will not **e** it for just one day,
11:21 them meat to **e** for a whole month!'
15:19 you **e** the food of the land, present
18:10 **E** it as something most holy; every
18:10 most holy; every male shall **e** it.
18:11 who is ceremonially clean may **e** it.
18:13 who is ceremonially clean may **e** it.
18:31 You and your households may **e** the
28:17 days **e** bread made without yeast.
Dt 2: 6 food you **e** and the water you drink.
2:28 Sell us food to **e** and water to drink
4:28 cannot see or hear or **e** or smell.
6:11 when you **e** and are satisfied,
8:12 Otherwise, when you **e** and are
8:16 He gave you manna to **e** in the desert,
11:15 and you will **e** and be satisfied.
12: 7 you and your families shall **e** and
12:15 **e** as much of the meat as you want,
12:16 you must not **e** the blood; pour it
12:17 You must not **e** in your own towns the
12:18 Instead, you are to **e** them in the
12:20 you may **e** as much of it as you want.
12:21 may **e** as much of them as you want.
12:22 **E** them as you would gazelle or deer.
12:22 unclean and the clean may **e**.
12:23 be sure you do not **e** the blood,
12:23 must not **e** the life with the meat.
12:24 You must not **e** the blood; pour it
12:25 Do not **e** it, so that it may go well
12:27 your God, but you may **e** the meat.
14: 3 Do not **e** any detestable thing.
14: 4 These are the animals you may **e**: the
14: 6 You may **e** any animal that has a
14: 7 **e** the camel, the rabbit or the coney.
14: 8 You are not to **e** their meat or touch
14: 9 may **e** any that has fins and scales.
14:10 may not **e**; for you it is unclean.
14:11 You may **e** any clean bird.
14:12 these you may not **e**: the eagle, the
14:19 are unclean to you; do not **e** them.
14:20 creature that is clean you may **e**.
14:21 Do not **e** anything you find already
14:21 and he may **e** it, or you may sell it
14:23 **E** the tithe of your grain, new wine
14:26 Then you and your household shall **e**
14:29 may come and **e** and be satisfied,
15:20 your family are to **e** them in the
15:22 You are to **e** it in your own towns.
15:22 **e** it, as if it were gazelle or deer.
15:23 you must not **e** the blood; pour it
16: 3 Do not **e** it with bread made with
16: 3 but for seven days **e** unleavened
16: 7 Roast it and **e** it at the place the
16: 8 For six days **e** unleavened bread and
20:19 them, because you can **e** their fruit.
23:24 you may **e** all the grapes you want,
26:12 **e** in your towns and be satisfied.
28:31 eyes, but you will **e** none of it.

Dt 28:33 A people that you do not know will **e**
28:39 grapes, because worms will **e** them.
28:53 you will **e** the fruit of the womb,
28:57 For she intends to **e** them secretly
31:20 and when they **e** their fill and
Jos 24:13 and you live in them and **e** from
Jdg 13: 4 that you do not **e** anything unclean,
13: 7 drink and do not **e** anything unclean,
13:14 She must not **e** anything that comes
13:14 drink nor **e** anything unclean.
13:16 me, I will not **e** any of your food.
14:14 "Out of the eater, something to **e**;
19: 5 something to **e**; then you can go."
19: 6 the two of them sat down to **e** and
19:21 they had something to **e** and drink.
1Sa 1: 7 till she wept and would not **e**.
1: 8 Why don't you **e**? Why are you
2:36 so that I can have food to **e**.
9:13 he goes up to the high place to **e**.
9:13 those who are invited will **e**.
9:19 for today you are to **e** with me, and
9:24 **E**, because it was set aside for you
14:34 and slaughter them here and **e** them.
20:24 the king sat down to **e**. He sat
20:34 day of the month he did not **e**,
28:22 that you may **e** and have the strength
28:23 He refused and said, "I will not **e**."
30:11 him water to drink and food to **e**—
2Sa 3:35 they all came and urged David to **e**
9: 7 and you will always **e** at my table."
9:10 master, will always **e** at my table.
11:11 How could I go to my house to **e** and
12:17 he would not **e** any food with them.
12:21 child is dead, you get up and **e**!"
13: 5 to come and give me something to **e**.
13: 5 her and then **e** it from her hand.'"
13: 6 so that I may **e** from her hand."
13: 9 him the bread, but he refused to **e**.
13:10 so that I may **e** from your hand.
13:11 when she took it to him to **e**, he
16: 2 and fruit are for the men to **e**,
17:29 milk for David and his people to **e**.
19:28 among those who **e** at your table.
1Ki 2: 7 be among those who **e** at your table.
13: 7 to **e**, and I will give you a gift."
13: 8 would I **e** bread or drink water here.
13: 9 'You must not **e** bread or drink water
13:15 to him, "Come home with me and **e**.
13:16 nor can I **e** bread or drink water
13:17 'You must not **e** bread or drink water
13:18 that he may **e** bread and drink water.'
13:22 where he told you not to **e** or drink.
14:11 Dogs will **e** those belonging to
16: 4 Dogs will **e** those belonging to
17:12 my son, that we may **e** it—and die."
18:19 Asherah, who **e** at Jezebel's table."
18:41 Elijah said to Ahab, "Go, **e** and
18:42 Ahab went off to **e** and drink, but
19: 5 touched him and said, "Get up and **e**.
19: 7 "Get up and **e**, for the journey is
21: 4 on his bed sulking and refused to **e**.
21: 5 are you so sullen? Why won't you **e**?"
21: 7 over Israel? Get up and **e**! Cheer up.
21:24 "Dogs will **e** those belonging to Ahab
2Ki 4: 8 he came by, he stopped there to **e**.
4:40 but as they began to **e** it, they
4:40 in the pot!" And they could not **e** it.
4:41 said, "Serve it to the people to **e**.
4:42 "Give it to the people to **e**," Elisha
4:43 "Give it to the people to **e**.
4:43 will **e** and have some left over.'"
6:22 water before them so that they may **e**
6:28 'Give up your son so that we may **e**
6:28 today, and tomorrow we'll **e** my son.'
6:29 may **e** him,' but she had hidden him."
7: 2 "but you will not **e** any of it!
7:19 eyes, but you will not **e** any of it!"
18:27 like you, will have to **e** their own
18:31 Then every one of you will **e** from
19:29 O Hezekiah: This year you will **e**
19:29 plant vineyards and **e** their fruit.
25: 3 there was no food for the people to **e**
2Ch 31:10 we have had enough to **e** and plenty
Ezr 2:63 The governor ordered them not to **e**
9:12 that you may be strong and **e** the
Ne 5: 2 **e** and stay alive, we must get grain."

Ne 7:65 therefore, ordered them not to **e** any
8:12 all the people went away to **e** and
9:36 so that they could **e** its fruit
Est 4:16 Do not **e** or drink for three days,
Job 1: 4 sisters to **e** and drink with them.
27:14 will never have enough to **e**.
31: 8 may others **e** what I have sown, and
Ps 14: 4 who devour my people as men **e** bread
22:26 The poor will **e** and be satisfied;
50:13 Do I **e** the flesh of bulls or drink
53: 4 who devour my people as men **e** bread
78:24 manna for the people to **e**,
78:25 sent them all the food they could **e**.
102: 4 like grass; I forget to **e** my food.
102: 9 For I **e** ashes as my food and mingle
127: 2 toiling for food to **e**—for he
128: 2 You will **e** the fruit of your labour;
141: 4 let me not **e** of their delicacies.
Pr 1:31 they will **e** the fruit of their ways
4:17 They **e** the bread of wickedness and
9: 5 "Come, **e** my food and drink the wine
13:25 The righteous **e** to their hearts'
18:21 those who love it will **e** its fruit.
23: 6 Do not **e** the food of a stingy man,
23: 7 "**E** and drink," he says to you, but
24:13 **E** honey, my son, for it is good;
25:16 If you find honey, **e** just enough—
25:21 give him food to **e**; if he is thirsty,
25:27 It is not good to **e** too much honey,
27:18 He who tends a fig-tree will **e** its
31:27 does not **e** the bread of idleness.
Ecc 2:24 A man can do nothing better than to **e**
2:25 for without him, who can **e** or find
3:13 That everyone may **e** and drink, and
5:18 and proper for a man to **e** and drink,
8:15 sun than to **e** and drink and be glad.
9: 7 Go, **e** your food with gladness, and
10:17 whose princes **e** at a proper time—
SS 5: 1 **E**, O friends, and drink; drink your
Isa 1:19 you will **e** the best from the land;
4: 1 "We will **e** our own food and provide
7:15 He will **e** curds and honey when he
7:22 they give, he will have curds to **e**.
7:22 in the land will **e** curds and honey.
9:20 they will **e**, but not be satisfied.
11: 7 the lion will **e** straw like the ox.
21: 5 they spread the rugs, they **e**, they
22:13 "Let us **e** and drink," you say, "for
30:24 will **e** fodder and mash, spread out
36:12 like you, will have to **e** their own
36:16 Then every one of you will **e** from
37:30 "This year you will **e** what grows by
37:30 plant vineyards and **e** their fruit.
49:26 I will make your oppressors **e** their
50: 9 a garment; the moths will **e** them up.
51: 8 For the moth will **e** them up like a
55: 1 come, buy and **e**! Come, buy wine and
55: 2 listen to me, and **e** what is good,
62: 9 those who harvest it will **e** it and
65: 4 who **e** the flesh of pigs, and whose
65:13 "My servants will **e**, but you will go
65:21 plant vineyards and **e** their fruit.
65:22 live in them, or plant and others **e**.
65:25 and the lion will **e** straw like the
66:17 of those who **e** the flesh of pigs
Jer 2: 7 to **e** its fruit and rich produce.
7:21 and **e** the meat yourselves!
9:15 "See, I will make this people **e**
16: 8 and sit down to **e** and drink.
19: 9 I will make them **e** the flesh of
19: 9 and they will **e** one another's flesh
23:15 "I will make them **e** bitter food and
29: 5 gardens and **e** what they produce.
29:28 gardens and **e** what they produce.'"
52: 6 was no food for the people to **e**.
Lam 2:20 Should women **e** their offspring,
Eze 2: 8 your mouth and **e** what I give you."
3: 1 he said to me, "Son of man, **e** what
3: 1 "Son of man, **e** what is before you, **e**
3: 2 and he gave me the scroll to **e**.
3: 3 he said to me, "Son of man, **e** this
4: 9 You are to **e** it during the 390 days
4:10 Weigh out twenty shekels of food to **e**
4:10 to **e** each day and **e** it at set times.
4:12 **E** the food as you would a barley
4:13 Israel will **e** defiled food among the
Eze 4:16 The people will **e** rationed food in
5:10 midst fathers will **e** their children,
5:10 and children will **e** their fathers.
12:18 "Son of man, tremble as you **e** your
12:19 They will **e** their food in anxiety
16:19 olive oil and honey I gave you to **e**—
18: 2 "'The fathers **e** sour grapes, and the
18: 6 He does not **e** at the mountain
18:15 "He does not **e** at the mountain
22: 9 in you are those who **e** at the
24:17 **e** the customary food of mourners."
24:22 or **e** the customary food of mourners.
25: 4 **e** your fruit and drink your milk.
33:25 Since you **e** meat with the blood
34: 3 You **e** the curds, clothe yourselves
39:17 you will **e** flesh and drink blood.
39:18 You will **e** the flesh of mighty men
39:19 you will **e** fat till you are glutted
39:20 At my table you will **e** your fill of
42:13 LORD will **e** the most holy offerings.
44: 3 to **e** in the presence of the LORD.
44:29 They will **e** the grain offerings, the
44:31 The priests must not **e** anything,
45:21 shall **e** bread made without yeast.
Da 1:12 vegetables to **e** and water to drink.
1:13 the young men who **e** the royal food,
4:25 you will **e** grass like cattle and be
4:32 you will **e** grass like cattle.
7: 5 'Get up and **e** your fill of flesh!'
11:26 Those who **e** from the king's
Hos 4:10 "They will **e** but not have enough;
8:13 given to me and they **e** the meat,
9: 3 Egypt and **e** unclean food in Assyria.
9: 4 all who **e** them will be unclean.
Joel 2:26 You will have plenty to **e**, until you
Am 9:14 will make gardens and **e** their fruit.
Ob : 7 those who **e** your bread will set a trap
Jnh 3: 7 do not let them **e** or drink.
Mic 3: 3 who **e** my people's flesh, strip off
6:14 You will **e** but not be satisfied;
7: 1 there is no cluster of grapes to **e**,
Zep 3:13 They will **e** and lie down and no-one
Hag 1: 6 You **e**, but never have enough. You
Zec 11: 9 who are left **e** one another's flesh."
11:16 but will **e** the meat of the choice
Mt 6:25 what you will **e** or drink; or about
6:31 'What shall we **e**?' or 'What shall we
9:11 **e** with tax collectors and 'sinners'?"
12: 1 pick some ears of corn and **e** them.
14:16 You give them something to **e**."
15: 2 wash their hands before they **e**!"
15:27 "but even the dogs **e** the crumbs that
15:32 me three days and have nothing to **e**.
24:49 and to **e** and drink with drunkards.
25:35 and you gave me something to **e**,
25:42 hungry and you gave me nothing to **e**,
26:17 for you to **e** the Passover?"
26:26 "Take and **e**; this is my body.
Mk 2:16 **e** with tax collectors and 'sinners'?"
2:26 is lawful only for priests to **e**.
3:20 disciples were not even able to **e**.
5:43 told them to give her something to **e**.
6:31 did not even have a chance to **e**,
6:36 and buy themselves something to **e**."
6:37 "You give them something to **e**.
6:37 on bread and give it to them to **e**?"
7: 3 all the Jews do not **e** unless they
7: 4 they do not **e** unless they wash.
7:27 "First let the children **e** all they
7:28 the table **e** the children's crumbs."
8: 1 Since they had nothing to **e**, Jesus
8: 2 me three days and have nothing to **e**.
11:14 no-one ever **e** fruit from you again.
14:12 for you to **e** the Passover?"
14:14 **e** the Passover with my disciples?'
Lk 5:30 "Why do you **e** and drink with tax
6: 1 them in their hands and **e** the grain.
6: 4 is lawful only for priests to **e**.
8:55 them to give her something to **e**.
9:13 "You give them something to **e**.
10: 8 welcomed, **e** what is set before you.
11:37 a Pharisee invited him to **e** with him;
12:19 Take life easy; **e**, drink and be merry.
12:22 what you will **e**; or about your body,
12:29 **e** or drink; do not worry about it.
12:45 and to **e** and drink and get drunk.
Lk 14: 1 One Sabbath, when Jesus went to **e** in
14:15 **e** at the feast in the kingdom of God.
16:21 longing to **e** what fell from the rich
17: 7 'Come along now and sit down to **e**'?
17: 8 and wait on me while I **e** and drink;
17: 8 after that you may **e** and drink'?
22: 8 for us to **e** the Passover."
22:11 **e** the Passover with my disciples?'
22:15 "I have eagerly desired to **e** this
22:16 For I tell you, I will not **e** it
22:30 that you may **e** and drink at my table
24:41 "Do you have anything here to **e**?
Jn 4:31 urged him, "Rabbi, **e** something.
4:32 he said to them, "I have food to **e**
6: 5 we buy bread for these people to **e**?"
6:12 they had all had enough to **e**, he
6:31 gave them bread from heaven to **e**.'"
6:50 which a man may **e** and not die.
6:52 this man give us his flesh to **e**?"
6:53 "I tell you the truth, unless you **e**
18:28 wanted to be able to **e** the Passover.
Ac 9: 9 and did not **e** or drink anything.
10:10 hungry and wanted something to **e**,
10:13 "Get up, Peter. Kill and **e**."
11: 7 'Get up, Peter. Kill and **e**.'
23:12 an oath not to **e** or drink until they
23:14 **e** anything until we have killed Paul.
23:21 They have taken an oath not to **e** or
27:33 dawn Paul urged them all to **e**.
27:35 Then he broke it and began to **e**.
Ro 14: 2 One man's faith allows him to **e**
14: 3 and the man who does not **e**
14:15 distressed because of what you **e**,
14:20 but it is wrong for a man to **e**
14:21 is better not to **e** meat or drink
1Co 5:11 With such a man do not even **e**.
8: 7 when they **e** such food they think
8: 8 we do not **e**, and no better if we do.
8:10 **e** what has been sacrificed to idols?
8:13 Therefore, if what I **e** causes my
8:13 I will never **e** meat again, so that I
9: 7 and does not **e** of its grapes?
10: 7 "The people sat down to **e** and drink
10:18 Do not those who **e** the sacrifices
10:25 **E** anything sold in the meat market
10:27 **e** whatever is put before you without
10:28 in sacrifice," then do not **e** it,
10:31 whether you **e** or drink or whatever
11:20 it is not the Lord's Supper you **e**,
11:21 for as you **e**, each of you goes ahead
11:22 Don't you have homes to **e** and drink
11:26 For whenever you **e** this bread and
11:33 together to **e**, wait for each other.
11:34 If anyone is hungry, he should **e** at
15:32 **e** and drink, for tomorrow we die."
Gal 2:12 he used to **e** with the Gentiles.
Col 2:16 judge you by what you **e** or drink,
2Th 3: 8 nor did we **e** anyone's food without
3:10 man will not work, he shall not **e**."
3:12 down and earn the bread they **e**.
Heb 13: 9 are of no value to those who **e** them.
13:10 the tabernacle have no right to **e**.
Jas 5: 3 against you and **e** your flesh
Rev 2: 7 I will give the right to **e** from the
3:20 in and **e** with him, and he with me.
10: 9 He said to me, "Take it and **e** it. It
17:16 **e** her flesh and burn her with fire.
19:18 that you may **e** the flesh of kings,

Eaten (Eat)

Ge 3:11 Have you **e** from the tree from which
6:21 every kind of food that is to be **e**
14:24 nothing but what my men have **e**
31:38 nor have I **e** rams from your flocks.
31:54 had **e**, they spent the night there.
43: 2 when they had **e** all the grain they
Ex 12:46 "It must be **e** inside one house; take
21:28 death, and its meat must not be **e**.
29:34 must not be **e**, because it is sacred.
Lev 6:16 but it is to be **e** without yeast in a
6:23 completely; it must not be **e**."
6:26 it; it is to be **e** in a holy place,
6:30 must not be **e**; it must be burned.
7: 6 **e** in a holy place; it is most holy.
7:15 must be **e** on the day it is offered;
7:16 the sacrifice shall be **e** on the day

Lev 7:16 left over may be **e** on the next day.
7:18 offering is **e** on the third day,
7:19 must not be **e**; it must be burned up.
10:18 you should have **e** the goat in the
10:19 if I had **e** the sin offering today?"
11:34 Any food that could be **e** but has
11:41 is detestable; it is not to be **e**.
11:47 be **e** and those that may not be **e**.'"
17:13 may be **e** must drain out the blood
19: 6 shall be **e** on the day you sacrifice
19: 7 If any of it is **e** on the third day,
19:23 it forbidden; it must not be **e**.
22:30 must be **e** that same day; leave none
25: 7 Whatever the land produces may be **e**.
Nu 12:12 womb with its flesh half **e** away."
Dt 8:10 you have **e** and are satisfied, praise
26:14 I have not **e** any of the sacred
Ru 2:18 left over after she had **e** enough.
1Sa 14:30 had **e** today some of the plunder they
28:20 **e** nothing all that day and night.
30:12 for he had not **e** any food or drunk
2Sa 19:42 Have we **e** any of the king's
1Ki 13:28 **e** the body nor mauled the donkey.
Job 6: 6 Is tasteless food **e** without salt, or
13:28 rotten, like a garment **e** by moths.
Pr 9:17 food **e** in secret is delicious!"
23: 8 will vomit up the little you have **e**
30:17 valley, will be **e** by the vultures.
SS 5: 1 I have **e** my honeycomb and my honey;
Jer 24: 2 so bad that they could not be **e**.
24: 3 are so bad that they cannot be **e**."
24: 8 are so bad that they cannot be **e**,'
29:17 that are so bad they cannot be **e**.
31:29 'The fathers have **e** sour grapes, and
Eze 4:14 I have never **e** anything found dead or
Hos 10:13 you have **e** the fruit of deception.
Joel 1: 4 has left the great locusts have **e**;
1: 4 have left the young locusts have **e**;
1: 4 have left other locusts have **e**.
2:25 locusts have **e**—the great locust
Mk 6:44 The number of the men who had **e** was
Jn 6:13 loaves left over by those who had **e**.
6:23 where the people had **e** the bread
Ac 10:14 never **e** anything impure or unclean."
12:23 and he was **e** by worms and died.
27:33 food—you haven't **e** anything.
27:38 they had **e** as much as they wanted,
Jas 5: 2 and moths have **e** your clothes.
Rev 10:10 I had **e** it, my stomach turned sour.

Eater (Eat)
Jdg 14:14 He replied, "Out of the **e**, something
Isa 55:10 for the sower and bread for the **e**,
Na 3:12 figs fall into the mouth of the **e**.

Eating (Eat)
Ge 40:17 **e** them out of the basket on my head."
Ex 34:28 without **e** bread or drinking water.
Lev 26:10 You will still be **e** last year's
Dt 27: 7 **e** them and rejoicing in the presence
28:55 flesh of his children that he is **e**.
Jdg 9:27 While they were **e** and drinking, they
19: 4 **e** and drinking, and sleeping there.
Ru 3: 3 he has finished **e** and drinking.
3: 7 Boaz had finished **e** and drinking and
1Sa 1: 9 Once when they had finished **e** and
9:13 The people will not begin **e** until he
14:33 LORD by **e** meat that has blood in it.
14:34 Do not sin against the LORD by **e**
30:16 scattered over the countryside, **e**,
1Ki 1:25 At this very moment they are **e** and
13:23 the man of God had finished **e** and
2Ki 6:23 and after they had finished **e** and
1Ch 12:39 **e** and drinking, for their families
Isa 22:13 **e** of meat and drinking of wine! "Let
29: 8 a hungry man dreams that he is **e**,
Jer 41: 1 While they were **e** together there,
Da 6:18 spent the night without **e** and
Zec 7: 6 you were **e** and drinking, were you
Mt 11:18 For John came neither **e** nor drinking,
11:19 The Son of Man came **e** and drinking,
15:20 'unclean'; but **e** with unwashed hands
24:38 people were **e** and drinking, marrying
26:21 while they were **e**, he said, "I tell
26:26 While they were **e**, Jesus took bread,
Mk 2:15 "sinners" were **e** with him and his
2:16 saw him **e** with the "sinners"
7: 2 saw some of his disciples **e** food
7: 5 **e** their food with 'unclean' hands?"
14:18 they were reclining at the table **e**,
14:18 betray me—one who is **e** with me."
14:22 While they were **e**, Jesus took bread,
16:14 to the Eleven as they were **e**;
Lk 5:29 and others were **e** with them.
5:33 but yours go on **e** and drinking."
7:33 For John the Baptist came neither **e**
7:34 The Son of Man came **e** and drinking,
7:37 Jesus was **e** at the Pharisee's house,
10: 7 Stay in that house, **e** and drinking
15:16 the pods that the pigs were **e**, but
17:27 People were **e**, drinking, marrying
17:28 People were **e** and drinking, buying
Jn 21:15 they had finished **e**, Jesus said to
Ac 1: 4 On one occasion, while he was **e** with
Ro 14:15 Do not by your **e** destroy your
14:17 is not a matter of **e** and drinking,
14:23 because his **e** is not from faith; and
1Co 8: 4 then, about **e** food sacrificed to
8:10 knowledge **e** in an idol's temple,
Jude :12 **e** with you without the slightest
Rev 2:14 sin by **e** food sacrificed to idols
2:20 the **e** of food sacrificed to idols.

Eats (Eat)
Ex 12:15 for whoever **e** anything with yeast in
12:19 And whoever **e** anything with yeast in
Lev 7:18 **e** any of it will be held responsible.
7:20 if anyone who is unclean **e** any meat
7:21 detestable thing—and then **e** any of
7:25 Anyone who **e** the fat of an animal
7:27 If anyone **e** blood, that person must
11:40 Anyone who **e** some of the carcass
14:47 Anyone who sleeps or **e** in the house
17:10 living among them who **e** any blood
17:10 against that person who **e** blood
17:14 anyone who **e** it must be cut off."
17:15 whether native-born or alien, who **e**
19: 8 Whoever **e** it will be held
22:14 "'If anyone **e** a sacred offering by
1Sa 14:24 "Cursed be any man who **e** food before
14:28 'Cursed be any man who **e** food today!'
2Sa 19:35 Can your servant taste what he **e** and
Job 18:13 It **e** away parts of his skin;
39:24 In frenzied excitement he **e** up the
Ps 106:20 an image of a bull, which **e** grass.
Pr 30:20 She **e** and wipes her mouth and says,
Ecc 5:12 whether he **e** little or much, but the
5:17 All his days he **e** in darkness, with
Isa 44:16 he roasts his meat and **e** his fill.
59: 5 Whoever **e** their eggs will die, and
Jer 31:30 whoever **e** sour grapes—his own teeth
Eze 18:11 "He **e** at the mountain shrines.
Lk 15: 2 welcomes sinners, and **e** with them."
Jn 6:51 If anyone **e** of this bread, he will
6:54 Whoever **e** my flesh and drinks my
6:56 Whoever **e** my flesh and drinks my
Ro 14: 2 faith is weak, **e** only vegetables.
14: 3 The man who **e** everything must not
14: 6 He who **e** meat, **e** to the Lord, for he
14:23 who has doubts is condemned if he **e**,
1Co 11:27 Therefore, whoever **e** the bread or
11:28 **e** of the bread and drinks of the cup.
11:29 For anyone who **e** and drinks without
11:29 **e** and drinks judgment on himself.

Eaves
1Ki 7: 9 courtyard and from foundation to **e**,

Ebal, Mount
North of Shechem, facing Mount Gerizim to the south. Highest peak of Samaria, at centre of Canaan. The LORD's curses were to be proclaimed from here (Dt 11:29), and an altar erected (Dt 27:4). Joshua carried out these instructions (Jos 8:30, 33).

Ge 36:23 Alvan, Manahath, **E**, Shepho and Onam.
Dt 11:29 and on Mount **E** the curses.
27: 4 set up these stones on Mount **E**, as I
27:13 these tribes shall stand on Mount **E**
Jos 8:30 Joshua built on Mount **E** an altar to
8:33 half of them in front of Mount **E**,
1Ch 1:40 Alvan, Manahath, **E**, Shepho and Onam.

Ebb (Ebbed, Ebbing, Ebbs)
Lam 2:12 lives **e** away in their mothers' arms.

Ebbed (Ebb)
Ps 107: 5 and thirsty, and their lives **e** away.

Ebbing (Ebb)
Jnh 2: 7 "When my life was **e** away, I

Ebbs (Ebb)
Job 30:16 "And now my life **e** away; days of

Ebed
Jdg 9:26 Now Gaal son of **E** moved with his
9:28 Gaal son of **E** said, "Who is
9:30 son of **E** said, he was very angry.
9:31 "Gaal son of **E** and his brothers have
9:35 Now Gaal son of **E** had gone out and
Ezr 8: 6 of the descendants of Adin, **E** son of

Ebed-Melech
Jer 38: 7 **E**, a Cushite, an official in the
38: 8 **E** went out of the palace and said to
38:10 the king commanded **E** the Cushite,
38:11 **E** took the men with him and went to
38:12 **E** the Cushite said to Jeremiah, "Put
39:16 "Go and tell **E** the Cushite, 'This is

Ebenezer
1Sa 4: 1 at **E**, and the Philistines at Aphek.
5: 1 God, they took it from **E** to Ashdod.
7:12 He named it **E**, saying, "Thus far has

Eber
Ge 10:21 the ancestor of all the sons of **E**.
10:24 Shelah, and Shelah the father of **E**.
10:25 Two sons were born to **E**: One was
11:14 30 years, he became the father of **E**.
11:15 after he became the father of **E**,
11:16 **E** had lived 34 years, he became the
11:17 **E** lived 430 years and had other sons
Nu 24:24 **E**, but they too will come to ruin."
1Ch 1:18 Shelah, and Shelah the father of **E**.
1:19 Two sons were born to **E**: One was
1:25 **E**, Peleg, Reu,
5:13 Jacan, Zia and **E**—seven in all.
8:12 The sons of Elpaal: **E**, Misham,
8:22 Ishpan, **E**, Eliel,
Ne 12:20 of Sallu's, Kallai; of Amok's, **E**;
Lk 3:35 the son of **E**, the son of Shelah,

Ebez
Jos 19:20 Rabbith, Kishion, **E**,

Ebiasaph
1Ch 6:23 Elkanah his son, **E** his son, Assir
6:37 the son of **E**, the son of Korah,
9:19 Shallum son of Kore, the son of **E**,

Ebony
Eze 27:15 paid you with ivory tusks and **e**.

Ecbatana
Ezr 6: 2 of **E** in the province of Media,

Echo (Echoes)
Hab 2:11 the beams of the woodwork will **e** it.
Zep 2:14 Their calls will **e** through the

Echoes (Echo)
Isa 15: 8 Their outcry **e** along the border of

Eden (*Garden of Eden*)
1. Wooded garden including Tree of Life and Tree of Knowledge of Good and Evil (Ge 2:9). First home of Adam and Eve (Ge 2:8) who took care of it (Ge 2:15). River flowed from Eden into the garden, and split into four (Ge 2:10–14). After disobeying God, Adam and

Eve banished from here (Ge 3:23–24). Used figuratively for God's paradise (Isa 51:3; Eze 28:13; 31:9; 36:35). Alluded to in vision of New Jerusalem (Rev 22:2–3). **2.** Market town providing Tyre with choice items (Eze 27:23), captured by Assyrians (2Ki 19:12; Isa 37:12). Probably in Mesopotamia.

Ge 2: 8 in **E**; and there he put the man he
2:10 watering the garden flowed from **E**;
4:16 lived in the land of Nod, east of **E**.
2Ki 19:12 people of **E** who were in Tel Assar?
2Ch 29:12 Joah son of Zimmah and **E** son of Joah;
31:15 **E**, Miniamin, Jeshua, Shemaiah,
Isa 37:12 people of **E** who were in Tel Assar?
51: 3 he will make her deserts like **E**,
Eze 27:23 "'Haran, Canneh and **E** and merchants
28:13 You were in **E**, the garden of God;
31: 9 the trees of **E** in the garden of God.
31:16 Then all the trees of **E**, the
31:18 "'Which of the trees of **E** can be
31:18 the trees of **E** to the earth below;

Eder

Jos 15:21 of Edom were: Kabzeel, **E**, Jagur,
1Ch 8:15 Zebadiah, Arad, **E**,
23:23 The sons of Mushi: Mahli, **E** and
24:30 the sons of Mushi: Mahli, **E** and

Edge (Double-edged, Edges)

Ex 13:20 at Etham on the **e** of the desert.
26: 4 the **e** of the end curtain in one set,
26:10 Make fifty loops along the **e** of the
26:10 also along the **e** of the end curtain
28:26 on the inside **e** next to the ephod.
28:32 There shall be a woven **e** like a
36:11 the **e** of the end curtain in one set,
36:17 they made fifty loops along the **e** of
36:17 also along the **e** of the end curtain
39:19 on the inside **e** next to the ephod.
Nu 20:16 a town on the **e** of your territory.
22:36 border, at the **e** of his territory.
33: 6 at Etham, on the **e** of the desert.
Jos 3: 8 'When you reach the **e** of the
3:15 their feet touched the water's **e**,
Jdg 7:17 **e** of the camp, do exactly as I do.
7:19 reached the **e** of the camp at the
1Sa 9:27 they were going down to the **e** of the
2Ki 7: 5 **e** of the camp, not a man was there,
7: 8 The men who had leprosy reached the **e**
1Ch 5: 9 the land up to the **e** of the desert
Ps 89:43 You have turned back the **e** of his
Ecc 10:10 If the axe is dull and its **e**
Jer 31:29 the children's teeth are set on **e**.'
31:30 own teeth will be set on **e**.
Eze 18: 2 the children's teeth are set on **e**'?
43:13 with a rim of one span around the **e**.
Am 3:12 those who sit in Samaria on the **e** of
Mt 9:20 him and touched the **e** of his cloak.
14:36 sick just touch the **e** of his cloak,
Mk 4: 1 along the shore at the water's **e**.
6:56 them touch even the **e** of his cloak,
Lk 5: 2 he saw at the water's **e** two boats,
8:44 him and touched the **e** of his cloak,
Heb 11:34 and escaped the **e** of the sword;

Edges (Edge)

Lev 19: 9 do not reap to the very **e** of your
19:27 or clip off the **e** of your beard.
21: 5 shave off the **e** of their beards or
23:22 do not reap to the very **e** of your
Job 38:13 that it might take the earth by the **e**

Edict (Dictate)

Ezr 6:11 that if anyone changes this **e**,
Est 1:20 the king's **e** is proclaimed
2: 8 the king's order and **e** had been
3:14 A copy of the text of the **e** was to
3:15 **e** was issued in the citadel of Susa.
4: 3 In every province to which the **e** and
4: 8 of the **e** for their annihilation,
8:11 The king's **e** granted the Jews in
8:13 A copy of the text of the **e** was to
8:14 And the **e** was also issued in the
8:17 wherever the **e** of the king went,
Est 9: 1 the month of Adar, the **e** commanded
9:13 carry out this day's **e** tomorrow
9:14 An **e** was issued in Susa, and they
Da 6: 7 that the king should issue an **e**
6:15 no decree or **e** that the king issues
Heb 11:23 were not afraid of the king's **e**.

Edification (Edified, Edifies)

Ro 14:19 what leads to peace and to mutual **e**.

Edified (Edification)

1Co 14: 5 so that the church may be **e**.
14:17 enough, but the other man is not **e**.

Edifies (Edification)

1Co 14: 4 He who speaks in a tongue **e** himself,
14: 4 but he who prophesies **e** the church.

Edom (Edom's, Edomite, Edomites, Esau)

1. Another name for *Esau*. **2.** Nation descended from Esau (Ge 36). **3.** Region south of Dead Sea and east of Arabah, known also as land of Seir and Esau. Home of Esau (also called Edom) (Ge 32:3; 38:8). Esau's descendants expelled the Horites (Dt 2:12, 22). During Exodus, Israel not permitted to pass through (Nu 20:14–21; 21:4; Jdg 11:17–18). Its people battled against Saul (1Sa 14:47), but were conquered by David (2Sa 8:13–14; 1Ki 11:15–16), enabling Solomon to develop a port here (1Ki 9:26). Revolted against Jehoram (2Ki 8:20–22), but retaken by Amaziah (2Ki 14:7). Azariah captured port of Elath (2Ki 14:22), but later recaptured (2Ki 16:6). Inhabitants joined with Babylonians against Judah (Ps 137:7; Eze 35:5; 36:5; Ob 10–16), and received prophetic judgment (Isa 34; 63:1–6; Jer 49:7–22; Eze 25:12–14; 35; Joel 3:19; Ob; Mal 1:3–5). Later referred to as Idumea (Mk 3:8).

Ge 25:30 (That is why he was also called **E**.
32: 3 the land of Seir, the country of **E**.
36: 1 is the account of Esau (that is, **E**).
36: 8 Esau (that is, **E**) settled in the
36:16 chiefs descended from Eliphaz in **E**;
36:17 chiefs descended from Reuel in **E**;
36:19 the sons of Esau (that is, **E**)
36:21 of Seir in **E** were Horite chiefs.
36:31 These were the kings who reigned in **E**
36:32 Bela son of Beor became king of **E**.
36:43 These were the chiefs of **E**,
Ex 15:15 The chiefs of **E** will be terrified,
Nu 20:14 from Kadesh to the king of **E**,
20:18 **E** answered: "You may not pass
20:20 Then **E** came out against them with a
20:21 Since **E** refused to let them go
20:23 At Mount Hor, near the border of **E**,
21: 4 route to the Red Sea, to go round **E**.
24:18 **E** will be conquered; Seir, his enemy,
33:37 at Mount Hor, on the border of **E**.
34: 3 Desert of Zin along the border of **E**.
Jos 15: 1 extended down to the territory of **E**,
15:21 the boundary of **E** were: Kabzeel, Eder
Jdg 5: 4 when you marched from the land of **E**,
11:17 sent messengers to the king of **E**,
11:17 but the king of **E** would not listen.
11:18 skirted the lands of **E** and Moab,
1Sa 14:47 the Ammonites, **E**, the kings of Zobah,
2Sa 8:12 **E** and Moab, the Ammonites and the
8:14 He put garrisons throughout **E**, and
1Ki 9:26 in **E**, on the shore of the Red Sea.
11:14 Edomite, from the royal line of **E**.
11:15 when David was fighting with **E**,
11:15 had struck down all the men in **E**.
11:16 they had destroyed all the men in **E**.
22:47 There was then no king in **E**; a
2Ki 3: 8 "Through the Desert of **E**," he
3: 9 the king of Judah and the king of **E**.
3:12 and the king of **E** went down to him.
3:20 flowing from the direction of **E**!
3:26 to the king of **E**, but they failed.
8:20 In the time of Jehoram, **E** rebelled
8:22 To this day **E** has been in rebellion
14:10 You have indeed defeated **E** and now
1Ch 1:43 These were the kings who reigned in **E**
1:51 The chiefs of **E** were: Timna, Alvah,
1:54 These were the chiefs of **E**.
18:11 from all these nations: **E** and Moab,
18:13 He put garrisons in **E**, and all the
2Ch 8:17 Geber and Elath on the coast of **E**.
20: 2 army is coming against you from **E**,
21: 8 In the time of Jehoram, **E** rebelled
21:10 To this day **E** has been in rebellion
25:19 yourself that you have defeated **E**,
25:20 because they sought the gods of **E**.
Ps 60: 8 Moab is my washbasin, upon **E** I toss
60: 9 city? Who will lead me to **E**?
83: 6 the tents of **E** and the Ishmaelites,
108: 9 Moab is my washbasin, upon **E** I toss
108:10 city? Who will lead me to **E**?
Isa 11:14 They will lay hands on **E** and Moab,
34: 5 it descends in judgment on **E**, the
34: 6 Bozrah and a great slaughter in **E**.
34:11 God will stretch out over **E** the
63: 1 Who is this coming from **E**, from
Jer 9:26 Egypt, Judah, **E**, Ammon, Moab and all
25:21 **E**, Moab and Ammon;
27: 3 send word to the kings of **E**, Moab,
40:11 all the Jews in Moab, Ammon, **E** and
49: 7 Concerning **E**: This is what the LORD
49:17 "**E** will become an object of horror;
49:19 chase **E** from its land in an instant.
49:20 what the LORD has planned against **E**,
Lam 4:21 Rejoice and be glad, O Daughter of **E**
4:22 But, O Daughter of **E**, he will punish
Eze 16:57 now scorned by the daughters of **E**
25:12 'Because **E** took revenge on the house
25:13 against **E** and kill its men and their
25:14 I will take vengeance on **E** by the
25:14 and they will deal with **E** in
32:29 "**E** is there, her kings and all her
35:15 O Mount Seir, you and all of **E**.
36: 5 and against **E**, for with glee and
Da 11:41 Many countries will fall, but **E**,
Joel 3:19 Egypt will be desolate, **E** a desert
Am 1: 6 communities and sold them to **E**,
1: 9 communities of captives to **E**,
1:11 "For three sins of **E**, even for four,
9:12 they may possess the remnant of **E**
Ob : 1 the Sovereign LORD says about **E**
: 8 I not destroy the wise men of **E**,
Mal 1: 4 **E** may say, "Though we have been

Edom's (Edom)

Isa 34: 9 **E** streams will be turned into pitch,
Jer 49:22 In that day the hearts of **E** warriors
Am 2: 1 as if to lime, the bones of **E** king,

Edomite (Edom)

Dt 23: 7 Do not abhor an **E**, for he is your
1Sa 21: 7 Doeg the **E**, Saul's head shepherd.
22: 9 Doeg the **E**, who was standing with
22:18 So Doeg the **E** turned and struck
22:22 "That day, when Doeg the **E** was there,
1Ki 11:14 Hadad the **E**, from the royal line of
11:17 fled to Egypt with some **E** officials
Ps 52: T When Doeg the **E** had gone to Saul and

Edomites (Edom)

Ge 36: 9 the **E** in the hill country of Seir.
36:43 This was Esau the father of the **E**.
2Sa 8:13 eighteen thousand **E** in the Valley
8:14 all the **E** became subject to David.
1Ki 11: 1 Ammonites, **E**, Sidonians and Hittites.
2Ki 8:21 The **E** surrounded him and his chariot
14: 7 ten thousand **E** in the Valley of Salt
16: 6 **E** then moved into Elath and have
1Ch 18:12 eighteen thousand **E** in the Valley
18:13 all the **E** became subject to David.
2Ch 21: 9 The **E** surrounded him and his chariot
25:14 returned from slaughtering the **E**,
28:17 The **E** had again come and attacked
Ps 60: T twelve thousand **E** in the Valley of
137: 7 Remember, O LORD, what the **E** did on

Edrei

Nu 21:33 out to meet them in battle at **E**.
Dt 1: 4 who reigned in Heshbon, and at **E** had
3: 1 out to meet us in battle at **E**.
3:10 Salecah and **E**, towns of Og's kingdom

Jos 12: 4 who reigned in Ashtaroth and **E**.
13:12 who had reigned in Ashtaroth and **E**
13:31 half of Gilead, and Ashtaroth and **E**
19:37 Kedesh, **E**, En Hazor,

Educated

Ac 7:22 Moses was **e** in all the wisdom of the

Effect (Effective, Effects)

Job 41:26 The sword that reaches him has no **e**,
Isa 32:17 the **e** of righteousness will be
Ac 7:53 that was put into **e** through angels
1Co 15:10 his grace to me was not without **e**.
Gal 3:19 into **e** through angels by a mediator.
Eph 1:10 to be put into **e** when the times will
Heb 9:17 it never takes **e** while the one who
9:18 was not put into **e** without blood.

Effective (Effect)

1Co 16: 9 a great door for **e** work has opened
Jas 5:16 a righteous man is powerful and **e**.

Effects (Effective)

Ac 28: 5 into the fire and suffered no ill **e**.

Effort (Efforts)

Ecc 2:19 poured my **e** and skill under the sun.
Da 6:14 every **e** until sundown to save him.
Lk 13:24 "Make every **e** to enter through the
Jn 5:44 yet make no **e** to obtain the praise
Ro 9:16 on man's desire or **e**, but on God's
14:19 Let us therefore make every **e** to do
Gal 3: 3 to attain your goal by human **e**?
Eph 4: 3 Make every **e** to keep the unity of
1Th 2:16 in their **e** to keep us from speaking
2:17 longing we made every **e** to see you.
Heb 4:11 Let us, therefore, make every **e** to
12:14 Make every **e** to live in peace with
2Pe 1: 5 For this very reason, make every **e**
1:15 I will make every **e** to see that
3:14 make every **e** to be found spotless,

Efforts (Effort)

Job 36:19 even all your mighty **e** sustain you
Ecc 6: 7 All man's **e** are for his mouth, yet
8:17 Despite all his **e** to search it out,
Eze 24:12 has frustrated all **e**; its heavy
29:20 as a reward for his **e** because he
Gal 4:11 somehow I have wasted my **e** on you.
1Th 3: 5 and our **e** might have been useless.

Egg (Eggs)

Job 6: 6 there flavour in the white of an **e**?
Lk 11:12 Or if he asks for an **e**, will give

Eggs (Egg)

Dt 22: 6 is sitting on the young or on the **e**,
Job 39:14 She lays her **e** on the ground and
Isa 10:14 nations; as men gather abandoned **e**,
34:15 The owl will nest there and lay **e**,
59: 5 They hatch the **e** of vipers and spin
59: 5 Whoever eats their **e** will die, and
Jer 17:11 Like a partridge that hatches **e** it

Eglah

2Sa 3: 5 Ithream the son of David's wife **E**.
1Ch 3: 3 the sixth, Ithream, by his wife **E**.

Eglaim

Isa 15: 8 their wailing reaches as far as **E**,

Eglath Shelishiyah

Isa 15: 5 flee as far as Zoar, as far as **E**.
Jer 48:34 from Zoar as far as Horonaim and **E**,

Eglon

Jos 10: 3 king of Lachish and Debir king of **E**.
10: 5 Lachish and **E**—joined forces.
10:23 Hebron, Jarmuth, Lachish and **E**.
10:34 with him moved on from Lachish to **E**;
10:36 up from **E** to Hebron and attacked it.
10:37 They left no survivors. Just as at **E**,
12:12 king of **E** one the king of Gezer one
15:39 Lachish, Bozkath, **E**,
Jdg 3:12 **E** king of Moab power over Israel.
3:13 **E** came and attacked Israel, and they
3:14 The Israelites were subject to **E**
3:15 him with tribute to **E** king of Moab.
3:17 He presented the tribute to **E** king

Egypt (Egypt's, Egyptian, Egyptian's, Egyptians)

Country lying south of Mediterranean Sea and south-west of Palestine. Habitable land limited to Valley of the River Nile. A place of refuge in time of famine or oppression for Abram (Ge 12:10), Jacob and his sons (Ge 42:1–3; 45:16–20), Hadad (1Ki 11:17), Jeroboam (1Ki 11:40), Uriah (Jer 26:21), Ishmael (Jer 41:15–18), and Mary, Joseph and Jesus (Mt 2:13). Also a place of oppression and servitude for many (e.g., Joseph (Ge 37:28), Jacob's descendants (Ex 1:1–11), Jehoahaz (2Ch 36:4), and the remnant of Judah (Jer 44:12–14, 27)). Jacob and Joseph both died here (Ge 50). Moses led Israelites out of slavery in Egypt (Ex 3–12). They were tempted to return to its relative security (Ex 13:17; 14:11–12; Nu 14:2–4; Ac 7:39). Figuratively a place of false security and hope (2Ki 18:21; Isa 20:5–6; 30:1–3; 31:1–3; 36:6; Jer 2:18; Eze 17:15–17). A centre of idolatry (Lev 18:3; Ezr 9:1; Isa 19:1, 3; Eze 20:7–8). Its downfall prophesied (Isa 19; Jer 46; Eze 29–32), but it will eventually turn to the LORD (Isa 19:19; Zec 14:16–19).

Ge 12:10 and Abram went down to **E** to live
12:11 he was about to enter **E**, he said to
12:14 Abram came to **E**, the Egyptians saw
13: 1 Abram went up from **E** to the Negev,
13:10 like the land of **E**, towards Zoar.
15:18 **E** to the great river, the Euphrates—
21:21 mother got a wife for him from **E**.
25:18 near the border of **E**, as you go
26: 2 "Do not go down to **E**; live in the
37:25 on their way to take them down to **E**.
37:28 the Ishmaelites, who took him to **E**.
37:36 the Midianites sold Joseph in **E** to
39: 1 Now Joseph had been taken down to **E**.
40: 1 the king of **E** offended their master,
40: 1 their master, the king of **E**.
40: 5 and the baker of the king of **E**,
41: 8 all the magicians and wise men of **E**.
41:19 such ugly cows in all the land of **E**.
41:29 are coming throughout the land of **E**,
41:30 Then all the abundance in **E** will be
41:33 put him in charge of the land of **E**.
41:34 a fifth of the harvest of **E** during
41:36 of famine that will come upon **E**,
41:41 in charge of the whole land of **E**."
41:43 in charge of the whole land of **E**.
41:44 will lift hand or foot in all **E**."
41:45 Joseph went throughout the land of **E**.
41:46 the service of Pharaoh king of **E**.
41:46 presence and travelled throughout **E**.
41:48 in **E** and stored it in the cities.
41:53 The seven years of abundance in **E**
41:54 the whole land of **E** there was food.
41:55 all **E** began to feel the famine, the
41:56 the famine was severe throughout **E**.
41:57 all the countries came to **E** to buy
42: 1 learned that there was grain in **E**,
42: 2 have heard that there is grain in **E**.
42: 3 went down to buy grain from **E**.
43: 2 the grain they had brought from **E**,
43:15 hurried down to **E** and presented
45: 4 Joseph, the one you sold into **E**!
45: 8 entire household and ruler of all **E**.
45: 9 says: God has made me lord of all **E**.
45:13 all the honour accorded me in **E**
45:18 give you the best of the land of **E**
45:19 'Do this: Take some carts from **E** for
45:20 the best of all **E** will be yours.'"
45:23 loaded with the best things of **E**,
45:25 they went up out of **E** and came to
45:26 In fact, he is ruler of all **E**.
46: 3 "Do not be afraid to go down to **E**,
46: 4 I will go down to **E** with you, and I
46: 6 and all his offspring went to **E**.
46: 7 He took with him to **E** his sons and
Ge 46: 8 who went to **E**: Reuben the firstborn
46:20 In **E**, Manasseh and Ephraim were born
46:26 All those who went to **E** with
46:27 who had been born to Joseph in **E**,
46:27 went to **E**, were seventy in all.
47: 6 the land of **E** is before you; settle
47:11 his brothers in **E** and gave them
47:13 both **E** and Canaan wasted away
47:14 the money that was to be found in **E**
47:15 the money of the people of **E** and
47:15 all **E** came to Joseph and said, "Give
47:20 Joseph bought all the land in **E** for
47:21 from one end of **E** to the other.
47:26 it as a law concerning land in **E**
47:27 Now the Israelites settled in **E** in
47:28 Jacob lived in **E** seventeen years,
47:29 Do not bury me in **E**,
47:30 carry me out of **E** and bury me where
48: 5 your two sons born to you in **E**
50: 7 court and all the dignitaries of **E**—
50:14 Joseph returned to **E**, together with
50:22 Joseph stayed in **E**, along with all
50:26 him, he was placed in a coffin in **E**.
Ex 1: 1 of Israel who went to **E** with Jacob,
1: 5 in all; Joseph was already in **E**.
1: 8 about Joseph, came to power in **E**.
1:15 The king of **E** said to the Hebrew
1:17 the king of **E** had told them to do;
1:18 the king of **E** summoned the midwives
2:23 long period, the king of **E** died.
3: 7 seen the misery of my people in **E**.
3:10 my people the Israelites out of **E**."
3:11 and bring the Israelites out of **E**?"
3:12 have brought the people out of **E**,
3:16 seen what has been done to you in **E**.
3:17 out of your misery in **E** into the land
3:18 go to the king of **E** and say to him,
3:19 I know that the king of **E** will not
4:18 "Let me go back to my own people in **E**
4:19 "Go back to **E**, for all the men who
4:20 on a donkey and started back to **E**.
4:21 "When you return to **E**, see that you
5: 4 the king of **E** said, "Moses and Aaron,
5:12 the people scattered all over **E** to
6:11 "Go, tell Pharaoh king of **E** to let
6:13 Israelites and Pharaoh king of **E**,
6:13 to bring the Israelites out of **E**.
6:26 out of **E** by their divisions."
6:27 who spoke to Pharaoh king of **E** about
6:27 bringing the Israelites out of **E**.
6:28 Now when the LORD spoke to Moses in **E**
6:29 king of **E** everything I tell you."
7: 3 miraculous signs and wonders in **E**,
7: 4 Then I will lay my hand on **E** and
7: 5 when I stretch out my hand against **E**
7:19 over the waters of **E**—over the
7:19 Blood will be everywhere in **E**, even
7:21 Blood was everywhere in **E**.
8: 5 frogs come up on the land of **E**.'"
8: 6 out his hand over the waters of **E**,
8: 7 made frogs come up on the land of **E**.
8:16 throughout the land of **E** the dust
8:17 the land of **E** became gnats.
8:24 throughout **E** the land was ruined by
9: 4 livestock of Israel and that of **E**,
9: 9 fine dust over the whole land of **E**,
9:18 hailstorm that has ever fallen on **E**,
9:22 hail will fall all over **E**—on men
9:22 growing in the fields of **E**."
9:23 LORD rained hail on the land of **E**;
9:24 the worst storm in all the land of **E**
9:25 Throughout **E** hail struck everything
10: 7 not yet realise that **E** is ruined?"
10:12 "Stretch out your hand over **E** so
10:13 Moses stretched out his staff over **E**,
10:14 they invaded all **E** and settled down
10:15 tree or plant in all the land of **E**.
10:19 Not a locust was left anywhere in **E**.
10:21 over **E**—darkness that can be felt."
10:22 covered all **E** for three days.
11: 1 one more plague on Pharaoh and on **E**.
11: 3 highly regarded in **E** by Pharaoh's
11: 4 midnight I will go throughout **E**.
11: 5 Every firstborn son in **E** will die,
11: 6 will be loud wailing throughout **E**
11: 7 a distinction between **E** and Israel.

Ex 11: 9 my wonders may be multiplied in E."
12: 1 The LORD said to Moses and Aaron in E
12:12 same night I will pass through E
12:12 bring judgment on all the gods of E.
12:13 will touch you when I strike E.
12:17 I brought your divisions out of E.
12:27 the houses of the Israelites in E
12:29 struck down all the firstborn in E,
12:30 and there was loud wailing in E, for
12:39 the dough they had brought from E,
12:39 they had been driven out of E
12:40 people lived in E was 430 years.
12:41 all the LORD's divisions left E.
12:42 that night to bring them out of E,
12:51 out of E by their divisions.
13: 3 the day you came out of E, out of
13: 8 did for me when I came out of E.'
13: 9 you out of E with his mighty hand.
13:14 the LORD brought us out of E, out of
13:15 firstborn in E, both man and animal.
13:16 us out of E with his mighty hand."
13:17 change their minds and return to E."
13:18 went up out of E armed for battle.
14: 5 the king of E was told that the
14: 7 other chariots of E, with officers
14: 8 the heart of Pharaoh king of E,
14:11 because there were no graves in E
14:11 done to us by bringing us out of E?
14:12 Didn't we say to you in E, 'Leave us
14:20 coming between the armies of E and
14:25 LORD is fighting for them against E."
16: 1 month after they had come out of E.
16: 3 we had died by the LORD's hand in E!
16: 6 the LORD who brought you out of E,
16:32 when I brought you out of E.'"
17: 3 "Why did you bring us up out of E to
18: 1 LORD had brought Israel out of E.
19: 1 month after the Israelites left E—
19: 4 what I did to E, and how I carried
20: 2 out of E, out of the land of slavery.
22:21 him, for you were aliens in E.
23: 9 because you were aliens in E.
23:15 for in that month you came out of E.
29:46 out of E so that I might dwell among
32: 1 Moses who brought us up out of E,
32: 4 Israel, who brought you up out of E."
32: 7 up out of E, have become corrupt.
32: 8 Israel, who brought you up out of E.'
32:11 brought out of E with great power
32:23 Moses who brought us up out of E,
33: 1 the people you brought up out of E,
34:18 for in that month you came out of E.
Lev 11:45 brought you up out of E to be your
18: 3 You must not do as they do in E,
19:34 yourself, for you were aliens in E.
19:36 your God, who brought you out of E.
22:33 who brought you out of E to be your
23:43 booths when I brought them out of E.
25:38 who brought you out of E to give you
25:42 servants, whom I brought out of E,
25:55 servants, whom I brought out of E.
26:13 who brought you out of E so that you
26:45 ancestors whom I brought out of E
Nu 1: 1 after the Israelites came out of E.
3:13 I struck down all the firstborn in E,
8:17 the firstborn in E, I set them apart
9: 1 year after they came out of E.
11: 5 We remember the fish we ate in E at
11:18 to eat! We were better off in E!"
11:20 "Why did we ever leave E?"'
13:22 built seven years before Zoan in E.)
14: 2 we had died in E! Or in this desert!
14: 3 be better for us to go back to E?"
14: 4 choose a leader and go back to E."
14:19 the time they left E until now."
14:22 miraculous signs I performed in E
15:41 brought you out of E to be your God.
20: 5 Why did you bring us up out of E to
20:15 Our forefathers went down into E,
20:16 an angel and brought us out of E.
21: 5 "Why have you brought us up out of E
22: 5 "A people has come out of E; they
22:11 'A people that has come out of E
23:22 God brought them out of E; they have
24: 8 "God brought them out of E; they
26: 4 the Israelites who came out of E:

Nu 26:59 who was born to the Levites in E.
32:11 who came up out of E will see the
33: 1 when they came out of E by divisions
33:38 after the Israelites came out of E.
34: 5 the Wadi of E and end at the Sea.
Dt 1:27 so he brought us out of E to deliver
1:30 for you in E, before your very eyes,
4:20 out of E, to be the people of his
4:34 for you in E before your very eyes?
4:37 he brought you out of E by his
4:45 gave them when they came out of E
4:46 Israelites as they came out of E.
5: 6 out of E, out of the land of slavery.
5:15 Remember that you were slaves in E
6:12 out of E, out of the land of slavery.
6:21 "We were slaves of Pharaoh in E, but
6:21 us out of E with a mighty hand.
6:22 wonders—great and terrible—upon E
7: 8 from the power of Pharaoh king of E.
7:15 the horrible diseases you knew in E,
7:18 God did to Pharaoh and to all E.
8:14 out of E, out of the land of slavery.
9: 7 From the day you left E until you
9:12 out of E have become corrupt.
9:26 brought out of E with a mighty hand.
10:19 for you yourselves were aliens in E.
10:22 Your forefathers who went down into E
11: 3 the things he did in the heart of E,
11: 3 king of E and to his whole country;
11:10 take over is not like the land of E,
13: 5 who brought you out of E and
13:10 out of E, out of the land of slavery.
15:15 Remember that you were slaves in E
16: 1 he brought you out of E by night.
16: 3 because you left E in haste—so that
16: 3 the time of your departure from E.
16: 6 of your departure from E.
16:12 Remember that you were slaves in E,
17:16 return to E to get more of them,
20: 1 you up out of E, will be with you.
23: 4 on your way when you came out of E,
24: 9 the way after you came out of E.
24:18 Remember that you were slaves in E
24:22 Remember that you were slaves in E.
25:17 the way when you came out of E.
26: 5 and he went down into E with a few
26: 8 the LORD brought us out of E with a
28:27 the boils of E and with tumours,
28:60 the diseases of E that you dreaded,
28:68 LORD will send you back in ships to E
29: 2 that the LORD did in E to Pharaoh,
29:16 You yourselves know how we lived in E
29:25 them when he brought them out of E.
34:11 wonders the LORD sent him to do in E
Jos 2:10 when you came out of E, and what you
5: 4 All those who came out of E—all the
5: 4 desert on the way after leaving E.
5: 5 during the journey from E had not.
5: 6 age when they left E had died,
5: 9 away the reproach of E from you.
9: 9 of him: all that he did in E,
13: 3 the Shihor River on the east of E
15: 4 the Wadi of E, ending at the sea.
15:47 the Wadi of E and the coastline of
24: 4 Jacob and his sons went down to E.
24: 6 I brought your fathers out of E, you
24:14 River and in E, and serve the LORD.
24:17 us and our fathers up out of E,
24:32 Israelites had brought up from E,
Jdg 2: 1 "I brought you up out of E and led
2:12 who had brought them out of E.
6: 8 out of E, out of the land of slavery.
6: 9 I snatched you from the power of E
6:13 did not the LORD bring us up out of E
11:13 "When Israel came up out of E, they
11:16 when they came up out of E, Israel
19:30 day the Israelites came up out of E.
1Sa 2:27 when they were in E under Pharaoh?
8: 8 them up out of E until this day,
10:18 'I brought Israel up out of E, and I
10:18 I delivered you from the power of E
12: 6 your forefathers up out of E.
12: 8 "After Jacob entered E, they cried
12: 8 out of E and settled them in this
15: 2 waylaid them as they came up from E.
15: 6 when they came up out of E.

1Sa 15: 7 Havilah to Shur, to the east of E.
27: 8 the land extending to Shur and E.)
2Sa 7: 6 Israelites up out of E to this day.
7:23 people, whom you redeemed from E?
1Ki 3: 1 king of E and married his daughter.
4:21 as far as the border of E.
4:30 greater than all the wisdom of E.
6: 1 the Israelites had come out of E,
8: 9 Israelites after they came out of E.
8:16 I brought my people Israel out of E,
8:21 when he brought them out of E."
8:51 out of E, out of that iron-smelting
8:53 LORD, brought our fathers out of E."
8:65 from Lebo Hamath to the Wadi of E.
9: 9 who brought their fathers out of E,
9:16 (Pharaoh king of E had attacked and
10:28 Solomon's horses were imported from E
10:29 They imported a chariot from E for
11:17 Hadad, still only a boy, fled to E
11:18 they went to E, to Pharaoh king of E,
11:21 While he was in E, Hadad heard that
11:40 but Jeroboam fled to E, to Shishak
12: 2 Nebat heard this (he was still in E,
12: 2 King Solomon), he returned from E.
12:28 Israel, who brought you up out of E."
14:25 Shishak king of E attacked Jerusalem.
2Ki 17: 4 he had sent envoys to So king of E,
17: 7 who had brought them up out of E
17: 7 the power of Pharaoh king of E.
17:36 the LORD, who brought you up out of E
18:21 Look now, you are depending on E,
18:21 king of E to all who depend on him.
18:24 depending on E for chariots and
19: 9 Tirhakah, the Cushite king ⌊of E⌋
19:24 have dried up all the streams of E."
21:15 came out of E until this day."
23:29 Pharaoh Neco king of E went up to
23:34 him off to E, and there he died.
24: 7 The king of E did not march out from
24: 7 Wadi of E to the Euphrates River.
25:26 fled to E for fear of the Babylonians
1Ch 13: 5 from the Shihor River in E to Lebo
17: 5 Israel up out of E to this day.
17:21 people, whom you redeemed from E?
2Ch 1:16 Solomon's horses were imported from E
1:17 They imported a chariot from E for
5:10 Israelites after they came out of E.
6: 5 day I brought my people out of E,
7: 8 from Lebo Hamath to the Wadi of E.
7:22 who brought them out of E, and have
9:26 as far as the border of E.
9:28 Solomon's horses were imported from E
10: 2 of Nebat heard this (he was in E,
10: 2 King Solomon), he returned from E.
12: 2 Shishak king of E attacked Jerusalem
12: 3 Cushites that came with him from E,
12: 9 Shishak king of E attacked Jerusalem,
20:10 to invade when they came from E;
26: 8 spread as far as the border of E,
35:20 Neco king of E went up to fight at
36: 3 The king of E dethroned him in
36: 4 The king of E made Eliakim, a
36: 4 Jehoahaz and carried him off to E.
Ne 9: 9 suffering of our forefathers in E;
9:18 your god, who brought you up out of E
Ps 68:31 Envoys will come from E; Cush will
78:12 land of E, in the region of Zoan.
78:43 his miraculous signs in E, his
78:51 He struck down all the firstborn of E
80: 8 You brought a vine out of E; you
81: 5 Joseph when he went out against E,
81:10 God, who brought you up out of E.
105:23 Israel entered E; Jacob lived as an
105:38 E was glad when they left, because
106: 7 our fathers were in E, they gave no
106:21 who had done great things in E,
114: 1 Israel came out of E, the house of
135: 8 He struck down the firstborn of E,
135: 9 and wonders into your midst, O E,
136:10 who struck down the firstborn of E
Pr 7:16 my bed with coloured linens from E.
Isa 7:18 flies from the distant streams of E
10:24 up a club against you, as E did.
10:26 over the waters, as he did in E.
11:11 from Lower E, from Upper E, from
11:16 for Israel when they came up from E.

Isa 19: 1 An oracle concerning E: See, the LORD
19: 1 on a swift cloud and is coming to E.
19: 1 The idols of E tremble before him,
19: 6 streams of E will dwindle and dry up.
19:12 LORD Almighty has planned against E.
19:13 of her peoples have led E astray.
19:14 make E stagger in all that she does,
19:15 There is nothing E can do—head or
19:18 In that day five cities in E will
19:19 altar to the LORD in the heart of E,
19:20 the LORD Almighty in the land of E.
19:22 The LORD will strike E with a plague;
19:23 will be a highway from E to Assyria.
19:23 The Assyrians will go to E and the
19:24 along with E and Assyria, a blessing
19:25 "Blessed be E my people, Assyria my
20: 3 sign and portent against E and Cush,
20: 5 E will be afraid and put to shame.
23: 5 When word comes to E, they will be
27:12 flowing Euphrates to the Wadi of E,
27:13 those who were exiled in E will come
30: 2 who go down to E without consulting
30: 7 to E, whose help is utterly useless.
31: 1 Woe to those who go down to E for
36: 6 Look now, you are depending on E,
36: 6 king of E to all who depend on him.
36: 9 depending on E for chariots and
37: 9 Tirhakah, the Cushite king ⌊of E⌋
37:25 have dried up all the streams of E.'
43: 3 I give E for your ransom, Cush and
45:14 "The products of E and the
52: 4 "At first my people went down to E
Jer 2: 6 who brought us up out of E and led
2:18 Now why go to E to drink water from
2:36 by E as you were by Assyria.
7:22 out of E and spoke to them, I did not
7:25 From the time your forefathers left E
9:26 E, Judah, Edom, Ammon, Moab and all
11: 4 out of E, out of the iron-smelting
11: 7 forefathers up from E until today,
16:14 brought the Israelites up out of E,'
23: 7 brought the Israelites up out of E,'
24: 8 remain in this land or live in E.
25:19 Pharaoh king of E, his attendants,
26:21 heard of it and fled in fear to E.
26:22 to E, along with some other men.
26:23 They brought Uriah out of E and took
31:32 by the hand to lead them out of E,
32:20 wonders in E and have continued them
32:21 out of E with signs and wonders,
34:13 out of E, out of the land of slavery.
37: 5 Pharaoh's army had marched out of E,
37: 7 will go back to its own land, to E.
41:17 near Bethlehem on their way to E
42:14 'No, we will go and live in E, where
42:15 determined to go to E and you do go
42:16 you into E, and there you will die.
42:17 all who are determined to go to E to
42:18 poured out on you when you go to E.
42:19 LORD has told you, 'Do not go to E.
43: 2 must not go to E to settle there.'
43: 7 they entered E in disobedience to
43:11 He will come and attack E, bringing
43:12 to the temples of the gods of E;
43:12 so will he wrap E round himself and
43:13 There in the temple of the sun in E
43:13 down the temples of the gods of E.'"
44: 1 Jews living in Lower E—in Migdol,
44: 1 and Memphis—and in Upper E:
44: 8 burning incense to other gods in E,
44:12 to go to E to settle there.
44:12 They will all perish in E; they will
44:13 I will punish those who live in E
44:14 have gone to live in E will escape
44:15 Lower and Upper E, said to Jeremiah,
44:24 LORD, all you people of Judah in E.
44:26 all Jews living in E: 'I swear by my
44:26 from Judah living anywhere in E
44:27 not for good; the Jews in E will
44:28 of Judah from E will be very few.
44:28 E will know whose word will stand
44:30 Hophra king of E over to his enemies
46: 2 Concerning E: This is the message
46: 2 the army of Pharaoh Neco king of E,
46: 8 E rises like the Nile, like rivers
46:11 get balm, O Virgin Daughter of E.
Jer 46:13 king of Babylon to attack E:
46:14 "Announce this in E, and proclaim it
46:17 'Pharaoh king of E is only a loud
46:19 you who live in E, for Memphis will
46:20 "E is a beautiful heifer, but a
46:22 E will hiss like a fleeing serpent
46:24 The Daughter of E will be put to
46:25 on Pharaoh, on E and her gods and
46:26 Later, however, E will be inhabited
Lam 5: 6 We submitted to E and Assyria to get
Eze 17:15 to E to get horses and a large army.
19: 4 led him with hooks to the land of E.
20: 5 and revealed myself to them in E.
20: 6 out of E into a land I had searched
20: 7 yourselves with the idols of E.
20: 8 nor did they forsake the idols of E.
20: 8 spend my anger against them in E.
20: 9 Israelites by bringing them out of E.
20:10 Therefore I led them out of E and
20:36 in the desert of the land of E,
23: 3 They became prostitutes in E,
23: 8 the prostitution she began in E,
23:19 when she was a prostitute in E.
23:21 when in E your bosom was caressed
23:27 and prostitution you began in E.
23:27 with longing or remember E any more.
27: 7 Fine embroidered linen from E was
29: 2 your face against Pharaoh king of E
29: 2 against him and against all E.
29: 3 Pharaoh king of E, you great monster
29: 6 all who live in E will know that I
29: 9 E will become a desolate wasteland.
29:10 and I will make the land of E a ruin
29:12 I will make the land of E desolate
29:14 Upper E, the land of their ancestry.
29:16 E will no longer be a source of
29:19 I am going to give E to Nebuchadnezzar
29:20 I have given him E as a reward for
30: 4 A sword will come against E, and
30: 4 When the slain fall in E, her wealth
30: 5 will fall by the sword along with E.
30: 6 "'The allies of E will fall and her
30: 8 E and all her helpers are crushed.
30:10 I will put an end to the hordes of E
30:11 will draw their swords against E and
30:13 longer will there be a prince in E,
30:14 I will lay waste Upper E, set fire
30:15 Pelusium, the stronghold of E,
30:16 I will set fire to E; Pelusium will
30:18 Tahpanhes when I break the yoke of E;
30:19 I will inflict punishment on E, and
30:21 broken the arm of Pharaoh king of E.
30:22 I am against Pharaoh king of E.
30:25 and he brandishes it against E.
31: 2 "Son of man, say to Pharaoh king of E
32: 2 Pharaoh king of E and say to him:
32:12 They will shatter the pride of E,
32:15 I make E desolate and strip the land
32:16 for E and all her hordes they will
32:18 "Son of man, wail for the hordes of E
32:21 will say of E and her allies,
47:19 along the Wadi ⌊of E⌋, to the Great
48:28 along the Wadi ⌊of E⌋, to the Great
Da 9:15 who brought your people out of E
11: 8 and gold and carry them off to E.
11:42 many countries; E will not escape.
11:43 and silver and all the riches of E,
Hos 2:15 as in the day she came up out of E.
7:11 now calling to E, now turning to
7:16 will be ridiculed in the land of E.
8:13 their sins: They will return to E.
9: 3 Ephraim will return to E and eat
9: 6 E will gather them, and Memphis will
11: 1 him, and out of E I called my son.
11: 5 "Will they not return to E and will
11:11 like birds from E, like doves from
12: 1 Assyria and sends olive oil to E.
12: 9 your God, ⌊who brought you⌋ out of E;
12:13 a prophet to bring Israel up from E,
13: 4 your God, ⌊who brought you⌋ out of E.
Joel 3:19 E will be desolate, Edom a desert
Am 2:10 "I brought you up out of E, and I
3: 1 whole family I brought up out of E:
3: 9 Ashdod and to the fortresses of E:
4:10 plagues among you as I did to E.
8: 8 and then sink like the river of E.
Am 9: 5 then sinks like the river of E—
9: 7 "Did I not bring Israel up from E,
Mic 6: 4 I brought you up out of E and
7:12 from Assyria and the cities of E,
7:12 even from E to the Euphrates and
7:15 in the days when you came out of E,
Na 3: 9 Cush and E were her boundless
Hag 2: 5 with you when you came out of E.
Zec 10:10 I will bring them back from E and
14:19 This will be the punishment of E and
Mt 2:13 and his mother and escape to E.
2:14 during the night and left for E,
2:15 said through the prophet: "Out of E I
2:19 appeared in a dream to Joseph in E
Ac 2:10 Phrygia and Pamphylia, E and the
7: 9 they sold him as a slave into E.
7:10 the goodwill of Pharaoh king of E;
7:10 him ruler over E and all his palace.
7:11 "Then a famine struck all E and
7:12 Jacob heard that there was grain in E
7:15 Jacob went down to E, where he and
7:17 our people in E greatly increased.
7:18 about Joseph, became ruler of E.
7:34 the oppression of my people in E.
7:34 Now come, I will send you back to E.'
7:36 He led them out of E and did wonders
7:36 wonders and miraculous signs in E,
7:39 in their hearts turned back to E.
7:40 fellow Moses who led us out of E
13:17 prosper during their stay in E,
Heb 3:16 not all those Moses led out of E?
8: 9 by the hand to lead them out of E,
11:22 the exodus of the Israelites from E
11:26 value than the treasures of E,
11:27 By faith he left E, not fearing the
Jude : 5 Lord delivered his people out of E,
Rev 11: 8 is figuratively called Sodom and E,

Egypt's (Egypt)

Isa 20: 4 with buttocks bared—to E shame.
30: 2 protection, to E shade for refuge.
30: 3 E shade will bring you disgrace.
Eze 30: 9 the day of E doom, for it is sure to
Zec 10:11 down and E sceptre will pass away.

Egyptian (Egypt)

Ge 16: 1 had an E maidservant named Hagar;
16: 3 his wife took her E maidservant Hagar
21: 9 the son whom Hagar the E had borne
25:12 Hagar the E, bore to Abraham.
39: 1 Potiphar, an E who was one of
39: 2 lived in the house of his E master.
39: 5 LORD blessed the household of the E
Ex 1:19 "Hebrew women are not like E women;
2:11 He saw an E beating a Hebrew, one of
2:12 killed the E and hid him in the sand.
2:14 of killing me as you killed the E?"
2:19 They answered, "An E rescued us from
7:11 and the E magicians also did the
7:22 the E magicians did the same things
14:24 E army and threw it into confusion.
Lev 24:10 an E father went out among the
Dt 11: 4 what he did to the E army, to its
23: 7 Do not abhor an E, because you lived
1Sa 30:11 They found an E in a field and
30:13 I am an E, the slave of an Amalekite.
2Sa 23:21 he struck down a huge E. Although
23:21 Although the E had a spear in his
2Ki 7: 6 Hittite and E kings to attack us!"
1Ch 2:34 He had an E servant named Jarha.
11:23 he struck down an E who was seven
11:23 Although the E had a spear like a
Isa 11:15 will dry up the gulf of the E sea;
19: 2 "I will stir up E against E—
20: 4 the E captives and Cushite exiles,
Zec 14:18 If the E people do not go up and
Ac 7:24 of them being ill-treated by an E,
7:24 and avenged him by killing the E.
7:28 me as you killed the E yesterday?'
21:38 "Aren't you the E who started a

Egyptian's (Egypt)

2Sa 23:21 He snatched the spear from the E
1Ch 11:23 He snatched the spear from the E

Egyptians (Egypt)
Ge 12:12 the E see you, they will say, 'This
12:14 Abram came to Egypt, the E saw that
41:55 Then Pharaoh told all the E, "Go to
41:56 storehouses and sold grain to the E,
43:32 and the E who ate with him by
43:32 because E could not eat with Hebrews,
43:32 Hebrews, for that is detestable to E.
45: 2 he wept so loudly that the E heard
46:34 shepherds are detestable to the E."
47:20 The E, one and all, sold their
50: 3 the E mourned for him seventy days.
50:11 "The E are holding a solemn ceremony
Ex 1:12 the E came to dread the Israelites
1:14 labour the E used them ruthlessly.
3: 8 rescue them from the hand of the E
3: 9 the way the E are oppressing them.
3:20 strike the E with all the wonders
3:21 "And I will make the E favourably
3:22 And so you will plunder the E."
6: 5 whom the E are enslaving, and I have
6: 6 out from under the yoke of the E.
6: 7 out from under the yoke of the E.
7: 5 the E will know that I am the LORD
7:18 the E will not be able to drink its
7:21 the E could not drink its water.
7:24 all the E dug along the Nile to get
8:21 The houses of the E will be full of
8:26 God would be detestable to the E.
9: 6 All the livestock of the E died, but
9:11 that were on them and on all the E.
10: 2 how I dealt harshly with the E
10: 6 all the E—something neither your
11: 3 (The LORD made the E favourably
12:23 the land to strike down the E,
12:27 our homes when he struck down the E.
12:30 all the E got up during the night,
12:33 The E urged the people to hurry and
12:35 asked the E for articles of silver
12:36 The LORD had made the E favourably
12:36 asked for; so they plundered the E.
14: 4 the E will know that I am the LORD.
14: 9 The E—all Pharaoh's horses and
14:10 were the E, marching after them.
14:12 'Leave us alone; let us serve the E'
14:12 better for us to serve the E than to
14:13 The E you see today you will never
14:17 I will harden the hearts of the E so
14:18 The E will know that I am the LORD
14:23 The E pursued them, and all
14:25 And the E said, "Let's get away from
14:26 waters may flow back over the E
14:27 The E were fleeing towards it, and
14:30 Israel from the hands of the E,
14:30 saw the E lying dead on the shore.
14:31 the LORD displayed against the E,
15:26 any of the diseases I brought on the E
18: 8 LORD had done to Pharoah and the E
18: 9 them from the hand of the E.
18:10 the hand of the E and of Pharaoh,
18:10 the people from the hand of the E.
32:12 Why should the E say, 'It was with
Lev 26:13 would no longer be slaves to the E;
Nu 14:13 Moses said to the LORD, "Then the E
20:15 The E ill-treated us and our fathers,
33: 3 boldly in full view of all the E,
Dt 26: 6 the E ill-treated us and made us
Jos 24: 5 and I afflicted the E by what I did
24: 6 you came to the sea, and the E
24: 7 put darkness between you and the E;
24: 7 your own eyes what I did to the E.
Jdg 10:11 The LORD replied, "When the E, the
1Sa 4: 8 They are the gods who struck the E
6: 6 you harden your hearts as the E and
Ezr 9: 1 Ammonites, Moabites, E and Amorites.
Ne 9:10 how arrogantly the E treated them.
Isa 19: 1 hearts of the E melt within them.
19: 3 The E will lose heart, and I will
19: 4 I will hand the E over to the power
19:16 In that day the E will be like women.
19:17 of Judah will bring terror to the E;
19:21 will make himself known to the E,
19:23 go to Egypt and the E to Assyria.
19:23 The E and Assyrians will worship
31: 3 the E are men and not God; their
Eze 16:26 engaged in prostitution with the E,
29:12 And I will disperse the E among the
29:13 I will gather the E from the nations
30:23 I will disperse the E among the
30:26 I will disperse the E among the
Ac 7:22 educated in all the wisdom of the E
Heb 11:29 E tried to do so, they were drowned.

Ehi
Ge 46:21 E, Rosh, Muppim, Huppim and Ard.

Ehud
Jdg 3:15 and he gave them a deliverer—E, a
3:16 Now E had made a double-edged sword
3:18 After E had presented the tribute,
3:20 E then approached him while he was
3:21 E reached with his left hand, drew
3:22 E did not pull the sword out, and
3:23 E went out to the porch; he shut the
3:26 While they waited, E got away. He
3:31 After E came Shamgar son of Anath,
4: 1 After E died, the Israelites once
1Ch 7:10 Benjamin, E, Kenaanah, Zethan,
8: 6 These were the descendants of E, who

Ejected
Ac 18:16 he had them e from the court.

Eker
1Ch 2:27 of Jerahmeel: Maaz, Jamin and E.

Ekron
Most northern of 5 principal Philistine cities, about 35 miles west of Jerusalem. Not conquered by Joshua (Jos 13:1–3), but allotted to Judah (Jos 15:45), and later Dan (Jos 19:43). Ark of covenant brought here (1Sa 5:10), and the 5 Philistine rulers return here (1Sa 6:16). Philistine army fled here from Israelite army (1Sa 17:52). Baal-Zebub worshipped, and consulted by Ahaziah who dies as a result (2Ki 1). Its judgment is pronounced (Jer 25:20; Am 1:8; Zep 2:4; Zec 9:5, 7).

Jos 13: 3 to the territory of E on the north,
13: 3 Gath and E—that of the Avvites);
15:11 went to the northern slope of E,
15:45 E, with its surrounding settlements
15:46 west of E, all that were in the
19:43 Elon, Timnah, E,
Jdg 1:18 and E—each city with its territory.
1Sa 5:10 they sent the ark of God to E. As
5:10 As the ark of God was entering E,
5:10 the people of E cried out, "They
6:16 then returned that same day to E.
6:17 Ashdod, Gaza, Ashkelon, Gath and E.
7:14 The towns from E to Gath that the
17:52 of Gath and to the gates of E.
17:52 the Shaaraim road to Gath and E.
2Ki 1: 2 the god of E, to see if I will
1: 3 consult Baal-Zebub, the god of E?'
1: 6 consult Baal-Zebub, the god of E?
1:16 consult Baal-Zebub, the god of E?
Jer 25:20 E, and the people left at Ashdod);
Am 1: 8 I will turn my hand against E, till
Zep 2: 4 will be emptied and E uprooted.
Zec 9: 5 and E too, for her hope will wither.
9: 7 and E will be like the Jebusites.

El Bethel
Ge 35: 7 and he called the place E, because

El Elohe Israel
Ge 33:20 he set up an altar and called it E.

El Paran
Ge 14: 6 Seir, as far as E near the desert.

Ela
1Ki 4:18 Shimei son of E—in Benjamin;

Elah (Elah's)
Ge 36:41 Oholibamah, E, Pinon,
1Sa 17: 2 camped in the Valley of E and drew
1Sa 17:19 in the Valley of E, fighting against
21: 9 whom you killed in the Valley of E,
1Ki 16: 6 And E his son succeeded him as king.
16: 8 E son of Baasha became king of
16: 9 E was in Tirzah at the time, getting
16:13 of all the sins Baasha and his son E
2Ki 15:30 Hoshea son of E conspired against
17: 1 Hoshea son of E became king of
18: 1 In the third year of Hoshea son of E
18: 9 of Hoshea son of E king of Israel,
1Ch 1:52 Oholibamah, E, Pinon,
4:15 son of Jephunneh: Iru, E and Naam.
4:15 The son of E: Kenaz.
9: 8 E son of Uzzi, the son of Micri;

Elah's (Elah)
1Ki 16:14 for the other events of E reign, and

Elam (Elam's, Elamites)
Region east of Babylonia, named after son of Shem, ancestor of the Elamites (Ge 10:22; 1Ch 1:17). Capital city is Susa or Shushan (Da 8:2). Its king captured Lot in Sodom (Ge 14:1–17). Some Israelites exiled here by Assyria (Isa 11:11; Ac 2:9) and Elamites settled in Samaria (Ezr 4:9). Its part in Babylon's downfall was prophesied (Isa 21:2; 22:6), but it too would receive God's judgment (Jer 25:15–26; 49:34–39; Eze 32:24–25).

Ge 10:22 The sons of Shem: E, Asshur,
14: 1 Kedorlaomer king of E and Tidal king
14: 9 against Kedorlaomer king of E, Tidal
1Ch 1:17 The sons of Shem: E, Asshur,
8:24 Hananiah, E, Anthothijah,
26: 3 E the fifth, Jehohanan the sixth and
Ezr 2: 7 of E 1,254
2:31 of the other E 1,254
8: 7 of the descendants of E, Jeshaiah
10: 2 one of the descendants of E, said to
10:26 From the descendants of E: Mattaniah,
Ne 7:12 of E 1,254
7:34 of the other E 1,254
10:14 Parosh, Pahath-Moab, E, Zattu, Bani,
12:42 Jehohanan, Malkijah, E and Ezer.
Isa 11:11 from Upper Egypt, from Cush, from E,
21: 2 E, attack! Media, lay siege! I will
22: 6 E takes up the quiver, with her
Jer 25:25 all the kings of Zimri, E and Media;
49:34 Jeremiah the prophet concerning E,
49:35 "See, I will break the bow of E, the
49:36 I will bring against E the four
49:37 I will shatter E before their foes,
49:38 I will set my throne in E and
49:39 "Yet I will restore the fortunes of E
Eze 32:24 "E is there, with all her hordes
Da 8: 2 of Susa in the province of E;

Elam's (Elam)
Jer 49:36 a nation where E exiles do not go.

Elamites (Elam)
Ezr 4: 9 Erech and Babylon, the E of Susa,
Ac 2: 9 Parthians, Medes and E; residents of

Elapsed
1Sa 18:26 So before the allotted time e,

Elasah
Ezr 10:22 Ishmael, Nethanel, Jozabad and E.
Jer 29: 3 the letter to E son of Shaphan and

Elated (Elation)
1Sa 11: 9 to the men of Jabesh, they were e.

Elath
Dt 2: 8 which comes up from E and Ezion
1Ki 9:26 which is near E in Edom, on the
2Ki 14:22 He was the one who rebuilt E and
16: 6 Rezin king of Aram recovered E for
16: 6 Edomites then moved into E and have
2Ch 8:17 Solomon went to Ezion Geber and E on
26: 2 He was the one who rebuilt E and

Elation (Elated)

Pr 28:12 righteous triumph, there is great **e**;

El-Berith

Jdg 9:46 the stronghold of the temple of **E**.

Eldaah

Ge 25: 4 Ephah, Epher, Hanoch, Abida and **E**.
1Ch 1:33 Ephah, Epher, Hanoch, Abida and **E**.

Eldad

Nu 11:26 two men, whose names were **E** and Medad
11:27 "**E** and Medad are prophesying in the

Elder (Elderly, Elders, Fellow-elder)

Isa 3: 2 and prophet, the soothsayer and **e**,
1Ti 5:19 an accusation against an **e** unless it
Tit 1: 6 An **e** must be blameless, the husband
2Jn : 1 The **e**, To the chosen lady and her
3Jn : 1 The **e**, To my dear friend Gaius, whom

Elderly (Elder)

Lev 19:32 show respect for the **e** and revere

Elders (Elder, *Elders of Israel*)

Ex 3:18 Then you and the **e** are to go to the
4:29 all the **e** of the Israelites,
19: 7 Moses went back and summoned the **e**
24:14 He said to the **e**, "Wait here for us
Lev 4:15 The **e** of the community are to lay
Nu 11:16 "Bring me seventy of Israel's **e** who
11:24 brought together seventy of their **e**
11:25 and put the Spirit on the seventy **e**.
11:26 They were listed among the **e**, but
22: 4 The Moabites said to the **e** of Midian,
22: 7 The **e** of Moab and Midian left,
Dt 5:23 your tribes and your **e** came to me.
19:12 the **e** of his town shall send for him,
21: 2 your **e** and judges shall go out and
21: 3 the **e** of the town nearest the body
21: 6 all the **e** of the town nearest the
21:19 to the **e** at the gate of his town.
21:20 They shall say to the **e**, "This son
22:15 a virgin to the town **e** at the gate.
22:16 The girl's father will say to the **e**,
22:17 the cloth before the **e** of the town,
22:18 the **e** shall take the man and punish
25: 7 she shall go to the **e** at the town
25: 8 the **e** of his town shall summon him
25: 9 up to him in the presence of the **e**,
29:10 your **e** and officials, and all the
31:28 Assemble before me all the **e** of your
32: 7 your **e**, and they will explain to you.
Jos 8:33 with their **e**, officials and judges,
9:11 our **e** and all those living in our
20: 4 his case before the **e** of that city.
23: 2 summoned all Israel—their **e**,
24: 1 He summoned the **e**, leaders, judges
24:31 of the **e** who outlived him and who
Jdg 2: 7 of the **e** who outlived him and who
8:14 of Succoth, the **e** of the town.
8:16 He took the **e** of the town and taught
11: 5 the **e** of Gilead went to get Jephthah
11: 8 The **e** of Gilead said to him,
11:10 The **e** of Gilead replied, "The LORD
11:11 Jephthah went with the **e** of Gilead,
21:16 the **e** of the assembly said, "With
Ru 4: 2 Boaz took ten of the **e** of the town
4: 4 the presence of the **e** of my people.
4: 9 Boaz announced to the **e** and all the
4:11 the **e** and all those at the gate said,
1Sa 11: 3 The **e** of Jabesh said to him, "Give
15:30 honour me before the **e** of my people
16: 4 When he arrived at Bethlehem, the **e**
30:26 of the plunder to the **e** of Judah,
2Sa 12:17 The **e** of his household stood beside
19:11 "Ask the **e** of Judah, 'Why should you
1Ki 12: 6 King Rehoboam consulted the **e** who
12: 8 Rehoboam rejected the advice the **e**
12:13 the advice given him by the **e**,
20: 7 The king of Israel summoned all the **e**
20: 8 The **e** and the people all answered,
1Ki 21: 8 and sent them to the **e** and nobles
21:11 **e** and nobles who lived in Naboth's
2Ki 6:32 and the **e** were sitting with him.
6:32 Elisha said to the **e**, "Don't you see
10: 1 to the **e** and to the guardians of
10: 5 the city governor, the **e** and the
23: 1 the king called together all the **e**
1Ch 21:16 Then David and the **e**, clothed in
2Ch 10: 6 King Rehoboam consulted the **e** who
10: 8 Rehoboam rejected the advice the **e**
10:13 Rejecting the advice of the **e**,
34:29 the king called together all the **e**
Ezr 5: 5 was watching over the **e** of the Jews,
5: 9 We questioned the **e** and asked them,
6: 7 the Jewish **e** rebuild this house of
6: 8 you are to do for these **e** of the Jews
6:14 the **e** of the Jews continued to build
10: 8 the decision of the officials and **e**,
10:14 along with the **e** and judges of each
Job 12:20 and takes away the discernment of **e**.
Ps 105:22 he pleased and teach his **e** wisdom.
107:32 praise him in the council of the **e**.
119:100 I have more understanding than the **e**,
Pr 31:23 his seat among the **e** of the land.
Isa 3:14 the **e** and leaders of his people:
9:15 the **e** and prominent men are the head,
24:23 and before its **e**, gloriously.
Jer 19: 1 Take along some of the **e** of the
26:17 Some of the **e** of the land stepped
29: 1 to the surviving **e** among the exiles
Lam 1:19 My priests and my **e** perished in the
2:10 The **e** of the Daughter of Zion sit on
4:16 shown no honour, the **e** no favour.
5:12 their hands; **e** are shown no respect.
5:14 The **e** are gone from the city gate;
Eze 7:26 lost, as will the counsel of the **e**.
8: 1 **e** of Judah were sitting before me,
8:11 In front of them stood seventy **e** of
8:12 have you seen what the **e** of the
9: 6 **e** who were in front of the temple.
Joel 1: 2 Hear this, you **e**; listen, all who
1:14 Summon the **e** and all who live in the
2:16 the assembly; bring together the **e**,
Mt 15: 2 break the tradition of the **e**?
16:21 many things at the hands of the **e**,
21:23 and the **e** of the people came to him.
26: 3 the chief priests and the **e** of the
26:47 priests and the **e** of the people.
26:57 of the law and the **e** had assembled.
27: 1 all the chief priests and the **e** of
27: 3 to the chief priests and the **e**.
27:12 and the **e**, he gave no answer.
27:20 the **e** persuaded the crowd to ask for
27:41 of the law and the **e** mocked him.
28:12 the chief priests had met with the **e**
Mk 7: 3 holding to the tradition of the **e**.
7: 5 according to the tradition of the **e**
8:31 things and be rejected by the **e**,
11:27 of the law and the **e** came to him.
14:43 the teachers of the law, and the **e**.
14:53 and all the chief priests, **e** and
15: 1 the chief priests, with the **e**, the
Lk 7: 3 and sent some **e** of the Jews to him,
9:22 things and be rejected by the **e**,
20: 1 together with the **e**, came up to him.
22:52 and the **e**, who had come for him, "Am
22:66 At daybreak the council of the **e** of
Ac 4: 5 The next day the rulers, **e** and
4: 8 "Rulers and **e** of the people!
4:23 priests and **e** had said to them.
6:12 they stirred up the people and the **e**
11:30 gift to the **e** by Barnabas and Saul.
14:23 Paul and Barnabas appointed **e** for
15: 2 apostles and **e** about this question.
15: 4 the church and the apostles and **e**,
15: 6 The apostles and **e** met to consider
15:22 the apostles and **e**, with the whole
15:23 following letter: The apostles and **e**,
16: 4 and **e** in Jerusalem for the people
20:17 to Ephesus for the **e** of the church.
21:18 James, and all the **e** were present.
23:14 They went to the chief priests and **e**
24: 1 the **e** and a lawyer named Tertullus,
25:15 the chief priests and **e** of the Jews
1Ti 4:14 body of **e** laid their hands on you.
5:17 The **e** who direct the affairs of the
Tit 1: 5 appoint **e** in every town, as I
Jas 5:14 He should call the **e** of the church
1Pe 5: 1 To the **e** among you, I appeal as a
Rev 4: 4 seated on them were twenty-four **e**.
4:10 the twenty-four **e** fall down before
5: 5 one of the **e** said to me, "Do not
5: 6 the four living creatures and the **e**.
5: 8 **e** fell down before the Lamb.
5:11 and the living creatures and the **e**.
5:14 and the **e** fell down and worshipped.
7:11 the **e** and the four living creatures.
7:13 one of the **e** asked me, "These in
11:16 the twenty-four **e**, who were seated
14: 3 the four living creatures and the **e**.
19: 4 The twenty-four **e** and the four

Elders of Israel

Ex 3:16 "Go, assemble the **e** and say to them,
3:18 "The **e** will listen to you. Then you
12:21 Moses summoned all the **e** and said to
17: 5 Take with you some of the **e** and take
17: 6 Moses did this in the sight of the **e**.
18:12 came with all the **e** to eat bread with
24: 1 and Abihu, and seventy of the **e**.
24: 9 the seventy **e** went up and saw the
Lev 9: 1 Aaron and his sons and the **e**.
Nu 11:30 Moses and the **e** returned to the camp.
16:25 and Abiram, and the **e** followed him.
Dt 27: 1 Moses and the **e** commanded the people:
31: 9 of the LORD, and to all the **e**.
Jos 7: 6 The **e** did the same, and sprinkled
1Sa 4: 3 returned to camp, the **e** asked, "Why
8: 4 all the **e** gathered together and came
2Sa 3:17 Abner conferred with the **e** and said,
5: 3 all the **e** had come to King David at
17: 4 good to Absalom and to all the **e**.
17:15 and the **e** to do such and such,
1Ki 8: 1 his presence at Jerusalem the **e**,
8: 3 all the **e** had arrived, the priests
1Ch 11: 3 all the **e** had come to King David at
15:25 David and the **e** and the commanders
2Ch 5: 2 Solomon summoned to Jerusalem the **e**,
5: 4 all the **e** had arrived, the Levites
Eze 14: 1 Some of the **e** came to me and sat
20: 1 some of the **e** came to enquire of the
20: 3 "Son of man, speak to the **e** and say
Ac 5:21 the full assembly of the **e**—and sent

Elead

1Ch 7:21 Ezer and **E** were killed by the

Eleadah

1Ch 7:20 his son, **E** his son, Tahath his son,

Elealeh

Nu 32: 3 Heshbon, **E**, Sebam, Nebo and Beon—
32:37 the Reubenites rebuilt Heshbon, **E**
Isa 15: 4 Heshbon and **E** cry out, their voices
16: 9 O Heshbon, O **E**, I drench you with
Jer 48:34 rises from Heshbon to **E** and Jahaz,

Eleasah

1Ch 2:39 of Helez, Helez the father of **E**,
2:40 **E** the father of Sismai, Sismai the
8:37 his son, **E** his son and Azel his son.
9:43 his son, **E** his son and Azel his son.

Eleazar (Eleazar's)

Third son of Aaron (Ex 6:23; Nu 3:2; 1Ch 6:3–4); anointed as priest (Lev 8–9; Nu 3:2–4); leader of Levites, responsible for care of sanctuary (Nu 3:32; 4:16). Succeeded Aaron (Nu 20:28; Dt 10:6); assisted Moses (Nu 26:1–4,63; 27:2; 31:12; 32:2). With Joshua, apportioned land (Nu 32:28; 34:17; Jos 14:1; 19:51). Death (Jos 24:33).

Ex 6:23 him Nadab and Abihu, **E** and Ithamar.
6:25 **E** son of Aaron married one of the
28: 1 with his sons Nadab and Abihu, **E** and
Lev 10: 6 Moses said to Aaron and his sons **E**
10:12 his remaining sons, **E** and Ithamar,
10:16 he was angry with **E** and Ithamar,
Nu 3: 2 firstborn and Abihu, **E** and Ithamar.
3: 4 They had no sons; so only **E** and
3:32 The chief leader of the Levites was **E**

Nu 4:16 "E son of Aaron, the priest, is to
16:37 "Tell E son of Aaron, the priest, to
16:39 E the priest collected the bronze
19: 3 Give it to E the priest; it is to be
19: 4 E the priest is to take some of its
20:25 Call Aaron and his son E and take
20:26 garments and put them on his son E,
20:28 garments and put them on his son E.
20:28 and E came down from the mountain,
25: 7 Phinehas son of E, the son of Aaron,
25:11 "Phinehas son of E, the son of Aaron,
26: 1 Moses and E son of Aaron, the priest,
26: 3 Moses and E the priest spoke with
26:60 of Nadab and Abihu, E and Ithamar.
26:63 the ones counted by Moses and E
27: 2 Moses, E the priest, the leaders and
27:19 Make him stand before E the priest
27:21 He is to stand before E the priest,
27:22 made him stand before E the priest
31: 6 along with Phinehas son of E, the
31:12 spoils and plunder to Moses and E
31:13 Moses, E the priest and all the
31:21 E the priest said to the soldiers
31:26 "You and E the priest and the family
31:29 to E the priest as the LORD's part.
31:31 Moses and E the priest did as the
31:41 Moses gave the tribute to E the
31:51 Moses and E the priest accepted from
31:52 E presented as a gift to the LORD
31:54 Moses and E the priest accepted the
32: 2 they came to Moses and E the priest
32:28 Moses gave orders about them to E
34:17 E the priest and Joshua son of Nun.
Dt 10: 6 E his son succeeded him as priest.
Jos 14: 1 which E the priest, Joshua son of
17: 4 They went to E the priest, Joshua
19:51 These are the territories that E the
21: 1 the Levites approached E the priest,
22:13 the Israelites sent Phinehas son of E
22:31 Phinehas son of E, the priest, said
22:32 Phinehas son of E, the priest, and
24:33 E son of Aaron died and was buried
Jdg 20:28 with Phinehas son of E, the son of
1Sa 7: 1 consecrated E his son to guard the
2Sa 23: 9 Next to him was E son of Dodai the
23:10 The troops returned to E, but only
1Ch 6: 3 Aaron: Nadab, Abihu, E and Ithamar.
6: 4 E was the father of Phinehas,
6:50 the descendants of Aaron: E his son,
9:20 In earlier times Phinehas son of E
11:12 Next to him was E son of Dodai the
23:21 The sons of Mahli: E and Kish.
23:22 E died without having sons: he had
24: 1 were Nadab, Abihu, E and Ithamar.
24: 2 E and Ithamar served as the priests.
24: 3 the help of Zadok a descendant of E
24: 5 descendants of both E and Ithamar.
24: 6 from E and then one from Ithamar.
24:28 From Mahli: E, who had no sons.
Ezr 7: 5 the son of Phinehas, the son of E,
8:33 E son of Phinehas was with him, and
10:25 Mijamin, E, Malkijah and Benaiah.
Ne 12:42 also Maaseiah, Shemaiah, E, Uzzi,
Mt 1:15 Eliud the father of E, E the father

Eleazar's (Eleazar)

1Ch 24: 4 were found among E descendants than
24: 4 heads of families from E descendants

Elect (Election)

Mt 24:22 for the sake of the e those days will
24:24 even the e—if that were possible.
24:31 and they will gather his e from the
Mk 13:20 But for the sake of the e, whom he
13:22 to deceive the e—if that were
13:27 gather his e from the four winds,
Ro 11: 7 it did not obtain, but the e did.
1Ti 5:21 and Christ Jesus and the e angels,
2Ti 2:10 everything for the sake of the e,
Tit 1: 1 Christ for the faith of God's e
1Pe 1: 1 To God's e, strangers in the world,

Election (Elect)

Ro 9:11 that God's purpose in e might stand:
11:28 but as far as e is concerned,
2Pe 1:10 to make your calling and e sure.

Elegance (Elegant)

SS 4: 4 built with e; on it hang a thousand

Elegant (Elegance)

Eze 23:41 You sat on an e couch, with a table
Lk 23:11 Dressing him in an e robe, they sent

Elementary (Elements)

Heb 5:12 someone to teach you the e truths
6: 1 let us leave the e teachings about

Elements (Elementary)

2Pe 3:10 the e will be destroyed by fire,
3:12 and the e will melt in the heat.

Elevate (Elevated, Elevating)

2Co 11: 7 to lower myself in order to e you by

Elevated (Elevate)

Est 5:11 had e him above the other nobles

Elevating (Elevate)

Est 3: 1 the Agagite, e him and giving him a

Elhanan

2Sa 21:19 E son of Jaare-Oregim the
23:24 Joab, E son of Dodo from Bethlehem,
1Ch 11:26 Joab, E son of Dodo from Bethlehem,
20: 5 E son of Jair killed Lahmi the

Eli (Eli's)

Priest at Shiloh; blessed Hannah (1Sa 1:9–17), who brought Samuel to him (1Sa 1:24–27); raised Samuel (1Sa 2:11,18–21,26). Wickedness of sons (1Sa 2:12–17,22–25); rebuked by prophet (1Sa 2:27–36). Directed Samuel to the Lord (1Sa 3). Death of Eli and his sons (1Sa 4:10–18).

1Sa 1: 3 sons of E, were priests of the LORD.
1: 9 Now E the priest was sitting on a
1:12 praying to the LORD, E observed her
1:13 E thought she was drunk
1:17 E answered, "Go in peace, and may
1:25 the bull, they brought the boy to E,
2:11 before the LORD under E the priest.
2:20 E would bless Elkanah and his wife,
2:22 Now E, who was very old, heard about
2:27 Now a man of God came to E and said
3: 1 ministered before the LORD under E.
3: 2 One night E, whose eyes were
3: 5 he ran to E and said, "Here I am;
3: 5 But E said, "I did not call; go
3: 6 Samuel got up and went to E and said,
3: 6 "My son," E said, "I did not call;
3: 8 and Samuel got up and went to E and
3: 8 Then E realised that the LORD was
3: 9 E told Samuel, "Go and lie down, and
3:12 I will carry out against E everything
3:14 I swore to the house of E, 'The guilt
3:15 He was afraid to tell E the vision,
3:16 E called him and said, "Samuel, my
3:17 "What was it he said to you?" E
3:18 Then E said, "He is the LORD; let
4:13 he arrived, there was E sitting on
4:14 E heard the outcry and asked, "What
4:14 uproar?" The man hurried over to E,
4:16 He told E, "I have just come from
4:16 E asked, "What happened, my son?"
4:18 he mentioned the ark of God, E fell
14: 3 the son of E, the LORD's priest in
1Ki 2:27 at Shiloh about the house of E.

Eli's (Eli)

1Sa 2:12 E sons were wicked men; they had no
3:14 'The guilt of E house will never be
4: 4 And E two sons, Hophni and Phinehas,
4:11 and E two sons, Hophni and Phinehas

Eliab

Nu 1: 9 from Zebulun, E son of Helon;
2: 7 people of Zebulun is E son of Helon.
7:24 On the third day, E son of Helon,
7:29 was the offering of E son of Helon.
10:16 E son of Helon was over the division
16: 1 Dathan and Abiram, sons of E,
16:12 Dathan and Abiram, the sons of E.
26: 8 The son of Pallu was E,
26: 9 the sons of E were Nemuel, Dathan
Dt 11: 6 sons of E the Reubenite, when the
1Sa 16: 6 they arrived, Samuel saw E and
17:13 The firstborn was E; the second,
17:28 E, David's oldest brother, heard him
1Ch 2:13 Jesse was the father of E his
6:27 E his son, Jeroham his son, Elkanah
12: 9 the second in command, E the third,
15:18 Shemiramoth, Jehiel, Unni, E,
15:20 Aziel, Shemiramoth, Jehiel, Unni, E,
16: 5 E, Benaiah, Obed-Edom and Jeiel.
2Ch 11:18 the daughter of Jesse's son E.

Eliada

2Sa 5:16 Elishama, E and Eliphelet.
1Ki 11:23 Rezon son of E, who had fled from
1Ch 3: 8 Elishama, E and Eliphelet—nine in
2Ch 17:17 From Benjamin: E, a valiant soldier,

Eliahba

2Sa 23:32 E the Shaalbonite, the sons of
1Ch 11:33 Azmaveth the Baharumite, E the

Eliakim (Eliakim's)

2Ki 18:18 They called for the king; and E son
18:26 E son of Hilkiah, and Shebna and
18:37 Then E son of Hilkiah the palace
19: 2 He sent E the palace administrator,
23:34 Pharaoh Neco made E son of Josiah
2Ch 36: 4 The king of Egypt made E, a brother
Ne 12:41 well as the priests—E, Maaseiah,
Isa 22:20 summon my servant, E son of Hilkiah.
36: 3 E son of Hilkiah the palace
36:11 E, Shebna and Joah said to the field
36:22 E son of Hilkiah the palace
37: 2 He sent E the palace administrator,
Mt 1:13 father of E, E the father of Azor,
Lk 3:30 the son of Jonam, the son of E,

Eliakim's (Eliakim)

2Ki 23:34 and changed E name to Jehoiakim.
2Ch 36: 4 and changed E name to Jehoiakim.
36: 4 But Neco took E brother Jehoahaz and

Eliam

2Sa 11: 3 daughter of E and the wife of Uriah
23:34 E son of Ahithophel the Gilonite,

Eliasaph

Nu 1:14 from Gad, E son of Deuel;
2:14 the people of Gad is E son of Deuel.
3:24 the Gershonites was E son of Lael.
7:42 On the sixth day E son of Deuel, the
7:47 was the offering of E son of Deuel.
10:20 E son of Deuel was over the division

Eliashib (Eliashib's)

1Ch 3:24 The sons of Elioenai: Hodaviah, E,
24:12 the eleventh to E, the twelfth to
Ezr 10: 6 to the room of Jehohanan son of E.
10:24 From the singers: E. From the
10:27 E, Mattaniah, Jeremoth, Zabad and
10:36 Vaniah, Meremoth, E,
Ne 3: 1 E the high priest and his fellow
3:20 of the house of E the high priest.
12:10 father of E, E the father of Joiada,
12:22 of the Levites in the days of E,
12:23 up to the time of Johanan son of E
13: 4 Before this, E the priest had been
13: 7 the evil thing E had done in
13:28 One of the sons of Joiada son of E

Eliashib's (Eliashib)

Ne 3:21 from the entrance of E house to the

Eliathah

1Ch 25: 4 Hanani, E, Giddalti and Romamti-Ezer;
25:27 the twentieth to E, his sons and

Elidad
Nu 34:21 **E** son of Kislon, from the tribe of

Eliehoenai
1Ch 26: 3 the sixth and **E** the seventh.
Ezr 8: 4 **E** son of Zerahiah, and with him

Eliel
1Ch 5:24 Ishi, **E**, Azriel, Jeremiah, Hodaviah
6:34 the son of **E**, the son of Toah,
8:20 Elienai, Zillethai, **E**,
8:22 Ishpan, Eber, **E**,
11:46 **E** the Mahavite, Jeribai and
11:47 **E**, Obed and Jaasiel the Mezobaite.
12:11 Attai the sixth, **E** the seventh,
15: 9 from the descendants of Hebron, **E**
15:11 **E** and Amminadab the Levites.
2Ch 31:13 Asahel, Jerimoth, Jozabad, **E**,

Elienai
1Ch 8:20 **E**, Zillethai, Eliel,

Eliezer
Ge 15: 2 inherit my estate is **E** of Damascus?"
Ex 18: 4 the other was named **E**, for he said,
1Ch 7: 8 The sons of Beker: Zemirah, Joash, **E**,
15:24 Zechariah, Benaiah and **E** the priests
23:15 The sons of Moses: Gershom and **E**.
23:17 The descendants of **E**: Rehabiah was
23:17 **E** had no other sons, but the sons of
26:25 His relatives through **E**: Rehabiah
27:16 over the Reubenites: **E** son of Zicri;
2Ch 20:37 **E** son of Dodavahu of Mareshah
Ezr 8:16 I summoned **E**, Ariel, Shemaiah,
10:18 Maaseiah, **E**, Jarib and Gedaliah.
10:23 is Kelita), Pethahiah, Judah and **E**.
10:31 From the descendants of Harim: **E**,
Lk 3:29 the son of Joshua, the son of **E**, the

Elihoreph
1Ki 4: 3 **E** and Ahijah, sons of Shisha

Elihu See Job[1] 2.
1Sa 1: 1 the son of **E**, the son of Tohu, the
1Ch 12:20 Jediael, Michael, Jozabad, **E** and
26: 7 **E** and Semakiah were also able men.
27:18 over Judah: **E**, a brother of David;
Job 32: 2 **E** son of Barakel the Buzite, of the
32: 4 Now **E** had waited before speaking to
32: 6 **E** son of Barakel the Buzite said: "I
34: 1 Then **E** said:
35: 1 Then **E** said:
36: 1 **E** continued:

Elijah (Elijah's)
Prophet; predicted drought in Israel (1Ki 17:1; Lk 4:25; Jas 5:17). Fed by ravens at brook Kerith (1Ki 17:2–6), and by widow of Zarephath (1Ki 17:9–16); raised widow's son (1Ki 17:17–24). Contest with prophets of Baal on Mt Carmel (1Ki 18:18–46). Fled from Jezebel to Horeb (1Ki 19); called Elisha (1Ki 19:19–21). Denounced Ahab over Naboth's vineyard (1Ki 21:17–29). Prophesied God's judgment on Ahaziah and called down fire (2Ki 1:1–17). Divided Jordan (2Ki 2:7–8); taken up to heaven in chariot of fire and whirlwind (2Ki 2:11–12); mantle taken by Elisha (2Ki 2:9–10,13–15).
Appeared with Moses at Jesus' transfiguration (Mt 17:2–3; Mk 9:2–4; Lk 9:28–31). Return prophesied (Mal 4:5–6; Mt 17:10; Mk 9:11); identified with John the Baptist (Mt 11:13–14; 17:11–13; Mk 9:12–13; Lk 1:17).

1Ki 17: 1 Now **E** the Tishbite, from Tishbe in
17: 2 the word of the LORD came to **E**:
17:13 **E** said to her, "Don't be afraid. Go
17:15 She went away and did as **E** had told
17:15 food every day for **E** and for the
17:16 the word of the LORD spoken by **E**.
17:18 She said to **E**, "What do you have
17:19 "Give me your son," **E** replied. He
17:23 **E** picked up the child and carried
17:24 the woman said to **E**, "Now I know
18: 1 the word of the LORD came to **E**: "Go
18: 2 **E** went to present himself to Ahab.
18: 7 Obadiah was walking along, **E** met him.
1Ki 18: 7 "Is it really you, my lord **E**?
18: 8 "Go tell your master, '**E** is here.'"
18:11 to my master and say, '**E** is here.'
18:14 go to my master and say, '**E** is here.
18:15 **E** said, "As the LORD Almighty lives,
18:16 told him, and Ahab went to meet **E**.
18:17 he saw **E**, he said to him, "Is that
18:18 made trouble for Israel," **E** replied.
18:21 **E** went before the people and said,
18:22 **E** said to them, "I am the only one
18:25 **E** said to the prophets of Baal,
18:27 At noon **E** began to taunt them.
18:30 **E** said to all the people, "Come here
18:31 **E** took twelve stones, one for each
18:36 the prophet **E** stepped forward and
18:40 **E** commanded them, "Seize the
18:40 and **E** had them brought down to the
18:41 **E** said to Ahab, "Go, eat and drink,
18:42 **E** climbed to the top of Carmel, bent
18:43 Seven times **E** said, "Go back."
18:44 So **E** said, "Go and tell Ahab,
18:46 The power of the LORD came upon **E**
19: 1 told Jezebel everything **E** had done
19: 2 Jezebel sent a messenger to **E** to say,
19: 3 **E** was afraid and ran for his life.
19: 9 "What are you doing here, **E**?
19:13 **E** heard it, he pulled his cloak over
19:13 "What are you doing here, **E**?
19:19 **E** went from there and found Elisha
19:19 **E** went up to him and threw his cloak
19:20 then left his oxen and ran after **E**.
19:20 "Go back," **E** replied. "What have I
19:21 follow **E** and became his attendant.
21:17 the word of the LORD came to **E** the
21:20 Ahab said to **E**, "So you have found
21:28 the word of the LORD came to **E** the
2Ki 1: 3 the angel of the LORD said to **E** the
1: 4 You will certainly die!" So **E** went.
1: 8 The king said, "That was **E** the
1: 9 he sent to **E** a captain with his
1: 9 The captain went up to **E**, who was
1:10 **E** answered the captain, "If I am a
1:11 At this the king sent to **E** another
1:12 "If I am a man of God," **E** replied,
1:13 up and fell on his knees before **E**.
1:15 The angel of the LORD said to **E**, "Go
1:15 So **E** got up and went down with him
1:17 word of the LORD that **E** had spoken.
2: 1 LORD was about to take **E** up to heaven
2: 1 **E** and Elisha were on their way from
2: 2 **E** said to Elisha, "Stay here; the
2: 4 **E** said to him, "Stay here, Elisha;
2: 6 **E** said to him, "Stay here; the LORD
2: 7 facing the place where **E** and Elisha
2: 8 **E** took his cloak, rolled it up and
2: 9 **E** said to Elisha, "Tell me, what can
2:10 have asked a difficult thing," **E** said
2:11 **E** went up to heaven in a whirlwind.
2:13 up the cloak that had fallen from **E**
2:14 "Where now is the LORD, the God of **E**?
2:15 The spirit of **E** is resting on Elisha.
3:11 to pour water on the hands of **E**."
9:36 through his servant **E** the Tishbite:
10:10 he promised through his servant **E**."
10:17 to the word of the LORD spoken to **E**.
1Ch 8:27 Jaareshiah, **E** and Zicri were the
2Ch 21:12 Jehoram received a letter from **E** the
Ezr 10:21 **E**, Shemaiah, Jehiel and Uzziah.
10:26 Jehiel, Abdi, Jeremoth and **E**.
Mal 4: 5 "See, I will send you the prophet **E**
Mt 11:14 it, he is the **E** who was to come.
16:14 others say **E**; and still others,
17: 3 Moses and **E**, talking with Jesus.
17: 4 you, one for Moses and one for **E**."
17:10 the law say that **E** must come first?"
17:11 Jesus replied, "To be sure, **E** comes
17:12 I tell you, **E** has already come, and
27:47 this, they said, "He's calling **E**.
27:49 Let's see if **E** comes to save him."
Mk 6:15 Others said, "He is **E**." And still
8:28 others say **E**; and still others,
9: 4 there appeared before them **E** and
9: 5 you, one for Moses and one for **E**."
9:11 the law say that **E** must come first?"
9:12 Jesus replied, "To be sure, **E** does
9:13 I tell you, **E** has come, and they
Mk 15:35 they said, "Listen, he's calling **E**.
15:36 "Now leave him alone. Let's see if **E**
Lk 1:17 in the spirit and power of **E**, to
4:26 Yet **E** was not sent to any of them,
9: 8 others that **E** had appeared, and
9:19 others say **E**; and still others,
9:30 Two men, Moses and **E**,
9:33 you, one for Moses and one for **E**.
Jn 1:21 you? Are you **E**?" He said, "I am not.
1:25 the Christ, nor **E**, nor the Prophet?"
Ro 11: 2 Scripture says in the passage about **E**
Jas 5:17 **E** was a man just like us. He prayed

Elijah's (Elijah)
1Ki 17:22 The LORD heard **E** cry, and the boy's
Lk 4:25 many widows in Israel in **E** time,

Elika
2Sa 23:25 Shammah the Harodite, **E** the Harodite,

Elim
Ex 15:27 they came to **E**, where there were
16: 1 set out from **E** and came to the Desert
Ex 16: 1 which is between **E** and Sinai, on the
Nu 33: 9 They left Marah and went to **E**, where
33:10 They left **E** and camped by the Red

Elimelech
Ru 1: 2 The man's name was **E**, his wife's
1: 3 Now **E**, Naomi's husband, died, and
2: 1 from the clan of **E**, a man of
2: 3 to Boaz, who was from the clan of **E**.
4: 3 land that belonged to our brother **E**.
4: 9 property of **E**, Kilion and Mahlon.

Eliminate (Eliminated)
Dt 7:22 You will not be allowed to **e** them

Eliminated (Eliminate)
Dt 2:15 had completely **e** them from the camp.

Elioenai
1Ch 3:23 The sons of Neariah: **E**, Hizkiah and
3:24 The sons of **E**: Hodaviah, Eliashib,
4:36 also **E**, Jaakobah, Jeshohaiah, Asaiah,
7: 8 Joash, Eliezer, **E**, Omri, Jeremoth,
Ezr 10:22 From the descendants of Pashhur: **E**,
10:27 From the descendants of Zattu: **E**,
Ne 12:41 Maaseiah, Miniamin, Micaiah, **E**,

Eliphal
1Ch 11:35 of Sacar the Hararite, **E** son of Ur,

Eliphaz See Job[1] 2.
Ge 36: 4 Adah bore **E** to Esau, Basemath bore
36:10 These are the names of Esau's sons: **E**
36:11 The sons of **E**: Teman, Omar, Zepho,
36:12 Esau's son **E** also had a concubine
36:15 The sons of **E** the firstborn of Esau:
36:16 the chiefs descended from **E** in Edom;
1Ch 1:35 The sons of Esau: **E**, Reuel, Jeush,
1:36 The sons of **E**: Teman, Omar, Zepho,
Job 2:11 Job's three friends, **E** the Temanite,
4: 1 Then **E** the Temanite replied:
15: 1 Then **E** the Temanite replied:
22: 1 Then **E** the Temanite replied:
42: 7 he said to **E** the Temanite, "I am
42: 9 **E** the Temanite, Bildad the Shuhite

Eliphelehu
1Ch 15:18 Benaiah, Maaseiah, Mattithiah, **E**,
15:21 Mattithiah, **E**, Mikneiah, Obed-Edom,

Eliphelet
2Sa 5:16 Elishama, Eliada and **E**.
23:34 **E** son of Ahasbai the Maacathite,
1Ch 3: 6 There were also Ibhar, Elishua, **E**,
3: 8 Elishama, Eliada and **E**—nine in all.
8:39 Jeush the second son and **E** the third.
14: 7 Elishama, Beeliada and **E**.

Ezr 8:13 the last ones, whose names were **E**,
10:33 **E**, Jeremai, Manasseh and Shimei.

Elisha (Elisha's)

Prophet; succeeded Elijah (1Ki 19:16–21); took his cloak and divided Jordan (2Ki 2:13–14). Purified bad water (2Ki 2:19–22); cursed youths who mocked him (2Ki 2:23–25); helped defeat Moab (2Ki 3:11–19); provided oil for widow (2Ki 4:1–7); raised Shunammite woman's son (2Ki 4:8–37); purified food (2Ki 4:38–41); fed 100 men with 20 loaves (2Ki 4:42–44); healed Naaman (2Ki 5); made axe-head float (2Ki 6:1–7). Captured Arameans (2Ki 6:8–23). Life threatened (2Ki 6:31–33). Prophesied end of siege of Samaria (2Ki 7:1–2). Visit to Damascus (2Ki 8:7–15). Sent prophet to anoint Jehu as king (2Ki 9:1–3). Death (2Ki 13:14–20); miracle with bones (2Ki 13:21).

1Ki 19:16 and anoint **E** son of Shaphat from
19:17 and **E** will put to death any who
19:19 Elijah went from there and found **E**
19:20 **E** then left his oxen and ran after
19:21 **E** left him and went back. He took
2Ki 2: 1 and **E** were on their way from Gilgal.
2: 2 Elijah said to **E**, "Stay here; the
2: 2 But **E** said, "As surely as the LORD
2: 3 at Bethel came out to **E** and asked,
2: 3 **E** replied, "but do not speak of it.
2: 4 Elijah said to him, "Stay here, **E**;
2: 5 Jericho went up to **E** and asked him,
2: 7 and **E** had stopped at the Jordan.
2: 9 they had crossed, Elijah said to **E**,
2: 9 portion of your spirit," **E** replied.
2:12 **E** saw this and cried out, "My father!
2:12 of Israel!" And **E** saw him no more.
2:15 The spirit of Elijah is resting on **E**.
2:16 "No," **E** replied, "do not send them."
2:18 they returned to **E**, who was staying
2:19 The men of the city said to **E**, "Look,
2:22 according to the word **E** had spoken.
2:23 From there **E** went up to Bethel. As
3:11 answered, "**E** son of Shaphat is here.
3:13 **E** said to the king of Israel, "What
3:14 **E** said, "As surely as the LORD
3:15 the hand of the LORD came upon **E**
4: 1 of the prophets cried out to **E**,
4: 2 **E** replied to her, "How can I help
4: 3 **E** said, "Go round and ask all your
4: 8 One day **E** went to Shunem. And a
4:11 One day when **E** came, he went up to
4:13 **E** said to him, "Tell her, 'You have
4:14 "What can be done for her?" **E** asked.
4:15 **E** said, "Call her." So he called her,
4:16 "About this time next year," **E** said,
4:17 to a son, just as **E** had told her.
4:29 **E** said to Gehazi, "Tuck your cloak
4:31 So Gehazi went back to meet **E** and
4:32 **E** reached the house, there was the
4:35 **E** turned away and walked back and
4:36 **E** summoned Gehazi and said, "Call
4:38 **E** returned to Gilgal and there was a
4:41 **E** said, "Get some flour." He put it
4:42 "Give it to the people to eat," **E**
4:43 But **E** answered, "Give it to the
5: 8 **E** the man of God heard that the king
5:10 **E** sent a messenger to say to him,
5:19 "Go in peace," **E** said. After Naaman
5:20 Gehazi, the servant of **E** the man of
5:25 in and stood before his master **E**.
5:25 "Where have you been, Gehazi?" **E**
5:26 **E** said to him, "Was not my spirit
6: 1 The company of the prophets said to **E**
6: 3 your servants?" "I will," **E** replied.
6: 6 **E** cut a stick and threw it there,
6:10 Time and again **E** warned the king, so
6:12 "but **E**, the prophet who is in Israel,
6:17 **E** prayed, "O LORD, open his eyes so
6:17 and chariots of fire all round **E**.
6:18 enemy came down towards him, **E** prayed
6:18 them with blindness, as **E** had asked.
6:19 **E** told them, "This is not the road
6:20 After they entered the city, **E** said,
6:21 he asked **E**, "Shall I kill them, my
6:31 if the head of **E** son of Shaphat
6:32 Now **E** was sitting in his house, and
6:32 but before he arrived, **E** said to the
2Ki 7: 1 **E** said, "Hear the word of the LORD.
7: 2 it with your own eyes," answered **E**,
8: 1 Now **E** had said to the woman whose
8: 4 all the great things **E** has done."
8: 5 how **E** had restored the dead to life,
8: 5 the woman whose son **E** had brought
8: 5 is her son whom **E** restored to life."
8: 7 **E** went to Damascus, and Ben-Hadad
8: 9 Hazael went to meet **E**, taking with
8:10 **E** answered, "Go and say to him, 'You
8:13 become king of Aram," answered **E**.
8:14 Hazael left **E** and returned to his
8:14 When Ben-Hadad asked, "What did **E**
9: 1 The prophet **E** summoned a man from
13:14 Now **E** was suffering from the illness
13:15 **E** said, "Get a bow and some arrows,"
13:16 **E** put his hands on the king's hands.
13:17 "Shoot!" **E** said, and he shot. "The
13:17 of victory over Aram!" **E** declared.
13:18 **E** told him, "Strike the ground." He
13:20 **E** died and was buried. Now Moabite
Lk 4:27 in the time of **E** the prophet,

Elisha's (Elisha)

2Ki 5: 9 and stopped at the door of **E** house.
5:27 Then Gehazi went from **E** presence
13:21 threw the man's body into **E** tomb.
13:21 When the body touched **E** bones, the

Elishah

Ge 10: 4 The sons of Javan: **E**, Tarshish, the
1Ch 1: 7 The sons of Javan: **E**, Tarshish, the
Eze 27: 7 and purple from the coasts of **E**.

Elishama

Nu 1:10 **E** son of Ammihud; from Manasseh,
2:18 of Ephraim is **E** son of Ammihud.
7:48 On the seventh day **E** son of Ammihud,
7:53 the offering of **E** son of Ammihud.
10:22 **E** son of Ammihud was in command.
2Sa 5:16 **E**, Eliada and Eliphelet.
2Ki 25:25 the son of **E**, who was of royal blood,
1Ch 2:41 and Jekamiah the father of **E**.
3: 8 **E**, Eliada and Eliphelet—nine in all.
7:26 Ladan his son, Ammihud his son, **E**
14: 7 **E**, Beeliada and Eliphelet.
2Ch 17: 8 the priests **E** and Jehoram.
Jer 36:12 were sitting: **E** the secretary,
36:20 in the room of **E** the secretary,
36:21 Jehudi brought it from the room of **E**
41: 1 the son of **E**, who was of royal blood

Elishaphat

2Ch 23: 1 son of Adaiah, and **E** son of Zicri.

Elisheba

Ex 6:23 Aaron married **E**, daughter of

Elishua

2Sa 5:15 Ibhar, **E**, Nepheg, Japhia,
1Ch 3: 6 There were also Ibhar, **E**, Eliphelet,
14: 5 Ibhar, **E**, Elpelet,

Elite

Eze 23: 7 to all the **e** of the Assyrians

Eliud

Mt 1:14 of Akim, Akim the father of **E**,
1:15 **E** the father of Eleazar, Eleazar the

Elizabeth

Wife of Zechariah; mother of John the Baptist (Lk 1:5–25,57–60). Related to Mary (Lk 1:36); blessed Mary when she visited (Lk 1:39–45).

Lk 1: 5 **E** was also a descendant of Aaron.
1: 7 they had no children, because **E** was
1:13 Your wife **E** will bear you a son, and
1:24 After this his wife **E** became
1:36 Even **E** your relative is going to
1:40 Zechariah's home and greeted **E**.
1:41 **E** heard Mary's greeting, the baby
1:41 **E** was filled with the Holy Spirit.
1:56 Mary stayed with **E** for about three
1:57 was time for **E** to have her baby, she

Elizaphan

Nu 3:30 Kohathite clans was **E** son of Uzziel.
34:25 **E** son of Parnach, the leader from
1Ch 15: 8 from the descendants of **E**, Shemaiah
2Ch 29:13 from the descendants of **E**, Shimri

Elizur

Nu 1: 5 you: from Reuben, **E** son of Shedeur;
2:10 of Reuben is **E** son of Shedeur.
7:30 On the fourth day **E** son of Shedeur,
7:35 the offering of **E** son of Shedeur.
10:18 **E** son of Shedeur was in command.

Elkanah

Ex 6:24 The sons of Korah were Assir, **E** and
1Sa 1: 1 whose name was **E** son of Jeroham, the
1: 4 Whenever the day came for **E** to
1: 8 **E** her husband would say to her,
1:19 **E** lay with Hannah his wife, and the
1:21 the man **E** went up with all his
1:23 "Do what seems best to you," **E** her
2:11 **E** went home to Ramah, but the boy
2:20 Eli would bless **E** and his wife,
1Ch 6:23 **E** his son, Ebiasaph his son, Assir
6:25 The descendants of **E**: Amasai,
6:26 **E** his son, Zophai his son, Nahath
6:27 Eliab his son, Jeroham his son, **E**
6:34 the son of **E**, the son of Jeroham,
6:35 the son of Zuph, the son of **E**, the
6:36 the son of **E**, the son of Joel, the
9:16 the son of **E**, who lived in the
12: 6 **E**, Isshiah, Azarel, Joezer and
15:23 Berekiah and **E** were to be
2Ch 28: 7 palace, and **E**, second to the king.

Elkoshite

Na 1: 1 book of the vision of Nahum the **E**.

Ellasar

Ge 14: 1 Arioch king of **E**, Kedorlaomer king
14: 9 king of **E**–four kings against five.

Elmadam

Lk 3:28 Cosam, the son of **E**, the son of Er,

Elnaam

1Ch 11:46 the sons of **E**, Ithmah the Moabite,

Elnathan

2Ki 24: 8 Nehushta daughter of **E**; she was from
Ezr 8:16 Ariel, Shemaiah, **E**, Jarib, **E**, Nathan,
8:16 and **E**, who were men of learning,
Jer 26:22 King Jehoiakim, however, sent **E** son
36:12 son of Shemaiah, **E** son of Acbor,
36:25 Even though **E**, Delaiah and Gemariah

Eloi

Mt 27:46 "**E**, **E**, lama sabachthani?"—which
Mk 15:34 "**E**, **E**, lama sabachthani?"—which

Elon (Elonite)

Ge 26:34 Basemath daughter of **E** the Hittite.
36: 2 Adah daughter of **E** the Hittite,
46:14 The sons of Zebulun: Sered, **E** and
Nu 26:26 the Seredite clan; through **E**, the
Jos 19:43 **E**, Timnah, Ekron,
Jdg 12:11 After him, **E** the Zebulunite led
12:12 **E** died, and was buried in Aijalon in

Elon Bethhanan

1Ki 4: 9 Makaz, Shaalbim, Beth Shemesh and **E**;

Elonite (Elon)

Nu 26:26 the **E** clan; through Jahleel, the

Eloquence (Eloquent)

1Co 2: 1 brothers, I did not come with **e** or

Eloquent (Eloquence)

Ex 4:10 "O Lord, I have never been **e**,

Elpaal
1Ch 8:11 By Hushim he had Abitub and **E**.
8:12 The sons of **E**: Eber, Misham, Shemed
8:18 Izliah and Jobab were the sons of **E**.

Elpelet
1Ch 14: 5 Ibhar, Elishua, **E**,

Eltekeh
Jos 19:44 **E**, Gibbethon, Baalath,
21:23 of Dan they received **E**, Gibbethon,

Eltekon
Jos 15:59 Maarath, Beth Anoth and **E**—six towns

Eltolad
Jos 15:30 **E**, Kesil, Hormah,
19: 4 **E**, Bethul, Hormah,

Elude (Eluded)
Job 11:20 and escape will **e** them; their hope
Rev 9: 6 long to die, but death will **e** them.

Eluded (Elude)
1Sa 18:11 But David **e** him twice.
19:10 but David **e** him as Saul drove the

Elul
Ne 6:15 completed on the twenty-fifth of **E**,

Eluzai
1Ch 12: 5 **E**, Jerimoth, Bealiah, Shemariah and

Elymas
Ac 13: 8 **E** the sorcerer (for that is what his
13: 9 looked straight at **E** and said,

Elzabad
1Ch 12:12 Johanan the eighth, **E** the ninth,
26: 7 Rephael, Obed and **E**; his relatives

Elzaphan
Ex 6:22 The sons of Uzziel were Mishael, **E**
Lev 10: 4 Moses summoned Mishael and **E**, sons

Emasculate (Emasculated)
Gal 5:12 go the whole way and **e** themselves!

Emasculated (Emasculate)
Dt 23: 1 No-one who has been **e** by crushing or

Embalm (Embalmed, Embalming)
Ge 50: 2 his service to **e** his father Israel.

Embalmed (Embalm)
Ge 50: 2 So the physicians **e** him,
50:26 And after they **e** him, he was placed

Embalming (Embalm)
Ge 50: 3 that was the time required for **e**.

Embankment (Bank)
Lk 19:43 enemies will build an **e** against you

Embarrass (Embarrassed, Embarrassment)
Ru 2:15 among the sheaves, don't **e** her.

Embarrassed (Embarrass)
2Co 7:14 about you, and you have not **e** me.

Embarrassment (Embarrass)
Jdg 3:25 They waited to the point of **e**, but

Embedded
Ecc 12:11 sayings, like firmly **e** nails—given

Embers
Ps 102: 3 smoke; my bones burn like glowing **e**.
Pr 26:21 As charcoal to **e** and as wood to fire,

Embitter (Embittered)
Col 3:21 Fathers, do not **e** your children, or

Embittered (Embitter)
Ps 73:21 my heart was grieved and my spirit **e**,

Embodiment (Body)
Ro 2:20 the law the **e** of knowledge and truth

Emboldened
1Co 8:10 won't he be **e** to eat what has been

Embrace (Embraced, Embraces, Embracing)
Pr 3:18 is a tree of life to those who **e** her
4: 8 **e** her, and she will honour you.
5:20 **e** the bosom of another man's wife?
Ecc 3: 5 a time to **e** and a time to refrain,
Mic 7: 5 in your **e** be careful of your words.

Embraced (Embrace)
Ge 29:13 He **e** him and kissed him and brought
33: 4 Esau ran to meet Jacob and **e** him; he
45:14 wept, and Benjamin **e** him, weeping.
48:10 his father kissed them and **e** them.
1Ki 9: 9 and have **e** other gods, worshipping
2Ch 7:22 and have **e** other gods, worshipping
Ac 20:37 They all wept as they **e** him and

Embraces (Embrace)
SS 2: 6 my head, and his right arm **e** me.
8: 3 my head and his right arm **e** me.

Embracing (Embrace)
Ecc 2: 3 myself with wine, and **e** folly—

Embroidered (Embroiderer, Embroiderers)
Jdg 5:30 colourful garments **e**, highly **e**
Ps 45:14 In **e** garments she is led to the king;
Eze 16:10 I clothed you with an **e** dress and
16:13 linen and costly fabric and **e** cloth.
16:18 you took your **e** clothes to put on
26:16 robes and take off their **e** garments.
27: 7 Fine **e** linen from Egypt was your
27:16 purple fabric, **e** work, fine linen,
27:24 garments, blue fabric, **e** work and

Embroiderer (Embroidered)
Ex 26:36 twisted linen—the work of an **e**.
27:16 twisted linen—the work of an **e**
28:39 The sash is to be the work of an **e**.
36:37 twisted linen—the work of an **e**;
38:18 twisted linen—the work of an **e**.
38:23 and an **e** in blue, purple and scarlet
39:29 an **e**—as the LORD commanded Moses.

Embroiderers (Embroidered)
Ex 35:35 designers, **e** in blue, purple and

Emek Keziz
Jos 18:21 cities: Jericho, Beth Hoglah, **E**,

Emerald
Ex 28:18 a turquoise, a sapphire and an **e**;
39:11 a turquoise, a sapphire and an **e**;
Eze 28:13 topaz and **e**, chrysolite, onyx and
Rev 4: 3 A rainbow, resembling an **e**, encircled
21:19 the third chalcedony, the fourth **e**,

Emerge
Da 8:22 four kingdoms that will **e** from

Emission
Lev 15:16 "When a man has an **e** of semen, he
15:18 a woman and there is an **e** of semen,
15:32 made unclean by an **e** of semen,
Lev 22: 4 or by anyone who has an **e** of semen,
Dt 23:10 is unclean because of a nocturnal **e**,
Eze 23:20 and whose **e** was like that of horses.

Emites
Ge 14: 5 in Ham, the **E** in Shaveh
Dt 2:10 (The **E** used to live there–a people
2:11 but the Moabites called them **E**.

Emmaus
Village in Judea about 7 miles from Jerusalem (Lk 24:13). After his resurrection, Jesus appeared to Cleopas and another disciple on the Emmaus road (Lk 24:15). He explained scriptures concerning himself but was not recognised until he broke bread at the evening meal (Lk 24:30–31). Exact location unknown.

Lk 24:13 **E**, about seven miles from Jerusalem.

Emperor (Empire)
Ac 25:25 the **E** I decided to send him to Rome.

Emperor's (Empire)
Ac 25:21 to be held over for the **E** decision,

Empire (Emperor, Emperor's, Imperial)
Est 10: 1 imposed tribute throughout the **e**,
Jer 34: 1 peoples in the **e** he ruled were
Da 11: 4 After he has appeared, his **e** will be
11: 4 because his **e** will be uprooted and

Employed
Eze 39:14 "Men will be regularly **e** to cleanse

Emptied (Empty)
Ge 24:20 she quickly **e** her jar into the
Lev 14:36 order the house to be **e** before he
Ne 5:13 may such a man be shaken out and **e**!"
Zep 2: 4 Ashdod will be **e** and Ekron uprooted.
1Co 1:17 cross of Christ be **e** of its power.

Empties (Empty)
Eze 47: 8 When it **e** into the Sea, the water

Empty (Emptied, Empties, Empty-handed, Emptying)
Ge 1: 2 Now the earth was formless and **e**,
37:24 was **e**; there was no water in it.
Jdg 7:16 he placed trumpets and **e** jars in the
Ru 1:21 but the LORD has brought me back **e**.
1Sa 6: 3 do not send it away **e**, but by all
20:18 missed, because your seat will be **e**.
20:25 to Saul, but David's place was **e**.
20:27 month, David's place was **e** again.
2Ki 4: 3 ask all your neighbours for **e** jars.
18:20 you speak only **e** words.
2Ch 24:11 **e** the chest and carry it back to its
Job 15: 2 a wise man answer with **e** notions
26: 7 over **e** space; he suspends the earth
35:13 God does not listen to their **e** plea;
35:16 Job opens his mouth with **e** talk;
Pr 14: 4 the manger is **e**, but from the
Isa 16: 6 insolence—but her boasts are **e**.
32: 6 the hungry he leaves **e** and from the
36: 5 but you speak only **e** words.
45:18 it; he did not create it to be **e**,
55:11 mouth: It will not return to me **e**,
59: 4 They rely on **e** arguments and speak
Jer 4:23 and it was formless and **e**; and at
48:12 will **e** her jars and smash her jugs.
51:34 confusion, he has made us an **e** jar.
Eze 24: 6 **E** it piece by piece without casting
24:11 set the **e** pot on the coals till it
Am 4: 6 "I gave you **e** stomachs in every city
Mic 6:14 your stomach will still be **e**.
Lk 1:53 things but has sent the rich away **e**.
Eph 5: 6 Let no-one deceive you with **e** words,
1Pe 1:18 redeemed from the **e** way of life
2Pe 2:18 For they mouth **e**, boastful words and,

Empty-handed (Empty, Hand)
Ge 31:42 would surely have sent me away **e**.
Ex 3:21 when you leave you will not go **e**.
23:15 "No-one is to appear before me **e**.
34:20 "No-one is to appear before me **e**.
Dt 15:13 release him, do not send him away **e**.
16:16 man should appear before the LORD **e**:
Ru 3:17 go back to your mother-in-law **e**.'"
Job 22: 9 you sent widows away **e** and broke the
Jer 50: 9 warriors who do not return **e**.
Mk 12: 3 him, beat him and sent him away **e**.
Lk 20:10 beat him and sent him away **e**.
20:11 treated shamefully and sent away **e**.

Emptying (Empty)
Ge 42:35 they were **e** their sacks, there in
Hab 1:17 Is he to keep on **e** his net,

En Eglaim
Eze 47:10 from En Gedi to **E** there will be

En Gannim
Jos 15:34 Zanoah, **E**, Tappuah, Enam,
19:21 Remeth, **E**, En Haddah and Beth Pazzez.
21:29 Jarmuth and **E**, together with their

En Gedi
Jos 15:62 Nibshan, the City of Salt and **E**—six
1Sa 23:29 and lived in the strongholds of **E**.
24: 1 told, "David is in the Desert of **E**.
2Ch 20: 2 in Hazezon Tamar" (that is, **E**).
SS 1:14 blossoms from the vineyards of **E**.
Eze 47:10 from **E** to En Eglaim there will be

En Haddah
Jos 19:21 Remeth, En Gannim, **E** and Beth Pazzez.

En Hakkore
Jdg 15:19 So the spring was called **E**, and it is

En Hazor
Jos 19:37 Kedesh, Edrei, **E**,

En Mishpat
Ge 14: 7 they turned back and went to **E** (that

En Rimmon
Ne 11:29 in **E**, in Zorah, in Jarmuth,

En Rogel
Jos 15: 7 of En Shemesh and came out at **E**.
18:16 of the Jebusite city and so to **E**.
2Sa 17:17 and Ahimaaz were staying at **E**.
1Ki 1: 9 at the Stone of Zoheleth near **E**.

En Shemesh
Jos 15: 7 of **E** and came out at En Rogel.
18:17 then curved north, went to **E**,

En Tappuah
Jos 17: 7 to include the people living at **E**.

Enable (Enabled, Enables, Enabling)
Ecc 6: 2 but God does not **e** him to enjoy them,
Lk 1:74 to **e** us to serve him without
Ac 4:29 Lord, consider their threats and **e**

Enabled (Enable)
Lev 26:13 **e** you to walk with heads held high.
Ru 4:13 the LORD **e** her to conceive, and she
Jn 6:65 to me unless the Father has **e** him."
Ac 2: 4 other tongues as the Spirit **e** them.
7:10 He gave Joseph wisdom and **e** him to
Heb 11:11 was **e** to become a father because he

Enables (Enable)
2Sa 22:34 he **e** me to stand on the heights.
Ps 18:33 he **e** me to stand on the heights.
Ecc 5:19 and **e** him to enjoy them, to accept
Hab 3:19 deer, he **e** me to go on the heights.
Php 3:21 who, by the power that **e** him to

Enabling (Enable)
Ac 14: 3 by **e** them to do miraculous signs

Enaim
Ge 38:14 **E**, which is on the road to Timnah.
38:21 who was beside the road at **E**?"

Enam
Jos 15:34 Zanoah, En Gannim, Tappuah, **E**,

Enan
Nu 1:15 from Naphtali, Ahira son of **E**."
2:29 of Naphtali is Ahira son of **E**.
7:78 On the twelfth day Ahira son of **E**,
7:83 was the offering of Ahira son of **E**.
10:27 Ahira son of **E** was over the division

Encamp (Camp)
Nu 1:50 to take care of it and **e** round it.
2: 3 Judah are to **e** under their standard.
2:17 set out in the same order as they **e**,
9:20 at the LORD's command they would **e**,
Job 19:12 against me and **e** around my tent.
Isa 29: 3 I will **e** against you all around; I
Jer 50:29 **E** all round her; let no-one escape.

Encamped (Camp)
Ge 26:17 Isaac moved away from there and **e** in
Nu 2:34 way they **e** under their standards,
9:17 the cloud settled, the Israelites **e**.
9:18 set out, and at his command they **e**.
9:23 At the LORD's command they **e**, and at
12:16 and **e** in the Desert of Paran.
24: 2 Balaam looked out and saw Israel **e**
Dt 23: 9 you are **e** against your enemies, keep
Jdg 11:20 **e** at Jahaz and fought with Israel.
1Sa 26: 5 camp, with the army **e** around him.
2Sa 23:13 was **e** in the Valley of Rephaim.
1Ki 16:15 **e** near Gibbethon, a Philistine town.
2Ki 25: 1 He **e** outside the city and built
1Ch 11:15 was **e** in the Valley of Rephaim.

Encamps (Camp)
Ps 34: 7 The angel of the LORD **e** around those

Enchanter (Enchanters)
Ps 58: 5 however skilful the **e** may be.
Isa 3: 3 skilled craftsman and clever **e**.
Da 2:10 of any magician or **e** or astrologer.
2:27 Daniel replied, "No wise man, **e**,

Enchanters (Enchanter)
Da 1:20 and **e** in his whole kingdom.
2: 2 the king summoned the magicians, **e**,
4: 7 the magicians, **e**, astrologers and
5: 7 The king called out for the **e**,
5:11 **e**, astrologers and diviners.
5:15 The wise men and **e** were brought

Encircle (Circle)
Ps 22:12 me; strong bulls of Bashan **e** me.
Isa 29: 3 I will **e** you with towers and set up
Lk 19:43 **e** you and hem you in on every side.

Encircled (Circle)
1Ki 7:24 Below the rim, gourds **e** it—ten to a
2Ch 4: 3 Below the rim, figures of bulls **e** it
Ps 22:16 me; a band of evil men has **e** me,
SS 7: 2 is a mound of wheat **e** by lilies.
Rev 4: 3 resembling an emerald, **e** the throne.
5: 6 **e** by the four living creatures and
5:11 They **e** the throne and the living

Encircling (Circle)
1Ki 7:18 He made pomegranates in two rows **e**
2Ch 33:14 Fish Gate and **e** the hill of Ophel;

Enclose (Close[1])
SS 8: 9 we will **e** her with panels of cedar.

Enclosed (Close[1])
Est 1: 5 lasting seven days, in the **e** garden
SS 4:12 are a spring **e**, a sealed fountain.
Eze 46:22 of the outer court were **e** courts,

Encounter
Ex 23:27 into confusion every nation you **e**.
2Sa 23: 8 men, whom he killed in one **e**.
1Ch 11:11 men, whom he killed in one **e**.

Encourage (Encouraged, Encouragement, Encourages, Encouraging)
Dt 1:38 **E** him, because he will lead Israel
3:28 commission Joshua, and **e** and
2Sa 11:25 Say this to **e** Joab."
19: 7 Now go out and **e** your men. I swear
Job 16: 5 my mouth would **e** you; comfort from
Ps 10:17 you **e** them, and you listen to their
64: 5 They **e** each other in evil plans,
Isa 1:17 learn to do right! Seek justice, **e**
Jer 29: 8 to the dreams you **e** them to have.
Ac 15:32 to **e** and strengthen the brothers.
Ro 12: 8 if it is encouraging, let him **e**; if
Eph 6:22 how we are, and that he may **e** you.
Col 4: 8 and that he may **e** your hearts.
1Th 3: 2 strengthen and **e** you in your faith,
4:18 Therefore **e** each other with these
1Th 5:11 Therefore **e** one another and build
5:14 warn those who are idle, **e** the timid,
2Th 2:17 **e** your hearts and strengthen you in
2Ti 4: 2 rebuke and **e**—with great patience
Tit 1: 9 so that he can **e** others by sound
2: 6 Similarly, **e** the young men to be
2:15 **E** and rebuke with all authority. Do
Heb 3:13 **e** one another daily, as long as it
10:25 but let us **e** one another—and all

Encouraged (Encourage)
Jdg 7:11 Afterwards, you will be **e** to attack
20:22 the men of Israel **e** one another and
2Ch 22: 3 for his mother **e** him in doing wrong.
32: 6 gate and **e** them with these words:
35: 2 **e** them in the service of the LORD's
Eze 13:22 and because you **e** the wicked not to
Ac 9:31 and **e** by the Holy Spirit, it grew in
11:23 he was glad and **e** them all to remain
16:40 met with the brothers and **e** them.
18:27 the brothers **e** him and wrote to the
27:36 They were all **e** and ate some food
28:15 men Paul thanked God and was **e**.
Ro 1:12 be mutually **e** by each other's faith.
1Co 14:31 everyone may be instructed and **e**.
2Co 7: 4 I am greatly **e**; in all our troubles
7:13 By all this we are **e**. In addition to
Php 1:14 have been **e** to speak the word of God
Col 2: 2 My purpose is that they may be **e** in
1Th 3: 7 **e** about you because of your faith.
Heb 6:18 hope offered to us may be greatly **e**.

Encouragement (Encourage)
Ac 4:36 Barnabas (which means Son of **E**),
13:15 if you have a message of **e** for the
20: 2 speaking many words of **e** to the
Ro 15: 4 so that through endurance and the **e**
15: 5 May the God who gives endurance and **e**
1Co 14: 3 their strengthening, **e** and comfort.
2Co 7:13 In addition to our own **e**, we were
Php 2: 1 If you have any **e** from being united
2Th 2:16 gave us eternal **e** and good hope,
Phm : 7 love has given me great joy and **e**,
Heb 12: 5 you have forgotten that word of **e**

Encourages (Encourage)
Isa 41: 7 The craftsman **e** the goldsmith, and

Encouraging (Encourage)
Ac 14:22 strengthening the disciples and **e**
15:31 it and were glad for its **e** message.
20: 1 after **e** them, said good-bye and set
Ro 12: 8 if it is **e**, let him encourage; if it
1Th 2:12 **e**, comforting and urging you to live
1Pe 5:12 I have written to you briefly, **e** you

Encroach
Dt 2:37 you did not **e** on any of the land of
Pr 23:10 **e** on the fields of the fatherless,

Encrusted (Crust)
Eze 24: 6 to the pot now **e**, whose deposit will

End (*End of the age*, Ended, Ending, Ends)
Ge 6:13 "I am going to put an **e** to all
8: 3 At the **e** of the hundred and fifty
23: 9 to him and is at the **e** of his field.
41:53 of abundance in Egypt came to an **e**,
47:21 from one **e** of Egypt to the other.
Ex 12:41 At the **e** of the 430 years, to the
23:16 of Ingathering at the **e** of the year,
25:19 Make one cherub on one **e** and the
26: 4 edge of the **e** curtain in one set,
26: 4 with the **e** curtain in the other set.
26: 5 on the **e** curtain of the other set,
26:10 edge of the **e** curtain in one set
26:10 of the **e** curtain in the other set.
26:22 Make six frames for the far **e**, that
26:22 is, the west **e** of the tabernacle,
26:23 frames for the corners at the far **e**.
26:27 at the far **e** of the tabernacle.
26:28 **e** to **e** at the middle of the frames.
27:12 "The west **e** of the courtyard shall
27:13 On the east **e**, towards the sunrise,
32:27 the camp from one **e** to the other,
36:11 edge of the **e** curtain in one set,
36:11 with the **e** curtain in the other set.
36:12 on the **e** curtain of the other set,
36:17 edge of the **e** curtain in one set
36:17 of the **e** curtain in the other set.
36:27 They made six frames for the far **e**,
36:27 is, the west **e** of the tabernacle,
36:28 of the tabernacle at the far **e**.
36:32 at the far **e** of the tabernacle.
36:33 **e** to **e** at the middle of the frames.
37: 8 He made one cherub on one **e** and the
38:12 The west **e** was fifty cubits wide and
38:13 The east **e**, towards the sunrise, was
Nu 13:25 At the **e** of forty days they returned
14:35 They will meet their **e** in this
16:21 I can put an **e** to them at once."
16:45 that I can put an **e** to them at once.
17:10 This will put an **e** to their
23:10 and may my **e** be like theirs!"
25:11 my zeal I did not put an **e** to them.
34: 3 start from the **e** of the Salt Sea,
34: 5 the Wadi of Egypt and **e** at the Sea.
34: 9 continue to Ziphron and **e** at Hazar
34:12 the Jordan and **e** at the Salt Sea.
Dt 4:32 one **e** of the heavens to the other.
8:16 in the **e** it might go well with you.
9:11 At the **e** of the forty days and forty
11:12 the beginning of the year to its **e**.
13: 7 one **e** of the land to the other),
14:28 At the **e** of every three years, bring
15: 1 At the **e** of every seven years you
28:64 one **e** of the earth to the other.
31:10 Moses commanded them: "At the **e** of
31:24 of this law from beginning to **e**,
31:30 from beginning to **e** in the hearing of
32:20 "and see what their **e** will be; for
32:29 and discern what their **e** will be!
Jos 13:27 to the **e** of the Sea of Kinnereth).
15: 2 at the southern **e** of the Salt Sea,
15: 8 northern **e** of the Valley of Rephaim.
24:20 on you and make an **e** of you,
Ru 3: 7 down at the far **e** of the grain pile.
1Sa 3:12 his family—from beginning to **e**.
14:27 so he reached out the **e** of the staff
14:43 little honey with the **e** of my staff.
2Sa 2:26 Don't you realise that this will **e**
15: 7 At the **e** of four years, Absalom said
24: 8 **e** of nine months and twenty days.
24:15 until the **e** of the time designated,
1Ki 9:10 At the **e** of twenty years, during
10:20 steps, one at either **e** of each step.
2Ki 8: 3 At the **e** of the seven years she came
10:21 it was full from one **e** to the other.
18:10 At the **e** of three years the
21:16 he filled Jerusalem from **e** to **e**—
24:20 in the **e** he thrust them from his
1Ch 29:29 from beginning to **e**, they are
2Ch 8: 1 At the **e** of twenty years, during
9:19 steps, one at either **e** of each step.
9:29 from beginning to **e**, are they not
12:15 from beginning to **e**, are they not
16:11 from beginning to **e**, are written in
20:16 and you will find them at the **e** of
20:34 from beginning to **e**, are written in
21:19 In the course of time, at the **e** of
25:26 from beginning to **e**, are they not
26:22 from beginning to **e**, are recorded by
28:26 from beginning to **e**, are written in
35:27 all the events, from beginning to **e**,
Ezr 9:11 impurity from one **e** to the other.
Ne 3:21 of Eliashib's house to the **e** of it.
4:11 kill them and put an **e** to the work."
9:31 put an **e** to them or abandon them,
Est 1:18 be no **e** of disrespect and discord.
8: 3 She begged him to put an **e** to the
Job 4:15 and the hair on my body stood on **e**.
7: 6 and they come to an **e** without hope.
16: 3 your long-winded speeches never **e**?
18: 2 "When will you **e** these speeches? Be
19:25 the **e** he will stand upon the earth.
21:21 his allotted months come to an **e**?
28: 3 Man puts an **e** to the darkness; he
Ps 7: 9 bring to an **e** the violence of the
19: 6 rises at one **e** of the heavens and
39: 4 "Show me, O LORD, my life's **e** and
48:14 he will be our guide even to the **e**.
89:44 You have put an **e** to his splendour
102:27 same, and your years will never **e**.
107:27 men; they were at their wits' **e**.
112: 8 in the **e** he will look in triumph on
119:33 then I will keep them to the **e**.
119:112 keeping your decrees to the very **e**.
Pr 1:19 Such is the **e** of all who go after
5: 4 in the **e** she is bitter as gall,
5:11 At the **e** of your life you will groan,
14:12 man, but in the **e** it leads to death.
14:13 may ache, and joy may **e** in grief.
16:25 man, but in the **e** it leads to death.
19:20 and in the **e** you will be wise.
20:21 will not be blessed at the **e**.
23:32 In the **e** it bites like a snake and
25: 8 for what will you do in the **e** if
28:23 He who rebukes a man will in the **e**
29:21 youth, he will bring grief in the **e**.
Ecc 3:11 God has done from beginning to **e**.
4: 8 There was no **e** to his toil, yet his
4:16 There was no **e** to all the people who
7: 8 The **e** of a matter is better than its
10:13 at the **e** they are wicked madness—
12:12 Of making many books there is no **e**,
Isa 2: 7 there is no **e** to their treasures.
2: 7 there is no **e** to the chariots.
7: 3 to meet Ahaz at the **e** of the
9: 7 and peace there will be no **e**.
10: 7 to put an **e** to many nations.
10:25 Very soon my anger against you will **e**
13:11 I will put an **e** to the arrogance of
14: 4 How the oppressor has come to an **e**!
16: 4 The oppressor will come to an **e**,
16:10 for I have put an **e** to the shouting.
21: 2 to an **e** all the groaning she caused.
21:16 the pomp of Kedar will come to an **e**.
23:15 But at the **e** of these seventy years,
23:17 At the **e** of seventy years, the LORD
38:12 day and night you made an **e** of me.
38:13 day and night you made an **e** of me.
46:10 I make known the **e** from the
60:20 and your days of sorrow will **e**.
66:17 meet their **e** together," declares the
Jer 5:31 But what will you do in the **e**?
7:34 I will bring an **e** to the sounds of
12:12 from one **e** of the land to the other;
16: 9 in your days I will bring an **e** to
17:11 in the **e** he will prove to be a fool.
20:18 sorrow and to **e** my days in shame?
25:33 one **e** of the earth to the other.
48: 2 Come, let us put an **e** to that nation.
48:35 In Moab I will put an **e** to those who
49:37 until I have made an **e** of them.
51:13 your **e** has come, the time for you to
51:64 The words of Jeremiah **e** here.
52: 3 **e** he thrust them from his presence.
Lam 3:53 They tried to **e** my life in a pit and
4:18 Our **e** was near, our days were
4:18 were numbered, for our **e** had come.
4:22 your punishment will **e**; he will not
Eze 3:16 At the **e** of seven days the word of
5: 2 the days of your siege come to an **e**,
7: 2 The **e**! The **e** has come upon the four
7: 3 The **e** is now upon you and I will
7: 6 The **e** has come! The **e** has come! It
7:24 put an **e** to the pride of the mighty,
12:23 going to put an **e** to this proverb,
20:17 or put an **e** to them in the desert.
22: 4 and the **e** of your years has come.
22:15 I will put an **e** to your uncleanness.
23:48 "So I will put an **e** to lewdness in
26:13 I will put an **e** to your noisy songs,
26:21 I will bring you to a horrible **e** and
27:36 a horrible **e** and will be no more.'"
28:19 a horrible **e** and will be no more.'"
29:13 At the **e** of forty years I will
30:10 "'I will put an **e** to the hordes of
30:13 put an **e** to the images in Memphis.
30:18 proud strength will come to an **e**.
33:28 proud strength will come to an **e**,
39:14 At the **e** of the seven months they
40:15 **e** of its portico was fifty cubits.
41: 4 across the **e** of the outer sanctuary.
43:27 At the **e** of these days, from the
46:19 showed me a place at the western **e**.
Da 1:15 At the **e** of the ten days they looked
1:18 At the **e** of the time set by the king
2:44 kingdoms and bring them to an **e**,
4:34 At the **e** of that time, I,
5:26 your reign and brought it to an **e**.
6:26 his dominion will never **e**.
7:28 "This is the **e** of the matter. I,
8:17 vision concerns the time of the **e**."
8:19 the appointed time of the **e**.
9:24 to put an **e** to sin, to atone for
9:26 The **e** will come like a flood: War
9:26 War will continue until the **e**, and
9:27 put an **e** to sacrifice and offering.
9:27 until the **e** that is decreed is
11:18 but a commander will put an **e** to his
11:27 but to no avail, because an **e** will
11:35 spotless until the time of the **e**,
11:40 "At the time of the **e** the king of
11:45 to his **e**, and no-one will help him.
12: 4 the scroll until the time of the **e**.
12: 9 and sealed until the time of the **e**.
12:12 reaches the **e** of the 1,335 days.
12:13 "As for you, go your way till the **e**.
12:13 You will rest, and then at the **e** of
Hos 1: 4 put an **e** to the kingdom of Israel.
11: 6 gates and put an **e** to their plans.
Am 6: 7 your feasting and lounging will **e**.
8:10 and the **e** of it like a bitter day.
Na 1: 8 flood he will make an **e** of Nineveh;
1: 9 the LORD he will bring to an **e**;
Hab 2: 3 of the **e** and will not prove false.
Zep 1:18 **e** of all who live in the earth."
Mt 10:22 stands firm to the **e** will be saved.
21:41 those wretches to a wretched **e**,"
24: 6 happen, but the **e** is still to come.
24:13 he who stands firm to the **e** will be
24:14 nations, and then the **e** will come.
24:31 one **e** of the heavens to the other.
Mk 3:26 he cannot stand; his **e** has come.
13: 7 happen, but the **e** is still to come.
13:13 stands firm to the **e** will be saved.
Lk 1:33 for ever; his kingdom will never **e**."
4: 2 and at the **e** of them he was hungry.
17:24 up the sky from one **e** to the other.
21: 9 but the **e** will not come right away."
Jn 11: 4 "This sickness will not **e** in death.
Ac 21:26 the days of purification would **e**
Ro 10: 4 Christ is the **e** of the law so that
1Co 1: 8 He will keep you strong to the **e**, so
4: 9 display at the **e** of the procession,
15:24 the **e** will come, when he hands over
2Co 11:15 **e** will be what their actions deserve.
Col 1:29 To this **e** I labour, struggling with
Heb 1:12 same, and your years will never **e**."
3:14 hold firmly to the **e** the confidence
6: 8 In the **e** it will be burned.
6:11 this same diligence to the very **e**,

Heb 6:16 said and puts an **e** to all argument.
7: 3 without beginning of days or **e** of
9:26 appeared once for all at the **e** of the
11:22 By faith Joseph, when his **e** was near,
1Pe 4: 7 The **e** of all things is near.
2Pe 2:20 worse off at the **e** than they were at
Rev 2:26 overcomes and does my will to the **e**,
21: 6 the Omega, the Beginning and the **E**.
22:13 the Last, the Beginning and the **E**.

End of the age
Mt 13:39 The harvest is the **e**, and the
13:40 in the fire, so it will be at the **e**.
13:49 This is how it will be at the **e**. The
24: 3 sign of your coming and of the **e**?"
28:20 I am with you always, to the very **e**."

Endanger (Danger)
Ru 4: 6 it because I might **e** my own estate.
1Co 15:30 for us, why do we **e** ourselves every

Endangered (Danger)
Ecc 10: 9 splits logs may be **e** by them.

Endangers (Danger)
Lev 19:16 "Do not do anything that **e** your

Ended (End)
Jos 15:11 The boundary **e** at the sea.
16: 8 the Kanah Ravine and **e** at the sea.
17: 9 side of the ravine and **e** at the sea.
19:14 and **e** at the Valley of Iphtah El.
19:22 Beth Shemesh, and **e** at the Jordan.
2Ch 31: 1 all this had **e**, the Israelites who
Job 31:40 The words of Job are **e**.
39: 3 young; their labour pains are **e**.
Ps 78:33 he **e** their days in futility and
Pr 22:10 strife; quarrels and insults are **e**.
Isa 14: 4 come to an end! How his fury has **e**!
Jer 8:20 summer has **e**, and we are not saved."
Am 8: 5 and the Sabbath be **e** that we may
Ac 20: 1 the uproar had **e**, Paul sent for the
Rev 20: 3 until the thousand years were **e**.
20: 5 until the thousand years were **e**.

Ending (End)
Ge 44:12 the oldest and **e** with the youngest.
Jos 15: 4 the Wadi of Egypt, **e** at the sea.
16: 3 Horon and on to Gezer, **e** at the sea.
19:33 to Lakkum and **e** at the Jordan.

Endless
Job 22: 5 great? Are not your sins **e**?
Ps 9: 6 **E** ruin has overtaken the enemy, you
49:11 their dwellings for **e** generations,
93: 5 your house for **e** days, O LORD.
106:31 for **e** generations to come.
Na 2: 9 The supply is **e**, the wealth from all
3:19 for who has not felt your **e** cruelty?
1Ti 1: 4 to myths and **e** genealogies.

Endor
Town about 4 miles south of Mount Tabor, allotted to tribe of Manasseh (Jos 17:11). Home of the medium whom Saul consulted (1Sa 28:7). Fleeing Midianites perished here (Ps 83:10).

Jos 17:11 Ibleam and the people of Dor, **E**,
1Sa 28: 7 "There is one in **E**," they said.
Ps 83:10 who perished at **E** and became like

Endow (Endowed)
Job 39:17 for God did not **e** her with wisdom or
Ps 72: 1 **E** the king with your justice, O God,

Endowed (Endow)
2Ch 2:12 **e** with intelligence and discernment,
Job 38:36 Who **e** the heart with wisdom or gave
Isa 55: 5 for he has **e** you with splendour."
60: 9 for he has **e** you with splendour.

Ends (End, *Ends of the earth*)
Ex 25:18 hammered gold at the **e** of the cover.
25:19 piece with the cover, at the two **e**.
28:25 the other **e** of the chains to the two
37: 7 hammered gold at the **e** of the cover.
37: 8 at the two **e** he made them of one
39:18 the other **e** of the chains to the two
1Ki 8: 8 These poles were so long that their **e**
2Ch 5: 9 These poles were so long that their **e**
Ps 19: 4 their words to the **e** of the world.
Pr 11:23 The desire of the righteous **e** only
12:24 but laziness **e** in slave labour.
16: 4 works out everything for his own **e**—
18: 1 An unfriendly man pursues selfish **e**;
20:17 he **e** up with a mouth full of gravel.
Isa 13: 5 from the **e** of the heavens—the LORD
58: 4 Your fasting **e** in quarrelling and
Jer 48:47 Here **e** the judgment on Moab.
Eze 15: 4 burns both **e** and chars the middle,
Ro 10:18 their words to the **e** of the world."

Ends of the earth
Dt 28:49 from the **e**, like an eagle swooping
33:17 the nations, even those at the **e**.
1Sa 2:10 heaven; the LORD will judge the **e**.
Job 28:24 for he views the **e** and sees
37: 3 whole heaven and sends it to the **e**.
Ps 2: 8 inheritance, the **e** your possession.
22:27 All the **e** will remember and turn to
46: 9 He makes wars cease to the **e**; he
48:10 O God, your praise reaches to the **e**;
59:13 Then it will be known to the **e** that
61: 2 From the **e** I call to you, I call as
65: 5 all the **e** and of the farthest seas,
67: 7 God will bless us, and all the **e**
72: 8 to sea and from the River to the **e**.
98: 3 **e** have seen the salvation of our God.
135: 7 He makes clouds rise from the **e**; he
Pr 17:24 but a fool's eyes wander to the **e**.
30: 4 Who has established all the **e**? What
Isa 5:26 he whistles for those at the **e**.
24:16 From the **e** we hear singing: "Glory
40:28 God, the Creator of the **e**.
41: 5 seen it and fear; the **e** tremble.
41: 9 I took you from the **e**, from its
42:10 his praise from the **e**, you who go
43: 6 afar and my daughters from the **e**—
45:22 "Turn to me and be saved, all you **e**;
48:20 Send it out to the **e**; say, "The LORD
49: 6 may bring my salvation to the **e**."
52:10 **e** will see the salvation of our God.
62:11 LORD has made proclamation to the **e**:
Jer 6:22 is being stirred up from the **e**.
10:13 he makes clouds rise from the **e**.
16:19 will come from the **e** and say,
25:31 The tumult will resound to the **e**,
25:32 mighty storm is rising from the **e**."
31: 8 north and gather them from the **e**.
50:41 are being stirred up from the **e**.
51:16 he makes clouds rise from the **e**.
Da 4:11 the sky; it was visible to the **e**.
Mic 5: 4 his greatness will reach to the **e**.
Zec 9:10 to sea and from the River to the **e**.
Mt 12:42 the **e** to listen to Solomon's wisdom,
Mk 13:27 the **e** to the ends of the heavens.
Lk 11:31 the **e** to listen to Solomon's wisdom,
Ac 1: 8 Judea and Samaria, and to the **e**."
13:47 you may bring salvation to the **e**.'"

Endued
Ps 89:13 Your arm is **e** with power; your hand

Endurance (Endure)
Ro 15: 4 so that through **e** and the
15: 5 May the God who gives **e** and
2Co 1: 6 which produces in you patient **e**
6: 4 every way: in great **e**; in troubles,
Col 1:11 may have great **e** and patience, and
1Th 1: 3 and your **e** inspired by hope in our
1Ti 6:11 faith, love, **e** and gentleness.
2Ti 3:10 purpose, faith, patience, love, **e**,
Tit 2: 2 sound in faith, in love and in **e**.
Rev 1: 9 patient **e** that are ours in Jesus,
13:10 This calls for patient **e** and
14:12 This calls for patient **e** on the part

Endure (Endurance, Endured, Endures, Enduring)
1Sa 13:14 now your kingdom will not **e**; the
2Sa 7:16 Your house and your kingdom shall **e**
Job 14: 2 a fleeting shadow, he does not **e**.
15:29 be rich and his wealth will not **e**,
20:21 devour; his prosperity will not **e**.
Ps 37:18 their inheritance will **e** for ever.
49:12 man, despite his riches, does not **e**;
55:12 I could **e** it; if a foe were raising
69: 7 For I **e** scorn for your sake, and
69:10 I weep and fast, I must **e** scorn;
72: 5 He will **e** as long as the sun, as
72:17 May his name **e** for ever; may it
89:29 his throne as long as the heavens **e**.
89:36 his throne **e** before me like the sun;
101: 5 and a proud heart, him will I not **e**.
104:31 May the glory of the LORD **e** for ever;
119:91 Your laws **e** to this day, for all
Pr 12:19 Truthful lips **e** for ever, but a
27:24 for riches do not **e** for ever, and a
Ecc 3:14 everything God does will **e** for ever;
Isa 66:22 earth that I make will **e** before me,"
66:22 so will your name and descendants **e**.
Jer 10:10 the nations cannot **e** his wrath.
10:19 is my sickness, and I must **e** it."
44:22 the LORD could no longer **e** your
Eze 22:14 Will your courage **e** or your hands be
Da 2:44 end, but it will itself **e** for ever.
Joel 2:11 it is dreadful. Who can **e** it?
Na 1: 6 Who can **e** his fierce anger? His
Mal 3: 2 who can **e** the day of his coming? Who
1Co 4:12 when we are persecuted, we **e** it;
2Co 1: 8 pressure, far beyond our ability to **e**,
2Ti 2: 3 **E** hardship with us like a good
2:10 Therefore I **e** everything for the
2:12 if we **e**, we will also reign with him.
4: 5 **e** hardship, do the work of an
Heb 12: 7 **E** hardship as discipline; God is
1Pe 2:20 a beating for doing wrong and **e** it?
2:20 and you **e** it, this is commendable
Rev 3:10 Since you have kept my command to **e**

Endured (Endure)
Ps 123: 3 on us, for we have **e** much contempt.
123: 4 We have **e** much ridicule from the
132: 1 David and all the hardships he **e**.
Ac 13:18 he **e** their conduct for about forty
2Ti 3:11 and Lystra, the persecutions I **e**.
Heb 12: 2 who for the joy set before him **e** the
12: 3 Consider him who **e** such opposition
Rev 2: 3 You have persevered and have **e**

Endures (Endure, *Love endures for ever*)
Ge 8:22 "As long as the earth **e**, seedtime
Ezr 3:11 good; his love to Israel **e** for ever.
Ps 102:12 renown **e** through all generations.
111: 3 and his righteousness **e** for ever.
112: 3 and his righteousness **e** for ever.
112: 9 his righteousness **e** for ever; his
117: 2 faithfulness of the LORD **e** for ever.
119:90 you established the earth, and it **e**.
125: 1 cannot be shaken but **e** for ever.
135:13 Your name, O LORD, **e** for ever, your
138: 8 Your love, O LORD, **e** for ever—
145:13 dominion **e** through all generations.
Lam 5:19 **e** from generation to generation.
Da 4: 3 **e** from generation to generation.
4:34 **e** from generation to generation.
6:26 "For he is the living God and he **e**
9:15 yourself a name that **e** to this day,
Jn 6:27 but for food that **e** to eternal life,
2Co 9: 9 poor; his righteousness **e** for ever."

Enduring (Endure)
1Ki 11:38 I will build you a dynasty as **e** as
Ps 19: 9 The fear of the LORD is pure, **e** for
Pr 8:18 riches and honour, **e** wealth and
Jer 5:15 you—an ancient and **e** nation,
2Th 1: 4 persecutions and trials you are **e**.
Heb 13:14 For here we do not have an **e** city,
1Pe 1:23 the living and **e** word of God.

Enemies (Enemy)

Ge 14:20 who delivered your **e** into your hand.
22:17 possession of the cities of their **e**,
24:60 possess the gates of their **e**."
49: 8 hand will be on the neck of your **e**;
Ex 1:10 if war breaks out, will join our **e**,
23:22 I will be an enemy to your **e** and
23:27 all your **e** turn their backs and run.
32:25 become a laughing-stock to their **e**.
Lev 26: 7 You will pursue your **e**, and they
26: 8 **e** will fall by the sword before you.
26:16 in vain, because your **e** will eat it.
26:17 that you will be defeated by your **e**;
26:32 **e** who live there will be appalled.
26:34 you are in the country of your **e**;
26:36 so fearful in the lands of their **e**
26:37 not be able to stand before your **e**.
26:38 the land of your **e** will devour you.
26:39 of their **e** because of their sins;
26:41 I sent them into the land of their **e**
26:44 they are in the land of their **e**,
Nu 10: 9 your God and rescued from your **e**.
10:35 O LORD! May your **e** be scattered;
14:42 You will be defeated by your **e**,
23:11 to me? I brought you to curse my **e**,
24:10 "I summoned you to curse my **e**, but
25:17 "Treat the Midianites as **e** and kill
25:18 they treated you as **e** when they
32:21 he has driven his **e** out before him—
Dt 1:42 You will be defeated by your **e**.'"
6:19 thrusting out all your **e** before you,
12:10 he will give you rest from all your **e**
20: 1 you go to war against your **e** and see
20: 3 going into battle against your **e**.
20: 4 against your **e** to give you victory."
20:14 LORD your God gives you from your **e**.
21:10 you go to war against your **e** and the
23: 9 you are encamped against your **e**,
23:14 you and to deliver your **e** to you.
25:19 God gives you rest from all the **e**
28: 7 The LORD will grant that the **e** who
28:25 you to be defeated before your **e**.
28:31 your **e**, and no-one will rescue them.
28:48 the **e** the LORD sends against you.
28:68 to your **e** as male and female slaves,
30: 7 your **e** who hate and persecute you.
32:31 our Rock, as even our **e** concede.
32:43 he will take vengeance on his **e** and
33:29 Your **e** will cower before you, and
Jos 5:13 "Are you for us or for our **e**?
7: 8 Israel has been routed by its **e**?
7:12 cannot stand against their **e**;
7:13 against your **e** until you remove it.
10:13 the nation avenged itself on its **e**,
10:19 don't stop! Pursue your **e**, attack
10:25 all the **e** you are going to fight."
21:44 Not one of their **e** withstood them;
21:44 LORD handed all their **e** over to them.
22: 8 brothers the plunder from your **e**."
23: 1 rest from all their **e** around them,
Jdg 2:14 He sold them to their **e** all around,
2:18 their **e** as long as the judge lived;
5:31 "So may all your **e** perish, O LORD!
8:34 hands of all their **e** on every side.
11:36 you of your **e**, the Ammonites.
1Sa 2: 1 My mouth boasts over my **e**, for I
4: 3 and save us from the hand of our **e**."
12:10 deliver us from the hands of our **e**,
12:11 the hands of your **e** on every side,
14:24 I have avenged myself on my **e**!"
14:30 the plunder they took from their **e**.
14:47 he fought against their **e** on every
18:25 foreskins, to take revenge on his **e**.
20:15 cut off every one of David's **e** from
20:16 the LORD call David's **e** to account."
25:26 may your **e** and all who intend to
25:29 But the lives of your **e** he will hurl
29: 8 against the **e** of my lord the king?"
30:26 from the plunder of the LORD's **e**."
2Sa 3:18 and from the hand of all their **e**.'"
5: 8 'lame and blind' who are David's **e**.
5:20 broken out against my **e** before me.
7: 1 him rest from all his **e** around him,
7: 9 cut off all your **e** from before you.
7:11 also give you rest from all your **e**.
2Sa 12:14 you have made the **e** of the LORD show
18:19 him from the hand of his **e**."
18:32 "May the **e** of my lord the king and
19: 9 delivered us from the hand of our **e**;
22: 1 all his **e** and from the hand of Saul.
22: 4 of praise, and I am saved from my **e**.
22:15 He shot arrows and scattered the ⌊**e**⌋
22:38 "I pursued my **e** and crushed them; I
22:41 You made my **e** turn their backs in
22:49 who sets me free from my **e**. You
24:13 from your **e** while they pursue you?
1Ki 3:11 have asked for the death of your **e**
5: 3 the LORD put his **e** under his feet.
8:44 people go to war against their **e**,
8:48 of their **e** who took them captive,
2Ki 17:39 you from the hand of all your **e**."
21:14 and hand them over to their **e**.
1Ch 12:17 to betray me to my **e** when my hands
14:11 broken out against my **e** by my hand.
17: 8 cut off all your **e** from before you.
17:10 I will also subdue all your **e**. "I
21:12 of being swept away before your **e**,
22: 9 rest from all his **e** on every side.
2Ch 1:11 nor for the death of your **e**, and
6:28 when **e** besiege them in any of their
6:34 people go to war against their **e**,
20:27 them cause to rejoice over their **e**.
20:29 had fought against the **e** of Israel.
26:13 to support the king against his **e**.
Ezr 4: 1 the **e** of Judah and Benjamin heard
8:22 to protect us from **e** on the road,
8:31 us from **e** and bandits along the way.
Ne 4:11 Also our **e** said, "Before they know
4:15 our **e** heard that we were aware of
5: 9 avoid the reproach of our Gentile **e**?
6: 1 the rest of our **e** that I had rebuilt
6:16 all our **e** heard about this, all the
9:27 you handed them over to their **e**, who
9:27 them from the hand of their **e**.
9:28 abandoned them to the hand of their **e**
Est 8:11 to plunder the property of their **e**.
8:13 day to avenge themselves on their **e**.
9: 1 On this day the **e** of the Jews had
9: 5 The Jews struck down all their **e**
9:16 and get relief from their **e**.
9:22 the Jews got relief from their **e**,
Job 8:22 Your **e** will be clothed in shame, and
19:11 me; he counts me among his **e**.
27: 7 "May my **e** be like the wicked, my
Ps 3: 7 O my God! Strike all my **e** on the jaw;
5: 8 because of my **e**—make straight your
6:10 All my **e** will be ashamed and
7: 6 rise up against the rage of my **e**.
8: 2 ordained praise because of your **e**,
9: 3 My **e** turn back; they stumble and
9:13 O LORD, see how my **e** persecute me!
10: 5 from him; he sneers at all his **e**.
17: 9 from my mortal **e** who surround me.
18: T all his **e** and from the hand of Saul.
18: 3 of praise, and I am saved from my **e**.
18:14 shot his arrows and scattered ⌊the **e**⌋
18:37 I pursued my **e** and overtook them; I
18:40 You made my **e** turn their backs in
18:48 who saves me from my **e**. You exalted
21: 8 Your hand will lay hold on all your **e**
23: 5 before me in the presence of my **e**.
25: 2 shame, nor let my **e** triumph over me.
25:19 See how my **e** have increased and how
27: 2 when my **e** and my foes attack me,
27: 6 my head will be exalted above the **e**
30: 1 and did not let my **e** gloat over me.
31:11 of all my **e**, I am the utter contempt
31:15 deliver me from my **e** and from those
35:19 over me who are my **e** without cause;
37:20 The LORD's **e** will be like the beauty
38:19 Many are those who are my vigorous **e**;
41: 5 My **e** say of me in malice, "When will
41: 7 All my **e** whisper together against me;
44: 5 Through you we push back our **e**;
44: 7 you give us victory over our **e**, you
45: 5 pierce the hearts of the king's **e**;
55:15 Let death take my **e** by surprise; let
56: 9 my **e** will turn back when I call for
59: 1 Deliver me from my **e**, O God;
60:12 and he will trample down our **e**.
66: 3 power that your **e** cringe before you.
Ps 68: 1 May God arise, may his **e** be
68:21 God will crush the heads of his **e**,
69: 4 head; many are my **e** without cause,
69:19 and shamed; all my **e** are before you.
71:10 For my **e** speak against me; those who
72: 9 him and his **e** will lick the dust.
74:23 of your **e**, which rises continually.
78:53 but the sea engulfed their **e**.
78:66 He beat back his **e**; he put them to
80: 6 our neighbours, and our **e** mock us.
81:14 how quickly would I subdue their **e**
83: 2 See how your **e** are astir, how your
86:17 that my **e** may see it and be put to
89:10 strong arm you scattered your **e**.
89:42 you have made all his **e** rejoice.
89:51 the taunts with which your **e** have
92: 9 For surely your **e**, O LORD, surely
92: 9 O LORD, surely your **e** will perish;
102: 8 All day long my **e** taunt me; those
106:42 Their **e** oppressed them and subjected
108:13 and he will trample down our **e**.
110: 1 your **e** a footstool for your feet."
110: 2 will rule in the midst of your **e**.
118: 7 I will look in triumph on my **e**.
119:98 Your commands make me wiser than my **e**
119:139 me out, for my **e** ignore your words
127: 5 contend with their **e** in the gate.
132:18 I will clothe his **e** with shame, but
136:24 and freed us from our **e**, His love
139:22 hatred for them; I count them my **e**.
143: 9 Rescue me from my **e**, O LORD, for I
143:12 In your unfailing love, silence my **e**;
144: 6 scatter ⌊the **e**⌋; shoot your arrows
Pr 16: 7 even his **e** live at peace with him.
Isa 1:24 my foes and avenge myself on my **e**.
9:11 them and has spurred their **e** on.
11:13 and Judah's **e** will be cut off;
26:11 reserved for your **e** consume them.
29: 5 your many **e** will become like fine
41:12 Though you search for your **e**, you
42:13 cry and will triumph over his **e**.
59:18 so will he repay wrath to his **e** and
62: 8 I give your grain as food for your **e**,
63:18 **e** have trampled down your sanctuary.
64: 2 to make your name known to your **e**
66: 6 LORD repaying his **e** all they deserve.
Jer 12: 7 one I love into the hands of her **e**.
15: 9 to the sword before their **e**,"
15:11 surely I will make your **e** plead with
15:14 I will enslave you to your **e** in a
17: 4 I will enslave you to your **e** in a
18:17 I will scatter them before their **e**;
19: 7 fall by the sword before their **e**,
19: 9 them by the **e** who seek their lives.'
20: 4 them fall by the sword of their **e**.
20: 5 I will hand over to their **e** all the
21: 7 and to their **e** who seek their lives.
30:16 all your **e** will go into exile.
34:20 I will hand over to their **e** who seek
34:21 to their **e** who seek their lives,
44:30 over to his **e** who seek his life,
50: 7 their **e** said, 'We are not guilty, for
51:55 Waves ⌊of enemies⌋ will rage like
Lam 1: 2 her; they have become her **e**.
1: 5 her masters; her **e** are at ease.
1: 7 Her **e** looked at her and laughed at
1:21 All my **e** have heard of my distress;
2:16 All your **e** open their mouths wide
3:46 "All our **e** have opened their mouths
3:52 Those who were my **e** without cause
3:62 what my **e** whisper and mutter against
4:12 that **e** and foes could enter the
Eze 16:27 you over to the greed of your **e**,
39:23 handed them over to their **e**, and they
39:27 them from the countries of their **e**,
Da 4:19 if only the dream applied to your **e**
Am 9: 4 are driven into exile by their **e**,
Mic 4:10 you out of the hand of your **e**.
5: 9 be lifted up in triumph over your **e**,
7: 6 a man's **e** are the members of his
Na 1: 2 maintains his wrath against his **e**.
3:13 are wide open to your **e**; fire has
Mt 5:44 I tell you: Love your **e** and pray for
10:36 a man's **e** will be the members of his
22:44 I put your **e** under your feet."'
Mk 12:36 I put your **e** under your feet."'

Lk 1:71 salvation from our **e** and from the
1:74 to rescue us from the hand of our **e**,
6:27 Love your **e**, do good to those who
6:35 love your **e**, do good to them, and
19:27 those **e** of mine who did not want me
19:43 when your **e** will build an embankment
20:43 until I make your **e** a footstool for
23:12 friends—before this they had been **e**.
Ac 2:35 until I make your **e** a footstool for
Ro 5:10 For if, when we were God's **e**, we
11:28 they are **e** on your account; but as
1Co 15:25 he has put all his **e** under his feet.
Php 3:18 live as **e** of the cross of Christ.
Col 1:21 were **e** in your minds because of your
Heb 1:13 your **e** a footstool for your feet"?
10:13 Since that time he waits for his **e**
10:27 fire that will consume the **e** of God.
Rev 11:5 their mouths and devours their **e**.
11:12 in a cloud, while their **e** looked on.

Enemy (Enemies, Enemy's, Enmity)
Ex 15:6 hand, O LORD, shattered the **e**.
15:9 "The **e** boasted, 'I will pursue, I
23:22 I will be an **e** to your enemies and
Lev 26:25 and you will be given into **e** hands.
Nu 10:9 against an **e** who is oppressing you,
24:18 Edom will be conquered; Seir, his **e**,
35:23 was not his **e** and he did not intend
Dt 28:53 of the suffering that your **e** will
28:55 suffering that your **e** will inflict
28:57 the distress that your **e** will inflict
32:27 I dreaded the taunt of the **e**, lest
32:42 the heads of the **e** leaders."
33:27 He will drive out your **e** before you
Jdg 3:28 given Moab, your **e**, into your hands.
16:23 Samson, our **e**, into our hands."
16:24 "Our god has delivered our **e** into
1Sa 18:29 remained his **e** for the rest of his
19:17 send my **e** away so that he escaped?"
24:4 'I will give your **e** into your hands
24:19 a man finds his **e**, does he let him
26:8 God has given your **e** into your hands.
28:16 away from you and become your **e**?
2Sa 4:8 your **e**, who tried to take your life.
22:18 He rescued me from my powerful **e**,
1Ki 8:33 defeated by an **e** because they have
8:37 or when an **e** besieges them in any of
8:46 them and give them over to the **e**,
21:20 "So you have found me, my **e**!" "I
2Ki 6:18 the **e** came down towards him, Elisha
2Ch 6:24 defeated by an **e** because they have
6:36 them and give them over to the **e**,
25:8 God will overthrow you before the **e**,
Est 3:10 the Agagite, the **e** of the Jews.
7:6 Esther said, "The adversary and **e** is
8:1 estate of Haman, the **e** of the Jews.
9:10 of Hammedatha, the **e** of the Jews.
9:24 the Agagite, the **e** of all the Jews,
Job 6:23 deliver me from the hand of the **e**,
13:24 your face and consider me your **e**?
33:10 with me; he considers me his **e**.
Ps 7:5 let my **e** pursue and overtake me; let
9:6 Endless ruin has overtaken the **e**,
13:2 How long will my **e** triumph over me?
13:4 my **e** will say, "I have overcome him,"
18:17 He rescued me from my powerful **e**,
31:8 You have not handed me over to the **e**
41:11 for my **e** does not triumph over me.
42:9 about mourning, oppressed by the **e**?"
43:2 about mourning, oppressed by the **e**?
44:10 You made us retreat before the **e**,
44:16 of the **e**, who is bent on revenge.
55:3 at the voice of the **e**, at the stares
55:12 If an **e** were insulting me, I could
60:11 Give us aid against the **e**, for the
64:1 my life from the threat of the **e**.
74:3 destruction the **e** has brought on the
74:10 How long will the **e** mock you, O God?
74:18 Remember how the **e** has mocked you,
78:61 his splendour into the hands of the **e**
89:22 No **e** will subject him to tribute; no
106:10 the hand of the **e** he redeemed them.
108:12 Give us aid against the **e**, for the
143:3 The **e** pursues me, he crushes me to
Pr 24:17 Do not gloat when your **e** falls; when
25:21 If your **e** is hungry, give him food
27:6 trusted, but an **e** multiplies kisses.
29:24 accomplice of a thief is his own **e**;
Isa 22:3 fled while the **e** was still far away.
63:10 he turned and became their **e** and he
Jer 6:25 for the **e** has a sword, and there is
30:14 I have struck you as an **e** would and
31:16 will return from the land of the **e**.
44:30 the **e** who was seeking his life."
46:22 serpent as the **e** advances in force;
47:3 at the noise of **e** chariots and the
Lam 1:7 When her people fell into **e** hands,
1:9 for the **e** has triumphed."
1:10 The **e** laid hands on all her
1:16 because the **e** has prevailed."
2:3 right hand at the approach of the **e**.
2:4 Like an **e** he has strung his bow; his
2:5 The Lord is like an **e**; he has
2:7 He has handed over to the **e** the
2:17 he has let the **e** gloat over you, he
2:22 for and reared, my **e** has destroyed.
Eze 36:2 LORD says: The **e** said of you,
Hos 8:3 what is good; an **e** will pursue him.
Am 3:11 "An **e** will overrun the land; he will
Mic 2:8 my people have risen up like an **e**.
7:8 Do not gloat over me, my **e**! Though I
7:10 my **e** will see it and will be covered
Na 3:11 hiding and seek refuge from the **e**.
Zep 3:15 he has turned back your **e**.
Zec 8:10 business safely because of his **e**,
Mt 5:43 Love your neighbour and hate your **e**.'
13:25 while everyone was sleeping, his **e**
13:28 "'An **e** did this,' he replied. "The
13:39 the **e** who sows them is the devil.
Lk 10:19 to overcome all the power of the **e**;
Ac 13:10 an **e** of everything that is right!
Ro 12:20 "If your **e** is hungry, feed him; if
1Co 15:26 The last **e** to be destroyed is death.
Gal 4:16 Have I now become your **e** by telling
2Th 3:15 Yet do not regard him as an **e**, but
1Ti 5:14 the **e** no opportunity for slander.
Jas 4:4 of the world becomes an **e** of God.
1Pe 5:8 Your **e** the devil prowls around like

Enemy's (Enemy)
Ex 23:4 "If you come across your **e** ox or
Job 31:29 I have rejoiced at my **e** misfortune
Jer 8:16 The snorting of the **e** horses is

Energy
Col 1:29 all his **e**, which so powerfully works

Enfolds (Fold)
Isa 25:7 the shroud that **e** all peoples,

Enforce (Force)
Da 6:7 **e** the decree that anyone who prays

Engage (Engaged, Engages, Engaging)
Ex 31:5 to **e** in all kinds of craftsmanship.
35:33 to work in wood and to **e** in all
Dt 2:24 of it and **e** him in battle.
20:12 make peace and they **e** you in battle,
1Sa 7:10 drew near to **e** Israel in battle.
2Ch 35:22 himself to **e** him in battle.
Jer 11:15 When you **e** in your wickedness, then
Da 11:40 of the South will **e** him in battle,
Hos 4:10 **e** in prostitution but not increase,

Engaged (Engage)
Jdg 12:2 "I and my people were **e** in a great
1Ki 14:24 the people **e** in all the detestable
Eze 16:17 and **e** in prostitution with them.
16:26 You **e** in prostitution with the
16:28 You **e** in prostitution with the
23:5 "Oholah **e** in prostitution while she
1Co 7:36 towards the virgin he is **e** to,

Engages (Engage)
Dt 18:10 interprets omens, **e** in witchcraft,

Engaging (Engage)
Eze 23:3 in Egypt, **e** in prostitution from

Engrave (Engraved, Engraves, Engraving)
Ex 28:9 " two onyx stones and **e** on them
28:11 **E** the names of the sons of Israel on
28:36 "Make a plate of pure gold and **e** on
Zec 3:9 and I will **e** an inscription on it,'

Engraved (Engrave)
Ex 28:21 each **e** like a seal with the name of
32:16 writing of God, **e** on the tablets.
39:6 **e** them like a seal with the names of
39:14 each **e** like a seal with the name of
39:30 out of pure gold and **e** on it, like
1Ki 7:36 He **e** cherubim, lions and palm trees
Job 19:24 tool on lead, or **e** in rock for ever!
Isa 49:16 See, I have **e** you on the palms of my
Jer 17:1 "Judah's sin is **e** with an iron tool,
2Co 3:7 which was **e** in letters on stone,

Engraves (Engrave)
Ex 28:11 the way a gem cutter **e** a seal.

Engraving (Engrave)
1Ki 7:31 Around its opening there was **e**. The
2Ch 2:7 and experienced in the art of **e**, to
2:14 He is experienced in all kinds of **e**

Engrossed
1Co 7:31 of the world, as if not **e** in them.

Engulf (Engulfed, Engulfing)
Ps 69:2 the deep waters; the floods **e** me.
69:15 Do not let the floodwaters **e** me or
Hos 7:2 Their sins **e** them; they are always

Engulfed (Engulf)
Ps 78:53 but the sea **e** their enemies.
88:17 a flood; they have completely **e** me.
124:4 the flood would have **e** us, the

Engulfing (Engulf)
Jnh 2:5 The **e** waters threatened me, the deep

Enhances
Ro 3:7 "If my falsehood **e** God's truthfulness

Enjoy (Enjoyed, Enjoying, Enjoyment, Enjoys)
Ge 45:18 and you can **e** the fat of the land.'
Ex 30:38 Whoever makes any like it to **e** its
Lev 26:34 the land will **e** its sabbath years
26:34 land will rest and **e** its sabbaths.
26:43 will **e** its sabbaths while it lies
Nu 14:31 in to **e** the land you have rejected.
Dt 6:2 and so that you may **e** long life.
20:6 not begun to **e** it? Let him go home,
20:6 die in battle and someone else **e** it.
28:30 will not even begin to **e** its fruit.
Jdg 19:6 "Please stay tonight and **e** yourself.
19:9 Stay and **e** yourself. Early tomorrow
Ne 8:10 Nehemiah said, "Go and **e** choice food
Job 3:18 Captives also **e** their ease; they no
20:17 He will not **e** the streams, the
20:18 not **e** the profit from his trading.
33:28 and I shall live to **e** the light.'
Ps 37:3 in the land and **e** safe pasture.
37:11 the meek will inherit the land and **e**
37:19 days of famine they will **e** plenty.
106:5 that I may **e** the prosperity of your
Pr 7:18 let's **e** ourselves with love!
28:16 ill-gotten gain will **e** a long life.
Ecc 3:22 **e** his work, because that is his lot.
5:19 and enables him to **e** them, to accept
6:2 God does not enable him to **e** them
6:3 if he cannot **e** his prosperity and
6:6 over but fails to **e** his prosperity.
9:9 **E** life with your wife, whom you love,
11:8 a man may live, let him **e** them all.
Isa 3:10 will **e** the fruit of their deeds.
65:22 long **e** the works of their hands.
Jer 31:5 will plant them and **e** their fruit.
33:6 them **e** abundant peace and security.

Jn 5:35 you chose for a time to e his light.
Ro 16:23 I and the whole church here e,
Eph 6: 3 you may e long life on the earth."
Heb 11:25 rather than to e the pleasures of sin
3Jn : 2 Dear friend, I pray that you may e

Enjoyed (Enjoy)
Jdg 8:28 the land e peace for forty years.
1Ch 29:28 He died at a good old age, having e
2Ch 36:21 The land e its sabbath rests; all
Job 21:25 soul, never having e anything good.
Ps 55:14 with whom I once e sweet fellowship
Ac 7:46 who e God's favour and asked that he
9:31 and Samaria e a time of peace.
24: 2 "We have e a long period of peace
Ro 15:24 I have e your company for a while.

Enjoying (Enjoy)
Jdg 19:22 While they were e themselves, some
Ne 9:35 e your great goodness to them in the
Ac 2:47 praising God and e the favour of all

Enjoyment (Enjoy)
Ecc 2:25 without him, who can eat or find e?
4: 8 "and why am I depriving myself of e?"
8:15 I commend the e of life, because
1Ti 6:17 us with everything for our e.

Enjoys (Enjoy)
Pr 13: 2 From the fruit of his lips a man e
Ecc 6: 2 them, and a stranger e them instead.
Hab 1:16 in luxury and e the choicest food.

Enlarge (Enlarged, Enlarges)
Ex 34:24 before you and e your territory,
1Ch 4:10 "Oh, that you would bless me and e
Isa 54: 2 "E the place of your tent, stretch
2Co 9:10 e the harvest of your righteousness.

Enlarged (Enlarge)
Dt 12:20 the LORD your God has e your
Isa 9: 3 You have e the nation and increased
26:15 You have e the nation, O LORD; you
26:15 O LORD; you have e the nation.
Jer 20:17 as my grave, her womb e for ever.

Enlarges (Enlarge)
Dt 19: 8 If the LORD your God e your
33:20 "Blessed is he who e Gad's domain!
Job 12:23 he e nations, and disperses them.
Isa 5:14 Therefore the grave e its appetite

Enlighten (Enlightened)
Isa 40:14 Whom did the LORD consult to e him,

Enlightened (Enlighten)
Eph 1:18 that the eyes of your heart may be e
Heb 6: 4 for those who have once been e,

Enmity (Enemy)
Ge 3:15 I will put e between you and the

Enoch
1. Cain's first son; city named after him (Ge 4:17–18). **2.** Descendant of Seth; father of Methuselah (Ge 5:18–21). Prophesied (Jude 14–15); walked with God, and taken by him (Ge 5:22–24).

Ge 4:17 became pregnant and gave birth to E.
4:17 and he named it after his son E.
4:18 To E was born Irad, and Irad was the
5:18 years, he became the father of E.
5:19 after he became the father of E,
5:21 E had lived 65 years, he became the
5:22 E walked with God 300 years and had
5:23 Altogether, E lived 365 years.
5:24 E walked with God; then he was no
1Ch 1: 3 E, Methuselah, Lamech, Noah.
Lk 3:37 the son of Methuselah, the son of E,
Heb 11: 5 By faith E was taken from this life,
Jude :14 E, the seventh from Adam, prophesied

Enormous
Da 2:31 an e, dazzling statue, awesome in
4:10 Its height was e.
Rev 12: 3 appeared in heaven: an e red dragon

Enosh
Ge 4:26 also had a son, and he named him E.
5: 6 years, he became the father of E.
5: 7 after he became the father of E,
5: 9 E had lived 90 years, he became the
5:10 E lived 815 years and had other sons
5:11 Altogether, E lived 905 years, and
1Ch 1: 1 Adam, Seth, E,
Lk 3:38 the son of E, the son of Seth, the

Enquire (Enquired, Enquires, Enquiring, Enquiry)
Ge 25:22 me?" So she went to e of the LORD.
Dt 13:14 you must e, probe and investigate it
17: 9 E of them and they will give you the
Jos 9:14 but did not e of the LORD.
Jdg 18: 5 they said to him, "Please e of God
1Sa 9: 9 if a man went to e of God, he would
14:36 But the priest said, "Let us e of
28: 7 so that I may go and e of her.
1Ki 22: 7 of the LORD here whom we can e of?"
22: 8 through whom we can e of the LORD,
2Ki 3:11 we may e of the LORD through him?"
22:13 "Go and e of the LORD for me and for
22:18 who sent you to e of the LORD, 'This
1Ch 10:14 did not e of the LORD. So the LORD
13: 3 e of it during the reign of Saul."
15:13 We did not e of him about how to do
21:30 David could not go before it to e of
2Ch 18: 6 of the LORD here whom we can e of?"
18: 7 through whom we can e of the LORD,
20: 3 Alarmed, Jehoshaphat resolved to e
34:21 "Go and e of the LORD for me and for
34:26 who sent you to e of the LORD, 'This
Ezr 7:14 his seven advisers to e about Judah
Isa 8:19 should not a people e of their God?
Jer 10:21 senseless and do not e of the LORD;
18:13 "E among the nations: Who has ever
21: 2 "E now of the LORD for us because
37: 7 king of Judah, who sent you to e of
Eze 14: 3 Should I let them e of me at all?
14: 7 then goes to a prophet to e of me,
20: 1 of Israel came to e of the LORD,
20: 3 LORD says: Have you come to e of me?
20: 3 e of me, declares the Sovereign LORD.
20:31 Am I to let you e of me, O house of
20:31 LORD, I will not let you e of me.
Zep 1: 6 neither seek the LORD nor e of him.
1Co 14:35 If they want to e about something,

Enquired (Enquire)
Lev 10:16 Moses e about the goat of the sin
Jdg 13:17 Manoah e of the angel of the LORD,
20:18 went up to Bethel and e of God.
20:23 evening, and they e of the LORD.
20:27 the Israelites e of the LORD. (In
1Sa 10:22 they e further of the LORD, "Has the
22:10 Ahimelech e of the LORD for him; he
22:15 Was that day the first time I e of
23: 2 he e of the LORD, saying, "Shall I
23: 4 Once again David e of the LORD, and
28: 6 He e of the LORD, but the LORD did
30: 8 David e of the LORD, "Shall I pursue
2Sa 2: 1 In the course of time, David e of
5:19 David e of the LORD, "Shall I go and
5:23 David e of the LORD, and he answered,
1Ch 14:10 David e of God: "Shall I go and
14:14 David e of God again, and God
2Ch 1: 5 and the assembly e of him there.
Ps 77: 6 My heart mused and my spirit e:
Mt 19:18 "Which ones?" the man e. Jesus
Jn 4:52 he e as to the time when his son got

Enquires (Enquire)
2Sa 16:23 was like that of one who e of God.

Enquiring (Enquire)
Ex 33: 7 Anyone e of the LORD would go to the
Nu 27:21 by e of the Urim before the LORD.
Dt 12:30 careful not to be ensnared by e about
1Sa 22:13 giving him bread and a sword and e

Enquiry (Enquire)
Job 34:24 Without e he shatters the mighty and

Enraged (Rage)
2Ki 6:11 This e the king of Aram. He summoned
2Ch 16:10 was so e that he put him in prison.
Est 3: 5 down or pay him honour, he was e.
Isa 8:21 they will become e and, looking
57:17 I was e by his sinful greed; I
Eze 16:43 but e me with all these things,
Mt 22: 7 The king was e. He sent his army and
Rev 12:17 the dragon was e at the woman and

Enrich (Enriched)
Ps 65: 9 and water it; you e it abundantly.
Pr 5:10 and your toil e another man's house.

Enriched (Enrich)
Isa 23: 2 of Sidon, whom the seafarers have e.
Eze 27:33 wares you e the kings of the earth.
1Co 1: 5 For in him you have been e in every

Enrol (Enrolled, Enrolment)
2Sa 24: 2 to Beersheba and e the fighting men,
24: 4 to e the fighting men of Israel.

Enrolled (Enrol)
2Ch 31:17 they distributed to the priests e by

Enrolment (Enrol)
2Ch 17:14 Their e by families was as follows:

Enslave (Enslaved, Enslaves, Enslaving)
Jer 15:14 I will e you to your enemies in a
17: 4 I will e you to your enemies in a
30: 8 no longer will foreigners e them.

Enslaved (Enslave)
Ge 15:13 e and ill-treated four hundred years.
Ne 5: 5 our daughters have already been e,
Jer 25:14 They themselves will be e by many
34:11 they had freed and e them again.
Eze 34:27 from the hands of those who e them.
Na 3: 4 the mistress of sorceries, who e
Ac 7: 6 and they will be e and ill-treated
Gal 4: 9 wish to be e by them all over again?
Tit 3: 3 disobedient, deceived and e by all

Enslaves (Enslave)
2Co 11:20 you even put up with anyone who e

Enslaving (Enslave)
Ex 6: 5 Israelites, whom the Egyptians are e,

Ensnare (Ensnared)
Pr 5:22 The evil deeds of a wicked man e him;
Ecc 7:26 her, but the sinner she will e.
Isa 29:21 who e the defender in court and with
Eze 13:18 their heads in order to e people.
13:18 Will you e the lives of my people
13:20 with which you e people like birds
13:20 the people that you e like birds.

Ensnared (Ensnare)
Dt 7:25 or you will be e by it, for it is
12:30 be careful not to be e by enquiring
Ps 9:16 are e by the work of their hands.
Pr 6: 2 said, e by the words of your mouth,
22:25 learn his ways and get yourself e.

Ensure
Ps 119:122 E your servant's well-being; let not

Entangle (Entangled, Entangles)
Ps 35: 8 may the net they hid e them,

Entangled (Entangle)

Ps 18: 4 The cords of death e me; the
116: 3 The cords of death e me, the anguish
Na 1:10 They will be e among thorns and
2Pe 2:20 and are again e in it and overcome,

Entangles (Entangle)

Heb 12: 1 and the sin that so easily e,

Enter (Entered, Entering, Enters, Entrance, Entrances, Re-entered)

Ge 6:18 and you will e the ark—you and your
12:11 he was about to e Egypt, he said to
49: 6 Let me not e their council, let me
Ex 12:23 e your houses and strike you down.
12:25 you e the land that the LORD will
28:43 whenever they e the Tent of Meeting
30:20 Whenever they e the Tent of Meeting,
40:35 Moses could not e the Tent of
Lev 14:34 "When you e the land of Canaan,
16: 3 "This is how Aaron is to e the
19:23 "'When you e the land and plant any
21:11 He must not e a place where there is
23:10 'When you e the land I am going to
25: 2 'When you e the land I am going to
Nu 5:22 May this water that brings a curse e
5:24 e her and cause bitter suffering.
14:30 Not one of you will e the land I
15: 2 e the land I am giving you as a
15:18 e the land to which I am taking
20:24 He will not e the land I give the
34: 2 'When you e Canaan, the land that
Dt 1:37 said, "You shall not e it, either.
1:38 Joshua son of Nun, will e it.
1:39 good from bad—they will e the land.
4:21 e the good land the LORD your God is
8: 1 increase and may e and possess the
10:11 so that they may e and possess the
11:31 are about to cross the Jordan to e
17:14 you e the land the LORD your God is
18: 9 you e the land the LORD your God is
23: 1 may e the assembly of the LORD.
23: 2 may e the assembly of the LORD,
23: 3 may e the assembly of the LORD,
23: 8 them may e the assembly of the LORD.
23:24 If you e your neighbour's vineyard,
23:25 If you e your neighbour's cornfield,
27: 3 you have crossed over to e the land
29:12 You are standing here in order to e
30:18 the Jordan to e and possess.
32:52 you will not e the land I am giving
Jos 2:18 unless, when we e the land, you have
Jdg 11:18 They did not e the territory of Moab,
1Sa 5: 5 who e Dagon's temple at Ashdod
9:13 soon as you e the town, you will
2Sa 5: 8 and lame' will not e the palace."
1Ki 22:30 "I will e the battle in disguise,
2Ki 11:16 the horses e the palace grounds,
13:20 used to e the country every spring.
19:32 He will not e this city or shoot
19:33 not e this city, declares the LORD.
2Ch 7: 2 The priests could not e the temple
18:29 "I will e the battle in disguise,
23: 6 No-one is to e the temple of the
23: 6 may e because they are consecrated,
23:19 who was in any way unclean might e.
27: 2 he did not e the temple of the LORD.
31:16 all who would e the temple of the
Ne 9:23 told their fathers to e and possess.
Est 1:19 to e the presence of King Xerxes.
4: 2 in sackcloth was allowed to e it.
Ps 45:15 they e the palace of the king.
95:11 anger, "They shall never e my rest.
100: 4 E his gates with thanksgiving and
118:19 I will e and give thanks to the LORD.
118:20 through which the righteous may e.
132: 3 "I will not e my house or go to my
Pr 2:10 For wisdom will e your heart, and
Isa 10:28 They e Aiath; they pass through
13: 2 them to e the gates of the nobles.
26: 2 that the righteous nation may e, the
26:20 Go, my people, e your rooms and shut
35:10 They will e Zion with singing;
37:33 e this city or shoot an arrow here.
37:34 he will not e this city," declares
Isa 51:11 They will e Zion with singing;
52: 1 and defiled will not e you again.
57: 2 Those who walk uprightly e into
59:14 in the streets, honesty cannot e.
Jer 3:16 It will never e their minds or be
7:31 not command, nor did it e my mind.
16: 5 "Do not e a house where there is a
16: 8 "And do not e a house where there is
19: 5 or mention, nor did it e my mind.
21:13 against us? Who can e our refuge?"
32:35 nor did it e my mind, that they
Lam 1:10 she saw pagan nations e her
1:10 had forbidden to e your assembly.
4:12 foes could e the gates of Jerusalem.
Eze 7:22 robbers will e it and desecrate it.
13: 9 nor will they e the land of Israel.
20:38 they will not e the land of Israel.
26:10 as men e a city whose walls have been
37: 5 I will make breath e you, and you
42:14 Once the priests e the holy
44: 2 It must not be opened; no-one may e
44: 3 He is to e by way of the portico of
44: 9 and flesh is to e my sanctuary,
44:16 They alone are to e my sanctuary;
44:17 "'When they e the gates of the inner
46: 2 The prince is to e from the outside
Da 1: 5 they were to e the king's service.
11: 7 of the North and e his fortress;
Joel 2: 9 thieves they e through the windows.
3: 2 There I will e into judgment against
Zec 5: 4 'I will send it out, and it will e
Mt 5:20 not e the kingdom of heaven.
7:13 "E through the narrow gate. For wide
7:13 destruction, and many e through it.
7:21 'Lord, Lord,' will e the kingdom of
10: 5 or e any town of the Samaritans.
10:11 "Whatever town or village you e,
10:12 you e the home, give it your
12:29 how can anyone e a strong man's house
18: 3 will never e the kingdom of heaven.
18: 8 It is better for you to e life
18: 9 It is better for you to e life with
19:17 to e life, obey the commandments."
19:23 rich man to e the kingdom of heaven.
19:24 a rich man to e the kingdom of God."
23:13 You yourselves do not e, nor will
23:13 you let those e who are trying to.
Mk 1:45 Jesus could no longer e a town openly
3:27 In fact, no-one can e a strong man's
6:10 Whenever you e a house, stay there
9:25 out of him and never e him again."
9:43 It is better for you to e life
9:45 It is better for you to e life
9:47 It is better for you to e the
10:15 like a little child will never e it."
10:23 the rich to e the kingdom of God!"
10:24 hard it is to e the kingdom of God!
10:25 a rich man to e the kingdom of God."
11: 2 and just as you e it, you will find
13:15 or e the house to take anything out.
Lk 9: 4 Whatever house you e, stay there
10: 5 "When you e a house, first say,
10: 8 "When you e a town and are welcomed,
10:10 when you e a town and are not
13:24 "Make every effort to e through the
13:24 try to e and will not be able to.
18:17 like a little child will never e it."
18:24 the rich to e the kingdom of God!
18:25 a rich man to e the kingdom of God."
19:30 and as you e it, you will find a
21:21 those in the country not e the city.
22:10 He replied, "As you e the city, a
24:26 these things and then e his glory?"
Jn 3: 4 "Surely he cannot e a second time
3: 5 no-one can e the kingdom of God
10: 1 the man who does not e the sheep pen
18:28 the Jews did not e the palace;
Ac 3: 3 he saw Peter and John about to e, he
14:22 to e the kingdom of God," they said.
16: 7 they tried to e Bithynia, but the
Heb 3:11 'They shall never e my rest.'"
3:18 swear that they would never e his
3:19 we see that they were not able to e,
4: 3 Now we who have believed e that rest,
4: 3 anger, 'They shall never e my rest.
4: 5 says, "They shall never e my rest.
Heb 4: 6 still remains that some will e that
4:11 make every effort to e that rest, so
9:12 He did not e by means of the blood
9:24 For Christ did not e a man-made
9:25 Nor did he e heaven to offer himself
10:19 since we have confidence to e the
Rev 15: 8 and no-one could e the temple until
21:27 Nothing impure will ever e it, nor

Entered (Enter)

Ge 7: 7 his wife and his sons' wives e the
7: 9 male and female, came to Noah and e
7:13 wives of his three sons, e the ark.
7:15 in them came to Noah and e the ark.
19: 3 did go with him and e his house.
31:33 of Leah's tent, he e Rachel's tent.
41:46 Joseph was thirty years old when he e
Ex 19: 2 they e the Desert of Sinai, and
24:18 Moses e the cloud as he went on up
33: 8 watching Moses until he e the tent.
34:34 whenever he e the LORD's presence to
40:32 They washed whenever they e the Tent
Lev 16:23 on before he e the Most Holy Place,
Nu 7:89 Moses e the Tent of Meeting to speak
17: 8 The next day Moses e the Tent of the
Dt 26: 1 you have e the land that the LORD
Jos 2: 1 So they went and e the house of a
2: 3 who came to you and e your house,
8:19 They e the city and captured it and
Jdg 4:18 Don't be afraid." So he e her tent,
18: 2 The men e the hill country of
1Sa 4:13 When the man e the town and told
12: 8 "After Jacob e Egypt, they cried to
14:25 The entire army e the woods, and
16:21 David came to Saul and e his service.
19:16 when the men e, there was the idol
1Ki 2:30 Benaiah e the tent of the LORD and
2Ki 6:20 After they e the city, Elisha said,
7: 8 of the camp and e one of the tents.
7: 8 They returned and e another tent and
9:31 Jehu e the gate, she asked, "Have
10:25 then e the inner shrine of the
1Ch 5:17 All these were e in the genealogical
24:19 when they e the temple of the LORD,
27:24 and the number was not e in the book
2Ch 8:11 the ark of the LORD has e are holy."
15:12 They e into a covenant to seek the
20:28 They e Jerusalem and went to the
26:16 and e the temple of the LORD to burn
Est 6: 4 Haman had just e the outer court of
6: 6 Haman e, the king asked him, "What
Job 3: 6 year nor be e in any of the months.
38:22 "Have you e the storehouses of the
Ps 73:17 till I e the sanctuary of God; then
105:23 Israel e Egypt; Jacob lived as an
109:18 it e into his body like water, into
Isa 28:15 You boast, "We have e into a
Jer 9:21 windows and has e our fortresses;
34:10 all the officials and people who e
43: 7 they e Egypt in disobedience to the
51:51 because foreigners have e the holy
Eze 4:14 No unclean meat has ever e my mouth."
16: 8 I gave you my solemn oath and e into
23:39 e my sanctuary and desecrated it.
37:10 and breath e them; they came to life
43: 4 The glory of the LORD e the temple
44: 2 the God of Israel, has e through it.
46: 9 through the gate by which he e,
Da 1:19 so they e the king's service.
Am 5:19 as though he e his house and rested
Ob :11 foreigners e his gates and cast lots
Mt 8: 5 Jesus had e Capernaum, a centurion
9:23 Jesus e the ruler's house and saw
12: 4 He e the house of God, and he and
21:10 Jesus e Jerusalem, the whole city
21:12 Jesus e the temple area and drove
21:23 Jesus e the temple courts, and,
24:38 up to the day Noah e the ark;
26:58 He e and sat down with the guards to
Mk 2: 1 A few days later, when Jesus again e
2:26 he e the house of God and ate the
3:20 Jesus e a house, and again a crowd
7:17 left the crowd and e the house,
7:24 He e a house and did not want anyone
11:11 Jesus e Jerusalem and went to the

Mk 11:15 On reaching Jerusalem, Jesus e the
16: 5 they e the tomb, they saw a young
Lk 1:40 where she e Zechariah's home and
6: 4 He e the house of God, and taking
7: 1 of the people, he e Capernaum.
7:45 from the time I e, has not stopped
9:34 were afraid as they e the cloud.
11:52 You yourselves have not e, and you
17:27 up to the day Noah e the ark.
19: 1 Jesus e Jericho and was passing
19:45 he e the temple area and began
22: 3 Satan e Judas, called Iscariot, one
24: 3 when they e, they did not find the
Jn 6:22 and that Jesus had not e it with his
11:30 Now Jesus had not yet e the village,
13:27 soon as Judas took the bread, Satan e
16:28 came from the Father and e the world
Ac 5:21 At daybreak they e the temple courts,
9:17 Ananias went to the house and e it.
10:25 Peter e the house, Cornelius met him
11: 8 or unclean has ever e my mouth.'
11:12 with me, and we e the man's house.
13:14 they e the synagogue and sat down.
19: 8 Paul e the synagogue and spoke
25:23 Bernice came with great pomp and e
Ro 5:12 Therefore, just as sin e the world
Heb 6:20 went before us, has e on our behalf.
9: 6 the priests e regularly into the
9: 7 only the high priest e the inner
9:12 but he e the Most Holy Place once
9:24 of the true one; he e heaven itself,
Rev 11:11 a breath of life from God e them,

Entering (Enter)

Nu 32: 9 e the land the LORD had given them.
Dt 4: 5 you are e to take possession of it.
7: 1 into the land you are e to possess
11:10 The land you are e to take over is
11:29 into the land you are e to possess,
23:20 to in the land you are e to possess.
28:21 from the land you are e to possess.
28:63 from the land you are e to possess.
30:16 in the land you are e to possess.
31:16 foreign gods of the land they are e.
1Sa 5:10 As the ark of God was e Ekron, the
9:14 and as they were e it, there was
23: 7 by e a town with gates and bars."
2Sa 6:16 the ark of the LORD was e the City
15:37 Jerusalem as Absalom was e the city.
17:17 not risk being seen e the city.
1Ki 15:17 e the territory of Asa king of Judah.
2Ki 11:19 e by way of the gate of the guards.
1Ch 15:29 of the LORD was e the City of David,
2Ch 16: 1 e the territory of Asa king of Judah.
Ezr 9:11 "The land you are e to possess is a
Mt 21:31 e the kingdom of God ahead of you.
Lk 11:52 you have hindered those who were e."
Heb 4: 1 the promise of e his rest still

Enters (Enter)

Ex 28:29 "Whenever Aaron e the Holy Place, he
28:30 he e the presence of the LORD.
28:35 he e the Holy Place before the LORD
Nu 19:14 Anyone who e the tent and anyone who
2Ki 5:18 When my master e the temple of
12: 9 as one e the temple of the LORD.
2Ch 23: 7 Anyone who e the temple must be put
Isa 3:14 The LORD e into judgment against the
Eze 26:10 wagons and chariots when he e your
42: 9 as one e them from the outer court.
42:12 eastward, by which one e the rooms.
44:21 No priest is to drink wine when he e
46: 8 the prince e, he is to go in through
46: 9 whoever e by the north gate to
46: 9 and whoever e by the south gate is
47: 8 into the Arabah, where it e the Sea.
Mt 15:17 "Don't you see that whatever e the
Mk 7:18 nothing that e a man from the outside
14:14 Say to the owner of the house he e,
Lk 22:10 Follow him to the house that he e,
Jn 10: 2 The man who e by the gate is the
10: 9 I am the gate; whoever e through me
Heb 4:10 for anyone who e God's rest also
6:19 It e the inner sanctuary behind the
9:25 the way the high priest e the Most

Entertain (Entertained, Entertainment)

Jdg 16:25 shouted, "Bring out Samson to e us.
Mt 9: 4 you e evil thoughts in your hearts?
1Ti 5:19 Do not e an accusation against an
Heb 13: 2 Do not forget to e strangers, for by

Entertained (Entertain)

Ac 28: 7 and for three days e us hospitably.
Heb 13: 2 have e angels without knowing it.

Entertainment (Entertain)

Da 6:18 without any e being brought to him.

Enthralled

Ps 45:11 The king is e by your beauty; honour

Enthroned (Enthrones)

1Sa 4: 4 who is e between the cherubim.
2Sa 6: 2 who is e between the cherubim that
2Ki 19:15 "O LORD, God of Israel, e between
1Ch 13: 6 who is e between the cherubim—the
Ps 2: 4 The One e in heaven laughs; the Lord
9:11 Sing praises to the LORD, e in Zion;
22: 3 Yet you are e as the Holy One; you
29:10 The LORD sits e over the flood; the
29:10 the LORD is e as King for ever.
55:19 God, who is e for ever, will hear
61: 7 May he be e in God's presence for
80: 1 you who sit e between the cherubim,
99: 1 let the nations tremble; he sits e
102:12 you, O LORD, sit e for ever; your
113: 5 our God, the One who sits e on high,
132:14 I will sit e, for I have desired it—
Isa 14:13 will sit e on the mount of assembly,
37:16 "O LORD Almighty, God of Israel, e
40:22 He sits e above the circle of the
52: 2 Shake off your dust; rise up, sit e,

Enthrones (Enthroned)

Job 36: 7 he e them with kings and exalts them

Enthusiasm

2Co 8:17 much e and on his own initiative.
9: 2 e has stirred most of them to action.

Entice (Enticed, Entices, Enticing)

1Ki 22:20 the LORD said, 'Who will e Ahab into
22:21 the LORD and said, 'I will e him.'
2Ch 18:19 the LORD said, 'Who will e Ahab king
18:20 the LORD and said, 'I will e him.
Pr 1:10 My son, if sinners e you, do not
2Pe 2:18 they e people who are just escaping
Rev 2:14 who taught Balak to e the Israelites

Enticed (Entice)

Dt 4:19 not be e into bowing down to them
11:16 Be careful, or you will be e to turn
2Ki 17:21 Jeroboam e Israel away from
Job 31: 9 "If my heart has been e by a woman,
31:27 that my heart was secretly e and my
Eze 14: 9 "'And if the prophet is e to utter a
14: 9 I the LORD have e that prophet, and
Jas 1:14 desire, he is dragged away and e.

Entices (Entice)

Dt 13: 6 or your closest friend secretly e
Job 36:18 Be careful that no-one e you by
Pr 16:29 A violent man e his neighbour and

Enticing (Entice)

1Ki 22:22 "'You will succeed in e him,' said
2Ch 18:21 "'You will succeed in e him,' said

Entire

Ge 2:11 winds through the e land of Havilah,
2:13 it winds through the e land of Cush.
7:19 under the e heavens were covered.
19:25 those cities and the e plain,
45: 8 e household and ruler of all Egypt.
Ex 14:28 horsemen—the e army of Pharaoh that
16: 3 to starve this e assembly to death."
16: 9 Moses told Aaron, "Say to the e
29:18 burn the e ram on the altar. It is a
Lev 3: 9 the e fat tail cut off close to the
8: 3 gather the e assembly at the
9: 5 and the e assembly came near and
19: 2 "Speak to the e assembly of Israel
24:14 and the e assembly is to stone him.
24:16 The e assembly must stone him.
27:32 The e tithe of the herd and
Nu 4:16 in charge of the e tabernacle and
5:30 and is to apply this e law to her.
6: 5 "'During the e period of his vow of
14: 7 said to the e Israelite assembly,
16:19 the LORD appeared to the e assembly.
16:22 will you be angry with the e assembly
20:29 the e house of Israel mourned for
21:23 He mustered his e army and marched
27:19 the e assembly and commission him in
27:21 At his command he and the e
Dt 2:14 By then, that e generation of
Jos 6:23 They brought out her e family and
8:11 The e force that was with him
9: 1 and along the e coast of the Great
9:21 water-carriers for the e community.
10: 7 up from Gilgal with his e army,
11:16 Joshua took this e land: the hill
11:23 Joshua took the e land, just as the
13:21 the e realm of Sihon king of the
13:30 the e realm of Og king of Bashan
24:17 He protected us on our e journey and
Jdg 8:12 captured them, routing their e army.
1Sa 14:25 The e army entered the woods, and
2Sa 6:11 LORD blessed him and his e household.
6:15 while he and the e house of Israel
7:17 all the words of this e revelation.
8: 9 defeated the e army of Hadadezer,
10: 7 out with the e army of fighting men.
12:29 David mustered the e army and went
12:31 his e army returned to Jerusalem.
15:16 set out, with his e household
20:14 through the e region of the Berites,
20:23 Joab was over Israel's e army;
24: 8 they had gone through the e land,
1Ki 8: 5 King Solomon and the e assembly of
20: 1 king of Aram mustered his e army.
2Ki 6:24 king of Aram mobilised his e army
15:18 During his e reign he did not turn
17: 5 king of Assyria invaded the e land,
17:13 in accordance with the e Law that I
24:16 deported to Babylon the e force of
1Ch 4:27 so their e clan did not become as
5:10 the e region east of Gilead.
17:15 all the words of this e revelation.
18: 9 e army of Hadadezer king of Zobah,
19: 8 out with the e army of fighting men.
20: 3 his e army returned to Jerusalem.
2Ch 5: 6 King Solomon and the e assembly of
26:14 bows and slingstones for the e army.
29:18 "We have purified the e temple of
30:25 The e assembly of Judah rejoiced,
34: 9 Ephraim and the e remnant of Israel
35:16 at that time the e service of the
Ezr 4: 5 frustrate their plans during the e
8:34 e weight was recorded at that time.
Job 16: 7 you have devastated my e household.
Isa 39: 2 the fine oil, his e armoury and
Jer 26:17 said to the e assembly of people,
36:23 the e scroll was burned in the fire.
37:10 were to defeat the e Babylonian
42: 2 LORD your God for this e remnant.
51:31 Babylon that his e city is captured,
Eze 9: 8 going to destroy the e remnant
10:12 Their e bodies, including their
20:40 there in the land the e house of
45: 1 wide; the e area will be holy.
48:20 The e portion will be a square,
Da 2:48 made him ruler over the e province
11:17 with the might of his e kingdom
Lk 2: 1 be taken of the e Roman world.
Ac 11:28 would spread over the e Roman world.
18: 8 his e household believed in the Lord
Gal 5:14 The e law is summed up in a single

Entrails

Zep 1:17 like dust and their e like filth.

Entrance (Enter)

Ge 18: 1 e to his tent in the heat of the day.
18: 2 he hurried from the e of his tent to
18:10 e to the tent, which was behind him.
38:14 and then sat down at the e to Enaim,
43:19 spoke to him at the e to the house.
Ex 26:36 "For the e to the tent make a
27:14 on one side of the e, with three
27:16 "For the e to the courtyard, provide
29: 4 bring Aaron and his sons to the e to
29:11 at the e to the Tent of Meeting.
29:32 At the e to the Tent of Meeting,
29:42 at the e to the Tent of Meeting
32:26 he stood at the e to the camp and
33: 9 would come down and stay at the e,
33:10 cloud standing at the e to the tent,
33:10 each at the e to his tent.
35:15 doorway at the e to the tabernacle;
35:17 curtain for the e to the courtyard;
36:37 For the e to the tent they made a
38: 8 at the e to the Tent of Meeting.
38:14 on one side of the e, with three
38:15 side of the e to the courtyard,
38:18 The curtain for the e to the
38:30 for the e to the Tent of Meeting,
38:31 those for its e and all the tent
39:38 the curtain for the e to the tent;
39:40 and the curtain for the e to the
40: 5 curtain at the e to the tabernacle.
40: 6 in front of the e to the tabernacle,
40: 8 curtain at the e to the courtyard.
40:12 "Bring Aaron and his sons to the e
40:28 he put up the curtain at the e to
40:29 near the e to the tabernacle,
40:33 curtain at the e to the courtyard.
Lev 1: 3 He must present it at the e to the
1: 5 at the e to the Tent of Meeting.
3: 2 it at the e to the Tent of Meeting.
4: 4 He is to present the bull at the e
4: 7 at the e to the Tent of Meeting.
4:18 at the e to the Tent of Meeting.
8: 3 gather the entire assembly at the e
8: 4 at the e to the Tent of Meeting.
8:31 "Cook the meat at the e to the Tent
8:33 Do not leave the e to the Tent of
8:35 You must stay at the e to the Tent
10: 7 Do not leave the e to the Tent of
12: 6 to the priest at the e to the Tent
14:11 LORD at the e to the Tent of Meeting.
14:23 at the e to the Tent of Meeting,
15:14 come before the LORD to the e to the
15:29 at the e to the Tent of Meeting.
16: 7 LORD at the e to the Tent of Meeting.
17: 4 instead of bringing it to the e to
17: 5 to the LORD, at the e to the Tent
17: 6 LORD at the e to the Tent of Meeting
17: 9 does not bring it to the e to the
19:21 must bring a ram to the e to the Tent
Nu 3:25 at the e to the Tent of Meeting,
3:26 curtain at the e to the courtyard
4:25 for the e to the Tent of Meeting,
4:26 the curtain for the e, the ropes and
6:10 at the e to the Tent of Meeting.
6:13 to the e to the Tent of Meeting.
6:18 "'Then at the e to the Tent of
10: 3 you at the e to the Tent of Meeting.
11:10 wailing, each at the e to his tent.
12: 5 he stood at the e to the Tent and
16:18 at the e to the Tent of Meeting.
16:19 at the e to the Tent of Meeting,
16:50 Aaron returned to Moses at the e to
20: 6 to the e to the Tent of Meeting
25: 6 at the e to the Tent of Meeting.
27: 2 the e to the Tent of Meeting and
Dt 31:15 cloud stood over the e to the Tent.
Jos 8:29 it down at the e of the city gate.
19:51 LORD at the e to the Tent of Meeting.
20: 4 he is to stand in the e of the city
Jdg 9:35 was standing at the e to the city
9:40 the way to the e to the gate.
9:44 position at the e to the city gate.
9:52 e to the tower to set it on fire,
18:16 battle, stood at the e to the gate.
18:17 men stood at the e to the gate.
1Sa 2:22 at the e to the Tent of Meeting.
17:52 e of Gath and to the gates of Ekron.
2Sa 10: 8 at the e to their city gate,
11: 9 Uriah slept at the e to the palace
11:23 them back to the e to the city gate.
1Ki 6: 8 The e to the lowest floor was on the
6:31 For the e of the inner sanctuary he
6:33 wood for the e to the main hall.
14:27 duty at the e to the royal palace.
22:10 by the e of the gate of Samaria,
2Ki 7: 3 leprosy at the e of the city gate.
10: 8 e of the city gate until morning."
12: 9 The priests who guarded the e put
16:18 the royal e outside the temple of the
23: 8 the e to the Gate of Joshua,
23:11 He removed from the e to the temple
1Ch 9:19 the e to the dwelling of the LORD.
9:21 at the e to the Tent of Meeting.
19: 9 formation at the e to their city,
2Ch 12:10 duty at the e to the royal palace.
18: 9 by the e to the gate of Samaria,
23:13 standing by his pillar at the e.
23:15 they seized her as she reached the e
33:14 as far as the e of the Fish Gate and
Ne 3:20 from the angle to the e of the house
3:21 from the e of Eliashib's house to
Est 5: 1 throne in the hall, facing the e.
Isa 24:10 the e to every house is barred
Jer 1:15 in the e of the gates of Jerusalem;
19: 2 near the e of the Potsherd Gate.
26:10 took their places at the e of the
36:10 the e of the New Gate of the temple,
38:14 third e to the temple of the LORD.
43: 9 e to Pharaoh's palace in Tahpanhes.
Eze 8: 3 to the e to the north gate of the
8: 5 So I looked, and in the e north of
8: 7 he brought me to the e to the court.
8:14 he brought me to the e to the north
8:16 and there at the e to the temple,
10:19 They stopped at the e to the east
11: 1 There at the e to the gate were
40:11 he measured the width of the e to
40:15 The distance from the e of the
40:40 near the steps at the e to the north
40:48 The width of the e was fourteen
41: 2 The e was ten cubits wide, and the
41: 3 measured the jambs of the e; each was
41: 3 The e was six cubits wide, and the
41:17 of the e to the inner sanctuary
41:20 the floor to the area above the e,
42: 9 The lower rooms had an e on the east
44: 5 Give attention to the e of the
46: 3 the LORD at the e to that gateway.
46:19 the man brought me through the e at
47: 1 The man brought me back to the e of
Mt 27:60 of the e to the tomb and went away.
Mk 14:68 he said, and went out into the e.
15:46 a stone against the e of the tomb.
16: 3 stone away from the e of the tomb?"
Jn 11:38 cave with a stone laid across the e.
20: 1 stone had been removed from the e.
Ac 12: 6 and sentries stood guard at the e.
12:13 Peter knocked at the outer e, and a

Entrances (Enter)

Ex 33: 8 and stood at the e to their tents,
Nu 16:27 little ones at the e to their tents.
Pr 8: 3 the city, at the e, she cries aloud:
Eze 41:11 There were e to the side rooms from
43:11 its exits and e—its whole design

Entreat (Entreaty)

Zec 7: 2 with their men, to e the LORD
8:21 'Let us go at once to e the LORD and
8:22 the LORD Almighty and to e him."

Entreaty (Entreat)

2Ch 33:13 the LORD was moved by his e and
33:19 and how God was moved by his e,

Entrust (Entrusted)

Ge 42:37 E him to my care, and I will bring
2Ki 22: 5 Make them e it to the men appointed
Jn 2:24 Jesus would not e himself to them,
2Ti 2: 2 e to reliable men who will also be

Entrusted (Entrust)

Ge 39: 4 e to his care everything he owned.
39: 8 he owns he has e to my care.
Lev 6: 2 neighbour about something e to him
6: 4 or what was e to him, or the lost
1Ki 15:18 He e it to his officials and sent
2Ki 22: 7 they need not account for the money e
22: 9 have e it to the workers and
1Ch 9:26 who were Levites, were e with the
9:31 was e with the responsibility for
2Ch 34:10 they e it to the men appointed to
34:17 e it to the supervisors and workers."
Ezr 7:19 the articles e to you for worship
Est 2: 8 to the king's palace and e to Hegai,
6: 9 let the robe and horse be e to one
Jer 13:20 Where is the flock that was e to you,
29: 3 He e the letter to Elasah son of
Mt 25:14 servants and e his property to them.
25:20 'Master,' he said, 'you e me with
25:22 'Master,' he said, 'you e me with
Lk 12:48 e with much, much more will be asked.
Jn 5:22 but has e all judgment to the Son,
Ro 3: 2 been e with the very words of God.
6:17 of teaching to which you were e.
1Co 4: 1 e with the secret things of God.
Gal 2: 7 they saw that I had been e with the
1Th 2: 4 by God to be e with the gospel.
1Ti 1:11 the blessed God, which he e to me.
6:20 Timothy, guard what has been e to
2Ti 1:12 what I have e to him for that day.
1:14 Guard the good deposit that was e to
Tit 1: 3 the preaching e to me by the command
Tit 1: 7 an overseer is e with God's work,
1Pe 2:23 e himself to him who judges justly.
5: 3 not lording it over those e to you,
Jude : 3 was once for all e to the saints.

Entwines

Job 8:17 e its roots around a pile of rocks

Enveloped

Isa 42:25 It e them in flames, yet they did
Mt 17: 5 a bright cloud e them, and a voice
Mk 9: 7 a cloud appeared and e them, and a
Lk 9:34 a cloud appeared and e them, and

Envied (Envy)

Ge 26:14 servants that the Philistines e him.
Ps 73: 3 For I e the arrogant when I saw the

Envies (Envy)

Jas 4: 5 he caused to live in us e intensely?

Envious (Envy)

Dt 32:21 I will make them e by those who are
Ps 37: 1 men or be e of those who do wrong;
106:16 In the camp they grew e of Moses and
Pr 24:19 of evil men or be e of the wicked,
Mt 20:15 Or are you e because I am generous?'
Ro 10:19 "I will make you e by those who are
11:11 to the Gentiles to make Israel e.

Envoy (Envoys)

Pr 13:17 but a trustworthy e brings healing.
Jer 49:14 An e was sent to the nations to say,
Ob : 1 An e was sent to the nations to say,

Envoys (Envoy)

1Ki 5: 1 he sent his e to Solomon, because he
2Ki 17: 4 he had sent e to So king of Egypt,
2Ch 32:31 when e were sent by the rulers of
Ps 68:31 E will come from Egypt; Cush will
Isa 14:32 What answer shall be given to the e
18: 2 which sends e by sea in papyrus
30: 4 and their e have arrived in Hanes,
30: 6 the e carry their riches on donkeys'
33: 7 the e of peace weep bitterly.
39: 2 Hezekiah received the e gladly and
Jer 27: 3 the e who have come to Jerusalem
Eze 17:15 his e to Egypt to get horses

Envy (Envied, Envies, Envious, Envying)
Job 5: 2 Resentment kills a fool, and **e** slays
Ps 68:16 Why gaze in **e**, O rugged mountains,
Pr 3:31 Do not **e** a violent man or choose any
14:30 to the body, but **e** rots the bones.
23:17 Do not let your heart **e** sinners, but
24: 1 Do not **e** wicked men, do not desire
Ecc 4: 4 from man's **e** of his neighbour.
Eze 31: 9 the **e** of all the trees of Eden in
Mt 27:18 For he knew it was out of **e** that
Mk 7:22 greed, malice, deceit, lewdness, **e**,
15:10 knowing it was out of **e** that the
Ro 1:29 They are full of **e**, murder, strife,
11:14 people to **e** and save some of them.
1Co 13: 4 It does not **e**, it does not boast, it
Gal 5:21 **e**; drunkenness, orgies, and the like.
Php 1:15 preach Christ out of **e** and rivalry,
1Ti 6: 4 about words that result in **e**,
Tit 3: 3 We lived in malice and **e**, being
Jas 3:14 if you harbour bitter **e** and selfish
3:16 For where you have **e** and selfish
1Pe 2: 1 **e**, and slander of every kind.

Envying (Envy)
Gal 5:26 provoking and **e** each other.

Epaphras
Col 1: 7 You learned it from **E**, our dear
4:12 **E**, who is one of you and a servant
Phm :23 **E**, my fellow-prisoner in Christ

Epaphroditus
Christian from Philippi; brought gifts from Philippians to Paul (Php 4:18); fellow-worker with Paul; almost died serving Christ (Php 2:25–29).

Php 2:25 is necessary to send back to you **E**,
4:18 received from **E** the gifts you sent.

Epenetus
Ro 16: 5 Greet my dear friend **E**, who was the

Ephah
Ge 25: 4 The sons of Midian were **E**, Epher,
Ex 16:36 (An omer is one tenth of an **e**.)
29:40 offer a tenth of an **e** of fine flour
Lev 5:11 **e** of fine flour for a sin offering.
6:20 a tenth of an **e** of fine flour as a
14:10 along with three-tenths of an **e** of
14:21 together with a tenth of an **e** of
19:36 an honest **e** and an honest hin.
23:13 an **e** of fine flour mixed with oil
23:17 of two-tenths of an **e** of fine flour,
24: 5 two-tenths of an **e** for each loaf.
Nu 5:15 an **e** of barley flour on her behalf.
15: 4 a tenth of an **e** of fine flour mixed
15: 6 two-tenths of an **e** of fine flour
15: 9 three-tenths of an **e** of fine flour
28: 5 a tenth of an **e** of fine flour mixed
28: 9 an **e** of fine flour mixed with oil.
28:12 three-tenths of an **e** of fine flour
28:12 two-tenths of an **e** of fine flour
28:13 an **e** of fine flour mixed with oil.
28:20 an **e** of fine flour mixed with oil;
28:28 an **e** of fine flour mixed with oil;
29: 3 an **e** of fine flour mixed with oil;
29: 9 an **e** of fine flour mixed with oil;
29:14 an **e** of fine flour mixed with oil;
Jdg 6:19 and from an **e** of flour he made bread
Ru 2:17 and it amounted to about an **e**.
1Sa 1:24 an **e** of flour and a skin of wine,
17:17 "Take this **e** of roasted grain and
1Ch 1:33 The sons of Midian: **E**, Epher, Hanoch,
2:46 Caleb's concubine **E** was the mother
2:47 Jotham, Geshan, Pelet, **E** and Shaaph.
Isa 5:10 a homer of seed only an **e** of grain."
60: 6 land, young camels of Midian and **E**.
Eze 45:10 an accurate **e** and an accurate bath.
45:11 The **e** and the bath are to be the
45:11 homer and the **e** a tenth of a homer;
45:13 a sixth of an **e** from each homer of
45:13 of an **e** from each homer of barley.
45:24 a grain offering an **e** for each bull
Eze 45:24 for each bull and an **e** for each ram,
45:24 along with a hin of oil for each **e**.
46: 5 given with the ram is to be an **e**,
46: 5 along with a hin of oil for each **e**.
46: 7 grain offering one **e** with the bull,
46: 7 one **e** with the ram, and with the
46: 7 along with a hin of oil with each **e**.
46:11 the grain offering is to be an **e**
46:11 an **e** with a ram, and with the lambs
46:11 along with a hin of oil for each **e**.
46:14 consisting of a sixth of an **e** with a
Mic 6:10 and the short **e**, which is accursed?

Ephai
Jer 40: 8 the sons of **E** the Netophathite, and

Epher
Ge 25: 4 The sons of Midian were Ephah, **E**,
1Ch 1:33 The sons of Midian: Ephah, **E**, Hanoch,
4:17 The sons of Ezrah: Jether, Mered, **E**
5:24 were the heads of their families: **E**,

Ephes Dammim
1Sa 17: 1 camp at **E**, between Socoh and Azekah.

Ephesian (Ephesus)
Ac 21:29 seen Trophimus the **E** in the city with

Ephesians (Ephesus)
Ac 19:28 "Great is Artemis of the **E**!
19:34 "Great is Artemis of the **E**!

Ephesus (Ephesian, Ephesians)
Capital city and important port of Asia Minor, opposite island of Samos. Famous for temple of Artemis (Ac 19:35). Paul visited on second missionary journey leaving Priscilla and Aquila here (Ac 18:19). Apollos joined them (Ac 18:24–26). Paul returned on third missionary journey (Ac 19:1) and stayed for between 2 and 3 years (Ac 19:10; 20:31), preaching in the synagogue (Ac 19:8), in the school of Tyrannus (Ac 19:9) and in private homes (Ac 20:20). His preaching threatened reputation of Artemis and associated trade (Ac 19:23–27), and trouble ensued (Ac 19:28–41). Paul wrote to Corinth from here (1Co 16:8; 15:32). He left Timothy, Onesimus and Tychicus to continue his work (1Ti 1:3; 2Ti 1:18; 4:12), and wrote to the church (Eph 1:1). One of the 7 letters of Revelation is addressed to Ephesus (Rev 1:11), in which the church receives praise and criticism (Rev 2:1–7).

Ac 18:19 They arrived at **E**, where Paul left
18:21 Then he set sail from **E**.
18:24 a native of Alexandria, came to **E**.
19: 1 the interior and arrived at **E**.
19:17 to the Jews and Greeks living in **E**,
19:26 large numbers of people here in **E**
19:35 "Men of **E**, doesn't all the world
19:35 **E** is the guardian of the temple of
20:16 Paul had decided to sail past **E** to
20:17 From Miletus, Paul sent to **E** for the
1Co 15:32 If I fought wild beasts in **E** for
16: 8 I will stay on at **E** until Pentecost,
Eph 1: 1 in **E**, the faithful in Christ Jesus:
1Ti 1: 3 stay there in **E** so that you may
2Ti 1:18 in how many ways he helped me in **E**.
4:12 I sent Tychicus to **E**.
Rev 1:11 send it to the seven churches: to **E**,
2: 1 "To the angel of the church in **E**

Ephlal
1Ch 2:37 Zabad the father of **E**, **E** the father

Ephod
Ex 25: 7 be mounted on the **e** and breastpiece.
28: 4 an **e**, a robe, a woven tunic, a
28: 6 "Make the **e** of gold, and of blue,
28: 8 piece with the **e** and made with gold,
28:12 them on the shoulder pieces of the **e**
28:15 Make it like the **e**: of gold, and of
28:25 pieces of the **e** at the front.
28:26 on the inside edge next to the **e**.
28:27 pieces on the front of the **e**,
28:27 just above the waistband of the **e**.
28:28 the rings of the **e** with blue cord,
Ex 28:28 will not swing out from the **e**.
28:31 "Make the robe of the **e** entirely of
29: 5 the robe of the **e**, the **e** itself
29: 5 Fasten the **e** on him by its skilfully
35: 9 be mounted on the **e** and breastpiece.
35:27 be mounted on the **e** and breastpiece.
39: 2 They made the **e** of gold, and of blue,
39: 4 They made shoulder pieces for the **e**,
39: 5 piece with the **e** and made with gold,
39: 7 on the shoulder pieces of the **e** as
39: 8 They made it like the **e**: of gold,
39:18 pieces of the **e** at the front.
39:19 on the inside edge next to the **e**.
39:20 pieces on the front of the **e**,
39:20 just above the waistband of the **e**.
39:21 the rings of the **e** with blue cord,
39:21 the **e**—as the LORD commanded Moses.
39:22 They made the robe of the **e** entirely
Lev 8: 7 with the robe and put the **e** on him.
8: 7 He also tied the **e** to him by its
Nu 34:23 Hanniel son of **E**, the leader from
Jdg 8:27 Gideon made the gold into an **e**,
17: 5 and he made an **e** and some idols and
18:14 that one of these houses has an **e**,
18:17 the **e**, the other household gods and
18:18 the **e**, the other household gods and
18:20 the priest was glad. He took the **e**,
1Sa 2:18 the LORD—a boy wearing a linen **e**.
2:28 and to wear an **e** in my presence.
14: 3 was Ahijah, who was wearing an **e**.
21: 9 is wrapped in a cloth behind the **e**.
22:18 men who wore the linen **e**.
23: 6 brought the **e** down with him when he
23: 9 Abiathar the priest, "Bring the **e**.
30: 7 son of Ahimelech, "Bring me the **e**.
2Sa 6:14 David, wearing a linen **e**, danced
1Ch 15:27 David also wore a linen **e**.
Hos 3: 4 or sacred stones, without **e** or idol.

Ephphatha
Mk 7:34 "**E**!" (which means, "Be opened!").

Ephraim (Ephraim's, Ephraimite, Ephraimites)
1. Joseph's second son (Ge 41:52); blessed by Jacob as firstborn (Ge 48:13-20). **2.** Tribe descended from Ephraim. Blessed by Moses (Dt 33:13-17). Included in census (Nu 1:32-33; 26:35-37). Apportioned land (Jos 16:1-9; Eze 48:5); unable to take full possession (Jos 16:10; Jdg 1:29). Occupied prestigious position among tribes (Jdg 8:2-3). **3.** Territory west of River Jordan, between Manasseh and Benjamin. Allotted to the descendants of Joseph's younger son. Territories of Ephraim and Manasseh, often treated together (Jos 16:1–17:2). Canaanites not driven out (Jos 16:10), but enslaved (Jos 17:13). Known for its beauty and fertility, contrasting with its moral decay (Isa 28:1, 4; Hos 9:13; 10:11; 12:8). **4.** Became synonym for northern kingdom (Ps 78:9-16, 67-68; Isa 7:1-17; Jer 7:15; Hos 5; 11). **5.** Town where Jesus withdrew with his disciples (Jn 11:54). Exact location unknown, probably also known as Ophrah.

Ge 41:52 The second son he named **E** and said,
46:20 In Egypt, Manasseh and **E** were born
48: 1 sons Manasseh and **E** along with him.
48: 5 mine; **E** and Manasseh will be mine,
48:13 Joseph took both of them, **E** on his
48:20 May God make you like **E** and Manasseh.
48:20 So he put **E** ahead of Manasseh.
Nu 1:10 from the sons of Joseph: from **E**,
1:32 From the descendants of **E**: All the
1:33 The number from the tribe of **E** was
2:18 the camp of **E** under their standard.
2:18 leader of the people of **E** is Elishama
2:24 All the men assigned to the camp of **E**
7:48 people of **E**, brought his offering.
10:22 The divisions of the camp of **E** went
13: 8 from the tribe of **E**, Hoshea son of
26:28 clans through Manasseh and **E** were:
26:35 These were the descendants of **E** by
26:37 These were the clans of **E**; those
34:24 from the tribe of **E** son of Joseph;
Dt 33:17 Such are the ten thousands of **E**;
34: 2 all of Naphtali, the territory of **E**
Jos 14: 4 become two tribes—Manasseh and **E**.

Jos 16: 4 Manasseh and **E**, the descendants of
16: 5 This was the territory of **E**, clan by
16:10 Canaanites live among the people of **E**
17: 9 There were towns belonging to **E**
17:10 On the south the land belonged to **E**,
17:15 "and if the hill country of **E** is too
17:17 said to the house of Joseph—to **E**
19:50 Serah in the hill country of **E**.
20: 7 Shechem in the hill country of **E**,
21: 5 the tribes of **E**, Dan and half of
21:20 allotted towns from the tribe of **E**:
21:21 In the hill country of **E** they were
24:30 country of **E**, north of Mount Gaash.
24:33 Phinehas in the hill country of **E**.
Jdg 1:29 Nor did **E** drive out the Canaanites
2: 9 country of **E**, north of Mount Gaash.
3:27 a trumpet in the hill country of **E**,
4: 5 and Bethel in the hill country of **E**,
5:14 Some came from **E**, whose roots were
7:24 throughout the hill country of **E**,
7:24 So all the men of **E** were called out
10: 1 in Shamir, in the hill country of **E**.
10: 9 Benjamin and the house of **E**; and
12: 1 The men of **E** called out their forces,
12: 4 men of Gilead and fought against **E**.
12: 4 are renegades from **E** and Manassah.
12: 5 fords of the Jordan leading to **E**,
12: 5 whenever a survivor of **E** said, "Let
12:15 and was buried at Pirathon in **E**, in
17: 1 Micah from the hill country of **E**
17: 8 house in the hill country of **E**.
18: 2 The men entered the hill country of **E**
18:13 to the hill country of **E** and came to
19: 1 country of **E** took a concubine from
19:16 old man from the hill country of **E**,
19:18 the hill country of **E** where I live.
1Sa 1: 1 Zuphite from the hill country of **E**,
9: 4 through the hill country of **E**
14:22 had hidden in the hill country of **E**
2Sa 2: 9 over **E**, Benjamin and all Israel.
13:23 at Baal Hazor near the border of **E**,
18: 6 took place in the forest of **E**.
20:21 from the hill country of **E**, has
1Ki 4: 8 Ben-Hur—in the hill country of **E**;
12:25 hill country of **E** and lived there.
2Ki 5:22 to me from the hill country of **E**.
14:13 from the **E** Gate to the Corner Gate
1Ch 6:66 territory towns from the tribe of **E**.
6:67 In the hill country of **E** they were
7:20 The descendants of **E**: Shuthelah,
7:22 Their father **E** mourned for them many
9: 3 from Benjamin, and from **E** and
12:30 men of **E**, brave warriors, famous in
2Ch 13: 4 in the hill country of **E**, and said,
15: 8 he had captured in the hills of **E**.
15: 9 and Benjamin and the people from **E**,
17: 2 the towns of **E** that his father Asa
19: 4 hill country of **E** and turned them
25: 7 with any of the people of **E**.
25:10 to him from **E** and sent them home.
25:23 from the **E** Gate to the Corner Gate
28:12 some of the leaders in **E**—Azariah
30: 1 wrote letters to **E** and Manasseh,
30:10 from town to town in **E** and Manasseh,
30:18 of the many people who came from **E**,
31: 1 and Benjamin and in **E** and Manasseh.
34: 6 In the towns of Manasseh, **E** and
34: 9 **E** and the entire remnant of Israel
Ne 8:16 Gate and the one by the Gate of **E**.
12:39 over the Gate of **E**, the Jeshanah
Ps 60: 7 **E** is my helmet, Judah my sceptre.
78: 9 The men of **E**, though armed with bows,
78:67 he did not choose the tribe of **E**;
80: 2 before **E**, Benjamin and Manasseh.
108: 8 Manasseh is mine; **E** is my helmet,
Isa 7: 2 "Aram has allied itself with **E**"; so
7: 5 Aram, **E** and Remaliah's son have
7: 8 Within sixty-five years **E** will be
7: 9 The head of **E** is Samaria, and the
7:17 any since **E** broke away from Judah
9: 9 All the people will know it—**E** and
9:21 Manasseh will feed on **E**, and **E** on
11:13 off; **E** will not be jealous of Judah,
11:13 Judah, nor Judah hostile towards **E**.
17: 3 city will disappear from **E**,
Jer 4:15 disaster from the hills of **E**.
7:15 all your brothers, the people of **E**.'
31: 6 watchmen cry out on the hills of **E**,
31: 9 father, and **E** is my firstborn son.
31:20 Is not **E** my dear son, the child in
50:19 on the hills of **E** and Gilead.
Eze 48: 5 "**E** will have one portion; it will
48: 6 territory of **E** from east to west.
Hos 4:17 **E** is joined to idols; leave him
5: 3 I know all about **E**; Israel is not
5: 3 **E**, you have now turned to
5: 5 even **E**, stumble in their sin; Judah
5: 9 **E** will be laid waste on the day of
5:11 **E** is oppressed, trampled in judgment,
5:12 I am like a moth to **E**, like rot to
5:13 "When **E** saw his sickness, and Judah
5:13 **E** turned to Assyria, and sent to the
5:14 For I will be like a lion to **E**, like
6: 4 "What can I do with you, **E**? What can
6:10 There **E** is given to prostitution and
7: 1 the sins of **E** are exposed and the
7: 8 "**E** mixes with the nations; **E** is a
7:11 "**E** is like a dove, easily deceived
8: 9 **E** has sold herself to lovers.
8:11 "Though **E** built many altars for sin
9: 3 **E** will return to Egypt and eat
9: 8 is the watchman over **E**, yet snares
9:13 I have seen **E**, like Tyre, planted in
9:13 But **E** will bring out their children
9:16 **E** is blighted, their root is
10: 6 **E** will be disgraced; Israel will be
10:11 **E** is a trained heifer that loves to
10:11 I will drive **E**, Judah must plough,
11: 3 It was I who taught **E** to walk, taking
11: 8 "How can I give you up, **E**? How can I
11: 9 nor will I turn and devastate **E**.
11:12 **E** has surrounded me with lies, the
12: 1 **E** feeds on the wind; he pursues the
12: 8 **E** boasts, "I am very rich; I have
12:14 **E** has bitterly provoked him to anger;
13: 1 **E** spoke, men trembled; he was
13:12 The guilt of **E** is stored up, his
14: 8 O **E**, what more have I to do with
Ob :19 They will occupy the fields of **E** and
Zec 9:10 I will take away the chariots from **E**
9:13 as I bend my bow and fill it with **E**.
Jn 11:54 to a village called **E**, where he

Ephraim's (Ephraim)

Ge 48:14 his right hand and put it on **E** head,
48:17 hand on **E** head he was displeased;
48:17 it from **E** head to Manasseh's head.
50:23 the third generation of **E** children.
Jdg 8: 2 Aren't the gleanings of **E** grapes
Isa 11:13 **E** jealousy will vanish, and Judah's
28: 1 Woe to that wreath, the pride of **E**
28: 3 That wreath, the pride of **E** drunkards
Jer 31:18 "I have surely heard **E** moaning:'You
Eze 37:16 '**E** stick, belonging to Joseph and
37:19 stick of Joseph—which is in **E** hand
Hos 9:11 **E** glory will fly away like a bird—

Ephraimite (Ephraim)

Jdg 12: 5 "Are you an **E**?" If he replied, "No,
1Sa 1: 1 son of Tohu, the son of Zuph, an **E**.
1Ki 11:26 an **E** from Zeredah, and his mother
1Ch 27:10 month, was Helez the Pelonite, an **E**.
27:14 was Benaiah the Pirathonite, an **E**.
2Ch 28: 7 Zicri, an **E** warrior, killed Maaseiah

Ephraimites (Ephraim)

Jos 16: 8 of the tribe of the **E**, clan by clan.
16: 9 that were set aside for the **E**
17: 8 of Manasseh, belonged to the **E**.)
Jdg 8: 1 Now the **E** asked Gideon, "Why have
12: 4 them down because the **E** had said,
12: 6 Forty-two thousand **E** were killed at
1Ch 27:20 over the **E**: Hoshea son of Azaziah;
Zec 10: 7 The **E** will become like mighty men,

Ephrath (Bethlehem 1., Ephrathite, Ephrathites)

Ge 35:16 were still some distance from **E**,
35:19 the way to **E** (that is, Bethlehem).
48: 7 the way, a little distance from **E**.
48: 7 the road to **E**" (that is, Bethlehem).
1Ch 2:19 Azubah died, Caleb married **E**, who

Ephrathah (Bethlehem 1.)

Ru 4:11 in **E** and be famous in Bethlehem.
1Ch 2:50 The sons of Hur the firstborn of **E**:
4: 4 the firstborn of **E** and father of
Ps 132: 6 We heard it in **E**, we came upon it in

Ephrathite (Ephrath)

1Sa 17:12 Now David was the son of an **E** named

Ephrathites (Ephrath)

Ru 1: 2 They were **E** from Bethlehem, Judah.

Ephron (Ephron's)

Ge 23: 8 with **E** son of Zohar on my
23:10 **E** the Hittite was sitting among his
23:13 he said to **E** in their hearing,
23:14 **E** answered Abraham,
25: 9 field of **E** son of Zohar the Hittite,
49:29 cave in the field of **E** the Hittite,
49:30 **E** the Hittite, along with the field.
50:13 **E** the Hittite, along with the field.
Jos 15: 9 came out at the towns of Mount **E** and
2Ch 13:19 **E**, with their surrounding villages.

Ephron's (Ephron)

Ge 23:16 Abraham agreed to **E** terms and
23:17 **E** field in Machpelah near

Epicurean

Ac 17:18 A group of **E** and Stoic philosophers

Equal (Equality, Equalled, Equally, Equity, Equivalent)

Ge 44:18 though you are **e** to Pharaoh himself.
47: 9 and they do not **e** the years of the
Ex 30:34 pure frankincense, all in **e** amounts,
Dt 33:25 and your strength will **e** your days.
1Sa 9: 2 an impressive young man without **e**
1Ki 3:13 you will have no **e** among kings.
Job 41:33 Nothing on earth is his **e**—a
Isa 40:25 Or who is my **e**?" says the Holy One.
46: 5 will you compare me or count me **e**?
Eze 31: 8 nor could the pine trees **e** its
45:12 plus fifteen shekels **e** one mina.
48: 8 will **e** one of the tribal portions;
Da 1:19 and he found none **e** to Daniel,
Mt 20:12 'and you have made them **e** to us who
Jn 5:18 Father, making himself **e** with God.
1Co 12:25 have **e** concern for each other.
2Co 2:16 And who is **e** to such a task?
11:12 an opportunity to be considered **e**

Equality (Equal)

2Co 8:13 pressed, but that there might be **e**.
8:14 Then there will be **e**,
Php 2: 6 **e** with God something to be grasped,

Equalled (Equal)

Mt 24:21 until now—and never to be **e** again.
Mk 13:19 until now—and never to be **e** again.

Equally (Equal)

Ex 21:35 the money and the dead animal **e**.
Lev 7:10 belongs **e** to all the sons of Aaron.
Dt 18: 8 He is to share **e** in their benefits
Ecc 11: 6 or whether both will do **e** well.
Eze 47:14 You are to divide it **e** among them.

Equip (Equipment, Equipped)

Heb 13:21 **e** you with everything good for doing

Equipment (Equip)

Nu 3:36 posts, bases, all its **e**, and
4:26 and all the **e** used in its service.
4:32 tent pegs, ropes, all their **e** and
Dt 23:13 part of your **e** have something to dig
1Sa 8:12 of war and **e** for his chariots.
1Ki 19:21 He burned the ploughing **e** to cook
2Ki 7:15 **e** the Arameans had thrown away in

2Ch 20:25 among them a great amount of **e**
Ne 13: 9 and then I put back into them the **e**
Zec 11:15 again the **e** of a foolish shepherd.

Equipped (Equip)
2Ch 14: 8 **e** with large shields and with spears,
Ne 4:16 the other half were **e** with spears,
Da 11:13 advance with a huge army fully **e**.
2Ti 3:17 be thoroughly **e** for every good work.

Equity (Equal)
Ps 96:10 he will judge the peoples with **e**.
98: 9 and the peoples with **e**.
99: 4 justice—you have established **e**;

Equivalent (Equal)
Lev 27: 2 to the LORD by giving **e** values,
Eze 45:14 for ten baths are **e** to a homer).

Er
Ge 38: 3 birth to a son, who was named **E**.
38: 6 Judah got a wife for **E**, his
38: 7 **E**, Judah's firstborn, was wicked in
46:12 The sons of Judah: **E**, Onan, Shelah,
46:12 Er and Onan had died in the land of
Nu 26:19 **E** and Onan were sons of Judah, but
1Ch 2: 3 The sons of Judah: **E**, Onan and
2: 3 **E**, Judah's firstborn, was wicked in
4:21 The sons of Shelah son of Judah: **E**
Lk 3:28 the son of Elmadam, the son of **E**,

Eran (Eranite)
Nu 26:36 through **E**, the Eranite clan.

Eranite (Eran)
Nu 26:36 Shuthelah: through Eran, the **E** clan.

Erastus
Ac 19:22 Timothy and **E**, to Macedonia, while
Ro 16:23 **E**, who is the city's director of
2Ti 4:20 **E** stayed in Corinth, and I left

Erech
Ge 10:10 **E**, Akkad and Calneh, in Shinar.
Ezr 4: 9 **E** and Babylon, the Elamites of Susa,

Erect (Erected)
Dt 16:22 do not **e** a sacred stone, for these
Eze 4: 2 lay siege to it: **E** siege works
21:22 build a ramp and to **e** siege works.

Erected (Erect)
Ex 40:18 put the bases in place, **e** the frames
2Sa 18:18 **e** it in the King's Valley as a
1Ki 7:21 He **e** the pillars at the portico of
2Ki 21: 3 he also **e** altars to Baal and made an
23:12 altars the kings of Judah had **e** on
2Ch 3:17 He **e** the pillars in the front of the
33: 3 he also **e** altars to the Baals and
Est 6: 4 on the gallows he had **e** for him.
Eze 17:17 siege works **e** to destroy many lives.

Eri (Erite)
Ge 46:16 Shuni, Ezbon, **E**, Arodi and Areli.
Nu 26:16 clan; through **E**, the Erite clan;

Erite (Eri)
Nu 26:16 Oznite clan; through Eri, the **E** clan;

Erodes
Job 14:18 "But as a mountain **e** and crumbles

Erred (Error)
Nu 15:28 who **e** by sinning unintentionally,
1Sa 26:21 like a fool and have **e** greatly."

Error (Erred, Errors)
Job 4:18 if he charges his angels with **e**,
19: 4 my **e** remains my concern alone.
Ecc 10: 5 sort of **e** that arises from a ruler:
Isa 32: 6 and spreads **e** concerning the LORD;
Isa 47:15 Each of them goes on in his **e**; there
Mt 22:29 Jesus replied, "You are in **e** because
Mk 12:24 Jesus replied, "Are you not in **e**
1Th 2: 3 not spring from **e** or impure motives,
Jas 5:20 turns a sinner from the **e** of his way
2Pe 2:18 escaping from those who live in **e**.
3:17 carried away by the **e** of lawless men
Jude :11 rushed for profit into Balaam's **e**;

Errors (Error)
Ps 19:12 Who can discern his **e**? Forgive my
Ecc 10: 4 calmness can lay great **e** to rest.

Esarhaddon
2Ki 19:37 And **E** his son succeeded him as king.
Ezr 4: 2 since the time of **E** king of Assyria,
Isa 37:38 And **E** his son succeeded him as king.

Esau (Edom, Esau's)
Also known as Edom (Ge 25:30). Son of Isaac; older twin of Jacob (Ge 25:24–26); hunter, favoured by Isaac (Ge 25:27–28). Sold birthright (Ge 25:29–34; Heb 12:6); lost blessing as eldest son (Ge 27). Married foreign wives (Ge 26:34–35; 28:8–9; 36:2–3). Reconciled to Jacob (Ge 32:3–21; 33:1–16). Occupied land of Seir (Ge 36:8; Dt 2:4–12); ancestor of Edomites (Ge 36:9–43). Rejection by God contrasted with gracious choice of Jacob (Mal 1:2–3; Ro 9:13).

Ge 25:25 hairy garment; so they named him **E**.
25:27 **E** became a skilful hunter, a man of
25:28 loved **E**, but Rebekah loved Jacob.
25:29 **E** came in from the open country,
25:32 "Look, I am about to die," **E** said.
25:34 Jacob gave **E** some bread and some
25:34 So **E** despised his birthright.
26:34 **E** was forty years old, he married
27: 1 he called for **E** his older son and
27: 5 as Isaac spoke to his son **E**. When **E**
27: 6 your father say to your brother **E**,
27:11 "But my brother **E** is a hairy man,
27:15 Rebekah took the best clothes of **E**
27:19 Jacob said to his father, "I am **E**
27:21 you really are my son **E** or not."
27:22 but the hands are the hands of **E**."
27:23 of his brother **E**; so he blessed him.
27:24 "Are you really my son **E**?" he asked.
27:30 his brother **E** came in from hunting.
27:32 he answered, "your firstborn, **E**.
27:34 **E** heard his father's words, he burst
27:36 **E** said, "Isn't he rightly named
27:37 Isaac answered **E**, "I have made him
27:38 **E** said to his father, "Do you have
27:38 too, my father!" Then **E** wept aloud.
27:41 **E** held a grudge against Jacob
27:42 Rebekah was told what her older son **E**
27:42 "Your brother **E** is consoling himself
28: 5 who was the mother of Jacob and **E**.
28: 6 Now **E** learned that Isaac had blessed
28: 8 **E** then realised how displeasing the
32: 3 his brother **E** in the land of Seir,
32: 4 say to my master **E**: 'Your servant
32: 6 "We went to your brother **E**, and now
32: 8 He thought, "If **E** comes and attacks
32:11 from the hand of my brother **E**, for I
32:13 selected a gift for his brother **E**:
32:17 "When my brother **E** meets you and
32:18 They are a gift sent to my lord **E**,
32:19 same thing to **E** when you meet him.
33: 1 Jacob looked up and there was **E**,
33: 4 **E** ran to meet Jacob and embraced him;
33: 5 **E** looked up and saw the women and
33: 8 **E** asked, "What do you mean by all
33: 9 **E** said, "I already have plenty, my
33:11 Jacob insisted, **E** accepted it.
33;12 **E** said, "Let us be on our way; I'll
33:15 **E** said, "Then let me leave some of
33:16 that day **E** started on his way back
35: 1 were fleeing from your brother **E**."
35:29 And his sons **E** and Jacob buried him.
36: 1 the account of **E** (that is, Edom).
36: 2 **E** took his wives from the women of
36: 4 Adah bore Eliphaz to **E**, Basemath
36: 5 sons of **E**, who were born to him in
36: 6 **E** took his wives and sons and
Ge 36: 8 **E** (that is, Edom) settled in the
36: 9 This is the account of **E** the father
36:14 bore to **E**: Jeush, Jalam and Korah.
36:15 sons of Eliphaz the firstborn of **E**:
36:19 These were the sons of **E** (that is,
36:40 were the chiefs descended from **E**,
36:43 was **E** the father of the Edomites.
Dt 2: 4 descendants of **E**, who live in Seir.
2: 5 I have given **E** the hill country of
2: 8 descendants of **E**, who live in Seir.
2:12 the descendants of **E** drove them out.
2:22 the same for the descendants of **E**,
2:29 the descendants of **E**, who live in
Jos 24: 4 to Isaac I gave Jacob and **E**. I
24: 4 the hill country of Seir to **E**,
1Ch 1:34 The sons of Isaac: **E** and Israel.
1:35 The sons of **E**: Eliphaz, Reuel, Jeush,
Jer 49: 8 on **E** at the time I punish him.
49:10 I will strip **E** bare; I will uncover
Ob : 6 how **E** will be ransacked, his hidden
: 8 understanding in the mountains of **E**?
:18 the house of **E** will be stubble,
:18 be no survivors from the house of **E**.
:19 Negev will occupy the mountains of **E**,
:21 Zion to govern the mountains of **E**.
Mal 1: 2 "Was not **E** Jacob's brother?" the LORD
1: 3 **E** I have hated, and I have turned
Ro 9:13 "Jacob I loved, but **E** I hated."
Heb 11:20 By faith Isaac blessed Jacob and **E**
12:16 or is godless like **E**, who for a

Esau's (Esau)
Ge 25:26 **E** heel; so he was named Jacob.
36:10 These are the names of **E** sons:
36:10 the son of **E** wife Adah, and Reuel,
36:10 Reuel, the son of **E** wife Basemath.
36:12 **E** son Eliphaz also had a concubine
36:12 These were grandsons of **E** wife Adah.
36:13 were grandsons of **E** wife Basemath.
36:14 The sons of **E** wife Oholibamah
36:15 were the chiefs among **E** descendants:
36:17 The sons of **E** son Reuel: Chiefs
36:17 were grandsons of **E** wife Basemath.
36:18 The sons of **E** wife Oholibamah:
36:18 **E** wife Oholibamah daughter of Anah.
Ob : 9 and everyone in **E** mountains will be

Escape (Escaped, Escapes, Escaping)
Ge 7: 7 ark to **e** the waters of the flood.
32: 8 the group that is left may **e**."
Jos 8:20 but they had no chance to **e** in any
Jdg 20:42 but they could not **e** the battle.
1Sa 19:10 That night David made good his **e**.
19:18 David had fled and made his **e**, he
27: 1 The best thing I can do is to **e** to
2Sa 15:14 or none of us will **e** from Absalom.
20: 6 fortified cities and **e** from us."
1Ki 12:18 into his chariot and **e** to Jerusalem.
19:17 any who **e** the sword of Hazael, and
19:17 death any who **e** the sword of Jehu.
2Ki 10:24 in your hands **e**, it will be your life
10:25 "Go in and kill them; let no-one **e**.
2Ch 10:18 into his chariot and **e** to Jerusalem.
Est 4:13 you alone of all the Jews will **e**.
Job 11:20 and **e** will elude them; their hope
15:30 He will not **e** the darkness; a flame
Ps 56: 7 On no account let them **e**; in your
68:20 Sovereign LORD comes **e** from death.
88: 8 I am confined and cannot **e**;
Pr 11: 9 through knowledge the righteous **e**.
Ecc 7:26 The man who pleases God will **e** her,
Isa 20: 6 of Assyria! How then can we **e**?'"
Jer 11:11 on them a disaster they cannot **e**.
21: 9 will live; he will **e** with his life.
25:35 leaders of the flock no place to **e**.
32: 4 Zedekiah king of Judah will not **e**
34: 3 You will not **e** from his grasp but
35:11 **e** the Babylonian and Aramean armies.
38: 2 will **e** with his life; he will live.'
38:18 will not **e** from their hands.'"
38:23 You yourself will not **e** from their
39:18 the sword but will **e** with your life,
41:18 to **e** the Babylonians. They were
42:17 **e** the disaster I will bring on them.'
44:14 will **e** or survive to return to the

Jer 44:28 Those who e the sword and return to
45: 5 I will let you e with your life.'"
46: 6 swift cannot flee nor the strong e.
48: 8 every town, and not a town will e.
50:29 Encamp all round her; let no-one e.
Lam 3: 7 has walled me in so that I cannot e;
Eze 6: 8 for some of you will e the sword
6: 9 those who e will remember me—how I
7:16 All who survive and e will be in the
17:15 Will he who does such things e? Will
17:15 Will he break the treaty and yet e?
17:18 all these things, he shall not e.
Da 11:42 many countries; Egypt will not e.
Hos 9: 6 Even if they e from destruction,
Am 2:14 The swift will not e, the strong
9: 1 Not one will get away, none will e.
Hab 2: 9 on high, to e the clutches of ruin!
Zec 2: 7 "Come, O Zion! E, you who live in
Mal 3:15 even those who challenge God e.'"
Mt 2:13 child and his mother and e to Egypt.
23:33 will you e being condemned to hell?
Lk 21:36 and pray that you may be able to e
Ac 27:30 In an attempt to e from the ship,
Ro 2: 3 you think you will e God's judgment?
1Th 5: 3 pregnant woman, and they will not e.
2Ti 2:26 and e from the trap of the devil,
Heb 2: 3 how shall we e if we ignore such a
12:25 If they did not e when they refused
2Pe 1: 4 e the corruption in the world caused

Escaped (Escape)
Ge 14:13 One who had e came and reported this
Jdg 3:26 passed by the idols and e to Seirah.
3:29 vigorous and strong; not a man e.
9: 5 son of Jerub-Baal, e by hiding.
1Sa 19:12 through a window, and he fled and e.
19:17 send my enemy away so that he e?"
22: 1 David left Gath and e to the cave of
22:20 of Ahitub, e and fled to join David.
23:13 told that David had e from Keilah,
2Sa 1: 3 He answered, "I have e from the
1Ki 20:20 But Ben-Hadad king of Aram e on
20:30 The rest of them e to the city of
2Ki 9:27 but he e to Megiddo and died there.
13: 5 and they e from the power of Aram.
19:37 and they e to the land of Ararat.
1Ch 4:43 the remaining Amalekites who had e,
2Ch 16: 7 king of Aram has e from your hand.
20:24 lying on the ground; no-one had e.
30: 6 who have e from the hand of the
36:20 the remnant who e from the sword,
Job 1:15 the only one who has e to tell you!"
1:16 the only one who has e to tell you!"
1:17 the only one who has e to tell you!"
1:19 the only one who has e to tell you!"
19:20 have e by only the skin of my teeth.
Ps 124: 7 We have e like a bird out of the
124: 7 has been broken, and we have e.
Isa 37:38 and they e to the land of Ararat.
Jer 41:15 eight of his men e from Johanan and
51:50 You who have e the sword, leave and
Lam 2:22 LORD's anger no-one e or survived;
Eze 33:21 a man who had e from Jerusalem came
Jn 10:39 to seize him, but he e their grasp.
Ac 16:27 he thought the prisoners had e.
26:26 that none of this has e his notice,
28: 4 for though he e from the sea,
Heb 11:34 and e the edge of the sword; whose
2Pe 2:20 If they have e the corruption of the

Escapes (Escape)
Ps 33:16 no warrior e by his great strength.
Pr 12:13 talk, but a righteous man e trouble.
Joel 2: 3 a desert waste—nothing e them.

Escaping (Escape)
Jdg 9:21 Jotham fled, e to Beer, and he lived
Job 15:22 He despairs of e the darkness; he is
Jer 48:19 and the woman e, ask them, 'What
Hos 13: 3 like smoke e through a window.
Ac 27:42 of them from swimming away and e.
1Co 3:15 only as one e through the flames.
2Pe 2:18 just e from those who live in error.

Escort (Escorted)
Da 11: 6 together with her royal e and her
Ac 16:37 them come themselves and e us out."

Escorted (Escort)
1Ki 1:38 King David's mule and e him to Gihon.
SS 3: 7 Solomon's carriage, e by sixty
Ac 16:39 They came to appease them and e them
17:15 The men who e Paul brought him to

Esek
Ge 26:20 So he named the well E, because

Eshan
Jos 15:52 Arab, Dumah, E,

Esh-Baal
1Ch 8:33 Jonathan, Malki-Shua, Abinadab and E.
9:39 Jonathan, Malki-Shua, Abinadab and E.

Eshban
Ge 36:26 The sons of Dishon: Hemdan, E,
1Ch 1:41 Dishon: Hemdan, E, Ithran and Keran.

Eshcol
Ge 14:13 a brother of E and Aner, all of whom
14:24 went with me—to Aner, E and Mamre.
Nu 13:23 they reached the Valley of E, they
13:24 That place was called the Valley of E
32: 9 After they went up to the Valley of E
Dt 1:24 to the Valley of E and explored it.

Eshek
1Ch 8:39 The sons of his brother E: Ulam his

Eshtaol (Eshtaolites)
Jos 15:33 In the western foothills: E, Zorah,
19:41 included: Zorah, E, Ir Shemesh,
Jdg 13:25 in Mahaneh Dan, between Zorah and E.
16:31 buried him between Zorah and E in the
18: 2 warriors from Zorah and E to spy
18: 8 they returned to Zorah and E, their
18:11 battle, set out from Zorah and E.

Eshtaolites (Eshtaol)
1Ch 2:53 descended the Zorathites and E.

Eshtemoa
Jos 21:14 Jattir, E,
1Sa 30:28 to those in Aroer, Siphmoth, E
1Ch 4:17 Shammai and Ishbah the father of E.
4:19 the Garmite, and E the Maacathite.
6:57 of refuge), and Libnah, Jattir, E,

Eshtemoh
Jos 15:50 Anab, E, Anim,

Eshton
1Ch 4:11 of Mehir, who was the father of E.
4:12 E was the father of Beth Rapha,

Esli
Lk 3:25 the son of E, the son of Naggai,

Establish (Established, Establishes, Establishing, Re-established)
Ge 6:18 I will e my covenant with you, and
9: 9 "I now e my covenant with you and
9:11 I e my covenant with you: Never
17: 7 I will e my covenant as an
17:19 I will e my covenant with him as an
17:21 my covenant I will e with Isaac,
Ex 23:31 "I will e your borders from the Red
Dt 28: 9 The LORD will e you as his holy
1Sa 2:35 I will firmly e his house, and he
2Sa 3:10 e David's throne over Israel and
7:11 LORD himself will e a house for you:
7:12 own body, and I will e his kingdom.
7:13 e the throne of his kingdom for ever.
1Ki 8:32 not guilty, and so e his innocence.
9: 5 I will e your royal throne over
1Ch 17:11 own sons, and I will e his kingdom.
17:12 and I will e his throne for ever.
18: 3 when he went to e his control along
22:10 And I will e the throne of his
28: 7 I will e his kingdom for ever if he
2Ch 6:23 not guilty and so e his innocence.
7:18 I will e your royal throne, as I
Est 9:27 the Jews took it upon themselves to e
9:31 to e these days of Purim at their
Ps 87: 5 the Most High himself will e her."
89: 4 'I will e your line for ever and
89:29 I will e his line for ever, his
90:17 e the work of our hands for us—yes,
90:17 us—yes, e the work of our hands.
Isa 26:12 LORD, you e peace for us; all that
Eze 16:60 e an everlasting covenant with you.
16:62 I will e my covenant with you, and
37:26 I will e them and increase their
Da 11:16 He will e himself in the Beautiful
Ro 10: 3 from God and sought to e their own,
16:25 Now to him who is able to e you by
Heb 10: 9 aside the first to e the second.

Established (Establish)
Ge 9:17 of the covenant I have e between me
47:26 Joseph e it as a law concerning land
Ex 6: 4 I also e my covenant with them to
15:17 the sanctuary, O Lord, your hands e.
Lev 26:46 the regulations that the LORD e on
Dt 19:15 A matter must be e by the testimony
1Sa 13:13 he would have e your kingdom over
20:31 you nor your kingdom will be e.
24:20 of Israel will be e in your hands.
2Sa 5:12 David knew that the LORD had e him
7:16 your throne shall be e for ever.'"
7:24 You have e your people Israel as
7:26 servant David will be e before you.
1Ki 2:12 David, and his rule was firmly e.
2:24 he who has e me securely on the
2:46 was now firmly e in Solomon's hands.
1Ch 14: 2 David knew that the LORD had e him
16:30 is firmly e; it cannot be moved.
17:14 his throne will be e for ever.'"
17:23 servant and his house be e for ever.
17:24 that it will be e and that your name
17:24 servant David will be e before you.
2Ch 1: 1 Solomon son of David e himself
2Ch 12: 1 king was e and he had become strong,
12:13 King Rehoboam e himself firmly in
17: 5 The LORD e the kingdom under his
21: 4 Jehoram e himself firmly over his
Ezr 8:20 had e to assist the Levites.
Est 9:31 and as they had e for themselves and
Job 12:19 stripped and overthrows men long e.
21: 8 They see their children e around
24:22 though they become e, they have no
28:25 he e the force of the wind and
Ps 9: 7 he has e his throne for judgment.
24: 2 founded it upon the seas and e it
74:16 the night; you e the sun and moon.
78: 5 for Jacob and e the law in Israel
78:69 like the earth that he e for ever.
81: 5 He e it as a statute for Joseph when
89: 2 e your faithfulness in heaven itself.
89:37 will be e for ever like the moon,
93: 1 is firmly e; it cannot be moved.
93: 2 Your throne was e long ago; you are
96:10 The world is firmly e, it cannot be
99: 4 he loves justice—you have e equity;
102:28 descendants will be e before you."
103:19 The LORD has e his throne in heaven,
119:90 you e the earth, and it endures.
119:152 that you e them to last for ever.
140:11 Let slanderers not be e in the land;
Pr 8:28 he e the clouds above and fixed
12: 3 A man cannot be e through wickedness,
16:12 a throne is e through righteousness.
24: 3 and through understanding it is e;
25: 5 will be e through righteousness.
30: 4 Who has e all the ends of the earth?
Isa 2: 2 be e as chief among the mountains;
14:32 "The LORD has e Zion, and in her his
16: 5 In love a throne will be e; in
44: 7 since I e my ancient people,
54:14 In righteousness you will be e:

Jer 12:16 they will be **e** among my people.
30:20 and their community will be **e** before
33: 2 it and **e** it—the LORD is his name:
33:25 'If I have not **e** my covenant with
Mic 4: 1 be **e** as chief among the mountains;
Mt 18:16 'every matter may be **e** by the
Ro 13: 1 except that which God has **e**.
13: 1 that exist have been **e** by God.
2Co 13: 1 "Every matter must be **e** by the
Gal 3:15 been duly **e**, so it is in this case.
3:17 the covenant previously **e** by God
Eph 3:17 you, being rooted and **e** in love,
Col 1:23 if you continue in your faith, **e** and
2Pe 1:12 firmly **e** in the truth you now have.

Establishes (Establish)

Job 25: 2 and awe belong to God; he **e** order
Isa 42: 4 till he **e** justice on earth.
62: 7 give him no rest till he **e** Jerusalem
Mic 7: 9 he pleads my case and **e** my right.
Hab 2:12 bloodshed and **e** a town by crime!

Establishing (Establish)

Isa 9: 7 **e** and upholding it with justice and

Estate

Ge 15: 2 who will inherit my **e** is Eliezer
31:14 the inheritance of our father's **e**?
Ru 4: 6 because I might endanger my own **e**.
Est 8: 1 gave Queen Esther the **e** of Haman,
8: 2 Esther appointed him over Haman's **e**.
8: 7 I have given his **e** to Esther, and
Ps 136:23 who remembered us in our low **e**
Lk 15:12 'Father, give me my share of the **e**.
Ac 28: 7 There was an **e** near by that belonged
Gal 4: 1 slave, although he owns the whole **e**.

Esteem (Esteemed)

Est 10: 3 and held in high **e** by his many
Pr 4: 8 **E** her, and she will exalt you;
Isa 66: 2 "This is the one I **e**: he who is

Esteemed (Esteem)

Pr 22: 1 be **e** is better than silver or gold.
Isa 53: 3 he was despised, and we **e** him not.
Da 9:23 to tell you, for you are highly **e**.
10:11 "Daniel, you who are highly **e**,
10:19 "Do not be afraid, O man highly **e**,"

Esther (Esther's)

Jewess living in Persia, also called Hadassah; brought up by cousin Mordecai (Est 2:7). Became Xerxes' queen (Est 2:8–18). Persuaded by Mordecai to help foil Haman's plot to destroy Jews (Est 3–4); risked life by approaching Xerxes (Est 4:9–11; 5:1–8); revealed Haman's plans (Est 7). Encouraged Jews to slaughter enemies; initiated feast of Purim in celebration (Est 9).

Est 2: 7 This girl, who was also known as **E**,
2: 8 **E** also was taken to the king's
2:10 **E** had not revealed her nationality
2:11 how **E** was and what was happening
2:15 When the turn came for **E** (the girl
2:15 And **E** won the favour of everyone who
2:17 Now the king was attracted to **E** more
2:20 **E** had kept secret her family
2:22 out about the plot and told Queen **E**,
4: 5 **E** summoned Hathach, one of the
4: 8 to show to **E** and explain it to her,
4: 9 Hathach went back and reported to **E**
4:15 **E** sent this reply to Mordecai:
5: 1 On the third day **E** put on her royal
5: 2 he saw Queen **E** standing in the court,
5: 2 So **E** approached and touched the tip
5: 3 the king asked, "What is it, Queen **E**?
5: 4 "If it pleases the king," replied **E**,
5: 5 "so that we may do what **E** asks.
5: 5 went to the banquet **E** had prepared.
5: 6 the king again asked **E**, "Now what is
5: 7 **E** replied, "My petition and my
5:12 "I'm the only person Queen **E** invited
6:14 away to the banquet **E** had prepared.
7: 1 and Haman went to dine with Queen **E**,
7: 2 "Queen **E**, what is your petition? It
Est 7: 3 Queen **E** answered, "If I have found
7: 5 King Xerxes asked Queen **E**, "Who is
7: 6 **E** said, "The adversary and enemy is
7: 7 behind to beg Queen **E** for his life.
7: 8 on the couch where **E** was reclining.
8: 1 gave Queen **E** the estate of Haman,
8: 1 **E** had told how he was related to her.
8: 2 **E** appointed him over Haman's estate.
8: 3 **E** again pleaded with the king,
8: 4 extended the gold sceptre to **E** and
8: 7 King Xerxes replied to Queen **E** and
8: 7 I have given his estate to **E**, and
9:12 The king said to Queen **E**, "The Jews
9:13 "If it pleases the king," **E** answered,
9:29 Queen **E**, daughter of Abihail, along
9:31 as Mordecai the Jew and Queen **E** had

Esther's (Esther)

Est 2:18 gave a great banquet, **E** banquet,
4: 4 **E** maids and eunuchs came and told
4:12 **E** words were reported to Mordecai,
4:17 carried out all of **E** instructions.
9:32 **E** decree confirmed these regulations

Estimate

Lk 14:28 Will he not first sit down and **e** the

Estranged

2Sa 14:14 person may not remain **e** from him.
Job 19:13 are completely **e** from me.

Etam

Jdg 15: 8 stayed in a cave in the rock of **E**.
15:11 in the rock of **E** and said to Samson,
1Ch 4: 3 These were the sons of **E**: Jezreel,
4:32 Their surrounding villages were **E**,
2Ch 11: 6 Bethlehem, **E**, Tekoa,

Eternal (*Eternal God, Eternal life,* Eternally, Eternity)

1Ki 10: 9 Because of the LORD's **e** love for
Ps 16:11 with **e** pleasures at your right hand.
21: 6 you have granted him **e** blessings
111:10 To him belongs **e** praise.
119:89 Your word, O LORD, is **e**; it stands
119:160 true; all your righteous laws are **e**.
Ecc 12: 5 Then man goes to his **e** home and
Isa 26: 4 the LORD, the LORD, is the Rock **e**.
47: 7 will continue for ever—the **e** queen
Jer 10:10 he is the living God, the **e** King.
Da 4: 3 His kingdom is an **e** kingdom;
4:34 His dominion is an **e** dominion; his
Hab 3: 6 His ways are **e**.
Mt 18: 8 two feet and be thrown into **e** fire.
25:41 you who are cursed, into the **e** fire
25:46 they will go away to **e** punishment
Mk 3:29 forgiven; he is guilty of an **e** sin."
Lk 16: 9 will be welcomed into **e** dwellings.
Ro 1:20 invisible qualities—his **e** power
2Co 4:17 **e** glory that far outweighs them all.
4:18 temporary, but what is unseen is **e**.
5: 1 a building from God, an **e** house in
Eph 3:11 according to his **e** purpose which he
2Th 2:16 us **e** encouragement and good hope,
1Ti 1:17 Now to the King **e**, immortal,
2Ti 2:10 is in Christ Jesus, with **e** glory.
Heb 5: 9 of **e** salvation for all who obey
6: 2 of the dead, and **e** judgment.
9:12 blood, having obtained **e** redemption.
9:14 who through the **e** Spirit offered
9:15 receive the promised **e** inheritance
13:20 through the blood of the **e** covenant
1Pe 5:10 who called you to his **e** glory in
2Pe 1:11 into the **e** kingdom of our Lord
Jude :7 who suffer the punishment of **e** fire.
Rev 14: 6 and he had the **e** gospel to proclaim

Eternal God

Ge 21:33 upon the name of the LORD, the **E**.
Dt 33:27 The **e** is your refuge, and underneath
Ro 16:26 writings by the command of the **e**,

Eternal life

Mt 19:16 what good thing must I do to get **e**?"
19:29 times as much and will inherit **e**.
25:46 punishment, but the righteous to **e**."
Mk 10:17 "what must I do to inherit **e**?
10:30 and in the age to come, **e**.
Lk 10:25 "what must I do to inherit **e**?
18:18 what must I do to inherit **e**?"
18:30 age and, in the age to come, **e**."
Jn 3:15 who believes in him may have **e**.
3:16 in him shall not perish but have **e**.
3:36 Whoever believes in the Son has **e**,
4:14 a spring of water welling up to **e**."
4:36 even now he harvests the crop for **e**,
5:24 me has **e** and will not be condemned;
5:39 think that by them you possess **e**.
6:27 but for food that endures to **e**,
6:40 Son and believes in him shall have **e**,
6:54 my flesh and drinks my blood has **e**,
6:68 we go? You have the words of **e**.
10:28 I give them **e**, and they shall never
12:25 in this world will keep it for **e**.
12:50 I know that his command leads to **e**.
17: 2 **e** to all those you have given him.
17: 3 Now this is **e**: that they may know
Ac 13:46 of **e**, we now turn to the Gentiles.
13:48 who were appointed for **e** believed.
Ro 2: 7 and immortality, he will give **e**.
5:21 **e** through Jesus Christ our Lord.
6:22 to holiness, and the result is **e**.
6:23 God is **e** in Christ Jesus our Lord.
Gal 6: 8 Spirit, from the Spirit will reap **e**.
1Ti 1:16 would believe on him and receive **e**.
6:12 Take hold of the **e** to which you were
Tit 1: 2 knowledge resting on the hope of **e**,
3: 7 become heirs having the hope of **e**.
1Jn 1: 2 and we proclaim to you the **e**, which
2:25 this is what he promised us—even **e**.
3:15 know that no murderer has **e** in him.
5:11 us **e**, and this life is in his Son.
5:13 that you may know that you have **e**.
5:20 He is the true God and **e**.
Jude :21 Lord Jesus Christ to bring you to **e**.

Eternally (Eternal)

Gal 1: 8 to you, let him be **e** condemned!
1: 9 accepted, let him be **e** condemned!

Eternity (Eternal)

Ps 93: 2 long ago; you are from all **e**.
Pr 8:23 I was appointed from **e**, from the
Ecc 3:11 He has also set **e** in the hearts of

Eth Kazin

Jos 19:13 eastward to Gath Hepher and **E**;

Etham

Ex 13:20 at **E** on the edge of the desert.
Nu 33: 6 They left Succoth and camped at **E**,
33: 7 They left **E**, turned back to Pi
33: 8 Desert of **E**, they camped at Marah.

Ethan

1Ki 4:31 including **E** the Ezrahite—wiser than
1Ch 2: 6 The sons of Zerah: Zimri, **E**, Heman,
2: 8 The son of **E**: Azariah.
6:42 the son of **E**, the son of Zimmah, the
6:44 at his left hand: **E** son of Kishi,
15:17 the Merarites, **E** son of Kushaiah;
15:19 The musicians Heman, Asaph and **E**
Ps 89: T A maskil of **E** the Ezrahite.

Ethanim

1Ki 8: 2 the month of **E**, the seventh month.

Ethbaal

1Ki 16:31 daughter of **E** king of the Sidonians,

Ether

Jos 15:42 Libnah, **E**, Ashan,
19: 7 Ain, Rimmon, **E** and Ashan—four towns

Ethiopia See Cush 1.

Ethiopian (Ethiopians)
Jer 13:23 Can the E change his skin or the
Ac 8:27 and on his way he met an E eunuch,

Ethiopians (Ethiopian)
Ac 8:27 treasury of Candace, queen of the E.

Ethnan
1Ch 4: 7 The sons of Helah: Zereth, Zohar, E,

Ethni
1Ch 6:41 the son of E, the son of Zerah, the

Eubulus
2Ti 4:21 E greets you, and so do Pudens,

Eunice
2Ti 1: 5 Lois and in your mother E and,

Eunuch (Eunuchs)
Est 2: 3 the king's e, who is in charge of
2:14 the king's e who was in charge of
2:15 the king's e who was in charge of
Isa 56: 3 And let not any e complain, "I am
Ac 8:27 on his way he met an Ethiopian e,
8:32 The e was reading this passage of
8:34 The e asked Philip, "Tell me, please,
8:36 the e said, "Look, here is water.
8:38 Then both Philip and the e went down
8:39 and the e did not see him again, but

Eunuchs (Eunuch)
2Ki 9:32 Two or three e looked down at him.
20:18 and they will become e in the palace
Est 1:10 he commanded the seven e who served
1:15 Xerxes that the e have taken to her."
4: 4 Esther's maids and e came and told
4: 5 one of the king's e assigned to
6:14 the king's e arrived and hurried
7: 9 Harbona, one of the e attending the
Isa 39: 7 and they will become e in the palace
56: 4 "To the e who keep my Sabbaths, who
Mt 19:12 For some are e because they were

Euodia
Php 4: 2 I plead with E and I plead with

Euphrates (Trans-Euphrates)
Longest river of western Asia (about 1,780 miles), which joins with the River Tigris. Known as the River (Ex 23:31) and the Great River (Ge 15:18). Babylon and Ur situated on its bank. One of the 4 rivers of Paradise (Ge 2:14); the north-east boundary of the promised land (Ge 15:18; Dt 1:7; Jos 1:4). David fought here (2Sa 8:3; 1Ch 18:3), and Josiah was killed here (2Ch 35:20–24). It features in prophecies about the exile (Isa 11:15; Jer 46:6; 51:63) and in John's vision (Rev 9:14; 16:12).

Ge 2:14 And the fourth river is the E.
15:18 of Egypt to the great river, the E—
Dt 1: 7 as far as the great river, the E.
11:24 from the E River to the western sea.
Jos 1: 4 and from the great river, the E—all
2Sa 8: 3 his control along the E River.
2Ki 23:29 to the E River to help the king
24: 7 the Wadi of Egypt to the E River.
1Ch 5: 9 desert that extends to the E River,
18: 3 his control along the E River.
2Ch 35:20 up to fight at Carchemish on the E,
Isa 11:15 sweep his hand over the E River.
27:12 the flowing E to the Wadi of Egypt,
Jer 46: 2 was defeated at Carchemish on the E
46: 6 the River E they stumble and fall.
46:10 land of the north by the River E.
51:63 stone to it and throw it into the E.
Mic 7:12 even from Egypt to the E and from
Rev 9:14 who are bound at the great river E."
16:12 out his bowl on the great river E,

Eutychus
Ac 20: 9 in a window was a young man named E,

Evangelist (Evangelists)
Ac 21: 8 of Philip the e, one of the Seven.
2Ti 4: 5 do the work of an e, discharge all

Evangelists (Evangelist)
Eph 4:11 some to be prophets, some to be e,

Eve
First woman; created from Adam as wife and helper (Ge 2:20–24). Deceived by serpent (Ge 3:1–6; 2Co 11:3; 1Ti 2:13–14). Punished (Ge 3:16). Mother of Cain and Abel (Ge 4:1–2).

Ge 3:20 Adam named his wife E, because she
4: 1 Adam lay with his wife E, and she
2Co 11: 3 I am afraid that just as E was
1Ti 2:13 For Adam was formed first, then E.

Evening (Evenings)
Ge 1: 5 And there was e, and there was
1: 8 And there was e, and there was
1:13 there was e, and there was morning
1:19 there was e, and there was morning
1:23 there was e, and there was morning
1:31 And there was e, and there was
8:11 the dove returned to him in the e,
19: 1 angels arrived at Sodom in the e,
24:11 outside the town; it was towards e,
24:63 He went out to the field one e to
29:23 when e came, he took his daughter
30:16 that e, Leah went out to meet him.
49:27 in the e he divides the plunder."
Ex 12:18 from the e of the fourteenth day
12:18 until the e of the twenty-first day.
16: 6 "In the e you will know that it was
16: 8 he gives you meat to eat in the e
16:13 That e quail came and covered the
18:13 stood round him from morning till e.
18:14 round you from morning till e?"
27:21 before the LORD from e till morning.
Lev 6:20 it in the morning and half in the e.
11:24 carcasses will be unclean till e.
11:25 and he will be unclean till e.
11:27 carcasses will be unclean till e.
11:28 and he will be unclean till e.
11:31 are dead will be unclean till e.
11:32 till e, and then it will be clean.
11:39 the carcass will be unclean till e.
11:40 and he will be unclean till e.
11:40 and he will be unclean till e.
14:46 is closed up will be unclean till e.
15: 5 and he will be unclean till e.
15: 6 and he will be unclean till e.
15: 7 and he will be unclean till e.
15: 8 and he will be unclean till e.
15:10 under him will be unclean till e;
15:10 and he will be unclean till e.
15:11 and he will be unclean till e.
15:16 and he will be unclean till e.
15:17 and it will be unclean till e.
15:18 and they will be unclean till e.
15:19 touches her will be unclean till e.
15:21 and he will be unclean till e.
15:22 and he will be unclean till e.
15:23 it, he will be unclean till e.
15:27 and he will be unclean till e.
17:15 till e; then he will be clean.
22: 6 such thing will be unclean till e.
23:32 From the e of the ninth day of the
23:32 the following e you are to observe
24: 3 from e till morning, continually.
Nu 9:15 From e till morning the cloud above
9:21 stayed only from e till morning,
19: 7 will be ceremonially unclean till e.
19: 8 and he too will be unclean till e.
19:10 and he too will be unclean till e.
19:19 water, and that e he will be clean.
19:21 of cleansing will be unclean till e.
19:22 touches it becomes unclean till e."
Dt 16: 4 the meat you sacrifice on the e of
16: 6 sacrifice the Passover in the e,
23:11 as e approaches he is to wash
28:67 "If only it were e!" and in the e,
Jos 5:10 On the e of the fourteenth day of
7: 6 of the LORD, remaining there till e.
8:29 a tree and left him there until e.
10:26 left hanging on the trees until e.
Jdg 19: 9 said, "Now look, it's almost e.
19:16 That e an old man from the hill
20:23 wept before the LORD until e, and
20:26 They fasted that day until e and
21: 2 where they sat before God until e,
Ru 2:17 Ruth gleaned in the field until e.
1Sa 14:24 man who eats food before e comes,
17:16 morning and e and took his stand.
20: 5 the e of the day after tomorrow.
20:19 The day after tomorrow, towards e,
30:17 dusk until the e of the next day,
2Sa 1:12 fasted till e for Saul and his son
11: 2 One e David got up from his bed and
11:13 But in the e Uriah went out to sleep
1Ki 17: 6 bread and meat in the e, and he drank
18:29 until the time for the e sacrifice.
22:35 of the chariot, and that e he died.
2Ki 16:15 offering and the e grain offering,
1Ch 16:40 morning and e, in accordance with
23:30 They were to do the same in the e
2Ch 2: 4 burnt offerings every morning and e
13:11 Every morning and e they present
13:11 lamps on the gold lampstand every e.
18:34 chariot facing the Arameans until e.
31: 3 for the morning and e burnt offerings
Ezr 3: 3 both the morning and e sacrifices.
9: 4 appalled until the e sacrifice.
9: 5 Then, at the e sacrifice, I rose
Ne 13:19 e shadows fell on the gates of
Est 2:14 In the e she would go there and in
Job 7: 2 Like a slave longing for the e
Ps 55:17 E, morning and noon I cry out in
59: 6 They return at e, snarling like dogs,
59:14 They return at e, snarling like dogs,
65: 8 e fades you call forth songs of joy.
90: 6 up new, by e it is dry and withered.
102:11 My days are like the e shadow; I
104:23 to his work, to his labour until e.
109:23 I fade away like an e shadow; I am
141: 2 of my hands be like the e sacrifice.
Ecc 11: 6 and at e let not your hands be idle,
Isa 17:14 In the e, sudden terror! Before the
Jer 6: 4 and the shadows of e grow long.
Eze 12: 4 Then in the e, while they are
12: 7 Then in the e I dug through the wall
24:18 morning, and in the e my wife died.
33:22 Now the e before the man arrived,
46: 2 the gate will not be shut until e.
Da 9:21 about the time of the e sacrifice.
Zep 2: 7 In the e they will lie down in the
3: 3 her rulers are e wolves, who leave
Zec 14: 7 When e comes, there will be light.
Mt 8:16 When e came, many who were
14:15 As e approached, the disciples came
14:23 When e came, he was there alone,
16: 2 He replied, "When e comes, you say,'
20: 8 "When e came, the owner of the
26:20 When e came, Jesus was reclining at
27:57 As e approached, there came a rich
Mk 1:32 That e after sunset the people
4:35 That day when e came, he said to his
6:47 When e came, the boat was in the
11:19 When e came, they went out of the
13:35 will come back—whether in the e,
14:17 When e came, Jesus arrived with the
15:42 the Sabbath). So as e approached,
Lk 21:37 and each e he went out to spend the
24:29 is nearly e; the day is almost over.
Jn 6:16 When e came, his disciples went down
13: 2 The e meal was being served, and the
20:19 On the e of that first day of the
Ac 4: 3 and because it was e, they put them
28:23 From morning till e he explained and

Evenings (Evening)
Da 8:14 He said to me, "It will take 2,300 e
8:26 "The vision of the e and mornings

Even-tempered (Temper)
Pr 17:27 and a man of understanding is e.

Events

1Ki 11:41 for the other **e** of Solomon's
12:15 for this turn of **e** was from the LORD,
14:19 The other **e** of Jeroboam's reign, his
14:29 for the other **e** of Rehoboam's reign,
15: 7 for the other **e** of Abijah's reign,
15:23 for all the other **e** of Asa's reign,
15:31 for the other **e** of Nadab's reign,
16: 5 for the other **e** of Baasha's reign,
16:14 for the other **e** of Elah's reign, and
16:20 for the other **e** of Zimri's reign,
16:27 for the other **e** of Omri's reign,
22:39 for the other **e** of Ahab's reign,
22:45 for the other **e** of Jehoshaphat's
2Ki 1:18 for all the other **e** of Ahaziah's
8:23 for the other **e** of Jehoram's reign,
10:34 for the other **e** of Jehu's reign, all
12:19 the other **e** of the reign of Joash
13: 8 the other **e** of the reign of Jehoahaz
13:12 the other **e** of the reign of Jehoash
14:15 the other **e** of the reign of Jehoash
14:18 for the other **e** of Amaziah's reign,
14:28 for the other **e** of Jeroboam's reign,
15: 6 for the other **e** of Azariah's reign,
15:11 The other **e** of Zechariah's reign are
15:15 The other **e** of Shallum's reign, and
15:21 for the other **e** of Menahem's reign,
15:26 The other **e** of Pekahiah's reign, and
15:31 for the other **e** of Pekah's reign,
15:36 for the other **e** of Jotham's reign,
16:19 for the other **e** of the reign of Ahaz,
20:20 for the other **e** of Hezekiah's reign,
21:17 for the other **e** of Manasseh's reign,
21:25 for the other **e** of Amon's reign, and
23:28 for the other **e** of Josiah's reign,
24: 5 for the other **e** of Jehoiakim's reign,
1Ch 29:29 for the **e** of King David's reign,
2Ch 9:29 for the other **e** of Solomon's reign,
10:15 for this turn of **e** was from God, to
12:15 for the **e** of Rehoboam's reign, from
13:22 The other **e** of Abijah's reign, what
16:11 The **e** of Asa's reign, from beginning
20:34 The other **e** of Jehoshaphat's reign,
25:26 for the other **e** of Amaziah's reign,
26:22 The other **e** of Uzziah's reign, from
27: 7 The other **e** in Jotham's reign,
28:26 The other **e** of his reign and all his
32:32 The other **e** of Hezekiah's reign and
33:18 The other **e** of Manasseh's reign,
35:26 The other **e** of Josiah's reign and
35:27 all the **e**, from beginning to end,
36: 8 The other **e** of Jehoiakim's reign,
Est 3: 1 After these **e**, King Xerxes honoured
9:20 Mordecai recorded these **e**, and he
Lk 21:11 fearful **e** and great signs from
Ac 5:11 and all who heard about these **e**.
19:40 with rioting because of today's **e**.

Ever (Everlasting, Evermore, *For ever and ever*, Forevermore, *Love endures for ever*)

Ge 3:22 of life and eat, and live for **e**."
6: 3 will not contend with man for **e**,
13:15 to you and your offspring for **e**.
24:16 virgin; no man had **e** lain with her.
Ex 3:15 This is my name for **e**, the name by
5:23 **E** since I went to Pharaoh to speak
9:18 that has **e** fallen on Egypt, from
10: 6 have **e** seen from the day they settled
10:14 locusts, nor will there **e** be again.
11: 6 there has **e** been or **e** will be again.
31:17 between me and the Israelites for **e**,
32:13 will be their inheritance for **e**.'"
Nu 11:20 "Why did we **e** leave Egypt?"'
14:23 not one of them will **e** see the land
14:23 me with contempt will **e** see it.
35:26 "But if the accused **e** goes outside
Dt 4:32 Has anything so great as this **e**
4:32 anything like it **e** been heard of?
4:34 Has any god **e** tried to take for
5:26 For what mortal man has **e** heard the
5:29 with them and their children for **e**!
8:19 If you **e** forget the LORD your God
9:24 the LORD **e** since I have known you.
13:16 a ruin for **e**, never to be rebuilt.
Dt 28:46 to you and your descendants for **e**.
29:29 to us and to our children for **e**,
32:40 declare: As surely as I live for **e**,
34:12 For no-one has **e** shown the mighty
Jos 4: 7 to the people of Israel for **e**."
7: 7 LORD, why did you **e** bring this
7:26 called the Valley of Achor **e** since.
14: 9 and that of your children for **e**,
14:14 of Jephunneh the Kenizzite **e** since,
22:28 "And we said, 'If they **e** say this to
Jdg 11:25 king of Moab? Did he **e** quarrel with
16:17 "No razor has **e** been used on my head,
Ru 1:17 May the LORD deal with me, be it **e**
1Sa 1:11 razor will **e** be used on his head."
2:30 would minister before me for **e**.
3:13 I would judge his family for **e**
3:17 May God deal with you, be it **e** so
14:44 "May God deal with me, be it **e** so
20:13 deal with me, be it **e** so severely
20:15 do not **e** cut off your kindness from
20:23 witness between you and me for **e**."
20:42 and my descendants for **e**.
25:22 May God deal with David, be it **e** so
27: 6 to the kings of Judah **e** since.
27:12 that he will be my servant for **e**."
2Sa 2:26 "Must the sword devour for **e**? Don't
3: 9 May God deal with Abner, be it **e** so
3:28 "I and my kingdom are for **e** innocent
3:35 "May God deal with me, be it **e** so
6: 9 the ark of the LORD **e** come to me?"
7: 7 did I **e** say to any of their rulers
7:11 have done **e** since the time I
7:13 the throne of his kingdom for **e**.
7:16 shall endure for **e** before me;
7:16 throne shall be established for **e**.'"
7:24 Israel as your very own for **e**,
7:25 "And now, LORD God, keep for **e** the
7:26 that your name will be great for **e**.
7:29 that it may continue for **e** in your
7:29 your servant will be blessed for **e**."
13:32 Absalom's expressed intention **e** since
19:13 be it **e** so severely, if from now on
22:51 to David and his descendants for **e**."
1Ki 1:31 "May my lord King David live for **e**!
2:23 "May God deal with me, be it **e** so
2:33 of Joab and his descendants for **e**.
2:33 there be the LORD's peace for **e**."
2:45 secure before the LORD for **e**."
3:12 like you, nor will there **e** be.
8:13 a place for you to dwell for **e**."
9: 3 by putting my Name there for **e**.
9: 5 your royal throne over Israel for **e**,
10:20 Nothing like it had **e** been made
11:39 because of this, but not for **e**.'"
19: 2 "May the gods deal with me, be it **e**
20:10 "May the gods deal with me, be it **e**
22:28 Micaiah declared, "If you **e** return
2Ki 5:27 you and to your descendants for **e**.
6:31 "May God deal with me, be it **e** so
8:19 for David and his descendants for **e**.
18:33 Has the god of any nation **e**
21: 7 of Israel, I will put my Name for **e**.
1Ch 13:12 can I **e** bring the ark of God to me?"
15: 2 and to minister before him for **e**."
16:15 He remembers his covenant for **e**, the
17: 6 did I **e** say to any of their leaders
17:10 have done **e** since the time I
17:12 I will establish his throne for **e**.
17:14 over my house and my kingdom for **e**;
17:14 throne will be established for **e**.'"
17:22 people Israel your very own for **e**,
17:23 and his house be established for **e**.
17:24 that your name will be great for **e**.
17:27 that it may continue for **e** in your
17:27 it, and it will be blessed for **e**."
22:10 of his kingdom over Israel for **e**.'
23:13 he and his descendants for **e**, to
23:13 blessings in his name for **e**.
23:25 come to dwell in Jerusalem for **e**,
28: 4 family to be king over Israel for **e**.
28: 7 I will establish his kingdom for **e**
28: 8 to your descendants for **e**.
28: 9 him, he will reject you for **e**.
29:18 in the hearts of your people for **e**,
29:25 as no king over Israel **e** had before.
2Ch 1:12 as no king before you **e** had
2Ch 6: 2 a place for you to dwell for **e**."
7:16 so that my Name may be there for **e**.
9: 8 and his desire to uphold them for **e**,
9:11 like them had **e** been seen in Judah.)
9:19 Nothing like it had **e** been made
13: 5 for **e** by a covenant of salt?
18:27 Micaiah declared, "If you **e** return
20: 7 give it for **e** to the descendants of
21: 7 for him and his descendants for **e**.
30: 8 which he has consecrated for **e**.
32:13 Were the gods of those nations **e**
33: 4 Name will remain in Jerusalem for **e**."
33: 7 of Israel, I will put my Name for **e**.
35:18 none of the kings of Israel had **e**
Ezr 3:11 his love to Israel endures for **e**.
Ne 2: 3 "May the king live for **e**! Why should
13: 1 **e** be admitted into the assembly
Job 4: 7 being innocent, has **e** perished?
4: 7 Where were the upright **e** destroyed?
4:20 unnoticed, they perish for **e**.
6:22 Have I **e** said, 'Give something on my
7:16 my life; I would not live for **e**.
15: 7 "Are you the first man **e** born? Were
19:24 on lead, or engraved in rock for **e**!
20: 4 **e** since man was placed on the earth,
20: 7 he will perish for **e**, like his own
23: 7 be delivered for **e** from my judge.
29:20 in me, the bow **e** new in my hand.'
36: 7 with kings and exalts them for **e**.
38:12 "Have you **e** given orders to the
Ps 5:11 be glad; let them **e** sing for joy.
9: 7 The LORD reigns for **e**; he has
9:18 the hope of the afflicted **e** perish.
12: 7 protect us from such people for **e**.
13: 1 O LORD? Will you forget me for **e**?
18:50 to David and his descendants for **e**.
19: 9 of the LORD is pure, enduring for **e**.
22:26 him—may your hearts live for **e**!
23: 6 in the house of the LORD for **e**.
25: 3 No-one whose hope is in you will **e**
25:15 My eyes are **e** on the LORD, for only
26: 3 for your love is **e** before me, and I
28: 9 their shepherd and carry them for **e**.
29:10 the LORD is enthroned as King for **e**.
30:12 God, I will give you thanks for **e**.
33:11 plans of the LORD stand firm for **e**,
37:18 their inheritance will endure for **e**.
37:27 you will dwell in the land for **e**.
37:28 They will be protected for **e**, but
37:29 the land and dwell in it for **e**.
38:17 to fall, and my pain is **e** with me.
41:12 and set me in your presence for **e**.
44: 8 and we will praise your name for **e**.
44:23 yourself! Do not reject us for **e**.
45: 2 since God has blessed you for **e**.
48: 8 our God: God makes her secure for **e**.
49: 8 is costly, no payment is **e** enough—
49: 9 that he should live on for **e** and not
49:11 will remain their houses for **e**,
50: 8 offerings, which are **e** before me.
52: 9 I will praise you for **e** for what you
55:19 God, who is enthroned for **e**, will
61: 4 I long to dwell in your tent for **e**
61: 7 enthroned in God's presence for **e**;
61: 8 will I **e** sing praise to your name
66: 7 He rules for **e** by his power, his
68:16 the LORD himself will dwell for **e**?
69:23 see, and their backs be bent for **e**.
71: 6 I will **e** praise you.
72:15 May people **e** pray for him and bless
72:17 May his name endure for **e**; may it
72:19 Praise be to his glorious name for **e**;
73:26 of my heart and my portion for **e**.
74: 1 Why have you rejected us for **e**,
74:10 Will the foe revile your name for **e**?
74:19 of your afflicted people for **e**.
75: 9 for me, I will declare this for **e**; I
77: 7 "Will the Lord reject for **e**? Will he
77: 8 Has his unfailing love vanished for **e**
78:69 the earth that he established for **e**.
79: 5 O LORD? Will you be angry for **e**?
79:13 will praise you for **e**; from
81:15 their punishment would last for **e**.
83:17 May they **e** be ashamed and dismayed;
84: 4 your house; they are **e** praising you.
85: 5 Will you be angry with us for **e**?

Ps 86:12 I will glorify your name for **e**.
89: 1 sing of the LORD's great love for **e**;
89: 2 that your love stands firm for **e**,
89: 4 'I will establish your line for **e**
89:28 I will maintain my love to him for **e**,
89:29 I will establish his line for **e**, his
89:33 nor will I **e** betray my faithfulness.
89:36 that his line will continue for **e**
89:37 will be established for **e** like the
89:46 Will you hide yourself for **e**? How
89:52 Praise be to the LORD for **e**! Amen
92: 7 they will be for **e** destroyed.
92: 8 you, O LORD, are exalted for **e**.
102:12 you, O LORD, sit enthroned for **e**;
103: 9 nor will he harbour his anger for **e**;
104:31 the glory of the LORD endure for **e**;
105: 8 He remembers his covenant for **e**, the
109:19 like a belt tied for **e** round him.
110: 4 a priest for **e**, in the order of
111: 3 and his righteousness endures for **e**.
111: 5 he remembers his covenant for **e**.
111: 9 he ordained his covenant for **e**—
112: 3 and his righteousness endures for **e**.
112: 6 man will be remembered for **e**.
112: 9 his righteousness endures for **e**; his
117: 2 of the LORD endures for **e**. Praise
119:98 my enemies, for they are **e** with me.
119:111 Your statutes are my heritage for **e**;
119:144 Your statutes are for **e** right; give
119:152 you established them to last for **e**.
125: 1 cannot be shaken but endures for **e**.
132:16 and her saints shall **e** sing for joy.
135:13 Your name, O LORD, endures for **e**,
138: 8 your love, O LORD, endures for **e**—
141: 5 is **e** against the deeds of evildoers;
146: 6 LORD, who remains faithful for **e**.
146:10 The LORD reigns for **e**, your God, O
Pr 4:18 shining **e** brighter till the full
5:19 may you **e** be captivated by her love.
6:21 Bind them upon your heart for **e**;
10:25 but the righteous stand firm for **e**.
12:19 Truthful lips endure for **e**, but a
21:28 to him will be destroyed for **e**.
27:24 for riches do not endure for **e**, and
30:13 those whose eyes are **e** so haughty,
Ecc 1: 4 go, but the earth remains for **e**.
1: 6 it goes, **e** returning on its course.
3:14 God does will endure for **e**;
Isa 6: 9 tell this people: "'Be **e** hearing
6: 9 **e** seeing, but never perceiving.'
9: 7 from that time on and for **e**.
25: 8 he will swallow up death for **e**. The
26: 4 Trust in the LORD for **e**, for the
28:28 does not go on threshing it for **e**.
32:14 will become a wasteland for **e**,
32:17 be quietness and confidence for **e**.
34:10 and day; its smoke will rise for **e**.
34:10 no-one will **e** pass through it again.
34:17 They will possess it for **e** and dwell
36:18 Has the god of any nation **e**
40: 8 the word of our God stands for **e**."
47: 7 You said,'I will continue for **e**—
49:16 hands; your walls are **e** before me.
51: 6 my salvation will last for **e**, my
51: 8 But my righteousness will last for **e**,
57:15 lofty One says–he who lives for **e**,
57:16 I will not accuse for **e**, nor will I
59:12 Our offences are **e** with us, and we
59:21 time on and for **e**," says the LORD.
60:21 they will possess the land for **e**.
64: 9 LORD; do not remember our sins for **e**.
65:18 be glad and rejoice for **e** in what I
66: 8 Who has **e** heard of such a thing? Who
66: 8 Who has **e** seen such things? Can a
Jer 2:10 there has **e** been anything like this:
2:11 Has a nation **e** changed its gods?
3: 5 Will your wrath continue for **e**?'
3:12 LORD,'I will not be angry for **e**.
6: 7 sickness and wounds are **e** before me.
17: 4 my anger, and it will burn for **e**."
17:25 this city will be inhabited for **e**.
18:13 Who has **e** heard anything like this?
18:14 Does the snow of Lebanon **e** vanish
18:14 distant sources **e** cease to flow?
19: 4 nor the kings of Judah **e** knew,
20:17 my grave, her womb enlarged for **e**.
Jer 20:18 Why did I **e** come out of the womb to
25:12 "and will make it desolate for **e**.
31:36 **e** cease to be a nation before me."
33:18 who are Levites, **e** fail to have a
35: 6 your descendants must **e** drink wine.
35: 8 sons and daughters have **e** drunk
44: 3 nor you nor your fathers **e** knew.
44:18 **e** since we stopped burning incense
44:26 **e** again invoke my name or swear,
49:13 its towns will be in ruins for **e**."
49:33 of jackals, a desolate place for **e**.
51:26 desolate for **e**," declares the LORD.
51:39 then sleep for **e** and not awake,"
51:57 will sleep for **e** and not awake,"
51:62 in it; it will be desolate for **e**.'
Lam 2:20 Whom have you **e** treated like
3:31 are not cast off by the Lord for **e**.
5:19 You, O LORD, reign for **e**; your
Eze 4:14 meat has **e** entered my mouth."
15: 3 Is wood **e** taken from it to make
16:16 not happen, nor should they **e** occur.
27:32 "Who was **e** silenced like Tyre,
31:14 are **e** to tower proudly on high,
31:14 No other trees so well-watered are **e**
35: 9 I will make you desolate for **e**; your
37:25 children will live there for **e**,
37:25 servant will be their prince for **e**.
37:26 put my sanctuary among them for **e**.
37:28 my sanctuary is among them for **e**.'"
43: 7 live among the Israelites for **e**.
43: 9 and I will live among them for **e**.
Da 2: 4 "O king, live for **e**! Tell your
2:10 has **e** asked such a thing of any
2:44 but it will itself endure for **e**.
3: 9 Nebuchadnezzar, "O king, live for **e**!
4:34 and glorified him who lives for **e**.
5:10 "O king, live for **e**!" she said.
6: 6 "O King Darius, live for **e**
6:21 Daniel answered, "O king, live for **e**!
6:22 Nor have I **e** done any wrong before
6:26 living God and he endures for **e**;
7:18 kingdom and possess it for **e**
7:26 away and completely destroyed for **e**.
9:12 Under the whole heaven nothing has **e**
12: 7 him swear by him who lives for **e**,
Hos 2:19 I will betroth you to me for **e**; I
Joel 1: 2 Has anything like this **e** happened in
2: 2 old nor **e** will be in ages to come.
3:20 Judah will be inhabited for **e** and
Ob :10 shame; you will be destroyed for **e**.
Jnh 2: 6 earth beneath barred me in for **e**.
Mic 2: 9 blessing from their children for **e**.
Mic 4: 7 Mount Zion from that day and for **e**.
7:18 for **e** but delight to show mercy.
Zep 2: 9 and salt pits, a wasteland for **e**.
Zec 1: 5 And the prophets, do they live for **e**?
Mal 3: 7 **E** since the time of your forefathers
Mt 9:33 this has **e** been seen in Israel."
13:14 "'You will be **e** hearing but never
Mk 4:12 **e** seeing but never perceiving.
11: 2 there, which no-one has **e** ridden.
11:14 he said to the tree, "May no-one **e**
Lk 1:33 reign over the house of Jacob for **e**
1:55 to Abraham and his descendants for **e**,
9:39 It scarcely **e** leaves him and is
19:30 there, which no-one has **e** ridden.
Jn 1:18 No-one has **e** seen God, but God the
3:13 No-one has **e** gone into heaven except
4:29 man who told me everything I **e** did.
4:39 "He told me everything I **e** did.
6:51 of this bread, he will live for **e**.
6:58 on this bread will live for **e**."
7:46 "No-one **e** spoke the way this man
8:35 but a son belongs to it for **e**.
9:32 Nobody has **e** heard of opening the
10: 8 All who **e** came before me were
12:34 that the Christ will remain for **e**,
14:16 Counsellor to be with you for **e**—
19:41 in which no-one had **e** been laid.
Ac 7:52 Was there **e** a prophet your fathers
11: 8 or unclean has **e** entered my mouth.'
20:25 the kingdom will **e** see me again.
26: 4 I have lived **e** since I was a child,
28:26 "You will be **e** hearing but never
28:26 **e** seeing but never perceiving.
Ro 1:25 the Creator—who is for **e** praised.
Ro 9: 5 God over all, for **e** praised! Amen.
11:10 see, and their backs be bent for **e**."
11:35 "Who has **e** given to God, that God
11:36 To him be the glory for **e**! Amen.
16:27 to the only wise God be glory for **e**
1Co 9:25 to get a crown that will last for ***e***
2Co 7: 7 so that my joy was greater than **e**.
9: 9 his righteousness endures for **e**."
11:31 Jesus, who is to be praised for **e**,
Eph 1:15 For this reason, **e** since I heard
5:29 After all, no-one **e** hated his own
1Th 4:17 so we will be with the Lord for **e**.
1Ti 6:16 To him be honour and might for **e**.
Heb 1: 5 For to which of the angels did God **e**
1:13 To which of the angels did God **e** say,
5: 6 for **e**, in the order of Melchizedek."
6:20 for **e**, in the order of Melchizedek.
7: 3 Son of God he remains a priest for **e**.
7:13 tribe has **e** served at the altar.
7:17 for **e**, in the order of Melchizedek."
7:21 his mind:'You are a priest for **e**.'"
7:24 Jesus lives for **e**, he has a
7:28 Son, who has been made perfect for **e**.
10:14 for **e** those who are being made holy.
13: 8 same yesterday and today and for **e**.
1Pe 1:25 the word of the Lord stands for **e**."
2Pe 3: 4 **E** since our fathers died, everything
3:18 be glory both now and for **e**! Amen.
1Jn 2:17 does the will of God lives for **e**.
4:12 No-one has **e** seen God; but if we
2Jn : 2 in us and will be with us for **e**:
Jude :13 darkness has been reserved for **e**.
Rev 16:18 No earthquake like it has **e** occurred
18:18 Was there **e** a city like this great
18:22 No workman of any trade will **e** be
21:25 On no day will its gates **e** be shut,
21:27 Nothing impure will **e** enter it, nor

Ever-flowing (Flow)

Ps 74:15 streams; you dried up the **e** rivers.

Ever-increasing (Increase)

Ro 6:19 to impurity and to **e** wickedness,
2Co 3:18 into his likeness with **e** glory,

Everlasting (Ever, *Everlasting covenant*)

Ge 17: 8 I will give as an **e** possession to
48: 4 give this land as an **e** possession
Dt 33:15 and the fruitfulness of the **e** hills;
33:27 and underneath are the **e** arms.
1Ch 16:36 LORD, the God of Israel, from **e** to **e**.
29:10 of our father Israel, from **e** to **e**.
Ezr 9:12 your children as an **e** inheritance.'
Ne 9: 5 LORD your God, who is from **e** to **e**.
Ps 41:13 LORD, the God of Israel, from **e** to **e**.
52: 5 God will bring you down to **e** ruin:
74: 3 your steps towards these **e** ruins
78:66 his enemies; he put them to **e** shame.
90: 2 the world, from **e** to **e** you are God.
103:17 from **e** to **e** the LORD's love is with
106:48 LORD, the God of Israel, from **e** to **e**.
119:142 Your righteousness is **e** and your law
139:24 way in me, and lead me in the way **e**.
145:13 Your kingdom is an **e** kingdom, and
Isa 9: 6 God, **E** Father, Prince of Peace.
30: 8 days to come it may be an **e** witness.
33:14 Who of us can dwell with **e** burning?"
35:10 enter Zion with singing; **e** joy will
40:28 not heard? The LORD is the **e** God,
45:17 by the LORD with an **e** salvation;
45:17 to shame or disgraced, to ages **e**.
51:11 will enter Zion with singing; **e** joy
54: 8 but with **e** kindness I will have
55:13 for an **e** sign, which will not be
56: 5 an **e** name that will not be cut off.
60:15 I will make you the **e** pride and the
60:19 for the LORD will be your **e** light,
60:20 more; the LORD will be your **e** light,
61: 7 land, and **e** joy will be theirs.
63:12 them, to gain for himself **e** renown,
Jer 5:22 sea, an **e** barrier it cannot cross.
23:40 bring upon you **e** disgrace—**e** shame
25: 9 of horror and scorn, and an **e** ruin.
31: 3 "I have loved you with an **e** love; I

Da 7:14 His dominion is an e dominion that
7:27 His kingdom will be an e kingdom,
9:24 to bring in e righteousness, to seal
12: 2 earth will awake: some to e life,
12: 2 others to shame and e contempt.
Mic 6: 2 you e foundations of the earth.
Hab 1:12 O LORD, are you not from e? My God,
Jn 6:47 truth, he who believes has e life.
2Th 1: 9 punished with e destruction and
Jude : 6 bound with e chains for judgment on

Everlasting covenant

Ge 9:16 I will see it and remember the e
17: 7 I will establish my covenant as an e
17:13 in your flesh is to be an e.
17:19 an e for his descendants after him.
Nu 18:19 It is an e of salt before the LORD
2Sa 23: 5 God? Has he not made with me an e,
1Ch 16:17 Jacob as a decree, to Israel as an e:
Ps 105:10 Jacob as a decree, to Israel as an e:
Isa 24: 5 the statutes and broken the e.
55: 3 I will make an e with you, my
61: 8 reward them and make an e with them.
Jer 32:40 I will make an e with them: I will
50: 5 in an e that will not be forgotten.
Eze 16:60 and I will establish an e with you.
37:26 of peace with them; it will be an e.

Evermore (Ever)

Ps 113: 2 LORD be praised, both now and for e.
115:18 extol the LORD, both now and for e.
121: 8 coming and going both now and for e.
125: 2 his people both now and for e.
131: 3 hope in the LORD both now and for e.
133: 3 his blessing, even life for e.
Jude :25 all ages, now and for e! Amen.

Ever-present (Present[1])

Ps 46: 1 our refuge and strength, an e help

Evi

Nu 31: 8 Among their victims were E, Rekem,
Jos 13:21 E, Rekem, Zur, Hur and Reba—princes

Evidence (Evident)

Ex 22:13 he shall bring in the remains as e
1Sa 12: 7 I am going to confront you with e
Mt 26:59 looking for false e against Jesus
Mk 14:55 looking for e against Jesus so that
Jn 14:11 on the e of the miracles themselves.
Ac 11:23 and saw the e of the grace of God
2Th 1: 5 All this is e that God's judgment is
Jas 2:20 do you want e that faith without

Evident (Evidence, Evidently)

1Ch 4:41 destroyed them, as is e to this day.
Gal 2:17 it becomes e that we ourselves are
Php 4: 5 Let your gentleness be e to all. The

Evidently (Evident)

Gal 1: 7 E some people are throwing you into

Evil (*Evil deeds, Evil in the eyes of the LORD, Evil one, Evil spirit, Evil spirits, Evil ways*, Evildoer, Evildoers, Evils, *Good and evil*)

Ge 6: 5 his heart was only e all the time.
8:21 of his heart is e from childhood.
44: 4 'Why have you repaid good with e?
Ex 10:10 children! Clearly you are bent on e.
32:12 'It was with e intent that he
32:22 how prone these people are to e.
Lev 5: 4 whether good or e—in any matter one
Nu 32:13 had done e in his sight was gone.
Dt 1:35 "Not a man of this e generation
9:18 doing what was e in the LORD's sight
13: 5 You must purge the e from among you.
13:11 you will do such an e thing again.
17: 5 done this e deed to your city gate
17: 7 You must purge the e from among you.
17:12 You must purge the e from Israel.
19:19 You must purge the e from among you.
19:20 such an e thing be done among you.
Dt 21:21 You must purge the e from among you.
22:21 You must purge the e from among you.
22:22 You must purge the e from Israel.
22:24 You must purge the e from among you.
24: 7 You must purge the e from among you.
28:20 ruin because of the e you have done
31:29 will do e in the sight of the LORD
Jos 23:15 on you all the e he has threatened,
Jdg 2:19 their e practices and stubborn ways.
3:12 and because they did this e the LORD
20:13 death and purge the e from Israel.
1Sa 12:17 And you will realise what an e thing
12:19 sins the e of asking for a king."
12:20 "You have done all this e; yet do
12:25 Yet if you persist in doing e, both
15:23 arrogance like the e of idolatry.
25:21 He has paid me back e for good.
30:22 all the e men and troublemakers
2Sa 12: 9 LORD by doing what is e in his eyes?
22:22 not done e by turning from my God.
23: 6 e men are all to be cast aside like
1Ki 1:52 if e is found in him, he will die."
14: 9 You have done more e than all who
16: 7 because of all the e he had done in
2Ki 21: 9 so that they did more e than the
21:11 He has done more e than the Amorites
21:15 they have done e in my eyes and have
1Ch 21: 7 This command was also e in the sight
2Ch 12:14 He did e because he had not set his
33: 9 so that they did more e than the
Ne 9:28 again did what was e in your sight.
13: 7 Here I learned about the e thing
Est 8: 3 to the e plan of Haman the Agagite,
9:25 the e scheme Haman had devised
Job 1: 1 he feared God and shunned e.
1: 8 a man who fears God and shuns e."
2: 3 a man who fears God and shuns e.
4: 8 those who plough e and those who
11:11 he sees e, does he not take note?
11:14 allow no e to dwell in your tent,
15:16 corrupt, who drinks up e like water!
15:35 conceive trouble and give birth to e
16:11 God has turned me over to e men and
18:21 such is the dwelling of an e man;
20:12 "Though e is sweet in his mouth and
21:30 that the e man is spared from the
22:15 the old path that e men have trod?
24:20 e men are no longer remembered but
28:28 and to shun e is understanding.'"
30:26 Yet when I hoped for good, e came;
34:10 Far be it from God to do e,
36:10 commands them to repent of their e.
36:21 Beware of turning to e, which you
Ps 5: 4 not a God who takes pleasure in e;
6: 8 Away from me, all you who do e, for
7: 4 if I have done e to him who is at
7:14 He who is pregnant with e and
10: 7 trouble and e are under his tongue.
10:15 Break the arm of the wicked and e
18:21 not done e by turning from my God.
21:11 Though they plot e against you and
22:16 a band of e men has encircled me,
23: 4 I will fear no e, for you are with
27: 2 e men advance against me to devour
28: 3 with those who do e, who speak
28: 4 their deeds and for their e work;
34:13 keep your tongue from e and your
34:14 Turn from e and do good; seek peace
34:16 the LORD is against those who do e,
34:21 E will slay the wicked; the foes of
35:12 They repay me e for good and leave
36: 4 Even on his bed he plots e; he
37: 1 Do not fret because of e men or be
37: 8 do not fret—it leads only to e.
37: 9 For e men will be cut off, but those
37:27 Turn from e and do good; then you
38:20 Those who repay my good with e
49: 5 Why should I fear when e days come,
50:19 You use your mouth for e and harness
51: 4 have I sinned and done what is e in
52: 1 Why do you boast of e, you mighty
52: 3 You love e rather than good,
54: 5 Let e recoil on those who slander me;
55:15 for e finds lodging among them.
64: 5 They encourage each other in e plans,
71: 4 from the grasp of e and cruel men.
Ps 73: 7 the e conceits of their minds know
97:10 Let those who love the LORD hate e,
101: 4 I will have nothing to do with e.
109: 5 They repay me e for good, and hatred
109: 6 Appoint an e man to oppose him; let
109:20 to those who speak e of me.
119:101 I have kept my feet from every e
125: 3 might use their hands to do e.
139:20 They speak of you with e intent;
140: 1 Rescue me, O LORD, from e men;
140: 2 who devise e plans in their hearts
141: 4 not my heart be drawn to what is e,
Pr 2:14 rejoice in the perverseness of e,
3: 7 own eyes; fear the LORD and shun e.
4:14 wicked or walk in the way of e men.
4:16 For they cannot sleep till they do e;
4:27 or the left; keep your foot from e.
6:14 who plots e with deceit in his heart
6:18 feet that are quick to rush into e,
8:13 To fear the LORD is to hate e; I
8:13 e behaviour and perverse speech.
10:23 A fool finds pleasure in e conduct,
10:29 it is the ruin of those who do e.
11: 6 unfaithful are trapped by e desires.
11:19 he who pursues e goes to his death.
11:27 e comes to him who searches for it.
12:12 The wicked desire the plunder of e
12:13 An e man is trapped by his sinful
12:20 in the hearts of those who plot e,
13:19 but fools detest turning from e.
14:16 A wise man fears the LORD and shuns e
14:19 E men will bow down in the presence
14:22 Do not those who plot e go astray?
15:28 the mouth of the wicked gushes e.
16: 6 the fear of the LORD a man avoids e.
16:17 The highway of the upright avoids e;
16:27 A scoundrel plots e, and his speech
16:30 he who purses his lips is bent on e.
17: 4 A wicked man listens to e lips; a
17:11 An e man is bent only on rebellion;
17:13 If a man pays back e for good, e
19:28 mouth of the wicked gulps down e.
20: 8 he winnows out all e with his eyes.
20:30 Blows and wounds cleanse away e, and
21:10 The wicked man craves e; his
21:27 more so when brought with e intent!
24: 8 He who plots e will be known as a
24:19 Do not fret because of e men or be
24:20 for the e man has no future hope,
26:23 are fervent lips with an e heart.
28: 5 E men do not understand justice, but
28:10 who leads the upright along an e path
29: 6 An e man is snared by his own sin,
30:32 if you have planned e, clap your
Ecc 4: 3 the e that is done under the sun.
5:13 I have seen a grievous e under the
5:16 This too is a grievous e: As a man
6: 1 I have seen another e under the sun,
6: 2 This is meaningless, a grievous e.
9: 3 This is the e in everything that
9: 3 moreover, are full of e and there is
9:12 so men are trapped by e times that
10: 5 There is an e I have seen under the
12:14 thing, whether it is good or e.
Isa 1:13 I cannot bear your e assemblies.
5:20 to those who call e good and good e,
13:11 I will punish the world for its e,
26:10 of uprightness they go on doing e
29:20 have an eye for e will be cut down—
32: 6 his mind is busy with e: He
32: 7 he makes up e schemes to destroy the
33:15 his eyes against contemplating e—
55: 7 his way and the e man his thoughts.
56: 2 keeps his hand from doing any e."
57: 1 are taken away to be spared from e.
59: 4 trouble and give birth to e.
59: 7 Their thoughts are e thoughts; ruin
59:15 and whoever shuns e becomes a prey.
65:12 You did e in my sight and chose what
66: 4 They did e in my sight and chose
Jer 2:19 realise how e and bitter it is for
3: 5 talk, but you do all the e you can."
3:17 the stubbornness of their e hearts.
4: 4 burn like fire because of the e you
4:14 O Jerusalem, wash the e from your
4:22 They are skilled in doing e;

Jer 7:24 inclinations of their **e** hearts.
7:26 did more **e** than their forefathers.'
7:30 Judah have done **e** in my eyes,
8: 3 all the survivors of this **e** nation
11: 8 the stubbornness of their **e** hearts.
11:15 works out her **e** schemes with many?
11:17 the house of Judah have done **e** and
13:23 good who are accustomed to doing **e**.
16:12 his **e** heart instead of obeying me.
18: 8 nation I warned repents of its **e**,
18:10 if it does **e** in my sight and does
18:12 the stubbornness of his **e** heart."
18:20 Should good be repaid with **e**? Yet
21:12 burn like fire because of the **e** you
23: 2 **e** you have done," declares the LORD.
23:10 The ⌊prophets⌋ follow an **e** course
25: 5 and your **e** practices, and you can
26: 3 and each will turn from his **e** way.
26: 3 because of the **e** they have done.
32:30 but **e** in my sight from their youth;
32:32 by all the **e** they have done—they,
44: 3 of the **e** they have done. They
Eze 3:20 from his righteousness and does **e**,
6: 9 themselves for the **e** they have done
11: 2 are the men who are plotting **e**
20:43 for all the **e** you have done.
30:12 the Nile and sell the land to **e** men;
33:13 in his righteousness and does **e**,
33:13 he will die for the **e** he has done.
33:15 and does no **e**, he will surely live;
33:18 and does **e**, he will die for it.
38:10 and you will devise an **e** scheme.
Da 11:27 with their hearts bent on **e**, will
Hos 7:15 them, but they plot **e** against me.
10:13 you have reaped **e**, you have eaten
Am 5:13 in such times, for the times are **e**.
5:14 Seek good, not **e**, that you may live.
5:15 Hate **e**, love good; maintain justice
6: 3 You put off the **e** day and bring near
9: 4 upon them for **e** and not for good."
Mic 2: 1 to those who plot **e** on their beds!
3: 2 you who hate good and love **e**; who
3: 4 because of the **e** they have done.
7: 3 Both hands are skilled in doing **e**;
Na 1:11 who plots **e** against the LORD
Hab 1:13 Your eyes are too pure to look on **e**;
Zec 1: 4 and your **e** practices.' But they would not
7:10 do not think **e** of each other.'
8:17 do not plot **e** against your neighbour,
Mal 2:17 By saying, "All who do **e** are good in
Mt 5:11 of **e** against you because of me.
5:39 Do not resist an **e** person.
5:45 He causes his sun to rise on the **e**
7:11 If you, then, though you are **e**, know
9: 4 entertain **e** thoughts in your hearts?
12:34 how can you who are **e** say anything
12:35 and the **e** man brings **e** things out of
12:35 out of the **e** stored up in him.
13:41 that causes sin and all who do **e**.
15:19 For out of the heart come **e** thoughts,
22:18 Jesus, knowing their **e** intent, said,
Mk 3: 4 to do **e**, to save life or to kill?"
7:21 out of men's hearts, come **e** thoughts,
Lk 3:19 all the other **e** things he had done,
6: 9 to do good or to do **e**, to save life
6:22 insult you and reject your name as **e**
6:45 and the **e** man brings **e** things out of
6:45 out of the **e** stored up in his heart.
11:13 If you then, though you are **e**, know
Jn 3:19 of light because their deeds were **e**.
3:20 Everyone who does **e** hates the light,
5:29 done **e** will rise to be condemned.
7: 7 I testify that what it does is **e**.
Ac 23: 5 **e** about the ruler of your people.'"
Ro 1:29 wickedness, **e**, greed and depravity.
1:30 doing **e**; they disobey their parents;
2: 8 and follow **e**, there will be wrath
2: 9 being who does **e**: first for the Jew,
3: 8 us do **e** that good may result"?
6:12 body so that you obey its **e** desires.
7:19 the **e** I do not want to do—this I
7:21 do good, **e** is right there with me.
12: 9 Love must be sincere. Hate what is **e**;
12:17 Do not repay anyone **e** for **e**. Be
12:21 by **e**, but overcome **e** with good.
14:16 consider good to be spoken of as **e**.
Ro 16:19 good, and innocent about what is **e**.
1Co 10: 6 our hearts on **e** things as they did.
13: 6 Love does not delight in **e** but
14:20 In regard to **e** be infants, but in
Gal 1: 4 to rescue us from the present **e** age,
Eph 5:16 opportunity, because the days are **e**.
6:12 forces of **e** in the heavenly realms.
6:13 so that when the day of **e** comes, you
Php 3: 2 men who do **e**, those mutilators of
Col 1:21 minds because of your **e** behaviour.
3: 5 impurity, lust, **e** desires and greed,
1Th 5:22 Avoid every kind of **e**.
2Th 2:10 in every sort of **e** that deceives
3: 2 delivered from wicked and **e** men,
1Ti 6: 4 malicious talk, **e** suspicions
6:10 money is a root of all kinds of **e**.
2Ti 2:22 Flee the **e** desires of youth, and
3: 6 swayed by all kinds of **e** desires,
3:13 while **e** men and impostors will go
4:18 The Lord will rescue me from every **e**
Tit 1:12 liars, **e** brutes, lazy gluttons."
Heb 5:14 to distinguish good from **e**.
Jas 1:13 God cannot be tempted by **e**,
1:14 by his own **e** desire, he is dragged
1:21 and the **e** that is so prevalent,
2: 4 and become judges with **e** thoughts?
3: 6 a world of **e** among the parts of the
3: 8 a restless **e**, full of deadly poison.
3:16 find disorder and every **e** practice.
4:16 All such boasting is **e**.
1Pe 1:14 do not conform to the **e** desires you
2:16 freedom as a cover-up for **e**;
3: 9 Do not repay **e** with **e** or insult with
3:10 must keep his tongue from **e** and his
3:11 He must turn from **e** and do good; he
3:12 the Lord is against those who do **e**."
3:17 for doing good than for doing **e**.
4: 2 earthly life for **e** human desires,
2Pe 1: 4 in the world caused by **e** desires.
3: 3 and following their own **e** desires.
1Jn 3:12 his own actions were **e** and his
3Jn :11 Dear friend, do not imitate what is **e**
:11 who does what is **e** has not seen God.
Jude :16 they follow their own **e** desires;

Evil deeds

1Sa 24:13 'From evildoers come **e**,'
2Sa 3:39 the evildoer according to his **e**!"
Ezr 9:13 result of our **e** and our great guilt,
Pr 5:22 The **e** of a wicked man ensnare him;
Isa 1:16 Take your **e** out of my sight!
59: 6 Their deeds are **e**, and acts of
Jer 5:28 Their **e** have no limit; they do not
23:22 their evil ways and from their **e**.
Hos 7: 2 realise that I remember all their **e**.
Ac 19:18 came and openly confessed their **e**.

Evil in the eyes of the LORD

Dt 4:25 doing **e** your God and provoking him
17: 2 found doing **e** your God in violation
Jdg 2:11 the Israelites did **e** and served the
3: 7 The Israelites did **e**; they forgot
3:12 Once again the Israelites did **e**, and
4: 1 the Israelites once again did **e**.
6: 1 Again the Israelites did **e**, and for
10: 6 Again the Israelites did **e**. They
13: 1 Again the Israelites did **e**, so the
1Sa 15:19 you pounce on the plunder and do **e**?"
1Ki 11: 6 Solomon did **e**; he did not follow the
14:22 Judah did **e**. By the sins they
15:26 He did **e**, walking in the ways of his
15:34 He did **e**, walking in the ways of
16:19 doing **e** and walking in the ways of
16:25 Omri did **e** and sinned more than all
16:30 Ahab son of Omri did more **e** than any
21:20 you have sold yourself to do **e**.
21:25 do **e**, urged on by Jezebel his wife.
22:52 He did **e**, because he walked in the
2Ki 3: 2 He did **e**, but not as his father and
8:18 married a daughter of Ahab. He did **e**.
8:27 ways of the house of Ahab and did **e**,
13: 2 He did **e** by following the sins of
13:11 He did **e** and did not turn away from
14:24 He did **e** and did not turn away from
15: 9 He did **e**, as his fathers had done.
2Ki 15:18 He did **e**. During his entire reign he
15:24 Pekahiah did **e**. He did not turn away
15:28 He did **e**. He did not turn away from
17: 2 He did **e**, but not like the kings of
17:17 to do **e**, provoking him to anger.
21: 2 He did **e**, following the detestable
21: 6 did much **e**, provoking him to anger.
21:16 Judah to commit, so that they did **e**.
21:20 He did **e**, as his father Manasseh had
23:32 He did **e**, just as his fathers had
23:37 he did **e**, just as his fathers had
24: 9 He did **e**, just as his father had
24:19 He did **e**, just as Jehoiakim had done.
2Ch 21: 6 married a daughter of Ahab. He did **e**.
22: 4 He did **e**, as the house of Ahab had
29: 6 they did **e** our God and forsook him.
33: 2 He did **e**, following the detestable
33: 6 did much **e**, provoking him to anger.
33:22 He did **e**, as his father Manasseh had
36: 5 He did **e** his God.
36: 9 He did **e**.
36:12 He did **e** his God and did not humble
Jer 52: 2 He did **e**, just as Jehoiakim had done.

Evil one

Mt 5:37 beyond this comes from the **e**.
6:13 but deliver us from the **e**.'
13:19 the **e** comes and snatches away what
13:38 The weeds are the sons of the **e**,
Jn 17:15 that you protect them from the **e**.
Eph 6:16 all the flaming arrows of the **e**.
2Th 3: 3 and protect you from the **e**.
1Jn 2:13 because you have overcome the **e**.
2:14 in you, and you have overcome the **e**.
3:12 to the **e** and murdered his brother.
5:18 him safe, and the **e** cannot harm him.
5:19 world is under the control of the **e**.

Evil spirit

Jdg 9:23 God sent an **e** between Abimelech and
1Sa 16:14 an **e** from the LORD tormented him.
16:15 See, an **e** from God is tormenting you.
16:16 He will play when the **e** from God
16:23 better, and the **e** would leave him.
18:10 The next day an **e** from God came
19: 9 an **e** from the LORD came upon Saul as
Mt 12:43 "When an **e** comes out of a man, it
Mk 1:23 who was possessed by an **e** cried out,
1:26 The **e** shook the man violently and
3:30 they were saying, "He has an **e**.
Mk 5: 2 **e** came from the tombs to meet him.
5: 8 "Come out of this man, you **e**!
7:25 by an **e** came and fell at his feet.
9:25 to the scene, he rebuked the **e**.
Lk 4:33 a man possessed by a demon, an **e**.
8:29 For Jesus had commanded the **e** to
9:42 But Jesus rebuked the **e**, healed the
11:24 "When an **e** comes out of a man, it
Ac 19:15 One day the **e** answered them, "Jesus
19:16 the man who had the **e** jumped on them
Rev 18: 2 for demons and a haunt for every **e**,

Evil spirits

Mt 10: 1 gave them authority to drive out **e**
Mk 1:27 orders to **e** and they obey him."
3:11 Whenever the **e** saw him, they fell
5:13 He gave them permission, and the **e**
6: 7 two and gave them authority over **e**.
Lk 4:36 orders to **e** and they come out!"
6:18 Those troubled by **e** were cured,
7:21 sicknesses and **e**, and gave sight to
8: 2 had been cured of **e** and diseases:
Ac 5:16 by **e**, and all of them were healed.
8: 7 With shrieks, **e** came out of many,
19:12 were cured and the **e** left them.
19:13 Jews who went around driving out **e**
Rev 16:13 I saw three **e** that looked like frogs;

Evil ways

1Ki 13:33 Jeroboam did not change his **e**, but
2Ki 17:13 and seers: "Turn from your **e**.
Ne 9:35 not serve you or turn from their **e**.
Jer 18:11 So turn from your **e**, each one of you,
23:22 their **e** and from their evil deeds.

Jer 25: 5 "Turn now, each of you, from your **e**
Eze 3:18 his **e** in order to save his life,
3:19 from his wickedness or from his **e**,
13:22 their **e** and so save their lives,
20:44 your **e** and your corrupt practices,
33:11 Turn! Turn from your **e**! Why will you
36:31 you will remember your **e** and wicked
Jnh 3: 8 give up their **e** and their violence.
3:10 and how they turned from their **e**,
Zec 1: 4 from your **e** and your evil practices.

Evildoer (Evil)
2Sa 3:39 the **e** according to his evil deeds!"
Ps 101: 8 I will cut off every **e** from the
Mal 4: 1 All the arrogant and every **e** will be

Evildoers (Evil)
1Sa 24:13 saying goes, 'From **e** come evil deeds
Job 8:20 man or strengthen the hands of **e**.
34: 8 He keeps company with **e**; he
34:22 no deep shadow, where **e** can hide.
Ps 14: 4 Will **e** never learn—those who
14: 6 You **e** frustrate the plans of the
26: 5 I abhor the assembly of **e** and refuse
36:12 See how the **e** lie fallen—thrown
53: 4 Will the **e** never learn—those who
59: 2 Deliver me from **e** and save me from
64: 2 wicked, from that noisy crowd of **e**.
92: 7 up like grass and all **e** flourish,
92: 9 perish; all **e** will be scattered.
94: 4 all the **e** are full of boasting.
94:16 will take a stand for me against **e**?
119:115 Away from me, you **e**, that I may keep
125: 5 the LORD will banish with the **e**.
141: 4 in wicked deeds with men who are **e**;
141: 5 is ever against the deeds of **e**;
141: 9 for me, from the traps set by **e**.
Pr 21:15 to the righteous but terror to **e**.
Isa 1: 4 a brood of **e**, children given to
31: 2 wicked, against those who help **e**.
Jer 23:14 They strengthen the hands of **e**, so
Hos 10: 9 Did not war overtake the **e** in Gibeah?
Mal 3:15 Certainly the **e** prosper, and even
Mt 7:23 never knew you. Away from me, you **e**
Lk 13:27 Away from me, all you **e**!'
18:11 not like other men—robbers, **e**,

Evil-Merodach
2Ki 25:27 in the year **E** became king of Babylon,
Jer 52:31 in the year **E** became king of Babylon,

Evils (Evil)
Mk 7:23 All these **e** come from inside and

Ewe (Ewes)
Ge 21:28 Abraham set apart seven **e** lambs from
21:29 these seven **e** lambs you have set
Lev 14:10 lambs and one **e** lamb a year old,
Nu 6:14 a year-old **e** lamb without defect for
2Sa 12: 3 little **e** lamb that he had bought.
12: 4 Instead, he took the **e** lamb that

Ewes (Ewe)
Ge 32:14 two hundred **e** and twenty rams,
33:13 that I must care for the **e** and cows

Exact (Exacted, Exacting, Exactly)
Ge 43:21 found his silver—the **e** weight—
Est 4: 7 including the **e** amount of money
Mt 2: 7 the **e** time the star had appeared.
Jn 4:53 the **e** time at which Jesus had said
Ac 17:26 the **e** places where they should live.
Heb 1: 3 the **e** representation of his being,

Exacted (Exact)
2Ki 15:20 Menahem **e** this money from Israel.
18:14 The king of Assyria **e** from Hezekiah
23:35 he taxed the land and **e** the silver

Exacting (Exact)
Ne 5: 7 I told them, "You are **e** usury from
5:10 But let the **e** of usury stop!

Exactly (Exact)
Ge 41:13 things turned out **e** as he
Ex 25: 9 **e** like the pattern I will show you.
Nu 8: 4 The lampstand was made **e** like the
15:14 to the LORD, he must do **e** as you do.
Dt 24: 8 very careful to do **e** as the priests,
Jdg 7:17 the edge of the camp, do **e** as I do.
2Ki 7:20 that is **e** what happened to him, for
Jn 14:31 **e** what my Father has commanded me.
Ac 22:30 **e** why Paul was being accused by the

Exalt (Exalted, Exalts)
Ex 15: 2 my father's God, and I will **e** him.
Jos 3: 7 "Today I will begin to **e** you in the
1Sa 2:10 and **e** the horn of his anointed."
1Ch 25: 5 the promises of God to **e** him.
29:12 power to **e** and give strength to all.
Job 19: 5 If indeed you would **e** yourselves
Ps 30: 1 I will **e** you, O LORD, for you
34: 3 Glorify the LORD with me: let us **e**
35:26 may all who **e** themselves over me be
37:34 He will **e** you to inherit the land;
38:16 gloat or **e** themselves over me
75: 6 west or from the desert can **e** a man.
89:17 and by your favour you **e** our horn.
99: 5 **E** the LORD our God and worship at
99: 9 **E** the LORD our God and worship at
107:32 Let them **e** him in the assembly of
118:28 you are my God, and I will **e** you.
145: 1 I will **e** you, my God the King; I
Pr 4: 8 Esteem her, and she will **e** you;
25: 6 Do not **e** yourself in the king's
Isa 24:15 to the LORD; **e** the name of the LORD,
25: 1 LORD, you are my God; I will **e** you
Eze 29:15 **e** itself above the other nations.
Da 4:37 I, Nebuchadnezzar, praise and **e** and
11:36 He will **e** and magnify himself above
11:37 but will **e** himself above them all.
Hos 11: 7 High, he will by no means **e** them.
2Th 2: 4 He will oppose and will **e** himself

Exalted (Exalt)
Ex 15: 1 to the LORD, for he is highly **e**.
15:21 Sing to the LORD, for he is highly **e**.
Nu 24: 7 than Agag; their kingdom will be **e**.
Jos 4:14 That day the LORD **e** Joshua in the
2Sa 5:12 had **e** his kingdom for the sake of
22:47 **E** be God, the Rock, my Saviour!
22:49 You **e** me above my foes; from violent
23: 1 the oracle of the man **e** by the Most
1Ch 14: 2 **e** for the sake of his people Israel.
17:17 were the most **e** of men, O LORD God.
1Ch 29:11 kingdom; you are **e** as head over all.
29:25 The LORD highly **e** Solomon in the
Ne 9: 5 be **e** above all blessing and praise.
Job 24:24 For a little while they are **e**, and
36:22 "God is **e** in his power. Who is a
37:23 is beyond our reach and **e** in power;
Ps 18:46 be to my Rock! **E** be God my Saviour!
18:48 You **e** me above my foes; from violent
21:13 Be **e**, O LORD, in your strength; we
27: 6 my head will be **e** above the enemies
35:27 "The LORD be **e**, who delights in the
40:16 always say, "The LORD be **e**!"
46:10 and know that I am God; I will be **e**
46:10 nations, I will be **e** in the earth."
47: 9 belong to God; he is greatly **e**.
57: 5 Be **e**, O God, above the heavens; let
57:11 Be **e**, O God, above the heavens; let
70: 4 always say, "Let God be **e**!"
89:13 hand is strong, your right hand **e**.
89:19 **e** a young man from among the people.
89:24 through my name his horn will be **e**.
89:27 most **e** of the kings of the earth.
89:42 You have **e** the right hand of his
92: 8 you, O LORD, are **e** for ever.
92:10 You have **e** my horn like that of a
97: 9 earth; you are **e** far above all gods.
99: 2 Great is the LORD in Zion; he is **e**
108: 5 Be **e**, O God, above the heavens, and
113: 4 The LORD is **e** over all the nations,
138: 2 for you have **e** above all things your
148:13 for his name alone is **e**; his
Pr 11:11 blessing of the upright a city is **e**,
30:32 have played the fool and **e** yourself
Isa 2:11 LORD alone will be **e** in that day.
2:12 is **e** (and they will be humbled),
2:17 LORD alone will be **e** in that day,
5:16 the LORD Almighty will be **e** by his
6: 1 high and **e**, and the train of his
12: 4 and proclaim that his name is **e**.
24: 4 the **e** of the earth languish.
33: 5 The LORD is **e**, for he dwells on high;
33:10 I be **e**; now will I be lifted up.
52:13 raised and lifted up and highly **e**.
Jer 17:12 A glorious throne, **e** from the
Lam 2:17 you, he has **e** the horn of your foes.
Eze 21:26 be **e** and the **e** will be brought low.
Hos 13: 1 Ephraim spoke, men trembled; he was **e**
Mic 6: 6 LORD and bow down before the **e** God?
Mt 23:12 whoever humbles himself will be **e**.
Lk 14:11 he who humbles himself will be **e**."
18:14 he who humbles himself will be **e**."
Ac 2:33 **E** to the right hand of God, he has
5:31 God **e** him to his own right hand as
Php 1:20 always Christ will be **e** in my body,
2: 9 Therefore God **e** him to the highest
Heb 7:26 from sinners, **e** above the heavens.

Exalts (Exalt)
1Sa 2: 7 and wealth; he humbles and he **e**.
Job 36: 7 them with kings and **e** them for ever.
Ps 75: 7 He brings one down, he **e** another.
Pr 14:34 Righteousness **e** a nation, but sin is
Mt 23:12 For whoever **e** himself will be
Lk 14:11 For everyone who **e** himself will be
18:14 For everyone who **e** himself will be

Examine (Cross-examine, Examined, Examines, Examining)
Ge 37:32 **E** it to see whether it is your son's
Lev 13: 3 The priest is to **e** the sore on his
13: 5 On the seventh day the priest is to **e**
13: 6 On the seventh day the priest is to **e**
13: 8 The priest is to **e** him, and if the
13:10 The priest is to **e** him, and if there
13:13 the priest is to **e** him, and if the
13:17 The priest is to **e** him, and if the
13:20 The priest is to **e** it, and if it
13:25 the priest is to **e** the spot, and if
13:27 On the seventh day the priest is to **e**
13:30 the priest is to **e** the sore, and if
13:32 On the seventh day the priest is to **e**
13:34 On the seventh day the priest is to **e**
13:36 the priest is to **e** him, and if the
13:39 the priest is to **e** them, and if the
13:43 The priest is to **e** him, and if the
Lev 13:50 The priest is to **e** the mildew and
13:51 On the seventh day he is to **e** it,
13:55 the priest is to **e** it, and if the
14: 3 is to go outside the camp and **e** him.
14:36 before he goes in to **e** the mildew,
14:37 He is to **e** the mildew on the walls,
14:44 the priest is to go and **e** it and, if
14:48 "But if the priest comes to **e** it and
Job 7:18 that you **e** him every morning and
34:23 God has no need to **e** men further,
Ps 11: 4 the sons of men; his eyes **e** them.
17: 3 Though you probe my heart and **e** me
26: 2 Test me, O LORD, and try me, **e** my
Jer 17:10 "I the LORD search the heart and **e**
20:12 O LORD Almighty, you who **e** the
Lam 3:40 Let us **e** our ways and test them, and
Eze 21:21 his idols, he will **e** the liver.
1Co 11:28 A man ought to **e** himself before he
2Co 13: 5 **E** yourselves to see whether you are

Examined (Examine)
Job 5:27 "We have **e** this, and it is true. So
13: 9 Would it turn out well if he **e** you?
Lk 23:14 I have **e** him in your presence and
Ac 17:11 **e** the Scriptures every day to see if
28:18 They **e** me and wanted to release me,

Examines (Examine)
Lev 13: 3 When the priest **e** him, he shall
13:21 if, when the priest **e** it, there is
13:26 if the priest **e** it and there is no
13:31 if, when the priest **e** this kind of

Lev 13:53 "But if, when the priest e it, the
13:56 If, when the priest e it, the mildew
Ps 11: 5 The LORD e the righteous, but the
Pr 5:21 of the LORD, and he e all his paths.

Examining (Examine)
Ne 2:13 e the walls of Jerusalem, which had
2:15 I went up the valley by night, e the
Ac 24: 8 By e him yourself you will be able

Example (Examples)
2Ki 14: 3 followed the e of his father Joash.
Ecc 9:13 saw under the sun this e of wisdom
Eze 14: 8 man and make him an e and a byword.
Jn 13:15 I have set you an e that you should
Ro 7: 2 For e, by law a married woman is
1Co 11: 1 Follow my e, as I follow the e of
Gal 3:15 let me take an e from everyday life
Php 3:17 Join with others in following my e,
2Th 3: 7 know how you ought to follow our e.
1Ti 1:16 as an e for those who would believe
4:12 but set an e for the believers in
Tit 2: 7 In everything set them an e by doing
Heb 4:11 following their e of disobedience.
Jas 3: 4 Or take ships as an e. Although they
5:10 Brothers, as an e of patience in the
1Pe 2:21 leaving you an e, that you should
2Pe 2: 6 and made them an e of what is going
Jude : 7 They serve as an e of those who

Examples (Example)
1Co 10: 6 Now these things occurred as e to
10:11 These things happened to them as e
1Pe 5: 3 to you, but being e to the flock.

Exasperate
Eph 6: 4 Fathers, do not e your children;

Exceed (Exceeded, Exceedingly, Excessive)
Nu 3:46 who e the number of the Levites,
Job 14: 5 and have set limits he cannot e.

Exceeded (Exceed)
Nu 3:49 e the number redeemed by the Levites.
1Ki 10: 7 you have far e the report I heard.
2Ch 9: 6 you have far e the report I heard.

Exceedingly (Exceed)
Ge 30:43 the man grew e prosperous and
Ex 1: 7 greatly and became e numerous,
Nu 11:10 e angry, and Moses was troubled.
14: 7 through and explored is e good.
2Ch 1: 1 was with him and made him e great.
Eze 9: 9 of Israel and Judah is e great;

Excel (Excelled, Excellency, Excellent, Excelling)
Ge 49: 4 you will no longer e, for you went
1Co 14:12 e in gifts that build up the church.
2Co 8: 7 just as you e in everything—in
8: 7 you also e in this grace of giving.

Excelled (Excel)
Isa 10:10 e those of Jerusalem and Samaria—

Excellency (Excel)
Ac 23:26 Claudius Lysias, To His E, Governor

Excellent (Excel)
Ps 45: 2 You are the most e of men and your
Lk 1: 3 account for you, most e Theophilus,
Ac 24: 3 and in every way, most e Felix,
26:25 "I am not insane, most e Festus,"
1Co 12:31 now I will show you the most e way.
Php 4: 8 if anything is e or praiseworthy
1Ti 3:13 have served well gain an e standing
Tit 3: 8 are e and profitable for everyone.

Excelling (Excel)
Ge 49: 3 strength, e in honour, e in power.

Exception (Exceptional)
Est 4:11 The only e to this is for the king

Exceptional (Exception)
Da 6: 3 the satraps by his e qualities that

Excessive (Exceed)
Eze 18: 8 lend at usury or take e interest.
18:13 lends at usury and takes e interest
18:17 and takes no usury or e interest.
22:12 you take usury and e interest and
2Co 2: 7 will not be overwhelmed by e sorrow.
Rev 18: 3 grew rich from her e luxuries."

Exchange (Exchanged, Exchanging)
Ge 47:16 "I will sell you food in e for your
47:17 gave them food in e for their horses
47:17 food in e for all their livestock.
47:19 Buy us and our land in e for food,
Lev 27:10 He must not e it or substitute a
Dt 14:25 e your tithe for silver, and take
1Ki 21: 2 In e I will give you a better
Isa 43: 4 I will give men in e for you, and
43: 4 you, and people in e for your life.
Eze 48:14 They must not sell or e any of it.
Mt 16:26 can a man give in e for his soul?
Mk 8:37 Or what can a man give in e for his
2Co 6:13 a fair e—I speak as to my children—

Exchanged (Exchange)
Ps 106:20 They e their Glory for an image of a
Jer 2:11 e their Glory for worthless idols.
Eze 27:12 wealth of goods; they e silver,
27:13 they e slaves and articles of bronze
27:14 "Men of Beth Togarmah e work horses,
27:16 many products; they e turquoise,
27:17 e wheat from Minnith and confections,
27:19 merchandise; they e wrought iron,
27:22 for your merchandise they e the
Hos 4: 7 they e their Glory for something
Ro 1:23 e the glory of the immortal God for
1:25 They e the truth of God for a lie,
1:26 Even their women e natural relations

Exchanging (Exchange)
Jn 2:14 others sitting at tables e money.

Excitement
Job 39:24 In frenzied e he eats up the ground;

Exclaim (Exclaimed, Exclaiming)
Ps 35:10 My whole being will e, "Who is like
Jer 46:17 There they will e,'Pharaoh king of
Rev 18:18 they will e,'Was there ever a city

Exclaimed (Exclaim)
Jdg 6:22 he e, "Ah, Sovereign LORD! I have
Ru 1:19 and the women e, "Can this be Naomi?"
2:10 She e, "Why have I found such favour
2Ki 3:10 "What!" e the king of Israel. "Has
Est 7: 8 The king e, "Will he even molest the
Mt 27:54 they were terrified, and e, "Surely
Mk 1:37 they found him, they e: "Everyone is
9:24 the boy's father e, "I do believe;
Lk 1:42 In a loud voice she e: "Blessed are
Jn 8:52 At this the Jews e, "Now we know
Ac 8:10 gave him their attention and e,
12:14 ran back without opening it and e,

Exclaiming (Exclaim)
1Co 14:25 e, "God is really among you!"

Exclude (Excluded, Exclusively)
Isa 56: 3 will surely e me from his people.
66: 5 "Your brothers who hate you, and e
Lk 6:22 when they e you and insult you and
Rev 11: 2 e the outer court; do not measure it,

Excluded (Exclude)
2Ch 26:21 and e from the temple of the LORD.
Ezr 2:62 e from the priesthood as unclean.
Ne 7:64 e from the priesthood as unclean.
Ne 13: 3 the people heard this law, they e
Ro 3:27 Where, then, is boasting? It is e.
Eph 2:12 e from citizenship in Israel and

Exclusively (Exclude)
Ac 18: 5 Paul devoted himself e to preaching,

Excrement
Dt 23:13 dig a hole and cover up your e.
Eze 4:12 the people, using human e for fuel."
4:15 over cow manure instead of human e."

Excuse (Excuses)
Ps 25: 3 shame who are treacherous without e.
Lk 14:18 I must go and see it. Please e me.'
14:19 to try them out. Please e me.'
Jn 15:22 they have no e for their sin.
Ro 1:20 made, so that men are without e.
2: 1 You, therefore, have no e, you who

Excuses (Excuse)
Lk 14:18 "But they all alike began to make e.

Execute (Executed, Executing, Execution, Executioner)
2Ch 2:14 and can e any design given to him.
Isa 66:16 LORD will e judgment upon all men,
Eze 11:10 and I will e judgment on you at the
11:11 I will e judgment on you at the
17:20 I will bring him to Babylon and e
20:35 to face, I will e judgment upon you.
38:22 I will e judgment upon him with
Da 2:24 had appointed to e the wise men
2:24 "Do not e the wise men of Babylon.
Hab 1:12 have appointed them to e judgment;
Jn 18:31 "But we have no right to e anyone,"

Executed (Execute)
2Ki 14: 5 he e the officials who had murdered
25:21 land of Hamath, the king had them e.
2Ch 24:24 fathers, judgment was e on Joash.
25: 3 he e the officials who had murdered
Jer 52:27 land of Hamath, the king had them e.
Da 2:18 his friends might not be e with the
Mt 27:20 for Barabbas and to have Jesus e.
Lk 23:32 were also led out with him to be e.
Ac 12:19 guards and ordered that they be e.
13:28 they asked Pilate to have him e.

Executing (Execute)
2Ch 22: 8 While Jehu was e judgment on the

Execution (Execute)
Da 2:12 e of all the wise men of Babylon.

Executioner (Execute)
Mk 6:27 he immediately sent an e with orders

Exempt
1Sa 17:25 will e his father's family from
1Ki 15:22 an order to all Judah—no-one was e
1Ch 9:33 were e from other duties because
Mt 17:26 "Then the sons are e," Jesus said to

Exercise (Exercised, Exercises)
Mt 20:25 officials e authority over them.
Mk 10:42 officials e authority over them.
Lk 22:25 and those who e authority over them
1Co 8: 9 that the e of your freedom does not
Rev 13: 5 e his authority for forty-two months.

Exercised (Exercise)
Da 11: 4 nor will it have the power he e,
Rev 13:12 He e all the authority of the first

Exercises (Exercise)
Jer 9:24 that I am the LORD, who e kindness,

Exerted
Eph 1:20 which he e in Christ when he raised

Exhaust (Exhausted)
Jer 51:58 peoples **e** themselves for nothing,
Hab 2:13 nations **e** themselves for nothing?

Exhausted (Exhaust)
Jdg 4:21 to him while he lay fast asleep, **e**.
8: 4 Gideon and his three hundred men, **e**
8:15 we give bread to your **e** men?"
1Sa 14:31 Michmash to Aijalon, they were **e**.
30:10 for two hundred men were too **e** to
30:21 who had been too **e** to follow him
2Sa 16: 2 those who become **e** in the desert."
16:14 him arrived at their destination **e**.
21:15 the Philistines, and he became **e**.
Jer 51:30 Their strength is **e**; they have
Da 8:27 I, Daniel, was **e** and lay ill for
Lk 12:33 in heaven that will not be **e**,
22:45 he found them asleep, **e** from sorrow.

Exhort (Exhortation, Exhorted)
1Ti 5: 1 but **e** him as if he were your father.

Exhortation (Exhort)
Heb 13:22 I urge you to bear with my word of **e**,

Exhorted (Exhort)
Lk 3:18 with many other words John **e** the

Exile (Exiled, Exiles, *Go into exile*)
2Sa 15:19 foreigner, an **e** from your homeland.
2Ki 17:23 their homeland into **e** in Assyria,
24:14 He carried into **e** all Jerusalem: all
25:11 carried into **e** the people who
25:27 In the thirty-seventh year of the **e**
1Ch 5: 6 king of Assyria took into **e**.
5:22 they occupied the land until the **e**.
5:26 the half-tribe of Manasseh into **e**.
6:15 **e** by the hand of Nebuchadnezzar.
2Ch 36:20 He carried into **e** to Babylon the
Ezr 6:21 who had returned from the **e** ate it,
Ne 1: 2 Jewish remnant that survived the **e**,
1: 3 "Those who survived the **e** and are
8:17 had returned from **e** built booths
Est 2: 6 who had been carried into **e** from
Isa 27: 8 By warfare and **e** you contend with
Jer 1: 3 the people of Jerusalem went into **e**.
13:19 All Judah will be carried into **e**,
24: 1 carried into **e** from Jerusalem to
27:20 into **e** from Jerusalem to Babylon,
29: 1 into **e** from Jerusalem to Babylon.
29: 2 had gone into **e** from Jerusalem.)
29: 4 into **e** from Jerusalem to Babylon:
29: 7 to which I have carried you into **e**.
29:14 from which I carried you into **e**."
29:16 who did not go with you into **e**—
30:10 from the land of their **e**.
39: 9 carried into **e** to Babylon
40: 1 being carried into **e** to Babylon.
40: 7 not been carried into **e** to Babylon,
43: 3 us or carry us into **e** to Babylon."
46:19 Pack your belongings for **e**, you who
46:27 from the land of their **e**.
48:11 another—she has not gone into **e**.
48:46 your sons are taken into **e** and your
52:15 into **e** some of the poorest people
52:28 people Nebuchadnezzar carried into **e**
52:30 745 Jews taken into **e** by Nebuzaradan
52:31 In the thirty-seventh year of the **e**
Lam 1: 3 harsh labour, Judah has gone into **e**.
1: 5 gone into **e**, captive before the foe.
1:18 men and maidens have gone into **e**.
4:22 end; he will not prolong your **e**.
Eze 1: 2 year of the **e** of King Jehoiachin—
3:11 Go now to your countrymen in **e** and
12: 3 pack your belongings for **e** and in
12: 4 out your belongings packed for **e**.
12: 7 I brought out my things packed for **e**.
25: 3 of Judah when they went into **e**,
33:21 In the twelfth year of our **e**, in the
39:23 of Israel went into **e** for their sin,
39:28 for though I sent them into **e** among
40: 1 In the twenty-fifth year of our **e**,
Hos 10: 5 it is taken from them into **e**.
Am 5:27 Therefore I will send you into **e**
9: 4 are driven into **e** by their enemies
Mic 1:16 for they will go from you into **e**.
Na 3:10 was taken captive and went into **e**.
Mt 1:11 at the time of the **e** to Babylon.
1:12 After the **e** to Babylon: Jeconiah was
1:17 fourteen from David to the **e** to
1:17 fourteen from the **e** to the Christ.
Ac 7:43 send you into **e**' beyond Babylon.

Exiled (Exile)
2Ki 17:28 one of the priests who had been **e**
Ne 1: 9 then even if your **e** people are at
Isa 27:13 those who were **e** in Egypt will come
49:21 and barren; I was **e** and rejected.
Jer 22:10 weep bitterly for him who is **e**,
Lam 2: 9 Her king and her princes are **e** among
Am 9:14 I will bring back my **e** people Israel;
Na 2: 7 is decreed that ⌊the city⌋ be **e**

Exiles (Exile)
Ezr 1:11 **e** came up from Babylon to Jerusalem.
2: 1 came up from the captivity of the **e**,
4: 1 Benjamin heard that the **e** were
6:16 the Levites and the rest of the **e**
6:19 the **e** celebrated the Passover.
6:20 the Passover lamb for all the **e**,
8:35 the **e** who had returned from
9: 4 of this unfaithfulness of the **e**.
10: 6 over the unfaithfulness of the **e**.
10: 7 all the **e** to assemble in Jerusalem.
10: 8 expelled from the assembly of the **e**.
10:16 the **e** did as was proposed. Ezra the
Ne 7: 6 came up from the captivity of the **e**
Ps 147: 2 he gathers the **e** of Israel.
Isa 11:12 nations and gather the **e** of Israel;
20: 4 the Egyptian captives and Cushite **e**,
45:13 He will rebuild my city and set my **e**
56: 8 he who gathers the **e** of Israel:
Jer 24: 5 I regard as good the **e** from Judah,
28: 4 **e** from Judah who went to Babylon,'
28: 6 **e** back to this place from Babylon.
29: 1 among the **e** and to the priests,
29:19 And you **e** have not listened either,"
29:20 all you **e** whom I have sent away from
29:22 of them, all the **e** from Judah who
29:31 "Send this message to all the **e**:
49:36 a nation where Elam's **e** do not go.
Eze 1: 1 while I was among the **e** by the Kebar
3:15 I came to the **e** who lived at Tel
11:24 brought me to the **e** in Babylonia in
11:25 I told the **e** everything the LORD had
Da 2:25 "I have found a man among the **e** from
5:13 "Are you Daniel, one of the **e** my
6:13 "Daniel, who is one of the **e** from
Ob :20 This company of Israelite **e** who are
:20 the **e** from Jerusalem who are in
Mic 4: 6 **e** and those I have brought to grief.
Zec 6:10 "Take ⌊silver and gold⌋ from the **e**

Exist (Existed, Exists)
Ro 13: 1 that **e** have been established by God.

Existed (Exist)
2Pe 3: 5 ago by God's word the heavens **e**

Exists (Exist)
Ecc 6:10 Whatever **e** has already been named,
Heb 2:10 whom and through whom everything **e**,
11: 6 comes to him must believe that he **e**

Exits
Eze 42:11 with similar **e** and dimensions.
43:11 its **e** and entrances—its whole
44: 5 and all the **e** of the sanctuary.
48:30 "These will be the **e** of the city:

Exodus
Heb 11:22 spoke about the **e** of the Israelites

Exorbitant
Pr 28: 8 increases his wealth by **e** interest

Expand (Expanse)
2Co 10:15 activity among you will greatly **e**,

Expanse (Expand, Expanses)
Ge 1: 6 God said, "Let there be an **e** between
1: 7 God made the **e** and separated the
1: 7 under the **e** from the water above it.
1: 8 God called the **e** "sky". And there
1:14 "Let there be lights in the **e** of the
1:15 let them be lights in the **e** of the
1:17 God set them in the **e** of the sky to
1:20 the earth across the **e** of the sky."
Eze 1:22 looked like an **e**, sparkling like ice
1:23 Under the **e** their wings were
1:25 there came a voice from above the **e**
1:26 Above the **e** over their heads was
10: 1 a throne of sapphire above the **e**

Expanses (Expanse)
Job 38:18 Have you comprehended the vast **e** of

Expect (Expectant, Expectantly, Expectation, Expected, Expecting)
Isa 58: 4 **e** your voice to be heard on high.
64: 3 awesome things that we did not **e**,
Eze 13: 6 they **e** their words to be fulfilled.
Mt 11: 3 come, or should we **e** someone else?"
24:44 at an hour when you do not **e** him.
24:50 on a day when he does not **e** him
Lk 6:34 if you lend to those from whom you **e**
7:19 come, or should we **e** someone else?"
7:20 come, or should we **e** someone else?'"
12:40 at an hour when you do not **e** him."
12:46 on a day when he does not **e** him
2Co 10: 2 have to be as bold as I **e** to be
Php 1:20 I eagerly **e** and hope that I will in

Expectant (Expect)
Jer 31: 8 **e** mothers and women in labour; a

Expectantly (Expect)
Job 29:21 "Men listened to me **e**, waiting in
Lk 3:15 The people were waiting **e** and were

Expectation (Expect)
Ps 5: 3 requests before you and wait in **e**.
Eze 19: 5 her **e** gone, she took another of her
Ro 8:19 The creation waits in eager **e** for
Heb 10:27 only a fearful **e** of judgment and of

Expected (Expect)
Ge 48:11 Israel said to Joseph, "I never **e** to
Pr 11: 7 **e** from his power comes to nothing.
Hag 1: 9 "You **e** much, but see, it turned out
Mt 20:10 hired first, they **e** to receive more.
Ac 16:13 we **e** to find a place of prayer.
25:18 him with any of the crimes I had **e**.
28: 6 The people **e** him to swell up or
2Co 8: 5 they did not do as we **e**, but they

Expecting (Expect)
Lk 2: 5 be married to him and was **e** a child.
6:34 'sinners', **e** to be repaid in full.
6:35 them without **e** to get anything back.
8:40 him, for they were all **e** him.
Ac 3: 5 the man gave them his attention, **e**
10:24 Cornelius was **e** them and had called
1Co 16:11 I am **e** him along with the brothers.

Expel (Expelled)
1Co 5:13 "**E** the wicked man from among you."

Expelled (Expel)
1Sa 28: 3 Saul had **e** the mediums and
1Ki 15:12 He **e** the male shrine-prostitutes
Ezr 10: 8 **e** from the assembly of the exiles.
Eze 28:16 and I **e** you, O guardian cherub,
Ac 13:50 and **e** them from their region.

Expend (Expense)
Dt 32:23 them and **e** my arrows against them.
2Co 12:15 I have and **e** myself as well.

Expense (Expend, Expenses, Expensive)
Lk 10:35 you for any extra e you may have.'
1Co 9: 7 Who serves as a soldier at his own e?

Expenses (Expense)
2Ki 12:12 the other e of restoring the temple.
Ezr 6: 8 The e of these men are to be fully
Ac 21:24 purification rites and pay their e,

Expensive (Expense)
Mt 26: 7 an alabaster jar of very e perfume,
Mk 14: 3 very e perfume, made of pure nard.
Lk 7:25 those who wear e clothes and indulge
Jn 12: 3 an e perfume; she poured it on Jesus'
1Ti 2: 9 hair or gold or pearls or e clothes,

Experience (Experienced)
Nu 16:29 e only what usually happens to men,
Jdg 3: 2 who had not had previous battle e):
Heb 11: 5 so that he did not e death; he could

Experienced (Experience)
Dt 11: 2 e the discipline of the LORD your
Jos 24:31 who had e everything the LORD had
Jdg 3: 1 had not e any of the wars in
2Sa 17: 8 Besides, your father is an e fighter;
1Ki 7:14 Huram was highly skilled and e in
1Ch 12:33 men of Zebulun, e soldiers prepared
12:36 men of Asher, e soldiers prepared
2Ch 2: 7 e in the art of engraving, to work
2:14 He is e in all kinds of engraving
17:13 kept e fighting men in Jerusalem.
Ecc 1:16 e much of wisdom and knowledge."
SS 3: 8 wearing the sword, all e in battle,
Ro 11:25 Israel has e a hardening in part

Expert (Experts)
Mt 22:35 One of them, an e in the law, tested
Lk 10:25 On one occasion an e in the law
10:37 The e in the law replied, "The one
1Co 3:10 I laid a foundation as an e builder,

Experts (Expert)
Est 1:13 e in matters of law and justice,
Lk 7:30 the Pharisees and e in the law
11:45 One of the e in the law answered him,
11:46 Jesus replied, "And you e in the law,
11:52 "Woe to you e in the law, because
14: 3 Jesus asked the Pharisees and e in
2Pe 2:14 are e in greed—an accursed brood!

Explain (Explained, Explaining, Explains, Explanation)
Ge 41:24 but none could e it to me."
Dt 32: 7 your elders, and they will e to you.
Jdg 14:16 "so why should I e it to you?
1Ki 10: 3 too hard for the king to e to her.
2Ch 9: 2 was too hard for him to e to her.
Est 4: 8 to show to Esther and e it to her,
Job 15:17 "Listen to me and I will e to you;
Jer 9:12 instructed by the LORD and can e it?
Da 2: 6 if you tell me the dream and e it,
2:27 magician or diviner can e to the
5:12 e riddles and solve difficult
5:15 it means, but they could not e it.
10:14 Now I have come to e to you what
Mt 13:36 "E to us the parable of the weeds in
15:15 Peter said, "E the parable to us."
16:21 From that time on Jesus began to e
Jn 4:25 comes, he will e everything to us."
Ac 2:14 let me e this to you; listen
Heb 5:11 hard to e because you are slow to
Rev 17: 7 I will e to you the mystery of the

Explained (Explain)
Jdg 14:16 "I haven't even e it to my father
14:17 in turn e the riddle to her people.
14:19 to those who had e the riddle.
1Sa 10:25 Samuel e to the people the
Da 2:15 Arioch then e the matter to Daniel.
2:17 Daniel returned to his house and e
Zec 1:10 standing among the myrtle trees e,
Mk 4:34 his own disciples, he e everything.
Lk 24:27 he e to them what was said in all
Ac 11: 4 Peter began and e everything to them
18:26 e to him the way of God more
28:23 From morning till evening he e and

Explaining (Explain)
Jdg 14:15 "Coax your husband into e the riddle
Isa 28: 9 To whom is he e his message? To
Ac 17: 3 e and proving that the Christ had to

Explains (Explain)
Ac 8:31 "unless someone e it to me?" So he

Explanation (Explain)
Ecc 8: 1 Who knows the e of things? Wisdom
Da 7:23 " gave me this e: 'The fourth

Exploit (Exploited, Exploiting, Exploits)
Pr 22:22 Do not e the poor because they are
Isa 58: 3 you please and e all your workers.
2Co 12:17 Did I e you through any of the men I
12:18 Titus did not e you, did he? Did we
2Pe 2: 3 In their greed these teachers will e

Exploited (Exploit)
2Co 7: 2 corrupted no-one, we have e no-one.

Exploiting (Exploit)
Jas 2: 6 Is it not the rich who are e you?

Exploits (Exploit)
2Sa 23:17 were the e of the three mighty men.
23:20 from Kabzeel, who performed great e.
23:22 Such were the e of Benaiah son of
1Ki 22:45 he achieved and his military e,
1Ch 11:19 were the e of the three mighty men.
11:22 from Kabzeel, who performed great e.
11:24 Such were the e of Benaiah son of
2Co 11:20 anyone who enslaves you or e you

Explore (Explored, Exploring)
Nu 13: 2 "Send some men to e the land of
13:16 of the men Moses sent to e the land.
13:17 Moses sent them to e Canaan, he said,
14:36 the men Moses had sent to e the land,
14:38 Of the men who went to e the land,
Jos 14: 7 me from Kadesh Barnea to e the land.
Jdg 18: 2 Eshtaol to spy out the land and e it.
18: 2 They told them, "Go, e the land."
2Sa 10: 3 sent them to you to e the city
1Ch 19: 3 Haven't his men come to you to e and
Ecc 1:13 myself to study and to e by wisdom

Explored (Explore)
Nu 13:21 they went up and e the land from the
13:32 report about the land they had e.
13:32 They said, "The land we e devours
14: 6 had e the land, tore their
14: 7 through and e is exceedingly good.
14:34 of the forty days you e the land
Dt 1:24 to the Valley of Eshcol and e it.

Exploring (Explore)
Nu 13:25 days they returned from e the land.

Exported
1Ki 10:29 They also e them to all the kings of
2Ch 1:17 They also e them to all the kings of

Expose (Exposed, Exposes, Exposing)
Nu 25: 4 kill them and e them in broad
Job 20:27 The heavens will e his guilt; the
Isa 57:12 I will e your righteousness and your
Lam 2:14 they did not e your sin to ward off
4:22 your sin and e your wickedness.
Eze 25: 9 therefore I will e the flank of Moab,
Hos 2:10 now I will e her lewdness before the
Mt 1:19 want to e her to public disgrace,
1Co 4: 5 will e the motives of men's hearts.
Eph 5:11 of darkness, but rather e them.

Exposed (Expose)
Ex 20:26 lest your nakedness be e on it.
Lev 20:18 he has e the source of her flow, and
2Sa 21: 6 e before the LORD at Gibeah of Saul—
21: 9 e them on a hill before the LORD.
21:13 been killed and e were gathered up.
22:16 The valleys of the sea were e and
Ne 4:13 points of the wall at the e places,
Est 6: 2 Mordecai had e Bigthana and Teresh,
Ps 18:15 The valleys of the sea were e and
Pr 26:26 will be e in the assembly.
Isa 47: 3 Your nakedness will be e and your
Jer 8: 2 They will be e to the sun and the
36:30 his body will be thrown out and e to
Eze 16:36 e your nakedness in your promiscuity
23:18 openly and e her nakedness,
23:29 of your prostitution will be e.
Hos 7: 1 the sins of Ephraim are e and the
Hab 2:16 Now it is your turn! Drink and be e!
Zep 2:14 the beams of cedar will be e.
Jn 3:20 for fear that his deeds will be e.
2Co 11:23 and been e to death again and again.
Eph 5:13 everything e by the light becomes
Heb 10:33 Sometimes you were publicly e to
Rev 16:15 not go naked and be shamefully e."

Exposes (Expose)
Pr 13:16 knowledge, but a fool e his folly.

Exposing (Expose)
Ge 30:37 e the white inner wood of the

Expound
Dt 1: 5 Moses began to e this law, saying:
Ps 49: 4 with the harp I will e my riddle:

Express (Expressed, Expresses, Expressing, Expression, Expressions)
2Sa 10: 2 So David sent a delegation to e his
10: 3 by sending men to you to e sympathy?
1Ch 19: 2 So David sent a delegation to e his
19: 2 the Ammonites to e sympathy to him,
19: 3 by sending men to you to e sympathy?
Eze 33:31 With their mouths they e devotion,
Ro 8:26 us with groans that words cannot e.
Col 4: 8 sending him to you for the e purpose

Expressed (Express)
2Sa 13:32 This has been Absalom's e intention
Eph 2: 7 e in his kindness to us in Christ

Expresses (Express)
Ps 7:11 a God who e his wrath every day.

Expressing (Express)
1Co 2:13 e spiritual truths in spiritual
Gal 5: 6 is faith e itself through love.

Expression (Express)
Lev 7:12 offers it as an e of thankfulness,
Job 9:27 I will change my e, and smile,'

Expressions (Express)
2Co 9:12 in many e of thanks to God.

Extend (Extended, Extending, Extends, Extensive, Extent)
Ge 9:27 May God e the territory of Japheth;
49:13 his border will e towards Sidon.
Ex 25:32 Six branches are to e from the sides
26:28 The centre crossbar is to e from end
Nu 35: 4 that you give the Levites will e
Dt 11:24 will e from the desert to Lebanon,
Jos 1: 4 Your territory will e from the
1Ch 11:10 support to e it over the whole land,
Est 4:11 king to e the gold sceptre to him
Ps 109:12 May no-one e kindness to him or take
110: 2 The LORD will e your mighty sceptre
Isa 66:12 "I will e peace to her like a river,

Eze 45: 7 It will **e** westward from the west
47:17 The boundary will **e** from the sea to
48:21 It will **e** eastward from the 25,000
48:23 it will **e** from the east side to the
Da 11:42 He will **e** his power over many
Am 1:13 in order to **e** his borders,
Zec 9:10 His rule will **e** from sea to sea and
14: 5 valley, for it will **e** to Azel.

Extended (Extend)

Ex 36:33 so that it **e** from end to end
37:18 Six branches **e** from the sides of the
Dt 4:48 This land **e** from Aroer on the rim of
Jos 13: 9 **e** from Aroer on the rim of the Arnon
15: 1 by clan, **e** down to the territory of
17: 7 The territory of Manasseh **e** from
19:11 and **e** to the ravine near Jokneam.
1Ki 6: 3 temple **e** the width of the temple,
6:21 and he **e** gold chains across the
1Ch 5:16 of Sharon as far as they **e**.
21:16 sword in his hand **e** over Jerusalem.
2Ch 3:13 The wings of these cherubim **e** twenty
Ezr 7:28 who has **e** his good favour to me
Est 8: 4 the king **e** the gold sceptre to
Isa 26:15 have **e** all the borders of the land.
Eze 42: 7 it **e** in front of the rooms for fifty

Extending (Extend)

Ex 25:33 six branches **e** from the lampstand.
25:35 of branches **e** from the lampstand,
37:19 six branches **e** from the lampstand.
37:21 of branches **e** from the lampstand,
Nu 21:13 the desert **e** into Amorite territory.
Dt 3:16 the Gadites I gave the territory **e**
Jos 13:30 The territory **e** from Mahanaim and
1Sa 27: 8 in the land **e** to Shur and Egypt.)
2Ch 5: 9 ends, **e** from the ark, could be seen
Eze 42:12 the corresponding wall **e** eastward,
Mic 7:11 come, the day for **e** your boundaries.

Extends (Extend)

Nu 21:30 far as Nophah, which **e** to Medeba."
1Ch 5: 9 that **e** to the Euphrates River,
Pr 31:20 She opens her arms to the poor and **e**
Da 4:22 **e** to distant parts of the earth.
Lk 1:50 His mercy **e** to those who fear him,

Extensive (Extend)

1Ch 22: 5 **e** preparations before his death.
2Ch 27: 3 did **e** work on the wall at the hill
Ne 4:19 "The work is **e** and spread out, and

Extent (Extend)

Jn 13: 1 showed them the full **e** of his love.
1Co 11:18 you, and to some **e** I believe it.
2Co 2: 5 grieved all of you, to some **e**—

Exterminate (Exterminating)

1Ki 9:21 whom the Israelites could not **e**
Eze 25: 7 and **e** you from the countries.

Exterminating (Exterminate)

Jos 11:20 **e** them without mercy, as the LORD

External

Gal 2: 6 God does not judge by **e** appearance
Heb 9:10 ceremonial washings—**e** regulations

Extinguish (Extinguished)

Eph 6:16 with which you can **e** all the flaming

Extinguished (Extinguish)

2Sa 21:17 the lamp of Israel will not be **e**."
Isa 43:17 again, **e**, snuffed out like a wick:

Extol

Job 36:24 Remember to **e** his work, which men
Ps 34: 1 I will **e** the LORD at all times; his
68: 4 sing praise to his name, **e** him who
95: 2 and **e** him with music and song.
109:30 With my mouth I will greatly **e** the
111: 1 Praise the LORD. I will **e** the LORD
115:18 is we who **e** the LORD, both now and
117: 1 you nations; **e** him, all you peoples
145: 2 I will praise you and **e** your name
145:10 O LORD; your saints will **e** you.
147:12 **E** the LORD, O Jerusalem; praise your

Extort (Extortion)

Lk 3:14 "Don't **e** money and don't accuse

Extortion (Extort)

Lev 6: 4 what he has stolen or taken by **e**,
Ps 62:10 Do not trust in **e** or take pride in
Ecc 7: 7 **E** turns a wise man into a fool, and
Isa 33:15 who rejects gain from **e** and keeps
Jer 22:17 blood and on oppression and **e**."
Eze 18:18 because he practised **e**, robbed his
22:12 gain from your neighbours by **e**.
22:29 The people of the land practise **e**
Hab 2: 6 and makes himself wealthy by **e**!

Extra

Mt 10:10 no bag for the journey, or **e** tunic
Mk 6: 9 Wear sandals but not an **e** tunic.
Lk 9: 3 bag, no bread, no money, no **e** tunic.
10:35 you for any **e** expense you may have.'

Extraordinary

Ac 19:11 God did **e** miracles through Paul,

Extreme (Extremes)

Jos 15: 1 to the Desert of Zin in the **e** south.
2Co 8: 2 overflowing joy and their **e** poverty

Extremes (Extreme)

Ecc 7:18 who fears God will avoid all ⌊**e**⌋

Exult

Ps 89:16 long; they **e** in your righteousness.
Isa 14: 8 of Lebanon **e** over you and say,
45:25 will be found righteous and will **e**.

Eye (*Eye for an eye*, Eyebrows, Eyed, Eyelids, Eyes, Eyesight)

Ge 2: 9 pleasing to the **e** and good for food.
3: 6 good for food and pleasing to the **e**,
Ex 21:26 in the **e** and destroys it, he must
21:26 go free to compensate for the **e**.
Lev 21:20 or who has any **e** defect, or who has
Nu 24: 3 oracle of one whose **e** sees clearly,
24:15 oracle of one whose **e** sees clearly,
Dt 32:10 guarded him as the apple of his **e**,
1Sa 11: 2 out the right **e** of every one of you
18: 9 on Saul kept a jealous **e** on David.
Ezr 5: 5 the **e** of their God was watching over
Job 7: 8 The **e** that now sees me will see me
10:18 wish I had died before any **e** saw me.
14: 3 Do you fix your **e** on such a one?
20: 9 The **e** that saw him will not see him
24:15 The **e** of the adulterer watches for
24:15 'No **e** will see me,' and he keeps his
28: 7 path, no falcon's **e** has seen it.
Ps 17: 8 Keep me as the apple of your **e**; hide
35:19 reason maliciously wink the **e**.
94: 9 Does he who formed the **e** not see?
Pr 6:13 who winks with his **e**, signals with
7: 2 my teachings as the apple of your **e**.
16:30 He who winks with his **e** is plotting
30:17 "The **e** that mocks a father, that
Ecc 1: 8 The **e** never has enough of seeing,
6: 9 Better what the **e** sees than the
Isa 29:20 an **e** for evil will be cut down—
64: 4 no ear has perceived, no **e** has seen
Lam 2: 4 all who were pleasing to the **e**;
Zec 2: 8 you touches the apple of his **e**—
11:17 strike his arm and his right **e**!
11:17 his right **e** totally blinded!"
12: 4 "I will keep a watchful **e** over the
Mt 5:29 If your right **e** causes you to sin,
6:22 "The **e** is the lamp of the body. If
7: 3 of sawdust in your brother's **e**
7: 3 to the plank in your own **e**?
7: 4 'Let me take the speck out of your **e**,
7: 4 time there is a plank in your own **e**?
7: 5 take the plank out of your own **e**,
7: 5 the speck from your brother's **e**.
18: 9 if your **e** causes you to sin, gouge
18: 9 with one **e** than to have two eyes
19:24 to go through the **e** of a needle
Mk 9:47 if your **e** causes you to sin, pluck
9:47 God with one **e** than to have two eyes
10:25 to go through the **e** of a needle
Lk 6:41 of sawdust in your brother's **e**
6:41 to the plank in your own **e**?
6:42 let me take the speck out of your **e**,'
6:42 plank in your own **e**? You hypocrite,
6:42 first take the plank out of your **e**,
6:42 the speck from your brother's **e**.
11:34 Your **e** is the lamp of your body.
18:25 to go through the **e** of a needle
1Co 2: 9 as it is written: "No **e** has seen,
12:16 "Because I am not an **e**, I do not
12:17 If the whole body were an **e**, where
12:21 The **e** cannot say to the hand, "I
15:52 in a flash, in the twinkling of an **e**,
Eph 6: 6 their favour when their **e** is on you,
Col 3:22 not only when their **e** is on you and
Rev 1: 7 and every **e** will see him, even those

Eye for eye

Ex 21:24 **e**, tooth for tooth, hand for hand,
Lev 24:20 fracture for fracture, **e**, tooth for
Dt 19:21 Show no pity: life for life, **e**,
Mt 5:38 "You have heard that it was said, 'E,

Eyebrows (Eye)

Lev 14: 9 his **e** and the rest of his hair.

Eyed (Eye)

Ecc 5: 8 one official is **e** by a higher one,

Eyelids (Eye)

Ps 132: 4 to my eyes, no slumber to my **e**,
Pr 6: 4 to your eyes, no slumber to your **e**.
Jer 9:18 tears and water streams from our **e**.

Eyes (*Evil in the eyes of the LORD, Eye, Right in the eyes of the LORD*)

Ge 3: 5 you eat of it your **e** will be opened,
3: 7 the **e** of both of them were opened,
6: 8 Noah found favour in the **e** of the
13:14 "Lift up your **e** from where you are
18: 3 "If I have found favour in your **e**,
19:19 servant has found favour in your **e**,
21:19 God opened her **e** and she saw a well
27: 1 Isaac was old and his **e** were so weak
29:17 Leah had weak **e**, but Rachel was
30:27 found favour in your **e**, please stay.
31:40 at night, and sleep fled from my **e**.
32: 5 that I may find favour in your **e**.'"
33: 8 favour in your **e**, my lord," he said.
33:10 "If I have found favour in your **e**,
33:15 me find favour in the **e** of my lord."
34:11 "Let me find favour in your **e**, and I
39: 4 Joseph found favour in his **e** and
39:21 in the **e** of the prison warder.
42:24 from them and bound before their **e**.
46: 4 Joseph's own hand will close your **e**."
47:15 Why should we die before your **e**?
47:19 Why should we perish before your **e**
47:25 "May we find favour in the **e** of our
47:29 "If I have found favour in your **e**,
48:10 Now Israel's **e** were failing because
49:12 His **e** will be darker than wine, his
50: 4 "If I have found favour in your **e**,
Ex 8:26 that are destestable in their **e**,
15:26 God and do what is right in his **e**,
34: 9 if I have found favour in your **e**,"
Lev 20: 4 community close their **e** when that
20:17 They must be cut off before the **e** of
Nu 10:31 in the desert, and you can be our **e**.
11:15 I have found favour in your **e**
13:33 like grasshoppers in our own **e**, and
15:39 the lusts of your own hearts and **e**.
16:14 Will you gouge out the **e** of these
20: 8 Speak to that rock before their **e**
22:31 the LORD opened Balaam's **e**, and he
24: 4 prostrate, and whose **e** are opened:

Nu 24:16 prostrate, and whose e are opened:
25: 6 woman right before the e of Moses
27:14 to honour me as holy before their e.
32: 5 If we have found favour in your e,"
33:55 in your e and thorns in your sides.
Dt 1:30 you in Egypt, before your very e,
3:21 "You have seen with your own e all
3:27 Look at the land with your own e,
4: 3 You saw with your own e what the
4: 9 not forget the things your e have
4:34 for you in Egypt before your very e?
6:22 Before our e the LORD sent
7:19 You saw with your own e the great
9:17 them to pieces before your e.
10:21 wonders you saw with your own e.
11: 7 was your own e that saw all these
11:12 the e of the LORD your God are
13:18 and doing what is right in his e.
16:19 for a bribe blinds the e of the wise
21: 7 blood, nor did our e see it done.
24: 4 That would be detestable in the e of
25: 3 brother will be degraded in your e.
28:31 before your e, but you will eat none
28:32 and you will wear out your e
28:65 e weary with longing, and a
28:67 and the sights that your e will see.
29: 2 Your e have seen all that the LORD
29: 3 With your own e you saw those great
29: 4 or e that see or ears that hear.
34: 4 I have let you see it with your e,
34: 7 yet his e were not weak nor his
Jos 3: 7 to exalt you in the e of all Israel,
23:13 on your backs and thorns in your e,
24: 7 You saw with your own e what I did
24:17 those great signs before our e.
Jdg 6:17 If now I have found favour in your e,
16:21 out his e and took him down to Gaza.
16:28 on the Philistines for my two e."
Ru 2: 2 anyone in whose e I find favour.
2:10 favour in your e that you notice me
2:13 find favour in your e, my lord,"
1Sa 1:18 your servant find favour in your e.
2:33 only to blind your e with tears
3: 2 One night Eli, whose e were becoming
3:18 let him do what is good in his e."
4:15 e were set so that he could not see.
12: 3 a bribe to make me shut my e?
12:16 LORD is about to do before your e!
12:17 evil thing you did in the e of the
14:27 to his mouth, and his e brightened.
14:29 See how my e brightened when I
15:17 you were once small in your own e,
20: 3 that I have found favour in your e,
20:29 If I have found favour in your e,
24:10 seen with your own e how the LORD
27: 5 "If I have found favour in your e,
29: 9 as pleasing in my e as an angel
2Sa 6:22 I will be humiliated in my own e.
12: 9 LORD by doing what is evil in his e?
12:11 Before your very e I will take your
14:22 that he has found favour in your e,
15:25 If I find favour in the LORD's e, he
16: 4 favour in your e, my lord the king."
22:28 your e are on the haughty to bring
24: 3 the e of my lord the king see it.
1Ki 1:20 the e of all Israel are on you,
1:48 who has allowed my e to see a
8:29 May your e be open towards this
8:52 "May your e be open to your
9: 3 My e and my heart will always be
10: 7 until I came and saw with my own e.
11:33 nor done what is right in my e, nor
11:38 do what is right in my e by keeping
14: 8 doing only what was right in my e.
16: 7 he had done in the e of the LORD,
20:38 with his headband down over his e.
20:41 removed the headband from his e,
2Ki 3:18 This is an easy thing in the e of
4:34 to mouth, e to e, hands to hands.
4:35 seven times and opened his e.
6:17 Elisha prayed, "O LORD, open his e
6:17 Then the LORD opened the servant's e,
6:20 e of these men so that they can see.
6:20 Then the LORD opened their e and
7: 2 "You will see it with your own e,"
7:19 see it with your own e, but you

2Ki 9:30 she painted her e, arranged her hair
10:30 accomplishing what is right in my e
19:16 O LORD, and hear; open your e,
19:22 voice and lifted your e in pride?
20: 3 have done what is good in your e.
21:15 they have done evil in my e and have
22:20 Your e will not see all the disaster
25: 7 the sons of Zedekiah before his e.
25: 7 Then they put out his e, bound him
2Ch 6:20 May your e be open towards this
6:40 "Now, my God, may your e be open and
7:15 Now my e will be open and my ears
7:16 My e and my heart will always be
9: 6 until I came and saw with my own e.
16: 9 For the e of the LORD range
20:12 what to do, but our e are upon you."
29: 8 as you can see with your own e.
34:28 Your e will not see all the disaster
Ezr 9: 8 our God gives light to our e and
Ne 1: 6 let your ear be attentive and your e
9:32 hardship seem trifling in your e
Job 3:10 on me to hide trouble from my e.
4:16 A form stood before my e, and I
7: 7 my e will never see happiness again.
10: 4 Do you have e of flesh? Do you see
11:20 the e of the wicked will fail, and
13: 1 "My e have seen all this, my ears
15:12 you away, and why do your e flash,
15:15 the heavens are not pure in his e,
16: 9 fastens on me his piercing e.
16:16 weeping, deep shadows ring my e;
16:20 as my e pour out tears to God;
17: 2 mockers surround me; my e must
17: 5 the e of his children will fail.
17: 7 My e have grown dim with grief; my
19:27 I myself will see him with my own e—
21: 8 their offspring before their e.
21:20 Let his own e see his destruction;
24:23 but his e are on their ways.
25: 5 and the stars are not pure in his e,
27:19 when he opens his e, all is gone.
28:10 rock; his e see all its treasures.
28:21 is hidden from the e of every living
29:15 I was e to the blind and feet to the
31: 1 "I made a covenant with my e not to
31: 7 if my heart has been led by my e,
31:16 let the e of the widow grow weary,
32: 1 he was righteous in his own e.
34:21 "His e are on the ways of men; he
36: 7 He does not take his e off the
39:29 his food; his e detect it from afar.
40:24 Can anyone capture him by the e, or
41:18 his e are like the rays of dawn.
42: 5 My ears had heard of you but now my e
Ps 6: 7 My e grow weak with sorrow; they
11: 4 the sons of men; his e examine them.
13: 3 Give light to my e, or I will sleep
17: 2 you; may your e see what is right.
17:11 surround me, with e alert, to
18:27 bring low those whose e are haughty.
19: 8 are radiant, giving light to the e.
25:15 My e are ever on the LORD, for only
31: 9 my e grow weak with sorrow,
33:18 the e of the LORD are on those who
34:15 The e of the LORD are on the
35:21 Aha! With our own e we have seen it."
36: 1 There is no fear of God before his e.
36: 2 For in his own e he flatters himself
38:10 even the light has gone from my e.
52: 1 who are a disgrace in the e of God?
54: 7 e have looked in triumph on my foes.
66: 7 his power, his e watch the nations
69: 3 My e fail, looking for my God.
69:23 May their e be darkened so that they
77: 4 You kept my e from closing; I was
79:10 Before our e, make known among the
88: 9 my e are dim with grief. I call to
91: 8 You will only observe with your e
92:11 My e have seen the defeat of my
101: 3 I will set before my e no vile thing.
101: 5 has haughty e and a proud heart,
101: 6 My e will be on the faithful in the
115: 5 cannot speak, e, but they cannot see
116: 8 e from tears, my feet from stumbling,
118:23 this, and it is marvellous in our e.
119:18 Open my e that I may see wonderful

Ps 119:37 Turn my e away from worthless things;
119:82 My e fail, looking for your promise;
119:123 My e fail, looking for your righteous
119:136 Streams of tears flow from my e, for
119:148 My e stay open through the watches
121: 1 I lift up my e to the hills—where
123: 1 I lift up my e to you, to you whose
123: 2 the e of slaves look to the hand of
123: 2 as the e of a maid look to the hand
123: 2 so our e look to the LORD our God,
131: 1 O LORD, my e are not haughty;
132: 4 I will allow no sleep to my e, no
135:16 They have mouths, but cannot speak, e
139:16 your e saw my unformed body. All the
141: 8 my e are fixed on you, O Sovereign
145:15 The e of all look to you, and you
Pr 3: 7 Do not be wise in your own e; fear
4:25 Let your e look straight ahead, fix
6: 4 Allow no sleep to your e, no slumber
6:17 haughty e, a lying tongue, hands
6:25 or let her captivate you with her e,
10:26 to the teeth and smoke to the e,
15: 3 The e of the LORD are everywhere,
17:24 e wander to the ends of the earth.
20: 8 he winnows out all evil with his e.
20:12 Ears that hear and e that see—the
21: 4 Haughty e and a proud heart, the
22:12 The e of the LORD keep watch over
23:26 and let your e keep to my ways,
23:29 bruises? Who has bloodshot e?
23:33 Your e will see strange sights and
25: 7 What you have seen with your e
26: 5 or he will be wise in his own e.
26:12 Do you see a man wise in his own e?
26:16 The sluggard is wiser in his own e
27:20 and neither are the e of man.
28:11 A rich man may be wise in his own e,
28:27 he who closes his e to them receives
29:13 LORD gives sight to the e of both.
30:12 those who are pure in their own e
30:13 those whose e are ever so haughty,
Ecc 2:10 I denied myself nothing my e desired;
2:14 The wise man has e in his head,
4: 8 e were not content with his wealth.
5:11 owner except to feast his e on them?
8:16 e not seeing sleep day or night–
11: 7 Light is sweet, and it pleases the e
11: 9 your heart and whatever your e see,
SS 1:15 Oh, how beautiful! Your e are doves.
4: 1 Your e behind your veil are doves.
4: 9 with one glance of your e,
5:12 His e are like doves by the water
6: 5 Turn your e from me; they overwhelm
7: 4 Your e are the pools of Heshbon by
8:10 his e like one bringing contentment.
Isa 1:15 I will hide my e from you; even if
2:11 The e of the arrogant man will be
3:16 flirting with their e, tripping
5:15 the e of the arrogant humbled.
5:21 own e and clever in their own sight.
6: 5 and my e have seen the King, the
6:10 their ears dull and close their e.
6:10 they might see with their e,
10:12 heart and the haughty look in his e.
11: 3 judge by what he sees with his e,
13:16 be dashed to pieces before their e;
17: 7 their e to the Holy One of Israel.
29:10 He has sealed your e (the prophets);
29:18 the e of the blind will see.
30:20 with your own e you will see them.
32: 3 the e of those who see will no
33:15 his e against contemplating evil–
33:17 Your e will see the king in his
33:20 your e will see Jerusalem,
35: 5 will the e of the blind be opened
37:17 O LORD, and hear; open your e,
37:23 voice and lifted your e in pride?
38: 3 have done what is good in your e.
38:14 My e grew weak as I looked to the
40:26 Lift your e and look to the heavens:
42: 7 to open e that are blind, to free
43: 8 Lead out those who have e but are
44:18 their e are plastered over so that
49: 5 I am honoured in the e of the LORD
49:18 Lift up your e and look around; all
51: 6 Lift up your e to the heavens, look

Isa 52: 8 they will see it with their own **e**.
59:10 feeling our way like men without **e**.
60: 4 "Lift up your **e** and look about you:
65:16 be forgotten and hidden from my **e**.
Jer 4:30 Why shade your **e** with paint? You
5: 3 LORD, do not your **e** look for truth
5:21 who have **e** but do not see, who have
7:30 evil in my **e**, declares the LORD.
9: 1 water and my **e** a fountain of tears!
9:18 wail over us till our **e** overflow
13:17 your pride; my **e** will weep bitterly,
13:20 Lift up your **e** and see those who are
14:17 "Let my **e** overflow with tears
16: 9 says: Before your **e** and in your days
16:17 My **e** are on all their ways; they are
16:17 is their sin concealed from my **e**.
20: 4 with your own **e** you will see them
22:17 "But your **e** and your heart are set
24: 6 My **e** will watch over them for their
29:21 them to death before your very **e**.
31:16 from weeping and your **e** from tears,
32: 4 to face and see him with his own **e**.
32:19 Your **e** are open to all the ways of
34: 3 the king of Babylon with your own **e**,
39: 6 the sons of Zedekiah before his **e**
39: 7 he put out Zedekiah's **e** and bound
39:16 will be fulfilled before your **e**.
51:24 "Before your **e** I will repay Babylon
52:10 the sons of Zedekiah before his **e**;
52:11 he put out Zedekiah's **e**, bound him
Lam 1:16 "This is why I weep and my **e**
2:11 My **e** fail from weeping, I am in
2:18 yourself no relief, your **e** no rest.
3:48 Streams of tears flow from my **e**
3:49 My **e** will flow unceasingly, without
4:17 Moreover, our **e** failed, looking in
5:17 of these things our **e** grow dim
Eze 1:18 four rims were full of **e** all around.
6: 9 and by their **e**, which have lusted
10:12 full of **e**, as were their four wheels
12: 2 They have **e** to see but do not see
20: 7 vile images you have set your **e** on,
20: 8 vile images they had set their **e** on,
20: 9 **e** of the nations they lived among
20:14 profaned in the **e** of the nations
20:22 profaned in the **e** of the nations
20:24 **e** lusted after their fathers' idols.
22:16 defiled in the **e** of the nations,
22:26 **e** to the keeping of my Sabbaths,
23:40 your **e** and put on your jewellery.
24:16 away from you the delight of your **e**.
24:21 the delight of your **e**, the object
24:25 the delight of their **e**, their
36:23 holy through you before their **e**.
37:20 Hold before their **e** the sticks you
38:16 holy through you before their **e**.
40: 4 "Son of man, look with your **e** and
Da 4:34 I, Nebuchadnezzar, raised my **e**
7: 8 This horn had **e** like the **e** of a man
7:20 **e** and a mouth that spoke boastfully.
8: 5 between his **e** came from the west,
8:21 between his **e** is the first king.
9:18 O God, and hear; open your **e** and see
10: 6 his **e** like flaming torches, his
Hos 2:10 lewdness before the **e** of her lovers;
Joel 1:16 cut off before our very **e**—joy
Am 9: 4 I will fix my **e** upon them for evil
9: 8 "Surely the **e** of the Sovereign LORD
Mic 4:11 defiled, let our **e** gloat over Zion!"
7:10 My **e** will see her downfall;
Hab 1:13 Your **e** are too pure to look on evil;
Zep 3:20 before your very **e**," says the LORD.
Zec 3: 9 There are seven **e** on that one stone,
4:10 "(These seven are the **e** of the LORD,
9: 1 upon Damascus—for the **e** of men
14:12 their **e** will rot in their sockets,
Mal 1: 5 You will see it with your own **e** and
2:17 "All who do evil are good in the **e**
Mt 6:22 If your **e** are good, your whole body
6:23 if your **e** are bad, your whole body
9:29 he touched their **e** and said,
13:15 ears, and they have closed their **e**.
13:15 they might see with their **e**,
13:16 blessed are your **e** because they see,
18: 9 with one eye than to have two **e**
20:34 on them and touched their **e**.
Mt 21:42 and it is marvellous in our **e**'?
26:43 because their **e** were heavy.
Mk 8:18 Do you have **e** but fail to see, and
8:23 When he had spat on the man's **e** and
8:25 Jesus put his hands on the man's **e**.
8:25 Then his **e** were opened, his sight
9:47 have two **e** and be thrown into hell,
12:11 and it is marvellous in our **e**'?"
14:40 because their **e** were heavy.
Lk 2:30 For my **e** have seen your salvation,
4:20 The **e** of everyone in the synagogue
10:23 are the **e** that see what you see.
11:34 When your **e** are good, your whole
16:15 justify yourselves in the **e** of men,
19:42 now it is hidden from your **e**.
24:31 their **e** were opened and they
Jn 4:35 open your **e** and look at the fields!
9: 6 saliva, and put it on the man's **e**.
9:10 "How then were your **e** opened?" they
9:11 made some mud and put it on my **e**.
9:14 opened the man's **e** was a Sabbath.
9:15 "He put mud on my **e**," the man
9:17 about him? It was your **e** he opened.
9:21 or who opened his **e**, we don't know.
9:26 do to you? How did he open your **e**?"
9:30 he comes from, yet he opened my **e**.
9:32 opening the **e** of a man born blind.
10:21 Can a demon open the **e** of the blind?"
11:37 "Could not he who opened the **e** of
12:40 "He has blinded their **e** and deadened
12:40 they can neither see with their **e**,
Ac 1: 9 he was taken up before their very **e**,
9: 8 opened his **e** he could see nothing.
9:18 Saul's **e**, and he could see again.
9:40 her **e**, and seeing Peter she sat up.
26:18 to open their **e** and turn them from
28:27 ears, and they have closed their **e**.
28:27 they might see with their **e**,
Ro 3:18 is no fear of God before their **e**."
11: 8 stupor, **e** so that they could not see
11:10 May their **e** be darkened so they
12:17 what is right in the **e** of everybody.
2Co 4:18 we fix our **e** not on what is seen,
8:21 not only in the **e** of the Lord but
8:21 the Lord but also in the **e** of men.
Gal 3: 1 Before your very **e** Jesus Christ was
4:15 out your **e** and given them to me.
Eph 1:18 I pray also that the **e** of your heart
Heb 4:13 laid bare before the **e** of him to
12: 2 Let us fix our **e** on Jesus, the
Jas 2: 5 who are poor in the **e** of the world
1Pe 3:12 For the **e** of the Lord are on the
2Pe 2:14 With **e** full of adultery, they never
1Jn 1: 1 which we have seen with our **e**, which
2:16 the lust of his **e** and the boasting
Rev 1:14 and his **e** were like blazing fire.
2:18 whose **e** are like blazing fire and
3:18 put on your **e**, so that you can see.
4: 6 covered with **e**, in front and behind.
4: 8 **e** all around, even under his wings.
5: 6 He had seven horns and seven **e**,
7:17 wipe away every tear from their **e**."
19:12 His **e** are like blazing fire, and on
21: 4 He will wipe every tear from their **e**.

Eyesight (Eye)

Jer 14: 6 their **e** fails for lack of pasture."

Eye-witnesses (Witness)

Lk 1: 2 were **e** and servants of the word.
2Pe 1:16 Christ, but we were **e** of his majesty.

Ezbai

1Ch 11:37 Hezro the Carmelite, Naarai son of **E**,

Ezbon

Ge 46:16 Shuni, **E**, Eri, Arodi and Areli.
1Ch 7: 7 The sons of Bela: **E**, Uzzi, Uzziel,

Ezekiel

Member of priestly family; deported to Babylon with Jehoiachin (Eze 1:1–3). Vision and call to be prophet to exiles (Eze 1:4–28; 2–3). Listened to, but words not acted upon (Eze 8:1; 14:1; 20:1; 33:30–32). Sudden death of wife (Eze 24:15–18). Visions: idolatry of Jerusalem (Eze 8–11); valley of dry bones (Eze 37); new temple (Eze 40–47). Prophetic symbolism (Eze 4–5; 12). Oracles: against Israel (Eze 13–24; 33); against nations (Eze 25–32; 35; 38–39); of restoration (Eze 34; 36).

Eze 1: 3 the word of the LORD came to **E** the
24:24 **E** will be a sign to you; you will do

Ezel

1Sa 20:19 began, and wait by the stone **E**.

Ezem

Jos 15:29 Baalah, Iim, **E**,
19: 3 Hazar Shual, Balah, **E**,
1Ch 4:29 Bilhah, **E**, Tolad,

Ezer

Ge 36:21 Dishon, **E** and Dishan. These sons of
36:27 The sons of **E**: Bilhan, Zaavan and
36:30 Dishon, **E** and Dishan. These were the
1Ch 1:38 Zibeon, Anah, Dishon, **E** and Dishan.
1:42 The sons of **E**: Bilhan, Zaavan and
4: 4 and **E** the father of Hushah.
7:21 **E** and Elead were killed by the
12: 9 **E** was the chief, Obadiah the second
Ne 3:19 Next to him, **E** son of Jeshua, ruler
12:42 Jehohanan, Malkijah, Elam and **E**.

Ezion Geber

Nu 33:35 They left Abronah and camped at **E**.
33:36 They left **E** and camped at Kadesh, in
Dt 2: 8 which comes up from Elath and **E**, and
1Ki 9:26 King Solomon also built ships at **E**,
22:48 set sail—they were wrecked at **E**.
2Ch 8:17 Solomon went to **E** and Elath on the
20:36 After these were built at **E**,

Ezra (Ezra's)

Priest and teacher of the Law of Moses (Ezr 7:6, 0–28); commissioned by Artaxerxes to lead a return of exiles to Jerusalem, to provide resources for temple worship and to establish observance of Law (Ezr 7–8). Addressed problem of intermarriage (Ezr 9–10); read Law at Feast of Tabernacles (Ne 8); took part in dedication of city walls (Ne 12:36).

Ezr 7: 1 **E** son of Seraiah, the son of Azariah,
7: 6 this **E** came up from Babylon. He was
7: 8 **E** arrived in Jerusalem in the fifth
7:10 For **E** had devoted himself to the
7:11 given to **E** the priest and teacher,
7:12 To **E** the priest, a teacher of the
7:21 diligence whatever **E** the priest,
7:25 you, **E**, in accordance with the
10: 1 While **E** was praying and confessing,
10: 2 said to **E**, "We have been unfaithful
10: 5 **E** rose up and put the leading
10: 6 **E** withdrew from before the house of
10:10 **E** the priest stood up and said to
10:16 **E** the priest selected men who were
Ne 8: 1 They told **E** the scribe to bring out
8: 2 **E** the priest brought the Law before
8: 4 **E** the scribe stood on a high wooden
8: 5 **E** opened the book. All the people
8: 6 **E** praised the LORD, the great God;
8: 9 Nehemiah the governor, **E** the priest
8:13 gathered round **E** the scribe to give
8:18 **E** read from the Book of the Law
12: 1 with Jeshua: Seraiah, Jeremiah, **E**,
12:26 and of **E** the priest and scribe.
12:33 along with Azariah, **E**, Meshullam,
12:36 **E** the scribe led the procession.

Ezra's (Ezra)

Ne 12:13 of **E**, Meshullam; of Amariah's,

Ezrah (Ezrahite)

1Ch 4:17 The sons of **E**: Jether, Mered, Epher

Ezrahite (Ezrah)

1Ki 4:31 including Ethan the E—wiser than
Ps 88: T A maskil of Heman the E.
89: T A maskil of Ethan the E.

Ezri

1Ch 27:26 E son of Kelub was in charge of the

Fabric

Jdg 16:13 of my head into the f ⌊on the loom⌋
16:13 of his head, wove them into the f
16:14 up the pin and the loom, with the f.
Eze 16:13 and costly f and embroidered cloth.
27:16 purple f, embroidered work, fine
27:24 blue f, embroidered work and

Face (*Face to face, Face to the ground*, Faced, Faces, Facing, *Hide your face, Set my face, Set your face*, Stern-faced)

Ge 1:29 plant on the f of the whole earth
4: 5 very angry, and his f was downcast.
4: 6 you angry? Why is your f downcast?
6: 7 whom I have created, from the f of
7: 4 will wipe from the f of the earth
7:23 Every living thing on the f of the
11: 4 over the f of the whole earth."
11: 9 them over the f of the whole earth.
17: 3 Abram fell f down, and God said to
17:17 Abraham fell f down; he laughed and
30:40 but made the rest f the streaked and
33:10 For to see your f is like seeing the
33:10 your f is like seeing the f of God,
38:15 for she had covered her f.
43: 3 'You will not see my f again unless
43: 5 'You will not see my f again unless
43:31 After he had washed his f, he came
44:23 you, you will not see my f again.'
44:26 We cannot see the man's f unless our
48:11 "I never expected to see your f
Ex 3: 6 At this, Moses hid his f, because
10: 5 They will cover the f of the ground
10:28 The day you see my f you will die."
13:17 For God said, "If they f war, they
25:20 The cherubim are to f each other,
32:12 wipe them off the f of the earth'?
33:16 other people on the f of the earth?"
33:20 But," he said, "you cannot see my f,
33:23 my back; but my f must not be seen."
34:29 not aware that his f was radiant
34:30 his f was radiant, and they were
34:33 to them, he put a veil over his f.
34:35 they saw that his f was radiant.
34:35 put the veil back over his f until
Lev 9:24 shouted for joy and fell f down.
13:45 cover the lower part of his f and
Nu 6:25 the LORD make his f shine upon you
6:26 the LORD turn his f towards you and
11:15 do not let me f my own ruin."
12: 3 anyone else on the f of the earth.)
12:14 "If her father had spat in her f,
14: 5 Moses and Aaron fell f down in front
14:43 and Canaanites will f you there.
16: 4 Moses heard this, he fell f down.
16:22 Moses and Aaron fell f down and
16:45 at once." And they fell f down.
20: 6 the Tent of Meeting and fell f down,
22: 5 they cover the f of the land and
22:11 of Egypt covers the f of the land.
22:31 So he bowed low and fell f down.
24: 1 but turned his f towards the desert.
Dt 6:15 destroy you from the f of the land.
7: 6 the f of the earth to be his people,
7:10 repay to their f by destruction;
7:10 repay to their f those who hate him.
14: 2 Out of all the peoples on the f of
25: 9 spit in his f and say, "This is what
31:17 them; I will hide my f from them,
31:18 I will certainly hide my f on that
32:20 "I will hide my f from them," he
Jos 5: 1 had the courage to f the Israelites.
5:14 Then Joshua fell f down to the
7: 6 Joshua tore his clothes and fell f
7:10 What are you doing down on your f?
1Sa 1:18 and her f was no longer downcast.
5: 3 there was Dagon, fallen on his f on
5: 4 there was Dagon, fallen on his f on
17:49 and he fell f down on the ground.
20:15 enemies from the f of the earth."
2Sa 2:22 I look your brother Joab in the f?"
14: 7 descendant on the f of the earth."
14:24 his own house; he must not see my f.
14:24 and did not see the f of the king.
14:28 without seeing the king's f.
14:32 I want to see the king's f, and if I
19: 4 The king covered his f and cried
21: 1 so David sought the f of the LORD.
1Ki 13:34 destruction from the f of the earth.
18:42 and put his f between his knees.
19:13 he pulled his cloak over his f and
22:24 up and slapped Micaiah in the f.
2Ki 4:29 Lay my staff on the boy's f."
4:31 and laid the staff on the boy's f,
8:15 over the king's f, so that he died.
20: 2 Hezekiah turned his f to the wall
1Ch 16:11 and his strength; seek his f always.
21:16 clothed in sackcloth, fell f down.
2Ch 7:14 seek my f and turn from their
18:23 up and slapped Micaiah in the f.
20:12 For we have no power to f this vast
20:17 Go out to f them tomorrow, and the
30: 9 He will not turn his f from you if
Ezr 9: 6 disgraced to lift up my f to you,
Ne 2: 2 "Why does your f look so sad when
2: 3 Why should my f not look sad when
4: 5 insults in the f of the builders.
Est 7: 8 mouth, they covered Haman's f.
Job 1:11 he will surely curse you to your f."
2: 5 he will surely curse you to your f."
4:15 A spirit glided past my f, and the
6:28 look at me. Would I lie to your f?
11:15 you will lift up your f without
13:15 will surely defend my ways to his f.
15:27 "Though his f is covered with fat
16:16 My f is red with weeping, deep
17: 6 a man in whose f people spit.
17:12 day; in the f of darkness they say,
21:31 Who denounces his conduct to his f?
22:26 and will lift up your f to God.
23:17 the thick darkness that covers my f.
24:15 me,' and he keeps his f concealed.
26: 9 He covers the f of the full moon,
26:10 He marks out the horizon on the f of
29:24 light of my f was precious to them.
30:10 do not hesitate to spit in my f.
33:26 he sees God's f and shouts for joy;
34:29 can condemn him? If he hides his f,
37:12 over the f of the whole earth to do
Ps 4: 6 light of your f shine upon us,
10:11 he covers his f and never sees."
11: 7 justice; upright men will see his f.
17:15 I shall see your f; when I awake,
22:24 he has not hidden his f from him but
24: 6 who seek your f, O God of Jacob.
27: 8 Seek his f!" Your f, LORD, I will
30: 7 when you hid your f, I was dismayed.
31:16 Let your f shine on your servant;
34:16 the f of the LORD is against those
44: 3 light of your f, for you loved them.
44:15 long, and my f is covered with
44:22 Yet for your sake we f death all day
50:21 rebuke you and accuse you to your f.
67: 1 make his f shine upon us.
69: 7 your sake, and shame covers my f.
80: 3 Restore us, O God; make your f shine
80: 7 O God Almighty; make your f shine
80:19 make your f shine upon us, that we
104:15 oil to make his f shine, and bread
104:30 and you renew the f of the earth.
105: 4 and his strength; seek his f always.
119:58 I have sought your f with all my
119:135 Make your f shine upon your servant
Pr 7:13 him and with a brazen f she said:
8:27 the horizon on the f of the deep,
15:13 A happy heart makes the f cheerful,
16:15 a king's f brightens, it means life;
27:19 water reflects a f, so a man's heart
Ecc 7: 3 a sad f is good for the heart.
8: 1 Wisdom brightens a man's f and
SS 2:14 show me your f, let me hear your
SS 2:14 is sweet, and your f is lovely.
Isa 8:17 hiding his f from the house
23:17 the kingdoms on the f of the earth.
24: 1 will ruin its f and scatter its
38: 2 Hezekiah turned his f to the wall
50: 6 hide my f from mocking and spitting.
50: 8 Let us f each other! Who is my
54: 8 In a surge of anger I hid my f from
57:17 and hid my f in anger, yet he kept
59: 2 your sins have hidden his f from
64: 7 for you have hidden your f from us
65: 3 continually provoke me to my very f,
Jer 13:26 pull up your skirts over your f
18:17 show them my back and not my f
25:26 the kingdoms on the f of the earth.
28:16 remove you from the f of the earth.
30: 6 labour, every f turned deathly pale?
33: 5 I will hide my f from this city
Lam 3:29 Let him bury his f in the dust—
Eze 1:10 Each of the four had the f of a man,
1:10 right side each had the f of a lion,
1:10 and on the left the f of an ox; each
1:10 ox; each also had the f of an eagle.
1:28 When I saw it, I fell f down, and I
3:23 the Kebar River, and I fell f down.
4: 3 the city and turn your f towards it.
4: 7 Turn your f towards the siege of
7:22 I will turn my f away from them, and
9: 8 I fell f down, crying out, "Ah,
10:14 faces: One f was that of a cherub,
10:14 the second the f of a man, the third
10:14 the third the f of a lion, and the
10:14 and the fourth the f of an eagle.
11:13 Then I fell f down and cried out in
12: 6 Cover your f so that you cannot see
12:12 will cover his f so that he cannot
14: 4 wicked stumbling-block before his f
14: 7 wicked stumbling-block before his f
20:47 and every f from south to north will
24:17 not cover the lower part of your f
24:22 not cover the lower part of your f
38:20 the people on the f of the earth
39:23 So I hid my f from them and handed
39:24 offences, and I hid my f from them.
39:29 I will no longer hide my f from them,
41:19 the f of a man towards the palm tree
41:19 the f of a lion towards the palm
43: 3 the Kebar River, and I fell f down.
43:17 The steps of the altar f east."
44: 4 of the LORD, and I fell f down.
Da 5: 6 His f turned pale and he was so
5: 9 terrified and his f grew more pale.
7:28 and my f turned pale, but I kept the
10: 6 chrysolite, his f like lightning,
10: 8 my f turned deathly pale and I was
10:15 I bowed with my f towards the ground
Hos 2: 2 the adulterous look from her f
5:15 And they will seek my f; in their
Joel 2: 6 are in anguish; every f turns pale.
Am 5: 8 pours them out over the f of the
9: 6 over the f of the land—the LORD
9: 8 destroy it from the f of the earth
Mic 3: 4 he will hide his f from them
Na 2:10 bodies tremble, every f grows pale.
3: 5 "I will lift your skirts over your f.
Zep 1: 2 everything from the f of the earth,
1: 3 cut off man from the f of the earth,
Mt 6:17 oil on your head and wash your f,
17: 2 His f shone like the sun, and his
17: 6 fell f down to the ground, terrified
18:10 see the f of my Father in heaven.
26:67 they spat in his f and struck him
Mk 10:22 At this the man's f fell. He went
Lk 9:29 the appearance of his f changed, and
21:35 live on the f of the whole earth.
Jn 11:44 of linen, and a cloth around his f.
18:22 near by struck him in the f.
19: 3 Jews!" And they struck him in the f.
Ac 6:15 his f was like the f of an angel.
16:19 market-place to f the authorities.
20:38 they would never see his f again.
Ro 8:36 "For your sake we f death all day
1Co 7:28 But those who marry will f many
2Co 3: 7 the f of Moses because of its glory,
3:13 who would put a veil over his f to
4: 6 the glory of God in the f of Christ.

2Co 11:20 forward or slaps you in the **f**.
11:28 I **f** daily the pressure of my
Gal 2:11 I opposed him to his **f**, because he
Heb 9:27 once, and after that to **f** judgment,
10:32 great contest in the **f** of suffering.
Jas 1: 2 whenever you **f** trials of many kinds,
1:23 who looks at his **f** in a mirror
5:10 patience in the **f** of suffering,
1Pe 3:12 but the **f** of the Lord is against
Rev 1:16 His **f** was like the sun shining in
4: 7 the third had a **f** like a man, the
6:16 hide us from the **f** of him who sits
10: 1 his head; his **f** was like the sun,
22: 4 They will see his **f**, and his name

Face to face

Ge 32:30 God **f**, and yet my life was spared."
Ex 33:11 The LORD would speak to Moses **f**, as
Nu 12: 8 With him I speak **f**, clearly and not
14:14 O LORD, have been seen **f**, that your
Dt 5: 4 The LORD spoke to you **f** out of the
34:10 like Moses, whom the LORD knew **f**,
Jdg 6:22 I have seen the angel of the LORD **f**!"
2Ki 14: 8 the challenge: "Come, meet me **f**.
2Ch 25:17 king of Israel: "Come, meet me **f**.
Jer 32: 4 him **f** and see him with his own eyes.
34: 3 eyes, and he will speak with you **f**.
Eze 20:35 there, **f**, I will execute judgment
1Co 13:12 as in a mirror; then we shall see **f**.
2Co 10: 1 "timid" when **f** with you, but "bold"
2Jn :12 to visit you and talk with you **f**,
3Jn :14 to see you soon, and we will talk **f**.

Face to the ground

Ge 19: 1 meet them and bowed down with his **f**.
48:12 knees and bowed down with his **f**.
Ru 2:10 At this, she bowed down with her **f**.
1Sa 20:41 Jonathan three times, with his **f**.
24: 8 and prostrated himself with his **f**.
25:23 bowed down before David with her **f**.
25:41 She bowed down with her **f** and said,
28:14 and prostrated himself with his **f**.
2Sa 14: 4 she fell with her **f** to pay him
14:22 Joab fell with his **f** to pay him
14:33 down with his **f** before the king.
18:28 before the king with his **f** and said,
24:20 down before the king with his **f**.
1Ki 1:23 the king and bowed with his **f**.
1:31 Bathsheba bowed low with her **f** and,
1Ch 21:21 bowed down before David with his **f**.
2Ch 20:18 Jehoshaphat bowed with his **f**, and
Da 8:18 I was in a deep sleep, with my **f**.
10: 9 him, I fell into a deep sleep, my **f**.
Mt 26:39 he fell with his **f** and prayed, "My
Lk 5:12 he fell with his **f** and begged him,

Faced (Face)

Ex 37: 9 The cherubim **f** each other, looking
Nu 8: 3 they **f** forward on the lampstand,
2Ki 14:11 He and Amaziah king of Judah **f** each
23:29 Neco **f** him and killed him at Megiddo.
2Ch 25:21 He and Amaziah king of Judah **f** each
Ne 8: 3 **f** the square before the Water Gate
Eze 1:17 the four directions the creatures **f**;
10:11 the four directions the cherubim **f**;
10:11 in whatever direction the head **f**,
40: 9 portico of the gateway **f** the temple.
40:16 the openings all round **f** inward.
40:31 Its portico **f** the outer court; palm
40:34 Its portico **f** the outer court; palm
40:37 Its portico **f** the outer court; palm
42: 2 The building whose door **f** north was
42: 3 gallery **f** gallery at the three levels
47: 1 the east (for the temple **f** east).
Ac 25:16 man before he has **f** his accusers
Ro 4:19 he **f** the fact that his body was
Heb 11:36 Some **f** jeers and flogging, while

Faces (Face)

Ge 9:23 Their **f** were turned the other way so
40: 7 "Why are your **f** so sad today?
42: 6 to him with their **f** to the ground.
Nu 21:11 that **f** Moab towards the sunrise.
Jos 15: 7 which **f** the Pass of Adummim south of
Jos 18:17 continued to Geliloth, which **f** the
Jdg 13:20 fell with their **f** to the ground.
16: 3 the top of the hill that **f** Hebron.
1Sa 26: 1 hill of Hakilah, which **f** Jeshimon?"
1Ki 7: 9 a saw on their inner and outer **f**.
1Ch 12: 8 Their **f** were the **f** of lions, and
2Ch 7: 3 pavement with their **f** to the ground,
29: 6 They turned their **f** away from the
Ne 8: 6 the LORD with their **f** to the ground.
Job 40:13 shroud their **f** in the grave.
Ps 34: 5 their **f** are never covered with shame
83:16 Cover their **f** with shame so that men
Isa 3: 9 The look on their **f** testifies
3:15 and grinding the **f** of the poor?"
6: 2 With two wings they covered their **f**,
13: 8 at each other, their **f** aflame.
25: 8 will wipe away the tears from all **f**;
29:22 no longer will their **f** grow pale.
49:23 you with their **f** to the ground;
53: 3 Like one from whom men hide their **f**
Jer 2:27 their backs to me and not their **f**;
5: 3 They made their **f** harder than stone
32:33 their backs to me and not their **f**;
50: 5 to Zion and turn their **f** towards it.
51:51 insulted and shame covers our **f**,
Eze 1: 6 each of them had four **f** and four
1: 8 All four of them had **f** and wings,
1:10 Their **f** looked like this: Each of
1:11 Such were their **f**. Their wings were
1:15 each creature with its four **f**.
7:18 Their **f** will be covered with shame
8:16 LORD and their **f** towards the east,
9: 2 which **f** north, each with a deadly
10:14 Each of the cherubim had four **f**: One
10:21 Each had four **f** and four wings, and
10:22 Their **f** had the same appearance as
11: 1 the house of the LORD that **f** east.
14: 3 stumbling-blocks before their **f**.
27:35 and their **f** are distorted with fear.
40:10 and the **f** of the projecting walls on
40:14 along the **f** of the projecting walls
40:16 The **f** of the projecting walls were
40:26 on the **f** of the projecting walls
41:18 Each cherub had two **f**:
Mic 3: 7 They will all cover their **f** because
Mal 2: 3 I will spread on your **f** the offal
Mt 6:16 disfigure their **f** to show men
23:13 the kingdom of heaven in men's **f**.
Lk 24: 5 down with their **f** to the ground,
24:17 They stood still, their **f** downcast.
2Co 3:18 we, who with unveiled **f** all reflect
Rev 7:11 They fell down on their **f** before the
9: 7 gold, and their **f** resembled human **f**.
11:16 fell on their **f** and worshipped God,

Facing (Face)

Jos 8:33 **f** those who carried it—the priests,
18:14 From the hill **f** Beth Horon on the
18:16 the hill **f** the Valley of Ben Hinnom,
19:46 and Rakkon, with the area **f** Joppa.
1Sa 13:18 the Valley of Zeboim **f** the desert.
17:21 drawing up their lines **f** each other.
26: 3 on the hill of Hakilah **f** Jeshimon,
1Ki 7: 4 high in sets of three, **f** each other.
7: 5 part in sets of three, **f** each other.
7:25 three **f** north, three **f** west,
7:25 three **f** south and three **f** east.
22:35 up in his chariot **f** the Arameans.
2Ki 2: 7 **f** the place where Elijah and Elisha
2Ch 3:13 on their feet, **f** the main hall.
4: 4 three **f** north, three **f** west,
4: 4 three **f** south and three **f** east.
18:34 **f** the Arameans until evening.
Ne 3:19 from a point **f** the ascent to the
Est 5: 1 throne in the hall, **f** the entrance.
Eze 40: 6 he went to the gate **f** east. He
40: 7 **f** the temple was one rod deep.
40:14 up to the portico **f** the courtyard.
40:20 and width of the gate **f** north,
40:22 as those of the gate **f** east.
40:23 a gate to the inner court **f** the north
40:24 south side and I saw a gate **f** south.
40:27 inner court also had a gate **f** south
40:44 side of the north gate and **f** south,
40:44 side of the south gate and **f** north.
Eze 40:45 He said to me, "The room **f** south is
40:46 the room **f** north is for the priests
41:12 The building **f** the temple courtyard
41:15 **f** the courtyard at the rear of the
41:15 and the portico **f** the court,
42:13 north and south rooms **f** the temple
43: 1 brought me to the gate **f** east,
43: 4 the temple through the gate **f** east.
44: 1 the one **f** east, and it was shut.
46: 1 The gate of the inner court **f** east
46:12 gate **f** east is to be opened for him.
46:19 gate to the sacred rooms **f** north,
47: 2 outside to the outer gate **f** east,
Ac 20:23 that prison and hardships are **f** me.
27:12 **f** both south-west and north-west.

Fact (Facts)

Ge 45:26 In **f**, he is ruler of all Egypt.
47:18 "We cannot hide from our lord the **f**
2Sa 13:15 In **f**, he hated her more than he had
2Ki 8:10 to me that he will in **f** die."
Ezr 5:17 to see if King Cyrus did in **f** issue
Mk 3:27 In **f**, no-one can enter a strong
7:25 In **f**, as soon as she heard about him,
12:22 In **f**, none of the seven left any
Jn 4: 2 although in **f** it was not Jesus who
4:18 The **f** is, you have had five husbands,
9:37 in **f**, he is the one speaking with you
10: 5 will never follow a stranger; in **f**,
16: 2 in **f**, a time is coming when
18:37 In **f**, for this reason I was born,
Ac 2:32 and we are all witnesses of the **f**.
13:34 The **f** that God raised him from the
Ro 4: 2 If, in **f**, Abraham was justified by
4:19 he faced the **f** that his body was as
1Co 6: 7 The very **f** that you have lawsuits
10: 1 want you to be ignorant of the **f**,
12:18 in **f** God has arranged the parts in
15:15 him if in **f** the dead are not raised.
2Co 11:20 In **f**, you even put up with anyone
1Th 3: 4 In **f**, when we were with you, we kept
4: 1 please God, as in **f** you are living.
4:10 in **f**, you do love all the brothers
5:11 up, just as in **f** you are doing.
1Ti 5:15 Some have in **f** already turned away
2Ti 3:12 In **f**, everyone who wants to live a
Tit 1:15 In **f**, both their minds and
Heb 5:12 In **f**, though by this time you ought
9:22 In **f**, the law requires that nearly
1Jn 3: 4 the law; in **f**, sin is lawlessness.

Factions

1Ki 16:21 of Israel were split into two **f**;
2Co 12:20 jealousy, outbursts of anger, **f**,
Gal 5:20 selfish ambition, dissensions, **f**

Facts (Fact)

Ac 19:36 Therefore, since these **f** are

Fade (Faded, Fades, Fading)

Ps 109:23 I **f** away like an evening shadow; I
Isa 17: 4 that day the glory of Jacob will **f**;
Na 1: 4 and the blossoms of Lebanon **f**.
Jas 1:11 the rich man will **f** away even
1Pe 1: 4 spoil or **f**—kept in heaven for you,
5: 4 of glory that will never **f** away.

Faded (Fade)

Lev 13: 6 and if the sore has **f** and has not
13:21 not more than skin deep and has **f**,
13:26 not more than skin deep and has **f**,
13:28 not spread in the skin but has **f**,
13:56 the mildew has **f** after the article

Fades (Fade)

Ps 65: 8 where morning dawns and evening **f**
Ecc 12: 4 closed and the sound of grinding **f**;

Fading (Fade)

Pr 7: 9 at twilight, as the day was **f**, as
Isa 1:30 be like an oak with **f** leaves
28: 1 to the **f** flower, his glorious beauty,
28: 4 That **f** flower, his glorious beauty,
Jer 6: 4 alas, the daylight is **f**, and the

2Co 3: 7 of its glory, f though it was,
3:11 if what was f away came with glory,
3:13 at it while the radiance was f away.

Fail (Failed, Failing, Failings, Fails, Failure)

Lev 20: 4 and they f to put him to death,
26:15 abhor my laws and f to carry out all
Nu 15:22 if you unintentionally f to keep
32:23 "But if you f to do this, you will
2Sa 17:16 in the desert; cross over without f,
1Ki 2: 4 you will never f to have a man on
8:25 'You shall never f to have a man to
9: 5 'You shall never f to have a man on
2Ki 10:10 against the house of Ahab will f.
1Ch 28:20 He will not f you or forsake you
2Ch 6:16 'You shall never f to have a man to
7:18 f to have a man to rule over Israel.'
34:33 he lived, they did not f to follow
Ezr 6: 9 be given them daily without f,
Est 9:27 without f observe these two days
Job 11:20 the eyes of the wicked will f, and
14: 7 and its new shoots will not f.
17: 5 the eyes of his children will f.
21:10 Their bulls never f to breed; their
41:12 "I will not f to speak of his limbs,
Ps 6: 7 My eyes grow weak with sorrow; they f
69: 3 My eyes f, looking for my God.
73:26 My flesh and my heart may f, but God
89:28 my covenant with him will never f.
89:31 decrees and f to keep my commands
119:82 My eyes f, looking for your promise;
119:123 My eyes f, looking for your
Pr 15:22 Plans f for lack of counsel, but
Isa 32:10 tremble; the grape harvest will f,
33:16 supplied, and water will not f him.
51: 6 ever, my righteousness will never f.
58:11 like a spring whose waters never f.
Jer 20:11 They will f and be thoroughly
33:17 'David will never f to have a man to
33:18 who are Levites, ever f to have a
35:19 never f to have a man to serve me.'"
Lam 2:11 My eyes f from weeping, I am in
3:22 for his compassions never f.
Eze 2: 5 whether they listen or f to listen
2: 7 whether they listen or f to listen,
3:11 whether they listen or f to listen."
30: 6 fall and her proud strength will f.
47:12 not wither, nor will their fruit f.
Hos 9: 2 people; the new wine will f them.
13:15 spring will f and his well dry up.
Zep 3: 5 every new day he does not f,
Mk 8:18 eyes but f to see, and ears but f
10:30 will f to receive a hundred times as
Lk 6:42 f to see the plank in your own eye?
18:30 will f to receive many times as much
22:32 Simon, that your faith may not f.
Jn 1:20 He did not f to confess, but
Ac 5:38 is of human origin, it will f.
2Co 13: 5 of course, you f the test?

Failed (Fail)

Lev 5:16 restitution for what he has f to do
Jos 2:11 everyone's courage f because of you,
21:45 promises to the House of Israel f;
23:14 the LORD your God gave you has f.
23:14 has been fulfilled; not one has f.
Jdg 1:21 f to dislodge the Jebusites, who
8:35 They also f to show kindness to the
21: 5 has f to assemble before the LORD?
21: 5 anyone who f to assemble before the
21: 8 "Which one of the tribes of Israel f
1Sa 3:13 and he f to restrain them.
25:37 his heart f him and he became like
1Ki 8:56 Not one word has f of all the good
15: 5 had not f to keep any of the LORD's
2Ki 3:26 to the king of Edom, but they f.
Ezr 10: 8 Anyone who f to appear within three
Ne 9:17 refused to listen and f to remember
Job 32:15 no more to say; words have f them.
Ps 77: 8 Has his promise f for all time?
Lam 4:17 Moreover, our eyes f, looking in
Ro 9: 6 is not as though God's word had f.
2Co 13: 6 that we have not f the test.
2Co 13: 7 even though we may seem to have f.
Jas 5: 4 The wages you f to pay the workmen

Failing (Fail)

Ge 48:10 Now Israel's eyes were f because of
Dt 8:11 f to observe his commands, his laws
1Sa 12:23 the LORD by f to pray for you.

Failings (Fail)

Ro 15: 1 to bear with the f of the weak

Fails (Fail)

Ex 21:33 digs one and f to cover it and an
Nu 9:13 journey f to celebrate the Passover,
19:13 f to purify himself defiles the LORD'
2Ki 10:19 Anyone who f to come will no longer
Ps 31:10 strength f because of my affliction,
38:10 My heart pounds, my strength f me;
40:12 my head, and my heart f within me.
143: 7 me quickly, O LORD; my spirit f.
Pr 8:36 whoever f to find me harms himself;
Ecc 6: 6 over but f to enjoy his prosperity.
Isa 65:20 he who f to reach a hundred will be
Jer 14: 6 eyesight f for lack of pasture."
15:18 brook, like a spring that f?
17: 8 drought and never f to bear fruit."
Joel 1:10 the new wine is dried up, the oil f.
Hab 3:17 though the olive crop f and the
1Co 13: 8 Love never f. But where there are

Failure (Fail)

1Th 2: 1 that our visit to you was not a f.

Faint (Fainted, Faint-hearted, Fainting, Faints)

1Sa 14:28 today!' That is why the men are f."
Job 23:16 God has made my heart f; the
26:14 how f the whisper we hear of him!
Ps 6: 2 Be merciful to me, LORD, for I am f;
61: 2 I call as my heart grows f; lead me
77: 3 I mused, and my spirit grew f.
102: T When he is f and pours out his
142: 3 my spirit grows f within me, it is
143: 4 my spirit grows f within me; my
Ecc 12: 4 birds, but all their songs grow f;
SS 2: 5 with apples, for I am f with love.
5: 8 tell him? Tell him I am f with love.
Isa 15: 4 Moab cry out, and their hearts are f.
29: 8 he awakens f, with his thirst
40:31 weary, they will walk and not be f.
44:12 he drinks no water and grows f.
57:10 your strength, and so you did not f.
57:16 spirit of man would grow f before me
Jer 8:18 in sorrow, my heart is f within me.
15: 9 The mother of seven will grow f and
31:25 the weary and satisfy the f."
Lam 1:13 me desolate, f all the day long.
1:22 My groans are many and my heart is f.
2:11 infants f in the streets of the city
2:12 they f like wounded men in the
2:19 who f from hunger at the head of
5:17 of this our hearts are f; because of
Eze 21: 7 every spirit will become f and every
Am 8:13 young men will f because of thirst.
Jnh 4: 8 on Jonah's head so that he grew f.
Lk 21:26 Men will f from terror, apprehensive

Fainted (Faint)

Isa 51:20 Your sons have f; they lie at the

Faint-hearted (Faint, Heart)

Dt 20: 3 Do not be f or afraid; do not be
20: 8 "Is any man afraid or f? Let him go

Fainting (Faint)

Jer 4:31 "Alas! I am f; my life is given over

Faints (Faint)

Ps 84: 2 My soul yearns, even f, for the
119:81 My soul f with longing for your

Fair (Fairly, Fairness)

Jdg 9:16 and if you have been f to Jerub-Baal
Job 26:13 By his breath the skies became f;
Pr 1: 3 doing what is right and just and f;
2: 9 and just and f—every good path.
SS 6:10 f as the moon, bright as the sun,
Hos 10:11 so I will put a yoke on her f neck.
Mt 16: 2 be f weather, for the sky is red,'
2Co 6:13 a f exchange—I speak as to my
Col 4: 1 slaves with what is right and f,

Fair Havens

Ac 27: 8 called F, near the town of Lasea.

Fairly (Fair)

Lev 19:15 great, but judge your neighbour f.
Dt 1:16 between your brothers and judge f,
16:18 and they shall judge the people f.
Pr 31: 9 Speak up and judge f; defend the
Eze 18: 8 and judges f between man and man.

Fairness (Fair)

Pr 29:14 If a king judges the poor with f,

Faith (*By faith*, Faithful, Faithfully, Faithfulness, *Great faith*, *Little faith*, *Live by faith*)

Ex 21: 8 because he has broken f with her.
Dt 32:51 This is because both of you broke f
Jos 22:16 'How could you break f with the God
Jdg 9:16 acted honourably and in good f
9:19 in good f towards Jerub-Baal and his
1Sa 14:33 "You have broken f," he said. "Roll
2Ch 20:20 Have f in the LORD your God and you
20:20 have f in his prophets and you will
Isa 7: 9 If you do not stand firm in your f,
26: 2 may enter, the nation that keeps f.
Hab 2: 4 the righteous will live by his f—
Mal 2:10 by breaking f with one another?
2:11 Judah has broken f. A detestable
2:14 because you have broken f with her,
2:15 do not break f with the wife of
2:16 in your spirit, and do not break f.
Mt 9: 2 When Jesus saw their f, he said to
9:22 he said, "your f has healed you.
9:29 According to your f will it be done
13:58 there because of their lack of f.
17:20 have f as small as a mustard seed,
21:21 if you have f and do not doubt,
24:10 time many will turn away from the f
Mk 2: 5 Jesus saw their f, he said to the
4:40 so afraid? Do you still have no f?"
5:34 "Daughter, your f has healed you.
6: 6 he was amazed at their lack of f.
10:52 "Go," said Jesus, "your f has healed
11:22 "Have f in God," Jesus answered.
16:14 he rebuked them for their lack of f
Lk 5:20 Jesus saw their f, he said, "Friend,
7:50 Jesus said to the woman, "Your f has
8:25 "Where is your f?" he asked his
8:48 "Daughter, your f has healed you.
17: 5 said to the Lord, "Increase our f!"
17: 6 have f as small as a mustard seed,
17:19 go; your f has made you well."
18: 8 comes, will he find f on the earth?"
18:42 your sight; your f has healed you."
22:32 Simon, that your f may not fail.
Jn 2:11 his disciples put their f in him.
7:31 many in the crowd put their f in him
8:30 as he spoke, many put their f in him
11:45 what Jesus did, put their f in him.
12:11 to Jesus and putting their f in him.
12:42 would not confess their f for fear
14:12 anyone who has f in me will do what
Ac 3:16 It is Jesus' name and the f that
6: 5 They chose Stephen, a man full of f
6: 7 of priests became obedient to the f.
11:24 man full of the Holy Spirit and f,
13: 8 to turn the proconsul from the f.
14: 9 saw that he had f to be healed
14:22 them to remain true to the f.
14:27 the door of f to the Gentiles.
16: 5 were strengthened in the f and grew
20:21 and have f in our Lord Jesus.

Ac 24:24 as he spoke about f in Christ Jesus.
27:25 courage, men, for I have f in God
Ro 1: 5 to the obedience that comes from f.
1: 8 because your f is being reported all
1:12 encouraged by each other's f.
3: 3 What if some did not have f? Will
3: 3 Will their lack of f nullify
3:22 comes through f in Jesus Christ to
3:25 atonement, through f in his blood.
3:26 justifies those who have f in Jesus.
3:27 the law? No, but on that of f.
3:30 uncircumcised through that same f.
3:31 then, nullify the law by this f? Not
4: 5 his f is credited as righteousness.
4: 9 Abraham's f was credited to him as
4:12 the f that our father Abraham had
4:14 f has no value and the promise is
4:16 those who are of the f of Abraham.
4:19 Without weakening in his f, he faced
4:20 was strengthened in his f and gave
5: 1 we have been justified through f,
10: 8 the word of f we are proclaiming:
10:17 Consequently, f comes from hearing
12: 3 the measure of f God has given you.
12: 6 him use it in proportion to his f.
14: 1 Accept him whose f is weak, without
14: 2 One man's f allows him to eat
14: 2 another man, whose f is weak, eats
14:23 because his eating is not from f;
14:23 that does not come from f is sin.
1Co 2: 5 that your f might not rest on men's
12: 9 to another f by the same Spirit, to
13: 2 and if I have a f that can move
13:13 now these three remain: f, hope and
15:14 is useless and so is your f.
15:17 not been raised, your f is futile;
16:13 Be on your guard; stand firm in the f
2Co 1:24 Not that we lord it over your f, but
4:13 With that same spirit of f we also
8: 7 just as you excel in everything—in f
10:15 that, as your f continues to grow,
13: 5 you are in the f; test yourselves.
Gal 1:23 the f he once tried to destroy."
2:16 So we, too, have put our f in Christ
3: 9 those who have f are blessed along
3: 9 along with Abraham, the man of f.
3:12 The law is not based on f; on the
3:22 being given through f in Jesus
3:23 Before this f came, we were held
3:23 up until f should be revealed.
3:25 Now that f has come, we are no
3:26 You are all sons of God through f in
5: 6 is f expressing itself through love.
Eph 1:15 ever since I heard about your f in
2: 8 through f—and this not from
3:12 In him and through f in him we may
3:17 may dwell in your hearts through f.
4: 5 one Lord, one f, one baptism;
4:13 until we all reach unity in the f
6:16 take up the shield of f, with which
6:23 and love with f from God the Father
Php 1:25 for your progress and joy in the f,
1:27 contending as one man for the f
2:17 and service coming from your f,
3: 9 but that which is through f in
Col 1: 4 we have heard of your f in Christ
1: 5 the f and love that spring from the
1:23 if you continue in your f,
2: 5 and how firm your f in Christ is.
2: 7 strengthened in the f as you were
2:12 through your f in the power of God,
1Th 1: 8 your f in God has become known
3: 2 and encourage you in your f,
3: 5 I sent to find out about your f.
3: 6 good news about your f and love.
3: 7 about you because of your f.
3:10 supply what is lacking in your f.
5: 8 putting on f and love as a
2Th 1: 3 your f is growing more and more,
1: 4 f in all the persecutions and trials
1:11 and every act prompted by your f.
3: 2 evil men, for not everyone has f.
1Ti 1: 2 To Timothy my true son in the f:
1: 5 a good conscience and a sincere f.
1:14 f and love that are in Christ Jesus.
1:19 holding on to f and a good
1Ti 1:19 and so have shipwrecked their f.
2: 7 of the true f to the Gentiles.
2:15 if they continue in f, love and
3: 9 of the f with a clear conscience.
3:13 assurance in their f in Christ
4: 1 later times some will abandon the f
4: 6 brought up in the truths of the f
4:12 life, in love, in f and in purity.
5: 8 has denied the f and is worse than
6:10 have wandered from the f and pierced
6:11 f, love, endurance and gentleness.
6:12 Fight the good fight of the f. Take
6:21 so doing have wandered from the f.
2Ti 1: 5 been reminded of your sincere f,
1:13 with f and love in Christ Jesus.
2:18 and they destroy the f of some.
2:22 and pursue righteousness, f, love
3: 8 as the f is concerned, are rejected.
3:10 f, patience, love, endurance,
3:15 salvation through f in Christ Jesus.
4: 7 the race, I have kept the f.
Tit 1: 1 an apostle of Jesus Christ for the f
1: 2 a f and knowledge resting on the
1: 4 To Titus, my true son in our common f
1:13 so that they will be sound in the f
2: 2 in f, in love and in endurance.
3:15 Greet those who love us in the f.
Phm : 5 I hear about your f in the Lord
: 6 you may be active in sharing your f,
Heb 4: 2 who heard did not combine it with f.
4:14 us hold firmly to the f we profess.
6: 1 that lead to death, and of f in God,
6:12 but to imitate those who through f
10:22 heart in full assurance of f,
11: 1 Now f is being sure of what we hope
11: 6 without f it is impossible to please
11: 7 By his f he condemned the world and
11:33 who through f conquered kingdoms,
11:39 These were all commended for their f,
12: 2 the author and perfecter of our f,
13: 7 way of life and imitate their f.
Jas 1: 3 you know that the testing of your f
2: 5 eyes of the world to be rich in f
2:14 if a man claims to have f but has no
2:14 has no deeds? Can such f save him?
2:17 In the same way, f by itself, if it
2:18 someone will say, "You have f; I
2:18 Show me your f without deeds, and I
2:18 I will show you my f by what I do.
2:20 that f without deeds is useless?
2:22 You see that his f and his actions
2:22 f was made complete by what he did.
2:26 is dead, so f without deeds is dead.
5:15 the prayer offered in f will make
1Pe 1: 5 who through f are shielded by God's
1: 7 These have come so that your f—of
1: 9 your f, the salvation of your souls.
1:21 and so your f and hope are in God.
5: 9 Resist him, standing firm in the f,
2Pe 1: 1 received a f as precious as ours:
1: 5 make every effort to add to your f
1Jn 5: 4 has overcome the world, even our f.
Jude : 3 urge you to contend for the f that
:20 holy f and pray in the Holy Spirit.
Rev 2:13 You did not renounce your f in me,
2:19 I know your deeds, your love and f,

Faithful (Faith, *Faithful witness*)

Nu 12: 7 Moses; he is f in all my house.
Dt 7: 9 your God is God; he is the f God,
32: 4 A f God who does no wrong, upright
1Sa 2:35 raise up for myself a f priest
2Sa 20:19 We are the peaceful and f in Israel.
22:26 "To the f you show yourself f, to
1Ki 3: 6 my father David, because he was f to
2Ch 31:18 were f in consecrating themselves.
31:20 right and f before the LORD his God.
Ne 9: 8 You found his heart f to you, and
Ps 12: 1 the f have vanished from among men.
18:25 To the f you show yourself f, to the
25:10 ways of the LORD are loving and f
31:23 saints! The LORD preserves the f,
33: 4 and true; he is f in all he does.
37:28 and will not forsake his f ones.
78: 8 God, whose spirits were not f to him.
Ps 78:37 they were not f to his covenant.
89:19 to your f people you said: "I have
89:24 My f love will be with him, and
97:10 he guards the lives of his f ones
101: 6 My eyes will be on the f in the land,
111: 7 The works of his hands are f and
145:13 The LORD is f to all his promises
146: 6 the LORD, who remains f for ever.
Pr 2: 8 and protects the way of his f ones.
20: 6 love, but a f man who can find?
28:20 A f man will be richly blessed, but
31:26 f instruction is on her tongue
Isa 1:21 See how the f city has become a
1:26 City of Righteousness, the F City."
49: 7 because of the LORD, who is f, the
55: 3 you, my f love promised to David.
Eze 43:11 so that they may be f to its design
48:11 the Zadokites, who were f in serving
Hos 11:12 God, even against the f Holy One.
Zec 8: 8 I will be f and righteous to them
Mt 24:45 "Who then is the f and wise servant,
25:21 good and f servant! You have been f
25:23 good and f servant! You have been f
Lk 12:42 "Who then is the f and wise manager
Ro 12:12 patient in affliction, f in prayer.
1Co 1: 9 his Son Jesus Christ our Lord, is f.
4: 2 been given a trust must prove f.
4:17 whom I love, who is f in the Lord.
10:13 And God is f; he will not let you be
2Co 1:18 as surely as God is f, our message
Eph 1: 1 in Ephesus, the f in Christ Jesus:
6:21 Tychicus, the dear brother and f
Col 1: 2 To the holy and f brothers in Christ
1: 7 f minister of Christ on our behalf,
4: 7 He is a dear brother, a f minister
4: 9 Onesimus, our f and dear brother,
1Th 5:24 The one who calls you is f and he
2Th 3: 3 the Lord is f, and he will
1Ti 1:12 he considered me f, appointing me
5: 9 sixty, has been f to her husband,
2Ti 2:13 if we are faithless, he will remain f
Heb 2:17 a merciful and f high priest in
3: 2 He was f to the one who appointed
3: 2 as Moses was f in all God's house.
3: 5 Moses was f as a servant in all
3: 6 Christ is f as a son over God's
8: 9 did not remain f to my covenant,
10:23 profess, for he who promised is f.
11:11 him f who had made the promise.
1Pe 4:19 commit themselves to their f Creator
5:12 whom I regard as a f brother, I have
1Jn 1: 9 If we confess our sins, he is f and
3Jn : 5 Dear friend, you are f in what you
Rev 2:10 Be f, even to the point of death,
3:14 the f and true witness, the ruler of
14:12 commandments and remain f to Jesus.
17:14 his called, chosen and f followers."
19:11 whose rider is called F and True.

Faithful witness

Ps 89:37 like the moon, the f in the sky.
Jer 42: 5 "May the LORD be a true and f
Rev 1: 5 from Jesus Christ, who is the f, the
2:13 even in the days of Antipas, my f,

Faithfully (Faith)

Dt 11:13 if you f obey the commands I am
Jos 2:14 we will treat you kindly and f when
1Sa 12:24 and serve him f with all your heart;
1Ki 2: 4 and if they walk f before me with
2Ki 20: 3 how I have walked before you f and
22: 7 to them, because they are acting f."
2Ch 19: 9 "You must serve f and wholeheartedly
31:12 they f brought in the contributions,
31:15 assisted him f in the towns of
32: 1 all that Hezekiah had so f done,
34:12 The men did the work f. Over them to
Ne 9:33 have acted f, while we did wrong.
13:14 do not blot out what I have so f
Isa 38: 3 how I have walked before you f and
Jer 23:28 the one who has my word speak it f.
Eze 18: 9 He follows my decrees and f keeps my
44:15 who f carried out the duties of
1Pe 4:10 f administering God's grace in its

Faithfulness (Faith)

Ge 24:27 his kindness and f to my master.
24:49 Now if you will show kindness and f
32:10 and f you have shown your servant.
47:29 you will show me kindness and f.
Ex 34: 6 to anger, abounding in love and f,
Jos 24:14 the LORD and serve him with all f.
1Sa 26:23 man for his righteousness and f.
2Sa 2: 6 LORD now show you kindness and f,
15:20 May kindness and f be with you."
Ps 30: 9 praise you? Will it proclaim your f?
36: 5 to the heavens, your f to the skies.
40:10 I speak of your f and salvation.
54: 5 slander me; in your f destroy them.
57: 3 God sends his love and his f.
57:10 your f reaches to the skies.
61: 7 your love and f to protect him.
71:22 praise you with the harp for your f,
85:10 Love and f meet together;
85:11 F springs forth from the earth, and
86:15 to anger, abounding in love and f.
88:11 in the grave, your f in Destruction?
89: 1 I will make your f known through
89: 2 established your f in heaven itself.
89: 5 O LORD, your f too, in the assembly
89: 8 O LORD, and your f surrounds you.
89:14 throne; love and f go before you.
89:33 him, nor will I ever betray my f.
89:49 which in your f you swore to David?
91: 4 f will be your shield and rampart.
92: 2 in the morning and your f at night,
98: 3 He has remembered his love and his f
100: 5 f continues through all generations.
108: 4 your f reaches to the skies.
111: 8 and ever, done in f and uprightness.
115: 1 glory, because of your love and f.
117: 2 the f of the LORD endures for ever.
119:75 and in f you have afflicted me.
119:90 Your f continues through all
138: 2 your name for your love and your f,
143: 1 in your f and righteousness come to
Pr 3: 3 Let love and f never leave you; bind
14:22 plan what is good find love and f.
16: 6 Through love and f sin is atoned for;
20:28 Love and f keep a king safe; through
Isa 11: 5 and f the sash round his waist.
16: 5 in f a man will sit on it—one from
25: 1 for in perfect f you have done
38:18 to the pit cannot hope for your f.
38:19 tell their children about your f.
42: 3 In f he will bring forth justice;
61: 8 In my f I will reward them and make
Lam 3:23 new every morning; great is your f.
Hos 2:20 I will betroth you in f, and you
4: 1 "There is no f, no love, no
Mt 23:23 of the law—justice, mercy and f.
Ro 3: 3 their lack of faith nullify God's f?
Gal 5:22 patience, kindness, goodness, f,
3Jn : 3 tell about your f to the truth and
Rev 13:10 and f on the part of the saints.

Faithless

Ps 78:57 f, as unreliable as a faulty bow.
101: 3 The deeds of f men I hate; they
119:158 I look on the f with loathing, for
Pr 14:14 The f will be fully repaid for their
Jer 3: 6 "Have you seen what f Israel has
3: 8 I gave f Israel her certificate of
3:11 The LORD said to me, "F Israel is
3:12 "'Return, f Israel,' declares the
3:14 "Return, f people," declares the
3:22 "Return, f people; I will cure you
12: 1 Why do all the f live at ease?
Ro 1:31 they are senseless, f, heartless,
2Ti 2:13 if we are f, he will remain faithful,

Falcon (Falcon's, Falcons)

Dt 14:13 kite, the black kite, any kind of f,

Falcon's (Falcon)

Job 28: 7 hidden path, no f eye has seen it.

Falcons (Falcon)

Isa 34:15 f will gather, each with its mate.

Fall (Downfall, Fallen, Falling, Falls, Fell, Felled, Felling)

Ge 2:21 the LORD God caused the man to f
9: 2 The fear and dread of you will f
27:13 him, "My son, let the curse f on me.
Ex 9:19 because the hail will f on every man
9:22 hail will f all over Egypt—on men
15:16 terror and dread will f upon them.
Lev 26: 7 they will f by the sword before you.
26: 8 will f by the sword before you.
26:36 and they will f, even though no-one
Nu 1:53 not f on the Israelite community.
14: 3 land only to let us f by the sword?
14:29 In this desert your bodies will f
14:32 your bodies will f in this desert.
14:43 you and you will f by the sword."
18: 5 will not f on the Israelites again.
Dt 28:52 walls in which you trust f down.
29:20 in this book will f upon him,
31:29 In days to come, disaster will f
32: 2 Let my teaching f like rain and my
Jos 9:20 so that wrath will not f on us for
Jdg 15:18 die of thirst and f into the hands
1Sa 3:19 none of his words f to the ground.
14:45 not a hair of his head shall f to
18:25 f by the hands of the Philistines.
26:20 Now do not let my blood f to the
2Sa 3:29 May his blood f upon the head of
14:11 son's head will f to the ground."
17:12 and we will f on him as dew settles
24:14 Let us f into the hands of the LORD,
24:14 not let me f into the hands of men."
24:17 your hand f upon me and my family."
1Ki 1:52 not a hair of his head will f to the
2Ki 6: 6 The man of God asked, "Where did it f
9:18 "F in behind me." The lookout
9:19 to do with peace? F in behind me."
1Ch 21:13 Let me f into the hands of the LORD,
21:13 not let me f into the hands of men."
21:17 let your hand f upon me and my
2Ch 34:11 of Judah had allowed to f into ruin.
Est 8: 6 For how can I bear to see disaster f
Job 13:11 Would not the dread of him f on you?
31:22 let my arm f from the shoulder, let
36:28 and abundant showers f on mankind.
37: 6 He says to the snow, 'F on the earth,
Ps 10:10 collapse; they f under his strength.
13: 4 and my foes will rejoice when I f.
20: 8 They are brought to their knees and f
27: 2 attack me, they will stumble and f.
35: 8 they f into the pit, to their ruin.
37:24 though he stumble, he will not f,
38:17 For I am about to f, and my pain is
45: 5 let the nations f beneath your feet.
46: 2 f into the heart of the sea,
46: 5 God is within her, she will not f;
46: 6 Nations are in uproar, kingdoms f;
55:22 he will never let the righteous f.
69: 9 of those who insult you f on me.
82: 7 you will f like every other ruler."
91: 7 A thousand may f at your side, ten
106:26 he would make them f in the desert,
106:27 make their descendants f among the
118:13 I was pushed back and about to f,
140:10 Let burning coals f upon them; may
141:10 Let the wicked f into their own nets,
145:14 The LORD upholds all those who f and
Pr 4:16 of slumber till they make someone f.
11:28 Whoever trusts in his riches will f,
16:18 a haughty spirit before a f.
22:14 the LORD's wrath will f into it.
26:27 If a man digs a pit, he will f into
28:10 evil path will f into his own trap,
28:18 ways are perverse will suddenly f.
Ecc 9:12 times that f unexpectedly upon them.
10: 8 Whoever digs a pit may f into it;
Isa 3:25 Your men will f by the sword, your
8:14 and a rock that makes them f.
8:15 stumble; they will f and be broken,
9: 8 against Jacob; it will f on Israel.
10: 4 the captives or f among the slain.
10:34 Lebanon will f before the Mighty One.
13:15 who are caught will f by the sword.
22:25 it will be sheared off and will f,
24:18 sound of terror will f into a pit;
28:13 that they will go and f backwards,
Isa 30:25 when the towers f, streams of water
31: 3 he who is helped will f; both will
31: 8 "Assyria will f by a sword that is
31: 9 Their stronghold will f because of
34: 4 f like withered leaves from the vine,
34: 7 the wild oxen will f with them, the
40: 7 The grass withers and the flowers f,
40: 8 The grass withers and the flowers f,
40:30 weary, and young men stumble and f;
47:11 A calamity will f upon you that you
51:23 'F prostrate that we may walk over
Jer 6:15 So they will f among the fallen;
8: 4 "'When men f down, do they not get
8:12 So they will f among the fallen;
13:18 crowns will f from your heads."
19: 7 I will make them f by the sword
20: 4 f by the sword of their enemies.
23:12 to darkness and there they will f.
25:27 vomit, and f to rise no more
25:34 f and be shattered like fine pottery.
34:17 f by the sword, plague and famine.
39:18 you will not f by the sword but
44:12 f by the sword or die from famine.
46: 6 River Euphrates they stumble and f.
46:12 another; both will f down together."
46:16 they will f over each other.
48:16 "The f of Moab is at hand; her
48:44 "Whoever flees from the terror will f
49:21 At the sound of their f the earth
49:26 her young men will f in the streets;
50:15 towers f, her walls are torn down.
50:30 her young men will f in the streets;
50:32 The arrogant one will stumble and f
51: 4 They will f down slain in Babylon,
51: 8 Babylon will suddenly f and be
51:44 And the wall of Babylon will f.
51:49 "Babylon must f because of Israel's
51:64 And her people will f.'" The words
Lam 1: 9 Her f was astounding; there was none
Eze 5:12 a third will f by the sword outside
6: 7 Your people will f slain among you,
6:11 f by the sword, famine and plague.
6:12 that is near will f by the sword
11:10 You will f by the sword, and I will
13:11 whitewash that it is going to f.
13:13 rain will f with destructive fury.
13:21 will no longer f prey to your power.
17:21 fleeing troops will f by the sword
23:25 who are left will f by the sword.
24:21 you left behind will f by the sword.
25:13 to Dedan they will f by the sword.
26:11 strong pillars will f to the ground.
26:15 tremble at the sound of your f,
26:18 tremble on the day of your f;
28:23 The slain will f within her, with
29: 5 You will f on the open field and not
30: 4 When the slain f in Egypt, her
30: 5 f by the sword along with Egypt.
30: 6 The allies of Egypt will f and her
30: 6 From Migdol to Aswan they will f by
30:17 and Bubastis will f by the sword,
30:22 and make the sword f from his hand.
30:25 but the arms of Pharaoh will f limp.
31:16 tremble at the sound of its f
32:12 I will cause your hordes to f by the
32:20 They will f among those killed by
33:12 him to f when he turns from it.
33:27 in the ruins will f by the sword,
35: 8 by the sword will f on your hills
36:15 or cause your nation to f, declares
38:20 and every wall will f to the ground.
39: 4 On the mountains of Israel you will f
39: 5 You will f in the open field, for I
40: 1 year after the f of the city—on
44:12 made the house of Israel f into sin,
Da 3: 5 you must f down and worship the
3: 6 Whoever does not f down and worship
3:10 f down and worship the image of gold,
3:11 that whoever does not f down and
3:15 if you are ready to f down and
11:19 stumble and f, to be seen no more.
11:26 away, and many will f in battle.
11:33 for a time they will f by the sword
11:34 When they f, they will receive a
11:41 Many countries will f, but Edom,
Hos 7: 7 All their kings f, and none of them

Hos 7:16 Their leaders will f by the sword
10: 8 and to the hills, "F on us!"
13:16 They will f by the sword; their
Am 3: 5 Does a bird f into a trap on the
3:14 will be cut off and f to the ground.
7:17 and daughters will f by the sword.
8:14 they will f, never to rise again."
Na 3:12 figs f into the mouth of the eater.
3:19 about you claps his hands at your f,
Hag 2:22 horses and their riders will f,
Mt 7:25 that house; yet it did not f,
10:29 Yet not one of them will f to the
11: 6 who does not f away on account of me
15:14 blind man, both will f into a pit."
15:27 that f from their masters' table."
24:29 the stars will f from the sky,
26:31 "This very night you will all f away
26:33 Peter replied, "Even if all f away
26:41 that you will not f into temptation.
Mk 4:17 of the word, they quickly f away.
13:25 the stars will f from the sky, and
14:27 "You will all f away," Jesus told
14:29 Peter declared, "Even if all f away,
14:38 Watch and pray so that you will not f
Lk 6:39 Will they not both f into a pit?
7:23 who does not f away on account of me
8:13 in the time of testing they f away.
10:18 "I saw Satan f like lightning
11:17 house divided against itself will f.
21:24 They will f by the sword and will be
22:40 you will not f into temptation."
22:46 you will not f into temptation."
23:30 will say to the mountains, "F on us!
Ac 5:15 Peter's shadow might f on some of
27:32 held the lifeboat and let it f away.
28: 6 him to swell up or suddenly f dead,
Ro 3:23 for all have sinned and f short of
9:33 and a rock that makes them f,
11:11 stumble so as to f beyond recovery?
14:21 that will cause your brother to f.
1Co 8:13 eat causes my brother to f into sin,
8:13 so that I will not cause him to f.
10:12 firm, be careful that you don't f!
14:25 So he will f down and worship God,
1Th 4:13 ignorant about those who f asleep,
1Ti 3: 6 may become conceited and f under
3: 7 so that he will not f into disgrace
6: 9 People who want to get rich f into
Heb 4:11 so that no-one will f by following
6: 6 if they f away, to be brought back
10:31 is a dreadful thing to f into the
1Pe 1:24 the grass withers and the flowers f,
2: 8 to stumble a rock that makes them f.
2Pe 1:10 do these things, you will never f,
3:17 men and f from your secure position.
Rev 3: 9 f down at your feet and acknowledge
4:10 the twenty-four elders f down before
6:16 "F on us and hide us from the face

Fallen (Fall)

Ge 15:17 the sun had set and darkness had f,
Ex 9:18 hailstorm that has ever f on Egypt,
23: 5 who hates you f down under its load,
Lev 19:10 or pick up the grapes that have f.
Dt 22: 4 ox f on the road, do not ignore it.
29:22 calamities that have f on the land
Jos 2: 9 a great fear of you has f on us,
Jdg 3:25 saw their lord f to the floor, dead.
8:10 and twenty thousand swordsmen had f.
19:27 his concubine, f in the doorway
1Sa 5: 3 there was Dagon, f on his face on
5: 4 there was Dagon, f on his face on
20:37 place where Jonathan's arrow had f,
31: 8 his three sons f on Mount Gilboa.
2Sa 1:10 after he had f he could not survive.
1:12 because they had f by the sword.
1:19 How the mighty have f!
1:25 "How the mighty have f in battle!
1:27 "How the mighty have f! The weapons
2:23 place where Asahel had f and died.
3:38 great man has f in Israel this day?
2Ki 1: 2 Now Ahaziah had f through the
1:14 See, fire has f from heaven and
2:13 He picked up the cloak that had f
2:14 took the cloak that had f from him
1Ch 10: 8 Saul and his sons f on Mount Gilboa.
2Ch 14:14 terror of the LORD had f upon them.
29: 8 the anger of the LORD has f on Judah
29: 9 our fathers have f by the sword
Ps 9:15 The nations have f into the pit they
16: 6 The boundary lines have f for me in
36:12 See how the evildoers lie f—thrown
57: 6 but they have f into it themselves.
68:14 land, it was like snow f on Zalmon.
105:38 dread of Israel had f on them.
Pr 6: 3 have f into your neighbour's hands:
Isa 9:10 "The bricks have f down, but we will
14:12 How you have f from heaven,
21: 9 'Babylon has f, has f! All the
Jer 3: 3 and no spring rains have f.
6:15 So they will fall among the f; they
8:12 So they will fall among the f; they
48:32 The destroyer has f on your ripened
51:47 her slain will all lie f within her.
51:49 the earth have f because of Babylon.
Lam 2:21 men and maidens have f by the sword.
5:16 The crown has f from our head. Woe
Eze 21:15 hearts may melt and the f be many
31:13 of the air settled on the f tree,
32:22 slain, all who have f by the sword.
32:23 living are slain, f by the sword.
32:24 are slain, f by the sword. All
32:27 uncircumcised warriors who have f,
33:21 to me and said, "The city has f!
Am 5: 2 "F is Virgin Israel, never to rise
9:11 I will restore David's f tent.
Mic 7: 8 enemy! Though I have f, I will rise.
Zec 11: 2 O pine tree, for the cedar has f;
Jn 11:11 "Our friend Lazarus has f asleep;
Ac 15:16 return and rebuild David's f tent.
Ro 15: 3 those who insult you have f on me."
1Co 11:30 and a number of you have f asleep.
15: 6 living, though some have f asleep.
15:18 those also who have f asleep in
15:20 of those who have f asleep.
Gal 5: 4 Christ; you have f away from grace.
1Th 4:14 Jesus those who have f asleep in him.
4:15 not precede those who have f asleep.
Heb 4: 1 you be found to have f short of it.
Rev 2: 5 the height from which you have f!
9: 1 had f from the sky to the earth.
14: 8 "F! F is Babylon the Great, which
17:10 Five have f, one is, the other has
18: 2 shouted: "F! F is Babylon the Great!

Falling (Fall)

Ge 8: 2 the rain had stopped f from the sky.
Est 7: 8 Haman was f on the couch where
8: 3 pleaded with the king, f at his feet
Ps 72: 6 be like rain f on a mown field
133: 3 dew of Hermon were f on Mount Zion
Isa 3: 8 Jerusalem staggers, Judah is f;
Mk 15:19 F on their knees, they paid homage
Lk 2:34 the f and rising of many in Israel,
22:44 like drops of blood f to the ground.
Heb 6: 7 Land that drinks in the rain often f
Jude :24 To him who is able to keep you from f

Falls (Fall)

Ex 21:33 it and an ox or a donkey f into it,
Lev 11:32 one of them dies and f on something,
11:33 If one of them f into a clay pot,
11:35 carcasses f on becomes unclean;
11:37 If a carcass f on any seeds that are
11:38 a carcass f on it, it is unclean
16: 9 the goat whose lot f to the LORD
Nu 24: 4 who f prostrate, and whose eyes are
24:16 who f prostrate, and whose eyes are
33:54 Whatever f to them by lot will be
Dt 20:20 until the city at war with you f.
22: 8 house if someone f from the roof.
2Sa 3:29 on a crutch or who f by the sword
3:34 You fell as one f before wicked men."
Job 4:13 the night, when deep sleep f on men,
9:24 a land f into the hands of the
18:12 disaster is ready for him when he f.
33:15 when deep sleep f on men as they
Ps 7:15 it out f into the pit he has made.
Pr 11:14 For lack of guidance a nation f, but
Pr 13:17 A wicked messenger f into trouble,
17:20 tongue is deceitful f into trouble.
24:16 for though a righteous man f seven
24:17 Do not gloat when your enemy f; when
28:14 hardens his heart f into trouble.
Ecc 4:10 If one f down, his friend can help
4:10 pity the man who f and has no-one
11: 3 Whether a tree f to the south or to
11: 3 place where it f, there will it lie.
Isa 24:20 that it f—never to rise again.
Eze 13:14 When it f, you will be destroyed in
Mt 12:11 a sheep and it f into a pit on
13:21 of the word, he quickly f away.
17:15 f into the fire or into the water.
21:44 He who f on this stone will be
21:44 he on whom it f will be crushed."
Lk 14: 5 f into a well on the Sabbath day,
20:18 Everyone who f on that stone will be
20:18 he on whom it f will be crushed."
Jn 12:24 unless a grain of wheat f to the
Ro 14: 4 To his own master he stands or f.
Jas 1:11 its blossom f and its beauty is

False (*False prophet, False prophets, False testimony, False witness,* Falsehood, Falsely)

Ex 23: 1 "Do not spread f reports. Do not
23: 7 Have nothing to do with a f charge
Job 24:25 who can prove me f and reduce my
36: 4 Be assured that my words are not f;
41: 9 Any hope of subduing him is f; the
Ps 4: 2 love delusions and seek f gods?
24: 4 to an idol or swear by what is f.
27:12 for f witnesses rise up against me,
35:20 but devise f accusations against
40: 4 to those who turn aside to f gods.
44:17 you or been f to your covenant.
Pr 13: 5 The righteous hate what is f, but
Isa 41:29 See, they are all f! Their deeds
57:11 feared that you have been f to me,
63: 8 sons who will not be f to me"; and
Jer 13:25 forgotten me and trusted in f gods.
14:14 prophesying to you f visions,
16:19 fathers possessed nothing but f gods
23:16 to you; they fill you with f hopes.
23:32 against those who prophesy f dreams,"
Lam 2:14 The visions of your prophets were f
2:14 they gave you were f and misleading.
Eze 12:24 For there will be no more f visions
13: 6 Their visions are f and their
13: 7 Have you not seen f visions and
13: 8 of your f words and lying visions,
13: 9 the prophets who see f visions
13:23 you will no longer see f visions
21:23 will seem like a f omen to those who
21:29 Despite f visions concerning you and
22:28 by f visions and lying divinations.
Hos 10: 4 make many promises, take f oaths
Am 2: 4 have been led astray by f gods,
Mic 6:11 scales, with a bag of f weights?
Hab 2: 3 of the end and will not prove f.
Zec 10: 2 they tell dreams that are f, they
Mal 2: 6 and nothing f was found on his lips.
Mt 24:24 For f Christs and f prophets will
26:59 looking for f evidence against Jesus
26:60 many f witnesses came forward.
Mk 13:22 For f Christs and f prophets will
Jn 1:47 in whom there is nothing f."
7:18 truth; there is nothing f about him.
Ac 6:13 They produced f witnesses, who
1Co 15:15 we are then found to be f witnesses
2Co 11:13 For such men are f apostles,
11:26 sea; and in danger from f brothers.
Gal 2: 4 some f brothers had infiltrated our
Php 1:18 whether from f motives or true,
Col 2:18 anyone who delights in f humility
2:23 their f humility and their harsh
1Ti 1: 3 not to teach f doctrines any
6: 3 If anyone teaches f doctrines and
2Pe 2: 1 there will be f teachers among you.
Rev 2: 2 but are not, and have found them f.

False prophet

Ac 13: 6 sorcerer and f named Bar-Jesus,
Rev 16:13 beast and out of the mouth of the f.

Rev 19:20 and with him the **f** who had performed
20:10 the beast and the **f** had been thrown.

False prophets

Isa 44:25 who foils the signs of **f** and makes
Jer 50:36 A sword against her **f**! They will
Mt 7:15 "Watch out for **f**. They come to you
24:11 many **f** will appear and deceive many
24:24 For false Christs and **f** will appear
Mk 13:22 For false Christs and **f** will appear
Lk 6:26 is how their fathers treated the **f**.
2Pe 2: 1 there were also **f** among the people,
1Jn 4: 1 many **f** have gone out into the world.

False testimony

Ex 20:16 "You shall not give **f** against your
Dt 5:20 "You shall not give **f** against your
19:18 liar, giving **f** against his brother,
Pr 25:18 who gives **f** against his neighbour.
Isa 29:21 with **f** deprive the innocent of
Mt 15:19 immorality, theft, **f**, slander.
19:18 do not steal, do not give **f**,
Mk 10:19 do not steal, do not give **f**, do not
14:57 some stood up and gave this **f**
Lk 18:20 do not give **f**, honour your father

False witness

Pr 6:19 a **f** who pours out lies and a man who
12:17 testimony, but a **f** tells lies.
14: 5 not deceive, but a **f** pours out lies.
14:25 saves lives, but a **f** is deceitful.
19: 5 A **f** will not go unpunished, and he
19: 9 A **f** will not go unpunished, and he
21:28 A **f** will perish, and whoever listens

Falsehood (False)

Job 21:34 is left of your answers but **f**!"
31: 5 "If I have walked in **f** or my foot
Ps 52: 3 evil rather than good, **f** rather
119:163 I hate and abhor **f** but I love your
Pr 30: 8 Keep **f** and lies far from me; give me
Isa 28:15 our refuge and **f** our hiding-place."
Ro 3: 7 might argue, "If my **f** enhances
Eph 4:25 Therefore each of you must put off **f**
1Jn 4: 6 Spirit of truth and the spirit of **f**.
Rev 22:15 everyone who loves and practises **f**.

Falsely (False)

Ge 21:23 that you will not deal **f** with me
Lev 6: 3 or if he swears **f**, or if he commits
6: 5 or whatever it was he swore **f** about.
19:12 "'Do not swear **f** by my name and so
Ps 41: 6 he speaks **f**, while his heart gathers
101: 7 speaks **f** will stand in my presence.
Jer 5: 2 lives,' still they are swearing **f**."
8: 8 pen of the scribes has handled it **f**?
Da 6:24 the men who had **f** accused Daniel
Zec 5: 3 who swears **f** will be banished.
5: 4 of him who swears **f** by my name.
8:17 and do not love to swear **f**.
Mt 5:11 persecute you and **f** say all kinds of
Mk 14:56 Many testified **f** against him, but
Lk 3:14 don't accuse people **f**—be content
1Ti 6:20 ideas of what is **f** called knowledge,

Falter (Faltered, Faltering, Falters)

Pr 24:10 If you **f** in times of trouble, how
Isa 42: 4 he will not **f** or be discouraged till

Faltered (Falter)

Ps 105:37 from among their tribes no-one **f**.

Faltering (Falter)

Ex 6:12 to me, since I speak with **f** lips?"
6:30 "Since I speak with **f** lips, why
Job 4: 4 you have strengthened **f** knees.

Falters (Falter)

Isa 21: 4 My heart **f**, fear makes me tremble;

Fame (Famous)

Dt 26:19 he will set you in praise, **f** and
Jos 6:27 was with Joshua, and his **f** spread
9: 9 of the **f** of the LORD your God.
1Ki 4:31 And his **f** spread to all the
10: 1 Sheba heard about the **f** of Solomon
1Ch 14:17 David's **f** spread throughout every
22: 5 **f** and splendour in the sight of all
2Ch 9: 1 queen of Sheba heard of Solomon's **f**,
26: 8 and his **f** spread as far as the
26:15 His **f** spread far and wide, for he
Isa 66:19 not heard of my **f** or seen my glory.
Jer 48:17 all who know her **f**; say, 'How broken
Eze 16:14 your **f** spread among the nations on
16:15 used your **f** to become a prostitute.
Hos 14: 7 his **f** will be like the wine from
Hab 3: 2 LORD, I have heard of your **f**; I

Familiar

Ps 139: 3 down; you are **f** with all my ways.
Isa 53: 3 of sorrows, and **f** with suffering.
Ac 26:26 The king is **f** with these things, and

Families (Family)

Ge 45:18 bring your father and your **f** back to
Ex 1:21 God, he gave them **f** of their own.
6:14 These were the heads of their **f**: The
6:25 heads of the Levite **f**, clan by clan.
12:21 select the animals for your **f** and
Nu 1: 2 community by their clans and **f**,
1:18 their ancestry by their clans and **f**,
1:20 to the records of their clans and **f**.
1:22 to the records of their clans and **f**.
1:24 to the records of their clans and **f**.
1:26 to the records of their clans and **f**.
1:28 to the records of their clans and **f**.
1:30 to the records of their clans and **f**.
1:32 to the records of their clans and **f**.
1:34 to the records of their clans and **f**.
1:36 to the records of their clans and **f**.
1:38 to the records of their clans and **f**.
1:40 to the records of their clans and **f**.
1:42 to the records of their clans and **f**.
1:45 were counted according to their **f**.
1:47 The **f** of the tribe of Levi, however,
2:32 counted according to their **f**.
3:15 "Count the Levites by their **f** and
3:20 Levite clans, according to their **f**.
3:24 leader of the **f** of the Gershonites
3:30 The leader of the **f** of the Kohathite
3:35 The leader of the **f** of the Merarite
4: 2 of the Levites by their clans and **f**.
4:22 Gershonites by their **f** and clans.
4:29 the Merarites by their clans and **f**.
4:34 the Kohathites by their clans and **f**.
4:38 were counted by their clans and **f**.
4:40 counted by their clans and **f**, were
4:42 were counted by their clans and **f**.
4:46 the Levites by their clans and **f**.
7: 2 leaders of Israel, the heads of **f**
26: 2 the whole Israelite community by **f**
34:14 the **f** of the tribe of Reuben, the
36: 1 the heads of the Israelite **f**.
Dt 12: 7 you and your **f** shall eat and shall
Jos 7:17 forward by **f**, and Zimri was taken.
21: 1 of the other tribal **f** of Israel
2Sa 15:22 men and the **f** that were with him.
1Ki 8: 1 and the chiefs of the Israelite **f**,
2Ki 10:13 come down to greet the **f** of the king
1Ch 4:38 Their **f** increased greatly,
5:13 Their relatives, by **f**, were: Michael,
5:24 These were the heads of their **f**:
5:24 famous men, and heads of their **f**.
7: 2 Ibsam and Samuel—heads of their **f**.
7: 7 and Iri, heads of **f**—five in all.
7: 9 heads of **f** and 20,200 fighting men.
7:11 sons of Jediael were heads of **f**.
7:40 descendants of Asher—heads of **f**,
8: 6 who were heads of **f** of those living
8:10 These were his sons, heads of **f**.
8:13 Beriah and Shema, who were heads of **f**
8:28 All these were heads of **f**, chiefs as
9: 9 All these men were heads of their **f**.
9:13 The priests, who were heads of **f**,
9:33 heads of Levite **f**, stayed in the
9:34 All these were heads of Levite **f**,
12:39 their **f** had supplied provisions for
15:12 You are the heads of the Levitical **f**;
16:28 Ascribe to the LORD, O **f** of nations,
23: 9 were the heads of the **f** of Ladan.
23:24 the descendants of Levi by their **f**
23:24 the heads of **f** as they were
24: 4 sixteen heads of **f** from Eleazar's
24: 4 eight heads of **f** from Ithamar's
24: 6 the heads of **f** of the priests and of
24:30 the Levites, according to their **f**.
24:31 heads of **f** of the priests and of the
24:31 The **f** of the oldest brother were
26:13 to their **f**, young and old alike.
26:21 heads of **f** belonging to Ladan the
26:26 by the heads of **f** who were the
26:31 the genealogical records of their **f**.
26:32 who were able men and heads of **f**,
27: 1 list of the Israelites—heads of **f**,
29: 6 the leaders of **f**, the officers of
2Ch 1: 2 leaders in Israel, the heads of **f**—
5: 2 and the chiefs of the Israelite **f**,
17:14 Their enrolment by **f** was as follows:
19: 8 priests and heads of Israelite **f** to
23: 2 of Israelite **f** from all the towns.
25: 5 assigned them according to their **f**
31:17 their **f** in the genealogical records
35: 4 Prepare yourselves by **f** in your
35: 5 of the **f** of your fellow countrymen,
35:12 subdivisions of the **f** of the people
Ezr 2:59 their **f** were descended from Israel:
2:68 some of the heads of the **f** gave
4: 2 and to the heads of the **f** and said,
4: 3 heads of the **f** of Israel answered,
Ne 4:13 posting them by **f**, with their swords,
7: 5 common people for registration by **f**.
7:61 their **f** were descended from Israel:
7:70 the heads of the **f** contributed to
7:71 Some of the heads of the **f** gave to
8:13 the heads of all the **f**, along with
10:34 when each of our **f** is to bring to
11:13 his associates, who were heads of **f**—
12:12 the priestly **f**: of Seraiah's family,
Ps 22:27 and all the **f** of the nations will
68: 6 God sets the lonely in **f**, he leads
96: 7 Ascribe to the LORD, O **f** of nations,
107:41 and increased their **f** like flocks.
Am 3: 2 chosen of all the **f** of the earth;

Family (Families)

Ge 7: 1 you and your whole **f**, because I have
16: 2 perhaps I can build a **f** through her.
19:32 our **f** line through our father."
19:34 our **f** line through our father."
24:38 go to my father's **f** and to my own
24:40 my own clan and from my father's **f**.
30: 3 through her I too can build a **f**."
43: 7 closely about ourselves and our **f**.
46:27 the members of Jacob's **f**, which went
50:22 Egypt, along with all his father's **f**.
Ex 1: 1 Egypt with Jacob, each with his **f**:
12: 3 for his **f**, one for each household.
Lev 6:29 Any male in a priest's **f** may eat it;
7: 6 Any male in a priest's **f** may eat it,
20: 5 his **f** and will cut off from their
22:10 No-one outside a priest's **f** may eat
25:10 is to return to his **f** property and
27:16 to the LORD part of his **f** land,
27:22 which is not part of his **f** land,
27:28 or **f** land—may be sold or redeemed;
Nu 1: 4 the head of his **f**, is to help you.
1:44 Israel, each one representing his **f**.
2: 2 standard with the banners of his **f**."
2:34 set out, each with his clan and **f**.
3: 1 the account of the **f** of Aaron
11:10 Moses heard the people of every **f**
18: 1 "You, your sons and your father's **f**
25: 6 brought to his **f** a Midianite woman
25:14 Salu, the leader of a Simeonite **f**.
25:15 Zur, a tribal chief of a Midianite **f**.
31:26 Eleazar the priest and the **f** heads
32:28 the **f** heads of the Israelite tribes.
36: 1 The **f** heads of the clan of Gilead
Dt 15:16 and your **f** and is well off with you,
15:20 Each year you and your **f** are to eat
18: 8 from the sale of **f** possessions.
25: 5 widow must not marry outside the **f**.
25: 9 not build up his brother's **f** line."

Dt 25:10 Israel as The **F** of the Unsandalled.
Jos 2:12 that you will show kindness to my **f**,
2:18 and all your **f** into your house.
6:23 They brought out her entire **f** and
6:25 with her **f** and all who belonged to
7:14 LORD takes shall come forward **f** by **f**;
7:14 and the **f** that the LORD takes shall
7:18 Joshua had his **f** come forward man by
13:29 half the **f** of the descendants of
21: 1 Now the **f** heads of the Levites
22:14 each the head of a **f** division among
Jdg 1:25 but spared the man and his whole **f**.
6:15 and I am the least in my **f**."
6:27 But because he was afraid of his **f**
8:27 became a snare to Gideon and his **f**.
8:35 to the **f** of Jerub-Baal (that is,
9:16 been fair to Jerub-Baal and his **f**,
9:18 have revolted against my father's **f**,
9:19 towards Jerub-Baal and his **f** today,
11: 2 to get any inheritance in our **f**,"
16:31 his brothers and his father's whole **f**
18:25 and your **f** will lose your lives."
Ru 4:10 will not disappear from among his **f**
4:12 may your **f** be like that of Perez,
4:18 This, then, is the **f** line of Perez:
1Sa 1:21 Elkanah went up with all his **f** to
2:31 not be an old man in your **f**
2:32 in your **f** line there will never be
2:36 everyone left in your **f** line will
3:12 everything I spoke against his **f**
3:13 would judge his **f** for ever because
9:20 not to you and all your father's **f**?"
17:25 exempt his father's **f** from taxes
18:18 "Who am I, and what is my **f** or my
20:15 cut off your kindness from my **f**
20:29 our **f** is observing a sacrifice in
22:11 of Ahitub and his father's whole **f**,
22:15 servant or any of his father's **f**,
22:16 you and your father's whole **f**."
22:22 the death of your father's whole **f**.
24:21 out my name from my father's **f**."
27: 3 Each man had his **f** with him, and
2Sa 2: 3 each with his **f**, and they settled in
3: 8 Saul and to his **f** and friends.
7:18 what is my **f**, that you have brought
9: 9 that belonged to Saul and his **f**.
14: 9 rest on me and on my father's **f**,
16: 5 as Saul's **f** came out from there.
21: 4 silver or gold from Saul or his **f**,
24:17 Let your hand fall upon me and my **f**."
1Ki 14:14 who will cut off the **f** of Jeroboam.
15:29 reign, he killed Jeroboam's whole **f**.
16:11 he killed off Baasha's whole **f**.
16:12 destroyed the whole **f** of Baasha,
17:15 Elijah and for the woman and her **f**.
18:18 "But you and your father's **f** have.
2Ki 8: 1 "Go away with your **f** and stay for a
8: 2 She and her **f** went away and stayed
8:27 was related by marriage to Ahab's **f**.
10:17 of Ahab's **f**; he destroyed them,
11: 1 to destroy the whole royal **f**.
1Ch 5:15 son of Guni, was head of their **f**.
7: 4 According to their **f** genealogy, they
7:23 there had been misfortune in his **f**.
9:19 his fellow gatekeepers from his **f**
12:27 Jehoiada, leader of the **f** of Aaron
12:28 with 22 officers from his **f**;
13:14 remained with the **f** of Obed-Edom
16:43 David returned home to bless his **f**.
17:16 what is my **f**, that you have brought
21:17 let your hand fall upon me and my **f**,
23:11 as one **f** with one assignment.
24: 6 of the Levites—one **f** being taken
26: 6 leaders in their father's **f** because
27:15 Netophathite, from the **f** of Othniel.
28: 4 chose me from my whole **f** to be king
28: 4 the house of Judah he chose my **f**,
2Ch 22:10 whole royal **f** of the house of Judah.
26:12 The total number of **f** leaders over
31:10 chief priest, from the **f** of Zadok,
Ezr 1: 5 the **f** heads of Judah and Benjamin,
2:36 Jedaiah (through the **f** of Jeshua) 973
2:62 These searched for their **f** records,
3:12 priests and Levites and **f** heads,
8: 1 These are the **f** heads and those
8:29 Levites and the **f** heads of Israel."
Ezr 10:16 selected men who were **f** heads,
10:16 one from each **f** division, and all of
Ne 7:39 Jedaiah (through the **f** of Jeshua) 973
7:64 These searched for their **f** records,
12:12 of Seraiah's **f**, Meraiah; of
12:22 The **f** heads of the Levites in the
12:23 The **f** heads among the descendants of
Est 2:10 her nationality and **f** background,
2:20 Esther had kept secret her **f**
4:14 you and your father's **f** will perish.
8: 6 to see the destruction of my **f**?"
9:28 in every generation by every **f**,
Job 21:21 care about the **f** he leaves behind
32: 2 of the **f** of Ram, became very angry
Pr 11:29 He who brings trouble on his **f** will
15:27 A greedy man brings trouble to his **f**,
27:27 milk to feed you and your **f** and to
31:15 she provides food for her **f** and
Isa 22:24 All the glory of his **f** will hang on
Jer 12: 6 Your brothers, your own **f**—even
35: 2 "Go to the Recabite **f** and invite
35: 3 sons—the whole **f** of the Recabites.
35: 5 the men of the Recabite **f** and said
35:18 Jeremiah said to the **f** of the
38:17 down; you and your **f** will live.
Eze 17:13 he took a member of the royal **f** and
43:19 who are Levites, of the **f** of Zadok,
Da 1: 3 from the royal **f** and the nobility—
11: 7 "One from her **f** line will arise to
Am 3: 1 whole **f** I brought up out of Egypt:
Mk 3:21 his **f** heard about this, they went to
5:19 "Go home to your **f** and tell them how
Lk 9:61 go back and say good-bye to my **f**."
12:52 in one **f** divided against each other,
Jn 7:42 from David's **f** and from Bethlehem,
8:35 has no permanent place in the **f**,
Ac 4: 6 other men of the high priest's **f**.
7:13 Pharaoh learned about Joseph's **f**.
7:14 his whole **f**, seventy-five in all.
10: 2 He and all his **f** were devout and
16:33 he and all his **f** were baptised.
16:34 believe in God—he and his whole **f**.
Gal 6:10 who belong to the **f** of believers.
Eph 3:15 from whom his whole **f** in heaven and
1Ti 3: 4 He must manage his own **f** well and
3: 5 not know how to manage his own **f**,
5: 4 practice by caring for their own **f**
5: 8 and especially for his immediate **f**,
5:16 is a believer has widows in her **f**,
Heb 2:11 who are made holy are of the same **f**.
11: 7 fear built an ark to save his **f**.
1Pe 4:17 judgment to begin with the **f** of God

Famine (Famines)

Ge 12:10 Now there was a **f** in the land, and
12:10 a while because the **f** was severe.
26: 1 Now there was a **f** in the land
26: 1 the earlier **f** of Abraham's time
41:27 wind: They are seven years of **f**.
41:30 seven years of **f** will follow them.
41:30 and the **f** will ravage the land.
41:31 **f** that follows it will be so severe.
41:36 years of **f** that will come upon Egypt
41:36 country may not be ruined by the **f**."
41:50 Before the years of **f** came, two sons
41:54 the seven years of **f** began, just as
41:54 There was **f** in all the other lands,
41:55 all Egypt began to feel the **f**, the
41:56 the **f** had spread over the whole
41:56 the **f** was severe throughout Egypt.
41:57 the **f** was severe in all the world.
42: 5 **f** was in the land of Canaan also.
43: 1 Now the **f** was still severe in the
45: 6 For two years now there has been **f**
45:11 five years of **f** are still to come.
47: 4 because the **f** is severe in Canaan
47:13 region because the **f** was severe;
47:13 Canaan wasted away because of the **f**.
47:20 the **f** was too severe for them.
Dt 32:24 I will send wasting **f** against them,
Ru 1: 1 there was a **f** in the land, and a man
2Sa 21: 1 there was a **f** for three successive
24:13 you three years of **f** in your land?
1Ki 8:37 "When **f** or plague comes to the land,
18: 2 Now the **f** was severe in Samaria,
2Ki 4:38 and there was a **f** in that region.
6:25 There was a great **f** in the city; the
7: 4 **f** is there, and we will die.
8: 1 the LORD has decreed a **f** in the land
25: 3 the **f** in the city had become so
1Ch 21:12 three years of **f**, three months of
2Ch 6:28 "When **f** or plague comes to the land,
20: 9 or plague or **f**, we will stand in
Ne 5: 3 homes to get grain during the **f**."
Job 5:20 In **f** he will ransom you from death,
5:22 You will laugh at destruction and **f**,
Ps 33:19 from death and keep them alive in **f**.
37:19 in days of **f** they will enjoy plenty.
105:16 He called down **f** on the land and
Isa 14:30 But your root I will destroy by **f**;
51:19 ruin and destruction, **f** and sword
Jer 5:12 to us; we will never see sword or **f**.
11:22 their sons and daughters by **f**.
14:12 them with the sword, **f** and plague."
14:13 will not see the sword or suffer **f**.
14:15 'No sword or **f** will touch this land.
14:15 prophets will perish by sword and **f**.
14:16 Jerusalem because of the **f** and sword.
14:18 the city, I see the ravages of **f**.
16: 4 They will perish by sword and **f**, and
18:21 give their children over to **f**; hand
21: 7 sword and **f**, to Nebuchadnezzar king
21: 9 will die by the sword, **f** or plague.
24:10 I will send the sword, **f** and plague
27: 8 that nation with the sword, **f** and
27:13 die by the sword, **f** and plague with
29:17 "I will send the sword, **f** and plague
29:18 I will pursue them with the sword, **f**
32:24 Because of the sword, **f** and plague,
32:36 'By the sword, **f** and plague it will
34:17 to fall by the sword, plague and **f**.
38: 2 will die by the sword, **f** or plague,
42:16 and the **f** you dread will follow you
42:17 will die by the sword, **f** and plague;
42:22 will die by the sword, **f** and plague
44:12 fall by the sword or die from **f**.
44:12 they will die by sword or **f**.
44:13 with the sword, **f** and plague, as I
44:18 have been perishing by sword and **f**."
44:27 and **f** until they are all destroyed.
52: 6 **f** in the city had become so severe
Lam 4: 9 who die of **f**; racked with hunger,
Eze 5:12 plague or perish by **f** inside you;
5:16 deadly and destructive arrows of **f**,
5:16 I will bring more and more **f** upon
5:17 I will send **f** and wild beasts
6:11 fall by the sword, **f** and plague.
6:12 and is spared will die of **f**.
7:15 inside are plague and **f**; those in
7:15 will be devoured by **f** and plague.
12:16 a few of them from the sword, **f** and
14:13 send **f** upon it and kill its men and
14:21 dreadful judgments—sword and **f** and
34:29 they will no longer be victims of **f**
36:29 and will not bring **f** upon you.
36:30 among the nations because of **f**.
Am 8:11 "when I will send a **f** through the
8:11 a **f** of food or a thirst for water,
8:11 **f** of hearing the words of the LORD.
Lk 4:25 was a severe **f** throughout the land.
15:14 there was a severe **f** in that whole
Ac 7:11 "Then a **f** struck all Egypt and
11:28 predicted that a severe **f** would
Ro 8:35 **f** or nakedness or danger or sword?
Rev 6: 8 to kill by sword, **f** and plague, and
18: 8 overtake her: death, mourning and **f**.

Famines (Famine)

Mt 24: 7 **f** and earthquakes in various places.
Mk 13: 8 in various places, and **f**.
Lk 21:11 There will be great earthquakes, **f**

Famished

Ge 25:29 came in from the open country, **f**.
25:30 have some of that red stew! I'm **f**!"
Isa 8:21 through the land; when they are **f**,

Famous (Fame)

Ru 4:11 in Ephrathah and be **f** in Bethlehem.
4:14 May he become **f** throughout Israel!

2Sa 8:13 David became **f** after he returned
23:18 and so he became as **f** as the Three.
23:22 was as **f** as the three mighty men.
1Ki 1:47 Solomon's name more **f** than yours
1Ch 5:24 They were brave warriors, **f** men,
11:20 and so he became as **f** as the Three.
11:24 was as **f** as the three mighty men.
12:30 men of Ephraim, brave warriors, **f** in
Isa 66:19 Libyans and Lydians (**f** as archers)

Fan (Fans)
2Ti 1: 6 **f** into flame the gift of God, which

Fangs
Dt 32:24 against them the **f** of wild beasts,
Job 20:16 the **f** of an adder will kill him.
29:17 I broke the **f** of the wicked and
Ps 58: 6 out, O LORD, the **f** of the lions!
Joel 1: 6 teeth of a lion, the **f** of a lioness.

Fans (Fan)
Isa 54:16 who **f** the coals into flame

Fantasies
Ps 73:20 O Lord, you will despise them as **f**.
Pr 12:11 but he who chases **f** lacks judgment.
28:19 the one who chases **f** will have his

Fare (Fared)
Isa 55: 2 will delight in the richest of **f**.
Jnh 1: 3 After paying the **f**, he went aboard

Fared (Fare)
Ge 30:29 your livestock has **f** under my care.
Isa 10: 9 'Has not Calno **f** like Carchemish? Is

Farewell
Ac 15:29 do well to avoid these things. **F**.

Farm (Farmed, Farmer, Farmers)
2Sa 9:10 and your servants are to **f** the land
2Ch 31:19 who lived on the **f** lands around
Eze 48:19 The workers from the city who **f** it

Farmed (Farm)
1Ch 27:26 of the field workers who **f** the land.
Heb 6: 7 useful to those for whom it is **f**

Farmer (Farm)
Isa 28:24 When a **f** ploughs for planting, does
Jer 51:23 with you I shatter **f** and oxen, with
Zec 13: 5 I am a **f**; the land has been my
Mt 13: 3 "A **f** went out to sow his seed.
Mk 4: 3 "Listen! A **f** went out to sow his
4:14 The **f** sows the word.
Lk 8: 5 "A **f** went out to sow his seed. As he
2Ti 2: 6 The hardworking **f** should be the
Jas 5: 7 See how the **f** waits for the land to

Farmers (Farm)
Jer 14: 4 **f** are dismayed and cover their heads.
31: 5 the **f** will plant them and enjoy
31:24 **f** and those who move about with
Joel 1:11 Despair, you **f**, wail, you vine
Am 5:16 The **f** will be summoned to weep and
Mt 21:33 he rented the vineyard to some **f**
Mk 12: 1 he rented the vineyard to some **f**
Lk 20: 9 rented it to some **f** and went away

Fashion (Fashioned, Fashioning, Fashions)
Ex 28:15 "**F** a breastpiece for making

Fashioned (Fashion)
Ex 39: 8 They **f** the breastpiece—the work of
2Ki 19:18 wood and stone, **f** by men's hands.
Isa 37:19 wood and stone, **f** by human hands.
45:18 God; he who **f** and made the earth
Hos 13: 2 cleverly **f** images, all of them the

Fashioning (Fashion)
Ex 32: 4 shape of a calf, **f** it with a tool.

Fashions (Fashion)
Job 15:35 birth to evil; their womb **f** deceit."
Isa 40:19 gold and **f** silver chains for it.
44:15 But he also **f** a god and worships it;

Fast[1]
Dt 4: 4 all of you who held **f** to the LORD
10:20 Hold **f** to him and take your oaths in
11:22 all his ways and to hold **f** to him—
13: 4 him; serve him and hold **f** to him.
30:20 to his voice, and hold **f** to him.
Jos 22: 5 obey his commands, to hold **f** to him
23: 8 you are to hold **f** to the LORD your
Jdg 4:21 while he lay **f** asleep, exhausted.
1Ki 11: 2 Solomon held **f** to them in love.
2Ki 18: 6 He held **f** to the LORD and did not
Est 8:10 who rode **f** horses especially bred
Job 18: 9 by the heel; a snare holds him **f**.
36: 8 bound in chains, held **f** by cords
41:17 They are joined **f** to one another;
Ps 119:31 I hold **f** to your statutes, O LORD;
139:10 me, your right hand will hold me **f**.
Pr 5:22 the cords of his sin hold him **f**.
Isa 56: 2 the man who holds it **f**, who keeps
56: 4 me and hold **f** to my covenant—
56: 6 it and who hold **f** to my covenant—
Jer 50:33 their captors hold them **f**, refusing
Ac 27:41 The bow stuck **f** and would not move,
1Pe 5:12 grace of God. Stand **f** in it.

Fast[2] (Fasted, Fasting, Fasts)
2Sa 12:23 now that he is dead, why should I **f**?
1Ki 21:12 They proclaimed a **f** and seated
2Ch 20: 3 and he proclaimed a **f** for all Judah.
Ezr 8:21 I proclaimed a **f**, so that we might
Est 4:16 Jews who are in Susa, and **f** for me.
4:16 I and my maids will **f** as you do.
Ps 69:10 I weep and **f**, I must endure scorn;
Isa 58: 4 You cannot **f** as you do today and
58: 5 Is this the kind of **f** I have chosen,
58: 5 Is that what you call a **f**, a day
Jer 14:12 Although they **f**, I will not listen
Joel 1:14 Declare a holy **f**; call a sacred
2:15 a holy **f**, call a sacred assembly.
Jnh 3: 5 They declared a **f**, and all of them,
Zec 7: 3 "Should I mourn and **f** in the fifth
Mt 6:16 "When you **f**, do not look sombre as
6:17 when you **f**, put oil on your head and
9:14 we and the Pharisees **f**, but your
9:14 but your disciples do not **f**?"
9:15 taken from them; then they will **f**.
Mk 2:19 bridegroom **f** while he is with them?
2:20 them, and on that day they will **f**.
Lk 5:33 "John's disciples often **f** and pray,
5:34 bridegroom **f** while he is with them?
5:35 them; in those days they will **f**."
18:12 I **f** twice a week and give a tenth of
Ac 27: 9 because by now it was after the **F**.

Fasted (Fast[2])
Jdg 20:26 They **f** that day until evening and
1Sa 7: 6 On that day they **f** and there they
31:13 at Jabesh, and they **f** seven days.
2Sa 1:12 They mourned and wept and **f** till
12:16 He **f** and went into his house and
12:21 you **f** and wept, but now that the
12:22 child was still alive, I **f** and wept.
1Ki 21:27 his clothes, put on sackcloth and **f**.
1Ch 10:12 in Jabesh, and they **f** seven days.
Ezr 8:23 we **f** and petitioned our God about
Ne 1: 4 For some days I mourned and **f** and
Isa 58: 3 'Why have we **f**,' they say, 'and you
Zec 7: 5 'When you **f** and mourned in the fifth
7: 5 was it really for me that you **f**?
Ac 13: 3 after they had **f** and prayed, they

Fasten (Fastened, Fastens)
Ex 25:12 Cast four gold rings for it and **f**
25:26 and **f** them to the four corners,
26: 6 use them to **f** the curtains together
26:11 to **f** the tent together as a unit.
28:12 **f** them on the shoulder pieces of the
28:23 Make two gold rings for it and **f**
28:24 **F** the two gold chains to the rings
28:37 **F** a blue cord to it to attach it to
29: 5 **F** the ephod on him by its skilfully
36:13 used them to **f** the two sets of
36:18 They made fifty bronze clasps to **f**
Job 13:27 You **f** my feet in shackles; you keep
Pr 6:21 for ever; **f** them around your neck.
Isa 22:21 **f** your sash around him and hand your
Jer 10: 4 they **f** it with hammer and nails so

Fastened (Fasten)
Ex 28: 7 of its corners, so that it can be **f**.
37: 3 He cast four gold rings for it and **f**
37:13 and **f** them to the four corners,
39: 4 its corners, so that it could be **f**.
39: 7 they **f** them on the shoulder pieces
39:16 and **f** the rings to two of the
39:17 They **f** the two gold chains to the
39:31 they **f** a blue cord to it to attach
Lev 8: 7 woven waistband; so it was **f** on him.
Nu 19:15 open container without a lid **f** on it
Jdg 15: 4 **f** a torch to every pair of tails,
1Sa 17:39 David **f** on his sword over the tunic
31:10 **f** his body to the wall of Beth Shan.
Est 1: 6 **f** with cords of white linen and
Eze 24:17 Keep your turban **f** and your sandals
Lk 4:20 in the synagogue were **f** on him,
Jn 19:19 Pilate had a notice prepared and **f**
Ac 16:24 cell and **f** their feet in the stocks.
28: 3 by the heat, **f** itself on his hand.

Fastens (Fasten)
Job 16: 9 opponent **f** on me his piercing eyes.
33:11 He **f** my feet in shackles; he keeps

Fasting (Fast[2])
1Ki 21: 9 "Proclaim a day of **f** and seat Naboth
Ne 9: 1 gathered together, **f** and wearing
Est 4: 3 Jews, with **f**, weeping and wailing.
9:31 to their times of **f** and lamentation.
Ps 35:13 sackcloth and humbled myself with **f**.
109:24 My knees give way from **f**; my body is
Isa 58: 3 "Yet on the day of your **f**, you do as
58: 4 Your **f** ends in quarrelling and
58: 6 "Is not this the kind of **f** I have
Jer 36: 6 the house of the LORD on a day of **f**
36: 9 a time of **f** before the LORD was
Da 9: 3 in **f**, and in sackcloth and ashes.
Joel 2:12 with **f** and weeping and mourning."
Mt 4: 2 After **f** for forty days and forty
6:16 their faces to show men they are **f**.
6:18 be obvious to men that you are **f**,
Mk 2:18 disciples and the Pharisees were **f**.
2:18 Pharisees are **f**, but yours are not?"
Lk 2:37 night and day, **f** and praying.
Ac 13: 2 were worshipping the Lord and **f**,
14:23 with prayer and **f**, committed them to

Fasts (Fast[2])
Zec 8:19 "The **f** of the fourth, fifth, seventh

Fat (Fattened, Fattening)
Ge 4: 4 Abel brought **f** portions from some of
41: 2 came up seven cows, sleek and **f**,
41: 4 ate up the seven sleek, **f** cows.
41:18 cows, **f** and sleek, and they grazed
41:20 the seven **f** cows that came up first.
45:18 you can enjoy the **f** of the land.'
Ex 23:18 "The **f** of my festival offerings must
29:13 take all the **f** around the inner
29:13 and both kidneys with the **f** on them,
29:22 the **f**, the **f** tail, the **f** around the
Lev 1: 8 including the head and the **f**, on the
1:12 including the head and the **f**, on the
3: 3 all the **f** that covers the inner
3: 4 both kidneys with the **f** on them near
3: 9 its **f**, the entire **f** tail cut off close
3: 9 all the **f** that covers the inner
3:10 both kidneys with the **f** on them near
3:14 all the **f** that covers the inner
3:15 both kidneys with the **f** on them near
3:16 All the **f** is the LORD's.

Lev 3:17 must not eat any **f** or any blood."
4: 8 He shall remove all the **f** from the
4: 8 the **f** that covers the inner parts or
4: 9 both kidneys with the **f** on them near
4:10 just as the **f** is removed from the ox
4:19 He shall remove all the **f** from it
4:26 He shall burn all the **f** on the altar
4:26 the **f** of the fellowship offering.
4:31 He shall remove all the **f**, just as
4:31 just as the **f** is removed from the
4:35 He shall remove all the **f**, just as
4:35 just as the **f** is removed from the
6:12 the **f** of the fellowship offerings
7: 3 All its **f** shall be offered:
7: 3 the **f** tail and the **f** that covers
7: 4 both kidneys with the **f** on them near
7:23 Do not eat any of the **f** of cattle,
7:24 The **f** of an animal found dead or
7:25 Anyone who eats the **f** of an animal
7:30 bring the **f**, together with the
7:31 The priest shall burn the **f** on the
7:33 the **f** of the fellowship offering
8:16 Moses also took all the **f** around the
8:16 kidneys and their **f**, and burned it
8:20 the head, the pieces and the **f**.
8:25 the **f**, the **f** tail, all the **f** around
8:25 both kidneys and their **f** and the
8:26 he put these on the **f** portions
9:10 On the altar he burned the **f**, the
9:19 the **f** portions of the ox and the ram
9:19 the **f** tail, the layer of **f**, the
9:20 Aaron burned the **f** on the altar.
9:24 and the **f** portions on the altar.
10:15 the **f** portions of the offerings
16:25 burn the **f** of the sin offering
17: 6 burn the **f** as an aroma pleasing to
Nu 18:17 burn their **f** as an offering made by
Dt 32:15 Jeshurun grew **f** and kicked; filled
32:38 the gods who ate the **f** of their
Jdg 3:17 king of Moab, who was a very **f** man.
3:22 out, and the **f** closed in over it.
1Sa 2:15 even before the **f** was burned, the
2:16 said to him, "Let the **f** be burned
15: 9 the **f** calves and lambs—everything
15:22 heed is better than the **f** of rams.
1Ki 8:64 the **f** of the fellowship offerings,
8:64 the **f** of the fellowship offerings.
2Ch 7: 7 the **f** of the fellowship offerings,
7: 7 grain offerings and the **f** portions.
29:35 the **f** of the fellowship offerings,
35:14 and the **f** portions until nightfall.
Job 15:27 "Though his face is covered with **f**
Ps 66:15 I will sacrifice **f** animals to you
Isa 1:11 rams and the **f** of fattened animals
10:27 broken because you have grown so **f**.
17: 4 the **f** of his body will waste away.
34: 6 it is covered with **f**—the blood of
34: 6 goats, **f** from the kidneys of rams.
34: 7 and the dust will be soaked with **f**.
43:24 on me the **f** of your sacrifices.
Jer 5:28 have grown **f** and sleek. Their evil
Eze 34:20 the **f** sheep and the lean sheep.
39:19 you will eat **f** till you are glutted
44: 7 you offered me food, **f** and blood,
44:15 to offer sacrifices of **f** and blood,

Fatal

Jer 42:20 that you made a **f** mistake when you
Na 3:19 heal your wound; your injury is **f**.
Rev 13: 3 beast seemed to have had a **f** wound,
13: 3 but the **f** wound had been healed.
13:12 whose **f** wound had been healed.

Fate

Est 7: 7 the king had already decided his **f**,
Job 12: 5 as the **f** of those whose feet are
18:20 Men of the west are appalled at his **f**
20:29 Such is the **f** God allots the wicked,
21:17 them, the **f** God allots in his anger?
27:13 "Here is the **f** God allots to the
27:14 their **f** is the sword; his offspring
Ps 49:13 This is the **f** of those who trust in
Ecc 2:14 that the same **f** overtakes them both.
2:15 The **f** of the fool will overtake me
3:19 Man's **f** is like that of the animals;
Ecc 3:19 the same **f** awaits them both: As
Isa 14:16 stare at you, they ponder your **f**:

Father (*Father Abraham, Father David, Father in heaven*, Father's, Fathered, Father-in-law, Fathers, Fathers', Forefather, Forefather's, Forefathers, *God of your father, God our Father, God the Father*, Grandfather, Grandfather's, *Heavenly Father*)

Ge 2:24 this reason a man will leave his **f**
4:18 and Irad was the **f** of Mehujael, and
4:18 and Mehujael was the **f** of Methushael,
4:18 and Methushael was the **f** of Lamech.
4:20 he was the **f** of those who live in
4:21 **f** of all who play the harp and flute.
5: 6 105 years, he became the **f** of Enosh.
5: 7 after he became the **f** of Enosh, Seth
5: 9 90 years, he became the **f** of Kenan.
5:10 after he became the **f** of Kenan,
5:12 years, he became the **f** of Mahalalel.
5:13 after he became the **f** of Mahalalel,
5:15 65 years, he became the **f** of Jared.
5:16 after he became the **f** of Jared,
5:18 162 years, he became the **f** of Enoch.
5:19 after he became the **f** of Enoch,
5:21 he became the **f** of Methuselah.
5:22 after he became the **f** of Methuselah,
5:25 years, he became the **f** of Lamech.
5:26 after he became the **f** of Lamech,
5:32 the **f** of Shem, Ham and Japheth.
9:18 (Ham was the **f** of Canaan.)
9:22 Ham, the **f** of Canaan, saw his
10: 8 Cush was the **f** of Nimrod, who grew
10:13 Mizraim was the **f** of the Ludites,
10:15 Canaan was the **f** of Sidon his
10:24 Arphaxad was the **f** of Shelah, and
10:24 of Shelah, and Shelah the **f** of Eber.
10:26 Joktan was the **f** of Almodad, Sheleph,
11:10 old, he became the **f** of Arphaxad.
11:11 after he became the **f** of Arphaxad,
11:12 35 years, he became the **f** of Shelah.
11:13 after he became the **f** of Shelah,
11:14 30 years, he became the **f** of Eber.
11:15 after he became the **f** of Eber,
11:16 34 years, he became the **f** of Peleg.
11:17 after he became the **f** of Peleg, Eber
11:18 30 years, he became the **f** of Reu.
11:19 after he became the **f** of Reu, Peleg
11:20 32 years, he became the **f** of Serug.
11:21 after he became the **f** of Serug, Reu
11:22 30 years, he became the **f** of Nahor.
11:23 after he became the **f** of Nahor,
11:24 29 years, he became the **f** of Terah.
11:25 after he became the **f** of Terah,
11:26 the **f** of Abram, Nahor and Haran.
11:27 Terah became the **f** of Abram, Nahor
11:27 And Haran became the **f** of Lot.
11:28 While his **f** Terah was still alive,
11:29 the **f** of both Milcah and Iscah.
17: 4 You will be the **f** of many nations.
17: 5 I have made you a **f** of many nations.
17:20 He will be the **f** of twelve rulers,
19:31 "Our **f** is old, and there is no man
19:32 Let's get our **f** to drink wine and
19:32 our family line through our **f**."
19:33 That night they got their **f** to drink
19:34 "Last night I lay with my **f**.
19:34 our family line through our **f**."
19:35 they got their **f** to drink wine that
19:36 became pregnant by their **f**.
19:37 is the **f** of the Moabites of today.
19:38 is the **f** of the Ammonites of today.
20:12 the daughter of my **f** though not of
22: 7 "**F**?" "Yes, my son?" Abraham replied.
22:21 his brother, Kemuel (the **f** of Aram),
22:23 Bethuel became the **f** of Rebekah.
25: 3 Jokshan was the **f** of Sheba and Dedan;
25:19 Abraham became the **f** of Isaac,
26:18 the same names his **f** had given them.
27: 6 overheard your **f** say to your brother
27: 9 prepare some tasty food for your **f**,
27:10 take it to your **f** to eat, so that he
27:12 What if my **f** touches me? I would
27:14 food, just the way his **f** liked it.
Ge 27:18 He went to his **f** and said, "My **f**."
27:19 Jacob said to his **f**, "I am Esau your
27:22 Jacob went close to his **f** Isaac, who
27:26 his **f** Isaac said to him, "Come here,
27:31 tasty food and brought it to his **f**.
27:31 Then he said to him, "My **f**, sit up
27:32 His **f** Isaac asked him, "Who are you?"
27:34 and bitter cry and said to his **f**,
27:34 "Bless me—me too, my **f**!
27:38 Esau said to his **f**, "Do you have
27:38 "Do you have only one blessing, my **f**?
27:38 me too, my **f**!" Then Esau wept aloud.
27:39 His **f** Isaac answered him, "Your
27:41 of the blessing his **f** had given him.
27:41 "The days of mourning for my **f** are
28: 2 house of your mother's **f** Bethuel.
28: 7 Jacob had obeyed his **f** and mother
28: 8 Canaanite women were to his **f** Isaac;
29:12 a relative of her **f** and a son of
29:12 So she ran and told her **f**.
31: 1 has taken everything our **f** owned
31: 1 wealth from what belonged to our **f**."
31: 5 the God of my **f** has been with me.
31: 6 You know that I've worked for your **f**
31: 7 yet your **f** has cheated me by
31:16 took away from our **f** belongs to us
31:18 his **f** Isaac in the land of Canaan.
31:35 Rachel said to her **f**, "Don't be
31:42 If the God of my **f**, the God of
31:53 God of their **f**, judge between us.
31:53 the name of the Fear of his **f** Isaac.
32: 9 God of my **f** Isaac, O LORD,
33:19 the **f** of Shechem, the plot of ground
34: 4 Shechem said to his **f** Hamor, "Get me
34: 6 Shechem's **f** Hamor went out to talk
34:11 Shechem said to Dinah's **f** and
34:13 spoke to Shechem and his **f** Hamor.
35:18 But his **f** named him Benjamin.
35:27 Jacob came home to his **f** Isaac in
36: 9 of Esau the **f** of the Edomites
36:24 grazing the donkeys of his **f** Zibeon.
36:43 This was Esau the **f** of the Edomites.
37: 1 Jacob lived in the land where his **f**
37: 2 their **f** a bad report about them.
37: 4 his brothers saw that their **f** loved
37:10 he told his **f** as well as his
37:10 his **f** rebuked him and said, "What is
37:11 but his **f** kept the matter in mind.
37:22 them and take him back to his **f**.
37:32 to their **f** and said, "We found this.
37:35 So his **f** wept for him.
42:13 The youngest is now with our **f**, and
42:29 they came to their **f** Jacob in the
42:32 were twelve brothers, sons of one **f**.
42:32 is now with our **f** in Canaan.'
42:35 and their **f** saw the money pouches,
42:36 Their **f** Jacob said to them, "You
42:37 Reuben said to his **f**, "You may put
43: 2 their **f** said to them, "Go back and
43: 7 'Is your **f** still living?' he asked
43: 8 Judah said to Israel his **f**, "Send
43:11 their **f** Israel said to them, "If it
43:27 "How is your aged **f** you told me
43:28 "Your servant our **f** is still alive
44:17 of you, go back to your **f** in peace."
44:19 'Do you have a **f** or a brother?'
44:20 we answered, 'We have an aged **f**, and
44:20 sons left, and his **f** loves him.'
44:22 'The boy cannot leave his **f**;
44:22 if he leaves him, his **f** will die.'
44:24 we went back to your servant my **f**,
44:25 "Then our **f** said, 'Go back and buy a
44:27 "Your servant my **f** said to us, 'You
44:30 to your servant my **f** and if my **f**,
44:31 our **f** down to the grave in sorrow.
44:32 guaranteed the boy's safety to my **f**.
44:32 before you, my **f**, all my life!'
44:34 How can I go back to my **f** if the boy
44:34 misery that would come upon my **f**."
45: 3 "I am Joseph! Is my **f** still living?"
45: 8 He made me **f** to Pharaoh, lord of his
45: 9 Now hurry back to my **f** and say to
45:13 Tell my **f** about all the honour
45:13 And bring my **f** down here quickly."
45:18 bring your **f** and your families back
45:19 your wives, and get your **f** and come.

Ge 45:23 this is what he sent to his **f**: ten
45:25 their **f** Jacob in the land of Canaan.
45:27 the spirit of their **f** Jacob revived.
46: 1 to the God of his **f** Isaac.
46: 5 and Israel's sons took their **f** Jacob
46:29 went to Goshen to meet his **f** Israel.
46:29 threw his arms around his **f** and wept
47: 1 Joseph went and told Pharaoh, "My **f**
47: 5 Pharaoh said to Joseph, "Your **f** and
47: 6 settle your **f** and your brothers in
47: 7 Joseph brought his **f** Jacob in and
47:11 Joseph settled his **f** and his
47:12 Joseph also provided his **f** and his
48: 1 Joseph was told, "Your **f** is ill.
48: 9 me here," Joseph said to his **f**.
48:10 his **f** kissed them and embraced them.
48:17 Joseph saw his **f** placing his right
48:18 Joseph said to him, "No, my **f**, this
48:19 his **f** refused and said, "I know, my
49: 2 of Jacob; listen to your **f** Israel.
49:28 and this is what their **f** said to
50: 1 Joseph threw himself upon his **f** and
50: 2 his service to embalm his **f** Israel.
50: 5 'My **f** made me swear an oath and said,
50: 5 and bury my **f**; then I will return.'"
50: 6 Pharaoh said, "Go up and bury your **f**,
50: 7 Joseph went up to bury his **f**. All
50:10 period of mourning for his **f**.
50:14 After burying his **f**, Joseph returned
50:14 who had gone with him to bury his **f**.
50:15 brothers saw that their **f** was dead
50:16 "Your **f** left these instructions
Ex 2:18 the girls returned to Reuel their **f**,
20:12 "Honour your **f** and your mother, so
21:15 "Anyone who attacks his **f** or his
21:17 "Anyone who curses his **f** or mother
22:17 If her **f** absolutely refuses to give
40:15 them just as you anointed their **f**,
Lev 16:32 ordained to succeed his **f** as high
18: 7 "'Do not dishonour your **f** by having
18: 8 wife; that would dishonour your **f**.
18:11 born to your **f**; she is your sister.
19: 3 must respect his mother and **f**, and
20: 9 "'If anyone curses his **f** or mother,
20: 9 He has cursed his **f** or his mother,
20:11 wife, he has dishonoured his **f**.
20:17 the daughter of either his **f** or his
20:19 of either your mother or your **f**,
21: 2 relative, such as his mother or **f**,
21: 9 a prostitute, she disgraces her **f**;
21:11 unclean, even for his **f** or mother,
24:10 mother and an Egyptian **f** went out
Nu 3: 4 the lifetime of their **f** Aaron.
6: 7 Even if his own **f** or mother or
12:14 "If her **f** had spat in her face,
26:29 Makir was the **f** of Gilead
26:60 Aaron was the **f** of Nadab and Abihu,
27: 3 "Our **f** died in the desert. He was
27:11 If his **f** had no brothers, give his
30: 4 her **f** hears about her vow or pledge
30: 5 if her **f** forbids her when he hears
30: 5 her because her **f** has forbidden her.
30:16 and between a **f** and his young
36: 6 within the tribal clan of their **f**.
Dt 1:31 as a **f** carries his son, all the way
5:16 "Honour your **f** and your mother, as
21:13 mourned her **f** and mother for a
21:18 son who does not obey his **f** and
21:19 his **f** and mother shall take hold of
22:15 the girl's **f** and mother shall bring
22:16 The girl's **f** will say to the elders,
22:19 and give them to the girl's **f**,
22:29 pay the girl's **f** fifty shekels of
26: 5 "My **f** was a wandering Aramean, and
27:16 who dishonours his **f** or his mother.
27:22 daughter of his **f** or the daughter
32: 6 Is he not your **F**, your Creator,
32: 7 Ask your **f** and he will tell you,
33: 9 He said of his **f** and mother, 'I have
Jos 2:13 spare the lives of my **f** and mother
2:18 and unless you have brought your **f**
6:23 brought out Rahab, her **f** and mother
15:18 urged him to ask her **f** for a field.
17: 4 along with the brothers of their **f**,
24: 2 including Terah the **f** of Abraham and
24:32 the sons of Hamor, the **f** of Shechem.
Jdg 1:14 urged him to ask her **f** for a field.
8:32 buried in the tomb of his **f** Joash
9:17 to think that my **f** fought for you,
9:28 the men of Hamor, Shechem's **f**!
9:56 that Abimelech had done to his **f**
11: 1 His **f** was Gilead; his mother was a
11:36 "My **f**," she replied, "you have given
11:39 she returned to her **f** and he did to
14: 2 he returned, he said to his **f** and
14: 3 His **f** and mother replied, "Isn't
14: 3 said to his **f**, "Get her for me.
14: 5 together with his **f** and mother.
14: 6 told neither his **f** nor his mother
14:10 Now his **f** went down to see the woman.
14:16 "I haven't even explained it to my **f**
15: 1 But her **f** would not let him go in.
15: 6 and burned her and her **f** to death.
16:31 Eshtaol in the tomb of Manoah his **f**.
17:10 "Live with me and be my **f** and priest,
18:19 Come with us, and be our **f** and
19: 3 when her father **f** saw him, he gladly
19: 4 His father-in-law, the girl's **f**,
19: 5 but the girl's **f** said to his
19: 6 Afterwards the girl's **f** said,
19: 8 girl's **f** said, "Refresh yourself.
19: 9 his father-in-law, the girl's **f**,
Ru 2:11 how you left your **f** and mother
4:17 was the **f** of Jesse, the **f** of David.
4:18 of Perez: Perez was the **f** of Hezron,
4:19 Hezron the **f** of Ram, Ram the **f** of
4:20 Amminadab the **f** of Nahshon, Nahshon
4:20 of Nahshon, Nahshon the **f** of Salmon,
4:21 Salmon the **f** of Boaz, Boaz the **f** of
4:22 Obed the **f** of Jesse, and Jesse the **f**
1Sa 2:28 I chose your **f** out of all the tribes
9: 3 Now the donkeys belonging to Saul's **f**
9: 5 "Come, let's go back, or my **f** will
10: 2 And now your **f** has stopped thinking
10:12 "And who is their **f**?" So it became a
14: 1 But he did not tell his **f**.
14:27 Jonathan had not heard that his **f**
14:28 told him, "Your **f** bound the army
14:29 Jonathan said, "My **f** has made
14:51 Saul's **f** Kish and Abner's **f** Ner were
19: 2 warned him, "My **f** Saul is looking
19: 3 I will go out and stand with my **f** in
19: 4 David to Saul his **f** and said to him,
20: 1 my crime? How have I wronged your **f**,
20: 2 my **f** doesn't do anything, great or
20: 3 David took an oath and said, "Your **f**
20: 6 If your **f** misses me at all, tell him,
20: 8 Why hand me over to your **f**?"
20: 9 my **f** was determined to harm you,
20:10 me if your **f** answers you harshly?"
20:12 I will surely sound out my **f** by this
20:13 if my **f** is inclined to harm you, may
20:13 with you as he has been with my **f**.
20:32 has he done?" Jonathan asked his **f**.
20:33 that his **f** intended to kill David.
22: 3 "Would you let my **f** and mother come
23:17 "My **f** Saul will not lay a hand on
23:17 Even my **f** Saul knows this."
24:11 See, my **f**, look at this piece of
2Sa 3: 8 loyal to the house of your **f** Saul
6:21 who chose me rather than your **f** or
7:14 I will be his **f**, and he shall be my
9: 7 for the sake of your **f** Jonathan.
10: 2 just as his **f** showed kindness to me.
10: 2 sympathy to Hanun concerning his **f**.
10: 3 think David is honouring your **f** by
13: 5 "When your **f** comes to see you, say
16:19 served your **f**, so I will serve you."
17: 8 You know your **f** and his men; they
17: 8 your **f** is an experienced fighter
17:10 knows that your **f** is a fighter
19:37 near the tomb of my **f** and mother.
21:14 in the tomb of Saul's **f** Kish,
1Ki 1: 6 (His **f** had never interfered with him
3:14 as David your **f** did, I will give
6:12 the promise I gave to David your **f**.
7:14 whose **f** was a man of Tyre and a
8:20 I have succeeded David my **f** and now
8:24 promise to your servant David my **f**;
8:25 keep for your servant David my **f** the
8:26 your servant David my **f** come true.
9: 4 as David your **f** did, and do all I
1Ki 9: 5 as I promised David your **f** when I
11: 4 the heart of David his **f** had been.
11: 6 completely, as David his **f** had done.
11:12 for the sake of David your **f**, I will
11:17 officials who had served his **f**.
11:27 the wall of the city of David his **f**.
11:33 and laws as David, Solomon's **f**, did.
11:43 buried in the city of David his **f**.
12: 4 "Your **f** put a heavy yoke on us, but
12: 6 his **f** Solomon during his lifetime.
12: 9 the yoke your **f** put on us'?"
12:10 'Your **f** put a heavy yoke on us, but
12:11 My **f** laid on you a heavy yoke; I
12:11 My **f** scourged you with whips; I will
12:14 "My **f** made your yoke heavy; I will
12:14 My **f** scourged you with whips; I will
13:11 told their **f** what he had said to
13:12 Their **f** asked them, "Which way did
15: 3 He committed all the sins his **f** had
15:15 that he and his **f** had dedicated.
15:19 there was between my **f** and your **f**.
15:26 walking in the ways of his **f** and in
19:20 "Let me kiss my **f** and mother
20:34 the cities my **f** took from your **f**,"
20:34 in Damascus, as my **f** did in Samaria.
22:43 he walked in the ways of his **f** Asa
22:46 even after the reign of his **f** Asa.
22:50 them in the city of David his **f**.
22:52 he walked in the ways of his **f**
22:53 to anger, just as his **f** had done.
2Ki 2:12 "My **f**! My **f**! The chariots and
3: 2 not as his **f** and mother had done.
3: 2 stone of Baal that his **f** had made.
3:13 Go to the prophets of your **f** and
4:18 to his **f**, who was with the reapers.
4:19 "My head! My head!" he said to his **f**.
4:19 His **f** told a servant, "Carry him to
5:13 "My **f**, if the prophet had told you
6:21 Shall I kill them, my **f**? Shall I
9:25 in chariots behind Ahab his **f** when
13:14 wept over him. "My **f**! My **f**!" he
13:25 taken in battle from his **f** Jehoahaz.
14: 3 followed the example of his **f** Joash.
14: 5 who had murdered his **f** the king.
14:21 him king in place of his **f** Amaziah.
15: 3 LORD, just as his **f** Amaziah had done.
15:34 LORD, just as his **f** Uzziah had done.
15:38 City of David, the city of his **f**.
16: 2 Unlike David his **f**, he did not do
21: 3 the high places his **f** Hezekiah
21:20 LORD, as his **f** Manasseh had done.
21:21 He walked in all the ways of his **f**;
21:21 the idols his **f** had worshipped,
23:30 and made him king in place of his **f**.
23:34 Josiah king in place of his **f** Josiah
24: 9 of the LORD, just as his **f** had done.
1Ch 1:10 Cush was the **f** of Nimrod, who grew
1:11 Mizraim was the **f** of the Ludites,
1:13 Canaan was the **f** of Sidon his
1:18 **f** of Shelah, and Shelah the **f** of
1:20 Joktan was the **f** of Almodad, Sheleph,
1:34 Abraham was the **f** of Isaac. The sons
2:10 Ram was the **f** of Amminadab, and
2:10 and Amminadab the **f** of Nahshon, the
2:11 Nahshon was the **f** of Salmon, Salmon
2:11 **f** of Salmon, Salmon the **f** of Boaz,
2:12 Boaz the **f** of Obed and Obed the **f** of
2:13 Jesse was the **f** of Eliab his
2:17 whose **f** was Jether the Ishmaelite.
2:20 Hur was the **f** of Uri, and Uri the **f**
2:21 daughter of Makir the **f** of Gilead
2:22 Segub was the **f** of Jair, who
2:23 of Makir the **f** of Gilead.
2:24 bore him Ashhur the **f** of Tekoa.
2:31 Ishi, who was the **f** of Sheshan.
2:31 Sheshan was the **f** of Ahlai.
2:36 **f** of Nathan, Nathan the **f** of Zabad,
2:37 Zabad the **f** of Ephlal, Ephlal the **f**
2:38 Obed the **f** of Jehu, Jehu the **f** of
2:39 Azariah the **f** of Helez, Helez the **f**
2:40 Eleasah the **f** of Sismai, Sismai the **f**
2:41 Shallum the **f** of Jekamiah, and
2:41 and Jekamiah the **f** of Elishama.
2:42 who was the **f** of Ziph, and his son
2:42 Mareshah, who was the **f** of Hebron.
2:44 the **f** of Raham, and Raham the **f** of

1Ch 2:44 Rekem was the **f** of Shammai.
2:45 Maon, and Maon was the **f** of Beth Zur.
2:46 Haran was the **f** of Gazez.
2:49 Shaaph the **f** of Madmannah
2:49 Sheva the **f** of Macbenah and Gibea.
2:50 Shobal the **f** of Kiriath Jearim,
2:51 Salma the **f** of Bethlehem, and Hareph
2:51 and Hareph the **f** of Beth Gader.
2:52 Shobal the **f** of Kiriath Jearim
2:55 Hammath, the **f** of the house of Recab.
4: 2 Reaiah son of Shobal was the **f** of
4: 2 Jahath the **f** of Ahumai and Lahad.
4: 4 Penuel was the **f** of Gedor, and Ezer
4: 4 **f** of Gedor, and Ezer the **f** of Hushah.
4: 5 Ashhur the **f** of Tekoa had two wives,
4: 8 Koz, who was the **f** of Anub and
4:11 Kelub, Shuhah's brother, was the **f**
4:11 **f** of Mehir, who was the **f** of Eshton.
4:12 Eshton was the **f** of Beth Rapha,
4:12 and Tehinnah the **f** of Ir Nahash.
4:14 Meonothai was the **f** of Ophrah.
4:14 Seraiah was the **f** of Joab, the **f** of
4:17 Shammai and Ishbah the **f** of Eshtemoa.
4:18 gave birth to Jered the **f** of Gedor,
4:18 Heber the **f** of Soco, and Jekuthiel
4:18 Soco, and Jekuthiel the **f** of Zanoah.
4:19 the sister of Naham: the **f** of Keilah
4:21 son of Judah: Er the **f** of Lecah,
4:21 Laadah the **f** of Mareshah and the
6: 4 Eleazar was the **f** of Phinehas,
6: 4 Phinehas, Phinehas the **f** of Abishua,
6: 5 Abishua the **f** of Bukki, Bukki the **f**
6: 6 Uzzi the **f** of Zerahiah, Zerahiah the
6: 6 Zerahiah, Zerahiah the **f** of Meraioth,
6: 7 Meraioth the **f** of Amariah, Amariah
6: 7 of Amariah, Amariah the **f** of Ahitub,
6: 8 Ahitub the **f** of Zadok, Zadok the **f**
6: 9 Ahimaaz the **f** of Azariah, Azariah
6: 9 Azariah, Azariah the **f** of Johanan,
6:10 Johanan the **f** of Azariah (it was he
6:11 Azariah the **f** of Amariah, Amariah
6:11 of Amariah, Amariah the **f** of Ahitub,
6:12 Ahitub the **f** of Zadok, Zadok the **f**
6:13 Shallum the **f** of Hilkiah, Hilkiah
6:13 Hilkiah, Hilkiah the **f** of Azariah,
6:14 Azariah the **f** of Seraiah, and
6:14 and Seraiah the **f** of Jehozadak.
7:14 gave birth to Makir the **f** of Gilead.
7:22 Their **f** Ephraim mourned for them
7:31 Malkiel, who was the **f** of Birzaith.
7:32 Heber was the **f** of Japhlet, Shomer
8: 1 Benjamin was the **f** of Bela his
8: 7 who was the **f** of Uzza and Ahihud.
8:29 Jeiel the **f** of Gibeon lived in
8:32 Mikloth, who was the **f** of Shimeah.
8:33 Ner was the **f** of Kish, Kish the **f** of
8:33 Saul the **f** of Jonathan,
8:34 Merib-Baal, who was the **f** of Micah.
8:36 Ahaz was the **f** of Jehoaddah,
8:36 Jehoaddah was the **f** of Alemeth,
8:36 Zimri, and Zimri was the **f** of Moza.
8:37 Moza was the **f** of Binea; Raphah was
9:35 Jeiel the **f** of Gibeon lived in
9:38 Mikloth was the **f** of Shimeam. They
9:39 Ner was the **f** of Kish, Kish the **f** of
9:39 Saul the **f** of Jonathan,
9:40 Merib-Baal, who was the **f** of Micah.
9:42 the **f** of Jadah, Jadah was the **f** of
9:42 Zimri, and Zimri was the **f** of Moza.
9:43 Moza was the **f** of Binea; Rephaiah
14: 3 the **f** of more sons and daughters.
17:13 I will be his **f**, and he will be my
19: 2 because his **f** showed kindness to me.
19: 2 sympathy to Hanun concerning his **f**.
19: 3 think David is honouring your **f** by
22:10 will be my son, and I will be his **f**.
24: 2 Nadab and Abihu died before their **f**
25: 3 under the supervision of their **f**
26:10 his **f** had appointed him the first),
28: 6 to be my son, and I will be his **f**.
29:10 O LORD, God of our **f** Israel, from
2Ch 1: 8 shown great kindness to David my **f**
2:14 from Dan and whose **f** was from Tyre.
2:14 with those of my lord, David your **f**.
6:10 I have succeeded David my **f** and now
6:15 promise to your servant David my **f**;
2Ch 6:16 keep for your servant David my **f** the
7:17 walk before me as David your **f** did,
7:18 as I covenanted with David your **f**
9:31 buried in the city of David his **f**.
10: 4 "Your **f** put a heavy yoke on us, but
10: 6 his **f** Solomon during his lifetime.
10: 9 the yoke your **f** put on us'?"
10:10 'Your **f** put a heavy yoke on us, but
10:11 My **f** laid on you a heavy yoke; I
10:11 My **f** scourged you with whips; I will
10:14 "My **f** made your yoke heavy; I will
10:14 My **f** scourged you with whips; I will
15:18 that he and his **f** had dedicated.
16: 3 there was between my **f** and your **f**.
17: 2 Ephraim that his **f** Asa had captured.
17: 4 sought the God of his **f** and followed
20:32 He walked in the ways of his **f** Asa
21: 3 Their **f** had given them many gifts of
21:12 the ways of your **f** Jehoshaphat or
24:22 kindness Zechariah's **f** Jehoiada had
25: 3 who had murdered his **f** the king.
26: 1 him king in place of his **f** Amaziah.
26: 4 LORD, just as his **f** Amaziah had done.
27: 2 just as his **f** Uzziah had done, but
28: 1 Unlike David his **f**, he did not do
33: 3 the high places his **f** Hezekiah
33:22 LORD, as his **f** Manasseh had done.
33:23 unlike his **f** Manasseh, he did not
36: 1 king in Jerusalem in place of his **f**.
Ne 12:10 Jeshua was the **f** of Joiakim, Joiakim
12:10 Joiakim the **f** of Eliashib, Eliashib
12:10 Eliashib, Eliashib the **f** of Joiada,
12:11 Joiada the **f** of Jonathan, and
12:11 and Jonathan the **f** of Jaddua.
Est 2: 7 she had neither **f** nor mother.
2: 7 daughter when her **f** and mother died.
Job 15:10 side, men even older than your **f**.
17:14 if I say to corruption, 'You are my **f**
29:16 I was a **f** to the needy; I took up
31:18 my youth I reared him as would a **f**,
38:28 Does the rain have a **f**? Who fathers
42:15 their **f** granted them an inheritance
Ps 2: 7 my Son; today I have become your **F**.
27:10 Though my **f** and mother forsake me,
68: 5 A **f** to the fatherless, a defender of
89:26 'You are my **F**, my God, the Rock
103:13 a **f** has compassion on his children,
Pr 3:12 as a **f** the son he delights in.
10: 1 A wise son brings joy to his **f**,
15:20 A wise son brings joy to his **f**, but
17:21 there is no joy for the **f** of a fool.
17:25 A foolish son brings grief to his **f**
19:26 He who robs his **f** and drives out his
20:20 If a man curses his **f** or mother, his
23:22 Listen to your **f**, who gave you life,
23:24 The **f** of a righteous man has great
23:25 May your **f** and mother be glad; may
27:10 friend and the friend of your **f**,
28: 7 of gluttons disgraces his **f**.
28:24 He who robs his **f** or mother and says,
29: 3 loves wisdom brings joy to his **f**,
30:17 "The eye that mocks a **f**, that scorns
Isa 7:17 on the house of your **f** a time unlike
9: 6 God, Everlasting **F**, Prince of Peace.
22:21 He will be a **f** to those who live in
22:23 of honour for the house of his **f**.
43:27 Your first **f** sinned; your spokesmen
45:10 Woe to him who says to his **f**, 'What
51: 2 look to Abraham, your **f**, and to
58:14 on the inheritance of your **f** Jacob.
63:16 you are our **F**, though Abraham does
63:16 O LORD, are our **F**, our Redeemer
64: 8 Yet, O LORD, you are our **F**. We are
Jer 2:27 They say to wood, 'You are my **f**,'
3: 4 called to me: 'My **F**, my friend
16: 7 not even for a **f** or a mother—nor
20:15 the man who brought my **f** the news
22:11 who succeeded his **f** as king of Judah
22:15 Did not your **f** have food and drink?
31: 9 I am Israel's **f**, and Ephraim is my
Eze 16: 3 your **f** was an Amorite and your
16:45 was a Hittite and your **f** an Amorite.
18: 4 the **f** as well as the son–both alike
18:11 (though the **f** has done none of them):
18:14 who sees all the sins his **f** commits,
18:18 his **f** will die for his own sin,
Eze 18:19 he son not share the guilt of his **f**?'
18:20 will not share the guilt of the **f**,
18:20 the **f** share the guilt of the son.
22: 7 treated **f** and mother with contempt;
44:25 if the dead person was his **f** or
Da 5: 2 that Nebuchadnezzar his **f** had taken
5:11 In the time of your **f** he was found
5:11 King Nebuchadnezzar your **f**—your **f**
5:13 the exiles my **f** the king brought
5:18 the Most High God gave your **f**
11: 6 her **f** and the one who supported her.
Am 2: 7 **F** and son use the same girl and so
Mic 7: 6 For a son dishonours his **f**, a
Zec 13: 3 if anyone still prophesies, his **f**
Mal 1: 6 "A son honours his **f**, and a servant
1: 6 If I am a **f**, where is the honour due
2:10 Have we not all one **F**? Did not one
Mt 1: 2 Abraham was the **f** of Isaac, Isaac
1: 2 Isaac the **f** of Jacob, Jacob the **f** of
1: 3 Judah the **f** of Perez and Zerah,
1: 3 **f** of Hezron, Hezron the **f** of Ram,
1: 4 Ram the **f** of Amminadab, Amminadab
1: 4 Amminadab the **f** of Nahshon, Nahshon
1: 4 of Nahshon, Nahshon the **f** of Salmon,
1: 5 Salmon the **f** of Boaz, whose mother
1: 5 Boaz the **f** of Obed, whose mother
1: 5 was Ruth, Obed the **f** of Jesse,
1: 6 Jesse the **f** of King David. David was
1: 6 David was the **f** of Solomon, whose
1: 7 Solomon the **f** of Rehoboam, Rehoboam
1: 7 **f** of Abijah, Abijah the **f** of Asa,
1: 8 Asa the **f** of Jehoshaphat,
1: 8 Jehoshaphat the **f** of Jehoram,
1: 8 Jehoram the **f** of Uzziah,
1: 9 Uzziah the **f** of Jotham, Jotham the
1: 9 **f** of Ahaz, Ahaz the **f** of Hezekiah,
1:10 Hezekiah the **f** of Manasseh, Manasseh
1:10 the **f** of Amon, Amon the **f** of Josiah,
1:11 Josiah the **f** of Jeconiah and his
1:12 Jeconiah was the **f** of Shealtiel,
1:12 Shealtiel the **f** of Zerubbabel,
1:13 Zerubbabel the **f** of Abiud, Abiud the
1:13 **f** of Eliakim, Eliakim the **f** of Azor,
1:14 Azor the **f** of Zadok, Zadok the **f** of
1:14 the **f** of Akim, Akim the **f** of Eliud,
1:15 Eliud the **f** of Eleazar, Eleazar the
1:15 **f** of Matthan, Matthan the **f** of Jacob,
1:16 Jacob the **f** of Joseph, the husband
2:22 reigning in Judea in place of his **f**
3: 9 'We have Abraham as our **f**.'
4:21 They were in a boat with their **f**
4:22 boat and their **f** and followed him.
6: 4 Then your **F**, who sees what is done
6: 6 and pray to your **F**, who is unseen.
6: 6 Then your **F**, who sees what is done
6: 8 your **F** knows what you need before
6:15 your **F** will not forgive your sins.
6:18 but only to your **F**, who is unseen;
6:18 who is unseen; and your **F**, who sees
7:21 the will of my **F** who is in heaven.
8:21 Lord, first let me go and bury my **f**."
10:20 the Spirit of your **F** speaking
10:21 to death and a **f** his child;
10:29 apart from the will of your **F**.
10:35 "'a man against his **f**, a daughter
10:37 "Anyone who loves his **f** or mother
11:25 "I praise you, **F**, Lord of heaven and
11:26 Yes, **F**, for this was your good
11:27 have been committed to me by my **F**.
11:27 No-one knows the Son except the **F**,
11:27 no-one knows the **F** except the Son
13:43 the sun in the kingdom of their **F**.
15: 4 For God said, 'Honour your **f** and
15: 4 'Anyone who curses his **f** or mother
15: 5 you say that if a man says to his **f**
19: 5 this reason a man will leave his **f**
19:19 honour your **f** and mother,' and 'love
19:29 brothers or sisters or **f** or mother
20:23 they have been prepared by my **F**."
21:30 "Then the **f** went to the other son
21:31 "Which of the two did what his **f**
23: 9 do not call anyone on earth '**f**',
24:36 heaven, nor the Son, but only the **F**.
25:34 'Come, you who are blessed by my **F**;
26:39 "My **F**, if it is possible, may this
26:42 "My **F**, if it is not possible for

Mt 26:53 Do you think I cannot call on my **F**,
28:19 baptising them in the name of the **F**
Mk 1:20 and they left their **f** Zebedee in the
5:40 he took the child's **f** and mother and
7:10 For Moses said, 'Honour your **f** and
7:10 'Anyone who curses his **f** or mother
7:11 you say that if a man says to his **f**
7:12 him do anything for his **f** or mother.
9:21 Jesus asked the boy's **f**, "How long
9:24 Immediately the boy's **f** exclaimed,
10: 7 this reason a man will leave his **f**
10:19 defraud, honour your **f** and mother.'"
10:29 or **f** or children or fields for me
13:12 brother to death, and a **f** his child.
13:32 heaven, nor the Son, but only the **F**.
14:36 "Abba, **F**," he said, "everything is
15:21 Simon, the **f** of Alexander and Rufus,
Lk 1:59 to name him after his **f** Zechariah,
1:62 they made signs to his **f**, to find
1:67 His **f** Zechariah was filled with the
2:33 The child's **f** and mother marvelled
2:48 Your **f** and I have been anxiously
3: 8 'We have Abraham as our **f**.
6:36 Be merciful, just as your **F** is
8:51 James, and the child's **f** and mother.
9:26 in the glory of the **F** and of the
9:42 the boy and gave him back to his **f**.
9:59 Lord, first let me go and bury my **f**."
10:21 "I praise you, **F**, Lord of heaven and
10:21 Yes, **F**, for this was your good
10:22 have been committed to me by my **F**.
10:22 knows who the Son is except the **F**,
10:22 and no-one knows who the **F** is except
11: 2 "When you pray, say: "'**F**, hallowed
12:30 and your **F** knows that you need them.
12:32 little flock, for your **F** has been
12:53 **f** against son and son against **f**,
14:26 and does not hate his **f** and mother,
15:12 The younger one said to his **f**, '**F**,
15:18 go back to my **f** and say to him: **F**,
15:20 he got up and went to his **f**. "But
15:20 his **f** saw him and was filled with
15:21 "The son said to him, '**F**, I have
15:22 "But the **f** said to his servants,
15:27 'and your **f** has killed the fattened
15:28 his **f** went out and pleaded with him.
15:29 he answered his **f**, 'Look! All these
15:31 "'My son,' the **f** said, 'you are
16:27 I beg you, **f**, send Lazarus to my
18:20 honour your **f** and mother.'"
22:29 just as my **F** conferred one on me,
22:42 "**F**, if you are willing, take this
23:34 Jesus said, "**F**, forgive them, for
23:46 "**F**, into your hands I commit my
24:49 I am going to send you what my **F** has
Jn 1:14 from the **F**, full of grace and truth.
3:35 The **F** loves the Son and has placed
4:12 Are you greater than our **f** Jacob,
4:21 worship the **F** neither on this
4:23 worship the **F** in spirit and truth,
4:23 the kind of worshippers the **F** seeks.
4:53 the **f** realised that this was the
5:17 Jesus said to them, "My **F** is always
5:18 he was even calling God his own **F**,
5:19 do only what he sees his **F** doing,
5:19 the **F** does the Son also does.
5:20 For the **F** loves the Son and shows
5:21 For just as the **F** raises the dead
5:22 Moreover, the **F** judges no-one, but
5:23 the Son just as they honour the **F**.
5:23 does not honour the **F**, who sent him.
5:26 For as the **F** has life in himself, so
5:36 For the very work that the **F** has
5:36 testifies that the **F** has sent me.
5:37 the **F** who sent me has himself
5:45 I will accuse you before the **F**.
6:32 but it is my **F** who gives you the
6:37 All that the **F** gives me will come to
6:42 the son of Joseph, whose **f** and
6:44 "No-one can come to me unless the **F**
6:45 Everyone who listens to the **F** and
6:46 No-one has seen the **F** except the one
6:46 is from God; only he has seen the **F**.
6:57 Just as the living **F** sent me and I
6:57 sent me and I live because of the **F**,
6:65 to me unless the **F** has enabled him."
Jn 8:16 I stand with the **F**, who sent me.
8:18 witness is the **F**, who sent me."
8:19 they asked him, "Where is your **f**?"
8:19 not know me or my **F**," Jesus replied.
8:19 knew me, you would know my **F** also."
8:27 he was telling them about his **F**.
8:28 speak just what the **F** has taught me.
8:38 what you have heard from your **f**.
8:39 "Abraham is our **f**," they answered.
8:41 doing the things your own **f** does.
8:41 "The only **F** we have is God himself."
8:42 "If God were your **F**, you would love
8:44 You belong to your **f**, the devil, and
8:44 he is a liar and the **f** of lies.
8:49 I honour my **F** and you dishonour me.
8:54 My **F**, whom you claim as your God,
10:15 the **F** knows me and I know the **F**—
10:17 The reason my **F** loves me is that I
10:18 This command I received from my **F**."
10:29 My **F**, who has given them to me, is
10:30 I and the **F** are one."
10:32 you many great miracles from the **F**.
10:36 about the one whom the **F** set apart
10:37 me unless I do what my **F** does.
10:38 the **F** is in me, and I in the **F**."
11:41 Then Jesus looked up and said, "**F**, I
12:26 My **F** will honour the one who serves
12:27 '**F**, save me from this hour'? No, it
12:28 **F**, glorify your name!" Then a voice
12:49 but the **F** who sent me commanded me
12:50 just what the **F** has told me to say."
13: 1 to leave this world and go to the **F**.
13: 3 Jesus knew that the **F** had put all
14: 6 comes to the **F** except through me.
14: 7 me, you would know my **F** as well.
14: 8 Philip said, "Lord, show us the **F**
14: 9 who has seen me has seen the **F**.
14:10 I am in the **F**, and that the **F** is in
14:10 Rather, it is the **F**, living in me,
14:11 I am in the **F** and the **F** is in me;
14:12 these, because I am going to the **F**.
14:13 the Son may bring glory to the **F**.
14:16 I will ask the **F**, and he will give
14:20 you will realise that I am in my **F**,
14:21 who loves me will be loved by my **F**,
14:23 My **F** will love him, and we will come
14:24 they belong to the **F** who sent me.
14:26 the Holy Spirit, whom the **F** will
14:28 the **F**, for the **F** is greater than I.
14:31 world must learn that I love the **F**
14:31 exactly what my **F** has commanded me.
15: 1 "I am the true vine, and my **F** is the
15: 9 "As the **F** has loved me, so have I
15:15 from my **F** I have made known to you.
15:16 Then the **F** will give you whatever
15:23 He who hates me hates my **F** as well.
15:24 they have hated both me and my **F**.
15:26 whom I will send to you from the **F**,
15:26 who goes out from the **F**, he will
16: 3 they have not known the **F** or me.
16:10 I am going to the **F**, where you can
16:15 All that belongs to the **F** is mine.
16:23 I tell you the truth, my **F** will give
16:25 will tell you plainly about my **F**.
16:26 I will ask the **F** on your behalf.
16:27 No, the **F** himself loves you because
16:28 I came from the **F** and entered the
16:28 the world and going back to the **F**."
16:32 I am not alone, for my **F** is with me.
17: 1 and prayed: "**F**, the time has come.
17: 5 now, **F**, glorify me in your presence
17:11 Holy **F**, protect them by the power of
17:21 that all of them may be one, **F**, just
17:24 "**F**, I want those you have given me
17:25 "Righteous **F**, though the world does
18:11 drink the cup the **F** has given me?"
20:17 I have not yet returned to the **F**.
20:17 I am returning to my **F** and your **F**,
20:21 As the **F** has sent me, I am sending
Ac 1: 4 but wait for the gift my **F** promised,
1: 7 the times or dates the **F** has set by
2:33 he has received from the **F** the
7: 4 After the death of his **f**, God sent
7: 8 And Abraham became the **f** of Isaac
7: 8 Later Isaac became the **f** of Jacob,
7: 8 the **f** of the twelve patriarchs.
Ac 7:14 After this, Joseph sent for his **f**
13:33 Son; today I have become your **F**.',
16: 1 a believer, but whose **f** was a Greek.
16: 3 all knew that his **f** was a Greek.
28: 8 His **f** was sick in bed, suffering
Ro 4:11 So then, he is the **f** of all who
4:12 he is also the **f** of the circumcised
4:16 He is the **f** of us all.
4:17 "I have made you a **f** of many nations
4:17 He is our **f** in the sight of God, in
4:18 and so became the **f** of many nations,
6: 4 through the glory of the **F**, we too
8:15 And by him we cry, "Abba, **F**."
9:10 had one and the same **f**, our **f** Isaac.
15: 6 God and **F** of our Lord Jesus Christ.
1Co 4:15 I became your **f** through the gospel.
2Co 1: 3 Praise be to the God and **F** of our
1: 3 the **F** of compassion and the God of
6:18 "I will be a **F** to you, and you will
11:31 The God and **F** of the Lord Jesus, who
Gal 1: 4 to the will of our God and **F**,
4: 2 until the time set by his **f**.
4: 6 Spirit who calls out, "Abba, **F**.
Eph 1: 3 Praise be to the God and **F** of our
1:17 the glorious **F**, may give you the
2:18 have access to the **F** by one Spirit.
3:14 For this reason I kneel before the **F**,
4: 6 one God and **F** of all, who is over
5:31 this reason a man will leave his **f**
6: 2 "Honour your **f** and mother"—which is
Php 2:22 because as a son with his **f** he has
4:20 To our God and **F** be glory for ever
Col 1:12 giving thanks to the **F**, who has
1Th 1: 3 remember before our God and **F** your
2:11 as a **f** deals with his own children,
3:11 Now may our God and **F** himself and
3:13 in the presence of our God and **F**
1Ti 5: 1 but exhort him as if he were your **f**.
Heb 1: 5 my Son; today I have become your **F**",
1: 5 be his **F**, and he will be my Son"?
5: 5 Son; today I have become your **F**.",
7: 3 Without **f** or mother, without
11:11 was enabled to become a **f** because he
12: 7 son is not disciplined by his **f**?
12: 9 submit to the **F** of our spirits and
Jas 1:17 coming down from the **F** of the
3: 9 the tongue we praise our Lord and **F**,
1Pe 1: 3 Praise be to the God and **F** of our
1:17 Since you call on a **F** who judges
1Jn 1: 2 with the **F** and has appeared to us.
1: 3 our fellowship is with the **F** and
2: 1 we have one who speaks to the **F** in
2:13 because you have known the **F**
2:15 the love of the **F** is not in him.
2:16 not from the **F** but from the world.
2:22 denies the **F** and the Son.
2:23 No-one who denies the Son has the **F**;
2:23 acknowledges the Son has the **F** also.
2:24 will remain in the Son and in the **F**.
3: 1 How great is the love the **F** has
4:14 testify that the **F** has sent his Son
5: 1 loves the **f** loves his child as well.
2Jn : 4 truth, just as the **F** commanded us.
: 9 teaching has both the **F** and the Son.
Rev 1: 6 priests to serve his God and **F**—to
2:27 I have received authority from my **F**.
3: 5 his name before my **F** and his angels.
3:21 sat down with my **F** on his throne.

Father Abraham

Ge 22: 7 Isaac spoke up and said to his **f**,
26: 3 confirm the oath I swore to your **f**.
26:15 had dug in the time of his **f**,
26:18 had been dug in the time of his **f**,
26:24 and said, "I am the God of your **f**.
28:13 God of your **f** and the God of Isaac.
32: 9 Jacob prayed, "O God of my **f**, God of
Jos 24: 3 I took your **f** from the land beyond
Lk 1:73 the oath he swore to our **f**:
16:24 he called to him, '**F**, have pity on
16:30 "'No, **f**,' he said, 'but if someone
Jn 8:53 Are you greater than our **f**? He died,
8:56 Your **f** rejoiced at the thought of
Ac 7: 2 appeared to our **f** while he was
Ro 4:12 our **f** had before he was circumcised.

Father David
1Ki 2:12 Solomon sat on the throne of his **f**,
2:24 me securely on the throne of my **f**
2:26 of the Sovereign LORD before my **f**
2:32 without the knowledge of my **f** he
2:44 heart all the wrong you did to my **f**.
3: 3 according to the statutes of his **f**,
3: 6 my **f**, because he was faithful to you
3: 7 your servant king in place of my **f**.
5: 1 been anointed king to succeed his **f**,
5: 3 waged against my **f** from all sides,
5: 5 as the LORD told my **f**, when he said,
7:51 the things his **f** had dedicated
8:15 promised with his own mouth to my **f**.
8:17 "My **f** had it in his heart to build a
8:18 the LORD said to my **f**, 'Because it
15:11 eyes of the LORD, as his **f** had done.
15:24 with them in the city of his **f**.
2Ki 14: 3 the LORD, but not as his **f** had done.
18: 3 of the LORD, just as his **f** had done.
20: 5 the God of your **f**, says: I have
22: 2 and walked in all the ways of his **f**,
1Ch 29:23 the LORD as king in place of his **f**.
2Ch 1: 9 LORD God, let your promise to my **f**
2: 3 cedar logs as you did for my **f** when
2: 7 craftsmen, whom my **f** provided.
2:17 after the census his **f** had taken;
3: 1 the LORD had appeared to his **f**.
5: 1 the things his **f** had dedicated
6: 4 he promised with his mouth to my **f**.
6: 7 "My **f** had it in his heart to build a
6: 8 the LORD said to my **f**, 'Because it
8:14 keeping with the ordinance of his **f**,
17: 3 in the ways that his **f** had followed.
21:12 the God of your **f**, says: 'You have
29: 2 of the LORD, just as his **f** had done.
34: 2 LORD and walked in the ways of his **f**,
34: 3 he began to seek the God of his **f**.
Isa 38: 5 the God of your **f**, says: I have
Mk 11:10 is the coming kingdom of our **f**!"
Lk 1:32 will give him the throne of his **f**,
Ac 4:25 the mouth of your servant, our **f**:

Father in heaven
Mt 5:16 your good deeds and praise your **F**.
5:45 that you may be sons of your **F**. He
6: 1 you will have no reward from your **F**.
6: 9 "'Our **F**, hallowed be your name,
7:11 how much more will your **F** give good
10:32 also acknowledge him before my **F**.
10:33 men, I will disown him before my **F**.
12:50 For whoever does the will of my **F** is
16:17 revealed to you by man, but by my **F**.
18:10 heaven always see the face of my **F**.
18:14 your **F** is not willing that any of
18:19 it will be done for you by my **F**.
Mk 11:25 your **F** may forgive you your sins."
Lk 11:13 how much more will your **F** give the

Father's (Father, *Father's house*)
Ge 9:22 saw his **f** nakedness and told his
9:23 and covered their **f** nakedness.
9:23 would not see their **f** nakedness.
12: 1 your people and your **f** household and
20:13 me to wander from my **f** household
24: 7 who brought me out of my **f** household
24:38 go to my **f** family and to my own clan,
24:40 my own clan and from my **f** family.
26:15 all the wells that his **f** servants
27:30 had scarcely left his **f** presence,
27:34 Esau heard his **f** words, he burst out
29: 9 Rachel came with her **f** sheep,
31: 5 your **f** attitude towards me is not
31: 9 God has taken away your **f** livestock
31:14 in the inheritance of our **f** estate?
31:19 Rachel stole her **f** household gods.
34:19 honoured of all his **f** household,
35:22 slept with his **f** concubine Bilhah,
37: 2 his **f** wives, and he brought their
37:12 graze their **f** flocks near Shechem,
41:51 my trouble and all my **f** household."
46:31 his brothers and to his **f** household,
46:31 'My brothers and my **f** household, who
47:12 and all his **f** household with food,
48:17 so he took hold of his **f** hand to
49: 4 you went up onto your **f** bed, onto
49: 8 your **f** sons will bow down to you.
49:25 because of your **f** God, who helps
49:26 Your **f** blessings are greater than
50: 8 those belonging to his **f** household.
50:22 Egypt, along with all his **f** family.
Ex 2:16 the troughs to water their **f** flock.
6:20 Amram married his **f** sister Jochebed,
15: 2 him, my **f** God, and I will exalt him.
18: 4 "My **f** God was my helper; he saved me
Lev 18: 8 sexual relations with your **f** wife;
18: 9 either your **f** daughter or your
18:11 with the daughter of your **f** wife,
18:12 sexual relations with your **f** sister;
18:12 she is your **f** close relative.
18:14 "'Do not dishonour your **f** brother by
20:11 "'If a man sleeps with his **f** wife,
22:13 youth, she may eat of her **f** food.
Nu 18: 1 "You, your sons and your **f** family
27: 4 Why should our **f** name disappear from
27: 4 us property among our **f** relatives."
27: 7 inheritance among their **f** relatives
27: 7 their **f** inheritance over to them.
27:10 his inheritance to his **f** brothers.
36: 8 marry someone in her **f** tribal clan,
36:11 their cousins on their **f** side.
36:12 remained in their **f** clan and tribe.
Dt 21:17 is the first sign of his **f** strength
22:30 A man is not to marry his **f** wife; he
22:30 he must not dishonour his **f** bed.
27:20 **f** wife, for he dishonours his **f** bed.
Jdg 6:25 the second bull from your **f** herd,
6:25 Tear down your **f** altar to Baal and
9: 5 He went to his **f** home in Ophrah and
9:18 have revolted against my **f** family,
14:15 you and your **f** household to death.
16:31 his brothers and his **f** whole family
1Sa 2:25 did not listen to their **f** rebuke,
9:20 not to you and all your **f** family?"
17:15 to tend his **f** sheep at Bethlehem.
17:25 exempt his **f** family from taxes in
17:34 has been keeping his **f** sheep.
18:18 and what is my family or my **f** clan
20:34 his **f** shameful treatment of David.
22: 1 his **f** household heard about it,
22:11 of Ahitub and his **f** whole family,
22:15 your servant or any of his **f** family,
22:16 you and your **f** whole family."
22:22 the death of your **f** whole family.
24:21 wipe out my name from my **f** family."
2Sa 2:32 him in his **f** tomb at Bethlehem.
3: 7 did you sleep with my **f** concubine?"
14: 9 blame rest on me and on my **f** family,
15:34 O king; I was your **f** servant in the
16:21 answered, "Lie with your **f** concubines
16:21 an offence to your **f** nostrils,
16:22 and he lay with his **f** concubines in
17:23 died and was buried in his **f** tomb.
1Ki 2:26 David and shared all my **f** hardships."
12:10 finger is thicker than my **f** waist.
18:18 "But you and your **f** family have. You
2Ki 10: 3 sons and set him on his **f** throne.
1Ch 5: 1 but when he defiled his **f** marriage
26: 6 who were leaders in their **f** family
28: 4 and from my **f** sons he was pleased to
2Ch 10:10 finger is thicker than my **f** waist.
21: 4 himself firmly over his **f** kingdom,
22: 4 for after his **f** death they became
Est 4:14 you and your **f** family will perish.
Pr 1: 8 my son, to your **f** instruction and
4: 1 Listen, my sons, to a **f** instruction;
6:20 My son, keep your **f** commands and do
13: 1 A wise son heeds his **f** instruction,
15: 5 A fool spurns his **f** discipline, but
19:13 A foolish son is his **f** ruin, and a
Isa 3: 6 one of his brothers at his **f** home,
Eze 18:17 He will not die for his **f** sin; he
22:11 his sister, his own **f** daughter.
Mt 16:27 come in his **F** glory with his angels,
26:29 it anew with you in my **F** kingdom."
Mk 8:38 his **F** glory with the holy angels."
Lk 15:17 'How many of my **f** hired men have
Jn 1:18 at the **F** side, has made him known.
5:43 I have come in my **F** name, and you do
6:40 For my **F** will is that everyone who
8:38 what I have seen in the **F** presence,
Jn 8:44 you want to carry out your **f** desire.
10:25 the miracles I do in my **F** name
10:29 can snatch them out of my **F** hand.
15: 8 This is to my **F** glory, that you bear
15:10 just as I have obeyed my **F** commands
1Co 5: 1 among pagans: A man has his **f** wife.
2Jn : 3 Jesus Christ, the **F** Son, will be
Rev 14: 1 and his **F** name written on their

Father's house
Ge 24:23 is there room in your **f** for us
28:21 that I return safely to my **f**, then
31:30 you longed to return to your **f**.
38:11 Live as a widow in your **f** until my
38:11 So Tamar went to live in her **f**.
Lev 22:13 and she returns to live in her **f** as
Nu 30: 3 living in her **f** makes a vow to the
Dt 22:21 be brought to the door of her **f**
22:21 promiscuous while still in her **f**.
Jdg 11: 7 hate me and drive me from my **f**?
14:19 with anger, he went up to his **f**.
19: 2 She left him and went back to her **f**
19: 3 She took him into her **f**, and when
1Sa 2:27 reveal myself to your **f** when they
2:28 I also gave your **f** all the offerings
2:30 your **f** would minister before me for
2:31 strength and the strength of your **f**,
18: 2 and did not let him return to his **f**.
2Sa 3:29 the head of Joab and upon all his **f**!
1Ki 2:31 clear me and my **f** of the guilt
2Ch 21:13 members of your **f**, men who were
Ne 1: 6 myself and my **f**, have committed
Ps 45:10 ear: Forget your people and your **f**.
Pr 4: 3 I was a boy in my **f**, still tender,
Lk 2:49 Didn't you know I had to be in my **F**?"
16:27 you, father, send Lazarus to my **f**,
Jn 2:16 dare you turn my **F** into a market!"
14: 2 In my **F** are many rooms; if it were
Ac 7:20 months he was cared for in his **f**.

Fathered (Father)
Dt 32:18 You deserted the Rock, who **f** you;

Father-in-law (Father)
Ge 38:13 Tamar was told, "Your **f** is on his
38:25 out, she sent a message to her **f**.
Ex 3: 1 tending the flock of Jethro his **f**,
4:18 Moses went back to Jethro his **f** and
18: 1 the priest of Midian and **f** of Moses,
18: 2 Zipporah, his **f** Jethro received her
18: 5 Jethro, Moses' **f**, together with
18: 6 "I, your **f** Jethro, am coming to you
18: 7 Moses went out to meet his **f** and
18: 8 Moses told his **f** about everything
18:12 Jethro, Moses' **f**, brought a burnt
18:12 Moses' **f** in the presence of God.
18:14 his **f** saw all that Moses was doing
18:17 Moses' **f** replied, "What you are
18:24 Moses listened to his **f** and did
18:27 Moses sent his **f** on his way, and
Nu 10:29 Moses' **f**, "We are setting out for
Jdg 1:16 The descendants of Moses' **f**, the
19: 4 His **f**, the girl's father, prevailed
19: 7 his **f** persuaded him, so he stayed
19: 9 got up to leave, his **f**, the girl's
1Sa 4:19 her **f** and her husband were dead,
4:21 the deaths of her **f** and her husband.
Jn 18:13 who was the **f** of Caiaphas, the high

Fatherless
Ex 22:24 become widows and your children **f**.
Dt 10:18 He defends the cause of the **f** and
14:29 the **f** and the widows who live in
16:11 **f** and the widows living among you.
16:14 and the Levites, the aliens, the **f**
24:17 Do not deprive the alien or the **f** of
24:19 Leave it for the alien, the **f** and
24:20 for the alien, the **f** and the widow.
24:21 for the alien, the **f** and the widow.
26:12 the alien, the **f** and the widow, so
26:13 the alien, the **f** and the widow,
27:19 from the alien, the **f** or the widow.
Job 6:27 You would even cast lots for the **f**
22: 9 and broke the strength of the **f**.

Job 24: 9 The **f** child is snatched from the
29:12 the **f** who had none to assist him.
31:17 myself, not sharing it with the **f**—
31:21 I have raised my hand against the **f**,
Ps 10:14 to you; you are the helper of the **f**.
10:18 defending the **f** and the oppressed,
68: 5 A father to the **f**, a defender of
82: 3 Defend the cause of the weak and **f**;
94: 6 and the alien; they murder the **f**.
109: 9 May his children be **f** and his wife a
109:12 him or take pity on his **f** children.
146: 9 and sustains the **f** and the widow,
Pr 23:10 or encroach on the fields of the **f**,
Isa 1:17 Defend the cause of the **f**, plead
1:23 do not defend the cause of the **f**;
9:17 nor will he pity the **f** and widows,
10: 2 widows their prey and robbing the **f**.
Jer 5:28 plead the case of the **f** to win it,
7: 6 do not oppress the alien, the **f** or
22: 3 violence to the alien, the **f** or the
Lam 5: 3 We have become orphans and **f**, our
Eze 22: 7 and ill-treated the **f** and the widow.
Hos 14: 3 for in you the **f** find compassion."
Zec 7:10 Do not oppress the widow or the **f**,
Mal 3: 5 who oppress the widows and the **f**,

Fathers (Father, *God of your fathers*)

Ge 15:15 will go to your **f** in peace and
31: 3 "Go back to the land of your **f** and
46:34 our boyhood on, just as our **f** did.
47: 3 to Pharaoh, "just as our **f** were.
47: 9 years of the pilgrimage of my **f**."
47:30 I rest with my **f**, carry me out of
48:15 God before whom my **f** Abraham and
48:16 the names of my **f** Abraham and Isaac,
48:21 take you back to the land of your **f**.
49:29 Bury me with my **f** in the cave in the
Ex 4: 5 the God of their **f**—the God of
10: 6 something neither your **f** nor your
20: 5 for the sin of the **f** to the third
34: 7 for the sin of the **f** to the third
Lev 26:40 the sins of their **f**—their treachery
Nu 14:18 for the sin of the **f** to the third
20:15 Egyptians ill-treated us and our **f**,
32: 8 This is what your **f** did when I sent
32:14 standing in the place of your **f** and
36: 8 possess the inheritance of his **f**.
Dt 1: 8 he would give to your **f**—to Abraham,
5: 3 It was not with our **f** that the LORD
5: 9 for the sin of the **f** to the third
6:10 into the land he swore to your **f**,
8: 3 neither you nor your **f** had known
8:16 something your **f** had never known, to
9: 5 what he swore to your **f**, to Abraham
10:11 I swore to their **f** to give them."
13: 6 neither you nor your **f** have known,
24:16 **F** shall not be put to death for
24:16 children put to death for their **f**;
26: 7 the God of our **f**, and the LORD heard
28:36 a nation unknown to you or your **f**.
28:64 neither you nor your **f** have known.
29:13 to your **f**, Abraham, Isaac and Jacob.
29:25 the God of their **f**, the covenant he
30: 5 to the land that belonged to your **f**,
30: 5 prosperous and numerous than your **f**.
30: 9 just as he delighted in your **f**,
30:20 to your **f**, Abraham, Isaac and Jacob.
31:16 "You are going to rest with your **f**,
32:17 appeared, gods your **f** did not fear.
Jos 4:21 when your descendants ask their **f**,
5: 6 promised their **f** to give us,
22:28 LORD's altar, which our **f** built,
24: 6 I brought your **f** out of Egypt, you
24:17 us and our **f** up out of Egypt,
Jdg 2:10 had been gathered to their **f**,
2:12 forsook the LORD, the God of their **f**
2:17 Unlike their **f**, they quickly turned
2:17 the way in which their **f** had walked,
2:19 more corrupt than those of their **f**,
6:13 our **f** told us about when they said,
21:22 their **f** or brothers complain to us,
1Sa 12: 7 by the LORD for you and your **f**.
12:15 you, as it was against your **f**.
2Sa 7:12 are over and you rest with your **f**,
1Ki 1:21 the king is laid to rest with his **f**,
1Ki 2:10 David rested with his **f** and was
8:21 that he made with our **f** when he
8:34 to the land you gave to their **f**.
8:40 live in the land you gave our **f**.
8:48 towards the land you gave their **f**,
8:53 LORD, brought our **f** out of Egypt."
8:57 God be with us as he was with our **f**;
8:58 and regulations he gave our **f**.
9: 9 who brought their **f** out of Egypt,
11:21 heard that David rested with his **f**
11:43 he rested with his **f** and was buried
13:22 be buried in the tomb of your **f**.'"
14:20 years and then rested with his **f**.
14:22 anger more than their **f** had done.
14:31 Rehoboam rested with his **f** and was
15: 8 Abijah rested with his **f** and was
15:12 rid of all the idols his **f** had made.
15:24 Asa rested with his **f** and was buried
16: 6 Baasha rested with his **f** and was
16:28 Omri rested with his **f** and was
21: 3 give you the inheritance of my **f**."
21: 4 give you the inheritance of my **f**.
22:40 Ahab rested with his **f**. And Ahaziah
22:50 Jehoshaphat rested with his **f** and
2Ki 8:24 Jehoram rested with his **f** and was
9:28 buried him with his **f** in his tomb
10:35 Jehu rested with his **f** and was
12:18 dedicated by his **f**—Jehoshaphat,
12:21 He died and was buried with his **f** in
13: 9 Jehoahaz rested with his **f** and was
13:13 Jehoash rested with his **f**, and
14: 6 "**F** shall not be put to death for
14: 6 children put to death for their **f**;
14:16 Jehoash rested with his **f** and was
14:20 with his **f**, in the City of David.
14:22 after Amaziah rested with his **f**.
14:29 Jeroboam rested with his **f**, the
15: 7 Azariah rested with his **f** and was
15: 9 eyes of the LORD, as his **f** had done.
15:22 Menahem rested with his **f**. And
15:38 Jotham rested with his **f** and was
16:20 Ahaz rested with his **f** and was
17:13 Law that I commanded your **f** to obey
17:14 and were as stiff-necked as their **f**,
17:15 covenant he had made with their **f**
17:41 continue to do as their **f** did.
20:17 and all that your **f** have stored up
20:21 Hezekiah rested with his **f**. And
21:18 Manasseh rested with his **f** and was
21:22 He forsook the LORD, the God of his **f**
22:13 our **f** have not obeyed the words of
22:20 Therefore I will gather you to your **f**
23:32 of the LORD, just as his **f** had done.
23:37 of the LORD, just as his **f** had done.
24: 6 Jehoiakim rested with his **f**. And
1Ch 5:25 unfaithful to the God of their **f**
6:19 Levites listed according to their **f**:
9:19 their **f** had been responsible for
12:17 God of our **f** see it and judge you."
17:11 over and you go to be with your **f**,
25: 6 under the supervision of their **f**
29:18 O LORD, God of our **f** Abraham, Isaac
29:20 the God of their **f**; they bowed low
2Ch 6:25 land you gave to them and their **f**.
6:31 in the land that you gave our **f**.
6:38 the land that you gave their **f**,
7:22 the God of their **f**, who brought them
9:31 he rested with his **f** and was buried
11:16 to the LORD, the God of their **f**.
12:16 Rehoboam rested with his **f** and was
13:18 on the LORD, the God of their **f**.
14: 1 Abijah rested with his **f** and was
14: 4 seek the LORD, the God of their **f**,
15:12 seek the LORD, the God of their **f**,
16:13 Asa died and rested with his **f**.
19: 4 to the LORD, the God of their **f**.
20: 6 said: "O LORD, God of our **f**, are
20:33 their hearts on the God of their **f**.
21: 1 Jehoshaphat rested with his **f** and
21:10 forsaken the LORD, the God of his **f**.
21:19 his honour, as they had for his **f**.
24:18 the God of their **f**, and worshipped
24:24 the God of their **f**, judgment was
25: 4 "**F** shall not be put to death for
25: 4 children put to death for their **f**;
25:28 with his **f** in the City of Judah.
2Ch 26: 2 after Amaziah rested with his **f**.
26:23 Uzziah rested with his **f** and was
27: 9 Jotham rested with his **f** and was
28: 6 the LORD, the God of their **f**.
28:25 LORD, the God of his **f**, to anger.
28:27 Ahaz rested with his **f** and was
29: 6 Our **f** were unfaithful; they did evil
29: 9 This is why our **f** have fallen by the
30: 7 Do not be like your **f** and brothers,
30: 7 the God of their **f**, so that he made
30: 8 Do not be stiff-necked, as your **f**
30:19 the God of his **f**—even if he is not
30:22 the LORD, the God of their **f**.
32:13 what I and my **f** have done to all
32:14 these nations that my **f** destroyed
32:15 from my hand or the hand of my **f**.
32:33 Hezekiah rested with his **f** and was
33:12 greatly before the God of his **f**.
33:20 Manasseh rested with his **f** and was
34:21 our **f** have not kept the word of the
34:28 Now I will gather you to your **f**, and
34:32 covenant of God, the God of their **f**.
34:33 follow the LORD, the God of their **f**.
35:24 He was buried in the tombs of his **f**,
36:15 The LORD, the God of their **f**, sent
Ezr 5:12 our **f** angered the God of heaven, he
7:27 the God of our **f**, who has put it
Ne 2: 3 where my **f** are buried lies in ruins,
2: 5 city in Judah where my **f** are buried
9: 2 sins and the wickedness of their **f**.
9:23 told their **f** to enter and possess.
9:32 upon our **f** and all your people, from
9:34 our leaders, our priests and our **f**
Job 8: 8 and find out what their **f** learned,
15:18 hiding nothing received from their **f**
30: 1 men younger than I, whose **f** I would
38:28 Who **f** the drops of dew?
Ps 22: 4 In you our **f** put their trust; they
39:12 alien, a stranger, as all my **f** were.
44: 1 O God; our **f** have told us what you
44: 2 out the nations and planted our **f**;
44: 2 the peoples and made our **f** flourish.
45:16 sons will take the place of your **f**;
49:19 he will join the generation of his **f**,
78: 3 and known, what our **f** have told us.
78:12 miracles in the sight of their **f**
78:57 Like their **f** they were disloyal and
79: 8 hold against us the sins of the **f**;
95: 9 where your **f** tested and tried me,
106: 6 We have sinned, even as our **f** did;
106: 7 When our **f** were in Egypt, they gave
109:14 May the iniquity of his **f** be
Pr 30:11 "There are those who curse their **f**
Isa 38:19 **f** tell their children about your
39: 6 and all that your **f** have stored up
49:23 Kings will be your foster **f**, and
64:11 where our **f** praised you, has been
65: 7 both your sins and the sins of your **f**
Jer 2: 5 "What fault did your **f** find in me,
3:25 both we and our **f**; from our youth
6:21 **F** and sons alike will stumble over
7:14 the place I gave to you and your **f**.
7:18 gather wood, the **f** light the fire,
9:14 the Baals, as their **f** taught them."
9:16 neither they nor their **f** have known,
13:14 **f** and sons alike, declares the LORD.
14:20 and the guilt of our **f**; we have
16: 3 mothers and the men who are their **f**:
16:11 'It is because your **f** forsook me,'
16:12 behaved more wickedly than your **f**.
16:13 neither you nor your **f** have known,
16:19 "Our **f** possessed nothing but false
19: 4 gods that neither they nor their **f**
23:27 just as their **f** forgot my name
23:39 the city I gave to you and your **f**.
24:10 land I gave to them and their **f**.'"
25: 5 to you and your **f** for ever and ever.
31:29 'The **f** have eaten sour grapes, and
34: 5 a funeral fire in honour of your **f**,
34:14 Your **f**, however, did not listen to
35:15 land I have given to you and your **f**.
44: 3 they nor you nor your **f** ever knew.
44: 9 the wickedness committed by your **f**
44:10 decrees I set before you and your **f**.
44:17 to her just as we and our **f**,
44:21 of Jerusalem by you and your **f**,

Jer 47: 3 **F** will not turn to help their
50: 7 the LORD, the hope of their **f**.'
Lam 5: 7 Our **f** sinned and are no more, and we
Eze 2: 3 they and their **f** have been in revolt
5:10 Therefore in your midst **f** will eat
5:10 and children will eat their **f**.
18: 2 "'The **f** eat sour grapes, and the
20: 4 the detestable practices of their **f**
20:18 Do not follow the statutes of your **f**
20:27 **f** blasphemed me by forsaking me:
20:30 yourselves the way your **f** did
20:36 I judged your **f** in the desert of the
20:42 uplifted hand to give to your **f**.
37:25 Jacob, the land where your **f** lived.
Da 2:23 O God of my **f**: You have given me
9: 6 to our kings, our princes and our **f**
9: 8 our princes and our **f** are covered
9:16 Our sins and the iniquities of our **f**
11:24 his **f** nor his forefathers did.
11:37 no regard for the gods of his **f** or
11:38 a god unknown to his **f** he will
Hos 9:10 in the desert; when I saw your **f**,
Mic 7:20 on oath to our **f** in days long ago.
Zec 8:14 no pity when your **f** angered me,"
Mal 2:10 profane the covenant of our **f** by
4: 6 He will turn the hearts of the **f** to
4: 6 hearts of the children to their **f**;
Lk 1:17 to turn the hearts of the **f** to their
1:55 for ever, even as he said to our **f**."
1:72 to show mercy to our **f** and to
6:23 is how their **f** treated the prophets.
6:26 their **f** treated the false prophets.
11:11 "Which of you **f**, if your son asks
Jn 4:20 Our **f** worshipped on this mountain,
Ac 3:13 the God of our **f**, has glorified his
3:25 the covenant God made with your **f**.
5:30 The God of our **f** raised Jesus from
7: 2 To this he replied: "Brothers and **f**,
7:11 and our **f** could not find food.
7:12 he sent our **f** on their first visit.
7:15 to Egypt, where he and our **f** died.
7:38 on Mount Sinai, and with our **f**;
7:39 "But our **f** refused to obey him.
7:45 the tabernacle, our **f** under Joshua
7:51 You are just like your **f**: You
7:52 a prophet your **f** did not persecute?
13:17 of the people of Israel chose our **f**;
13:32 good news: What God promised our **f**
13:36 with his **f** and his body decayed.
15:10 we nor our **f** have been able to bear?
22: 1 "Brothers and **f**, listen now to my
22: 3 trained in the law of our **f**
22:14 'The God of our **f** has chosen you
24:14 I worship the God of our **f** as a
26: 6 what God has promised our **f** that I
1Co 4:15 you do not have many **f**, for in
Gal 1:14 zealous for the traditions of my **f**.
Eph 6: 4 **F**, do not exasperate your children;
Col 3:21 **F**, do not embitter your children, or
1Ti 1: 9 those who kill their **f** or mothers,
Heb 3: 9 where your **f** tested and tried me and
12: 9 Moreover, we have all had human **f**
12:10 Our **f** disciplined us for a little
2Pe 3: 4 Ever since our **f** died, everything
1Jn 2:13 I write to you, **f**, because you have
2:14 I write to you, **f**, because you have

Fathers' (Father)

Lev 26:39 their **f** sins they will waste away.
Jer 3:24 the fruits of our **f** labour—their
32:18 the punishment for the **f** sins into
Eze 20:24 eyes ⌊lusted⌋ after their **f** idols.
22:10 are those who dishonour their **f** bed;

Fathom (Fathomed)

Job 11: 7 "Can you **f** the mysteries of God? Can
Ps 145: 3 praise; his greatness no-one can **f**.
Ecc 3:11 yet they cannot **f** what God has done
Isa 40:28 and his understanding no-one can **f**.
1Co 13: 2 and can **f** all mysteries and all

Fathomed (Fathom)

Job 5: 9 He performs wonders that cannot be **f**,
9:10 He performs wonders that cannot be **f**,

Fattened (Fat)

Dt 32:14 flock and with **f** lambs and goats,
1Sa 28:24 The woman had a **f** calf at the house,
2Sa 6:13 he sacrificed a bull and a **f** calf.
1Ki 1: 9 cattle and **f** calves at the Stone of
1:19 great numbers of cattle, **f** calves,
1:25 of cattle, **f** calves, and sheep.
Pr 15:17 is love than a **f** calf with hatred.
Isa 1:11 of rams and the fat of **f** animals; I
Jer 46:21 in her ranks are like **f** calves.
Eze 39:18 of them **f** animals from Bashan.
Am 6: 4 dine on choice lambs and **f** calves.
Mt 22: 4 and **f** cattle have been slaughtered,
Lk 15:23 Bring the **f** calf and kill it. Let's
15:27 your father has killed the **f** calf
15:30 home, you kill the **f** calf for him!'
Jas 5: 5 **f** yourselves in the day of slaughter.

Fattening (Fat)

1Sa 2:29 **f** yourselves on the choice parts

Fault (Fault-finders, Faults, Faulty)

Ex 5:16 but the **f** is with your own people."
1Sa 29: 3 now, I have found no **f** in him."
29: 6 I have found no **f** in you, but the
Job 33:10 Yet God has found **f** with me; he
Jer 2: 5 What **f** did your fathers find in me
17: 4 Through your own **f** you will lose the
Jnh 1:12 I know that it is my **f** that this
Mt 18:15 show him his **f**, just between the
Php 2:15 children of God without **f** in a
Heb 8: 8 God found **f** with the people and said:
Jas 1: 5 generously to all without finding **f**
3: 2 If anyone is never at **f** in what he
Jude :24 without **f** and with great joy—

Fault-finders (Fault)

Jude :16 These men are grumblers and **f**; they

Faultless

Pr 8: 9 are **f** to those who have knowledge.
Php 3: 6 as for legalistic righteousness, **f**.
Jas 1:27 Father accepts as pure and **f** is this:

Faults (Fault)

Job 10: 6 that you must search out my **f** and
Ps 19:12 his errors? Forgive my hidden **f**.

Faulty (Fault)

Ps 78:57 faithless, as unreliable as a **f** bow.
Hos 7:16 Most High; they are like a **f** bow.

Favour (Favourable, Favourably, Favoured, Favourite, Favouritism, Favours)

Ge 4: 4 with **f** on Abel and his offering,
4: 5 his offering he did not look with **f**.
6: 8 Noah found **f** in the eyes of the LORD.
18: 3 He said, "If I have found **f** in your
19:19 Your servant has found **f** in your
30:27 Laban said to him, "If I have found **f**
32: 5 that I may find **f** in your eyes.'"
33: 8 "To find **f** in your eyes, my lord,"
33:10 "If I have found **f** in your eyes,
33:15 me find **f** in the eyes of my lord."
34:11 "Let me find **f** in your eyes, and I
39: 4 Joseph found **f** in his eyes and
39:21 **f** in the eyes of the prison warder.
47:25 "May we find **f** in the eyes of our
47:29 "If I have found **f** in your eyes, put
50: 4 "If I have found **f** in your eyes,
Ex 32:11 Moses sought the **f** of the LORD his
33:12 name and you have found **f** with me.'
33:13 you and continue to find **f** with you.
34: 9 "O Lord, if I have found **f** in your
Lev 26: 9 "I will look on you with **f** and make
Nu 11:15 now—if I have found **f** in your eyes
32: 5 If we have found **f** in your eyes,"
Dt 33:16 and the **f** of him who dwelt in the
33:23 "Naphtali is abounding with the **f** of
Jos 15:19 She replied, "Do me a special **f**.
Jdg 1:15 She replied, "Do me a special **f**.
6:17 "If now I have found **f** in your eyes,
Ru 2: 2 anyone in whose eyes I find **f**.
2:10 "Why have I found such **f** in your
2:13 "May I continue to find **f** in your
1Sa 1:18 She said, "May your servant find **f**
2:26 and in **f** with the LORD and with men.
13:12 and I have not sought the LORD's **f**.
20: 3 that I have found **f** in your eyes,
20:29 If I have found **f** in your eyes, let
27: 5 "If I have found **f** in your eyes, let
29: 4 could he regain his master's **f**
2Sa 2: 6 I too will show you the same **f**
14:22 that he has found **f** in your eyes,
15:25 If I find **f** in the LORD's eyes, he
16: 4 **f** in your eyes, my lord the king."
2Ki 13: 4 Jehoahaz sought the LORD's **f**, and
2Ch 33:12 In his distress he sought the **f** of
Ezr 7:28 who has extended his good **f** to me
Ne 1:11 him **f** in the presence of this man.
2: 5 servant has found **f** in his sight,
5:19 Remember me with **f**, O my God, for
13:31 Remember me with **f**, O my God.
Est 2: 9 The girl pleased him and won his **f**.
2:15 won the **f** of everyone who saw her.
2:17 and she won his **f** and approval more
5: 8 If the king regards me with **f** and if
7: 3 "If I have found **f** with you, O king,
8: 5 "and if he regards me with **f** and
Job 11:19 afraid, and many will court your **f**.
33:26 He prays to God and finds **f** with him,
34:19 does not **f** the rich over the poor,
Ps 5:12 them with your **f** as with a shield.
30: 5 moment, but his **f** lasts a lifetime;
45:12 men of wealth will seek your **f**.
69:13 O LORD, in the time of your **f**; in
77: 7 Will he never show his **f** again?
84: 9 look with **f** on your anointed one.
84:11 the LORD bestows **f** and honour; no
85: 1 You showed **f** to your land, O LORD;
89:17 and by your **f** you exalt our horn.
90:17 May the **f** of the Lord our God rest
102:13 for it is time to show **f** to her; the
106: 4 Remember me, O LORD, when you show **f**
Pr 3: 4 you will win **f** and a good name in
8:35 life and receives **f** from the LORD.
12: 2 A good man obtains **f** from the LORD,
13:15 Good understanding wins **f**, but the
16:15 **f** is like a rain cloud in spring.
18:22 good and receives **f** from the LORD.
19: 6 Many curry **f** with a ruler, and
19:12 but his **f** is like dew on the grass.
28:23 will in the end gain more **f** than he
Ecc 9:11 the brilliant or **f** to the learned;
Isa 27:11 and their Creator shows them no **f**.
49: 8 "In the time of my **f** I will answer
60:10 in **f** I will show you compassion.
61: 2 to proclaim the year of the LORD's **f**
Jer 16:13 night, for I will show you no **f**.'
26:19 fear the LORD and seek his **f**?
31: 2 the sword will find **f** in the desert;
Lam 4:16 shown no honour, the elders no **f**.
Eze 5:11 I myself will withdraw my **f**; I will
36: 9 will look on you with **f**; you will
Da 1: 9 to show **f** and sympathy to Daniel,
7:22 judgment in **f** of the saints of
9:13 have not sought the **f** of the LORD
9:17 with **f** on your desolate sanctuary.
11:30 He will return and show **f** to those
Hos 12: 4 him; he wept and begged for his **f**.
Zec 11: 7 called one **F** and the other Union,
11:10 I took my staff called **F** and broke
Mt 20:20 kneeling down, asked a **f** of him.
Lk 1:25 "In these days he has shown his **f**
1:30 Mary, you have found **f** with God.
2:14 peace to men on whom his **f** rests."
2:52 stature, and in **f** with God and men.
4:19 to proclaim the year of the Lord's **f**.
Jn 5:32 is another who testifies in my **f**,
Ac 2:47 praising God and enjoying the **f** of
7:46 who enjoyed God's **f** and asked that
24:27 wanted to grant a **f** to the Jews,
25: 3 requested Festus, as a **f** to them,
25: 9 Festus, wishing to do the Jews a **f**,
2Co 1:11 the gracious **f** granted us in answer
6: 2 "In the time of my **f** I heard you,
6: 2 now is the time of God's **f**, now is
Eph 6: 6 Obey them not only to win their **f**

Col 3:22 eye is on you and to win their **f**,
Phm :14 so that any **f** you do will be
Rev 2: 6 you have this in your **f**: You hate

Favourable (Favour)
Ge 40:16 Joseph had given a **f** interpretation,
1Sa 25: 8 Therefore be **f** towards my young men,
1Ki 12: 7 serve them and give them a **f** answer,
2Ch 10: 7 them and give them a **f** answer,
Jer 42: 6 Whether it is **f** or unfavourable, we

Favourably (Favour)
Ge 33:10 God, now that you have received me **f**.
Ex 3:21 make the Egyptians **f** disposed
11: 3 LORD made the Egyptians **f** disposed
12:36 had made the Egyptians **f** disposed
1Sa 20:12 If he is **f** disposed towards you,
1Ki 22:13 agree with theirs, and speak **f**."
2Ch 18:12 agree with theirs, and speak **f**."

Favoured (Favour)
Dt 33: 8 and Urim belong to the man you **f**.
33:24 Asher; let him be **f** by his brothers,
Ps 30: 7 O LORD, when you **f** me, you made my
Eze 32:19 them, 'Are you more **f** than others?
Lk 1:28 are highly **f**! The Lord is with you."
1:43 why am I so **f**, that the mother of my

Favourite (Favour)
SS 6: 9 the **f** of the one who bore her.

Favouritism (Favour)
Ex 23: 3 do not show **f** to a poor man in his
Lev 19:15 to the poor or **f** to the great,
Ac 10:34 true it is that God does not show **f**
Ro 2:11 For God does not show **f**.
Eph 6: 9 heaven, and there is no **f** with him.
Col 3:25 for his wrong, and there is no **f**.
1Ti 5:21 and to do nothing out of **f**.
Jas 2: 1 Lord Jesus Christ, don't show **f**.
2: 9 if you show **f**, you sin and are

Favours (Favour)
2Sa 20:11 "Whoever **f** Joab, and whoever is for
Ecc 9: 7 it is now that God **f** what you do.
Jer 3:13 you have scattered your **f** to foreign
Eze 16:15 You lavished your **f** on anyone who
16:33 from everywhere for your illicit **f**.
16:34 no-one runs after you for your **f**.

Fawn (Fawns)
Job 39: 1 you watch when the doe bears her **f**?
Jer 14: 5 newborn **f** because there is no grass.

Fawns (Fawn)
Ge 49:21 doe set free that bears beautiful **f**.
SS 4: 5 Your two breasts are like two **f**,
4: 5 like twin **f** of a gazelle that browse
7: 3 Your breasts are like two **f**, twins

Fear (Afraid, *Do not fear, Fear and trembling, Fear God, Fear of God, Fear of the LORD, Fear the LORD,* Feared, Fearful, Fearfully, Fearing, Fears, Fearsome, Fright, Frighten, Frightened, Frightening, God-fearing)
Ge 9: 2 The **f** and dread of you will fall
31:42 God of Abraham and the **F** of Isaac,
31:53 name of the **F** of his father Isaac.
32: 7 In great **f** and distress Jacob
Ex 20:18 in smoke, they trembled with **f**.
Lev 19:14 front of the blind, but **f** your God.
25:17 of each other, but **f** your God.
25:36 but **f** your God, so that your
25:43 them ruthlessly, but **f** your God.
Dt 2:25 put the terror and **f** of you on all
5:29 **f** me and keep all my commands always,
7:19 same to all the peoples you now **f**.
11:25 will put the terror and **f** of you on
28:10 of the LORD, and they will **f** you.
32:17 gods your fathers did not **f**.
Jos 2: 9 a great **f** of you has fallen on us,
2: 9 are melting in **f** because of you.
2:24 are melting in **f** because of us."
22:24 "No! We did it for **f** that some day
Jdg 7: 3 'Anyone who trembles with **f** may turn
1Sa 13: 7 troops with him were quaking with **f**.
17:24 they all ran from him in great **f**.
28:20 with **f** because of Samuel's words.
2Sa 17:10 will melt with **f**, for all Israel
1Ki 1:50 Adonijah, in **f** of Solomon, went and
8:40 that they will **f** you all the time
8:43 earth may know your name and **f** you,
2Ki 25:26 to Egypt for **f** of the Babylonians.
1Ch 14:17 the LORD made all the nations **f** him.
2Ch 6:31 that they will **f** you and walk in
6:33 earth may know your name and **f** you,
12: 5 in Jerusalem for **f** of Shishak,
Ezr 3: 3 Despite their **f** of the peoples
10: 3 those who **f** the commands of our God.
Ne 5: 9 walk in the **f** of our God to avoid
Est 5: 9 rose nor showed **f** in his presence,
8:17 **f** of the Jews had seized them.
9: 3 **f** of Mordecai had seized them.
Job 5:21 need not **f** when destruction comes.
5:22 need not **f** the beasts of the earth.
6:14 he forsakes the **f** of the Almighty.
9:35 I would speak up without **f** of him,
11:15 you will stand firm and without **f**.
19:29 you should **f** the sword yourselves;
21: 9 Their homes are safe and free from **f**;
23:15 when I think of all this, I **f** him.
31:23 and for **f** of his splendour I could
33: 7 No **f** of me should alarm you, nor
39:22 He laughs at **f**, afraid of nothing;
41:33 is his equal—a creature without **f**.
Ps 2:11 Serve the LORD with **f** and rejoice
3: 6 I will not **f** the tens of thousands
22:25 who **f** you will I fulfil my vows.
23: 4 I will **f** no evil, for you are with
25:14 The LORD confides in those who **f** him;
27: 1 and my salvation—whom shall I **f**?
27: 3 my heart will not **f**; though war
31:19 have stored up for those who **f** you,
33:18 of the LORD are on those who **f** him,
34: 7 who **f** him, and he delivers them.
34: 9 for those who **f** him lack nothing.
40: 3 **f** and put their trust in the LORD.
46: 2 Therefore we will not **f**, though the
49: 5 Why should I **f** when evil days come,
52: 6 The righteous will see and **f**; they
60: 4 for those who **f** you, you have raised
61: 5 heritage of those who **f** your name.
64: 4 shoot at him suddenly, without **f**.
64: 9 All mankind will **f**; they will
65: 8 Those living far away **f** your wonders;
67: 7 the ends of the earth will **f** him.
85: 9 salvation is near those who **f** him,
86:11 heart, that I may **f** your name.
90:11 great as the **f** that is due to you.
91: 5 You will not **f** the terror of night,
102:15 The nations will **f** the name of the
103:11 is his love for those who **f** him;
103:13 has compassion on those who **f** him;
103:17 LORD's love is with those who **f** him,
111: 5 He provides food for those who **f** him;
112: 7 He will have no **f** of bad news; his
112: 8 he will have no **f**; in the end he
115:11 You who **f** him, trust in the LORD–
119:63 I am a friend to all who **f** you, to
119:74 May those who **f** you rejoice when
119:79 May those who **f** you turn to me,
119:120 My flesh trembles in **f** of you; I
135:20 LORD; you who **f** him, praise the LORD.
145:19 He fulfils the desires of those who **f**
147:11 the LORD delights in those who **f** him,
Pr 1:33 and be at ease, without **f** of harm."
3:25 Have no **f** of sudden disaster or of
29:25 **F** of man will prove to be a snare,
31:21 she has no **f** for her household,
Isa 7:25 go there for **f** of the briers and
8:12 what they **f**, and do not dread it.
8:13 he is the one you are to **f**, he is
19:16 They will shudder with **f** at the
21: 4 My heart falters, **f** makes me tremble;
41: 5 The islands have seen it and **f**; the
41:23 will be dismayed and filled with **f**.
43: 1 "**F** not, for I have redeemed you; I
51:12 Who are you that you **f** mortal men,
54:14 you; you will have nothing to **f**.
59:19 From the west, men will **f** the name
Jer 3: 8 unfaithful sister Judah had no **f**;
5:22 Should you not **f** me?" declares the
17: 8 It does not **f** when heat comes; its
22:25 those you **f**—to Nebuchadnezzar king
26:21 heard of it and fled in **f** to Egypt.
30: 5 Cries of **f** are heard—terror, not
32:39 will always **f** me for their own good
32:40 and I will inspire them to **f** me, so
36:16 they looked at each other in **f** and
36:24 showed no **f**, nor did they tear their
39:17 not be handed over to those you **f**.
42:11 the king of Babylon, whom you now **f**.
42:16 the sword you **f** will overtake you
Eze 11: 8 You **f** the sword, and the sword is
12:18 shudder in **f** as you drink your
27:35 their faces are distorted with **f**.
30:13 I will spread **f** throughout the land.
Da 6:26 **f** and reverence the God of Daniel.
Hos 10: 5 live in Samaria **f** for the calf-idol
Am 3: 8 The lion has roared—who will not **f**?
Mic 6: 9 to **f** your name is wisdom—"Heed the
7:17 they will turn in **f** to the LORD our
Na 2:11 and the cubs, with nothing to **f**?
Zep 3: 7 'Surely you will **f** me and accept
3:15 never again will you **f** any harm.
Zec 9: 5 Ashkelon will see it and **f**; Gaza
Mt 14:26 they said, and cried out in **f**.
Mk 5:33 trembling with **f**, told him the whole
Lk 1:12 was startled and was gripped with **f**.
1:50 His mercy extends to those who **f** him,
1:74 to enable us to serve him without **f**
8:25 In **f** and amazement they asked one
8:37 because they were overcome with **f**.
12: 5 whom you should **f**: **F** him who, after
12: 5 Yes, I tell you, **f** him.
Jn 3:20 **f** that his deeds will be exposed.
7:13 about him for **f** of the Jews.
12:42 for **f** they would be put out of the
20:19 the doors locked for **f** of the Jews
Ac 5: 5 And great **f** seized all who heard
5:11 Great **f** seized the whole church and
7:32 Moses trembled with **f** and did not
10: 4 Cornelius stared at him in **f**. "What
10:35 accepts men from every nation who **f**
19:17 they were all seized with **f**, and the
Ro 8:15 that makes you a slave again to **f**,
13: 3 free from **f** of the one in authority
1Co 2: 3 I came to you in weakness and **f**, and
16:10 see to it that he has nothing to **f**
2Co 12:20 I **f** that there may be quarrelling,
Gal 2: 2 for **f** that I was running or had run
4:11 I **f** for you, that somehow I have
Eph 6: 5 earthly masters with respect and **f**,
Heb 2:15 held in slavery by their **f** of death.
11: 7 in holy **f** built an ark to save his
12:21 Moses said, "I am trembling with **f**.
1Pe 1:17 as strangers here in reverent **f**.
3: 6 is right and do not give way to **f**.
3:14 what they **f**; do not be frightened."
1Jn 4:18 There is no **f** in love. But perfect
4:18 But perfect love drives out **f**,
4:18 because **f** has to do with punishment.
Jude :23 mixed with **f**—hating even the
Rev 15: 4 Who will not **f** you, O Lord, and
19: 5 who **f** him, both small and great!"

Fear and trembling
Job 4:14 **f** seized me and made all my bones
Ps 55: 5 **F** have beset me; horror has
2Co 7:15 all obedient, receiving him with **f**
Php 2:12 to work out your salvation with **f**,

Fear God
Ge 22:12 Now I know that you **f**, because you
42:18 "Do this and you will live, for I **f**
Ex 18:21 men from all the people—men who **f**,
Job 1: 9 "Does Job **f** for nothing?" Satan
Ps 66:16 Come and listen, all you who **f**; let
Ecc 8:13 Yet because the wicked do not **f**, it
12:13 matter: **F** and keep his commandments,
Lk 18: 4 though I don't **f** or care about men,
23:40 "Don't you **f**," he said, "since you

1Pe 2:17 of believers, f, honour the king.
Rev 14: 7 He said in a loud voice, "F and give

Fear of God
Ge 20:11 'There is surely no f in this place,
Ex 20:20 so that the f will be with you to
Dt 25:18 were lagging behind; they had no f.
2Sa 23: 3 when he rules in the f,
2Ch 20:29 The f came upon all the kingdoms of
26: 5 who instructed him in the f.
Ps 36: 1 There is no f before his eyes.
55:19 change their ways and have no f.
Ro 3:18 "There is no f before their eyes."

Fear of the Lord/Lord
2Ch 17:10 The f fell on all the kingdoms of
19: 7 Now let the f be upon you. Judge
19: 9 and wholeheartedly in the f.
Job 28:28 he said to man, 'The f—that is
Ps 19: 9 The f is pure, enduring for ever.
34:11 to me; I will teach you the f.
111:10 The f is the beginning of wisdom;
Pr 1: 7 The f is the beginning of knowledge,
2: 5 you will understand the f and find
9:10 "The f is the beginning of wisdom,
10:27 The f adds length to life, but the
14:27 The f is a fountain of life, turning
15:16 Better a little with the f than
15:33 The f teaches a man wisdom, and
16: 6 through the f a man avoids evil.
19:23 The f leads to life: Then one rests
22: 4 Humility and the f bring wealth and
23:17 but always be zealous for the f.
Isa 11: 2 Spirit of knowledge and of the f—
11: 3 he will delight in the f. He will
33: 6 the f is the key to this treasure.
Ac 9:31 it grew in numbers, living in the f.

Fear the Lord/Lord
Ex 9:30 your officials still do not f God
Dt 6: 2 children after them may f your God
6:13 F your God, serve him only and take
10:24 all these decrees and to f our God,
10:12 f your God, to walk in all his ways
31:20 F your God and serve him. Hold fast
31:12 to f your God and follow carefully
31:13 learn to f your god as long as you
Jos 4:24 so that you might always f your God
24:14 Now f and serve him with all
1Sa 12:14 If you f and serve and obey him
11:24 sure to f and serve him faithfully
Ps 15: 4 a vile man but honours those who f,
22:23 you who f, praise him! All you
32: 8 Let all the earth f; let all the
33: 9 F, you his saints, for those who
115:13 he will bless those who f—small and
118: 4 Let those who f say: "His love
128: 1 Blessed are all who f, who walk in
Pr 1:29 knowledge and did not choose to f
3: 7 f and shun evil.
8:13 To f is to hate evil; I hate pride
24:21 F and the king, my son, and do not
Jer 5:24 Let us f our God, who gives autumn
26:19 Did not Hezekiah f and seek his
2Co 5:11 Since, then, we know what it is to f

Feared (Fear)
Ex 1:17 The midwives, however, f God and did
1:21 the midwives f God, he gave them
9:20 Those officials of Pharaoh who f the
14:31 the people f the Lord and put their
Dt 9:19 I f the anger and wrath of the Lord,
Jos 9:24 So we f for our lives because of you,
1Sa 4:13 his heart f for the ark of God.
14:26 his mouth, because they f the oath.
1Ch 16:25 he is to be f above all gods.
Ne 7: 2 and f God more than most men do.
Job 1: 1 upright; he f God and shunned evil.
3:25 What I f has come upon me; what I
31:34 I so f the crowd and so dreaded the
Ps 76: 7 You alone are to be f. Who can stand
76: 8 and the land f and was quiet—
76:11 bring gifts to the One to be f.
76:12 he is f by the kings of the earth.
Ps 89: 7 of the holy ones God is greatly f;
96: 4 he is to be f above all gods.
119:38 your servant, so that you may be f.
130: 4 is forgiveness; therefore you are f.
Isa 18: 2 to a people f far and wide, an
18: 7 from a people f far and wide, an
57:11 "Whom have you so dreaded and f that
Da 5:19 of every language dreaded and f him.
Jnh 1:16 At this the men greatly f the Lord,
Hab 1: 7 They are a f and dreaded people;
Hag 1:12 And the people f the Lord.
Mal 1:14 name is to be f among the nations.
3:16 those who f the Lord talked with
3:16 f the Lord and honoured his name.
Mk 6:20 Herod f John and protected him,
11:18 for they f him, because the whole
11:32 They f the people, for everyone
Lk 18: 2 neither f God nor cared about men.
Jn 19:38 but secretly because he f the Jews.
Ac 5:26 f that the people would stone them.

Fearful (Fear)
Lev 26:36 I will make their hearts so f in the
Dt 28:59 the Lord will send f plagues on you
Job 32: 6 you are old; that is why I was f,
Isa 8:22 distress and darkness and f gloom,
35: 4 say to those with f hearts, "Be
Lk 21:11 f events and great signs from heaven.
Heb 10:27 only a f expectation of judgment and

Fearfully (Fear)
Ps 139:14 I am f and wonderfully made;

Fearing (Fear)
Jos 22:25 might cause ours to stop f the Lord.
Ac 27:17 F that they would run aground on the
27:29 F that we would be dashed against
Heb 11:27 left Egypt, not f the king's anger;

Fearlessly (Fear)
Ac 9:27 had preached f in the name of Jesus.
Eph 6:19 I will f make known the mystery
6:20 I may declare it f, as I should.
Php 1:14 word of God more courageously and f.

Fears (Fear)
Job 1: 8 a man who f God and shuns evil."
2: 3 a man who f God and shuns evil.
Ps 25:12 then, is the man that f the Lord
34: 4 me; he delivered me from all my f.
112: 1 Blessed is the man who f the Lord,
128: 4 is the man blessed who f the Lord
Pr 14: 2 He whose walk is upright f the Lord,
14:16 A wise man f the Lord and shuns evil,
14:26 He who f the Lord has a secure
28:14 Blessed is the man who always f the
31:30 who f the Lord is to be praised.
Ecc 7:18 who f God will avoid all extremes.
Isa 50:10 Who among you f the Lord and obeys
2Co 7: 5 on the outside, f within.
1Jn 4:18 who f is not made perfect in love.

Fearsome (Fear)
Job 41:14 ringed about with his f teeth?

Feast (*Feast of Dedication, Feast of Tabernacles, Feast of Unleavened Bread, Feast of Weeks,* Feasted, Feasting, Feasts, *Passover Feast*)
Ge 21: 8 was weaned Abraham held a great f.
26:30 Isaac then made a f for them, and
29:22 people of the place and gave a f.
40:20 he gave a f for all his officials.
Ex 23:16 "Celebrate the F of Harvest with the
23:16 "Celebrate the F of Ingathering at
34:22 and the F of Ingathering at the turn
Dt 16:14 Be joyful at your F—you, your sons
16:15 For seven days celebrate the F to
33:19 will f on the abundance of the seas,
Jdg 14:10 And Samson made a f there, as was
14:12 within the seven days of the f,
14:17 cried the whole seven days of the f.
2Sa 3:20 prepared a f for him and his men.
1Ki 1:41 it as they were finishing their f.
3:15 Then he gave a f for all his court.
2Ki 6:23 he prepared a great f for them, and
Ne 8:14 during the f of the seventh month
8:18 They celebrated the f for seven days,
Job 39:30 His young ones f on blood, and where
Ps 22:29 All the rich of the earth will f and
36: 8 They f in the abundance of your
81: 3 moon is full, on the day of our F;
Pr 5:10 lest strangers f on your wealth and
15:15 cheerful heart has a continual f.
Ecc 5:11 owner except to f his eyes on them?
10:16 and whose princes f in the morning.
10:19 A f is made for laughter, and wine
Isa 25: 6 a f of rich food for all peoples,
58:14 to f on the inheritance of your
Jer 51:39 I will set out a f for them and make
Lam 2: 7 Lord as on the day of an appointed f.
2:22 "As you summon to a f day, so you
Eze 45:21 the Passover, a f lasting seven days,
45:23 during the seven days of the F he
45:25 "'During the seven days of the F,
Mt 8:11 and will take their places at the f
26: 5 "But not during the F," they said,
27:15 at the F to release a prisoner
Mk 14: 2 "But not during the F," they said,
15: 6 Now it was the custom at the F to
Lk 2:41 Jerusalem for the F of the Passover.
2:42 they went up to the F, according
2:43 After the F was over, while his
13:29 at the f in the kingdom of God.
14: 8 someone invites you to a wedding f,
14:15 eat at the f in the kingdom of God."
15:23 Let's have a f and celebrate.
Jn 5: 1 up to Jerusalem for a f of the Jews.
7: 8 You go to the F. I am not yet going
7: 8 I am not yet going up to this F,
7:10 his brothers had left for the F,
7:11 Now at the F the Jews were watching
7:14 Not until halfway through the F did
7:37 On the last and greatest day of the F
11:56 Isn't he coming to the F at all?"
12:12 crowd that had come for the F heard
12:20 who went up to worship at the F.
13:29 to buy what ws needed for the F,
2Pe 2:13 pleasures while they f with you.

Feast of Dedication
Jn 10:22 Then came the F at Jerusalem.

Feast of Tabernacles
Lev 23:34 seventh month the Lord's F begins,
Dt 16:13 Celebrate the F for seven days after
16:16 Bread, the Feast of Weeks and the F.
31:10 for cancelling debts, during the F,
2Ch 8:13 Bread, the Feast of Weeks and the F.
Ezr 3: 4 they celebrated the F with the
Zec 14:16 Almighty, and to celebrate the F.
14:18 do not go up to celebrate the F.
14:19 do not go up to celebrate the F.
Jn 7: 2 when the Jewish F was near,

Feast Of Unleavened Bread
Ex 12:17 "Celebrate the F, because it was on
23:15 "Celebrate the F; for seven days eat
34:18 "Celebrate the F. For seven days eat
Lev 23: 6 of that month the Lord's F begins;
Dt 16:16 the place he will choose: at the F,
2Ch 8:13 and the three annual feasts—the F,
30:13 celebrate the F in the second month.
30:21 celebrated the F for seven days
35:17 and observed the F for seven days.
Ezr 6:22 days they celebrated with joy the F,
Mt 26:17 On the first day of the F, the
Mk 14: 1 Now the Passover and the F were only
14:12 On the first day of the F, when it
Lk 22: 1 Now the F, called the Passover, was
Ac 12: 3 This happened during the F.
20: 6 we sailed from Philippi after the F,

Feast of Weeks
Ex 34:22 Celebrate the F with the firstfruits
Nu 28:26 offering of new grain during the F,
Dt 16:10 celebrate the F to the Lord your God

Dt 16:16 the F and the Feast of Tabernacles.
2Ch 8:13 the F and the Feast of Tabernacles.

Feasted (Feast)

Ge 43:34 So they f and drank freely with him.

Feasting (Feast)

Est 8:17 the Jews, with f and celebrating.
9:17 and made it a day of f and joy.
9:18 and made it a day of f and joy.
9:19 month of Adar as a day of joy and f,
9:22 to observe the days as days of f
Job 1: 5 a period of f had run its course,
1:13 daughters were f and drinking wine
1:18 "Your sons and daughters were f and
Pr 17: 1 than a house full of f, with strife.
Ecc 7: 2 mourning than to go to a house of f,
Jer 16: 8 not enter a house where there is f
Am 6: 7 exile; your f and lounging will end.
Zec 7: 6 were you not just f for yourselves?

Feasts (Feast)

Lev 23: 2 'These are my appointed f, the
23: 2 the appointed f of the LORD, which
23: 4 "'These are the LORD's appointed f,
23:37 ("'These are the LORD's appointed f,
23:44 the appointed f of the LORD.
Nu 10:10 of rejoicing—your appointed f
29:39 appointed f: your burnt offerings,
1Ch 23:31 Moon festivals and at appointed f.
2Ch 2: 4 the appointed f of the LORD our God.
8:13 New Moons and the three annual f—
31: 3 and appointed f as written in the
Ezr 3: 5 the appointed sacred f of the LORD,
Ne 10:33 New Moon festivals and appointed f;
Job 1: 4 His sons used to take turns holding f
24:20 forgets them, the worm f on them;
Isa 1:14 and your appointed f my soul hates.
Lam 1: 4 for no-one comes to her appointed f.
2: 6 her appointed f and her Sabbaths;
Eze 36:38 at Jerusalem during her appointed f.
44:24 my decrees for all my appointed f,
45:17 appointed f of the house of Israel.
46: 9 before the LORD at the appointed f,
46:11 At the festivals and the appointed f,
Hos 2:11 Sabbath days—all her appointed f.
9: 5 your appointed f, on the festival
12: 9 as in the days of your appointed f.
Am 5:21 "I hate, I despise your religious f;
8:10 I will turn your religious f into
Zep 3:18 "The sorrows for the appointed f I
Jude :12 men are blemishes at your love f,

Feat

2Ki 8:13 a mere dog, accomplish such a f?"

Feathers

Job 39:13 with the pinions and f of the stork.
39:18 Yet when she spreads her f to run,
Ps 68:13 silver, its f with shining gold."
91: 4 He will cover you with his f, and
Eze 17: 3 eagle with powerful wings, long f
Da 4:33 hair grew like the f of an eagle

Features

1Sa 16:12 a fine appearance and handsome f.
Est 2: 7 was lovely in form and f, and
Job 38:14 f stand out like those of a garment.

Fed (Feed)

Dt 32:13 f him with the fruit of the fields.
Jdg 19:21 into his house and f his donkeys.
Ps 80: 5 You have f them with the bread of
81:16 you would be f with the finest of
Da 4:12 from it every creature was f.
Hos 13: 6 I f them, they were satisfied; when
Na 2:11 the place where they f their young,
Lk 6:25 Woe to you who are well f now, for
Php 4:12 whether well f or hungry, whether
Jas 2:16 you well; keep warm and well f,"

Fee

Nu 22: 7 with them the f for divination.
Eze 16:33 Every prostitute receives a f, but

Feeble (Feeblest)

Ne 4: 2 "What are those f Jews doing? Will
Job 4: 3 how you have strengthened f hands.
26: 2 How you have saved the arm that is f!
Ps 38: 8 I am f and utterly crushed; I groan
Isa 16:14 survivors will be very few and f."
35: 3 Strengthen the f hands, steady the
Jer 49:24 Damascus has become f, she has
Heb 12:12 Therefore, strengthen your f arms

Feeblest (Feeble)

Zec 12: 8 so that the f among them will be

Feed (Fed, Feeding, Feeds, Overfed, Pasture-fed, Stall-fed, Well-fed)

Ge 42:27 his sack to get f for his donkey,
1Ki 14:11 f on those who die in the country.
16: 4 f on those who die in the country."
17: 4 ordered the ravens to f you there."
21:24 f on those who die in the country."
Ps 49:14 the grave, and death will f on them.
80:13 the creatures of the field f on it.
Pr 27:27 have plenty of goats' milk to f you
Isa 5:17 will f among the ruins of the rich.
9:20 f on the flesh of his own offspring:
9:21 Manasseh will f on Ephraim, and
11: 7 The cow will f with the bear, their
18: 6 the birds will f on them all summer,
49: 9 "They will f beside the roads and
61: 6 You will f on the wealth of nations,
65:25 wolf and the lamb will f together
Eze 34:10 can no longer f themselves.
34:14 there they will f in a rich pasture
34:18 for you to f on the good pasture?
34:19 Must my flock f on what you have
Hos 4: 8 They f on the sins of my people and
9: 2 winepresses will not f the people;
11: 4 their neck and bent down to f them.
Mic 7:14 Let them f in Bashan and Gilead as
Zec 11:16 heal the injured, or f the healthy
Mt 15:33 remote place to f such a crowd?"
25:37 when did we see you hungry and f you,
Mk 8: 4 anyone get enough bread to f them?"
Lk 15:15 sent him to his fields to f pigs.
Jn 21:15 Jesus said, "F my lambs."
21:17 Jesus said, "F my sheep."
Ro 12:20 "If your enemy is hungry, f him; if
Jude :12 who f only themselves.

Feeding (Fed)

Dt 8: 3 causing you to hunger and then f you
Mt 8:30 them a large herd of pigs was f.
Mk 5:11 A large herd of pigs was f on the
Lk 8:32 A large herd of pigs was f there on

Feeds (Fed)

Job 40:15 you and which f on grass like an ox.
Pr 15:14 but the mouth of a fool f on folly.
Isa 44:20 He f on ashes, a deluded heart
Hos 12: 1 Ephraim f on the wind; he pursues
Mic 3: 5 if one f them, they proclaim 'peace';
Mt 6:26 and yet your heavenly Father f them.
Lk 12:24 storeroom or barn; yet God f them.
Jn 6:57 who f on me will live because of me.
6:58 he who f on this bread will live
Eph 5:29 but he f and cares for it, just as

Feel (Feeling, Feelings, Feels, Felt)

Ge 41:55 all Egypt began to f the famine, the
Jdg 16:26 "Put me where I can f the pillars
1Sa 16:16 upon you, and you will f better."
16:23 come to Saul; he would f better,
2Ki 9:15 "If this is the way you f, don't let
Ps 58: 9 Before your pots can f the heat of
115: 7 they have hands, but cannot f, feet,
Pr 23:35 They beat me, but I don't f it!
Isa 32: 9 you daughters who f secure, hear
32:10 you who f secure will tremble; the
32:11 you daughters who f secure! Strip
Da 8:25 When they f secure, he will destroy
Da 11:21 kingdom when its people f secure,
11:24 the richest provinces f secure, he
Am 6: 1 and to you who f secure on Mount
Zec 1:15 with the nations that f secure.
2Co 11:29 Who is weak, and I do not f weak?
Php 1: 7 is right for me to f this way about
2Th 3:14 him, in order that he may f ashamed.

Feeling (Feel)

Job 24:23 let them rest in a f of security,
Isa 59:10 f our way like men without eyes.

Feelings (Feel)

Nu 5:14 if f of jealousy come over her
5:30 or when f of jealousy come over a

Feels (Feel)

Ex 23: 9 know how it f to be aliens,
Job 14:22 He f but the pain of his own body
1Co 7:36 in years and he f he ought to marry,

Feet (Foot)

Ge 6:15 450 f long, 75 f wide and 45 f high.
7:20 to a depth of more than twenty f.
8: 9 could find no place to set its f
18: 4 wash your f and rest under this
19: 2 You can wash your f and spend the
24:32 for him and his men to wash their f.
43:24 gave them water to wash their f and
49:10 ruler's staff from between his f,
49:33 he drew his f up into the bed,
Ex 4:25 foreskin and touched ⌊Moses;⌋ f
12:11 sandals on your f and your staff in
24:10 saw the God of Israel. Under his f
25:12 it and fasten them to its four f,
29:20 on the big toes of their right f.
30:19 hands and f with water from it.
30:21 they shall wash their hands and f so
37: 3 it and fastened them to its four f,
40:31 used it to wash their hands and f.
Lev 8:24 on the big toes of their right f.
11:42 walks on all fours or on many f;
Nu 11:31 to about three f above the ground,
35: 4 hundred f from the town wall.
35: 5 measure three thousand f on the east
Dt 1:36 the land he set his f on,
3:11 than thirteen f long and six f wide.
8: 4 your f did not swell during these
22: 4 Help him to get it to its f.
28:35 of your f to the top of your head.
29: 5 out, nor did the sandals on your f.
33: 3 At your f they all bow down, and
33:24 and let him bathe his f in oil.
Jos 3:15 their f touched the water's edge,
4:18 No sooner had they set their f on
9: 5 patched sandals on their f and wore
10:24 your f on the necks of these kings.
10:24 and placed their f on their necks.
14: 9 'The land on which your f have
Jdg 5:27 At her f he sank, he fell; there he
5:27 At her f he sank, he fell; where he
19:21 After they had washed their f, they
Ru 3: 4 Then go and uncover his f and lie
3: 7 uncovered his f and lay down.
3: 8 discovered a woman lying at his f.
3:14 she lay at his f until morning, but
1Sa 2: 9 He will guard the f of his saints,
14:13 climbed up using his hands and f,
17: 4 He was over nine f tall.
25:24 She fell at his f and said: "My lord,
25:41 wash the f of my master's servants."
2Sa 3:34 bound, your f were not fettered.
4: 4 had a son who was lame in both f.
4:12 They cut off their hands and f and
9: 3 Jonathan; he is crippled in both f."
9:13 and he was crippled in both f.
11: 8 down to your house and wash your f.
19:24 He had not taken care of his f or
22:10 down; dark clouds were under his f.
22:34 He makes my f like the f of a deer;
22:39 not rise; they fell beneath my f.
22:40 you made my adversaries bow at my f.
1Ki 2: 5 his waist and the sandals on his f.
5: 3 LORD put his enemies under his f.

1Ki 15:23 age, however, his **f** became diseased.
2Ki 4:27 mountain, she took hold of his **f**.
4:37 She came in, fell at his **f** and bowed
9:35 her skull, her **f** and her hands.
13:21 came to life and stood up on his **f**.
14:13 section about six hundred **f** long.
19:24 With the soles of my **f** I have dried
21: 8 make the **f** of the Israelites wander
25:17 Each pillar was twenty-seven **f** high.
25:17 pillar was four and a half **f** high
1Ch 11:23 who was seven and a half **f** tall.
28: 2 King David rose to his **f** and said:
2Ch 3:13 on their **f**, facing the main hall.
16:12 afflicted with a disease in his **f**.
25:23 section about six hundred **f** long.
33: 8 make the **f** of the Israelites leave
Ezr 6: 3 be ninety **f** high and ninety **f** wide,
Ne 9:21 out nor did their **f** become swollen.
Est 5:14 gallows built, seventy-five **f** high,
7: 9 A gallows seventy-five **f** high
8: 3 king, falling at his **f** and weeping.
Job 2: 7 of his **f** to the top of his head.
9:13 cohorts of Rahab cowered at his **f**.
12: 5 fate of those whose **f** are slipping.
13:27 You fasten my **f** in shackles; you
13:27 putting marks on the soles of my **f**.
18: 8 His **f** thrust him into a net and he
23:11 My **f** have closely followed his steps;
29: 8 and the old men rose to their **f**;
29:15 eyes to the blind and **f** to the lame
30:12 attacks; they lay snares for my **f**,
33:11 He fastens my **f** in shackles; he
Ps 8: 6 you put everything under his **f**:
9:15 their **f** are caught in the net they
17: 5 your paths; my **f** have not slipped.
18: 9 down; dark clouds were under his **f**.
18:33 He makes my **f** like the **f** of a deer;
18:38 not rise; they fell beneath my **f**.
18:39 you made my adversaries bow at my **f**.
22:16 they have pierced my hands and my **f**.
25:15 he will release my **f** from the snare.
26:12 My **f** stand on level ground; in the
31: 8 have set my **f** in a spacious place.
37:31 is in his heart; his **f** do not slip.
40: 2 he set my **f** on a rock and gave me a
44:18 our **f** had not strayed from your
45: 5 let the nations fall beneath your **f**.
47: 3 under us, peoples under our **f**.
56:13 from death and my **f** from stumbling,
57: 6 They spread a net for my **f**—I was
58:10 they bathe their **f** in the blood of
66: 9 lives and kept our **f** from slipping.
68:23 may plunge your **f** in the blood of
73: 2 for me, my **f** had almost slipped; I
105:18 They bruised his **f** with shackles,
110: 1 enemies a footstool for your **f**."
115: 7 feel, **f**, but they cannot walk;
116: 8 from tears, my **f** from stumbling,
119:101 I have kept my **f** from every evil
119:105 Your word is a lamp to my **f** and a
122: 2 Our **f** are standing in your gates,
140: 4 of violence who plan to trip my **f**.
Pr 1:16 for their **f** rush into sin, they are
4:26 Make level paths for your **f** and take
5: 5 Her **f** go down to death; her steps
6:13 signals with his **f** and motions with
6:18 **f** that are quick to rush into evil,
6:28 coals without his **f** being scorched?
7:11 her **f** never stay at home;
26: 6 Like cutting off one's **f** or drinking
29: 5 is spreading a net for his **f**.
SS 5: 3 I have washed my **f**—must I soil
7: 1 How beautiful your sandalled **f**,
Isa 6: 2 with two they covered their **f**, and
20: 2 body and the sandals from your **f**.
23: 7 old city, whose **f** have taken her to
26: 6 **F** trample it down—the **f** of the
37:25 With the soles of my **f** I have dried
41: 3 his **f** have not travelled before.
49:23 they will lick the dust at your **f**.
52: 7 the **f** of those who bring good news,
58:13 "If you keep your **f** from breaking
59: 7 Their **f** rush into sin; they are
60:13 I will glorify the place of my **f**.
60:14 despise you will bow down at your **f**
Jer 2:25 Do not run until your **f** are bare and
Jer 13:16 **f** stumble on the darkening hills.
14:10 they do not restrain their **f**.
18:22 me and have hidden snares for my **f**.
38:22 Your **f** are sunk in the mud; your
Lam 1:13 He spread a net for my **f** and turned
Eze 1: 7 their **f** were like those of a calf
2: 1 "Son of man, stand up on your **f** and
2: 2 raised me to my **f**, and I heard him
3:24 came into me and raised me to my **f**.
6:11 and stamp your **f** and cry out "Alas!"
24:17 fastened and your sandals on your **f**;
24:23 heads and your sandals on your **f**.
25: 6 your hands and stamped your **f**,
32: 2 churning the water with your **f** and
34:18 rest of your pasture with your **f**?
34:18 you also muddy the rest with your **f**?
34:19 what you have muddied with your **f**?
37:10 stood up on their **f**—a vast army.
43: 7 and the place for the soles of my **f**.
Da 2:33 iron, its **f** partly of baked clay.
2:34 **f** of iron and clay and smashed them.
2:41 Just as you saw that the **f** and toes
3: 1 ninety **f** high and nine **f** wide, and
3:24 King Nebuchadnezzar leaped to his **f**
7: 4 that it stood on two **f** like a man,
8:18 he touched me and raised me to my **f**.
Na 1: 3 and clouds are the dust of his **f**.
1:15 the **f** of one who brings good news,
Hab 3:19 he makes my **f** like the **f** of a deer,
Zec 5: 2 thirty **f** long and fifteen **f** wide."
14: 4 On that day his **f** will stand on the
14:12 they are still standing on their **f**,
Mal 4: 3 be ashes under the soles of your **f**
Mt 7: 6 they may trample them under their **f**,
10:14 shake the dust off your **f** when you
15:30 them at his **f**; and he healed them.
18: 8 two **f** and be thrown into eternal
22:44 I put your enemies under your **f**."'
28: 9 clasped his **f** and worshipped him.
Mk 5: 4 apart and broke the irons on his **f**.
5:22 Seeing Jesus, he fell at his **f**
5:33 came and fell at his **f** and,
6:11 shake the dust off your **f** when you
7:25 evil spirit came and fell at his **f**.
9:27 by the hand and lifted him to his **f**
9:45 have two **f** and be thrown into hell.
10:49 up! On your **f**! He's calling you."
10:50 jumped to his **f** and came to Jesus.
12:36 I put your enemies under your **f**."'
Lk 1:79 guide our **f** into the path of peace."
7:38 she stood behind him at his **f**
7:38 began to wet his **f** with her tears.
7:44 did not give me any water for my **f**,
7:44 but she wet my **f** with her tears and
7:45 has not stopped kissing my **f**.
7:46 but she has poured perfume on my **f**.
8:28 he cried out and fell at his **f**,
8:35 sitting at Jesus' **f**, dressed and in
8:41 came and fell at Jesus' **f**, pleading
8:47 came trembling and fell at his **f**.
9: 5 shake the dust off your **f** when you
10:11 that sticks to our **f** we wipe off
10:39 sat at the Lord's **f** listening to
15:22 on his finger and sandals on his **f**.
17:16 He threw himself at Jesus' **f** and
20:43 enemies a footstool for your **f**."'
24:39 Look at my hands and my **f**. It is I
24:40 he showed them his hands and **f**.
Jn 11: 2 Lord and wiped his **f** with her hair.
11:32 she fell at his **f** and said, "Lord,
11:44 his hands and **f** wrapped with strips
12: 3 on Jesus' **f** and wiped his **f** with
13: 5 and began to wash his disciples' **f**,
13: 6 "Lord, are you going to wash my **f**?
13: 8 Peter, "you shall never wash my **f**.
13: 9 Peter replied, "not just my **f** but
13:10 wash his **f**; his whole body is clean.
13:12 he had finished washing their **f**, he
13:14 have washed your **f**, you also should
13:14 also should wash one another's **f**.
Ac 2:35 enemies a footstool for your **f**."'
3: 7 man's **f** and ankles became strong.
3: 8 He jumped to his **f** and began to walk.
4:35 put it at the apostles' **f**, and it
4:37 money and put it at the apostles' **f**.
5: 2 rest and put it at the apostles' **f**.
Ac 5: 9 Look! The **f** of the men who buried
5:10 At that moment she fell down at his **f**
7:58 at the **f** of a young man named Saul.
9:41 by the hand and helped her to her **f**.
10:25 him and fell at his **f** in reverence.
13:51 they shook the dust from their **f** in
14: 8 there sat a man crippled in his **f**,
14:10 called out, "Stand up on your **f**!" At
16:24 and fastened their **f** in the stocks.
21:11 tied his own hands and **f** with it and
26:16 'Now get up and stand on your **f**. I
27:28 was one hundred and twenty **f** deep.
27:28 and found it was ninety **f** deep.
Ro 3:15 "Their **f** are swift to shed blood;
10:15 the **f** of those who bring good news!"
16:20 will soon crush Satan under your **f**.
1Co 12:21 And the head cannot say to the **f**,
15:25 has put all his enemies under his **f**.
15:27 he "has put everything under his **f**".
Eph 1:22 God placed all things under his **f**
6:15 your **f** fitted with the readiness
1Ti 5:10 washing the **f** of the saints,
Heb 1:13 enemies a footstool for your **f**"?
2: 8 put everything under his **f**." In
12:13 "Make level paths for your **f**," so
Jas 2: 3 "Sit on the floor by my **f**,"
Rev 1:13 in a robe reaching down to his **f**
1:15 His **f** were like bronze glowing in a
1:17 I saw him, I fell at his **f** as though
2:18 whose **f** are like burnished bronze.
3: 9 fall down at your **f** and acknowledge
11:11 and they stood on their **f**, and
12: 1 with the moon under her **f** and a
13: 2 but had **f** like those of a bear and a
19:10 At this I fell at his **f** to worship
22: 8 I fell down to worship at the **f** of

Feigned

1Sa 21:13 he **f** insanity in their presence; and

Felix

Ac 23:24 may be taken safely to Governor **F**."
23:26 Excellency, Governor **F**: Greetings.
24: 2 presented his case before **F**:
24: 3 most excellent **F**, we acknowledge
24:22 **F**, who was well acquainted with the
24:24 Several days later **F** came with his
24:25 **F** was afraid and said, "That's
24:27 **F** was succeeded by Porcius Festus,
24:27 but because **F** wanted to grant a
25:14 man here whom **F** left as a prisoner.

Fell (Fall)

Ge 7:12 rain **f** on the earth for forty days
14:10 some of the men **f** into them and the
15:12 Abram **f** into a deep sleep, and a
17: 3 Abram **f** face down, and God said to
17:17 Abraham **f** face down; he laughed and
35: 5 the terror of God **f** upon the towns
41: 5 He **f** asleep again and had a second
Ex 9:24 hail **f** and lightning flashed back
Lev 9:24 shouted for joy and **f** face down.
Nu 3: 4 Nadab and Abihu, however, **f** dead
14: 5 Moses and Aaron **f** face down in front
16: 4 Moses heard this, he **f** face down.
16:22 Moses and Aaron **f** face down and
16:45 at once." And they **f** face down.
20: 3 our brothers **f** dead before the LORD!
20: 6 the Tent of Meeting and **f** face down,
22:31 So he bowed low and **f** face down.
Dt 9:18 again I **f** prostrate before the LORD
19: 5 and as he swings his axe to **f** a tree,
Jos 5:14 Then Joshua **f** face down to the
7: 6 Joshua tore his clothes and **f** face
8:25 Twelve thousand men and women **f** that
21:10 because the first lot **f** to them):
22:17 a plague **f** on the community of the
Jdg 4:16 the troops of Sisera **f** by the sword
5:27 At her feet he sank, he **f**; there he
5:27 he **f**; where he sank, there he **f**—dead
8:11 and **f** upon the unsuspecting army.
9:40 Abimelech chased him, and many **f**
13:20 **f** with their faces to the ground.
16: 4 Some time later, he **f** in love with a
19:26 **f** down at the door and lay there

Jdg 20:31 about thirty men f in the open
20:44 Eighteen thousand Benjamites f, all
20:46 Benjamite swordsmen f, all of them
1Sa 4:18 he mentioned the ark of God, Eli f
11: 7 terror of the LORD f on the people
14:13 The Philistines f before Jonathan,
17:49 and he f face down on the ground.
25:24 She f at his feet and said: "My lord,
28:20 Immediately Saul f full length on
31: 1 and many f slain on Mount Gilboa.
31: 4 Saul took his own sword and f on it.
31: 5 f on his sword and died with him.
2Sa 1: 2 f to the ground to pay him honour.
1: 4 Many of them f and died. And Saul
2:16 side, and they f down together.
2:23 He f there and died on the spot. And
3:34 You f as one falls before wicked men.
4: 4 to leave, he f and became crippled.
11:17 some of the men in David's army f;
13: 1 Amnon son of David f in love with
14: 4 she f with her face to the ground to
14:22 Joab f with his face to the ground
19:18 he f prostrate before the king
21: 9 All seven of them f together; they
21:22 f at the hands of David and his men.
22:39 not rise; they f beneath my feet.
1Ki 18:38 the fire of the LORD f and burned up
18:39 people saw this, they f prostrate
19: 5 down under the tree and f asleep.
2Ki 1:10 Then the fire f from heaven and
1:12 Then the fire of God f from heaven
1:13 captain went up and f on his knees
4:37 She came in, f at his feet and bowed
6: 5 the iron axe-head f into the water.
1Ch 5:22 many others f slain, because the
10: 1 and many f slain on Mount Gilboa.
10: 4 Saul took his own sword and f on it.
10: 5 he too f on his sword and died.
20: 8 f at the hands of David and his men.
21:14 seventy thousand men of Israel f
21:16 clothed in sackcloth, f face down.
24: 7 The first lot f to Jehoiarib, the
25: 9 which was for Asaph, f to Joseph,
26:14 the East Gate f to Shelemiah.
26:14 the lot for the North Gate f to him.
26:15 for the South Gate f to Obed-Edom
26:15 for the storehouse f to his sons.
26:16 upper road f to Shuppim and Hosah.
29:20 they bowed low and f prostrate
2Ch 14:13 Such a great number of Cushites f
17:10 The fear of the LORD f on all the
20:18 f down in worship before the LORD.
Ezr 9: 5 and cloak torn, and f on my knees
Ne 13:19 evening shadows f on the gates of
Est 3: 7 And the lot f on the twelfth month,
Job 1:16 "The fire of God f from the sky and
1:20 Then he f to the ground in worship
29:22 my words f gently on their ears.
Ps 18:38 not rise; they f beneath my feet.
105:44 and they f heir to what others had
137: 7 Edomites did on the day Jerusalem f.
Lam 1: 7 When her people f into enemy hands,
Eze 1:28 When I saw it, I f face down, and I
3:23 the Kebar River, and I f face down.
9: 8 I f face down, crying out, "Ah,
11:13 Then I f face down and cried out in
31:12 Its boughs f on the mountains and in
39:23 and they all f by the sword.
43: 3 the Kebar River, and I f face down.
44: 4 of the LORD, and I f face down.
Da 2:46 King Nebuchadnezzar f prostrate
3: 7 f down and worshipped the image
3:23 tied, f into the blazing furnace.
7:20 before which three of them f—the
8:17 I was terrified and f prostrate.
10: 9 and as I listened to him, I f into a
Jnh 1: 5 he lay down and f into a deep sleep.
1: 7 cast lots and the lot f on Jonah.
Mt 7:27 house, and it f with a great crash."
13: 4 the seed, some f along the path,
13: 5 Some f on rocky places, where it did
13: 7 Other seed f among thorns, which
13: 8 Still other seed f on good soil,
13:20 the seed that f on rocky places is
13:22 the seed that f among the thorns is
13:23 the seed that f on good soil is the
Mt 17: 6 they f face down to the ground,
18:26 "The servant f on his knees before
18:29 "His fellow-servant f to his knees
25: 5 they all became drowsy and f asleep.
26:39 Going a little farther, he f with
Mk 3:11 they f down before him and cried out,
4: 4 scattering the seed, some f along
4: 5 Some f on rocky places, where it did
4: 7 Other seed f among thorns, which
4: 8 Still other seed f on good soil. It
5: 6 and f on his knees in front of him.
5:22 Seeing Jesus, he f at his feet
5:33 came and f at his feet and,
7:25 evil spirit came and f at his feet.
9:20 He f to the ground and rolled around,
10:17 him and f on his knees before him.
10:22 At this the man's face f. He went
14:35 Going a little farther, he f to the
Lk 5: 8 Peter saw this, he f at Jesus' knees
5:12 When he saw Jesus, he f with his
8: 5 some f along the path; it was
8: 6 Some f on rock, and when it came up,
8: 7 Other seed f among thorns, which
8: 8 Still other seed f on good soil. It
8:14 The seed that f among thorns stands
8:23 they sailed, he f asleep. A squall
8:28 he saw Jesus, he cried out and f at
8:41 the synagogue, came and f at Jesus'
8:47 came trembling and f at his feet.
10:30 when he f into the hands of robbers.
10:36 who f into the hands of robbers?"
13: 4 when the tower in Siloam f on them
16:21 longing to eat what f from the rich
Jn 11:32 she f at his feet and said, "Lord,
18: 6 they drew back and f to the ground.
Ac 1:18 Judas bought a field; there he f
1:26 they cast lots, and the lot f to
5: 5 Ananias heard this, he f down and
5:10 At that moment she f down at his
7:60 he f on his knees and cried out,
7:60 When he had said this, he f asleep.
9: 4 He f to the ground and heard a voice
9:18 something like scales f from Saul's
10:10 being prepared, he f into a trance.
10:25 him and f at his feet in reverence.
12: 7 and the chains f off Peter's wrists.
13:36 he f asleep; he was buried with his
16:29 f trembling before Paul and Silas.
19:35 of her image, which f from heaven?
20: 9 sound asleep, he f to the ground
22: 7 I f to the ground and heard a voice
22:17 at the temple, I f into a trance
26:14 We all f to the ground, and I heard
Ro 11:22 sternness to those who f, but
Heb 3:17 whose bodies f in the desert?
11:30 By faith the walls of Jericho f,
Rev 1:17 I saw him, I f at his feet as though
5: 8 elders f down before the Lamb.
5:14 the elders f down and worshipped.
6:13 the stars in the sky f to earth, as
7:11 They f down on their faces before
8:10 blazing like a torch, f from the sky
11:16 f on their faces and worshipped God,
16:21 a hundred pounds each f upon men.
19: 4 creatures f down and worshipped God,
19:10 At this I f at his feet to worship
22: 8 I f down to worship at the feet of

Felled (Fall)

Isa 9:10 stone; the fig-trees have been f,
10:33 The lofty trees will be f, the

Felling (Fall)

1Ki 5: 6 in f timber as the Sidonians."

Fellow (Fellow's, Fellow-man, Fellow-men, Fellows, Fellowship)

Ge 9: 5 for the life of his f man.
19: 9 And they said, "This f came here as
34:20 city to speak to their f townsmen.
Ex 2:13 "Why are you hitting your f Hebrew?
32: 1 As for this f Moses who brought us
32:23 As for this f Moses who brought us
Lev 25:46 over your f Israelites ruthlessly.
Nu 16:10 brought you and all your f Levites
Nu 18: 2 Bring your f Levites from your
18: 6 have selected your f Levites from
Dt 15: 2 loan he has made to his f Israelite.
15: 2 from his f Israelite or brother,
15:12 If a f Hebrew, a man or woman, sells
18: 7 all his f Levites who serve there
Jdg 20:13 not listen to their f Israelites.
Ru 3:11 All my f townsmen know that you are
1Sa 10:27 "How can this f save us?" They
21:15 that you have to bring this f here to
2Sa 6:20 his servants as any vulgar f would."
1Ki 22:27 Put this f in prison and give him
2Ki 5: 7 Why does this f send someone to me
9:11 Jehu went out to his f officers, one
23: 9 bread with their f priests.
1Ch 6:48 Their f Levites were assigned to all
9:19 of Korah, and his f gatekeepers
15:12 you and your f Levites are to
16:39 Zadok the priest and his f priests
26:20 Their f Levites were in charge of
2Ch 18:26 Put this f in prison and give him
19:10 f countrymen who live in the cities
28:11 Send back your f countrymen
28:15 to their f countrymen at Jericho,
31:15 distributing to their f priests
35: 5 your f countrymen, the lay people.
35: 6 ⌊the lambs⌋ for your f countrymen,
35:15 because their f Levites made the
Ezr 3: 2 son of Jozadak and his f priests
6: 6 their f officials of that province,
Ne 3: 1 the high priest and his f priests
Est 10: 3 in high esteem by his many f Jews,
Jer 34: 9 was to hold a f Jew in bondage.
34:14 free any f Hebrew who has sold
34:17 freedom for your f countrymen.
Mt 9: 3 "This f is blaspheming!
12:24 that this f drives out demons."
26:61 declared, "This f said, 'I am able
26:71 "This f was with Jesus of Nazareth.
Mk 2: 7 "Why does this f talk like that?
14:69 around, "This f is one of them.
Lk 5:21 "Who is this f who speaks blasphemy?
14:10 the presence of all your f guests.
14:30 saying, 'This f began to build and
22:59 "Certainly this f was with him, for
Jn 5:12 they asked him, "Who is this f who
9:29 but as for this f, we don't even
Ac 2:14 "F Jews and all of you who live in
6:13 "This f never stops speaking against
7:23 decided to visit his f Israelites.
7:40 As for this f Moses who led us out
19:26 you see and hear how this f Paul has
19:38 Demetrius and his f craftsmen
2Co 12:16 Yet, crafty f that I am, I caught

Fellow's (Fellow)

1Sa 25:21 all my watching over this f property
Jn 9:28 "You are this f disciple! We are

Fellow-citizens (Citizen)

Eph 2:19 but f with God's people and members

Fellow-elder (Elder)

1Pe 5: 1 I appeal as a f, a witness of Christ'

Fellow-man (Fellow, Man)

Ps 15: 3 no wrong and casts no slur on his f,
Mic 2: 2 of his home, a f of his inheritance.
Ro 13: 8 loves his f has fulfilled the law.

Fellow-men (Fellow, Men)

Job 30: 5 They were banished from their f,

Fellow-prisoner (Prisoner)

Col 4:10 My f Aristarchus sends you his
Phm :23 Epaphras, my f in Christ Jesus,

Fellow-prisoners (Prisoner)

Heb 13: 3 in prison as if you were their f,

Fellows (Fellow)

1Sa 14: 6 outpost of those uncircumcised f.
31: 4 or these uncircumcised f will come
1Ch 10: 4 or these uncircumcised f will come

Fellow-servant (Servant)

Mt 18:29 "His f fell to his knees and begged
18:33 on your f just as I had on you?'
Col 1: 7 our dear f, who is a faithful
4: 7 faithful minister and f in the Lord
Rev 19:10 "Do not do it! I am a f with you and
22: 9 "Do not do it! I am a f with you and

Fellow-servants (Servant)

Mt 18:28 one of his f who owed him a hundred
24:49 he then begins to beat his f and to
Rev 6:11 until the number of their f and

Fellowship (Fellow, *Fellowship offering, Fellowship offerings*)

Ps 55:14 with whom I once enjoyed sweet f as
Ac 2:42 the apostles' teaching and to the f,
1Co 1: 9 God, who has called you into f with
5: 2 out of your f the man who did this?
2Co 6:14 what f can light have with darkness?
13:14 f of the Holy Spirit be with you all.
Gal 2: 9 Barnabas the right hand of f when
Php 2: 1 if any f with the Spirit, if any
3:10 the f of sharing in his sufferings,
1Jn 1: 3 so that you also may have f with us.
1: 3 And our f is with the Father and
1: 6 If we claim to have f with him yet
1: 7 light, we have f with one another,

Fellowship offering

Lev 3: 1 "'If someone's offering is a f, and
3: 3 From the f he is to bring a
3: 6 from the flock as a f to the LORD,
3: 9 From the f he is to bring a
4:10 from the ox sacrificed as a f.
4:26 altar as he burned the fat of the f.
4:31 as the fat is removed from the f,
4:35 is removed from the lamb of the f,
7:11 "'These are the regulations for the f
7:13 Along with his f of thanksgiving he
7:15 The meat of his f of thanksgiving
7:18 If any meat of the f is eaten on the
7:20 meat of the f belonging to the LORD,
7:21 meat of the f belonging to the LORD,
7:29 'Anyone who brings a f to the LORD
7:33 the fat of the f shall have the
7:37 the ordination offering and the f,
9: 4 an ox and a ram for a f to sacrifice
9:18 and the ram as the f for the people.
9:22 offering and the f, he stepped down.
19: 5 "'When you sacrifice a f to the LORD,
22:21 a f to the LORD to fulfil a special
23:19 two lambs, each a year old, for a f.
Nu 6:14 a ram without defect for a f,
6:17 the ram as a f to the LORD,
6:18 is under the sacrifice of the f.
7:17 a year old, to be sacrificed as a f.
7:23 a year old, to be sacrificed as a f.
7:29 a year old, to be sacrificed as a f.
7:35 a year old, to be sacrificed as a f.
7:41 a year old, to be sacrificed as a f.
7:47 a year old, to be sacrificed as a f.
7:53 a year old, to be sacrificed as a f.
7:59 a year old, to be sacrificed as a f.
7:65 a year old, to be sacrificed as a f.
7:71 a year old, to be sacrificed as a f.
7:77 a year old, to be sacrificed as a f.
7:83 a year old, to be sacrificed as a f.
7:88 of the f came to twenty-four oxen,
15: 8 a special vow or a f to the LORD,

Fellowship offerings

Ex 20:24 on it your burnt offerings and f,
24: 5 young bulls as f to the LORD.
29:28 to make to the LORD from their f.
32: 6 burnt offerings and presented f.
Lev 6:12 and burn the fat of the f on it.
7:14 who sprinkles the blood of the f.
7:32 f to the priest as a contribution.
Lev 7:34 From the f of the Israelites, I have
10:14 as your share of the Israelites' f.
17: 5 of Meeting and sacrifice them as f.
Nu 10:10 over your burnt offerings and f,
29:39 offerings, drink offerings and f.'"
Dt 27: 7 Sacrifice f there, eating them and
Jos 8:31 burnt offerings and sacrificed f.
22:23 or to sacrifice f on it, may the
22:27 burnt offerings, sacrifices and f.
Jdg 20:26 burnt offerings and f to the LORD.
21: 4 and presented burnt offerings and f.
1Sa 10: 8 to sacrifice burnt offerings and f,
11:15 There they sacrificed f before the
13: 9 me the burnt offering and the f.
2Sa 6:17 offerings and f before the LORD.
6:18 the burnt offerings and f,
24:25 sacrificed burnt offerings and f.
1Ki 3:15 sacrificed burnt offerings and f.
8:63 Solomon offered a sacrifice of f to
8:64 offerings and the fat of the f,
8:64 offerings and the fat of the f.
9:25 f on the altar he had built for the
2Ki 16:13 the blood of his f on the altar.
1Ch 16: 1 burnt offerings and f before God.
16: 2 the burnt offerings and f,
21:26 sacrificed burnt offerings and f.
2Ch 7: 7 offerings and the fat of the f,
29:35 together with the fat of the f and
30:22 and offered f and praised the LORD,
31: 2 offer burnt offerings and f,
33:16 f and thank-offerings on it,
Pr 7:14 "I have f at home; today I fulfilled
Eze 43:27 burnt offerings and f on the altar.
45:15 burnt offerings and f to make
45:17 burnt offerings and f to make
46: 2 his burnt offering and his f.
46:12 whether a burnt offering or f—the
46:12 his f as he does on the Sabbath day.
Am 5:22 f, I will have no regard for them.

Fellow-soldier (Soldier)

Php 2:25 my brother, fellow-worker and f, who
Phm : 2 Archippus our f and to the church

Fellow-worker (Worker)

Ro 16: 9 Greet Urbanus, our f in Christ, and
16:21 Timothy, my f, sends his greetings
2Co 8:23 for Titus, he is my partner and f
Php 2:25 my brother, f and fellow-soldier,
1Th 3: 2 God's f in spreading the gospel of
Phm : 1 To Philemon our dear friend and f,

Fellow-workers (Worker)

Ro 16: 3 Priscilla and Aquila, my f in Christ
1Co 3: 9 For we are God's f; you are God's
2Co 6: 1 God's f we urge you not to receive
Php 4: 3 with Clement and the rest of my f,
Col 4:11 These are the only Jews among my f
Phm :24 Aristarchus, Demas and Luke, my f.

Felt (Feel)

Ge 2:25 both naked, and they f no shame.
Ex 2: 6 He was crying, and she f sorry for
10:21 over Egypt—darkness that can be f."
1Sa 13:12 So I f compelled to offer the burnt
2Ki 8:11 a fixed gaze until Hazael f ashamed.
Ps 30: 6 I f secure, I said, "I shall never
Jer 5: 3 but they f no pain; you crushed them
22:21 I warned you when you f secure, but
Na 3:19 who has not f your endless cruelty?
Mk 5:29 she f in her body that she was freed
2Co 1: 9 Indeed, in our hearts we f the
Heb 10: 2 longer have f guilty for their sins.
Jude : 3 I f I had to write and urge you to

Female (Females)

Ge 1:27 him; male and f he created them.
5: 2 He created them male and f and
6:19 of all living creatures, male and f
7: 3 every kind of bird, male and f,
7: 9 male and f, came to Noah and entered
7:16 The animals going in were male and f
12:16 male and f donkeys, menservants and
20:14 f slaves and gave them to Abraham,
Ge 30:35 the speckled or spotted f goats
32:14 two hundred f goats and twenty male
32:15 thirty f camels with their young,
32:15 twenty f donkeys and ten male
45:23 and ten f donkeys loaded with grain
Ex 21:20 "If a man beats his male or f slave
21:32 If the bull gores a male or f slave,
Lev 3: 1 whether male or f, he is to present
3: 6 to offer a male or f without defect.
4:28 committed a f goat without defect.
4:32 he is to bring a f without defect.
5: 6 he must bring to the LORD a f lamb
25:44 "'Your male and f slaves are to come
27: 4 if it is a f, set her value at
27: 5 shekels and of a f at ten shekels.
27: 6 and that of a f at three shekels
27: 7 shekels and of a f at ten shekels.
Nu 5: 3 Send away male and f alike; send
15:27 year-old f goat for a sin offering.
Dt 23:18 the earnings of a f prostitute or
28:68 f slaves, but no-one will buy you.
Est 7: 4 been sold as male and f slaves,
Ecc 2: 7 I bought male and f slaves and had
Jer 34: 9 his Hebrew slaves, both male and f;
34:10 would free their male and f slaves
34:16 f slaves you had set free to go
Gal 3:28 slave nor free, male nor f, for you

Females (Female)

Ge 30:41 Whenever the stronger f were in heat,

Fence

Ps 62: 3 this leaning wall, this tottering f?

Fermented

Lev 10: 9 not to drink wine or other f drink
Nu 6: 3 abstain from wine and other f drink
6: 3 from wine or from other f drink.
28: 7 of a hin of f drink with each lamb.
Dt 14:26 wine or other f drink, or anything
29: 6 and drank no wine or other f drink.
Jdg 13: 4 you drink no wine or other f drink
13: 7 drink no wine or other f drink
13:14 nor drink any wine or other f drink
Lk 1:15 never to take wine or other f drink

Ferocious

Ge 37:20 say that a f animal devoured him.
37:33 Some f animal has devoured him.
Isa 35: 9 nor will any f beast get up on it;
Mt 7:15 but inwardly they are f wolves.

Fertile (Fertilise)

Nu 13:20 How is the soil? Is it f or poor?
2Ch 26:10 the f lands, for he loved the soil.
Ne 9:25 captured fortified cities and f land
9:35 spacious and f land you gave them,
Isa 5: 1 one had a vineyard on a f hillside.
10:18 his forests and f fields it will
28: 1 set on the head of a f valley—to
28: 4 set on the head of a f valley, will
29:17 Lebanon be turned into a f field
29:17 and the f field seem like a forest?
32:15 and the desert becomes a f field,
32:15 and the f field seems like a forest.
32:16 righteousness live in the f field.
Jer 2: 7 I brought you into a f land to eat
Eze 17: 5 of your land and put it in f soil.
Mic 7:14 in a forest, in f pasture-lands.

Fertilise (Fertile)

Lk 13: 8 and I'll dig round it and f it.

Fervent (Fervour)

Pr 26:23 are f lips with an evil heart.

Fervour (Fervent)

Ac 18:25 and he spoke with great f and taught
Ro 12:11 your spiritual f, serving the Lord.

Festal (Festival)

Ps 118:27 join in the f procession up to the

Fester (Festering)
Ps 38: 5 My wounds **f** and are loathsome

Festering (Fester)
Ex 9: 9 and **f** boils will break out on men
9:10 **f** boils broke out on men and animals.
Lev 21:20 or who has **f** or running sores or
22:22 with warts or **f** or running sores.
Dt 28:27 with tumour, **f** sores and the itch,
Job 7: 5 and scabs, my skin is broken and **f**.

Festival (Festal, Festivals, Festive)
Ex 5: 1 may hold a **f** to me in the desert.'"
10: 9 are to celebrate a **f** to the LORD."
12:14 celebrate it as a **f** to the LORD—
13: 6 seventh day hold a **f** to the LORD.
23:14 year you are to celebrate a **f** to me.
23:18 "The fat of my **f** offerings must not
32: 5 there will be a **f** to the LORD."
Lev 23:39 celebrate the **f** to the LORD for
23:41 Celebrate this as a **f** to the LORD
Nu 15: 3 freewill offerings or **f** offerings—
28:17 of this month there is to be a **f**;
29:12 a **f** to the LORD for seven days.
Jdg 9:27 held a **f** in the temple of their god.
21:19 the annual **f** of the LORD in Shiloh,
1Sa 20: 5 "Look, tomorrow is the New Moon **f**,
20:18 David: "Tomorrow is the New Moon **f**.
20:24 when the New Moon **f** came, the king
1Ki 8: 2 the time of the **f** in the month of
8:65 Solomon observed the **f** at that time,
12:32 He instituted a **f** on the fifteenth
12:32 like the **f** held in Judah, and
12:33 So he instituted the **f** for the
2Ch 5: 3 time of the **f** in the seventh month.
7: 8 Solomon observed the **f** at that time
7: 9 days and the **f** for seven days more.
30:23 to celebrate the **f** seven more days;
Isa 30:29 on the night you celebrate a holy **f**;
Hos 7: 5 On the day of the **f** of our king the
9: 5 feasts, on the **f** days of the LORD?
Mal 2: 3 the offal from your **f** sacrifices,
1Co 5: 8 Therefore let us keep the **F**, not
Col 2:16 or with regard to a religious **f**, a

Festivals (Festival)
Nu 10:10 New Moon **f**—you are to sound the
1Ch 23:31 New Moon **f** and at appointed feasts.
Ne 10:33 New Moon **f** and appointed feasts; for
Isa 1:14 Your New Moon **f** and your appointed
29: 1 year and let your cycle of **f** go on.
33:20 Look upon Zion, the city of our **f**;
Eze 45:17 and drink offerings at the **f**,
46:11 "'At the **f** and the appointed feasts,
Hos 2:11 all her celebrations: her yearly **f**,
5: 7 their New Moon **f** will devour them
Na 1:15 Celebrate your **f**, O Judah, and
Zec 8:19 occasions and happy **f** for Judah.

Festive (Festival)
1Sa 25: 8 men, since we come at a **f** time.
Ps 42: 4 and thanksgiving among the **f** throng.

Festooned
1Ki 7:17 interwoven chains **f** the capitals on

Festus
Ac 24:27 Felix was succeeded by Porcius **F**,
25: 1 **F** went up from Caesarea to Jerusalem,
25: 3 They urgently requested **F**, as a
25: 4 **F** answered, "Paul is being held at
25: 9 **F**, wishing to do the Jews a favour,
25:12 After **F** had conferred with his
25:13 Caesarea to pay their respects to **F**.
25:14 **F** discussed Paul's case with the
25:22 Agrippa said to **F**, "I would like to
25:23 command of **F**, Paul was brought in.
25:24 **F** said: "King Agrippa, and all who
26:24 At this point **F** interrupted Paul's
26:25 "I am not insane, most excellent **F**,"
26:32 Agrippa said to **F**, "This man could

Fettered (Fetters)
2Sa 3:34 not bound, your feet were not **f**.

Fetters (Fettered)
Job 36:13 he **f** them, they do not cry for help.
Ps 2: 3 they say, "and throw off their **f**.
149: 8 to bind their kings with **f**, their

Fever (Feverish)
Lev 26:16 wasting diseases and **f** that will
Dt 28:22 with **f** and inflammation, with
Job 30:30 and peels; my body burns with **f**.
Mt 8:14 mother-in-law lying in bed with a **f**.
8:15 He touched her hand and the **f** left
Mk 1:30 in bed with a **f**, and they told Jesus
1:31 The **f** left her and she began to wait
Lk 4:38 was suffering from a high **f**, and
4:39 he bent over her and rebuked the **f**,
Jn 4:52 "The **f** left him yesterday at the
Ac 28: 8 bed, suffering from **f** and dysentery.

Feverish (Fever)
Lam 5:10 is hot as an oven, **f** from hunger.

Field (Battlefield, Cornfield, Cornfields, Fields)
Ge 2: 5 no shrub of the **f** had yet appeared
2: 5 no plant of the **f** had yet sprung up,
2:19 all the beasts of the **f** and all the
2:20 the air and all the beasts of the **f**.
3:18 you will eat the plants of the **f**.
4: 8 Abel, "Let's go out to the **f**.
4: 8 And while they were in the **f**, Cain
23: 9 to him and is at the end of his **f**.
23:11 "Listen to me; I give you the **f**, and
23:13 I will pay the price of the **f**.
23:17 Ephron's **f** in Machpelah near Mamre
23:17 Mamre—both the **f** and the cave in it,
23:17 trees within the borders of the **f**
23:19 in the cave in the **f** of Machpelah
23:20 the **f** and the cave in it were
24:63 He went out to the **f** one evening to
24:65 "Who is that man in the **f** coming to
25: 9 **f** of Ephron son of Zohar the Hittite,
25:10 the **f** Abraham had bought from the
27:27 like the smell of a **f** that the LORD
29: 2 There he saw a well in the **f**, with
37: 7 sheaves of corn out in the **f** when
39: 5 had, both in the house and in the **f**.
49:29 cave in the **f** of Ephron the Hittite,
49:30 the cave in the **f** of Machpelah, near
49:30 Ephron the Hittite, along with the **f**.
49:32 The **f** and the cave in it were bought
50:13 in the cave in the **f** of Machpelah,
50:13 Ephron the Hittite, along with the **f**.
Ex 9: 3 plague on your livestock in the **f**
9:19 have in the **f** to a place of shelter,
9:19 out in the **f**, and they will die.'"
9:21 their slaves and livestock in the **f**.
22: 5 "If a man grazes his livestock in a **f**
22: 5 and they graze in another man's **f**,
22: 5 the best of his own **f** or vineyard.
22: 6 or standing corn or the whole **f**,
23:16 of the crops you sow in your **f**.
23:16 you gather in your crops from the **f**.
Lev 19: 9 reap to the very edges of your **f**
19:19 "'Do not plant your **f** with two kinds
23:22 reap to the very edges of your **f**
26: 4 and the trees of the **f** their fruit.
27:17 If he dedicates his **f** during the
27:18 if he dedicates his **f** after the
27:19 If the man who dedicates the **f**
27:19 and the **f** will again become his.
27:20 If, however, he does not redeem the **f**
27:21 the **f** is released in the Jubilee, it
27:21 holy, like a **f** devoted to the
27:22 "'If a man dedicates to the LORD a **f**
27:24 In the Year of Jubilee the **f** will
Nu 20:17 We will not go through any **f** or
21:22 We will not turn aside into any **f** or
22: 4 an ox licks up the grass of the **f**.
22:23 she turned off the road into a **f**.
23:14 he took him to the **f** of Zophim on
Dt 20:19 Are the trees of the **f** people, that
Dt 21: 1 If a man is found slain, lying in a **f**
24:19 you are harvesting in your **f** and you
27: 6 LORD your God with stones from the **f**
28:38 You will sow much seed in the **f** but
Jos 15:18 urged him to ask her father for a **f**.
Jdg 1:14 urged him to ask her father for a **f**.
5:18 Naphtali on the heights of the **f**.
13: 9 woman while she was out in the **f**;
20:31 about thirty men fell in the open **f**
Ru 2: 3 she found herself working in a **f**
2: 7 She went into the **f** and has worked
2: 8 Don't go and glean in another **f** and
2: 9 Watch the **f** where the men are
2:17 Ruth gleaned in the **f** until evening.
2:22 else's **f** you might be harmed."
1Sa 6:14 The cart came to the **f** of Joshua of
6:18 in the **f** of Joshua of Beth Shemesh.
14:15 whole army—those in the camp and **f**,
17:44 of the air and the beasts of the **f**!"
19: 3 my father in the **f** where you are.
20: 5 but let me go and hide in the **f**
20:11 said, "let's go out into the **f**.
20:24 David hid in the **f**, and when the New
20:35 to the **f** for his meeting with David.
30:11 They found an Egyptian in a **f** and
2Sa 14: 6 a fight with each other in the **f**,
14:30 "Look, Joab's **f** is next to mine, and
14:30 Absalom's servants set the **f** on fire.
14:31 your servants set my **f** on fire?"
18: 6 The army marched into the **f** to fight
20:12 dragged him from the road into a **f**
23:11 where there was a **f** full of lentils,
23:12 his stand in the middle of the **f**.
2Ki 3:19 and ruin every good **f** with stones."
3:25 every good **f** until it was covered.
9:25 "Pick him up and throw him on the **f**
18:17 chief officer and his **f** commander
18:17 on the road to the Washerman's **F**.
18:19 The **f** commander said to them, "Tell
18:26 and Joah said to the **f** commander
18:37 him what the **f** commander had said.
19: 4 all the words of the **f** commander,
19: 8 the **f** commander heard that the king
19:26 They are like plants in the **f**, like
1Ch 11:13 where there was a **f** full of barley
11:14 their stand in the middle of the **f**.
27:26 the **f** workers who farmed the land.
2Ch 26:23 buried near them in a **f** for burial
Job 5:23 a covenant with the stones of the **f**,
Ps 8: 7 and herds, and the beasts of the **f**,
50:11 and the creatures of the **f** are mine.
72: 6 like rain falling on a mown **f**,
72:16 it thrive like the grass of the **f**.
80:13 the creatures of the **f** feed on it.
103:15 flourishes like a flower of the **f**;
104:11 water to all the beasts of the **f**;
Pr 13:23 A poor man's **f** may produce abundant
24:30 I went past the **f** of the sluggard,
27:26 and the goats with the price of a **f**.
31:16 She considers a **f** and buys it; out
SS 2: 7 gazelles and by the does of the **f**:
3: 5 gazelles and by the does of the **f**:
Isa 1: 8 like a hut in a **f** of melons, like
5: 8 join **f** to **f** till no space is left
7: 3 on the road to the Washerman's **F**.
19: 7 Every sown **f** along the Nile will
28:25 in its plot, and spelt in its **f**?
29:17 Lebanon be turned into a fertile **f**
29:17 the fertile **f** seem like a forest?
32:15 and the desert becomes a fertile **f**,
32:15 the fertile **f** seems like a forest.
32:16 righteousness live in the fertile **f**.
36: 2 of Assyria sent his **f** commander
36: 2 on the road to the Washerman's **F**,
36: 4 The **f** commander said to them, "Tell
36:11 Joah said to the **f** commander
36:22 him what the **f** commander had said.
37: 4 hear the words of the **f** commander,
37: 8 the **f** commander heard that the king
37:27 They are like plants in the **f**, like
40: 6 glory is like the flowers of the **f**.
55:12 the trees of the **f** will clap their
56: 9 Come, all you beasts of the **f**, come
Jer 4:17 surround her like men guarding a **f**,
7:20 on the trees of the **f** and on the
9:22 will lie like refuse on the open **f**,

Jer 12: 4 the grass in every **f** be withered?
12:10 my vineyard and trample down my **f**;
12:10 will turn my pleasant **f** into a
14: 5 Even the doe in the **f** deserts her
26:18 "'Zion will be ploughed like a **f**,
32: 7 'Buy my **f** at Anathoth, because as
32: 8 'Buy my **f** at Anathoth in the
32: 9 I bought the **f** at Anathoth from my
32:25 'Buy the **f** with silver and have the
41: 8 oil and honey, hidden in a **f**.
Lam 4: 9 away for lack of food from the **f**.
Eze 16: 5 you were thrown out into the open **f**,
16: 7 I made you grow like a plant of the **f**
17:24 All the trees of the **f** will know
29: 5 You will fall on the open **f** and not
31: 4 channels to all the trees of the **f**.
31: 5 higher than all the trees of the **f**;
31: 6 all the beasts of the **f** gave birth
31:13 beasts of the **f** were among its
31:15 the trees of the **f** withered away.
32: 4 the land and hurl you on the open **f**.
34:27 The trees of the **f** will yield their
36:30 of the trees and the crops of the **f**,
38:20 the beasts of the **f**, every creature
39: 5 You will fall in the open **f**, for I
Da 2:38 beasts of the **f** and the birds of
4:12 Under it the beasts of the **f** found
4:15 the ground, in the grass of the **f**.
4:21 shelter to the beasts of the **f**,
4:23 in the grass of the **f**, while its
Hos 2:18 for them with the beasts of the **f**
4: 3 the beasts of the **f** and the birds of
10: 4 poisonous weeds in a ploughed **f**.
12:11 piles of stones on a ploughed **f**.
Joel 1:11 the harvest of the **f** is destroyed.
1:12 the trees of the **f**—are dried up.
1:19 burned up all the trees of the **f**.
Am 4: 7 One **f** had rain; another had none and
Mic 3:12 Zion will be ploughed like a **f**,
4:10 the city to camp in the open **f**.
Zec 10: 1 and plants of the **f** to everyone.
Mt 6:28 See how the lilies of the **f** grow.
6:30 how God clothes the grass of the **f**,
9:38 out workers into his harvest **f**."
13:24 a man who sowed good seed in his **f**.
13:27 didn't you sow good seed in your **f**?
13:31 a man took and planted in his **f**.
13:36 the parable of the weeds in the **f**."
13:38 The **f** is the world, and the good
13:44 is like treasure hidden in a **f**.
13:44 sold all he had and bought that **f**.
22: 5 and went off—one to his **f**, another
24:18 Let no-one in the **f** go back to get
24:40 Two men will be in the **f**; one will
27: 7 the potter's **f** as a burial place
27: 8 has been called the **F** of Blood to
27:10 they used them to buy the potter's **f**,
Mk 13:16 Let no-one in the **f** go back to get
Lk 10: 2 send out workers into his harvest **f**.
12:28 how God clothes the grass of the **f**,
14:18 'I have just bought a **f**, and I must
15:25 the older son was in the **f**.
17: 7 servant when he comes in from the **f**,
17:31 no-one in the **f** should go back
Ac 1:18 Judas bought a **f**; there he fell
1:19 so they called that **f** in their
1:19 Akeldama, that is, **F** of Blood.)
4:37 sold a **f** he owned and brought the
1Co 3: 9 you are God's **f**, God's building.
2Co 10:13 to the **f** God has assigned to us,
10:13 to us, a **f** that reaches even to you.
1Pe 1:24 glory is like the flowers of the **f**;

Fields (Field)

Ge 30:14 Reuben went out into the **f** and found
30:16 when Jacob came in from the **f** that
31: 4 out to the **f** where his flocks were.
34: 5 his sons were in the **f** with his
34: 7 Jacob's sons had come in from the **f**
34:28 theirs in the city and out in the **f**.
37:15 wandering around in the **f** and asked
41:48 food grown in the **f** surrounding it.
47:20 one and all, sold their **f**, because
47:24 you may keep as seed for the **f**
Ex 1:14 and with all kinds of work in the **f**;
8:13 in the courtyards and in the **f**.
9:22 growing in the **f** of Egypt."
9:25 in the **f**—both men and animals;
9:25 in the **f** and stripped every tree.
10: 5 tree that is growing in your **f**.
10:12 devour everything growing in the **f**,
10:15 in the **f** and the fruit on the trees.
23:10 "For six years you are to sow your **f**
Lev 14: 7 release the live bird in the open **f**.
14:53 bird in the open **f** outside the town.
17: 5 they are now making in the open **f**.
25: 3 For six years sow your **f**, and for
25: 4 sow your **f** or prune your vineyards.
25:12 what is taken directly from the **f**.
Nu 16:14 an inheritance of **f** and vineyards.
Dt 11:15 I will provide grass in the **f** for
14:22 all that your **f** produce each year.
32:13 and fed him with the fruit of the **f**.
32:32 of Sodom and from the **f** of Gomorrah.
Jos 8:24 killing all the men of Ai in the **f**
21:12 the **f** and villages around the city
Jdg 9:27 After they had gone out into the **f**
9:32 come and lie in wait in the **f**.
9:42 people of Shechem went out to the **f**,
9:43 and set an ambush in the **f**.
9:44 those in the **f** and struck them down.
19:16 came in from his work in the **f**.
Ru 2: 2 "Let me go to the **f** and pick up the
2: 3 in the **f** behind the harvesters.
1Sa 8:14 He will take the best of your **f** and
11: 5 then Saul was returning from the **f**,
22: 7 give all of you **f** and vineyards?
25:15 the **f** near them nothing was missing.
2Sa 1:21 nor **f** that yield offerings of grain.
11:11 lord's men are camped in the open **f**.
19:29 order you and Ziba to divide the **f**."
1Ki 2:26 "Go back to your **f** in Anathoth.
2Ki 4:39 One of them went out into the **f** to
23: 4 in the **f** of the Kidron Valley
25:12 land to work the vineyards and **f**.
1Ch 6:56 the **f** and villages around the city
16:32 let the **f** be jubilant, and
2Ch 26:10 He had people working his **f** and
31: 5 honey and all that the **f** produced.
Ne 5: 3 "We are mortgaging our **f**, our
5: 4 king's tax on our **f** and vineyards.
5: 5 **f** and our vineyards belong to others.
5:11 Give back to them immediately their **f**
11:25 for the villages with their **f**, some
11:30 in Lachish and its **f**, and in Azekah
12:44 From the **f** around the towns they
13:10 had gone back to their own **f**.
Job 24: 6 They gather fodder in the **f** and
Ps 37:20 will be like the beauty of the **f**,
96:12 let the **f** be jubilant, and
107:37 They sowed **f** and planted vineyards
132: 6 we came upon it in the **f** of Jaar:
144:13 by tens of thousands in our **f**;
Pr 8:26 before he made the earth or its **f** or
23:10 encroach on the **f** of the fatherless,
24:27 and get your **f** ready; after that,
Ecc 5: 9 the king himself profits from the **f**.
Isa 1: 7 your **f** are being stripped by
6:11 and the **f** ruined and ravaged,
10:18 forests and fertile **f** it will
16: 8 The **f** of Heshbon wither, the vines
32:12 Beat your breasts for the pleasant **f**,
61: 5 will work your **f** and vineyards.
Jer 6:12 together with their **f** and their
6:25 Do not go out to the **f** or walk on
8:10 other men and their **f** to new owners.
13:27 acts on the hills and in the **f**.
32:15 Houses, **f** and vineyards will again
32:43 Once more **f** will be bought in this
32:44 **F** will be bought for silver, and
35: 9 in or had vineyards, **f** or crops.
39:10 time he gave them vineyards and **f**.
48:33 from the orchards and **f** of Moab.
52:16 land to work the vineyards and **f**.
Eze 39:10 gather wood from the **f** or cut it
Hos 5: 7 will devour them and their **f**.
Joel 1:10 The **f** are ruined, the ground is
Ob :19 They will occupy the **f** of Ephraim
Mic 2: 2 They covet **f** and seize them, and
2: 4 me! He assigns our **f** to traitors.'"
Hab 3:17 fails and the **f** produce no food,
Hag 1:11 I called for a drought on the **f** and
Mal 3:11 your **f** will not cast their fruit,"
Mt 19:29 mother or children or **f** for my sake
Mk 10:29 children or **f** for me and the
10:30 sisters, mothers, children and **f**
11: 8 branches they had cut in the **f**.
Lk 2: 8 living out in the **f** near by,
15:15 who sent him to his **f** to feed pigs.
Jn 4:35 look at the **f**! They are ripe for
Jas 5: 4 your **f** are crying out against you.

Fierce (Fierce-looking, Fiercely, Fiercer, Fiercest)

Ge 49: 7 Cursed be their anger, so **f**, and
Ex 32:12 the earth'? Turn from your **f** anger;
Nu 25: 4 that the LORD's **f** anger may turn
Dt 13:17 his **f** anger; he will show you mercy,
29:23 which the LORD overthrew in **f** anger.
29:24 land? Why this **f**, burning anger?"
Jos 7:26 the LORD turned from his **f** anger.
1Sa 20:34 got up from the table in **f** anger;
28:18 his **f** wrath against the Amalekites,
31: 3 The fighting grew **f** around Saul, and
2Sa 2:17 The battle that day was very **f**, and
17: 8 **f** as a wild bear robbed of her cubs.
2Ki 23:26 away from the heat of his **f** anger,
1Ch 10: 3 The fighting grew **f** around Saul, and
2Ch 28:11 the LORD's **f** anger rests on you."
28:13 and his **f** anger rests on Israel."
29:10 his **f** anger will turn away from us.
30: 8 his **f** anger will turn away from you.
Ezr 10:14 until the **f** anger of our God in this
Job 41:10 No-one is **f** enough to rouse him. Who
Ps 59: 3 **F** men conspire against me for no
69:24 let your **f** anger overtake them.
85: 3 wrath and turned from your **f** anger.
Pr 26:13 road, a **f** lion roaming the streets!"
Isa 7: 4 because of the **f** anger of Rezin
13: 9 with wrath and **f** anger—to make the
19: 4 and a **f** king will rule over them,"
27: 1 his **f**, great and powerful sword,
27: 8 with his **f** blast he drives her out,
49:24 or captives rescued from the **f**?
49:25 and plunder retrieved from the **f**; I
Jer 4: 8 lament and wail, for the **f** anger of
4:26 before the LORD, before his **f** anger.
12:13 because of the LORD's **f** anger."
25:37 because of the **f** anger of the LORD.
25:38 and because of the LORD's **f** anger.
30:24 The **f** anger of the LORD will not
44: 6 Therefore, my **f** anger was poured out;
49:37 disaster upon them, even my **f** anger
51:45 Run from the **f** anger of the LORD.
Lam 1:12 on me in the day of his **f** anger?
2: 3 In **f** anger he has cut off every horn
2: 6 in his **f** anger he has spurned both
4:11 he has poured out his **f** anger.
Hos 11: 9 I will not carry out my **f** anger, nor
Jnh 3: 9 turn from his **f** anger so that we
Na 1: 6 Who can endure his **f** anger? His
Zep 2: 2 before the **f** anger of the LORD comes
3: 8 my wrath on them—all my **f** anger.

Fierce-looking (Fierce)

Dt 28:50 a **f** nation without respect for the

Fiercely (Fierce)

Job 39:21 He paws **f**, rejoicing in his strength,
Ps 25:19 increased and how **f** they hate me!
Jer 6:29 The bellows blow **f** to burn away the
Lk 11:53 began to oppose him **f** and to besiege

Fiercer (Fierce)

Hab 1: 8 leopards, **f** than wolves at dusk.

Fiercest (Fierce)

2Sa 11:15 front line where the fighting is **f**.

Fiery (Fire)

Ps 11: 6 On the wicked he will rain **f** coals
21: 9 you will make them like a **f** furnace.
Eze 21:31 breathe out my **f** anger against you;
22:20 a furnace to melt it with a **f** blast,
22:21 I will blow on you with my **f** wrath,

Eze 22:31 and consume them with my f anger,
28:14 God; you walked among the f stones.
28:16 cherub, from among the f stones.
38:19 In my zeal and f wrath I declare
Mt 13:42 will throw them into the f furnace,
13:50 throw them into the f furnace, where
Rev 6: 4 another horse came out, a f red one.
9:17 this: Their breastplates were f red,
10: 1 and his legs were like f pillars.
19:20 into the f lake of burning sulphur.
21: 8 be in the f lake of burning sulphur.

Fig (Figs, Fig-tree, Fig-trees, Sycamore-fig, Sycamore-figs)
Ge 3: 7 so they sewed f leaves together and
1Ch 12:40 f cakes, raisin cakes, wine, oil,
Isa 28: 4 will be like a f ripe before harvest
Am 4: 9 Locusts devoured your f and olive

Fight (Fighter, Fighters, Fighting, Fights, Fought)
Ex 1:10 f against us and leave the country."
14:14 The LORD will f for you; you need
17: 9 men and go out to f the Amalekites.
Lev 24:10 and a f broke out in the camp
Nu 22:11 to f them and drive them away.'"
32:27 will cross over to f before the LORD,
Dt 1:30 is going before you, will f for you,
1:41 We will go up and f, as the LORD our
1:42 'Do not go up and f, because I will
3:22 your God himself will f for you."
20: 4 goes with you to f for you against
29: 7 came out to f against us, but we
Jos 10:25 all the enemies you are going to f."
11: 5 Waters of Merom, to f against Israel.
24: 9 the king of Moab, prepared to f
Jdg 1: 1 f for us against the Canaanites?"
1: 3 to us, to f against the Canaanites.
1: 9 the men of Judah went down to f
2:15 Whenever Israel went out to f, the
8: 1 call us when you went to f Midian?"
9:38 you ridiculed? Go out and f them!"
10: 9 the Jordan to f against Judah,
11: 6 so we can f the Ammonites."
11: 8 come with us to f the Ammonites,
11: 9 take me back to f the Ammonites
11:25 quarrel with Israel or f with them?
11:32 Jephthah went over to f the
12: 1 "Why did you go to f the Ammonites
12: 3 and crossed over to f the Ammonites,
12: 3 why have you come up today to f me?"
15:10 "Why have you come to f us?" "We
18:23 that you called out your men to f?"
20:14 Gibeah to f against the Israelites.
20:18 "Who of us shall go first to f
20:20 Israel went out to f the Benjamites
1Sa 4: 1 Now the Israelites went out to f
4: 9 have been to you. Be men, and f!"
8:20 go out before us and f our battles."
13: 5 The Philistines assembled to f
17: 9 If he is able to f and kill me, we
17:10 me a man and let us f each other."
17:32 your servant will go and f him."
17:33 and f him; you are only a boy,
18:17 and f the battles of the LORD.
28: 1 their forces to f against Israel.
29: 8 Why can't I go and f against the
2Sa 2:14 and f hand to hand in front of us.
2:28 Israel, nor did they f any more.
10:12 Be strong and let us f bravely for
10:13 with him advanced to f the Arameans,
11:20 you get so close to the city to f?
14: 6 They got into a f with each other in
18: 6 The army marched into the field to f
21:15 David went down with his men to f
1Ki 12:24 go up to f against your brothers,
20:23 But if we f them on the plains,
20:25 we can f Israel on the plains.
20:26 up to Aphek to f against Israel.
22: 4 "Will you go with me to f against
22:31 "Do not f with anyone, small or
2Ki 3: 7 Will you go with me to f against
3:21 kings had come to f against them;
10: 3 Then f for your master's house."
16: 5 marched up to f against Jerusalem
2Ki 19: 9 was marching out to f against him.
1Ch 12:19 the Philistines to f against Saul.
19:13 let us f bravely for our people
19:14 with him advanced to f the Arameans,
2Ch 11: 4 go up to f against your brothers.
13:12 Israel, do not f against the LORD
18:30 "Do not f with anyone, small or
20:17 You will not have to f this battle.
25: 8 Even if you go and f courageously in
32: 8 God to help us and to f our battles.
35:20 Neco king of Egypt went up to f at
35:22 to f him on the plain of Megiddo.
Ne 4: 8 to come and f against Jerusalem
4:14 f for your brothers, your sons and
4:20 Our God will f for us!"
Ps 35: 1 f against those who f against me.
Isa 7: 1 marched up to f against Jerusalem,
19: 2 brother will f against brother,
29: 7 the hordes of all the nations that f
29: 8 nations that f against Mount Zion.
37: 9 was marching out to f against him.
Jer 1:19 They will f against you but will not
15:20 they will f against you but will not
21: 4 are using to f the king of Babylon
21: 5 I myself will f against you with an
32: 5 If you f against the Babylonians,
33: 5 in the f with the Babylonians: 'They
34:22 They will f against it, take it and
41:12 they took all their men and went to f
Da 10:20 to f against the prince of Persia,
11: 7 f against them and be victorious.
11:11 and f against the king of the North,
Zec 10: 5 will f and overthrow the horsemen.
14: 2 to Jerusalem to f against it;
14: 3 the LORD will go out and f against
14:14 Judah too will f at Jerusalem. The
Jn 18:36 If it were, my servants would f to
1Co 9:26 do not f like a man beating the air.
2Co 10: 4 The weapons we f with are not the
1Ti 1:18 following them you may f the good f,
6:12 F the good f of the faith. Take hold
2Ti 4: 7 I have fought the good f, I have
Jas 4: 2 You quarrel and f. You do not have,
Rev 2:16 and will f against them with the

Fighter (Fight)
2Sa 17: 8 your father is an experienced f; he
17:10 knows that your father is a f and
23:20 was a valiant f from Kabzeel,
1Ch 11:22 was a valiant f from Kabzeel,

Fighters (Fight)
Jos 10: 2 Ai, and all its men were good f.
Jdg 20:44 fell, all of them valiant f.
20:46 fell, all of them valiant f.
2Sa 17: 8 your father and his men; they are f,

Fighting (Fight)
Ex 2:13 he went out and saw two Hebrews f.
14:25 LORD is f for them against Egypt."
21:22 "If men who are f hit a pregnant
Nu 31:42 set apart from that of the f men—
Dt 2:14 that entire generation of f men had
2:16 Now when the last of these f men
20:19 f against it to capture it, do not
25:11 If two men are f and the wife of one
Jos 1:14 but all your f men, fully armed,
6: 2 along with its king and its f men.
8: 3 thirty thousand of his best f men
10: 7 army, including all the best f men.
10:14 Surely the LORD was f for Israel!
Jdg 20:17 swordsmen, all of them f men.
20:34 The f was so heavy that the
21:10 assembly sent twelve thousand f men
1Sa 17:19 of Elah, f against the Philistines."
17:33 he has been a f man from his youth."
23: 1 the Philistines are f against Keilah
28:15 "The Philistines are f against me,
29: 4 will turn against us during the f.
31: 3 The f grew fierce around Saul, and
2Sa 10: 7 out with the entire army of f men.
10:14 Joab returned from f the Ammonites
11:15 front line where the f is fiercest.
24: 2 Dan to Beersheba and enrol the f men,
24: 4 king to enrol the f men of Israel.
2Sa 24: 9 reported the number of the f men
24:10 after he had counted the f men,
1Ki 9:22 the Israelites; they were his f men,
11:15 Earlier when David was f with Edom,
12:21 eighty thousand f men—to make war
22:34 round and get me out of the f.
2Ki 19: 8 and found the king f against Libnah.
24:14 all the officers and f men,
24:16 force of seven thousand f men,
25:19 the f men and five royal advisers.
1Ch 5:20 They were helped in f them, and God
7: 2 descendants of Tola listed as f men
7: 5 The relatives who were f men
7: 7 record listed 22,034 f men.
7: 9 heads of families and 20,200 f men.
7:11 17,200 f men ready to go out to war.
10: 3 The f grew fierce around Saul, and
12:38 All these were f men who volunteered
19: 8 out with the entire army of f men.
21: 5 reported the number of the f men
21:17 "Was it not I who ordered the f men
2Ch 8: 9 for his work; they were his f men,
11: 1 eighty thousand f men—to make war
13: 3 of four hundred thousand able f men,
14: 8 All these were brave f men.
17:13 kept experienced f men in Jerusalem.
17:14 the commander, with 300,000 f men;
18:33 Wheel around and get me out of the f.
25: 6 also hired a hundred thousand f men
26:12 leaders over the f men was 2,600.
32:21 who annihilated all the f men and
Isa 37: 8 and found the king f against Libnah.
Jer 34: 1 he ruled were f against Jerusalem
34: 7 of Babylon was f against Jerusalem
51:30 Babylon's warriors have stopped f;
52:25 the f men, and seven royal advisers.
Joel 3: 9 all the f men draw near and attack.
Ac 5:39 only find yourselves f against God."
7:26 came upon two Israelites who were f.

Fights (Fight)
Jos 23:10 God f for you, just as he promised.
Jdg 6:31 Whoever f for him shall be put to
1Sa 25:28 because he f the LORD's battles.
Isa 30:32 as he f them in battle with the
Zec 14: 3 as he f in the day of battle.
Jas 4: 1 What causes f and quarrels among you?

Figs (Fig)
Nu 13:23 along with some pomegranates and f.
20: 5 or f, grapevines or pomegranates.
1Sa 25:18 two hundred cakes of pressed f,
30:12 part of a cake of pressed f and two
2Sa 16: 1 cakes of f and a skin of wine.
2Ki 20: 7 Isaiah said, "Prepare a poultice of f
Ne 13:15 wine, grapes, f and all other kinds
Isa 34: 4 like shrivelled f from the fig-tree.
38:21 "Prepare a poultice of f and apply
Jer 8:13 There will be no f on the tree, and
24: 1 the LORD showed me two baskets of f
24: 2 One basket had very good f, like
24: 2 the other basket had very poor f,
24: 3 you see, Jeremiah?" "F," I answered.
24: 5 'Like these good f, I regard as good
24: 8 "'But like the poor f, which are so
29:17 I will make them like poor f that
Mic 7: 1 none of the early f that I crave.
Na 3:12 f fall into the mouth of the eater.
Mt 7:16 thornbushes, or f from thistles?
Mk 11:13 because it was not the season for f.
Lk 6:44 do not pick f from thorn-bushes
Jas 3:12 bear olives, or a grapevine bear f?
Rev 6:13 as late f drop from a fig-tree when

Fig-tree (Fig, Tree)
Jdg 9:10 "Next, the trees said to the f,
9:11 "But the f replied, 'Should I give
1Ki 4:25 each man under his own vine and f.
2Ki 18:31 will eat from his own vine and f
Pr 27:18 He who tends a f will eat its fruit,
SS 2:13 The f forms its early fruit; the
Isa 34: 4 like shrivelled figs from the f.
36:16 will eat from his own vine and f
Hos 9:10 seeing the early fruit on the f.
Joel 1:12 dried up and the f is withered;

Joel 2:22 the f and the vine yield their
Mic 4: 4 his own vine and under his own f,
Hab 3:17 Though the f does not bud and there
Hag 2:19 the vine and the f, the pomegranate
Zec 3:10 to sit under his vine and f,'
Mt 21:19 Seeing a f by the road, he went up
21:20 "How did the f wither so quickly?"
21:21 can you do what was done to the f,
24:32 "Now learn this lesson from the f:
Mk 11:13 Seeing in the distance a f in leaf,
11:20 saw the f withered from the roots.
11:21 The f you cursed has withered!"
13:28 "Now learn this lesson from the f:
Lk 13: 6 he told this parable: "A man had a f,
13: 7 to look for fruit on this f and
21:29 "Look at the f and all the trees.
Jn 1:48 while you were still under the f
1:50 I told you I saw you under the f.
Jas 3:12 My brothers, can a f bear olives, or
Rev 6:13 as late figs drop from a f when

Fig-trees (Fig, Tree)

Dt 8: 8 f, pomegranates, olive oil and honey;
Ps 105:33 he struck down their vines and f and
Isa 9:10 stone; the f have been felled,
Jer 5:17 and herds, devour your vines and f.
Hos 2:12 I will ruin her vines and her f,
Joel 1: 7 laid waste my vines and ruined my f.
Na 3:12 All your fortresses are like f with

Figuratively (Figure)

Jn 16:25 "Though I have been speaking f, a
Gal 4:24 These things may be taken f, for the
Heb 11:19 and f speaking, he did receive Isaac
Rev 11: 8 which is f called Sodom and Egypt,

Figure (Figuratively, Figures)

Eze 1:26 throne was a f like that of a man.
8: 2 I looked, and I saw a f like that of
Jn 7: 4 No-one who wants to become a public f
10: 6 Jesus used this f of speech, but

Figurehead (Head)

Ac 28:11 ship with the f of the twin gods

Figures (Figure)

2Ch 4: 3 Below the rim, f of bulls encircled
Eze 23:14 f of Chaldeans portrayed in red,
Jn 16:29 clearly and without f of speech.

Filigree

Ex 28:11 mount the stones in gold f settings
28:13 Make gold f settings
28:20 Mount them in gold f settings.
39: 6 the onyx stones in gold f settings
39:13 They were mounted in gold f settings.
39:16 They made two gold f settings and

Fill (Filled, Filling, Fills, Full, Fully, Fulness)

Ge 1:22 number and f the water in the seas,
1:28 number; f the earth and subdue it.
9: 1 increase in number and f the earth.
42:25 Joseph gave orders to f their bags
44: 1 "F the men's sacks with as much food
Ex 2:16 to draw water and f the troughs
10: 6 They will f your houses and those of
Lev 25:19 eat your f and live there in safety.
Dt 28:67 the terror that will f your hearts
31:20 and when they eat their f and thrive,
1Sa 16: 1 F your horn with oil and be on your
1Ki 18:33 them, "F four large jars with water
Job 8:21 He will yet f your mouth with
15: 2 f his belly with the hot east wind?
15:21 Terrifying sounds f his ears; when
15:24 Distress and anguish f him with
23: 4 him and f my mouth with arguments.
31:31 has not had his f of Job's meat?'—
41: 7 Can you f his hide with harpoons or
Ps 16:11 will f me with joy in your presence,
74:20 f the dark places of the land.
81:10 Open wide your mouth and I will f it.
129: 7 the reaper cannot f his hands,
Ps 129: 7 nor the one who gathers f his arms.
Pr 1:13 and f our houses with plunder;
12:21 the wicked have their f of trouble.
26:25 for seven abominations f his heart.
28:19 will have his f of poverty.
Ecc 1: 8 nor the ear its f of hearing.
SS 5: 1 and drink; drink your f, O lovers.
Isa 13:21 jackals will f her houses; there the
27: 6 and f all the world with fruit.
33: 5 he will f Zion with justice and
34: 5 My sword has drunk its f in the
44:16 he roasts his meat and eats his f.
56:12 "let me get wine! Let us drink our f
65:11 f bowls of mixed wine for Destiny,
Jer 13:13 I am going to f with drunkenness all
23:16 to you; they f you with false hopes.
23:24 "Do not I f heaven and earth?"
46:12 shame; your cries will f the earth.
50:10 who plunder her will have their f,"
51:14 I will surely f you with men, as
Eze 3: 3 you and f your stomach with it.
7:19 hunger or f their stomachs with it,
8:17 Must they also f the land with
9: 7 and f the courts with the slain.
10: 2 F your hands with burning coals from
20:26 that I might f them with horror so
24: 4 F it with the best of these bones;
30:11 Egypt and f the land with the slain.
32: 5 and f the valleys with your remains.
35: 8 I will f your mountains with the
39:20 At my table you will eat your f of
Da 7: 5 'Get up and eat your f of flesh!'
Zep 1: 9 who f the temple of their gods with
Hag 1: 6 You drink, but never have your f.
2: 7 and I will f this house with glory,'
Zec 9:13 I bend my bow and f it with Ephraim.
Mt 23:32 F up, then, the measure of the sin
Lk 15:16 He longed to f his stomach with the
Jn 2: 7 said to the servants, "F the jars
6:26 you ate the loaves and had your f.
Ac 2:28 f me with joy in your presence.'
Ro 15:13 May the God of hope f you with all
Eph 4:10 in order to f the whole universe.)
Col 1: 9 asking God to f you with the
1:24 and I f up in my flesh what is still

Filled (Fill)

Ge 6: 6 and his heart was f with pain.
6:13 is f with violence because of them.
21:19 So she went and f the skin with
24:16 spring, f her jar and came up again.
34: 7 They were f with grief and fury,
Ex 1: 7 so that the land was f with them.
16:12 morning you will be f with bread.
31: 3 I have f him with the Spirit of God,
35:31 he has f him with the Spirit of God,
35:35 He has f them with skill to do all
40:34 glory of the LORD f the tabernacle.
40:35 glory of the LORD f the tabernacle.
Lev 19:29 and be f with wickedness.
Nu 7:13 each f with fine flour mixed with
7:14 ten shekels, f with incense;
7:19 each f with fine flour mixed with
7:20 ten shekels, f with incense;
7:25 each f with fine flour mixed with
7:26 ten shekels, f with incense;
7:31 each f with fine flour mixed with
7:32 ten shekels, f with incense;
7:37 each f with fine flour mixed with
7:38 ten shekels, f with incense;
7:43 each f with fine flour mixed with
7:44 ten shekels, f with incense;
7:49 each f with fine flour mixed with
7:50 ten shekels, f with incense;
7:55 each f with fine flour mixed with
7:56 ten shekels, f with incense;
7:61 each f with fine flour mixed with
7:62 ten shekels, f with incense;
7:67 each f with fine flour mixed with
7:68 ten shekels, f with incense;
7:73 each f with fine flour mixed with
7:74 ten shekels, f with incense;
7:79 each f with fine flour mixed with
7:80 ten shekels, f with incense;
7:86 twelve gold dishes f with incense
Nu 22: 3 Indeed, Moab was f with dread
22:18 if Balak gave me his palace f with
24:13 if Balak gave me his palace f with
Dt 6:11 houses f with all kinds of good
28:66 in constant suspense, f with dread
32:15 f with food, he became heavy and
32:32 Their grapes are f with poison, and
34: 9 son of Nun was f with the spirit of
Jos 9:13 these wineskins that we f were new,
Ru 2: 9 from the water jars the men have f."
1Sa 5:11 For death had f the city with panic;
28: 5 he was afraid; terror f his heart.
28:20 f with fear because of Samuel's
1Ki 3:26 was f with compassion for her son
8:10 the cloud f the temple of the LORD.
8:11 the glory of the LORD f his temple.
11:27 had f in the gap in the wall of the
18:35 the altar and even f the trench.
2Ki 3:17 yet this valley will be f with water,
3:20 Edom! And the land was f with water.
4: 4 as each is f, put it to one side."
4:39 gourds and f the fold of his cloak.
21:16 that he f Jerusalem from end to end
24: 4 had f Jerusalem with innocent blood
2Ch 5:13 of the LORD was f with a cloud,
5:14 of the LORD f the temple of God.
7: 1 the glory of the LORD f the temple.
7: 2 because the glory of the LORD f it.
Ezr 6:22 because the LORD had f them with joy
9:11 they have f it with their impurity
Ne 9:25 f with all kinds of good things,
Est 5: 9 he was f with rage against Mordecai.
Job 3:15 who f their houses with silver.
3:22 who are f with gladness and rejoice
20:23 he has f his belly, God will vent
22:18 Yet it was he who f their houses
Ps 4: 7 You have f my heart with greater joy
5: 9 their heart is f with destruction.
38: 7 My back is f with searing pain;
48:10 right hand is f with righteousness.
65: 4 f with the good things of your house,
65: 9 The streams of God are f with water
71: 8 My mouth is f with your praise,
72:19 the whole earth be f with his glory.
80: 9 it, and it took root and f the land.
119:64 The earth is f with your love,
126: 2 Our mouths were f with laughter, our
126: 3 for us, and we are f with joy.
144:13 Our barns will be f with every kind
Pr 1:31 f with the fruit of their schemes.
3:10 your barns will be f to overflowing,
7:20 He took his purse f with money and
8:30 I was f with delight day after day,
12:14 From the fruit of his lips a man is f
18:20 of his mouth a man's stomach is f;
24: 4 through knowledge its rooms are f
Ecc 8:11 are f with schemes to do wrong.
Isa 6: 1 the train of his robe f the temple.
6: 4 and the temple was f with smoke.
41:23 we will be dismayed and f with fear.
51:20 They are f with the wrath of the
Jer 6: 6 punished; it is f with oppression.
13:12 Every wineskin should be f with wine.
13:12 wineskin should be f with wine?'
15:17 and you had f me with indignation.
16:18 have f my inheritance with their
19: 4 and they have f this place with the
25:15 cup f with the wine of my wrath
31:14 my people will be f with my bounty,"
33: 5 'They will be f with the dead bodies
41: 9 son of Nethaniah f it with the dead.
50: 2 put to shame, Marduk f with terror.
50: 2 shame and her idols f with terror.'
50:36 They will be f with terror.
51:34 f his stomach with our delicacies,
Lam 3:15 He has f me with bitter herbs and
3:30 him, and let him be f with disgrace.
Eze 10: 3 in, and a cloud f the inner court.
10: 4 The cloud f the temple, and the
11: 6 and f its streets with the dead.
23:33 You will be f with drunkenness and
27:25 You are f with heavy cargo in the
28:16 you were f with violence, and you
32: 6 ravines will be f with your flesh.
36:38 cities be f with flocks of people.
43: 5 the glory of the LORD f the temple.

Da 2:35 huge mountain and f the whole earth.
11:12 of the South will be f with pride
Joel 2:24 will be f with grain; the vats will
Am 4:10 I f your nostrils with the stench of
Mic 3: 8 for me, I am f with power, with the
Na 1: 2 takes vengeance and is f with wrath.
Hab 2:14 For the earth will be f with the
2:16 You will be f with shame instead of
3: 3 heavens and his praise f the earth.
Zec 8: 5 The city streets will be f with boys
Mt 5: 6 righteousness, for they will be f.
9: 8 crowd saw this, they were f with awe
17:23 And the disciples were f with grief.
22:10 the wedding hall was f with guests.
27:48 He f it with wine vinegar, put it on
28: 8 afraid yet f with joy, and ran to
Mk 1:41 F with compassion, Jesus reached out
15:36 One man ran, f a sponge with wine
Lk 1:15 he will be f with the Holy Spirit
1:41 Elizabeth was f with the Holy Spirit.
1:53 He has f the hungry with good things
1:65 The neighbours were all f with awe,
1:67 Zechariah was f with the Holy
2:40 became strong; he was f with wisdom,
3: 5 Every valley shall be f in, every
5: 7 they came and f both boats so full
5:26 They were f with awe and said, "We
7:16 They were all f with awe and praised
15:20 saw him and was f with compassion
Jn 2: 7 water"; so they f them to the brim.
6:13 f twelve baskets with the pieces of
12: 3 f with the fragrance of the perfume.
16: 6 these things, you are f with grief.
Ac 2: 2 f the whole house where they were
2: 4 All of them were f with the Holy
2:43 Everyone was f with awe, and many
3:10 and they were f with wonder and
4: 8 Peter, f with the Holy Spirit, said
4:31 And they were all f with the Holy
5: 3 that Satan has so f your heart
5:17 the Sadducees, were f with jealousy.
5:28 "Yet you have f Jerusalem with your
9:17 and be f with the Holy Spirit."
13: 9 Paul, f with the Holy Spirit
13:45 they were f with jealousy and
13:52 the disciples were f with joy and
16:34 he was f with joy because he had
Ro 1:29 They have become f with every kind
1Co 5: 2 rather have been f with grief
Eph 3:19 that you may be f to the measure of
5:18 Instead, be f with the Spirit.
Php 1:11 f with the fruit of righteousness
2Ti 1: 4 you, so that I may be f with joy.
1Pe 1: 8 you believe in him and are f with an
Rev 8: 5 took the censer, f it with fire
12:12 gone down to you! He is f with fury,
15: 7 bowls f with the wrath of God,
15: 8 the temple was f with smoke from the
16:19 gave her the cup f with the wine of
17: 4 cup in her hand, f with abominable

Filling (Fill)

Ge 26:15 stopped up, f them with earth.
Eze 44: 4 the LORD f the temple of the LORD,
Na 2:12 f his lairs with the kill and his

Fills (Fill)

Nu 14:21 glory of the LORD f the whole earth,
Job 20:11 The youthful vigour that f his bones
36:32 He f his hands with lightning and
Ps 107: 9 and f the hungry with good things.
Ac 14:17 of food and f your hearts with joy."
Eph 1:23 him who f everything in every way.

Filth (Filthiness, Filthy)

2Ki 18:27 eat their own f and drink their own
Pr 30:12 and yet are not cleansed of their f;
Isa 4: 4 The Lord will wash away the f of the
28: 8 and there is not a spot without f.
36:12 eat their own f and drink their own
Na 3: 6 I will pelt you with f, I will treat
Zep 1:17 like dust and their entrails like f.
Jas 1:21 Therefore, get rid of all moral f
Rev 17: 4 things and the f of her adulteries.

Filthiness (Filth)

Lam 1: 9 Her f clung to her skirts; she did

Filthy (Filth)

Isa 64: 6 our righteous acts are like f rags;
Zec 3: 3 Now Joshua was dressed in f clothes
3: 4 before him, "Take off his f clothes.
Col 3: 8 and f language from your lips.
2Pe 2: 7 by the f lives of lawless men

Final (Finality)

Ru 4: 7 transfer of property to become f,
Ps 73:17 then I understood their f destiny.
Isa 41:22 them and know their f outcome.
Mt 12:45 And the f condition of that man is
Lk 11:26 And the f condition of that man is
Ac 28:25 Paul had made this f statement:

Finality (Final)

Ro 9:28 sentence on earth with speed and f."

Financial

1Ti 6: 5 that godliness is a means to f gain.

Find (Finding, Finds, Found)

Ge 8: 9 the dove could f no place to set its
18:26 LORD said, "If I f fifty righteous
18:28 "If I f forty-five there," he said,
18:30 will not do it if I f thirty there."
19:11 so that they could not f the door.
27:20 Isaac asked his son, "How did you f
31:32 if you f anyone who has your gods,
31:35 but could not f the household gods.
32: 5 that I may f favour in your eyes.'"
33: 8 "To f favour in your eyes, my lord,"
33:15 me f favour in the eyes of my lord."
34:11 "Let me f favour in your eyes, and I
38:20 the woman, but he did not f her.
38:22 to Judah and said, "I didn't f her.
38:23 young goat, but you didn't f her."
41:38 Pharaoh asked them, "Can we f anyone
44:15 me can f things out by divination?"
47:25 "May we f favour in the eyes of our
Ex 5:11 own straw wherever you can f it,
16:25 not f any of it on the ground today.
33:13 and continue to f favour with you.
Nu 9: 8 Moses answered them, "Wait until I f
10:33 days to f them a place to rest.
22:19 and I will f out what else the LORD
32:23 sure that your sin will f you out.
Dt 4:29 you will f him if you look for him
13: 3 God is testing you to f out whether
14:21 Do not eat anything you f already
22: 3 Do the same if you f your brother's
22:14 I did not f proof of her virginity,"
22:17 not f your daughter to be a virgin.
28:65 Among those nations you will f no
Jos 2:16 so that the pursuers will not f you.
20: 3 may flee there and f protection
Jdg 18: 8 asked them, "How did you f things?
18:10 you will f an unsuspecting people
Ru 1: 9 will f rest in the home of another
2: 2 anyone in whose eyes I f favour.
2:13 "May I continue to f favour in your
3: 1 should I not try to f a home for
3:18 until you f out what happens.
1Sa 1:18 She said, "May your servant f favour
9: 4 Shalisha, but they did not f them.
9: 4 Benjamin, but they did not f them.
9:13 you will f him before he goes up to
9:13 you should f him about this time."
14:38 and let us f out what sin has been
16:17 "F someone who plays well and bring
17:56 The king said, "F out whose son this
19: 3 you and will tell you what I f out."
20:21 a boy and say, 'Go, f the arrows.
20:36 to the boy, "Run and f the arrows
21: 3 of bread, or whatever you can f."
23:16 and helped him to f strength in God.
23:22 F out where David usually goes
23:23 F out about all the hiding-places he
25: 8 David whatever you can f for them.'"
28: 7 "F me a woman who is a medium, so
2Sa 3:25 and f out everything you are doing."
2Sa 11: 3 David sent someone to f out about
15:25 If I f favour in the LORD's eyes, he
16: 4 Ziba said. "May I f favour in your
20: 6 or he will f fortified cities and
1Ki 18: 5 Maybe we can f some grass to keep
18:10 them swear they could not f you.
18:12 he doesn't f you, he will kill me.
22:25 Micaiah replied, "You will f out on
2Ki 2:17 for three days but did not f him.
6:13 "Go, f out where he is," the king
7:13 send them to f out what happened."
7:14 He commanded the drivers, "Go and f
2Ch 18:24 Micaiah replied, "You will f out on
20:16 and you will f them at the end of
32: 4 and f plenty of water?" they said.
Ezr 2:62 but they could not f them and so
4:15 In these records you will f that
Ne 5: 8 because they could f nothing to say.
7:64 but they could not f them and so
Est 2:11 the harem to f out how Esther was
4: 5 and ordered him to f out what was
Job 5:24 your property and f nothing missing.
8: 8 f out what their fathers learned,
9:14 How can I f words to argue with him?
17:10 I will not f a wise man among you.
22:26 Surely then you will f delight in
23: 3 If only I knew where to f him; if
23: 5 I would f out what he would answer
23: 8 if I go to the west, I do not f him.
27:10 Will he f delight in the Almighty?
32:20 I must speak and f relief; I must
Ps 17: 3 test me, you will f nothing;
36: 7 f refuge in the shadow of your wings.
62: 5 F rest, O my soul, in God alone; my
91: 4 under his wings you will f refuge;
119:35 commands, for there I f delight.
119:52 O LORD, and I f comfort in them.
132: 5 till I f a place for the LORD, a
Pr 1:28 will look for me but will not f me.
2: 5 the LORD and f the knowledge of God.
4:22 they are life to those who f them
8:17 love me, and those who seek me f me.
8:36 whoever fails to f me harms himself;
14: 7 will not f knowledge on his lips.
14:22 is good f love and faithfulness.
20: 6 love, but a faithful man who can f?
23:35 I wake up so I can f another drink?"
24:14 is sweet to your soul; if you f it,
25:16 If you f honey, eat just enough—
31:10 A wife of noble character who can f?
Ecc 2: 1 with pleasure to f out what is good.
2:24 and f satisfaction in his work.
2:25 him, who can eat or f enjoyment?
3:13 and f satisfaction in all his toil
5:18 and to f satisfaction in his
7:26 I f more bitter than death the woman
11: 1 after many days you will f it again.
12: 1 will say, "I f no pleasure in them"
12:10 searched to f just the right words
SS 3: 1 I looked for him but did not f him.
3: 2 I looked for him but did not f him.
5: 6 I looked for him but did not f him.
5: 8 I charge you—if you f my lover,
Isa 14:30 poorest of the poor will f pasture,
14:32 his afflicted people will f refuge."
23:12 even there you will f no rest."
34:14 and f for themselves places of rest.
41:12 your enemies, you will not f them.
49: 9 and f pasture on every barren hill.
57: 2 they f rest as they lie in death.
58:14 you will f your joy in the LORD, and
59:11 We look for justice, but f none; for
Jer 2: 5 "What fault did your fathers f in me,
2:24 at mating time they will f her.
2:34 On your clothes men f the lifeblood
5: 1 If you can f but one person who
6:10 to them; they f no pleasure in it.
6:16 and you will f rest for your souls.
14: 3 go to the cisterns but f no water.
23:11 in my temple I f their wickedness,"
29: 6 have sons and daughters; f wives
29:13 You will seek me and f me when you
31: 2 sword will f favour in the desert;
45: 3 out with groaning and f no rest.'"
Lam 1: 6 are like deer that f no pasture;
2: 9 no longer f visions from the LORD.

Lam 5: 5 heels; we are weary and **f** no rest.
Eze 17:23 they will **f** shelter in the shade of
Da 6: 4 the satraps tried to **f** grounds for
6: 4 They could **f** no corruption in him,
6: 5 "We will never **f** any basis for
Hos 2: 6 her in so that she cannot **f** her way.
2: 7 will look for them but not **f** them.
5: 6 they will not **f** him; he has
12: 8 not **f** in me any iniquity or sin."
14: 3 in you the fatherless **f** compassion."
Am 8:12 of the LORD, but they will not **f** it.
Jnh 1: 7 "Come, let us cast lots to **f** out who
Na 3: 7 Where can I **f** anyone to comfort you?"
Zep 2: 7 of Judah; there they will **f** pasture.
Zec 2: 2 **f** out how wide and how long it is."
Mt 2: 8 As soon as you **f** him, report to me,
7: 7 seek and you will **f**; knock and the
7:14 leads to life, and only a few **f** it.
10:39 his life for my sake will **f** it.
11:29 and you will **f** rest for your souls.
12:43 seeking rest and does not **f** it.
16:25 loses his life for me will **f** it.
17:27 and you will **f** a four-drachma coin.
21: 2 and at once you will **f** a donkey tied
22: 9 invite to the banquet anyone you **f**.'
22:10 all the people they could **f**,
26:60 they did not **f** any, though many
Mk 11: 2 you will **f** a colt tied there, which
11:13 went to **f** out if it had any fruit.
13:36 do not let him **f** you sleeping.
14:55 to death, but they did not **f** any.
Lk 1:62 made signs to his father, to **f** out
2:12 You will **f** a baby wrapped in cloths
2:45 they did not **f** him, they went back
5:19 they could not **f** a way to do this
9:12 countryside and **f** food and lodging,
11: 9 seek and you will **f**; knock and the
11:24 seeking rest and does not **f** it.
13: 6 for fruit on it, but did not **f** any.
18: 8 will he **f** faith on the earth?"
19:15 **f** out what they had gained with it.
19:30 as you enter it, you will **f** a colt
19:48 Yet they could not **f** any way to do
23: 4 "I **f** no basis for a charge against
24: 3 they did not **f** the body of the Lord
24:23 didn't **f** his body. They came and
Jn 1:41 Andrew did was to **f** his brother
4:27 to **f** him talking with a woman.
7:17 he will **f** out whether my teaching
7:34 but you will not **f** me; and where I
7:35 intend to go that we cannot **f** him?
7:36 look for me, but you will not **f** me,'
7:51 him to **f** out what he is doing?"
7:52 you will **f** that a prophet does not
10: 9 come in and go out, and **f** pasture.
18:38 **f** no basis for a charge against him.
19: 4 **f** no basis for a charge against him."
19: 6 **f** no basis for a charge against him."
21: 6 of the boat and you will **f** some.
Ac 5:22 the officers did not **f** them there.
5:39 **f** yourselves fighting against God."
7:11 and our fathers could not **f** food.
12:19 made for him and did not **f** him,
16:13 we expected to **f** a place of prayer.
17: 6 when they did not **f** them, they
17:27 perhaps reach out for him and **f** him,
22:24 questioned in order to **f** out why the
22:30 since the commander wanted to **f** out
23: 9 "We **f** nothing wrong with this man,"
24:12 My accusers did not **f** me arguing
24:25 When I **f** it convenient, I will send
Ro 7:21 I **f** this law at work: When I want to
1Co 4:19 and then I will **f** out not only how
2Co 2:13 I did not **f** my brother Titus there.
9: 4 come with me and **f** you unprepared,
12:20 I may not **f** you as I want you to be,
12:20 may not **f** me as you want me to be.
Eph 5:10 **f** out what pleases the Lord.
1Th 3: 5 I sent to **f** out about your faith.
2Ti 1:18 Lord grant that he will **f** mercy
Heb 4:16 receive mercy and **f** grace to help
Jas 3:16 **f** disorder and every evil practice.
1Pe 1:11 trying to **f** out the time and
2Jn : 4 has given me great joy to **f** some of
Rev 9: 6 but will not **f** it; they will long to

Finding (Find)

Ex 15:22 in the desert without **f** water.
Jos 2:22 road and returned without **f** them.
Jdg 5:30 'Are they not **f** and dividing the
15:15 **F** a fresh jaw-bone of a donkey, he
Job 36:26 number of his years is past **f** out.
Ps 107: 4 in desert wastelands, **f** no way to a
Ecc 7:28 while I was still searching but not **f**
Hos 9:10 I found Israel, it was like **f** grapes
Jn 1:43 **F** Philip, he said to him, "Follow me.
Ac 5:10 young men came in and, **f** her dead,
21: 4 **F** the disciples there, we stayed
Jas 1: 5 generously to all without **f** fault,

Finds (Find)

Ge 4:14 and whoever **f** me will kill me."
Lev 6: 3 or if he **f** lost property and lies
Nu 35:27 the avenger of blood **f** him outside
Dt 24: 1 he **f** something indecent about her,
Jdg 9:33 you, do whatever your hand **f** to do."
1Sa 10: 7 hand **f** to do, for God is with you.
24:19 a man **f** his enemy, does he let him
Job 33:20 that his very being **f** food repulsive
33:26 He prays to God and **f** favour with
Ps 55:15 for evil **f** lodging among them.
62: 1 My soul **f** rest in God alone; my
112: 1 who **f** great delight in his commands.
119:162 promise like one who **f** great spoil.
Pr 3:13 Blessed is the man who **f** wisdom, the
8:35 For whoever **f** me **f** life and receives
10:23 A fool **f** pleasure in evil conduct,
11:27 He who seeks good **f** goodwill, but
14: 6 The mocker seeks wisdom and **f** none,
15:23 A man **f** joy in giving an apt reply—
18: 2 A fool **f** no pleasure in
18:22 He who **f** a wife **f** what is good and
20: 4 harvest time he looks but **f** nothing.
21:21 love **f** life, prosperity and honour.
28:13 and renounces them **f** mercy.
Ecc 9:10 Whatever your hand **f** to do, do it
Isa 38:16 and my spirit **f** life in them too.
Lam 1: 3 nations; she **f** no resting place.
Mt 7: 8 who seeks **f**; and to him who knocks,
10:39 Whoever **f** his life will lose it, and
12:44 When it arrives, it **f** the house
18:13 if he **f** it, I tell you the truth, he
24:46 servant whose master **f** him doing so
Lk 11:10 who seeks **f**; and to him who knocks,
11:25 arrives, it **f** the house swept clean
12:37 **f** them watching when he comes.
12:38 servants whose master **f** them ready,
12:43 master **f** doing so when he returns.
15: 4 after the lost sheep until he **f** it?
15: 5 he **f** it, he joyfully puts it on his
15: 8 and search carefully until she **f** it?
15: 9 she **f** it, she calls her friends and
22:16 **f** fulfilment in the kingdom of God."
1Co 14:16 how can one who **f** himself among

Fine[1] (Fine-looking, Finery, Fine-sounding, Finest)

Ge 18: 6 "get three seahs of **f** flour and
41:42 He dressed him in robes of **f** linen
Ex 2: 2 When she saw that he was a **f** child,
9: 9 will become **f** dust over the whole
25: 4 purple and scarlet yarn and **f** linen
28: 5 and scarlet yarn, and **f** linen.
28:39 "Weave the tunic of **f** linen and make
28:39 and make the turban of **f** linen.
29: 2 from **f** wheat flour, without yeast,
29:40 a tenth of an ephah of **f** flour
30:23 "Take the following **f** spices: 500
35: 6 purple and scarlet yarn and **f** linen
35:23 purple or scarlet yarn or **f** linen,
35:25 purple or scarlet yarn or **f** linen.
35:35 purple and scarlet yarn and **f** linen,
38:23 and scarlet yarn and **f** linen.)
39: 3 purple and scarlet yarn and **f** linen—
39:27 of **f** linen—the work of a weaver—
39:28 the turban of **f** linen, the linen
Lev 2: 1 his offering is to be of **f** flour.
2: 2 a handful of the **f** flour and oil,
2: 4 it is to consist of **f** flour: cakes
2: 5 it is to be made of **f** flour mixed
2: 7 it is to be made of **f** flour and oil.
Lev 5:11 ephah of **f** flour for a sin offering.
6:15 take a handful of **f** flour and oil,
6:20 **f** flour as a regular grain offering,
7:12 and cakes of **f** flour well-kneaded
14:10 three-tenths of an ephah of **f**
14:21 a tenth of an ephah of **f** flour
23:13 an ephah of **f** flour mixed with oil
23:17 two-tenths of an ephah of **f** flour,
24: 5 "Take **f** flour and bake twelve loaves
Nu 6:15 made of **f** flour mixed with oil,
7:13 each filled with **f** flour mixed with
7:19 each filled with **f** flour mixed with
7:25 each filled with **f** flour mixed with
7:31 each filled with **f** flour mixed with
7:37 each filled with **f** flour mixed with
7:43 each filled with **f** flour mixed with
7:49 each filled with **f** flour mixed with
7:55 each filled with **f** flour mixed with
7:61 each filled with **f** flour mixed with
7:67 each filled with **f** flour mixed with
7:73 each filled with **f** flour mixed with
7:79 each filled with **f** flour mixed with
8: 8 offering of **f** flour mixed with oil;
15: 4 a tenth of an ephah of **f** flour
15: 6 two-tenths of an ephah of **f** flour
15: 9 **f** flour mixed with half a hin of oil.
28: 5 a tenth of an ephah of **f** flour
28: 9 an ephah of **f** flour mixed with oil.
28:12 **f** flour mixed with oil; with the ram,
28:12 an ephah of **f** flour mixed with oil;
28:13 an ephah of **f** flour mixed with oil.
28:20 **f** flour mixed with oil; with the ram,
28:28 **f** flour mixed with oil; with the ram,
29: 3 **f** flour mixed with oil; with the ram,
29: 9 **f** flour mixed with oil; with the ram,
29:14 an ephah of **f** flour mixed with oil;
Dt 3:25 that **f** hill country and Lebanon."
8:12 you build **f** houses and settle down,
9:21 ground it to powder as **f** as dust and
1Sa 16:12 He was ruddy, with a **f** appearance
2Sa 22:43 I beat them as **f** as the dust of the
1Ki 4:22 of **f** flour and sixty cors of meal,
10:18 with ivory and overlaid with **f** gold.
2Ki 20:13 the gold, the spices and the **f** oil
1Ch 15:27 was clothed in a robe of **f** linen,
29: 2 and all kinds of **f** stone and marble—
2Ch 2:14 blue and crimson yarn and **f** linen.
3: 5 covered it with **f** gold and decorated
3: 8 with six hundred talents of **f** gold.
3:14 purple and crimson yarn and **f** linen,
5:12 dressed in **f** linen and playing
Ezr 8:27 and two **f** articles of polished
Est 8:15 gold and a purple robe of **f** linen.
Job 16: 4 I could make **f** speeches against you
Ps 18:42 I beat them as **f** as dust borne on
92:10 ox; **f** oils have been poured upon me.
Pr 8:19 My fruit is better than **f** gold; what
25:12 of **f** gold is a wise man's rebuke
31:22 is clothed in **f** linen and purple.
Ecc 7: 1 A good name is better than **f** perfume,
Isa 3:22 the **f** robes and the capes and cloaks,
3:24 baldness; instead of **f** clothing,
5: 9 **f** mansions left without occupants.
19: 9 weavers of **f** linen will lose hope.
23:18 for abundant food and **f** clothes.
29: 5 enemies will become like **f** dust,
39: 2 the gold, the spices, the **f** oil, his
40:15 islands as though they were **f** dust.
Jer 22: 7 and they will cut up your **f** cedar
25:34 and be shattered like **f** pottery.
Lam 4: 1 the **f** gold become dull! The sacred
Eze 16:10 I dressed you in **f** linen and covered
16:13 your clothes were of **f** linen and
16:13 Your food was **f** flour, honey and
16:17 You also took the **f** jewellery I gave
16:19 I provided for you—the **f** flour,
16:39 take your **f** jewellery and leave you
23:26 clothes and take your **f** jewellery.
26:12 your **f** houses and throw your stones,
27: 7 **F** embroidered linen from Egypt was
27:16 embroidered work, **f** linen, coral
Mt 11: 8 see? A man dressed in **f** clothes? No,
11: 8 **f** clothes are in kings' palaces.
13:45 a merchant looking for **f** pearls.
Mk 7: 9 he said to them: "You have a **f** way
Lk 7:25 see? A man dressed in **f** clothes? No,

Lk 13: 9 If it bears fruit next year, f! If
16:19 f linen and lived in luxury every
Gal 4:18 is f to be zealous, provided the
Jas 2: 2 wearing a gold ring and f clothes,
2: 3 the man wearing f clothes and say,
1Pe 3: 3 of gold jewellery and f clothes.
Rev 18:12 precious stones and pearls; f linen,
18:13 of wine and olive oil, of f flour
18:16 O great city, dressed in f linen,
19: 8 F linen, bright and clean, was given
19: 8 (F linen stands for the righteous
19:14 dressed in f linen, white and clean.

Fine[2] (Fined, Fines)
Dt 22:19 They shall f him a hundred shekels

Fined (Fine[2])
Ex 21:22 the offender must be f whatever the

Fine-looking (Fine[1], Look)
1Sa 16:18 He speaks well and is a f man. And

Finery (Fine[1])
2Sa 1:24 who clothed you in scarlet and f,
Isa 3:18 the Lord will snatch away their f:

Fines (Fine[2])
Am 2: 8 god they drink wine taken as f.

Fine-sounding (Fine[1], Sound)
Col 2: 4 may deceive you by f arguments.

Finest (Fine[1])
Nu 18:12 "I give you all the f olive oil and
18:12 all the f new wine and grain they
Dt 32:14 of Bashan and the f grains of wheat.
33:14 forth and the f the moon can yield;
Jdg 20:34 ten thousand of Israel's f men made
2Ki 8: 9 of all the f wares of Damascus.
19:23 parts, the f of its forests.
Job 28:15 cannot be bought with the f gold,
Ps 81:16 you would be fed with the f of wheat;
147:14 satisfies you with the f of wheat.
SS 4:14 and aloes and all the f spices.
Isa 17:10 f plants and plant imported vines,
25: 6 best of meats and the f of wines.
37:24 heights, the f of its forests.
Jer 48:15 her f young men will go down in the
Eze 27:22 the f of all kinds of spices
Da 10: 5 belt of the f gold round his waist.
Joel 3: 5 off my f treasures to your temples.
Am 6: 6 the bowlful and use the f lotions,

Finger (*Finger of God*, Fingers)
Ge 41:42 from his f and put it on Joseph's f.
Ex 29:12 the horns of the altar with your f,
Lev 4: 6 He is to dip his f into the blood
4:17 He shall dip his f into the blood
4:25 of the sin offering with his f
4:30 take some of the blood with his f
4:34 of the sin offering with his f
8:15 and with his f he put it on all the
9: 9 and he dipped his f into the blood
14:16 and with his f sprinkle some of it
16:14 with his f sprinkle it on the front
16:14 sprinkle some of it with his f
16:19 his f seven times to cleanse it
Nu 19: 4 to take some of its blood on his f
1Ki 12:10 f is thicker than my father's waist.
2Ch 10:10 f is thicker than my father's waist.
Est 3:10 took his signet ring from his f
Job 1:12 on the man himself do not lay a f.
Isa 58: 9 the pointing f and malicious talk,
Mt 23: 4 willing to lift a f to move them.
Lk 11:46 will not lift one f to help them.
15:22 put a ring on his f and sandals on
16:24 his f in water and cool my tongue,
Jn 8: 6 to write on the ground with his f.
20:25 and put my f where the nails were,
20:27 he said to Thomas, "Put your f here;

Finger of God
Ex 8:19 said to Pharaoh, "This is the f.
31:18 tablets of stone inscribed by the f.
Dt 9:10 stone tablets inscribed by the f.
Lk 11:20 if I drive out demons by the f, then

Fingers (Finger)
2Sa 21:20 a huge man with six f on each hand
1Ch 20: 6 a huge man with six f on each hand
Ps 8: 3 the work of your f, the moon and the
144: 1 my hands for war, my f for battle.
Pr 6:13 his feet and motions with his f,
7: 3 Bind them on your f; write them on
31:19 and grasps the spindle with her f.
SS 5: 5 my f with flowing myrrh, on the
Isa 2: 8 hands, to what their f have made.
17: 8 incense altars their f have made.
59: 3 with blood, your f with guilt.
Jer 52:21 each was four f thick, and hollow.
Da 5: 5 Suddenly the f of a human hand
Mk 7:33 Jesus put his f into the man's ears.

Finish (Finished, Finishing)
Ge 6:16 Make a roof for it and f the ark to
29:27 F this daughter's bridal week; then
Ru 2:21 they f harvesting all my grain.'"
1Ch 27:24 to count the men but did not f.
Ne 4: 2 Will they f in a day? Can they bring
Ps 90: 9 wrath; we f our years with a moan.
Pr 24:27 F your outdoor work and get your
Jer 51:63 you f reading this scroll, tie a
Da 9:24 your holy city to f transgression,
Mt 10:23 you will not f going through the
Lk 14:29 foundation and is not able to f it,
14:30 to build and was not able to f.'
Jn 4:34 him who sent me and to f his work.
5:36 that the Father has given me to f,
Ac 20:24 if only I may f the race and
2Co 8:11 Now f the work, so that your eager
9: 5 f the arrangements for the generous
Jas 1: 4 Perseverance must f its work so that

Finished (Finish)
Ge 2: 2 the seventh day God had f the work
17:22 he had f speaking with Abraham, God
18:33 the LORD had f speaking with Abraham,
24:15 Before he had f praying, Rebekah
24:19 too, until they have f drinking."
24:22 the camels had f drinking, the man
24:45 "Before I f praying in my heart,
27:30 After Isaac f blessing him and Jacob
29:28 He f the week with Leah, and then
49:33 Jacob had f giving instructions to
Ex 31:18 the LORD f speaking to Moses on
34:33 Moses f speaking to them, he put a
40:33 And so Moses f the work.
Lev 16:20 "When Aaron has f making atonement
Nu 4:15 "After Aaron and his sons have f
7: 1 Moses f setting up the tabernacle,
16:31 soon as he f saying all this, the
Dt 20: 9 the officers have f speaking to the
26:12 you have f setting aside a tenth of
31:24 After Moses f writing in a book the
32:45 Moses f reciting all these words to
Jos 4: 1 the whole nation had f crossing the
8:24 Israel had f killing all the men of
19:49 they had f dividing the land into
19:51 And so they f dividing the land.
Jdg 15:17 When he f speaking, he threw away the
Ru 2:23 barley and wheat harvests were f.
3: 3 until he has f eating and drinking.
3: 7 Boaz had f eating and drinking and
1Sa 1: 9 Once when they had f eating and
13:10 Just as he f making the offering,
18: 1 After David had f talking with Saul,
24:16 David f saying this, Saul asked, "Is
2Sa 6:18 After he had f sacrificing the burnt
11:19 "When you have f giving the king
13:36 he f speaking, the king's sons came
15:24 the people had f leaving the city.
1Ki 3: 1 David until he f building his palace
6:38 the eighth month, the temple was f
7:40 So Huram f all the work he had
7:51 for the temple of the LORD was f,
8:54 Solomon had f all these prayers and
1Ki 9: 1 Solomon had f building the temple of
13:23 the man of God had f eating and
2Ki 6:23 and after they had f eating and
10:25 soon as Jehu had f making the burnt
16:11 and f it before King Ahaz returned.
1Ch 16: 2 After David had f sacrificing the
28:20 of the temple of the LORD is f.
2Ch 4:11 So Huram f the work he had
5: 1 for the temple of the LORD was f,
7: 1 Solomon f praying, fire came down
7:11 Solomon had f the temple of the LORD
8:16 So the temple of the LORD was f.
20:23 After they f slaughtering the men
24:14 When they had f, they brought the
29:29 the offerings were f, the king and
29:34 helped them until the task was f
31: 7 month and f in the seventh month.
Ezr 5:11 a great king of Israel built and f.
5:16 construction but is not yet f."
6:14 They f building the temple according
10:17 they f dealing with all the men who
Isa 10:12 the Lord has f all his work against
Jer 26: 8 as soon as Jeremiah f telling all
43: 1 Jeremiah f telling the people all
Eze 4: 6 "After you have f this, lie down
4: 8 you have f the days of your siege.
42:15 he had f measuring what was inside
43:23 you have f purifying it, you are to
Mt 7:28 Jesus had f saying these things, the
11: 1 After Jesus had f instructing his
13:53 Jesus had f these parables, he moved
19: 1 Jesus had f saying these things, he
26: 1 Jesus had f saying all these things,
Lk 4:13 the devil had f all this tempting,
5: 4 he had f speaking, he said to Simon,
7: 1 Jesus had f saying all this in the
11: 1 When he f, one of his disciples said
11:37 Jesus had f speaking, a Pharisee
Jn 12:36 When he had f speaking, Jesus left
13:12 he had f washing their feet, he put
18: 1 he had f praying, Jesus left with
19:30 the drink, Jesus said, "It is f.
21:15 they had f eating, Jesus said to
Ac 12:25 and Saul had f their mission,
15:13 they f, James spoke up: "Brothers,
2Ti 4: 7 I have f the race, I have kept the
Heb 4: 3 f since the creation of the world.
Rev 11: 7 Now when they have f their testimony,

Finishing (Finish)
1Ki 1:41 heard it as they were f their feast.
2Ch 29:17 f in the sixteenth day of the first

Fins
Lev 11: 9 may eat any that have f and scales.
11:10 seas or streams that do not have f
11:12 in the water that does not have f
Dt 14: 9 may eat any that has f and scales.
14:10 anything that does not have f and

Fir (Firs)
Isa 41:19 the f and the cypress together,
60:13 the pine, the f and the cypress

Fire (Campfires, *Consuming fire*, Fiery, Firebrands, Firelight, Firepans, Fires, Firewood, *Pillar of fire*)
Ge 22: 6 himself carried the f and the knife.
22: 7 "The f and wood are here," Isaac
Ex 3: 2 in flames of f from within a bush.
3: 2 bush was on f it did not burn up.
12: 8 to eat the meat roasted over the f,
12: 9 roast it over the f—head, legs and
19:18 the LORD descended on it in f.
22: 6 "If a f breaks out and spreads into
22: 6 started the f must make restitution.
29:18 an offering made to the LORD by f.
29:25 an offering made to the LORD by f.
29:41 an offering made to the LORD by f.
30:20 an offering made to the LORD by f,
32:20 burned it in the f; then he ground
32:24 into the f, and out came this calf!"
35: 3 Do not light a f in any of your
40:38 and f was in the cloud by night, in

Lev 1: 7 priest are to put f on the altar
1: 7 the altar and arrange wood on the f.
1: 9 by f, an aroma pleasing to the LORD.
1:13 by f, an aroma pleasing to the LORD.
1:17 wood that is on the f on the altar.
1:17 by f, an aroma pleasing to the LORD.
2: 2 by f, an aroma pleasing to the LORD.
2: 3 the offerings made to the LORD by f.
2: 9 by f, an aroma pleasing to the LORD.
2:10 the offerings made to the LORD by f.
2:11 an offering made to the LORD by f.
2:14 heads of new grain roasted in the f.
2:16 an offering made to the LORD by f.
3: 3 a sacrifice made to the LORD by f:
3: 5 by f, an aroma pleasing to the LORD.
3: 9 made to the LORD by f: its fat,
3:11 an offering made to the LORD by f.
3:14 make this offering to the LORD by f:
3:16 made by f, a pleasing aroma.
4:12 burn it in a wood f on the ash heap.
4:35 the offerings made to the LORD by f.
5:12 the offerings made to the LORD by f.
6: 9 f must be kept burning on the altar.
6:10 offering that the f has consumed on
6:12 The f on the altar must be kept
6:12 arrange the burnt offering on the f
6:13 The f must be kept burning on the
6:17 of the offerings made to me by f.
6:18 the offerings made to the LORD by f
7: 5 an offering made to the LORD by f.
7:25 an offering by f may be made to
7:30 the offering made to the LORD by f
7:35 the offerings made to the LORD by f
8:21 by f, as the LORD commanded Moses.
8:28 an offering made to the LORD by f.
9:24 F came out from the presence of the
10: 1 put f in them and added incense; and
10: 1 unauthorised f before the LORD,
10: 2 f came out from the presence of the
10: 6 those the LORD has destroyed by f.
10:12 the offerings made to the LORD by f
10:13 by f; for so I have been commanded.
10:15 portions of the offerings made by f,
13:55 Burn it with f, whether the mildew
13:57 the mildew must be burned with f.
16:13 He is to put the incense on the f
20:14 he and they must be burned in the f,
21: 6 the offerings made to the LORD by f,
21: 9 father; she must be burned in the f.
21:21 the offerings made to the LORD by f.
22:22 an offering made to the LORD by f.
22:27 an offering made to the LORD by f.
23: 8 an offering made to the LORD by f.
23:13 offering made to the LORD by f,
23:18 by f, an aroma pleasing to the LORD.
23:25 an offering made to the LORD by f.'"
23:27 an offering made to the LORD by f.
23:36 offerings made to the LORD by f,
23:36 an offering made to the LORD by f.
23:37 the LORD by f—the burnt offerings
24: 7 an offering made to the LORD by f.
24: 9 offerings made to the LORD by f."
Nu 3: 4 an offering with unauthorised f
6:18 put it in the f that is under the
9:15 above the tabernacle looked like f.
9:16 it, and at night it looked like f.
11: 1 Then f from the LORD burned among
11: 2 to the LORD and the f died down.
11: 3 because f from the LORD had burned
15: 3 to the LORD offerings made by f,
15:10 by f, an aroma pleasing to the LORD.
15:13 an offering made by f as an aroma
15:14 an offering made by f as an aroma
15:25 made by f and a sin offering.
16: 7 tomorrow put f and incense in them
16:18 each man took his censer, put f and
16:35 f came out from the LORD and
16:46 along with f from the altar, and
18: 9 offerings that is kept from the f.
18:17 by f, an aroma pleasing to the LORD.
21:28 "F went out from Heshbon, a blaze
26:10 when the f devoured the 250 men.
26:61 the LORD with unauthorised f.)
28: 2 by f, as an aroma pleasing to me.'
28: 3 'This is the offering made by f that
28: 6 an offering made to the LORD by f.
Nu 28: 8 by f, an aroma pleasing to the LORD.
28:13 an offering made to the LORD by f.
28:19 to the LORD an offering made by f,
28:24 the food for the offering made by f
29: 6 to the LORD by f—a pleasing aroma.
29:13 Present an offering made by f as an
29:36 Present an offering made by f as an
31:23 anything else that can withstand f
31:23 must be put through the f, and then
31:23 whatever cannot withstand f must be
Dt 1:33 in f by night and in a cloud by day,
4:11 blazed with f to the very heavens,
4:12 the LORD spoke to you out of the f.
4:15 spoke to you at Horeb out of the f.
4:33 the voice of God speaking out of f,
4:36 On earth he showed you his great f,
4:36 heard his words from out of the f.
5: 4 face out of the f on the mountain.
5: 5 you were afraid of the f and did
5:22 on the mountain from out of the f,
5:23 the mountain was ablaze with f,
5:24 we have heard his voice from the f.
5:25 This great f will consume us, and
5:26 the living God speaking out of f,
7: 5 poles and burn their idols in the f.
7:25 their gods you are to burn in the f.
9: 3 ahead of you like a devouring f.
9:10 out of the f, on the day of the
9:15 mountain while it was ablaze with f.
9:21 had made, and burned it in the f.
10: 4 out of the f, on the day of the
12: 3 burn their Asherah poles in the f;
12:31 in the f as sacrifices to their gods.
18: 1 the offerings made to the LORD by f
18:10 his son or daughter in the f,
18:16 nor see this great f any more, or
32:22 For a f has been kindled by my wrath,
32:22 set on f the foundations of the
Jos 7:15 things shall be destroyed by f,
8: 8 you have taken the city, set it on f.
8:19 captured it and quickly set it on f.
13:14 since the offerings made by f to the
Jdg 1: 8 city to the sword and set it on f.
6:21 F flared from the rock, consuming
9:15 then let f come out of the thornbush
9:20 if you have not, let f come out from
9:20 and let f come out from you,
9:49 set it on f over the people inside.
9:52 to the tower to set it on f,
20:48 they came across they set on f.
1Sa 2:28 made with f by the Israelites.
30: 3 they found it destroyed by f and
2Sa 14:30 Go and set it on f." So Absalom's
14:30 servants set the field on f.
14:31 your servants set my field on f?"
1Ki 9:16 He had set it on f. He killed its
16:18 and set the palace on f around him.
18:23 it on the wood but not set f to it.
18:23 it on the wood but not set f to it.
18:24 The god who answers by f—he is God."
18:25 your god, but do not light the f."
18:38 the f of the LORD fell and burned up
19:12 a f, but the LORD was not in the f.
2Ki 1:10 may f come down from heaven and
1:10 your fifty men!" Then the f fell
1:12 "may f come down from heaven and
1:12 Then the f of God fell from heaven
1:14 See, f has fallen from heaven and
2:11 suddenly a chariot of f and horses
2:11 horses of f appeared and separated
6:17 and chariots of f all round Elisha.
8:12 "You will set f to their fortified
16: 3 even sacrificed his son in the f,
17:17 their sons and daughters in the f.
17:31 burned their children in the f as
19:18 gods into the f and destroyed them,
21: 6 He sacrificed his own son in the f,
23:10 son or daughter in the f to Molech.
25: 9 He set f to the temple of the LORD,
1Ch 14:12 gave orders to burn them in the f.
21:26 and the LORD answered him with f
2Ch 7: 1 Solomon finished praying, f came
7: 3 all the Israelites saw the f coming
16:14 they made a huge f in his honour.
21:19 His people made no f in his honour,
28: 3 and sacrificed his sons in the f,
2Ch 33: 6 He sacrificed his sons in the f in
35:13 animals over the f as prescribed,
36:19 They set f to God's temple and broke
Ne 1: 3 its gates have been burned with f."
2: 3 its gates have been destroyed by f?"
2:13 which had been destroyed by f.
2:17 its gates have been burned with f.
Job 1:16 "The f of God fell from the sky and
15:34 and f will consume the tents of
18: 5 the flame of his f stops burning.
18:15 F resides in his tent; burning
20:26 A f unfanned will consume him and
22:20 and f devours their wealth.'
28: 5 comes, is transformed below as by f;
31:12 is a f that burns to Destruction; it
41:19 his mouth; sparks of f shoot out.
41:20 a boiling pot over a f of reeds.
Ps 21: 9 up, and his f will consume them.
39: 3 and as I meditated, the f burned;
46: 9 spear, he burns the shields with f.
50: 3 be silent; a f devours before him,
66:12 heads; we went through f and water,
68: 2 as wax melts before the f, may
78:14 and with light from the f all night.
78:21 he was very angry; his f broke out
78:63 F consumed their young men, and
79: 5 long will your jealousy burn like f?
80:16 is cut down, it is burned with f;
83:14 f consumes the forest or a flame
89:46 How long will your wrath burn like f?
97: 3 F goes before him and consumes his
104: 4 flames of f his servants.
105:39 and a f to give light at night.
106:18 F blazed among their followers; a
140:10 may they be thrown into the f, into
Pr 6:27 Can a man scoop f into his lap
16:27 his speech is like a scorching f.
26:20 Without wood a f goes out; without
26:21 charcoal to embers and as wood to f,
30:16 and f, which never says, 'Enough!'
SS 8: 6 like blazing f, like a mighty flame.
Isa 1: 7 your cities burned with f; your
1:31 with no-one to quench the f."
4: 4 of judgment and a spirit of f.
4: 5 and a glow of flaming f by night;
5:24 as tongues of f lick up straw
9: 5 for burning, will be fuel for the f.
9:18 Surely wickedness burns like a f; it
9:19 the people will be fuel for the f;
10:16 under his pomp a f will be kindled
10:17 The Light of Israel will become a f,
26:11 let the f reserved for your enemies
27: 4 battle; I would set them all on f.
29: 6 tempest and flames of a devouring f.
30:33 Its f pit has been made deep and
30:33 with an abundance of f and wood; the
31: 9 whose f is in Zion, whose furnace is
33:11 breath is a f that consumes you.
37:19 gods into the f and destroyed them,
43: 2 When you walk through the f, you
44:15 he kindles a f and bakes bread.
44:16 Half of the wood he burns in the f;
44:16 says, "Ah! I am warm; I see the f.
47:14 like stubble; the f will burn them
47:14 warm anyone; here is no f to sit by.
64: 2 f sets twigs ablaze and causes water
64:11 has been burned with f, and all that
65: 5 a f that keeps burning all day.
66:15 See, the LORD is coming with f, and
66:15 and his rebuke with flames of f.
66:16 For with f and with his sword the
66:24 nor will their f be quenched, and
Jer 4: 4 burn like f because of the evil you
5:14 make my words in your mouth a f
6:29 to burn away the lead with f,
7:18 the fathers light the f, and the
7:31 their sons and daughters in the f
11:16 he will set it on f, and its
15:14 a f that will burn against you."
17:27 I will kindle an unquenchable f in
19: 5 sons in the f as offerings to Baal
20: 9 like a f, a f shut up in my bones.
21:10 and he will destroy it with f.'
21:12 burn like f because of the evil you
21:14 I will kindle a f in your forests
22: 7 beams and throw them into the f.

Jer 23:29 "Is not my word like **f**," declares
29:22 king of Babylon burned in the **f**.'
32:29 set it on **f**; they will burn it down,
34: 5 As people made a funeral **f** in honour
34: 5 so they will make a **f** in your honour
36:22 with a **f** burning in the brazier in
36:23 entire scroll was burned in the **f**.
36:32 king of Judah had burned in the **f**.
39: 8 The Babylonians set **f** to the royal
43:12 He will set **f** to the temples of the
48:45 for a **f** has gone out from Heshbon, a
49: 2 villages will be set on **f**.
49:27 "I will set **f** to the walls of
50:32 I will kindle a **f** in her towns that
51:30 Her dwellings are set on **f**; the
51:32 the marshes set on **f**, and the
51:58 and her high gates set on **f**;
52:13 He set **f** to the temple of the LORD,
Lam 1:13 "From on high he sent **f**, sent it
2: 3 a flaming **f** that consumes everything
2: 4 he has poured out his wrath like **f**
4:11 He kindled a **f** in Zion that consumed
Eze 1: 4 The centre of the **f** looked like
1: 5 in the **f** was what looked like four
1:13 burning coals of **f** or like torches.
1:13 **F** moved back and forth among the
1:27 as if full of **f**, and that from there
1:27 from there down he looked like **f**;
5: 2 of the hair with **f** inside the city.
5: 4 them into the **f** and burn them up.
5: 4 A **f** will spread from there to the
8: 2 to be his waist down he was like **f**,
10: 6 "Take **f** from among the wheels, from
10: 7 hand to the **f** that was among them.
15: 4 after it is thrown on the **f** as fuel
15: 4 the **f** burns both ends and chars the
15: 5 **f** has burned it and it is charred?
15: 6 of the forest as fuel for the **f**,
15: 7 the **f**, the **f** will yet consume them.
19:12 withered and **f** consumed them.
19:14 **F** spread from one of its main
20:31 the sacrifice of your sons in the **f**—
20:47 says: I am about to set **f** to you,
21:32 You will be fuel for the **f**, your
23:25 who are left will be consumed by **f**.
24:10 heap on the wood and kindle the **f**.
24:12 has not been removed, not even by **f**.
28:18 So I made a **f** come out from you, and
30: 8 when I set **f** to Egypt and all her
30:14 lay waste Upper Egypt, set **f** to Zoan
30:16 I will set **f** to Egypt; Pelusium will
39: 6 I will send **f** on Magog and on those
46:23 with places for **f** built all round
Da 3:22 flames of the **f** killed the soldiers
3:24 tied up and threw into the **f**?"
3:25 four men walking around in the **f**,
3:26 and Abednego came out of the **f**,
3:27 They saw that the **f** had not harmed
3:27 and there was no smell of **f** on them.
7: 9 His throne was flaming with **f**,
7:10 A river of **f** was flowing, coming out
7:11 and thrown into the blazing **f**.
Hos 7: 4 burning like an oven whose **f** the
7: 6 morning it blazes like a flaming **f**.
8:14 But I will send **f** upon their cities
Joel 1:19 O LORD, I call, for **f** has devoured
1:20 **f** has devoured the open pastures.
2: 3 Before them **f** devours, behind them a
2: 5 like a crackling **f** consuming stubble,
2:30 blood and **f** and billows of smoke.
Am 1: 4 I will send **f** upon the house of
1: 7 I will send **f** upon the walls of Gaza
1:10 I will send **f** upon the walls of Tyre
1:12 I will send **f** upon Teman that will
1:14 I will set **f** to the walls of Rabbah
2: 2 I will send **f** upon Moab that will
2: 5 I will send **f** upon Judah that will
4:11 a burning stick snatched from the **f**
5: 6 of Joseph like a **f**; it will devour,
7: 4 LORD was calling for judgment by **f**;
Ob :18 The house of Jacob will be a **f** and
:18 will set it on **f** and consume it.
Mic 1: 4 like wax before the **f**, like water
1: 7 temple gifts will be burned with **f**;
Na 1: 6 His wrath is poured out like **f**;
3:13 enemies; **f** has consumed their bars.
Na 3:15 There the **f** will devour you; the
Hab 2:13 labour is only fuel for the **f**,
Zep 1:18 In the **f** of his jealousy the whole
3: 8 by the **f** of my jealous anger.
Zec 2: 5 I myself will be a wall of **f** around
3: 2 burning stick snatched from the **f**?"
9: 4 sea, and she will be consumed by **f**.
11: 1 so that **f** may devour your cedars!
13: 9 This third I will bring into the **f**;
Mal 3: 2 a refiner's **f** or a launderer's soap.
4: 1 day that is coming will set them on **f**
Mt 3:10 be cut down and thrown into the **f**.
3:11 you with the Holy Spirit and with **f**.
3:12 up the chaff with unquenchable **f**."
5:22 will be in danger of the **f** of hell.
6:30 and tomorrow is thrown into the **f**,
7:19 is cut down and thrown into the **f**.
13:40 are pulled up and burned in the **f**,
17:15 falls into the **f** or into the water.
18: 8 feet and be thrown into eternal **f**.
18: 9 and be thrown into the **f** of hell.
25:41 into the eternal **f** prepared for the
Mk 9:22 "It has often thrown him into **f** or
9:43 hell, where the **f** never goes out.
9:48 not die, and the **f** is not quenched.'
9:49 Everyone will be salted with **f**.
14:54 guards and warmed himself at the **f**.
Lk 3: 9 be cut down and thrown into the **f**."
3:16 you with the Holy Spirit and with **f**.
3:17 up the chaff with unquenchable **f**."
9:54 Lord, do you want us to call **f** down
12:28 and tomorrow is thrown into the **f**,
12:49 "I have come to bring **f** on the earth,
16:24 because I am in agony in this **f**.'
17:29 Lot left Sodom, **f** and sulphur
22:55 when they had kindled a **f** in the
Jn 15: 6 up, thrown into the **f** and burned.
18:18 a **f** they had made to keep warm.
21: 9 they landed, they saw a **f** of burning
Ac 2: 3 to be tongues of **f** that separated
2:19 blood and **f** and billows of smoke.
28: 2 They built a **f** and welcomed us all
28: 3 as he put it on the **f**, a viper,
28: 5 Paul shook the snake off into the **f**
1Co 3:13 revealed with **f**, and the **f** will test
1Th 5:19 Do not put out the Spirit's **f**;
2Th 1: 7 blazing **f** with his powerful angels.
Heb 1: 7 winds, his servants flames of **f**."
10:27 of raging **f** that will consume the
12:18 that is burning with **f**; to darkness,
Jas 3: 5 forest is set on **f** by a small spark.
3: 6 The tongue also is a **f**, a world of
3: 6 on **f**, and is itself set on **f** by hell
5: 3 you and eat your flesh like **f**.
1Pe 1: 7 refined by **f**—may be proved genuine
2Pe 3: 7 and earth are reserved for **f**,
3:10 the elements will be destroyed by **f**,
3:12 the destruction of the heavens by **f**,
Jude : 7 suffer the punishment of eternal **f**.
:23 snatch others from the **f** and save
Rev 1:14 and his eyes were like blazing **f**.
2:18 whose eyes are like blazing **f** and
3:18 buy from me gold refined in the **f**,
8: 5 filled it with **f** from the altar, and
8: 7 and there came hail and **f** mixed with
9:17 mouths came **f**, smoke and sulphur.
9:18 killed by the three plagues of **f**,
11: 5 anyone tries to harm them, **f** comes
13:13 even causing **f** to come down from
14:18 who had charge of the **f**, came from
15: 2 a sea of glass mixed with **f** and,
16: 8 given power to scorch people with **f**.
17:16 eat her flesh and burn her with **f**.
18: 8 She will be consumed by **f**, for
19:12 His eyes are like blazing **f**, and on
20: 9 But **f** came down from heaven and
20:14 Hades were thrown into the lake of **f**.
20:14 The lake of **f** is the second death.
20:15 he was thrown into the lake of **f**.

Firebrands (Fire)

Job 41:19 **F** stream from his mouth; sparks of
Pr 26:18 Like a madman shooting **f** or deadly

Firelight (Fire)

Lk 22:56 girl saw him seated there in the **f**.

Firepans (Fire)

Ex 27: 3 sprinkling bowls, meat forks and **f**.
38: 3 sprinkling bowls, meat forks and **f**.
Nu 4:14 including the **f**, meat forks, shovels

Fires (Fire)

Isa 27:11 and women come and make **f** with them.
40:16 Lebanon is not sufficient for altar **f**
50:11 now, all you who light **f** and provide
50:11 go, walk in the light of your **f** and
Mal 1:10 not light useless **f** on my altar!

Firewood (Fire)

Lev 6:12 Every morning the priest is to add **f**
Isa 7: 4 of these two smouldering stubs of **f**—

Firm (Firmly, *Stand firm*)

Ex 15: 8 The surging waters stood **f** like a
Jos 3:17 stood **f** on dry ground in the middle
Ezr 9: 8 us a **f** place in his sanctuary,
Job 36: 5 he is mighty, and **f** in his purpose.
41:23 joined; they are **f** and immovable.
Ps 33: 9 to be; he commanded, and it stood **f**.
37:23 a man's way, he makes his steps **f**;
40: 2 rock and gave me a **f** place to stand.
75: 3 it is I who hold its pillars **f**.
89: 2 that your love stands **f** for ever,
89: 4 throne **f** through all generations.
119:89 eternal; it stands **f** in the heavens.
Pr 4:26 feet and take only ways that are **f**.
12: 7 the house of the righteous stands **f**.
Isa 22:17 the LORD is about to take **f** hold of
22:23 drive him like a peg into a **f** place
22:25 "the peg driven into the **f** place
Zec 8:23 nations will take **f** hold of one Jew
Mt 10:22 stands **f** to the end will be saved.
24:13 he who stands **f** to the end will be
Mk 13:13 stands **f** to the end will be saved.
Lk 21:19 By standing **f** you will gain life.
1Co 10:12 So, if you think you are standing **f**,
2Co 1: 7 our hope for you is **f**, because we
Col 1:23 established and **f**, not moved from
2: 5 and how **f** your faith in Christ is.
1Th 3: 8 you are standing **f** in the Lord.
1Ti 6:19 a **f** foundation for the coming age,
2Ti 2:19 God's solid foundation stands **f**,
Heb 6:19 anchor for the soul, **f** and secure.
1Pe 5: 9 Resist him, standing **f** in the faith,
5:10 make you strong, **f** and steadfast.

Firmly (Firm)

Ge 41:32 matter has been **f** decided by God,
1Sa 2:35 I will **f** establish his house, and he
1Ki 2:12 and his rule was **f** established.
2:46 **f** established in Solomon's hands.
2Ki 14: 5 After the kingdom was **f** in his grasp,
1Ch 16:30 **f** established; it cannot be moved.
2Ch 1: 1 himself **f** over his kingdom,
12:13 King Rehoboam established himself **f**
21: 4 Jehoram established himself **f** over
25: 3 After the kingdom was **f** in his
Ps 93: 1 **f** established; it cannot be moved.
96:10 The world is **f** established, it
Ecc 12:11 sayings like **f** embedded nails
Da 2: 5 "This is what I have **f** decided: If
2: 8 that this is what I have **f** decided:
3:23 these three men, **f** tied, fell into
11:32 know their God will **f** resist him.
1Co 15: 2 hold **f** to the word I preached to
Tit 1: 9 He must hold **f** to the trustworthy
Heb 3:14 if we hold **f** till the end the
4:14 us hold **f** to the faith we profess.
2Pe 1:12 you know them and are **f** established

Firs (Fir)

SS 1:17 house are cedars; our rafters are **f**.

First (*First and the last*, Firstborn, Firstfruits)

Ge 1: 5 and there was morning—the **f** day.
2:11 The name of the **f** is the Pishon; it
8: 5 and on the **f** day of the tenth month
8:13 By the **f** day of the **f** month of
8:13 of Noah's six hundred and **f** year,
10:10 The **f** centres of his kingdom were
13: 4 where he had **f** built an altar. There
25:25 The **f** to come out was red, and his
25:31 Jacob replied, "**F** sell me your
25:33 Jacob said, "Swear to me **f**." So he
38:28 and said, "This one came out **f**.
41:20 the seven fat cows that came up **f**.
43:18 put back into our sacks the **f** time.
43:20 down here the **f** time to buy food.
49: 3 my might, the **f** sign of my strength,
Ex 4: 8 attention to the **f** miraculous sign,
12: 2 **f** month, the **f** month of your year.
12:15 On the **f** day remove the yeast from
12:15 from the **f** day until the seventh
12:16 On the **f** day hold a sacred assembly,
12:18 In the **f** month you are to eat bread
13: 2 The **f** offspring of every womb among
13:12 LORD the **f** offspring of every womb.
13:15 the **f** male offspring of every womb
21:10 he must not deprive the **f** one of her
25:35 One bud shall be under the **f** pair of
28:17 In the **f** row there shall be a ruby,
29:40 With the **f** lamb offer a tenth of an
34: 1 two stone tablets like the **f** ones,
34: 1 on the **f** tablets, which you broke.
34: 4 two stone tablets like the **f** ones
34:19 "The **f** offspring of every womb
37:21 One bud was under the **f** pair of
39:10 In the **f** row there was a ruby, a
40: 2 Meeting, on the **f** day of the **f** month.
40:17 set up on the **f** day of the **f** month
Lev 4:21 and burn it as he burned the **f** bull.
5: 8 **f** offer the one for the sin offering.
9:15 offering as he did with the **f** one.
23: 5 the fourteenth day of the **f** month.
23: 7 On the **f** day hold a sacred assembly
23:10 a sheaf of the **f** grain you harvest.
23:24 'On the **f** day of the seventh month
23:35 The **f** day is a sacred assembly; do
23:39 days; the **f** day is a day of rest,
23:40 On the **f** day you are to take choice
Nu 1: 1 on the **f** day of the second month
1:18 on the **f** day of the second month.
2: 9 They will set out **f**.
3:12 in place of the **f** male offspring of
7:12 brought his offering on the **f** day
8:16 the **f** male offspring from every
9: 1 Desert of Sinai in the **f** month
9: 5 the fourteenth day of the **f** month.
10:13 They set out, this **f** time, at the
10:14 Judah went **f**, under their standard.
13:20 the season for the **f** ripe grapes.)
15:20 Present a cake from the **f** of your
15:21 LORD from the **f** of your ground meal.
18:15 The **f** offspring of every womb, both
20: 1 In the **f** month the whole Israelite
22:15 and more distinguished than the **f**.
24:20 "Amalek was **f** among the nations, but
28:11 "'On the **f** of every month, present
28:16 the fourteenth day of the **f** month
28:18 On the **f** day hold a sacred assembly
29: 1 "'On the **f** day of the seventh month
33: 3 on the fifteenth day of the **f** month
33:38 where he died on the **f** day of the
Dt 1: 3 In the fortieth year, on the **f** day
10: 1 two stone tablets like the **f** ones
10: 2 on the **f** tablets, which you broke.
10: 3 two stone tablets like the **f** ones,
10:10 as I did the **f** time, and the LORD
13: 9 Your hand must be the **f** in putting
16: 4 of the **f** day remain until morning.
17: 7 be the **f** in putting him to death,
18: 4 new wine and oil, and the **f** wool
21:17 the **f** sign of his father's strength.
24: 4 her **f** husband, who divorced her, is
25: 6 The **f** son she bears shall carry on
Jos 4:19 On the tenth day of the **f** month the
21: 4 The **f** lot came out for the
21:10 because the **f** lot fell to them):
Jdg 1: 1 "Who will be the **f** to go up and
20:18 They said, "Who of us shall go **f** to
20:18 The LORD replied, "Judah shall go **f**.
20:22 had stationed themselves the **f** day.
20:39 defeating them as in the **f** battle."
1Sa 2:16 "Let the fat be burned up **f**, and
14:14 In that **f** attack Jonathan and his
14:35 it was the **f** time he had done this.
22:15 Was that day the **f** time I enquired
2Sa 17: 9 If he should attack your troops **f**,
18:27 the **f** one runs like Ahimaaz son of
19:20 I have come here as the **f** of the
19:43 Were we not the **f** to speak of
21: 9 death during the **f** days of harvest,
1Ki 3:22 But the **f** one insisted, "No! The
3:27 the living baby to the **f** woman.
6:24 One wing of the **f** cherub was five
17:13 But **f** make a small cake of bread for
18:25 one of the bulls and prepare it **f**,
20: 9 will do all you demanded the **f** time,
20:17 provincial commanders went out **f**.
22: 5 "**F** seek the counsel of the LORD.
2Ki 1:14 consumed the **f** two captains and all
4:42 bread baked from the **f** ripe corn,
17:25 they **f** lived there, they did not
1Ch 6:54 because the **f** lot was for them):
9: 2 Now the **f** to resettle on their own
11: 6 Joab son of Zeruiah went up **f**,
12:15 crossed the Jordan in the **f** month
15:13 did not bring it up the **f** time that
16: 7 That day David **f** committed to Asaph
23: 8 The sons of Ladan: Jehiel the **f**,
23:11 Jahath was the **f** and Ziza the second,
23:16 of Gershom: Shubael was the **f**.
23:17 of Eliezer: Rehabiah was the **f**.
23:18 sons of Izhar: Shelomith was the **f**.
23:19 The sons of Hebron: Jeriah the **f**,
23:20 The sons of Uzziel: Micah the **f** and
24: 7 The **f** lot fell to Jehoiarib, the
24:21 from his sons: Isshiah was the **f**.
24:23 The sons of Hebron: Jeriah the **f**,
25: 9 The **f** lot, which was for Asaph, fell
26:10 the Merarite had sons: Shimri the **f**
26:10 father had approinted him the **f**)
27: 2 In charge of the **f** division, for the
27: 2 for the **f** month, was Jashobeam son
27: 3 the army officers for the **f** month.
2Ch 3:11 One wing of the **f** cherub was five
3:12 touched the wing of the **f** cherub.
18: 4 "**F** seek the counsel of the LORD.
29: 3 In the **f** month of the **f** year of his
29:17 on the **f** day of the **f** month, and by
35: 1 the fourteenth day of the **f** month.
36:22 In the **f** year of Cyrus king of
Ezr 1: 1 In the **f** year of Cyrus king of
3: 6 On the **f** day of the seventh month
5:13 "However, in the **f** year of Cyrus
6: 3 In the **f** year of King Cyrus, the
6:19 On the fourteenth day of the **f** month,
7: 9 Babylon on the **f** day of the **f** month,
7: 9 on the **f** day of the fifth month,
8:31 On the twelfth day of the **f** month we
10:16 On the **f** day of the tenth month they
10:17 by the **f** day of the **f** month they
Ne 4:21 from the **f** light of dawn till the
7: 5 those who had been the **f** to return.
8: 2 on the **f** day of the seventh month,
8:18 Day after day, from the **f** day to the
10:37 to the priests, the **f** of our ground
Est 3: 7 in the **f** month, the month of Nisan,
3:12 on the thirteenth day of the **f** month
Job 3: 9 vain and not see the **f** rays of dawn,
15: 7 "Are you the **f** man ever born? Were
40:19 He ranks **f** among the works of God,
42:12 part of Job's life more than the **f**.
42:14 The **f** daughter he named Jemimah, the
Pr 4:18 is like the **f** gleam of dawn,
8:22 "The LORD brought me forth as the **f**
18:17 The **f** to present his case seems
Isa 41: 4 I, the LORD—with the **f** of them and
41:27 I was the **f** to tell Zion, 'Look,
43:27 Your **f** father sinned; your spokesmen
44: 6 the LORD Almighty: I am the **f** and I
48:12 am he; I am the **f** and I am the last.
48:16 "From the **f** announcement I have not
52: 4 "At **f** my people went down to Egypt
Jer 4:31 groan as of one bearing her **f** child
7:12 I **f** made a dwelling for my Name,
25: 1 was the **f** year of Nebuchadnezzar
36:28 the words that were on the **f** scroll,
50:17 The **f** to devour him was the king of
Eze 26: 1 In the eleventh year, on the **f** day
29:17 in the **f** month on the **f** day, the
30:20 In the eleventh year, in the **f** month
31: 1 in the third month on the **f** day, the
32: 1 in the twelfth month on the **f** day,
40:21 as those of the **f** gateway.
44:30 You are to give them the **f** portion
45:18 In the **f** month on the **f** day you are
45:21 "'In the **f** month on the fourteenth
Da 1:21 until the **f** year of King Cyrus.
6:19 At the **f** light of dawn, the king got
7: 1 In the **f** year of Belshazzar king of
7: 4 "The **f** was like a lion, and it had
7: 8 the **f** horns were uprooted before it.
8:21 horn between his eyes is the **f** king.
9: 1 In the **f** year of Darius son of
9: 2 in the **f** year of his reign, I,
10: 4 twenty-fourth day of the **f** month
10:12 Since the **f** day that you set your
10:21 **f** I will tell you what is written in
11: 1 in the **f** year of Darius the Mede, I
11:13 larger than the **f**; and after several
Hos 2: 7 I will go back to my husband as at **f**,
Am 6: 7 Therefore you will be among the **f** to
Jnh 3: 4 On the **f** day, Jonah started into the
Na 3:12 fig-trees with their **f** ripe fruit;
Hag 1: 1 on the **f** day of the sixth month, the
Zec 6: 2 The **f** chariot had red horses, the
12: 7 will save the dwellings of Judah **f**,
14:10 Gate to the site of the **F** Gate,
Mt 5:24 **F** go and be reconciled to your
6:33 seek **f** his kingdom and his
7: 5 You hypocrite, **f** take the plank out
8:21 **f** let me go and bury my father."
10: 2 the twelve apostles: **f**, Simon
12:29 unless he **f** ties up the strong man?
12:45 of that man is worse than the **f**.
13:30 **F** collect the weeds and tie them in
17:10 law say that Elijah must come **f**?"
17:25 the house, Jesus was the **f** to speak.
17:27 Take the **f** fish you catch; open its
19:30 many who are **f** will be last, and
19:30 and many who are last will be **f**.
20: 8 ones hired and going on to the **f**.'
20:10 when those came who were hired **f**,
20:16 the last will be **f**, and the **f** will
20:27 whoever wants to be **f** must be your
21:28 He went to the **f** and said, 'Son, go
21:31 wanted?" "The **f**," they answered.
21:36 more than the **f** time, and the
22:25 The **f** one married and died, and
22:38 This is the **f** and greatest
23:26 Blind Pharisee! **F** clean the inside
26:17 On the **f** day of the Feast of
27:64 deception will be worse than the **f**."
28: 1 at dawn on the **f** day of the week,
Mk 3:27 unless he **f** ties up the strong man.
4:28 the soil produces corn—**f** the stalk,
7:27 "**F** let the children eat all they
9:11 law say that Elijah must come **f**?"
9:12 come **f**, and restores all things.
9:35 "If anyone wants to be **f**, he must be
10:31 are **f** will be last, and the last **f**."
10:44 whoever wants to be **f** must be slave
12:20 Now there were seven brothers. The **f**
13:10 the gospel must **f** be preached to all
14:12 On the **f** day of the Feast of
16: 2 Very early on the **f** day of the week,
16: 9 Jesus rose early on the **f** day of the
16: 9 he appeared **f** to Mary Magdalene, out
Lk 1: 2 who from the **f** were eye-witnesses
2: 2 This was the **f** census that took
6:42 **f** take the plank out of your eye,
9:59 **f** let me go and bury my father."
9:61 "I will follow you, Lord; but **f** let
10: 5 "When you enter a house, **f** say,
11:26 of that man is worse than the **f**."
11:38 noticing that Jesus did not **f** wash
12: 1 Jesus began to speak **f** to his
13:30 will be **f**, and **f** who will be last."
14:18 The **f** said, 'I have just bought a

Lk 14:28 Will he not **f** sit down and estimate
14:31 Will he not **f** sit down and consider
16: 5 asked the **f**, 'How much do you owe
17:25 **f** he must suffer many things and be
19:16 "The **f** one came and said, 'Sir, your
20:29 Now there were seven brothers. The **f**
21: 9 These things must happen **f**, but the
24: 1 On the **f** day of the week, very early
Jn 1:41 The **f** thing Andrew did was to find
2:10 brings out the choice wine **f**
2:11 This, the **f** of his miraculous signs,
7:51 "Does our law condemn a man without **f**
8: 7 be the **f** to throw a stone at her."
8: 9 the older ones **f**, until only Jesus
12:16 At **f** his disciples did not
15:18 keep in mind that it hated me **f**.
16: 4 this at **f** because I was with you.
18:13 brought him **f** to Annas, who was the
19:32 broke the legs of the **f** man who had
20: 1 Early on the **f** day of the week,
20: 4 outran Peter and reached the tomb **f**.
20: 8 had reached the tomb **f**, also went
20:19 On the evening of that **f** day of the
Ac 3:26 he sent him **f** to you to bless you by
7:12 sent our fathers on their **f** visit.
11:26 were called Christians **f** at Antioch.
12:10 They passed the **f** and second guards
13:46 to speak the word of God to you **f**.
15:14 how God at **f** showed his concern by
20: 7 On the **f** day of the week we came
20:18 from the **f** day I came into the
26:20 **F** to those in Damascus, then to
26:23 as the **f** to rise from the dead,
27:43 to jump overboard **f** and get to land.
Ro 1: 8 **F**, I thank my God through Jesus
1:16 **f** for the Jew, then for the Gentile.
1:17 that is by faith from **f** to last,
2: 9 **f** for the Jew, then for the Gentile;
2:10 **f** for the Jew, then for the Gentile.
3: 2 Much in every way! **F** of all, they
10:19 **F**, Moses says, "I will make you
13:11 nearer now than when we **f** believed.
16: 5 who was the **f** convert to Christ in
1Co 11:18 In the **f** place, I hear that when you
12:28 in the church God has appointed **f** of
14:30 down, the **f** speaker should stop.
15: 3 passed on to you as of **f** importance:
15:45 is written: "The **f** man Adam became a
15:46 The spiritual did not come **f**, but
15:47 The **f** man was of the dust of the
16: 2 On the **f** day of every week, each one
16:15 were the **f** converts in Achaia,
2Co 1:15 I planned to visit you **f** so that
8: 5 they gave themselves **f** to the Lord
8:10 Last year you were the **f** not only to
Gal 4:13 that I **f** preached the gospel to you.
Eph 1:12 that we, who were the **f** to hope in
6: 2 the **f** commandment with a promise—
Php 1: 5 the gospel from the **f** day until now,
1Th 4:16 and the dead in Christ will rise **f**.
1Ti 2: 1 I urge, then, **f** of all, that
2:13 For Adam was formed **f**, then Eve.
3:10 They must **f** be tested; and then if
5: 4 these should learn **f** of all to put
5:12 they have broken their **f** pledge.
2Ti 1: 5 which **f** lived in your grandmother
2: 6 should be the **f** to receive a share
4:16 At my **f** defence, no-one came to my
Heb 2: 3 which was **f** announced by the Lord,
3:14 the end the confidence we had at **f**.
7: 2 **F**, his name means "king of
7:27 **f** for his own sins, and then for the
8: 7 nothing wrong with that **f** covenant,
8:13 he has made the **f** one obsolete
9: 1 Now the **f** covenant had regulations
9: 2 In its **f** room were the lampstand,
9: 8 the **f** tabernacle was still standing.
9:15 sins committed under the **f** covenant.
9:18 This is why even the **f** covenant was
10: 8 **F** he said, "Sacrifices and offerings,
10: 9 aside the **f** to establish the second.
10:15 to us about this. **F** he says:
Jas 3:17 is **f** of all pure; then peace-loving,
2Pe 3: 3 **F** of all, you must understand that
1Jn 4:19 We love because he **f** loved us.
3Jn : 9 Diotrephes, who loves to be **f**,
Rev 2: 4 you: You have forsaken your **f** love.
2: 5 and do the things you did at **f**.
2:19 now doing more than you did at **f**.
4: 1 And the voice I had **f** heard speaking
4: 7 The **f** living creature was like a
6: 1 the Lamb opened the **f** of the seven
8: 7 The **f** angel sounded his trumpet, and
9:12 The **f** woe is past; two other woes
13:12 of the **f** beast on his behalf,
13:12 its inhabitants worship the **f** beast,
13:14 to do on behalf of the **f** beast,
13:15 breath to the image of the **f** beast,
16: 2 The **f** angel went and poured out his
20: 5 This is the **f** resurrection.
20: 6 who have part in the **f** resurrection.
21: 1 for the **f** heaven and the **f** earth had
21:19 The **f** foundation was jasper, the

First and the last

Rev 1:17 "Do not be afraid. I am the **F**.
2: 8 the **F**, who died and came to life
22:13 I am the Alpha and the Omega, the **F**,

Firstborn (*All the firstborn*, Bear[1], First)

Ge 4: 4 from some of the **f** of his flock.
10:15 Canaan was the father of Sidon his **f**,
22:21 Uz the **f**, Buz his brother, Kemuel
25:13 Nebaioth the **f** of Ishmael, Kedar,
27:19 to his father, "I am Esau your **f**.
27:32 son," he answered, "your **f**, Esau.
35:23 The sons of Leah: Reuben the **f** of
36:15 Eliphaz the **f** of Esau: Chiefs Teman,
38: 6 Judah got a wife for Er, his **f**, and
38: 7 Er, Judah's **f**, was wicked in the
41:51 Joseph named his **f** Manasseh and said,
43:33 from the **f** to the youngest; and they
46: 8 to Egypt: Reuben the **f** of Jacob.
48:14 even though Manasseh was the **f**.
48:18 "No, my father, this one is the **f**;
49: 3 "Reuben, you are my **f**, my might, the
Ex 4:22 the LORD says: Israel is my **f** son,
4:23 him go; so I will kill your **f** son.'"
6:14 of Reuben the **f** son of Israel
11: 5 Every **f** son in Egypt will die, from
11: 5 from the **f** son of Pharaoh, who sits
11: 5 to the **f** son of the slave girl,
12:12 strike down every **f**—both men and
12:29 from the **f** of Pharaoh, who sat on
12:29 to the **f** of the prisoner, who was
12:29 the **f** of all the livestock as well.
13: 2 "Consecrate to me every **f** male. The
13:13 Redeem with a lamb every **f** donkey,
13:13 Redeem every **f** among your sons.
13:15 the LORD killed every **f** in Egypt,
13:15 womb and redeem each of my **f** sons.'
22:29 "You must give me the **f** of your sons.
34:20 Redeem the **f** donkey with a lamb, but
34:20 Redeem all your **f** sons. "No-one is
Lev 27:26 "'No-one, however, may dedicate the **f**
27:26 the **f** already belongs to the LORD
Nu 1:20 From the descendants of Reuben the **f**
3: 2 sons of Aaron were Nadab the **f**
3:13 I set apart for myself every **f** in
3:43 The total number of **f** males a month
3:46 To redeem the 273 **f** Israelites who
3:50 From the **f** of the Israelites he
8:16 them as my own in place of the **f**,
8:17 Every **f** male in Israel, whether man
18:15 But you must redeem every **f** son and
18:15 and every **f** male of unclean animals.
18:17 you must not redeem the **f** of an ox,
26: 5 The descendants of Reuben, the **f** son
33: 4 who were burying all their **f**, whom
Dt 12: 6 and the **f** of your herds and flocks.
12:17 or the **f** of your herds and flocks,
14:23 and the **f** of your herds and flocks
15:19 every **f** male of your herds and
15:19 Do not put the **f** of your oxen to
15:19 do not shear the **f** of your sheep.
21:15 and both bear him sons but the **f** is
21:16 must not give the rights of the **f**
21:16 loves in preference to his actual **f**,
21:17 son of his unloved wife as the **f**
Dt 21:17 The right of the **f** belongs to him.
33:17 In majesty he is like a **f** bull; his
Jos 6:26 "At the cost of his **f** son will he
17: 1 **f**, that is, for Makir, Manasseh's **f**.
1Sa 8: 2 The name of his **f** was Joel and the
17:13 war: The **f** was Eliab; the second,
2Sa 3: 2 His **f** was Amnon the son of Ahinoam
1Ki 16:34 at the cost of his **f** son Abiram,
2Ki 3:27 he took his **f** son, who was to
1Ch 1:13 Canaan was the father of Sidon his **f**,
1:29 Nebaioth the **f** of Ishmael, Kedar,
2: 3 Er, Judah's **f**, was wicked in the
2:13 Jesse was the father of Eliab his **f**;
2:25 sons of Jerahmeel the **f** of Hezron:
2:25 Ram his **f**, Bunah, Oren, Ozem and
2:27 The sons of Ram the **f** of Jerahmeel:
2:42 brother of Jerahmeel: Mesha his **f**,
2:50 The sons of Hur the **f** of Ephrathah:
3: 1 The **f** was Amnon the son of Ahinoam
3:15 The sons of Josiah: Johanan the **f**,
4: 4 the **f** of Ephrathah and father of
5: 1 Reuben the **f** of Israel (he was the **f**,
5: 1 his rights as **f** were given to the
5: 2 rights of the **f** belonged to Joseph)
5: 3 the sons of Reuben the **f** of Israel:
6:28 The sons of Samuel: Joel the **f** and
8: 1 Benjamin was the father of Bela his **f**
8:30 his **f** son was Abdon, followed by Zur,
8:39 of his brother Eshek: Ulam his **f**,
9: 5 Of the Shilonites: Asaiah the **f** and
9:31 A Levite named Mattithiah, the **f** son
9:36 his **f** son was Abdon, followed by Zur,
26: 2 Meshelemiah had sons: Zechariah the **f**
26: 4 also had sons: Shemaiah the **f**,
26:10 first (although he was not the **f**,
2Ch 21: 3 to Jehoram because he was his **f** son.
Ne 10:36 we will bring the **f** of our sons and
Job 18:13 skin; death's **f** devours his limbs.
Ps 89:27 I will also appoint him my **f**, the
135: 8 He struck down the **f** of Egypt, the **f**
136:10 who struck down the **f** of Egypt
Jer 31: 9 father, and Ephraim is my **f** son.
Eze 20:26 the sacrifice of every **f**—that I
Mic 6: 7 I offer my **f** for my transgression,
Zec 12:10 for him as one grieves for a **f** son.
Lk 2: 7 she gave birth to her **f**, a son. She
2:23 "Every **f** male is to be consecrated
Ro 8:29 might be the **f** among many brothers.
Col 1:15 God, the **f** over all creation.
1:18 and the **f** from among the dead,
Heb 1: 6 again, when God brings his **f** into
11:28 **f** would not touch the **f** of Israel.
12:23 to the church of the **f**, whose names
Rev 1: 5 the **f** from the dead, and the ruler

Firstfruits (First, Fruit)

Ex 23:16 **f** of the crops you sow in your field.
23:19 "Bring the best of the **f** of your
34:22 with the **f** of the wheat harvest,
34:26 "Bring the best of the **f** of your
Lev 2:12 to the LORD as an offering of the **f**,
2:14 "'If you bring a grain offering of **f**
23:17 as a wave offering of **f** to the LORD.
23:20 together with the bread of the **f**.
Nu 18:12 the LORD as the **f** of their harvest.
18:13 All the land's **f** that they bring to
28:26 "'On the day of **f**, when you present
Dt 18: 4 You are to give them the **f** of your
26: 2 take some of the **f** of all that you
26:10 now I bring the **f** of the soil that
2Ch 31: 5 gave the **f** of their grain,
Ne 10:35 LORD each year the **f** of our crops
12:44 for the contributions, **f** and tithes.
13:31 at designated times, and for the **f**.
Ps 78:51 **f** of manhood in the tents of Ham.
105:36 land, the **f** of all their manhood.
Pr 3: 9 with the **f** of all your crops;
Jer 2: 3 Israel was holy to the LORD, the **f**
Eze 44:30 The best of all the **f** and of all
Ro 8:23 who have the **f** of the Spirit, groan
11:16 If the part of the dough offered as **f**
1Co 15:20 **f** of those who have fallen asleep.
15:23 each in his own turn: Christ, the **f**;
Jas 1:18 be a kind of **f** of all he created.
Rev 14: 4 offered as **f** to God and the Lamb.

Fish (Fishermen, Fishers, Fishhook, Fish-hooks, Fishing)
Ge 1:26 let them rule over the f of the sea
1:28 Rule over the f of the sea and the
9: 2 and upon all the f of the sea; they
Ex 7:18 The f in the Nile will die, and the
7:21 The f in the Nile died, and the
Nu 11: 5 We remember the f we ate in Egypt at
11:22 if all the f in the sea were caught
Dt 4:18 ground or any f in the waters below.
1Ki 4:33 animals and birds, reptiles and f.
2Ch 33:14 as far as the entrance of the F Gate
Ne 3: 3 The F Gate was rebuilt by the sons
12:39 the Jeshanah Gate, the F Gate, the
13:16 were bringing in f and all kinds of
Job 12: 8 or let the f of the sea inform you.
Ps 8: 8 the f of the sea, all that swim the
105:29 into blood, causing their f to die.
Ecc 9:12 As f are caught in a cruel net,
Isa 50: 2 their f rot for lack of water and
Eze 29: 4 make the f of your streams stick to
29: 4 all the f sticking to your scales.
29: 5 you and all the f of your streams.
38:20 The f of the sea, the birds of the
47: 9 There will be large numbers of f,
47:10 kinds—like the f of the Great Sea.
47:10 f will be of many kinds—like the f
Hos 4: 3 air and the f of the sea are dying.
Jnh 1:17 the LORD provided a great f to
1:17 Jonah was inside the f three days
2: 1 From inside the f Jonah prayed to
2:10 the LORD commanded the f, and it
Hab 1:14 You have made men like f in the sea,
Zep 1: 3 of the air and the f of the sea.
1:10 "a cry will go up from the F Gate,
Mt 7:10 Or if he asks for a f, will give him
12:40 nights in the belly of a huge f,
13:47 the lake and caught all kinds of f.
13:48 collected the good f in baskets,
14:17 of bread and two f," they answered.
14:19 Taking the five loaves and the two f
15:34 they replied, "and a few small f.
15:36 he took the seven loaves and the f,
17:27 Take the first f you catch; open its
Mk 6:38 out, they said, "Five—and two f.
6:41 Taking the five loaves and the two f
6:41 divided the two f among them all.
6:43 of broken pieces of bread and f.
8: 7 They had a few small f as well; he
Lk 5: 6 of f that their nets began to break.
5: 9 at the catch of f they had taken,
9:13 only five loaves of bread and two f
9:16 Taking the five loaves and the two f
11:11 if your son asks for a f, will
24:42 They gave him a piece of broiled f,
Jn 6: 9 small barley loaves and two small f,
6:11 He did the same with the f.
21: 3 "I'm going out to f," Simon Peter
21: 5 "Friends, haven't you any f?" "No,"
21: 6 in because of the large number of f.
21: 8 towing the net full of f, for they
21: 9 there with f on it, and some bread.
21:10 some of the f you have just caught."
21:11 It was full of large f, 153, but
21:13 them, and did the same with the f.
1Co 15:39 birds another and f another.

Fishermen (Fish)
Isa 19: 8 The f will groan and lament, all who
Jer 16:16 "But now I will send for many f,"
Eze 47:10 F will stand along the shore; from
Mt 4:18 net into the lake, for they were f.
13:48 was full, the f pulled it up on the
Mk 1:16 net into the lake, for they were f.
Lk 5: 2 the f, who were washing their nets.

Fishers (Fish)
Mt 4:19 said, "and I will make you f of men.
Mk 1:17 said, "and I will make you f of men.

Fishhook (Fish, Hook)
Job 41: 1 pull in the Leviathan with a f or

Fish-hooks (Fish, Hook)
Am 4: 2 with hooks, the last of you with f.

Fishing (Fish)
Job 41: 7 harpoons or his head with f spears?
Eze 26: 5 become a place to spread f nets,
26:14 become a place to spread f nets.

Fist (Fists, Tight-fisted)
Ex 21:18 other with a stone or with his f
Nu 35:21 hits him with his f so that he dies,
Job 15:25 he shakes his f at God and vaunts
Isa 10:32 they will shake their f at the mount

Fists (Fist)
Isa 58: 4 striking each other with wicked f.
Zep 2:15 pass by her scoff and shake their f.
Mt 26:67 face and struck him with their f.
Mk 14:65 struck him with their f, and said,

Fit (Fits, Fitted, Fitting, Fittings)
Ge 49:20 provide delicacies f for a king.
Dt 12: 8 here today, everyone as he sees f,
Jdg 5:25 milk; in a bowl f for nobles she
17: 6 no king; everyone did as he saw f.
21:25 no king; everyone did as he saw f.
2Ki 24:16 strong and f for war, and a thousand
Isa 54:16 and forges a weapon f for its work.
Eze 19:11 strong, f for a ruler's sceptre.
19:14 No strong branch is left on it f for
Mt 3:11 I, whose sandals I am not f to carry.
Lk 9:62 f for service in the kingdom of God."
14:35 It is f neither for the soil nor for
Ac 22:22 earth of him! He's not f to live!"

Fits (Fit)
Gal 5:20 discord, jealousy, f of rage,

Fitted (Fit)
Ex 26:24 to the top, and f into a single ring;
36:29 to the top and f into a single ring;
Eph 6:15 with your feet f with the readiness

Fitting (Fit)
Ps 33: 1 is f for the upright to praise him.
147: 1 how pleasant and f to praise him!
Pr 10:32 of the righteous know what is f,
19:10 not f for a fool to live in luxury
26: 1 harvest, honour is not f for a fool.
1Co 14:40 everything should be done in a f and
Col 3:18 your husbands, as is f in the Lord.
Heb 2:10 it was f that God, for whom and

Fittings (Fit)
1Ch 22: 3 doors of the gateways and for the f,

Fix (Affixing, Fixed)
Dt 11:18 F these words of mine in your hearts
Job 14: 3 Do you f your eye on such a one?
Pr 4:25 look straight ahead, f your gaze
Isa 46: 8 "Remember this, f it in mind, take
Am 9: 4 I will f my eyes upon them for evil
2Co 4:18 we f our eyes not on what is seen,
Heb 3: 1 f your thoughts on Jesus, the
12: 2 Let us f our eyes on Jesus, the

Fixed (Fix)
2Ki 8:11 He stared at him with a f gaze until
Job 38:10 I f limits for it and set its doors
Ps 141: 8 my eyes are f on you, O Sovereign
Pr 8:28 and f securely the fountains of the
Jer 33:25 and the f laws of heaven and earth,
Lk 16:26 us and you a great chasm has been f,

Flagstaff (Staff)
Isa 30:17 left like a f on a mountaintop,

Flakes
Ex 16:14 thin f like frost on the ground

Flame (Aflame, Flamed, Flames, Flaming)
Jdg 13:20 the f blazed up from the altar
13:20 angel of the LORD ascended in the f.
16: 9 snaps when it comes close to a f.
Job 15:30 a f will wither his shoots, and
18: 5 the f of his fire stops burning.
Ps 83:14 or a f sets the mountains ablaze,
106:18 followers; a f consumed the wicked.
SS 8: 6 like blazing fire, like a mighty f.
Isa 10:16 will be kindled like a blazing f.
10:17 become a fire, their Holy One a f;
47:14 themselves from the power of the f.
54:16 fans the coals into f and forges
Eze 20:47 The blazing f will not be quenched,
Joel 2: 3 devours, behind them a f blazes.
Ob :18 a fire and the house of Joseph a f;
2Ti 1: 6 you to fan into f the gift of God,

Flamed (Flame)
Am 1:11 and his fury f unchecked,

Flames (Flame)
Ex 3: 2 him in f of fire from within a bush.
Job 41:21 ablaze, and f dart from his mouth.
Ps 104: 4 messengers, f of fire his servants.
Isa 5:24 as dry grass sinks down in the f,
29: 6 tempest and f of a devouring fire.
42:25 It enveloped them in f, yet they did
43: 2 the f will not set you ablaze.
66:15 fury, and his rebuke with f of fire.
Jer 51:58 labour is only fuel for the f."
Da 3:22 the furnace so hot that the f of the
Joel 1:19 f have burned up all the trees of
Ac 7:30 an angel appeared to Moses in the f
1Co 3:15 only as one escaping through the f.
13: 3 surrender my body to the f, but
Heb 1: 7 winds, his servants f of fire."
11:34 quenched the fury of the f, and

Flaming (Flame)
Ge 3:24 a f sword flashing back and forth to
Ps 7:13 he makes ready his f arrows.
Isa 4: 5 day and a glow of f fire by night;
50:11 provide yourselves with f torches,
Lam 2: 3 He has burned in Jacob like a f fire
Da 7: 9 His throne was f with fire, and its
10: 6 his eyes like f torches, his arms
Hos 7: 6 the morning it blazes like a f fire.
Na 2: 4 They look like f torches; they dart
Zec 12: 6 like a f torch among sheaves.
Eph 6:16 all the f arrows of the evil one.

Flank
Eze 25: 9 therefore I will expose the f of
34:21 you shove with f and shoulder,

Flap (Flapped)
Job 39:13 "The wings of the ostrich f joyfully,

Flapped (Flap)
Isa 10:14 all the countries; not one f a wing,

Flare (Flared)
2Sa 11:20 the king's anger may f up, and he
Ps 2:12 for his wrath can f up in a moment.

Flared (Flare)
Jdg 6:21 Fire f from the rock, consuming the
1Sa 20:30 Saul's anger f up at Jonathan and he
Ps 124: 3 their anger f against us, they would

Flash (Flashed, Flashes, Flashing)
Job 15:12 you away, and why do your eyes f,
37:15 clouds and makes his lightning f?
Eze 21:10 polished to f like lightning!
21:15 Oh! It is made to f like lightning,
21:28 to consume and to f like lightning!
Hos 11: 6 Swords will f in their cities, will
Zec 9:14 his arrow will f like lightning.
Lk 9:29 as bright as a f of lightning.
1Co 15:52 in a f, in the twinkling of an eye,

Flashed (Flash)

Ex 9:23 and lightning f down to the ground.
9:24 hail fell and lightning f back and
Ps 77:17 your arrows f back and forth.
Eze 1:13 bright, and lightning f out of it.
Hos 6: 5 judgments f like lightning upon you.
Hab 3: 4 the sunrise; rays f from his hand,
Ac 9: 3 a light from heaven f around him.
22: 6 light from heaven f around me.

Flashes (Flash)

Job 41:18 His snorting throws out f of light;
Ps 29: 7 The voice of the LORD strikes with f
Eze 1:14 back and forth like f of lightning.
Am 5: 9 he f destruction on the stronghold
Na 2: 3 The metal on the chariots f on the
Lk 17:24 which f and lights up the sky from
Rev 4: 5 From the throne came f of lightning,
8: 5 f of lightning and an earthquake.
11:19 And there came f of lightning,
16:18 there came f of lightning, rumblings,

Flashing (Flash)

Ge 3:24 a flaming sword f back and forth to
Dt 32:41 I sharpen my f sword and my hand
Job 39:23 along with the f spear and lance.
Ps 76: 3 There he broke the f arrows, the
Eze 1: 4 immense cloud with f lightning
Na 3: 3 Charging cavalry, f swords and
Hab 3:11 at the lightning of your f spear.

Flask

1Sa 10: 1 Samuel took a f of oil and poured it
2Ki 9: 1 take this f of oil with you and go
9: 3 take the f and pour the oil on his

Flat (Flats, Flattens)

Hos 7: 8 Ephraim is a f cake not turned over.

Flats (Flat)

Job 39: 6 his home, the salt f as his habitat.

Flattens (Flat)

Isa 32:19 Though hail f the forest and the

Flatter (Flattering, Flatters, Flattery)

Job 32:21 to no-one, nor will I f any man;
Ps 78:36 they would f him with their mouths,
Jude :16 f others for their own advantage.

Flattering (Flatter)

Ps 12: 2 their f lips speak with deception.
12: 3 May the LORD cut off all f lips and
Pr 26:28 it hurts, and a f mouth works ruin.
28:23 favour than he who has a f tongue.
Eze 12:24 false visions or f divinations

Flatters (Flatter)

Ps 36: 2 For in his own eyes he f himself too
Pr 29: 5 Whoever f his neighbour is spreading

Flattery (Flatter)

Job 32:22 for if I were skilled in f, my Maker
Da 11:32 With f he will corrupt those who
Ro 16:18 By smooth talk and f they deceive
1Th 2: 5 You know we never used f, nor did we

Flavour

Job 6: 6 is there f in the white of an egg?

Flaw

Dt 15:21 or has any serious f, you must not
17: 1 that has any defect or f in it,
SS 4: 7 my darling; there is no f in you.

Flawless

2Sa 22:31 perfect; the word of the LORD is f.
Job 11: 4 You say to God, 'My beliefs are f
Ps 12: 6 the words of the LORD are f, like
18:30 perfect; the word of the LORD is f.
Pr 30: 5 "Every word of God is f; he is a
SS 5: 2 my darling, my dove, my f one.

Flax

Ex 9:31 (The f and barley were destroyed,
9:31 in the ear and the f was in bloom.
Jos 2: 6 hidden them under the stalks of f
Jdg 15:14 on his arms became like charred f,
Pr 31:13 She selects wool and f and works
Isa 19: 9 Those who work with combed f will

Flea

1Sa 24:14 are you pursuing? A dead dog? A f?
26:20 Israel has come out to look for a f

Fled (Flee)

Ge 14:10 the kings of Sodom and Gomorrah f,
14:10 them and the rest f to the hills.
16: 6 Hagar; so she f from her.
31:21 he f with all he had, and crossing
31:22 day Laban was told that Jacob had f.
31:40 at night, and sleep f from my eyes.
Ex 2:15 he tried to kill Moses, but Moses f
14: 5 Egypt was told that the people had f,
Nu 16:34 all the Israelites around them f,
35:25 to the city of refuge to which he f.
35:26 the city of refuge to which he has f
35:32 who has f to a city of refuge
Jos 8:15 them, and they f towards the desert.
10:11 they f before Israel on the road
10:16 Now the five kings had f and hidden
20: 6 home in the town from which he f."
Jdg 1: 6 Adoni-Bezek f, but they chased him
4:15 abandoned his chariot and f on foot.
4:17 Sisera, however, f on foot to the
7:21 Midianites ran, crying out as they f.
7:22 The army f to Beth Shittah towards
8:12 the two kings of Midian, f, but he
9:21 Jotham f, escaping to Beer, and he
9:51 the people of the city—f.
11: 3 Jephthah f from his brothers and
20:42 they f before the Israelites in the
20:45 they turned and f towards the desert
20:47 six hundred men turned and f into
1Sa 4:10 and every man f to his tent.
4:16 line; I f from it this very day.
4:17 "Israel f before the Philistines,
19: 8 such force that they f before him.
19:12 a window, and he f and escaped.
19:18 David had f and made his escape, he
20: 1 David f from Naioth at Ramah and
21:10 That day David f from Saul and went
22:20 Ahitub, escaped and f to join David.
23: 6 him when he f to David at Keilah.)
27: 4 Saul was told that David had f to
30:17 men who rode off on camels and f.
31: 1 Israel; the Israelites f before them,
31: 7 saw that the Israelite army had f
31: 7 they abandoned their towns and f.
2Sa 1: 4 He said, "The men f from the battle.
4: 3 the people of Beeroth f to Gittaim
4: 4 His nurse picked him up and f, but
10:13 the Arameans, and they f before him.
10:14 they f before Abishai and went
10:18 they f before Israel, and David
13:29 got up, mounted their mules and f.
13:34 Meanwhile, Absalom had f. Now the
13:37 Absalom f and went to Talmai son of
13:38 After Absalom f and went to Geshur,
18:17 all the Israelites f to their homes.
19: 8 the Israelites had f to their homes.
19: 9 f the country because of Absalom;
23:11 Israel's troops f from them.
1Ki 2: 7 when I f from your brother Absalom.
2:28 he f to the tent of the LORD and
2:29 King Solomon was told that Joab had f
11:17 Hadad, still only a boy, f to Egypt
11:23 Rezon son of Eliada, who had f from
11:40 but Jeroboam f to Egypt, to Shishak
12: 2 where he had f from King Solomon),
20:20 At that, the Arameans f, with the
20:30 And Ben-Hadad f to the city and hid
2Ki 3:24 up and fought them until they f.
7: 7 they got up and f in the dusk and
8:21 his army, however, f back home.
9:23 Joram turned about and f, calling
9:27 he f up the road to Beth Haggan.
14:12 Israel, and every man f to his home.
14:19 and he f to Lachish, but they sent
25: 4 and the whole army f at night
25: 4 They f towards the Arabah,
25:26 f to Egypt for fear of the
1Ch 10: 1 Israel; the Israelites f before them,
10: 7 the valley saw that the army had f
10: 7 they abandoned their towns and f.
11:13 the troops f from the Philistines.
19:14 the Arameans, and they f before him.
19:15 they too f before his brother
19:18 they f before Israel, and David
2Ch 10: 2 where he had f from King Solomon),
13:16 The Israelites f before Judah, and
14:12 before Asa and Judah. The Cushites f
25:22 Israel, and every man f to his home.
25:27 in Jerusalem and he f to Lachish,
Ps 3: T When he f from his son Absalom.
48: 5 were astounded; they f in terror.
57: T When he had f from Saul into the
104: 7 at your rebuke the waters f, at the
114: 3 The sea looked and f, the Jordan
114: 5 Why was it, O sea, that you f,
Isa 20: 6 those we f to for help and
22: 3 All your leaders have f together;
22: 3 f while the enemy was still far away.
Jer 9:10 The birds of the air have f and the
26:21 heard of it and f in fear to Egypt.
39: 4 they f; they left the city at night
41:15 from Johanan and f to the Ammonites.
52: 7 through, and the whole army f.
52: 7 They f towards the Arabah,
Lam 1: 6 they have f before the pursuer.
Da 10: 7 them that they f and hid themselves.
Hos 12:12 Jacob f to the country of Aram;
Am 5:19 be as though a man f from a lion
Zec 14: 5 You will flee as you f from the
Mt 26:56 the disciples deserted him and f.
Mk 14:50 everyone deserted him and f.
14:52 he f naked, leaving his garment
16: 8 women went out and f from the tomb.
Ac 7:29 Moses heard this, he f to Midian,
14: 6 they found out about it and f to the
Heb 6:18 who have f to take hold of the hope
Rev 12: 6 The woman f into the desert to a
16:20 Every island f away and the
20:11 Earth and sky f from his presence,

Flee (Fled, Fleeing, Flees)

Ge 19:17 "F for your lives! Don't look back,
19:17 F to the mountains or you will be
19:19 But I can't f to the mountains; this
19:20 Let me f to it—it is very small,
19:22 f there quickly, because I cannot do
27:43 F at once to my brother Laban in
Ex 21:13 is to f to a place I will designate.
Lev 26:17 f even when no-one is pursuing you.
Nu 10:35 may your foes f before you."
35: 6 person who has killed someone may f.
35:11 killed someone accidentally may f.
35:15 another accidentally can f there.
Dt 4:42 who had killed a person could f
4:42 He could f into one of these cities
19: 3 anyone who kills a man may f there.
19: 5 That man may f to one of these
28: 7 direction but f from you in seven.
28:25 direction but f from them in seven,
Jos 8: 5 did before, we will f from them.
8: 6 So when we f from them,
20: 3 unintentionally may f there and find
20: 9 could f to these designated cities
2Sa 15:14 "Come! We must f, or none of us will
17: 2 then all the people with him will f.
18: 3 if we are forced to f, they won't
19: 3 are ashamed when they f from battle.
2Ki 19:21 Jerusalem tosses her head as you f.
Job 41:28 Arrows do not make him f;
Ps 11: 1 say to me: "F like a bird to your
31:11 who see me on the street f from me.
55: 7 I would f far away and stay in the
68: 1 may his foes f before him.
68:12 "Kings and armies f in haste; in the
139: 7 Where can I f from your presence?

SS 2:17 the day breaks and the shadows **f**,
4: 6 the day breaks and the shadows **f**,
Isa 2:19 Men will **f** to caves in the rocks and
2:21 They will **f** to caverns in the rocks
13:14 each will **f** to his native land.
15: 5 Moab; her fugitives **f** as far as Zoar,
17:13 when he rebukes them they **f** far away,
21:15 They **f** from the sword, from the
30:16 You said, 'No, we will **f** on horses.'
30:16 Therefore you will **f**! You said, 'We
30:17 A thousand will **f** at the threat of
30:17 threat of five you will all **f** away,
31: 8 They will **f** before the sword and
33: 3 the peoples **f**; when you rise up, the
35:10 and sorrow and sighing will **f** away.
37:22 Jerusalem tosses her head as you **f**.
48:20 Leave Babylon, **f** from the
51:11 and sorrow and sighing will **f** away.
Jer 4: 5 Let us **f** to the fortified cities!'
4: 6 to Zion! **F** for safety without delay
6: 1 "**F** for safety, people of Benjamin! **F**
8:14 Let us **f** to the fortified cities
25:35 The shepherds will have nowhere to **f**,
46: 5 They **f** in haste without looking back,
46: 6 "The swift cannot **f** nor the strong
46:21 They too will turn and **f** together,
48: 6 **F**! Run for your lives; become like a
49: 8 Turn and **f**, hide in deep caves, you
49:24 she has turned to **f** and panic has
49:30 "**F** quickly away! Stay in deep caves,
50: 3 both men and animals will **f** away.
50: 8 "**F** out of Babylon; leave the land of
50:16 let everyone **f** to his own land.
51: 6 "**F** from Babylon! Run for your lives!
Lam 4:15 us!" When they **f** and wander about,
Da 4:14 Let the animals **f** from under it and
Am 2:16 Even the bravest warriors will **f**
Jnh 1: 3 for Tarshish to **f** from the LORD.
4: 2 why I was so quick to **f** to Tarshish.
Na 3: 7 All who see you will **f** from you and
Zec 2: 6 "Come! Come! **F** from the land of the
14: 5 You will **f** by my mountain valley,
14: 5 You will **f** as you fled from the
Mt 3: 7 you to **f** from the coming wrath?
10:23 are persecuted in one place, **f** to
24:16 let those who are in Judea **f** to the
Mk 13:14 who are in Judea **f** to the mountains.
Lk 3: 7 you to **f** from the coming wrath?
21:21 let those who are in Judea **f** to the
1Co 6:18 **F** from sexual immorality. All other
10:14 my dear friends, **f** from idolatry.
1Ti 6:11 you, man of God, **f** from all this,
2Ti 2:22 **F** the evil desires of youth, and
Jas 4: 7 the devil, and he will **f** from you.

Fleece

Jdg 6:37 look, I will place a wool **f** on the
6:37 If there is dew only on the **f** and
6:38 he squeezed the **f** and wrung out the
6:39 Allow me one more test with the **f**.
6:39 This time make the **f** dry and the
6:40 God did so. Only the **f** was dry;
Job 31:20 him with the **f** from my sheep,

Fleeing (Flee)

Ge 35: 1 you were **f** from your brother Esau."
35: 7 him when he was **f** from his brother.
Ex 14:27 The Egyptians were **f** towards it, and
Lev 26:36 They will run as though **f** from the
26:37 another as though **f** from the sword,
Jos 8:20 for the Israelites who had been **f**
1Sa 22:17 They knew he was **f**, yet they did not
2Sa 10:14 saw that the Arameans were **f**,
24:13 Or three months of **f** from your
1Ch 19:15 saw that the Arameans were **f**,
Jer 46:22 Egypt will hiss like a **f** serpent as
48:19 Ask the man **f** and the woman escaping,
Eze 17:21 All his **f** troops will fall by the

Flees (Flee)

Dt 19: 4 **f** there to save his life—one who
19:11 and then **f** to one of these cities,
Jos 20: 4 "When he **f** to one of these cities,
Job 20:24 Though he **f** from an iron weapon, a
27:22 as he **f** headlong from its power.
Pr 28: 1 The wicked man **f** though no-one
Isa 10:29 Ramah trembles; Gibeah of Saul **f**.
24:18 Whoever **f** at the sound of terror
Jer 48:44 "Whoever **f** from the terror will fall

Fleet

1Ki 9:27 serve in the **f** with Solomon's men.
10:22 The king had a **f** of trading ships at
22:48 Now Jehoshaphat built a **f** of trading
2Ch 9:21 The king had a **f** of trading ships
20:36 He agreed with him to construct a **f**
Da 11:40 and cavalry and a great **f** of ships.

Fleet-footed (Foot)

2Sa 2:18 Asahel was as **f** as a wild gazelle.
Am 2:15 the **f** soldier will not get away, and

Fleeting

Job 14: 2 like a **f** shadow, he does not endure.
Ps 39: 4 days; let me know how **f** is my life.
89:47 Remember how **f** is my life. For what
144: 4 his days are like a **f** shadow.
Pr 21: 6 is a **f** vapour and a deadly snare.
31:30 Charm is deceptive, and beauty is **f**;

Flesh (*Flesh and blood*)

Ge 2:21 ribs and closed up the place with **f**.
2:23 bone of my bones and **f** of my **f**;
2:24 wife, and they will become one **f**.
17:13 My covenant in your **f** is to be an
17:14 has not been circumcised in the **f**,
40:19 And the birds will eat away your **f**."
Ex 4: 7 restored, like the rest of his **f**.
29:14 burn the bull's **f** and its hide and
Lev 4:11 the hide of the bull and all its **f**,
6:27 Whatever touches any of the **f** will
8:17 the bull with its hide and its **f** and
9:11 the **f** and the hide he burned up
13:10 if there is raw **f** in the swelling,
13:14 whenever raw **f** appears on him, he
13:15 the priest sees the raw **f**, he shall
13:15 The raw **f** is unclean; he has an
13:16 Should the raw **f** change and turn
13:24 appears in the raw **f** of the burn,
16:27 **f** and offal are to be burned up.
26:29 the **f** of your sons and the **f** of
Nu 12:12 womb with its **f** half eaten away."
19: 5 hide, **f**, blood and offal.
Dt 28:53 the **f** of the sons and daughters the
28:55 **f** of his children that he is eating.
32:42 while my sword devours **f**: the blood
Jdg 8: 7 will tear your **f** with desert thorns
1Sa 17:44 "and I'll give your **f** to the birds
2Sa 1:22 from the **f** of the mighty, the bow of
16:11 my own **f**, is trying to take my life.
2Ki 5:10 and your **f** will be restored and you
5:14 and his **f** was restored and became
9:36 Jezreel dogs will devour Jezebel's **f**.
2Ch 32: 8 With him is only the arm of **f**, but
Job 2: 5 hand and strike his **f** and bones,
6:12 strength of stone? Is my **f** bronze?
10: 4 Do you have eyes of **f**? Do you see as
10:11 clothe me with skin and **f** and knit
15:27 fat and his waist bulges with **f**,
19:22 Will you never get enough of my **f**?
19:26 yet in my **f** I will see God;
33:21 His **f** wastes away to nothing, and
33:25 his **f** is renewed like a child's; it
41:23 The folds of his **f** are tightly
Ps 27: 2 advance against me to devour my **f**,
50:13 Do I eat the **f** of bulls or drink the
73:26 My **f** and my heart may fail, but God
78:39 He remembered that they were but **f**,
79: 2 the **f** of your saints to the beasts
84: 2 and my **f** cry out for the living God.
119:120 My **f** trembles in fear of you; I
Pr 5:11 when your **f** and body are spent.
Isa 9:20 feed on the **f** of his own offspring:
31: 3 their horses are **f** and not spirit.
49:26 your oppressors eat their own **f**;
65: 4 secret vigil; who eat the **f** of pigs,
66:17 of those who eat the **f** of pigs
Jer 9:25 who are circumcised only in the **f**—
17: 5 who depends on **f** for his strength
19: 9 I will make them eat the **f** of their
19: 9 and they will eat one another's **f**
51:35 May the violence done to our **f** be
Lam 3: 4 He has made my skin and my **f** grow
Eze 11:19 of stone and give them a heart of **f**.
32: 5 I will spread your **f** on the
32: 6 ravines will be filled with your **f**.
36:26 of stone and give you a heart of **f**.
37: 6 make **f** come upon you and cover you
37: 8 I looked, and tendons and **f** appeared
39:17 There you will eat **f** and drink blood.
39:18 You will eat the **f** of mighty men and
40:43 were for the **f** of the offerings.
44: 7 in heart and **f** into my sanctuary,
44: 9 and **f** is to enter my sanctuary,
Da 7: 5 'Get up and eat your fill of **f**!'
Mic 3: 2 people and the **f** from their bones;
3: 3 who eat my people's **f**, strip off
3: 3 for the pan, like **f** for the pot."
Zec 11: 9 who are left eat one another's **f**."
14:12 Their **f** will rot while they are
Mal 2:15 In **f** and spirit they are his.
Mk 10: 8 the two will become one **f**.' So they
Lk 24:39 a ghost does not have **f** and bones,
Jn 1:14 The Word became **f** and made his
3: 6 **F** gives birth to **f**, but the Spirit
6:51 This bread is my **f**, which I will
6:52 can this man give us his **f** to eat?"
6:53 unless you eat the **f** of the Son of
6:54 Whoever eats my **f** and drinks my
6:55 For my **f** is real food and my blood
6:56 Whoever eats my **f** and drinks my
6:63 The Spirit gives life; the **f** counts
1Co 6:16 is said, "The two will become one **f**.
15:39 All **f** is not the same: Men have one
15:39 the same: Men have one kind of **f**,
2Co 12: 7 there was given me a thorn in my **f**,
Gal 6:13 that they may boast about your **f**.
Eph 2:15 by abolishing in his **f** the law with
5:31 and the two will become one **f**."
Php 3: 2 do evil, those mutilators of the **f**.
3: 3 and who put no confidence in the **f**—
3: 4 confidence in the **f**, I have more:
Col 1:24 and I fill up in my **f** what is still
Jas 5: 3 you and eat your **f** like fire.
1Jn 4: 2 Christ has come in the **f** is from God,
2Jn : 7 Jesus Christ as coming in the **f**,
Jude :23 the clothing stained by corrupted **f**.
Rev 17:16 eat her **f** and burn her with fire.
19:18 that you may eat the **f** of kings,
19:18 riders, and the **f** of all people,
19:21 birds gorged themselves on their **f**.

Flesh and blood

Ge 29:14 Laban said to him, "You are my own **f**.
37:27 all, he is our brother, our own **f**.
Jdg 9: 2 one man?' Remember, I am your **f**."
2Sa 5: 1 Hebron and said, "We are your own **f**.
19:12 You are my brothers, my own **f**. So
19:13 say to Amasa, 'Are you not my own **f**?
1Ki 8:19 but your son, who is your own **f**—he
2Ki 20:18 some of your descendants, your own **f**,
1Ch 11: 1 Hebron and said, "We are your own **f**.
2Ch 6: 9 but your son, who is your own **f**—he
Ne 5: 5 Although we are of the same **f** as our
Isa 39: 7 some of your descendants, your own **f**
58: 7 not to turn away from your own **f**?
1Co 15:50 **f** cannot inherit the kingdom of God
Eph 6:12 For our struggle is not against **f**,
Heb 2:14 Since the children have **f**, he too

Flew (Fly[1])

2Sa 22:11 He mounted the cherubim and **f**; he
Ps 18:10 He mounted the cherubim and **f**; he
Isa 6: 6 one of the seraphs **f** to me with a
Ac 16:26 At once all the prison doors **f** open,

Flies[1] (Fly[1])

Dt 4:17 earth or any bird that **f** in the air,
Job 20: 8 Like a dream he **f** away, no more to
Ps 91: 5 night, nor the arrow that **f** by day,

Flies[2] (Fly[2])
Ex 8:21 I will send swarms of f on you and
8:21 of the Egyptians will be full of f,
8:22 live; no swarms of f will be there,
8:24 the LORD did this. Dense swarms of f
8:24 Egypt the land was ruined by the f.
8:29 and tomorrow the f will leave
8:31 The f left Pharaoh and his officials
Ps 78:45 He sent swarms of f that devoured
105:31 He spoke, and there came swarms of f,
Ecc 10: 1 dead f give perfume a bad smell, so
Isa 7:18 the LORD will whisper for f from
51: 6 and its inhabitants die like f.

Flight (Fly[1])
Lev 26:36 wind-blown leaf will put them to f.
Dt 32:30 or two put ten thousand to f, unless
Jdg 9:40 and many fell wounded in the f—all
2Sa 22:41 my enemies turn their backs in f,
2Ki 7:15 had thrown away in their headlong f.
1Ch 12:15 and they put to f everyone living in
Job 39:26 "Does the hawk take f by your wisdom
Ps 18:40 my enemies turn their backs in f,
104: 7 of your thunder they took to f;
Isa 10:31 Madmenah is in f; the people of
52:12 not leave in haste or go in f;
Jer 4:29 and archers every town takes to f.
Eze 40:49 It was reached by a f of stairs, and
Da 9:21 came to me in swift f about the time
Mt 24:20 Pray that your f will not take place

Flimsy
Eze 13:10 when a f wall is built, they cover

Flinging (Flung)
Ac 22:23 cloaks and f dust into the air,

Flint (Flinty)
Ex 4:25 Zipporah took a f knife, cut off her
Jos 5: 2 "Make f knives and circumcise the
5: 3 Joshua made f knives and circumcised
Isa 5:28 their horses' hoofs seem like f,
50: 7 Therefore have I set my face like f,
Jer 17: 1 inscribed with a f point, on the
Eze 3: 9 the hardest stone, harder than f.
Zec 7:12 They made their hearts as hard as f

Flinty (Flint)
Dt 32:13 rock, and with oil from the f crag,
Job 28: 9 Man's hand assaults the f rock and

Flirting
Isa 3:16 f with their eyes, tripping along

Float (Floated)
1Ki 5: 9 and I will f them in rafts by sea to
2Ki 6: 6 threw it there, and made the iron f.
2Ch 2:16 f them in rafts by sea down to Joppa.
Hos 10: 7 Samaria and its king will f away

Floated (Float)
Ge 7:18 ark f on the surface of the water.

Flock (Flocking, Flocks)
Ge 4: 4 from some of the firstborn of his f.
21:28 apart seven ewe lambs from the f,
27: 9 Go out to the f and bring me two
30:40 Jacob set apart the young of the f
31:10 mating with the f were streaked,
31:12 mating with the f are streaked,
38:17 "I'll send you a young goat from my f
Ex 2:16 troughs to water their father's f.
2:17 to their rescue and watered their f.
2:19 water for us and watered the f."
3: 1 Now Moses was tending the f of
3: 1 and he led the f to the far side of
34:19 livestock, whether from herd or f.
Lev 1: 2 from either the herd or the f.
1:10 is a burnt offering from the f,
3: 6 "If he offers an animal from the f
5: 6 goat from the f as a sin offering;
Lev 5:15 LORD as a penalty a ram from the f,
5:18 a guilt offering a ram from the f,
6: 6 a ram from the f, one without defect
22:21 anyone brings from the herd or f a
27:32 The entire tithe of the herd and f
Nu 15: 3 from the herd or the f, as an aroma
Dt 15:14 Supply him liberally from your f,
16: 2 an animal from your f or herd
32:14 with curds and milk from herd and f
1Sa 17:20 Early in the morning David left the f
17:34 and carried off a sheep from the f,
2Sa 7: 8 from following the f to be ruler
1Ch 17: 7 from following the f, to be ruler
Ezr 10:19 ram from the f as a guilt offering.)
Job 21:11 They send forth their children as a f
Ps 77:20 You led your people like a f by the
78:52 he brought his people out like a f;
80: 1 you who lead Joseph like a f; you
95: 7 his pasture, the f under his care.
SS 1: 7 where you graze your f and where you
4: 1 Your hair is like a f of goats
4: 2 Your teeth are like a f of sheep
6: 5 a f of goats descending from Gilead.
6: 6 Your teeth are like a f of sheep
Isa 40:11 He tends his f like a shepherd: He
63:11 the sea, with the shepherd of his f?
Jer 10:21 and all their f is scattered.
13:17 the LORD's f will be taken captive.
13:20 Where is the f that was entrusted to
23: 2 "Because you have scattered my f and
23: 3 will gather the remnant of my f
25:34 in the dust, you leaders of the f.
25:35 leaders of the f no place to escape.
25:36 the wailing of the leaders of the f,
31:10 watch over his f like a shepherd.'
49:20 The young of the f will be dragged
50: 8 be like the goats that lead the f.
50:17 "Israel is a scattered f that lions
50:45 The young of the f will be dragged
51:23 with you I shatter shepherd and f,
Eze 24: 5 take the pick of the f. Pile wood
34: 2 not shepherds take care of the f?
34: 3 but you do not take care of the f.
34: 8 because my f lacks a shepherd and so
34: 8 shepherds did not search for my f
34: 8 for themselves rather than for my f,
34:10 will hold them accountable for my f.
34:10 remove them from tending the f
34:10 I will rescue my f from their mouths,
34:12 scattered f when he is with them,
34:16 I will shepherd the f with justice.
34:17 "'As for you, my f, this is what the
34:19 Must my f feed on what you have
34:22 I will save my f, and they will no
43:23 ram from the f, both without defect.
43:25 ram from the f, both without defect.
45:15 taken from every f of two hundred
Am 7:15 the LORD took me from tending the f
Jnh 3: 7 beast, herd or f, taste anything;
Mic 2:12 like a f in its pasture; the place
4: 8 for you, O watchtower of the f,
5: 4 He will stand and shepherd his f in
7:14 the f of your inheritance, which
Zec 9:16 on that day as the f of his people.
10: 3 LORD Almighty will care for his f,
11: 4 "Pasture the f marked for slaughter.
11: 7 I pastured the f marked for
11: 7 particularly the oppressed of the f.
11: 7 other Union, and I pastured the f.
11: 8 The f detested me, and I grew weary
11:11 and so the afflicted of the f who
11:17 shepherd, who deserts the f!
Mal 1:14 male in his f and vows to give it,
Mt 26:31 sheep of the f will be scattered.'
Lk 12:32 "Do not be afraid, little f, for
Jn 10:12 wolf attacks the f and scatters it.
10:16 shall be one f and one shepherd.
Ac 20:28 all the f of which the Holy Spirit
20:29 among you and will not spare the f.
1Co 9: 7 Who tends a f and does not drink of
1Pe 5: 2 Be shepherds of God's f that is
5: 3 to you, but being examples to the f.

Flocking (Flock)
Hos 7:12 them f together, I will catch them.

Flocks (Flock)
Ge 4: 2 Abel kept f, and Cain worked the
13: 5 also had f and herds and tents.
26:14 He had so many f and herds and
29: 2 with three f of sheep lying near it
29: 2 the f were watered from that well.
29: 3 all the f were gathered there, the
29: 7 not time for the f to be gathered.
29: 8 "until all the f are gathered and
30:31 your f and watching over them:
30:32 Let me go through all your f today
30:36 to tend the rest of Laban's f.
30:38 of the f when they came to drink.
30:38 f were in heat and came to drink,
30:40 Thus he made separate f for himself
30:43 prosperous and came to own large f,
31: 4 out to the fields where his f were.
31: 8 the f gave birth to speckled young;
31: 8 then all the f bore streaked young.
31:38 nor have I eaten rams from your f.
31:41 daughters and six years for your f,
31:43 are my children, and the f are my f.
32: 7 the f and herds and camels as well.
34:28 They seized their f and herds and
37: 2 was tending the f with his brothers,
37:12 graze their father's f near Shechem,
37:13 are grazing the f near Shechem.
37:14 with your brothers and with the f,
37:16 me where they are grazing their f?"
45:10 your f and herds, and all you have.
46:32 f and herds and everything they own.'
47: 1 with their f and herds and
47: 4 your servants' f have no pasture.
50: 8 f and herds were left in Goshen.
Ex 10: 9 and with our f and herds, because we
10:24 only leave your f and herds behind."
12:32 Take your f and herds, as you have
12:38 of livestock, both f and herds.
34: 3 not even the f and herds may graze
Nu 11:22 Would they have enough if f and
31: 9 herds, f and goods as plunder.
32: 1 who had very large herds and f, saw
32:24 and pens for your f, but do what you
32:26 Our children and wives, our f and
32:36 cities, and built pens for their f.
35: 3 f and all their other livestock.
Dt 7:13 the lambs of your f in the land that
8:13 your herds and f grow large and your
12: 6 the firstborn of your herds and f.
12:17 the firstborn of your herds and f,
12:21 herds and f the LORD has given you,
14:23 the firstborn of your herds and f in
15:19 firstborn male of your herds and f.
28: 4 your herds and the lambs of your f.
28:18 your herds and the lambs of your f.
28:51 of your f until you are ruined.
Jos 14: 4 pasture-lands for their f and herds.
Jdg 5:16 to hear the whistling for the f?
1Sa 8:17 He will take a tenth of your f, and
30:20 He took all the f and herds, and his
1Ki 20:27 them like two small f of goats,
2Ki 5:26 olive groves, vineyards, f, herds,
1Ch 4:39 in search of pasture for their f.
4:41 there was pasture for their f.
27:31 the Hagrite was in charge of the f.
2Ch 17:11 and the Arabs brought him f: seven
31: 6 a tithe of their herds and f
32:28 kinds of cattle, and pens for the f.
32:29 great numbers of f and herds,
Ne 10:36 of our herds and of our f to the
Job 1:10 so that his f and herds are spread
24: 2 they pasture f they have stolen.
Ps 8: 7 all f and herds, and the beasts of
65:13 The meadows are covered with f and
107:41 and increased their families like f.
Pr 27:23 you know the condition of your f,
Ecc 2: 7 owned more herds and f than anyone
SS 1: 7 woman beside the f of your friends?
Isa 13:20 no shepherd will rest his f there.
17: 2 Aroer will be deserted and left to f,
32:14 delight of donkeys, a pasture for f,
60: 7 All Kedar's f will be gathered to
61: 5 Aliens will shepherd your f;
65:10 Sharon will become a pasture for f,
Jer 3:24 fathers' labour—their f and herds,
5:17 they will devour your f and herds,

Jer 6: 3 Shepherds with their f will come
31:12 oil, the young of the f and herds.
31:24 those who move about with their f.
33:12 for shepherds to rest their f.
33:13 f will again pass under the hand of
49:29 Their tents and their f will be
Eze 36:38 numerous as the f for offerings at
36:38 cities be filled with f of people.
Hos 5: 6 they go with their f and herds to
Joel 1:18 even the f of sheep are suffering.
Mic 5: 8 like a young lion among f of sheep,
Zep 2:14 F and herds will lie down there,
Lk 2: 8 keeping watch over their f at night.
Jn 4:12 also his sons and his f and herds?"

Flog (Flogged, Flogging, Floggings)
Pr 17:26 to f officials for their integrity.
19:25 F a mocker, and the simple will
Mt 10:17 and f you in their synagogues.
23:34 others you will f in your synagogues
Mk 10:34 will mock him and spit on him, f him
Lk 18:32 spit on him, f him and kill him.
Ac 22:25 they stretched him out to f him,
22:25 "Is it legal for you to f a Roman

Flogged (Flog)
Dt 25: 2 have him f in his presence with the
25: 3 If he is f more than that, your
Mt 20:19 to be mocked and f and crucified.
27:26 But he had Jesus f, and handed him
Mk 13: 9 councils and f in the synagogues.
15:15 He had Jesus f, and handed him over
Jn 19: 1 Pilate took Jesus and had him f.
Ac 5:40 the apostles in and had them f.
16:23 After they had been severely f, they
22:24 He directed that he be f and
2Co 11:23 been f more severely, and been

Flogging (Flog)
Ps 89:32 with the rod, their iniquity with f;
Heb 11:36 Some faced jeers and f, while still

Floggings (Flog)
2Sa 7:14 rod of men, with f inflicted by men.

Flood (Flooded, Floodgates, Flooding, Floods, Floodwaters)
Ge 7: 7 ark to escape the waters of the f.
7:17 For forty days the f kept coming on
9:11 be cut off by the waters of a f;
9:11 there be a f to destroy the earth."
9:15 become a f to destroy all life.
9:28 After the f Noah lived 350 years.
10: 1 who themselves had sons after the f.
10:32 out over the earth after the f.
11:10 Two years after the f, when Shem was
Jos 3:15 Now the Jordan is in f all during
4:18 their place and ran in f as before.
Job 20:28 A f will carry off his house,
22:11 and why a f of water covers you.
22:16 foundations washed away by a f.
27:20 Terrors overtake him like a f; a
38:34 cover yourself with a f of water?
Ps 6: 6 all night long I f my bed with
29:10 The LORD sits enthroned over the f;
88:17 they surround me like a f; they have
124: 4 the f would have engulfed us, the
Isa 59:19 For he will come like a pent-up f
Da 9:26 The end will come like a f: War will
11:10 sweep on like an irresistible f
11:40 and sweep through them like a f.
Hos 5:10 my wrath on them like a f of water.
Na 1: 8 with an overwhelming f he will make
Mal 2:13 You f the LORD's altar with tears.
Mt 24:38 For in the days before the f, people
24:39 the f came and took them all away.
Lk 6:48 When the f came, the torrent struck
17:27 the f came and destroyed them all.
1Pe 4: 4 them into the same f of dissipation,
2Pe 2: 5 brought the f on its ungodly people,

Flooded (Flood)
Ge 7:24 The waters f the earth for a hundred

Floodgates (Flood)
Ge 7:11 the f of the heavens were opened.
8: 2 the f of the heavens had been
2Ki 7: 2 even if the LORD should open the f
7:19 even if the LORD should open the f
Isa 24:18 The f of the heavens are opened, the
Mal 3:10 will not throw open the f of heaven

Flooding (Flood)
Isa 28: 2 like a driving rain and a f downpour,
66:12 wealth of nations like a f stream

Floods (Flood)
Ps 69: 2 the deep waters; the f engulf me.

Floodwaters (Flood)
Ge 6:17 I am going to bring f on the earth
7: 6 old when the f came on the earth.
7:10 after the seven days the f came on
Ps 69:15 Do not let the f engulf me or the
Isa 8: 7 them the mighty f of the River—

Floor (Floors, *Threshing-floor*, *Threshing-floors*)
Ex 16:14 the ground appeared on the desert f.
Nu 5:17 some dust from the tabernacle f
Jdg 3:25 their lord fallen to the f, dead.
1Ki 6: 6 The lowest f was five cubits wide,
6: 6 middle f six cubits and the third f
6: 8 The entrance to the lowest f was on
6:15 panelling them from the f of the
6:15 covered the f of the temple with
6:16 with cedar boards from f to ceiling
7: 7 it with cedar from f to ceiling.
22:35 wound ran onto the f of the chariot,
Eze 37: 2 many bones on the f of the valley,
41: 7 f to the top f through the middle f.
41:16 The f, the wall up to the windows,
41:20 From the f to the area above the
42: 6 The rooms on the third f had no
42: 6 so they were smaller in f space than
Da 6:24 before they reached the f of the den
Jas 2: 3 "You stand there" or "Sit on the f

Floors (Floor)
1Ki 6:30 He also covered the f of both the
Eze 42: 5 lower and middle f of the building.
42: 6 those on the lower and middle f.

Floral (Flower)
1Ki 7:49 the gold f work and lamps and tongs;
2Ch 4:21 the gold f work and lamps and tongs

Flour
Ge 18: 6 three seahs of fine f and knead it
Ex 29: 2 from fine wheat f, without yeast,
29:40 offer a tenth of an ephah of fine f
Lev 2: 1 his offering is to be of fine f.
2: 2 a handful of the fine f and oil,
2: 4 it is to consist of fine f: cakes
2: 5 f mixed with oil, and without yeast.
2: 7 it is to be made of fine f and oil.
5:11 ephah of fine f for a sin offering.
6:15 to take a handful of fine f and oil,
6:20 fine f as a regular grain offering,
7:12 f well-kneaded and mixed with oil.
14:10 fine f mixed with oil for a grain
14:21 fine f mixed with oil for a grain
23:13 an ephah of fine f mixed with oil
23:17 of two-tenths of an ephah of fine f,
24: 5 "Take fine f and bake twelve loaves
Nu 5:15 an ephah of barley f on her behalf.
6:15 made of fine f mixed with oil,
7:13 f mixed with oil as a grain offering;
7:19 f mixed with oil as a grain offering;
7:25 f mixed with oil as a grain offering;
7:31 f mixed with oil as a grain offering;
7:37 f mixed with oil as a grain offering;
7:43 f mixed with oil as a grain offering;
7:49 f mixed with oil as a grain offering;
7:55 f mixed with oil as a grain offering;
7:61 f mixed with oil as a grain offering;
7:67 f mixed with oil as a grain offering;
Nu 7:73 f mixed with oil as a grain offering;
7:79 f mixed with oil as a grain offering;
8: 8 offering of fine f mixed with oil;
15: 4 a tenth of an ephah of fine f mixed
15: 6 f mixed with a third of a hin of oil,
15: 9 fine f mixed with half a hin of oil.
28: 5 a tenth of an ephah of fine f mixed
28: 9 an ephah of fine f mixed with oil.
28:12 fine f mixed with oil; with the ram,
28:12 an ephah of fine f mixed with oil;
28:13 an ephah of fine f mixed with oil.
28:20 fine f mixed with oil; with the ram,
28:28 fine f mixed with oil; with the ram,
29: 3 fine f mixed with oil; with the ram,
29: 9 fine f mixed with oil; with the ram,
29:14 an ephah of fine f mixed with oil;
Jdg 6:19 of f he made bread without yeast.
1Sa 1:24 an ephah of f and a skin of wine,
28:24 She took some f, kneaded it and
2Sa 17:28 f and roasted grain, beans and
1Ki 4:22 of fine f and sixty cors of meal,
17:12 f in a jar and a little oil in a jug.
17:14 'The jar of f will not be used up
17:16 For the jar of f was not used up and
2Ki 4:41 Elisha said, "Get some f." He put it
7: 1 a seah of f will sell for a shekel
7:16 So a seah of f sold for a shekel,
7:18 a seah of f will sell for a shekel
1Ch 9:29 as well as the f and wine, and the
12:40 There were plentiful supplies of f,
23:29 the f for the grain offerings, the
Isa 47: 2 Take millstones and grind f; take
Eze 16:13 Your food was fine f, honey and
16:19 food I provided for you—the fine f,
46:14 of a hin of oil to moisten the f.
Hos 8: 7 has no head; it will produce no f.
Mt 13:33 mixed into a large amount of f until
Lk 13:21 mixed into a large amount of f until
Rev 18:13 of wine and olive oil, of fine f and

Flourish (Flourishes, Flourishing)
Ge 26:22 us room and we will f in the land."
Job 15:32 full, and his branches will not f.
Ps 44: 2 the peoples and made our fathers f.
72: 7 In his days the righteous will f;
72:16 Let its fruit f like Lebanon; let it
92: 7 evildoers f, they will be for ever
92:12 The righteous will f like a palm
92:13 will f in the courts of our God.
Pr 14:11 but the tent of the upright will f.
Isa 55:10 the earth and making it bud and f,
66:14 rejoice and you will f like grass;
Eze 17:24 green tree and make the dry tree f.
Hos 14: 7 He will f like the corn. He will

Flourishes (Flourish)
Ps 103:15 he f like a flower of the field;
Pr 12:12 but the root of the righteous f.

Flourishing (Flourish)
Dt 6:10 large, f cities you did not build,
Ps 37:35 ruthless man f like a green tree in
52: 8 I am like an olive tree f in the
Ecc 2: 6 to water groves of f trees.

Flow (Flowed, Flowing, Flows)
Ex 14:26 may f back over the Egyptians
Lev 12: 7 clean from her f of blood.
15:19 a woman has her regular f of blood
15:24 her and her monthly f touches him,
20:18 he has exposed the source of her f,
Nu 13:27 and it does f with milk and honey!
24: 7 Water will f from their buckets;
Jos 4: 7 tell them that the f of the Jordan
Job 6:17 that cease to f in the dry season,
Ps 78:16 and made water f down like rivers.
119:136 Streams of tears f from my eyes, for
147:18 up his breezes, and the waters f.
Ecc 1: 7 All streams f into the sea, yet the
Isa 30:25 streams of water will f on every
41:18 I will make rivers f on barren
48:21 he made water f for them from the
Jer 18:14 distant sources ever cease to f?
48:33 I have stopped the f of wine from

Lam 2:18 let your tears **f** like a river day
3:48 Streams of tears **f** from my eyes
3:49 My eyes will **f** unceasingly, without
Eze 28:23 her and make blood **f** in her streets.
32:14 and make her streams **f** like oil,
Joel 3:18 and the hills will **f** with milk; all
3:18 A fountain will **f** out of the LORD's
Am 9:13 mountains and **f** from all the hills.
Zec 14: 8 On that day living water will **f** out
Jn 7:38 water will **f** from within him."
19:34 a sudden **f** of blood and water.
2Co 1: 5 of Christ **f** over into our lives,
Jas 3:11 Can both fresh water and salt water **f**

Flowed (Flow)

Ge 2:10 A river watering the garden **f** from
Ex 14:28 The water **f** back and covered the
Dt 9:21 a stream that **f** down the mountain.
1Ki 18:28 their custom, until their blood **f**.
2Ch 32: 4 the stream that **f** through the land.
Ps 78:20 out, and streams **f** abundantly.
104: 8 they **f** over the mountains, they went
105:41 like a river it **f** in the desert.
Eze 31: 4 their streams **f** all around its base
Rev 14:20 and blood **f** out of the press, rising

Flower (Floral, Flowerlike, Flowers)

Job 14: 2 He springs up like a **f** and withers
Ps 103:15 he flourishes like a **f** of the field;
Isa 18: 5 and the **f** becomes a ripening grape,
28: 1 to the fading **f**, his glorious beauty,
28: 4 That fading **f**, his glorious beauty,
Jas 1:10 he will pass away like a wild **f**.

Flowerlike (Flower)

Ex 25:31 base and shaft; its **f** cups, buds and
37:17 base and shaft; its **f** cups, buds and

Flowers (Flower)

Ex 25:33 Three cups shaped like almond **f** with
25:34 almond **f** with buds and blossoms.
37:19 Three cups shaped like almond **f** with
37:20 almond **f** with buds and blossoms.
1Ki 6:18 carved with gourds and open **f**.
6:29 cherubim, palm trees and open **f**.
6:32 palm trees and open **f**, and overlaid
6:35 palm trees and open **f** on them and
SS 2:12 **F** appear on the earth; the season of
Isa 5:24 and their **f** blow away like dust;
40: 6 glory is like the **f** of the field.
40: 7 The grass withers and the **f** fall,
40: 8 The grass withers and the **f** fall,
1Pe 1:24 and all their glory is like the **f** of
1:24 the grass withers and the **f** fall,

Flowing (Flow, *Land flowing with milk and honey*)

Lev 15: 3 Whether it continues **f** from his body
Dt 8: 7 springs **f** in the valleys and hills;
21: 4 and where there is a **f** stream.
Jos 3:13 its waters **f** downstream will be cut
3:16 the water from upstream stopped **f**.
3:16 while the water **f** down to the Sea of
2Ki 3:20 there it was—water **f** from the
4: 6 Then the oil stopped **f**.
Job 20:17 the rivers **f** with honey and cream.
39:19 or clothe his neck with a **f** mane?
Ps 107:33 rivers into a desert, **f** springs
107:35 the parched ground into **f** springs;
SS 4:15 **f** water streaming down from Lebanon.
5: 5 **f** myrrh, on the handles of the lock.
7: 9 lover, **f** gently over lips and teeth.
Isa 8: 6 the gently **f** waters of Shiloah
27:12 from the **f** Euphrates to the Wadi of
44: 4 like poplar trees by **f** streams.
Eze 23:15 waists and **f** turbans on their heads
32: 6 drench the land with your **f** blood
47: 2 the water was **f** from the south side.
Da 7:10 A river of fire was **f**, coming out
Mk 12:38 They like to walk around in **f** robes
Lk 20:46 They like to walk around in **f** robes
Rev 22: 1 clear as crystal, **f** from the throne

Flown (Fly[1])

Jer 4:25 every bird in the sky had **f** away.

Flows (Flow)

Ezr 8:15 at the canal that **f** towards Ahava,
Ps 58: 7 them vanish like water that **f** away
104:10 ravines; it **f** between the mountains.
Eze 47: 8 He said to me, "This water **f** towards
47: 9 will live wherever the river **f**.
47: 9 because this water **f** there and makes
47: 9 the river **f** everything will live.
47:12 water from the sanctuary **f** to them.

Fluent

Isa 32: 4 tongue will be **f** and clear.

Flung (Flinging)

Am 8: 3 many bodies—**f** everywhere! Silence!"
Rev 12: 4 of the sky and **f** them to the earth.

Flute (Flutes)

Ge 4:21 of all who play the harp and **f**.
Job 21:12 make merry to the sound of the **f**.
30:31 and my **f** to the sound of wailing.
Ps 150: 4 praise him with the strings and **f**,
Jer 48:36 my heart laments for Moab like a **f**;
48:36 a **f** for the men of Kir Hareseth.
Da 3: 5 **f**, zither, lyre, harp, pipes and all
3: 7 **f**, zither, lyre, harp and all kinds
3:10 **f**, zither, lyre, harp, pipes and all
3:15 **f**, zither, lyre, harp, pipes and all
Mt 9:23 the **f** players and the noisy crowd,
11:17 "'We played the **f** for you, and you
Lk 7:32 "'We played the **f** for you, and you
1Co 14: 7 such as the **f** or harp, how will
Rev 18:22 **f** players and trumpeters, will never

Flutes (Flute)

1Sa 10: 5 tambourines, **f** and harps being
1Ki 1:40 playing **f** and rejoicing greatly, so
Ps 5: T For the director of music. For **f**. A
Isa 5:12 tambourines and **f** and wine, but they
30:29 with **f** to the mountain of the LORD,

Fluttering

Pr 26: 2 Like a **f** sparrow or a darting
Isa 16: 2 Like **f** birds pushed from the nest,

Fly[1] (Flew, Flies, Flight, Flown, Flying)

Ge 1:20 and let birds **f** above the earth
Dt 19: 5 the head may **f** off and hit his
Job 5: 7 as surely as sparks **f** upward.
9:25 **f** away without a glimpse of joy.
Ps 55: 6 I would **f** away and be at rest—
90:10 they quickly pass, and we **f** away.
Pr 23: 5 and **f** off to the sky like an eagle.
Isa 60: 8 "Who are these that **f** along like
Hos 9:11 Ephraim's glory will **f** away like a
Na 3:16 they strip the land and then **f** away.
3:17 they **f** away, and no-one knows where.
Hab 1: 8 **f** like a vulture swooping to devour;
Rev 12:14 so that she might **f** to the place

Fly[2] (Flies[2])

Ex 8:31 and his people; not a **f** remained.

Flying (Fly[1])

Ge 8: 7 sent out a raven, and it kept **f** back
Lev 11:20 "'All **f** insects that walk on all
Dt 14:19 All **f** insects that swarm are unclean
Ps 78:27 **f** birds like sand on the seashore.
148:10 cattle, small creatures and **f** birds,
Isa 6: 2 feet, and with two they were **f**.
Hab 3:11 at the glint of your **f** arrows,
Zec 5: 1 there before me was a **f** scroll!
5: 2 "I see a **f** scroll, thirty feet long
Rev 4: 7 man, the fourth was like a **f** eagle.
8:13 I heard an eagle that was **f** in
14: 6 I saw another angel **f** in mid-air,
19:17 voice to all the birds **f** in mid-air,

Foal

Zec 9: 9 on a colt, the **f** of a donkey.
Mt 21: 5 on a colt, the **f** of a donkey.'"

Foam (Foaming, Foams)

Job 24:18 "Yet they are **f** on the surface of
Ps 46: 3 though its waters roar and **f** and the

Foaming (Foam)

Dt 32:14 You drank the **f** blood of the grape.
Ps 75: 8 full of **f** wine mixed with spices;
Mk 9:20 and rolled around, **f** at the mouth.
Jude :13 They are wild waves of the sea, **f** up

Foams (Foam)

Mk 9:18 He **f** at the mouth, gnashes his teeth
Lk 9:39 so that he **f** at the mouth.

Fodder

Ge 24:25 "We have plenty of straw and **f**, as
24:32 Straw and **f** were brought for the
43:24 and provided **f** for their donkeys.
Jdg 19:19 We have both straw and **f** for our
Job 6: 5 or an ox bellow when it has **f**?
24: 6 They gather **f** in the fields and
Isa 30:24 work the soil will eat **f** and mash,

Foe (Foes)

Ps 7: 4 or without cause have robbed my **f**—
8: 2 to silence the **f** and the avenger.
55:12 I could endure it; if a **f** were
61: 3 a strong tower against the **f**.
74:10 Will the **f** revile your name for ever?
106:10 He saved them from the hand of the **f**;
107: 2 he redeemed from the hand of the **f**,
Lam 1: 5 into exile, captive before the **f**.
2: 4 Like a **f** he has slain all who were
Hab 1:15 The wicked **f** pulls all of them up

Foes (Foe)

Nu 10:35 may your **f** flee before you."
Dt 33: 7 Oh, be his help against his **f**!"
33:11 his **f** till they rise no more."
2Sa 22:18 my **f**, who were too strong for me.
22:41 in flight, and I destroyed my **f**.
22:49 You exalted me above my **f**; from
2Ki 21:14 looted and plundered by all their **f**,
Job 22:20 'Surely our **f** are destroyed, and
Ps 3: 1 O LORD, how many are my **f**! How many
6: 7 they fail because of all my **f**.
13: 4 and my **f** will rejoice when I fall.
17: 7 who take refuge in you from their **f**.
18:17 my **f**, who were too strong for me.
18:40 in flight, and I destroyed my **f**.
18:48 You exalted me above my **f**; from
21: 8 your right hand will seize your **f**.
27: 2 when my enemies and my **f** attack me,
27:12 hand me over to the desire of my **f**,
34:21 the **f** of the righteous will be
41: 2 him to the desire of his **f**.
42:10 suffer mortal agony as my **f** taunt me
44: 5 through your name we trample our **f**.
54: 7 eyes have looked in triumph on my **f**.
68: 1 may his **f** flee before him.
68:23 your feet in the blood of your **f**,
69:18 me; redeem me because of my **f**.
74: 4 Your **f** roared in the place where you
81:14 and turn my hand against their **f**!
83: 2 astir, how your **f** rear their heads.
89:23 I will crush his **f** before him and
89:42 exalted the right hand of his **f**;
92:11 have heard the rout of my wicked **f**.
97: 3 and consumes his **f** on every side.
105:24 made them too numerous for their **f**,
106:41 and their **f** ruled over them.
112: 8 he will look in triumph on his **f**.
119:157 Many are the **f** who persecute me, but
138: 7 your hand against the anger of my **f**,
143:12 my enemies; destroy all my **f**, for I
Isa 1:24 I will get relief from my **f** and
9:11 the LORD has strengthened Rezin's **f**
59:18 enemies and retribution to his **f**;
66:14 but his fury will be shown to his **f**.
Jer 46:10 vengeance, for vengeance on his **f**.

Jer 49:37 I will shatter Elam before their f,
Lam 1: 5 Her f have become her masters; her
1:17 that his neighbours become his f;
2:17 he has exalted the horn of your f.
4:12 enemies and f could enter the gates
Mic 5: 9 and all your f will be destroyed.
Na 1: 2 The LORD takes vengeance on his f
1: 8 he will pursue his f into darkness

Foils
Ps 33:10 The LORD f the plans of the nations;
Isa 44:25 who f the signs of false prophets

Fold (Enfolds, Folded, Folding, Folds)
Ex 26: 9 F the sixth curtain double at the
2Ki 4:39 and filled the f of his cloak.
Hag 2:12 meat in the f of his garment,
2:12 and that f touches some bread or

Folded (Fold)
Ex 28:16 long and a span wide—and f double.
39: 9 long and a span wide—and f double.
Jn 20: 7 The cloth was f up by itself,

Folding (Fold)
Pr 6:10 a little f of the hands to rest—
24:33 a little f of the hands to rest—

Folds (Fold)
Ne 5:13 I also shook out the f of my robe
Job 41:23 The f of his flesh are tightly
Ps 74:11 Take it from the f of your garment
Ecc 4: 5 The fool f his hands and ruins
Eze 5: 3 them away in the f of your garment.

Foliage
Eze 19:11 towered high above the thick f,
31: 3 on high, its top above the thick f.
31:10 lifting its top above the thick f,
31:14 their tops above the thick f.

Follow (Followed, Follower, Followers, Following, Follows)
Ge 41:30 seven years of famine will f them.
Ex 11: 8 Go, you and all the people who f you
16: 4 whether they will f my instructions.
23: 2 "Do not f the crowd in doing wrong.
23:24 worship them or f their practices.
Lev 18: 3 Do not f their practices.
18: 4 laws and be careful to f my decrees.
18:30 do not f any of the detestable
19:37 decrees and all my laws and f them.
20: 5 all who f him in prostituting
20: 8 Keep my decrees and f them. I am the
20:22 all my decrees and laws and f them
22:31 "Keep my commands and f them. I am
25:18 "F my decrees and be careful to
26: 3 "If you f my decrees and are
Nu 9:12 they must f all the regulations.
Dt 4: 1 F them so that you may live and may
4: 5 so that you may f them in the land
4:13 which he commanded you to f and then
4:14 laws you are to f in the land that
5: 1 Learn them and be sure to f them.
5:31 laws that you are to teach them to f
6:14 Do not f other gods, the gods of the
7:11 Therefore, take care to f the
7:12 laws and are careful to f them,
8: 1 Be careful to f every command I am
8:19 f other gods and worship and bow
11:22 you to f—to love the LORD your God,
12: 1 to f in the land that the LORD,
13: 2 "Let us f other gods" (gods you have
13: 4 is the LORD your God you must f, and
13: 5 LORD your God commanded you to f.
15: 5 are careful to f all these commands
16:12 Egypt, and f carefully these decrees.
16:20 F justice and justice alone, so that
17:19 f carefully all the words of this
19: 9 you carefully f all these laws I
20:18 teach you to f all the detestable
24: 8 You must f carefully what I have
26:16 day to f these decrees and laws;
Dt 27:10 Obey the LORD your God and f his
28: 1 carefully f all his commands that I
28:13 you this day and carefully f them,
28:15 do not carefully f all his commands
28:58 If you do not carefully f all the
29: 9 Carefully f the terms of this
29:22 Your children who f you in later
29:29 we may f all the words of this law.
30: 8 You will again obey the LORD and f
31:12 f carefully all the words of this
Jos 3: 3 out from your positions and f it.
22:27 and you and the generations that f,
Jdg 3:28 "F me," he ordered, "for the LORD
6:34 summoning the Abiezrites to f him.
7:17 "Watch me," he told them. "F my lead.
9: 3 they were inclined to f Abimelech,
Ru 2: 9 and f along after the girls.
1Sa 11: 7 who does not f Saul and Samuel.
12:14 reigns over you f the LORD your God
25:19 servants, "Go on ahead; I'll f you.
25:27 be given to the men who f you.
30:21 who had been too exhausted to f him
2Sa 17: 9 among the troops who f Absalom.'
20: 2 David to f Sheba son of Bicri.
20:11 is for David, let him f Joab!"
1Ki 6:12 if you f my decrees, carry out my
11: 6 he did not f the LORD completely,
11:10 forbidden Solomon to f other gods,
18:21 f him; but if Baal is God, f him.
19:21 he set out to f Elijah and became
2Ki 6:19 F me, and I will lead you to the man
18: 6 the LORD and did not cease to f him;
23: 3 f the LORD and keep his commands,
1Ch 28: 8 Be careful to f all the commands of
2Ch 34:31 f the LORD and keep his commands,
34:33 f the LORD, the God of their fathers.
Ne 9:34 and our fathers did not f your law;
10:29 an oath to f the Law of God given
Est 2:20 for she continued to f Mordecai's
Job 21:33 sweet to him; all men f after him,
Ps 23: 6 Surely goodness and love will f me
45:14 her virgin companions f her and are
81:12 hearts to f their own devices.
81:13 to me, if Israel would f my ways,
89:30 my law and do not f my statutes,
94:15 all the upright in heart will f it.
111:10 all who f his precepts have good
119:33 Teach me, O LORD, to f your decrees;
119:63 you, to all who f your precepts.
119:106 that I will f your righteous laws.
119:166 O LORD, and I f your commands.
Ecc 1:11 not be remembered by those who f.
11: 9 F the ways of your heart and
SS 1: 8 f the tracks of the sheep and graze
Isa 8:11 me not to f the way of this people.
42:24 For they would not f his ways;
Jer 3:17 No longer will they f the
7: 6 not f other gods to your own harm,
7: 9 and f other gods you have not known,
11: 6 terms of this covenant and f them.
11: 8 to f but that they did not keep.'"
13:10 who f the stubbornness of their
18:12 f the stubbornness of his evil heart.
23:10 The ⌊prophets⌋ f an evil course and
23:17 And to all who f the stubbornness
25: 6 Do not f other gods to serve and
26: 4 do not listen to me and f my law,
32:23 they did not obey you or f your law
35:15 do not f other gods to serve them.
42:16 and the famine you dread will f you
Eze 9: 5 "F him through the city and kill,
11:20 they will f my decrees and be
13: 3 prophets who f their own spirit
20:13 They did not f my decrees but
20:16 my laws and did not f my decrees
20:18 "Do not f the statutes of your
20:19 I am the LORD your God; f my decrees
20:21 me: They did not f my decrees,
36:27 move you to f my decrees and be
37:24 They will f my laws and be careful
43:11 design and f all its regulations.
48: 1 it will f the Hethlon road to Lebo
Hos 11:10 They will f the LORD; he will roar
Mt 4:19 "Come, f me," Jesus said, "and I
8:19 I will f you wherever you go."
8:22 Jesus told him, "F me, and let the
Mt 9: 9 "F me," he told him, and Matthew got
10:38 cross and f me is not worthy of me.
16:24 and take up his cross and f me.
19:21 treasure in heaven. Then come, f me
19:27 "We have left everything to f you!
Mk 1:17 "Come, f me," Jesus said, "and I
2:14 "F me," Jesus told him, and Levi got
5:37 He did not let anyone f him except
8:34 and take up his cross and f me.
10:21 treasure in heaven. Then come, f me
10:28 "We have left everything to f you!
14:13 will meet you. F him.
Lk 5:27 "F me," Jesus said to him,
9:23 take up his cross daily and f me.
9:57 him, "I will f you wherever you go.
9:59 He said to another man, "F me." But
9:61 Still another said, "I will f you,
14:27 and f me cannot be my disciple.
18:22 treasure in heaven. Then come, f me
18:28 "We have left all we had to f you!
21: 8 'The time is near.' Do not f them.
22:10 F him to the house that he enters,
Jn 1:43 Philip, he said to him, "F me."
10: 4 f him because they know his voice.
10: 5 they will never f a stranger; in
10:27 voice; I know them, and they f me.
12:26 Whoever serves me must f me; and
13:36 cannot f now, but you will f later."
13:37 Peter asked, "Lord, why can't I f
21:19 Then he said to him, "F me!"
21:22 what is that to you? You must f me."
Ac 12: 8 "Wrap your cloak around you and f me,
Ro 2: 8 and who reject the truth and f evil,
15: 5 yourselves as you f Christ Jesus,
1Co 1:12 One of you says, "I f Paul";
1:12 "I f Apollos"; another, "I f Cephas";
1:12 still another, "I f Christ."
3: 4 For when one says, "I f Paul," and
3: 4 and another, "I f Apollos," are you
11: 1 F my example, as I f the example of
14: 1 F the way of love and eagerly desire
2Co 12:18 same spirit and f the same course?
Gal 2:14 force Gentiles to f Jewish customs?
6:16 Peace and mercy to all who f this
2Th 3: 7 know how you ought to f our example.
3: 9 make ourselves a model for you to f.
1Ti 4: 1 f deceiving spirits and things
5:15 fact already turned away to f Satan.
1Pe 1:11 Christ and the glories that would f.
2:21 that you should f in his steps.
2Pe 1:16 We did not f cleverly invented
2: 2 Many will f their shameful ways and
2:10 f the corrupt desire of the sinful
2:15 to f the way of Balaam son of Beor,
Jude :16 they f their own evil desires; they
:18 will f their own ungodly desires."
:19 who f mere natural instincts and do
Rev 14: 4 They f the Lamb wherever he goes.
14:13 for their deeds will f them."

Followed (Follow)
Ge 32:19 and all the others who f the herds
Ex 14:23 and horsemen f them into the sea.
14:28 had f the Israelites into the sea.
15:20 f her, with tambourines and dancing.
Nu 16:25 and the elders of Israel f him.
25: 8 f the Israelite into the tent. He
31:16 'They were the ones who f Balaam's
32:11 'Because they have not f me
32:12 for they f the LORD wholeheartedly.'
Dt 1:36 he f the LORD wholeheartedly."
4: 3 you everyone who f the Baal of Peor,
Jos 6: 8 ark of the LORD's covenant f them.
6: 9 and the rear guard f the ark.
6:13 rear guard f the ark of the LORD,
14: 8 f the LORD my God wholeheartedly.
14: 9 f the LORD my God wholeheartedly.'
14:14 because he f the LORD, the God of
Jdg 2:12 They f and worshipped various gods
3:28 So they f him down and, taking
4:10 Ten thousand men f him, and Deborah
4:14 Mount Tabor, f by ten thousand men.
5:14 was with the people who f you.
9:49 men cut branches and f Abimelech.
10: 3 He was f by Jair of Gilead, who led

Jdg 11: 3 gathered around him and **f** him.
13:11 Manoah got up and **f** his wife. When
1Sa 6:12 The rulers of the Philistines **f** them
14:13 his armour-bearer **f** and killed
17:13 Jesse's three oldest sons had **f** Saul
17:14 The three oldest **f** Saul,
26: 3 he saw that Saul had **f** him there,
2Sa 2:10 The house of Judah, however, **f** David.
17:23 saw that his advice had not been **f**,
20:14 who gathered together and **f** him.
1Ki 11: 5 He **f** Ashtoreth the goddess of the
12:14 he **f** the advice of the young men and
14: 8 who kept my commands and **f** me with
18:18 LORD's commands and have **f** the Baals.
2Ki 4:30 So he got up and **f** her.
7:15 They **f** them as far as the Jordan,
14: 3 **f** the example of his father Joash.
17: 8 **f** the practices of the nations the
17:15 They **f** worthless idols and
17:19 They **f** the practices Israel had
1Ch 8:30 his firstborn son was Abdon, **f** by
9:36 his firstborn son was Abdon, **f** by
2Ch 10:14 he **f** the advice of the young men and
11:16 the God of Israel, **f** the Levites to
17: 3 ways that his father David had **f**.
17: 4 sought the God of his father and **f**
22: 5 He also **f** their counsel when he went
26:17 priests of the LORD **f** him in.
Ne 12:32 half the leaders of Judah **f** them,
12:38 I **f** them on top of the wall,
Est 2: 4 appealed to the king, and he **f** it.
Job 23:11 My feet have closely **f** his steps; I
Pr 7:22 All at once he **f** her like an ox
Ecc 4:15 **f** the youth, the king's successor.
Jer 2: 2 how as a bride you loved me and **f** me
2: 5 They **f** worthless idols and became
7:24 they **f** the stubborn inclinations of
8: 2 have **f** and consulted and worshipped.
9:13 they have not obeyed me or **f** my law.
9:14 they have **f** the stubbornness of
9:14 their hearts; they have **f** the Baals,
11: 8 they **f** the stubbornness of their
11:10 They have **f** other gods to serve them.
Eze 16:11 'and **f** other gods and served and
35:18 have **f** all his instructions and have
44:10 nor have they **f** my law and the
44:23 have not obeyed him or **f** his law or
5: 6 my laws and has not **f** my decrees.
5: 7 not **f** my decrees or kept my laws.
11:12 for you have not **f** my decrees or
Am 2: 4 the gods their ancestors **f**,
Mic 6:16 and you have **f** their traditions.
Hab 3: 5 before him; pestilence **f** his steps.
Mal 2: 9 because you have not **f** my ways but
Mt 4:20 they left their nets and **f** him.
4:22 the boat and their father and **f** him.
4:25 the region across the Jordan **f** him.
8: 1 mountainside, large crowds **f** him.
8:23 the boat and his disciples **f** him.
9: 9 him, and Matthew got up and **f** him.
9:27 two blind men **f** him, calling out,
12:15 **f** him, and he healed all their sick,
14:13 crowds **f** him on foot from the towns.
19: 2 Large crowds **f** him, and he healed
19:28 you who have **f** me will also sit on
20:29 Jericho, a large crowd **f** him.
20:34 they received their sight and **f** him.
21: 9 of him and those that **f** shouted,
26:58 Peter **f** him at a distance, right up
27:55 They had **f** Jesus from Galilee to
Mk 1:18 At once they left their nets and **f**
1:20 boat with the hired men and **f** him.
2:14 told him, and Levi got up and **f** him.
2:15 for there were many who **f** him.
3: 7 and a large crowd from Galilee **f**.
5:24 Jesus went with him. A large crowd **f**
10:32 while those who **f** were afraid.
10:52 sight and **f** Jesus along the road.
11: 9 those who **f** shouted, "Hosanna!"
14:54 Peter **f** him at a distance, right
15:41 In Galilee these women had **f** him and
Lk 5:11 on shore, left everything and **f** him.
5:28 Levi got up, left everything and **f**
9:11 crowds learned about it and **f** him.
18:43 his sight and **f** Jesus, praising God.
22:39 of Olives, and his disciples **f** him.
Lk 22:54 Peter **f** at a distance.
23:27 A large number of people **f** him,
23:49 including the women who had **f** him
23:55 with Jesus from Galilee **f** Joseph
Jn 1:37 heard him say this, they **f** Jesus.
1:40 John had said and who had **f** Jesus.
6: 2 a great crowd of people **f** him
6:66 turned back and no longer **f** him.
11:31 they **f** her, supposing she was going
21: 8 The other disciples **f** in the boat,
Ac 8:11 They **f** him because he had amazed
8:13 And he **f** Philip everywhere,
12: 9 Peter **f** him out of the prison, but
13:43 to Judaism **f** Paul and Barnabas,
16:17 This girl **f** Paul and the rest of us,
21:36 The crowd that **f** kept shouting,
27:11 **f** the advice of the pilot and of the
Ro 5:16 The judgment **f** one sin and brought
5:16 but the gift **f** many trespasses and
Eph 2: 2 when you **f** the ways of this world
1Ti 4: 6 the good teaching that you have **f**.
Rev 13: 3 was astonished and **f** the beast.
14: 8 A second angel **f** and said, "Fallen!
14: 9 A third angel **f** them and said in a

Follower (Follow)

Ac 24:14 **f** of the Way, which they call a sect.

Followers (Follow)

Nu 16: 5 he said to Korah and all his **f**: "In
16: 6 You, Korah, and all your **f** are to do
16:11 and all your **f** have banded together.
16:16 "You and all your **f** are to appear
16:19 Korah had gathered all his **f** in
16:40 would become like Korah and his **f**.
26: 9 Aaron and were among Korah's **f** when
26:10 whose **f** died when the fire devoured
27: 3 He was not among Korah's **f**, who
Jdg 9: 4 adventurers, who became his **f**.
1Sa 30:22 troublemakers among David's **f** said,
1Ki 16:22 Omri's **f** proved stronger than those
Ne 11: 8 his **f**, Gabbai and Sallai—928 men.
Ps 49:13 their **f**, who approve their sayings.
106:18 Fire blazed among their **f**; a flame
Da 11:24 loot and wealth among his **f**.
Lk 11:19 by whom do your **f** drive them out? So
22:49 Jesus' **f** saw what was going to
Ac 5:36 He was killed, all his **f** were
5:37 and all his **f** were scattered.
9:25 his **f** took him by night and lowered
17:34 A few men became **f** of Paul and
22: 4 I persecuted the **f** of this Way to
Rev 17:14 his called, chosen and faithful **f**."

Following (Follow)

Ge 47:18 they came to him the **f** year and said,
Ex 30:23 "Take the **f** fine spices: 500 shekels
Lev 20: 6 to prostitute himself by **f** them,
23:32 of the month until the **f** evening
Nu 32:15 If you turn away from **f** him, he will
Dt 7: 4 away from **f** me to serve other gods,
11:28 I command you today by **f** other gods,
28:14 left, **f** other gods and serving them.
Jos 18:21 clan by clan, had the **f** cities:
21: 3 gave the Levites the **f** towns and
21: 9 they allotted the **f** towns by
Jdg 2:19 **f** other gods and serving and
1Sa 5: 4 the **f** morning when they rose, there
2Sa 7: 8 from **f** the flock to be ruler over my
15:12 and Absalom's **f** kept on increasing.
15:16 with his entire household **f** him; but
15:17 with all the people **f** him, and they
1Ki 8:66 On the **f** day he sent the people away.
2Ki 13: 2 **f** the sins of Jeroboam son of Nebat,
16: 3 **f** the detestable ways of the nations
17:21 enticed Israel away from **f** the LORD
21: 2 **f** the detestable practices of the
1Ch 6:71 The Gershonites received the **f**: From
6:77 rest of the Levites) received the **f**:
17: 7 the pasture and from **f** the flock,
2Ch 25:27 Amaziah turned away from **f** the LORD,
28: 3 **f** the detestable ways of the nations
29:15 had ordered, **f** the word of the LORD.
30:12 had ordered, **f** the word of the LORD.
33: 2 **f** the detestable practices of the
2Ch 36:14 **f** all the detestable practices of
Ezr 2:59 The **f** came up from the towns of Tel
10:18 the **f** had married foreign women:
Ne 7:61 The **f** came up from the towns of Tel
Job 34:27 they turned from **f** him and had no
Ps 119:14 I rejoice in **f** your statutes as one
Isa 66:17 **f** the one in the midst of those who
Jer 2: 8 by Baal, **f** worthless idols.
3:19 and not turn away from **f** me.
16:12 See how each of you is **f** the
Zep 1: 6 those who turn back from **f** the LORD
Mt 8:10 astonished and said to those **f** him,
10: 5 sent out with the **f** instructions:
Mk 13:24 "But in those days, **f** that distress,
14:51 but a linen garment, was **f** Jesus.
Lk 7: 9 and turning to the crowd **f** him, he
Jn 1:38 Turning round, Jesus saw them **f** and
18:15 and another disciple were **f** Jesus.
21:20 whom Jesus loved was **f** them.
Ac 10: 9 About noon the **f** day as they were on
10:24 The **f** day he arrived in Caesarea.
15:23 With them they sent the **f** letter:
15:28 anything beyond the **f** requirements:
20:15 and on the **f** day arrived at Miletus.
23:11 The **f** night the Lord stood near Paul
28:13 and on the **f** day we reached Puteoli.
1Co 11:17 In the **f** directives I have no praise
Eph 2: 3 and **f** its desires and thoughts.
Php 3:17 Join with others in **f** my example,
1Ti 1:18 **f** them you may fight the good fight,
Heb 4:11 by **f** their example of disobedience.
2Pe 3: 3 and **f** their own evil desires.
Rev 6: 8 and Hades was **f** close behind him.
19:14 The armies of heaven were **f** him,

Follows (Follow)

Ge 41:31 famine that **f** it will be so severe.
Nu 14:24 spirit and **f** me wholeheartedly,
2Ki 11:15 put to the sword anyone who **f** her.
2Ch 17:14 Their enrolment by families was as **f**:
23:14 put to the sword anyone who **f** her.
Ezr 4: 8 to Artaxerxes the king as **f**:
5: 7 The report they sent him read as **f**:
Jer 4:20 Disaster **f** disaster; the whole land
51:31 One courier **f** another and messenger **f**
Eze 18: 9 He **f** my decrees and faithfully keeps
18:17 He keeps my laws and **f** my decrees.
33:15 **f** the decrees that give life, and
Hos 4: 2 bounds, and bloodshed **f** bloodshed.
Jn 8:12 Whoever **f** me will never walk in
Ac 23:25 He wrote a letter as **f**:

Folly (Fool)

1Sa 25:25 name is Fool, and **f** goes with him.
Job 42: 8 deal with you according to your **f**.
Ps 38: 5 loathsome because of my sinful **f**.
69: 5 You know my **f**, O God; my guilt is
85: 8 but let them not return to **f**.
Pr 5:23 led astray by his own great **f**.
9:13 The woman **F** is loud; she is
12:23 but the heart of fools blurts out **f**.
13:16 knowledge, but a fool exposes his **f**.
14: 8 but the **f** of fools is deception.
14:18 The simple inherit **f**, but the
14:24 crown, but the **f** of fools yields **f**.
14:29 but a quick-tempered man displays **f**.
15: 2 but the mouth of the fool gushes **f**.
15:14 but the mouth of a fool feeds on **f**.
15:21 **F** delights a man who lacks judgment,
16:22 but **f** brings punishment to fools.
17:12 of her cubs than a fool in his **f**.
18:13 that is his **f** and his shame.
19: 3 A man's own **f** ruins his life, yet
22:15 **F** is bound up in the heart of a
24: 9 The schemes of **f** are sin, and men
26: 4 answer a fool according to his **f**,
26: 5 Answer a fool according to his **f**, or
26:11 its vomit, so a fool repeats his **f**.
27:22 you will not remove his **f** from him.
Ecc 1:17 and also of madness and **f**, but I
2: 3 and embracing **f**—my mind still
2:12 wisdom, and also madness and **f**.
2:13 I saw that wisdom is better than **f**,
7:25 of wickedness and the madness of **f**.
10: 1 **f** outweighs wisdom and honour.

Ecc 10:13 At the beginning his words are f; at
Isa 32: 6 For the fool speaks f, his mind is
Mk 7:22 envy, slander, arrogance and f.
2Ti 3: 9 their f will be clear to everyone.

Fomenting

Isa 59:13 f oppression and revolt, uttering

Fond

1Sa 19: 1 Jonathan was very f of David

Fondled

Eze 23: 3 In that land their breasts were f
23:21 caressed and your young breasts f.

Food (Foods)

Ge 1:29 They will be yours for f.
1:30 it—I give every green plant for f.
2: 9 pleasing to the eye and good for f.
3: 6 good for f and pleasing to the eye,
3:19 will eat your f until you return
6:21 You are to take every kind of f that
6:21 it away as f for you and for them."
9: 3 lives and moves will be f for you.
14:11 all their f; then they went away.
21:14 next morning Abraham took some f
24:33 f was set before him, but he said,
27: 4 Prepare me the kind of tasty f I
27: 7 and prepare me some tasty f to eat,
27: 9 so that I can prepare some tasty f
27:14 f, just the way his father liked it.
27:17 tasty f and the bread she had made.
27:31 He too prepared some tasty f and
28:20 give me f to eat and clothes to
39: 6 with anything except the f he ate.
41:35 They should collect all the f of
41:35 to be kept in the cities for f.
41:36 This f should be held in reserve for
41:48 Joseph collected all the f produced
41:48 f grown in the fields surrounding it.
41:54 the whole land of Egypt there was f.
41:55 the people cried to Pharaoh for f.
42: 7 of Canaan," they replied, "to buy f.
42:10 "Your servants have come to buy f.
42:33 and take f for your starving
43: 2 "Go back and buy us a little more f.
43: 4 we will go down and buy f for you.
43:20 down here the first time to buy f.
43:22 additional silver with us to buy f.
43:31 himself, said, "Serve the f.
44: 1 "Fill the men's sacks with as much f
44:25 'Go back and buy a little more f.'
47:12 all his father's household with f,
47:13 There was no f, however, in the
47:15 came to Joseph and said, "Give us f.
47:16 "I will sell you f in exchange for
47:17 and he gave them f in exchange for
47:17 through that year with f in exchange
47:19 us and our land in exchange for f,
47:22 had f enough from the allotment
47:24 as f for yourselves and your
49:20 "Asher's f will be rich; he will
Ex 12:16 except to prepare f for everyone to
12:39 time to prepare f for themselves.
16: 3 of meat and ate all the f we wanted,
21:10 her f, clothing and marital rights.
23:11 among your people may get f from it,
23:25 will be on your f and water.
Lev 3:11 shall burn them on the altar as f,
3:16 shall burn them on the altar as f,
11:34 Any f that could be eaten but has
21: 6 f of their God, they are to be holy.
21: 8 they offer up the f of your God.
21:17 come near to offer the f of his God.
21:21 come near to offer the f of his God.
21:22 He may eat the most holy f of his
21:22 f of his God, as well as the holy f;
22: 7 offerings, for they are his f.
22:11 household, that slave may eat his f.
22:13 she may eat of her father's f.
22:25 and offer them as the f of your God.
25: 6 will be f for you—for yourself,
25:37 interest or sell him f at a profit.
26: 5 and you will eat all the f you want
Nu 11: 4 with them began to crave other f,
11:34 the people who had craved other f.
15:19 you eat the f of the land, present a
21: 5 And we detest this miserable f!"
28: 2 the f for my offerings made by fire,
28:24 In this way prepare the f for the
Dt 2: 6 f you eat and the water you drink.'"
2:28 Sell us f to eat and water to drink
10:18 alien, giving him f and clothing.
23:19 whether on money or f or anything
28:26 Your carcasses will be f for all the
32:15 with f, he became heavy and sleek.
Jos 5:12 after they ate this f from the land;
9: 5 their f supply was dry and mouldy.
Jdg 13:16 me, I will not eat any of your f.
17:10 a year, your clothes and your f."
Ru 1: 6 his people by providing f for them,
1Sa 2: 5 were full hire themselves out for f,
2:36 office so that I can have f to eat.
9: 7 the man? The f in our sacks is gone.
14:24 "Cursed be any man who eats f before
14:24 So none of the troops tasted f.
14:28 'Cursed be any man who eats f today!'
28:22 let me give you some f so that you
30:11 him water to drink and f to eat—
30:12 for he had not eaten any f or drunk
2Sa 3:29 falls by the sword or who lacks f."
12: 3 It shared his f, drank from his cup
12:17 he would not eat any f with them.
12:20 they served him f, and he ate.
13: 5 Let her prepare the f in my sight so
13: 7 Amnon and prepare some f for him."
13:10 Amnon said to Tamar, "Bring the f
1Ki 5: 9 providing f for my royal household."
5:11 of wheat as f for his household,
10: 5 the f on his table, the seating of
11:18 and land and provided him with f.
17: 9 in that place to supply you with f."
17:15 So there was f every day for Elijah
18: 4 had supplied them with f and water.)
18:13 and supplied them with f and water.
19: 8 Strengthened by that f, he travelled
2Ki 6:22 Set f and water before them so that
25: 3 so severe that there was no f for
1Ch 12:40 bringing f on donkeys, camels, mules
2Ch 9: 4 the f on his table, the seating of
11:11 supplies of f, olive oil and wine.
28:15 f and drink, and healing balm.
Ezr 2:63 eat any of the most sacred f until
3: 7 and gave f and drink and oil to the
10: 6 While he was there, he ate no f and
Ne 5:14 ate the f allotted to the governor.
5:15 from them in addition to f and wine.
5:18 I never demanded the f allotted to
7:65 eat any of the most sacred f until
8:10 Nehemiah said, "Go and enjoy choice f
8:12 to send portions of f and to
13: 2 had not met the Israelites with f
13:15 them against selling f on that day.
Est 2: 9 her beauty treatments and special f.
9:22 joy and giving presents of f to one
Job 3:24 For sighing comes to me instead of f;
6: 6 Is tasteless f eaten without salt,
6: 7 I refuse to touch it; such f makes
12:11 test words as the tongue tastes f?
15:23 He wanders about—f for vultures; he
20:14 yet his f will turn sour in his
22: 7 and you withheld f from the hungry,
24: 5 go about their labour of foraging f;
24: 5 provides f for their children.
28: 5 The earth, from which f comes, is
30: 4 their f was the root of the broom
33:20 that his very being finds f
34: 3 tests words as the tongue tastes f.
36:16 of your table laden with choice f.
36:31 nations and provides f in abundance.
38:41 Who provides f for the raven when
38:41 God and wander about for lack of f?
39:29 From there he seeks out his f; his
Ps 42: 3 My tears have been my f day and
59:15 They wander about for f and howl if
63:10 the sword and become f for jackals.
69:21 They put gall in my f and gave me
74:14 as f to the creatures of the desert.
78:18 test by demanding the f they craved.
78:20 But can he also give us f? Can he
Ps 78:25 sent them all the f they could eat.
78:30 before they turned from the f they
79: 2 as f to the birds of the air,
102: 4 like grass; I forget to eat my f.
102: 9 For I eat ashes as my f and mingle
104:14 bringing forth f from the earth:
104:21 prey and seek their f from God.
104:27 them their f at the proper time.
105:16 destroyed all their supplies of f;
107:18 They loathed all f and drew near the
111: 5 He provides f for those who fear him;
127: 2 toiling for f to eat—for he grants
132:15 her poor will I satisfy with f.
136:25 who gives f to every creature.
145:15 them their f at the proper time.
146: 7 oppressed and gives f to the hungry.
147: 9 He provides f for the cattle and for
Pr 6: 8 summer and gathers its f at harvest.
9: 5 "Come, eat my f and drink the wine I
9:17 f eaten in secret is delicious!
12: 9 to be somebody and have no f.
12:11 works his land will have abundant f,
13:23 produce abundant f, but injustice
20:13 awake and you will have f to spare.
20:17 F gained by fraud tastes sweet to a
21:20 wise are stores of choice f and oil,
22: 9 for he shares his f with the poor.
23: 3 delicacies, for that f is deceptive.
23: 6 Do not eat the f of a stingy man, do
25:21 If your enemy is hungry, give him f
28:19 works his land will have abundant f,
30:22 king, a fool who is full of f,
30:25 they store up their f in the summer;
31:14 ships, bringing her f from afar.
31:15 she provides f for her family and
Ecc 9: 7 Go, eat your f with gladness, and
9:11 nor does f come to the wise or
Isa 3: 1 all supplies of f and all supplies
3: 7 I have no f or clothing in my house;
4: 1 "We will eat our own f and provide
21:14 in Tema, bring f for the fugitives.
23:18 for abundant f and fine clothes.
25: 6 a feast of rich f for all peoples,
30:23 and the f that comes from the land
58: 7 Is it not to share your f with the
62: 8 your grain as f for your enemies,
65:25 but dust will be the serpent's f.
Jer 5:17 They will devour your harvests and f,
7:33 become f for the birds of the air
9:15 bitter f and drink poisoned water.
16: 4 and their dead bodies will become f
16: 7 No-one will offer f to comfort those
19: 7 I will give their carcasses as f to
22:15 Did not your father have f and drink?
23:15 "I will make them eat bitter f and
34:20 Their dead bodies will become f for
44:17 At that time we had plenty of f and
52: 6 was no f for the people to eat.
Lam 1:11 for f to keep themselves alive.
1:19 for f to keep themselves alive.
4: 9 away for lack of f from the field.
4:10 children, who became their f when
Eze 4:10 Weigh out twenty shekels of f to eat
4:12 Eat the f as you would a barley cake;
4:13 Israel will eat defiled f among the
4:16 off the supply of f in Jerusalem.
4:16 The people will eat rationed f in
4:17 for f and water will be scarce. They
5:16 you and cut off your supply of f.
12:18 tremble as you eat your f, and
12:19 They will eat their f in anxiety and
14:13 against it to cut off its f supply
16:13 Your f was fine flour, honey and
16:19 Also the f I provided for you—the
16:20 sacrificed them as f to the idols.
18: 7 but gives his f to the hungry and
18:16 but gives his f to the hungry and
23:37 whom they bore to me, as f for them.
24:17 or eat the customary f of mourners."
24:22 or eat the customary f of mourners.
29: 5 I will give you as f to the beasts
34: 5 became f for all the wild animals.
34: 8 become f for all the wild animals,
34:10 and it will no longer be f for them.
39: 4 I will give you as f to all kinds of
44: 7 my temple while you offered me f,

Eze 47:12 Their fruit will serve for f and
48:18 f for the workers of the city.
Da 1: 5 of f and wine from the king's table.
1: 8 himself with the royal f and wine,
1:10 who has assigned your f and drink.
1:13 the young men who eat the royal f,
1:15 the young men who ate the royal f.
1:16 the guard took away their choice f
4:12 abundant, and on it was f for all.
4:21 providing f for all, giving shelter
10: 3 I ate no choice f; no meat or wine
Hos 2: 5 who give me my f and my water, my
9: 3 Egypt and eat unclean f in Assyria.
9: 4 This f will be for themselves; it
Joel 1:16 Has not the f been cut off before
Am 8:11 a famine of f or a thirst for water,
Hab 1:16 in luxury and enjoys the choicest f.
3:17 fails and the fields produce no f,
Hag 2:12 or stew, some wine, oil or other f,
Zec 9: 7 f from between their teeth.
Mal 1: 7 "You place defiled f on my altar.
1:12 and of its f, 'It is contemptible.'
3:10 that there may be f in my house.
Mt 3: 4 His f was locusts and wild honey.
6:25 Is not life more important than f,
14:15 villages and buy themselves some f."
24:45 them their f at the proper time?
Mk 7: 2 saw some of his disciples eating f
7: 5 eating their f with 'unclean' hands
Lk 3:11 one who has f should do the same."
9:12 countryside and find f and lodging,
9:13 we go and buy f for all this crowd."
12:23 Life is more than f, and the body
12:42 f allowance at the proper time?
15:17 father's hired men have f to spare,
Jn 4: 8 had gone into the town to buy f.)
4:32 he said to them, "I have f to eat
4:33 "Could someone have brought him f?
4:34 "My f," said Jesus, "is to do the
6:27 Do not work for f that spoils, but
6:27 but for f that endures to eternal
6:55 For my flesh is real f and my blood
Ac 6: 1 in the daily distribution of f.
7:11 and our fathers could not find f.
9:19 after taking some f, he regained his
12:20 king's country for their f supply.
14:17 he provides you with plenty of f
15:20 telling them to abstain from f
15:29 You are to abstain from f sacrificed
21:25 abstain from f sacrificed to idols,
27:21 men had gone a long time without f,
27:33 without f—you haven't eaten
27:34 Now I urge you to take some f. You
27:36 and ate some f themselves.
Ro 14:14 that no f is unclean in itself.
14:20 the work of God for the sake of f.
14:20 All f is clean, but it is wrong for
1Co 3: 2 I gave you milk, not solid f, for
6:13 "F for the stomach and the stomach
6:13 the stomach for f"—but God will
8: 1 Now about f sacrificed to idols: We
8: 4 then, about eating f sacrificed to
8: 7 when they eat such f they think of
8: 8 f does not bring us near to God; we
9: 4 Don't we have the right to f and
9:13 temple get their f from the temple,
10: 3 They all ate the same spiritual f
2Co 9:10 seed to the sower and bread for f
11:27 and have often gone without f;
2Th 3: 8 nor did we eat anyone's f without
1Ti 6: 8 if we have f and clothing, we will
Heb 5:12 You need milk, not solid f!
5:14 solid f is for the mature, who by
9:10 They are only a matter of f and
Jas 2:15 is without clothes and daily f.
Rev 2:14 sin by eating f sacrificed to idols
2:20 the eating of f sacrificed to idols.

Foods (Food)

Ps 63: 5 satisfied as with the richest of f;
Mk 7:19 this, Jesus declared all f "clean".
1Ti 4: 3 them to abstain from certain f,
Heb 13: 9 not by ceremonial f, which are of no

Fool (Folly, Fool's, Foolish, Foolishly, Foolishness, Fools)

Nu 22:29 "You have made a f of me! If I had a
Jdg 16:10 have made a f of me; you lied to me.
16:13 making a f of me and lying to me.
16:15 third time you have made a f of me
1Sa 25:25 name is F, and folly goes with him.
26:21 like a f and have erred greatly."
Job 5: 2 Resentment kills a f, and envy slays
5: 3 I myself have seen a f taking root,
Ps 14: 1 The f says in his heart, "There is
53: 1 The f says in his heart, "There is
Pr 10: 8 but a chattering f comes to ruin.
10:10 and a chattering f comes to ruin.
10:14 but the mouth of a f invites ruin.
10:18 and whoever spreads slander is a f.
10:23 A f finds pleasure in evil conduct,
11:29 the f will be servant to the wise.
12:15 The way of a f seems right to him,
12:16 A f shows his annoyance at once, but
13:16 but a f exposes his folly.
14:16 but a f is hotheaded and reckless.
15: 2 but the mouth of the f gushes folly.
15: 5 A f spurns his father's discipline,
15:14 but the mouth of a f feeds on folly.
17: 7 Arrogant lips are unsuited to a f—
17:10 more than a hundred lashes a f.
17:12 of her cubs than a f in his folly.
17:16 use is money in the hand of a f,
17:21 To have a f for a son brings grief;
17:21 is no joy for the father of a f.
17:28 Even a f is thought wise if he keeps
18: 2 A f finds no pleasure in
19: 1 than a f whose lips are perverse.
19:10 is not fitting for a f to live in
20: 3 but every f is quick to quarrel.
23: 9 Do not speak to a f, for he will
24: 7 Wisdom is too high for a f; in the
26: 1 honour is not fitting for a f.
26: 4 Do not answer a f according to his
26: 5 Answer a f according to his folly,
26: 6 of a message by the hand of a f.
26: 7 is a proverb in the mouth of a f.
26: 8 is the giving of honour to a f.
26: 9 is a proverb in the mouth of a f.
26:10 he who hires a f or any passer-by.
26:11 so a f repeats his folly.
26:12 is more hope for a f than for him.
27: 3 but provocation by a f is
27:22 Though you grind a f in a mortar,
28:26 He who trusts in himself is a f, but
29: 9 If a wise man goes to court with a f,
29: 9 the f rages and scoffs, and there is
29:11 A f gives full vent to his anger,
29:20 is more hope for a f than for him.
30:22 king, a f who is full of food,
30:32 "If you have played the f and
Ecc 2:14 while the f walks in the darkness;
2:15 fate of the f will overtake me also.
2:16 For the wise man, like the f, will
2:16 Like the f, the wise man too must
2:19 he will be a wise man or a f?
4: 5 The f folds his hands and ruins
5: 3 so the speech of a f when there are
6: 8 advantage has a wise man over a f?
7: 7 Extortion turns a wise man into a f,
7:17 be a f—why die before your time?
10: 2 but the heart of the f to the left.
10: 3 the f lacks sense and shows everyone
10:12 but a f is consumed by his own lips.
10:14 the f multiplies words. No-one knows
Isa 32: 5 No longer will the f be called noble
32: 6 For the f speaks folly, his mind is
Jer 17:11 in the end he will prove to be a f.
Hos 9: 7 the prophet is considered a f,
Mt 5:22 But anyone who says, 'You f!' will
Lk 12:20 "But God said to him, 'You f! This
1Co 3:18 he should become a "f" so that he
2Co 11:16 I repeat: Let no-one take me for a f.
11:16 receive me just as you would a f,
11:17 as the Lord would, but as a f.
11:21 as a f—I also dare to boast about.
12: 6 I would not be a f, because I would
12:11 I have made a f of myself, but you

Fool's (Fool)

Pr 14: 3 A f talk brings a rod to his back,
17:24 but a f eyes wander to the ends of
18: 6 A f lips bring him strife, and his
18: 7 A f mouth is his undoing, and his
Ecc 10:15 A f work wearies him; he does not

Foolish (Fool)

Ge 31:28 You have done a f thing.
Dt 32: 6 O f and unwise people? Is he not
2Sa 24:10 I have done a very f thing."
1Ch 21: 8 I have done a very f thing."
2Ch 16: 9 You have done a f thing, and from
Job 2:10 "You are talking like a f woman.
Ps 49:10 the f and the senseless alike perish
74:18 how f people have reviled your name.
Pr 8: 5 you who are f, gain understanding.
10: 1 but a f son grief to his mother.
14: 1 own hands the f one tears hers down.
14: 7 Stay away from a f man, for you will
14:17 A quick-tempered man does f things,
15:20 but a f man despises his mother.
17:25 A f son brings grief to his father
19:13 A f son is his father's ruin, and a
21:20 oil, but a f man devours all he has.
Ecc 2: 2 "Laughter," I said, "is f. And what
4:13 than an old but f king who no
Jer 5: 4 "These are only the poor; they are f,
5:21 Hear this, you f and senseless
10: 8 They are all senseless and f; they
Eze 13: 3 Woe to the f prophets who follow
Zec 11:15 again the equipment of a f shepherd.
Mt 7:26 a f man who built his house on sand.
25: 2 Five of them were f and five were
25: 3 The f ones took their lamps but did
25: 8 The f ones said to the wise, 'Give
Lk 11:40 You f people! Did not the one who
24:25 He said to them, "How f you are, and
Ro 1:14 both to the wise and the f.
1:21 and their f hearts were darkened.
2:20 an instructor of the f, a teacher of
1Co 1:20 God made f the wisdom of the world?
1:27 God chose the f things of the world
15:36 How f! What you sow does not come to
Gal 3: 1 You f Galatians! Who has bewitched
3: 3 Are you so f? After beginning with
Eph 5: 4 obscenity, f talk or coarse joking,
5:17 Therefore do not be f, but
1Ti 6: 9 into many f and harmful desires
2Ti 2:23 Don't have anything to do with f and
Tit 3: 3 At one time we too were f,
3: 9 avoid f controversies and
Jas 2:20 You f man, do you want evidence that
1Pe 2:15 silence the ignorant talk of f men.

Foolishly (Fool)

Nu 12:11 us the sin we have so f committed.
1Sa 13:13 "You acted f," Samuel said. "You

Foolishness (Fool)

2Sa 15:31 turn Ahithophel's counsel into f."
1Co 1:18 For the message of the cross is f to
1:21 God was pleased through the f of
1:23 to Jews and f to Gentiles,
1:25 For the f of God is wiser than man's
2:14 for they are f to him, and he cannot
3:19 For the wisdom of this world is f in
2Co 11: 1 put up with a little of my f;

Fools (Fool)

2Sa 13:13 like one of the wicked f in Israel.
Job 12:17 away stripped and makes f of judges.
Ps 39: 8 do not make me the scorn of f.
74:22 how f mock you all day long.
92: 6 does not know, f do not understand,
94: 8 you f, when will you become wise?
107:17 Some became f through their
Pr 1: 7 but f despise wisdom and discipline.
1:22 in mockery and f hate knowledge?
1:32 complacency of f will destroy them;
3:35 honour, but f he holds up to shame.
10:21 but f die for lack of judgment.
12:23 but the heart of f blurts out folly.

Pr 13:19 but f detest turning from evil.
13:20 but a companion of f suffers harm.
14: 8 but the folly of f is deception.
14: 9 F mock at making amends for sin, but
14:24 but the folly of f yields folly.
14:33 among f she lets herself be known.
15: 7 knowledge; not so the hearts of f.
16:22 but folly brings punishment to f.
19:29 and beatings for the backs of f.
26: 3 and a rod for the backs of f!
Ecc 5: 1 than to offer the sacrifice of f,
5: 4 no pleasure in f; fulfil your vow.
7: 4 the heart of f is in the house of
7: 5 than to listen to the song of f.
7: 6 the pot, so is the laughter of f.
7: 9 for anger resides in the lap of f.
9:17 than the shouts of a ruler of f.
10: 6 F are put in many high positions,
Isa 19:11 officials of Zoan are nothing but f;
19:13 The officials of Zoan have become f,
35: 8 wicked f will not go about on it.
44:25 prophets and makes f of diviners,
Jer 4:22 "My people are f; they do not know
50:36 false prophets! They will become f.
Mt 23:17 You blind f! Which is greater: the
Ro 1:22 claimed to be wise, they became f
1Co 4:10 We are f for Christ, but you are so
2Co 11:19 You gladly put up with f since you

Foot (Afoot, Barefoot, Feet, Fleet-footed, Foothold, Footings, Footprints, Underfoot)

Ge 41:44 will lift hand or f in all Egypt."
Ex 12:37 on f, besides women and children.
19:12 the mountain or touch the f of it.
19:17 they stood at the f of the mountain.
21:24 for tooth, hand for hand, f for f,
24: 4 built an altar at the f of the
32:19 to pieces at the f of the mountain.
Lev 8:23 and on the big toe of his right f.
13:12 the infected person from head to f,
14:14 and on the big toe of his right f.
14:17 and on the big toe of his right f,
14:25 and on the big toe of his right f.
14:28 and on the big toe of his right f.
21:19 no man with a crippled f or hand,
Nu 11:21 among six hundred thousand men on f,
20:19 to pass through on f—nothing else."
22:25 crushing Balaam's f against it.
Dt 2: 5 not even enough to put your f on.
2:28 Only let us pass through on f—
4:11 You came near and stood at the f of
11:10 irrigated it by f as in a vegetable
11:24 Every place where you set your f
19:21 for tooth, hand for hand, f for f.
28:56 the ground with the sole of her f
28:65 place for the sole of your f.
32:35 In due time their f will slip; their
Jos 1: 3 you set your f, as I promised Moses.
3:13 all the earth—set f in the Jordan,
18:16 The boundary went down to the f of
Jdg 3:16 sword about a f and a half long,
4:15 abandoned his chariot and fled on f.
4:17 Sisera, however, fled on f to the
1Sa 4:10 lost thirty thousand f soldiers.
15: 4 hundred thousand f soldiers
2Sa 8: 4 and twenty thousand f soldiers.
10: 6 f soldiers from Beth Rehob and Zobah,
10:18 forty thousand of their f soldiers.
14:25 to the sole of his f there was no
21:20 toes on each f—twenty-four in all.
1Ki 14:12 When you set f in your city, the
20:29 the Aramean f soldiers in one day.
2Ki 13: 7 and ten thousand f soldiers,
1Ch 18: 4 and twenty thousand f soldiers.
19:18 forty thousand of their f soldiers.
20: 6 toes on each f—twenty-four in all.
Job 28: 4 in places forgotten by the f of man;
28: 8 Proud beasts do not set f on it, and
31: 5 or my f has hurried after deceit—
39:15 unmindful that a f may crush them,
Ps 36:11 May the f of the proud not come
38:16 themselves over me when my f slips."
66: 6 they passed through the waters on f
91:12 not strike your f against a stone.
94:18 I said, "My f is slipping," your
Ps 121: 3 He will not let your f slip—he who
Pr 1:15 them, do not set f on their paths;
3:23 safety, and your f will not stumble;
3:26 will keep your f from being snared.
4:14 Do not set f on the path of the
4:27 or the left; keep your f from evil.
25:17 Seldom set f in your neighbour's
25:19 Like a bad tooth or a lame f is
Ecc 10: 7 while princes go on f like slaves.
Isa 1: 6 From the sole of your f to the top
Jer 12: 5 "If you have raced with men on f and
Eze 29:11 No f of man or animal will pass
32:13 stirred by the f of man or muddied
Hab 3:13 you stripped him from head to f.
Mt 4: 6 not strike your f against a stone.'"
14:13 followed him on f from the towns.
18: 8 If your hand or your f causes you to
22:13 'Tie him hand and f, and throw him
Mk 5: 4 had often been chained hand and f,
6:33 ran on f from all the towns and got
9:45 if your f causes you to sin, cut it
Lk 4:11 not strike your f against a stone.'"
8:29 hand and f and kept under guard,
Jn 20:12 at the head and the other at the f.
Ac 7: 5 here, not even a f of ground.
20:13 because he was going there on f.
1Co 12:15 If the f should say, "Because I am
Heb 10:29 has trampled the Son of God under f,
Rev 10: 2 He planted his right f on the sea
10: 2 the sea and his left f on the land,

Foothills (Hill)

Dt 1: 7 in the mountains, in the western f,
Jos 9: 1 in the western f, and along the
10:40 the Negev, the western f and the
11: 2 in the western f and in Naphoth Dor
11:16 the western f, the Arabah and the
11:16 mountains of Israel with their f,
12: 8 the hill country, the western f, the
15:33 In the western f: Eshtaol, Zorah,
Jdg 1: 9 the Negev and the western f.
1Ki 10:27 as sycamore-fig trees in the f.
1Ch 27:28 sycamore-fig trees in the western f.
2Ch 1:15 as sycamore-fig trees in the f.
9:27 as sycamore-fig trees in the f.
26:10 livestock in the f and in the plain.
28:18 in the f and in the Negev of Judah.
Jer 17:26 of Benjamin and the western f,
32:44 of the western f and of the Negev,
33:13 of the western f and of the Negev,
Ob :19 and people from the f will possess
Zec 7: 7 and the western f were settled?'"

Foothold (Foot)

Ps 69: 2 miry depths, where there is no f.
73: 2 slipped; I had nearly lost my f.
Eph 4:27 do not give the devil a f.

Footings (Foot)

Job 38: 6 On what were its f set, or who laid

Footprints (Foot)

Ps 77:19 waters, though your f were not seen.
Hos 6: 8 wicked men, stained with f of blood.

Footsteps (Step)

1Ki 14: 6 when Ahijah heard the sound of her f
2Ki 6:32 sound of his master's f behind him?"
Ps 119:133 Direct my f according to your word;
Isa 26: 6 of the oppressed, the f of the poor.
Ro 4:12 walk in the f of the faith that our

Footstool (Stool)

1Ch 28: 2 for the f of our God, and I made
2Ch 9:18 had six steps, and a f of gold
Ps 99: 5 God and worship at his f; he is holy.
110: 1 your enemies a f for your feet."
132: 7 let us worship at his f—
Isa 66: 1 is my throne, and the earth is my f.
Lam 2: 1 has not remembered his f in the day
Mt 5:35 or by the earth, for it is his f; or
Lk 20:43 until I make your enemies a f for
Ac 2:35 until I make your enemies a f for
7:49 is my throne, and the earth is my f.
Heb 1:13 your enemies a f for your feet"?
10:13 for his enemies to be made his f,

For ever and ever

Ex 15:18; Ps 9:5; 10:16; 21:4; 45:6, 17; 48:14; 52:8 ; 111:8; 119:44; 132:12, 14; 145:1, 2, 21; 148:6; Jer 7:7; 25:5; Da 2:20; 7:18; 12:3; Mic 4:5; Gal 1:5; Eph 3:21; Php 4:20; 1Ti 1:17; 2Ti 4:18; Heb 1:8; 13:21; 1Pe 4:11; 5:11; Rev 1:6, 18; 4:9, 10; 5:13; 7:12; 10:6; 11:15; 14:11; 15:7; 19:3; 20:10; 22:5

Foraging

Job 24: 5 the poor go about their labour of f

Forbearance

Ro 3:25 because in his f he had left the

Forbid (Forbidden, Forbids)

Nu 30:11 nothing to her and does not f her,
1Sa 24: 6 He said to his men, "The LORD f that
26:11 the LORD f that I should lay a hand
1Ki 21: 3 Naboth replied, "The LORD f that I
1Ch 11:19 "God f that I should do this!" he
1Co 14:39 and do not f speaking in tongues.
1Ti 4: 3 They f people to marry and order

Forbidden (Forbid)

Lev 4: 2 is f in any of the LORD's commands—
4:13 is f in any of the LORD's commands,
4:22 does what is f in any of the
4:27 is f in any of the LORD's commands,
5:17 "If a person sins and does what is f
19:23 fruit tree, regard its fruit as f.
19:23 consider it f; it must not be eaten.
Nu 30: 5 her because her father has f her.
Dt 4:23 of anything the LORD your God has f.
23: 2 No-one born of a f marriage nor any
1Ki 11:10 Although he had f Solomon to follow
2Ki 17:15 things the LORD had f them to do.
Est 2:10 because Mordecai had f her to do so.
Lam 1:10 you had f to enter your assembly.
Zec 9: 7 the f food from between their teeth.

Forbids (Forbid)

Nu 30: 5 if her father f her when he hears
30: 8 if her husband f her when he hears
Jn 5:10 the law f you to carry your mat."

Force (Enforce, Forced, Forceful, Forcefully, Forces, Forcibly, Forcing)

Ge 31:31 your daughters away from me by f.
47:26 still in f today—that a fifth of
Ex 9:14 will send the full f of my plagues
19:21 warn the people so they do not f
19:24 the people must not f their way
Jos 8:11 The entire f that was with him
Jdg 7:13 It struck the tent with such f that
8:10 a f of about fifteen thousand men,
1Sa 2:16 if you don't, I'll take it by f."
19: 8 such f that they fled before him.
2Sa 5:17 they went up in full f to search for
13:12 "Don't f me. Such a thing should not
1Ki 9:21 conscripted for his slave labour f,
11:28 labour f of the house of Joseph.
2Ki 6:14 and chariots and a strong f there.
24:16 f of seven thousand fighting men,
1Ch 14: 8 they went up in full f to search for
2Ch 8: 8 conscripted for his slave labour f,
13: 3 Abijah went into battle with a f of
26:13 a powerful f to support the king
32: 4 A large f of men assembled, and they
Ezr 4:23 and compelled them by f to
Est 8:11 kill and annihilate any armed f of
Job 19:12 His troops advance in f; they build
20:22 full f of misery will come upon him.
24: 4 f all the poor of the land into
28:25 he established the f of the wind and
Jer 46:22 serpent as the enemy advances in f;
Am 5:11 You trample on the poor and f him to
Ob : 7 All your allies will f you to the
Jn 6:15 to come and make him king by f,
Ac 5:26 They did not use f, because they
23:10 away from them by f and bring him

Ac 26:11 and I tried to f them to blaspheme.
27:14 a wind of hurricane f, called the
Gal 2:14 f Gentiles to follow Jewish customs?
Heb 9:17 a will is in f only when somebody

Forced (Force)

Ge 49:15 the burden and submit to f labour.
Ex 1:11 them to oppress them with f labour,
Dt 20:11 shall be subject to f labour and
Jos 16:10 but are required to do f labour.
17:13 they subjected the Canaanites to f
Jdg 1:28 they pressed the Canaanites into f
1:30 they did subject them to f labour.
1:33 Anath became f labourers for them.
1:35 they too were pressed into f labour.
2Sa 18: 3 f to flee, they won't care about us.
20:24 Adoniram was in charge of f labour;
1Ki 4: 6 son of Abda—in charge of f labour.
5:14 was in charge of the f labour.
9:15 Here is the account of the f labour
12:18 who was in charge of f labour, but
2Ch 10:18 who was in charge of f labour, but
Job 30: 6 They were f to live in the dry
Ps 69: 4 f to restore what I did not steal.
Isa 31: 8 young men will be put to f labour.
Jer 34:16 f them to become your slaves again.
Mt 27:32 and they f him to carry the cross.
Mk 15:21 and they f him to carry the cross.
Phm :14 do will be spontaneous and not f.
Rev 13:16 He also f everyone, small and great,

Forceful (Force)

Mt 11:12 advancing, and f men lay hold of it.
2Co 10:10 "His letters are weighty and f, but

Forcefully (Force)

1Sa 18:10 spirit from God came f upon Saul.
Isa 28: 2 he will throw it f to the ground.
Mt 11:12 the kingdom of heaven has been f

Forces (Force)

Ge 14: 3 All these latter kings joined f in
21:22 commander of his f said to Abraham,
21:32 Phicol the commander of his f
26:26 and Phicol the commander of his f.
34:30 and if they join f against me and
Jos 10: 5 Jarmuth, Lachish and Eglon—joined f.
10: 6 country have joined f against us."
11: 5 All these kings joined f and made
Jdg 6:33 other eastern peoples joined f and
12: 1 The men of Ephraim called out their f
1Sa 4: 2 The Philistines deployed their f to
14:17 Muster the f and see who has left us.
17: 1 Now the Philistines gathered their f
23: 3 to Keilah against the Philistine f!"
23: 8 Saul called up all his f for battle,
23:26 As Saul and his f were closing in on
28: 1 the Philistines gathered their f to
29: 1 The Philistines gathered all their f
30:23 to us the f that came against us.
1Ki 11:24 when David destroyed the f of Zobah;
15:20 and sent the commanders of his f
1Ch 20: 1 to war, Joab led out the armed f.
2Ch 14:13 crushed before the LORD and his f.
16: 4 his f against the towns of Israel.
32: 9 his f were laying siege to Lachish,
Job 10:17 f come against me wave upon wave.
25: 3 Can his f be numbered? Upon whom
Ps 48: 4 the kings joined f, when they
55:11 Destructive f are at work in the
Da 11: 7 He will attack the f of the king of
11:15 The f of the South will be powerless
11:31 "His armed f will rise up to
Joel 2:11 his army; his f are beyond number,
Zec 9: 8 defend my house against marauding f.
Mt 5:41 If someone f you to go one mile, go
Eph 6:12 f of evil in the heavenly realms.

Forcibly (Force)

Ge 40:15 For I was f carried off from the
Dt 28:31 Your donkey will be f taken from you

Forcing (Force)

Lk 16:16 and everyone is f his way into it.
Ac 7:19 oppressed our forefathers by f them

Ford (Forded, Fords)

Ge 32:22 and crossed the f of the Jabbok.
2Sa 19:18 They crossed at the f to take the

Forded (Ford)

Jos 2:23 out of the hills, f the river and

Fords (Ford)

Jos 2: 7 that leads to the f of the Jordan,
Jdg 3:28 taking possession of the f of the
12: 5 The Gileadites captured the f of the
12: 6 killed him at the f of the Jordan.
2Sa 15:28 I will wait at the f in the desert
17:16 'Do not spend the night at the f in
Isa 16: 2 women of Moab at the f of the Arnon.

Forefather (Father)

Nu 26:58 (Kohath was the f of Amram;
Jos 15:13 (Arba was the f of Anak.)
19:47 and named it Dan after their f.)
21:11 (Arba was the f of Anak.)
Jdg 18:29 They named it Dan after their f Dan,
1Ki 15: 3 the heart of David his f had been.
1Ch 24:19 for them by their f Aaron,
Jer 35: 6 "We do not drink wine, because our f
35: 8 We have obeyed everything our f
35:10 our f Jonadab commanded us.
35:16 out the command their f gave them,
35:18 the command of your f Jonadab
Ro 4: 1 our f, discovered in this matter?

Forefather's (Father)

Jer 35:14 because they obey their f command.

Forefathers (Father)

Ex 10: 6 fathers nor your f have ever seen
13: 5 land he swore to your f to give you,
13:11 promised on oath to you and your f,
Lev 25:41 clan and to the property of his f.
Nu 11:12 you promised on oath to their f?
14:23 land I promised on oath to their f.
20:15 Our f went down into Egypt, and we
36: 4 the tribal inheritance of our f."
36: 7 tribal land inherited from his f.
Dt 1:35 good land I swore to give your f,
4:31 or forget the covenant with your f,
4:37 he loved your f and chose their
6:18 the LORD promised on oath to your f,
6:23 that he promised on oath to our f.
7: 8 kept the oath he swore to your f
7:12 with you, as he swore to your f.
7:13 that he swore to your f to give you.
8: 1 the LORD promised on oath to your f.
8:18 he swore to your f, as it is today.
10:15 affection on your f and loved them,
10:22 Your f who went down into Egypt were
11: 9 LORD swore to your f to give to them
11:21 that the LORD swore to give your f,
13:17 as he promised on oath to your f,
19: 8 as he promised on oath to your f,
26: 3 the LORD swore to our f to give us."
26:15 us as you promised on oath to our f,
28:11 land he swore to your f to give you.
31: 7 LORD swore to their f to give them,
31:20 land I promised on oath to their f,
Jos 1: 6 I swore to their f to give them.
21:43 land he had sworn to give their f,
21:44 just as he had sworn to their f.
24: 2 'Long ago your f, including Terah
24:14 Throw away the gods your f
24:15 whether the gods your f served
Jdg 2: 1 land that I swore to give to your f.
2:20 laid down for their f and has not
2:22 LORD and walk in it as their f did."
3: 4 he had given their f through Moses.
1Sa 12: 6 and brought your f up out of Egypt.
12: 8 who brought your f out of Egypt and
1Ki 14:15 good land that he gave to their f
2Ki 19:12 destroyed by my f deliver them: the
21: 8 wander from the land I gave their f,
2Ki 21:15 the day their f came out of Egypt
1Ch 29:15 in your sight, as were all our f.
2Ch 33: 8 leave the land I assigned to your f,
Ezr 9: 7 From the days of our f until now,
Ne 9: 9 "You saw the suffering of our f in
9:16 "But they, our f, became arrogant
9:36 slaves in the land you gave our f so
13:18 Didn't your f do the same things, so
Ps 78: 5 our f to teach their children,
78: 8 They would not be like their f—a
Pr 22:28 boundary stone set up by your f.
Isa 14:21 his sons for the sins of their f;
37:12 destroyed by my f deliver them—the
Jer 3:18 I gave your f as an inheritance.
7: 7 I gave to your f for ever and ever.
7:22 For when I brought your f out of
7:25 From the time your f left Egypt
7:26 and did more evil than their f.'
11: 4 the terms I commanded your f when I
11: 5 fulfil the oath I swore to your f,
11: 7 From the time I brought your f up
11:10 returned to the sins of their f,
11:10 the covenant I made with their f.
16:15 them to the land I gave to their f.
17:22 day holy, as I commanded your f.
30: 3 their f to possess,' says the LORD."
31:32 the covenant I made with their f
32:22 you had sworn to give to their f,
34:13 says: I made a covenant with your f
Eze 36:28 live in the land I gave your f;
47:14 uplifted hand to give it to your f,
Da 11:24 neither his fathers nor his f did.
Joel 1: 2 your days or in the days of your f?
Zec 1: 2 "The LORD was very angry with your f.
1: 4 Do not be like your f, to whom the
1: 5 Where are your f now? And the
1: 6 overtake your f? "Then they repented
Mal 3: 7 Ever since the time of your f you
Mt 23:30 If we had lived in the days of our f,
23:32 the measure of the sin of your f!
Lk 11:47 and it was your f who killed them.
11:48 f did; they killed the prophets,
Jn 6:31 Our f ate the manna in the desert;
6:49 Your f ate the manna in the desert,
6:58 Your f ate manna and died, but he
Ac 7:19 oppressed our f by forcing them to
7:44 "Our f had the tabernacle of the
28:25 spoke the truth to your f when he
1Co 10: 1 brothers, that our f were all under
2Ti 1: 3 I thank God, whom I serve, as my f
Heb 1: 1 In the past God spoke to our f
8: 9 the covenant I made with their f
1Pe 1:18 life handed down to you from your f,

Forefinger

Lev 14:16 dip his right f into the oil in his
14:27 with his right f sprinkle some of

Forehead (Foreheads)

Ex 13: 9 a reminder on your f that the law of
13:16 a symbol on your f that the LORD
28:38 will be on Aaron's f, and he will
28:38 It will be on Aaron's f continually
Lev 13:41 scalp and has a bald f, he is clean.
13:42 sore on his bald head or f,
13:42 breaking out on his head or f.
13:43 if the swollen sore on his head or f
1Sa 17:49 and struck the Philistine on the f.
17:49 The stone sank into his f, and he
2Ch 26:19 temple, leprosy broke out on his f.
26:20 he had leprosy on his f, so they
Isa 48: 4 neck were iron, your f was bronze.
Eze 3: 9 I will make your f like the hardest
Rev 13:16 mark on his right hand or on his f,
14: 9 his mark on the f or on the hand,
17: 5 This title was written on her f:

Foreheads (Forehead)

Nu 24:17 He will crush the f of Moab, the
Dt 6: 8 your hands and bind them on your f.
11:18 your hands and bind them on your f.
Jer 48:45 of Sihon; it burns the f of Moab,
Eze 9: 4 put a mark on the f of those who
Rev 7: 3 the f of the servants of our God."
9: 4 not have the seal of God on their f.

Rev 14: 1 Father's name written on their f.
20: 4 his mark on their f or their hands.
22: 4 and his name will be on their f.

Foreign (Foreigner, Foreigners, Foreigners')

Ge 35: 2 "Get rid of the f gods you have with
35: 4 they gave Jacob all the f gods they
Ex 2:22 "I have become an alien in a f land.
18: 3 "I have become an alien in a f land"
Dt 31:16 f gods of the land they are entering.
32:12 The LORD alone led him; no f god was
32:16 made him jealous with their f gods
Jos 24:20 forsake the LORD and serve f gods
24:23 "throw away the f gods that are
Jdg 10:16 they got rid of the f gods among
1Sa 7: 3 then rid yourselves of the f gods
1Ki 11: 1 Solomon, however, loved many f women
11: 8 He did the same for all his f wives,
2Ki 19:24 I have dug wells in f lands and
2Ch 14: 3 He removed the f altars and the high
33:15 He got rid of the f gods and removed
Ezr 9: 7 the hand of f kings, as it is today.
10: 2 marrying f women from the peoples
10:10 f women, adding to Israel's guilt.
10:11 around you and from your f wives."
10:14 a f woman come at a set time,
10:17 all the men who had married f women.
10:18 the following had married f women:
10:44 All these had married f women, and
Ne 13: 3 Israel all who were of f descent.
13:26 even he was led into sin by f women.
13:27 to our God by marrying f women?"
13:30 and the Levites of everything f,
Ps 44:20 or spread out our hands to a f god,
81: 9 You shall have no f god among you;
114: 1 of Jacob from a people of f tongue,
137: 4 songs of the LORD while in a f land?
Isa 28:11 Very well then, with f lips and
37:25 I have dug wells in f lands and
43:12 I, and not some f god among you.
Jer 2:25 said, 'It's no use! I love f gods,
3:13 f gods under every spreading tree,
5:19 and served f gods in your own land,
8:19 with their worthless f idols?"
19: 4 me and made this a place of f gods;
25:20 all the f people there; all the
25:24 the f people who live in the desert;
Eze 31:12 the most ruthless of f nations cut
Da 11:39 fortresses with the help of a f god
Zep 1: 8 and all those clad in f clothes.
Hag 2:22 shatter the power of the f kingdoms.
Mal 2:11 by marrying the daughter of a f god.
Ac 17:18 "He seems to be advocating f gods.
26:11 went to f cities to persecute them.
Heb 11: 9 in a f country; he lived in tents,
11:34 in battle and routed f armies.

Foreigner (Foreign)

Ge 17:12 or bought with money from a f—
17:27 from a f, was circumcised with him.
Ex 12:43 the Passover: "No f is to eat of it.
Lev 22:25 such animals from the hand of a f
Dt 14:21 eat it, or you may sell it to a f.
15: 3 You may require payment from a f,
17:15 Do not place a f over you, one who
23:20 You may charge a f interest, but not
Ru 2:10 your eyes that you notice me—a f?"
2Sa 15:19 a f, an exile from your homeland.
1Ki 8:41 "As for the f who does not belong to
8:43 and do whatever the f asks of you,
2Ch 6:32 "As for the f who does not belong to
6:33 and do whatever the f asks of you,
Isa 56: 3 Let no f who has bound himself to
Eze 44: 9 No f uncircumcised in heart and
Lk 17:18 give praise to God except this f?"
Ac 7:29 he settled as a f and had two sons.
1Co 14:11 I am a f to the speaker, and he is a
14:11 to the speaker, and he is a f to me.

Foreigners (Foreign)

Ge 31:15 Does he not regard us as f? Not only
Ex 21: 8 He has no right to sell her to f,
Dt 29:22 f who come from distant lands will
2Sa 22:45 f come cringing to me; as soon as
Ne 9: 2 had separated themselves from all f.
Ps 18:44 they obey me; f cringe before me.
144: 7 mighty waters, from the hands of f
144:11 of f whose mouths are full of lies,
Isa 1: 7 stripped by f right before you,
25: 5 You silence the uproar of f; as heat
56: 6 f who bind themselves to the LORD to
60:10 "F will rebuild your walls, and
61: 5 f will work your fields and
62: 8 and never again will f drink the new
Jer 5:19 serve f in a land not your own.'
30: 8 no longer will f enslave them.
50:37 chariots and all the f in her ranks!
51: 2 I will send f to Babylon to winnow
51:51 because f have entered the holy
Lam 5: 2 over to aliens, our homes to f.
Eze 7:21 hand it all over as plunder to f
11: 9 and hand you over to f and inflict
28: 7 I am going to bring f against you,
28:10 the uncircumcised at the hands of f.
30:12 by the hand of f I will lay waste
44: 7 you brought f uncircumcised in heart
44: 9 the f who live among the Israelites.
Hos 7: 9 F sap his strength, but he does not
8: 7 yield grain, f would swallow it up.
Joel 3:17 holy; never again will f invade her.
Ob 1:11 f entered his gates and cast lots
Zec 9: 6 F will occupy Ashdod, and I will cut
Mt 27: 7 field as a burial place for f.
Ac 17:21 (All the Athenians and the f who
1Co 14:21 through the lips of f I will speak
Eph 2:12 f to the covenants of the promise,
2:19 Consequently, you are no longer f

Foreigners' (Foreign)

Isa 25: 2 the f stronghold a city no more;

Foreknew (Know)

Ro 8:29 For those God f he also predestined
11: 2 not reject his people, whom he f.

Foreknowledge (Know)

Ac 2:23 by God's set purpose and f; and you,
1Pe 1: 2 to the f of God the Father,

Foreman (Foremen)

Ru 2: 5 Boaz asked the f of his harvesters,
2: 6 The f replied, "She is the Moabitess
Mt 20: 8 owner of the vineyard said to his f,

Foremen (Foreman)

Ex 5: 6 and f in charge of the people:
5:10 the slave drivers and the f went out
5:14 f appointed by Pharaoh's slave
5:15 the Israelite f went and appealed to
5:19 The Israelite f realised they were
1Ki 5:16 as well as thirty-three hundred f
2Ch 2: 2 thirty-six hundred as f over them.
2:18 with 3,600 f over them to keep the

Foresail (Sail)

Ac 27:40 they hoisted the f to the wind and

Foresaw (Foresee)

Gal 3: 8 The Scripture f that God would

Foresee (Foresaw, Foresight)

Isa 47:11 a catastrophe you cannot f will

Foresight (Foresee)

Ac 24: 2 and your f has brought about reforms

Foreskin (Foreskins)

Ex 4:25 her son's f and touched Moses' feet

Foreskins (Foreskin)

1Sa 18:25 a hundred Philistine f, to take
18:27 He brought their f and presented the
2Sa 3:14 price of a hundred Philistine f."

Forest (Forested, Forests)

Dt 19: 5 For instance, a man may go into the f
Jos 17:15 go up into the f and clear land for
1Sa 22: 5 left and went to the f of Hereth.
2Sa 18: 6 took place in the f of Ephraim.
18: 8 and the f claimed more lives that
18:17 threw him into a big pit in the f
1Ki 7: 2 He built the Palace of the F of
10:17 in the Palace of the F of Lebanon.
10:21 of the F of Lebanon were pure gold.
1Ch 16:33 the trees of the f will sing, they
2Ch 9:16 in the Palace of the F of Lebanon.
9:20 of the F of Lebanon were pure gold.
Ne 2: 8 keeper of the king's f, so he will
Ps 50:10 for every animal of the f is mine,
80:13 Boars from the f ravage it and the
83:14 fire consumes the f or a flame sets
96:12 trees of the f will sing for joy;
104:20 and all the beasts of the f prowl.
SS 2: 3 among the trees of the f is my
Isa 7: 2 as the trees of the f are shaken
9:18 it sets the f thickets ablaze, so
10:34 He will cut down the f thickets with
22: 8 the weapons in the Palace of the F;
29:17 and the fertile field seem like a f?
32:15 the fertile field seems like a f.
32:19 Though hail flattens the f and the
44:14 it grow among the trees of the f,
56: 9 and devour, all you beasts of the f!
Jer 5: 6 Therefore a lion from the f will
10: 3 they cut a tree out of the f,
12: 8 become to me like a lion in the f.
46:23 They will chop down her f,"
Eze 15: 2 branch on any of the trees in the f?
15: 6 trees of the f as fuel for the fire,
20:46 against the f of the southland.
20:47 Say to the southern f: 'Hear the
31: 3 branches overshadowing the f;
Mic 5: 8 a lion among the beasts of the f,
7:14 in a f, in fertile pasture-lands.
Zec 11: 2 the dense f has been cut down!
Jas 3: 5 f is set on fire by a small spark.

Forested (Forest)

Jos 17:18 the f hill country as well. Clear it,

Forests (Forest)

2Ki 19:23 remotest parts, the finest of its f.
Ps 29: 9 the oaks and strips the f bare.
Isa 10:18 The splendour of his f and fertile
10:19 the remaining trees of his f will be
37:24 heights, the finest of its f.
44:23 you mountains, you f and all your
Jer 21:14 I will kindle a fire in your f that
Eze 34:25 desert and sleep in the f in safety.
39:10 the fields or cut it from the f,

Foretell (Foretells, Foretold)

Isa 44: 7 yes, let him f what will come.
44: 8 Did I not proclaim this and f it

Foretells (Foretell)

Dt 13: 1 If a prophet, or one who f by dreams,

Foretold (Foretell)

2Ki 7:17 just as the man of God had f when
23:16 the man of God who f these things.
Ps 105:19 till what he f came to pass, till
Isa 41:26 no-one f it, no-one heard any words
43: 9 Which of them f this and proclaimed
45:21 Who f this long ago, who declared it
48: 3 I f the former things long ago, my
48:14 Which of ⌊the idols⌋ has f these
52: 6 will know that it is I who f it.
Ac 3:18 he had f through all the prophets,
3:24 as have spoken, have f these days.
Jude :17 apostles of our Lord Jesus Christ f.

Forfeit (Forfeiting, Forfeits)

Ezr 10: 8 three days would f all his property,
Jnh 2: 8 f the grace that could be theirs
Mk 8:36 the whole world, yet f his soul?
Lk 9:25 and yet lose or f his very self?

Forfeiting (Forfeit)
Hab 2:10 your own house and f your life.

Forfeits (Forfeit)
Pr 20: 2 lion; he who angers him f his life.
Mt 16:26 the whole world, yet f his soul?

Forgave (Forgive)
Ps 32: 5 and you f the guilt of my sin.
65: 3 by sins, you f our transgressions.
78:38 merciful; he f their iniquities
85: 2 You f the iniquity of your people
Eph 4:32 other, just as in Christ God f you.
Col 2:13 He f us all our sins,
3:13 Forgive as the Lord f you.

Forged (Forges)
Ge 4:22 Tubal-Cain, who f all kinds of tools
Isa 54:17 no weapon f against you will prevail,

Forges (Forged)
Isa 44:12 he f it with the might of his arm.
54:16 and f a weapon fit for its work.

Forget (Forgets, Forgetting, Forgot, Forgotten)
Ge 41:51 God has made me f all my trouble
Dt 4: 9 do not f the things your eyes have
4:23 Be careful not to f the covenant of
4:31 f the covenant with your forefathers,
6:12 be careful that you do not f the
8:11 Be careful that you do not f the
8:14 and you will f the LORD your God,
8:19 If you ever f the LORD your God and
9: 7 Remember this and never f how you
25:19 from under heaven. Do not f!
1Sa 1:11 and not f your servant but give her
2Ki 17:38 Do not f the covenant I have made
Job 8:13 Such is the destiny of all who f God;
9:27 If I say, 'I will f my complaint, I
11:16 You will surely f your trouble,
Ps 9:17 grave, all the nations that f God.
10:12 O God. Do not f the helpless.
13: 1 How long, O LORD? Will you f me for
44:24 you hide your face and f our misery
45:10 consider and give ear: F your people
50:22 "Consider this, you who f God, or I
59:11 Lord our shield, or my people will f.
74:19 do not f the lives of your afflicted
78: 7 would not f his deeds but would keep
102: 4 like grass; I f to eat my food.
103: 2 my soul, and f not all his benefits
119:61 with ropes, I will not f your law.
119:83 the smoke, I do not f your decrees.
119:93 I will never f your precepts, for by
119:109 in my hands, I will not f your law.
119:141 despised, I do not f your precepts.
137: 5 If I f you, O Jerusalem, may my
137: 5 may my right hand f its skill.
Pr 3: 1 My son, do not f my teaching, but
4: 5 not f my words or swerve from them.
31: 5 lest they drink and f what the law
31: 7 let them drink and f their poverty
Isa 43:18 "F the former things; do not dwell
44:21 servant; O Israel, I will not f you.
49:15 "Can a mother f the baby at her
49:15 Though she may f, I will not f you!
51:13 that you f the LORD your Maker, who
54: 4 You will f the shame of your youth
65:11 the LORD and f my holy mountain,
Jer 2:32 Does a maiden f her jewellery, a
23:27 will make my people f my name,
23:39 Therefore, I will surely f you and
Lam 2: 6 The LORD has made Zion f her
5:20 Why do you always f us? Why do you
Eze 39:26 They will f their shame and all the
Am 8: 7 never f anything they have done.
Mic 6:10 Am I still to f, O wicked house,
Heb 6:10 God is not unjust; he will not f
13: 2 Do not f to entertain strangers, for
13:16 do not f to do good and to share
2Pe 3: 5 they deliberately f that long ago by
3: 8 do not f this one thing, dear

Forgets (Forget)
Ge 27:45 with you and f what you did to him,
Job 24:20 The womb f them, the worm feasts on
Jn 16:21 her baby is born she f the anguish
Jas 1:24 immediately f what he looks like.

Forgetting (Forget)
Php 3:13 But one thing I do: F what is behind
Jas 1:25 and continues to do this, not f what

Forgive (Forgave, Forgiven, Forgiveness, Forgives, Forgiving)
Ge 50:17 I ask you to f your brothers the
50:17 Now please f the sins of the
Ex 10:17 Now f my sin once more and pray to
23:21 him; he will not f your rebellion,
32:32 now, please f their sin—but if not,
34: 9 f our wickedness and our sin, and
Nu 14:19 f the sin of these people, just as
Dt 29:20 The LORD will never be willing to f
Jos 24:19 not f your rebellion and your sins.
1Sa 15:25 Now I beg you, f my sin and come
25:28 Please f your servant's offence, for
1Ki 8:30 and when you hear, f.
8:34 hear from heaven and f the sin of
8:36 hear from heaven and f the sin of
8:39 F and act; deal with each man
8:50 f your people, who have sinned
8:50 f all the offences they have
2Ki 5:18 may the LORD f your servant for this
5:18 the LORD f your servant for this."
24: 4 and the LORD was not willing to f.
2Ch 6:21 and when you hear, f.
6:25 hear from heaven and f the sin of
6:27 hear from heaven and f the sin of
6:30 F, and deal with each man according
6:39 And f your people, who have sinned
7:14 f their sin and will heal their land.
Job 7:21 pardon my offences and f my sins?
Ps 19:12 his errors? F my hidden faults.
25:11 f my iniquity, though it is great
79: 9 and f our sins for your name's sake.
Isa 2: 9 and mankind humbled—do not f them.
Jer 5: 1 seeks the truth, I will f this city.
5: 7 "Why should I f you? Your children
18:23 Do not f their crimes or blot out
31:34 "For I will f their wickedness and
33: 8 will f all their sins of rebellion
36: 3 f their wickedness and their sin."
50:20 for I will f the remnant I spare.
Da 9:19 O Lord, listen! O Lord, f! O Lord,
Hos 1: 6 Israel, that I should at all f them.
14: 2 Say to him: "F all our sins and
Am 7: 2 "Sovereign LORD, f! How can Jacob
Mt 6:12 F us our debts, as we also have
6:14 For if you f men when they sin
6:14 heavenly Father will also f you.
6:15 if you do not f men their sins, your
6:15 your Father will not f your sins.
9: 6 Man has authority on earth to f sins.
18:21 how many times shall I f my brother
18:35 you f your brother from your heart."
Mk 2: 7 Who can f sins but God alone?"
2:10 has authority on earth to f sins .
11:25 f him, so that your Father in heaven
11:25 in heaven may f you your sins."
Lk 5:21 Who can f sins but God alone?"
5:24 Man has authority on earth to f sins.
6:37 F, and you will be forgiven.
11: 4 F us our sins, for we also f
17: 3 him, and if he repents, f him.
17: 4 to you and says, 'I repent,' f him."
23:34 Jesus said, "Father, f them, for
Jn 20:23 If you f anyone his sins, they are
20:23 If you f anyone his sins, they are
Ac 8:22 Perhaps he will f you for having
2Co 2: 7 Now instead, you ought to f and
2:10 If you f anyone, I also f him. And
2:10 if there was anything to f—I have
12:13 a burden to you? F me this wrong!
Col 3:13 f whatever grievances you may have
3:13 F as the Lord forgave you.
Heb 8:12 For I will f their wickedness and
1Jn 1: 9 he is faithful and just and will f

Forgiven (Forgive)
Lev 4:20 for them, and they will be f.
4:26 for the man's sin, and he will be f.
4:31 atonement for him, and he will be f.
4:35 he has committed, and he will be f.
5:10 he has committed, and he will be f.
5:13 he has committed, and he will be f.
5:16 a guilt offering, and he will be f.
5:18 unintentionally, and he will be f.
6: 7 and he will be f for any of these
19:22 committed, and his sin will be f.
Nu 14:20 The LORD replied, "I have f them, as
15:25 and they will be f, for it was not
15:26 aliens living among them will be f,
15:28 has been made for him, he will be f.
Ps 32: 1 whose transgressions are f, whose
Isa 33:24 of those who dwell there will be f.
Lam 3:42 and rebelled and you have not f.
Mt 6:12 as we also have f our debtors.
9: 2 "Take heart, son; your sins are f.
9: 5 to say, 'Your sins are f,' or to
12:31 every sin and blasphemy will be f
12:31 against the Spirit will not be f.
12:32 against the Son of Man will be f,
12:32 the Holy Spirit will not be f,
Mk 2: 5 paralytic, "Son, your sins are f.
2: 9 'Your sins are f,' or to say, 'Get
3:28 blasphemies of men will be f them.
3:29 will never be f; he is guilty of an
4:12 they might turn and be f!'"
Lk 5:20 he said, "Friend, your sins are f.
5:23 'Your sins are f,' or to say, 'Get
6:37 Forgive, and you will be f.
7:47 have been f—for she loved much.
7:47 who has been f little loves little."
7:48 Jesus said to her, "Your sins are f."
12:10 against the Son of Man will be f,
12:10 the Holy Spirit will not be f.
Jn 20:23 forgive anyone his sins, they are f
20:23 not forgive them, they are not f."
Ro 4: 7 whose transgressions are f, whose
2Co 2:10 And what I have f—if there was
2:10 I have f in the sight of Christ for
Heb 10:18 where these have been f, there is no
Jas 5:15 If he has sinned, he will be f.
1Jn 2:12 have been f on account of his name.

Forgiveness (Forgive, *Forgiveness of sins*)
Ps 130: 4 with you there is f; therefore you
Lk 1:77 through the f of their sins,
Ac 2:38 Jesus Christ for the f of your sins.
Heb 9:22 the shedding of blood there is no f.

Forgiveness of sins
Mt 26:28 is poured out for many for the f.
Mk 1: 4 a baptism of repentance for the f.
Lk 3: 3 a baptism of repentance for the f.
24:47 repentance and f will be preached in
Ac 5:31 give repentance and f to Israel.
10:43 in him receives f through his name."
13:38 Jesus the f is proclaimed to you.
26:18 so that they may receive f and a
Eph 1: 7 redemption through his blood, the f,
Col 1:14 in whom we have redemption, the f.

Forgives (Forgive)
Ps 103: 3 who f all your sins and heals all
Mic 7:18 pardons sin and f the transgression
Lk 7:49 "Who is this who even f sins?

Forgiving (Forgive)
Ex 34: 7 f wickedness, rebellion and sin
Nu 14:18 in love and f sin and rebellion.
Ne 9:17 But you are a f God, gracious and
Ps 86: 5 You are f and good, O Lord,
99: 8 them; you were to Israel a f God,
Da 9: 9 The Lord our God is merciful and f,
Eph 4:32 f each other, just as in Christ God

Forgo
Ne 10:31 Every seventh year we will f working

Forgot (Forget)
Ge 40:23 did not remember Joseph; he **f** him.
Dt 32:18 you **f** the God who gave you birth.
Jdg 3: 7 they **f** the LORD their God and served
1Sa 12: 9 "But they **f** the LORD their God; so
Ps 78:11 They **f** what he had done, the wonders
106:13 they soon **f** what he had done and did
106:21 They **f** the God who saved them, who
Jer 23:27 **f** my name through Baal worship.
50: 6 hill and **f** their own resting place.
Hos 2:13 went after her lovers, but me she **f**,"
13: 6 they became proud; then they **f** me.
Mt 16: 5 lake, the disciples **f** to take bread.

Forgotten (Forget)
Ge 41:30 the abundance in Egypt will be **f**,
Dt 26:13 commands nor have I **f** any of them.
31:21 will not be **f** by their descendants.
Job 11: 6 God has even **f** some of your sin.
19:14 gone away; my friends have **f** me.
28: 4 in places **f** by the foot of man; far
Ps 9:18 the needy will not always be **f**, nor
10:11 He says to himself, "God has **f**; he
31:12 I am **f** by them as though I were dead;
42: 9 to God my Rock, "Why have you **f** me?
44:17 we had not **f** you or been false
44:20 If we had **f** the name of our God or
77: 9 Has God **f** to be merciful? Has he in
119:153 me, for I have not **f** your law.
119:176 for I have not **f** your commands.
Ecc 2:16 in days to come both will be **f**.
9: 5 and even the memory of them is **f**.
Isa 17:10 You have **f** God your Saviour; you
23:15 At that time Tyre will be **f** for
23:16 O prostitute **f**; play the harp well,
49:14 has forsaken me, the Lord has **f** me."
65:16 will be **f** and hidden from my eyes.
Jer 2:32 Yet my people have **f** me, days
3:21 ways and have **f** the LORD their God.
13:25 have **f** me and trusted in false gods.
18:15 Yet my people have **f** me; they burn
20:11 their dishonour will never be **f**.
23:40 shame that will not be **f**."
30:14 All your allies have **f** you; they
44: 9 Have you **f** the wickedness committed
50: 5 covenant that will not be **f**.
Lam 3:17 peace; I have **f** what prosperity is.
Eze 22:12 you have **f** me, declares the
23:35 **f** me and thrust me behind your back,
Hos 8:14 Israel has **f** his Maker and built
Mk 8:14 The disciples had **f** to bring bread,
Lk 12: 6 Yet not one of them is **f** by God.
Heb 12: 5 have **f** that word of encouragement
2Pe 1: 9 and has **f** that he has been cleansed

Fork (Forks)
1Sa 2:13 with a three-pronged **f** in his hand.
2:14 himself whatever the **f** brought up.
Isa 30:24 mash, spread out with **f** and shovel.
Jer 15: 7 I will winnow them with a winnowing **f**
Eze 21:21 will stop at the **f** in the road,
Mt 3:12 His winnowing **f** is in his hand, and
Lk 3:17 His winnowing **f** is in his hand to

Forks (Fork)
Ex 27: 3 bowls, meat **f** and firepans.
38: 3 bowls, meat **f** and firepans.
Nu 4:14 **f**, shovels and sprinkling bowls.
1Sa 13:21 **f** and axes and for repointing goads.
1Ch 28:17 the weight of pure gold for the **f**,
2Ch 4:16 the pots, shovels, meat **f** and all

Forlorn
Ps 35:12 evil for good and leave my soul **f**.

Form (Deformed, Formation, Formed, Forming, Forms)
Ge 29:17 was lovely in **f**, and beautiful.
Ex 20: 4 an idol in the **f** of anything in
Nu 12: 8 riddles; he sees the **f** of the LORD.
Dt 4:12 saw no **f**; there was only a voice.
4:15 You saw no **f** of any kind the day the
4:23 an idol in the **f** of anything the
5: 8 in the **f** of anything in heaven
1Ki 6:16 to **f** within the temple an inner
Est 2: 7 was lovely in **f** and features, and
Job 4:16 A **f** stood before my eyes, and I
31:15 Did not the same one **f** us both
41:12 his strength and his graceful **f**.
Ps 83: 5 they **f** an alliance against you—
Isa 44:13 He shapes it in the **f** of man, of man
45: 7 I **f** the light and create darkness, I
52:14 his **f** marred beyond human likeness—
Jer 11:16 tree with fruit beautiful in **f**.
Eze 1: 5 their **f** was that of a man,
Mk 16:12 Jesus appeared in a different **f** to
Lk 3:22 on him in bodily **f** like a dove.
Jn 5:37 heard his voice nor seen his **f**,
Ac 7:41 made an idol in the **f** of a calf.
14:11 have come down to us in human **f**!"
Ro 6:17 obeyed the **f** of teaching to which
12: 5 in Christ we who are many **f** one body,
1Co 7:31 in its present **f** is passing away.
12:12 its parts are many, they **f** one body.
Eph 4:31 along with every **f** of malice.
Col 2: 9 of the Deity lives in bodily **f**,
2Ti 3: 5 having a **f** of godliness but denying

Formation (Form)
2Sa 10: 8 in battle **f** at the entrance to their
1Ch 19: 9 drew up in battle **f** at the entrance
Jer 6:23 like men in battle **f** to attack you,
50:42 like men in battle **f** to attack you,

Formed (Form)
Ge 2: 7 the LORD God **f** the man from the dust
2: 8 and there he put the man he had **f**.
2:19 Now the LORD God had **f** out of the
Dt 4:16 whether **f** like a man or a woman,
32: 6 Creator, who made you and **f** you?
Jos 18:20 The Jordan **f** the boundary on the
2Sa 2:25 They **f** themselves into a group and
10:17 The Arameans **f** their battle lines to
1Ch 19:17 **f** his battle lines opposite them.
19:17 David **f** his lines to meet the
Job 1:17 "The Chaldeans **f** three raiding
Ps 65: 6 who **f** the mountains by your power,
94: 9 hear? Does he who **f** the eye not see?
95: 5 it, and his hands **f** the dry land.
103:14 for he knows how we are **f**, he
104:26 which you **f** to frolic there.
119:73 Your hands made me and **f** me; give me
Ecc 11: 5 or how the body is **f** in a mother's
Isa 29:16 Shall what is **f** say to him who **f** it,
43: 1 O Jacob, he who **f** you, O Israel:
43: 7 for my glory, whom I **f** and made."
43:10 Before me no god was **f**, nor will
43:21 the people I **f** for myself that they
44: 2 who **f** you in the womb, and who will
44:24 who **f** you in the womb: I am the LORD,
45:18 but **f** it to be inhabited—he says:
49: 5 now the LORD says—he who **f** me in
Jer 1: 5 "Before I **f** you in the womb I knew
18: 4 so the potter **f** it into another pot,
33: 2 the LORD who **f** it and established it
Eze 16: 7 Your breasts were **f** and your hair
45: 7 the area **f** by the sacred district
48:21 of the area **f** by the sacred portion
Mt 13:26 the wheat sprouted and **f** ears, then
Ac 17: 5 **f** a mob and started a riot in the
23:12 the Jews **f** a conspiracy and
Ro 9:20 "Shall what is **f** say to him who **f** it,
Gal 4:19 childbirth until Christ is **f** in you,
1Ti 2:13 For Adam was **f** first, then Eve.
Heb 11: 3 the universe was **f** at God's command,
2Pe 3: 5 was **f** out of water and by water.

Forming (Form)
Isa 30: 1 **f** an alliance, but not by my Spirit,
Eze 41: 8 **f** the foundation of the side rooms.
Zec 14: 4 from east to west, **f** a great valley

Formless
Ge 1: 2 Now the earth was **f** and empty,
Jer 4:23 I looked at the earth, and it was **f**

Forms (Form)
Ge 41:32 dream was given to Pharaoh in two **f**
Lev 26:30 on the lifeless **f** of your idols,
Ps 33:15 he who **f** the hearts of all, who
49:14 their **f** will decay in the grave,
SS 2:13 The fig-tree **f** its early fruit; the
Jer 16:18 the lifeless **f** of their vile images
Am 4:13 He who **f** the mountains, creates the
Zec 12: 1 and who **f** the spirit of man within
1Pe 4:10 God's grace in its various **f**.

Formula
Ex 30:32 do not make any oil with the same **f**.
30:37 Do not make any incense with this **f**

Forsake (Forsaken, Forsakes, Forsaking, Forsook)
Dt 31: 6 he will never leave you nor **f** you."
31: 8 he will never leave you nor **f** you.
31:16 They will **f** me and break the
31:17 become angry with them and **f** them;
Jos 1: 5 I will never leave you nor **f** you.
24:16 to **f** the LORD to serve other gods!
24:20 If you **f** the LORD and serve foreign
1Ki 8:57 may he never leave us nor **f** us.
2Ki 21:14 I will **f** the remnant of my
1Ch 28: 9 **f** him, he will reject you for ever.
28:20 He will not fail you or **f** you until
2Ch 7:19 if you turn away and **f** the decrees
15: 2 but if you **f** him, he will **f** you.
Ezr 8:22 anger is against all who **f** him."
Ps 27: 9 reject me or **f** me, O God my Saviour.
27:10 Though my father and mother **f** me,
37:28 and will not **f** his faithful ones.
38:21 O LORD, do not **f** me; be not far
71: 9 not **f** me when my strength is gone.
71:18 when I am old and grey, do not **f** me,
89:30 "If his sons **f** my law and do not
94:14 he will never **f** his inheritance.
119: 8 your decrees; do not utterly **f** me.
Pr 1: 8 and do not **f** your mother's teaching.
4: 2 learning, so do not **f** my teaching.
4: 6 Do not **f** wisdom, and she will
6:20 and do not **f** your mother's teaching.
27:10 Do not **f** your friend and the friend
28: 4 Those who **f** the law praise the
Isa 1:28 those who **f** the LORD will perish.
41:17 the God of Israel, will not **f** them.
42:16 things I will do; I will not **f** them.
55: 7 Let the wicked **f** his way and the
65:11 "But as for you who **f** the LORD and
Jer 2:19 bitter it is for you when you **f** the
12: 7 "I will **f** my house, abandon my
14: 9 and we bear your name; do not **f** us!
17:13 all who **f** you will be put to shame.
23:33 I will **f** you, declares the LORD.'
Lam 5:20 forget us? Why do you **f** us so long?
Eze 20: 8 nor did they **f** the idols of Egypt.
Da 11:30 to those who **f** the holy covenant.
Heb 13: 5 I leave you; never will I **f** you."

Forsaken (Forsake)
Jdg 10:13 you have **f** me and served other gods,
1Sa 12:10 'We have sinned; we have **f** the LORD
1Ki 9: 9 'Because they have **f** the LORD their
11:33 will do this because they have **f** me
2Ki 22:17 they have **f** me and burned incense to
2Ch 7:22 'Because they have **f** the LORD, the
13:10 is our God, and we have not **f** him.
13:11 LORD our God. But you have **f** him.
21:10 **f** the LORD, the God of his fathers.
24:20 you have **f** the LORD, he has **f** you.'"
24:24 Because Judah had **f** the LORD, the
28: 6 **f** the LORD, the God of their fathers.
34:25 they have **f** me and burned incense to
Ps 9:10 have never **f** those who seek you.
22: 1 My God, my God, why have you **f** me?
37:25 I have never seen the righteous **f**
71:11 They say, "God has **f** him; pursue him
119:53 of the wicked, who have **f** your law.
119:87 but I have not **f** your precepts.
Isa 1: 4 to corruption! They have **f** the LORD;
6:12 far away and the land is utterly **f**.
27:10 an abandoned settlement, **f** like the
49:14 Zion said, "The LORD has **f** me, the

Isa 58: 2 has not f the commands of its God.
60:15 "Although you have been f and hated,
Jer 2:13 committed two sins: They have f me,
5: 7 Your children have f me and sworn by
5:19 'As you have f me and served foreign
9:13 "It is because they have f my law,
17:13 dust because they have f the LORD,
19: 4 For they have f me and made this a
22: 9 'Because they have f the covenant of
51: 5 For Israel and Judah have not been f
Eze 8:12 see us; the LORD has f the land.'"
9: 9 They say, 'The LORD has *f* the land
Mt 27:46 "My God, my God, why have you f me?
Mk 15:34 "My God, my God, why have you f me?
Rev 2: 4 you: You have f your first love.

Forsakes (Forsake)
Job 6:14 he f the fear of the Almighty.

Forsaking (Forsake)
Dt 28:20 of the evil you have done in f him.
Jdg 10:10 f our God and serving the Baals."
1Sa 8: 8 f me and serving other gods, so they
Isa 57: 8 F me, you uncovered your bed, you
Jer 1:16 because of their wickedness in f me,
2:17 this on yourselves by f the LORD
Eze 20:27 your fathers blasphemed me by f me:

Forsook (Forsake)
Jdg 2:12 They f the LORD, the God of their
2:13 they f him and served Baal and the
10: 6 f the LORD and no longer served him,
2Ki 17:16 They f all the commands of the LORD
21:22 He f the LORD, the God of his
2Ch 29: 6 eyes of the LORD our God and f him.
Jer 16:11 'It is because your fathers f me,'
16:11 They f me and did not keep my law.

Fortieth (Forty)
Nu 33:38 of the fifth month of the f year
Dt 1: 3 In the f year, on the first day of
1Ch 26:31 In the f year of David's reign a

Fortifications
2Sa 20:15 and it stood against the outer f.

Fortified (Fortifies)
Nu 13:19 live in? Are they unwalled or f?
13:28 and the cities are f and very large.
21:24 because their border was f.
32:17 and children will live in f cities,
32:36 and Beth Haran as f cities, and
Dt 3: 5 All these cities were f with high
28:52 f walls in which you trust fall down.
Jos 10:20 were left reached their f cities.
14:12 and their cities were large and f,
19:29 Ramah and went to the f city of Tyre,
19:35 The f cities were Ziddim, Zer,
1Sa 6:18 f towns with their country villages.
2Sa 20: 6 find f cities and escape from us."
1Ki 12:25 Jeroboam f Shechem in the hill
15:17 f Ramah to prevent anyone from
22:39 and the cities he f, are they not
2Ki 3:19 You will overthrow every f city and
8:12 "You will set fire to their f places,
10: 2 and horses, a f city and weapons,
17: 9 From watchtower to f city they built
18: 8 From watchtower to f city, he
18:13 f cities of Judah and captured them.
19:25 turned f cities into piles of stone.
2Ch 8: 5 and Lower Beth Horon as f cities,
11:10 were f cities in Judah and Benjamin.
11:23 Benjamin, and to all the f cities.
12: 4 he captured the f cities of Judah
14: 6 He built up the f cities of Judah,
16: 1 f Ramah to prevent anyone from
17: 2 stationed troops in all the f cities
17:19 in the f cities throughout Judah.
19: 5 in each of the f cities of Judah.
21: 3 as well as f cities in Judah, but he
26: 9 angle of the wall, and he f them.
32: 1 He laid siege to the f cities,
33:14 in all the f cities in Judah.
Ne 9:25 They captured f cities and fertile
Ps 60: 9 Who will bring me to the f city? Who
108:10 Who will bring me to the f city? Who
Pr 10:15 wealth of the rich is their f city
18:11 wealth of the rich is their f city
18:19 is more unyielding than a f city,
Isa 2:15 every lofty tower and every f wall
17: 3 The f city will disappear from
25: 2 a heap of rubble, the f town a ruin,
25:12 He will bring down your high f walls
27:10 The f city stands desolate, an
36: 1 f cities of Judah and captured them.
37:26 turned f cities into piles of stone.
Jer 1:18 Today I have made you a f city, an
4: 5 Let us flee to the f cities!'
5:17 the f cities in which you trust.
8:14 Let us flee to the f cities and
15:20 a f wall of bronze; they will fight
34: 7 the only f cities left in Judah.
48:18 against you and ruin your f cities.
Eze 21:20 against Judah and f Jerusalem.
36:35 destroyed, are now f and inhabited."
Da 11:15 ramps and will capture a f city.
Hos 8:14 palaces; Judah has f many towns.
Am 5: 9 and brings the f city to ruin),
Hab 1:10 They laugh at all f cities; they
Zep 1:16 battle cry against the f cities and

Fortifies (Fortified)
Jer 51:53 and f her lofty stronghold, I will

Fortress (Fortresses)
2Sa 5: 7 David captured the f of Zion,
5: 9 David then took up residence in the f
22: 2 He said: "The LORD is my rock, my f
24: 7 they went towards the f of Tyre and
1Ch 11: 5 the f of Zion, the City of David.
11: 7 David then took up residence in the f
Ps 18: 2 The LORD is my rock, my f and my
28: 8 a f of salvation for his anointed
31: 2 of refuge, a strong f to save me.
31: 3 Since you are my rock and my f, for
46: 7 with us; the God of Jacob is our f.
46:11 with us; the God of Jacob is our f.
48: 3 he has shown himself to be her f.
59: 9 watch for you; you, O God, are my f,
59:16 my f, my refuge in times of trouble.
59:17 you, O God, are my f, my loving God.
62: 2 he is my f, I shall never be shaken.
62: 6 he is my f, I shall not be shaken.
71: 3 me, for you are my rock and my f.
91: 2 and my f, my God, in whom I trust."
94:22 the LORD has become my f, and my God
144: 2 He is my loving God and my f, my
Pr 14:26 He who fears the LORD has a secure f,
Isa 17:10 not remembered the Rock, your f.
23: 4 O Sidon, and you, O f of the sea,
23:14 of Tarshish; your f is destroyed!
29: 7 that attack her and her f and
32:14 The f will be abandoned, the noisy
33:16 whose refuge will be the mountain f.
Jer 16:19 O LORD, my strength and my f, my
Da 11: 7 king of the North and enter his f;
11:10 carry the battle as far as his f.
11:31 rise up to desecrate the temple f
Na 2: 1 Guard the f, watch the road, brace
Zec 9:12 Return to your f, O prisoners of

Fortresses (Fortress)
Isa 23:11 Phoenicia that her f be destroyed.
23:13 they stripped its f bare and turned
Jer 6: 5 attack at night and destroy her f!"
9:21 our windows and has entered our f;
17:27 Jerusalem that will consume her f.'"
49:27 it will consume the f of Ben-Hadad."
Da 11:19 turn back towards the f of his own
11:24 overthrow of f—but only for a time.
11:38 he will honour a god of f; a god
11:39 He will attack the mightiest f with
Hos 8:14 cities that will consume their f."
10:14 so that all your f will be
Am 1: 4 will consume the f of Ben-Hadad.
1: 7 of Gaza that will consume her f.
1:10 of Tyre that will consume her f."
1:12 that will consume the f of Bozrah."
1:14 will consume her f amid war cries
Am 2: 2 that will consume the f of Kerioth.
2: 5 will consume the f of Jerusalem."
3: 9 Proclaim to the f of Ashdod and to
3: 9 f of Ashdod and to the f of Egypt:
3:10 hoard plunder and loot in their f."
3:11 strongholds and plunder your f."
6: 8 the pride of Jacob and detest his f;
Mic 5: 5 our land and marches through our f,
Na 3:12 All your f are like fig-trees with

Forts
2Ch 17:12 he built f and store cities in
27: 4 f and towers in the wooded areas.

Fortunate (Fortune)
Ac 26: 2 "King Agrippa, I consider myself f

Fortunatus
1Co 16:17 I was glad when Stephanas, F and

Fortune (Fortunate, Fortunes, Fortune-telling)
Ge 30:11 Leah said, "What good f!" So she
Job 31:25 wealth, the f my hands had gained,
Pr 21: 6 A f made by a lying tongue is a
Isa 65:11 who spread a table for F and fill

Fortunes (Fortune)
Dt 30: 3 the LORD your God will restore your f
Ps 14: 7 LORD restores the f of his people,
53: 6 God restores the f of his people,
85: 1 O LORD; you restored the f of Jacob.
126: 4 Restore our f, O LORD, like streams
Jer 30:18 "'I will restore the f of Jacob's
32:44 restore their f, declares the LORD."
33:11 For I will restore the f of the
33:26 restore their f and have compassion
48:47 "Yet I will restore the f of Moab in
49: 6 will restore the f of the Ammonites
49:39 "Yet I will restore the f of Elam in
Eze 16:53 I will restore the f of Sodom
16:53 and your f along with them,
Hos 6:11 I would restore the f of my people,
Joel 3: 1 the f of Judah and Jerusalem,
Mic 3:11 and her prophets tell f for money.
Zep 2: 7 for them; he will restore their f.
3:20 restore your f before your very eyes

Fortune-telling (Fortune)
Ac 16:16 deal of money for her owners by f.

Forty (Fortieth, *Forty days, Forty nights, Forty years*)
Ge 18:29 "What if only f are found there?" He
18:29 For the sake of f, I will not do it."
32:15 f cows and ten bulls, and twenty
Ex 26:19 make f silver bases to go under them
26:21 f silver bases—two under each frame.
36:24 made f silver bases to go under them
36:26 f silver bases—two under each frame.
Dt 25: 3 not give him more than f lashes.
Jos 4:13 About f thousand armed for battle
Jdg 5: 8 was seen among f thousand in Israel.
12:14 He had f sons and thirty grandsons,
2Sa 10:18 f thousand of their foot soldiers.
1Ki 6:17 of this room was f cubits long.
7:38 each holding f baths and measuring
2Ki 8: 9 with him as a gift f camel-loads
1Ch 19:18 f thousand of their foot soldiers.
Ne 5:15 took f shekels of silver from them
Eze 41: 2 f cubits long and twenty cubits wide.
46:22 f cubits long and thirty cubits wide;
Jnh 3: 4 He proclaimed: "F more days and
Ac 23:13 More than f men were involved in
23:21 because more than f of them are
2Co 11:24 the Jews the f lashes minus one.

Forty days
Ge 7: 4 on the earth for f and forty nights,
7:12 rain fell on the earth for f and
7:17 For f the flood kept coming on the
8: 6 After f Noah opened the window he
50: 3 taking a full f, for that was the
Ex 24:18 on the mountain f and forty nights.

Ex 34:28 Moses was there with the LORD **f** and
Nu 13:25 At the end of **f** they returned from
14:34 one year for each of the **f** you
Dt 9: 9 I stayed on the mountain **f** and forty
9:11 At the end of the **f** and forty nights,
9:18 the LORD for **f** and forty nights;
9:25 prostrate before the LORD those **f**
10:10 Now I had stayed on the mountain **f**
1Sa 17:16 For **f** the Philistine came forward
1Ki 19: 8 he travelled for **f** and forty nights
Mt 4: 2 After fasting for **f** and forty nights,
Mk 1:13 he was in the desert for **f**, being
Lk 4: 2 where for **f** he was tempted by the
Ac 1: 3 appeared to them over a period of **f**

Forty Nights

Ge 7: 4 on the earth for forty days and **f**,
7:12 on the earth for forty days and **f**.
Ex 24:18 on the mountain forty days and **f**.
34:28 **f** without eating bread or drinking
Dt 9: 9 on the mountain forty days and **f**;
9:11 At the end of the forty days and **f**,
9:18 forty days and **f**; I ate no bread
9:25 those forty days and **f** because the
1Ki 19: 8 he travelled for forty days and **f**
Mt 4: 2 After fasting for forty days and **f**,

Forty years

Ge 25:20 Isaac was **f** old when he married
26:34 Esau was **f** old, he married Judith
Ex 16:35 The Israelites ate manna for **f**,
Nu 14:33 will be shepherds here for **f**,
14:34 For **f**—one year for each of the
32:13 them wander in the desert for **f**,
Dt 2: 7 These **f** the LORD your God has been
8: 2 all the way in the desert these **f**,
8: 4 feet did not swell during these **f**.
29: 5 During the **f** that I led you through
Jos 5: 6 in the desert **f** until all the men
14: 7 I was **f** old when Moses the servant
Jdg 3:11 the land had peace for **f**, until
5:31 Then the land had peace for **f**.
8:28 the land enjoyed peace for **f**.
13: 1 the hands of the Philistines for **f**.
1Sa 4:18 He had led Israel for **f**.
2Sa 2:10 Ish-Bosheth son of Saul was **f** old
5: 4 became king, and he reigned for **f**.
1Ki 2:11 He had reigned for **f** over Israel
11:42 in Jerusalem over all Israel for **f**.
2Ki 12: 1 and he reigned in Jerusalem for **f**.
1Ch 29:27 He ruled over Israel for **f**—seven in
2Ch 9:30 in Jerusalem over all Israel for **f**.
24: 1 and he reigned in Jerusalem for **f**.
Ne 9:21 For **f** you sustained them in the
Job 42:16 After this, Job lived a hundred and **f**
Ps 95:10 For **f** I was angry with that
Eze 29:11 it; no-one will live there for **f**.
29:12 desolate for **f** among ruined cities.
29:13 At the end of **f** I will gather the
Am 2:10 and I led you for **f** in the desert to
5:25 and offerings for **f** in the desert,
Ac 4:22 miraculously healed was over **f** old.
7:23 "When Moses was **f** old, he decided to
7:30 "After **f** had passed, an angel
7:36 the Red Sea and for **f** in the desert.
7:42 and offerings for **f** in the desert,
13:18 he endured their conduct for about **f**
13:21 tribe of Benjamin, who ruled for **f**.
Heb 3: 9 tried me and for **f** saw what I did.
3:17 with whom was he angry for **f**? Was it

Forum

Ac 28:15 and they travelled as far as the **F**

Foster

Isa 49:23 Kings will be your **f** fathers, and

Fought (Fight)

Ex 17:10 Joshua **f** the Amalekites as Moses had
Nu 21:23 he reached Jahaz, he **f** with Israel.
21:26 who had **f** against the former king of
31: 7 They **f** against Midian, as the LORD
31:28 the soldiers who **f** in the battle
31:36 The half share of those who **f** in the
Jos 10:42 the God of Israel, **f** for Israel.
23: 3 was the LORD your God who **f** for you.
24: 8 They **f** against you, but I gave them
24:11 The citizens of Jericho **f** against
Jdg 1: 5 found Adoni-Bezek and **f** against him,
5:19 "Kings came, they **f**; the kings of
5:19 they **f**; the kings of Canaan **f** at
5:20 From the heavens the stars **f**, from
5:20 their courses they **f** against Sisera.
9:17 to think that my father **f** for you,
9:39 citizens of Shechem and **f** Abimelech.
11:20 encamped at Jahaz and **f** with Israel.
12: 4 men of Gilead and **f** against Ephraim.
1Sa 4:10 the Philistines **f**, and the
12: 9 king of Moab, who **f** against them.
14:47 he **f** against their enemies on every
14:48 He **f** valiantly and defeated the
19: 8 David went out and **f** the Philistines.
23: 5 went to Keilah, **f** the Philistines
30:17 David **f** them from dusk until the
31: 1 Now the Philistines **f** against Israel;
2Sa 8: 3 David **f** Hadadezer son of Rehob,
10:17 to meet David and **f** against him.
11:17 the men of the city came out and **f**
12:26 Meanwhile Joab **f** against Rabbah of
12:27 "I have **f** against Rabbah and taken
2Ki 3:23 "Those kings must have **f** and
3:24 rose up and **f** them until they fled.
1Ch 10: 1 Now the Philistines **f** against Israel;
18: 3 David **f** Hadadezer king of Zobah,
19:17 in battle, and they **f** against him.
22: 8 much blood and have **f** many wars.
2Ch 20:29 had **f** against the enemies of Israel.
Ps 60: T When he **f** Aram Naharaim and
Isa 63:10 enemy and he himself **f** against them.
Zec 14:12 nations that **f** against Jerusalem:
1Co 15:32 If I **f** wild beasts in Ephesus for
2Ti 4: 7 I have **f** the good fight, I have
Rev 12: 7 Michael and his angels **f** against the
12: 7 the dragon and his angels **f** back.

Found (Find)

Ge 2:20 for Adam no suitable helper was **f**.
4:15 no-one who **f** him would kill him.
6: 8 Noah **f** favour in the eyes of the
7: 1 **f** you righteous in this generation.
9:24 Noah awoke from his wine and **f** out
11: 2 men moved eastward, they **f** a plain
16: 7 The angel of the LORD **f** Hagar near a
18: 3 He said, "If I have **f** favour in your
18:29 "What if only forty are **f** there?" He
18:30 What if only thirty can be **f** there?"
18:31 what if only twenty can be **f** there?"
18:32 What if only ten can be **f** there?" He
19:19 Your servant has **f** favour in your
24:30 he went out to the man and **f** him
26:32 They said, "We've **f** water!"
30:14 fields and **f** some mandrake plants,
30:27 Laban said to him, "If I have **f**
31:33 two maidservants, but he **f** nothing.
31:34 in the tent but **f** nothing.
31:37 what have you **f** that belongs to your
33:10 "If I have **f** favour in your eyes,
37:15 a man **f** him wandering around in the
37:17 his brothers and **f** them near Dothan.
37:32 their father and said, "We **f** this.
39: 4 Joseph **f** favour in his eyes and
43:21 each of us **f** his silver—the exact
44: 8 we **f** inside the mouths of our sacks.
44: 9 If any of your servants is **f** to have
44:10 Whoever is **f** to have it will become
44:12 And the cup was **f** in Benjamin's sack.
44:16 the one who was **f** to have the cup."
44:17 Only the man who was **f** to have the
47:14 the money that was to be **f** in Egypt
47:29 "If I have **f** favour in your eyes,
50: 4 "If I have **f** favour in your eyes,
Ex 5:20 they left Pharaoh, they **f** Moses and
9: 7 Pharaoh sent men to investigate and **f**
12:19 For seven days no yeast is to be **f**
16:27 day to gather it, but they **f** none.
22: 4 "If the stolen animal is **f** alive in
22: 8 if the thief is not **f**, the owner of
33:12 name and you have **f** favour with me.'
34: 9 "O Lord, if I have **f** favour in your
Lev 6: 4 to him, or the lost property he **f**,
7:24 The fat of an animal **f** dead or torn
10:16 and **f** that it had been burned up,
17:15 who eats anything **f** dead or torn by
22: 8 He must not eat anything **f** dead or
Nu 11:15 if I have **f** favour in your eyes—
15:32 **f** gathering wood on the Sabbath day.
15:33 Those who **f** him gathering wood
23: 6 he went back to him and **f** him
23:17 he went to him and **f** him standing
32: 5 If we have **f** favour in your eyes,"
Dt 13:17 things shall be **f** in your hands,
15: 9 and you will be **f** guilty of sin.
16: 4 Let no yeast be **f** in your possession
17: 2 is **f** doing evil in the eyes of the
18:10 Let no-one be **f** among you who
21: 1 If a man is **f** slain, lying in a
22:20 of the girl's virginity can be **f**,
22:22 If a man is **f** sleeping with another
22:27 for the man **f** the girl out in the
32:10 In a desert land he **f** him, in a
Jos 10:17 **f** hiding in the cave at Makkedah,
Jdg 1: 5 was there that they **f** Adoni-Bezek
3:24 **f** the doors of the upper room locked.
6:17 Gideon replied, "If now I have **f**
20:48 animals and everything else they **f**.
21: 9 they **f** that none of the people of
21:12 They **f** among the people living in
Ru 2: 3 she **f** herself working in a field
2:10 She exclaimed, "Why have I **f** such
1Sa 9:20 worry about them; they have been **f**.
10: 2 you set out to look for have been **f**.
10:14 not to be **f**, we went to Samuel."
10:16 us that the donkeys had been **f**.
10:21 looked for him, he was not to be **f**.
12: 5 you have not **f** anything in my hand.
13:19 Not a blacksmith could be **f** in the
14:20 They **f** the Philistines in total
20: 3 that I have **f** favour in your eyes,
20:29 If I have **f** favour in your eyes, let
25:28 Let no wrongdoing be **f** in you
27: 5 David said to Achish, "If I have **f**
29: 3 now, I have **f** no fault in him."
29: 6 I have **f** no fault in you, but the
29: 8 "What have you **f** against your
30: 3 they **f** it destroyed by fire and
30: 6 David **f** strength in the LORD his God.
30:11 They **f** an Egyptian in a field and
31: 8 they **f** Saul and his three sons
2Sa 2:30 of David's men were **f** missing.
7:27 **f** courage to offer you this prayer.
14:22 that he has **f** favour in your eyes,
17:12 attack him wherever he may be **f**,
17:13 not even a piece of it can be **f**."
17:20 The men searched but **f** no-one, so
1Ki 1: 3 for a beautiful girl and **f** Abishag,
1:52 if evil is **f** in him, he will die."
13:14 rode after the man of God. He **f** him
13:28 he went out and **f** the body thrown
14:13 God of Israel, has **f** anything good.
19:19 Elijah went from there and **f** Elisha
20:36 away, a lion **f** him and killed him.
20:37 The prophet **f** another man and said,
21:20 Ahab said to Elijah, "So you have **f**
21:20 "I have **f** you," he answered,
2Ki 4:39 to gather herbs and **f** a wild vine.
7:15 and they **f** the whole road strewn
9: 5 he arrived, he **f** the army officers
9:35 they **f** nothing except her skull, her
12: 5 whatever damage is **f** in the temple."
12:18 all the gold **f** in the treasuries of
14:14 and all the articles **f** in the temple
16: 8 Ahaz took the silver and gold **f** in
18:15 was **f** in the temple of the LORD
19: 8 **f** the king fighting against Libnah.
20:13 everything **f** among his treasures.
22: 8 "I have **f** the Book of the Law in the
22:13 in this book that has been **f**.
23: 2 been **f** in the temple of the LORD.
25:19 of his men who were **f** in the city.
1Ch 4:40 They **f** rich, good pasture, and the
10: 8 they **f** Saul and his sons fallen on
17:25 has **f** courage to pray to you.
20: 2 weight was **f** to be a talent of gold,
24: 4 A larger number of leaders were **f**
26:31 Hebronites were **f** at Jazer in Gilead.

1Ch 28: 9 If you seek him, he will be **f** by you;
2Ch 2:17 and they were **f** to be 153,600.
15: 2 If you seek him, he will be **f** by you,
15: 4 sought him, and he was **f** by them.
15:15 God eagerly, and he was **f** by them.
20:25 and they **f** among them a great amount
21:17 the goods **f** in the king's palace,
22: 8 he **f** the princes of Judah and the
25: 5 **f** that there were three hundred
25:24 and all the articles **f** in the temple
29:16 they **f** in the temple of the LORD.
34:14 Hilkiah the priest **f** the Book of the
34:15 "I have **f** the Book of the Law in the
34:21 in this book that has been **f**.
34:30 been **f** in the temple of the LORD.
36: 8 did and all that was **f** against him,
Ezr 4:19 and it was **f** that this city has a
6: 2 A scroll was **f** in the citadel of
8:15 the priests, I **f** no Levites there.
Ne 2: 5 servant has **f**avour in his sight,
7: 5 I **f** the genealogical record of those
7: 5 This is what I **f** written there:
8:14 They **f** written in the Law, which the
9: 8 You **f** his heart faithful to you, and
13: 1 there it was **f** written that no
Est 2:22 Mordecai **f** out about the plot and
2:23 was investigated and **f** to be true,
6: 2 was **f** recorded there that Mordecai
7: 3 Queen Esther answered, "If I have **f**
Job 9:29 Since I am already **f** guilty, why
12:12 Is not wisdom **f** among the aged? Does
20: 8 no more to be **f**, banished like a
28:12 "But where can wisdom be **f**? Where
28:13 it cannot be **f** in the land
32: 3 because they had **f** no way to refute
32:13 Do not say, 'We have **f** wisdom; let
33:10 Yet God has **f** fault with me; he
33:24 pit; I have **f** a ransom for him'—
42:15 Nowhere in all the land were there **f**
Ps 10:15 wickedness that would not be **f** out.
32: 6 pray to you while you may be **f**;
37:10 look for them, they will not be **f**.
37:36 I looked for him, he could not be **f**.
69:20 none, for comforters, but I **f** none.
84: 3 Even the sparrow has **f** a home, and
89:20 I have **f** David my servant; with my
109: 7 he is tried, let him be **f** guilty,
109:17 he **f** no pleasure in blessing—may
Pr 7:15 I looked for you and have **f** you!
10: 9 takes crooked paths will be **f** out.
10:13 Wisdom is **f** on the lips of the
13:10 wisdom is **f** in those who take
14: 9 but goodwill is **f** among the upright.
19: 7 pleading, they are nowhere to be **f**.
30:28 hand, yet it is **f** in kings' palaces.
Ecc 7:28 I **f** one upright man among a thousand,
7:29 This only have I **f**: God made mankind
SS 3: 3 The watchmen **f** me as they made their
3: 4 when I **f** the one my heart loves.
5: 7 The watchmen **f** me as they made their
8: 1 if I **f** you outside, I would kiss you,
Isa 30:14 not a fragment will be **f** for taking
35: 9 up on it; they will not be **f** there.
37: 8 **f** the king fighting against Libnah.
39: 2 everything **f** among his treasures.
45:25 will be **f** righteous and will exult.
51: 3 Joy and gladness will be **f** in her,
55: 6 Seek the LORD while he may be **f**;
57:10 You **f** renewal of your strength, and
59:15 Truth is nowhere to be **f**, and
65: 1 I was **f** by those who did not seek me.
65: 8 when juice is still **f** in a cluster
Jer 29:14 I will be **f** by you," declares the
40: 1 He had **f** Jeremiah bound in chains
40: 2 commander of the guard **f** Jeremiah
50: 7 Whoever **f** them devoured them; their
50:20 but none will be **f**, for I will
50:24 you were **f** and captured because you
52:25 of his men who were **f** in the city.
Eze 4:14 **f** dead or torn by wild animals.
16:37 with whom you **f** pleasure, those you
22:30 have to destroy it, but I **f** none.
26:21 but you will never again be **f**,
28:15 till wickedness was **f** in you.
44:31 **f** dead or torn by wild animals.
Da 1:19 and he **f** none equal to Daniel,
Da 1:20 he **f** them ten times better than all
2:25 "I have **f** a man among the exiles
4:12 the beasts of the field **f** shelter
5:11 he was **f** to have insight and
5:12 was **f** to have a keen mind and
5:27 weighed on the scales and **f** wanting.
6:11 **f** Daniel praying and asking God
6:22 I was **f** innocent in his sight.
6:23 no wound was **f** on him, because he
12: 1 everyone whose name is **f** written in
Hos 9:10 "When I **f** Israel, it was like
12: 4 He **f** him at Bethel and talked with
Jnh 1: 3 down to Joppa, where he **f** a ship
Mic 1:13 of Israel were **f** in you.
Zep 3:13 will deceit be **f** in their mouths.
Zec 1:11 **f** the whole world at rest and in
Mal 2: 6 and nothing false was **f** on his lips.
Mt 1:18 she was **f** to be with child through
2: 7 **f** out from them the exact time the
8:10 I have not **f** anyone in Israel with
13:44 When a man **f** it, he hid it again,
13:46 he **f** one of great value, he went
18:28 he **f** one of his fellow-servants who
20: 6 and **f** still others standing around.
21:19 but **f** nothing on it except leaves.
26:40 his disciples and **f** them sleeping
26:43 came back, he again **f** them sleeping
Mk 1:37 when they **f** him, they exclaimed:
6:38 When they **f** out, they said, "Five—
7:30 She went home and **f** her child lying
11: 4 They went and **f** a colt outside in
11:13 reached it, he **f** nothing but leaves
14:16 **f** things just as Jesus had told them.
14:37 his disciples and **f** them sleeping
14:40 came back, he again **f** them sleeping
Lk 1:30 Mary, you have **f** favour with God.
2:16 they hurried off and **f** Mary and
2:46 After three days they **f** him in the
4:17 he **f** the place where it is written:
7: 9 **f** such great faith even in Israel."
7:10 to the house and **f** the servant well.
8:35 **f** the man from whom the demons had
9:36 spoken, they **f** that Jesus was alone
13: 7 on this fig-tree and haven't **f** any.
15: 6 with me; I have **f** my lost sheep.'
15: 9 with me; I have **f** my lost coin.'
15:24 alive again; he was lost and is **f**.
15:32 alive again; he was lost and is **f**.'"
17:18 Was no-one **f** to return and give
19:32 and **f** it just as he had told them
22:13 They left and **f** things just as Jesus
22:45 **f** them asleep, exhausted from sorrow.
23: 2 **f** this man subverting our nation.
23:14 have **f** no basis for your charges
23:22 I have **f** in him no grounds for the
24: 2 They **f** the stone rolled away from
24:24 and **f** it just as the women had said,
24:33 There they **f** the Eleven and those
Jn 1:41 "We have **f** the Messiah" (that is,
1:45 Philip **f** Nathanael and told him, "We
1:45 "We have **f** the one Moses wrote about
2:14 In the temple courts he **f** men
5:14 Later Jesus **f** him at the temple and
6:25 they **f** him on the other side of the
9:35 and when he **f** him, he said, "Do you
11:17 On his arrival, Jesus **f** that Lazarus
11:57 if anyone **f** out where Jesus was,
12: 9 a large crowd of Jews **f** out that
12:14 Jesus **f** a young donkey and sat upon
19:33 Jesus and **f** that he was already dead
Ac 4:12 Salvation is **f** in no-one else, for
5:23 "We **f** the jail securely locked, with
5:23 we opened them, we **f** no-one inside."
9: 2 so that if he **f** any there who
9:33 There he **f** a man named Aeneas, a
10:17 the men sent by Cornelius **f** out
10:27 and **f** a large gathering of people.
11:26 he **f** him, he brought him to Antioch.
13:22 'I have **f** David son of Jesse a man
13:28 Though they **f** no proper ground for a
14: 6 they **f** out about it and fled to the
17:23 I even **f** an altar with this
19: 1 Ephesus. There he **f** some disciples
21: 2 We **f** a ship crossing over to
22:25 who hasn't even been **f** guilty?"
23:29 I **f** that the accusation had to do
Ac 24: 5 "We have **f** this man to be a
24:18 ceremonially clean when they **f** me
24:20 state what crime they **f** in me
25:25 I **f** he had done nothing deserving of
27: 6 There the centurion **f** an Alexandrian
27:28 They took soundings and **f** that the
27:28 again and **f** it was ninety feet deep.
28: 1 we **f** out that the island was called
28:14 There we **f** some brothers who invited
Ro 7:10 I **f** that the very commandment that
10:20 Isaiah boldly says, "I was **f** by
1Co 15:15 we are then **f** to be false witnesses
2Co 2:12 **f** that the Lord had opened a door
5: 3 are clothed, we will not be **f** naked.
Php 2: 8 being **f** in appearance as a man, he
3: 9 be **f** in him, not having a
Col 2:17 reality, however, is **f** in Christ.
2Ti 1:17 searched hard for me until he **f** me.
Heb 3: 3 Jesus has been **f** worthy of greater
4: 1 you be **f** to have fallen short of it.
8: 8 God **f** fault with the people and said:
11: 5 he could not be **f**, because God had
Jas 2: 8 keep the royal law **f** in Scripture
1Pe 2:22 and no deceit was **f** in his mouth."
2Pe 3:14 make every effort to be **f** spotless,
Rev 2: 2 but are not, and have **f** them false.
3: 2 for I have not **f** your deeds complete
5: 4 I wept and wept because no-one was **f**
14: 5 No lie was **f** in their mouths; they
16:20 and the mountains could not be **f**.
18:21 be thrown down, never to be **f** again.
18:22 trade will ever be **f** in you again.
18:24 In her was **f** the blood of prophets
20:15 If anyone's name was not **f** written
21:16 city with the rod and **f** it to be

Foundation (Foundations, Founded)

1Ki 5:17 a **f** of dressed stone for the temple.
6:37 The **f** of the temple of the LORD was
7: 9 great courtyard and from **f** to eaves,
2Ch 3: 3 The **f** Solomon laid for building the
8:16 from the day the **f** of the temple of
23: 5 palace and a third at the **F** Gate,
Ezr 3: 3 they built the altar on its **f** and
3: 6 though the **f** of the LORD's temple
3:10 the builders laid the **f** of the
3:11 **f** of the house of the LORD was laid.
3:12 wept aloud when they saw the **f** of
Job 38: 4 when I laid the earth's **f**? Tell me,
Ps 87: 1 He has set his **f** on the holy
89:14 and justice are the **f** of your throne
97: 2 and justice are the **f** of his throne.
Isa 28:16 a precious cornerstone for a sure **f**;
33: 6 He will be the sure **f** for your times,
Jer 51:26 nor any stone for a **f**, for you will
Eze 13:14 so that its **f** will be laid bare.
41: 8 it, forming the **f** of the side rooms.
Am 9: 6 heavens and sets its **f** on the earth,
Hag 2:18 the **f** of the LORD's temple was laid.
Zec 4: 9 have laid the **f** of this temple;
8: 9 when the **f** was laid for the house
12: 1 who lays the **f** of the earth, and who
Mt 7:25 because it had its **f** on the rock.
Lk 6:48 down deep and laid the **f** on rock.
6:49 a house on the ground without a **f**.
14:29 For if he lays the **f** and is not able
Ro 15:20 not be building on someone else's **f**.
1Co 3:10 I laid a **f** as an expert builder, and
3:11 For no-one can lay any **f** other than
3:12 If any man builds on this **f** using
Eph 2:20 built on the **f** of the apostles and
1Ti 3:15 God, the pillar and **f** of the truth.
6:19 as a firm **f** for the coming age,
2Ti 2:19 God's solid **f** stands firm, sealed
Heb 6: 1 not laying again the **f** of repentance
Rev 21:19 The first **f** was jasper, the second

Foundations (Foundation)

Dt 32:22 set on fire the **f** of the mountains.
Jos 6:26 his firstborn son will he lay its **f**;
1Sa 2: 8 For the **f** of the earth are the LORD's
2Sa 22: 8 quaked, the **f** of the heavens shook;
22:16 the **f** of the earth laid bare at the
1Ki 7:10 The **f** were laid with large stones of
16:34 He laid its **f** at the cost of his

Ezr 4:12 the walls and repairing the **f**.
5:16 this Sheshbazzar came and laid the **f**
6: 3 sacrifices, and let its **f** be laid.
Job 4:19 whose **f** are in the dust, who are
22:16 their **f** washed away by a flood.
Ps 11: 3 the **f** are being destroyed, what can
18: 7 and the **f** of the mountains shook;
18:15 the **f** of the earth laid bare at your
82: 5 all the **f** of the earth are shaken.
102:25 In the beginning you laid the **f** of
104: 5 He set the earth on its **f**; it can
137: 7 "tear it down to its **f**!
Pr 3:19 By wisdom the LORD laid the earth's **f**
8:29 he marked out the **f** of the earth.
Isa 24:18 opened, the **f** of the earth shake.
44:28 of the temple, "Let its **f** be laid.
48:13 My own hand laid the **f** of the earth,
51:13 heavens and laid the **f** of the earth,
51:16 who laid the **f** of the earth, and who
54:11 of turquoise, your **f** with sapphires.
58:12 and will raise up the age-old **f**;
Jer 31:37 the **f** of the earth below be searched
Lam 4:11 a fire in Zion that consumed her **f**.
Eze 30: 4 be carried away and her **f** torn down.
Mic 1: 6 into the valley and lay bare her **f**.
6: 2 you everlasting **f** of the earth.
Ac 16:26 the **f** of the prison were shaken.
Heb 1:10 O Lord, you laid the **f** of the earth,
11:10 looking forward to the city with **f**,
Rev 21:14 The wall of the city had twelve **f**,
21:19 The **f** of the city walls were

Founded (Foundation)

Ex 9:18 from the day it was **f** till now.
1Ki 2:24 has **f** a dynasty for me as he
Ps 24: 2 for he **f** it upon the seas and
89:11 **f** the world and all that is in it.
94:15 Judgment will again be **f** on
107:36 **f** a city where they could settle.
Isa 40:21 understood since the earth was **f**?
45:18 he **f** it; he did not create it to be
Jer 10:12 he **f** the world by his wisdom
51:15 he **f** the world by his wisdom
Heb 8: 6 one, and it is **f** on better promises.

Fountain (*Fountain of life*, Fountains)

Ne 2:14 I moved on towards the **F** Gate and
3:15 The **F** Gate was repaired by Shallun
12:37 At the **F** Gate they continued
Pr 5:18 May your **f** be blessed, and may you
18: 4 the **f** of wisdom is a bubbling brook.
SS 4:12 are a spring enclosed, a sealed **f**.
4:15 You are a garden **f**, a well of
Jer 9: 1 of water and my eyes a **f** of tears!
Joel 3:18 A **f** will flow out of the LORD's
Zec 13: 1 "On that day a **f** will be opened to

Fountain of life

Ps 36: 9 For with you is the **f**; in your light
Pr 10:11 The mouth of the righteous is a **f**,
13:14 The teaching of the wise is a **f**,
14:27 The fear of the LORD is a **f**, turning
16:22 Understanding is a **f** to those who

Fountains (Fountain)

Ps 87: 7 will sing, "All my **f** are in you.
Pr 8:28 fixed securely the **f** of the deep,

Fowl (Fowler, Fowler's)

1Ki 4:23 gazelles, roebucks and choice **f**.

Fowler (Fowl)

Pr 6: 5 like a bird from the snare of the **f**.

Fowler's (Fowl)

Ps 91: 3 he will save you from the **f** snare
124: 7 like a bird out of the **f** snare;

Fox (Foxes)

Ne 4: 3 "What they are building—if even a **f**
Lk 13:32 He replied, "Go tell that **f**, 'I will

Foxes (Fox)

Jdg 15: 4 caught three hundred **f** and tied them
15: 5 lit the torches and let the **f** loose
SS 2:15 Catch for us the **f**, the little **f**
Mt 8:20 Jesus replied, "**F** have holes and
Lk 9:58 Jesus replied, "**F** have holes and

Fraction

Mk 12:42 coins, worth only a **f** of a penny.

Fracture (Fractures)

Lev 24:20 **f** for **f**, eye for eye, tooth for

Fractures (Fracture)

Ps 60: 2 open; mend its **f**, for it is quaking.

Fragile

Job 8:14 What he trusts in is **f**; what he

Fragment

Isa 30:14 not a **f** will be found for taking

Fragrance (Fragrant)

Ex 30:38 to enjoy its **f** must be cut off from
SS 1: 3 Pleasing is the **f** of your perfumes;
1:12 his table, my perfume spread its **f**.
2:13 the blossoming vines spread their **f**.
4:10 **f** of your perfume than any spice!
4:11 The **f** of your garments is like that
4:16 that its **f** may spread abroad.
7: 8 the **f** of your breath like apples,
7:13 The mandrakes send out their **f**, and
Isa 3:24 Instead of **f** there will be a stench;
Hos 14: 6 tree, his **f** like a cedar of Lebanon.
Jn 12: 3 filled with the **f** of the perfume.
2Co 2:14 the **f** of the knowledge of him.
2:16 death; to the other, the **f** of life.

Fragrant (Fragrance)

Ex 25: 6 anointing oil and for the **f** incense;
30: 7 "Aaron must burn **f** incense on the
30:23 **f** cinnamon, 250 shekels of **f** cane,
30:25 a **f** blend, the work of a perfumer.
30:34 LORD said to Moses, "Take **f** spices
30:35 make a **f** blend of incense, the work
31:11 the anointing oil and **f** incense for
35: 8 anointing oil and for the **f** incense;
35:15 the anointing oil and the **f** incense;
35:28 anointing oil and for the **f** incense.
37:29 **f** incense—the work of a perfumer.
39:38 the anointing oil, the **f** incense,
40:27 burned **f** incense on it, as the LORD
Lev 4: 7 the altar of **f** incense that is
16:12 of finely ground **f** incense and
Nu 4:16 the **f** incense, the regular grain
2Ch 2: 4 for burning **f** incense before him,
13:11 offerings and **f** incense to the LORD.
Ps 45: 8 All your robes are **f** with myrrh and
Isa 43:24 You have not bought any **f** calamus
Eze 6:13 **f** incense to all their idols.
8:11 and a **f** cloud of incense was rising.
16:19 offered as **f** incense before them.
20:28 presented their **f** incense and poured
20:41 I will accept you as **f** incense when
Eph 5: 2 a **f** offering and sacrifice to God.
Php 4:18 They are a **f** offering, an acceptable

Frame (Door-frame, Door-frames, Frames)

Ex 26:16 Each **f** is to be ten cubits long and
26:19 each **f**, one under each projection.
26:21 forty silver bases—two under each **f**.
26:25 silver bases—two under each **f**.
36:21 Each **f** was ten cubits long and a
36:24 each **f**, one under each projection.
36:26 forty silver bases—two under each **f**.
36:30 silver bases—two under each **f**.
Nu 4:10 sea cows and put it on a carrying **f**.
4:12 cows and put them on a carrying **f**.
1Ki 7:31 had a circular **f** one cubit deep.
Job 17: 7 grief; my whole **f** is but a shadow.
Ps 139:15 My **f** was not hidden from you when I
Isa 58:11 land and will strengthen your **f**.

Frames (Frame)

Ex 26:15 "Make upright **f** of acacia wood for
26:17 the **f** of the tabernacle in this way.
26:18 Make twenty **f** for the south side of
26:20 of the tabernacle, make twenty **f**
26:22 Make six **f** for the far end, that is,
26:23 make two **f** for the corners at the
26:25 there will be eight **f** and sixteen
26:26 the **f** on one side of the tabernacle,
26:27 and five for the **f** on the west, at
26:28 end to end at the middle of the **f**.
26:29 Overlay the **f** with gold and make
35:11 **f**, crossbars, posts and bases;
36:20 They made upright **f** of acacia wood
36:22 the **f** of the tabernacle in this way.
36:23 They made twenty **f** for the south
36:25 the tabernacle, they made twenty **f**
36:27 They made six **f** for the far end,
36:28 two **f** were made for the corners of
36:29 At these two corners the **f** were
36:30 there were eight **f** and sixteen
36:31 the **f** on one side of the tabernacle,
36:32 and five for the **f** on the west, at
36:33 end to end at the middle of the **f**.
36:34 They overlaid the **f** with gold and
39:33 **f**, crossbars, posts and bases;
40:18 erected the **f**, inserted the
Nu 3:36 care of the **f** of the tabernacle,
4:31 to carry the **f** of the tabernacle,
1Ki 7: 5 All the doorways had rectangular **f**;

Frankincense (Incense)

Ex 30:34 pure **f**, all in equal amounts,
Rev 18:13 of incense, myrrh and **f**, of wine and

Frantic

1Ki 18:29 continued their **f** prophesying until

Fraud (Defraud)

Pr 20:17 Food gained by **f** tastes sweet to a
Jer 10:14 His images are a **f**; they have no
51:17 His images are a **f**; they have no

Fray

Job 39:21 strength, and charges into the **f**.

Free (Freed, Freedman, Freedmen, Freedom, Freeing, Freely)

Ge 2:16 **f** to eat from any tree in the garden;
44:10 rest of you will be **f** from blame."
49:21 "Naphtali is a doe set **f** that bears
Ex 6: 6 I will **f** you from being slaves to
21: 2 shall go **f**, without paying anything.
21: 3 If he comes alone, he is to go **f**
21: 4 master, and only the man shall go **f**.
21: 5 children and do not want to go **f**,'
21: 7 is not to go **f** as menservants do.
21:11 go **f**, without any payment of money.
21:26 go **f** to compensate for the eye.
21:27 go **f** to compensate for the tooth.
Nu 5:28 herself and is **f** from impurity,
32:22 you may return and be **f** from your
Dt 7:15 The LORD will keep you **f** from every
15:12 seventh year you must let him go **f**.
15:18 it a hardship to set your servant **f**,
24: 5 For one year he is to be **f** to stay
32:36 gone and no-one is left, slave or **f**.
Jdg 16:20 go out as before and shake myself **f**.
2Sa 22:49 who sets me **f** from my enemies. You
1Ki 14:10 last male in Israel—slave or **f**.
20:34 basis of a treaty I will set you **f**.
20:42 **f** a man I had determined should die.
21:21 last male in Israel—slave or **f**.
2Ki 9: 8 last male in Israel—slave or **f**.
14:26 whether slave or **f**, was suffering;
1Ch 4:10 harm so that I will be **f** from pain.
12:17 when my hands are **f** from violence,
Job 10: 1 I will give **f** rein to my complaint
16:17 yet my hands have been **f** of violence
21: 9 Their homes are safe and **f** from fear;
33: 9 sin; I am clean and **f** from guilt.
36:16 a spacious place **f** from restriction,
39: 5 "Who let the wild donkey go **f**? Who
Ps 25:17 multiplied; **f** me from my anguish.

Ps 31: 4 F me from the trap that is set for
73: 5 They are f from the burdens common
81: 6 hands were set f from the basket.
105:20 him, the ruler of peoples set him f.
118: 5 and he answered by setting me f.
119:32 for you have set my heart f.
129: 4 he has cut me f from the cords of
142: 7 Set me f from my prison, that I may
146: 7 The LORD sets prisoners f,
Pr 6: 3 do this, my son, to f yourself,
6: 5 F yourself, like a gazelle from the
11:21 those who are righteous will go f.
19: 5 he who pours out lies will not go f.
Isa 32:20 your cattle and donkeys range f.
42: 7 blind, to f captives from prison
45:13 rebuild my city and set my exiles f,
49: 9 to those in darkness, 'Be f!'
51:14 prisoners will soon be set f;
52: 2 F yourself from the chains on your
58: 6 to set the oppressed f and break
Jer 2:31 'We are f to roam; we will come to
34: 9 Everyone was to f his Hebrew slaves,
34:10 agreed that they would f their male
34:10 They agreed, and set them f.
34:14 you must f any fellow Hebrew who
34:14 six years, you must let him go f.
34:16 had set f to go where they wished.
37: 4 Now Jeremiah was f to come and go
Lam 5: 8 is none to f us from their hands.
Eze 13:20 I will set f the people that you
Zec 9:11 I will f your prisoners from the
Lk 13:12 you are set f from your infirmity."
13:16 be set f on the Sabbath day from
Jn 8:32 and the truth will set you f."
8:33 can you say that we shall be set f?"
8:36 if the Son sets you f, you will be f
19:10 either to f you or to crucify you?"
19:12 Pilate tried to set Jesus f, but the
Ac 7:34 and have come down to set them f.
26:32 "This man could have been set f if
Ro 6:18 You have been set f from sin and
6:20 slaves to sin, you were f from the
6:22 you have been set f from sin and
8: 2 Spirit of life set me f from the
13: 3 Do you want to be f from fear of the
1Co 7:22 he who was a f man when he was
7:32 would like you to be f from concern
7:39 her husband dies, she is f to marry
9: 1 Am I not f? Am I not an apostle?
9:18 gospel I may offer it f of charge,
9:19 Though I am f and belong to no man,
9:21 (though I am not f from God's law
12:13 slave or f—and we were all given
2Co 11: 7 gospel of God to you f of charge?
Gal 3:28 neither slave nor f, male nor
4:22 woman and the other by the f woman.
4:23 but his son by the f woman was born
4:26 the Jerusalem that is above is f,
4:30 inheritance with the f woman's son."
4:31 the slave woman, but of the f woman.
5: 1 freedom that Christ has set us f.
5:13 You, my brothers, were called to be f
Eph 6: 8 he does, whether he is slave or f.
Col 1:22 blemish and f from accusation—
3:11 slave or f, but Christ is all, and
Heb 2:15 f those who all their lives were
9:15 has died as a ransom to set them f
13: 5 Keep your lives f from the love of
1Pe 2:16 Live as f men, but do not use your
Rev 6:15 and every slave and every f man hid
13:16 rich and poor, f and slave, to
19:18 f and slave, small and great."
20: 3 he must be set f for a short time.
22:17 the f gift of the water of life.

Freed (Free)

Lev 19:20 death, because she had not been f.
Job 3:19 and the slave is f from his master.
Ps 116:16 you have f me from my chains.
136:24 f us from our enemies, His love
Jer 34:11 they had f and enslaved them again.
52:31 f him from prison on the
Mk 5:29 that she was f from her suffering.
5:34 peace and be f from your suffering."

Ro 6: 7 who has died has been f from sin.
Rev 1: 5 has f us from our sins by his blood,

Freedman (Free)

1Co 7:22 called by the Lord is the Lord's f;

Freedmen (Free)

Ac 6: 9 members of the Synagogue of the F

Freedom (Free)

Lev 19:20 not been ransomed or given her f,
Ps 119:45 I will walk about in f, for I have
Isa 61: 1 to proclaim f for the captives and
Jer 34: 8 to proclaim f for the slaves.
34:15 you proclaimed f to his countrymen.
34:17 f for your fellow countrymen.
Eze 46:17 may keep it until the year of f;
Lk 4:18 to proclaim f for the prisoners
Ac 24:23 under guard but to give him some f
Ro 8:21 glorious f of the children of God.
1Co 7:21 if you can gain your f, do so.
8: 9 that the exercise of your f does not
10:29 why should my f be judged by
2Co 3:17 Spirit of the Lord is, there is f.
Gal 2: 4 to spy on the f we have in Christ
5: 1 is for f that Christ has set us free.
5:13 But do not use your f to indulge the
Eph 3:12 approach God with f and confidence.
Jas 1:25 into the perfect law that gives f,
2:12 be judged by the law that gives f,
1Pe 2:16 but do not use your f as a cover-up
2Pe 2:19 They promise them f, while they

Freeing (Free)

Jer 40: 4 today I am f you from the chains on
Ac 2:24 God raised him from the dead, f him

Freely (Free)

Ge 43:34 So they feasted and drank f with him.
Dt 15: 8 Rather be open-handed and f lend him
23:23 because you made your vow f to the
1Ch 29: 9 f and wholeheartedly to the LORD.
Ezr 7:15 have f given to the God of Israel,
Ps 12: 8 The wicked f strut about when what
37:26 They are always generous and lend f;
112: 5 to him who is generous and lends f,
Pr 11:24 One man gives f, yet gains even more;
Isa 55: 7 to our God, for he will f pardon.
Hos 14: 4 their waywardness and love them f,
Mt 10: 8 F you have received, f give.
Mk 1:45 began to talk f, spreading the news.
Jn 1:20 confessed f, "I am not the Christ.
Ac 9:28 them and moved about f in Jerusalem,
26:26 things, and I can speak f to him.
Ro 3:24 are justified f by his grace through
1Co 2:12 understand what God has f given us.
2Co 6:11 We have spoken f to you, Corinthians,
10: 8 For even if I boast somewhat f about
Eph 1: 6 has f given us in the One he loves.

Freewill offering

Lev 7:16; 22:18, 21, 23; Dt 16:10; Ezr 8:28; Ps 54:6; Eze 46:12

Freewill offerings

Ex 35:29; 36:3; Lev 23:38; Nu 15:3; 29:39; Dt 12:6, 17; 2Ch 31:14; Ezr 1:4, 6; 2:68; 3:5; 7:16; Am 4:5

Frenzied

Job 39:24 In f excitement he eats up the

Fresh (Fresh-cut)

Ge 26:19 discovered a well of f water there.
Lev 14: 5 killed over f water in a clay pot.
14: 6 that was killed over the f water.
14:50 kill one of the birds over f water
14:51 of the dead bird and the f water,
14:52 the f water, the live bird, the
15:13 with f water, and he will be clean.
Nu 19:17 a jar and pour f water over them.
Jdg 15:15 Finding a f jaw-bone of a donkey, he
16: 7 anyone ties me with seven f thongs
Jdg 16: 8 f thongs that had not been dried,
Job 29:20 My glory will remain f in me, the
Ps 92:14 old age, they will stay f and green,
Eze 47: 8 the Sea, the water there becomes f.
47: 9 there and makes the salt water f;
47:11 and marshes will not become f;
Jas 3:11 Can both f water and salt water flow
3:12 can a salt spring produce f water.

Fresh-cut (Cut, Fresh)

Ge 30:37 Jacob, however, took f branches from

Fret

Ps 37: 1 Do not f because of evil men or be
37: 7 do not f when men succeed in their
37: 8 do not f—it leads only to evil.
Pr 24:19 Do not f because of evil men or be

Friction

1Ti 6: 5 constant f between men of corrupt

Friend (Friendly, Friends, Friendship)

Ge 38:12 his f Hirah the Adullamite went with
38:20 Judah sent the young goat by his f
Ex 32:27 his brother and f and neighbour."
33:11 to face, as a man speaks with his f.
Dt 13: 6 or your closest f secretly entices
Jdg 7:13 as a man was telling a f his dream.
7:14 His f responded, "This can be
14:20 Samson's wife was given to the f who
15: 2 he said, "that I gave her to your f.
15: 6 because his wife was given to his f.
Ru 4: 1 "Come over here, my f, and sit down.
2Sa 13: 3 Now Amnon had a f named Jonadab son
15:37 David's f Hushai arrived at
16:16 Hushai the Arkite, David's f, went
16:17 "Is this the love you show your f?
16:17 Why didn't you go with your f?"
1Ki 16:11 single male, whether relative or f.
1Ch 27:33 Hushai the Arkite was the king's f.
2Ch 20: 7 the descendants of Abraham your f?
Job 6:27 fatherless and barter away your f.
16:20 My intercessor is my f as my eyes
16:21 with God as a man pleads for his f.
Ps 35:14 as though for my f or brother.
41: 9 Even my close f, whom I trusted, he
55:13 myself, my companion, my close f,
88:18 me; the darkness is my closest f.
119:63 I am a f to all who fear you, to all
Pr 17:17 A f loves at all times, and a
18:24 f who sticks closer than a brother.
19: 4 but a poor man's f deserts him.
19: 6 is the f of a man who gives gifts.
22:11 will have the king for his f.
27: 6 Wounds from a f can be trusted, but
27: 9 the pleasantness of one's f springs
27:10 Do not forsake your f and the f of
Ecc 4:10 If one falls down, his f can help
SS 5:16 This is my lover, this my f,
Isa 41: 8 you descendants of Abraham my f,
Jer 3: 4 me: 'My Father, my f from my youth,
9: 4 a deceiver, and every f a slanderer.
9: 5 F deceives f, and no-one speaks the
23:35 on saying to his f or relative:
Mic 7: 5 neighbour; put no confidence in a f.
Mt 11:19 a f of tax collectors and "sinners".
20:13 'F, I am not being unfair to you.
22:12 'F,' he asked, 'how did you get in
26:50 Jesus replied, "F, do what you came
Lk 5:20 he said, "F, your sins are forgiven
7:34 a f of tax collectors and "sinners".
11: 5 "Suppose one of you has a f, and he
11: 5 'F, lend me three loaves of bread,
11: 6 a f of mine on a journey has come to
11: 8 him the bread because he is his f,
14:10 you, 'F, move up to a better place.
Jn 3:29 The f who attends the bridegroom
11:11 "Our f Lazarus has fallen asleep;
19:12 this man go, you are no f of Caesar.
Ro 16: 5 Greet my dear f Epenetus, who was
16: 9 in Christ, and my dear f Stachys.
16:12 Greet my dear f Persis, another
Col 4:14 Our dear f Luke, the doctor, and
Phm : 1 our dear f and fellow-worker,

Jas 2:23 and he was called God's **f**.
4: 4 who chooses to be a **f** of the world
3Jn : 1 The elder, To my dear **f** Gaius, whom
: 2 Dear **f**, I pray that you may enjoy
: 5 Dear **f**, you are faithful in what you
:11 Dear **f**, do not imitate what is evil

Friendly (Friend)

Ge 34:21 "These men are **f** towards us," they
Jdg 4:17 because there were **f** relations
1Ki 5: 1 always been on **f** terms with David.

Friends (Friend)

Ge 19: 7 said, "No, my **f**. Don't do this
Jdg 11:37 weep with my **f**, because I will
19:23 them, "No, my **f**, don't be so vile.
1Sa 30:26 who were his **f**, saying, "Here is a
2Sa 3: 8 father Saul and to his family and **f**.
2Ki 10:11 his close **f** and his priests, leaving
Est 5:10 Calling together his **f** and Zeresh,
5:14 His wife Zeresh and all his **f** said
6:13 told Zeresh his wife and all his **f**
Job 2:11 Job's three **f**, Eliphaz the Temanite,
6:14 should have the devotion of his **f**,
12: 4 become a laughing-stock to my **f**,
17: 5 If a man denounces his **f** for reward,
19:14 gone away; my **f** have forgotten me.
19:19 All my intimate **f** detest me; those I
19:21 "Have pity on me, my **f**, have pity,
24:17 make **f** with the terrors of darkness.
32: 3 He was also angry with the three **f**,
35: 4 reply to you and to your **f** with you.
42: 7 "I am angry with you and your two **f**,
42:10 After Job had prayed for his **f**, the
Ps 31:11 I am a dread to my **f**—those who see
38:11 My **f** and companions avoid me because
55:20 My companion attacks his **f**; he
88: 8 You have taken from me my closest **f**
122: 8 For the sake of my brothers and **f**, I
Pr 14:20 but the rich have many **f**.
16:28 and a gossip separates close **f**.
17: 9 the matter separates close **f**.
19: 4 Wealth brings many **f**, but a poor
19: 7 how much more do his **f** avoid him!
22:24 Do not make **f** with a hot-tempered
SS 1: 7 woman beside the flocks of your **f**?
5: 1 Eat, O **f**, and drink; drink your fill,
8:13 You who dwell in the gardens with **f**
Jer 6:21 them; neighbours and **f** will perish."
9: 4 "Beware of your **f**; do not trust your
20: 4 to yourself and to all your **f**;
20: 6 **f** to whom you have prophesied lies.'"
20:10 All my **f** are waiting for me to slip,
38:22 you—those trusted **f** of yours.
38:22 the mud; your **f** have deserted you.'
Lam 1: 2 All her **f** have betrayed her; they
Da 2:13 and his **f** to put them to death.
2:17 his **f** Hananiah, Mishael and Azariah.
2:18 so that he and his **f** might not be
Ob : 7 your **f** will deceive and overpower
Zec 13: 6 I was given at the house of my **f**.'
Lk 2:44 for him among their relatives and **f**.
7: 6 sent **f** to say to him: "Lord,
12: 4 "I tell you, my **f**, do not be afraid
14:12 do not invite your **f**, your brothers
15: 6 goes home. Then he calls his **f** and
15: 9 she finds it, she calls her **f** and
15:29 goat so I could celebrate with my **f**.
16: 9 use worldly wealth to gain **f** for
21:16 brothers, relatives and **f**, and they
23:12 That day Herod and Pilate became **f**
Jn 15:13 that he lay down his life for his **f**.
15:14 You are my **f** if you do what I
15:15 Instead, I have called you **f**, for
21: 5 to them, "**F**, haven't you any fish?
Ac 10:24 together his relatives and close **f**.
15:25 with our dear **f** Barnabas and Paul—
19:31 **f** of Paul, sent him a message
24:23 his **f** to take care of his needs.
27: 3 allowed him to go to his **f** so they
Ro 12:19 Do not take revenge, my **f**, but leave
1Co 10:14 Therefore, my dear **f**, flee from
2Co 7: 1 Since we have these promises, dear **f**,
12:19 dear **f**, is for your strengthening.
Php 2:12 Therefore, my dear **f**, as you have
Php 4: 1 stand firm in the Lord, dear **f**!
Heb 6: 9 dear **f**, we are confident of better
1Pe 2:11 Dear **f**, I urge you, as aliens and
4:12 Dear **f**, do not be surprised at the
2Pe 3: 1 Dear **f**, this is now my second letter
3: 8 do not forget this one thing, dear **f**:
3:14 then, dear **f**, since you are looking
3:17 Therefore, dear **f**, since you already
1Jn 2: 7 Dear **f**, I am not writing you a new
3: 2 Dear **f**, now we are children of God,
3:21 Dear **f**, if our hearts do not condemn
4: 1 Dear **f**, do not believe every spirit,
4: 7 Dear **f**, let us love one another, for
4:11 Dear **f**, since God so loved us, we
3Jn :14 The **f** here send their greetings.
:14 Greet the **f** there by name.
Jude : 3 Dear **f**, although I was very eager to
:17 But, dear **f**, remember what the
:20 you, dear **f**, build yourselves up in

Friendship (Friend)

Dt 23: 6 Do not seek a treaty of **f** with them
1Sa 20:42 "Go in peace, for we have sworn **f**
Ezr 9:12 Do not seek a treaty of **f** with them
Job 29: 4 God's intimate **f** blessed my house,
Ps 109: 4 In return for my **f** they accuse me,
109: 5 evil for good, and hatred for my **f**.
Pr 12:26 A righteous man is cautious in **f**,
Jas 4: 4 don't you know that **f** with the world

Fright (Fear)

Lk 24: 5 In their **f** the women bowed down with

Frighten (Fear)

Dt 28:26 there will be no-one to **f** them away.
Ne 6: 9 They were all trying to **f** us,
Job 7:14 even then you **f** me with dreams and
9:34 that his terror would **f** me no more.
Jer 7:33 there will be no-one to **f** them away.
Eze 30: 9 to **f** Cush out of her complacency.
2Co 10: 9 be trying to **f** you with my letters.

Frightened (Fear)

Ge 42:35 saw the money pouches, they were **f**.
43:18 Now the men were **f** when they were
Isa 31: 4 he is not **f** by their shouts or
Da 5: 6 His face turned pale and he was so **f**
Mk 9: 6 know what to say, they were so **f**.)
Lk 21: 9 wars and revolutions, do not be **f**.
24:37 They were startled and **f**, thinking
Php 1:28 without being **f** in any way by those
1Pe 3:14 fear what they fear; do not be **f**."

Frightening (Fear)

Job 13:21 me, and stop **f** me with your terrors.
Da 7: 7 a fourth beast—terrifying and **f**

Fringe

Job 26:14 are but the outer **f** of his works

Frogs

Ex 8: 2 plague your whole country with **f**.
8: 3 The Nile will teem with **f**. They will
8: 4 The **f** will go up on you and your
8: 5 **f** come up on the land of Egypt.'"
8: 6 the **f** came up and covered the land.
8: 7 made **f** come up on the land of Egypt.
8: 8 "Pray to the LORD to take the **f** away
8: 9 and your houses may be rid of the **f**,
8:11 The **f** will leave you and your houses,
8:12 the **f** he had brought on Pharaoh.
8:13 did what Moses asked. The **f** died
Ps 78:45 them, and **f** that devastated them.
105:30 Their land teemed with **f**, which went
Rev 16:13 evil spirits that looked like **f**;

Frolic

Ps 104:26 which you formed to **f** there.
Jer 50:11 because you **f** like a heifer

From generation to generation

Ex 3:15; 17:16; Ps 79:13; Isa 34:10, 17; Jer 50:39; Lam 5:19; Da 4:3, 34; Lk 1:50

Fronds

Lev 23:40 and palm **f**, leafy branches and

Frontier (Frontiers)

Eze 25: 9 beginning at its **f** towns—
48: 1 listed by name: At the northern **f**,

Frontiers (Frontier)

Ne 9:22 to them even the remotest **f**.

Frost

Ex 16:14 thin flakes like **f** on the ground
Job 38:29 Who gives birth to the **f** from the
Ps 147:16 wool and scatters the **f** like ashes.
Jer 36:30 the heat by day and the **f** by night.
Zec 14: 6 will be no light, no cold or **f**.

Frown

Jer 3:12 'I will **f** on you no longer, for I am

Froze (Frozen)

2Sa 23:10 hand grew tired and **f** to the sword.

Frozen (Froze)

Job 37:10 ice, and the broad waters become **f**.
38:30 when the surface of the deep is **f**?

Fruit (Firstfruits, Fruitage, Fruitful, Fruitfulness, Fruition, Fruits)

Ge 1:11 land that bear **f** with seed in it,
1:12 trees bearing **f** with seed in it
1:29 tree that has **f** with seed in it.
3: 2 eat **f** from the trees in the garden,
3: 3 God did say, 'You must not eat **f**
3: 6 the woman saw that the **f** of the tree
3:12 some **f** from the tree, and I ate it."
Ex 10:15 the fields and the **f** on the trees.
Lev 19:23 **f** tree, regard its **f** as forbidden.
19:24 In the fourth year all its **f** will be
19:25 in the fifth year you may eat its **f**.
23:40 are to take choice **f** from the trees,
25:19 the land will yield its **f**, and you
26: 4 and the trees of the field their **f**.
26:20 the trees of the land yield their **f**.
27:30 from the soil or **f** from the trees
Nu 13:20 back some of the **f** of the land.
13:26 and showed them the **f** of the land.
13:27 with milk and honey! Here is its **f**.
Dt 1:25 Taking with them some of the **f** of
7:13 He will bless the **f** of your womb,
20:19 them, because you can eat their **f**.
20:20 trees that you know are not **f** trees
22: 9 **f** of the vineyard will be defiled.
28: 4 The **f** of your womb will be blessed,
28:11 prosperity—in the **f** of your womb,
28:18 The **f** of your womb will be cursed,
28:30 will not even begin to enjoy its **f**.
28:53 you will eat the **f** of the womb, the
30: 9 hands and in the **f** of your womb,
32:13 fed him with the **f** of the fields.
Jdg 9:11 'Should I give up my **f**, so good and
2Sa 16: 2 the bread and **f** are for the men to
2Ki 19:29 plant vineyards and eat their **f**.
19:30 take root below and bear **f** above.
Ne 9:25 groves and **f** trees in abundance.
9:36 so that they could eat its **f**
10:35 of our crops and of every **f** tree.
10:37 of the **f** of all our trees and of
Ps 1: 3 which yields its **f** in season and
72: 3 the hills the **f** of righteousness.
72:16 Let its **f** flourish like Lebanon; let
92:14 They will still bear **f** in old age,
104:13 is satisfied by the **f** of his work.
128: 2 You will eat the **f** of your labour;
148: 9 you mountains and all hills, **f** trees
Pr 1:31 they will eat the **f** of their ways
1:31 filled with the **f** of their schemes.
8:19 My **f** is better than fine gold; what
11:30 The **f** of the righteous is a tree of
12:14 From the **f** of his lips a man is
13: 2 From the **f** of his lips a man enjoys
18:20 From the **f** of his mouth a man's
18:21 those who love it will eat its **f**.

Pr 27:18 who tends a fig-tree will eat its **f**,
Ecc 2: 5 all kinds of **f** trees in them.
SS 2: 3 and his **f** is sweet to my taste.
2:13 The fig-tree forms its early **f**; the
7: 7 and your breasts like clusters of **f**.
7: 8 tree; I will take hold of its **f**.
8:11 bring for its **f** a thousand shekels
8:12 are for those who tend its **f**.
Isa 3:10 will enjoy the **f** of their deeds.
4: 2 and the **f** of the land will be the
5: 2 grapes, but it yielded only bad **f**.
11: 1 from his roots a Branch will bear **f**.
14:29 its **f** will be a darting, venomous
16: 9 shouts of joy over your ripened **f**
27: 6 and fill all the world with **f**.
32:10 and the harvest of **f** will not come.
32:17 The **f** of righteousness will be peace;
37:30 plant vineyards and eat their **f**.
37:31 take root below and bear **f** above.
65:21 plant vineyards and eat their **f**.
Jer 2: 7 land to eat its **f** and rich produce.
6:19 the **f** of their schemes, because they
7:20 field and on the **f** of the ground,
11:16 olive tree with **f** beautiful in form.
11:19 "Let us destroy the tree and its **f**;
12: 2 taken root; they grow and bear **f**.
17: 8 drought and never fails to bear **f**."
31: 5 will plant them and enjoy their **f**.
40:10 summer **f** and oil, and put them in
40:12 an abundance of wine and summer **f**.
48:32 fallen on your ripened **f** and grapes.
Eze 17: 8 bear **f** and become a splendid vine.'
17: 9 of its **f** so that it withers?
17:23 bear **f** and become a splendid cedar.
19:12 it was stripped of its **f**; its strong
19:14 main branches and consumed its **f**.
25: 4 will eat your **f** and drink your milk.
34:27 of the field will yield their **f**
36: 8 will produce branches and **f** for my
36:30 I will increase the **f** of the trees
47:12 **F** trees of all kinds will grow on
47:12 not wither, nor will their **f** fail.
47:12 Their **f** will serve for food and
Da 4:12 were beautiful, its **f** abundant,
4:14 off its leaves and scatter its **f**.
4:21 with beautiful leaves and abundant **f**,
Hos 9:10 seeing the early **f** on the fig-tree.
9:16 root is withered, they yield no **f**.
10: 1 he brought forth **f** for himself.
10: 1 As his **f** increased, he built more
10:12 reap the **f** of unfailing love, and
10:13 you have eaten the **f** of deception.
14: 2 that we may offer the **f** of our lips.
Joel 2:22 The trees are bearing their **f**; the
Am 2: 9 his **f** above and his roots below.
6:12 **f** of righteousness into bitterness—
8: 1 LORD showed me: a basket of ripe **f**.
8: 2 "A basket of ripe **f**," I answered.
9:14 will make gardens and eat their **f**.
Mic 6: 7 **f** of my body for the sin of my soul?
7: 1 **f** at the gleaning of the vineyard;
Na 3:12 first ripe **f**; when they are shaken,
Hag 2:19 and the olive tree have not borne **f**.
Zec 8:12 the vine will yield its **f**, the
Mal 3:11 your fields will not cost their **f**
Mt 3: 8 Produce **f** in keeping with repentance.
3:10 not produce good **f** will be cut down
7:16 By their **f** you will recognise them.
7:17 good **f**, but a bad tree bears bad **f**.
7:18 **f**, and a bad tree cannot bear good **f**.
7:19 Every tree that does not bear good **f**
7:20 Thus, by their **f** you will recognise
12:33 "Make a tree good and its **f** will be
12:33 or make a tree bad and its **f** will be
12:33 for a tree is recognised by its **f**.
21:19 "May you never bear **f** again!"
21:34 to the tenants to collect his **f**.
21:43 to a people who will produce its **f**.
26:29 I will not drink of this **f** of the
Mk 11:13 he went to find out if it had any **f**.
11:14 May no-one ever eat **f** from you again.
12: 2 them some of the **f** of the vineyard.
14:25 I will not drink again of the **f** of
Lk 3: 8 Produce **f** in keeping with repentance.
3: 9 not produce good **f** will be cut down
6:43 **f**, nor does a bad tree bear good **f**.
Lk 6:44 Each tree is recognised by its own **f**.
13: 6 for **f** on it, but did not find any.
13: 7 to look for **f** on this fig-tree
13: 9 If it bears **f** next year, fine! If
20:10 him some of the **f** of the vineyard.
22:18 not drink again of the **f** of the vine
Jn 15: 2 every branch in me that bears no **f**,
15: 2 while every branch that does bear **f**
15: 4 No branch can bear **f** by itself; it
15: 4 you bear **f** unless you remain in me.
15: 5 will bear much **f**; apart from me
15: 8 that you bear much **f**, showing
15:16 to go and bear **f**—**f** that will last.
Ro 7: 4 order that we might bear **f** to God.
7: 5 bodies, so that we bore **f** for death.
15:28 sure that they have received this **f**,
Gal 5:22 the **f** of the Spirit is love, joy,
Eph 5: 9 (for the **f** of the light consists in
Php 1:11 filled with the **f** of righteousness
Col 1: 6 gospel is bearing **f** and growing,
1:10 way: bearing **f** in every good work,
Heb 13:15 **f** of lips that confess his name.
Jas 3:17 and good **f**, impartial and sincere.
Jude :12 without **f** and uprooted—twice dead.
Rev 18:14 "They will say, 'The **f** you longed
22: 2 of **f**, yielding its **f** every month.

Fruitage (Fruit)
Isa 27: 9 the full **f** of the removal of his

Fruitful (Fruit)
Ge 1:22 God blessed them and said, "Be **f** and
1:28 "Be **f** and increase in number; fill
8:17 can multiply on earth and be **f**
9: 1 "Be **f** and increase in number and
9: 7 for you, be **f** and increase in number;
17: 6 I will make you very **f**; I will make
17:20 I will make him **f** and will greatly
28: 3 make you **f** and increase your numbers
35:11 be **f** and increase in number.
41:52 me **f** in the land of my suffering."
47:27 acquired property there and were **f**
48: 4 said to me, 'I am going to make you **f**
49:22 "Joseph is a **f** vine, a **f** vine near a
Ex 1: 7 the Israelites were **f** and multiplied
Lev 26: 9 make you **f** and increase your numbers
Ps 105:24 The LORD made his people very **f**; he
107:34 **f** land into a salt waste, because of
107:37 vineyards that yielded a **f** harvest;
128: 3 Your wife will be like a **f** vine
Isa 17: 6 four or five on the **f** boughs,"
27: 2 that day—"Sing about a **f** vineyard:
32:12 pleasant fields, for the **f** vines
Jer 4:26 the **f** land was a desert; all its
23: 3 will be **f** and increase in number.
49: 4 boast of your valleys so **f**?
Eze 19:10 it was **f** and full of branches
36:11 they will be **f** and become numerous.
Jn 15: 2 so that it will be even more **f**.
Php 1:22 this will mean **f** labour for me.

Fruitfulness (Fruit)
Dt 33:15 and the **f** of the everlasting hills;
Hos 14: 8 pine tree; your **f** comes from me."

Fruition (Fruit)
2Sa 23: 5 Will he not bring to **f** my salvation

Fruitless
Eph 5:11 Have nothing to do with the **f** deeds

Fruits (Fruit)
Ge 4: 3 brought some of the **f** of the soil
Ps 109:11 plunder the **f** of his labour.
SS 4:13 with choice **f**, with henna and nard,
4:16 his garden and taste its choice **f**.
Jer 3:24 consumed the **f** of our fathers' labour

Frustrate (Frustrated, Frustrates, Frustrating, Frustration)
2Sa 17:14 determined to **f** the good advice
Ezr 4: 5 **f** their plans during the entire
Ps 14: 6 You evildoers **f** the plans of the
1Co 1:19 of the intelligent I will **f**."

Frustrated (Frustrate)
2Sa 13: 2 Amnon became **f** to the point of
Ne 4:15 of their plot and that God had **f** it,
Eze 24:12 has **f** all efforts; its heavy deposit

Frustrates (Frustrate)
Ps 146: 9 but he **f** the ways of the wicked.
Pr 22:12 he **f** the words of the unfaithful.

Frustrating (Frustrate)
2Sa 15:34 help me by **f** Ahithophel's advice.

Frustration (Frustrate)
Ecc 5:17 with great **f**, affliction and anger.
Ro 8:20 For the creation was subjected to **f**,

Fuel
Isa 9: 5 for burning, will be **f** for the fire.
9:19 the people will be **f** for the fire;
44:15 is man's **f** for burning; some of it
44:19 "Half of it I used for **f**; I even
Jer 51:58 labour is only **f** for the flames."
Eze 4:12 using human excrement for **f**."
15: 4 after it is thrown on the fire as **f**
15: 6 of the forest as **f** for the fire,
21:32 You will be **f** for the fire, your
39: 9 use the weapons for **f** and burn them
39: 9 years they will use them for **f**.
39:10 they will use the weapons for **f**.
Hab 2:13 labour is only **f** for the fire,

Fugitive (Fugitives)
Pr 28:17 by the guilt of murder will be a **f**
Eze 24:26 on that day a **f** will come to tell

Fugitives (Fugitive)
Nu 21:29 He has given up his sons as **f** and
Jos 8:22 them neither survivors nor **f**.
Isa 15: 5 Moab; her **f** flee as far as Zoar,
15: 9 Dimon—a lion upon the **f** of Moab
16: 3 Hide the **f**, do not betray the
16: 4 Let the Moabite **f** stay with you; be
21:14 live in Tema, bring food for the **f**.
43:14 bring down as **f** all the Babylonians,
45:20 assemble, you **f** from the nations.
Jer 44:14 none will return except a few **f**."
48:45 of Heshbon the **f** stand helpless
49: 5 away, and no-one will gather the **f**.
50:28 Listen to the **f** and refugees from
Ob :14 the crossroads to cut down their **f**,

Fulfil (Fulfilled, Fulfilling, Fulfilment, Fulfils)
Ge 38: 8 your brother's wife and **f** your duty
Lev 22:18 **f** a vow or as a freewill offering,
22:21 to the LORD to **f** a special vow
Nu 6:21 He must **f** the vow he has made,
23:19 not act? Does he promise and not **f**?
Dt 25: 5 marry her and **f** the duty of a
25: 7 He will not **f** the duty of a
1Sa 1:21 to the LORD and to **f** his vow,
2Sa 15: 7 and **f** a vow I made to the LORD.
1Ki 6:12 I will **f** through you the promise I
12:15 to **f** the word the LORD had spoken to
2Ki 23:24 This he did to **f** the requirements of
2Ch 10:15 to **f** the word that the LORD had
36:22 in order to **f** the word of the LORD
Ezr 1: 1 in order to **f** the word of the LORD
Est 5: 8 grant my petition and **f** my request,
Job 22:27 hear you, and you will **f** your vows.
Ps 22:25 those who fear you will I **f** my vows.
50:14 God, **f** your vows to the Most High
61: 8 name and **f** my vows day after day.
66:13 offerings and **f** my vows to you—
76:11 vows to the LORD your God and **f** them
116:14 I will **f** my vows to the LORD in the
116:18 I will **f** my vows to the LORD in the
119:38 **F** your promise to your servant, so
138: 8 The LORD will **f** his purpose for me;
Ecc 5: 4 no pleasure in fools; **f** your vow.

Ecc 5: 5 vow than to make a vow and not **f** it.
Isa 46:11 far-off land, a man to **f** my purpose.
Jer 11: 5 I will **f** the oath I swore to your
28: 6 do so! May the LORD **f** the words you
29:10 I will come to you and **f** my gracious
33:14 'when I will **f** the gracious promise
39:16 says: I am about to **f** my words
Eze 12:25 I will **f** whatever I say,
Na 1:15 O Judah, and **f** your vows.
Mt 1:22 All this took place to **f** what the
3:15 to do this to **f** all righteousness.
4:14 to **f** what was said through the
5:17 come to abolish them but to **f** them.
8:17 This was to **f** what was spoken
12:17 This was to **f** what was spoken
21: 4 This took place to **f** what was spoken
Jn 12:38 This was to **f** the word of Isaiah the
13:18 But this is to **f** the scripture: 'He
15:25 this is to **f** what is written in
Ac 7:17 drew near for God to **f** his promise
1Co 7: 3 The husband should **f** his marital
Gal 6: 2 way you will **f** the law of Christ.
2Th 1:11 by his power he may **f** every good

Fulfilled (Fulfil)

Jos 21:45 of Israel failed; every one was **f**.
23:14 has been **f**; not one has failed.
Jdg 13:12 "When your words are **f**, what is to
1Sa 10: 7 Once these signs are **f**, do whatever
10: 9 and all these signs were **f** that day.
1Ki 8:15 who with his own hand has **f** what he
8:24 hand you have **f** it—as it is today.
9:25 and so **f** the temple obligations.
2Ki 15:12 of the LORD spoken to Jehu was **f**:
2Ch 6: 4 who with his hands has **f** what he
6:15 hand you have **f** it–as it is today.
Ps 65: 1 in Zion; to you our vows will be **f**.
Pr 7:14 at home; today I **f** my vows.
13:12 but a longing **f** is a tree of life.
13:19 A longing **f** is sweet to the soul,
Jer 1:12 watching to see that my word is **f**."
17:15 word of the LORD? Let it now be **f**!"
25:12 "But when the seventy years are **f**, I
34:18 have not **f** the terms of the covenant
39:16 they will be **f** before your eyes.
Lam 2:17 what he planned; he has **f** his word,
Eze 12:23 near when every vision will be **f**.
12:25 and it shall be **f** without delay.
12:28 whatever I say will be **f**,
13: 6 yet they expect their words to be **f**.
Da 4:33 said about Nebuchadnezzar was **f**.
8:13 will it take for the vision to be **f**
9:12 You have **f** the words spoken against
12: 6 these astonishing things are **f**?"
Mt 2:15 And so was **f** what the Lord had said
2:17 through the prophet Jeremiah was **f**:
2:23 So was **f** what was said through the
13:14 In them is **f** the prophecy of Isaiah:
13:35 was **f** what was spoken through the
26:54 how then would the Scriptures be **f**
26:56 writings of the prophets might be **f**.
27: 9 by Jeremiah the prophet was **f**:
Mk 13: 4 that they are all about to be **f**?"
14:49 But the Scriptures must be **f**."
Lk 1: 1 things that have been **f** among us,
4:21 scripture is **f** in your hearing."
18:31 about the Son of Man will be **f**.
21:24 the times of the Gentiles are **f**.
22:37 I tell you that this must be **f** in me.
24:44 Everything must be **f** that is written
Jn 17:12 so that Scripture would be **f**.
18: 9 the words he had spoken would be **f**:
18:32 he was going to die would be **f**.
19:24 the scripture might be **f** which said,
19:28 so that the Scripture would be **f**
19:36 so that the scripture would be **f**:
Ac 1:16 "Brothers, the Scripture had to be **f**
3:18 this is how God **f** what he had
13:27 in condemning him they **f** the words
13:33 he has **f** for us, their children, by
23: 1 "My brothers, I have **f** my duty to
26: 7 hoping to see **f** as they earnestly
Ro 13: 8 loves his fellow-man has **f** the law.
Jas 2:23 the scripture was **f** that says,
Rev 17:17 to rule, until God's words are **f**.

Fulfilling (Fulfil)

Nu 3: 8 **f** the obligations of the Israelites
1Ki 2:27 **f** the word the LORD had spoken at
Ecc 5: 4 a vow to God, do not delay in **f** it.

Fulfilment (Fulfil)

Lev 22:23 will not be accepted in **f** of a vow.
2Ch 36:21 in **f** of the word of the LORD spoken
Da 11:14 will rebel in **f** of the vision,
Lk 9:31 about to bring to **f** at Jerusalem.
21:22 in **f** of all that has been written.
22:16 it finds **f** in the kingdom of God."
22:37 written about me is reaching its **f**."
Ro 13:10 Therefore love is the **f** of the law.
1Co 10:11 on whom the **f** of the ages has come.
Eph 1:10 the times will have reached their **f**

Fulfils (Fulfil)

Ps 57: 2 to God, who **f** his purpose for me.
145:19 He **f** the desires of those who fear
Isa 44:26 **f** the predictions of his messengers,

Full (Fill)

Ge 6:11 God's sight and was **f** of violence.
14:10 the Valley of Siddim was **f** of tar
15:16 has not yet reached its **f** measure."
23: 9 for the **f** price as a burial site
25: 8 an old man and **f** of years; and he
35:29 to his people, old and **f** of years.
41: 1 two **f** years had passed, Pharaoh had
41: 7 up the seven healthy, **f** ears.
41:22 seven ears of corn, **f** and good,
50: 3 taking a **f** forty days, for that was
Ex 5:18 produce your **f** quota of bricks."
8:21 of the Egyptians will be **f** of flies,
9:14 or this time I will send the **f** force
16:20 was **f** of maggots and began to smell.
23:26 I will give you a **f** life span.
Lev 6: 5 He must make restitution in **f**, add a
16:12 He is to take a censer **f** of burning
23:15 offering, count off seven **f** weeks.
25:29 redemption a **f** year after its sale.
25:30 is not redeemed before a **f** year
Nu 5: 7 He must make **f** restitution for his
33: 3 in **f** view of all the Egyptians,
Dt 21:13 her father and mother for a **f** month,
33:23 the LORD and is **f** of his blessing;
Jos 10:13 delayed going down about a **f** day.
Jdg 8: 2 than the **f** grape harvest of Abiezer?
Ru 1:21 I went away **f**, but the LORD has
1Sa 2: 5 Those who were **f** hire themselves out
18:27 presented the **f** number to the king
28:20 Immediately Saul fell **f** length on
2Sa 5:17 they went up in **f** force to search
11:18 Joab sent David a **f** account of the
23:11 there was a field **f** of lentils,
2Ki 3:16 says: Make this valley **f** of ditches.
4: 6 all the jars were **f**, she said to her
6:17 looked and saw the hills **f** of horses
10:21 it was **f** from one end to the other.
1Ch 11:13 where there was a field **f** of barley
14: 8 they went up in **f** force to search
21:22 Sell it to me at the **f** price."
21:24 "No, I insist on paying the **f** price.
23: 1 David was old and **f** of years, he
2Ch 24:10 them into the chest until it was **f**.
24:15 Now Jehoiada was old and **f** of years,
Ne 9:25 They ate to the **f** and were
Est 1: 4 For a **f** 180 days he displayed the
9:29 wrote with **f** authority to confirm
10: 2 together with a **f** account of the
Job 5:26 will come to the grave in **f** vigour
10:15 lift my head, for I am **f** of shame
14: 1 is of few days and **f** of trouble.
15:32 Before his time he will be paid in **f**,
20:22 **f** force of misery will come upon him.
21:23 One man dies in **f** vigour, completely
21:27 "I know **f** well what you are thinking,
26: 9 He covers the face of the **f** moon,
32:12 I gave you my **f** attention. But not
32:18 For I am **f** of words, and the spirit
42:17 he died, old and **f** of years.
Ps 10: 7 His mouth is **f** of curses and lies
26:10 whose right hands are **f** of bribes.
31:23 but the proud he pays back in **f**.
33: 5 earth is **f** of his unfailing love.
75: 8 a cup **f** of foaming wine mixed
78:38 and did not stir up his **f** wrath.
81: 3 moon is **f**, on the day of our Feast;
88: 3 For my soul is **f** of trouble and my
94: 4 all the evildoers are **f** of boasting.
104:24 the earth is **f** of your creatures.
116: 5 our God is **f** of compassion.
127: 5 Blessed is the man whose quiver is **f**
130: 7 love and with him is **f** redemption.
139:14 are wonderful, I know that **f** well.
144: 8 whose mouths are **f** of lies, whose
144:11 whose mouths are **f** of lies,
Pr 1:17 a net in **f** view of all the birds!
4:18 brighter till the **f** light of day.
5:21 For a man's ways are in **f** view of
7:20 and will not be home till **f** moon."
8:21 me and making their treasuries **f**.
17: 1 a house **f** of feasting, with strife.
20:17 he ends up with a mouth **f** of gravel.
27: 7 He who is **f** loathes honey, but to
29:11 A fool gives **f** vent to his anger,
30:22 king, a fool who is **f** of food,
31:11 Her husband has **f** confidence in her
Ecc 1: 7 the sea, yet the sea is never **f**.
9: 3 of men, moreover, are **f** of evil
11: 3 If clouds are **f** of water, they pour
Isa 1:15 Your hands are **f** of blood;
1:21 a harlot! She once was **f** of justice;
2: 6 They are **f** of superstitions from the
2: 7 Their land is **f** of silver and gold;
2: 7 Their land is **f** of horses; there is
2: 8 Their land is **f** of idols; they bow
6: 3 the whole earth is **f** of his glory."
11: 9 for the earth will be **f** of the
15: 9 Dimon's waters are **f** of blood, but I
22: 2 O town **f** of commotion, O city of
22: 7 choicest valleys are **f** of chariots
27: 9 and this will be the **f** fruitage of
30:26 like the light of seven **f** days, when
30:27 of smoke; his lips are **f** of wrath,
47: 9 They will come upon you in **f** measure,
65: 6 keep silent but will pay back in **f**;
65: 7 **f** payment for their former deeds."
Jer 5:27 Like cages **f** of birds, their houses
5:27 their houses are **f** of deceit; they
6:11 I am **f** of the wrath of the LORD, and
23:10 The land is **f** of adulterers; because
35: 5 I set bowls **f** of wine and some cups
51: 5 though their land is **f** of guilt
51:56 of retribution; he will repay in **f**.
Lam 1: 1 How deserted lies the city, once so **f**
4:11 The LORD has given **f** vent to his
Eze 1:18 four rims were **f** of eyes all around.
1:27 as if **f** of fire, and that from there
7:23 because the land is **f** of bloodshed
7:23 and the city is **f** of violence.
9: 9 the land is **f** of bloodshed and the
9: 9 and the city is **f** of injustice.
10: 4 and the court was **f** of the radiance
10:12 **f** of eyes, as were their four wheels.
17: 3 long feathers and **f** plumage of
17: 7 with powerful wings and **f** plumage.
19:10 it was fruitful and **f** of branches
22: 5 you, O infamous city, **f** of turmoil.
23:12 warriors in **f** dress, mounted
28:12 **f** of wisdom and perfect in beauty.
37: 1 of a valley; it was **f** of bones.
Joel 2:26 until you are **f**, and you will praise
3:13 for the winepress is **f** and the vats
Na 3: 1 Woe to the city of blood, **f** of lies,
3: 1 **f** of plunder, never without victims!
Zec 9:15 they will be **f** like a bowl used for
Mt 6: 2 have received their reward in **f**.
6: 5 have received their reward in **f**.
6:16 have received their reward in **f**.
6:22 your whole body will be **f** of light.
6:23 whole body will be **f** of darkness.
13:48 When it was **f**, the fishermen pulled
23:25 are **f** of greed and self-indulgence.
23:27 inside are **f** of dead men's bones
23:28 are **f** of hypocrisy and wickedness.
Mk 2:12 walked out in **f** view of them all.
4:28 ear, then the **f** grain in the ear.
Lk 4: 1 Jesus, **f** of the Holy Spirit,
5: 7 boats so **f** that they began to sink.

Lk 6:34 expecting to be repaid in f.
10:21 At that time Jesus, f of joy through
11:34 your whole body also is f of light.
11:34 your body also is f of darkness.
11:36 if your whole body is f of light,
11:39 you are f of greed and wickedness.
14:23 come in, so that my house will be f.
Jn 1:14 the Father, f of grace and truth.
3:29 and is f of joy when he hears the
10:10 may have life, and have it to the f.
13: 1 them the f extent of his love.
17:13 the f measure of my joy within them.
21: 8 towing the net f of fish, for they
21:11 It was f of large fish, 153, but
Ac 5: 2 With his wife's f knowledge he kept
5:20 the f message of this new life."
5:21 the Sanhedrin—the f assembly of
6: 3 to be f of the Spirit and wisdom.
6: 5 They chose Stephen, a man f of faith
6: 8 Now Stephen, a man f of God's grace
7:55 Stephen, f of the Holy Spirit,
8:23 you are f of bitterness and
11:24 a good man, f of the Holy Spirit
13:10 You are f of all kinds of deceit and
17:16 to see that the city was f of idols.
Ro 1:29 They are f of envy, murder, strife,
3:14 "Their mouths are f of cursing and
11:25 until the f number of the Gentiles
13: 6 who give their f time to governing.
15:14 you yourselves are f of goodness
15:29 f measure of the blessing of Christ.
16:19 so I am f of joy over you; but I
Gal 4: 5 might receive the f rights of sons.
Eph 6:11 Put on the f armour of God so that
6:13 Therefore put on the f armour of God,
Php 4:18 I have received f payment and even
Col 2: 2 so that they may have the f riches
4: 6 conversation be always f of grace
1Ti 1:15 saying that deserves f acceptance:
2:11 learn in quietness and f submission.
4: 9 saying that deserves f acceptance
6: 1 their masters worthy of f respect,
Phm : 6 a f understanding of every good
Heb 10:22 heart in f assurance of faith,
Jas 3: 8 a restless evil, f of deadly poison.
3:17 considerate, submissive, f of mercy
5:11 Lord is f of compassion and mercy.
2Pe 2:14 With eyes f of adultery, they never
Rev 5: 8 holding golden bowls f of incense,
13:13 heaven to earth in f view of men.
14:10 poured f strength into the cup of
21: 9 bowls f of the seven last plagues

Full-grown (Grow)

Jas 1:15 sin, when it is f, gives birth to

Fully (Fill)

Ex 19: 5 Now if you obey me f and keep my
Dt 15: 5 if only you f obey the LORD your God
28: 1 If you f obey the LORD your God and
Jos 1:14 but all your fighting men, f armed,
1:17 Just as we f obeyed Moses, so we
1Ki 8:61 your hearts must be f committed to
11: 4 and his heart was not f devoted to
15: 3 not f devoted to the LORD his God,
15:14 f committed to the LORD all his life.
1Ch 12:38 They came to Hebron f determined to
2Ch 15:17 f committed to the LORD all his life.
16: 9 whose hearts are f committed to him.
Ezr 6: 8 be f paid out of the royal treasury,
Ps 62: 4 They f intend to topple him from his
106: 2 of the LORD or f declare his praise?
119: 4 precepts that are to be f obeyed.
119:138 righteous; they are f trustworthy.
Pr 13: 4 of the diligent are f satisfied.
14:14 The faithless will be f repaid for
28: 5 who seek the LORD understand it f.
Isa 21: 7 camels, let him be alert, f alert."
Jer 23:20 until he f accomplishes the purposes
30:24 until he f accomplishes the purposes
35:10 have f obeyed everything our
Eze 38: 4 your horsemen f armed, and a great
Da 11:13 advance with a huge army f equipped.
Joel 2:19 enough to satisfy you f; never again
Lk 6:40 f trained will be like his teacher.
Lk 9:32 but when they became f awake, they
11:21 "When a strong man, f armed, guards
Ro 4:21 being f persuaded that God had power
8: 4 of the law might be f met in us,
14: 5 be f convinced in his own mind.
14:14 I am f convinced that no food is
15:19 f proclaimed the gospel of Christ.
1Co 13:12 I shall know f, even as I am f known.
15:58 Always give yourselves f to the work
2Co 1:14 you will come to understand f that
Gal 4: 4 when the time had f come, God sent
Col 4:12 will of God, mature and f assured.
2Ti 4:17 the message might be f proclaimed
Tit 2:10 show that they can be f trusted
1Pe 1:13 set your hope f on the grace to be
2Jn : 8 for, but that you may be rewarded f.

Fulness (Fill)

Dt 33:16 best gifts of the earth and its f
Jn 1:16 From the f of his grace we have all
Ro 11:12 greater riches will their f bring!
Eph 1:23 which is his body, the f of him who
3:19 to the measure of all the f of God.
4:13 whole measure of the f of Christ.
Col 1:19 For God was pleased to have all his f
1:25 to you the word of God in its f—
2: 9 For in Christ all the f of the Deity
2:10 you have been given f in Christ, who

Fun

Ac 2:13 Some, however, made f of them and

Function

Ex 27:19 the tabernacle, whatever their f,
Ro 12: 4 members do not all have the same f,

Funeral

Jer 16: 5 a house where there is a f meal;
34: 5 As people made a f fire in honour of

Furious (Fury)

Dt 29:28 In f anger and in great wrath the
2Sa 13:21 King David heard all this, he was f.
2Ch 25:10 They were f with Judah and left for
Est 1:12 king became f and burned with anger.
Jer 32:37 them in my f anger and great wrath;
Da 2:12 This made the king so angry and f
3:13 F with rage, Nebuchadnezzar summoned
3:19 Nebuchadnezzar was f with Shadrach,
Mt 2:16 he was f, and he gave orders to kill
8:24 Without warning, a f storm came up
Mk 4:37 A f squall came up, and the waves
Lk 4:28 were f when they heard this.
6:11 they were f and began to discuss
Ac 5:33 When they heard this, they were f
7:54 they heard this, they were f and
19:28 they heard this, they were f and

Furiously (Fury)

Jer 46: 9 Charge, O horses! Drive f,
Da 8: 7 I saw him attack the ram f, striking

Furnace

Ge 19:28 from the land, like smoke from a f.
Ex 9: 8 "Take handfuls of soot from a f and
9:10 they took soot from a f and stood
19:18 up from it like smoke from a f,
Dt 4:20 you out of the iron-smelting f,
1Ki 8:51 Egypt, out of that iron-smelting f.
Ps 12: 6 a f of clay, purified seven times.
21: 9 you will make them like a fiery f.
Pr 17: 3 The crucible for silver and the f
27:21 for silver and the f for gold
Isa 31: 9 is in Zion, whose f is in Jerusalem.
48:10 tested you in the f of affliction.
Jer 11: 4 Egypt, out of the iron-smelting f.
Eze 22:18 tin, iron and lead left inside a f.
22:20 copper, iron, lead and tin into a f
22:22 silver is melted in a f, so you will
Da 3: 6 be thrown into a blazing f."
3:11 will be thrown into a blazing f.
3:15 thrown immediately into a blazing f.
3:17 If we are thrown into the blazing f,
3:19 He ordered the f to be heated seven
Da 3:20 and throw them into the blazing f.
3:21 bound and thrown into the blazing f.
3:22 the f so hot that the flames of the
3:23 tied, fell into the blazing f.
3:26 of the blazing f and shouted,
Mal 4: 1 is coming; it will burn like a f.
Mt 13:42 They will throw them into the fiery f
13:50 throw them into the fiery f, where
Rev 1:15 were like bronze glowing in a f,
9: 2 it like the smoke from a gigantic f.

Furnished (Furnishings)

Eze 16:52 you have f some justification for
Mk 14:15 you a large upper room, f and ready.
Lk 22:12 show you a large upper room, all f.
Ac 28:10 f us with the supplies we needed.

Furnishings (Furnished)

Ex 25: 9 Make this tabernacle and all its f
31: 7 and all the other f of the tent—
39:33 to Moses: the tent and all its f,
39:40 all the f for the tabernacle,
40: 9 and all its f, and it will be holy.
Nu 1:50 f and everything belonging to it.
1:50 carry the tabernacle and all its f;
3: 8 They are to take care of all the f
4:15 holy f and all the holy articles,
4:16 including its holy f and articles."
7: 1 it and consecrated it and all its f.
18: 3 but they must not go near the f of
19:18 the f and the people who were there.
1Ki 7:48 Solomon also made all the f that
7:51 gold and the f—and he placed them
8: 4 Meeting and all the sacred f in it.
1Ch 9:29 were assigned to take care of the f
2Ch 4:19 Solomon also made all the f that
5: 1 gold and all the f—and he placed
5: 5 Meeting and all the sacred f in it.
28:24 Ahaz gathered together the f from
Jer 27:18 f remaining in the house of the LORD
27:19 other f that are left in this city,

Furrow (Furrows)

Job 39:10 Can you hold him to the f with a

Furrows (Furrow)

Job 31:38 me and all its f are wet with tears,
Ps 65:10 You drench its f and level its
129: 3 my back and made their f long.

Fury (Furious, Furiously)

Ge 27:44 until your brother's f subsides.
34: 7 They were filled with grief and f,
49: 7 so fierce, and their f, so cruel! I
2Ki 3:27 The f against Israel was great; they
Est 7:10 Then the king's f subsided.
Job 40:11 Unleash the f of your wrath, look at
Pr 6:34 for jealousy arouses a husband's f,
22: 8 the rod of his f will be destroyed.
27: 4 Anger is cruel and f overwhelming,
Isa 14: 4 come to an end! How his f has ended!
14: 6 and in f subdued nations with
66:14 but his f will be shown to his foes.
66:15 he will bring down his anger with f,
Jer 21: 5 arm in anger and f and great wrath.
Eze 13:13 rain will fall with destructive f.
19:12 was uprooted in f and thrown to the
23:25 and they will deal with you in f.
Da 11:30 his f against the holy covenant.
Am 1:11 and his f flamed unchecked,
Heb 11:34 quenched the f of the flames, and
Rev 12:12 down to you! He is filled with f,
14:10 will drink of the wine of God's f,
16:19 with the wine of the f of his wrath.
19:15 the f of the wrath of God Almighty.

Futile (Futility)

Ps 94:11 of man; he knows that they are f.
Jer 48:30 I know her insolence but it is f,"
Mal 3:14 have said, 'It is f to serve God.
Ro 1:21 but their thinking became f and
1Co 3:20 the thoughts of the wise are f."
15:17 not been raised, your faith is f;

Futility (Futile)
Job 7: 3 I have been allotted months of **f**,
Ps 78:33 he ended their days in **f** and their
89:47 For what **f** you have created all men!
Eph 4:17 do, in the **f** of their thinking.

Future
Ge 30:33 will testify for me in the **f**,
Dt 6:20 In the **f**, when your son asks you,
Jos 4: 6 In the **f**, when your children ask you,
4:21 He said to the Israelites, "In the **f**
22:27 Then in the **f** your descendants will
2Sa 7:19 the **f** of the house of your servant.
1Ch 17:17 the **f** of the house of your servant.
Job 8: 7 so prosperous will your **f** be.
Ps 22:30 **f** generations will be told about
37:37 there is a **f** for the man of peace.
37:38 the **f** of the wicked will be cut off
102:18 this be written for a **f** generation
Pr 23:18 There is surely a **f** hope for you,
24:14 there is a **f** hope for you, and your
24:20 for the evil man has no **f** hope, and
Ecc 7:14 discover anything about his **f**.
8: 7 Since no man knows the **f**, who can
Isa 9: 1 but in the **f** he will honour Galilee
41:23 tell us what the **f** holds, so that we
Jer 29:11 you, plans to give you hope and a **f**.
31:17 there is hope for your **f**,"
Lam 1: 9 skirts; she did not consider her **f**.
Eze 12:27 he prophesies about the distant **f**.'
38: 8 In **f** years you will invade a land
Da 2:45 king what will take place in the **f**.
8:26 for it concerns the distant **f**."
10:14 will happen to your people in the **f**,
Mt 26:64 In the **f** you will see the Son of
Ac 16:16 spirit by which she predicted the **f**.
Ro 8:38 present nor the **f**, nor any powers,
1Co 3:22 the present or the **f**—all are yours,
Heb 3: 5 to what would be said in the **f**.
11:20 Jacob and Esau in regard to their **f**.

Gaal
Jdg 9:26 Now **G** son of Ebed moved with his
9:28 **G** son of Ebed said, "Who is
9:30 city heard what **G** son of Ebed said,
9:31 "**G** son of Ebed and his brothers have
9:33 When **G** and his men come out against
9:35 Now **G** son of Ebed had gone out and
9:36 **G** saw them, he said to Zebul, "Look,
9:37 **G** spoke up again: "Look, people are
9:39 **G** led out the citizens of Shechem
9:41 Zebul drove **G** and his brothers out

Gaash
Jos 24:30 of Ephraim, north of Mount **G**.
Jdg 2: 9 of Ephraim, north of Mount **G**.
2Sa 23:30 Hiddai from the ravines of **G**,
1Ch 11:32 Hurai from the ravines of **G**, Abiel

Gabbai
Ne 11: 8 his followers, **G** and Sallai—928 men.

Gabbatha
Jn 19:13 Pavement (which in Aramaic is **G**).

Gabriel
Angel; sent to Daniel to interpret vision (Da 8:15–26) and deliver prophetic message (Da 9:20–27); announced birth of John the Baptist (Lk 1:11–20) and of Jesus Lk 1:26–38).
Da 8:16 "**G**, tell this man the meaning of the
9:21 while I was still in prayer, **G**, the
Lk 1:19 The angel answered, "I am **G**. I stand
1:26 God sent the angel **G** to Nazareth

Gad (Gad's, Gadites)
1. Son of Jacob by Zilpah (Ge 30:9–11; 35:26); blessed by Jacob (Ge 49:19). **2.** Tribe descended from Gad. Blessed by Moses (Dt 33:20–21). Included in census (Nu 1:24–25; 26:15–18). Apportioned land east of Jordan (Nu 32; 34:14–15; Jos 18:7; 22); crossed into Canaan to fight alongside other tribes (Nu 32:16–32). Place in restored land (Eze 48:27–28). **3.** Territory east of River Jordan, with Manasseh to the north, and Reuben to the south. Its boundaries and towns were listed (Jos 13:24–28; Nu 32:34–36). Allotted to the descendants of Jacob's seventh son, who liked it for its good grazing (Nu 32:1). **4.** Seer at David's court (1Sa 22:5; 2Sa 24:11–19).

Ge 30:11 good fortune!" So she named him **G**.
35:26 maidservant Zilpah: **G** and Asher.
46:16 The sons of **G**: Zephon, Haggi, Shuni,
49:19 "**G** will be attacked by a band of
Ex 1: 4 Dan and Naphtali; **G** and Asher.
Nu 1:14 from **G**, Eliasaph son of Deuel;
1:24 From the descendants of **G**: All the
1:25 The number from the tribe of **G** was
2:14 The tribe of **G** will be next. The
2:14 leader of the people of **G** is
7:42 leader of the people of **G**, brought
10:20 over the division of the tribe of **G**.
13:15 from the tribe of **G**, Geuel son of
26:15 The descendants of **G** by their clans
26:18 These were the clans of **G**; those
34:14 the tribe of **G** and the half-tribe of
Dt 27:13 **G**, Asher, Zebulun, Dan and Naphtali.
33:20 About **G** he said: "Blessed is he who
Jos 4:12 The men of Reuben, **G** and the
13:24 to the tribe of **G**, clan by clan:
18: 7 And **G**, Reuben and the half-tribe of
20: 8 Ramoth in Gilead in the tribe of **G**,
21: 7 the tribes of Reuben, **G** and Zebulun.
21:38 from the tribe of **G**, Ramoth in
22:13 **G** and the half-tribe of Manasseh.
22:15 they went to Gilead—to Reuben, **G**
22:21 Reuben, **G** and the half-tribe of
22:30 **G** and Manasseh had to say, they were
22:31 the priest, said to Reuben, **G** and
1Sa 13: 7 Jordan to the land of **G** and Gilead.
22: 5 the prophet **G** said to David, "Do not
2Sa 24: 5 then went through **G** and on to Jazer.
24:11 come to **G** the prophet, David's seer:
24:13 **G** went to David and said to him,
24:14 David said to **G**, "I am in deep
24:18 On that day **G** went to David and said
24:19 as the LORD had commanded through **G**.
2Ki 10:33 the land of Gilead (the region of **G**,
1Ch 2: 2 Dan, Joseph, Benjamin, Naphtali, **G**
6:63 the tribes of Reuben, **G** and Zebulun.
6:80 from the tribe of **G** they received
12:37 men of Reuben, **G**, and the half-tribe
21: 9 The LORD said to **G**, David's seer,
21:11 **G** went to David and said to him,
21:13 David said to **G**, "I am in deep
21:18 the angel of the LORD ordered **G** to
21:19 **G** had spoken in the name of the LORD.
29:29 and the records of **G** the seer,
2Ch 29:25 **G** the king's seer and Nathan the
Jer 49: 1 has Molech taken possession of **G**?
Eze 48:27 "**G** will have one portion; it will
48:28 "The southern boundary of **G** will run
48:34 will be three gates: the gate of **G**
Rev 7: 5 12,000, from the tribe of **G** 12,000,

Gad's (Gad)
Dt 33:20 "Blessed is he who enlarges **G** domain!

Gadarenes
Mt 8:28 other side in the region of the **G**,

Gaddi
Nu 13:11 (a tribe of Joseph), **G** son of Susi;

Gaddiel
Nu 13:10 from the tribe of Zebulun, **G** son of

Gadfly
Jer 46:20 "Egypt is a beautiful heifer, but a **g**

Gadi
2Ki 15:14 Menahem son of **G** went from Tirzah up
15:17 Menahem son of **G** became king of

Gadites (Gad)
Nu 32: 1 The Reubenites and **G**, who had very
32: 6 Moses said to the **G** and Reubenites,
32:25 The **G** and Reubenites said to Moses,
32:29 He said to them, "If the **G** and
32:31 The **G** and Reubenites answered, "Your
32:33 Moses gave to the **G**, the Reubenites
32:34 The **G** built up Dibon, Ataroth, Aroer,
Dt 3:12 I gave the Reubenites and the **G** the
3:16 to the Reubenites and the **G** I gave
4:43 Ramoth in Gilead for the **G**;
29: 8 to the Reubenites, the **G** and the
Jos 1:12 to the Reubenites, the **G** and the
12: 6 to the Reubenites, the **G** and the
13: 8 the Reubenites and the **G** had
13:28 inheritance of the **G**, clan by clan.
22: 1 Joshua summoned the Reubenites, the **G**
22: 9 the Reubenites, the **G** and the
22:10 the Reubenites, the **G** and the
22:25 **G**! You have no share in the LORD.
22:32 **G** in Gilead and reported to the
22:33 the Reubenites and the **G** lived.
22:34 the Reubenites and the **G** gave the
1Ch 5:11 The **G** lived next to them in Bashan,
5:16 The **G** lived in Gilead, in Bashan and
5:18 The Reubenites, the **G** and the
5:26 who took the Reubenites, the **G** and
12: 8 Some **G** defected to David at his
12:14 These **G** were army commanders; the
26:32 the **G** and the half-tribe of Manasseh

Gaham
Ge 22:24 sons: Tebah, **G**, Tahash and Maacah.

Gahar
Ezr 2:47 Giddel, **G**, Reaiah,
Ne 7:49 Hanan, Giddel, **G**,

Gaiety
Isa 24: 8 The **g** of the tambourines is stilled,
24:11 all **g** is banished from the earth.

Gain (Gained, Gaining, Gains, Regain)
Ge 15: 8 that I shall **g** possession of it?"
37:26 "What will we **g** if we kill our
Ex 14: 4 But I will **g** glory for myself
14:17 And I will **g** glory through Pharaoh
14:18 LORD when I **g** glory through Pharaoh,
18:21 men who hate dishonest **g**
1Sa 8: 3 They turned aside after dishonest **g**
2Ki 15:19 talents of silver to **g** his support
Job 21:15 What would we **g** by praying to him?'
22: 3 he **g** if your ways were blameless?
35: 3 me, and what do I **g** by not sinning?'
Ps 30: 9 "What **g** is there in my destruction,
60:12 With God we shall **g** the victory, and
90:12 that we may **g** a heart of wisdom.
108:13 With God we shall **g** the victory, and
119:36 statutes and not towards selfish **g**.
119:104 I **g** understanding from your precepts;
Pr 1:19 of all who go after ill-gotten **g**;
4: 1 pay attention and **g** understanding.
8: 5 You who are simple, **g** prudence; you
8: 5 who are foolish, **g** understanding.
11:16 but ruthless men **g** only wealth.
16: 8 than much **g** with injustice.
19:25 man, and he will **g** knowledge.
21:11 is punished, the simple **g** wisdom;
28:16 he who hates ill-gotten **g** will enjoy
28:23 a man will in the end **g** more favour
Ecc 1: 3 What does man **g** from all his labour
2:15 What then do I **g** by being wise?" I
3: 9 What does the worker **g** from his toil?
5:16 he **g**, since he toils for the wind?
6: 8 What does a poor man **g** by knowing
Isa 29:24 in spirit will **g** understanding;
33:15 who rejects **g** from extortion and
56:11 their own way, each seeks his own **g**.
63:12 to **g** for himself everlasting renown,
Jer 6:13 the greatest, all are greedy for **g**
8:10 the greatest, all are greedy for **g**
12:13 wear themselves out but **g** nothing.
22:17 heart are set only on dishonest **g**,
Eze 22:12 make unjust **g** from your neighbours
22:13 at the unjust **g** you have made
22:27 and kill people to make unjust **g**.

Eze 28:22 Sidon, and I will **g** glory within you.
33:31 hearts are greedy for unjust **g**.
Da 2: 8 that you are trying to **g** time,
10:12 set your mind to **g** understanding
11:43 He will **g** control of the treasures
Hab 2: 9 by unjust **g** to set his nest on high,
Mal 3:14 What did we **g** by carrying out his
Mk 8:36 What good is it for a man to **g** the
Lk 9:25 What good is it for a man to **g** the
16: 9 I tell you, use worldly wealth to **g**
21:19 By standing firm you will **g** life.
Jn 7:18 He who speaks on his own does so to **g**
Ac 7:10 enabled him to **g** the goodwill of
1Co 7:21 if you can **g** your freedom, do so.
13: 3 but have not love, I **g** nothing.
Php 1:21 to live is Christ and to die is **g**.
3: 8 them rubbish, that I may **g** Christ
1Ti 3: 8 wine, and not pursuing dishonest **g**.
3:13 Those who have served well **g** an
6: 5 godliness is a means to financial **g**.
6: 6 godliness with contentment is great **g**
2Ti 3: 6 **g** control over weak-willed women,
Tit 1: 7 violent, not pursuing dishonest **g**.
1:11 that for the sake of dishonest **g**.
Heb 11:35 they might **g** a better resurrection.

Gained (Gain)
Ge 31: 1 has **g** all this wealth from what
2Sa 15:12 And so the conspiracy **g** strength,
2Ch 32: 8 And the people **g** confidence from
Job 31:25 wealth, the fortune my hands had **g**,
Ps 129: 2 they have not **g** the victory over me.
Pr 20:17 Food **g** by fraud tastes sweet to a
20:21 An inheritance quickly **g** at the
Ecc 2:11 wind; nothing was **g** under the sun.
Isa 26:15 You have **g** glory for yourself; you
Jer 32:20 **g** the renown that is still yours.
Eze 28: 4 understanding you have **g** wealth for
Da 11: 2 When he has **g** power by his wealth,
Mt 25:16 his money to work and **g** five more.
25:17 one with the two talents **g** two
Mt 25:20 See, I have **g** five more.'
25:22 talents; see, I have **g** two more.'
Lk 19:15 to find out what they had **g** with it.
Ro 5: 2 through whom we have **g** access by
1Co 15:32 what have I **g**? If the dead are not
2Co 12: 1 Although there is nothing to be **g**, I
Gal 2:21 for if righteousness could be **g**
Heb 11:33 administered justice, and **g** what was
Rev 18:15 **g** their wealth from her will stand

Gaining (Gain)
Ge 3: 6 **g** wisdom, she took some and ate it.
Ps 44:12 pittance, **g** nothing from their sale.
Jn 4: 1 The Pharisees heard that Jesus was **g**

Gains (Gain)
Pr 3:13 wisdom, the man who **g** understanding,
11:16 A kind-hearted woman **g** respect, but
11:24 One man gives freely, yet **g** even
15:32 heeds correction **g** understanding.
29:23 but a man of lowly spirit **g** honour.
Jer 17:11 man who **g** riches by unjust means.
Mic 4:13 You will devote their ill-gotten **g**
Mt 16:26 for a man if he **g** the whole world,

Gaius
Ac 19:29 The people seized **G** and Aristarchus,
20: 4 **G** from Derbe, Timothy also, and
Ro 16:23 **G**, whose hospitality I and the whole
1Co 1:14 any of you except Crispus and **G**,
3Jn : 1 The elder, To my dear friend **G**, whom

Galal
1Ch 9:15 Bakbakkar, Heresh, **G** and Mattaniah
9:16 Obadiah son of Shemaiah, the son of **G**
Ne 11:17 the son of **G**, the son of Jeduthun.

Galatia (Galatian, Galatians)
Central region of Asia Minor. Paul passed through on second missionary journey (Ac 16:6) and due to illness stayed and preached (Gal 4:13–14). Returned during third journey (Ac 18:23), and sent letter here (Gal 1:2; 3:1). Crescens left Paul to go here (2Ti 4:10). Peter addressed his first letter to Galatian church (1Pe 1:1).

Ac 16: 6 the region of Phrygia and **G**,
18:23 the region of **G** and Phrygia,
Gal 1: 2 with me, To the churches in **G**:
2Ti 4:10 Crescens has gone to **G**, and Titus to
1Pe 1: 1 **G**, Cappadocia, Asia and Bithynia,

Galatian (Galatia)
1Co 16: 1 Do what I told the **G** churches to do.

Galatians (Galatia)
Gal 3: 1 You foolish **G**! Who has bewitched you?

Galbanum
Ex 30:34 spices—gum resin, onycha and **g**

Gale
Job 21:18 wind, like chaff swept away by a **g**?
Isa 17:13 hills, like tumble-weed before a **g**.
41:16 up, and a **g** will blow them away.

Galeed
Ge 31:47 Sahadutha, and Jacob called it **G**.
31:48 That is why it was called **G**.

Galilean (Galilee)
Mk 14:70 are one of them, for you are a **G**."
Lk 22:59 fellow was with him, for he is a **G**."
23: 6 Pilate asked if the man was a **G**.
Ac 5:37 After him, Judas the **G** appeared in

Galileans (Galilee)
Lk 13: 1 **G** whose blood Pilate had mixed with
13: 2 "Do you think that these **G** were
13: 2 worse sinners than all the other **G**
Jn 4:45 the **G** welcomed him. They had seen
Ac 2: 7 all these men who are speaking **G**?

Galilee (Galilean, Galileans)
1. Lake situated 60 miles north of Jerusalem, measuring approximately 13 by 8 miles, fed by River Jordan. Known as Sea of Galilee (Mt 4:18), Sea of Kinnereth (Nu 34:11), Sea of Tiberias (Jn 6:1), and Lake of Gennesaret (Lk 5:1). In OT mentioned as a boundary (Nu 34:11; Jos 12:3; 13:27). Fishing industry thrived here: Jesus called some fishermen to become disciples (Mt 4:18; Mk 1:16); he made use of boats (Lk 5:3; Jn 6:1); he provided disciples with a large catch of fish (Jn 21:1–6); he calmed a storm (Mk 4:35–41). **2.** Region between the Lake and Mediterranean Sea. Contained refuge city of Kedesh (Jos 20:7; 21:32). Solomon gave 20 of its towns to Hiram (1Ki 9:11). It was later captured by Tiglath-Pileser of Assyria (2Ki 15:29), and flooded with immigrants (2Ki 17:24). It became known as Galilee of the Gentiles. It would be honoured through the coming Messiah (Isa 9:1; Mt 4:15). Jesus lived and ministered here (Mt 2:22; 4:12–13; Lk 23:5; Ac 10:37). He became known as Jesus of Galilee (Mt 26:69).

Jos 20: 7 they set apart Kedesh in **G** in the
21:32 Kedesh in **G** (a city of refuge for
1Ki 9:11 King Solomon gave twenty towns in **G**
2Ki 15:29 He took Gilead and **G**, including all
1Ch 6:76 Naphtali they received Kedesh in **G**,
Isa 9: 1 but in the future he will honour **G**
Mt 2:22 he withdrew to the district of **G**,
3:13 Jesus came from **G** to the Jordan to
4:12 put in prison, he returned to **G**.
4:15 the Jordan, **G** of the Gentiles—
4:18 Jesus was walking beside the Sea of **G**
4:23 Jesus went throughout **G**, teaching in
4:25 Large crowds from **G**, the Decapolis,
11: 1 teach and preach in the towns of **G**.
15:29 there and went along the Sea of **G**.
17:22 they came together in **G**, he said to
19: 1 he left **G** and went into the region
21:11 the prophet from Nazareth in **G**."
26:32 I will go ahead of you into **G**."
26:69 "You also were with Jesus of **G**," she
27:55 Jesus from **G** to care for his needs.
28: 7 and is going ahead of you into **G**.
Mt 28:10 to go to **G**; there they will see me."
28:16 the eleven disciples went to **G**, to
Mk 1: 9 Jesus came from Nazareth in **G**
1:14 Jesus went into **G**, proclaiming the
1:16 Jesus walked beside the Sea of **G**, he
1:28 quickly over the whole region of **G**.
1:39 he travelled throughout **G**, preaching
3: 7 and a large crowd from **G** followed.
6:21 commanders and the leading men of **G**.
7:31 down to the Sea of **G** and into the
9:30 that place and passed through **G**.
14:28 I will go ahead of you into **G**."
15:41 In **G** these women had followed him
16: 7 'He is going ahead of you into **G**.
Lk 1:26 Gabriel to Nazareth, a town in **G**,
2: 4 the town of Nazareth in **G** to Judea,
2:39 to **G** to their own town of Nazareth.
3: 1 Herod tetrarch of **G**, his brother
4:14 Jesus returned to **G** in the power of
4:31 a town in **G**, and on the Sabbath
5:17 had come from every village of **G**
8:26 which is across the lake from **G**.
17:11 the border between Samaria and **G**.
23: 5 started in **G** and has come all the
23:49 women who had followed him from **G**,
23:55 with Jesus from **G** followed Joseph
24: 6 while he was still with you in **G**:
Jn 1:43 day Jesus decided to leave for **G**.
2: 1 a wedding took place at Cana in **G**.
2:11 signs, Jesus performed at Cana in **G**.
4: 3 Judea and went back once more to **G**.
4:43 After the two days he left for **G**.
4:45 he arrived in **G**, the Galileans
4:46 Once more he visited Cana in **G**,
4:47 Jesus had arrived in **G** from Judea,
4:54 having come from Judea to **G**.
6: 1 the far shore of the Sea of **G**
7: 1 After this, Jesus went around in **G**,
7: 9 Having said this, he stayed in **G**.
7:41 "How can the Christ come from **G**
7:52 They replied, "Are you from **G**, too?
7:52 a prophet does not come out of **G**.
Jn 12:21 from Bethsaida in **G**, with a request.
21: 2 Nathanael from Cana in **G**, the sons
Ac 1:11 "Men of **G**," they said, "why do you
9:31 the church throughout Judea, **G** and
10:37 beginning in **G** after the baptism
13:31 with him from **G** to Jerusalem.

Gall
Job 16:13 and spills my **g** on the ground.
Ps 69:21 They put **g** in my food and gave me
Pr 5: 4 in the end she is bitter as **g**, sharp
Lam 3:15 bitter herbs and sated me with **g**.
3:19 wandering, the bitterness and the **g**.
Mt 27:34 Jesus wine to drink, mixed with **g**

Galled
1Sa 18: 8 Saul was very angry; this refrain **g**

Galleries (Gallery)
Eze 41:15 including its **g** on each side; it was
41:16 the narrow windows and **g** round the
42: 5 for the **g** took more space from them

Gallery (Galleries)
Eze 42: 3 **g** faced **g** at the three levels.

Galley
Isa 33:21 No **g** with oars will ride them, no

Gallim
1Sa 25:44 Paltiel son of Laish, who was from **G**.
Isa 10:30 Cry out, O Daughter of **G**! Listen,

Gallio
Ac 18:12 While **G** was proconsul of Achaia, the
18:14 Just as Paul was about to speak, **G**
18:17 But **G** showed no concern whatever.

Gallons
Lk 16: 6 "'Eight hundred **g** of olive oil,' he
Jn 2: 6 holding from twenty to thirty **g**.

Gallop (Galloping, Gallops)
Joel 2: 4 horses; they **g** along like cavalry.

Galloping (Gallop)
Jdg 5:22 hoofs—**g**, **g** go his mighty steeds.
Jer 47: 3 the sound of the hoofs of **g** steeds
Na 3: 2 **g** horses and jolting chariots!

Gallops (Gallop)
Hab 1: 8 Their cavalry **g** headlong; their

Gallows
Est 2:23 two officials were hanged on a **g**.
5:14 "Have a **g** built, seventy-five feet
5:14 Haman, and he had the **g** built.
6: 4 on the **g** he had erected for him.
7: 9 "A **g** seventy-five feet high stands
7:10 they hanged Haman on the **g** he had
8: 7 and they have hanged him on the **g**.
9:13 Haman's ten sons be hanged on **g**."
9:25 his sons should be hanged on the **g**.

Gamaliel
1. Leader from Manasseh; helped Moses with census (Nu 1:10; 2:20; 7:54–59; 10:23). **2.** Pharisee and respected Rabbi and teacher of the law who intervened in trial of apostles (Ac 5:34–40). Acknowledged by Paul as his teacher (Ac 22:3).

Nu 1:10 from Manasseh, **G** son of Pedahzur;
2:20 of Manasseh is **G** son of Pedahzur.
7:54 On the eighth day **G** son of Pedahzur,
7:59 the offering of **G** son of Pedahzur.
10:23 **G** son of Pedahzur was over the
Ac 5:34 a Pharisee named **G**, a teacher of the
22: 3 Under **G** I was thoroughly trained in

Game (Games)
Ge 25:28 Isaac, who had a taste for wild **g**,
27: 3 country to hunt some wild **g** for me.
Ge 27: 5 country to hunt **g** and bring it back,
27: 7 'Bring me some **g** and prepare me some
27:19 Please sit up and eat some of my **g**
27:25 "My son, bring me some of your **g** to
27:31 sit up and eat some of my **g**, so that
27:33 "Who was it, then, that hunted **g** and
Ps 76: 4 majestic than mountains rich with **g**.
Pr 12:27 The lazy man does not roast his **g**,

Games (Game)
1Co 9:25 Everyone who competes in the **g** goes

Gammad
Eze 27:11 side; men of **G** were in your towers.

Gamul
1Ch 24:17 to Jakin, the twenty-second to **G**,

Gangrene
2Ti 2:17 Their teaching will spread like **g**.

Gap (Gaps)
Jdg 21:15 made a **g** in the tribes of Israel.
1Ki 11:27 had filled in the **g** in the wall of
Ne 6: 1 rebuilt the wall and not a **g** was
Eze 22:30 stand before me in the **g** on behalf

Gape (Gaping)
Ps 35:21 They **g** at me and say, "Aha! Aha!

Gaping (Gape)
Job 30:14 They advance as through a **g** breach;

Gaps (Gap)
Ne 4: 7 and that the **g** were being closed,

Garden (*Garden of Eden*, Gardener, Gardens)
Ge 2: 8 Now the LORD God had planted a **g** in
2: 9 In the middle of the **g** were the tree
2:10 A river watering the **g** flowed from
2:16 free to eat from any tree in the **g**;
Ge 3: 1 not eat from any tree in the **g**'?"
3: 2 eat fruit from the trees in the **g**,
3: 3 tree that is in the middle of the **g**,
3: 8 in the **g** in the cool of the day,
3: 8 LORD God among the trees of the **g**.
3:10 He answered, "I heard you in the **g**,
13:10 like the **g** of the LORD, like the
Dt 11:10 it by foot as in a vegetable **g**.
1Ki 21: 2 vineyard to use for a vegetable **g**,
2Ki 21:18 in his palace **g**, the **g** of Uzza.
21:26 He was buried in his grave in the **g**
25: 4 the two walls near the king's **g**,
Ne 3:15 by the King's **G**, as far as the steps
Est 1: 5 in the enclosed **g** of the king's
1: 6 The **g** had hangings of white and blue
7: 7 wine and went out into the palace **g**.
7: 8 the palace **g** to the banquet hall,
Job 8:16 spreading its shoots over the **g**;
SS 4:12 You are a **g** locked up, my sister, my
4:15 You are a **g** fountain, a well of
4:16 and come, south wind! Blow on my **g**,
4:16 his **g** and taste its choice fruits.
5: 1 I have come into my **g**, my sister, my
6: 2 My lover has gone down to his **g**, to
Isa 1:30 leaves, like a **g** without water.
5: 7 of Judah are the **g** of his delight.
51: 3 wastelands like the **g** of the LORD.
58:11 You will be like a well-watered **g**,
61:11 up and a **g** causes seeds to grow,
Jer 31:12 They will be like a well-watered **g**,
39: 4 at night by way of the king's **g**,
52: 7 the two walls near the king's **g**,
Lam 2: 6 laid waste his dwelling like a **g**;
Eze 28:13 You were in Eden, the **g** of God;
31: 8 The cedars in the **g** of God could not
31: 8 no tree in the the **g** of God could match
31: 9 the trees of Eden in the **g** of God.
Mt 13:32 it is the largest of **g** plants and
Mk 4:32 becomes the largest of all **g** plants,
Lk 11:42 rue and all other kinds of **g** herbs,
13:19 a man took and planted in his **g**.
Jn 19:41 there was a **g**, and in the **g** a new

Garden of Eden
Ge 2:15 **G** to work it and take care of it.
3:23 the LORD God banished him from the **G**
3:24 he placed on the east side of the **G**
Eze 36:35 laid waste has become like the **g**;
Joel 2: 3 Before them the land is like the **g**,

Gardener (Garden)
Jn 15: 1 true vine, and my Father is the **g**.
20:15 looking for?" Thinking he was the **g**,

Gardens (Garden)
Nu 24: 6 "Like valleys they spread out, like **g**
Ecc 2: 5 I made **g** and parks and planted all
SS 6: 2 in the **g** and to gather lilies.
8:13 You who dwell in the **g** with friends
Isa 1:29 of the **g** that you have chosen.
65: 3 offering sacrifices in **g** and burning
66:17 purify themselves to go into the **g**,
Jer 29: 5 plant **g** and eat what they produce.
29:28 plant **g** and eat what they produce.'"
Am 4: 9 "Many times I struck your **g** and
9:14 will make **g** and eat their fruit.

Gareb
2Sa 23:38 Ira the Ithrite, **G** the Ithrite,
1Ch 11:40 Ira the Ithrite, **G** the Ithrite,
Jer 31:39 the hill of **G** and then turn to Goah.

Garland
Pr 1: 9 They will be a **g** to grace your head
4: 9 She will set a **g** of grace on your

Garlic
Nu 11: 5 melons, leeks, onions and **g**.

Garment (Garments, Undergarment, Undergarments)
Ge 9:23 Shem and Japheth took a **g** and laid
25:25 a hairy **g**; so they named him Esau.
Ex 22: 9 a donkey, a sheep, a **g**, or any other
Lev 6:27 **g**, you must wash it in a holy place.
Nu 31:20 Purify every **g** as well as everything
Jdg 8:25 So they spread out a **g**, and each
Ru 3: 9 "Spread the corner of your **g** over me,
1Sa 19:13 it with a **g** and putting some goats'
2Sa 13:18 for this was the kind of **g** the
20:12 into a field and threw a **g** over him.
2Ki 1: 8 "He was a man with a **g** of hair and
Job 13:28 rotten, like a **g** eaten by moths.
30:18 he binds me like the neck of my **g**.
31:19 or a needy man without a **g**,
38: 9 I made the clouds its **g** and wrapped
38:14 stand out like those of a **g**.
Ps 74:11 folds of your **g** and destroy them!
102:26 they will all wear out like a **g**.
104: 2 wraps himself in light as with a **g**
104: 6 it with the deep as with a **g**
109:18 He wore cursing as his **g**; it entered
Pr 20:16 Take the **g** of one who puts up
25:20 Like one who takes away a **g** on a
27:13 Take the **g** of one who puts up
Isa 9: 5 every **g** rolled in blood will be
50: 9 will all wear out like a **g**;
51: 6 the earth will wear out like a **g**
51: 8 moth will eat them up like a **g**;
61: 3 **g** of praise instead of a spirit of
Jer 43:12 As a shepherd wraps his **g** round him,
Eze 5: 3 them away in the folds of your **g**.
16: 8 I spread the corner of my **g** over you
44:17 they must not wear any woollen **g**
Hag 2:12 meat in the fold of his **g**,
Zec 13: 4 **g** of hair in order to deceive.
Mal 2:16 with violence as well as with his **g**
Mt 9:16 patch of unshrunk cloth on an old **g**,
9:16 the patch will pull away from the **g**
Mk 2:21 patch of unshrunk cloth on an old **g**.
14:51 man, wearing nothing but a linen **g**
14:52 he fled naked, leaving his **g** behind.
Lk 5:36 a new **g** and sews it on an old one.
5:36 he will have torn the new **g**, and the
Jn 19:23 This **g** was seamless, woven in one
21: 7 he wrapped his outer **g** around him
Heb 1:11 they will all wear out like a **g**.
1:12 robe; like a **g** they will be changed.

Garments (Garment)
Ge 3:21 The LORD God made **g** of skin for Adam
49:11 branch; he will wash his **g** in wine,
Ex 28: 2 Make sacred **g** for your brother Aaron,
28: 3 that they are to make **g** for Aaron,
28: 4 These are the **g** they are to make: a
28: 4 They are to make these sacred **g** for
29: 5 Take the **g** and dress Aaron with the
29:21 his **g** and on his sons and their **g**.
29:21 and their **g** will be consecrated.
29:29 "Aaron's sacred **g** will belong to his
31:10 also the woven **g**, both the sacred **g**
31:10 the **g** for his sons when they serve
35:19 the woven **g** worn for ministering in
35:19 the sacred **g** for Aaron the priest
35:19 the **g** for his sons when they serve
35:21 its service, and for the sacred **g**.
39: 1 **g** for ministering in the sanctuary.
39: 1 They also made sacred **g** for Aaron,
39:41 the woven **g** worn for ministering in
39:41 both the sacred **g** for Aaron the
39:41 the **g** for his sons when serving as
40:13 dress Aaron in the sacred **g**, anoint
Lev 8: 2 "Bring Aaron and his sons, their **g**,
8:30 his **g** and on his sons and their **g**.
8:30 and his **g** and his sons and their **g**.
16: 4 These are sacred **g**; so he must bathe
16:23 take off the linen **g** he put on
16:24 holy place and put on his regular **g**.
16:32 He is to put on the sacred linen **g**
21:10 ordained to wear the priestly **g**,
Nu 15:38 tassels on the corners of your **g**,
20:26 Remove Aaron's **g** and put them on his
20:28 Moses removed Aaron's **g** and put them
Jdg 5:30 colourful **g** as plunder for Sisera,
5:30 colourful **g** embroidered, highly
5:30 highly embroidered **g** for my neck—
8:26 the pendants and the purple **g** worn
14:12 linen **g** and thirty sets of clothes.

Jdg 14:13 linen **g** and thirty sets of clothes.
2Sa 1:24 your **g** with ornaments of gold.
10: 4 cut off their **g** in the middle at the
1Ch 19: 4 shaved them, cut off their **g** in the
Ezr 2:69 minas of silver and 100 priestly **g**
Ne 7:70 50 bowls and 530 **g** for priests.
7:72 minas of silver and 67 **g** for priests
Est 8:15 wearing royal **g** of blue and white,
Ps 22:18 They divide my **g** among them and cast
45:14 In embroidered **g** she is led to the
Pr 31:24 She makes linen **g** and sells them,
SS 4:11 of your **g** is like that of Lebanon.
Isa 3:23 mirrors, and the linen **g** and tiaras
52: 1 Put on your **g** of splendour,
59:17 he put on the **g** of vengeance and
61:10 clothed me with **g** of salvation.
63: 1 with his **g** stained crimson?
63: 2 Why are your **g** red, like those of
63: 3 their blood spattered my **g**, and
Lam 4:14 that no-one dares to touch their **g**.
Eze 16:10 linen and covered you with costly **g**.
16:16 You took some of your **g** to make
26:16 and take off their embroidered **g**.
27:24 they traded with you beautiful **g**,
42:14 behind the **g** in which they minister,
44:19 the people by means of their **g**.
Joel 2:13 Rend your heart and not your **g**.
Am 2: 8 They lie down beside every altar on **g**
Zec 3: 4 sin, and I will put rich **g** on you."
Mt 23: 5 and the tassels on their **g** long;
Jn 19:24 "They divided my **g** among them and

Garmite

1Ch 4:19 the **G**, and Eshtemoa the Maacathite.

Garrison (Garrisons)

2Sa 23:14 the Philistine **g** was at Bethlehem.
1Ch 11:16 the Philistine **g** was at Bethlehem.

Garrisons (Garrison)

2Sa 8: 6 He put **g** in the Aramean kingdom of
8:14 He put **g** throughout Edom, and all
1Ch 18: 6 He put **g** in the Aramean kingdom of
18:13 He put **g** in Edom, and all the
2Ch 17: 2 put **g** in Judah and in the towns of

Gasp (Gasping)

Job 11:20 their hope will become a dying **g**."
Isa 42:14 childbirth, I cry out, I **g** and pant.

Gasping (Gasp)

Jer 4:31 the Daughter of Zion **g** for breath,

Gatam

Ge 36:11 Teman, Omar, Zepho, **G** and Kenaz.
36:16 Korah, **G** and Amalek. These were the
1Ch 1:36 Zepho, **G** and Kenaz; by Timna: Amalek.

Gate (Gatekeepers, Gatepost, Gateposts, Gates, Gateway, Gateways)

Ge 23:10 who had come to the **g** of his city.
23:18 who had come to the **g** of the city.
28:17 of God; this is the **g** of heaven."
34:20 his son Shechem went to the **g** of
34:24 out of the city **g** agreed with Hamor
Dt 17: 5 to your city **g** and stone that person
21:19 to the elders at the **g** of his town.
22:15 virgin to the town elders at the **g**.
22:24 you shall take both of them to the **g**
25: 7 to the elders at the town **g** and say,
Jos 2: 5 to close the city **g**, the men left.
2: 7 had gone out, the **g** was shut.
7: 5 city **g** as far as the stone quarries
8:29 down at the entrance of the city **g**.
20: 4 stand in the entrance of the city **g**
Jdg 9:35 to the city **g** just as Abimelech
9:40 the way to the entrance to the **g**.
9:44 at the entrance to the city **g**.
16: 2 for him all night at the city **g**.
16: 3 hold of the doors of the city **g**,
18:16 stood at the entrance to the **g**.
18:17 men stood at the entrance to the **g**.
Ru 4: 1 Meanwhile Boaz went up to the town **g**
Ru 4:11 the elders and all those at the **g**
1Sa 4:18 off his chair by the side of the **g**.
21:13 making marks on the doors of the **g**
2Sa 10: 8 at the entrance to their city **g**,
11:23 back to the entrance to the city **g**.
15: 2 of the road leading to the city **g**.
18: 4 So the king stood beside the **g**
23:15 the well near the **g** of Bethlehem!"
23:16 drew water from the well near the **g**
1Ki 4:13 walled cities with bronze **g** bars);
17:10 When he came to the town **g**, a widow
22:10 by the entrance of the **g** of Samaria,
2Ki 7: 1 for a shekel at the **g** of Samaria."
7: 3 at the entrance of the city **g**.
7:17 arm he leaned in charge of the **g**,
7:18 for a shekel at the **g** of Samaria."
9:31 Jehu entered the **g**, she asked, "Have
10: 8 of the city **g** until morning."
11: 6 a third at the Sur **G**, and a third at
11: 6 and a third at the **g** behind the
11:19 by way of the **g** of the guards.
14:13 from the Ephraim **G** to the Corner **G**
15:35 Upper **G** of the temple of the LORD.
23: 8 at the entrance to the **G** of Joshua
23: 8 which is on the left of the city **g**
25: 4 through the **g** between the two walls
1Ch 9:18 being stationed at the King's **G** on
11:17 the well near the **g** of Bethlehem!"
11:18 drew water from the well near the **g**
16:42 of Jeduthun were stationed at the **g**.
26:13 Lots were cast for each **g**, according
26:14 The lot for the East **G** fell to
26:14 the lot for the North **G** fell to him.
26:15 The lot for the South **G** fell to
26:16 The lots for the West **G** and the
26:16 the Shalleketh **G** on the upper road
2Ch 18: 9 by the entrance to the **g** of Samaria,
23: 5 and a third at the Foundation **G**,
23:15 the Horse **G** on the palace grounds,
23:20 into the palace through the Upper **G**
24: 8 at the **g** of the temple of the LORD.
25:23 from the Ephraim **G** to the Corner **G**
26: 9 towers in Jerusalem at the Corner **G**,
26: 9 at the Valley **G** and at the angle of
27: 3 Jotham rebuilt the Upper **G** of the
31:14 keeper of the East **G**, was in charge
32: 6 him in the square at the city **g**
33:14 far as the entrance of the Fish **G**
35:15 The gatekeepers at each **g** did not
Ne 2:13 Valley **G** towards the Jackal Well
2:13 the Jackal Well and the Dung **G**,
2:14 I moved on towards the Fountain **G**
2:15 and re-entered through the Valley **G**.
3: 1 to work and rebuilt the Sheep **G**.
3: 3 The Fish **G** was rebuilt by the sons
3: 6 The Jeshanah **G** was repaired by
3:13 The Valley **G** was repaired by Hanun
3:13 of the wall as far as the Dung **G**.
3:14 The Dung **G** was repaired by Malkijah
3:15 The Fountain **G** was repaired by
3:26 the Water **G** towards the east
3:28 Above the Horse **G**, the priests made
3:29 guard at the East **G**, made repairs.
3:31 opposite the Inspection **G**, and as
3:32 above the corner and the Sheep **G**
8: 1 in the square before the Water **G**.
8: 3 Water **G** in the presence of the men,
8:16 **G** and the one by the **G** of Ephraim.
12:31 to the right, towards the Dung **G**.
12:37 At the Fountain **G** they continued
12:37 of David to the Water **G** on the east.
12:39 over the **G** of Ephraim, the Jeshanah **G**
12:39 the Jeshanah **G**, the Fish **G**, the
12:39 At the **G** of the Guard they stopped.
Est 2:19 Mordecai was sitting at the king's **g**.
2:21 Mordecai was sitting at the king's **g**,
3: 2 at the king's **g** knelt down
3: 3 the royal officials at the king's **g**
4: 2 he went only as far as the king's **g**,
4: 6 the city in front of the king's **g**.
5: 9 he saw Mordecai at the king's **g**
5:13 Mordecai sitting at the king's **g**."
6:10 the Jew, who sits at the king's **g**.
6:12 Mordecai returned to the king's **g**.
Job 29: 7 "When I went to the **g** of the city
Ps 69:12 Those who sit at the **g** mock me, and
Ps 118:20 This is the **g** of the LORD through
127: 5 contend with their enemies in the **g**.
Pr 17:19 builds a high **g** invites destruction.
24: 7 at the **g** he has nothing to say.
31:23 husband is respected at the city **g**,
31:31 bring her praise at the city **g**.
SS 7: 4 of Heshbon by the **g** of Bath Rabbim.
Isa 14:31 Wail, O **g**! Howl, O city! Melt away,
24:12 The city is left in ruins, its **g** is
28: 6 who turn back the battle at the **g**.
Jer 7: 2 "Stand at the **g** of the LORD's house
17:19 "Go and stand at the **g** of the people,
19: 2 near the entrance of the Potsherd **G**.
20: 2 **G** of Benjamin at the LORD's temple.
26:10 of the New **G** of the LORD's house.
31:38 Tower of Hananel to the Corner **G**.
31:40 Horse **G**, will be holy to the LORD.
36:10 entrance of the New **G** of the temple,
37:13 when he reached the Benjamin **G**, the
38: 7 king was sitting in the Benjamin **G**,
39: 3 came and took seats in the Middle **G**
39: 4 through the **g** between the two walls,
52: 7 left the city at night through the **g**
Lam 5:14 The elders are gone from the city **g**;
Eze 8: 3 to the entrance to the north **g** of
8: 5 and in the entrance north of the **g**
8:14 north **g** of the house of the LORD,
9: 2 from the direction of the upper **g**,
10:19 to the east **g** of the LORD's house,
11: 1 brought me to the **g** of the house of
11: 1 There at the entrance to the **g** were
26: 2 'Aha! The **g** to the nations is broken,
40: 6 he went to the **g** facing east. He
40: 6 measured the threshold of the **g**;
40: 7 And the threshold of the **g** next to
40:10 Inside the east **g** were three alcoves
40:20 and width of the **g** facing north,
40:22 as those of the **g** facing east.
40:23 There was a **g** to the inner court
40:23 **g**, just as there was on the east.
40:23 He measured from one **g** to the
40:24 side and I saw a **g** facing south.
40:27 The inner court also had a **g** facing
40:27 and he measured from this **g** to the
40:27 to the outer **g** on the south side;
40:28 the inner court through the south **g**,
40:28 and he measured the south **g**; it had
40:35 he brought me to the north **g** and
40:44 Outside the inner **g**, within the
40:44 one at the side of the north **g** and
40:44 of the south **g** and facing north.
42:15 by the east **g** and measured the area
43: 1 man brought me to the **g** facing east
43: 4 temple through the **g** facing east.
44: 1 to the outer **g** of the sanctuary,
44: 2 The LORD said to me, "This **g** is to
44: 4 north **g** to the front of the temple.
46: 1 The **g** of the inner court facing east
46: 2 **g** will not be shut until evening.
46: 9 whoever enters by the north **g** to
46: 9 worship is to go out by the south **g**;
46: 9 south **g** is to go out by the north **g**.
46: 9 No-one is to return through the **g** by
46: 9 each is to go out by the opposite **g**.
46:12 the **g** facing east is to be opened
46:12 he has gone out, the **g** will be shut.
46:19 **g** to the sacred rooms facing north,
47: 2 brought me out through the north **g**
47: 2 outside to the outer **g** facing east,
48:31 north side will be the **g** of Reuben,
48:31 the **g** of Judah and the **g** of Levi.
48:32 will be three gates: the **g** of Joseph,
48:32 the **g** of Benjamin and the **g** of Dan.
48:33 be three gates: the **g** of Simeon
48:33 **g** of Issachar and the **g** of Zebulun.
48:34 will be three gates: the **g** of Gad,
48:34 **g** of Asher and the **g** of Naphtali.
Am 1: 5 I will break down the **g** of Damascus;
Mic 1: 9 reached the very **g** of my people
1:12 LORD, even to the **g** of Jerusalem.
2:13 will break through the **g** and go out.
Zep 1:10 "a cry will go up from the Fish **G**,
Zec 14:10 from the Benjamin **G** to the site of
14:10 the First **G**, to the Corner **G**,
Mt 7:13 "Enter through the narrow **g**. For
7:13 For wide is the **g** and broad is the

Mt 7:14 small is the **g** and narrow the road
Lk 7:12 he approached the town **g**, a dead
16:20 At his **g** was laid a beggar named
Jn 5: 2 Jerusalem near the Sheep **G** a pool,
10: 1 not enter the sheep pen by the **g**,
10: 2 The man who enters by the **g** is the
10: 3 The watchman opens the **g** for him,
10: 7 the truth, I am the **g** for the sheep.
10: 9 I am the **g**; whoever enters through
Ac 3: 2 to the temple **g** called Beautiful,
3:10 at the temple **g** called Beautiful,
10:17 house was and stopped at the **g**.
12:10 to the iron **g** leading to the city.
16:13 outside the city **g** to the river,
Heb 13:12 also suffered outside the city **g**
Rev 21:21 each **g** made of a single pearl.

Gatekeeper (Gate, Keeper)

2Sa 18:26 he called down to the **g**, "Look,
1Ch 9:21 son of Meshelemiah was the **g** at the

Gatekeepers (Gate, Keeper)

2Ki 7:10 out to the city **g** and told them,
7:11 The **g** shouted the news, and it was
1Ch 9:17 The **g**: Shallum, Akkub, Talmon,
9:18 These were the **g** belonging to the
9:19 the son of Korah, and his fellow **g**
9:20 of Eleazer was in charge of the **g**
9:22 Altogether, those chosen to be **g** at
9:22 The **g** had been assigned to their
9:24 The **g** were on the four sides: east,
9:26 the four principal **g**, who were
15:18 Mikneiah, Obed-Edom and Jeiel, the **g**.
16:38 of Jeduthun, and also Hosah, were **g**.
23: 5 Four thousand are to be **g** and four
26: 1 The divisions of the **g**: From the
26:12 These divisions of the **g**, through
26:19 These were the divisions of the **g**
2Ch 8:14 He also appointed the **g** by divisions
35:15 The **g** at each gate did not need to
Ezr 2:42 The **g** of the temple: the descendants
2:70 the Levites, the singers, the **g** and
7: 7 Levites, singers, **g** and temple
7:24 Levites, singers, **g**, temple servants
10:24 From the **g**: Shallum, Telem and Uri.
Ne 7: 1 the **g** and the singers and the
7: 3 While the **g** are still on duty, make
7:45 The **g**: the descendants of Shallum,
7:73 The priests, the Levites, the **g**, the
10:28 Levites, **g**, singers, temple servants
10:39 priests, the **g** and the singers stay.
11:19 The **g**: Akkub, Talmon and their
12:25 Meshullam, Talmon and Akkub were **g**
12:45 as did also the singers and **g**,
12:47 portions for the singers and **g**.
13: 5 singers and **g**, as well as the

Gatepost (Gate, Posts[2])

Eze 46: 2 of the gateway and stand by the **g**.

Gateposts (Gate, Posts[2])

Eze 45:19 and on the **g** of the inner court.

Gates (Gate)

Ge 24:60 possess the **g** of their enemies."
Ex 20:10 nor the alien within your **g**.
Dt 3: 5 high walls and with **g** and bars,
5:14 nor the alien within your **g**, so
6: 9 of your houses and on your **g**.
11:20 of your houses and on your **g**,
20:11 If they accept and open their **g**,
33:25 The bolts of your **g** will be iron
Jos 6:26 his youngest will he set up its **g**."
Jdg 5: 8 war came to the city **g**, and not a
5:11 the LORD went down to the city **g**.
1Sa 17:52 of Gath and to the **g** of Ekron.
23: 7 entering a town with **g** and bars."
2Sa 18:24 between the inner and outer **g**,
1Ki 16:34 he set up its **g** at the cost of
2Ki 15:16 they refused to open their **g**.
23: 8 broke down the shrines at the **g**
1Ch 9:23 the **g** of the house of the LORD
2Ch 8: 5 with walls and with **g** and bars,
8:14 by divisions for the various **g**,
2Ch 14: 7 round them, with towers, **g** and bars.
23:19 stationed doorkeepers at the **g** of
31: 2 at the **g** of the LORD's dwelling.
Ne 1: 3 its **g** have been burned with fire."
2: 3 its **g** have been destroyed by fire?"
2: 8 make beams for the **g** of the citadel
2:13 **g**, which had been destroyed by fire.
2:17 its **g** have been burned with fire.
6: 1 I had not set the doors in the **g**—
7: 3 I said to them, "The **g** of Jerusalem
11:19 who kept watch at the **g**—172 men.
12:25 who guarded the storerooms at the **g**.
12:30 the people, the **g** and the wall.
13:19 shadows fell on the **g** of Jerusalem
13:19 stationed some of my own men at the **g**
13:22 go and guard the **g** in order to keep
Job 17:16 Will it go down to the **g** of death?
38:17 Have the **g** of death been shown to
38:17 seen the **g** of the shadow of death?
Ps 9:13 and lift me up from the **g** of death,
9:14 in the **g** of the Daughter of Zion
24: 7 Lift up your heads, O you **g**; be
24: 9 Lift up your heads, O you **g**; lift
87: 2 the LORD loves the **g** of Zion more
100: 4 Enter his **g** with thanksgiving and
107:16 for he breaks down **g** of bronze and
107:18 food and drew near the **g** of death.
118:19 Open for me the **g** of righteousness;
122: 2 Our feet are standing in your **g**,
147:13 for he strengthens the bars of your **g**
Pr 8: 3 beside the **g** leading into the city,
14:19 wicked at the **g** of the righteous.
18:19 are like the barred **g** of a citadel.
Isa 3:26 The **g** of Zion will lament and mourn;
13: 2 them to enter the **g** of the nobles.
22: 7 horsemen are posted at the city **g**;
26: 2 Open the **g** that the righteous nation
38:10 must I go through the **g** of death
45: 1 him so that **g** will not be shut:
45: 2 I will break down **g** of bronze and
54:12 your **g** of sparkling jewels, and all
60:11 Your **g** will always stand open, they
60:18 walls Salvation and your **g** Praise.
62:10 Pass through, pass through the **g**!
Jer 1:15 the entrance of the **g** of Jerusalem;
7: 2 through these **g** to worship the LORD.
15: 7 fork at the city **g** of the land.
17:19 at all the other **g** of Jerusalem.
17:20 Jerusalem who come through these **g**.
17:21 bring it through the **g** of Jerusalem.
17:24 and bring no load through the **g** of
17:25 **g** of this city with their officials.
17:27 **g** of Jerusalem on the Sabbath day,
17:27 fire in the **g** of Jerusalem that
22: 2 people who come through these **g**.
22: 4 come through the **g** of this palace,
22:19 thrown outside the **g** of Jerusalem."
49:31 a nation that has neither **g** nor bars
51:30 fire; the bars of her **g** are broken.
51:58 levelled and her high **g** set on fire;
Lam 2: 9 Her **g** have sunk into the ground;
4:12 foes could enter the **g** of Jerusalem.
Eze 21:15 sword for slaughter at all their **g**.
21:22 to set battering-rams against the **g**,
26:10 chariots when he enters your **g** as
38:11 walls and without **g** and bars.
44:11 having charge of the **g** of the temple
44:17 "When they enter the **g** of the inner
44:17 ministering at the **g** of the inner
48:31 the **g** of the city will be named
48:31 The three **g** on the north side will
48:32 will be three **g**: the gate of Joseph,
48:33 will be three **g**: the gate of Simeon,
48:34 will be three **g**: the gate of Gad,
Hos 11: 6 will destroy the bars of their **g**
Ob :11 his **g** and cast lots for Jerusalem,
:13 You should not march through the **g**
Na 2: 6 The river **g** are thrown open and the
3:13 The **g** of your land are wide open to
Mt 16:18 the **g** of Hades will not overcome it.
Ac 9:24 on the city **g** in order to kill him.
14:13 wreaths to the city **g** because he and
21:30 and immediately the **g** were shut.
Rev 21:12 had a great, high wall with twelve **g**,
21:12 **g**, and with twelve angels at the **g**.
21:13 There were three **g** on the east,
Rev 21:15 the city, its **g** and its walls.
21:21 The twelve **g** were twelve pearls,
21:25 On no day will its **g** ever be shut,
22:14 may go through the **g** into the city.

Gateway (Gate, Way)

Ge 19: 1 Lot was sitting in the **g** of the city.
1Sa 9:18 Saul approached Samuel in the **g** and
2Sa 3:27 Joab took him aside into the **g**, as
18:24 up to the roof of the **g** by the wall.
18:33 He went up to the room over the **g**
19: 8 got up and took his seat in the **g**.
19: 8 "The king is sitting in the **g**,"
2Ki 7:17 the people trampled him in the **g**,
7:20 trampled him in the **g**, and he died.
Eze 27: 3 Say to Tyre, situated at the **g** to
40: 3 he was standing in the **g** with a
40: 8 he measured the portico of the **g**;
40: 9 portico of the **g** faced the temple.
40:11 the width of the entrance to the **g**;
40:13 he measured the **g** from the top of
40:14 the inside of the **g**—sixty cubits.
40:15 distance from the entrance of the **g**
40:16 the projecting walls inside the **g**
40:19 **g** to the outside of the inner court;
40:21 as those of the first **g**.
40:25 The **g** and its portico had narrow
40:29 The **g** and its portico had openings
40:32 and he measured the **g**; it had the
40:33 The **g** and its portico had openings
40:39 In the portico of the **g** were two
40:40 wall of the portico of the **g**,
40:40 to the north **g** were two tables,
40:41 four tables on one side of the **g**
44: 3 **g** to eat in the presence of the LORD.
44: 3 of the **g** and go out the same way."
46: 2 of the **g** and stand by the gatepost.
46: 2 threshold of the **g** and then go out,
46: 3 the LORD at the entrance to that **g**.
46: 8 go in through the portico of the **g**,
Mt 26:71 he went out to the **g**, where another

Gateways (Gate, Way)

1Ch 22: 3 doors of the **g** and for the fittings,
Pr 1:21 **g** of the city she makes her speech:
Lam 1: 4 All her **g** are desolate, her priests
Eze 40:18 abutted the sides of the **g** and was
40:30 (The porticoes of the **g** around the
40:38 the portico in each of the inner **g**,

Gath

One of 5 chief cities of the Philistines, about 10 miles east of Ashdod (Jos 13:3; 1Sa 6:17). Inhabited by the Anakim, even after Joshua had driven them out of the hill country of Judah (Jos 11:22). Home to Goliath (1Sa 17:4) and another giant (2Sa 21:20). Its inhabitants were struck by plague when ark of covenant brought here (1Sa 5:8–9), so sent a guilt offering to Israel (1Sa 6:17). David took refuge here (1Sa 21:10; 27:2–4), and later captured it (1Ch 18:1). Rehoboam fortified it (2Ch 11:8), but Hazael of Aram captured it (2Ki 12:17). Was destroyed by the time of Amos (Am 6:2). Exact location unknown.

Jos 11:22 Gaza, **G** and Ashdod did any survive.
13: 3 **G** and Ekron—that of the Avvites);
1Sa 5: 8 ark of the god of Israel moved to **G**.
6:17 Ashdod, Gaza, Ashkelon, **G** and Ekron.
7:14 The towns from Ekron to **G** that the
17: 4 **G**, came out of the Philistine camp.
17:23 the Philistine champion from **G**,
17:52 of **G** and to the gates of Ekron.
17:52 the Shaaraim road to **G** and Ekron.
21:10 Saul and went to Achish king of **G**.
21:12 much afraid of Achish king of **G**.
22: 1 David left **G** and escaped to the cave
27: 2 to Achish son of Maoch king of **G**.
27: 3 David and his men settled in **G** with
27: 4 was told that David had fled to **G**,
27:11 or woman alive to be brought to **G**,
2Sa 1:20 "Tell it not in **G**, proclaim it not
15:18 him from **G** marched before the king.
21:20 another battle, which took place at **G**
21:22 four were descendants of Rapha in **G**,
1Ki 2:39 king of **G**, and Shimei was told,

1Ki 2:39 was told, "Your slaves are in **G**.
2:40 Achish at **G** in search of his slaves.
2:40 and brought the slaves back from **G**.
2:41 Jerusalem to **G** and had returned,
2Ki 12:17 up and attacked **G** and captured it.
1Ch 7:21 killed by the native-born men of **G**,
8:13 who drove out the inhabitants of **G**.
18: 1 and he took **G** and its surrounding
20: 6 another battle which took place at **G**
20: 8 These were descendants of Rapha in **G**,
2Ch 11: 8 **G**, Mareshah, Ziph,
26: 6 broke down the walls of **G**, Jabneh
Ps 56: T Philistines had seized him in **G**.
Am 6: 2 and then go down to **G** in Philistia.
Mic 1:10 Tell it not in **G**; weep not at all.

Gath Hepher

Jos 19:13 it continued eastward to **G** and
2Ki 14:25 son of Amittai, the prophet from **G**.

Gath Rimmon

Jos 19:45 Jehud, Bene Berak, **G**,
21:24 Aijalon and **G**, together with their
21:25 Manasseh they received Taanach and **G**,
1Ch 6:69 Aijalon and **G**, together with their

Gather (Gathered, Gathering, Gathers, Ingathering)

Ge 31:46 He said to his relatives, "**G** some
49: 1 "**G** round so that I can tell you what
Ex 5: 7 let them go and **g** their own straw.
5:12 Egypt to **g** stubble to use for straw.
16: 4 each day and **g** enough for that day.
16: 5 much as they **g** on the other days."
16:16 Each one is to **g** as much as he needs.
16:26 Six days you are to **g** it, but on the
16:27 went out on the seventh day to **g** it,
23:16 you **g** in your crops from the field.
Lev 8: 3 **g** the entire assembly at the
19: 9 or **g** the gleanings of your harvest.
23:22 or **g** the gleanings of your harvest.
25: 3 your vineyards and **g** their crops.
Nu 10: 7 To **g** the assembly, blow the trumpets,
19: 9 "A man who is clean shall **g** up the
20: 8 Aaron **g** the assembly together.
21:16 "**G** the people together and I will
Dt 11:14 **g** in your grain, new wine and oil.
13:16 **G** all the plunder of the town into
28:39 not drink the wine or **g** the grapes,
30: 3 have compassion on you and **g** you
30: 4 God will **g** you and bring you back.
Ru 2: 7 let me glean and **g** among the sheaves
2Ki 4:39 to **g** herbs and found a wild vine.
22:20 I will **g** you to your fathers, and
1Ch 16:35 "Save us, O God our Saviour; **g** us
2Ch 34:28 Now I will **g** you to your fathers,
Ne 1: 9 I will **g** them from there and bring
Est 4:16 "Go, **g** together all the Jews who are
Job 24: 6 They **g** fodder in the fields and
39:12 and **g** it to your threshing-floor?
Ps 2: 2 the rulers **g** together against the
7: 7 Let the assembled peoples **g** round
50: 5 "**G** to me my consecrated ones, who
104:28 you give it to them, they **g** it up;
106:47 Save us, O LORD our God, and **g** us
142: 7 Then the righteous will **g** about me
Ecc 3: 5 scatter stones and a time to **g** them,
SS 6: 2 in the gardens and to **g** lilies.
Isa 10:14 nations; as men **g** abandoned eggs,
11:12 nations and **g** the exiles of Israel;
34:15 falcons will **g**, each with its mate.
34:16 and his Spirit will **g** them together.
43: 5 the east and **g** you from the west.
43: 9 All the nations **g** together and the
45:20 "**G** together and come; assemble, you
49: 5 back to him and **g** Israel to himself,
49:18 all your sons **g** and come to you.
56: 8 "I will **g** still others to them
62: 9 and those who **g** the grapes will
66:18 am about to come and **g** all nations
Jer 3:17 and all nations will **g** in Jerusalem
4: 5 '**G** together! Let us flee to the
7:18 The children **g** wood, the fathers
8:14 "Why are we sitting here? **G** together!
9:22 the reaper, with no-one to **g** them.'"
Jer 10:17 **G** up your belongings to leave the
12: 9 Go and **g** all the wild beasts;
21: 4 And I will **g** them inside this city.
23: 3 "I myself will **g** the remnant of my
29:14 I will **g** you from all the nations
31: 8 **g** them from the ends of the earth.
31:10 'He who scattered Israel will **g** them
32:37 I will surely **g** them from all the
49: 5 and no-one will **g** the fugitives.
Eze 11:17 I will **g** you from the nations and
16:37 therefore I am going to **g** all your
16:37 I will **g** them against you from all
20:34 **g** you from the countries where you
20:41 **g** you from the countries where you
22:19 dross, I will **g** you into Jerusalem.
22:20 men **g** silver, copper, iron, lead and
22:20 so will I **g** you in my anger and my
22:21 I will **g** you and I will blow on you
28:25 When I **g** the people of Israel from
29:13 At the end of forty years I will **g**
34:13 and **g** them from the countries,
36:24 I will **g** you from all the countries
37:21 I will **g** them from all around and
39:10 They will not need to **g** wood from
39:28 I will **g** them to their own land, not
Hos 7:14 They **g** together for grain and new
8:10 nations, I will now **g** them together.
9: 6 Egypt will **g** them, and Memphis will
Joel 2:16 **G** the people, consecrate the
2:16 **g** the children, those nursing at the
3: 2 I will **g** all nations and bring them
Mic 2:12 "I will surely **g** all of you,
4: 6 "I will **g** the lame; I will assemble
Na 3:18 the mountains with no-one to **g** them.
Hab 1: 9 wind and **g** prisoners like sand.
Zep 2: 1 **G** together, **g** together, O shameful
3: 8 to **g** the kingdoms and to pour out my
3:19 and **g** those who have been scattered.
3:20 At that time I will **g** you; at that
Zec 10: 8 I will signal for them and **g** them in.
10:10 from Egypt and **g** them from Assyria.
14: 2 I will **g** all the nations to
Mt 12:30 he who does not **g** with me scatters.
13:30 then **g** the wheat and bring it into
23:37 how often I have longed to **g** your
24:28 carcass, there the vultures will **g**.
24:31 and they will **g** his elect from the
25:26 **g** where I have not scattered seed?
Mk 13:27 he will send his angels and **g** his
Lk 3:17 and to **g** the wheat into his barn,
11:23 he who does not **g** with me, scatters.
13:34 how often I have longed to **g** your
17:37 body, there the vultures will **g**."
Jn 6:12 "**G** the pieces that are left over.
Ac 4:26 the rulers **g** together against the
2Ti 4: 3 they will **g** around them a great
Rev 14:18 "Take your sharp sickle and **g** the
16:14 to **g** them for the battle on the
19:17 "Come, **g** together for the great
20: 8 and Magog—to **g** them for battle.

Gathered (Gather)

Ge 1: 9 "Let the water under the sky be **g** to
1:10 and the **g** waters he called "seas".
25: 8 years; and he was **g** to his people.
25:17 died, and he was **g** to his people.
29: 3 all the flocks were **g** there, the
29: 7 is not time for the flocks to be **g**.
29: 8 "until all the flocks are **g** and the
35:29 and died and was **g** to his people,
37: 7 **g** round mine and bowed down to it."
49:29 "I am about to be **g** to my people.
49:33 his last and was **g** to his people.
Ex 16:17 were told; some **g** much, some little.
16:18 he who **g** much did not have too much,
16:18 **g** little did not have too little.
16:18 Each one **g** as much as he needed.
16:21 Each morning everyone **g** as much as
16:22 On the sixth day, they **g** twice as
32: 1 they **g** round Aaron and said, "Come,
Lev 8: 4 and the assembly **g** at the entrance
23:39 after you have **g** the crops of the
Nu 11:32 day the people went out and **g** quail.
11:32 No-one **g** less than ten homers. Then
14: 5 whole Israelite assembly **g** there.
Nu 16:19 Korah had **g** all his followers in
16:42 when the assembly **g** in opposition to
20: 2 **g** in opposition to Moses and Aaron.
20:10 He and Aaron **g** the assembly together
20:24 "Aaron will be **g** to his people. He
20:26 Aaron will be **g** to his people; he
27:13 you too will be **g** to your people, as
31: 2 that, you will be **g** to your people."
Dt 16:13 after you have **g** the produce of your
32:50 will die and be **g** to your people,
32:50 Mount Hor and was **g** to his people.
Jos 18: 1 of the Israelites **g** at Shiloh
22:12 the whole assembly of Israel **g** at
Jdg 2:10 had been **g** to their fathers,
4:13 Sisera **g** together his nine hundred
9: 6 Beth Millo **g** beside the great tree
9:27 and **g** the grapes and trodden them,
11: 3 **g** around him and followed him.
Ru 2:17 she threshed the barley she had **g**
2:18 saw how much she had **g**.
1Sa 8: 4 all the elders of Israel **g** together
17: 1 Now the Philistines **g** their forces
17:47 All those **g** here will know that it
22: 2 in debt or discontented **g** round him,
28: 1 In those days the Philistines **g**
28: 4 while Saul **g** all the Israelites and
29: 1 The Philistines **g** all their forces
2Sa 10:17 David was told of this, he **g** all
17:11 sand on the seashore—be **g** to you,
20:14 who **g** together and followed him.
21:13 been killed and exposed were **g** up.
23: 6 which are not **g** with the hand.
23: 9 **g** at Pas Dammim for battle.
1Ki 8: 5 had **g** about him were before the ark,
11:24 He **g** men around him and became the
2Ki 4:39 He **g** some of its gourds and filled
1Ch 11:13 the Philistines **g** there for battle.
19:17 David was told of this, he **g** all
23: 2 He also **g** together all the leaders
2Ch 5: 6 had **g** about him were before the ark,
13: 7 Some worthless scoundrels **g** around
23: 2 They went throughout Judah and **g** the
28:24 Ahaz **g** together the furnishings from
29:20 **g** the city officials together
Ezr 7:28 I took courage and **g** leading men
9: 4 **g** round me because of this
10: 1 women and children—**g** round him.
10: 9 and Benjamin had **g** in Jerusalem.
Ne 8:13 **g** round Ezra the scribe to give
9: 1 the Israelites **g** together, fasting
Job 5:26 vigour, like sheaves **g** in season.
24:24 they are brought low and **g** up like
30: 4 In the brush they **g** salt herbs, and
Ps 35:15 I stumbled, they **g** in glee;
35:15 **g** against me when I was unaware.
107: 3 those he **g** from the lands, from east
Pr 27:25 the grass from the hills is **g** in,
30: 4 Who has **g** up the wind in the hollow
SS 5: 1 I have **g** my myrrh with my spice.
Isa 10:14 so I **g** all the countries; not one
27:12 Israelites, will be **g** up one by one.
56: 8 to them besides those already **g**."
60: 7 All Kedar's flocks will be **g** to you,
Jer 6:11 and on the young men **g** together;
8: 2 They will not be **g** up or buried, but
25:33 They will not be mourned or **g** up or
40:15 cause all the Jews who are **g** around
Eze 29: 5 field and not be **g** or picked up.
38: 7 you and all the hordes **g** about you,
38: 8 whose people were **g** from many
38:12 and the people **g** from the nations,
38:13 Have you **g** your hordes to loot,
39:27 have **g** them from the countries of
Hos 10:10 nations will be **g** against them to
Mic 1: 7 Since she **g** her gifts from the wages
4:11 now many nations are **g** against you.
Zec 12: 3 of the earth are **g** against her,
Mt 13: 2 Such large crowds **g** round him that
16: 9 and how many basketfuls you **g**?
16:10 and how many basketfuls you **g**?
22:10 **g** all the people they could find,
22:41 While the Pharisees were **g** together,
25:32 All the nations will be **g** before him,
27:17 when the crowd had **g**, Pilate asked
27:27 **g** the whole company of soldiers
Mk 1:33 The whole town **g** at the door,

Mk 2: 2 many **g** that there was no room left,
3:20 and again a crowd **g**, so that he and
4: 1 The crowd that **g** round him was so
5:21 **g** round him while he was by the lake.
6:30 The apostles **g** round Jesus and
7: 1 from Jerusalem **g** round Jesus
8: 1 those days another large crowd **g**.
Lk 12: 1 a crowd of many thousands had **g**,
23:48 all the people who had **g** to witness
Jn 6:13 they **g** them and filled twelve
8: 2 where all the people **g** round him,
10:24 The Jews **g** round him, saying, "How
Ac 5:16 Crowds **g** also from the towns around
6: 2 the Twelve **g** all the disciples
12:12 many people had **g** and were praying.
13:44 city **g** to hear the word of the Lord.
14:20 after the disciples had **g** round him,
14:27 On arriving there, they **g** the church
15:30 where they **g** the church together and
16:13 speak to the women who had **g** there.
28: 3 Paul **g** a pile of brushwood and, as
2Co 8:15 is written: "He who **g** much did not
8:15 **g** little did not have too little."
2Th 2: 1 Jesus Christ and our being **g** to him,
Rev 14:19 **g** its grapes and threw them into the
16:16 they **g** the kings together to the
19:19 their armies **g** together to make war

Gathering (Gather)

Nu 11: 8 The people went around **g** it, and
15:32 was found **g** wood on the Sabbath day.
15:33 Those who found him **g** wood brought
1Ki 17:10 gate, a widow was there **g** sticks.
17:12 I am **g** a few sticks to take home and
Ecc 2:26 the sinner he gives the task of **g**
Jer 6: 9 branches again, like one **g** grapes."
Mt 3:12 **g** his wheat into the barn and
25:24 **g** where you have not scattered seed.
Lk 8: 4 While a large crowd was **g** and people
15: 1 were all **g** round to hear him.
Ac 10:27 and found a large **g** of people.

Gathers (Gather)

Nu 19:10 The man who **g** up the ashes of the
Ru 2:15 "Even if she **g** among the sheaves,
Ps 33: 7 He **g** the waters of the sea into jars;
41: 6 while his heart **g** slander; then he
129: 7 nor the one who **g** fill his arms.
147: 2 he **g** the exiles of Israel.
Pr 6: 8 in summer and **g** its food at harvest.
10: 5 He who **g** crops in summer is a wise
13:11 but he who **g** money little by little
Isa 17: 5 will be as when a reaper **g** the
40:11 He **g** the lambs in his arms and
56: 8 he who **g** the exiles of Israel:
Mic 4:12 he who **g** them like sheaves to the
7: 1 I am like one who **g** summer fruit at
Hab 1:15 he **g** them up in his drag-net;
2: 5 he **g** to himself all the nations and
Mt 23:37 as a hen **g** her chicks under her
Lk 13:34 as a hen **g** her chicks under her

Gaudy

Eze 16:16 your garments to make **g** high places,

Gaunt (Gauntness)

Ge 41: 3 seven other cows, ugly and **g**, came
41: 4 the cows that were ugly and **g** ate up
Ps 109:24 from fasting; my body is thin and **g**.

Gauntness (Gaunt)

Job 16: 8 **g** rises up and testifies against me.

Gave (Give)

Ge 2:20 the man **g** names to all the livestock,
3: 6 She also **g** some to her husband, who
3:12 she **g** me some fruit from the tree,
4: 1 became pregnant and **g** birth to Cain.
4: 2 Later she **g** birth to his brother
4:17 pregnant and **g** birth to Enoch.
4:20 Adah **g** birth to Jabal; he was the
4:25 and she **g** birth to a son and named
9: 3 Just as I **g** you the green plants, I
12:20 Pharaoh **g** orders about Abram to his
Ge 14:20 Abram **g** him a tenth of everything.
16: 3 **g** her to her husband to be his wife.
16:13 She **g** this name to the LORD who
16:15 Hagar bore Abram a son, and Abram **g**
18: 7 tender calf and **g** it to a servant,
20:14 female slaves and **g** them to Abraham,
21: 3 Abraham **g** the name Isaac to the son
21:14 a skin of water and **g** them to Hagar.
21:19 with water and **g** the boy a drink.
21:27 and cattle and **g** them to Abimelech,
24:18 jar to her hands and **g** him a drink.
24:53 of clothing and **g** them to Rebekah;
24:53 he also **g** costly gifts to her
25: 6 **g** gifts to the sons of his
25:26 old when Rebekah **g** birth to them.
25:34 Jacob **g** Esau some bread and some
26:11 Abimelech **g** orders to all the people:
26:18 and he **g** them the same names his
27:20 your God **g** me success," he replied.
28: 4 alien, the land God **g** to Abraham."
29:22 people of the place and **g** a feast.
29:23 he took his daughter Leah and **g** her
29:24 Laban **g** his servant girl Zilpah to
29:28 and then Laban **g** him his daughter
29:29 Laban **g** his servant girl Bilhah to
29:32 Leah became pregnant and **g** birth to
29:33 She conceived again, and when she **g**
29:33 I am not loved, he **g** me this one too.
29:34 Again she conceived, and when she **g**
29:35 She conceived again, and when she **g**
30: 4 she **g** him her servant Bilhah as a
30: 9 Zilpah and **g** her to Jacob as a wife.
30:21 Some time later she **g** birth to a
30:23 She became pregnant and **g** birth to a
30:25 After Rachel **g** birth to Joseph,
31: 8 flocks **g** birth to speckled young;
35: 4 they **g** Jacob all the foreign gods
35:12 The land I **g** to Abraham and Isaac I
38: 3 she became pregnant and **g** birth to a
38: 4 She conceived again and **g** birth to a
38: 5 She **g** birth to still another son and
38: 5 at Kezib that she **g** birth to him.
38:18 So he **g** them to her and slept with
39: 3 **g** him success in everything he did,
39:23 **g** him success in whatever he did.
40:20 he **g** a feast for all his officials.
41:45 Pharaoh **g** Joseph the name
41:45 **g** him Asenath daughter of Potiphera,
42:25 Joseph **g** orders to fill their bags
43:24 **g** them water to wash their feet and
44: 1 Now Joseph **g** these instructions to
45:21 Joseph **g** them carts, as Pharaoh had
45:21 **g** them provisions for their journey.
45:22 To each of them he **g** new clothing,
45:22 Benjamin he **g** three hundred shekels
47:11 his brothers in Egypt and **g** them
47:17 and he **g** them food in exchange for
47:22 from the allotment Pharaoh **g** them.
49:29 he **g** them these instructions: "I am
Ex 1:21 the midwives feared God, he **g** them
1:22 Pharaoh **g** this order to all his
2: 2 she became pregnant and **g** birth to a
2:21 who **g** his daughter Zipporah to Moses
2:22 Zipporah **g** birth to a son, and Moses
4:11 The LORD said to him, "Who **g** man his
5: 6 That same day Pharaoh **g** this order
12:36 and they **g** them what they asked for;
16:32 so they can see the bread I **g** you to
31:18 he **g** him the two tablets of the
32:24 Then they **g** me the gold, and I
34:32 and he **g** them all the commands the
36: 6 Moses **g** an order and they sent this
Lev 7:38 which the LORD **g** Moses on Mount
27:34 These are the commands the LORD **g**
Nu 3:51 Moses **g** the redemption money to
7: 6 Moses took the carts and oxen and **g**
7: 7 He **g** two carts and four oxen to the
7: 8 he **g** four carts and eight oxen to
13:16 **g** Hoshea son of Nun the name Joshua.)
13:27 They **g** Moses this account: "We went
15:22 of these commands the LORD **g** Moses
15:23 from the day the LORD **g** them and
17: 6 their leaders **g** him twelve staffs,
21: 3 and **g** the Canaanites over to them.
22:18 "Even if Balak **g** me his palace
22:40 and **g** some to Balaam and the princes
Nu 24:13 'Even if Balak **g** me his palace
30:16 These are the regulations the LORD **g**
31:21 of the law that the LORD **g** Moses:
31:41 Moses **g** the tribute to Eleazar the
31:47 and **g** them to the Levites, who were
32:28 Moses **g** orders about them to Eleazar
32:33 Moses **g** to the Gadites, the
32:38 **g** names to the cities they rebuilt.
32:40 Moses **g** Gilead to the Makirites, the
36: 5 at the LORD's command Moses **g** this
36:13 regulations the LORD **g** through Moses
Dt 2:12 LORD **g** them as their possession.)
2:36 The LORD our God **g** us all of them.
3: 3 the LORD our God also **g** into our
3:12 I **g** the Reubenites and the Gadites
3:13 I **g** to the half-tribe of Manasseh.
3:15 I **g** Gilead to Makir.
3:16 to the Reubenites and the Gadites I **g**
4:45 **g** them when they came out of
5:22 two stone tablets and **g** them to me.
8:16 He **g** you manna to eat in the desert,
9:10 The LORD **g** me two stone tablets
9:11 the LORD **g** me the two stone tablets,
10: 4 And the LORD **g** them to me.
22:16 "I **g** my daughter in marriage to this
26: 9 He brought us to this place and **g** us
28:45 the commands and decrees he **g** you.
29: 8 We took their land and **g** it as an
31: 9 Moses wrote down this law and **g** it
31:23 The LORD **g** this command to Joshua
31:25 he **g** this command to the Levites who
32: 8 the Most High **g** the nations their
32:18 you forgot the God who **g** you birth.
33: 4 the law that Moses **g** us, the
Jos 1: 7 all the law my servant Moses **g** you;
1:13 Moses the servant of the LORD **g** you:
1:14 that Moses **g** you east of the Jordan,
1:15 Moses the servant of the LORD **g** you
6:20 when the people **g** a loud shout, the
8:33 he **g** instructions to bless the
10:12 On the day the LORD **g** the Amorites
10:27 At sunset Joshua **g** the order and
10:30 The LORD also **g** that city and its
11: 8 the LORD **g** them into the hand of
11:23 and he **g** it as an inheritance to
12: 6 And Moses the servant of the LORD **g**
12: 7 lands Joshua **g** as an inheritance to
13:14 to the tribe of Levi he **g** no
14:13 and **g** him Hebron as his inheritance.
15:13 Joshua **g** to Caleb son of Jephunneh a
15:17 so Caleb **g** his daughter Acsah
15:19 **g** her the upper and lower springs.
17: 4 So Joshua **g** them an inheritance
18: 7 servant of the LORD **g** it to them."
19:49 the Israelites **g** Joshua son of Nun
19:50 They **g** him the town he asked for
21: 3 the Israelites **g** the Levites the
21:11 They **g** them Kiriath Arba (that is,
21:13 they **g** Hebron (a city of refuge
21:17 from the tribe of Benjamin they **g**
21:43 the LORD **g** Israel all the land he
21:44 The LORD **g** them rest on every side,
22: 3 the mission the LORD your God **g** you.
22: 4 Moses the servant of the LORD **g** you
22: 5 Moses the servant of the LORD **g** you
22: 7 Joshua **g** land on the west side of
22:34 the Reubenites and the Gadites **g** the
23:14 the LORD your God **g** you has failed.
24: 3 Canaan and **g** him many descendants.
24: 3 I **g** him Isaac,
24: 4 to Isaac I **g** Jacob and Esau. I
24: 8 I **g** them into your hands. I
24:11 but I **g** them into your hands.
24:13 I **g** you a land on which you did not
Jdg 1: 4 When Judah attacked, the LORD **g** the
1:13 so Caleb **g** his daughter Acsah
1:15 **g** her the upper and lower springs.
3: 6 **g** their own daughters to their sons,
3:10 The LORD **g** Cushan-Rishathaim king of
3:12 the LORD **g** Eglon king of Moab power
3:15 and he **g** them a deliverer—Ehud, a
4:19 **g** him a drink, and covered him up.
5:25 He asked for water, and she **g** him
6: 1 and for seven years he **g** them into
6: 9 before you and **g** you their land.
8: 3 God **g** Oreb and Zeeb, the Midianite

Jdg 9: 4 They **g** him seventy shekels of silver
11:21 the LORD, the God of Israel, **g** Sihon
11:32 and the LORD **g** them into his hands.
12: 3 the LORD **g** me the victory over them.
12: 9 He **g** his daughters away in marriage
13:24 The woman **g** birth to a boy and named
14: 9 rejoined his parents, he **g** them some
14:19 **g** their clothes to those who had
15: 2 said, "that I **g** her to your friend.
17: 4 silver and **g** them to a silversmith,
Ru 1:12 tonight and then **g** birth to sons—
2:15 she got up to glean, Boaz **g** orders
2:18 Ruth also brought out and **g** her what
3:17 added, "He **g** me these six measures
4: 7 his sandal and **g** it to the other.
4:13 conceive, and she **g** birth to a son.
1Sa 1: 5 to Hannah he **g** a double portion
1:20 conceived and **g** birth to a son.
2:20 she prayed for and **g** to the LORD.
2:21 she conceived and **g** birth to three
2:28 I also **g** your father's house all the
4:19 she went into labour and **g** birth,
9:23 "Bring the piece of meat I **g** you,
13:13 the command the LORD your God **g** you
15:24 afraid of the people and so I **g** in
18: 4 he was wearing and **g** it to David,
18: 5 Saul **g** him a high rank in the army.
18:13 he sent David away from him and **g**
18:27 Then Saul **g** him his daughter Michal
20:40 Jonathan **g** his weapons to the boy
21: 6 the priest **g** him the consecrated
22:10 he also **g** him provisions and the
24:10 LORD **g** you into my hands in the cave.
24:18 the LORD **g** me into your hands, but
24:22 David **g** his oath to Saul. Then Saul
25: 9 David's men arrived, they **g** Nabal
26:23 The LORD **g** you into my hands today,
27: 6 on that day Achish **g** him Ziklag, and
30:11 They **g** him water to drink and food
2Sa 3:15 Ish-Bosheth **g** orders and had her
4:10 was the reward I **g** him for his news!
4:12 David **g** an order to his men, and
6:19 he **g** a loaf of bread, a cake of
8: 6 **g** David victory wherever he went.
8:14 **g** David victory wherever he went.
12: 8 I **g** your master's house to you, and
12: 8 I **g** you the house of Israel and
12:24 She **g** birth to a son, and they named
13:25 to go, but **g** him his blessing.
14:16 son from the inheritance God **g** us.'
16:23 the advice Ahithophel **g** was like that
19:28 but you **g** your servant a place among
19:39 The king kissed Barzillai and **g** him
1Ki 1: 7 and they **g** him their support.
2: 1 he **g** a charge to Solomon his son.
2:25 King Solomon **g** orders to Benaiah son
2:43 LORD and obey the command I **g** you?"
2:46 the king **g** the order to Benaiah son
3:15 Then he **g** a feast for all his court.
3:25 He then **g** an order: "Cut the living
3:27 the king **g** his ruling: "Give the
4:29 God **g** Solomon wisdom and very great
5:11 Solomon **g** Hiram twenty thousand cors
5:12 The LORD **g** Solomon wisdom, just as
6:12 promise I **g** to David your father.
8:34 to the land you **g** to their fathers.
8:36 **g** your people for an inheritance.
8:40 live in the land you **g** our fathers.
8:48 the land you **g** their fathers,
8:56 he **g** through his servant Moses.
8:58 and regulations he **g** our fathers.
9:11 King Solomon **g** twenty towns in
9:16 then **g** it as a wedding gift to his
10:10 she **g** the king 120 talents of gold,
10:10 queen of Sheba **g** to King Solomon.
10:13 King Solomon **g** the queen of Sheba
11:18 to Pharaoh king of Egypt, who **g**
11:19 he **g** him a sister of his own wife,
12: 8 rejected the advice the elders **g** him
13: 3 That same day the man of God **g** a
13:21 the command the LORD your God **g** you.
14: 8 the house of David and **g** it to you,
14:15 land that he **g** to their forefathers
15: 4 for David's sake the LORD his God **g**
17:23 He **g** him to his mother and said,
19:21 **g** it to the people, and they ate.
2Ki 4:17 that same time she **g** birth to a son,
5:23 He **g** them to two of his servants,
11:10 he **g** the commanders the spears and
12:11 **g** the money to the men appointed to
12:15 they **g** the money to pay the workers,
15:19 and Menahem **g** him a thousand talents
16:15 Ahaz then **g** these orders to Uriah
17:20 **g** them into the hands of plunderers,
17:27 the king of Assyria **g** this order:
17:34 the LORD **g** the descendants of Jacob,
18:15 Hezekiah **g** him all the silver that
18:16 and **g** it to the king of Assyria.
21: 8 from the land I **g** their forefathers,
21: 8 Law that my servant Moses **g** them."
22: 8 He **g** it to Shaphan, who read it.
22:12 He **g** these orders to Hilkiah the
23:21 The king **g** this order to all the
25:28 He spoke kindly to him and **g** him a
25:30 Day by day the king **g** Jehoiachin a
1Ch 2:35 Sheshan **g** his daughter in marriage
2:49 She also **g** birth to Shaaph the
4: 9 saying, "I **g** birth to him in pain.
4:17 One of Mered's wives **g** birth to
4:18 (His Judean wife **g** birth to Jered
6:64 the Israelites **g** the Levites these
6:70 the Israelites **g** Aner and Bileam,
7:14 She **g** birth to Makir the father of
7:16 Makir's wife Maacah **g** birth to a son
7:18 His sister Hammoleketh **g** birth to
7:23 pregnant and **g** birth to a son.
11:10 **g** his kingship strong support to
14:12 **g** orders to burn them in the fire.
16: 3 he **g** a loaf of bread, a cake of
18: 6 **g** David victory everywhere he went.
18:13 **g** David victory everywhere he went.
22: 2 David **g** orders to assemble the
22:13 that the LORD **g** to Moses for Israel.
25: 5 God **g** Heman fourteen sons and three
28:11 David **g** his son Solomon the plans
28:12 He **g** him the plans of all that the
28:13 He **g** him instructions for the
28:18 He also **g** him the plan for the
28:19 and he **g** me understanding in all the
29: 6 of the king's work **g** willingly.
29: 7 **g** towards the work on the temple
29: 8 Any who had precious stones **g** them
2Ch 2: 1 Solomon **g** orders to build a temple
6:25 you **g** to them and their fathers.
6:27 **g** your people for an inheritance.
6:31 in the land that you **g** our fathers.
6:38 the land that you **g** their fathers,
7: 3 and they worshipped and **g** thanks to
7: 6 which were used when he **g** thanks,
9: 9 she **g** the king 120 talents of gold,
9: 9 queen of Sheba **g** to King Solomon.
9:12 King Solomon **g** the queen of Sheba
9:12 he **g** her more than she had brought
10: 8 rejected the advice the elders **g**
11:23 He **g** them abundant provisions and
14: 6 years, for the LORD **g** him rest.
15:15 the LORD **g** them rest on every side.
19: 9 He **g** them these orders: "You must
20:11 you **g** us as an inheritance.
23: 9 he **g** the commanders of units of a
24:12 The king and Jehoiada **g** it to the
26: 5 sought the LORD, God **g** him success.
28: 9 Judah, he **g** them into your hand.
28:14 the soldiers **g** up the prisoners and
28:20 but **g** him trouble instead of help.
29:27 Hezekiah **g** the order to sacrifice
31: 5 the Israelites generously **g** the
31:11 Hezekiah **g** orders to prepare
32:24 him and **g** him a miraculous sign.
34: 9 **g** him the money that had been
34:11 They also **g** money to the carpenters
34:15 He **g** it to Shaphan.
34:20 He **g** these orders to Hilkiah, Ahikam
35: 8 administrators of God's temple, **g**
Ezr 2:68 some of the heads of the families **g**
2:69 According to their ability they **g** to
3: 7 they **g** money to the masons and
3: 7 and **g** food and drink and oil to the
3:11 And all the people **g** a great shout
5:11 This is the answer they **g** us: "We
5:14 "Then King Cyrus **g** them to a man
8:36 who then **g** assistance to the people
Ezr 9:11 you **g** through your servants the
10:19 (They all **g** their hands in pledge to
Ne 1: 7 and laws you **g** your servant Moses.
1: 8 "Remember the instruction you **g** your
2: 1 I took the wine and **g** it to the king.
2: 9 and **g** them the king's letters.
6: 4 each time I **g** them the same answer.
7:70 The governor **g** to the treasury 1,000
7:71 Some of the heads of the families **g**
9:13 You **g** them regulations and laws that
9:14 **g** them commands, decrees and laws
9:15 In their hunger you **g** them bread
9:20 You **g** your good Spirit to instruct
9:20 you **g** them water for their thirst.
9:22 "You **g** them kingdoms and nations,
9:27 you **g** them deliverers, who rescued
9:34 commands or the warnings you **g** them.
9:35 and fertile land you **g** them.
9:36 slaves in the land you **g** our
12:40 The two choirs that **g** thanks then
13: 9 I **g** orders to purify the rooms, and
Est 1: 3 in the third year of his reign he **g**
1: 5 days were over, the king **g** a banquet
1: 9 Queen Vashti also **g** a banquet for
2:18 the king **g** a great banquet, Esther's
3:10 and **g** it to Haman son of Hammedatha,
4: 8 He also **g** him a copy of the text of
5:12 the king to the banquet she **g**.
8: 1 That same day King Xerxes **g** Queen
Job 1:21 The LORD **g** and the LORD has taken
8: 4 he **g** them over to the penalty of
10:12 You **g** me life and showed me kindness,
22: 7 You **g** no water to the weary and you
32:12 I **g** you my full attention. But not
38:36 or **g** understanding to the mind?
39: 6 I **g** him the wasteland as his home,
42:10 **g** him twice as much as he had before.
42:11 and each one **g** him a piece of silver
Ps 21: 4 He asked you for life, and you **g** it
21: 5 Through the victories you **g**, his
40: 2 rock and **g** me a firm place to stand.
44:11 You **g** us up to be devoured like
68: 9 You **g** abundant showers, O God; you
69:21 They put gall in my food and **g** me
74:14 **g** him as food to the creatures of
78:15 **g** them water as abundant as the seas;
78:23 Yet he **g** a command to the skies
78:24 eat, he **g** them the grain of heaven.
78:46 He **g** their crops to the grasshopper,
78:48 He **g** over their cattle to the hail,
78:50 death but **g** them over to the plague.
78:62 He **g** his people over to the sword;
81:12 I **g** them over to their stubborn
99: 7 statutes and the decrees he **g** them.
105:44 he **g** them the lands of the nations,
106: 7 they **g** no thought to you miracles;
106:14 In the desert they **g** in to their
106:15 he **g** them what they asked for, but
135:12 he **g** their land as an inheritance,
136:21 **g** their land as an inheritance,
148: 6 **g** a decree that will never pass away.
Pr 1:24 **g** heed when I stretched out my hand,
8:29 he **g** the sea its boundary so that
23:22 Listen to your father, who **g** you
23:25 may she who **g** you birth rejoice!
Ecc 12: 7 the spirit returns to God who **g** it.
SS 8: 5 she who was in labour **g** you birth.
Isa 8: 3 she conceived and **g** birth to a son.
22:16 What are you doing here and who **g**
26:18 in pain, but we **g** birth to wind.
41:27 **g** to Jerusalem a messenger of good
47: 6 I **g** them into your hand, and you
51: 2 and to Sarah, who **g** you birth.
63: 5 I was appalled that no-one **g** support;
Jer 2:27 and to stone, 'You **g** me birth.
3: 8 I **g** faithless Israel her certificate
3:18 **g** your forefathers as an inheritance.
7: 7 in the land I **g** to your forefathers
7:14 place I **g** to you and your fathers.
7:23 I **g** them this command: Obey me, and
12:14 inheritance I **g** to my people Israel,
15:10 Alas, my mother, that you **g** me birth,
16:15 the land I **g** to their forefathers.
17: 4 will lose the inheritance I **g** you.
22:26 I will hurl you and the mother who **g**
23:39 city I **g** to you and your fathers.

Jer 24:10 I **g** to them and their fathers.'"
25: 5 you can stay in the land the LORD **g**
27:12 I **g** the same message to Zedekiah
30: 3 I **g** to their forefathers to possess,'
32:12 I **g** this deed to Baruch son of
32:13 "In their presence I **g** Baruch these
32:22 You **g** them this land you had sworn
35: 6 son of Recab **g** us this command:
35:16 the command their forefather **g** them,
36:32 Jeremiah took another scroll and **g**
37:21 King Zedekiah then **g** orders for
39:10 time he **g** them vineyards and fields.
40: 5 Then the commander **g** him provisions
50:12 who **g** you birth will be disgraced.
51:59 This is the message Jeremiah **g** to
52:32 He spoke kindly to him and **g** him a
52:34 Day by day the king of Babylon **g**
Lam 2:14 **g** you were false and misleading.
Eze 3: 2 I opened my mouth, and he **g** me the
16: 8 I **g** you my solemn oath and entered
16:17 You also took the fine jewellery I **g**
16:19 olive oil and honey I **g** you to
16:27 I **g** you over to the greed of your
16:36 you **g** them your children's blood,
20:11 I **g** them my decrees and made known
20:12 Also I **g** them my Sabbaths as a sign
20:25 I also **g** them over to statutes that
23: 4 They were mine and **g** birth to sons
23: 7 She **g** herself as a prostitute to all
28:25 land, which I **g** to my servant Jacob.
31: 6 all the beasts of the field **g** birth
36:28 You will live in the land I **g** your
37:25 They will live in the land I **g** to my
Da 1: 7 The chief official **g** them new names:
1:16 drink and **g** them vegetables instead.
1:17 To these four young men God **g**
5: 1 King Belshazzar **g** a great banquet
5: 2 he **g** orders to bring in the gold and
5: 6 knocked together and his legs **g** way.
5:18 "O king, the Most High God **g** your
5:19 of the high position he **g** him, all
6:16 the king **g** the order, and they
6:23 The king was overjoyed and **g** orders
7:16 "So he told me and **g** me the
7:23 "He **g** me this explanation: 'The
9:10 laws he **g** us through his servants
10:18 a man touched me and **g** me strength.
Hos 1: 6 Gomer conceived again and **g** birth to
2: 8 I was the one who **g** her the grain,
12:10 I spoke to the prophets, **g** them many
13:11 in my anger I **g** you a king, and in
Am 4: 6 "I **g** you empty stomachs in every
Hag 1:13 Haggai, the LORD's messenger, **g** this
Zec 3: 6 The angel of the LORD **g** this charge
Mal 2: 5 and I **g** them to him; this called for
4: 4 I **g** him at Horeb for all Israel.
Mt 1:25 he had no union with her until she **g**
1:25 And he **g** him the name Jesus.
2:16 he was furious, and he **g** orders to
8:18 Jesus saw the crowd around him, he **g**
10: 1 **g** them authority to drive out evil
14:19 he **g** thanks and broke the loaves.
14:19 Then he **g** them to the disciples, and
14:19 the disciples **g** them to the people.
15:36 he broke them and **g** them to the
20:14 was hired last the same as I **g** you.
21:23 "And who **g** you this authority?"
25:15 To one he **g** five talents of money,
25:35 For I was hungry and you **g** me
25:35 I was thirsty and you **g** me something
25:42 For I was hungry and you **g** me
25:42 and you **g** me nothing to drink,
26:26 **g** thanks and broke it, and **g** it to
26:27 he took the cup, **g** thanks and
27:12 and the elders, he **g** no answer.
27:50 in a loud voice, he **g** up his spirit.
28:12 **g** the soldiers a large sum of money,
Mk 2:26 he also **g** some to his companions."
3:12 he **g** them strict orders not to tell
3:16 Simon (to whom he **g** the name Peter);
3:17 (to them he **g** the name Boanerges,
5:13 He **g** them permission, and the evil
5:43 He **g** strict orders not to let anyone
6: 7 **g** them authority over evil spirits.
6:21 On his birthday Herod **g** a banquet
6:28 girl, and she **g** it to her mother.
Mk 6:41 he **g** thanks and broke the loaves.
6:41 Then he **g** them to his disciples to
8: 6 he broke them and **g** them to his
8: 7 he **g** thanks for them also and told
9: 9 Jesus **g** them orders not to tell
11:28 "And who **g** you authority to do this?"
12:44 They all **g** out of their wealth; but
14:22 **g** thanks and broke it, and **g** it to
14:23 he took the cup, **g** thanks and
14:57 some stood up and **g** this false
14:61 Jesus remained silent and **g** no
15:45 it was so, he **g** the body to Joseph.
Lk 1:57 have her baby, she **g** birth to a son.
2: 7 she **g** birth to her firstborn, a son.
2:38 she **g** thanks to God and spoke about
4:20 he rolled up the scroll, **g** it back
5:26 Everyone was amazed and **g** praise to
6: 4 he also **g** some to his companions."
7:15 and Jesus **g** him back to his mother.
7:21 and **g** sight to many who were blind.
8:32 into them, and he **g** them permission.
9: 1 he **g** them power and authority to
9:16 heaven, he **g** thanks and broke them.
9:16 Then he **g** them to the disciples to
9:42 boy and **g** him back to his father.
10:35 coins and **g** them to the innkeeper.
11:27 who **g** you birth and nursed you."
15:16 eating, but no-one **g** him anything.
15:29 Yet you never **g** me even a young goat
19:13 he called ten of his servants and **g**
20: 2 "Who **g** you this authority?"
21: 4 All these people **g** their gifts out
22:17 After taking the cup, he **g** thanks
22:19 **g** thanks and broke it, and **g** it to
23: 9 but Jesus **g** him no answer.
24:30 he took bread, **g** thanks, broke it
24:42 They **g** him a piece of broiled fish,
Jn 1:12 he **g** the right to become children of
1:32 John **g** this testimony: "I saw the
3:16 God so loved the world that he **g**
4:12 who **g** us the well and drank from it
5:19 Jesus **g** them this answer: "I tell
5:35 John was a lamp that burned and **g**
6:11 Jesus then took the loaves, **g** thanks,
6:31 He **g** them bread from heaven to eat.'"
7:22 because Moses **g** you circumcision
13:26 **g** it to Judas Iscariot, son of Simon.
17: 4 completing the work you **g** me to do.
17: 6 whom you **g** me out of the world.
17: 6 They were yours; you **g** them to me
17: 8 For I **g** them the words you **g** me and
17:11 the name you **g** me—so that they may
17:12 kept them safe by that name you **g**
17:22 given them the glory that you **g** me,
18: 9 not lost one of those you **g** me."
19: 9 Jesus, but Jesus **g** him no answer.
19:30 bowed his head and **g** up his spirit.
21:13 Jesus came, took the bread and **g** it
Ac 1: 3 **g** many convincing proofs that he was
1: 4 while he was eating with them, he **g**
2:45 they **g** to anyone as he had need.
3: 5 the man **g** them his attention,
5:28 "We **g** you strict orders not to teach
7: 5 He **g** him no inheritance here, not
7: 8 he **g** Abraham the covenant of
7:10 He **g** Joseph wisdom and enabled him
7:42 God turned away and **g** them over to
8:10 all the people, both high and low, **g**
8:38 he **g** orders to stop the chariot.
10: 2 he **g** generously to those in need and
11:17 if God **g** them the same gift as he **g**
13:19 **g** their land to his people as their
13:20 "After this, God **g** them judges until
13:21 the people asked for a king, and he **g**
19:16 He **g** them such a beating that they
21:14 he would not be dissuaded, we **g** up
27:15 **g** way to it and were driven along.
27:20 **g** up all hope of being saved.
27:35 **g** thanks to God in front of them all.
Ro 1:21 him as God nor **g** thanks to him,
1:24 Therefore God **g** them over in the
1:26 of this, God **g** them over to shameful
1:28 he **g** them over to a depraved mind,
4:20 in his faith and **g** glory to God,
8:32 his own Son, but **g** him up for us all
11: 8 is written: "God **g** them a spirit of
Ro 15:15 again, because of the grace God **g**
1Co 3: 2 I **g** you milk, not solid food, for
2Co 5:18 **g** us the ministry of reconciliation:
8: 3 For I testify that they **g** as much as
8: 5 but they **g** themselves first to the
10: 8 the Lord **g** us for building you up
13: 2 I already **g** you a warning when I was
13:10 the Lord **g** me for building you up,
Gal 1: 4 who **g** himself for our sins to rescue
2: 9 those reputed to be pillars, **g** me
2:20 who loved me and **g** himself for me.
3:18 **g** it to Abraham through a promise.
Eph 4: 8 in his train and **g** gifts to men."
4:11 was he who **g** some to be apostles,
5: 2 Christ loved us and **g** himself up
5:25 the church and **g** himself up for
Php 2: 9 **g** him the name that is above every
3:17 according to the pattern we **g** you.
Col 1:25 the commission God **g** me to present
1Th 1: 9 what kind of reception you **g** us.
4: 2 For you know what instructions we **g**
2Th 2:16 who loved us and by his grace **g** us
3:10 we **g** you this rule: "If a man will
1Ti 2: 6 who **g** himself as a ransom for all
2Ti 4:17 the Lord stood at my side and **g** me
Tit 2:14 who **g** himself for us to redeem us
Heb 7: 2 Abraham **g** him a tenth of everything.
7: 4 Abraham **g** him a tenth of the plunder!
11:22 and **g** instructions about his bones.
Jas 2:25 did when she **g** lodging to the spies
5:18 he prayed, and the heavens **g** rain
2Pe 3:15 you with the wisdom that God **g** him.
1Jn 3:24 We know it by the Spirit he **g** us.
3Jn : 3 **g** me great joy to have some brothers
Jude : 7 Gomorrah and the surrounding towns **g**
Rev 1: 1 which God **g** him to show his servants
10: 3 he **g** a loud shout like the roar of a
11:13 and **g** glory to the God of heaven.
12: 5 She **g** birth to a son, a male child,
13: 2 The dragon **g** the beast his power and
15: 7 one of the four living creatures **g**
16:19 **g** her the cup filled with the wine
18: 7 the glory and luxury she **g** herself.
20:13 The sea **g** up the dead that were in
20:13 and death and Hades **g** up the dead

Gaza

Most southern of 5 principal Philistine cities, and the oldest, having been a Canaanite border town (Ge 10:19). Reached during Joshua's conquests (Jos 10:41), but not subdued (Jos 11:22). Captured briefly by men of Judah (Jdg 1:18), but back in Philistine hands when Samson tormented its people (Jdg 16:3, 21, 30). Destruction was prophesied (Jer 25:20; Am 1:6–7; Zep 2:4; Zec 9:5). Ethiopian eunuch converted on road from Jerusalem to here (Ac 8:26).

Ge 10:19 Sidon towards Gerar as far as **G**,
Dt 2:23 who lived in villages as far as **G**,
Jos 10:41 them from Kadesh Barnea to **G**
11:22 **G**, Gath and Ashdod did any survive.
13: 3 of the five Philistine rulers in **G**,
15:47 and **G**, its settlements and villages
Jdg 1:18 The men of Judah also took **G**,
6: 4 ruined the crops all the way to **G**
16: 1 One day Samson went to **G**, where he
16: 2 The people of **G** were told, "Samson
16:21 out his eyes and took him down to **G**.
1Sa 6:17 Ashdod, **G**, Ashkelon, Gath and Ekron.
1Ki 4:24 to **G**, and had peace on all sides.
2Ki 18: 8 as far as **G** and its territory.
Jer 25:20 those of Ashkelon, **G**, Ekron, and
47: 1 before Pharaoh attacked **G**:
47: 5 **G** will shave her head in mourning;
Am 1: 6 "For three sins of **G**, even for four,
1: 7 I will send fire upon the walls of **G**
Zep 2: 4 **G** will be abandoned and Ashkelon
Zec 9: 5 **G** will writhe in agony, and Ekron
9: 5 **G** will lose her king and Ashkelon
Ac 8:26 goes down from Jerusalem to **G**."

Gaze (Gazing)

2Ki 8:11 He stared at him with a fixed **g**
Job 35: 5 **g** at the clouds so high above you.
36:25 All mankind has seen it; men **g** on it

Ps 27: 4 to **g** upon the beauty of the LORD and
68:16 Why **g** in envy, O rugged mountains,
Pr 4:25 fix your **g** directly before you.
23:31 Do not **g** at wine when it is red,
SS 6:13 come back, that we may **g** on you! Why
6:13 Why would you **g** on the Shulammite as
Hab 2:15 that he can **g** on their naked bodies.
Rev 11: 9 tribe, language and nation will **g** on

Gazelle (Gazelles)
Dt 12:15 as if it were **g** or deer, according
12:22 Eat them as you would **g** or deer.
14: 5 the deer, the **g**, the roe deer, the
15:22 may eat it, as if it were **g** or deer.
2Sa 2:18 was as fleet-footed as a wild **g**.
Pr 6: 5 Free yourself, like a **g** from the
SS 2: 9 My lover is like a **g** or a young stag.
2:17 turn, my lover, and be like a **g** or
4: 5 like twin fawns of a **g** that browse
7: 3 are like two fawns, twins of a **g**.
8:14 Come away, my lover, and be like a **g**
Isa 13:14 Like a hunted **g**, like sheep without

Gazelles (Gazelle)
1Ki 4:23 deer, **g**, roebucks and choice fowl.
1Ch 12: 8 were as swift as **g** in the mountains.
SS 2: 7 I charge you by the **g** and by the
3: 5 I charge you by the **g** and by the

Gazez
1Ch 2:46 was the mother of Haran, Moza and **G**.
2:46 Haran was the father of **G**.

Gazing (Gaze)
SS 2: 9 **g** through the windows, peering
Da 10: 8 I was left alone, **g** at this great
2Co 3:13 to keep the Israelites from **g** at it

Gazzam
Ezr 2:48 Rezin, Nekoda, **G**,
Ne 7:51 **G**, Uzza, Paseah,

Ge Harashim
1Ch 4:14 the father of Joab, the father of **G**.

Geba
Jos 18:24 Kephar Ammoni, Ophni and **G**—twelve
21:17 they gave them Gibeon, **G**, Anathoth
1Sa 13: 3 the Philistine outpost at **G**,
14: 5 the other to the south towards **G**.
1Ki 15:22 King Asa built up **G** in Benjamin,
2Ki 23: 8 from **G** to Beersheba, where the
1Ch 6:60 **G**, Alemeth and Anathoth, together
8: 6 in **G** and were deported to Manahath:
2Ch 16: 6 With them he built up **G** and Mizpah.
Ezr 2:26 of Ramah and **G** 621
Ne 7:30 of Ramah and **G** 621
11:31 Benjamites from **G** lived in Michmash,
12:29 and from the area of **G** and Azmaveth,
Isa 10:29 say, "We will camp overnight at **G**.
Zec 14:10 The whole land, from **G** to Rimmon,

Gebal (Gebalites)
1Ki 5:18 Hiram and the men of **G** cut and
Ps 83: 7 **G**, Ammon and Amalek, Philistia, with
Eze 27: 9 Veteran craftsmen of **G** were on board

Gebalites (Gebal)
Jos 13: 5 the area of the **G**; and all Lebanon

Geber
1Ki 4:19 **G** son of Uri—in Gilead (the country

Gebim
Isa 10:31 flight; the people of **G** take cover.

Gecko
Lev 11:30 the **g**, the monitor lizard, the wall

Gedaliah (Gedaliah's)
2Ki 25:22 Babylon appointed **G** son of Ahikam,
25:23 Babylon had appointed **G** as governor,
25:23 they came to **G** at Mizpah—Ishmael
25:24 **G** took an oath to reassure them and
25:25 assassinated **G** and also the men of
1Ch 25: 3 for Jeduthun, from his sons: **G**, Zeri,
25: 9 **G**, he and his relatives and sons, 12
Ezr 10:18 Maaseiah, Eliezer, Jarib and **G**.
Jer 38: 1 son of Mattan, **G** son of Passhur,
39:14 handed him over to **G** son of Ahikam,
40: 5 "Go back to **G** son of Ahikam, the son
40: 6 Jeremiah went to **G** son of Ahikam at
40: 7 had appointed **G** son of Ahikam as
40: 8 they came to **G** at Mizpah—Ishmael
40: 9 **G** son of Ahikam, the son of Shaphan,
40:11 and had appointed **G** son of Ahikam,
40:12 to **G** at Mizpah, from all the
40:13 the open country came to **G** at
40:14 **G** son of Ahikam did not believe them.
40:15 Kareah said privately to **G** in Mizpah,
40:16 **G** son of Ahikam said to Johanan son
41: 1 men to **G** son of Ahikam at Mizpah.
41: 2 up and struck down **G** son of Ahikam,
41: 3 the Jews who were with **G** at Mizpah,
41: 6 he said, "Come to **G** son of Ahikam.
41: 9 the men he had killed along with **G**
41:10 guard had appointed **G** son of Ahikam.
41:16 he had assassinated **G** son of Ahikam
41:18 Nethaniah had killed **G** son of Ahikam,
43: 6 guard had left with **G** son of Ahikam,
Zep 1: 1 the son of **G**, the son of Amariah,

Gedaliah's (Gedaliah)
Jer 41: 4 The day after **G** assassination,

Geder (Gederite)
Jos 12:13 king of Debir one the king of **G** one

Gederah (Gederathite)
Jos 15:36 Shaaraim, Adithaim and **G** (or
1Ch 4:23 potters who lived at Netaim and **G**;

Gederathite (Gederah)
1Ch 12: 4 Jahaziel, Johanan, Jozabad the **G**,

Gederite (Geder)
1Ch 27:28 Baal-Hanan the **G** was in charge of

Gederoth
Jos 15:41 **G**, Beth Dagon, Naamah and
2Ch 28:18 Aijalon and **G**, as well as Soco,

Gederothaim
Jos 15:36 Shaaraim, Adithaim and Gederah (or **G**)

Gedor
Jos 15:58 Halhul, Beth Zur, **G**,
1Ch 4: 4 Penuel was the father of **G**, and Ezer
4:18 gave birth to Jered the father of **G**,
4:39 they went to the outskirts of **G** to
8:31 **G**, Ahio, Zeker
9:37 **G**, Ahio, Zechariah and Mikloth.
12: 7 Zebadiah the sons of Jeroham from **G**.

Gehazi
Elisha's servant. Suggested Shunammite woman be rewarded with a son (2Ki 4:14); obtained money from Naaman falsely, contracted leprosy as punishment (2Ki 5:19–27); recounted Elisha's raising of Shunammite's son (2Ki 8:1–6). May be unnamed servant (2Ki 4:43; 6:15).

2Ki 4:12 He said to his servant **G**, "Call the
4:14 **G** said, "Well, she has no son and
4:25 man of God said to his servant **G**,
4:27 **G** came over to push her away, but
4:29 Elisha said to **G**, "Tuck your cloak
4:31 **G** went on ahead and laid the staff
4:31 So **G** went back to meet Elisha and
4:36 Elisha summoned **G** and said, "Call
5:20 **G**, the servant of Elisha the man of
5:21 **G** hurried after Naaman. When Naaman
5:22 "Everything is all right," **G**
5:23 He urged **G** to accept them, and then
5:23 and they carried them ahead of **G**.
5:24 **G** came to the hill, he took the
5:25 "Where have you been, **G**?" Elisha
5:25 "Your servant didn't go anywhere," **G**
5:27 Then **G** went from Elisha's presence
8: 4 The king was talking to **G**, the
8: 5 Just as **G** was telling the king how
8: 5 **G** said, "This is the woman, my lord

Geliloth
Jos 18:17 went to En Shemesh, continued to **G**,
22:10 they came to **G** near the Jordan in
22:11 on the border of Canaan at **G** near

Gem (Gems)
Ex 28:11 the way a **g** cutter engraves a seal.

Gemalli
Nu 13:12 the tribe of Dan, Ammiel son of **G**;

Gemariah
Jer 29: 3 of Shaphan and to **G** son of Hilkiah,
36:10 From the room of **G** son of Shaphan
36:11 Micaiah son of **G**, the son of Shaphan,
36:12 son of Acbor, **G** son of Shaphan,
36:25 Even though Elnathan, Delaiah and **G**

Gems (Gem)
Ex 25: 7 onyx stones and other **g** to be
35: 9 onyx stones and other **g** to be
35:27 other **g** to be mounted on the ephod
Lam 4: 1 The sacred **g** are scattered at the

Genealogical (Genealogy)
1Ch 4:33 And they kept a **g** record.
5: 1 so he could not be listed in the **g**
5: 7 listed according to their **g** records:
5:17 All these were entered in the **g**
7: 7 **g** record listed 22,034 fighting men.
7: 9 Their **g** record listed the heads of
26:31 to the **g** records of their families.
2Ch 31:16 whose names were in the **g** records
31:17 by their families in the **g** records
31:18 community listed in these **g** records.
Ne 7: 5 I found the **g** record of those who

Genealogies (Genealogy)
1Ch 9: 1 All Israel was listed in the **g** in
2Ch 12:15 of Iddo the seer that deal with **g**?
31:19 recorded in the **g** of the Levites.
1Ti 1: 4 themselves to myths and endless **g**.
Tit 3: 9 avoid foolish controversies and **g**

Genealogy (Genealogical, Genealogies)
1Ch 7: 2 men in their **g** numbered 22,600.
7: 4 According to their family **g**, they
7: 5 in their **g**, were 87,000 in all.
7:40 as listed in their **g**, was 26,000.
8:28 chiefs as listed in their **g**,
9: 9 as listed in their **g**, numbered 956.
9:22 They were registered by **g** in their
9:34 chiefs as listed in their **g**,
Mt 1: 1 A record of the **g** of Jesus Christ
Heb 7: 3 Without father or mother, without **g**,

Generals
Rev 6:15 the princes, the **g**, the rich, the
19:18 **g**, and mighty men, of horses and

Generation (*From generation to generation*, Generations)
Ge 7: 1 I have found you righteous in this **g**.
15:16 In the fourth **g** your descendants
50:23 saw the third **g** of Ephraim's
Ex 1: 6 his brothers and all that **g** died,
20: 5 and fourth **g** of those who hate me,
34: 7 fathers to the third and fourth **g**."
Nu 14:18 fathers to the third and fourth **g**.'
32:13 until the whole **g** of those who had
Dt 1:35 "Not a man of this evil **g** shall see
2:14 By then, that entire **g** of fighting
5: 9 and fourth **g** of those who hate me,
23: 2 the LORD, even down to the tenth **g**.

Dt 23: 3 the LORD, even down to the tenth g.
23: 8 The third g of children born to them
32: 5 but a warped and crooked g.
32:20 they are a perverse g, children who
Jdg 2:10 After that whole g had been gathered
2:10 another g grew up, who knew neither
2Ki 10:30 throne of Israel to the fourth g."
15:12 throne of Israel to the fourth g."
Est 9:28 observed in every g by every family,
Job 42:16 and their children to the fourth g.
Ps 24: 6 Such is the g of those who seek him,
48:13 you may tell of them to the next g.
49:19 he will join the g of his fathers,
71:18 I declare your power to the next g,
78: 4 we will tell the next g the
78: 6 that the next g would know them,
78: 8 a stubborn and rebellious g,
95:10 I was angry with that g; I said,
102:18 Let this be written for a future g,
109:13 names blotted out from the next g.
112: 2 g of the upright will be blessed.
145: 4 One g will commend your works to
Jer 2:31 "You of this g, consider the word of
7:29 this g that is under his wrath.
Joel 1: 3 and their children to the next g.
Mt 11:16 "To what can I compare this g? They
12:39 "A wicked and adulterous g asks for
12:41 judgment with this g and condemn it;
12:42 judgment with this g and condemn it;
12:45 how it will be with this wicked g."
16: 4 A wicked and adulterous g looks for
17:17 "O unbelieving and perverse g,"
23:36 all this will come upon this g.
24:34 I tell you the truth, this g will
Mk 8:12 "Why does this g ask for a
8:38 in this adulterous and sinful g,
9:19 "O unbelieving g," Jesus replied,
13:30 I tell you the truth, this g will
Lk 7:31 of this g? What are they like?
9:41 "O unbelieving and perverse g,"
11:29 Jesus said, "This is a wicked g.
11:30 will the Son of Man be to this g.
11:31 the men of this g and condemn them;
11:32 judgment with this g and condemn it;
11:50 Therefore this g will be held
11:51 Yes, I tell you, this g will be held
17:25 things and be rejected by this g.
21:32 "I tell you the truth, this g will
Ac 2:40 Save yourselves from this corrupt g."
13:36 served God's purpose in his own g,
Php 2:15 fault in a crooked and depraved g,
Heb 3:10 That is why I was angry with that g,

Generations (*All generations*, Generation)

Ge 17: 7 after you for the g to come,
17: 9 after you for the g to come.
17:12 For the g to come every male among
Ex 12:14 for the g to come you shall
12:17 lasting ordinance for the g to come.
12:42 honour the LORD for the g to come.
16:32 manna and keep it for the g to come,
16:33 LORD to be kept for the g to come."
20: 6 showing love to a thousand ⌊g⌋ of
27:21 the Israelites for the g to come.
29:42 "For the g to come this burnt
30: 8 before the LORD for the g to come.
30:10 sin offering for the g to come.
30:21 his descendants for the g to come."
30:31 anointing oil for the g to come.
31:13 between me and you for the g to come
31:16 celebrating it for the g to come as
Lev 3:17 lasting ordinance for the g to come,
6:18 the LORD by fire for the g to come.
7:36 regular share for the g to come.
10: 9 lasting ordinance for the g to come.
17: 7 for them and for the g to come.'
21:17 "Say to Aaron: 'For the g to come
22: 3 "Say to them: 'For the g to come, if
23:14 a lasting ordinance for the g to come
23:21 a lasting ordinance for the g to come
23:31 a lasting ordinance for the g to come
23:41 lasting ordinance for the g to come;
24: 3 lasting ordinance for the g to come.
Nu 10: 8 ordinance for you and the g to come.
Nu 15:14 For the g to come, whenever an alien
15:15 lasting ordinance for the g to come.
15:21 Throughout the g to come you are to
15:23 continuing through the g to come—
15:38 'Throughout the g to come you are to
18:23 lasting ordinance for the g to come.
35:29 the g to come, wherever you live.
Dt 5:10 showing love to a thousand ⌊g⌋ of
7: 9 a thousand g of those who love him
29:22 children who follow you in later g
32: 7 of old; consider the g long past.
Jos 22:27 us and you and the g that follow,
1Ch 16:15 word he commanded, for a thousand g,
Job 8: 8 "Ask the former g and find out what
Ps 22:30 future g will be told about the Lord
49:11 their dwellings for endless g,
61: 6 king's life, his years for many g.
105: 8 word he commanded, for a thousand g,
106:31 righteousness for endless g to come.
Ecc 1: 4 G come and g go, but the earth
Isa 41: 4 calling forth the g from the
51: 9 as in days gone by, as in g of old.
61: 4 that have been devastated for g.
Mt 1:17 Thus there were fourteen g in all
Eph 3: 5 not made known to men in other g
Col 1:26 has been kept hidden for ages and g,

Generosity (Generous)

2Co 8: 2 extreme poverty welled up in rich g.
9:11 g will result in thanksgiving to God.
9:13 and for your g in sharing with them

Generous (Generosity, Generously)

Ps 37:26 They are always g and lend freely;
112: 5 Good will come to him who is g and
Pr 11:25 A g man will prosper; he who
22: 9 A g man will himself be blessed, for
Mt 20:15 Or are you envious because I am g?'
2Co 9: 5 for the g gift you had promised.
9: 5 g gift, not as one grudgingly given.
9:11 that you can be g on every occasion,
1Ti 6:18 and to be g and willing to share.

Generously (Generous)

Dt 15:10 Give g to him and do so without a
1Ch 29:14 that we should be able to give as g
2Ch 31: 5 the Israelites g gave the
Ps 37:21 not repay, but the righteous give g;
Ac 10: 2 he gave g to those in need and
Ro 12: 8 let him give g; if it is leadership,
2Co 9: 6 and whoever sows g will also reap g.
Tit 3: 6 whom he poured out on us g through
Jas 1: 5 he should ask God, who gives g to

Genitals

Eze 23:20 whose g were like those of donkeys

Gennesaret

Mt 14:34 had crossed over, they landed at G.
Mk 6:53 they landed at G and anchored there.
Lk 5: 1 Jesus was standing by the Lake of G,

Gentile (Gentiles)

Ezr 6:21 the unclean practices of their G
Ne 5: 9 avoid the reproach of our G enemies?
Ac 10:28 to associate with a G or visit him.
15:23 To the G believers in Antioch, Syria
21:25 for the G believers, we have written
Ro 1:16 first for the Jew, then for the G.
2: 9 first for the Jew, then for the G;
2:10 first for the Jew, then for the G.
10:12 is no difference between Jew and G
Gal 2:14 live like a G and not like a Jew.
2:15 are Jews by birth and not 'G sinners

Gentiles(Gentile)

Ne 5: 8 brothers who were sold to the G.
Isa 9: 1 he will honour Galilee of the G,
42: 6 the people and a light for the G,
49: 6 also make you a light for the G,
49:22 "See, I will beckon to the G, I will
Mt 4:15 along the Jordan, Galilee of the G—
Mt 10: 5 "Do not go among the G or enter any
10:18 as witnesses to them and to the G.
20:19 will turn him over to the G to be
20:25 "You know that the rulers of the G
Mk 10:33 and will hand him over to the G,
10:42 rulers of the G lord it over them,
Lk 2:32 a light for revelation to the G and
18:32 He will be turned over to the G.
21:24 will be trampled on by the G until
21:24 the times of the G are fulfilled.
22:25 "The kings of the G lord it over
Ac 4:27 Pilate met together with the G
9:15 to carry my name before the G
10:45 had been poured out even on the G.
11: 1 G also had received the word of God.
11:18 God has granted even the G repentance
13:16 you G who worship God, listen to me!
13:26 and you God-fearing G, it is to us
13:46 eternal life, we now turn to the G.
13:47 "'I have made you a light for the G,
13:48 the G heard this, they were glad and
14: 1 great number of Jews and G believed.
14: 2 refused to believe stirred up the G
14: 5 There was a plot afoot among the G
14:27 opened the door of faith to the G.
15: 3 told how the G had been converted.
15: 5 "The G must be circumcised and
15: 7 the G might hear from my lips
15:12 had done among the G through them.
15:14 from the G a people for himself.
15:17 and all the G who bear my name, says
15:19 for the G who are turning to God.
18: 6 From now on I will go to the G."
21:11 and will hand him over to the G.'"
21:19 among the G through his ministry.
21:21 among the G to turn away from Moses,
22:21 I will send you far away to the G.'"
26:17 from your own people and from the G.
26:20 and to the G also, I preached that
26:23 to his own people and to the G."
28:28 to the G, and they will listen!"
Ro 1: 5 call people from among all the G
1:13 as I have had among the other G.
2:14 (Indeed, when G, who do not have the
2:24 among the G because of you."
3: 9 Jews and G alike are all under sin.
3:29 not the God of G too? Yes, of G too,
9:24 from the Jews but also from the G?
9:30 What then shall we say? That the G,
11:11 to the G to make Israel envious.
11:12 their loss means riches for the G,
11:13 I am talking to you G. Inasmuch as I
11:13 to the G, I make much of my
11:25 full number of the G has come in.
15: 9 that the G may glorify God for his
15: 9 I will praise you among the G; I
15:10 Again, it says, "Rejoice, O G, with
15:11 again, "Praise the Lord, all you G,
15:12 nations; the G will hope in him."
15:16 a minister of Christ Jesus to the G
15:16 so that the G might become an
15:18 leading the G to obey God by what I
15:27 For if the G have shared in the Jews'
16: 4 churches of the G are grateful
1Co 1:23 to Jews and foolishness to G,
2Co 11:26 in danger from G; in danger in the
Gal 1:16 that I might preach among the G,
2: 2 gospel that I preach among the G.
2: 7 of preaching the gospel to the G,
2: 8 my ministry as an apostle to the G.
2: 9 go to the G, and they to the Jews.
2:12 James, he used to eat with the G.
2:12 separate himself from the G because
2:14 force G to follow Jewish customs?
3: 8 God would justify the G by faith,
3:14 come to the G through Christ Jesus,
Eph 2:11 G by birth and called "uncircumcised"
3: 1 Christ Jesus for the sake of you G—
3: 6 G are heirs together with Israel,
3: 8 to preach to the G the unsearchable
4:17 you must no longer live as the G do,
Col 1:27 make known among the G the glorious
1Th 2:16 to the G so that they may be saved.
1Ti 2: 7 teacher of the true faith to the G.
2Ti 4:17 and all the G might hear it.
Rev 11: 2 because it has been given to the G.

Gentle (Gentleness, Gently)

Dt 28:54 Even the most **g** and sensitive man
28:56 The most **g** and sensitive woman among
28:56 and **g** that she would not venture to
2Sa 18: 5 "Be **g** with the young man Absalom for
1Ki 19:12 And after the fire came a **g** whisper.
Job 41: 3 Will he speak to you with **g** words?
Pr 15: 1 A **g** answer turns away wrath, but a
25:15 and a **g** tongue can break a bone.
Jer 11:19 I had been like a **g** lamb led to the
Zec 9: 9 righteous and having salvation, **g**
Mt 11:29 for I am **g** and humble in heart, and
21: 5 'See, your king comes to you, **g** and
Ac 27:13 a **g** south wind began to blow, they
1Co 4:21 or in love and with a **g** spirit?
Eph 4: 2 Be completely humble and **g**; be
1Th 2: 7 we were **g** among you, like a mother
1Ti 3: 3 not violent but **g**, not quarrelsome,
1Pe 3: 4 the unfading beauty of a **g** and quiet

Gentleness (Gentle)

2Co 10: 1 By the meekness and **g** of Christ, I
Gal 5:23 **g** and self-control. Against such
Php 4: 5 Let your **g** be evident to all. The
Col 3:12 kindness, humility, **g** and patience.
1Ti 6:11 faith, love, endurance and **g**.
1Pe 3:15 But do this with **g** and respect,

Gently (Gentle)

Job 15:11 for you, words spoken **g** to you?
29:22 more; my words fell **g** on their ears.
SS 7: 9 flowing **g** over lips and teeth.
Isa 8: 6 the **g** flowing waters of Shiloah
40:11 he **g** leads those that have young.
Gal 6: 1 are spiritual should restore him **g**.
2Ti 2:25 Those who oppose him he must **g**
Heb 5: 2 He is able to deal **g** with those who

Genubath

1Ki 11:20 of Tahpenes bore him a son named **G**,
11:20 **G** lived with Pharaoh's own children.

Genuine

2Co 6: 8 **g**, yet regarded as impostors;
Php 2:20 takes a **g** interest in your welfare.
1Pe 1: 7 proved **g** and may result in praise,

Gera

Ge 46:21 Beker, Ashbel, **G**, Naaman, Ehi, Rosh,
Jdg 3:15 man, the son of **G** the Benjamite.
2Sa 16: 5 His name was Shimei son of **G**, and
19:16 Shimei son of **G**, the Benjamite from
19:18 When Shimei son of **G** crossed the
1Ki 2: 8 you have with you Shimei son of **G**,
1Ch 8: 3 The sons of Bela were: Addar, **G**,
8: 5 **G**, Shephuphan and Huram.
8: 7 Naaman, Ahijah and **G**, who deported.

Gerahs

Ex 30:13 shekel, which weighs twenty **g**.
Lev 27:25 shekel, twenty **g** to the shekel.
Nu 3:47 shekel, which weighs twenty **g**.
18:16 shekel, which weighs twenty **g**.
Eze 45:12 The shekel is to consist of twenty **g**.

Gerar

Border town between Egypt and Philistia (Ge 10:19), where Abraham stayed and pretended Sarah was his sister (Ge 20:1–7). Isaac dug wells here (Ge 26). Asa's army pursued the Cushites to here, killing them and plundering the surrounding villages (2Ch 14:13–14).

Ge 10:19 from Sidon towards **G** as far as Gaza,
20: 1 For a while he stayed in **G**,
20: 2 king of **G** sent for Sarah and took
26: 1 king of the Philistines in **G**.
26: 6 Isaac stayed in **G**.
26:17 the Valley of **G** and settled there.
26:20 the herdsmen of **G** quarrelled with
26:26 Abimelech had come to him from **G**,
2Ch 14:13 his army pursued them as far as **G**.
14:14 destroyed all the villages around **G**,

Gerasenes

Mk 5: 1 the lake to the region of the **G**.
Lk 8:26 They sailed to the region of the **G**,
8:37 all the people of the region of the **G**

Gerizim, Mount

South of Shechem, facing Mount Ebal to the north. Place where the LORD's blessings were to be announced (Dt 11:29; 27:12), fulfilled by Joshua (Jos 8:33–35). Place where Jotham addressed the people of Shechem (Jdg 9:7). In Jesus' day the Samaritans worshipped here (Jn 4:20–21).

Dt 11:29 you are to proclaim on Mount **G** the
27:12 these tribes shall stand on Mount **G**
Jos 8:33 people stood in front of Mount **G**
Jdg 9: 7 he climbed up on the top of Mount **G**

Gershom

Ex 2:22 and Moses named him **G**, saying, "I
18: 3 her two sons. One son was named **G**,
Jdg 18:30 and Jonathan son of **G**, the son of
1Ch 23:15 The sons of Moses: **G** and Eliezer.
23:16 The descendants of **G**: Shubael was
26:24 Shubael, a descendant of **G** son of
Ezr 8: 2 of the descendants of Phinehas, **G**;

Gershon (Gershonite, Gershonites)

Ge 46:11 The sons of Levi: **G**, Kohath and
Ex 6:16 their records: **G**, Kohath and Merari.
6:17 The sons of **G**, by clans, were Libni
Nu 3:17 sons of Levi: **G**, Kohath and Merari.
3:21 To **G** belonged the clans of the
26:57 counted by their clans: through **G**,
Jos 21: 6 The descendants of **G** were allotted
1Ch 6: 1 The sons of Levi: **G**, Kohath and
6:16 The sons of Levi: **G**, Kohath and
6:17 These are the names of the sons of **G**:
6:20 Of **G**: Libni his son, Jehath his son,
6:43 the son of Jahath, the son of **G**, the
6:62 The descendants of **G**, clan by clan,
15: 7 from the descendants of **G**, Joel the
23: 6 sons of Levi: **G**, Kohath and Merari.

Gershonite (Gershon)

Nu 3:18 These were the names of the **G** clans:
3:21 Shimeites; these were the **G** clans.
3:23 The **G** clans were to camp on the west,
Nu 4:24 "This is the service of the **G** clans
4:28 This is the service of the **G** clans
4:41 the total of those in the **G** clans
26:57 through Gershon, the **G** clan
Jos 21:33 All the towns of the **G** clans were
1Ch 26:21 to Ladan the **G**, were Jehieli,
29: 8 LORD in the custody of Jehiel the **G**.

Gershonites (Gershon)

Nu 3:24 The leader of the families of the **G**
3:25 At the Tent of Meeting the **G** were
4:22 "Take a census also of the **G** by
4:26 The **G** are to do all that needs to be
4:38 The **G** were counted by their clans
7: 7 to the **G**, as their work required,
10:17 and the **G** and Merarites, who carried
Jos 21:27 The Levite clans of the **G** were given:
1Ch 6:71 The **G** received the following: From
23: 7 Belonging to the **G**: Ladan and Shimei.
26:21 The descendants of Ladan, who were **G**
2Ch 29:12 son of Jehallelel; from the **G**,

Geruth Kimham

Jer 41:17 they went on, stopping at **G** near

Geshan

1Ch 2:47 The sons of Jahdai: Regem, Jotham, **G**,

Geshem

Ne 2:19 Tobiah the Ammonite official and **G**
6: 1 word came to Sanballat, Tobiah, **G**
6: 2 Sanballat and **G** sent me this message
6: 6 **G** says it is true—that you and the

Geshur (Geshurites)

Jos 12: 5 of the people of **G** and Maacah,
13:11 the territory of the people of **G** and
13:13 out the people of **G** and Maacah,
2Sa 3: 3 Maacah daughter of Talmai king of **G**;
13:37 Talmai son of Ammihud, the king of **G**.
13:38 After Absalom fled and went to **G**, he
14:23 Joab went to **G** and brought Absalom
14:32 "Why have I come from **G**? It would be
15: 8 While your servant was living at **G**
1Ch 2:23 (But **G** and Aram captured Havvoth
3: 2 of Talmai king of **G**; the fourth,

Geshurites (Geshur)

Dt 3:14 border of the **G** and the Maacathites;
Jos 13: 2 regions of the Philistines and **G**:
1Sa 27: 8 **G**, the Girzites and the Amalekites.

Gether

Ge 10:23 The sons of Aram: Uz, Hul, **G** and
1Ch 1:17 of Aram: Uz, Hul, **G** and Meshech.

Gethsemane

Mt 26:36 his disciples to a place called **G**,
Mk 14:32 They went to a place called **G**, and

Geuel

Nu 13:15 from the tribe of Gad, **G** son of Maki.

Gezer

Jos 10:33 Meanwhile, Horam king of **G** had come
12:12 king of Eglon one the king of **G** one
16: 3 Horon and on to **G**, ending at the sea.
16:10 dislodge the Canaanites living in **G**;
21:21 for one accused of murder) and **G**,
Jdg 1:29 out the Canaanites living in **G**,
2Sa 5:25 all the way from Gibeon to **G**.
1Ki 9:15 Jerusalem, and Hazor, Megiddo and **G**.
9:16 Egypt had attacked and captured **G**.
9:17 Solomon rebuilt **G**.) He built up
1Ch 6:67 Shechem (a city of refuge), and **G**,
7:28 Naaran to the east, **G** and its
14:16 army, all the way from Gibeon to **G**.
20: 4 out with the Philistines, at **G**.

Ghost (Ghostlike)

Mt 14:26 "It's a **g**," they said, and cried out
Mk 6:49 the lake, they thought he was a **g**.
Lk 24:37 frightened, thinking they saw a **g**.
24:39 a **g** does not have flesh and bones,

Ghostlike (Ghost)

Isa 29: 4 Your voice will come **g** from the

Giah

2Sa 2:24 near **G** on the way to the wasteland

Gibbar

Ezr 2:20 of **G** 95

Gibbethon

Jos 19:44 Eltekeh, **G**, Baalath,
21:23 of Dan they received Eltekeh, **G**,
1Ki 15:27 and he struck him down at **G**, a
16:15 encamped near **G**, a Philistine town.
16:17 from **G** and laid siege to Tirzah.

Gibea (Gibeathite)

1Ch 2:49 Sheva the father of Macbenah and **G**.

Gibeah

1. City in territory of Benjamin (Jos 18:28; Jdg 19:14); inhabitants brutalised the concubine of a Levite of Ephraim (Jdg 19:22–25). War with the Benjamites ensued (Jdg 20:12–48). Occupied by Philistines for a while (1Sa 10:5). Also Saul's home (1Sa 10:26; 15:34), and base (1Sa 11:4; 22:6; 23:19; 26:1). Spirit of God came upon Saul here (1Sa 10:10) and seven of his descendants killed here by Gibeonites (2Sa 21:6). **2.** Town south-east of Hebron in territory of Judah (Jos 15:57). Exact location unknown. **3.** Town in territory

of Phinehas, where Aaron's son Eleazar was buried (Jos 24:33).

Jos 15:57 Kain, G and Timnah—ten towns and
18:28 Jerusalem), G and Kiriath—fourteen
24:33 of Aaron died and was buried at G,
Jdg 19:12 We will go on to G."
19:13 He added, "Come, let's try to reach G
19:14 set as they neared G in Benjamin.
19:16 who was living in G (the men of the
20: 4 to G in Benjamin to spend the night.
20: 5 During the night the men of G came
20: 9 now this is what we'll do to G:
20:10 Then, when the army arrives at G in
20:13 Now surrender those wicked men of G
20:14 came together at G to fight against
20:15 chosen men from those living in G.
20:19 got up and pitched camp near G.
20:20 battle positions against them at G.
20:21 The Benjamites came out of G and cut
20:25 when the Benjamites came out from G
20:29 Israel set an ambush around G.
20:30 against G as they had done before.
20:31 to Bethel and the other to G.
20:33 out of its place on the west of G.
20:34 men made a frontal attack on G.
20:36 on the ambush they had set near G.
20:37 in ambush made a sudden dash into G,
20:43 in the vicinity of G on the east.
1Sa 10: 5 "After that you will go to G of God,
10:10 they arrived at G, a procession of
10:26 Saul also went to his home in G,
11: 4 the messengers came to G of Saul and
13: 2 were with Jonathan at G in Benjamin.
13:15 Samuel left Gilgal and went up to G
13:16 them were staying in G of Benjamin,
14: 2 was staying on the outskirts of G
14:16 Saul's lookouts at G in Benjamin saw
15:34 went up to his home in G of Saul.
22: 6 the tamarisk tree on the hill at G,
23:19 The Ziphites went up to Saul at G
26: 1 The Ziphites went to Saul at G and
2Sa 21: 6 at G of Saul—the LORD's chosen one.
23:29 son of Ribai from G in Benjamin,
1Ch 11:31 Ithai son of Ribai from G in
2Ch 13: 2 Maacah, a daughter of Uriel of G.
Isa 10:29 Ramah trembles; G of Saul flees.
Hos 5: 8 "Sound the trumpet in G, the horn in
9: 9 corruption, as in the days of G.
10: 9 "Since the days of G, you have
10: 9 not war overtake the evildoers in G?

Gibeath Haaraloth

Jos 5: 3 and circumcised the Israelites at G.

Gibeathite (Gibea)

1Ch 12: 3 and Joash the sons of Shemaah the G;

Gibeon (Gibeonite, Gibeonites)

Chief of 4 fortress cities, inhabited by the Hivites (Jos 9:17) and allotted to the tribe of Benjamin (Jos 21:17). Gibeonites tricked Joshua into signing a peace treaty, but they became Israel's woodcutters and watercarriers (Jos 9). Joshua defended them from the Amorite alliance; during the battle the sun stood still (Jos 10:1–14). Saul violated treaty (2Sa 21:1), so his descendants killed by Gibeonites (2Sa 21:9). Place where Saul's and David's men fought (2Sa 2:12–16); David slaughtered the Philistines (2Sa 5:25; 1Ch 14:6) and Solomon offered sacrifices (1Ki 3:3–5; 1Ch 16:39; 21:29; 2Ch 1:3–5, 13). Inhabitants helped rebuild Jerusalem (Ne 3:7; 7:25). Home of Hananiah (Jer 28:1).

Jos 9: 3 However, when the people of G heard
9:17 third day came to their cities: G,
10: 1 the people of G had made a treaty
10: 2 because G was an important city,
10: 4 "Come up and help me attack G," he
10: 5 positions against G and attacked it.
10:10 them in a great victory at G.
10:12 "O sun, stand still over G, O moon,
10:41 the whole region of Goshen to G.
11:19 Except for the Hivites living in G,
18:25 G, Ramah, Beeroth,
21:17 of Benjamin they gave them G, Geba,
2Sa 2:12 Saul, left Mahanaim and went to G.
2:13 out and met them at the pool of G.
2:16 in G was called Helkath Hazzurim.
2:24 on the way to the wasteland of G.
3:30 brother Asahel in the battle of G.)
5:25 all the way from G to Gezer.
20: 8 rock in G, Amasa came to meet them.
1Ki 3: 4 The king went to G to offer
3: 5 At G the LORD appeared to Solomon
9: 2 as he had appeared to him at G.
1Ch 6:60 tribe of Benjamin they were given G,
8:29 Jeiel the father of G lived in G.
9:35 Jeiel the father of G lived in G.
14:16 army, all the way from G to Gezer.
16:39 of the LORD at the high place in G
21:29 at that time on the high place at G.
2Ch 1: 3 went to the high place at G,
1: 5 the son of Hur, had made was in G in
1:13 from the high place at G, from before
Ne 3: 7 repairs were made by men from G and
3: 7 Mizpah—Melatiah of G and Jadon of
7:25 of G 95
Isa 28:21 rouse himself as in the Valley of G
Jer 28: 1 who was from G, said to me in the
41:12 with him near the great pool in G.
41:16 officials he had brought from G.

Gibeonite (Gibeon)

1Ch 12: 4 Ishmaiah the G, a mighty man among.

Gibeonites (Gibeon)

Jos 9:16 they made the treaty with the G,
9:22 Joshua summoned the G and said, "Why
9:27 That day he made the G woodcutters
10: 6 The G then sent word to Joshua in
2Sa 21: 1 is because he put the G to death."
21: 2 The king summoned the G and spoke to
21: 2 (Now the G were not a part of Israel
21: 3 David asked the G, "What shall I do
21: 4 The G answered him, "We have no
21: 9 He handed them over to the G, who

Giddalti

1Ch 25: 4 Hanani, Eliathah, G and Romamti-Ezer;
25:29 the twenty-second to G, his sons and

Giddel

Ezr 2:47 G, Gahar, Reaiah,
2:56 Jaala, Darkon, G,
Ne 7:49 Hanan, G, Gahar,
7:58 Jaala, Darkon, G,

Gideon (Gideon's)

Judge, called to save Israel from Midianites (Jdg 6:11–24). Broke down altar of Baal (Jdg 6:25–32). Sign of fleece (Jdg 6:36–40); army reduced to 300 (Jdg 7:2–8); defeated Midianites (Jdg 7:16–8:28). Refused throne (Jdg 8:22–23); ephod made from spoil became source of idolatry (Jdg 8:24–27). Death (Jdg 8:32).

Jdg 6:11 where his son G was threshing wheat
6:12 the angel of the LORD appeared to G,
6:13 "But sir," G replied, "if the LORD
6:15 "But Lord," G asked, "how can I save
6:17 G replied, "If now I have found
6:19 G went in, prepared a young goat,
6:20 pour out the broth." And G did so.
6:22 G realised that it was the angel of
6:24 G built an altar to the LORD there
6:27 G took ten of his servants and did
6:29 were told, "G son of Joash did it.
6:32 that day they called G "Jerub-Baal,"
6:34 the Spirit of the LORD came upon G,
6:36 G said to God, "If you will save
6:38 that is what happened. G rose early
6:39 G said to God, "Do not be angry with
7: 1 Jerub-Baal (that is, G) and all his
7: 2 The LORD said to G, "You have too
7: 4 the LORD said to G, "There are still
7: 5 G took the men down to the water.
7: 7 The LORD said to G, "With the three
7: 8 G sent the rest of the Israelites to
7: 9 During that night the LORD said to G,
7:13 G arrived just as a man was telling
Jdg 7:14 the sword of G son of Joash,
7:15 G heard the dream and its
7:18 shout, 'For the LORD and for G.'"
7:19 G and the hundred men with him
7:20 "A sword for the LORD and for G!
7:24 G sent messengers throughout the
7:25 the heads of Oreb and Zeeb to G,
8: 1 Now the Ephraimites asked G, "Why
8: 4 G and his three hundred men,
8: 7 G replied, "Just for that, when the
8:11 G went up by the route of the nomads
8:13 G son of Joash then returned from
8:15 G came and said to the men of
8:19 G replied, "Those were my brothers,
8:21 So G stepped forward and killed
8:22 The Israelites said to G, "Rule over
8:23 G told them, "I will not rule over
8:27 G made the gold into an ephod, which
8:27 became a snare to G and his family.
8:32 G son of Joash died at a good old
8:33 No sooner had G died than the
8:35 the family of Jerub-Baal (that is, G)
Heb 11:32 I do not have time to tell about G,

Gideon's (Gideon)

Jdg 8:28 During G lifetime, the land enjoyed

Gideoni

Nu 1:11 from Benjamin, Abidan son of G;
2:22 of Benjamin is Abidan son of G.
7:60 On the ninth day Abidan son of G,
7:65 was the offering of Abidan son of G.
10:24 Abidan son of G was over the

Gidom

Jdg 20:45 after the Benjamites as far as G

Gift (Gifted, Gifts)

Ge 30:20 has presented me with a precious g.
32:13 selected a g for his brother Esau:
32:18 They are a g sent to my lord Esau,
33:10 in your eyes, accept this g from me.
34:12 g I am to bring as great as you like,
43:11 g—a little balm and a little honey,
Lev 22:18 g for a burnt offering to the LORD,
Nu 18: 6 among the Israelites as a g to you,
18: 7 service of the priesthood as a g.
31:52 g to the LORD weighed 16,750 shekels.
Dt 16:17 Each of you must bring a g in
1Sa 9: 7 We have no g to take to the man of
25:27 let this g, which your servant has
2Sa 11: 8 g from the king was sent after him.
1Ki 9:16 g to his daughter, Solomon's wife.
10:25 everyone who came brought a g
13: 7 to eat, and I will give you a g."
15:19 See, I am sending you a g of silver
2Ki 5:15 accept now a g from your servant."
8: 8 he said to Hazael, "Take a g with
8: 9 taking with him as a g forty
16: 8 it as a g to the king of Assyria.
20:12 sent Hezekiah letters and a g,
2Ch 9:24 everyone who came brought a g—
Ps 45:12 Daughter of Tyre will come with a g,
Pr 18:16 A g opens the way for the giver and
21:14 A g given in secret soothes anger,
Ecc 3:13 all his toil—this is the g of God.
5:19 in his work—this is a g of God.
Isa 39: 1 sent Hezekiah letters and a g,
Eze 45:13 "'This is the special g you are to
45:16 will participate in this special g
46:16 If the prince makes a g from his
46:17 If, however, he makes a g from his
48: 8 you are to present as a special g.
48:12 will be a special g to them from the
48:20 As a special g you will set aside
Mt 5:23 if you are offering your g at the
5:24 leave your g there in front of the
5:24 brother; then come and offer your g.
8: 4 and offer the g Moses commanded,
15: 5 from me is a g devoted to God,'
23:18 swears by the g on it, he is bound
23:19 blind men! Which is greater: the g,
23:19 the altar that makes the g sacred?
Mk 7:11 (that is, a g devoted to God),

Jn 4:10 "If you knew the **g** of God and who it
Ac 1: 4 but wait for the **g** my Father
2:38 receive the **g** of the Holy Spirit.
8:20 could buy the **g** of God with money!
10:45 **g** of the Holy Spirit had been poured
11:17 if God gave them the same **g** as he
11:30 This they did, sending their **g** to
Ro 1:11 spiritual **g** to make you strong—
4: 4 to him as a **g**, but as an obligation.
5:15 the **g** is not like the trespass. For
5:15 the **g** that came by the grace of the
5:16 Again, the **g** of God is not like the
5:16 but the **g** followed many trespasses
5:17 of the **g** of righteousness reign in
6:23 but the **g** of God is eternal life in
12: 6 If a man's **g** is prophesying, let him
1Co 1: 7 you do not lack any spiritual **g** as
7: 7 But each man has his own **g** from God;
7: 7 one has this **g**, another has that.
13: 2 If I have the **g** of prophecy and can
14: 1 gifts, especially the **g** of prophecy.
16: 3 send them with your **g** to Jerusalem.
2Co 8:12 the **g** is acceptable according to
8:20 way we administer this liberal **g**.
9: 5 for the generous **g** you had promised.
9: 5 **g**, not as one grudgingly given.
9:15 be to God for his indescribable **g**!
Eph 2: 8 yourselves, it is the **g** of God—
3: 7 by the **g** of God's grace given me
Php 4:17 Not that I am looking for a **g**, but I
1Ti 4:14 Do not neglect your **g**, which was
2Ti 1: 6 you to fan into flame the **g** of God,
Heb 6: 4 who have tasted the heavenly **g**, who
Jas 1:17 Every good and perfect **g** is from
1Pe 3: 7 with you of the gracious **g** of life,
4:10 Each one should use whatever **g** he
Rev 22:17 the free **g** of the water of life.

Gifted (Gift)

1Co 14:37 he is a prophet or spiritually **g**,

Gifts (Gift, *Spiritual gifts*)

Ge 24:53 **g** to her brother and to her mother.
25: 6 while he was still living, he gave **g**
32:20 "I will pacify him with these **g** I am
32:21 Jacob's **g** went on ahead of him, but
43:15 the men took the **g** and double the
43:25 They prepared their **g** for Joseph's
43:26 they presented to him the **g** they had
Ex 28:38 sacred **g** the Israelites consecrate,
28:38 consecrate, whatever their **g** may be.
Lev 23:38 in addition to your **g** and whatever
Nu 5:10 Each man's sacred **g** are his own, but
7: 3 They brought as their **g** before the
8:19 I have given the Levites as **g** to
18: 9 From all the **g** they bring me as most
18:11 whatever is set aside from the **g** of
Dt 12: 6 your tithes and special **g**, what you
12:11 your tithes and special **g**, and all
12:17 freewill offerings or special **g**.
33:15 with the choicest **g** of the ancient
33:16 with the best **g** of the earth and its
1Sa 10:27 despised him and brought him no **g**.
2Ki 12:18 and the **g** he himself had dedicated
2Ch 17: 5 all Judah brought **g** to Jehoshaphat,
17:11 Jehoshaphat **g** and silver as tribute,
21: 3 Their father had given them many **g**
31:12 tithes and dedicated **g**.
31:14 the LORD and also the consecrated **g**.
32:23 **g** for Hezekiah king of Judah.
Ezr 1: 6 and with valuable **g**, in addition to
Est 2:18 distributed **g** with royal liberality.
9:22 to one another and **g** to the poor.
Ps 68:18 you received **g** from men, even from
68:29 at Jerusalem kings will bring you **g**.
72:10 Sheba and Seba will present him **g**.
76:11 bring **g** to the One to be feared.
112: 9 He has scattered abroad his **g** to the
Pr 19: 6 is the friend of a man who gives **g**.
22:16 **g** to the rich—both come to poverty.
25:14 who boasts of **g** he does not give.
Isa 1:23 all love bribes and chase after **g**.
18: 7 At that time **g** will be brought to
18: 7 the **g** will be brought to Mount Zion,
Eze 16:33 but you give **g** to all your lovers,
Eze 20:26 them become defiled through their **g**
20:31 you offer your **g**—the sacrifice of
20:39 my holy name with your **g** and idols.
20:40 your offerings and your choice **g**,
44:30 **g** will belong to the priests.
Da 2: 6 me **g** and rewards and great honour.
2:48 position and lavished many **g** on him.
5:17 "You may keep your **g** for yourself
11:38 with precious stones and costly **g**.
Mic 1: 7 all her temple **g** will be burned with
1: 7 Since she gathered her **g** from the
1:14 Therefore you will give parting **g** to
7: 3 the ruler demands **g**, the judge
Mt 2:11 presented him with **g** of gold and of
7:11 know how to give good **g** to your
7:11 give good **g** to those who ask him!
Lk 11:13 know how to give good **g** to your
21: 1 their **g** into the temple treasury.
21: 4 All these people gave their **g** out of
21: 5 stones and with **g** dedicated to God.
Ac 10: 4 "Your prayers and **g** to the poor have
10:31 and remembered your **g** to the poor.
24:17 to bring my people **g** for the poor
Ro 11:29 for God's **g** and his call are
12: 6 We have different **g**, according to
1Co 12: 4 There are different kinds of **g**, but
12: 9 **g** of healing by that one Spirit,
12:28 also those having **g** of healing,
12:28 those with **g** of administration, and
12:30 Do all have **g** of healing? Do all
12:31 eagerly desire the greater **g**. And
14:12 excel in **g** that build up the church.
2Co 9: 9 "He has scattered abroad his **g** to
Eph 4: 8 in his train and gave **g** to men."
Php 4:18 from Epaphroditus the **g** you sent.
Heb 2: 4 miracles, and **g** of the Holy Spirit
5: 1 to offer **g** and sacrifices for sins.
8: 3 to offer both **g** and sacrifices,
8: 4 offer the **g** prescribed by the law.
9: 9 indicating that the **g** and sacrifices
Rev 11:10 celebrate by sending each other **g**,

Gigantic

Rev 9: 2 it like the smoke from a **g** furnace.

Gihon

Ge 2:13 The name of the second river is the **G**
1Ki 1:33 my own mule and take him down to **G**.
1:38 David's mule and escorted him to **G**.
1:45 prophet have anointed him king at **G**.
2Ch 32:30 the upper outlet of the **G** spring
33:14 west of the **G** spring in the valley,

Gilalai

Ne 12:36 Azarel, Milalai, **G**, Maai, Nethanel,

Gilboa, Mount

Range between plain of Jezreel and River Jordan. Site of battle between Israelites and Philistines (1Sa 28:4), when Israel was defeated (1Sa 31:1; 1Ch 10:1), and Saul and his sons killed (1Sa 31:8; 1Ch 10:8). Cursed by David (2Sa 1:21).

1Sa 28: 4 the Israelites and set up camp at **G**.
31: 1 and many fell slain on Mount **G**.
31: 8 his three sons fallen on Mount **G**.
2Sa 1: 6 "I happened to be on Mount **G**," the
1:21 "O mountains of **G**, may you have
21:12 after they struck Saul down on **G**.)
1Ch 10: 1 and many fell slain on Mount **G**.
10: 8 Saul and his sons fallen on Mount **G**.

Gilead (Gilead's, Gileadite, Gileadites)

1. Mountainous region east of River Jordan, between Sea of Galilee and Dead Sea. Place of refuge for Jacob from Laban (Ge 31:21), Israelites from the Philistines (1Sa 13:7), and David from Absalom (2Sa 17:22, 26). Midianite merchants, who bought Joseph, were travelling from here (Ge 37:25). Ideal region for raising livestock, so Reuben and Gad desired it (Nu 32:1). Half was allotted to them and the rest to Manasseh (Dt 3:12–13). **2.** A city of wicked men (Hos 6:8). Location unknown. **3.** Mountain in the Jezreel valley, where Gideon had to reduce the size of his army (Jdg 6:2–3).

Ge 31:21 he headed for the hill country of **G**.
31:23 with him in the hill country of **G**.
31:25 of **G** when Laban overtook him,
37:25 of Ishmaelites coming from **G**.
Nu 26:29 **G**); through **G**, the Gileadite clan.
26:30 These were the descendants of **G**:
27: 1 the son of **G**, the son of Makir, the
32: 1 and **G** were suitable for livestock.
32:26 will remain here in the cities of **G**.
32:29 the land of **G** as their possession.
32:39 of Makir son of Manasseh went to **G**,
32:40 Moses gave **G** to the Makirites, the
36: 1 The family heads of the clan of **G**
Dt 2:36 even as far as **G**, not one town was
3:10 and all **G**, and all Bashan as far as
3:12 of **G**, together with its towns.
3:13 The rest of **G** and also all of Bashan,
3:15 I gave **G** to Makir.
3:16 from **G** down to the Arnon Gorge
4:43 Ramoth in **G**, for the Gadites; and
34: 1 him the whole land—from **G** to Dan,
Jos 12: 2 This included half of **G**.
12: 5 and half of **G** to the border of Sihon
13:11 also included **G**, the territory of
13:25 all the towns of **G** and half the
13:31 half of **G**, and Ashtaroth and Edrei
17: 1 who had received **G** and Bashan
17: 3 the son of **G**, the son of Makir, the
17: 5 **G** and Bashan east of the Jordan,
17: 6 The land of **G** belonged to the rest
20: 8 Ramoth in **G** in the tribe of Gad, and
21:38 from the tribe of Gad, Ramoth in **G**
22: 9 at Shiloh in Canaan to return to **G**,
22:13 the priest, to the land of **G**—to
22:15 they went to **G**—to Reuben, Gad and
22:32 in **G** and reported to the Israelites.
Jdg 5:17 **G** stayed beyond the Jordan. And Dan,
7: 3 may turn back and leave Mount **G**.
10: 3 He was followed by Jair of **G**, who
10: 4 They controlled thirty towns in **G**,
10: 8 in **G**, the land of the Amorites.
10:17 were called to arms and camped in **G**,
10:18 The leaders of the people of **G** said
10:18 the head of all those living in **G**."
11: 1 His father was **G**; his mother was a
11: 5 the elders of **G** went to get Jephthah
11: 8 The elders of **G** said to him,
11: 8 be our head over all who live in **G**."
11:10 The elders of **G** replied, "The LORD
11:11 Jephthah went with the elders of **G**,
11:29 He crossed **G** and Manasseh, passed
11:29 passed through Mizpah of **G**, and from
12: 4 called together the men of **G** and
12: 5 "Let me cross over," the men of **G**
12: 7 died, and was buried in a town in **G**.
20: 1 from the land of **G** came out as one
1Sa 13: 7 the Jordan to the land of Gad and **G**.
2Sa 2: 9 He made him king over **G**, Ashuri and
17:26 and Absalom camped in the land of **G**.
24: 6 They went to **G** and the region of
1Ki 2: 7 to the sons of Barzillai of **G**
4:13 Jair son of Manasseh in **G** were his,
4:19 Geber son of Uri—in **G** (the country
17: 1 from Tishbe in **G**, said to Ahab, "As
2Ki 10:33 the land of **G** (the region of Gad,
10:33 the Arnon Gorge through **G** to Bashan.
15:25 Taking fifty men of **G** with him, he
15:29 He took **G** and Galilee, including all
1Ch 2:21 daughter of Makir the father of **G**
2:22 controlled twenty-three towns in **G**.
2:23 of Makir the father of **G**.
5: 9 their livestock had increased in **G**.
5:10 the entire region east of **G**.
5:14 the son of Jaroah, the son of **G**, the
5:16 The Gadites lived in **G**, in Bashan
6:80 they received Ramoth in **G**, Mahanaim,
7:14 gave birth to Makir the father of **G**.
7:17 **G** son of Makir, the son of Manasseh.
26:31 Hebronites were found at Jazer in **G**.
27:21 over the half-tribe of Manasseh in **G**:
Ps 60: 7 **G** is mine, and Manasseh is mine;
108: 8 **G** is mine, Manasseh is mine; Ephraim

SS 4: 1 of goats descending from Mount **G**.
6: 5 a flock of goats descending from **G**.
Jer 8:22 Is there no balm in **G**? Is there no
22: 6 "Though you are like **G** to me, like
46:11 "Go up to **G** and get balm, O Virgin
50:19 on the hills of Ephraim and **G**.
Eze 47:18 along the Jordan between **G** and the
Hos 6: 8 **G** is a city of wicked men, stained
12:11 Is **G** wicked? Its people are
Am 1: 3 Because she threshed **G** with sledges
1:13 ripped open the pregnant women of **G**
Ob :19 Samaria, and Benjamin will possess **G**.
Mic 7:14 in Bashan and **G** as in days long ago.
Zec 10:10 I will bring them to **G** and Lebanon,

Gilead's (Gilead)
Jdg 11: 2 **G** wife also bore him sons, and when

Gileadite (Gilead)
Nu 26:29 Gilead); through Gilead, the **G** clan.
Jdg 11: 1 Jephthah the **G** was a mighty warrior.
11:40 the daughter of Jephthah the **G**.
12: 7 Then Jephthah the **G** died, and was
2Sa 17:27 and Barzillai the **G** from
19:31 Barzillai the **G** also came down from
Ezr 2:61 the **G** and was called by that name).
Ne 7:63 the **G** and was called by that name).

Gileadites (Gilead)
Jos 17: 1 Makir was the ancestor of the **G**, who
Jdg 12: 4 The **G** struck them down because the
12: 4 "You **G** are renegades from Ephraim
12: 5 The **G** captured the fords of the

Gilgal
1. First encampment for Israelites in promised land, on the eastern side of Jericho (Jos 4:19). Monument set up as a memorial (Jos 4:19–20): here Israelites were circumcised and celebrated Passover (Jos 5:2–10). Israelite base camp for Joshua's conquest (Jos 6:11; 10:15; 14:6), until it moved to Shiloh (Jos 18:1). Here the Gibeonites tricked Joshua (Jos 9:6), and from here he marched to their aid (Jos 10:7). Samuel held court here (1Sa 7:15–16), it became a sanctuary (1Sa 10:8; 13:8–10; 15:21). Here Agag died (1Sa 15:33), and Saul was both proclaimed king (1Sa 11:15) and rejected as king (1Sa 15:12–23). David was greeted here by the men of Judah (2Sa 19:15). Became a centre of idolatry (Hos 4:15; 9:15; 12:11; Am 4:4; 5:5). **2.** Village from which Elijah travelled (2Ki 2:1). Elisha visited here (2Ki 4:8). Probably in hill country of Ephraim, near Bethel and Shiloh. **3.** Royal city associated with Dor (Jos 12:23), about 5 miles north of Antipatris.

Dt 11:30 in the Arabah in the vicinity of **G**.
Jos 4:19 **G** on the eastern border of Jericho.
4:20 Joshua set up at **G** the twelve stones
5: 9 place has been called **G** to this day.
5:10 while camped at **G** on the plains of
9: 6 they went to Joshua in the camp at **G**
10: 6 at **G**: "Do not abandon your servants.
10: 7 Joshua marched up from **G** with his
10: 9 After an all-night march from **G**,
10:15 with all Israel to the camp at **G**.
10:43 with all Israel to the camp at **G**.
12:23 the king of Goyim in **G** one
14: 6 men of Judah approached Joshua at **G**,
15: 7 of Achor and turned north to **G**,
Jdg 2: 1 The angel of the LORD went up from **G**
3:19 At the idols near **G** he himself
1Sa 7:16 circuit from Bethel to **G** to Mizpah,
10: 8 "Go down ahead of me to **G**. I will
11:14 let us go to **G** and there reaffirm
11:15 all the people went to **G** and
13: 4 were summoned to join Saul at **G**.
13: 7 Saul remained at **G**, and all the
13: 8 Samuel did not come to **G**, and Saul's
13:12 will come down against me at **G**,
13:15 Samuel left **G** and went up to Gibeah
15:12 has turned and gone on down to **G**."
15:21 them to the LORD your God at **G**."
15:33 Agag to death before the LORD at **G**.
2Sa 19:15 Now the men of Judah had come to **G**
19:40 the king crossed over to **G**, Kimham
2Ki 2: 1 and Elisha were on their way from **G**.
4:38 Elisha returned to **G** and there was a
Hos 4:15 "Do not go to **G**; do not go up to
9:15 "Because of all their wickedness in **G**
12:11 Do they sacrifice bulls in **G**?
Am 4: 4 "Go to Bethel and sin; go to **G** and
5: 5 do not seek Bethel, do not go to **G**,
5: 5 For **G** will surely go into exile, and
Mic 6: 5 ⌊your journey⌋ from Shittim to **G**

Giloh
Jos 15:51 Goshen, Holon and **G**—eleven towns
2Sa 15:12 to come from **G**, his home town.

Gilonite
2Sa 15:12 he also sent for Ahithophel the **G**,
23:34 Eliam son of Ahithophel the **G**,

Gimzo
2Ch 28:18 **G**, with their surrounding villages.

Ginath
1Ki 16:21 supported Tibni son of **G** for king,
16:22 than those of Tibni son of **G**.

Ginnethon (Ginnethon's)
Ne 10: 6 Daniel, **G**, Baruch,
12: 4 Iddo, **G**, Abijah,

Ginnethon's (Ginnethon)
Ne 12:16 Zechariah; of **G**, Meshullam;

Gird
Ps 45: 3 **G** your sword upon your side,

Girgashites
Ge 10:16 Jebusites, Amorites, **G**,
15:21 Amorites, Canaanites, **G** and
Dt 7: 1 **G**, Amorites, Canaanites, Perizzites,
Jos 3:10 **G**, Amorites and Jebusites.
24:11 Perizzites, Canaanites, Hittites, **G**,
1Ch 1:14 Jebusites, Amorites, **G**,
Ne 9: 8 Perizzites, Jebusites and **G**.

Girl (Girl's, Girls)
Ge 24:14 May it be that when I say to a **g**,
24:16 The **g** was very beautiful, a virgin;
24:28 The **g** ran and told her mother's
24:55 "Let the **g** remain with us ten days
24:57 they said, "Let's call the **g** and ask
29:24 Laban gave his servant **g** Zilpah to
29:29 Laban gave his servant **g** Bilhah to
34: 3 loved the **g** and spoke tenderly to her
34: 4 Hamor, "Get me this **g** as my wife.
34:12 Only give me the **g** as my wife."
Ex 1:16 but if it is a **g**, let her live."
1:22 the Nile, but let every **g** live."
2: 5 and sent her slave **g** to get it.
2: 8 Yes, go," she answered. And the **g**
11: 5 the firstborn son of the slave **g**,
Lev 12: 7 who gives birth to a boy or a **g**.
19:20 a woman who is a slave **g** promised
Nu 31:18 save for yourselves every **g** who has
Dt 22:24 stone them to death—the **g** because
22:25 to meet a **g** pledged to be married
22:26 Do nothing to the **g**; she has
22:27 for the man found the **g** out in the
22:27 and though the betrothed **g** screamed,
22:29 He must marry the **g**, for he has
Jdg 5:30 the spoils: a **g** or two for each man,
9:18 the son of his slave **g**, king over
1Sa 30:19 boy or **g**, plunder or anything else
2Sa 17:17 A servant **g** was to go and inform
1Ki 1: 3 for a beautiful **g** and found Abishag,
1: 4 The **g** was very beautiful; she took
2Ki 5: 2 taken captive a young **g** from Israel,
5: 4 him what the **g** from Israel had said.
Est 2: 4 let the **g** who pleases the king be
2: 7 This **g**, who was also known as Esther,
2: 9 The **g** pleased him and won his favour.
2:15 the turn came for Esther (the **g**
Job 31: 1 eyes not to look lustfully at a **g**.
Am 2: 7 Father and son use the same **g** and so
Mt 9:24 he said, "Go away. The **g** is not dead
9:25 the **g** by the hand, and she got up.
14:11 the **g**, who carried it to her mother.
26:69 and a servant **g** came to him.
26:71 where another **g** saw him and said to
Mk 5:41 "Little **g**, I say to you, get up!").
5:42 Immediately the **g** stood up and
6:22 The king said to the **g**, "Ask me for
6:25 At once the **g** hurried in to the king
6:28 He presented it to the **g**, and she
14:69 the servant **g** saw him there, she
Lk 8:42 his only daughter, a **g** of about
22:56 A servant **g** saw him seated there in
Jn 18:16 **g** on duty there and brought Peter in.
18:17 you?" the **g** at the door asked Peter.
Ac 12:13 and a servant **g** named Rhoda came to
16:16 we were met by a slave **g** who had a
16:17 This **g** followed Paul and the rest of
16:19 the owners of the slave **g** realised

Girl's (Girl)
Dt 22:15 the **g** father and mother shall bring
22:16 The **g** father will say to the elders,
22:19 and give them to the **g** father,
22:20 of the **g** virginity can be found,
22:29 he shall pay the **g** father fifty
Jdg 19: 4 His father-in-law, the **g** father,
19: 5 but the **g** father said to his
19: 6 Afterwards the **g** father said,
19: 8 **g** father said, "Refresh yourself.
19: 9 his father-in-law, the **g** father,
Est 2:12 Before a **g** turn came to go in to

Girls (Girl)
Ge 20:17 **g** so they could have children again,
Ex 2:18 the **g** returned to Reuel their father,
Jdg 11:38 She and the **g** went into the hills
21:21 When the **g** of Shiloh come out to join
21:21 each of you seize a wife from the **g**
21:23 While the **g** were dancing, each man
Ru 2: 8 Stay here with my servant **g**.
2: 9 and follow along after the **g**.
2:13 standing of one of your servant **g**."
2:22 my daughter, to go with his **g**,
2:23 Ruth stayed close to the servant **g**
3: 2 Is not Boaz, with whose servant **g**
1Sa 9:11 they met some **g** coming out to draw
2Sa 6:20 in the sight of the slave **g** of his
6:22 But by these slave **g** you spoke of,
Est 2: 3 to bring all these beautiful **g** into
2: 8 many **g** were brought to the citadel
Job 41: 5 or put him on a leash for your **g**?
Pr 27:27 and to nourish your servant **g**.
31:15 and portions for her servant **g**.
Joel 3: 3 sold **g** for wine that they might
Na 2: 7 Its slave **g** moan like doves and beat
Zec 8: 5 with boys and **g** playing there."
Mk 14:66 **g** of the high priest came by.

Girzites
1Sa 27: 8 Geshurites, the **G** and the Amalekites.

Gishpa
Ne 11:21 Ziha and **G** were in charge of them.

Gittaim
2Sa 4: 3 the people of Beeroth fled to **G** and
Ne 11:33 in Hazor, Ramah and **G**,

Gittite (Gittites)
2Sa 6:10 to the house of Obed-Edom the **G**.
6:11 of Obed-Edom the **G** for three months,
15:19 The king said to Ittai the **G**, "Why
15:22 So Ittai the **G** marched on with all
18: 2 and a third under Ittai the **G**.
21:19 Bethlehemite killed Goliath the **G**,
1Ch 13:13 to the house of Obed-Edom the **G**.
20: 5 Lahmi the brother of Goliath the **G**,

Gittites (Gittite)
2Sa 15:18 and all the six hundred **G** who had

Gittith

Ps 8: T According to g. A psalm of David.
81: T According to g. Of Asaph.
84: T According to g. Of the Sons of

Give (Gave, *Give thanks*, Given, Giver, Gives, Giving, Life-giving)

Ge 1:15 of the sky to g light on the earth.
1:17 of the sky to g light on the earth,
1:29 God said, "I g you every seed-bearing
1:30 I g every green plant for food.
3:16 pain you will g birth to children.
9: 3 plants, I now g you everything.
12: 7 To your offspring I will g this land.
13:15 All the land that you see I will g
14:21 The king of Sodom said to Abram, "G
15: 2 "O Sovereign LORD, what can you g me
15: 7 to g you this land to take possession
15:18 "To your descendants I g this land,
17: 8 I will g as an everlasting
17:16 I will bless her and will surely g
23:11 "Listen to me; I g you the field,
23:11 and I g you the cave that is in it.
23:11 I g it to you in the presence of my
24: 7 'To your offspring I will g this
24:12 God of my master Abraham, g me
24:17 g me a little water from your jar."
24:41 even if they refuse to g her to you
24:45 I said to her, 'Please g me a drink.'
25:24 the time came for her to g birth,
26: 3 your descendants I will g all these
26: 4 sky and will g them all these lands,
27: 4 may g you my blessing before I die."
27: 7 so that I may g you my blessing in
27:10 g you his blessing before he dies."
27:19 so that you may g me your blessing."
27:25 so that I may g you my blessing.
27:28 May God g you of heaven's dew and of
27:31 so that you may g me your blessing."
28: 4 May he g you and your descendants
28:13 I will g you and your descendants
28:20 g me food to eat and clothes to
28:22 that you g me I will g you a tenth."
29:19 Laban said, "It's better that I g
29:21 Jacob said to Laban, "G me my wife.
29:26 "It is not our custom here to g the
29:27 we will g you the younger one also,
30: 1 So she said to Jacob, "G me children,
30:14 g me some of your son's mandrakes."
30:26 G me my wives and children, for whom
30:31 What shall I g you?" he asked. "Don't
30:31 "Don't g me anything," Jacob replied.
34: 8 Please g her to him as his wife.
34: 9 Intermarry with us; g us your
34:11 and I will g you whatever you ask.
34:12 Only g me the girl as my wife."
34:14 we can't g our sister to a man who
34:15 We will g our consent to you on one
34:16 we will g you our daughters and take
34:23 So let us g our consent to them,
35:12 Abraham and Isaac I also g to you,
35:12 and I will g this land to your
35:16 to g birth and had great difficulty.
38:16 "And what will you g me to sleep
38:17 "Will you g me something as a pledge
38:18 He said, "What pledge should I g you?
38:26 I wouldn't g her to my son Shelah.
38:27 the time came for her to g birth,
41:16 g Pharaoh the answer he desires."
42:22 must g an accounting for his blood."
42:25 g them provisions for their journey.
42:34 Then I will g your brother back to
45:18 I will g you the best of the land of
47:15 came to Joseph and said, "G us food.
47:19 G us seed so that we may live and
47:24 when the crop comes in, g a fifth of
48: 4 and I will g this land as an
48:22 I g the ridge of land I took from
Ex 1:19 g birth before the midwives arrive."
5:10 'I will not g you any more straw.
6: 4 g them the land of Canaan, where
6: 8 g to Abraham, to Isaac and to Jacob.
6: 8 I will g it to you as a possession.
9:19 G an order now to bring your
12:25 the LORD will g you as he promised,
Ex 13: 5 swore to your forefathers to g you,
13:12 you are to g over to the LORD the
13:21 in a pillar of fire to g them light,
17: 2 Moses and said, "G us water to drink.
18:19 Listen now to me and I will g you
20:16 "You shall not g false testimony
22:17 If her father absolutely refuses to g
22:29 g me the firstborn of your sons.
22:30 but g them to me on the eighth day.
23: 2 When you g testimony in a lawsuit,
23:26 I will g you a full life span.
24:12 and I will g you the tablets of
25: 2 man whose heart prompts him to g.
25:16 the Testimony, which I will g you.
25:21 the Testimony, which I will g you.
25:22 I will meet with you and g you all
28: 2 Aaron, to g him dignity and honour.
28:40 sons, to g them dignity and honour.
30:13 counted is to g a half shekel,
30:14 are to g an offering to the LORD.
30:15 The rich are not to g more than a
30:15 the poor are not to g less when you
32:13 I will g your descendants all this
33: 1 'I will g it to your descendants.'
33:14 go with you, and I will g you rest."
Lev 5:16 to that and g it all to the priest,
6: 5 g it all to the owner on the day he
6: 9 "G Aaron and his sons this command:
7:32 You are to g the right thigh of your
7:36 the Israelites g this to them as
15:14 of Meeting and g them to the priest.
18:21 "'Do not g any of your children to
20:24 I will g it to you as an inheritance,
23:10 to g you and you reap its harvest,
23:38 offerings you g to the LORD.)
25: 2 enter the land I am going to g you,
25:38 who brought you out of Egypt to g
Nu 3: 9 G the Levites to Aaron and his sons;
3:48 G the money for the redemption of
5: 7 add one fifth to it and g it all to
6:26 face towards you and g you peace."'
7: 5 G them to the Levites as each man's
7: 9 Moses did not g any to the
10:29 the LORD said, 'I will g it to you.
11:12 Did I g them birth? Why do you tell
11:13 wailing to me, 'G us meat to eat!'
11:18 g you meat, and you will eat it.
11:21 'I will g them meat to eat for a
14: 8 milk and honey, and will g it to us.
15:21 you are to g this offering to the
18: 8 the Israelites g me I g to you
18:11 I g this to you and your sons and
18:12 "I g you all the finest olive oil
18:12 grain they g to the LORD as the
18:19 present to the LORD I g to you
18:21 "I g to the Levites all the tithes
18:24 Instead, I g to the Levites as their
18:26 tithe I g you as your inheritance,
18:28 From these tithes you must g the
19: 3 G it to Eleazar the priest; it is to
20:12 community into the land I g them."
20:24 He will not enter the land I g the
21:16 together and I will g them water."
23: 5 to Balak and g him this message."
23:16 to Balak and g him this message."
26:54 To a larger group g a larger
27: 4 G us property among our father's
27: 7 You must certainly g them property
27: 7 g their father's inheritance over to
27: 8 'If a man dies and leaves no son, g
27: 9 If he has no daughter, g his
27:10 If he has no brothers, g his
27:11 If his father had no brothers, g his
27:20 G him some of your authority so that
28: 2 "G this command to the Israelites
31:29 g it to Eleazar the priest as the
31:30 G them to the Levites, who are
32:29 g them the land of Gilead as their
33:54 To a larger group g a larger
33:55 They will g you trouble in the land
35: 2 "Command the Israelites to g the
35: 2 And g them pasture-lands around the
35: 4 the towns that you g the Levites will
35: 6 "Six of the towns you g the Levites
35: 6 g them forty-two other towns.
35: 7 In all you must g the Levites
Nu 35: 8 The towns you g the Levites from the
35:13 These six towns you g will be your
35:14 G three on this side of the Jordan
36: 2 LORD commanded my lord to g the land
36: 2 he ordered you to g the inheritance
Dt 1: 8 would g to your fathers—to Abraham,
1:35 land I swore to g your forefathers,
1:36 He will see it, and I will g him and
1:39 I will g it to them and they will
2: 4 G the people these orders: 'You are
2: 5 for I will not g you any of their
2: 9 not g you any part of their land.
2:19 for I will not g you possession of
2:30 in order to g him into your hands,
4: 2 of the LORD your God that I g you.
4:38 to g it to you for your inheritance,
5:20 "You shall not g false testimony
5:31 you stay here with me so that I may g
6: 2 decrees and commands that I g you,
6: 6 These commandments that I g you
6:10 to Abraham, Isaac and Jacob, to g
6:23 g us the land that he promised on
7: 3 Do not intermarry with them. Do not g
7:11 decrees and laws I g you today.
7:13 swore to your forefathers to g you.
7:24 He will g their kings into your hand,
10:11 I swore to their fathers to g them."
11: 9 to g to them and their descendants,
11:21 LORD swore to g your forefathers,
12: 6 what you have vowed to g and your
12:10 and he will g you rest from all your
12:17 or whatever you have vowed to g, or
12:26 and whatever you have vowed to g,
14:21 You may g it to an alien living in
15: 9 needy brother and g him nothing.
15:10 G generously to him and do so
15:14 G to him as the LORD your God has
15:15 is why I g you this command today.
17: 9 and they will g you the verdict.
17:10 decisions they g you at the place
17:11 you and the decisions they g you.
18: 4 You are to g them the firstfruits of
20: 3 or g way to panic before them.
20: 4 your enemies to g you victory."
21:16 he must not g the rights of the
22: 2 Then g it back to him.
22:19 and g them to the girl's father,
25: 3 he must not g him more than forty
26: 3 swore to our forefathers to g us."
26:12 the year of the tithe, you shall g
27: 1 these commands that I g you today.
27:10 and decrees that I g you today."
28: 1 all his commands that I g you today,
28:11 swore to your forefathers to g you.
28:13 LORD your God that I g you this day
28:14 any of the commands I g you today,
28:55 he will not g to one of them any of
28:65 There the LORD will g you an anxious
30:20 and he will g you many years in the
30:20 land he swore to g to your fathers,
31: 7 to their forefathers to g them,
32:38 to help you! Let them g you shelter!
34: 4 'I will g it to your descendants.
Jos 1: 2 the land I am about to g to them
1: 3 I will g you every place where you
1: 6 to their forefathers to g them.
2:12 G me a sure sign.
5: 6 promised their fathers to g us,
6: 5 make all the people g a loud shout;
6:10 "Do not g a war cry, do not raise
7:19 Joshua said to Achan, "My son, g
7:19 God of Israel, and g him the praise.
8: 7 your God will g it into your hand.
9:24 Moses to g you the whole land
14:12 Now g me this hill country that the
15:16 Caleb said, "I will g my daughter
15:19 Negev, g me also springs of water.
17: 4 "The LORD commanded Moses to g us an
20: 4 and g him a place to live with them.
21: 2 that you g us towns to live in, with
21:43 he had sworn to g their forefathers,
Jdg 1:12 Caleb said, "I will g my daughter
1:15 Negev, g me also springs of water.
2: 1 I swore to g to your forefathers.
2:19 They refused to g up their evil
4: 7 Kishon River and g him into your

Jdg 4:19 “I'm thirsty,” he said. “Please **g** me
6:17 **g** me a sign that it is really you
7: 7 **g** the Midianites into your hands.
7: 9 I am going to **g** it into your hands.
8: 5 He said to the men of Succoth, “**G** my
8: 6 should we **g** bread to your troops?”
8:15 we **g** bread to your exhausted men?'”
8:24 that each of you **g** me an ear-ring
8:25 They answered, “We'll be glad to **g**
9: 9 ‘Should I **g** up my oil, by which both
9:11 ‘Should I **g** up my fruit, so good and
9:13 “But the vine answered, ‘Should I **g**
11:13 Now **g** it back peaceably.”
11:17 ‘**G** us permission to go through your
11:30 If you **g** the Ammonites into my hands,
11:37 “**G** me two months to roam the hills
13: 5 you will conceive and **g** birth to a
13: 7 will conceive and **g** birth to a son.
14:12 “If you can **g** me the answer within
14:12 I will **g** you thirty linen garments
14:13 you must **g** me thirty linen garments
14:14 days they could not **g** the answer.
16: 5 Each one of us will **g** you eleven
17: 3 I will **g** it back to you.”
17:10 and I'll **g** you ten shekels of silver
20: 7 speak up and **g** your verdict.”
20:10 it can **g** them what they deserve for
20:28 I will **g** them into your hands.”
21: 1 “Not one of us will **g** his daughter
21: 7 taken an oath by the LORD not to **g**
21:18 We can't **g** them our daughters as
21:22 did not **g** your daughters to them.'”
1Sa 1: 4 he would **g** portions of the meat to
1:11 and not forget your servant but **g**
1:11 then I will **g** him to the LORD for
1:28 now I **g** him to the LORD. For his
2:10 “He will **g** strength to his king and
2:15 “**G** the priest some meat to roast; he
2:20 “May the LORD **g** you children by this
8: 6 when they said, “**G** us a king to lead
8:14 groves and **g** them to his attendants.
8:15 **g** it to his officials and attendants.
8:22 “Listen to them and **g** them a king.
9: 7 “If we go, what can we **g** the man?
9: 8 I will **g** it to the man of God so
9:27 I may **g** you a message from God.”
11: 3 elders of Jabesh said to him, “**G** us
14:37 Will you **g** them into Israel's hand?”
14:41 of Israel, “**G** me the right answer.
17:10 **G** me a man and let us fight each
17:25 The king will **g** great wealth to the
17:25 He will also **g** him his daughter in
17:44 “Come here,” he said, “and I'll **g**
17:46 Today I will **g** the carcasses of the
17:47 will **g** all of you into our hands.”
18:17 I will **g** her to you in marriage;
18:21 “I will **g** her to him,” he thought,
21: 3 what have you to hand? **G** me five
21: 9 “There is none like it; **g** it to me.
22: 7 **g** all of you fields and vineyards?
23: 4 **g** the Philistines into your hand.”
23:14 God did not **g** David into his hands.
24: 4 ‘I will **g** your enemy into your hands
25: 8 Please **g** your servants and your son
25:11 **g** it to men coming from who knows
25:14 to **g** our master his greetings, but
27: 1 Then Saul will **g** up searching for me
28:22 let me **g** you some food so that you
2Sa 2:23 Asahel refused to **g** up the pursuit;
3:14 “**G** me my wife Michal, whom I
7:11 I will also **g** you rest from all your
12:11 **g** them to one who is close to you,
13: 5 to come and **g** me something to eat.
16: 3 **g** me back my grandfather's kingdom.'”
16:20 Absalom said to Ahithophel, “**G** us
17: 6 he says? If not, **g** us your opinion.”
18: 3 you to **g** us support from the city.”
18:11 I would have had to **g** you ten shekels
21: 6 So the king said, “I will **g** them to
22:36 You **g** me your shield of victory; you
1Ki 2:17 he will not refuse you—to **g** me
3: 5 for whatever you want me to **g** you.”
3: 9 **g** your servant a discerning heart to
3:12 I will **g** you a wise and discerning
3:13 Moreover, I will **g** you what you have
3:14 did, I will **g** you a long life.”

1Ki 3:25 **g** half to one and half to the other.”
3:26 “Please, my lord, **g** her the living
3:27 the king gave his ruling: “**G** the
5: 6 “So **g** orders that cedars of Lebanon
8:28 Yet **g** attention to your servant's
8:46 them and **g** them over to the enemy,
11:11 **g** it to one of your subordinates.
11:13 but will **g** him one tribe for the
11:31 Solomon's hand and **g** you ten tribes.
11:35 son's hands and **g** you ten tribes.
11:36 I will **g** one tribe to his son so
11:38 for David and will **g** Israel to you.
12: 7 them and **g** them a favourable answer,
12:27 they will again **g** their allegiance
13: 7 to eat, and I will **g** you a gift.”
13: 8 “Even if you were to **g** me half your
14: 5 to **g** her such and such an answer.
14:16 he will **g** Israel up because of the
17:19 “**G** me your son,” Elijah replied. He
20:10 to **g** each of my men a handful.”
20:13 ‘Do you see this vast army? I will **g**
21: 2 In exchange I will **g** you a better
21: 3 **g** you the inheritance of my fathers.”
21: 4 **g** you the inheritance of my fathers.
21: 6 **g** you another vineyard in its place.
21: 6 ‘I will not **g** you my vineyard.'”
22: 6 Lord will **g** it into the king's hand.”
22:12 LORD will **g** it into the king's hand.”
22:15 LORD will **g** it into the king's hand.”
22:27 Put this fellow in prison and **g** him
2Ki 4:42 “**G** it to the people to eat,” Elisha
4:43 But Elisha answered, “**G** it to the
5:22 Please **g** them a talent of silver and
6:28 ‘**G** up your son so that we may eat
6:29 The next day I said to her, ‘**G** up
8: 6 “**G** back everything that belonged to
10:15 “If so,” said Jehu, “**g** me your hand.”
14: 9 ‘**G** your daughter to my son in
18:23 I will **g** you two thousand horses
19:16 **G** ear, O LORD, and hear; open your
1Ch 16:18 “To you I will **g** the land of Canaan
21:23 Look, I will **g** the oxen for the
21:23 grain offering. I will **g** all this
22: 9 and I will **g** him rest from all his
22:12 May the LORD **g** you discretion and
29: 3 now **g** my personal treasures of gold
29:12 to exalt and **g** strength to all.
29:13 Now, our God, we **g** you thanks, and
29:14 that we should be able to **g** as
29:19 **g** my son Solomon the wholehearted
2Ch 1: 7 for whatever you want me to **g** you.”
1:10 **G** me wisdom and knowledge, that I
1:12 And I will also **g** you wealth, riches
2:10 I will **g** your servants, the woodsmen
5:13 to **g** praise and thanks to the LORD.
6:19 Yet **g** attention to your servant's
6:36 them and **g** them over to the enemy,
10: 7 them and **g** them a favourable answer,
12: 7 but will soon **g** them deliverance.
15: 7 for you, be strong and do not **g**
18: 5 God will **g** it into the king's hand.”
18:11 LORD will **g** it into the king's hand.”
18:26 Put this fellow in prison and **g** him
19: 6 with you whenever you **g** a verdict.
20: 7 **g** it for ever to the descendants of
20:17 will **g** you, O Judah and Jerusalem.
25: 9 LORD can **g** you much more than that.”
25:18 ‘**G** your daughter to my son in
30:12 to **g** them unity of mind to carry out
31: 4 to **g** the portion due to the priests
35:12 set aside the burnt offerings to **g**
Ezr 9:12 Therefore, do not **g** your daughters
Ne 1:11 **G** your servant success today by
2: 8 so he will **g** me timber to make beams
2:20 God of heaven will **g** us success.
4: 4 **G** them over as plunder in a land of
5:11 **G** back to them immediately their
5:12 “We will **g** it back,” they said. “And
6:13 **g** me a bad name to discredit me.
8:13 **g** attention to the words of the Law.
9: 6 You **g** life to everything, and the
9: 8 you made a covenant with him to **g** to
9:12 by night with a pillar of fire to **g**
9:15 sworn with uplifted hand to **g** them.
10:30 “We promise not to **g** our daughters
10:32 to **g** a third of a shekel each year

Ne 12:24 who stood opposite them to **g** praise
13:25 “You are not to **g** your daughters in
Est 1:19 Also let the king **g** her royal
9:13 “**g** the Jews in Susa permission to
Job 2: 4 will **g** all he has for his own life.
6:22 Have I ever said, ‘**G** something on my
7:17 that you **g** him so much attention,
9:16 not believe he would **g** me a hearing.
10: 1 therefore I will **g** free rein to my
15:35 They conceive trouble and **g** birth to
17: 3 “**G** me, O God, the pledge you demand.
20:10 own hands must **g** back his wealth.
20:18 What he toiled for he must **g** back
21: 2 this be the consolation you **g** me.
22: 3 What pleasure would it **g** the
31:37 I would **g** him an account of my every
35: 7 If you are righteous, what do you **g**
39: 1 when the mountain goats **g** birth?
39: 2 Do you know the time they **g** birth?
39:17 or **g** her a share of good sense.
39:19 “Do you **g** the horse his strength or
Ps 4: 1 **G** me relief from my distress; be
5: 1 **G** ear to my words, O LORD, consider
13: 3 **G** light to my eyes, or I will sleep
17: 1 **G** ear to my prayer—it does not
17: 6 me; **g** ear to me and hear my prayer.
18:35 You **g** me your shield of victory, and
20: 4 May he **g** you the desire of your
21: 1 is his joy in the victories you **g**!
30:12 God, I will **g** you thanks for ever.
35:18 I will **g** you thanks in the great
36: 8 you **g** them drink from your river of
37: 4 **g** you the desires of your heart.
37:21 but the righteous **g** generously;
44: 7 you **g** us victory over our enemies,
45:10 Listen, O daughter, consider and **g**
46: 2 though the earth **g** way and the
49: 3 from my heart will **g** understanding.
49: 7 or **g** to God a ransom for him—
60:11 **G** us aid against the enemy, for the
71: 3 **g** the command to save me, for you
78:20 But can he also **g** us food? Can he
85:12 The LORD will indeed **g** what is good,
86:11 **g** me an undivided heart, that I may
86:17 **G** me a sign of your goodness, that
104:11 They **g** water to all the beasts of
104:27 These all look to you to **g** them
104:28 you **g** it to them, they gather it up;
105:11 “To you I will **g** the land of Canaan
105:39 and a fire to **g** light at night.
106:47 that we may **g** thanks to your holy
108:12 **G** us aid against the enemy, for the
109:24 My knees **g** way from fasting; my body
118:21 I will **g** you thanks, for you
119:34 **G** me understanding, and I will keep
119:62 At midnight I rise to **g** you thanks
119:73 **g** me understanding to learn your
119:125 **g** me discernment that I may
119:144 **g** me understanding that I may live.
119:169 **g** me understanding according to your
141: 8 refuge—do not **g** me over to death.
145:15 **g** them their food at the proper time.
Pr 1:10 entice you, do not **g** in to them.
3:28 “Come back later; I'll **g** it tomorrow”
4: 2 I **g** you sound learning, so do not
5: 9 lest you **g** your best strength to
14: 8 The wisdom of the prudent is to **g**
21:26 but the righteous **g** without sparing.
22:21 **g** sound answers to him who sent you?
23:26 My son, **g** me your heart and let your
25:14 who boasts of gifts he does not **g**.
25:21 If your enemy is hungry, **g** him food
25:21 he is thirsty, **g** him water to drink.
27:23 **g** careful attention to your herds;
29:17 Discipline your son, and he will **g**
30: 8 me; **g** me neither poverty nor riches,
30: 8 but **g** me only my daily bread.
30:15 “The leech has two daughters. ‘**G**! **G**!’
31: 6 **G** beer to those who are perishing,
31:31 **G** her the reward she has earned, and
Ecc 3: 6 a time to search and a time to **g** up,
10: 1 dead flies **g** perfume a bad smell, so
11: 2 **G** portions to seven, yes to eight,
11: 9 **g** you joy in the days of your youth.
SS 7:12 bloom—there I will **g** you my love.
8: 2 I would **g** you spiced wine to drink,

SS 8: 7 If one were to **g** all the wealth of
8:12 my own vineyard is mine to **g**; the
Isa 7:14 Therefore the Lord himself will **g**
7:14 child and will **g** birth to a son,
7:22 of the abundance of the milk they **g**,
11: 4 with justice he will **g** decisions for
13:10 and the moon will not **g** its light.
16: 3 "**G** us counsel, render a decision.
19:11 of Pharaoh **g** senseless advice.
22:25 into the firm place will **g** way;
24:15 Therefore in the east **g** glory to the
26:17 a woman with child and about to **g**
26:19 the earth will **g** birth to her dead.
29:11 And if you **g** the scroll to someone
29:12 Or if you **g** the scroll to someone
30:10 "**G** us no more visions of what is
33:11 You conceive chaff, you **g** birth to
34: 2 he will **g** them over to slaughter.
35: 3 hands, steady the knees that **g** way;
36: 8 I will **g** you two thousand horses
37:17 **G** ear, O LORD, and hear; open your
41:28 no-one among them to **g** counsel,
41:28 no-one to **g** answer when I ask them.
42: 8 I will not **g** my glory to another or
42:12 Let them **g** glory to the LORD and
43: 3 I **g** Egypt for your ransom, Cush and
43: 4 and because I love you, I will **g** men
43: 6 I will say to the north, '**G** them up!'
43:20 to **g** drink to my people, my chosen,
45: 3 I will **g** you the treasures of
45:11 or **g** me orders about the work of my
49:20 for us; **g** us more space to live in.'
53:12 Therefore I will **g** him a portion
55: 3 **G** ear and come to me; hear me, that
56: 5 to them I will **g** within my temple
56: 5 I will **g** them an everlasting name
56: 7 **g** them joy in my house of prayer.
59: 4 trouble and **g** birth to evil.
62: 6 on the LORD, **g** yourselves no rest,
62: 7 **g** him no rest till he establishes
62: 8 "Never again will I **g** your grain as
65:15 his servants he will **g** another name.
66: 9 and not **g** delivery?" says the LORD.
Jer 3:15 I will **g** you shepherds after my own
3:19 sons and **g** you a desirable land,
6:10 To whom can I speak and **g** warning?
7:22 I did not just **g** them commands about
8:10 Therefore I will **g** their wives to
11: 5 to **g** them a land flowing with milk
12: 7 I will **g** the one I love into the
13:16 **G** glory to the LORD your God before
14:13 **g** you lasting peace in this place.'"
15:13 your treasures I will **g** as plunder,
16: 7 **g** them a drink to console them.
17: 3 treasures I will **g** away as plunder,
18: 2 and there I will **g** you my message."
18:21 **g** their children over to famine;
19: 7 and I will **g** their carcasses as food
20:13 Sing to the LORD! **G** praise to the
24: 7 I will **g** them a heart to know me,
27: 4 **G** them a message for their masters
27: 5 it, and I **g** it to anyone I please.
28:14 I will even **g** him control over the
29: 6 and **g** your daughters in marriage,
29:11 plans to **g** you hope and a future.
31: 2 I will come to **g** rest to Israel."
31:13 I will **g** them comfort and joy
32:22 had sworn to **g** to their forefathers,
32:39 I will **g** them singleness of heart
32:42 so I will **g** them all the prosperity
34:22 I am going to **g** the order, declares
35: 2 the LORD and **g** them wine to drink."
38:15 Jeremiah said to Zedekiah, "If I **g**
38:15 me? Even if I did **g** you counsel,
Lam 2:18 **g** yourself no relief, your eyes no
Eze 2: 8 your mouth and eat what I **g** you."
3:17 I speak and **g** them warning from me.
11:17 **g** you back the land of Israel again.'
11:19 I will **g** them an undivided heart and
11:19 stone and **g** them a heart of flesh.
16:33 but you **g** gifts to all your lovers,
16:34 **g** payment and none is given to you.
16:61 I will **g** them to you as daughters,
20:28 into the land I had sworn to **g** them
20:42 uplifted hand to **g** to your fathers.
21:22 to **g** the command to slaughter, to
Eze 21:27 belongs; to him I will **g** it.'
23: 8 She did not **g** up the prostitution
23:46 **g** them over to terror and plunder.
25: 4 therefore I am going to **g** you to the
25: 7 and **g** you as plunder to the nations.
25:10 I will **g** Moab along with the
29: 5 I will **g** you as food to the beasts
29:19 I am going to **g** Egypt to
32: 7 and the moon will not **g** its light.
33: 7 I speak and **g** them warning from me.
33:15 follows the decrees that **g** life, and
33:27 those out in the country I will **g** to
35: 6 I will **g** you over to bloodshed and
36:26 I will **g** you a new heart and put a
36:26 of stone and **g** you a heart of flesh.
39: 4 I will **g** you as food to all kinds of
39:11 "'On that day I will **g** Gog a burial
43:19 You are to **g** a young bull as a sin
44: 5 listen closely and **g** attention to
44: 5 **G** attention to the entrance of the
44:28 You are to **g** them no possession in
44:30 You are to **g** them the first portion
45: 6 "'You are to **g** the city as its
45: 9 O princes of Israel! **G** up your
46: 7 the lambs as much as he wants to **g**,
46:18 He is to **g** his sons their
47:14 hand to **g** it to your forefathers,
47:23 you are to **g** him his inheritance,"
Da 1:12 **G** us nothing but vegetables to eat
3:28 were willing to **g** up their lives
5:16 you are able to **g** interpretations
5:17 and **g** your rewards to someone else.
9:18 **G** ear, O God, and hear; open your
9:22 to **g** you insight and understanding.
11:17 And he will **g** him a daughter in
Hos 2: 5 'I will go after my lovers, who **g** me
2:15 There I will **g** her back her
4:10 deserted the LORD to **g**
5: 7 **g** birth to illegitimate children.
9:14 **G** them, O LORD—what will you **g**
9:14 **G** them wombs that miscarry and
11: 8 "How can I **g** you up, Ephraim? How
13:10 you said, '**G** me a king and princes'?
Am 2:10 to **g** you the land of the Amorites.
5:11 poor and force him to **g** you grain.
9: 9 "For I will **g** the command, and I
Jnh 3: 2 proclaim to it the message I **g** you."
3: 8 Let them **g** up their evil ways and
4: 6 made it grow up over Jonah to **g**
Mic 1:14 Therefore you will **g** parting gifts
4:13 O Daughter of Zion, for I will **g**
4:13 I will **g** you hoofs of bronze and you
6:14 what you save I will **g** to the sword.
6:16 Therefore I will **g** you over to ruin
Na 2:10 Hearts melt, knees **g** way, bodies
Hab 2: 1 answer I am to **g** to this complaint.
2:19 'Wake up!' Can it **g** guidance? It is
Zep 3:19 I will **g** them praise and honour in
3:20 I will **g** you honour and praise among
Hag 1: 5 "**G** careful thought to your ways.
1: 7 "**G** careful thought to your ways.
2:15 "Now **g** careful thought to this from
2:18 **g** careful thought to the day when
2:18 **G** careful thought:
Zec 3: 7 and I will **g** you a place among these
8:12 I will **g** all these things as an
10: 2 are false, they **g** comfort in vain.
11:12 I told them, "If you think it best, **g**
Mal 1:14 male in his flock and vows to **g** it,
Mt 1:21 She will **g** birth to a son, and you
1:21 and you are to **g** him the name Jesus,
1:23 child and will **g** birth to a son,
4: 9 "All this I will **g** you," he said,
5:31 **g** her a certificate of divorce.'
5:42 **G** to the one who asks you, and do
6: 2 "So when you **g** to the needy, do not
6: 3 when you **g** to the needy, do not let
6:11 **G** us today our daily bread.
7: 6 "Do not **g** dogs what is sacred; do
7: 9 asks for bread, will **g** him a stone?
7:10 Or if he asks for a fish, will **g** him
7:11 though you are evil, know how to **g**
7:11 **g** good gifts to those who ask him!
10: 8 Freely you have received, freely **g**.
10:12 you enter the home, **g** it your
11:28 and burdened, and I will **g** you rest.
Mt 12:36 I tell you that men will have to **g**
14: 7 that he promised with an oath to **g**
14: 8 Prompted by her mother, she said, "**G**
14:16 You **g** them something to eat."
16:19 I will **g** you the keys of the kingdom
16:26 a man **g** in exchange for his soul?
17:27 **g** it to them for my tax and yours."
19: 7 "did Moses command that a man **g** his
19:18 not steal, do not **g** false testimony,
19:21 go, sell your possessions and **g** to
20:14 I want to **g** the man who was hired
20:28 to **g** his life as a ransom for many."
21:41 who will **g** him his share of the crop
22:21 Then he said to them, "**G** to Caesar
23:23 you hypocrites! You **g** a tenth of
24:29 and the moon will not **g** its light;
24:45 **g** them their food at the proper time?
25: 8 The foolish ones said to the wise, '**G**
25:28 "'Take the talent from him and **g** it
25:37 and **g** you something to drink?
26:15 asked, "What are you willing to **g** me
27:64 **g** the order for the tomb to be made
Mk 5:43 told them to **g** her something to eat.
6:22 you want, and I'll **g** it to you."
6:23 I will **g** you, up to half my kingdom."
6:25 "I want you to **g** me right now the
6:37 he answered, "You **g** them something
6:37 on bread and **g** it to them to eat?"
7: 3 **g** their hands a ceremonial washing,
8:37 Or what can a man **g** in exchange for
10:19 do not steal, do not **g** false
10:21 "Go, sell everything you have and **g**
10:45 to **g** his life as a ransom for many."
12: 9 and **g** the vineyard to others.
12:17 Jesus said to them, "**G** to Caesar
13:24 and the moon will not **g** its light;
14:11 this and promised to **g** him money.
Lk 1:13 and you are to **g** him the name John.
1:31 You will be with child and **g** birth
1:31 and you are to **g** him the name Jesus.
1:32 **g** him the throne of his father David,
1:77 to **g** his people the knowledge of
4: 6 he said to him, "I will **g** you all
4: 6 I can **g** it to anyone I want to.
6:30 **G** to everyone who asks you, and if
6:38 **G**, and it will be given to you. A
7:44 You did not **g** me any water for my
7:45 You did not **g** me a kiss, but this
8:55 told them to **g** her something to eat.
9:13 He replied, "You **g** them something to
10: 7 eating and drinking whatever they **g**
11: 3 **G** us each day our daily bread.
11: 7 I can't get up and **g** you anything.'
11: 8 though he will not get up and **g** him
11: 8 up and **g** him as much as he needs.
11:11 a fish, will **g** him a snake instead?
11:12 Or if he asks for an egg, will **g** him
11:13 though you are evil, know how to **g**
11:13 Father in heaven **g** the Holy Spirit
11:41 **g** what is inside the dish to the
11:42 "Woe to you Pharisees, because you **g**
12:32 been pleased to **g** you the kingdom.
12:33 Sell your possessions and **g** to the
12:42 in charge of his servants to **g** them
13:15 stall and lead it out to **g** it water?
14: 9 say to you, '**G** this man your seat.
14:12 Jesus said to his host, "When you **g**
14:13 when you **g** a banquet, invite the
14:33 any of you who does not **g** up
15:12 **g** me my share of the estate.
16: 2 **G** an account of your management,
16:12 who will **g** you property of your own?
17:18 Was no-one found to return and **g**
18: 1 should always pray and not **g** up.
18:12 I fast twice a week and **g** a tenth of
18:20 do not steal, do not **g** false
18:22 Sell everything you have and **g** to
19: 8 "Look, Lord! Here and now I **g** half
19:24 **g** it to the one who has ten minas.'
20:10 would **g** him some of the fruit of the
20:16 and **g** the vineyard to others.
20:25 He said to them, "Then **g** to Caesar
21:15 For I will **g** you words and wisdom
22: 5 They were delighted and agreed to **g**
24:30 broke it and began to **g** it to them.
Jn 1:22 Finally they said, "Who are you? **G**

Jn 4: 7 “Will you **g** me a drink?
4:14 whoever drinks the water I **g** him
4:14 Indeed, the water I **g** him will
4:15 The woman said to him, “Sir, **g** me
5:21 life to whom he is pleased to **g** it.
6:27 which the Son of Man will **g** you.
6:30 **g** that we may see it and believe you?
6:34 “Sir,” they said, “from now on **g** us
6:51 I will **g** for the life of the world.”
6:52 can this man **g** us his flesh to eat?”
9:24 “**G** glory to God,” they said. “We
10:28 I **g** them eternal life, and they
11:22 I know that even now God will **g** you
13:26 “It is the one to whom I will **g** this
13:29 Feast, or to **g** something to the poor.
13:34 “A new command I **g** you: Love one
14:16 I will ask the Father, and he will **g**
14:27 Peace I leave with you; my peace I **g**
14:27 I do not **g** to you as the world gives.
15:16 **g** you whatever you ask in my name.
16:23 **g** you whatever you ask in my name.
17: 2 he might **g** eternal life to all those
18:40 They shouted back, “No, not him! **G**
Ac 3: 6 not have, but what I have I **g** you.
5:31 Saviour that he might **g** repentance
6: 4 will **g** our attention to prayer and
8:19 said, “**G** me also this ability so
12:23 Immediately, because Herod did not **g**
13:34 “‘I will **g** you the holy and sure
20:32 which can build you up and **g** you an
20:35 more blessed to **g** than to receive.’”
21:26 Then he went to the temple to **g**
23:21 Don’t **g** in to them, because more
24:23 guard but to **g** him some freedom
Ro 2: 6 God “will **g** to each person according
2: 7 immortality, he will **g** eternal life.
8:11 **g** life to your mortal bodies through
8:32 him, graciously **g** us all things?
12: 8 let him **g** generously; if it is
12:20 thirsty, **g** him something to drink.
13: 6 who **g** their full time to governing.
13: 7 **G** everyone what you owe him: If you
14:12 then, each of us will **g** an account
15: 5 encouragement **g** you a spirit of
16: 2 **g** her any help she may need from you,
1Co 7:10 To the married I **g** this command (not
7:25 but I **g** a judgment as one who by the
11:34 I come I will **g** further directions.
13: 3 If I **g** all I possess to the poor and
15:58 Let nothing move you. Always **g**
16: 3 Then, when I arrive, I will **g**
2Co 4: 6 to **g** us the light of the knowledge
8:10 first not only to **g** but also to have
9: 2 year you in Achaia were ready to **g**;
9: 7 Each man should **g** what he has
9: 7 he has decided in his heart to **g**,
Gal 2: 5 We did not **g** in to them for a moment,
3: 5 Does God **g** you his Spirit and work
6: 9 reap a harvest if we do not **g** up.
Eph 1:17 the glorious Father, may **g** you the
4:27 do not **g** the devil a foothold.
Php 2:30 up for the help you could not **g** me.
Col 4:15 **G** my greetings to the brothers at
2Th 1: 7 **g** relief to you who are troubled,
3:16 Now may the Lord of peace himself **g**
1Ti 1:18 Timothy, my son, I **g** you this
4:15 **g** yourself wholly to them, so that
5: 3 **G** proper recognition to those widows
5: 7 **G** the people these instructions, too,
5:14 to manage their homes and to **g** the
2Ti 1: 7 For God did not **g** us a spirit of
2: 7 will **g** you insight into all this.
4: 1 his kingdom, I **g** you this charge:
Heb 4:13 of him to whom we must **g** account.
6:14 you and **g** you many descendants.”
10:25 Let us not **g** up meeting together, as
13:17 you as men who must **g** an account.
Jas 1:18 He chose to **g** us birth through the
1Pe 3: 6 is right and do not **g** way to fear.
3:15 Always be prepared to **g** an answer to
3:15 asks you to **g** the reason for the
4: 5 they will have to **g** account to him
1Jn 5:16 should pray and God will **g** him life.
Rev 2: 7 To him who overcomes, I will **g** the
2:10 and I will **g** you the crown of life.
2:17 To him who overcomes, I will **g** some
Rev 2:17 I will also **g** him a white stone with
2:26 I will **g** authority over the nations—
2:28 I will also **g** him the morning star.
3:21 To him who overcomes, I will **g** the
4: 9 Whenever the living creatures **g**
10: 9 asked him to **g** me the little scroll.
11: 3 I will **g** power to my two witnesses,
12: 2 in pain as she was about to **g** birth.
12: 4 the woman who was about to **g** birth,
13:15 He was given power to **g** breath to
14: 7 “Fear God and **g** him glory, because
17:13 They have one purpose and will **g**
17:17 to **g** the beast their power to rule,
18: 6 **G** back to her as she has given; pay
18: 7 **G** her as much torture and grief as
19: 7 Let us rejoice and be glad and **g** him
21: 6 To him who is thirsty I will **g** to
22: 5 for the Lord God will **g** them light.
22:12 and I will **g** to everyone according
22:16 “I, Jesus, have sent my angel to **g**

Give thanks

1Ch 16: 4 to make petition, to **g**, and to
16: 8 **G** to the LORD, call on his name;
16:34 **G** to the LORD, for he is good; his
16:35 that we may **g** to your holy name,
16:41 designated by name to **g** to the LORD,
2Ch 20:21 “**G** to the LORD, for his love endures
31: 2 to minister, to **g** and to sing
Ne 12:31 also assigned two large choirs to **g**.
Ps 7:17 I will **g** to the LORD because of his
28: 7 for joy and I will **g** to him in song.
75: 1 We **g** to you, O God, we **g**, for your
100: 4 **g** to him and praise his name.
105: 1 **G** to the LORD, call on his name;
106: 1 Praise the LORD. **G** to the LORD, for
106:47 that we may **g** to your holy name and
107: 1 **G** to the LORD, for he is good; his
107: 8 Let them **g** to the LORD for his
107:15 Let them **g** to the LORD for his
107:21 Let them **g** to the LORD for his
107:31 Let them **g** to the LORD for his
118: 1 **G** to the LORD, for he is good; his
118:19 I will enter and **g** to the LORD.
118:28 You are my God, and I will **g**; you
118:29 **G** to the LORD, for he is good; his
136: 1 **G** to the LORD, for he is good.
136: 2 **G** to the God of gods. His love
136: 3 **G** to the Lord of lords: His love
136:26 **G** to the God of heaven. His love
Isa 12: 4 In that day you will say: “**G** to the
Jer 33:11 “**G** to the LORD Almighty, for the
1Co 10:16 cup of thanksgiving for which we **g**
2Co 1:11 Then many will **g** on our behalf for
1Th 5:18 **g** in all circumstances, for this is
Rev 11:17 saying: “We **g** to you, Lord God

Given (Give)

Ge 9: 2 the sea; they are **g** into your hands.
15: 3 Abram said, “You have **g** me no
24:19 After she had **g** him a drink, she
24:35 He has **g** him sheep and cattle,
24:36 and he has **g** him everything he owns.
26:18 same names his father had **g** them.
26:22 “Now the LORD has **g** us room and we
27:41 the blessing his father had **g** him.
28: 4 the blessing **g** to Abraham,
30: 6 listened to my plea and **g** me a son.
31: 9 livestock and has **g** them to me.
33: 5 God has graciously **g** your servant.”
38:14 had not been **g** to him as his wife.
38:30 out and he was **g** the name Zerah.
40:16 the chief baker saw that Joseph had **g**
41:32 The reason the dream was **g** to
43:23 the God of your father, has **g** you
46:18 whom Laban had **g** to his daughter
46:25 whom Laban had **g** to his daughter
48: 9 “They are the sons God has **g** me here,
Ex 4:21 I have **g** you the power to do.
5:16 Your servants are **g** no straw, yet we
5:18 You will not be **g** any straw, yet you
16:15 the bread the LORD has **g** you to eat.
16:29 Bear in mind that the LORD has **g** you
28: 3 I have **g** wisdom in such matters that
31: 6 Also I have **g** skill to all the
Ex 34:32 the LORD had **g** him on Mount Sinai.
35:34 he has **g** both him and Oholiab son of
36: 1 person to whom the LORD has **g** skill
36: 2 to whom the LORD had **g** ability
Lev 6:17 I have **g** it as their share of the
7:34 have **g** them to Aaron the priest and
10:11 the LORD has **g** them through Moses.”
10:14 they have been **g** to you and your
10:17 it was **g** to you to take away the
17:11 and I have **g** it to you to make
19:20 not been ransomed or **g** her freedom,
26:25 and you will be **g** into enemy hands.
27: 9 animal **g** to the LORD becomes holy.
Nu 1:17 these men whose names had been **g**,
3: 9 who are to be **g** wholly to him.
5: 8 LORD and must be **g** to the priest,
8:16 who are to be **g** wholly to me.
8:19 Of all the Israelites, I have **g** the
16:14 or **g** us an inheritance of fields and
18:29 part of everything **g** to you.’
21:29 O people of Chemosh! He has **g** up
27:12 the land I have **g** the Israelites.
32: 5 **g** to your servants as our possession.
32: 7 into the land the LORD has **g** them?
32: 9 the land the LORD had **g** them.
33:53 I have **g** you the land to possess.
34:13 be **g** to the nine and a half tribes,
35: 8 **g** in proportion to the inheritance
Dt 1: 8 See, I have **g** you this land. Go in
1:21 See, the LORD your God has **g** you the
2: 5 I have **g** Esau the hill country of
2: 9 I have **g** Ar to the descendants of
2:19 I have **g** it as a possession to the
2:24 See, I have **g** into your hand Sihon
3:18 “The LORD your God has **g** you this
3:19 may stay in the towns I have **g** you,
3:20 to the possession I have **g** you.”
6:17 and decrees he has **g** you.
8:10 God for the good land he has **g** you.
9:23 possession of the land I have **g** you.
12: 1 the God of your fathers, has **g** you
12:21 herds and flocks the LORD has **g** you,
16:10 the LORD your God has **g** you.
22:19 **g** an Israelite virgin a bad name.
26:10 soil that you, O LORD, have **g** me.
26:11 God has **g** to you and your household.
26:13 portion and have **g** it to the Levite,
26:15 the land you have **g** us as you
28:31 Your sheep will be **g** to your enemies,
28:32 Your sons and daughters will be **g** to
28:53 the LORD your God has **g** you.
29: 4 to this day the LORD has not **g** you a
29:26 not know, gods he had not **g** them.
32:30 them, unless the LORD had **g** them up?
Jos 2: 9 “I know that the LORD has **g** this
2:24 “The LORD has surely **g** the whole
6:16 For the LORD has **g** you the city!
9:19 the leaders answered, “We have **g**
10: 8 them; I have **g** them into your hand.
10:19 your God has **g** them into your hand.”
13: 8 Moses had **g** them east of the Jordan,
13:15 This is what Moses had **g** to the
13:24 This is what Moses had **g** to the
13:29 This is what Moses had **g** to the
13:32 This is the inheritance Moses had **g**
13:33 to the tribe of Levi, Moses had **g** no
15:19 Since you have **g** me land in the
17:14 “Why have you **g** us only one
18: 3 the God of your fathers, has **g** you?
21:12 villages around the city they had **g**
21:21 **g** Shechem (a city of refuge for one
21:26 **g** to the rest of the Kohathite clans.
21:27 clans of the Gershonites were **g**
21:34 (the rest of the Levites) were **g**
22: 4 Now that the LORD your God has **g**
22: 7 Manasseh Moses had **g** land in Bashan,
23: 1 the LORD had **g** Israel rest from all
23:13 which the LORD your God has **g** you.
23:15 from this good land he has **g** you.
23:16 from the good land he has **g** you.”
Jdg 1: 2 I have **g** the land into their hands.”
1:15 Since you have **g** me land in the
1:20 Moses had promised, Hebron was **g** to
3: 4 **g** their forefathers through Moses.
3:28 **g** Moab, your enemy, into your hands.
4:14 LORD has **g** Sisera into your hands.

Jdg 7:14 God has **g** the Midianites and the
7:15 **g** the Midianite camp into your hands.
8: 7 "Just for that, when the LORD has **g**
11:24 our God has **g** us, we will possess.
11:36 "My father," she replied, "you have **g**
14:11 he appeared, he was **g** thirty
14:16 You've **g** my people a riddle, but you
14:20 Samson's wife was **g** to the friend
15: 6 his wife was **g** to his friend.
15:18 **g** your servant this great victory.
20:36 Now the men of Israel had **g** way
21:14 were **g** the women of Jabesh Gilead
Ru 2:13 "You have **g** me comfort and have
4:15 than seven sons, has **g** him birth."
1Sa 1:28 For his whole life he shall be **g**
4:20 despair; you have **g** birth to a son.
14:10 the LORD has **g** them into our hands."
14:12 has **g** them into the hand of Israel."
15:28 has **g** it to one of your
18:19 Saul's daughter, to be **g** to David,
18:19 **g** in marriage to Adriel of Meholah.
25:27 be **g** to the men who follow you.
25:44 Saul had **g** his daughter Michal,
26: 8 God has **g** your enemy into your hands.
28:17 **g** it to one of your neighbours—to
30:23 do that with what the LORD has **g** us.
2Sa 7: 1 the LORD had **g** him rest from all his
9: 9 "I have **g** your master's grandson
12: 8 I would have **g** you even more.
13:28 Don't be afraid. Have not I **g** you
17: 6 said, "Ahithophel has **g** this advice.
17: 7 has **g** is not good this time.
21: 6 descendants be **g** to us to be killed
1Ki 2:21 "Let Abishag the Shunammite be **g** in
3: 6 have **g** him a son to sit on his
3:28 heard the verdict the king had **g**,
5: 4 now the LORD my God has **g** me rest on
5: 7 for he has **g** David a wise son to
8:56 "Praise be to the LORD, who has **g**
9: 6 decrees I have **g** you and go off to
9: 7 Israel from the land I have **g** them
9:12 see the towns that Solomon had **g** him
9:13 have **g** me, my brother?" he asked.
10:13 had **g** her out of his royal bounty.
12:13 the advice **g** him by the elders,
13: 5 according to the sign **g** by the man
13:26 The LORD has **g** him over to the lion,
15:29 according to the word of the LORD **g**
18:26 they took the bull **g** them and
20:27 were also mustered and **g** provisions,
2Ki 5: 1 him the LORD had **g** victory to Aram.
5:17 "please let me, your servant, be **g**
15:20 to be **g** to the king of Assyria.
17:15 and the warnings he had **g** them.
18: 6 the commands the LORD had **g** Moses.
18:30 this city will not be **g** into the
22:10 "Hilkiah the priest has **g** me a book.
1Ch 5: 1 his rights as firstborn were **g** to
6:55 They were **g** Hebron in Judah with its
6:56 were **g** to Caleb son of Jephunneh.
6:57 the descendants of Aaron were **g**
6:60 of Benjamin they were **g** Gibeon,
6:66 Some of the Kohathite clans were **g**
6:67 were **g** Shechem (a city of refuge),
16:40 of the LORD, which he had **g** Israel.
25: 5 They were **g** to him through the
28: 5 Of all my sons–and the LORD has **g**
29: 9 for they had **g** freely and
29:14 **g** you only what comes from your hand.
29:17 All these things have I **g** willingly
29:17 people who are here have **g** to you.
2Ch 1:12 wisdom and knowledge will be **g** you.
2:12 He has **g** King David a wise son,
2:14 and can execute any design **g** to him.
7:19 commands I have **g** you and go off to
7:20 which I have **g** them, and will reject
8: 2 the villages that Hiram had **g** him,
13: 5 the God of Israel, has **g** the
14: 7 and he has **g** us rest on every side.
18:14 "for they will be **g** into your hand.
20:27 for the LORD had **g** them cause to
20:30 God had **g** him rest on every side.
21: 3 Their father had **g** them many gifts
21: 3 but he had **g** the kingdom to Jehoram
28: 5 He was also **g** into the hands of the
31:14 of the freewill offerings **g** to God,
2Ch 32:29 for God had **g** him very great riches.
33: 8 and ordinances **g** through Moses."
34:14 LORD that had been **g** through Moses.
34:18 "Hilkiah the priest has **g** me a book.
36:23 has **g** me all the kingdoms of the
Ezr 1: 2 has **g** me all the kingdoms of the
6: 9 be **g** them daily without fail,
7: 6 the LORD, the God of Israel, had **g**.
7:11 **g** to Ezra the priest and teacher,
7:15 have freely **g** to the God of Israel,
9: 9 and he has **g** us a wall of protection
9:13 and have **g** us a remnant like this.
Ne 7:72 The total **g** by the rest of the
10:29 an oath to follow the Law of God **g**
12:43 because God had **g** them great joy.
13:10 the Levites had not been **g** to them,
Est 2: 3 let beauty treatments be **g** to them.
2:13 Anything she wanted was **g** to her to
5: 3 half the kingdom, it will be **g** you."
5: 6 is your petition? It will be **g** you.
7: 2 is your petition? It will be **g** you.
8: 7 I have **g** his estate to Esther, and
9:12 is your petition? It will be **g** you.
Job 3:20 "Why is light **g** to those in misery,
3:23 Why is life **g** to a man whose way is
15:19 (to whom alone the land was **g** when
38:12 "Have you ever **g** orders to the
Ps 60: 3 **g** us wine that makes us stagger.
61: 5 you have **g** me the heritage of those
63:10 They will be **g** over to the sword and
72:15 May gold from Sheba be **g** to him.
74: 9 We are **g** no miraculous signs; no
78:29 for he had **g** them what they craved.
79: 2 They have **g** the dead bodies of your
94:17 Unless the LORD had **g** me help, I
105:42 For he remembered his holy promise **g**
115:16 LORD, but the earth he has **g** to man.
118:18 but he has not **g** me over to death.
119:49 servant, for you have **g** me hope.
122: 4 to the statute **g** to Israel.
Pr 8:24 there were no oceans, I was **g** birth,
8:25 before the hills, I was **g** birth,
21:14 A gift **g** in secret soothes anger,
23: 2 throat if you are **g** to gluttony.
Ecc 5:18 God has **g** him—for this is his lot.
8:15 life God has **g** him under the sun.
9: 9 that God has **g** you under the sun
12:11 embedded nails—**g** by one Shepherd.
Isa 1: 4 evildoers, children **g** to corruption!
8:18 and the children the LORD has **g** me.
9: 6 to us a son is **g**, and the government
14:32 What answer shall be **g** to the envoys
23: 4 "I have neither been in labour nor **g**
23:11 He has **g** an order concerning
26:18 not **g** birth to people of the world.
34:16 For it is his mouth that has **g** the
35: 2 The glory of Lebanon will be **g** to it,
36:15 this city will not be **g** into the
50: 4 The Sovereign LORD has **g** me an
63:14 **g** rest by the Spirit of the LORD.
Jer 4:31 my life is **g** over to murderers."
8:13 **g** them will be taken from them.'"
8:14 and **g** us poisoned water to drink,
21:10 It will be **g** into the hands of the
32:16 "After I had **g** the deed of purchase
35:15 I have **g** to you and your fathers.
37:21 **g** bread from the street of the
38:16 who has **g** us breath, I will neither
39:11 had **g** these orders about Jeremiah
Lam 4:11 The LORD has **g** full vent to his
Eze 11:15 land was **g** to us as our possession.'
11:24 the vision **g** by the Spirit of God.
15: 6 As I have **g** the wood of the vine
16:14 because the splendour I had **g** you
16:34 give payment and none is **g** to you.
17:18 Because he had **g** his hand in pledge
20:15 **g** them—a land flowing with milk
29:20 I have **g** him Egypt as a reward for
33:24 has been **g** to us as our possession.'
35:12 have been **g** over to us to devour."
46: 5 The grain offering **g** with the ram is
Da 2:23 O God of my fathers: You have **g** me
2:37 The God of heaven has **g** you dominion
4:16 let him be **g** the mind of an animal,
5:21 He was driven away from people and **g**
5:28 and **g** to the Medes and Persians."
Da 7: 4 and the heart of a man was **g** to it.
7: 6 and it was **g** authority to rule.
7:14 He was **g** authority, glory and
8:12 of rebellion, the host of the saints
8:26 that has been **g** you is true,
9: 2 according to the word of the LORD **g**
9:23 an answer was **g**, which I have come
10: 1 a revelation was **g** to Daniel (who
10:19 lord, since you have **g** me strength."
11: 4 will be uprooted and **g** to others.
11:21 not been **g** the honour of royalty.
Hos 6:10 There Ephraim is **g** to prostitution
8:13 They offer sacrifices **g** to me and
Joel 2:23 for he has **g** you the autumn rains in
Am 6:11 For the LORD has **g** the command, and
9:15 uprooted from the land I have **g** them
Na 1:14 The LORD has **g** a command concerning
Zec 6: 8 **g** my Spirit rest in the land of the
6:14 The crown will be **g** to Heldai,
13: 6 I was **g** at the house of my friends.'
Mt 6:33 things will be **g** to you as well.
7: 7 "Ask and it will be **g** to you; seek
9: 8 God, who had **g** such authority to men.
10:19 that time you will be **g** what to say,
12:39 But none will be **g** it except the
13:11 has been **g** to you, but not to them.
13:12 Whoever has will be **g** more, and he
14:11 in on a platter and **g** to the girl,
15:36 and when he had **g** thanks, he broke
16: 4 be **g** it except the sign of Jonah.
19:11 only those to whom it has been **g**.
21:43 **g** to a people who will produce its
22:30 neither marry nor be **g** in marriage;
25:29 For everyone who has will be **g** more,
26: 9 price and the money **g** to the poor."
27:58 Pilate ordered that it be **g** to him.
28:18 and on earth has been **g** to me.
Mk 4:11 kingdom of God has been **g** to you.
4:25 Whoever has will be **g** more; whoever
6: 2 this wisdom that has been **g** him,
6:17 For Herod himself had **g** orders to
8: 6 taken the seven loaves and **g** thanks,
8:12 the truth, no sign will be **g** to it."
12:25 they will neither marry nor be **g** in
12:28 Noticing that Jesus had **g** them a
13:11 Just say whatever is **g** you at the
14: 5 wages and the money **g** to the poor.
Lk 2:21 **g** him before he had been conceived.
4: 6 for it has been **g** to me, and I can
6:38 Give, and it will be **g** to you. A
8:10 kingdom of God has been **g** to you,
8:18 Whoever has will be **g** more; whoever
10:19 I have **g** you authority to trample on
11: 9 Ask and it will be **g** to you; seek
11:29 be **g** it except the sign of Jonah.
12:31 things will be **g** to you as well.
12:48 From everyone who has been **g** much,
17:27 drinking, marrying and being **g** in
19:15 servants to whom he had **g** the money,
19:26 more will be **g**, but as for the one
20:34 age marry and are **g** in marriage.
20:35 neither marry nor be **g** in marriage,
22:19 "This is my body **g** for you; do this
Jn 1:17 For the law was **g** through Moses;
3:27 only what is **g** him from heaven.
4: 5 Jacob had **g** to his son Joseph.
4:10 he would have **g** you living water."
5:27 he has **g** him authority to judge
5:36 that the Father has **g** me to finish,
6:23 bread after the Lord had **g** thanks.
6:32 it is not Moses who has **g** you the
6:39 lose none of all that he has **g** me,
7:19 Has not Moses **g** you the law? Yet not
7:39 that time the Spirit had not been **g**,
10:29 My Father, who has **g** them to me, is
11:57 the chief priests and Pharisees had **g**
12: 2 Here a dinner was **g** in Jesus' honour.
12: 5 sold and the money **g** to the poor?
12:18 that he had **g** this miraculous sign,
15: 7 you wish, and it will be **g** you.
17: 2 life to all those you have **g** him.
17: 7 you have **g** me comes from you.
17: 9 you have **g** me, for they are yours.
17:14 I have **g** them your word and the
17:22 I have **g** them the glory that you
17:24 "Father, I want those you have **g** me

Jn 17:24 the glory you have g me because you
18:11 drink the cup the Father has g me?"
19:11 if it were not g to you from above.
19:35 The man who saw it has g testimony,
Ac 3:16 has g this complete healing to him,
4:12 g to men by which we must be saved."
5:32 God has g to those who obey him."
8:18 Simon saw that the Spirit was g at
17:31 He has g proof of this to all men by
20:24 the task the Lord Jesus has g me
27:24 and God has graciously g you the
Ro 5: 5 the Holy Spirit, whom he has g us.
5:13 for before the law was g, sin was in
11:35 "Who has ever g to God, that God
12: 3 For by the grace g me I say to every
12: 3 the measure of faith God has g you.
12: 6 gifts, according to the grace g us.
1Co 1: 4 of his grace g you in Christ Jesus.
2:12 understand what God has freely g us.
3:10 By the grace God has g me, I laid a
4: 2 been g a trust must prove faithful.
11:15 long hair is g to her as a covering.
11:24 he had g thanks, he broke it and
12: 7 the Spirit is g for the common good.
12: 8 To one there is g through the Spirit
12:13 were all g the one Spirit to drink.
12:24 has g greater honour to the parts
2Co 4:11 g over to death for Jesus' sake
5: 5 has g us the Spirit as a deposit,
7: 7 also by the comfort you had g him.
8: 1 God has g the Macedonian churches.
9: 5 gift, not as one grudgingly g.
9:14 the surpassing grace God has g you.
12: 7 there was g me a thorn in my flesh,
Gal 2: 9 they recognised the grace g to me.
3:14 blessing g to Abraham might come
3:21 had been g that could impart life,
3:22 being g through faith in Jesus Christ
3:22 might be g to those who believe.
4:15 torn out your eyes and g them to me.
Eph 1: 6 has freely g us in the One he loves.
1:21 and every title that can be g, not
3: 2 God's grace that was g to me for you,
3: 7 by the gift of God's grace g me
3: 8 this grace was g me: to preach to
4: 7 to each one of us grace has been g
4:19 they have g themselves over to
6:19 words may be g me so that I will
Php 1:19 g by the Spirit of Jesus Christ,
Col 2:10 you have been g fulness in Christ,
1Th 1: 6 with the joy g by the Holy Spirit.
1Ti 1:12 who has g me strength, that he
2: 6 testimony g in its proper time.
3: 3 not g to drunkenness, not violent
4:14 Do not neglect your gift, which was g
2Ti 1: 9 This grace was g us in Christ Jesus
Tit 1: 7 not quick-tempered, not g to
Phm : 7 Your love has g me great joy and
Heb 2:13 I, and the children God has g me."
4: 8 For if Joshua had g them rest, God
7:11 of it the law was g to the people),
Jas 1: 5 fault, and it will be g to him.
1Pe 1: 3 In his great mercy he has g us new
1:13 g you when Jesus Christ is revealed.
2Pe 1: 3 His divine power has g us everything
1: 4 Through these he has g us his very
3: 2 the command g by our Lord and
1Jn 4:13 because he has g us of his Spirit.
4:21 he has g us this command: Whoever
5: 9 God, which he has g about his Son.
5:10 testimony God has g about his Son.
5:11 this is the testimony: God has g us
5:20 has come and has g us understanding,
2Jn : 4 has g me great joy to find some of
Rev 2:21 I have g her time to repent of her
6: 2 and he was g a crown, and he rode
6: 4 Its rider was g power to take peace
6: 4 To him was g a large sword.
6: 8 They were g power over a fourth of
6:11 each of them was g a white robe, and
7: 2 g power to harm the land and the sea:
8: 2 and to them were g seven trumpets.
8: 3 He was g much incense to offer, with
9: 1 g the key to the shaft of the Abyss.
9: 3 were g power like that of scorpions
9: 5 They were not g power to kill them,
Rev 11: 1 I was g a reed like a measuring rod
11: 2 it has been g to the Gentiles.
12:13 who had g birth to the male child.
12:14 The woman was g the two wings of a
13: 4 he had g authority to the beast,
13: 5 The beast was g a mouth to utter
13: 7 He was g power to make war against
13: 7 And he was g authority over every
13:14 of the signs he was g power to do on
13:15 He was g power to give breath to the
15: 2 They held harps g them by
16: 6 and you have g them blood to drink
16: 8 g power to scorch people with fire.
18: 6 Give back to her as she has g; pay
19: 8 Fine linen, bright and clean, was g
20: 4 who had been g authority to judge.

Giver (Give)

Pr 18:16 A gift opens the way for the g and
2Co 9: 7 for God loves a cheerful g.

Gives (Give)

Ex 4:11 Who g him sight or makes him blind?
13:11 of the Canaanites and g it to you,
16: 8 he g you meat to eat in the evening
16:29 day he g you bread for two days.
21: 4 If his master g him a wife and she
21:22 she g birth prematurely but there is
22: 7 "If a man g his neighbour silver or
22:10 "If a man g a donkey, an ox, a sheep
Lev 12: 2 'A woman who becomes pregnant and g
12: 5 If she g birth to a daughter, for
12: 7 who g birth to a boy or a girl.
20: 2 who g any of his children to Molech
20: 4 man g one of his children to Molech
Nu 5:10 but what he g to the priest will
10:32 whatever good things the LORD g us."
22: 8 you back the answer the LORD g me.
Dt 3:20 until the LORD g rest to your
4:40 LORD your God g you for all time.
7:16 the LORD your God g over to you.
8:18 for it is he who g you the ability
12:15 blessing the LORD your God g you.
16: 5 in any town the LORD your God g
17: 2 in one of the towns the LORD g you
19: 8 and g you the whole land he promised
20:14 your God g you from your enemies.
22:14 slanders her and g her a bad name,
24: 1 g it to her and sends her from his
24: 3 g it to her and sends her from his
25:19 the LORD your God g you rest from
Jos 1:15 until the LORD g them rest, as he
2:14 when the LORD g us the land."
Jdg 11: 9 the LORD g them to me—will I really
11:24 take what your god Chemosh g you?
21:18 anyone who g a wife to a Benjamite.'
Ru 4:12 Through the offspring the LORD g you
2Sa 22:51 He g his king great victories; he
24:23 O king, Araunah g all this to the
1Ki 17:14 day the LORD g rain on the land.'"
Ezr 9: 8 and so our God g light to our eyes
Est 5:13 all this g me no satisfaction as
Job 8:15 He leans on his web, but it g way;
32: 8 Almighty, that g him understanding.
33: 4 breath of the Almighty g me life.
35:10 my Maker, who g songs in the night,
36: 6 but g the afflicted their rights.
38:29 Who g birth to the frost from the
Ps 7:14 trouble g birth to disillusionment.
18:50 He g his king great victories; he
29:11 The LORD g strength to his people;
68:35 g power and strength to his people.
82: 1 he g judgment among the "gods":
119:130 The unfolding of your words g light;
119:130 it g understanding to the simple.
136:25 who g food to every creature.
144:10 to the One who g victory to kings,
146: 7 oppressed and g food to the hungry.
146: 8 the LORD g sight to the blind, the
Pr 2: 6 For the LORD g wisdom, and from his
3:34 He mocks proud mockers but g grace
5: 6 She g no thought to the way of life;
11:24 One man g freely, yet gains even
12:17 A truthful witness g honest
14:15 prudent man g thought to his steps.
Pr 14:30 A heart at peace g life to the body,
15:30 and good news g health to the bones.
16:20 Whoever g heed to instruction
17: 8 A bribe is a charm to the one who g
19: 6 is the friend of a man who g gifts.
19:11 A man's wisdom g him patience; it is
21:29 upright man g thought to his ways.
22:16 he who g gifts to the rich—both
25:18 sharp arrow is the man who g false
25:26 man who g way to the wicked.
28:27 He who g to the poor will lack
29: 4 By justice a king g a country
29:11 A fool g full vent to his anger, but
29:13 The LORD g sight to the eyes of both.
Ecc 2:26 To the man who pleases him, God g
2:26 but to the sinner he g the task of
5:19 Moreover, when God g any man wealth
6: 2 God g a man wealth, possessions and
Isa 14: 3 On the day the LORD g you relief
21: 9 And he g back the answer: 'Babylon
30:20 Although the Lord g you the bread of
40:29 He g strength to the weary and
42: 5 who g breath to its people, and life
66: 7 "Before she goes into labour, she g
66: 8 than she g birth to her children.
Jer 5:24 'Let us fear the LORD our God, who g
Lam 4: 4 for bread, but no-one g it to them.
Eze 18: 7 but g his food to the hungry
18:16 but g his food to the hungry
33:15 if he g back what he took in pledge
Da 2:21 He g wisdom to the wise and
4:17 g them to anyone he wishes and sets
4:25 men and g them to anyone he wishes.
4:32 men and g them to anyone he wishes."
Mic 5: 3 when she who is in labour g birth
Hab 2:15 "Woe to him who g drink to his
Zec 10: 1 He g showers of rain to men, and
Mt 5:15 it g light to everyone in the house.
10:42 if anyone g even a cup of cold water
26:73 them, for your accent g you away."
Mk 1:27 He even g orders to evil spirits and
9:41 who g you a cup of water in my
Lk 4:36 With authority and power he g orders
Jn 1: 9 The true light that g light to every
3: 6 Flesh g birth to flesh, but the
3: 6 but the Spirit g birth to spirit.
3:34 for God g the Spirit without limit.
5:21 raises the dead and g them life,
5:21 even so the Son g life to whom he is
6:32 g you the true bread from heaven.
6:33 heaven and g life to the world."
6:37 All that the Father g me will come
6:63 The Spirit g life; the flesh counts
14:27 I do not give to you as the world g.
Ac 17:25 because he himself g all men life
Ro 4:17 in whom he believed—the God who g
14: 6 eats to the Lord, for he g thanks to
14: 6 so to the Lord and g thanks to God.
15: 5 May the God who g endurance and
1Co 12:11 and he g them to each one, just as
15:38 God g it a body as he has determined,
15:38 each kind of seed he g its own body.
15:57 thanks be to God! He g us the
2Co 3: 6 letter kills, but the Spirit g life.
Php 4:13 I can do everything through him who g
1Th 4: 8 but God, who g you his Holy Spirit.
1Ti 6:13 In the sight of God, who g life to
Jas 1: 5 he should ask God, who g generously
1:15 after desire has conceived, it g
1:15 it is full-grown, g birth to death.
1:25 into the perfect law that g freedom,
2:12 be judged by the law that g freedom,
4: 6 he g us more grace. That is why
4: 6 proud but g grace to the humble."
1Pe 5: 5 proud but g grace to the humble."
Rev 21:23 g it light, and the Lamb is its lamp.

Giving (Give)

Ge 13:17 of the land, for I am g it to you."
20:16 To Sarah he said, "I am g your
30:18 Leah said, "God has rewarded me for g
38:28 she was g birth, one of them put out
41:12 interpreted them for us, g each man
49:28 g each the blessing appropriate to
49:33 Jacob had finished g instructions to

Ex 20:12 the land the LORD your God is **g** you.
Lev 14:34 which I am **g** you as your possession,
20: 3 for by **g** his children to Molech,
27: 2 to the LORD by **g** equivalent values,
Nu 13: 2 which I am **g** to the Israelites.
15: 2 enter the land I am **g** you as a
18: 7 I am **g** you the service of the
Dt 1:20 which the LORD our God is **g** us.
1:25 land that the LORD our God is **g** us."
2:29 the land the LORD our God is **g** us."
3:20 God is **g** them, across the Jordan.
4: 1 the God of your fathers, is **g** you.
4:21 God is **g** you as your inheritance.
4:40 which I am **g** you today, so that it
5:16 the land the LORD your God is **g** you.
5:31 in the land I am **g** them to possess."
8: 1 every command I am **g** you today,
8:11 decrees that I am **g** you this day.
9: 6 is **g** you this good land to possess,
10:13 I am **g** you today for your own good?
10:18 the alien, **g** him food and clothing.
11: 8 all the commands I am **g** you today,
11:13 obey the commands I am **g** you today
11:17 the good land the LORD is **g** you.
11:22 these commands I am **g** you to follow
11:27 LORD your God that I am **g** you today;
11:31 the land the LORD your God is **g** you.
12: 9 the LORD your God is **g** you.
12:10 your God is **g** you as an inheritance,
12:28 all these regulations I am **g** you,
13:12 LORD your God is **g** you to live
13:18 his commands that I am **g** you today
15: 4 **g** you to possess as your inheritance,
15: 5 all these commands I am **g** you today.
15: 7 that the LORD your God is **g** you,
16:10 **g** a freewill offering in proportion
16:18 town the LORD your God is **g** you,
16:20 the land the LORD your God is **g** you.
17:14 the land the LORD your God is **g** you
18: 9 the land the LORD your God is **g** you,
19: 1 the nations whose land he is **g** you,
19: 2 LORD your God is **g** you to possess.
19: 3 your God is **g** you as an inheritance,
19:10 which the LORD your God is **g** you as
19:14 LORD your God is **g** you to possess.
19:18 **g** false testimony against his
20:16 your God is **g** you as an inheritance,
21: 1 LORD your God is **g** you to possess,
21:17 **g** him a double share of all he has.
21:23 your God is **g** you as an inheritance.
24: 4 your God is **g** you as an inheritance.
25:15 the land the LORD your God is **g** you.
25:19 **g** you to possess as an inheritance,
26: 1 your God is **g** you as an inheritance
26: 2 is **g** you and put them in a basket.
27: 2 the land the LORD your God is **g** you,
27: 3 the land the LORD your God is **g** you,
28: 8 bless you in the land he is **g** you.
28:15 and decrees I am **g** you today,
28:52 the land the LORD your God is **g** you.
30: 8 all his commands I am **g** you today.
32:49 and view Canaan, the land I am **g** the
32:52 I am **g** to the people of Israel."
Jos 1:11 your God is **g** you for your own.'"
1:13 'The LORD your God is **g** you rest and
1:15 that the LORD your God is **g** them.
3: 3 **g** orders to the people: "When you
Jdg 2:23 by **g** them into the hands of Joshua.
1Sa 22:13 you and the son of Jesse, **g** him
2Sa 11:19 "When you have finished **g** the king
18: 5 And all the troops heard the king **g**
24:12 LORD says: I am **g** you three options.
1Ch 21:10 LORD says: I am **g** you three options.
Ezr 9: 8 **g** us a firm place in his sanctuary,
Ne 4:10 "The strength of the labourers is **g**
8: 8 making it clear and **g** the meaning so
Est 2:22 to the king, **g** credit to Mordecai.
3: 1 the Agagite, elevating him and **g** him
9:19 a day for **g** presents to each other.
9:22 joy and **g** presents of food to one
Ps 19: 8 The precepts of the LORD are right, **g**
19: 8 are radiant, **g** light to the eyes.
100: T A psalm. For **g** thanks.
106: 5 join your inheritance in **g** praise.
111: 6 **g** them the lands of other nations.
Pr 1: 4 for **g** prudence to the simple,
15:23 A man finds joy in **g** an apt reply—
26: 8 sling is the **g** of honour to a fool.
Eze 3: 3 **g** you and fill your stomach with it.
11: 2 and **g** wicked advice in this city.
16:54 all you have done in **g** them comfort.
Da 4:21 providing food for all, **g** shelter to
6:10 **g** thanks to his God, just as he had
9:13 sins and **g** attention to your truth.
Mt 6: 4 that your **g** may be in secret. Then
24:38 marrying and **g** in marriage, up to
Jn 16:21 A woman **g** birth to a child has pain
Ac 1: 2 after **g** instructions through the
8: 1 Saul was there, **g** approval to his
14:17 He has shown kindness by **g** you rain
15: 8 showed that he accepted them by **g**
22:20 I stood there **g** my approval and
1Co 14:17 You may be **g** thanks well enough, but
2Co 5:12 but are **g** you an opportunity to take
8: 7 you also excel in this grace of **g**.
Eph 1:16 I have not stopped **g** thanks for you,
5:20 always **g** thanks to God the Father
Php 4:15 of **g** and receiving, except you only;
Col 1:12 **g** thanks to the Father, who has
3:17 **g** thanks to God the Father through

Gizonite
1Ch 11:34 the sons of Hashem the **G**, Jonathan

Glad (Gladdens, Gladly, Gladness)
Ex 4:14 heart will be **g** when he sees you.
Jos 22:33 They were **g** to hear the report and
Jdg 8:25 They answered, "We'll be **g** to give
18:20 the priest was **g**. He took the ephod,
1Sa 19: 5 Israel, and you saw it and were **g**.
2Sa 1:20 daughters of the Philistines be **g**,
1Ki 8:66 joyful and **g** in heart for all the
1Ch 16:31 heavens rejoice, let the earth be **g**
2Ch 7:10 joyful and **g** in heart for the good
Ps 5:11 let all who take refuge in you be **g**;
9: 2 I will be **g** and rejoice in you; I
14: 7 let Jacob rejoice and Israel be **g**!
16: 9 Therefore my heart is **g** and my
21: 6 him **g** with the joy of your presence.
31: 7 I will be **g** and rejoice in your love,
32:11 Rejoice in the LORD and be **g**, you
40:16 may all who seek you rejoice and be **g**
45: 8 music of the strings makes you **g**.
46: 4 There is a river whose streams make **g**
48:11 are **g** because of your judgments.
53: 6 let Jacob rejoice and Israel be **g**!
58:10 The righteous will be **g** when they
67: 4 May the nations be **g** and sing for
68: 3 may the righteous be **g** and rejoice
69:32 The poor will see and be **g**—you who
70: 4 may all who seek you rejoice and be **g**
90:14 sing for joy and be **g** all our days.
90:15 Make us **g** for as many days as you
92: 4 For you make me **g** by your deeds,
96:11 let the earth be **g**; let the sea
97: 1 The LORD reigns, let the earth be **g**;
97: 8 **g** because of your judgments, O LORD.
105:38 Egypt was **g** when they left, because
107:30 They were **g** when it grew calm, and
118:24 made; let us rejoice and be **g** in it.
149: 2 people of Zion be **g** in their King.
Pr 23:15 is wise, then my heart will be **g**;
23:25 May your father and mother be **g**; may
29: 6 a righteous one can sing and be **g**.
Ecc 8:15 sun than to eat and drink and be **g**.
Isa 25: 9 rejoice and be **g** in his salvation."
35: 1 and the parched land will be **g**;
65:18 be **g** and rejoice for ever in what I
66:10 "Rejoice with Jerusalem and be **g** for
Jer 20:15 who made him very **g**, saying, "A
31:13 maidens will dance and be **g**, young
41:13 who were with him, they were **g**.
50:11 "Because you rejoice and are **g**, you
Lam 4:21 Rejoice and be **g**, O Daughter of
Joel 2:21 Be not afraid, O land; be **g** and
2:23 Be **g**, O people of Zion, rejoice in
Hab 1:15 and so he rejoices and is **g**.
Zep 3:14 O Israel! Be **g** and rejoice with all
Zec 2:10 "Shout and be **g**, O Daughter of Zion.
8:19 **g** occasions and happy festivals for
10: 7 their hearts will be **g** as with wine.
Mt 5:12 Rejoice and be **g**, because great is
Lk 15:32 we had to celebrate and be **g**,
Jn 4:36 and the reaper may be **g** together.
8:56 seeing my day; he saw it and was **g**."
11:15 for your sake I am **g** I was not there,
14:28 If you loved me, you would be **g**
Ac 2:26 Therefore my heart is **g** and my
2:46 together with **g** and sincere hearts,
11:23 he was **g** and encouraged them all to
13:48 the Gentiles heard this, they were **g**
15: 3 news made all the brothers very **g**.
15:31 The people read it and were **g** for
1Co 16:17 I was **g** when Stephanas, Fortunatus
2Co 2: 2 who is left to make me **g** but you
7:16 I am **g** I can have complete
13: 9 We are **g** whenever we are weak but
Gal 4:27 For it is written: "Be **g**, O barren
Php 2:17 I am **g** and rejoice with all of you.
2:18 you too should be **g** and rejoice with
2:28 be **g** and I may have less anxiety.
Rev 19: 7 Let us rejoice and be **g** and give him

Gladdens (Glad)
Ps 104:15 wine that **g** the heart of man, oil to

Gladly (Glad)
Dt 28:47 and **g** in the time of prosperity,
Jdg 19: 3 father saw him, he **g** welcomed him.
2Ch 24:10 brought their contributions **g**,
Isa 39: 2 Hezekiah received the envoys **g** and
64: 5 to the help of those who **g** do right.
Jer 3:19 "I myself said, "'How **g** would I
Lk 19: 6 down at once and welcomed him **g**.
Ac 24:10 this nation; so I **g** make my defence.
2Co 11:19 You **g** put up with fools since you
12: 9 all the more **g** about my weaknesses,
12:15 I will very **g** spend for you

Gladness (Glad)
2Ch 29:30 So they sang praises with **g** and
Est 8:16 of happiness and joy, **g** and honour.
8:17 there was joy and **g** among the Jews,
Job 3:22 who are filled with **g** and rejoice
Ps 35:27 for joy and **g**; may they always say,
45:15 They are led in with joy and **g**; they
51: 8 Let me hear joy and **g**; let the bones
65:12 the hills are clothed with **g**.
100: 2 Worship the LORD with **g**; come before
Ecc 5:20 keeps him occupied with **g** of heart.
9: 7 Go, eat your food with **g**, and drink
Isa 16:10 Joy and **g** are taken away from the
35:10 **G** and joy will overtake them, and
51: 3 Joy and **g** will be found in her,
51:11 **G** and joy will overtake them, and
61: 3 the oil of **g** instead of mourning,
Jer 7:34 an end to the sounds of joy and **g**
16: 9 an end to the sounds of joy and **g**
25:10 from them the sounds of joy and **g**,
31:13 I will turn their mourning into **g**; I
33:11 the sounds of joy and **g**, the voices
48:33 Joy and **g** are gone from the orchards
Joel 1:16 joy and **g** from the house of our God?

Glance (Glances, Glancing)
Pr 23: 5 Cast but a **g** at riches, and they are
SS 4: 9 my heart with one **g** of your eyes,

Glances (Glance)
Pr 30:13 haughty, whose **g** are so disdainful;

Glancing (Glance)
Ex 2:12 **G** this way and that and seeing

Glass
Rev 4: 6 like a sea of **g**, clear as crystal.
15: 2 I saw what looked like a sea of **g**
21:18 the city of pure gold, as pure as **g**.
21:21 of pure gold, like transparent **g**.

Glaze
Pr 26:23 Like a coating of **g** over earthenware

Gleam (Gleamed, Gleaming)
Pr 4:18 is like the first g of dawn,
Da 10: 6 his arms and legs like the g of

Gleamed (Gleam)
Eze 1: 7 a calf and g like burnished bronze.
Lk 24: 4 clothes that g like lightning stood

Gleaming (Gleam)
Job 20:25 He pulls it out of his back, the g

Glean (Gleaned, Gleaning, Gleanings, Gleans)
Ru 2: 3 she went out and began to g in the
2: 7 She said, 'Please let me g and
2: 8 Don't go and g in another field and
2:15 she got up to g, Boaz gave orders to
2:19 "Where did you g today? Where did
2:23 girls of Boaz to g until the barley
Job 24: 6 g in the vineyards of the wicked.
Jer 6: 9 "Let them g the remnant of Israel as

Gleaned (Glean)
Ru 2:17 Ruth g in the field until evening.

Gleaning (Glean)
Mic 7: 1 fruit at the g of the vineyard;

Gleanings (Glean)
Lev 19: 9 or gather the g of your harvest.
23:22 or gather the g of your harvest.
Jdg 8: 2 Aren't the g of Ephraim's grapes
Isa 17: 6 Yet some g will remain, as when an
24:13 g are left after the grape harvest.

Gleans (Glean)
Isa 17: 5 as when a man g ears of corn in the

Glee
Ps 35:15 I stumbled, they gathered in g;
Eze 36: 5 g and malice in their hearts they

Glide (Glided, Gliding)
Dt 32:24 venom of vipers that g in the dust.

Glided (Glide)
Job 4:15 A spirit g past my face, and the

Gliding (Glide)
Job 26:13 his hand pierced the g serpent.
Isa 27: 1 Leviathan the g serpent, Leviathan

Glimpse
Job 9:25 they fly away without a g of joy.
23: 9 to the south, I catch no g of him.

Glint
Hab 3:11 at the g of your flying arrows,

Glistening
Job 41:32 Behind him he leaves a g wake; one

Glittering
Na 3: 3 flashing swords and g spears! Many
Rev 17: 4 and was g with gold, precious stones
18:16 purple and scarlet, and g with gold,

Gloat (Gloated, Gloating, Gloats)
Ps 22:17 bones; people stare and g over me.
30: 1 did not let my enemies g over me.
35:19 Let not those g over me who are my
35:24 my God; do not let them g over me.
35:26 May all who g over my distress be
38:16 For I said, "Do not let them g or
59:10 let me g over those who slander me.
Pr 24:17 Do not g when your enemy falls; when
Lam 2:17 he has let the enemy g over you, he
Mic 4:11 defiled, let our eyes g over Zion!"
7: 8 Do not g over me, my enemy! Though I
Rev 11:10 The inhabitants of the earth will g

Gloated (Gloat)
Job 31:29 g over the trouble that came to him—

Gloating (Gloat)
Hab 3:14 g as though about to devour the

Gloats (Gloat)
Pr 17: 5 whoever g over disaster will not go

Gloom (Gloomy)
Job 10:21 to the land of g and deep shadow,
Ps 107:10 sat in darkness and the deepest g,
107:14 out of darkness and the deepest g
Isa 8:22 distress and darkness and fearful g,
9: 1 Nevertheless, there will be no more g
24:11 all joy turns to g, all gaiety is
29:18 and out of g and darkness the eyes
Jer 13:16 darkness and change it to deep g.
Eze 31:15 I clothed Lebanon with g, and all
Joel 2: 2 a day of darkness and g, a day of
Zep 1:15 a day of darkness and g, a day of
Heb 12:18 with fire; to darkness, g and storm;
Jas 4: 9 to mourning and your joy to g.

Gloomy (Gloom)
2Pe 2: 4 g dungeons to be held for judgment;

Glories (Glory)
1Pe 1:11 Christ and the g that would follow.

Glorified (Glory)
Isa 66: 5 'Let the LORD be g, that we may see
Eze 39:13 and the day I am g will be a
Da 4:34 and g him who lives for ever.
Jn 7:39 since Jesus had not yet been g.
11: 4 that God's Son may be g through it."
12:16 Only after Jesus was g did they
12:23 has come for the Son of Man to be g.
12:28 g it, and will glorify it again."
13:31 Son of Man g and God is g in him.
13:32 If God is g in him, God will glorify
Ac 3:13 fathers, has g his servant Jesus.
Ro 1:21 they neither g him as God nor gave
8:30 those he justified, he also g.
2Th 1:10 on the day he comes to be g in his
1:12 of our Lord Jesus may be g in you,
1Pe 1:21 who raised him from the dead and g

Glorifies (Glory)
Lk 1:46 Mary said: "My soul g the
Jn 8:54 as your God, is the one who g me.

Glorify (Glory)
Ps 34: 3 G the LORD with me: let us exalt his
63: 3 than life, my lips will g you.
69:30 in song and g him with thanksgiving.
86:12 heart; I will g your name for ever.
Isa 60:13 and I will g the place of my feet.
Da 4:37 praise and exalt and g the King of
Jn 8:54 Jesus replied, "If I g myself, my
12:28 Father, g your name!" Then a voice
12:28 glorified it, and will g it again."
13:32 God will g the Son in himself, and
13:32 in himself, and will g him at once.
17: 1 G your Son, that your Son may g you.
17: 5 now, Father, g me in your presence
21:19 of death by which Peter would g God.
Ro 15: 6 mouth you may g the God and Father
15: 9 that the Gentiles may g God for his
1Pe 2:12 and g God on the day he visits us.
Rev 16: 9 they refused to repent and g him.

Glorifying (Glory)
Lk 2:20 The shepherds returned, g and

Glorious (Glory)
Dt 28:58 do not revere this g and awesome
33:29 shield and helper and your g sword.
1Ch 29:13 you thanks, and praise your g name.
Ne 9: 5 "Blessed be your g name, and may it
Ps 16: 3 g ones in whom is all my delight.
45:13 All g is the princess within her
66: 2 of his name; make his praise g!
72:19 Praise be to his g name for ever;
87: 3 G things are said of you, O city of
111: 3 G and majestic are his deeds, and
145: 5 They will speak of the g splendour
145:12 and the g splendour of your kingdom.
Isa 3: 8 the LORD, defying his g presence.
4: 2 of the LORD will be beautiful and g,
11:10 and his place of rest will be g.
12: 5 Sing to the LORD, for he has done g
28: 1 to the fading flower, his g beauty,
28: 4 That fading flower, his g beauty,
28: 5 the LORD Almighty will be a g crown,
42:21 to make his law great and g.
60: 7 altar, and I will adorn my g temple.
63:12 who sent his g arm of power to be at
63:14 to make for yourself a g name.
63:15 from your lofty throne, holy and g.
64:11 Our holy and g temple, where our
Jer 13:18 g crowns will fall from your heads."
14:21 us; do not dishonour your g throne.
17:12 A g throne, exalted from the
48:17 sceptre, how broken the g staff!'
Mt 19:28 when the Son of Man sits on his g
Lk 9:31 appeared in g splendour, talking
Ac 2:20 of the great and g day of the Lord.
Ro 8:21 g freedom of the children of God.
2Co 3: 8 of the Spirit be even more g?
3: 9 the ministry that condemns men is g,
3: 9 how much more g is the ministry that
3:10 For what was g has no glory now in
Eph 1: 6 to the praise of his g grace, which
1:17 the g Father, may give you the
1:18 of his g inheritance in the saints,
3:16 I pray that out of his g riches he
Php 3:21 that they will be like his g body.
4:19 to his g riches in Christ Jesus.
Col 1:11 according to his g might so that
1:27 the g riches of this mystery,
1Ti 1:11 that conforms to the g gospel of the
Tit 2:13 g appearing of our great God
Jas 2: 1 My brothers, as believers in our g
1Pe 1: 8 with an inexpressible and g joy,
Jude :24 to present you before his g presence

Gloriously (Glory)
Isa 24:23 Jerusalem, and before its elders, g.

Glory (Glories, Glorified, Glorifies, Glorify, Glorifying, Glorious, Gloriously, *Glory of God, Glory of the LORD*)
Ex 14: 4 But I will gain g for myself through
14:17 And I will gain g through Pharaoh
14:18 LORD when I gain g through Pharaoh,
15:11 awesome in g, working wonders?
29:43 place will be consecrated by my g.
33:18 Moses said, "Now show me your g."
33:22 my g passes by, I will put you in a
Nu 14:22 not one of the men who saw my g and
Dt 5:24 "The LORD our God has shown us his g
Jos 7:19 Joshua said to Achan, "My son, give g
1Sa 4:21 "The g has departed from Israel"
4:22 She said, "The g has departed from
15:29 He who is the G of Israel does not
2Sa 1:19 "Your g, O Israel, lies slain on
2Ki 14:10 G in your victory, but stay at home!
1Ch 16:10 G in his holy name; let the hearts
16:24 Declare his g among the nations, his
16:28 ascribe to the LORD g and strength,
16:29 ascribe to the LORD the g due to his
16:35 name, that we may g in your praise."
29:11 g and the majesty and the splendour,
Est 1: 4 the splendour and g of his majesty.
Job 29:20 My g will remain fresh in me, the
40:10 adorn yourself with g and splendour,
Ps 3: 3 bestow g on me and lift up my head.
4: 2 How long, O men, will you turn my g
8: 1 have set your g above the heavens.
8: 5 and crowned him with g and honour.
19: 1 The heavens declare the g of God;
21: 5 Through the victories you gave, his g
24: 7 that the King of g may come in.
24: 8 Who is this King of g? The LORD
24: 9 that the King of g may come in.
24:10 Who is he, this King of g? The LORD
24:10 LORD Almighty—he is the King of g.

Ps 26: 8 the place where your **g** dwells.
29: 1 ascribe to the LORD **g** and strength.
29: 2 Ascribe to the LORD the **g** due to his
29: 3 the God of **g** thunders, the LORD
29: 9 And in his temple all cry, "**G**!"
57: 5 let your **g** be over all the earth.
57:11 let your **g** be over all the earth.
63: 2 and beheld your power and your **g**.
66: 2 Sing the **g** of his name; make his
72:19 whole earth be filled with his **g**.
73:24 afterwards you will take me into **g**.
79: 9 Help us, O God our Saviour, for the **g**
85: 9 that his **g** may dwell in our land.
86: 9 Lord; they will bring **g** to your name.
89:17 For you are their **g** and strength,
96: 3 Declare his **g** among the nations, his
96: 6 strength and **g** are in his sanctuary.
96: 7 ascribe to the LORD **g** and strength.
96: 8 Ascribe to the LORD the **g** due to his
97: 6 and all the peoples see his **g**.
102:15 of the earth will revere your **g**.
102:16 rebuild Zion and appear in his **g**.
105: 3 **G** in his holy name; let the hearts
106:20 They exchanged their **G** for an image
106:47 your holy name and **g** in your praise.
108: 5 let your **g** be over all the earth.
113: 4 nations, his **g** above the heavens.
115: 1 not to us but to your name be the **g**,
145:11 They will tell of the **g** of your
149: 9 This is the **g** of all his saints.
Pr 14:28 A large population is a king's **g**,
19:11 is to his **g** to overlook an offence.
20:29 The **g** of young men is their strength,
25: 2 is the **g** of God to conceal a matter;
25: 2 out a matter is the **g** of kings.
Isa 4: 2 and **g** of the survivors in Israel.
4: 5 over all the **g** will be a canopy.
6: 3 the whole earth is full of his **g**."
13:19 Babylon, the jewel of kingdoms, the **g**
17: 3 be like the **g** of the Israelites,"
17: 4 "In that day the **g** of Jacob will
22:24 All the **g** of his family will hang on
23: 9 to bring low the pride of all **g** and
24:15 Therefore in the east give **g** to the
24:16 singing: "**G** to the Righteous One."
26:15 You have gained **g** for yourself; you
35: 2 The **g** of Lebanon will be given to it,
40: 6 **g** is like the flowers of the field.
41:16 LORD and **g** in the Holy One of Israel.
42: 8 **g** to another or my praise to idols.
42:12 Let them give **g** to the LORD and
43: 7 whom I created for my **g**, whom I
44:13 of man in all his **g**, that it may
44:23 Jacob, he displays his **g** in Israel.
48:11 I will not yield my **g** to another.
59:19 of the sun, they will revere his **g**.
60: 2 upon you and his **g** appears over you.
60:13 "The **g** of Lebanon will come to you,
60:19 light, and your God will be your **g**.
62: 2 and all kings your **g**; you will be
66:18 and they will come and see my **g**.
66:19 not heard of my fame or seen my **g**.
66:19 proclaim my **g** among the nations.
Jer 2:11 their **G** for worthless idols.
4: 2 by him and in him they will **g**."
13:16 Give **g** to the LORD your God before
48:18 "Come down from your **g** and sit on
Eze 3:23 like the **g** I had seen by the Kebar
8: 4 there before me was the **g** of the God
9: 3 Now the **g** of the God of Israel went
10:19 and the **g** of the God of Israel was
11:22 spread their wings, and the **g** of the
24:25 their joy and **g**, the delight of
25: 9 and Kiriathaim—the **g** of that land.
28:22 and I will gain **g** within you.
39:21 "I will display my **g** among the
43: 2 I saw the **g** of the God of Israel
43: 2 and the land was radiant with his **g**.
Da 2:37 dominion and power and might and **g**;
4:30 power and for the **g** of my majesty?"
4:36 to me for the **g** of my kingdom.
5:18 and greatness and **g** and splendour.
5:20 royal throne and stripped of his **g**.
7:14 He was given authority, **g** and
Hos 4: 7 their **G** for something disgraceful.
9:11 Ephraim's **g** will fly away like a
Mic 1:15 **g** of Israel will come to Adullam.
Hab 2:16 be filled with shame instead of **g**.
2:16 you, and disgrace will cover your **g**.
3: 3 His **g** covered the heavens and his
Hag 2: 3 who saw this house in its former **g**?
2: 7 with **g**,' says the LORD Almighty.
2: 9 'The **g** of this present house will be
2: 9 than the **g** of the former house,' says
Zec 2: 5 LORD, 'and I will be its **g** within.'
Mt 16:27 in his Father's **g** with his angels,
24:30 of the sky, with power and great **g**.
25:31 "When the Son of Man comes in his **g**,
25:31 sit on his throne in heavenly **g**.
Mk 8:38 Father's **g** with the holy angels."
10:37 the other at your left in your **g**."
13:26 in clouds with great power and **g**.
Lk 2:14 "**G** to God in the highest, and on
2:32 and for **g** to your people Israel."
9:26 of him when he comes in his **g**
9:26 in the **g** of the Father and of the
9:32 saw his **g** and the two men standing
19:38 in heaven and **g** in the highest!"
21:27 in a cloud with power and great **g**.
24:26 these things and then enter his **g**?"
Jn 1:14 We have seen his **g**, the **g** of the One
2:11 He thus revealed his **g**, and his
8:50 I am not seeking **g** for myself; but
8:54 I glorify myself, my **g** means nothing.
9:24 "Give **g** to God," they said. "We know
11: 4 No, it is for God's **g** so that God's
11:40 you would see the **g** of God?"
12:41 he saw Jesus' **g** and spoke about him.
14:13 the Son may bring **g** to the Father.
15: 8 This is to my Father's **g**, that you
16:14 He will bring **g** to me by taking from
17: 4 I have brought you **g** on earth by
17: 5 with the **g** I had with you before
17:10 And **g** has come to me through them.
17:22 I have given them the **g** that you
17:24 and to see my **g**, the **g** you have
Ac 7: 2 listen to me! The God of **g** appeared
7:55 looked up to heaven and saw the **g** of
Ro 1:23 exchanged the **g** of the immortal God
2: 7 by persistence in doing good seek **g**,
2:10 **g**, honour and peace for everyone who
3: 7 truthfulness and so increases his **g**,
3:23 and fall short of the **g** of God,
4:20 in his faith and gave **g** to God,
5: 2 rejoice in the hope of the **g** of God.
6: 4 dead through the **g** of the Father,
8:17 that we may also share in his **g**.
8:18 the **g** that will be revealed in us.
9: 4 as sons; theirs the divine **g**, the
9:23 **g** known to the objects of his mercy,
9:23 whom he prepared in advance for **g**—
11:36 To him be the **g** for ever! Amen.
15:17 Therefore I **g** in Christ Jesus in my
16:27 to the only wise God be **g** for ever
1Co 2: 7 for our **g** before time began.
2: 8 not have crucified the Lord of **g**.
10:31 you do, do it all for the **g** of God.
11: 7 since he is the image and **g** of God;
11: 7 God; but the woman is the **g** of man.
11:15 it is her **g**? For long hair is given
15:31 **g** over you in Christ Jesus our Lord.
15:43 it is raised in **g**; it is sown in
2Co 1:20 is spoken by us to the **g** of God.
3: 7 came with **g**, so that the Israelites
3: 7 of its **g**, fading though it was,
3:10 For what was glorious has no **g** now
3:10 in comparison with the surpassing **g**.
3:11 if what was fading away came with **g**,
3:11 greater is the **g** of that which lasts
3:18 faces all reflect the Lord's **g**,
3:18 his likeness with ever-increasing **g**,
4: 4 **g** of Christ, who is the image of God.
4: 6 the **g** of God in the face of Christ.
4:15 to overflow to the **g** of God.
4:17 **g** that far outweighs them all.
6: 8 through **g** and dishonour, bad report
Gal 1: 5 to whom be **g** for ever and ever. Amen.
Eph 1:12 might be for the praise of his **g**.
1:14 possession—to the praise of his **g**.
3:13 for you, which are your **g**.
3:21 to him be **g** in the church and in
Php 1:11 Christ—to the **g** and praise of God.
Php 2:11 is Lord, to the **g** of God the Father.
3: 3 who **g** in Christ Jesus, and who put
3:19 and their **g** is in their shame.
4:20 To our God and Father be **g** for ever
Col 1:27 is Christ in you, the hope of **g**.
3: 4 you also will appear with him in **g**.
1Th 2:12 calls you into his kingdom and **g**.
2:19 or the crown in which we will **g** in
2:20 Indeed, you are our **g** and joy.
2Th 2:14 in the **g** of our Lord Jesus Christ.
1Ti 1:17 be honour and **g** for ever and ever.
3:16 on in the world, was taken up in **g**.
2Ti 2:10 is in Christ Jesus, with eternal **g**.
4:18 To him be **g** for ever and ever. Amen.
Heb 1: 3 The Son is the radiance of God's **g**
2: 7 you crowned him with **g** and honour
2: 9 now crowned with **g** and honour
2:10 In bringing many sons to **g**, it was
5: 5 the **g** of becoming a high priest.
9: 5 **G**, overshadowing the atonement cover.
13:21 to whom be **g** for ever and ever.
1Pe 1: 7 **g** and honour when Jesus Christ is
1:24 and all their **g** is like the flowers
4:11 To him be the **g** and the power for
4:13 be overjoyed when his **g** is revealed.
4:14 Spirit of **g** and of God rests on you.
5: 1 will share in the **g** to be revealed:
5: 4 of **g** that will never fade away.
5:10 who called you to his eternal **g** in
2Pe 1: 3 called us by his own **g** and goodness.
1:17 For he received honour and **g** from
1:17 came to him from the Majestic **G**,
3:18 be **g** both now and for ever! Amen.
Jude :25 to the only God our Saviour be **g**,
Rev 1: 6 **g** and power for ever and ever! Amen.
4: 9 Whenever the living creatures give **g**,
4:11 our Lord and God, to receive **g** and
5:12 and honour and **g** and praise!"
5:13 and **g** and power, for ever and ever!"
7:12 saying: "Amen! Praise and **g** and
11:13 and gave **g** to the God of heaven.
14: 7 "Fear God and give him **g**, because
15: 4 O Lord, and bring **g** to your name?
15: 8 the **g** of God and from his power,
18: 7 the **g** and luxury she gave herself.
19: 1 and **g** and power belong to our God,
19: 7 rejoice and be glad and give him **g**!
21:11 shone with the **g** of God, and its
21:23 for the **g** of God gives it light, and
21:26 The **g** and honour of the nations will

Glory of God

Ps 19: 1 The heavens declare the **g**; the skies
Pr 25: 2 It is the **g** to conceal a matter;
Jn 11:40 you believed, you would see the **g**?"
Ac 7:55 looked up to heaven and saw the **g**,
Ro 3:23 have sinned and fall short of the **g**,
5: 2 And we rejoice in the hope of the **g**.
1Co 10:31 you do, do it all for the **g**.
11: 7 since he is the image and **g**; but
2Co 1:20 the "Amen" is spoken by us to the **g**.
4: 6 of the **g** in the face of Christ.
4:15 thanksgiving to overflow to the **g**.
Php 2:11 Christ is Lord, to the **g** the Father.
Rev 15: 8 smoke from the **g** and from his power,
21:11 shone with the **g**, and its brilliance
21:23 for the **g** gives it light, and the

Glory of the LORD/Lord

Ex 16: 7 in the morning you will see the **g**,
16:10 was the **g** appearing in the cloud.
24:16 the **g** settled on Mount Sinai. For
24:17 To the Israelites the **g** looked like
40:34 and the **g** filled the tabernacle.
40:35 it, and the **g** filled the tabernacle.
Lev 9: 6 so that the **g** may appear to you."
9:23 the **g** appeared to all the people.
Nu 14:10 Then the **g** appeared at the Tent of
14:21 as the **g** fills the whole earth,
16:19 **g** appeared to the entire assembly.
16:42 cloud covered it and the **g** appeared.
20: 6 down, and the **g** appeared to them.
1Ki 8:11 cloud, for the **g** filled his temple.
2Ch 5:14 for the **g** filled the temple of God.
7: 1 and the **g** filled the temple.

2Ch 7: 2 of the LORD because the g filled it.
7: 3 the g above the temple, they knelt
Ps 104:31 May the g endure for ever; may the
138: 5 of the LORD, for the g is great.
Isa 35: 2 see the g, the splendour of our God.
40: 5 the g will be revealed, and all
58: 8 and the g will be your rear guard.
60: 1 has come, and the g rises upon you.
Eze 1:28 appearance of the likeness of the g.
3:12 g be praised in his dwelling-place!
3:23 And the g was standing there, like
10: 4 the g rose from above the cherubim
10: 4 was full of the radiance of the g.
10:18 g departed from over the threshold
11:23 The g went up from within the city
43: 4 The g entered the temple through the
43: 5 court, and the g filled the temple.
44: 4 I looked and saw the g filling the
Hab 2:14 filled with the knowledge of the g,
Lk 2: 9 and the g shone around them, and

Glow (Glowing, Glows)
Isa 4: 5 and a g of flaming fire by night;

Glowing (Glow)
Ps 102: 3 smoke; my bones burn like g embers.
Eze 1: 4 of the fire looked like g metal,
1:27 his waist up he looked like g metal,
8: 2 appearance was as bright as g metal.
Rev 1:15 His feet were like bronze g in a

Glows (Glow)
Eze 24:11 its copper g so its impurities may

Glutted
Eze 39:19 g and drink blood till you are drunk.

Glutton (Gluttons, Gluttony)
Mt 11:19 'Here is a g and a drunkard, a
Lk 7:34 'Here is a g and a drunkard, a

Gluttons (Glutton)
Pr 23:21 for drunkards and g become poor, and
28: 7 companion of g disgraces his father.
Tit 1:12 always liars, evil brutes, lazy g."

Gluttony (Glutton)
Pr 23: 2 your throat if you are given to g.

Gnash (Gnashed, Gnashes, Gnashing)
Ps 37:12 righteous and g their teeth at them;
112:10 he will g his teeth and waste away;
Lam 2:16 scoff and g their teeth and say,

Gnashed (Gnash)
Ps 35:16 mocked; they g their teeth at me.
Ac 7:54 furious and g their teeth at him.

Gnashes (Gnash)
Job 16: 9 in his anger and g his teeth at me;
Mk 9:18 He foams at the mouth, g his teeth

Gnashing (Gnash, *Weeping and gnashing of teeth*)
Lk 13:28 will be weeping there, and g of teeth

Gnat (Gnats)
Mt 23:24 blind guides! You strain out a g

Gnats (Gnat)
Ex 8:16 of Egypt the dust will become g."
8:17 ground, g came upon men and animals.
8:17 the land of Egypt became g.
8:18 the magicians tried to produce g
8:18 And the g were on men and animals.
Ps 105:31 and g throughout their country.

Gnawed (Gnawing)
Rev 16:10 Men g their tongues in

Gnawing (Gnawed)
Job 30:17 my bones; my g pains never rest.

Go down to the grave
Ge 37:35; 1Ki 2:6; Job 21:13

Go down to the pit
Ps 88:4; 143:7; Pr 1:12; Isa 38:18; Eze 26:20; 31:14, 16; 32:18, 24, 25, 29, 30

Go into exile
Isa 5:13; Jer 20:6; 22:22; 30:16; 48:7; 49:3; Eze 12:4, 11; Am 1:5, 15; 5:5; 6:7; 7:11, 17; Zec 14:2

Goads
1Sa 13:21 forks and axes and for repointing g.
Ecc 12:11 The words of the wise are like g,
Ac 26:14 hard for you to kick against the g.'

Goah
Jer 31:39 hill of Gareb and then turn to G.

Goal
Lk 13:32 on the third day I will reach my g.'
2Co 5: 9 we make it our g to please him,
Gal 3: 3 to attain your g by human effort?
Php 3:14 I press on towards the g to win the
1Ti 1: 5 The g of this command is love, which
1Pe 1: 9 for you are receiving the g of your

Goat (Goat's, Goats, Goats', Goatskins, He-goat, Scapegoat)
Ge 15: 9 "Bring me a heifer, a g and a ram,
30:32 and every spotted or speckled g.
30:33 Any g in my possession that is not
37:31 slaughtered a g and dipped the robe
38:17 "I'll send you a young g from my
38:20 Meanwhile Judah sent the young g by
38:23 I did send her this young g, but you
Ex 23:19 cook a young g in its mother's milk.
25: 4 scarlet yarn and fine linen; g hair;
26: 7 "Make curtains of g hair for the
34:26 a young g in its mother's milk."
35: 6 scarlet yarn and fine linen; g hair;
35:23 or g hair, ram skins dyed red or
35:26 and had the skill spun the g hair.
36:14 They made curtains of g hair for the
Lev 3:12 "'If his offering is a g, he is to
4:23 offering a male g without defect.
4:28 committed a female g without defect.
5: 6 g from the flock as a sin offering;
9: 3 say to the Israelites: 'Take a male g
9:15 He took the g for the people's sin
10:16 Moses enquired about the g of the
10:18 you should have eaten the g in the
16: 9 Aaron shall bring the g whose lot
16:10 the g chosen by lot as the scapegoat
16:15 "He shall then slaughter the g for
16:20 he shall bring forward the live g.
16:21 hands on the head of the live g
16:22 The g will carry on itself all their
16:26 "The man who releases the g as a
16:27 The bull and the g for the sin
17: 3 or a g in the camp or outside of
17: 7 the g idols to whom they prostitute
22:27 "When a calf, a lamb or a g is born,
23:19 sacrifice one male g for a sin
Nu 7:16 one male g for a sin offering;
7:22 one male g for a sin offering;
7:28 one male g for a sin offering;
7:34 one male g for a sin offering;
7:40 one male g for a sin offering;
7:46 one male g for a sin offering;
7:52 one male g for a sin offering;
7:58 one male g for a sin offering;
7:64 one male g for a sin offering;
7:70 one male g for a sin offering;
7:76 one male g for a sin offering;
7:82 one male g for a sin offering;
15:11 bull or ram, each lamb or young g
15:24 and a male g for a sin offering.
15:27 female g for a sin offering.
18:17 ox, a sheep or a g; they are holy.
28:15 one male g is to be presented to the
28:22 Include one male g as a sin offering
28:30 Include one male g to make atonement
29: 5 Include one male g as a sin offering
29:11 Include one male g as a sin offering,
Nu 29:16 Include one male g as a sin offering,
29:19 Include one male g as a sin offering,
29:22 Include one male g as a sin offering,
29:25 Include one male g as a sin offering,
29:28 Include one male g as a sin offering,
29:31 Include one male g as a sin offering,
29:34 Include one male g as a sin offering,
29:38 Include one male g as a sin offering,
31:20 made of leather, g hair or wood."
Dt 14: 4 may eat: the ox, the sheep, the g,
14: 5 the roe deer, the wild g, the ibex,
14:21 cook a young g in its mother's milk.
Jdg 6:19 Gideon went in, prepared a young g,
13:15 until we prepare a young g for you."
13:19 Manoah took a young g, together with
14: 6 as he might have torn a young g.
15: 1 young g and went to visit his wife.
1Sa 16:20 a skin of wine and a young g and
2Ch 11:15 the g and calf idols he had made.
Isa 11: 6 leopard will lie down with the g,
Eze 43:22 g without defect for a sin offering,
43:25 a male g daily for a sin offering;
45:23 and a male g for a sin offering.
Da 8: 5 suddenly a g with a prominent horn
8: 7 the g knocked him to the ground and
8: 8 The g became very great, but at the
8:21 The shaggy g is the king of Greece,
Lk 15:29 Yet you never gave me even a young g
Rev 6:12 black like sackcloth made of g hair,

Goat's (Goat)
Lev 4:24 He is to lay his hand on the g head
16:18 some of the g blood and put it on
16:21 sins—and put them on the g head.

Goats (Goat)
Ge 27: 9 and bring me two choice young g,
30:35 g that were streaked or spotted,
30:35 all the speckled or spotted female g
31:10 saw that the male g mating with the
31:12 'Look up and see that all the male g
31:38 Your sheep and g have not miscarried,
32: 5 and g, menservants and maidservants.
32:14 two hundred female g and twenty male
32:14 g, two hundred ewes and twenty rams,
47:17 and g, their cattle and donkeys.
Ex 9: 3 and on your cattle and sheep and g.
12: 5 take them from the sheep or the g.
20:24 your sheep and g and your cattle.
Lev 1:10 from either the sheep or the g, he
7:23 of the fat of cattle, sheep or g.
16: 5 take two male g for a sin offering
16: 7 he is to take the two g and present
16: 8 He is to cast lots for the two g
22:19 sheep or g in order that it may be
Nu 7:17 two oxen, five rams, five male g and
7:23 two oxen, five rams, five male g and
7:29 two oxen, five rams, five male g and
7:35 two oxen, five rams, five male g and
7:41 two oxen, five rams, five male g and
7:47 two oxen, five rams, five male g and
7:53 two oxen, five rams, five male g and
7:59 two oxen, five rams, five male g and
7:65 two oxen, five rams, five male g and
7:71 two oxen, five rams, five male g and
7:77 two oxen, five rams, five male g and
7:83 two oxen, five rams, five male g and
7:87 Twelve male g were used for the sin
7:88 sixty male g and sixty male lambs a
31:28 cattle, donkeys, sheep or g.
31:30 donkeys, sheep, g or other animals.
Dt 32:14 flock and with fattened lambs and g,
1Sa 10: 3 One will be carrying three young g,
24: 2 men near the Crags of the Wild G.
25: 2 He had a thousand g and three
1Ki 4:23 cattle and a hundred sheep and g,
8:63 and twenty thousand sheep and g.
20:27 them like two small flocks of g,
2Ch 7: 5 and twenty thousand sheep and g.
14:15 droves of sheep and g and camels.
15:11 seven thousand sheep and g from the
17:11 and seven thousand seven hundred g.
29:21 seven male lambs and seven male g as
29:23 The g for the sin offering were
29:24 The priests then slaughtered the g
29:33 and three thousand sheep and g.

2Ch 30:24 sheep and g for the assembly,
30:24 bulls and ten thousand sheep and g.
35: 7 and g for the Passover offerings,
Ezr 6:17 twelve male g, one for each of the
8:35 as a sin offering, twelve male g.
Job 39: 1 "Do you know when the mountain g
Ps 50: 9 your stall or of g from your pens,
50:13 of bulls or drink the blood of g?
66:15 of rams; I will offer bulls and g.
104:18 high mountains belong to the wild g;
Pr 27:26 and the g with the price of a field.
SS 1: 8 g by the tents of the shepherds.
4: 1 of g descending from Mount Gilead.
6: 5 a flock of g descending from Gilead.
Isa 1:11 the blood of bulls and lambs and g.
7:21 keep alive a young cow and two g.
13:21 there the wild g will leap about.
34: 6 the blood of lambs and g, fat from
34:14 and wild g will bleat to each other;
Jer 50: 8 be like the g that lead the flock.
51:40 to the slaughter, like rams and g.
Eze 27:21 with you in lambs, rams and g.
34:17 and another, and between rams and g.
39:18 g and bulls—all of them fattened
Mt 25:32 separates the sheep from the g.
25:33 on his right and the g on his left.
Heb 9:12 means of the blood of g and calves;
9:13 The blood of g and bulls and the
10: 4 of bulls and g to take away sins.

Goats' (Goat)

1Sa 19:13 and putting some g hair at the head.
19:16 and at the head was some g hair.
Pr 27:27 You will have plenty of g milk to

Goatskins (Goat, Skin)

Ge 27:16 smooth part of his neck with the g.
Heb 11:37 They went about in sheepskins and g,

Gob

2Sa 21:18 battle with the Philistines, at G.
21:19 battle with the Philistines at G,

Goblet (Goblets)

SS 7: 2 Your navel is a rounded g that never
Isa 51:17 dregs the g that makes men stagger.
51:22 the g of my wrath, you will never

Goblets (Goblet)

1Ki 10:21 All King Solomon's g were gold, and
2Ch 9:20 All King Solomon's g were gold, and
Est 1: 7 Wine was served in g of gold, each
Da 5: 2 silver g that Nebuchadnezzar his
5: 3 they brought in the gold g that had
5:23 You had the g from his temple

God (*Angel of God, Ark of God, Before God, Children of God, City of God, Eternal God, Fear God, Fear of God, Finger of God, Glory of God, God Almighty, God blessed, God is my rock, God Most High, God of Abraham, God of gods, God of heaven, God of Israel, God of Jacob, God of your father, God of your fathers, God our father, God the Father*, God's, God-breathed, goddess, God-fearing, God-haters, Godliness, Godly, Gods, *Grace of God, Hand of God, House of God, I will be their God, I will be your God, Image of God, Jealous God, Kingdom of God, Lamb of God, Law of God, Living God, LORD God, Lord God, LORD God Almighty, Lord God Almighty, LORD your God, Lord your God, Love of God, Man of God, Mountain of God, One God, Peace with God, People of God, Power of God, Servant of God, Son of God, Sons of God, Spirit of God, True God, Will of God, Word of God, Work of God, Wrath of God*)

Ge 1: 1 In the beginning G created the
1: 3 G said, "Let there be light," and
1: 4 G saw that the light was good, and
1: 5 G called the light "day", and the
1: 6 G said, "Let there be an expanse
1: 7 G made the expanse and separated the
1: 8 G called the expanse "sky". And
1: 9 G said, "Let the water under the sky
1:10 G called the dry ground "land", and
1:10 And G saw that it was good.
1:11 G said, "Let the land produce
1:12 And G saw that it was good.
1:14 G said, "Let there be lights in the
1:16 G made two great lights—the greater
1:17 G set them in the expanse of the sky
1:18 And G saw that it was good.
1:20 G said, "Let the water teem with
1:21 G created the great creatures of the
1:21 And G saw that it was good.
1:24 G said, "Let the land produce living
1:25 G made the wild animals according to
1:25 And G saw that it was good.
1:26 G said, "Let us make man in our
1:27 G created man in his own image, in
1:29 Then G said, "I give you every
1:31 G saw all that he had made, and it
2: 2 By the seventh day G had finished
3: 1 He said to the woman, "Did G really
3: 3 G did say, 'You must not eat fruit
3: 5 "For G knows that when you eat of it
3: 5 be like G, knowing good and evil."
4:25 "G has granted me another child in
5: 1 When G created man, he made him in
5: 1 he made him in the likeness of G.
5:22 Enoch walked with G 300 years and
5:24 Enoch walked with G; then he was no
5:24 no more, because G took him away.
6: 9 of his time, and he walked with G.
6:12 G saw how corrupt the earth had
6:13 G said to Noah, "I am going to put
6:22 Noah did everything just as G
7: 9 the ark, as G had commanded Noah.
7:16 thing, as G had commanded Noah.
8: 1 G remembered Noah and all the wild
8:15 Then G said to Noah,
9: 6 in the image of G has G made man.
9: 8 G said to Noah and to his sons with
9:12 G said, "This is the sign of the
9:16 the everlasting covenant between G
9:17 G said to Noah, "This is the sign of
9:26 "Blessed be the LORD, the G of Shem!
9:27 May G extend the territory of
16:13 "You are the G who sees me," for she
17: 3 Abram fell face down, and G said to
17: 7 to be your G and the G of your
17: 9 G said to Abraham, "As for you, you
17:15 G also said to Abraham, "As for
17:18 Abraham said to G, "If only Ishmael
17:19 G said, "Yes, but your wife Sarah
17:22 with Abraham, G went up from him.
17:23 and circumcised them, as G told him.
19:29 when G destroyed the cities of the
20: 3 G came to Abimelech in a dream one
20: 6 G said to him in the dream, "Yes, I
20:13 G caused me to wander from my father'
20:17 Abraham prayed to G, and G healed
21: 2 at the very time G had promised him.
21: 4 circumcised him, as G commanded him.
21: 6 Sarah said, "G has brought me
21:12 G said to him, "Do not be so
21:17 G heard the boy crying, and the
21:17 Do not be afraid; G has heard the
21:19 G opened her eyes and she saw a well
21:20 G was with the boy as he grew up. He
21:22 "G is with you in everything you do.
22: 1 Some time later G tested Abraham. He
22: 2 G said, "Take your son, your only
22: 3 for the place G had told him about.
22: 8 Abraham answered, "G himself will
22: 9 they reached the place G had told
24: 3 the G of heaven and the G of earth,
24:12 he prayed, "O LORD, G of my master
24:27 saying, "Praise be to the LORD, the G
24:42 'O LORD, G of my master Abraham, if
24:48 I praised the LORD, the G of my
27:28 May G give you of heaven's dew and
28: 4 alien, the land G gave to Abraham."
28:12 and the angels of G were ascending
Ge 28:13 father Abraham and the G of Isaac.
28:20 Jacob made a vow, saying, "If G will
28:21 house, then the LORD will be my G
30: 2 "Am I in the place of G, who has
30: 6 Rachel said, "G has vindicated me;
30:17 G listened to Leah, and she became
30:18 Leah said, "G has rewarded me for
30:20 Leah said, "G has presented me with
30:22 G remembered Rachel; he listened to
30:23 said, "G has taken away my disgrace.
31: 5 the G of my father has been with me.
31: 7 G has not allowed him to harm me.
31: 9 G has taken away your father's
31:13 I am the G of Bethel, where you
31:16 Surely all the wealth that G took
31:16 So do whatever G has told you."
31:24 G came to Laban the Aramean in a
31:42 If the G of my father, the G of
31:42 But G has seen my hardship and the
31:50 G is a witness between you and me."
31:53 G of Abraham and the G of Nahor,
31:53 G of their father, judge between us.
32: 1 way, and the angels of G met him.
32: 2 he said, "This is the camp of G!"
32: 9 Jacob prayed, "O G of my father
32: 9 G of my father, Isaac, O LORD who
32:28 you have struggled with G and with
32:30 "It is because I saw G face to face,
33: 5 children G has graciously given your
33:10 face is like seeing the face of G,
33:11 for G has been gracious to me and I
35: 1 G said to Jacob, "Go up to Bethel
35: 1 and build an altar there to G, who
35: 3 where I will build an altar to G,
35: 5 they set out, and the terror of G
35: 7 because it was there that G revealed
35: 9 G appeared to him again and blessed
35:10 G said to him, "Your name is Jacob,
35:11 G said to him, "I am G Almighty; be
35:13 G went up from him at the place
35:14 place where G had talked with him,
35:15 Jacob called the place where G had
39: 9 a wicked thing and sin against G?"
40: 8 Do not interpretations belong to G?
41:16 "but G will give Pharaoh the answer
41:25 G has revealed to Pharaoh what he is
41:28 as I said to Pharaoh: G has shown
41:32 decided by G, and G will do it soon.
41:39 Pharaoh said to Joseph, "Since G has
41:51 "It is because G has made me forget
41:52 "It is because G has made me
42:28 "What is this that G has done to us?
43:23 "Don't be afraid. Your G, the G of
43:29 said, "G be gracious to you, my son.
44:16 G has uncovered your servants' guilt.
45: 5 to save lives that G sent me ahead
45: 7 G sent me ahead of you to preserve
45: 8 was not you who sent me here, but G.
45: 9 G has made me lord of all Egypt.
46: 1 to the G of his father Isaac.
46: 2 G spoke to Israel in a vision at
46: 3 "I am G, the G of your father," he
48: 9 "They are the sons G has given me
48:11 and now G has allowed me to see your
48:15 "May the G before whom my fathers
48:15 the G who has been my shepherd all
48:20 G make you like Ephraim and Manasseh.
48:21 "I am about to die, but G will be
49:25 because of your father's G, who
50:19 Am I in the place of G?
50:20 You intended to harm me, but G
50:24 But G will surely come to your aid
50:25 "G will surely come to your aid, and
Ex 1:17 The midwives, however, feared G and
1:20 G was kind to the midwives and the
1:21 the midwives feared G, he gave them
2:23 of their slavery went up to G.
2:24 G heard their groaning and he
2:25 G looked on the Israelites and was
3: 4 G called to him from within the bush,
3: 5 "Do not come any closer," G said.
3: 6 the G of Isaac and the G of Jacob.
3:11 Moses said to G, "Who am I, that I
3:12 G said, "I will be with you. And
3:12 will worship G on this mountain."
3:13 Moses said to G, "Suppose I go to

Ex 3:14 **G** said to Moses, "I AM WHO I AM
3:15 **G** also said to Moses, "Say to the
3:15 the **G** of Isaac and the **G** of Jacob
3:18 **G** of the Hebrews, has met with us.
3:18 offer sacrifices to the LORD our **G**.'
4: 5 the **G** of their fathers—the **G** of
4: 5 the **G** of Isaac and the **G** of
4:16 mouth and as if you were **G** to him.
4:20 he took the staff of **G** in his hand.
5: 3 they said, "The **G** of the Hebrews has
5: 3 offer sacrifices to the LORD our **G**,
5: 8 'Let us go and sacrifice to our **G**.'
6: 2 **G** also said to Moses, "I am the LORD.
7: 1 "See, I have made you like **G** to
7:16 say to him, 'The LORD, the **G** of the
8:10 there is no-one like the LORD our **G**.
8:25 to your **G** here in the land."
8:26 sacrifices we offer the LORD our **G**
8:27 offer sacrifices to the LORD our **G**,
9: 1 what the LORD, the **G** of the Hebrews
9:13 what the LORD, the **G** of the Hebrews
10: 3 what the LORD, the **G** of the Hebrews
10: 7 they may worship the LORD their **G**.
10:25 to present to the LORD our **G**.
10:26 them in worshipping the LORD our **G**,
13:17 Pharaoh let the people go, **G** did not
13:17 For **G** said, "If they face war, they
13:18 **G** led the people around by the
13:19 He had said, "**G** will surely come to
15: 2 He is my **G**, and I will praise him,
15: 2 my father's **G**, and I will exalt him.
17: 9 with the staff of **G** in my hands."
18: 1 heard of everything **G** had done for
18: 4 "My father's **G** was my helper; he
18:12 offering and other sacrifices to **G**,
18:12 father-in-law in the presence of **G**.
18:19 some advice, and may **G** be with you.
18:23 If you do this and **G** so commands,
19: 3 Moses went up to **G**, and the LORD
19:17 out of the camp to meet with **G**,
19:19 and the voice of **G** answered him.
20: 1 And **G** spoke all these words:
20:19 have **G** speak to us or we will die."
20:20 **G** has come to test you, so that the
20:21 the thick darkness where **G** was.
21:13 but **G** lets it happen, he is to flee
22:20 "Whoever sacrifices to any **g** other
22:28 "Do not blaspheme **G** or curse the
24:11 **G** did not raise his hand against
24:11 they saw **G**, and they ate and drank.
29:45 among the Israelites and be their **G**.
29:46 know that I am the LORD their **G**,
29:46 I am the LORD their **G**.
32:11 sought the favour of the LORD his **G**.
32:16 the writing was the writing of **G**,
34: 6 the compassionate and gracious **G**,
34:14 Do not worship any other **g**, for the
Lev 2:13 the salt of the covenant of your **G**
4:22 of the commands of the LORD his **G**,
11:45 you, up out of Egypt to be your **G**
18:21 must not profane the name of your **G**.
19:12 and so profane the name of your **G**.
19:14 front of the blind, but fear your **G**.
19:32 for the elderly and revere your **G**.
21: 6 They must be holy to their **G** and
21: 6 not profane the name of their **G**.
21: 6 the food of their **G**, they are to be
21: 7 because priests are holy to their **G**.
21: 8 they offer up the food of your **G**.
21:12 nor leave the sanctuary of his **G** or
21:12 by the anointing oil of his **G**.
21:17 near to offer the food of his **G**.
21:21 near to offer the food of his **G**.
21:22 of his **G**, as well as the holy food;
22:25 offer them as the food of your **G**.
22:33 you out of Egypt to be your **G**.
23:14 you bring this offering to your **G**.
24:15 if anyone curses his **G**, he will be
25:17 of each other, but fear your **G**.
25:36 but fear your **G**, so that your
25:38 the land of Canaan and to be your **G**.
25:43 them ruthlessly, but fear your **G**.
26:12 I will walk among you and be your **G**,
26:44 I am the LORD their **G**.
26:45 sight of the nations to be their **G**.
Nu 6: 7 his separation to **G** is on his head.
Nu 10:10 be a memorial for you before your **G**.
12:13 Moses cried out to the LORD, "O **G**,
15:40 and will be consecrated to your **G**.
15:41 I am the LORD your **G**, who brought
15:41 you out of Egypt to be your **G**.
16:22 "O **G**, **G** of the spirits of all
21: 5 they spoke against **G** and against
22: 9 **G** came to Balaam and asked, "Who are
22:10 Balaam said to **G**, "Balak son of
22:12 **G** said to Balaam, "Do not go with
22:18 beyond the command of the LORD my **G**.
22:20 That night **G** came to Balaam and said,
22:22 **G** was very angry when he went, and
22:38 speak only what **G** puts in my mouth."
23: 4 **G** met with him, and Balaam said, "I
23: 8 How can I curse those whom **G** has not
23:19 **G** is not a man, that he should lie,
23:21 The LORD their **G** is with them; the
23:22 **G** brought them out of Egypt; they
23:23 of Israel, 'See what **G** has done!'
23:27 Perhaps it will please **G** to let you
24: 4 of one who hears the words of **G**,
24: 8 "**G** brought them out of Egypt; they
24:16 of one who hears the words of **G**,
24:23 "Ah, who can live when **G** does
25:13 was zealous for the honour of his **G**
27:16 "May the LORD, the **G** of the spirits
Dt 1: 6 The LORD our **G** said to us at Horeb,
1:17 any man, for judgment belongs to **G**.
1:19 Then, as the LORD our **G** commanded us,
1:20 which the LORD our **G** is giving us.
1:25 that the LORD our **G** is giving us."
1:41 as the LORD our **G** commanded us.
2: 7 These forty years the LORD your **G**
2:29 land the LORD our **G** is giving us."
2:33 the LORD our **G** delivered him over to
2:36 The LORD our **G** gave us all of them.
2:37 with the command of the LORD our **G**,
3: 3 the LORD our **G** also gave into our
3:24 For what **g** is there in heaven or on
4: 5 laws as the LORD my **G** commanded me,
4: 7 the way the LORD our **G** is near us
4:31 For the LORD your **G** is a merciful **G**;
4:32 from the day **G** created man on the
4:33 the voice of **G** speaking out of fire
4:34 Has any **g** ever tried to take for
4:35 you might know that the LORD is **G**;
4:39 that the LORD is **G** in heaven above
5: 2 The LORD our **G** made a covenant with
5:24 you said, "The LORD our **G** has shown
5:24 can live even if **G** speaks with him.
5:25 if we hear the voice of the LORD our **G**
5:27 to all that the LORD our **G** says.
5:27 Then tell us whatever the LORD our **G**
6: 4 Hear, O Israel: The LORD our **G**, the
6:20 the LORD our **G** has commanded you?"
6:24 decrees and to fear the LORD our **G**,
6:25 all this law before the LORD our **G**,
7: 9 your **G** is **G**; he is the faithful **G**,
7:21 among you, is a great and awesome **G**.
10:21 He is your praise; he is your **G**, who
17:19 may learn to revere the LORD his **G**
18: 7 in the name of the LORD his **G** like
18:16 not hear the voice of the LORD our **G**
26: 7 we cried out to the LORD, the **G** of
26:14 I have obeyed the LORD my **G**; I have
26:17 this day that the LORD is your **G**
29:13 that he may be your **G** as he promised
29:15 in the presence of the LORD our **G**
29:18 away from the LORD our **G** to go
29:25 the **G** of their fathers, the covenant
29:29 things belong to the LORD our **G**,
31:17 us because our **G** is not with us?'
32: 3 Oh, praise the greatness of our **G**!
32: 4 A faithful **G** who does no wrong,
32:12 The LORD alone led him; no foreign **g**
32:15 He abandoned the **G** who made him and
32:17 sacrificed to demons which are not **G**
32:18 you forgot the **G** who gave you birth.
32:21 They made me jealous by what is no **g**
32:39 am He! There is no **g** besides me.
33:26 is no-one like the **G** of Jeshurun,
Jos 9:23 for the house of my **G**."
14: 8 the LORD my **G** wholeheartedly.
14: 9 the LORD my **G** wholeheartedly.'
18: 6 in the presence of the LORD our **G**.
Jos 22:19 than the altar of the LORD our **G**.
22:22 "The Mighty One, **G**, the LORD! The
22:22 Mighty One, **G**, the LORD! He knows
22:29 **G** that stands before his tabernacle."
22:33 to hear the report and praised **G**.
22:34 Between Us that the LORD is **G**.
24:17 was the LORD our **G** himself who
24:18 the LORD, because he is our **G**."
24:24 serve the LORD our **G** and obey him."
24:27 you if you are untrue to your **G**."
Jdg 1: 7 Now **G** has paid me back for what I
2:12 They forsook the LORD, the **G** of
3: 7 they forgot the LORD their **G** and
3:20 "I have a message from **G** for you.
4:23 On that day **G** subdued Jabin, the
6:31 If Baal really is a **g**, he can defend
6:36 Gideon said to **G**, "If you will save
6:39 Gideon said to **G**, "Do not be angry
6:40 That night **G** did so. Only the fleece
7:14 **G** has given the Midianites and the
7:15 its interpretation, he worshipped **G**.
8: 3 **G** gave Oreb and Zeeb, the Midianite
8:33 set up Baal-Berith as their **g**
8:34 did not remember the LORD their **G**,
9: 7 Shechem, so that **G** may listen to you.
9:23 **G** sent an evil spirit between
9:24 **G** did this in order that the crime
9:27 a festival in the temple of their **g**.
9:56 Thus **G** repaid the wickedness that
9:57 **G** also made the men of Shechem pay
10:10 our **G** and serving the Baals."
11:24 Will you not take what your **g**
11:24 our **G** has given us, we will possess.
13: 5 set apart to **G** from birth, and he
13: 7 will be a Nazirite of **G** from birth
13: 9 **G** heard Manoah, and the angel of **G**
13:22 said to his wife. "We have seen **G**!"
15:19 **G** opened up the hollow place in Lehi,
16:17 Nazirite set apart to **G** since birth.
16:23 to Dagon their **g** and to celebrate,
16:23 "Our **g** has delivered Samson, our
16:24 they praised their **g**, saying, "Our **g**
16:28 O **G**, please strengthen me just once
18: 5 "Please enquire of **G** to learn
18:10 land that **G** has put into your hands,
20:18 went up to Bethel and enquired of **G**.
20:27 ark of the covenant of **G** was there,
Ru 1:16 will be my people and your **G** my **G**.
1Sa 2: 2 you; there is no Rock like our **G**.
2: 3 for the LORD is a **G** who knows, and
2:25 If a man sins against another man, **G**
3: 3 The lamp of **G** had not yet gone out,
3:17 May **G** deal with you, be it ever so
4: 4 with the ark of the covenant of **G**.
4: 7 "A **g** has come into the camp," they
5: 7 heavy upon us and upon Dagon our **g**."
6: 5 and pay honour to Israel's **g**.
6:19 **G** struck down some of the men of
6:20 presence of the LORD, this holy **G**?
7: 8 crying out to the LORD our **G** for us,
9: 9 if a man went to enquire of **G**, he
9:27 I may give you a message from **G**."
10: 3 Three men going up to **G** at Bethel
10: 5 that you will go to Gibeah of **G**,
10: 7 hand finds to do, for **G** is with you.
10: 9 **G** changed Saul's heart, and all
10:19 you have now rejected your **G**, who
10:26 men whose hearts **G** had touched.
12: 9 "But they forgot the LORD their **G**;
14:15 It was a panic sent by **G**.
14:36 said, "Let us enquire of **G** here.
14:37 Saul asked **G**, "Shall I go down after
14:37 But **G** did not answer him that day.
14:44 Saul said, "May **G** deal with me, be
15:21 the best of what was devoted to **G**,
16:15 spirit from **G** is tormenting you.
16:16 evil spirit from **G** comes upon you,
16:23 Whenever the spirit from **G** came upon
17:45 the **G** of the armies of Israel, whom
17:46 know that there is a **G** in Israel.
18:10 The next day an evil spirit from **G**
22: 3 I learn what **G** will do for me?"
22:13 a sword and enquiring of **G** for him,
22:15 first time I enquired of **G** for him?
23: 7 "**G** has handed him over to me, for
23:14 **G** did not give David into his hands.

1Sa 23:16 helped him to find strength in **G**.
25:22 May **G** deal with David, be it ever so
26: 8 Abishai said to David, "Today **G** has
28:15 me, and **G** has turned away from me.
30: 6 found strength in the Lord his **G**.
2Sa 2:27 Joab answered, "As surely as **G** lives,
3: 9 May **G** deal with Abner, be it ever so
3:35 "May **G** deal with me, be it ever so
6: 7 therefore **G** struck him down and he
7:22 and there is no **G** but you, as we
7:23 the one nation on earth that **G** went
7:24 you, O Lord, have become their **G**.
7:26 'The Lord Almighty is **G** over Israel!'
7:28 O Sovereign Lord, you are **G**! Your
10:12 our people and the cities of our **G**.
12:16 David pleaded with **G** for the child.
14:11 let the king invoke the Lord his **G**
14:14 But **G** does not take away life;
14:16 son from the inheritance **G** gave us.'
15:24 the ark of the covenant of **G**.
15:32 where people used to worship **G**,
16:23 like that of one who enquires of **G**.
19:13 May **G** deal with me, be it ever so
21:14 After that, **G** answered prayer on
22: 7 to the Lord; I called out to my **G**.
22:22 not done evil by turning from my **G**.
22:30 troop; with my **G** I can scale a wall.
22:31 "As for **G**, his way is perfect; the
22:32 For who is **G** besides the Lord? And
22:32 And who is the Rock except our **G**?
22:33 It is **G** who arms me with strength
22:47 Exalted be **G**, the Rock, my Saviour!
22:48 He is the **G** who avenges me, who puts
23: 5 "Is not my house right with **G**? Has
24:24 will not sacrifice to the Lord my **G**
1Ki 1:36 **G** of my lord the king, so declare it.
1:47 'May your **G** make Solomon's name more
2:23 "May **G** deal with me, be it ever so
3: 5 and **G** said, "Ask for whatever you
3: 7 "Now, O Lord my **G**, you have made
3:11 **G** said to him, "Since you have asked
3:28 wisdom from **G** to administer justice.
4:29 **G** gave Solomon wisdom and very great
5: 3 for the Name of the Lord his **G**
5: 4 now the Lord my **G** has given me rest
5: 5 for the Name of the Lord my **G**,
8:23 there is no **G** like you in heaven
8:27 "But will **G** really dwell on earth?
8:28 his plea for mercy, O Lord my **G**.
8:57 May the Lord our **G** be with us as he
8:59 be near to the Lord our **G** day and
8:60 Lord is **G** and that there is no other.
8:61 fully committed to the Lord our **G**,
8:65 **G** for seven days and seven days more,
9: 9 they have forsaken the Lord their **G**,
10:24 the wisdom **G** had put in his heart.
11: 4 not fully devoted to the Lord his **G**
11: 5 the detestable **g** of the Ammonites.
11: 7 Chemosh the detestable **g** of Moab,
11: 7 the detestable **g** of the Ammonites.
11:23 **G** raised up against Solomon another
11:33 Chemosh the **g** of the Moabites, and
11:33 and Molech the **g** of the Ammonites,
15: 3 not fully devoted to the Lord his **G**,
15: 4 for David's sake the Lord his **G** gave
17:20 "O Lord my **G**, have you brought
17:21 "O Lord my **G**, let this boy's life
18:21 If the Lord is **G**, follow him;
18:21 him; but if Baal is **G**, follow him.
18:24 you call on the name of your **g**,
18:24 **g** who answers by fire—he is **G**."
18:25 Call on the name of your **g**, but do
18:27 "Surely he is a **g**! Perhaps he is
18:36 today that you are **G** in Israel
18:37 you, O Lord, are **G**, and that you
18:39 Lord—he is **G**! The Lord—he is **G**!"
20:28 think the Lord is a **g** of the hills
20:28 hills and not a **g** of the valleys,
21:10 he has cursed both **G** and the king.
21:13 has cursed both **G** and the king.
2Ki 1: 2 consult Baal-Zebub, the **g** of Ekron
1: 3 because there is no **G** in Israel
1: 3 consult Baal-Zebub, the **g** of Ekron?'
1: 6 because there is no **G** in Israel
1: 6 consult Baal-Zebub, the **g** of Ekron?
1:12 Then the fire of **G** fell from heaven

2Ki 1:16 because there is no **G** in Israel
1:16 consult Baal-Zebub, the **g** of Ekron?
2:14 now is the Lord, the **G** of Elijah?
5: 7 "Am I **G**? Can I kill and bring back
5:11 call on the name of the Lord his **G**,
5:15 **G** in all the world except in Israel.
5:17 to any other **g** but the Lord.
6:31 He said, "May **G** deal with me, be it
16: 2 right in the eyes of the Lord his **G**.
17: 7 had sinned against the Lord their **G**,
17: 9 Lord their **G** that were not right.
17:14 did not trust in the Lord their **G**.
17:16 the commands of the Lord their **G**
17:19 the commands of the Lord their **G**.
17:26 what the **g** of that country requires.
17:27 what the **g** of the land requires."
18:12 had not obeyed the Lord their **G**,
18:22 We are depending on the Lord our **G**
18:33 Has the **g** of any nation ever
19: 4 may be that the Lord your **G** will
19:10 Do not let the **g** you depend on
19:15 **G** over all the kingdoms of the earth.
19:19 Now, O Lord our **G**, deliver us from
19:19 that you alone, O Lord, are **G**."
19:37 in the temple of his **g** Nisroch,
21:22 He forsook the Lord, the **G** of his
23:13 for Chemosh the vile **g** of Moab, and
23:13 detestable **g** of the people of Ammon.
1Ch 4:10 And **G** granted his request.
5:20 and **G** handed the Hagrites and all
5:25 they were unfaithful to the **G** of
5:25 whom **G** had destroyed before them.
6:48 of the tabernacle, the house of **G**.
11:19 "**G** forbid that I should do this!" he
12:17 may the **G** of our fathers see it and
12:18 help you, for your **G** will help you.
12:22 a great army, like the army of **G**.
13: 2 if it is the will of the Lord our **G**,
13: 3 Let us bring the ark of our **G** back
13:12 David was afraid of **G** that day and
14:10 David enquired of **G**: "Shall I go and
14:11 As waters break out, **G** has broken
14:14 David enquired of **G** again, and **G**
14:15 because that will mean **G** has gone
14:16 David did as **G** commanded him, and
15:13 our **G** broke out in anger against us.
15:26 **G** had helped the Levites who were
16: 6 before the ark of the covenant of **G**.
16:14 He is the Lord our **G**; his judgments
16:35 Cry out, "Save us, O **G** our Saviour;
17: 2 in mind, do it, for **G** is with you."
17:17 O **G**, you have spoken about the
17:20 O Lord, and there is no **G** but you,
17:21 the one nation on earth whose **G** went
17:22 you, O Lord, have become their **G**.
17:24 'The Lord Almighty, the **G** over
17:24 the **G** over Israel, is Israel's **G**!'
17:25 "You, my **G**, have revealed to your
17:26 O Lord, you are **G**! You have
19:13 our people and the cities of our **G**.
21: 7 was also evil in the sight of **G**;
21: 8 David said to **G**, "I have sinned
21:15 **G** sent an angel to destroy Jerusalem.
21:17 David said to **G**, "Was it not I who
21:17 Lord my **G**, let your hand fall upon
21:30 not go before it to enquire of **G**,
22: 7 house for the Name of the Lord my **G**.
22:19 the sacred articles belonging to **G**
24: 5 officials of **G** among the descendants
25: 5 the promises of **G** to exalt him.
25: 5 **G** gave Heman fourteen sons and three
26: 5 (For **G** had blessed Obed-Edom.)
26:32 **G** and for the affairs of the king.
28: 2 for the footstool of our **G**, and I
28: 3 **G** said to me, 'You are not to build
28: 8 and in the hearing of our **G**: Be
28:12 the treasuries of the temple of **G**
28:20 my **G**, is with you. He will not fail
28:21 for all the work on the temple of **G**,
29: 1 Solomon, the one whom **G** has chosen,
29: 2 have provided for the temple of my **G**
29: 3 in my devotion to the temple of my **G**
29: 3 and silver for the temple of my **G**,
29: 7 temple of **G** five thousand talents
29:10 "Praise be to you, O Lord, **G** of our
29:13 Now, our **G**, we give you thanks, and

1Ch 29:16 O Lord our **G**, as for all this
29:17 I know, my **G**, that you test the
29:18 O Lord, **G** of our fathers Abraham,
29:20 So they all praised the Lord, the **G**
2Ch 1: 1 for the Lord his **G** was with him and
1: 7 That night **G** appeared to Solomon and
1: 8 Solomon answered **G**, "You have shown
1:11 **G** said to Solomon, "Since this is
2: 4 for the Name of the Lord my **G**
2: 4 appointed feasts of the Lord our **G**.
2: 5 **G** is greater than all other gods.
3: 3 temple of **G** was sixty cubits long
4:11 for King Solomon in the temple of **G**:
5:14 of the Lord filled the temple of **G**.
6:14 there is no **G** like you in heaven
6:18 "But will **G** really dwell on earth
6:19 his plea for mercy, O Lord my **G**.
6:40 "Now, my **G**, may your eyes be open
7: 5 people dedicated the temple of **G**.
7:22 the **G** of their fathers, who brought
9: 8 Because of the love of your **G** for
9:23 the wisdom **G** had put in his heart.
10:15 for this turn of events was from **G**,
11:16 to the Lord, the **G** of their fathers.
13:10 "As for us, the Lord is our **G**, and
13:11 the requirements of the Lord our **G**.
13:12 **G** is with us; he is our leader. His
13:15 At the sound of their battle cry, **G**
13:16 **G** delivered them into their hands.
13:18 on the Lord, the **G** of their fathers.
14: 2 right in the eyes of the Lord his **G**.
14: 4 the **G** of their fathers, and to obey
14: 7 we have sought the Lord our **G**;
14:11 Asa called to the Lord his **G** and
14:11 Help us, O Lord our **G**, for we rely
14:11 O Lord, you are our **G**; do not let
15: 6 because **G** was troubling them with
15: 9 that the Lord his **G** was with him.
15:12 the **G** of their fathers, with all
15:15 They sought **G** eagerly, and he was
15:18 He brought into the temple of **G** the
17: 4 sought the **G** of his father and
18: 5 **G** will give it into the king's hand."
18:13 I can tell him only what my **G** says."
18:31 **G** drew them away from him,
19: 3 have set your heart on seeking **G**."
19: 4 to the Lord, the **G** of their fathers.
19: 7 for with the Lord our **G** there is no
20: 6 said: "O Lord, **G** of our fathers,
20: 6 are you not the **G** who is in heaven?
20: 7 O our **G**, did you not drive out the
20:12 O our **G**, will you not judge them?
20:30 **G** had given him rest on every side.
20:33 hearts on the **G** of their fathers.
21:10 the Lord, the **G** of his fathers.
22: 7 Through Ahaziah's visit to Joram, **G**
22:12 hidden with them at the temple of **G**
23: 3 with the king at the temple of **G**.
23: 9 and that were in the temple of **G**.
24: 5 to repair the temple of your **G**.
24: 7 had broken into the temple of **G**
24:13 They rebuilt the temple of **G**
24:16 done in Israel for **G** and his temple.
24:18 the **G** of their fathers, and
24:20 "This is what **G** says: 'Why do you
24:24 the Lord, the **G** of their fathers,
24:27 the restoration of the temple of **G**
25: 8 **G** will overthrow you before the
25: 8 for **G** has the power to help or to
25:16 "I know that **G** has determined to
25:20 **G** so worked that he might hand them
25:24 articles found in the temple of **G**
26: 5 He sought **G** during the days of
26: 5 sought the Lord, **G** gave him success.
26: 7 **G** helped him against the Philistines
26:16 He was unfaithful to the Lord his **G**,
27: 6 steadfastly before the Lord his **G**.
28: 5 Therefore the Lord his **G** handed him
28: 6 the Lord, the **G** of their fathers.
28:10 of sins against the Lord your **G**?
28:24 the temple of **G** and took them away.
28:25 provoked the Lord, the **G** of his
29: 6 of the Lord our **G** and forsook him.
29:36 **G** had brought about for his people,
30: 7 the **G** of their fathers, so that he
30:19 who sets his heart on seeking **G**—the

2Ch 30:19 the LORD, the **G** of his fathers—even
30:22 the LORD, the **G** of their fathers.
30:27 and **G** heard them, for their prayer
31: 6 things dedicated to the LORD their **G**
31:13 in charge of the temple of **G**.
31:14 the freewill offerings given to **G**,
31:20 and faithful before the LORD his **G**.
31:21 his **G** and worked wholeheartedly.
32: 8 with us is the LORD our **G** to help us
32:11 Hezekiah says, 'The LORD our **G** will
32:14 can your **g** deliver you from my hand?
32:15 Do not believe him, for no **g** of any
32:15 your **g** deliver you from my hand!"
32:17 the **g** of Hezekiah will not rescue
32:19 the **g** of Hezekiah will not rescue
32:21 he went into the temple of his **g**,
32:29 **G** had given him very great riches.
32:31 **G** left him to test him and to know
33: 7 of which **G** had said to David and to
33:12 sought the favour of the LORD his **G**
33:12 greatly before the **G** of his fathers.
33:13 Manasseh knew that the LORD is **G**.
33:17 but only to the LORD their **G**.
33:18 including his prayer to his **G** and
33:19 His prayer and how **G** was moved by
34: 3 to seek the **G** of his father David.
34: 8 repair the temple of the LORD his **G**.
34: 9 been brought into the temple of **G**,
34:32 of **G**, the **G** of their fathers.
34:33 in Israel serve the LORD their **G**.
34:33 the LORD, the **G** of their fathers.
35:21 **G** has told me to hurry; so stop
35:21 me to hurry; so stop opposing **G**,
36: 5 evil in the eyes of the LORD his **G**.
36:12 evil in the eyes of the LORD his **G**
36:15 The LORD, the **G** of their fathers,
36:17 **G** handed all of them over to
36:18 the articles from the temple of **G**,
36:23 **G** be with him, and let him go up.'"
Ezr 1: 3 among you—may his **G** be with him,
1: 3 the **G** who is in Jerusalem.
1: 4 for the temple of **G** in Jerusalem.'"
1: 5 everyone whose heart **G** had moved
1: 7 had placed in the temple of his **g**.
4: 2 like you, we seek your **G** and have
4: 3 us in building a temple to our **G**.
5: 2 prophets of **G** were with them,
5: 5 the eye of their **G** was watching over
5: 8 Judah, to the temple of the great **G**.
6: 3 the temple of **G** in Jerusalem:
6: 7 with the work on this temple of **G**.
6:12 May **G**, who has caused his Name to
6:18 for the service of **G** at Jerusalem,
7: 6 hand of the LORD his **G** was on him.
7: 9 gracious hand of his **G** was on him.
7:14 Law of your **G**, which is in your hand.
7:16 the temple of their **G** in Jerusalem.
7:17 the temple of your **G** in Jerusalem.
7:18 accordance with the will of your **G**.
7:19 Deliver to the **G** of Jerusalem all
7:19 for worship in the temple of your **G**.
7:20 needed for the temple of your **G**
7:25 with the wisdom of your **G**,
7:25 who know the laws of your **G**.
7:26 does not obey the law of your **G**
7:27 Praise be to the LORD, the **G** of our
7:28 Because the hand of the LORD my **G**
8:17 to us for the house of our **G**.
8:18 the gracious hand of our **G** was on us,
8:21 might humble ourselves before our **G**
8:22 "The gracious hand of our **G** is on
8:23 we fasted and petitioned our **G** about
8:25 had donated for the house of our **G**.
8:30 to the house of our **G** in Jerusalem.
8:31 The hand of our **G** was on us, and he
8:33 in the house of our **G**, we weighed
9: 5 my hands spread out to the LORD my **G**
9: 6 my **G**, I am too ashamed and disgraced
9: 6 to lift up my face to you, my **G**
9: 8 the LORD our **G** has been gracious in
9: 8 and so our **G** gives light to our eyes
9: 9 Though we are slaves, our **G** has not
9: 9 house of our **G** and repair its ruins,
9:10 "But now, O our **G**, what can we say
9:13 and yet, our **G**, you have punished us
10: 2 "We have been unfaithful to our **G** by
Ezr 10: 3 our **G** to send away all these women
10: 3 who fear the commands of our **G**.
10:14 until the fierce anger of our **G** in
Ne 1: 5 the great and awesome **G**, who keeps
2: 8 gracious hand of my **G** was upon me,
2:12 I had not told anyone what my **G** had
2:18 the gracious hand of my **G** upon me
4: 4 Hear us, O our **G**, for we are
4: 9 we prayed to our **G** and posted a
4:15 plot and that **G** had frustrated it,
4:20 Our **G** will fight for us!"
5: 9 walk in the fear of our **G** to avoid
5:13 "In this way may **G** shake out of his
5:15 for **G** I did not act like that.
5:19 Remember me with favour, O my **G**, for
6:12 I realised that **G** had not sent him,
6:14 Remember Tobiah and Sanballat, O my **G**
6:16 been done with the help of our **G**.
7: 2 and feared **G** more than most men do.
7: 5 my **G** put it into my heart to
8: 6 Ezra praised the LORD, the great **G**;
9: 3 their **G** for a quarter of the day,
9: 3 and in worshipping the LORD their **G**.
9: 4 loud voices to the LORD their **G**.
9:17 But you are a forgiving **G**, gracious
9:18 'This is your **g**, who brought you up
9:31 you are a gracious and merciful **G**.
9:32 "Now therefore, O our **G**, the great,
9:32 the great, mighty and awesome **G**, who
10:32 the service of the house of our **G**:
10:33 the duties of the house of our **G**.
10:34 is to bring to the house of our **G**
10:34 our **G**, as it is written in the Law.
10:36 the house of our **G**, to the priests
10:37 storerooms of the house of our **G**,
10:38 house of our **G**, to the storerooms
10:39 not neglect the house of our **G**."
12:43 because **G** had given them great joy.
12:45 They performed the service of their **G**
12:46 of praise and thanksgiving to **G**.
13: 1 be admitted into the assembly of **G**,
13: 2 (Our **G**, however, turned the curse
13: 4 storerooms of the house of our **G**.
13:14 Remember me for this, O my **G**, and do
13:14 the house of my **G** and its services.
13:18 so that our **G** brought all this
13:22 Remember me for this also, O my **G**,
13:26 He was loved by his **G**, and **G** made
13:27 to our **G** by marrying foreign women?"
13:29 Remember them, O my **G**, because they
13:31 Remember me with favour, O my **G**.
Job 1: 1 he feared **G** and shunned evil.
1: 5 sinned and cursed **G** in their hearts.
1: 8 a man who fears **G** and shuns evil."
1:16 "The fire of **G** fell from the sky and
1:22 sin by charging **G** with wrongdoing.
2: 3 a man who fears **G** and shuns evil.
2: 9 to your integrity? Curse **G** and die!"
2:10 Shall we accept good from **G**, and not
3: 4 may **G** above not care about it; may
3:23 way is hidden, whom **G** has hedged in?
4: 9 At the breath of **G** they are
4:17 a mortal be more righteous than **G**?
4:18 If **G** places no trust in his servants,
5: 8 if it were I, I would appeal to **G**;
5:17 "Blessed is the man whom **G** corrects;
6: 8 that **G** would grant what I hope for,
6: 9 that **G** would be willing to crush me,
7: 7 Remember, O **G**, that my life is but a
8: 3 Does **G** pervert justice? Does the
8: 5 if you will look to **G** and plead with
8:13 is the destiny of all who forget **G**;
8:20 "Surely **G** does not reject a
9:13 **G** does not restrain his anger; even
10: 2 I will say to **G**: Do not condemn me,
11: 4 You say to **G**, 'My beliefs are
11: 5 Oh, how I wish that **G** would speak,
11: 6 Know this: **G** has even forgotten some
11: 7 "Can you fathom the mysteries of **G**?
12: 4 though I called upon **G** and he
12: 6 and those who provoke **G** are secure—
12: 6 who carry their **g** in their hands.
12:13 "To **G** belong wisdom and power;
13: 3 Almighty and to argue my case with **G**.
13: 8 Will you argue the case for **G**?
13:20 "Only grant me these two things, O **G**
Job 15: 4 piety and hinder devotion to **G**.
15:13 that you vent your rage against **G**
15:15 If **G** places no trust in his holy
15:25 he shakes his fist at **G** and vaunts
16: 7 Surely, O **G**, you have worn me out;
16: 9 **G** assails me and tears me in his
16:11 **G** has turned me over to evil men and
16:20 as my eyes pour out tears to **G**;
16:21 on behalf of a man he pleads with **G**
17: 3 "Give me, O **G**, the pledge you demand.
17: 6 "**G** has made me a byword to everyone,
18:21 the place of one who knows not **G**."
19: 6 know that **G** has wronged me and drawn
19:22 Why do you pursue me as **G** does? Will
19:26 yet in my flesh I will see **G**;
20:15 **G** will make his stomach vomit them
20:23 he has filled his belly, **G** will vent
20:29 Such is the fate **G** allots the wicked,
20:29 heritage appointed for them by **G**."
21: 9 fear; the rod of **G** is not upon them.
21:14 Yet they say to **G**, 'Leave us alone!
21:17 the fate **G** allots in his anger?
21:19 **G** stores up a man's punishment for
21:22 "Can anyone teach knowledge to **G**,
22: 2 "Can a man be of benefit to **G**? Can
22:12 "Is not **G** in the heights of heaven?
22:13 Yet you say, 'What does **G** know? Does
22:17 They said to **G**, 'Leave us alone!
22:21 "Submit to **G** and be at peace with
22:26 and will lift up your face to **G**.
23:16 **G** has made my heart faint; the
24:12 But **G** charges no-one with wrongdoing.
24:22 **G** drags away the mighty by his power;
25: 2 "Dominion and awe belong to **G**; he
27: 2 "As surely as **G** lives, who has
27: 3 me, the breath of **G** in my nostrils,
27: 8 cut off, when **G** takes away his life
27: 9 Does **G** listen to his cry when
27:10 Will he call upon **G** at all times?
27:13 "Here is the fate **G** allots to the
28:23 **G** understands the way to it and he
29: 2 for the days when **G** watched over me,
30:11 Now that **G** has unstrung my bow and
30:18 In his great power ⌊**G**⌋ ***becomes like***
30:20 "I cry out to you, O **G**, but you do
31: 2 For what is man's lot from **G** above,
31: 6 let **G** weigh me in honest scales and
31:14 what will I do when **G** confronts me?
31:23 For I dreaded destruction from **G**,
31:28 have been unfaithful to **G** on high.
32: 2 justifying himself rather than **G**.
32:13 wisdom; let **G** refute him, not man.'
33:10 Yet **G** has found fault with me; he
33:12 right, for **G** is greater than man.
33:14 For **G** does speak—now one way, now
33:26 He prays to **G** and finds favour with
33:26 is restored by **G** to his righteous
33:29 "**G** does all these things to a man—
34: 5 "Job says, 'I am innocent, but **G**
34: 9 nothing when he tries to please **G**.'
34:10 Far be it from **G** to do evil, from
34:12 is unthinkable that **G** would do wrong,
34:23 **G** has no need to examine men further,
34:31 "Suppose a man says to **G**, 'I am
34:33 Should **G** then reward you on your
34:37 and multiplies his words against **G**.
35: 2 You say, 'I shall be cleared by **G**.'
35:10 no-one says, 'Where is **G** my Maker,
35:13 Indeed, **G** does not listen to their
36: 5 "**G** is mighty, but does not despise
36:22 "**G** is exalted in his power. Who is a
36:26 How great is **G**—beyond our
37:10 The breath of **G** produces ice, and
37:15 Do you know how **G** controls the
37:22 **G** comes in awesome majesty.
38:41 its young cry out to **G** and wander
39:17 for **G** did not endow her with wisdom
40: 2 Let him who accuses **G** answer him!"
40:19 He ranks first among the works of **G**,
Ps 3: 2 Many are saying of me, "**G** will not
3: 7 Arise, O LORD! Deliver me, O my **G**!
4: 1 I call to you, O my righteous **G**.
5: 2 my King and my **G**, for to you I pray.
5: 4 You are not a **G** who takes pleasure
5:10 Declare them guilty, O **G**! Let their
7: 1 O LORD my **G**, I take refuge in you;

Ps 7: 3 O LORD my **G**, if I have done this
7: 6 Awake, my **G**; decree justice.
7: 9 O righteous **G**, who searches minds
7:11 **G** is a righteous judge, a **G** who
9:17 all the nations that forget **G**.
10: 4 his thoughts there is no room for **G**.
10:11 He says to himself, "**G** has forgotten;
10:12 Arise, LORD! Lift up your hand, O **G**.
10:13 Why does the wicked man revile **G**?
10:14 you, O **G**, do see trouble and grief;
13: 3 Look on me and answer, O LORD my **G**.
14: 1 says in his heart, "There is no **G**.
14: 2 any who understand, any who seek **G**.
14: 5 overwhelmed with dread, for **G** is
16: 1 Keep me safe, O **G**, for in you I take
17: 6 I call on you, O **G**, for you will
18: 6 the LORD; I cried to my **G** for help.
18:21 not done evil by turning from my **G**.
18:28 my **G** turns my darkness into light.
18:29 troop; with my **G** I can scale a wall.
18:30 As for **G**, his way is perfect; the
18:31 For who is **G** besides the LORD? And
18:31 And who is the Rock except our **G**?
18:32 It is **G** who arms me with strength
18:46 to my Rock! Exalted be **G** my Saviour!
18:47 He is the **G** who avenges me, who
20: 5 up our banners in the name of our **G**.
20: 7 trust in the name of the LORD our **G**.
22: 1 My **G**, my **G**, why have you forsaken me?
22: 2 O my **G**, I cry out by day, but you do
22:10 my mother's womb you have been my **G**.
24: 5 and vindication from **G** his Saviour.
25: 2 in you I trust, O my **G**. Do not let
25: 5 for you are **G** my Saviour, and my
25:22 Redeem Israel, O **G**, from all their
27: 9 me or forsake me, O **G** my Saviour.
29: 3 the waters; the **G** of glory thunders,
30: 2 O LORD my **G**, I called to you for
30:12 **G**, I will give you thanks for ever.
31: 5 redeem me, O LORD, the **G** of truth.
31:14 you, O LORD; I say, "You are my **G**.
33:12 Blessed is the nation whose **G** is the
35:23 Contend for me, my **G** and Lord.
35:24 my **G**; do not let them gloat over me.
37:31 The law of his **G** is in his heart;
38:15 you will answer, O Lord my **G**.
38:21 me; be not far from me, O my **G**.
40: 3 my mouth, a hymn of praise to our **G**.
40: 5 Many, O LORD my **G**, are the wonders
40: 8 I desire to do your will, O my **G**;
40:17 my deliverer; O my **G**, do not delay.
42: 1 so my soul pants for you, O **G**.
42: 2 My soul thirsts for **G**, for the
42: 2 When can I go and meet with **G**?
42: 3 "Where is your **G**?
42: 5 within me? Put your hope in **G**,
42: 6 my **G**. My soul is downcast within me;
42: 8 a prayer to the **G** of my life.
42: 9 I say to **G** my Rock, "Why have you
42:10 "Where is your **G**?
42:11 Put your hope in **G**, for I will yet
42:11 yet praise him, my Saviour and my **G**.
43: 1 Vindicate me, O **G**, and plead my
43: 2 You are **G** my stronghold. Why have
43: 4 will I go to the altar of **G**, to **G**,
43: 4 praise you with the harp, O **G**, my **G**.
43: 5 Put your hope in **G**, for I will yet
43: 5 yet praise him, my Saviour and my **G**.
44: 1 We have heard with our ears, O **G**;
44: 4 You are my King and my **G**, who
44: 8 In **G** we make our boast all day long,
44:20 If we had forgotten the name of our **G**
44:20 spread out our hands to a foreign **g**,
44:21 would not **G** have discovered it,
45: 2 since **G** has blessed you for ever.
45: 6 Your throne, O **G**, will last for ever
45: 7 and hate wickedness; therefore **G**,
45: 7 your **G**, has set you above your
46: 1 **G** is our refuge and strength, an
46: 5 **G** is within her, she will not fall; **G**
46:10 "Be still, and know that I am **G**; I
47: 1 shout to **G** with cries of joy.
47: 5 **G** has ascended amid shouts of joy,
47: 6 Sing praises to **G**, sing praises;
47: 7 For **G** is the King of all the earth;
47: 8 **G** reigns over the nations; **G** is

Ps 47: 9 belong to **G**; he is greatly exalted
48: 1 city of our **G**, his holy mountain.
48: 3 **G** is in her citadels; he has shown
48: 8 our **G**: **G** makes her secure for ever.
48: 9 Within your temple, O **G**, we meditate
48:10 Like your name, O **G**, your praise
48:14 For this **G** is our **G** for ever and
49: 7 or give to **G** a ransom for him—
49:15 **G** will redeem my life from the grave;
50: 1 The Mighty One, **G**, the LORD, speaks
50: 2 perfect in beauty, **G** shines forth
50: 3 Our **G** comes and will not be silent;
50: 6 for **G** himself is judge.
50: 7 testify against you: I am **G**, your **G**.
50:14 Sacrifice thank-offerings to **G**,
50:16 to the wicked, **G** says: "What right
50:22 "Consider this, you who forget **G**, or
50:23 I may show him the salvation of **G**."
51: 1 Have mercy on me, O **G**, according to
51:10 Create in me a pure heart, O **G**, and
51:14 Save me from bloodguilt, O **G**, the **G**
51:17 sacrifices of **G** are a broken spirit
51:17 heart, O **G**, you will not despise.
52: 1 who are a disgrace in the eyes of **G**?
52: 5 Surely **G** will bring you down to
52: 7 who did not make **G** his stronghold
53: 1 says in his heart, "There is no **G**.
53: 2 **G** looks down from heaven on the sons
53: 2 any who understand, any who seek **G**.
53: 4 eat bread and who do not call on **G**?
53: 5 **G** scattered the bones of those who
53: 5 them to shame, for **G** despised them.
53: 6 When **G** restores the fortunes of his
54: 1 Save me, O **G**, by your name;
54: 2 Hear my prayer, O **G**; listen to the
54: 3 my life—men without regard for **G**.
54: 4 Surely **G** is my help; the Lord is the
55: 1 Listen to my prayer, O **G**, do not
55:16 I call to **G**, and the LORD saves me.
55:19 **G**, who is enthroned for ever, will
55:23 you, O **G**, will bring down the wicked
56: 1 Be merciful to me, O **G**, for men
56: 4 In **G**, whose word I praise, in **G** I
56: 7 anger, O **G**, bring down the nations.
56: 9 By this I will know that **G** is for me.
56:10 In **G**, whose word I praise, in the
56:11 in **G** I trust; I will not be afraid.
56:12 I am under vows to you, O **G**; I will
57: 1 Have mercy on me, O **G**, have mercy on
57: 2 to **G**, who fulfils his ⌊purpose⌋ for
57: 3 **G** sends his love and his faithfulness
57: 5 Be exalted, O **G**, above the heavens;
57: 7 My heart is steadfast, O **G**, my
57:11 Be exalted, O **G**, above the heavens;
58: 6 Break the teeth in their mouths, O **G**
58:11 there is a **G** who judges the earth."
59: 1 Deliver me from my enemies, O **G**;
59: 9 for you; you, O **G**, are my fortress,
59:10 my loving **G**. **G** will go before me and
59:13 the earth that **G** rules over Jacob.
59:17 O **G**, are my fortress, my loving **G**.
60: 1 You have rejected us, O **G**, and
60: 6 **G** has spoken from his sanctuary: "In
60:10 Is it not you, O **G**, you who have
60:12 With **G** we shall gain the victory,
61: 1 Hear my cry, O **G**; listen to my
61: 5 For you have heard my vows, O **G**;
62: 1 My soul finds rest in **G** alone; my
62: 5 Find rest, O my soul, in **G** alone; my
62: 7 salvation and my honour depend on **G**
62: 8 hearts to him, for **G** is our refuge.
62:11 One thing **G** has spoken, two things
62:11 I heard: that you, O **G**, are strong,
63: 1 O **G**, you are my **G**, earnestly I seek
63:11 the king will rejoice in **G**; all who
64: 1 Hear me, O **G**, as I voice my
64: 7 **G** will shoot them with arrows;
64: 9 of **G** and ponder what he has done.
65: 1 Praise awaits you, O **G**, in Zion; to
65: 5 O **G** our Saviour, the hope of all the
65: 9 The streams of **G** are filled with
66: 1 Shout with joy to **G**, all the earth!
66: 3 Say to **G**, "How awesome are your
66: 5 Come and see what **G** has done, how
66: 8 Praise our **G**, O peoples, let the
66:10 For you, O **G**, tested us; you refined

Ps 66:19 **G** has surely listened and heard my
66:20 Praise be to **G**, who has not rejected
67: 1 May **G** be gracious to us and bless us
67: 3 May the peoples praise you, O **G**;
67: 5 May the peoples praise you, O **G**;
67: 6 and **G**, our **G**, will bless us.
67: 7 **G** will bless us, and all the ends of
68: 1 May **G** arise, may his enemies be
68: 4 Sing to **G**, sing praise to his name,
68: 5 widows, is **G** in his holy dwelling.
68: 6 **G** sets the lonely in families, he
68: 7 you went out before your people, O **G**,
68: 9 You gave abundant showers, O **G**; you
68:10 O **G**, you provided for the poor.
68:16 at the mountain where **G** chooses to
68:17 The chariots of **G** are tens of
68:19 Praise be to the Lord, to **G** our
68:20 Our **G** is a **G** who saves; from the
68:21 Surely **G** will crush the heads of his
68:24 O **G**, the procession of my **G** and
68:26 Praise **G** in the great congregation;
68:28 Summon your power, O **G**; show us
68:28 O **G**, as you have done before.
68:31 Egypt; Cush will submit herself to **G**.
68:32 Sing to **G**, O kingdoms of the earth,
68:35 You are awesome, O **G**, in your
69: 1 Save me, O **G**, for the waters have
69: 3 My eyes fail, looking for my **G**.
69: 5 You know my folly, O **G**; my guilt is
69:13 O **G**, answer me with your sure
69:29 your salvation, O **G**, protect me.
69:32 who seek **G**, may your hearts live!
69:35 for **G** will save Zion and rebuild the
70: 1 Hasten, O **G**, to save me; O LORD,
70: 4 "Let **G** be exalted!
70: 5 and needy; come quickly to me, O **G**.
71: 4 Deliver me, O my **G**, from the hand of
71:11 They say, "**G** has forsaken him;
71:12 Be not far from me, O **G**; come
71:12 come quickly, O my **G**, to help me.
71:17 Since my youth, O **G**, you have taught
71:18 do not forsake me, O **G**, till I
71:19 O **G**, you who have done great things.
71:19 Who, O **G**, is like you?
71:22 O my **G**; I will sing praise to you
72: 1 O **G**, the royal son with your
73: 1 Surely **G** is good to Israel, to those
73:11 They say, "How can **G** know? Does the
73:17 till I entered the sanctuary of **G**;
73:26 flesh and my heart may fail, but **G**
73:28 for me, it is good to be near **G**. I
74: 1 have rejected me for ever, O **G**?
74: 8 where **G** was worshipped in the land.
74:10 long will the enemy mock you, O **G**?
74:12 you, O **G**, are my king from of old;
74:22 Rise up, O **G**, and defend your cause;
75: 1 We give thanks to you, O **G**, we give
75: 7 is **G** who judges: He brings one down,
76: 1 In Judah **G** is known; his name is
76: 9 you, O **G**, rose up to judge, to save
77: 1 I cried out to **G** for help; I cried
77: 1 help; I cried out to **G** to hear me.
77: 3 I remembered you, O **G**, and I groaned;
77: 9 Has **G** forgotten to be merciful? Has
77:13 Your ways, O **G**, are holy. What **g** is
77:13 What **g** is so great as our **G**?
77:14 You are the **G** who performs miracles;
77:16 The waters saw you, O **G**, the waters
78: 7 they would put their trust in **G** and
78: 8 whose hearts were not loyal to **G**,
78:18 They wilfully put **G** to the test by
78:19 They spoke against **G**, saying, "Can **G**
78:22 for they did not believe in **G** or
78:34 Whenever **G** slew them, they would
78:35 They remembered that **G** was their
78:41 Again and again they put **G** to the
78:56 they put **G** to the test and rebelled
78:59 **G** heard them, he was very angry; he
79: 1 O **G**, the nations have invaded your
79: 9 Help us, O **G** our Saviour, for the
79:10 "Where is their **G**?" Before our eyes,
80: 3 Restore us, O **G**; make your face
81: 1 Sing for joy to **G** our strength;
81: 9 You shall have no foreign **g** among
81: 9 shall not bow down to an alien **g**.
82: 1 **G** presides in the great assembly; he

Ps 82: 8 Rise up, O **G**, judge the earth, for
83: 1 O **G**, do not keep silent; be not
83: 1 be not quiet, O **G**, be not still.
83:12 of the pasture-lands of **G**."
83:13 Make them like tumble-weed, O my **G**,
84: 3 O LORD Almighty, my King and my **G**.
84: 9 Look upon our shield, O **G**; look
84:10 doorkeeper in the house of my **G**
85: 4 Restore us again, O **G** our Saviour,
85: 8 I will listen to what **G** the LORD
86: 2 You are my **G**; save your servant who
86:10 marvellous deeds; you alone are **G**.
86:12 I will praise you, O Lord my **G**, with
86:14 The arrogant are attacking me, O **G**;
86:15 are a compassionate and gracious **G**,
87: 3 said of you, O city of **G**:
88: 1 O LORD, the **G** who saves me, day and
89: 7 In the council of the holy ones **G** is
89:26 Father, my **G**, the Rock my Saviour.'
90: 2 to everlasting you are **G**.
90:17 May the favour of the Lord our **G**
91: 2 my fortress, my **G**, in whom I trust."
92:13 flourish in the courts of our **G**.
94: 1 O LORD, the **G** who avenges, O **G** who
94:22 my **G** the rock in whom I take refuge.
94:23 the LORD our **G** will destroy them.
95: 3 For the LORD is the great **G**, the
95: 7 for he is our **G** and we are the
98: 3 have seen the salvation of our **G**.
99: 5 Exalt the LORD our **G** and worship at
99: 8 O LORD our **G**, you answered them;
99: 8 you were to Israel a forgiving **G**,
99: 9 Exalt the LORD our **G** and worship at
99: 9 for the LORD our **G** is holy.
100: 3 Know that the LORD is **G**. It is he
102:24 I said: "Do not take me away, O my **G**
104: 1 O LORD my **G**, you are very great;
104:21 prey and seek their food from **G**.
104:33 praise to my **G** as long as I live.
105: 7 He is the LORD our **G**; his judgments
106:14 wasteland they put **G** to the test.
106:21 They forgot the **G** who saved them,
106:47 Save us, O LORD our **G**, and gather
107:11 had rebelled against the words of **G**
108: 1 My heart is steadfast, O **G**; I will
108: 5 Be exalted, O **G**, above the heavens,
108: 7 **G** has spoken from his sanctuary: "In
108:11 Is it not you, O **G**, you who have
108:13 With **G** we shall gain the victory,
109: 1 O **G**, whom I praise, do not remain
109:26 Help me, O LORD my **G**; save me in
113: 5 Who is like the LORD our **G**, the One
115: 2 the nations say, "Where is their **G**?
115: 3 Our **G** is in heaven; he does whatever
116: 5 our **G** is full of compassion.
118:27 The LORD is **G**, and he has made his
118:28 You are my **G**, and I will give thanks;
118:28 you are my **G**, and I will exalt you.
119:115 I may keep the commands of my **G**!
122: 9 our **G**, I will seek your prosperity.
123: 2 our **G**, till he shows us his mercy.
135: 2 in the courts of the house of our **G**.
139:17 O **G**! How vast is the sum of them!
139:19 you would slay the wicked, O **G**!
139:23 Search me, O **G**, and know my heart;
140: 6 O LORD, I say to you, "You are my **G**.
143:10 for you are my **G**; may your good
144: 2 He is my loving **G** and my fortress,
144: 9 I will sing a new song to you, O **G**;
144:15 are the people whose **G** is the LORD.
145: 1 I will exalt you, my **G** the King; I
146: 2 praise to my **G** as long as I live.
146: 5 whose hope is in the LORD his **G**,
146:10 The LORD reigns for ever, your **G**,
147: 1 good it is to sing praises to our **G**,
147: 7 make music to our **G** on the harp.
147:12 O Jerusalem; praise your **G**, O Zion,
149: 6 May the praise of **G** be in their
150: 1 Praise **G** in his sanctuary; praise
Pr 2: 5 LORD and find the knowledge of **G**.
3: 4 good name in the sight of **G** and man.
14:31 is kind to the needy honours **G**.
30: 9 and so dishonour the name of my **G**.
Ecc 1:13 a heavy burden **G** has laid on men!
2:26 To the man who pleases him, **G** gives
2:26 it over to the one who pleases **G**.
Ecc 3:10 I have seen the burden **G** has laid on
3:11 **G** has done from beginning to end.
3:13 all his toil—this is the gift of **G**.
3:14 I know that everything **G** does will
3:14 **G** does it so that men will revere
3:15 and **G** will call the past to account.
3:17 I thought in my heart, "**G** will bring
3:18 I also thought, "As for men, **G** tests
5: 2 **G** is in heaven and you are on earth,
5: 4 you make a vow to **G**, do not delay in
5: 6 Why should **G** be angry at what you
5: 7 Therefore stand in awe of **G**.
5:18 the few days of life **G** has given
5:19 Moreover, when **G** gives any man
5:19 in his work—this is a gift of **G**.
5:20 because **G** keeps him occupied with
6: 2 **G** gives a man wealth, possessions
6: 2 but **G** does not enable him to enjoy
7:13 Consider what **G** has done: Who can
7:14 consider: **G** has made the one as well
7:18 who fears **G** will avoid all extremes.
7:26 The man who pleases **G** will escape
7:29 This only have I found: **G** made
8:15 life **G** has given him under the sun.
8:17 I saw all that **G** has done. No-one
9: 7 is now that **G** favours what you do.
9: 9 that **G** has given you under the sun
11: 9 things **G** will bring you to judgment.
12: 7 the spirit returns to **G** who gave it.
12:14 For **G** will bring every deed into
Isa 1:10 of our **G**, you people of Gomorrah!
5:16 and the holy **G** will show himself
5:19 to those who say, "Let **G** hurry, let
7:13 you try the patience of my **G** also?
8:10 it will not stand, for **G** is with us.
8:19 not a people enquire of their **G**?
8:21 will curse their king and their **G**.
9: 6 Mighty **G**, Everlasting Father, Prince
10:21 Jacob will return to the Mighty **G**.
12: 2 Surely **G** is my salvation; I will
13:19 by **G** like Sodom and Gomorrah.
14:13 my throne above the stars of **G**;
17:10 You have forgotten **G** your Saviour;
25: 1 O LORD, you are my **G**; I will exalt
25: 9 "Surely this is our **G**; we trusted in
25:11 **G** will bring down their pride
26: 1 We have a strong city; **G** makes
26:13 O LORD, our **G**, other lords besides
28:11 tongues **G** will speak to this people,
28:26 His **G** instructs him and teaches him
30:18 For the LORD is a **G** of justice.
31: 3 the Egyptians are men and not **G**;
34:11 **G** will stretch out over Edom the
35: 2 of the LORD, the splendour of our **G**.
35: 4 "Be strong, do not fear; your **G** will
36: 7 "We are depending on the LORD our **G**"—
36:18 Has the **g** of any nation ever
37:10 Do not let the **g** you depend on
37:16 **G** over all the kingdoms of the earth.
37:20 Now, O LORD our **G**, deliver us from
37:20 that you alone, O LORD, are **G**."
37:38 in the temple of his **g** Nisroch,
40: 1 comfort my people, says your **G**.
40: 3 the wilderness a highway for our **G**.
40: 8 the word of our **G** stands for ever."
40: 9 towns of Judah, "Here is your **G**!
40:18 To whom, then, will you compare **G**?
40:27 my cause is disregarded by my **G**"?
40:28 The LORD is the everlasting **G**,
41:10 do not be dismayed, for I am your **G**.
41:13 For I am the LORD, your **G**, who takes
42: 5 This is what **G** the LORD says—he
43:10 Before me no **g** was formed, nor will
43:12 I, and not some foreign **g** among you.
43:12 declares the LORD, "that I am **G**.
44: 6 last; apart from me there is no **G**.
44: 8 Is there any **G** besides me? No, there
44:10 Who shapes a **g** and casts an idol,
44:15 But he also fashions a **g** and
44:17 From the rest he makes a **g**, his idol;
44:17 it and says, "Save me; you are my **g**.
45: 5 other; apart from me there is no **G**.
45:14 'Surely **G** is with you, and there is
45:14 is no other; there is no other **g**.'"
45:15 Truly you are a **G** who hides himself,
45:15 himself, O **G** and Saviour of Israel.
Isa 45:18 he is **G**; he who fashioned and made
45:21 the LORD? And there is no **G** apart
45:21 a righteous **G** and a Saviour; there
45:22 for I am **G**, and there is no other.
46: 6 a **g**, and they bow down and worship
46: 9 I am **G**, and there is no other;
46: 9 I am **G**, and there is none like me.
48: 5 image and metal **g** ordained them.'
49: 4 hand, and my reward is with my **G**."
49: 5 LORD and my **G** has been my strength—
50:10 name of the LORD and rely on his **G**.
51:20 the LORD and the rebuke of your **G**.
51:22 your **G**, who defends his people: "See,
52: 7 who say to Zion "Your **G** reigns! "
52:10 will see the salvation of our **G**.
53: 4 by **G**, smitten by him, and afflicted.
54: 5 he is called the **G** of all the earth.
54: 6 only to be rejected," says your **G**.
55: 7 to our **G**, for he will freely pardon.
57:21 "There is no peace," says my **G**, "for
58: 2 not forsaken the commands of its **G**.
58: 2 seem eager for **G** to come near them.
59: 2 have separated you from your **G**;
59:13 turning our backs on our **G**,
60:19 and your **G** will be your glory.
61: 2 of our **G**, to comfort all who mourn,
61: 6 will be named ministers of our **G**.
61:10 the LORD; my soul rejoices in my **G**.
62: 3 royal diadem in the hand of your **G**.
62: 5 so will your **G** rejoice over you.
64: 4 no eye has seen any **G** besides you,
65:16 land will do so by the **G** of truth;
65:16 land will swear by the **G** of truth.
66: 9 I bring to delivery?" says your **G**.
Jer 3:21 have forgotten the LORD their **G**.
3:22 to you, for you are the LORD our **G**.
3:23 our **G** is the salvation of Israel
3:25 have sinned against the LORD our **G**,
3:25 we have not obeyed the LORD our **G**.
5: 4 LORD, the requirements of their **G**.
5: 5 LORD, the requirements of their **G**.
5:19 'Why has the LORD our **G** done all
5:24 'Let us fear the LORD our **G**, who
7:28 its **G** or responded to correction.
8:14 For the LORD our **G** has doomed us to
10:12 **G** made the earth by his power; he
11:13 burn incense to that shameful **g**
14:22 No, it is you, O LORD our **G**.
16:10 committed against the LORD our **G**?'
22: 9 the covenant of the LORD their **G**
23:23 "Am I only a **G** nearby," declares
23:23 "and not a **G** far away?
23:36 living **G**, the LORD Almighty, our **G**.
26:16 us in the name of the LORD our **G**."
30: 9 they will serve the LORD their **G** and
31: 1 "I will be the **G** of all the clans of
31: 6 go up to Zion, to the LORD our **G**.'"
31:18 because you are the LORD my **G**.
32:18 **G**, whose name is the LORD Almighty,
32:27 "I am the LORD, the **G** of all mankind.
37: 3 pray to the LORD our **G** for us."
42: 6 we will obey the LORD our **G**, to whom
42: 6 for we will obey the LORD our **G**."
43: 1 all the words of the LORD their **G**
43: 2 "You are lying! The LORD our **G** has
46:25 punishment on Amon **g** of Thebes,
50: 4 in tears to seek the LORD their **G**.
50:28 the LORD our **G** has taken vengeance,
50:40 **G** overthrew Sodom and Gomorrah along
51: 5 have not been forsaken by their **G**,
51:10 Zion what the LORD our **G** has done.'
51:56 For the LORD is a **G** of retribution;
Lam 3:41 our hands to **G** in heaven, and say:
Eze 1: 1 were opened and I saw visions of **G**.
8: 3 of **G** he took me to Jerusalem,
28: 2 I am a **g**; I sit on the throne of a **g**
28: 2 But you are a man and not a **g**,
28: 2 you think you are as wise as a **g**.
28: 6 think you are wise, as wise as a **g**,
28: 9 Will you then say, "I am a **g**," in
28: 9 You will be a man, not a **g**, in the
28:13 You were in Eden, the garden of **G**;
28:14 You were on the holy mount of **G**;
28:16 you in disgrace from the mount of **G**,
28:26 know that I am the LORD their **G**.'"
31: 8 The cedars in the garden of **G** could

Eze 31: 8 garden of **G** could match its beauty.
31: 9 trees of Eden in the garden of **G**.
34:24 I the LORD will be their **G**, and my
34:30 the LORD their **G**, am with them and
34:31 I am your **G**, declares the Sovereign
39:22 know that I am the LORD their **G**.
39:28 know that I am the LORD their **G**,
40: 2 In visions of **G** he took me to the
Da 1: 2 the articles from the temple of **G**.
1: 2 to the temple of his **g** in Babylonia
1: 2 put in the treasure-house of his **g**.
1: 9 Now **G** had caused the official to
1:17 To these four young men **G** gave
2:20 said: "Praise be to the name of **G**
2:23 I thank and praise you, O **G** of my
2:28 there is a **G** in heaven who reveals
2:45 "The great **G** has shown the king what
2:47 "Surely your **G** is the **G** of gods and
3:15 Then what **g** will be able to rescue
3:17 the **G** we serve is able to save us
3:26 Most High **G**, come out! Come here!"
3:28 "Praise be to the **G** of Shadrach,
3:28 or worship any **g** except their own **G**.
3:29 anything against the **G** of Shadrach,
3:29 no other **g** can save in this way."
4: 2 Most High **G** has performed for me.
4: 8 after the name of my **g**, and the
5: 3 from the temple of **G** in Jerusalem,
5:18 "O king, the Most High **G** gave your
5:21 the Most High **G** is sovereign over
5:23 did not honour the **G** who holds in
5:26 **G** has numbered the days of your
6: 5 to do with the law of his **G**."
6: 7 **g** or man during the next thirty days,
6:10 giving thanks to his **G**, just as he
6:11 Daniel praying and asking **G** for help.
6:12 prays to any **g** or man except to you,
6:16 The king said to Daniel, "May your **G**,
6:20 your **G**, whom you serve continually,
6:22 My **G** sent his angel, and he shut the
6:23 because he had trusted in his **G**.
6:26 fear and reverence the **G** of Daniel.
9: 4 I prayed to the LORD my **G** and
9: 4 "O Lord, the great and awesome **G**,
9: 9 The Lord our **G** is merciful and
9:10 we have not obeyed the LORD our **G** or
9:13 LORD our **G** by turning from our sins
9:14 for the LORD our **G** is righteous in
9:15 "Now, O Lord our **G**, who brought your
9:17 "Now, our **G**, hear the prayers and
9:18 Give ear, O **G**, and hear; open your
9:19 For your sake, O my **G**, do not delay
9:20 to the LORD my **G** for his holy hill—
10:12 to humble yourself before your **G**,
11:32 know their **G** will firmly resist him.
11:36 magnify himself above every **g** and
11:37 nor will he regard any **g**, but will
11:38 Instead of them, he will honour a **g**
11:38 a **g** unknown to his fathers he will
11:39 with the help of a foreign **g**
Hos 1: 7 horsemen, but by the LORD their **G**."
1: 9 not my people, and I am not your **G**.
2:23 and they will say, 'You are my **G**.'"
3: 5 LORD their **G** and David their king.
4: 1 no acknowledgment of **G** in the land.
4: 6 you have ignored the law of your **G**
4:12 they are unfaithful to their **G**.
5: 4 permit them to return to their **G**.
6: 6 acknowledgment of **G** rather than
7:10 to the LORD his **G** or search for him.
8: 2 Israel cries out to me, 'O our **G**, we
8: 6 craftsman has made it; it is not **G**.
9: 1 you have been unfaithful to your **G**;
9: 8 The prophet, along with my **G**, is the
9: 8 and hostility in the house of his **G**.
9: 9 **G** will remember their wickedness and
9:17 My **G** will reject them because they
11: 9 For I am **G**, and not man—the Holy
11:12 And Judah is unruly against **G**, even
12: 3 heel; as a man he struggled with **G**.
12: 6 you must return to your **G**; maintain
12: 6 justice, and wait for your **G** always.
13: 4 no **G** but me, no Saviour except me.
13:16 they have rebelled against their **G**.
Joel 1:13 you who minister before my **G**; for
1:13 withheld from the house of your **G**.
Joel 1:16 gladness from the house of our **G**?
2:17 the peoples, 'Where is their **G**?'"
Am 2: 8 the house of their **g** they drink
4:12 prepare to meet your **G**, O Israel."
5:26 the star of your **g**—which you made
8:14 'As surely as your **g** lives, O Dan',
8:14 'As surely as the **g** of Beersheba
Jnh 1: 5 and each cried out to his own **g**.
1: 6 Get up and call on your **g**! Maybe he
2: 1 fish Jonah prayed to the LORD his **G**.
2: 6 life up from the pit, O LORD my **G**.
3: 5 The Ninevites believed **G**. They
3: 8 Let everyone call urgently on **G**. Let
3: 9 Who knows? **G** may yet relent and with
3:10 **G** saw what they did and how they
4: 2 are a gracious and compassionate **G**,
4: 2 **G** who relents from sending calamity.
4: 7 at dawn the next day **G** provided a
4: 8 the sun rose, **G** provided a scorching
4: 9 **G** said to Jonah, "Do you have a
Mic 3: 7 because there is no answer from **G**."
4: 5 Walk in the name of the LORD our **G**
5: 4 of the name of the LORD his **G**.
6: 6 and bow down before the exalted **G**?
6: 8 and to walk humbly with your **G**.
7: 4 has come, the day **G** visits you.
7: 7 for **G** my Saviour; my **G** will hear me.
7:17 LORD our **G** and will be afraid of you.
7:18 Who is a **G** like you, who pardons sin
Na 1: 2 The LORD is a jealous and avenging **G**;
Hab 1:11 men, whose own strength is their **g**."
1:12 My **G**, my Holy One, we will not die.
3: 3 **G** came from Teman, the Holy One from
3:18 I will be joyful in **G** my Saviour.
Zep 2: 7 The LORD their **G** will care for them;
3: 2 she does not draw near to her **G**.
Hag 1:12 the voice of the LORD their **G**
1:12 the LORD their **G** had sent him.
1:14 house of the LORD Almighty, their **G**,
Zec 4: 7 shouts of '**G** bless it! **G** bless it!'"
8: 8 and righteous to them as their **G**."
8:23 we have heard that **G** is with you.
9: 7 our **G** and become leaders in Judah,
9:16 The LORD their **G** will save them on
10: 6 LORD their **G** and I will answer them.
11: 4 This is what the LORD my **G** says:
12: 5 the LORD Almighty is their **G**.'
12: 8 the house of David will be like **G**,
13: 9 they will say, 'The LORD is our **G**.'"
14: 5 Then the LORD my **G** will come, and
Mal 1: 9 "Now implore **G** to be gracious to us.
2:11 the daughter of a foreign **g**.
2:17 "Where is the **G** of justice?
3: 8 "Will a man rob **G**? Yet you rob me.
3:14 have said, 'It is futile to serve **G**.
3:15 even those who challenge **G** escape.'"
3:18 who serve **G** and those who do not.
Mt 1:23 Immanuel"—which means, "**G** with us.
3: 9 **G** can raise up children for Abraham.
4: 4 that comes from the mouth of **G**.'"
5: 8 pure in heart, for they will see **G**.
6:24 You cannot serve both **G** and Money.
6:30 If that is how **G** clothes the grass
9: 8 filled with awe; and they praised **G**,
15: 3 of **G** for the sake of your tradition?
15: 4 For **G** said, 'Honour your father and
15: 5 from me is a gift devoted to **G**,'
16:23 things of **G**, but the things of men."
19: 6 Therefore what **G** has joined together,
19:26 but with **G** all things are possible."
22:16 of **G** in accordance with the truth.
22:21 Caesar's, and to **G** what is God's."
22:31 you not read what **G** said to you,
22:32 the **G** of Isaac, and the **G** of Jacob'?
22:32 He is not the **G** of the dead but of
26:61 am able to destroy the temple of **G**
27:43 He trusts in **G**. Let **G** rescue him now
27:46 **G**, my **G**, why have you forsaken me?"
Mk 1:14 proclaiming the good news of **G**.
1:24 who you are—the Holy One of **G**!"
2: 7 Who can forgive sins but **G** alone?"
2:12 amazed everyone and they praised **G**,
5: 7 Jesus, Son of the Most High **G**? Swear
5: 7 to **G** that you won't torture me!"
7: 8 You have let go of the commands of **G**
7: 9 setting aside the commands of **G** in
Mk 7:11 (that is, a gift devoted to **G**),
8:33 things of **G**, but the things of men."
10: 6 "But at the beginning of creation **G**
10: 9 Therefore what **G** has joined together,
10:18 "No-one is good—except **G** alone.
10:27 **G**; all things are possible with **G**."
11:22 "Have faith in **G**," Jesus answered.
12:14 of **G** in accordance with the truth.
12:17 is Caesar's and to **G** what is God's.
12:26 in the account of the bush, how **G**
12:26 the **G** of Isaac, and the **G** of Jacob'?
12:27 He is not the **G** of the dead, but of
12:29 the Lord our **G**, the Lord is one.
12:32 "You are right in saying that **G** is
13:19 when **G** created the world, until now—
15:34 **G**, my **G**, why have you forsaken me?"
Lk 1: 6 them were upright in the sight of **G**,
1:16 he bring back to the Lord their **G**.
1:19 I stand in the presence of **G**, and I
1:26 In the sixth month, **G** sent the angel
1:30 Mary, you have found favour with **G**.
1:37 For nothing is impossible with **G**."
1:47 my spirit rejoices in **G** my Saviour,
1:64 and he began to speak, praising **G**.
1:78 of the tender mercy of our **G**, by
2:13 the angel, praising **G** and saying,
2:14 "Glory to **G** in the highest, and on
2:20 glorifying and praising **G** for all
2:28 in his arms and praised **G**, saying:
2:38 she gave thanks to **G** and spoke about
2:52 and in favour with **G** and men.
3: 8 **G** can raise up children for Abraham.
4:34 who you are—the Holy One of **G**!"
5:21 Who can forgive sins but **G** alone?"
5:25 lying on and went home praising **G**.
5:26 was amazed and gave praise to **G**.
6:12 and spent the night praying to **G**.
7:16 all filled with awe and praised **G**.
7:16 "**G** has come to help his people."
8:28 Jesus, Son of the Most High **G**?
8:39 "Return home and tell how much **G** has
9:20 Peter answered, "The Christ of **G**.
9:43 all amazed at the greatness of **G**.
11:42 because you give **G** a tenth of your
11:49 **G** in his wisdom said, 'I will send
12: 6 not one of them is forgotten by **G**.
12: 8 him before the angels of **G**.
12: 9 be disowned before the angels of **G**.
12:20 "But **G** said to him, 'You fool! This
12:21 himself but is not rich towards **G**."
12:24 storeroom or barn; yet **G** feeds them.
12:28 If that is how **G** clothes the grass
13:13 she straightened up and praised **G**.
15:10 of **G** over one sinner who repents."
16:13 You cannot serve both **G** and Money."
16:15 of men, but **G** knows your hearts.
17:15 back, praising **G** in a loud voice.
17:18 praise to **G** except this foreigner?"
18: 2 feared **G** nor cared about men.
18: 7 will not **G** bring about justice for
18:11 '**G**, I thank you that I am not like
18:13 '**G**, have mercy on me, a sinner.'
18:19 "No-one is good—except **G** alone.
18:27 with men is possible with **G**."
18:43 and followed Jesus, praising **G**.
18:43 people saw it, they also praised **G**.
19:37 began joyfully to praise **G** in loud
20:21 of **G** in accordance with the truth.
20:25 Caesar's, and to **G** what is God's."
20:37 the **G** of Isaac, and the **G** of Jacob'.
20:38 He is not the **G** of the dead, but of
21: 5 and with gifts dedicated to **G**.
22:69 at the right hand of the mighty **G**."
23:35 is the Christ of **G**, the Chosen One."
23:47 seeing what had happened, praised **G**
24:53 at the temple, praising **G**.
Jn 1: 1 Word was with **G**, and the Word was **G**.
1: 2 He was with **G** in the beginning.
1: 6 There came a man who was sent from **G**;
1:13 or a husband's will, but born of **G**.
1:18 No-one has ever seen **G**, but **G** the
1:51 and the angels of **G** ascending and
3: 2 are a teacher who has come from **G**.
3: 2 are doing if **G** were not with him."
3:16 "For **G** so loved the world that he
3:17 For **G** did not send his Son into the

Jn 3:21 has done has been done through **G**."
3:33 it has certified that **G** is truthful.
3:34 **G** has sent speaks the words of **G**,
3:34 For **G** gives the Spirit without limit
4:10 "If you knew the gift of **G** and who
4:24 **G** is spirit, and his worshippers
5:18 but he was even calling **G** his own
5:18 Father, making himself equal with **G**.
5:44 praise that comes from the only **G**?
6:28 we do to do the works **G** requires?"
6:33 For the bread of **G** is he who comes
6:45 'They will all be taught by **G**.
6:46 from **G**; only he has seen the Father.
6:69 that you are the Holy One of **G**."
7:17 from **G** or whether I speak on my own.
8:40 you the truth that I heard from **G**.
8:41 only Father we have is **G** himself."
8:42 Jesus said to them, "If **G** were your
8:42 for I came from **G** and now am here.
8:47 He who belongs to **G** hears what **G**
8:47 is that you do not belong to **G**."
8:54 your **G**, is the one who glorifies me.
9:16 This man is not from **G**, for he does
9:24 "Give glory to **G**," they said. "We
9:29 We know that **G** spoke to Moses, but
9:31 We know that **G** does not listen to
9:33 If this man were not from **G**, he
10:33 you, a mere man, claim to be **G**."
11:22 I know that even now **G** will give you
12:43 from men more than praise from **G**.
13: 3 come from **G** and was returning to **G**;
13:31 glorified and **G** is glorified in him.
13:32 If **G** is glorified in him, **G** will
14: 1 Trust in **G**; trust also in me.
16: 2 think he is offering a service to **G**.
16:27 have believed that I came from **G**.
16:30 us believe that you came from **G**."
20:17 your Father, to my **G** and your **G**.'"
20:28 Thomas said to him, "My Lord and my **G**
21:19 by which Peter would glorify **G**.
Ac 2:11 wonders of **G** in our own tongues!"
2:17 "In the last days, **G** says, I will
2:22 accredited by **G** to you by miracles,
2:22 wonders and signs, which **G** did among
2:24 **G** raised him from the dead, freeing
2:30 he was a prophet and knew that **G** had
2:32 **G** has raised this Jesus to life, and
2:36 **G** has made this Jesus, whom you
2:39 all whom the Lord our **G** will call."
2:47 praising **G** and enjoying the favour
3: 8 walking and jumping, and praising **G**.
3: 9 saw him walking and praising **G**,
3:13 the **G** of our fathers, has glorified
3:15 You killed the author of life, but **G**
3:18 this is how **G** fulfilled what he had
3:19 Repent, then, and turn to **G**, so that
3:21 comes for **G** to restore everything,
3:25 covenant **G** made with your fathers.
3:26 **G** raised up his servant, he sent him
4:10 whom you crucified but whom **G** raised
4:19 sight to obey you rather than **G**.
4:21 praising **G** for what had happened.
4:24 voices together in prayer to **G**.
5: 4 You have not lied to men but to **G**."
5:29 "We must obey **G** rather than
5:30 The **G** of our fathers raised Jesus
5:31 **G** exalted him to his own right hand
5:32 **G** has given to those who obey him."
5:39 if it is from **G**, you will not be
5:39 find yourselves fighting against **G**."
6:11 against Moses and against **G**."
7: 2 listen to me! The **G** of glory
7: 3 country and your people,' **G** said,
7: 4 After the death of his father, **G**
7: 5 But **G** promised him that he and his
7: 6 **G** spoke to him in this way: 'Your
7: 7 they serve as slaves,' **G** said,
7: 9 slave into Egypt. But **G** was with
7:17 "As the time drew near for **G** to
7:25 that **G** was using him to rescue them,
7:35 ruler and deliverer by **G** himself,
7:37 '**G** will send you a prophet like me
7:42 **G** turned away and gave them over to
7:43 Molech and the star of your **g** Rephan,
7:44 It had been made as **G** directed Moses,
7:45 the nations **G** drove out before them.
Ac 8:20 could buy the gift of **G** with money!
10: 2 in need and prayed to **G** regularly.
10:15 impure that **G** has made clean."
10:28 **G** has shown me that I should not
10:31 Cornelius, **G** has heard your prayer
10:33 are all here in the presence of **G**
10:34 that **G** does not show favouritism
10:36 You know the message **G** sent to the
10:38 how **G** anointed Jesus of Nazareth
10:38 the devil, because **G** was with him.
10:40 **G** raised him from the dead on the
10:41 but by witnesses whom **G** had already
10:42 to testify that he is the one whom **G**
10:46 speaking in tongues and praising **G**.
11: 9 impure that **G** has made clean.'
11:17 if **G** gave them the same gift as he
11:17 I to think that I could oppose **G**?"
11:18 no further objections and praised **G**,
11:18 **G** has granted even the Gentiles
12: 5 was earnestly praying to **G** for him.
12:22 is the voice of a **g**, not of a man."
12:23 Herod did not give praise to **G**,
13:16 Gentiles who worship **G**, listen to me!
13:17 The **G** of the people of Israel chose
13:20 "After this, **G** gave them judges
13:23 "From this man's descendants **G** has
13:30 But **G** raised him from the dead,
13:32 "We tell you the good news: What **G**
13:34 The fact that **G** raised him from the
13:37 the one whom **G** raised from the dead
14:27 reported all that **G** had done through
15: 4 everything **G** had done through them.
15: 7 you know that some time ago **G** made a
15: 8 **G**, who knows the heart, showed that
15:10 Now then, why do you try to test **G**
15:12 wonders **G** had done among the
15:14 Simon has described to us how **G** at
15:19 the Gentiles who are turning to **G**.
16:10 concluding that **G** had called us to
16:14 Thyatira, who was a worshipper of **G**.
16:17 men are servants of the Most High **G**,
16:25 were praying and singing hymns to **G**,
16:34 because he had come to believe in **G**
17:23 inscription: TO AN UNKNOWN **G**.
17:24 "The **G** who made the world and
17:27 **G** did this so that men would seek
17:30 In the past **G** overlooked such
18: 7 of Titius Justus, a worshipper of **G**
18:13 persuading the people to worship **G**
18:26 to him the way of **G** more adequately.
19:11 **G** did extraordinary miracles through
20:21 they must turn to **G** in repentance
20:28 Be shepherds of the church of **G**,
20:32 "Now I commit you to **G** and to the
21:19 reported in detail what **G** had done
21:20 they heard this, they praised **G**.
22: 3 just as zealous for **G** as any of you
22:14 "Then he said: 'The **G** of our fathers
23: 1 **G** in all good conscience to this day.
23: 3 Paul said to him, "**G** will strike you,
24:14 However, I admit that I worship the **G**
24:15 I have the same hope in **G** as these
26: 6 my hope in what **G** has promised our
26: 7 earnestly serve **G** day and night.
26: 8 incredible that **G** raises the dead?
26:18 and from the power of Satan to **G**, so
26:20 turn to **G** and prove their repentance
26:29 "Short time or long—I pray **G** that
27:23 Last night an angel of the **G** whose I
27:24 **G** has graciously given you the lives
27:25 have faith in **G** that it will happen
27:35 thanks to **G** in front of them all.
28: 6 their minds and said he was a **g**.
28:15 Paul thanked **G** and was encouraged.
Ro 1: 1 and set apart for the gospel of **G**—
1: 7 To all in Rome who are loved by **G**
1: 8 First, I thank my **G** through Jesus
1: 9 **G**, whom I serve with my whole heart
1:17 a righteousness from **G** is revealed,
1:19 since what may be known about **G** is
1:19 because **G** has made it plain to them.
1:21 For although they knew **G**, they
1:21 they neither glorified him as **G** nor
1:23 exchanged the glory of the immortal **G**
1:24 Therefore **G** gave them over in the
1:25 They exchanged the truth of **G** for
Ro 1:26 **G** gave them over to shameful lusts
1:28 while to retain the knowledge of **G**,
2: 6 **G** "will give to each person
2:11 For **G** does not show favouritism.
2:16 on the day when **G** will judge men's
2:17 brag about your relationship to **G**;
2:23 you dishonour **G** by breaking the law?
2:29 praise is not from men, but from **G**.
3: 2 entrusted with the very words of **G**.
3: 4 Let **G** be true, and every man a liar
3: 5 what shall we say? That **G** is unjust
3: 6 so, how could **G** judge the world?
3:11 who understands, no-one who seeks **G**.
3:19 whole world held accountable to **G**.
3:21 now a righteousness from **G**, apart
3:22 This righteousness from **G** comes
3:25 **G** presented him as a sacrifice of
3:29 Is **G** the **G** of Jews only? Is he not
3:29 Is he not the **G** of Gentiles too? Yes,
4: 3 "Abraham believed **G**, and it was
4: 5 trusts **G** who justifies the wicked,
4: 6 to whom **G** credits righteousness
4:17 He is our father in the sight of **G**,
4:17 the **G** who gives life to the dead
4:20 unbelief regarding the promise of **G**,
4:20 in his faith and gave glory to **G**,
4:21 being fully persuaded that **G** had
4:24 also for us, to whom **G** will credit
5: 5 because **G** has poured out his love
5: 8 **G** demonstrates his own love for us
5:11 but we also rejoice in **G** through our
5:16 the gift of **G** is not like the result
6:10 the life he lives, he lives to **G**.
6:11 sin but alive to **G** in Christ Jesus.
6:13 but rather offer yourselves to **G**, as
6:17 thanks be to **G** that, though you used
6:22 sin and have become slaves to **G**,
6:23 but the gift of **G** is eternal life in
7: 4 order that we might bear fruit to **G**.
7:25 Thanks be to **G**—through Jesus Christ
8: 3 **G** did by sending his own Son in the
8: 7 the sinful mind is hostile to **G**. It
8: 8 the sinful nature cannot please **G**.
8:17 are heirs—heirs of **G** and co-heirs
8:28 we know that in all things **G** works
8:29 For those **G** foreknew he also
8:31 **G** is for us, who can be against us?
8:33 **G** has chosen? It is **G** who justifies.
9: 5 who is **G** over all, for ever praised
9:14 What then shall we say? Is **G** unjust?
9:18 Therefore **G** has mercy on whom he
9:19 "Then why does **G** still blame us? For
9:20 who are you, O man, to talk back to **G**
9:22 What if **G**, choosing to show his
10: 1 my heart's desire and prayer to **G**
10: 2 them that they are zealous for **G**,
10: 3 **G** and sought to establish their own,
10: 9 that **G** raised him from the dead,
11: 1 I ask then: Did **G** reject his people?
11: 2 **G** did not reject his people, whom he
11: 2 he appealed to **G** against Israel:
11: 8 "**G** gave them a spirit of stupor,
11:21 For if **G** did not spare the natural
11:22 of **G**: sternness to those who fell,
11:23 **G** is able to graft them in again.
11:30 were at one time disobedient to **G**
11:32 For **G** has bound all men over to
11:33 of the wisdom and knowledge of **G**!
11:35 "Who has ever given to **G**, that **G**
12: 1 holy and pleasing to **G**—this is your
12: 3 measure of faith **G** has given you.
13: 1 except that which **G** has established.
13: 1 exist have been established by **G**.
13: 2 against what **G** has instituted,
14: 3 who does, for **G** has accepted him.
14: 6 for he gives thanks to **G**; and he
14: 6 to the Lord and gives thanks to **G**.
14:11 every tongue will confess to **G**.'"
14:12 give an account of himself to **G**.
14:18 pleasing to **G** and approved by men.
14:22 things keep between yourself and **G**.
15: 5 May the **G** who gives endurance and
15: 6 mouth you may glorify the **G** and
15: 7 you, in order to bring praise to **G**.
15: 9 that the Gentiles may glorify **G** for
15:13 May the **G** of hope fill you with all

Ro 15:15 because of the grace **G** gave me
15:16 duty of proclaiming the gospel of **G**,
15:16 become an offering acceptable to **G**,
15:17 in Christ Jesus in my service to **G**.
15:18 to obey **G** by what I have said and
15:30 my struggle by praying to **G** for me.
15:33 The **G** of peace be with you all. Amen.
16:20 The **G** of peace will soon crush Satan
16:27 to the only wise **G** be glory for ever
1Co 1: 2 To the church of **G** in Corinth, to
1: 4 I always thank **G** for you because
1: 9 **G**, who has called you into
1:20 Has not **G** made foolish the wisdom
1:21 For since in the wisdom of **G** the
1:21 **G** was pleased through the
1:24 to those whom **G** has called, both
1:24 the power of **G** and the wisdom of **G**.
1:25 For the foolishness of **G** is wiser
1:25 **G** is stronger than man's strength.
1:27 **G** chose the foolish things of the
1:27 **G** chose the weak things of the world
1:30 who has become for us wisdom from **G**
2: 1 to you the testimony about **G**.
2: 7 that **G** destined for our glory before
2: 9 no mind has conceived what **G** has
2:10 **G** has revealed it to us by his
2:10 things, even the deep things of **G**.
2:11 no-one knows the thoughts of **G** except
2:12 world but the Spirit who is from **G**,
2:12 what **G** has freely given us.
3: 6 watered it, but **G** made it grow.
3: 7 but only **G**, who makes things grow.
3:10 By the grace **G** has given me, I laid
3:17 If anyone destroys God's temple, **G**
3:23 you are of Christ, and Christ is of **G**
4: 1 with the secret things of **G**.
4: 5 each will receive his praise from **G**.
4: 9 For it seems to me that **G** has put us
5:13 **G** will judge those outside. "Expel
6:11 Christ and by the Spirit of our **G**.
6:13 food"—but **G** will destroy them both.
6:14 By his power **G** raised the Lord from
6:19 from **G**? You are not your own;
6:20 Therefore honour **G** with your body.
7: 7 But each man has his own gift from **G**;
7:15 **G** has called us to live in peace.
7:17 him and to which **G** has called him.
7:20 which he was in when **G** called him.
7:24 each man, as responsible to **G**,
7:24 in the situation **G** called him to.
8: 3 the man who loves **G** is known by **G**.
8: 4 and that there is no **G** but one.
8: 8 food does not bring us near to **G**; we
9: 9 Is it about oxen that **G** is concerned?
10: 5 Nevertheless, **G** was not pleased with
10:13 And **G** is faithful; he will not let
10:20 not to **G**, and I do not want you to
10:30 because of something I thank **G** for?
10:32 Jews, Greeks or the church of **G**—
11: 3 is man, and the head of Christ is **G**.
11:12 But everything comes from **G**.
11:13 pray to **G** with her head uncovered?
11:16 practice—nor do the churches of **G**.
11:22 Or do you despise the church of **G**
12: 6 same **G** works all of them in all men.
12:18 in fact **G** has arranged the parts in
12:24 But **G** has combined the members of
12:28 in the church **G** has appointed first
14: 2 does not speak to men but to **G**.
14:16 If you are praising **G** with your
14:18 I thank **G** that I speak in tongues
14:25 So he will fall down and worship **G**,
14:25 "**G** is really among you!
14:28 church and speak to himself and **G**.
14:33 For **G** is not a **G** of disorder but of
15: 9 I persecuted the church of **G**.
15:15 found to be false witnesses about **G**,
15:15 for we have testified about **G** that
15:27 this does not include **G** himself,
15:28 him, so that **G** may be all in all.
15:34 are some who are ignorant of **G**
15:38 **G** gives it a body as he has
15:57 thanks be to **G**! He gives us the
2Co 1: 1 To the church of **G** in Corinth,
1: 3 Praise be to the **G** and Father of our
1: 3 compassion and the **G** of all comfort,
2Co 1: 4 we ourselves have received from **G**.
1: 9 but on **G**, who raises the dead.
1:12 and sincerity that are from **G**.
1:18 as surely as **G** is faithful, our
1:20 For no matter how many promises **G**
1:21 Now it is **G** who makes both us and
1:23 I call **G** as my witness that it was
2:14 thanks be to **G**, who always leads us
2:15 For we are to **G** the aroma of Christ
2:17 sincerity, like men sent from **G**.
3: 5 but our competence comes from **G**.
4: 2 man's conscience in the sight of **G**.
4: 4 The **g** of this age has blinded the
4: 6 For **G**, who said, "Let light shine
4: 7 power is from **G** and not from us.
5: 1 we have a building from **G**, an
5: 5 Now it is **G** who has made us for this
5:11 What we are is plain to **G**, and I
5:13 it is for the sake of **G**; if we are
5:18 All this is from **G**, who reconciled
5:19 that **G** was reconciling the world to
5:20 **G** were making his appeal through us.
5:20 Christ's behalf: Be reconciled to **G**.
5:21 **G** made him who had no sin to be sin
5:21 might become the righteousness of **G**.
6: 4 Rather, as servants of **G** we commend
6:16 between the temple of **G** and idols?
6:16 As **G** has said: "I will live with
7: 1 holiness out of reverence for **G**.
7: 6 **G**, who comforts the downcast,
7: 9 For you became sorrowful as **G**
8: 1 **G** has given the Macedonian churches.
8:16 I thank **G**, who put into the heart of
9: 7 for **G** loves a cheerful giver.
9: 8 **G** is able to make all grace abound
9:11 will result in thanksgiving to **G**.
9:12 in many expressions of thanks to **G**.
9:13 men will praise **G** for the obedience
9:14 surpassing grace **G** has given you.
9:15 Thanks be to **G** for his indescribable
10: 5 up against the knowledge of **G**, and
10:13 to the field **G** has assigned to us,
11: 7 gospel of **G** to you free of charge?
11:11 I do not love you? **G** knows I do!
11:31 The **G** and Father of the Lord Jesus,
12: 2 of the body I do not know—**G** knows.
12: 3 body I do not know, but **G** knows—
12:19 the sight of **G** as those in Christ;
12:21 my **G** will humble me before you,
13: 7 Now we pray to **G** that you will not
13:11 **G** of love and peace will be with you.
Gal 1: 4 to the will of our **G** and Father,
1:10 win the approval of men, or of **G**?
1:13 church of **G** and tried to destroy it.
1:15 when **G**, who set me apart from birth
1:24 they praised **G** because of me.
2: 6 **G** does not judge by external
2: 8 For **G**, who was at work in the
2:19 the law so that I might live for **G**.
3: 5 Does **G** give you his Spirit and work
3: 6 Consider Abraham: "He believed **G**,
3: 8 The Scripture foresaw that **G** would
3:17 covenant previously established by **G**
3:18 but **G** in his grace gave it to
3:20 just one party; but **G** is one.
3:21 opposed to the promises of **G**?
4: 4 when the time had fully come, **G** sent
4: 6 you are sons, **G** sent the Spirit of
4: 7 a son, **G** has made you also an heir.
4: 8 Formerly, when you did not know **G**,
4: 9 now that you know **G**—or rather are
4: 9 or rather are known by **G**—how is it
6: 7 Do not be deceived: **G** cannot be
6:16 this rule, even to the Israel of **G**.
Eph 1: 3 Praise be to the **G** and Father of our
1:17 I keep asking that the **G** of our Lord
1:22 **G** placed all things under his feet
2: 4 of his great love for us, **G**, who is
2: 6 **G** raised us up with Christ and
2: 8 yourselves, it is the gift of **G**—
2:10 **G** prepared in advance for us to do.
2:12 hope and without **G** in the world.
2:16 reconcile both of them to **G** through
2:22 in which **G** lives by his Spirit.
3: 9 hidden in **G**, who created all things.
3:10 the manifold wisdom of **G** should be
Eph 3:12 **G** with freedom and confidence.
3:19 the measure of all the fulness of **G**.
4:18 separated from the life of **G** because
4:24 to be like **G** in true righteousness
4:32 just as in Christ **G** forgave you.
5: 1 Be imitators of **G**, therefore, as
5: 2 offering and sacrifice to **G**.
5: 5 in the kingdom of Christ and of **G**.
6:11 Put on the full armour of **G** so that
6:13 Therefore put on the full armour of **G**
Php 1: 3 I thank my **G** every time I remember
1: 8 **G** can testify how I long for all of
1:11 Christ—to the glory and praise of **G**.
1:28 you will be saved—and that by **G**.
2: 6 Who, being in very nature **G**, did not
2: 6 with **G** something to be grasped,
2: 9 Therefore **G** exalted him to the
2:13 for it is **G** who works in you to will
2:27 But **G** had mercy on him, and not on
3: 9 that comes from **G** and is by faith.
3:14 the prize for which **G** has called me
3:15 that too **G** will make clear to you.
3:19 destruction, their **g** is their stomach
4: 6 present your requests to **G**.
4: 7 the peace of **G**, which transcends all
4: 9 And the **G** of peace will be with you.
4:18 acceptable sacrifice, pleasing to **G**.
4:19 my **G** will meet all your needs
4:20 To our **G** and Father be glory for
Col 1: 3 We always thank **G**, the Father of our
1: 9 asking **G** to fill you with the
1:10 work, growing in the knowledge of **G**,
1:15 He is the image of the invisible **G**,
1:19 For **G** was pleased to have all his
1:21 Once you were alienated from **G** and
1:25 its servant by the commission **G** gave
1:25 you the word of **G** in its fulness—
1:27 To them **G** has chosen to make known
2: 2 the mystery of **G**, namely, Christ,
2:13 **G** made you alive with Christ.
2:19 grows as **G** causes it to grow.
3: 3 life is now hidden with Christ in **G**.
3:16 with gratitude in your hearts to **G**.
4: 3 pray for us, too, that **G** may open a
1Th 1: 2 We always thank **G** for all of you,
1: 3 We continually remember before our **G**
1: 4 For we know, brothers loved by **G**,
1: 8 your faith in **G** has become known
1: 9 They tell how you turned to **G** from
2: 2 but with the help of our **G** we dared
2: 4 approved by **G** to be entrusted with
2: 4 are not trying to please men but **G**,
2: 5 to cover up greed—**G** is our witness.
2: 8 gospel of **G** but our lives as well,
2: 9 we preached the gospel of **G** to you.
2:10 You are witnesses, and so is **G**, of
2:12 you to live lives worthy of **G**,
2:13 we also thank **G** continually because,
2:13 the word of **G**, which is at work in
2:15 They displease **G** and are hostile
3: 9 How can we thank **G** enough for you
3: 9 presence of our **G** because of you?
3:11 Now may our **G** and Father himself and
3:13 holy in the presence of our **G** and
4: 1 please **G**, as in fact you are living.
4: 5 like the heathen, who do not know **G**;
4: 7 For **G** did not call us to be impure,
4: 8 **G**, who gives you his Holy Spirit.
4: 9 been taught by **G** to love each other.
4:14 rose again and so we believe that **G**
4:16 and with the trumpet call of **G**,
5: 9 For **G** did not appoint us to suffer
5:23 May **G** himself, the **G** of peace,
2Th 1: 2 Grace and peace to you from **G** the
1: 3 We ought always to thank **G** for you,
1: 6 **G** is just: He will pay back trouble
1: 8 will punish those who do not know **G**
1:11 that our **G** may count you worthy of
1:12 of our **G** and the Lord Jesus Christ.
2: 4 that is called **G** or is worshipped,
2: 4 temple, proclaiming himself to be **G**
2:11 For this reason **G** sends them a
2:13 we ought always to thank **G** for you,
2:13 because from the beginning **G** chose
1Ti 1: 1 by the command of **G** our Saviour
1:11 blessed **G**, which he entrusted to me.

1Ti 1:17 immortal, invisible, the only **G**, be
2: 3 This is good, and pleases **G** our
2: 5 **G** and men, the man Christ Jesus,
2:10 for women who profess to worship **G**.
4: 3 which **G** created to be received with
4: 4 For everything **G** created is good,
5: 4 for this is pleasing to **G**.
5: 5 left all alone puts her hope in **G**
5: 5 day to pray and to ask **G** for help.
5:21 I charge you, in the sight of **G** and
6:13 In the sight of **G**, who gives life
6:15 which **G** will bring about in his own
6:15 **G**, the blessed and only Ruler, the
6:17 but to put their hope in **G**, who
2Ti 1: 3 I thank **G**, whom I serve, as my
1: 6 you to fan into flame the gift of **G**,
1: 7 For **G** did not give us a spirit of
2:15 your best to present yourself to **G**
2:25 in the hope that **G** will grant them
3: 4 pleasure rather than lovers of **G**—
4: 1 In the presence of **G** and of Christ
Tit 1: 2 which **G**, who does not lie, promised
1: 3 me by the command of **G** our Saviour,
1:16 They claim to know **G**, but by their
2:10 about **G** our Saviour attractive.
2:13 great **G** and Saviour, Jesus Christ,
3: 8 so that those who have trusted in **G**
Phm : 4 I always thank my **G** as I remember
Heb 1: 1 In the past **G** spoke to our
1: 5 For to which of the angels did **G**
1: 6 again, when **G** brings his firstborn
1: 8 "Your throne, O **G**, will last for
1: 9 therefore **G**, your **G**, has set you
1:13 To which of the angels did **G** ever
2: 4 **G** also testified to it by signs,
2: 8 In putting everything under him, **G**
2:10 it was fitting that **G**, for whom and
2:13 I, and the children **G** has given me."
2:17 high priest in service to **G**,
3: 4 but **G** is the builder of everything.
3:18 to whom did **G** swear that they would
4: 3 just as **G** has said, "So I declared
4: 4 day **G** rested from all his work."
4: 7 Therefore **G** again set a certain day,
4: 8 **G** would not have spoken later about
4:10 own work, just as **G** did from his.
5: 1 them in matters related to **G**,
5: 4 be called by **G**, just as Aaron was.
5: 5 But **G** said to him, "You are my Son;
5:10 was designated by **G** to be high
6: 1 lead to death, and of faith in **G**,
6: 3 **G** permitting, we will do so.
6: 7 farmed receives the blessing of **G**.
6:10 **G** is not unjust; he will not forget
6:13 **G** made his promise to Abraham, since
6:17 **G** wanted to make the unchanging
6:18 **G** did this so that, by two
6:18 which it is impossible for **G** to lie,
7:19 by which we draw near to **G**.
7:21 with an oath when **G** said to him:
7:25 those who come to **G** through him,
8: 8 **G** found fault with the people and
9:14 offered himself unblemished to **G**,
9:20 which **G** has commanded you to keep."
10: 7 I have come to do your will, O **G**.'"
10:22 let us draw near to **G** with a sincere
10:27 that will consume the enemies of **G**.
11: 4 By faith Abel offered **G** a better
11: 4 when **G** spoke well of his offerings.
11: 5 found, because **G** had taken him away.
11: 5 was commended as one who pleased **G**.
11: 6 faith it is impossible to please **G**,
11:10 whose architect and builder is **G**.
11:16 Therefore **G** is not ashamed to be
11:16 is not ashamed to be called their **G**,
11:17 By faith Abraham, when **G** tested him,
11:18 even though **G** had said to him, "It
11:19 Abraham reasoned that **G** could raise
11:40 **G** had planned something better for
12: 2 the right hand of the throne of **G**.
12: 7 **G** is treating you as sons. For what
12:10 but **G** disciplines us for our good,
12:23 You have come to **G**, the judge of all
12:28 worship **G** acceptably with reverence
12:29 for our "**G** is a consuming fire."
13: 4 for **G** will judge the adulterer and
Heb 13: 5 **G** has said, "Never will I leave you;
13:15 let us continually offer to **G** a
13:16 with such sacrifices **G** is pleased.
13:20 May the **G** of peace, who through the
Jas 1: 5 he should ask **G**, who gives
1:12 **G** has promised to those who love him.
1:13 tempted, no-one should say, "**G** is
1:13 For **G** cannot be tempted by evil,
1:20 the righteous life that **G** desires.
2: 5 Listen, my dear brothers: Has not **G**
2:23 "Abraham believed **G**, and it was
4: 2 not have, because you do not ask **G**.
4: 4 with the world is hatred towards **G**?
4: 4 of the world becomes an enemy of **G**.
4: 6 Scripture says: "**G** opposes the proud
4: 7 Submit yourselves, then, to **G**.
4: 8 Come near to **G** and he will come near
1Pe 1: 3 Praise be to the **G** and Father of our
1:21 Through him you believe in **G**, who
1:21 and so your faith and hope are in **G**.
2: 4 chosen by **G** and precious to him—
2: 5 to **G** through Jesus Christ.
2: 9 a people belonging to **G**, that you
2:12 glorify **G** on the day he visits us.
2:16 for evil; live as servants of **G**.
2:19 because he is conscious of **G**.
3: 5 the past who put their hope in **G**
3:18 the unrighteous, to bring you to **G**.
3:20 who disobeyed long ago when **G** waited
3:21 of a good conscience towards **G**.
4: 6 to **G** in regard to the spirit.
4:11 as one speaking the very words of **G**.
4:11 he should do it with the strength **G**
4:11 so that in all things **G** may be
4:14 of glory and of **G** rests on you.
4:16 praise **G** that you bear that name.
4:17 to begin with the family of **G**;
4:17 who do not obey the gospel of **G**?
5: 2 because you are willing, as **G** wants
5: 5 "**G** opposes the proud but gives grace
5:10 the **G** of all grace, who called you
2Pe 1: 1 through the righteousness of our **G**
1: 2 of **G** and of Jesus our Lord.
1:21 but men spoke from **G** as they were
2: 4 For if **G** did not spare angels when
3:12 you look forward to the day of **G** and
3:15 you with the wisdom that **G** gave him.
1Jn 1: 5 **G** is light; in him there is no
3: 9 No-one who is born of **G** will continue
3: 9 because **G**'s seed remains in him; he
3:10 what is right is not a child of **G**;
3:20 For **G** is greater than our hearts,
4: 1 to see whether they are from **G**,
4: 2 has come in the flesh is from **G**,
4: 3 not acknowledge Jesus is not from **G**.
4: 4 You, dear children, are from **G** and
4: 6 We are from **G**, and whoever knows **G**
4: 6 is not from **G** does not listen to us.
4: 7 one another, for love comes from **G**.
4: 7 has been born of **G** and knows **G**.
4: 8 Whoever does not love does not know **G**
4: 8 does not know **G**, because **G** is love.
4: 9 This is how **G** showed his love among
4:10 This is love: not that we loved **G**,
4:11 Dear friends, since **G** so loved us,
4:12 No-one has ever seen **G**; but if we
4:12 **G** lives in us and his love is made
4:15 Son of **G**, **G** lives in him and he in **G**.
4:16 we know and rely on the love **G** has
4:16 **G** is love. Whoever lives in love
4:16 in love lives in **G**, and **G** in him.
4:20 If anyone says, "I love **G**," yet
4:20 cannot love **G**, whom he has not seen.
4:21 loves **G** must also love his brother.
5: 1 Jesus is the Christ is born of **G**,
5: 2 by loving **G** and carrying out his
5: 3 This is love for **G**: to obey his
5: 4 for everyone born of **G** overcomes the
5: 9 testimony of **G**, which he has given
5:10 Anyone who does not believe **G** has
5:10 testimony **G** has given about his Son.
5:11 this is the testimony: **G** has given
5:14 confidence we have in approaching **G**:
5:16 pray and **G** will give him life.
5:18 We know that anyone born of **G** does
5:18 who was born of **G** keeps him safe,
2Jn : 9 teaching of Christ does not have **G**;
3Jn : 6 their way in a manner worthy of **G**.
:11 who does what is good is from **G**.
:11 does what is evil has not seen **G**.
Jude : 4 who change the grace of our **G** into
:25 to the only **G** our Saviour be glory,
Rev 1: 1 which **G** gave him to show his
1: 6 priests to serve his **G** and Father
2: 7 life, which is in the paradise of **G**.
3: 1 spirits of **G** and the seven stars.
3: 2 deeds complete in the sight of my **G**.
3:12 make a pillar in the temple of my **G**.
3:12 I will write on him the name of my **G**
3:12 and the name of the city of my **G**,
4: 5 These are the seven spirits of **G**.
4:11 "You are worthy, our Lord and **G**,
5: 6 seven spirits of **G** sent out into all
5: 9 you purchased men for **G** from every
5:10 a kingdom and priests to serve our **G**
7: 3 foreheads of the servants of our **G**."
7:10 "Salvation belongs to our **G**, who
7:11 before the throne and worshipped **G**,
7:12 power and strength be to our **G** for
7:15 "they are before the throne of **G** and
7:17 And **G** will wipe away every tear from
9: 4 the seal of **G** on their foreheads.
10: 7 the mystery of **G** will be
11: 1 "Go and measure the temple of **G** and
11:11 breath of life from **G** entered them,
11:16 on their faces and worshipped **G**,
12: 5 snatched up to **G** and to his throne.
12: 6 to a place prepared for her by **G**,
12:10 the power and the kingdom of our **G**
12:10 who accuses them before our **G** day
13: 6 He opened his mouth to blaspheme **G**,
14: 4 as firstfruits to **G** and the Lamb.
15: 2 They held harps given them by **G**
16: 9 heat and they cursed the name of **G**,
16:19 **G** remembered Babylon the Great and
16:21 And they cursed **G** on account of the
17:17 For **G** has put it into their hearts
18: 5 and **G** has remembered her crimes.
18:20 **G** has judged here for the way she
19: 1 and glory and power belong to our **G**,
19: 4 **G**, who was seated on the throne.
19: 5 "Praise our **G**, all you his servants,
19: 9 "These are the true words of **G**.
19:10 Worship **G**! For the testimony of
19:17 together for the great supper of **G**,
20: 6 but they will be priests of **G** and of
21: 2 coming down out of heaven from **G**,
21: 3 "Now the dwelling of **G** is with men,
21: 3 They will be his people, and **G**
21: 3 will be with them and be their **G**.
21: 7 will be his **G** and he will be my son.
21:10 coming down out of heaven from **G**.
22: 1 from the throne of **G** and of the
22: 3 The throne of **G** and of the Lamb will
22: 6 The Lord, the **G** of the spirits of
22: 9 Worship **G**!"
22:18 **G** will add to him the plagues
22:19 **G** will take away from him his share

God Almighty (*Lord God Almighty, Lord God Almighty*)

Ge 17: 1 I am **G**; walk before me and be
28: 3 May **G** bless you and make you
35:11 God said to him, "I am **G**; be
43:14 may **G** grant you mercy before the man
48: 3 Jacob said to Joseph, "**G** appeared to
Ex 6: 3 to Isaac and to Jacob as **G**, but by
Ps 80: 7 Restore us, O **G**; make your face
80:14 Return to us, O **G**! Look down from
Eze 10: 5 like the voice of **G** when he speaks.
Am 5:27 says the LORD, whose name is **G**.
Rev 16:14 the battle on the great day of **G**.
19:15 of the fury of the wrath of **G**.

God blessed

Ge 1:22 **G** them and said, "Be fruitful and
1:28 **G** them and said to them, "Be
2: 3 **G** the seventh day and made it holy,
9: 1 **G** Noah and his sons, saying to them,
25:11 After Abraham's death, **G** his son

God is my rock

2Sa 22: 3 my **G**, in whom I take refuge, my
Ps 18: 2 my **G**, in whom I take refuge.

God Most High

Ge 14:18 He was priest of **G**,
14:19 by **G**, Creator of heaven and earth.
14:20 blessed be **G**, who delivered your
14:22 **G**, Creator of heaven and earth, and
Ps 7:10 My shield is **G**, who saves the
57: 2 I cry out to **G**, to God, who fulfils
78:35 Rock, that **G** was their Redeemer.
Heb 7: 1 was king of Salem and priest of **G**.

God of Abraham

Ge 31:42 If the God of my father, the **G** and
31:53 May the **G** and the God of Nahor, the
Ex 3: 6 "I am the God of your father, the **G**,
3:15 the God of your fathers—the **G**, the
3:16 the God of your fathers—the **G**,
4: 5 the God of their fathers—the **G**, the
1Ki 18:36 "O LORD, **G**, Isaac and Israel, let
2Ch 30: 6 return to the LORD, the **G**, Isaac and
Ps 47: 9 assemble as the people of the **G**,
Mt 22:32 'I am the **G**, the God of Isaac, and
Mk 12:26 'I am the **G**, the God of Isaac, and
Lk 20:37 'the **G**, and the God of Isaac, and
Ac 3:13 The **G**, Isaac and Jacob, the God of
7:32 'I am the God of your fathers, the **G**,

God of gods

Dt 10:17 For the LORD your God is **G** and Lord
Ps 136: 2 Give thanks to the **G**. His love
Da 2:47 "Surely your God is the **G** and the
11:36 say unheard-of things against the **G**.

God of heaven

Ge 24: 3 the **G** and the God of earth, that you
24: 7 "The LORD, the **G**, who brought me out
2Ch 36:23 "The LORD, the **G**, has given me all
Ezr 1: 2 "The LORD, the **G**, has given me all
5:11 "We are the servants of the **G** and
5:12 our fathers angered the **G**, he handed
6: 9 lambs for burnt offerings to the **G**,
6:10 offer sacrifices pleasing to the **G**
7:12 a teacher of the Law of the **G**
7:21 the Law of the **G**, may ask of you—
7:23 Whatever the **G** has prescribed, let
7:23 diligence for the temple of the **G**.
Ne 1: 4 and fasted and prayed before the **G**.
1: 5 I said: "O LORD, **G**, the great and
2: 4 Then I prayed to the **G**,
2:20 I answered them by saying, "The **G**
Ps 136:26 Give thanks to the **G**. His love
Da 2:18 from the **G** concerning this mystery,
2:19 Then Daniel praised the **G**
2:37 The **G** has given you dominion and
2:44 "In the time of those kings, the **G**
Jnh 1: 9 **G**, who made the sea and the land."
Rev 11:13 terrified and gave glory to the **G**.
16:11 cursed the **G** because of their pains

God of Israel

Ex 5: 1 "This is what the LORD, the **G**, says:
24:10 saw the **G**. Under his feet was
32:27 "This is what the LORD, the **G**, says:
34:23 before the Sovereign LORD, the **G**.
Nu 16: 9 Isn't it enough for you that the **G**
Jos 7:13 the **G**, says: That which is devoted
7:19 LORD, the **G**, and give him the praise.
7:20 have sinned against the LORD, the **G**.
8:30 Ebal an altar to the LORD, the **G**,
9:18 an oath to them by the LORD, the **G**.
9:19 them our oath by the LORD, the **G**,
10:40 as the LORD, the **G**, had commanded.
10:42 the LORD, the **G**, fought for Israel.
13:14 made by fire to the LORD, the **G**,
13:33 the **G**, is their inheritance, as he
14:14 because he followed the LORD, the **G**,
22:16 break faith with the **G** like this?
22:24 you have to do with the LORD, the **G**?
24: 2 "This is what the LORD, the **G**, says:
24:23 your hearts to the LORD, the **G**."
Jdg 4: 6 "The LORD, the **G**, commands you: 'Go,
5: 3 I will make music to the LORD, the **G**.
5: 5 One of Sinai, before the LORD, the **G**.
6: 8 "This is what the LORD, the **G**, says:
11:21 "Then the LORD, the **G**, gave Sihon
11:23 "Now since the LORD, the **G**, has
21: 3 "O LORD, the **G**," they cried, "why
Ru 2:12 the **G**, under whose wings you have
1Sa 1:17 "Go in peace, and may the **G** grant
2:30 "Therefore the LORD, the **G**, declares:
5: 7 "The ark of the **g** must not stay here
5: 8 shall we do with the ark of the **g**?"
5: 8 the ark of the **g** moved to Gath.
5: 8 So they moved the ark of the **G**.
5:10 "They have brought the ark of the **g**
5:11 "Send the ark of the **g** away; let it
6: 3 "If you return the ark of the **g**, do
10:18 "This is what the LORD, the **G**, says:
14:41 Saul prayed to the LORD, the **G**,
20:12 "By the LORD, the **G**, I will surely
23:10 David said, "O LORD, **G**, your
23:11 O LORD, **G**, tell your servant.
25:32 Praise be to the LORD, the **G**, who
25:34 as surely as the LORD, the **G**, lives,
2Sa 7:27 "O LORD Almighty, **G**, you have
12: 7 the **G**, says: 'I anointed you king
23: 3 The **G** spoke, the Rock of Israel said
1Ki 1:30 I swore to you by the LORD, the **G**:
1:48 said, 'Praise be to the LORD, the **G**,
8:15 "Praise be to the LORD, the **G**, who
8:17 for the Name of the LORD, the **G**.
8:20 for the Name of the LORD, the **G**.
8:23 said: "O LORD, **G**, there is no God
8:25 "Now LORD, **G**, keep for your servant
8:26 now, O **G**, let your word that you
11: 9 **G**, who had appeared to him twice.
11:31 for this is what the LORD, the **G**,
14: 7 the **G**, says: 'I raised you up from
14:13 LORD, the **G**, has found anything good.
15:30 provoked the LORD, the **G**, to anger.
16:13 provoked the LORD, the **G**, to anger by
16:26 provoked the LORD, the **G**, to anger by
16:33 provoke the LORD, the **G**, to anger
17: 1 "As the LORD, the **G**, lives, whom I
17:14 For this is what the LORD, the **G**,
22:53 provoked the LORD, the **G**, to anger,
2Ki 9: 6 "This is what the LORD, the **G**, says:
10:31 keep the law of the LORD, the **G**,
14:25 the word of the **G**, spoken
18: 5 Hezekiah trusted in the LORD, the **G**.
19:15 "O LORD, **G**, enthroned between the
19:20 "This is what the LORD, the **G**, says:
21:12 the **G**, says: I am going to bring
22:15 "This is what the LORD, the **G**, says:
22:18 'This is what the LORD, the **G**, says
1Ch 4:10 Jabez cried out to the **G**, "Oh, that
5:26 the **G** stirred up the spirit of Pul
15:12 the ark of the LORD, the **G**, to the
15:14 bring up the ark of the LORD, the **G**.
16: 4 and to praise the LORD, the **G**:
16:36 Praise be to the LORD, the **G**, from
22: 6 build a house for the LORD, the **G**.
23:25 "Since the LORD, the **G**, has granted
24:19 the LORD, the **G**, had commanded him.
28: 4 "Yet the LORD, the **G**, chose me from
2Ch 2:12 "Praise be to the LORD, the **G**, who
6: 4 "Praise be to the LORD, the **G**, who
6: 7 for the Name of the LORD, the **G**.
6:10 for the Name of the LORD, the **G**.
6:14 He said: "O LORD, **G**, there is no
6:16 "Now LORD, **G**, keep for your servant
6:17 now, O LORD, **G**, let your word that
11:16 the **G**, followed the Levites to
13: 5 Don't you know that the LORD, the **G**,
15: 4 they turned to the LORD, the **G**,
15:13 whho would not seek the LORD, the **G**,
20:19 praised LORD, the **G**, with a very
29: 7 offerings at the sanctuary to the **G**.
29:10 a covenant with the LORD, the **G**,
30: 1 the Passover to the LORD, the **G**.
30: 5 the Passover to the LORD, the **G**.
32:17 insulting the LORD, the **G**, and saying
33:16 told Judah to serve the LORD, the **G**.
33:18 in the name of the LORD, the **G**, are
34:23 "This is what the LORD, the **G**, says:
34:26 'This is what the LORD, the **G**, says
36:13 would not turn to the LORD, the **G**.
Ezr 1: 3 the **G**, the God who is in Jerusalem.
3: 2 altar of the **G** to sacrifice burnt
4: 1 a temple for the LORD, the **G**,
4: 3 the **G**, as King Cyrus, the king of
5: 1 name of the **G**, who was over them.
6:14 of the **G** and the decrees of Cyrus,
6:21 in order to seek the LORD, the **G**.
6:22 the work on the house of God, the **G**.
7: 6 which the LORD, the **G**, had given.
7:15 **G**, whose dwelling is in Jerusalem,
8:35 sacrificed burnt offerings to the **G**
9: 4 trembled at the words of the **G**
9:15 O LORD, **G**, you are righteous! We
Ps 41:13 Praise be to the LORD, the **G**, from
59: 5 O LORD God Almighty, the **G**, rouse
68: 8 the One of Sinai, before God, the **G**.
68:35 the **G** gives power and strength
69: 6 be put to shame because of me, O **G**.
72:18 Praise be to the LORD God, the **G**,
106:48 Praise be to the LORD, the **G**, from
Isa 17: 6 declares the LORD, the **G**.
21:10 from the LORD Almighty, from the **G**.
21:17 The LORD, the **G**, has spoken.
24:15 exalt the name of the LORD, the **G**,
29:23 and will stand in awe of the **G**.
37:16 "O LORD Almighty, **G**, enthroned
37:21 "This is what the LORD, the **G**, says:
41:17 I, the **G**, will not forsake them.
45: 3 LORD, the **G**, who summons you by name.
48: 1 invoke the **G**—but not in truth or
48: 2 rely on the **G**—the LORD Almighty
52:12 you, the **G** will be your rear guard.
Jer 7: 3 This is what the LORD Almighty, the **G**
7:21 the **G**, says: Go ahead, add your
9:15 the **G**, says: "See, I will make this
11: 3 the **G**, says: 'Cursed is the man who
13:12 'This is what the LORD, the **G**, says:
16: 9 the **G**, says: Before your eyes and in
19: 3 the **G**, says: Listen! I am going to
19:15 the **G**, says: 'Listen! I am going to
21: 4 'This is what the LORD, the **G**, says:
23: 2 the **G**, says to the shepherds who
24: 5 "This is what the LORD, the **G**, says:
25:15 This is what the LORD, the **G**, said
25:27 the **G**, says: Drink, get drunk and
27: 4 the **G**, says: "Tell this to your
27:21 the **G**, says about the things that
28: 2 the **G**, says: 'I will break the yoke
28:14 This is what the LORD Almighty, the **G**
29: 4 This is what the LORD Almighty, the **G**
29: 8 the **G**, says: "Do not let the
29:21 This is what the LORD Almighty, the **G**
29:25 the **G**, says: You sent letters in
30: 2 "This is what the LORD, the **G**, says:
31:23 This is what the LORD Almighty, the **G**
32:14 the **G**, says: Take these documents,
32:15 the **G**, says: Houses, fields and
32:36 this is what the LORD, the **G**, says:
33: 4 For this is what the LORD, the **G**,
34: 2 "This is what the LORD, the **G**, says:
34:13 "This is what the LORD, the **G**, says:
35:13 the **G**, says: Go and tell the men of
35:17 the **G**, says: 'Listen! I am going to
35:18 the **G**, says: 'You have obeyed the
35:19 the **G**, says: 'Jonadab son of Recab
37: 7 "This is what the LORD, the **G**, says:
38:17 the **G**, says: 'If you surrender to
39:16 the **G**, says: I am about to fulfil my
42: 9 "This is what the LORD, the **G**, to
42:15 the **G**, says: 'If you are determined
42:18 This is what the LORD Almighty, the **G**
43:10 the **G**, says: I will send for my
44: 2 the **G**, says: You saw the great
44: 7 the **G**, says: Why bring such great
44:11 the **G**, says: I am determined to
44:25 This is what the LORD Almighty, the **G**
45: 2 "This is what the LORD, the **G**, says
46:25 The LORD Almighty, the **G**, says: "I
48: 1 the **G**, says: "Woe to Nebo, for it
50:18 the **G**, says: "I will punish the king
51:33 This is what the LORD Almighty, the **G**
Eze 8: 4 before me was the glory of the **G**,
9: 3 Now the glory of the **G** went up from
10:19 the glory of the **G** was above them.
10:20 beneath the **G** by the Kebar River,
11:22 the glory of the **G** was above them.

Eze 43: 2 I saw the glory of the **G** coming from
44: 2 LORD, the **G**, has entered through it.
Zep 2: 9 the **G**, "surely Moab will become like
Mal 2:16 "I hate divorce," says the LORD **G**,
Mt 15:31 And they praised the **G**.
Lk 1:68 "Praise be to the Lord, the **G**,

God of Jacob

Ex 3: 6 Abraham, the God of Isaac and the **G**.
3:15 Isaac and the **G**—has sent me to you.
4: 5 and the **G**—has appeared to you."
2Sa 23: 1 anointed by the **G**, Israel's singer
Ps 20: 1 may the name of the **G** protect you.
24: 6 seek him, who seek your face, O **G**.
46: 7 the **G** is our fortress
46:11 the **G** is our fortress
75: 9 ever; I will sing praise to the **G**.
76: 6 At your rebuke, O **G**, both horse and
81: 1 our strength; shout aloud to the **G**!
81: 4 for Israel, an ordinance of the **G**.
84: 8 LORD God Almighty; listen to me, O **G**.
94: 7 does not see; the **G** pays no heed."
114: 7 the Lord, at the presence of the **G**,
146: 5 Blessed is he whose help is the **G**,
Isa 2: 3 of the LORD, to the house of the **G**.
Mic 4: 2 of the LORD, to the house of the **G**.
Mt 22:32 the God of Isaac, and the **G**'? He
Mk 12:26 the God of Isaac, and the **G**'?
Lk 20:37 and the God of Isaac, and the **G**'.
Ac 7:46 provide a dwelling-place for the **G**.

God of your father

Ge 26:24 him and said, "I am the **G** Abraham.
28:13 the **G** Abraham and the God of Isaac.
31:29 but last night the **G** said to me,
43:23 "Don't be afraid. Your God, the **G**,
46: 3 "I am God, the **G**," he said. "Do not
50:17 the sins of the servants of the **G**.
Ex 3: 6 he said, "I am the **G**, the God of
2Ki 20: 5 'This is what the LORD, the **G** David,
1Ch 28: 9 my son Solomon, acknowledge the **G**,
2Ch 21:12 "This is what the LORD, the **G** David,
Isa 38: 5 'This is what the LORD, the **G** David,

God of your fathers

Ex 3:13 'The **G** has sent me to you,' and they
3:15 'The LORD, the **G**—the God of Abraham,
3:16 'The LORD, the **G**—the God of Abraham,
Dt 1:11 May the LORD, the **G**, increase you a
1:21 of it as the LORD, the **G**, told you.
4: 1 that the LORD, the **G**, is giving you.
6: 3 as the LORD, the **G**, promised you.
12: 1 land that the LORD, the **G**, has given
27: 3 as the LORD, the **G**, promised you.
Jos 18: 3 land that the LORD, the **G**, has given
2Ch 13:12 do not fight against the LORD, the **G**,
28: 9 "Because the LORD, the **G**, was angry
29: 5 the temple of the LORD, the **G**.
Ezr 8:28 offering to the LORD, the **G**.
10:11 confession to the LORD, the **G**,
Ac 7:32 'I am the **G**, the God of Abraham,

God our father

Ro 1: 7 from **G** and from the Lord Jesus
1Co 1: 3 Grace and peace to you from **G** and
2Co 1: 2 Grace and peace to you from **G** and
Gal 1: 3 Grace and peace to you from **G** and
Eph 1: 2 Grace and peace to you from **G** and
Php 1: 2 Grace and peace to you from **G** and
Col 1: 2 Grace and peace to you from **G**.
2Th 1: 1 in **G** and the Lord Jesus Christ:
2:16 our Lord Jesus Christ himself and **G**,
Phm : 3 Grace to you and peace from **G** and
Jas 1:27 Religion that **G** accepts as pure and

God the Father

Jn 6:27 On him **G** has placed his seal of
1Co 15:24 when he hands over the kingdom to **G**
Gal 1: 1 **G**, who raised him from the dead—
Eph 5:20 always giving thanks to **G** for
6:23 from **G** and the Lord Jesus Christ.
Php 2:11 Christ is Lord, to the glory of **G**.
Col 3:17 giving thanks to **G** through him.
1Th 1: 1 in **G** and the Lord Jesus Christ:
2Th 1: 2 Grace and peace to you from **G** and
1Ti 1: 2 from **G** and Christ Jesus our Lord.
2Ti 1: 2 from **G** and Christ Jesus our Lord.
Tit 1: 4 from **G** and Christ Jesus our Saviour.
1Pe 1: 2 according to the foreknowledge of **G**,
2Pe 1:17 glory from **G** when the voice came to
2Jn : 3 Grace, mercy and peace from **G** and
Jude : 1 loved by **G** and kept by Jesus Christ:

God's (God, *God's wrath*)

Ge 6:11 Now the earth was corrupt in **G** sight
28:22 set up as a pillar will be **G** house,
Ex 18:15 people come to me to seek **G** will.
18:16 inform them of **G** decrees and laws."
Dt 21:23 is hung on a tree is under **G** curse.
1Sa 5:11 **G** hand was very heavy upon it.
14:45 for he did this today with **G** help.
2Sa 9: 3 Saul to whom I can show **G** kindness?"
1Ch 5:22 slain, because the battle was **G**.
2Ch 1: 3 for **G** Tent of Meeting was there,
4:19 furnishings that were in **G** temple:
5: 1 them in the treasuries of **G** temple.
20:15 For the battle is not yours, but **G**.
24:18 Because of their guilt, **G** anger came
31:21 in the service of **G** temple
32:12 this **g** high places and altars,
33: 7 he had made and put it in **G** temple,
35: 8 the administrators of **G** temple, gave
35:22 to what Neco had said at **G** command
36:13 had made him take an oath in **G** name.
36:16 they mocked **G** messengers, despised
36:19 They set fire to **G** temple and broke
Ne 13:25 I made them take an oath in **G** name
Job 6: 4 **G** terrors are marshalled against me.
9:34 someone to remove **G** rod from me,
13: 7 Will you speak wickedly on **G** behalf?
15: 8 Do you listen in on **G** council? Do
15:11 Are **G** consolations not enough for
15:30 breath of **G** mouth will carry him
29: 4 when **G** intimate friendship blessed
33:26 he sees **G** face and shouts for joy;
36: 2 is more to be said on **G** behalf.
37: 5 **G** voice thunders in marvellous ways;
37:14 Job; stop and consider **G** wonders.
38:33 Can you set up ⌊**G**⌋ dominion over
40: 9 Do you have an arm like **G**, and can
Ps 52: 8 **G** unfailing love for ever and ever.
61: 7 May he be enthroned in **G** presence
63:11 who swear by **G** name will praise him,
69:30 I will praise **G** name in song and
78:10 they did not keep **G** covenant and
78:31 **G** anger rose against them; he put to
114: 2 Judah became **G** sanctuary, Israel his
Ecc 9: 1 and what they do are in **G** hands,
Mt 5:34 by heaven, for it is **G** throne;
22:21 is Caesar's, and to God what is **G**."
23:22 he who swears by heaven swears by **G**
Mk 3:35 Whoever does **G** will is my brother
12:17 is Caesar's and to God what is **G**.
Lk 3: 6 all mankind will see **G** salvation.'"
7:29 acknowledged that **G** way was right,
7:30 rejected **G** purpose for themselves,
8:21 who hear **G** word and put it into
16:15 among men is detestable in **G** sight.
19:44 the time of **G** coming to you."
20:25 is Caesar's, and to God what is **G**."
20:36 They are **G** children, since they are
Jn 3:18 in the name of **G** one and only Son.
7:17 If anyone chooses to do **G** will, he
10:36 because I said, 'I am **G** Son'?
11: 4 No, it is for **G** glory so that **G** Son
Ac 2:23 handed over to you by **G** set purpose
4:19 right in **G** sight to obey you rather
6: 8 Now Stephen, a man full of **G** grace
7:46 who enjoyed **G** favour and asked that
13:36 "For when David had served **G** purpose
17:29 "Therefore since we are **G** offspring,
18:21 "I will come back if it is **G** will.
20:24 testifying to the gospel of **G** grace.
23: 4 "You dare to insult **G** high priest?
26:22 I have had **G** help to this very day,
28:28 I want you to know that **G** salvation
Ro 1:10 I pray that now at last by **G** will
1:20 For since the creation of the world **G**
1:32 Although they know **G** righteous
Ro 2: 2 Now we know that **G** judgment against
2: 3 think you will escape **G** judgment?
2: 4 not realising that **G** kindness leads
2:13 law who are righteous in **G** sight,
2:24 is written: "**G** name is blasphemed
3: 3 of faith nullify **G** faithfulness?
3: 5 if our unrighteousness brings out **G**
3: 7 "If my falsehood enhances **G**
5:10 For if, when we were **G** enemies, we
5:15 how much more did **G** grace and the
5:17 **G** abundant provision of grace
7:22 my inner being I delight in **G** law
7:25 in my mind am a slave to **G** law
8: 7 It does not submit to **G** law, nor
8:16 our spirit that we are **G** children.
8:27 saints in accordance with **G** will.
9: 6 is not as though **G** word had failed.
9: 8 natural children who are **G** children,
9:11 **G** purpose in election might stand:
9:16 desire or effort, but on **G** mercy.
10: 3 did not submit to **G** righteousness.
11: 4 what was **G** answer to him? "I have
11:29 for **G** gifts and his call are
11:31 mercy as a result of **G** mercy to you.
12: 1 brothers, in view of **G** mercy
12: 2 approve what **G** will is—his good,
12:13 Share with **G** people who are in need.
13: 4 For he is **G** servant to do you good.
13: 4 He is **G** servant, an agent of wrath
13: 6 for the authorities are **G** servants,
14:10 all stand before **G** judgment seat.
15: 8 of the Jews on behalf of **G** truth,
15:32 that by **G** will I may come to you
1Co 2: 5 on men's wisdom, but on **G** power.
2: 7 No, we speak of **G** secret wisdom, a
3: 9 For we are **G** fellow-workers; you are
3: 9 you are **G** field, **G** building.
3:16 that you yourselves are **G** temple
3:16 and that **G** Spirit lives in you?
3:17 If anyone destroys **G** temple, God
3:17 God will destroy him; for **G** temple
3:19 world is foolishness in **G** sight.
7:19 Keeping **G** commands is what counts.
9:21 **G** law but am under Christ's law),
11:19 show which of you have **G** approval.
16: 1 the collection for **G** people:
2Co 1:12 wisdom but according to **G** grace.
4: 1 Therefore, since through **G** mercy we
6: 1 **G** fellow-workers we urge you not to
6: 1 you not to receive **G** grace in vain.
6: 2 now is the time of **G** father
8: 5 then to us in keeping with **G** will.
9:12 supplying the needs of **G** people
13: 4 weakness, yet he lives by **G** power.
13: 4 we are weak in him, yet by **G** power
Eph 1: 7 with the riches of **G** grace
1:14 of those who are **G** possession
2:10 For we are **G** workmanship, created in
2:19 **G** people and members of **G** household,
3: 2 **G** grace that was given to me for you,
3: 5 to **G** holy apostles and prophets.
3: 7 by the gift of **G** grace given me
3: 8 less than the least of all **G** people,
4:12 to prepare **G** people for works of
5: 3 are improper for **G** holy people.
Php 1: 7 all of you share in **G** grace with me.
Col 1: 6 understood **G** grace in all its truth.
3:12 Therefore, as **G** chosen people, holy
1Th 2:14 became imitators of **G** churches in
3: 2 our brother and **G** fellow-worker
4: 3 is **G** will that you should be
5:18 is **G** will for you in Christ Jesus.
2Th 1: 4 Therefore, among **G** churches we boast
1: 5 All this is evidence that **G** judgment
2: 4 he sets himself up in **G** temple
3: 5 **G** love and Christ's perseverance.
1Ti 1: 4 than **G** work—which is by faith.
3: 5 how can he take care of **G** church?)
3:15 conduct themselves in **G** household,
6: 1 so that **G** name and our teaching may
2Ti 2: 9 But **G** word is not chained.
2:19 Nevertheless, **G** solid foundation
Tit 1: 1 Christ for the faith of **G** elect
1: 7 an overseer is entrusted with **G** work
Heb 1: 3 The Son is the radiance of **G** glory
1: 6 says, "Let all **G** angels worship him.

Heb 3: 2 Moses was faithful in all **G** house.
3: 5 as a servant in all **G** house,
3: 6 faithful as a son over **G** house
4:10 for anyone who enters **G** rest also
4:13 all creation is hidden from **G** sight.
5:12 truths of **G** word all over again.
9:24 now to appear for us in **G** presence.
11: 3 universe was formed at **G** command,
13:24 your leaders and all **G** people
Jas 2:23 and he was called **G** friend.
3: 9 who have been made in **G** likeness.
1Pe 1: 1 apostle of Jesus Christ, To **G** elect
1: 5 through faith are shielded by **G** power
2:15 For it is **G** will that by doing good
3: 4 which is of great worth in **G** sight.
3:17 is better, if it is **G** will, to
3:22 into heaven and is at **G** right hand
4:10 **G** grace in its various forms.
4:19 those who suffer according to **G** will
5: 2 Be shepherds of **G** flock that is
5: 6 therefore, under **G** mighty hand
2Pe 3: 5 ago by **G** word the heavens existed
1Jn 2: 5 if anyone obeys his word, **G** love is
3: 9 because **G** seed remains in him; he
5: 9 man's testimony, but **G** testimony is
Jude :21 Keep yourselves in **G** love as you
Rev 3:14 witness, the ruler of **G** creation.
11:19 **G** temple in heaven was opened, and
12:17 who obey **G** commandments
14:10 will drink of the wine of **G** fury
14:12 the saints who obey **G** commandments
17:17 rule, until **G** words are fulfilled.
20: 9 camp of **G** people, the city he loves.
22:21 of the Lord Jesus be with **G** people

God's wrath

Job 20:28 rushing waters on the day of **G**.
Jn 3:36 not see life, for **G** remains on him."
Ro 2: 5 against yourself for the day of **G**,
5: 9 we be saved from **G** through him!
12:19 my friends, but leave room for **G**,
Eph 5: 6 **G** comes on those who are disobedient.
Rev 14:19 them into the great winepress of **G**.
15: 1 because with them **G** is completed.
16: 1 the seven bowls of **G** on the earth."

God-breathed (Breath, God)

2Ti 3:16 All Scripture is **G** and is useful for

Goddess (God)

1Ki 11: 5 He followed Ashtoreth the **g** of the
11:33 Ashtoreth the **g** of the Sidonians,
2Ki 23:13 the vile **g** of the Sidonians,
Ac 19:27 great **g** Artemis will be discredited,
19:27 and the **g** herself, who is worshipped
19:37 robbed temples nor blasphemed our **g**.

God-fearing (Fear, God)

Ecc 8:12 **G** men, who are reverent before God.
Ac 2: 5 Now there were staying in Jerusalem **G**
10: 2 all his family were devout and **G**;
10:22 He is a righteous and **G** man, who is
13:26 of Abraham, and you **G** Gentiles,
13:50 the Jews incited the **G** women of high
17: 4 as did a large number of **G** Greeks
17:17 with the Jews and the **G** Greeks,

God-haters (God, Hate)

Ro 1:30 slanderers, **G**, insolent, arrogant

Godless (Godlessness)

Job 8:13 God; so perishes the hope of the **g**.
13:16 no **g** man would dare come before him!
15:34 For the company of the **g** will be
20: 5 the joy of the **g** lasts but a moment.
27: 8 For what hope has the **g** when he is
34:30 to keep a **g** man from ruling, from
36:13 "The **g** in heart harbour resentment;
Pr 11: 9 With his mouth the **g** destroys his
Isa 10: 6 I send him against a **g** nation, I
33:14 terrified; trembling grips the **g**:
Jer 23:11 "Both prophet and priest are **g**; even
1Ti 4: 7 Have nothing to do with **g** myths and
6:20 Turn away from **g** chatter and the
2Ti 2:16 Avoid **g** chatter, because those who
Heb 12:16 or is **g** like Esau, who for a single
Jude : 4 They are **g** men, who change the grace

Godlessness (Godless)

Ro 1:18 from heaven against all the **g**
11:26 Zion; he will turn **g** away from Jacob.

Godliness (God)

Ac 3:12 as if by our own power or **g** we had
1Ti 2: 2 quiet lives in all **g** and holiness.
3:16 the mystery of **g** is great:
4: 8 but **g** has value for all things,
6: 5 that **g** is a means to financial gain.
6: 6 **g** with contentment is great gain.
6:11 and pursue righteousness, **g**, faith,
2Ti 3: 5 having a form of **g** but denying its
Tit 1: 1 of the truth that leads to **g**—
2Pe 1: 3 **g** through our knowledge of him who
1: 6 and to perseverance, **g**;
1: 7 to **g**, brotherly kindness; and to

Godly (God)

Ps 4: 3 LORD has set apart the **g** for himself;
12: 1 Help, LORD, for the **g** are no more;
32: 6 Therefore let everyone who is **g** pray
Mic 7: 2 The **g** have been swept from the land;
Mal 2:15 Because he was seeking **g** offspring
Jn 9:31 to the **g** man who does his will.
Ac 8: 2 **G** men buried Stephen and mourned
2Co 7:10 **G** sorrow brings repentance that
7:11 See what this **g** sorrow has produced
11: 2 jealous for you with a **g** jealous
1Ti 4: 7 rather, train yourself to be **g**.
6: 3 Lord Jesus Christ and to **g** teaching,
2Ti 3:12 everyone who wants to live a **g** life
Tit 2:12 and **g** lives in this present age,
2Pe 2: 9 the Lord knows how to rescue **g** men
3:11 You ought to live holy and **g** lives

Gods (God, *God of Gods*, *Other gods*)

Ge 31:19 stole her father's household **g**.
31:30 But why did you steal my **g**?"
31:32 if you find anyone who has your **g**,
31:32 know that Rachel had stolen the **g**.
31:34 Now Rachel had taken the household **g**
31:35 but could not find the household **g**.
35: 2 "Get rid of the foreign **g** you have
35: 4 they gave Jacob all the foreign **g**
Ex 12:12 judgment on all the **g** of Egypt.
15:11 "Who among the **g** is like you,
20:23 Do not make any **g** to be alongside me;
20:23 yourselves **g** of silver or **g** of gold.
23:24 Do not bow down before their **g** or
23:32 covenant with them or with their **g**.
23:33 **g** will certainly be a snare to you."
32: 1 make us **g** who will go before us.
32: 4 Then they said, "These are your **g**, O
32: 8 'These are your **g**, O Israel, who
32:23 They said to me, 'Make us **g** who will
32:31 They have made themselves **g** of gold.
34:15 to their **g** and sacrifice to them,
34:16 prostitute themselves to their **g**,
Lev 19: 4 "'Do not turn to idols or make **g** of
Nu 25: 2 them to the sacrifices to their **g**.
25: 2 ate and bowed down before these **g**.
33: 4 LORD had brought judgment on their **g**.
Dt 4: 7 so great as to have their **g** near
4:28 There you will worship man-made **g** of
6:14 the **g** of the people around you
7: 4 from following me to serve other **g**,
7:16 do not serve their **g**, for that will
7:25 The images of their **g** you are to
12: 2 are dispossessing worship their **g**.
12: 3 cut down the idols of their **g** and
12:30 ensnared by enquiring about their **g**,
12:30 serve their **g**? We will do the same."
12:31 because in worshipping their **g**, they
12:31 the fire as sacrifices to their **g**.
13: 2 (**g** you have not known)
13: 6 (**g** that neither you nor your fathers
13: 7 **g** of the peoples around you, whether
13:13 (**g** you have not known),
Dt 20:18 they do in worshipping their **g**,
28:36 **g** of wood and stone.
28:64 **g** of wood and stone, which neither
29:18 and worship the **g** of those nations;
29:26 **g** they did not know, **g** he had not
31:16 **g** of the land they are entering.
32:16 him jealous with their foreign **g**
32:17 **g** they had not know, **g** that
32:17 **g** your fathers did not fear.
32:37 He will say: "Now where are their **g**,
32:38 the **g** who ate the fat of their
Jos 23: 7 names of their **g** or swear by them.
24:14 Throw away the **g** your forefathers
24:15 whether the **g** your forefathers
24:15 or the **g** of the Amorites, in whose
24:20 the LORD and serve foreign **g**,
24:23 "throw away the foreign **g** that are
Jdg 2: 3 Now therefore I tell you that I will
2:12 various **g** of the peoples around them
3: 6 to their sons, and served their **g**.
5: 8 they chose new **g**, war came to the
6:10 not worship the **g** of the Amorites,
9: 9 by which both **g** and men are honoured,
9:13 which cheers both **g** and men, to hold
10: 6 and the **g** of Aram, the **g** of Sidon,
10: 6 **g** of Moab, the **g** of the Ammonites
10: 6 the **g** of the Philistines.
10:14 Go and cry out to the **g** you have
10:16 they got rid of the foreign **g** among
18:14 other household **g**, a carved image
18:17 the ephod, the other household **g**
18:18 the ephod, the other household **g**
18:20 the other household **g** and the carved
18:24 He replied, "You took the **g** I made,
Ru 1:15 going back to her people and her **g**.
1Sa 4: 8 us from the hand of these mighty **g**?
4: 8 They are the **g** who struck the
6: 5 from you and your **g** and your land.
7: 3 rid yourselves of the foreign **g**
17:43 Philistine cursed David by his **g**.
2Sa 7:23 and their **g** from before your people,
1Ki 11: 2 turn your hearts after their **g**.
11: 8 and offered sacrifices to their **g**.
12:28 Here are your **g**, O Israel, who
19: 2 "May the **g** deal with me, be it ever
20:10 "May the **g** deal with me, be it ever
20:23 him, "Their **g** are **g** of the hills.
2Ki 17:29 each national group made its own **g**
17:31 and Anammelech, the **g** of Sepharvaim.
17:33 but they also served their own **g** in
18:34 Where are the **g** of Hamath and Arpad?
18:34 Arpad? Where are the **g** of Sepharvaim,
18:35 Who of all the **g** of these countries
19:12 Did the **g** of the nations that were
19:12 the **g** of Gozan, Haran, Rezeph,
19:18 They have thrown their **g** into the
19:18 for they were not **g** but only wood
23:24 the household **g**, the idols and all
1Ch 5:25 to the **g** of the peoples of the land,
10:10 his armour in the temple of their **g**
14:12 The Philistines had abandoned their **g**
16:25 he is to be feared above all **g**.
16:26 For all the **g** of the nations are
2Ch 13: 8 that Jeroboam made to be your **g**.
13: 9 become a priest of what are not **g**.
25:14 back the **g** of the people of Seir.
25:14 He set them up as his own **g**, bowed
25:15 "Why do you consult this people's **g**,
25:20 because they sought the **g** of Edom.
28:23 He offered sacrifices to the **g** of
28:23 "Since the **g** of the kings of Aram
32:13 Were the **g** of those nations ever
32:14 Who of all the **g** of these nations
32:17 "Just as the **g** of the peoples of the
32:19 **g** of the other peoples of the world
33:15 He got rid of the foreign **g** and
Ps 4: 2 love delusions and seek false **g**?
40: 4 to those who turn aside to false **g**.
82: 1 he gives judgment among the "**g**":
82: 6 "I said, 'You are "**g**"; you are all
86: 8 Among the **g** there is none like you,
95: 3 God, the great King above all **g**.
96: 4 he is to be feared above all **g**.
96: 5 For all the **g** of the nations are
97: 7 in idols—worship him, all you **g**!
97: 9 you are exalted far above all **g**.

Ps 106:28 sacrifices offered to lifeless **g**;
135: 5 that our Lord is greater than all **g**.
138: 1 the "**g**" I will sing your praise.
Isa 21: 9 its **g** lie shattered on the ground!'"
36:19 Where are the **g** of Hamath and Arpad?
36:19 Where are the **g** of Sepharvaim? Have
36:20 Who of all the **g** of these countries
37:12 Did the **g** of the nations that were
37:12 the **g** of Gozan, Haran, Rezeph
37:19 They have thrown their **g** into the
37:19 for they were not **g** but only wood
41:23 so that we may know you are **g**.
42:17 say to images, 'You are our **g**,'
45:20 who pray to **g** that cannot save.
Jer 2:11 Has a nation ever changed its **g**?
2:11 (Yet they are not **g** at all.)
2:25 I love foreign **g**, and I must go
2:28 Where then are the **g** you made for
2:28 have as many **g** as you have towns,
3:13 scattered your favours to foreign **g**
3:24 From our youth shameful **g** have
5: 7 me and sworn by **g** that are not **g**.
5:19 served foreign **g** in your own land,
10:11 "Tell them this: 'These **g**, who did
11:12 to the **g** to whom they burn incense,
11:13 You have as many **g** as you have towns,
13:25 forgotten me and trusted in false **g**.
16:19 possessed nothing but false **g**,
16:20 Do men make their own **g**? Yes, but
16:20 own **g**? Yes, but they are not **g**!"
19: 4 and made this a place of foreign **g**;
19: 4 have burned sacrifices in it to **g**
43:12 to the temples of the **g** of Egypt;
43:12 temples and take their **g** captive.
43:13 the temples of the **g** of Egypt.'"
46:25 on Pharaoh, on Egypt and her **g** and
48:35 burn incense to their **g**,"
Da 2:11 **g**, and they do not live among men."
3:12 They neither serve your **g** nor
3:14 that you do not serve my **g** or
3:18 that we will not serve your **g** or
3:25 fourth looks like a son of the **g**."
4: 8 the spirit of the holy **g** is in him.)
4: 9 the spirit of the holy **g** is in you,
4:18 the spirit of the holy **g** is in you."
5: 4 they praised the **g** of gold and
5:11 has the spirit of the holy **g** in him.
5:11 and wisdom like that of the **g**.
5:14 I have heard that the spirit of the **g**
5:23 You praised the **g** of silver and gold,
11: 8 He will also seize their **g**, their
11:37 He will show no regard for the **g** of
Hos 14: 3 We will never again say 'our **g**' to
Am 2: 4 have been led astray by false **g**
2: 4 the **g** their ancestors followed,
Mic 4: 5 may walk in the name of their **g**;
Na 1:14 that are in the temple of your **g**.
Zep 1: 9 fill the temple of their **g** with
2:11 he destroys all the **g** of the land.
Jn 10:34 your Law, 'I have said you are **g**'?
10:35 If he called them '**g**', to whom the
Ac 7:40 They told Aaron, 'Make us **g** who will
14:11 "The **g** have come down to us in human
17:18 seems to be advocating foreign **g**.
19:26 that man-made **g** are no **g** at all.
28:11 of the twin **g** Castor and Pollux.
1Co 8: 5 For even if there are so-called **g**,
8: 5 there are many "**g**" and many "lords
Gal 4: 8 to those who by nature are not **g**.

Gog

1Ch 5: 4 his son, **G** his son, Shimei his son,
Eze 38: 2 "Son of man, set your face against **G**,
38: 3 **G**, chief prince of Meshech and Tubal.
38:14 son of man, prophesy and say to **G**:
38:16 In days to come, O **G**, I will bring
38:18 When **G** attacks the land of Israel,
38:21 I will summon a sword against **G** on
39: 1 "Son of man, prophesy against **G** and
39: 1 **G**, chief prince of Meshech and Tubal.
39:11 "On that day I will give **G** a burial
39:11 because **G** and all his hordes will be
Rev 20: 8 corners of the earth—**G** and Magog—

Goiim

Ge 14: 1 king of Elam and Tidal king of **G**
14: 9 Tidal king of **G**, Amraphel king of

Golan

Dt 4:43 and **G** in Bashan, for the Manassites.
Jos 20: 8 **G** in Bashan in the tribe of Manasseh.
21:27 **G** in Bashan (a city of refuge for
1Ch 6:71 **G** in Bashan and also Ashtaroth,

Gold (Gold-covered, Golden, Goldsmith, Goldsmiths, *Silver and gold*)

Ge 2:11 land of Havilah, where there is **g**.
2:12 (The **g** of that land is good;
24:22 the man took out a **g** nose ring
24:22 **g** bracelets weighing ten shekels.
24:53 the servant brought out **g** and silver
41:42 and put a **g** chain around his neck.
44: 8 or **g** from your master's house?
Ex 20:23 gods of silver or gods of **g**.
25: 3 from them: **g**, silver and bronze;
25:11 Overlay it with pure **g**, both inside
25:11 and make a **g** moulding around it.
25:12 Cast four **g** rings for it and fasten
25:13 acacia wood and overlay them with **g**.
25:17 "Make an atonement cover of pure **g**
25:18 make two cherubim out of hammered **g**
25:24 Overlay it with pure **g** and make a **g**
25:25 and put a **g** moulding on the rim.
25:26 Make four **g** rings for the table and
25:28 **g** and carry the table with them.
25:29 make its plates and dishes of pure **g**,
25:31 "Make a lampstand of pure **g** and
25:36 lampstand, hammered out of pure **g**.
25:38 and trays are to be of pure **g**.
25:39 A talent of pure **g** is to be used for
26: 6 make fifty **g** clasps and use them to
26:29 Overlay the frames with **g** and make **g**
26:29 Also overlay the crossbars with **g**.
26:32 Hang it with **g** hooks on four posts
26:32 wood overlaid with **g** and standing
26:37 Make **g** hooks for this curtain and
26:37 of acacia wood overlaid with **g**.
28: 5 Make them use **g**, and blue, purple
28: 6 "Make the ephod of **g**, and of blue,
28: 8 with the ephod and made with **g**,
28:11 the stones in **g** filigree
28:13 Make **g** filigree settings .
28:14 two braided chains of pure **g**, like a
28:15 Make it like the ephod: of **g**, and of
28:20 Mount them in **g** filigree settings.
28:22 chains of pure **g**, like a rope.
28:23 Make two **g** rings for it and fasten
28:24 Fasten the two **g** chains to the rings
28:26 Make two **g** rings and attach them to
28:27 Make two more **g** rings and attach
28:33 the robe, with **g** bells between them.
28:34 The **g** bells and the pomegranates are
28:36 "Make a plate of pure **g** and engrave
30: 3 pure **g**, and make a **g** moulding
30: 4 Make two **g** rings for the altar below
30: 5 acacia wood and overlay them with **g**.
31: 4 for work in **g**, silver and bronze,
31: 8 the pure **g** lampstand and all its
32: 2 Aaron answered them, "Take off the **g**
32:24 I told them, 'Whoever has any **g**
32:24 Then they gave me the **g**, and I
32:31 They have made themselves gods of **g**.
35: 5 an offering of **g**, silver and bronze;
35:22 came and brought **g** jewellery of all
35:22 **g** as a wave offering to the LORD.
35:32 for work in **g**, silver and bronze,
36:13 they made fifty **g** clasps and used
36:34 They overlaid the frames with **g** and
36:34 made **g** rings to hold the crossbars.
36:34 also overlaid the crossbars with **g**.
36:36 for it and overlaid them with **g**.
36:36 They made **g** hooks for them and cast
36:38 their bands with **g** and made their
37: 2 He overlaid it with pure **g**, both
37: 2 and made a **g** moulding around it.
37: 3 He cast four **g** rings for it and
37: 4 wood and overlaid them with **g**.
37: 6 He made the atonement cover of pure **g**
Ex 37: 7 hammered **g** at the ends of the cover.
37:11 they overlaid it with pure **g** and
37:11 made a **g** moulding around it.
37:12 and put a **g** moulding on the rim.
37:13 They cast four **g** rings for the table
37:15 wood and were overlaid with **g**.
37:16 they made from pure **g** the articles
37:17 They made the lampstand of pure **g**
37:22 lampstand, hammered out of pure **g**.
37:23 wick trimmers and trays, of pure **g**.
37:24 from one talent of pure **g**.
37:26 **g**, and made a **g** moulding around it.
37:27 They made two **g** rings below the
37:28 wood and overlaid them with **g**.
38:24 The total amount of the **g** from the
39: 2 They made the ephod of **g**, and of
39: 3 They hammered out thin sheets of **g**
39: 5 with the ephod and made with **g**,
39: 6 They mounted the onyx stones in **g**
39: 8 They made it like the ephod: of **g**,
39:13 were mounted in **g** filigree settings.
39:15 chains of pure **g**, like a rope.
39:16 They made two **g** filigree settings
39:16 two **g** rings, and fastened
39:17 They fastened the two **g** chains to
39:19 They made two **g** rings and attached
39:20 they made two more **g** rings and
39:25 they made bells of pure **g** and
39:30 the sacred diadem, out of pure **g** and
39:37 the pure **g** lampstand with its row of
39:38 the **g** altar, the anointing oil, the
40: 5 Place the **g** altar of incense in
40:26 Moses placed the **g** altar in the Tent
Lev 8: 9 on Aaron's head and set the **g** plate,
24: 4 The lamps on the pure **g** lampstand
24: 6 the table of pure **g** before the LORD.
Nu 4:11 "Over the **g** altar they are to spread
7:14 one **g** dish weighing ten shekels,
7:20 one **g** dish weighing ten shekels,
7:26 one **g** dish weighing ten shekels,
7:32 one **g** dish weighing ten shekels,
7:38 one **g** dish weighing ten shekels,
7:44 one **g** dish weighing ten shekels,
7:50 one **g** dish weighing ten shekels,
7:56 one **g** dish weighing ten shekels,
7:62 one **g** dish weighing ten shekels,
7:68 one **g** dish weighing ten shekels,
7:74 one **g** dish weighing ten shekels,
7:80 one **g** dish weighing ten shekels,
7:84 bowls and twelve **g** dishes.
7:86 The twelve **g** dishes filled with
7:86 Altogether, the **g** dishes weighed a
8: 4 It was made of hammered **g**—from its
31:22 **G**, silver, bronze, iron, tin,
31:50 the **g** articles each of us acquired
31:51 accepted from them the **g**—all the
31:52 All the **g** from the commanders of
31:54 Eleazar the priest accepted the **g**
Jos 7:21 a wedge of **g** weighing fifty shekels,
7:24 the silver, the robe, the **g** wedge,
22: 8 with silver, **g**, bronze and iron, and
Jdg 8:24 Ishmaelites to wear **g** ear-rings.)
8:26 The weight of the **g** rings he asked
8:27 Gideon made the **g** into an ephod,
1Sa 6: 4 "Five **g** tumours and five **g** rats,
6: 8 and in a chest beside it put the **g**
6:11 **g** rats and the models of the tumours.
6:15 the chest containing the **g** objects,
6:17 These are the **g** tumours the
6:18 the number of the **g** rats was
2Sa 1:24 your garments with ornaments of **g**.
8: 7 David took the **g** shields that
12:30 king—its weight was a talent of **g**,
21: 4 silver or **g** from Saul or his family,
1Ki 6:20 He overlaid the inside with pure **g**,
6:21 inside of the temple with pure **g**,
6:21 and he extended **g** chains across the
6:21 which was overlaid with **g**.
6:22 he overlaid the whole interior with **g**
6:22 He also overlaid with **g** the altar
6:28 He overlaid the cherubim with **g**.
6:30 outer rooms of the temple with **g**.
6:32 and palm trees with beaten **g**.
6:35 **g** hammered evenly over the carvings.
7:49 the lampstands of pure **g** (five on
7:49 **g** floral work and lamps and tongs;

1Ki 7:50 the pure g dishes, wick trimmers,
7:50 the g sockets from the doors of the
9:11 the cedar and pine and g he wanted.
9:14 sent to the king 120 talents of g.
9:28 and brought back 420 talents of g,
10: 2 large quantities of g, and precious
10:10 she gave the king 120 talents of g,
10:11 (Hiram's ships brought g from Ophir;
10:14 The weight of the g that Solomon
10:16 hundred large shields of hammered g;
10:16 bekas of g went into each shield.
10:17 hundred small shields of hammered g,
10:17 three minas of g in each shield.
10:18 with ivory and overlaid with fine g.
10:21 All King Solomon's goblets were g,
10:21 the Forest of Lebanon were pure g.
10:22 three years it returned carrying g,
14:26 all the g shields Solomon had made.
20: 7 silver and my g, I did not refuse
22:48 trading ships to go to Ophir for g,
2Ki 5: 5 six thousand shekels of g and ten
7: 8 and carried away silver, g and
12:13 trumpets or any other articles of g
12:18 all the g found in the treasuries
14:14 He took all the g and silver and
18:14 of silver and thirty talents of g.
18:16 king of Judah stripped off the g
20:13 the silver, the g, the spices and
23:33 talents of silver and a talent of g.
24:13 and took away all the g articles
25:15 that were made of pure g or silver.
1Ch 18: 7 David took the g shields carried by
18:10 articles of g and silver and bronze.
20: 2 was found to be a talent of g,
21:25 hundred shekels of g for the site.
22:14 a hundred thousand talents of g,
22:16 in g and silver, bronze and
28:14 He designated the weight of g for
28:14 g articles to be used in various
28:15 the weight of g for the g lampstands
28:16 the weight of g for each table for
28:17 the weight of pure g for the forks,
28:17 the weight of g for each g dish; the
28:18 the weight of the refined g for the
28:18 that is, the cherubim of g that
29: 2 g for the g work, silver for the
29: 3 now give my personal treasures of g
29: 4 three thousand talents of g (g of
29: 5 for the g work and the silver work,
29: 7 and ten thousand darics of g,
2Ch 2: 7 a man skilled to work in g and
2:14 He is trained to work in g and
3: 4 He overlaid the inside with pure g.
3: 5 covered it with fine g and decorated
3: 6 And the g he used was g of Parvaim.
3: 7 and doors of the temple with g,
3: 8 with six hundred talents of fine g.
3: 9 The g nails weighed fifty shekels.
3: 9 overlaid the upper parts with g.
3:10 cherubim and overlaid them with g.
4: 7 He made ten g lampstands according
4: 8 made a hundred g sprinkling bowls.
4:20 the lampstands of pure g with their
4:21 the g floral work and lamps and
4:21 lamps and tongs (they were solid g)
4:22 the pure g wick trimmers, sprinkling
4:22 the g doors of the temple: the inner
8:18 four hundred and fifty talents of g,
9: 1 large quantities of g, and precious
9: 9 she gave the king 120 talents of g,
9:10 men of Solomon brought g from Ophir;
9:13 The weight of the g that Solomon
9:14 brought g and silver to Solomon.
9:15 hundred large shields of hammered g;
9:15 of hammered g went into each shield.
9:16 hundred small shields of hammered g,
9:16 hundred bekas of g in each shield.
9:17 with ivory and overlaid with pure g.
9:18 a footstool of g was attached to it.
9:20 All King Solomon's goblets were g,
9:20 the Forest of Lebanon were pure g.
9:21 carrying g, silver and ivory, and
12: 9 the g shields that Solomon had made.
13:11 on the g lampstand every evening.
24:14 and other objects of g and silver.
25:24 He took all the g and silver and all

2Ch 36: 3 talents of silver and a talent of g.
Ezr 1: 9 This was the inventory: g dishes 30
1:10 g bowls 30 matching silver bowls 410
1:11 5,400 articles of g and of silver.
2:69 for this work 61,000 drachmas of g,
5:14 from the temple of Babylon the g
6: 5 Also, the g and silver articles of
8:26 100 talents, 100 talents of g,
8:27 20 bowls of g valued at 1,000
8:27 polished bronze, as precious as g.
Ne 7:70 to the treasury 1,000 drachmas of g
7:71 20,000 drachmas of g and 2,200 minas
7:72 the people was 20,000 drachmas of g,
Est 1: 6 There were couches of g and silver
1: 7 Wine was served in goblets of g,
4:11 extend the g sceptre to him and
5: 2 the g sceptre that was in his hand.
8: 4 the king extended the g sceptre to
8:15 large crown of g and a purple robe
Job 3:15 with rulers who had g, who filled
22:24 your g of Ophir to the rocks in the
22:25 the Almighty will be your g, the
23:10 tested me, I shall come forth as g.
28: 1 and a place where g is refined.
28: 6 and its dust contains nuggets of g.
28:15 cannot be bought with the finest g,
28:16 cannot be bought with the g of Ophir,
28:17 Neither g nor crystal can compare
28:17 nor can it be had for jewels of g.
28:19 it; it cannot be bought with pure g.
31:24 "If I have put my trust in g or said
31:24 to pure g, 'You are my security,'
42:11 him a piece of silver and a g ring.
Ps 19:10 They are more precious than g, than
19:10 than much pure g; they are sweeter
21: 3 a crown of pure g on his head.
45: 9 is the royal bride in g of Ophir.
45:13 her gown is interwoven with g
68:13 its feathers with shining g
72:15 May g from Sheba be given to him.
119:127 I love your commands more than g,
119:127 more than g, more than pure g,
Pr 3:14 and yields better returns than g.
8:10 knowledge rather than choice g,
8:19 My fruit is better than fine g; what
11:22 Like a g ring in a pig's snout is a
16:16 How much better to get wisdom than g,
17: 3 for silver and the furnace for g,
20:15 G there is, and rubies in abundance,
22: 1 esteemed is better than silver or g.
25:11 apples of g in settings of silver.
25:12 Like an ear-ring of g or an ornament
25:12 ornament of fine g is a wise man's
27:21 for silver and the furnace for g,
SS 1:11 We will make you ear-rings of g,
3:10 he made of silver, its base of g.
5:11 His head is purest g; his hair is
5:14 His arms are rods of g set with
5:15 of marble set on bases of pure g.
Isa 2:20 idols of silver and idols of g,
13:12 I will make man scarcer than pure g
13:12 more rare than the g of Ophir.
13:17 for silver and have no delight in g.
30:22 and your images covered with g;
39: 2 the g, the spices, the fine oil, his
40:19 a goldsmith overlays it with g
46: 6 Some pour out g from their bags and
60: 6 bearing g and incense and
60:17 Instead of bronze I will bring you g,
Jer 4:30 in scarlet and put on jewels of g?
10: 9 from Tarshish and g from Uphaz.
51: 7 Babylon was a g cup in the LORD's
52:19 that were made of pure g or silver.
Lam 4: 1 How the g has lost its lustre, the
4: 1 the fine g become dull! The sacred
4: 2 once worth their weight in g, are
Eze 7:19 their g will be an unclean thing.
16:13 you were adorned with g and silver;
16:17 the jewellery made of my g and
27:22 spices and precious stones, and g.
28: 4 g and silver in your treasuries.
28:13 and mountings were made of g;
Da 2:32 of the statue was made of pure g,
2:35 the bronze, the silver and the g
2:38 You are that head of g.
2:45 the silver and the g to pieces.

Da 3: 1 Nebuchadnezzar made an image of g,
3: 5 worship the image of g that King
3: 7 worshipped the image of g that King
3:10 down and worship the image of g,
3:12 the image of g you have set up."
3:14 the image of g I have set up?
3:18 the image of g you have set up."
5: 2 he gave orders to bring in the g and
5: 3 they brought in the g goblets that
5: 4 they praised the gods of g and
5: 7 a g chain placed around his neck,
5:16 a g chain placed around your neck,
5:29 a g chain was placed around his
10: 5 of the finest g round his waist.
11:38 he will honour with g and silver,
11:43 gain control of the treasures of g
Joel 3: 5 For you took my silver and my g and
Na 2: 9 Plunder the silver! Plunder the g!
Hab 2:19 It is covered with g and silver;
Zep 1:18 Neither their silver nor their g
Hag 2: 8 'The silver is mine and the g is
Zec 4: 2 "I see a solid g lampstand with a
4:12 g pipes that pour out golden oil?"
9: 3 and g like the dirt of the streets.
13: 9 like silver and test them like g.
14:14 great quantities of g and silver
Mal 3: 3 and refine them like g and silver.
Mt 2:11 gifts of g and of incense and of
10: 9 Do not take along any g or silver or
23:16 swears by the g of the temple,
23:17 fools! Which is greater: the g,
23:17 the temple that makes the g sacred?
Ac 3: 6 Peter said, "Silver or g I do not
17:29 divine being is like g or silver
20:33 anyone's silver or g or clothing.
1Co 3:12 builds on this foundation using g,
1Ti 2: 9 or g or pearls or expensive clothes,
2Ti 2:20 articles not only of g and silver,
Heb 9: 4 This ark contained the g jar of
Jas 2: 2 wearing a g ring and fine clothes,
5: 3 Your g and silver are corroded.
1Pe 1: 7 your faith—of greater worth than g,
1:18 things such as silver or g that you
3: 3 wearing of g jewellery and fine
Rev 3:18 I counsel you to buy from me g
4: 4 and had crowns of g on their heads.
9: 7 wore something like crowns of g,
9:20 and idols of g, silver, bronze,
14:14 man" with a crown of g on his head
17: 4 with g, precious stones and pearls.
18:12 cargoes of g, silver, precious
18:16 with g, precious stones and pearls!
21:15 rod of g to measure the city,
21:18 city of pure g, as pure as glass.
21:21 of pure g, like transparent glass.

Gold-covered (Gold, Cover)

Heb 9: 4 and the g ark of the covenant.

Golden (Gold)

1Ki 7:48 the g altar; the g table on which
12:28 advice, the king made two g calves.
2Ki 10:29 of the g calves at Bethel and Dan.
2Ch 4:19 the g altar; the tables on which was
13: 8 have with you the g calves that
Job 37:22 Out of the north he comes in g
Ecc 12: 6 or the g bowl is broken; before the
Zec 4:12 two gold pipes that pour out g oil?
Heb 9: 4 which had the g altar of incense and
Rev 1:12 I turned I saw seven g lampstands,
1:13 and with a g sash round his chest.
1:20 of the seven g lampstands is this:
2: 1 walks among the seven g lampstands:
5: 8 holding g bowls full of incense,
8: 3 Another angel, who had a g censer,
8: 3 on the g altar before the throne.
9:13 of the g altar that is before God.
15: 6 wore g sashes round their chests.
15: 7 g bowls filled with the wrath of God,
17: 4 She held a g cup in her hand, filled

Goldsmith (Gold)

Isa 40:19 and a g overlays it with gold
41: 7 The craftsman encourages the g, and
46: 6 they hire a g to make it into a god,

Jer 10: 9 What the craftsman and **g** have made
10:14 every **g** is shamed by his idols.
51:17 every **g** is shamed by his idols.

Goldsmiths (Gold)

Ne 3: 8 Uzziel son of Harhaiah, one of the **g**,
3:31 Next to him, Malkijah, one of the **g**,
3:32 the **g** and merchants made repairs.

Golgotha

Mt 27:33 They came to a place called **G** (which
Mk 15:22 brought Jesus to the place called **G**
Jn 19:17 Skull (which in Aramaic is called **G**).

Goliath

Philistine giant (1Sa 17:4–7); challenged Israel (1Sa 17:8–11,23–26); killed by David (1Sa 17:32–50). Sword kept at sanctuary at Nob; given to David (1Sa 21:9).

1Sa 17: 4 A champion named **G**, who was from
17: 8 **G** stood and shouted to the ranks of
17:23 **G**, the Philistine champion from
21: 9 The priest replied, "The sword of **G**
22:10 and the sword of **G** the Philistine."
2Sa 21:19 Bethlehemite killed **G** the Gittite,
1Ch 20: 5 Lahmi the brother of **G** the Gittite,

Gomer

Ge 10: 2 The sons of Japheth: **G**, Magog, Madai,
10: 3 The sons of **G**: Ashkenaz, Riphath and
1Ch 1: 5 The sons of Japheth: **G**, Magog, Madai,
1: 6 The sons of **G**: Ashkenaz, Riphath and
Eze 38: 6 also **G** with all its troops, and
Hos 1: 3 he married **G** daughter of Diblaim,
1: 6 **G** conceived again and gave birth to
1: 8 After she had weaned Lo-Ruhamah, **G**

Gomorrah (Sodom and Gomorrah)

City in Valley of Siddim (Ge 14:2–3), usually paired with Sodom. Its king and army were defeated by a Mesopotamian alliance (Ge 14:8–11). Faced God's judgment on account of gross sin (Ge 18:20–21; 19:24–25). Used to exemplify human depravity and God's judgment (Dt 29:23; Isa 13:19; Jer 23:14; 49:18; Am 4:11; Mt 10:15; Ro 9:29; 2Pe 2:6). See *Sodom*.

Ge 10:19 and then towards Sodom, **G**, Admah and
14: 2 Birsha king of **G**, Shinab king of
14: 8 the king of Sodom, the king of **G**,
Dt 32:32 of Sodom and from the fields of **G**.
Isa 1: 9 Sodom, we would have been like **G**.
1:10 the law of our God, you people of **G**!
Jer 23:14 the people of Jerusalem are like **G**."
Zep 2: 9 the Ammonites like **G**—a place of
Ro 9:29 Sodom, we would have been like **G**."

Gong

1Co 13: 1 a resounding **g** or a clanging cymbal.

Good (Best, Better, *Good and evil, Good deeds, Good land, Good news, Good shepherd, Good work*, Goodness, Goodwill)

Ge 1: 4 God saw that the light was **g**, and he
1:10 And God saw that it was **g**.
1:12 And God saw that it was **g**.
1:18 And God saw that it was **g**.
1:21 And God saw that it was **g**.
1:25 And God saw that it was **g**.
1:31 that he had made, and it was very **g**.
2: 9 pleasing to the eye and **g** for food.
2:12 (The gold of that land is **g**;
2:18 The LORD God said, "It is not **g** for
3: 6 **g** for food and pleasing to the eye,
15:15 peace and be buried at a **g** old age.
20: 3 "You are as **g** as dead because of the
24:10 kinds of **g** things from his master.
25: 8 his last and died at a **g** old age,
25:32 "What **g** is the birthright to me?"
30:11 Leah said, "What **g** fortune!" So she
31:24 anything to Jacob, either **g** or bad.
31:29 anything to Jacob, either **g** or bad.
34:18 Their proposal seemed **g** to Hamor
41: 5 Seven ears of corn, healthy and **g**,
41:22 seven ears of corn, full and **g**,
Ge 41:24 corn swallowed up the seven **g** ears.
41:26 The seven **g** cows are seven years,
41:26 and the seven **g** ears of corn are
41:35 of these **g** years that are coming
41:37 The plan seemed **g** to Pharaoh and
44: 4 'Why have you repaid **g** with evil?
49:15 he sees how **g** is his resting place
50:20 but God intended it for **g** to
Ex 3: 8 land into a **g** and spacious land,
18: 9 the **g** things the LORD had done for
18:17 "What you are doing is not **g**.
Lev 5: 4 to do anything whether **g** or evil
27:10 or substitute a **g** one for a bad one,
27:10 or a bad one for a **g** one; if he
27:12 who will judge its quality as **g** or
27:14 will judge its quality as **g** or bad.
27:33 He must not pick out the **g** from the
Nu 10:29 has promised **g** things to Israel."
10:32 **g** things the LORD gives us."
13:19 Is it **g** or bad? What kind of towns
14: 7 and explored is exceedingly **g**.
24:13 **g** or bad, to go beyond the command
Dt 1:14 me, "What you propose to do is **g**.
1:23 The idea seemed **g** to me; so I
1:39 children who do not yet know **g** from
5:28 Everything they said was **g**.
6:11 houses filled with all kinds of **g**
6:18 Do what is right and **g** in the LORD's
10:13 am giving you today for your own **g**?
12:28 because you will be doing what is **g**
18:17 LORD said to me: "What they say is **g**.
26:11 shall rejoice in all the **g** things
Jos 9:25 whatever seems **g** and right to you."
10: 2 Ai, and all its men were **g** fighters.
21:45 Not one of all the LORD's **g** promises
23:14 that not one of all the **g** promises
23:15 just as every **g** promise of the LORD
24:20 of you, after he has been **g** to you."
Jdg 8:32 Gideon son of Joash died at a **g** old
8:35 the **g** things he had done for them.
9:11 'Should I give up my fruit, so **g** and
9:16 **g** faith when you made Abimelech king,
9:19 in **g** faith towards Jerub-Baal and
17:13 "Now I know that the LORD will be **g**
18: 9 We have seen that the land is very **g**.
Ru 2:22 "It will be **g** for you, my daughter,
3: 7 and drinking and was in **g** spirits,
3:13 wants to redeem, **g**; let him redeem.
1Sa 1:23 only may the LORD make **g** his word.
2:24 No, my sons; it is not a **g** report
2:32 Although **g** will be done to Israel,
3:18 let him do what is **g** in his eyes."
9:10 "**G**," Saul said to his servant. "Come,
11:10 do to us whatever seems **g** to you."
12:14 you follow the LORD your God—**g**!
12:21 They can do you no **g**, nor can they
12:23 you the way that is **g** and right.
15: 9 and lambs—everything that was **g**.
19:10 That night David made **g** his escape.
24:18 You have just now told me of the **g**
25: 6 'Long life to you! **G** health to you
25: 6 And **g** health to all that is yours!
25:15 Yet these men were very **g** to us.
25:21 He has paid me back evil for **g**.
25:30 **g** thing he promised concerning
25:33 be blessed for your **g** judgment
26:16 What you have done is not **g**. As
2Sa 3:13 "**G**," said David. "I will make an
7:28 these **g** things to your servant.
10:12 LORD will do what is **g** in his sight."
13:22 a word to Amnon, either **g** or bad;
15:26 do to me whatever seems **g** to him."
16:12 repay me with **g** for the cursing I am
17: 4 This plan seemed **g** to Absalom and to
17: 7 has given is not **g** this time.
17:14 to frustrate the **g** advice of
18:27 "He's a **g** man," the king said. "He
19:35 between what is **g** and what is not?
1Ki 2:38 the king, "What you say is **g**.
2:42 you said to me, 'What you say is **g**.
7:10 laid with large stones of **g** quality,
8:56 Not one word has failed of all the **g**
8:66 glad in heart for all the **g** things
14:13 God of Israel, has found anything **g**.
18:24 the people said, "What you say is **g**.
20:33 The men took this as a **g** sign and
1Ki 22: 8 anything **g** about me, but always bad.
22:18 anything **g** about me, but only bad?"
2Ki 3:19 You will cut down every **g** tree, stop
3:19 and ruin every **g** field with stones."
3:25 every **g** field until it was covered.
3:25 springs and cut down every **g** tree.
20: 3 have done what is **g** in your eyes.
20:19 have spoken is **g**," Hezekiah replied.
1Ch 4:40 They found rich, **g** pasture, and the
13: 2 "If it seems **g** to you and if it is
16:34 Give thanks to the LORD, for he is **g**;
17:26 these **g** things to your servant.
19:13 LORD will do what is **g** in his sight."
29:28 He died at a **g** old age, having
2Ch 5:13 He is **g**; his love endures for ever
7: 3 He is **g**; his love endures for ever
7:10 joyful and glad in heart for the **g**
12:12 Indeed, there was some **g** in Judah.
14: 2 Asa did what was **g** and right in the
18: 7 anything **g** about me, but always bad.
18:17 anything **g** about me, but only bad?"
19: 3 There is, however, some **g** in you,
24:16 because of the **g** he had done in
30:18 the LORD, who is **g**, pardon
30:22 who showed **g** understanding of the
31:20 doing what was **g** and right and
Ezr 3:11 He is **g**; his love to Israel endures
7:28 who has extended his **g** favour to me
9:12 eat the **g** things of the land and
Ne 5: 5 though our sons are as **g** as theirs,
9:13 and decrees and commands that are **g**.
9:20 You gave your **g** Spirit to instruct
9:25 filled with all kinds of **g** things,
9:36 and the other **g** things it produces.
Est 10: 3 because he worked for the **g** of his
Job 2:10 Shall we accept **g** from God, and not
21:25 never having enjoyed anything **g**.
22:18 filled their houses with **g** things,
30:26 Yet when I hoped for **g**, evil came;
34: 4 let us learn together what is **g**.
39:17 or give her a share of **g** sense.
Ps 4: 6 "Who can show us any **g**?" Let the
13: 6 the LORD, for he has been **g** to me.
14: 1 vile; there is no-one who does **g**.
14: 3 is no-one who does **g**, not even one.
16: 2 apart from you I have no **g** thing."
25: 7 remember me, for you are **g**, O LORD.
25: 8 **G** and upright is the LORD; therefore
34: 8 Taste and see that the LORD is **g**;
34:10 who seek the LORD lack no **g** thing.
34:12 life and desires to see many **g** days,
34:14 Turn from evil and do **g**; seek peace
35:12 They repay me evil for **g** and leave
36: 3 has ceased to be wise and to do **g**.
37: 3 Trust in the LORD and do **g**; dwell in
37:27 Turn from evil and do **g**; then you
38:20 Those who repay my **g** with evil
38:20 slander me when I pursue what is **g**.
39: 2 anything **g**, my anguish increased.
51:18 In your **g** pleasure make Zion prosper;
52: 3 You love evil rather than **g**,
52: 9 I will hope, for your name is **g**.
53: 1 vile; there is no-one who does **g**.
53: 3 is no-one who does **g**, not even one.
54: 6 your name, O LORD, for it is **g**.
65: 4 with the **g** things of your house,
73: 1 Surely God is **g** to Israel, to those
73:28 for me, it is **g** to be near God. I
84:11 no **g** thing does he withhold from
85:12 The LORD will indeed give what is **g**,
86: 5 You are forgiving and **g**, O Lord,
92: 1 is **g** to praise the LORD and make
100: 5 For the LORD is **g** and his love
103: 5 who satisfies your desires with **g**
104:28 they are satisfied with **g** things.
106: 1 he is **g**; his love endures for ever.
107: 1 Give thanks to the LORD, for he is **g**;
107: 9 and fills the hungry with **g** things.
109: 5 They repay me evil for **g**, and hatred
111:10 his precepts have **g** understanding.
112: 5 **G** will come to him who is generous
116: 7 for the LORD has been **g** to you.
118: 1 Give thanks to the LORD, for he is **g**
118:29 Give thanks to the LORD, for he is **g**
119:17 Do **g** to your servant, and I will
119:39 I dread, for your laws are **g**.

Ps 119:65 Do g to your servant according to
119:66 Teach me knowledge and g judgment,
119:68 You are g, and what you do is g;
119:71 was g for me to be afflicted so that
125: 4 Do g, O LORD, to those who are g,
133: 1 How g and pleasant it is when
135: 3 Praise the LORD, for the LORD is g;
136: 1 Give thanks to the LORD, for he is g.
143:10 g Spirit lead me on level ground.
145: 9 The LORD is g to all; he has
147: 1 Praise the LORD. How g it is to sing
Pr 2: 9 and just and fair—every g path.
2:20 Thus you will walk in the ways of g
3: 4 you will win favour and a g name in
3:27 Do not withhold g from those who
11:23 of the righteous ends only in g,
11:27 He who seeks g finds goodwill, but
12: 2 A g man obtains favour from the LORD,
12:14 man is filled with g things as
13: 2 of his lips a man enjoys g things,
13:15 G understanding wins favour, but the
13:22 A g man leaves an inheritance for
14:14 and the g man rewarded for his.
14:19 bow down in the presence of the g,
14:22 is g find love and faithfulness.
15: 3 watch on the wicked and the g.
15:23 reply—and how g is a timely word!
16:29 leads him down a path that is not g
17:13 If a man pays back evil for g, evil
17:22 A cheerful heart is g medicine, but
17:26 is not g to punish an innocent man,
18: 5 is not g to be partial to the wicked
18:22 He who finds a wife finds what is g
19: 2 is not g to have zeal without
20:14 "It's no g, it's no g!" says the
22: 1 A g name is more desirable than
24:13 Eat honey, my son, for it is g;
24:23 show partiality in judging is not g:
25:27 is not g to eat too much honey, nor
28:10 will receive a g inheritance.
28:21 To show partiality is not g—yet a
31:12 She brings him g, not harm, all the
Ecc 2: 1 with pleasure to find out what is g.
3:12 be happy and do g while they live.
4: 9 they have a g return for their work
5:18 I realised that it is g and proper
6:12 For who knows what is g for a man in
7: 1 A g name is better than fine perfume,
7: 3 a sad face is g for the heart.
7:11 Wisdom, like an inheritance, is a g
7:14 times are g, be happy; but when
7:18 is g to grasp the one and not let go
9: 2 the g and the bad, the clean and the
9: 2 As it is with the g man, so with the
9:18 war, but one sinner destroys much g.
12:14 thing, whether it is g or evil.
Isa 5: 2 Then he looked for a crop of g
5: 4 I looked for g grapes, why did it
5:20 Woe to those who call evil g and g
38: 3 have done what is g in your eyes.
39: 8 have spoken is g," Hezekiah replied.
40: 9 You who bring g tidings to Zion, go
40: 9 You who bring g tidings to Jerusalem
41: 7 He says of the welding, "It is g."
41:23 Do something, whether g or bad, so
41:27 Jerusalem a messenger of g tidings.
52: 7 proclaim peace, who bring g tidings
55: 2 listen to me, and eat what is g,
63: 7 the many g things he has done for
65: 2 who walk in ways not g, pursuing
65: 8 it, there is yet some g in it,'
Jer 4:22 evil; they know not how to do g."
5:25 your sins have deprived you of g.
6:16 ask where the g way is, and walk in
8:15 We hoped for peace but no g has come
10: 5 do no harm nor can they do any g."
13:23 Neither can you do g who are
14:19 hoped for peace but no g has come
15:11 I will deliver you for a g purpose
16:19 worthless idols that did them no g.
18:10 the g I had intended to do for it.
18:20 Should g be repaid with evil? Yet
21:10 harm and not g, declares the LORD.
24: 2 One basket had very g figs, like
24: 3 "The g ones are very g, but the poor
24: 5 'Like these g figs, I regard as g
Jer 24: 6 will watch over them for their g,
26:14 whatever you think is g and right.
29:32 nor will he see the g things I will
32:39 will always fear me for their own g
32:39 the g of their children after them.
32:40 I will never stop doing g to them,
32:41 I will rejoice in doing them g and
33: 9 of all the g things I do for it;
33:11 LORD is g; his love endures for ever.
38: 4 g of these people but their ruin."
44:27 over them for harm not for g;
Lam 3:25 The LORD is g to those whose hope is
3:26 it is g to wait quietly for the
3:27 It is g for a man to bear the yoke
3:38 both calamities and g things come?
Eze 17: 8 had been planted in g soil by
20:25 not g and laws they could not live
30:22 I will break both his arms, the g
34:14 I will tend them in a g pasture, and
34:14 will lie down in g grazing land
34:18 for you to feed on the g pasture?
Da 3:15 worship the image I made, very g.
Hos 8: 3 Israel has rejected what is g; an
Am 5:14 Seek g, not evil, that you may live.
5:15 Hate evil, love g; maintain justice
9: 4 upon them for evil and not for g."
Jnh 2: 9 What I have vowed I will make g.
Mic 2: 7 do g to him whose ways are upright?
3: 2 you who hate g and love evil; who
6: 8 He has showed you, O man, what is g.
Na 1: 7 The LORD is g, a refuge in times of
Zep 1:12 will do nothing, either g or bad.'
Zec 8:15 "so now I have determined to do g
Mal 2:17 By saying, "All who do evil are g in
Mt 3:10 every tree that does not produce g
5:13 It is no longer g for anything,
5:45 sun to rise on the evil and the g,
6:22 If your eyes are g, your whole body
7:11 know how to give g gifts to your
7:11 give g gifts to those who ask him!
7:17 Likewise every g tree bears g fruit,
7:18 A g tree cannot bear bad fruit, and
7:18 and a bad tree cannot bear g fruit.
7:19 tree that does not bear g fruit
11:26 for this was your g pleasure
12:12 is lawful to do g on the Sabbath."
12:33 "Make a tree g and its fruit will be
12:33 a tree g and its fruit will be g,
12:34 can you who are evil say anything g?
12:35 The g man brings g things out of the
12:35 out of the g stored up in him,
13: 8 Still other seed fell on g soil,
13:23 g soil is the man who hears the word
13:24 a man who sowed g seed in his field.
13:27 'Sir, didn't you sow g seed in your
13:37 "The one who sowed the g seed is
13:38 field is the world, and the g seed
13:48 and collected the g fish in baskets,
16:26 What g will it be for a man if he
17: 4 Peter said to Jesus, "Lord, it is g
19:16 "Teacher, what g thing must I do to
19:17 "Why do you ask me about what is g?"
19:17 "There is only One who is g. If you
22:10 both g and bad, and the wedding hall
24:46 will be g for that servant whose
25:21 "His master replied, 'Well done, g
25:23 "His master replied, 'Well done, g
Mk 3: 4 the Sabbath: to do g or to do evil,
4: 8 Still other seed fell on g soil. It
4:20 Others, like seed sown on g soil,
8:36 What g is it for a man to gain the
9: 5 Peter said to Jesus, "Rabbi, it is g
9:50 "Salt is g, but if it loses its
10:17 "G teacher," he asked, "what must I
10:18 "Why do you call me g?" Jesus
10:18 "No-one is g—except God alone.
12:28 Jesus had given them a g answer,
Lk 1: 3 it seemed g also to me to write an
1:53 He has filled the hungry with g
3: 9 every tree that does not produce g
6: 9 the Sabbath: to do g or to do evil,
6:27 enemies, do g to those who hate you,
6:33 if you do g to those who are g to
6:35 love your enemies, do g to them, and
6:38 A g measure, pressed down, shaken
6:43 "No g tree bears bad fruit, nor does
Lk 6:43 nor does a bad tree bear g fruit.
6:45 The g man brings g things out of the
6:45 out of the g stored up in his heart,
8: 8 Still other seed fell on g soil. It
8:15 the seed on g soil stands for those
8:15 for those with a noble and g heart,
9:25 What g is it for a man to gain the
9:33 "Master, it is g for us to be here.
10:21 Father, for this was your g pleasure.
11:13 know how to give g gifts to your
11:34 When your eyes are g, your whole
12:16 certain rich man produced a g crop.
12:19 of g things laid up for many years.
12:37 will be g for those servants whose
12:38 will be g for those servants whose
12:43 will be g for that servant whom the
14:34 "Salt is g, but if it loses its
16:25 lifetime you received your g things,
18:18 ruler asked him, "G teacher, what
18:19 "Why do you call me g?" Jesus
18:19 "No-one is g—except God alone.
19:17 "'Well done, my g servant!' his
23:50 of the Council, a g and upright man,
Jn 1:46 "Nazareth! Can anything g come from
5:29 come out—those who have done g will
7:12 Some said, "He is a g man." Others
16: 7 is for your g that I am going away.
18:14 be g if one man died for the people.
Ac 9:36 always doing g and helping the poor.
10:33 and it was g of you to come.
10:38 and how he went around doing g and
11:24 He was a g man, full of the Holy
15:28 seemed g to the Holy Spirit and to
19:25 a g income from this business.
19:27 that our trade will lose its g name,
23: 1 God in all g conscience to this day
Ro 2: 7 persistence in doing g seek glory,
2:10 who does g: first for the Jew,
3: 8 us do evil that g may result"?
3:12 is no-one who does g, not even one
4:19 fact that his body was as g as dead
5: 7 though for a g man someone might
7:12 is holy, righteous and g.
7:13 Did that which is g, then, become
7:13 death in me through what was g,
7:16 to do, I agree that the law is g.
7:18 I know that nothing g lives in me,
7:18 desire to do what is g, but I cannot
7:19 For what I do is not the g I want to
7:21 do g, evil is right there with me.
8:28 for the g of those who love him,
9:11 born or had done anything g or bad
12: 2 g, pleasing and perfect will.
12: 9 what is evil; cling to what is g.
12:21 by evil, but overcome evil with g.
13: 4 For he is God's servant to do you g.
14:16 Do not allow what you consider g to
15: 2 for his g, to build him up.
16:19 wise about what is g, and innocent
1Co 5: 6 Your boasting is not g. Don't you
7: 1 It is g for a man not to marry.
7: 8 It is g for them to stay unmarried,
7:26 is g for you to remain as you are.
7:35 I am saying this for your own g, not
10:24 seek his own g, but the g of others
10:33 not seeking my own g but the g of
11:17 your meetings do more harm than g.
12: 7 Spirit is given for the common g.
14: 6 what g will I be to you, unless I
15:33 "Bad company corrupts g character.
2Co 5:10 while in the body, whether g or bad.
6: 8 bad report and g report; genuine,
Gal 4:17 to win you over, but for no g.
4:18 provided the purpose is g, and to be
5: 7 You were running a g race. Who cut
6: 6 all g things with his instructor.
6: 9 Let us not become weary in doing g,
6:10 as we have opportunity, let us do g
6:12 Those who want to make a g
Eph 1: 9 will according to his g pleasure,
2:10 created in Christ Jesus to do g
6: 8 everyone for whatever g he does,
Php 2:13 to act according to his g purpose.
4:14 Yet it was g of you to share in my
1Th 5:21 Test everything. Hold on to the g.
2Th 1:11 may fulfil every g purpose of yours

2Th 2:16 us eternal encouragement and g hope,
2:17 you in every g deed and word.
1Ti 1: 5 a g conscience and a sincere faith.
1: 8 We know that the law is g if one
1:18 them you may fight the g fight,
1:19 on to faith and a g conscience
2: 3 This is g, and pleases God our
3: 7 He must also have a g reputation
4: 4 For everything God created is g,
4: 6 you will be a g minister of Christ
4: 6 g teaching that you have followed.
6:12 Fight the g fight of the faith. Take
6:12 when you made your g confession in
6:13 made the g confession, I charge
6:18 Command them to do g, to be rich in
2Ti 1:14 Guard the g deposit that was
2: 3 hardship with us like a g solider of
3: 3 brutal, not lovers of the g,
4: 7 I have fought the g fight, I have
Tit 1: 8 one who loves what is g, who is
1:16 and unfit for doing anything g.
2: 3 much wine, but to teach what is g.
2: 7 them an example by doing what is g.
2:14 his very own, eager to do what is g
3: 1 to be ready to do whatever is g,
3: 8 themselves to doing what is g.
3:14 themselves to doing what is g,
Phm : 6 of every g thing we have in Christ.
:15 that you might have him back for g
Heb 5:14 to distinguish g from evil.
9:11 Christ came as high priest of the g
10: 1 The law is only a shadow of the g
11:12 this one man, and he as g as dead
12:10 God disciplines us for our g, that
13: 9 It is g for our hearts to be
13:16 do not forget to do g and to share
13:21 equip you with everything g for
Jas 1:17 Every g and perfect gift is from
2: 3 "Here's a g seat for you," but say
2:14 What g is it, my brothers, if a man
2:16 his physical needs, what g is it?
2:19 You believe that there is one God. G!
3:13 you? Let him show it by his g life,
3:17 and g fruit, impartial and sincere.
4:17 who knows the g he ought to do
1Pe 2: 3 you have tasted that the Lord is g.
2:12 Live such g lives among the pagans
2:15 it is God's will that by doing g
2:18 not only to those who are g and
2:20 for doing g and you endure it,
3:10 would love life and see g days
3:11 He must turn from evil and do g; he
3:13 harm you if you are eager to do g?
3:16 maliciously against your g behaviour
3:17 for doing g than for doing evil.
3:21 of a g conscience towards God.
4:19 Creator and continue to do g.
3Jn : 2 I pray that you may enjoy g health
:11 imitate what is evil but what is g.
:11 Anyone who does what is g is from

Good and evil
Ge 2: 9 and the tree of the knowledge of g.
2:17 from the tree of the knowledge of g,
3: 5 you will be like God, knowing g."
3:22 become like one of us, knowing g.
2Sa 14:17 an angel of God in discerning g.

Good deeds
Ne 6:19 reporting to me his g and then
Mt 5:16 See your g and praise your Father
1Ti 2:10 with g, appropriate for women who
5:10 is well known for her g, such as
5:10 devoting herself to all kinds of g.
5:25 In the same way, g are obvious, and
6:18 to be rich in g, and to be generous
Heb 10:24 one another on towards love and g.
1Pe 2:12 they may see your g and glorify God

Good land
Dt 1:25 g that the LORD our God is giving us.
1:35 g I swore to give your forefathers,
3:25 Let me go over and see the g beyond
4:21 enter the g the LORD your God is
4:22 over and take possession of that g.
6:18 you may go in and take over the g
8: 7 you into a g—a land with streams
8:10 your God for the g he has given you.
9: 6 God is giving you this g to possess,
11:17 from the g the LORD is giving you.
Jos 23:13 until you perish from this g, which
23:15 you from this g he has given you.
23:16 perish from the g he has given you."
1Ki 14:15 He will uproot Israel from this g
1Ch 28: 8 that you may possess this g and pass

Good news
2Sa 4:10 and thought he was bringing g,
18:25 "If he is alone, he must have g.
18:26 said, "He must be bringing g, too.
18:27 "He comes with g."
18:31 "My lord the king, hear the g! The
1Ki 1:42 man like you must be bringing g."
2Ki 7: 9 This is a day of g and we are
Pr 15:30 and g gives health to the bones.
25:25 Like cold water to a weary soul is g
Isa 52: 7 are the feet of those who bring g,
61: 1 anointed me to preach g to the poor.
Na 1:15 the feet of one who brings g, who
Mt 4:23 preaching the g of the kingdom, and
9:35 preaching the g of the kingdom and
11: 5 and the g is preached to the poor.
Mk 1:14 Galilee, proclaiming the g of God.
1:15 Repent and believe the g!"
16:15 and preach the g to all creation.
Lk 1:19 speak to you and to tell you this g.
2:10 I bring you g of great joy that will
3:18 people and preached the g to them.
4:18 anointed me to preach g to the poor.
4:43 he said, "I must preach the g of the
7:22 and the g is preached to the poor.
8: 1 the g of the kingdom of God.
16:16 Since that time, the g of the
Ac 5:42 the g that Jesus is the Christ.
8:12 the g of the kingdom of God
8:35 and told him the g about Jesus.
10:36 telling the g of peace through Jesus
11:20 them the g about the Lord Jesus.
13:32 "We tell you the g: What God
14: 7 where they continued to preach the g.
14:15 We are bringing you g, telling you
14:21 They preached the g in that city and
17:18 g about Jesus and the resurrection.
Ro 10:15 are the feet of those who bring g!"
10:16 not all the Israelites accepted the g
1Th 3: 6 brought g about your faith and love.

Good shepherd
Jn 10:11 "I am the g. The g lays down his
10:14 "I am the g; I know my sheep and my

Good work
Ne 2:18 So they began this g.
2Co 9: 8 need, you will abound in every g.
Php 1: 6 that he who began a g in you will
Col 1:10 bearing fruit in every g, growing
2Ti 2:21 the Master and prepared to do any g.
3:17 be thoroughly equipped for every g.

Good-bye
Ge 31:28 my grandchildren and my daughters g.
Ru 1:14 g, but Ruth clung to her.
1Ki 19:20 "Let me kiss my father and mother g,"
Lk 9:61 me go back and say g to my family."
Ac 20: 1 said g and set out for Macedonia.
21: 6 After saying g to each other, we
2Co 2:13 g to them and went on to Macedonia.
13:11 Finally, brothers, g. Aim for

Goodness (Good)
Ex 33:19 the LORD said, "I will cause all my g
2Ch 6:41 may your saints rejoice in your g.
Ne 9:25 they revelled in your great g.
9:35 enjoying your great g to them in the
Ps 23: 6 Surely g and love will follow me all
27:13 I will see the g of the LORD in the
31:19 How great is your g, which you have
69:16 Answer me, O LORD, out of the g of
86:17 Give me a sign of your g, that my
Ps 109:21 of the g of your love, deliver me.
116:12 I repay the LORD for all his g to me?
142: 7 about me because of your g to me.
145: 7 They will celebrate your abundant g
Ro 15:14 that you yourselves are full of g,
Gal 5:22 patience, kindness, g, faithfulness,
Eph 5: 9 in all g, righteousness and truth)
Heb 6: 5 who have tasted the g of the word of
2Pe 1: 3 called us by his own glory and g.
1: 5 your faith g; and to g, knowledge;

Goods
Ge 14:11 The four kings seized all the g of
14:16 He recovered all the g and brought
14:21 people and keep the g for yourself."
31:18 along with all the g he had
31:37 you have searched through all my g,
36: 6 all the g he had acquired in Canaan,
40:17 all kinds of baked g for Pharaoh,
Ex 22: 7 silver or g for safekeeping
Nu 31: 9 herds, flocks and g as plunder.
2Ch 21:17 the g found in the king's palace,
Ezr 1: 4 with g and livestock, and with
1: 6 with g and livestock, and with
Ne 13: 8 Tobiah's household g out of the room
13:20 sellers of all kinds of g spent the
Est 3:13 of Adar, and to plunder their g.
Ps 62:10 or take pride in stolen g; though
Ecc 5:11 g increase, so do those who consume
Jer 49:29 off with all their g and camels.
Eze 27:12 wealth of g; they exchanged silver,
27:18 many products and great wealth of g,
38:12 rich in livestock and g, living at
38:13 and g and to seize much plunder?"'
Hab 2: 6 "'Woe to him who piles up stolen g
Lk 12:18 I will store all my grain and my g.
17:31 g inside, should go down to get them.
Ac 2:45 Selling their possessions and g,

Goodwill (Good)
Est 9:30 Xerxes—words of g and assurance—
Pr 11:27 He who seeks good finds g, but evil
14: 9 but g is found among the upright.
Ac 7:10 gain the g of Pharaoh king of Egypt;
Php 1:15 and rivalry, but others out of g.

Gore (Gores, Goring)
Dt 33:17 With them he will g the nations,
1Ki 22:11 With these you will g the Arameans
2Ch 18:10 With these you will g the Arameans

Gores (Gore)
Ex 21:28 "If a bull g a man or a woman to
21:31 This law also applies if the bull g
21:32 If the bull g a male or female slave,

Gorge (Gorged)
Ex 15: 9 divide the spoils; I will g myself
Dt 2:24 "Set out now and cross the Arnon G.
2:36 From Aroer on the rim of the Arnon G
2:36 and from the town in the g, even as
3: 8 the Arnon G as far as Mount Hermon.
3:12 north of Aroer by the Arnon G,
3:16 Arnon G (the middle of the G being
4:48 rim of the Arnon G to Mount Siyon
Jos 12: 1 from the Arnon G to Mount Hermon,
12: 2 Aroer on the rim of the Arnon G
12: 2 of the g—to the Jabbok River,
13: 9 Aroer on the rim of the Arnon G,
13: 9 the town in the middle of the g,
13:16 Aroer on the rim of the Arnon G,
13:16 middle of the g, and the whole
15: 7 the Pass of Adummim south of the g.
2Sa 24: 5 south of the town in the g, and then
2Ki 10:33 Arnon G through Gilead to Bashan.
2Ch 20:16 of the g in the Desert of Jeruel.
Pr 23:20 much wine or g themselves on meat,
Eze 32: 4 of the earth g themselves on you.

Gorged (Gorge)
Rev 19:21 birds g themselves on their flesh.

Goring (Gore)
Ex 21:29 the bull has had the habit of **g** and
21:36 that the bull had the habit of **g**,

Goshen
1. North-eastern region of Nile Delta in Egypt. Jacob's family brought here by Joseph during famine (Ge 45:10; 46:28–29, 34; 47:1, 4, 6). They flourished here (Ge 47:27), and Jacob died here (Ge 49:33). It was protected from the plagues (Ex 8:22; 9:26). **2.** Region of southern Palestine, between Gaza and Gibeon. Joshua's conquests reached to here (Jos 10:41; 11:16). **3.** Town in the mountains of south-west Judah (Jos 15:51).

Ge 45:10 You shall live in the region of **G**
46:28 to Joseph to get directions to **G**.
46:28 When they arrived in the region of **G**,
46:29 went to **G** to meet his father Israel.
46:34 to settle in the region of **G**,
47: 1 land of Canaan and are now in **G**."
47: 4 let your servants settle in **G**."
47: 6 Let them live in **G**. And if you know
47:27 settled in Egypt in the region of **G**.
50: 8 flocks and herds were left in **G**.
Ex 8:22 deal differently with the land of **G**,
9:26 of **G**, where the Israelites were.
Jos 10:41 the whole region of **G** to Gibeon.
11:16 the whole region of **G**, the western
15:51 **G**, Holon and Giloh—eleven towns and

Gospel
Mt 24:14 this **g** of the kingdom will be
26:13 truth, wherever this **g** is preached
Mk 1: 1 The beginning of the **g** about Jesus
8:35 for me and for the **g** will save it.
10:29 children or fields for me and the **g**
13:10 the **g** must first be preached to all
14: 9 truth, wherever the **g** is preached
Lk 9: 6 preaching the **g** and healing people
20: 1 temple courts and preaching the **g**,
Ac 8:25 the **g** in many Samaritan villages.
8:40 preaching the **g** in all the towns
15: 7 the message of the **g** and believe.
16:10 called us to preach the **g** to them.
20:24 testifying to the **g** of God's grace.
Ro 1: 1 and set apart for the **g** of God—
1: 2 the **g** he promised beforehand through
1: 9 heart in preaching the **g** of his Son,
1:15 the **g** also to you who are at Rome.
1:16 I am not ashamed of the **g**, because
1:17 For in the **g** a righteousness from
2:16 Jesus Christ, as my **g** declares.
11:28 far as the **g** is concerned, they are
15:16 duty of proclaiming the **g** of God,
15:19 fully proclaimed the **g** of Christ.
15:20 the **g** where Christ was not known,
16:25 is able to establish you by my **g**
1Co 1:17 but to preach the **g**—not with words
4:15 I became your father through the **g**.
9:12 rather than hinder the **g** of Christ.
9:14 that those who preach the **g** should
9:14 receive their living from the **g**.
9:16 Yet when I preach the **g**, I cannot
9:16 Woe to me if I do not preach the **g**!
9:18 preaching the **g** I may offer it free
9:23 I do all this for the sake of the **g**,
15: 1 I want to remind you of the **g** I
15: 2 By this **g** you are saved, if you hold
2Co 2:12 to Troas to preach the **g** of Christ
4: 3 even if our **g** is veiled, it is
4: 4 of the **g** of the glory of Christ,
8:18 churches for his service to the **g**.
9:13 your confession of the **g** of Christ,
10:14 as far as you with the **g** of Christ.
10:16 that we can preach the **g** in the
11: 4 or a different **g** from the one you
11: 7 the **g** of God to you free of charge?
Gal 1: 6 and are turning to a different **g**—
1: 7 which is really no **g** at all.
1: 7 trying to pervert the **g** of Christ.
1: 8 a **g** other than the one we preached
1: 9 a **g** other than what you accepted,
1:11 brothers, that the **g** I preached is
2: 2 **g** that I preach among the Gentiles.
Gal 2: 5 truth of the **g** might remain with you
2: 7 of preaching the **g** to the Gentiles,
2:14 in line with the truth of the **g**,
3: 8 and announced the **g** in advance to
4:13 that I first preached the **g** to you.
Eph 1:13 of truth, the **g** of your salvation.
3: 6 through the **g** the Gentiles are heirs
3: 7 I became a servant of this **g** by the
6:15 that comes from the **g** of peace.
6:19 make known the mystery of the **g**,
Php 1: 5 of your partnership in the **g** from
1: 7 or defending and confirming the **g**,
1:12 has really served to advance the **g**.
1:16 put here for the defence of the **g**.
1:27 a manner worthy of the **g** of Christ.
1:27 as one man for the faith of the **g**
2:22 served with me in the work of the **g**
4: 3 at my side in the cause of the **g**,
4:15 of your acquaintance with the **g**,
Col 1: 5 about in the word of truth, the **g**
1: 6 All over the world this **g** is bearing
1:23 from the hope held out in the **g**.
1:23 This is the **g** that you heard and
1Th 1: 5 our **g** came to you not simply with
2: 2 his **g** in spite of strong opposition.
2: 4 by God to be entrusted with the **g**.
2: 8 the **g** of God but our lives as well,
2: 9 we preached the **g** of God to you.
3: 2 in spreading the **g** of Christ,
2Th 1: 8 do not obey the **g** of our Lord Jesus.
2:14 He called you to this through our **g**,
1Ti 1:11 that conforms to the glorious **g** of
2Ti 1: 8 for the **g**, by the power of God,
1:10 immortality to light through the **g**.
1:11 of this **g** I was appointed a herald
2: 8 This is my **g**,
Phm :13 me while I am in chains for the **g**.
Heb 4: 2 For we also have had the **g** preached
4: 6 and those who formerly had the **g**
1Pe 1:12 those who have preached the **g** to
4: 6 is the reason the **g** was preached
4:17 those who do not obey the **g** of God?
Rev 14: 6 and he had the eternal **g** to proclaim

Gossip (Gossiping, Gossips)
Pr 11:13 A **g** betrays a confidence, but a
16:28 and a **g** separates close friends.
18: 8 words of a **g** are like choice morsels
20:19 A **g** betrays a confidence; so avoid a
26:20 out; without **g** a quarrel dies down.
26:22 words of a **g** are like choice morsels
2Co 12:20 slander, **g**, arrogance and disorder.

Gossiping (Gossip)
3Jn :10 he is doing, **g** maliciously about us.

Gossips (Gossip)
Ro 1:29 deceit and malice. They are **g**,
1Ti 5:13 but also **g** and busybodies, saying

Gouge (Gouged)
Nu 16:14 you **g** out the eyes of these men?
1Sa 11: 2 I **g** out the right eye of every one
Mt 5:29 to sin, **g** it out and throw it away.
18: 9 if your eye causes you to sin, **g** it

Gouged (Gouge)
Jdg 16:21 the Philistines seized him, **g** out

Gourds
1Ki 6:18 carved with **g** and open flowers.
7:24 Below the rim, **g** encircled it—ten
7:24 The **g** were cast in two rows in one
2Ki 4:39 He gathered some of its **g** and filled

Govern (Governed, Governing, Government, Governor, Governor's, Governors, Governs)
Ge 1:16 greater light to **g** the day
1:16 and the lesser light to **g** the night.
1:18 to **g** the day and the night, and to
1Sa 9:17 to you about; he will **g** my people."
1Ki 3: 9 a discerning heart to **g** your people
1Ki 3: 9 to **g** this great people of yours?"
2Ch 1:10 to **g** this great people of yours?"
1:11 knowledge to **g** my people over whom I
Job 34:17 Can he who hates justice **g**? Will you
Ps 9: 8 he will **g** the peoples with justice.
136: 8 the sun to **g** the day, His love
136: 9 the moon and stars to **g** the night;
Pr 8:16 by me princes **g**, and all nobles who
Isa 3: 4 mere children will **g** them.
Ob :21 Zion to **g** the mountains of Esau.
Zec 3: 7 then you will **g** my house and have
Ro 12: 8 let him **g** diligently; if it is

Governed (Govern)
Jdg 9:22 After Abimelech had **g** Israel for
2Ki 15: 5 palace and **g** the people of the land
2Ch 26:21 palace and **g** the people of the land

Governing (Govern)
Ro 13: 1 submit himself to the **g** authorities
13: 6 who give their full time to **g**.

Government (Govern)
1Ki 9:22 his **g** officials, his officers, his
Isa 9: 6 and the **g** will be on his shoulders.
9: 7 Of the increase of his **g** and peace
Da 6: 4 Daniel in his conduct of **g** affairs,

Governor (Govern)
Ge 42: 6 Now Joseph was the **g** of the land,
Jdg 9:30 Zebul the **g** of the city heard what
1Ki 4:19 He was the only **g** over the district.
2Ki 10: 5 the palace administrator, the city **g**,
23: 8 the city **g**, which is on the left of
25:23 Babylon had appointed Gedaliah as **g**,
Ezr 2:63 The **g** ordered them not to eat any of
5: 3 At that time Tattenai, **g** of
5: 6 **g** of Trans-Euphrates, and
5:14 Sheshbazzar, whom he had appointed **g**,
6: 6 Now then, Tattenai, **g** of
6: 7 Let the **g** of the Jews and the Jewish
6:13 Tattenai, **g** of Trans-Euphrates, and
Ne 3: 7 of the **g** of Trans-Euphrates.
5:14 when I was appointed to be their **g**
5:14 ate the food allotted to the **g**.
5:18 demanded the food allotted to the **g**,
7:65 The **g**, therefore, ordered them not
7:70 The **g** gave to the treasury 1,000
8: 9 Nehemiah the **g**, Ezra the priest and
10: 1 Nehemiah the **g**, the son of Hacaliah.
12:26 Nehemiah the **g** and of Ezra the priest
Isa 60:17 your **g** and righteousness your ruler.
Jer 40: 7 son of Ahikam as **g** over the land
40:11 the son of Shaphan, as **g** over them,
41: 2 had appointed as **g** over the land.
41:18 had appointed as **g** over the land.
Hag 1: 1 **g** of Judah, and to Joshua son of
1:14 **g** of Judah, and the spirit of Joshua
2: 2 **g** of Judah, to Joshua son of
2:21 "Tell Zerubbabel **g** of Judah that I
Mal 1: 8 Try offering them to your **g**! Would
Mt 27: 2 handed him over to Pilate, the **g**.
27:11 Meanwhile Jesus stood before the **g**,
27:11 and the **g** asked him, "Are you the
27:14 the great amazement of the **g**.
27:21 me to release to you?" asked the **g**.
28:14 If this report gets to the **g**, we
Lk 2: 2 while Quirinius was **g** of Syria.)
3: 1 Pontius Pilate was **g** of Judea,
20:20 to the power and authority of the **g**.
Jn 18:28 to the palace of the Roman **g**.
Ac 23:24 he may be taken safely to **G** Felix."
23:26 Claudius Lysias, To His Excellency, **G**
23:33 the **g** and handed Paul over to him.
23:34 The **g** read the letter and asked what
24: 1 charges against Paul before the **g**.
24:10 the **g** motioned for him to speak,
26:30 The king rose, and with him the **g**
2Co 11:32 In Damascus the **g** under King Aretas

Governor's (Govern)
Mt 27:15 Now it was the **g** custom at the Feast
27:27 the **g** soldiers took Jesus into the

Governors (Govern)
1Ki 4: 7 Solomon also had twelve district **g**
10:15 Arabian kings and the **g** of the land.
2Ch 9:14 the **g** of the land brought gold and
Ezr 8:36 to the **g** of Trans-Euphrates who then
Ne 2: 7 may I have letters to the **g** of
2: 9 I went to the **g** of Trans-Euphrates
5:15 the earlier **g**—those preceding
Est 3:12 the **g** of the various provinces and
8: 9 and to the satraps, **g** and nobles of
9: 3 the satraps, the **g** and the king's
Jer 51:23 with you I shatter **g** and officials.
51:28 their **g** and all their officials, and
51:57 her **g**, officers and warriors as well;
Eze 23: 6 clothed in blue, **g** and commanders,
23:12 too lusted after the Assyrians—**g**
23:23 handsome young men, all of them **g**
Da 3: 2 prefects, **g**, advisers, treasurers,
3: 3 the satraps, prefects, **g**, advisers,
3:27 the satraps, prefects, **g** and royal
6: 7 prefects, satraps, advisers and **g**
Mt 10:18 you will be brought before **g**
Mk 13: 9 **g** and kings as witnesses to them.
Lk 21:12 brought before kings and **g**, and all
1Pe 2:14 or to **g**, who are sent by him to

Governs (Govern)
Job 36:31 This is the way he **g** the nations and

Gown
Ps 45:13 her **g** is interwoven with gold.

Goyim
Jos 12:23 Dor) one the king of **G** in Gilgal

Gozan
2Ki 17: 6 He settled them in Halah, in **G** on
18:11 in **G** on the Habor River, and in
19:12 deliver them: the gods of **G**,
1Ch 5:26 the river of **G**, where they are to
Isa 37:12 deliver them—the gods of **G**,

Grabbed
Jdg 15:15 **g** it and struck down a thousand men.
2Sa 2:16 each man **g** his opponent by the head
13:11 she took it to him to eat, he **g** her
Mt 18:28 He **g** him and began to choke him.

Grace (*Grace and peace, Grace of God*, Graceful, Gracious, Graciously)
Ps 45: 2 your lips have been anointed with **g**,
Pr 1: 9 will be a garland to **g** your head
3:22 for you, an ornament to **g** your neck.
3:34 He mocks proud mockers but gives **g**
4: 9 She will set a garland of **g** on your
Isa 26:10 Though **g** is shown to the wicked,
Jnh 2: 8 forfeit the **g** that could be theirs.
Zec 12:10 a spirit of **g** and supplication.
Jn 1:14 the Father, full of **g** and truth.
1:16 From the fulness of his **g** we have
1:17 **g** and truth came through Jesus
Ac 4:33 Jesus, and much **g** was upon them all.
6: 8 Now Stephen, a man full of God's **g**
14: 3 who confirmed the message of his **g**
15:11 No! We believe it is through the **g**
15:40 the brothers to the **g** of the Lord.
18:27 help to those who by **g** had believed.
20:24 testifying to the gospel of God's **g**.
20:32 you to God and to the word of his **g**,
Ro 1: 5 we received **g** and apostleship to
3:24 are justified freely by his **g**
4:16 so that it may be by **g** and may be
5: 2 into this **g** in which we now stand.
5:15 how much more did God's **g** and the
5:15 that came by the **g** of the one man,
5:17 God's abundant provision of **g**
5:20 increased, **g** increased all the more,
5:21 so also **g** might reign through
6: 1 on sinning, so that **g** may increase?
6:14 you are not under law, but under **g**.
6:15 under law but under **g**? By no means!
11: 5 time there is a remnant chosen by **g**.
11: 6 if by **g**, then it is no longer by
11: 6 if it were, **g** would no longer be **g**.
12: 3 For by the **g** given me I say to every
12: 6 gifts, according to the **g** given us.
15:15 again, because of the **g** God gave
16:20 The **g** of our Lord Jesus be with you.
1Co 1: 4 of his **g** given you in Christ Jesus.
3:10 By the **g** God has given me, I laid a
15:10 his **g** to me was not without effect.
16:23 The **g** of the Lord Jesus be with you.
2Co 1:12 wisdom but according to God's **g**.
4:15 so that the **g** that is reaching more
6: 1 you not to receive God's **g** in vain.
8: 1 we want you to know about the **g** that
8: 6 this act of **g** on your part.
8: 7 you also excel in this **g** of giving.
8: 9 For you know the **g** of our Lord Jesus
9: 8 God is able to make all **g** abound to
9:14 the surpassing **g** God has given you.
12: 9 he said to me, "My **g** is sufficient
13:14 May the **g** of the Lord Jesus Christ,
Gal 1: 6 who called you by the **g** of Christ
1:15 and called me by his **g**, was
2: 9 they recognised the **g** given to me.
3:18 but God in his **g** gave it to Abraham
5: 4 Christ; you have fallen away from **g**.
6:18 The **g** of our Lord Jesus Christ be
Eph 1: 6 to the praise of his glorious **g**,
1: 7 with the riches of God's **g**
2: 5 it is by **g** you have been saved.
2: 7 the incomparable riches of his **g**,
2: 8 For it is by **g** you have been saved,
3: 2 God's **g** that was given to me for you,
3: 7 by the gift of God's **g** given me
3: 8 this **g** was given me: to preach to
4: 7 to each one of us **g** has been given
6:24 **G** to all who love our Lord Jesus
Php 1: 7 all of you share in God's **g** with me.
4:23 The **g** of the Lord Jesus Christ be
Col 1: 6 understood God's **g** in all its truth.
4: 6 conversation be always full of **g**,
4:18 Remember my chains. **G** be with you.
1Th 5:28 The **g** of our Lord Jesus Christ be
2Th 1:12 and you in him, according to the **g**
2:16 who loved us and by his **g** gave us
3:18 The **g** of our Lord Jesus Christ be
1Ti 1: 2 Timothy my true son in the faith: **G**,
1:14 The **g** of our Lord was poured out on
6:21 **G** be with you.
2Ti 1: 2 To Timothy, my dear son: **G**, mercy
1: 9 because of his own purpose and **g**.
1: 9 This **g** was given us in Christ Jesus
2: 1 You then, my son, be strong in the **g**
4:22 be with your spirit. **G** be with you.
Tit 3: 7 that, having been justified by his **g**,
3:15 **G** be with you all.
Phm : 3 **G** to you and peace from God our
:25 The **g** of the Lord Jesus Christ be
Heb 4:16 Let us then approach the throne of **g**
4:16 **g** to help us in our time of need.
10:29 who has insulted the Spirit of **g**?
13: 9 our hearts to be strengthened by **g**,
13:25 **G** be with you all.
Jas 4: 6 he gives us more **g**. That is why
4: 6 proud but gives **g** to the humble."
1Pe 1:10 the prophets, who spoke of the **g**
1:13 set your hope fully on the **g** to be
4:10 God's **g** in its various forms.
5: 5 proud but gives **g** to the humble."
5:10 the God of all **g**, who called you to
2Pe 1: 2 **G** and peace be yours in abundance
3:18 grow in the **g** and knowledge of our
2Jn : 3 **G**, mercy and peace from God the
Jude : 4 who change the **g** of our God into a
Rev 22:21 The **g** of the Lord Jesus be with

Grace and peace
Ro 1: 7 **G** to you from God our Father and
1Co 1: 3 **G** to you from God our Father and the
2Co 1: 2 **G** to you from God our Father and the
Gal 1: 3 **G** to you from God our Father and the
Eph 1: 2 **G** to you from God our Father and the
Php 1: 2 **G** to you from God our Father and the
Col 1: 2 **G** to you from God our Father.
1Th 1: 1 and the Lord Jesus Christ: **G** to you.
2Th 1: 2 **G** to you from God the Father and the
Tit 1: 4 my true son in our common faith: **G**
1Pe 1: 2 his blood: **G** be yours in abundance.
2Pe 1: 2 **G** be yours in abundance through the
Rev 1: 4 of Asia: **G** to you from him who is,

Grace of God
Lk 2:40 with wisdom, and the **g** was upon him.
Ac 11:23 and saw the evidence of the **g**,
13:43 and urged them to continue in the **g**.
14:26 had been committed to the **g** for the
1Co 15:10 by the **g** I am what I am, and his
15:10 not I, but the **g** that was with me.
Gal 2:21 I do not set aside the **g**, for if
Tit 2:11 For the **g** that brings salvation has
Heb 2: 9 by the **g** he might taste death for
12:15 See to it that no-one misses the **g**
1Pe 5:12 testifying that this is the true **g**.

Graceful (Grace)
Job 41:12 limbs, his strength and his **g** form.
Pr 5:19 A loving doe, a **g** deer—may her
SS 7: 1 Your **g** legs are like jewels, the

Gracious (Grace)
Ge 21: 1 Now the LORD was **g** to Sarah as he
33:11 been **g** to me and I have all I need.
43:29 he said, "God be **g** to you, my son.
Ex 34: 6 the LORD, the compassionate and **g**
Nu 6:25 face shine upon you and be **g** to you;
1Sa 2:21 the LORD was **g** to Hannah; she
2Sa 1:23 in life they were loved and **g**, and
12:22 be **g** to me and let the child live.'
2Ki 13:23 the LORD was **g** to them and had
2Ch 30: 9 LORD your God is **g** and compassionate.
Ezr 7: 9 the **g** hand of his God was on him.
8:18 the **g** hand of our God was on us,
8:22 "The **g** hand of our God is on
9: 8 the LORD our God has been **g** in
Ne 2: 8 the **g** hand of my God was upon me,
2:18 I also told them about the **g** hand of
9:17 But you are a forgiving God, **g** and
9:31 for you are a **g** and merciful God.
Job 33:24 to be **g** to him and say, 'Spare him
Ps 25:16 Turn to me and be **g** to me, for I am
67: 1 May God be **g** to us and bless us and
86:15 O Lord, are a compassionate and **g**
103: 8 The LORD is compassionate and **g**,
111: 4 the LORD is **g** and compassionate.
112: 4 for the **g** and compassionate and
116: 5 The LORD is **g** and righteous; our God
119:29 me from deceitful ways; be **g** to me
119:58 **g** to me according to your promise.
145: 8 The LORD is **g** and compassionate,
Pr 22:11 whose speech is **g** will have the king
Ecc 10:12 Words from a wise man's mouth are **g**,
Isa 30:18 Yet the LORD longs to be **g** to you;
30:19 How **g** he will be when you cry for
33: 2 O LORD, be **g** to us; we long for you.
Jer 29:10 come to you and fulfil my **g** promise
33:14 'when I will fulfil the **g** promise I
Joel 2:13 for he is **g** and compassionate, slow
Jnh 4: 2 I knew that you are a **g** and
Mal 1: 9 "Now implore God to be **g** to us. With
Lk 4:22 the **g** words that came from his lips.
2Co 1:11 for the **g** favour granted us in
1Pe 3: 7 with you of the **g** gift of life,

Graciously (Grace)
Ge 33: 5 God has **g** given your servant."
Hos 14: 2 all our sins and receive us **g**,
Ac 27:24 and God has **g** given you the lives of
Ro 8:32 with him, **g** give us all things?

Graft (Grafted)
Ro 11:23 for God is able to **g** them in again.

Grafted (Graft)
Ro 11:17 have been **g** in among the others and
11:19 broken off so that I could be **g** in."
11:23 they will be **g** in, for God is able
11:24 and contrary to nature were **g** into a
11:24 be **g** into their own olive tree!

Grain (*Grain offering, Grain offerings*, Grains, Granaries)

Ge 27:28 an abundance of g and new wine.
27:37 sustained him with g and new wine.
41:35 store up g under the authority of
41:49 Joseph stored up huge quantities of g
41:56 and sold g to the Egyptians,
41:57 came to Egypt to buy g from Joseph,
42: 1 Jacob learned that there was g in
42: 2 have heard that there is g in Egypt.
42: 3 went down to buy g from Egypt.
42: 5 were among those who went to buy g,
42: 6 one who sold g to all its people.
42:19 go and take g back for your starving
42:25 orders to fill their bags with g,
42:26 they loaded their g on their donkeys
43: 2 when they had eaten all the g they
44: 2 along with the silver for his g.
45:23 ten female donkeys loaded with g and
47:14 payment for the g they were buying,
Ex 22: 6 it burns shocks of g or standing
Lev 2:14 heads of new g roasted in the fire.
2:16 of the crushed g and the oil,
23:10 a sheaf of the first g you harvest.
23:14 or roasted or new g, until the very
23:16 an offering of new g to the LORD.
23:18 together with their g offerings and
23:37 burnt offerings and g offerings,
27:30 whether g from the soil or fruit
Nu 18: 9 whether g or sin or guilt offerings
18:12 all the finest new wine and g they
18:27 g from the threshing-floor or juice
20: 5 terrible place? It has no g or figs
28:26 of new g during the Feast of Weeks,
Dt 7:13 the crops of your land—your g, new
11:14 gather in your g, new wine and oil.
12:17 of your g and new wine and oil,
14:23 Eat the tithe of your g, new wine
18: 4 give them the firstfruits of your g,
25: 4 ox while it is treading out the g.
28:51 They will leave you no g, new wine
33:28 secure in a land of g and new wine,
Jos 5:11 unleavened bread and roasted g.
Ru 2: 2 pick up the leftover g behind anyone
2:14 he offered her some roasted g.
2:21 they finish harvesting all my g.'"
3: 7 down at the far end of the g pile.
1Sa 8:15 He will take a tenth of your g and
17:17 "Take this ephah of roasted g and
25:18 five seahs of roasted g, a hundred
2Sa 1:21 field that yield offerings ⌊of g⌋
17:19 of the well and scattered g over it.
17:28 and roasted g, beans and lentils,
2Ki 18:32 a land of g and new wine, a land of
2Ch 31: 5 gave the firstfruits of their g,
32:28 buildings to store the harvest of g,
Ne 5: 2 eat and stay alive, we must get g."
5: 3 homes to get g during the famine."
5:10 also lending the people money and g.
5:11 of the money, g, new wine and oil."
10:31 or g to sell on the Sabbath,
10:39 to bring their contributions of g,
13: 5 and also the tithes of g, new wine
13:12 All Judah brought the tithes of g,
13:15 bringing in g and loading it on
Job 31:10 may my wife grind another man's g,
39:12 Can you trust him to bring in your g
Ps 4: 7 when their g and new wine abound.
78:24 eat, he gave them the g of heaven.
Pr 11:26 People curse the man who hoards g,
27:22 grinding him like g with a pestle,
Isa 5:10 a homer of seed only an ephah of g."
23: 3 On the great waters came the g of
28:28 G must be ground to make bread; so
62: 8 "Never again will I give your g as
Jer 23:28 For what has straw to do with g?"
31:12 the g, the new wine and the oil,
50:26 pile her up like heaps of g.
Hos 2: 8 I was the one who gave her the g,
2: 9 "Therefore I will take away my g
2:22 the earth will respond to the g, the
7:14 They gather together for g and new
8: 7 Were it to yield g, foreigners would
Joel 1:10 the g is destroyed, the new wine is
1:17 broken down, for the g has dried up.
2:19 "I am sending you g, new wine and
2:24 will be filled with g;
Am 2:13 a cart crushes when loaded with g.
5:11 poor and force him to give you g.
8: 5 New Moon be over that we may sell g,
9: 9 nations as g is shaken in a sieve,
Hag 1:11 on the g, the new wine, the oil and
Zec 9:17 G will make the young men thrive,
Mk 4: 7 plants, so that they did not bear g.
4:28 the ear, then the full g in the ear.
4:29 soon as the g is ripe, he puts the
Lk 6: 1 them in their hands and eat the g.
12:18 I will store all my g and my goods.
17:35 Two women will be grinding g
Jn 12:24 I tell you the truth, unless a g of
Ac 7:12 Jacob heard that there was g in
27:38 ship by throwing the g into the sea.
1Co 9: 9 ox while it is treading out the g.
1Ti 5:18 ox while it is treading out the g,"

Grain offering

Ex 29:41 lamb at twilight with the same g
30: 9 incense or any burnt offering or g,
Lev 2: 1 "When someone brings a g to the
2: 3 The rest of the g belongs to Aaron
2: 4 "If you bring a g baked in an oven,
2: 5 If your g is prepared on a griddle,
2: 6 it and pour oil on it; it is a g.
2: 7 If your g is cooked in a pan, it is
2: 8 Bring the g made of these things to
2: 9 out the memorial portion from the g
2:10 The rest of the g belongs to Aaron
2:11 "Every g you bring to the LORD must
2:14 "If you bring a g of firstfruits to
2:15 Put oil and incense on it; it is a g.
5:13 priest, as in the case of the g.'"
6:14 "'These are the regulations for the g
6:15 with all the incense on the g,
6:20 ephah of fine flour as a regular g,
6:21 present the g broken in pieces as an
6:23 Every g of a priest shall be burned
7: 9 Every g baked in an oven or cooked
7:10 every g, whether mixed with oil or
7:37 the g, the sin offering, the guilt
9: 4 together with a g mixed with oil.
9:17 He also brought the g, took a
10:12 "Take the g left over from the
14:10 oil for a g, and one log of oil.
14:20 together with the g, and make
14:21 with oil for a g, a log of oil,
14:31 burnt offering, together with the g
23:13 together with its g of two-tenths
Nu 4:16 the regular g and the anointing oil.
5:15 because it is a g for jealousy, a
5:18 the g for jealousy, while he himself
5:25 from her hands the g for jealousy,
5:26 of the g as a memorial offering
6:17 with its g and drink offering.
7:13 fine flour mixed with oil as a g;
7:19 fine flour mixed with oil as a g;
7:25 fine flour mixed with oil as a g;
7:31 fine flour mixed with oil as a g;
7:37 fine flour mixed with oil as a g;
7:43 fine flour mixed with oil as a g;
7:49 fine flour mixed with oil as a g;
7:55 fine flour mixed with oil as a g;
7:61 fine flour mixed with oil as a g;
7:67 fine flour mixed with oil as a g;
7:73 fine flour mixed with oil as a g;
7:79 fine flour mixed with oil as a g;
7:87 a year old, together with their g.
8: 8 its g of fine flour mixed with oil;
15: 4 shall present to the LORD a g of a
15: 6 "'With a ram prepare a g of
15: 9 bring with the bull a g of
15:24 along with its prescribed g and
28: 5 together with a g of a tenth of an
28: 8 along with the same kind of g and
28: 9 a g of two-tenths of an ephah of
28:12 With each bull there is to be a g
28:12 a g of two-tenths of an ephah of
28:13 with each lamb, a g of a tenth of
28:20 With each bull prepare a g of
28:28 With each bull there is to be a g
28:31 regular burnt offering and its g.
Nu 29: 3 With the bull prepare a g of
29: 9 With the bull prepare a g of
29:11 its g, and their drink offerings.
29:14 prepare a g of three-tenths of an
29:16 with its g and drink offering.
29:19 its g, and their drink offerings.
29:22 with its g and drink offering.
29:25 with its g and drink offering.
29:28 with its g and drink offering.
29:31 with its g and drink offering.
29:34 with its g and drink offering.
29:38 with its g and drink offering.
Jdg 13:19 together with the g, and sacrificed
13:23 burnt offering and g from our hands
2Ki 16:13 offered up his burnt offering and g
16:15 burnt offering and the evening g,
16:15 the king's burnt offering and his g
16:15 their g and their drink offering.
1Ch 21:23 the wood, and the wheat for the g.
Isa 66: 3 whoever makes a g is like one who
Eze 45:24 He is to provide as a g an ephah for
46: 5 The g given with the ram is to be an
46: 5 and the g with the lambs is to be as
46: 7 He is to provide as a g one ephah
46:11 the g is to be an ephah with a bull,
46:14 with it morning by morning a g,
46:14 g to the LORD is a lasting ordinance.
46:15 the lamb and the g and the oil shall
46:20 and the sin offering and bake the g,

Grain offerings

Ex 40:29 and g, as the LORD commanded him.
Lev 2:13 Season all your g with salt. Do not
2:13 g; add salt to all your offerings.
23:18 together with their g and drink
23:37 by fire—the burnt offerings and g,
Nu 6:15 together with their g and drink
29: 6 g and drink offerings as specified.
29:18 rams and lambs, prepare their g and
29:21 rams and lambs, prepare their g and
29:24 rams and lambs, prepare their g and
29:27 rams and lambs, prepare their g and
29:30 rams and lambs, prepare their g and
29:33 rams and lambs, prepare their g and
29:37 prepare their g and drink offerings
29:39 g, drink offerings and fellowship
Jos 22:23 and to offer burnt offerings and g,
22:29 g and sacrifices, other than the
1Ki 8:64 g and the fat of the fellowship
8:64 the g and the fat of the fellowship
1Ch 23:29 the flour for the g, the unleavened
2Ch 7: 7 the g and the fat portions.
Ezr 7:17 together with their g and drink
Ne 10:33 for the regular g and burnt
13: 5 g and incense and temple articles,
13: 9 of God, with the g and the incense.
Isa 19:21 will worship with sacrifices and g;
43:23 I have not burdened you with g nor
57: 6 out drink offerings and offered g.
66:20 as the Israelites bring their g, to
Jer 14:12 and g, I will not accept them.
17:26 g, incense and thank-offerings to
33:18 burn g and to present sacrifices.'"
41: 5 Shiloh and Samaria, bringing g and
Eze 42:13 put the most holy offerings—the g,
44:29 They will eat the g, the sin
45:15 These will be used for the g, burnt
45:17 g and drink offerings at the
45:17 will provide the sin offerings, g,
45:25 burnt offerings, g and oil.
Joel 1: 9 G and drink offerings are cut off
1:13 for the g and drink offerings are
2:14 g and drink offerings for the LORD
Am 5:22 and g, I will not accept them.

Grains (Grain)

Dt 32:14 of Bashan and the finest g of wheat.
Job 29:18 days as numerous as the g of sand.
Ps 139:18 they would outnumber the g of sand.
Isa 48:19 your children like its numberless g;

Granaries (Grain)

Ex 22:29 offerings from your g or your vats.
Jer 50:26 Break open her g; pile her up like
Joel 1:17 the g have been broken down,

Grandchildren (Child)
Ge 31:28 You didn't even let me kiss my g and
31:55 g and his daughters and blessed them.
45:10 your children and g, your flocks and
Ex 10: 2 that you may tell your children and g
Dt 4:25 After you have had children and g
2Ki 17:41 To this day their children and g
1Ti 5: 4 if a widow has children or g, these

Granddaughter (Daughter)
Ge 24:48 g of my master's brother for his son.
36: 2 of Anah and g of Zibeon the Hivite—
36:14 daughter of Anah and g of Zibeon,
2Ki 8:26 Athaliah, a g of Omri king of Israel.
2Ch 22: 2 name was Athaliah, a g of Omri.

Granddaughters (Daughter)
Ge 46: 7 daughters and g—all his offspring.

Grandfather (Father)
2Sa 9: 7 land that belonged to your g Saul,

Grandfather's (Father)
2Sa 16: 3 will give me back my g kingdom.'"
19:28 All my g descendants deserved

Grandmother (Mother)
1Ki 15:13 He even deposed his g Maacah from
2Ch 15:16 King Asa also deposed his g Maacah
2Ti 1: 5 which first lived in your g Lois and

Grandmother's (Mother)
1Ki 15:10 His g name was Maacah daughter of

Grandparents (Parents)
1Ti 5: 4 repaying their parents and g,

Grandson (Son)
Ge 11:31 Terah took his son Abram, his g Lot
29: 5 "Do you know Laban, Nahor's g?" "Yes,
Jdg 8:22 your son and your g—because you
2Sa 9: 9 "I have given your master's g
9:10 your master's g may be provided for.
9:10 And Mephibosheth, g of your master,
16: 3 "Where is your master's g?" Ziba
19:24 Mephibosheth, Saul's g, also went
Jer 27: 7 serve him and his son and his g

Grandsons (Son)
Ge 36:12 These were g of Esau's wife Adah.
36:13 These were g of Esau's wife Basemath.
36:16 Eliphaz in Edom; they were g of Adah.
36:17 they were g of Esau's wife Basemath.
46: 7 his sons and g and his daughters
Jdg 12:14 He had forty sons and thirty g, who
1Ch 8:40 They had many sons and g—150 in all.

Grant (Granted, Granting, Grants)
Ge 19:21 "Very well, I will g this request
24:42 if you will, please g success to the
43:14 may God Almighty g you mercy before
Ex 21: 9 must g her the rights of a daughter.
Lev 26: 6 "I will g peace in the land, and
Dt 28: 7 The—will g that the enemies who
28:11 The LORD will g you abundant
Jdg 11:37 g me this one request," she said.
Ru 1: 9 May the LORD g that each of you will
1Sa 1:17 g you what you have asked of him."
2Sa 23: 5 salvation and g me my every desire?
1Ki 5: 9 And you are to g my wish by
1Ch 22: 9 and I will g Israel peace and quiet
Est 5: 8 g my petition and fulfil my request,
7: 3 g me my life—this is my petition.
Job 6: 8 that God would g what I hope for,
13:20 "Only g me these two things, O God,
Ps 20: 2 and g you support from Zion.
20: 5 May the LORD g all your requests.
51:12 g me a willing spirit, to sustain me.
85: 7 O LORD, and g us your salvation.
86:16 g your strength to your servant
94:13 you g him relief from days of
118:25 save us; O LORD, g us success.
140: 8 do not g the wicked their desires,
Isa 46:13 I will g salvation to Zion, my
Hag 2: 9 'And in this place I will g peace,'
Mt 20:21 She said, "G that one of these two
20:23 my right or left is not for me to g
Mk 10:40 my right or left is not for me to g
Lk 18: 3 'G me justice against my adversary.
23:24 Pilate decided to g their demand.
Ac 24:27 but because Felix wanted to g a
2Ti 1:18 May the Lord g that he will find
2:25 in the hope that God will g them

Granted (Grant)
Ge 4:25 "God has g me another child in place
24:56 LORD has g success to my journey.
39:21 he showed him kindness and g him
Jos 1:13 you rest and has g you this land.
14: 3 Moses had g the two-and-a-half
14: 3 not g the Levites an inheritance
1Sa 1:27 LORD has g me what I asked of him.
25:35 your words and g your request."
2Sa 14:22 king has g his servant's request
1Ch 4:10 And God g his request.
22:18 And has he not g you rest on every
23:25 the God of Israel, has g rest to his
Ezr 7: 6 The king had g him everything he
9: 9 He has g us new life to rebuild the
Ne 2: 8 was upon me, the king g my requests
Est 5: 6 to half the kingdom, it will be g
7: 2 to half the kingdom, it will be g
8:11 king's edict g the Jews in every
9:12 is your request? It will also be g
Job 42:15 and their father g them an
Ps 21: 2 You have g him the desire of his
21: 6 Surely you have g him eternal
Pr 10:24 what the righteous desire will be g
Mt 14: 9 he ordered that her request be g
15:28 have great faith! Your request is g
Jn 5:26 g the Son to have life in himself.
17: 2 For you g him authority over all
Ac 11:18 "So then, God has g even the
Ro 11:20 G. But they were broken off because
2Co 1:11 the gracious favour g us in answer
Php 1:29 For it has been g to you on behalf

Granting (Grant)
Ne 1:11 success today by g him favour

Grants (Grant)
Ps 127: 2 for he g sleep to those he loves.
147:14 He g peace to your borders and

Grape (Grapes, Grape-pickers, Grapevine, Grapevines)
Lev 26: 5 threshing will continue until g
26: 5 the g harvest will continue until
Nu 6: 3 g juice or eat grapes or raisins.
Dt 32:14 You drank the foaming blood of the g
Jdg 8: 2 than the full g harvest of Abiezer?
Isa 18: 5 and the flower becomes a ripening g,
24:13 are left after the g harvest.
32:10 tremble; the g harvest will fail,
Ob : 5 wanted? If g pickers came to you,

Grape-pickers (Grape)
Jer 49: 9 If g came to you, would they not

Grapes (Grape)
Ge 40:10 and its clusters ripened into g.
40:11 and I took the g, squeezed them into
49:11 wine, his robes in the blood of g.
Lev 19:10 or pick up the g that have fallen.
25: 5 the g of your untended vines.
Nu 6: 3 grape juice or eat g or raisins.
13:20 the season for the first ripe g.)
13:23 bearing a single cluster of g.
13:24 of g the Israelites cut off there.
Dt 23:24 you may eat all the g you want, but
24:21 you harvest the g in your vineyard,
28:39 not drink the wine or gather the g,
32:32 Their g are filled with poison, and
Jdg 8: 2 Aren't the gleanings of Ephraim's g
9:27 and gathered the g and trodden them,
Ne 13:15 g, figs and all other kinds of loads.
Job 15:33 a vine stripped of its unripe g,
Ps 80:12 so that all who pass by pick its g?
Isa 5: 2 looked for a crop of good g, but it
5: 4 good g, why did it yield only bad?
62: 9 and those who gather the g will
65: 8 found in a cluster of g and men say,
Jer 6: 9 again, like one gathering g."
8:13 There will be no g on the vine.
25:30 shout like those who tread the g,
31:29 'The fathers have eaten sour g, and
31:30 whoever eats sour g—his own teeth
48:32 fallen on your ripened fruit and g.
49: 9 would they not leave a few g? If
Eze 18: 2 "'The fathers eat sour g, and the
Hos 9:10 it was like finding g in the desert;
Joel 3:13 Come, trample the g, for the
Am 9:13 the planter by the one treading g.
Ob : 5 you, would they not leave a few g?
Mic 6:15 will crush g but not drink the wine.
7: 1 there is no cluster of g to eat,
Hab 3:17 bud and there are no g on the vines,
Mt 7:16 Do people pick g from thornbushes,
Lk 6:44 from thorn-bushes, or g from briers.
1Co 9: 7 vineyard and does not eat of its g?
Rev 14:18 clusters of g from the earth's vine,
14:18 vine, because its g are ripe."
14:19 gathered its g and threw them into

Grapevine (Grape, Vine)
Nu 6: 4 the g, not even the seeds or skins.
Jdg 13:14 eat anything that comes from the g,
Jas 3:12 fig-tree bear olives, or a g bear

Grapevines (Grape, Vine)
Nu 20: 5 no grain or figs, g or pomegranates.

Grasp (Grasped, Grasping, Grasps)
2Ki 14: 5 After the kingdom was firmly in his g
Ps 71: 4 from the g of evil and cruel men.
Ecc 7:18 is good to g the one and not let go
Jer 15:21 redeem you from the g of the cruel."
34: 3 You will not escape from his g but
Lk 9:45 so that they did not g it, and they
Jn 10:39 seize him, but he escaped their g.
1Co 14:11 If then I do not g the meaning of
Eph 3:18 to g how wide and long and high and

Grasped (Grasp)
Ge 19:16 he hesitated, the men g his hand and
Eze 21:11 to be g with the hand; it is
21:15 lightning, it is g for slaughter.
29: 7 they g you with their hands, you
Hos 12: 3 In the womb he g his brother's heel;
Php 2: 6 equality with God something to be g,

Grasping (Grasp)
Ge 25:26 g Esau's heel; so he was named Jacob.
Jdg 7:20 G the torches in their left hands
Pr 27:16 the wind or g oil with the hand.

Grasps (Grasp)
Dt 32:41 sword and my hand g it in judgment,
Pr 31:19 and g the spindle with her fingers.

Grass (Grasslands)
Nu 22: 4 an ox licks up the g of the field.
Dt 11:15 I will provide g in the fields for
32: 2 like showers on new g, like abundant
2Sa 23: 4 that brings the g from the earth.'
1Ki 18: 5 Maybe we can find some g to keep the
2Ki 19:26 like tender green shoots, like g
Job 5:25 descendants like the g of the earth.
6: 5 Does a wild donkey bray when it has g
8:12 they wither more quickly than g.
38:27 wasteland and make it sprout with g?
40:15 you and which feeds on g like an ox.
Ps 37: 2 for like the g they will soon wither,
72:16 it thrive like the g of the field.
90: 5 are like the new g of the morning—
92: 7 like g and all evildoers flourish,
102: 4 is blighted and withered like g;
102:11 shadow; I wither away like g.
103:15 for man, his days are like g, he
104:14 He makes g grow for the cattle, and
106:20 an image of a bull, which eats g.

Ps 129: 6 May they be like g on the roof,
147: 8 rain and makes g grow on the hills.
Pr 19:12 but his favour is like dew on the g.
27:25 the g from the hills is gathered in,
Isa 5:24 as dry g sinks down in the flames,
15: 6 are dried up and the g is withered;
35: 7 g and reeds and papyrus will grow.
37:27 like g sprouting on the roof,
40: 6 "All men are like g, and all their
40: 7 The g withers and the flowers fall,
40: 7 Surely the people are g.
40: 8 The g withers and the flowers fall,
44: 4 They will spring up like g in a
51:12 the sons of men, who are but g,
66:14 and you will flourish like g;
Jer 12: 4 the g in every field be withered?
14: 5 newborn fawn because there is no g.
Da 4:15 the ground, in the g of the field.
4:23 in the g of the field, while its
4:25 you will eat g like cattle and be
4:32 animals; you will eat g like cattle.
4:33 from people and ate g like cattle.
5:21 wild donkeys and ate g like cattle;
Mic 5: 7 like showers on the g, which do not
Mt 6:30 If that is how God clothes the g of
14:19 the people to sit down on the g.
Mk 6:39 sit down in groups on the green g.
Lk 12:28 If that is how God clothes the g of
Jn 6:10 There was plenty of g in that place,
1Pe 1:24 For, "All men are like g, and all
1:24 the g withers and the flowers fall,
Rev 8: 7 and all the green g was burned up.
9: 4 They were told not to harm the g of

Grasshopper (Grasshoppers)
Lev 11:22 of locust, katydid, cricket or g.
Ps 78:46 He gave their crops to the g, their
Ecc 12: 5 the g drags himself along and desire

Grasshoppers (Grasshopper)
Nu 13:33 We seemed like g in our own eyes,
1Ki 8:37 or blight or mildew, locusts or g,
2Ch 6:28 or blight or mildew, locusts or g,
Ps 105:34 He spoke, and the locusts came, g
Isa 40:22 earth, and its people are like g.
Na 3:15 you down and, like g, consume you.
3:15 like g, multiply like locusts!

Grasslands (Grass, Land)
Ps 65:12 The g of the desert overflow; the

Grateful (Gratify, Gratifying, Gratitude)
Ro 16: 4 of the Gentiles are g to them.

Gratify (Grateful)
Ro 13:14 g the desires of the sinful nature
Gal 5:16 g the desires of the sinful nature

Gratifying (Grateful)
Eph 2: 3 g the cravings of our sinful nature

Grating
Ex 27: 4 Make a g for it, a bronze network,
35:16 burnt offering with its bronze g,
38: 4 They made a g for the altar, a
38: 5 the four corners of the bronze g.
38:30 its bronze g and all its utensils,
39:39 the bronze altar with its bronze g,

Gratitude (Grateful)
Ac 24: 3 acknowledge this with profound g.
Col 3:16 songs with g in your hearts to God.

Grave (*Go down to the grave*, Graves)
Ge 42:38 grey head down to the g in sorrow."
44:29 grey head down to the g in misery.'
44:31 our father down to the g in sorrow.
Nu 16:30 and they go down alive into the g,
16:33 They went down alive into the g,
19:16 a g, will be unclean for seven days.
19:18 who has touched a human bone or a g
Dt 34: 6 day no-one knows where his g is.
1Sa 2: 6 brings down to the g and raises up.
2Sa 22: 6 The cords of the g coiled around me;
1Ki 2: 9 grey head down to the g in blood."
13:31 "When I die, bury me in the g where
2Ki 21:26 He was buried in his g in the garden
Job 3:22 and rejoice when they reach the g?
5:26 You will come to the g in full
7: 9 goes down to the g does not return.
10:19 straight from the womb to the g!
11: 8 depths of the g—what can you know?
14:13 "If only you would hide me in the g
17: 1 days are cut short, the g awaits me.
17:13 If the only home I hope for is the g,
21:32 He is carried to the g, and watch is
24:19 so the g snatches away those who
40:13 shroud their faces in the g.
Ps 5: 9 Their throat is an open g; with
6: 5 Who praises you from his g?
9:17 The wicked return to the g, all the
16:10 you will not abandon me to the g,
18: 5 The cords of the g coiled around me;
30: 3 Lord, you brought me up from the g
31:17 to shame and lie silent in the g.
49:14 sleep they are destined for the g,
49:14 their forms will decay in the g, far
49:15 God will redeem my life from the g;
55:15 let them go down alive to the g,
86:13 me from the depths of the g.
88: 3 and my life draws near the g.
88: 5 like the slain who lie in the g,
88:11 Is your love declared in the g, your
89:48 from the power of the g?
107:20 them; he rescued them from the g.
116: 3 the anguish of the g came upon me; I
141: 7 scattered at the mouth of the g."
Pr 1:12 let's swallow them alive, like the g,
5: 5 her steps lead straight to the g.
7:27 Her house is a highway to the g,
9:18 guests are in the depths of the g.
15:24 keep him from going down to the g.
30:16 the g, the barren womb, land, which
Ecc 9:10 for in the g, where you are going,
SS 8: 6 its jealousy unyielding as the g.
Isa 5:14 Therefore the g enlarges its
14: 9 The g below is all astir to meet you
14:11 pomp has been brought down to the g,
14:15 you are brought down to the g, to
22:16 to cut out a g for yourself here,
22:16 hewing your g on the height and
28:15 the g we have made an agreement.
28:18 agreement with the g will not stand.
38:18 For the g cannot praise you, death
53: 9 He was assigned a g with the wicked,
57: 9 away; you descended to the g itself!
Jer 5:16 Their quivers are like an open g;
20:17 my mother as my g, her womb
Eze 31:15 it was brought down to the g I
31:16 down to the g with those who go down
31:17 had also gone down to the g with it,
32:21 From within the g the mighty leaders
32:23 pit and her army lies around her g.
32:24 with all her hordes around her g.
32:25 with all her hordes around her g.
32:27 who went down to the g with their
Hos 13:14 from the power of the g; I will
13:14 Where, O g, is your destruction?
Am 9: 2 dig down to the depths of the g,
Jnh 2: 2 From the depths of the g I called
Na 1:14 I will prepare your g, for you
Hab 2: 5 Because he is as greedy as the g and
Jn 11:44 Take off the g clothes and let him
Ac 2:27 you will not abandon me to the g,
2:31 not abandoned to the g, nor did his

Gravediggers (Dig)
Eze 39:15 until the g have buried it in the

Gravel
Pr 20:17 he ends up with a mouth full of g.
Lam 3:16 He has broken my teeth with g; he

Graves (Grave)
Ex 14:11 "Was it because there were no g in
2Ki 23: 6 over the g of the common people.
2Ch 34: 4 scattered over the g of those who
Isa 65: 4 who sit among the g and spend their
Jer 8: 1 will be removed from their g.
Eze 32:22 by the g of all her slain,
32:23 Their g are in the depths of the pit
32:26 all their hordes around their g.
37:12 I am going to open your g and bring
37:13 your g and bring you up from them.
Mt 23:29 and decorate the g of the righteous.
Lk 11:44 because you are like unmarked g,
Jn 5:28 are in their g will hear his
Ro 3:13 "Their throats are open g; their

Graze (Grazed, Grazes, Grazing)
Ge 37:12 Now his brothers had gone to g their
Ex 22: 5 and they g in another man's field,
34: 3 may g in front of the mountain."
SS 1: 7 Tell me, you whom I love, where you g
1: 8 g your young goats by the tents of
Isa 5:17 sheep will g as in their own pasture;
27:10 like the desert; there the calves g,
30:23 your cattle will g in broad meadows.
Jer 50:19 and he will g on Carmel and Bashan;

Grazed (Graze)
Ge 41: 2 and fat, and they g among the reeds.
41:18 sleek, and they g among the reeds.

Grazes (Graze)
Ex 22: 5 "If a man g his livestock in a field

Grazing (Graze)
Ge 36:24 g the donkeys of his father Zibeon.
37:13 are g the flocks near Shechem.
37:16 me where they are g their flocks?"
1Ch 27:29 in charge of the herds g in Sharon.
Job 1:14 and the donkeys were g nearby,
Eze 34:14 of Israel will be their g land.
34:14 There they will lie down in good g

Great (*Great faith*, Great Sea, Greater, Greatest, Greatly, Greatness)
Ge 1:16 God made two g lights—the greater
1:21 God created the g creatures of the
6: 5 The Lord saw how g man's wickedness
7:11 springs of the g deep burst forth,
10:12 and Calah; that is the g city.
12: 2 "I will make you into a g nation and
12: 2 name g, and you will be a blessing.
12: 6 of the g tree of Moreh at Shechem.
13: 6 for their possessions were so g that
13:18 near the g trees of Mamre at Hebron,
14:13 Now Abram was living near the g
15: 1 am your shield, your very g reward."
15:14 will come out with g possessions.
15:18 Egypt to the g river, the Euphrates
17:20 and I will make him into a g nation.
18: 1 near the g trees of Mamre while he
18:18 Abraham will surely become a g and
18:20 is so g and their sin so
19:13 g that he has sent us to destroy it
19:19 g kindness to me in sparing my life
20: 9 such g guilt upon me and my kingdom?
21: 8 was weaned Abraham held a g feast.
21:18 I will make him into a g nation."
30: 8 Rachel said, "I have had a g
32: 7 In g fear and distress Jacob divided
34:12 gift I am to bring as g as you like,
35:16 to give birth and had g difficulty.
35:17 she was having g difficulty in
36: 7 Their possessions were too g for
41:29 Seven years of g abundance are
45: 7 save your lives by a g deliverance.
46: 3 will make you into a g nation there.
48:19 a people, and he too will become g.
Ex 10:14 area of the country in g numbers.
14:31 the Israelites saw the g power the
32:10 I will make you into a g nation."
32:11 Egypt with g power and a mighty hand?
32:21 that you led them into such g sin?"
32:30 people, "You have committed a g sin.
32:31 "Oh, what a g sin these people have
Lev 11:17 little owl, the cormorant, the g owl
11:29 the rat, any kind of g lizard,

Lev 19:15 favouritism to the **g**, but judge your
Nu 13:32 people we saw there are of **g** size.
14:19 In accordance with your **g** love,
22:18 I could not do anything **g** or small
Dt 1: 7 far as the **g** river, the Euphrates.
1:17 hear both small and **g** alike.
3: 5 also a **g** many unwalled villages.
4: 6 "Surely this **g** nation is a wise and
4: 7 What other nation is so **g** as to have
4: 8 what other nation is so **g** as to have
4:32 Has anything so **g** as this ever
4:34 or by **g** and awesome deeds, like all
4:36 On earth he showed you his **g** fire,
4:37 by his Presence and his **g** strength,
5:25 This **g** fire will consume us, and
6:22 wonders—**g** and terrible—upon Egypt
7:19 You saw with your own eyes the **g**
7:21 among you, is a **g** and awesome God.
7:23 **g** confusion until they are destroyed.
9:26 that you redeemed by your **g** power
9:29 **g** power and your outstretched arm."
10:17 the **g** God, mighty and awesome, who
10:21 who performed for you those **g** and
11: 7 these **g** things the LORD has done.
11:30 near the **g** trees of Moreh, in the
14:16 the little owl, the **g** owl, the white
17:16 moreover, must not acquire **g** numbers
18:16 **g** fire any more, or we will die."
19: 6 him if the distance is too **g**,
26: 5 a **g** nation, powerful and numerous.
26: 8 with **g** terror and with miraculous
29: 3 With your own eyes you saw those **g**
29: 3 miraculous signs and **g** wonders.
29:28 In furious anger and in **g** wrath the
Jos 1: 4 and from the **g** river, the Euphrates
2: 9 a **g** fear of you has fallen on us,
3:16 It piled up in a heap a **g** distance
7: 9 will you do for your own **g** name?"
10:10 them in a **g** victory at Gibeon.
17: 1 the Makirites were **g** soldiers.
22: 8 to your homes with your **g** wealth
22: 8 iron, and a **g** quantity of clothing
23: 9 "The LORD has driven out before you **g**
24:17 those **g** signs before our eyes.
Jdg 2: 7 who had seen all the **g** things the
2:15 They were in **g** distress.
4:11 the **g** tree in Zaanannim near Kedesh.
9: 6 gathered beside the **g** tree at the
10: 9 and Israel was in **g** distress.
12: 2 people were engaged in a **g** struggle
15:18 given your servant this **g** victory.
16: 5 you the secret of his **g** strength
16: 6 me the secret of your **g** strength
16:15 me the secret of your **g** strength."
16:23 a **g** sacrifice to Dagon their god
20:38 up a **g** cloud of smoke from the city,
1Sa 1:16 here out of my **g** anguish and grief."
2:17 This sin of the young men was very **g**
4: 5 a **g** shout that the ground shook.
4:10 The slaughter was very **g**; Israel
5: 9 city, throwing it into a **g** panic.
6: 9 has brought this **g** disaster on us.
10: 3 until you reach the **g** tree of Tabor.
11:15 the Israelites held a **g** celebration.
12:16 stand still and see this **g** thing
12:22 For the sake of his **g** name the LORD
12:24 what **g** things he has done for you.
14:45 about this **g** deliverance in Israel?
17:24 they all ran from him in **g** fear.
17:25 The king will give **g** wealth to the
18:14 everything he did he had **g** success
19: 5 The LORD won a **g** victory for all
19:22 and went to the **g** cistern at Secu.
20: 2 **g** or small, without confiding in me.
26:25 will do **g** things and surely triumph.
28:15 "I am in **g** distress," Saul said.
30:16 because of the **g** amount of plunder
2Sa 3:22 with them a **g** deal of plunder.
3:38 **g** man has fallen in Israel this day?
7: 9 Now I will make your name **g**, like
7:21 you have done this **g** thing and made
7:22 "How **g** you are, O Sovereign LORD!
7:23 and to perform **g** and awesome wonders
7:26 that your name will be **g** for ever.
8: 8 David took a **g** quantity of bronze.
12:30 **g** quantity of plunder from the
2Sa 18: 7 the casualties that day were **g**
18:29 "I saw **g** confusion just as Joab
20: 8 While they were at the **g** rock in
22:36 you stoop down to make me **g**.
22:51 He gives his king **g** victories; he
23:10 The LORD brought about a **g** victory
23:12 the LORD brought about a **g** victory.
23:20 Kabzeel, who performed **g** exploits.
24:14 for his mercy is **g**; but do not let
1Ki 1:19 He has sacrificed **g** numbers of
1:25 and sacrificed **g** numbers of cattle,
3: 6 Solomon answered, "You have shown **g**
3: 6 You have continued this **g** kindness
3: 8 a **g** people, too numerous to count or
3: 9 to govern this **g** people of yours?"
4:29 God gave Solomon wisdom and very **g**
5: 7 son to rule over this **g** nation."
7: 9 from the outside to the **g** courtyard
7:12 The **g** courtyard was surrounded by a
8:42 for men will hear of your **g** name and
10: 2 Arriving at Jerusalem with a very **g**
10:11 and from there they brought **g**
10:18 the king made a **g** throne inlaid with
19:11 Then a **g** and powerful wind tore the
22:31 Do not fight with anyone, small or **g**
2Ki 3:27 The fury against Israel was **g**; they
5: 1 He was a **g** man in the sight of his
5:13 had told you to do some **g** thing,
6:23 he prepared a **g** feast for them, and
6:25 There was a **g** famine in the city;
7: 6 of chariots and horses and a **g** army,
8: 4 all the **g** things Elisha has done."
10:19 to hold a **g** sacrifice for Baal.
17:21 and caused them to commit a **g** sin.
18:19 Hezekiah: "'This is what the **g** king
18:28 of the **g** king, the king of Assyria!
22:13 **G** is the LORD's anger that burns
1Ch 10:12 bones under the **g** tree in Jabesh,
11:14 the LORD brought about a **g** victory.
11:22 Kabzeel, who performed **g** exploits.
12:22 had a **g** army, like the army of God.
16:25 For **g** is the LORD and most worthy of
17:19 you have done this **g** thing and made
17:19 and made known all these **g** promises.
17:21 and to perform **g** and awesome wonders
17:24 that your name will be **g** for ever.
18: 8 David took a **g** quantity of bronze,
20: 2 **g** quantity of plunder from the
21:13 for his mercy is very **g**; but do not
22: 5 LORD should be of **g** magnificence
22:14 "I have taken **g** pains to provide for
22:14 too **g** to be weighed, and wood and
29: 1 The task is **g**, because this palatial
29:22 They ate and drank with **g** joy in the
2Ch 1: 1 with him and made him exceedingly **g**.
1: 8 "You have shown **g** kindness to David
1:10 to govern this **g** people of yours?"
2: 5 I am going to build will be **g**,
2:13 you Huram-Abi, a man of **g** skill,
6:32 distant land because of your **g** name
6:42 Remember the **g** love promised to
9: 1 Arriving with a very **g** caravan—with
9:17 the king made a **g** throne inlaid with
14:13 Such a **g** number of Cushites fell
15: 5 of the lands were in **g** turmoil.
15:13 whether small or **g**, man or woman.
16: 8 **g** numbers of chariots and horsemen?
17: 5 so that he had **g** wealth and honour.
18: 1 Now Jehoshaphat had **g** wealth and
18:30 not fight with anyone, small or **g**,
20:25 and they found among them a **g** amount
21:19 the disease, and he died in **g** pain.
24:11 and collected a **g** amount of money.
25:10 Judah and left for home in a **g** rage
25:13 carried off **g** quantities of plunder
28: 8 They also took a **g** deal of plunder,
28:13 guilt? For our guilt is already **g**,
30:21 for seven days with **g** rejoicing,
30:24 A **g** number of priests consecrated
30:26 There was **g** joy in Jerusalem, for
31: 5 a **g** amount, a tithe of everything.
31:10 and this **g** amount is left over."
32:27 Hezekiah had very **g** riches and
32:29 He built villages and acquired **g**
32:29 God had given him very **g** riches.
34:21 **G** is the LORD's anger that is poured
Ezr 3:11 And all the people gave a **g** shout
4:10 the other people whom the **g** and
5: 8 Judah, to the temple of the **g** God.
5:11 **g** king of Israel built and finished.
8:22 but his **g** anger is against all who
9: 7 until now, our guilt has been **g**.
9:13 of our evil deeds and our **g** guilt,
Ne 1: 3 are in **g** trouble and disgrace.
1: 5 "O LORD, God of heaven, the **g** and
1:10 **g** strength and your mighty hand.
3:27 from the **g** projecting tower to the
4:14 Remember the Lord, who is **g** and
5: 1 their wives raised a **g** outcry
6: 3 on a **g** project and cannot go down.
8: 6 Ezra praised the LORD, the **g** God;
8:12 food and to celebrate with **g** joy,
8:17 And their joy was very **g**.
9:19 "Because of your **g** compassion you
9:25 they revelled in your **g** goodness.
9:27 and in your **g** compassion you gave
9:31 in your **g** mercy you did not put an
9:32 "Now therefore, O our God, the **g**,
9:35 enjoying your **g** goodness to them in
9:37 We are in **g** distress.
12:43 that day they offered **g** sacrifices
12:43 because God had given them **g** joy.
13:22 to me according to your **g** love.
Est 2:18 the king gave a **g** banquet, Esther's
4: 3 there was **g** mourning among the Jews,
4: 4 Mordecai, she was in **g** distress.
Job 2:13 they saw how **g** his suffering was.
3:19 The small and the **g** are there, and
4:10 the teeth of the **g** lions are broken.
12:23 He makes nations **g**, and destroys
21:28 You say, 'Where now is the **g** man's
22: 5 Is not your wickedness **g**? Are not
23: 6 Would he oppose me with **g** power? No,
26: 3 what **g** insight you have displayed!
30:18 In his **g** power God becomes like
31:25 if I have rejoiced over my **g** wealth,
36:26 How **g** is God—beyond our
37: 5 **g** things beyond our understanding.
37:23 **g** righteousness, he does not oppress
39:11 rely on him for his **g** strength?
Ps 5: 7 I, by your **g** mercy, will come into
17: 7 Show the wonder of your **g** love, you
17:12 like a **g** lion crouching in cover.
18:14 great bolts of lightning and routed
18:35 me; you stoop down to make me **g**.
18:50 He gives his king **g** victories; he
19:11 in keeping them there is **g** reward.
19:13 innocent of **g** transgression.
21: 1 How **g** is his joy in the victories
21: 5 his glory is **g**; you have bestowed
22:25 of my praise in the **g** assembly;
25: 6 Remember, O LORD, your **g** mercy and
25:11 forgive my iniquity, though it is **g**
26:12 **g** assembly I will praise the LORD.
31:19 How **g** is your goodness, which you
33:16 warrior escapes by his **g** strength.
33:17 all its **g** strength it cannot save.
35:18 give you thanks in the **g** assembly
36: 6 your justice like the **g** deep.
37:11 inherit the land and enjoy **g** peace.
40: 9 righteousness in the **g** assembly
40:10 and your truth from the **g** assembly.
47: 2 High, the **g** King over all the earth!
48: 1 **G** is the LORD, and most worthy of
48: 2 Mount Zion, the city of the **G** King.
49: 6 wealth and boast of their **g** riches?
51: 1 according to your **g** compassion blot
52: 7 but trusted in his **g** wealth
57:10 For **g** is your love, reaching to the
66: 3 So **g** is your power that your enemies
68:11 The Lord announced the word, and **g**
68:26 Praise God in the **g** congregation;
68:27 them, there the **g** throng of Judah's
69:13 time of your favour; in your **g** love,
69:16 love; in your **g** mercy turn to me.
71:19 O God, you who have done **g** things.
76: 1 In Judah God is known; his name is **g**
77:13 What god is so **g** as our God?
82: 1 God presides in the **g** assembly; he
86:10 For you are **g** and do marvellous
86:13 For **g** is your love towards me; you
89: 1 I will sing of the LORD's **g** love for

Ps 89:49 O Lord, where is your former **g** love,
90:11 as **g** as the fear that is due to you.
91:13 trample the **g** lion and the serpent.
92: 5 How **g** are your works, O LORD, how
93: 4 than the thunder of the **g** waters
94:19 anxiety was **g** within me, your
95: 3 LORD is the **g** God, the **g** King
96: 4 For **g** is the LORD and most worthy of
99: 2 **G** is the LORD in Zion; he is exalted
99: 3 Let them praise your **g** and awesome
102:10 of your **g** wrath, for you have taken
103:11 **g** is his love for those who fear him;
104: 1 O LORD my God, you are very **g**; you
106:21 who had done **g** things in Egypt,
106:45 and out of his **g** love he relented.
107:43 and consider the **g** love of the LORD.
108: 4 For **g** is your love, higher than the
109:30 in the **g** throng I will praise him.
111: 2 **G** are the works of the LORD; they
112: 1 who finds **g** delight in his commands.
115:13 fear the LORD—small and **g** alike.
116: 6 when I was in **g** need, he saved me.
117: 2 For **g** is his love towards us, and
119:14 as one rejoices in **g** riches.
119:156 Your compassion is **g**, O LORD;
119:162 promise like one who finds **g** spoil.
119:165 **G** peace have they who love your law,
126: 2 The LORD has done **g** things for them
126: 3 The LORD has done **g** things for us,
131: 1 not concern myself with **g** matters
135: 5 I know that the LORD is **g**, that our
136: 4 to him who alone does **g** wonders,
136: 7 who made the **g** lights—His love
136:17 who struck down **g** kings, His love
138: 5 for the glory of the LORD is **g**.
145: 3 **G** is the LORD and most worthy of
145: 6 and I will proclaim your **g** deeds.
147: 5 **G** is our Lord and mighty in power;
148: 7 you **g** sea creatures and all ocean
Pr 5:23 led astray by his own **g** folly.
6:35 refuse the bribe, however **g** it is.
13: 7 to be poor, yet has **g** wealth.
14:29 A patient man has **g** understanding,
15: 6 house of the righteous contains **g**
15:16 the LORD than **g** wealth with turmoil.
18:16 him into the presence of the **g**.
21:14 in the cloak pacifies **g** wrath.
22: 1 A good name is more desirable than **g**
23:24 father of a righteous man has **g** joy
24: 5 A wise man has **g** power, and a man of
25: 6 do not claim a place among **g** men;
28:12 the righteous triumph, there is **g**
Ecc 2: 4 I undertook **g** projects: I built
2:21 is meaningless and a **g** misfortune.
5:17 **g** frustration, affliction and anger.
10: 4 calmness can lay **g** errors to rest.
Isa 5: 9 "Surely the **g** houses will become
9: 2 in darkness have seen a **g** light;
10:33 lop off the boughs with **g** power.
12: 6 people of Zion, for **g** is the Holy
13: 4 like that of a **g** multitude! Listen,
17:12 roar like the roaring of **g** waters!
23: 3 On the **g** waters came the grain of
27: 1 his fierce, **g** and powerful sword,
27:13 in that day a **g** trumpet will sound.
29: 6 thunder and earthquake and **g** noise,
29:15 Woe to those who go to **g** depths to
30:25 In the day of **g** slaughter, when the
31: 1 in the **g** strength of their horsemen,
31: 4 "As a lion growls, a **g** lion over his
32: 2 of a **g** rock in a thirsty land.
34: 6 in Bozrah and a **g** slaughter in Edom.
34: 7 the bull calves and the **g** bulls.
34:11 **g** owl and the raven will nest there.
36: 4 Hezekiah, "'This is what the **g** king,
36:13 of the **g** king, the king of Assyria!
40:26 Because of his **g** power and mighty
42:21 to make his law **g** and glorious.
51:10 the waters of the **g** deep, who made a
53:12 will give him a portion among the **g**,
54:13 and **g** will be your children's peace.
Jer 2:12 with **g** horror," declares the LORD.
2:31 or a land of **g** darkness? Why do my
5: 6 their rebellion is **g** and their
6:22 a **g** nation is being stirred up from
9:19 ruined we are! How **g** is our shame
Jer 10: 6 your are **g**, and your name is mighty
10:22 The report is coming—a **g** commotion
13: 9 Judah and the **g** pride of Jerusalem.
14: 7 our backsliding is **g**; we have sinned
16:10 the LORD decreed such a **g** disaster
21: 5 arm in anger and fury and **g** wrath.
22: 8 done such a thing to this **g** city?'
22:14 'I will build myself a **g** palace
25:14 by many nations and **g** kings;
27: 5 With my **g** power and outstretched arm
27: 7 and **g** kings will subjugate him.
28: 8 many countries and **g** kingdoms.
30:14 guilt is so **g** and your sins so many.
30:15 Because of your **g** guilt and many
31: 8 in labour; a **g** throng will return.
31:15 mourning and **g** weeping, Rachel
31:20 him; I have **g** compassion for him,"
32:17 your **g** power and outstretched arm.
32:18 O **g** and powerful God, whose name is
32:19 **g** are your purposes and mighty are
32:21 outstretched arm and with **g** terror.
32:37 in my furious anger and **g** wrath;
32:42 all this **g** calamity on this people,
33: 3 I will answer you and tell you **g** and
36: 7 this people by the LORD are **g**."
41:12 with him near the **g** pool in Gibeon.
44: 2 says: You saw the **g** disaster I
44: 7 says: Why bring such **g** disaster on
44:26 'I swear by my **g** name,' says the
45: 5 Should you then seek **g** things for
48: 3 cries of **g** havoc and destruction.
50: 9 **g** nations from the land of the north.
50:22 land, the noise of **g** destruction!
50:41 a **g** nation and many kings are being
51:54 the sound of **g** destruction from the
51:55 enemies⌋ will rage like **g** waters
Lam 1: 1 who once was **g** among the nations!
3:22 of the LORD's **g** love we are not
3:23 **g** is your faithfulness
3:32 so **g** is his unfailing love.
Eze 9: 9 Israel and Judah is exceedingly **g**;
14: 4 in keeping with his **g** idolatry.
17: 3 says: A **g** eagle with powerful wings,
17: 7 "'But there was another **g** eagle with
17:17 with his mighty army and **g** horde
21:14 slaughter—a sword for **g** slaughter,
25:17 I will carry out **g** vengeance on them
26: 7 with horsemen and a **g** army.
27:12 because of your **g** wealth of goods;
27:18 of your many products and **g** wealth
27:33 with your **g** wealth and your wares
28: 5 By your **g** skill in trading you have
29: 3 **g** monster lying among your streams.
31: 6 the **g** nations lived in its shade.
32: 3 "'With a **g** throng of people I will
36:23 show the holiness of my **g** name
37: 2 and I saw a **g** many bones on the
38: 4 horsemen fully armed, and a **g** horde
38:15 on horses, a **g** horde, a mighty army.
38:19 **g** earthquake in the land of Israel.
39:17 the **g** sacrifice on the mountains of
47: 7 I saw a **g** number of trees on each
Da 2: 6 me gifts and rewards and **g** honour.
2:10 however **g** and mighty, has ever asked
2:45 "The **g** God has shown the king what
4: 3 How **g** are his signs, how mighty his
4:22 are that tree! You have become **g** and
4:30 he said, "Is not this the **g** Babylon
5: 1 King Belshazzar gave a **g** banquet for
7: 2 of heaven churning up the **g** sea.
7: 3 Four **g** beasts, each different from
7:17 'The four **g** beasts are four kingdoms
8: 4 He did as he pleased and became **g**.
8: 6 canal and charged at him in **g** rage.
8: 8 The goat became very **g**, but at the
8:11 set itself up to be as **g** as the
9: 4 "O Lord, the **g** and awesome God, who
9:12 by bringing upon us **g** disaster.
9:18 but because of your **g** mercy.
10: 1 was true and it concerned a **g** war.
10: 4 the bank of the **g** river, the Tigris,
10: 8 left alone, gazing at this **g** vision
11: 3 with **g** power and do as he pleases.
11: 5 rule his own kingdom with **g** power.
11:10 for war and assemble a **g** army,
11:28 to his own country with **g** wealth,
Da 11:40 and cavalry and a **g** fleet of ships.
11:44 and he will set out in a **g** rage to
12: 1 "At that time Michael, the **g** prince
Hos 1:11 for **g** will be the day of Jezreel.
5:13 and sent to the **g** king for help.
5:14 to Ephraim, like a **g** lion to Judah.
9: 7 are so many and your hostility so **g**,
10: 6 Assyria as tribute for the **g** king.
10:15 Bethel, because your wickedness is **g**.
Joel 1: 4 What the locust swarm has left the **g**
1: 4 what the **g** locusts have left the
2:11 The day of the LORD is **g**; it is
2:20 Surely he has done **g** things.
2:21 Surely the LORD has done **g** things.
2:25 the **g** locust and the young locust,
2:25 my **g** army that I sent among you.
2:31 the **g** and dreadful day of the LORD.
3:13 so **g** is their wickedness!"
Am 2: 2 Moab will go down in **g** tumult amid
3: 9 see the **g** unrest within her and the
5:12 your offences and how **g** your sins.
6: 2 at it; go from there to **g** Hamath,
6:11 and he will smash the **g** house into
7: 4 up the **g** deep and devoured the land.
Jnh 1: 2 "Go to the **g** city of Nineveh and
1: 4 the LORD sent a **g** wind on the sea,
1:12 this **g** storm has come upon you."
1:17 the LORD provided a **g** fish to
3: 2 "Go to the **g** city of Nineveh and
4:11 not be concerned about that **g** city?"
Na 1: 3 The LORD is slow to anger and **g** in
3:10 all her **g** men were put in chains.
Hab 3:15 your horses, churning the **g** waters.
Zep 1:14 "The **g** day of the LORD is near—
3:17 He will take **g** delight in you, he
Zec 2: 4 **g** number of men and livestock in it.
12:11 the weeping in Jerusalem will be **g**,
14: 4 forming a **g** valley, with half of the
14:13 stricken by the LORD with **g** panic.
14:14 be collected—**g** quantities of gold
Mal 1: 5 '**G** is the LORD—even beyond the
1:11 My name will be **g** among the nations,
1:11 name will be **g** among the nations,"
1:14 For I am a **g** king," says the LORD
4: 5 **g** and dreadful day of the LORD comes.
Mt 2:18 weeping and **g** mourning, Rachel
4:16 in darkness have seen a **g** light;
5:12 Rejoice and be glad, because **g** is
5:19 called **g** in the kingdom of heaven.
5:35 for it is the city of the **G** King.
6:23 is darkness, how **g** is that darkness!
7:27 house, and it fell with a **g** crash."
13:46 he found one of **g** value, he went
15:30 **G** crowds came to him, bringing the
19:22 away sad, because he had **g** wealth.
20:26 **g** among you must be your servant,
24:21 For then there will be **g** distress,
24:24 perform **g** signs and miracles to
24:30 of the sky, with power and **g** glory.
27:14 the **g** amazement of the governor.
27:19 for I have suffered a **g** deal today
Mk 5:26 She had suffered a **g** deal under the
10:22 away sad, because he had **g** wealth.
10:43 **g** among you must be your servant,
13: 2 "Do you see all these **g** buildings?"
13:26 in clouds with **g** power and glory.
Lk 1:15 for he will be **g** in the sight of the
1:32 He will be **g** and will be called the
1:49 for the Mighty One has done **g** things
1:58 the Lord has shown her **g** mercy,
2:10 I bring you good news of **g** joy that
2:13 Suddenly a **g** company of the heavenly
5:29 Levi held a **g** banquet for Jesus at
6:17 a **g** number of people from all over
6:23 because **g** is your reward in heaven.
6:35 Then your reward will be **g**, and you
7:16 "A **g** prophet has appeared among us,"
8:23 swamped, and they were in **g** danger.
14:16 a **g** banquet and invited many guests.
16:26 between us and you a **g** chasm has
18:23 because he was a man of **g** wealth.
21:11 There will be **g** earthquakes, famines
21:11 events and **g** signs from heaven.
21:23 There will be **g** distress in the land
21:27 in a cloud with power and **g** glory.
24:52 returned to Jerusalem with **g** joy.

Jn 5: 3 Here a g number of disabled people
6: 2 a g crowd of people followed him
6: 5 Jesus looked up and saw a g crowd
10:32 you many g miracles from the Father.
12:12 The next day the g crowd that had
Ac 2:20 the g and glorious day of the Lord.
4:29 to speak your word with g boldness.
4:33 With g power the apostles continued
5: 5 And g fear seized all who heard what
5:11 G fear seized the whole church and
6: 8 did g wonders and miraculous signs
7:11 bringing g suffering, and our
8: 1 On that day a g persecution broke
8: 8 there was g joy in that city.
8: 9 He boasted that he was someone g,
8:10 divine power known as the G Power."
8:13 by the g signs and miracles he saw.
11:21 and a g number of people believed
11:24 and a g number of people were
11:26 and taught g numbers of people.
14: 1 a g number of Jews and Gentiles
16:16 She earned a g deal of money for her
17:11 the message with g eagerness
18:25 and he spoke with g fervour and
18:27 On arriving, he was a g help to
19:23 there arose a g disturbance about
19:27 that the temple of the g goddess
19:28 "G is Artemis of the Ephesians!
19:34 "G is Artemis of the Ephesians!
19:35 of the g Artemis and of her image,
20:19 I served the Lord with g humility
21:35 the violence of the mob was so g he
23: 9 There was a g uproar, and some of
25:23 Bernice came with g pomp and entered
26:22 and testify to small and g alike.
26:24 g learning is driving you insane."
27:10 and bring g loss to ship and cargo,
Ro 9: 2 I have g sorrow and unceasing
9:22 bore with g patience the objects of
16: 2 g help to many people, including me.
1Co 16: 9 a g door for effective work has
2Co 1: 8 We were under g pressure, far beyond
2: 4 For I wrote to you out of g distress
6: 4 way: in g endurance; in troubles,
7: 4 I have g confidence in you; I take g
8:22 because of his g confidence in you.
12: 7 of these surpassingly g revelations,
12:12 done among you with g perseverance.
Eph 1:19 his incomparably g power for us who
2: 4 of his g love for us, God, who is
Php 2:29 Welcome him in the Lord with g joy,
Col 1:11 may have g endurance and patience,
2:18 Such a person goes into g detail
1Ti 3:13 g assurance in their faith in Christ
3:16 the mystery of godliness is g: He
6: 6 godliness with contentment is g gain.
2Ti 4: 2 g patience and careful instruction.
4: 3 they will gather around them a g
4:14 Alexander the metalworker did me a g
Tit 2:13 our g God and Saviour, Jesus Christ,
Phm : 7 Your love has given me g joy and
Heb 2: 3 such a g salvation? This salvation,
4:14 since we have a g high priest
7: 4 Just think how g he was: Even the
10:21 since we have a g priest over the
10:32 g contest in the face of suffering.
12: 1 are surrounded by such a g cloud of
13:20 Jesus, that g Shepherd of the sheep,
Jas 3: 5 of the body, but it makes g boasts.
3: 5 Consider what a g forest is set on
1Pe 1: 3 In his g mercy he has given us new
3: 4 which is of g worth in God's sight.
2Pe 1: 4 us his very g and precious promises,
1Jn 3: 1 How g is the love the Father has
2Jn : 4 has given me g joy to find some of
3Jn : 3 gave me g joy to have some brothers
Jude : 6 chains for judgment on the g Day.
:24 without fault and with g joy—
Rev 6:12 There was a g earthquake. The sun
6:17 For the g day of their wrath has
7: 9 g multitude that no-one could count,
7:14 have come out of the g tribulation;
8:10 and a g star, blazing like a torch,
9:14 are bound at the g river Euphrates."
11: 8 lie in the street of the g city,
11:17 g power and have begun to reign.
Rev 11:18 both small and g—and for
11:19 an earthquake and a g hailstorm.
12: 1 A g and wondrous sign appeared in
12: 9 The g dragon was hurled down—that
12:14 given the two wings of a g eagle,
13: 2 and his throne and g authority.
13:13 he performed g and miraculous signs,
13:16 He also forced everyone, small and g,
14: 8 "Fallen! Fallen is Babylon the G,
14:19 into the g winepress of God's wrath.
15: 1 I saw in heaven another g and
15: 3 "G and marvellous are your deeds,
16:12 his bowl on the g river Euphrates,
16:14 battle on the g day of God Almighty.
16:19 The g city split into three parts,
16:19 God remembered Babylon the G and
17: 1 the punishment of the g prostitute,
17: 5 BABYLON THE G THE MOTHER OF
17:18 The woman you saw is the g city that
18: 1 He had g authority, and the earth
18: 2 "Fallen! Fallen is Babylon the G!
18:10 "'Woe! Woe, O g city, O Babylon,
18:16 cry out: "'Woe! Woe, O g city,
18:17 In one hour such g wealth has been
18:18 there ever a city like this g city?'
18:19 "'Woe! Woe, O g city, where all who
18:21 "With such violence the g city of
18:23 merchants were the world's g men
19: 1 of a g multitude in heaven shouting:
19: 2 He has condemned the g prostitute
19: 5 you who fear him, both small and g!"
19: 6 I heard what sounded like a g
19:17 together for the g supper of God,
19:18 free and slave, small and g."
20: 1 and holding in his hand a g chain.
20:11 I saw a g white throne and him who
20:12 I saw the dead, g and small,
21:10 the Spirit to a mountain g and high,
21:12 had a g, high wall with twelve gates,
21:21 The g street of the city was of pure
22: 2 down the middle of the g street of

Great Faith

Mt 8:10 found anyone in Israel with such g.
15:28 Jesus answered, "Woman, you have g!
Lk 7: 9 not found such g even in Israel."

Great Sea

Known today as the Mediterranean Sea, it was called the Great Sea (Nu 34:6–7; Jos 1:4; 9:1; 15:12, 47; 23:4; Eze 47:10–20; 48:28), the Western Sea (Dt 11:24; 34:2; Joel 2:20; Zec 14:8), and the Sea of the Philistines (Ex 23:31). Formed a natural boundary so often used as a territorial marker.

Nu 34: 6 boundary will be the coast of the G
34: 7 run a line from the G to Mount
Jos 1: 4 country—to the G on the west.
9: 1 along the entire coast of the G
15:12 is the coastline of the G.
15:47 Egypt and the coastline of the G
23: 4 the Jordan and the G in the west
Eze 47:10 many kinds—like the fish of the G.
47:15 it will run from the G by the Hethlon
47:19 the Wadi ⌊of Egypt⌋ to the G
47:20 "On the west side, the G will be the
48:28 the Wadi ⌊of Egypt⌋ to the G

Greater (Great)

Ge 1:16 God made two great lights—the g
39: 9 No-one is g in this house than I am.
41:40 to the throne will I be g than you."
48:19 his younger brother will be g than
49:26 Your father's blessings are g than
Ex 18:11 Now I know that the LORD is g than
Nu 14:12 a nation g and stronger than they."
24: 7 "Their king will be g than Agag;
Dt 4:38 to drive out before you nations g
9: 1 nations g and stronger than you,
20: 1 chariots and an army g than yours,
Ru 3:10 "This kindness is g than that which
1Sa 14:30 the Philistines have been even g?"
2Sa 13:16 "Sending me away would be a g wrong
2Sa 19:43 a g claim on David than you have.
23:19 Was he not held in g honour than the
23:23 He was held in g honour than any of
1Ki 1:37 to make his throne even g than the
1:47 yours and his throne g than yours!'
4:30 Solomon's wisdom was g than the
4:30 and g than all the wisdom of Egypt.
10:23 King Solomon was g in riches and
1Ch 11:25 He was held in g honour than any of
2Ch 2: 5 our God is g than all other gods.
9:22 King Solomon was g in riches and
32: 7 is a g power with us than with him.
Job 33:12 not right, for God is g than man.
Ps 4: 7 You have filled my heart with g joy
135: 5 that our Lord is g than all gods.
Ecc 2: 9 I became g by far than anyone in
Lam 4: 6 The punishment of my people is g
Da 2:30 not because I have g wisdom than
4:36 and became even g than before.
Hag 2: 9 g than the glory of the former
Zec 12: 7 may not be g than that of Judah.
Mt 11:11 anyone g than John the Baptist;
11:11 the kingdom of heaven is g than he.
12: 6 I tell you that one g than the
12:41 and now one g than Jonah is here.
12:42 and now one g than Solomon is here.
23:17 You blind fools! Which is g: the
23:19 You blind men! Which is g: the gift,
Mk 12:31 is no commandment g than these."
Lk 7:28 women there is no-one g than John;
7:28 in the kingdom of God is g than he.
11:31 and now one g than Solomon is here.
11:32 and now one g than Jonah is here.
22:27 For who is g, the one who is at the
Jn 1:50 You shall see g things than that."
3:30 He must become g; I must become less.
4:12 Are you g than our father Jacob, who
5:20 show him even g things than these.
8:53 Are you g than our father Abraham?
10:29 who has given them to me, is g than
13:16 I tell you the truth, no servant is g
13:16 g than the one who sent him.
14:12 He will do even g things than these,
14:28 Father, for the Father is g than I.
15:13 G love has no-one than this, that he
15:20 'No servant is g than his master.
19:11 over to you is guilty of a g sin."
Ro 11:12 g riches will their fulness bring!
1Co 12:24 g honour to the parts that lacked it,
12:31 eagerly desire the g gifts. And now
14: 5 He who prophesies is g than one who
2Co 3:11 g is the glory of that which lasts!
7: 7 me, so that my joy was g than ever.
7:15 his affection for you is all the g
Heb 3: 3 Jesus has been found worthy of g
3: 3 has g honour than the house itself.
6:13 since there was no-one g for him to
6:16 Men swear by someone g than
7: 7 lesser person is blessed by the g.
9:11 he went through the g and more
11:26 g value than the treasures of Egypt,
1Pe 1: 7 your faith—of g worth than gold,
1Jn 3:20 For God is g than our hearts, and he
4: 4 g than the one who is in the world.
5: 9 but God's testimony is g because it
3Jn : 4 I have no g joy than to hear that my

Greater Sidon

Jos 11: 8 and pursued them all the way to G,
19:28 Rehob, Hammon and Kanah, as far as G.

Greatest (Great)

Jos 14:15 was the g man among the Anakites.
2Sa 7: 9 the names of the g men of the earth.
2Ki 23: 2 the people from the least to the g.
25:26 the people from the least to the g,
1Ch 12:14 a hundred, and the g for a thousand.
17: 8 the names of the g men of the earth.
2Ch 34:30 the people from the least to the g.
Est 1: 5 to the g, who were in the citadel
1:20 husbands, from the least to the g."
Job 1: 3 He was the g man among all the
Jer 6:13 "From the least to the g, all are
8:10 From the least to the g, all are

Jer 31:34 from the least of them to the g,"
42: 1 from the least to the g
42: 8 the people from the least to the g.
44:12 From the least to the g, they will
Jnh 3: 5 g to the least, put on sackcloth.
Mt 18: 1 is the g in the kingdom of heaven?"
18: 4 is the g in the kingdom of heaven.
22:36 "Teacher, which is the g commandment
22:38 This is the first and g commandment.
23:11 The g among you will be your servant.
Mk 9:34 they had argued about who was the g.
Lk 9:46 as to which of them would be the g.
9:48 least among you all—he is the g."
22:24 of them was considered to be g.
22:26 Instead, the g among you should be
Jn 7:37 On the last and g day of the Feast,
1Co 13:13 But the g of these is love.
Heb 8:11 me, from the least of them to the g.
1Pe 1:10 intently and with the g care,

Greatly (Great)

Ge 3:16 To the woman he said, "I will g
7:18 The waters rose and increased g on
7:19 They rose g on the earth, and all
13:13 and were sinning g against the LORD.
17: 2 and will g increase your numbers."
17:20 and will g increase his numbers.
21:11 The matter distressed Abraham g
30:30 had before I came has increased g,
47:27 fruitful and increased g in number.
48:16 may they increase g upon the earth."
Ex 1: 7 g and became exceedingly numerous,
Dt 6: 3 that you may increase g in a land
1Sa 19: 4 he has done has benefited you g.
26:21 acted like a fool and have erred g."
28:21 Saul and saw that he was g shaken,
30: 6 David was g distressed because the
2Sa 10: 5 the men, for they were g humiliated.
24:10 have sinned g in what I have done.
1Ki 1:40 playing flutes and rejoicing g, so
5: 7 he was g pleased and said, "Praise
1Ch 4:38 Their families increased g,
19: 5 them, for they were g humiliated.
21: 8 David said to God, "I have sinned g
29: 9 David the king also rejoiced g.
2Ch 26:15 g helped until he became powerful.
33:12 humbled himself g before the God of
Ezr 10: 9 g distressed by the occasion and
10:13 we have sinned g in this thing.
Ne 4: 1 he became angry and was g incensed.
13: 8 I was g displeased and threw all
Job 20: 2 to answer because I am g disturbed.
Ps 47: 9 belong to God; he is g exalted.
89: 7 of the holy ones God is g feared;
107:38 he blessed them, and their numbers g
109:30 With my mouth I will g extol the
116:10 therefore I said, "I am g afflicted
119:167 your statutes, for I love them g.
129: 1 They have g oppressed me from my
129: 2 they have g oppressed me from my
Ecc 9:13 of wisdom that g impressed me:
Isa 31: 6 Return to him you have so g revolted
35: 2 it will rejoice g and shout for joy.
61:10 I delight g in the LORD; my soul
66:10 all you who love her; rejoice g with
Jer 3:16 have increased g in the land,"
14:10 "They g love to wander; they do not
50:12 your mother will be g ashamed; she
Lam 1: 8 Jerusalem has sinned g and so has
Da 4: 1 in all the world: May you prosper g!
4:19 was g perplexed for a time,
6:14 the king heard this, he was g
6:25 "May you prosper g!
11:39 g honour those who acknowledge him.
Jnh 1:16 At this the men g feared the LORD,
4: 1 Jonah was g displeased and became
Zec 9: 9 Rejoice g, O Daughter of Zion!
Mt 17:15 "He has seizures and is suffering g.
18:31 they were g distressed and went and
19:25 the disciples heard this, they were g
Mk 6:20 Herod heard John, he was g puzzled
6:26 The king was g distressed, but
Lk 1:29 Mary was g troubled at his words and
23: 8 Herod saw Jesus, he was g pleased,
Ac 4: 2 They were g disturbed because the
Ac 7:17 of our people in Egypt g increased.
17:16 he was g distressed to see that the
20:12 man home alive and were g comforted.
2Co 7: 4 I am g encouraged; in all our
10:15 of activity among you will g expand,
Php 4:10 I rejoice g in the Lord that at last
Heb 6:18 offered to us may be g encouraged.
1Pe 1: 6 In this you g rejoice, though now
Rev 17: 6 When I saw her, I was g astonished.

Greatness (Great)

Ex 15: 7 In the g of your majesty you threw
Dt 3:24 servant your g and your strong hand.
32: 3 Oh, praise the g of our God!
1Ch 29:11 Yours, O LORD, is the g and the
2Ch 9: 6 Indeed, not even half the g of your
Est 10: 2 a full account of the g of Mordecai
Ps 145: 3 of praise; his g no-one can fathom.
150: 2 praise him for his surpassing g.
Isa 63: 1 striding forward in the g of his
Eze 38:23 I will show my g and my holiness,
Da 4:22 g has grown until it reaches the sky,
5:18 and g and glory and splendour.
7:27 the sovereignty, power and g of the
Mic 5: 4 for then his g will reach to the
Lk 9:43 they were all amazed at the g of God.
Php 3: 8 g of knowing Christ Jesus my Lord,

Greaves

1Sa 17: 6 on his legs he wore bronze g, and a

Grecian (Greece)

Ac 6: 1 the G Jews among them complained
9:29 He talked and debated with the G

Greece (Grecian, Greek, Greeks)

Isa 66:19 to Tubal and G, and to the distant
Eze 27:13 "'G, Tubal and Meshech traded with
Da 8:21 The shaggy goat is the king of G,
10:20 I go, the prince of G will come;
11: 2 everyone against the kingdom of G.
Zec 9:13 O Zion, against your sons, O G,
Ac 20: 2 people, and finally arrived in G,

Greed (Greedy)

Isa 57:17 I was enraged by his sinful g; I
Eze 16:27 you over to the g of your enemies,
Mt 23:25 are full of g and self-indulgence.
Mk 7:22 g, malice, deceit, lewdness, envy,
Lk 11:39 you are full of g and wickedness.
12:15 your guard against all kinds of g;
Ro 1:29 wickedness, evil, g and depravity.
Eph 5: 3 or of any kind of impurity, or of g,
Col 3: 5 desires and g, which is idolatry.
1Th 2: 5 to cover up g—God is our witness.
2Pe 2: 3 In their g these teachers will
2:14 are experts in g—an accursed brood!

Greedy (Greed)

Ps 10: 3 blesses the g and reviles the LORD.
Pr 15:27 A g man brings trouble to his family,
28:25 A g man stirs up dissension, but he
29: 4 who is g for bribes tears it down.
Jer 6:13 all are g for gain; prophets and
8:10 all are g for gain; prophets and
Eze 33:31 their hearts are g for unjust gain.
Hab 2: 5 Because he is as g as the grave and
1Co 5:10 the g and swindlers, or idolaters.
5:11 but is sexually immoral or g,
6:10 nor thieves nor the g nor drunkards
Eph 5: 5 impure or g person—such a man is an
1Pe 5: 2 not g for money, but eager to serve;

Greek (Greece)

Mk 7:26 The woman was a G, born in Syrian
Jn 19:20 was written in Aramaic, Latin and G.
Ac 16: 1 believer, but whose father was a G.
16: 3 all knew that his father was a G.
17:12 of prominent G women and many G men.
21:37 you?" "Do you speak G?" he replied.
Gal 2: 3 circumcised, even though he was a G.
3:28 There is neither Jew nor G, slave
Col 3:11 Here there is no G or Jew,
Rev 9:11 is Abaddon, and in G, Apollyon.

Greeks (Greece)

Eze 27:19 "'Danites and G from Uzal bought
Joel 3: 6 of Judah and Jerusalem to the G,
Jn 7:35 among the G, and teach the G?
12:20 Now there were some G among those
Ac 11:20 Antioch and began to speak to G also,
17: 4 G and not a few prominent women.
17:17 with the Jews and the God-fearing G,
18: 4 trying to persuade Jews and G.
19:10 so that all the Jews and G who lived
19:17 this became known to the Jews and G
20:21 I have declared to both Jews and G
21:28 And besides, he has brought G into
Ro 1:14 I am bound both to G and non-Greeks,
1Co 1:22 Jews demand miraculous signs and G
1:24 both Jews and G, Christ the power of
10:32 Jews, G or the church of God—
12:13 into one body—whether Jews or G,

Green (Greenish)

Ge 1:30 it—I give every g plant for food.
9: 3 g plants, I now give you everything.
Ex 10:15 Nothing g remained on tree or plant
2Ki 19:26 like tender g shoots, like grass
Job 39: 8 and searches for any g thing.
Ps 23: 2 He makes me lie down in g pastures,
37: 2 g plants they will soon die away.
37:35 like a g tree in its native soil,
58: 9 whether they be g or dry
92:14 old age, they will stay fresh and g,
105:35 they ate up every g thing in their
Pr 11:28 righteous will thrive like a g leaf.
Isa 15: 6 is gone and nothing g is left.
37:27 like tender g shoots, like grass
Jer 17: 8 heat comes; its leaves are always g.
Eze 17:24 I dry up the g tree and make the dry
20:47 all your trees, both g and dry.
Hos 14: 8 I am like a g pine tree; your
Joel 2:22 the open pastures are becoming g.
Mk 6:39 sit down in groups on the g grass.
Lk 23:31 g, what will happen when it is dry?"
Rev 8: 7 and all the g grass was burned up.

Greenish (Green)

Lev 13:49 or any leather article, is g or
14:37 and if it has g or reddish

Greet (Greeted, Greeting, Greetings, Greets)

1Sa 10: 4 They will g you and offer you two
13:10 arrived, and Saul went out to g him.
25: 5 Nabal at Carmel and g him in my name.
2Sa 8:10 son Joram to King David to g him
2Ki 4:29 If you meet anyone, do not g him,
10:13 and we have come down to g the
1Ch 18:10 son Hadoram to King David to g him
Isa 14: 9 spirits of the departed to g you
Mt 5:47 if you g only your brothers, what
Mk 9:15 with wonder and ran to g him.
Lk 10: 4 and do not g anyone on the road.
Ro 16: 3 G Priscilla and Aquila, my
16: 5 G also the church that meets at
16: 5 G my dear friend Epenetus, who was
16: 6 G Mary, who worked very hard for
16: 7 G Andronicus and Junias, my
16: 8 G Ampliatus, whom I love in the
16: 9 G Urbanus, our fellow-worker in
16:10 G Apelles, tested and approved in
16:10 G those who belong to the household
16:11 G Herodion, my relative. G those in
16:12 G Tryphena and Tryphosa, those women
16:12 G my dear friend Persis, another
16:13 G Rufus, chosen in the Lord, and his
16:14 G Asyncritus, Phlegon, Hermes,
16:15 G Philologus, Julia, Nereus and his
16:16 G one another with a holy kiss. All
16:22 down this letter, g you in the Lord.
1Co 16:19 Aquila and Priscilla g you warmly in
16:20 G one another with a holy kiss.
2Co 13:12 G one another with a holy kiss.
Php 4:21 G all the saints in Christ Jesus.
1Th 5:26 G all the brothers with a holy kiss.
2Ti 4:19 G Priscilla and Aquila and the
Tit 3:15 G those who love us in the faith.
Heb 13:24 G all your leaders and all God's

1Pe 5:14 **G** one another with a kiss of love.
3Jn :14 **G** the friends there by name.

Greeted (Greet)

Ex 18: 7 They **g** each other and then went into
Jdg 18:15 Levite at Micah's place and **g** him.
Ru 2: 4 from Bethlehem and **g** the harvesters,
1Sa 17:22 the battle lines and **g** his brothers.
30:21 and his men approached, he **g** them.
2Ki 10:15 Jehu **g** him and said, "Are you in
Mt 23: 7 they love to be **g** in the
Mk 12:38 robes and be **g** in the market-places,
Lk 1:40 Zechariah's home and **g** Elizabeth.
20:46 love to be **g** in the market-places
Ac 18:22 he went up and **g** the church and then
21: 7 where we **g** the brothers and stayed
21:19 Paul **g** them and reported in detail

Greeting (Greet)

Mt 10:12 you enter the home, give it your **g**.
Lk 1:29 what kind of **g** this might be.
1:41 Elizabeth heard Mary's **g**, the baby
1:44 soon as the sound of your **g** reached
1Co 16:21 Paul, write this **g** in my own hand
Col 4:18 Paul, write this **g** in my own hand
2Th 3:17 Paul, write this **g** in my own hand

Greetings (Greet)

1Sa 25:14 **g**, but he hurled insults at them.
Ezr 4:17 and elsewhere in Trans-Euphrates: **G**.
5: 7 follows: To King Darius: Cordial **g**.
7:12 of the Law of the God of heaven: **G**.
Mt 26:49 said, "**G**, Rabbi!" and kissed him.
28: 9 Suddenly Jesus met them. "**G**," he
Lk 1:28 The angel went to her and said, "**G**,
11:43 and **g** in the market-places.
Ac 15:23 in Antioch, Syria and Cilicia: **G**.
23:26 To His Excellency, Governor Felix: **G**.
Ro 16:16 All the churches of Christ send **g**.
16:21 my fellow-worker, sends his **g** to you,
16:23 church here enjoy, sends you his **g**.
16:23 brother Quartus send you their **g**.
1Co 16:19 in the province of Asia send you **g**.
16:20 All the brothers here send you **g**.
2Co 13:13 All the saints send their **g**.
Php 4:21 The brothers who are with me send **g**.
4:22 All the saints send you **g**,
Col 4:10 Aristarchus sends you his **g**,
4:11 who is called Justus, also sends **g**.
4:12 a servant of Christ Jesus, sends **g**.
4:14 Luke, the doctor, and Demas send **g**.
4:15 Give my **g** to the brothers at
Tit 3:15 Everyone with me sends you **g**. Greet
Phm :23 in Christ Jesus, sends you **g**.
Heb 13:24 Those from Italy send you their **g**.
Jas 1: 1 scattered among the nations: **G**.
1Pe 5:13 you her **g**, and so does my son Mark.
2Jn :13 of your chosen sister send their **g**.
3Jn :14 The friends here send their **g**. Greet

Greets (Greet)

2Ki 4:29 and if anyone **g** you, do not answer.
2Ti 4:21 Eubulus **g** you, and so do Pudens,

Grew (Grow)

Ge 10: 8 Cush was the father of Nimrod, who **g**
21: 8 The child **g** and was weaned, and on
21:20 God was with the boy as he **g** up. He
25:27 The boys **g** up, and Esau became a
30:43 In this way the man **g** exceedingly
Ex 2:10 the child **g** older, she took him to
16:21 when the sun **g** hot, it melted away.
17:12 Moses' hands **g** tired, they took a
19:19 the sound of the trumpet **g** louder
Nu 21: 4 the people **g** impatient on the way;
Dt 32:15 Jeshurun **g** fat and kicked; filled
Jos 17:13 when the Israelites **g** stronger
Jdg 2:10 another generation **g** up, who knew
4:24 hand of the Israelites **g** stronger
13:24 He **g** and the LORD blessed him,
Ru 1:13 would you wait until they **g** up?
1Sa 2:21 **g** up in the presence of the LORD.
3:19 The LORD was with Samuel as he **g** up,
8: 1 Samuel **g** old, he appointed his sons
1Sa 31: 3 The fighting **g** fierce around Saul,
2Sa 3: 1 David **g** stronger and stronger, while
3: 1 house of Saul **g** weaker and weaker.
12: 3 He raised it, and it **g** up with him
23:10 hand **g** tired and froze to the sword.
1Ki 11: 4 Solomon **g** old, his wives turned his
17:17 He **g** worse and worse, and finally
18:45 Meanwhile, the sky **g** black with
2Ki 4:18 The child **g**, and one day he went out
4:34 out upon him, the boy's body **g** warm.
1Ch 1:10 Cush was the father of Nimrod, who **g**
10: 3 The fighting **g** fierce around Saul,
2Ch 13:21 Abijah **g** in strength. He married
27: 6 Jotham **g** powerful because he walked
Ps 39: 3 My heart **g** hot within me, and as I
52: 7 and **g** strong by destroying others!"
77: 3 I mused, and my spirit **g** faint.
106:16 In the camp they **g** envious of Moses
107:30 They were glad when it **g** calm, and
Isa 38:14 My eyes **g** weak as I looked to the
53: 2 He **g** up before him like a tender
Eze 16: 7 You **g** up and developed and became
16: 7 hair **g**, you who were naked and bare.
17:10 away in the plot where it **g**?'"
31: 5 increased and its branches **g** long,
Da 4:11 The tree **g** large and strong and its
4:20 The tree you saw, which **g** large and
4:33 **g** like the feathers of an eagle
5: 9 terrified and his face **g** more pale.
8: 3 than the other but **g** up later.
8: 8 in its place four prominent horns **g**
8: 9 which started small but **g** in power
8:10 **g** until it reached the host of the
Jnh 1:13 the sea **g** even wilder than before.
1:15 and the raging sea **g** calm.
4: 8 on Jonah's head so that he **g** faint.
Zec 11: 8 detested me, and I **g** weary of
Mt 13: 7 Other seed fell among thorns, which **g**
Mk 4: 7 Other seed fell among thorns, which **g**
4: 8 It came up, **g** and produced a crop,
5:26 of getting better she **g** worse.
Lk 1:80 the child **g** and became strong in
2:40 the child **g** and became strong; he
2:52 Jesus **g** in wisdom and stature, and
8: 7 Other seed fell among thorns, which **g**
13:19 It **g** and became a tree, and the
Jn 6:18 was blowing and the waters **g** rough.
Ac 4: 4 of men **g** to about five thousand.
9:22 Yet Saul **g** more and more powerful
9:31 it **g** in numbers, living in the fear
16: 5 in the faith and **g** daily in numbers.
19:20 Lord spread widely and **g** in power.
Rev 18: 3 **g** rich from her excessive luxuries."

Grey (Grey-haired)

Ge 42:38 **g** head down to the grave in sorrow."
44:29 **g** head down to the grave in misery.'
44:31 Your servants will bring the **g** head
1Sa 12: 2 As for me, I am old and **g**, and my
1Ki 2: 6 **g** head go down to the grave in peace.
2: 9 **g** head down to the grave in blood."
Ps 71:18 Even when I am old and **g**, do not
Pr 16:31 **G** hair is a crown of splendour; it
20:29 **g** hair the splendour of the old.
Isa 46: 4 Even to your old age and **g** hairs I
Hos 7: 9 with **g**, but he does not notice.

Grey-haired (Grey, Hair)

Dt 32:25 will perish, infants and **g** men.
Job 15:10 The **g** and the aged are on our side,

Griddle

Lev 2: 5 grain offering is prepared on a **g**,
6:21 Prepare it with oil on a **g**; bring
7: 9 or cooked in a pan or on a **g**

Grief (Griefs, Grievance, Grievances, Grieve, Grieved, Grieves, Grieving, Grievous)

Ge 26:35 They were a source of **g** to Isaac and
34: 7 They were filled with **g** and fury,
38:12 When Judah had recovered from his **g**,
1Sa 1:16 here out of my great anguish and **g**."
Est 6:12 home, with his head covered, in **g**,
Job 17: 7 My eyes have grown dim with **g**; my
Ps 10:14 you, O God, do see trouble and **g**;
31: 9 sorrow, my soul and my body with **g**.
35:14 **g** as though weeping for my mother.
88: 9 my eyes are dim with **g**. I call to
Pr 10: 1 but a foolish son **g** to his mother.
10:10 He who winks maliciously causes **g**,
14:13 may ache, and joy may end in **g**.
17:21 To have a fool for a son brings **g**;
17:25 A foolish son brings **g** to his father
29:21 youth, he will bring **g** in the end.
Ecc 1:18 the more knowledge, the more **g**.
2:23 All his days his work is pain and **g**;
Lam 1: 5 The LORD has brought her **g** because
3:32 Though he brings **g**, he will show
3:33 or **g** to the children of men.
3:51 What I see brings **g** to my soul
Eze 13:22 when I had brought them no **g**, and
21: 6 them with broken heart and bitter **g**.
Mic 4: 6 and those I have brought to **g**.
Mt 17:23 And the disciples were filled with **g**.
Jn 16: 6 these things, you are filled with **g**.
16:20 grieve, but your **g** will turn to joy.
16:22 with you: Now is your time of **g**, but
1Co 5: 2 you rather have been filled with **g**
2Co 2: 5 If anyone has caused **g**, he has not
1Pe 1: 6 to suffer **g** in all kinds of trials.
Rev 18: 7 Give her as much torture and **g** as

Griefs (Grief)

1Ti 6:10 and pierced themselves with many **g**.

Grievance (Grief)

Job 31:13 when they had a **g** against me,
Ac 19:38 craftsmen have a **g** against anybody,

Grievances (Grief)

Col 3:13 **g** you may have against one another.

Grieve (Grief)

1Sa 2:33 eyes with tears and to **g** your heart,
2Sa 1:26 I **g** for you, Jonathan my brother;
Ne 8:10 Do not **g**, for the joy of the LORD
8:11 This is a sacred day. Do not **g**."
Isa 16: 7 and **g** for the men of Kir Hareseth.
61: 3 provide for those who **g** in Zion—
Lam 1: 4 **g**, and she is in bitter anguish.
Eze 7:12 **g**, for wrath is upon the whole crowd
9: 4 on the foreheads of those who **g**
Joel 1:11 wail, you vine growers; **g** for the
Am 6: 6 do not **g** over the ruin of Joseph.
Zec 12:10 and **g** bitterly for him as one
Jn 16:20 **g**, but your grief will turn to joy.
2Co 2: 2 For if I **g** you, who is left to make
2: 4 not to **g** you but to let you know the
Eph 4:30 do not **g** the Holy Spirit of God,
1Th 4:13 or to **g** like the rest of men, who
Jas 4: 9 **G**, mourn and wail. Change your

Grieved (Grief)

Ge 6: 6 The LORD was **g** that he had made man
6: 7 I am **g** that I have made them."
Dt 34: 8 The Israelites **g** for Moses in the
Jdg 21: 6 Now the Israelites **g** for their
21:15 The people **g** for Benjamin, because
1Sa 15:11 "I am **g** that I have made Saul king,
15:35 And the LORD was **g** that he had made
20: 3 must not know this or he will be **g**.
20:34 because he was **g** at his father's
2Sa 24:16 the LORD was **g** because of the
1Ch 21:15 the LORD saw it and was **g** because of
Job 30:25 Has not my soul **g** for the poor?
Ps 73:21 my heart was **g** and my spirit
78:40 desert and **g** him in the wasteland!
Isa 63:10 they rebelled and **g** his Holy Spirit
Jer 42:10 for I am **g** over the disaster I have
Eze 6: 9 been **g** by their adulterous hearts,
Ac 20:38 What **g** them most was his statement
2Co 2: 2 make me glad but you whom I have **g**?
2: 5 he has not so much **g** me as he has **g**
12:21 and I will be **g** over many who have

Grieves (Grief)

Zec 12:10 him as one **g** for a firstborn son.

Grieving (Grief)
2Sa 14: 2 has spent many days **g** for the dead.
19: 2 it said, "The king is **g** for his son.
Joel 1: 8 Mourn like a virgin in sackcloth **g**

Grievous (Grief)
Ge 18:20 is so great and their sin so **g**
Ecc 2:17 is done under the sun was **g** to me.
5:13 I have seen a **g** evil under the sun:
5:16 This too is a **g** evil: As a man comes,
6: 2 This is meaningless, a **g** evil.
Jer 14:17 suffered a **g** wound, a crushing blow.
15:18 and my wound **g** and incurable?

Grind (Grinders, Grinding)
Ex 30:36 **G** some of it to powder and place it
Job 31:10 may my wife **g** another man's grain,
Pr 27:22 Though you **g** a fool in a mortar,
Isa 28:28 over it, his horses do not **g** it.
47: 2 Take millstones and **g** flour; take

Grinders (Grind)
Ecc 12: 3 when the **g** cease because they are

Grinding (Grind)
Jdg 16:21 they set him to **g** in the prison.
Pr 27:22 **g** him like grain with a pestle, you
Ecc 12: 4 are closed and the sound of **g** fades;
Isa 3:15 people and **g** the faces of the poor?"
Mt 24:41 Two women will be **g** with a hand mill;
Lk 17:35 Two women will be **g** grain together;

Grip (Gripped, Grips)
Ex 15:14 will **g** the people of Philistia.
Job 30:16 ebbs away; days of suffering **g** me.
Isa 13: 8 pain and anguish will **g** them; they
Jer 13:21 What will you say when the LORD sets

Gripped (Grip)
Jer 6:24 Anguish has **g** us, pain like that of
49:24 turned to flee and panic has **g** her;
50:43 Anguish has **g** him, pain like that of
Lk 1:12 he was startled and was **g** with fear.

Grips (Grip)
Ps 119:53 Indignation **g** me because of the
Isa 33:14 terrified; trembling **g** the godless:
Jer 8:21 crushed; I mourn, and horror **g** me.

Groan (Groaned, Groaning, Groans)
Ps 38: 8 I am feeble and utterly crushed; I **g**
Pr 5:11 At the end of your life you will **g**,
29: 2 when the wicked rule, the people **g**.
Isa 19: 8 The fishermen will **g** and lament, all
24: 7 vine withers; all the merrymakers **g**.
Jer 4:31 a **g** as of one bearing her first
22:23 how you will **g** when pangs come upon
51:52 her land the wounded will **g**.
Lam 1: 4 her priests **g**, her maidens grieve,
1:11 All her people **g** as they search for
Eze 21: 6 "Therefore **g**, son of man! **G** before
24:17 **G** quietly; do not mourn for the dead.
24:23 of your sins and **g** among yourselves.
26:15 when the wounded **g** and the slaughter
30:24 and he will **g** before him like a
Ro 8:23 **g** inwardly as we wait eagerly for
2Co 5: 2 Meanwhile we **g**, longing to be
5: 4 For while we are in this tent, we **g**

Groaned (Groan)
Ex 2:23 The Israelites **g** in their slavery
Jdg 2:18 as they **g** under those who oppressed
Ps 77: 3 I remembered you, O God, and I **g**; I

Groaning (Groan)
Ex 2:24 God heard their **g** and he remembered
6: 5 Moreover, I have heard the **g** of the
Job 23: 2 his hand is heavy in spite of my **g**.
Ps 6: 6 I am worn out from **g**; all night long
12: 5 **g** of the needy, I will now arise,"
22: 1 me, so far from the words of my **g**?
31:10 by anguish and my years by **g**;
32: 3 away through my **g** all day long.
102: 5 of my loud **g** I am reduced to skin
Isa 21: 2 to an end all the **g** she caused.
Jer 45: 3 worn out with **g** and find no rest.'"
Lam 1:21 "People have heard my **g**, but there
Eze 21: 7 they ask you, 'Why are you **g**?' you
Ac 7:34 I have heard their **g** and have come
Ro 8:22 the whole creation has been **g** as in

Groans (Groan)
Job 3:24 of food; my **g** pour out like water.
24:12 The **g** of the dying rise from the
Ps 79:11 May the **g** of the prisoners come
102:20 to hear the **g** of the prisoners and
Lam 1: 8 she herself **g** and turns away.
1:22 My **g** are many and my heart is faint."
Ro 8:26 us with **g** that words cannot express.

Grope (Groped)
Dt 28:29 At midday you will **g** about like a
Job 5:14 at noon they **g** as in the night.
12:25 They **g** in darkness with no light; he
Isa 59:10 Like the blind we **g** along the wall,
Lam 4:14 Now they **g** through the streets like

Groped (Grope)
Ac 13:11 and he **g** about, seeking someone to

Ground (Aground, *Face to the ground*, Grounds)
Ge 1: 9 to one place, and let dry **g** appear.
1:10 God called the dry **g** "land", and the
1:24 creatures that move along the **g**, and
1:25 the **g** according to their kinds.
1:26 creatures that move along the **g**."
1:28 creature that moves on the **g**."
1:30 the creatures that move on the **g**
2: 5 and there was no man to work the **g**,
2: 6 watered the whole surface of the **g**
2: 7 the man from the dust of the **g**
2: 9 kinds of trees grow out of the **g**
2:19 formed out of the **g** all the beasts
3:17 "Cursed is the **g** because of you;
3:19 your food until you return to the **g**,
3:23 the **g** from which he had been taken.
4:10 blood cries out to me from the **g**.
4:11 under a curse and driven from the **g**,
4:12 you work the **g**, it will no longer
5:29 by the **g** the LORD has cursed."
6: 7 and creatures that move along the **g**,
6:20 creature that moves along the **g**
7: 8 all creatures that move along the **g**,
7:14 along the **g** according to its kind
7:23 the creatures that move along the **g**
8: 8 receded from the surface of the **g**.
8:13 that the surface of the **g** was dry.
8:17 creatures that move along the **g**
8:19 the creatures that move along the **g**
8:21 "Never again will I curse the **g**
9: 2 creature that moves along the **g**,
18: 2 meet them and bowed low to the **g**
24:52 bowed down to the **g** before the LORD.
33: 3 bowed down to the **g** seven times as
33:19 plot of **g** where he pitched his tent.
37:10 and bow down to the **g** before you?"
38: 9 he spilled his semen on the **g** to
42: 6 to him with their faces to the **g**.
43:26 they bowed down before him to the **g**.
44:11 his sack to the **g** and opened it.
44:14 themselves to the **g** before him.
47:23 seed for you so you can plant the **g**
Ex 3: 5 where you are standing is holy **g**."
4: 3 The LORD said, "Throw it on the **g**."
4: 3 Moses threw it on the **g** and it
4: 9 the Nile and pour it on the dry **g**.
4: 9 river will become blood on the **g**."
8:16 staff and strike the dust of the **g**
8:17 struck the dust of the **g**, gnats came
8:21 and even the **g** where they are.
9:23 and lightning flashed down to the **g**.
10: 5 They will cover the face of the **g** so
10:15 They covered all the **g** until it was
14:16 can go through the sea on dry **g**.
14:22 went through the sea on dry **g**,
14:29 went through the sea on dry **g**,
15:19 walked through the sea on dry **g**.
16:14 the **g** appeared on the desert floor.
16:25 not find any of it on the **g** today.
32:20 in the fire; then he **g** it to powder,
34: 8 Moses bowed to the **g** at once and
Lev 5: 2 creatures that move along the **g**
11:21 jointed legs for hopping on the **g**.
11:29 animals that move about on the **g**,
11:31 Of all those that move along the **g**,
11:41 moves about on the **g** is detestable;
11:42 creature that moves about on the **g**,
11:44 creature that moves about on the **g**.
11:46 creature that moves about on the **g**.
16:12 two handfuls of finely **g** fragrant
20:25 anything that moves along the **g**
26: 4 and the **g** will yield its crops and
26:19 and the **g** beneath you like bronze.
Nu 11: 8 and then **g** it in a hand mill or
11:31 to about three feet above the **g**,
15:20 cake from the first of your **g** meal
15:21 LORD from the first of your **g** meal.
16:31 this, the **g** under them split
Dt 4:18 creature that moves along the **g**
9:21 Then I crushed it and **g** it to powder
11:17 and the **g** will yield no produce,
12:16 pour it out on the **g** like water.
12:24 pour it out on the **g** like water.
15:23 pour it out on the **g** like water.
22: 6 either in a tree or on the **g**, and
28:11 the crops of your **g**—in the land he
28:23 be bronze, the **g** beneath you iron.
28:56 the **g** with the sole of her foot
Jos 3:17 dry **g** in the middle of the Jordan,
3:17 completed the crossing on dry **g**.
4:18 set their feet on the dry **g** than
4:22 crossed the Jordan on dry **g**.'
5:14 Then Joshua fell face down to the **g**
7: 6 to the **g** before the ark of the LORD,
7:21 They are hidden in the **g** inside my
Jdg 4:21 his temple into the **g**, and he died.
6:37 on the fleece and all the **g** is dry,
6:39 dry and the **g** covered with dew."
6:40 dry; all the **g** was covered with dew.
13:20 wife fell with their faces to the **g**.
1Sa 3:19 let none of his words fall to the **g**
4: 5 such a great shout that the **g** shook.
5: 3 fallen on his face on the **g** before
5: 4 fallen on his face on the **g** before
8:12 and others to plough his **g** and reap
14:15 raiding parties—and the **g** shook.
14:25 woods, and there was honey on the **g**.
14:32 they butchered them on the **g** and ate
14:45 of his head shall fall to the **g**,
17:49 and he fell face down on the **g**.
26: 7 spear stuck in the **g** near his head.
26: 8 Now let me pin him to the **g** with one
26:20 Now do not let my blood fall to the **g**
28:13 a spirit coming up out of the **g**."
28:20 Saul fell full length on the **g**,
28:23 up from the **g** and sat on the couch.
2Sa 1: 2 he fell to the **g** to pay him honour.
8: 2 He made them lie down on the **g** and
12:16 and spent the nights lying on the **g**.
12:17 beside him to get him up from the **g**,
12:20 David got up from the **g**. After he
13:31 his clothes and lay down on the **g**;
14:11 your son's head will fall to the **g**."
14:14 Like water spilled on the **g**, which
17:12 fall on him as dew settles on the **g**.
18:11 Why didn't you strike him to the **g**
20:10 his intestines spilled out on the **g**.
23:10 he stood his **g** and struck down the
1Ki 1:40 so that the **g** shook with the sound.
1:52 fall to the **g**; but if evil is found
18: 7 bowed down to the **g**, and said, "Is
18:42 bent down to the **g** and put his face
2Ki 2: 8 two of them crossed over on dry **g**.
2:15 him and bowed to the **g** before him.
4:37 fell at his feet and bowed to the **g**.
8:12 dash their little children to the **g**,
9:10 her on the plot of **g** at Jezreel,
9:21 They met him at the plot of **g** that
9:26 this plot of **g**, declares the LORD.
9:36 On the plot of **g** at Jezreel dogs
9:37 on the **g** in the plot at Jezreel,
13:18 Elisha told him, "Strike the **g**." He

2Ki 13:19 "You should have struck the **g** five
23: 6 He **g** it to powder and scattered the
23:15 He burned the high place and **g** it to
2Ch 2:10 twenty thousand cors of **g** wheat,
7: 3 pavement with their faces to the **g**,
20:24 lying on the **g**; no-one had escaped.
Ne 8: 6 the LORD with their faces to the **g**.
9:11 they passed through it on dry **g**,
10:37 priests, the first of our **g** meal
Job 1:20 Then he fell to the **g** in
2:13 they sat on the **g** with him for seven
3:16 Or why was I not hidden in the **g**
5: 6 nor does trouble sprout from the **g**.
14: 8 Its roots may grow old in the **g** and
16:13 kidneys and spills my gall on the **g**
18:10 A noose is hidden for him on the **g**;
30: 6 the rocks and in holes in the **g**.
39:14 She lays her eggs on the **g** and lets
39:24 excitement he eats up the **g**;
Ps 7: 5 the **g** and make me sleep in the dust.
17:11 eyes alert, to throw me to the **g**.
26:12 My feet stand on level **g**; in the
44:25 the dust; our bodies cling to the **g**
73:18 Surely you place them on slippery **g**
74: 7 They burned your sanctuary to the **g**
80: 9 You cleared the **g** for it, and it
83:10 and became like refuse on the **g**.
89:44 and cast his throne to the **g**.
107:33 flowing springs into thirsty **g**,
107:35 the parched **g** into flowing springs;
143: 3 he crushes me to the **g**; he makes me
143:10 your good Spirit lead me on level **g**
146: 4 they return to the **g**; on that very
147: 6 but casts the wicked to the **g**.
Pr 24:31 the **g** was covered with weeds, and
Ecc 12: 7 the dust returns to the **g** it came
Isa 2:10 Go into the rocks, hide in the **g**
2:19 to holes in the **g** from the dread of
3:26 destitute, she will sit on the **g**.
21: 9 its gods lie shattered on the **g**!'"
25:12 down to the **g**, to the very dust.
26: 5 the **g** and casts it down to the dust.
28: 2 will throw it forcefully to the **g**.
28:28 Grain must be **g** to make bread; so
29: 4 you will speak from the **g**; your
30:23 rain for the seed you sow in the **g**,
35: 7 the thirsty **g** bubbling springs.
40: 4 low; the rough **g** shall become level,
40:24 sooner do they take root in the **g**,
41:18 and the parched **g** into springs.
44: 3 and streams on the dry **g**; I will
45: 9 among the potsherds on the **g**.
47: 1 sit on the **g** without a throne,
49:23 you with their faces to the **g**;
51:23 And you made your back like the **g**,
53: 2 shoot, and like a root out of dry **g**.
63: 6 and poured their blood on the **g**."
Jer 4: 3 "Break up your unploughed **g** and do
7:20 the field and on the fruit of the **g**,
8: 2 will be like refuse lying on the **g**.
14: 4 The **g** is cracked because there is no
16: 4 will be like refuse lying on the **g**.
25:33 will be like refuse lying on the **g**.
46:21 they will not stand their **g**, for the
48:18 your glory and sit on the parched **g**,
Lam 2: 2 princes down to the **g** in dishonour.
2: 9 Her gates have sunk into the **g**;
2:10 of Zion sit on the **g** in silence;
2:10 have bowed their heads to the **g**.
2:11 my heart is poured out on the **g**
Eze 1:15 I saw a wheel on the **g** beside each
1:19 from the **g**, the wheels also rose.
1:21 when the creatures rose from the **g**,
10:16 their wings to rise from the **g**,
10:19 their wings and rose from the **g**,
13:14 will level it to the **g** so that its
19:12 in fury and thrown to the **g**.
24: 7 she did not pour it on the **g**,
26:11 strong pillars will fall to the **g**.
26:16 they will sit on the **g**, trembling
28:18 I reduced you to ashes on the **g**
34:27 and the **g** will yield its crops;
38:20 creature that moves along the **g**,
38:20 and every wall will fall to the **g**.
39:14 bury those that remain on the **g**.
43:14 From the gutter on the **g** up to the
44:30 first portion of your **g** meal so
Da 4:15 in the **g**, in the grass of the field.
4:23 while its roots remain in the **g**.
7: 4 it was lifted from the **g** so that it
8: 5 whole earth without touching the **g**.
8: 7 him to the **g** and trampled on him,
8:12 and truth was thrown to the **g**.
10:15 towards the **g** and was speechless.
Hos 2:18 the creatures that move along the **g**.
10:11 and Jacob must break up the **g**.
10:12 and break up your unploughed **g**; for
10:14 dashed to the **g** with their children.
13:16 little ones will be dashed to the **g**,
Joel 1:10 The fields are ruined, the **g** is
Am 2: 7 as upon the dust of the **g** and deny
2:15 The archer will not stand his **g**, the
3: 5 Does a bird fall into a trap on the **g**
3:14 will be cut off and fall to the **g**.
5: 7 and cast righteousness to the **g**
9: 9 and not a pebble will reach the **g**.
Ob : 3 'Who can bring me down to the **g**?'
Mic 7:17 like creatures that crawl on the **g**.
Hag 1:11 the oil and whatever the **g** produces,
Zec 4: 7 Zerubbabel you will become level **g**.
8:12 the **g** will produce its crops, and
Mt 10:29 not one of them will fall to the **g**
15:35 told the crowd to sit down on the **g**.
17: 6 fell face down to the **g**, terrified.
25:18 in the **g** and hid his master's money.
25:25 out and hid your talent in the **g**.
Mk 4:26 A man scatters seed on the **g**.
4:31 smallest seed you plant in the **g**.
8: 6 told the crowd to sit down on the **g**.
9:18 seizes him, it throws him to the **g**.
9:20 He fell to the **g** and rolled around,
14:35 he fell to the **g** and prayed that if
Lk 6:49 house on the **g** without a foundation.
9:42 threw him to the **g** in a convulsion.
12:16 he told them this parable: "The **g** of
19:44 They will dash you to the **g**, you and
22:44 drops of blood falling to the **g**.
24: 5 down with their faces to the **g**,
Jn 4: 5 **g** Jacob had given to his son Joseph.
8: 6 to write on the **g** with his finger.
8: 8 he stooped down and wrote on the **g**.
9: 6 Having said this, he spat on the **g**,
12:24 of wheat falls to the **g** and dies,
18: 6 they drew back and fell to the **g**.
Ac 7: 5 here, not even a foot of **g**.
7:33 where you are standing is holy **g**.
9: 4 He fell to the **g** and heard a voice
9: 8 Saul got up from the **g**, but when he
13:28 Though they found no proper **g** for a
20: 9 he fell to the **g** from the third
22: 7 I fell to the **g** and heard a voice
26:14 We all fell to the **g**, and I heard a
2Co 11:12 in order to cut the **g** from under
Eph 6:13 you may be able to stand your **g**, and
Heb 10:32 when you stood your **g** in a great
11:38 and in caves and holes in the **g**.

Grounds (Ground)

2Ki 11:16 palace **g**, and there she was put to
2Ch 23:15 palace **g**, and there they put her
Da 6: 4 the satraps tried to find **g** for
Lk 23:22 in him no **g** for the death penalty.
Jn 8:59 slipping away from the temple **g**.

Group (Groups, Regrouped)

Ge 32: 8 **g**, the **g** that is left may escape."
48:19 will become a **g** of nations."
Nu 16: 3 They came as a **g** to oppose Moses
26:54 To a larger **g** give a larger
26:54 and to a smaller **g** a smaller one;
26:55 What each **g** inherits will be
33:54 To a larger **g** give a larger
33:54 and to a smaller **g** a smaller one.
Jdg 11: 3 where a **g** of adventurers gathered
1Sa 19:20 But when they saw a **g** of prophets
2Sa 2:13 One **g** sat down on one side of the
2:13 pool and one **g** on the other side.
2:25 They formed themselves into a **g** and
2Ki 17:29 Nevertheless, each national **g** made
2Ch 35: 5 "Stand in the holy place with a **g**
Da 6: 6 went as a **g** to the king and said:
6:11 these men went as a **g** and found
6:15 the men went as a **g** to the king and
Jn 8: 3 They made her stand before the **g**
Ac 1:15 (a **g** numbering about a hundred
6: 5 This proposal pleased the whole **g**.
17:18 A **g** of Epicurean and Stoic
Gal 2:12 who belonged to the circumcision **g**
Tit 1:10 those of the circumcision **g**.

Groups (Group)

Ge 32: 7 people who were with him into two **g**
32:10 Jordan, but now I have become two **g**
Nu 26:56 lot among the larger and smaller **g**
1Ch 23: 6 David divided the Levites into **g**
Ezr 6:18 the Levites in their **g** for the
Mk 6:39 sit down in **g** on the green grass.
6:40 they sat down in **g** of hundreds and
Lk 9:14 sit down in **g** of about fifty each."

Grove (Groves)

Ex 23:11 with your vineyard and your olive **g**.
SS 6:11 I went down to the **g** of nut trees to
Jn 18: 1 the other side there was an olive **g**,
18: 3 Judas came to the **g**, guiding a
18:26 I see you with him in the olive **g**?"

Groves (Grove)

Dt 6:11 and vineyards and olive **g** you did
Jos 24:13 and olive **g** that you did not plant
Jdg 15: 5 with the vineyards and olive **g**.
1Sa 8:14 **g** and give them to his attendants.
2Ki 5:26 or to accept clothes, olive **g**,
Ne 5:11 vineyards, olive **g** and houses, and
9:25 **g** and fruit trees in abundance.
Ecc 2: 6 I made reservoirs to water **g** of

Grow (Full-grown, Grew, Growers, Growing, Grown, Grows, Growth, Overgrown)

Ge 2: 9 kinds of trees **g** out of the ground
26:13 to **g** until he became very wealthy.
27:40 But when you **g** restless, you will
Nu 6: 5 let the hair of his head **g** long.
24:18 conquered, but Israel will **g** strong.
Dt 8:13 your herds and flocks **g** large and
Jdg 16:22 the hair on his head began to **g**
1Sa 2:26 the boy Samuel continued to **g** in
Ezr 4:22 Why let this threat **g**, to the
Job 8:11 Can papyrus **g** tall where there is no
8:19 and from the soil other plants **g**.
14: 8 Its roots may **g** old in the ground
17: 9 with clean hands will **g** stronger.
31:16 let the eyes of the widow **g** weary,
39: 4 Their young thrive and **g** strong in
Ps 6: 7 My eyes **g** weak with sorrow; they
31: 9 I am in distress; my eyes **g** weak
31:10 my affliction, and my bones **g** weak.
34:10 The lions may **g** weak and hungry,
92:12 they will **g** like a cedar of Lebanon;
104:14 He makes grass **g** for the cattle,
129: 6 roof, which withers before it can **g**
132:17 Here I will make a horn **g** for David
147: 8 rain and makes grass **g** on the hills
Pr 13:11 money little by little makes it **g**.
20:13 not love sleep or you will **g** poor
Ecc 12: 2 and the moon and the stars **g** dark,
12: 3 looking through the windows **g** dim;
12: 4 birds, but all their songs **g** faint;
Isa 5: 6 and briers and thorns will **g** there.
17:11 you make them **g**, and on the morning
29:22 no longer will their faces **g** pale.
35: 7 grass and reeds and papyrus will **g**.
40:28 He will not **g** tired or weary, and
40:30 Even youths **g** tired and weary, and
40:31 they will run and not **g** weary,
44:14 He let it **g** among the trees of the
44:14 a pine, and the rain made it **g**.
45: 8 let righteousness **g** with it; I, the
55:13 Instead of the thornbush will **g** the
55:13 instead of briers the myrtle will **g**
57:16 for then the spirit of man would **g**
61:11 up and a garden causes seeds to **g**,
Jer 4:28 mourn and the heavens above **g** dark,
6: 4 and the shadows of evening **g** long.

Jer 12: 2 taken root; they g and bear fruit.
15: 9 The mother of seven will g faint
Lam 3: 4 He has made my skin and my flesh g
5:17 of these things our eyes g
Eze 16: 7 I made you g like a plant of the
17:24 tree and make the low tree g tall.
29:21 "On that day I will make a horn g
31: 4 deep springs made it g tall; their
44:20 heads or let their hair g long,
47:12 Fruit trees of all kinds will g on
Hos 10: 8 Thorns and thistles will g up and
14: 6 his young shoots will g. His
Jnh 4: 6 made it g up over Jonah to give
4:10 you did not tend it or make it g.
Zec 8:12 "The seed will g well, the vine will
Mt 6:28 See how the lilies of the field g.
13:30 Let both g together until the
24:12 the love of most will g cold,
Lk 12:27 "Consider how the lilies g. They do
1Co 3: 6 watered it, but God made it g.
3: 7 but only God, who makes things g.
2Co 10:15 as your faith continues to g, our
Eph 4:15 we will in all things g up into him
Col 2:19 sinews, grows as God causes it to g
Heb 12: 3 you will not g weary and lose heart
1Pe 2: 2 it you may g up in your salvation,
2Pe 3:18 g in the grace and knowledge of our

Growers (Grow)
Joel 1:11 you farmers, wail, you vine g;

Growing (Grow)
Ge 41: 5 and good, were g on a single stalk
41:22 full and good, g on a single stalk
Ex 9:22 g in the fields of Egypt."
9:25 it beat down everything g in the
10: 5 every tree that is g in your fields.
10:12 devour everything g in the fields,
10:15 hail—everything g in the fields
Dt 29:23 sprouting, no vegetation g on it.
Job 8:12 still g and uncut, they wither
21: 7 Why do the wicked live on, g old
Col 1: 6 this gospel is bearing fruit and g
1:10 work, g in the knowledge of God,
2Th 1: 3 because your faith is g more and

Growl (Growled, Growls)
Job 4:10 The lions may roar and g, yet the
Isa 5:29 they roar like young lions; they g
59:11 We all g like bears; we moan
Jer 51:38 young lions, they g like lion cubs.
Am 3: 4 Does he g in his den when he has

Growled (Growl)
Jer 2:15 Lions have roared; they have g at

Growls (Growl)
Isa 31: 4 "As a lion g, a great lion over his

Grown (Grow)
Ge 38:14 though Shelah had now g up, she had
41:48 food g in the fields surrounding it.
Ex 2:11 One day, after Moses had g up, he
Lev 13:37 has g in it, the itch is healed.
Jdg 11: 2 were g up, they drove Jephthah away.
2Sa 10: 5 beards have g, and then come back."
1Ki 12: 8 g up with him and were serving him.
12:10 The young men who had g up with him
1Ch 19: 5 beards have g, and then come back."
2Ch 10: 8 g up with him and were serving him.
10:10 The young men who had g up with him
Job 17: 7 My eyes have g dim with grief; my
Ecc 1:16 thought to myself, "Look, I have g
SS 8: 8 and her breasts are not yet g.
Isa 10:27 be broken because you have g so fat.
Jer 5:28 have g fat and sleek. Their evil
Eze 7:11 Violence has g into a rod to punish
28: 5 your wealth your heart has g proud.
Da 4:22 has g until it reaches the sky,
Heb 11:24 By faith Moses, when he had g up,
Rev 2: 3 for my name, and have not g weary.

Grows (Grow)
Ge 38:11 house until my son Shelah g up.
Lev 25: 5 Do not reap what g of itself or
25:11 do not sow and do not reap what g
1Ki 4:33 to the hyssop that g out of walls.
2Ki 19:26 the roof, scorched before it g up.
19:29 year you will eat what g by itself,
Job 30:30 My skin g black and peels; my body
Ps 49:16 not be overawed when a man g rich,
61: 2 I call as my heart g faint; lead me
142: 3 my spirit g faint within me, it is
143: 4 my spirit g faint within me; my
Pr 13:20 He who walks with the wise g wise,
Isa 5:27 Not one of them g tired or stumbles,
37:27 the roof, scorched before it g up.
37:30 "This year you will eat what g by
44:12 he drinks no water and g faint.
Na 2:10 bodies tremble, every face g pale.
Mt 13:32 yet when it g, it is the largest
Mk 4:27 g, though he does not know how.
4:32 Yet when planted, it g and becomes
Eph 4:16 g and builds itself up in love, as
Col 2:19 sinews, g as God causes it to grow
Heb 12:15 that no bitter root g up to cause

Growth (Grow, Undergrowth)
Pr 27:25 the hay is removed and new g appears
SS 6:11 to look at the new g in the valley,
Eze 17: 9 withers? All its new g will wither.

Grudge (Grudging)
Ge 27:41 Esau held a g against Jacob because
50:15 "What if Joseph holds a g against
Lev 19:18 "'Do not seek revenge or bear a g
Mk 6:19 Herodias nursed a g against John

Grudging (Grudge)
Dt 15:10 to him and do so without a g heart;

Grumble (Grumbled, Grumblers, Grumbling)
Ex 16: 7 we, that you should g against us?"
Nu 14:27 this wicked community g against me?
14:36 made the whole community g against
16:11 that you should g against him?"
Mt 20:11 they received it, they began to g
Jn 6:41 At this the Jews began to g about
1Co 10:10 do not g, as some of them did—and
Jas 5: 9 Don't g against each other, brothers

Grumbled (Grumble)
Ex 15:24 the people g against Moses, saying,
16: 2 In the desert the whole community g
17: 3 there, and they g against Moses.
Nu 14: 2 All the Israelites g against Moses
14:29 the census and who has g against me.
16:41 community g against Moses and Aaron.
Dt 1:27 You g in your tents and said, "The
Jos 9:18 assembly g against the leaders,
Ps 106:25 They g in their tents and did not

Grumblers (Grumble)
Jude :16 These men are g and fault-finders

Grumbling (Grumble)
Ex 16: 7 he has heard your g against him.
16: 8 he has heard your g against him.
16: 8 g against us, but against the LORD
16: 9 the LORD, for he has heard your g
16:12 "I have heard the g of the
Nu 14:27 complaints of these g Israelites.
17: 5 g against you by the Israelites."
17:10 This will put an end to their g
Jn 6:43 "Stop g among yourselves," Jesus
6:61 Aware that his disciples were g
1Pe 4: 9 to one another without g.

Guarantee (Guaranteed, Guaranteeing)
Ge 43: 9 I myself will g his safety; you can
Heb 7:22 this oath, Jesus has become the g

Guaranteed (Guarantee)
Ge 44:32 Your servant g the boy's safety to
Ro 4:16 may be g to all Abraham's offspring

Guaranteeing (Guarantee)
2Co 1:22 as a deposit, g what is to come.
5: 5 as a deposit, g what is to come.
Eph 1:14 who is a deposit g our inheritance

Guard (Bodyguard, Guarded, Guardian, Guardians, Guarding, Guardroom, Guards, Safeguard)
Ge 3:24 to g the way to the tree of life.
37:36 officials, the captain of the g.
39: 1 the captain of the g, bought him
40: 3 the house of the captain of the g,
40: 4 The captain of the g assigned them
41:10 the house of the captain of the g.
41:12 a servant of the captain of the g.
Ex 23:20 ahead of you to g you along the way
Nu 10:25 Finally, as the rear g for all the
Jos 6: 7 g going ahead of the ark of the
6: 9 The armed g marched ahead of the
6: 9 and the rear g followed the ark.
6:13 rear g followed the ark of the LORD
10:18 and post some men there to g it.
Jdg 7:19 just after they had changed the g.
1Sa 2: 9 He will g the feet of his saints,
7: 1 his son to g the ark of the LORD.
19: 2 Be on your g tomorrow morning; go
26:15 didn't you g your lord the king?
26:16 g your master, the LORD's anointed.
2Sa 16: 6 g were on David's right and left.
20: 3 and put them in a house under g.
20:10 Amasa was not on his g against
1Ki 1: 8 special g did not join Adonijah.
1:10 special g or his brother Solomon.
14:27 the commanders of the g on duty at
20:39 a captive and said, 'G this man.
2Ki 6:10 he was on his g in such places.
11: 6 a third at the gate behind the g,
11: 7 all to g the temple for the king.
25: 8 commander of the imperial g,
25:10 the commander of the imperial g,
25:11 Nebuzaradan the commander of the g
25:15 commander of the imperial g took
25:18 The commander of the g took as
1Ch 9:27 because they had to g it; and they
26:16 G was alongside g:
2Ch 12:10 the commanders of the g on duty at
23: 6 g what the LORD has assigned to
Ezr 8:29 G them carefully until you weigh
Ne 3:25 palace near the court of the g.
3:29 g at the East Gate, made repairs.
4: 9 prayed to our God and posted a g
12:39 At the Gate of the G they stopped.
13:22 go and g the gates in order to keep
Job 7:12 the deep, that you put me under g?
Ps 25:20 G my life and rescue me; let me not
86: 2 G my life, for I am devoted to you.
91:11 you to g you in all your ways;
127: 1 city, the watchmen stand g in vain.
141: 3 Set a g over my mouth, O LORD; keep
Pr 2:11 you, and understanding will g you.
4:13 go; g it well, for it is your life.
4:23 Above all else, g your heart, for it
7: 2 g my teachings as the apple of
Ecc 5: 1 G your steps when you go to the
Isa 27: 3 I g it day and night so that no-one
52:12 God of Israel will be your rear g.
58: 8 of the LORD will be your rear g.
Jer 32: 2 the g in the royal palace of Judah.
32: 8 in the courtyard of the g and said,
32:12 sitting in the courtyard of the g.
33: 1 confined in the courtyard of the g,
37:13 the captain of the g, whose name was
37:21 be placed in the courtyard of the g
37:21 remained in the courtyard of the g.
38: 6 which was in the courtyard of the g.
38:13 remained in the courtyard of the g.
38:28 remained in the courtyard of the g
39: 9 commander of the imperial g
39:10 Nebuzaradan the commander of the g
39:11 commander of the imperial g:
39:13 Nebuzaradan the commander of the g,

Jer 39:14 taken out of the courtyard of the **g**.
39:15 confined in the courtyard of the **g**
40: 1 **g** had released him at Ramah.
40: 2 the commander of the **g** found
41:10 commander of the imperial **g**
43: 6 commander of the imperial **g**
51:12 walls of Babylon! Reinforce the **g**,
52:12 commander of the imperial **g**,
52:14 the commander of the imperial **g**
52:15 Nebuzaradan the commander of the **g**
52:19 The commander of the imperial **g** took
52:24 The commander of the **g** took as
52:30 the commander of the imperial **g**.
Da 1:11 Daniel then said to the **g** whom the
1:16 the **g** took away their choice food
2:14 the commander of the king's **g**
Na 2: 1 **G** the fortress, watch the road,
Mal 2:15 **g** yourself in your spirit, and do
2:16 **g** yourself in your spirit, and do
Mt 10:17 "Be on your **g** against men; they will
16: 6 "Be on your **g** against the yeast of
16:11 But be on your **g** against the yeast
16:12 **g** against the yeast used in bread,
27:65 "Take a **g**," Pilate answered. "Go,
27:66 on the stone and posting the **g**.
Mk 13: 9 "You must be on your **g**. You will be
13:23 be on your **g**; I have told you
13:33 Be on **g**! Be alert! You do not know
14:44 him and lead him away under **g**."
Lk 4:10 concerning you to **g** you carefully;
8:29 hand and foot and kept under **g**,
12: 1 "Be on your **g** against the yeast of
12:15 "Watch out! Be on your **g** against all
22: 4 the officers of the temple **g** and
22:52 the officers of the temple **g**, and
Ac 4: 1 the captain of the temple **g** and the
5:24 the captain of the temple **g** and the
12: 6 sentries stood **g** at the entrance.
16:23 was commanded to **g** them carefully.
20:31 be on your **g**! Remember that for
23:35 be kept under **g** in Herod's palace.
24:23 **g** but to give him some freedom
28:16 by himself, with a soldier to **g** him.
1Co 16:13 Be on your **g**; stand firm in the
Php 1:13 clear throughout the whole palace **g**
4: 7 will **g** your hearts and your minds in
1Ti 6:20 Timothy, **g** what has been entrusted
2Ti 1:12 am convinced that he is able to **g**
1:14 **G** the good deposit that was
1:14 **g** it with the help of the Holy
4:15 You too should be on your **g** against
2Pe 3:17 be on your **g** so that you may not be

Guarded (Guard)
Dt 32:10 he **g** him as the apple of his eye,
33: 9 over your word and **g** your covenant.
2Ki 12: 9 The priests who **g** the entrance put
Ne 12:25 who **g** the storerooms at the gates.
Est 2:21 two of the king's officers who **g**
6: 2 two of the king's officers who **g**
Ac 12: 4 handing him over to be **g** by four
2Co 11:32 city of the Damascenes **g** in order

Guardian (Guard)
Eze 28:14 You were anointed as a **g** cherub,
28:16 and I expelled you, O **g** cherub,
Ac 19:35 **g** of the temple of the great Artemis

Guardians (Guard)
2Ki 10: 1 and to the **g** of Ahab's children.
10: 5 the elders and the **g** sent this
1Co 4:15 though you have ten thousand **g**
Gal 4: 2 He is subject to **g** and trustees

Guarding (Guard)
2Ki 11: 5 third of you **g** the royal palace,
11: 6 guard, who take turns **g** the temple
1Ch 9:19 responsible for **g** the thresholds
9:19 responsible for **g** the entrance to
9:23 **g** the gates of the house of the LORD
Jer 4:17 surround her like men **g** a field,
Mt 27:54 those with him who were **g** Jesus saw
Lk 22:63 The men who were **g** Jesus began
Ac 22:20 **g** the clothes of those who were

Guardroom (Guard)
1Ki 14:28 they returned them to the **g**.
2Ch 12:11 they returned them to the **g**.

Guards (Guard)
1Sa 22:17 the king ordered the **g** at his side:
1Ki 14:28 the **g** bore the shields, and
2Ki 10:25 he ordered the **g** and officers: "Go
10:25 The **g** and officers threw the bodies
11: 4 the Carites and the **g** and had them
11:11 The **g**, each with his weapon in his
11:13 noise made by the **g** and the people,
11:18 posted **g** at the temple of the LORD.
11:19 the Carites, the **g** and all the
11:19 by way of the gate of the **g**.
2Ch 12:11 the **g** went with him, bearing the
Ne 4:22 as **g** by night and workmen by day."
4:23 the **g** with me took off our clothes;
7: 3 appoint residents of Jerusalem as **g**,
Ps 97:10 for he **g** the lives of his faithful
Pr 2: 8 for he **g** the course of the just and
13: 3 He who **g** his lips **g** his life, but he
13: 6 Righteousness **g** the man of integrity,
16:17 evil; he who **g** his way **g** his life.
19:16 He who obeys instructions **g** his life,
21:23 He who **g** his mouth and his tongue
22: 5 who **g** his soul stays far from them.
24:12 Does not he who **g** your life know it?
Eze 9: 1 "Bring the **g** of the city here, each
40: 7 The alcoves for the **g** were one rod
Na 3:17 Your **g** are like locusts, your
Mt 26:58 down with the **g** to see the outcome.
28: 4 The **g** were so afraid of him that
28:11 some of the **g** went into the city
Mk 14:54 sat with the **g** and warmed himself
14:65 And the **g** took him and beat him.
Lk 11:21 "When a strong man, fully armed, **g**
Jn 7:32 sent temple **g** to arrest him.
7:45 Finally the temple **g** went back to
7:46 way this man does," the **g** declared
Ac 5:23 with the **g** standing at the doors;
12:10 They passed the first and second **g**
12:19 cross-examined the **g** and ordered

Gudgodah
Dt 10: 7 From there they travelled to **G** and

Guest (Guests)
Lev 22:10 nor may the **g** of a priest or his
Jdg 19:23 is my **g**, don't do this disgraceful
Est 1: 8 By the king's command each **g** was
Mk 14:14 'The Teacher asks: Where is my **g**
Lk 19: 7 has gone to be the **g** of a 'sinner'."
22:11 'The Teacher asks: Where is the **g**
Ac 10:32 He is a **g** in the home of Simon the
Phm :22 one thing more: Prepare a **g** room for

Guests (Guest)
1Sa 9:24 the time I said, 'I have invited **g**.
2Sa 15:11 They had been invited as **g** and went
1Ki 1:41 Adonijah and all the **g** who were with
1:49 At this, all Adonijah's **g** rose in
Job 19:15 My **g** and my maidservants count me a
Pr 9:18 **g** are in the depths of the grave.
Mt 9:15 Jesus answered, "How can the **g** of
14: 9 of his oaths and his dinner **g**,
22:10 the wedding hall was filled with **g**.
22:11 when the king came in to see the **g**,
Mk 2:19 Jesus answered, "How can the **g** of
6:22 she pleased Herod and his dinner **g**.
6:26 **g**, he did not want to refuse her.
Lk 5:34 Jesus answered, "Can you make the **g**
7:49 The other **g** began to say among
14: 7 he noticed how the **g** picked the
14:10 the presence of all your fellow **g**.
14:16 a great banquet and invited many **g**.
Jn 2:10 the **g** have had too much to drink;
Ac 10:23 the men into the house to be his **g**.

Guidance (Guide)
2Ki 16:15 use the bronze altar for seeking **g**."
1Ch 10:13 and even consulted a medium for **g**,
Pr 1: 5 and let the discerning get **g**—
11:14 For lack of **g** a nation falls, but
20:18 advice; if you wage war, obtain **g**.
24: 6 for waging war you need **g**, and for
Hab 2:19 'Wake up!' Can it give **g**? It is

Guide (Guidance, Guided, Guideposts, Guides, Guiding)
Ex 13:21 of cloud to **g** them on their way
15:13 will **g** them to your holy dwelling.
Ne 9:19 not cease to **g** them on their path,
Ps 25: 5 **g** me in your truth and teach me, for
31: 3 the sake of your name lead and **g** me.
43: 3 let them **g** me; let them bring me to
48:14 he will be our **g** even to the end.
67: 4 and **g** the nations of the earth.
73:24 You **g** me with your counsel, and
139:10 even there your hand will **g** me, your
Pr 4:11 I **g** you in the way of wisdom and
6:22 you walk, they will **g** you; when you
Isa 9:16 Those who **g** this people mislead them,
42:16 along unfamiliar paths I will **g** them;
49:10 He who has compassion on them will **g**
51:18 she bore there was none to **g** her;
57:18 **g** him and restore comfort to him,
58:11 The LORD will **g** you always; he will
Lk 1:79 **g** our feet into the path of peace."
Jn 16:13 comes, he will **g** you into all truth.
Ac 1:16 as **g** for those who arrested Jesus—
Ro 2:19 if you are convinced that you are a **g**

Guided (Guide)
Job 31:18 and from my birth I **g** the widow—
Ps 78:14 He **g** them with the cloud by day and
78:53 He **g** them safely, so they were
107:30 he **g** them to their desired haven.
Isa 9:16 and those who are **g** are led astray.
63:14 This is how you **g** your people to

Guideposts (Guide)
Jer 31:21 "Set up road signs; put up **g**. Take

Guides (Guide)
Ps 23: 3 he restores my soul. He **g** me in
25: 9 He **g** the humble in what is right and
Pr 11: 3 The integrity of the upright **g** them,
16:23 A wise man's heart **g** his mouth, and
Isa 3:12 O my people, your **g** lead you astray;
Mt 15:14 Leave them; they are blind **g**. If a
23:16 "Woe to you, blind **g**! You say, 'If
23:24 You blind **g**! You strain out a gnat

Guiding (Guide)
2Sa 6: 3 of Abinadab, were **g** the new
1Ch 13: 7 new cart, with Uzzah and Ahio **g** it.
Ecc 2: 3 mind still **g** me with wisdom.
Jn 18: 3 Judas came to the grove, **g** a

Guilt (Bloodguilt, *Guilt offering, Guilt offerings*, Guilty)
Ge 20: 9 such great **g** upon me and my kingdom?
26:10 you would have brought **g** upon us."
44:16 God has uncovered your servants' **g**.
Ex 28:38 and he will bear the **g** involved in
28:43 that they will not incur **g** and die.
Lev 4: 3 bringing **g** on the people, he must
10:17 to take away the **g** of the community
19:17 so that you will not share in his **g**.
22:16 bring upon them **g** requiring payment.
Nu 5:15 offering to draw attention to **g**.
5:28 **g** and will be able to have children.
15:31 be cut off; his **g** remains on him.'"
30:15 then he is responsible for her **g**."
Dt 19:13 You must purge from Israel the **g** of
21: 9 will purge from yourselves the **g**
22: 8 may not bring the **g** of bloodshed
1Sa 3:14 'The **g** of Eli's house will never be
2Sa 14: 9 king and his throne be without **g**."
24:10 take away the **g** of your servant.
1Ki 2:31 my father's house of the **g** of the
2:33 May the **g** of their blood rest on
1Ch 21: 3 Why should he bring **g** on Israel?"
21: 8 Now, I beg you, take away the **g** of
2Ch 24:18 Because of their **g**, God's anger came
28:13 and **g**? For our **g** is already great,
33:23 the LORD; Amon increased his **g**.

Ezr 9: 6 our **g** has reached to the heavens.
9: 7 until now, our **g** has been great.
9:13 of our evil deeds and our great **g**,
9:15 Here we are before you in our **g**,
10:10 foreign women, adding to Israel's **g**.
10:19 and for their **g** they each presented
Ne 4: 5 Do not cover up their **g** or blot out
Job 20:27 The heavens will expose his **g**; the
31:33 men do, by hiding my **g** in my
33: 9 sin; I am clean and free from **g**.
Ps 7: 3 this and there is **g** on my hands—
32: 5 and you forgave the **g** of my sin.
38: 4 My **g** has overwhelmed me like a
69: 5 You know my folly, O God; my **g** is
Pr 28:17 A man tormented by the **g** of murder
Isa 1: 4 a people loaded with **g**, a brood of
6: 7 this has touched your lips; your **g**
24: 6 earth; its people must bear their **g**.
24:20 so heavy upon it is the **g** of its
27: 9 By this, then, will Jacob's **g** be
59: 3 with blood, your fingers with **g**.
Jer 2:22 stain of your **g** is still before me,"
3:13 Only acknowledge your **g**—you have
14:20 wickedness and the **g** of our fathers
25:12 of the Babylonians, for their **g**,"
26:15 you will bring the **g** of innocent
30:14 **g** is so great and your sins so many
30:15 Because of your great **g** and many
50:20 search will be made for Israel's **g**
51: 5 of **g** before the Holy One of Israel.
Eze 14:10 They will bear their **g**—the prophet
18:19 'Why does the son not share the **g**
18:20 The son will not share the **g** of the
18:20 the father share the **g** of the son.
21:23 of their **g** and take them captive.
21:24 mind your **g** by your open rebellion,
Hos 5:15 my place until they admit their **g**.
10: 2 and now they must bear their **g**.
12:14 his Lord will leave upon him the **g**
13:12 The **g** of Ephraim is stored up, his
13:16 people of Samaria must bear their **g**
Jn 9:41 claim you can see, your **g** remains.
16: 8 he will convict the world of **g** in

Guilt offering

Lev 5:15 It is a **g**.
5:16 ram as a **g**, and he will be forgiven.
5:18 He is to bring to the priest as a **g**
5:19 It is a **g**; he has been guilty of
6: 5 owner on the day he presents his **g**.
6: 6 that is, to the LORD, his **g**, a ram
6:17 offering and the **g**, it is most holy.
7: 1 These are the regulations for the **g**
7: 2 The **g** is to be slaughtered in the
7: 5 It is a **g**.
7: 7 to both the sin offering and the **g**:
7:37 the sin offering, the **g**, the
14:12 the male lambs and offer it as a **g**,
14:13 Like the sin offering, the **g** belongs
14:14 to take some of the blood of the **g**
14:17 foot, on top of the blood of the **g**.
14:21 he must take one male lamb as a **g**
14:24 is to take the lamb for the **g**,
14:25 shall slaughter the lamb for the **g**
14:28 places he put the blood of the **g**
19:21 Tent of Meeting for a **g** to the LORD.
19:22 With the ram of the **g** the priest is
Nu 6:12 bring a year-old male lamb as a **g**.
1Sa 6: 3 but by all means send a **g** to him.
6: 4 The Philistines asked, "What **g**
6: 8 you are sending back to him as a **g**.
6:17 **g** to the LORD—one each for Ashdod,
Ezr 10:19 a ram from the flock as a **g**.)
Isa 53:10 though the LORD makes his life a **g**,
Eze 46:20 where the priests will cook the **g**

Guilt offerings

Nu 18: 9 whether grain or sin or **g**, that part
2Ki 12:16 The money from the **g** and sin
Eze 40:39 offerings and **g** were slaughtered.
42:13 and the **g**—for the place is holy.
44:29 the sin offerings and the **g**; and

Guiltless

Ex 20: 7 hold anyone **g** who misuses his name.
Dt 5:11 hold anyone **g** who misuses his name.
1Sa 26: 9 on the LORD's anointed and be **g**?
Job 34: 6 considered a liar; although I am **g**,

Guilty (Guilt)

Ge 38:24 "Your daughter-in-law Tamar is **g** of
Ex 22: 2 the defender is not **g** of bloodshed;
22: 3 if it happens after sunrise, he is **g**
22: 9 The one whom the judges declare **g**
23: 7 death, for I will not acquit the **g**.
34: 7 Yet he does not leave the **g**
Lev 4:13 unaware of the matter, they are **g**.
4:22 of the LORD his God, he is **g**.
4:27 any of the LORD's commands, he is **g**
5: 2 it, he has become unclean and is **g**
5: 3 when he learns of it he will be **g**.
5: 4 when he learns of it he will be **g**.
5: 5 "'When anyone is **g** in any of these
5:17 is **g** and will be held responsible.
5:19 is a guilt offering; he has been **g**
6: 4 he thus sins and becomes **g**, he must
6: 7 things he did that made him **g**."
17: 4 shall be considered **g** of bloodshed;
22: 9 so that they do not become **g**
Nu 5: 6 to the LORD, that person is **g**
14:18 Yet he does not leave the **g**
18:32 you will not be **g** in this matter
35:27 accused without being **g** of murder.
Dt 15: 9 you, and you will be found **g** of sin
19:10 that you will not be **g** of bloodshed
21: 8 **g** of the blood of an innocent man.
21:22 If a man **g** of a capital offence is
23:21 it of you and you will be **g** of sin.
23:22 making a vow, you will not be **g**.
24:15 you, and you will be **g** of sin.
25: 1 the innocent and condemning the **g**.
25: 2 If the **g** man deserves to be beaten,
1Sa 20: 8 If I am **g**, then kill me yourself!
24:11 am not **g** of wrongdoing or rebellion.
26:18 I done, and what wrong am I **g** of?
2Sa 14:32 and if I am **g** of anything, let him
19:19 to him, "May my lord not hold me **g**.
1Ki 8:32 condemning the **g** and bringing down
8:32 **g**, and so establish his innocence.
2Ch 6:23 repaying the **g** by bringing down on
6:23 **g** and so establish his innocence.
20:35 of Israel, who was **g** of wickedness.
28:10 **g** of sins against the LORD your God?
28:13 "or we will be **g** before the LORD.
Job 9:20 blameless, it would pronounce me **g**
9:29 Since I am already found **g**, why
10: 7 though you know that I am not **g**
10:15 If I am **g**—woe to me! Even if I am
34:31 "Suppose a man says to God, 'I am **g**
Ps 5:10 Declare them **g**, O God! Let their
109: 7 he is tried, let him be found **g**,
Pr 17:15 Acquitting the **g** and condemning the
21: 8 The way of the **g** is devious, but the
24:24 Whoever says to the **g**, "You are
24:25 well with those who convict the **g**,
Isa 5:23 who acquit the **g** for a bribe, but
29:21 with a word make a man out to be **g**,
Jer 2: 3 held **g**, and disaster overtook them
50: 7 'We are not **g**, for they sinned
Eze 14:10 as **g** as the one who consults him.
18:24 of the unfaithfulness he is **g** of
22: 4 you have become **g** because of the
25:12 Judah and became very **g** by doing so
Hos 1: 2 because the land is **g** of the vilest
4:15 O Israel, let not Judah become **g**.
13: 1 became **g** of Baal worship and died.
Na 1: 3 LORD will not leave the **g** unpunished.
Hab 1:11 **g** men, whose own strength is their
Mk 3:29 he is **g** of an eternal sin."
Lk 13: 4 do you think they were more **g** than
Jn 8:46 Can any of you prove me **g** of sin?
9:41 you would not be **g** of sin; but now
15:22 to them, they would not be **g** of sin
15:24 did, they would not be **g** of sin.
19:11 over to you is **g** of a greater sin."
Ac 5:28 to make us **g** of this man's blood."
22:25 who hasn't even been found **g**?"
25:11 If, however, I am **g** of doing
Ac 28:18 not **g** of any crime deserving death.
1Co 11:27 be **g** of sinning against the body
Heb 10: 2 longer have felt **g** for their sins.
10:22 to cleanse us from a **g** conscience
Jas 2:10 point is **g** of breaking all of it.

Gulf

Isa 11:15 The LORD will dry up the **g** of the

Gull

Lev 11:16 owl, the **g**, any kind of hawk,
Dt 14:15 owl, the **g**, any kind of hawk,

Gulps

Pr 19:28 the mouth of the wicked **g** down evil.

Gum

Ex 30:34 "Take fragrant spices—**g** resin,

Guni (Gunite)

Ge 46:24 The sons of Naphtali: Jahziel, **G**,
Nu 26:48 clan; through **G**, the Gunite clan;
1Ch 5:15 Ahi son of Abdiel, the son of **G**, was
7:13 The sons of Naphtali: Jahziel, **G**,

Gunite (Guni)

Nu 26:48 clan; through Guni, the **G** clan;

Gur

2Ki 9:27 on the way up to **G** near Ibleam,

Gur Baal

2Ch 26: 7 lived in **G** and against the Meunites.

Gush (Gushed, Gushes)

Isa 35: 6 Water will **g** forth in the wilderness

Gushed (Gush)

Nu 20:11 Water **g** out, and the community and
Ps 78:20 he struck the rock, water **g** out, and
105:41 He opened the rock, and water **g** out;
Isa 48:21 he split the rock and water **g** out.

Gushes (Gush)

Pr 15: 2 but the mouth of the fool **g** folly.
15:28 but the mouth of the wicked **g** evil.

Gutter

Eze 43:13 **g** is a cubit deep and a cubit wide,
43:14 From the **g** on the ground up to the
43:17 cubit and a **g** of a cubit all round.

Haahashtari

1Ch 4: 6 him Ahuzzam, Hepher, Temeni and **H**.

Habakkuk

Prophet to Judah (Hab 1:1; 3:1).

Hab 1: 1 The oracle that **H** the prophet
3: 1 A prayer of **H** the prophet. On

Habazziniah

Jer 35: 3 Jeremiah, the son of **H**, and his

Habit

Ex 21:29 the bull has had the **h** of goring
21:36 that the bull had the **h** of goring,
Nu 22:30 been in the **h** of doing this to you?"
1Ti 5:13 they get into the **h** of being idle
Heb 10:25 as some are in the **h** of doing, but

Habitat (Inhabit)

Job 39: 6 his home, the salt flats as his **h**.

Habor

2Ki 17: 6 in Gozan on the **H** River and in the
18:11 in Gozan on the **H** River and in the
1Ch 5:26 He took them to Halah, **H**, Hara and

Hacaliah
Ne 1: 1 The words of Nehemiah son of **H**: In
10: 1 Nehemiah the governor, the son of **H**.

Hack
Eze 16:40 **h** you to pieces with their swords.

Hacmoni (Hacmonite)
1Ch 27:32 Jehiel son of **H** took care of the

Hacmonite (Hacmoni)
1Ch 11:11 Jashobeam, a **H**, was chief of the

Hadad
Ge 25:15 **H**, Tema, Jetur, Naphish and Kedemah.
36:35 When Husham died, **H** son of Bedad,
36:36 When **H** died, Samlah from Masrekah
36:39 Acbor died, **H** succeeded him as king.
1Ki 11:14 an adversary, **H** the Edomite,
11:17 **H**, still only a boy, fled to Egypt
11:18 who gave **H** a house and land and
11:19 Pharaoh was so pleased with **H** that
11:21 While he was in Egypt, **H** heard that
11:21 Then **H** said to Pharaoh, "Let me go,
11:22 "Nothing," **H** replied, "but do let
11:25 adding to the trouble caused by **H**.
1Ch 1:30 Mishma, Dumah, Massa, **H**, Tema,
1:46 When Husham died, **H** son of Bedad,
1:47 When **H** died, Samlah from Masrekah
1:50 Baal-Hanan died, **H** succeeded him as
1:51 **H** also died. The chiefs of Edom were:

Hadad Rimmon
Zec 12:11 like the weeping of **H** in the plain

Hadadezer (Hadadezer's)
2Sa 8: 3 David fought **H** son of Rehob,
8: 5 came to help **H** king of Zobah,
8: 7 of **H** and brought them to Jerusalem.
8: 8 towns that belonged to **H**, King David
8: 9 had defeated the entire army of **H**,
8:10 on his victory in battle over **H**,
8:12 plunder taken from **H** son of Rehob
10:16 **H** had Arameans brought from beyond
10:19 the kings who were vassals of **H**
1Ki 11:23 from his master, **H** king of Zobah.
1Ch 18: 3 David fought **H** king of Zobah
18: 5 came to help **H** king of Zobah,
18: 7 of **H** and brought them to Jerusalem.
18: 8 towns that belonged to **H**, David took
18: 9 the entire army of **H** king of Zobah,
18:10 on his victory in battle over **H**,
19:19 the vassals of **H** saw that they had

Hadadezer's (Hadadezer)
2Sa 10:16 commander of **H** army leading them.
1Ch 19:16 commander of **H** army leading them.

Hadashah
Jos 15:37 Zenan, **H**, Migdal Gad,

Hadassah
Est 2: 7 Mordecai had a cousin named **H**, whom

Hades
Mt 16:18 gates of **H** will not overcome it.
Rev 1:18 And I hold the keys of death and **H**.
6: 8 **H** was following close behind him.
20:13 and death and **H** gave up the dead
20:14 death and **H** were thrown into the

Hadid
Ezr 2:33 of Lod, **H** and Ono 725
Ne 7:37 of Lod, **H** and Ono 721
11:34 in **H**, Zeboim and Neballat,

Hadlai
2Ch 28:12 and Amasa son of **H**—confronted those

Hadoram
Ge 10:27 **H**, Uzal, Diklah,
1Ch 1:21 **H**, Uzal, Diklah,

1Ch 18:10 he sent his son **H** to King David to
18:10 **H** brought all kinds of articles of

Hadrach
Zec 9: 1 the LORD is against the land of **H**

Haeleph
Jos 18:28 Zelah, **H**, the Jebusite city (that is,

Hagab
Ezr 2:46 **H**, Shalmai, Hanan,

Hagaba
Ne 7:48 Lebana, **H**, Shalmai,

Hagabah
Ezr 2:45 Lebanah, **H**, Akkub,

Hagar
Sarah's Egyptian maidservant given to Abraham as his wife (Ge 16:1–3). Became pregnant; fled from Sarah (Ge 16:4–8); encouraged by God (Ge 16:9–14). Gave birth to Ishmael (Ge 16:15–16; 25:12); driven away by Sarah (Ge 21:9–21). Symbol of those in slavery through dependence on law for justification (Gal 4:21–31).

Ge 16: 1 had an Egyptian maidservant named **H**;
16: 3 took her Egyptian maidservant **H**
16: 4 He slept with **H**, and she conceived.
16: 6 Sarai ill-treated **H**; so she fled
16: 7 The angel of the LORD found **H** near a
16: 8 he said, "**H**, servant of Sarai, where
16:15 **H** bore Abram a son, and Abram gave
16:16 Abram was eighty-six years old when **H**
21: 9 Sarah saw that the son whom **H** the
21:14 a skin of water and gave them to **H**.
21:17 and the angel of God called to **H**
21:17 "What is the matter, **H**? Do not be
25:12 **H** the Egyptian, bore to Abraham.
Gal 4:24 who are to be slaves: This is **H**.
4:25 Now **H** stands for Mount Sinai in

Haggai
Prophet; encouraged returned exiles to continue rebuilding temple (Ezr 5:1; 6:14; Hag 1:1–11; 2).

Ezr 5: 1 Now **H** the prophet and Zechariah
6:14 of **H** the prophet and Zechariah,
Hag 1: 1 through the prophet **H** to Zerubbabel
1: 3 the LORD came through the prophet **H**:
1:12 and the message of the prophet **H**,
1:13 **H**, the LORD's messenger, gave this
2: 1 the LORD came through the prophet **H**:
2:10 of the LORD came to the prophet **H**:
2:13 **H** said, "If a person defiled by
2:14 **H** said, "'So it is with this people
2:20 The word of the LORD came to **H** a

Haggard
2Sa 13: 4 look so **h** morning after morning?
Job 30: 3 **H** from want and hunger, they roamed

Haggedolim
Ne 11:14 chief officer was Zabdiel son of **H**.

Haggi (Haggite)
Ge 46:16 The sons of Gad: Zephon, **H**, Shuni,
Nu 26:15 through **H**, the Haggite clan;

Haggiah
1Ch 6:30 Shimea his son, **H** his son and Asaiah

Haggite (Haggi)
Nu 26:15 through Haggi, the **H** clan; through

Haggith
2Sa 3: 4 the fourth, Adonijah the son of **H**;
1Ki 1: 5 Now Adonijah, whose mother was **H**,
1:11 the son of **H**, has become king
2:13 Now Adonijah, the son of **H**, went to
1Ch 3: 2 the fourth, Adonijah the son of **H**;

Hagri (Hagrite, Hagrites)
2Sa 23:36 of Nathan from Zobah, the son of **H**,
1Ch 11:38 brother of Nathan, Mibhar son of **H**,

Hagrite (Hagri)
1Ch 27:31 Jaziz the **H** was in charge of the

Hagrites (Hagri)
1Ch 5:10 reign they waged war against the **H**,
5:10 occupied the dwellings of the **H**
5:19 They waged war against the **H**, Jetur,
5:20 and God handed the **H** and all their
5:21 They seized the livestock of the **H**
Ps 83: 6 the Ishmaelites, of Moab and the **H**,

Hail[1] (Hailstones, Hailstorm)
Ex 9:19 because the **h** will fall on every man
9:22 **h** will fall all over Egypt—on men
9:23 the LORD sent thunder and **h**, and
9:23 LORD rained **h** on the land of Egypt;
9:24 **h** fell and lightning flashed back
9:25 Throughout Egypt **h** struck everything
9:26 The only place it did not **h** was the
9:28 we have had enough thunder and **h**.
9:29 stop and there will be no more **h**,
9:33 the thunder and **h** stopped, and the
9:34 Pharaoh saw that the rain and **h** and
10: 5 little you have left after the **h**,
10:12 fields, everything left by the **h**."
10:15 all that was left after the **h**
Job 38:22 or seen the storehouses of the **h**,
Ps 78:47 He destroyed their vines with **h** and
78:48 He gave over their cattle to the **h**,
105:32 He turned their rain into **h**, with
147:17 He hurls down **h** like pebbles. Who
148: 8 lightning and **h**, snow and clouds,
Isa 28:17 **h** will sweep away your refuge,
30:30 with cloudburst, thunderstorm and **h**.
32:19 Though **h** flattens the forest and the
Hag 2:17 and **h**, yet you did not turn to me,'
Rev 8: 7 and there came **h** and fire mixed with
16:21 God on account of the plague of **h**,

Hail[2]
Mt 27:29 "**H**, king of the Jews!" they said.
Mk 15:18 they began to call out to him, "**H**,
Jn 19: 3 "**H**, king of the Jews!" And they

Hailstones (Hail[1])
Jos 10:11 the LORD hurled large **h** down on them
10:11 and more of them died from the **h**
Ps 18:12 with **h** and bolts of lightning.
Eze 13:11 and I will send **h** hurtling down,
13:13 and in my anger **h** and torrents of
38:22 **h** and burning sulphur on him and on
Rev 16:21 From the sky huge **h** of about a

Hailstorm (Hail[1])
Ex 9:18 **h** that has ever fallen on Egypt,
Isa 28: 2 Like a **h** and a destructive wind,
Rev 11:19 an earthquake and a great **h**.

Hair (Grey-haired, Hairs, Hairy)
Ex 25: 4 scarlet yarn and fine linen; goat **h**;
26: 7 "Make curtains of goat **h** for the
35: 6 scarlet yarn and fine linen; goat **h**;
35:23 or goat **h**, ram skins dyed red or
35:26 and had the skill spun the goat **h**.
36:14 They made curtains of goat **h** for the
Lev 10: 6 "Do not let your **h** become unkempt,
13: 3 and if the **h** in the sore has turned
13: 4 the **h** in it has not turned white,
13:10 skin that has turned the **h** white
13:20 and the **h** in it has turned white,
13:21 there is no white **h** in it and it is
13:25 and if the **h** in it has turned white,
13:26 there is no white **h** in the spot and
13:30 and the **h** in it is yellow and thin,
13:31 deep and there is no black **h** in it,
13:32 there is no yellow **h** in it and it
13:36 does not need to look for yellow **h**
13:37 and black **h** has grown in it,
13:40 "When a man has lost his **h** and is

Lev 13:41 If he has lost his **h** from the front
13:45 let his **h** be unkempt, cover the
14: 8 shave off all his **h** and bathe with
14: 9 shave off all his **h**; he must shave
14: 9 his eyebrows and the rest of his **h**.
19:27 "Do not cut the **h** at the sides of
21:10 let his **h** become unkempt or tear his
Nu 5:18 he shall loosen her **h** and place in
6: 5 let the **h** of his head grow long.
6: 9 thus defiling the **h** he has dedicated,
6:18 shave off the **h** that he dedicated.
6:18 He is to take the **h** and put it in
6:19 shaved off the **h** of his dedication,
31:20 made of leather, goat **h** or wood."
Jdg 16:19 shave off the seven braids of his **h**
16:22 the **h** on his head began to grow
20:16 sling a stone at a **h** and not miss.
1Sa 14:45 not a **h** of his head shall fall to
17:35 seized it by its **h**, struck it and
19:13 putting some goats' **h** at the head.
19:16 and at the head was some goats' **h**.
2Sa 14:11 "not one **h** of your son's head will
14:26 Whenever he cut the **h** of his
14:26 he used to cut his **h** from time to
1Ki 1:52 not a **h** of his head will fall to the
2Ki 1: 8 "He was a man with a garment of **h**
9:30 arranged her **h** and looked out of a
Ezr 9: 3 pulled **h** from my head and beard
Ne 13:25 of the men and pulled out their **h**.
Job 4:15 and the **h** on my body stood on end.
41:32 would think the deep had white **h**.
Pr 16:31 Grey **h** is a crown of splendour; it
20:29 grey **h** the splendour of the old.
SS 4: 1 Your **h** is like a flock of goats
5: 2 my **h** with the dampness of the night
5:11 his **h** is wavy and black as a raven
6: 5 Your **h** is like a flock of goats
7: 5 Your **h** is like royal tapestry;
Isa 3:24 instead of well-dressed **h**, baldness
7:20 your head and the **h** of your legs,
22:12 to tear out your **h** and put on
Jer 7:29 Cut off your **h** and throw it away;
Eze 5: 1 a set of scales and divide up the **h**.
5: 2 burn a third of the **h** with fire
5: 3 take a few strands of **h** and tuck
8: 3 and took me by the **h** of my head.
16: 7 breasts were formed and your **h** grew
44:20 heads or let their **h** grow long,
44:20 keep the **h** of their heads trimmed.
Da 3:27 nor was a **h** of their heads singed;
4:33 **h** grew like the feathers of an eagle
7: 9 **h** of his head was white like wool.
Hos 7: 9 His **h** is sprinkled with grey, but he
Zec 13: 4 garment of **h** in order to deceive.
Mt 3: 4 clothes were made of camel's **h**
5:36 make even one **h** white or black.
Mk 1: 6 John wore clothing made of camel's **h**
Lk 7:38 Then she wiped them with her **h**,
7:44 her tears and wiped them with her **h**.
21:18 not a **h** of your head will perish.
Jn 11: 2 Lord and wiped his feet with her **h**.
12: 3 feet and wiped his feet with her **h**.
Ac 18:18 Before he sailed, he had his **h** cut
27:34 will lose a single **h** from his head."
1Co 11: 6 she should have her **h** cut off;
11: 6 to have her **h** cut or shaved off,
11:14 has long **h**, it is a disgrace to him,
11:15 that if a woman has long **h**, it is
11:15 **h** is given to her as a covering.
1Ti 2: 9 not with braided **h** or gold or pearls
1Pe 3: 3 such as braided **h** and the wearing of
Rev 1:14 His head and **h** were white like wool,
6:12 black like sackcloth made of goat **h**
9: 8 Their **h** was like women's **h**, and

Hairs (Hair)

Ps 40:12 They are more than the **h** of my head,
69: 4 reason outnumber the **h** of my head;
Isa 46: 4 to your old age and grey **h** I am he
Mt 10:30 very **h** of your head are all numbered
Lk 12: 7 very **h** of your head are all numbered

Hairy (Hair)

Ge 25:25 his whole body was like a **h** garment
27:11 "But my brother Esau is a **h** man, and
27:23 his hands were **h** like those of his
Ps 68:21 the **h** crowns of those who go on in

Hakilah

1Sa 23:19 on the hill of **H**, south of Jeshimon?
26: 1 hill of **H**, which faces Jeshimon?"
26: 3 on the hill of **H** facing Jeshimon,

Hakkatan

Ezr 8:12 son of **H**, and with him 110 men;

Hakkoz

1Ch 24:10 the seventh to **H**, the eighth to
Ezr 2:61 **H** and Barzillai (a man who had
Ne 3: 4 Meremoth son of Uriah, the son of **H**
3:21 Meremoth son of Uriah, the son of **H**
7:63 **H** and Barzillai (a man who had

Hakupha

Ezr 2:51 Bakbuk, **H**, Harhur,
Ne 7:53 Bakbuk, **H**, Harhur,

Halah

2Ki 17: 6 He settled them in **H**, in Gozan on
18:11 to Assyria and settled them in **H**,
1Ch 5:26 He took them to **H**, Habor, Hara and

Halak

Jos 11:17 from Mount **H**, which rises towards
12: 7 in the Valley of Lebanon to Mount **H**,

Half-dead (Dead)

Lk 10:30 him and went away, leaving him **h**.

Halhul

Jos 15:58 **H**, Beth Zur, Gedor,

Hali

Jos 19:25 Their territory included: Helkath, **H**,

Hall

1Sa 9:22 his servant into the **h** and seated
1Ki 6: 3 portico at the front of the main **h**
6: 5 Against the walls of the main **h** and
6:17 The main **h** in front of this room was
6:33 wood for the entrance to the main **h**.
7: 7 He built the throne **h**, the **H** of
7: 8 like this **h** for Pharaoh's daughter,
7:50 doors of the main **h** of the temple.
2Ch 3: 5 He panelled the main **h** with pine
3:13 on their feet, facing the main **h**.
4:22 and the doors of the main **h**.
Est 5: 1 palace, in front of the king's **h**.
5: 1 in the **h**, facing the entrance.
7: 8 the palace garden to the banquet **h**,
SS 2: 4 He has taken me to the banquet **h**,
Da 5:10 his nobles, came into the banquet **h**.
Mt 22:10 wedding **h** was filled with guests.
Ac 19: 9 daily in the lecture **h** of Tyrannus.

Hallelujah

Rev 19: 1 "**H**! Salvation and glory and power
19: 3 again they shouted: "**H**! The smoke
19: 4 And they cried: "Amen, **H**!"
19: 6 "**H**! For our Lord God Almighty

Hallohesh

Ne 3:12 Shallum son of **H**, ruler of a
10:24 **H**, Pilha, Shobek,

Hallowed (Holy)

Mt 6: 9 Our Father in heaven, **h** be your name,
Lk 11: 2 **h** be your name, your kingdom come.

Halt (Halted)

2Sa 2:28 and all the men came to a **h**;
20:12 all the troops came to a **h** there.
Job 38:11 here is where your proud waves **h**'?
Isa 10:32 This day they will **h** at Nob;

Halted (Halt)

2Sa 15:17 **h** at a place some distance away.
18:16 pursuing Israel, for Joab **h** them.

Halter

Pr 26: 3 for the horse, a **h** for the donkey

Ham (Hamites)

Son of Noah (Ge 5:32; 6:10; 1Ch 1:4). Saved in ark (Ge 7:13; 9:18–19). Father of Canaan, Cush (Ethiopia), Put (Libya) and Mizraim (Egypt) (Ge 9:18; 10:6; 1Ch 1:8). Dishonoured Noah by looking at his nakedness; brought curse on Canaan (Ge 9:20–27). Associated with Egypt (Ps 78:51; 105:23,27; 106:22).

Ge 5:32 the father of Shem, **H** and Japheth.
6:10 Noah had three sons: Shem, **H** and
7:13 Shem, **H** and Japheth, together with
9:18 of the ark were Shem, **H** and Japheth.
9:18 (**H** was the father of Canaan.)
9:22 **H**, the father of Canaan, saw his
10: 1 This is the account of Shem, **H** and
10: 6 The sons of **H**: Cush, Mizraim, Put
10:20 These are the sons of **H** by their
14: 5 the Zuzites in **H**, the Emites in
1Ch 1: 4 The sons of Noah: Shem, **H** and
1: 8 The sons of **H**: Cush, Mizraim, Put
Ps 78:51 of manhood in the tents of **H**.
105:23 lived as an alien in the land of **H**.
105:27 them, his wonders in the land of **H**.
106:22 miracles in the land of **H** and

Haman (Haman's)

Agagite, honoured by Xerxes (Est 3:1–2). Angered by Mordecai's defiance (Est 3:3–5; 5:9–14); planned to exterminate Jewish people (Est 3:6–15). Ordered to honour Mordecai (Est 6:1–12). Plot exposed by Esther (Est 7:1–7); hanged on gallows built for Mordecai (Est 7:9–10).

Est 3: 1 honoured **H** son of Hammedatha
3: 2 knelt down and paid honour to **H**,
3: 4 Therefore they told **H** about it to
3: 5 **H** saw that Mordecai would not kneel
3: 6 Instead **H** looked for a way to
3: 7 in the presence of **H** to select a
3: 8 **H** said to King Xerxes, "There is a
3:10 and gave it to **H** son of Hammedatha,
3:11 Keep the money," the king said to **H**
3:15 The king and **H** sat down to drink,
4: 7 the exact amount of money **H**
5: 4 "let the king, together with **H**, come
5: 5 "Bring **H** at once," the king said,
5: 5 So the king and **H** went to the
5: 8 let the king and **H** come tomorrow to
5: 9 **H** went out that day happy and in
5:10 Nevertheless, **H** restrained himself
5:11 **H** boasted to them about his vast
5:12 And that's not all," **H** added. "I'm
5:14 suggestion delighted **H**, and he had
6: 4 **H** had just entered the outer court
6: 5 "**H** is standing in the court."
6: 6 **H** entered, the king asked him,
6: 6 Now **H** thought to himself, "Who is
6:10 "Go at once," the king commanded **H**.
6:11 **H** got the robe and the horse. He
6:12 But **H** rushed home, with his head
6:14 hurried **H** away to the banquet Esther
7: 1 the king and **H** went to dine with
7: 6 adversary and enemy is this vile **H**.
7: 6 Then **H** was terrified before the
7: 7 But **H**, realising that the king had
7: 8 **H** was falling on the couch where
7:10 they hanged **H** on the gallows he had
8: 1 estate of **H**, the enemy of the Jews.
8: 2 ring which he had reclaimed from **H**
8: 3 to the evil plan of **H** the Agagite,
8: 5 dispatches that **H** son of Hammedatha,
8: 7 Because **H** attacked the Jews, I have
9:10 the ten sons of **H** son of Hammedatha,
9:12 ten sons of **H** in the citadel of Susa
9:14 and they hanged the ten sons of **H**.
9:24 For **H** son of Hammedatha, the Agagite,
9:25 the evil scheme **H** had devised

Haman's (Haman)

Est 3:12 all **H** orders to the king's satraps,
7: 8 king's mouth, they covered **H** face.
7: 9 feet high stands by **H** house.
8: 2 Esther appointed him over **H** estate.
9:13 **H** ten sons be hanged on gallows."

Hamath (Hamathites)

City and region in Syria on southern bank of River Orontes. Its king congratulated David for defeat of Hadadezer (2Sa 8:9–10; 1Ch 18:9–10). Solomon controlled it, and built storage depot there (2Ch 8:4). Was lost to Israel but recovered by Jeroboam (2Ki 14:28). After Assyrian capture, some inhabitants moved to Samaria (2Ki 17:24; Isa 36:18–19; 37:13), and some Israelites moved to Hamath (Isa 11:11). Its people worshipped Ashima (2Ki 17:30), and were guilty of syncretism (2Ki 17:29–33). In Amos' time the city was in ruins (Am 6:2).

2Sa 8: 9 Tou king of **H** heard that David had
2Ki 14:28 for Israel both Damascus and **H**,
17:24 Cuthah, Avva, **H** and Sepharvaim and
17:30 and the men from **H** made Ashima;
18:34 Where are the gods of **H** and Arpad?
19:13 Where is the king of **H**, the king of
23:33 at Riblah in the land of **H** so that
25:21 There at Riblah, in the land of **H**,
1Ch 18: 3 as far as **H**, when he went to
18: 9 Tou king of **H** heard that David had
2Ch 8: 4 the store cities he had built in **H**.
Isa 10: 9 Is not **H** like Arpad, and Samaria
11:11 from **H** and from the islands of the
36:19 Where are the gods of **H** and Arpad?
37:13 Where is the king of **H**, the king of
Jer 39: 5 Babylon at Riblah in the land of **H**,
49:23 Concerning Damascus: "**H** and Arpad
52: 9 Babylon at Riblah in the land of **H**,
52:27 There at Riblah, in the land of **H**,
Eze 47:16 the border between Damascus and **H**)
47:17 with the border of **H** to the north.
48: 1 border of Damascus next to **H** will
Am 6: 2 go from there to great **H**, and then
Zec 9: 2 upon **H** too, which borders on it, and

Hamath Zobah

2Ch 8: 3 Solomon then went to **H** and captured

Hamathites (Hamath)

Ge 10:18 Arvadites, Zemarites and **H**. Later
1Ch 1:16 Arvadites, Zemarites and **H**.

Hamites (Ham)

1Ch 4:40 Some **H** had lived there formerly.
4:41 They attacked the **H** in their

Hammath

Jos 19:35 Ziddim, Zer, **H**, Rakkath, Kinnereth,
1Ch 2:55 **H**, the father of the house of Recab.

Hammedatha

Est 3: 1 King Xerxes honoured Haman son of **H**,
3:10 and gave it to Haman son of **H**,
8: 5 the dispatches that Haman son of **H**,
9:10 the ten sons of Haman son of **H**, the
9:24 For Haman son of **H**, the Agagite, the

Hammer (Hammered, Hammers)

Ex 25:31 lampstand of pure gold and **h** it out
Nu 16:38 **H** the censers into sheets to overlay
Jdg 4:21 picked up a tent peg and a **h** and
5:26 her right hand for the workman's **h**.
1Ki 6: 7 and no **h**, chisel or any other iron
Isa 41: 7 he who smooths with the **h** spurs on
Jer 10: 4 they fasten it with **h** and nails so
23:29 a **h** that breaks a rock in pieces?
50:23 is the **h** of the whole earth!

Hammered (Hammer)

Ex 25:18 make two cherubim out of **h** gold at
25:36 the lampstand, **h** out of pure gold.
37: 7 he made two cherubim out of **h** gold
37:17 lampstand of pure gold and **h** it out,
37:22 the lampstand, **h** out of pure gold.
39: 3 They **h** out thin sheets of gold and
Nu 8: 4 It was made of **h** gold—from its base
10: 2 "Make two trumpets of **h** silver, and
16:39 had them **h** out to overlay the altar,
1Ki 6:35 gold **h** evenly over the carvings.
7:29 and bulls were wreaths of **h** work.
10:16 two hundred large shields of **h** gold;
10:17 hundred small shields of **h** gold,
2Ch 9:15 two hundred large shields of **h** gold;
9:15 of **h** gold went into each shield.
9:16 hundred small shields of **h** gold,
Jer 10: 9 **H** silver is brought from Tarshish

Hammers (Hammer)

Isa 44:12 the coals; he shapes an idol with **h**,

Hammoleketh

1Ch 7:18 His sister **H** gave birth to Ishhod,

Hammon

Jos 19:28 went to Abdon, Rehob, **H** and Kanah,
1Ch 6:76 **H** and Kiriathaim, together with

Hammoth Dor

Jos 21:32 **H** and Kartan, together with their

Hammuel

1Ch 4:26 The descendants of Mishma: **H** his son

Hamon Gog

Eze 39:11 So it will be called the Valley of **H**
39:15 have buried it in the Valley of **H**.

Hamonah

Eze 39:16 (Also a town called **H** will be there.

Hamor

Ge 33:19 he bought from the sons of **H**, the
34: 2 Shechem son of **H** the Hivite, the
34: 4 Shechem said to his father **H**, "Get
34: 6 Shechem's father **H** went out to talk
34: 8 **H** said to them, "My son Shechem has
34:13 spoke to Shechem and his father **H**.
34:18 Their proposal seemed good to **H** and
34:20 **H** and his son Shechem went to the
34:24 agreed with **H** and his son Shechem,
34:26 They put **H** and his son Shechem to
Jos 24:32 sons of **H**, the father of Shechem.
Jdg 9:28 Serve the men of **H**, Shechem's father
Ac 7:16 had bought from the sons of **H** at

Hampered

Pr 4:12 you walk, your steps will not be **h**

Hamstring (Hamstrung)

Jos 11: 6 You are to **h** their horses and burn

Hamstrung (Hamstring)

Ge 49: 6 anger and **h** oxen as they pleased.
Jos 11: 9 He **h** their horses and burned their
2Sa 8: 4 He **h** all but a hundred of the
1Ch 18: 4 He **h** all but a hundred of the

Hamul (Hamulite)

Ge 46:12 The sons of Perez: Hezron and H.
Nu 26:21 through **H**, the Hamulite clan.
1Ch 2: 5 The sons of Perez: Hezron and **H**.

Hamulite (Hamul)

Nu 26:21 through Hamul, the **H** clan.

Hamutal

2Ki 23:31 His mother's name was **H** daughter of
24:18 His mother's name was **H** daughter of
Jer 52: 1 His mother's name was **H** daughter of

Hanamel

Jer 32: 7 **H** son of Shallum your uncle is going
32: 8 my cousin **H** came to me in the
32: 9 field at Anathoth from my cousin **H**
32:12 in the presence of my cousin **H** and

Hanan

1Ch 8:23 Abdon, Zicri, **H**,
8:38 Ishmael, Sheariah, Obadiah and **H**.
9:44 Ishmael, Sheariah, Obadiah and **H**.
11:43 **H** son of Maacah, Joshaphat the
Ezr 2:46 Hagab, Shalmai, **H**,
Ne 7:49 **H**, Giddel, Gahar,
8: 7 Kelita, Azariah, Jozabad, **H** and
10:10 Hodiah, Kelita, Pelaiah, **H**,
10:22 Pelatiah, **H**, Anaiah,
10:26 Ahiah, **H**, Anan,
13:13 storerooms and made **H** son of Zaccur,
Jer 35: 4 of **H** son of Igdaliah the man of God.

Hananel

Ne 3: 1 and as far as the Tower of **H**.
12:39 the Fish Gate, the Tower of **H** and
Jer 31:38 the Tower of **H** to the Corner Gate.
Zec 14:10 Tower of **H** to the royal winepresses.

Hanani

1Ki 16: 1 to Jehu son of **H** against Baasha:
16: 7 son of **H** to Baasha and his house,
1Ch 25: 4 Shubael and Jerimoth; Hananiah, **H**,
25:25 the eighteenth to **H**, his sons and
2Ch 16: 7 At that time **H** the seer came to Asa
19: 2 Jehu the seer, the son of **H**, went
20:34 in the annals of Jehu son of **H**,
Ezr 10:20 From the descendants of Immer: **H** and
Ne 1: 2 **H**, one of my brothers, came from
7: 2 in charge of Jerusalem my brother **H**,
12:36 Maai, Nethanel, Judah and **H**—with

Hananiah

1Ch 3:19 sons of Zerubbabel: Meshullam and **H**.
3:21 The descendants of **H**: Pelatiah and
8:24 **H**, Elam, Anthothijah,
25: 4 Uzziel, Shubael and Jerimoth; **H**,
25:23 the sixteenth to **H**, his sons and
2Ch 26:11 **H**, one of the royal officials.
Ezr 10:28 Jehohanan, **H**, Zabbai and Athlai.
Ne 3: 8 **H**, one of the perfume-makers,
3:30 Next to him, **H** son of Shelemiah, and
7: 2 along with **H** the commander of the
10:23 Hoshea, **H**, Hasshub,
12:12 family, Meraiah; of Jeremiah's, **H**;
12:41 Zechariah and **H** with their trumpets
Jer 28: 1 the prophet **H** son of Azzur, who was
28: 5 to the prophet **H** before the priests
28:10 the prophet **H** took the yoke off the
28:12 Shortly after the prophet **H** had
28:13 "Go and tell **H**, 'This is what the
28:15 Jeremiah said to **H** the prophet,
28:15 "Listen, **H**! The LORD has not sent
28:17 that same year, **H** the prophet died.
36:12 Zedekiah, son of **H**,
37:13 the son of **H**, arrested him and said,
Da 1: 6 Daniel, **H**, Mishael and Azariah.
1: 7 to **H**, Shadrach;
1:11 over Daniel, **H**, Mishael and Azariah,
1:19 Daniel, **H**, Mishael and Azariah;
2:17 his friends **H**, Mishael and Azariah.

Hand (*Hand of God, Hand of the LORD*, Handbreadth, Handed, Handful, Handfuls, Handing, Hands, Left-handed, *Mighty hand*, Open-handed, *Right hand*, Right-handed)

Ge 3:22 not be allowed to reach out his **h**
4:11 your brother's blood from your **h**.
8: 9 He reached out his **h** and took the
14:20 delivered your enemies into your **h**.
14:22 "I have raised my **h** to the LORD,
16:12 his **h** will be against everyone and
16:12 and everyone's **h** against him,
19:16 he hesitated, the men grasped his **h**
21:18 Lift the boy up and take him by the **h**
21:30 Accept these seven lambs from my **h**
22:10 he reached out his **h** and took the
22:12 "Do not lay a **h** on the boy," he said.
24: 2 "Put your **h** under my thigh.
24: 9 servant put his **h** under the thigh
25:26 with his **h** grasping Esau's heel
32:11 Save me, I pray, from the **h** of my

Ge 37:22 desert, but don't lay a **h** on him.
38:18 the staff in your **h**," she answered.
38:28 one of them put out his **h**; so the
38:29 when he drew back his **h**, his brother
39:12 in her **h** and ran out of the house.
39:13 her **h** and had run out of the house,
40:11 Pharaoh's cup was in my **h**, and I
40:11 cup and put the cup in his **h**."
40:13 will put Pharaoh's cup in his **h**,
40:21 again put the cup into Pharaoh's **h**,
41:44 will lift **h** or foot in all Egypt."
46: 4 Joseph's own **h** will close your eyes."
47:29 put your **h** under my thigh and
48:13 his right towards Israel's left **h**
48:14 he put his left **h** on Manasseh's head,
48:17 he took hold of his father's **h** to
49: 8 your **h** will be on the neck of your
49:24 because of the **h** of the Mighty One
Ex 3: 8 them from the **h** of the Egyptians
3:20 I will stretch out my **h** and strike
4: 2 in your **h**?" "A staff," he replied.
4: 4 Reach out your **h** and take it
4: 4 turned back into a staff in his **h**.
4: 6 "Put your **h** inside your cloak
4: 6 Moses put his **h** into his cloak,
4: 7 Moses put his **h** back into his
4:17 take this staff in your **h** so that
4:20 he took the staff of God in his **h**.
5:21 put a sword in their **h** to kill us."
6: 8 with uplifted **h** to give to Abraham,
7: 4 Then I will lay my **h** on Egypt and
7: 5 I stretch out my **h** against Egypt
7:15 and take in your **h** the staff that
7:17 With the staff that is in my **h** I
7:19 stretch out your **h** over the waters
8: 5 'Stretch out your **h** with your staff
8: 6 Aaron stretched out his **h** over the
8:17 and when Aaron stretched out his **h**
9:15 now I could have stretched out my **h**
9:22 "Stretch out your **h** towards the sky
10:12 "Stretch out your **h** over Egypt so
10:21 "Stretch out your **h** towards the sky
10:22 Moses stretched out his **h** towards
11: 5 slave girl, who is at her **h** mill
12:11 your feet and your staff in your **h**.
13: 9 be for you like a sign on your **h**
13:16 will be like a sign on your **h** and
14:16 stretch out your **h** over the sea
14:21 Moses stretched out his **h** over the
14:26 "Stretch out your **h** over the sea
14:27 Moses stretched out his **h** over the
15: 9 sword and my **h** will destroy them.'
15:20 took a tambourine in her **h**, and
16: 3 only we had died by the LORD's **h**
17: 5 take in your **h** the staff with which
18: 9 them from the **h** of the Egyptians.
18:10 who rescued you from the **h** of the
18:10 people from the **h** of the Egyptians.
19:13 not a **h** is to be laid on him.
21:24 for eye, tooth for tooth, **h** for **h**
23:31 I will **h** over to you the people
24:11 God did not raise his **h** against
33:22 cover you with my **h** until I have
33:23 I will remove my **h** and you will
Lev 1: 4 He is to lay his **h** on the head of
3: 2 He is to lay his **h** on the head of
3: 8 He is to lay his **h** on the head of
3:13 He is to lay his **h** on its head
4: 4 He is to lay his **h** on its head
4:24 He is to lay his **h** on the goat's
4:29 He is to lay his **h** on the head of
4:33 He is to lay his **h** on its head
14:15 it in the palm of his own left **h**,
14:26 oil into the palm of his own left **h**,
21:19 no man with a crippled foot or **h**,
22:25 animals from the **h** of a foreigner
Nu 11: 8 ground it in a **h** mill or crushed
14:30 I swore with uplifted **h** to make
22:23 road with a drawn sword in his **h**,
22:29 If I had a sword in my **h**, I would
25: 7 the assembly, took a spear in his **h**
27:18 the spirit, and lay your **h** on him.
35:17 Or if anyone has a stone in his **h**
35:18 object in his **h** that could kill,
Dt 2:15 The LORD's **h** was against them until
2:24 See, I have given into your **h** Sihon
Dt 3:24 your greatness and your strong **h**.
7:24 will give their kings into your **h**,
12: 7 everything you have put your **h** to,
12:18 God in everything you put your **h** to.
13: 9 Your **h** must be the first in putting
15:10 and in everything you put your **h** to.
15:18 twice as much as that of a hired **h**.
19:12 **h** him over to the avenger of blood
19:21 for tooth, **h** for **h**, foot for foot.
20:13 your God delivers it into your **h**,
23:15 do not **h** him over to his master.
23:20 in everything you put your **h** to
25:12 you shall cut off her **h**. Show her
28: 8 and on everything you put your **h** to.
28:20 in everything you put your **h** to,
28:32 after day, powerless to lift a **h**.
32:27 'Our **h** has triumphed; the LORD has
32:39 and no-one can deliver out of my **h**.
32:40 I lift my **h** to heaven and declare:
32:41 sharpen my flashing sword and my **h**
33: 3 all the holy ones are in your **h**.
Jos 2:19 on our head if a **h** is laid on him.
5:13 of him with a drawn sword in his **h**.
8: 7 your God will give it into your **h**.
8:18 the javelin that is in your **h**,
8:18 into your **h** I will deliver the city.
8:26 For Joshua did not draw back the **h**
10: 8 them; I have given them into your **h**.
10:19 God has given them into your **h**."
10:30 city and its king into Israel's **h**.
11: 6 **h** all of them over to Israel, slain.
11: 8 LORD gave them into the **h** of Israel
22:31 the Israelites from the LORD's **h**.
24:10 and I delivered you out of his **h**.
Jdg 3:21 Ehud reached with his left **h**, drew
4: 9 LORD will **h** Sisera over to a woman.
4:24 the **h** of the Israelites grew
5:26 Her **h** reached for the tent peg,
6: 9 from the **h** of all your oppressors.
6:13 and put us into the **h** of Midian."
6:14 and save Israel out of Midian's **h**.
6:21 tip of the staff that was in his **h**,
6:36 Israel by my **h** as you have promised
6:37 save Israel by my **h**, as you said."
8: 7 given Zebah and Zalmunna into my **h**,
8:22 saved us out of the **h** of Midian."
9:17 to rescue you from the **h** of
9:33 do whatever your **h** finds to do."
15:12 and **h** you over to the Philistines.
15:13 will only tie you up and **h** you over
16:26 said to the servant who held his **h**,
16:29 his left **h** on the other,
Ru 1:13 LORD's **h** has gone out against me!"
1Sa 2:13 a three-pronged fork in his **h**.
2:16 "No, **h** it over now; if you don't,
4: 3 save us from the **h** of our enemies."
4: 8 us from the **h** of these mighty gods?
5: 6 The LORD's **h** was heavy upon the
5: 7 because his **h** is heavy upon us and
5: 9 the LORD's **h** was against that city,
5:11 God's **h** was very heavy upon it.
6: 3 his **h** has not been lifted from you."
6: 5 Perhaps he will lift his **h** from you
6: 9 it was not his **h** that struck us
7: 3 out of the **h** of the Philistines."
7: 8 from the **h** of the Philistines."
9:16 from the **h** of the Philistines.
10: 7 whatever your **h** finds to do,
12: 3 From whose **h** have I accepted a
12: 4 not taken anything from anyone's **h**.
12: 5 have not found anything in my **h**.
12:15 his **h** will be against you, as it was
13:22 had a sword or spear in his **h**;
14:12 given them into the **h** of Israel."
14:19 to the priest, "Withdraw your **h**.
14:26 yet no-one put his **h** to his mouth,
14:27 **h** and dipped it into the honeycomb.
14:27 He raised his **h** to his mouth, and
14:37 Will you give them into Israel's **h**
17:37 me from the **h** of this Philistine.
17:40 he took his staff in his **h**, chose
17:40 in his **h**, approached the Philistine.
17:46 This day the LORD will **h** you over
17:50 without a sword in his **h** he struck
18:10 Saul had a spear in his **h**
18:17 "I will not raise a **h** against him.
1Sa 18:21 that the **h** of the Philistines may
19: 9 his house with his spear in his **h**.
20: 8 Why **h** me over to your father?"
21: 3 Now then, what have you to **h**?
21: 4 any ordinary bread to **h**; however,
22: 6 And Saul, spear in **h**, was seated
22:17 raise a **h** to strike the priests
23: 4 give the Philistines into your **h**."
23:17 "My father Saul will not lay a **h** on
24: 6 or lift my **h** against him; for he
24:10 'I will not lift my **h** against my
24:11 at this piece of your robe in my **h**!
24:12 to me, but my **h** will not touch you.
24:13 deeds,' so my **h** will not touch you.
24:15 me by delivering me from your **h**."
25:35 David accepted from her **h** what she
26: 9 Who can lay a **h** on the LORD's
26:11 LORD forbid that I should lay a **h**
26:23 not lay a **h** on the LORD's anointed.
27: 1 shall be destroyed by the **h** of Saul.
27: 1 and I will slip out of his **h**."
28:19 The LORD will **h** over both Israel and
28:19 The LORD will also **h** over the army
30:15 kill me or **h** me over to my master,
2Sa 1:14 lift your **h** to destroy the LORD's
2:14 up and fight **h** to **h** in front of us.
3:18 Israel from the **h** of the Philistines
3:18 and from the **h** of all their enemies.
4:11 demand his blood from your **h** and rid
5:19 Will you **h** them over to me?"
5:19 **h** the Philistines over to you."
12: 7 delivered you from the **h** of Saul.
13: 5 her and then eat it from her **h**.
13: 6 so that I may eat from her **h**."
13:10 so that I may eat from your **h**.
13:19 She put her **h** on her head and went
14: 7 '**H** over the one who struck his
14:16 deliver his servant from the **h** of
14:19 king asked, "Isn't the **h** of Joab
15: 5 Absalom would reach out his **h**,
18:12 lift my **h** against the king's son.
18:14 he took three javelins in his **h**
18:19 him from the **h** of his enemies."
19: 9 "The king delivered us from the **h**
19: 9 us from the **h** of the Philistines.
20:10 against the dagger in Joab's **h**,
20:21 lifted up his **h** against the king,
20:21 **H** over this one man, and I'll
21:20 huge man with six fingers on each **h**
22: 1 him from the **h** of all his enemies
22: 1 his enemies and from the **h** of Saul.
23: 6 which are not gathered with the **h**.
23:10 **h** grew tired and froze to the sword.
23:21 the Egyptian had a spear in his **h**,
23:21 the spear from the Egyptian's **h**
24:16 the angel stretched out his **h** to
24:16 people, "Enough! Withdraw your **h**.
24:17 your **h** fall upon me and my family."
1Ki 8:15 who with his own **h** has fulfilled
8:24 with your **h** you have fulfilled
11:12 tear it out of the **h** of your son.
11:31 Solomon's **h** and give you ten tribes.
11:34 whole kingdom out of Solomon's **h**;
13: 4 he stretched out his **h** from the
13: 4 "Seize him!" But the **h** he stretched
13: 6 for me that my **h** may be restored.
13: 6 and the king's **h** was restored and
18:44 A cloud as small as a man's **h** is
20:13 I will give it into your **h** today,
22: 6 will give it into the king's **h**."
22:12 will give it into the king's **h**."
22:15 will give it into the king's **h**."
2Ki 3:10 together only to **h** us over to Moab?"
3:13 together to **h** us over to Moab."
3:18 he will also **h** Moab over to you.
4:29 take my staff in your **h** and run.
5:11 wave his **h** over the spot and cure me
6: 7 man reached out his **h** and took it.
10:15 If so," said Jehu, "give me your **h**.
11: 8 each man with his weapon in his **h**.
11:11 each with his weapon in his **h**,
12: 7 **h** it over for repairing the temple.
14:27 by the **h** of Jeroboam son of Jehoash.
16: 7 Come up and save me out of the **h**
17:39 you from the **h** of all your enemies."
18:21 which pierces a man's **h** and wounds

2Ki 18:29 He cannot deliver you from my **h**.
18:30 into the **h** of the king of Assyria
18:33 from the **h** of the king of Assyria
18:34 Have they rescued Samaria from my **h**?
18:35 LORD deliver Jerusalem from my **h**?"
19:19 LORD our God, deliver us from his **h**
20: 6 from the **h** of the king of Assyria.
21:14 and **h** them over to their enemies.
1Ch 4:10 territory! Let your **h** be with me,
6:15 exile by the **h** of Nebuchadnezzar.
6:44 the Merarites, at his left **h**: Ethan
11:23 spear like a weaver's rod in his **h**,
11:23 the spear from the Egyptian's **h**
13: 9 Uzzah reached out his **h** to steady
13:10 because he had put his **h** on the ark.
14:10 Will you **h** them over to me?"
14:10 "Go, I will **h** them over to you.
14:11 out against my enemies by my **h**.
20: 6 huge man with six fingers on each **h**
21:15 people, "Enough! Withdraw your **h**.
21:16 in his **h** extended over Jerusalem.
21:17 let your **h** fall upon me and my
29:14 you only what comes from your **h**.
29:16 it comes from your **h**,
2Ch 6:15 with your **h** you have fulfilled
16: 7 of Aram has escaped from your **h**.
16: 8 he delivered them into your **h**.
18: 5 will give it into the king's **h**."
18:11 will give it into the king's **h**."
18:14 they will be given into your **h**.
20: 6 Power and might are in your **h**
23: 7 each man with his weapons in his **h**.
23:10 each with his weapon in his **h**,
25:15 save their own people from your **h**?"
25:20 for God so worked that he might **h**
26:19 Uzziah, who had a censer in his **h**
28: 9 Judah, he gave them into your **h**.
30: 6 from the **h** of the kings of Assyria.
32:11 from the **h** of the king of Assyria,
32:13 to deliver their land from my **h**?
32:14 can your god deliver you from my **h**?
32:15 from my **h** or the **h** of my fathers.
32:15 your god deliver you from my **h**!"
32:17 not rescue their people from my **h**,
32:17 not rescue his people from my **h**."
32:22 from the **h** of Sennacherib king of
32:22 and from the **h** of all others.
Ezr 6:12 who lifts a **h** to change this decree
7: 9 gracious **h** of his God was on him.
7:14 of your God, which is in your **h**.
8:18 the gracious **h** of our God was on us,
8:22 "The gracious **h** of our God is on
8:31 The **h** of our God was on us, and he
9: 7 **h** of foreign kings, as it is today.
Ne 2: 8 gracious **h** of my God was upon me,
2:18 told them about the gracious **h**
4:17 work with one **h** and held a weapon in
6: 5 in his **h** was an unsealed letter
9:15 sworn with uplifted **h** to give them.
9:27 them from the **h** of their enemies.
9:28 you abandoned them to the **h** of
Est 5: 2 the gold sceptre that was in his **h**.
9: 1 upper **h** over those who hated them.
Job 1:11 stretch out your **h** and strike
2: 5 stretch out your **h** and strike his
6: 9 let loose his **h** and cut me off!
6:23 deliver me from the **h** of the enemy,
9:33 us, to lay his **h** upon us both,
10: 7 no-one can rescue me from your **h**?
11:14 put away the sin that is in your **h**
12:10 In his **h** is the life of every
13:21 Withdraw your **h** far from me, and
15:23 knows the day of darkness is at **h**.
21: 5 clap your **h** over your mouth.
23: 2 **h** is heavy in spite of my groaning.
26:13 his **h** pierced the gliding serpent.
28: 9 Man's **h** assaults the flinty rock
29:20 in me, the bow ever new in my **h**.'
30:21 the might of your **h** you attack me.
30:24 no-one lays a **h** on a broken man
31:21 raised my **h** against the fatherless
31:27 my **h** offered them a kiss of homage,
33: 7 nor should my **h** be heavy upon you.
34:20 mighty are removed without human **h**.
35: 7 or what does he receive from your **h**?
40: 4 to you? I put my **h** over my mouth.
Job 41: 8 If you lay a **h** on him, you will
Ps 10:12 Arise, LORD! Lift up your **h**, O God.
10:14 you consider it to take it in **h**.
17:14 O LORD, by your **h** save me from such
18: T LORD delivered him from the **h** of
18: T his enemies and from the **h** of Saul
21: 8 Your **h** will lay hold on all your
27:12 Do not **h** me over to the desire of my
32: 4 For day and night your **h** was heavy
36:11 the **h** of the wicked drive me away.
37:24 the LORD upholds him with his **h**.
38: 2 and your **h** has come down upon me.
39:10 I am overcome by the blow of your **h**
44: 2 With your **h** you drove out the
71: 4 my God, from the **h** of the wicked
74:11 Why do you hold back your **h**, your
74:19 Do not **h** over the life of your dove
77:20 like a flock by the **h** of Moses and
80:17 Let your **h** rest on the man at your
81:14 and turn my **h** against their foes!
82: 4 them from the **h** of the wicked.
89:13 with power; your **h** is strong,
89:21 My **h** will sustain him; surely my arm
89:25 I will set his **h** over the sea, his
95: 4 In his **h** are the depths of the earth,
97:10 them from the **h** of the wicked.
104:28 gather it up; when you open your **h**,
106:10 He saved them from the **h** of the foe;
106:10 from the **h** of the enemy he redeemed
106:26 he swore to them with uplifted **h**
107: 2 he redeemed from the **h** of the foe,
109:27 Let them know that it is your **h**,
118:27 With boughs in **h**, join in the festal
119:173 May your **h** be ready to help me, for
123: 2 look to the **h** of their master
123: 2 look to the **h** her mistress
138: 7 your **h** against the anger of my foes,
139: 5 you have laid your **h** upon me.
139:10 even there your **h** will guide me,
144: 7 Reach down your **h** from on high;
145:16 You open your **h** and satisfy the
Pr 1:24 gave heed when I stretched out my **h**
3:16 in her left **h** are riches and honour.
6: 5 a gazelle from the **h** of the hunter
17:16 use is money in the **h** of a fool,
19:24 sluggard buries his **h** in the dish
26: 6 of a message by the **h** of a fool.
26: 9 Like a thornbush in a drunkard's **h**
26:15 sluggard buries his **h** in the dish
27:16 the wind or grasping oil with the **h**.
30:28 a lizard can be caught with the **h**,
30:32 evil, clap your **h** over your mouth!
31:19 In her **h** she holds the distaff and
Ecc 2:26 **h** it over to the one who pleases God.
5:15 labour that he can carry in his **h**.
9:10 Whatever your **h** finds to do, do it
SS 5: 4 My lover thrust his **h** through the
Isa 1:25 I will turn my **h** against you; I will
5:25 **h** is raised and he strikes them down.
5:25 away, his **h** is still upraised.
6: 6 to me with a live coal in his **h**,
8:11 to me with his strong **h** upon me,
9:12 away, his **h** is still upraised.
9:17 away, his **h** is still upraised.
9:21 away, his **h** is still upraised.
10: 4 away, his **h** is still upraised.
10: 5 in whose **h** is the club of my wrath!
10:10 my **h** seized the kingdoms of the
10:13 'By the strength of my **h** I have
10:14 my **h** reached for the wealth of
11: 8 put his **h** into the viper's nest.
11:11 the Lord will reach out his **h**
11:15 sweep his **h** over the Euphrates
13:22 Her time is at **h**, and her days will
14:26 **h** stretched out over all nations.
14:27 His **h** is stretched out, and who
19: 4 I will **h** the Egyptians over to the
19:16 the uplifted **h** that the LORD
22:21 and **h** your authority over to him.
23:11 The LORD has stretched out his **h**
26:11 O LORD, your **h** is lifted high, but
28: 4 takes it in his **h**, he swallows it.
31: 3 When the LORD stretches out his **h**,
33:15 keeps his **h** from accepting bribes,
34:17 his **h** distributes them by measure
36: 6 which pierces a man's **h** and wounds
Isa 36:15 into the **h** of the king of Assyria.
36:18 from the **h** of the king of Assyria?
36:19 they rescued Samaria from my **h**?
36:20 LORD deliver Jerusalem from my **h**?"
37:20 LORD our God, deliver us from his **h**
38: 6 from the **h** of the king of Assyria.
40: 2 received from the LORD's **h** double
40:12 the waters in the hollow of his **h**,
40:12 or with the breadth of his **h** marked
42: 6 I will take hold of your **h**.
43:13 No-one can deliver out of my **h**.
44: 5 still another will write on his **h**,
47: 6 I gave them into your **h**, and you
48:13 My own **h** laid the foundations of
49: 2 in the shadow of his **h** he hid me;
49: 4 is due to me is in the LORD's **h**,
50:11 what you shall receive from my **h**:
51:16 covered you with the shadow of my **h**
51:18 there was none to take her by the **h**.
51:22 "See, I have taken out of your **h** the
53:10 of the LORD will prosper in his **h**.
56: 1 for my salvation is close at **h** and
56: 2 keeps his **h** from doing any evil."
62: 3 crown of splendour in the LORD's **h**,
62: 3 a royal diadem in the **h** of your God.
64: 8 we are all the work of your **h**.
66: 2 Has not my **h** made all these things,
Jer 1: 9 the LORD reached out his **h** and
6: 9 pass your **h** over the branches again,
6:12 when I stretch out my **h** against
15:17 I sat alone because your **h** was on
18: 6 "Like clay in the **h** of the potter,
18: 6 are you in my **h**, O house of Israel.
18:21 **h** them over to the power of the
20: 4 I will **h** all Judah over to the king
20: 5 I will **h** over to their enemies all
21: 5 against you with an outstretched **h**
21: 7 I will **h** over Zedekiah
21:12 rescue from the **h** of his oppressor
22: 3 Rescue from the **h** of his oppressor
22:25 I will **h** you over to those who seek
25:15 "Take from my **h** this cup filled with
25:17 I took the cup from the LORD's **h** and
25:28 take the cup from your **h** and drink,
27: 6 Now I will **h** all your countries over
27: 8 LORD, until I destroy it by his **h**.
29:21 "I will **h** them over to
31:11 from the **h** of those stronger than
31:32 by the **h** to lead them out of Egypt
32: 3 I am about to **h** this city over to
32:28 I am about to **h** this city over to
33:13 under the **h** of the one who counts
34: 2 I am about to **h** this city over to
34:20 I will **h** over to their enemies who
34:21 "I will **h** Zedekiah king of Judah
36:14 to them with the scroll in his **h**.
38:16 I will neither kill you nor **h** you
38:19 for the Babylonians may **h** me over
38:20 "They will not **h** you over," Jeremiah
43: 3 us to **h** us over to the Babylonians,
44:30 'I am going to **h** Pharaoh Hophra king
46:26 I will **h** them over to those who seek
48:16 "The fall of Moab is at **h**; her
48:37 every **h** is slashed and every waist
51: 7 was a gold cup in the LORD's **h**
51:25 "I will stretch out my **h** against you,
Lam 2: 8 not withhold his **h** from destroying.
3: 3 indeed, he has turned his **h** against
4: 6 without a **h** turned to help her.
Eze 2: 9 I saw a **h** stretched out to me.
6:14 I will stretch out my **h** against them
7:17 Every **h** will go limp, and every knee
7:21 I will **h** it all over as plunder to
8: 1 the **h** of the Sovereign LORD came
8: 3 stretched out what looked like a **h**
8:11 Each had a censer in his **h**, and a
9: 1 here, each with a weapon in his **h**."
9: 2 each with a deadly weapon in his **h**.
10: 7 one of the cherubim reached out his **h**
11: 9 **h** you over to foreigners and inflict
13: 9 My **h** will be against the prophets
14: 9 I will stretch out my **h** against him
14:13 I stretch out my **h** against it to cut
16:27 I stretched out my **h** against you and
16:39 I will **h** you over to your lovers,
17:18 Because he had given his **h** in pledge

Eze 18: 8 He withholds his **h** from doing wrong
18:17 He withholds his **h** from sin and
20: 5 I swore with uplifted **h** to the
20: 5 With uplifted **h** I said to them, "I
20:15 Also with uplifted **h** I swore to them
20:22 I withheld my **h**, and for the sake of
20:23 Also with uplifted **h** I swore to them
20:42 uplifted **h** to give to your fathers.
21: 7 heart will melt and every **h** go limp
21:11 to be grasped with the **h**; it is
21:11 made ready for the **h** of the slayer.
21:31 I will **h** you over to brutal men,
23:28 to **h** you over to those you hate,
23:31 so I will put her cup into your **h**.
25: 7 therefore I will stretch out my **h**
25:13 will stretch out my **h** against Edom
25:14 Edom by the **h** of my people Israel,
25:16 out my **h** against the Philistines,
30:10 by the **h** of Nebuchadnezzar king of
30:12 by the **h** of foreigners I will lay
30:22 and make the sword fall from his **h**.
30:24 Babylon and put my sword in his **h**,
30:25 when I put my sword into the **h** of
35: 3 and I will stretch out my **h** against
36: 7 I swear with uplifted **h** that the
37:17 that they will become one in your **h**.
37:19 of Joseph—which is in Ephraim's **h**
37:19 and they will become one in my **h**.'
38:12 will plunder and loot and turn my **h**
39: 3 strike your bow from your left **h**
39:21 I inflict and the **h** I lay upon them.
40: 3 cord and a measuring rod in his **h**.
40: 5 in the man's **h** was six long cubits,
44:12 I have sworn with uplifted **h** that
47: 3 with a measuring line in his **h**,
47:14 Because I swore with uplifted **h** to
Da 1: 2 Jehoiakim king of Judah into his **h**,
3:15 be able to rescue you from my **h**?"
3:17 will rescue us from your **h**, O king.
4:35 No-one can hold back his **h** or say
5: 5 Suddenly the fingers of a human **h**
5: 5 The king watched the **h** as it wrote.
5:23 God who holds in his **h** your life
5:24 Therefore he sent the **h** that wrote
10:10 A **h** touched me and set me trembling
11:41 Ammon will be delivered from his **h**.
12: 7 lifted his right **h** and his left **h**
Hos 9: 7 the days of reckoning are at **h**.
11: 8 Ephraim? How can I **h** you over,
Joel 2: 1 It is close at **h**—
Am 1: 8 I will turn my **h** against Ekron,
5:19 rested his **h** on the wall only to
7: 7 plumb, with a plumb-line in his **h**.
9: 2 from there my **h** will take them.
Ob :14 nor **h** over their survivors in the
Mic 4:10 you out of the **h** of your enemies.
5: 9 Your **h** will be lifted up in triumph
Hab 3: 4 rays flashed from his **h**, where
Zep 1: 4 "I will stretch out my **h** against
2:13 He will stretch out his **h** against
Zec 2: 1 with a measuring line in his **h**!
2: 9 I will surely raise my **h** against
4:10 plumb-line in the **h** of Zerubbabel.
8: 4 with cane in **h** because of his age.
11: 6 "I will **h** everyone over to his
13: 7 turn my **h** against the little ones.
14:13 Each man will seize the **h** of another,
Mt 3:12 His winnowing fork is in his **h**, and
5:25 or he may **h** you over to the judge,
5:25 and the judge may **h** you over to the
6: 3 do not let your left **h** know what
8: 3 Jesus reached out his **h** and touched
8:15 He touched her **h** and the fever left
9:18 come and put your **h** on her, and she
9:25 took the girl by the **h**, and she
10:17 they will **h** you over to the local
12:10 a man with a shrivelled **h** was there.
12:13 to the man, "Stretch out your **h**.
14:31 Immediately Jesus reached out his **h**
18: 8 If your **h** or your foot causes you to
22:13 'Tie him **h** and foot, and throw him
24:41 women will be grinding with a **h** mill
26:15 to give me if I **h** him over to you?"
26:16 for an opportunity to **h** him over.
26:23 "The one who has dipped his **h** into
Mk 1:31 he went to her, took her **h** and
Mk 1:41 reached out his **h** and touched the
3: 1 a man with a shrivelled **h** was there.
3: 3 to the man with the shrivelled **h**,
3: 5 to the man, "Stretch out your **h**.
3: 5 and his **h** was completely restored.
5: 4 had often been chained **h** and foot
5:41 He took her by the **h** and said to her,
7:32 him to place his **h** on the man.
8:23 He took the blind man by the **h** and
9:27 Jesus took him by the **h** and lifted
9:43 If your **h** causes you to sin, cut it
10:33 and will **h** him over to the Gentiles,
14:11 for an opportunity to **h** him over.
Lk 1:66 For the Lord's **h** was with him.
1:71 and from the **h** of all who hate us
1:74 to rescue us from the **h** of our
3:17 His winnowing fork is in his **h** to
5:13 Jesus reached out his **h** and touched
6: 8 to the man with the shrivelled **h**,
6:10 to the man, "Stretch out your **h**.
6:10 and his **h** was completely restored.
8:29 and though he was chained **h** and foot
8:54 he took her by the **h** and said, "My
9:62 Jesus replied, "No-one who puts his **h**
20:20 they might **h** him over to the power
22: 6 watched for an opportunity to **h**
22:21 the **h** of him who is going to betray
22:53 and you did not lay a **h** on me.
Jn 7:30 no-one laid a **h** on him, because
7:44 him, but no-one laid a **h** on him.
10:12 The hired **h** is not the shepherd
10:13 he is a hired **h** and cares nothing
10:28 no-one can snatch them out of my **h**.
10:29 snatch them out of my Father's **h**.
20:25 and put my **h** into his side, I will
20:27 Reach out your **h** and put it into my
Ac 4:30 Stretch out your **h** to heal and
7:50 Has not my **h** made all these things?
9: 8 they led him by the **h** into Damascus.
9:41 He took her by the **h** and helped her
11:21 The Lord's **h** was with them, and a
12:17 Peter motioned with his **h** for them
13:11 someone to lead him by the **h**.
13:16 Paul motioned with his **h** and said
21:11 will **h** him over to the Gentiles.'
22:11 My companions led me by the **h** into
23:19 took the young man by the **h**,
25:11 has the right to **h** me over to them.
25:16 is not the Roman custom to **h** over
26: 1 Paul motioned with his **h** and began
28: 3 the heat, fastened itself on his **h**.
28: 4 saw the snake hanging from his **h**,
1Co 5: 5 **h** this man over to Satan, so that
12:15 "Because I am not a **h**, I do not
12:21 The eye cannot say to the **h**, "I
16:21 write this greeting in my own **h**.
Gal 6:11 as I write to you with my own **h**!
Col 4:18 write this greeting in my own **h**.
2Th 3:17 write this greeting in my own **h**,
Phm :19 Paul, am writing this with my own **h**.
Heb 8: 9 by the **h** to lead them out of Egypt,
Rev 6: 5 holding a pair of scales in his **h**.
8: 4 up before God from the angel's **h**.
10: 2 scroll, which lay open in his **h**.
10: 8 lies open in the **h** of the angel who
10:10 from the angel's **h** and ate it.
14: 9 mark on the forehead or on the **h**,
14:14 head and a sharp sickle in his **h**.
17: 4 She held a golden cup in her **h**,
20: 1 holding in his **h** a great chain.

Hand of God

2Ch 30:12 Also in Judah the **h** was on the
Job 19:21 have pity, for the **h** has struck me.
Ecc 2:24 This too, I see, is from the **h**,
Mk 16:19 heaven and he sat at the right **h**.
Ac 2:33 Exalted to the right **h**, he has
7:55 and Jesus standing at the right **h**.
7:56 Son of Man standing at the right **h**.
Ro 8:34 is at the right **h** and is also
Col 3: 1 Christ is seated at the right **h**.
Heb 10:12 sins, he sat down at the right **h**.

Hand of the LORD/Lord

Ex 9: 3 the **h** will bring a terrible plague
Jos 4:24 might know that the **h** is powerful
Jdg 2:15 the **h** was against them to defeat
1Sa 7:13 the **h** was against the Philistines.
2Ki 3:15 was playing, the **h** came upon Elisha
1Ch 28:19 "I have in writing from the **h** upon
Ezr 7: 6 asked, for the **h** his God was on him.
7:28 Because the **h** my God was on me, I
Job 12: 9 not know that the **h** has done this?
Ps 75: 8 In the **h** is a cup full of foaming
Pr 21: 1 The king's heart is in the **h**; he
Isa 25:10 The **h** will rest on this mountain;
41:20 that the **h** has done this, that
51:17 you who have drunk from the **h** the
66:14 **h** will be made known to his servants,
Eze 1: 3 There the **h** was upon him.
3:14 spirit, with the strong **h** upon me.
3:22 The **h** was upon me there, and he said
33:22 the **h** was upon me, and he opened my
37: 1 The **h** was upon me, and he brought me
40: 1 **h** was upon me and he took me there.
Ac 13:11 Now the **h** is against you. You are

Handbreadth (Hand)

Ex 25:25 Also make around it a rim a **h** wide
37:12 They also made around it a rim a **h**
1Ki 7:26 was a **h** in thickness, and its rim
2Ch 4: 5 was a **h** in thickness, and its rim
Ps 39: 5 You have made my days a mere **h**; the
Eze 40: 5 each of which was a cubit and a **h**.
40:43 double-pronged hooks, each a **h** long,
43:13 that cubit being a cubit and a **h**:

Handcrafted (Craft)

Nu 31:51 them the gold—all the **h** articles.

Handed (Hand)

Ge 27:17 she **h** to her son Jacob the tasty
Ex 32: 4 He took what they **h** him and made
Lev 9:12 His sons **h** him the blood, and he
9:13 They **h** him the burnt offering piece
9:18 His sons **h** him the blood, and he
Nu 21:34 for I have **h** him over to you, with
Dt 3: 2 for I have **h** him over to you with
Jos 10:32 The LORD **h** Lachish over to Israel,
21:44 **h** all their enemies over to them.
Jdg 2:14 the LORD **h** them over to raiders
1Sa 23: 7 "God has **h** him over to me,
30:23 He has protected us and **h** over
2Sa 3: 8 I haven't **h** you over to David.
16: 8 The LORD has **h** the kingdom over to
21: 9 He **h** them over to the Gibeonites,
2Ki 19:10 be **h** over to the king of Assyria.
1Ch 5:20 and God **h** the Hagrites and all
22:18 For he has **h** the inhabitants of
2Ch 28: 5 the LORD his God **h** him over to
30:16 the blood **h** to them by the Levites.
35:11 sprinkled the blood **h** to them,
36:17 **h** all of them over to Nebuchadnezzar
Ezr 5:12 he **h** them over to Nebuchadnezzar the
Ne 9:24 you **h** the Canaanites over to
9:27 you **h** them over to their enemies,
9:30 so you **h** them over to the
Ps 31: 8 You have not **h** me over to the enemy
106:41 He **h** them over to the nations, and
Isa 37:10 be **h** over to the king of Assyria.'
42:24 Who **h** Jacob over to become loot,
Jer 26:24 and so he was not **h** over to the
32: 4 be **h** over to the king of Babylon,
32:24 the city will be **h** over to the
32:25 though the city will be **h** over to
32:36 famine and plague it will be **h** over
32:43 has been **h** over to the Babylonians.
34: 3 be captured and **h** over to him.
37:17 be **h** over to the king of Babylon."
38: 3 'This city will certainly be **h** over
38:18 this city will be **h** over to the
39:14 They **h** him over to Gedaliah son
39:17 not be **h** over to those you fear.
44:30 just as I **h** Zedekiah king of Judah
46:24 **h** over to the people of the north.
Lam 1:14 He has **h** me over to those I cannot
2: 7 has **h** over to the enemy the walls
Eze 23: 9 "Therefore I **h** her over to her

Eze 31:11 I **h** it over to the ruler of the
39:23 and **h** them over to their enemies
Da 7:25 The saints will be **h** over to him
7:27 heaven will be **h** over to the saints,
11: 6 In those days she will be **h** over,
Mt 24: 9 "Then you will be **h** over to be
26: 2 Man will be **h** over to be crucified.
27: 2 They bound him, led him away and **h**
27:18 that they had **h** Jesus over to him.
27:26 and **h** him over to be crucified.
Mk 7:13 tradition that you have **h** down.
13: 9 You will be **h** over to the local
15:10 priests had **h** Jesus over to him.
15:15 and **h** him over to be crucified.
Lk 1: 2 just as they were **h** down to us by
4:17 of the prophet Isaiah was **h** to him.
24:20 **h** him over to be sentenced to
Jn 18:30 would not have **h** him over to you.
18:35 chief priests who **h** you over to me.
19:11 the one who **h** me over to you is
19:16 Finally Pilate **h** him over to them to
Ac 2:23 **h** over to you by God's set purpose
3:13 You **h** him over to be killed, and you
6:14 the customs Moses **h** down to us."
23:33 the governor and **h** Paul over to him.
27: 1 **h** over to a centurion named Julius,
28:17 Jerusalem and **h** over to the Romans.
1Ti 1:20 whom I have **h** over to Satan to be
1Pe 1:18 **h** down to you from your forefathers,

Handful (Hand)

Lev 2: 2 The priest shall take a **h** of the
5:12 who shall take a **h** of it as a
6:15 The priest is to take a **h** of fine
9:17 took a **h** of it and burned it on the
Nu 5:26 The priest is then to take a **h** of
1Ki 17:12 only a **h** of flour in a jar and a
20:10 Samaria to give each of my men a **h**."
Ecc 4: 6 Better one **h** with tranquillity than

Handfuls (Hand)

Ex 9: 8 "Take **h** of soot from a furnace and
Lev 16:12 two **h** of finely ground fragrant
Ecc 4: 6 tranquillity than two **h** with toil
Eze 13:19 few **h** of barley and scraps of bread.

Handing (Hand)

1Sa 23:20 for **h** him over to the king."
1Ki 18: 9 "that you are **h** your servant over
Ac 12: 4 he put him in prison, **h** him over

Handiwork

Isa 19:25 Assyria my **h**, and Israel my

Handkerchiefs

Ac 19:12 that even **h** and aprons that had

Handle (Handled, Handles, Handling)

Ex 18:18 for you; you cannot **h** it alone.
Jdg 3:22 Even the **h** sank in after the blade,
2Sa 24: 9 able-bodied men who could **h** a sword,
1Ch 5:18 men who could **h** shield and sword,
8:40 brave warriors who could **h** the bow.
12: 8 and able to **h** the shield and spear.
21: 5 thousand men who could **h** a sword,
2Ch 25: 5 able to **h** the spear and shield.
Eze 27:29 All who **h** the oars will abandon
Col 2:21 "Do not **h**! Do not taste! Do not

Handled (Handle)

Jer 8: 8 pen of the scribes has **h** it falsely?

Handles (Handle)

1Ki 7:34 Each stand had four **h**, one on each
SS 5: 5 flowing myrrh, on the **h** of the lock.
2Ti 2:15 who correctly **h** the word of truth.

Handling (Handle)

Lk 16:11 you have not been trustworthy in **h**

Hands (Hand)

Ge 5:29 painful toil of our **h** caused by the
9: 2 the sea; they are given into your **h**.
16: 6 "Your servant is in your **h**," Abram
19:16 his hand and the **h** of his wife
20: 5 a clear conscience and clean **h**."
24:18 jar to her **h** and gave him a drink.
27:16 She also covered his **h** and the
27:22 but the **h** are the **h** of Esau."
27:23 for his **h** were hairy like those of
31:42 my hardship and the toil of my **h**
37:21 tried to rescue him from their **h**.
37:27 and not lay our **h** on him; after all,
Ex 9:29 out my **h** in prayer to the LORD.
9:33 He spread out his **h** towards the LORD;
14:30 Israel from the **h** of the Egyptians,
15:17 O Lord, your **h** established.
17: 9 with the staff of God in my **h**."
17:11 long as Moses held up his **h**, the
17:11 lowered his **h**, the Amalekites were
17:12 Moses' **h** grew tired, they took a
17:12 Aaron and Hur held his **h** up—one on
17:12 his **h** remained steady till sunset.
17:16 He said, "For **h** were lifted up to
22: 8 his **h** on the other man's property.
22:11 **h** on the other person's property.
29:10 sons shall lay their **h** on its head.
29:15 sons shall lay their **h** on its head.
29:19 sons shall lay their **h** on its head.
29:20 on the thumbs of their right **h**, and
29:24 Put all these in the **h** of Aaron and
29:25 take them from their **h** and burn them
30:19 wash their **h** and feet with water
30:21 they shall wash their **h** and feet
32:15 tablets of the Testimony in his **h**.
32:19 he threw the tablets out of his **h**,
34: 4 the two stone tablets in his **h**.
34:29 tablets of the Testimony in his **h**,
35:25 Every skilled woman spun with her **h**
40:31 used it to wash their **h** and feet.
Lev 4:15 lay their **h** on the bull's head
7:30 With his own **h** he is to bring the
8:14 his sons laid their **h** on its head.
8:18 his sons laid their **h** on its head.
8:22 his sons laid their **h** on its head.
8:24 on the thumbs of their right **h** and
8:27 He put all these in the **h** of Aaron
8:28 Moses took them from their **h** and
9:22 Aaron lifted his **h** towards the
15:11 rinsing his **h** with water must wash
16:21 He is to lay both **h** on the head of
24:14 are to lay their **h** on his head,
26:25 and you will be given into enemy **h**.
Nu 5:18 in her **h** the reminder offering,
5:25 The priest is to take from her **h**
6:19 the priest is to place in his **h**
8:10 are to lay their **h** on them.
8:12 "After the Levites lay their **h** on
21: 2 deliver these people into our **h**,
24:10 He struck his **h** together and said
27:23 he laid his **h** on him and
Dt 1:27 the **h** of the Amorites to destroy us.
2: 7 you in all the work of your **h**.
2:30 him into your **h**, as he has now done.
3: 3 LORD our God also gave into our **h**
6: 8 Tie them as symbols on your **h** and
8:17 strength of my **h** have produced this
9:15 of the covenant were in my **h**.
9:17 tablets and threw them out of my **h**,
10: 3 with the two tablets in my **h**.
11:18 tie them as symbols on your **h** and
13: 9 and then the **h** of all the people.
13:17 things shall be found in your **h**,
14:29 in all the work of your **h**.
16:15 in all the work of your **h**,
17: 7 The **h** of the witnesses must be the
17: 7 and then the **h** of all the people.
21: 6 wash their **h** over the heifer
21: 7 "Our **h** did not shed this blood
21:10 into your **h** and you take captives,
23:25 you may pick the ears with your **h**,
24:19 in all the work of your **h**.
26: 4 shall take the basket from your **h**
27:15 the work of the craftsman's **h**
28:12 to bless all the work of your **h**.
Dt 30: 9 in all the work of your **h**
31:29 to anger by what your **h** have made
33: 7 With his own **h** he defends his cause.
33:11 be pleased with the work of his **h**.
34: 9 because Moses had laid his **h** on him.
Jos 2:24 given the whole land into our **h**;
6: 2 I have delivered Jericho into your **h**,
7: 7 the **h** of the Amorites to destroy us?
8: 1 I have delivered into your **h** the
9:25 We are now in your **h**. Do to us
24: 8 you, but I gave them into your **h**.
24:11 but I gave them into your **h**.
Jdg 1: 2 I have given the land into their **h**
1: 4 Perizzites into their **h** and they
2:16 them out of the **h** of these raiders.
2:18 saved them out of the **h** of their
2:23 by giving them into the **h** of Joshua.
3: 8 he sold them into the **h** of
3:10 king of Aram in the **h** of Othniel
3:28 given Moab, your enemy, into your **h**.
4: 2 the LORD sold them into the **h** of
4: 7 River and give him into your **h**.
4:14 LORD has given Sisera into your **h**.
6: 1 them into the **h** of the Midianites.
7: 2 me to deliver Midian into their **h**.
7: 6 Three hundred men lapped with their **h**
7: 7 and give the Midianites into your **h**.
7: 9 I am going to give it into your **h**.
7:14 and the whole camp into his **h**."
7:15 the Midianite camp into your **h**."
7:16 empty jars in the **h** of all of them,
7:19 broke the jars that were in their **h**.
7:20 Grasping the torches in their left **h**
7:20 holding in their right **h** the trumpets
8: 3 the Midianite leaders, into your **h**.
8: 6 "Do you already have the **h** of Zebah
8:15 'Do you already have the **h** of Zebah
8:34 **h** of all their enemies on every side.
10: 7 He sold them into the **h** of the
10:12 did I not save you from their **h**?
11:21 into Israel's **h**, and they defeated
11:30 you give the Ammonites into my **h**
11:32 and the LORD gave them into his **h**.
12: 2 you didn't save me out of their **h**.
12: 3 I took my life in my **h** and crossed
13: 1 into the **h** of the Philistines for
13: 5 from the **h** of the Philistines."
13:23 and grain offering from our **h**,
14: 6 tore the lion apart with his bare **h**
14: 9 which he scooped out with his **h** and
15:14 and the bindings dropped from his **h**.
15:18 into the **h** of the uncircumcised?"
16:18 returned with the silver in their **h**.
16:23 Samson, our enemy, into our **h**."
16:24 has delivered our enemy into our **h**,
18:10 land that God has put into your **h**,
19:27 house, with her **h** on the threshold.
20:28 I will give them into your **h**."
1Sa 5: 4 His head and **h** had been broken off
12: 9 he sold them into the **h** of Sisera,
12: 9 and into the **h** of the Philistines
12:10 now deliver us from the **h** of our
12:11 and he delivered you from the **h** of
14:10 the LORD has given them into our **h**."
14:13 Jonathan climbed up, using his **h** and
14:48 **h** of those who had plundered them.
17:47 will give all of you into our **h**."
18:25 fall by the **h** of the Philistines.
19: 5 He took his life in his **h** when he
21:13 in their **h** he acted like a madman,
23:14 God did not give David into his **h**.
24: 4 I will give your enemy into your **h**
24:10 LORD gave you into my **h** in the cave.
24:18 the LORD gave me into your **h**,
24:20 Israel will be established in your **h**.
25:26 avenging yourself with your own **h**,
25:33 from avenging myself with my own **h**.
26: 8 has given your enemy into your **h**.
26:23 The LORD gave you into my **h** today,
28:17 has torn the kingdom out of your **h**
28:21 I took my life in my **h** and did
2Sa 3:34 Your **h** were not bound, your feet
4:12 They cut off their **h** and feet and
16:21 and the **h** of everyone with you will
18:12 shekels were weighed out into my **h**,
18:28 their **h** against my lord the king."

2Sa 21:22 fell at the **h** of David and his men.
22:21 of my **h** he has rewarded me.
22:35 He trains my **h** for battle; my arms
24:14 Let us fall into the **h** of the LORD,
24:14 not let me fall into the **h** of men
1Ki 2:46 firmly established in Solomon's **h**.
8:22 spread out his **h** towards
8:38 out his **h** towards this temple—
8:54 his **h** spread out towards heaven.
11:35 take the kingdom from his son's **h**
20:28 deliver this vast army into your **h**,
2Ki 3:11 to pour water on the **h** of Elijah."
4:34 to mouth, eyes to eyes, **h** to **h**.
9:35 her skull, her feet and her **h**.
10:24 men I am placing in your **h** escape,
11:12 and the people clapped their **h** and
13:16 "Take the bow in your **h**," he said
13:16 Elisha put his **h** on the king's **h**.
17:20 gave them into the **h** of plunderers,
19:18 and stone, fashioned by men's **h**.
22:17 by all the idols their **h** have made,
1Ch 5:10 who were defeated at their **h**; they
12:17 when my **h** are free from violence,
20: 8 fell at the **h** of David and his men.
21:13 Let me fall into the **h** of the LORD,
21:13 not let me fall into the **h** of men
29:12 In your **h** are strength and power
2Ch 6: 4 who with his **h** has fulfilled what
6:12 of Israel and spread out his **h**.
6:13 and spread out his **h** towards heaven.
6:29 out his **h** towards this temple—
13: 8 is in the **h** of David's descendants.
13:16 God delivered them into their **h**.
23:18 of the LORD in the **h** of the priests,
24:24 into their **h** a much larger army.
28: 5 He was also given into the **h** of the
29:23 and they laid their **h** on them.
32:19 of the world—the work of men's **h**.
34:25 anger by all that their **h** have made,
Ezr 8:33 into the **h** of Meremoth son of Uriah,
9: 5 my **h** spread out to the LORD my
10: 4 Rise up; this matter is in your **h**.
10:19 (They all gave their **h** in pledge to
Ne 6: 9 "Their **h** will get too weak for the
6: 9 I prayed, "Now strengthen my **h**."
8: 6 lifted their **h** and responded,
13:21 do this again, I will lay **h** on you.
Est 9:10 did not lay their **h** on the plunder.
9:15 did not lay their **h** on the plunder.
9:16 did not lay their **h** on the plunder.
Job 1:10 You have blessed the work of his **h**,
1:12 everything he has is in your **h**,
2: 6 he is in your **h**; but you must
4: 3 how you have strengthened feeble **h**.
5:12 so that their **h** achieve no success.
5:18 up; he injures, but his **h** also heal.
8:20 or strengthen the **h** of evildoers.
9:24 a land falls into the **h** of the
9:30 soap and my **h** with washing soda,
10: 3 to spurn the work of your **h**, while
10: 8 "Your **h** shaped me and made me. Will
11:13 him and stretch out your **h** to him,
12: 6 who carry their god in their **h**.
13:14 jeopardy and take my life in my **h**?
14:15 for the creature your **h** have made.
16:17 yet my **h** have been free of violence
17: 9 with clean **h** will grow stronger.
20:10 his own **h** must give back his wealth.
21:16 prosperity is not in their own **h**,
22:30 through the cleanness of your **h**."
27:23 claps its **h** in derision and hisses
29: 9 covered their mouths with their **h**;
30: 2 was the strength of their **h** to me,
31: 7 eyes, or if my **h** have been defiled,
31:25 wealth, the fortune my **h** had gained,
34:19 for they are all the work of his **h**?
34:37 scornfully he claps his **h** among us
36:32 He fills his **h** with lightning and
Ps 7: 3 this and there is guilt on my **h**—
8: 6 ruler over the works of your **h**;
9:16 are ensnared by the work of their **h**.
18:20 of my **h** he has rewarded me.
18:24 the cleanness of my **h** in his sight.
18:34 He trains my **h** for battle; my arms
19: 1 skies proclaim the work of his **h**.
22:16 they have pierced my **h** and my feet.
Ps 24: 4 He who has clean **h** and a pure heart,
26: 6 I wash my **h** in innocence, and go
26:10 in whose **h** are wicked schemes, whose
26:10 whose right **h** are full of bribes.
28: 2 my **h** towards your Most Holy Place.
28: 4 repay them for what their **h** have
28: 5 the LORD and what his **h** have done,
31: 5 Into your **h** I commit my spirit;
31:15 My times are in your **h**; deliver me
44:20 spread out our **h** to a foreign god,
47: 1 Clap your **h**, all you nations; shout
58: 2 **h** mete out violence on the earth.
63: 4 in your name I will lift up my **h**.
73:13 have I washed my **h** in innocence.
76: 5 one of the warriors can lift his **h**.
77: 2 at night I stretched out untiring **h**
78:61 splendour into the **h** of the enemy.
78:72 heart; with skilful **h** he led them.
81: 6 **h** were set free from the basket.
88: 9 every day; I spread out my **h** to you.
90:17 establish the work of our **h** for us
90:17 yes, establish the work of our **h**.
91:12 they will lift you up in their **h**,
92: 4 sing for joy at the work of your **h**.
95: 5 it, and his **h** formed the dry land.
98: 8 Let the rivers clap their **h**, let the
102:25 the heavens are the work of your **h**.
111: 7 The works of his **h** are faithful and
115: 4 and gold, made by the **h** of men.
115: 7 they have **h**, but cannot feel, feet,
119:48 I lift up my **h** to your commands,
119:73 Your **h** made me and formed me; give
119:109 I constantly take my life in my **h**,
125: 3 might use their **h** to do evil.
127: 4 Like arrows in the **h** of a warrior
129: 7 with it the reaper cannot fill his **h**,
134: 2 Lift up your **h** in the sanctuary and
135:15 and gold, made by the **h** of men.
138: 8 do not abandon the works of your **h**.
140: 4 Keep me, O LORD, from the **h** of the
141: 2 may the lifting up of my **h** be like
143: 5 consider what your **h** have done.
143: 6 I spread out my **h** to you; my soul
144: 1 trains my **h** for war, my fingers for
144: 7 from the **h** of foreigners
144: 8 lies, whose right **h** are deceitful.
144:11 rescue me from the **h** foreigners
144:11 lies, whose right **h** are deceitful.
149: 6 a double-edged sword in their **h**,
Pr 6: 1 have struck **h** in pledge for another,
6: 3 fallen into your neighbour's **h**:
6:10 a little folding of the **h** to rest
6:17 **h** that shed innocent blood,
10: 4 Lazy **h** make a man poor, but diligent
10: 4 poor, but diligent **h** bring wealth.
11:15 to strike **h** in pledge is safe.
12:14 as the work of his **h** rewards him.
12:24 Diligent **h** will rule, but laziness
14: 1 own **h** the foolish one tears hers
17:18 A man lacking in judgment strikes **h**
21:25 him, because his **h** refuse to work.
22:26 Do not be a man who strikes **h** in
24:33 a little folding of the **h** to rest
30: 4 the wind in the hollow of his **h**?
31:13 and flax and works with eager **h**.
31:20 poor and extends her **h** to the needy.
Ecc 2:11 I surveyed all that my **h** had done
4: 5 The fool folds his **h** and ruins
5: 6 destroy the work of your **h**?
7:26 is a trap and whose **h** are chains.
9: 1 and what they do are in God's **h**,
10:18 if his **h** are idle, the house leaks.
11: 6 at evening let not your **h** be idle
SS 5: 5 and my **h** dripped with myrrh, my
7: 1 the work of a craftsman's **h**.
Isa 1:15 you spread out your **h** in prayer,
1:15 Your **h** are full of blood;
2: 6 Philistines and clasp **h** with pagans.
2: 8 bow down to the work of their **h**,
3:11 back for what their **h** have done.
5:12 no respect for the work of his **h**.
11:14 They will lay **h** on Edom and Moab,
13: 7 of this, all **h** will go limp, every
17: 8 the work of their **h**, and they will
25:11 They will spread out their **h** in it,
25:11 a swimmer spreads out his **h** to swim.
Isa 25:11 despite the cleverness of their **h**.
29:23 the work of my **h**, they will keep my
31: 7 and gold your sinful **h** have made.
35: 3 Strengthen the feeble **h**, steady the
37:19 and stone, fashioned by human **h**.
41: 2 He **h** nations over to him and subdues
45: 9 Does your work say, 'He has no **h**'?
45:11 me orders about the work of my **h**?
45:12 My own **h** stretched out the heavens;
49:16 engraved you on the palms of my **h**.
51:23 I will put it into the **h** of your
55:12 of the field will clap their **h**.
59: 3 For your **h** are stained with blood,
59: 6 and acts of violence are in their **h**.
60:21 the work of my **h**, for the
65: 2 All day long I have held out my **h**
65:22 long enjoy the works of their **h**.
Jer 1:16 worshipping what their **h** have made.
2:37 that place with your **h** on your head,
4:31 stretching out her **h** and saying,
6:24 about them, and our **h** hang limp.
11:21 the LORD or you will die by our **h**
12: 7 I love into the **h** of her enemies.
15: 6 So I will lay **h** on you and destroy
15:21 "I will save you from the **h** of the
18: 4 from the clay was marred in his **h**;
19: 7 at the **h** of those who seek their
20:13 the needy from the **h** of the wicked.
21: 4 weapons of war that are in your **h**,
21:10 It will be given into the **h** of the
23:14 They strengthen the **h** of evildoers,
25: 6 to anger with what your **h** have made.
25: 7 me with what your **h** have made,
25:14 deeds and the work of their **h**."
26:14 for me, I am in your **h**; do with me
30: 6 every strong man with his **h** on his
32: 4 out of the **h** of the Babylonians
32:30 with what their **h** have made,
38: 5 "He is in your **h**," King Zedekiah
38:18 will not escape from their **h**.
38:23 will not escape from their **h** but
42:11 save you and deliver you from his **h**.
44: 8 to anger with what your **h** have made,
47: 3 children; their **h** will hang limp.
50:43 about them, and his **h** hang limp.
Lam 1: 7 When her people fell into enemy **h**,
1:10 The enemy laid **h** on all her
1:14 by his **h** they were woven together.
1:17 Zion stretches out her **h**, but there
2:15 All who pass your way clap their **h**
2:19 Lift up your **h** to him for the lives
3:41 Let us lift up our hearts and our **h**
3:64 O LORD, for what their **h** have done.
4: 2 of clay, the work of a potter's **h**!
4:10 With their own **h** compassionate women
5: 8 is none to free us from their **h**.
5:12 Princes have been hung up by their **h**;
Eze 1: 8 four sides they had the **h** of a man.
6:11 Strike your **h** together and stamp
7:27 and the **h** of the people of the land
10: 2 Fill your **h** with burning coals from
10: 7 it into the **h** of the man in linen,
10: 8 what looked like the **h** of a man.)
10:12 including their backs, their **h** and
10:21 was what looked like the **h** of a man.
12: 7 I dug through the wall with my **h**.
13:21 and save my people from your **h**,
13:23 I will save my people from your **h**.
21:14 prophesy and strike your **h** together.
21:17 I too will strike my **h** together,
22:13 I will surely strike my **h**
22:14 courage endure or your **h** be strong
23:37 adultery and blood is on their **h**.
23:45 adulterous and blood is on their **h**.
25: 6 your **h** and stamped your feet,
28: 9 in the **h** of those who slay you.
28:10 at the **h** of foreigners.
29: 7 they grasped you with their **h**, you
34:27 the **h** of those who enslaved them.
48:14 must not pass into other **h**,
Da 2:34 was cut out, but not by human **h**.
2:38 in your **h** he has placed mankind
2:45 but not by human **h**—a rock that
10:10 set me trembling on my **h** and knees.
Hos 2:10 no-one will take her out of my **h**.
7: 5 and he joins **h** with the mockers.

Hos 14: 3 'Our gods' to what our own **h** have
Mic 5:13 bow down to the work of your **h**.
7: 3 Both **h** are skilled in doing evil;
7:16 They will lay their **h** on their
Na 3:19 about you claps his **h** at your fall,
Zep 3:16 do not let your **h** hang limp.
Hag 1:11 and on the labour of your **h**."
2:17 I struck all the work of your **h** with
Zec 4: 9 "The **h** of Zerubbabel have laid the
4: 9 temple; his **h** will also complete it.
8: 9 let your **h** be strong so that the
8:13 afraid, but let your **h** be strong."
11: 6 will not rescue them from their **h**
Mal 1: 9 With such offerings from your **h**,
1:10 will accept no offering from your **h**.
1:13 them from your **h**?" says the LORD.
2:13 them with pleasure from your **h**.
Mt 4: 6 they will lift you up in their **h**,
15: 2 don't wash their **h** before they eat
15:20 eating with unwashed **h** does not
16:21 many things at the **h** of the elders,
17:12 Man is going to suffer at their **h**."
17:22 to be betrayed into the **h** of men.
18: 8 than to have two **h** or two feet
19:13 his **h** on them and pray for them.
19:15 had placed his **h** on them, he went
26:45 is betrayed into the **h** of sinners.
27:24 washed his **h** in front of the crowd.
Mk 5:23 Please come and put your **h** on her
6: 5 lay his **h** on a few sick people
7: 2 food with **h** that were "unclean",
7: 3 give their **h** a ceremonial washing,
7: 5 eating their food with 'unclean' **h**
8:23 the man's eyes and put his **h** on him,
8:25 Jesus put his **h** on the man's eyes
9:31 to be betrayed into the **h** of men.
9:43 than with two **h** to go into hell,
10:16 put his **h** on them and blessed them.
14:41 is betrayed into the **h** of sinners.
16:18 they will pick up snakes with their **h**
16:18 will place their **h** on sick people,
Lk 4:11 they will lift you up in their **h**,
4:40 his **h** on each one, he healed them.
6: 1 them in their **h** and eat the grain.
9:44 to be betrayed into the **h** of men."
10:30 when he fell into the **h** of robbers.
10:36 man who fell into the **h** of robbers?"
13:13 he put his **h** on her, and immediately
21:12 all this, they will lay **h** on you
23:46 into your **h** I commit my spirit.
24: 7 delivered into the **h** of sinful men,
24:39 Look at my **h** and my feet. It is I
24:40 he showed them his **h** and feet.
24:50 he lifted up his **h** and blessed them.
Jn 3:35 and has placed everything in his **h**.
11:44 his **h** and feet wrapped with linen
13: 9 feet but my **h** and my head as well!"
20:20 this, he showed them his **h** and side.
20:25 Unless I see the nail marks in his **h**
20:27 "Put your finger here; see my **h**.
21:18 are old you will stretch out your **h**,
Ac 6: 6 who prayed and laid their **h** on them.
7:41 in honour of what their **h** had made.
8:17 Peter and John placed their **h** on
8:18 at the laying on of the apostles' **h**
8:19 my **h** may receive the Holy Spirit."
9:12 his **h** on him to restore his sight."
9:17 Placing his **h** on Saul, he said,
13: 3 their **h** on them and sent them off.
17:24 does not live in temples built by **h**.
17:25 he is not served by human **h**, as if
19: 6 Paul placed his **h** on them, the Holy
20:34 these **h** of mine have supplied
21:11 tied his own **h** and feet with it
27:19 tackle overboard with their own **h**.
28: 8 placed his **h** on him and healed him.
Ro 10:21 "All day long I have held out my **h**
1Co 4:12 We work hard with our own **h**. When we
15:24 the end will come, when he **h** over
2Co 5: 1 in heaven, not built by human **h**.
11:33 the wall and slipped through his **h**.
Eph 2:11 done in the body by the **h** of men)—
4:28 something useful with his own **h**,
Col 2:11 circumcision done by the **h** of men
1Th 4:11 to work with your **h**, just as we
1Ti 2: 8 to lift up holy **h** in prayer,
1Ti 4:14 body of elders laid their **h** on you.
5:22 Do not be hasty in the laying on of **h**
2Ti 1: 6 you through the laying on of my **h**.
Heb 1:10 the heavens are the work of your **h**.
6: 2 the laying on of **h**, the resurrection
10:31 fall into the **h** of the living God.
Jas 4: 8 Wash your **h**, you sinners, and purify
1Jn 1: 1 looked at and our **h** have touched
Rev 7: 9 holding palm branches in their **h**.
9:20 not repent of the work of their **h**;
20: 4 mark on their foreheads or their **h**.

Handsome (Handsomely)

Ge 39: 6 Now Joseph was well-built and **h**,
1Sa 16:12 a fine appearance and **h** features.
17:42 he was only a boy, ruddy and **h**,
2Sa 14:25 praised for his **h** appearance
1Ki 1: 6 **h** and was born next after Absalom.)
SS 1:16 How **h** you are, my lover! Oh, how
Eze 23: 6 **h** young men, and mounted horsemen.
23:12 mounted horsemen, all **h** young men.
23:23 **h** young men, all of them governors
Da 1: 4 **h**, showing aptitude for every kind
Zec 11:13 **h** price at which they priced me!

Handsomely (Handsome)

Nu 22:17 I will reward you **h** and do whatever
24:11 home! I said I would reward you **h**,

Hanes

Isa 30: 4 and their envoys have arrived in **H**,

Hang (Hanged, Hanging, Hangings, Hangs, Hung, Overhang, Overhanging, Overhangs)

Ge 40:19 off your head and **h** you on a tree.
Ex 26:12 **h** down at the rear of the tabernacle.
26:13 what is left will **h** over the sides
26:32 **H** it with gold hooks on four posts
26:33 **H** the curtain from the clasps and
Est 7: 9 The king said, "**H** him on it!"
Job 37:16 Do you know how the clouds **h** poised,
Pr 26: 7 Like a lame man's legs that **h** limp
SS 4: 4 on it **h** a thousand shields,
Isa 22:24 glory of his family will **h** on him
Jer 6:24 about them, and our hands **h** limp.
47: 3 children; their hands will **h** limp.
50:43 about them, and his hands **h** limp.
Eze 15: 3 make pegs from it to **h** things on?
Zep 3:16 O Zion; do not let your hands **h** limp.
Mt 22:40 All the Law and the Prophets **h** on

Hanged (Hang)

Ge 40:22 he **h** the chief baker, just as Joseph
41:13 position, and the other man was **h**."
2Sa 17:23 house in order and then **h** himself
Est 2:23 two officials were **h** on a gallows.
5:14 morning to have Mordecai **h** on it.
7:10 they **h** Haman on the gallows he had
8: 7 and they have **h** him on the gallows.
9:13 Haman's ten sons be **h** on gallows."
9:14 and they **h** the ten sons of Haman.
9:25 his sons should be **h** on the gallows.
Mt 27: 5 Then he went away and **h** himself.

Hanging (Hang)

Jos 10:26 left **h** on the trees until evening.
1Sa 25:17 disaster is **h** over our master
2Sa 18: 9 He was left **h** in mid-air, while the
18:10 just seen Absalom **h** in an oak tree."
Est 6: 4 speak to the king about **h** Mordecai
Isa 22:25 the load **h** on it will be cut down.
Ac 5:30 you had killed by **h** him on a tree.
10:39 They killed him by **h** him on a tree,
28: 4 saw the snake **h** from his hand
2Pe 2: 3 has long been **h** over them,

Hangings (Hang)

Est 1: 6 The garden had **h** of white and blue

Hangs (Hang)

Isa 33:23 Your rigging **h** loose: The mast is

Hannah

Wife of Elkanah; childless (1Sa 1:1–8). Prayed for a child (1Sa 1:9–18); gave birth to Samuel (1Sa 1:19–20); dedicated Samuel to God (1Sa 1:21–28). Her prayer (1Sa 2:1–10). Blessed with other children (1Sa 2:19–21).

1Sa 1: 2 He had two wives; one was called **H**
1: 2 had children, but **H** had none.
1: 5 to **H** he gave a double portion
1: 7 Whenever **H** went up to the house of
1: 8 "**H**, why are you weeping? Why don't
1: 9 and drinking in Shiloh, **H** stood up.
1:10 In bitterness of soul **H** wept much
1:13 **H** was praying in her heart, and her
1:15 "Not so, my lord," **H** replied, "I am
1:19 Elkanah lay with **H** his wife, and the
1:20 in the course of time **H** conceived
1:22 **H** did not go. She said to her
2: 1 **H** prayed and said: "My heart
2:21 the LORD was gracious to **H**; she

Hannathon

Jos 19:14 went round on the north to **H**

Hanniel

Nu 34:23 **H** son of Ephod, the leader from the
1Ch 7:39 The sons of Ulla: Arah, **H** and Rizia.

Hanoch (Hanochite)

Ge 25: 4 Ephah, Epher, **H**, Abida and Eldaah.
46: 9 The sons of Reuben: **H**, Pallu, Hezron
Ex 6:14 were **H** and Pallu, Hezron and Carmi.
Nu 26: 5 were: through **H**, the Hanochite clan;
1Ch 1:33 The sons of Midian: Ephah, Epher, **H**,
5: 3 Israel: **H**, Pallu, Hezron and Carmi.

Hanochite (Hanoch)

Nu 26: 5 were: through Hanoch, the **H** clan;

Hanun

2Sa 10: 1 and his son **H** succeeded him as king.
10: 2 show kindness to **H** son of Nahash
10: 2 sympathy to **H** concerning his father.
10: 3 the Ammonite nobles said to **H** their
10: 4 **H** seized David's men, shaved off
1Ch 19: 2 "I will show kindness to **H** son of
19: 2 sympathy to **H** concerning his father.
19: 2 When David's men came to **H** in the
19: 3 the Ammonite nobles said to **H**, "Do
19: 4 **H** seized David's men, shaved them,
19: 6 **H** and the Ammonites sent a thousand
Ne 3:13 The Valley Gate was repaired by **H**
3:30 **H**, the sixth son of Zalaph

Hapharaim

Jos 19:19 **H**, Shion, Anaharath,

Happen (Happened, Happening, Happens)

Ge 49: 1 what will **h** to you in days to come.
Ex 2: 4 distance to see what would **h** to him.
21:13 but God lets it **h**, he is to flee to
1Ki 14: 3 tell you what will **h** to the boy."
2Ki 7: 2 of the heavens, could this **h**?"
7:19 of the heavens, could this **h**?"
Ecc 3:22 him to see what will **h** after him?
6:12 Who can tell him what will **h**
9:11 but time and chance **h** to them all.
10:14 can tell him what will **h** after him?
Isa 7: 7 will not take place, it will not **h**,
23:15 it will **h** to Tyre as in the song of
41:22 idols to tell us what is going to **h**.
47: 7 things or reflect on what might **h**.
Jer 6:18 O witnesses, what will **h** to them.
Lam 3:37 Who can speak and have it **h** if the
Eze 16:16 Such things should not **h**, nor
20:32 what you have in mind will never **h**.
38:18 This is what will **h** in that day:
Da 2:28 what will **h** in days to come.
2:29 showed you what is going to **h**.
8:19 "I am going to tell you what will **h**
10:14 will **h** to your people in the future,
Hos 10:15 Thus will it **h** to you, O Bethel,

Am 7: 3 the LORD relented. "This will not **h**
7: 6 the LORD relented. "This will not **h**
Jnh 4: 5 to see what would **h** to the city.
Zec 6:15 This will **h** if you diligently obey
Mt 16:22 "This shall never **h** to you!"
24: 3 "when will this **h**, and what will be
24: 6 Such things must **h**, but the end is
24:39 they knew nothing about what would **h**
26:54 that say it must **h** in this way?"
Mk 10:32 them what was going to **h** to him.
11:23 what he says will **h**, it will be
13: 4 "Tell us, when will these things **h**?
13: 7 Such things must **h**, but the end is
Lk 21: 7 "when will these things **h**? And what
21: 9 These things must **h** first, but the
21:36 to escape all that is about to **h**,
22:49 followers saw what was going to **h**,
23:31 green, what will **h** when it is dry?"
Jn 5:14 or something worse may **h** to you."
13:19 when it does **h** you will believe
14:29 when it does **h** you will believe.
18: 4 knowing all that was going to **h**
Ac 4:28 had decided beforehand should **h**.
8:24 nothing you have said may **h** to me."
13:40 have said does not **h** to you:
20:22 not knowing what will **h** to me there.
26:22 prophets and Moses said would **h**—
27:25 that it will **h** just as he told me.
28: 6 seeing nothing unusual **h** to him,
Ro 9:26 and, "It will **h** that in the very
2Th 1: 7 This will **h** when the Lord Jesus is
Jas 4:14 you do not even know what will **h**
2Pe 2: 6 what is going to **h** to the ungodly;

Happened (Happen)

Ge 20: 8 had **h**, they were very much afraid.
34: 7 as soon as they heard what had **h**.
42:29 told him all that had **h** to them.
Ex 32: 1 we don't know what has **h** to him.
32:23 we don't know what has **h** to him.
Lev 10:19 such things as this have **h** to me.
Nu 31:16 from the LORD in what **h** at Peor,
Dt 4:30 and all these things have **h** to you,
4:32 anything so great as this ever **h**,
Jos 2:23 him everything that had **h** to them.
Jdg 6:13 why has all this **h** to us? Where are
6:38 that is what **h**. Gideon rose early
20: 3 "Tell us how this awful thing **h**.
21: 3 why has this **h** to Israel?
1Sa 4: 7 Nothing like this has **h** before.
4:13 had **h**, the whole town sent up a cry.
4:16 Eli asked, "What **h**, my son?"
6: 9 and that it **h** to us by chance."
10:11 "What is this that has **h** to the son
20:26 "Something must have **h** to David to
2Sa 1: 4 "What **h**?" David asked. "Tell me." He
1: 6 "I **h** to be on Mount Gilboa," the
13:35 it has **h** just as your servant said."
18: 9 Now Absalom **h** to meet David's men.
20: 1 Bicri, a Benjamite, **h** to be there.
2Ki 7:13 us send them to find out what **h**."
7:14 "Go and find out what has **h**.
7:18 **h** as the man of God had said to the
7:20 that is exactly what **h** to him, for
9:27 Ahaziah king of Judah saw what had **h**,
18:12 This **h** because they had not obeyed
24: 3 Surely these things **h** to Judah
24:20 all this **h** to Jerusalem and Judah,
Ezr 9:13 "What has **h** to us is a result of
Ne 9:33 In all that has **h** to us, you have
Est 1: 1 This is what **h** during the time of
4: 7 him everything that had **h** to him,
6:13 everything that had **h** to him.
9:17 This **h** on the thirteenth day of the
9:26 had seen and what had **h** to them,
Job 3:25 upon me; what I dreaded has **h** to me.
Ps 44:17 All this **h** to us, though we had not
Isa 20: 6 'See what has **h** to those we relied
44: 7 lay out before me what has **h** since
48: 5 before they **h** I announced them to
Jer 5:30 A horrible and shocking thing has **h**
13:22 if you ask yourself, "Why has this **h**
32:24 What you said has **h**, as you now see.
40: 3 All this **h** because you people sinned
48:19 escaping, ask them, 'What has **h**?'
Jer 52: 3 all this **h** to Jerusalem and Judah,
Lam 4:13 **h** because of the sins of her
5: 1 Remember, O LORD, what has **h** to us;
Eze 16:19 what **h**, declares the Sovereign LORD.
Da 4:28 All this **h** to King Nebuchadnezzar.
12: 1 has not **h** from the beginning
Joel 1: 2 Has anything like this ever **h** in
Mt 8:33 had **h** to the demon-possessed men.
14:13 Jesus heard what had **h**, he withdrew
18:31 the other servants saw what had **h**,
18:31 their master everything that had **h**.
22:26 The same thing **h** to the second and
24:34 away until all these things have **h**.
27:54 the earthquake and all that had **h**,
28:11 chief priests everything that had **h**.
Mk 5:14 people went out to see what had **h**.
5:16 had **h** to the demon-possessed man
5:33 the woman, knowing what had **h** to her,
13:30 away until all these things have **h**.
Lk 2:15 see this thing that has **h**, which
8:34 those tending the pigs saw what had **h**
8:35 the people went out to see what had **h**
8:56 them not to tell anyone what had **h**.
10:31 A priest **h** to be going down the same
21:32 away until all these things have **h**.
23:47 The centurion, seeing what had **h**,
24:12 wondering to himself what had **h**.
24:14 other about everything that had **h**.
24:18 do not know the things that have **h**
24:35 the two told what had **h** on the way,
Jn 1:28 This all **h** at Bethany on the other
9: 3 "but this **h** so that the work of God
18: 9 This **h** so that the words he had
18:32 This **h** so that the words Jesus had
19:24 This **h** that the scripture might be
19:36 These things **h** so that the scripture
21: 1 It **h** this way:
Ac 3:10 amazement at what had **h** to him.
4:21 were praising God for what had **h**.
5: 5 seized all who heard what had **h**.
5: 7 came in, not knowing what had **h**.
7:40 don't know what has **h** to him!'
10: 8 He told them everything that had **h**
10:16 This **h** three times, and immediately
10:37 You know what has **h** throughout Judea,
11: 4 to them precisely as it had **h**:
11:10 This **h** three times, and then it was
11:28 This **h** during the reign of Claudius
12: 3 This **h** during the Feast of
13:12 the proconsul saw what had **h**, he
17:17 by day with those who **h** to be there.
19:21 After all this had **h**, Paul decided
28: 9 this had **h**, the rest of the sick
1Co 10:11 These things **h** to them as examples
2Co 1: 9 But this **h** that we might not rely on
Gal 4:15 What has **h** to all your joy? I can
Php 1:12 brothers, that what has **h** to me has
1:19 what has **h** to me will turn out for
2Ti 3:11 what kinds of things **h** to me

Happening (Happen)

Ge 25:22 "Why is this **h** to me?" So she went
1Sa 5: 7 the men of Ashdod saw what was **h**,
Ne 6: 8 like what you are saying is **h**;
Est 2:11 Esther was and what was **h** to her.
Mk 13:29 Even so, when you see these things **h**,
Lk 18:36 crowd going by, he asked what was **h**.
21:31 Even so, when you see these things **h**,
Ac 12: 9 the angel was doing was really **h**;
Col 4: 9 tell you everything that is **h** here.
1Pe 4:12 something strange were **h** to you.

Happens (Happen)

Ex 22: 3 if it **h** after sunrise, he is guilty
Nu 16:29 only what usually **h** to men,
Dt 22:23 If a man **h** to meet in a town a
22:25 a man **h** to meet a girl pledged
22:28 If a man **h** to meet a virgin who is
Ru 3:18 daughter, until you find out what **h**.
1Sa 2:34 "'And what **h** to your two sons,
2Sa 14:20 everything that **h** in the land."
Ecc 9: 3 is the evil in everything that **h**
9: 6 in anything that **h** under the sun.
Isa 48:16 at the time it **h**, I am there.
Jer 12: 4 "He will not see what **h** to us.
Eze 24:24 When this **h**, you will know that I am
Lk 1:20 able to speak until the day this **h**,
Jn 13:19 "I am telling you now before it **h**,
14:29 I have told you now before it **h**, so
Php 1:27 Whatever **h**, conduct yourselves in a

Happier (Happy)

Ecc 4: 2 already died, are **h** than the living
Mt 18:13 he is **h** about that one sheep
1Co 7:40 she is **h** if she stays as she is

Happiness (Happy)

Dt 24: 5 bring **h** to the wife he has married.
Est 8:16 For the Jews it was a time of **h** and
Job 7: 7 my eyes will never see **h** again.
Ecc 2:26 God gives wisdom, knowledge and **h**,
Mt 25:21 Come and share your master's **h**!'
25:23 Come and share your master's **h**!'

Happizzez

1Ch 24:15 to Hezir, the eighteenth to **H**,

Happy (Happier, Happiness)

Ge 30:13 **h** I am! The women will call me **h**.
1Ki 4:20 ate, they drank and they were **h**.
10: 8 How **h** your men must be! How **h** your
2Ch 9: 7 How **h** your men must be! How **h** your
Est 5: 9 Haman went out that day **h** and in
5:14 the king to the dinner and be **h**.
Ps 10: 6 always be **h** and never have trouble
68: 3 God; may they be **h** and joyful.
113: 9 her home as a **h** mother of children.
137: 8 **h** is he who repays you for what you
Pr 15:13 A **h** heart makes the face cheerful,
Ecc 3:12 to be **h** and do good while they live.
5:19 **h** in his work—this is a gift of God.
7:14 times are good, be **h**; but when times
11: 9 Be **h**, young man, while you are young,
Jnh 4: 6 and Jonah was very **h** about the vine.
Zec 8:19 occasions and **h** festivals for Judah.
1Co 7:30 those who are **h**, as if they were not
2Co 7: 9 yet now I am **h**, not because you were
7:13 delighted to see how **h** Titus was,
Jas 5:13 Is anyone **h**? Let him sing songs

Hara

1Ch 5:26 He took them to Halah, Habor, **H** and

Haradah

Nu 33:24 left Mount Shepher and camped at **H**.
33:25 They left **H** and camped at Makheloth.

Haran

City in northern Mesopotamia, where Terah and Abram stayed and Terah died (Ge 11:31–32; Ac 7:2, 4). Abram received God's promise here (Ge 12:1–4). Here Jacob fled (Ge 28:10), then found and married Rachel (Ge 29:4–28). Captured by Assyrians (2Ki 19:12; Isa 37:12). Its merchants traded with Tyre (Eze 27:23–24).

Ge 11:26 the father of Abram, Nahor and **H**.
11:27 the father of Abram, Nahor and **H**.
11:27 And **H** became the father of Lot.
11:28 **H** died in Ur of the Chaldeans, in
11:29 Milcah; she was the daughter of **H**,
11:31 his grandson Lot son of **H**, and his
11:31 they came to **H**, they settled there.
11:32 lived 205 years, and he died in **H**.
12: 4 years old when he set out from **H**.
12: 5 the people they had acquired in **H**,
27:43 at once to my brother Laban in **H**.
28:10 left Beersheba and set out for **H**.
29: 4 from?" "We're from **H**," they replied.
2Ki 19:12 the gods of Gozon, **H**, Rezeph and
1Ch 2:46 was the mother of **H**, Moza and Gazez.
2:46 **H** was the father of Gazez.
23: 9 Haziel and **H**—three in all.
Isa 37:12 the gods of Gozon, **H**, Rezeph and
Eze 27:23 **H**, Canneh and Eden and merchants
Ac 7: 2 Mesopotamia, before he lived in **H**.
7: 4 of the Chaldeans and settled in **H**.

Hararite
2Sa 23:11 him was Shammah son of Agee the **H**.
23:33 son of Shammah the **H**, Ahiam son of
23:33 the **H**, Ahiam son of Sharar the **H**,
1Ch 11:34 Jonathan son of Shagee the **H**,
11:35 Ahiam son of Sacar the **H**, Eliphal

Harass (Harassed)
Dt 2: 9 "Do not **h** the Moabites or provoke
2:19 do not **h** them or provoke them

Harassed (Harass)
Mt 9:36 because they were **h** and helpless,
2Co 7: 5 but we were **h** at every

Harbona
Est 1:10 Biztha, **H**, Bigtha, Abagtha, Zethar
7: 9 **H**, one of the eunuchs attending the

Harbour (Harboured, Harbours)
Dt 15: 9 Be careful not to **h** this wicked
Job 36:13 "The godless in heart **h** resentment;
Ps 28: 3 but **h** malice in their hearts.
103: 9 nor will he **h** his anger for ever;
Isa 23: 1 and left without house or **h**.
23:10 Tarshish, for you no longer have a **h**.
Jer 4:14 How long will you **h** wicked thoughts?
Ac 27:12 the **h** was unsuitable to winter in,
27:12 This was a **h** in Crete, facing both
Jas 3:14 if you **h** bitter envy and selfish

Harboured (Harbour)
Eze 35: 5 you **h** an ancient hostility

Harbours (Harbour)
Pr 26:24 but in his heart he **h** deceit.

Hard (Harden, Hardened, Hardening, Hardens, Harder, Hardest, Hardship, Hardships)
Ge 18:14 Is anything too **h** for the LORD?
33:13 If they are driven **h** just one day,
Ex 1:14 their lives bitter with **h** labour
1:14 in all their **h** labour the Egyptians
2:11 and watched them at their **h** labour.
7:13 Yet Pharaoh's heart became **h** and he
7:22 and Pharaoh's heart became **h**; he
8:19 But Pharaoh's heart was **h** and he
9:35 Pharaoh's heart was **h** and he would
Dt 1:17 Bring me any case too **h** for you,
8:15 He brought you water out of **h** rock.
26: 6 us suffer, putting us to **h** labour.
1Sa 13: 6 and that their army was **h** pressed,
31: 2 The Philistines pressed **h** after Saul
1Ki 10: 1 came to test him with **h** questions.
10: 3 **h** for the king to explain to her.
1Ch 10: 2 The Philistines pressed **h** after Saul
2Ch 9: 1 to test him with **h** questions.
9: 2 was too **h** for him to explain to her.
32: 5 he worked **h** repairing all the broken
Job 7: 1 "Does not man have **h** service on
14:14 All the days of my **h** service I will
37:18 skies, **h** as a mirror of cast bronze?
38:30 the waters become **h** as stone, when
38:38 the dust becomes **h** and the clods of
41:24 His chest is **h** as rock, **h** as a lower
Ps 114: 8 the **h** rock into springs of water.
Pr 13:15 but the way of the unfaithful is **h**.
14:23 All **h** work brings a profit, but mere
Ecc 8: 1 face and changes its **h** appearance.
Isa 40: 2 her **h** service has been completed
Jer 32:17 Nothing is too **h** for you.
32:27 Is anything too **h** for me?
Eze 29:18 army in a **h** campaign against Tyre;
Zec 7:12 They made their hearts as **h** as flint
Mt 19: 8 wives because your hearts were **h**.
19:23 it is **h** for a rich man to enter
25:24 'I knew that you are a **h** man,
Mk 10: 5 "It was because your hearts were **h**
10:23 "How **h** it is for the rich to enter
10:24 **h** it is to enter the kingdom of God!
Lk 5: 5 "Master, we've worked **h** all night
12:58 try **h** to be reconciled to him on the
Lk 18:24 "How **h** it is for the rich to enter
19:21 of you, because you are a **h** man.
19:22 did you, that I am a **h** man, taking
Jn 4:38 Others have done the **h** work, and you
6:60 said, "This is a **h** teaching.
Ac 20:35 by this kind of **h** work we must help
26:14 **h** for you to kick against the goads
Ro 16: 6 Greet Mary, who worked very **h** for
16:12 those women who work **h** in the Lord.
16:12 who has worked very **h** in the Lord.
1Co 4:12 We work **h** with our own hands. When
2Co 4: 8 We are **h** pressed on every side, but
6: 5 **h** work, sleepless nights and hunger;
8:13 be relieved while you are **h** pressed,
Col 4:13 I vouch for him that he is working **h**
1Th 5:12 to respect those who work **h** among
2Ti 1:17 searched **h** for me until he found me.
Heb 5:11 but it is **h** to explain because you
1Pe 4:18 And, "If it is **h** for the righteous
2Pe 3:16 things that are **h** to understand,
Rev 2: 2 I know your deeds, your **h** work and

Harden (Hard)
Ex 4:21 But I will **h** his heart so that he
7: 3 I will **h** Pharaoh's heart, and though
14: 4 I will **h** Pharaoh's heart, and he
14:17 I will **h** the hearts of the Egyptians
1Sa 6: 6 Why do you **h** your hearts as the
Ps 95: 8 do not **h** your hearts as you did at
Isa 63:17 **h** our hearts so we do not revere you?
Ro 9:18 and he hardens whom he wants to **h**.
Heb 3: 8 do not **h** your hearts as you did in
3:15 do not **h** your hearts as you did
4: 7 his voice, do not **h** your hearts."

Hardened (Hard)
Ex 8:15 he **h** his heart and would not listen
8:32 this time also Pharaoh **h** his heart
9:12 the LORD **h** Pharaoh's heart and he
9:34 He and his officials **h** their hearts.
10: 1 Pharaoh, for I have **h** his heart
10:20 the LORD **h** Pharaoh's heart, and he
10:27 the LORD **h** Pharaoh's heart, and he
11:10 but the LORD **h** Pharaoh's heart, and
14: 8 The LORD **h** the heart of Pharaoh king
Jos 11:20 LORD himself who **h** their hearts
2Ch 36:13 stiff-necked and **h** his heart
Jer 6:28 They are all **h** rebels, going about
Eze 3: 7 house of Israel is **h** and obstinate.
3: 8 I will make you as unyielding and **h**
Da 5:20 when his heart became arrogant and **h**
Mk 6:52 the loaves; their hearts were **h**.
8:17 or understand? Are your hearts **h**?
Ro 11: 7 The others were **h**,
Heb 3:13 you may be **h** by sin's deceitfulness.

Hardening (Hard)
Ro 11:25 Israel has experienced a **h** in part
Eph 4:18 them due to the **h** of their hearts.

Hardens (Hard)
Pr 28:14 who **h** his heart falls into trouble.
Ro 9:18 and he **h** whom he wants to harden.

Harder (Hard)
Ex 5: 9 Make the work **h** for the men so that
Jer 5: 3 **h** than stone and refused to repent.
Eze 3: 9 the hardest stone, **h** than flint.
Jn 5:18 Jews tried all the **h** to kill him;
1Co 15:10 No, I worked **h** than all of them—
2Co 11:23 I am more. I have worked much **h**,

Hardest (Hard)
Eze 3: 9 make your forehead like the **h** stone,

Hard-hearted (Heart)
Dt 15: 7 do not be **h** or tight-fisted towards

Hardship (Hard)
Ge 31:42 But God has seen my **h** and the toil
Dt 15:18 Do not consider it a **h** to set your
Ne 9:32 do not let all this **h** seem trifling
9:32 eyes—the **h** that has come upon us,
Job 5: 6 For **h** does not spring from the soil,
Isa 30: 6 Through a land of **h** and distress,
Lam 3: 5 surrounded me with bitterness and **h**.
Ro 8:35 Shall trouble or **h** or persecution or
1Th 2: 9 brothers, our toil and **h**; we worked
2Ti 2: 3 Endure **h** with us like a good soldier
4: 5 endure **h**, do the work of an
Heb 12: 7 Endure **h** as discipline; God is

Hardships (Hard)
Ex 18: 8 about all the **h** they had met along
Nu 11: 1 the people complained about their **h**
20:14 all the **h** that have come upon us.
1Ki 2:26 David and shared all my father's **h**.
Ps 132: 1 David and all the **h** he endured.
Ac 14:22 "We must go through many **h** to enter
20:23 me that prison and **h** are facing me.
2Co 1: 8 brothers, about the **h** we suffered in
6: 4 in troubles, **h** and distresses;
12:10 **h**, in persecutions, in difficulties.
Rev 2: 3 and have endured **h** for my name,

Hardworking (Work)
2Ti 2: 6 The **h** farmer should be the first to

Harem
Est 2: 3 into the **h** at the citadel of Susa.
2: 8 to Hegai, who had charge of the **h**.
2: 9 maids into the best place in the **h**.
2:11 fro near the courtyard of the **h** to
2:13 her from the **h** to the king's palace.
2:14 return to another part of the **h**
2:15 was in charge of the **h**, suggested.
Ecc 2: 8 and a **h** as well—the delights of the

Hareph
1Ch 2:51 **H** the father of Beth Gader.

Harhaiah
Ne 3: 8 Uzziel son of **H**, one of the

Harhas
2Ki 22:14 son of **H**, keeper of the wardrobe.

Harhur
Ezr 2:51 Bakbuk, Hakupha, **H**,
Ne 7:53 Bakbuk, Hakupha, **H**,

Harim (Harim's)
1Ch 24: 8 the third to **H**, the fourth to Seorim,
Ezr 2:32 of **H** 320
2:39 of **H** 1,017
10:21 From the descendants of **H**: Maaseiah,
10:31 From the descendants of **H**: Eliezer,
Ne 3:11 Malkijah son of **H** and Hasshub son of
7:35 of **H** 320
7:42 of **H** 1,017
10: 5 **H**, Meremoth, Obadiah,
10:27 Malluch, **H** and Baanah.

Harim's (Harim)
Ne 12:15 of **H**, Adna; of Meremoth's, Helkai;

Hariph
Ne 7:24 of **H** 112
10:19 **H**, Anathoth, Nebai,

Harlot (Harlots)
Isa 1:21 the faithful city has become a **h**!
Na 3: 4 because of the wanton lust of a **h**

Harlots (Harlot)
Hos 4:14 the men themselves consort with **h**

Harm (Harmed, Harmful, Harming, Harms)
Ge 26:29 that you will do us no **h**, just as we
31: 7 God has not allowed him to **h** me.
31:29 I have the power to **h** you; but last
31:52 this heap to your side to **h** you
31:52 heap and pillar to my side to **h** me.
42: 4 was afraid that **h** might come to him.

Ge 42:38 If **h** comes to him on the journey you
44:29 one from me too and **h** comes to him,
48:16 who has delivered me from all **h**
50:20 You intended to **h** me, but God
Nu 5:19 water that brings a curse not **h** you.
35:23 and he did not intend to **h** him,
Jdg 15: 3 Philistines; I will really **h** them."
1Sa 20: 7 sure that he is determined to **h** me.
20: 9 to **h** you, wouldn't I tell you?"
20:13 if my father is inclined to **h** you,
25:26 all who intend to **h** my master be
26:21 I will not try to **h** you again.
2Sa 18:32 all who rise up to **h** you be like
20: 6 will do us more **h** than Absalom did.
2Ki 8:12 "Because I know the **h** you will do
1Ch 4:10 keep me from **h** so that I will be
16:22 anointed ones; do my prophets no **h**."
Ne 6: 2 But they were scheming to **h** me;
Job 5:19 you; in seven no **h** will befall you.
Ps 38:12 those who would **h** me talk of my ruin;
56: 5 they are always plotting to **h** me.
71:13 may those who want to **h** me be
71:24 for those who wanted to **h** me have
91:10 no **h** will befall you, no disaster
105:15 anointed ones; do my prophets no **h**.
121: 6 the sun will not **h** you by day, nor
121: 7 The LORD will keep you from all **h**—
Pr 1:33 and be at ease, without fear of **h**.
3:29 Do not plot **h** against your neighbour,
3:30 reason—when he has done you no **h**.
12:21 No **h** befalls the righteous, but the
13:20 but a companion of fools suffers **h**.
31:12 She brings him good, not **h**, all the
Ecc 5:13 hoarded to the **h** of its owner,
8: 5 obeys his command will come to no **h**,
Isa 11: 9 They will neither **h** nor destroy
27: 3 and night so that no-one may **h** it.
65:25 They will neither **h** nor destroy on
Jer 5:12 No **h** will come to us; we will never
7: 6 not follow other gods to your own **h**,
10: 5 do no **h** nor can they do any good."
21:10 I have determined to do this city **h**
23:17 they say, 'No **h** will come to you.'
25: 6 Then I will not **h** you."
25: 7 you have brought **h** to yourselves."
29:11 plans to prosper you and not to **h**
39:12 don't **h** him but do for him
44:17 and were well off and suffered no **h**.
44:27 For I am watching over them for **h**,
44:29 threats of **h** against you will surely
Zep 3:15 never again will you fear any **h**.
Lk 10:19 of the enemy; nothing will **h** you.
Ac 9:13 all the **h** he has done to your saints
16:28 Paul shouted, "Don't **h** yourself! We
18:10 no-one is going to attack and **h** you
Ro 13:10 Love does no **h** to its neighbour.
1Co 11:17 your meetings do more **h** than good.
2Ti 4:14 did me a great deal of **h**.
1Pe 3:13 Who is going to **h** you if you are
2Pe 2:13 with **h** for the **h** they have done.
1Jn 5:18 safe, and the evil one cannot **h** him.
Rev 7: 2 power to **h** the land and the sea:
7: 3 "Do not **h** the land or the sea or the
9: 4 told not to **h** the grass of the earth
11: 5 If anyone tries to **h** them, fire
11: 5 anyone who wants to **h** them must die.

Harmed (Harm)
Ru 2:22 else's field you might be **h**."
Da 3:27 the fire had not **h** their bodies,
2Co 7: 9 and so were not **h** in any way by us.

Harmful (Harm)
2Ki 4:41 And there was nothing **h** in the pot.
Ps 52: 4 You love every **h** word, O you
1Ti 6: 9 into many foolish and **h** desires

Harming (Harm)
1Sa 24: 9 men say, 'David is bent on **h** you'?
25:34 lives, who has kept me from **h** you,
Jer 7:19 **h** themselves, to their own shame?

Harmless
Lev 13:39 it is a **h** rash that has broken out
Pr 1:11 blood, let's waylay some **h** soul;

Harmon
Am 4: 3 out towards **H**," declares the LORD.

Harmony
Zec 6:13 And there will be **h** between the two
Ro 12:16 Live in **h** with one another. Do not
2Co 6:15 What **h** is there between Christ and
1Pe 3: 8 Finally, all of you, live in **h** with

Harms (Harm)
Pr 8:36 whoever fails to find me **h** himself;

Harnepher
1Ch 7:36 The sons of Zophah: Suah, **H**, Shual,

Harness (Harnessed)
Job 39:10 you hold him to the furrow with a **h**?
Ps 50:19 and **h** your tongue to deceit
Jer 46: 4 **H** the horses, mount the steeds! Take
Mic 1:13 **h** the team to the chariot.

Harnessed (Harness)
SS 1: 9 to a mare **h** to one of the chariots

Harod (Harodite)
Jdg 7: 1 his men camped at the spring of **H**.

Harodite (Harod)
2Sa 23:25 Shammah the **H**, Elika the **H**,

Haroeh
1Ch 2:52 were: **H**, half the Manahathites,

Harorite
1Ch 11:27 Shammoth the **H**, Helez the Pelonite,

Harosheth Haggoyim
Jdg 4: 2 his army was Sisera, who lived in **H**.
4:13 him, from **H** to the Kishon River.
4:16 the chariots and army as far as **H**.

Harp (Harpist, Harpists, Harps)
Ge 4:21 of all who play the **h** and flute.
1Sa 16:16 for someone who can play the **h**.
16:18 who knows how to play the **h**.
16:23 David would take his **h** and play.
18:10 playing the **h**, as he usually did.
19: 9 While David was playing the **h**,
1Ch 25: 3 prophesied, used the **h** in thanking
Job 21:12 to the music of tambourine and **h**;
30:31 My **h** is tuned to mourning, and my
Ps 33: 2 Praise the LORD with the **h**; make
43: 4 I will praise you with the **h**, O God
49: 4 with the **h** I will expound my riddle
57: 8 Awake, my soul! Awake, **h** and lyre!
71:22 I will praise you with the **h** for
81: 2 play the melodious **h** and lyre.
92: 3 lyre and the melody of the **h**.
98: 5 make music to the LORD with the **h**,
98: 5 with the **h** and the sound of singing,
108: 2 Awake, **h** and lyre! I will awaken the
147: 7 make music to our God on the **h**.
149: 3 music to him with tambourine and **h**.
150: 3 praise him with the **h** and lyre,
Isa 16:11 My heart laments for Moab like a **h**,
23:16 "Take up a **h**, walk through the city,
23:16 play the **h** well, sing many a song,
24: 8 has stopped, the joyful **h** is silent.
Da 3: 5 flute, zither, lyre, **h**, pipes and
3: 7 flute, zither, lyre, **h** and all kinds
3:10 flute, zither, lyre, **h**, pipes and
3:15 flute, zither, lyre, **h**, pipes and
1Co 14: 7 such as the flute or **h**, how will
Rev 5: 8 Each one had a **h** and they were

Harpist (Harp)
2Ki 3:15 now bring me a **h**." While the **h** was

Harpists (Harp)
Rev 14: 2 like that of **h** playing their harps.
18:22 The music of **h** and musicians, flute

Harpoons
Job 41: 7 Can you fill his hide with **h** or his

Harps (Harp)
Ge 31:27 to the music of tambourines and **h**?
1Sa 10: 5 and **h** being played before them,
2Sa 6: 5 with songs and with **h**, lyres,
1Ki 10:12 make **h** and lyres for the musicians.
1Ch 13: 8 with songs and with **h**, lyres,
15:16 instruments: lyres, **h** and cymbals.
15:21 **h**, directing according to sheminith.
15:28 and the playing of lyres and **h**.
16: 5 They were to play the lyres and **h**,
25: 1 accompanied by **h**, lyres and cymbals.
25: 6 with cymbals, lyres and **h**, for the
2Ch 5:12 and playing cymbals, **h** and lyres.
9:11 make **h** and lyres for the musicians.
20:28 LORD with **h** and lutes and trumpets.
29:25 **h** and lyres in the way prescribed by
Ne 12:27 the music of cymbals, **h** and lyres.
Ps 137: 2 There on the poplars we hung our **h**,
Isa 5:12 They have **h** and lyres at their
14:11 along with the noise of your **h**;
30:32 to the music of tambourines and **h**,
Eze 26:13 of your **h** will be heard no more.
Am 5:23 not listen to the music of your **h**.
6: 5 You strum away on your **h** like David
Rev 14: 2 that of harpists playing their **h**.
15: 2 They held **h** given them by

Harrowing
Isa 28:24 keep on breaking up and **h** the soil?

Harsh
Dt 28:59 **h** and prolonged disasters, and
1Ki 12: 4 but now lighten the **h** labour and the
2Ch 10: 4 but now lighten the **h** labour and the
Pr 15: 1 wrath, but a **h** word stirs up anger.
Isa 66: 4 I also will choose **h** treatment for
Lam 1: 3 After affliction and **h** labour, Judah
Da 2:15 the king issue such a **h** decree?
Mal 3:13 "You have said **h** things against me,"
2Co 13:10 have to be **h** in my use of authority
Col 2:23 their **h** treatment of the body,
3:19 wives and do not be **h** with them.
1Pe 2:18 but also to those who are **h**.
Jude :15 **h** words ungodly sinners have spoken

Harsha
Ezr 2:52 Bazluth, Mehida, **H**,
Ne 7:54 Bazluth, Mehida, **H**,

Harum
1Ch 4: 8 of the clans of Aharhel son of **H**.

Harumaph
Ne 3:10 Adjoining this, Jedaiah son of **H**

Haruphite
1Ch 12: 5 Shemariah and Shephatiah the **H**;

Haruz
2Ki 21:19 daughter of **H**; she was from Jotbah.

Harvest (Harvested, Harvesters, Harvesting, Harvests)
Ge 8:22 seedtime and **h**, cold and heat,
30:14 During wheat **h**, Reuben went out
41:34 to take a fifth of the **h** of Egypt
Ex 23:10 to sow your fields and **h** the crops,
23:16 "Celebrate the Feast of **H** with the
34:21 season and **h** you must rest.
34:22 with the firstfruits of the wheat **h**,
Lev 19: 9 'When you reap the **h** of your land,
19: 9 or gather the gleanings of your **h**.
19:25 In this way your **h** will be increased.
23:10 to give you and you reap its **h**,
23:10 a sheaf of the first grain you **h**.
23:22 "'When you reap the **h** of your land,

Lev 23:22 or gather the gleanings of your **h**.
25: 5 or **h** the grapes of your untended
25:11 of itself or **h** the untended vines.
25:20 if we do not plant or **h** our crops?"
25:22 the **h** of the ninth year comes in.
26: 5 will continue until grape **h**
26: 5 **h** will continue until planting,
26:10 still be eating last year's **h**
Nu 18:12 as the firstfruits of their **h**.
Dt 16:15 God will bless you in all your **h**
24:21 you **h** the grapes in your vineyard,
28:38 in the field but you will **h** little,
Jos 3:15 the Jordan is in flood all during **h**.
Jdg 8: 2 than the full grape **h** of Abiezer?
15: 1 Later on, at the time of wheat **h**,
Ru 1:22 as the barley **h** was beginning.
1Sa 8:12 to plough his ground and reap his **h**,
12:17 Is it not wheat **h** now? I will call
2Sa 21: 9 to death during the first days of **h**,
21: 9 just as the barley **h** was beginning.
21:10 From the beginning of the **h** till the
23:13 During **h** time, three of the thirty
2Ch 32:28 He also made buildings to store the **h**
Ne 9:37 its abundant **h** goes to the kings
Job 5: 5 The hungry consume his **h**, taking it
31:12 it would have uprooted my **h**.
Ps 67: 6 the land will yield its **h**, and God,
85:12 good, and our land will yield its **h**.
107:37 vineyards that yielded a fruitful **h**;
Pr 6: 8 in summer and gathers its food at **h**.
10: 5 he who sleeps during **h** is a
14: 4 of an ox comes an abundant **h**.
18:20 the **h** from his lips he is satisfied.
20: 4 **h** time he looks but finds nothing.
25:13 Like the coolness of snow at **h** time
26: 1 Like snow in summer or rain in **h**,
Isa 9: 3 you as people rejoice at the **h**,
17:11 yet the **h** will be as nothing
18: 4 a cloud of dew in the heat of **h**."
18: 5 For, before the **h**, when the blossom
23: 3 the **h** of the Nile was the revenue of
24:13 are left after the grape **h**.
28: 4 will be like a fig ripe before **h**—
32:10 will tremble; the grape **h** will fail,
32:10 and the **h** of fruit will not come.
62: 9 those who **h** it will eat it and
Jer 2: 3 the firstfruits of his **h**; all who
5:24 us of the regular weeks of **h**'
8:13 "'I will take away their **h**,
8:20 "The **h** is past, the summer has ended,
12:13 So bear the shame of your **h** because
40:10 but you are to **h** the wine, summer
50:16 the reaper with his sickle at **h**.
51:33 the time to **h** her will soon come."
Hos 6:11 "Also for you, Judah, a **h** is
Joel 1:11 the **h** of the field is destroyed.
3:13 Swing the sickle, for the **h** is ripe.
Am 4: 7 the **h** was still three months away.
Mic 6:15 You will plant but not **h**; you will
Mt 9:37 "The **h** is plentiful but the
9:38 Ask the Lord of the **h**, therefore,
9:38 send out workers into his **h** field.
13:30 Let both grow together until the **h**.
13:39 The **h** is the end of the age, and
21:34 the **h** time approached, he sent his
21:41 his share of the crop at **h** time."
25:26 you knew that I **h** were I have not
Mk 4:29 to it, because the **h** has come."
12: 2 At **h** time he sent a servant to the
Lk 10: 2 He told them, "The **h** is plentiful,
10: 2 Ask the Lord of the **h**, therefore,
10: 2 send out workers into his **h** field.
20:10 At **h** time he sent a servant to the
Jn 4:35 'Four months more and then the **h**'?
4:35 at the fields! They are ripe for **h**.
Ro 1:13 that I might have a **h** among you,
1Co 9:10 so in the hope of sharing in the **h**.
9:11 if we reap a material **h** from you?
2Co 9:10 enlarge the **h** of your righteousness.
Gal 6: 9 will reap a **h** if we do not give up.
Heb 12:11 Later on, however, it produces a **h**
Jas 3:18 in peace raise a **h** of righteousness.
Rev 14:15 for the **h** of the earth is ripe."

Harvested (Harvest)

Isa 33: 4 Your plunder, O nations, is **h** as by
Jer 40:12 And they **h** an abundance of wine and
Am 7: 1 after the king's share had been **h**
Hag 1: 6 planted much, but have **h** little.
Rev 14:16 over the earth, and the earth was **h**.

Harvesters (Harvest)

Ru 2: 3 to glean in the fields behind the **h**.
2: 4 greeted the **h**, "The LORD be with
2: 5 Boaz asked the foreman of his **h**,
2: 7 among the sheaves behind the **h**.
2:14 When she sat down with the **h**, he
Mt 13:30 At that time I will tell the **h**:
13:39 of the age, and the **h** are angels.
Jas 5: 4 The cries of the **h** have reached the

Harvesting (Harvest)

Lev 25:15 number of years left for **h** crops.
Dt 24:19 you are **h** in your field and you
Ru 2: 9 Watch the field where the men are **h**,
2:21 until they finish **h** all my grain.
1Sa 6:13 the people of Beth Shemesh were **h**
Mt 25:24 **h** where you have not sown

Harvests (Harvest)

Dt 32:22 It will devour the earth and its **h**
Ru 2:23 barley and wheat **h** were finished.
Isa 16: 9 and over your **h** have been stilled.
17: 5 **h** the corn with his arm—as when a
Jer 5:17 They will devour your **h** and food,
Jn 4:36 even now he **h** the crop for eternal

Hasadiah

1Ch 3:20 Ohel, Berekiah, **H** and Jushab-Hesed.

Hashabiah

1Ch 6:45 the son of **H**, the son of Amaziah,
9:14 Azrikam, the son of **H**, a Merarite;
25: 3 Zeri, Jeshaiah, Shimei, **H** and
25:19 the twelfth to **H**, his sons and
26:30 From the Hebronites: **H** and his
27:17 over Levi: **H** son of Kemuel; over
2Ch 35: 9 his brothers, and **H**, Jeiel and
Ezr 8:19 **H**, together with Jeshaiah from the
8:24 **H** and ten of their brothers,
Ne 3:17 Beside him, **H**, ruler of half the
10:11 Mica, Rehob, **H**,
11:15 the son of **H**, the son of Bunni;
11:22 the son of **H**, the son of Mattaniah,
12:21 of Hilkiah's, **H**; of Jedaiah's,
12:24 the leaders of the Levites were **H**,

Hashabnah

Ne 10:25 Rehum, **H**, Maaseiah,

Hashabneiah

Ne 3:10 son of **H** made repairs next to him.
9: 5 the Levites—Jeshua, Kadmiel, Bani, **H**

Hashbaddanah

Ne 8: 4 Hashum, **H**, Zechariah and Meshullam.

Hashem

1Ch 11:34 the sons of **H** the Gizonite, Jonathan

Hashmonah

Nu 33:29 They left Mithcah and camped at **H**.
33:30 They left **H** and camped at Moseroth.

Hashubah

1Ch 3:20 There were also five others: **H**, Ohel,

Hashum

Ezr 2:19 of **H** 223
10:33 From the descendants of **H**: Mattenai,
Ne 7:22 of **H** 328
8: 4 Mishael, Malkijah, **H**, Hashbaddanah,
10:18 Hodiah, **H**, Bezai,

Hasrah

2Ch 34:22 son of **H**, keeper of the wardrobe.

Hassenaah

Ne 3: 3 Gate was rebuilt by the sons of **H**.

Hassenuah

1Ch 9: 7 the son of Hodaviah, the son of **H**;
Ne 11: 9 and Judah son of **H** was over the

Hasshub

1Ch 9:14 Of the Levites: Shemaiah son of **H**,
Ne 3:11 and **H** son of Pahath-Moab
3:23 Benjamin and **H** made repairs
10:23 Hoshea, Hananiah, **H**,
11:15 From the Levites: Shemaiah son of **H**,

Hassophereth

Ezr 2:55 the descendants of Sotai, **H**, Peruda,

Haste (Hasten, Hastily, Hasty)

Ex 12:11 Eat it in **h**; it is the LORD's
Dt 16: 3 because you left Egypt in **h**—
Ps 68:12 "Kings and armies flee in **h**; in the
Pr 21: 5 as surely as **h** leads to poverty.
29:20 Do you see a man who speaks in **h**?
Isa 52:12 you will not leave in **h** or go in
Jer 46: 5 They flee in **h** without looking back,

Hasten (Haste)

Ps 70: 1 **H**, O God, to save me; O LORD, come
119:60 I will **h** and not delay to obey your
Isa 5:19 let him **h** his work so that we may
49:17 Your sons **h** back, and those who laid
55: 5 that do not know you will **h** to you,

Hastily (Haste)

Pr 25: 8 do not bring **h** to court, for what

Hasty (Haste)

Pr 19: 2 nor to be **h** and miss the way.
Ecc 5: 2 do not be **h** in your heart to utter
1Ti 5:22 Do not be **h** in the laying on of

Hasupha

Ezr 2:43 descendants of Ziha, **H**, Tabbaoth,
Ne 7:46 descendants of Ziha, **H**, Tabbaoth,

Hatch (Hatched, Hatches)

Isa 34:15 she will **h** them, and care for her
59: 5 They **h** the eggs of vipers and spin

Hatched (Hatch)

Isa 59: 5 when one is broken, an adder is **h**.

Hatches (Hatch)

Jer 17:11 partridge that **h** eggs it did not lay

Hatchets

Ps 74: 6 panelling with their axes and **h**.

Hate (God-haters, Hated, Hates, Hating, Hatred)

Ex 18:21 trustworthy men who **h** dishonest gain
20: 5 fourth generation of those who **h** me,
Lev 19:17 'Do not **h** your brother in your
26:17 those who **h** you will rule over you,
Dt 5: 9 fourth generation of those who **h** me,
7:10 those who **h** him he will repay to
7:10 repay to their face those who **h** him.
7:15 will inflict them on all who **h** you.
30: 7 enemies who **h** and persecute you.
32:41 and repay those who **h** me.
Jdg 11: 7 "Didn't you **h** me and drive me
14:16 "You **h** me! You don't really love me.
2Sa 19: 6 You love those who **h** you and **h** those
1Ki 22: 8 but I **h** him because he never
2Ch 18: 7 but I **h** him because he never
19: 2 and love those who **h** the LORD?
Ps 5: 5 presence; you **h** all who do wrong.
25:19 and how fiercely they **h** me!
31: 6 I **h** those who cling to worthless
35:19 let not those who **h** me without
36: 2 too much to detect or **h** his sin.
38:19 **h** me without reason are numerous.

Ps 45: 7 and **h** wickedness; therefore God,
50:17 You **h** my instruction and cast my
69: 4 Those who **h** me without reason
69:14 deliver me from those who **h** me,
81:15 Those who **h** the LORD would cringe
97:10 Let those who love the LORD **h** evil,
101: 3 The deeds of faithless men I **h**;
105:25 whose hearts he turned to **h**
119:104 therefore I **h** every wrong path.
119:113 I **h** double-minded men, but I love
119:128 right, I **h** every wrong path.
119:163 I **h** and abhor falsehood but I love
120: 6 I lived among those who **h** peace.
129: 5 May all who **h** Zion be turned back
139:21 Do I not **h** those who **h** you, O LORD,
Pr 1:22 in mockery and fools **h** knowledge?
8:13 To fear the LORD is to **h** evil; I **h**
8:36 himself; all who **h** me love death."
9: 8 not rebuke a mocker or he will **h** you
13: 5 The righteous **h** what is false, but
25:17 too much of you, and he will **h** you.
29:10 Bloodthirsty men **h** a man of
Ecc 3: 8 a time to love and a time to **h**,
9: 1 knows whether love or **h** awaits him.
9: 6 Their love, their **h** and their
Isa 61: 8 I **h** robbery and iniquity.
66: 5 "Your brothers who **h** you, and
Jer 12: 8 She roars at me; therefore I **h** her.
44: 4 do this detestable thing that I **h**!
Eze 23:28 to hand you over to those you **h**,
35: 6 Since you did not **h** bloodshed,
Am 5:10 you **h** the one who reproves in court
5:15 **H** evil, love good; maintain justice
5:21 "I **h**, I despise your religious
Mic 3: 2 you who **h** good and love evil; who
Zec 8:17 I **h** all this," declares the LORD.
Mal 2:16 "I **h** divorce," says the LORD God
2:16 "and I **h** a man's covering himself
Mt 5:43 your neighbour and **h** your enemy.
6:24 Either he will **h** the one and love
10:22 All men will **h** you because of me,
24:10 and will betray and **h** each other,
Mk 13:13 All men will **h** you because of me,
Lk 1:71 and from the hand of all who **h** us
6:22 Blessed are you when men **h** you, when
6:27 enemies, do good to those who **h** you,
14:26 If anyone comes to me and does not **h**
16:13 Either he will **h** the one and love
21:17 All men will **h** you because of me.
Jn 7: 7 The world cannot **h** you, but it hates
Ro 7:15 I do not do, but what I **h** I do.
12: 9 Love must be sincere. **H** what is evil;
Rev 2: 6 You **h** the practices of the
2: 6 of the Nicolaitans, which I also **h**.
17:16 horns you saw will **h** the prostitute.

Hated (Hate)

Ge 37: 4 they **h** him and could not speak
37: 5 brothers, they **h** him all the more.
37: 8 And they **h** him all the more
Dt 9:28 and because he **h** them, he brought
Jdg 15: 2 "I was so sure you thoroughly **h** her
2Sa 13:15 Amnon **h** her with intense hatred.
13:15 In fact, he **h** her more than he had
13:22 he **h** Amnon because he had disgraced
Est 9: 1 upper hand over those who **h** them.
9: 5 they pleased to those who **h** them.
Pr 1:29 Since they **h** knowledge and did not
5:12 You will say, "How I **h** discipline!
14:17 things, and a crafty man is **h**.
Ecc 2:17 I **h** life, because the work that is
2:18 I **h** all the things I had toiled for
Isa 60:15 you have been forsaken and **h**,
Eze 16:37 you loved as well as those you **h**.
Hos 9:15 in Gilgal, I **h** them there.
Mal 1: 3 Esau I have **h**, and I have turned his
Mt 24: 9 be **h** by all nations because of me.
Lk 19:14 "But his subjects **h** him and sent a
Jn 15:18 keep in mind that it **h** me first.
15:24 they have **h** both me and my Father.
15:25 Law: 'They **h** me without reason.'
17:14 your word and the world has **h** them,
Ro 9:13 "Jacob I loved, but Esau I **h**.
Eph 5:29 no-one ever **h** his own body,
Tit 3: 3 being **h** and hating one another.
Heb 1: 9 righteousness and **h** wickedness;

Hates (Hate)

Ex 23: 5 donkey of someone who **h** you fallen
Dt 1:27 "The LORD **h** us; so he brought us out
12:31 of detestable things the LORD **h**.
16:22 for these the LORD your God **h**.
19:11 if a man **h** his neighbour and lies in
Job 34:17 Can he who **h** justice govern?
Ps 11: 5 those who love violence his soul **h**.
Pr 6:16 There are six things the LORD **h**,
12: 1 but he who **h** correction is stupid.
13:24 He who spares the rod **h** his son,
15:10 path; he who **h** correction will die.
15:27 but he who **h** bribes will live.
26:28 A lying tongue **h** those it hurts,
28:16 but he who **h** ill-gotten gain will
Isa 1:14 and your appointed feasts my soul **h**.
Jn 3:20 Everyone who does evil **h** the light,
7: 7 world cannot hate you, but it **h** me
12:25 the man who **h** his life in this world
15:18 "If the world **h** you, keep in mind
15:19 That is why the world **h** you.
15:23 He who **h** me **h** my Father as well.
1Jn 2: 9 **h** his brother is still in the
2:11 whoever **h** his brother is in the
3:13 my brothers, if the world **h** you.
3:15 Anyone who **h** his brother is a
4:20 yet **h** his brother, he is a liar.

Hathach

Est 4: 5 Esther summoned **H**, one of the king's
4: 6 **H** went out to Mordecai in the open
4: 9 **H** went back and reported to Esther

Hathath

1Ch 4:13 The sons of Othniel: **H** and Meonothai.

Hating (Hate)

Tit 3: 3 envy, being hated and **h** one another.
Jude :23 **h** even the clothing stained by

Hatipha

Ezr 2:54 Neziah and **H**
Ne 7:56 Neziah and **H**

Hatita

Ezr 2:42 Ater, Talmon, Akkub, **H** and Shobai 139
Ne 7:45 Ater, Talmon, Akkub, **H** and Shobai 138

Hatred (Hate)

2Sa 13:15 Amnon hated her with intense **h**.
Ps 109: 3 With words of **h** they surround me;
109: 5 for good, and **h** for my friendship.
139:22 I have nothing but **h** for them;
Pr 10:12 **H** stirs up dissension, but love
10:18 He who conceals his **h** has lying lips,
15:17 is love than a fattened calf with **h**.
Eze 23:29 They will deal with you in **h** and
35:11 you showed in your **h** of them
Gal 5:20 **h**, discord, jealousy, fits of rage,
Jas 4: 4 with the world is **h** towards God?

Hattil

Ezr 2:57 Shephatiah, **H**, Pokereth-Hazzebaim
Ne 7:59 Shephatiah, **H**, Pokereth-Hazzebaim

Hattush

1Ch 3:22 Shemaiah and his sons: **H**,
Ezr 8: 2 of the descendants of David, **H**
Ne 3:10 and **H** son of Hashabneiah made
10: 4 **H**, Shebaniah, Malluch,
12: 2 Amariah, Malluch, **H**,

Haughtiness (Haughty)

Jer 48:29 arrogance and the **h** of her heart.

Haughty (Haughtiness)

2Sa 22:28 eyes are on the **h** to bring them low.
Job 41:34 He looks down on all that are **h**; he
Ps 10: 5 he is **h** and your laws are far from
18:27 bring low those whose eyes are **h**.
101: 5 has **h** eyes and a proud heart,
131: 1 O LORD, my eyes are not **h**; I do not
Pr 6:17 **h** eyes, a lying tongue, hands that
16:18 a **h** spirit before a fall.
21: 4 **H** eyes and a proud heart, the lamp
30:13 those whose eyes are ever so **h**,
Isa 3:16 "The women of Zion are **h**, walking
10:12 heart and the **h** look in his eyes.
13:11 an end to the arrogance of the **h**
Eze 16:50 were **h** and did detestable things
Zep 3:11 again will you be **h** on my holy hill.

Haul

1Ki 5: 9 My men will **h** them down from Lebanon
Eze 32: 3 and they will **h** you up in my net.
Jn 21: 6 they were unable to **h** the net in

Haunt (Haunts)

Ps 44:19 and made us a **h** for jackals
Isa 34:13 a **h** for jackals, a home for owls.
Jer 9:11 a **h** of jackals; and I will lay waste
10:22 of Judah desolate, a **h** of jackals.
49:33 "Hazor will become a **h** of jackals,
51:37 be a heap of ruins, a **h** of jackals
Rev 18: 2 and a **h** for every evil spirit,
18: 2 a **h** for every unclean and detestable

Haunts (Haunt)

Ps 74:20 because **h** of violence fill the dark
SS 4: 8 and the mountain **h** of the leopards.
Isa 35: 7 In the **h** where jackals once lay,

Hauran

Eze 47:16 which is on the border of **H**.
47:18 will run between **H** and Damascus,

Haven

Ge 49:13 seashore and become a **h** for ships;
Ps 107:30 he guided them to their desired **h**.

Havilah

Ge 2:11 land of **H**, where there is gold.
10: 7 The sons of Cush: Seba, **H**, Sabtah,
10:29 Ophir, **H** and Jobab. All these were
25:18 settled in the area from **H** to Shur,
1Sa 15: 7 **H** to Shur, to the east of Egypt.
1Ch 1: 9 The sons of Cush: Seba, **H**, Sabta,
1:23 Ophir, **H** and Jobab. All these were

Havoc

Isa 54:16 created the destroyer to work **h**;
Jer 48: 3 cries of great **h** and destruction.
Ac 9:21 "Isn't he the man who caused **h** in

Havvoth Jair

Nu 32:41 their settlements and called them **H**.
Dt 3:14 to this day Bashan is called **H**.)
Jdg 10: 4 which to this day are called **H**.
1Ch 2:23 (But Geshur and Aram captured **H**,

Hawk

Lev 11:16 owl, the gull, any kind of **h**,
Dt 14:15 owl, the gull, any kind of **h**,
Job 39:26 "Does the **h** take flight by your

Hay

Pr 27:25 the **h** is removed and new growth
1Co 3:12 costly stones, wood, **h** or straw,

Hazael

1Ki 19:15 get there, anoint **H** king over Aram.
19:17 death any who escape the sword of **H**,
2Ki 8: 8 he said to **H**, "Take a gift with you
8: 9 **H** went to meet Elisha, taking with
8:11 a fixed gaze until **H** felt ashamed.
8:12 "Why is my lord weeping?" asked **H**.
8:13 **H** said, "How could your servant, a
8:14 **H** left Elisha and returned to his
8:14 **H** replied, "He told me that you
8:15 Then **H** succeeded him as king.
8:28 **H** king of Aram at Ramoth Gilead.

2Ki 8:29 in his battle with **H** king of Aram.
9:14 Ramoth Gilead against **H** king of Aram,
9:15 in the battle with **H** king of Aram.
10:32 **H** overpowered the Israelites
12:17 About this time **H** king of Aram went
12:18 and he sent them to **H** king of Aram,
13: 3 **H** king of Aram and Ben-Hadad his son.
13:22 **H** king of Aram oppressed Israel
13:24 **H** king of Aram died, and Ben-Hadad
13:25 recaptured from Ben-Hadad son of **H**
2Ch 22: 5 **H** king of Aram at Ramoth Gilead.
22: 6 in his battle with **H** king of Aram.
Am 1: 4 I will send fire upon the house of **H**

Hazaiah
Ne 11: 5 the son of Col-Hozeh, the son of **H**,

Hazar Addar
Nu 34: 4 it will go to **H** and over to Azmon,

Hazar Enan
Nu 34: 9 continue to Ziphron and end at **H**.
34:10 run a line from **H** to Shepham.
Eze 47:17 will extend from the sea to **H**,
48: 1 **H** and the northern border of

Hazar Gaddah
Jos 15:27 **H**, Heshmon, Beth Pelet,

Hazer Hatticon
Eze 47:16 **H**, which is on the border of Hauran.

Hazar Shual
Jos 15:28 **H**, Beersheba, Biziothiah,
19: 3 **H**, Balah, Ezem,
1Ch 4:28 They lived in Beersheba, Moladah, **H**,
Ne 11:27 in **H**, in Beersheba and its

Hazar Susah
Jos 19: 5 Ziklag, Beth Marcaboth, **H**,

Hazar Susim
1Ch 4:31 Beth Marcaboth, **H**, Beth Biri and

Hazarmaveth
Ge 10:26 of Almodad, Sheleph, **H**, Jerah,
1Ch 1:20 of Almodad, Sheleph, **H**, Jerah,

Hazer Hatticon
Eze 47:16 **H**, which is on the border of Hauran.

Hazeroth
Nu 11:35 travelled to **H** and stayed there.
12:16 After that, the people left **H** and
33:17 Kibroth Hattaavah and camped at **H**.
33:18 They left **H** and camped at Rithmah.
Dt 1: 1 and Tophel, Laban, **H** and Dizahab.

Hazezon Tamar
Ge 14: 7 the Amorites who were living in **H**.
2Ch 20: 2 It is already in **H**" (that is, En

Haziel
1Ch 23: 9 The sons of Shimei: Shelomoth, **H** and

Hazo
Ge 22:22 Kesed, **H**, Pildash, Jidlaph and

Hazor
Jos 11: 1 Jabin king of **H** heard of this, he
11:10 Joshua turned back and captured **H** and
11:10 (**H** had been the head of all these
11:11 breathed, and he burned up **H** itself.
11:13 **H**, which Joshua burned.
12:19 the king of **H** one
15:23 Kedesh, **H**, Ithnan,
15:25 Kerioth Hezron (that is, **H**),
19:36 Adamah, Ramah, **H**,
Jdg 4: 2 a king of Canaan, who reigned in **H**.
4:17 **H** and the clan of Heber the Kenite.
1Sa 12: 9 the commander of the army of **H**, and
1Ki 9:15 Jerusalem, and **H**, Megiddo and Gezer.
2Ki 15:29 Beth Maacah, Janoah, Kedesh and **H**.
Ne 11:33 in **H**, Ramah and Gittaim,
Jer 49:28 Kedar and the kingdoms of **H**,
49:30 in deep caves, you who live in **H**
49:33 "**H** will become a haunt of jackals,

Hazor Hadattah
Jos 15:25 **H**, Kerioth Hezron (that is, Hazor),

Hazzelelponi
1Ch 4: 3 Their sister was named **H**.

Hazzobebah
1Ch 4: 8 Koz, who was the father of Anub and **H**

Head (Figurehead, Headed, Heading, Heads, Hotheaded)
Ge 3:15 he will crush your **h**, and you will
28:11 under his **h** and lay down to sleep.
28:18 the stone he had placed under his **h**
40:13 will lift up your **h** and restore you
40:16 On my **h** were three baskets of bread.
40:17 them out of the basket on my **h**."
40:19 off your **h** and hang you on a tree.
42:38 grey **h** down to the grave in sorrow.
44:29 grey **h** down to the grave in misery.
44:31 Your servants will bring the grey **h**
48:14 hand and put it on Ephraim's **h**,
48:14 put his left hand on Manasseh's **h**,
48:17 on Ephraim's **h** he was displeased;
48:17 from Ephraim's **h** to Manasseh's **h**.
48:18 put your right hand on his **h**."
49:26 all these rest on the **h** of Joseph
Ex 12: 9 the fire—**h**, legs and inner parts.
22: 1 he must pay back five **h** of cattle
28:32 an opening for the **h** in its centre
29: 6 Put the turban on his **h** and attach
29: 7 anoint him by pouring it on his **h**.
29:10 shall lay their hands on its **h**.
29:15 shall lay their hands on its **h**.
29:17 with the **h** and the other pieces.
29:19 shall lay their hands on its **h**.
Lev 1: 4 He is to lay his hand on the **h** of
1: 8 including the **h** and the fat, on the
1:12 including the **h** and the fat, on the
1:15 wring off the **h** and burn it on the
3: 2 He is to lay his hand on the **h** of
3: 8 He is to lay his hand on the **h** of
3:13 He is to lay his hand on its **h** and
4: 4 He is to lay his hand on its **h** and
4:11 as well as the **h** and legs, the inner
4:15 on the bull's **h** before the LORD,
4:24 is to lay his hand on the goat's **h**
4:29 He is to lay his hand on the **h** of
4:33 He is to lay his hand on its **h** and
5: 8 He is to wring its **h** from its neck,
8: 9 he placed the turban on Aaron's **h**
8:12 anointing oil on Aaron's **h** and
8:14 his sons laid their hands on its **h**.
8:18 his sons laid their hands on its **h**.
8:20 the **h**, the pieces and the fat.
8:22 his sons laid their hands on its **h**.
9:13 **h**, and he burned them on the altar.
13:12 the infected person from **h** to foot,
13:29 has a sore on the **h** or on the chin,
13:30 infectious disease of the **h** or chin.
13:42 sore on his bald **h** or forehead,
13:42 breaking out on his **h** or forehead.
13:43 and if the swollen sore on his **h**
13:44 because of the sore on his **h**.
14: 9 all his hair; he must shave his **h**,
14:18 on the **h** of the one to be cleansed
14:29 on the **h** of the one to be cleansed,
16:21 He is to lay both hands on the **h** of
16:21 sins—and put them on the goat's **h**.
19:27 the hair at the sides of your **h** or
20: 9 and his blood will be on his own **h**.
21:10 the anointing oil poured on his **h**
24:14 him are to lay their hands on his **h**,
Nu 1: 4 One man from each tribe, each the **h**
6: 5 no razor may be used on his **h**.
6: 5 let the hair of his **h** grow long.
6: 7 his separation to God is on his **h**.
Nu 6: 9 he must shave his **h** on the day of
6:11 same day he is to consecrate his **h**.
17: 3 for the **h** of each ancestral tribe.
Dt 19: 5 the **h** may fly off and hit his
21:12 make her shave her **h**, trim her
28:13 The LORD will make you the **h**, not
28:23 The sky over your **h** will be bronze,
28:35 of your feet to the top of your **h**.
28:44 be the **h**, but you will be the tail.
33:16 all these rest on the **h** of Joseph
33:20 like a lion, tearing at arm or **h**.
Jos 2:19 his blood will be on his own **h**;
2:19 on our **h** if a hand is laid on him.
11:10 been the **h** of all these kingdoms.)
22:14 each the **h** of a family division
Jdg 5:26 She struck Sisera, she crushed his **h**,
8:28 and did not raise its **h** again.
9:53 on his **h** and cracked his skull.
10:18 **h** of all those living in Gilead."
11: 8 our **h** over all who live in Gilead."
11: 9 to me—will I really be your **h**?"
11:11 made him **h** and commander over them.
12: 1 burn down your house over your **h**."
13: 5 No razor may be used on his **h**,
16:13 braids of my **h** into the fabric
16:13 braids of his **h**, wove them into the
16:17 No razor has ever been used on my **h**,
16:17 If my **h** were shaved, my strength
16:22 the hair on his **h** began to grow
1Sa 1:11 no razor will ever be used on his **h**
4:12 his clothes torn and dust on his **h**.
5: 4 His **h** and hands had been broken off
9: 2 **h** taller than any of the others.
9:22 seated them at the **h** of those who
10: 1 it on Saul's **h** and kissed him,
10:23 a **h** taller than any of the others.
14:45 not a hair of his **h** shall fall to
15:17 the **h** of the tribes of Israel?
17: 5 He had a bronze helmet on his **h** and
17:38 on him and a bronze helmet on his **h**.
17:46 strike you down and cut off your **h**.
17:51 he cut off his **h** with the sword.
17:54 David took the Philistine's **h** and
17:57 still holding the Philistine's **h**.
19:13 putting some goats' hair at the **h**.
19:16 and at the **h** was some goats' hair.
21: 7 Doeg the Edomite, Saul's **h** shepherd.
25:39 Nabal's wrongdoing down on his own **h**.
26: 7 stuck in the ground near his **h**.
26:11 that are near his **h**, and let's go."
26:12 jug near Saul's **h**, and they left.
26:16 and water jug that were near his **h**?"
31: 9 They cut off his **h** and stripped off
2Sa 1: 2 clothes torn and with dust on his **h**.
1:10 I took the crown that was on his **h**
1:16 him, "Your blood be on your own **h**.
2:16 man grabbed his opponent by the **h**
3: 8 "Am I a dog's **h**—on Judah's side?
3:29 May his blood fall upon the **h** of
4: 7 and killed him, they cut off his **h**.
4: 8 They brought the **h** of Ish-Bosheth to
4: 8 "Here is the **h** of Ish-Bosheth son of
4:12 But they took the **h** of Ish-Bosheth
12:30 He took the crown from the **h** of
12:30 it was placed on David's **h**.
13:19 Tamar put ashes on her **h** and tore
13:19 She put her hand on her **h** and went
14:11 not one hair of your son's **h** will
14:25 From the top of his **h** to the sole
14:26 Whenever he cut the hair of his **h**
15:30 **h** was covered and he was barefoot.
15:32 his robe torn and dust on his **h**.
16: 9 Let me go over and cut off his **h**."
18: 9 Absalom's **h** got caught in the tree.
20:21 His **h** will be thrown to you
20:22 cut off the **h** of Sheba son of Bicri
22:44 preserved me as the **h** of nations.
1Ki 1:52 not a hair of his **h** will fall to the
2: 6 **h** go down to the grave in peace.
2: 9 grey **h** down to the grave in blood."
2:33 their blood rest on the **h** of Joab
2:37 your blood will be on your own **h**."
4:23 ten **h** of stall-fed cattle, twenty of
8:32 down on his own **h** what he has done.
19: 6 He looked around, and there by his **h**
2Ki 4:19 "My **h**! My **h**!" he said to his father.

2Ki 6:25 **h** sold for eighty shekels of silver,
6:31 the **h** of Elisha son of Shaphat
6:32 someone to cut off my **h**? Look,
9: 3 pour the oil on his **h** and declare,
9: 6 the oil on Jehu's **h** and declared,
19:21 Jerusalem tosses her **h** as you flee.
1Ch 5:15 son of Guni, was **h** of their family.
10: 9 They stripped him and took his **h**
10:10 up his **h** in the temple of Dagon.
15:22 Kenaniah the **h** Levite was in charge
20: 2 David took the crown from the **h** of
20: 2 it was placed on David's **h**.
29:11 you are exalted as **h** over all.
2Ch 6:23 down on his own **h** what he has done.
7: 5 of twenty-two thousand **h** of cattle
15:11 the LORD seven hundred **h** of cattle
20:21 they went out at the **h** of the army,
35: 9 hundred **h** of cattle for the Levites.
Ezr 9: 3 pulled hair from my **h** and beard
Ne 6: 8 just making it up out of your **h**."
Est 2:17 So he set a royal crown on her **h**
6: 8 with a royal crest placed on its **h**.
6:12 home, with his **h** covered, in grief,
9:25 should come back on to his own **h**,
Job 1:20 and tore his robe and shaved his **h**.
2: 7 of his feet to the top of his **h**.
10:15 I cannot lift my **h**, for I am full of
10:16 If I hold my **h** high, you stalk me
16: 4 against you and shake my **h** at you.
19: 9 and removed the crown from my **h**.
20: 6 and his **h** touches the clouds,
29: 3 his lamp shone upon my **h** and by his
41: 7 or his **h** with fishing spears?
Ps 3: 3 bestow glory on me and lift up my **h**.
7:16 violence comes down on his own **h**.
18:43 you have made me the **h** of nations;
21: 3 a crown of pure gold on his **h**.
23: 5 You anoint my **h** with oil; my cup
27: 6 my **h** will be exalted above the
35:14 I bowed my **h** in grief as though
40:12 are more than the hairs of my **h**,
69: 4 outnumber the hairs of my **h**;
110: 7 therefore he will lift up his **h**.
132:18 crown on his **h** shall be resplendent
133: 2 like precious oil poured on the **h**,
140: 7 shields my **h** in the day of battle
141: 5 him rebuke me—it is oil on my **h**.
141: 5 My **h** will not refuse it. Yet my
Pr 1: 9 will be a garland to grace your **h**
1:21 at the **h** of the noisy streets she
4: 9 set a garland of grace on your **h**
10: 6 Blessings crown the **h** of the
25:22 will heap burning coals on his **h**
Ecc 2:14 The wise man has eyes in his **h**,
9: 8 and always anoint your **h** with oil.
SS 2: 6 His left arm is under my **h**, and his
5: 2 My **h** is drenched with dew, my hair
5:11 His **h** is purest gold; his hair is
7: 5 Your **h** crowns you like Mount Carmel.
8: 3 His left arm is under my **h** and his
Isa 1: 5 rebellion? Your whole **h** is injured,
1: 6 top of your **h** there is no soundness
7: 8 for the **h** of Aram is Damascus, and
7: 8 and the **h** of Damascus is only Rezin.
7: 9 The **h** of Ephraim is Samaria, and the
7: 9 **h** of Samaria is only Remaliah's son.
7:20 to shave your **h** and the hair of
9:14 cut off from Israel both **h** and tail,
9:15 elders and prominent men are the **h**,
15: 2 **h** is shaved and every beard cut off.
19:15 **h** or tail, palm branch or reed.
28: 1 set on the **h** of a fertile valley
28: 4 set on the **h** of a fertile valley
37:22 Jerusalem tosses her **h** as you flee.
51:20 they lie at the **h** of every street,
58: 5 Is it only for bowing one's **h** like a
59:17 the helmet of salvation on his **h**;
61:10 as a bridegroom adorns his **h** like a
Jer 2:16 have shaved the crown of your **h**.
2:37 place with your hands on your **h**,
9: 1 Oh, that my **h** were a spring of water
16: 6 cut himself or shave his **h** for them.
47: 5 Gaza will shave her **h** in mourning;
48:27 **h** in scorn whenever you speak of her?
48:37 Every **h** is shaved and every beard
Lam 2:19 hunger at the **h** of every street.
Lam 3:54 the waters closed over my **h**, and I
4: 1 scattered at the **h** of every street.
5:16 The crown has fallen from our **h**.
Eze 5: 1 to shave your **h** and your beard.
8: 3 and took me by the hair of my **h**.
10:11 in whatever direction the **h** faced,
16:12 and a beautiful crown on your **h**.
16:25 At the **h** of every street you built
16:31 mounds at the **h** of every street
16:43 I will surely bring down on your **h**
17:19 I will bring down on his **h** my oath
18:13 and his blood will be on his own **h**.
29:18 every **h** was rubbed bare and every
33: 4 his blood will be on his own **h**.
33: 5 his blood will be on his own **h**.
Da 1:10 then have my **h** because of you."
2:32 The **h** of the statue was made of pure
2:38 You are that **h** of gold.
7: 9 hair of his **h** was white like wool.
7:20 know about the ten horns on its **h**
Hos 8: 7 The stalk has no **h**; it will produce
Joel 2:11 LORD thunders at the **h** of his army
Ob :15 deeds will return upon your own **h**.
Jnh 2: 5 seaweed was wrapped around my **h**.
4: 6 for his **h** to ease his discomfort,
4: 8 on Jonah's **h** so that he grew faint.
Mic 2:13 before them, the LORD at their **h**."
Na 3:10 to pieces at the **h** of every street.
Hab 3:13 you stripped him from **h** to foot.
3:14 With his own spear you pierced his **h**
Zec 1:21 so that no-one could raise his **h**,
3: 5 I said, "Put a clean turban on his **h**.
3: 5 So they put a clean turban on his **h**
6:11 and set it on the **h** of the high
Mt 5:36 do not swear by your **h**, for you
6:17 when you fast, put oil on your **h**
8:20 Son of Man has nowhere to lay his **h**
10:25 If the **h** of the house has been
10:30 even the very hairs of your **h** are
14: 8 platter the **h** of John the Baptist."
14:11 His **h** was brought in on a platter
26: 7 poured on his **h** as he was reclining
27:29 crown of thorns and set it on his **h**.
27:30 struck him on the **h** again and again.
27:37 Above his **h** they placed the written
Mk 6:24 **h** of John the Baptist," she answered.
6:25 **h** of John the Baptist on a platter."
6:27 with orders to bring John's **h**.
6:28 brought back his **h** on a platter.
12: 4 on the **h** and treated him shamefully.
14: 3 jar and poured the perfume on his **h**.
15:19 the **h** with a staff and spat on him.
Lk 7:46 You did not put oil on my **h**, but
9:58 Son of Man has nowhere to lay his **h**
12: 7 Indeed, the very hairs of your **h** are
21:18 not a hair of your **h** will perish.
Jn 13: 9 feet but my hands and my **h** as well!"
19: 2 crown of thorns and put it on his **h**.
19:30 bowed his **h** and gave up his spirit.
20: 7 cloth that had been around Jesus' **h**.
20:12 at the **h** and the other at the foot.
Ac 27:15 storm and could not **h** into the wind;
27:34 will lose a single hair from his **h**."
Ro 12:20 will heap burning coals on his **h**."
1Co 11: 3 the **h** of every man is Christ,
11: 3 and the **h** of the woman is man, and
11: 3 is man, and the **h** of Christ is God.
11: 4 with his **h** covered dishonours his **h**.
11: 5 her **h** uncovered dishonours her **h**
11: 5 is just as though her **h** were shaved.
11: 6 If a woman does not cover her **h**, she
11: 6 shaved off, she should cover her **h**.
11: 7 A man ought not to cover his **h**,
11:10 have a sign of authority on her **h**.
11:13 to pray to God with her **h** uncovered?
12:21 the **h** cannot say to the feet,
Eph 1:10 together under one **h**, even Christ.
1:22 be **h** over everything for the church,
4:15 him who is the **H**, that is, Christ.
5:23 For the husband is the **h** of the wife
5:23 as Christ is the **h** of the church,
Col 1:18 he is the **h** of the body, the church;
2:10 **H** over every power and authority.
2:19 He has lost connection with the **H**,
2Ti 4: 5 you, keep your **h** in all situations,
Rev 1:14 His **h** and hair were white like wool,
Rev 10: 1 with a rainbow above his **h**; his face
12: 1 a crown of twelve stars on her **h**.
13: 1 and on each **h** a blasphemous name.
14:14 with a crown of gold on his **h** and
19:12 fire, and on his **h** are many crowns.

Headband (Headbands)

1Ki 20:38 with his **h** down over his eyes.
20:41 the prophet quickly removed the **h**

Headbands (Headband)

Ex 28:40 Make tunics, sashes and **h** for
29: 9 put **h** on them. Then tie sashes on
39:28 turban of fine linen, the linen **h**
Lev 8:13 tied sashes around them and put **h** on
Isa 3:18 and **h** and crescent necklaces,

Head-dresses

Isa 3:20 the **h** and ankle chains and sashes,

Headed (Head)

Ge 31:21 he **h** for the hill country of Gilead.
Jos 15: 9 From the hilltop the boundary **h**
18:12 and **h** west into the hill country,
Jer 39: 4 two walls, and **h** towards the Arabah.
Jnh 1: 3 Jonah ran away from the LORD and **h**

Heading (Head)

Lk 9:53 him, because he was **h** for Jerusalem.
Jn 6:21 reached the shore where they were **h**.

Headlong

2Ki 7:15 had thrown away in their **h** flight.
Job 27:22 mercy as he flees **h** from its power.
Hab 1: 8 Their cavalry gallops **h**; their
Ac 1:18 bought a field; there he fell **h**,

Heads (Head)

Ge 40:20 He lifted up the **h** of the chief
Ex 6:14 These were the **h** of their families:
6:25 These were the **h** of the Levite
Lev 2:14 **h** of new grain roasted in the fire.
20:11 their blood will be on their own **h**.
20:12 their blood will be on their own **h**.
20:13 their blood will be on their own **h**.
20:16 their blood will be on their own **h**.
20:27 their blood will be on their own **h**.
21: 5 Priests must not shave their **h** or
26:13 you to walk with **h** held high.
Nu 1:16 were the **h** of the clans of Israel.
7: 2 the **h** of families who were the
8:12 their hands on the **h** of the bulls,
10: 4 —the **h** of the clans of Israel—
30: 1 Moses said to the **h** of the tribes of
31:26 Eleazar the priest and the family **h**
32:28 family **h** of the Israelite tribes.
36: 1 The family **h** of the clan of Gilead
36: 1 the **h** of the Israelite families.
Dt 14: 1 the front of your **h** for the dead,
32:42 the **h** of the enemy leaders."
33:21 When the **h** of the people assembled,
Jos 7: 6 same, and sprinkled dust on their **h**.
14: 1 Joshua son of Nun and the **h** of the
19:51 Joshua son of Nun and the **h** of the
21: 1 Now the family **h** of the Levites
21: 1 Joshua son of Nun, and the **h** of the
22:21 to the **h** of the clans of Israel:
22:30 **h** of the clans of the Israelites
Jdg 7:25 the **h** of Oreb and Zeeb to Gideon,
1Sa 29: 4 by taking the **h** of our own men?
2Sa 15:30 people with him covered their **h** too
1Ki 8: 1 all the **h** of the tribes and the
20:31 our waists and ropes round our **h**.
20:32 waists and ropes round their **h**,
2Ki 10: 6 take the **h** of your master's sons
10: 7 They put their **h** in baskets and sent
10: 8 have brought the **h** of the princes.
1Ch 5:24 These were the **h** of their families:
5:24 famous men, and **h** of their families.
7: 2 and Samuel—**h** of their families.
7: 7 and Iri, **h** of families—five in all.
7: 9 listed the **h** of families and
7:11 sons of Jediael were **h** of families
7:40 descendants of Asher—**h** of families,

1Ch 8: 6 who were **h** of families of those
8:10 These were his sons, **h** of families.
8:13 Beriah and Shema, who were **h** of
8:28 All these were **h** of families, chiefs
9: 9 these men were **h** of their families.
9:13 The priests, who were **h** of families,
9:33 musicians, **h** of Levite families
9:34 All these were **h** of Levite families,
12:19 It will cost us our **h** if he deserts
15:12 He said to them, "You are the **h** of
23: 9 were the **h** of the families of Ladan.
23:24 the **h** of families as they were
24: 4 sixteen **h** of families from Eleazar's
24: 4 eight **h** of families from Ithamar's
24: 6 son of Abiathar and the **h** families
24:31 Ahimelech, and the **h** of families of
26:21 who were **h** of families belonging to
26:26 by the **h** of families who were the
26:32 who were able men and **h** of families,
27: 1 **h** of families, commanders of
2Ch 1: 2 in Israel, the **h** of families—
5: 2 all the **h** of the tribes and the
19: 8 priests and **h** of Israelite families
23: 2 the **h** of Israelite families
29:30 and bowed their **h** and worshipped.
Ezr 1: 5 the family **h** of Judah and Benjamin,
2:68 some of the **h** of the families gave
3:12 priests and Levites and family **h**,
4: 2 to the **h** of families and said,
4: 3 and the rest of the **h** of the families
8: 1 These are the family **h** and those
8:29 Levites and the family **h** of Israel."
9: 6 our sins are higher than our **h**
10:16 selected men who were family **h**,
Ne 4: 4 their insults back on their own **h**.
7:70 Some of the **h** of the families
7:71 Some of the **h** of the families gave
8:13 the **h** of all the families,
9: 1 and having dust on their **h**.
11:13 associates, who were **h** of families
11:16 two of the **h** of the Levites,
12:12 the **h** of the priestly families:
12:22 The family **h** of the Levites in the
12:23 The family **h** among the descendants
Job 2:12 robes and sprinkled dust on their **h**.
Ps 22: 7 they hurl insults, shaking their **h**:
24: 7 Lift up your **h**, O you gates; be
24: 9 Lift up your **h**, O you gates; lift
44:14 the peoples shake their **h** at us.
64: 8 them will shake their **h** in scorn.
66:12 You let men ride over our **h**; we went
68:21 Surely God will crush the **h** of his
74:13 you broke the the **h** of the monster
74:14 It was you who crushed the **h** of
83: 2 astir, how your foes rear their **h**.
109:25 they see me, they shake their **h**.
140: 9 Let the **h** of those who surround me
Isa 3:17 sores on the **h** of the women of Zion;
29:10 he has covered your **h** (the seers).
35:10 everlasting joy will crown their **h**
51:11 everlasting joy will crown their **h**
Jer 13:18 crowns will fall from your **h**."
14: 3 and despairing, they cover their **h**.
14: 4 are dismayed and cover their **h**.
18:16 be appalled and will shake their **h**.
23:19 down on the **h** of the wicked.
30:23 down on the **h** of the wicked.
Lam 2:10 on their **h** and put on sackcloth.
2:10 have bowed their **h** to the ground.
2:15 they scoff and shake their **h** at
Eze 1:22 Spread out above the **h** of the living
1:25 above the expanse over their **h**
1:26 Above the expanse over their **h** was
7:18 shame and their **h** will be shaved.
9:10 on their own **h** what they have done
10: 1 that was over the **h** of the cherubim
11:21 I will bring down on their own **h**
13:18 their **h** in order to ensnare people.
22:31 bringing down on their own **h** all
23:15 and flowing turbans on their **h**;
23:42 and beautiful crowns on their **h**.
24:23 You will keep your turbans on your **h**
27:30 dust on their **h** and roll in ashes.
27:31 They will shave their **h** because of
32:27 swords were placed under their **h**?
44:18 to wear linen turbans on their **h**
Eze 44:20 They must not shave their **h** or
44:20 to keep the hair of their **h** trimmed.
Da 3:27 nor was a hair of their **h** singed;
7: 6 This beast had four **h**, and it was
Joel 3: 4 on your own **h** what you have done.
3: 7 on your own **h** what you have done.
Am 2: 7 They trample on the **h** of the poor
8:10 you wear sackcloth and shave your **h**.
9: 1 Bring them down on the **h** of all the
Mic 1:16 Shave your **h** in mourning for the
Mt 27:39 insults at him, shaking their **h**
Mk 15:29 shaking their **h** and saying, "So! You
Lk 21:28 stand up and lift up your **h**, because
Ac 18: 6 Your blood be on your own **h**!
21:24 that they can have their **h** shaved.
Rev 4: 4 and had crowns of gold on their **h**.
9: 7 On their **h** they wore something like
9:17 The **h** of the horses resembled the **h**
9:19 **h** with which they inflict injury.
12: 3 an enormous red dragon with seven **h**
12: 3 ten horns and seven crowns on his **h**.
13: 1 He had ten horns and seven **h**, with
13: 3 One of the **h** of the beast seemed to
17: 3 names and had seven **h** and ten horns.
17: 7 which has the seven **h** and ten horns.
17: 9 The seven **h** are seven hills on which
18:19 They will throw dust on their **h**, and

Headwaters (Water)

Ge 2:10 there it was separated into four **h**.

Headway

Ac 27: 7 We made slow **h** for many days and had

Heal (Healed, Healing, Heals)

Nu 12:13 "O God, please **h** her!
Dt 32:39 I have wounded and I will **h**, and
2Ki 20: 5 and seen your tears; I will **h** you.
20: 8 be the sign that the LORD will **h** me
2Ch 7:14 their sin and will **h** their land.
Job 5:18 he injures, but his hands also **h**.
Ps 6: 2 O LORD, **h** me, for my bones are
41: 4 **h** me, for I have sinned against
Ecc 3: 3 a time to kill and a time to **h**,
Isa 19:22 he will strike them and **h** them.
19:22 respond to their pleas and **h** them.
57:18 I have seen his ways, but I will **h**
57:19 "And I will **h** them."
Jer 17:14 **H** me, O LORD, and I shall be healed;
30:17 I will restore you to health and **h**
33: 6 I will **h** my people and will let them
Lam 2:13 Who can **h** you?
Hos 5:13 cure you, not able to **h** your sores.
6: 1 torn us to pieces but he will **h** us;
7: 1 whenever I would **h** Israel, the sins
14: 4 "I will **h** their waywardness and love
Na 3:19 Nothing can **h** your wound; your
Zec 11:16 or seek the young, or **h** the injured,
Mt 8: 7 Jesus said to him, "I will go and **h**
10: 1 and to **h** every disease and sickness.
10: 8 **H** the sick, raise the dead, cleanse
12:10 "Is it lawful to **h** on the Sabbath?
13:15 and turn, and I would **h** them.'
17:16 but they could not **h** him."
Mk 3: 2 if he would **h** him on the Sabbath.
6: 5 on a few sick people and **h** them.
Lk 4:23 'Physician, **h** yourself! Do here in
5:17 was present for him to **h** the sick.
6: 7 to see if he would **h** on the Sabbath.
7: 3 him to come and **h** his servant.
8:43 years, but no-one could **h** her.
9: 2 kingdom of God and to **h** the sick.
10: 9 **H** the sick who are there and tell
13:32 'I will drive out demons and **h**
14: 3 Is it lawful to **h** on the Sabbath or
Jn 4:47 **h** his son, who was close to death.
12:40 nor turn—and I would **h** them."
Ac 4:30 Stretch out your hand to **h** and
28:27 and turn, and I would **h** them.'

Healed (Heal)

Ge 20:17 Abraham prayed to God, and God **h**
Ex 21:19 and see that he is completely **h**.
Lev 13:37 hair has grown in it, the itch is **h**.
Lev 14: 3 **h** of his infectious skin disease,
Jos 5: 8 they were in camp until they were **h**.
1Sa 6: 3 Then you will be **h**, and you will
2Ki 2:21 the LORD says: 'I have **h** this water.
2Ch 30:20 the LORD heard Hezekiah and **h** the
Ps 30: 2 called to you for help and you **h** me.
107:20 He sent forth his word and **h** them;
Isa 6:10 their hearts, and turn and be **h**."
53: 5 him, and by his wounds we are **h**.
Jer 14:19 afflicted us so that we cannot be **h**?
17:14 Heal me, O LORD, and I shall be **h**;
51: 8 for her pain; perhaps she can be **h**.
51: 9 **h** Babylon, but she cannot be **h**;
Eze 34: 4 **h** the sick or bound up the injured.
Hos 11: 3 did not realise it was I who **h** them.
Mt 4:24 and the paralysed, and he **h** them.
8: 8 the word, and my servant will be **h**.
8:13 his servant was **h** at that very hour.
8:16 with a word and **h** all the sick.
9:21 only touch his cloak, I will be **h**.
9:22 he said, "your faith has **h** you.
9:22 the woman was **h** from that moment.
12:15 him, and he **h** all their sick,
12:22 and Jesus **h** him, so that he could
14:14 compassion on them and **h** their sick.
14:36 and all who touched him were **h**.
15:28 daughter was **h** from that very hour.
15:30 them at his feet; and he **h** them.
17:18 boy, and he was **h** from that moment.
19: 2 crowds followed him, and he **h** them
21:14 to him at the temple, and he **h** them.
Mk 1:34 Jesus **h** many who had various
3:10 For he had **h** many, so that those
5:23 her so that she will be **h** and live.
5:28 touch his clothes, I will be **h**."
5:34 "Daughter, your faith has **h** you.
6:13 sick people with oil and **h** them.
6:56 and all who touched him were **h**.
10:52 "Go," said Jesus, "your faith has **h**
Lk 4:40 his hands on each one, he **h** them.
5:15 him and to be **h** of their sicknesses.
6:18 who had come to hear him and to be **h**
7: 7 the word, and my servant will be **h**.
8:47 and how she had been instantly **h**.
8:48 "Daughter, your faith has **h** you.
8:50 just believe, and she will be **h**."
9:11 God, and **h** those who needed healing.
9:42 rebuked the evil spirit, **h** the boy
13:14 because Jesus had **h** on the Sabbath
13:14 **h** on those days, not on the Sabbath."
14: 4 the man, he **h** him and sent him away.
17:15 One of them, when he saw he was **h**,
18:42 your sight; your faith has **h** you."
22:51 he touched the man's ear and **h** him.
Jn 5:10 Jews said to the man who had been **h**,
5:13 The man who was **h** had no idea who it
Ac 4: 9 cripple and are asked how he was **h**,
4:10 that this man stands before you **h**.
4:14 had been **h** standing there with them,
4:22 For the man who was miraculously **h**
5:16 spirits, and all of them were **h**.
8: 7 many paralytics and cripples were **h**.
14: 9 him, saw that he had faith to be **h**
28: 8 placed his hands on him and **h** him.
Heb 12:13 may not be disabled, but rather **h**.
Jas 5:16 for each other so that you may be **h**.
1Pe 2:24 by his wounds you have been **h**.
Rev 13: 3 but the fatal wound had been **h**.
13:12 beast, whose fatal wound had been **h**.

Healing (Heal)

2Ch 28:15 sandals, food and drink, and **h** balm.
Pr 12:18 but the tongue of the wise brings **h**.
13:17 but a trustworthy envoy brings **h**.
15: 4 The tongue that brings **h** is a tree
16:24 to the soul and **h** to the bones.
Isa 58: 8 and your **h** will quickly appear; then
Jer 8:15 time of **h** but there was only terror.
8:22 no **h** for the wound of my people?
14:19 time of **h** but there is only terror.
30:12 is incurable, your injury beyond **h**.
30:13 remedy for your sore, no **h** for you.
33: 6 I will bring health and **h** to it;
46:11 in vain; there is no **h** for you.
Eze 30:21 It has not been bound up for **h** or

Eze 47:12 for food and their leaves for **h**."
Mal 4: 2 will rise with **h** in its wings.
Mt 4:23 and **h** every disease and sickness
9:35 and **h** every disease and sickness.
Lk 6:19 was coming from him and **h** them all.
9: 6 the gospel and **h** people everywhere.
9:11 God, and healed those who needed **h**.
Jn 7:23 for **h** the whole man on the Sabbath?
Ac 3:16 has given this complete **h** to him,
10:38 he went around doing good and **h** all
1Co 12: 9 gifts of **h** by that one Spirit,
12:28 also those having gifts of **h**, those
12:30 Do all have gifts of **h**? Do all speak
Rev 22: 2 tree are for the **h** of the nations.

Heals (Heal)

Ex 15:26 for I am the LORD, who **h** you."
Lev 13:18 has a boil on his skin and it **h**,
Ps 103: 3 your sins and **h** all your diseases,
147: 3 He **h** the broken-hearted and binds up
Isa 30:26 and **h** the wounds he inflicted.
Ac 9:34 said to him, "Jesus Christ **h** you.

Health (Healthier, Healthy)

1Sa 25: 6 Say to him: 'Long life to you! Good **h**
25: 6 And good **h** to all that is yours!
Ps 38: 3 of your wrath there is no **h** in my
38: 7 pain; there is no **h** in my body.
Pr 3: 8 This will bring **h** to your body and
4:22 them and **h** to a man's whole body.
15:30 and good news gives **h** to the bones.
Isa 38:16 You restored me to **h** and let me live.
Jer 30:17 I will restore you to **h** and heal
33: 6 'Nevertheless, I will bring **h** and
3Jn : 2 I pray that you may enjoy good **h** and

Healthier (Health)

Da 1:15 end of the ten days they looked **h**

Healthy (Health)

Ge 41: 5 Seven ears of corn, **h** and good, were
41: 7 swallowed up the seven **h**, full ears.
Ps 73: 4 their bodies are **h** and strong.
Zec 11:16 or heal the injured, or feed the **h**,
Mt 9:12 **h** who need a doctor, but the sick.
Mk 2:17 **h** who need a doctor, but the sick.
Lk 5:31 "It is not the **h** who need a doctor

Heap (Heaped, Heaping, Heaps)

Ge 31:46 in a **h**, and they ate there by the **h**.
31:48 Laban said, "This **h** is a witness
31:51 "Here is this **h**, and here is this
31:52 This **h** is a witness, and this pillar
31:52 that I will not go past this **h** to
31:52 you will not go past this **h** and
Lev 4:12 burn it in a wood fire on the ash **h**.
Dt 32:23 "I will **h** calamities upon them and
Jos 3:13 be cut off and stand up in a **h**."
3:16 It piled up in a **h** a great distance
8:28 and made it a permanent **h** of ruins,
1Sa 2: 8 and lifts the needy from the ash **h**;
2Sa 18:17 up a large **h** of rocks over him.
Ps 113: 7 and lifts the needy from the ash **h**;
Pr 25:22 In doing this, you will **h** burning
Isa 3: 6 take charge of this **h** of ruins!"
17: 1 a city but will become a **h** of ruins.
25: 2 You have made the city a **h** of rubble,
Jer 9:11 "I will make Jerusalem a **h** of ruins,
26:18 Jerusalem will become a **h** of rubble,
51:37 Babylon will be a **h** of ruins, a
Eze 24:10 **h** on the wood and kindle the fire.
Mic 1: 6 I will make Samaria a **h** of rubble
3:12 Jerusalem will become a **h** of rubble,
Hag 2:16 anyone came to a **h** of twenty
Lk 14:35 for the manure **h**; it is thrown out.
Ro 12:20 will **h** burning coals on his head."
1Th 2:16 In this way they always **h** up their
1Pe 4: 4 and they **h** abuse on you.

Heaped (Heap)

Jos 7:26 Over Achan they **h** up a large pile of
2Ki 19:23 By your messengers you have **h**
Isa 37:24 By your messengers you have **h**
Zec 9: 3 she has **h** up silver like dust,
Mt 27:44 with him also **h** insults on him.
Mk 15:32 with him also **h** insults on him.

Heaping (Heap)

Ps 110: 6 He will judge nations, **h** up the dead
Isa 30: 1 not by my Spirit, **h** sin upon sin;

Heaps (Heap)

Ex 8:14 They were piled into **h**, and the land
2Ch 31: 6 their God, and they piled them in **h**.
31: 8 his officials came and saw the **h**,
31: 9 the priests and Levites about the **h**;
Ne 4: 2 **h** of rubble—burned as they are?"
Job 27:16 Though he **h** up silver like dust and
Ps 39: 6 he **h** up wealth, not knowing who
Jer 50:26 pile her up like **h** of grain.
Lam 4: 5 nurtured in purple now lie on ash **h**.
Zep 1: 3 wicked will have only **h** of rubble

Hear (*Ears to hear*, Heard, Hearers, Hearing, Hears, Overheard)

Ge 4:23 to me; wives of Lamech, **h** my words.
41:15 you **h** a dream you can interpret it."
Ex 15:14 The nations will **h** and tremble;
18: 9 Jethro was delighted to **h** about all
19: 9 so that the people will **h** me
22:23 to me, I will certainly **h** their cry.
22:27 I will **h**, for I am compassionate.
32:18 is the sound of singing that I **h**."
Nu 14:13 "Then the Egyptians will **h** about it!
23:18 and listen; **h** me, son of Zippor.
Dt 1:16 **H** the disputes between your
1:17 **h** both small and great alike
1:17 too hard for you, and I will **h** it.
2:25 They will **h** reports of you and will
4: 1 **H** now, O Israel, the decrees and
4: 6 who will **h** about all these decrees
4:10 "Assemble the people before me to **h**
4:28 cannot see or **h** or eat or smell.
4:36 From heaven he made you **h** his voice
5: 1 **H**, O Israel, the decrees and the
5:25 and we will die if we **h** the voice of
6: 3 **H**, O Israel, and be careful to obey
6: 4 **H**, O Israel: The LORD our God, the
9: 1 **H**, O Israel. You are now about to
13:11 all Israel will **h** and be afraid,
13:12 If you **h** it said about one of the
17:13 All the people will **h** and be afraid,
18:16 "Let us not **h** the voice of the LORD
19:20 rest of the people will **h** of this
20: 3 He shall say: "**H**, O Israel, today
21:21 Israel will **h** of it and be afraid.
29: 4 or eyes that see or ears that **h**.
31:13 who do not know this law, must **h** it
32: 1 **h**, O earth, the words of my mouth.
33: 7 this he said about Judah: "**H**, O LORD,
Jos 6: 5 you **h** them sound a long blast on the
7: 9 of the country will **h** about this
22:33 They were glad to **h** the report and
Jdg 5: 3 "**H** this, you kings! Listen, you
5:16 to **h** the whistling for the flocks?
14:13 "Let's **h** it."
1Sa 2:23 I **h** from all the people about
2:24 it is not a good report that I **h**
13: 3 "Let the Hebrews **h**!
15:14 is this lowing of cattle that I **h**?"
16: 2 Saul will **h** about it and kill me.
25: 7 Now I **h** that it is sheep-shearing
25:24 you; **h** what your servant has to say.
2Sa 5:24 soon as you **h** the sound of marching
15: 3 of the king to **h** you."
15:10 "As soon as you **h** the sound of the
15:35 anything you **h** in the king's palace.
15:36 Send them to me with anything you **h**.
16:21 Then all Israel will **h** that you have
17: 5 that we can **h** what he has to say."
18:31 "My lord the king, **h** the good news!
19:35 Can I still **h** the voices of men and
22:45 as soon as they **h** me, they obey me.
1Ki 1:45 That's the noise you **h**.
8:28 **H** the cry and the prayer that your
8:29 **h** the prayer your servant prays
8:30 **H** the supplication of your servant
8:30 **H** from heaven, your dwelling-place,
8:30 and when you **h**, forgive.
1Ki 8:32 **h** from heaven and act. Judge between
8:34 **h** from heaven and forgive the sin of
8:36 **h** from heaven and forgive the sin of
8:39 **h** from heaven, your dwelling-place.
8:42 for men will **h** of your great name
8:43 **h** from heaven, your dwelling-place,
8:45 **h** from heaven their prayer and their
8:49 **h** their prayer and their plea,
10: 8 stand before you and **h** your wisdom!
10:24 to **h** the wisdom God had put in his
22:19 "Therefore **h** the word of the LORD
2Ki 7: 1 Elisha said, "**H** the word of the LORD.
7: 6 Arameans to **h** the sound of chariots
18:28 "**H** the word of the great king, the
19: 4 may be that the LORD your God will **h**
19:16 Give ear, O LORD, and **h**; open your
20:16 "**H** the word of the LORD:
1Ch 14:15 soon as you **h** the sound of marching
2Ch 6:19 **H** the cry and the prayer that your
6:20 May you **h** the prayer your servant
6:21 **H** the supplications of your servant
6:21 **H** from heaven, your dwelling-place;
6:21 and when you **h**, forgive.
6:23 **h** from heaven and act. Judge between
6:25 **h** from heaven and forgive the sin of
6:27 **h** from heaven and forgive the sin of
6:30 **h** from heaven, your dwelling-place.
6:33 **h** from heaven, your dwelling-place,
6:35 **h** from heaven their prayer and their
6:39 **h** their prayer and their pleas,
7:14 then will I **h** from heaven and will
9: 7 stand before you and **h** your wisdom!
9:23 to **h** the wisdom God had put in his
18:18 "Therefore **h** the word of the LORD
20: 9 and you will **h** us and save us.'
Ne 1: 6 your eyes open to **h** the prayer your
4: 4 **H** us, O our God, for we are despised.
4:20 Wherever you **h** the sound of the
13:27 Must we **h** now that you too are doing
Job 3:18 no longer **h** the slave driver's shout
5:27 So **h** it and apply it to yourself."
13: 6 **H** now my argument; listen to the
20: 3 I **h** a rebuke that dishonours me,
22:27 You will pray to him, and he will **h**
26:14 how faint the whisper we **h** of him!
31:35 ("Oh, that I had someone to **h** me!
34: 2 "**H** my words, you wise men; listen
34:16 "If you have understanding, **h** this;
34:34 wise men who **h** me say to me,
39: 7 he does not **h** a driver's shout.
Ps 4: 1 be merciful to me and **h** my prayer.
4: 3 the LORD will **h** when I call to him.
5: 3 morning, O LORD, you **h** my voice
10:17 You **h**, O LORD, the desire of the
17: 1 **H**, O LORD, my righteous plea; listen
17: 6 give ear to me and **h** my prayer.
18:44 soon as they **h** me, they obey me;
27: 7 **H** my voice when I call, O LORD;
28: 2 **H** my cry for mercy as I call to you
30:10 **H**, O LORD, and be merciful to me;
31:13 For I **h** the slander of many; there
34: 2 let the afflicted **h** and rejoice.
38:13 I am like a deaf man, who cannot **h**,
38:14 became like a man who does not **h**,
39:12 "**H** my prayer, O LORD, listen to my
49: 1 **H** this, all you peoples; listen, all
50: 7 "**H**, O my people, and I will speak,
51: 8 Let me **h** joy and gladness; let the
54: 2 **H** my prayer, O God; listen to the
55: 2 **h** me and answer me. My thoughts
55:19 will **h** them and afflict them
59: 7 "Who can **h** us?
61: 1 **H** my cry, O God; listen to my prayer.
64: 1 **H** me, O God, as I voice my complaint;
65: 2 O you who **h** prayer, to you all men
77: 1 help; I cried out to God to **h** me.
78: 1 O my people, **h** my teaching; listen
80: 1 **H** us, O Shepherd of Israel, you who
81: 8 "**H**, O my people, and I will warn you
84: 8 **H** my prayer, O LORD God Almighty;
86: 1 **H**, O LORD, and answer me, for I am
86: 6 **H** my prayer, O LORD; listen to my
94: 9 Does he who implanted the ear not **h**?
95: 7 Today, if you **h** his voice,
102: 1 **H** my prayer, O LORD; let my cry for
102:20 to **h** the groans of the prisoners and

Ps 115: 6 they have ears, but cannot **h**, noses,
119:149 **H** my voice in accordance with your
130: 2 O Lord, **h** my voice. Let your ears be
135:17 they have ears, but cannot **h**, nor is
138: 4 when they **h** the words of your mouth.
140: 6 **H**, O LORD, my cry for mercy.
141: 1 **H** my voice when I call to you.
143: 1 O LORD, **h** my prayer, listen to my
Pr 20:12 Ears that **h** and eyes that see—
Ecc 7:21 you may **h** your servant cursing you
SS 2:14 your face, let me **h** your voice;
8:13 in attendance, let me **h** your voice!
Isa 1: 2 **H**, O heavens! Listen, O earth! For
1:10 **H** the word of the LORD, you rulers
6:10 **h** with their ears, understand with
7:13 Isaiah said, "**H** now, you house of
18: 3 a trumpet sounds, you will **h** it.
21: 3 I **h**, I am bewildered by what I see.
24:16 From the ends of the earth we **h**
28:14 Therefore **h** the word of the LORD,
28:23 and **h** my voice; pay attention and **h**
29:18 In that day the deaf will **h** the
30:21 your ears will **h** a voice behind you,
30:30 The LORD will cause men to **h** his
32: 3 the ears of those who **h** will listen.
32: 9 feel secure, **h** what I have to say!
33:13 You who are far away, **h** what I have
34: 1 you peoples! Let the earth **h**, and
36:13 "**H** the words of the great king, the
37: 4 may be that the LORD your God will **h**
37:17 Give ear, O LORD, and **h**; open
39: 5 "**H** the word of the LORD Almighty:
42:18 "**H**, you deaf; look, you blind, and
42:20 ears are open, but you **h** nothing."
43: 9 others may **h** and say, "It is true.
49: 1 **h** this, you distant nations:
51: 4 to me, my people; **h** me, my nation:
51: 7 "**H** me, you who know what is right,
51:21 Therefore **h** this, you afflicted one,
55: 3 **h** me, that your soul may live.
59: 1 to save, nor his ear too dull to **h**.
59: 2 from you, so that he will not **h**.
65:24 they are still speaking I will **h**.
66: 5 **H** the word of the LORD, you who
66: 6 **H** that uproar from the city, **h** that
Jer 2: 4 **H** the word of the LORD, O house of
4:21 and **h** the sound of the trumpet?
4:31 I **h** a cry as of a woman in labour,
5:21 **H** this, you foolish and senseless
5:21 not see, who have ears but do not **h**
6:10 are closed so that they cannot **h**.
6:18 Therefore **h**, O nations; observe,
6:19 **H**, O earth: I am bringing disaster
7: 2 '**H** the word of the LORD, all you
9:20 Now, O women, **h** the word of the LORD
10: 1 **H** what the LORD says to you, O house
13:15 **H** and pay attention, do not be
17:20 Say to them, '**H** the word of the LORD,
18:19 **h** what my accusers are saying
19: 3 '**H** the word of the LORD, O kings
20:10 I **h** many whispering, "Terror on
20:16 May he **h** wailing in the morning,
21:11 of Judah, '**H** the word of the LORD;
22: 2 '**H** the word of the LORD, O king of
22:29 O land, land, land, **h** the word of
23:18 of the LORD to see or to **h** his word?
25:36 **H** the cry of the shepherds, the
29:20 Therefore, **h** the word of the LORD,
31:10 "**H** the word of the LORD, O nations;
33: 9 **h** of all the good things I do for it;
34: 4 'Yet **h** the promise of the LORD,
36: 3 Perhaps when the people of Judah **h**
38:25 If the officials **h** that I talked
42: 2 "Please **h** our petition and pray to
42:14 will not see war or **h** the trumpet
42:15 **h** the word of the LORD, O remnant of
44:24 "**H** the word of the LORD, all you
44:26 **h** the word of the LORD, all Jews
46:12 The nations will **h** of your shame;
49:20 Therefore, **h** what the LORD has
50:45 Therefore, **h** what the LORD has
Eze 3:17 so **h** the word I speak and give them
6: 3 'O mountains of Israel, **h** the word
12: 2 but do not **h** for they are a
13: 2 '**H** the word of the LORD!
16:35 Therefore, you prostitute, **h** the
Eze 18:25 **H**, O house of Israel: Is my way
20:47 Say to the southern forest: '**H** the
25: 3 Say to them, '**H** the word of the
33: 7 so **h** the word I speak and give them
33:30 'Come and **h** the message that has
33:32 for they **h** your words but do not put
34: 7 'Therefore, you shepherds, **h** the
34: 9 therefore, O shepherds, **h** the word
36: 1 of Israel, **h** the word of the LORD.
36: 4 O mountains of Israel, **h** the word
36:15 No longer will I make you **h** the
37: 4 'Dry bones, **h** the word of the LORD!
40: 4 with your eyes and **h** with your ears
Da 3: 5 soon as you **h** the sound of the horn,
3:15 Now when you **h** the sound of the horn,
5:23 which cannot see or **h** or understand.
9:17 "Now, our God, **h** the prayers and
9:18 Give ear, O God, and **h**; open your
9:19 listen! O Lord, forgive! O Lord, **h**
Hos 4: 1 **H** the word of the LORD, you
5: 1 "**H** this, you priests! Pay attention,
7:12 When I **h** them flocking together, I
Joel 1: 2 **H** this, you elders; listen, all who
Am 3: 1 **H** this word the LORD has spoken
3:13 "**H** this and testify against the
4: 1 **H** this word, you cows of Bashan on
5: 1 **H** this word, O house of Israel, this
7:16 Now then, **h** the word of the LORD.
8: 4 **H** this, you who trample the needy
Mic 1: 2 **H**, O peoples, all of you, listen,
3: 9 **H** this, you leaders of the house of
6: 1 the hills **h** what you have to say.
6: 2 **H**, O mountains, the LORD's
7: 7 God my Saviour; my God will **h** me.
Zec 8: 9 "You who now **h** these words spoken by
Mt 11: 4 report to John what you **h** and see:
11: 5 the deaf **h**, the dead are raised, and
11:15 He who has ears, let him **h**.
12:19 will **h** his voice in the streets.
13: 9 He who has ears, let him **h**."
13:13 they do not **h** or understand.
13:15 they hardly **h** with their ears,
13:15 **h** with their ears, understand with
13:16 see, and your ears because they **h**.
13:17 to **h** what you **h** but did not **h** it.
13:43 He who has ears, let him **h**.
21:16 "Do you **h** what these children are
24: 6 You will **h** of wars and rumours of
27:13 Pilate asked him, "Don't you **h** the
Mk 4: 9 "He who has ears to **h**, let him **h**.
4:15 As soon as they **h** it, Satan comes
4:16 **h** the word and at once receive it
4:18 seed sown among thorns, **h** the word;
4:20 **h** the word, accept it, and produce
4:23 If anyone has ears to **h**, let him **h**
4:24 "Consider carefully what you **h**,"
7:37 the deaf **h** and the mute speak."
8:18 and ears but fail to **h**?
12:29 '**H**, O Israel, the Lord our God, the
13: 7 you **h** of wars and rumours of wars,
14:11 They were delighted to **h** this and
15:44 Pilate was surprised to **h** that he
Lk 5:15 so that crowds of people came to **h**
6:18 who had come to **h** him and to be
6:27 "But I tell you who **h** me: Love your
7:22 the deaf **h**, the dead are raised, and
8: 8 "He who has ears to **h**, let him **h**.
8:12 along the path are the ones who **h**,
8:13 they **h** it, but they have no root.
8:14 among thorns stands for those who **h**,
8:15 who **h** the word, retain it, and by
8:21 brothers are those who **h** God's word
9: 9 Who, then, is this I **h** such things
10:24 to **h** what you **h** but did not **h** it."
11:28 who **h** the word of God and obey it."
14:35 "He who has ears to **h**, let him **h**."
15: 1 were all gathering round to **h** him.
16: 2 'What is this I **h** about you? Give an
21: 9 you **h** of wars and revolutions, do
21:38 the morning to **h** him at the temple.
Jn 3: 8 You **h** its sound, but you cannot tell
5:25 has now come when the dead will **h**
5:25 Son of God and those who **h** will live.
5:28 are in their graves will **h** his
5:30 can do nothing; I judge only as I **h**,
8:43 you are unable to **h** what I say.
Jn 8:47 reason you do not **h** is that you do
9:27 Why do you want to **h** it again? Do
11:42 I knew that you always **h** me, but I
14:24 These words you **h** are not my own;
Ac 2:11 Cretans and Arabs—we **h** them
2:33 poured out what you now see and **h**.
10:22 he could **h** what you have to say."
13: 7 he wanted to **h** the word of God.
13:44 gathered to **h** the word of the Lord.
15: 7 the Gentiles might **h** from my lips
17:32 to **h** you again on this subject."
19:26 you see and **h** how this fellow Paul
21:22 will certainly **h** that you have come,
22:14 One and to **h** words from his mouth.
23:35 he said, "I will **h** your case when
24: 4 you be kind enough to **h** us briefly.
25:22 "I would like to **h** this man myself.
25:22 He replied, "Tomorrow you will **h**
28:22 we want to **h** what your views are,
28:27 they hardly **h** with their ears,
28:27 **h** with their ears, understand with
Ro 2:13 For it is not those who **h** the law
10:14 **h** without someone preaching to them?
10:18 I ask: Did they not **h**? Of course
11: 8 they could not **h**, to this very day."
1Co 11:18 In the first place, I **h** that when
Php 1:27 or only **h** about you in my absence,
1:30 I had, and now **h** that I still have.
2Th 3:11 We **h** that some among you are idle.
2Ti 4: 3 what their itching ears want to **h**.
4:17 and all the Gentiles might **h** it.
Phm : 5 I **h** about your faith in the Lord
Heb 3: 7 "Today, if you **h** his
3:15 has just been said: "Today, if you **h**
4: 7 "Today, if you **h** his voice, do not
3Jn : 4 I have no greater joy than to **h** that
Rev 1: 3 and blessed are those who **h** it and
2: 7 He who has an ear, let him **h** what
2:11 He who has an ear, let him **h** what
2:17 He who has an ear, let him **h** what
2:29 He who has an ear, let him **h** what
3: 6 He who has an ear, let him **h** what
3:13 He who has an ear, let him **h** what
3:22 He who has an ear, let him **h** what
9:20 that cannot see or **h** or walk.
13: 9 He who has an ear, let him **h**.

Heard (Hear)

Ge 3: 8 the man and his wife **h** the sound of
3:10 He answered, "I **h** you in the garden,
14:14 Abram **h** that his relative had been
16:11 for the LORD has **h** of your misery.
17:20 as for Ishmael, I have **h** you:
21:17 God **h** the boy crying, and the angel
21:17 **h** the boy crying as he lies there.
21:26 me, and I **h** about it only today."
24:30 and had **h** Rebekah tell what the man
24:52 Abraham's servant **h** what they said,
27:34 Esau **h** his father's words, he burst
29:13 soon as Laban **h** the news about Jacob,
29:33 "Because the LORD **h** that I am not
31: 1 Jacob **h** that Laban's sons were
34: 5 Jacob **h** that his daughter Dinah had
34: 7 as soon as they **h** what had happened.
35:22 Bilhah, and Israel **h** of it.
37:17 "I **h** them say, 'Let's go to Dothan
37:21 Reuben **h** this, he tried to rescue
39:15 he **h** me scream for help, he left his
39:19 his master **h** the story his wife told
41:15 But I have **h** it said of you that
42: 2 He continued, "I have **h** that there
43:25 had **h** that they were to eat there.
45: 2 so loudly that the Egyptians **h** him,
45: 2 and Pharaoh's household **h** about it.
Ex 2:15 Pharaoh **h** of this, he tried to kill
2:24 God **h** their groaning and he
3: 7 I have **h** them crying out because of
4:31 when they **h** that the LORD was
6: 5 Moreover, I have **h** the groaning of
16: 7 he has **h** your grumbling against him
16: 8 he has **h** your grumbling against him
16: 9 LORD, for he has **h** your grumbling.
16:12 "I have **h** the grumbling of the
18: 1 **h** of everything God had done for
20:18 lightning and **h** the trumpet and saw

Ex 23:13 do not let them be **h** on your lips.
28:35 The sound of the bells will be **h**
32:17 Joshua **h** the noise of the people
33: 4 the people **h** these distressing words,
Lev 10:20 Moses **h** this, he was satisfied.
24:14 All those who **h** him are to lay their
Nu 7:89 he **h** the voice speaking to him from
11: 1 when he **h** them his anger was aroused
11:10 Moses **h** the people of every family
11:18 The LORD **h** you when you wailed, "If
12: 2 through us?" And the LORD **h** this.
14:14 They have already **h** that you,
14:15 **h** this report about you will say,
14:27 I have **h** the complaints of these
14:28 the very things I **h** you say:
16: 4 Moses **h** this, he fell face down.
20:16 we cried out to the LORD, he **h** our
21: 1 **h** that Israel was coming along the
22:36 Balak **h** that Balaam was coming, he
33:40 **h** that the Israelites were coming.
Dt 1:34 the LORD **h** what you said, he was
4:12 You **h** the sound of words but saw no
4:32 has anything like it ever been **h** of?
4:33 Has any other people **h** the voice of
4:36 **h** his words from out of the fire.
5:23 you **h** the voice out of the darkness,
5:24 we have **h** his voice from the fire.
5:26 For what mortal man has ever **h** the
5:28 The LORD **h** you when you spoke to me
5:28 have **h** what this people said to you.
9: 2 know about them and have **h** it said:
26: 7 and the LORD **h** our voice and saw our
Jos 2:10 We have **h** how the LORD dried up the
2:11 we **h** of it, our hearts sank and
5: 1 **h** how the LORD had dried up the
9: 1 of the Jordan **h** about these things
9: 3 However, when the people of Gibeon **h**
9: 9 For we have **h** reports of him: all
9:16 the Israelites **h** that they were
10: 1 Adoni-Zedek king of Jerusalem **h**
11: 1 Jabin king of Hazor **h** of this, he
14:12 You yourself **h** then that the
22:11 the Israelites **h** that they had built
22:30 **h** what Reuben, Gad and Manasseh
24:27 It has **h** all the words the LORD has
Jdg 7:15 Gideon **h** the dream and its
9:30 Zebul the governor of the city **h**
9:47 Abimelech **h** that they had assembled
13: 9 God **h** Manoah, and the angel of God
17: 2 about which I **h** you utter a curse
20: 3 (The Benjamites **h** that the
Ru 1: 6 she **h** in Moab that the LORD had come
1Sa 1:13 were moving but her voice was not **h**.
2:22 Now Eli, who was very old, **h** about
4:14 Eli **h** the outcry and asked, "What is
4:19 When she **h** the news that the ark of
7: 7 the Philistines **h** that Israel had
7: 7 And when the Israelites **h** of it,
8:21 Samuel **h** all that the people said,
11: 6 Saul **h** their words, the Spirit of
13: 3 and the Philistines **h** about it.
13: 4 all Israel **h** the news: "Saul has
14:22 **h** that the Philistines were on the
14:27 Jonathan had not **h** that his father
17:23 his usual defiance, and David **h** it.
17:28 Eliab, David's oldest brother, **h** him
22: 1 his father's household **h** about it,
22: 6 Now Saul **h** that David and his men
23:10 your servant has **h** definitely that
23:11 come down as your servant has **h**?
23:25 When Saul **h** this, he went into the
25: 4 he **h** that Nabal was shearing sheep
25:35 I have **h** your words and granted your
25:39 David **h** that Nabal was dead, he said,
31:11 the people of Jabesh Gilead **h** of
2Sa 3:28 Later, when David **h** about this, he
4: 1 Ish-Bosheth son of Saul **h** that Abner
5:17 the Philistines **h** that David had
5:17 but David **h** about it and went down
7:22 you, as we have **h** with our own ears.
8: 9 Tou king of Hamath **h** that David had
11:26 Uriah's wife **h** that her husband was
13:21 King David **h** all this, he was
18: 5 And all the troops **h** the king
19: 2 because on that day the troops **h** it
22: 7 From his temple he **h** my voice;
1Ki 1:11 "Have you not **h** that Adonijah, the
1:41 all the guests who were with him **h**
3:28 all Israel **h** the verdict the king
4:34 the world, who had **h** of his wisdom.
5: 1 Hiram king of Tyre **h** that Solomon
5: 7 Hiram **h** Solomon's message, he was
6: 7 chisel or any other iron tool was **h**
9: 3 The LORD said to him: "I have **h** the
10: 1 the queen of Sheba **h** about the fame
10: 6 She said to the king, "The report I **h**
10: 7 have far exceeded the report I **h**.
11:21 While he was in Egypt, Hadad **h** that
12: 2 Jeroboam son of Nebat **h** this (he was
12:20 all the Israelites **h** that Jeroboam
13: 4 King Jeroboam **h** what the man of God
13:26 him back from his journey **h** of it,
14: 6 when Ahijah **h** the sound of her
15:21 Baasha **h** this, he stopped building
16:16 the Israelites in the camp **h** that
17:22 The LORD **h** Elijah's cry, and the
18:13 Haven't you **h**, my lord, what I did
19:13 Elijah **h** it, he pulled his cloak
20:12 Ben-Hadad **h** this message while he
20:31 "Look, we have **h** that the kings of
21:15 soon as Jezebel **h** that Naboth had
21:16 Ahab **h** that Naboth was dead, he got
21:27 Ahab **h** these words, he tore his
2Ki 3:21 Now all the Moabites had **h** that
5: 8 Elisha the man of God **h** that the
6:30 the king **h** the woman's words, he
9:30 When Jezebel **h** about it, she
11:13 Athaliah **h** the noise made by the
19: 1 King Hezekiah **h** this, he tore his
19: 4 the words the LORD your God has **h**.
19: 6 Do not be afraid of what you have **h**
19: 8 the field commander **h** that the king
19:11 Surely you have **h** what the kings of
19:20 the God of Israel, says: I have **h**
19:25 'Have you not **h**? Long ago I
20: 5 says: I have **h** your prayer and seen
20:12 he had **h** of Hezekiah's illness.
22:11 the king **h** the words of the Book of
22:18 says concerning the words you **h**:
22:19 when you **h** what I have spoken
22:19 I have **h** you, declares the LORD.
25:23 all the army officers and their men **h**
1Ch 10:11 the inhabitants of Jabesh Gilead **h**
14: 8 the Philistines **h** that David had
14: 8 **h** about it and went out to meet them
17:20 as we have **h** with our own ears
18: 9 Tou king of Hamath **h** that David had
2Ch 7:12 "I have **h** your prayer and have
9: 1 the queen of Sheba **h** of Solomon's
9: 5 She said to the king, "The report I **h**
9: 6 have far exceeded the report I **h**.
10: 2 Jeroboam son of Nebat **h** this (he was
15: 8 Asa **h** these words and the prophecy
16: 5 Baasha **h** this, he stopped building
20:29 when they **h** how the LORD had fought
23:12 Athaliah **h** the noise of the people
30:20 the LORD **h** Hezekiah and healed the
30:27 and God **h** them, for their prayer
34:19 the king **h** the words of the Law, he
34:26 says concerning the words you **h**:
34:27 **h** what he spoke against this place
34:27 I have **h** you, declares the LORD.
Ezr 3:13 And the sound was **h** far away.
4: 1 the enemies of Judah and Benjamin **h**
9: 3 I **h** this, I tore my tunic and cloak,
Ne 1: 4 I **h** these things, I sat down and
2:10 the Ammonite official **h** about this,
2:19 and Geshem the Arab **h** about it,
4: 1 Sanballat **h** that we were rebuilding
4: 7 the men of Ashdod **h** that the repairs
4:15 our enemies **h** that we were aware of
5: 6 I **h** their outcry and these charges,
6:16 all our enemies **h** about this, all
9: 9 you **h** their cry at the Red Sea.
9:27 From heaven you **h** them, and in your
9:28 you **h** from heaven, and in your
12:43 in Jerusalem could be **h** far away.
13: 3 the people **h** this law, they excluded
Est 1:18 have **h** about the queen's conduct
Job 2:11 **h** about all the troubles that had
3: 7 may no shout of joy be **h** in it.
4:16 my eyes, and I **h** a hushed voice:
Job 13: 1 my ears have **h** and understood it.
16: 2 "I have **h** many things like these;
29:11 Whoever **h** me spoke well of me, and
33: 8 in my hearing—I **h** the very words—
34:28 so that he **h** the cry of the needy.
42: 5 My ears had **h** of you but now my eyes
Ps 6: 8 evil, for the LORD has **h** my weeping.
6: 9 The LORD has **h** my cry for mercy;
18: 6 From his temple he **h** my voice;
19: 3 language where their voice is not **h**.
28: 6 Praise be to the LORD, for he has **h**
31:22 **h** my cry for mercy when I called
34: 6 This poor man called, and the LORD **h**
40: 1 he turned to me and **h** my cry.
44: 1 We have **h** with our ears, O God;
48: 8 As we have **h**, so have we seen
61: 5 For you have **h** my vows, O God;
62:11 I **h**: that you, O God, are strong,
66: 8 let the sound of his praise be **h**;
66:19 God has surely listened and **h** my
77:18 Your thunder was **h** in the whirlwind,
78: 3 what we have **h** and known, what our
78:21 the LORD **h** them, he was very angry;
78:59 God **h** them, he was very angry;
81: 5 **h** a language we did not understand.
92:11 have **h** the rout of my wicked foes.
106:44 their distress when he **h** their cry;
116: 1 I love the LORD, for he **h** my voice;
116: 1 **h** my voice; he **h** my cry for mercy.
132: 6 We **h** it in Ephrathah, we came upon
Ecc 12:13 Now all has been **h**; here is the
SS 2:12 cooing of doves is **h** in our land.
Isa 5: 7 but **h** cries of distress.
6: 8 I **h** the voice of the Lord saying,
15: 4 voices are **h** all the way to Jahaz.
16: 6 We have **h** of Moab's pride—her
21:10 I tell you what I have **h** from the
37: 1 King Hezekiah **h** this, he tore his
37: 4 the words the LORD your God has **h**.
37: 6 Do not be afraid of what you have **h**
37: 8 the field commander **h** that the king
37: 9 When he **h** it, he sent messengers
37:11 Surely you have **h** what the kings of
37:26 "Have you not **h**? Long ago I ordained
38: 5 says: I have **h** your prayer and seen
39: 1 had **h** of his illness and recovery.
40:21 Do you not know? Have you not **h**?
40:28 Do you not know? Have you not **h**?
41:26 it, no-one **h** any words from you.
48: 6 You have **h** these things; look at
48: 7 you have not **h** of them before today.
48: 8 You have neither **h** nor understood;
52:15 have not **h**, they will understand.
58: 4 expect your voice to be **h** on high.
60:18 No longer will violence be **h** in your
64: 4 Since ancient times no-one has **h**,
65:19 of crying will be **h** in it no more.
66: 8 Who has ever **h** of such a thing?
66:19 not **h** of my fame or seen my glory.
Jer 3:21 A cry is **h** on the barren heights,
4:19 For I have **h** the sound of the
4:19 I have **h** the battle cry.
6:24 We have **h** reports about them, and
8:16 of the enemy's horses is **h** from Dan;
9:10 and the lowing of cattle is not **h**.
9:19 The sound of wailing is **h** from Zion:
18:13 Who has ever **h** anything like this?
18:22 Let a cry be **h** from their houses
20: 1 **h** Jeremiah prophesying these things,
22:20 let your voice be **h** in Bashan,
23:18 Who has listened and **h** his word?
23:25 "I have **h** what the prophets say who
26: 7 the prophets and all the people **h**
26:10 the officials of Judah **h** about these
26:11 You have **h** it with your own ears!"
26:12 this city all the things you have **h**.
26:21 officers and officials **h** his words,
26:21 Uriah **h** of it and fled in fear
30: 5 Cries of fear are **h**—terror, not
31: 7 Make your praises **h**, and say,
31:15 "A voice is **h** in Ramah, mourning
31:18 "I have surely **h** Ephraim's moaning:
33:10 animals, there will be **h** once
36:11 the son of Shaphan, **h** all the words
36:13 everything he had **h** Baruch read
36:16 they **h** all these words, they looked

Jer 36:24 The king and all his attendants who **h**
37: 5 Jerusalem **h** the report about them,
38: 1 and Pashhur son of Malkijah **h** what
38: 7 **h** that they had put Jeremiah into
38:27 **h** his conversation with the king.
40: 7 **h** that the king of Babylon had
40:11 Edom and all the other countries **h**
41:11 **h** about all the crimes Ishmael son
42: 4 "I have **h** you," replied Jeremiah
48: 5 cries over the destruction are **h**.
48:29 "We have **h** of Moab's pride—her
49:14 I have **h** a message from the LORD:
49:23 dismayed, for they have **h** bad news.
50:43 The king of Babylon has **h** reports
51:46 when rumours are **h** in the land;
Lam 1:21 "People have **h** my groaning, but
1:21 my enemies have **h** of my distress;
3:56 You **h** my plea: "Do not close your
3:61 O LORD, you have **h** their insults,
Eze 1:24 the creatures moved, I **h** the sound
1:28 and I **h** the voice of one speaking.
2: 2 my feet, and I **h** him speaking to me.
3:12 I **h** behind me a loud rumbling sound
9: 1 I **h** him call out in a loud voice,
10: 5 wings of the cherubim could be **h**
10:13 I **h** the wheels being called "the
19: 4 The nations **h** about him, and he was
19: 9 so his roar was **h** no longer on the
26:13 of your harps will be **h** no more.
33: 5 Since he **h** the sound of the trumpet
35:12 you will know that I the LORD have **h**
35:13 me without restraint, and I **h** it.
43: 6 I **h** someone speaking to me from
Da 3: 7 as soon as they **h** the sound of
5:14 I have **h** that the spirit of the gods
5:16 Now I have **h** that you are able to
6:14 the king **h** this, he was greatly
8:13 I **h** a holy one speaking, and another
8:16 I **h** a man's voice from the Ulai
10: 9 I **h** him speaking, and as I listened
10:12 your words were **h**, and I have come
12: 7 and I **h** him swear by him who lives
12: 8 I **h**, but I did not understand.
Ob : 1 We have **h** a message from the LORD:
Na 2:13 messengers will no longer be **h**."
Hab 3: 2 LORD, I have **h** of your fame; I stand
3:16 I **h** and my heart pounded, my lips
Zep 2: 8 "I have **h** the insults of Moab and
Zec 8:23 we have **h** that God is with you.
Mal 3:16 and the LORD listened and **h**.
Mt 2: 3 King Herod **h** this he was disturbed,
2: 9 After they had **h** the king, they went
2:18 "A voice is **h** in Ramah, weeping and
2:22 when he **h** that Archelaus was
4:12 Jesus **h** that John had been put in
5:21 "You have **h** that it was said to the
5:27 "You have **h** that it was said, 'Do
5:33 "Again, you have **h** that it was said
5:38 "You have **h** that it was said, 'Eye
5:43 "You have **h** that it was said, 'Love
6: 7 be **h** because of their many words.
8:10 Jesus **h** this, he was astonished and
11: 2 John **h** in prison what Christ was
12:24 when the Pharisees **h** this, they said,
14: 1 At that time Herod the tetrarch **h**
14:13 Jesus **h** what had happened, he
15:12 were offended when they **h** this?"
17: 6 the disciples **h** this, they fell face
19:22 the young man **h** this, he went away
19:25 the disciples **h** this, they were
20:24 the ten **h** about this, they were
20:30 and when they **h** that Jesus was going
21:45 the chief priests and the Pharisees **h**
22:22 they **h** this, they were amazed. So
22:33 the crowds **h** this, they were
26:65 Look, now you have **h** the blasphemy.
27:47 some of those standing there **h** this,
Mk 2: 1 the people **h** that he had come home.
3: 8 they **h** all he was doing, many people
3:21 his family **h** about this, they went
5:27 she **h** about Jesus, she came up
6: 2 and many who **h** him were amazed.
6:14 King Herod **h** about this, for
6:16 when Herod **h** this, he said, "John
6:20 When Herod **h** John, he was greatly
6:55 on mats to wherever they **h** he was.
Mk 7:25 In fact, as soon as she **h** about him,
10:41 the ten **h** about this, they became
10:47 he **h** that it was Jesus of Nazareth,
11:14 And his disciples **h** him say it.
11:18 the teachers of the law **h** this and
12:28 of the law came and **h** them debating.
14:58 "We **h** him say, 'I will destroy this
14:64 "You have **h** the blasphemy. What do
15:35 some of those standing near **h** this,
15:39 **h** his cry and saw how he died, he
16:11 they **h** that Jesus was alive and that
Lk 1:13 Zechariah; your prayer has been **h**.
1:41 Elizabeth **h** Mary's greeting, the
1:58 Her neighbours and relatives **h** that
1:66 Everyone who **h** this wondered about
2:18 all who **h** it were amazed at what the
2:20 all the things they had **h** and seen,
2:47 Everyone who **h** him was amazed at his
4:23 we have **h** that you did in Capernaum.
4:28 were furious when they **h** this.
7: 3 The centurion **h** of Jesus and sent
7: 9 Jesus **h** this, he was amazed at him,
7:22 to John what you have seen and **h**:
7:29 tax collectors, when they **h** Jesus'
9: 7 Now Herod the tetrarch **h** about all
12: 3 the dark will be **h** in the daylight,
14:15 one of those at the table with him **h**
15:25 the house, he **h** music and dancing.
16:14 The Pharisees, who loved money, **h**
18:22 Jesus **h** this, he said to him, "You
18:23 he **h** this, he became very sad,
18:26 Those who **h** this asked, "Who then
18:36 he **h** the crowd going by, he asked
20:16 When the people **h** this, they said,
22:71 We have **h** it from his own lips."
23: 8 From what he had **h** about him, he
Jn 1:37 the two disciples **h** him say this,
1:40 was one of the two who **h** what John
3:32 testifies to what he has seen and **h**
4: 1 The Pharisees **h** that Jesus was
4:42 said; now we have **h** for ourselves,
4:47 this man **h** that Jesus had arrived
5:37 never **h** his voice nor seen his form,
7:32 The Pharisees **h** the crowd whispering
8: 9 At this, those who **h** began to go
8:26 I have **h** from him I tell the world."
8:38 what you have **h** from your father."
8:40 you the truth that I **h** from God.
9:32 Nobody has ever **h** of opening the
9:35 Jesus **h** that they had thrown him out,
9:40 Some Pharisees who were with him **h**
11: 4 he **h** this, Jesus said, "This
11: 6 Yet when he **h** that Lazarus was sick,
11:20 Martha **h** that Jesus was coming, she
11:29 Mary **h** this, she got up quickly and
11:41 I thank you that you have **h** me.
12:12 **h** that Jesus was on his way to
12:18 Many people, because they had **h** that
12:29 The crowd that was there and **h** it
12:34 The crowd spoke up, "We have **h** from
14:28 "You **h** me say, 'I am going away and
18:21 Why question me? Ask those who **h** me.
19: 8 Pilate **h** this, he was even more
19:13 Pilate **h** this, he brought Jesus out
21: 7 Peter **h** him say, "It is the Lord,"
Ac 1: 4 which you have **h** me speak about.
1:19 Everyone in Jerusalem **h** about this,
2: 6 they **h** this sound, a crowd came
2: 6 **h** them speaking in his own language.
2:37 the people **h** this, they were cut to
4: 4 many who **h** the message believed, and
4:20 about what we have seen and **h**."
4:24 they **h** this, they raised their
5: 5 Ananias **h** this, he fell down and
5: 5 seized all who **h** what had happened.
5:11 and all who **h** about these events.
5:33 they **h** this, they were furious and
6:11 "We have **h** Stephen speak words of
6:14 For we have **h** him say that this
7:12 Jacob **h** that there was grain in
7:29 Moses **h** this, he fled to Midian,
7:31 more closely, he **h** the Lord's voice:
7:34 I have **h** their groaning and have
7:54 they **h** this, they were furious and
8: 6 the crowds **h** Philip and saw the
8:14 the apostles in Jerusalem **h** that
Ac 8:30 Philip ran up to the chariot and **h**
9: 4 He fell to the ground and **h** a voice
9: 7 **h** the sound but did not see anyone.
9:13 "Lord," Ananias answered, "I have **h**
9:21 All those who **h** him were astonished
9:38 disciples **h** that Peter was in Lydda,
10:31 said, 'Cornelius, God has **h** your
10:44 Spirit came on all who **h** the message.
10:46 For they **h** them speaking in tongues
11: 1 the brothers throughout Judea **h** that
11: 7 I **h** a voice telling me, 'Get up,
11:18 they **h** this, they had no further
13:48 the Gentiles **h** this, they were glad
14:14 the apostles Barnabas and Paul **h**
15:24 We have **h** that some went out from us
16:38 and when they **h** that Paul and Silas
17: 8 they **h** this, the crowd and the city
17:32 they **h** about the resurrection of the
18: 8 **h** him believed and were baptised.
18:26 When Priscilla and Aquila **h** him,
19: 2 even **h** that there is a Holy Spirit.
19:10 of Asia **h** the word of the Lord.
19:28 they **h** this, they were furious and
21:12 we **h** this, we and the people there
21:20 they **h** this, they praised God. Then
22: 2 they **h** him speak to them in Aramaic,
22: 7 I fell to the ground and **h** a voice
22:15 all men of what you have seen and **h**.
22:26 the centurion **h** this, he went to the
23:16 when the son of Paul's sister **h** of
26:14 We all fell to the ground, and I **h**
28:15 The brothers there had **h** that we
Ro 10:14 the one of whom they have not **h**?
10:17 is **h** through the word of Christ.
15:21 who have not **h** will understand."
16:19 Everyone has **h** about your obedience
1Co 2: 9 "No eye has seen, no ear has **h**,
2Co 6: 2 "In the time of my favour I **h** you,
12: 4 He **h** inexpressible things, things
Gal 1:13 For you have **h** of my previous way
1:23 They only **h** the report: "The man who
3: 2 the law, or by believing what you **h**?
3: 5 or because you believe what you **h**?
Eph 1:13 Christ when you **h** the word of truth,
1:15 For this reason, ever since I **h**
3: 2 Surely you have **h** about the
4:21 Surely you **h** of him and were taught
Php 2:26 distressed because you **h** he was ill.
4: 9 learned or received or **h** from me,
Col 1: 4 we have **h** of your faith in Christ
1: 5 **h** about in the word of truth,
1: 6 among you since the day you **h** it
1: 9 For this reason, since the day we **h**
1:23 This is the gospel that you **h** and
1Th 2:13 which you **h** from us, you accepted
2Ti 1:13 What you **h** from me, keep as the
2: 2 the things you have **h** me say in the
Heb 2: 1 to what we have **h**, so that we
2: 3 confirmed to us by those who **h** him.
3:16 Who were they who **h** and rebelled?
4: 2 they **h** was of no value to them,
4: 2 who **h** did not combine it with faith.
5: 7 **h** because of his reverent submission.
12:19 that those who **h** it begged that no
Jas 1:25 not forgetting what he has **h**, but
5:11 You have **h** of Job's perseverance and
2Pe 1:18 We ourselves **h** this voice that came
2: 8 by the lawless deeds he saw and **h**)
1Jn 1: 1 which we have **h**, which we have seen
1: 3 to you what we have seen and **h**,
1: 5 This is the message we have **h** from
2: 7 command is the message you have **h**.
2:18 **h** that the antichrist is coming,
2:24 See that what you have **h** from the
3:11 This is the message you **h** from the
4: 3 which you have **h** is coming and even
2Jn : 6 As you have **h** from the beginning,
Rev 1:10 and I **h** behind me a loud voice like
3: 3 received and **h**; obey it, and repent.
4: 1 And the voice I had first **h** speaking
5:11 I looked and **h** the voice of many
5:13 I **h** every creature in heaven and on
6: 1 Then I **h** one of the four living
6: 3 Lamb opened the second seal, I **h**
6: 5 Lamb opened the third seal, I **h**
6: 6 I **h** what sounded like a voice among

Rev 6: 7 Lamb opened the fourth seal, I **h**
7: 4 I **h** the number of those who were
8:13 I watched, I **h** an eagle that was
9:13 and I **h** a voice coming from the
9:16 I **h** their number.
10: 4 I was about to write; but I **h** a
10: 8 the voice that I had **h** from heaven
11:12 they **h** a loud voice from heaven
12:10 I **h** a loud voice in heaven say:
14: 2 I **h** a sound from heaven like the
14: 2 The sound I **h** was like that of
14:13 **h** a voice from heaven say, "Write
16: 1 I **h** a loud voice from the temple
16: 5 I **h** the angel in charge of the
16: 7 I **h** the altar respond: "Yes, Lord
18: 4 I **h** another voice from heaven say:
18:22 will never be **h** in you again.
18:22 will never be **h** in you again.
18:23 bride will never be **h** in you again.
19: 1 After this I **h** what sounded like
19: 6 I **h** what sounded like a great
21: 3 I **h** a loud voice from the throne
22: 8 I, John, am the one who **h** and saw
22: 8 And when I had **h** and seen them, I

Hearers (Hear)

1Ti 4:16 will save both yourself and your **h**.

Hearing (Hear)

Ge 23:10 he replied to Abraham in the **h** of
23:13 he said to Ephron in their **h**,
23:16 had named in the **h** of the Hittites:
Nu 11: 1 hardships in the **h** of the LORD,
Dt 5: 1 the laws I declare in your **h** today.
31:11 this law before them in their **h**.
31:28 I can speak these words in their **h**
31:30 **h** of the whole assembly of Israel:
32:44 of this song in the **h** of the people.
Jdg 9:46 On **h** this, the citizens in the tower
1Sa 4: 6 **H** the uproar, the Philistines asked,
17:11 On **h** the Philistine's words, Saul
2Sa 10: 7 On **h** this, David sent Joab out with
18:12 In our **h** the king commanded you and
1Ki 1:41 On **h** the sound of the trumpet, Joab
2Ki 18:26 in the **h** of the people on the wall.
23: 2 He read in their **h** all the words of
1Ch 19: 8 On **h** this, David sent Joab out with
28: 8 and in the **h** of our God: Be careful
2Ch 34:30 He read in their **h** all the words of
Ne 13: 1 read aloud in the **h** of the people
Job 9:16 do not believe he would give me a **h**.
33: 8 "But you have said in my **h**—I heard
Ecc 1: 8 seeing, nor the ear its fill of **h**.
Isa 5: 9 LORD Almighty has declared in my **h**:
6: 9 Be ever **h**, but never understanding;
22:14 Almighty has revealed this in my **h**:
36:11 in the **h** of the people on the wall.
49:20 bereavement will yet say in your **h**,
Jer 2: 2 "Go and proclaim in the **h** of
26:15 speak all these words in your **h**."
28: 7 **h** and in the **h** of all the people:
Da 5:10 The queen, **h** the voices of the king
Am 8:11 a famine of **h** the words of the LORD.
Mt 9:12 On **h** this, Jesus said, "It is not
13:13 though **h**, they do not hear or
13:14 'You will be ever **h** but never
14:13 **H** of this, the crowds followed him
22:34 **H** that Jesus had silenced the
Mk 2:17 On **h** this, Jesus said to them, "It
4:12 and ever **h** but never understanding;
6:29 On **h** of this, John's disciples came
Lk 4:21 scripture is fulfilled in your **h**."
7: 1 all this in the **h** of the people,
8:10 though **h**, they may not understand.
8:50 **H** this, Jesus said to Jairus, "Don't
23: 6 On **h** this, Pilate asked if the man
Jn 6:60 On **h** it, many of his disciples said,
7:40 On **h** his words, some of the people
7:51 **h** him to find out what he is doing?"
Ac 5:24 On **h** this report, the captain of the
19: 5 On **h** this, they were baptised into
28:26 "You will be ever **h** but never
Ro 10:17 Consequently, faith comes from **h** the
1Co 12:17 where would the sense of **h** be? If

Hears (Hear)

Ge 21: 6 **h** about this will laugh with me."
Ex 17:14 and make sure that Joshua **h** it,
Lev 5: 1 he **h** a public charge to testify
Nu 24: 4 the oracle of one who **h** the words of
24:16 the oracle of one who **h** the words of
30: 4 her father **h** about her vow or pledge
30: 5 if her father forbids her when he **h**
30: 7 her husband **h** about it but says
30: 8 if her husband forbids her when he **h**
30:11 her husband **h** about it but says
30:12 nullifies them when he **h** about them,
30:14 nothing to her when he **h** about them.
30:15 some time after he **h** about them,
Dt 29:19 such a person **h** the words of this
1Sa 3:11 ears of everyone who **h** of it tingle
2Sa 17: 9 whoever **h** about it will say, 'There
2Ki 19: 7 him that when he **h** a certain report,
21:12 of everyone who **h** of it will tingle.
Ps 34:17 righteous cry out, and the LORD **h**
55:17 out in distress, and he **h** my voice.
69:33 The LORD **h** the needy and does not
97: 8 Zion **h** and rejoices and the villages
145:19 him; he **h** their cry and saves them.
Pr 13: 8 life, but a poor man **h** no threat.
15:29 he **h** the prayer of the righteous.
25:10 he who **h** it may shame you and you
Isa 11: 3 decide by what he **h** with his ears;
30:19 As soon as he **h**, he will answer you.
37: 7 so that when he **h** a certain report,
Jer 19: 3 ears of everyone who **h** of it tingle.
Eze 33: 4 if anyone **h** the trumpet but does not
Da 3:10 O king, that everyone who **h** the
Na 3:19 Everyone who **h** the news about you
Mt 7:24 "Therefore everyone who **h** these
7:26 everyone who **h** these words of mine
13:19 anyone **h** the message about the
13:20 places is the man who **h** the word
13:22 thorns is the man who **h** the word,
13:23 who **h** the word and understands it.
Lk 6:47 **h** my words and puts them into
6:49 the one who **h** my words and does not
Jn 3:29 when he **h** the bridegroom's voice.
5:24 whoever **h** my word and believes him
8:47 He who belongs to God **h** what God
12:47 "As for the person who **h** my words
16:13 he will speak only what he **h**,
Ac 2: 8 how is it that each of us **h** them
1Jn 5:14 according to his will, he **h** us.
5:15 if we know that he **h** us—whatever
Rev 3:20 If anyone **h** my voice and opens the
22:17 And let him who **h** say, "Come!
22:18 I warn everyone who **h** the words of

Heart (Broken-hearted, Disheartened, Downhearted, Faint-hearted, Hard-hearted, Heart's, Heartache, Hearts, Hearts', Kind-hearted, *New heart*, Simple-hearted, Stout-hearted, Stubborn-hearted, Wholehearted, Wholeheartedly)

Ge 6: 5 his **h** was only evil all the time.
6: 6 and his **h** was filled with pain.
8:21 pleasing aroma and said in his **h**:
8:21 inclination of his **h** is evil
24:45 Before I finished praying in my **h**,
34: 3 His **h** was drawn to Dinah daughter of
34: 8 has his **h** set on your daughter.
Ex 4:14 his **h** will be glad when he sees you.
4:21 But I will harden his **h** so that he
7: 3 I will harden Pharaoh's **h**, and
7:13 Yet Pharaoh's **h** became hard and he
7:14 "Pharaoh's **h** is unyielding; he
7:22 and Pharaoh's **h** became hard; he
7:23 and did not take even this to **h**.
8:15 he hardened his **h** and would not
8:19 But Pharaoh's **h** was hard and he
8:32 this time also Pharaoh hardened his **h**
9: 7 Yet his **h** was unyielding and he
9:12 the LORD hardened Pharaoh's **h** and he
9:35 Pharaoh's **h** was hard and he would
10: 1 for I have hardened his **h** and the
10:20 the LORD hardened Pharaoh's **h**, and
10:27 the LORD hardened Pharaoh's **h**, and
11:10 but the LORD hardened Pharaoh's **h**,
Ex 14: 4 I will harden Pharaoh's **h**, and he
14: 8 The LORD hardened the **h** of Pharaoh
15: 8 congealed in the **h** of the sea.
25: 2 man whose **h** prompts him to give.
28:29 of the sons of Israel over his **h**
28:30 so they may be over Aaron's **h**
28:30 over his **h** before the LORD.
35:21 was willing and whose **h** moved him
Lev 19:17 Do not hate your brother in your **h**
Dt 1:28 Our brothers have made us lose **h**.
2:30 his **h** obstinate in order to give him
4: 9 from your **h** as long as you live.
4:29 all your **h** and with all your soul.
4:39 Acknowledge and take to **h** this day
6: 5 the LORD your God with all your **h**
8: 2 in order to know what was in your **h**,
8: 5 Know then in your **h** that as a man
8:14 your **h** will become proud and you
10:12 all your **h** and with all your soul,
11: 3 the things he did in the **h** of Egypt,
11:13 all your **h** and with all your soul—
13: 3 all your **h** and with all your soul.
15:10 him and do so without a grudging **h**;
17:17 or his **h** will be led astray
26:16 all your **h** and with all your soul.
28:65 with longing, and a despairing **h**.
29:18 whose **h** turns away from the LORD
30: 1 you take them to **h** wherever the LORD
30: 2 obey him with all your **h** and with
30: 6 **h** and with all your soul, and live.
30:10 all your **h** and with all your soul.
30:14 in your **h** so that you may obey it.
30:17 if your **h** turns away and you are not
32:46 he said to them, "Take to **h** all the
Jos 22: 5 with all your **h** and all your soul."
23:14 You know with all your **h** and soul
Jdg 5: 9 My **h** is with Israel's princes, with
5:15 Reuben there was much searching of **h**
5:16 Reuben there was much searching of **h**
1Sa 1:13 Hannah was praying in her **h**, and her
2: 1 Hannah prayed and said: "My **h**
2:33 with tears and to grieve your **h**,
2:35 to what is in my **h** and mind.
4:13 his **h** feared for the ark of God.
9:19 will tell you all that is in your **h**.
10: 9 God changed Saul's **h**, and all these
12:20 but serve the LORD with all your **h**.
12:24 him faithfully with all your **h**;
13:14 sought out a man after his own **h**
14: 7 "Go ahead; I am with you **h** and soul
16: 7 but the LORD looks at the **h**."
17:28 you are and how wicked your **h** is;
17:32 "Let no-one lose **h** on account of
21:12 David took these words to **h** and was
25:37 and his **h** failed him and he became
28: 5 he was afraid; terror filled his **h**.
2Sa 3:21 rule over all that your **h** desires.
6:16 the LORD, she despised him in her **h**.
13:20 Don't take this thing to **h**." And
14: 1 the king's **h** longed for Absalom.
17:10 whose **h** is like the **h** of a lion,
18:14 plunged them into Absalom's **h** while
22:46 They all lose **h**; they come trembling
1Ki 2: 4 before me with all their **h** and soul,
2:44 "You know in your **h** all the wrong
3: 6 you and righteous and upright in **h**.
3: 9 give your servant a discerning **h** to
3:12 give you a wise and discerning **h**,
8:17 "My father David had it in his **h** to
8:18 'Because it was in your **h** to build a
8:18 you did well to have this in your **h**.
8:38 of the afflictions of his own **h**,
8:39 since you know his **h** (for you alone
8:47 if they have a change of **h** in the
8:48 turn back to you with all their **h**
8:66 joyful and glad in **h** for all the
9: 3 eyes and my **h** will always be there.
9: 4 in integrity of **h** and uprightness,
10:24 the wisdom God had put in his **h**.
11: 4 his wives turned his **h** after other
11: 4 and his **h** was not fully devoted to
11: 4 the **h** of David his father had been.
11: 9 his **h** had turned away from the LORD,
11:37 rule over all that your **h** desires;
14: 8 and followed me with all his **h**,
15: 3 his **h** was not fully devoted to the

1Ki 15: 3 **h** of David his forefather had been.
15:14 Asa's **h** was fully committed to the
2Ki 9:24 arrow pierced his **h** and he slumped
10:31 the God of Israel, with all his **h**.
22:19 your **h** was responsive and you
23: 3 with all his **h** and all his soul,
23:25 all his **h** and with all his soul
1Ch 15:29 she despised him in her **h**.
22: 7 "My son, I had it in my **h** to build
22:19 Now devote your **h** and soul to
28: 2 I had it in my **h** to build a house
28: 9 for the LORD searches every **h** and
29:17 I know, my God, that you test the **h**
2Ch 6: 7 "My father David had it in his **h** to
6: 8 'Because it was in your **h** to build a
6: 8 you did well to have this in your **h**.
6:30 since you know his **h** (for you alone
6:37 if they have a change of **h** in the
6:38 turn back to you with all their **h**
7:10 joyful and glad in **h** for the good
7:16 eyes and my **h** will always be there.
9:23 the wisdom God had put in his **h**.
12:14 not set his **h** on seeking the LORD.
15:12 fathers, with all their **h** and soul.
15:17 Asa's **h** was fully committed to the
17: 6 His **h** was devoted to the ways of
19: 3 and have set your **h** on seeking God.
22: 9 who sought the LORD with all his **h**.
30:19 who sets his **h** on seeking God—the
32:25 Hezekiah's **h** was proud and he did
32:26 repented of the pride of his **h**,
32:31 know everything that was in his **h**.
34:27 your **h** was responsive and you
34:31 with all his **h** and all his soul,
36:13 hardened his **h** and would not turn
36:22 the LORD moved the **h** of Cyrus king
Ezr 1: 1 the LORD moved the **h** of Cyrus king
1: 5 everyone whose **h** God had moved
7:27 who has put it into the king's **h** to
Ne 2: 2 This can be nothing but sadness of **h**.
2:12 had put in my **h** to do for Jerusalem.
4: 6 the people worked with all their **h**.
7: 5 my God put it into my **h** to assemble
9: 8 You found his **h** faithful to you, and
Job 10:13 is what you concealed in your **h**,
11:13 "Yet if you devote your **h** to him and
15:12 Why has your **h** carried you away, and
17:11 and so are the desires of my **h**.
19:27 How my **h** yearns within me!
22:22 and lay up his words in your **h**.
23:16 God has made my **h** faint; the
29:13 me; I made the widow's **h** sing.
31: 7 if my **h** has been led by my eyes, or
31: 9 "If my **h** has been enticed by a woman,
31:20 his **h** did not bless me for warming
31:27 that my **h** was secretly enticed and
31:33 men do, by hiding my guilt in my **h**
33: 3 My words come from an upright **h**; my
36:13 The godless in **h** harbour resentment
37: 1 "At this my **h** pounds and leaps from
37:24 have regard for all the wise in **h**?"
38:36 Who endowed the **h** with wisdom or
Ps 4: 7 You have filled my **h** with greater
5: 9 their **h** is filled with destruction.
7:10 High, who saves the upright in **h**.
9: 1 praise you, O LORD, with all my **h**;
10: 3 He boasts of the cravings of his **h**;
11: 2 the shadows at the upright in **h**.
13: 2 and every day have sorrow in my **h**?
13: 5 my **h** rejoices in your salvation
14: 1 The fool says in his **h**, "There is no
15: 2 who speaks the truth from his **h**
16: 7 even at night my **h** instructs me.
16: 9 Therefore my **h** is glad and my tongue
17: 3 Though you probe my **h** and examine me
18:45 They all lose **h**; they come trembling
19: 8 LORD are right, giving joy to the **h**.
19:14 of my **h** be pleasing in your sight,
20: 4 May he give you the desire of your **h**
21: 2 granted him the desire of his **h**
22:14 My **h** has turned to wax; it has
24: 4 He who has clean hands and a pure **h**,
25:17 The troubles of my **h** have multiplied;
26: 2 try me, examine my **h** and my mind;
27: 3 army besiege me, my **h** will not fear
27: 8 My **h** says of you, "Seek his face!"
Ps 27:14 and take **h** and wait for the LORD.
28: 7 my **h** trusts in him, and I am helped.
28: 7 My **h** leaps for joy and I will give
30:12 my **h** may sing to you and not be
31:24 Be strong and take **h**, all you who
32:11 sing, all you who are upright in **h**!
33:11 of his **h** through all generations.
36: 1 An oracle is within my **h** concerning
36:10 righteousness to the upright in **h**.
37: 4 will give you the desires of your **h**.
37:31 The law of his God is in his **h**; his
38: 8 crushed; I groan in anguish of **h**.
38:10 My **h** pounds, my strength fails me;
39: 3 My **h** grew hot within me, and as I
40: 8 O my God; your law is within my **h**.
40:10 not hide your righteousness in my **h**
40:12 my head, and my **h** fails within me.
41: 6 while his **h** gathers slander
44:21 since he knows the secrets of the **h**?
45: 1 My **h** is stirred by a noble theme
46: 2 fall into the **h** of the sea,
49: 3 from my **h** will give understanding.
51:10 Create in me a pure **h**, O God, and
51:17 a broken and contrite **h**, O God,
53: 1 fool says in his **h**, "There is no
55: 4 My **h** is in anguish within me; the
55:21 yet war is in his **h**; his words are
57: 7 My **h** is steadfast, O God, my **h** is
58: 2 No, in your **h** you devise injustice,
61: 2 I call as my **h** grows faint; lead me
62:10 increase, do not set your **h** on them.
64: 6 the mind and **h** of man are cunning.
64:10 let all the upright in **h** praise him!
66:18 If I had cherished sin in my **h**, the
69:20 Scorn has broken my **h** and has left
73: 1 Israel, to those who are pure in **h**.
73:13 Surely in vain have I kept my **h** pure;
73:21 my **h** was grieved and my spirit
73:26 My flesh and my **h** may fail, but God
73:26 of my **h** and my portion for ever.
77: 6 My **h** mused and my spirit enquired:
78:72 shepherded them with integrity of **h**;
84: 2 my **h** and my flesh cry out for the
86:11 give me an undivided **h**, that I may
86:12 O LORD my God, with all my **h**;
89:50 bear in my **h** the taunts of all the
90:12 that we may gain a **h** of wisdom.
94:15 all the upright in **h** will follow it.
97:11 and joy on the upright in **h**.
101: 2 walk in my house with blameless **h**.
101: 4 Men of perverse **h** shall be far from
101: 5 a proud **h**, him will I not endure.
102: 4 My **h** is blighted and withered like
104:15 wine that gladdens the **h** of man,
104:15 and bread that sustains his **h**.
108: 1 My **h** is steadfast, O God; I will
109:22 I am poor and needy, and my **h** is
111: 1 I will extol the LORD with all my **h**
112: 7 **h** is steadfast, trusting in the LORD.
112: 8 His **h** is secure, he will have no
119: 2 and seek him with all their **h**.
119: 7 I will praise you with an upright **h**
119:10 I seek you with all my **h**; do not let
119:11 I have hidden your word in my **h** that
119:30 I have set my **h** on your laws.
119:32 for you have set my **h** free.
119:34 your law and obey it with all my **h**.
119:36 Turn my **h** towards your statutes and
119:58 I have sought your face with all my **h**
119:69 I keep your precepts with all my **h**.
119:80 May my **h** be blameless towards your
119:111 for ever; they are the joy of my **h**.
119:112 My **h** is set on keeping your decrees
119:145 I call with all my **h**; answer me,
119:161 but my **h** trembles at your word.
125: 4 good, to those who are upright in **h**.
131: 1 My **h** is not proud, O LORD, my eyes
138: 1 praise you, O LORD, with all my **h**
139:23 Search me, O God, and know my **h**;
141: 4 Let not my **h** be drawn to what is
143: 4 my **h** within me is dismayed
148:14 Israel, the people close to his **h**.
Pr 1:23 I would have poured out my **h** to you
2: 2 applying your **h** to understanding,
2:10 For wisdom will enter your **h**, and
3: 1 but keep my commands in your **h**,
Pr 3: 3 write them on the tablet of your **h**.
3: 5 Trust in the LORD with all your **h**
4: 4 Lay hold of my words with all your **h**;
4:21 your sight, keep them within your **h**;
4:23 Above all else, guard your **h**, for it
5:12 How my **h** spurned correction!
6:14 who plots evil with deceit in his **h**
6:18 a **h** that devises wicked schemes,
6:21 Bind them upon your **h** for ever;
6:25 Do not lust in your **h** after her
7: 3 write them on the tablet of your **h**.
7:25 Do not let your **h** turn to her ways
10: 8 The wise in **h** accept commands, but
10:20 **h** of the wicked is of little value.
11:20 The LORD detests men of perverse **h**
12:23 but the **h** of fools blurts out folly.
12:25 An anxious **h** weighs a man down, but
13:12 Hope deferred makes the **h** sick, but
14:10 Each **h** knows its own bitterness, and
14:13 Even in laughter the **h** may ache, and
14:30 A **h** at peace gives life to the body,
14:33 Wisdom reposes in the **h** of the
15:13 A happy **h** makes the face cheerful,
15:14 The discerning **h** seeks knowledge,
15:15 cheerful **h** has a continual feast.
15:28 The **h** of the righteous weighs its
15:30 A cheerful look brings joy to the **h**,
16: 1 To man belong the plans of the **h**,
16: 5 The LORD detests all the proud of **h**.
16: 9 In his **h** a man plans his course, but
16:21 The wise in **h** are called discerning,
16:23 A wise man's **h** guides his mouth, and
17: 3 for gold, but the LORD tests the **h**.
17:20 A man of perverse **h** does not prosper;
17:22 A cheerful **h** is good medicine, but a
18:12 his downfall a man's **h** is proud
18:15 The **h** of the discerning acquires
19: 3 yet his **h** rages against the LORD.
19:21 Many are the plans in a man's **h**,
20: 5 The purposes of a man's **h** are deep
20: 9 Who can say, "I have kept my **h** pure
21: 1 The king's **h** is in the hand of the
21: 2 to him, but the LORD weighs the **h**.
21: 4 Haughty eyes and a proud **h**, the lamp
22:11 He who loves a pure **h** and whose
22:15 Folly is bound up in the **h** of a
22:17 wise; apply your **h** to what I teach,
22:18 when you keep them in your **h**
23: 7 to you, but his **h** is not with you.
23:12 Apply your **h** to instruction and your
23:15 if your **h** is wise, then my **h** will be
23:17 Do not let your **h** envy sinners, but
23:19 and keep your **h** on the right path.
23:26 My son, give me your **h** and let your
24:12 not he who weighs the **h** perceive it?
24:17 stumbles, do not let your **h** rejoice,
24:32 I applied my **h** to what I observed
25:20 one who sings songs to a heavy **h**.
26:23 are fervent lips with an evil **h**.
26:24 but in his **h** he harbours deceit.
26:25 for seven abominations fill his **h**.
27: 9 and incense bring joy to the **h**,
27:11 my son, and bring joy to my **h**; then
27:19 water reflects a face, so a man's **h**
28:14 hardens his **h** falls into trouble.
Ecc 2: 1 I thought in my **h**, "Come now, I will
2: 8 well—the delights of the **h** of man.
2:10 desired; I refused my **h** no pleasure.
2:10 My **h** took delight in all my work,
2:15 I thought in my **h**, "The fate of the
2:15 I said in my **h**, "This too is
2:20 my **h** began to despair over all my
3:17 I thought in my **h**, "God will bring
5: 2 hasty in your **h** to utter anything
5:20 him occupied with gladness of **h**.
6: 2 he lacks nothing his **h** desires
7: 2 the living should take this to **h**.
7: 3 a sad face is good for the **h**.
7: 4 The **h** of the wise is in the house
7: 4 but the **h** of fools is in the house
7: 7 a fool, and a bribe corrupts the **h**.
7:22 for you know in your **h** that many
7:26 whose **h** is a trap and whose hands
8: 5 and the wise **h** will know the proper
9: 7 and drink your wine with a joyful **h**,
10: 2 The **h** of the wise inclines to the

Ecc 10: 2 but the **h** of the fool to the left.
11: 9 let your **h** give you joy in the days
11: 9 Follow the ways of your **h** and
11:10 banish anxiety from your **h** and
SS 3: 1 I looked for the one my **h** loves;
3: 2 I will search for the one my **h** loves.
3: 3 "Have you seen the one my **h** loves?"
3: 4 when I found the one my **h** loves.
3:11 his wedding, the day his **h** rejoiced.
4: 9 You have stolen my **h**, my sister, my
4: 9 my bride; you have stolen my **h** with
5: 2 I slept but my **h** was awake. Listen!
5: 4 my **h** began to pound for him.
5: 6 My **h** sank at his departure. I looked
8: 6 Place me like a seal over your **h**,
Isa 1: 5 is injured, your whole **h** afflicted.
6:10 Make the **h** of this people calloused;
7: 4 Do not lose **h** because of these two
9: 9 say with pride and arrogance of **h**,
10:12 for the wilful pride of his **h**
13: 7 go limp, every man's **h** will melt.
14:13 You said in your **h**, "I will ascend
15: 5 My **h** cries out over Moab; her
16:11 My **h** laments for Moab like a harp,
19: 3 The Egyptians will lose **h**, and I
19:10 the wage earners will be sick at **h**.
19:19 altar to the LORD in the **h** of Egypt,
21: 4 My **h** falters, fear makes me tremble;
40:11 and carries them close to his **h**;
42:25 but they did not take it to **h**.
44:20 a deluded **h** misleads him;
46: 8 in mind, take it to **h**, you rebels.
49:21 you will say in your **h**, 'Who bore me
57: 1 and no-one ponders it in his **h**;
57:15 and to revive the **h** of the contrite.
60: 5 your **h** will throb and swell with joy
63: 4 For the day of vengeance was in my **h**,
65:14 you will cry out from anguish of **h**
66:14 you see this, your **h** will rejoice
Jer 3:10 did not return to me with all her **h**
3:15 give you shepherds after my own **h**,
4: 9 king and the officials will lose **h**,
4:14 the evil from your **h** and be saved.
4:18 it is! How it pierces to the **h**!"
4:19 Oh, the agony of my **h**! My **h** pounds
8:18 my **h** is faint within me.
9: 8 but in his **h** he sets a trap for him.
9:26 of Israel is uncircumcised in **h**."
11:20 righteously and test the **h** and mind,
15: 1 **h** would not go out to this people.
16:12 of his evil **h** instead of obeying me.
17: 5 whose **h** turns away from the LORD.
17: 9 The **h** is deceitful above all things
17:10 "I the LORD search the **h** and examine
18:12 the stubbornness of his evil **h**.
20: 9 his word is in my **h** like a fire,
20:12 righteous and probe the **h** and mind,
22:17 "But your eyes and your **h** are set
23: 9 My **h** is broken within me; all my
23:20 accomplishes the purposes of his **h**.
24: 7 I will give them a **h** to know me,
24: 7 will return to me with all their **h**.
29:13 when you seek me with all your **h**.
30:24 accomplishes the purposes of his **h**.
31:20 Therefore my **h** yearns for him;
32:39 I will give them singleness of **h**
32:41 in this land with all my **h** and soul.
48:29 and the haughtiness of her **h**.
48:36 "So my **h** laments for Moab like a
48:41 be like the **h** of a woman in labour.
49:16 pride of your **h** have deceived you,
49:22 be like the **h** of a woman in labour.
51:46 Do not lose **h** or be afraid when
Lam 1:20 and in my **h** I am disturbed, for I
1:22 groans are many and my **h** is faint."
2:11 my **h** is poured out on the ground
2:19 pour out your **h** like water in the
3:13 He pierced my **h** with arrows from
Eze 3:10 take to **h** all the words I speak
11:19 I will give them an undivided **h** and
11:19 remove from them their **h** of stone
11:19 and give them a **h** of flesh.
14: 4 Israelite sets up idols in his **h**
14: 7 sets up idols in his **h** and puts a
21: 6 them with broken **h** and bitter grief.
21: 7 Every **h** will melt and every hand go
Eze 25: 6 your **h** against the land of Israel,
27:25 heavy cargo in the **h** of the sea.
27:26 you to pieces in the **h** of the sea.
27:27 will sink into the **h** of the sea
28: 2 'In the pride of your **h** you say,
28: 2 of a god in the **h** of the seas.
28: 5 your wealth your **h** has grown proud.
28: 8 violent death in the **h** of the seas.
28:17 Your **h** became proud on account of
36:26 **h** of stone and give you a **h** of flesh.
44: 7 uncircumcised in **h** and flesh
44: 9 uncircumcised in **h** and flesh
Da 5:20 when his **h** became arrogant and
7: 4 and the **h** of a man was given to it.
11:28 but his **h** will be set against the
11:30 will oppose him, and he will lose **h**.
Hos 5: 4 of prostitution is in their **h**;
10: 2 Their **h** is deceitful, and now they
11: 8 Zeboiim? My **h** is changed within me;
Joel 2:12 "return to me with all your **h**, with
2:13 Rend your **h** and not your garments.
Am 7:10 against you in the very **h** of Israel.
Ob : 3 The pride of your **h** has deceived you,
Jnh 2: 3 into the very **h** of the seas, and the
Hab 3:16 I heard and my **h** pounded, my lips
Zep 3:14 rejoice with all your **h**, O Daughter
Mal 2: 2 not set your **h** to honour my name
2: 2 have not set your **h** to honour me.
Mt 5: 8 Blessed are the pure in **h**, for they
5:28 adultery with her in his **h**.
6:21 is, there your **h** will be also.
9: 2 Take **h**, son; your sins are forgiven.
9:22 Jesus turned and saw her. "Take **h**,
11:29 for I am gentle and humble in **h**, and
12:34 overflow of the **h** the mouth speaks.
12:40 three nights in the **h** of the earth.
13:15 For this people's **h** has become
13:19 away what was sown in his **h**.
15:18 out of the mouth come from the **h**,
15:19 out of the **h** come evil thoughts,
18:35 forgive your brother from your **h**."
22:37 the Lord your God with all your **h**
Mk 7:19 For it doesn't go into his **h** but
11:23 does not doubt in his **h** but believes
12:30 the Lord your God with all your **h**
12:33 To love him with all your **h**, with
Lk 2:19 things and pondered them in her **h**.
2:51 treasured all these things in her **h**
6:45 out of the good stored up in his **h**,
6:45 out of the evil stored up in his **h**.
6:45 overflow of his **h** his mouth speaks.
7:13 the Lord saw her, his **h** went out
8:15 for those with a noble and good **h**,
10:27 the Lord your God with all your **h**
12:29 do not set your **h** on what you will
12:34 is, there your **h** will be also.
24:25 and how slow of **h** to believe all
Jn 12:27 "Now my **h** is troubled, and what
16:33 take **h**! I have overcome the world."
Ac 1:24 "Lord, you know everyone's **h**.
2:26 Therefore my **h** is glad and my tongue
2:37 they were cut to the **h** and said to
4:32 All the believers were one in **h** and
5: 3 Satan has so filled your **h** that you
8:21 your **h** is not right before God.
8:22 having such a thought in your **h**.
13:22 son of Jesse a man after my own **h**;
15: 8 God, who knows the **h**, showed that
16:14 her **h** to respond to Paul's message.
21:13 are you weeping and breaking my **h**?
28:27 For this people's **h** has become
Ro 1: 9 God, whom I serve with my whole **h**
2: 5 stubbornness and your unrepentant **h**
2:29 is circumcision of the **h**,
9: 2 and unceasing anguish in my **h**.
10: 6 "Do not say in your **h**, 'Who will
10: 8 it is in your mouth and in your **h**,
10: 9 believe in your **h** that God raised
10:10 For it is with your **h** that you
15: 6 that with one **h** and mouth you may
1Co 14:25 the secrets of his **h** will be laid
2Co 2: 4 anguish of **h** and with many tears,
4: 1 this ministry, we do not lose **h**.
4:16 Therefore we do not lose **h**. Though
5:12 rather than in what is in the **h**.
8:16 God, who put into the **h** of Titus
2Co 9: 7 he has decided in his **h** to give,
Eph 1:18 pray also that the eyes of your **h**
5:19 make music in your **h** to the Lord,
6: 5 sincerity of **h**, just as you would
6: 6 doing the will of God from your **h**.
Php 1: 7 since I have you in my **h**; for
Col 2: 2 encouraged in **h** and united in love,
3:22 sincerity of **h** and reverence
3:23 work at it with all your **h**, as
1Ti 1: 5 which comes from a pure **h** and
3: 1 sets his **h** on being an overseer,
2Ti 2:22 call on the Lord out of a pure **h**.
Phm :12 am sending him—who is my very **h**
:20 in the Lord; refresh my **h** in Christ.
Heb 3:12 unbelieving **h** that turns away from
4:12 thoughts and attitudes of the **h**.
10:22 a sincere **h** in full assurance
12: 3 you will not grow weary and lose **h**.
12: 5 do not lose **h** when he rebukes you,
1Pe 1:22 love one another deeply, from the **h**.
1Jn 5:10 of God has this testimony in his **h**.
Rev 1: 3 and take to **h** what is written in it,
18: 7 In her **h** she boasts, 'I sit as queen;

Heart's (Heart)

2Ch 1:11 "Since this is your **h** desire and you
Jer 15:16 they were my joy and my **h** delight,
Eze 24:25 of their eyes, their **h** desire,
Ro 10: 1 Brothers, my **h** desire and prayer to

Heartache (Heart)

Pr 15:13 cheerful, but **h** crushes the spirit.

Hearth

Lev 6: 9 on the altar **h** throughout the night,
Isa 29: 2 she will be to me like an altar **h**.
30:14 for taking coals from a **h** or
Eze 43:15 The altar **h** is four cubits high, and
43:15 horns project upward from the **h**.
43:16 The altar **h** is square, twelve cubits

Heartless

Lam 4: 3 **h** like ostriches in the desert.
Ro 1:31 they are senseless, faithless, **h**,

Hearts (Heart)

Ge 42:28 Their **h** sank and they turned to
Ex 9:34 and his officials hardened their **h**.
10: 1 the **h** of his officials so that I may
14:17 I will harden the **h** of the Egyptians
Lev 26:36 I will make their **h** so fearful in
26:41 their uncircumcised **h** are humbled
Nu 15:39 the lusts of your own **h** and eyes.
Dt 5:29 Oh, that their **h** would be inclined
6: 6 you today are to be upon your **h**.
10:16 Circumcise your **h**, therefore, and
11:18 Fix these words of mine in your **h**
28:67 the terror that will fill your **h**
30: 6 circumcise your **h** and the **h** of
Jos 2:11 we heard of it, our **h** sank and
5: 1 their **h** sank and they no longer had
7: 5 At this the **h** of the people melted
11:20 hardened their **h** to wage war
14: 8 made the **h** of the people sink.
24:23 yield your **h** to the LORD, the God
1Sa 6: 6 Why do you harden your **h** as the
7: 3 to the LORD with all your **h**,
10:26 valiant men whose **h** God had touched.
2Sa 15: 6 he stole the **h** of the men of Israel.
15:13 "The **h** of the men of Israel are with
19:14 He won over the **h** of all the men of
1Ki 8:39 you alone know the **h** of all men),
8:58 May he turn our **h** to him, to walk in
8:61 your **h** must be fully committed to
11: 2 surely turn your **h** after their gods.
18:37 you are turning their **h** back again
1Ch 16:10 let the **h** of those who seek the
29:18 ever, and keep their **h** loyal to you.
29:18 this desire in the **h** of your people
2Ch 6:30 (for you alone know the **h** of men),
11:16 who set their **h** on seeking the LORD,
16: 9 whose **h** are fully committed to him.
20:33 their **h** on the God of their fathers.

2Ch 29:31 and all whose **h** were willing brought
Job 1: 5 sinned and cursed God in their **h**.
Ps 4: 4 beds, search your **h** and be silent.
7: 9 who searches minds and **h**, bring to
17:10 They close up their callous **h**, and
22:26 may your **h** live for ever!
28: 3 but harbour malice in their **h**.
33:15 he who forms the **h** of all, who
33:21 In him our **h** rejoice, for we trust
37:15 their swords will pierce their own **h**,
44:18 Our **h** had not turned back; our feet
45: 5 Let your sharp arrows pierce the **h**
62: 4 bless, but in their **h** they curse.
62: 8 pour out your **h** to him,
69:32 you who seek God, may your **h** live!
73: 7 From their callous **h** comes iniquity;
74: 8 They said in their **h**, "We will crush
78: 8 whose **h** were not loyal to God, whose
78:37 their **h** were not loyal to him, they
81:12 gave them over to their stubborn **h**
84: 5 who have set their **h** on pilgrimage.
95: 8 do not harden your **h** as you did at
95:10 "They are a people whose **h** go astray,
105: 3 let the **h** of those who seek the
105:25 whose **h** he turned to hate his people,
119:70 Their **h** are callous and unfeeling,
140: 2 who devise evil plans in their **h**
Pr 12:20 There is deceit in the **h** of those
15: 7 knowledge; not so the **h** of fools.
15:11 how much more the **h** of men!
24: 2 for their **h** plot violence, and their
25: 3 so the **h** of kings are unsearchable.
Ecc 3:11 also set eternity in the **h** of men
8:11 the **h** of the people are filled with
9: 3 The **h** of men, moreover, are full of
9: 3 madness in their **h** while they live,
Isa 6:10 understand with their **h**, and turn
7: 2 **h** of Ahaz and his people were shaken,
15: 4 Moab cry out, and their **h** are faint.
19: 1 **h** of the Egyptians melt within them.
26: 8 and renown are the desire of our **h**.
29:13 lips, but their **h** are far from me.
30:29 your **h** will rejoice as when people
35: 4 say to those with fearful **h**, "Be
51: 7 people who have my law in your **h**:
57:11 me nor pondered this in your **h**?
59:13 uttering lies our **h** have conceived.
63:17 harden our **h** so we do not revere
65:14 will sing out of the joy of their **h**,
Jer 3:17 the stubbornness of their evil **h**.
4: 4 circumcise your **h**, you men of Judah
5:23 have stubborn and rebellious **h**;
7:24 inclinations of their evil **h**.
9:14 the stubbornness of their **h**;
11: 8 the stubbornness of their evil **h**.
12: 2 on their lips but far from their **h**.
13:10 follow the stubbornness of their **h**
17: 1 on the tablets of their **h** and on the
23:17 stubbornness of their **h** they say,
23:26 How long will this continue in the **h**
31:33 their minds and write it on their **h**.
48:41 In that day the **h** of Moab's warriors
49:22 In that day the **h** of Edom's warriors
Lam 2:18 The **h** of the people cry out to the
3:41 Let us lift up our **h** and our hands
3:65 Put a veil over their **h**, and may
5:15 Joy is gone from our **h**; our dancing
5:17 of this our **h** are faint; because of
Eze 6: 9 been grieved by their adulterous **h**,
11:21 as for those whose **h** are devoted to
14: 3 men have set up idols in their **h**
14: 5 to recapture the **h** of the people
20:16 their **h** were devoted to their idols.
21:15 that **h** may melt and the fallen be
25:15 took revenge with malice in their **h**,
32: 9 I will trouble the **h** of many peoples
33:31 their **h** are greedy for unjust gain.
36: 5 with malice in their **h** they made my
Da 11:27 kings, with their **h** bent on evil
Hos 7: 6 Their **h** are like an oven; they
7:14 do not cry out to me from their **h**
Na 2:10 **H** melt, knees give way, bodies
Zec 7:10 **h** do not think evil of each other.
7:12 They made their **h** as hard as flint
10: 7 their **h** will be glad as with wine.
10: 7 their **h** will rejoice in the LORD.
Zec 12: 5 of Judah will say in their **h**,
Mal 4: 6 He will turn the **h** of the fathers
4: 6 and the **h** of the children to their
Mt 9: 4 entertain evil thoughts in your **h**?
13:15 understand with their **h** and turn,
15: 8 lips, but their **h** are far from me.
19: 8 your wives because your **h** were hard.
Mk 2: 8 what they were thinking in their **h**,
3: 5 distressed at their stubborn **h**,
6:52 the loaves; their **h** were hardened.
7: 6 lips, but their **h** are far from me.
7:21 For from within, out of men's **h**,
8:17 or understand? Are your **h** hardened?
10: 5 "It was because your **h** were hard
Lk 1:17 to turn the **h** of the fathers to
2:35 the thoughts of many **h** will be
3:15 were all wondering in their **h** if
5:22 you thinking these things in your **h**?
8:12 takes away the word from their **h**,
16:15 eyes of men, but God knows your **h**.
21:34 "Be careful, or your **h** will be
24:32 "Were not our **h** burning within us
Jn 5:42 not have the love of God in your **h**.
12:40 their eyes and deadened their **h**,
12:40 nor understand with their **h**, nor
14: 1 "Do not let your **h** be troubled.
14:27 "Do not let your **h** be troubled.
Ac 2:46 together with glad and sincere **h**,
7:39 and in their **h** turned back to Egypt.
7:51 with uncircumcised **h** and ears!
11:23 true to the Lord with all their **h**.
14:17 of food and fills your **h** with joy.
15: 9 for he purified their **h** by faith.
28:27 understand with their **h** and turn,
Ro 1:21 and their foolish **h** were darkened.
1:24 in the sinful desires of their **h**
2:15 of the law are written on their **h**,
5: 5 love into our **h** by the Holy Spirit,
8:27 he who searches our **h** knows the mind
1Co 4: 5 will expose the motives of men's **h**.
10: 6 setting our **h** on evil things
2Co 1: 9 in our **h** we felt the sentence of
1:22 and put his Spirit in our **h** as a
3: 2 written on our **h**, known and read
3: 3 of stone but on tablets of human **h**.
3:15 Moses is read, a veil covers their **h**.
4: 6 made his light shine in our **h** to
6:11 and opened wide our **h** to you.
6:13 my children—open wide your **h** also.
7: 2 Make room for us in your **h**. We have
7: 3 place in our **h** that we would live or
9:14 in their prayers for you their **h**
Gal 4: 6 the Spirit of his Son into our **h**,
Eph 3:17 that Christ may dwell in your **h**
4:18 due to the hardening of their **h**.
Php 4: 7 **h** and your minds in Christ Jesus.
Col 3: 1 set your **h** on things above, where
3:15 the peace of Christ rule in your **h**,
3:16 with gratitude in your **h** to God.
4: 8 and that he may encourage your **h**.
1Th 2: 4 please men but God, who tests our **h**.
3:13 May he strengthen your **h** so that you
2Th 2:17 encourage your **h** and strengthen you
3: 5 May the Lord direct your **h** into
Phm : 7 have refreshed the **h** of the saints.
Heb 3: 8 do not harden your **h** as you did in
3:10 'Their **h** are always going astray,
3:15 do not harden your **h** as you did
4: 7 his voice, do not harden your **h**."
8:10 minds and write them on their **h**.
10:16 I will put my laws in their **h**, and
10:22 having our **h** sprinkled to cleanse us
13: 9 It is good for our **h** to be
Jas 3:14 envy and selfish ambition in your **h**,
4: 8 purify your **h**, you double-minded.
1Pe 3:15 in your **h** set apart Christ as Lord.
2Pe 1:19 the morning star rises in your **h**.
1Jn 3:19 we set our **h** at rest in his
3:20 whenever our **h** condemn us. For God
3:20 than our **h**, and he knows everything.
3:21 if our **h** do not condemn us,
Rev 2:23 I am he who searches **h** and minds,
17:17 For God has put it into their **h** to

Hearts' (Heart)
Pr 13:25 The righteous eat to their **h** content,

Heat (Heated)
Ge 8:22 seedtime and harvest, cold and **h**,
18: 1 to his tent in the **h** of the day.
30:38 flocks were in **h** and came to drink,
30:41 the stronger females were in **h**,
31:40 The **h** consumed me in the daytime
Dt 28:22 with scorching **h** and drought, with
1Sa 11:11 them until the **h** of the day.
2Sa 4: 5 arrived there in the **h** of the day
2Ki 23:26 away from the **h** of his fierce anger,
Job 6:17 in the **h** vanish from their channels.
24:19 **h** and drought snatch away the melted
Ps 19: 6 other; nothing is hidden from its **h**.
32: 4 was sapped as in the **h** of summer.
58: 9 Before your pots can feel the **h** of
Isa 4: 6 and shade from the **h** of the day,
18: 4 like shimmering **h** in the sunshine,
18: 4 a cloud of dew in the **h** of harvest
21:15 bent bow and from the **h** of battle.
25: 4 the storm and a shade from the **h**.
25: 5 like the **h** of the desert. You
25: 5 as **h** is reduced by the shadow of a
49:10 desert **h** or the sun beat upon them.
Jer 2:24 in her **h** who can restrain her?
17: 8 It does not fear when **h** comes;
36:30 the **h** by day and the frost by night.
Hos 13: 5 desert, in the land of burning **h**.
Mt 20:12 of the work and the **h** of the day.
Ac 28: 3 the **h**, fastened itself on his hand.
Jas 1:11 the sun rises with scorching **h**
2Pe 3:12 the elements will melt in the **h**
Rev 7:16 beat upon them, nor any scorching **h**.
16: 9 They were seared by the intense **h**

Heated (Heat)
Da 3:19 be **h** seven times hotter than

Heathen
1Th 4: 5 not in passionate lust like the **h**,

Heaven (*Father in heaven, God of heaven, Heaven and earth,* Heaven's, Heavenly, Heavens, Heavenwards, *Host of heaven, Kingdom of heaven, New heaven*)
Ge 21:17 to Hagar from **h** and said to her,
22:11 to him from **h**, "Abraham! Abraham!"
22:15 to Abraham from **h** a second
27:39 away from the dew of **h** above.
28:12 with its top reaching to **h**, and the
28:17 of God; this is the gate of **h**."
Ex 16: 4 will rain down bread from **h** for you.
17:14 the memory of Amalek from under **h**."
20: 4 idol in the form of anything in **h**
20:22 that I have spoken to you from **h**:
Dt 2:25 of you on all the nations under **h**.
3:24 For what god is there in **h** or on
4:19 to all the nations under **h**.
4:36 From **h** he made you hear his voice
4:39 in **h** above and on the earth below.
5: 8 idol in the form of anything in **h**
7:24 wipe out their names from under **h**.
9:14 blot out their name from under **h**.
11:11 and valleys that drinks rain from **h**.
25:19 the memory of Amalek from under **h**.
26:15 Look down from **h**, your holy
29:20 will blot out his name from under **h**.
30:12 is not up in **h**, so that you have to
30:12 "Who will ascend into **h** to get it
32:40 I lift my hand to **h** and declare: As
33:13 with the precious dew from **h** above
Jos 2:11 in **h** above and on the earth below.
Jdg 13:20 blazed up from the altar towards **h**,
1Sa 2:10 He will thunder against them from **h**;
5:12 the outcry of the city went up to **h**.
2Sa 22:14 The LORD thundered from **h**; the voice
1Ki 8:22 spread out his hands towards **h**
8:23 there is no God like you in **h** above
8:27 the highest **h**, cannot contain you.
8:30 Hear from **h**, your dwelling-place,
8:32 hear from **h** and act. Judge between

1Ki 8:34 hear from **h** and forgive the sin of
8:36 hear from **h** and forgive the sin of
8:39 hear from **h**, your dwelling-place.
8:43 hear from **h**, your dwelling-place,
8:45 hear from **h** their prayer and their
8:49 from **h**, your dwelling-place, hear
8:54 with his hands spread out towards **h**.
2Ki 1:10 may fire come down from **h** and
1:10 Then the fire fell from **h** and
1:12 "may fire come down from **h** and
1:12 the fire of God fell from **h** and
1:14 See, fire has fallen from **h** and
2: 1 take Elijah up to **h** in a whirlwind,
2:11 Elijah went up to **h** in a whirlwind.
14:27 the name of Israel from under **h**,
1Ch 21:26 LORD answered him with fire from **h**
2Ch 6:13 and spread out his hands towards **h**.
6:14 no God like you in **h** or on earth
6:21 Hear from **h**, your dwelling-place;
6:23 hear from **h** and act. Judge between
6:25 hear from **h** and forgive the sin of
6:27 hear from **h** and forgive the sin of
6:30 hear from **h**, your dwelling-place.
6:33 hear from **h**, your dwelling-place,
6:35 hear from **h** their prayer and their
6:39 from **h**, your dwelling-place, hear
7: 1 fire came down from **h** and consumed
7:14 then will I hear from **h** and will
20: 6 are you not the God who is in **h**?
28: 9 them in a rage that reaches to **h**.
30:27 reached **h**, his holy dwelling-place.
32:20 cried out in prayer to **h** about this.
Ne 9: 6 and the multitudes of **h** worship you.
9:13 Sinai; you spoke to them from **h**.
9:15 hunger you gave them bread from **h**
9:27 From **h** you heard them, and in your
9:28 you heard from **h**, and in your
Job 16:19 Even now my witness is in **h**; my
22:12 "Is not God in the heights of **h**?
25: 2 order in the heights of **h**.
37: 3 his lightning beneath the whole **h**
41:11 Everything under **h** belongs to me.
Ps 2: 4 The One enthroned in **h** laughs; the
14: 2 The LORD looks down from **h** on the
18:13 The LORD thundered from **h**; the voice
20: 6 he answers him from his holy **h** with
33:13 From **h** the LORD looks down and sees
53: 2 God looks down from **h** on the sons of
57: 3 He sends from **h** and saves me,
73: 9 Their mouths lay claim to **h**, and
73:25 Whom have I in **h** but you? And earth
75: 5 Do not lift your horns against **h**;
76: 8 From **h** you pronounced judgment, and
78:24 to eat, he gave them the grain of **h**.
80:14 Look down from **h** and see!
85:11 and righteousness looks down from **h**.
89: 2 your faithfulness in **h** itself.
102:19 on high, from **h** he viewed the earth,
103:19 has established his throne in **h**,
105:40 satisfied them with the bread of **h**.
115: 3 Our God is in **h**; he does whatever
123: 1 to you, to you whose throne is in **h**.
Pr 30: 4 Who has gone up to **h** and come down?
Ecc 1:13 by wisdom all that is done under **h**.
2: 3 worth while for men to do under **h**
3: 1 a season for every activity under **h**:
5: 2 God is in **h** and you are on earth,
Isa 13:10 The stars of **h** and their
14:12 How you have fallen from **h**,
14:13 "I will ascend to **h**; I will raise
55:10 rain and the snow come down from **h**,
63:15 Look down from **h** and see from your
66: 1 "**H** is my throne, and the earth is
Jer 7:18 cakes of bread for the Queen of **H**.
44:17 will burn incense to the Queen of **H**
44:18 burning incense to the Queen of **H**
44:19 we burned incense to the Queen of **H**
44:25 drink offerings to the Queen of **H**.
Lam 2: 1 splendour of Israel from **h** to earth;
3:41 and our hands to God in **h**, and say:
3:50 until the LORD looks down from **h** and
Eze 8: 3 lifted me up between earth and **h**
Da 2:28 there is a God in **h** who reveals
4:13 a holy one, coming down from **h**.
4:15 him be drenched with the dew of **h**,
4:23 a holy one, coming down from **h**
Da 4:23 him be drenched with the dew of **h**;
4:25 and be drenched with the dew of **h**.
4:26 when you acknowledge that **H** rules.
4:31 his lips when a voice came from **h**,
4:33 body was drenched with the dew of **h**
4:34 raised my eyes towards **h**, and my
4:35 with the powers of **h** and the
4:37 exalt and glorify the King of **h**,
5:21 body was drenched with the dew of **h**,
5:23 yourself up against the Lord of **h**.
7: 2 four winds of **h** churning up the
7:13 of man, coming with the clouds of **h**.
7:27 **h** will be handed over to the saints,
8: 8 grew up towards the four winds of **h**.
9:12 Under the whole **h** nothing has ever
11: 4 out towards the four winds of **h**.
12: 7 hand and his left hand towards **h**,
Zec 2: 6 four winds of **h**," declares the LORD.
6: 5 "These are the four spirits of **h**,
Mal 3:10 not throw open the floodgates of **h**
Mt 3:16 At that moment **h** was opened, and he
3:17 a voice from **h** said, "This is my Son,
5:12 because great is your reward in **h**,
5:34 either by **h**, for it is God's throne;
6:10 will be done on earth as it is in **h**.
6:20 up for yourselves treasures in **h**,
7:21 the will of my Father who is in **h**.
14:19 the two fish and looking up to **h**,
16: 1 him to show them a sign from **h**.
16:19 bind on earth will be bound in **h**,
16:19 loose on earth will be loosed in **h**.
18:10 their angels in **h** always see the
18:18 bind on earth will be bound in **h**,
18:18 loose on earth will be loosed in **h**.
19:21 and you will have treasure in **h**.
21:25 Was it from **h**, or from men?"
21:25 'From **h**', he will ask, 'Then why
22:30 they will be like the angels in **h**.
23: 9 you have one Father, and he is in **h**.
23:22 he who swears by **h** swears by God's
24:36 not even the angels in **h**, nor the
26:64 One and coming on the clouds of **h**."
28: 2 of the Lord came down from **h** and,
28:18 All authority in **h** and on earth has
Mk 1:10 he saw **h** being torn open and the
1:11 a voice came from **h**: "You are my Son,
6:41 the two fish and looking up to **h**,
7:34 He looked up to **h** and with a deep
8:11 they asked him for a sign from **h**.
10:21 and you will have treasure in **h**.
11:30 John's baptism—was it from **h**, or
11:31 'From **h**', he will ask, 'Then why
12:25 they will be like the angels in **h**.
13:32 not even the angels in **h**, nor the
14:62 One and coming on the clouds of **h**."
16:19 he was taken up into **h** and he sat
Lk 1:78 rising sun will come to us from **h**
2:15 had left them and gone into **h**,
3:21 he was praying, **h** was opened
3:22 a voice came from **h**: "You are my
6:23 because great is your reward in **h**.
9:16 looking up to **h**, he gave thanks and
9:51 for him to be taken up to **h**,
9:54 fire down from **h** to destroy them?"
10:18 Satan fall like lightning from **h**.
10:20 that your names are written in **h**."
11:16 him by asking for a sign from **h**.
12:33 a treasure in **h** that will not be
15: 7 there will be more rejoicing in **h**
15:18 sinned against **h** and against you.
15:21 sinned against **h** and against you.
17:29 down from **h** and destroyed them all.
18:13 He would not even look up to **h**, but
18:22 and you will have treasure in **h**.
19:38 Peace in **h** and glory in the highest
20: 4 John's baptism—was it from **h**, or
20: 5 'From **h**', he will ask, 'Why didn't
21:11 events and great signs from **h**.
22:43 An angel from **h** appeared to him and
24:51 left them and was taken up into **h**.
Jn 1:32 from **h** as a dove and remain on him.
1:51 you shall see **h** open, and the angels
3:13 No-one has ever gone into **h** except
3:13 one who came from **h**—the Son of Man.
3:27 only what is given him from **h**.
3:31 one who comes from **h** is above all.
Jn 6:31 'He gave them bread from **h** to eat.'"
6:32 who has given you the bread from **h**,
6:32 who gives you the true bread from **h**.
6:33 from **h** and gives life to the world."
6:38 For I have come down from **h** not to
6:41 the bread that came down from **h**."
6:42 he now say, 'I came down from **h**'?"
6:50 the bread that comes down from **h**,
6:51 living bread that came down from **h**.
6:58 is the bread that came down from **h**.
12:28 name!" Then a voice came from **h**,
17: 1 he looked towards **h** and prayed:
Ac 1: 2 until the day he was taken up to **h**,
1:11 who has been taken from you into **h**,
1:11 way you have seen him go into **h**."
2: 2 of a violent wind came from **h**
2: 5 Jews from every nation under **h**.
2:19 I will show wonders in the **h** above
2:34 For David did not ascend to **h**, and
3:21 He must remain in **h** until the time
4:12 for there is no other name under **h**
4:24 "you made the **h** and the earth and
7:49 '**H** is my throne, and the earth is
7:55 looked up to **h** and saw the glory of
7:56 "Look," he said, "I see **h** open and
9: 3 a light from **h** flashed around him.
10:11 He saw **h** opened and something like
10:16 the sheet was taken back to **h**.
11: 5 let down from **h** by its four corners
11: 9 "The voice spoke from **h** a second
11:10 then it was pulled up to **h** again.
14:17 rain from **h** and crops in their
19:35 of her image, which fell from **h**?
22: 6 light from **h** flashed around me.
26:13 I saw a light from **h**, brighter than
26:19 disobedient to the vision from **h**.
Ro 1:18 from **h** against all the godlessness
10: 6 'Who will ascend into **h**?'" (that is,
1Co 8: 5 whether in **h** or on earth (as indeed
15:47 of the earth, the second man from **h**.
15:48 **h**, so also are those who are of **h**.
15:49 bear the likeness of the man from **h**.
2Co 5: 1 an eternal house in **h**, not built
12: 2 ago was caught up to the third **h**.
Gal 1: 8 if we or an angel from **h** should
Eph 1:10 all things in **h** and on earth
3:15 from whom his whole family in **h** and
6: 9 both their Master and yours is in **h**,
Php 2:10 in **h** and on earth and under the
3:20 our citizenship is in **h**. And we
Col 1: 5 hope that is stored up for you in **h**
1:16 created: things in **h** and on earth,
1:20 things on earth or things in **h**,
1:23 to every creature under **h**,
4: 1 that you also have a Master in **h**.
1Th 1:10 to wait for his Son from **h**, whom he
4:16 Lord himself will come down from **h**,
2Th 1: 7 the Lord Jesus is revealed from **h**
Heb 1: 3 the right hand of the Majesty in **h**.
8: 1 of the throne of the Majesty in **h**,
8: 5 a copy and shadow of what is in **h**.
9:24 the true one; he entered **h** itself,
9:25 Nor did he enter **h** to offer himself
12:23 whose names are written in **h**.
12:25 away from him who warns us from **h**?
Jas 3:15 "wisdom" does not come down from **h**
3:17 the wisdom that comes from **h** is
5:12 not by **h** or by earth or by
1Pe 1: 4 spoil or fade—kept in **h** for you,
1:12 you by the Holy Spirit sent from **h**.
3:22 who has gone into **h** and is at God's
2Pe 1:18 heard this voice that came from **h**
Rev 3:12 which is coming down out of **h** from
4: 1 me was a door standing open in **h**.
4: 2 a throne in **h** with someone sitting
5: 3 no-one in **h** or on earth or under
5:13 I heard every creature in **h** and on
8: 1 silence in **h** for about half an hour.
10: 1 mighty angel coming down from **h**.
10: 4 but I heard a voice from **h** say,
10: 5 raised his right hand to **h**.
10: 8 the voice that I had heard from **h**
11:12 they heard a loud voice from **h**
11:12 And they went up to **h** in a cloud,
11:15 and there were loud voices in **h**,
11:19 God's temple in **h** was opened, and

Rev 12: 1 and wondrous sign appeared in **h**:
12: 3 another sign appeared in **h**: an
12: 7 there was war in **h**. Michael and his
12: 8 and they lost their place in **h**.
12:10 I heard a loud voice in **h** say: "Now
13: 6 and those who live in **h**.
13:13 from **h** to earth in full view of men.
14: 2 I heard a sound from **h** like the roar
14:13 I heard a voice from **h** say, "Write:
14:17 angel came out of the temple in **h**,
15: 1 I saw in **h** another great and
15: 5 After this I looked and in **h** the
18: 1 another angel coming down from **h**.
18: 4 I heard another voice from **h** say:
18: 5 for her sins are piled up to **h**, and
18:20 Rejoice over her, O **h**! Rejoice,
19: 1 of a great multitude in **h** shouting:
19:11 I saw **h** standing open and there
19:14 The armies of **h** were following him,
20: 1 I saw an angel coming down out of **h**,
20: 9 came down from **h** and devoured them.
21: 1 for the first **h** and the first earth
21: 2 coming down out of **h** from God,
21:10 coming down out of **h** from God.

Heaven and earth

Ge 14:19 Abram by God Most High, Creator of **h**.
14:22 Creator of **h**, and have taken an
Dt 4:26 I call **h** as witnesses against you
30:19 This day I call **h** as witnesses
31:28 and call **h** to testify against them.
2Ki 19:15 You have made **h**.
1Ch 21:16 of the LORD standing between **h**,
29:11 for everything in **h** is yours.
2Ch 2:12 the God of Israel, who made **h**! He
Ezr 5:11 We are the servants of the God of **h**
Ps 69:34 Let **h** praise him, the seas and all
115:15 blessed by the LORD, the Maker of **h**
121: 2 comes from the LORD, the Maker of **h**
124: 8 name of the LORD, the Maker of **h**.
134: 3 May the LORD, the Maker of **h**, bless
146: 6 the Maker of **h**, the sea, and
Isa 37:16 You have made **h**.
Jer 23:24 Do not I fill **h**?" declares the LORD
33:25 and night and the fixed laws of **h**,
51:48 **h** and all that is in them will shout
Zec 5: 9 they lifted up the basket between **h**.
Mt 5:18 until **h** disappear, not the smallest
11:25 "I praise you, Father, Lord of **h**,
24:35 **H** will pass away, but my words will
Mk 13:31 **H** will pass away, but my words will
Lk 10:21 "I praise you, Father, Lord of **h**,
16:17 is easier for **h** to disappear than
21:33 **H** will pass away, but my words will
Ac 14:15 **h** and sea and everything in them.
17:24 everything in it is the Lord of **h**

Heaven's (Heaven)

Ge 27:28 May God give you of **h** dew and of

Heavenly (Heaven, *Heavenly Father*)

Dt 4:19 and the stars—all the **h** array
Ps 8: 5 a little lower than the **h** beings
11: 4 temple; the LORD is on his **h** throne.
89: 6 is like the LORD among the **h** beings?
103:21 Praise the LORD, all his **h** hosts,
148: 2 angels, praise him, all his **h** hosts.
Mt 24:29 and the **h** bodies will be shaken.
25:31 will sit on his throne in **h** glory.
Mk 13:25 and the **h** bodies will be shaken.
Lk 2:13 a great company of the **h** host
21:26 for the **h** bodies will be shaken.
Jn 3:12 you believe if I speak of **h** things?
Ac 7:42 over to the worship of the **h** bodies.
1Co 15:40 There are also **h** bodies and there
15:40 of the **h** bodies is one kind,
2Co 5: 2 to be clothed with our **h** dwelling,
5: 4 to be clothed with our **h** dwelling,
Eph 1: 3 who has blessed us in the **h** realms
1:20 at his right hand in the **h** realms,
2: 6 him in the **h** realms in Christ Jesus,
3:10 and authorities in the **h** realms,
6:12 forces of evil in the **h** realms.
2Ti 4:18 bring me safely to his **h** kingdom.
Heb 3: 1 who share in the **h** calling, fix
Heb 6: 4 who have tasted the **h** gift, who have
9:23 for the copies of the **h** things
9:23 but the **h** things themselves with
11:16 for a better country—a **h** one.
12:22 to Mount Zion, to the **h** Jerusalem
Jas 1:17 from the Father of the **h** lights,

Heavenly Father

Mt 5:48 Be perfect, therefore, as your **h** is
6:14 you, your **h** will also forgive you.
6:26 in barns, and yet your **h** feeds them.
6:32 and your **h** knows that you need them.
15:13 "Every plant that my **h** has not
18:35 "This is how my **h** will treat each of

Heavens (Heaven, *New heavens*)

Ge 1: 1 In the beginning God created the **h**
2: 1 Thus the **h** and the earth were
2: 4 This is the account of the **h** and
2: 4 LORD God made the earth and the **h**—
6:17 to destroy all life under the **h**,
7:11 the floodgates of the **h** were opened.
7:19 under the entire **h** were covered.
8: 2 floodgates of the **h** had been closed,
11: 4 with a tower that reaches to the **h**,
15: 5 "Look up at the **h** and count the
19:24 —from the LORD out of the **h**.
49:25 you with blessings of the **h** above,
Ex 20:11 For in six days the LORD made the **h**
31:17 for in six days the LORD made the **h**
Dt 4:11 it blazed with fire to the very **h**,
4:32 from one end of the **h** to the other.
10:14 To the LORD your God belong the **h**,
10:14 even the highest **h**, the earth and
11:17 and he will shut the **h** so that it
11:21 that the **h** are above the earth.
28:12 The LORD will open the **h**, the
30: 4 the most distant land under the **h**,
32: 1 Listen, O **h**, and I will speak;
33:26 who rides on the **h** to help you and
33:28 and new wine, where the **h** drop dew.
Jdg 5: 4 the earth shook, the **h** poured, the
5:20 From the **h** the stars fought, from
2Sa 21:10 down from the **h** on the bodies,
22: 8 the foundations of the **h** shook;
22:10 He parted the **h** and came down;
1Ki 8:27 The **h**, even the highest heaven,
8:35 "When the **h** are shut up and there is
2Ki 7: 2 open the floodgates of the **h**,
7:19 open the floodgates of the **h**,
1Ch 16:26 are idols, but the LORD made the **h**.
16:31 Let the **h** rejoice, let the earth
2Ch 2: 6 since the **h**, even the highest **h**,
6:18 The **h**, even the highest **h**,
6:26 the **h** are shut up and there is
7:13 "When I shut up the **h** so that there
Ezr 9: 6 and our guilt has reached to the **h**.
Ne 9: 6 You made the **h**, even the highest **h**,
Job 9: 8 He alone stretches out the **h** and
11: 8 They are higher than the **h**—what
14:12 till the **h** are no more,
15:15 even the **h** are not pure in his eyes,
20: 6 Though his pride reaches to the **h**
20:27 The **h** will expose his guilt;
22:14 he goes about in the vaulted **h**.'
26:11 The pillars of the **h** quake, aghast
28:24 and sees everything under the **h**.
35: 5 Look up at the **h** and see; gaze at
38:29 gives birth to the frost from the **h**
38:33 Do you know the laws of the **h**?
38:37 tip over the water jars of the **h**
Ps 8: 1 You have set your glory above the **h**.
8: 3 I consider your **h**, the work of your
18: 9 He parted the **h** and came down; dark
19: 1 The **h** declare the glory of God;
19: 4 In the **h** he has pitched a tent for
19: 6 rises at one end of the **h** and makes
33: 6 By the word of the LORD were the **h**
36: 5 Your love, O LORD, reaches to the **h**
50: 4 He summons the **h** above, and the
50: 6 the **h** proclaim his righteousness,
57: 5 Be exalted, O God, above the **h**;
57:10 is your love, reaching to the **h**
57:11 Be exalted, O God, above the **h**;
68: 8 the earth shook, the **h** poured down
Ps 78:23 and opened the doors of the **h**;
78:26 let loose the east wind from the **h**
89: 5 The **h** praise your wonders, O LORD,
89:11 The **h** are yours, and yours also the
89:29 his throne as long as the **h** endure.
96: 5 are idols, but the LORD made the **h**.
96:11 Let the **h** rejoice, let the earth
97: 6 The **h** proclaim his righteousness,
102:25 the **h** are the work of your hands.
103:11 For as high as the **h** are above the
104: 2 he stretches out the **h** like a
107:26 They mounted up to the **h** and went
108: 4 is your love, higher than the **h**;
108: 5 Be exalted, O God, above the **h**,
113: 4 the nations, his glory above the **h**
113: 6 who stoops down to look on the **h**
115:16 The highest **h** belong to the LORD,
119:89 eternal; it stands firm in the **h**.
135: 6 in the **h** and on the earth, in the
136: 5 by his understanding made the **h**,
139: 8 If I go up to the **h**, you are there;
144: 5 Part your **h**, O LORD, and come down;
148: 1 Praise the LORD from the **h**, praise
148: 4 Praise him, you highest **h** and you
148:13 is above the earth and the **h**.
150: 1 praise him in his mighty **h**.
Pr 3:19 understanding he set the **h** in place
8:27 I was there when he set the **h** in
25: 3 the **h** are high and the earth is deep,
Isa 1: 2 Hear, O **h**! Listen, O earth! For the
13: 5 from the ends of the **h**—the LORD
13:13 Therefore I will make the **h** tremble;
24:18 The floodgates of the **h** are opened,
24:21 punish the powers in the **h** above
34: 4 All the stars of the **h** will be
34: 5 sword has drunk its fill in the **h**;
38:14 eyes grew weak as I looked to the **h**.
40:12 of his hand marked off the **h**?
40:22 stretches out the **h** like a canopy,
40:26 Lift your eyes and look to the **h**:
42: 5 he who created the **h** and
44:23 Sing for joy, O **h**, for the LORD
44:24 who alone stretched out the **h**, who
45: 8 "You **h** above, rain down
45:12 My own hands stretched out the **h**;
45:18 he who created the **h**, he is God
48:13 and my right hand spread out the **h**;
49:13 Shout for joy, O **h**; rejoice, O earth;
51: 6 Lift up your eyes to the **h**, look at
51: 6 the **h** will vanish like smoke,
51:13 who stretched out the **h** and laid the
51:16 my hand—I who set the **h** in place,
55: 9 "As the **h** are higher than the earth,
64: 1 Oh, that you would rend the **h** and
Jer 2:12 Be appalled at this, O **h**, and
4:23 at the **h**, and their light was gone.
4:28 mourn and the **h** above grow dark,
8: 2 moon and all the stars of the **h**,
10:11 These gods, who did not make the **h**
10:11 from the earth and from under the **h**
10:12 out the **h** by his understanding.
10:13 thunders, the waters in the **h** roar
31:37 Only if the **h** above can be measured
32:17 Sovereign LORD, you have made the **h**
49:36 from the four quarters of the **h**;
51:15 stretched out the **h** by his
51:16 thunders, the waters in the **h** roar
Lam 3:66 them from under the **h** of the LORD.
Eze 1: 1 the **h** were opened and I saw visions
32: 7 I snuff you out, I will cover the **h**
32: 8 All the shining lights in the **h** I
Da 6:27 wonders in the **h** and on the earth.
8:10 until it reached the host of the **h**,
12: 3 shine like the brightness of the **h**,
Joel 2:30 I will show wonders in the **h** and on
Am 9: 2 they climb up to the **h**, from there
9: 6 builds his lofty palace in the **h**
Hab 3: 3 His glory covered the **h** and his
3:11 Sun and moon stood still in the **h**
Hag 1:10 Therefore, because of you the **h** have
2: 6 once more shake the **h** and the earth,
2:21 I will shake the **h** and the earth.
Zec 8:12 and the **h** will drop their dew.
12: 1 The LORD, who stretches out the **h**,
Mt 24:31 from one end of the **h** to the other.
Mk 13:27 of the earth to the ends of the **h**.

Eph 4:10 who ascended higher than all the **h**,
Heb 1:10 the **h** are the work of your hands.
4:14 priest who has gone through the **h**,
7:26 from sinners, exalted above the **h**.
12:26 not only the earth but also the **h**.
Jas 5:18 he prayed, and the **h** gave rain,
2Pe 3: 5 ago by God's word the **h** existed
3: 7 By the same word the present **h** and
3:10 The **h** will disappear with a roar;
3:12 the destruction of the **h** by fire,
Rev 10: 6 created the **h** and all that is in
12:12 Therefore rejoice, you **h** and you who
14: 7 Worship him who made the **h**, the

Heavenwards (Heaven)

Php 3:14 God has called me **h** in Christ Jesus

Heavier (Heavy)

1Ki 12:11 a heavy yoke; I will make it even **h**.
12:14 yoke heavy; I will make it even **h**.
2Ch 10:11 a heavy yoke; I will make it even **h**.
10:14 yoke heavy; I will make it even **h**.
Pr 27: 3 provocation by a fool is **h**
Isa 28:22 or your chains will become **h**; the

Heavily (Heavy)

Ps 88: 7 Your wrath lies **h** upon me; you have
Ecc 6: 1 the sun, and it weighs **h** on men:
8: 6 a man's misery weighs **h** upon him.

Heavy (Heavier, Heavily)

Ex 18:18 The work is too **h** for you; you
Nu 11:14 the burden is too **h** for me.
Dt 1: 9 too **h** a burden for me to carry
25:13 in your bag—one **h**, one light.
32:15 with food, he became **h** and sleek.
Jdg 20:34 The fighting was so **h** that the
1Sa 4:17 the army has suffered **h** losses.
4:18 died, for he was an old man and **h**.
5: 6 The LORD's hand was **h** upon the
5: 7 his hand is **h** upon us and upon Dagon
5:11 God's hand was very **h** upon it.
6:19 **h** blow the LORD had dealt them,
23: 5 He inflicted **h** losses on the
2Sa 14:26 when it became too **h** for him
1Ki 12: 4 "Your father put a **h** yoke on us,
12: 4 labour and the **h** yoke he put on us,
12:10 'Your father put a **h** yoke on us,
12:11 My father laid on you a **h** yoke;
12:14 My father made your yoke **h**;
18:41 there is the sound of a **h** rain."
18:45 the wind rose, a **h** rain came on and
20:21 inflicted **h** losses on the Arameans.
2Ch 10: 4 "Your father put a **h** yoke on us,
10: 4 labour and the **h** yoke he put on us,
10:10 'Your father put a **h** yoke on us,
10:11 My father laid on you a **h** yoke;
10:14 My father made your yoke **h**;
13:17 his men inflicted **h** losses
21:14 that is yours, with a **h** blow.
28: 5 who inflicted **h** casualties on him.
Ne 5:15 placed a **h** burden on the people
5:18 the demands were **h** on these people.
Job 23: 2 hand is **h** in spite of my groaning.
33: 7 nor should my hand be **h** upon you.
39:11 Will you leave your **h** work to him?
Ps 32: 4 For day and night your hand was **h**
38: 4 me like a burden too **h** to bear.
144:14 our oxen will draw **h** loads. There
Pr 25:20 is one who sings songs to a **h** heart.
27: 3 Stone is **h** and sand a burden, but
Ecc 1:13 What a **h** burden God has laid on men
Isa 24:20 so **h** upon it is the guilt of its
47: 6 on the aged you laid a very **h** yoke.
Eze 24:12 its **h** deposit has not been removed
27:25 **h** cargo in the heart of the sea.
Mt 23: 4 They tie up **h** loads and put them
26:43 sleeping, because their eyes were **h**
Mk 14:40 sleeping, because their eyes were **h**

Heber (Heber's, Heberite)

Ge 46:17 The sons of Beriah: **H** and Malkiel.
Nu 26:45 through **H**, the Heberite clan;
Jdg 4:11 Now **H** the Kenite had left the other
4:17 the wife of **H** the Kenite, because
4:17 Hazor and the clan of **H** the Kenite.
5:24 the wife of **H** the Kenite, most
1Ch 4:18 **H** the father of Soco, and Jekuthiel
7:31 The sons of Beriah: **H** and Malkiel,
7:32 **H** was the father of Japhlet, Shomer
8:17 Zebadiah, Meshullam, Hizki, **H**,

Heber's (Heber)

Jdg 4:21 Jael, **H** wife, picked up a tent peg

Heberite (Heber)

Nu 26:45 through Heber, the **H** clan;

Hebraic (Hebrew)

Ac 6: 1 complained against the **H** Jews

Hebrew (Hebraic, Hebrews)

Ge 14:13 and reported this to Abram the **H**.
39:14 "Look," she said to them, "this **H**
39:17 told him this story: "That **H** slave
41:12 Now a young **H** was there with us, a
Ex 1:15 The king of Egypt said to the **H**
1:16 "When you help the **H** women in
1:19 "**H** women are not like Egyptian women
2: 6 "This is one of the **H** babies," she
2: 7 **H** women to nurse the baby for you?
2:11 beating a **H**, one of his own people.
2:13 "Why are you hitting your fellow **H**?
21: 2 "If you buy a **H** servant, he is to
Dt 15:12 If a fellow **H**, a man or woman, sells
1Sa 4: 6 all this shouting in the **H** camp?
2Ki 18:26 Don't speak to us in **H** in the
18:28 called out in **H**: "Hear the word of
2Ch 32:18 they called out in **H** to the people
Isa 36:11 Don't speak to us in **H** in the
36:13 commander stood and called out in **H**,
Jer 34: 9 Everyone was to free his **H** slaves,
34:14 you must free any fellow **H** who
Jnh 1: 9 He answered, "I am a **H** and I worship
Php 3: 5 tribe of Benjamin, a **H** of Hebrews
Rev 9:11 name in **H** is Abaddon, and in Greek
16:16 that in **H** is called Armageddon.

Hebrews (Hebrew)

Ge 40:15 carried off from the land of the **H**,
43:32 Egyptians could not eat with **H**,
Ex 2:13 he went out and saw two **H** fighting.
3:18 the God of the **H**, has met with us.
5: 3 said, "The God of the **H** has met
7:16 'The LORD, the God of the **H**, has
9: 1 the God of the **H**, says: "Let my
9:13 the God of the **H**, says: Let my
10: 3 the God of the **H**, says: 'How long
1Sa 4: 9 or you will be subject to the **H**,
13: 3 "Let the **H** hear!
13: 7 Some **H** even crossed the Jordan to
13:19 the **H** will make swords or spears!"
14:11 "The **H** are crawling out of the holes
14:21 Those **H** who had previously been with
29: 3 "What about these **H**?" Achish replied,
2Co 11:22 Are they **H**? So am I. Are they
Php 3: 5 tribe of Benjamin, a Hebrew of **H**;

Hebron (Hebronite, Hebronites)

Town in the highlands of Judah, between Beersheba and Jerusalem. Originally known as Kiriath Arba (Ge 23:2; Jos 14:15). Abram's home, where he built an altar (Ge 13:18), received promise of birth of Isaac (Ge 18:1–15), and where Sarah died (Ge 23:2). Isaac and Jacob lived here (Ge 35:27) and Moses' spies came here (Nu 13:22). Joshua killed its king (Jos 10:3–27), Caleb drove out its inhabitants (Jos 14:12–15). Designated a city of refuge (Jos 20:7). Abner killed and buried here (2Sa 3:27–32). David made king here (2Sa 5:1–5); base for Absalom's rebellion (2Sa 15:7–12). Fortified by Rehoboam (2Ch 11:10–12).

Ge 13:18 near the great trees of Mamre at **H**,
23: 2 She died at Kiriath Arba (that is, **H**)
23:19 is at **H**) in the land of Canaan.
35:27 near Kiriath Arba (that is, **H**),
37:14 sent him off from the Valley of **H**.
Ex 6:18 were Amram, Izhar, **H** and Uzziel.
Nu 3:19 The Kohathite clans: Amram, Izhar, **H**
13:22 up through the Negev and came to **H**,
13:22 (**H** had been built seven years before
Jos 10: 3 appealed to Hoham king of **H**,
10: 5 **H**, Jarmuth, Lachish and
10:23 **H**, Jarmuth, Lachish and Eglon.
10:36 up from Eglon to **H** and attacked it.
10:39 to Libnah and its king and to **H**.
11:21 from the hill country: from **H**,
12:10 the king of **H** one
14:13 and gave him **H** as his inheritance.
14:14 **H** has belonged to Caleb son of
14:15 (**H** used to be called Kiriath Arba
15:13 Kiriath Arba, that is, **H**.
15:14 From **H** Caleb drove out the three
15:54 Humtah, Kiriath Arba (that is, **H**)
20: 7 and Kiriath Arba (that is, **H**)
21:11 Kiriath Arba (that is, **H**),
21:13 they gave **H** (a city of refuge for
Jdg 1:10 in **H** (formerly called Kiriath Arba)
1:20 Moses had promised, **H** was given to
16: 3 to the top of the hill that faces **H**.
1Sa 30:31 **H**; and to those in all the other
2Sa 2: 1 I go?" "To **H**," the LORD answered.
2: 3 and they settled in **H** and its towns.
2: 4 the men of Judah came to **H** and there
2:11 length of time David was king in **H**
2:32 night and arrived at **H** by daybreak.
3: 2 Sons were born to David in **H**:
3: 5 These were born to David in **H**.
3:19 Then he went to **H** to tell David
3:20 came to David at **H**, David prepared a
3:22 Abner was no longer with David in **H**,
3:27 Now when Abner returned to **H**, Joab
3:32 They buried Abner in **H**, and the king
4: 1 Saul heard that Abner had died in **H**,
4: 8 to David at **H** and said to the king,
4:12 hung the bodies by the pool in **H**.
4:12 and buried it in Abner's tomb at **H**.
5: 1 Israel came to David at **H** and said,
5: 3 Israel had come to King David at **H**,
5: 3 with them at **H** before the LORD,
5: 5 In **H** he reigned over Judah for
5:13 After he left **H**, David took more
15: 7 "Let me go to **H** and fulfil a vow I
15: 8 I will worship the LORD in **H**.
15: 9 So he went to **H**.
15:10 then say, 'Absalom is king in **H**.
1Ki 2:11 seven years in **H** and thirty-three
1Ch 2:42 Mareshah, who was the father of **H**.
2:43 The sons of **H**: Korah, Tappuah, Rekem
3: 1 the sons of David born to him in **H**:
3: 4 These six were born to David in **H**,
6: 2 The sons of Kohath: Amram, Izhar, **H**
6:18 The sons of Kohath: Amram, Izhar, **H**
6:55 They were given **H** in Judah with its
6:57 descendants of Aaron were given **H**
11: 1 together to David at **H** and said,
11: 3 Israel had come to King David at **H**,
11: 3 he made a compact with them at **H**
12:23 who came to David at **H** to turn
12:38 They came to **H** fully determined to
15: 9 from the descendants of **H**, Eliel the
23:12 The sons of Kohath: Amram, Izhar, **H**
23:19 The sons of **H**: Jeriah the first,
24:23 The sons of **H**: Jeriah the first,
29:27 seven in **H** and thirty-three in
2Ch 11:10 Zorah, Aijalon and **H**. These were

Hebronite (Hebron)

Nu 26:58 the **H** clan, the Mahlite clan, the

Hebronites (Hebron)

Nu 3:27 Izharites, **H** and Uzzielites; these
1Ch 26:23 Izharites, the **H** and the Uzzielites:
26:30 From the **H**: Hashabiah and his
26:31 for the **H**, Jeriah was their chief
26:31 capable men among the **H** were found

Hedge (Hedged)

Job 1:10 "Have you not put a **h** around him and
Isa 5: 5 I will take away its **h**, and it will
Mic 7: 4 most upright worse than a thorn **h**.

Hedged (Hedge)
Job 3:23 way is hidden, whom God has **h** in?

Heed (Heeded, Heeds)
1Sa 15:22 to **h** is better than the fat of rams
Ps 58: 5 that will not **h** the tune of the
94: 7 see; the God of Jacob pays no **h**."
94: 8 Take **h**, you senseless ones among the
107:43 Whoever is wise, let him **h** these
Pr 1:24 gave **h** when I stretched out my hand,
16:20 Whoever gives **h** to instruction
Ecc 7: 5 is better to **h** a wise man's rebuke
Mic 6: 9 **H** the rod and the One who appointed

Heeded (Heed)
Ecc 9:16 and his words are no longer **h**.
9:17 more to be **h** than the shouts of

Heeds (Heed)
Pr 10:17 He who **h** discipline shows the way
13: 1 A wise son **h** his father's
13:18 whoever **h** correction is honoured.
15: 5 whoever **h** correction shows prudence.
15:32 whoever **h** correction gains

Heel (Heels)
Ge 3:15 head, and you will strike his **h**."
25:26 with his hand grasping Esau's **h**;
Job 18: 9 A trap seizes him by the **h**;
Ps 41: 9 has lifted up his **h** against me.
Hos 12: 3 he grasped his brother's **h**;
Jn 13:18 has lifted up his **h** against me.'

Heels (Heel)
Ge 49:17 that bites the horse's **h** so that
49:19 but he will attack them at their **h**.
Lam 5: 5 Those who pursue us are at our **h**;

Hegai
Est 2: 3 them be placed under the care of **H**,
2: 8 of Susa and put under the care of **H**.
2: 8 to **H**, who had charge of the harem.
2:15 asked for nothing other than what **H**,

He-goat (Goat)
Pr 30:31 a strutting cock, a **h**, and a king

Heifer (Heifer's)
Ge 15: 9 the LORD said to him, "Bring me a **h**,
Nu 19: 2 a red **h** without defect or blemish
19: 5 the **h** is to be burned
19: 6 and throw them onto the burning **h**.
19: 9 shall gather up the ashes of the **h**
19:10 of the **h** must also wash his clothes,
Dt 21: 3 take a **h** that has never been worked
21: 6 wash their hands over the **h** whose
Jdg 14:18 "If you had not ploughed with my **h**,
1Sa 16: 2 The LORD said, "Take a **h** with you
Jer 46:20 "Egypt is a beautiful **h**, but a
50:11 because you frolic like a **h**
Hos 4:16 are stubborn, like a stubborn **h**.
10:11 Ephraim is a trained **h** that loves to
Heb 9:13 bulls and the ashes of a **h** sprinkled

Heifer's (Heifer)
Dt 21: 4 valley they are to break the **h** neck.

Height (Heights)
Nu 23: 3 Then he went off to a barren **h**.
Jdg 6:26 LORD your God on the top of this **h**.
1Sa 16: 7 consider his appearance or his **h**,
1Ki 6:10 The **h** of each was five cubits, and
6:26 The **h** of each cherub was ten cubits.
Ne 4: 6 till all of it reached half its **h**,
Isa 22:16 hewing your grave on the **h** and
Eze 19:11 conspicuous for its **h** and for its
31:10 and because it was proud of its **h**,
31:14 are ever to reach such a **h**;
43:13 And this is the **h** of the altar:
Da 4:10 Its **h** was enormous.
8: 8 but at the **h** of his power his large
Ro 8:39 neither **h** nor depth, nor anything
Rev 2: 5 Remember the **h** from which you have

Heights (Height)
Nu 21:28 of Moab, the citizens of Arnon's **h**.
23: 9 I see them, from the **h** I view them.
Dt 32:13 He made him ride on the **h** of the
Jdg 5:18 did Naphtali on the **h** of the field.
2Sa 1:19 O Israel, lies slain on your **h**.
1:25 Jonathan lies slain on your **h**.
22:34 he enables me to stand on the **h**.
2Ki 19:23 ascended the **h** of the mountains,
19:23 mountains, the utmost **h** of Lebanon.
Job 22:12 "Is not God in the **h** of heaven?
25: 2 order in the **h** of heaven.
Ps 18:33 he enables me to stand on the **h**.
42: 6 the **h** of Hermon—from Mount Mizar.
48: 2 Like the utmost **h** of Zaphon is Mount
78:69 He built his sanctuary like the **h**,
148: 1 heavens, praise him in the **h** above.
Pr 8: 2 On the **h** along the way, where the
Ecc 12: 5 men are afraid of **h** and of dangers
Isa 7:11 deepest depths or in the highest **h**
14:13 the utmost **h** of the sacred mountain.
31: 4 battle on Mount Zion and on its **h**.
33:16 is the man who will dwell on the **h**,
37:24 ascended the **h** of the mountains,
37:24 mountains, the utmost **h** of Lebanon
37:24 I have reached its remotest **h**,
41:18 I will make rivers flow on barren **h**,
58:14 I will cause you to ride on the **h** of
Jer 3: 2 "Look up to the barren **h** and see.
3:21 A cry is heard on the barren **h**, the
4:11 A scorching wind from the barren **h**
7:29 take up a lament on the barren **h**,
12:12 Over all the barren **h** in the desert
14: 6 Wild donkeys stand on the barren **h**
31:12 and shout for joy on the **h** of Zion;
49:16 rocks, who occupy the **h** of the hill.
Eze 17:23 On the mountain **h** of Israel I will
34:14 and the mountain **h** of Israel will be
36: 2 The ancient **h** have become our
Ob : 3 rocks and make your home on the **h**,
Hab 3:19 he enables me to go on the **h**.

Heir (Inherit)
Ge 15: 3 in my household will be my **h**."
15: 4 "This man will not be your **h**, but
15: 4 from your own body will be your **h**.
2Sa 14: 7 we will get rid of the **h** as well.
Ps 105:44 **h** to what others had toiled for—
Mt 21:38 said to each other, 'This is the **h**.
Mk 12: 7 said to one another, 'This is the **h**.
Lk 20:14 'This is the **h**,' they said. 'Let's
Ro 4:13 that he would be **h** of the world,
Gal 4: 1 is that as long as the **h** is a child,
4: 7 a son, God has made you also an **h**.
Heb 1: 2 whom he appointed **h** of all things,
11: 7 became **h** of the righteousness that

Heirs (Inherit)
Jdg 21:17 The Benjamite survivors must have **h**,
Jer 49: 1 "Has Israel no sons? Has she no **h**?
Ac 3:25 you are **h** of the prophets and of the
Ro 4:14 For if those who live by law are **h**,
8:17 if we are children, then we are **h**
8:17 then we are **h**—**h** of God and co-heirs
Gal 3:29 and **h** according to the promise.
Eph 3: 6 Gentiles are **h** together with Israel,
Tit 3: 7 **h** having the hope of eternal life.
Heb 6:17 clear to the **h** of what was promised,
11: 9 were **h** with him of the same promise.
1Pe 3: 7 as **h** with you of the gracious gift

Helah
1Ch 4: 5 Tekoa had two wives, **H** and Naarah.
4: 7 The sons of **H**: Zereth, Zohar, Ethnan,

Helam
2Sa 10:16 beyond the River; they went to **H**,
10:17 crossed the Jordan and went to **H**.

Helbah
Jdg 1:31 or Aczib or **H** or Aphek or Rehob,

Helbon
Eze 27:18 in wine from **H** and wool from Zahar.

Held (Hold)
Ge 21: 8 was weaned Abraham **h** a great feast.
27:41 Esau **h** a grudge against Jacob
39:22 charge of all those **h** in the prison,
40: 5 who were being **h** in prison—had a
41:36 This food should be **h** in reserve for
Ex 17:11 long as Moses **h** up his hands, the
17:12 Aaron and Hur **h** his hands up—one on
21:19 **h** responsible if the other gets up
21:28 the bull will not be **h** responsible.
Lev 5: 1 about, he will be **h** responsible.
5:17 is guilty and will be **h** responsible.
7:18 any of it will be **h** responsible.
17:16 himself, he will be **h** responsible.
19: 8 Whoever eats it will be **h**
20:17 sister and will be **h** responsible.
20:19 both of you would be **h** responsible.
20:20 They will be **h** responsible; they
24:15 his God, he will be **h** responsible;
26:13 you to walk with heads **h** high.
Nu 28:16 the LORD's Passover is to be **h**.
Dt 4: 4 all of you who **h** fast to the LORD
Jos 8:18 Joshua **h** out his javelin towards Ai.
8:26 not draw back the hand that **h** out
21:41 the territory **h** by the Israelites
Jdg 4: 5 She **h** court under the Palm of
7:21 While each man **h** his position around
9:27 they **h** a festival in the temple of
16:26 Samson said to the servant who **h** his
1Sa 11:15 Israelites **h** a great celebration.
2Sa 6:22 spoke of, I will be **h** in honour."
23:19 Was he not **h** in greater honour than
23:23 He was **h** in greater honour than any
1Ki 3:28 they **h** the king in awe, because they
7:26 It **h** two thousand baths.
8:47 the land where they are **h** captive,
11: 2 Solomon **h** fast to them in love.
12:32 like the festival **h** in Judah, and
2Ki 18: 6 He **h** fast to the LORD and did not
1Ch 11:25 He was **h** in greater honour than any
2Ch 4: 5 It **h** three thousand baths.
6:37 the land where they are **h** captive,
7: 9 On the eighth day they **h** an assembly,
Ne 4:17 hand and **h** a weapon in the other,
Est 5: 2 he was pleased with her and **h** out to
8:15 city of Susa **h** a joyous celebration.
10: 3 and **h** in high esteem by his many
Job 36: 8 **h** fast by cords of affliction,
Ps 17: 5 My steps have **h** to your paths;
106:46 pitied by all who **h** them captive.
SS 3: 4 I **h** him and would not let him go
7: 5 king is **h** captive by its tresses.
Isa 33:23 mast is not **h** secure, the sail
40:12 **h** the dust of the earth in a basket,
42:14 I have been quiet and **h** myself back.
65: 2 All day long I have **h** out my hands
Jer 2: 3 all who devoured her were **h** guilty,
Eze 31:15 for it; I **h** back its streams,
Mt 21:46 the people **h** that he was a prophet.
Mk 11:32 **h** that John really was a prophet.)
Lk 5:29 Levi **h** a great banquet for Jesus at
11:50 generation will be **h** responsible
11:51 will be **h** responsible for it all.
Ac 3:11 While the beggar **h** on to Peter and
7:41 sacrifices to it and **h** a celebration
19:17 the Lord Jesus was **h** in high honour.
25: 4 Festus answered, "Paul is being **h**
25:21 Paul made his appeal to be **h** over
25:21 **h** until I could send him to Caesar.
27:32 the soldiers cut the ropes that **h**
27:40 untied the ropes that **h** the rudders.
Ro 3:19 whole world **h** accountable to God.
10:21 "All day long I have **h** out my hands
Gal 3:23 we were **h** prisoners by the law
Eph 4:16 joined and **h** together by every
Col 1:23 from the hope **h** out in the gospel.
2:19 supported and **h** together by its
2Ti 4:16 May it not be **h** against them.
Heb 2:15 who all their lives were **h** in slavery
2Pe 2: 4 dungeons to be **h** for judgment;
Rev 1:16 In his right hand he **h** seven stars,
6: 2 a white horse! Its rider **h** a bow,
15: 2 They **h** harps given them by
17: 4 She **h** a golden cup in her hand,

Heldai
1Ch 27:15 for the twelfth month, was **H** the
Zec 6:10 and gold⌋ from the exiles Heldai,
6:14 The crown will be given to **H**,

Helech
Eze 27:11 Men of Arvad and **H** manned your walls

Heled
2Sa 23:29 **H** son of Baanah the Netophathite,
1Ch 11:30 the Netophathite, **H** son of Baanah

Helek (Helekite)
Nu 26:30 clan; through **H**, the Helekite clan;
Jos 17:2 **H**, Asriel, Shechem, Hepher and

Helekite (Helek)
Nu 26:30 clan; through Helek, the **H** clan;

Helem
1Ch 7:35 The sons of his brother **H**: Zophah,

Heleph
Jos 19:33 Their boundary went from **H** and the

Helez
2Sa 23:26 **H** the Paltite, Ira son of Ikkesh
1Ch 2:39 Azariah the father of **H**, **H** the
11:27 the Harorite, **H** the Pelonite
27:10 was **H** the Pelonite, an Ephraimite.

Heli
Lk 3:23 thought, of Joseph, the son of **H**,

Heliopolis
Eze 30:17 The young men of **H** and Bubastis will

Helkai
Ne 12:15 of Harim's, Adna; of Meremoth's, **H**;

Helkath
Jos 19:25 Their territory included: **H**, Hali,
21:31 **H** and Rehob, together with their

Helkath Hazzurim
2Sa 2:16 that place in Gibeon was called **H**.

Hell
Mt 5:22 will be in danger of the fire of **h**.
5:29 your whole body to be thrown into **h**.
5:30 for your whole body to go into **h**.
10:28 can destroy both soul and body in **h**.
18:9 and be thrown into the fire of **h**.
23:15 twice as much a son of **h** as you are.
23:33 you escape being condemned to **h**?
Mk 9:43 **h**, where the fire never goes out.
9:45 have two feet and be thrown into **h**.
9:47 have two eyes and be thrown into **h**,
Lk 12:5 body, has power to throw you into **h**.
16:23 In **h**, where he was in torment, he
Jas 3:6 and is itself set on fire by **h**.
2Pe 2:4 but sent them to **h**, putting them

Helmet (Helmets)
1Sa 17:5 He had a bronze **h** on his head and
17:38 on him and a bronze **h** on his head.
Ps 60:7 Ephraim is my **h**, Judah my sceptre.
108:8 Ephraim is my **h**, Judah my sceptre.
Isa 59:17 and the **h** of salvation on his head;
Eph 6:17 Take the **h** of salvation and the
1Th 5:8 and the hope of salvation as a **h**.

Helmets (Helmet)
2Ch 26:14 Uzziah provided shields, spears, **h**,
Jer 46:4 Take your positions with **h** on!
Eze 23:24 large and small shields and with **h**.
27:10 They hung their shields and **h** on
38:5 with them, all with shields and **h**,

Helon
Nu 1:9 from Zebulun, Eliab son of **H**;
2:7 people of Zebulun is Eliab son of **H**
7:24 On the third day, Eliab son of **H**,
7:29 was the offering of Eliab son of **H**.
10:16 Eliab son of **H** was over the division

Help (Helped, Helper, Helpers, Helpful, Helping, Helps)
Ge 4:1 "With the **h** of the LORD I have
39:15 he heard me scream for **h**, he left
39:18 as soon as I screamed for **h**, he left
Ex 1:16 "When you **h** the Hebrew women in
2:23 and their cry for **h** because of their
4:12 Now go; I will **h** you speak and will
4:15 I will **h** both of you speak and will
23:1 Do not **h** a wicked man by being a
23:5 be sure you **h** him with it.
31:6 of the tribe of Dan, to **h** him.
Lev 25:35 **h** him as you would an alien or a
Nu 1:4 the head of his family, is to **h** you.
11:17 They will **h** you carry the burden of
34:18 each tribe to **h** assign the land.
Dt 22:4 **H** him to get it to its feet.
22:24 in a town and did not scream for **h**,
32:38 Let them rise up to **h** you! Let them
33:7 Oh, be his **h** against his foes!"
33:26 who rides on the heavens to **h** you
Jos 1:14 You are to **h** your brothers
10:4 "Come up and **h** me attack Gibeon,"
10:6 **H** us, because all the Amorite kings
10:33 of Gezer had come up to **h** Lachish,
24:7 they cried to the LORD for **h**, and he
Jdg 4:3 years, they cried to the LORD for **h**.
5:23 they did not come to **h** the LORD
5:23 to **h** the LORD against the mighty.'
6:6 they cried out to the LORD for **h**.
10:12 you and you cried to me for **h**,
12:3 I saw that you wouldn't **h**, I took my
1Sa 12:8 they cried to the LORD for **h**, and
14:45 for he did this today with God's **h**.
2Sa 3:12 **h** you bring all Israel over to you.
8:5 the Arameans of Damascus came to **h**
10:19 afraid to **h** the Ammonites any more.
14:4 she said, "**H** me, O king!"
15:34 **h** me by frustrating Ahithophel's
22:30 With your **h** I can advance against
22:42 They cried for **h**, but there was
2Ki 4:2 Elisha replied to her, "How can I **h**
6:26 "**H** me, my lord the king!
6:27 not **h** you, where can I get **h**
14:26 there was no-one to **h** them.
23:29 River to **h** the king of Assyria.
1Ch 12:17 have come to me in peace, to **h** me,
12:18 who **h** you, for your God will **h** you.
12:19 (He and his men did not **h** the
12:22 Day after day men came to **h** David,
12:33 to **h** David with undivided loyalty
18:5 the Arameans of Damascus came to **h**
19:19 willing to **h** the Ammonites any more.
22:17 of Israel to **h** his son Solomon.
23:28 The duty of the Levites was to **h**
24:3 With the **h** of Zadok a descendant of
28:21 craft will **h** you in all the work.
2Ch 14:11 **h** the powerless against the mighty.
14:11 **H** us, O LORD our God, for we rely on
16:12 he did not seek **h** from the LORD,
19:2 "Should you **h** the wicked and love
20:4 to seek **h** from the LORD; indeed,
25:8 has the power to **h** or to overthrow."
28:16 sent to the king of Assyria for **h**.
28:20 but gave him trouble instead of **h**.
28:21 of Assyria, but that did not **h** him.
28:23 to them so that they will **h** me.
32:8 LORD our God to **h** us and to fight
Ezr 4:2 "Let us **h** you build because, like
Ne 3:12 section with the **h** of his daughters.
6:16 had been done with the **h** of our God.
Est 7:9 Mordecai, who spoke up to **h** the king.
Job 6:13 Do I have any power to **h** myself, now
6:21 you too have proved to be of no **h**
19:7 I call for **h**, there is no justice.
24:12 souls of the wounded cry out for **h**.
29:12 I rescued the poor who cried for **h**,
30:24 when he cries for **h** in his distress.
Job 30:28 up in the assembly and cry for **h**.
36:13 fetters them, they do not cry for **h**.
Ps 5:2 Listen to my cry for **h**, my King and
12:1 **H**, LORD, for the godly are no more;
18:6 the LORD; I cried to my God for **h**.
18:29 With your **h** I can advance against
18:41 They cried for **h**, but there was
20:2 May he send you **h** from the sanctuary
22:11 is near and there is no-one to **h**.
22:19 O my Strength, come quickly to **h** me.
22:24 but has listened to his cry for **h**.
28:2 for mercy as I call to you for **h**,
30:2 LORD my God, I called to you for **h**
30:10 Hear, O LORD, and be merciful to me;
31:22 mercy when I called to you for **h**.
33:20 he is our **h** and our shield.
38:22 Come quickly to **h** me, O Lord my
39:12 listen to me cry for **h**; be not deaf
40:13 O LORD, come quickly to **h** me.
40:17 You are my **h** and my deliverer;
44:26 Rise up and **h** us; redeem us because
46:1 an ever-present **h** in trouble.
46:5 God will **h** her at break of day.
54:4 Surely God is my **h**; the Lord is
56:9 will turn back when I call for **h**.
59:4 Arise to **h** me; look on my plight!
60:5 Save us and **h** us with your right
60:11 for the **h** of man is worthless.
63:7 you are my **h**, I sing in the shadow
69:3 I am worn out calling for **h**; my
70:1 O LORD, come quickly to **h** me.
70:5 You are my **h** and my deliverer;
71:12 come quickly, O my God, to **h** me.
72:12 the afflicted who have no-one to **h**.
77:1 I cried out to God for **h**; I cried
79:9 **H** us, O God our Saviour, for the
88:13 I cry to you for **h**, O LORD; in the
94:17 Unless the LORD had given me **h**, I
102:1 let my cry for **h** come to you.
107:12 stumbled, and there was no-one to **h**.
108:6 Save us and **h** us with your right
108:12 for the **h** of man is worthless.
109:26 **H** me, O LORD my God; save me in
115:9 the LORD—he is their **h** and shield
115:10 the LORD—he is their **h** and shield
115:11 the LORD—he is their **h** and shield
119:86 **h** me for men persecute me without
119:147 I rise before dawn and cry for **h**;
119:173 May your hand be ready to **h** me, for
121:1 hills—where does my **h** come from?
121:2 My **h** comes from the LORD, the Maker
124:8 Our **h** is in the name of the LORD,
146:5 Blessed is he whose **h** is the God
Ecc 4:10 If one falls down, his friend can **h**
4:10 falls and has no-one to **h** him up!
Isa 10:3 To whom will you run for **h**?
20:6 those we fled to for **h** and
30:2 look for **h** to Pharaoh's protection,
30:5 who bring neither **h** nor advantage,
30:7 to Egypt, whose **h** is utterly useless.
30:19 gracious he will be when you cry for **h**
31:1 those who go down to Egypt for **h**,
31:1 of Israel, or seek **h** from the LORD.
31:2 against those who **h** evildoers.
41:10 I will strengthen you and **h** you;
41:13 to you, Do not fear; I will **h** you.
41:14 Israel, for I myself will **h** you,"
44:2 in the womb, and who will **h** you:
49:8 in the day of salvation I will **h**
57:13 When you cry out for **h**, let your
58:9 you will cry for **h**, and he will say
63:5 I looked, but there was no-one to **h**,
64:5 You come to the **h** of those who
Jer 11:12 they will not **h** them at all when
47:3 Fathers will not turn to **h** their
47:4 who could **h** Tyre and Sidon.
50:32 and fall and no-one will **h** her up;
Lam 1:7 hands, there was no-one to **h** her.
3:8 Even when I call out or cry for **h**,
3:11 mangled me and left me without **h**.
4:6 without a hand turned to **h** her.
4:17 looking in vain for **h**; from our
Eze 16:49 they did not **h** the poor and needy.
17:17 will be of no **h** to him in war,
29:16 their sin in turning to her for **h**.
Da 6:11 Daniel praying and asking God for **h**

Da 10:13 one of the chief princes, came to **h**
11:17 his plans will not succeed or **h** him
11:34 they will receive a little **h**, and
11:39 with the **h** of a foreign god
11:45 to his end, and no-one will **h** him.
Hos 5:13 and sent to the great king for **h**.
Jnh 2: 2 for **h**, and you listened to my cry.
Hab 1: 2 How long, O LORD, must I call for **h**,
Zec 6:15 **h** to build the temple of the LORD,
Mt 8: 5 centurion came to him, asking for **h**.
15: 5 'Whatever **h** you might otherwise have
15:25 "Lord, **h** me!" she said.
25:44 or in prison, and did not **h** you?'
Mk 7:11 'Whatever **h** you might otherwise have
9:22 anything, take pity on us and **h** us."
9:24 believe; **h** me overcome my unbelief!"
14: 7 you can **h** them any time you want.
Lk 4:38 and they asked Jesus to **h** her.
5: 7 the other boat to come and **h** them,
7:16 "God has come to **h** his people."
10:40 work by myself? Tell her to **h** me!"
11:46 will not lift one finger to **h** them.
Jn 5: 7 "I have no-one to **h** me into the pool
12: 6 he used to **h** himself to what was
Ac 2:23 with the **h** of wicked men, put him
4:20 For we cannot **h** speaking about what
11:29 **h** for the brothers living in Judea.
16: 9 "Come over to Macedonia and **h** us.
18:27 **h** to those who by grace had believed.
20:35 of hard work we must **h** the weak,
21:28 shouting, "Men of Israel, **h** us!
26:22 have had God's **h** to this very day,
Ro 16: 2 her any **h** she may need from you,
16: 2 **h** to many people, including me.
1Co 12:28 those able to **h** others, those with
16: 6 **h** me on my journey, wherever I go.
2Co 1:11 you **h** us by your prayers. Then many
8:19 and to show our eagerness to **h**.
9: 2 For I know your eagerness to **h**,
Php 1:19 the **h** given by the Spirit of Jesus
2:30 up for the **h** you could not give me.
4: 3 **h** these women who have contended
1Th 2: 2 with the **h** of our God we dared to
5:14 **h** the weak, be patient with everyone.
2Th 3: 9 we do not have the right to such **h**,
1Ti 5: 5 day to pray and to ask God for **h**.
5:16 she should **h** them and not let the
5:16 so that the church can **h** those
2Ti 1:14 **h** of the Holy Spirit who lives in us.
Tit 3:13 Do everything you can to **h** Zenas the
Heb 2:18 to **h** those who are being tempted.
4:16 grace to **h** us in our time of need.
6:10 his people and continue to **h** them.
1Pe 5:12 With the **h** of Silas, whom I regard
3Jn : 7 out, receiving no **h** from the pagans.

Helped (Help)

Jdg 9:24 who had **h** him murder his brothers.
1Sa 7:12 saying, "Thus far has the LORD **h** us.
23:16 and **h** him to find strength in God.
2Ki 10:15 and Jehu **h** him up into the chariot.
1Ch 5:20 They were **h** in fighting them, and
12: 1 the warriors who **h** him in battle;
12:21 They **h** David against raiding bands,
15:26 God had **h** the Levites who were
2Ch 18:31 cried out, and the LORD **h** him.
20:23 Seir, they **h** to destroy one another.
26: 7 God **h** him against the Philistines
26:15 greatly **h** until he became powerful.
28:23 of the kings of Aram have **h** them,
29:34 so their kinsmen the Levites **h** them
32: 3 outside the city, and they **h** him.
Est 9: 3 king's administrators **h** the Jews,
Job 26: 2 "How you have **h** the powerless!
26: 4 Who has **h** you utter these words?
Ps 28: 7 my heart trusts in him, and I am **h**.
86:17 Give me a sign of your goodness,
118:13 about to fall, but the LORD **h** me.
Isa 31: 3 he who is **h** will fall; both will
Jer 2:37 trust; you will not be **h** by them.
Mk 1:31 to her, took her hand and **h** her up
Lk 1:54 He has **h** his servant Israel,
Ac 3: 7 by the right hand, he **h** him up
9:41 by the hand and **h** her to her feet.
2Co 6: 2 and in the day of salvation I **h** you.
2Ti 1:18 in how many ways he **h** me in Ephesus.
Heb 6:10 shown him as you have **h** his people
Rev 12:16 the earth **h** the woman by opening its

Helper (Help)

Ge 2:18 I will make a **h** suitable for him."
2:20 But for Adam no suitable **h** was found.
Ex 18: 4 "My father's God was my **h**; he saved
Dt 33:29 He is your shield and **h** and your
Ne 4:22 "Have every man and his **h** stay
Ps 10:14 you are the **h** of the fatherless.
27: 9 away in anger; you have been my **h**.
118: 7 The LORD is with me; he is my **h**.
Hos 13: 9 you are against me, against your **h**.
Ac 13: 5 John was with them as their **h**.
Heb 13: 6 Lord is my **h**; I will not be afraid.

Helpers (Help)

Eze 30: 8 to Egypt and all her **h** are crushed.
Ac 19:22 two of his **h**, Timothy and Erastus

Helpful (Help)

Ac 20:20 anything that would be **h** to you
Eph 4:29 but only what is **h** for building
2Ti 4:11 he is **h** to me in my ministry.

Helping (Help)

Jos 14:12 but, the LORD **h** me, I will drive
Jdg 21:22 'Do us a kindness by **h** them, because
Ezr 5: 2 of God were with them, **h** them.
Job 30:13 me—without anyone's **h** them.
Lk 8: 3 These women were **h** to support them
Ac 9:36 always doing good and **h** the poor.
1Ti 5:10 **h** those in trouble and
Phm :13 he could take your place in **h** me

Helpless

Ps 10: 9 he lies in wait to catch the **h**;
10: 9 the **h** and drags them off in his net.
10:12 Do not forget the **h**.
69:20 broken my heart and has left me **h**;
Pr 28:15 a wicked man ruling over a **h** people.
Jer 48:45 of Heshbon the fugitives stand **h**,
Da 10: 8 turned deathly pale and I was **h**.
10:16 of the vision, my lord, and I am **h**.
Mt 9:36 **h**, like sheep without a shepherd.

Helps (Help)

Ge 49:25 of your father's God, who **h** you,
Ps 37:40 The LORD **h** them and delivers them;
Isa 31: 3 he who **h** will stumble, he who is
41: 6 each **h** the other and says to his
50: 7 the Sovereign LORD **h** me, I will not
50: 9 is the Sovereign LORD who **h** me.
Ro 8:26 In the same way, the Spirit **h** us in
Heb 2:16 For surely it is not angels he **h**,

Hem (Hemmed)

Ex 28:33 yarn around the **h** of the robe,
28:34 alternate around the **h** of the robe.
39:24 linen around the **h** of the robe.
39:25 the **h** between the pomegranates.
39:26 pomegranates alternated around the **h**
1Sa 15:27 of the **h** of his robe, and it tore.
Ps 139: 5 You **h** me in—behind and before;
Hab 1: 4 The wicked **h** in the righteous,
Zec 8:23 Jew by the **h** of his robe and say,
Lk 19:43 you and **h** you in on every side.

Heman (Heman's)

1Ki 4:31 Ethan the Ezrahite—wiser than **H**,
1Ch 2: 6 The sons of Zerah: Zimri, Ethan, **H**,
6:33 the Kohathites: **H**, the musician,
15:17 the Levites appointed **H** son of Joel;
15:19 The musicians **H**, Asaph and Ethan
16:41 With them were **H** and Jeduthun and
16:42 **H** and Jeduthun were responsible for
25: 1 **H** and Jeduthun for the ministry of
25: 4 As for **H**, from his sons: Bukkiah,
25: 5 were sons of **H** the king's seer.
25: 5 God gave **H** fourteen sons and three
25: 6 Asaph, Jeduthun and **H** were under the
2Ch 5:12 **H**, Jeduthun and their sons and
2Ch 29:14 from the descendants of **H**, Jehiel
35:15 **H** and Jeduthun the king's seer.
Ps 88: T A maskil of **H** the Ezrahite.

Heman's (Heman)

1Ch 6:39 **H** associate Asaph, who served at his

Hemdan

Ge 36:26 The sons of Dishon: **H**, Eshban,
1Ch 1:41 Dishon: **H**, Eshban, Ithran and Keran.

Hemmed (Hem)

Ex 14: 3 in confusion, **h** in by the desert.'

Hen

Zec 6:14 Tobijah, Jedaiah and **H** son of
Mt 23:37 as a **h** gathers her chicks under her
Lk 13:34 as a **h** gathers her chicks under her

Hena

2Ki 18:34 **H** and Ivvah? Have they rescued
19:13 of Sepharvaim, or of **H** or Ivvah?"
Isa 37:13 of Sepharvaim, or of **H** or Ivvah?"

Henadad

Ezr 3: 9 the sons of **H** and their sons and
Ne 3:18 countrymen under Binnui son of **H**,
3:24 Next to him, Binnui son of **H**
10: 9 Binnui of the sons of **H**, Kadmiel,

Henna

SS 1:14 My lover is to me a cluster of **h**
4:13 with choice fruits, with **h** and nard,

Hepher (Hepherite)

Nu 26:32 through **H**, the Hepherite clan.
26:33 (Zelophehad son of **H** had no sons;
27: 1 The daughters of Zelophehad son of **H**,
Jos 12:17 the king of **H** one
17: 2 Asriel, Shechem, **H** and Shemida.
17: 3 Now Zelophehad son of **H**, the son of
1Ki 4:10 and all the land of **H** were his);
1Ch 4: 6 Naarah bore him Ahuzzam, **H**, Temeni
11:36 **H** the Mekerathite, Ahijah the

Hepherite (Hepher)

Nu 26:32 through Hepher, the **H** clan.

Hephzibah

2Ki 21: 1 His mother's name was **H**.
Isa 62: 4 But you will be called **H**, and your

Herald

Da 3: 4 the **h** loudly proclaimed, "This is
Hab 2: 2 tablets so that a **h** may run with it.
1Ti 2: 7 for this purpose I was appointed a **h**
2Ti 1:11 of this gospel I was appointed a **h**

Herbs

Ex 12: 8 **h**, and bread made without yeast.
Nu 9:11 with unleavened bread and bitter **h**.
2Ki 4:39 to gather **h** and found a wild vine.
Job 30: 4 In the brush they gathered salt **h**,
Lam 3:15 He has filled me with bitter **h** and
Lk 11:42 rue and all other kinds of garden **h**,

Herd (Herded, Herding, Herds, Herdsmen)

Ge 18: 7 he ran to the **h** and selected a
32:16 each **h** by itself, and said to his
Ex 34:19 livestock, whether from **h** or flock.
Lev 1: 2 from either the **h** or the flock.
1: 3 is a burnt offering from the **h**,
3: 1 he offers an animal from the **h**,
22:21 anyone brings from the **h** or flock a
27:32 The entire tithe of the **h** and flock
Nu 15: 3 from the **h** or the flock, as an aroma
Dt 16: 2 an animal from your flock or **h**
32:14 with curds and milk from **h** and flock
Jdg 6:25 father's **h**, the one seven years old.
Ps 68:30 the **h** of bulls among the calves of
Jnh 3: 7 beast, **h** or flock, taste anything;

Mt 8:30 Some distance from them a large **h** of
8:31 us out, send us into the **h** of pigs."
8:32 and the whole **h** rushed down the
Mk 5:11 A large **h** of pigs was feeding on the
5:13 The **h**, about two thousand in number,
Lk 8:32 A large **h** of pigs was feeding there
8:33 they went into the pigs, and the **h**

Herded (Herd)
Isa 24:22 They will be **h** together like

Herding (Herd)
1Sa 25:16 time we were **h** our sheep near them.

Herds (Herd)
Ge 13: 5 also had flocks and **h** and tents.
26:14 He had so many flocks and **h** and
32: 7 the flocks and **h** and camels as well.
32:16 and keep some space between the **h**."
32:19 all the others who followed the **h**:
34:28 They seized their flocks and **h** and
45:10 your flocks and **h**, and all you have.
46:32 and **h** and everything they own.'
47: 1 with their flocks and **h** and
50: 8 flocks and **h** were left in Goshen.
Ex 10: 9 and with our flocks and **h**, because
10:24 leave your flocks and **h** behind."
12:32 Take your flocks and **h**, as you have
12:38 of livestock, both flocks and **h**.
34: 3 **h** may graze in front of the mountain.
Nu 11:22 and **h** were slaughtered for them?
31: 9 **h**, flocks and goods as plunder.
32: 1 who had very large **h** and flocks,
32:26 our flocks and **h** will remain here
Dt 7:13 oil—the calves of your **h** and the
8:13 your **h** and flocks grow large and
12: 6 the firstborn of your **h** and flocks.
12:17 or the firstborn of your **h** and
12:21 **h** and flocks the LORD has given you,
14:23 and the firstborn of your **h** and
15:19 firstborn male of your **h** and flocks.
28: 4 your **h** and the lambs of your flocks.
28:18 your **h** and the lambs of your flocks.
28:51 nor any calves of your **h** or lambs of
Jos 14: 4 for their flocks and **h**.
22: 8 wealth—with large **h** of livestock,
1Sa 30:20 He took all the flocks and **h**, and
2Ki 5:26 **h**, or menservants and maidservants?
1Ch 27:29 charge of the **h** grazing in Sharon.
27:29 in charge of the **h** in the valleys.
2Ch 31: 6 also brought a tithe of their **h**
32:29 great numbers of flocks and **h**,
Ne 10:36 of our **h** and of our flocks to the
Job 1:10 **h** are spread throughout the land.
Ps 8: 7 all flocks and **h**, and the beasts of
107:38 and he did not let their **h** diminish.
Pr 27:23 give careful attention to your **h**;
Ecc 2: 7 I also owned more **h** and flocks than
Isa 60: 6 **H** of camels will cover your land,
65:10 a resting place for **h**,
Jer 3:24 and **h**, their sons and daughters.
5:17 they will devour your flocks and **h**,
31:12 the young of the flocks and **h**.
49:32 and their large **h** will be booty.
Hos 5: 6 they go with their flocks and **h**
Joel 1:18 The **h** mill about because they
Zep 2:14 Flocks and **h** will lie down there,
Jn 4:12 his sons and his flocks and **h**?"

Herdsmen (Herd)
Ge 13: 7 between Abram's **h** and the **h** of Lot.
13: 8 between your **h** and mine,
26:20 **h** of Gerar quarrelled with Isaac's
26:20 **h** and said, "The water is ours!"
2Ch 14:15 They also attacked the camps of the **h**

Heres
Jdg 1:35 also to hold out in Mount **H**,
8:13 from the battle by the Pass of **H**.

Heresh
1Ch 9:15 Bakbakkar, **H**, Galal and Mattaniah

Heresies
2Pe 2: 1 secretly introduce destructive **h**,

Hereth
1Sa 22: 5 left and went to the forest of **H**.

Heritage (Inherit)
Job 20:29 the **h** appointed for them by God."
27:13 the **h** a ruthless man receives from
31: 2 his **h** from the Almighty on high?
Ps 61: 5 the **h** of those who fear your name.
119:111 Your statutes are my **h** for ever;
127: 3 Sons are a **h** from the LORD, children
Isa 54:17 This is the **h** of the servants of the

Hermas
Ro 16:14 **H** and the brothers with them.

Hermes
Ac 14:12 **H** because he was the chief speaker.
Ro 16:14 Greet Asyncritus, Phlegon, **H**,

Hermogenes
2Ti 1:15 me, including Phygelus and **H**.

Hermon, Mount
At the most northerly point conquered by Joshua (Dt 3:8; Jos 11:3,17; 12:1, 5; 13:5, 11), also known as Mount Sirion, Mount Senir (Dt 3:9; 1Ch 5:23), Mount Siyon (Dt 4:48) and Mount Baal Hermon (Jdg 3:3; 1Ch 5:23) because of its role in Baal worship. Used figuratively in Hebrew poetry (Ps 42:6; 89:12; 133:3; SS 4:8). (Possibly the site of Jesus' transfiguration.)

Dt 3: 8 the Arnon Gorge as far as Mount **H**.
3: 9 (**H** is called Sirion by the Sidonians;
4:48 Gorge to Mount Siyon (that is, **H**),
Jos 11: 3 below **H** in the region of Mizpah.
11:17 the Valley of Lebanon below Mount **H**.
12: 1 from the Arnon Gorge to Mount **H**,
12: 5 He ruled over Mount **H**, Salecah, all
13: 5 Gad below Mount **H** to Lebo Hamath.
13:11 **H** and all Bashan as far as Salecah—
1Ch 5:23 that is, to Senir (Mount **H**).
Ps 42: 6 the heights of **H**—from Mount Mizar.
89:12 and **H** sing for joy at your name.
133: 3 is as if the dew of **H** were falling
SS 4: 8 the top of Senir, the summit of **H**,

Hero (Heroes)
1Sa 17:51 **h** was dead, they turned and ran.
Isa 3: 2 the **h** and warrior, the judge and

Herod (Herod's, Herodians)
1. Herod the Great. King of Judea at time of Jesus' birth (Mt 2:1; Lk 1:5). Received Magi (Mt 2:1–8); slaughtered infants in attempt to kill Jesus (Mt 2:16–18). **2.** Son of Herod the Great, also called Antipas. Tetrarch of Galilee. Arrested and executed John the Baptist (Mt 14:1–12; Mk 6:14–29; Lk 3:19–20; 9:7–9); questioned Jesus (Lk 23:6–12,15). **3.** See *Agrippa*.

Mt 2: 1 during the time of King **H**, Magi from
2: 3 King **H** heard this he was disturbed,
2: 7 **H** called the Magi secretly and found
2:12 in a dream not to go back to **H**,
2:13 **H** is going to search for the child
2:15 where he stayed until the death of **H**.
2:16 **H** realised that he had been
2:19 After **H** died, an angel of the Lord
2:22 in place of his father **H**, he was
14: 1 At that time **H** the tetrarch heard
14: 3 Now **H** had arrested John and bound
14: 5 **H** wanted to kill John, but he was
14: 6 danced for them and pleased **H**
Mk 6:14 **H** heard about this, for Jesus' name
6:16 when **H** heard this, he said, "John,
6:17 For **H** himself had given orders to
6:18 For John had been saying to **H**, "It
6:20 **H** feared John and protected him,
6:20 When **H** heard John, he was greatly
6:21 On his birthday **H** gave a banquet for
6:22 she pleased **H** and his dinner guests.
8:15 of the Pharisees and that of **H**."
Lk 1: 5 In the time of **H** king of Judea there
3: 1 **H** tetrarch of Galilee, his brother
3:19 when John rebuked **H** the tetrarch
3:20 **H** added this to them all: He locked
9: 7 Now **H** the tetrarch heard about all
9: 9 **H** said, "I beheaded John. Who, then,
13:31 **H** wants to kill you."
23: 7 he sent him to **H**, who was also in
23: 8 **H** saw Jesus, he was greatly pleased,
23:11 **H** and his soldiers ridiculed and
23:12 That day **H** and Pilate became friends
23:15 Neither has **H**, for he sent him back
Ac 4:27 Indeed **H** and Pontius Pilate met
12: 1 was about this time that King **H**
12: 4 **H** intended to bring him out for
12: 6 The night before **H** was to bring him
12:19 After **H** had a thorough search made
12:19 Then **H** went from Judea to Caesarea
12:21 On the appointed day **H**, wearing his
12:23 Immediately, because **H** did not give
13: 1 brought up with **H** the tetrarch)

Herod's (Herod)
Mt 14: 6 On **H** birthday the daughter of
Lk 8: 3 the manager of **H** household; Susanna;
23: 7 that Jesus was under **H** jurisdiction
Ac 12:11 rescued me from **H** clutches and from
23:35 Paul be kept under guard in **H** palace.

Herodians (Herod)
Mt 22:16 disciples to him along with the **H**.
Mk 3: 6 plot with the **H** how they might
12:13 **H** to Jesus to catch him in his words.

Herodias
Granddaughter of Herod the Great. Divorced Philip to marry his brother Herod Antipas, bringing condemnation from John the Baptist (Mt 14:3–4; Mk 6:17–19); prompted daughter to ask for John's head (Mt 14:6–12; Mk 6:21–29).

Mt 14: 3 of **H**, his brother Philip's wife,
14: 6 On Herod's birthday the daughter of **H**
Mk 6:17 He did this because of **H**, his
6:19 **H** nursed a grudge against John and
6:22 the daughter of **H** came in and danced,
Lk 3:19 Herod the tetrarch because of **H**,

Herodion
Ro 16:11 Greet **H**, my relative. Greet those in

Heroes (Hero)
Ge 6: 4 were the **h** of old, men of renown.
Ne 3:16 pool and the House of the **H**.
Isa 5:22 Woe to those who are **h** at drinking

Heron
Lev 11:19 stork, any kind of **h**, the hoopoe
Dt 14:18 stork, any kind of **h**, the hoopoe

Heshbon
Capital city of Sihon, king of Amorites (Nu 21:26), situated about 25 miles east of northern Dead Sea. Captured by Israelites when Sihon blocked their path (Nu 21:25–30; Dt 2:24–33; Jos 13:10–27). Allotted to Gad and Reuben, who rebuilt it (Nu 32:37), became a Levite town for the Merarites (Jos 21:39). Occupied by Moabites (Isa 15:4; Jer 48:34, 45) and Ammonites (Jer 48:2; 49:3). Known for its pastures (Nu 32:1–4), vineyards (Isa 16:8–9) and pools (SS 7:4).

Nu 21:25 including **H** and all its surrounding
21:26 **H** was the city of Sihon king of the
21:27 That is why the poets say: "Come to **H**
21:28 "Fire went out from **H**, a blaze from
21:30 **H** is destroyed all the way to
21:34 of the Amorites, who reigned in **H**.
32: 3 "Ataroth, Dibon, Jazer, Nimrah, **H**,
32:37 the Reubenites rebuilt **H**, Elealeh
Dt 1: 4 who reigned in **H**, and at Edrei had
2:24 Amorite, king of **H**, and his country.
2:26 king of **H** offering peace and saying,
2:30 Sihon king of **H** refused to let us
3: 2 of the Amorites, who reigned in **H**.

Dt 3: 6 we had done with Sihon king of **H**
4:46 who reigned in **H** and was defeated by
29: 7 Sihon king of **H** and Og king of
Jos 9:10 east of the Jordan—Sihon king of **H**,
12: 2 of the Amorites, who reigned in **H**.
12: 5 to the border of Sihon king of **H**.
13:10 who ruled in **H**, out to the border
13:17 to **H** and all its towns on the
13:21 of the Amorites, who ruled at **H**.
13:26 from **H** to Ramath Mizpah and Betonim,
13:27 of the realm of Sihon king of **H**
21:39 **H** and Jazer, together with their
Jdg 11:19 who ruled in **H**, and said to him,
11:26 hundred years Israel occupied **H**,
1Ch 6:81 **H** and Jazer, together with their
Ne 9:22 over the country of Sihon king of **H**
SS 7: 4 Your eyes are the pools of **H** by the
Isa 15: 4 **H** and Elealeh cry out, their voices
16: 8 The fields of **H** wither, the vines of
16: 9 O **H**, O Elealeh, I drench you with
Jer 48: 2 in **H** men will plot her downfall:
48:34 The sound of their cry rises from **H**
48:45 "In the shadow of **H** the fugitives
48:45 for a fire has gone out from **H**, a
49: 3 "Wail, O **H**, for Ai is destroyed!

Heshmon
Jos 15:27 Hazar Gaddah, **H**, Beth Pelet,

Hesitate (Hesitated, Hesitation)
Jdg 18: 9 Don't **h** to go there and take it over.
Job 30:10 they do not **h** to spit in my face.
Da 9:14 The Lord did not **h** to bring the
Ac 10:20 Do not **h** to go with them, for I

Hesitated (Hesitate)
Ge 19:16 he **h**, the men grasped his hand and
Ac 20:20 You know that I have not **h** to preach
20:27 For I have not **h** to proclaim to you

Hesitation (Hesitate)
Ac 11:12 The Spirit told me to have no **h**

Hethlon
Eze 47:15 by the **H** road past Lebo Hamath to
48: 1 it will follow the **H** road to Lebo

Hewing (Hewn)
Isa 22:16 **h** your grave on the height and

Hewn (Hewing)
Pr 9: 1 she has **h** out its seven pillars.
Isa 51: 1 to the quarry from which you were **h**;

Hezekiah (Hezekiah's)
King of Judah; outstanding for piety (2Ki 18:5–6; 2Ch 31:20–21). Reformed Judah's religious life (2Ki 18:3–4; 2Ch 29–31). Rebelled against Assyria (2Ki 18:7); sought and received help from God (2Ki 19:1–4, 14–37; Isa 37:1–7,14–38). Healed (2Ki 20:1–11; Isa 38:1–22; 2Ch 32:24). Built up Jerusalem's defences (2Ch 32:2–5,30). Isaiah challenged dependence on human resources (Isa 22:8–11) and pride in displaying wealth to envoys from Babylon (2Ki 20:12–18; 2Ch 32:31; Isa 39:1–8); repented (2Ch 32:26). Included in Jesus' genealogy (Mt 1:9–10).

2Ki 16:20 And **H** his son succeeded him as king.
18: 1 **H** son of Ahaz king of Judah began to
18: 5 **H** trusted in the Lord, the God of
18:14 **H** king of Judah sent this message to
18:14 The king of Assyria exacted from **H**
18:15 **H** gave him all the silver that was
18:16 At this time **H** king of Judah
18:17 from Lachish to King **H** at Jerusalem.
18:19 "Tell **H**: "'This is what the great
18:22 high places and altars **H** removed,
18:29 king says: Do not let **H** deceive you.
18:30 Do not let **H** persuade you to trust
18:31 "Do not listen to **H**. This is what
18:32 "Do not listen to **H**, for he is
18:37 son of Asaph the recorder went to **H**,
19: 1 King **H** heard this, he tore his
19: 3 They told him, "This is what **H** says:
2Ki 19: 9 he again sent messengers to **H**
19:10 "Say to **H** king of Judah: Do not let
19:14 **H** received the letter from the
19:15 **H** prayed to the Lord: "O Lord, God
19:20 son of Amoz sent a message to **H**:
19:29 "This will be the sign for you, O **H**:
20: 1 In those days **H** became ill and was
20: 2 **H** turned his face to the wall and
20: 3 And **H** wept bitterly.
20: 5 "Go back and tell **H**, the leader of
20: 8 **H** had asked Isaiah, "What will be
20:10 to go forward ten steps," said **H**.
20:12 Babylon sent **H** letters and a gift,
20:13 **H** received the messengers and showed
20:13 kingdom that **H** did not show them.
20:14 Isaiah the prophet went to King **H**
20:14 "From a distant land," **H** replied.
20:15 everything in my palace," **H** said.
20:16 Isaiah said to **H**, "Hear the word of
20:19 you have spoken is good," **H** replied.
20:21 **H** rested with his fathers. And
21: 3 places his father **H** had destroyed;
1Ch 3:13 Ahaz his son, **H** his son, Manasseh
4:41 came in the days of **H** king of Judah.
2Ch 28:27 And **H** his son succeeded him as king.
29: 1 **H** was twenty-five years old when he
29:18 they went in to King **H** and reported:
29:20 Early the next morning King **H**
29:27 **H** gave the order to sacrifice the
29:30 King **H** and his officials ordered the
29:31 **H** said, "You have now dedicated
29:36 **H** and all the people rejoiced at
30: 1 **H** sent word to all Israel and Judah
30:18 But **H** prayed for them, saying, "May
30:20 the Lord heard **H** and healed the
30:22 **H** spoke encouragingly to all the
30:24 **H** king of Judah provided a thousand
31: 2 **H** assigned the priests and Levites
31: 8 **H** and his officials came and saw the
31: 9 **H** asked the priests and Levites
31:11 **H** gave orders to prepare storerooms
31:13 by appointment of King **H** and Azariah
31:20 This is what **H** did throughout Judah,
32: 1 After all that **H** had so faithfully
32: 2 **H** saw that Sennacherib had come and
32: 8 from what **H** the king of Judah said.
32: 9 this message for **H** king of Judah
32:11 **H** says, 'The Lord our God will save
32:12 Did not **H** himself remove this god's
32:15 Now do not let **H** deceive you and
32:16 Lord God and against his servant **H**.
32:17 so the god of **H** will not rescue his
32:20 King **H** and the prophet Isaiah son of
32:22 the Lord saved **H** and the people of
32:23 valuable gifts for **H** king of Judah.
32:24 In those days **H** became ill and was
32:26 **H** repented of the pride of his heart,
32:26 come upon them during the days of **H**.
32:27 **H** had very great riches and honour,
32:30 was **H** who blocked the upper outlet
32:33 **H** rested with his fathers and was
33: 3 places his father **H** had demolished;
Ezr 2:16 of Ater (through **H**) 98
Ne 7:21 of Ater (through **H**) 98
10:17 Ater, **H**, Azzur,
Pr 25: 1 by the men of **H** king of Judah:
Isa 1: 1 Jotham, Ahaz and **H**, kings of Judah.
36: 2 from Lachish to King **H** at Jerusalem.
36: 4 "Tell **H**, "'This is what the great
36: 7 high places and altars **H** removed,
36:14 king says: Do not let **H** deceive you.
36:15 Do not let **H** persuade you to trust
36:16 "Do not listen to **H**. This is what
36:18 "Do not let **H** mislead you when he
36:22 son of Asaph the recorder went to **H**
37: 1 King **H** heard this, he tore his
37: 3 They told him, "This is what **H** says:
37: 9 he sent messengers to **H** with this
37:10 "Say to **H** king of Judah: Do not let
37:14 **H** received the letter from the
37:15 **H** prayed to the Lord:
37:21 to **H**: "This is what the Lord,
37:30 This will be the sign for you, O **H**
38: 1 In those days **H** became ill and was
38: 2 **H** turned his face to the wall and
38: 3 And **H** wept bitterly.
Isa 38: 5 "Go and tell **H**, 'This is what the
38: 9 A writing of **H** king of Judah after
38:22 **H** had asked, "What will be the sign
39: 1 Babylon sent **H** letters and a gift,
39: 2 **H** received the envoys gladly and
39: 2 kingdom that **H** did not show them.
39: 3 Isaiah the prophet went to King **H**
39: 3 "From a distant land," **H** replied.
39: 4 everything in my palace," **H** said.
39: 5 Isaiah said to **H**, "Hear the word of
39: 8 you have spoken is good," **H** replied.
Jer 15: 4 of **H** king of Judah did in Jerusalem.
26:18 in the days of **H** king of Judah.
26:19 "Did **H** king of Judah or anyone else
26:19 Did not **H** fear the Lord and seek his
Hos 1: 1 Jotham, Ahaz and **H**, kings of Judah,
Mic 1: 1 Ahaz and **H**, kings of Judah—the
Zep 1: 1 the son of Amariah, the son of **H**,
Mt 1: 9 of Ahaz, Ahaz the father of **H**,
1:10 **H** the father of Manasseh, Manasseh

Hezekiah's (Hezekiah)
2Ki 18: 9 In King **H** fourth year, which was the
18:10 So Samaria was captured in **H** sixth
18:13 fourteenth year of King **H** reign
19: 5 King **H** officials came to Isaiah,
20:12 because he had heard of **H** illness.
20:20 for the other events of **H** reign, all
2Ch 32:25 **H** heart was proud and he did not
32:32 The other events of **H** reign and his
Isa 36: 1 fourteenth year of King **H** reign
37: 5 King **H** officials came to Isaiah,

Hezion
1Ki 15:18 the son of **H**, the king of Aram,

Hezir
1Ch 24:15 the seventeenth to **H**, the eighteenth
Ne 10:20 Magpiash, Meshullam, **H**,

Hezro
2Sa 23:35 **H** the Carmelite, Paarai the Arbite,
1Ch 11:37 **H** the Carmelite, Naarai son of Ezbai,

Hezron (Hezronite)
Ge 46: 9 The sons of Reuben: Hanoch, Pallu, **H**
46:12 The sons of Perez: **H** and Hamul.
Ex 6:14 were Hanoch and Pallu, **H** and Carmi.
Nu 26: 6 through **H**, the Hezronite clan;
26:21 of Perez were: through **H**,
Jos 15: 3 Then it ran past **H** up to Addar and
Ru 4:18 of Perez: Perez was the father of **H**,
4:19 **H** the father of Ram, Ram the father
1Ch 2: 5 The sons of Perez: **H** and Hamul.
2: 9 The sons born to **H** were: Jerahmeel,
2:18 Caleb son of **H** had children by his
2:21 **H** lay with the daughter of Makir
2:24 After **H** died in Caleb Ephrathah,
2:24 Abijah the wife of **H** bore him Ashhur
2:25 firstborn of **H**: Ram his firstborn,
4: 1 The descendants of Judah: Perez, **H**,
5: 3 Israel: Hanoch, Pallu, **H** and Carmi.
Mt 1: 3 father of **H**, **H** the father of Ram,
Lk 3:33 the son of Ram, the son of **H**, the

Hezronite (Hezron)
Nu 26: 6 through Hezron, the **H** clan; through
26:21 the **H** clan; through Hamul, the

Hid (Hide)
Ge 3: 8 and they **h** from the Lord God among
3:10 afraid because I was naked; so I **h**.
Ex 2: 2 child, she **h** him for three months.
2:12 killed the Egyptian and **h** him
3: 6 At this, Moses **h** his face, because
Jos 6:17 because she **h** the spies we sent.
6:25 because she **h** the men Joshua had
1Sa 13: 6 they **h** in caves and thickets, among
20:19 go to the place where you **h** when
20:24 David **h** in the field, and when the
1Ki 18:13 I **h** a hundred of the Lord's prophets
20:30 to the city and **h** in an inner room.
2Ki 7: 8 clothes, and went off and **h** them.
7: 8 some things from it and **h** them also.

1Ch 21:20 sons who were with him **h** themselves.
2Ch 22:11 she **h** the child from Athaliah
Ps 30: 7 you **h** your face, I was dismayed.
35: 7 Since they **h** their net for me
35: 8 may the net they **h** entangle them,
Isa 49: 2 in the shadow of his hand he **h** me;
54: 8 In a surge of anger I **h** my face from
57:17 and **h** my face in anger, yet he kept
Jer 13: 5 I went and **h** it at Perath, as the
Eze 39:23 So I **h** my face from them and handed
39:24 offences, and I **h** my face from them.
Da 10: 7 that they fled and **h** themselves.
Mt 13:44 When a man found it, he **h** it again,
25:18 the ground and **h** his master's money.
25:25 I was afraid and went out and **h** your
Jn 8:59 but Jesus **h** himself, slipping away
12:36 Jesus left and **h** himself from them.
Ac 1: 9 and a cloud **h** him from their sight.
Heb 11:23 By faith Moses' parents **h** him for
Rev 6:15 every slave and every free man **h** in

Hiddai

2Sa 23:30 **H** from the ravines of Gaash,

Hidden (Hide)

Ge 4:14 and I will be **h** from your presence;
Nu 5:13 and this is **h** from her husband and
Dt 33:19 on the treasures **h** in the sand."
Jos 2: 4 had taken the two men and **h** them.
2: 6 **h** them under the stalks of flax she
7:21 They are **h** in the ground inside my
7:22 and there it was, **h** in his tent,
10:16 Now the five kings had fled and **h**
Jdg 16: 9 With men **h** in the room, she called
16:12 Then, with men **h** in the room, she
1Sa 10:22 he has **h** himself among the baggage.
14:22 all the Israelites who had **h** in the
2Sa 17: 9 Even now, he is **h** in a cave or some
18:13 nothing is **h** from the king—you
1Ki 18: 4 prophets and **h** them in two caves,
2Ki 4:27 **h** it from me and has not told me why.
6:29 we may eat him,' but she had **h** him."
11: 3 He remained **h** with his nurse at the
2Ch 22:12 He remained **h** with them at the
Job 3:16 Or why was I not **h** in the ground
3:21 for it more than for **h** treasure,
3:23 life given to a man whose way is **h**
18:10 A noose is **h** for him on the ground;
28: 7 No bird of prey knows that **h** path,
28:11 rivers and brings **h** things to light.
28:21 is **h** from the eyes of every living
33:21 his bones, once **h**, now stick out.
40:21 **h** among the reeds in the marsh.
Ps 9:15 are caught in the net they have **h**.
19: 6 other; nothing is **h** from its heat.
19:12 his errors? Forgive my **h** faults.
22:24 he has not **h** his face from him but
38: 9 my sighing is not **h** from you.
69: 5 my guilt is not **h** from you.
78: 2 utter **h** things, things from of old
119:11 I have **h** your word in my heart that
139:15 My frame was not **h** from you when I
140: 5 Proud men have **h** a snare for me;
142: 3 men have **h** a snare for me.
Pr 2: 4 and search for it as for **h** treasure,
27: 5 Better is open rebuke than **h** love.
Ecc 12:14 including every **h** thing, whether
Isa 30:20 your teachers will be **h** no more;
40:27 "My way is **h** from the LORD;
42:22 in pits or **h** away in prisons.
48: 6 of **h** things unknown to you.
59: 2 your sins have **h** his face from you,
64: 7 for you have **h** your face from us
65:16 be forgotten and **h** from my eyes.
Jer 13: 7 from the place where I had **h** it,
16:17 their ways; they are not **h** from me,
18:22 and have **h** snares for my feet.
36:26 But the LORD had **h** them.
41: 8 barley, oil and honey, **h** in a field.
Eze 28: 3 Daniel? Is no secret **h** from you?
Da 2:22 He reveals deep and **h** things;
Hos 5: 3 Israel is not **h** from me.
Ob : 6 his **h** treasures pillaged!
Hab 3: 4 his hand, where his power was **h**.
Mt 5:14 A city on a hill cannot be **h**.
10:26 or **h** that will not be made known.
11:25 because you have **h** these things
13:35 **h** since the creation of the world.
13:44 is like treasure **h** in a field.
Mk 4:22 For whatever is **h** is meant to be
Lk 8:17 there is nothing **h** that will not
9:45 It was **h** from them, so that they
10:21 because you have **h** these things
11:33 where it will be **h**, or under a bowl
12: 2 or **h** that will not be made known.
18:34 Its meaning was **h** from them, and
19:42 now it is **h** from your eyes.
Ro 16:25 the mystery **h** for long ages past,
1Co 2: 7 a wisdom that has been **h** and that
4: 5 He will bring to light what is **h** in
Eph 3: 9 **h** in God, who created all things.
Col 1:26 the mystery that has been kept **h** for
2: 3 in whom are **h** all the treasures of
3: 3 you died, and your life is now **h**
1Ti 5:25 even those that are not cannot be **h**
Heb 4:13 Nothing in all creation is **h** from
Rev 2:17 I will give some of the **h** manna.

Hide (Hid, Hidden, *Hide your face*, Hides, Hiding)

Ge 18:17 said, "Shall I **h** from Abraham
47:18 We cannot **h** from our lord the fact
Ex 2: 3 when she could **h** him no longer,
29:14 burn the bull's flesh and its **h** and
Lev 4:11 **h** of the bull and all its flesh,
7: 8 anyone may keep its **h** for himself.
8:17 the bull with its **h** and its flesh
9:11 the flesh and the **h** he burned up
11:32 made of wood, cloth, **h** or sackcloth
Nu 19: 5 **h**, flesh, blood and offal.
Dt 7:20 who **h** from you have perished.
31:17 I will **h** my face from them,
31:18 I will certainly **h** my face on that
32:20 "I will **h** my face from them," he
Jos 2:16 **H** yourselves there three days until
7:19 you have done; do not **h** it from me.
Jdg 21:20 "Go and **h** in the vineyards
1Sa 3:17 "Do not **h** it from me. May God deal
3:17 you **h** from me anything he told you.
20: 2 Why should he **h** this from me?
20: 5 but let me go and **h** in the field
1Ki 17: 3 "Leave here, turn eastward and **h**
22:25 day you go to **h** in an inner room."
2Ki 7:12 the camp to **h** in the countryside,
11: 2 in a bedroom to **h** him from Athaliah
2Ch 18:24 day you go to **h** in an inner room."
Job 3:10 on me to **h** trouble from my eyes.
13:20 and then I will not **h** from you:
14:13 If only you would **h** me in the grave
34:22 deep shadow, where evildoers can **h**.
41: 7 Can you fill his **h** with harpoons or
Ps 10: 1 you **h** yourself in times of trouble?
17: 8 **h** me in the shadow of your wings
27: 5 he will **h** me in the shelter of his
31:20 you **h** them from the intrigues of men
40:10 I do not **h** your righteousness in my
55:12 against me, I could **h** from him.
64: 2 **H** me from the conspiracy of the
78: 4 We will not **h** them from their
89:46 Will you **h** yourself for ever?
119:19 do not **h** your commands from me.
139:11 "Surely the darkness will **h** me
143: 9 O LORD, for I **h** myself in you.
Isa 1:15 I will **h** my eyes from you;
2:10 Go into the rocks, **h** in the ground
3: 9 sin like Sodom; they do not **h** it.
16: 3 **H** the fugitives, do not betray the
26:20 **h** yourselves for a little while
29:15 to **h** their plans from the LORD,
50: 6 **h** my face from mocking and spitting.
53: 3 Like one from whom men **h** their faces
Jer 13: 4 **h** it there in a crevice in the rocks.
13: 6 get the belt I told you to **h** there.
23:24 Can anyone **h** in secret places so
33: 5 I will **h** my face from this city
36:19 Baruch, "You and Jeremiah, go and **h**
38:14 "Do not **h** anything from me."
38:25 **h** it from us or we will kill you,'
49: 8 Turn and flee, **h** in deep caves, you
Eze 39:29 will no longer **h** my face from them
Am 9: 3 Though they **h** themselves on the top
9: 3 Though they **h** from me at the bottom
Mic 3: 4 At that time he will **h** his face
Rev 6:16 "Fall on us and **h** us from the face

Hide your face

Job 13:24 Why do you **h** and consider me your
Ps 13: 1 How long will you **h** from me?
27: 9 Do not **h** from me, do not turn your
44:24 Why do you **h** and forget our misery
51: 9 **H** from my sins and blot out all my
69:17 Do not **h** from your servant;
88:14 Why, O LORD, do you reject me and **h**
102: 2 Do not **h** from me when I am in
104:29 When you **h**, they are terrified;
143: 7 Do not **h** from me or I will be like

Hides (Hide)

Ex 25: 5 skins dyed red and **h** of sea cows;
26:14 that a covering of **h** of sea cows.
35: 7 skins dyed red and **h** of sea cows;
35:23 or **h** of sea cows brought them.
36:19 that a covering of **h** of sea cows.
39:34 the covering of **h** of sea cows and
Lev 16:27 their **h**, flesh and offal are to be
Nu 4: 6 are to cover this with **h** of sea cows
4: 8 cover that with **h** of sea cows and
4:10 in a covering of **h** of sea cows
4:11 cover that with **h** of sea cows and
4:12 cover that with **h** of sea cows and
4:14 spread a covering of **h** of sea cows
4:25 the outer covering of **h** of sea cows
Job 20:12 mouth and he **h** it under his tongue,
34:29 If he **h** his face, who can see him?
Isa 45:15 Truly you are a God who **h** himself,
Lk 8:16 "No-one lights a lamp and **h** it in a

Hiding (Hide)

Jos 10:17 found **h** in the cave at Makkedah,
10:27 into the cave where they had been **h**.
Jdg 9: 5 son of Jerub-Baal, escaped by **h**.
1Sa 3:18 told him everything, **h** nothing
14:11 out of the holes they were **h** in."
19: 2 go into **h** and stay there.
23:19 "Is not David **h** among us in the
26: 1 "Is not David **h** on the hill of
2Ch 22: 9 him while he was **h** in Samaria.
Job 15:18 **h** nothing received from their
24: 4 all the poor of the land into **h**.
31:33 by **h** my guilt in my heart
Ps 54: T said, "Is not David **h** among us?"
64: 5 they talk about **h** their snares;
Pr 28:12 wicked rise to power, men go into **h**
28:28 rise to power, people go into **h**;
Isa 8:17 I will wait for the LORD, who is **h**
Lam 3:10 lying in wait, like a lion in **h**,
Am 6:10 and asks anyone still **h** there,
Na 3:11 will go into **h** and seek refuge
Hab 3:14 devour the wretched who were in **h**.

Hiding-place (Hiding-places)

Jdg 9:35 his soldiers came out from their **h**.
Ps 32: 7 You are my **h**; you will protect me
Isa 4: 6 and **h** from the storm and rain.
28:15 lie our refuge and falsehood our **h**.
28:17 and water will overflow your **h**

Hiding-places (Hiding-place)

1Sa 23:23 Find out about all the **h** he uses
SS 2:14 in the **h** on the mountainside, show
Jer 49:10 Esau bare; I will uncover his **h**,

Hiel

1Ki 16:34 In Ahab's time, **H** of Bethel rebuilt

Hierapolis

Col 4:13 you and for those at Laodicea and **H**.

Higgaion

Ps 9:16 by the work of their hands. **H**.

High (*God Most High, High place, High places, High priest*, Highborn, Higher, Highest, High-grade, *Most high*)

Ge 6:15 long, 75 feet wide and 45 feet **h**.
7:17 lifted the ark **h** above the earth.
7:19 and all the **h** mountains under the
29: 7 Look," he said, "the sun is still **h**
Ex 25:10 and a cubit and a half **h**.
25:23 cubit wide and a cubit and a half **h**.
27: 1 three cubits **h**; it is to be square,
27:18 cubits **h**, and with bronze bases.
30: 2 a cubit wide, and two cubits **h**
37: 1 and a cubit and a half **h**.
37:10 and a cubit and a half **h**.
37:25 a cubit wide, and two cubits **h**
38: 1 three cubits **h**; it was square,
38:18 of the courtyard, five cubits **h**,
Lev 26:13 you to walk with heads held **h**.
Nu 14:40 went up towards the **h** hill country
14:44 went up towards the **h** hill country
Dt 3: 5 **h** walls and with gates and bars,
12: 2 all the places on the **h** mountains
26:19 fame and honour **h** above all the
28: 1 **h** above all the nations on earth.
28:52 until the **h** fortified walls
Jdg 16:25 While they were in **h** spirits, they
1Sa 2: 1 in the LORD my horn is lifted **h**.
18: 5 Saul gave him a **h** rank in the army.
25:36 He was in **h** spirits and very drunk.
2Sa 13:28 "Listen! When Amnon is in **h** spirits
22:17 "He reached down from on **h** and took
1Ki 6: 2 long, twenty wide and thirty **h**.
6:20 long, twenty wide and twenty **h**.
6:23 of olive wood, each ten cubits **h**.
7: 2 fifty wide and thirty **h**, with four
7: 4 Its windows were placed **h** in sets of
7:15 each eight cubits **h** and twelve
7:16 each capital was five cubits **h**.
7:19 shape of lilies, four cubits **h**.
7:23 from rim to rim and five cubits **h**.
7:27 cubits long, four wide and three **h**.
14:23 Asherah poles on every **h** hill and
2Ki 17:10 Asherah poles on every **h** hill and
25:17 Each pillar was twenty-seven feet **h**
25:17 pillar was four and a half feet **h**
2Ch 3: 4 of the building and twenty cubits **h**
4: 1 twenty cubits wide and ten cubits **h**
4: 2 from rim to rim and five cubits **h**.
6:13 five cubits wide and three cubits **h**
Ezr 6: 3 ninety feet **h** and ninety feet wide
Ne 8: 4 Ezra the scribe stood on a **h** wooden
Est 1:10 when King Xerxes was in **h** spirits
5: 9 that day happy and in **h** spirits.
5:14 gallows built, seventy-five feet **h**
7: 9 A gallows seventy-five feet **h**
10: 3 and held in **h** esteem by his many
Job 5:11 The lowly he sets on **h**, and those
10:16 If I hold my head **h**, you stalk me
16:19 is in heaven; my advocate is on **h**.
31: 2 his heritage from the Almighty on **h**
31:28 have been unfaithful to God on **h**.
35: 5 gaze at the clouds so **h** above you.
39:27 command and build his nest on **h**?
Ps 7: 7 Rule over them from on **h**;
18:16 He reached down from on **h** and took
27: 5 tabernacle and set me **h** upon a rock.
36: 7 Both **h** and low among men find refuge
49: 2 both low and **h**, rich and poor alike:
68:18 you ascended on **h**, you led captives
93: 4 the LORD on **h** is mighty.
102:19 looked down from his sanctuary on **h**,
103:11 For as **h** as the heavens are above
104:18 The **h** mountains belong to the wild
107:25 a tempest that lifted **h** the waves.
112: 9 his horn will be lifted **h** in honour
113: 5 the One who sits enthroned on **h**,
118:16 The LORD's right hand is lifted **h**;
138: 6 Though the LORD is on **h**, he looks
144: 7 Reach down your hand from on **h**;
Pr 17:19 He who builds a **h** gate invites
23:34 like one sleeping on the **h** seas,
24: 7 Wisdom is too **h** for a fool;
25: 3 the heavens are **h** and the earth is
30:19 the way of a ship on the **h** seas,
Ecc 10: 6 Fools are put in many **h** positions,
Isa 2:14 mountains and all the **h** hills,
6: 1 saw the Lord seated on a throne, **h**
16: 3 your shadow like night—at **h** noon
25:12 bring down your **h** fortified walls
26: 5 He humbles those who dwell on **h**,
26:11 O LORD, your hand is lifted **h**,
30:13 sin will become for you like a **h** wall
30:25 **h** mountain and every lofty hill.
32:15 Spirit is poured upon us from on **h**,
33: 5 is exalted, for he dwells on **h**;
40: 9 to Zion, go up on a **h** mountain.
57: 7 made your bed on a **h** and lofty hill
57:15 this is what the **h** and lofty One
57:15 "I live in a **h** and holy place, but
58: 4 expect your voice to be heard on **h**.
Jer 2:20 on every **h** hill and under every
3: 6 She has gone up on every **h** hill
16: 6 "Both **h** and low will die in this
17: 2 spreading trees and on the **h** hills.
25:30 'The LORD will roar from on **h**;
39: 3 Nergal-Sharezer a **h** official and all
39:13 Nergal-Sharezer a **h** official and all
49:16 Though you build your nest as **h** as
51: 9 skies, it rises as **h** as the clouds.'
51:58 and her **h** gates set on fire;
52:21 the pillars was eighteen cubits **h**
52:22 of the one pillar was five cubits **h**
Lam 1:13 "From on **h** he sent fire, sent it
Eze 1:18 Their rims were **h** and awesome, and
1:26 and **h** above on the throne was a
6:13 on every **h** hill and on all the
17:22 plant it on a **h** and lofty mountain.
19:11 towered **h** above the thick foliage,
20:28 saw any **h** hill or any leafy tree,
20:40 the **h** mountain of Israel,
23:23 and men of **h** rank, all mounted
24: 9 I, too, will pile the wood **h**.
27: 4 Your domain was on the **h** seas;
27:26 oarsmen take you out to the **h** seas
31: 3 **h**, its top above the thick foliage.
31:10 LORD says: Because it towered on **h**,
31:14 are ever to tower proudly on **h**,
34: 6 the mountains and on every **h** hill.
40: 2 and set me on a very **h** mountain,
40: 5 measuring rod thick and one rod **h**.
40:12 each alcove was a wall one cubit **h**,
40:42 cubit and a half wide and a cubit **h**.
41:22 three cubits **h** and two cubits square
43:14 it is two cubits **h** and a cubit wide
43:14 is four cubits **h** ând a cubit wide.
43:15 The altar hearth is four cubits **h**,
Da 2:48 placed Daniel in a **h** position
3: 1 ninety feet **h** and nine feet wide,
5:19 of the **h** position he gave him,
Hab 2: 9 to set his nest on **h**, to escape
3:10 roared and lifted its waves on **h**.
Mt 4: 8 devil took him to a very **h** mountain
17: 1 them up a **h** mountain by themselves.
20:25 and their **h** officials exercise
Mk 6:21 gave a banquet for his **h** officials
9: 2 him and led them up a **h** mountain,
10:42 and their **h** officials exercise
Lk 3: 2 during the **h** priesthood of Annas and
4:38 was suffering from a **h** fever,
24:49 been clothed with power from on **h**."
Jn 18:10 and struck the **h** priest's servant,
18:15 Jesus into the **h** priest's courtyard,
18:26 One of the **h** priest's servants, a
Ac 4: 6 other men of the **h** priest's family.
8:10 all the people, both **h** and low, gave
13:50 the God-fearing women of **h** standing
19:17 the Lord Jesus was held in **h** honour.
25:23 **h** ranking officers and the leading
Eph 3:18 **h** and deep is the love of Christ,
4: 8 "When he ascended on **h**, he led
Heb 7:27 Unlike the other **h** priests, he does
7:28 For the law appoints as **h** priests
Jas 1: 9 to take pride in his **h** position.
Rev 14:20 rising as **h** as the horses' bridles
21:10 Spirit to a mountain great and **h**,
21:12 a great, **h** wall with twelve gates
21:16 and as wide and **h** as it is long.

High place

1Sa 9:12 people have a sacrifice at the **h**.
9:13 before he goes up to the **h** to eat.
9:14 towards them on his way up to the **h**
9:19 "Go up ahead of me to the **h**,
9:25 After they came down from the **h**
10: 5 coming down from the **h** with lyres,
10:13 prophesying, he went to the **h**.
1Ki 3: 4 for that was the most important **h**,
11: 7 Solomon built a **h** for Chemosh the
2Ki 17:11 At every **h** they burned incense, as
23:15 the **h** made by Jeroboam son of Nebat
23:15 that altar and **h** he demolished.
23:15 He burned the **h** and ground it to
1Ch 16:39 of the LORD at the **h** in Gibeon
21:29 at that time on the **h** at Gibeon.
2Ch 1: 3 assembly went to the **h** at Gibeon,
1:13 to Jerusalem from the **h** at Gibeon
Isa 16:12 Moab appears at her **h**, she only
Eze 20:29 What is this **h** you go to?'"
Mic 1: 5 is Judah's **h**? Is it not Jerusalem?
Lk 4: 5 The devil led him up to a **h** and

High places

Lev 26:30 will destroy your **h**, cut down your
Nu 33:52 idols, and demolish all their **h**.
Dt 33:29 and you will trample down their **h**.
1Ki 3: 2 were still sacrificing at the **h**,
3: 3 and burned incense on the **h**.
12:31 Jeroboam built shrines on **h** and
12:32 priests at the **h** he had made.
13: 2 will sacrifice the priests of the **h**
13:32 against all the shrines on the **h**
13:33 appointed priests for the **h** from
13:33 a priest he consecrated for the **h**.
14:23 They also set up for themselves **h**,
15:14 Although he did not remove the **h**,
22:43 The **h**, however, were not removed,
2Ki 12: 3 The **h**, however, were not removed;
14: 4 The **h**, however, were not removed;
15: 4 The **h**, however, were not removed;
15:35 The **h**, however, were not removed;
16: 4 and burned incense at the **h**,
17: 9 themselves **h** in all their towns.
17:29 people of Samaria had made at the **h**
17:32 as priests in the shrines at the **h**.
18: 4 removed the **h**, smashed the sacred
18:22 whose **h** and altars Hezekiah removed
21: 3 rebuilt the **h** his father Hezekiah
23: 5 on the **h** of the towns of Judah
23: 8 towns of Judah and desecrated the **h**
23: 9 priests of the **h** did not serve
23:13 The king also desecrated the **h** that
23:19 defiled all the shrines at the **h**
23:20 priests of those **h** on the altars
2Ch 11:15 appointed his own priests for the **h**
14: 3 the foreign altars and the **h**,
14: 5 He removed the **h** and incense altars
15:17 Although he did not remove the **h**
17: 6 removed the **h** and the Asherah poles
20:33 The **h**, however, were not removed,
21:11 He had also built **h** on the hills
28: 4 and burned incense at the **h**,
28:25 In every town in Judah he built **h**
31: 1 They destroyed the **h** and the altars
32:12 remove this god's **h** and altars,
33: 3 rebuilt the **h** his father Hezekiah
33:17 continued to sacrifice at **h**,
33:19 and the sites where he built **h**
34: 3 to purge Judah and Jerusalem of **h**,
Ps 78:58 They angered him with their **h**;
Isa 15: 2 goes up to its temple, to its **h**
36: 7 whose **h** and altars Hezekiah removed,
Jer 7:31 They have built the **h** of Topheth in
17: 3 together with your **h**, because of sin
19: 5 They have built the **h** of Baal to
32:35 They built **h** for Baal in the Valley
48:35 those who make offerings on the **h**
Eze 6: 3 and I will destroy your **h**.
6: 6 be laid waste and the **h** demolished,
16:16 of your garments to make gaudy **h**,
43: 7 idols of their kings at their **h**.
Hos 10: 8 The **h** of wickedness will be
Am 4:13 and treads the **h** of the earth

Am 7: 9 “The **h** of Isaac will be destroyed
Mic 1: 3 down and treads the **h** of the earth.

High priest

Lev 16:32 father as **h** is to make atonement.
21:10 The **h**, the one among his brothers
Nu 35:25 until the death of the **h**, who
35:28 of refuge until the death of the **h**;
35:28 after the death of the **h** may he
35:32 own land before the death of the **h**.
Jos 20: 6 the **h** who is serving at that time.
2Ki 12:10 the royal secretary and the **h** came,
22: 4 “Go up to Hilkiah the **h** and make him
22: 8 Hilkiah the **h** said to Shaphan the
23: 4 The king ordered Hilkiah the **h**,
2Ch 34: 9 They went to Hilkiah the **h** and gave
Ne 3: 1 Eliashib the **h** and his fellow
3:20 of the house of Eliashib the **h**.
13:28 Joiada son of Eliashib the **h**
Hag 1: 1 to Joshua son of Jehozadak, the **h**:
1:12 Joshua son of Jehozadak, the **h**,
1:14 of Joshua, son of Jehozadak, the **h**,
2: 2 to Joshua, son of Jehozadak, the **h**,
2: 4 O Joshua son of Jehozadak, the **h**.
Zec 3: 1 he showed me Joshua the **h** standing
3: 8 “‘Listen, O **h** Joshua and your
6:11 of the **h**, Joshua son of Jehozadak.
Mt 26: 3 assembled in the palace of the **h**,
26:51 struck the servant of the **h**,
26:57 took him to Caiaphas, the **h**,
26:58 right up to the courtyard of the **h**.
26:62 the **h** stood up and said to Jesus,
26:63 Jesus remained silent. The **h** said
26:65 the **h** tore his clothes and said,
Mk 2:26 In the days of Abiathar the **h**, he
14:47 struck the servant of the **h**,
14:53 They took Jesus to the **h**, and all
14:54 right into the courtyard of the **h**.
14:60 the **h** stood up before them and asked
14:61 Again the **h** asked him, “Are you the
14:63 The **h** tore his clothes. “Why do we
14:66 the servant girls of the **h** came by.
Lk 22:50 struck the servant of the **h**,
22:54 took him into the house of the **h**.
Jn 11:49 named Caiaphas, who was **h** that year,
11:51 but as **h** that year he prophesied
18:13 of Caiaphas, the **h** that year.
18:15 this disciple was known to the **h**,
18:16 disciple who was known to the **h**,
18:19 Meanwhile, the **h** questioned Jesus
18:22 “Is this the way you answer the **h**?”
18:24 him, still bound, to Caiaphas the **h**.
Ac 4: 6 Annas the **h** was there, and so were
5:17 the **h** and all his associates, who
5:21 When the **h** and his associates
5:27 Sanhedrin to be questioned by the **h**.
7: 1 the **h** asked him, “Are these charges
9: 1 He went to the **h**
22: 5 **h** and all the Council can testify
23: 2 At this the **h** Ananias ordered those
23: 4 “You dare to insult God’s **h**?
23: 5 I did not realise that he was the **h**;
24: 1 Five days later the **h** Ananias went
Heb 2:17 and faithful **h** in service to God,
3: 1 the apostle and **h** whom we confess.
4:14 Therefore, since we have a great **h**
4:15 For we do not have a **h** who is unable
5: 1 Every **h** is selected from among men
5: 5 himself the glory of becoming a **h**.
5:10 was designated by God to be **h** in the
6:20 He has become a **h** for ever, in the
7:26 Such a **h** meets our need—one who is
8: 1 We do have such a **h**, who sat down
8: 3 Every **h** is appointed to offer both
9: 7 only the **h** entered the inner room,
9:11 Christ came as **h** of the good things
9:25 the **h** enters the Most Holy Place
13:11 The **h** carries the blood of animals

Highborn (Bear[1], High)

Ps 62: 9 the **h** are but a lie; if weighed

Higher (High)

Dt 28:43 you will rise above you **h** and **h**,
2Ki 25:28 gave him a seat of honour **h** than
2Ch 33:14 of Ophel; he also made it much **h**.
Ezr 9: 6 our sins are **h** than our heads
Est 3: 1 **h** than that of all the other nobles.
Job 11: 8 They are **h** than the heavens—what
Ps 61: 2 me to the rock that is **h** than I.
108: 4 is your love, **h** than the heavens;
Ecc 5: 8 for one official is eyed by a **h** one,
5: 8 over them both are others **h** still.
Isa 55: 9 the heavens are **h** than the earth,
55: 9 so are my ways **h** than your ways and
Jer 52:32 gave him a seat of honour **h** than
Eze 31: 5 towered **h** than all the trees of the
Eph 4:10 who ascended **h** than all the heavens,

Highest (High)

Dt 10:14 even the **h** heavens, the earth and
1Ki 8:27 the **h** heaven, cannot contain you.
2Ch 2: 6 since the heavens, even the **h**
6:18 the **h** heavens, cannot contain you.
Ne 9: 6 You made the heavens, even the **h**
Est 1:14 the king and were **h** in the kingdom.
Job 21:22 to God, since he judges even the **h**?
22:12 And see how lofty are the **h** stars!
Ps 115:16 The **h** heavens belong to the LORD,
137: 6 I do not consider Jerusalem my **h** joy.
148: 4 Praise him, you **h** heavens and you
Pr 9: 3 calls from the **h** point of the city.
9:14 a seat at the **h** point of the city,
Isa 7:11 deepest depths or in the **h** heights
Da 5: 7 the third **h** ruler in the kingdom.”
5:16 the third **h** ruler in the kingdom.”
5:29 the third **h** ruler in the kingdom.
Mt 4: 5 stand on the **h** point of the temple
21: 9 “Hosanna in the **h**!
Mk 11:10 “Hosanna in the **h**!
Lk 2:14 “Glory to God in the **h**, and on earth
4: 9 stand on the **h** point of the temple.
19:38 Peace in heaven and glory in the **h**
Php 2: 9 God exalted him to the **h** place
1Th 5:13 Hold them in the **h** regard in love

High-grade (High)

1Ki 7: 9 were made of blocks of **h** stone cut
7:11 Above were **h** stones, cut to size,

Highway (Highways)

Nu 20:17 We will travel along the king’s **h**
21:22 We will travel along the king’s **h**
Pr 7:27 Her house is a **h** to the grave,
15:19 but the path of the upright is a **h**.
16:17 The **h** of the upright avoids evil;
Isa 11:16 There will be a **h** for the remnant of
19:23 In that day there will be a **h** from
35: 8 a **h** will be there; it will be called
40: 3 in the wilderness a **h** for our God.
62:10 Build up, build up the **h**! Remove the
Jer 31:21 Take note of the **h**, the road that

Highways (Highway)

Isa 33: 8 The **h** are deserted, no travellers
49:11 roads, and my **h** will be raised up.

Hilen

1Ch 6:58 **H**, Debir,

Hilkiah (Hilkiah's)

2Ki 18:18 son of **H** the palace administrator,
18:26 Eliakim son of **H**, and Shebna and
18:37 Eliakim son of **H** the palace
22: 4 “Go up to **H** the high priest and make
22: 8 **H** the high priest said to Shaphan
22:10 “**H** the priest has given me a book.
22:12 He gave these orders to **H** the priest,
22:14 **H** the priest, Ahikam, Acbor, Shaphan
23: 4 The king ordered **H** the high priest,
23:24 that **H** the priest had discovered
1Ch 6:13 Shallum the father of **H**, **H** the
6:45 the son of Amaziah, the son of **H**,
9:11 Azariah son of **H**, the son of
26:11 **H** the second, Tabaliah the third
2Ch 34: 9 They went to **H** the high priest and
34:14 **H** the priest found the Book of the
34:15 **H** said to Shaphan the secretary, “I
34:18 “**H** the priest has given me a book.
34:20 He gave these orders to **H**, Ahikam
34:22 **H** and those the king had sent with
35: 8 **H**, Zechariah and Jehiel, the
Ezr 7: 1 the son of Azariah, the son of **H**,
Ne 8: 4 Anaiah, Uriah, **H** and Maaseiah;
11:11 Seraiah son of **H**, the son of
12: 7 Sallu, Amok, **H** and Jedaiah. These
Isa 22:20 summon my servant, Eliakim son of **H**.
36: 3 Eliakim son of **H** the palace
36:22 Eliakim son of **H** the palace
Jer 1: 1 The words of Jeremiah son of **H**, one
29: 3 Shaphan and to Gemariah son of **H**,

Hilkiah's (Hilkiah)

Ne 12:21 of **H**, Hashabiah; of Jedaiah’s,

Hill (Foothills, Hills, Hillside, Hilltop, Hilltops)

Ge 10:30 Sephar, in the eastern **h** country.
14: 6 the Horites in the **h** country of Seir,
31:21 headed for the **h** country of Gilead.
31:23 with him in the **h** country of Gilead.
31:25 pitched his tent in the **h** country
31:54 a sacrifice there in the **h** country
36: 8 is, Edom) settled in the **h** country
36: 9 Edomites in the **h** country of Seir.
Ex 17: 9 top of the **h** with the staff of God
17:10 and Hur went to the top of the **h**.
Nu 13:17 the Negev and on into the **h** country.
13:29 and Amorites live in the **h** country;
14:40 went up towards the high **h** country.
14:44 went up towards the high **h** country,
14:45 who lived in that **h** country
Dt 1: 7 and advance into the **h** country
1:19 went towards the **h** country of the
1:20 “You have reached the **h** country of
1:24 and went up into the **h** country
1:41 it easy to go up into the **h** country.
1:43 you marched up into the **h** country.
2: 1 way around the **h** country of Seir.
2: 3 made your way around this **h** country
2: 5 the **h** country of Seir as his own.
3:12 including half the **h** country of
3:25 fine **h** country and Lebanon.”
Jos 9: 1 things—those in the **h** country,
10: 6 Amorite kings from the **h** country
10:40 including the **h** country, the Negev,
11: 3 and Jebusites in the **h** country
11:16 the **h** country, all the Negev,
11:21 Anakites from the **h** country:
11:21 from all the **h** country of Judah,
11:21 from all the **h** country of Israel.
12: 8 the **h** country, the western foothills,
13:19 Zereth Shahar on the **h** in the valley,
14:12 Now give me this **h** country that the
15: 8 climbed to the top of the **h** west of
15:48 In the **h** country: Shamir, Jattir,
16: 1 desert into the **h** country of Bethel.
17:15 “and if the **h** country of Ephraim is
17:16 The **h** country is not enough for us
17:18 the forested **h** country as well.
18:12 and headed west into the **h** country,
18:13 on the **h** south of Lower Beth Horon.
18:14 From the **h** facing Beth Horon on the
18:16 **h** facing the Valley of Ben Hinnom,
19:50 Serah in the **h** country of Ephraim.
20: 7 Galilee in the **h** country of Naphtali,
20: 7 Shechem in the **h** country of Ephraim,
20: 7 Hebron) in the **h** country of Judah.
21:11 in the **h** country of Judah.
21:21 In the **h** country of Ephraim they
24: 4 I assigned the **h** country of Seir to
24:30 at Timnath Serah in the **h** country of
24:33 Phinehas in the **h** country of Ephraim.
Jdg 1: 9 Canaanites living in the **h** country,
1:19 took possession of the **h** country
1:34 the Danites to the **h** country,
2: 9 at Timnath Heres in the **h** country of
3:27 he blew a trumpet in the **h** country
4: 5 Bethel in the **h** country of Ephraim,
7: 1 in the valley near the **h** of Moreh.
7:24 throughout the **h** country of Ephraim,
10: 1 Shamir, in the **h** country of Ephraim.
12:15 in the **h** of the Amalekites
16: 3 the top of the **h** that faces Hebron.

Jdg 17: 1 man named Micah from the **h** country
17: 8 house in the **h** country of Ephraim.
18: 2 The men entered the **h** country of
18:13 they went on to the **h** country
19: 1 in the **h** country of Ephraim
19:16 an old man from the **h** country of
19:18 **h** country of Ephraim where I live.
1Sa 1: 1 a Zuphite from the **h** country of
7: 1 it to Abinadab's house on the **h**
9: 4 he passed through the **h** country of
9:11 they were going up the **h** to the town,
13: 2 and in the **h** country of Bethel,
14:22 in the **h** country of Ephraim
17: 3 The Philistines occupied one **h** and
22: 6 tamarisk tree on the **h** at Gibeah,
23:19 the **h** of Hakilah, south of Jeshimon
26: 1 **h** of Hakilah, which faces Jeshimon?
26: 3 on the **h** of Hakilah facing Jeshimon
26:13 on top of the **h** some distance away;
2Sa 2:24 they came to the **h** of Ammah, near
2:25 and took their stand on top of a **h**.
6: 3 of Abinadab, which was on the **h**.
13:34 him, coming down the side of the **h**.
13:34 of Horonaim, on the side of the **h**."
20:21 from the **h** country of Ephraim, has
21: 9 exposed them on a **h** before the LORD.
1Ki 4: 8 Ben-Hur—in the **h** country of Ephraim;
11: 7 On a **h** east of Jerusalem, Solomon
12:25 fortified Shechem in the **h** country
14:23 on every high **h** and under every
16:24 He bought the **h** of Samaria from
16:24 of silver and built a city on the **h**
16:24 name of the former owner of the **h**.
2Ki 1: 9 who was sitting on the top of a **h**,
5:22 to me from the **h** country of Ephraim
5:24 Gehazi came to the **h**, he took the
17:10 on every high **h** and under every
23:13 on the south of the **H** of Corruption
1Ch 4:42 Ishi, invaded the **h** country of Seir
6:67 In the **h** country of Ephraim they
2Ch 13: 4 in the **h** country of Ephraim, and
19: 4 to the **h** country of Ephraim
27: 3 work on the wall at the **h** of Ophel
32:33 buried on the **h** where the tombs
33:14 Gate and encircling the **h** of Ophel
33:15 on the temple **h** and in Jerusalem;
Ne 3:26 the temple servants living on the **h**
8:15 "Go out into the **h** country and bring
11:21 The temple servants lived on the **h**
Ps 2: 6 my King on Zion, my holy **h**."
3: 4 and he answers me from his holy **h**.
15: 1 Who may live on your holy **h**?
24: 3 Who may ascend the **h** of the LORD?
78:54 **h** country his right hand had taken.
SS 4: 6 of myrrh and to the **h** of incense.
Isa 10:32 of Zion, at the **h** of Jerusalem.
30:17 mountaintop, like a banner on a **h**.
30:25 high mountain and every lofty **h**.
40: 4 every mountain and **h** made low;
49: 9 and find pasture on every barren **h**.
57: 7 made your bed on a high and lofty **h**
Jer 2:20 on every high **h** and under every
3: 6 She has gone up on every high **h** and
16:16 every mountain and **h** and from the
17:26 from the **h** country and the Negev,
26:18 the temple **h** a mound overgrown with
31:39 to the **h** of Gareb and then turn
32:44 and in the towns of the **h** country,
33:13 In the towns of the **h** country, of
49:16 who occupy the heights of the **h**.
50: 6 They wandered over mountain and **h**
Eze 6:13 on every high **h** and on all the
20:28 saw any high **h** or any leafy tree,
34: 6 the mountains and on every high **h**.
34:26 and the places surrounding my **h**.
Da 9:16 Jerusalem, your city, your holy **h**.
9:20 to the LORD my God for his holy **h**—
Joel 2: 1 Zion; sound the alarm on my holy **h**.
3:17 your God, dwell in Zion, my holy **h**.
Ob :16 Just as you drank on my holy **h**, so
Mic 3:12 the temple **h** a mound overgrown with
Zep 3:11 will you be haughty on my holy **h**.
Mt 5:14 A city on a **h** cannot be hidden.
Lk 1:39 to a town in the **h** country of Judea
1:65 and throughout the **h** country of
3: 5 in, every mountain and **h** made low.
Lk 4:29 and took him to the brow of the **h**
19:29 at the **h** called the Mount of Olives
21:37 on the **h** called the Mount of Olives
Ac 1:12 they returned to Jerusalem from the **h**

Hillel

Jdg 12:13 After him, Abdon son of **H**, from
12:15 Abdon son of **H** died, and was buried

Hills (Hill)

Ge 12: 8 From there he went on towards the **h**
14:10 them and the rest fled to the **h**.
49:26 than the bounty of the age-old **h**.
Dt 1:44 The Amorites who lived in those **h**
2:37 nor that around the towns in the **h**.
8: 7 flowing in the valleys and **h**;
8: 9 and you can dig copper out of the **h**.
12: 2 on the **h** and under every spreading
33:15 fruitfulness of the everlasting **h**;
Jos 2:16 "Go to the **h** so that the pursuers
2:22 they left, they went into the **h** and
2:23 They went down out of the **h**, forded
Jdg 3:27 from the **h**, with him leading them.
11:37 "Give me two months to roam the **h**
11:38 She and the girls went into the **h**
1Sa 23:14 and in the **h** of the Desert of Ziph.
1Ki 5:15 thousand stonecutters in the **h**,
20:23 "Their gods are gods of the **h**.
20:28 the LORD is a god of the **h** and not
22:17 I saw all Israel scattered on the **h**
2Ki 6:17 and saw the **h** full of horses
2Ch 2: 2 as stonecutters in the **h**
2:18 80,000 to be stonecutters in the **h**,
15: 8 had captured in the **h** of Ephraim.
18:16 I saw all Israel scattered on the **h**
21:11 built high places on the **h** of Judah
26:10 in the **h** and in the fertile lands,
27: 4 He built towns in the Judean **h** and
Job 15: 7 Were you brought forth before the **h**?
39: 8 He ranges the **h** for his pasture and
40:20 The **h** bring him their produce, and
Ps 50:10 and the cattle on a thousand **h**.
65:12 the **h** are clothed with gladness.
72: 3 the **h** the fruit of righteousness.
72:16 on the tops of the **h** may it sway.
114: 4 skipped like rams, the **h** like lambs.
114: 6 like rams, you **h**, like lambs?
121: 1 I lift up my eyes to the **h**—where
147: 8 rain and makes grass grow on the **h**.
148: 9 you mountains and all **h**, fruit trees
Pr 8:25 before the **h**, I was given birth,
27:25 the grass from the **h** is gathered in,
SS 2: 8 the mountains, bounding over the **h**.
2:17 like a young stag on the rugged **h**.
Isa 2: 2 it will be raised above the **h**, and
2:14 mountains and all the high **h**,
7:25 for all the **h** once cultivated by the
17:13 before the wind like chaff on the **h**
40:12 the scales and the **h** in a balance?
41:15 them, and reduce the **h** to chaff.
42:15 will lay waste the mountains and **h**
54:10 be shaken and the **h** be removed,
55:12 **h** will burst into song before you,
65: 7 mountains and defied me on the **h**,
Jer 3:23 commotion on the **h** and mountains
4:15 disaster from the **h** of Ephraim.
4:24 quaking; all the **h** were swaying.
13:16 feet stumble on the darkening **h**.
13:27 seen your detestable acts on the **h**
17: 2 spreading trees and on the high **h**.
31: 5 plant vineyards on the **h** of Samaria
31: 6 cry out on the **h** of Ephraim,
50:19 on the **h** of Ephraim and Gilead.
Eze 6: 3 LORD says to the mountains and **h**,
35: 8 by the sword will fall on your **h**
36: 4 LORD says to the mountains and **h**,
36: 6 and say to the mountains and **h**,
Hos 4:13 and burn offerings on the **h**,
10: 8 and to the **h**, "Fall on us!"
Joel 3:18 and the **h** will flow with milk;
Am 9:13 mountains and flow from all the **h**.
Mic 4: 1 it will be raised above the **h**,
6: 1 let the **h** hear what you have to say.
Na 1: 5 before him and the **h** melt away.
Hab 3: 6 and the age-old **h** collapsed.
Zep 1:10 and a loud crash from the **h**.
Mt 18:12 not leave the ninety-nine on the **h**
Mk 5: 5 day among the tombs and in the **h**
Lk 23:30 "Fall on us!" and to the **h** "Cover us!
Rev 17: 9 are seven **h** on which the woman sits.

Hillside (Hill)

2Sa 16:13 was going along the **h** opposite him,
2Ki 23:16 the tombs that were there on the **h**,
Isa 5: 1 one had a vineyard on a fertile **h**.
Mk 5:11 of pigs was feeding on the nearby **h**.
Lk 8:32 of pigs was feeding there on the **h**.

Hilltop (Hill)

Jos 15: 9 From the **h** the boundary headed
Isa 13: 2 Raise a banner on a bare **h**, shout

Hilltops (Hill)

Jdg 9:25 Shechem set men on the **h** to ambush
2Ki 16: 4 the high places, on the **h** and under
2Ch 28: 4 the high places, on the **h** and under

Hin

Ex 29:40 quarter of a **h** of oil from pressed
29:40 quarter of a **h** of wine as a drink
30:24 shekel—and a **h** of olive oil.
Lev 19:36 an honest ephah and an honest **h**.
23:13 of a quarter of a **h** of wine.
Nu 15: 4 mixed with a quarter of a **h** of oil.
15: 5 quarter of a **h** of wine as a drink
15: 6 mixed with a third of a **h** of oil,
15: 7 a third of a **h** of wine as a drink
15: 9 flour mixed with half a **h** of oil.
15:10 Also bring half a **h** of wine as a
28: 5 quarter of a **h** of oil from pressed
28: 7 quarter of a **h** of fermented drink
28:14 drink offering of half a **h** of wine
28:14 with the ram, a third of a **h**;
28:14 with each lamb, a quarter of a **h**.
Eze 4:11 measure out a sixth of a **h** of water
45:24 with a **h** of oil for each ephah.
46: 5 with a **h** of oil for each ephah.
46: 7 with a **h** of oil with each ephah.
46:11 with a **h** of oil for each ephah.
46:14 third of a **h** of oil to moisten the

Hinder (Hindered, Hinders, Hindrance)

1Sa 14: 6 Nothing can **h** the LORD from saving,
Job 15: 4 and **h** devotion to God.
Mt 19:14 and do not **h** them, for the kingdom
Mk 10:14 and do not **h** them, for the kingdom
Lk 18:16 and do not **h** them, for the kingdom
1Co 9:12 rather than **h** the gospel of Christ.
1Pe 3: 7 so that nothing will **h** your prayers.

Hindered (Hinder)

Lk 11:52 you have **h** those who were entering."
Ro 15:22 often been **h** from coming to you.

Hinders (Hinder)

Heb 12: 1 let us throw off everything that **h**

Hindquarters

1Ki 7:25 and their **h** were towards the centre
2Ch 4: 4 and their **h** were towards the centre

Hindrance (Hinder)

Ac 28:31 Boldly and without **h** he preached the

Hinged (Hinges)

Eze 41:24 two **h** leaves for each door.

Hinges (Hinged)

Pr 26:14 a door turns on its **h**, so a sluggard

Hinnom

Deep ravine on southern slope of Jerusalem, known also as Ben Hinnom. Part of boundary between Judah and Benjamin (Jos 15:8; 18:16; Ne 11:30). Scene of abominable practice of sacrificing children to Molech (2Ch 28:3; 33:6; Jer 7:31–32; 19:6; 32:35), which

Josiah tried to prevent (2Ki 23:10) and Jeremiah denounced (Jer 19:2–6).

Jos 15: 8 the hill west of the **H** Valley
18:16 It continued down the **H** Valley along
Ne 11:30 from Beersheba to the Valley of **H**.

Hint

Eph 5: 3 among you there must not be even a **h**

Hip

Ge 32:25 he touched the socket of Jacob's **h**
32:25 his **h** was wrenched as he wrestled
32:31 and he was limping because of his **h**.
32:32 attached to the socket of the **h**,
32:32 Jacob's **h** was touched near the

Hirah

Ge 38: 1 stay with a man of Adullam named **H**.
38:12 **H** the Adullamite went with him.

Hiram (Hiram's)

King of Tyre. Helped with building of David's palace (2Sa 5:11–12; 1Ch 14:1). Made treaty with Solomon (1Ki 5:12); provided materials and expertise for building temple (1Ki 5; 2Ch 2) and navy (1Ki 9:26–27; 2Ch 8:18; 1Ki 10:22; 2Ch 9:21).

2Sa 5:11 Now **H** king of Tyre sent messengers
1Ki 5: 1 **H** king of Tyre heard that Solomon
5: 2 Solomon sent back this message to **H**
5: 7 **H** heard Solomon's message, he was
5: 8 **H** sent word to Solomon: "I have
5:10 In this way **H** kept Solomon supplied
5:11 Solomon gave **H** twenty thousand cors
5:11 to do this for **H** year after year.
5:12 relations between **H** and Solomon,
5:18 The craftsmen of Solomon and **H** and
9:11 towns in Galilee to **H** king of Tyre,
9:11 because **H** had supplied him with all
9:12 when **H** went from Tyre to see the
9:14 **H** had sent to the king 120 talents
9:27 **H** sent his men—sailors who knew the
10:22 at sea along with the ships of **H**.
1Ch 14: 1 Now **H** king of Tyre sent messengers
2Ch 2: 3 Solomon sent this message to **H** king
2:11 **H** king of Tyre replied by letter to
2:12 **H** added: "Praise be to the LORD, the
8: 2 the villages that **H** had given him
8:18 **H** sent him ships commanded by his
9:10 (The men of **H** and the men of Solomon

Hiram's (Hiram)

1Ki 10:11 (**H** ships brought gold from Ophir;
2Ch 9:21 of trading ships manned by **H** men.

Hire (Hired, Hires)

Ex 22:15 paid for the **h** covers the loss.
Jdg 9: 4 and Abimelech used it to **h** reckless
1Sa 2: 5 Those who were full **h** themselves out
1Ch 19: 6 talents of silver to **h** chariots
Isa 23:17 She will return to her **h** as a
46: 6 **h** a goldsmith to make it into a god,
Mt 20: 1 to **h** men to work in his vineyard.

Hired (Hire)

Ge 30:16 "I have **h** you with my son's
Ex 12:45 a temporary resident and a **h** worker
22:15 If the animal was **h**, the money paid
Lev 19:13 back the wages of a **h** man overnight.
22:10 of a priest or his **h** worker eat it.
25: 6 and the **h** worker and temporary
25:40 He is to be treated as a **h** worker or
25:50 to a **h** man for that number of years.
25:53 He is to be treated as a man **h** from
Dt 15:18 twice as much as that of a **h** hand.
23: 4 and they **h** Balaam son of Beor from
24:14 Do not take advantage of a **h** man who
Jdg 18: 4 "He has **h** me and I am his priest.
2Sa 10: 6 they **h** twenty thousand Aramean foot
2Ki 7: 6 the king of Israel has **h** the Hittite
1Ch 19: 7 They **h** thirty-two thousand chariots
2Ch 24:12 They **h** masons and carpenters to
25: 6 He also **h** a hundred thousand
Ezr 4: 5 They **h** counsellors to work against
Ne 6:12 Tobiah and Sanballat had **h** him.
6:13 He had been **h** to intimidate me so
13: 2 water but had **h** Balaam to call a
Job 7: 1 not his days like those of a **h** man?
7: 2 **h** man waiting eagerly for his wages,
14: 6 he has put in his time like a **h** man.
Isa 7:20 use a razor **h** from beyond the River
Mt 20: 7 'Because no-one has **h** us,' they
20: 8 last ones **h** and going on to the
20: 9 "The workers who were **h** about the
20:10 when those came who were **h** first,
20:12 'These men who were **h** last worked
20:14 was **h** last the same as I gave you.
Mk 1:20 with the **h** men and followed him.
Lk 15:15 he went and **h** himself out to a
15:17 How many of my father's **h** men have
15:19 make me like one of your **h** men.'
Jn 10:12 The **h** hand is not the shepherd who
10:13 runs away because he is a **h** hand

Hires (Hire)

Pr 26:10 is he who **h** a fool or any passer-by.

Hiss (Hisses)

Jer 46:22 Egypt will **h** like a fleeing serpent
Eze 27:36 The merchants among the nations **h** at

Hisses (Hiss)

Job 27:23 claps its hands in derision and **h**

Historic (History)

Ne 2:20 or any claim or **h** right to it."

History (Historic)

Ezr 4:19 a long **h** of revolt against kings

Hit (Hits, Hitting)

Ex 21:22 "If men who are fighting **h** a
Dt 19: 5 and **h** his neighbour and kill him.
1Ki 22:34 someone drew his bow at random and **h**
2Ch 18:33 someone drew his bow at random and **h**
Pr 23:35 "They **h** me," you will say, "but I'm
Mt 26:68 "Prophesy to us, Christ. Who **h** you?
Lk 22:64 "Prophesy! Who **h** you?"

Hitch (Hitched)

1Sa 6: 7 **H** the cows to the cart, but take
1Ki 18:44 '**H** up your chariot and go down
2Ki 9:21 "**H** up my chariot," Joram ordered.

Hitched (Hitch)

1Sa 6:10 They took two such cows and **h** them
2Ki 9:21 And when it was **h** up, Joram king of

Hits (Hit)

Ex 21:18 "If men quarrel and one **h** the other
21:26 "If a man **h** a manservant or
Nu 35:18 and he **h** someone so that he dies, he
35:21 or if in hostility he **h** him with his

Hitting (Hit)

Ex 2:13 "Why are you **h** your fellow Hebrew?

Hittite (Hittites)

Ge 23:10 Ephron the **H** was sitting among his
25: 9 field of Ephron son of Zohar the **H**,
26:34 Judith daughter of Beeri the **H**,
26:34 Basemath daughter of Elon the **H**.
27:46 living because of these **H** women.
27:46 from **H** women like these, my life
36: 2 Canaan: Adah daughter of Elon the **H**,
49:29 cave in the field of Ephron the **H**,
49:30 Ephron the **H**, along with the field.
50:13 Ephron the **H**, along with the field.
Jos 1: 4 the Euphrates—all the **H** country—
1Sa 26: 6 David then asked Ahimelech the **H** and
2Sa 11: 3 Eliam and the wife of Uriah the **H**?"
11: 6 word to Joab: "Send me Uriah the **H**.
11:17 moreover, Uriah the **H** died.
11:21 your servant Uriah the **H** is dead.
11:24 your servant Uriah the **H** is dead."
2Sa 12: 9 You struck down Uriah the **H** with the
12:10 wife of Uriah the **H** to be your own.'
23:39 and Uriah the **H**. There were
1Ki 15: 5 in the case of Uriah the **H**.
2Ki 7: 6 the king of Israel has hired the **H**
1Ch 11:41 Uriah the **H**, Zabad son of Ahlai,
Eze 16: 3 was an Amorite and your mother a **H**.
16:45 was a **H** and your father an Amorite.

Hittites (Hittite)

Ge 10:15 Sidon his firstborn, and of the **H**,
15:20 **H**, Perizzites, Rephaites,
23: 3 his dead wife and spoke to the **H**.
23: 5 The **H** replied to Abraham,
23: 7 the people of the land, the **H**.
23:10 in the hearing of all the **H** who
23:16 had named in the hearing of the **H**:
23:18 in the presence of all the **H** who
23:20 made over to Abraham by the **H**
25:10 field Abraham had bought from the **H**.
49:32 cave in it were bought from the **H**."
Ex 3: 8 **H**, Amorites, Perizzites, Hivites and
3:17 **H**, Amorites, Perizzites, Hivites and
13: 5 **H**, Amorites, Hivites and
23:23 **H**, Perizzites, Canaanites, Hivites
23:28 Canaanites and **H** out of your way.
33: 2 **H**, Perizzites, Hivites and Jebusites.
34:11 **H**, Perizzites, Hivites and Jebusites.
Nu 13:29 **H**, Jebusites and Amorites live
Dt 7: 1 out before you many nations—the **H**,
20:17 Completely destroy them—the **H**,
Jos 3:10 **H**, Hivites, Perizzites, Girgashites,
9: 1 far as Lebanon (the kings of the **H**,
11: 3 **H**, Perizzites and Jebusites in the
12: 8 and the Negev—the lands of the **H**,
24:11 Perizzites, Canaanites, **H**,
Jdg 1:26 He then went to the land of the **H**,
3: 5 **H**, Amorites, Perizzites, Hivites and
1Ki 9:20 **H**, Perizzites, Hivites and Jebusites
10:29 kings of the **H** and of the Arameans.
11: 1 Ammonites, Edomites, Sidonians and **H**.
1Ch 1:13 Sidon his firstborn, and of the **H**,
2Ch 1:17 kings of the **H** and of the Arameans.
8: 7 All the people left from the **H**,
Ezr 9: 1 like those of the Canaanites, **H**,
Ne 9: 8 **H**, Amorites, Perizzites, Jebusites

Hivite (Hivites)

Ge 34: 2 Shechem son of Hamor the **H**, the
36: 2 and granddaughter of Zibeon the **H**

Hivites (Hivite)

Ge 10:17 **H**, Arkites, Sinites,
Ex 3: 8 Perizzites, **H** and Jebusites.
3:17 Hittites, Amorites, Perizzites, **H**
13: 5 Hittites, Amorites, **H** and Jebusites
23:23 Hittites, Perizzites, Canaanites, **H**
23:28 hornet ahead of you to drive the **H**,
33: 2 Perizzites, **H** and Jebusites.
34:11 Perizzites, **H** and Jebusites.
Dt 7: 1 Amorites, Canaanites, Perizzites, **H**
20:17 Amorites, Canaanites, Perizzites, **H**
Jos 3:10 Hittites, **H**, Perizzites, Girgashites,
9: 1 Perizzites, **H** and Jebusites)
9: 7 The men of Israel said to the **H**,
11: 3 and to the **H** below Hermon in the
11:19 Except for the **H** living in Gibeon,
12: 8 Perizzites, **H** and Jebusites):
24:11 Hittites, Girgashites, **H** and
Jdg 3: 3 the Sidonians, and the **H** living in
3: 5 Perizzites, **H** and Jebusites.
2Sa 24: 7 the towns of the **H** and Canaanites.
1Ki 9:20 Hittites, Perizzites, **H** and
1Ch 1:15 **H**, Arkites, Sinites,
2Ch 8: 7 Amorites, Perizzites, **H** and

Hizki

1Ch 8:17 Zebadiah, Meshullam, **H**, Heber,

Hizkiah

1Ch 3:23 The sons of Neariah: Elioenai, **H**

Hoard (Hoarded, Hoards)

Am 3:10 "who **h** plunder and loot in their

Hoarded (Hoard)
Ecc 5:13 wealth **h** to the harm of its owner,
Isa 23:18 they will not be stored up or **h**.
Jas 5: 3 You have **h** wealth in the last days.

Hoards (Hoard)
Pr 11:26 People curse the man who **h** grain,

Hobab
Nu 10:29 Now Moses said to **H** son of Reuel the
Jdg 4:11 Kenites, the descendants of **H**,

Hobah
Ge 14:15 them as far as **H**, north of Damascus.

Hobaiah
Ezr 2:61 the priests: The descendants of **H**,
Ne 7:63 the priests: the descendants of **H**,

Hod
1Ch 7:37 Bezer, **H**, Shamma, Shilshah, Ithran

Hodaviah
1Ch 3:24 The sons of Elioenai: **H**, Eliashib,
5:24 Azriel, Jeremiah, **H** and Jahdiel.
9: 7 the son of **H**, the son of Hassenuah;
Ezr 2:40 Kadmiel (through the line of **H**) 74
3: 9 his sons (descendants of **H**) and the
Ne 7:43 Kadmiel through the line of **H**) 74

Hodesh
1Ch 8: 9 By his wife **H** he had Jobab, Zibia,

Hodiah (Hodiah's)
Ne 8: 7 Jamin, Akkub, Shabbethai, **H**,
9: 5 Bani, Hashabneiah, Sherebiah, **H**,
10:10 their associates: Shebaniah, **H**,
10:13 **H**, Bani and Beninu.
10:18 **H**, Hashum, Bezai,

Hodiah's (Hodiah)
1Ch 4:19 The sons of **H** wife, the sister of

Hoe
Isa 7:25 the hills once cultivated by the **h**,

Hoglah
Nu 26:33 Mahlah, Noah, **H**, Milcah and Tirzah.)
27: 1 Mahlah, Noah, **H**, Milcah and Tirzah.
36:11 Tirzah, **H**, Milcah and Noah—married
Jos 17: 3 Mahlah, Noah, **H**, Milcah and Tirzah.

Hoham
Jos 10: 3 appealed to **H** king of Hebron,

Hoisted
Ac 27:17 the men had **h** it aboard, they passed
27:40 Then they **h** the foresail to the wind

Hold (Held, Holding, Holds)
Ge 43: 9 **h** me personally responsible for him.
48:17 so he took **h** of his father's hand to
Ex 4: 4 So Moses reached out and took **h** of
5: 1 **h** a festival to me in the desert.
9: 2 them go and continue to **h** them back,
12:16 On the first day **h** a sacred assembly,
13: 6 on the seventh day **h** a festival to
20: 7 LORD will not **h** anyone guiltless
22:29 "Do not **h** back offerings from your
25:27 to **h** the poles used in carrying
26:29 make gold rings to **h** the crossbars.
30: 4 **h** the poles used to carry it.
36:34 made gold rings to **h** the crossbars.
37:14 to **h** the poles used in carrying
37:27 **h** the poles used to carry it.
38: 5 cast bronze rings to **h** the poles
Lev 19:13 'Do not **h** back the wages of a
23: 7 On the first day **h** a sacred assembly
23: 8 And on the seventh day **h** a sacred
23:27 **H** a sacred assembly and deny
23:36 and on the eighth day **h** a sacred
Lev 25:24 Throughout the country that you **h** as
25:33 a house sold in any town they **h**—and
Nu 12:11 my lord, do not **h** against us
28:18 On the first day **h** a sacred assembly
28:25 On the seventh day **h** a sacred
28:26 **h** a sacred assembly and do no
29: 1 seventh month **h** a sacred assembly
29: 7 seventh month **h** a sacred assembly.
29:12 **h** a sacred assembly and do no
29:35 'On the eighth day **h** an assembly
Dt 5:11 LORD will not **h** anyone guiltless
10:20 **H** fast to him and take your oaths in
11:22 all his ways and to **h** fast to him—
13: 4 serve him and **h** fast to him.
16: 8 on the seventh day **h** an assembly to
21: 8 do not **h** your people guilty of the
21:19 his father and mother shall take **h**
30:20 to his voice, and **h** fast to him.
Jos 8:18 the LORD said to Joshua, "**H** out
22: 5 to obey his commands, to **h** fast to
23: 8 you are to **h** fast to the LORD your
Jdg 1:35 also to **h** out in Mount Heres,
9: 9 honoured, to **h** sway over the trees?
9:11 sweet, to **h** sway over the trees?'
9:13 and men, to **h** sway over the trees?
16: 3 Then he got up and took **h** of the
Ru 3:15 shawl you are wearing and **h** it out.
1Sa 15:27 Saul caught **h** of the hem of his
17:51 He took **h** of the Philistine's sword
2Sa 1:11 took **h** of their clothes and tore
6: 6 Uzzah reached out and took **h** of the
15: 5 hand, take **h** of him and kiss him.
19:19 "May my lord not **h** me guilty.
22:17 down from on high and took **h** of me;
1Ki 1:50 took **h** of the horns of the altar.
2:28 took **h** of the horns of the altar.
8:64 too small to **h** the burnt offerings,
11:30 Ahijah took **h** of the new cloak he
18:32 large enough to **h** two seahs of seed.
2Ki 2:12 Then he took **h** of his own clothes
4:16 "you will **h** a son in your arms."
4:27 mountain, she took **h** of his feet.
6:32 the door and **h** it shut against him.
10:19 to **h** a great sacrifice for Baal.
15:19 strengthen his own **h** on the kingdom.
2Ch 7: 7 could not **h** the burnt offerings,
Job 8:15 he clings to it, but it does not **h**.
9:28 I know you will not **h** me innocent.
10:16 If I **h** my head high, you stalk me
17: 9 the righteous will **h** to their ways
36:17 and justice have taken **h** of you.
39:10 Can you **h** him to the furrow with a
Ps 18:16 down from on high and took **h** of me;
21: 8 Your hand will lay **h** on all your
73:23 you **h** me by my right hand
74:11 Why do you **h** back your hand, your
75: 3 it is I who **h** its pillars firm.
79: 8 Do not **h** against us the sins of the
119:31 I **h** fast to your statutes, O LORD;
139:10 your right hand will **h** me fast.
Pr 3:18 who lay **h** of her will be blessed.
4: 4 "Lay **h** of my words with all your
4:13 **H** on to instruction, do not let it
5:22 the cords of his sin **h** him fast.
7:13 She took **h** of him and kissed him
20:16 **h** it in pledge if he does it for a
24:11 **h** back those staggering towards
27:13 **h** it in pledge if he does it for a
SS 7: 8 I will take **h** of its fruit.
Isa 4: 1 In that day seven women will take **h**
22:17 LORD is about to take firm **h** of you
41:13 God, who takes **h** of your right hand
42: 6 I will take **h** of your hand.
43: 6 to the south, 'Do not **h** them back.
45: 1 to Cyrus, whose right hand I take **h**
48: 9 of my praise I **h** it back from you,
54: 2 do not **h** back; lengthen your cords,
56: 4 and **h** fast to my covenant—
56: 6 and who **h** fast to my covenant—
58: 1 "Shout it aloud, do not **h** back.
64: 7 name or strives to lay **h** of you;
64:12 O LORD, will you **h** yourself back?
65: 4 whose pots **h** broth of unclean meat;
Jer 2:13 broken cisterns that cannot **h** water.
6:11 of the LORD, and I cannot **h** it in.
34: 9 was to **h** a fellow Jew in bondage.
Jer 34:10 and no longer **h** them in bondage.
50:33 **h** them fast, refusing to let them go.
Eze 3:18 **h** you accountable for his blood.
3:20 **h** you accountable for his blood.
17: 3 Taking **h** of the top of a cedar,
24:14 I will not **h** back; I will not have
30: 9 Anguish will take **h** of them on the
30:21 become strong enough to **h** a sword.
33: 6 but I will **h** the watchman
33: 8 **h** you accountable for his blood.
34:10 **h** them accountable for my flock.
37:20 **H** before their eyes the sticks you
Da 4:35 No-one can **h** back his hand or say to
Jnh 1:14 Do not **h** us accountable for killing
Zec 8:23 nations will take firm **h** of one Jew
Mt 11:12 and forceful men lay **h** of it.
12:11 not take **h** of it and lift it out?
21:26 they all **h** that John was a prophet.
Mk 11:25 if you **h** anything against anyone,
Lk 14: 4 So taking **h** of the man, he healed him
Jn 8:31 "If you **h** to my teaching, you are
14:30 He has no **h** on me,
20:17 Jesus said, "Do not **h** on to me, for
Ac 2:24 for death to keep its **h** on him.
7:60 Lord, do not **h** this sin against them.
27: 7 When the wind did not allow us to **h**
27:17 the ship itself to **h** it together.
Ro 13: 3 For rulers **h** no terror for those who
1Co 15: 2 if you **h** firmly to the word I
Php 2:16 you **h** out the word of life—in order
3:12 but I press on to take **h** of that for
3:12 for which Christ Jesus took **h** of me.
3:13 myself yet to have taken **h** of it.
Col 1:17 and in him all things **h** together.
1Th 5:13 **H** them in the highest regard in love
5:21 Test everything. **H** on to the good.
2Th 2:15 stand firm and **h** to the teachings
1Ti 3: 9 They must keep **h** of the deep truths
6:12 Take **h** of the eternal life to which
6:19 **h** of the life that is truly life.
Tit 1: 9 He must **h** firmly to the trustworthy
Heb 3: 6 And we are his house, if we **h** on to
3:14 if we **h** firmly till the end the
4:14 us **h** firmly to the faith we profess.
6:18 we who have fled to take **h** of the
10:23 Let us **h** unswervingly to the hope we
2Pe 2: 9 to **h** the unrighteous for the day of
Rev 1:18 And I **h** the keys of death and Hades.
2: 4 Yet I **h** this against you: You have
2:14 who **h** to the teaching of Balaam,
2:15 Likewise you also have those who **h**
2:24 to you who do not **h** to her teaching
2:25 Only **h** on to what you have until I
3:11 **H** on to what you have, so that
12:17 and **h** to the testimony of Jesus.
19:10 who **h** to the testimony of Jesus.

Holding (Hold)
Ge 50:11 are **h** a solemn ceremony of mourning.
Jdg 7:20 **h** in their right hands the trumpets
1Sa 17:57 David still **h** the Philistine's head.
25:36 **h** a banquet like that of a king.
1Ki 7:38 each **h** forty baths and measuring
Ne 4:21 the work with half the men **h** spears,
Job 1: 4 His sons used to take turns **h** feasts
2: 9 "Are you still **h** on to your
Jer 20: 9 I am weary of **h** it in;
34: 7 still **h** out—Lachish and Azekah.
Mk 7: 3 **h** to the tradition of the elders.
7: 8 are **h** on to the traditions of men."
Jn 2: 6 **h** from twenty to thirty gallons.
8:44 not **h** to the truth, for there is no
1Co 11: 2 and for **h** to the teachings,
2Th 2: 6 now you know what is **h** him back,
1Ti 1:19 **h** on to faith and a good conscience.
4: 8 **h** promise for both the present life
Rev 5: 8 **h** golden bowls full of incense
6: 5 was **h** a pair of scales in his hand.
7: 1 **h** back the four winds of the earth
7: 9 were **h** palm branches in their hands.
10: 2 He was **h** a little scroll, which lay
20: 1 and **h** in his hand a great chain.

Holds (Hold)

Ge 50:15 "What if Joseph **h** a grudge against
Nu 5:18 while he himself **h** the bitter water
Job 12:15 If he **h** back the waters, there is
18: 9 him by the heel; a snare **h** him fast.
37: 4 voice resounds, he **h** nothing back.
Pr 2: 7 He **h** victory in store for the
3:35 honour, but fools he **h** up to shame.
10:19 but he who **h** his tongue is wise.
11:12 a man of understanding **h** his tongue.
17:28 and discerning if he **h** his tongue.
31:19 In her hand she **h** the distaff and
Isa 41:23 tell us what the future **h**, so that
56: 2 the man who **h** it fast, who keeps the
Eze 23:32 and derision, for it **h** so much.
Da 5:23 God who **h** in his hand your life
Am 1: 5 one who **h** the sceptre in Beth Eden.
1: 8 one who **h** the sceptre in Ashkelon.
2Th 2: 7 but the one who now **h** it back will
Heb 2:14 who **h** the power of death—that is,
Rev 2: 1 words of him who **h** the seven stars
3: 1 words of him who **h** the seven spirits
3: 7 and true, who **h** the key of David.

Hole (Holes)

Dt 23:13 dig a **h** and cover up your excrement.
2Ki 12: 9 a chest and bored a **h** in its lid.
Ps 7:15 He who digs a **h** and scoops it out
Isa 11: 8 The infant will play near the **h** of
Eze 8: 7 I looked, and I saw a **h** in the wall.
12:12 and a **h** will be dug in the wall for
Mt 25:18 dug a **h** in the ground and hid his

Holes (Hole)

1Sa 14:11 out of the **h** they were hiding in."
Job 30: 6 the rocks and in **h** in the ground.
Isa 2:19 to **h** in the ground from the dread of
7:19 thornbushes and at all the water **h**.
Hag 1: 6 put them in a purse with **h** in it."
Mt 8:20 Jesus replied, "Foxes have **h** and
Lk 9:58 Jesus replied, "Foxes have **h** and
Heb 11:38 and in caves and **h** in the ground.

Holiday

Est 2:18 He proclaimed a **h** throughout the

Holiest (Holy)

Nu 18:29 **h** part of everything given to you.'

Holiness (Holy)

Ex 15:11 majestic in **h**, awesome in glory,
Dt 32:51 uphold my **h** among the Israelites.
1Ch 16:29 the LORD in the splendour of his **h**.
2Ch 20:21 for the splendour of his **h**
Ps 29: 2 the LORD in the splendour of his **h**.
89:35 Once for all, I have sworn by my **h**
93: 5 **h** adorns your house for endless
96: 9 in the splendour of his **h**;
Isa 29:23 the **h** of the Holy One of Jacob,
35: 8 it will be called the Way of **H**.
Eze 36:23 I will show the **h** of my great name,
38:23 I will show my greatness and my **h**,
Am 4: 2 The Sovereign LORD has sworn by his **h**
Lk 1:75 in **h** and righteousness before him
Ro 1: 4 who through the Spirit of **h** was
6:19 to righteousness leading to **h**.
6:22 the benefit you reap leads to **h**,
1Co 1:30 our righteousness, **h** and redemption.
2Co 1:12 **h** and sincerity that are from God.
7: 1 perfecting **h** out of reverence for
Eph 4:24 God in true righteousness and **h**.
1Ti 2: 2 quiet lives in all godliness and **h**.
2:15 in faith, love and **h** with propriety.
Heb 12:10 good, that we may share in his **h**.
12:14 without **h** no-one will see the Lord.

Hollow

Ex 27: 8 Make the altar **h**, out of boards.
38: 7 They made it **h**, out of boards.
Jdg 15:19 God opened up the **h** place in Lehi,
Pr 30: 4 up the wind in the **h** of his hands?
Isa 40:12 the waters in the **h** of his hand,
Jer 52:21 each was four fingers thick, and **h**.
2Co 9: 3 in this matter should not prove **h**,
Col 2: 8 through **h** and deceptive philosophy,

Holon

Jos 15:51 Goshen, **H** and Giloh—eleven towns
21:15 **H**, Debir,
Jer 48:21 to **H**, Jahzah and Mephaath,

Holy (Hallowed, Holiest, Holiness, *Holy city, Holy name, Holy One of Israel, Holy people, Holy place, Holy Spirit, Holy to the LORD, Most holy, Most Holy Place*)

Ge 2: 3 the seventh day and made it **h**,
Ex 3: 5 where you are standing is **h** ground."
15:13 will guide them to your **h** dwelling.
16:23 of rest, a **h** Sabbath to the LORD.
19: 6 kingdom of priests and a **h** nation.
19:23 the mountain and set it apart as **h**.
20: 8 the Sabbath day by keeping it **h**.
20:11 the Sabbath day and made it **h**.
29:37 whatever touches it will be **h**.
30:29 and whatever touches them will be **h**.
31:13 that I am the LORD, who makes you **h**.
31:14 the Sabbath, because it is **h** to you.
35: 2 **h** day, a Sabbath of rest to the LORD.
40: 9 its furnishings, and it will be **h**.
Lev 5:15 to any of the LORD's **h** things,
5:16 to do in regard to the **h** things,
6:18 Whatever touches it will become **h**.'
6:27 any of the flesh will become **h**,
10: 3 approach me I will show myself **h**;
10:10 between the **h** and the common
11:44 yourselves and be **h**, because I am **h**.
11:45 therefore be **h**, because I am **h**.
19: 2 **h** because I, the LORD your God, am **h**
19:24 all its fruit will be **h**, an offering
20: 7 'Consecrate yourselves and be **h**,
20: 8 I am the LORD, who makes you **h**.
20:26 You are to be **h** to me because I,
20:26 the LORD, am **h**, and I have set you
21: 6 They must be **h** to their God and must
21: 6 food of their God, they are to be **h**.
21: 7 because priests are **h** to their God.
21: 8 Regard them as **h**, because they offer
21: 8 Consider them **h**, because I the LORD
21: 8 I the LORD am **h**—I who make you **h**.
21:15 I am the LORD, who makes him **h**.'
21:22 of his God, as well as the **h** food;
21:23 I am the LORD, who makes them **h**.'
22: 9 I am the LORD, who makes them **h**.
22:16 I am the LORD, who makes them **h**.'
22:32 I must be acknowledged as **h** by the
22:32 I am the LORD, who makes you **h**
25:12 For it is a jubilee and is to be **h**
27: 9 animal given to the LORD becomes **h**.
27:10 both it and the substitute become **h**.
27:21 it will become **h**, like a field
27:33 become **h** and cannot be redeemed.
Nu 4:15 **h** furnishings and all the **h** articles
4:15 But they must not touch the **h** things
4:16 its **h** furnishings and articles."
4:20 not go in to look at the **h** things,
5:17 take some **h** water in a clay jar
6: 5 He must be **h** until the period of his
6:20 they are **h** and belong to the priest,
7: 9 on their shoulders the **h** things,
10:21 set out, carrying the **h** things.
16: 3 The whole community is **h**, every one
16: 5 who belongs to him and who is **h**,
16: 7 chooses will be the one who is **h**.
16:37 away, for the censers are **h**—
16:38 before the LORD and have become **h**.
18: 8 all the **h** offerings the Israelites
18:10 You must regard it as **h**.
18:17 ox, a sheep or a goat; they are **h**.
18:19 set aside from the **h** offerings
18:32 the **h** offerings of the Israelites,
20:12 as **h** in the sight of the Israelites,
20:13 he showed himself **h** among them.
27:14 to honour me as **h** before their eyes.
35:25 priest, who was anointed with **h** oil.
Dt 5:12 the Sabbath day by keeping it **h**,
23:14 Your camp must be **h**, so that he will
26:15 from heaven, your **h** dwelling-place
33: 2 He came with myriads of **h** ones from
33: 3 all the **h** ones are in your hand.
Jos 5:15 place where you are standing is **h**.
24:19 He is a **h** God; he is a jealous God.
1Sa 2: 2 "There is no-one **h** like the LORD;
6:20 presence of the LORD, this **h** God?
21: 5 **h** even on missions that are not **h**
2Ki 4: 9 comes our way is a **h** man of God.
1Ch 29: 3 I have provided for this **h** temple:
2Ch 30:27 heaven, his **h** dwelling-place.
31: 6 flocks and a tithe of the **h** things
35:13 and boiled the **h** offerings in pots,
Ezr 9: 2 mingled the **h** race with the peoples
Ne 9:14 known to them your **h** Sabbath
10:31 them on the Sabbath or on any **h** day.
10:33 for the **h** offerings; for sin
13:22 in order to keep the Sabbath day **h**.
Job 5: 1 To which of the **h** ones will you turn?
6:10 not denied the words of the **H** One.
15:15 If God places no trust in his **h** ones,
Ps 2: 6 my King on Zion, my **h** hill."
3: 4 and he answers me from his **h** hill.
5: 7 I bow down towards your **h** temple.
11: 4 The LORD is in his **h** temple;
15: 1 Who may live on your **h** hill?
16:10 will you let your **H** One see decay.
20: 6 he answers him from his **h** heaven
22: 3 Yet you are enthroned as the **H** One;
43: 3 them bring me to your **h** mountain,
47: 8 God is seated on his **h** throne.
48: 1 the city of our God, his **h** mountain.
65: 4 of your house, of your **h** temple.
68: 5 of widows, is God in his **h** dwelling.
77:13 Your ways, O God, are **h**. What god is
78:54 them to the border of his **h** land,
79: 1 they have defiled your **h** temple,
87: 1 his foundation on the **h** mountain
89: 5 in the assembly of the **h** ones.
89: 7 In the council of the **h** ones God is
98: 1 **h** arm have worked salvation for him.
99: 3 great and awesome name—he is **h**.
99: 5 worship at his footstool; he is **h**.
99: 9 God and worship at his **h** mountain,
99: 9 for the LORD our God is **h**.
105:42 For he remembered his **h** promise
110: 3 Arrayed in **h** majesty, from the womb
111: 9 **h** and awesome is his name.
138: 2 will bow down towards your **h** temple
Pr 9:10 of the **H** One is understanding.
30: 3 nor have I knowledge of the **H** One.
Isa 4: 3 will be called **h**, all who are
5:16 and the **h** God will show himself **h**
6: 3 "**H**, **H**, **H** is the LORD Almighty; the
6:13 **h** seed will be the stump in the land.
8:13 is the one you are to regard as **h**,
10:17 a fire, their **H** One a flame;
11: 9 nor destroy on all my **h** mountain,
13: 3 I have commanded my **h** ones;
27:13 LORD on the **h** mountain in Jerusalem.
29:23 they will keep my name **h**;
29:23 the holiness of the **H** One of Jacob,
30:29 night you celebrate a **h** festival;
40:25 Or who is my equal?" says the **H** One.
43:15 I am the LORD, your **H** One, Israel's
52:10 The LORD will lay bare his **h** arm in
56: 7 these I will bring to my **h** mountain
57:13 the land and possess my **h** mountain."
57:15 who lives for ever, whose name is **h**
58:13 doing as you please on my **h** day,
58:13 and the LORD's **h** day honourable,
63:15 your lofty throne, **h** and glorious.
64:11 Our **h** and glorious temple, where our
65:11 the LORD and forget my **h** mountain,
65:25 all my **h** mountain," says the LORD.
66:20 to my **h** mountain in Jerusalem
Jer 17:22 keep the Sabbath day **h**, as I
17:24 day **h** by not doing any work on it,
17:27 to keep the Sabbath day **h** by not
23: 9 because of the LORD and his **h** words.
25:30 he will thunder from his **h** dwelling
51:51 the **h** places of the LORD's house."
Eze 20:12 know that I the LORD made them **h**.
20:20 Keep my Sabbaths **h**, that they may be
20:40 For on my **h** mountain, the high
20:40 along with all your **h** sacrifices.

Eze 20:41 and I will show myself **h** among you
22: 8 You have despised my **h** things and
22:26 to my law and profane my **h** things;
22:26 between the **h** and the common;
28:14 You were on the **h** mount of God;
28:22 on her and show myself **h** within her.
28:25 I will show myself **h** among them in
36:23 I show myself **h** through you
37:28 know that I the LORD make Israel **h**,
38:16 I show myself **h** through you
39: 7 I the LORD am the **H** One in Israel.
39:27 I will show myself **h** through them
42:13 guilt offerings—for the place is **h**.
42:14 priests enter the **h** precincts
42:14 they minister, for these are **h**.
42:20 to separate the **h** from the common.
44: 8 your duty in regard to my **h** things,
44:23 between the **h** and the common
44:24 they are to keep my Sabbaths **h**.
45: 1 the entire area will be **h**.
Da 4: 8 the spirit of the **h** gods is in him
4: 9 I know that the spirit of the **h** gods
4:13 a **h** one, coming down from heaven.
4:17 the **h** ones declare the verdict,
4:18 the spirit of the **h** gods is in you.
4:23 a **h** one, coming down from heaven
5:11 the spirit of the **h** gods in him.
8:13 I heard a **h** one speaking, and
8:13 another **h** one said to him, "How
9:16 Jerusalem, your city, your **h** hill.
9:20 to the LORD my God for his **h** hill
9:24 prophecy and to anoint the most **h**.
11:28 will be set against the **h** covenant.
11:30 his fury against the **h** covenant.
11:30 to those who forsake the **h** covenant
11:45 seas at the beautiful **h** mountain.
Hos 11: 9 not man—the **H** One among you.
11:12 even against the faithful **H** One.
Joel 1:14 Declare a **h** fast; call a sacred
2: 1 Zion; sound the alarm on my **h** hill.
2:15 trumpet in Zion, declare a **h** fast,
3:17 your God, dwell in Zion, my **h** hill.
3:17 Jerusalem will be **h**; never again
Ob :16 Just as you drank on my **h** hill, so
:17 will be deliverance; it will be **h**,
Jnh 2: 4 look again towards your **h** temple.'
2: 7 rose to you, to your **h** temple.
Mic 1: 2 you, the Lord from his **h** temple.
Hab 1:12 My God, my **H** One, we will not die.
2:20 the LORD is in his **h** temple;
3: 3 God came from Teman, the **H** One from
Zep 3:11 will you be haughty on my **h** hill.
Zec 2:12 Judah as his portion in the **h** land
2:13 roused himself from his **h** dwelling.
8: 3 will be called the **H** Mountain."
14: 5 come, and all the **h** ones with him.
Mk 1:24 know who you are—the **H** One of God
6:20 him to be a righteous and **h** man.
8:38 Father's glory with the **h** angels
Lk 1:35 So the **h** one to be born will be
1:49 great things for me—**h** is his name.
1:70 (as he said through his **h** prophets
1:72 and to remember his **h** covenant,
4:34 know who you are—the **H** One of God
9:26 of the Father and of the **h** angels.
Jn 6:69 know that you are the **H** One of God
17:11 **H** Father, protect them by the power
Ac 2:27 will you let your **H** One see decay.
3:14 You disowned the **H** and Righteous
3:21 long ago through his **h** prophets.
4:27 against your **h** servant Jesus
4:30 the name of your **h** servant Jesus."
7:33 where you are standing is **h** ground.
13:34 'I will give you the **h** and sure
13:35 will not let your **H** One see decay.'
Ro 1: 2 his prophets in the **H** Scriptures
7:12 then, the law is **h**, and the
7:12 the commandment is **h**, righteous
11:16 dough offered as firstfruits is **h**,
11:16 whole batch is **h**; if the root is **h**
12: 1 **h** and pleasing to God—this is your
16:16 Greet one another with a **h** kiss.
1Co 1: 2 in Christ Jesus and called to be **h**,
7:14 unclean, but as it is, they are **h**.
16:20 Greet one another with a **h** kiss.
2Co 13:12 Greet one another with a **h** kiss.
Eph 1: 4 to be **h** and blameless in his sight.
2:21 to become a **h** temple in the Lord.
3: 5 to God's **h** apostles and prophets.
5:26 to make her **h**, cleansing her by the
5:27 other blemish, but **h** and blameless.
Col 1: 2 To the **h** and faithful brothers in
1:22 death to present you **h** in his sight,
3:12 chosen people, **h** and dearly loved
1Th 2:10 witnesses, and so is God, of how **h**
3:13 **h** in the presence of our God and
3:13 Lord Jesus comes with all his **h** ones
4: 4 in a way that is **h** and honourable,
4: 7 to be impure, but to live a **h** life.
5:26 Greet all the brothers with a **h** kiss
1Ti 2: 8 men everywhere to lift up **h** hands
2Ti 1: 9 saved us and called us to a **h** life
2:21 made **h**, useful to the Master and
3:15 you have known the **h** Scriptures,
Tit 1: 8 upright, **h** and disciplined.
Heb 2:11 Both the one who makes men **h** and
2:11 are made **h** are of the same family.
3: 1 Therefore, **h** brothers, who share in
7:26 one who is **h**, blameless, pure,
10:10 by that will, we have been made **h**
10:14 for ever those who are being made **h**.
11: 7 in **h** fear built an ark to save his
12:14 in peace with all men and to be **h**;
13:12 the people **h** through his own blood.
1Pe 1:15 you is **h**, so be **h** in all you do;
1:16 is written: "Be **h**, because I am **h**.
2: 5 house to be a **h** priesthood,
2: 9 a royal priesthood, a **h** nation, a
3: 5 For this is the way the **h** women of
2Pe 3: 2 in the past by the **h** prophets
3:11 You ought to live **h** and godly lives
1Jn 2:20 you have an anointing from the **H** One
Jude :14 upon thousands of his **h** ones
Rev 3: 7 the words of him who is **h** and true,
4: 8 "**H**, **h**, **h** is the Lord God Almighty,
6:10 "How long, Sovereign Lord, **h** and
14:10 of the **h** angels and of the Lamb.
15: 4 to your name? For you alone are **h**.
16: 5 who are and who were, **H** One,
20: 6 Blessed and **h** are those who have
22:11 let him who is **h** continue to be **h**.

Holy city

Ne 11: 1 to live in Jerusalem, the **h**,
11:18 The Levites in the **h** totalled 284.
Isa 48: 2 call yourselves citizens of the **h**
52: 1 of splendour, O Jerusalem, the **h**.
Da 9:24 and your **h** to finish transgression,
Mt 4: 5 the devil took him to the **h** and had
27:53 into the **h** and appeared to many
Rev 11: 2 will trample on the **h** for 42 months.
21: 2 I saw the **H**, the new Jerusalem,
21:10 and showed me the **H**, Jerusalem,
22:19 in the tree of life and in the **h**,

Holy name

Lev 20: 3 my sanctuary and profaned my **h**.
22: 2 so that they will not profane my **h**.
22:32 Do not profane my **h**. I must be
1Ch 16:10 Glory in his **h**; let the hearts of
16:35 that we may give thanks to your **h**,
29:16 building you a temple for your **H**,
Ps 30: 4 you saints of his; praise his **h**.
33:21 rejoice, for we trust in his **h**.
97:12 who are righteous, and praise his **h**.
103: 1 all my inmost being, praise his **h**.
105: 3 Glory in his **h**; let the hearts of
106:47 to your **h** and glory in your praise.
145:21 praise his **h** for ever and ever.
Eze 20:39 no longer profane my **h** with your
36:20 the nations they profaned my **h**,
36:21 I had concern for my **h**, which the
36:22 but for the sake of my **h**, which you
39: 7 'I will make known my **h** among my
39: 7 I will no longer let my **h** be
39:25 and I will be zealous for my **h**.
43: 7 Israel will never again defile my **h**
43: 8 defiled my **h** by their detestable
Am 2: 7 the same girl and so profane my **h**.

Holy One of Israel

2Ki 19:22 your eyes in pride? Against the **H**!
Ps 71:22 praise to you with the lyre, O **H**.
78:41 God to the test; they vexed the **H**.
89:18 to the LORD, our king to the **H**.
Isa 1: 4 they have spurned the **H** and turned
5:19 let the plan of the **H** come, so that
5:24 and spurned the word of the **H**.
10:20 will truly rely on the LORD, the **H**.
12: 6 Zion, for great is the **H** among you."
17: 7 Maker and turn their eyes to the **H**.
29:19 the needy will rejoice in the **H**.
30:11 and stop confronting us with the **H**!"
30:12 Therefore, this is what the **H** says:
30:15 the **H**, says: "In repentance and rest
31: 1 but do not look to the **H**, or seek
37:23 your eyes in pride? Against the **H**!
41:14 the LORD, your Redeemer, the **H**.
41:16 in the LORD and glory in the **H**.
41:20 this, that the **H** has created it.
43: 3 For I am the LORD, your God, the **H**,
43:14 your Redeemer, the **H**:
45:11 the **H**, and its Maker
47: 4 LORD Almighty is his name—is the **H**
48:17 your Redeemer, the **H**:
49: 7 the Redeemer and **H**—
49: 7 the **H**, who has chosen you."
54: 5 his name—the **H** is your Redeemer;
55: 5 because of the LORD your God, the **H**,
60: 9 the **H**, for he has endowed you with
60:14 the City of the LORD, Zion of the **H**.
Jer 50:29 For she defied the LORD, the **H**.
51: 5 land is full of guilt before the **H**.

Holy people

Ex 22:31 "You are to be my **h**. So do not eat
Dt 28: 9 The LORD will establish you as his **h**,
Isa 62:12 They will be called the **H**, the
Da 8:24 destroy the mighty men and the **h**.
12: 7 When the power of the **h** has been
Mt 27:52 **h** who had died were raised to life.
Eph 5: 3 these are improper for God's **h**.
2Th 1:10 he comes to be glorified in his **h**

Holy place (Most holy place)

Ex 28:29 "Whenever Aaron enters the **H**, he
28:35 he enters the **H** before the LORD
28:43 the altar to minister in the **H**,
29:30 in the **H** is to wear them seven days.
31:11 oil and fragrant incense for the **H**.
Lev 6:16 is to be eaten without yeast in a **h**;
6:26 eat it; it is to be eaten in a **h**,
6:27 a garment, you must wash it in a **h**.
6:30 in the **H** must not be eaten;
7: 6 it must be eaten in a **h**;
10:13 Eat it in a **h**, because it is your
10:18 its blood was not taken into the **H**,
14:13 He is to slaughter the lamb in the **h**
16:23 he put on before he entered the **H**,
16:24 bathe himself with water in a **h**
24: 9 who are to eat it in a **h**, because it
Jos 24:26 the oak near the **h** of the LORD.
1Ki 8: 8 **H** in front of the inner sanctuary,
8: 8 but not from outside the **H**;
8:10 the priests withdrew from the **H**,
1Ch 23:32 for the **H** and, under their brothers
2Ch 5: 9 but not from outside the **H**;
5:11 The priests then withdrew from the **H**.
35: 5 "Stand in the **h** with a group of
Ps 24: 3 of the LORD? Who may stand in his **h**?
46: 4 the **h** where the Most High dwells.
Ecc 8:10 go from the **h** and receive praise
Isa 57:15 "I live in a high and **h**, but also
63:18 while your people possessed your **h**,
Eze 45: 4 as well as a **h** for the sanctuary.
Mt 24:15 "So when you see standing in the **h**
Ac 6:13 against this **h** and against the law.
21:28 the temple area and defiled this **h**.
Heb 9: 2 bread; this was called the **H**.

Holy Spirit

Ps 51:11 presence or take your **H** from me.
Isa 63:10 they rebelled and grieved his **H**.
63:11 Where is he who set his **H** among
Mt 1:18 to be with child through the **H**.

Mt 1:20 is conceived in her is from the **H**.
3:11 you with the **H** and with fire.
12:32 anyone who speaks against the **H**
28:19 Father and of the Son and of the **H**
Mk 1: 8 but he will baptise you with the **H**
3:29 whoever blasphemes against the **H**
12:36 David himself, speaking by the **H**,
13:11 it is not you speaking, but the **H**.
Lk 1:15 filled with the **H** even from birth.
1:35 angel answered, "The **H** will come
1:41 and Elizabeth was filled with the **H**.
1:67 filled with the **H** and prophesied:
2:25 of Israel, and the **H** was upon him.
2:26 had been revealed to him by the **H**
3:16 you with the **H** and with fire.
3:22 the **H** descended on him in bodily
4: 1 Jesus, full of the **H**, returned from
10:21 full of joy through the **H**, said,
11:13 give the **H** to those who ask him!"
12:10 against the **H** will not be forgiven.
12:12 the **H** will teach you at that time
Jn 1:33 is he who will baptise with the **H**'
14:26 the Counsellor, the **H**, whom the
20:22 on them and said, "Receive the **H**.
Ac 1: 2 through the **H** to the apostles
1: 5 you will be baptised with the **H**."
1: 8 you will receive power when the **H**
1:16 the **H** spoke long ago through the
2: 4 All of them were filled with the **H**
2:33 from the Father the promised **H**
2:38 you will receive the gift of the **H**.
4: 8 Peter, filled with the **H**, said to
4:25 You spoke by the **H** through the mouth
4:31 they were all filled with the **H**
5: 3 heart that you have lied to the **H**
5:32 and so is the **H**, whom God has given
6: 5 a man full of faith and of the **H**;
7:51 fathers: You always resist the **H**!
7:55 Stephen, full of the **H**, looked up to
8:15 them that they might receive the **H**,
8:16 the **H** had not yet come upon any of
8:17 on them, and they received the **H**.
8:19 I lay my hands may receive the **H**."
9:17 see again and be filled with the **H**
9:31 and encouraged by the **H**,
10:38 of Nazareth with the **H** and power,
10:44 **H** came on all who heard the message.
10:45 gift of the **H** had been poured out
10:47 received the **H** just as we have."
11:15 "As I began to speak, the **H** came on
11:16 you will be baptised with the **H**'
11:24 He was a good man, full of the **H**
13: 2 the **H** said, "Set apart for me
13: 4 sent on their way by the **H**, went
13: 9 filled with the **H**, looked straight
13:52 were filled with joy and with the **H**.
15: 8 by giving the **H** to them, just as
15:28 seemed good to the **H** and to us not
16: 6 having been kept by the **H** from
19: 2 asked them, "Did you receive the **H**
19: 2 not even heard that there is a **H**."
19: 6 the **H** came on them and they spoke
20:23 in every city the **H** warns me
20:28 which the **H** has made you overseers.
21:11 "The **H** says, 'In this way the Jews
28:25 "The **H** spoke the truth to your
Ro 5: 5 by the **H**, whom he has given us.
9: 1 my conscience confirms it in the **H**
14:17 peace and joy in the **H**,
15:13 with hope by the power of the **H**.
15:16 to God, sanctified by the **H**.
1Co 6:19 that your body is a temple of the **H**,
12: 3 "Jesus is Lord," except by the **H**.
2Co 6: 6 in the **H** and in sincere love;
13:14 fellowship of the **H** be with you all.
Eph 1:13 in him with a seal, the promised **H**,
4:30 do not grieve the **H** of God, with
1Th 1: 5 with the **H** and with deep conviction.
1: 6 message with the joy given by the **H**.
4: 8 man but God, who gives you his **H**.
2Ti 1:14 the help of the **H** who lives in us.
Tit 3: 5 of rebirth and renewal by the **H**,
Heb 2: 4 gifts of the **H** distributed
3: 7 So, as the **H** says: "Today, if you
6: 4 gift, who have shared in the **H**,
9: 8 The **H** was showing by this that the
Heb 10:15 The **H** also testifies to us about
1Pe 1:12 to you by the **H** sent from heaven.
2Pe 1:21 they were carried along by the **H**.
Jude :20 most holy faith and pray in the **H**.

Holy to the LORD

Ex 28:36 and engrave on it as on a seal: **H**
30:10 It is most **h**."
30:37 for yourselves; consider it **h**.
31:15 seventh day is a Sabbath of rest, **h**.
39:30 like an inscription on a seal: **H**
Lev 19: 8 because he has desecrated what is **h**;
27:14 dedicates his house as something **h**,
27:23 value on that day as something **h**.
27:28 everything so devoted is most **h**.
27:30 trees, belongs to the LORD; it is **h**.
27:32 under the shepherd's rod—will be **h**.
Dt 7: 6 For you are a people **h** your God.
14: 2 for you are a people **h** your God.
14:21 But you are a people **h** your God.
26:19 a people **h** your God, as he promised.
Jer 2: 3 Israel was **h**, the firstfruits of his
31:40 corner of the Horse Gate, will be **h**.
Eze 48:14 into other hands, because it is **h**.
Zec 14:20 On that day **H** will be inscribed on
14:21 and Judah will be **h** Almighty,

Homage

2Ch 24:17 Judah came and paid **h** to the king,
Job 31:27 my hand offered them a kiss of **h**,
Mk 15:19 on their knees, they paid **h** to him.

Homam

Ge 36:22 The sons of Lotan: Hori and **H**.
1Ch 1:39 The sons of Lotan: Hori and **H**.

Home (Homeland, Homes)

Ge 18:33 he left, and Abraham returned **h**.
29:13 kissed him and brought him to his **h**,
31:55 Then he left and returned **h**.
34: 5 quiet about it until they came **h**.
35:27 Jacob came **h** to his father Isaac in
39:16 beside her until his master came **h**.
43:26 Joseph came **h**, they presented to him
Ex 3: 8 and honey—the **h** of the Canaanites,
18:23 these people will go **h** satisfied."
Lev 18: 9 born in the same **h** or elsewhere.
Nu 14:30 with uplifted hand to make your **h**,
15: 2 the land I am giving you as a **h**
24:11 Now leave at once and go **h**!
24:25 Balaam got up and returned **h** and
Dt 6: 7 Talk about them when you sit at **h**
11:19 sit at **h** and when you walk along
20: 5 Let him go **h**, or he may die
20: 6 Let him go **h**, or he may die
20: 7 Let him go **h**, or he may die
20: 8 Let him go **h** so that his brothers
21:12 Bring her into your **h** and make her
22: 2 take it **h** with you and keep it until
24: 5 year he is to be free to stay at **h**
Jos 9:12 at **h** on the day we left to come
20: 6 go back to his own **h** in the town
22: 7 Joshua sent them **h**, he blessed them,
Jdg 8:29 Jerub-Baal son of Joash went back **h**
9: 5 He went to his father's **h** in Ophrah
9:55 Abimelech was dead, they went **h**.
11:34 Jephthah returned to his **h** in Mizpah,
18:26 him, turned round and went back **h**.
19: 9 can get up and be on your way **h**."
19:15 took them into his **h** for the night.
19:28 her on his donkey and set out for **h**.
19:29 he reached **h**, he took a knife and
20: 8 man, saying, "None of us will go **h**.
21:24 went **h** to their tribes and clans,
Ru 1: 6 prepared to return **h** from there.
1: 8 each of you, to your mother's **h**.
1: 9 rest in the **h** of another husband.
1:11 Naomi said, "Return **h**, my daughters.
1:12 Return **h**, my daughters; I am too old
3: 1 should I not try to find a **h** for you,
4:11 into your **h** like Rachel and Leah,
1Sa 1:19 then went back to their **h** at Ramah.
1:23 So the woman stayed at **h** and nursed
2:11 Elkanah went **h** to Ramah, but the boy
1Sa 2:20 Then they would go **h**.
7:17 Ramah, where his **h** was, and there
10:25 the people, each to his own **h**.
10:26 Saul also went to his **h** in Gibeah,
15:34 went up to his **h** in Gibeah of Saul.
18: 6 the men were returning **h** after David
20: 6 Bethlehem, his **h** town,
23:18 Jonathan went **h**; but David
24:22 Then Saul returned **h**, but David and
25: 1 they buried him at his **h** in Ramah.
25:35 to him and said, "Go **h** in peace.
26:25 on his way, and Saul returned **h**.
2Sa 3:16 Then Abner said to him, "Go back **h**!
6:20 David returned **h** to bless his
7:10 that they can have a **h** of their own
11: 4 Then she went back **h**.
11:10 David was told, "Uriah did not go **h**,
11:10 a distance? Why didn't you go **h**?"
11:13 master's servants; he did not go **h**.
12:15 After Nathan had gone **h**, the LORD
14: 8 The king said to the woman, "Go **h**,
15:12 to come from Giloh, his **h** town.
17:23 set out for his house in his **h** town.
19:30 lord the king has arrived **h** safely."
19:39 and Barzillai returned to his **h**.
20:22 the city, each returning to his **h**.
1Ki 1:53 and Solomon said, "Go to your **h**.
5:14 in Lebanon and two months at **h**.
8:66 blessed the king and then went **h**,
12:16 So the Israelites went **h**.
12:24 Go **h**, every one of you, for this is
12:24 **h** again, as the LORD had ordered.
13: 7 "Come **h** with me and have something
13:15 the prophet said to him, "Come **h**
14:12 "As for you, go back **h**. When you set
16: 9 getting drunk in the **h** of Arza, the
17:12 am gathering a few sticks to take **h**
17:13 Go **h** and do as you have said. But
21: 4 Ahab went **h**, sullen and angry
22:17 Let each one go **h** in peace.'
2Ki 4:13 "I have a **h** among my own people.
8:21 his army, however, fled back **h**.
14:10 Glory in your victory, but stay at **h**!
14:12 Israel, and every man fled to his **h**.
1Ch 16:43 left, each for his own **h**, and David
16:43 David returned **h** to bless his family.
17: 9 that they can have a **h** of their own
2Ch 10:16 So all the Israelites went **h**.
11: 4 Go **h**, every one of you, for this is
18:16 Let each one go **h** in peace.'
25:10 to him from Ephraim and sent them **h**.
25:10 Judah and left for **h** in a great rage.
25:19 But stay at **h**! Why ask for trouble
25:22 Israel, and every man fled to his **h**.
Ne 6:10 Mehetabel, who was shut in at his **h**.
Est 5:10 Haman restrained himself and went **h**.
6:12 Haman rushed **h**, with his head
Job 17:13 If the only **h** I hope for is the
39: 6 I gave him the wasteland as his **h**,
Ps 84: 3 Even the sparrow has found a **h**, and
104:17 stork has its **h** in the pine trees.
113: 9 He settles the barren woman in her **h**
Pr 3:33 he blesses the **h** of the righteous.
7:11 defiant, her feet never stay at **h**;
7:14 "I have fellowship offerings at **h**;
7:19 My husband is not at **h**; he has gone
7:20 and will not be **h** till full moon."
15:31 rebuke will be at **h** among the wise.
27: 8 nest is a man who strays from his **h**.
30:26 yet they make their **h** in the crags;
Ecc 12: 5 Then man goes to his eternal **h** and
Isa 3: 6 of his brothers at his father's **h**,
14:17 would not let his captives go **h**?"
34:13 a haunt for jackals, a **h** for owls.
Jer 39:14 Shaphan, to take him back to his **h**.
Eze 36: 8 Israel, for they will soon come **h**.
Da 4: 4 I, Nebuchadnezzar, was at **h** in my
6:10 went **h** to his upstairs room where
Ob :3 and make your **h** on the heights,
Jnh 4: 2 what I said when I was still at **h**?
Mic 2: 2 They defraud a man of his **h**, a
Zep 3:20 at that time I will bring you **h**.
Hag 1: 9 What you brought **h**, I blew away.
Mt 1:20 do not be afraid to take Mary **h**
1:24 him and took Mary **h** as his wife.
8: 6 "my servant lies at **h** paralysed

Mt 9: 6 "Get up, take your mat and go **h**.
9: 7 the man got up and went **h**.
10:12 you enter the **h**, give it your
10:13 If the **h** is deserving, let your
10:14 feet when you leave that **h** or town.
13:54 Coming to his **h** town, he began
13:57 "Only in his **h** town and in his own
26: 6 While Jesus was in Bethany in the **h**
Mk 1:29 John to the **h** of Simon and Andrew.
2: 1 the people heard that he had come **h**.
2:11 get up, take your mat and go **h**."
5:19 "Go **h** to your family and tell them
5:38 the **h** of the synagogue ruler
6: 1 Jesus left there and went to his **h**
6: 4 said to them, "Only in his **h** town,
7:30 She went **h** and found her child lying
8: 3 If I send them **h** hungry, they will
8:26 Jesus sent him **h**, saying, "Don't go
10:29 "no-one who has left **h** or brothers
14: 3 reclining at the table in the **h** of a
Lk 1:23 was completed, he returned **h**.
1:40 where she entered Zechariah's **h** and
1:56 three months and then returned **h**.
2:43 while his parents were returning **h**,
4:23 Do here in your **h** town what we
4:24 prophet is accepted in his **h** town.
4:38 and went to the **h** of Simon.
5:24 get up, take your mat and go **h**."
5:25 lying on and went **h** praising God.
8:39 "Return **h** and tell how much God has
10:38 named Martha opened her **h** to him.
15: 6 goes **h**. Then he calls his friends
15:30 property with prostitutes comes **h**,
18:14 other, went **h** justified before God.
18:29 "no-one who has left **h** or wife or
19:15 made king, however, and returned **h**.
23:56 they went **h** and prepared spices and
Jn 7:53 each went to his own **h**.
9: 7 went and washed, and came **h** seeing.
11:20 to meet him, but Mary stayed at **h**.
14:23 come to him and make our **h** with him.
16:32 be scattered, each to his own **h**.
19:27 this disciple took her into his **h**.
Ac 8:28 on his way **h** was sitting in his
10:32 He is a guest in the **h** of Simon the
16:15 baptised, she invited us to her **h**.
18:26 they invited him to their **h** and
20:12 The people took the young man **h**
21: 6 the ship, and they returned **h**.
21:16 **h** of Mnason, where we were to stay.
28: 7 He welcomed us to his **h** and for
1Co 11:34 he should eat at **h**, so that when you
14:35 should ask their own husbands at **h**;
2Co 5: 6 know that as long as we are at **h** in
5: 8 the body and at **h** with the Lord.
5: 9 at **h** in the body or away from it.
Tit 2: 5 to be busy at **h**, to be kind, and to
Phm : 2 to the church that meets in your **h**:
Heb 11: 9 By faith he made his **h** in the
2Pe 3:13 a new earth, the **h** of righteousness.
Jude : 6 abandoned their own **h**—these he has
Rev 18: 2 She has become a **h** for demons and

Homeland (Home)
Ge 30:25 so that I can go back to my own **h**.
Ru 2:11 mother and your **h** and came to live
2Sa 15:19 a foreigner, an exile from your **h**.
2Ki 17:23 from their **h** into exile in Assyria,
Ps 79: 7 devoured Jacob and destroyed his **h**.
Jer 10:25 him completely and destroyed his **h**.
Joel 3: 6 might send them far from their **h**.

Homeless
1Co 4:11 we are brutally treated, we are **h**.

Homer (Homers)
Lev 27:16 of silver to a **h** of barley seed.
Isa 5:10 a **h** of seed only an ephah of grain.
Eze 45:11 the bath containing a tenth of a **h**
45:11 the **h** is to be the tenth of a **h**
45:13 of an ephah from each **h** of wheat
45:13 of an ephah from each **h** of barley.
45:14 consists of ten baths or one **h**,
45:14 ten baths are equivalent to a **h**).
Hos 3: 2 about a **h** and a lethek of barley.

Homers (Homer)
Nu 11:32 No-one gathered less than ten **h**.

Homes (Home)
Ex 12:27 spared our **h** when he struck down
Nu 32:18 We will not return to our **h** until
Dt 32:25 in their **h** terror will reign.
Jos 22: 4 return to your **h** in the land that
22: 6 them away, and they went to their **h**.
22: 8 saying, "Return to your **h** with your
1Sa 13: 2 of the men he sent back to their **h**.
2Sa 6:19 And all the people went to their **h**.
18:17 all the Israelites fled to their **h**.
19: 8 the Israelites had fled to their **h**.
2Ki 13: 5 in their own **h** as they had before.
2Ch 7:10 he sent the people to their **h**,
Ne 4:14 daughters, your wives and your **h**."
5: 3 **h** to get grain during the famine."
Job 1: 4 turns holding feasts in their **h**,
2:11 they set out from their **h** and met
21: 9 Their **h** are safe and free from fear;
36:20 to drag people away from their **h**.
Ps 78:55 the tribes of Israel in their **h**.
109:10 they be driven from their ruined **h**.
Isa 32:18 in secure **h**, in undisturbed places
Lam 5: 2 over to aliens, our **h** to foreigners.
Hos 11:11 I will settle them in their **h**,"
Mic 2: 9 of my people from their pleasant **h**.
Mk 10:30 (**h**, brothers, sisters, mothers,
Jn 20:10 the disciples went back to their **h**,
Ac 2:46 They broke bread in their **h** and ate
1Co 11:22 Don't you have **h** to eat and drink in?
1Ti 5:14 to have children, to manage their **h**
2Ti 3: 6 the kind who worm their way into **h**

Homosexual
1Co 6: 9 nor male prostitutes nor **h**

Honest (Honestly, Honesty)
Ge 42:11 Your servants are **h** men, not spies."
42:19 If you are **h** men, let one of your
42:31 we said to him, 'We are **h** men; we
42:33 I will know whether you are **h** men:
42:34 that you are not spies but **h** men.
Ex 23: 7 an innocent or **h** person to death,
Lev 19:36 Use **h** scales and **h** weights,
19:36 an **h** ephah and an **h** hin.
Dt 25:15 You must have accurate and **h** weights
1Ch 29:17 I given willingly and with **h** intent.
Job 6:25 How painful are **h** words! But what do
31: 6 let God weigh me in **h** scales and he
Pr 12:17 A truthful witness gives **h** testimony,
16:11 **H** scales and balances are from the
16:13 Kings take pleasure in **h** lips; they
24:26 An **h** answer is like a kiss on the
Lk 20:20 sent spies, who pretended to be **h**.

Honestly (Honest)
Jer 5: 1 who deals **h** and seeks the truth,

Honesty (Honest)
Ge 30:33 my **h** will testify for me in the
2Ki 12:15 because they acted with complete **h**.
Isa 59:14 in the streets, **h** cannot enter.

Honey (Honeycomb, *Land flowing with milk and honey*)
Ge 43:11 gift—a little balm and a little **h**,
Ex 16:31 and tasted like wafers made with **h**.
Lev 2:11 not to burn any yeast or **h** in an
Nu 13:27 it does flow with milk and **h**!
Dt 8: 8 pomegranates, olive oil and **h**;
32:13 He nourished him with **h** from the
Jdg 14: 8 In it was a swarm of bees and some **h**
14: 9 taken the **h** from the lion's carcass.
14:18 "What is sweeter than **h**? What is
1Sa 14:25 and there was **h** on the ground.
14:26 they saw the **h** oozing out, yet
14:29 when I tasted a little of this **h**.
14:43 a little **h** with the end of my staff.
2Sa 17:29 **h** and curds, sheep, and cheese from
1Ki 14: 3 cakes and a jar of **h**, and go to him.
2Ki 18:32 a land of olive trees and **h**.
2Ch 31: 5 **h** and all that the fields produced.
Job 20:17 the rivers flowing with **h** and cream.
Ps 19:10 than **h**, than **h** from the comb.
81:16 **h** from the rock I would satisfy you.
119:103 taste, sweeter than **h** to my mouth!
Pr 5: 3 For the lips of an adulteress drip **h**
24:13 Eat **h**, my son, for it is good; **h**
25:16 If you find **h**, eat just enough—
25:27 is not good to eat too much **h**, nor
27: 7 He who is full loathes **h**, but to the
SS 4:11 milk and **h** are under your tongue.
5: 1 I have eaten my honeycomb and my **h**;
Isa 7:15 He will eat curds and **h** when he
7:22 in the land will eat curds and **h**.
Jer 41: 8 oil and **h**, hidden in a field.
Eze 3: 3 it tasted as sweet as **h** in my mouth.
16:13 Your food was fine flour, **h** and
16:19 olive oil and **h** I gave you to
27:17 **h**, oil and balm for your wares.
Mt 3: 4 His food was locusts and wild **h**.
Mk 1: 6 and he ate locusts and wild **h**.
Rev 10: 9 mouth it will be as sweet as **h**."
10:10 It tasted as sweet as **h** in my mouth,

Honeycomb (Honey)
1Sa 14:27 his hand and dipped it into the **h**.
Pr 16:24 Pleasant words are a **h**, sweet to the
SS 4:11 Your lips drop sweetness as the **h**,
5: 1 I have eaten my **h** and my honey; I

Honour (Honourable, Honourably, Honoured, Honouring, Honours)
Ge 30:20 my husband will treat me with **h**,
43:28 And they bowed low to pay him **h**.
45:13 Tell my father about all the **h**
49: 3 excelling in **h**, excelling in power.
Ex 8: 9 "I leave to you the **h** of setting the
12:42 to keep vigil to **h** the LORD for the
20:12 "**H** your father and your mother,
28: 2 Aaron, to give him dignity and **h**.
28:40 sons, to give them dignity and **h**.
Nu 20:12 to **h** me as holy in the sight of
25:11 zealous as I am for my **h** among them,
25:13 he was zealous for the **h** of his God
27:14 to **h** me as holy before their eyes.
Dt 5:16 "**H** your father and your mother,
26:19 fame and **h** high above all the
Jdg 4: 9 the **h** will not be yours, for the
13:17 **h** you when your word comes true?"
1Sa 2: 8 and has them inherit a throne of **h**.
2:29 Why do you **h** your sons more than me
2:30 it from me! Those who **h** me I will **h**,
6: 5 country, and pay **h** to Israel's god.
15:12 has set up a monument in his own **h**
15:30 But please **h** me before the elders
2Sa 1: 2 he fell to the ground to pay him **h**.
6:22 you spoke of, I will be held in **h**.
9: 6 David, he bowed down to pay him **h**.
14: 4 face to the ground to pay him **h**,
14:22 pay him **h**, and he blessed the king.
23:19 Was he not held in greater **h** than
23:23 He was held in greater **h** than any of
1Ki 3:13 both riches and **h**—so that in your
2Ki 10:20 "Call an assembly in **h** of Baal
25:28 gave him a seat of **h** higher than
1Ch 11:25 He was held in greater **h** than any
29:12 Wealth and **h** come from you; you are
29:28 enjoyed long life, wealth and **h**.
2Ch 1:11 not asked for wealth, riches or **h**,
1:12 give you wealth, riches and **h**,
16:14 and they made a huge fire in his **h**.
17: 5 so that he had great wealth and **h**.
18: 1 Jehoshaphat had great wealth and **h**,
21:19 His people made no fire in his **h**,
32:27 Hezekiah had very great riches and **h**,
Ezr 7:27 to bring **h** to the house of the LORD
Est 3: 1 giving him a seat of **h** higher than
3: 2 gate knelt down and paid **h** to Haman,
3: 2 would not kneel down or pay him **h**.
3: 5 would not kneel down or pay him **h**.
6: 3 "What **h** and recognition has Mordecai
6: 6 for the man the king delights to **h**?"
6: 6 the king would rather **h** than me?"
6: 7 the man the king delights to **h**
6: 9 the man the king delights to **h**,
6: 9 the man the king delights to **h**!'

Est 6:11 the man the king delights to **h**!"
8:16 happiness and joy, gladness and **h**.
Job 19: 9 He has stripped me of my **h** and
40:10 clothe yourself in **h** and majesty.
Ps 8: 5 and crowned him with glory and **h**.
22:23 All you descendants of Jacob, **h** him
45:11 **h** him, for he is your lord.
50:15 deliver you, and you will **h** me."
62: 7 My salvation and my **h** depend on God;
71:21 You will increase my **h** and comfort
84:11 the LORD bestows favour and **h**; no
91:15 I will deliver him and **h** him.
112: 9 his horn will be lifted high in **h**.
149: 5 Let the saints rejoice in this **h**
Pr 3: 9 **H** the LORD with your wealth, with
3:16 in her left hand are riches and **h**.
3:35 The wise inherit **h**, but fools he
4: 8 embrace her, and she will **h** you.
8:18 With me are riches and **h**, enduring
15:33 wisdom, and humility comes before **h**.
18:12 proud, but humility comes before **h**.
20: 3 It is to a man's **h** to avoid strife,
21:21 love finds life, prosperity and **h**.
22: 4 LORD bring wealth and **h** and life.
25:27 honourable to seek one's own **h**.
26: 1 **h** is not fitting for a fool.
26: 8 is the giving of **h** to a fool.
29:23 but a man of lowly spirit gains **h**.
Ecc 6: 2 possessions and **h**, so that he lacks
10: 1 little folly outweighs wisdom and **h**.
Isa 9: 1 but in the future he will **h** Galilee
22:23 a seat of **h** for the house of his
25: 3 Therefore strong peoples will **h** you;
26:13 but your name alone do we **h**.
29:13 mouth and **h** me with their lips,
43:20 The wild animals **h** me, the jackals
45: 4 bestow on you a title of **h**,
58:13 and if you **h** it by not going your
60: 9 to the **h** of the LORD your God,
Jer 3:17 Jerusalem to **h** the name of the LORD.
13:11 for my renown and praise and **h**.
30:19 I will bring them **h**, and they will
33: 9 joy, praise and **h** before all nations
34: 5 funeral fire in **h** of your fathers
34: 5 a fire in your **h** and lament, "Alas,
52:32 gave him a seat of **h** higher than
Lam 4:16 shown no **h**, the elders no favour.
Da 2: 6 me gifts and rewards and great **h**.
2:46 paid him **h** and ordered that an
4:36 my **h** and splendour were returned to
5:23 But you did not **h** the God who holds
11:21 has not been given the **h** of royalty.
11:38 he will **h** a god of fortresses
11:38 he will **h** with gold and silver,
11:39 greatly **h** those who acknowledge him.
Hab 1: 7 themselves and promote their own **h**.
Zep 3:19 I will give them praise and **h** in
3:20 I will give you **h** and praise among
Zec 12: 7 so that the **h** of the house of David
Mal 1: 6 If I am a father, where is the **h** due
2: 2 do not set your heart to **h** my name,"
2: 2 you have not set your heart to **h** me.
Mt 13:57 own house is a prophet without **h**."
15: 4 For God said, '**H** your father and
15: 6 he is not to '**h** his father' with it.
15: 8 'These people **h** me with their lips,
19:19 **h** your father and mother,' and 'love
23: 6 they love the place of **h** at banquets
Mk 6: 4 own house is a prophet without **h**."
7: 6 'These people **h** me with their lips,
7:10 For Moses said, '**H** your father and
10:19 defraud, **h** your father and mother.
12:39 and the places of **h** at banquets.
Lk 14: 7 picked the places of **h** at the table,
14: 8 do not take the place of **h**, for a
18:20 **h** your father and mother.'"
20:46 and the places of **h** at banquets.
Jn 4:44 has no **h** in his own country.)
5:23 all may **h** the Son just as they **h**
5:23 He who does not **h** the Son does not **h**
7:18 own does so to gain **h** for himself,
7:18 but he who works for the **h** of the
8:49 I **h** my Father and you dishonour me.
12: 2 a dinner was given in Jesus' **h**.
12:26 Father will **h** the one who serves me.
Ac 7:41 in **h** of what their hands had made.
19:17 the Lord Jesus was held in high **h**.
Ro 2: 7 **h** and immortality, he will give
2:10 **h** and peace for everyone who
12:10 **H** one another above yourselves.
13: 7 respect, then respect; if **h**, then **h**.
1Co 6:20 Therefore **h** God with your body.
12:23 honourable we treat with special **h**.
12:24 **h** to the parts that lacked it,
2Co 8:19 in order to **h** the Lord himself
8:23 of the churches and an **h** to Christ.
Eph 6: 2 "**H** your father and mother"—which
Php 2:29 with great joy, and **h** men like him,
1Ti 1:17 be **h** and glory for ever and ever.
5:17 church well are worthy of double **h**,
6:16 To him be **h** and might for ever.
Heb 2: 7 you crowned him with glory and **h**
2: 9 now crowned with glory and **h** because
3: 3 worthy of greater **h** than Moses,
3: 3 has greater **h** than the house itself.
5: 4 No-one takes this **h** upon himself;
1Pe 1: 7 and **h** when Jesus Christ is revealed.
2:17 of believers, fear God, **h** the king.
2Pe 1:17 For he received **h** and glory from God
Rev 4: 9 **h** and thanks to him who sits on the
4:11 to receive glory and **h** and power,
5:12 and **h** and glory and praise!"
5:13 praise and **h** and glory and power,
7:12 glory and wisdom and thanks and **h**
13:14 set up an image in **h** of the beast
21:26 The glory and **h** of the nations will

Honourable (Honour)

1Ch 4: 9 Jabez was more **h** than his brothers.
Ezr 4:10 whom the great and **h** Ashurbanipal
Pr 25:27 is it **h** to seek one's own honour.
Isa 3: 5 the old, the base against the **h**.
58:13 a delight and the LORD's holy day **h**,
1Co 12:23 the parts that we think are less **h**
1Th 4: 4 body in a way that is holy and **h**,

Honourably (Honour)

Jdg 9:16 Now if you have acted **h** and in good
9:19 then you have acted **h** and in good
Heb 13:18 and desire to live **h** in every way.

Honoured (Honour)

Ge 34:19 The young man, who was the most **h** of
Ex 20:24 Wherever I cause my name to be **h**,
Lev 10: 3 sight of all the people I will be **h**.
Jdg 9: 9 by which both gods and men are **h**,
1Ch 11:21 He was doubly **h** above the Three and
2Ch 26:18 you will not be **h** by the LORD God."
32:33 of Jerusalem **h** him when he died.
Est 3: 1 King Xerxes **h** Haman son of
5:11 and all the ways the king had **h** him
Job 14:21 If his sons are **h**, he does not know
22: 8 an **h** man, living on it.
Ps 12: 8 when what is vile is **h** among men.
45: 9 Daughters of kings are among your **h**
Pr 13:18 but whoever heeds correction is **h**.
27:18 looks after his master will be **h**.
Isa 43: 4 you are precious and **h** in my sight
43:23 nor **h** me with your sacrifices.
49: 5 for I am **h** in the eyes of the LORD
Lam 1: 8 All who **h** her despise her, for they
Da 4:34 I **h** and glorified him who lives
Hag 1: 8 in it and be **h**," says the LORD.
Zec 2: 8 "After he has **h** me and has sent me
Mal 3:16 who feared the LORD and **h** his name.
Mt 6: 2 and on the streets, to be **h** by men.
Lk 14:10 Then you will be **h** in the presence
Ac 5:34 a teacher of the law, who was **h** by
13:48 they were glad and **h** the word of the
28:10 They **h** us in many ways and when we
1Co 4:10 You are **h**, we are dishonoured!
12:26 one part is **h**, every part rejoices
2Th 3: 1 and be **h**, just as it was with you.
Heb 13: 4 Marriage should be **h** by all, and the

Honouring (Honour)

2Sa 10: 3 "Do you think David is **h** your father
1Ch 17:18 David say to you for **h** your servant?
19: 3 "Do you think David is **h** your father

Honours (Honour)

Ps 15: 4 who despises a vile man but **h** those
50:23 who sacrifices thank-offerings **h** me
Pr 14:31 whoever is kind to the needy **h** God.
Mal 1: 6 "A son **h** his father, and a servant

Hoof (Hoofs)

Ex 10:26 not a **h** is to be left behind.
Lev 11: 3 has a split **h** completely divided
11: 4 split **h**, but you must not eat them.
11: 4 does not have a split **h**; it is
11: 5 a split **h**; it is unclean for you.
11: 6 a split **h**; it is unclean for you.
11: 7 the pig, though it has a split **h**
11:26 'Every animal that has a split **h**
Dt 14: 6 that has a split **h** divided in two
14: 7 split **h** completely divided you may
14: 7 they do not have a split **h**; they are
14: 8 a split **h**, it does not chew the cud.

Hoofs (Hoof)

Jdg 5:22 thundered the horses' **h**—galloping,
Ps 69:31 than a bull with its horns and **h**.
Isa 5:28 their horses' **h** seem like flint,
Jer 47: 3 at the sound of the **h** of galloping
Eze 26:11 The **h** of his horses will trample all
32:13 man or muddied by the **h** of cattle.
Mic 4:13 I will give you **h** of bronze and you
Zec 11:16 choice sheep, tearing off their **h**.

Hook (Fishhook, Fish-hooks, Hooks)

2Ki 19:28 I will put my **h** in your nose and my
2Ch 33:11 prisoner, put a **h** in his nose
Job 41: 2 his nose or pierce his jaw with a **h**?
Isa 37:29 I will put my **h** in your nose and my

Hooks (Hook)

Ex 26:32 Hang it with gold **h** on four posts
26:37 Make gold **h** for this curtain and
27:10 silver **h** and bands on the posts.
27:11 silver **h** and bands on the posts.
27:17 bands and **h**, and bronze bases.
36:36 They made gold **h** for them and cast
36:38 they made five posts with **h** for them.
38:10 silver **h** and bands on the posts.
38:11 silver **h** and bands on the posts.
38:12 silver **h** and bands on the posts.
38:17 The **h** and bands on the posts were
38:19 Their **h** and bands were silver, and
38:28 shekels to make the **h** for the posts,
Isa 2: 4 and their spears into pruning **h**.
19: 8 all who cast **h** into the Nile;
Eze 19: 4 led him with **h** to the land of Egypt.
19: 9 With **h** they pulled him into a cage
29: 4 I will put **h** in your jaws and make
38: 4 I will turn you around, put **h** in
40:43 double-pronged **h**, each a handbreadth
Joel 3:10 and your pruning **h** into spears.
Am 4: 2 you will be taken away with **h**,
Mic 4: 3 and their spears into pruning **h**.
Hab 1:15 foe pulls all of them up with **h**,

Hoopoe

Lev 11:19 stork, any kind of heron, the **h**
Dt 14:18 stork, any kind of heron, the **h**

Hope (Hoped, Hopes, Hoping)

Ru 1:12 Even if I thought there was still **h**
1Ch 29:15 earth are like a shadow, without **h**.
Ezr 10: 2 this, there is still **h** for Israel.
Job 4: 6 and your blameless ways your **h**?
5:16 the poor have **h**, and injustice shuts
6: 8 that God would grant what I **h** for,
6:11 that I should still **h**? What
6:19 merchants of Sheba look in **h**.
7: 6 and they come to an end without **h**.
8:13 so perishes the **h** of the godless.
11:18 because there is **h**; you will look
11:20 their **h** will become a dying gasp."
13:15 he slay me, yet will I **h** in him
14: 7 "At least there is **h** for a tree:
14:19 the soil, so you destroy man's **h**.
17:13 If the only home I **h** for is the
17:15 then is my **h**? Who can see any **h**

Job 19:10 gone; he uproots my **h** like a tree.
27: 8 For what **h** has the godless when he
41: 9 Any **h** of subduing him is false;
Ps 9:18 the **h** of the afflicted ever perish.
25: 3 No-one whose **h** is in you will ever
25: 5 and my **h** is in you all day long.
25:21 protect me, because my **h** is in you.
31:24 heart, all you who **h** in the LORD.
33:17 horse is a vain **h** for deliverance
33:18 whose **h** is in his unfailing love,
33:20 We wait in **h** for the LORD; he is our
33:22 O LORD, even as we put our **h** in you.
37: 9 **h** in the LORD will inherit the land.
39: 7 what do I look for? My **h** is in you.
42: 5 Put your **h** in God, for I will
42:11 Put your **h** in God, for I will
43: 5 Put your **h** in God, for I will
52: 9 I will **h**, for your name is good.
62: 5 in God alone; my **h** comes from him.
65: 5 the **h** of all the ends of the earth
69: 6 May those who **h** in you not be
71: 5 For you have been my **h**, O Sovereign
71:14 for me, I shall always have **h**;
119:43 for I have put my **h** in your laws.
119:49 servant, for you have given me **h**.
119:74 for I have put my **h** in your word.
119:81 but I have put my **h** in your word.
119:114 I have put my **h** in your word.
119:147 I have put my **h** in your word.
130: 5 waits, and in his word I put my **h**.
130: 7 O Israel, put your **h** in the LORD,
131: 3 O Israel, put your **h** in the LORD
146: 5 whose **h** is in the LORD his God,
147:11 put their **h** in his unfailing love.
Pr 11: 7 a wicked man dies, his **h** perishes;
11:23 the **h** of the wicked only in wrath.
13:12 **H** deferred makes the heart sick,
19:18 for in that there is **h**; do not be
23:18 There is surely a future **h** for you,
23:18 and your **h** will not be cut off.
24:14 there is a future **h** for you, and
24:14 and your **h** will not be cut off.
24:20 for the evil man has no future **h**,
26:12 is more **h** for a fool than for him.
29:20 is more **h** for a fool than for him.
Ecc 9: 4 Anyone who is among the living has **h**
Isa 19: 9 weavers of fine linen will lose **h**.
38:18 pit cannot **h** for your faithfulness.
40:31 those who **h** in the LORD will renew
42: 4 law the islands will put their **h**."
49:23 **h** in me will not be disappointed."
51: 5 look to me and wait in **h** for my arm.
Jer 13:16 You **h** for light, but he will turn it
14: 8 O **H** of Israel, its Saviour in times
14:22 Therefore our **h** is in you, for you
17:13 O LORD, the **h** of Israel, all who
29:11 plans to give you **h** and a future.
31:17 there is **h** for your future,"
50: 7 the LORD, the **h** of their fathers.'
Lam 3:21 call to mind and therefore I have **h**
3:25 The LORD is good to those whose **h** is
3:29 in the dust—there may yet be **h**.
Eze 19: 5 'When she saw her **h** unfulfilled,
37:11 and our **h** is gone; we are cut off.
Hos 2:15 the Valley of Achor a door of **h**.
Mic 7: 7 for me, I watch in **h** for the LORD,
Zec 9: 5 Ekron too, for her **h** will wither.
9:12 O prisoners of **h**; even now I
Mt 12:21 name the nations will put their **h**.
Ac 2:26 my body also will live in **h**,
16:19 their **h** of making money was gone,
23: 6 **h** in the resurrection of the dead.
24:15 I have the same **h** in God as these
26: 6 now it is because of my **h** in what
26: 7 **h** that the Jews are accusing me.
27:20 gave up all **h** of being saved.
28:20 It is because of the **h** of Israel
Ro 4:18 all **h**, Abraham in **h** believed
5: 2 in the **h** of the glory of God.
5: 4 character; and character, **h**.
5: 5 **h** does not disappoint us, because
8:20 of the one who subjected it, in **h**
8:24 For in this **h** we were saved.
8:24 But **h** that is seen is no **h** at all.
8:25 if we **h** for what we do not yet have,
11:14 in the **h** that I may somehow arouse
Ro 12:12 Be joyful in **h**, patient in
15: 4 of the Scriptures we might have **h**.
15:12 the Gentiles will **h** in him."
15:13 May the God of **h** fill you with all
15:13 **h** by the power of the Holy Spirit.
15:24 I **h** to visit you while passing
1Co 9:10 in the **h** of sharing in the harvest.
9:15 And I am not writing this in the **h**
13:13 now these three remain: faith, **h** and
15:19 for this life we have **h** in Christ
16: 7 I **h** to spend some time with you,
2Co 1: 7 our **h** for you is firm, because we
1:10 On him we have set our **h** that he
1:13 And I **h** that,
3:12 Therefore, since we have such a **h**,
5:11 I **h** it is also plain to your
10:15 Our **h** is that, as your faith
11: 1 I **h** you will put up with a little
Gal 5: 5 the righteousness for which we **h**.
Eph 1:12 who were the first to **h** in Christ,
1:18 the **h** to which he has called you,
2:12 **h** and without God in the world.
4: 4 to one **h** when you were called—
Php 1:20 I eagerly expect and **h** that I will
2:19 I **h** in the Lord Jesus to send
2:23 I **h**, therefore, to send him as soon
Col 1: 5 love that spring from the **h** that is
1:23 from the **h** held out in the gospel.
1:27 is Christ in you, the **h** of glory.
1Th 1: 3 by **h** in our Lord Jesus Christ.
2:19 For what is our **h**, our joy, or the
4:13 like the rest of men, who have no **h**
5: 8 and the **h** of salvation as a helmet.
2Th 2:16 eternal encouragement and good **h**,
1Ti 1: 1 Saviour and of Christ Jesus our **h**,
3:14 Although I **h** to come to you soon, I
4:10 we have put our **h** in the living God
5: 5 left all alone puts her **h** in God
6:17 nor to put their **h** in wealth,
6:17 but to put their **h** in God, who
2Ti 2:25 in the **h** that God will grant them
Tit 1: 2 resting on the **h** of eternal life,
2:13 while we wait for the blessed **h**—
3: 7 heirs having the **h** of eternal life.
Phm :22 because I **h** to be restored to you
Heb 3: 6 courage and the **h** of which we boast.
6:11 end, in order to make your **h** sure.
6:18 to take hold of the **h** offered to us
6:19 We have this **h** as an anchor for the
7:19 and a better **h** is introduced, by
10:23 Let us hold unswervingly to the **h** we
11: 1 faith is being sure of what we **h** for
1Pe 1: 3 given us new birth into a living **h**
1:13 set your **h** fully on the grace to be
1:21 and so your faith and **h** are in God.
3: 5 who put their **h** in God used to make
3:15 the reason for the **h** that you have.
1Jn 3: 3 Everyone who has this **h** in him
2Jn :12 Instead, I **h** to visit you and talk
3Jn :14 I **h** to see you soon, and we will

Hoped (Hope)

Est 9: 1 of the Jews had **h** to overpower them
Job 30:26 Yet when I **h** for good, evil came;
Jer 8:15 We **h** for peace but no good has come
14:19 We **h** for peace but no good has come
Lam 3:18 and all that I had **h** from the LORD.
Lk 20:20 They **h** to catch Jesus in something
23: 8 **h** to see him perform some miracle.
24:21 had **h** that he was the one who was

Hopeless

Isa 57:10 but you would not say, 'It is **h**.

Hopes (Hope)

2Ki 4:28 I tell you, 'Don't raise my **h**'?"
Ps 119:116 do not let my **h** be dashed.
Pr 10:28 the **h** of the wicked come to nothing.
Jer 23:16 to you; they fill you with false **h**.
Jn 5:45 is Moses, on whom your **h** are set.
Ro 8:24 Who **h** for what he already has?
1Co 13: 7 trusts, always **h**, always perseveres.

Hophni

1Sa 1: 3 where **H** and Phinehas, the two sons
2:34 **H** and Phinehas, will be a sign to
4: 4 And Eli's two sons, **H** and Phinehas,
4:11 Eli's two sons, **H** and Phinehas, died.
4:17 Also your two sons, **H** and Phinehas,

Hophra

Jer 44:30 'I am going to hand Pharaoh **H** king

Hoping (Hope)

Da 2: 9 things, **h** the situation will change.
Ac 24:26 At the same time he was **h** that Paul
26: 7 are **h** to see fulfilled as they
27:12 **h** to reach Phoenix and winter there.

Hopping

Lev 11:21 jointed legs for **h** on the ground.

Hor, Mount

1. On border of Edom (Nu 20:23; 33:37), where Aaron died (Nu 20:22–29; 33:38–39; Dt 32:50).
2. On northern border of Palestine, exact location unknown (Nu 34:7–8).

Nu 20:22 out from Kadesh and came to Mount **H**.
20:23 At Mount **H**, near the border of Edom,
20:25 Eleazar and take them up Mount **H**.
20:27 They went up Mount **H** in the sight of
21: 4 They travelled from Mount **H** along
33:37 at Mount **H**, on the border of Edom.
33:38 Aaron the priest went up Mount **H**,
33:39 years old when he died on Mount **H**.
33:41 They left Mount **H** and camped at
34: 7 a line from the Great Sea to Mount **H**
34: 8 from Mount **H** to Lebo Hamath. Then
Dt 32:50 your brother Aaron died on Mount **H**

Hor Haggidgad

Nu 33:32 left Bene Jaakan and camped at **H**
33:33 They left **H** and camped at Jotbathah.

Horam

Jos 10:33 Meanwhile, **H** king of Gezer had come

Horde (Hordes)

Nu 22: 4 "This **h** is going to lick up
Eze 17:17 **h** will be of no help to him in war,
38: 4 and a great **h** with large and small
38:15 on horses, a great **h**, a mighty army.

Hordes (Horde)

Isa 29: 5 the ruthless **h** like blown chaff.
29: 7 the **h** of all the nations that fight
29: 8 So will it be with the **h** of all the
Eze 30:10 'I will put an end to the **h** of Egypt
30:15 Egypt, and cut off the **h** of Thebes.
31: 2 Pharaoh king of Egypt and to his **h**:
31:18 'This is Pharaoh and all his **h**,
32:12 I will cause your **h** to fall by the
32:12 and all her **h** will be overthrown.
32:16 and all her **h** they will chant it,
32:18 "Son of man, wail for the **h** of Egypt
32:20 her be dragged off with all her **h**.
32:24 "Elam is there, with all her **h**
32:25 with all her **h** around her grave.
32:26 all their **h** around their graves.
32:31 **h** that were killed by the sword,
32:32 Pharaoh and all his **h** will be laid
38: 7 and all the **h** gathered about you,
38:13 Have you gathered your **h** to loot,
39:11 and all his **h** will be buried there.
Hab 1: 9 Their **h** advance like a desert wind

Horeb See Sinai 1.

Ex 3: 1 and came to **H**, the mountain of God.
17: 6 there before you by the rock at **H**.
33: 6 off their ornaments at Mount **H**.
Dt 1: 2 (It takes eleven days to go from **H**
1: 6 The LORD our God said to us at **H**,
1:19 we set out from **H** and went towards
4:10 stood before the LORD your God at **H**
4:15 spoke to you at **H** out of the fire.

Dt 5: 2 God made a covenant with us at **H**.
9: 8 At **H** you aroused the LORD's wrath so
18:16 asked of the LORD your God at **H**
29: 1 covenant he had made with them at **H**
1Ki 8: 9 that Moses had placed in it at **H**,
19: 8 he reached **H**, the mountain of God.
2Ch 5:10 that Moses had placed in it at **H**,
Ps 106:19 **H** they made a calf and worshipped
Mal 4: 4 laws I gave him at **H** for all Israel.

Horem

Jos 19:38 Iron, Migdal El, **H**, Beth Anath and

Horesh

1Sa 23:15 While David was at **H** in the Desert
23:16 son Jonathan went to David at **H**
23:18 went home, but David remained at **H**
23:19 among us in the strongholds at **H**,

Hori (Horite, Horites)

Ge 36:22 The sons of Lotan: **H** and Homam.
Nu 13: 5 tribe of Simeon, Shaphat son of **H**;
1Ch 1:39 The sons of Lotan: **H** and Homam.

Horite (Hori)

Ge 36:20 These were the sons of Seir the **H**,
36:21 sons of Seir in Edom were **H** chiefs.
36:29 These were the **H** chiefs: Lotan,
36:30 These were the **H** chiefs, according

Horites (Hori)

Ge 14: 6 the **H** in the hill country of Seir,
Dt 2:12 **H** used to live in Seir, but the
2:12 They destroyed the **H** from before
2:22 he destroyed the **H** from before them.

Horizon

Ne 1: 9 exiled people are at the farthest **h**
Job 26:10 He marks out the **h** on the face of
Pr 8:27 out the **h** on the face of the deep,

Hormah

Canaanite town near Ziklag in southern Judah (Jos 12:14). Originally called Zephath, until renamed by either the Israelites (Nu 21:3) or the men of Judah and Simeon (Jdg 1:17). Israelites defeated near here by the Amalekites and Canaanites (Nu 14:45; Dt 1:44). Allotted to Simeon, though in the territory of Judah (Jos 19:14; 1Ch 4:30). David sent a share of Amalekite spoils to here (1Sa 30:30).

Nu 14:45 and beat them down all the way to **H**.
21: 3 so the place was named **H**.
Dt 1:44 down from Seir all the way to **H**.
Jos 12:14 the king of **H** one the king of Arad
15:30 Eltolad, Kesil, **H**,
19: 4 Eltolad, Bethul, **H**,
Jdg 1:17 Therefore it was called **H**.
1Sa 30:30 to those in **H**, Bor Ashan,
1Ch 4:30 Bethuel, **H**, Ziklag,

Horn (Horned, Horns)

Ex 19:13 Only when the ram's **h** sounds a long
27: 2 Make a **h** at each of the four corners,
38: 2 They made a **h** at each of the four
1Sa 2: 1 in the LORD my **h** is lifted high.
2:10 and exalt the **h** of his anointed."
16: 1 your **h** with oil and be on your way;
16:13 Samuel took the **h** of oil and
2Sa 22: 3 my shield and the **h** of my salvation
1Ki 1:39 Zadok the priest took the **h** of oil
Ps 18: 2 **h** of my salvation, my stronghold.
81: 3 Sound the ram's **h** at the New Moon,
89:17 by your favour you exalt our **h**.
89:24 my name his **h** will be exalted.
92:10 You have exalted my **h** like that of
98: 6 and the blast of the ram's **h**
112: 9 his **h** will be lifted high in honour.
132:17 I will make a **h** grow for David
148:14 has raised up for his people a **h**,
Jer 48:25 Moab's **h** is cut off; her arm is
Lam 2: 3 he has cut off every **h** of Israel.
2:17 he has exalted the **h** of your foes.
Eze 29:21 "On that day I will make a **h** grow
Da 3: 5 soon as you hear the sound of the **h**
3: 7 as they heard the sound of the **h**,
3:10 who hears the sound of the **h**,
3:15 when you hear the sound of the **h**,
7: 8 there before me was another **h**, a
7: 8 **h** had eyes like the eyes of a man
7:11 boastful words the **h** was speaking.
7:20 and about the other **h** that came up,
7:20 **h** that looked more imposing than
7:21 I watched, this **h** was waging war
8: 5 suddenly a goat with a prominent **h**
8: 8 power his large **h** was broken off,
8: 9 Out of one of them came another **h**,
8:21 **h** between his eyes is the first king
Hos 5: 8 trumpet in Gibeah, the **h** in Ramah.
Lk 1:69 He has raised up a **h** of salvation

Horned (Horn)

Lev 11:16 **h** owl, the screech owl, the gull,
Dt 14:15 **h** owl, the screech owl, the gull,

Hornet

Ex 23:28 I will send the **h** ahead of you to
Dt 7:20 the LORD your God will send the **h**
Jos 24:12 I sent the **h** ahead of you, which

Horns (Horn, *Horns of the altar*)

Ge 22:13 he saw a ram caught by its **h**.
Ex 27: 2 so that the **h** and the altar are of
30: 2 high—its **h** of one piece with it.
30: 3 the sides and the **h** with pure gold,
30:10 Aaron shall make atonement on its **h**.
37:25 high—its **h** of one piece with it.
37:26 the sides and the **h** with pure gold,
38: 2 so that the **h** and the altar were of
Dt 33:17 his **h** are the **h** of a wild ox.
Jos 6: 4 of rams' **h** in front of the ark.
1Ki 22:11 had made iron **h** and he declared,
1Ch 15:28 with the sounding of rams' **h** and
2Ch 15:14 shouting and with trumpets and **h**.
18:10 son of Kenaanah had made iron **h**,
Ps 22:21 save me from the **h** of the wild
69:31 than a bull with its **h** and hoofs.
75: 4 the wicked, 'Do not lift up your **h**.
75: 5 Do not lift your **h** against heaven;
75:10 I will cut off the **h** of all the
75:10 but the **h** of the righteous shall be
Jer 17: 1 hearts and on the **h** of their altars.
Eze 34:21 all the weak sheep with your **h**
43:15 four **h** project upward from the
Da 7: 7 former beasts, and it had ten **h**.
7: 8 "While I was thinking about the **h**,
7: 8 the first **h** were uprooted before it.
7:20 also wanted to know about the ten **h**
7:24 The ten **h** are ten kings who will
8: 3 before me was a ram with two **h**,
8: 3 the canal, and the **h** were long.
8: 3 One of the **h** was longer than the
8: 7 the ram and shattering his two **h**.
8: 8 and in its place four prominent **h**
8:22 The four **h** that replaced the one
Mic 4:13 for I will give you **h** of iron;
Zec 1:18 and there before me were four **h**!
1:19 "These are the **h** that scattered
1:21 "These are the **h** that scattered
1:21 throw down these **h** of the nations
1:21 who lifted up their **h** against the
Rev 5: 6 He had seven **h** and seven eyes,
9:13 I heard a voice coming from the **h**
12: 3 ten **h** and seven crowns on his heads.
13: 1 He had ten **h** and seven heads,
13: 1 with ten crowns on his **h**, and on
13:11 He had two **h** like a lamb, but he
17: 3 and had seven heads and ten **h**.
17: 7 has the seven heads and ten **h**.
17:12 "The ten **h** you saw are ten kings who
17:16 The beast and the ten **h** you saw will

Horns of the altar

Ex 29:12 put it on the **h** with your finger,
Lev 4: 7 blood on the **h** of fragrant incense
4:18 put some of the blood on the **h** that
4:25 put it on the **h** of burnt offering
4:30 put it on the **h** of burnt offering
Lev 4:34 put it on the **h** of burnt offering
8:15 it on all the **h** to purify the altar.
9: 9 into the blood and put it on the **h**;
16:18 blood and put it on all the **h**.
1Ki 1:50 Solomon, went and took hold of the **h**.
1:51 Solomon and is clinging to the **h**.
2:28 of the LORD and took hold of the **h**.
Ps 118:27 the festal procession up to the **h**.
Eze 43:20 put it on the four **h** and on the four
Am 3:14 the **h** will be cut off and fall to

Horonaim

2Sa 13:34 I see men in the direction of **H**,
Isa 15: 5 to **H** they lament their destruction.
Jer 48: 3 Listen to the cries from **H**, cries
48: 5 on the road down to **H** anguished
48:34 from Zoar as far as **H** and Eglath

Horonite

Ne 2:10 Sanballat the **H** and Tobiah the
2:19 when Sanballat the **H**, Tobiah the
13:28 son-in-law to Sanballat the **H**.

Horrible (Horror)

Dt 7:15 He will not inflict on you the **h**
Jer 5:30 **h** and shocking thing has happened
18:13 A most **h** thing has been done by
23:14 Jerusalem I have seen something **h**:
Eze 26:21 I will bring you to a **h** end and you
27:36 come to a **h** end and will be no more.
28:19 come to a **h** end and will be no more.
Hos 6:10 I have seen a **h** thing in the house

Horrified (Horror)

Jer 4: 9 the priests will be **h**, and the
50:13 All who pass Babylon will be **h** and

Horror (Horrible, Horrified)

Dt 28:25 you will become a thing of **h** to all
28:37 You will become a thing of **h** and an
2Ch 29: 8 an object of dread and **h** and scorn,
30: 7 them an object of **h**, as you see.
Job 18:20 men of the east are seized with **h**.
Ps 55: 5 **h** has overwhelmed me.
Isa 21: 4 I longed for has become a **h** to me.
Jer 2:12 shudder with great **h**," declares
8:21 am crushed; I mourn, and **h** grips me.
25: 9 make them an object of **h** and scorn,
25:18 object of **h** and scorn and cursing,
29:18 and an object of cursing and **h**,
42:18 will be an object of cursing and **h**,
44:12 become an object of cursing and **h**,
48:39 an object of **h** to all those around
49:13 become a ruin and an object of **h**,
49:17 "Edom will become an object of **h**;
51:37 a haunt of jackals, an object of **h**
51:41 **h** Babylon will be among the nations
Eze 5:15 a warning and an object of **h** to the
20:26 that I might fill them with **h** so
27:35 their kings shudder with **h** and their
32:10 and their kings will shudder with **h**

Horse (Horse's, Horseback, Horseman, Horsemen, Horses, Horses', War-horses)

Ex 15: 1 The **h** and its rider he has hurled
15:21 The **h** and its rider he has hurled
1Ki 10:29 and a **h** for a hundred and fifty.
20:25 **h** for **h** and chariot for chariot
2Ki 14:20 He was brought back by **h** and was
2Ch 1:17 and a **h** for a hundred and fifty.
23:15 the **H** Gate on the palace grounds,
25:28 He was brought back by **h** and was
Ne 3:28 Above the **H** Gate, the priests made
Est 6: 8 worn and a **h** the king has ridden,
6: 9 the robe and **h** be entrusted to
6: 9 and lead him on the **h** through the
6:10 "Get the robe and the **h** and do
6:11 Haman got the robe and the **h**.
Job 39:18 to run, she laughs at **h** and rider.
39:19 "Do you give the **h** his strength
Ps 32: 9 Do not be like the **h** or the mule,
33:17 A **h** is a vain hope for deliverance;
76: 6 both **h** and chariot lie still.

Ps 147:10 is not in the strength of the **h**,
Pr 21:31 The **h** is made ready for the day of
26: 3 A whip for the **h**, a halter for the
Isa 63:13 Like a **h** in open country,
Jer 8: 6 like a **h** charging into battle.
31:40 as far as the corner of the **H** Gate,
51:21 with you I shatter **h** and rider,
Zec 1: 8 before me was a man riding a red **h**!
10: 3 make them like a proud **h** in battle.
12: 4 On that day I will strike every **h**
Rev 6: 2 and there before me was a white **h**!
6: 4 another **h** came out, a fiery red one
6: 5 and there before me was a black **h**!
6: 8 and there before me was a pale **h**!
19:11 and there before me was a white **h**,
19:19 the rider on the **h** and his army.
19:21 of the mouth of the rider on the **h**

Horse's (Horse)

Ge 49:17 that bites the **h** heels so that its

Horseback (Horse)

1Ki 20:20 on **h** with some of his horsemen.
Est 6:11 robed Mordecai, and led him on **h**
Ecc 10: 7 I have seen slaves on **h**, while

Horseman (Horse, Man)

2Ki 9:17 "Get a **h**," Joram ordered. "Send him
9:18 The **h** rode off to meet Jehu and said,
9:19 the king sent out a second **h**.
Am 2:15 and the **h** will not save his life.

Horsemen (Horse, Man)

Ge 50: 9 Chariots and **h** also went up with him.
Ex 14: 9 **h** and troops—pursued the Israelites
14:17 through his chariots and his **h**.
14:18 Pharaoh, his chariots and his **h**."
14:23 and **h** followed them into the sea.
14:26 Egyptians and their chariots and **h**."
14:28 covered the chariots and **h**—the
15:19 Pharaoh's horses, chariots and **h**
Jos 24: 6 and **h** as far as the Red Sea.
1Ki 20:20 on horseback with some of his **h**.
2Ki 2:12 The chariots and **h** of Israel!"
13: 7 army of Jehoahaz except fifty **h**,
13:14 "The chariots and **h** of Israel!"
18:24 on Egypt for chariots and **h**?
2Ch 12: 3 sixty thousand **h** and the innumerable
16: 8 great numbers of chariots and **h**?
Ezr 8:22 **h** to protect us from enemies on the
Isa 22: 7 and **h** are posted at the city gates;
31: 1 in the great strength of their **h**,
36: 9 on Egypt for chariots and **h**?
Jer 4:29 At the sound of **h** and archers every
Eze 23: 6 handsome young men, and mounted **h**.
23:12 mounted **h**, all handsome young men.
26: 7 chariots, with **h** and a great army.
38: 4 your **h** fully armed, and a great
Hos 1: 7 by horse and **h**, but by the LORD
Hab 1: 8 their **h** come from afar.
Zec 10: 5 they will fight and overthrow the **h**.
Ac 23:23 seventy **h** and two hundred spearmen

Horses (Horse)

Ge 47:17 them food in exchange for their **h**,
Ex 9: 3 —on your **h** and donkeys and camels
14: 9 all Pharaoh's **h** and chariots,
14:23 all Pharaoh's **h** and chariots and
15:19 Pharaoh's **h**, chariots and horsemen
Dt 11: 4 to its **h** and chariots, how he
17:16 must not acquire great numbers of **h**
20: 1 see **h** and chariots and an army
Jos 11: 4 of **h** and chariots—a huge army,
11: 6 their **h** and burn their chariots."
11: 9 their **h** and burned their chariots.
1Sa 8:11 them serve with his chariots and **h**,
2Sa 8: 4 all but a hundred of the chariot **h**.
15: 1 provided himself with a chariot and **h**
1Ki 1: 5 So he got chariots and **h** ready,
4:26 chariot **h**, and twelve thousand **h**.
4:28 for the chariot **h** and the other **h**.
9:19 for his **h**—whatever he desired to
10:25 weapons and spices, and **h** and mules.
10:26 Solomon accumulated chariots and **h**;
1Ki 10:26 chariots and twelve thousand **h**,
10:28 Solomon's **h** were imported from Egypt
18: 5 can find some grass to keep the **h**
20: 1 kings with their **h** and chariots,
20:21 overpowered the **h** and chariots and
22: 4 as your people, my **h** as your **h**."
2Ki 2:11 suddenly a chariot of fire and **h**
3: 7 as your people, my **h** as your **h**."
5: 9 Naaman went with his **h** and chariots
6:14 he sent **h** and chariots and a strong
6:15 an army with **h** and chariots had
6:17 looked and saw the hills full of **h**
7: 6 of chariots and **h** and a great army,
7: 7 their tents and their **h** and donkeys.
7:10 anyone—only tethered **h** and donkeys,
7:13 of the **h** that are left in the city.
7:14 selected two chariots with their **h**,
9:33 spattered the wall and the **h**
10: 2 you have chariots and **h**, a
11:16 the **h** enter the palace grounds,
18:23 I will give you two thousand **h**
23:11 the **h** that the kings of Judah had
1Ch 18: 4 all but a hundred of the chariot **h**.
2Ch 1:14 Solomon accumulated chariots and **h**;
1:14 chariots and twelve thousand **h**,
1:16 Solomon's **h** were imported from Egypt
8: 6 for his **h**—whatever he desired to
9:24 weapons and spices, and **h** and mules.
9:25 thousand stalls for **h** and chariots,
9:25 twelve thousand **h**, which he kept
9:28 Solomon's **h** were imported from Egypt
Ezr 2:66 They had 736 **h**, 245 mules,
Ne 7:68 There were 736 **h**, 245 mules,
Est 8:10 fast **h** especially bred for the king.
8:14 The couriers, riding the royal **h**,
Ps 20: 7 Some trust in chariots and some in **h**,
Isa 2: 7 Their land is full of **h**;
21: 7 he sees chariots with teams of **h**,
21: 9 man in a chariot with a team of **h**.
22: 6 with her charioteers and **h**;
28:28 over it, his **h** do not grind it.
30:16 You said, 'No, we will flee on **h**'
30:16 'We will ride off on swift **h**.
31: 1 who rely on **h**, who trust in the
31: 3 their **h** are flesh and not spirit.
36: 8 I will give you two thousand **h**
43:17 who drew out the chariots and **h**,
66:20 on **h**, in chariots and wagons,
Jer 4:13 his **h** are swifter than eagles.
6:23 roaring sea as they ride on their **h**;
8:16 The snorting of the enemy's **h** is
12: 5 how can you compete with **h**?
17:25 come riding in chariots and on **h**,
22: 4 riding in chariots and on **h**,
46: 4 Harness the **h**, mount the steeds!
46: 9 Charge, O **h**! Drive furiously,
50:37 A sword against her **h** and chariots
50:42 roaring sea as they ride on their **h**;
51:27 send up **h** like a swarm of locusts.
Eze 17:15 to Egypt to get **h** and a large army.
23:20 whose emission was like that of **h**.
23:23 men of high rank, all mounted on **h**.
26: 7 king of kings, with **h** and chariots,
26:10 His **h** will be so many that they will
26:10 tremble at the noise of the war **h**,
26:11 The hoofs of his **h** will trample all
27:14 of Beth Togarmah exchanged work **h**,
27:14 **h** and mules for your merchandise.
38: 4 out with your whole army—your **h**,
38:15 riding on **h**, a great horde,
39:20 will eat your fill of **h** and riders
Hos 1: 7 or by **h** and horsemen, but by the
Joel 2: 4 They have the appearance of **h**;
Am 4:10 sword, along with your captured **h**.
6:12 Do **h** run on the rocky crags?
Mic 5:10 "I will destroy your **h** from among
Na 3: 2 galloping **h** and jolting chariots!
Hab 1: 8 Their **h** are swifter than leopards,
3: 8 your **h** and your victorious chariots?
3:15 You trampled the sea with your **h**,
Hag 2:22 **h** and their riders will fall,
Zec 1: 8 him were red, brown and white **h**.
6: 2 The first chariot had red **h**, the
6: 6 The one with the black **h** is going
6: 6 the one with the white **h** towards the
6: 6 the dappled **h** towards the south."
Zec 6: 7 the powerful **h** went out, they were
12: 4 will blind all the **h** of the nations.
14:15 A similar plague will strike the **h**
14:20 be inscribed on the bells of the **h**,
Jas 3: 3 we put bits into the mouths of **h** to
Rev 9: 7 The locusts looked like **h** prepared
9: 9 **h** and chariots rushing into battle.
9:17 The **h** and riders I saw in my vision
9:17 The heads of the **h** resembled the
9:19 The power of the **h** was in their
18:13 cattle and sheep; **h** and carriages;
19:14 riding on white **h** and dressed in
19:18 generals, and mighty men, of **h** and

Horses' (Horse)

Jdg 5:22 thundered the **h** hoofs—galloping,
Isa 5:28 their **h** hoofs seem like flint,
Rev 14:20 rising as high as the **h** bridles for

Hosah

Jos 19:29 turned towards **H** and came out at
1Ch 16:38 and also **H**, were gatekeepers.
26:10 **H** the Merarite had sons: Shimri the
26:11 and relatives of **H** were 13 in all.
26:16 upper road fell to Shuppim and **H**.

Hosanna

Mt 21: 9 "**H** to the Son of David!" "Blessed is
21: 9 "**H** in the highest!
21:15 "**H** to the Son of David," they were
Mk 11: 9 "**H**!" "Blessed is he who comes in the
11:10 "**H** in the highest!
Jn 12:13 "**H**!" "Blessed is he who comes in the

Hosea

Prophet to Israel. Relationship with unfaithful wife, Gomer, and readiness to forgive her mirrored relationship between God and unfaithful Israel (Hos 1–3).

Hos 1: 1 The word of the LORD that came to **H**
1: 2 the LORD began to speak through **H**,
1: 4 the LORD said to **H**, "Call him
1: 6 Then the LORD said to **H**, "Call her
Ro 9:25 he says in **H**: "I will call them 'my

Hoshaiah

Ne 12:32 **H** and half the leaders of Judah
Jer 42: 1 son of Kareah and Jezaniah son of **H**,
43: 2 Azariah son of **H** and Johanan son of

Hoshama

1Ch 3:18 Shenazzar, Jekamiah, **H** and Nedabiah.

Hoshea (Joshua)

1. Former name of *Joshua*. **2.** Last king of Israel. Assassinated and succeeded Pekah (2Ki 15:30). Imprisoned when withheld tribute from Assyria; Israel was invaded and king and people exiled (2Ki 17:3–6; 18:9–12).

Nu 13: 8 tribe of Ephraim, **H** son of Nun;
13:16 gave **H** son of Nun the name Joshua.)
2Ki 15:30 **H** son of Elah conspired against
17: 1 **H** son of Elah became king of Israel
17: 3 king of Assyria came up to attack **H**,
17: 4 the king of Assyria discovered that **H**
17: 6 In the ninth year of **H**, the king of
18: 1 In the third year of **H** son of Elah
18: 9 the seventh year of **H** son of Elah
18:10 the ninth year of **H** king of Israel.
1Ch 27:20 Ephraimites: **H** son of Azaziah;
Ne 10:23 **H**, Hananiah, Hasshub,

Hospitable (Hospitality)

1Ti 3: 2 respectable, **h**, able to teach,
Tit 1: 8 Rather he must be **h**, one who loves

Hospitably (Hospitality)

Ac 28: 7 and for three days entertained us **h**.

Hospitality (Hospitable, Hospitably)

Ro 12:13 Practise **h**.
16:23 Gaius, whose **h** I and the whole

1Ti 5:10 showing **h**, washing the feet of the
1Pe 4: 9 Offer **h** to one another without
3Jn : 8 We ought therefore to show **h** to such

Host (*Host of heaven*, Hosts)

Ne 9: 6 and all their starry **h**, the earth
Ps 33: 6 starry **h** by the breath of his mouth.
Isa 34: 4 all the starry **h** will fall like
40:26 brings out the starry **h** one by one,
Da 8:10 it reached the **h** of the heavens
8:10 and it threw some of the starry **h**
8:11 be as great as the Prince of the **h**;
8:12 of rebellion, the **h** of the saints
8:13 **h** that will be trampled underfoot?"
Zep 1: 5 the roofs to worship the starry **h**,
Lk 2:13 heavenly **h** appeared with the angel,
14: 9 If so, the **h** who invited both of you
14:10 so that when your **h** comes, he will
14:12 Jesus said to his **h**, "When you give

Host of heaven

1Ki 22:19 **h** standing round him on his right
2Ch 18:18 all the **h** standing on his right

Hostages

2Ki 14:14 also took **h** and returned to Samaria.
2Ch 25:24 and the **h**, and returned to Samaria.

Hostile (Hostility)

Ge 26:27 you were **h** to me and sent me away?"
Lev 26:21 "'If you remain **h** towards me and
26:23 but continue to be **h** towards me,
26:24 I myself will be **h** towards you and
26:27 me but continue to be **h** towards me,
26:28 in my anger I will be **h** towards you,
26:41 which made me **h** towards them so that
Nu 24: 8 They devour **h** nations and break
Jdg 6:31 Joash replied to the **h** crowd around
1Ki 11:25 in Aram and was **h** towards Israel.
Isa 11:13 Judah, nor Judah **h** towards Ephraim.
Ro 8: 7 the sinful mind is **h** to God. It does
1Th 2:15 displease God and are **h** to all

Hostility (Hostile)

Ge 16:12 live in **h** towards all his brothers.
25:18 in **h** towards all their brothers.
49:23 they shot at him with **h**.
Lev 26:40 against me and their **h** towards me,
Nu 35:21 or if in **h** he hits him with his fist
35:22 'But if without **h** someone suddenly
2Ch 21:16 Jehoram the **h** of the Philistines
Job 17: 2 my eyes must dwell on their **h**.
Ps 78:49 his wrath, indignation and **h**
Eze 25:15 ancient **h** sought to destroy Judah,
35: 5 Because you harboured an ancient **h**
Hos 9: 7 are so many and your **h** so great,
9: 8 and **h** in the house of his God.
Eph 2:14 barrier, the dividing wall of **h**,
2:16 by which he put to death their **h**.

Hosts (Host)

2Ki 17:16 bowed down to all the starry **h**,
21: 3 the starry **h** and worshipped them.
21: 5 he built altars to all the starry **h**.
23: 4 and Asherah and all the starry **h**.
23: 5 and to all the starry **h**.
2Ch 33: 3 bowed down to all the starry **h**
33: 5 he built altars to all the starry **h**.
Ps 103:21 Praise the LORD, all his heavenly **h**,
148: 2 praise him, all his heavenly **h**.
Isa 45:12 I marshalled their starry **h**.
Jer 19:13 on the roofs to all the starry **h**

Hot (Hotheaded, Hot-tempered, Hotter)

Ge 36:24 Anah who discovered the **h** springs
Ex 11: 8 Moses, **h** with anger, left Pharaoh.
16:21 when the sun grew **h**, it melted away.
1Sa 11: 9 By the time the sun is **h** tomorrow,
14:22 they joined the battle in **h** pursuit.
21: 6 replaced by **h** bread on the day it
1Ki 19: 6 over **h** coals, and a jar of water.
Ne 7: 3 not to be opened until the sun is **h**.
Job 15: 2 fill his belly with the **h** east wind?
Ps 39: 3 My heart grew **h** within me, and as I
78:49 unleashed against them his **h** anger
Pr 6:28 Can a man walk on **h** coals without
Lam 5:10 Our skin is **h** as an oven, feverish
Eze 24:11 pot on the coals till it becomes **h**
38:18 my **h** anger will be aroused, declares
Da 3:22 the furnace so **h** that the flames of
Hos 7: 7 All of them are **h** as an oven;
Lk 12:55 'It's going to be **h**,' and it is.
1Ti 4: 2 have been seared as with a **h** iron.
Rev 3:15 that you are neither cold nor **h**.
3:16 because you are lukewarm—neither **h**

Hotham

1Ch 7:32 and **H** and of their sister Shua.
11:44 Jeiel the sons of **H** the Aroerite,

Hotheaded (Head, Hot)

Pr 14:16 evil, but a fool is **h** and reckless.

Hothir

1Ch 25: 4 Mallothi, **H** and Mahazioth.
25:28 the twenty-first to **H**, his sons and

Hot-tempered (Hot, Temper)

Jdg 18:25 "Don't argue with us, or some **h** men
Pr 15:18 A **h** man stirs up dissension, but a
19:19 A **h** man must pay the penalty; if you
22:24 Do not make friends with a **h** man,
29:22 and a **h** one commits many sins.

Hotter (Hot)

Da 3:19 be heated seven times **h** than

Hound (Hounded)

Job 19:28 "If you say, 'How we will **h** him,

Hounded (Hound)

Ps 109:16 but **h** to death the poor and the
Eze 36: 3 Because they ravaged and **h** you

Hour (Hours)

Ecc 9:12 no man knows when his **h** will come
Mt 6:27 can add a single **h** to his life?
8:13 servant was healed at that very **h**.
15:28 was healed from that very **h**.
20: 3 "About the third **h** he went out and
20: 5 went out again about the sixth **h**
20: 5 the ninth **h** and did the same thing.
20: 6 About the eleventh **h** he went out and
20: 9 eleventh **h** came and each received a
20:12 were hired last worked only one **h**,'
24:36 "No-one knows about that day or **h**,
24:44 at an **h** when you do not expect him.
24:50 him and at an **h** he is not aware of.
25:13 you do not know the day or the **h**.
26:40 with me for one **h**?" he asked Peter.
26:45 the **h** is near, and the Son of Man
27:45 From the sixth **h** until the ninth **h**
27:46 About the ninth **h** Jesus cried out
Mk 13:32 "No-one knows about that day or **h**,
14:35 possible the **h** might pass from him.
14:37 Could you not keep watch for one **h**?
14:41 and resting? Enough! The **h** has come.
15:25 was the third **h** when they crucified
15:33 At the sixth **h** darkness came over
15:33 the whole land until the ninth **h**.
15:34 at the ninth **h** Jesus cried out in a
Lk 12:25 can add a single **h** to his life?
12:39 at what **h** the thief was coming,
12:40 an **h** when you do not expect him."
12:46 him and at an **h** he is not aware of
22:14 the **h** came, Jesus and his apostles
22:53 is your **h**—when darkness reigns."
22:59 About an **h** later another asserted,
23:44 was now about the sixth **h**, and
23:44 the whole land until the ninth **h**,
Jn 1:39 It was about the tenth **h**.
4: 6 It was about the sixth **h**.
4:52 him yesterday at the seventh **h**."
12:23 Jesus replied, "The **h** has come for
12:27 'Father, save me from this **h**'? No,
Jn 12:27 this very reason I came to this **h**.
19:14 Passover Week, about the sixth **h**.
Ac 10:30 this **h**, at three in the afternoon.
16:33 At that **h** of the night the jailer
Ro 13:11 The **h** has come for you to wake up
1Co 4:11 To this very **h** we go hungry and
15:30 do we endanger ourselves every **h**?
1Jn 2:18 Dear children, this is the last **h**;
2:18 is how we know it is the last **h**.
Rev 3:10 also keep you from the **h** of trial
8: 1 in heaven for about half an **h**.
9:15 had been kept ready for this very **h**
11:13 At that very **h** there was a severe
14: 7 the **h** of his judgment has come.
17:12 but who for one **h** will receive
18:10 In one **h** your doom has come!'
18:17 In one **h** such great wealth has been
18:19 one **h** she has been brought to ruin!

Hours (Hour)

Jn 11: 9 "Are there not twelve **h** of daylight?
Ac 5: 7 About three **h** later his wife came in,
19:34 shouted in unison for about two **h**:

House (*Father's house, House of David, House of God, House of Israel, House of Judah, House of the LORD*, Household, Households, Houses, *Rebellious house*, Storehouse, Storehouses, Treasure-house)

Ge 19: 2 turn aside to your servant's **h**.
19: 3 did go with him and entered his **h**.
19: 4 young and old—surrounded the **h**.
19:10 back into the **h** and shut the door.
19:11 men who were at the door of the **h**,
24:27 to the **h** of my master's relatives."
24:31 prepared the **h** and a place for
24:32 the man went to the **h**, and the
27:15 which she had in the **h**, and put them
28: 2 to the **h** of your mother's father
28:22 set up as a pillar will be God's **h**,
34:26 Dinah from Shechem's **h** and left.
39: 2 in the **h** of his Egyptian master.
39: 5 both in the **h** and in the field.
39: 8 himself with anything in the **h**;
39: 9 No-one is greater in this **h** than I
39:11 One day he went into the **h** to attend
39:12 in her hand and ran out of the **h**.
39:13 her hand and had run out of the **h**,
39:15 beside me and ran out of the **h**."
39:18 beside me and ran out of the **h**."
40: 3 put them in custody in the **h** of the
40: 7 custody with him in his master's **h**,
41:10 the **h** of the captain of the guard.
43:16 he said to the steward of his **h**,
43:16 Take these men to my **h**, slaughter
43:17 him and took the men to Joseph's **h**.
43:18 when they were taken to his **h**.
43:19 to him at the entrance to the **h**.
43:24 took the men into Joseph's **h**,
43:26 gifts they had brought into the **h**,
44: 1 to the steward of his **h**:
44: 8 silver or gold from your master's **h**?
44:14 Joseph was still in the **h** when Judah
Ex 2: 1 a man of the **h** of Levi married a
3:22 any woman living in her **h** for
12:22 of the door of his **h** until morning.
12:30 was not a **h** without someone dead.
12:46 "It must be eaten inside one **h**;
12:46 take none of the meat outside the **h**.
19: 3 you are to say to the **h** of Jacob
20:17 shall not covet your neighbour's **h**.
22: 7 are stolen from the neighbour's **h**,
22: 8 the owner of the **h** must appear
Lev 14:34 mildew in a **h** in that land,
14:35 the owner of the **h** must go and tell
14:35 that looks like mildew in my **h**'
14:36 The priest is to order the **h** to be
14:36 in the **h** will be pronounced unclean.
14:36 is to go in and inspect the **h**.
14:38 **h** and close it up for seven days.
14:39 shall return to inspect the **h**.
14:41 the inside walls of the **h** scraped
14:42 take new clay and plaster the **h**.
14:43 "If the mildew reappears in the **h**

Lev 14:43 and the **h** scraped and plastered,
14:44 if the mildew has spread in the **h**,
14:44 mildew; the **h** is unclean.
14:46 "Anyone who goes into the **h** while
14:47 Anyone who sleeps or eats in the **h**
14:48 after the **h** has been plastered,
14:48 he shall pronounce the **h** clean,
14:49 To purify the **h** he is to take two
14:51 and sprinkle the **h** seven times.
14:52 He shall purify the **h** with the
14:53 make atonement for the **h**,
14:55 mildew in clothing or in a **h**,
25:29 'If a man sells a **h** in a walled
25:30 the **h** in the walled city shall
25:33 a **h** sold in any town they hold
27:14 'If a man dedicates his **h** as
27:15 If the man who dedicates his **h**
27:15 and the **h** will again become his.
Nu 12: 7 he is faithful in all my **h**.
17: 8 which represented the **h** of Levi,
30:16 daughter still living in his **h**.
Dt 5:21 on your neighbour's **h** or land,
7:26 detestable thing into your **h** or
20: 5 "Has anyone built a new **h** and not
21:13 After she has lived in your **h** and
22: 8 you build a new **h**, make a parapet
22: 8 the guilt of bloodshed on your **h**
24: 1 to her and sends her from his **h**,
24: 2 if after she leaves his **h** she
24: 3 sends her from his **h**, or if he dies,
24:10 do not go into his **h** to get what he
25:14 two different measures in your **h**
26:13 have removed from my **h** the sacred
28:30 You will build a **h**, but you will
Jos 2: 1 entered the **h** of a prostitute
2: 3 who came to you and entered your **h**,
2:15 for the **h** she lived in was part of
2:18 and all your family into your **h**.
2:19 If anyone goes outside your **h** into
2:19 As for anyone who is in the **h** with
6:17 with her in her **h** shall be spared,
6:22 "Go into the prostitute's **h** and
6:24 into the treasury of the LORD's **h**.
9:23 water-carriers for the **h** of my God
17:17 Joshua said to the **h** of Joseph—to
18: 5 the **h** of Joseph in its territory on
Jdg 1:22 Now the **h** of Joseph attacked Bethel,
1:35 the power of the **h** of Joseph
3:24 himself in the inner room of the **h**
10: 9 Benjamin and the **h** of Ephraim;
11:31 out of the door of my **h** to meet me
12: 1 burn down your **h** over your head."
17: 4 And they were put in Micah's **h**.
17: 8 Micah's **h** in the hill country of
17:12 his priest and lived in his **h**.
18: 2 Ephraim and came to the **h** of Micah,
18: 3 they were near Micah's **h**, they
18:13 of Ephraim and came to Micah's **h**.
18:15 went to the **h** of the young Levite
18:18 these men went into Micah's **h** and
18:22 gone some distance from Micah's **h**,
19:18 No-one has taken me into his **h**.
19:20 You are welcome at my **h**," the old
19:21 he took him into his **h** and fed his
19:22 men of the city surrounded the **h**.
19:22 to the old man who owned the **h**,
19:22 your **h** so we can have sex with him
19:23 The owner of the **h** went outside and
19:26 the **h** where her master was staying,
19:27 opened the door of the **h** and
19:27 fallen in the doorway of the **h**,
20: 5 surrounded the **h**, intending to
20: 8 not one of us will return to his **h**.
1Sa 2:30 'I promised that your **h** and your
2:35 I will firmly establish his **h**, and
3:14 Therefore, I swore to the **h** of Eli,
3:14 'The guilt of Eli's **h** will never be
7: 1 They took it to Abinadab's **h** on the
9:18 tell me where the seer's **h** is?"
9:25 with Saul on the roof of his **h**.
18:10 He was prophesying in his **h**, while
19: 9 in his **h** with his spear in his hand.
19:11 Saul sent men to David's **h** to watch
21:15 Must this man come into my **h**?"
25:36 he was in the **h** holding a banquet
28:24 woman had a fattened calf at the **h**,
2Sa 3: 1 The war between the **h** of Saul and
3: 1 **h** of Saul grew weaker and weaker.
3: 6 the war between the **h** of Saul
3: 8 This very day I am loyal to the **h**
3:10 the kingdom from the **h** of Saul
3:19 whole **h** of Benjamin wanted to do.
3:29 May Joab's **h** never be without
4: 5 set out for the **h** of Ish-Bosheth,
4: 6 went into the inner part of the **h**
4: 7 They had gone into the **h** while he
4:11 killed an innocent man in his own **h**
6: 3 **h** of Abinadab, which was on the hill.
6:10 to the **h** of Obed-Edom the Gittite.
6:11 ark of the LORD remained in the **h**
6:12 brought up the ark of God from the **h**
6:21 your father or anyone from his **h**
7: 5 the one to build me a **h** to dwell in?
7: 6 I have not dwelt in a **h** from the day
7: 7 you not built me a **h** of cedar?"
7:11 himself will establish a **h** for you:
7:13 who will build a **h** for my Name,
7:16 Your **h** and your kingdom shall endure
7:19 the future of the **h** of your servant.
7:25 concerning your servant and his **h**.
7:26 the **h** of your servant David will be
7:27 saying, 'I will build a **h** for you.
7:29 Now be pleased to bless the **h** of
7:29 and with your blessing the **h** of your
9: 1 "Is there anyone still left of the **h**
9: 3 "Is there no-one still left of the **h**
9: 4 Ziba answered, "He is at the **h** of
9: 5 from the **h** of Makir son of Ammiel.
11: 8 down to your **h** and wash your feet.
11: 9 and did not go down to his **h**.
11:11 How could I go to my **h** to eat and
11:27 David had her brought to his **h**,
12: 8 I gave your master's **h** to you,
12:10 shall never depart from your **h**,
12:16 He fasted and went into his **h**
12:20 Then he went to his own **h**,
13: 7 "Go to the **h** of your brother Amnon
13: 8 Tamar went to the **h** of her brother
13:20 Absalom's **h**, a desolate woman.
14:24 He must go to his own **h**; he must
14:24 So Absalom went to his own **h** and
14:31 Joab did go to Absalom's **h** and he
17:18 went to the **h** of a man in Bahurim.
17:20 men came to the woman at the **h**,
17:23 set out for his **h** in his home town.
17:23 He put his **h** in order and then
19: 5 Joab went into the **h** to the king
19:20 the whole **h** of Joseph to come down
20: 3 and put them in a **h** under guard.
21: 1 of Saul and his blood-stained **h**;
23: 5 "Is not my **h** right with God?
1Ki 2:27 spoken at Shiloh about the **h** of Eli
2:33 his **h** and his throne, may there be
2:36 "Build yourself a **h** in Jerusalem
3:17 this woman and I live in the same **h**
3:18 no-one in the **h** but the two of us.
8:43 **h** I have built bears your Name.
11:18 who gave Hadad a **h** and land and
11:28 labour force of the **h** of Joseph.
12:16 Look after your own **h**, O David!"
13:18 Bring him back with you to your **h**
13:19 with him and ate and drank in his **h**
13:34 the sin of the **h** of Jeroboam
14: 4 and went to Ahijah's **h** in Shiloh.
14:10 bring disaster on the **h** of Jeroboam
14:10 I will burn up the **h** of Jeroboam as
14:13 the only one in the **h** of Jeroboam
14:17 over the threshold of the **h**,
15:27 Baasha son of Ahijah of the **h** of
16: 3 about to consume Baasha and his **h**,
16: 3 make your **h** like that of Jeroboam
16: 7 son of Hanani to Baasha and his **h**,
16: 7 and becoming like the **h** of Jeroboam
17:17 woman who owned the **h** became ill.
17:23 him down from the room into the **h**.
21:22 I will make your **h** like that of
21:29 will bring it on his **h** in the days
2Ki 4: 2 Tell me, what do you have in your **h**
4:32 Elisha reached the **h**, there was the
5: 9 stopped at the door of Elisha's **h**.
5:24 servants and put them away in the **h**.
6:32 Now Elisha was sitting in his **h**,
2Ki 7:17 when the king came down to his **h**.
8: 3 the king to beg for her **h** and land.
8: 5 to beg the king for her **h** and land.
8:18 as the **h** of Ahab had done, for he
8:27 He walked in the ways of the **h** of
8:27 as the **h** of Ahab had done, for he
9: 6 Jehu got up and went into the **h**.
9: 7 You are to destroy the **h** of Ahab
9: 8 The whole **h** of Ahab will perish.
9: 9 will make the **h** of Ahab like the **h**
9: 9 like the **h** of Baasha son of Ahijah.
10: 1 seventy sons of the **h** of Ahab.
10: 3 Then fight for your master's **h**."
10:10 against the **h** of Ahab will fail.
10:11 who remained of the **h** of Ahab,
10:30 have done to the **h** of Ahab all I
13: 6 from the sins of the **h** of Jeroboam,
15: 5 died, and he lived in a separate **h**.
20: 1 the LORD says: Put your **h** in order,
21:13 used against the **h** of Ahab.
1Ch 2:55 the father of the **h** of Recab.
9:23 the **h** called the Tent.
10: 6 and all his **h** died together.
12:29 loyal to Saul's **h** until then;
13: 7 from Abinadab's **h** on a new cart,
13:13 to the **h** of Obed-Edom the Gittite.
13:14 Obed-Edom in his **h** for three months,
15:25 from the **h** of Obed-Edom,
17: 4 the one to build me a **h** to dwell in.
17: 5 have not dwelt in a **h** from the day
17: 6 you not built me a **h** of cedar?"
17:10 the LORD will build a **h** for you:
17:12 He is the one who will build a **h**
17:14 I will set him over my **h** and my
17:17 the future of the **h** of your servant.
17:23 and his **h** be established for ever.
17:24 the **h** of your servant David will be
17:25 that you will build a **h** for him.
17:27 to bless the **h** of your servant,
22: 5 and the **h** to be built for the LORD
22: 6 a **h** for the LORD, the God of Israel
22: 7 a **h** for the Name of the LORD my God
22: 8 are not to build a **h** for my Name,
22:10 He is the one who will build a **h**
28: 2 I had it in my heart to build a **h**
28: 3 'You are not to build a **h** for my
28: 6 who will build my **h** and my courts,
2Ch 6:33 **h** that I have built bears your Name
10:16 Look after your own **h**, O David!"
21: 6 as the **h** of Ahab had done, for he
21:13 just as the **h** of Ahab did.
22: 3 in the ways of the **h** of Ahab,
22: 4 as the **h** of Ahab had done,
22: 7 anointed to destroy the **h** of Ahab.
22: 8 executing judgment on the **h** of Ahab,
22: 9 was no-one in the **h** of Ahaziah
26:21 He lived in a separate **h**—leprous,
35:21 but the **h** with which I am at war.
Ezr 6:11 a beam is to be pulled from his **h**
6:11 **h** is to be made a pile of rubble.
8:17 to us for the **h** of our God.
8:25 had donated for the **h** of our God.
8:30 to the **h** of our God in Jerusalem.
8:33 fourth day, in the **h** of our God
9: 9 **h** of our God and repair its ruins,
Ne 3:10 Harumaph made repairs opposite his **h**,
3:16 pool and the **H** of the Heroes.
3:20 the **h** of Eliashib the high priest.
3:21 of Eliashib's **h** to the end of it.
3:23 made repairs in front of their **h**;
3:23 Ananiah, made repairs beside his **h**.
3:24 from Azariah's **h** to the angle
3:28 repairs, each in front of his own **h**.
3:29 Immer made repairs opposite his **h**.
3:31 far as the **h** of the temple servants
5:13 this way may God shake out of his **h**
6:10 One day I went to the **h** of Shemaiah
10:32 for the service of the **h** of our God:
10:33 all the duties of the **h** of our God.
10:34 is to bring to the **h** of our God
10:36 of our flocks to the **h** of our God,
10:37 the storerooms of the **h** of our God,
10:38 the tithes up to the **h** of our God,
10:39 will not neglect the **h** of our God.
13: 4 the storerooms of the **h** of our God.
13:14 the **h** of my God and its services.

Est 4:13 because you are in the king's **h** you
7: 8 while she is with me in the **h**?"
7: 9 feet high stands by Haman's **h**.
Job 1:13 wine at the oldest brother's **h**,
1:18 wine at the oldest brother's **h**,
1:19 struck the four corners of the **h**.
5: 3 but suddenly his **h** was cursed.
7:10 He will never come to his **h** again;
20:28 A flood will carry off his **h**,
21:28 'Where now is the great man's **h**,
27:18 The **h** he builds is like a moth's
29: 4 intimate friendship blessed my **h**,
29:18 I thought, 'I shall die in my own **h**
42:11 came and ate with him in his **h**.
Ps 5: 7 will come into your **h**; in reverence
26: 8 I love the **h** where you live, O LORD,
36: 8 They feast in the abundance of your **h**
49:16 the splendour of his **h** increases;
52: T David has gone to the **h** of Ahimelech
59: T Saul had sent men to watch David's **h**
65: 4 with the good things of your **h**,
69: 9 for zeal for your **h** consumes me,
84: 4 Blessed are those who dwell in your **h**
84:10 be a doorkeeper in the **h** of my God
93: 5 adorns your **h** for endless days,
101: 2 walk in my **h** with blameless heart.
101: 7 practises deceit will dwell in my **h**
112: 3 Wealth and riches are in his **h**,
114: 1 the **h** of Jacob from a people of
115:10 O **h** of Aaron, trust in the LORD—
115:12 he will bless the **h** of Aaron,
118: 3 Let the **h** of Aaron say: "His love
127: 1 Unless the LORD builds the **h**,
128: 3 like a fruitful vine within your **h**;
132: 3 "I will not enter my **h** or go to my
135: 2 in the courts of the **h** of our God.
135:19 O **h** of Aaron, praise the LORD;
135:20 O **h** of Levi, praise the LORD; you
Pr 2:18 For her **h** leads down to death and
3:33 The LORD's curse is on the **h** of the
5: 8 do not go near the door of her **h**,
5:10 your toil enrich another man's **h**.
6:31 costs him all the wealth of his **h**.
7: 6 At the window of my **h** I looked out
7: 8 along in the direction of her **h**
7:27 Her **h** is a highway to the grave,
9: 1 Wisdom has built her **h**; she has hewn
9:14 She sits at the door of her **h**, on a
12: 7 the **h** of the righteous stands firm.
14: 1 The wise woman builds her **h**, but
14:11 The **h** of the wicked will be
15: 6 The **h** of the righteous contains
15:25 LORD tears down the proud man's **h**
17: 1 a **h** full of feasting, with strife.
17:13 evil will never leave his **h**.
21: 9 share a **h** with a quarrelsome wife.
21:12 takes note of the **h** of the wicked
21:20 In the **h** of the wise are stores of
24: 3 By wisdom a **h** is built, and through
24:15 outlaw against a righteous man's **h**
24:27 after that, build your **h**.
25:17 Seldom set foot in your neighbour's **h**
25:24 share a **h** with a quarrelsome wife.
27:10 and do not go to your brother's **h**
Ecc 2: 7 other slaves who were born in my **h**.
7: 2 is better to go to a **h** of mourning
7: 2 than to go to a **h** of feasting,
7: 4 the wise is in the **h** of mourning
7: 4 of fools is in the **h** of pleasure.
10:18 if his hands are idle, the **h** leaks.
12: 3 the keepers of the **h** tremble, and
SS 1:17 The beams of our **h** are cedars;
3: 4 I had brought him to my mother's **h**,
8: 2 and bring you to my mother's **h**
8: 7 all the wealth of his **h** for love,
Isa 2: 3 to the **h** of the God of Jacob.
2: 5 Come, O **h** of Jacob, let us walk in
2: 6 abandoned your people, the **h** of Jacob
3: 7 I have no food or clothing in my **h**;
5: 8 Woe to you who add **h** to **h** and join
7:17 and on the **h** of your father
8:17 hiding his face from the **h** of Jacob.
10:20 the survivors of the **h** of Jacob,
14: 1 them and unite with the **h** of Jacob.
22:18 you disgrace to your master's **h**!
22:23 of honour for the **h** of his father.

Isa 23: 1 and left without **h** or harbour.
24:10 the entrance to every **h** is barred.
29:22 says to the **h** of Jacob: "No longer
31: 2 rise up against the **h** of the wicked
38: 1 the LORD says: Put your **h** in order,
38:12 Like a shepherd's tent my **h** has been
46: 3 "Listen to me, O **h** of Jacob, all you
48: 1 "Listen to this, O **h** of Jacob, you
56: 7 and give them joy in my **h** of prayer.
56: 7 my **h** will be called a **h** of prayer
58: 1 and to the **h** of Jacob their sins.
66: 1 Where is the **h** you will build for me?
Jer 2: 4 word of the LORD, O **h** of Jacob,
5:20 "Announce this to the **h** of Jacob
7: 2 "Stand at the gate of the LORD's **h**
7:10 come and stand before me in this **h**,
7:11 Has this **h**, which bears my Name,
7:14 now do to the **h** that bears my Name,
7:30 idols in the **h** that bears my Name
12: 7 "I will forsake my **h**, abandon my
16: 5 "Do not enter a **h** where there is a
16: 8 do not enter a **h** where there is
18: 2 "Go down to the potter's **h**, and
18: 3 I went down to the potter's **h**,
20: 6 all who live in your **h** will go into
26: 2 in the courtyard of the LORD's **h**
26: 6 I will make this **h** like Shiloh and
26: 9 that this **h** will be like Shiloh
26:10 of the New Gate of the LORD's **h**.
26:12 sent me to prophesy against this **h**
27:16 the articles from the LORD's **h** will
28: 3 all the articles of the LORD's **h**
28: 6 the articles of the LORD's **h**
32:34 in the **h** that bears my Name and
34:15 me in the **h** that bears my Name.
37:15 in the **h** of Jonathan the secretary,
37:20 to the **h** of Jonathan the secretary,
38:26 back to Jonathan's **h** to die there.
51:51 the holy places of the LORD's **h**."
Eze 3:24 "Go, shut yourself inside your **h**.
8: 1 while I was sitting in my **h** and the
10:19 to the east gate of the LORD's **h**,
20: 5 the descendants of the **h** of Jacob
23:39 That is what they did in my **h**.
Da 2:17 Daniel returned to his **h** and
Hos 1: 4 I will soon punish the **h** of Jehu
5: 1 you Israelites! Listen, O royal **h**!
9: 8 and hostility in the **h** of his God.
9:15 I will drive them out of my **h**.
Joel 1:13 are withheld from the **h** of your God.
1:16 and gladness from the **h** of our God?
3:18 will flow out of the LORD's **h**
Am 1: 4 send fire upon the **h** of Hazael
2: 8 In the **h** of their god they drink
3:13 and testify against the **h** of Jacob,"
3:15 winter **h** along with the summer **h**;
5: 6 sweep through the **h** of Joseph
5:19 as though he entered his **h** and
6: 9 If ten men are left in one **h**, they
6:10 comes to carry them out of the **h**
6:11 great **h** into pieces and the small **h**
7: 9 rise against the **h** of Jeroboam."
7:16 preaching against the **h** of Isaac.'
9: 8 not totally destroy the **h** of Jacob
Ob :17 the **h** of Jacob will possess its
:18 The **h** of Jacob will be a fire and
:18 a fire and the **h** of Joseph a flame;
:18 the **h** of Esau will be stubble,
:18 be no survivors from the **h** of Esau.
Mic 2: 7 Should it be said, O **h** of Jacob:
3: 9 you leaders of the **h** of Jacob,
4: 2 to the **h** of the God of Jacob.
6:10 Am I still to forget, O wicked **h**,
6:16 and all the practices of Ahab's **h**,
Hab 2:10 shaming your own **h** and forfeiting
Hag 1: 2 come for the LORD's **h** to be built.
1: 4 while this **h** remains a ruin?"
1: 8 bring down timber and build the **h**,
1: 9 "Because of my **h**, which remains a
1: 9 each of you is busy with his own **h**.
2: 3 'Who of you is left who saw this **h**
2: 7 and I will fill this **h** with glory,'
2: 9 'The glory of this present **h** will be
2: 9 than the glory of the former **h**,'
Zec 1:16 and there my **h** will be rebuilt.
3: 7 then you will govern my **h** and have

Zec 5: 4 it will enter the **h** of the thief
5: 4 the **h** of him who swears falsely by
5: 4 It will remain in his **h** and destroy
5:11 of Babylonia to build a **h** for it.
6:10 Go the same day to the **h** of Josiah
9: 8 I will defend my **h** against marauding
10: 6 **h** of Judah and save the **h** of Joseph.
12:12 of the **h** of Nathan and their wives,
12:13 the clan of the **h** of Levi and their
13: 6 I was given at the **h** of my friends.'
14:20 the cooking pots in the LORD's **h**
Mal 3:10 that there may be food in my **h**.
Mt 2:11 On coming to the **h**, they saw the
5:15 gives light to everyone in the **h**.
7:24 man who built his **h** on the rock.
7:25 winds blew and beat against that **h**
7:26 foolish man who built his **h** on sand.
7:27 winds blew and beat against that **h**,
8:14 Jesus came into Peter's **h**, he saw
9:10 was having dinner at Matthew's **h**
9:23 Jesus entered the ruler's **h** and saw
10:11 and stay at his **h** until you leave.
10:25 If the head of the **h** has been called
12:29 can anyone enter a strong man's **h**
12:29 strong man? Then he can rob his **h**.
12:44 'I will return to the **h** I left.
12:44 it finds the **h** unoccupied,
13: 1 That same day Jesus went out of the **h**
13:36 he left the crowd and went into the **h**
13:52 is like the owner of a **h** who
13:57 own **h** is a prophet without honour."
17:25 When Peter came into the **h**, Jesus
21:13 'My **h** will be called a **h** of prayer,'
23:38 Look, your **h** is left to you desolate.
24:17 Let no-one on the roof of his **h** go
24:17 down to take anything out of the **h**.
24:43 If the owner of the **h** had known at
24:43 not have let his **h** be broken into.
26:18 Passover with my disciples at your **h**.
Mk 1:35 Jesus got up, left the **h** and went
2:15 Jesus was having dinner at Levi's **h**
3:20 Jesus entered a **h**, and again a crowd
3:25 If a **h** is divided against itself,
3:25 against itself, that **h** cannot stand.
3:27 no-one can enter a strong man's **h**
3:27 Then he can rob his **h**.
5:35 **h** of Jairus, the synagogue ruler.
6: 4 own **h** is a prophet without honour."
6:10 Whenever you enter a **h**, stay there
7:17 left the crowd and entered the **h**,
7:24 He entered a **h** and did not want
9:33 When he was in the **h**, he asked them,
10:10 they were in the **h** again, the
11:17 'My **h** will be called a **h** of prayer
13:15 Let no-one on the roof of his **h** go
13:15 or enter the **h** to take anything out.
13:34 He leaves his **h** and puts his servants
13:35 the owner of the **h** will come back
14:14 Say to the owner of the **h** he enters,
Lk 1:33 he will reign over the **h** of Jacob
1:69 for us in the **h** of his servant
2: 4 belonged to the **h** and line of David.
5:18 into the **h** to lay him before Jesus.
5:29 a great banquet for Jesus at his **h**,
6:48 He is like a man building a **h**, who
6:48 the torrent struck that **h** but could
6:49 who built a **h** on the ground without
6:49 The moment the torrent struck that **h**,
7: 6 He was not far from the **h** when the
7:10 to the **h** and found the servant well.
7:36 so he went to the Pharisee's **h** and
7:37 Jesus was eating at the Pharisee's **h**,
7:44 see this woman? I came into your **h**.
8:27 in a **h**, but had lived in the tombs.
8:41 pleading with him to come to his **h**
8:49 **h** of Jairus, the synagogue ruler.
8:51 he arrived at the **h** of Jairus, he
9: 4 Whatever **h** you enter, stay there
10: 5 a **h**, first say, 'Peace to this **h**.'
10: 7 Stay in that **h**, eating and drinking
10: 7 Do not move around from **h** to **h**.
11:17 **h** divided against itself will fall.
11:21 fully armed, guards his own **h**
11:24 'I will return to the **h** I left.'
11:25 it finds the **h** swept clean
12:39 If the owner of the **h** had known at

Lk 12:39 not have let his **h** be broken into.
13:25 Once the owner of the **h** gets up and
13:35 Look, your **h** is left to you desolate.
14: 1 in the **h** of a prominent Pharisee
14:21 Then the owner of the **h** became angry
14:23 come in, so that my **h** will be full.
15: 8 sweep the **h** and search carefully
15:25 came near the **h**, he heard music and
17:31 no-one who is on the roof of his **h**,
19: 5 I must stay at your **h** today."
19: 9 Today salvation has come to this **h**
19:46 'My **h** will be a **h** of prayer'; but
22:10 Follow him to the **h** that he enters,
22:11 say to the owner of the **h**, 'The
22:54 him into the **h** of the high priest.
Jn 2:17 "Zeal for your **h** will consume me.
11:31 Jews who had been with Mary in the **h**,
12: 3 And the **h** was filled with the
20:26 his disciples were in the **h** again,
Ac 2: 2 the whole **h** where they were sitting.
5:42 in the temple courts and from **h** to **h**,
7:47 was Solomon who built the **h** for him.
7:49 What kind of **h** will you build for me?
8: 3 Going from **h** to **h**, he dragged off
9:11 The Lord told him, "Go to the **h** of
9:17 Ananias went to the **h** and entered it.
10: 6 the tanner, whose **h** is by the sea."
10:17 where Simon's **h** was and stopped at
10:22 told him to have you come to his **h**
10:23 Peter invited the men into the **h** to
10:25 Peter entered the **h**, Cornelius met
10:30 "Four days ago I was in my **h** praying
11: 3 into the **h** of uncircumcised men
11:11 at the **h** where I was staying.
11:12 with me, and we entered the man's **h**.
11:13 an angel appear in his **h** and say,
12:12 he went to the **h** of Mary the mother
16:15 she said, "come and stay at my **h**.
16:32 him and to all the others in his **h**.
16:34 The jailer brought them into his **h**
16:40 they went to Lydia's **h**, where they
17: 5 They rushed to Jason's **h** in search
17: 7 Jason has welcomed them into his **h**.
18: 7 next door to the **h** of Titius Justus,
19:16 ran out of the **h** naked and bleeding.
20:20 taught you publicly and from **h** to **h**.
21: 8 at the **h** of Philip the evangelist,
28:30 stayed there in his own rented **h**
Ro 16: 5 the church that meets at their **h**.
1Co 16:19 the church that meets at their **h**.
2Co 5: 1 an eternal **h** in heaven, not built by
Col 4:15 to Nympha and the church in her **h**.
1Ti 5:13 idle and going about from **h** to **h**.
2Ti 2:20 In a large **h** there are articles not
Heb 3: 2 Moses was faithful in all God's **h**.
3: 3 just as the builder of a **h** has
3: 3 greater honour than the **h** itself.
3: 4 For every **h** is built by someone, but
3: 5 as a servant in all God's **h**,
3: 6 is faithful as a son over God's **h**.
3: 6 And we are his **h**, if we hold on to
1Pe 2: 5 are being built into a spiritual **h**
2Jn :10 take him into your **h** or welcome him.

House of David

1Sa 20:16 Jonathan made a covenant with the **h**,
2Sa 3: 1 Saul and the **h** lasted a long time.
3: 6 between the house of Saul and the **h**,
1Ki 12:19 rebellion against the **h** to this day.
12:20 of Judah remained loyal to the **h**.
12:26 is now likely to revert to the **h**.
13: 2 named Josiah will be born to the **h**.
14: 8 I tore the kingdom away from the **h**
2Ki 17:21 he tore Israel away from the **h**, they
2Ch 10:19 rebellion against the **h** to this day.
21: 7 was not willing to destroy the **h**.
Ne 12:37 passed above the **h** to the Water Gate
Ps 122: 5 stand, the thrones of the **h**.
Isa 7: 2 Now the **h** was told, "Aram has allied
7:13 Isaiah said, "Hear now, you **h**! Is it
16: 5 one from the **h**—one who in judging
22:22 on his shoulder the key to the **h**;
Jer 21:12 O **h**, this is what the LORD says:
Zec 12: 7 so that the honour of the **h** and of
12: 8 and the **h** will be like God, like the
Zec 12:10 "And I will pour out on the **h** and
12:12 the clan of the **h** and their wives,
13: 1 **h** and the inhabitants of Jerusalem,

House of God

Ge 28:17 This is none other than the **h**;
Jdg 18:31 all the time the **h** was in Shiloh.
1Ch 6:48 duties of the tabernacle, the **h**.
9:11 the official in charge of the **h**;
9:13 for ministering in the **h**.
9:26 the rooms and treasuries in the **h**.
9:27 the night stationed round the **h**,
22: 2 dressed stone for building the **h**.
23:28 of other duties at the **h**.
25: 6 harps, for the ministry at the **h**.
26:20 charge of the treasuries of the **h**
Ezr 2:68 the rebuilding of the **h** on its site.
3: 8 their arrival at the **h** in Jerusalem,
3: 9 supervising those working on the **h**.
4:24 Thus the work on the **h** in Jerusalem
5: 2 work to rebuild the **h** in Jerusalem.
5:13 issued a decree to rebuild this **h**.
5:14 gold and silver articles of the **h**,
5:15 And rebuild the **h** on its site.'
5:16 foundations of the **h** in Jerusalem.
5:17 to rebuild this **h** in Jerusalem.
6: 5 gold and silver articles of the **h**,
6: 5 they are to be deposited in the **h**.
6: 7 elders rebuild this **h** on its site.
6: 8 Jews in the construction of this **h**:
6:16 the dedication of the **h** with joy.
6:17 For the dedication of this **h** they
6:22 work on the **h**, the God of Israel.
7:24 servants or other workers at this **h**.
8:36 to the people and to the **h**.
10: 1 throwing himself down before the **h**,
10: 6 Ezra withdrew from before the **h** and
10: 9 sitting in the square before the **h**,
Ne 6:10 He said, "Let us meet in the **h**,
8:16 in the courts of the **h** and in the
11:11 son of Ahitub, supervisor in the **h**,
11:16 charge of the outside work of the **h**;
11:22 for the service of the **h**.
12:40 then took their places in the **h**;
13: 7 Tobiah a room in the courts of the **h**.
13: 9 into them the equipment of the **h**,
13:11 "Why is the **h** neglected?" Then I
Ps 42: 4 leading the procession to the **h**,
52: 8 an olive tree flourishing in the **h**;
55:14 we walked with the throng at the **h**.
Ecc 5: 1 Guard your steps when you go to the **h**
Mt 12: 4 He entered the **h**, and he and his
Mk 2:26 he entered the **h** and ate the
Lk 6: 4 He entered the **h**, and taking the
Heb 10:21 we have a great priest over the **h**,

House of Israel

Ex 40:38 in the sight of all the **h** during
Lev 10: 6 But your relatives, all the **h**, may
Nu 20:29 **h** mourned for him thirty days.
Jos 21:45 good promises to the **h** failed;
Ru 4:11 Leah, who together built up the **h**.
1Sa 7: 3 Samuel said to the whole **h**, "If you
2Sa 1:12 for the army of the LORD and the **h**,
6: 5 David and the whole **h** were
6:15 while he and the entire **h** brought up
12: 8 I gave you the **h** and Judah. And if
16: 3 'Today the **h** will give me back my
1Ki 12:21 men—to make war against the **h**
20:31 the kings of the **h** are merciful.
Ps 98: 3 love and his faithfulness to the **h**;
115: 9 O **h**, trust in the LORD—he is their
115:12 He will bless the **h**,
135:19 O **h**, praise the LORD; O house of
Isa 5: 7 of the LORD Almighty is the **h**,
14: 2 And the **h** will possess the nations
46: 3 all you who remain of the **h**, you
63: 7 good things he has done for the **h**,
Jer 2: 4 of Jacob, all you clans of the **h**.
2:26 so the **h** is disgraced—they, their
3:18 the house of Judah will join the **h**,
3:20 have been unfaithful to me, O **h**,"
5:11 The **h** and the house of Judah have
5:15 O **h**," declares the LORD, "I am
Jer 9:26 whole **h** is uncircumcised in heart.
10: 1 Hear what the LORD says to you, O **h**.
11:10 Both the **h** and the house of Judah
11:17 because the **h** and the house of Judah
13:11 so I bound the whole **h** and the whole
18: 6 "O **h**, can I not do with you as this
18: 6 potter, so are you in my hand, O **h**.
31:27 "when I will plant the **h** and the
31:31 the **h** and with the house of Judah.
31:33 make with the **h** after that time,"
33:14 to the **h** and to the house of Judah.
33:17 a man to sit on the throne of the **h**,
48:13 as the **h** was ashamed when they
Eze 3: 1 then go and speak to the **h**."
3: 4 to the **h** and speak my words to them.
3: 5 difficult language, but to the **h**—
3: 7 the **h** is not willing to listen to
3: 7 whole **h** is hardened and obstinate.
3:17 I have made you a watchman for the **h**;
4: 3 This will be a sign to the **h**.
4: 4 put the sin of the **h** upon yourself.
4: 5 days you will bear the sin of the **h**.
5: 4 spread from there to the whole **h**.
6:11 and detestable practices of the **h**,
8: 6 things the **h** is doing here,
8:10 animals and all the idols of the **h**.
8:11 them stood seventy elders of the **h**,
8:12 of the **h** are doing in the darkness,
9: 9 He answered me, "The sin of the **h**
11: 5 O **h**, but I know what is going
11:15 the whole **h**—are those of whom the
12: 6 I have made you a sign to the **h**."
12: 9 did not that rebellious **h** ask you,
12:10 and the whole **h** who are there.'
12:27 "Son of man, the **h** is saying, 'The
13: 5 in the wall to repair it for the **h**
13: 9 be listed in the records of the **h**,
14: 6 "Therefore say to the **h**, 'This is
17: 2 allegory and tell the **h** a parable.
18: 6 or look to the idols of the **h**.
18:15 or look to the idols of the **h**.
18:25 Hear, O **h**: Is my way unjust? Is it
18:29 Yet the **h** says, 'The way of the Lord
18:29 Are my ways unjust, O **h**? Is it not
18:30 "Therefore, O **h**, I will judge you,
18:31 Why will you die, O **h**?
20:30 "Therefore say to the **h**: 'This is
20:31 Am I to let you enquire of me, O **h**?
20:39 "'As for you, O **h**, this is what the
20:40 there in the land the entire **h** will
20:44 O **h**, declares the Sovereign LORD
22:18 "Son of man, the **h** has become dross
24:21 Say to the **h**, 'This is what the
29: 6 have been a staff of reed for the **h**.
29:21 I will make a horn grow for the **h**,
33: 7 have made you a watchman for the **h**;
33:10 "Son of man, say to the **h**, 'This is
33:11 evil ways! Why will you die, O **h**?'
33:20 Yet, O **h**, you say, 'The way of the
34:30 am with them and that they, the **h**,
35:15 of the **h** became desolate,
36:10 people upon you, even the whole **h**.
36:21 which the **h** profaned among the
36:22 "Therefore say to the **h**, 'This is
36:22 O **h**, that I am going to do these
36:32 and disgraced for your conduct, O **h**!
36:37 plea of the **h** and do this for them:
37:11 of man, these bones are the whole **h**.
37:16 and all the **h** associated with him.'
39:12 "'For seven months the **h** will be
39:22 From that day forward the **h** will
39:29 the **h**, declares the Sovereign LORD."
40: 4 Tell the **h** everything you see."
43: 7 The **h** will never again defile my
44: 6 Say to the rebellious **h**, 'This is
44: 6 of your detestable practices, O **h**!
44:12 idols and made the **h** fall into sin,
45: 6 it will belong to the whole **h**.
45: 8 allow the **h** to possess the land
45:17 all the appointed feasts of the **h**.
45:17 to make atonement for the **h**.
Hos 1: 6 will no longer show love to the **h**,
6:10 have seen a horrible thing in the **h**
11:12 me with lies, the **h** with deceit.
Am 5: 1 Hear this word, O **h**, this lament I
5: 4 This is what the LORD says to the **h**:

Am 5:25 for forty years in the desert, O **h**?
6:14 O **h**, that will oppress you all the
9: 9 and I will shake the **h** among all the
Mic 1: 5 because of the sins of the **h**.
3: 1 of Jacob, you rulers of the **h**.
3: 9 you rulers of the **h**, who despise
Ac 7:42 for forty years in the desert, O **h**?
Heb 8: 8 will make a new covenant with the **h**
8:10 the covenant I will make with the **h**

House of Judah

2Sa 2: 4 they anointed David king over the **h**.
2: 7 **h** has anointed me king over them."
2:10 The **h**, however, followed David.
2:11 David was king in Hebron over the **h**
1Ki 12:21 he mustered the whole **h** and the
12:23 to the whole **h** and Benjamin, and to
2Ki 19:30 Once more a remnant of the **h** will
1Ch 28: 4 and from the **h** he chose my family,
2Ch 11: 1 he mustered the **h** and Benjamin—
22:10 the whole royal family of the **h**.
Isa 22:21 who live in Jerusalem and to the **h**.
37:31 Once more a remnant of the **h** will
Jer 3:18 In those days the **h** will join the
5:11 The house of Israel and the **h** have
11:10 Both the house of Israel and the **h**
11:17 the **h** have done evil and provoked me
12:14 I will uproot the **h** from among them.
13:11 use of Israel and the whole **h** to me,
21:11 "Moreover, say to the royal **h**, 'Hear
31:27 the **h** with the offspring of men and
31:31 the house of Israel and with the **h**.
33:14 to the house of Israel and to the **h**.
Eze 4: 6 side, and bear the sin of the **h**.
8:17 Is it a trivial matter for the **h** to
25: 8 "Look, the **h** has become like all the
25:12 Edom took revenge on the **h** and
Hos 1: 7 Yet I will show love to the **h**; and I
Zep 2: 7 will belong to the remnant of the **h**;
Zec 10: 3 will care for his flock, the **h**,
10: 6 "I will strengthen the **h** and save
12: 4 will keep a watchful eye over the **h**,
Heb 8: 8 the house of Israel and with the **h**.

House of the Lord

Ex 23:19 of your soil to the **h** your God.
34:26 of your soil to the **h** your God.
Dt 23:18 into the **h** your God to pay any vow,
Jdg 19:18 Judah and now I am going to the **h**.
1Sa 1: 7 Whenever Hannah went up to the **h**,
1:24 and brought him to the **h** at Shiloh.
3:15 and then opened the doors of the **h**.
2Sa 12:20 he went into the **h** and worshipped.
1Ch 6:31 put in charge of the music in the **h**
9:23 of the **h**—the house called the Tent.
22: 1 David said, "The **h** God is to be here,
22:11 may you have success and build the **h**
Ezr 1: 5 go up and build the **h** in Jerusalem.
2:68 they arrived at the **h** in Jerusalem,
3: 8 to supervise the building of the **h**.
3:11 the foundation of the **h** was laid.
7:27 to the **h** in Jerusalem in this
8:29 in the chambers of the **h** in
Ne 10:35 bringing to the **h** each year the
Ps 23: 6 and I will dwell in the **h** for ever.
27: 4 in the **h** all the days of my life,
92:13 planted in the **h**, they will flourish
116:19 in the courts of the **h**—in your
118:26 From the **h** we bless you.
122: 1 who said to me, "Let us go to the **h**.
122: 9 For the sake of the **h** our God, I
134: 1 LORD who minister by night in the **h**.
135: 2 you who minister in the **h**, in the
Jer 17:26 and thank-offerings to the **h**.
26: 2 Judah who come to worship in the **h**.
26: 7 Jeremiah speak these words in the **h**.
26: 9 crowded around Jeremiah in the **h**.
26:10 up from the royal palace to the **h**
27:18 the furnishings remaining in the **h**
27:21 the things that are left in the **h**
28: 1 said to me in the **h** in the presence
28: 5 people who were standing in the **h**.
29:26 Jehoiada to be in charge of the **h**;
33:11 who bring thank-offerings to the **h**,
35: 2 to one of the side rooms of the **h**
Jer 35: 4 I brought them into the **h**, into the
36: 6 you go to the **h** on a day of fasting
41: 5 and incense with them to the **h**.
Lam 2: 7 they have raised a shout in the **h**
Eze 8:14 entrance to the north gate of the **h**
8:16 me into the inner court of the **h**,
11: 1 the gate of the **h** that faces east.
Hos 8: 1 An eagle is over the **h** because the
Joel 1: 9 offerings are cut off from the **h**.
1:14 to the **h** your God, and cry out
Hag 1:14 work on the **h** Almighty, their God,
Zec 7: 3 by asking the priests of the **h**
8: 9 was laid for the **h** Almighty,
11:13 threw them into the **h** to the potter.
14:21 be a Canaanite in the **h** Almighty.

Household (House)

Ge 12: 1 **h** and go to the land I will show you.
12:17 diseases on Pharoah and his **h**
14:14 the 318 trained men born in his **h**
15: 3 a servant in my **h** will be my heir."
17:12 including those born in your **h** or
17:13 Whether born in your **h** or bought
17:23 in his **h** or bought with his money,
17:23 every male in his **h**, and circumcised
17:27 every male in Abraham's **h**, including
17:27 including those born in his **h** or
18:19 his **h** after him to keep the way of
20:13 me to wander from my father's **h**,
20:18 **h** because of Abraham's wife Sarah.
24: 2 said to the chief servant in his **h**
24: 7 who brought me out of my father's **h**
24:28 girl ran and told her mother's **h**
30:30 may I do something for my own **h**?"
31:19 Rachel stole her father's **h** gods.
31:34 Now Rachel had taken the **h** gods and
31:35 but could not find the **h** gods.
31:37 you found that belongs to your **h**?
31:41 the twenty years I was in your **h**.
34:19 most honoured of all his father's **h**,
34:30 I and my **h** will be destroyed."
35: 2 Jacob said to his **h** and to all who
36: 6 and all the members of his **h**,
39: 4 Potiphar put him in charge of his **h**,
39: 5 in charge of his **h** and of all
39: 5 blessed the **h** of the Egyptian
39:11 none of the **h** servants was inside.
39:14 she called her **h** servants. "Look,"
41:51 my trouble and all my father's **h**."
45: 2 and Pharaoh's **h** heard about it.
45: 8 his entire **h** and ruler of all Egypt.
45:11 Otherwise you and your **h** and all who
46:31 his brothers and to his father's **h**,
46:31 'My brothers and my father's **h**, who
47:12 and all his father's **h** with food,
50: 8 besides all the members of Joseph's **h**
50: 8 those belonging to his father's **h**.
Ex 12: 3 lamb for his family, one for each **h**.
12: 4 If any **h** is too small for a whole
12:48 all the males in his **h** circumcised;
23:12 rest and the slave born in your **h**,
Lev 16: 6 atonement for himself and his **h**.
16:11 atonement for himself and his **h**,
16:17 made atonement for himself, his **h**
22:11 or if a slave is born in his **h**,
Nu 18:11 Everyone in your **h** who is
18:13 Everyone in your **h** who is
Dt 6:22 Egypt and Pharaoh and his whole **h**.
14:26 Then you and your **h** shall eat there
26:11 God has given to you and your **h**.
Jos 24:15 and my **h**, we will serve the LORD."
Jdg 14:15 you and your father's **h** to death.
18:14 other **h** gods, a carved image and a
18:17 the ephod, the other **h** gods and the
18:18 the ephod, the other **h** gods and the
18:19 rather than just one man's **h**?"
18:20 He took the ephod, the other **h** gods
1Sa 22: 1 When his brothers and his father's **h**
22:14 and highly respected in your **h**?
25: 6 Good health to you and your **h**!
25:17 over our master and his whole **h**.
2Sa 6:11 LORD blessed him and his entire **h**.
6:12 "The LORD has blessed the **h** of
6:20 David returned home to bless his **h**,
9: 2 Now there was a servant of Saul's **h**
2Sa 9:12 all the members of Ziba's **h** were
12:11 'Out of your own **h** I am going to
12:17 The elders of his **h** stood beside him
15:16 The king set out, with his entire **h**
16: 2 "The donkeys are for the king's **h**
16: 8 the blood you shed in the **h** of Saul,
19:17 the steward of Saul's **h**, and his
19:18 to take the king's **h** over and to
19:41 him and his **h** across the Jordan,
1Ki 4: 7 for the king and the royal **h**.
5: 9 by providing food for my royal **h**."
5:11 cors of wheat as food for his **h**,
10:21 and all the **h** articles in the Palace
2Ki 23:24 the **h** gods, the idols and all the
1Ch 13:14 blessed his **h** and everything he had.
2Ch 9:20 and all the **h** articles in the Palace
Ne 13: 8 Tobiah's **h** goods out of the room.
Est 1:22 man should be ruler over his own **h**.
Job 1:10 him and his **h** and everything he has?
16: 7 you have devastated my entire **h**.
31:31 if the men of my **h** have never said,
Ps 105:21 He made him master of his **h**, ruler
Pr 31:21 snows, she has no fear for her **h**;
31:27 watches over the affairs of her **h**
Jer 23:34 I will punish that man and his **h**.
Eze 44:30 that a blessing may rest on your **h**.
Mic 7: 6 are the members of his own **h**.
Mt 10:25 how much more the members of his **h**!
10:36 will be the members of his own **h**'
12:25 and every city or **h** divided against
24:45 in charge of the servants in his **h**
Lk 8: 3 the manager of Herod's **h**; Susanna
Jn 4:53 So he and all his **h** believed.
Ac 11:14 you and all your **h** will be saved.'
16:15 she and the members of her **h** were
16:31 you will be saved—you and your **h**.
18: 8 and his entire **h** believed in the
Ro 16:10 who belong to the **h** of Aristobulus.
16:11 Greet those in the **h** of Narcissus
1Co 1:11 My brothers, some from Chloe's **h**
1:16 baptised the **h** of Stephanas
16:15 You know that the **h** of Stephanas
Eph 2:19 God's people and members of God's **h**
Php 4:22 those who belong to Caesar's **h**.
1Ti 3:12 manage his children and his **h** well.
3:15 to conduct themselves in God's **h**,
2Ti 1:16 show mercy to the **h** of Onesiphorus
4:19 Aquila and the **h** of Onesiphorus

Households (House)

Ge 42:19 take grain back for your starving **h**.
42:33 food for your starving **h** and go.
47:24 and your **h** and your children."
Nu 16:32 with their **h** and all Korah's men and
18:31 You and your **h** may eat the rest of
Dt 11: 6 and swallowed them up with their **h**,
Tit 1:11 because they are ruining whole **h** by

Houses (House)

Ge 34:29 as plunder everything in the **h**.
Ex 8: 3 into the **h** of your officials and on
8: 9 and your **h** may be rid of the frogs,
8:11 The frogs will leave you and your **h**,
8:13 The frogs died in the **h**, in the
8:21 on your people and into your **h**.
8:21 The **h** of the Egyptians will be full
8:24 and into the **h** of his officials,
10: 6 They will fill your **h** and those of
12: 7 of the **h** where they eat the lambs.
12:13 sign for you on the **h** where you are;
12:15 day remove the yeast from your **h**,
12:19 no yeast is to be found in your **h**.
12:23 to enter your **h** and strike you down.
12:27 who passed over the **h** of the
Lev 25:31 **h** in villages without walls round
25:32 their **h** in the Levitical towns,
25:33 because the **h** in the towns of the
Dt 6: 9 of your **h** and on your gates.
6:11 **h** filled with all kinds of good
8:12 you build fine **h** and settle down,
11:20 of your **h** and on your gates,
19: 1 and settled in their towns and **h**,
Jdg 18:14 "Do you know that one of these **h** has
1Ki 20: 6 palace and the **h** of your officials.
2Ki 25: 9 palace and all the **h** of Jerusalem.

Ne 5:11 vineyards, olive groves and **h**, and
7: 3 posts and some near their own **h**."
7: 4 and the **h** had not yet been rebuilt.
9:25 they took possession of **h** filled
Job 3:15 who filled their **h** with silver.
4:19 those who live in **h** of clay,
15:28 he will inhabit ruined towns and **h**
15:28 no-one lives, **h** crumbling to rubble.
20:19 he has seized **h** he did not build.
22:18 Yet it was he who filled their **h**
24:16 In the dark, men break into **h**, but
Ps 49:11 tombs will remain their **h** for ever,
Pr 1:13 things and fill our **h** with plunder;
19:14 **H** and wealth are inherited from
Ecc 2: 4 great projects: I built **h** for myself
Isa 3:14 plunder from the poor is in your **h**.
5: 9 great **h** will become desolate,
6:11 until the **h** are left deserted and
8:14 but for both **h** of Israel he will be
13:16 their **h** will be looted and their
13:21 jackals will fill her **h**; there the
22:10 tore down **h** to strengthen the wall.
32:13 mourn for all **h** of merriment and for
65:21 They will build **h** and dwell in them;
65:22 No longer will they build **h** and
Jer 5: 7 thronged to the **h** of prostitutes.
5:27 their **h** are full of deceit;
6:12 **h** will be turned over to others
9:19 our land because our **h** are in ruins.
17:22 Do not bring a load out of your **h**
18:22 Let a cry be heard from their **h** when
19:13 The **h** in Jerusalem and those of the
19:13 all the **h** where they burned incense
29: 5 "Build **h** and settle down; plant
29:28 Therefore build **h** and settle down;
32:15 the God of Israel, says: **H**, fields
32:29 along with the **h** where the people
33: 4 about the **h** in this city and the
35: 7 Also you must never build **h**, sow
35: 9 or built **h** to live in or had
39: 8 the **h** of the people and broke down
52:13 palace and all the **h** of Jerusalem.
Eze 7:24 to take possession of their **h**;
11: 3 Will it not soon be time to build **h**?
16:41 They will burn down your **h** and
23:47 daughters and burn down their **h**.
26:12 demolish your fine **h** and throw your
28:26 will build **h** and plant vineyards;
33:30 the walls and at the doors of the **h**,
45: 4 It will be a place for their **h** as
48:15 city, for **h** and for pasture-land.
Da 2: 5 your **h** turned into piles of rubble.
3:29 **h** be turned into piles of rubble,
Hos 7: 1 thieves break into **h**, bandits rob
Joel 2: 9 They climb into the **h**; like thieves
Am 3:15 the **h** adorned with ivory will be
Mic 2: 2 seize them, and **h**, and take them.
Zep 1:13 be plundered, their **h** demolished.
1:13 They will build **h** but not live in
2: 7 will lie down in the **h** of Ashkelon.
Hag 1: 4 to be living in your panelled **h**,
Zec 14: 2 **h** ransacked, and the women raped.
Mt 19:29 everyone who has left **h** or brothers
Mk 12:40 devour widows' **h** and for a show
Lk 16: 4 will welcome me into their **h**'
20:47 devour widows' **h** and for a show
Ac 4:34 who owned lands or **h** sold them,
7:48 does not live in **h** made by men.

Hovering (Hovers)

Ge 1: 2 Spirit of God was **h** over the waters.
Isa 31: 5 Like birds **h** overhead, the LORD

Hovers (Hovering)

Dt 32:11 up its nest and **h** over its young,

Howl (Howling)

Ps 59:15 They wander about for food and **h**
Isa 13:22 Hyenas will **h** in her strongholds,
14:31 Wail, O gate! **H**, O city! Melt away,
Mic 1: 8 **h** like a jackal and moan like an owl

Howling (Howl)

Dt 32:10 found him, in a barren and **h** waste.

Hubbah

1Ch 7:34 The sons of Shomer: Ahi, Rohgah, **H**

Hubs

1Ki 7:33 spokes and **h** were all of cast metal.

Huddled

Job 30: 7 They brayed among the bushes and **h**

Hug

Job 24: 8 and **h** the rocks for lack of shelter.

Huge

Ge 41:49 Joseph stored up **h** quantities of
Jos 11: 4 of horses and chariots—a **h** army,
2Sa 21:20 there was a **h** man with six fingers
23:21 he struck down a **h** Egyptian.
1Ch 20: 6 there was a **h** man with six fingers
2Ch 16:14 they made a **h** fire in his honour.
Ecc 9:14 and built **h** siegeworks against it.
Da 2:35 the statue became a **h** mountain
11:13 with a **h** army fully equipped.
Mt 12:40 nights in the belly of a **h** fish,
Rev 8: 8 and something like a **h** mountain,
16:21 From the sky **h** hailstones of about

Hukkok

Jos 19:34 Aznoth Tabor and came out at **H**.

Hukok

1Ch 6:75 **H** and Rehob, together with their

Hul

Ge 10:23 The sons of Aram: Uz, **H**, Gether and
1Ch 1:17 of Aram: Uz, **H**, Gether and Meshech.

Huldah

2Ki 22:14 went to speak to the prophetess **H**,
2Ch 34:22 went to speak to the prophetess **H**,

Human (Humanity)

Lev 5: 3 if he touches **h** uncleanness
7:21 whether **h** uncleanness or an unclean
24:17 "'If anyone takes the life of a **h**
Nu 19:16 or anyone who touches a **h** bone or a
19:18 anyone who has touched a **h** bone
1Ki 13: 2 and **h** bones will be burned on you.
2Ki 23:14 and covered the sites with **h** bones.
23:20 altars and burned **h** bones on them.
Job 34:20 mighty are removed without **h** hand.
Ps 73: 5 they are not plagued by **h** ills.
Isa 37:19 and stone, fashioned by **h** hands.
52:14 his form marred beyond **h** likeness—
Eze 4:12 people, using **h** excrement for fuel."
4:15 cow manure instead of **h** excrement."
39:15 land and one of them sees a **h** bone,
Da 2:34 was cut out, but not by **h** hands.
2:45 but not by **h** hands—a rock that
5: 5 Suddenly the fingers of a **h** hand
8:25 be destroyed, but not by **h** power.
Hos 11: 4 I led them with cords of **h** kindness,
13: 2 **h** sacrifice and kiss the calf-idols."
Jn 1:13 nor of **h** decision or a husband's
5:34 Not that I accept **h** testimony;
8:15 You judge by **h** standards; I pass
Ac 5:38 is of **h** origin, it will fail.
14:11 have come down to us in **h** form!"
14:15 We too are only men, **h** like you.
17:25 he is not served by **h** hands,
Ro 1: 3 his Son, who as to his **h** nature
2: 9 for every **h** being who does evil:
3: 5 on us? (I am using a **h** argument.)
6:19 I put this in **h** terms because you
9: 5 from them is traced the **h** ancestry
1Co 1:17 gospel—not with words of **h** wisdom,
1:26 Not many of you were wise by **h**
2:13 not in words taught us by **h** wisdom
4: 3 by you or by any **h** court; indeed,
9: 8 Do I say this merely from a **h** point
15:32 in Ephesus for merely **h** reasons,
2Co 3: 3 of stone but on tablets of **h** hearts.
5: 1 in heaven, not built by **h** hands.
Gal 3: 3 to attain your goal by **h** effort?
Gal 3:15 set aside or add to a **h** covenant
Php 2: 7 a servant, being made in **h** likeness.
Col 2: 8 which depends on **h** tradition and the
2:22 based on **h** commands and teachings.
Heb 12: 9 Moreover, we have all had **h** fathers
1Pe 4: 2 his earthly life for evil **h** desires,
2Pe 2:18 lustful desires of sinful **h** nature,
Rev 9: 7 and their faces resembled **h** faces.

Humanity (Human)

Heb 2:14 he too shared in their **h** so that by

Humble (Humbled, Humbles, Humbly, Humiliate, Humiliated, Humiliation, Humility)

Ex 10: 3 will you refuse to **h** yourself
Nu 12: 3 Moses was a very **h** man, more **h**
Dt 8: 2 to **h** you and to test you in order to
8:16 to **h** and to test you so that in the
2Sa 22:28 You save the **h**, but your eyes are on
1Ki 11:39 I will **h** David's descendants because
2Ch 7:14 will **h** themselves and pray
33:23 he did not **h** himself before the LORD;
36:12 did not **h** himself before Jeremiah
Ezr 8:21 so that we might **h** ourselves before
Job 8: 7 Your beginnings will seem **h**, so
40:12 look at every proud man and **h** him,
Ps 18:27 You save the **h** but bring low those
25: 9 He guides the **h** in what is right and
147: 6 The LORD sustains the **h** but casts
149: 4 he crowns the **h** with salvation.
Pr 3:34 mockers but gives grace to the **h**.
6: 3 Go and **h** yourself; press your plea
Isa 13:11 will **h** the pride of the ruthless.
23: 9 **h** all who are renowned on the earth.
29:19 Once more the **h** will rejoice in the
58: 5 only a day for a man to **h** himself?
66: 2 he who is **h** and contrite in spirit,
Da 4:37 who walk in pride he is able to **h**.
5:19 those he wanted to **h**, he humbled.
10:12 and to **h** yourself before your God,
Zep 2: 3 Seek the LORD, all you **h** of the land,
3:12 leave within you the meek and **h**,
Mt 11:29 for I am gentle and **h** in heart, and
Lk 1:48 for he has been mindful of the **h**
1:52 thrones but has lifted up the **h**.
2Co 12:21 again my God will **h** me before you,
Eph 4: 2 Be completely **h** and gentle; be
Jas 1: 9 The brother in **h** circumstances ought
4: 6 the proud but gives grace to the **h**."
4:10 **H** yourselves before the Lord, and he
1Pe 3: 8 as brothers, be compassionate and **h**.
5: 5 the proud but gives grace to the **h**."
5: 6 **H** yourselves, therefore, under God's

Humbled (Humble)

Lev 26:41 their uncircumcised hearts are **h**
Dt 8: 3 He **h** you, causing you to hunger and
1Ki 21:29 noticed how Ahab has **h** himself
21:29 before me? Because he has **h** himself,
2Ki 22:19 your heart was responsive and you **h**
2Ch 12: 6 The leaders of Israel and the king **h**
12: 7 the LORD saw that they **h** themselves,
12: 7 "Since they have **h** themselves, I
12:12 Rehoboam **h** himself, the LORD's anger
28:19 The LORD had **h** Judah because of Ahaz
30:11 **h** themselves and went to Jerusalem.
33:12 **h** himself greatly before the God of
33:19 idols before he **h** himself—all are
34:27 your heart was responsive and you **h**
34:27 and because you **h** yourself before me
Ps 35:13 sackcloth and **h** myself with fasting.
44: 9 now you have rejected and **h** us; you
68:30 **H**, may it bring bars of silver.
107:39 **h** by oppression, calamity and sorrow;
Isa 2: 9 man will be brought low and mankind **h**
2:11 eyes of the arrogant man will be **h**
2:12 is exalted (and they will be **h**),
2:17 brought low and the pride of men **h**;
5:15 **h**, the eyes of the arrogant **h**.
9: 1 In the past he **h** the land of Zebulun
58: 3 seen it? Why have we **h** ourselves,
Jer 44:10 they have not **h** themselves
Da 5:19 and those he wanted to humble, he **h**.
5:22 have not **h** yourself, though you knew

Mt 23:12 For whoever exalts himself will be **h**,
Lk 14:11 who exalts himself will be **h**,
18:14 who exalts himself will be **h**,
Php 2: 8 he **h** himself and became obedient to

Humbles (Humble)
1Sa 2: 7 and wealth; he **h** and he exalts.
Isa 26: 5 He **h** those who dwell on high, he
Mt 18: 4 Therefore, whoever **h** himself like
23:12 whoever **h** himself will be exalted.
Lk 14:11 he who **h** himself will be exalted."
18:14 he who **h** himself will be exalted."

Humbly (Humble)
2Sa 16: 4 "I **h** bow," Ziba said. "May I find
Isa 38:15 I will walk **h** all my years because
Mic 6: 8 mercy and to walk **h** with your God.
Jas 1:21 and **h** accept the word planted in you,

Humiliate (Humble)
Pr 25: 7 for him to **h** you before a nobleman.
1Co 11:22 of God and **h** those who have nothing?

Humiliated (Humble)
2Sa 6:22 and I will be **h** in my own eyes.
10: 5 the men, for they were greatly **h**.
19: 5 "Today you have **h** all your men, who
1Ch 19: 5 meet them, for they were greatly **h**.
Isa 54: 4 fear disgrace; you will not be **h**.
Jer 15: 9 day; she will be disgraced and **h**.
31:19 I was ashamed and **h** because I bore
Mal 2: 9 and **h** before all the people,
Lk 13:17 all his opponents were **h**, but the
14: 9 Then, **h**, you will have to take the

Humiliation (Humble)
Ezr 9: 7 to pillage and **h** at the hand of
Job 19: 5 above me and use my **h** against me,
Eze 16:63 open your mouth because of your **h**,
Ac 8:33 In his **h** he was deprived of justice.

Humility (Humble)
Ps 45: 4 on behalf of truth, **h** and
Pr 11: 2 disgrace, but with **h** comes wisdom.
15:33 wisdom, and **h** comes before honour.
18:12 is proud, but **h** comes before honour.
22: 4 **H** and the fear of the LORD bring
Zep 2: 3 Seek righteousness, seek **h**;
Ac 20:19 I served the Lord with great **h** and
Php 2: 3 but in **h** consider others better than
Col 2:18 let anyone who delights in false **h**
2:23 their false **h** and their harsh
3:12 **h**, gentleness and patience.
Tit 3: 2 and to show true **h** towards all men.
Jas 3:13 in the **h** that comes from wisdom.
1Pe 5: 5 All of you, clothe yourselves with **h**

Humps
Isa 30: 6 their treasures on the **h** of camels,

Humtah
Jos 15:54 **H**, Kiriath Arba (that is, Hebron)

Hunchbacked
Lev 21:20 or who is **h** or dwarfed, or who has

Hundred (Hundredfold, Hundreds, Hundredth)
Ge 6: 3 days will be a **h** and twenty years."
7: 6 Noah was six **h** years old when the
7:24 the earth for a **h** and fifty days
8: 3 At the end of the **h** and fifty days
8:13 of Noah's six **h** and first year,
15:13 and ill-treated four **h** years.
17:17 son be born to a man a **h** years old
21: 5 Abraham was a **h** years old when his
23: 1 Sarah lived to be a **h** and
23:15 the land is worth four **h** shekels
23:16 Hittites: four **h** shekels of silver,
25: 7 Abraham lived a **h** and seventy-five
25:17 Ishmael lived a **h** and thirty-seven
32: 6 you, and four **h** men are with him."
32:14 two **h** female goats and twenty male
Ge 32:14 goats, two **h** ewes and twenty rams,
33: 1 coming with his four **h** men; so he
33:19 For a **h** pieces of silver, he bought
35:28 Isaac lived a **h** and eighty years.
45:22 Benjamin he gave three **h** shekels
47: 9 of my pilgrimage are a **h** and thirty.
47:28 his life were a **h** and forty-seven.
50:22 He lived a **h** and ten years
50:26 Joseph died at the age of a **h** and
Ex 12:37 There were about six **h** thousand men
14: 7 He took six **h** of the best chariots,
27: 9 The south side shall be a **h** cubits
27:11 north side shall also be a **h** cubits
27:18 The courtyard shall be a **h** cubits
38: 9 The south side was a **h** cubits long
38:11 The north side was also a **h** cubits
Lev 26: 8 Five of you will chase a **h**, and a **h**
Nu 7:13 weighing a **h** and thirty shekels,
7:19 weighing a **h** and thirty shekels,
7:25 weighing a **h** and thirty shekels,
7:31 weighing a **h** and thirty shekels,
7:37 weighing a **h** and thirty shekels,
7:43 weighing a **h** and thirty shekels,
7:49 weighing a **h** and thirty shekels,
7:55 weighing a **h** and thirty shekels,
7:61 weighing a **h** and thirty shekels,
7:67 weighing a **h** and thirty shekels,
7:73 weighing a **h** and thirty shekels,
7:79 weighing a **h** and thirty shekels,
7:85 silver plate weighed a **h** and thirty
7:85 weighed two thousand four **h** shekels,
7:86 weighed a **h** and twenty shekels.
11:21 I am among six **h** thousand men
31:28 the LORD one out of every five **h**,
33:39 Aaron was a **h** and twenty-three years
35: 4 fifteen **h** feet from the town wall.
Dt 22:19 They shall fine him a **h** shekels of
31: 2 "I am now a **h** and twenty years old
34: 7 Moses was a **h** and twenty years old
Jos 7:21 two **h** shekels of silver and a wedge
24:29 LORD, died at the age of a **h** and ten.
24:32 bought for a **h** pieces of silver
Jdg 2: 8 LORD, died at the age of a **h** and ten.
3:31 six **h** Philistines with an ox-goad.
4: 3 he had nine **h** iron chariots and had
4:13 Sisera gathered together his nine **h**
7: 6 Three **h** men lapped with their hands
7: 7 "With the three **h** men that lapped I
7: 8 to their tents but kept the three **h**,
7:16 Dividing the three **h** men into three
7:19 Gideon and the **h** men with him
7:22 the three **h** trumpets sounded, the
8: 4 Gideon and his three **h** men,
8:10 a **h** and twenty thousand swordsmen
8:26 for came to seventeen **h** shekels,
11:26 For three **h** years Israel occupied
15: 4 he went out and caught three **h** foxes
16: 5 you eleven **h** shekels of silver."
17: 2 "The eleven **h** shekels of silver
17: 3 he returned the eleven **h** shekels of
17: 4 and she took two **h** shekels of silver
18:11 six **h** men from the clan of the
18:16 The six **h** Danites, armed for battle,
18:17 the six **h** armed men stood at the
20: 2 four **h** thousand soldiers armed with
20:10 We'll take ten men out of every **h**
20:10 and a **h** from a thousand, and a
20:15 in addition to seven **h** chosen men
20:16 seven **h** chosen men who were
20:17 mustered four **h** thousand swordsmen,
20:47 six **h** men turned and fled into the
21:12 four **h** young women who had never
1Sa 11: 8 of Israel numbered three **h** thousand
13:15 They numbered about six **h**.
14: 2 With him were about six **h** men,
15: 4 two **h** thousand foot soldiers
17: 7 iron point weighed six **h** shekels.
18:25 bride than a **h** Philistine foreskins,
18:27 out and killed two **h** Philistines.
22: 2 About four **h** men were with him.
23:13 David and his men, about six **h** in
25:13 About four **h** men went up with David,
25:13 two **h** stayed with the supplies.
25:18 She took two **h** loaves of bread
25:18 a **h** cakes of raisins and two **h** cakes
27: 2 David and the six **h** men with him
1Sa 30: 9 David and the six **h** men with him
30:10 for two **h** men were too exhausted to
30:10 four **h** men continued the pursuit.
30:17 except four **h** young men who rode off
30:21 David came to the two **h** men who had
2Sa 3:14 price of a **h** Philistine foreskins."
8: 4 all but a **h** of the chariot horses.
10:18 and David killed seven **h** of their
14:26 two **h** shekels by the royal standard.
15:11 Two **h** men from Jerusalem had
15:18 and all the six **h** Gittites who had
16: 1 loaded with two **h** loaves of bread,
16: 1 a **h** cakes of raisins, a **h** cakes of
21:16 spearhead weighed three **h** shekels
23: 8 his spear against eight **h** men,
23:18 He raised his spear against three **h**
24: 3 multiply the troops a **h** times over,
24: 9 there were eight **h** thousand
24: 9 sword, and in Judah five **h** thousand.
1Ki 4:23 cattle and a **h** sheep and goats,
5:16 well as thirty-three **h** foremen who
6: 1 In the four **h** and eightieth year
7: 2 Forest of Lebanon a **h** cubits long,
7:20 two **h** pomegranates in rows all
7:42 the four **h** pomegranates for the two
8:63 a **h** and twenty thousand sheep
10:16 King Solomon made two **h** large
10:16 six **h** bekas of gold went into each
10:17 He also made three **h** small shields
10:26 he had fourteen **h** chariots and
10:29 Egypt for six **h** shekels of silver,
10:29 and a horse for a **h** and fifty.
11: 3 He had seven **h** wives of royal birth
11: 3 royal birth and three **h** concubines,
12:21 a **h** and eighty thousand fighting
18: 4 Obadiah had taken a **h** prophets and
18:13 I hid a **h** of the LORD's prophets in
18:19 And bring the four **h** and fifty
18:19 and the four **h** prophets of Asherah,
18:22 Baal has four **h** and fifty prophets.
20:29 inflicted a **h** thousand casualties
22: 6 four **h** men—and asked them,
2Ki 3: 4 of Israel with a **h** thousand lambs
3: 4 with the wool of a **h** thousand rams.
3:26 he took with him seven **h** swordsmen
4:43 "How can I set this before a **h** men?"
11: 4 for the commanders of units of a **h**,
11: 9 The commanders of units of a **h** did
11:15 the commanders of units of a **h**,
14:13 section about six **h** feet long.
18:14 of Judah three **h** talents of silver
19:35 a **h** and eighty-five thousand
23:33 on Judah a levy of a **h** talents of
1Ch 4:42 five **h** of these Simeonites, led by
5:21 two **h** and fifty thousand sheep and
5:21 took one **h** thousand people captive,
11:11 his spear against three **h** men,
11:20 He raised his spear against three **h**
12:14 the least was a match for a **h**
18: 4 all but a **h** of the chariot horses.
21: 3 multiply his troops a **h** times over.
21: 5 one million one **h** thousand men who
21: 5 four **h** and seventy thousand in
21:25 David paid Araunah six **h** shekels of
22:14 LORD a **h** thousand talents of gold,
26:30 relatives—seventeen **h** able men—
26:32 Jeriah had two thousand seven **h**
29: 7 and a **h** thousand talents of iron.
2Ch 1:14 he had fourteen **h** chariots and
1:17 Egypt for six **h** shekels of silver,
1:17 and a horse for a **h** and fifty.
2: 2 thirty-six **h** as foremen over them.
3: 8 with six **h** talents of fine gold.
3:16 He also made a **h** pomegranates and
4: 8 also made a **h** gold sprinkling bowls.
4:13 the four **h** pomegranates for the two
7: 5 a **h** and twenty thousand sheep and
8:10 two **h** and fifty officials
8:18 four **h** and fifty talents of gold,
9:15 King Solomon made two **h** large
9:15 six **h** bekas of hammered gold went
9:16 He also made three **h** small shields
9:16 three **h** bekas of gold in each
11: 1 Benjamin—a **h** and eighty thousand
12: 3 With twelve **h** chariots and sixty
13: 3 four **h** thousand able fighting men,

2Ch 13: 3 with eight **h** thousand able troops.
13:17 so that there were five **h** thousand
14: 8 Asa had an army of three **h** thousand
14: 8 and two **h** and eighty thousand from
14: 9 a vast army and three **h** chariots,
15:11 to the LORD seven **h** head of cattle
17:11 seven thousand seven **h** rams and
17:11 and seven thousand seven **h** goats.
18: 5 the prophets—four **h** men—and
23: 1 the commanders of units of a **h**
23: 9 of units of a **h** the spears
23:14 out the commanders of units of a **h**,
24:15 died at the age of a **h** and thirty.
25: 5 were three **h** thousand men
25: 6 hired a **h** thousand fighting men
25: 6 Israel for a **h** talents of silver.
25: 9 what about the **h** talents I paid
25:23 section about six **h** feet long.
27: 5 Ammonites paid him a **h** talents of
28: 6 killed a **h** and twenty thousand
28: 8 two **h** thousand wives, sons and
29:32 a **h** rams and two **h** male lambs—all
29:33 sacrifices amounted to six **h** bulls
35: 8 gave the priests two thousand six **h**
35: 8 offerings and three **h** cattle.
35: 9 five **h** head of cattle for the
36: 3 on Judah a levy of a **h** talents
Ezr 6:17 house of God they offered a **h** bulls,
6:17 two **h** rams, four **h** male lambs and,
7:22 up to a **h** talents of silver, a **h**
7:22 a **h** cors of wheat, a **h** baths of wine,
Ne 3: 1 as far as the Tower of the **H**,
3:13 They also repaired five **h** yards of
5:17 Furthermore, a **h** and fifty Jews and
12:39 the Tower of the **H**, as far as the
Est 9: 6 Jews killed and destroyed five **h** men.
9:12 destroyed five **h** men and the ten
9:15 put to death in Susa three **h** men,
Job 1: 3 five **h** yoke of oxen and five **h**
42:16 After this, Job lived a **h** and forty
Pr 17:10 more than a **h** lashes a fool.
Ecc 6: 3 A man may have a **h** children and live
8:12 a wicked man commits a **h** crimes
SS 8:12 two **h** are for those who tend its
Isa 37:36 a **h** and eighty-five thousand
65:20 he who dies at a **h** will be thought
65:20 a **h** will be considered accursed.
Jer 52:23 the surrounding network was a **h**.
Eze 40:19 it was a **h** cubits on the east side
40:23 the opposite one; it was a **h** cubits.
40:27 the south side; it was a **h** cubits.
40:47 **h** cubits long and a **h** cubits wide.
41:13 the temple; it was a **h** cubits long
41:13 its walls were also a **h** cubits long.
41:14 front of the temple, was a **h** cubits.
41:15 on each side; it was a **h** cubits.
42: 2 **h** cubits long and fifty cubits wide.
42: 4 ten cubits wide and a **h** cubits long.
42: 8 the sanctuary was a **h** cubits long.
42:16 measuring rod; it was five **h** cubits.
42:17 five **h** cubits by the measuring rod.
42:18 five **h** cubits by the measuring rod.
42:19 five **h** cubits by the measuring rod.
42:20 five **h** cubits long and five **h** cubits
45:15 taken from every flock of two **h**
Am 5: 3 for Israel will have only a **h** left;
5: 3 a **h** strong will have only ten left."
Jnh 4:11 more than a **h** and twenty thousand
Mt 13: 8 where it produced a crop—a **h**, sixty
13:23 He produces a crop, yielding a **h**,
18:12 you think? If a man owns a **h** sheep,
18:28 who owed him a **h** denarii.
19:29 sake will receive a **h** times as much
Mk 4: 8 thirty, sixty, or even a **h** times."
4:20 or even a **h** times what was sown."
10:30 will fail to receive a **h** times as
Lk 7:41 five **h** denarii, and the other fifty.
8: 8 yielded a crop, a **h** times more
15: 4 "Suppose one of you has a **h** sheep
16: 6 'Eight **h** gallons of olive oil,'
16: 6 down quickly, and make it four **h**'
16: 7 your bill and make it eight **h**'
Jn 21: 8 not far from shore, about a **h** yards.
Ac 1:15 numbering about a **h** and twenty)
5:36 and about four **h** men rallied to him.
7: 6 and ill-treated for four **h** years.
Ac 23:23 a detachment of two **h** soldiers
23:23 seventy horsemen and two **h** spearmen
27:28 was one **h** and twenty feet deep.
Ro 4:19 he was about a **h** years old
1Co 15: 6 he appeared to more than five **h** of
Rev 9:16 mounted troops was two **h** million.
16:21 about a **h** pounds each fell upon men.

Hundredfold (Hundred)

Ge 26:12 a **h**, because the LORD blessed him.

Hundreds (Hundred)

Ex 18:21 over thousands, **h**, fifties and tens.
18:25 over thousands, **h**, fifties and tens.
Nu 31:14 and commanders of **h**—who
31:48 and commanders of **h**—went to
31:52 commanders of **h** that Moses and
31:54 commanders of **h** and brought it into
Dt 1:15 of **h**, of fifties and of tens and as
1Sa 22: 7 of thousands and commanders of **h**?
29: 2 with their units of **h** and thousands,
2Sa 18: 1 of thousands and commanders of **h**.
18: 4 out in units of **h** and of thousands.
2Ki 11:19 He took with him the commanders of **h**,
1Ch 13: 1 of thousands and commanders of **h**.
26:26 and commanders of **h**, and
27: 1 of thousands and commanders of **h**,
28: 1 of thousands and commanders of **h**,
29: 6 of thousands and commanders of **h**,
2Ch 1: 2 of thousands and commanders of **h**,
23:20 He took with him the commanders of **h**,
25: 5 commanders of **h** for all Judah and
Mk 6:40 they sat down in groups of **h** and

Hundredth (Hundred)

Ge 7:11 In the six **h** year of Noah's life,
Ne 5:11 them—the **h** part of the money,

Hung (Hang)

Ex 40:21 **h** the shielding curtain and shielded
Dt 21:22 death and his body is **h** on a tree,
21:23 is **h** on a tree is under God's curse.
Jos 8:29 He **h** the king of Ai on a tree and
10:26 the kings and **h** them on five trees,
2Sa 4:12 **h** the bodies by the pool in Hebron.
21:12 where the Philistines had **h** them
1Ch 10:10 **h** up his head in the temple of Dagon.
Ps 137: 2 There on the poplars we **h** our harps,
Lam 5:12 Princes have been **h** up by their
Eze 27:10 They **h** their shields and helmets on
27:11 They **h** their shields around your
Mt 18: 6 a large millstone **h** around his neck
Lk 19:48 all the people **h** on his words.
23:39 One of the criminals who **h** there
Gal 3:13 is everyone who is **h** on a tree."

Hunger (Hungry)

Dt 8: 3 He humbled you, causing you to **h** and
28:48 therefore in **h** and thirst, in
1Sa 2: 5 but those who were hungry **h** no more.
2Ch 32:11 you, to let you die of **h** and thirst.
Ne 9:15 In their **h** you gave them bread from
Job 30: 3 Haggard from want and **h**, they roamed
38:39 and satisfy the **h** of the
Ps 17:14 You still the **h** of those you cherish;
Pr 6:30 satisfy his **h** when he is starving.
16:26 works for him; his **h** drives him on.
Isa 5:13 their men of rank will die of **h** and
29: 8 but he awakens, and his **h** remains;
49:10 They will neither **h** nor thirst, nor
Lam 2:19 from **h** at the head of every street.
4: 9 who die of famine; racked with **h**,
5:10 is hot as an oven, feverish from **h**.
Eze 7:19 They will not satisfy their **h** or
Mt 5: 6 Blessed are those who **h** and thirst
Lk 6:21 Blessed are you who **h** now, for you
2Co 6: 5 hard work, sleepless nights and **h**;
11:27 I have known **h** and thirst and have
Rev 7:16 Never again will they **h**; never again

Hungry (Hunger)

1Sa 2: 5 but those who were **h** hunger no more.
2Sa 17:29 "The people have become **h** and tired
Job 5: 5 The **h** consume his harvest, taking it
Job 18:12 Calamity is **h** for him; disaster is
22: 7 and you withheld food from the **h**,
24:10 carry the sheaves, but still go **h**.
Ps 17:12 They are like a lion **h** for prey,
34:10 The lions may grow weak and **h**, but
50:12 If I were **h** I would not tell you,
107: 5 They were **h** and thirsty, and their
107: 9 and fills the **h** with good things.
107:36 there he brought the **h** to live, and
146: 7 oppressed and gives food to the **h**.
Pr 10: 3 not let the righteous go **h** but he
13:25 the stomach of the wicked goes **h**.
19:15 sleep, and the shiftless man goes **h**.
25:21 If your enemy is **h**, give him food to
27: 7 **h** even what is bitter tastes sweet.
Isa 8:21 Distressed and **h**, they will roam
9:20 will devour, but still be **h**;
29: 8 a **h** man dreams that he is eating,
32: 6 the **h** he leaves empty and from the
44:12 He gets **h** and loses his strength;
58: 7 not to share your food with the **h**
58:10 spend yourselves on behalf of the **h**
65:13 but you will go **h**; my servants will
Jer 42:14 hear the trumpet or be **h** for bread,
Eze 18: 7 but gives his food to the **h** and
18:16 but gives his food to the **h** and
Mt 4: 2 days and forty nights, he was **h**.
12: 1 His disciples were **h** and began to
12: 3 when he and his companions were **h**?
15:32 I do not want to send them away **h**
21:18 his way back to the city, he was **h**.
25:35 For I was **h** and you gave me
25:37 'Lord, when did we see you **h** and
25:42 For I was **h** and you gave me nothing
25:44 'Lord, when did we see you **h** or
Mk 2:25 his companions were **h** and in need?
8: 3 If I send them home **h**, they will
11:12 were leaving Bethany, Jesus was **h**.
Lk 1:53 He has filled the **h** with good things
4: 2 and at the end of them he was **h**.
6: 3 when he and his companions were **h**?
6:25 are well fed now, for you will go **h**.
Jn 6:35 He who comes to me will never go **h**,
Ac 10:10 He became **h** and wanted something to
Ro 12:20 On the contrary: "If your enemy is **h**,
1Co 4:11 To this very hour we go **h** and
11:21 One remains **h**, another gets drunk.
11:34 If anyone is **h**, he should eat at
Php 4:12 whether well fed or **h**, whether

Hunt (Hunted, Hunter, Hunters, Hunting, Hunts)

Ge 27: 3 country to **h** some wild game for me.
27: 5 country to **h** game and bring it back,
31:36 have I committed that you **h** me down?
Job 38:39 "Do you **h** the prey for the lioness
Ps 140:11 may disaster **h** down men of violence.
Jer 16:16 and they will **h** them down on every
Am 9: 3 I will **h** them down and seize them.

Hunted (Hunt)

Ge 27:33 "Who was it, then, that **h** game and
Isa 13:14 Like a **h** gazelle, like sheep without
Lam 3:52 without cause **h** me like a bird.

Hunter (Hunt)

Ge 10: 9 He was a mighty **h** before the LORD;
10: 9 Nimrod, a mighty **h** before the LORD."
25:27 and Esau became a skilful **h**, a man
Pr 6: 5 a gazelle from the hand of the **h**,

Hunters (Hunt)

Jer 16:16 After that I will send for many **h**,

Hunting (Hunt)

Ge 27:30 his brother Esau came in from **h**.
1Sa 24:11 you are **h** me down to take my life.

Hunts (Hunt)

Lev 17:13 **h** any animal or bird that may be
1Sa 26:20 one **h** a partridge in the mountains."
Ps 10: 2 In his arrogance the wicked man **h**
Mic 7: 2 each **h** his brother with a net.

Hupham (Huphamite)
Nu 26:39 through **H**, the Huphamite clan;

Huphamite (Hupham)
Nu 26:39 through Hupham, the **H** clan;

Huppah
1Ch 24:13 the thirteenth to **H**, the fourteenth

Huppim
Ge 46:21 Naaman, Ehi, Rosh, Muppim, **H** and Ard.

Huppites
1Ch 7:12 The Shuppites and **H** were the
7:15 Makir took a wife from among the **H**

Hur
Ex 17:10 and **H** went to the top of the hill.
17:12 Aaron and **H** held his hands up—one
24:14 Aaron and **H** are with you, and anyone
31: 2 the son of **H**, of the tribe of Judah,
35:30 the son of **H**, of the tribe of Judah,
38:22 (Bezalel son of Uri, the son of **H**,
Nu 31: 8 **H** and Reba—the five kings of Midian.
Jos 13:21 Evi, Rekem, Zur, **H** and Reba—princes
1Ch 2:19 married Ephrath, who bore him **H**.
2:20 **H** was the father of Uri, and Uri the
2:50 The sons of **H** the firstborn of
4: 1 Perez, Hezron, Carmi, **H** and Shobal.
4: 4 These were the descendants of **H**, the
2Ch 1: 5 the son of **H**, had made was in Gibeon
Ne 3: 9 Rephaiah son of **H**, ruler of a

Hurai
1Ch 11:32 **H** from the ravines of Gaash, Abiel

Huram
1Ki 7:13 Solomon sent to Tyre and brought **H**,
7:14 **H** was highly skilled and experienced
7:40 So **H** finished all the work he had
7:45 All these objects that **H** made for
1Ch 8: 5 Gera, Shephuphan and **H**.
2Ch 4:11 So **H** finished the work he had

Huram-abi
2Ch 2:13 "I am sending you **H**, a man of great
4:16 All the objects that **H** made for King

Huri
1Ch 5:14 were the sons of Abihail son of **H**,

Hurl (Hurled, Hurls)
1Sa 25:29 **h** away as from the pocket of a sling.
2Ch 26:15 to shoot arrows and **h** large stones.
Ps 22: 7 **h** insults, shaking their heads
Isa 22:17 and **h** you away, O you mighty man.
Jer 10:18 "At this time I will **h** out those who
22:26 I will **h** you and the mother who gave
Eze 32: 4 and **h** you on the open field.
Mic 7:19 **h** all our iniquities into the depths

Hurled (Hurl)
Ex 15: 1 and its rider he has **h** into the sea.
15: 4 and his army he has **h** into the sea.
15:21 its rider he has **h** into the sea."
Jos 10:11 the LORD **h** large hailstones down on
1Sa 18:11 he **h** it, saying to himself, "I'll
20:33 Saul **h** his spear at him to kill him.
25:14 greetings, but he **h** insults at them.
Ne 9:11 but you **h** their pursuers into the
Ps 79:12 reproach they have **h** at you, O Lord.
Jer 22:28 will he and his children be **h** out,
Lam 2: 1 He has **h** down the splendour of
Jnh 2: 3 You **h** me into the deep, into the
Mt 27:39 Those who passed by **h** insults at him,
Mk 15:29 Those who passed by **h** insults at him,
Lk 23:39 who hung there **h** insults at him:
Jn 9:28 they **h** insults at him and said, "You
1Pe 2:23 they **h** their insults at him, he did
Rev 8: 5 and **h** it on the earth; and there
8: 7 and it was **h** down upon the earth.
12: 9 The great dragon was **h** down—that
Rev 12: 9 He was **h** to the earth, and his
12:10 God day and night, has been **h** down.
12:13 saw that he had been **h** to the earth

Hurls (Hurl)
Job 27:22 **h** itself against him without mercy
Ps 147:17 He **h** down hail like pebbles. Who can

Hurricane
Ac 27:14 Before very long, a wind of **h** force,

Hurried (Hurry)
Ge 18: 2 When he saw them, he **h** from the
18: 6 Abraham **h** into the tent to Sarah.
18: 7 to a servant, who **h** to prepare it.
24:17 The servant **h** to meet her and said,
24:29 he **h** out to the man at the spring.
29:13 his sister's son, he **h** to meet him.
43:15 They **h** down to Egypt and presented
43:30 **h** out and looked for a place to weep.
Ex 9:20 of the LORD **h** to bring their slaves
Jos 4:10 The people **h** over,
8:14 he and all the men of the city **h** out
Jdg 13:10 The woman **h** to tell her husband,
1Sa 4:14 this uproar?" The man **h** over to Eli,
2Sa 4: 4 but as she **h** to leave, he fell and
19:16 the Benjamite from Bahurim, **h** down
2Ki 5:21 Gehazi **h** after Naaman. When Naaman
9:13 They **h** and took their cloaks and
2Ch 26:20 on his forehead, so they **h** him out.
Est 6:14 eunuchs arrived and **h** Haman away
Job 31: 5 or my foot has **h** after deceit—
Da 6:19 king got up and **h** to the lions' den.
Mt 28: 8 the women **h** away from the tomb,
Mk 6:25 At once the girl **h** in to the king
Lk 1:39 Mary got ready and **h** to a town
2:16 they **h** off and found Mary and Joseph,

Hurries (Hurry)
Ecc 1: 5 and **h** back to where it rises.

Hurry (Hurried, Hurries, Hurrying)
Ge 19:14 He said, "**H** and get out of this
19:15 "**H**! Take your wife and your two
45: 9 Now **h** back to my father and say to
Ex 12:33 The Egyptians urged the people to **h**
Nu 16:46 and **h** to the assembly to make
1Sa 9:12 "He's ahead of you. **H** now; he has
17:17 your brothers and **h** to their camp.
20: 6 my permission to **h** to Bethlehem,
20:38 he shouted, "**H**! Go quickly! Don't
2Ch 35:21 God has told me to **h**; so stop
Ps 55: 8 I would **h** to my place of shelter,
Ecc 8: 3 Do not be in a **h** to leave the king's
SS 1: 4 Take me away with you—let us **h**!
Isa 5:19 to those who say, "Let God **h**, let
Ac 20:16 for he was in a **h** to reach Jerusalem,

Hurrying (Hurry)
1Sa 23:26 other side, **h** to get away from Saul.

Hurt (Hurts)
Ps 69:26 talk about the pain of those you **h**.
Pr 23:35 "but I'm not **h**! They beat me, but I
Ecc 8: 9 lords it over others to his own **h**.
Da 6:22 They have not **h** me, because I was
Mk 16:18 it will not **h** them at all; they will
Jn 21:17 Peter was **h** because Jesus asked
Ac 7:26 why do you want to **h** each other?'
2Co 7: 8 I see that my letter **h** you, but
Rev 2:11 not be **h** at all by the second death.

Hurtling
Eze 13:11 and I will send hailstones **h** down,

Hurts (Hurt)
Ps 15: 4 who keeps his oath even when it **h**,
Pr 26:28 A lying tongue hates those it **h**,

Husband (Husband's, Husbands)
Ge 3: 6 **h**, who was with her, and he ate it.
3:16 your **h**, and he will rule over you."
16: 3 gave her to her **h** to be his wife.
Ge 29:32 Surely my **h** will love me now."
29:34 "Now at last my **h** will become
30:15 it enough that you took away my **h**?
30:18 for giving my maidservant to my **h**.
30:20 This time my **h** will treat me with
Ex 21:22 the woman's **h** demands and the court
Lev 21: 3 dependent on him since she has no **h**
Nu 5:13 and this is hidden from her **h** and
5:14 of jealousy come over her **h**
5:19 impure while married to your **h**,
5:20 gone astray while married to your **h**
5:20 with a man other than your **h**"—
5:27 and been unfaithful to her **h**,
5:29 herself while married to her **h**,
5:31 The **h** will be innocent of any
30: 7 her **h** hears about it but says
30: 8 if her **h** forbids her when he hears
30:10 "If a woman living with her **h** makes
30:11 her **h** hears about it but says
30:12 if her **h** nullifies them when he
30:12 Her **h** has nullified them, and the
30:13 Her **h** may confirm or nullify any vow
30:14 if her **h** says nothing to her about
Dt 21:13 be her **h** and she shall be your wife.
24: 3 her second **h** dislikes her and writes
24: 4 her first **h**, who divorced her, is
25:11 to rescue her **h** from his assailant,
28:56 foot—will begrudge the **h** she loves
Jdg 13: 6 the woman went to her **h** and told him,
13: 9 but her **h** Manoah was not with her.
13:10 The woman hurried to tell her **h**,
14:15 "Coax your **h** into explaining the
19: 3 her **h** went to her to persuade her to
20: 4 the Levite, the **h** of the murdered
Ru 1: 3 Now Elimelech, Naomi's **h**, died, and
1: 5 left without her two sons and her **h**.
1: 9 find rest in the home of another **h**.
1:12 I am too old to have another **h**.
1:12 for me—even if I had a **h** tonight
2:11 of your **h**—how you left your father
1Sa 1: 8 Elkanah her **h** would say to her,
1:22 Hannah did not go. She said to her **h**,
1:23 to you," Elkanah her **h** told her.
2:19 her **h** to offer the annual sacrifice.
4:19 father-in-law and her **h** were dead,
4:21 of her father-in-law and her **h**.
25: 3 but her **h**, a Calebite, was surly and
25:19 But she did not tell her **h** Nabal.
2Sa 3:15 from her **h** Paltiel son of Laish.
3:16 Her **h**, however, went with her,
11:26 Uriah's wife heard that her **h** was
14: 5 "I am indeed a widow; my **h** is dead.
14: 7 leaving my **h** neither name nor
2Ki 4: 1 "Your servant my **h** is dead, and you
4: 9 She said to her **h**, "I know that this
4:14 she has no son and her **h** is old."
4:22 She called her **h** and said, "Please
4:26 all right? Is your **h** all right?
Pr 7:19 My **h** is not at home; he has gone on
31:11 Her **h** has full confidence in her and
31:23 Her **h** is respected at the city gate,
31:28 her **h** also, and he praises her:
Isa 54: 1 of her who has a **h**," says the LORD.
54: 5 For your Maker is your **h**—the LORD
Jer 3:14 declares the LORD, "for I am your **h**.
3:20 like a woman unfaithful to her **h**,
6:11 **h** and wife will be caught in it,
31:32 was a **h** to them," declares the LORD.
Eze 16:32 You prefer strangers to your own **h**!
16:45 who despised her **h** and her children;
Hos 2: 2 is not my wife, and I am not her **h**.
2: 7 I will go back to my **h** as at first,
2:16 "you will call me 'my **h**'; you will
Joel 1: 8 grieving for the **h** of her youth.
Mt 1:16 the father of Joseph, the **h** of Mary
1:19 Joseph her **h** was a righteous man and
19:10 the situation between a **h** and wife,
Mk 10:12 if she divorces her **h** and marries
Lk 2:36 **h** seven years after her marriage,
Jn 4:16 He told her, "Go, call your **h** and
4:17 "I have no **h**," she replied. Jesus
4:17 right when you say you have no **h**.
4:18 the man you now have is not your **h**.
Ac 5: 9 who buried your **h** are at the door,
5:10 her out and buried her beside her **h**.
Ro 7: 2 to her **h** as long as he is alive,

Ro 7: 2 but if her **h** dies, she is released
7: 3 man while her **h** is still alive,
7: 3 But if her **h** dies, she is released
1Co 7: 2 own wife, and each woman her own **h**.
7: 3 The **h** should fulfil his marital duty
7: 3 and likewise the wife to her **h**.
7: 4 to her alone but also to her **h**.
7:10 wife must not separate from her **h**.
7:11 or else be reconciled to her **h**.
7:11 And a **h** must not divorce his wife.
7:13 if a woman has a **h** who is not a
7:14 For the unbelieving **h** has been
7:14 sanctified through her believing **h**.
7:16 wife, whether you will save your **h**?
7:16 **h**, whether you will save your wife?
7:34 world—how she can please her **h**.
7:39 A woman is bound to her **h** as long as
7:39 But if her **h** dies, she is free to
2Co 11: 2 I promised you to one **h**, to Christ,
Gal 4:27 woman than of her who has a **h**."
Eph 5:23 For the **h** is the head of the wife as
5:33 and the wife must respect her **h**.
1Ti 3: 2 the **h** of but one wife, temperate,
3:12 A deacon must be the **h** of but one
5: 9 sixty, has been faithful to her **h**,
Tit 1: 6 the **h** of but one wife, a man
Rev 21: 2 bride beautifully dressed for her **h**.

Husband's (Husband)
Dt 25: 5 Her **h** brother shall take her and
25: 7 "My **h** brother refuses to carry on
Ru 2: 1 Naomi had a relative on her **h** side
Pr 6:34 for jealousy arouses a **h** fury, and
12: 4 of noble character is her **h** crown
Jn 1:13 or a **h** will, but born of God.
1Co 7: 4 the **h** body does not belong to him

Husbands (Husband)
Lev 21: 7 or divorced from their **h**,
Ru 1:11 more sons, who could become your **h**?
Est 1:17 and so they will despise their **h** and
1:20 all the women will respect their **h**
Jer 44:19 did not our **h** know that we were
Eze 16:45 despised their **h** and their children.
Am 4: 1 crush the needy and say to your **h**,
Jn 4:18 The fact is, you have had five **h**,
1Co 14:35 they should ask their own **h** at home;
Eph 5:22 Wives, submit to your **h** as to the
5:24 submit to their **h** in everything.
5:25 **H**, love your wives, just as Christ
5:28 In this same way, **h** ought to love
Col 3:18 Wives, submit to your **h**, as is
3:19 **H**, love your wives and do not be
Tit 2: 4 women to love their **h** and children,
2: 5 and to be subject to their **h**, so
1Pe 3: 1 way be submissive to your **h** so that,
3: 5 They were submissive to their own **h**,
3: 7 **H**, in the same way be considerate as

Hush (Hushed)
Am 6:10 "No," then he will say, "**H**! We must

Hushah
1Ch 4: 4 of Gedor, and Ezer the father of **H**.

Hushai
2Sa 15:32 **H** the Arkite was there to meet
15:37 David's friend **H** arrived at
16:16 **H** the Arkite, David's friend, went
16:17 Absalom asked **H**, "Is this the love
16:18 **H** said to Absalom, "No, the one
17: 5 said, "Summon also **H** the Arkite
17: 6 **H** came to him, Absalom said,
17: 7 **H** replied to Absalom, "The advice
17:14 "The advice of **H** the Arkite is
17:15 **H** told Zadok and Abiathar, the
1Ki 4:16 Baana son of **H**—in Asher and in
1Ch 27:33 **H** the Arkite was the king's friend.

Husham
Ge 36:34 Jobab died, **H** from the land of the
36:35 **H** died, Hadad son of Bedad, who
1Ch 1:45 Jobab died, **H** from the land of the
1:46 **H** died, Hadad son of Bedad, who

Hushathite
2Sa 21:18 At that time Sibbecai the **H** killed
23:27 Abiezer from Anathoth, Mebunnai the **H**
1Ch 11:29 Sibbecai the **H**, Ilai the Ahohite,
20: 4 At that time Sibbecai the **H** killed
27:11 was Sibbecai the **H**, a Zerahite.

Hushed (Hush)
Job 4:16 my eyes, and I heard a **h** voice:
29:10 the voices of the nobles were **h**,
37:17 land lies **h** under the south wind,
Ps 107:29 the waves of the sea were **h**.

Hushim
Ge 46:23 The son of Dan: **H**.
1Ch 8: 8 had divorced his wives **H** and Baara.
8:11 By **H** he had Abitub and Elpaal.

Hushites
1Ch 7:12 and the **H** the descendants of Aher.

Hut
Job 27:18 cocoon, like a **h** made by a watchman.
Isa 1: 8 like a **h** in a field of melons, like
24:20 it sways like a **h** in the wind; so

Hyenas
Isa 13:22 **H** will howl in her strongholds,
34:14 Desert creatures will meet with **h**,
Jer 50:39 "So desert creatures and **h** will live

Hymenaeus
1Ti 1:20 Among them are **H** and Alexander, whom
2Ti 2:17 Among them are **H** and Philetus,

Hymn (Hymns)
Ps 40: 3 a **h** of praise to our God.
Mt 26:30 they had sung a **h**, they went out to
Mk 14:26 they had sung a **h**, they went out to
1Co 14:26 everyone has a **h**, or a word of

Hymns (Hymn)
Ac 16:25 were praying and singing **h** to God,
Ro 15: 9 I will sing **h** to your name."
Eph 5:19 psalms, **h** and spiritual songs.
Col 3:16 and as you sing psalms, **h** and

Hypocrisy (Hypocrite, Hypocrites, Hypocritical)
Mt 23:28 you are full of **h** and wickedness.
Mk 12:15 we?" But Jesus knew their **h**.
Lk 12: 1 yeast of the Pharisees, which is **h**.
Gal 2:13 The other Jews joined him in his **h**,
2:13 other Jews joined him in his **h**
1Pe 2: 1 **h**, envy, and slander of every kind.

Hypocrite (Hypocrisy)
Mt 7: 5 You **h**, first take the plank out of
Lk 6:42 the plank in your own eye? You **h**,

Hypocrites (Hypocrisy)
Ps 26: 4 men, nor do I consort with **h**;
Mt 6: 2 as the **h** do in the synagogues and on
6: 5 do not be like the **h**, for they love
6:16 do not look sombre as the **h** do, for
15: 7 You **h**! Isaiah was right when he
22:18 You **h**, why are you trying to trap me?
23:13 you **h**! You shut the kingdom of
23:15 you **h**! You travel over land and sea
23:23 you **h**! You give a tenth of your
23:25 you **h**! You clean the outside of the
23:27 you **h**! You are like whitewashed
23:29 you **h**! You build tombs for the
24:51 and assign him a place with the **h**,
Mk 7: 6 about you **h**; as it is written:
Lk 12:56 **H**! You know how to interpret the
13:15 The Lord answered him, "You **h**!

Hypocritical (Hypocrisy)
1Ti 4: 2 Such teachings come through **h** liars,

Hyssop
Ex 12:22 Take a bunch of **h**, dip it into the
Lev 14: 4 scarlet yarn and **h** be brought for
14: 6 the scarlet yarn and the **h**, into the
14:49 some cedar wood, scarlet yarn and **h**.
14:51 he is to take the cedar wood, the **h**,
14:52 wood, the **h** and the scarlet yarn.
Nu 19: 6 **h** and scarlet wool and throw them
19:18 clean is to take some **h**,
1Ki 4:33 to the **h** that grows out of walls.
Ps 51: 7 Cleanse me with **h**, and I shall be
Jn 19:29 the **h** plant, and lifted it to Jesus'
Heb 9:19 scarlet wool and branches of **h**, and

I am (*I am the Lord, I am the Lord, I am with you, Know that I am the Lord*)
Ge 6:7, 13, 17; 9:12; 13:17; 15:1, 7; 16:5; 17:1; 18:12, 13, 17, 27; 20:16; 22:1, 11; 23:4; 24:3, 13, 24, 34, 43; 25:32; 26:24; 27:1, 2, 19, 24, 32; 28:13, 15; 29:33; 30:13; 31:11, 13; 32:5, 10, 11, 20; 34:12; 35:11; 37:13; 38:25; 39:9; 41:9, 44; 43:14; 45:3, 4; 46:2, 3, 30; 48:4, 21; 49:29; 50:5, 24; Ex 3:4, 6, 7, 10, 14, 15; 4:10; 6:2, 6, 7, 8, 29; 7:5, 17; 10:2; 12:12; 14:4, 18; 15:26; 16:12; 19:9; 20:2; 22:27; 23:20; 29:46; 31:13; 33:17; 34:10; Lev 11:44, 45; 14:34; 18:2, 3, 4, 5, 6, 21, 24, 30; 19:3, 4, 10, 12, 14, 16, 18, 25, 28, 30, 31, 32, 34, 36, 37; 20:7, 8, 22, 23, 24; 21:12, 15, 23; 22:2, 3, 8, 9, 16, 30, 31, 32, 33; 23:10, 22, 43; 24:22; 25:2, 17, 38, 55; 26:1, 2, 13, 44, 45; Nu 3:13, 41, 45; 10:10, 30; 11:21; 13:2; 15:2, 18, 41; 18:7, 20; 24:14; 25:11, 12; Dt 4:1, 8, 40; 5:6, 31, ; 8:1, 11; 10:13; 11:8, 13, 22, 26, 27, 32; 12:28; 13:18; 15:5; 28:15; 29:6, 14; 30:8, 11; 31:2, 27; 32:49, 52; Jos 1:2; 3:7; 14:10, 11; 23:2; 23:14; Jdg 6:10; 6:15; 7:9; 8:5; 9:2; 13:11; 18:4; 19:18; Ru 1:12; 3:9, 12; 4:4; 1Sa 1:15, 26; 3:4, 5, 6, 8, 11, 16; 9:19; 12:2, 7; 14:7; 15:1, 11; 16:1, 22; 17:39, 58; 20:5, 8; 22:22; 23:4; 24:11; 28:15; 30:13; 2Sa 1:9, 13; 3:8, 39; 7:2; 11:5; 12:11; 14:5, 18, 32; 15:20, 26; 16:12; 18:14; 19:22, 35; 20:17; 22:4; 24:12, 14, 17; 1Ki 2:2; 3:7; 11:31; 13:14; 14:10; 15:19; 16:3; 17:12, 20; 18:22, 36; 19:4, 10, 14; 20:6, 13, 28; 21:21; 22:4; 2Ki 1:10, 12; 2:9, 10; 3:7; 5:6; 10:15; 10:19; 10:24; 16:7; 19:7; 21:12; 22:16; 22:20; 1Ch 12:17; 17:1; 21:10, 13, 17; 2Ch 2:4, 5, 13; 16:3; 18:3; 34:24, 28; 35:21, 23; Ezr 9:6; Ne 6:3; Job 1:15, 16, 17, 19; 9:21, 29; 10:7, 15; 11:4; 12:3; 13:2; 19:10, 17, 20; 20:2; 21:6; 23:15, 17; 30:19; 31:6; 32:6, 18, 19, ; 33:2, 6, 9; 34:5, 6, 31; 40:4; 42:7; Ps 6:2, 6; 18:3; 22:6, 14; 25:16; 27:13; 28:7; 31:9, 11, 12, 22; 35:3; 37:25; 38:6, 8, 13, 17, 18; 39:10; 40:7, 17; 46:10; 50:7; 52:8; 55:2; 56:3, 12; 57:4; 69:3, 4, 8, 12, 17, 19, 29; 70:5; 71:9, 18; 73:23; 81:10; 86:1, 2; 88:4, 5, 8; 102:2, 5, 6; 109:4, 22, 23, 25; 116:10, 16; 119:19, 25, 63, 83, 94, 125, 141; 120:7; 139:14, 18; 142:6; 143:12; Pr 20:9; 30:2; Ecc 7:23; SS 1:6; 2:1, 5, 16; 5:8; 6:3; 8:10; Isa 1:14; 5:5; 6:5; 19:11; 21:3; 27:4; 33:24; 37:7; 38:14, 19; 41:4, 10, 13; 42:8; 43:3, 5, 10, 12, 13, 15, 19; 44:6, 16, 24; 45:3, 5, 6, 18, 22; 46:4, 9, 13; 47:8, 10; 48:12, 16, 17; 49:5, 23; 51:15; 56:3; 60:22; 65:5; Jer 1:6, 7, 8, 12, 15, 19; 2:23, 35; 3:12, 14; 4:6, 31; 5:15; 6:11, 19; 8:21; 9:24; 13:13; 15:20; 18:11; 19:3, 15; 20:7, 9; 21:4, 8, 13; 23:9, 30, 31, 32; 24:7; 25:29; 26:14; 28:16; 30:11; 31:9; 32:3, 27, 28; 34:2, 22; 35:17; 36:5; 37:14; 38:14, 19; 39:16; 40:4; 42:10, 11; 44: 11, 27, 30; 45:3; 46:25, 28; 50:31; 51:25; Lam 1:11, 20, ; 2:11; 3:1; Eze 2:3, 4; 3:3; 6:3, 7, 10, 13, 14; 7:4, 8, 27; 11:10, 12; 12:11, 15, 16, 20, 23; 13:8, 9, 14, 20, 21, 23; 14:8; 15:7; 16:37, 62; 20:5, 7, 19, 20, 26, 38, 42, 44, 47; 21:3, 4; 22:16, 26; 23:28, 49; 24:16, 21, 24, 27; 25:4, 5, 7, 11, 16, 17; 26:3, 6, 7; 27:3; 28:2, 7, 9, 22, 23, 24, 26; 29:3, 6, 9, 10, 16, 19, 21; 30:8, 19, 22, 25, 26; 32:15; 33:29; 34:10, 27, 31; 35:3, 4, 9, 15; 36:9, 11, 22, 23, 32, 38; 37:6, 12, 13, 19; 38:3, 23; 39:1, 6, 13, 17, 19, 22, 28; 40:4; 44:28; Da 1:10; 2:8; 8:19; 10:11, 16; Hos 1:9; 2:2, 14; 5:12; 11:9; 12:8, 9; 13:4; 14:8; Joel 2:19, 27; 3:7, 10; Am 7:8; Jnh 1:9; 4:9; Mic 2:3; 3:8; 7:1; Na 2:13; 3:5; Hab 1:5, 6; 2:1; Zep 2:15; Hag 1:13; 2:4; Zec 1:14, 15; 2:10; 3:8; 8:2; 9:8; 10:6; 11:5, 16; 12:2; 13:5; Mal 1:6, 10, 14; Mt 3:11, 17; 8:3; 9:28; 10:16; 11:29; 16:15; 17:5; 20:13, 15, 22; 21:24, 27; 22:32; 23:34; 24:5; 26:18, 61; 27:24, 43; 28:20; Mk 1:7, 11, 41; 8:27, 29; 10:38, 39; 11:29, 33; 12:26; 13:6; 14:62; Lk 1:18, 19, 34, 38; 3:16, 22; 5:8, 13; 9:18, 20, 44; 10:3; 12:50; 15:17, 19, 21; 16:24; 18:11; 19:22; 20:8; 21:8; 22:27, 33, 58, 70; 24:49; Jn 1:20, 21, 23, 27;

3:28; 4:9; 5:7, 36; 6:35, 41, 48, 51; 7:8, 28, 29, 33, 34, 36; 8:12, 14, 16, 18, 21, 23, 24, 28, 38, 46, 49, 50, 58; 9:5, 9; 10:7, 9, 11, 14, 36; 11:11, 15, 25; 12:26, 32; 13:7, 13, 18, 19, 33, 36; 14:2, 3, 4, 6, 10, 11, 12, 20, 28; 15:1, 5; 16:5, 7, 10, 17, 26, 28, 32; 17:9, 11, 13, 14, 16, 21, 24; 18:5, 6, 8, 17, 25, 37; 19:4, 28; 20:17, 21; Ac 7:32; 9:5; 10:26; 13:25, 41; 17:3, 23; 18:6, 10; 20:22, 26; 21:13, 39; 22:3, 8, 27; 23:6; 24:21; 25:10, 11; 26:6, 15, 17, 22, 25, 26, 29; 27:23; 28:20; Ro 1:14, 15, 16; 3:5; 7:1, 14, 24; 8:38; 9:1; 11:1, 3, 13, ; 14:14; 15:25; 16:19; 1Co 1:14; 4:3, 14, 17; 5:3, 4, 11; 7:7, 8, 35; 9:2, 15, 16, 17, 19, 21; 10:33; 12:15, 16; 13:1, 2, 12; 14:11, 37; 15:9, 10; 16:10, 11; 2Co 7:4, 9, 16; 8:8; 9:3; 11:2, 3, 5, 12, 17, 21, 23, 31; 12:10, 11, 14, 16, 20, 21; 13:10; Gal 1:6, 20; 2:18; 4:1, 18, 19, 20; 5:10, 11; Eph 3:8; 5:32; 6:20, 21, 22; Php 1:7, 13, 16, 17, 22, 23; 2:17, 24, 28; 4:11, 17, 18; Col 2:1, 5; 4:3, 8; 1Ti 1:15; 2:7; 3:14, 15; 2Ti 1:5, 12; 2:7, 9; 4:6; Phm 12, 13; Heb 10:7, 9; 12:21; 1Pe 1:16; 2Pe 1:17; 1Jn 2:7, 8, 26; 5:16; 2Jn 5; Rev 1:8, 17, 18; 2:23; 3:11, 16, 17, 20; 18:7; 19:10; 21:5, 6; 22:7, 9, 12, 13, 16, 20

I am the LORD
Ge 15:7; 28:13; Ex 6:2, 6, 7, 29; 7:5, 17; 10:2; 12:12; 14:4, 18; 15:26; 16:12; 20:2; 29:46; 31:13; Lev 11:44, 45; 18:2, 4, 5, 6, 21, 30; 19:3, 4, 10, 12, 14, 16, 18, 25, 28, 30, 31, 32, 34, 36, 37; 20:7, 8, 24; 21:12, 15, 23; 22:2, 3, 8, 9, 16, 30, 31, 32, 33; 23:22, 43; 24:22; 25:17, 38, 55; 26:1, 2, 13, 44, 45; Nu 3:13, 41, 45; 10:10; 15:41; Dt 5:6; 29:6; Jdg 6:10; Ps 81:10; Isa 41:13; 42:8; 43:3, 15; 44:24; 45:3, 5, 6, 18; 48:17; 49:23; 51:15; 60:22; Jer 9:24; 24:7; 32:27; Eze 6:7, 10, 13; 7:4, 27; 11:10, 12; 12:15, 16; 13:14, 21; 14:8; 15:7; 16:62; 20:5, 7, 19, 20, 26, 38, 42, 44; 24:27; 25:5, 17; 26:6; 28:22, 23, 26; 29:6, 9, 21; 30:8, 25, 26; 32:15; 33:29; 34:27; 35:4, 9; 36:11, 23, 38; 37:13; 38:23; 39:6, 22, 28; Hos 12:9; 13:4; Joel 2:27; Zec 10:6

I am the Lord
Ex 6:8; 1Ki 20:13, 28; Eze 6:14; 12:20; 13:23; 22:16; 25:7, 11; 30:19; 35:15; 37:6

I am with you
Ge 26:24; 28:15; Jos 3:7; 1Sa 14:7; 2Ki 10:15; Isa 41:10; 43:5; Jer 1:8, 19; 15:20; 30:11; 42:11; 46:28; Hag 1:13; 2:4; Mt 28:20; Jn 7:33; Ac 18:10; 1Co 5:3, 4; Gal 4:18

I tell you the truth
Da 11:2; Mt 5:18, 26; 6:2, 5, 16; 8:10; 10:15, 23, 42; 11:11; 13:17; 16:28; 17:20; 18:3, 13, 18; 19:23, 28; 21:21, 31; 23:36; 24:2, 34, 47; 25:12, 40, 45; 26:13, 21, 34; Mk 3:28; 8:12; 9:1, 41; 10:15, 29; 11:23; 12:43; 13:30; 14:9, 18, 25, 30; Lk 4:24; 9:27; 12:37, 44; 18:17, 29; 21:3, 32; 23:43; Jn 1:51; 3:3, 5, 11; 5:19, 24, 25; 6:26, 32, 47, 53; 8:34, 51, 58; 10:1, 7; 12:24; 13:16, 20, 21, 38; 14:12; 16:7, 20, 23; 21:18

I will be their God
Ge 17:8; Jer 24:7; 31:33; 32:38; Eze 11:20; 14:11; 37:23, 27; 2Co 6:16; Heb 8:10

I will be with you
Ge 26:3; 31:3; Ex 3:12; Jos 1:5; Jdg 6:16; 1Ki 11:38; Isa 43:2; Jn 13:33

I will be your God
Ex 6:7; Jer 7:23; 11:4; 30:22; Eze 36:28

Ibex
Dt 14: 5 roe deer, the wild goat, the **i**,

Ibhar
2Sa 5:15 **I**, Elishua, Nepheg, Japhia,
1Ch 3: 6 There were also **I**, Elishua,
14: 5 **I**, Elishua, Elpelet,

Ibleam
Jos 17:11 Manasseh also had Beth Shan, **I** and
Jdg 1:27 or Taanach or Dor or **I** or Megiddo
2Ki 9:27 chariot on the way up to Gur near **I**

Ibneiah
1Ch 9: 8 **I** son of Jeroham; Elah son of Uzzi,

Ibnijah
1Ch 9: 8 the son of Reuel, the son of **I**.

Ibri
1Ch 24:27 Jaaziah: Beno, Shoham, Zaccur and **I**

Ibsam
1Ch 7: 2 Rephaiah, Jeriel, Jahmai, **I** and

Ibzan
Jdg 12: 8 After him, **I** of Bethlehem led Israel
12: 9 **I** led Israel for seven years.
12:10 **I** died, and was buried in Bethlehem.

Ice (Icy)
Job 6:16 darkened by thawing **i** and swollen
37:10 The breath of God produces **i**, and
38:29 From whose womb comes the **i**? Who
Eze 1:22 sparkling like **i**, and awesome.

Ichabod (Ichabod's)
1Sa 4:21 She named the boy **I**, saying, "The

Ichabod's (Ichabod)
1Sa 14: 3 He was a son of **I** brother Ahitub

Iconium
Capital city of Lycaonia in Asia Minor. Visited by Paul and Barnabas who enjoyed successful ministry here until Jews forced them out (Ac 14:1–7) and pursued Paul to Lystra to stone him (Ac 14:19). Paul later returned (Ac 14:21) and was well received (Ac 16:2), but he remembered the persecution (2Ti 3:11).

Ac 13:51 protest against them and went to **I**.
14: 1 At **I** Paul and Barnabas went as usual
14:19 some Jews came from Antioch and **I**
14:21 returned to Lystra, **I** and Antioch,
16: 2 The brothers at Lystra and **I** spoke
2Ti 3:11 **I** and Lystra, the persecutions I

Icy (Ice)
Ps 147:17 Who can withstand his **i** blast?

Idalah
Jos 19:15 Nahalal, Shimron, **I** and Bethlehem.

Idbash
1Ch 4: 3 sons of Etam: Jezreel, Ishma and **I**.

Iddo (Iddo's)
1Ki 4:14 Ahinadab son of **I**—in Mahanaim;
1Ch 6:21 Joah his son, **I** his son, Zerah his
27:21 **I** son of Zechariah; over Benjamin:
2Ch 9:29 in the visions of **I** the seer
12:15 of **I** the seer that deal with
13:22 in the annotations of the prophet **I**.
Ezr 5: 1 a descendant of **I**, prophesied to the
6:14 and Zechariah, a descendant of **I**.
8:17 I sent them to **I**, the leader in
8:17 I told them what to say to **I** and his
Ne 12: 4 **I**, Ginnethon, Abijah,
Zec 1: 1 son of Berekiah, the son of **I**:
1: 7 son of Berekiah, the son of **I**.

Iddo's (Iddo)
Ne 12:16 of **I**, Zechariah; of Ginnethon's,

Idea (Ideas)
Nu 16:28 things and that it was not my **i**:
Dt 1:23 The **i** seemed good to me; so I
Est 3: 6 the **i** of killing only Mordecai.
Jn 5:13 The man who was healed had no **i** who
8:14 But you have no **i** where I come from
18:34 "Is that your own **i**," Jesus asked,
Ac 12: 9 but he had no **i** that what the angel
2Pe 2:13 Their **i** of pleasure is to carouse

Ideas (Idea)
Ac 17:20 You are bringing some strange **i**
17:21 and listening to the latest **i**.)
1Ti 6:20 the opposing **i** of what is falsely

Identical
1Ki 6:25 cherubim were **i** in size and shape.
7:37 moulds and were **i** in size and shape

Idle (Idleness, Idlers)
Dt 32:47 They are not just **i** words for
Job 11: 3 Will your **i** talk reduce men to
Ecc 10:18 if his hands are **i**, the house leaks
11: 6 at evening let not your hands be **i**,
Isa 58:13 as you please or speaking **i** words,
Col 2:18 mind puffs him up with **i** notions.
1Th 5:14 brothers, warn those who are **i**,
2Th 3: 6 away from every brother who is **i**
3: 7 We were not **i** when we were with you,
3:11 We hear that some among you are **i**.
1Ti 5:13 they get into the habit of being **i**

Idleness (Idle)
Pr 31:27 and does not eat the bread of **i**.

Idlers (Idle)
1Ti 5:13 And not only do they become **i**, but

Idol (Calf-idol, Calf-idols, Idol's, Idolater, Idolaters, Idolatries, Idolatrous, Idolatry, Idols)
Ex 20: 4 You shall not make for yourself an **i**
32: 4 an **i** cast in the shape of a calf,
32: 8 an **i** cast in the shape of a calf.
Dt 4:16 and make for yourselves an **i**,
4:23 do not make for yourselves an **i** in
4:25 corrupt and make any kind of **i**,
5: 8 You shall not make for yourself an **i**
9:12 have made a cast **i** for themselves."
9:16 an **i** cast in the shape of a calf.
27:15 who carves an image or casts an **i**
Jdg 17: 3 to make a carved image and a cast **i**
17: 4 made them into the image and the **i**.
18:14 a carved image and a cast **i**?
18:17 took the cast **i** while the priest
18:18 other household gods and the cast **i**,
1Sa 19:13 Michal took an **i** and laid it on the
19:16 the men entered, there was the **i**
Ps 24: 4 to an **i** or swear by what is false.
106:19 and worshipped an **i** cast from metal.
Isa 40:19 for an **i**, a craftsman casts it, and
40:20 to set up an **i** that will not topple.
41: 7 the **i** so that it will not topple.
44:10 Who shapes a god and casts an **i**,
44:12 he shapes an **i** with hammers,
44:15 he makes an **i** and bows down to it.
44:17 From the rest he makes a god, his **i**
66: 3 incense, like one who worships an **i**.
Eze 8: 3 **i** that provokes to jealousy stood.
8: 5 the altar I saw this **i** of jealousy.
8:12 each at the shrine of his own **i**?
Hos 3: 4 sacred stones, without ephod or **i**.
4:12 They consult a wooden **i** and are
9:10 themselves to that shameful **i**
Hab 2:18 "Of what value is an **i**, since a man
Ac 7:41 That was the time they made an **i** in
1Co 8: 4 We know that an **i** is nothing at all
8: 7 as having been sacrificed to an **i**,
10:19 a sacrifice offered to an **i**
10:19 anything, or that an **i** is anything?

Idol's (Idol)
1Co 8:10 knowledge eating in an **i** temple,

Idolater (Idol)
1Co 5:11 an **i** or a slanderer, a drunkard or a
Eph 5: 5 such a man is an **i**—has any

Idolaters (Idol)
1Co 5:10 or the greedy and swindlers, or **i**.
6: 9 Neither the sexually immoral nor **i**
10: 7 Do not be **i**, as some of them were;

Rev 21: 8 the **i** and all liars—their place
22:15 the murderers, the **i** and everyone

Idolatries (Idol)

Jer 14:14 divinations, **i** and the delusions of

Idolatrous (Idol)

Jer 3:23 Surely the **i** commotion on the hills
Hos 10: 5 so will its **i** priests, those who
Zep 1: 4 of the pagan and the **i** priests—

Idolatry (Idol)

1Sa 15:23 and arrogance like the evil of **i**.
2Ki 9:22 as long as all the **i** and witchcraft
Eze 14: 4 myself in keeping with his great **i**.
23:49 the consequences of your sins of **i**.
1Co 10:14 my dear friends, flee from **i**.
Gal 5:20 **i** and witchcraft; hatred, discord,
Col 3: 5 evil desires and greed, which is **i**.
1Pe 4: 3 orgies, carousing and detestable **i**.

Idols (Idol)

Ex 34:17 "Do not make cast **i**.
Lev 17: 7 the goat **i** to whom they prostitute
19: 4 "'Do not turn to **i** or make gods of
26: 1 "'Do not make **i** or set up an image
26:30 on the lifeless forms of your **i**,
Nu 33:52 carved images and their cast **i**,
Dt 7: 5 poles and burn their **i** in the fire.
12: 3 cut down the **i** of their gods and
29:17 images and **i** of wood and stone,
32:16 angered him with their detestable **i**
32:21 angered me with their worthless **i**.
Jdg 3:19 At the **i** near Gilgal he himself
3:26 He passed by the **i** and escaped
17: 5 he made an ephod and some **i** and
18:30 Danites set up for themselves the **i**,
18:31 They continued to use the **i** Micah
1Sa 12:21 Do not turn away after useless **i**.
31: 9 in the temple of their **i** and among
2Sa 5:21 The Philistines abandoned their **i**
1Ki 14: 9 other gods, **i** made of metal;
15:12 of all the **i** his fathers had made.
16:13 to anger by their worthless **i**.
16:26 to anger by their worthless **i**.
21:26 vilest manner by going after **i**,
2Ki 11:18 They smashed the altars and **i** to
17:12 They worshipped **i**, though the LORD
17:15 They followed worthless **i** and
17:16 two **i** cast in the shape of calves,
17:41 they were serving their **i**.
21:11 has led Judah into sin with his **i**.
21:21 the **i** his father had worshipped,
22:17 by all the **i** their hands have made,
23:24 the household gods, the **i** and all
1Ch 10: 9 news among their **i** and their people.
16:26 all the gods of the nations are **i**
2Ch 11:15 for the goat and calf **i** he had made.
15: 8 He removed the detestable **i** from the
23:17 They smashed the altars and **i** and
24:18 and worshipped Asherah poles and **i**.
28: 2 cast **i** for worshipping the Baals.
33:19 set up Asherah poles and **i** before
33:22 to all the **i** Manasseh had made.
34: 3 poles, carved **i** and cast images.
34: 4 Asherah poles, the **i** and the images.
34: 7 the Asherah poles and crushed the **i**
34:33 Josiah removed all the detestable **i**
Ps 31: 6 hate those who cling to worthless **i**
78:58 aroused his jealousy with their **i**.
96: 5 all the gods of the nations are **i**
97: 7 those who boast in **i**—worship him,
106:36 They worshipped their **i**, which
106:38 whom they sacrificed to the **i** of
115: 4 their **i** are silver and gold, made by
135:15 The **i** of the nations are silver and
Isa 2: 8 Their land is full of **i**; they bow
2:18 the **i** will totally disappear.
2:20 their **i** of silver and **i** of gold,
10:10 my hand seized the kingdoms of the **i**
10:11 I dealt with Samaria and her **i**?'
19: 1 The **i** of Egypt tremble before him,
19: 3 the **i** and the spirits of the dead,
30:22 you will defile your **i** overlaid with
Isa 31: 7 you will reject the **i** of silver
41:22 "Bring in your **i** to tell us what is
42: 8 glory to another or my praise to **i**.
42:17 those who trust in **i**, who say to
44: 9 All who make **i** are nothing, and the
45:16 All the makers of **i** will be put to
45:20 Ignorant are those who carry about **i**
46: 1 **i** are borne by beasts of burden.
48: 5 'My **i** did them; my wooden image and
48:14 Which of ⌊the **i**⌋ has foretold
57: 6 The **i** among the smooth stones of the
57:13 let your collection of **i** save you!
Jer 2: 5 followed worthless **i** and became
2: 8 by Baal, following worthless **i**.
2:11 their Glory for worthless **i**.
4: 1 "If you put your detestable **i** out
7:30 They have set up their detestable **i**
8:19 with their worthless foreign **i**?"
10: 5 their **i** cannot speak; they must be
10: 8 are taught by worthless wooden **i**.
10:14 every goldsmith is shamed by his **i**.
14:22 Do any of the worthless **i** of the
16:18 with their detestable **i**."
16:19 worthless **i** that did them no good.
18:15 they burn incense to worthless **i**,
32:34 They set up their abominable **i** in
50: 2 and her **i** filled with terror.'
50:38 a land of **i**, **i** that will go mad
51:17 every goldsmith is shamed by his **i**.
51:47 when I will punish the **i** of Babylon;
51:52 "when I will punish her **i**, and
Eze 5: 9 of all your detestable **i**, I will
6: 4 slay your people in front of your **i**
6: 5 the Israelites in front of their **i**,
6: 6 your **i** smashed and ruined, your
6: 9 which have lusted after their **i**.
6:13 among their **i** around their altars,
6:13 fragrant incense to all their **i**.
7:20 their detestable **i** and vile images
8:10 all the **i** of the house of Israel.
11:18 its vile images and detestable **i**.
11:21 their vile images and detestable **i**,
14: 3 Son of man, these men have set up **i**
14: 4 When any Israelite sets up **i** in his
14: 5 have all deserted me for their **i**.'
14: 6 Repent! Turn from your **i** and
14: 7 sets up **i** in his heart and puts a
16:17 and you made for yourself male **i** and
16:20 sacrificed them as food to the **i**.
16:21 and sacrificed them to the **i**.
16:36 because of all your detestable **i**,
18: 6 to the **i** of the house of Israel.
18:12 He looks to the **i**. He does
18:15 to the **i** of the house of Israel.
20: 7 yourselves with the **i** of Egypt.
20: 8 nor did they forsake the **i** of Egypt.
20:16 hearts were devoted to their **i**.
20:18 or defile yourselves with their **i**.
20:24 they had not obeyed my laws but had
20:31 with all your **i** to this day.
20:39 LORD says: Go and serve your **i**,
20:39 my holy name with your gifts and **i**.
21:21 he will consult his **i**, he will
22: 3 and defiles herself by making **i**,
22: 4 defiled by the **i** you have made.
23: 7 the **i** of everyone she lusted after.
23:30 and defiled yourself with their **i**.
23:37 They committed adultery with their **i**
23:39 their children to their **i**,
30:13 I will destroy the **i** and put an end
33:25 and look to your **i** and shed blood,
36:18 they had defiled it with their **i**.
36:25 your impurities and from all your **i**
37:23 defile themselves with their **i**
43: 7 the lifeless **i** of their kings at
43: 9 and the lifeless **i** of their kings,
44:10 who wandered from me after their **i**
44:12 them in the presence of their **i**
Hos 4:17 Ephraim is joined to **i**; leave him
5:11 in judgment, intent on pursuing **i**.
8: 4 gold they make **i** for themselves to
10: 6 will be ashamed of its wooden **i**.
13: 2 **i** for themselves from their silver,
14: 8 what more have I to do with **i**? I
Am 5:26 the pedestal of your **i**, the star of
Jnh 2: 8 "Those who cling to worthless **i**
Mic 1: 7 All her **i** will be broken to pieces;
Na 1:14 cast **i** that are in the temple of
Hab 2:18 he makes **i** that cannot speak.
Zec 10: 2 The **i** speak deceit, diviners see
13: 2 I will banish the names of the **i**
Ac 7:43 Rephan, the **i** you made to worship.
15:20 to abstain from food polluted by **i**,
15:29 abstain from food sacrificed to **i**,
17:16 to see that the city was full of **i**.
21:25 abstain from food sacrificed to **i**,
Ro 2:22 You who abhor **i**, do you rob temples?
1Co 8: 1 Now about food sacrificed to **i**: We
8: 4 about eating food sacrificed to **i**:
8: 7 people are still so accustomed to **i**
8:10 eat what has been sacrificed to **i**?
12: 2 influenced and led astray to mute **i**.
2Co 6:16 between the temple of God and **i**?
1Th 1: 9 **i** to serve the living and true God,
1Jn 5:21 Dear children, keep yourselves from **i**
Rev 2:14 sin by eating food sacrificed to **i**
2:20 the eating of food sacrificed to **i**.
9:20 and **i** of gold, silver, bronze, stone
9:20 **i** that cannot see or hear or walk.

Idumea

Mk 3: 8 Jerusalem, **I**, and the regions across

Iezer (Iezerite)

Nu 26:30 descendants of Gilead: through **I**,

Iezerite (Iezer)

Nu 26:30 through Iezer, the **I** clan;

Igal

Nu 13: 7 tribe of Issachar, **I** son of Joseph;
2Sa 23:36 **I** son of Nathan from Zobah, the son
1Ch 3:22 **I**, Bariah, Neariah and Shaphat—six

Igdaliah

Jer 35: 4 of Hanan son of **I** the man of God.

Ignoble

2Ti 2:20 for noble purposes and some for **i**.

Ignorance (Ignore)

Eze 45:20 sins unintentionally or through **i**;
Ac 3:17 you acted in **i**, as did your leaders.
17:30 In the past God overlooked such **i**,
Eph 4:18 because of the **i** that is in them
1Ti 1:13 because I acted in **i** and unbelief.
Heb 9: 7 sins the people had committed in **i**.
1Pe 1:14 desires you had when you lived in **i**

Ignorant (Ignore)

Ps 73:22 I was senseless and **i**; I was a brute
Pr 30: 2 "I am the most **i** of men; I do not
Isa 44: 9 they are **i**, to their own shame.
45:20 **I** are those who carry about idols of
Ro 11:25 I do not want you to be **i** of this
1Co 10: 1 For I do not want you to be **i** of the
12: 1 brothers, I do not want you to be **i**.
15:34 there are some who are **i** of God
1Th 4:13 Brothers, we do not want you to be **i**
Heb 5: 2 who are **i** and are going astray,
1Pe 2:15 silence the **i** talk of foolish men.
2Pe 3:16 which **i** and unstable people distort,

Ignore (Ignorance, Ignorant, Ignored, Ignores, Ignoring)

Dt 22: 1 do not **i** it but be sure to take it
22: 3 Do not **i** it.
22: 4 ox fallen on the road, do not **i** it.
Ps 9:12 does not **i** the cry of the afflicted.
55: 1 my prayer, O God, do not **i** my plea
74:23 Do not **i** the clamour of your
119:139 me out, for my enemies **i** your words.
Pr 8:33 and be wise; do not **i** it.
Hos 4: 6 God, I also will **i** your children.
Heb 2: 3 if we **i** such a great salvation?

Ignored (Ignore)

Ex 9:21 those who **i** the word of the LORD
Pr 1:25 since you **i** all my advice and would

Pr 2:17 **i** the covenant she made before God.
Hos 4: 6 you have **i** the law of your God,
1Co 14:38 ignores this, he himself will be **i**.

Ignores (Ignore)
Pr 10:17 **i** correction leads others astray.
13:18 He who **i** discipline comes to poverty
15:32 He who **i** discipline despises himself,
1Co 14:38 If he **i** this, he himself will be

Ignoring (Ignore)
Mk 5:36 **I** what they said, Jesus told the

Iim
Jos 15:29 Baalah, **I**, Ezem,

Ijon
1Ki 15:20 He conquered **I**, Dan, Abel Beth
2Ki 15:29 king of Assyria came and took **I**,
2Ch 16: 4 They conquered **I**, Dan, Abel Maim and

Ikkesh
2Sa 23:26 the Paltite, Ira son of **I** from Tekoa
1Ch 11:28 Ira son of **I** from Tekoa, Abiezer
27: 9 was Ira the son of **I** the Tekoite.

Ilai
1Ch 11:29 the Hushathite, **I** the Ahohite,

Ill (Illness, Illnesses, Ills)
Ge 48: 1 Joseph was told, "Your father is **i**.
Dt 15: 9 so that you do not show **i** will
1Sa 19:14 David, Michal said, "He is **i**.
30:13 me when I became **i** three days ago.
2Sa 12:15 had borne to David, and he became **i**.
13: 5 "Go to bed and pretend to be **i**,"
13: 6 Amnon lay down and pretended to be **i**.
1Ki 14: 1 Abijah son of Jeroboam became **i**,
14: 5 for he is **i**, and you are to give her
17:17 woman who owned the house became **i**.
2Ki 8: 7 and Ben-Hadad king of Aram was **i**.
20: 1 In those days Hezekiah became **i** and
2Ch 21:15 You yourself will be very **i** with a
32:24 In those days Hezekiah became **i** and
Ne 2: 2 face look so sad when you are not **i**?
Job 6: 7 to touch it; such food makes me **i**.
Ps 35:13 Yet when they were **i**, I put on
Isa 33:24 "I am **i**"; and the sins of those who
38: 1 In those days Hezekiah became **i** and
Da 8:27 I, Daniel, was exhausted and lay **i**
Mt 4:24 who were **i** with various diseases,
Ac 28: 5 the fire and suffered no **i** effects.
Php 2:26 because you heard he was **i**.
2:27 Indeed he was **i**, and almost died.

Illegal
Ex 22: 9 In all cases of **i** possession of an

Illegitimate
Hos 5: 7 they give birth to **i** children.
Jn 8:41 "We are not **i** children," they
Heb 12: 8 are **i** children and not true sons.

Ill-gotten
Pr 1:19 the end of all who go after **i** gain
10: 2 **I** treasures are of no value, but
28:16 hates **i** gain will enjoy a long life.
Mic 4:13 You will devote their **i** gains to
6:10 O wicked house, your **i** treasures and

Illicit
Eze 16:33 from everywhere for your **i** favours.

Illness (Ill)
2Sa 13: 2 became frustrated to the point of **i**
2Ki 8: 8 him, 'Will I recover from this **i**?'
8: 9 ask, 'Will I recover from this **i**?'
13:14 Now Elisha was suffering from the **i**
20:12 he had heard of Hezekiah's **i**.
2Ch 16:12 even in his **i** he did not seek help
Ps 41: 3 and restore him from his bed of **i**.
Isa 38: 9 of Judah after his **i** and recovery:
39: 1 he had heard of his **i** and recovery.
Gal 4:13 you know, it was because of an **i**
4:14 Even though my **i** was a trial to you,

Illnesses (Ill)
Dt 28:59 and severe and lingering **i**.
Ac 19:12 and their **i** were cured and the evil
1Ti 5:23 of your stomach and your frequent **i**.

Ills (Ill)
Ps 73: 5 they are not plagued by human **i**.

Ill-tempered (Temper)
Pr 21:19 than with a quarrelsome and **i** wife.

Ill-treat (Ill-treated, Ill-treating)
Ge 31:50 If you **i** my daughters or if you take
Ex 22:21 "Do not **i** an alien or oppress him,
Lev 19:33 with you in your land, do not **i** him.
1Sa 25: 7 we did not **i** them, and the whole
25:15 They did not **i** us, and the whole
Jer 38:19 me over to them and they will **i** me."
Eze 22:29 **i** the alien, denying them justice.
Lk 6:28 curse you, pray for those who **i** you.
Ac 14: 5 leaders, to **i** them and stone them.

Ill-treated (Ill-treat)
Ge 15:13 enslaved and **i** four hundred years.
16: 6 Sarai **i** Hagar; so she fled from her.
Nu 20:15 The Egyptians **i** us and our fathers,
Dt 26: 6 the Egyptians **i** us and made us
Jer 13:22 have been torn off and your body **i**.
Eze 22: 7 and **i** the fatherless and the widow.
Mt 22: 6 The rest seized his servants, **i** them
Ac 7: 6 and **i** for four hundred years.
7:24 He saw one of them being **i** by an
Heb 11:25 He chose to be **i** along with the
11:37 destitute, persecuted and **i**—
13: 3 and those who are **i** as if you

Ill-treating (Ill-treat)
Ac 7:27 "But the man who was **i** the other

Illuminated
Rev 18: 1 the earth was **i** by his splendour.

Illusions
Isa 30:10 Tell us pleasant things, prophesy **i**.

Illustration
Heb 9: 9 This is an **i** for the present time,

Illyricum
Ro 15:19 Jerusalem all the way round to **I**,

Image (*Image of God*, Images)
Ge 1:26 God said, "Let us make man in our **i**,
1:27 God created man in his own **i**, in the
5: 3 in his own **i**; and he named him Seth.
Lev 26: 1 "'Do not make idols or set up an **i**
Dt 4:16 an **i** of any shape, whether formed
27:15 "Cursed is the man who carves an **i**
Jdg 17: 3 to make a carved **i** and a cast idol.
17: 4 made them into the **i** and the idol.
18:14 other household gods, a carved **i** and
18:17 went inside and took the carved **i**,
18:18 Micah's house and took the carved **i**,
18:20 household gods and the carved **i**
2Ch 33: 7 He took the carved **i** he had made
33:15 the **i** from the temple of the LORD,
Ne 9:18 themselves an **i** of a calf and said,
Ps 106:20 They exchanged their Glory for an **i**
Isa 40:18 What **i** will you compare him to?
48: 5 my wooden **i** and metal god ordained
Jer 44:19 we were making cakes like her **i**
Da 3: 1 King Nebuchadnezzar made an **i** of
3: 2 dedication of the **i** he had set up.
3: 3 for the dedication of the **i** that
3: 5 worship the **i** of gold that King
3: 7 worshipped the **i** of gold that King
3:10 fall down and worship the **i** of gold,
3:12 the **i** of gold you have set up."
Da 3:14 worship the **i** of gold I have set up?
3:15 and worship the **i** I made, very good.
3:18 the **i** of gold you have set up."
Hab 2:18 Or an **i** that teaches lies?
Ac 17:29 **i** made by man's design and skill.
19:35 of her **i**, which fell from heaven?
1Co 11: 7 since he is the **i** and glory of God;
Col 1:15 He is the **i** of the invisible God,
3:10 knowledge in the **i** of its Creator.
Rev 13:14 He ordered them to set up an **i** in
13:15 breath to the **i** of the first beast,
13:15 to worship the **i** to be killed.
14: 9 his **i** and receives his mark on the
14:11 who worship the beast and his **i**,
15: 2 victorious over the beast and his **i**
16: 2 of the beast and worshipped his **i**.
19:20 of the beast and worshipped his **i**.
20: 4 not worshipped the beast or his **i**

Image of God
Ge 1:27 in the **i** he created him; male and
9: 6 shed; for in the **i** has God made man.
2Co 4: 4 the glory of Christ, who is the **i**.

Images (Image)
Nu 33:52 Destroy all their carved **i** and their
Dt 7:25 The **i** of their gods you are to burn
29:17 You saw among them their detestable **i**
2Ch 34: 3 poles, carved idols and cast **i**.
34: 4 Asherah poles, the idols and the **i**.
Ps 97: 7 All who worship **i** are put to shame,
Isa 10:10 kingdoms whose **i** excelled those of
10:11 her **i** as I dealt with Samaria and
21: 9 the **i** of its gods lie shattered
30:22 silver and your **i** covered with gold;
41:29 their **i** are but wind and confusion.
42:17 who say to **i**, 'You are our gods,'
46: 1 The **i** that are carried about are
Jer 8:19 provoked me to anger with their **i**,
10:14 His **i** are a fraud; they have no
16:18 the lifeless forms of their vile **i**
50: 2 Her **i** will be put to shame and her
51:17 His **i** are a fraud; they have no
Eze 5:11 vile **i** and detestable practices,
7:20 their detestable idols and vile **i**.
11:18 all its vile **i** and detestable idols.
11:21 their vile **i** and detestable idols,
20: 7 Each of you, get rid of the vile **i**
20: 8 vile **i** they had set their eyes on,
20:30 did and lust after their vile **i**?
30:13 and put an end to the **i** in Memphis.
37:23 defile themselves with their **i**
Da 4: 5 As I was lying in my bed, the **i** and
11: 8 their metal **i** and their valuable
Hos 11: 2 Baals and they burned incense to **i**.
13: 2 cleverly fashioned **i**, all of them
Mic 1: 7 I will destroy all her **i**.
5:13 I will destroy your carved **i** and
Na 1:14 I will destroy the carved **i** and
Ro 1:23 for **i** made to look like mortal man

Imagination (Imagine)
Eze 13: 2 who prophesy out of their own **i**:
13:17 who prophesy out of their own **i**.

Imaginations (Imagine)
Isa 65: 2 not good, pursuing their own **i**—
66:18 of their actions and their **i**,

Imagine (Imagination, Imaginations)
Ps 41: 7 they **i** the worst for me, saying,
Pr 18:11 they **i** it an unscalable wall.
23:33 and your mind **i** confusing things.
Eph 3:20 more than all we ask or **i**,

Imitate (Imitated, Imitators)
Dt 18: 9 do not learn to **i** the detestable
Eze 23:48 may take warning and not **i** you.
1Co 4:16 Therefore I urge you to **i** me.
Heb 6:12 but to **i** those who through faith
13: 7 their way of life and **i** their faith.
3Jn :11 Dear friend, do not **i** what is evil

Imitated (Imitate)
2Ki 17:15 They **i** the nations around them

Imitators (Imitate)
Eph 5: 1 Be **i** of God, therefore, as dearly
1Th 1: 6 You became **i** of us and of the Lord
2:14 became **i** of God's churches in Judea

Imlah
1Ki 22: 8 He is Micaiah son of **I**." "The king
22: 9 "Bring Micaiah son of **I** at once.
2Ch 18: 7 He is Micaiah son of **I**." "The king
18: 8 "Bring Micaiah son of **I** at once.

Immanuel
Isa 7:14 birth to a son, and will call him **I**.
8: 8 the breadth of your land, O **I**!"
Mt 1:23 him **I**"—which means, "God with us.

Immeasurably
Eph 3:20 Now to him who is able to do **i** more

Immediate (Immediately)
1Ti 5: 8 and especially for his **i** family,

Immediately (Immediate)
1Sa 28:20 **I** Saul fell full length on the
2Sa 15:14 We must leave **i**, or he will move
17:16 Now send a message **i** and tell David,
Ezr 4:23 they went **i** to the Jews in Jerusalem
Ne 5:11 Give back to them **i** their fields,
Est 2: 9 **I** he provided her with her beauty
Da 3: 6 **i** be thrown into a blazing furnace.
3:15 be thrown **i** into a blazing furnace.
4:33 **I** what had been said about
Mt 4:22 **i** they left the boat and their
8: 3 "Be clean!" **I** he was cured of his
14:22 **I** Jesus made the disciples get into
14:27 Jesus **i** said to them: "Take courage!
14:31 **I** Jesus reached out his hand and
20:34 **I** they received their sight and
21:19 fruit again!" **I** the tree withered.
24:29 "**I** after the distress of those
26:74 know the man!" **I** a cock crowed.
27:48 **I** one of them ran and got a sponge.
Mk 1:42 **I** the leprosy left him and he was
2: 8 **I** Jesus knew in his spirit that this
5:29 **I** her bleeding stopped and she felt
5:42 **I** the girl stood up and walked
6:27 he **i** sent an executioner with orders
6:45 **I** Jesus made his disciples get into
6:50 **I** he spoke to them and said, "Take
9:20 **i** threw the boy into a convulsion
9:24 **I** the boy's father exclaimed, "I do
10:52 **I** he received his sight and
14:72 **I** the cock crowed the second time.
Lk 1:64 **I** his mouth was opened and his
5:13 "Be clean!" And **i** the leprosy left
5:25 **I** he stood up in front of them, took
8:44 cloak, and **i** her bleeding stopped.
12:36 they can **i** open the door for him.
12:54 **i** you say, 'It's going to rain,'
13:13 **i** she straightened up and praised
14: 5 day, will you not **i** pull him out?"
18:43 **I** he received his sight and followed
19: 5 to him, "Zacchaeus, come down **i**.
20:19 looked for a way to arrest him **i**,
Jn 6:21 and **i** the boat reached the shore
Ac 9:18 **I**, something like scales fell from
9:34 up your mat." **I** Aeneas got up.
10:16 **i** the sheet was taken back to
10:33 I sent for you **i**, and it was good of
12:23 **I**, because Herod did not give praise
13:11 **I** mist and darkness came over him,
16:33 then **i** he and all his family were
17:14 The brothers **i** sent Paul to the
21:30 temple, and **i** the gates were shut.
22:18 'Leave Jerusalem **i**, because they
22:29 about to question him withdrew **i**.
Gal 1:17 but I went **i** into Arabia and later
Jas 1:24 **i** forgets what he looks like.

Immense
Eze 1: 4 **i** cloud with flashing lightning

Immer
1Ch 9:12 son of Meshillemith, the son of **I**.
24:14 to Bilgah, the sixteenth to **I**,
Ezr 2:37 of **I** 1,052
2:59 Tel Harsha, Kerub, Addon and **I**,
10:20 From the descendants of **I**: Hanani
Ne 3:29 Next to them, Zadok son of **I** made
7:40 of **I** 1,052
7:61 Tel Harsha, Kerub, Addon and **I**,
11:13 son of Meshillemoth, the son of **I**,
Jer 20: 1 the priest Pashhur son of **I**, the

Immoral (Immorality)
Pr 6:24 keeping you from the **i** woman, from
1Co 5: 9 associate with sexually **i** people—
5:10 the people of this world who are **i**,
5:11 brother but is sexually **i** or greedy,
6: 9 Neither the sexually **i** nor idolaters
Eph 5: 5 No **i**, impure or greedy person—
Heb 12:16 See that no-one is sexually **i**, or is
13: 4 adulterer and all the sexually **i**.
Rev 21: 8 the murderers, the sexually **i**, those
22:15 the sexually **i**, the murderers, the

Immorality (Immoral)
Nu 25: 1 in sexual **i** with Moabite women,
Jer 3: 9 Israel's **i** mattered so little to her,
Mt 15:19 **i**, theft, false testimony, slander.
Mk 7:21 sexual **i**, theft, murder, adultery,
Ac 15:20 from sexual **i**, from the meat of
15:29 strangled animals and from sexual **i**.
21:25 animals and from sexual **i**."
Ro 13:13 not in sexual **i** and debauchery, not
1Co 5: 1 that there is sexual **i** among you,
6:13 The body is not meant for sexual **i**,
6:18 Flee from sexual **i**. All other sins
7: 2 since there is so much **i**, each man
10: 8 We should not commit sexual **i**, as
Gal 5:19 sexual **i**, impurity and debauchery;
Eph 5: 3 must not be even a hint of sexual **i**
Col 3: 5 to your earthly nature: sexual **i**,
1Th 4: 3 that you should avoid sexual **i**;
Jude : 4 of our God into a licence for **i**
: 7 up to sexual **i** and perversion.
Rev 2:14 to idols and by committing sexual **i**
2:20 misleads my servants into sexual **i**
2:21 of her **i**, but she is unwilling.
9:21 their sexual **i** or their thefts.

Immortal (Immortality)
Ro 1:23 exchanged the glory of the **i** God
1Ti 1:17 Now to the King eternal, **i**,
6:16 who alone is **i** and who lives in

Immortality (Immortal)
Pr 12:28 there is life; along that path is **i**.
Ro 2: 7 seek glory, honour and **i**, he will
1Co 15:53 imperishable, and the mortal with **i**.
15:54 and the mortal with **i**, then the
2Ti 1:10 and **i** to light through the gospel.

Immovable
Job 41:23 tightly joined; they are firm and **i**.
Zec 12: 3 an **i** rock for all the nations.

Imna
1Ch 7:35 Helem: Zophah, **I**, Shelesh and Amal.

Imnah (Imnite)
Ge 46:17 The sons of Asher: **I**, Ishvah, Ishvi
Nu 26:44 Asher by their clans were: through **I**,
1Ch 7:30 The sons of Asher: **I**, Ishvah, Ishvi
2Ch 31:14 Kore son of **I** the Levite, keeper of

Imnite (Imnah)
Nu 26:44 through Imnah, the **I** clan;

Impaled
Ezr 6:11 he is to be lifted up and **i** on it.

Impart (Imparted, Imparts)
Ro 1:11 I long to see you so that I may **i**
Gal 3:21 had been given that could **i** life,

Imparted (Impart)
Ecc 12: 9 also he **i** knowledge to the people.

Impartial (Impartially)
Jas 3:17 mercy and good fruit, **i** and sincere.

Impartially (Impartial)
1Ch 24: 5 They divided them **i** by drawing lots,
1Pe 1:17 Father who judges each man's work **i**,

Imparts (Impart)
Pr 29:15 The rod of correction **i** wisdom, but

Impatient
Nu 21: 4 But the people grew **i** on the way;
Job 4: 2 a word with you, will you be **i**?
21: 4 to man? Why should I not be **i**?

Imperfect
1Co 13:10 perfection comes, the **i** disappears

Imperial (Empire)
2Ki 25: 8 Nebuzaradan commander of the **i** guard
25:10 under the commander of the **i** guard,
25:15 The commander of the **i** guard took
Jer 39: 9 Nebuzaradan commander of the **i** guard
39:11 Nebuzaradan commander of the **i** guard
40: 1 Nebuzaradan commander of the **i** guard
41:10 Nebuzaradan commander of the **i** guard
43: 6 Nebuzaradan commander of the **i** guard
52:12 Nebuzaradan commander of the **i** guard
52:14 under the commander of the **i** guard
52:19 The commander of the **i** guard took
52:30 the commander of the **i** guard.
Ac 27: 1 who belonged to the **I** Regiment.

Imperishable
1Co 15:42 sown is perishable, it is raised **i**;
15:50 does the perishable inherit the **i**.
15:52 be raised **i**, and we will be changed.
15:53 must clothe itself with the **i**,
15:54 has been clothed with the **i**,
1Pe 1:23 not of perishable seed, but of **i**,

Impetuous
Job 6: 3 no wonder my words have been **i**.
Hab 1: 6 that ruthless and **i** people, who

Implanted
Ps 94: 9 Does he who **i** the ear not hear?

Implore
Mal 1: 9 "Now **i** God to be gracious to us.
2Co 5:20 We **i** you on Christ's behalf: Be

Importance (Important)
1Co 15: 3 I passed on to you as of first **i**:

Important (Importance)
Jos 10: 2 because Gibeon was an **i** city, like
1Ki 3: 4 for that was the most **i** high place,
2Ki 25: 9 Every **i** building he burned down.
Jer 52:13 Every **i** building he burned down.
Jnh 3: 3 Nineveh was a very **i** city
Mt 6:25 Is not life more **i** than food, and
6:25 and the body more **i** than clothes?
23: 6 the most **i** seats in the synagogues;
23:23 But you have neglected the more **i**
Mk 12:28 commandments, which is the most **i**?
12:29 "The most **i** one," answered Jesus,
12:33 is more **i** than all burnt offerings
12:39 have the most **i** seats in the
Lk 11:43 because you love the most **i** seats
14: 9 will have to take the least **i** place
20:46 have the most **i** seats in the
Ac 8:27 an **i** official in charge of all the
Gal 2: 6 As for those who seemed to be **i**
Php 1:18 The **i** thing is that in every way,

Imported
1Ki 10:12 been **i** or seen since that day.)
10:28 Solomon's horses were **i** from Egypt
10:29 They **i** a chariot from Egypt for
2Ch 1:16 Solomon's horses were **i** from Egypt
1:17 They **i** a chariot from Egypt for
9:28 Solomon's horses were **i** from Egypt
Isa 17:10 the finest plants and plant **i** vines,

Impose (Imposed, Imposing, Self-imposed)
Ezr 7:24 you have no authority to **i** taxes,
Rev 2:24 will not **i** any other burden on you)

Imposed (Impose)
2Ki 23:33 and he **i** on Judah a levy of a
2Ch 24: 6 Jerusalem the tax **i** by Moses the
36: 3 **i** on Judah a levy of a hundred
Est 10: 1 King Xerxes **i** tribute throughout the
Jer 19: 9 siege **i** on them by the enemies who

Imposing (Impose)
Jos 22:10 an **i** altar there by the Jordan.
1Ki 9: 8 though this temple is now **i**, all who
2Ch 7:21 though this temple is now so **i**, all
Da 7:20 that looked more **i** than the others

Impossible
Ge 11: 6 they plan to do will be **i** for them.
Jdg 6: 5 It was **i** to count the men and their
2Sa 13: 2 **i** for him to do anything to her.
Mt 17:20 Nothing will be **i** for you."
19:26 "With man this is **i**, but with God
Mk 10:27 "With man this is **i**, but not with
Lk 1:37 For nothing is **i** with God."
18:27 Jesus replied, "What is **i** with men
Ac 2:24 **i** for death to keep its hold on him.
Heb 6: 4 It is **i** for those who have once
6:18 in which it is **i** for God to lie,
10: 4 it is **i** for the blood of bulls and
11: 6 without faith it is **i** to please God,

Impostors
2Co 6: 8 report; genuine, yet regarded as **i**;
2Ti 3:13 while evil men and **i** will go from

Impoverished (Poor)
Jdg 6: 6 Midian so **i** the Israelites that they

Impress (Impressed, Impresses, Impression, Impressive)
Dt 6: 7 **I** them on your children. Talk about

Impressed (Impress)
Ecc 9:13 example of wisdom that greatly **i** me:

Impresses (Impress)
Pr 17:10 A rebuke **i** a man of discernment more

Impression (Impress)
Gal 6:12 Those who want to make a good **i**

Impressive (Impress)
1Sa 9: 2 a son named Saul, an **i** young man

Imprison (Imprisoned, Imprisonment, Imprisonments, Imprisons)
Ac 22:19 **i** and beat those who believe in you.

Imprisoned (Imprison)
Ge 41:10 and he **i** me and the chief baker in
1Sa 23: 7 for David has **i** himself by entering
Jer 32: 3 Now Zedekiah king of Judah had **i** him
37:15 had him beaten and **i** in the house of

Imprisonment (Imprison)
Ezr 7:26 confiscation of property, or **i**.
Ac 23:29 him that deserved death or **i**.
26:31 anything that deserves death or **i**."

Imprisonments (Imprison)
2Co 6: 5 in beatings, **i** and riots; in hard

Imprisons (Imprison)
Job 12:14 the man he **i** cannot be released.

Improper
Eph 5: 3 these are **i** for God's holy people.

Improvise
Am 6: 5 David and **i** on musical instruments.

Impure (Impurities, Impurity)
Lev 7:18 for it is **i**; the person who eats any
19: 7 it is **i** and will not be accepted.
Nu 5:14 he suspects his wife and she is **i**
5:14 her even though she is not **i**—
5:19 **i** while married to your husband,
Dt 23: 9 keep away from everything **i**.
Job 14: 4 can bring what is pure from the **i**
Ac 10:14 never eaten anything **i** or unclean."
10:15 anything **i** that God has made clean.
10:28 not call any man **i** or unclean.
11: 8 'Surely not, Lord! Nothing **i** or
11: 9 anything **i** that God has made clean.
Eph 5: 5 **i** or greedy person—such a man is
1Th 2: 3 not spring from error or **i** motives,
4: 7 For God did not call us to be **i**, but
Rev 21:27 Nothing **i** will ever enter it, nor

Impurities (Impure)
Isa 1:25 your dross and remove all your **i**.
Eze 24:11 its copper glows so its **i** may be
36:25 all your **i** and from all your idols.

Impurity (Impure)
Lev 15:19 the **i** of her monthly period will
20:21 **i**; he has dishonoured his brother.
Nu 5:13 her **i** is undetected (since there is
5:28 defiled herself and is free from **i**,
Ezr 9:11 their **i** from one end to the other.
Eze 24:13 "'Now your **i** is lewdness. Because
24:13 would not be cleansed from your **i**,
Zec 13: 1 to cleanse them from sin and **i**.
13: 2 and the spirit of **i** from the land.
Ro 1:24 to sexual **i** for the degrading of
6:19 parts of your body in slavery to **i**
2Co 12:21 and have not repented of the **i**,
Gal 5:19 sexual immorality, **i** and debauchery
Eph 4:19 to indulge in every kind of **i**,
5: 3 or of any kind of **i**, or of greed,
Col 3: 5 **i**, lust, evil desires and greed,

Imrah
1Ch 7:36 Suah, Harnepher, Shual, Beri, **I**,

Imri
1Ch 9: 4 the son of Omri, the son of **I**, the
Ne 3: 2 Zaccur son of **I** built next to them.

In Christ
Ac 24:24; Ro 6:11, 23; 8:1, 39; 9:1; 12:5; 15:17; 16:3, 7, 9, 10; 1Co 1:2, 4, 30; 3:1; 4:10, 15, 17; 15:18, 19, 22, 31; 16:24; 2Co 1:20, 21; 2:14, 17; 3:14; 5:17, 19; 12:2, 19; Gal 1:22; 2:4, 16, 17; 3:26, 28; 5:6; Eph 1:1, 3, 9, 12, 13, 20; 2:6, 7, 10, 13; 3:6, 11, 21; 4:32; Php 1:1, 26; 3:3, 9, 14; 4:7, 19, 21; Col 1:2, 4, 28; 2:5, 9, 10, 17; 1Th 2:14; 4:16; 5:18; 1Ti 1:14; 3:13; 2Ti 1:1, 9, 13; 2:1, 10; 3:12, 15; Phm 6, 8, 20, 23; Heb 3:14; 1Pe 3:16; 5:10, 14

In peace
Ge 15:15; 26:29, 31; 44:17; Jdg 18:6; 1Sa 1:17; 16:4, 5; 20:42; 25:35; 29:7; 2Sa 3:21, 22, 23; 15:9, 27; 1Ki 2:6; 22:17; 2Ki 5:19; 9:17, 18, 19, 22, 31; 22:20; 1Ch 12:17; 2Ch 18:16; 34:28; Job 3:13; 21:13; Ps 4:8; Isa 55:12; Zec 1:11; Mal 2:6; Mk 5:34; Lk 2:29; 7:50; 8:48; Ac 16:36; 1Co 7:15; 16:11; 2Co1 3:11; 1Th 5:13; Heb 12:14; Jas 3:18

Incapable
Hos 8: 5 How long will they be **i** of purity?

Incense (*Altar of incense*, Frankincense)
Ex 25: 6 oil and for the fragrant **i**;
30: 1 altar of acacia wood for burning **i**.
30: 7 "Aaron must burn fragrant **i** on the
30: 8 He must burn **i** again when he lights
30: 8 **i** will burn regularly before the
30: 9 not offer on this altar any other **i**
30:35 make a fragrant blend of **i**, the work
30:37 Do not make any **i** with this formula
31:11 the anointing oil and fragrant **i** for
35: 8 oil and for the fragrant **i**;
35:15 anointing oil and the fragrant **i**;
35:28 oil and for the fragrant **i**.
37:29 fragrant **i**—the work of a perfumer.
39:38 the anointing oil, the fragrant **i**,
40:27 burned fragrant **i** on it, as the LORD
Lev 2: 1 is to pour oil on it, put **i** on it
2: 2 together with all the **i**, and burn
2:15 Put oil and **i** on it; it is a grain
2:16 together with all the **i**, as an
4: 7 horns of the altar of fragrant **i**
5:11 He must not put oil or **i** on it,
6:15 together with all the **i** on the grain
10: 1 put fire in them and added **i**; and
16:12 finely ground fragrant **i** and take
16:13 He is to put the **i** on the fire
16:13 and the smoke of the **i** will conceal
24: 7 Along each row put some pure **i** as a
26:30 cut down your **i** altars and pile your
Nu 4:16 the fragrant **i**, the regular grain
5:15 He must not pour oil on it or put **i**
7:14 weighing ten shekels, filled with **i**
7:20 weighing ten shekels, filled with **i**
7:26 weighing ten shekels, filled with **i**
7:32 weighing ten shekels, filled with **i**
7:38 weighing ten shekels, filled with **i**
7:44 weighing ten shekels, filled with **i**
7:50 weighing ten shekels, filled with **i**
7:56 weighing ten shekels, filled with **i**
7:62 weighing ten shekels, filled with **i**
7:68 weighing ten shekels, filled with **i**
7:74 weighing ten shekels, filled with **i**
7:80 weighing ten shekels, filled with **i**
7:86 twelve gold dishes filled with **i**
16: 7 tomorrow put fire and **i** in them
16:17 put **i** in it—250 censers in all—
16:18 put fire and **i** in it, and stood
16:35 the 250 men who were offering the **i**.
16:40 come to burn **i** before the LORD,
16:46 "Take your censer and put **i** in it,
16:47 offered the **i** and made atonement
Dt 33:10 He offers **i** before you and whole
1Sa 2:28 to go up to my altar, to burn **i**,
1Ki 3: 3 and burned **i** on the high places.
9:25 burning **i** before the LORD along with
11: 8 who burned **i** and offered sacrifices
22:43 offer sacrifices and burn **i** there.
2Ki 12: 3 offer sacrifices and burn **i** there.
14: 4 offer sacrifices and burn **i** there.
15: 4 offer sacrifices and burn **i** there.
15:35 offer sacrifices and burn **i** there.
16: 4 He offered sacrifices and burned **i**
17:11 At every high place they burned **i**,
18: 4 Israelites had been burning **i** to it.
22:17 they have forsaken me and burned **i**
23: 5 to burn **i** on the high places of the
23: 5 who burned **i** to Baal,
23: 8 where the priests had burned **i**.
1Ch 9:29 and wine, and the oil, **i** and spices.
2Ch 2: 4 for burning fragrant **i** before him,
13:11 and fragrant **i** to the LORD.
14: 5 He removed the high places and **i**
26:16 LORD to burn **i** on the altar of **i**.
26:18 you, Uzziah, to burn **i** to the LORD.
26:18 who have been consecrated to burn **i**.
26:19 in his hand ready to burn **i**,
26:19 the **i** altar in the LORD's temple,
28: 4 He offered sacrifices and burned **i**
29: 7 They did not burn **i** or present any
29:11 minister before him and to burn **i**."
30:14 cleared away the **i** altars and threw
34: 4 he cut to pieces the **i** altars that
34: 7 cut to pieces all the **i** altars
34:25 they have forsaken me and burned **i**

Ne 13: 5 offerings and **i** and temple articles,
13: 9 with the grain offerings and the **i**.
Ps 141: 2 my prayer be set before you like **i**;
Pr 27: 9 Perfume and **i** bring joy to the heart,
SS 3: 6 perfumed with myrrh and **i** made from
4: 6 of myrrh and to the hill of **i**.
4:14 with every kind of **i** tree, with
Isa 1:13 Your **i** is detestable to me.
17: 8 **i** altars their fingers have made.
27: 9 or **i** altars will be left standing.
43:23 nor wearied you with demands for **i**.
60: 6 bearing gold and **i** and proclaiming
65: 3 and burning **i** on altars of brick;
66: 3 whoever burns memorial **i**, like one
Jer 1:16 in burning **i** to other gods and in
6:20 What do I care about **i** from Sheba or
7: 9 commit adultery and perjury, burn **i**
11:12 out to the gods to whom they burn **i**,
11:13 the altars you have set up to burn **i**
11:17 me to anger by burning **i** to Baal.
17:26 grain offerings, **i** and
18:15 they burn **i** to worthless idols,
19:13 all the houses where they burned **i**
32:29 by burning **i** on the roofs to Baal
41: 5 **i** with them to the house of the LORD.
44: 3 provoked me to anger by burning **i**
44: 5 or stop burning **i** to other gods.
44: 8 burning **i** to other gods in Egypt,
44:15 wives were burning **i** to other gods,
44:17 We will burn **i** to the Queen of
44:18 ever since we stopped burning **i** to
44:19 The women added, "When we burned **i**
44:21 think about the **i** burned in the
44:23 you have burned **i** and have sinned
44:25 out the vows we made to burn **i**
48:35 **i** to their gods," declares the LORD.
Eze 6: 4 and your **i** altars will be smashed;
6: 6 your **i** altars broken down, and what
6:13 fragrant **i** to all their idols.
8:11 a fragrant cloud of **i** was rising.
16:18 offered my oil and **i** before them.
16:19 offered as fragrant **i** before them.
20:28 presented their fragrant **i** and
20:41 I will accept you as fragrant **i** when
23:41 the **i** and oil that belonged to me.
Da 2:46 offering and **i** be presented to him.
Hos 2:13 the days she burned **i** to the Baals;
11: 2 Baals and they burned **i** to images.
Hab 1:16 his net and burns **i** to his drag-net,
Mal 1:11 In every place **i** and pure offerings
Mt 2:11 gifts of gold and of **i** and of myrrh.
Lk 1: 9 the temple of the Lord and burn **i**.
1:10 the time for the burning of **i** came,
Rev 5: 8 were holding golden bowls full of **i**,
8: 3 He was given much **i** to offer, with
8: 4 The smoke of the **i**, together with
18:13 cargoes of cinnamon and spice, of **i**,

Incensed

Ne 4: 1 he became angry and was greatly **i**.

Inches

Ge 6:16 the ark to within 18 **i** of the top.

Incident

1Ki 21: 1 Some time later there was an **i**

Incited (Inciting)

1Sa 22: 8 **i** my servant to lie in wait for me,
26:19 If the LORD has **i** you against me,
2Sa 24: 1 and he **i** David against them, saying,
1Ch 21: 1 Satan rose up against Israel and **i**
Job 2: 3 you **i** me against him to ruin him
Ac 13:50 the Jews **i** the God-fearing women of

Inciting (Incited)

Jer 43: 3 Baruch son of Neriah is **i** you
Lk 23:14 who was **i** the people to rebellion.

Inclination (Inclinations, Inclined, Inclines)

Ge 6: 5 and that every **i** of the thoughts of
8:21 even though every **i** of his heart is

Inclinations (Inclination)

Jer 7:24 the stubborn **i** of their evil hearts.

Inclined (Inclination)

Dt 5:29 their hearts would be **i** to fear me
Jdg 9: 3 they were **i** to follow Abimelech, for
1Sa 20:13 if my father is **i** to harm you, may

Inclines (Inclination)

Ecc 10: 2 The heart of the wise **i** to the right,

Income

2Ki 8: 6 including all the **i** from her land
Pr 10:16 but the **i** of the wicked brings them
15: 6 **i** of the wicked brings them trouble.
Ecc 5:10 is never satisfied with his **i**.
Ac 19:25 receive a good **i** from this business.
1Co 16: 2 sum of money in keeping with his **i**,

Incomparable

Eph 2: 7 show the **i** riches of his grace,

Incomprehensible

Isa 33:19 with their strange, **i** tongue.

Increase (Ever-increasing, Increased, Increases, Increasing)

Ge 1:22 "Be fruitful and **i** in number and
1:22 and let the birds **i** on the earth."
1:28 "Be fruitful and **i** in number; fill
3:16 "I will greatly **i** your pains in
6: 1 men began to **i** in number on the
8:17 fruitful and **i** in number upon it."
9: 1 and **i** in number and fill the earth.
9: 7 for you, be fruitful and **i** in number;
9: 7 on the earth and **i** upon it."
16:10 "I will so **i** your descendants
17: 2 and will greatly **i** your numbers."
17:20 and will greatly **i** his numbers.
24:60 "Our sister, may you **i** to thousands
26:24 I will bless you and will **i** the
28: 3 make you fruitful and **i** your numbers
35:11 be fruitful and **i** in number.
48: 4 fruitful and will **i** your numbers.
48:16 may they **i** greatly upon the earth."
Lev 25:16 are many, you are to **i** the price
26: 9 you fruitful and **i** your numbers,
Dt 1:11 **i** you a thousand times and bless you
6: 3 that you may **i** greatly in a land
7:13 and bless you and **i** your numbers
8: 1 so that you may live and **i** and may
8:13 **i** and all you have is multiplied,
13:17 **i** your numbers, as he promised on
28:63 to make you prosper and **i** in number,
30:16 and laws; then you will live and **i**,
Job 10:17 me and **i** your anger towards me;
Ps 16: 4 The sorrows of those will **i** who run
61: 6 **I** the days of the king's life, his
62:10 **i**, do not set your heart on them.
71:21 You will **i** my honour and comfort me
73:12 always carefree, they **i** in wealth.
115:14 May the LORD make you **i**, both you
144:13 Our sheep will **i** by thousands, by
Pr 22:16 He who oppresses the poor to **i** his
Ecc 5: 9 The **i** from the land is taken by all;
5:11 goods **i**, so do those who consume
Isa 9: 7 Of the **i** of his government and peace
Jer 23: 3 will be fruitful and **i** in number.
29: 6 **I** in number there; do not decrease.
Eze 36:11 I will **i** the number of men and
36:30 I will **i** the fruit of the trees and
37:26 I will establish them and **i** their
Da 12: 4 go here and there to **i** knowledge."
Hos 4:10 engage in prostitution but not **i**,
Mt 24:12 of the **i** of wickedness, the love
Lk 17: 5 said to the Lord, "**I** our faith!"
Ac 12:24 the word of God continued to **i** and
Ro 5:20 added so that the trespass might **i**.
6: 1 go on sinning, so that grace may **i**?
2Co 9:10 **i** your store of seed and will
1Th 3:12 May the Lord make your love **i** and

Increased (Increase)

Ge 7:17 and as the waters **i** they lifted the
7:18 The waters rose and **i** greatly on the
30:30 you had before I came has **i** greatly,
47:27 fruitful and **i** greatly in number.
Ex 1:20 **i** and became even more numerous.
23:30 until you have **i** enough to take
Lev 19:25 In this way your harvest will be **i**.
Dt 1:10 The LORD your God has **i** your numbers
Jdg 1:35 the power of the house of Joseph **i**,
1Sa 14:19 the Philistine camp **i** more and more.
1Ch 4:38 Their families **i** greatly,
5: 9 their livestock had **i** in Gilead.
2Ch 33:23 before the LORD; Amon **i** his guilt.
Ps 25:19 See how my enemies have **i** and how
39: 2 saying anything good, my anguish **i**.
107:38 and their numbers greatly **i**, and he
107:41 and **i** their families like flocks.
Ecc 1:16 "Look, I have grown and **i** in wisdom
Isa 9: 3 enlarged the nation and **i** their joy
57: 9 with olive oil and **i** your perfumes.
Jer 3:16 numbers have **i** greatly in the land,"
Eze 16:29 you **i** your promiscuity to include
28: 5 in trading you have **i** your wealth,
31: 5 boughs **i** and its branches grew long,
Hos 4: 7 The more the priests **i**, the more
10: 1 As his fruit **i**, he built more altars
Na 3:16 You have **i** the number of your
Lk 11:29 the crowds **i**, Jesus said, "This is
Ac 6: 7 of disciples in Jerusalem **i** rapidly,
7:17 of our people in Egypt greatly **i**.
Ro 5:20 where sin **i**, grace **i** all the more,

Increases (Increase)

Ps 49:16 when the splendour of his house **i**;
Pr 24: 5 and a man of knowledge **i** strength;
28: 8 He who **i** his wealth by exorbitant
Isa 40:29 and **i** the power of the weak
Ro 3: 7 truthfulness and so **i** his glory,

Increasing (Increase)

2Sa 15:12 and Absalom's following kept on **i**.
Job 21: 7 live on, growing old and **i** in power
Eze 16:25 offering your body with **i**
16:26 me to anger with your **i** promiscuity
Ac 6: 1 when the number of disciples was **i**,
2Th 1: 3 one of you has for each other is **i**.
2Pe 1: 8 these qualities in **i** measure,

Incredible

Ac 26: 8 Why should any of you consider it **i**

Incur (Incurs)

Ex 28:43 that they will not **i** guilt and die.

Incurable

2Ch 21:18 with an **i** disease of the bowels.
Job 34: 6 his arrow inflicts an **i** wound.'
Isa 17:11 in the day of disease and **i** pain.
Jer 10:19 My wound is **i**! Yet I said to myself,
15:18 and my wound grievous and **i**?
30:12 is **i**, your injury beyond healing.
Mic 1: 9 For her wound is **i**; it has come to

Incurs (Incur)

Pr 9: 7 rebukes a wicked man **i** abuse.
14:35 but a shameful servant **i** his wrath.

Indecent

Dt 23:14 will not see among you anything **i**
24: 1 he finds something **i** about her,
Ro 1:27 Men committed **i** acts with other men,

Indecisive

2Ch 13: 7 he was young and **i** and not strong

Independent

1Co 11:11 not **i** of man, nor is man **i** of woman.

Indescribable

2Co 9:15 Thanks be to God for his **i** gift!

Indestructible
Heb 7:16 the basis of the power of an **i** life

India
Est 1: 1 provinces stretching from **I** to Cush
8: 9 provinces stretching from **I** to Cush

Indicate (Indicated, Indicating)
1Sa 16: 3 are to anoint for me the one I **i**."
Jn 21:19 Jesus said this to **i** the kind of
Heb 12:27 The words "once more" **i** the removing

Indicated (Indicate)
Nu 1:18 The people **i** their ancestry by their
2Ki 6:10 on the place **i** by the man of God.

Indicating (Indicate)
Jn 18:32 the words Jesus had spoken **i** the
Heb 9: 9 **i** that the gifts and sacrifices

Indictment
Job 31:35 let my accuser put his **i** in writing.

Indignant (Indignation)
Mt 20:24 the ten heard about this, they were **i**
21:15 to the Son of David," they were **i**.
26: 8 the disciples saw this, they were **i**.
Mk 10:14 Jesus saw this, he was **i**. He said to
10:41 they became **i** with James and John.
Lk 13:14 **I** because Jesus had healed on the

Indignation (Indignant)
Ps 78:49 hot anger, his wrath, **i** and hostility
90: 7 your anger and terrified by your **i**.
119:53 **I** grips me because of the wicked,
Jer 15:17 on me and you had filled me with **i**.
Na 1: 6 Who can withstand his **i**? Who can
2Co 7:11 what **i**, what alarm, what longing,

Indispensable
1Co 12:22 body that seem to be weaker are **i**,

Indulge (Indulged, Indulgence, Indulging, Self-indulgence)
Ex 32: 6 drink and got up to **i** in revelry.
Nu 25: 1 the men began to **i** in sexual
Lk 7:25 and **i** in luxury are in palaces.
1Co 10: 7 and got up to **i** in pagan revelry."
Gal 5:13 But do not use your freedom to **i** the
Eph 4:19 so as to **i** in every kind of impurity
2Ti 2:16 because those who **i** in it will

Indulged (Indulge)
2Co 12:21 and debauchery in which they have **i**

Indulgence (Indulge)
Col 2:23 any value in restraining sensual **i**

Indulging (Indulge)
1Ti 3: 8 sincere, not **i** in much wine, and not

Ineffective
2Pe 1: 8 they will keep you from being **i** and

Inexperienced
1Ch 22: 5 "My son Solomon is young and **i**, and
29: 1 whom God has chosen, is young and **i**.

Inexpressible
2Co 12: 4 He heard **i** things, things that men
1Pe 1: 8 filled with an **i** and glorious joy,

Infamous (Infamy)
Eze 22: 5 mock you, O **i** city, full of turmoil.

Infamy (Infamous)
Isa 44:11 be brought down to terror and **i**.

Infancy (Infant)
2Ti 3:15 how from **i** you have known the holy

Infant (Infancy, Infant's, Infants)
Nu 11:12 as a nurse carries an **i**, to the land
12:12 Do not let her be like a stillborn **i**
Job 3:16 an **i** who never saw the light of day?
24: 9 **i** of the poor is seized for a debt.
Isa 11: 8 The **i** will play near the hole of the
65:20 "Never again will there be in it an **i**
Heb 5:13 being still an **i**, is not acquainted

Infant's (Infant)
Lam 4: 4 of thirst the **i** tongue sticks to the

Infants (Infant)
Dt 32:25 will perish, **i** and grey-haired men.
1Sa 15: 3 children and **i**, cattle and sheep,
22:19 its children and **i**, and its cattle,
Ps 8: 2 From the lips of children and **i** you
137: 9 he who seizes your **i** and dashes them
Isa 13:16 Their **i** will be dashed to pieces
13:18 they will have no mercy on **i** nor
Jer 44: 7 the children and **i**, and so leave
Lam 2:11 **i** faint in the streets of the city.
Na 3:10 Her **i** were dashed to pieces at the
Mt 21:16 and **i** you have ordained praise'?"
Ro 2:20 a teacher of **i**, because you have in
1Co 3: 1 but as worldly—mere **i** in Christ.
14:20 in regard to evil be **i**, but in your
Eph 4:14 we will no longer be **i**, tossed back

Infected (Infection)
Lev 13: 4 **i** person in isolation for seven days.
13:12 covers all the skin of the **i** person
13:17 shall pronounce the **i** person
13:31 **i** person in isolation for seven days.

Infection (Infected, Infectious)
Lev 13:46 long as he has the **i** he remains

Infectious (Infection)
Lev 13: 2 that may become an **i** skin disease,
13: 3 skin deep, it is an **i** skin disease.
13: 8 him unclean; it is an **i** disease.
13: 9 "When anyone has an **i** skin disease,
13:15 is unclean; he has an **i** disease.
13:20 It is an **i** skin disease that has
13:22 pronounce him unclean; it is **i**.
13:25 it is an **i** disease that has broken
13:25 unclean; it is an **i** skin disease.
13:27 unclean; it is an **i** skin disease.
13:30 an **i** disease of the head or chin.
13:42 it is an **i** disease breaking out on
13:43 like an **i** skin disease,
13:45 "The person with such an **i** disease
14: 3 been healed of his **i** skin disease,
14: 7 **i** disease and pronounce him clean.
14:32 anyone who has an **i** skin disease
14:54 regulations for any **i** skin disease
14:57 for **i** skin diseases and mildew.
22: 4 of Aaron has an **i** skin disease or
Nu 5: 2 anyone who has an **i** skin disease

Inferior
Job 12: 3 as well as you; I am not **i** to you.
13: 2 I also know; I am not **i** to you.
Da 2:39 kingdom will rise, **i** to yours.
2Co 11: 5 I do not think I am in the least **i**
12:11 for I am not in the least **i** to the
12:13 How were you **i** to the other churches,

Infiltrated
Gal 2: 4 some false brothers had **i** our ranks

Infirmities (Infirmity)
Isa 53: 4 Surely he took up our **i** and carried
Mt 8:17 up our **i** and carried our diseases."

Infirmity (Infirmities)
Lk 13:12 Woman, you are set free from your **i**."

Inflamed (Inflammation)
Isa 5:11 at night till they are **i** with wine.
Hos 7: 5 king the princes become **i** with wine,
Ro 1:27 were **i** with lust for one another.

Inflammation (Inflamed)
Dt 28:22 with fever and **i**, with scorching

Inflict (Inflicted, Inflicts)
Dt 7:15 He will not **i** on you the horrible
7:15 he will **i** them on all who hate you.
28:53 will **i** on you during the siege,
28:55 suffering that your enemy will **i**
28:57 enemy will **i** on you in your cities.
Jdg 20:31 They began to **i** casualties on the
20:39 The Benjamites had begun to **i**
Ps 149: 7 to **i** vengeance on the nations and
Jer 18: 8 **i** on it the disaster I had planned.
36: 3 every disaster I plan to **i** on them,
Eze 5: 8 Jerusalem, and I will **i** punishment
5:10 I will **i** punishment on you and will
5:15 when I **i** punishment on you in anger
11: 9 foreigners and **i** punishment on you.
16:41 **i** punishment on you in the sight of
25:11 I will **i** punishment on Moab. Then
28:22 when I **i** punishment on her and show
28:26 live in safety when I **i** punishment
30:14 to Zoan and **i** punishment on Thebes.
30:19 I will **i** punishment on Egypt, and
39:21 the punishment I **i** and the hand
Rev 9:19 heads with which they **i** injury.

Inflicted (Inflict)
Ge 12:17 the LORD **i** serious diseases on
1Sa 14:47 he turned, he **i** punishment on them.
23: 5 He **i** heavy losses on the Philistines
2Sa 7:14 rod of men, with floggings **i** by men.
1Ki 20:21 and **i** heavy losses on the Arameans.
20:29 The Israelites **i** a hundred thousand
2Ki 8:29 wounds the Arameans had **i** on him
9:15 wounds the Arameans had **i** on him
2Ch 13:17 Abijah and his men **i** heavy losses on
22: 6 wounds they had **i** on him
28: 5 who **i** heavy casualties on him.
Isa 30:26 people and heals the wounds he **i**.
Jer 42:10 over the disaster I have **i** on you.
Lam 1:12 like my suffering that was **i** on me,
Eze 23:10 women, and punishment was **i** on her.
2Co 2: 6 The punishment **i** on him by the

Inflicts (Inflict)
Job 34: 6 his arrow **i** an incurable wound.'
Zec 14:18 the plague he **i** on the nations

Influence (Influenced, Influential)
Job 31:21 knowing that I had **i** in court,

Influenced (Influence)
1Co 12: 2 were **i** and led astray to mute idols.

Influential (Influence)
1Co 1:26 not many were **i**; not many were of

Inform (Information, Informed)
Ex 18:16 **i** them of God's decrees and laws."
1Sa 27:11 "They might **i** on us and say, 'This
2Sa 15:28 until word comes from you to **i** me."
17:17 A servant girl was to go and **i** them,
17:21 the well and went to **i** King David.
Ezr 4:14 sending this message to **i** the king,
4:16 We **i** the king that if this city is
Job 12: 8 or let the fish of the sea **i** you.

Information (Inform)
1Sa 23:23 and come back to me with definite **i**
Ezr 5:10 names of their leaders for your **i**.
Ac 23:15 more accurate **i** about his case.
23:20 wanting more accurate **i** about him.

Informed (Inform)
2Ki 22:10 Shaphan the secretary **i** the king,
2Ch 34:18 Shaphan the secretary **i** the king,
Da 1: 4 well **i**, quick to understand, and
Ac 21:21 They have been **i** that you teach all
23:30 I was **i** of a plot to be carried out
1Co 1:11 some from Chloe's household have **i**

Ingathering (Gather)
Ex 23:16 "Celebrate the Feast of **I** at the end
34:22 Feast of **I** at the turn of the year.

Inhabit (Habitat, Inhabitant, Inhabitants, Inhabited)
Job 15:28 he will **i** ruined towns and houses
Ac 17:26 that they should **i** the whole earth;

Inhabitant (Inhabit)
Isa 6:11 the cities lie ruined and without **i**,
Jer 4: 7 towns will lie in ruins without **i**.
46:19 waste and lie in ruins without **i**.

Inhabitants (Inhabit)
Lev 18:25 sin, and the land vomited out its **i**.
25:10 throughout the land to all its **i**.
Nu 14:14 they will tell the **i** of this land
32:17 protection from the **i** of the land.
33:52 drive out all the **i** of the land
33:55 But if you do not drive out the **i**
Jos 9:24 wipe out all its **i** from before you.
13: 6 "As for all the **i** of the mountain
Jdg 1:32 among the Canaanite **i** of the land.
1:33 among the Canaanite **i** of the land,
1Ki 9:16 He killed its Canaanite **i** and then
2Ki 16: 9 He deported its **i** to Kir and put
1Ch 8:13 and who drove out the **i** of Gath.
10:11 all the **i** of Jabesh Gilead heard of
22:18 handed the **i** of the land over to me,
2Ch 15: 5 **i** of the lands were in great turmoil.
20: 7 did you not drive out the **i** of this
34: 9 and Benjamin and the **i** of Jerusalem.
Isa 9: 9 the **i** of Samaria—who say with
24: 1 ruin its face and scatter its **i**—
24: 6 Therefore earth's **i** are burned up,
51: 6 a garment and its **i** die like flies.
Jer 25: 9 its **i** and against all the
44:22 waste without **i**, as it is today.
48:18 O **i** of the Daughter of Dibon, for he
49: 3 Cry out, O **i** of Rabbah! Put on
51:35 be upon Babylon," say the **i** of Zion.
Mic 7:13 become desolate because of its **i**,
Zec 8:20 the **i** of many cities will yet come,
8:21 the **i** of one city will go to another
12: 7 of Jerusalem's **i** may not be greater
12:10 the **i** of Jerusalem a spirit of grace
13: 1 of David and the **i** of Jerusalem,
Rev 6:10 until you judge the **i** of the earth
8:13 "Woe! Woe! Woe to the **i** of the earth,
11:10 The **i** of the earth will gloat over
13: 8 All **i** of the earth will worship the
13:12 and made the earth and its **i** worship
13:14 he deceived the **i** of the earth.
17: 2 the **i** of the earth were intoxicated
17: 8 The **i** of the earth whose names have

Inhabited (Inhabit)
Isa 13:20 She will never be **i** or lived in
44:26 'It shall be **i**,' of the towns of
45:18 but formed it to be **i**—he says:
Jer 17:25 and this city will be **i** for ever.
22: 6 you like a desert, like towns not **i**.
33:10 **i** by neither men nor animals, there
46:26 Later, however, Egypt will be **i** as
50:13 of the LORD's anger she will not be **i**
50:39 It will never again be **i** or lived in
Eze 12:20 The **i** towns will be laid waste and
26:19 like cities no longer **i**, and when I
35: 9 for ever; your towns will not be **i**.
36:10 will be **i** and the ruins rebuilt.
36:35 destroyed, are now fortified and **i**.
Joel 3:20 Judah will be **i** for ever and
Zec 14:11 will be **i**; never again will it be

Inherit (Co-heirs, Heir, Heirs, Heritage, Inheritance, Inheritances, Inherited, Inherits)
Ge 15: 2 **i** my estate is Eliezer of Damascus?
48: 6 in the territory they **i** they will
Nu 14:24 to, and his descendants will **i** it.
32:32 property we **i** will be on this side
Dt 1:38 because he will lead Israel to **i** it.
3:28 to **i** the land that you will see."
Dt 33:23 he will **i** southward to the lake."
Jos 1: 6 lead these people to **i** the land
1Sa 2: 8 and has them **i** a throne of honour.
2Ki 2: 9 "Let me **i** a double portion of your
1Ch 16:18 Canaan as the portion you will **i**."
Job 13:26 and make me **i** the sins of my youth.
Ps 25:13 and his descendants will **i** the land.
37: 9 hope in the LORD will **i** the land.
37:11 the meek will **i** the land and enjoy
37:22 those the LORD blesses will **i** the
37:29 the righteous will **i** the land and
37:34 He will exalt you to **i** the land;
69:36 children of his servants will **i**
105:11 Canaan as the portion you will **i**."
Pr 3:35 The wise **i** honour, but fools he
11:29 on his family will **i** only wind,
14:18 The simple **i** folly, but the prudent
Isa 14:21 they are not to rise to **i** the land
57:13 makes me his refuge will **i** the land
61: 7 **i** a double portion in their land,
65: 9 my chosen people will **i** them,
Zep 2: 9 of my nation will **i** their land."
Zec 2:12 The LORD will **i** Judah as his portion
Mt 5: 5 Blessed are the meek, for they will **i**
19:29 as much and will **i** eternal life.
Mk 10:17 "what must I do to **i** eternal life?
Lk 10:25 "what must I do to **i** eternal life?
18:18 what must I do to **i** eternal life?"
1Co 6: 9 will not **i** the kingdom of God?
6:10 swindlers will **i** the kingdom of God
15:50 that flesh and blood cannot **i** the
15:50 the perishable **i** the imperishable.
Gal 5:21 this will not **i** the kingdom of God.
Heb 1:14 to serve those who will **i** salvation?
6:12 patience **i** what has been promised.
12:17 to **i** this blessing, he was rejected.
Jas 2: 5 to **i** the kingdom he promised those
1Pe 3: 9 called so that you may **i** a blessing.
Rev 21: 7 He who overcomes will **i** all this,

Inheritance (Inherit)
Ge 21:10 share in the **i** with my son Isaac."
31:14 in the **i** of our father's estate?
Ex 15:17 the mountain of your **i**—the place,
32:13 and it will be their **i** for ever.
34: 9 our sin, and take us as your **i**."
Lev 20:24 I will give it to you as an **i**,
Nu 16:14 us an **i** of fields and vineyards.
18:20 "You will have no **i** in their land,
18:20 and your **i** among the Israelites.
18:21 all the tithes in Israel as their **i**
18:23 receive no **i** among the Israelites.
18:24 I give to the Levites as their **i** the
18:24 will have no **i** among the Israelites.
18:26 the tithe I give you as your **i**,
26:53 an **i** based on the number of names.
26:54 To a larger group give a larger **i**,
26:54 each is to receive its **i** according
26:56 Each **i** is to be distributed by lot
26:62 they received no **i** among them.
27: 7 **i** among their father's relatives
27: 7 give their father's **i** over to them.
27: 8 give his **i** over to his daughter.
27: 9 give his **i** to his brothers.
27:10 give his **i** to his father's brothers
27:11 give his **i** to the nearest relative
32:18 every Israelite has received his **i**.
32:19 We will not receive any **i** with them
32:19 because our **i** has come to us on the
33:54 To a larger group give a larger **i**,
34: 2 as an **i** will have these boundaries:
34:13 "Assign this land by lot as an **i**.
34:14 of Manasseh have received their **i**.
34:15 a half tribes have received their **i**
34:17 to assign the land for you as an **i**:
34:29 to assign the **i** to the Israelites
35: 2 the **i** the Israelites will possess.
35: 8 proportion to the **i** of each tribe:
36: 2 as an **i** to the Israelites by lot,
36: 2 he ordered you to give the **i** of our
36: 3 then their **i** will be taken from our
36: 3 from our ancestral **i** and added to
36: 4 their **i** will be added to that of the
36: 4 the tribal **i** of our forefathers."
36: 7 No **i** in Israel is to pass from tribe
Nu 36: 8 will possess the **i** of his fathers.
36: 9 No **i** may pass from tribe to tribe,
36:12 **i** remained in their father's clan
Dt 4:20 the people of his **i**, as you now are.
4:21 your God is giving you as your **i**.
4:38 to you for your **i**, as it is today.
9:26 your own **i** that you redeemed by your
9:29 they are your people, your **i** that
10: 9 no share or **i** among their brothers;
10: 9 the LORD is their **i**,
12: 9 **i** the LORD your God is giving you.
12:10 LORD your God is giving you as an **i**,
12:12 have no allotment or **i** of their own.
14:27 have no allotment or **i** of their own.
14:29 have no allotment or **i** of their own
15: 4 as your **i**, he will richly bless you,
18: 1 have no allotment or **i** with Israel.
18: 1 LORD by fire, for that is their **i**.
18: 2 They shall have no **i** among their
18: 2 LORD is their **i**, as he promised them.
19: 3 LORD your God is giving you as an **i**,
19:10 your God is giving you as your **i**,
19:14 in the **i** you receive in the land
20:16 LORD your God is giving you as an **i**
21:23 LORD your God is giving you as an **i**
24: 4 LORD your God is giving you as an **i**
25:19 is giving you to possess as an **i**,
26: 1 LORD your God is giving you as an **i**
29: 8 gave it as an **i** to the Reubenites,
31: 7 divide it among them as their **i**.
32: 8 Most High gave the nations their **i**
32: 9 his people, Jacob his allotted **i**.
Jos 11:23 and he gave it as an **i** to Israel
12: 7 (their lands Joshua gave as an **i** to
13: 6 for an **i**, as I have instructed you,
13: 7 as an **i** among the nine tribes
13: 8 the Gadites had received the **i** that
13:14 to the tribe of Levi he gave no **i**,
13:14 are their **i**, as he promised them.
13:23 **i** of the Reubenites, clan by clan.
13:28 the **i** of the Gadites, clan by clan.
13:32 This is the **i** Moses had given when
13:33 Moses had given no **i**; the LORD, the
13:33 is their **i**, as he promised them.
14: 1 as an **i** in the land of Canaan,
14: 3 their **i** east of the Jordan but had
14: 3 the Levites an **i** among the rest,
14: 9 **i** and that of your children for ever,
14:13 and gave him Hebron as his **i**.
15:20 This is the **i** of the tribe of Judah,
16: 4 of Joseph, received their **i**.
16: 5 The boundary of their **i** went from
16: 8 This was the **i** of the tribe of the
16: 9 within the **i** of the Manassites.
17: 4 to give us an **i** among our brothers.
17: 4 So Joshua gave them an **i** along with
17: 6 received an **i** among the sons.
17:14 allotment and one portion for an **i**?
18: 2 who had not yet received their **i**.
18: 4 of it, according to the **i** of each.
18: 7 service of the LORD is their **i**.
18: 7 **i** on the east side of the Jordan.
18:20 the **i** of the clans of Benjamin
18:28 was the **i** of Benjamin for its clans.
19: 1 **i** lay within the territory of Judah.
19: 8 This was the **i** of the tribe of the
19: 9 The **i** of the Simeonites was taken
19: 9 **i** within the territory of Judah.
19:10 of their **i** went as far as Sarid.
19:16 were the **i** of Zebulun, clan by clan.
19:23 were the **i** of the tribe of Issachar,
19:31 were the **i** of the tribe of Asher,
19:39 were the **i** of the tribe of Naphtali,
19:41 The territory of their **i** included:
19:48 **i** of the tribe of Dan, clan by clan.
19:49 Joshua son of Nun an **i** among them,
21: 3 pasture-lands out of their own **i**:
23: 4 Remember how I have allotted as an **i**
24:28 the people away, each to his own **i**.
24:30 they buried him in the land of his **i**,
24:32 the **i** of Joseph's descendants.
Jdg 2: 6 of the land, each to his own **i**.
2: 9 they buried him in the land of his **i**,
11: 2 "You are not going to get any **i** in
18: 1 an **i** among the tribes of Israel.
20: 6 piece to each region of Israel's **i**,

Jdg 21:23 Then they returned to their **i** and
21:24 tribes and clans, each to his own **i**.
1Sa 10: 1 LORD anointed you leader over his **i**?
26:19 share in the LORD's **i** and have said,
2Sa 14:16 and my son from the **i** God gave us.'
20:19 want to swallow up the LORD's **i**?"
21: 3 that you will bless the LORD's **i**?"
1Ki 8:36 land you gave your people for an **i**.
8:51 for they are your people and your **i**,
8:53 of the world to be your own **i**,
21: 3 give you the **i** of my fathers."
21: 4 not give you the **i** of my fathers.
2Ki 21:14 I will forsake the remnant of my **i**
1Ch 28: 8 an **i** to your descendants for ever.
2Ch 6:27 that you gave your people for an **i**.
20:11 the possession you gave us as an **i**.
Ezr 9:12 your children as an everlasting **i**.'
Job 42:15 them an **i** along with their brothers.
Ps 2: 8 and I will make the nations your **i**,
16: 6 surely I have a delightful **i**.
28: 9 Save your people and bless your **i**;
33:12 LORD, the people he chose for his **i**.
37:18 and their **i** will endure for ever.
47: 4 He chose our **i** for us, the pride of
68: 9 O God; you refreshed your weary **i**.
74: 2 the tribe of your **i**, whom you
78:55 their lands to them as an **i**;
78:62 he was very angry with his **i**.
78:71 his people Jacob, of Israel his **i**.
79: 1 the nations have invaded your **i**;
82: 8 for all the nations are your **i**.
94: 5 people, O LORD; they oppress your **i**.
94:14 people; he will never forsake his **i**.
106: 5 and join your **i** in giving praise.
106:40 with his people and abhorred his **i**.
135:12 he gave their land as an **i**, an **i** to
136:21 gave their land as an **i**, His love
136:22 an **i** to his servant Israel; His
Pr 13:22 A good man leaves an **i** for his
17: 2 share the **i** as one of the brothers.
20:21 An **i** quickly gained at the beginning
28:10 the blameless will receive a good **i**.
Ecc 7:11 Wisdom, like an **i**, is a good thing
Isa 19:25 my handiwork, and Israel my **i**."
47: 6 and desecrated my **i**;
58:14 feast on the **i** of your father Jacob.
61: 7 they will rejoice in their **i**;
63:17 the tribes that are your **i**.
Jer 2: 7 my land and made my **i** detestable.
3:18 I gave your forefathers as an **i**.
3:19 the most beautiful **i** of any nation.
10:16 including Israel, the tribe of his **i**
12: 7 forsake my house, abandon my **i**;
12: 8 My **i** has become to me like a lion
12: 9 Has not my **i** become to me like a
12:14 the **i** I gave to my people Israel,
12:15 to his own **i** and his own country.
16:18 my **i** with their detestable idols.
17: 4 you will lose the **i** I gave you.
50:11 you who pillage my **i**, because you
51:19 including the tribe of his **i**—
Lam 5: 2 Our **i** has been turned over to aliens
Eze 35:15 you rejoiced when the **i** of the house
36:12 and you will be their **i**; you will
44:28 I am to be the only **i** the priests
45: 1 "When you allot the land as an **i**,
46:16 gift from his **i** to one of his sons,
46:16 it is to be their property by **i**.
46:17 however, he makes a gift from his **i**
46:17 His **i** belongs to his sons only; it
46:18 prince must not take any of the **i**
46:18 He is to give his sons their **i** out
47:13 **i** among the twelve tribes of Israel,
47:14 this land will become your **i**.
47:22 You are to allot it as an **i** for
47:22 an **i** among the tribes of Israel.
47:23 there you are to give him his **i**,"
48:29 as an **i** to the tribes of Israel,
Da 12:13 rise to receive your allotted **i**."
Joel 2:17 Do not make your **i** an object of
3: 2 against them concerning my **i**,
Ob :17 house of Jacob will possess its **i**.
Mic 2: 2 his home, a fellow-man of his **i**.
7:14 the flock of your **i**, which lives
7:18 of the remnant of his **i**?
Zec 8:12 an **i** to the remnant of this people.
Mal 1: 3 left his **i** to the desert jackals."
Mt 21:38 Come, let's kill him and take his **i**.
25:34 blessed by my Father; take your **i**,
Mk 12: 7 kill him, and the **i** will be ours.'
Lk 12:13 my brother to divide the **i** with me.
20:14 kill him, and the **i** will be ours.'
Ac 7: 5 He gave him no **i** here, not even a
13:19 their land to his people as their **i**.
20:32 give you an **i** among all those who
Gal 3:18 For if the **i** depends on the law,
4:30 in the **i** with the free woman's son.
Eph 1:14 is a deposit guaranteeing our **i**
1:18 of his glorious **i** in the saints,
5: 5 any **i** in the kingdom of Christ
Col 1:12 to share in the **i** of the saints in
3:24 an **i** from the Lord as a reward.
Heb 9:15 may receive the promised eternal **i**
11: 8 he would later receive as his **i**,
12:16 sold his **i** rights as the oldest son
1Pe 1: 4 into an **i** that can never perish,

Inheritances (Inherit)

Jos 14: 2 Their **i** were assigned by lot to the
Isa 49: 8 land and to reassign its desolate **i**,

Inherited (Inherit)

Lev 25:46 them to your children as **i** property
Nu 36: 7 tribal land **i** from his forefathers.
Pr 19:14 Houses and wealth are **i** from parents,
Heb 1: 4 name he has **i** is superior to theirs.

Inherits (Inherit)

Nu 26:55 What each group **i** will be according
36: 8 Every daughter who **i** land in any
36: 9 tribe is to keep the land it **i**."

Iniquities (Iniquity)

Ps 78:38 he was merciful and forgave their **i**
90: 8 You have set our **i** before you,
103:10 or repay us according to our **i**.
107:17 affliction because of their **i**.
Isa 53: 5 he was crushed for our **i**; the
53:11 many, and he will bear their **i**.
59: 2 your **i** have separated you from
59:12 with us, and we acknowledge our **i**:
Lam 4:13 prophets and the **i** of her priests,
Da 9:16 Our sins and the **i** of our fathers
Mic 7:19 our **i** into the depths of the sea.

Iniquity (Iniquities)

Ps 25:11 forgive my **i**, though it is great.
32: 5 to you and did not cover up my **i**.
38:18 I confess my **i**; I am troubled by my
51: 2 Wash away all my **i** and cleanse me
51: 9 from my sins and blot out all my **i**.
73: 7 From their callous hearts comes **i**;
85: 2 You forgave the **i** of your people
89:32 with the rod, their **i** with flogging
109:14 May the **i** of his fathers be
Isa 53: 6 LORD has laid on him the **i** of us all.
61: 8 love justice; I hate robbery and **i**.
Hos 12: 8 will not find in me any **i** or sin."
Mic 2: 1 Woe to those who plan **i**, to those
Zec 5: 6 **i** of the people throughout the land.

Initiative

2Co 8:17 much enthusiasm and on his own **i**.

Injure (Injured, Injures, Injuring, Injury)

Zec 12: 3 try to move it will **i** themselves.

Injured (Injure)

Ex 21:19 he must pay the **i** man for the loss
22:10 it dies or is **i** or is taken away
22:14 it is **i** or dies while the owner is
Lev 22:22 the **i** or the maimed, or anything
24:20 has **i** the other, so he is to be **i**.
2Ki 1: 2 upper room in Samaria and **i** himself.
Ecc 10: 9 Whoever quarries stones may be **i** by
Isa 1: 5 Your whole head is **i**, your whole
28:13 be **i** and snared and captured.
Eze 34: 4 healed the sick or bound up the **i**.
Eze 34:16 I will bind up the **i** and strengthen
Hos 6: 1 **i** us but he will bind up our wounds.
Zec 11:16 or seek the young, or heal the **i**, or
Mal 1:13 "When you bring **i**, crippled or
2Co 7:12 who did the wrong or of the **i** party,

Injures (Injure)

Ex 21:35 "If a man's bull **i** the bull of
Lev 24:19 If anyone **i** his neighbour, whatever
Job 5:18 he **i**, but his hands also heal.

Injuring (Injure)

Ge 4:23 wounding me, a young man for **i** me.
Lk 4:35 them all and came out without **i** him.

Injury (Injure)

Ex 21:22 but there is no serious **i**,
21:23 if there is serious **i**, you are to
2Ki 1: 2 see if I will recover from this **i**."
Jer 10:19 Woe to me because of my **i**! My wound
30:12 is incurable, your **i** beyond healing.
Na 3:19 heal your wound; your **i** is fatal.
Rev 9:19 heads with which they inflict **i**.

Injustice

2Ch 19: 7 is no **i** or partiality or bribery."
Job 5:16 have hope, and **i** shuts its mouth.
Ps 58: 2 No, in your heart you devise **i**, and
64: 6 They plot **i** and say, "We have
Pr 13:23 abundant food, but **i** sweeps it away.
16: 8 righteousness than much gain with **i**.
Isa 58: 6 loose the chains of **i** and untie the
Jer 22:13 his upper rooms by **i**, making his
Eze 9: 9 bloodshed and the city is full of **i**
Hab 1: 3 Why do you make me look at **i**? Why

Ink

Jer 36:18 I wrote them in **i** on the scroll."
2Co 3: 3 written not with **i** but with the
2Jn :12 I do not want to use paper and **i**.
3Jn :13 do not want to do so with pen and **i**

Inkling

1Sa 20: 9 I had the least **i** that my father

Inlaid

1Ki 10:18 the king made a great throne **i** with
22:39 the palace he built and **i** with ivory,
2Ch 9:17 the king made a great throne **i** with
SS 3:10 **i** by the daughters of Jerusalem.
Eze 27: 6 they made your deck, **i** with ivory.
Am 6: 4 You lie on beds **i** with ivory and

Inmost (Innermost)

Ps 51: 6 you teach me wisdom in the **i** place.
103: 1 my **i** being, praise his holy name
139:13 For you created my **i** being; you knit
Pr 18: 8 they go down to a man's **i** parts.
20:27 it searches out his **i** being.
20:30 and beatings purge the **i** being.
23:16 my **i** being will rejoice when your
26:22 they go down to a man's **i** parts.
Isa 16:11 a harp, my **i** being for Kir Hareseth
Lk 1:51 who are proud in their **i** thoughts.

Inn (Innkeeper)

Lk 2: 7 there was no room for them in the **i**
10:34 him to an **i** and took care of him.

Inner

Ge 30:37 the white **i** wood of the branches.
Ex 12: 9 the fire—head, legs and **i** parts.
29:13 take all the fat around the **i** parts
29:17 and wash the **i** parts and the legs,
29:22 tail, the fat around the **i** parts
Lev 1: 9 He is to wash the **i** parts and the
1:13 He is to wash the **i** parts and the
3: 3 fat that covers the **i** parts or is
3: 9 the **i** parts or is connected to them
3:14 the **i** parts or is connected to them
4: 8 the **i** parts or is connected to them
4:11 and legs, the **i** parts and offal—
7: 3 and the fat that covers the **i** parts

Lev 8:16 took all the fat around the **i** parts
8:21 He washed the **i** parts and the legs
8:25 all the fat around the **i** parts, the
9:14 He washed the **i** parts and the legs
Dt 18: 3 shoulder, the jowls and the **i** parts
Jdg 3:24 himself in the **i** room of the house.
2Sa 4: 6 into the **i** part of the house
18:24 between the **i** and outer gates,
1Ki 6: 5 **i** sanctuary he built a structure
6:16 an **i** sanctuary, the Most Holy Place.
6:19 He prepared the **i** sanctuary within
6:20 The **i** sanctuary was twenty cubits
6:21 across the front of the **i** sanctuary
6:22 that belonged to the **i** sanctuary.
6:23 In the **i** sanctuary he made a pair
6:29 in both the **i** and outer rooms, he
6:30 covered the floors of both the **i**
6:31 the entrance of the **i** sanctuary
6:36 he built the **i** courtyard of three
7: 9 a saw on their **i** and outer faces.
7:12 was the **i** courtyard of the temple
7:49 in front of the **i** sanctuary);
8: 6 in the **i** sanctuary of the temple,
8: 8 Place in front of the **i** sanctuary,
20:30 to the city and hid in an **i** room.
22:25 day you go to hide in an **i** room."
2Ki 9: 2 and take him into an **i** room.
10:25 the **i** shrine of the temple of Baal
1Ch 28:11 **i** rooms and the place of atonement
2Ch 4:20 of the **i** sanctuary as prescribed;
4:22 the **i** doors to the Most Holy Place
5: 7 in the **i** sanctuary of the temple,
5: 9 from in front of the **i** sanctuary,
18:24 day you go to hide in an **i** room."
Est 4:11 approaches the king in the **i** court
5: 1 stood in the **i** court of the palace,
Ps 51: 6 you desire truth in the **i** parts
Eze 8: 3 to the north gate of the **i** court,
8:16 then brought me into the **i** court
10: 3 and a cloud filled the **i** court.
40:19 to the outside of the **i** court;
40:23 There was a gate to the **i** court
40:27 The **i** court also had a gate facing
40:28 he brought me into the **i** court
40:30 **i** court were twenty-five cubits wide
40:32 he brought me to the **i** court on the
40:38 portico in each of the **i** gateways,
40:44 Outside the **i** gate, within the **i**
41: 3 he went into the **i** sanctuary and
41: 4 the length of the **i** sanctuary
41:15 The outer sanctuary, the **i** sanctuary
41:17 the entrance to the **i** sanctuary
41:17 the **i** and outer sanctuary
42: 3 twenty cubits from the **i** court
42: 4 an **i** passageway ten cubits wide
43: 5 up and brought me into the **i** court,
44:17 enter the gates of the **i** court,
44:17 of the **i** court or inside the temple.
44:21 wine when he enters the **i** court.
44:27 On the day he goes into the **i** court
45:19 and on the gateposts of the **i** court.
46: 1 The gate of the **i** court facing east
Mt 24:26 in the **i** rooms,' do not believe it.
Lk 12: 3 whispered in the ear in the **i** rooms
Ac 16:24 he put them in the **i** cell and
Ro 7:22 in my **i** being I delight in God's law
Eph 3:16 through his Spirit in your **i** being,
Heb 6:19 the **i** sanctuary behind the curtain,
9: 7 the high priest entered the **i** room
1Pe 3: 4 it should be that of your **i** self,

Innermost (Inmost)
1Ki 6:27 cherubim inside the **i** room of the
7:50 sockets for the doors of the **i** room,

Innkeeper (Inn)
Lk 10:35 silver coins and gave them to the **i**

Innocence (Innocent)
Ge 44:16 How can we our **i**? God has
1Ki 8:32 not guilty, and so establish his **i**.
2Ch 6:23 not guilty and so establish his **i**.
Ps 26: 6 I wash my hands in **i**, and go about
73:13 in vain have I washed my hands in **i**
Isa 43:26 together; state the case for your **i**

Innocent (Innocence)
Ge 20: 4 will you destroy an **i** nation?
Ex 23: 7 put an **i** or honest person to death,
Nu 5:31 The husband will be **i** of any
Dt 19:10 Do this so that **i** blood will not
19:13 Israel the guilt of shedding **i** blood
21: 8 guilty of the blood of an **i** man.
21: 9 the guilt of shedding **i** blood,
25: 1 acquitting the **i** and condemning the
27:25 accepts a bribe to kill an **i** person
Jdg 21:22 and you are **i**, since you did not
1Sa 19: 5 do wrong to an **i** man like David
2Sa 3:28 "I and my kingdom are for ever **i**
4:11 killed an **i** man in his own house
1Ki 2: 9 now, do not consider him **i**. You are
2:31 guilt of the **i** blood that Joab shed
8:32 Declare the **i** not guilty, and so
2Ki 10: 9 all the people and said, "You are **i**
21:16 Manasseh also shed so much **i** blood
24: 4 including the shedding of **i** blood.
24: 4 filled Jerusalem with **i** blood
2Ch 6:23 Declare the **i** not guilty and so
Job 4: 7 "Consider now: Who, being **i**, has
9:15 Though I were **i**, I could not answer
9:20 Even if I were **i**, my mouth would
9:23 he mocks the despair of the **i**.
9:28 for I know you will not hold me **i**.
10:15 if I am **i**, I cannot lift my head,
17: 8 **i** are aroused against the ungodly.
22:19 rejoice; the **i** mock them, saying,
22:30 will deliver even one who is not **i**
27:17 and the **i** will divide his silver.
34: 5 "Job says, 'I am **i**, but God denies
Ps 10: 8 from ambush he murders the **i**,
15: 5 not accept a bribe against the **i**.
19:13 blameless, **i** of great transgression.
64: 4 They shoot from ambush at the **i** man
94:21 and condemn the **i** to death.
106:38 They shed **i** blood, the blood of
Pr 6:17 tongue, hands that shed **i** blood,
16: 2 All a man's ways seem **i** to him, but
17:15 the **i**—the LORD detests them both.
17:26 is not good to punish an **i** man,
18: 5 or to deprive the **i** of justice.
21: 8 but the conduct of the **i** is upright
24:24 "You are **i**"—peoples will curse him
Isa 5:23 a bribe, but deny justice to the **i**.
29:21 testimony deprive the **i** of justice.
59: 7 they are swift to shed **i** blood.
Jer 2:34 find the lifeblood of the **i** poor,
2:35 you say, 'I am **i**; he is not angry
7: 6 do not shed **i** blood in this place,
19: 4 this place with the blood of the **i**.
22: 3 do not shed **i** blood in this place.
22:17 on shedding **i** blood and on
26:15 you will bring the guilt of **i** blood
Da 6:22 because I was found **i** in his sight.
Joel 3:19 in whose land they shed **i** blood.
Jnh 1:14 accountable for killing an **i** man,
Mt 10:16 shrewd as snakes and as **i** as doves
12: 5 desecrate the day and yet are **i**?
12: 7 you would not have condemned the **i**
27: 4 said, "for I have betrayed **i** blood.
27:19 have anything to do with that **i** man,
27:24 "I am **i** of this man's blood," he
Ac 20:26 I am **i** of the blood of all men.
Ro 16:19 is good, and **i** about what is evil.
1Co 4: 4 clear, but that does not make me **i**.
2Co 7:11 yourselves to be **i** in this matter.
Jas 5: 6 have condemned and murdered **i** men

Innumerable
2Ch 12: 3 and the **i** troops of Libyans,

Insane
1Sa 21:14 He is **i**! Why bring him to me?
Ps 34: T pretended to be **i** before Abimelech
Ac 26:24 great learning is driving you **i**."
26:25 "I am not **i**, most excellent Festus

Insanity
1Sa 21:13 he feigned **i** in their presence;

Insatiable
Eze 16:28 because you were **i**; and even after

Inscribe (Inscribed, Inscription)
Isa 30: 8 write it on a tablet for them, **i** it

Inscribed (Inscribe)
Ex 31:18 of stone **i** by the finger of God.
32:15 **i** on both sides, front and back.
Dt 9:10 The LORD gave me two stone tablets **i**
Job 19:24 that they were **i** with an iron tool
Jer 17: 1 **i** with a flint point, on the tablets
Zec 14:20 be **i** on the bells of the horses,

Inscription (Inscribe)
Ex 39:30 like an **i** on a seal: HOLY TO THE LORD.
Da 5:24 he sent the hand that wrote the **i**.
5:25 "This is the **i** that was written:
Zec 3: 9 and I will engrave an **i** on it,'
Mt 22:20 Whose portrait is this? And whose **i**?"
Mk 12:16 whose **i**?" "Caesar's," they replied.
Lk 20:24 Whose portrait and **i** are on it?"
Ac 17:23 with this **i**: TO AN UNKNOWN GOD.
2Ti 2:19 sealed with this **i**: "The Lord knows

Insects
Lev 11:20 "'All flying **i** that walk on all
Dt 14:19 All flying **i** that swarm are unclean

Insert (Inserted)
Ex 25:14 **I** the poles into the rings on the

Inserted (Insert)
Ex 27: 7 The poles are to be **i** into the rings
37: 5 he **i** the poles into the rings on the
38: 7 They **i** the poles into the rings so
40:18 **i** the crossbars and set up the posts.
1Ki 6: 6 would be **i** into the temple walls.
Eze 41: 6 not **i** into the wall of the temple.

Insight (Insights)
1Ki 4:29 Solomon wisdom and very great **i**,
1Ch 27:32 counsellor, a man of **i** and a scribe.
Job 26: 3 And what great **i** you have displayed!
34:35 knowledge; his words lack **i**.'
Ps 119:99 I have more **i** than all my teachers,
Pr 1: 2 for understanding words of **i**;
2: 3 if you call out for **i** and cry aloud
5: 1 listen well to my words of **i**,
21:30 There is no wisdom, no **i**, no plan
Da 5:11 your father he was found to have **i**
5:14 gods is in you and that you have **i**,
9:22 to give you **i** and understanding.
Eph 3: 4 my **i** into the mystery of Christ,
Php 1: 9 more in knowledge and depth of **i**,
2Ti 2: 7 Lord will give you **i** into all this.
Rev 13:18 If anyone has **i**, let him calculate

Insights (Insight)
Job 15: 9 **i** do you have that we do not have?

Insist (Insisted, Insisting)
2Sa 24:24 "No, I **i** on paying for it.
1Ch 21:24 "No, I **i** on paying the full price.
Eph 4:17 this, and **i** on it in the Lord,

Insisted (Insist)
Ge 19: 3 he **i** so strongly that they did go
33:11 because Jacob **i**, Esau accepted it.
1Ki 3:22 But the first one **i**, "No! The dead
Mk 14:31 Peter **i** emphatically, "Even if I
Lk 23: 5 they **i**, "He stirs up the people all
Jn 9: 9 But he himself **i**, "I am the man."
19: 7 The Jews **i**, "We have a law, and

Insisting (Insist)
Ac 12:15 When she kept **i** that it was so, they

Insolence (Insolent)
2Ki 19:28 and your **i** has reached my ears,
Isa 16: 6 and conceit, her pride and her **i**
37:29 because your **i** has reached my ears,

Jer 48:30 I know her i but it is futile,”
Da 11:18 i and will turn his i back upon him.

Insolent (Insolence)

Nu 16: 1 and On son of Peleth—became i
Hos 7:16 the sword because of their i words.
Ro 1:30 slanderers, God-haters, i, arrogant

Inspect (Inspected, Inspection)

Lev 14:36 priest is to go in and i the house.
14:39 priest shall return to i the house.

Inspected (Inspect)

Ex 39:43 Moses i the work and saw that they

Inspection (Inspect)

Ne 3:31 opposite the I Gate, and as far as

Inspire (Inspired, Inspires)

Jer 32:40 and I will i them to fear me, so
49:16 The terror you i and the pride of

Inspired (Inspire)

Hos 9: 7 a fool, the i man a maniac.
1Th 1: 3 i by hope in our Lord Jesus Christ

Inspires (Inspire)

Job 20: 3 and my understanding i me to reply

Installed

Jdg 17: 5 and i one of his sons as his priest
17:12 Micah i the Levite, and the young
1Ki 12:32 And at Bethel he also i priests at
Ezr 6:18 they i the priests in their
Ps 2: 6 “I have i my King on Zion, my holy

Instance

Dt 19: 5 For i, a man may go into the forest

Instant (Instantly)

Job 7:19 me, or let me alone even for an i?
34:20 They die in an i, in the middle of
Pr 6:15 disaster will overtake him in an i;
Isa 29: 5 Suddenly, in an i,
30:13 that collapses suddenly, in an i.
Jer 4:20 In an i my tents are destroyed, my
49:19 chase Edom from its land in an i.
50:44 chase Babylon from its land in an i.
Lk 4: 5 showed him in an i all the kingdoms

Instantly (Instant)

Lk 8:47 and how she had been i healed.
Ac 3: 7 i the man’s feet and ankles became

Instinct (Instincts)

2Pe 2:12 creatures of i, born only to be
Jude :10 what things they do understand by i

Instincts (Instinct)

Jude :19 follow mere natural i and do not

Instituted

Nu 28: 6 burnt offering i at Mount Sinai
1Ki 12:32 He i a festival on the fifteenth day
12:33 So he i the festival for the
Ro 13: 2 is rebelling against what God has i,
1Pe 2:13 to every authority i among men:

Instruct (Instructed, Instructing, Instruction, Instructions, Instructor, Instructors, Instructs)

Dt 24: 8 the priests, who are Levites, i you.
Ne 9:20 You gave your good Spirit to i them.
Job 8:10 Will they not i you and tell you?
Ps 25:12 i him in the way chosen for him.
32: 8 I will i you and teach you in the
105:22 to i his princes as he pleased and
Pr 9: 9 I a wise man and he will be wiser
Da 11:33 “Those who are wise will i many,
Ro 15:14 and competent to i one another.
1Co 2:16 mind of the Lord that he may i him
1Co 14:19 five intelligible words to i others
2Ti 2:25 Those who oppose him he must gently i

Instructed (Instruct)

Ge 32: 4 He i them: “This is what you are to
32:17 He i the one in the lead: “When my
32:19 He also i the second, the third and
Ex 12:35 The Israelites did as Moses i and
Nu 5: 4 did just as the LORD had i Moses.
27:23 as the LORD i through Moses.
Jos 8:27 this city, as the LORD had i Joshua.
13: 6 for an inheritance, as I have i you,
18: 8 Joshua i them, “Go and make a survey
20: 2 of refuge, as I i you through Moses,
Jdg 21:20 they i the Benjamites, saying, “Go
2Sa 11:19 He i the messenger: “When you have
14:19 it was your servant Joab who i me
2Ki 12: 2 the years Jehoiada the priest i him.
2Ch 26: 5 who i him in the fear of God.
35: 3 to the Levites, who i all Israel
Ne 8: 7 i the people in the Law while the
Est 1: 8 for the king i all the wine stewards
4:10 she i him to say to Mordecai,
Job 4: 3 Think how you have i many, how you
Pr 21:11 a wise man is i, he gets knowledge.
Isa 40:13 or i him as his counsellor?
50: 4 has given me an i tongue, to know
Jer 9:12 Who has been i by the LORD and can
Da 9:22 He i me and said to me, “Daniel, I
Mt 13:52 i about the kingdom of heaven is
17: 9 Jesus i them, “Don’t tell anyone
21: 6 went and did as Jesus had i them.
28:15 the money and did as they were i.
Ac 18:25 had been i in the way of the Lord,
Ro 2:18 because you are i by the law;
1Co 14:31 everyone may be i and encouraged.
1Th 4: 1 brothers, we i you how to live

Instructing (Instruct)

Ne 8: 9 and the Levites who were i the
Mt 11: 1 After Jesus had finished i his

Instruction (Instruct)

Ex 24:12 I have written for their i.”
Dt 33: 3 bow down, and from you receive i,
Ne 1: 8 “Remember the i you gave your
Job 22:22 Accept i from his mouth and lay up
Ps 50:17 You hate my i and cast my words
Pr 1: 8 Listen, my son, to your father’s i
4: 1 Listen, my sons, to a father’s i;
4:13 Hold on to i, do not let it go;
8:10 Choose my i instead of silver,
8:33 Listen to my i and be wise; do not
13: 1 A wise son heeds his father’s i,
13:13 He who scorns i will pay for it,
16:20 Whoever gives heed to i prospers,
16:21 and pleasant words promote i.
16:23 his mouth, and his lips promote i.
19:20 Listen to advice and accept i,
19:27 Stop listening to i, my son, and you
23:12 Apply your heart to i and your ears
31:26 and faithful i is on her tongue.
Isa 29:24 those who complain will accept i.”
30: 9 unwilling to listen to the LORD’s i
Mal 2: 6 True i was in his mouth and nothing
2: 7 from his mouth men should seek i
1Co 14: 6 knowledge or prophecy or word of i?
14:26 everyone has a hymn, or a word of i
Gal 6: 6 Anyone who receives i in the word
Eph 6: 4 in the training and i of the Lord.
1Th 4: 8 Therefore, he who rejects this i
2Th 3:14 does not obey our i in this letter,
1Ti 1:18 Timothy, my son, I give you this i
6: 3 does not agree to the sound i of our
2Ti 4: 2 great patience and careful i.
Heb 6: 2 i about baptisms, the laying on of

Instructions (Instruct)

Ge 44: 1 Now Joseph gave these i to the
49:29 he gave them these i: “I am about to
49:33 Jacob had finished giving i to his
50:16 father left these i before he died:
Ex 12:24 “Obey these i as a lasting ordinance
16: 4 see whether they will follow my i.
Ex 16:28 refuse to keep my commands and my i
Jos 8:33 i to bless the people of Israel.
Jdg 21:10 men with i to go to Jabesh Gilead
1Sa 15:11 me and has not carried out my i.
15:13 I have carried out the LORD’s i.”
15:24 the LORD’s command and your i.
21: 2 about your mission and your i.
1Ch 23:27 According to the last i of David,
28:13 He gave him i for the divisions of
Est 2:20 continued to follow Mordecai’s i
4:17 and carried out all of Esther’s i.
Pr 19:16 He who obeys i guards his life,
Jer 32:13 presence I gave Baruch these i:
35:18 have followed all his i and have
Mt 10: 5 Jesus sent out with the following i
Mk 6: 8 These were his i: “Take nothing for
Ac 1: 2 after giving i through the Holy
17:15 then left with i for Silas and
19:33 some of the crowd shouted i to him
Col 4:10 (You have received i about him;
1Th 4: 2 For you know what i we gave you by
1Ti 3:14 I am writing you these i so that,
5: 7 Give the people these i, too, so
5:21 to keep these i without partiality,
Heb 11:22 Egypt and gave i about his bones.

Instructor (Instruct)

Ro 2:20 an i of the foolish, a teacher of
Gal 6: 6 share all good things with his i.

Instructors (Instruct)

Pr 5:13 obey my teachers or listen to my i

Instructs (Instruct)

Ps 16: 7 even at night my heart i me.
25: 8 therefore he i sinners in his ways
Isa 28:26 His God i him and teaches him the

Instrument (Instruments)

Eze 33:32 beautiful voice and plays an i well
Ac 9:15 “Go! This man is my chosen i to
2Ti 2:21 he will be an i for noble purposes,

Instruments (Instrument)

1Ch 15:16 musical i: lyres, harps and cymbals
16:42 of the other i for sacred song.
23: 5 i I have provided for that purpose.
2Ch 5:13 cymbals and other i, they raised
7: 6 Levites with the LORD’s musical i,
23:13 musical i were leading the praises.
29:26 Levites stood ready with David’s i,
29:27 and the i of David king of Israel.
30:21 by the LORD’s i of praise.
34:12 were skilled in playing musical i
Ne 12:36 Judah and Hanani—with musical I
Ps 4: T director of music. With stringed i.
6: T director of music. With stringed i.
54: T director of music. With stringed i.
55: T director of music. With stringed i.
61: T director of music. With stringed i.
67: T director of music. With stringed i.
76: T director of music. With stringed i.
Isa 38:20 and we will sing with stringed i
Am 6: 5 David and improvise on musical i.
Hab 3:19 On my stringed i.
Ro 6:13 your body to sin, as i of wickedness
6:13 body to him as i of righteousness.

Insult (Insulted, Insulting, Insults)

2Ki 19:16 has sent to i the living God.
Ps 69: 9 the insults of those who i you
Pr 9: 7 Whoever corrects a mocker invites i
12:16 but a prudent man overlooks an i.
Isa 37:17 has sent to i the living God.
Jer 20: 8 word of the LORD has brought me i
Mt 5:11 “Blessed are you when people i you,
Lk 6:22 when they exclude you and i you and
11:45 say these things, you i us also.”
18:32 They will mock him, i him, spit on
Ac 23: 4 “You dare to i God’s high priest?
Ro 15: 3 those who i you have fallen on me.
Heb 10:33 exposed to i and persecution;
1Pe 3: 9 repay evil with evil or i with i,

Insulted (Insult)
2Ki 19:22 Who is it you have **i** and blasphemed?
Isa 37:23 Who is it you have **i** and blasphemed?
Jer 51:51 are disgraced, for we have been **i**
Zep 2: 8 who **i** my people and made threats
1Th 2: 2 had previously suffered and been **i**
Heb 10:29 and who has **i** the Spirit of grace?
Jas 2: 6 you have **i** the poor. Is it not the
1Pe 4:14 If you are **i** because of the name of

Insulting (Insult)
2Ch 32:17 The king also wrote letters **i** the
Ps 55:12 If an enemy were **i** me, I could
Zep 2:10 for **i** and mocking the people of the
Lk 22:65 they said many other **i** things to him.

Insults (Insult)
1Sa 25:14 greetings, but he hurled **i** at them.
2Ki 19:23 you have heaped **i** on the Lord
Ne 4: 4 Turn their **i** back on their own heads.
4: 5 **i** in the face of the builders.
Ps 22: 7 they hurl **i**, shaking their heads
69: 9 **i** of those who insult you fall on me
Pr 22:10 strife; quarrels and **i** are ended.
Isa 37:24 you have heaped **i** on the Lord
51: 7 of men or be terrified by their **i**.
Lam 3:61 O LORD, you have heard their **i**,
Eze 21:28 about the Ammonites and their **i**:
Zep 2: 8 "I have heard the **i** of Moab and the
Mt 27:39 Those who passed by hurled **i** at him,
27:44 with him also heaped **i** on him.
Mk 15:29 Those who passed by hurled **i** at him,
15:32 with him also heaped **i** on him.
Lk 23:39 who hung there hurled **i** at him:
Jn 9:28 they hurled **i** at him and said, "You
Ro 15: 3 "The **i** of those who insult you have
2Co 12:10 I delight in weaknesses, in **i**, in
1Pe 2:23 they hurled their **i** at him, he did

Insurrection (Insurrectionists)
Lk 23:19 an **i** in the city, and for murder.)
23:25 thrown into prison for **i** and murder,

Insurrectionists (Insurrection)
Mk 15: 7 was in prison with the **i** who had

Intact
Pr 15:25 he keeps the widow's boundaries **i**.
Zec 12: 6 Jerusalem will remain **i** in her place

Integrity
Dt 9: 5 or your **i** that you are going in to
1Ki 9: 4 if you walk before me in **i** of heart
1Ch 29:17 the heart and are pleased with **i**.
Ne 7: 2 because he was a man of **i** and feared
Job 2: 3 And he still maintains his **i**, though
2: 9 Are you still holding on to your **i**?
6:29 reconsider, for my **i** is at stake.
27: 5 till I die, I will not deny my **i**.
Ps 7: 8 according to my **i**, O Most High.
25:21 May **i** and uprightness protect me,
41:12 In my **i** you uphold me and set me
78:72 David shepherded them with **i** of
Pr 10: 9 The man of **i** walks securely, but
11: 3 The **i** of the upright guides them,
13: 6 Righteousness guards the man of **i**,
17:26 or to flog officials for their **i**.
29:10 Bloodthirsty men hate a man of **i**
Isa 45:23 my mouth has uttered in all **i** a word
59: 4 no-one pleads his case with **i**.
Mt 22:16 "we know you are a man of **i** and that
Mk 12:14 we know you are a man of **i**.
Tit 2: 7 In your teaching show **i**,

Intelligence (Intelligent)
2Ch 2:12 endowed with **i** and discernment,
Isa 29:14 **i** of the intelligent will vanish."
Da 5:11 **i** and wisdom like that of the gods.
5:14 insight, **i** and outstanding wisdom.
1Co 1:19 the **i** of the intelligent I will

Intelligent (Intelligence)
1Sa 25: 3 She was an **i** and beautiful woman,
Isa 29:14 intelligence of the **i** will vanish."
Ac 13: 7 The proconsul, an **i** man, sent for
1Co 1:19 of the **i** I will frustrate."

Intelligible
1Co 14: 9 you speak **i** words with your tongue
14:19 speak five **i** words to instruct

Intend (Intended, Intending, Intends, Intent, Intention, Intentional, Intentionally, Intently)
Ge 37: 8 "Do you **i** to reign over us?"
Nu 35:23 enemy and he did not **i** to harm him,
1Sa 25:26 **i** to harm my master be like Nabal.
1Ki 5: 5 I **i**, therefore, to build a temple
2Ch 28:10 now you **i** to make the men and women
28:13 Do you **i** to add to our sin and guilt?
29:10 Now I **i** to make a covenant with the
Ps 62: 4 They fully **i** to topple him from his
Jn 7:35 "Where does this man **i** to go that we
14:22 why do you **i** to show yourself
Ac 5:35 what you **i** to do to these men.

Intended (Intend)
Ge 50:20 You **i** to harm me, but God **i** it for
Dt 19:19 do to him as he **i** to do to his
1Sa 14: 4 Jonathan **i** to cross to reach the
20:33 that his father **i** to kill David.
2Ch 32: 2 he **i** to make war on Jerusalem,
Jer 18:10 the good I had **i** to do for it.
Hos 2: 9 my linen, **i** to cover her nakedness.
Jn 6:15 Jesus, knowing that they **i** to come
12: 7 was **i**⌋ that she should save this
Ac 12: 4 Herod **i** to bring him out for public
20: 7 because he **i** to leave the next day,
Ro 7:10 commandment that was **i** to bring
2Co 7: 9 For you became sorrowful as God **i**

Intending (Intend)
Jdg 20: 5 surrounded the house, **i** to kill me.
Ac 12: 1 to the church, **i** to persecute them.

Intends (Intend)
Dt 28:57 For she **i** to eat them secretly
Isa 10: 7 this is not what he **i**, this is not

Intense (Intensely)
2Sa 13:15 Amnon hated her with **i** hatred.
1Th 2:17 out of our **i** longing we made every
Rev 16: 9 They were seared by the **i** heat and

Intensely (Intense)
Gal 1:13 how **i** I persecuted the church of God
Jas 4: 5 he caused to live in us envies **i**?
Rev 2:22 suffer **i**, unless they repent of her

Intent (Intend)
Ex 32:12 'It was with evil **i** that he brought
1Ch 29:17 given willingly and with honest **i**.
Ps 139:20 They speak of you with evil **i**; your
Pr 7:10 like a prostitute and with crafty **i**.
21:27 more so when brought with evil **i**!
Hos 5:11 in judgment, **i** on pursuing idols.
Mt 22:18 Jesus, knowing their evil **i**, said,
Eph 3:10 His **i** was that now, through the

Intention (Intend)
2Sa 13:32 This has been Absalom's expressed **i**
Job 34:14 If it were his **i** and he withdrew

Intentional (Intend)
Nu 15:25 for it was not **i** and they have

Intentionally (Intend)
Ex 21:13 However, if he does not do it **i**,
Nu 35:20 something at him **i** so that he

Intently (Intend)
Ac 1:10 They were looking **i** up into the sky
6:15 the Sanhedrin looked **i** at Stephen,
Jas 1:25 who looks **i** into the perfect law
1Pe 1:10 **i** and with the greatest care,

Intercede (Interceded, Intercedes, Interceding, Intercession, Intercessor)
Ge 23: 8 listen to me and **i** with Ephron
1Sa 2:25 the LORD, who will **i** for him?"
7: 5 I will **i** with the LORD for you."
1Ki 13: 6 "I with the LORD your God and
Heb 7:25 he always lives to **i** for them.

Interceded (Intercede)
1Ki 13: 6 So the man of God **i** with the LORD,

Intercedes (Intercede)
Ro 8:26 but the Spirit himself **i** for us with
8:27 because the Spirit **i** for the saints

Interceding (Intercede)
Ro 8:34 hand of God and is also **i** for us.

Intercession (Intercede)
Isa 53:12 and made **i** for the transgressors.
1Ti 2: 1 that requests, prayers, **i** and

Intercessor (Intercede)
Job 16:20 My **i** is my friend as my eyes pour

Interest (Interests)
Ex 22:25 a money-lender; charge him no **i**.
Lev 25:36 Do not take **i** of any kind from him,
25:37 You must not lend him money at **i** or
Dt 23:19 Do not charge your brother **i**,
23:19 or anything else that may earn **i**.
23:20 You may charge a foreigner **i**, but
Est 3: 8 the king's best **i** to tolerate them.
Pr 28: 8 exorbitant **i** amasses it for another,
Eze 18: 8 lend at usury or take excessive **i**.
18:13 at usury and takes excessive **i**.
18:17 and takes no usury or excessive **i**.
22:12 you take usury and excessive **i** and
Mt 25:27 would have received it back with **i**.
Lk 19:23 I could have collected it with **i**?'
Php 2:20 takes a genuine **i** in your welfare.
1Ti 6: 4 an unhealthy **i** in controversies

Interests (Interest)
Ezr 4:22 to the detriment of the royal **i**?
1Co 7:34 his **i** are divided. An unmarried
Php 2: 4 own **i**, but also to the **i** of others.
2:21 everyone looks out for his own **i**,

Interfere (Interfered)
Ezr 6: 7 Do not **i** with the work on this

Interfered (Interfere)
1Ki 1: 6 (His father had never **i** with him

Interior
1Ki 6:15 He lined its **i** walls with cedar
6:22 he overlaid the whole **i** with gold.
SS 3:10 its **i** lovingly inlaid by the
Ac 19: 1 the **i** and arrived at Ephesus.

Intermarry (Marry)
Ge 34: 9 **I** with us; give us your daughters
Dt 7: 3 Do not **i** with them. Do not give your
Jos 23:12 **i** with them and associate with them,
1Ki 11: 2 "You must not **i** with them, because
Ezr 9:14 **i** with the peoples who commit such

Intermittent
Job 6:15 are as undependable as **i** streams,

Interpret (Interpretation, Interpretations, Interpreted, Interpreter, Interpreters, Interprets)
Ge 40: 8 "but there is no-one to **i** them.
41: 8 but no-one could **i** them for him.
41:15 had a dream, and no-one can **i** it.
41:15 when you hear a dream you can **i** it

Da 2: 4 the dream, and we will i it."
2: 5 tell me what my dream was and i it
2: 6 tell me the dream and i it for me.
2: 7 the dream, and we will i it."
2: 9 will know that you can i it for me
2:16 that he might i the dream for him.
2:24 and I will i his dream for him."
2:26 what I saw in my dream and i it?"
2:36 and now we will i it to the king.
4: 6 before me to i the dream for me.
4: 7 but they could not i it for me.
4: 9 Here is my dream; i it for me.
4:18 men in my kingdom can i it for me.
5:12 and also the ability to i dreams,
Mt 16: 3 You know how to i the appearance
16: 3 cannot i the signs of the times.
Lk 12:56 You know how to i the appearance
12:56 know how to i this present time?
1Co 12:30 Do all speak in tongues? Do all i?
14:13 pray that he may i what he says.
14:27 one at a time, and someone must i.

Interpretation (Interpret)
Ge 40:16 Joseph had given a favourable i,
40:22 Joseph had said to them in his i.
41:12 giving each man the i of his dream.
Jdg 7:15 Gideon heard the dream and its i,
Da 2:30 O king, may know the i and that you
2:45 is true and the i is trustworthy."
4:24 "This is the i, O king, and this is
7:16 and gave me the i of these things:
1Co 12:10 to still another the i of tongues.
14:26 a revelation, a tongue or an i.
2Pe 1:20 came about by the prophet's own i.

Interpretations (Interpret)
Ge 40: 8 to them, "Do not i belong to God?
Da 5:16 you are able to give i and to solve

Interpreted (Interpret)
Ge 41:12 our dreams, and he i them for us
41:13 out exactly as he i them to us

Interpreter (Interpret)
Ge 42:23 them, since he was using an i.
1Co 14:28 If there is no i, the speaker should

Interpreters (Interpret)
Jer 27: 9 your diviners, your i of dreams,

Interprets (Interpret)
Dt 18:10 i omens, engages in witchcraft,
1Co 14: 5 i, so that the church may be edified.

Interrupted
Ac 26:24 At this point Festus i Paul's

Intersecting
Eze 1:16 to be made like a wheel i a wheel
10:10 each was like a wheel i a wheel.

Intervals
Eze 41:17 on the walls at regular i all round

Intervene (Intervened)
Isa 59:16 appalled that there was no-one to i

Intervened (Intervene)
Ps 106:30 Phinehas stood up and i, and the

Interwoven (Weave)
1Ki 7:17 A network of i chains festooned the
2Ch 3:16 He made i chains and put them on top
Ps 45:13 chamber; her gown is i with gold.

Intestines
2Sa 20:10 and his i spilled out on the ground.
Ac 1:18 open and all his i spilled out.

Intimate
1Ki 1: 4 king had no i relations with her.
Job 19:19 All my i friends detest me; those I
Job 29: 4 God's i friendship blessed my house,
Hos 3: 3 a prostitute or be i with any man,

Intimidate
Ne 6:13 He had been hired to i me so that
6:14 who have been trying to i me.
6:19 And Tobiah sent letters to i me.

Intoxicated
Rev 17: 2 i with the wine of her adulteries.

Intrigue (Intrigues)
Da 8:23 king, a master of i, will arise.
11:21 and he will seize it through i.
Hos 7: 6 they approach him with i.

Intrigues (Intrigue)
Ps 5:10 O God! Let their i be their downfall
31:20 you hide them from the i of men;

Introduce (Introduced, Introduction)
2Pe 2: 1 secretly i destructive heresies,

Introduced (Introduce)
2Ki 17: 8 that the kings of Israel had i.
17:19 followed the practices Israel had i.
Gal 3:17 The law, i 430 years later,
Heb 7:19 a better hope is i, by which we

Introduction (Introduce)
1Co 16: 3 I will give letters of i to the men

Invade (Invaded, Invader, Invaders, Invades, Invading)
Dt 12:29 you are about to i and dispossess.
1Sa 7:13 did not i Israelite territory again.
2Ch 20:10 to i when they came from Egypt;
Isa 7: 6 "Let us i Judah; let us tear it
Eze 38: 8 In future years you will i a land
38:11 You will say, "I will i a land of
Da 11: 9 the king of the North will i the
11:21 He will i the kingdom when its
11:24 he will i them and will achieve what
11:29 "At the appointed time he will i the
11:40 He will i many countries and sweep
11:41 He will also i the Beautiful Land.
Joel 3:17 never again will foreigners i her.
Na 1:15 No more will the wicked i you;

Invaded (Invade)
Ex 10:14 they i all Egypt and settled down in
Jdg 6: 3 other eastern peoples i the country.
6: 5 they i the land to ravage it.
2Ki 3:24 And the Israelites i the land and
15:19 Pul king of Assyria i the land, and
17: 5 The king of Assyria i the entire
24: 1 Nebuchadnezzar king of Babylon i the
1Ch 4:42 of Ishi, i the hill country of Seir.
2Ch 21:17 They attacked Judah, i it and
24:23 it i Judah and Jerusalem and killed
32: 1 king of Assyria came and i Judah.
Ps 79: 1 the nations have i your inheritance
Jer 35:11 when Nebuchadnezzar king of Babylon i
48:15 will be destroyed and her towns i;
Joel 1: 6 A nation has i my land, powerful and

Invader (Invade)
Isa 21: 1 an i comes from the desert, from a
Da 11:16 The i will do as he pleases; no-one

Invaders (Invade)
Jer 18:22 you suddenly bring i against them,

Invades (Invade)
Mic 5: 5 When the Assyrian i our land and
5: 6 the Assyrian when he i our land

Invading (Invade)
2Ch 20:22 i Judah, and they were defeated.
Hab 3:16 calamity to come on the nation i us.

Invalid
Jn 5: 5 been an i for thirty-eight years.
5: 7 "Sir," the i replied, "I have no-one

Invent (Invented)
Ro 1:30 they i ways of doing evil;

Invented (Invent)
2Pe 1:16 We did not follow cleverly i stories

Inventory
Ezr 1: 9 This was the i: gold dishes 30

Investigate (Investigated, Investigation)
Ex 9: 7 Pharaoh sent men to i and found that
Dt 13:14 you must enquire, probe and i it
17: 4 then you must i it thoroughly.
Ezr 10:16 month they sat down to i the cases,
Ecc 7:25 to i and to search out wisdom and
Ac 25:20 a loss how to i such matters;

Investigated (Investigate)
Jdg 6:29 they carefully i, they were told,
Est 2:23 the report was i and found to be
Lk 1: 3 since I myself have carefully i

Investigation (Investigate)
Dt 19:18 The judges must make a thorough i,
Ac 25:26 as a result of this i I may have

Invisible
Ro 1:20 God's i qualities—his eternal power
Col 1:15 He is the image of the i God, the
1:16 visible and i, whether thrones or
1Ti 1:17 to the King eternal, immortal, i,
Heb 11:27 because he saw him who is i.

Invitation (Invite)
2Sa 11:13 At David's i, he ate and drank with

Invite (Invitation, Invited, Invites, Inviting)
Ex 2:20 I him to have something to eat."
34:15 they will i you and you will eat
Jdg 14:15 Did you i us here to rob us?"
1Sa 16: 3 I Jesse to the sacrifice, and I will
1Ki 1:10 he did not i Nathan the prophet or
1:26 your servant Solomon he did not i.
Job 1: 4 and they would i their three sisters
Jer 35: 2 "Go to the Recabite family and i
Zec 3:10 each of you will i his neighbour
Mt 22: 9 Go to the street corners and i to
25:38 did we see you a stranger and i you
25:43 a stranger and you did not i me in
Lk 14:12 do not i your friends, your brothers
14:12 i you back and so you will be repaid.
14:13 when you give a banquet, i the poor,

Invited (Invite)
Ge 31:54 and i his relatives to a meal.
Nu 25: 2 who i them to the sacrifices to
1Sa 9:13 those who are i will eat.
9:22 who were i—about thirty in number.
9:24 the time I said, 'I have i guests.
16: 5 sons and i them to the sacrifice.
2Sa 13:23 i all the king's sons to come there.
15:11 They had been i as guests and went
1Ki 1: 9 He i all his brothers, the king's
1:19 and has i all the king's sons,
1:19 he has not i Solomon your servant.
1:25 He has i all the king's sons, the
Est 5:12 I'm the only person Queen Esther i
5:12 i me along with the king tomorrow.
Zep 1: 7 he has consecrated those he has i.
Mt 22: 3 those who had been i to the banquet
22: 4 'Tell those who have been i that I
22: 8 those I i did not deserve to come.
22:14 "For many are i, but few are chosen
25:35 I was a stranger and you i me in,
Lk 7:36 Now one of the Pharisees i Jesus to
7:39 the Pharisee who had i him saw this,

Lk 11:37 a Pharisee **i** him to eat with him;
14: 8 than you may have been **i**.
14: 9 If so, the host who **i** both of you
14:10 when you are **i**, take the lowest
14:16 a great banquet and **i** many guests.
14:17 to tell those who had been **i**,
14:24 **i** will get a taste of my banquet.
Jn 2: 2 had also been **i** to the wedding.
Ac 8:31 **i** Philip to come up and sit with him.
10:23 Peter **i** the men into the house to be
13:42 the people **i** them to speak further
16:15 were baptised, she **i** us to her home.
18:26 they **i** him to their home and
28:14 brothers who **i** us to spend a week
Rev 19: 9 'Blessed are those who are **i** to the

Invites (Invite)
Pr 9: 7 Whoever corrects a mocker **i** insult
10:14 but the mouth of a fool **i** ruin.
17:19 builds a high gate **i** destruction.
18: 6 strife, and his mouth **i** a beating.
Lk 14: 8 "When someone **i** you to a wedding
1Co 10:27 If some unbeliever **i** you to a meal

Inviting (Invite)
2Ch 30: 1 **i** them to come to the temple of the

Invoke (Invoked, Invokes, Invoking)
Ex 23:13 Do not **i** the names of other gods;
Jos 23: 7 do not **i** the names of their gods or
2Sa 14:11 "Then let the king **i** the LORD
Isa 48: 1 **i** the God of Israel—but not in
Jer 44:26 shall ever again **i** my name or swear,
Ac 19:13 to **i** the name of the Lord Jesus

Invoked (Invoke)
Hos 2:17 no longer will their names be **i**.

Invokes (Invoke)
Dt 29:19 he **i** a blessing on himself and
Isa 65:16 Whoever **i** a blessing in the land

Invoking (Invoke)
Job 31:30 sin by **i** a curse against his life—

Involve (Involved, Involves, Involving)
Jn 2: 4 "Dear woman, why do you **i** me?"

Involved (Involve)
Ex 24:14 **i** in a dispute can go to them."
28:38 and he will bear the guilt **i** in the
Nu 15:26 were **i** in the unintentional wrong.
Dt 19:17 the two men **i** in the dispute must
Ac 23:13 More than forty men were **i** in this
24:18 me, nor was I **i** in any disturbance.
2Ti 2: 4 No-one serving as a soldier gets **i**

Involves (Involve)
Ac 18:15 since it **i** questions about words and

Involving (Involve)
2Sa 3: 8 me of an offence **i** this woman!
1Ki 21: 1 an incident **i** a vineyard belonging

Inward (Inwardly)
2Sa 5: 9 from the supporting terraces **i**.
Eze 40:16 the openings all round faced **i**.

Inwardly (Inward)
Mt 7:15 but **i** they are ferocious wolves.
Ro 2:29 No, a man is a Jew if he is one **i**;
8:23 groan **i** as we wait eagerly for our
2Co 4:16 **i** we are being renewed day by day.
11:29 led into sin, and I do not **i** burn?

Iphdeiah
1Ch 8:25 **I** and Penuel were the sons of

Iphtah
Jos 15:43 **I**, Ashnah, Nezib,

Iphtah El
Jos 19:14 and ended at the Valley of **I**.
19:27 touched Zebulun and the Valley of **I**

Ir
1Ch 7:12 Huppites were the descendants of **I**,

Ir Nahash
1Ch 4:12 Paseah and Tehinnah the father of **I**

Ir Shemesh
Jos 19:41 included: Zorah, Eshtaol, **I**,

Ira
2Sa 20:26 **I** the Jairite was David's priest.
23:26 Helez the Paltite, **I** son of Ikkesh
23:38 **I** the Ithrite, Gareb the
1Ch 11:28 **I** son of Ikkesh from Tekoa, Abiezer
11:40 **I** the Ithrite, Gareb the Ithrite,
27: 9 sixth, for the sixth month, was **I**

Irad
Ge 4:18 To Enoch was born **I**, and **I** was the

Iram
Ge 36:43 Magdiel and **I**. These were the chiefs
1Ch 1:54 Magdiel and **I**. These were the chiefs

Iri
1Ch 7: 7 **I**, heads of families—five in all.

Irijah
Jer 37:13 whose name was **I** son of Shelemiah,
37:14 But **I** would not listen to him;

Iron (Iron-smelting, Irons, Neck-irons)
Ge 4:22 kinds of tools out of bronze and **i**.
Lev 26:19 make the sky above you like **i** and
Nu 31:22 Gold, silver, bronze, **i**, tin,
35:16 If a man strikes someone with an **i**
Dt 3:11 His bed was made of **i** and was more
8: 9 a land where the rocks are **i** and you
27: 5 Do not use any **i** tool upon them.
28:23 be bronze, the ground beneath you **i**.
28:48 He will put an **i** yoke on your neck
33:25 The bolts of your gates will be **i**
Jos 6:19 the articles of bronze and **i** are
6:24 the articles of bronze and **i** into
8:31 on which no **i** tool had been used.
17:16 live in the plain have **i** chariots,
17:18 though the Canaanites have **i**
19:38 **I**, Migdal El, Horem, Beth Anath and
22: 8 with silver, gold, bronze and **i**,
Jdg 1:19 plains, because they had **i** chariots.
4: 3 he had nine hundred **i** chariots and
4:13 **i** chariots and all the men with him,
1Sa 17: 7 **i** point weighed six hundred shekels.
2Sa 12:31 with saws and with **i** picks and axes,
23: 7 a tool of **i** or the shaft of a spear;
1Ki 6: 7 chisel or any other **i** tool was heard
22:11 had made **i** horns and he declared,
2Ki 6: 5 the **i** axe-head fell into the water.
6: 6 it there, and made the **i** float.
1Ch 20: 3 with saws and with **i** picks and axes.
22: 3 He provided a large amount of **i** to
22:14 quantities of bronze and **i** too great
22:16 in gold and silver, bronze and **i**
29: 2 bronze for the bronze, **i** for the **i**
29: 7 a hundred thousand talents of **i**.
2Ch 2: 7 bronze and **i**, and in purple, crimson
2:14 bronze and **i**, stone and wood, and
18:10 son of Kenaanah had made **i** horns,
24:12 **i** and bronze to repair the temple.
Job 19:24 that they were inscribed with an **i**
20:24 Though he flees from an **i** weapon,
28: 2 **I** is taken from the earth, and
40:18 of bronze, his limbs like rods of **i**
41:27 **I** he treats like straw and bronze
Ps 2: 9 will rule them with an **i** sceptre;
107:10 prisoners suffering in **i** chains,
107:16 bronze and cuts through bars of **i**.
149: 8 their nobles with shackles of **i**,
Pr 27:17 **i** sharpens **i**, so one man sharpens
Isa 45: 2 of bronze and cut through bars of **i**
48: 4 were **i**, your forehead was bronze.
60:17 you gold, and silver in place of **i**
60:17 bronze, and **i** in place of stones.
Jer 1:18 an **i** pillar and a bronze wall to
6:28 They are bronze and **i**; they all act
15:12 "Can a man break **i**—**i** from the
17: 1 "Judah's sin is engraved with an **i**
28:13 its place you will get a yoke of **i**.
28:14 says: I will put an **i** yoke on the
Eze 4: 3 take an **i** pan, place it as an **i** wall
22:18 **i** and lead left inside a furnace.
22:20 men gather silver, copper, **i**, lead
27:12 **i**, tin and lead for your merchandise.
27:19 **i**, cassia and calamus for your wares.
Da 2:33 its legs of **i**, its feet partly of **i**
2:34 feet of **i** and clay and smashed them.
2:35 the **i**, the clay, the bronze, the
2:40 strong as **i**—for **i** breaks and
2:40 as **i** breaks things to pieces,
2:41 of baked clay and partly of **i**,
2:41 some of the strength of **i** in it,
2:41 even as you saw **i** mixed with clay.
2:42 the toes were partly **i** and partly
2:43 just as you saw the **i** mixed with
2:43 any more than **i** mixes with clay.
2:45 hands—a rock that broke the **i**,
4:15 bound with **i** and bronze, remain in
4:23 but leave the stump, bound with **i**
5: 4 of bronze, **i**, wood and stone.
5:23 of bronze, **i**, wood and stone, which
7: 7 It had large **i** teeth; it crushed
7:19 with its **i** teeth and bronze
Am 1: 3 Gilead with sledges having **i** teeth,
Mic 4:13 for I will give you horns of **i**;
Ac 12:10 to the **i** gate leading to the city.
1Ti 4: 2 have been seared as with a hot **i**.
Rev 2:27 He will rule them with an **i** sceptre
9: 9 breastplates like breastplates of **i**,
12: 5 all the nations with an **i** sceptre.
18:12 costly wood, bronze, **i** and marble;
19:15 He will rule them with an **i** sceptre

Irons (Iron)
Ps 105:18 shackles, his neck was put in **i**,
Mk 5: 4 apart and broke the **i** on his feet.

Iron-smelting (Iron)
Dt 4:20 brought you out of the **i** furnace,
1Ki 8:51 out of Egypt, out of that **i** furnace
Jer 11: 4 out of Egypt, out of the **i** furnace.

Irpeel
Jos 18:27 Rekem, **I**, Taralah,

Irreligious
1Ti 1: 9 and sinful, the unholy and **i**;

Irresistible
Da 11:10 which will sweep on like an **i** flood

Irreverent
2Sa 6: 7 against Uzzah because of his **i** act;

Irrevocable
Ro 11:29 for God's gifts and his call are **i**.

Irrigated
Dt 11:10 you planted your seed and **i** it

Irritate
1Sa 1: 6 provoking her in order to **i** her.

Iru
1Ch 4:15 sons of Caleb son of Jephunneh: **I**

Isaac (Isaac's)
Son of Abraham and Sarah. Birth announced by God (Ge 17:15–19; 18:10–15; 21:1–7); heir through whom God's promises to Abraham continued (Ge 17:19, 21; 21:12; 26:2–5; Ro 9:6–9;

Heb 11:9); patriarch (Ge 50:24; Ex 3:6; Dt 29:13; Mt 8:11).
Offered by Abraham (Ge 22; Heb 11:17–19; Jas 2:21). Married Rebekah (Ge 24); father of Esau and Jacob (Ge 25:21–26; 1Ch 1:34). In Gerar, passed Rebekah off as his sister (Ge 26:6–11). Made treaty with Abimelech (Ge 26:26–31). Deceived by Rebekah; blessed Jacob as firstborn (Ge 27:1–29; 28:1–4). Death (Ge 35:28–29).

Ge 17:19 you a son, and you will call him **I.**
17:21 my covenant I will establish with **I,**
21: 3 Abraham gave the name **I** to the son
21: 4 his son **I** was eight days old,
21: 5 old when his son **I** was born to him.
21: 8 and on the day **I** was weaned Abraham
21:10 in the inheritance with my son **I.**"
21:12 because it is through **I** that your
22: 2 "Take your son, your only son, **I,**
22: 3 two of his servants and his son **I.**
22: 6 offering and placed it on his son **I,**
22: 7 **I** spoke up and said to his father
22: 7 "The fire and wood are here," **I** said,
22: 9 He bound his son **I** and laid him on
24: 4 and get a wife for my son **I.**"
24:14 you have chosen for your servant **I.**
24:62 Now **I** had come from Beer Lahai Roi,
24:64 Rebekah also looked up and saw **I.**
24:66 the servant told **I** all he had done.
24:67 **I** brought her into the tent of his
24:67 **I** was comforted after his mother's
25: 5 Abraham left everything he owned to **I**
25: 6 his son **I** to the land of the east.
25: 9 His sons **I** and Ishmael buried him in
25:11 God blessed his son **I,** who then
25:19 is the account of Abraham's son **I.**
25:19 Abraham became the father of **I,**
25:20 **I** was forty years old when he
25:21 **I** prayed to the LORD on behalf of
25:26 **I** was sixty years old when Rebekah
25:28 **I,** who had a taste for wild game,
26: 1 **I** went to Abimelech king of the
26: 2 The LORD appeared to **I** and said,
26: 6 **I** stayed in Gerar.
26: 8 **I** had been there a long time,
26: 8 saw **I** caressing his wife Rebekah.
26: 9 Abimelech summoned **I** and said,
26: 9 She is my sister'?" **I** answered him
26:12 **I** planted crops in that land and the
26:16 Abimelech said to **I,** "Move away from
26:17 **I** moved away from there and encamped
26:18 **I** reopened the wells that had been
26:25 **I** built an altar there and called on
26:27 **I** asked them, "Why have you come to
26:30 **I** then made a feast for them, and
26:31 Then **I** sent them on their way, and
26:35 They were a source of grief to **I** and
27: 1 **I** was old and his eyes were so weak
27: 2 **I** said, "I am now an old man and
27: 5 Now Rebekah was listening as **I** spoke
27:20 **I** asked his son, "How did you find
27:21 **I** said to Jacob, "Come near so I
27:22 Jacob went close to his father **I,**
27:26 his father **I** said to him, "Come here,
27:27 **I** caught the smell of his clothes
27:30 After **I** finished blessing him and
27:32 His father **I** asked him, "Who are you?
27:33 **I** trembled violently and said, "Who
27:37 **I** answered Esau, "I have made him
27:39 His father **I** answered him, "Your
27:46 Rebekah said to **I,** "I'm disgusted
28: 1 **I** called for Jacob and blessed him
28: 5 **I** sent Jacob on his way, and he went
28: 6 Now Esau learned that **I** had blessed
28: 8 Canaanite women were to his father **I**
28:13 father Abraham and the God of **I.**
31:18 his father **I** in the land of Canaan.
31:42 God of Abraham and the Fear of **I,**
31:53 name of the Fear of his father **I.**
32: 9 God of my father **I,** O LORD, who said
35:12 The land I gave to Abraham and **I** I
35:27 Jacob came home to his father **I** in
35:27 where Abraham and **I** had stayed.
35:28 **I** lived a hundred and eighty years.
46: 1 to the God of his father **I.**
48:15 my fathers Abraham and **I** walked,
48:16 names of my fathers Abraham and **I,**
49:31 there **I** and his wife Rebekah were
50:24 on oath to Abraham, **I** and Jacob."
Ex 2:24 with Abraham, with **I** and with Jacob
3: 6 the God of **I** and the God of Jacob.
3:15 the God of **I** and the God of
3:16 **I** and Jacob—appeared to me and
4: 5 the God of **I** and the God of
6: 3 I appeared to Abraham, to **I** and to
6: 8 give to Abraham, to **I** and to Jacob.
32:13 Remember your servants Abraham, **I**
33: 1 **I** and Jacob, saying, 'I will give
Lev 26:42 with **I** and my covenant with Abraham
Nu 32:11 on oath to Abraham, **I** and Jacob—
Dt 1: 8 **I** and Jacob—and to their
6:10 to Abraham, **I** and Jacob, to give you
9: 5 fathers, to Abraham, **I** and Jacob.
9:27 Remember your servants Abraham, **I**
29:13 your fathers, Abraham, **I** and Jacob.
30:20 your fathers, Abraham, **I** and Jacob.
34: 4 **I** and Jacob when I said, 'I will
Jos 24: 3 I gave him **I,**
24: 4 to **I** I gave Jacob and Esau.
1Ki 18:36 "O LORD, God of Abraham, **I** and
2Ki 13:23 covenant with Abraham, **I** and Jacob.
1Ch 1:28 The sons of Abraham: **I** and Ishmael.
1:34 was the father of **I.** The sons of **I:**
16:16 Abraham, the oath he swore to **I.**
29:18 God of our fathers Abraham, **I** and
2Ch 30: 6 the God of Abraham, **I** and Israel,
Ps 105: 9 Abraham, the oath he swore to **I.**
Jer 33:26 descendants of Abraham, **I** and Jacob.
Am 7: 9 "The high places of **I** will be
7:16 preaching against the house of **I.**'
Mt 1: 2 Abraham was the father of **I,** **I** the
8:11 **I** and Jacob in the kingdom of heaven.
22:32 God of **I,** and the God of Jacob'?
Mk 12:26 God of **I,** and the God of Jacob'?
Lk 3:34 son of Jacob, the son of **I,** the
13:28 when you see Abraham, **I** and Jacob
20:37 the God of **I,** and the God of Jacob'
Ac 3:13 The God of Abraham, **I** and Jacob, the
7: 8 And Abraham became the father of **I**
7: 8 Later **I** became the father of Jacob,
7:32 the God of Abraham, **I** and Jacob.
Ro 9: 7 It is through **I** that your offspring
9:10 and the same father, our father **I.**
Gal 4:28 Now you, brothers, like **I,** are
Heb 11: 9 as did **I** and Jacob, who were heirs
11:17 him, offered **I** as a sacrifice.
11:18 It is through **I** that your offspring
11:19 he did receive **I** back from death.
11:20 By faith **I** blessed Jacob and Esau
Jas 2:21 he offered his son **I** on the altar?

Isaac's (Isaac)

Ge 26:19 **I** servants dug in the valley and
26:20 quarrelled with **I** herdsmen and said,
26:32 That day **I** servants came and told

Isaiah

Prophet to Judah (Isa 1:1); commissioned by God (Isa 6). Married prophetess (Isa 8:3), had two sons whose names were clues to message (Isa 7:3; 8:3). Warned Ahaz; gave sign of Immanuel (Isa 7). Called for trust in God rather than human resources (Isa 7:9; 22:7–11; 31:1); rebuked Hezekiah's pride (2Ki 20:12–18; 2Ch 32:31; Isa 39:1–8). Announced deliverance from Assyria (Isa 10:12–19,24–27; 14:24–27; 36–37; 2Ki 19). Hezekiah's sickness and recovery (2Ki 20:1–11; 2Ch 32:24–26; Isa 38). Recorded Judah's history (2Ch 26:22; 32:32).

2Ki 19: 2 to the prophet **I** son of Amoz.
19: 5 King Hezekiah's officials came to **I,**
19: 6 **I** said to them, "Tell your master,
19:20 **I** son of Amoz sent a message to
20: 1 The prophet **I** son of Amoz went to
20: 4 Before **I** had left the middle court,
20: 7 **I** said, "Prepare a poultice of figs
20: 8 Hezekiah had asked **I,** "What will be
20: 9 **I** answered, "This is the LORD's sign
20:11 the prophet **I** called upon the LORD,
20:14 **I** the prophet went to King Hezekiah
20:16 **I** said to Hezekiah, "Hear the word
2Ch 26:22 by the prophet **I** son of Amoz.
32:20 King Hezekiah and the prophet **I** son
32:32 vision of the prophet **I** son of Amoz
Isa 1: 1 Jerusalem that **I** son of Amoz saw
2: 1 This is what **I** son of Amoz saw
7: 3 the LORD said to **I,** "Go out, you
7:13 **I** said, "Hear now, you house of
13: 1 An oracle concerning Babylon that **I**
20: 2 that time the LORD spoke through **I**
20: 3 the LORD said, "Just as my servant **I**
37: 2 to the prophet **I** son of Amoz.
37: 5 King Hezekiah's officials came to **I**
37: 6 **I** said to them, "Tell your master,
37:21 **I** son of Amoz sent a message to
38: 1 The prophet **I** son of Amoz went to
38: 4 the word of the LORD came to **I:**
38:21 **I** had said, "Prepare a poultice of
39: 3 **I** the prophet went to King Hezekiah
39: 5 **I** said to Hezekiah, "Hear the word
Mt 3: 3 spoken of through the prophet **I:**
4:14 was said through the prophet **I:**
8:17 was spoken through the prophet **I:**
12:17 was spoken through the prophet **I:**
13:14 is fulfilled the prophecy of **I:**
15: 7 **I** was right when he prophesied
Mk 1: 2 is written in **I** the prophet: "I will
7: 6 He replied, "**I** was right when he
Lk 3: 4 book of the words of **I** the prophet:
4:17 The scroll of the prophet **I** was
Jn 1:23 in the words of **I** the prophet,
12:38 to fulfil the word of **I** the prophet
12:39 because, as **I** says elsewhere:
12:41 **I** said this because he saw Jesus'
Ac 8:28 reading the book of **I** the prophet.
8:30 heard the man reading **I** the prophet.
28:25 when he said through **I** the prophet:
Ro 9:27 **I** cries out concerning Israel:
9:29 is just as **I** said previously:
10:16 For **I** says, "Lord, who has believed
10:20 **I** boldly says, "I was found by those
15:12 again, **I** says, "The Root of Jesse

Iscah

Ge 11:29 the father of both Milcah and **I.**

Iscariot

Mt 10: 4 Simon the Zealot and Judas **I,** who
26:14 Judas **I**—went to the chief
Mk 3:19 Judas **I,** who betrayed him.
14:10 Judas **I,** one of the Twelve, went to
Lk 6:16 Judas son of James, and Judas **I,** who
22: 3 Satan entered Judas, called **I,** one
Jn 6:71 (He meant Judas, the son of Simon **I,**
12: 4 one of his disciples, Judas **I,** who
13: 2 Judas **I,** son of Simon, to betray
13:26 he gave it to Judas **I,** son of Simon.
14:22 Judas (not Judas **I**) said, "But,

Ishbah

1Ch 4:17 Shammai and **I** the father of Eshtemoa

Ishbak

Ge 25: 2 Jokshan, Medan, Midian, **I** and Shuah
1Ch 1:32 Jokshan, Medan, Midian, **I** and Shuah

Ishbi-Benob

2Sa 21:16 **I,** one of the descendants of Rapha,

Ish-Bosheth

2Sa 2: 8 had taken **I** son of Saul and brought
2:10 **I** son of Saul was forty years old
2:12 with the men of **I** son of Saul,
2:15 **I** son of Saul, and twelve for David.
3: 7 And **I** said to Abner, "Why did you
3: 8 of what **I** said and he answered,
3:11 **I** did not dare to say another word
3:14 sent messengers to **I** son of Saul,
3:15 **I** gave orders and had her taken away
4: 1 **I** son of Saul heard that Abner had
4: 5 set out for the house of **I,** and they
4: 8 They brought the head of **I** to David
4: 8 "Here is the head of **I** son of Saul,
4:12 But they took the head of **I** and

Ishhod

1Ch 7:18 gave birth to **I**, Abiezer and Mahlah

Ishi

1Ch 2:31 The son of Appaim: **I**, who was the
4:20 The descendants of **I**: Zoheth and
4:42 the sons of **I**, invaded the hill
5:24 **I**, Eliel, Azriel, Jeremiah, Hodaviah

Ishijah

Ezr 10:31 **I**, Malkijah, Shemaiah, Shimeon,

Ishma

1Ch 4: 3 sons of Etam: Jezreel, **I** and Idbash.

Ishmael (Ishmaelite, Ishmaelites)

1. Son of Abraham by Hagar (Ge 16:15; 1Ch 1:28); circumcised (Ge 17:23–26); blessed by God, but not as heir of promise (Ge 17:19–21; 21:10–13; Gal 4:21–30). Hostility towards Isaac (Ge 16:12; 21:9; 25:18; Gal 4:29); driven away by Sarah (Ge 21:10–14); cry heard by God (Ge 21:15–21). With Isaac, buried Abraham (Ge 25:9). Children (Ge 25:12–16; 1Ch 1:29–31). Death (Ge 25:17). **2.** Son of Nethaniah; killed Gedaliah, governor of Judah, and his followers (2Ki 25:22–26; Jer 40:7–9; 41:1–16). Pursued by Johanan; escaped to Ammon (Jer 41:10–15).

Ge 16:11 You shall name him **I**, for the LORD
16:15 the name **I** to the son she had borne.
16:16 years old when Hagar bore him **I**.
17:18 **I** might live under your blessing!
17:20 And as for **I**, I have heard you:
17:23 very day Abraham took his son **I**
17:25 his son **I** was thirteen;
17:26 Abraham and his son **I** were both
25: 9 His sons Isaac and **I** buried him in
25:12 is the account of Abraham's son **I**,
25:13 are the names of the sons of **I**,
25:13 of **I**, Kedar, Adbeel, Mibsam,
25:16 These were the sons of **I**, and these
25:17 **I** lived a hundred and thirty-seven
28: 9 he went to **I** and married Mahalath,
28: 9 and daughter of **I** son of Abraham,
36: 3 also Basemath daughter of **I** and
2Ki 25:23 **I** son of Nethaniah, Johanan son
25:25 **I** son of Nethaniah, the son of
1Ch 1:28 The sons of Abraham: Isaac and **I**.
1:29 of **I**, Kedar, Adbeel, Mibsam,
1:31 These were the sons of **I**.
8:38 **I**, Sheariah, Obadiah and Hanan.
9:44 **I**, Sheariah, Obadiah and Hanan.
2Ch 19:11 and Zebadiah son of **I**, the leader of
23: 1 **I** son of Jehohanan, Azariah son of
Ezr 10:22 **I**, Nethanel, Jozabad and Elasah.
Jer 40: 8 **I** son of Nethaniah, Johanan and
40:14 **I** son of Nethaniah to take your life
40:15 "Let me go and kill **I** son of
40:16 you are saying about **I** is not true.
41: 1 In the seventh month **I** son of
41: 2 **I** son of Nethaniah and the ten men
41: 3 **I** also killed all the Jews who were
41: 6 **I** son of Nethaniah went out from
41: 7 **I** son of Nethaniah and the men who
41: 8 ten of them said to **I**, "Don't kill
41: 9 **I** son of Nethaniah filled it with
41:10 **I** made captives of all the rest of
41:10 **I** son of Nethaniah took them captive
41:11 **I** son of Nethaniah had committed,
41:12 went to fight **I** son of Nethaniah.
41:13 all the people **I** had with him saw
41:14 All the people **I** had taken captive
41:15 **I** son of Nethaniah and eight of his
41:16 recovered from **I** son of Nethaniah
41:18 **I** son of Nethaniah had killed

Ishmaelite (Ishmael)

1Ch 2:17 Amasa, whose father was Jether the **I**.
27:30 Obil the **I** was in charge of the

Ishmaelites (Ishmael)

Ge 37:25 a caravan of **I** coming from Gilead.
37:27 Come, let's sell him to the **I** and
37:28 to the **I**, who took him to Egypt.
39: 1 from the **I** who had taken him there.
Jdg 8:24 of the **I** to wear gold ear-rings.)
Ps 83: 6 the tents of Edom and the **I**, of Moab

Ishmaiah

1Ch 12: 4 **I** the Gibeonite, a mighty man among
27:19 over Zebulun: **I** son of Obadiah; over

Ishmerai

1Ch 8:18 **I**, Izliah and Jobab were the sons of

Ishpah

1Ch 8:16 Michael, **I** and Joha were the sons of

Ishpan

1Ch 8:22 **I**, Eber, Eliel,

Ishvah

Ge 46:17 The sons of Asher: Imnah, **I**, Ishvi
1Ch 7:30 The sons of Asher: Imnah, **I**, Ishvi

Ishvi (Ishvite)

Ge 46:17 sons of Asher: Imnah, Ishvah, **I**
Nu 26:44 through **I**, the Ishvite clan;
1Sa 14:49 Saul's sons were Jonathan, **I** and
1Ch 7:30 sons of Asher: Imnah, Ishvah, **I**

Ishvite (Ishvi)

Nu 26:44 through Ishvi, the **I** clan;

Island (Islanders, Islands)

Isa 23: 2 Be silent, you people of the **i** and
23: 6 Tarshish; wail, you people of the **i**.
Ac 13: 6 They travelled through the whole **i**
27:14 swept down from the **i**.
27:16 we passed to the lee of a small **i**
27:26 we must run aground on some **i**."
28: 1 out that the **i** was called Malta.
28: 7 the chief official of the **i**.
28: 9 sick on the **i** came and were cured.
28:11 a ship that had wintered in the **i**.
Rev 1: 9 was on the **i** of Patmos because of
6:14 and **i** was removed from its place.
16:20 Every **i** fled away and the mountains

Islanders (Island)

Ac 28: 2 The **i** showed us unusual kindness.
28: 4 **i** saw the snake hanging from his

Islands (Island)

Isa 11:11 Hamath and from the **i** of the sea.
24:15 God of Israel, in the **i** of the sea.
40:15 the **i** as though they were fine dust.
41: 1 "Be silent before me, you **i**! Let the
41: 5 The **i** have seen it and fear; the
42: 4 his law the **i** will put their hope."
42:10 it, you **i**, and all who live in them.
42:12 and proclaim his praise in the **i**.
42:15 rivers into **i** and dry up the pools.
49: 1 Listen to me, you **i**; hear this, you
51: 5 The **i** will look to me and wait in
59:18 he will repay the **i** their due.
60: 9 Surely the **i** look to me; in the lead
66:19 and to the distant **i** that have not
Eze 26:18 the **i** in the sea are terrified at

Ismakiah

2Ch 31:13 Jerimoth, Jozabad, Eliel, **I**,

Isolate (Isolation)

Lev 13:50 **i** the affected article for seven
13:54 is to **i** it for another seven days.

Isolation (Isolate)

Lev 13: 4 infected person in **i** for seven days.
13: 5 to keep him in **i** another seven days.
13:11 in **i**, because he is already unclean.
13:21 is to put him in **i** for seven days.
13:26 is to put him in **i** for seven days.
13:31 infected person in **i** for seven days.
13:33 to keep him in **i** another seven days.

Israel (*All Israel, Elders of Israel, God of Israel, Holy One of Israel, House of Israel, Israel and Judah,* Israel's, Israelite, Israelites, Israelites', *Kings of Israel, Men of Israel, My people Israel, People of Israel*)

The new name given to Jacob (Ge 32:28; 35:10), was soon used of the land where his descendants settled (Ge 34:7; 49:7), giving rise to the 12 tribes of Israel (Ge 49:28). While in Egypt and the wilderness, it was used only of the people (Ex 5:2), but once resettled in Canaan it was used of the land and kingdom (Lev 20:2; 22:18; Dt 17:4, 20; 18:6; Jdg 5:2, 7). It reached its full potential (Nu 34:1–15; Eze 47:13–21) under the reigns of David and Solomon. After the kingdom divided it designated the ten tribes of the northern kingdom (1Ki 11:31, 35), as opposed to Judah in the south (which had absorbed Simeon). For 2 centuries Israel was in conflict with Judah (1Ki 12:19), until it fell to the Assyrians (2Ki 17). Re-unification was prophesied (Jer 3:18; Eze 37:16–17).

Ge 32:28 name will no longer be Jacob, but **I**
33:20 an altar and called it El Elohe **I**.
34: 7 had done a disgraceful thing in **I** by
35:10 name will be **I**. So he named him **I**.
35:21 **I** moved on again and pitched his
35:22 While **I** was living in that region,
35:22 concubine Bilhah, and **I** heard of it.
37: 3 Now **I** loved Joseph more than any of
37:13 **I** said to Joseph, "As you know, your
43: 6 **I** asked, "Why did you bring this
43: 8 Judah said to **I** his father, "Send
43:11 their father **I** said to them, "If it
45:21 the sons of **I** did this. Joseph gave
45:28 **I** said, "I'm convinced! My son
46: 1 **I** set out with all that was his,
46: 2 God spoke to **I** in a vision at night
46: 8 These are the names of the sons of **I**
46:29 went to Goshen to meet his father **I**.
46:30 **I** said to Joseph, "Now I am ready to
47:29 the time drew near for **I** to die, he
47:31 Then Joseph swore to him, and **I**
48: 2 **I** rallied his strength and sat up
48: 8 **I** saw the sons of Joseph, he asked,
48: 9 Then **I** said, "Bring them to me so
48:11 **I** said to Joseph, "I never expected
48:14 **I** reached out his right hand and put
48:20 "In your name will **I** pronounce this
48:21 **I** said to Joseph, "I am about to die,
49: 2 of Jacob; listen to your father **I**.
49: 7 in Jacob and disperse them in **I**.
49:16 people as one of the tribes of **I**.
49:24 of the Shepherd, the Rock of **I**,
49:28 these are the twelve tribes of **I**,
50: 2 his service to embalm his father **I**.
50:25 Joseph made the sons of **I** swear an
Ex 1: 1 are the names of the sons of **I**
4:22 LORD says: **I** is my firstborn son,
5: 2 that I should obey him and let **I** go?
5: 2 the LORD and I will not let **I** go."
6:14 of Reuben the firstborn son of **I**
9: 4 livestock of **I** and that of Egypt,
11: 7 a distinction between Egypt and **I**.
12: 3 Tell the whole community of **I** that
12: 6 **I** must slaughter them at twilight.
12:15 the seventh must be cut off from **I**.
12:19 be cut off from the community of **I**,
12:47 The whole community of **I** must
13:19 made the sons of **I** swear an oath.
14:20 between the armies of Egypt and **I**.
14:30 That day the LORD saved **I** from the
14:30 and **I** saw the Egyptians lying dead
15:22 Moses led **I** from the Red Sea and
18: 1 done for Moses and for his people **I**,
18: 1 the LORD had brought **I** out of Egypt.
18: 9 good things the LORD had done for **I**
18:11 those who had treated **I** arrogantly."
19: 2 and **I** camped there in the desert in
24: 4 representing the twelve tribes of **I**.
28: 9 on them the names of the sons of **I**
28:11 Engrave the names of the sons of **I**
28:12 memorial stones for the sons of **I**.
28:21 each of the names of the sons of **I**,
28:29 bear the names of the sons of **I**
32: 4 said, "These are your gods, O **I**,

Ex 32: 8 said, 'These are your gods, O I,
32:13 Isaac and I, to whom you swore by
34:27 a covenant with you and with I."
39: 6 with the names of the sons of I.
39: 7 memorial stones for the sons of I,
39:14 each of the names of the sons of I,
Lev 16:17 and the whole community of I.
19: 2 Speak to the entire assembly of I
20: 2 Israelite or any alien living in I
22:18 Israelite or an alien living in I
Nu 1: 3 all the men in I twenty years old
1:16 were the heads of the clans of I.
1:20 of Reuben the firstborn son of I:
1:44 and the twelve leaders of I, each
3:13 in I, whether man or animal.
3:45 in place of all the firstborn of I
4:46 Moses, Aaron and the leaders of I
7: 2 the leaders of I, the heads of
8:17 Every firstborn male in I, whether
8:18 of all the firstborn sons in I.
10: 4 —the heads of the clans of I—
10:29 LORD has promised good things to I.
10:36 to the countless thousands of I."
18:14 "Everything in I that is devoted to
18:21 tithes in I as their inheritance
19:13 That person must be cut off from I.
20:14 "This is what your brother I says:
20:21 territory, I turned away from them.
21: 1 heard that I was coming along the
21: 2 I made this vow to the LORD: "If you
21:17 I sang this song: "Spring up, O well!
21:21 I sent messengers to say to Sihon
21:23 Sihon would not let I pass through
21:23 out into the desert against I.
21:23 he reached Jahaz, he fought with I.
21:24 I, however, put him to the sword and
21:25 I captured all the cities of the
21:31 I settled in the land of the
22: 2 all that I had done to the Amorites,
23: 7 Jacob for me; come, denounce I.'
23:10 Jacob or number the fourth part of I?
23:21 in Jacob, no misery observed in I.
23:23 Jacob, no divination against I.
23:23 and of I, 'See what God has done!'
24: 1 that it pleased the LORD to bless I,
24: 2 Balaam looked out and saw I encamped
24: 5 your dwelling-places, O I!
24:17 a sceptre will rise out of I.
24:18 conquered, but I will grow strong.
25: 1 While I was staying in Shittim, the
25: 3 I joined in worshipping the Baal of
25: 4 fierce anger may turn away from I."
25: 6 the whole assembly of I while they
26: 2 are able to serve in the army of I."
26: 5 the firstborn son of I, were:
30: 1 to the heads of the tribes of I:
31: 4 men from each of the tribes of I."
31: 5 were supplied from the clans of I.
32:13 The LORD's anger burned against I
32:14 the LORD even more angry with I.
32:22 obligation to the LORD and to I.
36: 7 No inheritance in I is to pass from
Dt 1:38 he will lead I to inherit it.
2:12 just as I did in the land the LORD
4: 1 Hear now, O I, the decrees and laws
5: 1 Hear, O I, the decrees and the laws
6: 3 Hear, O I, and be careful to obey
6: 4 Hear, O I: The LORD our God, the
9: 1 Hear, O I. You are now about to
10:12 now, O I, what does the LORD your
17: 4 detestable thing has been done in I
17:12 You must purge the evil from I.
17:20 a long time over his kingdom in I.
18: 1 no allotment or inheritance with I.
18: 6 anywhere in I where he is living,
19:13 You must purge from I the guilt of
20: 3 He shall say: "Hear, O I, today you
21: 8 this atonement for your people I,
22:21 has done a disgraceful thing in I
22:22 You must purge the evil from I.
25: 6 name will not be blotted out from I.
25: 7 to carry on his brother's name in I.
25:10 That man's line shall be known in I
26:15 and bless your people I and the land
27: 9 "Be silent, O I, and listen! You
29:21 all the tribes of I for disaster,
Dt 31:30 hearing of the whole assembly of I
32: 8 to the number of the sons of I.
33: 5 along with the tribes of I.
33:10 precepts to Jacob and your law to I
33:21 and his judgments concerning I."
33:28 I will live in safety alone;
33:29 Blessed are you, O I! Who is like
34:10 Since then, no prophet has risen in I
Jos 3:12 tribes of I, one from each tribe.
4:22 tell them, 'I crossed the Jordan on
6:18 the camp of I liable to destruction
6:23 in a place outside the camp of I.
7: 1 So the LORD's anger burned against I.
7: 8 I has been routed by its enemies?
7:11 I has sinned; they have violated my
7:13 which is devoted is among you, O I.
7:15 done a disgraceful thing in I!'
7:16 Joshua had I come forward by tribes
8:10 of I marched before them to Ai.
8:14 meet I in battle at a certain place
8:17 or Bethel who did not go after I.
8:17 city open and went in pursuit of I.
8:22 I cut them down, leaving them
8:24 I had finished killing all the men
8:27 I did carry off for themselves the
8:35 not read to the whole assembly of I,
9: 2 to make war against Joshua and I.
10: 1 with I and were living near them.
10:10 threw them into confusion before I,
10:10 I pursued them along the road going
10:11 they fled before I on the road down
10:12 LORD gave the Amorites over to I,
10:12 LORD in the presence of I: "O sun,
10:14 Surely the LORD was fighting for I!
10:32 The LORD handed Lachish over to I,
10:42 LORD, the God of I, fought for I.
11: 5 Waters of Merom, to fight against I.
11: 6 hand all of them over to I, slain.
11: 8 LORD gave them into the hand of I
11:13 Yet I did not burn any of the cities
11:16 mountains of I with their foothills,
11:20 their hearts to wage war against I,
11:21 and from all the hill country of I.
11:23 he gave it as an inheritance to I
12: 7 inheritance to the tribes of I
13: 6 Be sure to allocate this land to I
14: 1 tribal clans of I allotted to them.
14:10 while I moved about in the desert.
19:51 the heads of the tribal clans of I
21: 1 of the other tribal families of I
21:43 the LORD gave I all the land he had
22:12 the whole assembly of I gathered at
22:14 one for each of the tribes of I,
22:18 angry with the whole community of I
22:20 come upon the whole community of I?
22:21 to the heads of the clans of I:
22:22 the LORD! He knows! And let I know!
23: 1 the LORD had given I rest from all
24: 1 Joshua assembled all the tribes of I
24: 1 leaders, judges and officials of I,
24: 9 prepared to fight against I, he sent
24:31 I served the LORD throughout the
24:31 everything the LORD had done for I.
Jdg 1:28 I became strong, they pressed the
2: 7 things the LORD had done for I.
2:10 the LORD nor what he had done for I.
2:14 In his anger against I the LORD
2:15 Whenever I went out to fight, the
2:20 LORD was very angry with I and said,
2:22 I will use them to test I and see
3: 8 anger of the LORD burned against I
3:12 Eglon king of Moab power over I.
3:13 Eglon came and attacked I, and they
3:30 That day Moab was made subject to I,
3:31 He too saved I.
4: 4 was leading I at that time.
5: 2 When the princes in I take the lead,
5: 7 Village life in I ceased, ceased
5: 7 Deborah, arose, arose a mother in I
5: 8 was seen among forty thousand in I.
5:11 righteous acts of his warriors in I
6: 4 did not spare a living thing for I,
6:14 and save I out of Midian's hand.
6:15 "how can I save I? My clan is the
6:36 save I by my hand as you have
6:37 save I by my hand, as you said."
Jdg 7: 2 In order that I may not boast
7:15 He returned to the camp of I and
9:22 After Abimelech had governed I for
10: 1 the son of Dodo, rose to save I.
10: 2 He led I for twenty-three years;
10: 3 who led I for twenty-two years.
10: 9 and I was in great distress.
11: 4 when the Ammonites made war on I,
11:13 "When I came up out of Egypt, they
11:15 I did not take the land of Moab or
11:16 I went through the desert to the
11:17 I sent messengers to the king of
11:17 So I stayed at Kadesh.
11:19 "Then I sent messengers to Sihon
11:20 Sihon, however, did not trust I to
11:20 encamped at Jahaz and fought with I.
11:21 I took over all the land of the
11:23 Amorites out before his people I,
11:25 quarrel with I or fight with them?
11:26 For three hundred years I occupied
11:33 Thus I subdued Ammon.
11:40 that each year the young women of I
12: 7 Jephthah led I for six years.
12: 8 After him, Ibzan of Bethlehem led I.
12: 9 Ibzan led I for seven years.
12:11 After him, Elon the Zebulunite led I
12:13 son of Hillel, from Pirathon, led I.
12:14 He led I for eight years.
13: 5 deliverance of I from the hands of
14: 4 that time they were ruling over I.)
15:20 Samson led I for twenty years in the
16:31 He had led I for twenty years.
17: 6 In those days I had no king;
18: 1 In those days I had no king.
18: 1 inheritance among the tribes of I.
18:19 you serve a tribe and clan in I
18:29 who was born to I—though the city
19: 1 In those days I had no king.
19:29 sent them into all the areas of I.
20: 2 the tribes of I took their places
20: 6 this lewd and disgraceful act in I.
20:10 hundred from all the tribes of I,
20:10 for all this vileness done in I."
20:12 The tribes of I sent men throughout
20:13 to death and purge the evil from I.
20:17 I, apart from Benjamin, mustered
20:29 I set an ambush around Gibeah.
20:35 LORD defeated Benjamin before I,
21: 3 "why has this happened to I?
21: 3 one tribe be missing from I today?"
21: 5 "Who from all the tribes of I has
21: 6 "Today one tribe is cut off from I,"
21: 8 Which one of the tribes of I failed
21:15 had made a gap in the tribes of I.
21:17 a tribe of I will not be wiped out.
21:25 In those days I had no king;
Ru 4: 7 (Now in earlier times in I, for the
4: 7 of legalising transactions in I.)
4:14 May he become famous throughout I!
1Sa 2:28 all the tribes of I to be my priest
2:32 Although good will be done to I, in
3:11 I am about to do something in I that
4: 2 deployed their forces to meet I,
4: 2 I was defeated by the Philistines,
4:10 I lost thirty thousand foot soldiers
4:17 "I fled before the Philistines, and
4:18 He had led I for forty years.
4:21 "The glory has departed from I"
4:22 "The glory has departed from I,
7: 6 Samuel was leader of I at Mizpah.
7: 7 the Philistines heard that I had
7:10 drew near to engage I in battle.
7:14 from I were restored to her,
7:14 and I delivered the neighbouring
7:14 peace between I and the Amorites.
7:15 Samuel continued as judge over I
7:16 judging I in all those places.
7:17 and there he also judged I.
8: 1 appointed his sons as judges for I.
9: 9 (Formerly in I, if a man went to
9:20 And to whom is all the desire of I
9:21 from the smallest tribe of I,
10:18 'I brought I up out of Egypt, and I
10:20 Samuel brought all the tribes of I
11: 3 send messengers throughout I;
11: 7 pieces by messengers throughout I,

1Sa 11:13 this day the LORD has rescued I."
13: 1 over I for ⌊forty-⌋ two years.
13: 2 Saul chose three thousand men from I
13: 4 and now I has become an offence to
13: 5 Philistines assembled to fight I,
13:13 your kingdom over I for all time.
13:19 be found in the whole land of I,
14:12 has given them into the hand of I.
14:23 the LORD rescued I that day, and
14:39 as the LORD who rescues I lives,
14:45 about this great deliverance in I?
14:47 After Saul had assumed rule over I,
14:48 delivering I from the hands of those
15: 1 anoint you king over his people I;
15: 2 for what they did to I when they
15:17 become the head of the tribes of I?
15:17 The LORD anointed you king over I.
15:26 has rejected you as king over I!"
15:28 The LORD has torn the kingdom of I
15:29 He who is the Glory of I does not
15:30 and before I; come back with me,
15:35 that he had made Saul king over I.
16: 1 I have rejected him as king over I?
17: 8 stood and shouted to the ranks of I
17:10 "This day I defy the ranks of I!
17:21 I and the Philistines were drawing
17:25 coming out? He comes out to defy I.
17:25 father's family from taxes in I."
17:26 and removes this disgrace from I?
17:45 armies of I, whom you have defied.
17:46 will know that there is a God in I.
18: 6 of I to meet King Saul with singing
18:18 my family or my father's clan in I,
23:17 You shall be king over I, and I will
24:14 "Against whom has the king of I come
24:20 I will be established in your hands.
25:30 and has appointed him leader over I,
26:15 And who is like you in I? Why didn't
26:20 The king of I has come out to look
27: 1 searching for me anywhere in I,
28: 1 their forces to fight against I.
28:19 The LORD will hand over both I and
28:19 the army of I to the Philistines."
29: 1 I camped by the spring in Jezreel.
29: 3 was an officer of Saul king of I?
30:25 for I from that day to this.
31: 1 the Philistines fought against I;
2Sa 1:19 "Your glory, O I, lies slain on your
1:24 "O daughters of I, weep for Saul,
2:10 over I, and he reigned two years.
2:28 no longer pursued I, nor did they
3:19 to tell David everything that I
3:38 great man has fallen in I this day?
5: 1 All the tribes of I came to David at
5: 2 led I on their military campaigns.
5: 3 and they anointed David king over I.
5:12 had established him as king over I
5:12 for the sake of his people I.
5:17 David had been anointed king over I,
6: 1 David again brought together out of I
6:20 How the king of I has distinguished
6:21 mw ruler over the LORD's people I
7:23 who is like your people I—the one
7:24 You have established your people I
7:26 'The LORD Almighty is God over I!'
10: 9 some of the best troops in I
10:15 been routed by I, they regrouped.
10:18 they fled before I, and David killed
10:19 that they had been defeated by I,
12: 7 'I anointed you king over I, and I
13:12 a thing should not be done in I!
13:13 like one of the wicked fools in I.
15: 2 is from one of the tribes of I."
15:10 throughout the tribes of I to say,
18: 6 marched into the field to fight I,
18: 7 There the army of I was defeated by
18:16 pursuing I, for Joab halted them.
19: 9 Throughout the tribes of I, the
19:11 what is being said throughout I has
19:22 anyone be put to death in I today?
19:22 know that today I am king over I?"
19:40 troops of I had taken the king over.
20: 1 Every man to his tent O I!"
20:14 the tribes of I to Abel Beth Maacah
20:19 are the peaceful and faithful in I
20:19 a city that is a mother in I.

2Sa 21: 2 Gibeonites were not a part of I
21: 4 right to put anyone in I to death.
21: 5 and have no place anywhere in I,
21:15 between the Philistines and I.
21:17 lamp of I will not be extinguished
21:21 he taunted I, Jonathan son of
23: 3 the Rock of I said to me: 'When one
24: 1 anger of the LORD burned against I,
24: 2 "Go throughout the tribes of I from
24: 9 In I there were eight hundred
24:15 the LORD sent a plague on I from
24:25 and the plague on I was stopped.
1Ki 1: 3 they searched throughout I for a
1:34 the prophet anoint him king over I.
2: 4 to have a man on the throne of I.'
2:11 had reigned for forty years over I
4:20 The people of Judah and I were as
4:25 Solomon's lifetime Judah and I
6: 1 year of Solomon's reign over I,
8: 5 the entire assembly of I that had
8:14 While the whole assembly of I was
8:16 not chosen a city in any tribe of I
8:20 and now I sit on the throne of I,
8:22 in front of the whole assembly of I
8:25 sit before me on the throne of I,
8:30 your servant and your people I
8:33 "When your people I have been
8:34 forgive the sin of your people I
8:36 sin of your servants, your people I
8:38 is made by any of your people I
8:41 does not belong to your people I
8:43 for you, as do your own people I
8:52 and to the plea of your people I,
8:55 and blessed the whole assembly of I
8:56 to his people I just as he promised
8:59 the cause of his people I according
8:66 his servant David and his people I
9: 5 your royal throne over I for ever,
9: 5 to have a man on the throne of I.'
9: 7 I will cut off I from the land I
9: 7 I will then become a byword and an
10: 9 and placed you on the throne of I.
10: 9 of the LORD's eternal love for I,
11:25 in Aram and was hostile towards I.
11:32 chosen out of all the tribes of I,
11:37 desires; you will be king over I.
11:38 for David and will give I to you.
12: 3 I went to Rehoboam and said to him
12:16 To your tents, O I! Look after your
12:19 I has been in rebellion against
12:28 Here are your gods, O I, who
14:10 every last male in I—slave or free.
14:14 raise up for himself a king over I
14:15 the LORD will strike I, so that it
14:15 will uproot I from this good land
14:16 he will give I up because of the
14:16 and has caused I to commit."
14:21 of I in which to put his Name.
15: 9 Jeroboam king of I, Asa became
15:16 king of I throughout their reigns.
15:17 Baasha king of I went up against
15:19 your treaty with Baasha king of I
15:20 his forces against the towns of I.
15:25 son of Jeroboam became king of I in
15:25 he reigned over I for two years.
15:26 which he had caused I to commit.
15:30 and had caused I to commit,
15:32 king of I throughout their reigns.
15:34 which he had caused I to commit.
16: 8 Elah son of Baasha became king of I
16:13 and had caused I to commit,
16:16 king over I that very day there in
16:19 and had caused I to commit.
16:23 Omri became king of I, and he
16:26 which he had caused I to commit,
16:29 Ahab son of Omri became king of I,
16:29 Samaria over I for twenty-two years
18:17 "Is that you, you troubler of I?
18:18 "I have not made trouble for I,"
18:19 summon the people from all over I
18:31 come, saying, "Your name shall be I.
18:36 LORD, God of Abraham, Isaac and I
18:36 known today that you are God in I
19:16 Jehu son of Nimshi king over I,
19:18 Yet I reserve seven thousand in I
20: 2 into the city to Ahab king of I,

1Ki 20: 4 king of I answered, "Just as you
20: 7 The king of I summoned all the
20:11 The king of I answered, "Tell him:
20:13 to Ahab king of I and announced,
20:21 The king of I advanced and
20:22 the prophet came to the king of I
20:25 we can fight I on the plains.
20:26 went up to Aphek to fight against I.
20:28 God came up and told the king of I,
20:31 Let us go to the king of I with
20:32 went to the king of I and said,
20:40 your sentence," the king of I said.
20:41 and the king of I recognised him as
20:43 Sullen and angry, the king of I went
21: 7 Is this how you act as king over I?
21:18 "Go down to meet Ahab king of I,
21:21 every last male in I—slave or free.
21:22 to anger and have caused I to sin.'
21:26 the LORD drove out before I.)
22: 1 there was no war between Aram and I.
22: 2 Judah went down to see the king of I
22: 3 The king of I had said to his
22: 4 Jehoshaphat replied to the king of I
22: 5 also said to the king of I,
22: 6 the king of I brought together the
22: 8 The king of I answered Jehoshaphat,
22: 9 the king of I called one of his
22:10 the king of I and Jehoshaphat king
22:18 The king of I said to Jehoshaphat,
22:26 The king of I then ordered, "Take
22:29 the king of I and Jehoshaphat king
22:30 The king of I said to Jehoshaphat,
22:30 So the king of I disguised himself
22:31 or great, except the king of I."
22:32 "Surely this is the king of I.
22:33 saw that he was not the king of I
22:34 hit the king of I between the
22:41 the fourth year of Ahab king of I.
22:44 also at peace with the king of I.
22:51 son of Ahab became king of I
22:51 and he reigned over I for two years.
22:52 son of Nebat, who caused I to sin.
2Ki 1: 1 death, Moab rebelled against I.
1: 3 Is it because there is no God in I
1: 6 Is it because there is no God in I
1:16 Is it because there is no God in I
2:12 The chariots and horsemen of I!"
3: 1 Joram son of Ahab became king of I
3: 3 which he had caused I to commit;
3: 4 and he had to supply the king of I
3: 5 Moab rebelled against the king of I
3: 9 the king of I set out with the king
3:10 "What!" exclaimed the king of I.
3:11 officer of the king of I answered,
3:12 So the king of I and Jehoshaphat
3:13 Elisha said to the king of I, "What
3:13 "No," the king of I answered,
3:24 the Moabites came to the camp of I,
3:27 The fury against I was great; they
5: 2 taken captive a young girl from I,
5: 4 him what the girl from I had said.
5: 5 will send a letter to the king of I
5: 6 that he took to the king of I read:
5: 7 soon as the king of I read the
5: 8 the king of I had torn his robes,
5: 8 know that there is a prophet in I."
5:12 better than any of the waters of I?
5:15 no God in all the world except in I.
6: 8 the king of Aram was at war with I.
6: 9 sent word to the king of I: "Beware
6:10 the king of I checked on the place
6:11 us is on the side of the king of I?"
6:12 but Elisha, the prophet who is in I,
6:12 tells the king of I the very words
6:21 the king of I saw them, he asked
6:26 the king of I was passing by on the
7: 6 "Look, the king of I has hired the
8:16 year of Joram son of Ahab king of I,
8:25 year of Joram son of Ahab king of I,
8:26 a granddaughter of Omri king of I.
9: 3 LORD says: I anoint you king over I.
9: 6 you king over the LORD's people I.
9: 8 every last male in I—slave or free.
9:12 LORD says: I anoint you king over I.
9:21 Joram king of I and Ahaziah king of
10:21 he sent word throughout I, and all

2Ki 10:28 Jehu destroyed Baal worship in I.
10:29 which he had caused I to commit—
10:30 of I to the fourth generation."
10:31 which he had caused I to commit.
10:32 LORD began to reduce the size of I.
10:36 The time that Jehu reigned over I in
13: 1 of Jehu became king of I in Samaria,
13: 2 which he had caused I to commit,
13: 3 the LORD's anger burned against I,
13: 4 the king of Aram was oppressing I.
13: 5 The LORD provided a deliverer for I,
13: 6 I to commit; they continued in them.
13:10 Jehoahaz became king of I in Samaria,
13:11 which he had caused I to commit;
13:14 Jehoash king of I went down to see
13:14 "The chariots and horsemen of I!"
13:16 hands," he said to the king of I.
13:22 Hazael king of Aram oppressed I
14: 1 Jehoash son of Jehoahaz king of I,
14: 8 the son of Jehu, king of I, with the
14: 9 Jehoash king of I replied to Amaziah
14:11 so Jehoash king of I attacked.
14:12 Judah was routed by I, and every
14:13 Jehoash king of I captured Amaziah
14:17 Jehoash son of Jehoahaz king of I.
14:23 Jeroboam son of Jehoash king of I
14:24 which he had caused I to commit.
14:25 who restored the boundaries of I
14:26 had seen how bitterly everyone in I
14:27 out the name of I from under heaven,
14:28 including how he recovered for I
15: 1 year of Jeroboam king of I,
15: 8 Jeroboam became king of I in Samaria
15: 9 which he had caused I to commit.
15:12 of I to the fourth generation."
15:17 Menahem son of Gadi became king of I
15:18 which he had caused I to commit.
15:20 Menahem exacted this money from I.
15:23 Menahem became king of I in Samaria
15:24 which he had caused I to commit.
15:27 Remaliah became king of I in Samaria
15:28 which he had caused I to commit.
15:29 In the time of Pekah king of I,
15:32 Pekah son of Remaliah king of I,
16: 5 Pekah son of Remaliah king of I
16: 7 the king of I who are attacking me.
17: 1 Hoshea son of Elah became king of I
17:18 the LORD was very angry with I and
17:19 the practices I had introduced.
17:20 LORD rejected all the people of I;
17:21 he tore I away from the house of
17:21 Jeroboam enticed I away from
17:34 of Jacob, whom he named I.
18: 1 of Hoshea son of Elah king of I,
18: 9 of Hoshea son of Elah king of I,
18:10 ninth year of Hoshea king of I.
18:11 The king of Assyria deported I to
21: 3 pole, as Ahab king of I had done.
21: 7 chosen out of all the tribes of I,
23:13 the ones Solomon king of I had built
23:15 who had caused I to sin—even that
23:22 the days of the judges who led I,
23:27 from my presence as I removed I,
24:13 gold articles that Solomon king of I
1Ch 1:34 The sons of Isaac: Esau and I.
2: 1 These were the sons of I: Reuben,
2: 7 who brought trouble on I by
5: 1 sons of Reuben the firstborn of I
5: 1 to the sons of Joseph son of I;
5: 3 sons of Reuben the firstborn of I
5:17 of Judah and Jeroboam king of I.
6:38 the son of Levi, the son of I;
6:49 making atonement for I, in
7:29 Joseph son of I lived in these towns
10: 1 Now the Philistines fought against I
11: 2 led I on their military campaigns.
11: 3 and they anointed David king over I
12:32 knew what I should do—200 chiefs,
12:40 and sheep, for there was joy in I.
13: 2 said to the whole assembly of I,
13: 2 throughout the territories of I,
14: 2 had established him as king over I
14: 2 for the sake of his people I.
16:13 O descendants of I his servant,
16:17 to I as an everlasting covenant:
16:40 of the LORD, which he had given I.
1Ch 17: 5 I up out of Egypt to this day.
17:21 who is like your people I—the one
17:22 made your people I your very own
17:24 'The LORD Almighty, the God over I,
19:10 some of the best troops in I
19:16 saw that they had been routed by I,
19:18 they fled before I, and David killed
19:19 that they had been defeated by I,
20: 7 he taunted I, Jonathan son of Shimea,
21: 1 Satan rose up against I and incited
21: 1 incited David to take a census of I.
21: 3 Why should he bring guilt on I?"
21: 4 Joab left and went throughout I
21: 7 the sight of God; so he punished I.
21:12 the LORD ravaging every part of I.
21:14 the LORD sent a plague on I, and
22: 1 the altar of burnt offering for I."
22: 2 to assemble the aliens living in I,
22: 9 I will grant I peace and quiet
22:10 of his kingdom over I for ever.'
22:12 when he puts you in command over I,
22:13 that the LORD gave to Moses for I.
22:17 David ordered all the leaders of I
23: 1 made his son Solomon king over I.
23: 2 together all the leaders of I,
26:29 as officials and judges over I.
26:30 responsible in I west of the Jordan
27:16 The officers over the tribes of I:
27:22 the officers over the tribes of I.
27:23 had promised to make I as numerous
27:24 Wrath came on I on account of this
28: 1 summoned all the officials of I
28: 4 family to be king over I for ever.
28: 5 of the kingdom of the LORD over I.
29: 6 the officers of the tribes of I,
29:10 God of our father I, from
29:18 of our fathers Abraham, Isaac and I
29:25 as no king over I ever had before.
29:27 He ruled over I for forty years
29:30 I and the kingdoms of all the other
2Ch 1: 2 to all the leaders in I, the heads
1:13 And he reigned over I.
2: 4 This is a lasting ordinance for I.
2:17 of all the aliens who were in I,
5: 6 the entire assembly of I that had
6: 3 While the whole assembly of I was
6: 5 not chosen a city in any tribe of I
6:10 and now I sit on the throne of I,
6:12 in front of the whole assembly of I
6:13 down before the whole assembly of I
6:16 to sit before me on the throne of I
6:21 your servant and of your people I
6:24 "When your people I have been
6:25 forgive the sin of your people I
6:27 sin of your servants, your people I
6:29 is made by any of your people I
6:32 does not belong to your people I
6:33 fear you, as do your own people I
7:10 and Solomon and for his people I.
7:18 fail to have a man to rule over I.'
7:20 I will uproot I from my land,
8:11 in the palace of David king of I,
9: 8 of the love of your God for I
10:16 To your tents, O I! Look after your
10:19 I has been in rebellion against the
11: 1 fighting men—to make war against I
11:13 throughout I sided with him.
11:16 Those from every tribe of I who set
12: 6 The leaders of I and the king
12:13 chosen out of all the tribes of I
13: 5 given the kingship of I to David
15: 3 For a long time I was without the
15: 9 numbers had come over to him from I
15:17 not remove the high places from I,
16: 1 king of I went up against Judah
16: 3 your treaty with Baasha King of I
16: 4 his forces against the towns of I.
16:11 book of the kings of Judah and I.
17: 1 and strengthened himself against I.
17: 4 rather than the practices of I.
18: 3 Ahab king of I asked Jehoshaphat
18: 4 also said to the king of I,
18: 5 the king of I brought together the
18: 7 The king of I answered Jehoshaphat,
18: 8 the king of I called one of his
18: 9 the king of I and Jehoshaphat king
2Ch 18:17 The king of I said to Jehoshaphat,
18:19 Who will entice Ahab king of I into
18:25 The king of I then ordered, "Take
18:28 the king of I and Jehoshaphat king
18:29 The king of I said to Jehoshaphat,
18:29 So the king of I disguised himself
18:30 or great, except the king of I."
18:31 thought, "This is the king of I.
18:32 saw that he was not the king of I,
18:33 hit the king of I between the
18:34 and the king of I propped himself up
20: 7 of this land before your people I
20:10 you would not allow I to invade
20:29 had fought against the enemies of I.
20:35 an alliance with Ahaziah king of I
21: 2 were sons of Jehoshaphat king of I.
21: 4 along with some of the princes of I
22: 5 with Joram son of Ahab king of I to
24: 6 by the assembly of I for the Tent
24: 9 God had required of I in the desert.
24:16 done in I for God and his temple.
25: 6 fighting men from I for a hundred
25: 7 "O king, these troops from I must
25: 7 for the LORD is not with I—not with
25:17 king of I: "Come, meet me face to
25:18 Jehoash king of I replied to Amaziah
25:21 Jehoash king of I attacked. He and
25:22 Judah was routed by I, and every man
25:23 Jehoash king of I captured Amaziah
25:25 Jehoash son of Jehoahaz king of I.
25:26 book of the kings of Judah and I?
28: 5 into the hands of the king of I,
28:13 and his fierce anger rests on I."
28:19 Judah because of Ahaz king of I,
28:26 book of the kings of Judah and I.
29:27 the instruments of David king of I.
30: 5 to send a proclamation throughout I
30: 6 the God of Abraham, Isaac and I,
30:25 and all who had assembled from I,
30:25 the aliens who had come from I and
30:26 Solomon son of David king of I
31: 8 the LORD and blessed his people I.
32:32 book of the kings of Judah and I.
33: 7 chosen out of all the tribes of I,
34: 7 all the incense altars throughout I.
34: 9 Ephraim and the entire remnant of I
34:33 in I serve the LORD their God.
35: 3 Solomon son of David king of I built
35: 3 the LORD your God and his people I.
35: 4 king of I and by his son Solomon.
35:18 not been observed like this in I
35:18 the Levites and all Judah and I who
35:25 These became a tradition in I and
Ezr 2:59 families were descended from I:
3:10 as prescribed by David king of I.
3:11 his love to I endures for ever.
4: 3 heads of the families of I answered,
5:11 great king of I built and finished.
6:17 one for each of the tribes of I.
7:10 teaching its decrees and laws in I
7:11 and decrees of the LORD for I:
7:28 leading men from I to go up with me.
8:18 Mahli, son of Levi, the son of I,
8:29 Levites and the family heads of I.
10: 2 of this, there is still hope for I.
Ne 7:61 families were descended from I:
8: 1 which the LORD had commanded for I
10:33 offerings to make atonement for I
13: 3 excluded from I all who were of
13:18 I by desecrating the Sabbath."
13:26 that Solomon king of I sinned?
Ps 14: 7 Oh, that salvation for I would come
14: 7 let Jacob rejoice and I be glad!
22: 3 Holy One; you are the praise of I.
22:23 Revere him, all you descendants of I!
25:22 Redeem I, O God, from all their
50: 7 O I, and I will testify against you
53: 6 Oh, that salvation for I would come
53: 6 let Jacob rejoice and I be glad!
68:26 the LORD in the assembly of I.
68:34 whose majesty is over I, whose
73: 1 Surely God is good to I, to those
76: 1 God is known; his name is great in I
78: 5 Jacob and established the law in I,
78:21 Jacob, and his wrath rose against I,
78:55 the tribes of I in their homes.

Ps 78:59 he rejected I completely.
78:71 people Jacob, of I his inheritance.
80: 1 Hear us, O Shepherd of I, you who
81: 4 is a decree for I, an ordinance
81: 8 if you would but listen to me, O I!
81:11 I would not submit to me.
81:13 to me, if I would follow my ways,
83: 4 name of I be remembered no more."
99: 8 you were to I a forgiving God,
105:10 to I as an everlasting covenant:
105:23 I entered Egypt; Jacob lived as an
105:37 He brought out I, laden with silver
105:38 dread of I had fallen on them.
114: 1 I came out of Egypt, the house of
114: 2 God's sanctuary, I his dominion.
115:12 He will bless the house of I,
118: 2 Let I say: "His love endures for
121: 4 he who watches over I will neither
122: 4 according to the statute given to I.
124: 1 not been on our side—let I say—
125: 5 Peace be upon I.
128: 6 Peace be upon I.
129: 1 me from my youth—let I say—
130: 7 O I, put your hope in the LORD,
130: 8 He himself will redeem I from all
131: 3 O I, put your hope in the LORD both
135: 4 I to be his treasured possession.
135:12 an inheritance to his people I.
136:11 brought I out from among them
136:14 brought I through the midst of it,
136:22 an inheritance to his servant I;
147: 2 he gathers the exiles of I.
147:19 Jacob, his laws and decrees to I.
148:14 of I, the people close to his heart.
149: 2 Let I rejoice in their Maker;
Pr 1: 1 of Solomon son of David, king of I:
Ecc 1:12 I, the Teacher, was king over I in
SS 3: 7 by sixty warriors, the noblest of I,
Isa 1: 3 but I does not know, my people do
1:24 the Mighty One of I, declares: "Ah,
4: 2 and glory of the survivors in I.
7: 1 Pekah son of Remaliah king of I
8:14 but for both houses of I he will be
8:18 We are signs and symbols in I from
9: 8 against Jacob; it will fall on I.
9:12 have devoured I with open mouth.
9:14 the LORD will cut off from I both
10:17 The Light of I will become a fire,
10:20 In that day the remnant of I, the
10:22 Though your people, O I, be like the
11:12 nations and gather the exiles of I;
11:16 for I when they came up from Egypt.
14: 1 once again he will choose I and will
19:24 In that day I will be the third,
19:25 my handiwork, and I my inheritance."
27: 6 I will bud and blossom and fill all
30:29 of the LORD, to the Rock of I.
40:27 complain, O I, "My way is hidden
41: 8 "But you, O I, my servant, Jacob,
41:14 I, for I myself will help you,"
42:24 and I to the plunderers? Was it not
43: 1 he who formed you, O I: "Fear not,
43:22 not wearied yourselves for me, O I
43:28 Jacob to destruction and I to scorn.
44: 1 my servant, I, whom I have chosen.
44: 5 LORD's', and will take the name I.
44:21 Jacob, for you are my servant, O I.
44:21 servant; O I, I will not forget you.
44:23 Jacob, he displays his glory in I.
45: 4 of I my chosen, I summon you by name
45:15 himself, O God and Saviour of I.
45:17 I will be saved by the LORD with an
45:25 in the LORD all the descendants of I
46:13 to Zion, my splendour to I.
48: 1 you who are called by the name of I
48:12 "Listen to me, O Jacob, I, whom I
49: 3 said to me, "You are my servant, I
49: 5 back to him and gather I to himself,
49: 6 bring back those of I I have kept.
56: 8 he who gathers the exiles of I:
57:19 on the lips of the mourners in I.
63:16 know us or I acknowledge us; you,
Jer 2: 3 I was holy to the LORD, the
2:14 Is I a servant, a slave by birth?
2:31 Have I been a desert to I or a land
3: 6 you seen what faithless I has done?
Jer 3: 8 I gave faithless I her certificate
3:11 The LORD said to me, "Faithless I is
3:12 'Return, faithless I,' declares the
3:23 LORD our God is the salvation of I.
4: 1 "If you will return, O I, return to
6: 9 "Let them glean the remnant of I as
10:16 including I, the tribe of his
14: 8 O Hope of I, its Saviour in times of
17:13 O LORD, the hope of I, all who
18:13 thing has been done by Virgin I.
23: 6 be saved and I will live in safety.
23: 8 who brought the descendants of I up
29:23 have done outrageous things in I;
30:10 do not be dismayed, O I,'
31: 1 be the God of all the clans of I,
31: 2 I will come to give rest to I."
31: 4 you will be rebuilt, O Virgin I.
31: 7 save your people, the remnant of I.'
31:10 'He who scattered I will gather them
31:21 O Virgin I, return to your towns.
31:36 the descendants of I ever cease
31:37 I reject all the descendants of I
32:20 both in I and among all mankind,
32:21 brought your people I out of Egypt
33: 7 I will bring Judah and I back from
36: 2 I have spoken to you concerning I,
41: 9 defence against Baasha king of I.
46:27 my servant; do not be dismayed, O I.
48:27 Was not I the object of your
49: 1 "Has I no sons? Has she no heirs?
49: 2 Then I will drive out those who
50:17 "I is a scattered flock that lions
50:19 I will bring I back to his own
Lam 2: 1 splendour of I from heaven to earth
2: 3 he has cut off every horn of I.
2: 5 an enemy; he has swallowed up I.
Eze 6: 2 face against the mountains of I;
6: 3 say: 'O mountains of I, hear the
7: 2 Sovereign LORD says to the land of I
9: 8 to destroy the entire remnant of I
11:10 judgment on you at the borders of I
11:11 judgment on you at the borders of I
11:13 destroy the remnant of I?"
11:15 the whole house of I—are those of
11:17 give you back the land of I again.'
12:19 in Jerusalem and in the land of I:
12:22 proverb you have in the land of I:
12:23 they will no longer quote it in I.
13: 2 of I who are now prophesying.
13: 4 Your prophets, O I, are like jackals
13: 9 nor will they enter the land of I.
13:16 those prophets of I who prophesied
14: 7 or any alien living in I separates
17:23 On the mountain heights of I I will
18: 2 this proverb about the land of I:
18: 3 no longer quote this proverb in I.
19: 1 lament concerning the princes of I
19: 9 no longer on the mountains of I.
20: 5 LORD says: On the day I chose I,
20:38 they will not enter the land of I.
20:40 the high mountain of I, declares the
20:42 when I bring you into the land of I,
21: 2 Prophesy against the land of I
21:12 it is against all the princes of I.
21:25 "'O profane and wicked prince of I,
22: 6 "'See how each of the princes of I
25: 3 over the land of I when it was laid
25: 6 of your heart against the land of I,
27:17 "'Judah and I traded with you;
33:24 ruins in the land of I are saying,
33:28 and the mountains of I will become
34: 2 prophesy against the shepherds of I
34: 2 Woe to the shepherds of I who only
34:13 pasture them on the mountains of I,
34:14 of I will be their grazing land.
34:14 rich pasture on the mountains of I.
35:12 said against the mountains of I.
36: 1 prophesy to the mountains of I and
36: 1 O mountains of I, hear the word
36: 4 therefore, O mountains of I, hear
36: 6 prophesy concerning the land of I
36: 8 "'But you, O mountains of I, will
37:12 bring you back to the land of I.
37:22 in the land, on the mountains of I.
37:28 know that I the LORD make I holy,
38: 8 to the mountains of I, which had
Eze 38:17 by my servants the prophets of I?
38:18 When Gog attacks the land of I,
38:19 a great earthquake in the land of I.
39: 2 send you against the mountains of I.
39: 4 On the mountains of I you will fall,
39: 7 I the LORD am the Holy One in I.
39: 9 live in the towns of I will go out
39:11 I will give Gog a burial place in I,
39:17 sacrifice on the mountains of I.
40: 2 he took me to the land of I and set
44:10 went far from me when I went astray
44:28 are to give them no possession in I
44:29 and everything in I devoted to the
45: 8 This land will be his possession in I
45: 9 gone far enough O princes of I!
45:15 from the well-watered pastures of I.
45:16 gift for the use of the prince in I.
47:13 among the twelve tribes of I, with
47:18 between Gilead and the land of I,
47:21 according to the tribes of I.
47:22 inheritance among the tribes of I.
48:19 will come from all the tribes of I.
48:29 an inheritance to the tribes of I,
48:31 will be named after the tribes of I
Hos 1: 1 of Jeroboam son of Joash king of I:
1: 4 will put an end to the kingdom of I.
4:15 "Though you commit adultery, O I,
5: 3 I is not hidden from me.
5: 3 to prostitution; I is corrupt.
5: 9 of I I proclaim what is certain.
6:10 to prostitution and I is defiled.
7: 1 whenever I would heal I, the sins
8: 2 I cries out to me, 'O our God, we
8: 3 I has rejected what is good;
8: 6 They are from I! This calf—a
8: 8 I is swallowed up; now she is among
8:14 I has forgotten his Maker and built
9: 1 Do not rejoice, O I; do not be
9: 7 Let I know this. Because your sins
9:10 "When I found I, it was like finding
10: 1 I was a spreading vine; he brought
10: 6 I will be ashamed of its wooden
10: 8 be destroyed—it is the sin of I.
10: 9 of Gibeah, you have sinned, O I,
10:15 the king of I will be completely
11: 1 "When I was a child, I loved him,
11: 2 the more I called I, the further
11: 8 Ephraim? How can I hand you over, I?
12:12 I served to get a wife, and to pay
12:13 The LORD used a prophet to bring I
13: 1 men trembled; he was exalted in I.
13: 9 "You are destroyed, O I, because you
14: 1 Return, O I, to the LORD your God.
14: 5 I will be like the dew to I; he will
Joel 2:27 you will know that I am in I, that I
Am 1: 1 what he saw concerning I two years
1: 1 son of Jehoash was king of I.
2: 6 For three sins of I, even for four
3:14 "On the day I punish I for her sins
4:12 this is what I will do to you, I,
4:12 prepare to meet your God, O I."
5: 2 "Fallen is Virgin I, never to rise
5: 3 for I will have only a hundred left;
7: 9 the sanctuaries of I will be ruined
7:10 a message to Jeroboam king of I:
7:10 against you in the very heart of I.
7:11 and I will surely go into exile,
7:16 'Do not prophesy against I, and stop
7:17 And I will certainly go into exile,
9: 7 "Did I not bring I up from Egypt,
9:14 will bring back my exiled people I;
9:15 I will plant I in their own land,
Mic 1:13 of I were found in you.
1:15 the glory of I will come to Adullam
2:12 bring together the remnant of I.
3: 8 his transgression, to I his sin.
5: 2 for me one who will be ruler over I
5: 3 Therefore I will be abandoned until
6: 2 he is lodging a charge against I.
Na 2: 2 of Jacob like the splendour of I,
Zep 3:13 The remnant of I will do no wrong;
3:14 shout aloud, O I! Be glad and
3:15 LORD, the King of I, is with you;
Zec 1:19 scattered Judah, I and Jerusalem."
8:13 O Judah and I, so will I save you,
9: 1 the tribes of I are on the LORD—

Zec 11:14 brotherhood between Judah and **I**.
12: 1 the word of the LORD concerning **I**.
Mal 1: 1 An oracle: The word of the LORD to **I**
1: 5 LORD—even beyond the borders of **I**!'
2:11 committed in **I** and in Jerusalem:
Mt 2:20 his mother and go to the land of **I**,
2:21 mother and went to the land of **I**.
8:10 anyone in **I** with such great faith.
9:33 like this has ever been seen in **I**."
10: 6 Go rather to the lost sheep of **I**.
10:23 of **I** before the Son of Man comes.
15:24 sent only to the lost sheep of **I**."
19:28 judging the twelve tribes of **I**.
27:42 He's the King of **I**! Let him come
Mk 12:29 Hear, O **I**, the Lord our God, the
15:32 Let this Christ, this King of **I**,
Lk 1:54 He has helped his servant **I**,
1:80 until he appeared publicly to **I**.
2:25 waiting for the consolation of **I**,
2:32 and for glory to your people **I**."
2:34 falling and rising of many in **I**,
4:25 many widows in **I** in Elijah's time,
4:27 there were many in **I** with leprosy
7: 9 found such great faith even in **I**."
22:30 judging the twelve tribes of **I**.
24:21 the one who was going to redeem **I**.
Jn 1:31 was that he might be revealed to **I**.
1:49 Son of God; you are the King of **I**."
12:13 "Blessed is the King of **I**!
Ac 1: 6 going to restore the kingdom to **I**?"
5:31 and forgiveness of sins to **I**.
13:23 brought to **I** the Saviour Jesus,
28:20 It is because of the hope of **I** that
Ro 9: 6 all who are descended from **I** are **I**
9:27 Isaiah cries out concerning **I**:
9:31 **I**, who pursued a law of
10:19 Again I ask: Did **I** not understand?
10:21 concerning **I** he says, "All day long
11: 2 he appealed to God against **I**:
11: 7 What **I** sought so earnestly
11:11 to the Gentiles to make **I** envious.
11:25 **I** has experienced a hardening in
Gal 6:16 this rule, even to the **I** of God.
Eph 2:12 excluded from citizenship in **I** and
3: 6 Gentiles are heirs together with **I**,
Heb 11:28 would not touch the firstborn of **I**.
Rev 7: 4 144,000 from all the tribes of **I**.
21:12 the names of the twelve tribes of **I**

Israel and Judah

1Sa 17:52 the men of **I** surged forward with a
18:16 all **I** loved David, because he led
2Sa 3:10 establish David's throne over **I**
5: 5 over all **I** for thirty-three years.
11:11 The ark and **I** are staying in tents,
12: 8 I gave you the house of **I**. And if
21: 2 for **I** had tried to annihilate them.
24: 1 saying, "Go and take a census of **I**.
1Ki 1:35 I have appointed him ruler over **I**."
2Ki 17:13 The LORD warned **I** through all his
2Ch 27: 7 in the book of the kings of **I**.
30: 1 Hezekiah sent word to all **I** and also
30: 6 couriers went throughout **I** with
31: 6 The men of **I** who lived in the towns
34:21 for the remnant in **I** about what is
35:27 in the book of the kings of **I**.
36: 8 in the book of the kings of **I**.
Jer 30: 3 'when I will bring my people **I** back
30: 4 words the LORD spoke concerning **I**:
32:30 "The people of **I** have done nothing
32:32 The people of **I** have provoked me by
51: 5 For **I** have not been forsaken by
Eze 9: 9 "The sin of the house of **I** is

Israel's (Israel)

Ge 42: 5 **I** sons were among those who went to
46: 5 **I** sons took their father Jacob and
48:10 Now **I** eyes were failing because of
48:12 Joseph removed them from **I** knees and
48:13 Ephraim on his right towards **I** left
48:13 on his left towards **I** right hand,
Ex 14:19 been travelling in front of **I** army,
18: 8 the Egyptians for **I** sake and about
Nu 1:45 who were able to serve in **I** army
11:16 "Bring me seventy of **I** elders who
21: 3 The LORD listened to **I** plea and gave
25: 5 Moses said to **I** judges, "Each of you
Jos 10:30 that city and its king into **I** hand.
Jdg 3:10 he became **I** judge and went to war.
5: 9 My heart is with **I** princes, with the
10:16 And he could bear **I** misery no longer.
11:21 Sihon and all his men into **I** hands,
20: 6 to each region of **I** inheritance,
20:34 ten thousand of **I** finest men made a
1Sa 6: 5 country, and pay honour to **I** god.
7: 9 cried out to the LORD on **I** behalf,
14:37 Will you give them into **I** hand?"
2Sa 20:23 Joab was over **I** entire army; Benaiah
23: 1 the God of Jacob, **I** singer of songs:
23:11 of lentils, **I** troops fled from them.
1Ki 2: 5 to the two commanders of **I** armies,
2:32 commander of **I** army, and Amasa son
11:25 Rezon was **I** adversary as long as
2Ki 6:23 Aram stopped raiding **I** territory.
1Ch 17:24 the God over Israel, is **I** God!'
2Ch 13:17 casualties among **I** able men.
Ezr 10:10 foreign women, adding to **I** guilt.
Isa 43:15 your Holy One, **I** Creator, your King
44: 6 **I** King and Redeemer, the LORD
56:10 **I** watchmen are blind, they all lack
Jer 3: 9 **I** immorality mattered so little to
31: 9 because I am **I** father, and Ephraim
50:20 "search will be made for **I** guilt,
51:49 must fall because of **I** slain,
Hos 1: 5 In that day I will break **I** bow
5: 5 **I** arrogance testifies against them;
7:10 **I** arrogance testifies against him,
Mic 5: 1 will strike **I** ruler on the cheek
Jn 3:10 "You are **I** teacher," said Jesus,

Israelite (Israel)

Ge 36:31 in Edom before any **I** king reigned:
Ex 5:14 The **I** foremen appointed by Pharaoh's
5:15 the **I** foremen went and appealed to
5:19 The **I** foremen realised they were in
12:40 Now the length of time the **I** people
16: 1 The whole **I** community set out from
16: 9 "Say to the entire **I** community,
16:10 speaking to the whole **I** community,
17: 1 The whole **I** community set out from
24: 5 he sent young **I** men, and they
35: 1 assembled the whole **I** community
35: 4 Moses said to the whole **I** community,
35:20 the whole **I** community withdrew from
35:29 All the **I** men and women who were
Lev 4:13 "'If the whole **I** community sins
16: 5 From the **I** community he is to take
17: 3 Any **I** who sacrifices an ox, a lamb
17: 8 "Say to them: 'Any **I** or any alien
17:10 "'Any **I** or any alien living among
17:13 "'Any **I** or any alien living among
20: 2 "Say to the Israelites: 'Any **I** or
22:18 'If any of you—either an **I** or an
24:10 Now the son of an **I** mother and an
24:10 in the camp between him and an **I**.
24:11 The son of the **I** woman blasphemed
Nu 1: 2 a census of the whole **I** community
1:53 will not fall on the **I** community.
3:12 male offspring of every **I** woman.
3:40 Count all the firstborn **I** males who
7:84 the offerings of the **I** leaders
8: 9 and assemble the whole **I** community.
8:16 male offspring from every **I** woman.
8:20 Aaron and the whole **I** community
10:28 order of march for the **I** divisions
13:26 Aaron and the whole **I** community at
14: 5 the whole **I** assembly gathered there.
14: 7 said to the entire **I** assembly, "The
15:25 atonement for the whole **I** community,
15:26 The whole **I** community and the aliens
15:29 he is a native-born **I** or an alien.
16: 2 With them were 250 **I** men, well-known
16: 9 from the rest of the **I** community
16:41 The next day the whole **I** community
19: 9 be kept by the **I** community
20: 1 first month the whole **I** community
20:22 The whole **I** community set out from
25: 6 an **I** man brought to his family a
25: 8 followed the **I** into the tent. He
25: 8 the **I** and into the woman's body.
Nu 25:14 The name of the **I** who was killed
26: 2 a census of the whole **I** community
27:20 whole **I** community will obey him.
31:12 the priest and the **I** assembly at
32:18 **I** has received his inheritance.
32:28 to the family heads of the **I** tribes.
36: 1 the heads of the **I** families.
36: 3 they marry men from other **I** tribes;
36: 7 for every **I** shall keep the tribal
36: 8 who inherits land in any **I** tribe
36: 8 so that every **I** will possess the
36: 9 for each **I** tribe is to keep the land
Dt 15: 2 loan he has made to his fellow **I**.
15: 2 from his fellow **I** or brother,
17:15 you, one who is not a brother **I**.
22:19 has given an **I** virgin a bad name.
23:17 No **I** man or woman is to become a
23:20 but not a brother **I**, so that the
24:14 whether he is a brother **I** or an
Jos 11:22 No Anakites were left in **I** territory
18: 2 there were still seven **I** tribes who
22:11 near the Jordan on the **I** side,
22:14 a family division among the **I** clans.
Jdg 7:14 sword of Gideon son of Joash, the **I**.
11:39 From this comes the **I** custom
20:33 and the **I** ambush charged out of its
1Sa 7:13 did not invade **I** territory again.
31: 7 Jordan saw that the **I** army had fled
2Sa 1: 3 "I have escaped from the **I** camp.
11: 1 the king's men and the whole **I** army
17:25 an **I** who had married Abigail, the
1Ki 8: 1 and the chiefs of the **I** families,
2Ki 13:25 and so he recovered the **I** towns.
1Ch 1:43 **I** king reigned: Bela son of Beor,
16: 3 of raisins to each **I** man and woman.
2Ch 5: 2 and the chiefs of the **I** families,
19: 8 priests and heads of **I** families to
23: 2 of **I** families from all the towns.
25: 9 talents I paid for these **I** troops?"
Ne 9: 2 Those of **I** descent had separated
Eze 14: 4 When any **I** sets up idols in his
14: 7 "'When any **I** or any alien living in
37:19 of the **I** tribes associated with him,
44:22 of **I** descent or widows of priests.
Ob :20 This company of **I** exiles who are in
Jn 1:47 **I**, in whom there is nothing false."
Ro 11: 1 By no means! I am an **I** myself,

Israelites (*All the Israelites*, Israel)

Ge 32:32 Therefore to this day the **I** do not
47:27 Now the **I** settled in Egypt in the
Ex 1: 7 the **I** were fruitful and multiplied
1: 9 the **I** have become too numerous for us
1:12 so the Egyptians came to dread the **I**
2:23 The **I** groaned in their slavery and
2:25 God looked on the **I** and was
3: 9 now the cry of the **I** has reached me,
3:10 bring my people the **I** out of Egypt."
3:11 and bring the **I** out of Egypt?"
3:13 "Suppose I go to the **I** and say to
3:14 This is what you are to say to the **I**
3:15 God also said to Moses, "Say to the **I**
4:29 together all the elders of the **I**,
6: 5 I have heard the groaning of the **I**,
6: 6 "Therefore, say to the **I**: 'I am the
6: 9 Moses reported this to the **I**, but
6:11 to let the **I** go out of his country."
6:12 "If the **I** will not listen to me,
6:13 the **I** and Pharaoh king of Egypt,
6:13 them to bring the **I** out of Egypt.
6:26 **I** out of Egypt by their divisions."
6:27 about bringing the **I** out of Egypt.
7: 2 to let the **I** go out of his country.
7: 4 out my divisions, my people the **I**.
7: 5 Egypt and bring the **I** out of it."
9: 4 animal belonging to the **I** will die.
9: 6 one animal belonging to the **I** died.
9: 7 of the animals of the **I** had died.
9:26 land of Goshen, where the **I** were.
9:35 and he would not let the **I** go,
10:20 and he would not let the **I** go.
11: 7 among the **I** not a dog will bark at
11:10 not let the **I** go out of his country.
12:27 who passed over the houses of the **I**
12:28 The **I** did just what the LORD

Ex 12:31 Leave my people, you and the **I**!
12:35 The **I** did as Moses instructed and
12:37 The **I** journeyed from Rameses to
12:51 LORD brought the **I** out of Egypt
13: 2 womb among the **I** belongs to me,
13:18 The **I** went up out of Egypt armed for
14: 2 "Tell the **I** to turn back and camp
14: 3 Pharaoh will think, 'The **I** are
14: 4 So the **I** did this.
14: 5 **I** go and have lost their services!"
14: 8 the **I**, who were marching out boldly.
14: 9 horsemen and troops—pursued the **I**
14:10 Pharaoh approached, the **I** looked up,
14:15 out to me? Tell the **I** to move on.
14:16 the **I** can go through the sea on dry
14:22 the **I** went through the sea on dry
14:25 "Let's get away from the **I**! The LORD
14:28 had followed the **I** into the sea.
14:29 the **I** went through the sea on dry
14:31 the **I** saw the great power the LORD
15: 1 Moses and the **I** sang this song to
15:19 but the **I** walked through the sea on
16: 3 The **I** said to them, "If only we had
16:12 "I have heard the grumbling of the **I**.
16:15 the **I** saw it, they said to each
16:17 The **I** did as they were told; some
16:35 The **I** ate manna for forty years,
17: 7 Meribah because the **I** quarrelled and
17: 8 came and attacked the **I** at Rephidim.
17:11 the **I** were winning, but whenever he
19: 1 In the third month after the **I** left
19: 6 words you are to speak to the **I**."
20:22 the LORD said to Moses, "Tell the **I**
24:11 hand against these leaders of the **I**
24:17 To the **I** the glory of the LORD
25: 2 Tell the **I** to bring me an offering
25:22 give you all my commands for the **I**.
27:20 "Command the **I** to bring you clear
27:21 a lasting ordinance among the **I**
28: 1 brought to you from among the **I**,
28:30 means of making decisions for the **I**
28:38 the sacred gifts the **I** consecrate,
29:28 from the **I** for Aaron and his sons.
29:28 is the contribution the **I** are to
29:43 there also I will meet with the **I**,
29:45 I will dwell among the **I** and be
30:12 "When you take a census of the **I**
30:16 the atonement money from the **I**
30:16 It will be a memorial for the **I**
30:31 Say to the **I**, 'This is to be my
31:13 Say to the **I**, 'You must observe my
31:16 The **I** are to observe the Sabbath,
31:17 will be a sign between me and the **I**
32:20 the water and made the **I** drink it.
33: 5 **I**, 'You are a stiff-necked people.
33: 6 the **I** stripped off their ornaments
34:34 the **I** what he had been commanded,
35:30 Moses said to the **I**, "See, the LORD
36: 3 from Moses all the offerings the **I**
39:32 The **I** did everything just as the
39:42 The **I** had done all the work just as
40:36 In all the travels of the **I**,
Lev 1: 2 "Speak to the **I** and say to them:
4: 2 "Say to the **I**: 'When anyone sins
7:23 "Say to the **I**: 'Do not eat any of
7:29 "Say to the **I**: 'Anyone who brings a
7:34 the fellowship offerings of the **I**,
7:34 as their regular share from the **I**.
7:36 the LORD commanded that the **I** give
7:38 he commanded the **I** to bring their
9: 3 say to the **I**: 'Take a male goat for
10:11 you must teach the **I** all the decrees
11: 2 "Say to the **I**: 'Of all the animals
12: 2 "Say to the **I**: 'A woman who becomes
15: 2 "Speak to the **I** and say to them:
15:31 "'You must keep the **I** separate from
16:16 uncleanness and rebellion of the **I**
16:19 it from the uncleanness of the **I**.
16:21 wickedness and rebellion of the **I**
16:34 a year for all the sins of the **I**.
17: 5 This is so that the **I** will bring to
17:12 Therefore I say to the **I**, "None of
17:14 That is why I have said to the **I**,
18: 2 "Speak to the **I** and say to them:
20: 2 Say to the **I**: 'Any Israelite or any
22: 2 offerings the **I** consecrate to me,
Lev 22: 3 that the **I** consecrate to the LORD,
22:15 offerings the **I** present to the
22:32 be acknowledged as holy by the **I**.
23: 2 "Speak to the **I** and say to them:
23:10 "Speak to the **I** and say to them:
23:24 "Say to the **I**: 'On the first day of
23:34 to the **I**: 'On the fifteenth day
23:42 native-born **I** are to live in
23:43 I made the **I** live in booths when I
23:44 Moses announced to the **I** the
24: 2 "Command the **I** to bring you clear
24: 8 of the **I**, as a lasting covenant.
24:10 Egyptian father went out among the **I**,
24:15 Say to the **I**: 'If anyone curses his
24:23 Moses spoke to the **I**, and they took
24:23 **I** did as the LORD commanded Moses.
25: 2 "Speak to the **I** and say to them:
25:33 are their property among the **I**.
25:42 the **I** are my servants, whom I
25:46 rule over your fellow **I** ruthlessly.
25:55 for the **I** belong to me as servants.
26:46 himself and the **I** through Moses.
27: 2 "Speak to the **I** and say to them:
27:34 gave Moses on Mount Sinai for the **I**
Nu 1: 1 year after the **I** came out of Egypt.
1:49 them in the census of the other **I**.
1:52 The **I** are to set up their tents by
1:54 The **I** did all this just as the LORD
2: 2 "The **I** are to camp round the Tent of
2:32 These are the **I**, counted according
2:33 not counted along with the other **I**,
2:34 the **I** did everything the LORD
3: 8 fulfilling the obligations of the **I**
3: 9 **I** who are to be given wholly to him.
3:12 taken the Levites from among the **I**
3:38 of the sanctuary on behalf of the **I**.
3:41 place of all the firstborn of the **I**,
3:41 firstborn of the livestock of the **I**.
3:42 counted all the firstborn of the **I**,
3:46 To redeem the 273 firstborn **I** who
3:48 additional **I** to Aaron and his sons."
3:50 From the firstborn of the **I** he
5: 2 "Command the **I** to send away from the
5: 4 The **I** did this; they sent them
5: 6 "Say to the **I**: 'When a man or woman
5: 9 sacred contributions the **I** bring
5:12 "Speak to the **I** and say to them: 'If
6: 2 "Speak to the **I** and say to them: 'If
6:23 'This is how you are to bless the **I**.
6:27 "So they will put my name on the **I**,
8: 6 the Levites from among the other **I**
8:10 **I** are to lay their hands on them.
8:11 LORD as a wave offering from the **I**,
8:14 the Levites apart from the other **I**,
8:16 They are the **I** who are to be given
8:19 Tent of Meeting on behalf of the **I**
8:19 no plague will strike the **I** when
9: 2 "Make the **I** celebrate the Passover
9: 4 Moses told the **I** to celebrate the
9: 5 The **I** did everything just as the
9: 7 the other **I** at the appointed time?"
9:10 "Tell the **I**: 'When any of you or
9:17 the **I** set out; wherever the cloud
9:17 the cloud settled, the **I** encamped.
9:18 At the LORD's command the **I** set out,
9:19 the **I** obeyed the LORD's order and
9:22 the **I** would remain in camp and not
10:12 the **I** set out from the Desert of
11: 4 again the **I** started wailing and
13: 2 Canaan, which I am giving to the **I**.
13: 3 All of them were leaders of the **I**.
13:24 of grapes the **I** cut off there.
13:32 they spread among the **I** a bad report
14:27 the complaints of these grumbling **I**.
15: 2 "Speak to the **I** and say to them:
15:18 "Speak to the **I** and say to them:
15:32 While the **I** were in the desert, a
15:38 "Speak to the **I** and say to them:
16:38 Let them be a sign to the **I**."
16:40 This was to remind the **I** that no-one
17: 2 "Speak to the **I** and get twelve
17: 5 grumbling against you by the **I**."
17: 6 Moses spoke to the **I**, and their
17:12 The **I** said to Moses, "We shall die!
18: 5 wrath will not fall on the **I** again.
18: 6 from among the **I** as a gift to you,
Nu 18: 8 all the holy offerings the **I** give me
18:11 of all the wave offerings of the **I**.
18:19 offerings the **I** present to the LORD
18:20 and your inheritance among the **I**.
18:22 From now on the **I** must not go near
18:23 receive no inheritance among the **I**.
18:24 **I** present as an offering to the LORD.
18:24 have no inheritance among the **I**.
18:26 'When you receive from the **I** the
18:28 the tithes you receive from the **I**.
18:32 of the **I**, and you will not die.
19: 2 Tell the **I** to bring you a red heifer
19:10 a lasting ordinance both for the **I**
20:12 me as holy in the sight of the **I**,
20:13 where the **I** quarrelled with the LORD
20:19 The **I** replied: "We will go along the
20:24 not enter the land I give the **I**,
21: 1 he attacked the **I** and captured
21: 6 they bit the people and many **I** died.
21:10 The **I** moved on and camped at Oboth.
21:32 the **I** captured its surrounding
22: 1 the **I** travelled to the plains of
22: 3 filled with dread because of the **I**.
25: 8 plague against the **I** was stopped;
25:11 has turned my anger away from the **I**;
25:13 God and made atonement for the **I**."
26: 4 were the **I** who came out of Egypt:
26:62 not counted along with the other **I**
26:63 counted the **I** on the plains of Moab
26:64 counted the **I** in the Desert of
26:65 For the LORD had told those **I** they
27: 8 "Say to the **I**, 'If a man dies and
27:11 to be a legal requirement for the **I**
27:12 see the land I have given the **I**.
27:21 community of the **I** will go out,
28: 2 Give this command to the **I** and say
29:40 Moses told the **I** all that the LORD
31: 2 on the Midianites for the **I**.
31: 9 The **I** captured the Midianite women
31:16 were the means of turning the **I** away
31:42 The half belonging to the **I**, which
31:54 memorial for the **I** before the LORD.
32: 7 Why do you discourage the **I** from
32: 9 they discouraged the **I** from entering
32:17 go ahead of the **I** until we have
33: 1 the stages in the journey of the **I**
33: 3 The **I** set out from Rameses on the
33: 5 The **I** left Rameses and camped at
33:38 year after the **I** came out of Egypt.
33:40 Canaan, heard that the **I** were coming
33:51 "Speak to the **I** and say to them:
34: 2 "Command the **I** and say to them:
34:13 Moses commanded the **I**: "Assign this
34:29 to the **I** in the land of Canaan.
35: 2 "Command the **I** to give the Levites
35: 2 the inheritance the **I** will possess.
35: 8 from the land the **I** possess are to
35:10 "Speak to the **I** and say to them:
35:15 will be a place of refuge for **I**,
35:34 for I, the LORD, dwell among the **I**.
36: 2 as an inheritance to the **I** by lot,
36: 4 the Year of Jubilee for the **I** comes,
36: 5 Moses gave this order to the **I**:
36:13 LORD gave through Moses to the **I**
Dt 1: 3 Moses proclaimed to the **I** all that
1:16 brother **I** or between one of them
3:18 cross over ahead of your brother **I**.
4:44 is the law Moses set before the **I**.
4:46 defeated by Moses and the **I** as they
10: 6 (The **I** travelled from the wells of
24: 7 kidnapping one of his brother **I**
29: 1 Moses to make with the **I** in Moab,
31:19 it to the **I** and make them sing it,
31:22 that day and taught it to the **I**.
31:23 for you will bring the **I** into the
32:49 the **I** as their own possession.
32:51 in the presence of the **I** at the
32:51 not uphold my holiness among the **I**.
33: 1 on the **I** before his death.
34: 8 The **I** grieved for Moses in the
34: 9 So the **I** listened to him and did
Jos 1: 2 am about to give to them—to the **I**.
2: 2 "Look! Some of the **I** have come here
3: 9 Joshua said to the **I**, "Come here and
4: 4 from the **I**, one from each tribe,
4: 5 the number of the tribes of the **I**,

Jos 4: 8 the **I** did as Joshua commanded them.
4: 8 the number of the tribes of the **I**,
4:12 the **I**, as Moses had directed them.
4:21 He said to the **I**, "In the future
5: 1 dried up the Jordan before the **I**
5: 1 had the courage to face the **I**.
5: 2 knives and circumcise the **I** again.
5: 3 the **I** at Gibeath Haaraloth.
5: 6 The **I** had moved about in the desert
5:10 the **I** celebrated the Passover.
5:12 was no longer any manna for the **I**,
6: 1 tightly shut up because of the **I**.
6:25 she lives among the **I** to this day.
7: 1 the **I** acted unfaithfully in regard
7: 5 They chased the **I** from the city gate
7:12 That is why the **I** cannot stand
8:20 for the **I** who had been fleeing
8:22 in the middle, with **I** on both sides.
8:31 of the LORD had commanded the **I**.
8:32 There, in the presence of the **I**,
9:16 the **I** heard that they were
9:17 the **I** set out and on the third day
9:18 the **I** did not attack them, because
9:26 Joshua saved them from the **I**, and
10: 4 made peace with Joshua and the **I**."
10:11 were killed by the swords of the **I**.
10:20 Joshua and the **I** destroyed them
10:21 no-one uttered a word against the **I**.
11:14 The **I** carried off for themselves all
11:19 made a treaty of peace with the **I**
12: 1 of the land whom the **I** had defeated
12: 6 the LORD, and the **I** conquered them.
12: 7 the **I** conquered on the west side of
13: 6 will drive them out before the **I**.
13:13 the **I** did not drive out the people
13:13 to live among the **I** to this day.
13:22 the **I** had put to the sword Balaam
14: 1 the areas the **I** received as an
14: 5 the **I** divided the land, just as the
17:13 However, when the **I** grew stronger,
18: 1 The whole assembly of the **I** gathered
18: 3 Joshua said to the **I**: "How long will
18:10 he distributed the land to the **I**
19:49 the **I** gave Joshua son of Nun an
20: 2 "Tell the **I** to designate the cities
20: 9 Any of the **I** or any alien living
21: 3 the **I** gave the Levites the
21: 8 the **I** allotted to the Levites these
21:41 by the **I** were forty-eight in all,
22: 9 left the **I** at Shiloh in Canaan to
22:11 the **I** heard that they had built the
22:13 the **I** sent Phinehas son of Eleazar,
22:30 the heads of the clans of the **I**
22:31 rescued the **I** from the LORD's hand.
22:32 in Gilead and reported to the **I**.
24:32 Joseph's bones, which the **I** had
Jdg 1: 1 After the death of Joshua, the **I**
2: 6 After Joshua had dismissed the **I**,
2:11 the **I** did evil in the eyes of the
3: 1 to test all those **I** who had not
3: 2 to the descendants of the **I** who
3: 4 They were left to test the **I** to see
3: 5 The **I** lived among the Canaanites,
3: 7 The **I** did evil in the eyes of the
3: 8 the **I** were subject for eight years.
3:12 Once again the **I** did evil in the
3:14 The **I** were subject to Eglon king of
3:15 Again the **I** cried out to the LORD,
3:15 The **I** sent him with tribute to Eglon
3:27 and the **I** went down with him from
4: 1 After Ehud died, the **I** once again
4: 3 oppressed the **I** for twenty years,
4: 5 and the **I** came to her to have their
4:23 the Canaanite king, before the **I**.
4:24 the hand of the **I** grew stronger and
6: 1 Again the **I** did evil in the eyes of
6: 2 the **I** prepared shelters for
6: 3 Whenever the **I** planted their crops,
6: 6 Midian so impoverished the **I** that
6: 7 the **I** cried to the LORD because of
7: 8 Gideon sent the rest of the **I** to
7:23 **I** from Naphtali, Asher and all
8:22 The **I** said to Gideon, "Rule over us
8:28 Thus Midian was subdued before the **I**
8:33 No sooner had Gideon died than the **I**
9:55 the **I** saw that Abimelech was dead,
Jdg 10: 6 **I** did evil in the eyes of the LORD
10: 6 And because the **I** forsook the LORD
10:10 the **I** cried out to the LORD, "We
10:15 the **I** said to the LORD, "We have
10:17 **I** assembled and camped at Mizpah.
11:27 between the **I** and the Ammonites."
13: 1 **I** did evil in the eyes of the LORD
19:12 alien city, whose people are not **I**.
19:30 the day the **I** came up out of Egypt.
20: 3 that the **I** had gone up to Mizpah.)
20: 3 Then the **I** said, "Tell us how this
20: 7 Now, all you **I**, speak up and give
20:13 would not listen to their fellow **I**
20:14 at Gibeah to fight against the **I**.
20:18 **I** went up to Bethel and enquired
20:19 The next morning the **I** got up and
20:21 cut down twenty-two thousand **I** on
20:23 The **I** went up and wept before the
20:24 the **I** drew near to Benjamin the
20:25 **I**, all of them armed with swords.
20:26 the **I**, all the people, went up to
20:27 the **I** enquired of the LORD. (In
20:31 casualties on the **I** as before,
20:32 the **I** were saying, "Let's retreat
20:35 on that day the **I** struck down 25,100
20:42 they fled before the **I** in the
20:45 the **I** cut down five thousand men
21: 5 the **I** asked, "Who from all the
21: 6 the **I** grieved for their brothers,
21:18 since we **I** have taken this oath:
21:24 At that time the **I** left that place
1Sa 2:28 offerings made with fire by the **I**.
4: 1 Now the **I** went out to fight against
4: 1 The **I** camped at Ebenezer, and the
4:10 the Philistines fought, and the **I**
6: 6 did they not send the **I** out so that
7: 4 the **I** put away their Baals and
7: 7 And when the **I** heard of it, they
7:10 that they were routed before the **I**.
9: 2 young man without equal among the **I**
14:18 (At that time it was with the **I**.)
14:21 went over to the **I** who were with
14:31 That day, after the **I** had struck
17: 2 Saul and the **I** assembled and camped
17: 3 occupied one hill and the **I** another,
17:24 the **I** saw the man, they all ran from
17:25 Now the **I** had been saying, "Do you
17:53 the **I** returned from chasing the
27:12 so odious to his people, the **I**,
31: 1 the **I** fled before them, and many
31: 7 the **I** along the valley and those
2Sa 6:19 crowd of **I**, both men and women.
7: 6 I brought the **I** up out of Egypt
10:19 they made peace with the **I** and
17:26 The **I** and Absalom camped in the land
19: 8 the **I** had fled to their homes.
21: 2 the **I** had sworn to spare them,
1Ki 6: 1 after the **I** had come out of Egypt,
6:13 I will live among the **I** and will not
8: 9 the LORD made a covenant with the **I**
9:20 Jebusites (these peoples were not **I**)
9:21 whom the **I** could not exterminate
9:22 did not make slaves of any of the **I**
11: 2 about which the LORD had told the **I**,
12:16 house, O David!" So the **I** went home.
12:17 as for the **I** who were living in the
12:24 fight against your brothers, the **I**.
12:33 instituted the festival for the **I**
14:24 LORD had driven out before the **I**.
16:16 the **I** in the camp heard that Zimri
19:10 The **I** have rejected your covenant,
19:14 The **I** have rejected your covenant,
20:15 the rest of the **I**, 7,000 in all.
20:20 Arameans fled, with the **I** in pursuit.
20:27 the **I** were also mustered and given
20:27 The **I** camped opposite them like two
20:29 The **I** inflicted a hundred thousand
2Ki 3:24 the **I** rose up and fought them until
3:24 And the **I** invaded the land and
7:13 be like all these **I** who are doomed.
8:12 the harm you will do to the **I**,"
10:32 the **I** throughout their territory
13: 5 So the **I** lived in their own homes as
13:21 Once while some **I** were burying a man,
16: 3 LORD had driven out before the **I**.
17: 6 and deported the **I** to Assyria.
2Ki 17: 7 All this took place because the **I**
17: 9 The **I** secretly did things against
17:22 The **I** persisted in all the sins of
17:24 towns of Samaria to replace the **I**.
17:35 the LORD made a covenant with the **I**,
18: 4 **I** had been burning incense to it.
21: 2 LORD had driven out before the **I**.
21: 8 not again make the feet of the **I**
21: 9 the LORD had destroyed before the **I**.
1Ch 6:64 the **I** gave the Levites these towns
6:70 half the tribe of Manasseh the **I**
9: 2 in their own towns were some **I**,
10: 1 the **I** fled before them, and many fell
12:38 All the rest of the **I** were also of
21: 2 count the **I** from Beersheba to Dan.
27: 1 This is the list of the **I**—heads of
2Ch 5:10 LORD made a covenant with the **I**
8: 2 given him, and settled **I** in them.
8: 7 Jebusites (these peoples were not **I**)
8: 8 whom the **I** had not destroyed—these
8: 9 Solomon did not make slaves of the **I**
10:17 as for the **I** who were living in the
10:18 but the **I** stoned him to death.
13:16 The **I** fled before Judah, and God
28: 3 LORD had driven out before the **I**.
28: 8 The **I** took captive from their
30:21 The **I** who were present in Jerusalem
31: 1 the **I** who were there went out to
31: 1 the **I** returned to their own towns
31: 5 **I** generously gave the firstfruits
33: 2 LORD had driven out before the **I**.
33: 8 not again make the feet of the **I**
33: 9 LORD had destroyed before the **I**.
34:33 the territory belonging to the **I**,
35:17 The **I** who were present celebrated
Ezr 2:70 of the **I** settled in their towns.
3: 1 seventh month came and the **I** had
6:21 the **I** who had returned from the
7: 7 Some of the **I**, including priests,
7:13 I decree that any of the **I** in my
10: 1 a large crowd of **I**—men, women and
10:25 among the other **I**: From the
Ne 1: 6 I confess the sins we **I**, including
2:10 to promote the welfare of the **I**.
7:73 the **I**, settled in their own towns.
7:73 the **I** had settled in their towns,
8:14 that the **I** were to live in booths
8:17 **I** had not celebrated it like this.
9: 1 the **I** gathered together, fasting and
11: 3 settled in Jerusalem (now some **I**,
11:20 The rest of the **I**, with the priests
13: 2 they had not met the **I** with food and
Isa 17: 3 will be like the glory of the **I**,"
17: 9 which they left because of the **I**,
27:12 O **I**, will be gathered up one by one.
31: 6 so greatly revolted against, O **I**.
66:20 the **I** bring their grain offerings,
Jer 16:14 who brought the **I** up out of Egypt,'
16:15 brought the **I** up out of the land
23: 7 who brought the **I** up out of Egypt,'
Eze 2: 3 I am sending you to the **I**, to a
6: 5 I will lay the dead bodies of the **I**
20: 9 had revealed myself to the **I** by
35: 5 delivered the **I** over to the sword at
37:16 Judah and the **I** associated with him.
37:21 I will take the **I** out of the nations
43: 7 I will live among the **I** for ever.
44: 9 foreigners who live among the **I**.
44:15 when the **I** went astray from me,
47:22 to consider them as native-born **I**;
48:11 Levites did when the **I** went astray.
Da 1: 3 to bring in some of the **I** from the
Hos 1:10 "Yet the **I** will be like the sand on
3: 1 Love her as the LORD loves the **I**,
3: 4 For the **I** will live for many days
3: 5 Afterwards the **I** will return and
4: 1 Hear the word of the LORD, you **I**,
4:16 The **I** are stubborn, like a stubborn
5: 1 you priests! Pay attention, you **I**!
5: 5 the **I**, even Ephraim, stumble in
Am 3:12 so will the **I** be saved, those who
4: 5 boast about them, you **I**, for this is
9: 7 "Are not you **I** the same to me as the
Mic 5: 3 his brothers return to join the **I**.
Ac 7:23 he decided to visit his fellow **I**.
7:26 The next day Moses came upon two **I**

Ac 7:37 "This is that Moses who told the **I**,
Ro 9:27 "Though the number of the **I** be like
10: 1 for the **I** is that they may be saved.
2Co 3: 7 came with glory, so that the **I** could
3:13 to keep the **I** from gazing at it
11:22 Are they **I**? So am I.
Heb 11:22 about the exodus of the **I** from Egypt
Rev 2:14 taught Balak to entice the **I** to sin

Israelites' (Israel)
Lev 10:14 share of the **I** fellowship offerings.
Nu 31:30 From the **I** half, select one out of
31:47 From the **I** half, Moses selected one

Issachar
1. Son of Jacob by Leah (Ge 30:17–18; 35:23); blessed by Jacob (Ge 49:14–15). **2.** Tribe descended from Issachar. Blessed by Moses (Dt 33:18–19). Included in census (Nu 1:28–29; 26:23–25). Apportioned land (Jos 19:17–23; Eze 48:25). **3.** Fertile territory south-east of Sea of Galilee, with Naphtali to the north, and Manasseh to the south. Allotted to the descendants of Jacob's ninth son. Its towns were listed, but its borders were rather vague (Jos 19:17–23).
Ge 30:18 So she named him **I**.
35:23 Simeon, Levi, Judah, **I** and Zebulun.
46:13 The sons of **I**: Tola, Puah, Jashub
49:14 "**I** is a scrawny donkey lying down
Ex 1: 3 **I**, Zebulun and Benjamin;
Nu 1: 8 from **I**, Nethanel son of Zuar;
1:28 From the descendants of **I**: All the
1:29 number from the tribe of **I** was 54,400
2: 5 The tribe of **I** will camp next to
2: 5 people of **I** is Nethanel son of Zuar.
7:18 leader of **I**, brought his offering.
10:15 over the division of the tribe of **I**,
13: 7 from the tribe of **I**, Igal son of
26:23 The descendants of **I** by their clans
26:25 These were the clans of **I**; those
34:26 the leader from the tribe of **I**;
Dt 27:12 Levi, Judah, **I**, Joseph and Benjamin.
33:18 out, and you, **I**, in your tents.
Jos 17:10 Asher on the north and **I** on the east
17:11 Within **I** and Asher, Manasseh also
19:17 The fourth lot came out for **I**, clan
19:23 of the tribe of **I**, clan by clan.
21: 6 from the clans of the tribes of **I**,
21:28 from the tribe of **I**, Kishion,
Jdg 5:15 The princes of **I** were with Deborah;
5:15 **I** was with Barak, rushing after him
10: 1 the time of Abimelech a man of **I**,
1Ki 4:17 Jehoshaphat son of Paruah—in **I**;
15:27 the house of **I** plotted against him,
1Ch 2: 1 Simeon, Levi, Judah, **I**, Zebulun,
6:62 thirteen towns from the tribes of **I**
6:72 from the tribe of **I** they received
7: 1 The sons of **I**: Tola, Puah, Jashub
7: 5 men belonging to all the clans of **I**
12:32 men of **I**, who understood the times
12:40 neighbours from as far away as **I**,
26: 5 Ammiel the sixth, **I** the seventh and
27:18 David; over **I**: Omri son of Michael;
2Ch 30:18 Manasseh, **I** and Zebulun had not
Eze 48:25 "**I** will have one portion; it will
48:26 territory of **I** from east to west.
48:33 gate of **I** and the gate of Zebulun.
Rev 7: 7 from the tribe of **I** 12,000,

Isshiah
1Ch 7: 3 Michael, Obadiah, Joel and **I**.
12: 6 Elkanah, **I**, Azarel, Joezer and
23:20 Micah the first and **I** the second.
24:21 from his sons: **I** was the first.
24:25 **I**; from the sons of **I**: Zechariah.

Issue (Issued, Issues, Issuing)
Ex 22:11 the **i** between them will be settled
2Sa 14: 8 I will **i** an order on your behalf."
Ezr 4:21 Now **i** an order to these men to stop
5:17 King Cyrus did in fact **i** a decree
Est 1:19 let him **i** a royal decree and let it
Isa 10: 1 to those who **i** oppressive decrees,
Da 2:15 "Why did the king **i** such a harsh
6: 7 that the king should **i** an edict
Da 6: 8 Now, O king, **i** the decree and put it
6:26 "I **i** a decree that in every part of

Issued (Issue)
1Ki 15:22 King Asa **i** an order to all Judah—
2Ch 24: 9 A proclamation was then **i** in Judah
Ezr 4:19 I **i** an order and a search was made,
5:13 King Cyrus **i** a decree to rebuild
6: 1 King Darius then **i** an order, and
6: 3 the king **i** a decree concerning the
10: 7 A proclamation was then **i** throughout
Est 3: 9 let a decree be **i** to destroy them,
3:14 to be **i** as law in every province
3:15 edict was **i** in the citadel of Susa.
8:13 to be **i** as law in every province
8:14 was also **i** in the citadel of Susa.
9:14 An edict was **i** in Susa, and they
9:25 he **i** written orders that the evil
Da 2:13 the decree was **i** to put the wise men
3:10 You have **i** a decree, O king, that
4:24 has **i** against my lord the king:
Jnh 3: 7 he **i** a proclamation in Nineveh: "By
Lk 2: 1 Caesar Augustus **i** a decree that a

Issues (Issue)
Da 6:15 that the king **i** can be changed."

Issuing (Issue)
Da 9:25 From the **i** of the decree to restore

It is written
Jos 8:34; 10:13; 2Sa 1:18; 2Ki 23:21; Ne 8:15; 10:34; Ps 40:7; Da 9:13; Mt 4:4, 6, 10; 11:10; 21:13; 26:24, 31; Mk 7:6; 9:13; 14:21, 27; Lk 2:23; 4:4, 8, 10, 17; 7:27; 19:46; Jn 2:17; 6:31; 8:17; 12:14; Ac 1:20; 13:33; 15:15; 23:5; Ro 1:17; 3:4; 9:13; 10:15; 11:26; 12:19; 15:3, 9, 21 1Co 1:19, 31; 2:9; 3:19; 9:9; 10:7; 14:21; Gal 3:10, 13; 4:22, 27; Heb 10:7; 1Pe 1:16

Italian (Italy)
Ac 10: 1 what was known as the **I** Regiment.

Italy (Italian)
Ac 18: 2 who had recently come from **I** with
27: 1 decided that we would sail for **I**,
27: 6 sailing for **I** and put us on board.
Heb 13:24 from **I** send you their greetings.

Itch (Itching)
Lev 13:30 is an **i**, an infectious disease
13:32 and if the **i** has not spread and
13:34 day the priest is to examine the **i**,
13:35 if the **i** does spread in the skin
13:36 and if the **i** has spread in the skin,
13:37 has grown in it, the **i** is healed.
14:54 infectious skin disease, for an **i**,
Dt 28:27 **i**, from which you cannot be cured.

Itching (Itch)
2Ti 4: 3 say what their **i** ears want to hear

Ithai
2Sa 23:29 **I** son of Ribai from Gibeah in
1Ch 11:31 **I** son of Ribai from Gibeah in

Ithamar (Ithamar's)
Ex 6:23 him Nadab and Abihu, Eleazar and **I**.
28: 1 Eleazar and **I**, so that they may
38:21 of **I** son of Aaron, the priest.
Lev 10: 6 to Aaron and his sons Eleazar and **I**,
10:12 Eleazar and **I**, "Take the grain
10:16 angry with **I**, Aaron's remaining sons
Nu 3: 2 firstborn and Abihu, Eleazar and **I**.
3: 4 so only Eleazar and **I** served as
4:28 of **I** son of Aaron, the priest.
4:33 of **I** son of Aaron, the priest."
7: 8 of **I** son of Aaron, the priest.
26:60 of Nadab and Abihu, Eleazar and **I**.
1Ch 6: 3 Aaron: Nadab, Abihu, Eleazar and **I**.
24: 1 were Nadab, Abihu, Eleazar and **I**.
24: 2 Eleazar and **I** served as the priests.
24: 3 and Ahimelech a descendant of **I**,
1Ch 24: 5 descendants of both Eleazar and **I**.
24: 6 from Eleazar and then one from **I**.
Ezr 8: 2 of the descendants of **I**, Daniel;

Ithamar's (Ithamar)
1Ch 24: 4 Eleazar's descendants than among **I**
24: 4 of families from **I** descendants.

Ithiel
Ne 11: 7 the son of **I**, the son of Jeshaiah,
Pr 30: 1 man declared to **I**, to **I** and to Ucal:

Ithlah
Jos 19:42 Shaalabbin, Aijalon, **I**,

Ithmah
1Ch 11:46 the sons of Elnaam, **I** the Moabite,

Ithnan
Jos 15:23 Kedesh, Hazor, **I**,

Ithran
Ge 36:26 sons of Dishon: Hemdan, Eshban, **I**
1Ch 1:41 Dishon: Hemdan, Eshban, **I** and Keran.
7:37 Bezer, Hod, Shamma, Shilshah, **I** and

Ithream
2Sa 3: 5 the sixth, **I** the son of David's wife
1Ch 3: 3 and the sixth, **I**, by his wife Eglah.

Ithrite (Ithrites)
2Sa 23:38 Ira the **I**, Gareb the **I**
1Ch 11:40 Ira the **I**, Gareb the **I**,

Ithrites (Ithrite)
1Ch 2:53 the clans of Kiriath Jearim: the **I**,

Ittai
2Sa 15:19 The king said to **I** the Gittite, "Why
15:21 **I** replied to the king, "As surely as
15:22 David said to **I**, "Go ahead, march on."
15:22 So **I** the Gittite marched on with
18: 2 and a third under **I** the Gittite.
18: 5 Abishai and **I**, "Be gentle with the
18:12 commanded you and Abishai and **I**,

Iturea
Lk 3: 1 his brother Philip tetrarch of **I** and

Ivory
1Ki 10:18 with **i** and overlaid with fine gold.
10:22 silver and **i**, and apes and baboons.
22:39 palace he built and inlaid with **i**,
2Ch 9:17 with **i** and overlaid with pure gold.
9:21 silver and **i**, and apes and baboons.
Ps 45: 8 from palaces adorned with **i** the
SS 5:14 polished **i** decorated with sapphires.
7: 4 Your neck is like an **i** tower. Your
Eze 27: 6 they made your deck, inlaid with **i**.
27:15 paid you with **i** tusks and ebony.
Am 3:15 the houses adorned with **i** will be
6: 4 You lie on beds inlaid with **i** and
Rev 18:12 articles of every kind made of **i**,

Ivvah
2Ki 18:34 the gods of Sepharvaim, Hena and **I**?
19:13 of Sepharvaim, or of Hena or **I**?"
Isa 37:13 of Sepharvaim, or of Hena or **I**?"

Iye Abarim
Nu 21:11 set out from Oboth and camped in **I**,
33:44 They left Oboth and camped at **I**, on

Iyim
Nu 33:45 They left **I** and camped at Dibon Gad.

Izhar (Izharites)
Ex 6:18 The sons of Kohath were Amram, **I**,
6:21 The sons of **I** were Korah, Nepheg and
Nu 3:19 The Kohathite clans: Amram, **I**,
16: 1 Korah son of **I**, the son of Kohath,

1Ch 6: 2 The sons of Kohath: Amram, **I**, Hebron
6:18 The sons of Kohath: Amram, **I**, Hebron
6:38 the son of **I**, the son of Kohath, the
23:12 The sons of Kohath: Amram, **I**, Hebron
23:18 The sons of **I**: Shelomith was the

Izharites (Izhar)
Nu 3:27 **I**, Hebronites and Uzzielites; these
1Ch 24:22 From the **I**: Shelomoth; from the sons
26:23 From the Amramites, the **I**, the
26:29 From the **I**: Kenaniah and his sons

Izliah
1Ch 8:18 Ishmerai, **I** and Jobab were the sons

Izrahiah
1Ch 7: 3 The son of Uzzi: **I**. The sons of **I**:

Izrahite
1Ch 27: 8 was the commander Shamhuth the **I**.

Izri
1Ch 25:11 the fourth to **I**, his sons and

Izziah
Ezr 10:25 **I**, Malkijah, Mijamin, Eleazar,

Jaakanites
Dt 10: 6 from the wells of the **J** to Moserah.

Jaakobah
1Ch 4:36 Elioenai, **J**, Jeshohaiah, Asaiah,

Jaala
Ezr 2:56 **J**, Darkon, Giddel,
Ne 7:58 **J**, Darkon, Giddel,

Jaar
Ps 132: 6 we came upon it in the fields of **J**:

Jaare-Oregim
2Sa 21:19 Elhanan son of **J** the Bethlehemite

Jaareshiah
1Ch 8:27 **J**, Elijah and Zicri were the sons of

Jaasiel
1Ch 11:47 Eliel, Obed and **J** the Mezobaite.
27:21 over Benjamin: **J** son of Abner;

Jaasu
Ezr 10:37 Mattaniah, Mattenai and **J**.

Jaazaniah
2Ki 25:23 **J** the son of the Maacathite, and
Jer 35: 3 I went to get **J** son of Jeremiah,
40: 8 and **J** the son of the Maacathite,
Eze 8:11 and **J** son of Shaphan was standing
11: 1 and I saw among them **J** son of Azzur

Jaaziah
1Ch 24:26 The son of **J**: Beno.
24:27 The sons of Merari: from **J**: Beno,

Jaaziel
1Ch 15:18 **J**, Shemiramoth, Jehiel, Unni, Eliab,

Jabal
Ge 4:20 Adah gave birth to **J**; he was the

Jabbok, River
An eastern tributary of River Jordan, about 22 miles north of Dead Sea. Jacob crossed at its ford, before wrestling with an angel (Ge 32:22–24). It was a natural boundary (Nu 21:24; Dt 2:37; 3:16; Jos 12:2; Jdg 11:13, 22).

Ge 32:22 sons and crossed the ford of the **J**.
Nu 21:24 his land from the Arnon to the **J**,
Dt 2:37 land along the course of the **J** nor
3:16 the border) and out to the **J** River,
Jos 12: 2 middle of the gorge—to the **J** River,
Jdg 11:13 to the **J**, all the way to the Jordan.
11:22 from the Arnon to the **J** and from

Jabesh
1Sa 11: 1 And all the men of **J** said to him,
11: 3 The elders of **J** said to him, "Give
11: 5 to him what the men of **J** had said.
11: 9 reported this to the men of **J**, they
31:12 went to **J**, where they burned them.
31:13 under a tamarisk tree at **J**,
2Ki 15:10 Shallum son of **J** conspired against
15:13 Shallum son of **J** became king in the
15:14 He attacked Shallum son of **J** in
1Ch 10:12 and his sons and brought them to **J**.
10:12 bones under the great tree in **J**,

Jabesh Gilead
Town in Gilead about 10 miles south-east of Beth Shan, 2 miles east of the Jordan. Its people would not fight against Benjamin, so they were put to the sword (Jdg 21:8–15). It was besieged by the Ammonites, but rescued by Saul (1Sa 11:1–11). Its people later rescued Saul's body from the Philistines and gave him a proper burial here (1Sa 31:1–13; 1Ch 10:11–12). Also known by abbreviated name Jabesh (1Ch 10:12).

Jdg 21: 8 no-one from **J** had come to the camp
21: 9 none of the people of **J** were there.
21:10 men with instructions to go to **J**
21:12 found among the people living in **J**
21:14 the women of **J** who had been spared.
1Sa 11: 1 the Ammonite went up and besieged **J**.
11: 9 "Say to the men of **J**, 'By the time
31:11 the people of **J** heard of what the
2Sa 2: 4 the men of **J** who had buried Saul,
2: 5 he sent messengers to the men of **J**
21:12 son Jonathan from the citizens of **J**.
1Ch 10:11 all the inhabitants of **J** heard of

Jabez
1Ch 2:55 the clans of scribes who lived at **J**:
4: 9 **J** was more honourable than his
4: 9 His mother had named him **J**, saying,
4:10 **J** cried out to the God of Israel,

Jabin (Jabin's)
Jos 11: 1 **J** king of Hazor heard of this, he
Jdg 4: 2 LORD sold them into the hands of **J**,
4:17 relations between **J** king of Hazor
4:23 On that day God subdued **J**, the
4:24 stronger and stronger against **J**,
Ps 83: 9 to Sisera and **J** at the river Kishon,

Jabin's (Jabin)
Jdg 4: 7 the commander of **J** army, with his

Jabneel
Jos 15:11 along to Mount Baalah and reached **J**.
19:33 **J** to Lakkum and ending at the Jordan.

Jabneh
2Ch 26: 6 the walls of Gath, **J** and Ashdod.

Jacan
1Ch 5:13 **J**, Zia and Eber—seven in all.

Jacinth
Ex 28:19 in the third row a **j**, an agate and
39:12 in the third row a **j**, an agate and
Rev 21:20 the eleventh **j**, and the twelfth

Jackal (Jackals)
Ne 2:13 the **J** Well and the Dung Gate,
Mic 1: 8 howl like a **j** and moan like an owl.

Jackals (Jackal)
Job 30:29 I have become a brother of **j**, a
Ps 44:19 made us a haunt for **j** and covered us
63:10 to the sword and become food for **j**.
Isa 13:21 **j** will fill her houses;
13:22 **j** in her luxurious palaces.
34:13 a haunt for **j**, a home for owls.
Isa 35: 7 In the haunts where **j** once lay,
43:20 The wild animals honour me, the **j**
Jer 9:11 a heap of ruins, a haunt of **j**;
10:22 of Judah desolate, a haunt of **j**.
14: 6 the barren heights and pant like **j**;
49:33 "Hazor will become a haunt of **j**,
51:37 a haunt of **j**, an object of horror
Lam 4: 3 Even **j** offer their breasts to nurse
5:18 desolate, with **j** prowling over it.
Eze 13: 4 Your prophets, O Israel, are like **j**
Mal 1: 3 his inheritance to the desert **j**."

Jacob (*God of Jacob*, Jacob's)
Son of Isaac; younger twin of Esau (Ge 25:21–26). Favoured by Rebekah (Ge 25:27–28). Bought birthright from Esau (Ge 25:29–34); tricked Isaac into blessing him as firstborn (Ge 27); fled to Haran (Ge 27:41–28:5).

Dream at Bethel (Ge 28:10–22); heir to promises of Abrahamic covenant (Ge 28:13–15; 48:3–4; Lev 26:42; Heb 11:9); patriarch (Ex 3:15–16; Jer 33:26; Mt 22:32; Mk 12:26). Gracious choice by God contrasted with rejection of Esau (Mal 1:2–3; Ro 9:13).

Worked for Laban to win Rachel; tricked into marrying Leah; married Rachel in return for further labour (Ge 29:16–30). Children (Ge 29:31–30:24; 35:23–26; 1Ch 2–9). Wealth increased (Ge 30:25–43); returned to Canaan (Ge 31); wrestled with God; called Israel (Ge 32:22–32); reconciled to Esau (Ge 33). Returned to Bethel (Ge 35:1–15).

Showed favouritism to Joseph (Ge 37:3–4). Sent sons to Egypt for food (Ge 42:1–5). Settled in Egypt with family (Ge 46; Ex 1:1–5). Blessed Ephraim and Manasseh (Ge 48:8–20; Heb 11:21); blessed sons (Ge 49:1–28). Death (Ge 49:29–33); burial in Canaan (Ge 50:1–14).

Ge 25:26 Esau's heel; so he was named **J**.
25:27 while **J** was a quiet man, staying
25:28 loved Esau, but Rebekah loved **J**.
25:29 Once when **J** was cooking some stew,
25:30 He said to **J**, "Quick, let me have
25:31 **J** replied, "First sell me your
25:33 **J** said, "Swear to me first." So he
25:33 to him, selling his birthright to **J**.
25:34 **J** gave Esau some bread and some
27: 6 Rebekah said to her son **J**, "Look,
27:11 **J** said to Rebekah his mother, "But
27:15 and put them on her younger son **J**.
27:17 she handed to her son **J** the tasty
27:19 **J** said to his father, "I am Esau
27:21 Isaac said to **J**, "Come near so I can
27:22 **J** went close to his father Isaac,
27:22 "The voice is the voice of **J**, but
27:25 **J** brought it to him and he ate; and
27:30 **J** had scarcely left his father's
27:36 Esau said, "Isn't he rightly named **J**?
27:41 Esau held a grudge against **J** because
27:41 then I will kill my brother **J**."
27:42 she sent for her younger son **J** and
27:46 If **J** takes a wife from among the
28: 1 Isaac called for **J** and blessed him
28: 5 Isaac sent **J** on his way, and he went
28: 5 who was the mother of **J** and Esau.
28: 6 learned that Isaac had blessed **J**
28: 7 that **J** had obeyed his father and
28:10 **J** left Beersheba and set out for
28:16 **J** awoke from his sleep, he thought,
28:18 **J** took the stone he had placed
28:20 **J** made a vow, saying, "If God will
29: 1 **J** continued on his journey and came
29: 4 **J** asked the shepherds, "My brothers,
29: 6 **J** asked them, "Is he well?" "Yes, he
29:10 **J** saw Rachel daughter of Laban, his
29:11 **J** kissed Rachel and began to weep
29:13 soon as Laban heard the news about **J**,
29:13 there **J** told him all these things.
29:14 After **J** had stayed with him for a
29:18 **J** was in love with Rachel and said,
29:20 **J** served seven years to get Rachel,
29:21 **J** said to Laban, "Give me my wife.
29:23 gave her to **J**, and **J** lay with her.
29:25 there was Leah! So **J** said to Laban,
29:28 **J** did so. He finished the week with
29:30 **J** lay with Rachel also, and he loved
30: 1 she was not bearing **J** any children

Ge 30: 1 So she said to J, "Give me children,
30: 2 J became angry with her and said,
30: 4 Bilhah as a wife. J slept with her
30: 7 again and bore J a second son.
30: 9 Zilpah and gave her to J as a wife.
30:10 Leah's servant Zilpah bore J a son.
30:12 Leah's servant Zilpah bore J a
30:16 when J came in from the fields that
30:17 pregnant and bore J a fifth son.
30:19 Leah conceived again and bore J a
30:25 gave birth to Joseph, J said to Laban
30:29 J said to him, "You know how I have
30:31 "Don't give me anything," J replied.
30:36 journey between himself and J,
30:36 while J continued to tend the rest
30:37 J, however, took fresh-cut branches
30:40 J set apart the young of the flock
30:41 J would place the branches in the
30:42 to Laban and the strong ones to J.
31: 1 J heard that Laban's sons were
31: 1 "J has taken everything our father
31: 2 J noticed that Laban's attitude
31: 3 the LORD said to J, "Go back to the
31: 4 J sent word to Rachel and Leah to
31:11 of God said to me in the dream, 'J.
31:17 J put his children and his wives on
31:20 Moreover, J deceived Laban the
31:22 day Laban was told that J had fled.
31:23 he pursued J for seven days and
31:24 not to say anything to J, either
31:25 J had pitched his tent in the hill
31:26 Laban said to J, "What have you done?
31:29 anything to J, either good or bad.'
31:31 J answered Laban, "I was afraid,
31:32 Now J did not know that Rachel had
31:36 J was angry and took Laban to task.
31:43 Laban answered J, "The women are my
31:45 J took a stone and set it up as a
31:47 Sahadutha, and J called it Galeed.
31:51 Laban also said to J, "Here is this
31:53 So J took an oath in the name of
32: 1 J also went on his way, and the
32: 2 J saw them, he said, "This is the
32: 3 J sent messengers ahead of him to
32: 4 'Your servant J says, I have been
32: 6 the messengers returned to J, they
32: 7 In great fear and distress J divided
32: 9 J prayed, "O God of my father
32:18 say, 'They belong to your servant J.
32:20 Your servant J is coming behind us
32:22 J got up and took his two wives, his
32:24 J was left alone, and a man wrestled
32:26 But J replied, "I will not let you
32:27 What is your name?" "J," he answered.
32:28 "Your name will no longer be J, but
32:29 J said, "Please tell me your name."
32:30 J called the place Peniel, saying,
33: 1 J looked up and there was Esau,
33: 4 Esau ran to meet J and embraced him;
33: 5 J answered, "They are the children
33:10 "No, please!" said J. "If I have
33:11 J insisted, Esau accepted it.
33:13 J said to him, "My lord knows that
33:15 "But why do that?" J asked. "Just
33:17 J, however, went to Succoth, where
33:18 After J came from Paddan Aram, he
34: 1 the daughter Leah had borne to J,
34: 3 was drawn to Dinah daughter of J,
34: 5 J heard that his daughter Dinah had
34: 6 Hamor went out to talk with J.
34:27 The sons of J came upon the dead
34:30 J said to Simeon and Levi, "You have
35: 1 God said to J, "Go up to Bethel and
35: 2 J said to his household and to all
35: 4 they gave J all the foreign gods
35: 4 and J buried them under the oak at
35: 6 J and all the people with him came
35: 9 After J returned from Paddan Aram,
35:10 God said to him, "Your name is J,
35:10 no longer be called J; your name
35:14 J set up a stone pillar at the place
35:15 J called the place where God had
35:20 Over her tomb J set up a pillar,
35:22 J had twelve sons:
35:23 of Leah: Reuben the firstborn of J,
35:26 These were the sons of J, who were

Ge 35:27 J came home to his father Isaac in
35:29 And his sons Esau and J buried him.
36: 6 some distance from his brother J.
37: 1 J lived in the land where his father
37: 2 This is the account of J. Joseph, a
37:34 J tore his clothes, put on sackcloth
42: 1 J learned that there was grain in
42: 4 J did not send Benjamin, Joseph's
42:29 they came to their father J in the
42:36 Their father J said to them, "You
42:38 J said, "My son will not go down
45:25 came to their father J in the land
45:26 J was stunned; he did not believe
45:27 spirit of their father J revived.
46: 2 "J! J!" "Here I am," he replied.
46: 5 J left Beersheba, and Israel's sons
46: 5 Israel's sons took their father J
46: 6 and J and all his offspring went to
46: 8 the names of the sons of Israel (J
46: 8 to Egypt: Reuben the firstborn of J.
46:15 These were the sons Leah bore to J
46:18 the children born to J by Zilpah,
46:22 who were born to J—fourteen in all.
46:25 were the sons born to J by Bilhah,
46:26 All those who went to Egypt with J
46:28 Now J sent Judah ahead of him to
47: 7 Joseph brought his father J in and
47: 7 After J blessed Pharaoh,
47: 9 J said to Pharaoh, "The years of my
47:10 J blessed Pharaoh and went out from
47:28 J lived in Egypt seventeen years,
48: 2 J was told, "Your son Joseph has
48: 3 J said to Joseph, "God Almighty
49: 1 J called for his sons and said:
49: 2 "Assemble and listen, sons of J;
49: 7 in J and disperse them in Israel.
49:24 of the hand of the Mighty One of J,
49:33 J had finished giving instructions
50:24 on oath to Abraham, Isaac and J."
Ex 1: 1 went to Egypt with J, each with his
1: 5 The descendants of J numbered
2:24 with Abraham, with Isaac and with J.
3:16 the God of Abraham, Isaac and J—
6: 3 to Isaac and to J as God Almighty,
6: 8 give to Abraham, to Isaac and to J.
19: 3 you are to say to the house of J
33: 1 Isaac and J, saying, 'I will give it
Lev 26:42 I will remember my covenant with J
Nu 23: 7 'Come,' he said, 'curse J for me;
23:10 Who can count the dust of J or
23:21 "No misfortune is seen in J, no
23:23 There is no sorcery against J, no
23:23 It will now be said of J and of
24: 5 "How beautiful are your tents, O J,
24:17 A star will come out of J; a sceptre
24:19 A ruler will come out of J and
32:11 on oath to Abraham, Isaac and J—
Dt 1: 8 to Abraham, Isaac and J—and to
6:10 to Abraham, Isaac and J, to give you—
9: 5 fathers, to Abraham, Isaac and J.
9:27 your servants Abraham, Isaac and J.
29:13 your fathers, Abraham, Isaac and J.
30:20 your fathers, Abraham, Isaac and J.
32: 9 J his allotted inheritance.
33: 4 the possession of the assembly of J
33:10 He teaches your precepts to J and
34: 4 Isaac and J when I said, 'I will
Jos 24: 4 to Isaac I gave J and Esau.
24: 4 J and his sons went down to Egypt.
24:32 in the tract of land that J bought
1Sa 12: 8 "After J entered Egypt, they cried
1Ki 18:31 each of the tribes descended from J
2Ki 13:23 covenant with Abraham, Isaac and J.
17:34 of J, whom he named Israel.
1Ch 16:13 O sons of J, his chosen ones.
16:17 He confirmed it to J as a decree,
Ps 14: 7 let J rejoice and Israel be glad!
22:23 you descendants of J, honour him!
44: 4 my God, who decrees victories for J.
47: 4 us, the pride of J, whom he loved.
53: 6 let J rejoice and Israel be glad!
59:13 of the earth that God rules over J.
77:15 the descendants of J and Joseph.
78: 5 He decreed statutes for J and
78:21 his fire broke out against J,
78:71 to be the shepherd of his people J,

Ps 79: 7 for they have devoured J and
85: 1 you restored the fortunes of J.
87: 2 more than all the dwellings of J.
99: 4 in J you have done what is just and
105: 6 O sons of J, his chosen ones.
105:10 He confirmed it to J as a decree,
105:23 J lived as an alien in the land of
114: 1 the house of J from a people of
132: 2 made a vow to the Mighty One of J:
132: 5 a dwelling for the Mighty One of J
135: 4 the LORD has chosen J to be his own
147:19 He has revealed his word to J, his
Isa 2: 5 Come, O house of J, let us walk in
2: 6 your people, the house of J.
8:17 hiding his face from the house of J.
9: 8 Lord has sent a message against J
10:20 the survivors of the house of J,
10:21 remnant will return, a remnant of J
14: 1 The LORD will have compassion on J;
14: 1 them and unite with the house of J.
17: 4 "In that day the glory of J will
27: 6 In days to come J will take root,
29:22 says to the house of J: "No longer
29:22 "No longer will J be ashamed; no
29:23 the holiness of the Holy One of J,
40:27 Why do you say, O J, and complain,
41: 8 "But you, O Israel, my servant, J,
41:14 Do not be afraid, O worm J, O little
42:24 Who handed J over to become loot,
43: 1 O J, he who formed you, O Israel:
43:22 you have not called upon me, O J,
43:28 I will consign J to destruction and
44: 1 "But now listen, O J, my servant,
44: 2 O J, my servant, Jeshurun, whom I
44: 5 will call himself by the name of J;
44:21 "Remember these things, O J, for you
44:23 for the LORD has redeemed J,
45: 4 For the sake of J my servant, of
46: 3 "Listen to me, O house of J, all you
48: 1 "Listen to this, O house of J, you
48:12 "Listen to me, O J, Israel, whom I
48:20 The LORD has redeemed his servant J
49: 5 his servant to bring J back to him
49: 6 servant to restore the tribes of J
49:26 your Redeemer, the Mighty One of J
58: 1 and to the house of J their sins.
58:14 on the inheritance of your father J.
59:20 in J who repent of their sins,"
60:16 your Redeemer, the Mighty One of J.
65: 9 will bring forth descendants from J
Jer 2: 4 O house of J, all you clans of the
5:20 "Announce this to the house of J and
10:16 He who is the Portion of J is not
10:25 For they have devoured J; they have
30: 7 It will be a time of trouble for J,
30:10 "'So do not fear, O J my servant;
30:10 J will again have peace and security,
31: 7 "Sing with joy for J; shout for the
31:11 For the LORD will ransom J and
33:26 I will reject the descendants of J
33:26 descendants of Abraham, Isaac and J.
46:27 "Do not fear, O J my servant; do not
46:27 J will again have peace and security,
46:28 Do not fear, O J my servant, for I
51:19 He who is the Portion of J is not
Lam 1:17 The LORD has decreed for J that his
2: 2 swallowed up all the dwellings of J;
2: 3 He has burned in J like a flaming
Eze 20: 5 the descendants of the house of J
28:25 land, which I gave to my servant J.
37:25 the land I gave to my servant J,
39:25 I will now bring J back from
Hos 10:11 and J must break up the ground.
12: 2 he will punish J according to his
12:12 J fled to the country of Aram;
Am 3:13 and testify against the house of J,"
6: 8 "I abhor the pride of J and detest
7: 2 How can J survive? He is so small!"
7: 5 How can J survive? He is so small!"
8: 7 LORD has sworn by the Pride of J:
9: 8 not totally destroy the house of J
Ob :10 the violence against your brother J,
:17 the house of J will possess its
:18 The house of J will be a fire and
Mic 2: 7 Should it be said, O house of J:
2:12 will surely gather all of you, O J

Mic 3: 1 I said, "Listen, you leaders of J,
3: 8 to declare to J his transgression,
3: 9 you leaders of the house of J, you
5: 7 The remnant of J will be in the
5: 8 The remnant of J will be among the
7:20 You will be true to J, and show
Na 2: 2 will restore the splendour of J
Mal 1: 2 LORD says. "Yet I have loved J,
2:12 LORD cut him off from the tents of J
3: 6 descendants of J, are not destroyed.
Mt 1: 2 Isaac the father of J, J the father
1:15 of Matthan, Matthan the father of J,
1:16 J the father of Joseph, the husband
8:11 Isaac and J in the kingdom of heaven.
Lk 1:33 he will reign over the house of J
3:34 the son of J, the son of Isaac, the
13:28 when you see Abraham, Isaac and J
Jn 4: 5 J had given to his son Joseph.
4:12 Are you greater than our father J,
Ac 3:13 The God of Abraham, Isaac and J, the
7: 8 Later Isaac became the father of J,
7: 8 and J became the father of the
7:12 J heard that there was grain in
7:14 Joseph sent for his father J and his
7:15 J went down to Egypt, where he and
7:32 the God of Abraham, Isaac and J.
Ro 9:13 Just as it is written: "J I loved,
11:26 will turn godlessness away from J.
Heb 11: 9 as did Isaac and J, who were heirs
11:20 By faith Isaac blessed J and Esau
11:21 By faith J, when he was dying,

Jacob's (Jacob)
Ge 31:33 Laban went into J tent and into
32:21 J gifts went on ahead of him, but he
32:25 he touched the socket of J hip so
32:32 J hip was touched near the tendon.
34: 7 Now J sons had come in from the
34: 7 in Israel by lying with J daughter
34:13 J sons replied deceitfully as they
34:19 he was delighted with J daughter.
34:25 two of J sons, Simeon and Levi,
46:19 The sons of J wife Rachel: Joseph
46:27 the members of J family, which went
50:12 J sons did as he had commanded them:
Dt 33:28 J spring is secure in a land of
Isa 27: 9 then, will J guilt be atoned for
41:21 "Set forth your arguments," says J
45:19 to J descendants, 'Seek me in vain.
Jer 30:18 restore the fortunes of J tents
Mic 1: 5 this is because of J transgression
1: 5 What is J transgression? Is it not
Mal 1: 2 not Esau J brother?" the LORD says.
Jn 4: 6 J well was there, and Jesus, tired

Jada
1Ch 2:28 The sons of Onam: Shammai and J.
2:32 The sons of J, Shammai's brother:

Jadah
1Ch 9:42 Ahaz was the father of J, J was the

Jaddai
Ezr 10:43 Zabad, Zebina, J, Joel and Benaiah.

Jaddua
Ne 10:21 Meshezabel, Zadok, J,
12:11 and Jonathan the father of J.
12:22 Joiada, Johanan and J, as well as

Jadon
Ne 3: 7 Melatiah of Gibeon and J of Meronoth

Jael
Wife of Heber the Kenite; killed Sisera, commander of Canaanite army, after his defeat by Deborah and Barak (Jdg 4:17–22; 5:24–27).

Jdg 4:17 fled on foot to the tent of J, the
4:18 J went out to meet Sisera and said
4:21 J, Heber's wife, picked up a tent
4:22 Sisera, and J went out to meet him.
5: 6 in the days of J, the roads were
5:24 "Most blessed of women be J, the

Jagged
Job 41:30 His undersides are j potsherds,

Jagur
Jos 15:21 of Edom were: Kabzeel, Eder, J,

Jahath
1Ch 4: 2 son of Shobal was the father of J,
4: 2 J the father of Ahumai and Lahad.
6:43 the son of J, the son of Gershon,
23:10 the sons of Shimei: J, Ziza, Jeush
23:11 J was the first and Ziza the second,
24:22 from the sons of Shelomoth: J.
2Ch 34:12 Over them to direct them were J and

Jahaz
Town on plains of Moab about 17 miles east of Dead Sea. Sihon the Amorite was defeated by Israel here (Nu 21:23–24; Dt 2:32–33; Jdg 11:20). Allotted to tribe of Reuben (Jos 13:18) and set aside for the Levites (Jos 21:34–36). Became part of Moab, about which the prophets proclaimed disaster (Isa 15:4; Jer 48:34). Variant name Jahzah (1Ch 6:78; Jer 48:21).

Nu 21:23 he reached J, he fought with Israel.
Dt 2:32 came out to meet us in battle at J,
Jos 13:18 J, Kedemoth, Mephaath,
21:36 from the tribe of Reuben, Bezer, J,
Jdg 11:20 at J and fought with Israel.
Isa 15: 4 voices are heard all the way to J.
Jer 48:34 rises from Heshbon to Elealeh and J,

Jahaziel
1Ch 12: 4 J, Johanan, Jozabad the Gederathite,
16: 6 Benaiah and J the priests were to
23:19 J the third and Jekameam the fourth.
24:23 J the third and Jekameam the fourth.
2Ch 20:14 the Spirit of the LORD came upon J
Ezr 8: 5 Shecaniah son of J, and with him

Jahdai
1Ch 2:47 The sons of J: Regem, Jotham, Geshan,

Jahdiel
1Ch 5:24 Azriel, Jeremiah, Hodaviah and J.

Jahdo
1Ch 5:14 the son of J, the son of Buz.

Jahleel (Jahleelite)
Ge 46:14 sons of Zebulun: Sered, Elon and J.
Nu 26:26 through J, the Jahleelite clan.

Jahleelite (Jahleel)
Nu 26:26 through Jahleel, the J clan.

Jahmai
1Ch 7: 2 Rephaiah, Jeriel, J, Ibsam and

Jahzah
1Ch 6:78 received Bezer in the desert, J,
Jer 48:21 plateau—to Holon, J and Mephaath

Jahzeel (Jahzeelite)
Nu 26:48 by their clans were: through J,

Jahzeelite (Jahzeel)
Nu 26:48 through Jahzeel, the J clan;

Jahzeiah
Ezr 10:15 son of Asahel and J son of Tikvah,

Jahzerah
1Ch 9:12 the son of J, the son of Meshullam,

Jahziel
Ge 46:24 The sons of Naphtali: J, Guni, Jezer
1Ch 7:13 The sons of Naphtali: J, Guni, Jezer

Jail (Jailer, Jailers)
Ac 4: 3 put them in j until the next day.
5:18 and put them in the public j.
5:19 opened the doors of the j and
5:21 sent to the j for the apostles.
5:22 on arriving at the j, the officers
5:23 "We found the j securely locked,
5:25 "Look! The men you put in j are

Jailer (Jail)
Ac 16:23 and the j was commanded to guard
16:27 The j woke up, and when he saw the
16:29 The j called for lights, rushed in
16:33 the j took them and washed their
16:34 The j brought them into his house
16:35 j with the order: "Release those men.
16:36 The j told Paul, "The magistrates

Jailers (Jail)
Mt 18:34 him over to the j to be tortured,

Jair (Jairite)
Nu 32:41 J, a descendant of Manasseh,
Dt 3:14 J, a descendant of Manasseh, took
Jos 13:30 of J in Bashan, sixty towns,
Jdg 10: 3 He was followed by J of Gilead, who
10: 5 J died, he was buried in Kamon.
1Ki 4:13 of J son of Manasseh in Gilead were
1Ch 2:22 Segub was the father of J, who
20: 5 Elhanan son of J killed Lahmi the
Est 2: 5 named Mordecai son of J, the son of

Jairite (Jair)
2Sa 20:26 Ira the J was David's priest.

Jairus
Synagogue ruler whose daughter was raised to life by Jesus (Mt 9:18–26; Mk 5:22–43; Lk 8:41–56).

Mk 5:22 one of the synagogue rulers, named J,
5:35 the house of J, the synagogue ruler.
Lk 8:41 a man named J, a ruler of the
8:49 the house of J, the synagogue ruler.
8:50 Hearing this, Jesus said to J,
8:51 he arrived at the house of J, he did

Jakeh
Pr 30: 1 The sayings of Agur son of J—an

Jakim
1Ch 8:19 J, Zicri, Zabdi,
24:12 to Eliashib, the twelfth to J,

Jakin (Jakinite)
Ge 46:10 Jamin, Ohad, J, Zohar and Shaul the
Ex 6:15 Jamin, Ohad, J, Zohar and Shaul the
Nu 26:12 clan; through J, the Jakinite clan;
1Ki 7:21 The pillar to the south he named J
1Ch 9:10 the priests: Jedaiah; Jehoiarib; J
24:17 the twenty-first to J, the
2Ch 3:17 The one to the south he named J
Ne 11:10 Jedaiah; the son of Joiarib; J;

Jakinite (Jakin)
Nu 26:12 clan; through Jakin, the J clan;

Jalam
Ge 36: 5 Oholibamah bore Jeush, J and Korah.
36:14 bore to Esau: Jeush, J and Korah.
36:18 Chiefs Jeush, J and Korah.
1Ch 1:35 Eliphaz, Reuel, Jeush, J and Korah.

Jalon
1Ch 4:17 Jether, Mered, Epher and J.

Jambres
2Ti 3: 8 Just as Jannes and J opposed Moses,

Jambs
1Ki 6:31 of olive wood with five-sided j.
6:33 In the same way he made four-sided j
Eze 40: 9 and its j were two cubits thick.
40:24 He measured its j and its portico,

Eze 40:31 palm trees decorated its **j**, and
40:34 decorated the **j** on either side,
40:37 decorated the **j** on either side,
40:48 and measured the **j** of the portico;
40:49 were pillars on each side of the **j**.
41: 1 outer sanctuary and measured the **j**;
41: 1 the **j** was six cubits on each side.
41: 3 and measured the **j** of the entrance;

James

1. Apostle; son of Zebedee, brother of John (Mt 4:21–22; 10:2; Mk 1:19–20; 3:17; Lk 5:10). With Peter and John, especially close to Jesus: at raising of Jairus' daughter (Mk 5:37; Lk 8:51); transfiguration (Mt 17:1–2; Mk 9:2; Lk 9:28–29); in Gethsemane (Mt 26:36–38; Mk 14:32–34). Mother's request (Mt 20:20–28; Mk 10:35–45). Killed by Herod (Ac 12:2). **2.** Apostle; son of Alphaeus (Mt 10:3; Mk 3:18; Lk 6:15; Ac 1:13). **3.** Brother of Jesus and Jude (Mt 13:55; Mk 6:3; Gal 1:19; Jude 1); saw risen Lord (1Co 15:7) and with disciples before Pentecost (Ac 1:13); leader of church in Jerusalem (Ac 12:17; 15:13–21; 21:18; Gal 2:9); wrote letter (Jas 1:1).

Mt 4:21 other brothers, **J** son of Zebedee
10: 2 brother Andrew; **J** son of Zebedee,
10: 3 **J** son of Alphaeus, and Thaddaeus;
13:55 brothers **J**, Joseph, Simon and Judas?
17: 1 Peter, **J** and John the brother of **J**,
27:56 Mary the mother of **J** and Joses, and
Mk 1:19 he saw **J** son of Zebedee and his
1:29 they went with **J** and John to the
3:17 **J** son of Zebedee and his brother
3:18 Matthew, Thomas, **J** son of Alphaeus
5:37 Peter, **J** and John the brother of **J**.
6: 3 Mary's son and the brother of **J**,
9: 2 After six days Jesus took Peter, **J**
10:35 **J** and John, the sons of Zebedee,
10:41 became indignant with **J** and John.
13: 3 Peter, **J**, John and Andrew asked him
14:33 He took Peter, **J** and John along with
15:40 Mary the mother of **J** the younger and
16: 1 Mary the mother of **J**, and Salome
Lk 5:10 were **J** and John, the sons of Zebedee,
6:14 Andrew, **J**, John, Philip, Bartholomew,
6:15 Matthew, Thomas, **J** son of Alphaeus,
6:16 Judas son of **J**, and Judas Iscariot,
8:51 **J**, and the child's father and mother.
9:28 he took Peter, John and **J** with him
9:54 the disciples **J** and John saw this,
24:10 Joanna, Mary the mother of **J**, and
Ac 1:13 Those present were Peter, John, **J**
1:13 and Matthew; **J** son of Alphaeus
1:13 Simon the Zealot, and Judas son of **J**.
12: 2 He had **J**, the brother of John, put
12:17 "Tell **J** and the brothers about this,"
15:13 they finished, **J** spoke up: "Brothers,
21:18 **J**, and all the elders were present.
1Co 15: 7 he appeared to **J**, then to all the
Gal 1:19 —only **J**, the Lord's brother.
2: 9 **J**, Peter and John, those reputed to
2:12 Before certain men came from **J**, he
Jas 1: 1 **J**, a servant of God and of the Lord
Jude : 1 of Jesus Christ and a brother of **J**,

Jamin (Jaminite)

Ge 46:10 The sons of Simeon: Jemuel, **J**, Ohad,
Ex 6:15 The sons of Simeon were Jemuel, **J**,
Nu 26:12 through **J**, the Jaminite clan
1Ch 2:27 of Jerahmeel: Maaz, **J** and Eker.
4:24 The descendants of Simeon: Nemuel, **J**,
Ne 8: 7 Bani, Sherebiah, **J**, Akkub,

Jaminite (Jamin)

Nu 26:12 the **J** clan; through Jakin, the

Jamlech

1Ch 4:34 Meshobab, **J**, Joshah son of Amaziah,

Janai

1Ch 5:12 then **J** and Shaphat, in Bashan.

Janim

Jos 15:53 **J**, Beth Tappuah, Aphekah,

Jannai

Lk 3:24 the son of **J**, the son of Joseph,

Jannes

2Ti 3: 8 Just as **J** and Jambres opposed Moses,

Janoah

Jos 16: 6 passing by it to **J** on the east.
16: 7 went down from **J** to Ataroth and
2Ki 15:29 Beth Maacah, **J**, Kedesh and Hazor.

Japheth

Son of Noah (Ge 5:32; 6:10; 1Ch 1:4). Saved in ark (Ge 7:13; 9:18–19). Blessed by Noah (Ge 9:27); descendants (Ge 10:2–5; 1Ch 1:5–7).

Ge 5:32 the father of Shem, Ham and **J**.
6:10 Noah had three sons: Shem, Ham and **J**
7:13 Shem, Ham and **J**, together with his
9:18 out of the ark were Shem, Ham and **J**.
9:23 Shem and **J** took a garment and laid
9:27 May God extend the territory of **J**;
9:27 may **J** live in the tents of Shem,
10: 1 Ham and **J**, Noah's sons, who
10: 2 The sons of **J**: Gomer, Magog, Madai,
10:21 to Shem, whose older brother was **J**;
1Ch 1: 4 The sons of Noah: Shem, Ham and **J**.
1: 5 The sons of **J**: Gomer, Magog, Madai,

Japhia

Jos 10: 3 king of Jarmuth, **J** king of Lachish
19:12 and went on to Daberath and up to **J**.
2Sa 5:15 Ibhar, Elishua, Nepheg, **J**,
1Ch 3: 7 Nogah, Nepheg, **J**,
14: 6 Nogah, Nepheg, **J**,

Japhlet (Japhlet's, Japhletites)

1Ch 7:32 Heber was the father of **J**, Shomer
7:33 The sons of **J**: Pasach, Bimhal and

Japhlet's (Japhlet)

1Ch 7:33 These were **J** sons.

Japhletites (Japhlet)

Jos 16: 3 westward to the territory of the **J**

Jar (Jars)

Ge 24:14 'Please let down your **j** that I may
24:15 came out with her **j** on her shoulder.
24:16 filled her **j** and came up again.
24:17 give me a little water from your **j**."
24:18 quickly lowered the **j** to her hands
24:20 she quickly emptied her **j** into the
24:43 drink a little water from your **j**,"
24:45 Rebekah came out, with her **j** on
24:46 "She quickly lowered her **j** from her
Ex 16:33 Moses said to Aaron, "Take a **j** and
Nu 5:17 take some holy water in a clay **j**
19:17 into a **j** and pour fresh water over
1Ki 14: 3 and a **j** of honey, and go to him.
17:10 water in a **j** so I may have a drink?"
17:12 in a **j** and a little oil in a jug.
17:14 'The **j** of flour will not be used up
17:16 For the **j** of flour was not used up
19: 6 over hot coals, and a **j** of water.
2Ki 4: 6 he replied, "There is not a **j** left
Jer 19: 1 "Go and buy a clay **j** from a potter.
19:10 "Then break the **j** while those who go
19:11 **j** is smashed and cannot be repaired.
32:14 put them in a clay **j** so that they
48:11 not poured from one **j** to another—
48:38 Moab like a **j** that no-one wants,"
51:34 he has made us an empty **j**.
Eze 4: 9 put them in a storage **j** and use them
Mt 26: 7 **j** of very expensive perfume,
Mk 14: 3 an alabaster **j** of very expensive
14: 3 broke the **j** and poured the perfume
14:13 carrying a **j** of water will meet you.
Lk 7:37 brought an alabaster **j** of perfume,
8:16 hides it in a **j** or puts it under
22:10 carrying a **j** of water will meet you.
Jn 4:28 Then, leaving her water **j**, the woman
19:29 A **j** of wine vinegar was there, so
Heb 9: 4 ark contained the gold **j** of manna

Jared

Ge 5:15 years, he became the father of **J**.
5:16 after he became the father of **J**,
5:18 **J** had lived 162 years, he became
5:19 **J** lived 800 years and had other sons
5:20 Altogether, **J** lived 962 years, and
1Ch 1: 2 Kenan, Mahalalel, **J**,
Lk 3:37 the son of Enoch, the son of **J**, the

Jarha

1Ch 2:34 He had an Egyptian servant named **J**.
2:35 servant **J**, and she bore him Attai.

Jarib

1Ch 4:24 Nemuel, Jamin, **J**, Zerah and Shaul;
Ezr 8:16 Ariel, Shemaiah, Elnathan, **J**,
10:18 Maaseiah, Eliezer, **J** and Gedaliah.

Jarmuth

Jos 10: 3 Piram king of **J**, Japhia king of
10: 5 **J**, Lachish and Eglon—joined forces.
10:23 Hebron, **J**, Lachish and Eglon.
12:11 the king of **J** one the king of
15:35 **J**, Adullam, Socoh, Azekah,
21:29 **J** and En Gannim, together with their
Ne 11:29 in En Rimmon, in Zorah, in **J**,

Jaroah

1Ch 5:14 the son of **J**, the son of Gilead, the

Jars (Jar)

Ex 7:19 in the wooden buckets and stone **j**."
Nu 4: 7 and the **j** for drink offerings,
4: 9 its **j** for the oil used to supply it.
Jdg 7:16 and empty **j** in the hands of all
7:19 the **j** that were in their hands.
7:20 blew the trumpets and smashed the **j**.
Ru 2: 9 the water **j** the men have filled."
1Ki 18:33 "Fill four large **j** with water and
2Ki 4: 3 ask all your neighbours for empty **j**.
4: 4 Pour oil into all the **j**, and as each
4: 5 brought the **j** to her and she kept
4: 6 all the **j** were full, she said to her
Job 38:37 tip over the water **j** of the
Ps 33: 7 the waters of the sea into **j**;
Isa 22:24 from the bowls to all the **j**.
Jer 14: 3 They return with their **j** unfilled;
40:10 and put them in your storage **j**, and
48:12 I will send men who pour from **j**,
48:12 will empty her **j** and smash her jugs.
Mt 25: 4 The wise, however, took oil in **j**
Jn 2: 6 Nearby stood six stone water **j**, the
2: 7 "Fill the **j** with water"; so they
2Co 4: 7 we have this treasure in **j** of clay

Jashar

Jos 10:13 as it is written in the Book of **J**.
2Sa 1:18 (it is written in the Book of **J**):

Jashen

2Sa 23:32 Shaalbonite, the sons of **J**,

Jashobeam

1Ch 11:11 the list of David's mighty men: **J**,
12: 6 Azarel, Joezer and **J** the Korahites;
27: 2 first month, was **J** son of Zabdiel.

Jashub (Jashubite)

Ge 46:13 The sons of Issachar: Tola, Puah, **J**
Nu 26:24 through **J**, the Jashubite clan;
1Ch 7: 1 The sons of Issachar: Tola, Puah, **J**
Ezr 10:29 Adaiah, **J**, Sheal and Jeremoth.

Jashubi Lehem

1Ch 4:22 Saraph, who ruled in Moab and **J**.

Jashubite (Jashub)

Nu 26:24 through Jashub, the **J** clan; through

Jason (Jason's)

Ac 17: 6 they dragged **J** and some other
17: 7 **J** has welcomed them into his house.

Ac 17: 9 they put J and the others on bail
Ro 16:21 J and Sosipater, my relatives.

Jason's (Jason)

Ac 17: 5 They rushed to J house in search of

Jasper

Ex 28:20 a chrysolite, an onyx and a j.
39:13 a chrysolite, an onyx and a j.
Job 28:18 Coral and j are not worthy of
Eze 28:13 j, sapphire, turquoise and beryl.
Rev 4: 3 the appearance of j and carnelian.
21:11 jewel, like a j, clear as crystal.
21:18 The wall was made of j, and the city
21:19 The first foundation was j, the

Jathniel

1Ch 26: 2 Zebadiah the third, J the fourth,

Jattir

Jos 15:48 In the hill country: Shamir, J,
21:14 J, Eshtemoa,
1Sa 30:27 were in Bethel, Ramoth Negev and J;
1Ch 6:57 of refuge), and Libnah, J, Eshtemoa,

Javan

Ge 10: 2 Madai, J, Tubal, Meshech and Tiras.
10: 4 The sons of J: Elishah, Tarshish,
1Ch 1: 5 Madai, J, Tubal, Meshech and Tiras.
1: 7 The sons of J: Elishah, Tarshish,

Javelin (Javelins)

Jos 8:18 "Hold out towards Ai the j that is
8:18 So Joshua held out his j towards Ai.
8:26 the hand that held out his j until
1Sa 17: 6 a bronze j was slung on his back.
17:45 me with sword and spear and j,
Job 41:26 does the spear or the dart or the j.
Ps 35: 3 Brandish spear and j against those

Javelins (Javelin)

2Sa 18:14 So he took three j in his hand and

Jaw (Jaw-bone, Jaws)

Job 41: 2 nose or pierce his j with a hook?
Ps 3: 7 Strike all my enemies on the j;

Jaw-bone (Jaw)

Jdg 15:15 Finding a fresh j of a donkey, he
15:16 Samson said, "With a donkey's j I
15:16 With a donkey's j I have killed a
15:17 he threw away the j; and the place

Jaws (Jaw)

Job 36:16 wooing you from the j of distress
Pr 30:14 whose j are set with knives to
Isa 30:28 he places in the j of the peoples a
Eze 29: 4 I will put hooks in your j and make
38: 4 put hooks in your j and bring you

Jazer

Town east of the Jordan, in the south of Gilead. Captured by Israel from Amorites (Nu 21:32). Both Gad and Reuben laid claim to it (Nu 32:1–3), but Gad was given it, and fortified it (Nu 32:35; Jos 13:25). Later designated as a Levite town (Jos 21:39; 1Ch 6:81). Included in David's census (2Sa 24:5; 1Ch 26:31). Became part of Moab, about which the prophets proclaimed disaster (Isa 16:8–9; Jer 48:32).

Nu 21:32 After Moses had sent spies to J, the
32: 1 saw that the lands of J and Gilead
32: 3 "Ataroth, Dibon, J, Nimrah, Heshbon,
32:35 Atroth Shophan, J, Jogbehah,
Jos 13:25 The territory of J, all the towns of
21:39 Heshbon and J, together with their
2Sa 24: 5 then went through Gad and on to J.
1Ch 6:81 Heshbon and J, together with their
26:31 Hebronites were found at J in Gilead.
Isa 16: 8 which once reached J and spread
16: 9 I weep, as J weeps, for the vines of
Jer 48:32 I weep for you, as J weeps, O vines
48:32 they reached as far as the sea of J.

Jaziz

1Ch 27:31 J the Hagrite was in charge of the

Jealous (*Jealous God*, Jealousy)

Ge 30: 1 she became j of her sister.
37:11 His brothers were j of him, but his
Ex 34:14 for the LORD, whose name is J,
Nu 5:14 or if he is j and suspects her even
11:29 replied, "Are you j for my sake?
Dt 32:16 They made him j with their foreign
32:21 They made me j by what is no god and
1Sa 18: 9 Saul kept a j eye on David.
1Ki 14:22 they stirred up his j anger more
Isa 11:13 Ephraim will not be j of Judah,
Eze 16:38 vengeance of my wrath and j anger.
16:42 my j anger will turn away from you;
23:25 I will direct my j anger against you,
36: 6 I speak in my j wrath because you
Joel 2:18 the LORD will be j for his land and
Na 1: 2 The LORD is a j and avenging God;
Zep 3: 8 consumed by the fire of my j anger.
Zec 1:14 'I am very j for Jerusalem and Zion,
8: 2 "I am very j for Zion; I am burning
Ac 7: 9 the patriarchs were j of Joseph,
17: 5 the Jews were j; so they rounded up
2Co 11: 2 I am j for you with a godly jealousy.

Jealous God

Ex 20: 5 the LORD your God, am a j, punishing
34:14 LORD, whose name is Jealous, is a j.
Dt 4:24 your God is a consuming fire, a j.
5: 9 the LORD your God, am a j, punishing
6:15 who is among you, is a j and his
Jos 24:19 He is a holy God; he is a j. He will

Jealousy (Jealous)

Nu 5:14 if feelings of j come over her
5:15 it is a grain offering for j,
5:18 the grain offering for j, while he
5:25 her hands the grain offering for j,
5:29 "'This, then, is the law of j when
5:30 or when feelings of j come over a
Ps 78:58 they aroused his j with their idols.
79: 5 How long will your j burn like fire?
Pr 6:34 for j arouses a husband's fury, and
27: 4 but who can stand before j?
Ecc 9: 6 Their love, their hate and their j
SS 8: 6 its j unyielding as the grave.
Isa 11:13 Ephraim's j will vanish, and Judah's
Eze 8: 3 the idol that provokes to j stood.
8: 5 of the altar I saw this idol of j.
35:11 j you showed in your hatred of them
Zep 1:18 In the fire of his j the whole world
Zec 8: 2 I am burning with j for her."
Ac 5:17 the Sadducees, were filled with j.
13:45 they were filled with j and talked
Ro 13:13 debauchery, not in dissension and j.
1Co 3: 3 For since there is j and quarrelling
10:22 Are we trying to arouse the Lord's j?
2Co 11: 2 I am jealous for you with a godly j.
12:20 j, outbursts of anger, factions,
Gal 5:20 discord, j, fits of rage, selfish

Jearim

Jos 15:10 northern slope of Mount J (that is,

Jeatherai

1Ch 6:21 son, Zerah his son and J his son.

Jeberekiah

Isa 8: 2 son of J as reliable witnesses for

Jebus (Jebusite, Jebusites)

Jdg 19:10 the man left and went towards J
19:11 they were near J and the day was
1Ch 11: 4 marched to Jerusalem (that is, J).

Jebusite (Jebus)

Jos 15: 8 of the J city (that is, Jerusalem).
18:16 of the J city and so to En Rogel.
18:28 Zelah, Haeleph, the J city (that is,
2Sa 24:16 threshing-floor of Araunah the J.
24:18 threshing-floor of Araunah the J."
1Ch 21:15 threshing-floor of Araunah the J.
21:18 threshing-floor of Araunah the J.
21:28 threshing-floor of Araunah the J,
2Ch 3: 1 threshing-floor of Araunah the J,

Jebusites (Jebus)

Ge 10:16 J, Amorites, Girgashites,
15:21 Canaanites, Girgashites and J."
Ex 3: 8 Amorites, Perizzites, Hivites and J
3:17 Amorites, Perizzites, Hivites and J
13: 5 Hittites, Amorites, Hivites and J
23:23 and J, and I will wipe them out.
33: 2 Hittites, Perizzites, Hivites and J
34:11 Hittites, Perizzites, Hivites and J
Nu 13:29 J and Amorites live in the hill
Dt 7: 1 Perizzites, Hivites and J, seven
20:17 Perizzites, Hivites and J—as the
Jos 3:10 Girgashites, Amorites and J.
9: 1 Perizzites, Hivites and J)—
11: 3 Hittites, Perizzites and J in the
12: 8 Perizzites, Hivites and J):
15:63 Judah could not dislodge the J, who
15:63 to this day the J live there with
24:11 J, but I gave them into your hands.
Jdg 1:21 however, failed to dislodge the J,
1:21 J live there with the Benjamites.
3: 5 Amorites, Perizzites, Hivites and J
19:11 city of the J and spend the night."
2Sa 5: 6 to attack the J, who lived there.
5: 6 The J said to David, "You will not
5: 8 Anyone who conquers the J will have
1Ki 9:20 Hittites, Perizzites, Hivites and J
1Ch 1:14 J, Amorites, Girgashites,
11: 4 Jebus). The J who lived there
11: 6 J will become commander-in-chief.
2Ch 8: 7 Amorites, Perizzites, Hivites and J
Ezr 9: 1 Hittites, Perizzites, J, Ammonites,
Ne 9: 8 Perizzites, J and Girgashites.
Zec 9: 7 Judah, and Ekron will be like the J

Jecoliah

2Ki 15: 2 name was J; she was from Jerusalem.
2Ch 26: 3 name was J; she was from Jerusalem.

Jeconiah

Mt 1:11 Josiah the father of J and his
1:12 J was the father of Shealtiel,

Jedaiah (Jedaiah's)

1Ch 4:37 the son of Allon, the son of J, the
9:10 Of the priests: J; Jehoiarib; Jakin;
24: 7 fell to Jehoiarib, the second to J,
Ezr 2:36 The priests: the descendants of J
Ne 3:10 Adjoining this, J son of Harumaph
7:39 The priests: the descendants of J
11:10 From the priests: J; the son of
12: 6 Shemaiah, Joiarib, J,
12: 7 Sallu, Amok, Hilkiah and J. These
Zec 6:10 the exiles Heldai, Tobijah and J
6:14 Tobijah, J and Hen son of Zephaniah

Jedaiah's (Jedaiah)

Ne 12:19 of Joiarib's, Mattenai; of J, Uzzi;
12:21 Hashabiah; of J, Nethanel

Jediael

1Ch 7: 6 sons of Benjamin: Bela, Beker and J.
7:10 The son of J: Bilhan. The sons of
7:11 All these sons of J were heads of
11:45 J son of Shimri, his brother Joha
12:20 Jozabad, J, Michael, Jozabad, Elihu
26: 2 J the second, Zebadiah the third,

Jedidah

2Ki 22: 1 His mother's name was J daughter of

Jedidiah

2Sa 12:25 Nathan the prophet to name him J.

Jeduthun

1Ch 9:16 the son of Galal, the son of J;
16:38 J, and also Hosah, were gatekeepers.
16:41 With them were Heman and J and the

1Ch 16:42 Heman and J were responsible for the
16:42 sons of J were stationed at the
25: 1 J for the ministry of prophesying,
25: 3 As for J, from his sons: Gedaliah,
25: 3 the supervision of their father J,
25: 6 Asaph, J and Heman were under the
2Ch 5:12 Heman, J and their sons and
29:14 from the descendants of J, Shemaiah
35:15 Asaph, Heman and J the king's seer.
Ne 11:17 the son of Galal, the son of J.62
Ps 39: T For the director of music. For J.
62: T For the director of music. For J.
77: T For the director of music. For J.

Jeer (Jeered, Jeers)
Job 16:10 Men open their mouths to j at me;

Jeered (Jeer)
2Ki 2:23 came out of the town and j at him.

Jeers (Jeer)
Heb 11:36 Some faced j and flogging, while

Jegar Sahadutha
Ge 31:47 Laban called it J, and Jacob called

Jehallelel
1Ch 4:16 The sons of J: Ziph, Ziphah, Tiria
2Ch 29:12 Azariah son of J; from the

Jehath
1Ch 6:20 Of Gershon: Libni his son, J his son

Jehdeiah
1Ch 24:20 from the sons of Shubael: J.
27:30 J the Meronothite was in charge of

Jehezkel
1Ch 24:16 to Pethahiah, the twentieth to J,

Jehiah
1Ch 15:24 Obed-Edom and J were also to be

Jehiel
1Ch 15:18 Jaaziel, Shemiramoth, J, Unni, Eliab,
15:20 Zechariah, Aziel, Shemiramoth, J,
16: 5 then Jeiel, Shemiramoth, J,
23: 8 The sons of Ladan: J the first,
27:32 J son of Hacmoni took care of the
29: 8 in the custody of J the Gershonite.
2Ch 21: 2 were Azariah, J, Zechariah, Azariahu,
29:14 from the descendants of Heman, J and
31:13 J, Azaziah, Nahath, Asahel, Jerimoth,
35: 8 Hilkiah, Zechariah and J, the
Ezr 8: 9 Obadiah son of J, and with him
10: 2 Shecaniah son of J, one of the
10:21 Elijah, Shemaiah, J and Uzziah.
10:26 J, Abdi, Jeremoth and Elijah.

Jehieli
1Ch 26:21 to Ladan the Gershonite, were J,
26:22 the sons of J, Zetham and his

Jehizkiah
2Ch 28:12 son of Meshillemoth, J son of Shallum,

Jehoaddah
1Ch 8:36 Ahaz was the father of J, J was the

Jehoaddin
2Ki 14: 2 name was J; she was from Jerusalem.
2Ch 25: 1 name was J; she was from Jerusalem.

Jehoahaz
2Ki 10:35 And J his son succeeded him as king.
13: 1 J son of Jehu became king of Israel
13: 4 J sought the LORD's favour, and the
13: 7 left of the army of J except fifty
13: 8 the other events of the reign of J,
13: 9 J rested with his fathers and was
13:10 Jehoash son of J became king of
2Ki 13:22 Israel throughout the reign of J.
13:25 Jehoash son of J recaptured from
13:25 taken in battle from his father J.
14: 1 of Jehoash son of J king of Israel,
14: 8 sent messengers to Jehoash son of J,
14:17 of Jehoash son of J king of Israel.
23:30 And the people of the land took J
23:31 J was twenty-three years old when he
23:34 But he took J and carried him off to
2Ch 25:17 this challenge to Jehoash son of J,
25:25 of Jehoash son of J king of Israel.
36: 1 of the land took J son of Josiah and
36: 2 J was twenty-three years old when he
36: 4 Eliakim, a brother of J, king over
36: 4 took Eliakim's brother J and

Jehoash
2Ki 13: 9 And J his son succeeded him as king.
13:10 J son of Jehoahaz became king of
13:12 the other events of the reign of J,
13:13 J rested with his fathers, and
13:13 J was buried in Samaria with the
13:14 J king of Israel went down to see
13:25 J son of Jehoahaz recaptured from
13:25 Three times J defeated him, and so
14: 1 In the second year of J son of
14: 8 Amaziah sent messengers to J son of
14: 9 J king of Israel replied to Amaziah
14:11 so J king of Israel attacked.
14:13 J king of Israel captured Amaziah
14:13 Then J went to Jerusalem and broke
14:15 the other events of the reign of J,
14:16 J rested with his fathers and was
14:17 death of J son of Jehoahaz king of
14:23 Jeroboam son of J king of Israel
14:27 by the hand of Jeroboam son of J.
2Ch 25:17 this challenge to J son of Jehoahaz
25:18 J king of Israel replied to Amaziah
25:20 that he might hand them over to ⌊J⌋
25:21 J king of Israel attacked. He and
25:23 J king of Israel captured Amaziah
25:23 Then J brought him to Jerusalem and
25:25 death of J son of Jehoahaz king of
Am 1: 1 Jeroboam son of J was king of Israel.

Jehohanan
1Ch 26: 3 Elam the fifth, J the sixth and
2Ch 17:15 J the commander, with 280,000;
23: 1 Ishmael son of J, Azariah son of
28:12 in Ephraim—Azariah son of J,
Ezr 10: 6 to the room of J son of Eliashib.
10:28 From the descendants of Bebai: J,
Ne 6:18 and his son J had married the
12:13 Ezra's, Meshullam; of Amariah's, J
12:42 Uzzi, J, Malkijah, Elam and Ezer.

Jehoiachin (Jehoiachin's)
King of Judah; succeeded father, Jehoiakim; after three months taken as captive to Babylon (2Ki 24:8–17; 2Ch 36:8–10); removed from prison to royal palace (2Ki 25:27–30; Jer 52:31–34).

2Ki 24: 6 J his son succeeded him as king.
24: 8 J was eighteen years old when he
24:12 J king of Judah, his mother, his
24:12 king of Babylon, he took J prisoner.
24:15 Nebuchadnezzar took J captive to
25:27 of the exile of J king of Judah,
25:27 he released J from prison on the
25:29 J put aside his prison clothes and
25:30 the king gave J a regular allowance
1Ch 3:16 successors of Jehoiakim: J his son
3:17 The descendants of J the captive:
2Ch 36: 8 And J his son succeeded him as king.
36: 9 J was eighteen years old when he
Est 2: 6 taken captive with J king of Judah.
Jer 22:24 "even if you, J son of Jehoiakim
22:28 this man J a despised, broken pot,
24: 1 After J son of Jehoiakim king of
27:20 J son of Jehoiakim king of Judah
28: 4 J son of Jehoiakim king of Judah
29: 2 (This was after King J and the queen
37: 1 in place of J son of Jehoiakim.
52:31 of the exile of J king of Judah,
52:31 he released J king of Judah and
Jer 52:33 J put aside his prison clothes and
52:34 the king of Babylon gave J a regular
Eze 1: 2 fifth year of the exile of King J—

Jehoiachin's (Jehoiachin)
2Ki 24:17 He made Mattaniah, J uncle, king in
2Ch 36:10 and he made J uncle, Zedekiah, king

Jehoiada
2Sa 8:18 Benaiah son of J was over the
20:23 Benaiah son of J was over the
23:20 Benaiah son of J was a valiant
23:22 the exploits of Benaiah son of J;
1Ki 1: 8 Zadok the priest, Benaiah son of J,
1:26 and Benaiah son of J, and your
1:32 the prophet and Benaiah son of J.
1:36 Benaiah son of J answered the king,
1:38 Benaiah son of J, the Kerethites and
1:44 Benaiah son of J, the Kerethites and
2:25 gave orders to Benaiah son of J,
2:29 Solomon ordered Benaiah son of J,
2:34 Benaiah son of J went up and struck
2:35 The king put Benaiah son of J over
2:46 gave the order to Benaiah son of J,
4: 4 Benaiah son of J—commander-in-chief;
2Ki 11: 4 In the seventh year J sent for the
11: 9 did just as J the priest ordered.
11: 9 off duty—and came to J the priest.
11:12 J brought out the king's son and put
11:15 J the priest ordered the commanders
11:17 J then made a covenant between the
11:18 Then J the priest posted guards at
12: 2 years J the priest instructed him.
12: 7 King Joash summoned J the priest
12: 9 J the priest took a chest and bored
1Ch 11:22 Benaiah son of J was a valiant
11:24 the exploits of Benaiah son of J;
12:27 including J, leader of the family of
18:17 Benaiah son of J was over the
27: 5 was Benaiah son of J the priest.
27:34 was succeeded by J son of Benaiah
2Ch 22:11 Jehoram and wife of the priest J,
23: 1 In the seventh year J showed his
23: 3 J said to them, "The king's son
23: 8 did just as J the priest ordered.
23: 8 J the priest had not released any
23:11 J and his sons brought out the
23:14 J the priest sent out the commanders
23:16 J then made a covenant that he and
23:18 J placed the oversight of the temple
24: 2 LORD all the years of J the priest.
24: 3 J chose two wives for him, and he
24: 6 king summoned J the chief priest
24:12 The king and J gave it to the men
24:14 rest of the money to the king and J
24:14 As long as J lived, burnt offerings
24:15 Now J was old and full of years,
24:17 After the death of J, the officials
24:20 upon Zechariah son of J the priest.
24:22 J had shown him but killed his son,
24:25 murdering the son of J the priest,
Jer 29:26 appointed you priest in place of J

Jehoiakim (Jehoiakim's)
King of Judah. Son of Josiah, formerly called Eliakim; made king by Pharaoh Neco (2Ki 23:33–36; 2Ch 36:4). Killed prophet Uriah (Jer 26:20–23; burned Jeremiah's scroll (Jer 36). Became Babylonian vassal; subsequent rebellion brought invasion; died on way into captivity (2Ki 24:1–4; 2Ch 36:5–8; Da 1:1–2).

2Ki 23:34 and changed Eliakim's name to J.
23:35 J paid Pharaoh Neco the silver and
23:36 J was twenty-five years old when he
24: 1 J became his vassal for three years.
24: 6 J rested with his fathers.
24:19 of the LORD, just as J had done.
1Ch 3:15 J the second son, Zedekiah the third,
3:16 The successors of J: Jehoiachin his
2Ch 36: 4 and changed Eliakim's name to J.
36: 5 J was twenty-five years old when he
Jer 1: 3 through the reign of J son of Josiah
22:18 about J son of Josiah king of Judah:
22:24 "even if you, Jehoiachin son of J
24: 1 Jehoiachin son of J king of Judah

Jer 25: 1 of J son of Josiah king of Judah,
26: 1 in the reign of J son of Josiah
26:21 King J and all his officers and
26:22 King J, however, sent Elnathan son
26:23 out of Egypt and took him to King J
27:20 Jehoiachin son of J king of Judah
28: 4 Jehoiachin son of J king of Judah
35: 1 of J son of Josiah king of Judah:
36: 1 fourth year of J son of Josiah
36: 9 of J son of Josiah king of Judah,
36:28 which J king of Judah burned up.
36:29 Also tell J king of Judah, 'This is
36:30 this is what the LORD says about J
36:32 that J king of Judah had burned in
37: 1 in place of Jehoiachin son of J.
45: 1 of J son of Josiah king of Judah,
46: 2 of J son of Josiah king of Judah:
52: 2 of the LORD, just as J had done.
Da 1: 1 In the third year of the reign of J
1: 2 the Lord delivered J king of Judah

Jehoiakim's (Jehoiakim)

2Ki 24: 1 During J reign, Nebuchadnezzar king
24: 5 for the other events of J reign, and
2Ch 36: 8 The other events of J reign, the

Jehoiarib

1Ch 9:10 Of the priests: Jedaiah; J; Jakin;
24: 7 The first lot fell to J, the second

Jehonadab

2Ki 10:15 After he left there, he came upon J
10:15 I am with you?" "I am," J answered.
10:23 Jehu and J son of Recab went into

Jehonathan

2Ch 17: 8 Zebadiah, Asahel, Shemiramoth, J,
Ne 12:18 Bilgah's, Shammua; of Shemaiah's, J;

Jehoram (Jehoram's)

1Ki 22:50 And J his son succeeded him.
2Ki 1:17 J son of Jehoshaphat king of Judah.
8:16 J son of Jehoshaphat began his reign
8:20 In the time of J, Edom rebelled
8:21 J went to Zair with all his chariots.
8:24 J rested with his fathers and was
8:25 of J king of Judah began to reign.
8:29 Then Ahaziah son of J king of Judah
11: 2 Jehosheba, the daughter of King J
12:18 J and Ahaziah, the kings of
1Ch 3:11 J his son, Ahaziah his son, Joash
2Ch 17: 8 the priests Elishama and J.
21: 1 And J his son succeeded him as king.
21: 3 J because he was his firstborn son.
21: 4 J established himself firmly over
21: 5 J was thirty-two years old when he
21: 8 In the time of J, Edom rebelled
21: 9 J went there with his officers and
21:10 because J had forsaken the LORD, the
21:12 J received a letter from Elijah the
21:16 The LORD aroused against J the
21:18 After all this, the LORD afflicted J
21:20 J was thirty-two years old when he
22: 1 of J king of Judah began to reign.
22: 6 Then Ahaziah son of J king of Judah
22:11 Jehosheba, the daughter of King J,
22:11 the daughter of King J and wife of
Mt 1: 8 father of J, J the father of Uzziah,

Jehoram's (Jehoram)

2Ki 8:23 for the other events of J reign, and
2Ch 21: 2 J brothers, the sons of Jehoshaphat,
22: 1 J youngest son, king in his place,

Jehoshaphat (Jehoshaphat's)

King of Judah; son of Asa (1Ki 22:41). Devoted to God; removed idols; sent officials to teach Law (2Ch 17:3–9). Strengthened kingdom (2Ch 17:2,10–19). Allied with Israel (1Ki 22:44; 2Ch 18:1; 20:35–36); helped Ahab against Aram (1Ki 22:1–33; 2Ch 18:1–19:1), Joram against Moab (2Ki 3). Alliances rebuked (2Ch 19:1–2; 2Ch 20:35–37). Appointed judges (2Ch 19:4–11). Trusted God for victory over Moab and Ammon (2Ch 20:1–30). Death (2Ch 21:1).

2Sa 8:16 J son of Ahilud was recorder;
20:24 J son of Ahilud was recorder;
1Ki 4: 3 J son of Ahilud—recorder;
4:17 J son of Paruah—in Issachar;
15:24 And J his son succeeded him as king.
22: 2 in the third year J king of Judah
22: 4 he asked J, "Will you go with me to
22: 4 J replied to the king of Israel,
22: 5 J also said to the king of Israel,
22: 7 J asked, "Is there not a prophet of
22: 8 The king of Israel answered J,
22: 8 "The king should not say that," J
22:10 king of Israel and J king of Judah
22:18 The king of Israel said to J,
22:29 king of Israel and J king of Judah
22:30 The king of Israel said to J, "I
22:32 the chariot commanders saw J, they
22:32 to attack him, but when J cried out,
22:41 J son of Asa became king of Judah in
22:42 J was thirty-five years old when he
22:44 J was also at peace with the king of
22:48 Now J built a fleet of trading ships
22:49 Ahaziah son of Ahab said to J, "Let
22:49 sail with your men," but J refused.
22:50 J rested with his fathers and was
22:51 seventeenth year of J king of Judah,
2Ki 1:17 of Jehoram son of J king of Judah.
3: 1 eighteenth year of J king of Judah,
3: 7 this message to J king of Judah
3:11 J asked, "Is there no prophet of the
3:12 J said, "The word of the LORD is
3:12 So the king of Israel and J and the
3:14 for the presence of J king of Judah,
8:16 when J was king of Judah, Jehoram
8:16 J began his reign as king of Judah.
9: 2 get there, look for Jehu son of J
9:14 Jehu son of J, the son of Nimshi,
12:18 J, Jehoram and Ahaziah, the kings of
1Ch 3:10 his son, Asa his son, J his son,
18:15 J son of Ahilud was recorder;
2Ch 17: 1 J his son succeeded him as king and
17: 3 The LORD was with J because in his
17: 5 and all Judah brought gifts to J,
17:10 that they did not make war with J.
17:11 Some Philistines brought J gifts
17:12 J became more and more powerful;
18: 1 Now J had great wealth and honour,
18: 3 Ahab king of Israel asked J king of
18: 3 against Ramoth Gilead?" J replied,
18: 4 J also said to the king of Israel,
18: 6 J asked, "Is there not a prophet of
18: 7 The king of Israel answered J,
18: 7 "The king should not say that," J
18: 9 king of Israel and J king of Judah
18:17 The king of Israel said to J,
18:28 king of Israel and J king of Judah
18:29 The king of Israel said to J, "I
18:31 the chariot commanders saw J, they
18:31 to attack him, but J cried out,
19: 1 J king of Judah returned safely to
19: 4 J lived in Jerusalem, and he went
19: 8 J appointed some of the Levites,
20: 1 the Meunites came to make war on J.
20: 2 Some men came and told J, "A vast
20: 3 Alarmed, J resolved to enquire of
20: 5 J stood up in the assembly of Judah
20:15 He said: "Listen, King J and all who
20:18 J bowed with his face to the ground,
20:20 As they set out, J stood and said,
20:21 J appointed men to sing to the LORD
20:25 J and his men went to carry off
20:27 led by J, all the men of Judah
20:30 the kingdom of J was at peace, for
20:31 J reigned over Judah. He was
20:35 J king of Judah made an alliance
20:37 of Mareshah prophesied against J,
21: 1 J rested with his fathers and was
21: 2 Jehoram's brothers, the sons of J,
21: 2 these were sons of J king of Israel.
21:12 of your father J or of Asa king of
22: 9 "He was a son of J, who sought the
Joel 3: 2 bring them down to the Valley of J.
3:12 them advance into the Valley of J,
Mt 1: 8 Asa the father of J, J the father

Jehoshaphat's (Jehoshaphat)

1Ki 22:45 for the other events of J reign, the
2Ch 20:34 The other events of J reign, from

Jehosheba

2Ki 11: 2 J, the daughter of King Jehoram
2Ch 22:11 J, the daughter of King Jehoram,
22:11 J, the daughter of King Jehoram

Jehozabad

2Ki 12:21 son of Shimeath and J son of Shomer.
1Ch 26: 4 J the second, Joah the third, Sacar
2Ch 17:18 J, with 180,000 men armed for battle
24:26 J, son of Shimrith a Moabite woman.

Jehozadak

1Ch 6:14 Seraiah, and Seraiah the father of J.
6:15 J was deported when the LORD sent
Hag 1: 1 to Joshua son of J, the high priest:
1:12 Joshua son of J, the high priest,
1:14 and the spirit of Joshua son of J,
2: 2 to Joshua son of J, the high priest,
2: 4 'Be strong, O Joshua son of J, the
Zec 6:11 of the high priest, Joshua son of J.

Jehu (Jehu's)

1. Prophet; rebuked Baasha (1Ki 16:1–7) and Jehoshaphat (2Ch 19:1–2). **2.** King of Israel. Choice by God announced to Elijah (1Ki 19:16–17); anointed by servant of Elisha; instructed to destroy Ahab's house (2Ki 9:1–13). Killed Joram, Ahaziah (2Ki 9:14–29), Jezebel (2Ki 9:30–37), Ahab's family (2Ki 10:1–17), ministers of Baal (2Ki 10:18–29). Succession promised for four generations (2Ki 10:30). Death (2Ki 10: 34–36).

1Ki 16: 1 the word of the LORD came to J
16: 7 prophet J son of Hanani to Baasha
16:12 Baasha through the prophet J—
19:16 Also, anoint J son of Nimshi king
19:17 J will put to death any who escape
19:17 death any who escape the sword of J.
2Ki 9: 2 look for J son of Jehoshaphat,
9: 5 For which of us?" asked J. "For you
9: 6 J got up and went into the house.
9:11 J went out to his fellow officers,
9:11 sort of things he says," J replied.
9:12 "Tell us." J said, "Here is what he
9:13 and shouted, "J is king!
9:14 J son of Jehoshaphat, the son of
9:15 J said, "If this is the way you
9:18 The horseman rode off to meet J and
9:18 have to do with peace?" J replied.
9:19 'Do you come in peace?' " J replied,
9:20 is like that of J son of Nimshi—
9:21 each in his own chariot, to meet J.
9:22 Joram saw J he asked, "Have you
9:22 "Have you come in peace, J?"
9:22 "How can there be peace," J replied,
9:24 J drew his bow and shot Joram
9:25 J said to Bidkar, his chariot
9:27 J chased him, shouting, "Kill him
9:30 J went to Jezreel. When Jezebel
9:31 J entered the gate, she asked, "Have
9:33 "Throw her down!" J said. So they
9:34 J went in and ate and drank. "Take
9:36 They went back and told J, who said,
10: 1 So J wrote letters and sent them to
10: 5 guardians sent this message to J:
10: 6 J wrote them a second letter, saying,
10: 7 and sent them to J in Jezreel.
10: 8 the messenger arrived, he told J,
10: 8 J ordered, "Put them in two piles
10: 9 The next morning J went out. He
10:11 J killed everyone in Jezreel who
10:12 J then set out and went towards
10:15 J greeted him and said, "Are you in
10:15 "If so," said J, "give me your hand."
10:15 J helped him up into the chariot.
10:16 J said, "Come with me and see my
10:17 J came to Samaria, he killed all who
10:18 J brought all the people together
10:18 J will serve him much.
10:19 J was acting deceptively in order
10:20 J said, "Call an assembly in honour

2Ki 10:22 J said to the keeper of the wardrobe,
10:23 J and Jehonadab son of Recab went
10:23 J said to the ministers of Baal,
10:24 Now J had posted eighty men outside
10:25 soon as J had finished making the
10:28 J destroyed Baal worship in Israel.
10:30 The LORD said to J, "Because you
10:31 Yet J was not careful to keep the
10:35 J rested with his fathers and was
10:36 The time that J reigned over Israel
12: 1 In the seventh year of J, Joash
13: 1 Jehoahaz son of J became king of
14: 8 the son of J, king of Israel, with
15:12 the word of the LORD spoken to J was
1Ch 2:38 Obed the father of J, J the father
4:35 Joel, J son of Joshibiah, the son of
12: 3 Azmaveth; Beracah, J the Anathothite,
2Ch 19: 2 J the seer, the son of Hanani, went
20:34 are written in the annals of J son
22: 7 with Joram to meet J son of Nimshi
22: 8 While J was executing judgment on
22: 9 He was brought to J and put to death.
25:17 the son of J, king of Israel: "Come,
Hos 1: 4 soon punish the house of J for the

Jehu's (Jehu)

2Ki 9: 6 the prophet poured the oil on J head
9:17 in Jezreel saw J troops approaching,
10:34 for the other events of J reign, all

Jehucal

Jer 37: 3 however, sent J son of Shelemiah
38: 1 son of Pashhur, J son of Shelemiah

Jehud

Jos 19:45 J, Bene Berak, Gath Rimmon,

Jehudi

Jer 36:14 officials sent J son of Nethaniah,
36:21 The king sent J to get the scroll,
36:21 and J brought it from the room of
36:23 Whenever J had read three or four

Jeiel

1Ch 5: 7 records: J the chief, Zechariah,
8:29 J the father of Gibeon lived in
9:35 J the father of Gibeon lived in
11:44 Uzzia the Ashterathite, Shama and J
15:18 Obed-Edom and J, the gatekeepers.
15:21 Eliphelehu, Mikneiah, Obed-Edom, J
16: 5 Zechariah second, then J,
16: 5 Eliab, Benaiah, Obed-Edom and J.
2Ch 20:14 the son of Benaiah, the son of J,
26:11 as mustered by J the secretary
29:13 of Elizaphan, Shimri and J;
35: 9 his brothers, and Hashabiah, J and
Ezr 10:43 From the descendants of Nebo: J,

Jekabzeel

Ne 11:25 settlements, in J and its villages,

Jekameam

1Ch 23:19 Jahaziel the third and J the fourth
24:23 Jahaziel the third and J the fourth

Jekamiah

1Ch 2:41 Shallum the father of J, and J the
3:18 Malkiram, Pedaiah, Shenazzar, J,

Jekuthiel

1Ch 4:18 of Soco, and J the father of Zanoah

Jemimah

Job 42:14 The first daughter he named J, the

Jemuel

Ge 46:10 The sons of Simeon: J, Jamin, Ohad,
Ex 6:15 The sons of Simeon were J, Jamin,

Jeopardy

2Sa 18:13 if I had put my life in j—and
Job 13:14 Why do I put myself in j and take my

Jephthah (Jephthah's)

Judge. Social outcast, called on to deliver Israel from Ammonites (Jdg 11:1–32). Rash vow led to sacrifice of daughter (Jdg 11:30–40). Victory over Ephraim (Jdg 12:1–6). Death (Jdg 12:7). Example of faith (Heb 11:32–34).

Jdg 11: 1 J the Gileadite was a mighty warrior.
11: 2 were grown up, they drove J away.
11: 3 J fled from his brothers and settled
11: 5 the elders of Gilead went to get J
11: 7 J said to them, "Didn't you hate me
11: 9 J answered, "Suppose you take me
11:11 J went with the elders of Gilead,
11:12 J sent messengers to the Ammonite
11:14 J sent back messengers to the
11:15 saying: "This is what J says: Israel
11:28 attention to the message J sent him.
11:29 the Spirit of the LORD came upon J.
11:30 J made a vow to the LORD: "If you
11:32 J went over to fight the Ammonites,
11:34 J returned to his home in Mizpah,
11:40 the daughter of J the Gileadite.
12: 1 over to Zaphon and said to J,
12: 2 J answered, "I and my people were
12: 4 J then called together the men of
12: 7 J led Israel for six years. Then J
1Sa 12:11 the LORD sent Jerub-Baal, Barak, J
Heb 11:32 J, David, Samuel and the prophets,

Jephthah's (Jephthah)

Jdg 11:13 The king of the Ammonites answered J

Jephunneh

Nu 13: 6 the tribe of Judah, Caleb son of J;
14: 6 Joshua son of Nun and Caleb son of J,
14:30 Caleb son of J and Joshua son of Nun.
14:38 of Nun and Caleb son of J survived.
26:65 Caleb son of J and Joshua son of Nun.
32:12 except Caleb son of J the Kenizzite
34:19 These are their names: Caleb son of J
Dt 1:36 except Caleb son of J. He will see
Jos 14: 6 and Caleb son of J the Kenizzite
14:13 Joshua blessed Caleb son of J and
14:14 Hebron has belonged to Caleb son of J
15:13 Joshua gave to Caleb son of J a
21:12 to Caleb son of J as his possession.
1Ch 4:15 The sons of Caleb son of J: Iru,
6:56 city were given to Caleb son of J.
7:38 The sons of Jether: J, Pispah and

Jerah

Ge 10:26 of Almodad, Sheleph, Hazarmaveth, J,
1Ch 1:20 of Almodad, Sheleph, Hazarmaveth, J,

Jerahmeel (Jerahmeelites)

1Sa 27:10 "Against the Negev of J" or "Against
1Ch 2: 9 The sons born to Hezron were: J, Ram
2:25 The sons of J the firstborn of
2:26 J had another wife, whose name was
2:27 The sons of Ram the firstborn of J:
2:33 These were the descendants of J.
2:42 The sons of Caleb the brother of J:
24:29 From Kish: the son of Kish: J.
Jer 36:26 Instead, the king commanded J, a son

Jerahmeelites (Jerahmeel)

1Sa 30:29 to those in the towns of the J

Jered

1Ch 4:18 (His Judean wife gave birth to J the

Jeremai

Ezr 10:33 Eliphelet, J, Manasseh and Shimei.

Jeremiah (Jeremiah's)

Prophet to Judah (Jer 1:1–3). Called by God while still young (Jer 1). Persecuted (Jer 11:18–23; 12:6; 18:18); put in stocks (Jer 20:2); threatened with death (Jer 26:7–11); scroll burned (Jer 36); imprisoned (Jer 37); thrown into cistern (Jer 38:6–13). Warned of Babylonian exile (Jer 25:8–11; 34:1–3); challenged false prophets (Jer 6:10–15; 23:9–40; 28). Promised restoration (Jer 25:12–14; 30; 33); announced new covenant (Jer 31); bought field (Jer 32). Taken to Egypt with fleeing remnant (Jer 43).

2Ki 23:31 daughter of J; she was from Libnah.
24:18 daughter of J; she was from Libnah.
1Ch 5:24 Azriel, J, Hodaviah and Jahdiel.
12: 4 who was a leader of the Thirty; J,
12:10 Mishmannah the fourth, J the fifth,
12:13 J the tenth and Macbannai the
2Ch 35:25 J composed laments for Josiah, and
36:12 humble himself before J the prophet,
36:21 of the word of the LORD spoken by J.
36:22 the word of the LORD spoken by J,
Ezr 1: 1 the word of the LORD spoken by J,
Ne 10: 2 Seraiah, Azariah, J,
12: 1 and with Jeshua: Seraiah, J, Ezra,
12:34 Judah, Benjamin, Shemaiah, J,
Jer 1: 1 The words of J son of Hilkiah, one
1:11 "What do you see, J?" "I see the
7: 1 This is the word that came to J from
11: 1 This is the word that came to J from
14: 1 This is the word of the LORD to J
18: 1 This is the word that came to J from
18:18 "Come, let's make plans against J;
19:14 J then returned from Topheth, where
20: 1 heard J prophesying these things,
20: 2 he had J the prophet beaten and put
20: 3 J said to him, "The LORD's name for
21: 1 The word came to J from the LORD
21: 3 J answered them, "Tell Zedekiah,
24: 3 asked me, "What do you see, J?"
25: 1 The word came to J concerning all
25: 2 J the prophet said to all the people
25:13 prophesied by J against all the
26: 7 all the people heard J speak these
26: 8 as soon as J finished telling all
26: 9 around J in the house of the LORD.
26:12 J said to all the officials and all
26:20 this city and this land as J did.
26:24 Ahikam son of Shaphan supported J,
27: 1 this word came to J from the LORD:
28: 5 the prophet J replied to the prophet
28:10 neck of the prophet J and broke it,
28:11 this, the prophet J went on his way.
28:12 yoke off the neck of the prophet J,
28:12 the word of the LORD came to J:
28:15 the prophet J said to Hananiah the
29: 1 the letter that the prophet J sent
29:27 not reprimanded J from Anathoth,
29:29 read the letter to J the prophet.
29:30 the word of the LORD came to J:
30: 1 This is the word that came to J from
32: 1 This is the word that came to J from
32: 2 and J the prophet was confined in
32: 6 J said, "The word of the LORD came
32:26 the word of the LORD came to J:
33: 1 While J was still confined in the
33:19 The word of the LORD came to J:
33:23 The word of the LORD came to J:
34: 1 this word came to J from the LORD:
34: 6 J the prophet told all this to
34: 8 The word came to J from the LORD
34:12 the word of the LORD came to J:
35: 1 This is the word that came to J from
35: 3 I went to get Jaazaniah son of J,
35:12 the word of the LORD came to J,
35:18 J said to the family of the
36: 1 this word came to J from the LORD:
36: 4 J called Baruch son of Neriah, and
36: 4 and while J dictated all the words
36: 5 J told Baruch, "I am restricted; I
36: 8 everything J the prophet told him
36:10 the words of J from the scroll.
36:17 write all this? Did J dictate it?"
36:19 to Baruch, "You and J, go and hide.
36:26 Baruch the scribe and J the prophet.
36:27 the word of the LORD came to J:
36:32 J took another scroll and gave it to
36:32 and as J dictated, Baruch wrote on
37: 2 had spoken through J the prophet.
37: 3 to J the prophet with this message:
37: 4 Now J was free to come and go among
37: 6 the word of the LORD came to J the
37:12 J started to leave the city to go to
37:14 "That's not true!" J said. "I am not
37:14 he arrested J and brought him to

Jer 37:15 They were angry with J and had him
37:16 J was put into a vaulted cell in a
37:17 "Yes," J replied, "you will be
37:18 J said to King Zedekiah, "What crime
37:21 gave orders for J to be placed in
37:21 So J remained in the courtyard of
38: 1 Malkijah heard what J was telling
38: 6 they took J and put him into the
38: 6 lowered J by ropes into the cistern
38: 6 and J sank down into the mud.
38: 7 they had put J into the cistern.
38: 9 all they have done to J the prophet.
38:10 lift J the prophet out of the
38:11 down with ropes to J in the cistern.
38:12 Ebed-Melech the Cushite said to J,
38:12 to pad the ropes." J did so,
38:13 And J remained in the courtyard of
38:14 King Zedekiah sent for J the prophet
38:14 you something," the king said to J.
38:15 J said to Zedekiah, "If I give you
38:16 to J: "As surely as the LORD lives,
38:17 J said to Zedekiah, "This is what
38:19 King Zedekiah said to J, "I am
38:20 will not hand you over," J replied
38:24 Zedekiah said to J, "Do not let
38:27 All the officials did come to J and
38:28 J remained in the courtyard of the
39:11 had given these orders about J
39:14 had J taken out of the courtyard
39:15 While J had been confined in the
40: 1 The word came to J from the LORD
40: 1 He had found J bound in chains among
40: 2 the commander of the guard found J,
40: 5 However, before J turned to go,
40: 6 J went to Gedaliah son of Ahikam at
42: 2 J the prophet and said to him,
42: 4 "I have heard you," replied J the
42: 5 they said to J, "May the LORD be a
42: 7 the word of the LORD came to J.
43: 1 J finished telling the people all
43: 2 and all the arrogant men said to J,
43: 6 the son of Shaphan, and J the
43: 8 the word of the LORD came to J:
44: 1 This word came to J concerning all
44:15 in Lower and Upper Egypt, said to J,
44:20 J said to all the people, both men
44:24 J said to all the people, including
45: 1 This is what J the prophet told
45: 1 the words J was then dictating:
46: 1 J the prophet concerning the nations:
46:13 the LORD spoke to J the prophet
47: 1 the word of the LORD that came to J
49:34 to J the prophet concerning Elam,
50: 1 J the prophet concerning Babylon
51:59 This is the message J gave to the
51:60 J had written on a scroll about all
51:64 The words of J end here.
52: 1 daughter of J; she was from Libnah.
Da 9: 2 of the LORD given to J the prophet,
Mt 2:17 what was said through the prophet J
16:14 others, J or one of the prophets."
27: 9 what was spoken by J the prophet was

Jeremiah's (Jeremiah)

Ne 12:12 family, Meraiah; of J, Hananiah;
Jer 36:27 Baruch had written at J dictation,

Jeremoth

1Ch 7: 8 J, Abijah, Anathoth and Alemeth.
8:14 Ahio, Shashak, J,
Ezr 10:26 Jehiel, Abdi, J and Elijah.
10:27 Mattaniah, J, Zabad and Aziza.
10:29 Malluch, Adaiah, Jashub, Sheal and J.

Jeriah

1Ch 23:19 The sons of Hebron: J the first,
24:23 The sons of Hebron: J the first,
26:31 for the Hebronites, J was their
26:32 J had two thousand seven hundred

Jeribai

1Ch 11:46 Eliel the Mahavite, J and Joshaviah

Jericho

One of the oldest and lowest-lying cities in the world, situated in Jordan Valley, about 15 miles north-east of Jerusalem. The Israelites camped opposite here, before crossing the Jordan (Nu 22:1; 26:3, 63; 31:12; 33:48, 50; 35:1; 36:13; Dt 32:49; 34:1, 3; Jos 3:16; 13:32). Joshua's spies focused on this city and escaped with Rahab's help (Jos 2:1–7). Israel's army camped near here to prepare for battle (Jos 4:13), and defeated the city (Jos 6). Allotted to the tribe of Benjamin (Jos 18:21). David's men waited here while their beards grew back (2Sa 10:5; 1Ch 19:5). Joshua's curse was fulfilled on Hiel who rebuilt Jericho (Jos 6:26; 1Ki 16:34). It became a community of prophets (2Ki 2:5). Known also as the City of Palms (2Ch 28:15). Zedekiah was captured by the Babylonians near here (Jer 39:5; 52:8). Place where Jesus healed blind men (Mt 20:29; Mk 10:46; Lk 18:35) and met with Zacchaeus (Lk 19:1). Referred to in a parable (Lk 10:30).

Nu 22: 1 along the Jordan across from J.
26: 3 of Moab by the Jordan across from J,
26:63 of Moab by the Jordan across from J.
31:12 Moab, by the Jordan across from J.
33:48 of Moab by the Jordan across from J.
33:50 across from J the LORD said to
34:15 the east side of the Jordan of J,
35: 1 across from J, the LORD said to
36:13 of Moab by the Jordan across from J.
Dt 32:49 across from J, and view Canaan, the
34: 1 to the top of Pisgah, across from J.
34: 3 the Valley of J, the City of Palms,
Jos 2: 1 the land," he said, "especially J.
2: 2 The king of J was told, "Look! Some
2: 3 the king of J sent this message to
3:16 the people crossed over opposite J.
4:13 the LORD to the plains of J for war.
4:19 Gilgal on the eastern border of J.
5:10 camped at Gilgal on the plains of J,
5:13 Now when Joshua was near J, he
6: 1 Now J was tightly shut up because of
6: 2 I have delivered J into your hands
6:25 men Joshua had sent as spies to J
6:26 undertakes to rebuild this city, J
7: 2 Now Joshua sent men from J to Ai,
8: 2 as you did to J and its king,
9: 3 what Joshua had done to J and Ai,
10: 1 as he had done to J and its king,
10:28 as he had done to the king of J.
10:30 as he had done to the king of J.
12: 9 the king of J one the king of Ai
13:32 of Moab across the Jordan east of J.
16: 1 for Joseph began at the Jordan of J,
16: 1 east of the waters of J, and went up
16: 7 touched J and came out at the
18:12 passed the northern slope of J and
18:21 cities: J, Beth Hoglah, Emek Keziz,
20: 8 On the east side of the Jordan of J
24:11 crossed the Jordan and came to J.
24:11 The citizens of J fought against you,
2Sa 10: 5 "Stay at J till your beards have
1Ki 16:34 time, Hiel of Bethel rebuilt J.
2Ki 2: 4 the LORD has sent me to J.
2: 4 not leave you. So they went to J.
2: 5 The company of the prophets at J
2:15 The company of the prophets from J,
2:18 who was staying in J, he said to
25: 5 and overtook him in the plains of J.
1Ch 6:78 across the Jordan east of J
19: 5 "Stay at J till your beards have
2Ch 28:15 to their fellow countrymen at J,
Ezr 2:34 of J 345
Ne 3: 2 The men of J built the adjoining
7:36 of J 345
Jer 39: 5 Zedekiah in the plains of J.
52: 8 and overtook him in the plains of J.
Mt 20:29 and his disciples were leaving J,
Mk 10:46 they came to J. As Jesus and his
Lk 10:30 was going down from Jerusalem to J,
18:35 Jesus approached J, a blind man was
19: 1 Jesus entered J and was passing
Heb 11:30 By faith the walls of J fell, after

Jeriel

1Ch 7: 2 The sons of Tola: Uzzi, Rephaiah, J,

Jerimoth

1Ch 7: 7 Uzzi, Uzziel, J and Iri, heads of
12: 5 Eluzai, J, Bealiah, Shemariah and
23:23 The sons of Mushi: Mahli, Eder and J
24:30 the sons of Mushi: Mahli, Eder and J
25: 4 Mattaniah, Uzziel, Shubael and J;
25:22 the fifteenth to J, his sons and
27:19 over Naphtali: J son of Azriel;
2Ch 11:18 of David's son J and of Abihail,
31:13 Jehiel, Azaziah, Nahath, Asahel, J,

Jerioth

1Ch 2:18 by his wife Azubah (and by J).

Jeroboam (Jeroboam's)

1. Israel's first king. Former official of Solomon; rebelled and fled to Egypt (1Ki 11:26–40). After Solomon's death, led northern tribes in rebellion against Rehoboam (1Ki 12:1–20; 2Ch 10). Established idolatrous worship (1Ki 12:25–33); set evil example for successors (1Ki 15:34; 16:19,26,31; 22:52). Rebuked by prophets (1Ki 13–14). Death (2Ch 13:20).
2. Jeroboam II. Son of Jehoash. Restored Israel's boundaries; brought economic prosperity (2Ki 14:23–29). Spiritual decay challenged by Amos (Am 1:1; 2:6–8; 5:21–24; 6:1–8; 7:9–11).

1Ki 11:26 Also, J son of Nebat rebelled
11:28 Now J was a man of standing, and
11:29 J was going out of Jerusalem, and
11:31 he said to J, "Take ten pieces for
11:40 Solomon tried to kill J, but J fled
12: 2 J son of Nebat heard this (he was
12: 3 they sent for J, and he and the
12:12 Three days later J and all the
12:15 the word the LORD had spoken to J
12:20 all the Israelites heard that J had
12:25 J fortified Shechem in the hill
12:26 J thought to himself, "The kingdom
12:31 J built shrines on high places and
13: 1 as J was standing by the altar to
13: 4 King J heard what the man of God
13:33 J did not change his evil ways,
13:34 This was the sin of the house of J
14: 1 Abijah son of J became ill,
14: 2 J said to his wife, "Go, disguise
14: 2 be recognised as the wife of J.
14: 6 he said, "Come in, wife of J.
14: 7 Go, tell J that this is what the
14:10 to bring disaster on the house of J.
14:10 I will cut off from J every last
14:10 I will burn up the house of J as one
14:11 Dogs will eat those belonging to J
14:13 He is the only one belonging to J
14:13 in the house of J in whom the LORD,
14:14 who will cut off the family of J.
14:16 because of the sins J has committed
14:30 warfare between Rehoboam and J.
15: 1 year of the reign of J son of Nebat,
15: 6 There was war between Rehoboam and J
15: 7 There was war between Abijah and J.
15: 9 twentieth year of J king of Israel
15:25 Nadab son of J became king of Israel
15:29 He did not leave J anyone that
15:30 of the sins J had committed and had
15:34 walking in the ways of J and in his
16: 2 but you walked in the ways of J and
16: 3 house like that of J son of Nebat.
16: 7 and becoming like the house of J
16:19 walking in the ways of J and in the
16:26 walked in all the ways of J son of
16:31 commit the sins of J son of Nebat,
21:22 I will make your house like that of J
22:52 and in the ways of J son of Nebat,
2Ki 3: 3 clung to the sins of J son of Nebat,
9: 9 like the house of J son of Nebat
10:29 from the sins of J son of Nebat,
10:31 not turn away from the sins of J,
13: 2 the sins of J son of Nebat,
13: 6 from the sins of the house of J,
13:11 any of the sins of J son of Nebat,
13:13 and J succeeded him on the throne.
14:16 And J his son succeeded him as king.
14:23 J son of Jehoash king of Israel
14:24 any of the sins of J son of Nebat,

2Ki 14:27 by the hand of J son of Jehoash.
14:29 J rested with his fathers, the kings
15: 1 In the twenty-seventh year of J king
15: 8 Zechariah son of J became king of
15: 9 from the sins of J son of Nebat,
15:18 from the sins of J son of Nebat,
15:24 from the sins of J son of Nebat,
15:28 from the sins of J son of Nebat,
17:21 they made J son of Nebat their king.
17:21 J enticed Israel away from following
17:22 persisted in all the sins of J
23:15 the high place made by J son of
1Ch 5:17 king of Judah and J king of Israel.
2Ch 9:29 the seer concerning J son of Nebat?
10: 2 J son of Nebat heard this (he was in
10: 3 they sent for J, and he and all
10:12 Three days later J and all the
10:15 had spoken to J son of Nebat
11: 4 turned back from marching against J.
11:14 J and his sons had rejected them
12:15 warfare between Rehoboam and J.
13: 1 eighteenth year of the reign of J,
13: 2 There was war between Abijah and J.
13: 3 J drew up a battle line against him
13: 4 "J and all Israel, listen to me!
13: 6 Yet J son of Nebat, an official of
13: 8 calves that J made to be your gods.
13:13 J had sent troops round to the rear
13:15 God routed J and all Israel before
13:19 Abijah pursued J and took from him
13:20 J did not regain power during the
Hos 1: 1 of J son of Joash king of Israel:
Am 1: 1 J son of Jehoash was king of Israel.
7: 9 I will rise against the house of J."
7:10 sent a message to J king of Israel:
7:11 saying: " 'J will die by the sword,

Jeroboam's (Jeroboam)

1Ki 14: 4 J wife did what he said and went to
14: 5 "J wife is coming to ask you about
14:17 J wife got up and left and went to
14:19 The other events of J reign, his
15:29 to reign, he killed J whole family.
2Ki 14:28 for the other events of J reign, all

Jeroham

1Sa 1: 1 whose name was Elkanah son of J, the
1Ch 6:27 Eliab his son, J his son, Elkanah
6:34 the son of Elkanah, the son of J,
8:27 Elijah and Zicri were the sons of J.
9: 8 Ibneiah son of J; Elah son of Uzzi,
9:12 Adaiah son of J, the son of Pashhur,
12: 7 Joelah and Zebadiah the sons of J
27:22 over Dan: Azarel son of J.
2Ch 23: 1 of a hundred: Azariah son of J,
Ne 11:12 Adaiah son of J, the son of

Jerub-Baal (Jerub-Baal's)

Jdg 6:32 that day they called Gideon "J,"
7: 1 J (that is, Gideon) and all his
8:29 J son of Joash went back home to
8:35 the family of J (that is, Gideon)
9: 1 Abimelech son of J went to his
9: 5 his seventy brothers, the sons of J.
9: 5 son of J, escaped by hiding.
9:16 and if you have been fair to J and
9:19 towards J and his family today,
9:57 of Jotham son of J came on them.
1Sa 12:11 the LORD sent J, Barak, Jephthah and

Jerub-Baal's (Jerub-Baal)

Jdg 9: 2 all seventy of J sons rule over you,
9:24 the crime against J seventy sons,
9:28 Isn't he J son, and isn't Zebul

Jerub-Besheth

2Sa 11:21 Who killed Abimelech son of J?

Jeruel

2Ch 20:16 end of the gorge in the Desert of J.

Jerusalem (Jerusalem's, *New Jerusalem*)

City in northern Judea, about 18 miles west of Dead Sea. Its king was defeated by Joshua (Jos 10:1–26; 12:10). Allotted to tribe of Judah, and later Benjamin, but they could not expel the Jebusites (Jos 15:63; 18:28; Jdg 1:21). Chosen by David as capital of his kingdom (2Sa 5:5; 1Ch 3:4) and captured from the Jebusites. He put the ark of the covenant here (2Sa 6:12–15). He planned to build a great temple for the LORD here (2Sa 7; 1Ch 17), but this was Solomon's task (2Ch 2–7). Known as the City of David (2Sa 5:7) it remained capital of Judah after the kingdom split, until it was destroyed by the Babylonians (2Ki 25:10). Since the time of David the word "Zion" has been used to refer to either the hill on which the temple stood or Jerusalem in its entirety. The prophets and the Psalms use "Zion" to convey the idea that Jerusalem is the central place of Israelite religion and as a special place of God's presence it has security and renown (Ps 48; Isa 2:2–4). Historically the city of Jerusalem was rebuilt by Nehemiah after the exile (Ne 2:5); the temple rebuilt by Zerubbabel (Ezr 6:13–15). In NT times Jerusalem was associated with kings (Mt 2:1–2), and another temple stood in place of Zerubbabel's. Jesus came here at 12 years old (Lk 2:41–42), and later confronted the temple sellers (Lk 19:45–46). He entered the city triumphantly (Lk 19:28), but was soon arrested (Lk 22:47), tried (Lk 22:66–23:25) and crucified (Lk 23:26–55). After Stephen was martyred here (Ac 7:59) many believers left and scattered (Ac 8:1). It remained the place for settling disputes (Ac 15:2). In AD 70 the city was destroyed fulfilling Jesus' prophecy (Lk 19:41–44). A new Jerusalem is envisioned at the heart of God's new kingdom on earth inhabited by Christ and the church (Rev 3:12; 21:2, 10).

Jos 10: 1 Now Adoni-Zedek king of J heard that
10: 3 Adoni-Zedek king of J appealed to
10: 5 of the Amorites—the kings of J,
10:23 out of the cave—the kings of J,
12:10 the king of J one the king of Hebron
15: 8 of the Jebusite city (that is, J).
15:63 Jebusites, who were living in J;
18:28 the Jebusite city (that is, J),
Jdg 1: 7 brought him to J, and he died there.
1: 8 The men of Judah attacked J also and
1:21 Jebusites, who were living in J;
19:10 went towards Jebus (that is, J),
1Sa 17:54 head and brought it to J,
2Sa 5: 5 and in J he reigned over all Israel
5: 6 The king and his men marched to J
5:13 took more concubines and wives in J,
8: 7 of Hadadezer and brought them to J.
9:13 Mephibosheth lived in J, because he
10:14 the Ammonites and came to J.
11: 1 But David remained in J.
11:12 remained in J that day and the next.
12:31 and his entire army returned to J.
14:23 Geshur and brought Absalom back to J.
14:28 Absalom lived for two years in J
15: 8 If the LORD takes me back to J,
15:11 Two hundred men from J had
15:14 officials who were with him in J,
15:29 took the ark of God back to J
15:37 David's friend Hushai arrived at J
16: 3 "He is staying in J, because he
16:15 all the men of Israel came to J,
17:20 found no-one, so they returned to J.
19:19 on the day my lord the king left J.
19:25 he came from J to meet the king,
19:33 with me and stay with me in J,
19:34 I should go up to J with the king?
20: 2 all the way from the Jordan to J.
20: 3 David returned to his palace in J,
20: 7 They marched out from J to pursue
20:22 And Joab went back to the king in J.
24: 8 they came back to J at the end of
24:16 stretched out his hand to destroy J,
1Ki 2:11 in Hebron and thirty-three in J.
2:36 "Build yourself a house in J and
2:38 Shimei stayed in J for a long time.
2:41 Shimei had gone from J to Gath
3: 1 of the LORD, and the wall around J.
3:15 He returned to J, stood before the
8: 1 summoned into his presence at J
9:15 the wall of J, and Hazor, Megiddo
9:19 he desired to build in J,

1Ki 10: 2 Arriving at J with a very great
10:26 cities and also with him in J.
10:27 The king made silver as common in J
11: 7 On a hill east of J, Solomon built a
11:13 the sake of J, which I have chosen."
11:29 Jeroboam was going out of J, and
11:32 my servant David and the city of J,
11:36 always have a lamp before me in J,
11:42 Solomon reigned in J over all Israel
12:18 into his chariot and escape to J.
12:21 Rehoboam arrived in J, he mustered
12:27 at the temple of the LORD in J,
12:28 It is too much for you to go up to J.
14:21 he reigned for seventeen years in J,
14:25 Shishak king of Egypt attacked J.
15: 2 he reigned in J for three years. His
15: 4 lamp in J by raising up a son to
15: 4 succeed him and by making J strong.
15:10 he reigned in J for forty-one years.
22:42 reigned in J for twenty-five years.
2Ki 8:17 and he reigned in J for eight years.
8:26 and he reigned in J for one year.
9:28 His servants took him by chariot to J
12: 1 and he reigned in J for forty years.
12:17 Then he turned to attack J.
12:18 of Aram, who then withdrew from J.
14: 2 reigned in J for twenty-nine years.
14: 2 name was Jehoaddin; she was from J.
14:13 Then Jehoash went to J and broke
14:13 broke down the wall of J from the
14:19 They conspired against him in J, and
14:20 was buried in J with his fathers,
15: 2 he reigned in J for fifty-two years.
15: 2 name was Jecoliah; she was from J.
15:33 he reigned in J for sixteen years.
16: 2 he reigned in J for sixteen years.
16: 5 fight against J and besieged Ahaz,
18: 2 reigned in J for twenty-nine years.
18:17 from Lachish to King Hezekiah at J.
18:17 They came up to J and stopped at the
18:22 saying to Judah and J, "You must
18:22 worship before this altar in J"?
18:35 the LORD deliver J from my hand?"
19:10 'J will not be handed over to the
19:21 the Daughter of J tosses her head
19:31 For out of J will come a remnant,
21: 1 reigned in J for fifty-five years.
21: 4 had said, "In J I will put my Name.
21: 7 "In this temple and in J, which I
21:12 going to bring such disaster on J
21:13 I will stretch out over J the
21:13 wipe out J as one wipes out a dish,
21:16 that he filled J from end to end—
21:19 and he reigned in J for two years.
22: 1 reigned in J for thirty-one years.
22:14 lived in J, in the Second District.
23: 1 all the elders of Judah and J.
23: 2 the people of J, the priests and the
23: 4 He burned them outside J in the
23: 5 those around J—those who burned
23: 6 Valley outside J and burned it there.
23: 9 serve at the altar of the LORD in J,
23:13 were east of J on the south of the
23:20 Then he went back to J.
23:23 was celebrated to the LORD in J.
23:24 things seen in Judah and J.
23:27 and I will reject J, the city I
23:30 to J and buried him in his own tomb.
23:31 he reigned in J for three months.
23:33 so that he might not reign in J,
23:36 he reigned in J for eleven years.
24: 4 had filled J with innocent blood
24: 8 he reigned in J for three months.
24: 8 of Elnathan; she was from J.
24:10 advanced on J and laid siege to it,
24:14 He carried into exile all J: all the
24:15 He also took from J to Babylon the
24:18 he reigned in J for eleven years.
24:20 all this happened to J and Judah,
25: 1 against J with his whole army.
25: 8 of the king of Babylon, came to J.
25: 9 palace and all the houses of J.
25:10 broke down the walls around J.
1Ch 3: 4 reigned in J for thirty-three years,
6:10 in the temple Solomon built in J),
6:15 LORD sent Judah and J into exile

1Ch 6:32 built the temple of the LORD in J.
8:28 genealogy, and they lived in J.
8:32 lived near their relatives in J.
9: 3 and Manasseh who lived in J were:
9:34 genealogy, and they lived in J.
9:38 lived near their relatives in J.
11: 4 marched to J (that is, Jebus).
14: 3 In J David took more wives and
15: 3 David assembled all Israel in J to
18: 7 of Hadadezer and brought them to J.
19:15 So Joab went back to J.
20: 1 but David remained in J.
20: 3 and his entire army returned to J.
21: 4 Israel and then came back to J.
21:15 God sent an angel to destroy J. But
21:16 sword in his hand extended over J.
23:25 and has come to dwell in J for ever,
28: 1 of Israel to assemble at J:
29:27 in Hebron and thirty-three in J.
2Ch 1: 4 he had pitched a tent for it in J.
1:13 Solomon went to J from the high
1:14 cities and also with him in J.
1:15 and gold as common in J as stones,
2: 7 to work in Judah and J with my
2:16 You can then take them up to J."
3: 1 of the LORD in J on Mount Moriah,
5: 2 Solomon summoned to J the elders of
6: 6 now I have chosen J for my Name to
8: 6 he desired to build in J,
9: 1 came to J to test him with hard
9:25 cities and also with him in J.
9:27 silver as common in J as stones,
9:30 Solomon reigned in J over all Israel
10:18 into his chariot and escape to J.
11: 1 Rehoboam arrived in J, he mustered
11: 5 Rehoboam lived in J and built up
11:14 and came to Judah and J because
11:16 followed the Levites to J to offer
12: 2 Shishak king of Egypt attacked J
12: 4 of Judah and came as far as J.
12: 5 assembled in J for fear of Shishak,
12: 7 wrath will not be poured out on J
12: 9 Shishak king of Egypt attacked J, he
12:13 established himself firmly in J
12:13 he reigned for seventeen years in J,
13: 2 he reigned in J for three years. His
14:15 Then they returned to J.
15:10 They assembled at J in the third
17:13 kept experienced fighting men in J.
19: 1 returned safely to his palace in J,
19: 4 Jehoshaphat lived in J, and he went
19: 8 In J also, Jehoshaphat appointed
19: 8 And they lived in J.
20: 5 in the assembly of Judah and J at
20:15 and all who live in Judah and J!
20:17 LORD will give you, O Judah and J.
20:18 and all the people of Judah and J
20:20 "Listen to me, Judah and people of J!
20:27 all the men of Judah and J returned
20:27 Judah and J returned joyfully to J,
20:28 They entered J and went to the
20:31 reigned in J for twenty-five years.
21: 5 and he reigned in J for eight years.
21:11 had caused the people of J to
21:13 of J to prostitute themselves,
21:20 and he reigned in J for eight years.
22: 1 The people of J made Ahaziah,
22: 2 and he reigned in J for one year.
23: 2 When they came to J,
24: 1 and he reigned in J for forty years.
24: 6 bring in from Judah and J the tax
24: 9 in Judah and J that they should
24:18 God's anger came upon Judah and J.
24:23 it invaded Judah and J and killed
25: 1 reigned in J for twenty-nine years.
25: 1 name was Jehoaddin; she was from J.
25:23 Then Jehoash brought him to J and
25:23 broke down the wall of J from the
25:27 they conspired against him in J and
26: 3 he reigned in J for fifty-two years.
26: 3 name was Jecoliah; she was from J.
26: 9 Uzziah built towers in J at the
26:15 In J he made machines designed by
27: 1 he reigned in J for sixteen years.
27: 8 he reigned in J for sixteen years.
28: 1 he reigned in J for sixteen years.
2Ch 28:10 women of Judah and J your slaves.
28:24 altars at every street corner in J.
28:27 and was buried in the city of J,
29: 1 reigned in J for twenty-nine years.
29: 8 the LORD has fallen on Judah and J;
30: 1 come to the temple of the LORD in J
30: 2 the whole assembly in J decided to
30: 3 the people had not assembled in J.
30: 5 calling the people to come to J and
30:11 humbled themselves and went to J.
30:13 people assembled in J to celebrate
30:14 They removed the altars in J and
30:21 The Israelites who were present in J
30:26 There was great joy in J, for since
30:26 had been nothing like this in J.
31: 4 He ordered the people living in J to
32: 2 that he intended to make war on J,
32: 9 he sent his officers to J with this
32:10 that you remain in J under siege?
32:12 saying to Judah and J, 'You must
32:18 people of J who were on the wall,
32:19 They spoke about the God of J as
32:22 the people of J from the hand of
32:23 Many brought offerings to J for the
32:25 wrath was on him and on Judah and J.
32:26 as did the people of J; therefore
32:33 All Judah and the people of J
33: 1 reigned in J for fifty-five years.
33: 4 "My Name will remain in J for ever.
33: 7 "In this temple and in J, which I
33: 9 Judah and the people of J astray,
33:13 him back to J and to his kingdom.
33:15 built on the temple hill and in J;
33:21 and he reigned in J for two years.
34: 1 reigned in J for thirty-one years.
34: 3 to purge Judah and J of high places,
34: 5 and so he purged Judah and J.
34: 7 Then he went back to J.
34: 9 Benjamin and the inhabitants of J.
34:22 lived in J, in the Second District.
34:29 all the elders of Judah and J.
34:30 the people of J, the priests and the
34:32 he made everyone in J and Benjamin
34:32 the people of J did this in
35: 1 the Passover to the LORD in J,
35:18 who were there with the people of J.
35:24 and brought him to J, where he died.
35:24 and all Judah and J mourned for him.
36: 1 king in J in place of his father.
36: 2 he reigned in J for three months.
36: 3 The king of Egypt dethroned him in J
36: 4 king over Judah and J and changed
36: 5 he reigned in J for eleven years.
36: 9 reigned in J for three months and
36:10 Zedekiah, king over Judah and J.
36:11 he reigned in J for eleven years.
36:14 LORD, which he had consecrated in J.
36:19 temple and broke down the wall of J;
36:23 a temple for him at J in Judah.
Ezr 1: 2 a temple for him at J in Judah.
1: 3 let him go up to J in Judah and
1: 3 God of Israel, the God who is in J.
1: 4 for the temple of God in J.
1: 5 build the house of the LORD in J.
1: 7 had carried away from J
1:11 exiles came up from Babylon to J.
2: 1 returned to J and Judah, each to
2:68 at the house of the LORD in J,
3: 1 people assembled as one man in J.
3: 8 arrival at the house of God in J,
3: 8 returned from the captivity to J)
4: 6 against the people of Judah and J.
4: 8 secretary wrote a letter against J
4:12 up to us from you have gone to J
4:20 J has had powerful kings ruling over
4:23 went immediately to the Jews in J
4:24 the work on the house of God in J
5: 1 to the Jews in Judah and J in
5: 2 to rebuild the house of God in J.
5:14 had taken from the temple in J
5:15 and deposit them in the temple in J.
5:16 of the house of God in J.
5:17 to rebuild this house of God in J.
6: 3 concerning the temple of God in J:
6: 5 from the temple in J and brought
6: 5 to their places in the temple in J;
Ezr 6: 9 as requested by the priests in J
6:12 or to destroy this temple in J.
6:18 groups for the service of God at J,
7: 7 came up to J in the seventh year
7: 8 Ezra arrived in J in the fifth month
7: 9 and he arrived in J on the first day
7:13 wish to go to J with you, may go.
7:14 to enquire about Judah and J with
7:15 of Israel, whose dwelling is in J,
7:16 for the temple of their God in J.
7:17 of the temple of your God in J.
7:19 Deliver to the God of J all the
7:27 house of the LORD in J in this
8:29 of the house of the LORD in J
8:30 taken to the house of our God in J.
8:31 out from the Ahava Canal to go to J.
8:32 we arrived in J, where we rested
9: 9 a wall of protection in Judah and J.
10: 7 issued throughout Judah and J
10: 7 for all the exiles to assemble in J
10: 9 Judah and Benjamin had gathered in J.
Ne 1: 2 the exile, and also about J.
1: 3 The wall of J is broken down, and
2:11 I went to J, and after staying there
2:12 God had put in my heart to do for J.
2:13 examining the walls of J, which had
2:17 J lies in ruins, and its gates have
2:17 Come, let us rebuild the wall of J,
2:20 you have no share in J or any claim
3: 8 restored J as far as the Broad Wall.
3: 9 ruler of a half-district of J,
3:12 ruler of a half-district of J,
4: 8 to come and fight against J and
4:22 his helper stay inside J at night,
6: 7 this proclamation about you in J:
7: 2 I put in charge of J my brother
7: 3 I said to them, "The gates of J are
7: 3 appoint residents of J as guards
7: 6 returned to J and Judah, each to
8:15 it throughout their towns and in J:
11: 1 leaders of the people settled in J,
11: 1 one out of every ten to live in J,
11: 2 men who volunteered to live in J.
11: 3 leaders who settled in J (now some
11: 4 both Judah and Benjamin lived in J)
11: 6 lived in J totalled 468 able men.
11:22 The chief officer of the Levites in J
12:27 At the dedication of the wall of J,
12:27 were brought to J to celebrate
12:28 together from the region around J
12:29 villages for themselves around J.
12:43 sound of rejoicing in J could be
13: 6 I was not in J, for in the
13: 7 came back to J. Here I learned about
13:15 all this into J on the Sabbath.
13:16 Men from Tyre who lived in J were
13:16 selling them in J on the Sabbath to
13:19 the gates of J before the Sabbath,
13:20 of goods spent the night outside J.
Est 2: 6 had been carried into exile from J
Ps 51:18 prosper; build up the walls of J.
68:29 of your temple at J kings will bring
79: 1 they have reduced J to rubble.
79: 3 out blood like water all around J,
102:21 declared in Zion and his praise in J
116:19 of the LORD—in your midst, O J.
122: 2 are standing in your gates, O J
122: 3 J is built like a city that is
122: 6 Pray for the peace of J: "May those
125: 2 the mountains surround J, so the
128: 5 may you see the prosperity of J,
135:21 from Zion, to him who dwells in J.
137: 5 If I forget you, O J, may my right
137: 6 I do not consider J my highest joy.
137: 7 the Edomites did on the day J fell.
147: 2 The LORD builds up J; he gathers the
147:12 Extol the LORD, O J; praise your God,
Ecc 1: 1 Teacher, son of David, king of J:
1:12 Teacher, was king over Israel in J.
1:16 who has ruled over J before me;
2: 7 flocks than anyone in J before me.
2: 9 by far than anyone in J before me.
SS 1: 5 yet lovely, O daughters of J, dark
2: 7 Daughters of J, I charge you by the
3: 5 Daughters of J, I charge you by the
3:10 inlaid by the daughters of J.

SS 5: 8 O daughters of J, I charge you—if
5:16 this my friend, O daughters of J.
6: 4 lovely as J, majestic as troops with
8: 4 Daughters of J, I charge you: Do not
Isa 1: 1 The vision concerning Judah and J
2: 1 of Amoz saw concerning Judah and J:
2: 3 Zion, the word of the LORD from J.
3: 1 is about to take from J and Judah
3: 8 J staggers, Judah is falling; their
4: 3 who remain in J, will be called holy,
4: 3 are recorded among the living in J.
4: 4 will cleanse the bloodstains from J
5: 3 "Now you dwellers in J and men of
7: 1 marched up to fight against J, but
8:14 for the people of J he will be a
10:10 excelled those of J and Samaria—
10:11 shall I not deal with J and her
10:12 his work against Mount Zion and J,
10:32 Daughter of Zion, at the hill of J.
22:10 You counted the buildings in J and
22:21 be a father to those who live in J
24:23 will reign on Mount Zion and in J,
27:13 the LORD on the holy mountain in J.
28:14 scoffers who rule this people in J.
30:19 O people of Zion, who live in J, you
31: 5 the LORD Almighty will shield J;
31: 9 is in Zion, whose furnace is in J.
33:20 your eyes will see J, a peaceful
36: 2 from Lachish to King Hezekiah at J.
36: 7 saying to Judah and J, "You must
36:20 the LORD deliver J from my hand?"
37:10 'J will not be handed over to the
37:22 Daughter of J tosses her head as
37:32 For out of J will come a remnant,
40: 2 Speak tenderly to J, and proclaim to
40: 9 You who bring good tidings to J,
41:27 I gave to J a messenger of good
44:26 says of J, 'It shall be inhabited,'
44:28 will say of J, "Let it be rebuilt,"
51:17 Awake, awake! Rise up, O J, you who
52: 1 of splendour, O J, the holy city.
52: 2 rise up, sit enthroned, O J.
52: 9 you ruins of J, for the LORD has
52: 9 his people, he has redeemed J.
62: 6 posted watchmen on your walls, O J;
62: 7 him no rest till he establishes J
64:10 Zion is a desert, J a desolation.
65:18 for I will create J to be a delight
65:19 I will rejoice over J and take
66:10 "Rejoice with J and be glad for her,
66:13 and you will be comforted over J."
66:20 to my holy mountain in J as an
Jer 1: 3 the people of J went into exile.
1:15 in the entrance of the gates of J;
2: 2 Go and proclaim in the hearing of J
3:17 they will call J The Throne of
3:17 gather in J to honour the name of
4: 3 says to the men of Judah and to J:
4: 4 you men of Judah and people of J,
4: 5 "Announce in Judah and proclaim in J
4:10 deceived this people and J by
4:11 this people and J will be told,
4:14 O J, wash the evil from your heart
4:16 to the nations, proclaim it to J:
5: 1 "Go up and down the streets of J,
6: 1 people of Benjamin! Flee from J!
6: 6 and build siege ramps against J.
6: 8 Take warning, O J, or I will turn
7:17 of Judah and in the streets of J?
7:34 towns of Judah and the streets of J
8: 1 bones of the people of J will be
8: 5 Why does J always turn away? They
9:11 "I will make J a heap of ruins, a
11: 2 of Judah and to those who live in J.
11: 6 of Judah and in the streets of J:
11: 9 of Judah and those who live in J.
11:12 the people of J will go and cry out
11:13 are as many as the streets of J.'
13: 9 of Judah and the great pride of J.
13:13 prophets and all those living in J.
13:27 Woe to you, O J! How long will you
14: 2 the land, and a cry goes up from J.
14:16 thrown out in the streets of J
15: 4 of Hezekiah king of Judah did in J.
15: 5 "Who will have pity on you, O J?
17:19 also at all the other gates of J.
Jer 17:20 everyone living in J who come
17:21 or bring it through the gates of J.
17:25 men of Judah and those living in J,
17:26 of Judah and the villages around J,
17:27 the gates of J on the Sabbath day,
17:27 fire in the gates of J that will
18:11 of Judah and those living in J,
19: 3 O kings of Judah and people of J.
19: 7 I will ruin the plans of Judah and J.
19:13 The houses in J and those of the
21:13 I am against you, J, you who live
22:19 and thrown outside the gates of J."
23:14 among the prophets of J I have seen
23:14 the people of J are like Gomorrah."
23:15 because from the prophets of J
24: 1 were carried into exile from J to
24: 8 officials and the survivors from J,
25: 2 Judah and to all those living in J:
25:18 J and the towns of Judah, its kings
26:18 J will become a heap of rubble, the
27: 3 the envoys who have come to J to
27:18 and in J not be taken to Babylon.
27:20 Judah into exile from J to Babylon,
27:20 with all the nobles of Judah and J—
27:21 of the king of Judah and in J:
29: 1 the prophet Jeremiah sent from J
29: 1 into exile from J to Babylon.
29: 2 and the leaders of Judah and J,
29: 2 had gone into exile from J.)
29: 4 into exile from J to Babylon:
29:20 I have sent away from J to Babylon.
29:25 own name to all the people in J,
32: 2 of Babylon was then besieging J,
32:32 men of Judah and the people of J.
32:44 in the villages around J, in the
33:10 the streets of J that are deserted,
33:13 in the villages around J and in the
33:16 be saved and J will live in safety.
34: 1 J and all its surrounding towns,
34: 6 to Zedekiah king of Judah, in J,
34: 7 of Babylon was fighting against J
34: 8 covenant with all the people in J
34:19 The leaders of Judah and J, the
35:11 'Come, we must go to J to escape the
35:11 So we have remained in J."
35:13 men of Judah and the people of J,
35:17 on everyone living in J every
36: 9 proclaimed for all the people in J
36:31 those living in J and the people of
37: 5 J heard the report about them,
37: 5 about them, they withdrew from J.
37:11 from J because of Pharaoh's army,
38:28 guard until the day J was captured.
39: 1 This is how J was taken:
39: 1 against J with his whole army
39: 8 and broke down the walls of J.
40: 1 among all the captives from J
42:18 poured out on those who lived in J,
44: 2 on J and on all the towns of Judah.
44: 6 the streets of J and made them the
44: 9 land of Judah and the streets of J?
44:13 famine and plague, as I punished J.
44:17 of Judah and in the streets of J.
44:21 towns of Judah and the streets of J
51:35 who live in Babylonia," says J.
51:50 in a distant land, and think on J."
52: 1 he reigned in J for eleven years.
52: 3 all this happened to J and Judah,
52: 4 against J with his whole army.
52:12 the king of Babylon, came to J.
52:13 palace and all the houses of J.
52:14 broke down all the walls around J.
52:29 eighteenth year, 832 people from J;
Lam 1: 7 wandering J remembers all the
1: 8 J has sinned greatly and so has
1:17 J has become an unclean thing among
2:10 The young women of J have bowed
2:13 can I compare you, O Daughter of J?
2:15 their heads at the Daughter of J:
4:12 and foes could enter the gates of J.
Eze 4: 1 of you and draw the city of J on it.
4: 7 Turn your face towards the siege of J
4:16 cut off the supply of food in J.
5: 5 the Sovereign LORD says: This is J,
5: 8 I myself am against you J, and I
8: 3 in visions of God he took me to J,
Eze 9: 4 "Go throughout the city of J and put
9: 8 this outpouring of your wrath on J?"
11:15 of whom the people of J have said,
12:10 This oracle concerns the prince in J
12:19 living in J and in the land of
13:16 of Israel who prophesied to J
14:21 I send against J my four dreadful
14:22 the disaster I have brought upon J
15: 6 will I treat the people living in J.
16: 2 "Son of man, confront J with her
16: 3 what the Sovereign LORD says to J:
17:12 'The king of Babylon went to J and
21: 2 Son of man, set your face against J
21:20 against Judah and fortified J.
21:22 right hand will come the lot for J,
22:19 dross, I will gather you into J.
23: 4 Oholah is Samaria, and Oholibah is J.
24: 2 has laid siege to J this very day.
26: 2 because Tyre has said of J, 'Aha!
33:21 a man who had escaped from J came to
36:38 at J during her appointed feasts.
Da 1: 1 Babylon came to J and besieged it.
5: 2 had taken from the temple in J,
5: 3 taken from the temple of God in J,
6:10 where the windows opened towards J.
9: 2 the desolation of J would last
9: 7 Judah and people of J and all Israel,
9:12 done like what has been done to J.
9:16 from J, your city, your holy hill.
9:16 have made J and your people an
9:25 rebuild J until the Anointed One,
Joel 2:32 and in J there will be deliverance,
3: 1 restore the fortunes of Judah and J,
3: 6 You sold the people of Judah and J
3:16 roar from Zion and thunder from J;
3:17 J will be holy; never again will
3:20 will be inhabited for ever and J
Am 1: 2 roars from Zion and thunders from J;
2: 5 will consume the fortresses of J."
Ob :11 cast lots for J, you were like one
:20 the exiles from J who are in
Mic 1: 1 he saw concerning Samaria and J.
1: 5 is Judah's high place? Is it not J?
1: 9 gate of my people, even to J itself.
1:12 the LORD, even to the gate of J.
3:10 bloodshed, and J with wickedness.
3:12 J will become a heap of rubble, the
4: 2 Zion, the word of the LORD from J.
4: 8 will come to the Daughter of J."
Zep 1: 4 Judah and against all who live in J.
1:12 I will search J with lamps and
3:14 all your heart, O Daughter of J!
3:16 On that day they will say to J, "Do
Zec 1:12 from J and from the towns of Judah,
1:14 'I am very jealous for J and Zion,
1:16 'I will return to J with mercy, and
1:16 line will be stretched out over J,'
1:17 again comfort Zion and choose J.
1:19 that scattered Judah, Israel and J."
2: 2 "To measure J, to find out how wide
2: 4 'J will be a city without walls
2:12 holy land and will again choose J.
3: 2 The LORD, who has chosen J, rebuke
7: 7 through the earlier prophets when J
8: 3 I will return to Zion and dwell in J.
8: 3 J will be called the City of Truth
8: 4 age will sit in the streets of J,
8: 8 I will bring them back to live in J;
8:15 to do good again to J and Judah.
8:22 powerful nations will come to J to
9: 9 Shout, Daughter of J! See, your king
9:10 war-horses from J, and the
12: 2 "I am going to make J a cup that
12: 2 Judah will be besieged as well as J.
12: 3 I will make J an immovable rock for
12: 5 'The people of J are strong, because
12: 6 J will remain intact in her place.
12: 8 LORD will shield those who live in J,
12: 9 all the nations that attack J.
12:10 J a spirit of grace and supplication.
12:11 the weeping in J will be great, like
13: 1 of David and the inhabitants of J,
14: 2 I will gather all the nations to J
14: 4 on the Mount of Olives, east of J,
14: 8 living water will flow out from J,
14:10 from Geba to Rimmon, south of J,

Zec 14:10 But J will be raised up and remain
14:11 J will be secure.
14:12 the nations that fought against J:
14:14 Judah too will fight at J. The
14:16 the nations that have attacked J
14:17 not go up to J to worship the King,
14:21 Every pot in J and Judah will be
Mal 2:11 been committed in Israel and in J:
3: 4 the offerings of Judah and J will be
Mt 2: 1 Magi from the east came to J
2: 3 was disturbed, and all J with him.
3: 5 People went out to him from J and
4:25 the Decapolis, J, Judea and the
5:35 or by J, for it is the city of
15: 1 law came to Jesus from J and asked,
16:21 his disciples that he must go to J
20:17 Now as Jesus was going up to J, he
20:18 "We are going up to J, and the Son
21: 1 they approached J and came to
21:10 Jesus entered J, the whole city was
23:37 "O J, J, you who kill the prophets
Mk 1: 5 all the people of J went out to him.
3: 8 J, Idumea, and the regions across
3:22 who came down from J said, "He is
7: 1 come from J gathered round Jesus
10:32 They were on their way up to J, with
10:33 "We are going up to J," he said,
11: 1 they approached J and came to
11:11 Jesus entered J and went to the
11:15 On reaching J, Jesus entered the
11:27 They arrived again in J, and while
15:41 up with him to J were also there.
Lk 2:22 him to J to present him to the
2:25 Now there was a man in J called
2:38 forward to the redemption of J.
2:41 Every year his parents went to J for
2:43 in J, but they were unaware of it.
2:45 they went back to J to look for him.
4: 9 The devil led him to J and had him
5:17 of Galilee and from Judea and J,
6:17 from J, and from the coast of Tyre
9:31 about to bring to fulfilment at J.
9:51 Jesus resolutely set out for J.
9:53 him, because he was heading for J.
10:30 "A man was going down from J to
13: 4 than all the others living in J?
13:22 teaching as he made his way to J.
13:33 surely no prophet can die outside J!
13:34 "O J, J, you who kill the prophets
17:11 Now on his way to J, Jesus travelled
18:31 "We are going up to J, and
19:11 because he was near J and the people
19:28 he went on ahead, going up to J.
19:41 he approached J and saw the city, he
21:20 "When you see J being surrounded by
21:24 J will be trampled on by the
23: 7 who was also in J at that time.
23:28 "Daughters of J, do not weep for me;
24:13 Emmaus, about seven miles from J.
24:18 "Are you only a visitor to J and do
24:33 They got up and returned at once to J
24:47 name to all nations, beginning at J.
24:52 they worshipped him and returned to J
Jn 1:19 when the Jews of J sent priests
2:13 Jewish Passover, Jesus went up to J.
2:23 Now while he was in J at the
4:20 where we must worship is in J."
4:21 neither on this mountain nor in J.
4:45 had done in J at the Passover Feast,
5: 1 Some time later, Jesus went up to J
5: 2 there is in J near the Sheep Gate
7:25 At that point some of the people of J
10:22 came the Feast of Dedication at J.
11:18 was less than two miles from J,
11:55 many went up from the country to J
12:12 that Jesus was on his way to J.
Ac 1: 4 "Do not leave J, but wait for the
1: 8 and you will be my witnesses in J,
1:12 they returned to J from the hill
1:19 Everyone in J heard about this,
2: 5 Now there were staying in J
2:14 Jews and all of you who live in J,
4: 5 and teachers of the law met in J.
4:16 "Everybody living in J knows they
5:16 also from the towns around J,
5:28 "Yet you have filled J with your
Ac 6: 7 The number of disciples in J
8: 1 broke out against the church at J,
8:14 the apostles in J heard that Samaria
8:25 Peter and John returned to J,
8:26 goes down from J to Gaza."
8:27 This man had gone to J to worship,
9: 2 he might take them prisoners to J.
9:13 he has done to your saints in J.
9:21 he the man who caused havoc in J
9:26 he came to J, he tried to join the
9:28 them and moved about freely in J,
10:39 in the country of the Jews and in J.
11: 2 when Peter went up to J, the
11:22 reached the ears of the church at J
11:27 came down from J to Antioch.
12:25 they returned from J, taking with
13:13 where John left them to return to J.
13:27 The people of J and their rulers did
13:31 with him from Galilee to J.
15: 2 to go up to J to see the apostles
15: 4 they came to J, they were welcomed
16: 4 elders in J for the people to obey.
19:21 Paul decided to go to J, passing
20:16 for he was in a hurry to reach J,
20:22 I am going to J, not knowing what
21: 4 they urged Paul not to go on to J.
21:11 'In this way the Jews of J will bind
21:12 pleaded with Paul not to go up to J.
21:13 to die in J for the name of the
21:15 we got ready and went up to J.
21:17 we arrived at J, the brothers
21:31 whole city of J was in an uproar.
22: 5 as prisoners to J to be punished.
22:17 I returned to J and was praying
22:18 'Quick!' he said to me. 'Leave J
23:11 As you have testified about me in J
24:11 days ago I went up to J to worship.
24:17 I came to J to bring my people gifts
25: 1 Festus went up from Caesarea to J,
25: 3 to have Paul transferred to J, for
25: 7 the Jews who had come down from J
25: 9 "Are you willing to go up to J and
25:15 I went to J, the chief priests and
25:20 if he would be willing to go to J
25:24 about him in J and here in Caesarea,
26: 4 in my own country, and also in J.
26:10 that is just what I did in J. On the
26:20 then to those in J and in all Judea,
28:17 I was arrested in J and handed over
Ro 15:19 So from J all the way round to
15:25 I am on my way to J in the service
15:26 for the poor among the saints in J.
15:31 that my service in J may be
1Co 16: 3 and send them with your gift to J.
Gal 1:17 nor did I go up to J to see those
1:18 I went up to J to get acquainted
2: 1 again to J, this time with Barnabas.
4:25 to the present city of J,
4:26 the J that is above is free, and she
Heb 12:22 J, the city of the living God.
Rev 21:10 and showed me the Holy City, J,

Jerusalem's (Jerusalem)

Ne 4: 7 repairs to J walls had gone ahead
Isa 62: 1 for J sake I will not remain quiet,
Zec 12: 7 of J inhabitants may not be greater

Jerusha

2Ki 15:33 name was J daughter of Zadok.
2Ch 27: 1 name was J daughter of Zadok.

Jesarelah

1Ch 25:14 the seventh to J, his sons and

Jeshaiah

1Ch 3:21 of Hananiah: Pelatiah and J,
25: 3 from his sons: Gedaliah, Zeri, J,
25:15 the eighth to J, his sons and
26:25 J his son, Joram his son, Zicri his
Ezr 8: 7 of Elam, J son of Athaliah, and
8:19 with J from the descendants of
Ne 11: 7 the son of Ithiel, the son of J,

Jeshanah

2Ch 13:19 J and Ephron, with their surrounding
Ne 3: 6 The J Gate was repaired by Joiada
12:39 over the Gate of Ephraim, the J Gate,

Jeshebeab

1Ch 24:13 to Huppah, the fourteenth to J,

Jesher

1Ch 2:18 were her sons: J, Shobab and Ardon.

Jeshimon

1Sa 23:19 on the hill of Hakilah, south of J?
23:24 of Maon, in the Arabah south of J.
26: 1 the hill of Hakilah, which faces J?"
26: 3 on the hill of Hakilah facing J,

Jeshishai

1Ch 5:14 the son of J, the son of Jahdo,

Jeshohaiah

1Ch 4:36 also Elioenai, Jaakobah, J, Asaiah,

Jeshua

1Ch 24:11 the ninth to J, the tenth to
2Ch 31:15 Eden, Miniamin, J, Shemaiah, Amariah
Ezr 2: 2 in company with Zerubbabel, J,
2: 6 of Pahath-Moab (through the line of J
2:36 Jedaiah (through the family of J) 973
2:40 The Levites: the descendants of J
3: 2 J son of Jozadak and his fellow
3: 8 son of Shealtiel, J son of Jozadak
3: 9 J and his sons and brothers and
4: 3 Zerubbabel, J and the rest of the
5: 2 Zerubbabel son of Shealtiel and J
8:33 son of J and Noadiah son of Binnui.
10:18 the descendants of J son of Jozadak,
Ne 3:19 Ezer son of J, ruler of Mizpah,
7: 7 in company with Zerubbabel, J,
7:11 (through the line of J and Joab)
7:39 Jedaiah (through the family of J) 973
7:43 The Levites: the descendants of J
8: 7 The Levites—J, Bani, Sherebiah,
9: 4 on the stairs were the Levites—J,
9: 5 the Levites—J, Kadmiel, Bani,
10: 9 The Levites: J son of Azaniah,
11:26 in J, in Moladah, in Beth Pelet,
12: 1 and with J: Seraiah, Jeremiah, Ezra,
12: 7 their associates in the days of J.
12: 8 The Levites were J, Binnui, Kadmiel,
12:10 J was the father of Joiakim, Joiakim
12:24 Sherebiah, J son of Kadmiel, and
12:26 in the days of Joiakim son of J,

Jeshurun

Dt 32:15 J grew fat and kicked; filled with
33: 5 He was king over J when the leaders
33:26 "There is no-one like the God of J,
Isa 44: 2 my servant, J, whom I have chosen.

Jesimiel

1Ch 4:36 Asaiah, Adiel, J, Benaiah,

Jesse (Jesse's)

From Bethlehem; father of David (Ru 4:17,22; 1Sa 16; 17:12–20; 1Ch 2:12–17; Isa 11:1,10; Ro 15:12).

Ru 4:17 father of J, the father of David.
4:22 Obed the father of J, and J the
1Sa 16: 1 I am sending you to J of Bethlehem.
16: 3 Invite J to the sacrifice, and I
16: 5 Then he consecrated J and his sons
16: 8 J called Abinadab and made him pass
16: 9 J then made Shammah pass by, but
16:10 J made seven of his sons pass before
16:11 he asked J, "Are these all the sons
16:11 still the youngest," J answered,
16:18 "I have seen a son of J of Bethlehem
16:19 Saul sent messengers to J and said,
16:20 J took a donkey loaded with bread,
16:22 Saul sent word to J, saying, "Allow
17:12 J, who was from Bethlehem in Judah.
17:12 J had eight sons, and in Saul's time
17:17 Now J said to his son David, "Take
17:20 up and set out, as J had directed.

1Sa 17:58 son of your servant **J** of Bethlehem."
20:27 "Why hasn't the son of **J** come to the
20:30 with the son of **J** to your own shame
20:31 long as the son of **J** lives on this
22: 7 Will the son of **J** give all of you
22: 8 makes a covenant with the son of **J**.
22: 9 "I saw the son of **J** come to
22:13 you and the son of **J**, giving him
25:10 Who is this son of **J**? Many servants
2Sa 23: 1 "The oracle of David son of **J**, the
1Ch 2:12 of Obed and Obed the father of **J**.
2:13 **J** was the father of Eliab his
10:14 the kingdom over to David son of **J**.
12:18 We are with you, O son of **J**!
29:26 David son of **J** was king over all
Ps 72:20 the prayers of David son of **J**.
Isa 11: 1 will come up from the stump of **J**;
11:10 In that day the Root of **J** will stand
Mt 1: 5 was Ruth, Obed the father of **J**,
1: 6 **J** the father of King David. David
Lk 3:32 the son of **J**, the son of Obed, the
Ac 13:22 'I have found David son of **J** a man
Ro 15:12 "The Root of **J** will spring up,

Jesse's (Jesse)

1Sa 17:13 **J** three oldest sons had followed
2Sa 20: 1 no share in David, no part in **J** son!
1Ki 12:16 what part in **J** son? To your tents, O
2Ch 10:16 what part in **J** son? To your tents, O
11:18 Abihail, the daughter of **J** son Eliab.

Jesus (*Christ Jesus, Jesus Christ, Jesus of Nazareth*, Jesus', *Lord Jesus, Lord Jesus Christ, Name of Jesus*)

LIFE: Genealogy (Mt 1:1–17; Lk 3:23–38); birth (Mt 1:18–2:12; Lk 1:26–38; 2:1–20); presented in temple (Lk 2:21–40); fled to Egypt (Mt 2:13–18). Brought up in Nazareth (Mt 2:19–23); visited Jerusalem temple (Lk 2:41–52).

Baptised by John (Mt 3:13–17; Mk 1:9–11; Lk 3:21–23; Jn 1:29–34); tempted (Mt 4:1–11; Mk 1:12–13; Lk 4:1–13); began public ministry (Mt 4:12–17; Mk 1:14–15; Lk 4:14–30); called first disciples (Mt 4:18–22; Mk 1:16–20; Lk 5:2–11; Jn 1:35–51); preached in Galilee (Mt 4:23–25; Mk 1:39). Appointed and sent out disciples (Mt 9:35–10:16; Mk 3:13–18; 6:7–11; Lk 9:1–6; 10:1–17).

Acknowledged by Peter as Christ (Mt 16:13–23; Mk 8:27–33; Lk 9:18–22). Transfigured (Mt 17:1–8; Mk 9:2–8; Lk 9:28–36). Set out for Jerusalem (Mt 16:21; 20:17–19; Mk 10:32–34; Lk 18:31–34). Last week in Jerusalem: entered city (Mt 21:1–11; Mk 11:1–11; Lk 19:29–44; Jn 12:12–15); cleared temple (Mt 21:12–13; Mk 11:15–19; Lk 19:45–48; Jn 2:13–16); anointed at Bethany (Mt 26:6–13; Mk 14:3–9); shared Last Supper (Mt 26:17–30; Mk 14:12–26; Lk 22:7–23); washed disciples' feet (Jn 13:1–17); prayed in Gethsemane (Mt 26:36–46; Mk 14:32–42; Lk 22:40–46); arrested and tried (Mt 26:47–68; 27:11–26; Mk 14:43–65; 15:1–15; Lk 22:47–53; 22:66–23:25; Jn 18:1–19:16); crucified and buried (Mt 27:27–66; Mk 15:16–47; Lk 23:26–56; Jn 19:17–42). Raised to life; appeared to followers (Mt 28; Mk 16; Lk 24; Jn 20–21; Ac 1:1–4; 1Co 15:1–8); commissioned disciples (Mt 28:16–20; Ac 1:4–8); ascended (Lk 24:50–53; Ac 1:9).

MIRACLES: Healed: crowds (Mt 4:23–24; 8:16; Mk 1:32–34; Lk 4:40–41; Mt 14:14; Lk 9:11; Mt 15:29–31; Lk 6:17–18); those with leprosy (Mt 8:2–4; Mk 1:40–45; Lk 5:12–16; Lk 17:11–19); centurion's servant (Mt 8:5–13; Lk 7:1–10); Peter's mother-in-law (Mt 8:14–15; Mk 1:29–31; Lk 4:38–39); demon-possessed (Mt 8:28–34; Mk 5:1–20; Lk 8:26–39; Mt 9:32–34; 12:22; Lk 11:14; Mt 17:14–18; Mk 9:17–27; Lk 9:38–43; Mk 1:23–26; Lk 4:33–35); paralysed man (Mt 9:1–8; Mk 2:3–12; Lk 5:18–26); woman with bleeding (Mt 9:20–22; Mk 5:25–34; Lk 8:43–48); blind (Mt 9:27–31; 20:29–34; Mk 10:46–52; Lk 18:35–43; Mk 8:22–26; Jn 9:1–7); man with shrivelled hand (Mt 12:9–14; Mk 3:1–6; Lk 6:6–11); deaf mute (Mk 7:31–37); crippled woman (Lk 13:10–17); man with dropsy (Lk 14:1–4); high priest's servant (Lk 22:50–51); official's son (Jn 4:46–54); man at pool of Bethesda (Jn 5:1–9).

Raised to life: Jairus' daughter (Mt 9:18–26; Mk 5:22–43; Lk 8:41–56); widow of Nain's son (Lk 7:11–17); Lazarus (Jn 11:1–44). Stilled storm (Mt 8:23–27; Mk 4:35–41; Lk 8:22–25); fed 5,000 (Mt 14:15–21; Mk 6:35–44; Lk 9:12–17; Jn 6:5–13); walked on water (Mt 14:25–33; Mk 6:47–52; Jn 6:18–20); fed 4,000 (Mt 15:32–39; Mk 8:1–10); money from fish (Mt 17:24–27); cursed fig-tree (Mt 21:18–19; Mk 11:12–14,20–22); catches of fish (Lk 5:1–11; Jn 21:4–6); changed water to wine (Jn 2:1–11).

TEACHING: Announced God's kingdom (Mt 4:17; 10:7; 12:24–29; Lk 11:14–22; Mt 16:28; Mk 9:1; Mk 1:15; Lk 4:43; 9:11); Sermon on the Mount (Mt 5–7; Lk 6:20–49); pronounced woe on Pharisees (Mt 23; Lk 11:37–54); signs of the end of the age (Mt 24; Mk 13; Lk 21); conversations with Nicodemus (Jn 3), Samaritan woman (Jn 4); the bread of life (Jn 6:25–58); the good shepherd (Jn 10:1–20); discourse in Upper Room (Jn 13–17).

PARABLES: wise and foolish builders (Mt 7:24–27; Lk 6:47–49); sower (Mt 13:3–23; Mk 4:2–20; Lk 8:4–8); weeds (Mt 13:24–30); mustard seed and yeast (Mt 13:31–33; Mk 4:30–32; Lk 13:18–21); hidden treasure, pearl, net, houseowner (Mt 13:44–52); lost sheep (Mt 18:12–14; Lk 15:4–7); unmerciful servant (Mt 18:23–34); workers in vineyard (Mt 20:1–16); two sons (Mt 21:28–32); tenants (Mt 21:33–41; Mk 12:1–9; Lk 20:9–16); banquet (Mt 22:2–14; Lk 14:16–24); ten virgins (Mt 25:1–13); talents (Mt 25:14–30; Lk 19:12–27); sheep and goats (Mt 25:31–46); growing seed (Mk 4:26–29); good Samaritan (Lk 10:30–37); rich fool (Lk 12:16–21); cost of discipleship (Lk 14:28–33); lost coin, lost son (Lk 15:8–32); shrewd manager (Lk 16:1–8); rich man and Lazarus (Lk 16:19–31); persistent widow (Lk 18:2–8); Pharisee and tax collector (Lk 18:10–14).

Mt 1:16 was born **J**, who is called Christ.
1:21 and you are to give him the name **J**,
1:25 And he gave him the name **J**.
2: 1 After **J** was born in Bethlehem in
3:13 **J** came from Galilee to the Jordan to
3:15 **J** replied, "Let it be so now; it is
3:16 soon as **J** was baptised, he went up
4: 1 **J** was led by the Spirit into the
4: 4 **J** answered, "It is written: 'Man
4: 7 **J** answered him, "It is also written:
4:10 **J** said to him, "Away from me, Satan!
4:12 **J** heard that John had been put in
4:17 From that time on **J** began to preach,
4:18 **J** was walking beside the Sea of
4:19 "Come, follow me," **J** said, "and I
4:21 preparing their nets. **J** called them,
4:23 **J** went throughout Galilee, teaching
7:28 **J** had finished saying these things,
8: 3 **J** reached out his hand and touched
8: 4 **J** said to him, "See that you don't
8: 5 **J** had entered Capernaum, a centurion
8: 7 **J** said to him, "I will go and heal
8:10 **J** heard this, he was astonished and
8:13 **J** said to the centurion, "Go! It
8:14 **J** came into Peter's house, he saw
8:18 **J** saw the crowd around him, he gave
8:20 **J** replied, "Foxes have holes and
8:22 **J** told him, "Follow me, and let the
8:24 over the boat. But **J** was sleeping.
8:31 The demons begged **J**, "If you drive
8:34 the whole town went out to meet **J**.
9: 1 **J** stepped into a boat, crossed over
9: 2 When **J** saw their faith, he said to
9: 4 Knowing their thoughts, **J** said, "Why
9: 9 **J** went on from there, he saw a man
9:10 **J** was having dinner at Matthew's
9:12 **J** said, "It is not the healthy who
9:15 **J** answered, "How can the guests of
9:19 **J** got up and went with him, and so
9:22 **J** turned and saw her. "Take heart,
9:23 **J** entered the ruler's house and saw
9:27 **J** went on from there, two blind men
9:30 **J** warned them sternly, "See that
9:32 and could not talk was brought to **J**.
9:35 **J** went through all the towns and
10: 5 These twelve **J** sent out with the
11: 1 After **J** had finished instructing his
11: 4 **J** replied, "Go back and report to
11: 7 **J** began to speak to the crowd
11:20 **J** began to denounce the cities in
11:25 At that time **J** said, "I praise you,
12: 1 **J** went through the cornfields on
12:10 Looking for a reason to accuse **J**,

Mt 12:14 and plotted how they might kill **J**.
12:15 of this, **J** withdrew from that place.
12:22 and **J** healed him, so that he could
12:25 **J** knew their thoughts and said to
12:46 While **J** was still talking to the
13: 1 **J** went out of the house and sat
13:24 **J** told them another parable: "The
13:34 **J** spoke all these things to the
13:51 all these things?" **J** asked.
13:53 **J** had finished these parables, he
13:57 But **J** said to them, "Only in his
14: 1 tetrarch heard the reports about **J**,
14:12 Then they went and told **J**.
14:13 **J** heard what had happened, he
14:14 **J** landed and saw a large crowd, he
14:16 **J** replied, "They do not need to go
14:22 Immediately **J** made the disciples get
14:25 **J** went out to them, walking on
14:27 **J** immediately said to them: "Take
14:29 on the water and came towards **J**.
14:31 Immediately **J** reached out his hand
14:35 the men of that place recognised **J**,
15: 1 came to **J** from Jerusalem and asked,
15: 3 **J** replied, "And why do you break the
15:10 **J** called the crowd to him and said,
15:16 "Are you still so dull?" **J** asked
15:21 Leaving that place, **J** withdrew to
15:23 **J** did not answer a word. So his
15:28 **J** answered, "Woman, you have great
15:29 **J** left there and went along the Sea
15:32 **J** called his disciples to him and
15:34 many loaves do you have?" **J** replied
15:39 After **J** had sent the crowd away, he
16: 1 Pharisees and Sadducees came to **J**
16: 4 **J** then left them and went away.
16: 6 "Be careful," **J** said to them. "Be on
16: 8 Aware of their discussion, **J** asked,
16:13 **J** came to the region of Caesarea
16:17 **J** replied, "Blessed are you, Simon
16:21 From that time on **J** began to explain
16:23 **J** turned and said to Peter, "Get
16:24 **J** said to his disciples, "If anyone
17: 1 After six days **J** took with him Peter,
17: 3 Moses and Elijah, talking with **J**.
17: 4 Peter said to **J**, "Lord, it is good
17: 7 **J** came and touched them. "Get up,"
17: 8 looked up, they saw no-one except **J**.
17: 9 they were coming down the mountain, **J**
17:11 **J** replied, "To be sure, Elijah comes
17:14 approached **J** and knelt before him.
17:17 and perverse generation," **J** replied,
17:18 **J** rebuked the demon, and it came out
17:19 the disciples came to **J** in private
17:24 After **J** and his disciples arrived in
17:25 Peter came into the house, **J** was
17:26 "Then the sons are exempt," **J** said
18: 1 At that time the disciples came to **J**
18:21 Peter came to **J** and asked, "Lord,
18:22 **J** answered, "I tell you, not seven
19: 1 **J** had finished saying these things,
19: 8 **J** replied, "Moses permitted you to
19:11 **J** replied, "Not everyone can accept
19:13 little children were brought to **J**
19:14 **J** said, "Let the little children
19:16 Now a man came up to **J** and asked,
19:17 me about what is good?" **J** replied.
19:18 **J** replied, "'Do not murder, do not
19:21 **J** answered, "If you want to be
19:23 **J** said to his disciples, "I tell you
19:26 **J** looked at them and said, "With man
19:28 **J** said to them, "I tell you the
20:17 Now as **J** was going up to Jerusalem,
20:20 sons came to **J** with her sons and,
20:22 you are asking," **J** said to them.
20:23 **J** said to them, "You will indeed
20:25 **J** called them together and said,
20:29 **J** and his disciples were leaving
20:30 and when they heard that **J** was going
20:32 **J** stopped and called them. "What do
20:34 **J** had compassion on them and touched
21: 1 of Olives, **J** sent two disciples,
21: 6 The disciples went and did as **J** had
21: 7 cloaks on them, and **J** sat on them.
21:10 **J** entered Jerusalem, the whole city
21:11 The crowds answered, "This is **J**, the
21:12 **J** entered the temple area and drove

Mt 21:16 "Yes," replied J, "have you never
21:21 J replied, "I tell you the truth, if
21:23 J entered the temple courts, and,
21:24 J replied, "I will also ask you one
21:27 they answered J, "We don't know."
21:31 J said to them, "I tell you the
21:42 J said to them, "Have you never read
22: 1 J spoke to them again in parables,
22:18 J, knowing their evil intent, said,
22:29 J replied, "You are in error because
22:34 Hearing that J had silenced the
22:37 J replied: "'Love the Lord your God
22:41 gathered together, J asked them,
23: 1 J said to the crowds and to his
24: 1 J left the temple and was walking
24: 3 J was sitting on the Mount of Olives,
24: 4 J answered: "Watch out that no-one
26: 1 J had finished saying all these
26: 4 they plotted to arrest J in some sly
26: 6 While J was in Bethany in the home
26:10 Aware of this, J said to them, "Why
26:17 the disciples came to J and asked,
26:19 the disciples did as J had directed
26:20 evening came, J was reclining at the
26:23 J replied, "The one who has dipped
26:25 Rabbi?" J answered, "Yes, it is you.
26:26 While they were eating, J took bread,
26:31 J told them, "This very night you
26:34 "I tell you the truth," J answered,
26:36 J went with his disciples to a place
26:49 Going at once to J, Judas said,
26:50 J replied, "Friend, do what you came
26:50 forward, seized J and arrested him.
26:52 your sword back in its place," J said
26:55 At that time J said to the crowd,
26:57 Those who had arrested J took him to
26:59 looking for false evidence against J
26:62 high priest stood up and said to J,
26:63 J remained silent. The high priest
26:64 "Yes, it is as you say," J replied.
26:69 "You also were with J of Galilee,"
26:75 remembered the word J had spoken
27: 1 to the decision to put J to death.
27: 3 saw that J was condemned, he was
27:11 Meanwhile J stood before the
27:11 "Yes, it is as you say," J replied.
27:14 J made no reply, not even to a
27:17 Barabbas, or J who is called Christ?"
27:18 that they had handed J over to him.
27:20 for Barabbas and to have J executed.
27:22 "What shall I do, then, with J who
27:26 But he had J flogged, and handed him
27:27 the governor's soldiers took J into
27:34 There they offered J wine to drink,
27:37 THIS IS J, THE KING OF THE JEWS.
27:46 About the ninth hour J cried out in
27:48 stick, and offered it to J to drink.
27:50 J had cried out again in a loud
27:54 those with him who were guarding J
27:55 J from Galilee to care for his needs.
27:57 had himself become a disciple of J.
28: 5 looking for J, who was crucified.
28: 9 Suddenly J met them. "Greetings," he
28:10 J said to them, "Do not be afraid.
28:16 where J had told them to go.
28:18 J came to them and said, "All
Mk 1: 9 At that time J came from Nazareth in
1:10 J was coming up out of the water, he
1:14 After John was put in prison, J went
1:16 J walked beside the Sea of Galilee,
1:17 "Come, follow me," J said, "and I
1:21 and when the Sabbath came, J went
1:25 "Be quiet!" said J sternly. "Come
1:30 a fever, and they told J about her.
1:32 people brought to J all the sick
1:34 J healed many who had various
1:35 while it was still dark, J got up,
1:38 J replied, "Let us go somewhere else
1:41 Filled with compassion, J reached
1:43 J sent him away at once with a
1:45 J could no longer enter a town openly
2: 1 few days later, when J again entered
2: 4 Since they could not get him to J
2: 4 an opening in the roof above J and,
2: 5 J saw their faith, he said to the
2: 8 Immediately J knew in his spirit

Mk 2:13 Once again J went out beside the
2:14 "Follow me," J told him, and Levi
2:15 While J was having dinner at Levi's
2:17 On hearing this, J said to them, "It
2:18 Some people came and asked J, "How
2:19 J answered, "How can the guests of
2:23 One Sabbath J was going through the
3: 2 looking for a reason to accuse J,
3: 3 J said to the man with the
3: 4 J asked them, "Which is lawful on
3: 6 the Herodians how they might kill J.
3: 7 J withdrew with his disciples to the
3:13 J went up on a mountainside and
3:20 J entered a house, and again a crowd
3:23 J called them and spoke to them in
4: 1 Again J began to teach by the lake.
4: 9 J said, "He who has ears to hear,
4:13 J said to them, "Don't you
4:33 With many similar parables J spoke
4:38 J was in the stern, sleeping on a
5: 2 J got out of the boat, a man with an
5: 6 he saw J from a distance, he ran and
5: 7 "What do you want with me, J, Son of
5: 8 For J had said to him, "Come out of
5: 9 J asked him, "What is your name?"
5:10 he begged J again and again not to
5:12 The demons begged J, "Send us among
5:15 they came to J, they saw the man who
5:17 the people began to plead with J to
5:18 J was getting into the boat, the man
5:19 J did not let him, but said, "Go
5:20 how much J had done for him.
5:21 J had again crossed over by boat to
5:22 Seeing J, he fell at his feet
5:24 J went with him. A large crowd
5:27 she heard about J, she came up
5:30 At once J realised that power had
5:32 J kept looking around to see who had
5:35 While J was still speaking, some men
5:36 Ignoring what they said, J told the
5:38 J saw a commotion, with people
6: 1 J left there and went to his home
6: 4 J said to them, "Only in his home
6: 6 Then J went round teaching from
6:30 The apostles gathered round J and
6:34 J landed and saw a large crowd, he
6:39 J directed them to have all the
6:45 Immediately J made his disciples get
6:54 of the boat, people recognised J.
7: 1 from Jerusalem gathered round J
7: 5 and teachers of the law asked J,
7:14 Again J called the crowd to him and
7:19 J declared all foods "clean".)
7:24 J left that place and went to the
7:26 She begged J to drive the demon out
7:31 J left the vicinity of Tyre and went
7:33 J put his fingers into the man's
7:36 J commanded them not to tell anyone.
8: 1 J called his disciples to him and
8: 5 many loaves do you have?" J asked
8:11 came and began to question J.
8:15 "Be careful," J warned them. "Watch
8:17 Aware of their discussion, J asked
8:22 blind man and begged J to touch him.
8:23 J asked, "Do you see anything?"
8:25 J put his hands on the man's eyes.
8:26 J sent him home, saying, "Don't go
8:27 J and his disciples went on to the
8:30 J warned them not to tell anyone
8:33 when J turned and looked at his
9: 2 After six days J took Peter, James
9: 4 and Moses, who were talking with J.
9: 5 Peter said to J, "Rabbi, it is good
9: 8 saw anyone with them except J.
9: 9 J gave them orders not to tell
9:12 J replied, "To be sure, Elijah does
9:15 soon as all the people saw J, they
9:19 unbelieving generation," J replied
9:20 When the spirit saw J, it
9:21 J asked the boy's father, "How long
9:23 "'If you can'?" said J. "Everything
9:25 J saw that a crowd was running to
9:27 J took him by the hand and lifted
9:28 After J had gone indoors, his
9:30 J did not want anyone to know where
9:35 Sitting down, J called the Twelve

Mk 9:39 "Do not stop him," J said. "No-one
10: 1 J then left that place and went into
10: 5 Moses wrote you this law," J replied.
10:10 the disciples asked J about this.
10:13 to J to have him touch them,
10:14 J saw this, he was indignant. He
10:17 J started on his way, a man ran up
10:18 "Why do you call me good?" J
10:21 J looked at him and loved him. "One
10:23 J looked around and said to his
10:24 But J said again, "Children, how
10:27 J looked at them and said, "With man
10:29 "I tell you the truth," J replied,
10:32 with J leading the way, and the
10:38 know what you are asking," J said.
10:39 J said to them, "You will drink the
10:42 J called them together and said,
10:46 As J and his disciples, together
10:47 "J, Son of David, have mercy on me!
10:49 J stopped and said, "Call him." So
10:50 he jumped to his feet and came to J.
10:51 want me to do for you?" J asked him.
10:52 "Go," said J, "your faith has healed
10:52 sight and followed J along the road.
11: 1 J sent two of his disciples,
11: 6 They answered as J had told them to,
11: 7 they brought the colt to J and threw
11:11 J entered Jerusalem and went to the
11:12 were leaving Bethany, J was hungry.
11:15 On reaching Jerusalem, J entered the
11:21 Peter remembered and said to J,
11:22 "Have faith in God," J answered.
11:27 J was walking in the temple courts,
11:29 J replied, "I will ask you one
11:33 answered J, "We don't know." J said
12:13 to J to catch him in his words.
12:15 But J knew their hypocrisy.
12:17 J said to them, "Give to Caesar what
12:24 J replied, "Are you not in error
12:28 Noticing that J had given them a
12:29 The most important one," answered J,
12:34 J saw that he had answered wisely,
12:35 While J was teaching in the temple
12:38 J said, "Watch out for the teachers
12:41 J sat down opposite the place where
12:43 Calling his disciples to him, J said,
13: 2 these great buildings?" replied J.
13: 3 J was sitting on the Mount of Olives
13: 5 J said to them: "Watch out that
14: 1 sly way to arrest J and kill him.
14: 6 "Leave her alone," said J. "Why are
14:10 chief priests to betray J to them.
14:16 things just as J had told them.
14:17 evening came, J arrived with the
14:22 While they were eating, J took bread
14:27 "You will all fall away," J told
14:30 "I tell you the truth," J answered,
14:32 and J said to his disciples, "Sit
14:45 Going at once to J, Judas said,
14:46 The men seized J and arrested him.
14:48 "Am I leading a rebellion," said J,
14:51 a linen garment, was following J.
14:53 They took J to the high priest, and
14:55 were looking for evidence against J
14:60 stood up before them and asked J,
14:61 J remained silent and gave no answer
14:62 "I am," said J. "And you will see
14:67 You also were with that Nazarene, J,
14:72 Then Peter remembered the word J had
15: 1 They bound J, led him away and
15: 2 "Yes, it is as you say," J replied.
15: 5 J still made no reply, and Pilate
15:10 priests had handed J over to him.
15:15 He had J flogged, and handed him
15:16 The soldiers led J away into the
15:22 They brought J to the place called
15:34 at the ninth hour J cried out in a
15:36 stick, and offered it to J to drink.
15:37 With a loud cry, J breathed his last.
15:39 who stood there in front of J, heard
15:44 he asked him if J had already died.
16: 6 "You are looking for J the Nazarene,
16: 9 J rose early on the first day of the
16:11 they heard that J was alive and that
16:12 Afterwards J appeared in a different
16:14 Later J appeared to the Eleven as

Lk 1:31 and you are to give him the name J.
2:21 he was named J, the name the angel
2:27 the parents brought in the child J
2:43 the boy J stayed behind in Jerusalem,
2:52 J grew in wisdom and stature, and in
3:21 being baptised, J was baptised too.
3:23 Now J himself was about thirty years
4: 1 J, full of the Holy Spirit, returned
4: 4 J answered, "It is written: 'Man
4: 8 J answered, "It is written: 'Worship
4:12 J answered, "It says: 'Do not put
4:14 J returned to Galilee in the power
4:23 J said to them, "Surely you will
4:35 "Be quiet!" J said sternly. "Come
4:38 J left the synagogue and went to the
4:38 fever, and they asked J to help her.
4:40 the people brought to J all who had
4:42 At daybreak J went out to a solitary
5: 1 One day as J was standing by the
5:10 Then J said to Simon, "Don't be
5:12 While J was in one of the towns, a
5:12 When he saw J, he fell with his face
5:13 J reached out his hand and touched
5:14 J ordered him, "Don't tell anyone,
5:16 J often withdrew to lonely places
5:18 into the house to lay him before J.
5:19 of the crowd, right in front of J.
5:20 J saw their faith, he said, "Friend,
5:22 J knew what they were thinking and
5:27 J went out and saw a tax collector
5:27 "Follow me," J said to him,
5:29 Levi held a great banquet for J at
5:31 J answered them, "It is not the
5:34 J answered, "Can you make the guests
6: 1 One Sabbath J was going through the
6: 3 J answered them, "Have you never
6: 5 J said to them, "The Son of Man is
6: 7 looking for a reason to accuse J,
6: 8 J knew what they were thinking and
6: 9 J said to them, "I ask you, which is
6:11 one another what they might do to J.
6:12 One of those days J went out to a
7: 1 J had finished saying all this in
7: 3 The centurion heard of J and sent
7: 4 they came to J, they pleaded
7: 6 J went with them. He was not far
7: 9 J heard this, he was amazed at him,
7:11 Soon afterwards, J went to a town
7:15 and J gave him back to his mother.
7:17 This news about J spread throughout
7:20 the men came to J, they said, "John
7:21 At that very time J cured many who
7:24 J began to speak to the crowd
7:36 Now one of the Pharisees invited J
7:37 J was eating at the Pharisee's house,
7:40 J answered him, "Simon, I have
7:43 "You have judged correctly," J said.
7:48 J said to her, "Your sins are
7:50 J said to the woman, "Your faith has
8: 1 After this, J travelled about from
8: 4 coming to J from town after town,
8:22 One day J said to his disciples,
8:27 J stepped ashore, he was met by a
8:28 he saw J, he cried out and fell at
8:28 "What do you want with me, J, Son of
8:29 For J had commanded the evil spirit
8:30 J asked him, "What is your name?"
8:32 The demons begged J to let them go
8:35 When they came to J, they found the
8:37 the Gerasenes asked J to leave them,
8:38 him, but J sent him away, saying,
8:39 town how much J had done for him.
8:40 Now when J returned, a crowd
8:42 As J was on his way, the crowds
8:45 "Who touched me?" J asked. When they
8:46 J said, "Someone touched me; I know
8:49 While J was still speaking, someone
8:50 J said to Jairus, "Don't be afraid;
8:52 "Stop wailing," J said. "She is not
8:55 Then J told them to give her
9: 1 J had called the Twelve together, he
9:10 reported to J what they had done.
9:18 Once when J was praying in private
9:21 J strictly warned them not to tell
9:28 About eight days after J said this,
9:31 glorious splendour, talking with J.

Lk 9:33 the men were leaving J, Peter said
9:36 spoken, they found that J was alone.
9:41 and perverse generation," J replied,
9:42 But J rebuked the evil spirit,
9:43 was marvelling at all that J did, he
9:47 J, knowing their thoughts, took a
9:50 "Do not stop him," J said, "for
9:51 J resolutely set out for Jerusalem.
9:55 J turned and rebuked them,
9:58 J replied, "Foxes have holes and
9:60 J said to him, "Let the dead bury
9:62 J replied, "No-one who puts his hand
10:21 At that time J, full of joy through
10:25 in the law stood up to test J.
10:28 have answered correctly," J replied
10:29 so he asked J, "And who is my
10:30 In reply J said: "A man was going
10:37 J told him, "Go and do likewise."
10:38 J and his disciples were on their
11: 1 One day J was praying in a certain
11:14 J was driving out a demon that was
11:17 J knew their thoughts and said to
11:27 J was saying these things, a woman
11:29 J said, "This is a wicked
11:37 J had finished speaking, a Pharisee
11:38 noticing that J did not first wash
11:46 J replied, "And you experts in the
11:53 J left there, the Pharisees and the
12: 1 J began to speak first to his
12:14 J replied, "Man, who appointed me a
12:22 J said to his disciples: "Therefore
13: 1 who told J about the Galileans
13: 2 J answered, "Do you think that these
13:10 On a Sabbath J was teaching in one
13:12 J saw her, he called her forward and
13:14 Indignant because J had healed on
13:18 J asked, "What is the kingdom of God
13:22 J went through the towns and
13:31 At that time some Pharisees came to J
14: 1 One Sabbath, when J went to eat in
14: 3 J asked the Pharisees and experts in
14:12 J said to his host, "When you give a
14:15 he said to J, "Blessed is the man
14:16 J replied: "A certain man was
14:25 Large crowds were travelling with J,
15: 3 J told them this parable:
15:11 J continued: "There was a man who
16: 1 J told his disciples: "There was a
16:14 all this and were sneering at J.
17: 1 J said to his disciples: "Things
17:11 J travelled along the border
17:13 called out in a loud voice, "J,
17:17 J asked, "Were not all ten cleansed?
17:20 J replied, "The kingdom of God does
18: 1 J told his disciples a parable to
18: 9 everybody else, J told this parable:
18:15 People were also bringing babies to J
18:16 J called the children to him and
18:19 "Why do you call me good?" J
18:22 J heard this, he said to him, "You
18:24 J looked at him and said, "How hard
18:27 J replied, "What is impossible with
18:29 "I tell you the truth," J said to
18:31 J took the Twelve aside and told
18:35 J approached Jericho, a blind man
18:38 He called out, "J, Son of David,
18:40 J stopped and ordered the man to be
18:40 When he came near, J asked him,
18:42 J said to him, "Receive your sight;
18:43 received his sight and followed J,
19: 1 J entered Jericho and was passing
19: 3 He wanted to see who J was, but
19: 4 him, since J was coming that way.
19: 5 J reached the spot, he looked up and
19: 9 J said to him, "Today salvation has
19:28 After J had said this, he went on
19:35 They brought it to J, threw their
19:35 cloaks on the colt and put J on it.
19:39 Pharisees in the crowd said to J,
20: 8 J said, "Neither will I tell you by
20:17 J looked directly at them and asked,
20:20 They hoped to catch J in something
20:27 came to J with a question.
20:34 J replied, "The people of this age
20:41 J said to them, "How is it that they
20:45 listening, J said to his disciples,

Lk 21: 1 J saw the rich putting their gifts
21: 5 gifts dedicated to God. But J said,
21:37 Each day J was teaching at the
22: 2 for some way to get rid of J,
22: 4 with them how he might betray J.
22: 6 for an opportunity to hand J over
22: 8 J sent Peter and John, saying, "Go
22:13 found things just as J had told them
22:14 J and his apostles reclined at
22:25 J said to them, "The kings of the
22:34 J answered, "I tell you, Peter,
22:35 J asked them, "When I sent you
22:39 J went out as usual to the Mount of
22:47 He approached J to kiss him,
22:48 J asked him, "Judas, are you
22:51 J answered, "No more of this!" And
22:52 J said to the chief priests, the
22:63 The men who were guarding J began
22:66 together, and J was led before them.
22:67 J answered, "If I tell you, you
23: 3 Pilate asked J, "Are you the king of
23: 3 "Yes, it is as you say," J replied.
23: 7 he learned that J was under Herod's
23: 8 Herod saw J, he was greatly pleased,
23: 9 questions, but J gave him no answer.
23:20 Wanting to release J, Pilate
23:25 and surrendered J to their will.
23:26 him and made him carry it behind J.
23:28 J turned and said to them,
23:34 J said, "Father, forgive them, for
23:42 he said, "J, remember me when you
23:43 J answered him, "I tell you the
23:46 J called out with a loud voice,
23:55 The women who had come with J from
24:15 J himself came up and walked along
24:28 J acted as if he were going further.
24:35 and how J was recognised by them
24:36 J himself stood among them and said

Jn 1:29 The next day John saw J coming
1:36 he saw J passing by, he said, "Look,
1:37 heard him say this, they followed J.
1:38 Turning round, J saw them following
1:40 John had said and who had followed J.
1:42 he brought him to J. J looked at him
1:43 The next day J decided to leave for
1:47 J saw Nathanael approaching, he said
1:48 J answered, "I saw you while you
1:50 J said, "You believe because I told
2: 2 J and his disciples had also been
2: 4 why do you involve me?" J replied.
2: 7 J said to the servants, "Fill the
2:11 signs J performed at Cana in
2:13 Passover, J went up to Jerusalem.
2:19 J answered them, "Destroy this
2:22 and the words that J had spoken.
2:24 J would not entrust himself to them,
3: 2 He came to J at night and said,
3: 3 In reply J declared, "I tell you the
3: 5 J answered, "I tell you the truth,
3:10 "You are Israel's teacher," said J,
3:22 After this, J and his disciples went
4: 1 The Pharisees heard that J was
4: 2 in fact it was not J who baptised,
4: 6 J, tired as he was from the journey
4: 7 J said to her, "Will you give me a
4:10 J answered her, "If you knew the
4:13 J answered, "Everyone who drinks
4:17 J said to her, "You are right when
4:21 J declared, "Believe me, woman, a
4:26 J declared, "I who speak to you am
4:34 "My food," said J, "is to do the
4:44 (Now J himself had pointed out that
4:47 this man heard that J had arrived in
4:48 J told him, "you will never believe.
4:50 J replied, "You may go. Your son
4:50 man took J at his word and departed.
4:53 time at which J had said to him,
4:54 miraculous sign that J performed,
5: 1 J went up to Jerusalem for a
5: 6 J saw him lying there and learned
5: 8 J said to him, "Get up! Pick up your
5:13 for J had slipped away into the
5:14 Later J found him at the temple and
5:15 that it was J who had made him well.
5:16 So, because J was doing these things
5:17 J said to them, "My Father is always

Jn 5:19 **J** gave them this answer: "I tell you
6: 1 **J** crossed to the far shore of the
6: 3 **J** went up on a mountainside and sat
6: 5 **J** looked up and saw a great crowd
6:10 **J** said, "Make the people sit down."
6:11 **J** then took the loaves, gave thanks,
6:14 saw the miraculous sign that **J** did,
6:15 **J**, knowing that they intended to
6:17 dark, and **J** had not yet joined them.
6:19 they saw **J** approaching the boat,
6:22 and that **J** had not entered it with
6:24 **J** nor his disciples were there,
6:24 went to Capernaum in search of **J**.
6:26 **J** answered, "I tell you the truth,
6:29 **J** answered, "The work of God is this:
6:32 **J** said to them, "I tell you the
6:35 **J** declared, "I am the bread of life.
6:42 They said, "Is this not **J**, the son
6:43 "Stop grumbling among yourselves," **J**
6:53 **J** said to them, "I tell you the
6:61 **J** said to them, "Does this offend
6:64 For **J** had known from the beginning
6:67 too, do you?" **J** asked the Twelve.
6:70 **J** replied, "Have I not chosen you,
7: 1 After this, **J** went around in Galilee,
7: 6 Therefore **J** told them, "The right
7:14 did **J** go up to the temple courts
7:16 **J** answered, "My teaching is not my
7:21 **J** said to them, "I did one miracle,
7:28 **J**, still teaching in the temple
7:33 **J** said, "I am with you for only a
7:37 **J** stood and said in a loud voice,
7:39 since **J** had not yet been glorified.
7:43 people were divided because of **J**.
7:50 Nicodemus, who had gone to **J** earlier
8: 1 **J** went to the Mount of Olives.
8: 4 said to **J**, "Teacher, this woman was
8: 6 But **J** bent down and started to write
8: 9 only **J** was left, with the woman
8:10 **J** straightened up and asked her,
8:11 "Then neither do I condemn you," **J**
8:12 **J** spoke again to the people, he said,
8:14 **J** answered, "Even if I testify on my
8:19 know me or my Father," **J** replied.
8:21 Once more **J** said to them, "I am
8:25 been claiming all along," **J** replied.
8:28 **J** said, "When you have lifted up the
8:31 **J** said, "If you hold to my teaching
8:34 **J** replied, "I tell you the truth,
8:39 were Abraham's children," said **J**,
8:42 **J** said to them, "If God were your
8:49 not possessed by a demon," said **J**,
8:54 **J** replied, "If I glorify myself, my
8:58 "I tell you the truth," **J** answered,
8:59 but **J** hid himself, slipping away
9: 3 man nor his parents sinned," said **J**,
9:11 He replied, "The man they call **J**
9:14 the day on which **J** had made the mud
9:22 acknowledged that **J** was the Christ
9:35 **J** heard that they had thrown him out,
9:37 **J** said, "You have now seen him; in
9:39 **J** said, "For judgment I have come
9:41 **J** said, "If you were blind, you
10: 6 **J** used this figure of speech, but
10: 7 Therefore **J** said again, "I tell you
10:23 **J** was in the temple area walking in
10:25 **J** answered, "I did tell you, but you
10:32 **J** said to them, "I have shown you
10:34 **J** answered them, "Is it not written
10:40 **J** went back across the Jordan to the
10:42 in that place many believed in **J**.
11: 3 the sisters sent word to **J**, "Lord,
11: 4 **J** said, "This sickness will not
11: 5 **J** loved Martha and her sister and
11: 9 **J** answered, "Are there not twelve
11:13 **J** had been speaking of his death,
11:17 On his arrival, **J** found that Lazarus
11:20 Martha heard that **J** was coming, she
11:21 "Lord," Martha said to **J**, "if you
11:23 **J** said to her, "Your brother will
11:25 **J** said to her, "I am the
11:30 Now **J** had not yet entered the
11:32 Mary reached the place where **J** was
11:33 **J** saw her weeping, and the Jews who
11:35 **J** wept.
11:38 **J**, once more deeply moved, came to

Jn 11:40 **J** said, "Did I not tell you that if
11:41 **J** looked up and said, "Father, I
11:43 **J** called in a loud voice, "Lazarus,
11:44 **J** said to them, "Take off the grave
11:45 and had seen what **J** did, put their
11:46 and told them what **J** had done.
11:51 **J** would die for the Jewish nation,
11:54 **J** no longer moved about publicly
11:56 They kept looking for **J**, and as they
11:57 if anyone found out where **J** was,
12: 1 **J** arrived at Bethany, where Lazarus
12: 1 whom **J** had raised from the dead.
12: 7 "Leave her alone," **J** replied. "It
12: 9 found out that **J** was there and came,
12:11 to **J** and putting their faith in him.
12:12 that **J** was on his way to Jerusalem.
12:14 **J** found a young donkey and sat upon
12:16 Only after **J** was glorified did they
12:21 they said, "we would like to see **J**.
12:22 Andrew and Philip in turn told **J**.
12:23 **J** replied, "The hour has come for
12:30 **J** said, "This voice was for your
12:35 **J** told them, "You are going to have
12:36 **J** left and hid himself from them.
12:37 Even after **J** had done all these
12:44 **J** cried out, "When a man believes in
13: 1 **J** knew that the time had come for
13: 2 Iscariot, son of Simon, to betray **J**.
13: 3 **J** knew that the Father had put all
13: 7 **J** replied, "You do not realise now
13: 8 **J** answered, "Unless I wash you, you
13:10 **J** answered, "A person who has had a
13:21 **J** was troubled in spirit and
13:23 the disciple whom **J** loved, was
13:25 Leaning back against **J**, he asked him,
13:26 **J** answered, "It is the one to whom I
13:27 to do, do quickly," **J** told him,
13:28 understood why **J** said this to him.
13:29 some thought **J** was telling him to
13:31 he was gone, **J** said, "Now is the Son
13:36 **J** replied, "Where I am going, you
13:38 **J** answered, "Will you really lay
14: 6 **J** answered, "I am the way and the
14: 9 **J** answered: "Don't you know me,
14:23 **J** replied, "If anyone loves me, he
16:19 **J** saw that they wanted to ask him
16:31 "You believe at last!" **J** answered.
17: 1 After **J** said this, he looked towards
18: 1 he had finished praying, **J** left with
18: 2 **J** had often meet there with his
18: 4 **J**, knowing all that was going to
18: 5 "I am he," **J** said. (And Judas the
18: 6 **J** said, "I am he," they drew back
18: 8 told you that I am he," **J** answered,
18:11 **J** commanded Peter, "Put your sword
18:12 and the Jewish officials arrested **J**.
18:15 another disciple were following **J**.
18:15 went with **J** into the high priest's
18:19 the high priest questioned **J** about
18:20 openly to the world," **J** replied.
18:22 **J** said this, one of the officials
18:23 I said something wrong," **J** replied
18:28 the Jews led **J** from Caiaphas to the
18:32 so that the words **J** had spoken
18:33 summoned **J** and asked him, "Are you
18:34 "Is that your own idea," **J** asked,
18:36 **J** said, "My kingdom is not of this
18:37 **J** answered, "You are right in saying
19: 1 Pilate took **J** and had him flogged.
19: 5 **J** came out wearing the crown of
19: 9 asked **J**, but **J** gave him no answer.
Jn 19:11 **J** answered, "You would have no power
19:12 then on, Pilate tried to set **J** free,
19:13 Pilate heard this, he brought **J** out
19:16 So the soldiers took charge of **J**.
19:18 on each side and **J** in the middle.
19:20 for the place where **J** was crucified
19:23 the soldiers crucified **J**, they took
19:25 Near the cross of **J** stood his mother,
19:26 **J** saw his mother there, and the
19:28 be fulfilled, **J** said, "I am thirsty.
19:30 **J** said, "It is finished." With that
19:32 man who had been crucified with **J**,
19:33 when they came to **J** and found that
19:38 asked Pilate for the body of **J**.
19:38 Now Joseph was a disciple of **J**, but

Jn 19:39 who earlier had visited **J** at night.
19:41 At the place where **J** was crucified,
19:42 tomb was near by, they laid **J** there.
20: 2 the one **J** loved, and said, "They
20: 9 that **J** had to rise from the dead.)
20:14 At this, she turned round and saw **J**
20:14 she did not realise that it was **J**.
20:16 **J** said to her, "Mary." She turned
20:17 **J** said, "Do not hold on to me, for I
20:19 **J** came and stood among them and said,
20:21 Again **J** said, "Peace be with you! As
20:24 not with the disciples when **J** came.
20:26 **J** came and stood among them
20:29 **J** told him, "Because you have seen
20:30 **J** did many other miraculous signs in
20:31 may believe that **J** is the Christ,
21: 1 **J** appeared again to his disciples
21: 4 **J** stood on the shore, but the
21: 4 did not realise that it was **J**.
21: 7 the disciple whom **J** loved said to
21:10 **J** said to them, "Bring some of the
21:12 **J** said to them, "Come and have
21:13 **J** came, took the bread and gave it
21:14 the third time **J** appeared to his
21:15 **J** said to Simon Peter, "Simon son
21:15 **J** said, "Feed my lambs."
21:16 Again **J** said, "Simon son of John, do
21:16 **J** said, "Take care of my sheep."
21:17 because **J** asked him the third time,
21:17 **J** said, "Feed my sheep.
21:19 **J** said this to indicate the kind of
21:20 whom **J** loved was following them.
21:20 one who had leaned back against **J** at
21:22 **J** answered, "If I want him to remain
21:23 But **J** did not say that he would not
21:25 **J** did many other things as well.
Ac 1: 1 all that **J** began to do and to
1:11 This same **J**, who has been taken from
1:14 mother of **J**, and with his brothers.
1:16 as guide for those who arrested **J**—
1:22 time when **J** was taken up from us.
2:32 God has raised this **J** to life, and
2:36 God has made this **J**, whom you
3:13 has glorified his servant **J**.
3:20 has been appointed for you—even **J**.
4: 2 in **J** the resurrection of the dead.
4:13 note that these men had been with **J**.
4:27 holy servant **J**, whom you anointed.
4:30 the name of your holy servant **J**."
5:30 The God of our fathers raised **J** from
5:42 the good news that **J** is the Christ.
7:55 **J** standing at the right hand of God.
8:35 and told him the good news about **J**.
9: 5 "I am **J**, whom you are persecuting,"
9:17 "Brother Saul, the Lord—**J**, who
9:20 synagogues that **J** is the Son of God.
9:22 by proving that **J** is the Christ.
13:23 Israel the Saviour **J**, as he promised.
13:24 Before the coming of **J**, John
13:27 their rulers did not recognise **J**,
13:33 us, their children, by raising up **J**.
13:38 I want you to know that through **J**
16: 7 Spirit of **J** would not allow them to.
17: 3 "This **J** I am proclaiming to you is
17: 7 is another king, one called **J**."
17:18 news about **J** and the resurrection.
18: 5 to the Jews that **J** was the Christ.
18:25 and taught about **J** accurately,
18:28 Scriptures that **J** was the Christ.
19: 4 coming after him, that is, in **J**."
19:15 **J** I know, and I know about Paul,
25:19 named **J** whom Paul claimed was alive.
26:15 'Who are you, Lord?' "'I am **J**, whom
28:23 tried to convince them about **J** from
Ro 3:26 justifies those who have faith in **J**.
4:24 who raised **J** our Lord from the dead.
8:11 if the Spirit of him who raised **J**
10: 9 "**J** is Lord," and believe in your
1Co 9: 1 Have I not seen **J** our Lord? Are you
12: 3 "**J** be cursed," and no-one can say,
12: 3 "**J** is Lord," except by the Holy
2Co 4:10 around in our body the death of **J**,
4:10 **J** may also be revealed in our body.
4:14 the dead will also raise us with **J**
11: 4 a **J** other than the **J** we preached,
Gal 6:17 I bear on my body the marks of **J**.

Eph 4:21 with the truth that is in J.
Col 4:11 J, who is called Justus, also sends
1Th 1:10 J, who rescues us from the coming
4:14 We believe that J died and rose
4:14 believe that God will bring with J
Heb 2: 9 we see J, who was made a little
2:11 So J is not ashamed to call them
3: 1 fix your thoughts on J, the apostle
3: 3 J has been found worthy of greater
4:14 J the Son of God, let us hold firmly
6:20 where J, who went before us, has
7:22 of this oath, J has become the
7:24 J lives for ever, he has a permanent
8: 6 the ministry J has received is as
10:19 Most Holy Place by the blood of J,
12: 2 Let us fix our eyes on J, the author
12:24 to J the mediator of a new covenant,
13:12 J also suffered outside the city
13:15 Through J, therefore, let us
2Pe 1: 2 knowledge of God and of J our Lord.
1Jn 1: 7 the blood of J, his Son, purifies us
2: 6 to live in him must walk as J did.
2:22 man who denies that J is the Christ.
4: 3 not acknowledge J is not from God.
4:15 If anyone acknowledges that J is the
5: 1 Everyone who believes that J is the
5: 5 believes that J is the Son of God.
Rev 1: 9 endurance that are ours in J,
1: 9 word of God and the testimony of J.
12:17 and hold to the testimony of J.
14:12 and remain faithful to J.
17: 6 of those who bore testimony to J.
19:10 who hold to the testimony of J.
19:10 the testimony of J is the spirit of
20: 4 because of their testimony for J and
22:16 "I, J, have sent my angel to give

Jesus Christ (Lord Jesus Christ)

Mt 1: 1 genealogy of J the son of David,
1:18 how the birth of J came about:
Mk 1: 1 The beginning of the gospel about J,
Jn 1:17 grace and truth came through J.
17: 3 true God, and J, whom you have sent.
Ac 2:38 in the name of J for the forgiveness
3: 6 In the name of J of Nazareth, walk."
4:10 It is by the name of J of Nazareth,
8:12 kingdom of God and the name of J,
9:34 said to him, "J heals you. Get up
10:36 peace through J, who is Lord of all.
10:48 they be baptised in the name of J.
16:18 "In the name of J I command you to
Ro 1: 4 from the dead: J our Lord.
1: 6 those who are called to belong to J.
1: 8 First, I thank my God through J for
2:16 will judge men's secrets through J,
3:22 faith in J to all who believe.
5:15 one man, J, overflow to the many!
5:17 in life through the one man, J.
5:21 eternal life through J our Lord.
7:25 Thanks be to God—through J our Lord!
16:25 my gospel and the proclamation of J,
16:27 be glory for ever through J! Amen.
1Co 1: 9 his Son J our Lord, is faithful.
2: 2 with you except J and him crucified.
3:11 the one already laid, which is J.
8: 6 J, through whom all things came and
2Co 1:19 For the Son of God, J, who was
4: 5 For we do not preach ourselves, but J
Gal 1: 1 but by J and God the Father, who
1:12 I received it by revelation from J.
2:16 the law, but by faith in J.
3: 1 J was clearly portrayed as crucified.
3:22 being given through faith in J,
Eph 1: 5 to be adopted as his sons through J,
Php 1:11 righteousness that comes through J
1:19 the help given by the Spirit of J,
2:11 every tongue confess that J is Lord,
2:21 his own interests, not those of J.
2Ti 2: 8 Remember J, raised from the dead,
Tit 1: 1 apostle of J for the faith of God's
2:13 of our great God and Saviour, J,
3: 6 us generously through J our Saviour,
Heb 10:10 of the body of J once for all.
13: 8 J is the same yesterday and today
13:21 through J, to whom be glory for ever
1Pe 1: 1 Peter, an apostle of J, To God's
1: 2 for obedience to J and sprinkling by
1: 3 the resurrection of J from the dead,
1: 7 glory and honour when J is revealed.
1:13 to be given you when J is revealed.
2: 5 acceptable to God through J.
3:21 saves you by the resurrection of J,
4:11 things God may be praised through J.
2Pe 1: 1 a servant and apostle of J, To those
1: 1 our God and Saviour J have received
1:11 kingdom of our Lord and Saviour J.
2:20 by knowing our Lord and Saviour J
3:18 knowledge of our Lord and Saviour J.
1Jn 1: 3 with the Father and with his Son, J.
2: 1 our defence—J, the Righteous One.
3:16 J laid down his life for us.
3:23 believe in the name of his Son, J,
4: 2 that acknowledges that J has come
5: 6 one who came by water and blood—J.
5:20 him who is true—even in his Son J.
2Jn : 3 from God the Father and from J,
: 7 who do not acknowledge J as coming
Jude : 1 Jude, a servant of J and a brother
: 1 by God the Father and kept by J:
: 4 deny J our only Sovereign and Lord.
:25 and authority, through J our Lord,
Rev 1: 1 The revelation of J, which God gave
1: 2 word of God and the testimony of J.
1: 5 from J, who is the faithful witness,

Jesus of Nazareth

Mt 26:71 there, "This fellow was with J.
Mk 1:24 "What do you want with us, J? Have
10:47 he heard that it was J, he began to
Lk 4:34 "Ha! What do you want with us, J?
18:37 They told him, "J is passing by."
24:19 "What things?" he asked. "About J,"
Jn 1:45 also wrote—J, the son of Joseph."
18: 5 "J," they replied. "I am he," Jesus
18: 7 is it you want?" And they said, "J.
19:19 It read: J, THE KING OF THE JEWS.
Ac 2:22 "Men of Israel, listen to this: J
6:14 have heard him say that this J will
10:38 how God anointed J with the Holy
22: 8 "'I am J, whom you are persecuting,'
26: 9 possible to oppose the name of J.

Jesus' (Jesus)

Mt 21:45 and the Pharisees heard J parables,
26:51 one of J companions reached for
27:53 and after J resurrection they went
27:58 Going to Pilate, he asked for J body,
Mk 3:31 J mother and brothers arrived.
6:14 for J name had become well known.
14:12 J disciples asked him, "Where do you
15:43 to Pilate and asked for J body.
16: 1 that they might go to anoint J body.
Lk 5: 8 he fell at J knees and said,
7:29 when they heard J words,
8:19 Now J mother and brothers came to
8:35 sitting at J feet, dressed and in
8:41 came and fell at J feet, pleading
17:16 He threw himself at J feet and
22:49 J followers saw what was going to
23:52 Going to Pilate, he asked for J body.
Jn 2: 1 Cana in Galilee. J mother was there,
2: 3 wine was gone, J mother said to him
7: 3 J brothers said to him, "You ought
12: 2 Here a dinner was given in J honour.
12: 3 she poured it on J feet and wiped
12:41 because he saw J glory and spoke
16:29 J disciples said, "Now you are
19:29 plant, and lifted it to J lips.
19:34 one of the soldiers pierced J side
19:40 Taking J body, the two of them
20: 7 cloth that had been around J head.
20:12 seated where J body had been, one at
Ac 3:16 It is J name and the faith that
2Co 4: 5 as your servants for J sake.
4:11 given over to death for J sake,
Heb 5: 7 During the days of J life on earth,

Jether

Jdg 8:20 Turning to J, his oldest son, he
8:20 "Kill them!" But J did not draw his
2Sa 17:25 Amasa was the son of a man named J,
1Ki 2: 5 Abner son of Ner and Amasa son of J.
2:32 and Amasa son of J, commander of
1Ch 2:17 whose father was J the Ishmaelite.
2:32 Shammai's brother: J and Jonathan.
2:32 J died without children.
4:17 The sons of Ezrah: J, Mered, Epher
7:38 The sons of J: Jephunneh, Pispah and

Jetheth

Ge 36:40 clans and regions: Timna, Alvah, J,
1Ch 1:51 of Edom were: Timna, Alvah, J,

Jethro

Father-in-law of Moses (Ex 3:1; 4:18), also called Reuel (Ex 2:18). Visited Moses at Horeb; advised him to delegate administration of justice (Ex 18).

Ex 3: 1 Now Moses was tending the flock of J
4:18 Moses went back to J his
4:18 J said, "Go, and I wish you well."
18: 1 Now J, the priest of Midian and
18: 2 his father-in-law J received
18: 5 J, Moses' father-in-law, together
18: 6 J had sent word to him, "I, your
18: 6 "I, your father-in-law J, am coming
18: 9 J was delighted to hear about all
18:12 J, Moses' father-in-law, brought a
18:27 and J returned to his own country.

Jetur

Ge 25:15 Hadad, Tema, J, Naphish and Kedemah.
1Ch 1:31 J, Naphish and Kedemah. These were
5:19 the Hagrites, J, Naphish and Nodab.

Jeuel

1Ch 9: 6 Of the Zerahites: J. The people from
Ezr 8:13 J and Shemaiah, and with them 60 men;

Jeush

Ge 36: 5 Oholibamah bore J, Jalam and Korah.
36:14 bore to Esau: J, Jalam and Korah.
36:18 Chiefs J, Jalam and Korah.
1Ch 1:35 The sons of Esau: Eliphaz, Reuel, J,
7:10 The sons of Bilhan: J, Benjamin,
8:39 J the second son and Eliphelet the
23:10 the sons of Shimei: Jahath, Ziza, J
23:11 J and Beriah did not have many sons
2Ch 11:19 She bore him sons: J, Shemariah and

Jeuz

1Ch 8:10 J, Sakia and Mirmah. These were his

Jew (Jewess, Jewish, Jews, Jews', Judaism)

Est 2: 5 Susa a J of the tribe of Benjamin,
3: 4 for he had told them he was a J.
5:13 as long as I see that J Mordecai
6:10 the J, who sits at the king's gate.
8: 7 Queen Esther and to Mordecai the J,
9:29 along with Mordecai the J, wrote
9:31 as Mordecai the J and Queen Esther
10: 3 Mordecai the J was second in rank to
Jer 34: 9 was to hold a fellow J in bondage.
Zec 8:23 take firm hold of one J by the hem
Jn 3:25 a certain J over the matter of
4: 9 are a J and I am a Samaritan woman.
18:35 "Am I a J?" Pilate replied. "It was
Ac 10:28 it is against our law for a J to
18: 2 There he met a J named Aquila, a
18:24 Meanwhile a J named Apollos, a
19:34 when they realised he was a J, they
21:39 Paul answered, "I am a J, from
22: 3 "I am a J, born in Tarsus of Cilicia,
Ro 1:16 for the J, then for the Gentile.
2: 9 for the J, then for the Gentile;
2:10 for the J, then for the Gentile.
2:17 Now you, if you call yourself a J;
2:28 A man is not a J if he is only one
2:29 No, a man is a J if he is one
3: 1 is there in being a J, or what value
10:12 no difference between J and Gentile
1Co 9:20 To the Jews I became like a J, to
Gal 2:14 "You are a J, yet you live like a

Gal 2:14 like a Gentile and not like a **J**.
3:28 There is neither **J** nor Greek, slave
Col 3:11 Here there is no Greek or **J**,

Jewel (Jewellery, Jewels)

Pr 20:15 that speak knowledge are a rare **j**.
SS 4: 9 eyes, with one **j** of your necklace.
Isa 13:19 Babylon, the **j** of kingdoms, the
Rev 21:11 **j**, like a jasper, clear as crystal.

Jewellery (Jewel)

Ge 24:53 silver **j** and articles of clothing
Ex 32:24 I told them, 'Whoever has any gold **j**,
35:22 came and brought gold **j** of all kinds:
Jer 2:32 Does a maiden forget her **j**, a bride
Eze 7:20 They were proud of their beautiful **j**
16:11 I adorned you with **j**: I put
16:17 You also took the fine **j** I gave you,
16:17 the **j** made of my gold and silver,
16:39 fine **j** and leave you naked and bare.
23:26 your clothes and take your fine **j**.
23:40 painted your eyes and put on your **j**.
Hos 2:13 she decked herself with rings and **j**,
1Pe 3: 3 wearing of gold **j** and fine clothes.

Jewels (Jewel)

Job 28:17 nor can it be had for **j** of gold.
SS 1:10 your neck with strings of **j**.
5:12 washed in milk, mounted like **j**.
7: 1 **j**, the work of a craftsman's hands.
Isa 54:12 your gates of sparkling **j**, and all
61:10 a bride adorns herself with her **j**.
Jer 4:30 in scarlet and put on **j** of gold?
Eze 16: 7 and became the most beautiful of **j**.
Zec 9:16 in his land like **j** in a crown.

Jewess (Jew)

Ac 16: 1 whose mother was a **J** and a believer,
24:24 with his wife Drusilla, who was a **J**.

Jewish (Jew)

Ezr 6: 7 the **J** elders rebuild this house of
Ne 1: 2 questioned them about the **J** remnant
5: 1 outcry against their **J** brothers.
5: 8 we have bought back our **J** brothers
Est 6:13 is of **J** origin, you cannot stand
Jn 2:13 was almost time for the **J** Passover,
3: 1 a member of the **J** ruling council.
6: 4 The **J** Passover Feast was near.
7: 2 when the **J** Feast of Tabernacles was
11:51 Jesus would die for the **J** nation,
11:55 was almost time for the **J** Passover,
18:12 and the **J** officials arrested Jesus.
19:40 in accordance with **J** burial customs.
19:42 it was the **J** day of Preparation and
Ac 10:22 is respected by all the **J** people.
12:11 the **J** people were anticipating."
13: 5 the word of God in the **J** synagogues.
13: 6 There they met a **J** sorcerer and
14: 1 went as usual into the **J** synagogue.
17: 1 where there was a **J** synagogue.
17:10 there, they went to the **J** synagogue.
19:14 a **J** chief priest, were doing this
25: 2 the chief priests and **J** leaders
25:24 whole **J** community has petitioned me
26: 3 all the **J** customs and controversies.
Gal 2:14 force Gentiles to follow **J** customs?
Tit 1:14 will pay no attention to **J** myths or

Jews (Jew, *King of the Jews*)

Ezr 4:12 should know that the **J** who come up
4:23 immediately to the **J** in Jerusalem
5: 1 prophesied to the **J** in Judah and
5: 5 watching over the elders of the **J**,
6: 7 Let the governor of the **J** and the
6: 8 to do for these elders of the **J** in
6:14 the elders of the **J** continued to
7:18 You and your brother **J** may then do
Ne 2:16 I had said nothing to the **J** or the
4: 1 incensed. He ridiculed the **J**,
4: 2 "What are those feeble **J** doing? Will
4:12 the **J** who lived near them came and
5:17 Furthermore, a hundred and fifty **J**
6: 6 and the **J** are plotting to revolt,
Est 3: 6 the **J**, throughout the whole kingdom
3:10 the Agagite, the enemy of the **J**.
3:13 kill and annihilate all the **J**—young
4: 3 great mourning among the **J**, with
4: 7 for the destruction of the **J**.
4:13 you alone of all the **J** will escape.
4:14 relief and deliverance for the **J**
4:16 "Go, gather together all the **J** who
8: 1 estate of Haman, the enemy of the **J**.
8: 3 which he had devised against the **J**.
8: 5 the **J** in all the king's provinces.
8: 7 "Because Haman attacked the **J**, I
8: 8 on behalf of the **J** as seems best
8: 9 out all Mordecai's orders to the **J**,
8: 9 to the **J** in their own script and
8:11 The king's edict granted the **J** in
8:12 The day appointed for the **J** to do
8:13 so that the **J** would be ready on
8:16 For the **J** it was a time of happiness
8:17 was joy and gladness among the **J**,
8:17 became **J** because fear of the **J** had
9: 1 On this day the enemies of the **J** had
9: 1 the **J** got the upper hand over those
9: 2 The **J** assembled in their cities in
9: 3 king's administrators helped the **J**,
9: 5 The **J** struck down all their enemies
9: 6 In the citadel of Susa, the **J** killed
9:10 of Hammedatha, the enemy of the **J**.
9:12 "The **J** have killed and destroyed
9:13 "give the **J** in Susa permission to
9:15 The **J** in Susa came together on the
9:16 Meanwhile, the remainder of the **J**
9:18 The **J** in Susa, however, had
9:19 That is why rural **J**—those living in
9:20 and he sent letters to all the **J**
9:22 the **J** got relief from their enemies
9:23 the **J** agreed to continue the
9:24 the Agagite, the enemy of all the **J**,
9:24 had plotted against the **J** to destroy
9:25 Haman had devised against the **J**
9:27 the **J** took it upon themselves to
9:28 cease to be celebrated by the **J**,
9:30 Mordecai sent letters to all the **J**
10: 3 pre-eminent among the **J**, and held
10: 3 in high esteem by his many fellow **J**,
10: 3 up for the welfare of all the **J**.
Jer 32:12 of all the **J** sitting in the
38:19 "I am afraid of the **J** who have gone
40:11 all the **J** in Moab, Ammon, Edom and
40:15 cause all the **J** who are gathered
41: 3 Ishmael also killed all the **J** who
43: 9 "While the **J** are watching, take some
44: 1 **J** living in Lower Egypt—in Migdol,
44:26 hear the word of the LORD, all **J**
44:27 the **J** in Egypt will perish by sword
52:28 in the seventh year, 3,023 **J**;
52:30 745 **J** taken into exile by
Da 3: 8 came forward and denounced the **J**.
3:12 are some **J** whom you have set over
Mt 28:15 among the **J** to this very day.
Mk 7: 3 Pharisees and all the **J** do not eat
Lk 7: 3 sent some elders of the **J** to him,
Jn 1:19 the **J** of Jerusalem sent priests
2: 6 the kind used by the **J** for
2:18 the **J** demanded of him, "What
2:20 The **J** replied, "It has taken
4: 9 **J** do not associate with Samaritans.)
4:20 but you **J** claim that the place where
4:22 know, for salvation is from the **J**.
5: 1 to Jerusalem for a feast of the **J**.
5:10 the **J** said to the man who had been
5:15 The man went away and told the **J**
5:16 the Sabbath, the **J** persecuted him.
5:18 **J** tried all the harder to kill him;
6:41 At this the **J** began to grumble about
6:52 the **J** began to argue sharply among
7: 1 because the **J** there were waiting to
7:11 Now at the Feast the **J** were watching
7:13 about him for fear of the **J**.
7:15 The **J** were amazed and asked, "How
7:35 The **J** said to one another, "Where
8:22 This made the **J** ask, "Will he kill
8:31 To the **J** who had believed him, Jesus
8:48 The **J** answered him, "Aren't we right
8:52 At this the **J** exclaimed, "Now we
8:57 fifty years old," the **J** said to him,
Jn 9:18 The **J** still did not believe that he
9:22 because they were afraid of the **J**,
9:22 for already the **J** had decided that
10:19 words the **J** were again divided.
10:24 The **J** gathered round him, saying,
10:31 Again the **J** picked up stones to
10:33 for any of these," replied the **J**,
11: 8 "a short while ago the **J** tried to
11:19 many **J** had come to Martha and Mary
11:31 the **J** who had been with Mary in the
11:33 Jesus saw her weeping, and the **J** who
11:36 the **J** said, "See how he loved him!"
11:45 many of the **J** who had come to visit
11:54 moved about publicly among the **J**.
12: 9 a large crowd of **J** found out that
12:11 many of the **J** were going over to
13:33 and just as I told the **J**, so I tell
18:14 the one who had advised the **J** that
18:20 where all the **J** come together.
18:28 the **J** led Jesus from Caiaphas to the
18:28 the **J** did not enter the palace;
18:31 to execute anyone," the **J** objected.
18:36 fight to prevent my arrest by the **J**.
18:38 With this he went out again to the **J**
19: 4 Pilate came out and said to the **J**,
19: 7 The **J** insisted, "We have a law, and
19:12 but the **J** kept shouting, "If you let
19:14 is your king," Pilate said to the **J**.
19:20 Many of the **J** read this sign, for
19:21 The chief priests of the **J** protested
19:31 the **J** did not want the bodies left
19:38 secretly because he feared the **J**.
20:19 the doors locked for fear of the **J**,
Ac 2: 5 **J** from every nation under heaven.
2:11 (both **J** and converts to Judaism);
2:14 "Fellow **J** and all of you who live in
6: 1 the Grecian **J** among them complained
6: 1 against the Hebraic **J** because their
6: 9 **J** of Cyrene and Alexandria as well
9:22 baffled the **J** living in Damascus
9:23 the **J** conspired to kill him
9:29 and debated with the Grecian **J**,
10:39 country of the **J** and in Jerusalem.
11:19 telling the message only to **J**.
12: 3 he saw that this pleased the **J**, he
13:43 many of the **J** and devout converts to
13:45 the **J** saw the crowds, they were
13:50 the **J** incited the God-fearing women
14: 1 number of **J** and Gentiles believed.
14: 2 the **J** who refused to believe stirred
14: 4 some sided with the **J**, others with
14: 5 plot afoot among the Gentiles and **J**,
14:19 some **J** came from Antioch and Iconium
16: 3 of the **J** who lived in that area,
16:20 "These men are **J**, and are throwing
17: 4 Some of the **J** were persuaded and
17: 5 the **J** were jealous; so they rounded
17:12 Many of the **J** believed, as did also
17:13 the **J** in Thessalonica learned that
17:17 the **J** and the God-fearing Greeks,
18: 2 had ordered all the **J** to leave Rome.
18: 4 trying to persuade **J** and Greeks.
18: 5 to the **J** that Jesus was the Christ.
18: 6 **J** opposed Paul and became abusive
18:12 the **J** made a united attack on Paul
18:14 Gallio said to the **J**, "If you **J** were
18:19 synagogue and reasoned with the **J**.
18:28 vigorously refuted the **J** in public
19:10 so that all the **J** and Greeks who
19:13 Some **J** who went around driving out
19:17 this became known to the **J** and
19:33 The **J** pushed Alexander to the front,
20: 3 the **J** made a plot against him
20:19 tested by the plots of the **J**.
20:21 I have declared to both **J** and Greeks
21:11 'In this way the **J** of Jerusalem will
21:20 brother, how many thousands of **J**
21:21 you teach all the **J** who live among
21:27 some **J** from the province of Asia saw
22:12 respected by all the **J** living there.
22:30 why Paul was being accused by the **J**,
23:12 the **J** formed a conspiracy
23:20 He said: "The **J** have agreed to ask
23:27 This man was seized by the **J** and
24: 5 among the **J** all over the world.
24: 9 The **J** joined in the accusation,

Ac 24:19 there are some J from the province
24:27 wanted to grant a favour to the J,
25: 7 Paul appeared, the J who had come
25: 8 wrong against the law of the J or
25: 9 Festus, wishing to do the J a favour,
25:10 I have not done any wrong to the J
25:11 against me by these J are not true,
25:15 elders of the J brought charges
26: 2 all the accusations of the J,
26: 4 "The J all know the way I have lived
26: 7 hope that the J are accusing me.
26:21 That is why the J seized me in the
28:17 together the leaders of the J.
28:19 when the J objected, I was compelled
Ro 3: 9 the charge that J and Gentiles alike
3:29 Is God the God of J only? Is he not
9:24 not only from the J but also from
15: 8 has become a servant of the J on
15:27 they owe it to the J to share with
1Co 1:22 J demand miraculous signs and Greeks
1:23 to J and foolishness to Gentiles,
1:24 to those whom God has called, both J
9:20 J I became like a Jew, to win the J.
10:32 J, Greeks or the church of God—
12:13 into one body—whether J or Greeks,
2Co 11:24 Five times I received from the J the
Gal 1:14 Judaism beyond many J of my own age
2: 7 just as Peter had been to the J.
2: 8 of Peter as an apostle to the J,
2: 9 to the Gentiles, and they to the J.
2:13 The other J joined him in his
2:15 "We who are J by birth and not
Col 4:11 the only J among my fellow-workers
1Th 2:14 those churches suffered from the J,
Rev 2: 9 who say they are J and are not,
3: 9 claim to be J though they are not

Jews' (Jew)

Ro 15:27 shared in the J spiritual blessings,

Jezaniah

Jer 42: 1 son of Kareah and J son of Hoshaiah,

Jezebel (Jezebel's)

1. Daughter of Sidonian king; wife of Ahab (1Ki 16:31). Encouraged his sin (1Ki 21:25): promoted worship of native god, Baal (1Ki 16:32–33; 18:19); killed Lord's prophets (1Ki 18:4,13); threatened Elijah (1Ki 19:1–2); had Naboth killed (1Ki 21). Death prophesied by Elijah (1Ki 21:23); killed by Jehu (2Ki 9:30–37). **2.** Designation of prophetess in church at Thyatira who was leading believers astray (Rev 2:20).

1Ki 16:31 also married J daughter of Ethbaal
18: 4 While J was killing off the LORD's
18:13 what I did while J was killing
19: 1 Now Ahab told J everything Elijah
19: 2 J sent a messenger to Elijah to say,
21: 5 His wife J came in and asked him,
21: 7 J his wife said, "Is this how you
21:11 did as J directed in the letters
21:14 they sent word to J: "Naboth has
21:15 soon as J heard that Naboth had been
21:23 "And also concerning J the LORD says:
21:23 devour J by the wall of Jezreel.'
21:25 of the LORD, urged on by J his wife.
2Ki 9: 7 all the LORD's servants shed by J.
9:10 As for J, dogs will devour her on
9:22 witchcraft of your mother J abound?"
9:30 When J heard about it, she painted
9:37 will be able to say, 'This is J.
Rev 2:20 J, who calls herself a prophetess.

Jezebel's (Jezebel)

1Ki 18:19 of Asherah, who eat at J table."
2Ki 9:36 at Jezreel dogs will devour J flesh.
9:37 J body will be like refuse on the

Jezer (Jezerite)

Ge 46:24 Jahziel, Guni, J and Shillem.
Nu 26:49 through J, the Jezerite clan;
1Ch 7:13 Guni, J and Shillem—the descendants

Jezerite (Jezer)

Nu 26:49 through Jezer, the J clan; through

Jeziel

1Ch 12: 3 J and Pelet the sons of Azmaveth;

Jezrahiah

Ne 12:42 sang under the direction of J.

Jezreel (Jezreelite)

1. City in hill country of Judah (Jos 15:56), where Ahinoam was probably born (1Sa 25:43; 27:3). Exact location uncertain. **2.** City in northern Israel, about 56 miles north of Jerusalem (Jos 19:18), in a valley named after it (Jos 17:16), with nearby spring (1Sa 29:1). Ahab had a palace here, overlooking Naboth's vineyard (1Ki 21:1–16). Joram recovering from battle was visited by Ahaziah here (2Ki 8:29; 2Ch 22:6). Place of bloodshed during Jehu's revolt (2Ki 9:1–10:11). Hosea's son named Jezreel to announce God's judgment on the house of Jehu (Hos 1:4–5).

Jos 15:56 J, Jokdeam, Zanoah,
17:16 and those in the Valley of J."
19:18 Their territory included: J,
Jdg 6:33 Jordan and camped in the Valley of J.
1Sa 25:43 David had also married Ahinoam of J,
27: 3 Ahinoam of J and Abigail of Carmel,
29: 1 Israel camped by the spring in J.
29:11 and the Philistines went up to J.
30: 5 captured—Ahinoam of J and Abigail,
2Sa 2: 2 Ahinoam of J and Abigail, the widow
2: 9 king over Gilead, Ashuri and J,
3: 2 was Amnon the son of Ahinoam of J;
4: 4 about Saul and Jonathan came from J.
1Ki 4:12 Beth Shan next to Zarethan below J,
18:45 rain came on and Ahab rode off to J.
18:46 ran ahead of Ahab all the way to J.
21: 1 The vineyard was in J, close to the
21:23 devour Jezebel by the wall of J.'
2Ki 8:29 King Joram returned to J to recover
8:29 down to J to see Joram son of Ahab,
9:10 her on the plot of ground at J,
9:15 King Joram had returned to J to
9:15 city to go and tell the news in J."
9:16 he got into his chariot and rode to J
9:17 in J saw Jehu's troops approaching,
9:30 Jehu went to J. When Jezebel heard
9:36 at J dogs will devour Jezebel's flesh
9:37 on the ground in the plot at J,
10: 1 to Samaria: to the officials of J,
10: 6 to me in J by this time tomorrow.
10: 7 baskets and sent them to Jehu in J.
10:11 Jehu killed everyone in J who
1Ch 3: 1 was Amnon the son of Ahinoam of J;
4: 3 These were the sons of Etam: J,
2Ch 22: 6 he returned to J to recover from the
22: 6 king of Judah went down to J to see
Hos 1: 4 the LORD said to Hosea, "Call him J,
1: 4 house of Jehu for the massacre at J,
1: 5 Israel's bow in the Valley of J."
1:11 for great will be the day of J.
2:22 and oil, and they will respond to J.

Jezreelite (Jezreel)

1Ki 21: 1 vineyard belonging to Naboth the J.
21: 4 angry because Naboth the J had said,
21: 6 "Because I said to Naboth the J,
21: 7 you the vineyard of Naboth the J."
21:15 of Naboth the J that he refused to
2Ki 9:21 that had belonged to Naboth the J.
9:25 field that belonged to Naboth the J.

Jidlaph

Ge 22:22 Kesed, Hazo, Pildash, J and Bethuel."

Jingling

Isa 3:16 with ornaments j on their ankles.

Joab (Joab's)

Nephew of David; brother of Abishai and Asahel (1Ch 2:16). Led David's army against Abner (2Sa 2:13–32); killed Abner to avenge death of Asahel (2Sa 3:26–27, 30). Led attack on Jerusalem (1Ch 11:4–6); made commander-in-chief (2Sa 8:16; 18:2; 20:23). Defeated Ammon (2Sa 10:7–14; 1Ch 19:8–15), Rabbah (2Sa 12:26–27). Followed David's order to kill Uriah (2Sa 11:14–17); killed Absalom (2Sa 18:14–15); killed Amasa (2Sa 20:9–10). Supported Adonijah (1Ki 1:17–19); killed by Benaiah (1Ki 2:5–6,28–34).

2Sa 2:13 J son of Zeruiah and David's men
2:14 Abner said to J, "Let's have some of
2:14 "All right, let them do it," J said.
2:18 were there: J, Abishai and Asahel.
2:22 I look your brother J in the face?"
2:24 J and Abishai pursued Abner, and as
2:26 Abner called out to J, "Must the
2:27 J answered, "As surely as God lives,
2:28 J blew the trumpet, and all the men
2:30 J returned from pursuing Abner and
2:32 Then J and his men marched all night
3:22 Just then David's men and J returned
3:23 J and all the soldiers with him
3:24 J went to the king and said, "What
3:26 J then left David and sent
3:27 J took him aside into the gateway,
3:27 J stabbed him in the stomach, and he
3:29 May his blood fall upon the head of J
3:30 (J and his brother Abishai murdered
3:31 David said to J and all the people
8:16 J son of Zeruiah was over the army;
10: 7 On hearing this, David sent J out
10: 9 J saw that there were battle lines
10:11 J said, "If the Arameans are too
10:13 J and the troops with him advanced
10:14 So J returned from fighting the
11: 1 David sent J out with the king's men
11: 6 David sent this word to J: "Send me
11: 6 And J sent him to David.
11: 7 David asked him how J was, how the
11:11 and my master J and my lord's men
11:14 letter to J and sent it with Uriah.
11:16 while J had the city under siege, he
11:17 city came out and fought against J,
11:18 J sent David a full account of the
11:22 everything J had sent him to say.
11:25 "Say this to J: 'Don't let this
11:25 Say this to encourage J."
12:26 Meanwhile J fought against Rabbah of
12:27 J then sent messengers to David,
14: 1 J son of Zeruiah knew that the
14: 2 J sent someone to Tekoa and had a
14: 3 And J put the words in her mouth.
14:19 "Isn't the hand of J with you in
14:19 Yes, it was your servant J who
14:20 Your servant J did this to change
14:21 The king said to J, "Very well, I
14:22 J fell with his face to the ground
14:22 J said, "Today your servant knows
14:23 J went to Geshur and brought Absalom
14:29 Absalom sent for J in order to send
14:29 king, but J refused to come to him.
14:31 J did go to Absalom's house and he
14:32 Absalom said to J, "Look, I sent
14:33 J went to the king and told him this.
17:25 Amasa over the army in place of J.
17:25 sister of Zeruiah the mother of J.
18: 2 a third under the command of J, a
18: 5 The king commanded J, Abishai and
18:10 one of the men saw this, he told J,
18:11 J said to the man who had told him
18:14 J said, "I am not going to wait like
18:16 J sounded the trumpet, and the
18:16 pursuing Israel, for J halted them.
18:20 to take the news today," J told him.
18:21 J said to a Cushite, "Go, tell the
18:21 bowed down before J and ran off.
18:22 Ahimaaz son of Zadok again said to J,
18:22 But J replied, "My son, why do you
18:23 So J said, "Run!" Then Ahimaaz ran
18:29 confusion just as J was about to send
19: 1 J was told, "The king is weeping and
19: 5 J went into the house to the king
19:13 commander of my army in place of J.
20: 8 J was wearing his military tunic,
20: 9 J said to Amasa, "How are you, my
20: 9 Then J took Amasa by the beard
20:10 and J plunged it into his belly, and
20:10 Then J and his brother Abishai

2Sa 20:11 "Whoever favours J, and whoever is
20:11 is for David, let him follow J!"
20:13 with J to pursue Sheba son of Bicri.
20:15 All the troops with J came and
20:16 "Listen! Listen! Tell J to come here
20:17 "Are you J?" "I am," he answered.
20:20 "Far be it from me!" J replied, "Far
20:21 The woman said to J, "His head will
20:22 Sheba son of Bicri and threw it to J.
20:22 J went back to the king in Jerusalem.
20:23 J was over Israel's entire army;
23:18 the brother of J son of Zeruiah
23:24 Asahel the brother of J, Elhanan son
23:37 armour-bearer of J son of Zeruiah,
24: 2 the king said to J and the army
24: 3 J replied to the king, "May the LORD
24: 4 The king's word, however, overruled J
24: 9 J reported the number of the
1Ki 1: 7 conferred with J son of Zeruiah,
1:19 the priest and J the commander of
1:41 J asked, "What's the meaning of all
2: 5 know what J son of Zeruiah did to me
2:22 the priest and J son of Zeruiah!"
2:28 the news reached J, who had
2:29 King Solomon was told that J had
2:30 said to J, "The king says, 'Come out
2:30 king, "This is how J answered me.
2:31 of the innocent blood that J shed.
2:33 of J and his descendants for ever.
2:34 up and struck down J and killed him,
11:15 J the commander of the army, who had
11:16 J and all the Israelites stayed
11:21 that J the commander of the army was
1Ch 2:16 sons were Abishai, J and Asahel.
4:14 Seraiah was the father of J, the
11: 6 J son of Zeruiah went up first, and
11: 8 J restored the rest of the city.
11:20 Abishai the brother of J was chief
11:26 men were: Asahel the brother of J,
11:39 armour-bearer of J son of Zeruiah,
18:15 J son of Zeruiah was over the army;
19: 8 On hearing this, David sent J out
19:10 J saw that there were battle lines
19:12 J said, "If the Arameans are too
19:14 J and the troops with him advanced
19:15 So J went back to Jerusalem.
20: 1 to war, J led out the armed forces.
20: 1 J attacked Rabbah and left it in
21: 2 David said to J and the commanders
21: 3 J replied, "May the LORD multiply
21: 4 The king's word, however, overruled J
21: 4 however, overruled J; so J left and
21: 5 J reported the number of the
21: 6 J did not include Levi and Benjamin
26:28 son of Ner and J son of Zeruiah
27: 7 was Asahel the brother of J; his son
27:24 J son of Zeruiah began to count the
27:34 J was the commander of the royal
Ezr 2: 6 the line of Jeshua and J) 2,812
8: 9 of the descendants of J, Obadiah son
Ne 7:11 the line of Jeshua and J) 2,818
Ps 60: T and when J returned and struck down

Joab's (Joab)

1Sa 26: 6 Abishai son of Zeruiah, J brother,
2Sa 3:29 May J house never be without someone
14:30 said to his servants, "Look, J field
18: 2 a third under J brother Abishai son
18:15 ten of J armour-bearers surrounded
20: 7 J men and the Kerethites and
20:10 guard against the dagger in J hand,
20:11 One of J men stood beside Amasa and
1Ki 2:35 Jehoiada over the army in J position

Joah

2Ki 18:18 the secretary, and J son of Asaph
18:26 and Shebna and J said to the field
18:37 the secretary and J son of Asaph
1Ch 6:21 J his son, Iddo his son, Zerah his
26: 4 Jehozabad the second, J the third,
2Ch 29:12 J son of Zimmah and Eden son of J;
34: 8 with J son of Joahaz, the recorder,
Isa 36: 3 the secretary, and J son of Asaph
36:11 Eliakim, Shebna and J said to the
36:22 the secretary, and J son of Asaph

Joahaz

2Ch 34: 8 with Joah son of J, the recorder, to

Joanan

Lk 3:27 the son of J, the son of Rhesa, the

Joanna

Lk 8: 3 J the wife of Chuza, the manager of
24:10 was Mary Magdalene, J, Mary the

Joash

1. Father of Gideon (Jdg 6:11,29–31; 8:32). **2.** King of Judah; son of Ahaziah. Hidden from Athaliah (2Ki 11:1–3; 2Ch 22:10–12); crowned king by Jehoida (2Ki 11:4–21; 2Ch 23). Repaired temple (2Ki 12; 2Ch 24:1–14); returned to idolatry after Jehoiada's death (2Ch 24:17–24). Defeated by Aram (2Ch 24:23–24); murdered by officials (2Ki 12:20; 2Ch 24:25).

Jdg 6:11 that belonged to J the Abiezrite,
6:29 were told, "Gideon son of J did it.
6:30 The men of the town demanded of J,
6:31 J replied to the hostile crowd
7:14 of Gideon son of J, the Israelite.
8:13 Gideon son of J then returned from
8:29 Jerub-Baal son of J went back home
8:32 Gideon son of J died at a good old
8:32 buried in the tomb of his father J
1Ki 22:26 the city and to J the king's son
2Ki 11: 2 took J son of Ahaziah and stole him
11:21 J was seven years old when he began
12: 1 J became king and he reigned in
12: 2 J did what was right in the eyes of
12: 4 J said to the priests, "Collect all
12: 6 by the twenty-third year of King J
12: 7 Therefore King J summoned Jehoiada
12:18 J king of Judah took all the sacred
12:19 the other events of the reign of J,
13: 1 In the twenty-third year of J son of
13:10 In the thirty-seventh year of J king
14: 1 of J king of Judah began to reign.
14: 3 the example of his father J.
14:13 the son of J, the son of Ahaziah, at
14:17 Amaziah son of J king of Judah lived
14:23 of Amaziah son of J king of Judah,
1Ch 3:11 his son, Ahaziah his son, J his son
4:22 Jokim, the men of Cozeba, and J and
7: 8 The sons of Beker: Zemirah, J,
12: 3 Ahiezer their chief and J the sons
27:28 J was in charge of the supplies of
2Ch 18:25 of the city and to J the king's son,
22:11 took J son of Ahaziah and stole him
24: 1 J was seven years old when he became
24: 2 J did what was right in the eyes of
24: 4 J decided to restore the temple of
24:22 King J did not remember the kindness
24:23 the army of Aram marched against J;
24:24 fathers, judgment was executed on J.
24:25 the Arameans withdrew, they left J
25:23 the son of J, the son of Ahaziah, at
25:25 Amaziah son of J king of Judah lived
Hos 1: 1 of Jeroboam son of J king of Israel:

Job[1] (Job's)

1. Wealthy, God-fearing man from Uz (Job 1:1–8). Uprightness tested by Satan, with God's permission (Job 1:6–12; 2:1–6). Suffered loss of family and wealth (Job 1:13–19), and physical affliction (Job 2:7–8). Remained patient (Job 1:20–22; 2:9–10); protested when innocence challenged by friends (Job 3–31). Rebuked by the LORD (Job 38–41); finally vindicated, healed and restored to greater wealth (Job 42:7–17). **2.** Job's friends: Eliphaz (Job 4–5; 15; 22), Bildad (Job 8; 18; 25) Zophar (Job 11; 20) and Elihu (Job 32–37). Came to offer sympathy (Job 2:11–13); tried and failed to explain Job's suffering in terms of conventional wisdom.

Job 1: 1 there lived a man whose name was J.
1: 5 J would send and have them purified.
1: 8 "Have you considered my servant J?
1: 9 "Does J fear God for nothing?" Satan
1:14 a messenger came to J and said, "The
1:20 At this, J got up and tore his robe
1:22 J did not sin by charging God
2: 3 "Have you considered my servant J?
2: 7 afflicted J with painful sores from
2: 8 J took a piece of broken pottery and
2:10 this, J did not sin in what he said.
3: 1 After this, J opened his mouth and
6: 1 Then J replied:
9: 1 Then J replied:
12: 1 Then J replied:
16: 1 Then J replied:
19: 1 Then J replied:
21: 1 Then J replied:
23: 1 Then J replied:
26: 1 Then J replied:
27: 1 And J continued his discourse:
29: 1 J continued his discourse:
31:40 The words of J are ended.
32: 1 these three men stopped answering J,
32: 2 became very angry with J for
32: 3 they had found not way to refute J,
32: 4 had waited before speaking to J
32:12 not one of you has proved J wrong
32:14 J has not marshalled his words
33: 1 "But now, J, listen to my words; pay
33:31 "Pay attention, J, and listen to me;
34: 5 "J says, 'I am innocent, but God
34: 7 What man is like J, who drinks scorn
34:35 'J speaks without knowledge; his
34:36 Oh, that J might be tested to the
35:16 J opens his mouth with empty talk;
37:14 "Listen to this, J; stop and
38: 1 the LORD answered J out of the storm.
40: 1 The LORD said to J:
40: 3 Then J answered the LORD:
40: 6 the LORD spoke to J out of the storm:
42: 1 Then J replied to the LORD:
42: 7 the LORD had said these things to J,
42: 7 what is right, as my servant J has.
42: 8 seven rams and go to my servant J
42: 8 My servant J will pray for you, and
42: 8 what is right, as my servant J has."
42:10 After J had prayed for his friends,
42:16 After this, J lived a hundred and
Eze 14:14 Noah, Daniel and J—were in it, they
14:20 even if Noah, Daniel and J were in

Job's (Job[1])

Job 1: 5 This was J regular custom.
1:13 One day when J sons and daughters
2:11 J three friends, Eliphaz the
31:31 has not had his fill of J meat?'—
42: 9 and the LORD accepted J prayer.
42:12 blessed the latter part of J life
42:15 women as beautiful as J daughters,
Jas 5:11 You have heard of J perseverance and

Job[2]

2Ch 34:13 all the workers from j to j.
Lk 16: 3 now? My master is taking away my j.
16: 4 when I lose my j here, people will

Jobab

Ge 10:29 Ophir, Havilah and J. All these were
36:33 J son of Zerah from Bozrah
36:34 J died, Husham from the land of the
Jos 11: 1 he sent word to J king of Madon, to
1Ch 1:23 Ophir, Havilah and J. All these were
1:44 Bela died, J son of Zerah from
1:45 J died, Husham from the land of the
8: 9 By his wife Hodesh he had J, Zibia,
8:18 Ishmerai, Izliah and J were the sons

Jochebed

Ex 6:20 Amram married his father's sister J
Nu 26:59 the name of Amram's wife was J, a

Joda

Lk 3:26 the son of Josech, the son of J,

Joed

Ne 11: 7 the son of J, the son of Pedaiah,

Joel

Prophet (Joel 1:1). Saw plague of locusts as depiction of God's judgment (Joel 1:2–2:12); called for

repentance (Joel 2:13–17). Future blessing included pouring out of Spirit (Joel 2:18–32; Ac 2:16–21).

1Sa 8: 2 The name of his firstborn was J and
1Ch 4:35 J, Jehu son of Joshibiah, the son of
5: 4 The descendants of J: Shemaiah his
5: 8 Azaz, the son of Shema, the son of J.
5:12 J was the chief, Shapham the second,
6:28 The sons of Samuel: J the firstborn
6:33 the son of J, the son of Samuel,
6:36 the son of Elkanah, the son of J,
7: 3 Michael, Obadiah, J and Isshiah.
11:38 J the brother of Nathan, Mibhar son
15: 7 J the leader and 130 relatives
15:11 and Uriel, Asaiah, J, Shemaiah,
15:17 the Levites appointed Heman son of J;
23: 8 first, Zetham and J—three in all.
26:22 Jehieli, Zetham and his brother J.
27:20 tribe of Manasseh: J son of Pedaiah;
2Ch 29:12 son of Amasai and J son of Azariah
Ezr 10:43 Zabad, Zebina, Jaddai, J and Benaiah.
Ne 11: 9 J son of Zicri was their chief
Joel 1: 1 The word of the LORD that came to J
Ac 2:16 is what was spoken by the prophet J:

Joelah
1Ch 12: 7 J and Zebadiah the sons of Jeroham

Joezer
1Ch 12: 6 Elkanah, Isshiah, Azarel, J and

Jogbehah
Nu 32:35 Atroth Shophan, Jazer, J,
Jdg 8:11 east of Nobah and J and fell upon

Jogli
Nu 34:22 Bukki son of J, the leader from the

Joha
1Ch 8:16 and J were the sons of Beriah.
11:45 Jediael son of Shimri, his brother J

Johanan
2Ki 25:23 J son of Kareah, Seraiah son of
1Ch 3:15 The sons of Josiah: J the firstborn,
3:24 J, Delaiah and Anani—seven in all.
6: 9 of Azariah, Azariah the father of J,
6:10 J the father of Azariah (it was he
12: 4 Jahaziel, J, Jozabad the Gederathite,
12:12 J the eighth, Elzabad the ninth,
Ezr 8:12 J son of Hakkatan, and with him
Ne 12:22 Joiada, J and Jaddua, as well as
12:23 up to the time of J son of Eliashib
Jer 40: 8 J and Jonathan the sons of Kareah,
40:13 J son of Kareah and all the army
40:15 J son of Kareah said privately to
40:16 of Ahikam said to J son of Kareah
41:11 J son of Kareah and all the army
41:13 had with him saw J son of Kareah
41:14 and went over to J son of Kareah.
41:15 escaped from J and fled to the
41:16 J son of Kareah and all the army
42: 1 all the army officers, including J
42: 8 he called together J son of Kareah
43: 2 son of Hoshaiah and J son of Kareah
43: 4 J son of Kareah and all the army
43: 5 Instead, J son of Kareah and all the

John (John's)
1. The Baptist; son of Zechariah and Elizabeth (Lk 1:5–25,57–80). Prepared way for Jesus (Mt 3:1–12; Mk 1:3–8; Lk 3:2–17; Jn 1:6–8,15,19–36; 3:27–30); baptised Jesus (Mt 3:13–15; Mk 1:9; Lk 3:21). Opposed Herod's marriage to Herodias; arrested (Mt 14:3–5; Mk 6:17–18); reassured and commended by Jesus (Mt 11:2–19; Lk 7:18–35). Executed (Mt 14:6–12; Mk 6:21–29). Identified with Elijah (Mt 11:14; 17:11–13; Mk 9:12–13; Lk 1:17). **2.** Apostle; son of Zebedee; brother of James. With Peter and James, especially close to Jesus: at raising of Jairus' daughter (Mk 5:37; Lk 8:51); transfiguration (Mt 17:1–2; Mk 9:2; Lk 9:28–29); in Gethsemane (Mt 26:36–38; Mk 14:32–34). Mother's request (Mt 20:20–28; Mk 10:35–45). Called "the disciple whom Jesus loved": close to Jesus at Last Supper (Jn 13:23; 21:20); at crucifixion (Jn 19:25–27). Leader in Jerusalem church (Gal 2:9; 2Jn 1; 3Jn 1). Wrote fourth gospel, letters, book of Revelation (Rev 1:1,9; 22:8; Jn 20:2; 21:7,24). **3.** See *Mark*.

Mt 3: 1 In those days J the Baptist came,
3:13 to the Jordan to be baptised by J.
3:14 J tried to deter him, saying, "I
3:15 Then J consented.
4:12 Jesus heard that J had been put in
4:21 son of Zebedee and his brother J.
10: 2 son of Zebedee, and his brother J;
11: 2 J heard in prison what Christ was
11: 4 report to J what you hear and see:
11: 7 began to speak to the crowd about J:
11:11 anyone greater than J the Baptist;
11:12 From the days of J the Baptist until
11:13 and the Law prophesied until J.
11:18 For J came neither eating nor
14: 2 he said to his attendants, "This is J
14: 3 Now Herod had arrested J and bound
14: 4 for J had been saying to him: "It is
14: 5 Herod wanted to kill J, but he was
14: 8 platter the head of J the Baptist."
14:10 had J beheaded in the prison.
16:14 replied, "Some say J the Baptist
17: 1 James and J the brother of James,
17:13 talking to them about J the Baptist.
21:26 they all hold that J was a prophet."
21:32 For J came to you to show you the
Mk 1: 4 J came, baptising in the desert
1: 6 J wore clothing made of camel's hair,
1: 9 and was baptised by J in the Jordan.
1:14 After J was put in prison, Jesus
1:19 his brother J in a boat, preparing
1:29 with James and J to the home of
3:17 his brother J (to them he gave the
5:37 James and J the brother of James.
6:14 Some were saying, "J the Baptist has
6:16 when Herod heard this, he said, "J,
6:17 had given orders to have J arrested,
6:18 For J had been saying to Herod, "It
6:19 Herodias nursed a grudge against J
6:20 Herod feared J and protected him,
6:20 When Herod heard J, he was greatly
6:24 of J the Baptist," she answered.
6:25 head of J the Baptist on a platter."
6:27 man went, beheaded J in the prison,
8:28 replied, "Some say J the Baptist
9: 2 James and J with him and led them up
9:38 "Teacher," said J, "we saw a man
10:35 James and J, the sons of Zebedee,
10:41 became indignant with James and J.
11:32 held that J really was a prophet.)
13: 3 J and Andrew asked him privately,
14:33 He took Peter, James and J along
Lk 1:13 and you are to give him the name J.
1:60 and said, "No! He is to be called J.
1:63 he wrote, "His name is J.
3: 2 to J son of Zechariah in the desert.
3: 7 J said to the crowds coming out to
3:11 J answered, "The man with two tunics
3:15 if J might possibly be the Christ.
3:16 J answered them all, "I baptise you
3:18 with many other words J exhorted the
3:19 when J rebuked Herod the tetrarch
3:20 them all: He locked J up in prison.
5:10 James and J, the sons of Zebedee,
6:14 James, J, Philip, Bartholomew,
7:20 they said, "J the Baptist sent us to
7:22 "Go back and report to J what you
7:24 began to speak to the crowd about J:
7:28 there is no-one greater than J;
7:29 because they had been baptised by J.
7:30 they had not been baptised by J.)
7:33 For J the Baptist came neither
8:51 J and James, and the child's father
9: 7 J had been raised from the dead,
9: 9 Herod said, "I beheaded J. Who, then,
9:19 replied, "Some say J the Baptist
9:28 he took Peter, J and James with him
9:49 "Master," said J, "we saw a man
9:54 the disciples James and J saw this,
11: 1 just as J taught his disciples."
16:16 Prophets were proclaimed until J.
20: 6 are persuaded that J was a prophet."
22: 8 Jesus sent Peter and J, saying, "Go
Jn 1: 6 was sent from God; his name was J.
1:15 J testifies concerning him. He cries
1:23 J replied in the words of Isaiah the
1:26 "I baptise with water," J replied,
1:28 the Jordan, where J was baptising.
1:29 The next day J saw Jesus coming
1:32 J gave this testimony: "I saw the
1:35 The next day J was there again with
1:40 the two who heard what J had said
1:42 and said, "You are Simon son of J.
3:23 Now J also was baptising at Aenon
3:24 (This was before J was put in prison.
3:26 They came to J and said to him,
3:27 To this J replied, "A man can
4: 1 and baptising more disciples than J,
5:33 "You have sent to J and he has
5:35 J was a lamp that burned and gave
5:36 testimony weightier than that of J.
10:40 place where J had been baptising
10:41 They said, "Though J never performed
10:41 J said about this man was true."
21:15 "Simon son of J, do you truly love
21:16 Again Jesus said, "Simon son of J,
21:17 "Simon son of J, do you love me?"
Ac 1: 5 For J baptised with water, but in a
1:13 Those present were Peter, J, James
3: 1 One day Peter and J were going up to
3: 3 he saw Peter and J about to enter,
3: 4 looked straight at him, as did J.
3:11 the beggar held on to Peter and J,
4: 1 the Sadducees came up to Peter and J
4: 3 They seized Peter and J, and because
4: 6 and so were Caiaphas, J, Alexander
4: 7 They had Peter and J brought before
4:13 they saw the courage of Peter and J
4:19 Peter and J replied, "Judge for
4:23 On their release, Peter and J went
8:14 God, they sent Peter and J to them.
8:17 Peter and J placed their hands on
8:25 Peter and J returned to Jerusalem,
10:37 after the baptism that J preached—
11:16 'J baptised with water, but you will
12: 2 He had James, the brother of J, put
12:12 the house of Mary the mother of J,
12:25 with them J, also called Mark.
13: 5 J was with them as their helper.
13:13 J left them to return to Jerusalem.
13:24 J preached repentance and baptism
13:25 J was completing his work, he said:
15:37 Barnabas wanted to take J, also
18:25 he knew only the baptism of J.
Gal 2: 9 James, Peter and J, those reputed to
Rev 1: 1 sending his angel to his servant J,
1: 4 J, To the seven churches in the
1: 9 I, J, your brother and companion in
22: 8 I, J, am the one who heard and saw

John's (John)
Mt 3: 4 J clothes were made of camel's hair,
9:14 J disciples came and asked him, "How
11: 7 J disciples were leaving, Jesus
14:12 J disciples came and took his body
21:25 J baptism—where did it come from?
Mk 2:18 Now J disciples and the Pharisees
2:18 "How is it that J disciples and the
6:27 with orders to bring J head.
6:29 On hearing of this, J disciples came
11:30 J baptism—was it from heaven, or
Lk 5:33 They said to him, "J disciples often
7:18 J disciples told him about all these
7:24 After J messengers left, Jesus began
20: 4 J baptism—was it from heaven, or
Jn 1:19 Now this was J testimony when the
3:25 between some of J disciples
Ac 1:22 beginning from J baptism to the time
19: 3 receive?" "J baptism," they replied.
19: 4 Paul said, "J baptism was a baptism

Joiada
Ne 3: 6 The Jeshanah Gate was repaired by J
12:10 Eliashib, Eliashib the father of J,
12:11 J the father of Jonathan, and

Ne 12:22 J, Johanan and Jaddua, as well as
13:28 One of the sons of J son of Eliashib

Joiakim

Ne 12:10 Jeshua was the father of J, J the
12:12 In the days of J, these were the
12:26 in the days of J son of Jeshua

Joiarib (Joiarib's)

Ezr 8:16 who were leaders, and J and Elnathan,
Ne 11: 5 the son of Adaiah, the son of J, the
11:10 Jedaiah; the son of J; Jakin;
12: 6 Shemaiah, J, Jedaiah,

Joiarib's (Joiarib)

Ne 12:19 Jehonathan; of J, Mattenai;

Join (Joined, Joining, Joins, Junction, Rejoined)

Ge 34:30 and if they j forces against me
49: 6 let me not j their assembly, for
Ex 1:10 war breaks out, will j our enemies
26: 3 J five of the curtains together, and
26: 9 J five of the curtains together into
Nu 18: 2 from your ancestral tribe to j you
18: 4 They are to j you and be responsible
34: 5 j the Wadi of Egypt and end at the
Jdg 3:13 Ammonites and Amalekites to j him,
21:21 Shiloh come out to j in the dancing,
1Sa 13: 4 were summoned to j Saul at Gilgal.
22:20 Ahitub, escaped and fled to j David.
2Sa 13:24 king and his officials please j me?"
1Ki 1: 8 special guard did not j Adonijah.
1Ch 13: 2 and pasture-lands, to come and j us.
2Ch 18: 3 we will j you in the war."
Ne 4:20 sound of the trumpet, j us there.
10:29 all these now j their brothers the
Est 9:27 their descendants and all who j them
Job 37:18 can you j him in spreading out the
Ps 49:19 he will j the generation of his
50:18 you see a thief, you j with him; you
106: 5 j your inheritance in giving praise.
118:27 j in the festal procession up to
Pr 23:20 Do not j those who drink too much
24:21 and do not j with the rebellious,
Ecc 9: 3 and afterwards they j the dead.
Isa 5: 8 j field to field till no space is
14: 1 Aliens will j them and unite with
14:20 you will not j them in burial, for
Jer 3:18 of Judah will j the house of Israel,
Eze 37:17 J them together into one stick so
37:19 and j it to Judah's stick, making
Da 11:34 who are not sincere will j them.
Mic 5: 3 brothers return to j the Israelites.
Ac 5:13 No-one else dared j them, even
9:26 he came to Jerusalem, he tried to j
17:15 Timothy to j him as soon as possible.
21:24 j in their purification rites and
Ro 15:30 to j me in my struggle by praying to
Php 3:17 J with others in following my
2Ti 1: 8 But j with me in suffering for the

Joined (Join)

Ge 14: 3 All these latter kings j forces in
Ex 36:10 They j five of the curtains together
36:16 They j five of the curtains into one
Nu 25: 3 Israel j in worshipping the Baal of
25: 5 j in worshipping the Baal of Peor."
Jos 10: 5 Jarmuth, Lachish and Eglon—j forces.
10: 6 country have j forces against us."
11: 5 All these kings j forces and made
15: 4 to Azmon and j the Wadi of Egypt
Jdg 6:33 other eastern peoples j forces and
1Sa 10:10 and he j in their prophesying.
14:22 they j the battle in hot pursuit.
28:23 But his men j the woman in urging
1Ki 20:29 on the seventh day the battle was j.
2Ch 5:13 The trumpeters and singers j in
Ezr 3: 9 Levites—j together in supervising
Job 41:17 They are j fast to one another; they
41:23 The folds of his flesh are tightly j;
Ps 48: 4 the kings j forces, when they
83: 8 Even Assyria has j them to lend
Hos 4:17 Ephraim is j to idols; leave him
Zec 2:11 nations will be j with the LORD
Mt 19: 6 j together, let man not separate."
Mk 10: 9 Therefore what God has j together,
Jn 6:17 dark, and Jesus had not yet j them.
Ac 1:14 They all j together constantly in
12:20 they now j together and sought an
16:22 The crowd j in the attack against
17: 4 were persuaded and j Paul and Silas
20: 6 and five days later j the others at
24: 9 The Jews j in the accusation,
Gal 2:13 The other Jews j him in his
Eph 2:21 In him the whole building is j
4:16 the whole body, j and held together

Joining (Join)

Eze 31:17 it, j those killed by the sword.

Joins (Join)

Hos 7: 5 and he j hands with the mockers.
1Co 16:16 j in the work, and labours at it.

Joint (Jointed, Joints)

Job 31:22 let it be broken off at the j.
Ps 22:14 and all my bones are out of j.

Jointed (Joint)

Lev 11:21 j legs for hopping on the ground.

Joints (Joint)

Heb 4:12 soul and spirit, j and marrow;

Joists

2Ch 34:11 and timber for j and beams for the

Jokdeam

Jos 15:56 Jezreel, J, Zanoah,

Jokim

1Ch 4:22 J, the men of Cozeba, and Joash and

Joking

Ge 19:14 But his sons-in-law thought he was j.
Pr 26:19 and says, "I was only j!"
Eph 5: 4 foolish talk or coarse j, which are

Jokmeam

1Ki 4:12 Shan to Abel Meholah across to J;
1Ch 6:68 J, Beth Horon,

Jokneam

Jos 12:22 the king of J in Carmel one
19:11 and extended to the ravine near J.
21:34 the tribe of Zebulun, J, Kartah,
1Ch 6:77 tribe of Zebulun they received J,

Jokshan

Ge 25: 2 She bore him Zimran, J, Medan,
25: 3 J was the father of Sheba and Dedan;
1Ch 1:32 J, Medan, Midian, Ishbak and Shuah.
1:32 The sons of J: Sheba and Dedan.

Joktan

Ge 10:25 divided; his brother was named J.
10:26 J was the father of Almodad, Sheleph,
10:29 All these were sons of J.
1Ch 1:19 divided; his brother was named J.
1:20 J was the father of Almodad, Sheleph,
1:23 All these were sons of J.

Joktheel

Jos 15:38 Dilean, Mizpah, J,
2Ki 14: 7 it J, the name it has to this day.

Jolting

Na 3: 2 galloping horses and j chariots!

Jonadab

2Sa 13: 3 a friend named J son of Shimeah,
13: 3 J was a very shrewd man.
13: 5 to bed and pretend to be ill," J said
13:32 J son of Shimeah, David's brother,
13:35 J said to the king, "See, the king's
Jer 35: 6 our forefather J son of Recab gave
35: 8 J son of Recab commanded us.
35:10 our forefather J commanded us.
35:14 'J son of Recab ordered his sons not
35:16 The descendants of J son of Recab
35:18 the command of your forefather J
35:19 'J son of Recab shall never fail to

Jonah (Jonah's)

Prophet during reign of Jeroboam II (2Ki 14:25). Ran from God's call to preach against Nineveh (Jnh 1:2–3,10). God sent storm; thrown overboard; swallowed by fish (Jnh 1:4–17). Prayed; disgorged onto dry land (Jnh 2); deliverance a "sign" prefiguring Jesus' death and resurrection (Mt 12:39–41; Lk 11:29–32). Obeyed second call (Jnh 3); response to Nineveh's repentance rebuked (Jnh 4).

2Ki 14:25 through his servant J son of Amittai
Jnh 1: 1 of the LORD came to J son of Amittai
1: 3 J ran away from the LORD and headed
1: 5 But J had gone below deck, where he
1: 7 They cast lots and the lot fell on J.
1:15 they took J and threw him overboard,
1:17 provided a great fish to swallow J,
1:17 and J was inside the fish three days
2: 1 From inside the fish J prayed to the
2:10 and it vomited J onto dry land.
3: 1 the word of the LORD came to J a
3: 3 J obeyed the word of the LORD and
3: 4 On the first day, J started into the
4: 1 J was greatly displeased and became
4: 5 J went out and sat down at a place
4: 6 made it grow up over J to give shade
4: 6 and J was very happy about the vine.
4: 9 God said to J, "Do you have a right
Mt 12:39 except the sign of the prophet J.
12:40 J was three days and three nights
12:41 they repented at the preaching of J,
12:41 and now one greater than J is here.
16: 4 be given it except the sign of J.
16:17 "Blessed are you, Simon son of J,
Lk 11:29 be given it except the sign of J.
11:30 For as J was a sign to the Ninevites,
11:32 they repented at the preaching of J,
11:32 and now one greater than J is here.

Jonah's (Jonah)

Jnh 4: 8 the sun blazed on J head so that

Jonam

Lk 3:30 the son of J, the son of Eliakim,

Jonathan (Jonathan's)

Eldest son of Saul (1Sa 13:16; 14:49; 1Ch 8:33). Courageous warrior (1Sa 14:1–23; 2Sa 1:22–23). Violated Saul's oath (1Sa 14:24–45). Friendship with David (1Sa 18:1–4; 19–20; 23:16–18; 2Sa 1:26). Killed (1Sa 31:1–2); mourned by David (2Sa 1:19–27).

Jdg 18:30 and J son of Gershom, the son of
1Sa 13: 2 were with J at Gibeah in Benjamin.
13: 3 J attacked the Philistine outpost at
13:16 Saul and his son J and the men with
13:22 J had a sword or spear in his hand;
13:22 only Saul and his son J had them.
14: 1 One day J son of Saul said to the
14: 3 No-one was aware that J had left.
14: 4 the pass that J intended to cross
14: 6 J said to his young armour-bearer,
14: 8 J said, "Come, then; we will cross
14:12 The men of the outpost shouted to J
14:12 So J said to his armour-bearer,
14:13 J climbed up, using his hands and
14:13 The Philistines fell before J, and
14:14 In that first attack J and his
14:17 When they did, it was J and his
14:21 Israelites who were with Saul and J.
14:27 J had not heard that his father had
14:29 J said, "My father has made trouble
14:39 it lies with my son J, he must die.
14:40 I and J my son will stand over here.
14:41 And J and Saul were taken by lot,

1Sa 14:42 lot between me and J my son. And J
14:43 Saul said to J, "Tell me what you
14:43 So J told him, "I merely tasted a
14:44 so severely, if you do not die, J."
14:45 the men said to Saul, "Should J die
14:45 rescued J, and he was not put to
14:49 Saul's sons were J, Ishvi and
18: 1 J became one in spirit with David,
18: 3 J made a covenant with David because
18: 4 J took off the robe he was wearing
19: 1 Saul told his son J and all the
19: 1 But J was very fond of David
19: 4 J spoke well of David to Saul his
19: 6 Saul listened to J and took this
19: 7 J called David and told him the
20: 1 at Ramah and went to J and asked,
20: 2 "Never!" J replied. "You are not
20: 3 'J must not know this or he will be
20: 4 J said to David, "Whatever you want
20: 9 "Never!" J said. "If I had the least
20:11 "Come," J said, "let's go out into
20:12 J said to David: "By the LORD, the
20:16 J made a covenant with the house of
20:17 J made David reaffirm his oath out
20:18 J said to David: "Tomorrow is the
20:25 opposite J, and Abner sat next to
20:27 Then Saul said to his son J, "Why
20:28 J answered, "David earnestly asked
20:30 Saul's anger flared up at J and he
20:32 has he done?" J asked his father.
20:33 Then J knew that his father intended
20:34 J got up from the table in fierce
20:35 In the morning J went out to the
20:37 J called out after him, "Isn't the
20:39 of all this; only J and David knew.)
20:40 J gave his weapons to the boy and
20:41 bowed down before J three times,
20:42 J said to David, "Go in peace, for
20:42 left, and J went back to the town.
23:16 Saul's son J went to David at Horesh
23:18 Then J went home, but David remained
31: 2 his sons J, Abinadab and Malki-Shua.
2Sa 1: 4 And Saul and his son J are dead."
1: 5 that Saul and his son J are dead?"
1:12 till evening for Saul and his son J,
1:17 concerning Saul and his son J,
1:22 the bow of J did not turn back, the
1:23 "Saul and J—in life they were
1:25 J lies slain on your heights.
1:26 I grieve for you, J my brother;
4: 4 (J son of Saul had a son who was
4: 4 about Saul and J came from Jezreel.
9: 3 "There is still a son of J; he is
9: 6 Mephibosheth son of J, the son of
9: 7 for the sake of your father J.
15:27 son Ahimaaz and J son of Abiathar.
15:36 of Zadok and J son of Abaithar,
17:17 J and Ahimaaz were staying at
17:20 "Where are Ahimaaz and J?" The woman
21: 7 The king spared Mephibosheth son of J
21: 7 LORD between David and J son of Saul.
21:12 J from the citizens of Jabesh Gilead.
21:13 of Saul and his son J from there,
21:14 J in the tomb of Saul's father Kish,
21:21 he taunted Israel, J son of Shimeah,
23:32 J son of Shammah the Hararite,
1Ki 1:42 he was speaking, J son of Abiathar
1:43 "Not at all!" J answered. "Our lord
1Ch 2:32 Shammai's brother: Jether and J.
2:33 The sons of J: Peleth and Zaza.
8:33 J, Malki-Shua, Abinadab and Esh-Baal.
8:34 The son of J: Merib-Baal, who was
9:39 J, Malki-Shua, Abinadab and Esh-Baal.
9:40 The son of J: Merib-Baal, who was
10: 2 his sons J, Abinadab and Malki-Shua.
11:34 J son of Shagee the Hararite,
20: 7 he taunted Israel, J son of Shimea,
27:25 J son of Uzziah was in charge of the
27:32 J, David's uncle, was a counsellor,
Ezr 8: 6 Ebed son of J, and with him 50 men;
10:15 Only J son of Asahel and Jahzeiah
Ne 12:11 Joiada the father of J, and J the
12:14 of Malluch's, J; of Shecaniah's,
12:35 and also Zechariah son of J, the son
Jer 37:15 in the house of J the secretary,
37:20 to the house of J the secretary,
40: 8 Johanan and J the sons of Kareah,

Jonathan's (Jonathan)

1Sa 20:37 the place where J arrow had fallen,
2Sa 9: 1 I can show kindness for J sake?"
Jer 38:26 me back to J house to die there.

Joppa

Mediterranean seaport about 35 miles north-west of Jerusalem, important for trade. Allotted to the tribe of Dan who had difficulty possessing it (Jos 19:46–47). Solomon and Zerubbabel used the port when building their temples (2Ch 2:16; Ezr 3:7). Jonah sailed from here when fleeing the LORD (Jnh 1:3). Home of Tabitha, whom Peter restored to life (Ac 9:36–40). While staying with Simon the tanner, Peter had a vision from God (Ac 10:5–17).

Jos 19:46 and Rakkon, with the area facing J.
2Ch 2:16 them in rafts by sea down to J.
Ezr 3: 7 cedar logs by sea from Lebanon to J,
Jnh 1: 3 He went down to J, where he found a
Ac 9:36 In J there was a disciple named
9:38 Lydda was near J; so when the
9:42 This became known all over J, and
9:43 Peter stayed in J for some time with
10: 5 Now send men to J to bring back a
10: 8 had happened and sent them to J.
10:23 of the brothers from J went along.
10:32 Send to J for Simon who is called
11: 5 "I was in the city of J praying, and
11:13 to J for Simon who is called Peter.

Jorah

Ezr 2:18 of J 112

Jorai

1Ch 5:13 J, Jacan, Zia and Eber—seven in all.

Joram

2Sa 8:10 he sent his son J to King David to
8:10 J brought with him articles of
2Ki 1:17 Ahaziah had no son, J succeeded him
3: 1 J son of Ahab became king of Israel
3: 6 at that time King J set out from
8:16 In the fifth year of J son of Ahab
8:25 In the twelfth year of J son of Ahab
8:28 Ahaziah went with J son of Ahab to
8:28 The Arameans wounded J;
8:29 King J returned to Jezreel to
8:29 to Jezreel to see J son of Ahab,
9:14 son of Nimshi, conspired against J.
9:14 (Now J and all Israel had been
9:15 King J had returned to Jezreel to
9:16 because J was resting there and
9:17 "Get a horseman," J ordered. "Send
9:21 "Hitch up my chariot," J ordered.
9:21 it was hitched up, J king of Israel
9:22 J saw Jehu he asked, "Have you come
9:23 J turned about and fled, calling out
9:24 and shot J between the shoulders.
9:29 the eleventh year of J son of Ahab
1Ch 26:25 Jeshaiah his son, J his son, Zicri
2Ch 22: 5 he went with J son of Ahab king of
22: 5 The Arameans wounded J;
22: 6 down to Jezreel to see J son of Ahab
22: 7 Through Ahaziah's visit to J, God
22: 7 he went out with J to meet Jehu son

Jordan, River (Jordan's)

Largest river in Palestine, with principal source near Mount Hermon. Flows southwards from Sea of Galilee through a deep valley into the Dead Sea. Lot desired the fertile land around it (Ge 13:10–11). A natural boundary crossed to escape enemies, e.g. by Jacob (Ge 32:10), and David (2Sa 17:21–22). Israelites camped to its east (Jos 3:1), before crossing it on dry ground to take the promised land (Jos 3:11–17). Used strategically in battle by Ehud (Jdg 3:28), Gideon (Jdg 7:24) and the Gileadites (Jdg 12:5). Elijah and Elisha crossed it on dry ground (2Ki 2:8, 14), and Elisha instructed Naaman to wash in it (2Ki 5:10). Mentioned in Isaiah's Messianic prophecy (Isa 9:1), and is the site of Jesus' baptism (Mt 3:13; Mk 1:9).

Ge 13:10 plain of the J was well watered,
13:11 the whole plain of the J and set out
32:10 only my staff when I crossed this J,
50:10 near the J, they lamented loudly and
50:11 near the J is called Abel Mizraim.
Nu 13:29 live near the sea and along the J."
22: 1 along the J across from Jericho.
26: 3 on the plains of Moab by the J
26:63 by the J across from Jericho.
31:12 by the J across from Jericho.
32: 5 Do not make us cross the J."
32:19 them on the other side of the J,
32:19 to us on the east side of the J."
32:21 you will go armed over the J before
32:29 cross over the J with you before the
32:32 will be on this side of the J."
33:48 by the J across from Jericho.
33:49 they camped along the J from
33:50 On the plains of Moab by the J
33:51 'When you cross the J into Canaan,
34:12 the boundary will go down along the J
34:15 the east side of the J of Jericho,
35: 1 On the plains of Moab by the J
35:10 'When you cross the J into Canaan,
35:14 Give three on this side of the J and
36:13 by the J across from Jericho.
Dt 1: 1 the desert east of the J—that is,
1: 5 East of the J in the territory of
2:29 did for us—until we cross the J
3: 8 Amorites the territory east of the J,
3:17 Its western border was the J in the
3:20 God is giving them, across the J.
3:25 see the good land beyond the J—that
3:27 you are not going to cross this J.
4:14 you are crossing the J to possess.
4:21 swore that I would not cross the J
4:22 I will not cross the J; but you are
4:26 you are crossing the J to possess.
4:41 aside three cities east of the J,
4:46 valley near Beth Peor east of the J,
4:47 the two Amorite kings east of the J.
4:49 included all the Arabah east of the J
6: 1 you are crossing the J to possess,
9: 1 You are now about to cross the J to
11: 8 you are crossing the J to possess,
11:11 the land you are crossing the J to
11:30 these mountains are across the J,
11:31 You are about to cross the J to
12:10 you will cross the J and settle in
27: 2 you have crossed the J into the land
27: 4 you have crossed the J, set up these
27:12 you have crossed the J, these tribes
30:18 crossing the J to enter and possess.
31: 2 to me, 'You shall not cross the J.'
31:13 you are crossing the J to possess."
32:47 you are crossing the J to possess."
Jos 1: 2 get ready to cross the J River into
1:11 you will cross the J here to go in
1:14 that Moses gave you east of the J,
1:15 east of the J towards the sunrise."
2: 7 that leads to the fords of the J,
2:10 kings of the Amorites east of the J
3: 1 out from Shittim and went to the J,
3:11 will go into the J ahead of you.
3:13 of all the earth—set foot in the J,
3:14 people broke camp to cross the J,
3:15 Now the J is in flood all during
3:15 who carried the ark reached the J
3:17 dry ground in the middle of the J,
4: 1 nation had finished crossing the J
4: 3 from the middle of the J from right
4: 5 your God into the middle of the J.
4: 7 tell them that the flow of the J was
4: 7 crossed the J, the waters of the J
4: 8 stones from the middle of the J,
4: 9 that had been in the middle of the J
4:10 standing in the middle of the J
4:16 Testimony to come up out of the J."
4:17 the priests, "Come up out of the J.
4:18 the waters of the J returned to
4:19 month the people went up from the J
4:20 stones they had taken out of the J.
4:22 tell them, 'Israel crossed the J on

Jos 4:23 For the LORD your God dried up the J
4:23 The LORD your God did to the J just
5: 1 all the Amorite kings west of the J
5: 1 how the LORD had dried up the J
7: 7 bring this people across the J to
7: 7 to stay on the other side of the J!
9: 1 Now when all the kings west of the J
9:10 kings of the Amorites east of the J
12: 1 they took over east of the J,
12: 7 conquered on the west side of the J,
13: 8 Moses had given them east of the J,
13:23 Reubenites was the bank of the J.
13:27 of Heshbon (the east side of the J,
13:32 across the J east of Jericho.
14: 3 their inheritance east of the J
15: 5 as far as the mouth of the J.
15: 5 of the sea at the mouth of the J,
16: 1 Joseph began at the J of Jericho
16: 7 Jericho and came out at the J.
17: 5 Gilead and Bashan east of the J,
18: 7 on the east side of the J.
18:12 side their boundary began at the J,
18:19 at the mouth of the J in the south.
18:20 The J formed the boundary on the
19:22 Beth Shemesh, and ended at the J.
19:33 to Lakkum and ending at the J.
19:34 on the west and the J on the east.
20: 8 On the east side of the J of Jericho
22: 4 gave you on the other side of the J.
22: 7 side of the J with their brothers.
22:10 they came to Geliloth near the J in
22:10 an imposing altar there by the J.
22:11 near the J on the Israelite side,
22:25 The LORD has made the J a boundary
23: 4 the J and the Great Sea in the west.
24: 8 Amorites who lived east of the J.
24:11 crossed the J and came to Jericho
Jdg 3:28 the fords of the J that led to Moab,
5:17 Gilead stayed beyond the J. And Dan,
6:33 crossed over the J and camped in the
7:24 J ahead of them as far as Beth Barah.
7:24 of the J as far as Beth Barah.
7:25 Zeeb to Gideon, who was by the J.
8: 4 came to the J and crossed it.
10: 8 on the east side of the J in Gilead,
10: 9 The Ammonites also crossed the J to
11:13 to the Jabbok, all the way to the J.
11:22 Jabbok and from the desert to the J.
12: 5 fords of the J leading to Ephraim,
12: 6 killed him at the fords of the J.
1Sa 13: 7 Some Hebrews even crossed the J to
31: 7 those across the J saw that the
2Sa 2:29 They crossed the J, continued
10:17 crossed the J and went to Helam.
17:22 with him set out and crossed the J.
17:22 was left who had not crossed the J.
17:24 crossed the J with all the men of
19:15 returned and went as far as the J.
19:15 the king and bring him across the J.
19:17 rushed to the J, where the king was.
19:18 crossed the J, he fell prostrate
19:31 from Rogelim to cross the J with the
19:36 Your servant will cross over the J
19:39 all the people crossed the J, and
19:41 across the J, together with all his
20: 2 all the way from the J to Jerusalem.
24: 5 After crossing the J, they camped
1Ki 2: 8 he came down to meet me at the J,
7:46 in the plain of the J between
17: 3 in the Kerith Ravine, east of the J.
17: 5 east of the J, and stayed there.
2Ki 2: 6 the LORD has sent me to the J.
2: 7 and Elisha had stopped at the J.
2:13 back and stood on the bank of the J.
5:10 wash yourself seven times in the J,
5:14 dipped himself in the J seven times,
6: 2 Let us go to the J, where each of us
6: 4 They went to the J and began to cut
7:15 They followed them as far as the J,
10:33 east of the J in all the land of
1Ch 6:78 from the tribe of Reuben across the J
12:15 was they who crossed the J in the
12:37 from east of the J, men of Reuben,
19:17 all Israel and crossed the J;
26:30 west of the J for all the work of
2Ch 4:17 in the plain of the J between
Job 40:23 though the J should surge against
Ps 42: 6 remember you from the land of the J,
114: 3 looked and fled, the J turned back;
114: 5 O J, that you turned back,
Isa 9: 1 by the way of the sea, along the J—
Jer 12: 5 you manage in the thickets by the J?
Eze 47:18 along the J between Gilead and the
Zec 11: 3 the lush thicket of the J is ruined!
Mt 3: 5 Judea and the whole region of the J.
3: 6 were baptised by him in the J River.
3:13 Jesus came from Galilee to the J to
4:15 the way to the sea, along the J,
4:25 region across the J followed him.
19: 1 of Judea to the other side of the J.
Mk 1: 5 were baptised by him in the J River.
1: 9 and was baptised by John in the J.
3: 8 the J and around Tyre and Sidon.
10: 1 region of Judea and across the J.
Lk 3: 3 into all the country around the J,
4: 1 returned from the J and was led by
Jn 1:28 of the J, where John was baptising.
3:26 with you on the other side of the J
10:40 Jesus went back across the J to the

Jordan's (Jordan)

Jos 3: 8 you reach the edge of the J waters,
Jer 49:19 a lion coming up from J thickets
50:44 a lion coming up from J thickets

Jorim

Lk 3:29 the son of Eliezer, the son of J,

Jorkeam

1Ch 2:44 of Raham, and Raham the father of J.

Josech

Lk 3:26 the son of J, the son of Joda,

Joseph (Joseph's)

1. Son of Jacob by Rachel (Ge 30:22–24; 35:24; 1Ch 2:2). Father's favouritism aroused brothers' hostility (Ge 37:3–4). Dreams (Ge 37:5–11). Sold by brothers (Ge 37:12–36); became slave of Potiphar (Ge 39:1–6). Resisted attentions of Potiphar's wife; falsely accused; imprisoned (Ge 39:7–23). Interpreted dreams of cupbearer and baker (Ge 40); Pharaoh (Ge 41:1–36). Put in charge of Egypt (Ge 41:37–57). Tested brothers when came to buy grain (Ge 42–44); made himself known (Ge 45:1–15); settled family in Egypt (Ge 45:16–47:12). Sons blessed (Ge 48); received Jacob's blessing (Ge 49:22–26). Death (Ge 50:22–26; Ex 13:19; Jos 24:32; Heb 11:22). Descendants divided into tribes of Ephraim and Manasseh (Jos 14:4; 16–17; Eze 47:13); blessed by Moses (Dt 33:13–17).
2. Husband of Jesus' mother, Mary (Mt 1:16,18–25; Lk 1:27); descendant of David (Lk 2:4); carpenter (Mt 13:55). Dreams (Mt 1:20–23; 2:13,19–20). **3.** Disciple from Arimathea; member of Jewish council. Asked for Jesus' body; gave tomb for burial (Mt 27:57–60; Mk 15:42–46; Lk 23:50–54; Jn 19:38–42). **4.** See *Barnabas*.

Ge 30:24 She named him J, and said, "May the
30:25 After Rachel gave birth to J, Jacob
33: 2 next, and Rachel and J in the rear.
33: 7 Last of all came J and Rachel, and
35:24 The sons of Rachel: J and Benjamin.
37: 2 J, a young man of seventeen, was
37: 3 Now Israel loved J more than any of
37: 5 J had a dream, and when he told it
37:13 Israel said to J, "As you know, your
37:14 When J arrived at Shechem,
37:17 So J went after his brothers and
37:23 when J came to his brothers, they
37:28 his brothers pulled J up out of the
37:29 J was not there, he tore his clothes.
37:33 J has surely been torn to pieces."
37:36 the Midianites sold J in Egypt to
39: 1 Now J had been taken down to Egypt.
39: 2 The LORD was with J and he prospered,
39: 4 J found favour in his eyes and
39: 5 of the Egyptian because of J.
39: 6 with J in charge, he did not concern
39: 6 Now J was well-built and handsome,
39: 7 wife took notice of J and said,
39:10 though she spoke to J day after day,
39:20 But while J was there in the prison,
39:22 the warder put J in charge of all
39:23 because the LORD was with J and gave
40: 3 same prison where J was confined.
40: 4 assigned them to J, and he attended
40: 6 J came to them the next morning, he
40: 8 Then J said to them, "Do not
40: 9 the chief cupbearer told J his dream.
40:12 "This is what it means," J said to
40:16 the chief baker saw that J had given
40:16 he said to J, "I too had a dream: On
40:18 "This is what it means," J said.
40:22 the chief baker, just as J had said
40:23 did not remember J; he forgot him.
41:14 Pharaoh sent for J, and he was
41:15 Pharaoh said to J, "I had a dream,
41:16 "I cannot do it," J replied to
41:17 Pharaoh said to J, "In my dream I
41:25 J said to Pharaoh, "The dreams of
41:39 Pharaoh said to J, "Since God has
41:41 Pharaoh said to J, "I hereby put you
41:44 Pharaoh said to J, "I am Pharaoh,
41:45 Pharaoh gave J the name
41:45 J went throughout the land of Egypt.
41:46 J was thirty years old when he
41:46 J went out from Pharaoh's presence
41:48 J collected all the food produced in
41:49 J stored up huge quantities of grain,
41:50 two sons were born to J by Asenath
41:51 J named his firstborn Manasseh and
41:54 of famine began, just as J had said.
41:55 "Go to J and do what he tells you.
41:56 J opened the storehouses and sold
41:57 came to Egypt to buy grain from J,
42: 6 Now J was the governor of the land,
42: 7 soon as J saw his brothers, he
42: 8 Although J recognised his brothers,
42:14 J said to them, "It is just as I
42:18 On the third day, J said to them,
42:23 They did not realise that J could
42:25 J gave orders to fill their bags
42:36 J is no more and Simeon is no more,
43:15 Egypt and presented themselves to J.
43:16 J saw Benjamin with them, he said to
43:17 The man did as J told him and took
43:26 J came home, they presented to him
43:30 J hurried out and looked for a place
44: 1 Now J gave these instructions to the
44: 2 And he did as J said.
44: 4 when J said to his steward, "Go after
44:14 J was still in the house when Judah
44:15 J said to them, "What is this you
44:17 J said, "Far be it from me to do
45: 1 J could no longer control himself
45: 1 there was no-one with J when he
45: 3 J said to his brothers, "I am J! Is
45: 4 J said to his brothers, "Come close
45: 4 J, the one you sold into Egypt!
45: 9 'This is what your son J says: God
45:17 Pharaoh said to J, "Tell your
45:21 J gave them carts, as Pharaoh had
45:26 They told him, "J is still alive! In
45:27 they told him everything J had said
45:27 and when he saw the carts J had sent
45:28 convinced! My son J is still alive.
46:19 The sons of Jacob's wife Rachel: J
46:20 Manasseh and Ephraim were born to J
46:27 who had been born to J in Egypt,
46:28 to J to get directions to Goshen.
46:29 J had his chariot made ready and
46:29 As soon as J appeared before him, he
46:30 Israel said to J, "Now I am ready to
46:31 J said to his brothers and to his
47: 1 J went and told Pharaoh, "My father
47: 5 Pharaoh said to J, "Your father and
47: 7 J brought his father Jacob in and
47:11 J settled his father and his
47:12 J also provided his father and his
47:14 J collected all the money that was
47:15 came to J and said, "Give us food.
47:16 "Then bring your livestock," said J.
47:17 they brought their livestock to J,
47:20 J bought all the land in Egypt for
47:21 J reduced the people to servitude,
47:23 J said to the people, "Now that I

Ge 47:26 J established it as a law concerning
47:29 he called for his son J and said to
47:31 "Swear to me," he said. Then J swore
48: 1 Some time later J was told, "Your
48: 2 Jacob was told, "Your son J has come
48: 3 Jacob said to J, "God Almighty
48: 8 Israel saw the sons of J, he asked,
48: 9 me here," J said to his father.
48:10 So J brought his sons close to him,
48:11 Israel said to J, "I never expected
48:12 J removed them from Israel's knees
48:13 J took both of them, Ephraim on his
48:15 he blessed J and said, "May the God
48:17 J saw his father placing his right
48:18 J said to him, "No, my father, this
48:21 Israel said to J, "I am about to die,
49:22 "J is a fruitful vine, a fruitful
49:26 Let all these rest on the head of J,
50: 1 J threw himself upon his father and
50: 2 J directed the physicians in his
50: 4 passed, J said to Pharaoh's court,
50: 7 J went up to bury his father.
50:10 J observed a seven-day period of
50:14 After burying his father, J returned
50:15 "What if J holds a grudge against us
50:16 they sent word to J, saying, "Your
50:17 'This is what you are to say to J:
50:17 their message came to him, J wept.
50:19 J said to them, "Don't be afraid.
50:22 J stayed in Egypt, along with all
50:24 J said to his brothers, "I am about
50:25 J made the sons of Israel swear an
50:26 J died at the age of a hundred and
Ex 1: 5 J was already in Egypt.
1: 6 Now J and all his brothers and all
1: 8 a new king, who did not know about J,
13:19 Moses took the bones of J with him
13:19 J had made the sons of Israel
Nu 1:10 from the sons of J: from Ephraim,
1:32 From the sons of J: From the
13: 7 tribe of Issachar, Igal son of J;
13:11 tribe of Manasseh (a tribe of J)
26:28 The descendants of J by their clans
26:37 the descendants of J by their clans.
27: 1 to the clans of Manasseh son of J.
32:33 the half-tribe of Manasseh son of J
34:23 from the tribe of Manasseh son of J;
34:24 from the tribe of Ephraim son of J;
36: 1 the clans of the descendants of J,
36: 5 descendants of J is saying is right.
36:12 descendants of Manasseh son of J,
Dt 27:12 Judah, Issachar, J and Benjamin.
33:13 About J he said: "May the LORD bless
33:16 Let all these rest on the head of J,
Jos 14: 4 for the sons of J had become two
16: 1 The allotment for J began at the
16: 4 descendants of J, received their
17: 2 of Manasseh son of J by their clans.
17:14 The people of J said to Joshua, "Why
17:16 The people of J replied, "The hill
17:17 Joshua said to the house of J—
18: 5 house of J in its territory on the
18:11 between the tribes of Judah and J:
Jdg 1:22 Now the house of J attacked Bethel,
1:35 power of the house of J increased,
2Sa 19:20 the whole house of J to come down
1Ki 11:28 labour force of the house of J.
1Ch 2: 2 Dan, J, Benjamin, Naphtali, Gad and
5: 1 to the sons of J son of Israel;
5: 2 of the firstborn belonged to J)
7:29 J son of Israel lived in these towns.
25: 2 From the sons of Asaph: Zaccur, J,
25: 9 fell to J, his sons and relatives,
Ezr 10:42 Shallum, Amariah and J.
Ne 12:14 Jonathan; of Shecaniah's, J;
Ps 77:15 the descendants of Jacob and J.
78:67 he rejected the tents of J, he did
80: 1 you who lead J like a flock; you who
81: 5 He established it as a statute for J
105:17 before them—J, sold as a slave.
Eze 37:16 'Ephraim's stick, belonging to J and
37:19 I am going to take the stick of J
47:13 of Israel, with two portions for J.
48:32 gates: the gate of J, the gate of
Am 5: 6 through the house of J like a fire;
5:15 will have mercy on the remnant of J.
Am 6: 6 do not grieve over the ruin of J.
Ob :18 a fire and the house of J a flame;
Zec 10: 6 of Judah and save the house of J.
Mt 1:16 Jacob the father of J, the husband
1:18 Mary was pledged to be married to J,
1:19 J her husband was a righteous man
1:20 "J son of David, do not be afraid to
1:24 J woke up, he did what the angel of
2:13 the Lord appeared to J in a dream.
2:19 appeared in a dream to J in
13:55 brothers James, J, Simon and Judas?
27:57 a rich man from Arimathea, named J,
27:59 J took the body, wrapped it in a
Mk 6: 3 of James, J, Judas and Simon?
15:43 J of Arimathea, a prominent member
15:45 it was so, he gave the body to J.
15:46 J bought some linen cloth, took down
Lk 1:27 man named J, a descendant of David.
2: 4 J also went up from the town of
2:16 they hurried off and found Mary and J
2:22 J and Mary took him to Jerusalem to
2:39 J and Mary had done everything
3:23 the son, so it was thought, of J,
3:24 the son of Jannai, the son of J,
3:30 the son of Judah, the son of J, the
23:50 Now there was a man named J, a
23:55 with Jesus from Galilee followed J
Jn 1:45 of Nazareth, the son of J."
4: 5 ground Jacob had given to his son J.
6:42 "Is this not Jesus, the son of J,
19:38 Later, J of Arimathea asked Pilate
19:38 Now J was a disciple of Jesus, but
Ac 1:23 proposed two men: J called Barsabbas
4:36 J, a Levite from Cyprus, whom the
7: 9 the patriarchs were jealous of J,
7:10 He gave J wisdom and enabled him to
7:13 On their second visit, J told his
7:14 After this, J sent for his father
7:18 king, who knew nothing about J,
Heb 11:22 By faith J, when his end was near,
Rev 7: 8 from the tribe of J 12,000,

Joseph's (Joseph)

Ge 37:31 they got J robe, slaughtered a goat
39: 6 he left in J care everything he had;
39:20 J master took him and put him in
39:23 attention to anything under J care,
41:42 his finger and put it on J finger.
42: 3 ten of J brothers went down to buy
42: 4 did not send Benjamin, J brother
42: 6 So when J brothers arrived, they
43:17 him and took the men to J house.
43:19 they went up to J steward and spoke
43:24 steward took the men into J house
43:25 prepared their gifts for J arrival
43:34 were served to them from J table,
45:16 palace that J brothers had come,
46: 4 And J own hand will close your eyes."
50: 8 all the members of J household
50:15 J brothers saw that their father was
50:23 were placed at birth on J knees.
Jos 17: 1 tribe of Manasseh as J firstborn,
24:32 J bones, which the Israelites had
24:32 the inheritance of J descendants.
Lk 4:22 "Isn't this J son?" they asked.
Ac 7:13 and Pharaoh learned about J family.
Heb 11:21 blessed each of J sons, and

Joses

Mt 27:56 J, and the mother of Zebedee's sons.
Mk 15:40 the younger and of J, and Salome.
15:47 mother of J saw where he was laid.

Joshah

1Ch 4:34 Meshobab, Jamlech, J son of Amaziah,

Joshaphat

1Ch 11:43 Hanan son of Maacah, J the Mithnite,
15:24 Shebaniah, J, Nethanel, Amasai,

Joshaviah

1Ch 11:46 Eliel the Mahavite, Jeribai and J

Joshbekashah

1Ch 25: 4 J, Mallothi, Hothir and Mahazioth.
25:24 the seventeenth to J, his sons and

Josheb-Basshebeth

2Sa 23: 8 the names of David's mighty men: J,

Joshibiah

1Ch 4:35 Joel, Jehu son of J, the son of

Joshua (Hoshea)

1. Son of Nun, formerly called Hoshea (Nu 13:8,16; 1Ch 7:27). Fought Amalekites (Ex 17:9–14). Moses' assistant: on Sinai (Ex 24:13; 32:17); at tent of meeting (Ex 33:11). One of spies sent to explore Canaan (Nu 13:8); with Caleb encouraged people to go in (Nu 14:6–9); so allowed to enter land (Nu 26:65; 32:12). Succeeded Moses (Dt 1:38; 3:28; 31:1–8; 34:9). Commissioned and encouraged by God (Jos 1:1–9). crossed Jordan (Jos 3–4). Victory at Jericho (Jos 5:13–6:27); defeat then victory at Ai (Jos 7–8); renewed covenant at Mt Ebal (Jos 8:30–35); deceived by Gibeonites (Jos 9); sun stood still to enable victory over five kings at Gibeon (Jos 10); conquered southern Canaan (Jos 10:29–43), northern Canaan (Jos 11). Apportioned land among tribes (Jos 13–22). Gave final instructions (Jos 23); renewed covenant at Shechem (Jos 24:1–27); death (Jos 24:29–31; Jdg 2:8–9).
2. High priest at time of restoration (Hag 1:1); encouraged by Haggai to finish work on temple (Hag 1:12–2:9). Representative of sinful Israel saved by God's grace (Zec 3); crowning foreshadowed reign of Messiah (Zec 6:9–15).

Ex 17: 9 Moses said to J, "Choose some of our
17:10 J fought the Amalekites as Moses had
17:13 J overcame the Amalekite army with
17:14 and make sure that J hears it,
24:13 Moses set out with J his assistant,
32:17 J heard the noise of the people
33:11 J son of Nun did not leave the tent.
Nu 11:28 J son of Nun, who had been Moses'
13:16 gave Hoshea son of Nun the name J.)
14: 6 J son of Nun and Caleb son of
14:30 son of Jephunneh and J son of Nun.
14:38 only J son of Nun and Caleb son of
26:65 son of Jephunneh and J son of Nun.
27:18 said to Moses, "Take J son of Nun
27:22 He took J and made him stand before
32:12 the Kenizzite and J son of Nun,
32:28 J son of Nun and to the family heads
34:17 Eleazar the priest and J son of Nun.
Dt 1:38 your assistant, J son of Nun, will
3:21 At that time I commanded J: "You
3:28 commission J, and encourage and
31: 3 J also will cross over ahead of you,
31: 7 Moses summoned J and said to him in
31:14 Call J and present yourselves at the
31:14 So Moses and J came and presented
31:23 gave this command to J son of Nun:
32:44 Moses came with J son of Nun and
34: 9 Now J son of Nun was filled with the
Jos 1: 1 to J son of Nun, Moses' assistant:
1:10 J ordered the officers of the people:
1:12 the half-tribe of Manasseh, J said,
1:16 they answered J, "Whatever you have
2: 1 J son of Nun secretly sent two spies
2:23 the river and came to J son of Nun
2:24 They said to J, "The LORD has surely
3: 1 Early in the morning J and all the
3: 5 J told the people, "Consecrate
3: 6 J said to the priests, "Take up the
3: 7 the LORD said to J, "Today I will
3: 9 J said to the Israelites, "Come here
4: 1 the Jordan, the LORD said to J,
4: 4 J called together the twelve men he
4: 8 the Israelites did as J commanded
4: 8 as the LORD had told J; and they
4: 9 J set up the twelve stones that had
4:10 commanded J was done by the people,
4:10 just as Moses had directed J.
4:14 That day the LORD exalted J in the
4:15 Then the LORD said to J,
4:17 J commanded the priests, "Come up
4:20 J set up at Gilgal the twelve stones

Jos 5: 2 At that time the LORD said to J,
5: 3 J made flint knives and circumcised
5: 7 these were the ones J circumcised.
5: 9 the LORD said to J, "Today I have
5:13 Now when J was near Jericho, he
5:13 J went up to him and asked, "Are you
5:14 Then J fell face down to the ground
5:15 standing is holy. And J did so.
6: 2 the LORD said to J, "See, I have
6: 6 J son of Nun called the priests and
6: 8 J had spoken to the people, the
6:10 J had commanded the people, "Do not
6:12 J got up early the next morning and
6:16 J commanded the people, "Shout! For
6:22 J said to the two men who had spied
6:25 J spared Rahab the prostitute, with
6:25 because she hid the men J had sent
6:26 At that time J pronounced this
6:27 the LORD was with J, and his fame
7: 2 Now J sent men from Jericho to Ai,
7: 3 they returned to J, they said, "Not
7: 6 J tore his clothes and fell face
7: 7 J said, "Ah, Sovereign LORD, why did
7:10 The LORD said to J, "Stand up! What
7:16 Early the next morning J had Israel
7:18 J had his family come forward man by
7:19 J said to Achan, "My son, give glory
7:22 J sent messengers, and they ran to
7:23 brought them to J and all the
7:24 J, together with all Israel, took
7:25 J said, "Why have you brought this
8: 1 the LORD said to J, "Do not be
8: 3 J and the whole army moved out to
8: 9 J sent them off, and they went to
8: 9 J spent that night with the people.
8:10 Early the next morning J mustered
8:12 J had taken about five thousand men
8:13 That night J went into the valley.
8:15 J and all Israel let themselves be
8:16 pursued J and were lured away from
8:18 the LORD said to J, "Hold out
8:18 So J held out his javelin towards Ai.
8:21 For when J and all Israel saw that
8:23 of Ai alive and brought him to J.
8:26 For J did not draw back the hand
8:27 city, as the LORD had instructed J.
8:28 J burned Ai and made it a permanent
8:29 At sunset, J ordered them to take
8:30 J built on Mount Ebal an altar to
8:32 J copied on stones the law of Moses,
8:34 Afterwards, J read all the words of
8:35 had commanded that J did not read
9: 2 to make war against J and Israel.
9: 3 what J had done to Jericho and Ai,
9: 6 they went to J in the camp at Gilgal
9: 8 are your servants," they said to J.
9: 8 But J asked, "Who are you and where
9:15 J made a treaty of peace with them
9:22 J summoned the Gibeonites and said,
9:24 They answered J, "Your servants were
9:26 J saved them from the Israelites,
10: 1 Jerusalem heard that J had taken Ai
10: 4 peace with J and the Israelites."
10: 6 The Gibeonites then sent word to J
10: 7 J marched up from Gilgal with his
10: 8 The LORD said to J, "Do not be
10: 9 Gilgal, J took them by surprise.
10:12 J said to the LORD in the presence
10:15 J returned with all Israel to the
10:17 J was told that the five kings had
10:20 J and the Israelites destroyed them
10:21 safely to J in the camp at Makkedah,
10:22 J said, "Open the mouth of the cave
10:24 they had brought these kings to J,
10:25 J said to them, "Do not be afraid;
10:26 J struck and killed the kings and
10:27 At sunset J gave the order and they
10:28 That day J took Makkedah. He put the
10:29 J and all Israel with him moved on
10:30 and everyone in it J put to the sword
10:31 J and all Israel with him moved on
10:32 and J took it on the second day.
10:33 but J defeated him and his
10:34 J and all Israel with him moved on
10:36 J and all Israel with him went up
10:38 J and all Israel with him turned
Jos 10:40 J subdued the whole region,
10:41 J subdued them from Kadesh Barnea to
10:42 kings and their lands J conquered
10:43 J returned with all Israel to the
11: 6 The LORD said to J, "Do not be
11: 7 J and his whole army came against
11: 9 J did to them as the LORD had
11:10 At that time J turned back and
11:12 J took all these royal cities and
11:13 Hazor, which J burned.
11:15 so Moses commanded J, and J did it;
11:16 J took this entire land: the hill
11:18 J waged war against all these kings
11:21 At that time J went and destroyed
11:21 J totally destroyed them and their
11:23 J took the entire land, just as the
12: 7 are the kings of the land that J
12: 7 their lands J gave as an inheritance
13: 1 J was old and well advanced in years,
14: 1 Eleazar the priest, J son of Nun
14: 6 Now the men of Judah approached J at
14:13 J blessed Caleb son of Jephunneh and
15:13 J gave to Caleb son of Jephunneh a
17: 4 to Eleazar the priest, J son of Nun,
17: 4 So J gave them an inheritance along
17:14 The people of Joseph said to J, "Why
17:15 "If you are so numerous," J answered,
17:17 J said to the house of Joseph—to
18: 3 J said to the Israelites: "How long
18: 8 J instructed them, "Go and make a
18: 9 returned to J in the camp at Shiloh.
18:10 J then cast lots for them in Shiloh
19:49 the Israelites gave J son of Nun an
19:51 J son of Nun and the heads of the
20: 1 Then the LORD said to J:
21: 1 J son of Nun, and the heads of the
22: 1 J summoned the Reubenites, the
22: 6 J blessed them and sent them away,
22: 7 other half of the tribe J gave
22: 7 J sent them home, he blessed them,
23: 1 J, by then old and well advanced in
24: 1 J assembled all the tribes of Israel
24: 2 J said to all the people, "This is
24:19 J said to the people, "You are not
24:21 the people said to J, "No! We will
24:22 J said, "You are witnesses against
24:23 "Now then," said J, "throw away the
24:24 the people said to J, "We will serve
24:25 On that day J made a covenant for
24:26 J recorded these things in the Book
24:28 J sent the people away, each to his
24:29 After these things, J son of Nun,
24:31 LORD throughout the lifetime of J
Jdg 1: 1 After the death of J, the Israelites
2: 6 After J had dismissed the Israelites,
2: 7 LORD throughout the lifetime of J
2: 8 J son of Nun, the servant of the
2:21 of the nations J left when he died.
2:23 by giving them into the hands of J.
1Sa 6:14 to the field of J of Beth Shemesh
6:18 in the field of J of Beth Shemesh.
1Ki 16:34 of the LORD spoken by J son of Nun.
2Ki 23: 8 the entrance to the Gate of J,
1Ch 7:27 Nun his son and J his son.
Ne 8:17 From the days of J son of Nun until
Hag 1: 1 J son of Jehozadak, the high priest:
1:12 son of Shealtiel, J son of Jehozadak
1:14 and the spirit of J son of Jehozadak,
2: 2 of Judah, to J son of Jehozadak
2: 4 'Be strong, O J son of Jehozadak,
Zec 3: 1 he showed me J the high priest
3: 3 Now J was dressed in filthy clothes
3: 4 Then he said to J, "See, I have
3: 6 of the LORD gave this charge to J:
3: 8 " 'Listen, O high priest J and your
3: 9 the stone I have set in front of J!
6:11 the high priest, J son of Jehozadak.
Lk 3:29 the son of J, the son of Eliezer,
Ac 7:45 our fathers under J brought it with
Heb 4: 8 For if J had given them rest, God

Josiah (Josiah's)

King of Judah; son of Amon (2Ki 21:26; 1Ch 3:14; 2Ch 33:25). Birth prophesied (1Ki 13:2). Godliness commended (2Ki 22:2; 2Ch 34:2–3; Jer 22:15–16). Removed idols (2Ch 34:3–7); repaired temple (2Ki 22:3–7; 2Ch 34:8–13). Repented, following discovery of Book of the Law (2Ki 22:8–20; 2Ch 34:14–28); renewed covenant (2Ki 23:1–3; 2Ch 34:29–32); purified temple (2Ki 23:4–12); destroyed high places (2Ki 23:13–20,24–25; 2Ch 34:33). Celebrated Passover (2Ki 23:21–23; 2Ch 35:1–19). Killed fighting Pharaoh Neco (2Ki 23:29–30; 2Ch 35:20–27).

1Ki 13: 2 J will be born to the house of David.
2Ki 21:24 made J his son king in his place.
21:26 And J his son succeeded him as king.
22: 1 J was eight years old when he became
22: 3 King J sent the secretary, Shaphan
23: 8 J brought all the priests from the
23:11 J then burned the chariots dedicated
23:14 J smashed the sacred stones and cut
23:16 J looked around, and when he saw the
23:19 J removed and defiled all the
23:20 J slaughtered all the priests of
23:23 in the eighteenth year of King J,
23:24 J got rid of the mediums
23:25 Neither before nor after J was there
23:29 While J was king, Pharaoh Neco king
23:29 King J marched out to meet him in
23:30 of the land took Jehoahaz son of J
23:34 of J king in place of his father J
1Ch 3:14 Amon his son, J his son.
3:15 The sons of J: Johanan the firstborn,
2Ch 33:25 made J his son king in his place.
34: 1 J was eight years old when he became
34:33 J removed all the detestable idols
35: 1 J celebrated the Passover to the
35: 7 J provided for all the lay people
35:16 of the LORD, as King J had ordered.
35:18 celebrated such a Passover as did J,
35:20 when J had set the temple in order
35:20 J marched out to meet him in battle.
35:22 J, however, would not turn away from
35:23 Archers shot King J, and he told his
35:25 Jeremiah composed laments for J, and
35:25 commemorate J in the laments.
36: 1 of the land took Jehoahaz son of J
Jer 1: 2 of J son of Amon king of Judah,
1: 3 of Jehoiakim son of J king of Judah,
1: 3 of Zedekiah son of J king of Judah,
3: 6 During the reign of King J, the LORD
22:11 LORD says about Shallum son of J,
22:18 Jehoiakim son of J king of Judah:
25: 1 of Jehoiakim son of J king of Judah,
25: 3 the thirteenth year of J son of Amon
26: 1 of Jehoiakim son of J king of Judah,
27: 1 of Zedekiah son of J king of Judah,
35: 1 of Jehoiakim son of J king of Judah:
36: 1 of Jehoiakim son of J king of Judah,
36: 2 to you in the reign of J till now.
36: 9 of Jehoiakim son of J king of Judah,
37: 1 Zedekiah son of J was made king of
45: 1 of Jehoiakim son of J king of Judah,
46: 2 of Jehoiakim son of J king of Judah:
Zep 1: 1 the reign of J son of Amon king of
Zec 6:10 Go the same day to the house of J
Mt 1:10 of Amon, Amon the father of J,
1:11 J the father of Jeconiah and his

Josiah's (Josiah)

2Ki 23:28 for the other events of J reign, and
23:30 J servants brought his body in a
2Ch 34: 8 In the eighteenth year of J reign,
35:19 in the eighteenth year of J reign.
35:26 The other events of J reign and his

Josiphiah

Ezr 8:10 son of J, and with him 160 men;

Jostle (Jostled)

Joel 2: 8 They do not j each other; each

Jostled (Jostle)

Ge 25:22 The babies j each other within her,

Jotbah

2Ki 21:19 daughter of Haruz; she was from J.

Jotbathah
Nu 33:33 left Hor Haggidgad and camped at **J**.
33:34 They left **J** and camped at Abronah.
Dt 10: 7 to **J**, a land with streams of water.

Jotham (Jotham's)
Jdg 9: 5 But **J**, the youngest son of
9: 7 **J** was told about this, he climbed up
9:21 **J** fled, escaping to Beer, and he
9:57 curse of **J** son of Jerub-Baal came on
2Ki 15: 5 **J** the king's son had charge of the
15: 7 And **J** his son succeeded him as king.
15:30 twentieth year of **J** son of Uzziah.
15:32 **J** son of Uzziah king of Judah began
15:35 **J** rebuilt the Upper Gate of the
15:38 **J** rested with his fathers and was
16: 1 son of **J** king of Judah began to reign
1Ch 2:47 The sons of Jahdai: Regem, **J**, Geshan,
3:12 his son, Azariah his son, **J** his son
5:17 the reigns of **J** king of Judah
2Ch 26:21 **J** his son had charge of the palace
26:23 And **J** his son succeeded him as king.
27: 1 **J** was twenty-five years old when he
27: 3 **J** rebuilt the Upper Gate of the
27: 5 **J** made war on the king of the
27: 6 **J** grew powerful because he walked
27: 9 **J** rested with his fathers and was
Isa 1: 1 **J**, Ahaz and Hezekiah, kings of Judah.
7: 1 Ahaz son of **J**, the son of Uzziah,
Hos 1: 1 **J**, Ahaz and Hezekiah, kings of Judah,
Mic 1: 1 of Moresheth during the reigns of **J**,
Mt 1: 9 Uzziah the father of **J**, **J** the father

Jotham's (Jotham)
2Ki 15:36 for the other events of **J** reign, and
2Ch 27: 7 The other events in **J** reign,

Journey (Journeyed, Journeys)
Ge 24:21 the LORD had made his **j** successful.
24:27 the LORD has led me on the **j** to the
24:40 with you and make your **j** a success,
24:42 to the **j** on which I have come.
24:56 LORD has granted success to my **j**.
28:20 will watch over me on this **j** I am
29: 1 Jacob continued on his **j** and came to
30:36 he put a three-day **j** between himself
42:25 to give them provisions for their **j**.
42:38 If harm comes to him on the **j** you
45:21 gave them provisions for their **j**.
45:23 and other provisions for his **j**.
Ex 3:18 Let us take a three-day **j** into the
5: 3 Now let us take a three-day **j** into
8:27 We must take a three-day **j** into the
Nu 9:10 of a dead body or are away on a **j**,
9:13 not on a **j** fails to celebrate the
33: 1 Here are the stages in the **j** of the
33: 2 Moses recorded the stages in their **j**.
33: 2 This is their **j** by stages:
Dt 1:33 who went ahead of you on your **j**, in
2: 7 He has watched over your **j** through
25:18 they met you on your **j** and cut off
28:68 **j** I said you should never make again.
Jos 5: 5 during the **j** from Egypt had not.
9:11 'Take provisions for your **j**; go and
9:13 are worn out by the very long **j**."
24:17 He protected us on our entire **j** and
Jdg 18: 5 whether our **j** will be successful."
18: 6 Your **j** has the LORD's approval."
1Ki 13:26 him back from his **j** heard of it,
19: 4 while he himself went a day's **j** into
19: 7 eat, for the **j** is too much for you."
Ezr 7: 9 He had begun his **j** from Babylon on
8:21 a safe **j** for us and our children,
Ne 2: 6 "How long will your **j** take, and when
Job 16:22 before I go on the **j** of no return.
Pr 7:19 he has gone on a long **j**.
Isa 35: 8 The unclean will not **j** on it;
Am 5: 5 go to Gilgal, do not **j** to Beersheba.
Mic 6: 5 Remember your **j** from Shittim to
Mt 10:10 take no bag for the **j**, or extra
21:33 some farmers and went away on a **j**.
25:14 it will be like a man going on a **j**,
25:15 Then he went on his **j**.
Mk 6: 8 "Take nothing for the **j** except a
12: 1 some farmers and went away on a **j**.
Lk 9: 3 He told them: "Take nothing for the **j**
11: 6 a friend of mine on a **j** has come to
Jn 4: 6 tired as he was from the **j**, sat down
Ac 9: 3 he neared Damascus on his **j**,
9:27 He told them how Saul on his **j** had
10: 9 on their **j** and approaching the city,
16: 3 wanted to take him along on the **j**,
Ro 15:24 to have you assist me on my **j** there,
1Co 16: 6 can help me on my **j**, wherever I go.

Journeyed (Journey)
Ex 12:37 The Israelites **j** from Rameses to
1Sa 31:12 all their valiant men **j** through the
Job 38:16 "Have you **j** to the springs of the

Journeys (Journey)
Ac 26:12 "On one of these **j** I was going to

Jowls
Dt 18: 3 shoulder, the **j** and the inner parts.

Joy (Joyful, Joyfully, Joyous, Overjoyed, Rejoice)
Ge 31:27 that I could send you away with **j**
Lev 9:24 shouted for **j** and fell face down.
Dt 16:15 hands, and your **j** will be complete.
Jdg 9:19 be your **j**, and may you be his, too!
1Ch 12:40 sheep, for there was **j** in Israel.
16:27 and **j** in his dwelling-place.
16:33 they will sing for **j** before the LORD,
29:17 And now I have seen with **j** how
29:22 They ate and drank with great **j** in
2Ch 30:26 There was great **j** in Jerusalem, for
Ezr 3:12 while many others shouted for **j**.
3:13 the sound of the shouts of **j** from
6:16 of the house of God with **j**.
6:22 For seven days they celebrated with **j**
6:22 the LORD had filled them with **j** by
Ne 8:10 the **j** of the LORD is your strength."
8:12 food and to celebrate with great **j**,
8:17 And their **j** was very great.
12:43 because God had given them great **j**.
Est 8:16 and **j**, gladness and honour.
8:17 there was **j** and gladness among the
9:17 and made it a day of feasting and **j**.
9:18 and made it a day of feasting and **j**.
9:19 of Adar as a day of **j** and feasting,
9:22 when their sorrow was turned into **j**
9:22 **j** and giving presents of food to one
Job 3: 7 may no shout of **j** be heard in it.
6:10 my **j** in unrelenting pain—
8:21 and your lips with shouts of **j**.
9:25 fly away without a glimpse of **j**.
10:20 so that I can have a moment's **j**
20: 5 **j** of the godless lasts but a moment.
33:26 he sees God's face and shouts for **j**;
38: 7 and all the angels shouted for **j**?
Ps 4: 7 greater **j** than when their grain
5:11 be glad; let them ever sing for **j**.
16:11 fill me with **j** in your presence,
19: 8 are right, giving **j** to the heart.
20: 5 We will shout for **j** when you are
21: 1 is his **j** in the victories you give!
21: 6 glad with the **j** of your presence.
27: 6 will I sacrifice with shouts of **j**;
28: 7 My heart leaps for **j** and I will give
30:11 my sackcloth and clothed me with **j**,
33: 3 play skilfully, and shout for **j**.
35:27 shout for **j** and gladness; may they
42: 4 with shouts of **j** and thanksgiving
43: 4 of God, to God, my **j** and my delight.
45: 7 by anointing you with the oil of **j**.
45:15 They are led in with **j** and gladness;
47: 1 shout to God with cries of **j**.
47: 5 God has ascended amid shouts of **j**,
48: 2 the **j** of the whole earth.
51: 8 Let me hear **j** and gladness; let the
51:12 Restore to me the **j** of your
65: 8 fades you call forth songs of **j**.
65:13 corn; they shout for **j** and sing.
66: 1 Shout with **j** to God, all the earth!
67: 4 the nations be glad and sing for **j**,
71:23 My lips will shout for **j** when I sing
81: 1 Sing for **j** to God our strength;
86: 4 Bring **j** to your servant, for to you,
89:12 and Hermon sing for **j** at your name.
90:14 sing for **j** and be glad all our days.
92: 4 for **j** at the work of your hands.
94:19 consolation brought **j** to my soul.
95: 1 Come, let us sing for **j** to the LORD;
96:12 trees of the forest will sing for **j**
97:11 and **j** on the upright in heart.
98: 4 Shout for **j** to the LORD, all the
98: 6 for **j** before the LORD, the King.
98: 8 the mountains sing together for **j**;
100: 1 Shout for **j** to the LORD, all the
105:43 his chosen ones with shouts of **j**;
106: 5 that I may share in the **j** of your
107:22 tell of his works with songs of **j**.
118:15 Shouts of **j** and victory resound in
119:111 they are the **j** of my heart.
126: 2 our tongues with songs of **j**.
126: 3 for us, and we are filled with **j**.
126: 5 in tears will reap with songs of **j**.
126: 6 will return with songs of **j**,
132: 9 may your saints sing for **j**."
132:16 her saints shall ever sing for **j**.
137: 3 our tormentors demanded songs of **j**;
137: 6 not consider Jerusalem my highest **j**
149: 5 honour and sing for **j** on their beds
Pr 10: 1 A wise son brings **j** to his father,
10:28 The prospect of the righteous is **j**,
11:10 perish, there are shouts of **j**.
12:20 but **j** for those who promote peace.
14:10 and no-one else can share its **j**.
14:13 may ache, and **j** may end in grief.
15:20 A wise son brings **j** to his father,
15:23 A man finds **j** in giving an apt reply
15:30 A cheerful look brings **j** to the
17:21 is no **j** for the father of a fool.
21:15 it brings **j** to the righteous but
23:24 of a righteous man has great **j**;
27: 9 Perfume and incense bring **j** to the
27:11 Be wise, my son, and bring **j** to my
29: 3 A man who loves wisdom brings **j** to
Ecc 8:15 Then **j** will accompany him in his
11: 9 you **j** in the days of your youth.
Isa 9: 3 the nation and increased their **j**;
12: 3 With **j** you will draw water from the
12: 6 Shout aloud and sing for **j**, people
16: 9 The shouts of **j** over your ripened
16:10 **J** and gladness are taken away from
22:13 see, there is **j** and revelry,
24:11 all **j** turns to gloom, all gaiety is
24:14 raise their voices, they shout for **j**
26:19 the dust, wake up and shout for **j**.
35: 2 rejoice greatly and shout for **j**.
35: 6 and the mute tongue shout for **j**.
35:10 **j** will crown their heads.
35:10 Gladness and **j** will overtake them,
42:11 Let the people of Sela sing for **j**;
44:23 Sing for **j**, O heavens, for the LORD
48:20 with shouts of **j** and proclaim it.
49:13 Shout for **j**, O heavens; rejoice,
51: 3 **J** and gladness will be found in her,
51:11 **j** will crown their heads.
51:11 Gladness and **j** will overtake them,
52: 8 voices; together they shout for **j**.
52: 9 Burst into songs of **j** together, you
54: 1 shout for **j**, you who were never in
55:12 You will go out in **j** and be led
56: 7 give them **j** in my house of prayer.
58:14 you will find your **j** in the LORD,
60: 5 heart will throb and swell with **j**;
60:15 pride and the **j** of all generations.
61: 7 and everlasting **j** will be theirs.
65:14 My servants will sing out of the **j**
65:18 to be a delight and its people a **j**.
66: 5 that we may see your **j**!'
Jer 7:34 bring an end to the sounds of **j**
15:16 were my **j** and my heart's delight,
16: 9 bring an end to the sounds of **j**
25:10 them the sounds of **j** and gladness,
31: 7 "Sing with **j** for Jacob; shout for
31:12 They will come and shout for **j** on
31:13 comfort and **j** instead of sorrow.
33: 9 this city will bring me renown, **j**,
33:11 the sounds of **j** and gladness, the
48:33 **J** and gladness are gone from the
48:33 no-one treads them with shouts of **j**.

Jer 48:33 shouts, they are not shouts of **j**.
51:48 them will shout for **j** over Babylon,
Lam 2:15 beauty, the **j** of the whole earth?"
5:15 **J** is gone from our hearts; our
Eze 7: 7 is panic, not **j**, upon the mountains.
24:25 their **j** and glory, the delight of
Joel 1:12 the **j** of mankind is withered away.
1:16 **j** and gladness from the house of
Mt 13:20 word and at once receives it with **j**.
13:44 he hid it again, and then in his **j**
28: 8 afraid yet filled with **j**, and ran
Mk 4:16 word and at once receive it with **j**.
Lk 1:14 He will be a **j** and delight to you,
1:44 the baby in my womb leaped for **j**.
1:58 great mercy, and they shared her **j**.
2:10 **j** that will be for all the people.
6:23 "Rejoice in that day and leap for **j**,
8:13 the word with **j** when they hear it,
10:17 The seventy-two returned with **j** and
10:21 At that time Jesus, full of **j**
24:41 it because of **j** and amazement,
24:52 returned to Jerusalem with great **j**.
Jn 3:29 and is full of **j** when he hears the
3:29 **j** is mine, and it is now complete.
15:11 my **j** may be in you and that your **j**
16:20 but your grief will turn to **j**.
16:21 her **j** that a child is born into the
16:22 and no-one will take away your **j**.
16:24 and your **j** will be complete.
17:13 full measure of my **j** within them.
Ac 2:28 fill me with **j** in your presence.'
8: 8 there was great **j** in that city.
13:52 the disciples were filled with **j** and
14:17 food and fills your hearts with **j**."
16:34 he was filled with **j** because he had
Ro 14:17 peace and **j** in the Holy Spirit,
15:13 all **j** and peace as you trust in him,
15:32 come to you with **j** and together with
16:19 so I am full of **j** over you; but I
2Co 1:24 but we work with you for your **j**,
2: 3 you, that you would all share my **j**.
7: 4 our troubles my **j** knows no bounds.
7: 7 so that my **j** was greater than ever.
8: 2 their overflowing **j** and their
Gal 4:15 What has happened to all your **j**?
5:22 the fruit of the Spirit is love, **j**,
Php 1: 4 for all of you, I always pray with **j**
1:25 your progress and **j** in the faith,
1:26 your **j** in Christ Jesus will overflow
2: 2 make my **j** complete by being
2:29 Welcome him in the Lord with great **j**
4: 1 love and long for, my **j** and crown,
1Th 1: 6 with the **j** given by the Holy Spirit.
2:19 For what is our hope, our **j**, or the
2:20 Indeed, you are our glory and **j**.
3: 9 in return for all the **j** we have in
2Ti 1: 4 you, so that I may be filled with **j**.
Phm : 7 Your love has given me great **j** and
Heb 1: 9 by anointing you with the oil of **j**."
12: 2 who for the **j** set before him endured
13:17 them so that their work will be a **j**,
Jas 1: 2 Consider it pure **j**, my brothers,
4: 9 to mourning and your **j** to gloom.
1Pe 1: 8 an inexpressible and glorious **j**,
1Jn 1: 4 We write this to make our **j** complete.
2Jn : 4 has given me great **j** to find some of
:12 so that our **j** may be complete.
3Jn : 3 gave me great **j** to have some
: 4 I have no greater **j** than to hear
Jude :24 without fault and with great **j**—

Joyful (Joy)

Dt 16:14 Be **j** at your Feast—you, your sons
1Sa 18: 6 with **j** songs and with tambourines
1Ki 8:66 **j** and glad in heart for all the good
1Ch 15:16 brothers as singers to sing **j** songs,
2Ch 7:10 **j** and glad in heart for the good
Ps 68: 3 before God; may they be happy and **j**.
100: 2 come before him with **j** songs.
Ecc 9: 7 and drink your wine with a **j** heart,
Isa 24: 8 has stopped, the **j** harp is silent.
Jer 31: 4 and go out to dance with the **j**.
Hab 3:18 LORD, I will be **j** in God my Saviour.
Zec 8:19 tenth months will become **j** and glad
10: 7 Their children will see it and be **j**;
Ro 12:12 Be **j** in hope, patient in affliction,
1Th 5:16 Be **j** always;
Heb 12:22 thousands of angels in **j** assembly,

Joyfully (Joy)

Dt 28:47 did not serve the LORD your God **j**
2Ch 20:27 Jerusalem returned **j** to Jerusalem,
30:23 seven days they celebrated **j**.
Ne 12:27 to celebrate **j** the dedication with
Job 39:13 "The wings of the ostrich flap **j**,
Ps 33: 1 Sing **j** to the LORD, you righteous;
145: 7 and **j** sing of your righteousness.
Lk 15: 5 he finds it, he **j** puts it on his
19:37 disciples began **j** to praise God in
Col 1:11 great endurance and patience, and **j**
Heb 10:34 **j** accepted the confiscation of your

Joyous (Joy)

Est 8:15 city of Susa held a **j** celebration.

Jozabad

2Ki 12:21 The officials who murdered him were **J**
1Ch 12: 4 Jahaziel, Johanan, **J** the Gederathite,
12:20 **J**, Jediael, Michael, **J**, Elihu and
2Ch 31:13 Nahath, Asahel, Jerimoth, **J**, Eliel,
35: 9 and Hashabiah, Jeiel and **J**, the
Ezr 8:33 were the Levites **J** son of Jeshua
10:22 Ishmael, Nethanel, **J** and Elasah.
10:23 Among the Levites: **J**, Shimei,
Ne 8: 7 Maaseiah, Kelita, Azariah, **J**, Hanan
11:16 Shabbethai and **J**, two of the heads

Jozadak

Ezr 3: 2 Jeshua son of **J** and his fellow
3: 8 Jeshua son of **J** and the rest of
5: 2 Jeshua son of **J** set to work to
10:18 the descendants of Jeshua son of **J**,
Ne 12:26 the son of **J**, and in the days of

Jubal

Ge 4:21 His brother's name was **J**; he was the

Jubilant

1Ch 16:32 fields be **j**, and everything in them!
Ps 94: 3 LORD, how long will the wicked be **j**?
96:12 let the fields be **j**, and everything
98: 4 earth, burst into **j** song with music;
Hos 9: 1 Do not rejoice, O Israel; do not be **j**

Jubilee

Lev 25:10 It shall be a **j** for you; each one of
25:11 The fiftieth year shall be a **j** for
25:12 For it is a **j** and is to be holy for
25:13 "'In this Year of **J** everyone is to
25:15 of the number of years since the **J**.
25:28 of the buyer until the Year of **J**.
25:28 It will be returned in the **J**, and he
25:30 It is not to be returned in the **J**.
25:31 they are to be returned in the **J**.
25:33 is to be returned in the **J**,
25:40 to work for you until the Year of **J**.
25:50 he sold himself up to the Year of **J**.
25:52 years remain until the Year of **J**,
25:54 are to be released in the Year of **J**,
27:17 his field during the Year of **J**,
27:18 if he dedicates his field after the **J**
27:18 until the next Year of **J**, and its
27:21 the field is released in the **J**, it
27:23 its value up to the Year of **J**,
27:24 In the Year of **J** the field will
Nu 36: 4 the Year of **J** for the Israelites

Judah (*House of Judah, Israel and Judah*, Judah's, Judea, Judean)

1. Son of Jacob by Leah (Ge 29:35; 35:23; 1Ch 2:1). Urged brothers to sell, not kill, Joseph (Ge 37:26–27). Father of Perez and Zerah, by daughter-in-law, Tamar (Ge 38). Offered himself in place of Benjamin (Ge 44:18–34). Blessed by Jacob as ruler (Ge 49:8–12).
2. Tribe descended from Judah. Blessed by Moses (Dt 33:7). Included in census (Nu 1:26–27; 26:19–22). Apportioned land (Jos 15; Eze 48:7); unable to take full possession (Jos 15:63; Jdg 1:1–20). Anointed David as king (2Sa 2:4); remained loyal to Davidic kings (1Ki 12:21; 2Ch 11:12). Tribe of Jesus (Mt 1:3; Heb 7:14).
3. Southern kingdom of Judah. Following the breakdown of relationships between the northern and southern tribes, Palestine was divided (about 931 BC) and Judah suffered 2 centuries of conflict with the northern kingdom of Israel (1Ki 12–2Ki 17). Judah survived because Israel fell to the Assyrians (2Ki 17:18). But Judah itself fell to the Babylonians about 134 years later (2Ki 25) and the people of Judah were exiled. Following the fall of Jerusalem (586 BC) Judah lost its kingdom status and became a small province of the Persian empire. By NT times this area was known as Judea, an annex of the Roman province of Syria, in which Jesus was born (Mt 2:1).

Ge 29:35 So she named him **J**. Then she
35:23 Levi, **J**, Issachar and Zebulun.
37:26 **J** said to his brothers, "What will
38: 1 At that time, **J** left his brothers
38: 2 There **J** met the daughter of a
38: 6 **J** got a wife for Er, his firstborn,
38: 8 **J** said to Onan, "Lie with your
38:11 **J** then said to his daughter-in-law
38:12 When **J** had recovered from his grief,
38:15 **J** saw her, he thought she was a
38:20 Meanwhile **J** sent the young goat by
38:22 went back to **J** and said, "I didn't
38:23 **J** said, "Let her keep what she has,
38:24 About three months later **J** was told,
38:24 **J** said, "Bring her out and have her
38:26 **J** recognised them and said, "She is
43: 3 **J** said to him, "The man warned us
43: 8 **J** said to Israel his father, "Send
44:14 when **J** and his brothers came in,
44:16 can we say to my lord?" **J** replied
44:18 **J** went up to him and said: "Please,
46:12 The sons of **J**: Er, Onan, Shelah,
46:28 Now Jacob sent **J** ahead of him to
49: 8 "**J**, your brothers will praise you;
49: 9 You are a lion's cub, O **J**; you
49:10 The sceptre will not depart from **J**,
Ex 1: 2 Reuben, Simeon, Levi and **J**;
31: 2 the son of Hur, of the tribe of **J**,
35:30 the son of Hur, of the tribe of **J**,
38:22 the son of Hur, of the tribe of **J**,
Nu 1: 7 from **J**, Nahshon son of Amminadab;
1:26 From the descendants of **J**: All the
1:27 The number from the tribe of **J** was 74
2: 3 camp of **J** are to encamp under their
2: 3 of **J** is Nahshon son of Amminadab.
2: 9 All the men assigned to the camp of **J**
7:12 son of Amminadab of the tribe of **J**.
10:14 The divisions of the camp of **J** went
13: 6 from the tribe of **J**, Caleb son of
26:19 Er and Onan were sons of **J**, but they
26:20 The descendants of **J** by their clans
26:22 These were the clans of **J**; those
34:19 of Jephunneh, from the tribe of **J**;
Dt 27:12 **J**, Issachar, Joseph and Benjamin.
33: 7 about **J**: "Hear, O LORD, the cry of **J**
34: 2 land of **J** as far as the western sea,
Jos 7: 1 the tribe of **J**, took some of them.
7:16 forward by tribes, and **J** was taken.
7:17 The clans of **J** came forward, and he
7:18 Zerah, of the tribe of **J**, was taken.
11:21 from all the hill country of **J**, and
14: 6 Now the men of **J** approached Joshua
15: 1 The allotment for the tribe of **J**,
15:12 the people of **J** by their clans.
15:13 in **J**—Kiriath Arba, that is, Hebron.
15:20 of the tribe of **J**, clan by clan:
15:21 towns of the tribe of **J** in the Negev
15:63 **J** could not dislodge the Jebusites,
15:63 live there with the people of **J**.
18: 5 **J** is to remain in its territory on
18:11 between the tribes of **J** and Joseph:
18:14 a town of the people of **J**.
19: 1 lay within the territory of **J**.
19: 9 was taken from the share of **J**,
19: 9 within the territory of **J**.
20: 7 Hebron) in the hill country of **J**.
21: 4 tribes of **J**, Simeon and Benjamin.
21: 9 From the tribes of **J** and Simeon they
21:11 in the hill country of **J**.
Jdg 1: 2 The LORD answered, "**J** is to go;

Jdg 1: 3 the men of J said to the Simeonites
1: 4 J attacked, the LORD gave the
1: 8 The men of J attacked Jerusalem also
1: 9 After that, the men of J went down
1:16 with the men of J to live among the
1:16 Desert of J in the Negev near Arad.
1:17 the men of J went with the
1:18 The men of J also took Gaza,
1:19 The LORD was with the men of J.
10: 9 the Jordan to fight against J,
15: 9 Philistines went up and camped in J
15:10 The men of J asked, "Why have you
15:11 three thousand men from J went down
17: 7 A young Levite from Bethlehem in J,
17: 7 been living within the clan of J,
17: 9 "I'm a Levite from Bethlehem in J,"
18:12 up camp near Kiriath Jearim in J.
19: 1 a concubine from Bethlehem in J.
19: 2 her father's house in Bethlehem, J.
19:18 on our way from Bethlehem in J to a
19:18 I have been to Bethlehem in J and
20:18 The LORD replied, "J shall go first.
Ru 1: 1 and a man from Bethlehem in J,
1: 2 were Ephrathites from Bethlehem, J.
1: 7 take them back to the land of J.
4:12 of Perez, whom Tamar bore to J."
1Sa 11: 8 and the men of J thirty thousand.
15: 4 and ten thousand men from J.
17: 1 for war and assembled at Socoh in J.
17:12 Jesse, who was from Bethlehem in J.
22: 5 Go into the land of J." So David
23: 3 David's men said to him, "Here in J
23:23 him down among all the clans of J."
27: 6 to the kings of J ever since.
27:10 "Against the Negev of J" or "Against
30:14 belonging to J and the Negev of Caleb
30:16 land of the Philistines and from J.
30:26 of the plunder to the elders of J,
2Sa 1:18 ordered that the men of J be taught
2: 1 to one of the towns of J?" he asked.
2: 4 the men of J came to Hebron and
5: 5 In Hebron he reigned over J for
6: 2 all his men set out from Baalah of J
19:11 "Ask the elders of J, 'Why should
19:14 of all the men of J as though they
19:15 Now the men of J had come to Gilgal
19:16 the men of J to meet King David.
19:40 All the troops of J and half the
19:41 "Why did our brothers, the men of J,
19:42 All the men of J answered the men of
19:43 men of Israel answered the men of J,
19:43 the men of J responded even more
20: 2 the men of J stayed by their king
20: 4 "Summon the men of J to come to me
20: 5 when Amasa went to summon J, he took
24: 7 on to Beersheba in the Negev of J.
24: 9 and in J five hundred thousand.
1Ki 1: 9 men of J who were royal officials,
4:20 The people of J and Israel were as
4:25 During Solomon's lifetime J and
12:17 were still living in the towns of J,
12:20 Only the tribe of J remained loyal
12:23 Rehoboam son of Solomon king of J,
12:27 to their lord, Rehoboam king of J.
12:32 like the festival held in J, and
13: 1 a man of God came from J to Bethel,
13:12 the man of God from J had taken.
13:14 came from J?" "I am," he replied.
13:21 the man of God who had come from J,
14:21 Rehoboam son of Solomon was king in J
14:22 J did evil in the eyes of the LORD.
14:29 of the annals of the kings of J?
15: 1 of Nebat, Abijah became king of J,
15: 7 of the annals of the kings of J?
15: 9 of Israel, Asa became king of J,
15:17 king of Israel went up against J
15:17 the territory of Asa king of J.
15:22 King Asa issued an order to all J
15:23 of the annals of the kings of J?
15:25 in the second year of Asa king of J,
15:28 king of J and succeeded him as king.
15:33 In the third year of Asa king of J,
16: 8 twenty-sixth year of Asa king of J,
16:10 year of Asa king of J.
16:15 year of Asa king of J,
16:23 thirty-first year of Asa king of J,
1Ki 16:29 thirty-eighth year of Asa king of J,
19: 3 Beersheba in J, he left his servant
22: 2 third year Jehoshaphat king of J
22:10 Jehoshaphat king of J were sitting
22:29 king of J went up to Ramoth Gilead.
22:41 son of Asa became king of J in the
22:45 of the annals of the kings of J?
22:51 year of Jehoshaphat king of J,
2Ki 1:17 Jehoram son of Jehoshaphat king of J.
3: 1 Jehoshaphat king of J, and he
3: 7 message to Jehoshaphat king of J:
3: 9 the king of J and the king of Edom.
3:14 presence of Jehoshaphat king of J,
8:16 when Jehoshaphat was king of J,
8:16 began his reign as king of J.
8:19 LORD was not willing to destroy J.
8:20 against J and set up its own king.
8:22 Edom has been in rebellion against J.
8:23 of the annals of the kings of J?
8:25 of Jehoram king of J began to reign.
8:29 Ahaziah son of Jehoram king of J
9:16 king of J had gone down to see him.
9:21 and Ahaziah king of J rode out,
9:27 Ahaziah king of J saw what had
9:29 Ahaziah had become king of J.)
10:13 king of J and asked, "Who are you?"
12:18 Joash king of J took all the sacred
12:18 Jehoram and Ahaziah, the kings of J
12:19 of the annals of the kings of J?
13: 1 of Joash son of Ahaziah king of J,
13:10 year of Joash king of J,
13:12 his war against Amaziah king of J,
14: 1 of Joash king of J began to reign.
14: 9 Israel replied to Amaziah king of J:
14:10 own downfall and that of J also?"
14:11 He and Amaziah king of J faced each
14:11 each other at Beth Shemesh in J.
14:12 J was routed by Israel, and every
14:13 Israel captured Amaziah king of J,
14:15 his war against Amaziah king of J,
14:17 Amaziah son of Joash king of J lived
14:18 of the annals of the kings of J?
14:21 all the people of J took Azariah,
14:22 restored it to J after Amaziah
14:23 of Amaziah son of Joash king of J,
15: 1 of Amaziah king of J began to reign.
15: 6 of the annals of the kings of J?
15: 8 year of Azariah king of J,
15:13 year of Uzziah king of J,
15:17 year of Azariah king of J,
15:23 fiftieth year of Azariah king of J,
15:27 year of Azariah king of J,
15:32 of Uzziah king of J began to reign.
15:36 of the annals of the kings of J?
15:37 Pekah son of Remaliah against J.)
16: 1 of Jotham king of J began to reign.
16: 6 Aram by driving out the men of J.
16:19 of the annals of the kings of J?
17: 1 In the twelfth year of Ahaz king of J
17:18 Only the tribe of J was left,
17:19 even J did not keep the commands of
18: 1 of Ahaz king of J began to reign.
18: 5 among all the kings of J, either
18:13 cities of J and captured them.
18:14 Hezekiah king of J sent this message
18:14 exacted from Hezekiah king of J
18:16 At this time Hezekiah king of J
18:22 saying to J and Jerusalem, "You must
19:10 "Say to Hezekiah king of J: Do not
20:20 of the annals of the kings of J?
21:11 "Manasseh king of J has committed
21:11 has led J into sin with his idols.
21:12 such disaster on Jerusalem and J
21:16 sin that he had caused J to commit,
21:17 of the annals of the kings of J?
21:25 of the annals of the kings of J?
22:13 for the people and for all J about
22:16 in the book the king of J has read.
22:18 Tell the king of J, who sent you to
23: 1 all the elders of J and Jerusalem.
23: 2 of the LORD with the men of J,
23: 5 appointed by the kings of J to burn
23: 5 the high places of the towns of J
23: 8 all the priests from the towns of J
23:11 kings of J had dedicated to the sun.
23:12 altars the kings of J had erected
2Ki 23:17 of the man of God who came from J
23:22 kings of Israel and the kings of J,
23:24 things seen in J and Jerusalem.
23:26 which burned against J because of
23:27 the LORD said, "I will remove J also
23:28 of the annals of the kings of J?
23:33 and he imposed on J a levy of a
24: 2 He sent them to destroy J, in
24: 3 Surely these things happened to J
24: 5 of the annals of the kings of J?
24:12 Jehoiachin king of J, his mother,
24:20 this happened to Jerusalem and J,
25:21 So J went into captivity, away from
25:22 the people he had left behind in J.
25:25 also the men of J and the
25:27 the exile of Jehoiachin king of J,
1Ch 2: 1 Simeon, Levi, J, Issachar, Zebulun,
2: 3 The sons of J: Er, Onan and Shelah.
2: 4 J had five sons in all.
2:10 the leader of the people of J.
4: 1 The descendants of J: Perez, Hezron,
4:21 The sons of Shelah son of J: Er the
4:27 as numerous as the people of J.
4:41 in the days of Hezekiah king of J.
5: 2 though J was the strongest of his
5:17 Jotham king of J and Jeroboam king
6:15 deported when the LORD sent J and
6:55 They were given Hebron in J with its
6:65 From the tribes of J, Simeon and
9: 1 The people of J were taken captive
9: 3 Those from J, from Benjamin, and
9: 4 Bani, a descendant of Perez son of J.
9: 6 The people from J numbered 690.
12:16 Other Benjamites and some men from J
12:24 men of J, carrying shield and spear—
13: 6 went to Baalah of J (Kiriath Jearim)
21: 5 hundred and seventy thousand in J.
27:18 over J: Elihu, a brother of David;
28: 4 He chose J as leader, and from the
2Ch 2: 7 to work in J and Jerusalem with my
9:11 like them had ever been seen in J.)
10:17 were still living in the towns of J,
11: 3 Rehoboam son of Solomon king of J
11: 3 the Israelites in J and Benjamin,
11: 5 and built up towns for defence in J:
11:10 fortified cities in J and Benjamin.
11:12 So J and Benjamin were his.
11:14 and came to J and Jerusalem because
11:17 They strengthened the kingdom of J
11:23 the districts of J and Benjamin,
12: 4 he captured the fortified cities of J
12: 5 to the leaders of J who had
12:12 Indeed, there was some good in J.
13: 1 Jeroboam, Abijah became king of J,
13:13 in front of J the ambush was behind
13:14 J turned and saw that they were
13:15 the men of J raised the battle cry.
13:15 and all Israel before Abijah and J.
13:16 The Israelites fled before J, and
13:18 and the men of J were victorious
14: 4 He commanded J to seek the LORD, the
14: 5 incense altars in every town in J,
14: 6 He built up the fortified cities of J
14: 7 build up these towns," he said to J,
14: 8 three hundred thousand men from J,
14:12 down the Cushites before Asa and J.
14:13 The men of J carried off a large
15: 2 to me, Asa and all J and Benjamin.
15: 8 idols from the whole land of J
15: 9 he assembled all J and Benjamin and
15:15 All J rejoiced about the oath
16: 1 king of Israel went up against J
16: 1 the territory of Asa king of J.
16: 6 King Asa brought all the men of J,
16: 7 to Asa king of J and said to him:
16:11 book of the kings of J and Israel.
17: 2 in all the fortified cities of J
17: 2 put garrisons in J and in the towns
17: 5 all J brought gifts to Jehoshaphat,
17: 6 places and the Asherah poles from J.
17: 7 Micaiah to teach in the towns of J.
17: 9 They taught throughout J, taking
17: 9 towns of J and taught the people.
17:10 kingdoms of the lands surrounding J,
17:12 he built forts and store cities in J
17:13 had large supplies in the towns of J.

2Ch 17:14 by families was as follows: From J,
17:19 the fortified cities throughout J.
18: 3 Israel asked Jehoshaphat king of J,
18: 9 Jehoshaphat king of J were sitting
18:28 king of J went up to Ramoth Gilead.
19: 1 Jehoshaphat king of J returned
19: 5 each of the fortified cities of J.
19:11 the leader of the tribe of J, will
20: 3 and he proclaimed a fast for all J.
20: 4 The people of J came together to
20: 4 from every town in J to seek him.
20: 5 stood up in the assembly of J
20:13 All the men of J, with their wives
20:15 and all who live in J and Jerusalem!
20:17 will give you, O J and Jerusalem.
20:18 and all the people of J and
20:20 "Listen to me, J and people of
20:22 invading J, and they were defeated.
20:24 the men of J came to the place that
20:27 all the men of J and Jerusalem
20:31 Jehoshaphat reigned over J. He was
20:31 years old when he became king of J,
20:35 Later, Jehoshaphat king of J made an
21: 3 as well as fortified cities in J,
21: 8 against J and set up its own king.
21:10 Edom has been in rebellion against J.
21:11 built high places on the hills of J
21:11 themselves and had led J astray.
21:12 Jehoshaphat or of Asa king of J.
21:13 and you have led J and the people of
21:17 They attacked J, invaded it and
22: 1 of Jehoram king of J began to reign.
22: 6 son of Jehoram king of J went down
22: 8 he found the princes of J and the
23: 2 They went throughout J and gathered
23: 8 The Levites and all the men of J did
24: 5 "Go to the towns of J and collect
24: 6 the Levites to bring in from J
24: 9 A proclamation was then issued in J
24:17 the officials of J came and paid
24:18 anger came upon J and Jerusalem.
24:23 it invaded J and Jerusalem and
24:24 Because J had forsaken the LORD, the
25: 5 Amaziah called the people of J
25: 5 of hundreds for all J and Benjamin.
25:10 furious with J and left for home in
25:12 The army of J also captured ten
25:17 Amaziah king of J consulted his
25:18 Israel replied to Amaziah king of J,
25:19 own downfall and that of J also?"
25:21 He and Amaziah king of J faced each
25:21 each other at Beth Shemesh in J.
25:22 J was routed by Israel, and every
25:23 Israel captured Amaziah king of J,
25:25 Amaziah son of Joash king of J lived
25:26 book of the kings of J and Israel?
25:28 with his fathers in the City of J.
26: 1 all the people of J took Uzziah, who
26: 2 restored it to J after Amaziah
28: 6 J—because J had forsaken the LORD,
28: 9 with J, he gave them into your hand.
28:10 men and women of J and Jerusalem
28:17 came and attacked J and carried away
28:18 the foothills and in the Negev of J.
28:19 The LORD had humbled J because of
28:19 for he had promoted wickedness in J
28:25 In every town in J he built high
28:26 book of the kings of J and Israel.
29: 8 LORD has fallen on J and Jerusalem;
29:21 for the sanctuary and for J.
30:12 Also in J the hand of God was on the
30:24 Hezekiah king of J provided a
30:25 The entire assembly of J rejoiced,
30:25 Israel and those who lived in J.
31: 1 there went out to the towns of J,
31: 1 the altars throughout J and Benjamin
31: 6 and J who lived in the towns of J
31:20 is what Hezekiah did throughout J,
32: 1 king of Assyria came and invaded J.
32: 8 what Hezekiah the king of J said.
32: 9 this message for Hezekiah king of J
32: 9 all the people of J who were there:
32:12 saying to J and Jerusalem, 'You must
32:23 gifts for Hezekiah king of J.
32:25 was on him and on J and Jerusalem.
32:32 book of the kings of J and Israel.
2Ch 32:33 All J and the people of Jerusalem
33: 9 Manasseh led J and the people of
33:14 in all the fortified cities in J.
33:16 and told J to serve the LORD, the
34: 3 purge J and Jerusalem of high places
34: 5 and so he purged J and Jerusalem.
34: 9 from all the people of J and
34:11 kings of J had allowed to fall into
34:24 in the presence of the king of J.
34:26 Tell the king of J, who sent you to
34:29 all the elders of J and Jerusalem.
34:30 of the LORD with the men of J,
35:18 the Levites and all J and Israel who
35:21 between you and me, O king of J?
35:24 all J and Jerusalem mourned for him.
36: 3 imposed on J a levy of a hundred
36: 4 a brother of Jehoahaz, king over J
36:10 Zedekiah, king over J and Jerusalem.
36:23 a temple for him at Jerusalem in J.
Ezr 1: 2 a temple for him at Jerusalem in J.
1: 3 and let him go up to Jerusalem in J
1: 5 the family heads of J and Benjamin,
1: 8 out to Sheshbazzar the prince of J.
2: 1 and J, each to his own town,
4: 1 the enemies of J and Benjamin heard
4: 4 out to discourage the people of J
4: 6 the people of J and Jerusalem.
5: 1 prophesied to the Jews in J and
5: 8 went to the district of J, to the
7:14 seven advisers to enquire about J
9: 9 of protection in J and Jerusalem.
10: 7 was then issued throughout J
10: 9 all the men of J and Benjamin had
10:23 Kelita), Pethahiah, J and Eliezer.
Ne 1: 2 one of my brothers, came from J with
2: 5 let him send me to the city in J
2: 7 me safe-conduct until I arrive in J?
4:10 Meanwhile, the people in J said,
4:16 behind all the people of J
5:14 be their governor in the land of J,
6: 7 'There is a king in J!' Now this
6:17 Also, in those days the nobles of J
6:18 For many in J were under oath to him,
7: 6 and J, each to his own town,
11: 3 servants lived in the towns of J,
11: 4 while other people from both J and
11: 4 of J: Athaiah son of Uzziah,
11: 9 and J son of Hassenuah was over the
11:20 in all the towns of J, each on his
11:24 the descendants of Zerah son of J,
11:25 some of the people of J lived in
11:36 Levites of J settled in Benjamin.
12: 8 Binnui, Kadmiel, Sherebiah, J, and
12:31 I had the leaders of J go up on top
12:32 Hoshaiah and half the leaders of J
12:34 J, Benjamin, Shemaiah, Jeremiah,
12:36 Milalai, Gilalai, Maai, Nethanel, J
12:44 for J was pleased with the
13:12 All J brought the tithes of grain,
13:15 In those days I saw men in J
13:16 on the Sabbath to the people of J.
13:17 I rebuked the nobles of J and said
13:23 in those days I saw men of J who had
13:24 know how to speak the language of J.
Est 2: 6 captive with Jehoiachin king of J.
Ps 48:11 villages of J are glad because of
60: 7 Ephraim is my helmet, J my sceptre.
63: T When he was in the Desert of J.
69:35 Zion and rebuild the cities of J.
76: 1 In J God is known; his name is great
78:68 he chose the tribe of J, Mount Zion,
97: 8 villages of J are glad because of
108: 8 Ephraim is my helmet, J my sceptre.
114: 2 J became God's sanctuary, Israel his
Pr 25: 1 by the men of Hezekiah king of J:
Isa 1: 1 The vision concerning J and
1: 1 Ahaz and Hezekiah, kings of J.
2: 1 Amoz saw concerning J and Jerusalem:
3: 1 take from Jerusalem and J both
3: 8 Jerusalem staggers, J is falling;
5: 3 J, judge between me and my vineyard.
5: 7 of J are the garden of his delight.
7: 1 the son of Uzziah, was king of J,
7: 6 "Let us invade J; let us tear it
7:17 since Ephraim broke away from J
8: 8 sweep on into J, swirling over it,
Isa 9:21 together they will turn against J.
11:12 assemble the scattered people of J
11:13 not be jealous of J, nor J hostile
19:17 the land of J will bring terror to
19:17 everyone to whom J is mentioned
22: 8 the defences of J are stripped away.
26: 1 song will be sung in the land of J:
36: 1 cities of J and captured them.
36: 7 saying to J and Jerusalem, "You must
37:10 "Say to Hezekiah king of J: Do not
38: 9 A writing of Hezekiah king of J
40: 9 say to the towns of J, "Here is
44:26 towns of J, 'They shall be built,'
48: 1 Israel and come from the line of J,
65: 9 and from J those who will possess my
Jer 1: 2 of Josiah son of Amon king of J,
1: 3 Jehoiakim son of Josiah king of J,
1: 3 of Zedekiah son of Josiah king of J,
1:15 and against all the towns of J.
1:18 whole land—against the kings of J,
2:28 as many gods as you have towns, O J.
3: 7 and her unfaithful sister J saw it.
3: 8 her unfaithful sister J had no fear;
3:10 her unfaithful sister J did not
3:11 is more righteous than unfaithful J.
4: 3 to the men of J and to Jerusalem:
4: 4 you men of J and people of Jerusalem,
4: 5 "Announce in J and proclaim in
4:16 a war cry against the cities of J.
5:20 house of Jacob and proclaim it in J:
7: 2 all you people of J who come through
7:17 in the towns of J and in the streets
7:30 people of J have done evil in my eyes
7:34 in the towns of J and the streets
8: 1 of the kings and officials of J,
9:11 I will lay waste the towns of J so
9:26 Egypt, J, Edom, Ammon, Moab and all
10:22 I will make the towns of J desolate,
11: 2 tell them to the people of J and to
11: 6 in the towns of J and in the streets
11: 9 a conspiracy among the people of J
11:12 The towns of J and the people of
11:13 as many gods as you have towns, O J
13: 9 I will ruin the pride of J and the
13:19 All J will be carried into exile,
14: 2 "J mourns, her cities languish;
14:19 Have you rejected J completely?
15: 4 Hezekiah king of J did in Jerusalem.
17:19 through which the kings of J go in
17:20 O kings of J and all people of J and
17:25 accompanied by the men of J and
17:26 People will come from the towns of J
18:11 "Now therefore say to the people of J
19: 3 O kings of J and people of Jerusalem.
19: 4 nor the kings of J ever knew,
19: 7 ruin the plans of J and Jerusalem.
19:13 J will be defiled like this place,
20: 4 I will hand all J over to the king
20: 5 all the treasures of the kings of J.
21: 7 I will hand over Zedekiah king of J,
22: 1 of the king of J and proclaim this
22: 2 O king of J, you who sit on David's
22: 6 about the palace of the king of J:
22:11 king of J but has gone from this
22:18 Jehoiakim son of Josiah king of J:
22:24 son of Jehoiakim king of J,
22:30 of David or rule any more in J."
23: 6 In his days J will be saved and
24: 1 king of J and the officials,
24: 1 the craftsmen and the artisans of J
24: 5 I regard as good the exiles from J,
24: 8 will I deal with Zedekiah king of J,
25: 1 concerning all the people of J
25: 1 Jehoiakim son of Josiah king of J,
25: 2 prophet said to all the people of J
25: 3 Amon king of J until this very day
25:18 Jerusalem and the towns of J, its
26: 1 king of J, this word came from the
26: 2 all the people of the towns of J who
26:10 the officials of J heard about these
26:18 in the days of Hezekiah king of J.
26:18 He told all the people of J, 'This
26:19 "Did Hezekiah king of J or anyone
26:19 anyone else in J put him to death?
27: 1 of Zedekiah son of Josiah king of J,
27: 3 to Jerusalem to Zedekiah king of J.

Jer 27:12 same message to Zedekiah king of J.
27:18 in the palace of the king of J and
27:20 son of Jehoiakim king of J into
27:20 all the nobles of J and Jerusalem—
27:21 of the king of J and in Jerusalem:
28: 1 in the reign of Zedekiah king of J,
28: 4 son of Jehoiakim king of J
28: 4 exiles from J who went to Babylon,
29: 2 and the leaders of J and Jerusalem,
29: 3 whom Zedekiah king of J sent to King
29:22 all the exiles from J who are in
31:23 the people in the land of J and in
31:24 People will live together in J and
32: 1 tenth year of Zedekiah king of J,
32: 2 the guard in the royal palace of J.
32: 3 Now Zedekiah king of J had
32: 4 Zedekiah king of J will not escape
32:32 the men of J and the people of
32:35 detestable thing and so make J sin.
32:44 in the towns of J and in the towns
33: 4 the royal palaces of J that have
33: 7 I will bring J and Israel back from
33:10 Yet in the towns of J and the
33:13 Jerusalem and in the towns of J,
33:16 In those days J will be saved and
34: 2 says: Go to Zedekiah king of J and
34: 4 of the LORD, O Zedekiah king of J.
34: 6 to Zedekiah king of J, in Jerusalem,
34: 7 the other cities of J that were
34: 7 the only fortified cities left in J.
34:19 The leaders of J and Jerusalem, the
34:21 "I will hand Zedekiah king of J and
34:22 I will lay waste the towns of J so
35: 1 Jehoiakim son of Josiah king of J:
35:13 says: Go and tell the men of J and
35:17 'Listen! I am going to bring on J
36: 1 Jehoiakim son of Josiah king of J,
36: 2 J and all the other nations from the
36: 3 Perhaps when the people of J hear
36: 6 people of J who come in from their
36: 9 Jehoiakim son of Josiah king of J,
36: 9 who had come from the towns of J.
36:28 which Jehoiakim king of J burned up.
36:29 Also tell Jehoiakim king of J, 'This
36:30 LORD says about Jehoiakim king of J:
36:31 the people of J every disaster I
36:32 king of J had burned in the fire.
37: 1 made king of J by Nebuchadnezzar
37: 7 says: Tell the king of J, who sent
38:22 left in the palace of the king of J
39: 1 ninth year of Zedekiah king of J,
39: 4 Zedekiah king of J and all the
39: 6 and also killed all the nobles of J.
39:10 in the land of J some of the poor
40: 1 J who were being carried into exile
40: 5 has appointed over the towns of J,
40:11 of Babylon had left a remnant in J
40:12 they all came back to the land of J,
40:15 and the remnant of J to perish?"
42:15 word of the LORD, O remnant of J.
42:19 "O remnant of J, the LORD has told
43: 4 command to stay in the land of J.
43: 5 led away all the remnant of J
43: 5 come back to live in the land of J
44: 2 Jerusalem and on all the towns of J.
44: 6 it raged against the towns of J and
44: 7 off from J the men and women,
44: 9 by the kings and queens of J and the
44: 9 in the land of J and the streets of
44:11 on you and to destroy all J.
44:12 I will take away the remnant of J
44:14 None of the remnant of J who have
44:14 survive to return to the land of J,
44:17 in the towns of J and in the streets
44:21 incense burned in the towns of J
44:24 LORD, all you people of J in Egypt.
44:26 'that no-one from J living anywhere
44:28 return to the land of J from Egypt
44:28 Then the whole remnant of J who came
44:30 just as I handed Zedekiah king of J
45: 1 Jehoiakim son of Josiah king of J,
46: 2 Jehoiakim son of Josiah king of J:
49:34 in the reign of Zedekiah king of J:
50: 4 the people of J together will go in
50:20 and for the sins of J, but none will
50:33 and the people of J as well.

Jer 51:59 with Zedekiah king of J in the
52: 3 this happened to Jerusalem and J,
52:10 also killed all the officials of J.
52:27 So J went into captivity, away from
52:31 the exile of Jehoiachin king of J,
52:31 he released Jehoiachin king of J and
Lam 1: 3 harsh labour, J has gone into exile
1:15 trampled the Virgin Daughter of J.
2: 2 strongholds of the Daughter of J.
2: 5 lamentation for the Daughter of J.
5:11 Zion, and virgins in the towns of J.
Eze 8: 1 elders of J were sitting before me,
21:10 rejoice in the sceptre of my son J?
21:13 And what if the sceptre of J, which
21:20 against J and fortified Jerusalem.
25: 3 over the people of J when they went
25:15 hostility sought to destroy J,
27:17 "'J and Israel traded with you;
37:16 'Belonging to J and the Israelites
48: 7 "J will have one portion; it will
48: 8 "Bordering the territory of J from
48:22 between the border of J and the
48:31 the gate of J and the gate of Levi.
Da 1: 1 of the reign of Jehoiakim king of J,
1: 2 Jehoiakim king of J into his hand,
1: 6 Among these were some from J: Daniel,
2:25 found a man among the exiles from J
5:13 my father the king brought from J?
6:13 who is one of the exiles from J,
9: 7 shame—the men of J and people of
Hos 1: 1 Ahaz and Hezekiah, kings of J, and
1:11 The people of J and the people of
4:15 O Israel, let not J become guilty.
5: 5 J also stumbles with them.
5:12 Ephraim, like rot to the people of J
5:13 saw his sickness, and J his sores,
5:14 to Ephraim, like a great lion to J.
6: 4 Ephraim? What can I do with you, J?
6:11 "Also for you, J, a harvest is
8:14 J has fortified many towns. But I
10:11 I will drive Ephraim, J must plough,
11:12 And J is unruly against God, even
12: 2 LORD has a charge to bring against J;
Joel 3: 1 the fortunes of J and Jerusalem,
3: 6 You sold the people of J and
3: 8 and daughters to the people of J,
3:18 ravines of J will run with water.
3:19 of violence done to the people of J,
3:20 J will be inhabited for ever and
Am 1: 1 when Uzziah was king of J and
2: 4 "For three sins of J, even for four,
2: 5 I will send fire upon J that will
7:12 you seer! Go back to the land of J.
Ob :12 nor rejoice over the people of J in
Mic 1: 1 Ahaz and Hezekiah, kings of J—the
1: 9 is incurable; it has come to J.
5: 2 you are small among the clans of J,
Na 1:12 Although I have afflicted you, ⌊O J
1:15 Celebrate your festivals, O J, and
Zep 1: 1 of Josiah son of Amon king of J:
1: 4 I will stretch out my hand against J
Hag 1: 1 governor of J, and to Joshua son of
1:14 governor of J, and the spirit of
2: 2 governor of J, to Joshua son of
2:21 "Tell Zerubbabel governor of J that
Zec 1:12 Jerusalem and from the towns of J,
1:19 scattered J, Israel and Jerusalem."
1:21 These are the horns that scattered J
1:21 against the land of J to scatter
2:12 The LORD will inherit J as his
8:13 O J and Israel, so will I save you,
8:15 to do good again to Jerusalem and J.
8:19 occasions and happy festivals for J.
9: 7 to our God and become leaders in J,
9:13 I will bend J as I bend my bow and
10: 4 From J will come the cornerstone,
11:14 brotherhood between J and Israel.
12: 2 J will be besieged as well as
12: 5 the leaders of J will say in their
12: 6 the leaders of J like a brazier in
12: 7 will save the dwellings of J first,
12: 7 may not be greater than that of J.
14: 5 in the days of Uzziah king of J.
14:14 J too will fight at Jerusalem. The
14:21 Every pot in Jerusalem and J will be
Mal 2:11 J has broken faith. A detestable

Mal 2:11 J has desecrated the sanctuary the
3: 4 the offerings of J and Jerusalem
Mt 1: 2 the father of J and his brothers,
1: 3 J the father of Perez and Zerah,
2: 6 Bethlehem, in the land of J, are by
2: 6 means least among the rulers of J;
Lk 3:30 the son of Simeon, the son of J, the
3:33 the son of Perez, the son of J,
Heb 7:14 that our Lord descended from J,
Rev 5: 5 Lion of the tribe of J, the Root of
7: 5 From the tribe of J 12,000 were

Judah's (Judah)

Ge 38: 7 Er, J firstborn, was wicked in the
38:12 After a long time J wife, the
Jos 19: 9 J portion was more than they needed.
2Sa 3: 8 "Am I a dog's head—on J side? This
1Ki 2:32 commander of J army—were better men
1Ch 2: 3 Er, J firstborn, was wicked in the
2: 4 Tamar, J daughter-in-law, bore him
Ps 68:27 there the great throng of J princes,
Isa 11:13 and J enemies will be cut off;
Jer 17: 1 "J sin is engraved with an iron tool,
Eze 37:19 and join it to J stick, making them
Hos 5:10 J leaders are like those who move
Mic 1: 5 J high place? Is it not Jerusalem?

Judaism (Jew)

Ac 2:11 (both Jews and converts to J);
6: 5 Nicolas from Antioch, a convert to J.
13:43 devout converts to J followed Paul
Gal 1:13 of my previous way of life in J,
1:14 I was advancing in J beyond many

Judas

1. Brother of Jesus (Mt 13:55; Mk 6:3); also called Jude, author of letter (Jude 1). **2.** Apostle; son of James (Lk 6:16; Jn 14:22; Ac 1:13); also known as Thaddaeus (Mt 10:3; Mk 3:18). **3.** Apostle; also called Iscariot; known as Jesus' betrayer (Mt 10:4; Mk 3:19; Lk 6:16; Jn 6:71; 12:4); treasurer for disciples (Jn 12:6; 13:29). Agreed to betray Jesus for 30 silver pieces (Mt 26:14–16; Mk 14:10–11; Lk 22:3–6); kissed Jesus to identify him (Mt 26:47–49; Mk 14:43–45; Lk 22:47–48); filled with remorse; committed suicide (Mt 27:3–5; Ac 1:16–25). **4.** Prophet; also called Barsabbas. Sent, with Silas, by apostles in Jerusalem to Antioch with decision about circumcision (Ac 15:22–34).

Mt 10: 4 Simon the Zealot and J Iscariot, who
13:55 brothers James, Joseph, Simon and J?
26:14 one of the Twelve—the one called J
26:16 From then on J watched for an
26:25 J, the one who would betray him,
26:47 J, one of the Twelve arrived.
26:49 J said, "Greetings, Rabbi!" and
27: 3 J, who had betrayed him, saw that
27: 5 J threw the money into the temple
Mk 3:19 J Iscariot, who betrayed him.
6: 3 of James, Joseph, J and Simon?
14:10 J Iscariot, one of the Twelve, went
14:43 J, one of the Twelve, appeared.
14:45 at once to Jesus, J said, "Rabbi!"
Lk 6:16 J son of James, and J Iscariot, who
22: 3 Satan entered J, called Iscariot,
22: 4 J went to the chief priests and the
22:47 and the man who was called J, one of
22:48 Jesus asked him, "J, are you
Jn 6:71 (He meant J, the son of Simon
12: 4 one of his disciples, J Iscariot,
13: 2 had already prompted J Iscariot,
13:26 gave it to J Iscariot, son of Simon.
13:27 soon as J took the bread, Satan
13:29 Since J had charge of the money,
13:30 soon as J had taken the bread, he
14:22 J (not J Iscariot) said, "But, Lord,
18: 2 Now J, who betrayed him, knew the
18: 3 J came to the grove, guiding a
18: 5 J the traitor was standing there
Ac 1:13 Simon the Zealot, and J son of James.
1:16 the mouth of David concerning J,
1:18 J bought a field; there he fell
1:25 J left to go where he belongs."
5:37 After him, J the Galilean appeared

Ac 9:11 the house of J on Straight Street
15:22 They chose J (called Barsabbas) and
15:27 Therefore we are sending J and Silas
15:32 J and Silas, who themselves were

Jude See **Judas 1.**
Jude :1 J, a servant of Jesus Christ and

Judea See **Judah 3.**
Mt 2:1 Jesus was born in Bethlehem in J,
2:5 "In Bethlehem in J," they replied,
2:22 reigning in J in place of his father
3:1 came, preaching in the Desert of J
3:5 J and the whole region of the Jordan.
4:25 the Decapolis, Jerusalem, J and the
19:1 J to the other side of the Jordan.
24:16 let those who are in J flee to the
Mk 3:8 many people came to him from J,
10:1 region of J and across the Jordan.
13:14 who are in J flee to the mountains.
Lk 1:5 In the time of Herod king of J there
1:39 to a town in the hill country of J,
1:65 throughout the hill country of J
2:4 town of Nazareth in Galilee to J,
3:1 Pontius Pilate was governor of J,
4:44 preaching in the synagogues of J.
5:17 J and Jerusalem, were sitting there.
6:17 number of people from all over J,
7:17 J and the surrounding country.
21:21 let those who are in J flee to the
23:5 people all over J by his teaching.
Jn 4:3 the Lord learned of this, he left J
4:47 Jesus had arrived in Galilee from J,
4:54 having come from J to Galilee.
7:1 purposely staying away from J
7:3 "You ought to leave here and go to J,
11:7 his disciples, "Let us go back to J.
Ac 1:8 and in all J and Samaria, and to the
2:9 J and Cappadocia, Pontus and Asia,
8:1 scattered throughout J and Samaria.
9:31 the church throughout J, Galilee and
10:37 know what has happened throughout J,
11:1 the brothers throughout J heard that
11:29 help for the brothers living in J.
12:19 Then Herod went from J to Caesarea
15:1 Some men came down from J to Antioch
21:10 named Agabus came down from J.
26:20 to those in Jerusalem and in all J,
28:21 any letters from J concerning you,
Ro 15:31 rescued from the unbelievers in J
2Co 1:16 to have you send me on my way to J.
Gal 1:22 churches of J that are in Christ.
1Th 2:14 imitators of God's churches in J,

Judean (Judah)
1Ch 4:18 (His J wife gave birth to Jered the
2Ch 25:13 J towns from Samaria to Beth Horon.
27:4 He built towns in the J hills and
Mk 1:5 The whole J countryside and all the
Lk 23:51 He came from the J town of Arimathea
Jn 3:22 went out into the J countryside,

Judge (Judge's, Judged, Judges, Judging, Judgment, Judgments)
Ge 16:5 May the LORD j between you and me."
18:25 the J of all the earth do right?"
19:9 now he wants to play the j!
31:37 let them j between the two of us.
31:53 God of their father, j between us.
Ex 2:14 "Who made you ruler and j over us?
5:21 the LORD look upon you and j you!
18:13 seat to serve as j for the people,
18:14 Why do you alone sit as j, while
Lev 19:15 great, but j your neighbour fairly.
27:12 who will j its quality as good or
27:14 will j its quality as good or bad.
Nu 35:24 the assembly must j between him and
Dt 1:16 between your brothers and j fairly,
16:18 and they shall j the people fairly.
17:8 are too difficult for you to j
17:9 the j who is in office at that time.
17:12 The man who shows contempt for the j
25:2 the j shall make him lie down and
32:36 The LORD will j his people and have
Jdg 2:18 a j for them, he was with the j and
2:18 enemies as long as the j lived;
2:19 when the j died, the people returned
3:10 became Israel's j and went to war.
11:27 Let the LORD, the J, decide the
1Sa 2:10 LORD will j the ends of the earth.
3:13 For I told him that I would j his
7:15 Samuel continued as j over Israel
24:12 May the LORD j between you and me.
24:15 May the LORD be our j and decide
2Sa 15:4 "If only I were appointed j in the
1Ki 7:7 where he was to j, and he covered it
8:32 hear from heaven and act. J between
1Ch 12:17 God of our fathers see it and j you."
16:33 LORD, for he comes to j the earth.
2Ch 6:23 J between your servants, condemning
19:7 J carefully, for with the LORD our
20:12 O our God, will you not j them?
Job 9:15 only plead with my J for mercy.
22:13 Does he j through such darkness?
23:7 be delivered for ever from my j.
Ps 7:8 let the LORD j the peoples. J me,
7:11 God is a righteous j, a God who
9:8 He will j the world in righteousness;
50:4 the earth, that he may j his people:
50:6 righteousness, for God himself is j.
51:4 you speak and justified when you j.
58:1 Do you j uprightly among men?
72:2 will j your people in righteousness
75:2 it is I who j uprightly.
76:9 you, O God, rose up to j, to save
82:8 Rise up, O God, j the earth, for all
94:2 Rise up, O J of the earth; pay back
96:10 he will j the peoples with equity.
96:13 he comes, he comes to j the earth.
96:13 He will j the world in righteousness
98:9 LORD, for he comes to j the earth.
98:9 He will j the world in righteousness
110:6 He will j nations, heaping up the
Pr 20:8 a king sits on his throne to j, he
31:9 Speak up and j fairly; defend the
Isa 2:4 He will j between the nations and
3:2 the hero and warrior, the j and
3:13 in court; he rises to j the people.
5:3 men of Judah, j between me and my
11:3 He will not j by what he sees with
11:4 with righteousness he will j the
33:22 For the LORD is our j, the LORD is
Jer 11:20 LORD Almighty, you who j righteously
Eze 7:3 I will j you according to your
7:8 I will j you according to your
7:27 their own standards I will j them.
18:30 O house of Israel, I will j you,
20:4 "Will you j them? Will you j them,
20:36 so I will j you, declares the
21:30 land of your ancestry, I will j you.
22:2 will you j her? Will you j this city
23:36 "Son of man, will you j Oholah and
33:20 But I will j each of you according
34:17 j between one sheep and another,
34:20 I myself will j between the fat
34:22 j between one sheep and another.
35:11 known among them when I j you.
Joel 3:12 to j all the nations on every side.
Mic 3:11 Her leaders j for a bribe, her
4:3 He will j between many peoples and
7:3 the j accepts bribes, the powerful
Mt 5:25 or he may hand you over to the j,
5:25 and the j may hand you over to the
7:1 "Do not j, or you too will be judged.
7:2 For in the same way as you j others,
Lk 6:37 "Do not j, and you will not be
12:14 me a j or an arbiter between you?"
12:57 "Why don't you j for yourselves what
12:58 or he may drag you off to the j, and
12:58 and the j turn you over to the
18:2 "In a certain town there was a j who
18:6 "Listen to what the unjust j says.
19:22 "His master replied, 'I will j you
Jn 5:27 he has given him authority to j
5:30 I j only as I hear, and my judgment
8:15 You j by human standards; I pass
8:16 if I do j, my decisions are right,
8:50 one who seeks it, and he is the j.
12:47 does not keep them, I do not j him.
12:47 come to j the world, but to save it.
Jn 12:48 There is a j for the one who rejects
18:31 and j him by your own law.
Ac 4:19 Peter and John replied, "J for
7:27 'Who made you ruler and j over us?
7:35 'Who made you ruler and j?' He was
10:42 as j of the living and the dead.
17:31 For he has set a day when he will j
18:15 I will not be a j of such things."
23:3 there to j me according to the law,
24:10 you have been a j over this nation;
Ro 2:1 at whatever point you j the other
2:16 j men's secrets through Jesus Christ,
3:4 you speak and prevail when you j."
3:6 were so, how could God j the world?
14:4 Who are you to j someone else's
14:10 You, then, why do you j your brother?
1Co 4:3 indeed, I do not even j myself.
4:5 Therefore j nothing before the
5:12 What business is it of mine to j
5:12 Are you not to j those inside?
5:13 God will j those outside. "Expel the
6:2 that the saints will j the world?
6:2 And if you are to j the world,
6:2 not competent to j trivial cases?
6:3 Do you not know that we will j
6:5 to j a dispute between believers?
10:15 j for yourselves what I say.
11:13 J for yourselves: Is it proper for a
Gal 2:6 God does not j by external
Col 2:16 Therefore do not let anyone j you by
2Ti 4:1 who will j the living and the dead,
4:8 which the Lord, the righteous J,
Heb 10:30 again, "The Lord will j his people.
12:23 You have come to God, the j of all
13:4 for God will j the adulterer and all
Jas 4:11 When you j the law, you are not
4:12 There is only one Lawgiver and J,
4:12 are you to j your neighbour?
5:9 The J is standing at the door!
1Pe 4:5 ready to j the living and the dead.
Jude :15 to j everyone, and to convict all
Rev 6:10 holy and true, until you j the
20:4 who had been given authority to j.

Judge's (Judge)
Mt 27:19 Pilate was sitting on the j seat,
Jn 19:13 sat down on the j seat at a place

Judged (Judge)
1Sa 7:17 was, and there he also j Israel.
Job 31:11 have been shameful, a sin to be j.
31:28 these also would be sins to be j,
Ps 9:19 the nations be j in your presence.
Eze 20:36 I j your fathers in the desert of
24:14 You will be j according to your
36:19 I j them according to their conduct
Mt 7:1 "Do not judge, or you too will be j.
7:2 you will be j, and with the measure
Lk 6:37 "Do not judge, and you will not be j.
7:43 "You have j correctly," Jesus said.
Ro 2:12 under the law will be j by the law.
1Co 4:3 I care very little if I am j by you
10:29 be j by another's conscience?
11:31 if we j ourselves, we would not come
11:32 we are j by the Lord, we are being
14:24 he is a sinner and will be j by all,
Jas 2:12 be j by the law that gives freedom,
3:1 who teach will be j more strictly.
5:9 brothers, or you will be j. The Judge
1Pe 4:6 so that they might be j according to
Rev 16:5 the Holy One, because you have so j;
18:20 j her for the way she treated you.
20:12 The dead were j according to what
20:13 was j according to what he had done.

Judges (Judge)
Ex 18:22 Have them serve as j for the people
18:26 They served as j for the people at
21:6 his master must take him before the j
22:8 appear before the j to determine
22:9 to bring their cases before the j.
22:9 The one whom the j declare guilty
Nu 25:5 Moses said to Israel's j, "Each of
Dt 1:16 I charged your j at that time: Hear
16:18 Appoint j and officials for each of

Dt 19:17 the j who are in office at the time.
19:18 The j must make a thorough
21: 2 your elders and j shall go out and
25: 1 and the j will decide the case,
Jos 8:33 with their elders, officials and j,
23: 2 leaders, j and officials—and said
24: 1 He summoned the elders, leaders, j
Jdg 2:16 the LORD raised up j, who saved them
2:17 Yet they would not listen to their j
Ru 1: 1 In the days when the j ruled, there
1Sa 8: 1 appointed his sons as j for Israel.
2Ki 23:22 Not since the days of the j who led
1Ch 23: 4 thousand are to be officials and j.
26:29 as officials and j over Israel.
2Ch 1: 2 to the j and to all the leaders in
19: 5 He appointed j in the land, in each
Ezr 4: 9 the rest of their associates—the j
7:25 appoint magistrates and j to
10:14 along with the elders and j of each
Job 9:24 of the wicked, he blindfolds its j.
12:17 away stripped and makes fools of j.
21:22 to God, since he j even the highest?
Ps 58:11 there is a God who j the earth."
75: 7 But it is God who j: He brings one
Pr 29:14 If a king j the poor with fairness,
Isa 1:26 I will restore your j as in days of
Eze 18: 8 and j fairly between man and man.
44:24 the priests are to serve as j and
Da 3: 2 governors, advisers, treasurers, j,
3: 3 governors, advisers, treasurers, j,
Mt 12:27 So then, they will be your j.
Lk 11:19 So then, they will be your j.
Jn 5:22 Moreover, the Father j no-one, but
Ac 13:20 "After this, God gave them j until
1Co 4: 4 It is the Lord who j me.
6: 4 appoint as j even men of little
Heb 4:12 it j the thoughts and attitudes of
Jas 2: 4 and become j with evil thoughts?
4:11 j him speaks against the law and j it
1Pe 1:17 a Father who j each man's work
2:23 himself to him who j justly.
Rev 18: 8 mighty is the Lord God who j her.
19:11 With justice he j and makes war.

Judging (Judge)

Dt 1:17 Do not show partiality in j; hear
1Sa 7:16 Mizpah, j Israel in all those places.
2Ch 19: 6 because you are not j for man but
Ps 9: 4 sat on your throne, j righteously.
Pr 24:23 To show partiality in j is not good:
Isa 16: 5 one who in j seeks justice and
Mt 19:28 j the twelve tribes of Israel.
Lk 22:30 j the twelve tribes of Israel.
Jn 7:24 Stop j by mere appearances, and make
Rev 11:18 The time has come for j the dead,

Judgment (*Day of Judgment*, Judge)

Ex 6: 6 arm and with mighty acts of j.
7: 4 with mighty acts of j I will bring
12:12 bring j on all the gods of Egypt.
Lev 13:37 in his j it is unchanged and
Nu 33: 4 LORD had brought j on their gods.
Dt 1:17 of any man, for j belongs to God.
32:41 sword and my hand grasps it in j,
1Sa 25:33 May you be blessed for your good j
2Ch 20: 9 whether the sword of j, or plague or
22: 8 While Jehu was executing j on the
24:24 fathers, j was executed on Joash.
Job 14: 3 Will you bring him before you for j?
19:29 then you will know that there is j."
24: 1 the Almighty not set times for j?
34:23 they should come before him for j.
36:17 j due to the wicked; j and justice
Ps 1: 5 the wicked will not stand in the j,
9: 7 he has established his throne for j.
76: 8 From heaven you pronounced j, and
82: 1 he gives j among the "gods":
94:15 J will again be founded on
119:66 Teach me knowledge and good j, for I
122: 5 There the thrones for j stand, the
143: 2 Do not bring your servant into j,
Pr 3:21 My son, preserve sound j and
6:32 a man who commits adultery lacks j;
7: 7 the young men, a youth who lacked j.
8:14 Counsel and sound j are mine; I have
Pr 9: 4 here!" she says to those who lack j.
9:16 here!" she says to those who lack j.
10:13 is for the back of him who lacks j.
10:21 many, but fools die for lack of j.
11:12 A man who lacks j derides his
12:11 but he who chases fantasies lacks j.
15:21 Folly delights a man who lacks j,
17:18 A man lacking in j strikes hands in
18: 1 selfish ends; he defies all sound j.
24:30 the vineyard of the man who lacks j;
28:16 A tyrannical ruler lacks j, but he
Ecc 3:16 in the place of j—wickedness was
3:17 "God will bring to j both the
11: 9 things God will bring you to j.
12:14 For God will bring every deed into j,
Isa 3:14 The LORD enters into j against the
4: 4 a spirit of j and a spirit of fire.
28: 6 of justice to him who sits in j,
34: 5 it descends in j on Edom, the people
41: 1 us meet together at the place of j.
53: 8 By oppression and j he was taken
66:16 LORD will execute j upon all men,
Jer 2:35 But I will pass j on you because
10:15 their j comes, they will perish.
25:31 he will bring j on all mankind and
48:21 J has come to the plateau—to Holon,
48:47 Here ends the j on Moab.
51: 9 for her j reaches to the skies, it
51:18 their j comes, they will perish.
Eze 11:10 j on you at the borders of Israel.
11:11 j on you at the borders of Israel.
17:20 execute j upon him there because he
20:35 to face, I will execute j upon you.
38:22 I will execute j upon him with
Da 7:22 pronounced j in favour of the saints
Hos 5: 1 O royal house! This j is against you:
5:11 Ephraim is oppressed, trampled in j,
Joel 3: 2 I will enter into j against them
Am 7: 4 LORD was calling for j by fire;
Hab 1:12 you have appointed them to execute j
Zec 8:16 true and sound j in your courts;
Mal 3: 5 "So I will come near to you for j. I
Mt 5:21 who murders will be subject to j.'
5:22 his brother will be subject to j.
12:41 up at the j with this generation
12:42 rise at the j with this generation
Lk 10:14 Tyre and Sidon at the j than for you.
11:31 j with the men of this generation
11:32 up at the j with this generation
Jn 5:22 but has entrusted all j to the Son,
5:30 and my j is just, for I seek not to
7:24 appearances, and make a right j."
8:15 human standards; I pass j on no-one.
8:26 "I have much to say in j of you. But
9:39 Jesus said, "For j I have come into
12:31 Now is the time for j on this world;
16: 8 to sin and righteousness and j:
16:11 in regard to j, because the prince
Ac 15:19 "It is my j, therefore, that we
24:25 self-control and the j to come,
Ro 2: 1 you who pass j on someone else,
2: 1 you who pass j do the same things.
2: 2 Now we know that God's j against
2: 3 when you, a mere man, pass j on them
2: 3 you think you will escape God's j?
2: 5 his righteous j will be revealed.
5:16 The j followed one sin and brought
12: 3 think of yourself with sober j,
13: 2 do so will bring j on themselves.
14: 1 passing j on disputable matters.
14:10 will all stand before God's j seat.
14:13 Therefore let us stop passing j on
1Co 2:15 is not subject to any man's j:
5: 3 And I have already passed j on the
6: 1 for j instead of before the saints?
7:25 but I give a j as one who by the
7:40 In my j, she is happier if she stays
9: 3 defence to those who sit in j on me.
11:29 Lord eats and drinks j on himself.
11:31 we would not come under j.
11:34 together it may not result in j.
2Co 5:10 For we must all appear before the j
2Th 1: 5 is evidence that God's j is right,
1Ti 3: 6 fall under the same j as the devil.
5:12 Thus they bring j on themselves,
5:24 reaching the place of j ahead of
Heb 6: 2 of the dead, and eternal j.
9:27 die once, and after that to face j,
10:27 only a fearful expectation of j and
Jas 2:13 j without mercy will be shown to
2:13 Mercy triumphs over j!
4:11 keeping it, but sitting in j on it.
1Pe 4:17 For it is time for j to begin with
2Pe 2: 4 gloomy dungeons to be held for j;
Jude : 6 chains for j on the great Day.
Rev 14: 7 because the hour of his j has come.

Judgments (Judge)

Dt 33:21 will, and his j concerning Israel."
1Ch 16:12 miracles, and the j he pronounced,
16:14 God; his j are in all the earth.
Ps 48:11 of Judah are glad because of your j.
97: 8 are glad because of your j, O LORD.
105: 5 miracles, and the j he pronounced,
105: 7 God; his j are in all the earth.
Isa 26: 9 When your j come upon the earth, the
Jer 1:16 I will pronounce my j on my people
4:12 Now I pronounce my j against them."
Eze 14:21 Jerusalem my four dreadful j—sword
Da 9:11 sworn j written in the Law of Moses
Hos 6: 5 j flashed like lightning upon you.
Ro 11:33 How unsearchable his j, and his
1Co 2:15 The spiritual man makes j about all
Rev 16: 5 "You are just in these j, you who
16: 7 Almighty, true and just are your j."
19: 2 for true and just are his j. He has

Judith

Ge 26:34 he married J daughter of Beeri the

Jug (Jugs)

1Sa 26:11 Now get the spear and water j that
26:12 David took the spear and water j
26:16 water j that were near his head?"
1Ki 17:12 in a jar and a little oil in a j.
17:14 the j of oil will not run dry until
17:16 up and the j of oil did not run dry,

Jugs (Jug)

Jer 48:12 will empty her jars and smash her j.

Juice

Nu 6: 3 He must not drink grape j or eat
18:27 or j from the winepress.
Isa 65: 8 "As when j is still found in a

Julia

Ro 16:15 Greet Philologus, J, Nereus and his

Julius

Ac 27: 1 handed over to a centurion named J,
27: 3 next day we landed at Sidon; and J,

Jump (Jumped, Jumping)

Ac 27:43 j overboard first and get to land.

Jumped (Jump)

Mk 10:50 he j to his feet and came to Jesus
Jn 21: 7 taken it off) and j into the water.
Ac 3: 8 He j to his feet and began to walk.
14:10 the man j up and began to walk.
19:16 who had the evil spirit j on them

Jumping (Jump)

Ac 3: 8 walking and j, and praising God.

Junction (Join)

Eze 21:21 at the j of the two roads, to seek

Junias

Ro 16: 7 Greet Andronicus and J, my relatives

Jurisdiction

Lk 23: 7 that Jesus was under Herod's j,

Jushab-Hesed

1Ch 3:20 Ohel, Berekiah, Hasadiah and J.

Just (Justice, Justification, Justified, Justifies, Justify, Justifying, Justly)

Dt 32: 4 are perfect, and all his ways are **j**.
32: 4 does no wrong, upright and **j** is he.
2Sa 8:15 was **j** and right for all his people.
1Ch 18:14 was **j** and right for all his people.
2Ch 12: 6 themselves and said, "The LORD is **j**.
Ne 9:13 and laws that are **j** and right,
9:33 you have been **j**; you have acted
Job 34:17 you condemn the **j** and mighty One?
35: 2 "Do you think this is **j**? You say,
Ps 37:28 For the LORD loves the **j** and will
37:30 and his tongue speaks what is **j**.
99: 4 you have done what is **j** and right.
111: 7 of his hands are faithful and **j**;
119:121 I have done what is righteous and **j**;
Pr 1: 3 doing what is right and **j** and fair;
2: 8 for he guards the course of the **j**
2: 9 and **j** and fair—every good path.
8: 8 All the words of my mouth are **j**;
8:15 and rulers make laws that are **j**;
12: 5 The plans of the righteous are **j**,
21: 3 To do what is right and **j** is more
Isa 32: 7 when the plea of the needy is **j**.
58: 2 They ask me for **j** decisions and seem
Jer 4: 2 in a truthful, **j** and righteous way
22: 3 LORD says: Do what is **j** and right.
22:15 He did what was right and **j**, so all
23: 5 do what is **j** and right in the land.
33:15 do what is **j** and right in the land.
Eze 18: 5 man who does what is **j** and right.
18:19 Since the son has done what is **j**
18:21 and does what is **j** and right,
18:25 say, 'The way of the Lord is not **j**.
18:27 **j** and right, he will save his life.
18:29 says, 'The way of the Lord is not **j**.
33:14 sin and does what is **j** and right—
33:16 is **j** and right; he will surely live.
33:17 say, 'The way of the Lord is not **j**.
33:17 But it is their way that is not **j**.
33:19 and does what is **j** and right,
33:20 say, 'The way of the Lord is not **j**.
45: 9 and do what is **j** and right.
Da 4:37 is right and all his ways are **j**.
Jn 5:30 and my judgment is **j**, for I seek not
Ro 3:26 so as to be **j** and the one who
2Th 1: 6 God is **j**: He will pay back trouble
1Jn 1: 9 he is faithful and **j** and will
Rev 15: 3 **J** and true are your ways, King of
16: 5 "You are **j** in these judgments, you
16: 7 true and **j** are your judgments."
19: 2 for true and **j** are his judgments. He

Justice (Just, *Righteousness and Justice*)

Ge 49:16 "Dan will provide **j** for his people
Ex 23: 2 pervert **j** by siding with the crowd,
23: 6 "Do not deny **j** to your poor people
Lev 19:15 "'Do not pervert **j**; do not show
Dt 16:19 Do not pervert **j** or show partiality.
16:20 Follow **j** and **j** alone, so that you
24:17 the alien or the fatherless of **j**,
27:19 "Cursed is the man who withholds **j**
1Sa 8: 3 and accepted bribes and perverted **j**.
2Sa 15: 4 and I would see that he receives **j**."
15: 6 who came to the king asking for **j**,
1Ki 3:11 for discernment in administering **j**,
3:28 had wisdom from God to administer **j**.
7: 7 the Hall of **J**, where he was to judge,
10: 9 to maintain **j** and righteousness."
2Ch 9: 8 to maintain **j** and righteousness."
Ezr 7:25 judges to administer **j** to all the
Est 1:13 experts in matters of law and **j**,
Job 8: 3 Does God pervert **j**? Does the
9:19 it is a matter of **j**, who will summon
19: 7 I call for help, there is no **j**.
27: 2 who has denied me **j**, the Almighty,
29:14 **j** was my robe and my turban.
31:13 "If I have denied **j** to my
34: 5 'I am innocent, but God denies me **j**.
34:12 that the Almighty would pervert **j**.
34:17 Can he who hates **j** govern? Will you
36: 3 I will ascribe **j** to my Maker.
36:17 and **j** have taken hold of you.
Job 37:23 in his **j** and great righteousness,
40: 8 "Would you discredit my **j**? Would you
Ps 7: 6 Awake, my God; decree **j**.
9: 8 he will govern the peoples with **j**.
9:16 The LORD is known by his **j**; the
11: 7 For the LORD is righteous, he loves **j**
36: 6 your **j** like the great deep.
37: 6 **j** of your cause like the noonday sun.
45: 6 a sceptre of **j** will be the sceptre
72: 1 Endow the king with your **j**, O God,
72: 2 your afflicted ones with **j**.
99: 4 The King is mighty, he loves **j**—
101: 1 I will sing of your love and **j**;
106: 3 Blessed are they who maintain **j**,
112: 5 who conducts his affairs with **j**.
140:12 I know that the LORD secures **j** for
Pr 8:20 righteousness, along the paths of **j**,
16:10 and his mouth should not betray **j**.
17:23 secret to pervert the course of **j**.
18: 5 or to deprive the innocent of **j**.
19:28 A corrupt witness mocks at **j**, and
21:15 **j** is done, it brings joy to the
28: 5 Evil men do not understand **j**, but
29: 4 By **j** a king gives a country
29: 7 righteous care about **j** for the poor
29:26 it is from the LORD that man gets **j**.
Ecc 3:16 In the place of **j**—wickedness was
5: 8 and **j** and rights denied, do not be
Isa 1:17 Seek **j**, encourage the oppressed.
1:21 a harlot! She once was full of **j**;
1:27 Zion will be redeemed with **j**, her
5: 7 And he looked for **j**, but saw
5:16 Almighty will be exalted by his **j**,
5:23 a bribe, but deny **j** to the innocent.
9: 7 upholding it with **j** and
10: 2 withhold **j** from the oppressed of my
11: 4 with **j** he will give decisions for
16: 5 one who in judging seeks **j** and
28: 6 He will be a spirit of **j** to him who
28:17 I will make **j** the measuring line and
29:21 testimony deprive the innocent of **j**.
30:18 For the LORD is a God of **j**. Blessed
32: 1 and rulers will rule with **j**.
32:16 **J** will dwell in the desert and
33: 5 fill Zion with **j** and righteousness.
42: 1 and he will bring **j** to the nations.
42: 3 faithfulness he will bring forth **j**;
42: 4 till he establishes **j** on earth.
51: 4 **j** will become a light to the nations.
51: 5 my arm will bring **j** to the nations.
56: 1 "Maintain **j** and do what is right,
59: 4 No-one calls for **j**; no-one pleads
59: 8 there is no **j** in their paths.
59: 9 **j** is far from us, and righteousness
59:11 We look for **j**, but find none; for
59:14 **j** is driven back, and righteousness
59:15 was displeased that there was no **j**.
61: 8 "For I, the LORD, love **j**; I hate
Jer 9:24 who exercises kindness, **j** and
10:24 Correct me, LORD, but only with **j**—
12: 1 I would speak with you about your **j**:
21:12 'Administer **j** every morning; rescue
30:11 will discipline you but only with **j**;
46:28 will discipline you but only with **j**;
Lam 3:36 to deprive a man of **j**—would not
Eze 22:29 ill-treat the alien, denying them **j**.
34:16 I will shepherd the flock with **j**.
Hos 12: 6 maintain love and **j**, and wait for
Am 2: 7 ground and deny **j** to the oppressed.
5: 7 You who turn **j** into bitterness and
5:12 deprive the poor of **j** in the courts.
5:15 love good; maintain **j** in the courts
5:24 let **j** roll on like a river,
6:12 But you have turned **j** into poison
Mic 3: 1 Should you not know **j**,
3: 8 and with **j** and might, to declare to
3: 9 despise **j** and distort all that is
Hab 1: 4 is paralysed, and **j** never prevails.
1: 4 righteous, so that **j** is perverted.
Zep 3: 5 by morning he dispenses his **j**,
Zec 7: 9 'Administer true **j**; show mercy and
Mal 2:17 "Where is the God of **j**?
3: 5 deprive aliens of **j**, but do not fear
Mt 12:18 he will proclaim **j** to the nations.
12:20 out, till he leads **j** to victory.
23:23 the law—**j**, mercy and faithfulness.
Lk 11:42 you neglect **j** and the love of God.
18: 3 'Grant me **j** against my adversary.'
18: 5 I will see that she gets **j**, so that
18: 7 will not God bring about **j** for his
18: 8 see that they get **j**, and quickly.
Ac 8:33 humiliation he was deprived of **j**.
17:31 with **j** by the man he has appointed.
28: 4 **J** has not allowed him to live."
Ro 3:25 He did this to demonstrate his **j**,
3:26 —he did it to demonstrate his **j** at
2Co 7:11 what readiness to see **j** done.
Heb 11:33 administered **j**, and gained what was
Rev 19:11 With **j** he judges and makes war.

Justification (Just)

Eze 16:52 furnished some **j** for your sisters.
Ro 4:25 and was raised to life for our **j**.
5:16 many trespasses and brought **j**.
5:18 was **j** that brings life for all men.

Justified (Just)

Ps 51: 4 when you speak and **j** when you judge.
Lk 18:14 the other, went home **j** before God.
Ac 13:39 everyone who believes is **j** from
13:39 not be **j** from by the law of Moses.
Ro 3:24 are **j** freely by his grace through
3:28 maintain that a man is **j** by faith
4: 2 If, in fact, Abraham was **j** by works,
5: 1 we have been **j** through faith, we
5: 9 we have now been **j** by his blood
8:30 he also **j**; those he **j**, he also
10:10 heart that you believe and are **j**,
1Co 6:11 you were **j** in the name of the Lord
Gal 2:16 know that a man is not **j** by
2:16 that we may be **j** by faith in Christ
2:16 observing the law no-one will be **j**.
2:17 "If, while we seek to be **j** in Christ,
3:11 no-one is **j** before God by the law
3:24 Christ that we might be **j** by faith.
5: 4 You who are trying to be **j** by law
Tit 3: 7 that, having been **j** by his grace, we
Jas 2:24 a person is **j** by what he does and

Justifies (Just)

Ro 3:26 who **j** those who have faith in Jesus.
4: 5 but trusts God who **j** the wicked,
8:33 God has chosen? It is God who **j**.

Justify (Just)

Est 7: 4 would **j** disturbing the king."
Job 40: 8 Would you condemn me to **j** yourself?
Isa 53:11 my righteous servant will **j** many,
Lk 10:29 he wanted to **j** himself, so he asked
16:15 "You are the ones who **j** yourselves
Ro 3:30 who will **j** the circumcised by faith
Gal 3: 8 God would **j** the Gentiles by faith,

Justifying (Just)

Job 32: 2 angry with Job for **j** himself rather

Justly (Just)

Ps 58: 1 Do you rulers indeed speak **j**? Do you
67: 4 you rule the peoples **j** and guide
Jer 7: 5 actions and deal with each other **j**,
Mic 6: 8 To act **j** and to love mercy and to
Lk 23:41 We are punished **j**, for we are
1Pe 2:23 himself to him who judges **j**.

Justus

Ac 1:23 (also known as **J**) and Matthias.
18: 7 of Titius **J**, a worshipper of God.
Col 4:11 Jesus, who is called **J**, also sends

Juttah

Jos 15:55 Maon, Carmel, Ziph, **J**,
21:16 Ain, **J** and Beth Shemesh, together
1Ch 6:59 Ashan, **J** and Beth Shemesh, together

Kabzeel

Jos 15:21 of Edom were: **K**, Eder, Jagur,
2Sa 23:20 was a valiant fighter from **K**,
1Ch 11:22 was a valiant fighter from **K**,

Kadesh
Ge 14: 7 and went to En Mishpat (that is, **K**)
16:14 still there, between **K** and Bered.
20: 1 Negev and lived between **K** and Shur.
Nu 13:26 at **K** in the Desert of Paran.
20: 1 Desert of Zin, and they stayed at **K**.
20:14 Moses sent messengers from **K** to the
20:16 "Now we are here at **K**, a town on the
20:22 out from **K** and came to Mount Hor.
33:36 They left Ezion Geber and camped at **K**
33:37 They left **K** and camped at Mount Hor,
Dt 1:46 you stayed in **K** many days—all the
Jdg 11:16 desert to the Red Sea and on to **K**.
11:17 So Israel stayed at **K**.
Ps 29: 8 the LORD shakes the Desert of **K**.

Kadesh Barnea
Oasis town in northern Sinai 50 miles south of Beersheba. Originally known as En Mishpat and abbreviated to Kadesh. Kedorlaomer defeated the Amalekites and Amorites here (Ge 14:7). An angel appeared to Hagar near here (Ge 16:14), Abram settled close by (Ge 20:1) and the people camped here during the exodus (Nu 20:1; 33:36; Dt 1:19, 46). Here Miriam died and was buried (Nu 20:1), the spies reported back (Nu 13:26; Jos 14:7), the people complained (Nu 20:2–5) and messengers were dispatched to Edom and Moab (Jdg 11:17).

Nu 32: 8 them from **K** to look over the land.
34: 4 on to Zin and go south of **K**.
Dt 1: 2 Horeb to **K** by the Mount Seir road.)
1:19 you have seen, and so we reached **K**.
2:14 from the time we left **K** until we
9:23 the LORD sent you out from **K**, he
Jos 10:41 Joshua subdued them from **K** to Gaza
14: 6 man of God at **K** about you and me.
14: 7 sent me from **K** to explore the land.
15: 3 Zin and went over to the south of **K**.

Kadmiel
Ezr 2:40 the descendants of Jeshua and **K**
3: 9 his sons and brothers and **K** and his
Ne 7:43 descendants of Jeshua (through **K**
9: 4 Bani, **K**, Shebaniah, Bunni, Sherebiah,
9: 5 the Levites—Jeshua, **K**, Bani,
10: 9 Binnui of the sons of Henadad, **K**,
12: 8 The Levites were Jeshua, Binnui, **K**,
12:24 Sherebiah, Jeshua son of **K**, and

Kadmonites
Ge 15:19 land of the Kenites, Kenizzites, **K**,

Kain
Jos 15:57 **K**, Gibeah and Timnah—ten towns and

Kallai
Ne 12:20 of Sallu's, **K**; of Amok's, Eber;

Kamon
Jdg 10: 5 Jair died, he was buried in **K**.

Kanah
Jos 16: 8 the **K** Ravine and ended at the sea.
17: 9 continued south to the **K** Ravine.
19:28 went to Abdon, Rehob, Hammon and **K**,

Kareah
2Ki 25:23 Johanan son of **K**, Seraiah son of
Jer 40: 8 Johanan and Jonathan the sons of **K**,
40:13 Johanan son of **K** and all the army
40:15 Johanan son of **K** said privately to
40:16 of Ahikam said to Johanan son of **K**,
41:11 Johanan son of **K** and all the army
41:13 had with him saw Johanan son of **K**
41:14 and went over to Johanan son of **K**.
41:16 Johanan son of **K** and all the army
42: 1 including Johanan son of **K** and
42: 8 he called together Johanan son of **K**
43: 2 Johanan son of **K** and all the
43: 4 Johanan son of **K** and all the army
43: 5 Instead, Johanan son of **K** and all

Karka
Jos 15: 3 up to Addar and curved around to **K**.

Karkor
Jdg 8:10 Now Zebah and Zalmunna were in **K**

Karnaim
Am 6:13 we not take **K** by our own strength?"

Kartah
Jos 21:34 the tribe of Zebulun, Jokneam, **K**,
1Ch 6:77 **K**, Rimmono and Tabor, together with

Kartan
Jos 21:32 Hammoth Dor and **K**, together with

Kattath
Jos 19:15 Included were **K**, Nahalal, Shimron,

Katydid
Lev 11:22 locust, **k**, cricket or grasshopper.

Kebar River
Runs through Babylonia; the exiled people lived along its banks (Eze 1:1; 3:15); Ezekiel received his vision here (Eze 1:3; 3:23; 10:15, 20, 22; 43:3).

Eze 1: 1 was among the exiles by the **K**,
1: 3 the son of Buzi, by the **K** in
3:15 lived at Tel Abib near the **K**.
3:23 the glory I had seen by the **K**
10:15 creatures I had seen by the **K**
10:20 the God of Israel by the **K**,
10:22 as those I had seen by the **K**.
43: 3 visions I had seen by the **K**,

Kedar (Kedar's)
Ge 25:13 of Ishmael, **K**, Adbeel, Mibsam,
1Ch 1:29 of Ishmael, **K**, Adbeel, Mibsam,
Ps 120: 5 that I live among the tents of **K**!
SS 1: 5 dark like the tents of **K**, like the
Isa 21:16 the pomp of **K** will come to an end.
21:17 the warriors of **K**, will be few.
42:11 settlements where **K** lives rejoice.
Jer 2:10 send to **K** and observe closely; see
49:28 Concerning **K** and the kingdoms of
49:28 "Arise, and attack **K** and destroy
Eze 27:21 "'Arabia and all the princes of **K**

Kedar's (Kedar)
Isa 60: 7 All **K** flocks will be gathered to you,

Kedemah
Ge 25:15 Hadad, Tema, Jetur, Naphish and **K**.
1Ch 1:31 Jetur, Naphish and **K**. These were the

Kedemoth
Dt 2:26 From the desert of **K** I sent
Jos 13:18 Jahaz, **K**, Mephaath,
21:37 **K** and Mephaath, together with their
1Ch 6:79 **K** and Mephaath, together with their

Kedesh
Jos 12:22 the king of **K** one the king of
15:23 **K**, Hazor, Ithnan,
19:37 **K**, Edrei, En Hazor,
20: 7 they set apart **K** in Galilee in the
21:32 **K** in Galilee (a city of refuge for
Jdg 4: 6 from **K** in Naphtali and said to him,
4: 9 So Deborah went with Barak to **K**,
4:11 the great tree in Zaanannim near **K**.
2Ki 15:29 Beth Maacah, Janoah, **K** and Hazor.
1Ch 6:72 Issachar they received **K**, Daberath,
6:76 Naphtali they received **K** in Galilee,

Kedorlaomer
Ge 14: 1 king of Ellasar, **K** king of Elam
14: 4 years they had been subject to **K**,
14: 5 In the fourteenth year, **K** and the
14: 9 against **K** king of Elam, Tidal king
14:17 After Abram returned from defeating **K**

Keen
Da 5:12 was found to have a **k** mind and

Keep (Keeper, Keepers, Keeping, Keeps, Kept, Safekeeping)
Ge 6:19 female, to **k** them alive with you.
7: 3 to **k** their various kinds alive
14:21 and **k** the goods for yourself."
17: 9 As for you, you must **k** my covenant
17:10 the covenant you are to **k**: Every
18:19 to **k** the way of the LORD by doing
31:49 "May the LORD **k** watch between you
32:16 and **k** some space between the herds."
33: 9 **K** what you have for yourself."
38: 9 to **k** from producing offspring for
38:23 Judah said, "Let her **k** what she has,
42: 1 you just **k** looking at each other?"
47:24 The other four-fifths you may **k** as
Ex 5: 9 for the men so that they **k** working
5:17 That is why you **k** saying, 'Let us go
12:42 all the Israelites are to **k** vigil to
13:10 You must **k** this ordinance at the
15:26 his commands and **k** all his decrees,
16:19 "No-one is to **k** any of it until
16:23 Save whatever is left and **k** it until
16:28 **k** my commands and my instructions?
16:32 'Take an omer of manna and **k** it for
19: 5 obey me fully and **k** my covenant
20: 6 who love me and **k** my commandments.
20:20 be with you to **k** you from sinning."
21:36 yet the owner did not **k** it penned up,
27:21 his sons are to **k** the lamps burning
Lev 7: 8 anyone may **k** its hide for himself.
13: 5 he is to **k** him in isolation another
13:33 is to **k** him in isolation another
15:31 You must **k** the Israelites separate
18: 5 **K** my decrees and laws, for the man
18:26 you must **k** my decrees and my laws.
18:30 **K** my requirements and do not follow
19:19 "'**K** my decrees. "'Do not mate
19:37 "'**K** all my decrees and all my laws
20: 8 **K** my decrees and follow them. I am
20:22 "'**K** all my decrees and laws and
22: 9 are to **k** my requirements so that
22:31 "**K** my commands and follow them.
26: 9 and I will **k** my covenant with you.
Nu 6:24 "'"The LORD bless you and **k** you;
11:13 these people? They **k** wailing to me,
15:22 fail to **k** any of these commands
22:16 Do not let anything **k** you from
36: 7 Israelite shall **k** the tribal land
36: 9 tribe is to **k** the land it inherits."
Dt 4: 2 but **k** the commands of the LORD your
4:40 **K** his decrees and commands, which I
5:10 who love me and **k** my commandments
5:29 and **k** all my commands always,
6:17 Be sure to **k** the commands of the
7: 9 who love him and **k** his commands.
7:12 **k** his covenant of love with you
7:15 will **k** you free from every disease
8: 2 or not you would **k** his commands.
11: 1 your God and **k** his requirements,
13: 4 **K** his commands and obey him; serve
22: 2 **k** it until he comes looking for it.
23: 9 **k** away from everything impure.
26:17 that you will **k** his decrees,
26:18 that you are to **k** all his commands.
27: 1 "**K** all these commands that I give
28: 9 if you **k** the commands of the LORD
28:41 daughters but you will not **k** them,
30:10 God and **k** his commands and decrees
30:16 **k** his commands, decrees and laws;
Jos 3: 4 But **k** a distance of about a thousand
6:18 **k** away from the devoted things, so
7:11 which I commanded them to **k**.
22: 5 be very careful to **k** the commandment
Jdg 2:22 they will **k** the way of the LORD
6:11 to **k** it from the Midianites.
1Sa 1:14 How long will you **k** on getting drunk
2: 3 "Do not **k** talking so proudly or let
6: 9 **k** watching it. If it goes up to its
2Sa 7:25 "And now, LORD God, **k** for ever the
13:13 not **k** me from being married to you."
14:18 said to the woman, "Do not **k** from me
1Ki 1: 1 he could not **k** warm even when they

1Ki 1: 2 that our lord the king may **k** warm."
2: 3 and **k** his decrees and commands, his
2: 4 that the LORD may **k** his promise to
2:43 Why then did you not **k** your oath to
6:12 regulations and **k** all my commands
8:23 you who **k** your covenant of love with
8:25 of Israel, **k** for your servant David
8:58 all his ways and to **k** the commands,
11:10 Solomon did not **k** the LORD's command.
15: 5 **k** any of the LORD's commands
18: 5 Maybe we can find some grass to **k**
2Ki 10:31 to **k** the horses and mules alive
17:19 even Judah did not **k** the commands of
17:37 be careful to **k** the decrees and
21: 8 will **k** the whole Law that my servant
23: 3 follow the LORD and **k** his commands,
1Ch 4:10 and **k** me from harm so that I will be
10:13 he did not **k** the word of the LORD,
22:12 may **k** the law of the LORD your God.
29:18 **k** this desire in the hearts of your
29:18 and **k** their hearts loyal to you.
29:19 devotion to **k** your commands,
2Ch 2:18 over them to **k** the people working.
6:14 you who **k** your covenant of love with
6:16 of Israel, **k** for your servant David
23: 4 Sabbath are to **k** watch at the doors,
34:31 follow the LORD and **k** his commands,
Ne 5:13 man who does not **k** this promise.
13:22 in order to **k** the Sabbath day holy.
Est 3:11 "**K** the money," the king said to
Job 4: 2 But who can **k** from speaking?
7:11 "Therefore I will not **k** silent;
13:13 "**K** silent and let me speak; then let
13:27 you **k** close watch on all my paths
14:16 my steps but not **k** track of my sin.
16: 3 What ails you that you **k** on arguing?
22:15 Will you **k** to the old path that evil
30:10 They detest me and **k** their distance;
33:17 wrongdoing and **k** him from pride,
34:30 to **k** a godless man from ruling, from
36: 6 He does not **k** the wicked alive but
41: 3 Will he **k** begging you for mercy?
Ps 12: 7 O LORD, you will **k** us safe and
16: 1 **K** me safe, O God, for in you I take
17: 8 **K** me as the apple of your eye; hide
18:28 You, O LORD, **k** my lamp burning; my
19:13 **K** your servant also from wilful sins;
22:29 those who cannot **k** themselves alive.
25:10 who **k** the demands of his covenant.
27: 5 he will **k** me safe in his dwelling;
31:20 **k** them safe from accusing tongues.
33:19 death and **k** them alive in famine.
34:13 **k** your tongue from evil and your
37:34 Wait for the LORD and **k** his way.
39: 1 my ways and **k** my tongue from sin;
78: 7 his deeds but would **k** his commands.
78:10 they did not **k** God's covenant and
78:56 they did not **k** his statutes.
83: 1 O God, do not **k** silent; be not quiet,
89:31 decrees and fail to **k** my commands,
103:18 with those who **k** his covenant and
105:45 that they might **k** his precepts and
106:23 to **k** his wrath from destroying them.
119: 2 Blessed are they who **k** his statutes
119: 9 How can a young man **k** his way pure?
119:22 and contempt, for I **k** your statutes.
119:29 **K** me from deceitful ways;
119:33 then I will **k** them to the end.
119:34 and I will **k** your law and obey it
119:55 name, O LORD, and I will **k** your law.
119:69 I **k** your precepts with all my heart.
119:115 that I may **k** the commands of my God!
119:146 save me and I will **k** your statutes.
121: 7 The LORD will **k** you from all harm—
132:12 if your sons **k** my covenant and the
140: 4 **K** me, O LORD, from the hands of the
141: 3 **k** watch over the door of my lips.
141: 9 **K** me from the snares they have laid
Pr 2:20 and **k** to the paths of the righteous.
3: 1 but **k** my commands in your heart,
3:26 will **k** your foot from being snared.
4: 4 **k** my commands and you will live.
4:21 **k** them within your heart;
4:24 **k** corrupt talk far from your lips.
4:27 or the left; **k** your foot from evil.
5: 8 **K** to a path far from her, do not go
Pr 6:20 My son, **k** your father's commands and
7: 1 My son, **k** my words and store up my
7: 2 **K** my commands and you will live;
7: 5 they will **k** you from the adulteress,
8:32 blessed are those who **k** my ways.
15:24 **k** him from going down to the grave.
20:28 Love and faithfulness **k** a king safe;
22: 3 the simple **k** going and suffer
22:12 The eyes of the LORD **k** watch over
22:18 for it is pleasing when you **k** them
23:19 **k** your heart on the right path.
23:26 and let your eyes **k** to my ways,
27:12 the simple **k** going and suffer
28: 4 but those who **k** the law resist them.
30: 8 **K** falsehood and lies far from me;
Ecc 3: 6 time to **k** and a time to throw away,
4:11 lie down together, they will **k** warm.
4:11 But how can one **k** warm alone?
12:13 Fear God and **k** his commandments,
Isa 7: 4 Say to him, 'Be careful, **k** calm
7:21 In that day, a man will **k** alive
19:21 make vows to the LORD and **k** them.
26: 3 will **k** in perfect peace him whose
28:24 Does he **k** on breaking up and
29:23 they will **k** my holy name;
42: 6 I will **k** you and will make you to be
47:12 "**K** on, then, with your magic spells
49: 8 I will **k** you and will make you to be
56: 4 "To the eunuchs who **k** my Sabbaths,
56: 6 all who **k** the Sabbath without
58:13 "If you **k** your feet from breaking
62: 1 For Zion's sake I will not **k** silent,
64:12 Will you **k** silent and punish us
65: 5 who say, '**K** away; don't come near me,
65: 6 I will not **k** silent but will pay
Jer 4:19 pounds within me, I cannot **k** silent.
11: 8 to follow but that they did not **k**.
13:14 to **k** me from destroying them.
14:13 the prophets **k** telling them, 'You
15: 6 "You **k** on backsliding. So I will lay
16:11 They forsook me and did not **k** my law.
17:15 They **k** saying to me, "Where is the
17:18 but **k** me from shame; let them be
17:18 be terrified, but **k** me from terror.
17:22 but **k** the Sabbath day holy, as I
17:24 but **k** the Sabbath day holy by not
17:27 to **k** the Sabbath day holy by not
23:17 They **k** saying to those who despise
23:37 This is what you **k** saying to a
42: 4 and will **k** nothing back from you."
44:25 do what you promised! **K** your vows!
50: 2 **k** nothing back, but say, 'Babylon
Lam 1:11 for food to **k** themselves alive.
1:19 for food to **k** themselves alive.
Eze 11:20 decrees and be careful to **k** my laws.
18:19 been careful to **k** all my decrees,
20: 9 I did what would **k** it from being
20:14 I did what would **k** it from being
20:18 **k** their laws or defile yourselves
20:19 decrees and be careful to **k** my laws.
20:20 **K** my Sabbaths holy, that they may be
20:21 they were not careful to **k** my laws
20:22 I did what would **k** it from being
24:17 **K** your turban fastened and your
24:23 You will **k** your turbans on your
36:27 decrees and be careful to **k** my laws.
37:24 laws and be careful to **k** my decrees.
44:20 **k** the hair of their heads trimmed.
44:24 They are to **k** my laws and my decrees
44:24 and they are to **k** my Sabbaths holy.
46:17 the servant may **k** it until the year
Da 5:17 "You may **k** your gifts for yourself
Hab 1:17 Is he to **k** on emptying his net,
Zec 3: 7 in my ways and **k** my requirements
11:12 give me my pay; but if not, **k** it.
12: 4 "I will **k** a watchful eye over the
Mt 5:33 but **k** the oaths you have made to
6: 7 you pray, do not **k** on babbling like
10:10 for the worker is worth his **k**.
24:42 "Therefore **k** watch, because you do
25:13 "Therefore **k** watch, because you do
26:38 Stay here and **k** watch with me."
26:40 "Could you men not **k** watch with me
28:14 him and **k** you out of trouble."
Mk 3: 9 to **k** the people from crowding him.
7:24 he could not **k** his presence secret.
Mk 13:34 the one at the door to **k** watch.
13:35 "Therefore **k** watch because you do
14:34 "Stay here and **k** watch."
14:37 Could you not **k** watch for one hour?
Lk 4:42 tried to **k** him from leaving them.
12:35 service and **k** your lamps burning,
13:33 In any case, I must **k** going today
17:33 Whoever tries to **k** his life will
18: 7 Will he **k** putting them off?
19:40 "if they **k** quiet, the stones will
Jn 4:15 to **k** coming here to draw water."
8:55 but I do know him and **k** his word.
9:16 for he does not **k** the Sabbath.
10:24 "How long will you **k** us in suspense?
12:25 world will **k** it for eternal life.
12:47 does not **k** them, I do not judge him.
15:18 **k** in mind that it hated me first.
18:18 a fire they had made to **k** warm.
Ac 2:24 for death to **k** its hold on him.
10:47 "Can anyone **k** these people from
18: 9 **k** on speaking, do not be silent.
20:28 **K** watch over yourselves and all the
24:16 I strive always to **k** my conscience
24:23 centurion to **k** Paul under guard
27:22 now I urge you to **k** up your courage,
27:25 **k** up your courage, men, for I have
Ro 2:26 are not circumcised **k** the law's
7:19 not want to do—this I **k** on doing.
12:11 but **k** your spiritual fervour,
14:22 things **k** between yourself and God.
16:17 **K** away from them.
1Co 1: 8 He will **k** you strong to the end,
5: 8 Therefore let us **k** the Festival,
7:30 as if it were not theirs to **k**;
10: 6 to **k** us from setting our hearts on
14:28 the speaker should **k** quiet in the
2Co 3:13 **k** the Israelites from gazing at it
11:12 I will **k** on doing what I am doing
12: 7 To **k** me from becoming conceited
Gal 5:15 If you **k** on biting and devouring
5:25 let us **k** in step with the Spirit.
Eph 1:17 I **k** asking that the God of our Lord
4: 3 Make every effort to **k** the unity of
6:18 **k** on praying for all the saints.
1Th 2:16 in their effort to **k** us from
2Th 3: 6 to **k** away from every brother who is
1Ti 3: 9 They must **k** hold of the deep truths
5:21 to **k** these instructions without
5:22 **K** yourself pure.
6:14 to **k** this command without spot or
2Ti 1:13 **k** as the pattern of sound teaching
2:14 **K** reminding them of these things.
4: 5 you, **k** your head in all situations,
Phm :13 I would have liked to **k** him with me
Heb 9:20 which God has commanded you to **k**."
10:26 If we deliberately **k** on sinning
13: 1 **K** on loving each other as brothers.
13: 5 **K** your lives free from the love of
13:17 They **k** watch over you as men who
Jas 1:26 not **k** a tight rein on his tongue,
1:27 widows in their distress and to **k**
2: 8 If you really **k** the royal law found
2:16 "Go, I wish you well; **k** warm and
3: 2 able to **k** his whole body in check.
1Pe 3:10 see good days must **k** his tongue from
2Pe 1: 8 they will **k** you from being
1Jn 5:21 children, **k** yourselves from idols
Jude : 6 who did not **k** their positions
:21 **K** yourselves in God's love as you
:24 is able to **k** you from falling
Rev 3:10 also **k** you from the hour of trial
20: 3 to **k** him from deceiving the nations
22: 9 of all who **k** the words of this book.

Keeper (Keep)

Ge 4: 9 "Am I my brother's **k**?"
1Sa 17:22 his things with the **k** of supplies,
2Ki 10:22 Jehu said to the **k** of the wardrobe,
22:14 son of Harhas, **k** of the wardrobe.
2Ch 31:14 the Levite, **k** of the East Gate
34:22 son of Hasrah, **k** of the wardrobe.
Ne 2: 8 Asaph, **k** of the king's forest,
Jn 12: 6 was a thief; as **k** of the money bag,

Keepers (Keep)
Ecc 12: 3 the **k** of the house tremble, and the

Keeping (Keep)
Ge 41:49 he stopped **k** records because
Ex 20: 8 the Sabbath day by **k** it holy.
Dt 5:12 the Sabbath day by **k** it holy,
6: 2 as you live by **k** all his decrees
7: 9 **k** his covenant of love to a thousand
13:18 LORD your God, **k** all his commands
Jdg 8: 4 exhausted yet **k** up the pursuit, came
1Sa 6:12 **k** on the road and lowing all the way;
17:34 has been **k** his father's sheep.
25:33 for **k** me from bloodshed this day and
1Ki 11:38 eyes by **k** my statutes and commands,
17:16 in **k** with the word of the LORD
2Ki 7: 9 news and we are **k** it to ourselves.
2Ch 8:14 In **k** with the ordinance of his
Est 1: 7 in **k** with the king's liberality.
Ps 19:11 in **k** them there is great reward.
119:112 My heart is set on **k** your decrees to
Pr 6:24 **k** you from the immoral woman, from
15: 3 **k** watch on the wicked and the good.
Isa 65: 4 spend their nights **k** secret vigil;
Eze 14: 4 myself in **k** with his great idolatry.
17:14 surviving only by **k** his treaty.
22:26 their eyes to the **k** of my Sabbaths,
Da 9:16 in **k** with all your righteous acts
Zec 9: 8 my people, for now I am **k** watch.
Mt 3: 8 Produce fruit in **k** with repentance.
Lk 2: 8 **k** watch over their flocks at night.
2:24 in **k** with what is said in the Law
3: 8 Produce fruit in **k** with repentance.
20:20 **K** a close watch on him, they sent
Ac 14:18 **k** the crowd from sacrificing to them.
1Co 7:19 **K** God's commands is what counts.
16: 2 a sum of money in **k** with his income,
2Co 8: 5 and then to us in **k** with God's will.
1Ti 1:18 in **k** with the prophecies once made
Jas 4:11 not **k** it, but sitting in judgment
1Pe 3:16 **k** a clear conscience, so that those
2Pe 3: 9 is not slow in **k** his promise
3:13 in **k** with his promise we are looking

Keeps (Keep)
Jdg 5:29 indeed, she **k** saying to herself,
1Sa 17:25 "Do you see how this man **k** coming
Ne 1: 5 who **k** his covenant of love with
9:32 God, who **k** his covenant of love,
Job 20:13 to let it go and **k** it in his mouth,
24:15 and he **k** his face concealed.
33:11 he **k** close watch on all my paths.
34: 8 He **k** company with evildoers; he
Ps 15: 4 who **k** his oath even when it hurts,
Pr 11:13 but a trustworthy man **k** a secret.
12:23 A prudent man **k** his knowledge to
15:21 understanding **k** a straight course.
15:25 he **k** the widow's boundaries intact.
17:24 A discerning man **k** wisdom in view,
17:28 fool is thought wise if he **k** silent
18:18 and **k** strong opponents apart.
21:23 his tongue **k** himself from calamity.
28: 7 He who **k** the law is a discerning son,
29:11 a wise man **k** himself under control.
29:18 but blessed is he who **k** the law.
Ecc 5:20 because God **k** him occupied with
Isa 26: 2 may enter, the nation that **k** faith.
33:15 **k** his hand from accepting bribes,
56: 2 who **k** the Sabbath without
56: 2 and **k** his hand from doing any evil."
65: 5 a fire that **k** burning all day.
Jer 23:35 This is what each of you **k** on saying
48:10 him who **k** his sword from bloodshed!
Eze 18: 9 my decrees and faithfully **k** my laws.
18:17 He **k** my laws and follows my decrees.
18:21 **k** all my decrees and does what is
Da 9: 4 God, who **k** his covenant of love
Am 5:13 Therefore the prudent man **k** quiet in
Mt 15:23 for she **k** crying out after us."
Lk 18: 5 because this widow **k** bothering me
Jn 7:19 Yet not one of you **k** the law.
8:51 if anyone **k** my word, he will never
8:52 say that if anyone **k** your word,
1Co 13: 5 angered, it **k** no record of wrongs.
Jas 2:10 For whoever **k** the whole law and yet
1Jn 3: 6 No-one who lives in him **k** on sinning.
5:18 one who was born of God **k** him safe,
Rev 16:15 awake and **k** his clothes with him,
22: 7 Blessed is he who **k** the words of the

Kehelathah
Nu 33:22 They left Rissah and camped at **K**.
33:23 They left **K** and camped at Mount

Keilah
Town about 18 miles south-west of Jerusalem allotted to Judah (Jos 15:44). David rescued it from Philistine attack (1Sa 23:1–5), then left here to escape from Saul (1Sa 23:7–14). In Nehemiah's time it had two rulers who helped rebuild Jerusalem (Ne 3:17–18).

Jos 15:44 **K**, Aczib and Mareshah—nine towns
1Sa 23: 1 Philistines are fighting against **K**
23: 2 attack the Philistines and save **K**."
23: 3 we go to **K** against the Philistine
23: 4 "Go down to **K**, for I am going to
23: 5 David and his men went to **K**, fought
23: 5 and saved the people of **K**.
23: 6 him when he fled to David at **K**.)
23: 7 was told that David had gone to **K**,
23: 8 to **K** to besiege David and his men.
23:10 Saul plans to come to **k** and
23:11 Will the citizens of **K** surrender me
23:12 Will the citizens of **K** surrender me
23:13 about six hundred in number, left **K**
23:13 escaped from **K**, he did not go there.
1Ch 4:19 Naham: the father of **K** the Garmite,
Ne 3:17 ruler of half the district of **K**,
3:18 of the other half-district of **K**.

Kelaiah
Ezr 10:23 Among the Levites: Jozabad, Shimei, **K**

Kelal
Ezr 10:30 **K**, Benaiah, Maaseiah, Mattaniah,

Kelita
Ezr 10:23 Kelaiah, (that is **K**), Pethahiah,
Ne 8: 7 Shabbethai, Hodiah, Maaseiah, **K**,
10:10 Shebaniah, Hodiah, **K**, Pelaiah, Hanan,

Kelub
1Ch 4:11 **K**, Shuhah's brother, was the father
27:26 Ezri son of **K** was in charge of the

Keluhi
Ezr 10:35 Benaiah, Bedeiah, **K**,

Kemuel
Ge 22:21 **K** (the father of Aram),
Nu 34:24 **K** son of Shiphtan, the leader from
1Ch 27:17 over Levi: Hashabiah son of **K**; over

Kenaanah
1Ki 22:11 Now Zedekiah son of **K** had made iron
22:24 Zedekiah son of **K** went up and
1Ch 7:10 **K**, Zethan, Tarshish and Ahishahar.
2Ch 18:10 Now Zedekiah son of **K** had made iron
18:23 Zedekiah son of **K** went up and

Kenan
Ge 5: 9 90 years, he became the father of **K**.
5:10 after he became the father of **K**,
5:12 **K** had lived 70 years, he became the
5:13 **K** lived 840 years and had other sons
5:14 Altogether, **K** lived 910 years, and
1Ch 1: 2 **K**, Mahalalel, Jared,
Lk 3:37 the son of Mahalalel, the son of **K**,

Kenani
Ne 9: 4 Bunni, Sherebiah, Bani and **K**—who

Kenaniah
1Ch 15:22 **K** the head Levite was in charge of
15:27 and as were the singers, and **K**, who
26:29 From the Izharites: **K** and his sons

Kenath
Nu 32:42 Nobah captured **K** and its surrounding
1Ch 2:23 as well as **K** with its surrounding

Kenaz
Ge 36:11 Teman, Omar, Zepho, Gatam and **K**.
36:15 Esau: Chiefs Teman, Omar, Zepho, **K**,
36:42 **K**, Teman, Mibzar,
Jos 15:17 Othniel son of **K**, Caleb's brother,
Jdg 1:13 Othniel son of **K**, Caleb's younger
3: 9 Othniel son of **K**, Caleb's younger
3:11 years, until Othniel son of **K** died.
1Ch 1:36 Zepho, Gatam and **K**; by Timna: Amalek.
1:53 **K**, Teman, Mibzar,
4:13 The sons of **K**: Othniel and Seraiah.
4:15 The son of Elah: **K**.

Kenite (Kenites)
Jdg 1:16 the **K**, went up from the City of
4:11 Now Heber the **K** had left the other
4:17 the wife of Heber the **K**, because
4:17 Hazor and the clan of Heber the **K**.
5:24 the wife of Heber the **K**, most

Kenites (Kenite)
Ge 15:19 the land of the **K**, Kenizzites,
Nu 24:21 he saw the **K** and uttered his oracle:
24:22 yet you **K** will be destroyed when
Jdg 4:11 had left the other **K**, the descendants
1Sa 15: 6 he said to the **K**, "Go away, leave
15: 6 **K** moved away from the Amalekites.
27:10 or "Against the Negev of the **K**.
30:29 of the Jerahmeelites and the **K**;
1Ch 2:55 These are the **K** who came from

Kenizzite (Kenizzites)
Nu 32:12 the **K** and Joshua son of Nun,
Jos 14: 6 and Caleb son of Jephunneh the **K**
14:14 son of Jephunneh the **K** ever since,

Kenizzites (Kenizzite)
Ge 15:19 the land of the Kenites, **K**,

Kephar Ammoni
Jos 18:24 **K**, Ophni and Geba—twelve towns and

Kephirah
Jos 9:17 **K**, Beeroth and Kiriath Jearim.
18:26 Mizpah, **K**, Mozah,
Ezr 2:25 of Kiriath Jearim, **K** and Beeroth 743
Ne 7:29 of Kiriath Jearim, **K** and Beeroth 743

Kept (Keep)
Ge 4: 2 Abel **k** flocks, and Cain worked the
6:20 will come to you to be **k** alive.
7:17 For forty days the flood **k** coming on
8: 7 a raven, and it **k** flying back and
16: 2 LORD has **k** me from having children.
19: 9 They **k** bringing pressure on Lot and
20: 6 I have **k** you from sinning against me.
26: 5 obeyed me and **k** my requirements
30: 2 who has **k** you from having children?
34: 5 so he **k** quiet about it until they
37:11 but his father **k** the matter in mind.
39:16 She **k** his cloak beside her until his
41:35 to be **k** in the cities for food.
42:16 the rest of you will be **k** in prison,
Ex 5:13 The slave drivers **k** pressing them,
12:42 the LORD **k** vigil that night to bring
16:20 they **k** part of it until morning,
16:33 be **k** for the generations to come."
16:34 the Testimony, that it might be **k**.
21:29 warned but has not **k** it penned up
23:18 must not be **k** until morning.
27:20 so that the lamps may be **k** burning.
Lev 6: 9 fire must be **k** burning on the altar.
6:12 on the altar must be **k** burning;
6:13 The fire must be **k** burning on the
24: 2 lamps may be **k** burning continually.
Nu 9: 7 why should we be **k** from presenting
15:34 they **k** him in custody, because it
17:10 to be **k** as a sign to the rebellious.
18: 9 offerings that is **k** from the fire.

Nu 19: 9 be **k** by the Israelite community
24:11 LORD has **k** you from being rewarded."
Dt 6:24 always prosper and be **k** alive,
7: 8 the LORD loved you and **k** the oath he
32:34 "Have I not **k** this in reserve and
33:21 the leader's portion was **k** for him.
Jos 6:13 LORD, while the trumpets **k** sounding.
9:21 the leaders' promise to them was **k**.
14:10 LORD promised, he has **k** me alive
Jdg 7: 8 their tents but **k** the three hundred,
20:45 They **k** pressing after the Benjamites
1Sa 1: 6 her rival **k** provoking her in order
1:12 As she **k** on praying to the LORD,
9:24 "Here is what has been **k** for you.
10:27 no gifts. But Saul **k** silent.
13:13 You have not **k** the command the LORD
13:14 you have not **k** the LORD's command."
17:41 of him, **k** coming closer to David.
18: 2 From that day Saul **k** David with him
18: 9 Saul **k** a jealous eye on David.
21: 4 men have **k** themselves from women."
21: 5 "Indeed women have been **k** from us,
23:13 and **k** moving from place to place.
25:26 "Now since the LORD has **k** you, my
25:34 who has **k** me from harming you,
25:39 **k** his servant from doing wrong
2Sa 15:12 Absalom's following **k** on increasing.
18: 9 the mule he was riding **k** on going.
18:13 would have **k** your distance from me."
20: 3 They were **k** in confinement till the
22:22 For I have **k** the ways of the LORD;
22:24 him and have **k** myself from sin.
1Ki 5:10 In this way Hiram **k** Solomon supplied
8:20 "The LORD has **k** the promise he made:
8:24 You have **k** your promise to your
10:26 which he **k** in the chariot cities and
11:11 not **k** my covenant and my decrees,
11:33 nor **k** my statutes and laws as David,
13:21 have not **k** the command the LORD your
14: 8 who **k** my commands and followed me
2Ki 4: 5 the jars to her and she **k** pouring.
13: 3 and for a long time he **k** them under
18: 6 he **k** the commands the LORD had given
25: 2 The city was **k** under siege until the
1Ch 4:33 And they **k** a genealogical record.
2Ch 1:14 which he **k** in the chariot cities and
6:10 "The LORD has **k** the promise he made.
6:15 You have **k** your promise to your
9:25 which he **k** in the chariot cities and
17:13 He also **k** experienced fighting men
34:21 have not **k** the word of the LORD;
Ezr 9: 1 have not **k** themselves separate from
Ne 5: 8 They **k** quiet, because they could
6:17 from Tobiah **k** coming to them.
6:19 **k** reporting to me his good deeds
9: 8 You have **k** your promise because you
10:39 **k** and where the ministering priests,
11:19 who **k** watch at the gates—172 men.
Est 2:20 Esther had **k** secret her family
7: 4 I would have **k** quiet, because no
Job 21:32 grave, and watch is **k** over his tomb.
23:11 **k** to his way without turning aside.
31:17 if I have **k** my bread to myself, not
31:34 I **k** silent and would not go outside—
Ps 17: 4 I have **k** myself from the ways of the
18:21 For I have **k** the ways of the LORD;
18:23 him and have **k** myself from sin.
32: 3 I **k** silent, my bones wasted away
50:21 you have done and I **k** silent;
66: 9 and **k** our feet from slipping.
73:13 in vain have I **k** my heart pure
77: 4 You **k** my eyes from closing; I was
78:32 of all this, they **k** on sinning
99: 7 they **k** his statutes and the decrees
119:101 I have **k** my feet from every evil
130: 3 If you, O LORD, **k** a record of sins,
Pr 20: 9 Who can say, "I have **k** my heart pure;
28:18 He whose walk is blameless is **k** safe,
28:26 he who walks in wisdom is **k** safe.
29:25 trusts in the LORD is **k** safe.
Isa 38:17 In your love you **k** me from the pit
42:14 "For a long time I have **k** silent,
49: 6 bring back those of Israel I have **k**.
57:17 yet he **k** on in his wilful ways.
Jer 5:25 Your wrongdoings have **k** these away;
35:14 wine and this command has been **k**.
Jer 52: 5 The city was **k** under siege until the
Eze 5: 7 followed my decrees or **k** my laws.
11:12 not followed my decrees or **k** my laws
Da 7:11 I **k** looking until the beast was
7:28 but I **k** the matter to myself."
9:10 not obeyed the LORD our God or **k** the
Hos 13:12 stored up, his sins are **k** on record.
Am 2: 4 the LORD and have not **k** his decrees,
Mal 3: 7 from my decrees and have not **k** them.
Mt 19:20 "All these I have **k**," the young man
24:43 he would have **k** watch and would not
27:36 sitting down, they **k** watch over him
Mk 5:32 Jesus **k** looking around to see who
7:36 the more they **k** talking about it.
9:10 They **k** the matter to themselves,
9:34 they **k** quiet because on the way they
10:20 these I have **k** since I was a boy."
Lk 1:22 for he **k** making signs to them but
4:44 he **k** on preaching in the synagogues
8:29 hand and foot and **k** under guard,
9:36 The disciples **k** this to themselves,
13:16 has **k** bound for eighteen long years
18: 3 a widow in that town who **k** coming
18:21 "All these I have **k** since I was a
19:20 **k** it laid away in a piece of cloth.
23:21 they **k** shouting, "Crucify him!
24:16 they were **k** from recognising him.
Jn 8: 7 they **k** on questioning him, he
11:37 man have **k** this man from dying?"
11:56 They **k** looking for Jesus, and as
16:18 They **k** asking, "What does he mean by
17:12 **k** them safe by that name you gave me.
19:12 but the Jews **k** shouting, "If you let
Ac 5: 2 he **k** back part of the money for
5: 3 have **k** for yourself some of the
9:24 Day and night they **k** close watch on
12: 5 Peter was **k** in prison, but the
12:15 When she **k** insisting that it was so,
12:16 Peter **k** on knocking, and when they
16: 6 having been **k** by the Holy Spirit
16:18 She **k** this up for many days. Finally
20: 7 day, **k** on talking until midnight.
21:36 The crowd that followed **k** shouting,
23:35 be **k** under guard in Herod's palace.
27:43 **k** them from carrying out their plan.
2Co 11: 9 I have **k** myself from being a burden
Gal 5: 7 and **k** you from obeying the truth?
Eph 3: 9 which for ages past was **k** hidden in
Col 1:26 the mystery that has been **k** hidden
1Th 3: 4 we were with you, we **k** telling you
5:23 soul and body be **k** blameless at the
2Ti 4: 7 the race, I have **k** the faith.
Heb 11:28 By faith he **k** the Passover and the
13: 4 and the marriage bed **k** pure, for God
1Pe 1: 4 spoil or fade—**k** in heaven for you,
2Pe 3: 7 being **k** for the day of judgment and
Jude : 1 God the Father and **k** by Jesus Christ:
: 6 these he has **k** in darkness, bound
Rev 3: 8 yet you have **k** my word and have not
3:10 Since you have **k** my command to
9:15 the four angels who had been **k** ready
14: 4 women, for they **k** themselves pure.

Keran
Ge 36:26 Hemdan, Eshban, Ithran and **K**.
1Ch 1:41 Hemdan, Eshban, Ithran and **K**.

Keren-Happuch
Job 42:14 the second Keziah and the third **K**.

Kerethite (Kerethites)
Zep 2: 5 who live by the sea, O **K** people;

Kerethites (Kerethite)
1Sa 30:14 We raided the Negev of the **K** and the
2Sa 8:18 was over the **K** and Pelethites;
15:18 along with all the **K** and Pelethites;
20: 7 Joab's men and the **K** and Pelethites
20:23 was over the **K** and Pelethites;
1Ki 1:38 Benaiah son of Jehoiada, the **K** and
1:44 Benaiah son of Jehoiada, the **K** and
1Ch 18:17 was over the **K** and Pelethites;
Eze 25:16 I will cut off the **K** and destroy
Zep 2: 6 land by the sea, where the **K** dwell,

Kerioth
Jer 48:24 to **K** and Bozrah—to all the towns
48:41 **K** will be captured and the
Am 2: 2 will consume the fortresses of **K**.

Kerioth Hezron
Jos 15:25 Hazor Hadattah, **K** (that is, Hazor),

Kerith Ravine
An almost dry river bed east of the Jordan. Elijah hid here (1Ki 17:2–3, 5), was fed by ravens and drank from the small brook (1Ki 17:4). When the brook dried up, he went to Zarephath (1Sa 17:7–9).

1Ki 17: 3 in the **K**, east of the Jordan.
17: 5 He went to the **K**, east of the

Keros
Ezr 2:44 **K**, Siaha, Padon,
Ne 7:47 **K**, Sia, Padon,

Kerub
Ezr 2:59 Tel Harsha, **K**, Addon and Immer, but
Ne 7:61 Tel Harsha, **K**, Addon and Immer, but

Kesalon
Jos 15:10 slope of Mount Jearim (that is, **K**

Kesed
Ge 22:22 **K**, Hazo, Pildash, Jidlaph and

Kesil
Jos 15:30 Eltolad, **K**, Hormah,

Kesulloth
Jos 19:18 Their territory included: Jezreel, **K**,

Kettle (Kettles)
1Sa 2:14 He would plunge it into the pan or **k**

Kettles (Kettle)
Mk 7: 4 washing of cups, pitchers and **k**.)

Keturah
Ge 25: 1 took another wife, whose name was **K**.
25: 4 All these were descendants of **K**.
1Ch 1:32 The sons born to **K**, Abraham's
1:33 All these were descendants of **K**.

Key (Keys)
Jdg 3:25 they took a **k** and unlocked them.
1Ch 9:27 the **k** for opening it each morning.
Isa 22:22 the **k** to the house of David
33: 6 the LORD is the **k** to this treasure.
Lk 11:52 have taken away the **k** to knowledge.
Rev 3: 7 and true, who holds the **k** of David.
9: 1 the **k** to the shaft of the Abyss.
20: 1 having the **k** to the Abyss and

Keys (Key)
Mt 16:19 I will give you the **k** of the kingdom
Rev 1:18 And I hold the **k** of death and Hades.

Keziah
Job 42:14 **K** and the third Keren-Happuch.

Kezib
Ge 38: 5 was at **K** that she gave birth to him.

Kibroth Hattaavah
Nu 11:34 Therefore the place was named **K**,
11:35 From **K** the people travelled to
33:16 the Desert of Sinai and camped at **K**.
33:17 They left **K** and camped at Hazeroth.
Dt 9:22 at Taberah, at Massah and at **K**.

Kibzaim
Jos 21:22 **K** and Beth Horon, together with

Kick (Kicked, Kicking)
Ac 26:14 for you to **k** against the goads.'

Kicked (Kick)
Dt 32:15 Jeshurun grew fat and **k**; filled with

Kicking (Kick)
Eze 16: 6 "'Then I passed by and saw you **k**
16:22 and bare, **k** about in your blood.

Kidnapper (Kidnapping, Kidnaps)
Dt 24: 7 slave or sells him, the **k** must die.

Kidnapping (Kidnapper)
Dt 24: 7 If a man is caught **k** one of his

Kidnaps (Kidnapper)
Ex 21:16 "Anyone who **k** another and either

Kidneys
Ex 29:13 and both **k** with the fat on them, and
29:22 both **k** with the fat on them,
Lev 3: 4 both **k** with the fat on them near the
3: 4 which he will remove with the **k**.
3:10 both **k** with the fat on them near the
3:10 which he will remove with the **k**.
3:15 both **k** with the fat on them near the
3:15 which he will remove with the **k**.
4: 9 both **k** with the fat on them near the
4: 9 which he will remove with the **k**—
7: 4 both **k** with the fat on them near the
7: 4 which is to be removed with the **k**.
8:16 and both **k** and their fat, and burned
8:25 both **k** and their fat and the right
9:10 the **k** and the covering of the liver
9:19 **k** and the covering of the liver—
Job 16:13 Without pity, he pierces my **k**
Isa 34: 6 and goats, fat from the **k** of rams.

Kidon
1Ch 13: 9 they came to the threshing-floor of **K**

Kidron Valley
On eastern slope of Jerusalem, towards Mount of Olives, through which flows a small brook. David crossed here to escape from Absalom (2Sa 15:23), and so did Shimei, in disobedience of Solomon (1Ki 2:37–46). Here Asa burned Maacah's Asherah pole (1Ki 15:13; 2Ch 15:16), and the priests burned and tipped articles dedicated to Baal and Asherah (2Ki 23:4, 6, 12; 2Ch 29:16; 30:14). It became the site of a cemetery (2Ki 23:6; Jer 31:40). Nehemiah inspected the walls of Jerusalem from here (Ne 2:15). Jesus crossed it to reach Gethsemane (Jn 18:1).

2Sa 15:23 The king also crossed the **K**,
1Ki 2:37 you leave and cross the **K**,
15:13 down and burned it in the **K**.
2Ki 23: 4 in the fields of the **K**
23: 6 to the **K** outside Jerusalem
23:12 threw the rubble into the **K**.
2Ch 15:16 it up and burned it in the **K**.
29:16 and carried it out to the **K**.
30:14 and threw them into the **K**.
Jer 31:40 the terraces out to the **K**
Jn 18: 1 disciples and crossed the **K**.

Kileab
2Sa 3: 3 his second, **K** the son of Abigail the

Kilion
Ru 1: 2 of his two sons were Mahlon and **K**.
1: 5 both Mahlon and **K** also died, and
4: 9 property of Elimelech, **K** and Mahlon.

Kill (Killed, Killing, Kills)
Ge 4:14 and whoever finds me will **k** me."
4:15 no-one who found him would **k** him.
12:12 will **k** me but will let you live.
18:25 **k** the righteous with the wicked,
20:11 they will **k** me because of my wife.'
26: 7 "The men of this place might **k** me
27:41 then I will **k** my brother Jacob."
37:18 reached them, they plotted to **k** him.
37:20 "Come now, let's **k** him and throw him
Ge 37:26 **k** our brother and cover up his blood?
Ex 1:16 if it is a boy, **k** him; but if it is
2:15 heard of this, he tried to **k** Moses,
4:19 men who wanted to **k** you are dead."
4:23 so I will **k** your firstborn son.
4:24 met ⌊Moses⌋ and was about to **k** him.
5:21 put a sword in their hand to **k** us."
22:24 and I will **k** you with the sword;
32:12 to **k** them in the mountains and to
Lev 14:50 He shall **k** one of the birds over
20:15 to death, and you must **k** the animal.
20:16 **k** both the woman and the animal.
Nu 16:13 and honey to **k** us in the desert?
22:29 my hand, I would **k** you right now."
25: 4 **k** them and expose them in broad
25:17 Midianites as enemies and **k** them,
31:17 Now **k** all the boys. And **k** every
35:17 a stone in his hand that could **k**,
35:18 object in his hand that could **k**,
35:23 drops a stone on him that could **k**
35:27 the avenger of blood may **k** the
Dt 19: 5 and hit his neighbour and **k** him.
19: 6 and **k** him even though he is not
27:25 a bribe to **k** an innocent person.
Jos 9:26 Israelites, and they did not **k** them
Jdg 8:18 What kind of men did you **k** at Tabor
8:19 their lives, I would not **k** you."
8:20 "**K** them!" But Jether did not draw
9:54 "Draw your sword and **k** me, so that
13:23 "If the LORD had meant to **k** us, he
15:12 me that you won't **k** me yourselves.
15:13 We will not **k** you." So they bound
16: 2 night, saying, "At dawn we'll **k** him.
20: 5 the house, intending to **k** me.
21:11 "**K** every male and every woman who
1Sa 5:10 round to us to **k** us and our people
5:11 or it will **k** us and our people.
16: 2 Saul will hear about it and **k** me.
17: 9 If he is able to fight and **k** me,
17: 9 but if I overcome him and **k** him,
19: 1 and all the attendants to **k** David.
19: 2 is looking for a chance to **k** you.
19:11 it and to **k** him in the morning.
19:15 me in his bed so that I may **k** him."
19:17 Why should I **k** you?'
20: 8 If I am guilty, then **k** me yourself!
20:33 hurled his spear at him to **k** him
20:33 that his father intended to **k** David.
22:17 "Turn and **k** the priests of the LORD,
24:10 Some urged me to **k** you, but I spared
24:11 of your robe but did not **k** you.
24:18 your hands, but you did not **k** me.
30:15 **k** me or hand me over to my master,
2Sa 1: 9 'Stand over me and **k** me! I am in the
13:28 'Strike Amnon down,' then **k** him.
21:16 new ⌊sword⌋, said he would **k** David
1Ki 3:26 her the living baby! Don't **k** him!"
3:27 Do not **k** him; she is his mother."
11:40 Solomon tried to **k** Jeroboam, but
12:27 **k** me and return to King Rehoboam."
17:18 remind me of my sin and **k** my son?"
18: 5 not have to **k** any of our animals."
18:12 he doesn't find you, he will **k** me.
18:14 He will **k** me!"
19:10 now they are trying to **k** me too."
19:14 now they are trying to **k** me too."
20:36 as you leave me a lion will **k** you.
2Ki 5: 7 "Am I God? Can I **k** and bring back to
6:21 I **k** them, my father? Shall I **k** them?"
6:22 "Do not **k** them," he answered. "Would
6:22 "Would you **k** men you have captured
7: 4 we live; if they **k** us, then we die."
8:12 **k** their young men with the sword,
9:27 Jehu chased him, shouting, "**K** him
10:25 "Go in and **k** them; let no-one
2Ch 22:11 Athaliah so that she could not **k** him.
30:17 the Levites had to **k** the Passover
Ne 4:11 **k** them and put an end to the work."
6:10 because men are coming to **k** you—
6:10 by night they are coming to **k** you."
Est 3:13 **k** and annihilate all the Jews—
8:11 **k** and annihilate any armed force
Job 20:16 the fangs of an adder will **k** him.
Ps 59: T David's house in order to **k** him.
59:11 do not **k** them, O Lord our shield,
71:10 who wait to **k** me conspire together.
Pr 1:32 of the simple will **k** them,
29:10 integrity and seek to **k** the upright.
Ecc 3: 3 a time to **k** and a time to heal,
Jer 15: 3 "the sword to **k** and the dogs to drag
18:23 O LORD, all their plots to **k** me.
20:17 For he did not **k** me in the womb,
38:15 you an answer, will you not **k** me?
38:16 I will neither **k** you nor hand you
38:25 hide it from us or we will **k** you,'
40:15 "Let me go and **k** Ishmael son of
41: 8 them said to Ishmael, "Don't **k** us!
41: 8 and did not **k** them with the others.
43: 3 so that they may **k** us or carry us
50:21 Pursue, **k** and completely destroy
50:27 **K** all her young bulls; let them go
Eze 9: 5 "Follow him through the city and **k**,
14:13 it and **k** its men and their animals,
14:17 and I **k** its men and their animals,
14:21 **k** its men and their animals!
22:27 and **k** people to make unjust gain.
23:47 they will **k** their sons and daughters
25:13 Edom and **k** its men and their animals.
26:11 will **k** your people with the sword,
28: 9 presence of those who **k** you?
29: 8 and **k** your men and their animals.
Am 2: 3 I will destroy her ruler and **k** all
9: 1 are left I will **k** with the sword.
Na 2:12 the **k** and his dens with the prey.
Mt 2:13 to search for the child to **k** him."
2:16 he gave orders to **k** all the boys
10:28 **k** the body but cannot **k** the soul.
12:14 and plotted how they might **k** Jesus.
14: 5 Herod wanted to **k** John, but he was
17:23 They will **k** him, and on the third
21:38 **k** him and take his inheritance.'
23:34 Some of them you will **k** and crucify;
23:37 Jerusalem, you who **k** the prophets
26: 4 Jesus in some sly way and **k** him.
Mk 3: 4 to save life or to **k**?" But they
3: 6 Herodians how they might **k** Jesus.
6:19 against John and wanted to **k** him.
9:22 him into fire or water to **k** him.
9:31 They will **k** him, and after three
10:34 spit on him, flog him and **k** him.
11:18 began looking for a way to **k** him,
12: 7 Come, let's **k** him, and the
12: 9 He will come and **k** those tenants
14: 1 sly way to arrest Jesus and **k** him.
Lk 11:49 some of whom they will **k** and others
12: 4 afraid of those who **k** the body
13:31 Herod wants to **k** you."
13:34 Jerusalem, you who **k** the prophets
15:23 Bring the fattened calf and **k** it.
15:30 you **k** the fattened calf for him!'
18:32 spit on him, flog him and **k** him.
19:27 here and **k** them in front of me.
19:47 the people were trying to **k** him.
20:14 'Let's **k** him, and the inheritance
20:16 He will come and **k** those tenants
Jn 5:18 Jews tried all the harder to **k** him;
7:19 Why are you trying to **k** me?"
7:20 "Who is trying to **k** you?"
7:25 this the man they are trying to **k**?
8:22 the Jews ask, "Will he **k** himself?
8:37 Yet you are ready to **k** me, because
8:40 As it is, you are determined to **k** me
10:10 The thief comes only to steal and **k**
12:10 made plans to **k** Lazarus as well,
Ac 7:28 Do you want to **k** me as you killed
9:23 the Jews conspired to **k** him,
9:24 on the city gates in order to **k** him.
9:29 Jews, but they tried to **k** him.
10:13 told him, "Get up, Peter. **K** and eat
11: 7 'Get up, Peter. **K** and eat.'
16:27 was about to **k** himself because he
21:31 While they were trying to **k** him,
23:15 ready to **k** him before he gets here."
23:27 Jews and they were about to **k** him,
25: 3 an ambush to **k** him along the way.
26:21 the temple courts and tried to **k** me.
27:42 planned to **k** the prisoners
Ro 11: 3 and they are trying to **k** me"?
1Ti 1: 9 who **k** their fathers or mothers,
Jas 4: 2 You **k** and covet, but you cannot have
Rev 6: 8 a fourth of the earth to **k** by sword,
9: 5 They were not given power to **k** them,

Rev 9:15 released to **k** a third of mankind.
11: 7 them, and overpower and **k** them.

Killed (Kill)

Ge 4: 8 attacked his brother Abel and **k** him.
4:23 I have **k** a man for wounding me,
4:25 in place of Abel, since Cain **k** him."
49: 6 for they have **k** men in their anger
Ex 2:12 he **k** the Egyptian and hid him in the
2:14 killing me as you **k** the Egyptian?"
13:15 the LORD **k** every firstborn in Egypt,
Lev 14: 5 of the birds be **k** over fresh water
14: 6 the bird that was **k** over the
Nu 16:41 "You have **k** the LORD's people," they
19:16 someone who has been **k** with a sword
19:18 someone who has been **k** or someone
22:33 I would certainly have **k** you by now,
25:14 The name of the Israelite who was **k**
25:18 the woman who was **k** when the plague
31: 7 commanded Moses, and **k** every man.
31: 8 **k** Balaam son of Beor with the sword.
31:19 "All of you who have **k** anyone or
31:19 or touched anyone who was **k** must
35: 6 a person who has **k** someone may flee.
35:11 has **k** someone accidentally may flee.
35:15 so that anyone who has **k** another
Dt 4:42 to which anyone who had **k** a person
4:42 had unintentionally **k** his neighbour
21: 1 and it is not known who **k** him,
Jos 7: 5 who **k** about thirty-six of them.
8:24 to Ai and **k** those who were in it.
10:11 **k** by the swords of the Israelites.
10:26 Joshua struck and **k** the kings and
20: 5 because he **k** his neighbour
20: 9 who **k** someone accidentally could
20: 9 not be **k** by the avenger of blood
Jdg 7:25 They **k** Oreb at the rock of Oreb,
8:17 of Peniel and **k** the men of the town.
8:21 Gideon stepped forward and **k** them
9:45 he had captured it and **k** its people.
9:54 that they can't say, 'A woman **k** him.
12: 6 **k** him at the fords of the Jordan.
12: 6 Ephraimites were **k** at that time.
15:16 jaw-bone I have **k** a thousand men."
16:30 Thus he **k** many more when he died
1Sa 4: 2 who **k** about four thousand of them
14:13 followed and **k** behind him.
14:14 his armour-bearer **k** some twenty men
17:35 it by its hair, struck it and **k** it.
17:36 Your servant has **k** both the lion and
17:50 down the Philistine and **k** him.
17:51 After he **k** him, he cut off his head
18: 6 after David had **k** the Philistine,
18:27 David and his men went out and **k**
19: 5 his hands when he **k** the Philistine.
19:11 life tonight, tomorrow you'll be **k**."
20:14 as I live, so that I may not be **k**,
21: 9 whom you **k** in the Valley of Elah,
22:18 That day he **k** eighty-five men who
22:21 Saul had **k** the priests of the
30: 2 They **k** none of them, but carried
31: 2 and they **k** his sons Jonathan,
2Sa 1:10 "So I stood over him and **k** him,
1:16 you said, 'I **k** the LORD's anointed.
2:31 David's men had **k** 360 Benjamites who
3:30 he had **k** their brother Asahel in
4: 7 After they stabbed and **k** him, they
4:11 wicked men have **k** an innocent man
4:12 order to his men, and they **k** them.
10:18 and David **k** seven hundred of their
11:21 **k** Abimelech son of Jerub-Besheth?
12: 9 You **k** him with the sword of the
13:32 think that they **k** all the princes;
14: 6 One struck the other and **k** him.
14: 7 the life of his brother whom he **k**;
18:15 Absalom, struck him and **k** him.
21: 6 descendants be given to us to be **k**
21: 9 who **k** and exposed them on a hill
21:13 been **k** and exposed were gathered up.
21:17 the Philistine down and **k** him.
21:18 time Sibbecai the Hushathite **k** Saph,
21:19 Bethlehemite **k** Goliath the Gittite,
21:21 of Shimeah, David's brother, **k** him.
23: 8 men, whom he **k** in one encounter.
23:18 whom he **k**, and so he became as
2Sa 23:20 a pit on a snowy day and **k** a lion.
23:21 hand and **k** him with his own spear.
1Ki 2: 5 He **k** them, shedding their blood in
2:32 two men and **k** them with the sword.
2:34 up and struck down Joab and **k** him,
2:46 and struck Shimei down and **k** him.
9:16 He **k** its Canaanite inhabitants
13:24 lion met him on the road and **k** him
13:26 which has mauled him and **k** him,
15:28 Baasha **k** Nadab in the third year of
15:29 he **k** Jeroboam's whole family.
16:10 came in, struck him down and **k** him
16:11 he **k** off Baasha's whole family.
19: 1 **k** all the prophets with the sword.
20:36 away, a lion found him and **k** him.
2Ki 10: 9 and **k** him, but who **k** all these?
10:11 Jehu **k** everyone in Jezreel who
10:17 he **k** all who were left there
11: 2 from Athaliah; so he was not **k**.
11:18 and **k** Mattan the priest of Baal
14:19 him to Lachish and **k** him there.
15:25 **k** Pekahiah and succeeded him as king.
17:25 them and they **k** some of the people.
21:24 the people of the land **k** all who had
23:29 Neco faced him and **k** him at Megiddo.
25: 7 They **k** the sons of Zedekiah before
1Ch 4:43 They **k** the remaining Amalekites who
7:21 Ezer and Elead were **k** by the
10: 2 and they **k** his sons Jonathan,
11:11 men, whom he **k** in one encounter.
11:20 whom he **k**, and so he became as
11:22 a pit on a snowy day and **k** a lion.
11:23 hand and **k** him with his own spear.
19:18 and David **k** seven hundred of their
19:18 He also **k** Shophach the commander of
20: 4 Sibbecai the Hushathite **k** Sippai,
20: 5 Elhanan son of Jair **k** Lahmi the
20: 7 of Shimea, David's brother, **k** him.
2Ch 22: 1 the camp, had **k** all the older sons.
22: 8 attending Ahaziah, and he **k** them.
23:17 and **k** Mattan the priest of Baal
24:22 Jehoiada had shown him but **k** his son,
24:23 and **k** all the leaders of the people.
24:25 priest, and they **k** him in his bed.
25:11 where he **k** ten thousand men of Seir.
25:13 They **k** three thousand people and
25:27 him to Lachish and **k** him there.
28: 6 In one day Pekah son of Remaliah **k**
28: 7 Zicri, an Ephraimite warrior, **k**
33:25 the people of the land **k** all who had
36:17 who **k** their young men with the sword
Ne 9:26 They **k** your prophets, who had
Est 9: 6 In the citadel of Susa, the Jews **k**
9: 7 They also **k** Parshandatha, Dalphon,
9:12 "The Jews have **k** and destroyed five
9:16 They **k** seventy-five thousand of them
Ps 135:10 many nations and **k** mighty kings
136:18 and **k** mighty kings—
Isa 14:20 your land and **k** your people.
22: 2 Your slain were not **k** by the sword,
27: 7 been **k** as those were **k** who **k** her?
Jer 39: 6 and also **k** all the nobles of Judah.
41: 3 Ishmael also **k** all the Jews who were
41: 9 all the bodies of the men he had **k**
41:18 had **k** Gedaliah son of Ahikam,
52:10 also **k** all the officials of Judah.
Lam 2:20 be **k** in the sanctuary of the Lord?
4: 9 Those **k** by the sword are better off
Eze 11: 6 You have **k** many people in this city
13:19 you have **k** those who should not
23:10 daughters and **k** her with the sword.
31:17 joining those **k** by the sword.
31:18 with those **k** by the sword.
32:20 fall among those **k** by the sword
32:21 with those **k** by the sword.'
32:25 are uncircumcised, **k** by the sword.
32:26 are uncircumcised, **k** by the sword
32:28 with those **k** by the sword.
32:29 are laid with those **k** by the sword.
32:30 with those **k** by the sword and
32:31 his hordes that were **k** by the sword,
32:32 with those **k** by the sword, declares
35: 8 those **k** by the sword will fall on
Da 3:22 **k** the soldiers who took up Shadrach,
Hos 6: 5 I **k** you with the words of my mouth;
Am 4:10 I **k** your young men with the sword,
Na 2:12 The lion **k** enough for his cubs and
Mt 16:21 and that he must be **k** and on the
21:35 one, **k** another, and stoned a third.
21:39 him out of the vineyard and **k** him.
22: 6 ill-treated them and **k** them.
Mk 8:31 **k** and after three days rise again.
12: 5 still another, and that one they **k**.
12: 5 of them they beat, others they **k**.
12: 8 they took him and **k** him, and threw
Lk 9:22 and he must be **k** and on the third
11:47 it was your forefathers who **k** them.
11:48 they **k** the prophets, and you build
11:51 who was **k** between the altar and the
15:27 your father has **k** the fattened calf
20:15 him out of the vineyard and **k** him.
Ac 3:13 You handed him over to be **k**, and you
3:15 You **k** the author of life, but God
5:30 you had **k** by hanging him on a tree.
5:36 He was **k**, all his followers were
5:37 He too was **k**, and all his followers
7:28 Do you want to kill me as you **k** the
7:52 They even **k** those who predicted the
10:39 They **k** him by hanging him on a tree,
23:12 eat or drink until they had **k** Paul.
23:14 eat anything until we have **k** Paul.
23:21 eat or drink until they have **k** him.
Ro 11: 3 "Lord, they have **k** your prophets and
1Co 10: 9 of them did—and were **k** by snakes.
10:10 were **k** by the destroying angel.
2Co 6: 9 we live on; beaten, and yet not **k**;
1Th 2:15 who **k** the Lord Jesus and the
Heb 11:31 **k** with those who were disobedient.
Rev 6:11 be **k** as they had been was completed.
9:18 A third of mankind was **k** by the
9:20 The rest of mankind that were not **k**
11:13 Seven thousand people were **k** in the
13:10 If anyone is to be **k** with the sword,
13:10 sword, with the sword he will be **k**.
13:15 to worship the image to be **k**.
18:24 all who have been **k** on the earth."
19:21 The rest of them were **k** with the

Killing (Kill)

Ge 27:42 himself with the thought of **k** you.
34:25 the unsuspecting city, **k** every male.
Ex 2:14 **k** me as you killed the Egyptian?"
32:27 each **k** his brother and friend and
Jos 8:24 Israel had finished **k** all the men
1Sa 17:57 soon as David returned from **k** the
19: 5 like David by **k** him for no reason?"
1Ki 18: 4 While Jezebel was **k** off the LORD's
18:13 while Jezebel was **k** the prophets
2Ki 17:26 which are **k** them off, because the
Est 3: 6 scorned the idea of **k** only Mordecai.
9: 5 **k** and destroying them, and they did
Isa 22:13 of cattle and **k** of sheep,
Jer 41: 2 with the sword, **k** the one whom the
Eze 9: 7 out and began **k** throughout the city.
9: 8 While they were **k** and I was left
14:19 **k** its men and their animals,
Jnh 1:14 accountable for **k** an innocent man
Lk 12: 5 after the **k** of the body, has power
Ac 7:24 and avenged him by **k** the Egyptian.
22:20 clothes of those who were **k** him.'

Kills (Kill)

Ge 4:15 "Not so; if anyone **k** Cain, he will
Ex 21:12 "Anyone who strikes a man and **k** him
21:14 if a man schemes and **k** another man
21:29 penned up and it **k** a man or woman,
Lev 24:21 Whoever **k** an animal must make
24:21 **k** a man must be put to death.
Nu 35:30 "'Anyone who **k** a person is to be
Dt 19: 3 anyone who **k** a man may flee there.
19: 4 concerning the man who **k** another
19: 4 who **k** his neighbour unintentionally,
19:11 assaults and **k** him, and then flees
27:24 "Cursed is the man who **k** his
Jos 20: 3 that anyone who **k** a person
1Sa 17:25 great wealth to the man who **k** him.
17:26 "What will be done for the man who **k**
17:27 will be done for the man who **k** him."
Job 5: 2 Resentment **k** a fool, and envy slays
24:14 the murderer rises up and **k** the poor
Isa 66: 3 a bull is like one who **k** a man,

Jn 16: 2 is coming when anyone who **k** you
2Co 3: 6 letter **k**, but the Spirit gives life.

Kilmad
Eze 27:23 Sheba, Asshur and **K** traded with you.

Kimham
2Sa 19:37 But here is your servant **K**. Let him
19:38 The king said, "**K** shall cross over
19:40 over to Gilgal, **K** crossed with him.

Kin (Kinsman, Kinsmen)
Ru 3:12 it is true that I am near of **k**,

Kinah
Jos 15:22 **K**, Dimonah, Adadah,

Kind[1] (Kinds)
Ge 1:21 winged bird according to its **k**.
1:24 animals, each according to its **k**.
6:20 Two of every **k** of bird, of every
6:20 of every **k** of animal and of every **k**
6:21 You are to take every **k** of food that
7: 2 seven of every **k** of clean animal
7: 2 and two of every **k** of unclean animal,
7: 3 also seven of every **k** of bird, male
7:14 wild animal according to its **k**,
7:14 along the ground according to its **k**
7:14 every bird according to its **k**
8:17 Bring out every **k** of living creature
8:19 out of the ark, one **k** after another.
9:15 and all living creatures of every **k**.
9:16 creatures of every **k** on the earth."
27: 4 Prepare me the **k** of tasty food I
Lev 7:14 He is to bring one of each **k** as an
11:14 the red kite, any **k** of black kite,
11:15 any **k** of raven,
11:16 owl, the gull, any **k** of hawk,
11:19 the stork, any **k** of heron, the
11:22 Of these you may eat any **k** of locust,
11:29 the rat, any **k** of great lizard,
13:31 priest examines this **k** of sore
19:23 land and plant any **k** of fruit tree,
25:36 Do not take interest of any **k** from
Nu 5: 2 disease or a discharge of any **k**,
13:19 What **k** of land do they live in?
13:19 What **k** of towns do they live in?
28: 8 along with the same **k** of grain
Dt 4:15 You saw no form of any **k** the day the
4:25 corrupt and make any **k** of idol,
14:13 the black kite, any **k** of falcon,
14:14 any **k** of raven,
14:15 owl, the gull, any **k** of hawk,
14:18 the stork, any **k** of heron, the
24:10 you make a loan of any **k** to your
28:61 bring on you every **k** of sickness
Jdg 6:26 build a proper **k** of altar to the
8:18 "What **k** of men did you kill at
2Sa 13:18 for this was the **k** of garment the
1Ki 9:13 "What **k** of towns are these you have
2Ki 1: 7 The king asked them, "What **k** of man
1Ch 22:15 as men skilled in every **k** of work
2Ch 15: 6 them with every **k** of distress.
Ps 144:13 filled with every **k** of provision.
Pr 23: 7 he is the **k** of man who is always
SS 4:14 with every **k** of incense tree,
Isa 44:11 He and his **k** will be put to shame;
58: 5 Is this the **k** of fast I have chosen,
58: 6 "Is not this the **k** of fasting I have
Jer 8: 9 LORD, what **k** of wisdom do they have?
Eze 17:23 Birds of every **k** will nest in it;
39:17 Call out to every **k** of bird and all
39:20 mighty men and soldiers of every **k**
Da 1: 4 aptitude for every **k** of learning
Zep 2:14 down there, creatures of every **k**.
Mt 8:27 "What **k** of man is this? Even the
Mk 9:29 He replied, "This **k** can come out
Lk 1:29 what **k** of greeting this might be.
7:39 what **k** of woman she is—that she
16: 8 shrewd in dealing with their own **k**
Jn 2: 6 the **k** used by the Jews for
4:23 **k** of worshippers the Father seeks.
12:33 He said this to show the **k** of death
16:25 I will no longer use this **k** of
Jn 18:32 indicating the **k** of death he was
21:19 to indicate the **k** of death by which
Ac 7:49 What **k** of house will you build for
20:35 by this **k** of hard work we must help
Ro 1:29 every **k** of wickedness, evil, greed
7: 8 in me every **k** of covetous desire.
1Co 5: 1 and of a **k** that does not occur even
15:35 With what **k** of body will they come?"
15:38 to each **k** of seed he gives its own
15:39 Men have one **k** of flesh, animals
15:40 of the heavenly bodies is one **k**,
15:41 The sun has one **k** of splendour,
Gal 5: 8 That **k** of persuasion does not come
Eph 4:19 to indulge in every **k** of impurity,
5: 3 or of any **k** of impurity, or of greed,
1Th 1: 9 report what **k** of reception you gave
5:22 Avoid every **k** of evil.
2Ti 3: 6 They are the **k** who worm their way
Jas 1:18 **k** of firstfruits of all he created.
1Pe 2: 1 envy, and slander of every **k**.
4:15 or any other **k** of criminal, or
5: 9 undergoing the same **k** of sufferings.
2Pe 3:11 what **k** of people ought you to be?
Rev 11: 6 the earth with every **k** of plague
18:12 and articles of every **k** made of
21:19 with every **k** of precious stone.

Kind[2] (Kindest, Kind-hearted, Kindly, Kindness, Kindnesses)
Ge 37: 4 could not speak a **k** word to him.
Ex 1:20 God was **k** to the midwives and the
2Ch 10: 7 They replied, "If you will be **k** to
Job 6:28 "But now be so **k** as to look at me.
Pr 11:17 A **k** man benefits himself, but a
12:25 down, but a **k** word cheers him up.
14:21 blessed is he who is **k** to the needy.
14:31 is **k** to the needy honours God.
19:17 He who is **k** to the poor lends to the
28: 8 another, who will be **k** to the poor.
Da 4:27 by being **k** to the oppressed.
Zec 1:13 the LORD spoke **k** and comforting
Lk 6:35 is **k** to the ungrateful and wicked.
Ac 24: 4 you be **k** enough to hear us briefly.
1Co 13: 4 Love is patient, love is **k**. It does
Eph 4:32 Be **k** and compassionate to one
1Th 5:15 **k** to each other and to everyone else.
2Ti 2:24 he must be **k** to everyone, able to
Tit 2: 5 to be busy at home, to be **k**, and to

Kindest (Kind[2])
Pr 12:10 the **k** acts of the wicked are cruel.

Kind-hearted (Kind[2])
Pr 11:16 A **k** woman gains respect, but

Kindle (Kindled, Kindles, Kindling)
Jer 15:14 **k** a fire that will burn against you."
17:27 then I will **k** an unquenchable fire
21:14 I will **k** a fire in your forests that
50:32 I will **k** a fire in her towns that
Eze 24:10 heap on the wood and **k** the fire.

Kindled (Kindle)
Dt 32:22 For a fire has been **k** by my wrath,
Isa 10:16 fire will be **k** like a blazing flame.
Jer 17: 4 for you have **k** my anger, and it will
Lam 4:11 He **k** a fire in Zion that consumed
Eze 20:48 will see that I the LORD have **k** it;
Lk 12:49 and how I wish it were already **k**!
22:55 when they had **k** a fire in the middle

Kindles (Kindle)
Isa 44:15 he **k** a fire and bakes bread.

Kindling (Kindle)
Pr 26:21 is a quarrelsome man for **k** strife.

Kindly (Kind[2])
Ge 50:21 reassured them and spoke **k** to them.
Jos 2:14 we will treat you **k** and faithfully
Ru 2:13 have spoken **k** to your
2Ki 25:28 He spoke **k** to him and gave him a
Jer 52:32 He spoke **k** to him and gave him a
1Co 4:13 we are slandered, we answer **k**.

Kindness (Kind[2])
Ge 19:19 great **k** to me in sparing my life.
21:23 the same **k** I have shown to you."
24:12 and show **k** to my master Abraham.
24:14 that you have shown **k** to my master."
24:27 his **k** and faithfulness to my master.
24:49 Now if you will show **k** and
32:10 I am unworthy of all the **k** and
39:21 he showed him **k** and granted him
40:14 remember me and show me **k**; mention
47:29 you will show me **k** and faithfulness.
Jos 2:12 that you will show **k** to my family,
2:12 because I have shown **k** to you.
Jdg 8:35 They also failed to show **k** to the
21:22 'Do us a **k** by helping them, because
Ru 1: 8 May the LORD show **k** to you, as you
2:20 "He has not stopped showing his **k**
3:10 "This **k** is greater than that which
1Sa 15: 6 for you showed **k** to all the
20: 8 for you, show **k** to your servant, for
20:14 show me unfailing **k** like that of the
20:15 do not ever cut off your **k** from my
2Sa 2: 5 **k** to Saul your master by burying him.
2: 6 May the LORD now show you **k** and
9: 1 I can show **k** for Jonathan's sake?"
9: 3 of Saul to whom I can show God's **k**?"
9: 7 "for I will surely show you **k** for
10: 2 David thought, "I will show **k** to
10: 2 just as his father showed **k** to me.
15:20 May **k** and faithfulness be with you."
22:51 shows unfailing **k** to his anointed,
1Ki 2: 7 "But show **k** to the sons of Barzillai
3: 6 "You have shown great **k** to your
3: 6 You have continued this great **k** to
1Ch 19: 2 David thought, "I will show **k** to
19: 2 because his father showed **k** to me.
2Ch 1: 8 "You have shown great **k** to David my
24:22 King Joash did not remember the **k**
32:25 did not respond to the **k** shown him;
Ezr 9: 9 He has shown us **k** in the sight of
Job 10:12 You gave me life and showed me **k**,
24:21 woman, and to the widow show no **k**.
Ps 18:50 shows unfailing **k** to his anointed,
109:12 May no-one extend **k** to him or take
109:16 For he never thought of doing a **k**,
141: 5 righteous man strike me—it is a **k**;
Isa 54: 8 with everlasting **k** I will have
Jer 9:24 I am the LORD, who exercises **k**,
Hos 11: 4 I led them with cords of human **k**,
Ac 4: 9 for an act of **k** shown to a cripple
14:17 He has shown **k** by giving you rain
27: 3 in **k** to Paul, allowed him to go
28: 2 The islanders showed us unusual **k**.
Ro 2: 4 contempt for the riches of his **k**,
2: 4 God's **k** leads you towards repentance?
11:22 Consider therefore the **k** and
11:22 to those who fell, but **k** to you,
11:22 provided that you continue in his **k**.
2Co 6: 6 understanding, patience and **k**;
Gal 5:22 patience, **k**, goodness, faithfulness,
Eph 2: 7 in his **k** to us in Christ Jesus.
Col 3:12 **k**, humility, gentleness and patience.
Tit 3: 4 when the **k** and love of God our
2Pe 1: 7 and to godliness, brotherly **k**;
1: 7 and to brotherly **k**, love.

Kindnesses (Kind[2])
Ps 106: 7 they did not remember your many **k**,
Isa 63: 7 I will tell of the **k** of the LORD,
63: 7 to his compassion and many **k**.

Kinds (Kind[1])
Ge 1:11 in it, according to their various **k**.
1:12 bearing seed according to their **k**
1:12 seed in it according to their **k**.
1:21 according to their **k**, and every
1:24 according to their **k**: livestock,
1:25 wild animals according to their **k**,
1:25 the livestock according to their **k**,
1:25 the ground according to their **k**.
2: 9 the LORD God made all **k** of trees
4:22 **k** of tools out of bronze and iron.

Ge 7: 3 to keep their various **k** alive
7:14 all livestock according to their **k**,
24:10 with him all **k** of good things
40:17 were all **k** of baked goods for
Ex 1:14 with all **k** of work in the fields;
31: 3 and knowledge in all **k** of crafts—
31: 5 to engage in all **k** of craftsmanship.
35:22 gold jewellery of all **k**: brooches,
35:31 and knowledge in all **k** of crafts—
35:33 in all **k** of artistic craftsmanship.
35:35 to do all **k** of work as craftsmen,
Lev 19:19 mate different **k** of animals.
19:19 plant your field with two **k** of seed.
19:19 clothing woven of two **k** of material.
Dt 6:11 filled with all **k** of good things
12:31 they do all **k** of detestable things
22: 9 Do not plant two **k** of seed in your
1Sa 4: 8 with all **k** of plagues in the desert.
1Ki 7:14 experienced in all **k** of bronze work.
1Ch 18:10 Hadoram brought all **k** of articles
28:14 to be used in various **k** of service,
28:14 to be used in various **k** of service:
29: 2 and all **k** of fine stone and
2Ch 2:14 experienced in all **k** of engraving
32:27 shields and all **k** of valuables.
32:28 stalls for various **k** of cattle,
Ne 5:18 an abundant supply of wine of all **k**.
9:25 filled with all **k** of good things,
13:15 figs and all other **k** of loads.
13:16 all **k** of merchandise and selling
13:20 sellers of all **k** of goods spent the
Ecc 2: 5 all **k** of fruit trees in them.
Jer 15: 3 "I will send four **k** of destroyers
Eze 8:10 the walls all **k** of crawling things
27:22 all **k** of spices and precious stones,
39: 4 as food to all **k** of carrion birds
47:10 The fish will be of many **k**—like the
47:12 Fruit trees of all **k** will grow on
Da 1:17 of all **k** of literature and learning.
1:17 visions and dreams of all **k**.
3: 5 harp, pipes and all **k** of music,
3: 7 lyre, harp and all **k** of music,
3:10 harp, pipes and all **k** of music
3:15 harp, pipes and all **k** of music,
Mt 5:11 all **k** of evil against you because
13:47 the lake and caught all **k** of fish.
Lk 4:40 all who had various **k** of sickness,
11:42 rue and all other **k** of garden herbs,
12:15 your guard against all **k** of greed;
Ac 10:12 contained all **k** of four-footed
13:10 of all **k** of deceit and trickery.
1Co 12: 4 There are different **k** of gifts, but
12: 5 There are different **k** of service,
12: 6 There are different **k** of working,
12:10 speaking in different **k** of tongues
12:28 speaking in different **k** of tongues.
Eph 6:18 with all **k** of prayers and requests.
2Th 2: 9 in all **k** of counterfeit miracles,
1Ti 5:10 herself to all **k** of good deeds.
6:10 money is a root of all **k** of evil.
2Ti 3: 6 are swayed by all **k** of evil desires,
3:11 what **k** of things happened to me in
Tit 3: 3 by all **k** of passions and pleasures.
Heb 13: 9 by all **k** of strange teachings.
Jas 1: 2 whenever you face trials of many **k**,
3: 7 All **k** of animals, birds, reptiles
1Pe 1: 6 to suffer grief in all **k** of trials.

King (*King of kings, King of the Jews*, King's, Kingdom, Kingdoms, Kings, Kings', Kingship, *Lord the king*)

Ge 14: 1 At this time Amraphel **k** of Shinar,
14: 1 Arioch **k** of Ellasar, Kedorlaomer **k**
14: 1 of Elam and Tidal **k** of Goiim
14: 2 went to war against Bera **k** of Sodom,
14: 2 Birsha **k** of Gomorrah, Shinab **k** of
14: 2 of Admah, Shemeber **k** of
14: 8 the **k** of Sodom, the **k** of Gomorrah,
14: 8 the **k** of Admah, the **k** of Zeboiim
14: 8 the **k** of Bela (that is, Zoar)
14: 9 Kedorlaomer **k** of Elam, Tidal **k**
14: 9 Amraphel **k** of Shinar and Arioch **k**
14:17 the **k** of Sodom came out to meet him
14:18 Melchizedek **k** of Salem brought out
14:21 The **k** of Sodom said to Abram, "Give
Ge 14:22 Abram said to the **k** of Sodom, "I
20: 2 Then Abimelech **k** of Gerar sent for
26: 1 **k** of the Philistines in Gerar.
26: 8 Abimelech **k** of the Philistines
36:31 Edom before any Israelite **k** reigned:
36:32 Bela son of Beor became **k** of Edom.
36:33 Zerah from Bozrah succeeded him as **k**.
36:34 of the Temanites succeeded him as **k**.
36:35 country of Moab, succeeded him as **k**.
36:36 from Masrekah succeeded him as **k**.
36:37 on the river succeeded him as **k**.
36:38 son of Acbor succeeded him as **k**.
36:39 Acbor died, Hadad succeeded him as **k**.
40: 1 **k** of Egypt offended their master,
40: 1 their master, the **k** of Egypt.
40: 5 and the baker of the **k** of Egypt,
41:46 the service of Pharaoh **k** of Egypt.
49:20 will provide delicacies fit for a **k**.
Ex 1: 8 a new **k**, who did not know about
1:15 The **k** of Egypt said to the Hebrew
1:17 the **k** of Egypt had told them to do;
1:18 the **k** of Egypt summoned the midwives
2:23 long period, the **k** of Egypt died.
3:18 go to the **k** of Egypt and say to him,
3:19 I know that the **k** of Egypt will not
5: 4 the **k** of Egypt said, "Moses and
6:11 "Go, tell Pharaoh **k** of Egypt to let
6:13 Israelites and Pharaoh **k** of Egypt,
6:27 who spoke to Pharaoh **k** of Egypt
6:29 Tell Pharoah **k** of Egypt everything
14: 5 the **k** of Egypt was told that the
14: 8 the heart of Pharaoh **k** of Egypt,
Nu 20:14 from Kadesh to the **k** of Edom,
21: 1 the Canaanite **k** of Arad, who lived
21:21 to say to Sihon **k** of the Amorites:
21:26 city of Sihon **k** of the Amorites
21:26 fought against the former **k** of Moab
21:29 captives to Sihon **k** of the Amorites.
21:33 and Og **k** of Bashan and his whole
21:34 Do to him what you did to Sihon **k** of
22: 4 who was **k** of Moab at that time,
22:10 **k** of Moab, sent me this message:
23: 7 **k** of Moab from the eastern mountains.
23:21 the shout of the **K** is among them.
24: 7 "Their **k** will be greater than Agag;
32:33 kingdom of Sihon **k** of the Amorites
32:33 the kingdom of Og **k** of Bashan—
33:40 The Canaanite **k** of Arad, who lived
Dt 1: 4 defeated Sihon **k** of the Amorites,
1: 4 had defeated Og **k** of Bashan, who
2:24 **k** of Heshbon, and his country.
2:26 Sihon **k** of Heshbon offering peace
2:30 Sihon **k** of Heshbon refused to let us
3: 1 and Og **k** of Bashan with his whole
3: 2 Do to him what you did to Sihon **k** of
3: 3 Og **k** of Bashan and all his army.
3: 6 done with Sihon **k** of Heshbon
3:11 (Only Og **k** of Bashan was left of the
4:46 of Sihon **k** of the Amorites
4:47 land and the land of Og **k** of Bashan,
7: 8 the power of Pharaoh **k** of Egypt.
11: 3 to Pharoah **k** of Egypt and to his
17:14 "Let us set a **k** over us like all the
17:15 be sure to appoint over you the **k**
17:16 The **k**, moreover, must not acquire
28:36 The LORD will drive you and the **k**
29: 7 Sihon **k** of Heshbon and Og **k** of
33: 5 He was **k** over Jeshurun when the
Jos 2: 2 The **k** of Jericho was told, "Look!
2: 3 the **k** of Jericho sent this message
6: 2 with its **k** and its fighting men.
8: 1 into your hands the **k** of Ai,
8: 2 You shall do to Ai and its **k**
8: 2 as you did to Jericho and its **k**,
8:14 the **k** of Ai saw this, he and all the
8:23 they took the **k** of Ai alive and
8:29 He hung the **k** of Ai on a tree and
9:10 of the Jordan—Sihon **k** of Heshbon,
9:10 and Og **k** of Bashan, who reigned in
10: 1 Now Adoni-Zedek **k** of Jerusalem heard
10: 1 doing to Ai and its **k** as he had done
10: 1 as he had done to Jericho and its **k**,
10: 3 Adoni-Zedek **k** of Jerusalem appealed
10: 3 appealed to Hoham **k** of Hebron,
10: 3 Piram **k** of Jarmuth, Japhia **k** of
10: 3 Lachish and Debir **k** of Eglon.
Jos 10:28 the city and its **k** to the sword
10:28 And he did to the **k** of Makkedah
10:28 as he had done to the **k** of Jericho.
10:30 city and its **k** into Israel's hand.
10:30 **k** as he had done to the **k** of Jericho.
10:33 Meanwhile, Horam **k** of Gezer had come
10:37 together with its **k**, its villages
10:39 They took the city, its **k** and its
10:39 They did to Debir and its **k** as they
10:39 to Libnah and its **k** and to Hebron.
11: 1 Jabin **k** of Hazor heard of this,
11: 1 he sent word to Jobab **k** of Madon,
11:10 Hazor and put its **k** to the sword.
12: 2 Sihon **k** of the Amorites, who reigned
12: 4 the territory of Og **k** of Bashan,
12: 5 to the border of Sihon **k** of Heshbon.
12: 9 the **k** of Jericho one the **k** of Ai
12:10 **k** of Jerusalem one the **k** of Hebron
12:11 the **k** of Jarmuth one the **k** of
12:12 the **k** of Eglon one the **k** of Gezer
12:13 the **k** of Debir one the **k** of Geder
12:14 the **k** of Hormah one the **k** of Arad
12:15 **k** of Libnah one the **k** of Adullam
12:16 the **k** of Makkedah one the **k** of
12:17 **k** of Tappuah one the **k** of Hepher
12:18 **k** of Aphek one the **k** of Lasharon
12:19 the **k** of Madon one the **k** of Hazor
12:20 the **k** of Shimron Meron one the **k** of
12:21 the **k** of Taanach one the **k** of
12:22 **k** of Kedesh one the **k** of Jokneam
12:23 the **k** of Dor (in Naphoth Dor) one
12:23 the **k** of Goyim in Gilgal one
12:24 **k** of Tirzah one thirty-one kings
13:10 of Sihon **k** of the Amorites
13:21 realm of Sihon **k** of the Amorites,
13:27 the realm of Sihon **k** of Heshbon
13:30 entire realm of Og **k** of Bashan
24: 9 Balak son of Zippor, the **k** of Moab,
Jdg 3: 8 Cushan-Rishathaim **k** of Aram Naharaim,
3:10 gave Cushan-Rishathaim **k** of Aram
3:12 Eglon **k** of Moab power over Israel.
3:14 Eglon **k** of Moab for eighteen years.
3:15 him with tribute to Eglon **k** of Moab.
3:17 the tribute to Eglon **k** of Moab.
3:19 have a secret message for you, O **k**.
3:19 The **k** said, "Quiet!" And all his
3:20 As the **k** rose from his seat,
4: 2 Jabin, a **k** of Canaan, who reigned in
4:17 relations between Jabin **k** of Hazor
4:23 subdued Jabin, the Canaanite **k**,
4:24 against Jabin, the Canaanite **k**,
9: 6 in Shechem to crown Abimelech **k**.
9: 8 out to anoint a **k** for themselves.
9: 8 said to the olive tree, 'Be our **k**.'
9:10 the fig-tree, 'Come and be our **k**.'
9:12 to the vine, 'Come and be our **k**.'
9:14 the thornbush, 'Come and be our **k**.'
9:15 'If you really want to anoint me **k**
9:16 faith when you made Abimelech **k**,
9:18 **k** over the citizens of Shechem
11:12 to the Ammonite **k** with the question:
11:13 The **k** of the Ammonites answered
11:14 back messengers to the Ammonite **k**,
11:17 sent messengers to the **k** of Edom
11:17 but the **k** of Edom would not listen.
11:17 They sent also to the **k** of Moab, and
11:19 to Sihon **k** of the Amorites,
11:25 Balak son of Zippor, **k** of Moab?
11:28 The **k** of Ammon, however, paid no
17: 6 In those days Israel had no **k**;
18: 1 In those days Israel had no **k**.
19: 1 In those days Israel had no **k**.
21:25 In those days Israel had no **k**;
1Sa 2:10 "He will give strength to his **k** and
8: 5 now appoint a **k** to lead us,
8: 6 they said, "Give us a **k** to lead us
8: 7 they have rejected me as their **k**.
8: 9 **k** who will reign over them will do."
8:10 people who were asking him for a **k**.
8:11 what the **k** who will reign over you
8:18 relief from the **k** you have chosen,
8:19 "No!" they said. "We want a **k** over
8:20 with a **k** to lead us and to go out
8:22 "Listen to them and give them a **k**.
10:19 have said, 'No, set a **k** over us.'
10:24 people shouted, "Long live the **k**!

1Sa 11:15 as **k** in the presence of the LORD.
12: 1 to me and have set a **k** over you.
12: 2 Now you have a **k** as your leader.
12: 9 **k** of Moab, who fought against them.
12:12 "But when you saw that Nahash **k** of
12:12 'No, we want a **k** to rule over us
12:12 though the LORD your God was your **k**.
12:13 Now here is the **k** you have chosen,
12:13 see, the LORD has set a **k** over you.
12:14 and if both you and the **k** who reigns
12:17 of the LORD when you asked for a **k**."
12:19 sins the evil of asking for a **k**."
12:25 you and your **k** will be swept away."
13: 1 Saul was thirty years old when he
15: 1 anoint you **k** over his people Israel;
15: 8 He took Agag **k** of the Amalekites
15:11 am grieved that I have made Saul **k**
15:17 The LORD anointed you **k** over Israel.
15:20 and brought back Agag their **k**.
15:23 the LORD, he has rejected you as **k**."
15:26 has rejected you as **k** over Israel!"
15:32 Samuel said, "Bring me Agag **k** of the
15:35 that he had made Saul **k** over Israel.
16: 1 have rejected him as **k** over Israel?
16: 1 chosen one of his sons to be **k**."
17:25 The **k** will give great wealth to the
17:55 as you live, O **k**, I don't know."
17:56 The **k** said, "Find out whose son this
18: 6 to meet **K** Saul with singing and
18:22 'Look, the **k** is pleased with you,
18:25 Say to David, 'The **k** wants no other
18:27 presented the full number to the **k**
19: 4 "Let not the **k** do wrong to his
20: 5 I am supposed to dine with the **k**;
20:24 came, the **k** sat down to eat.
21: 2 "The **k** charged me with a certain
21:10 Saul and went to Achish **k** of Gath.
21:11 Isn't this David, the **k** of the land
21:12 much afraid of Achish **k** of Gath.
22: 3 in Moab and said to the **k** of Moab,
22: 4 he left them with the **k** of Moab,
22:11 the **k** sent for the priest Ahimelech
22:11 at Nob, and they all came to the **k**.
22:14 Ahimelech answered the **k**, "Who of
22:15 Let not the **k** accuse your servant
22:16 the **k** said, "You shall surely die,
22:17 the **k** ordered the guards at his side:
22:18 The **k** then ordered Doeg, "You turn
23:17 You shall be **k** over Israel, and I
23:20 Now, O **k**, come down whenever it
23:20 for handing him over to the **k**."
24:14 "Against whom has the **k** of Israel
24:20 I know that you will surely be **k**
25:36 holding a banquet like that of a **k**.
26:14 "Who are you who calls to the **k**?
26:15 came to destroy your lord the **k**.
26:20 The **k** of Israel has come out to look
27: 2 to Achish son of Maoch **k** of Gath.
28:13 **k** said to her, "Don't be afraid.
29: 3 an officer of Saul **k** of Israel
2Sa 2: 4 David **k** over the house of Judah.
2: 7 Judah has anointed me **k** over them.
2: 9 He made him **k** over Gilead, Ashuri
2:10 old when he became **k** over Israel,
2:11 The length of time David was **k** in
3: 3 daughter of Talmai **k** of Geshur;
3:17 have wanted to make David your **k**.
3:23 Abner son of Ner had come to the **k**
3:23 that the **k** had sent him away and
3:24 Joab went to the **k** and said, "What
3:31 **K** David himself walked behind the
3:32 the **k** wept aloud at Abner's tomb.
3:33 The **k** sang this lament for Abner:
3:36 everything the **k** did pleased them.
3:37 all Israel knew that the **k** had no
3:38 the **k** said to his men, "Do you not
3:39 today, though I am the anointed **k**,
4: 8 David at Hebron and said to the **k**,
5: 2 while Saul was **k** over us, you
5: 3 Israel had come to **K** David at Hebron,
5: 3 the **k** made a compact with them at
5: 3 they anointed David **k** over Israel.
5: 4 **k**, and he reigned for forty years.
5: 6 The **k** and his men marched to
5:11 Now Hiram **k** of Tyre sent messengers
5:12 established him as **k** over Israel

2Sa 5:17 had been anointed **k** over Israel,
6:12 Now **K** David was told, "The LORD has
6:16 And when she saw **K** David leaping
6:20 "How the **k** of Israel has
7: 1 After the **k** was settled in his
7: 3 Nathan replied to the **k**, "Whatever
7:18 **K** David went in and sat before the
8: 3 **k** of Zobah, when he went to restore
8: 5 came to help Hadadezer **k** of Zobah,
8: 8 **K** David took a great quantity of
8: 9 Tou **k** of Hamath heard that David had
8:10 he sent his son Joram to **K** David to
8:11 **K** David dedicated these articles to
8:12 Hadadezer son of Rehob, **k** of Zobah.
9: 2 the **k** said to him, "Are you Ziba?"
9: 3 The **k** asked, "Is there no-one still
9: 3 Ziba answered the **k**, "There is still
9: 4 "Where is he?" the **k** asked. Ziba
9: 5 **K** David had him brought from
9: 9 the **k** summoned Ziba, Saul's servant,
9:11 Ziba said to the **k**, "Your servant
10: 1 the **k** of the Ammonites died,
10: 1 his son Hanun succeeded him as **k**.
10: 5 The **k** said, "Stay at Jericho till
10: 6 as well as the **k** of Maacah with a
11: 8 gift from the **k** was sent after him.
11:19 giving the **k** this account of the
12: 7 'I anointed you **k** over Israel, and
12:30 the crown from the head of their **k**
13: 6 When the **k** came to see him, Amnon
13:13 Please speak to the **k**; he will not
13:18 the virgin daughters of the **k** wore.
13:21 **K** David heard all this, he was
13:24 Absalom went to the **k** and said,
13:24 **k** and his officials please join me
13:25 "No, my son," the **k** replied. "All
13:26 The **k** asked him, "Why should he go
13:31 The **k** stood up, tore his clothes
13:34 The watchman went and told the **k**,
13:35 Jonadab said to the **k**, "See, the
13:36 The **k**, too, and all his servants
13:37 son of Ammihud, the **k** of Geshur.
13:37 But **K** David mourned for his son
13:39 the spirit of the **k** longed to go to
14: 3 go to the **k** and speak these words
14: 4 the woman from Tekoa went to the **k**,
14: 4 and she said, "Help me, O **k**!
14: 5 The **k** asked her, "What is troubling
14: 8 The **k** said to the woman, "Go home,
14: 9 **k** and his throne be without guilt."
14:10 The **k** replied, "If anyone says
14:11 She said, "Then let the **k** invoke the
14:13 When the **k** says this, does he not
14:13 for the **k** has not brought back his
14:15 'I will speak to the **k**; perhaps he
14:16 Perhaps the **k** will agree to deliver
14:18 the **k** said to the woman, "Do not
14:19 **k** asked, "Isn't the hand of Joab
14:21 The **k** said to Joab, "Very well,
14:22 him honour, and he blessed the **k**.
14:24 the **k** said, "He must go to his own
14:24 and did not see the face of the **k**.
14:29 in order to send him to the **k**,
14:32 I can send you to the **k** to ask,
14:33 Joab went to the **k** and told him this.
14:33 Then the **k** summoned Absalom, and he
14:33 his face to the ground before the **k**.
14:33 And the **k** kissed Absalom.
15: 2 placed before the **k** for a decision,
15: 3 of the **k** to hear you."
15: 6 came to the **k** asking for justice,
15: 7 Absalom said to the **k**, "Let me go
15: 9 The **k** said to him, "Go in peace."
15:10 then say, 'Absalom is **k** in Hebron.
15:16 The **k** set out, with his entire
15:17 the **k** set out, with all the people
15:18 from Gath marched before the **k**.
15:19 The **k** said to Ittai the Gittite,
15:19 Go back and stay with **K** Absalom.
15:21 Ittai replied to the **k**, "As surely
15:23 The **k** also crossed the Kidron Valley,
15:25 the **k** said to Zadok, "Take the ark
15:27 The **k** also said to Zadok the priest,
15:34 'I will be your servant, O **k**; I was
16: 2 The **k** asked Ziba, "Why have you
16: 3 The **k** then asked, "Where is your

2Sa 16: 4 the **k** said to Ziba, "All that
16: 5 **K** David approached Bahurim, a man
16: 9 Abishai son of Zeruiah said to the **k**,
16:10 the **k** said, "What do you and I have
16:14 The **k** and all the people with him
16:16 "Long live the **k**! Long live the **k**!
17: 2 I would strike down only the **k**
17:16 or the **k** and all the people with him
17:17 and they were to go and tell **K** David,
17:21 and went to inform **K** David.
18: 2 The **k** told the troops, "I myself
18: 4 The **k** answered, "I will do whatever
18: 4 So the **k** stood beside the gate
18: 5 The **k** commanded Joab, Abishai and
18: 5 And all the troops heard the **k**
18:12 In our hearing the **k** commanded you
18:13 nothing is hidden from the **k**—you
18:19 take the news to the **k** that the LORD
18:21 "Go, tell the **k** what you have seen.
18:25 The watchman called out to the **k** and
18:25 The **k** said, "If he is alone, he must
18:26 The **k** said, "He must be bringing
18:27 "He's a good man," the **k** said. "He
18:28 Ahimaaz called out to the **k**, "All
18:28 the **k** with his face to the ground
18:29 The **k** asked, "Is the young man
18:30 The **k** said, "Stand aside and wait
18:32 The **k** asked the Cushite, "Is the
18:33 The **k** was shaken. He went up to the
19: 1 Joab was told, "The **k** is weeping and
19: 2 "The **k** is grieving for his son.
19: 4 The **k** covered his face and cried
19: 5 Joab went into the house to the **k**
19: 8 the **k** got up and took his seat in
19: 8 When the men were told, "The **k** is
19: 9 "The **k** delivered us from the hand of
19:10 nothing about bringing the **k** back?"
19:11 **K** David sent this message to Zadok
19:11 to bring the **k** back to his palace,
19:11 has reached the **k** at his quarters?
19:12 be the last to bring back the **k**?'
19:14 They sent word to the **k**, "Return,
19:15 the **k** returned and went as far as
19:15 **k** and bring him across the Jordan.
19:16 the men of Judah to meet **K** David.
19:17 to the Jordan, where the **k** was.
19:18 he fell prostrate before the **k**
19:19 May the **k** put it out of his mind.
19:22 know that today I am **k** over Israel?"
19:23 **k** said to Shimei, "You shall not
19:23 And the **k** promised him on oath.
19:24 also went down to meet the **k**.
19:24 from the day the **k** left until the
19:25 came from Jerusalem to meet the **k**,
19:25 the **k** asked him, "Why didn't you go
19:26 so that I can go with the **k**.
19:28 to make any more appeals to the **k**?"
19:29 The **k** said to him, "Why say more?
19:30 Mephibosheth said to the **k**, "Let him
19:31 to cross the Jordan with the **k**
19:32 He had provided for the **k** during his
19:33 The **k** said to Barzillai, "Cross over
19:34 Barzillai answered the **k**, "How many
19:34 go up to Jerusalem with the **k**?
19:36 with the **k** for a short distance,
19:36 should the **k** reward me in this way?
19:38 The **k** said, "Kimham shall cross over
19:39 Jordan, and then the **k** crossed over.
19:39 The **k** kissed Barzillai and gave him
19:40 the **k** crossed over to Gilgal, Kimham
19:40 of Israel had taken the **k** over.
19:41 coming to the **k** and saying to him,
19:41 the men of Judah, steal the **k** away
19:42 the **k** is closely related to us.
19:43 "We have ten shares in the **k**;
19:43 to speak of bringing back our **k**?"
20: 2 the men of Judah stayed by their **k**
20: 4 the **k** said to Amasa, "Summon the men
20: 5 than the time the **k** had set for him.
20:21 hand against the **k**, against David.
20:22 Joab went back to the **k** in Jerusalem.
21: 2 The **k** summoned the Gibeonites and
21: 5 They answered the **k**, "As for the man
21: 6 So the **k** said, "I will give them to
21: 7 The **k** spared Mephibosheth son of
21: 8 the **k** took Armoni and Mephibosheth,

2Sa 21:14 and did everything the **k** commanded.
22:51 He gives his **k** great victories;
24: 2 the **k** said to Joab and the army
24: 3 Joab replied to the **k**, "May the LORD
24: 4 so they left the presence of the **k**
24: 9 number of the fighting men to the **k**:
24:20 Araunah looked and saw the **k** and his
24:20 the **k** with his face to the ground.
24:23 O **k**, Araunah gives all this to the **k**
24:24 the **k** replied to Araunah, "No, I
1Ki 1: 1 **K** David was old and well advanced in
1: 2 attend the **k** and take care of him.
1: 3 Shunammite, and brought her to the **k**.
1: 4 care of the **k** and waited on him,
1: 4 **k** had no intimate relations with her.
1: 5 forward and said, "I will be **k**.
1:11 the son of Haggith, has become **k**
1:13 Go in to **K** David and say to him, 'My
1:13 "Surely Solomon your son shall be **k**
1:13 Why then has Adonijah become **k**?'
1:14 are still there talking to the **k**,
1:15 Bathsheba went to see the aged **k**
1:16 bowed low and knelt before the **k**.
1:16 "What is it you want?" the **k** asked.
1:17 'Solomon your son shall become **k**
1:18 now Adonijah has become **k**, and you,
1:22 she was still speaking with the **k**,
1:23 told the **k**, "Nathan the prophet
1:23 So he went before the **k** and bowed
1:24 declared that Adonijah shall be **k**
1:25 and saying, 'Long live King Adonijah!
1:27 throne of my lord the **k** after him?
1:28 **K** David said, "Call in Bathsheba."
1:29 The **k** then took an oath: "As surely
1:30 Solomon your son shall be **k** after me,
1:31 kneeling before the **k**, said, "May my
1:31 "May my lord **K** David live for ever!
1:32 **K** David said, "Call in Zadok the
1:32 When they came before the **k**,
1:34 prophet anoint him **k** over Israel.
1:34 and shout, 'Long live **K** Solomon!'
1:36 son of Jehoiada answered the **k**,
1:37 than the throne of my lord **K** David!"
1:38 put Solomon on **K** David's mule and
1:39 shouted, "Long live **K** Solomon!
1:43 lord **K** David has made Solomon **k**.
1:44 The **k** has sent with him Zadok the
1:45 have anointed him **k** at Gihon.
1:47 to congratulate our lord **K** David,
1:47 And the **k** bowed in worship on his
1:51 "Adonijah is afraid of **K** Solomon
1:51 He says, 'Let **K** Solomon swear to me
1:53 **K** Solomon sent men, and they brought
1:53 came and bowed down to **K** Solomon,
2:15 All Israel looked to me as their **k**.
2:17 he continued, "Please ask **K** Solomon
2:18 "I will speak to the **k** for you.
2:19 Bathsheba went to **K** Solomon to speak
2:19 the **k** stood up to meet her, bowed
2:20 "Do not refuse me." The **k** replied,
2:22 **K** Solomon answered his mother, "Why
2:23 **K** Solomon swore by the LORD: "May
2:25 **K** Solomon gave orders to Benaiah
2:26 To Abiathar the priest the **k** said,
2:29 **K** Solomon was told that Joab had
2:30 "The **k** says, 'Come out!'" But he
2:30 Benaiah reported to the **k**, "This is
2:31 the **k** commanded Benaiah, "Do as he
2:35 The **k** put Benaiah son of Jehoiada
2:36 the **k** sent for Shimei and said to
2:38 Shimei answered the **k**, "What you say
2:39 **k** of Gath, and Shimei was told,
2:42 the **k** summoned Shimei and said to
2:44 The **k** also said to Shimei, "You know
2:45 **K** Solomon will be blessed, and
2:46 the **k** gave the order to Benaiah
3: 1 an alliance with Pharoah **k** of Egypt
3: 4 The **k** went to Gibeon to offer
3: 7 you have made your servant **k** in
3:16 Now two prostitutes came to the **k**
3:22 And so they argued before the **k**.
3:23 The **k** said, "This one says, 'My son
3:24 the **k** said, "Bring me a sword."
3:24 So they brought a sword for the **k**.
3:26 for her son and said to the **k**,
3:27 the **k** gave his ruling: "Give the

1Ki 3:28 heard the verdict the **k** had given
3:28 they held the **k** in awe, because they
4: 1 **K** Solomon ruled over all Israel.
4: 5 and personal adviser to the **k**;
4: 7 for the **k** and the royal household.
4:19 country of Sihon **k** of the Amorites
4:19 and the country of Og **k** of Bashan).
4:27 supplied provisions for **K** Solomon
5: 1 Hiram **k** of Tyre heard that Solomon
5: 1 **k** to succeed his father David,
5:13 **K** Solomon conscripted labourers from
6: 2 The temple that **K** Solomon built for
7:13 **K** Solomon sent to Tyre and brought
7:14 He came to **K** Solomon and did all the
7:40 **K** Solomon in the temple of the LORD:
7:45 that Huram made for **K** Solomon
7:46 The **k** had them cast in clay moulds
7:51 all the work **K** Solomon had done for
8: 1 **K** Solomon summoned into his presence
8: 2 came together to **K** Solomon at the
8: 5 **K** Solomon and the entire assembly of
8:14 the **k** turned round and blessed them.
8:62 the **k** and all Israel with him
8:63 the **k** and all the Israelites
8:64 On that same day the **k** consecrated
8:66 They blessed the **k** and then went
9:11 **K** Solomon gave twenty towns in
9:11 towns in Galilee to Hiram **k** of Tyre,
9:14 Hiram had sent to the **k** 120 talents
9:15 forced labour **K** Solomon conscripted
9:16 (Pharaoh **k** of Egypt had attacked
9:26 **K** Solomon also built ships at Ezion
9:28 which they delivered to **K** Solomon.
10: 3 hard for the **k** to explain to her.
10: 6 She said to the **k**, "The report I
10: 9 he has made you **k**, to maintain
10:10 she gave the **k** 120 talents of gold
10:10 queen of Sheba gave to **K** Solomon.
10:12 The **k** used the almug-wood to make
10:13 **K** Solomon gave the queen of Sheba
10:16 **K** Solomon made two hundred large
10:17 The **k** put them in the Palace of the
10:18 the **k** made a great throne inlaid
10:21 All **K** Solomon's goblets were gold,
10:22 The **k** had a fleet of trading ships
10:23 **K** Solomon was greater in riches and
10:27 The **k** made silver as common in
11: 1 **K** Solomon, however, loved many
11:18 to Egypt, to Pharaoh **k** of Egypt
11:23 his master, Hadadezer **k** of Zobah.
11:26 son of Nebat rebelled against the **k**.
11:27 of how he rebelled against the **k**:
11:37 you will be **k** over Israel.
11:40 to Shishak the **k**, and stayed there
11:43 Rehoboam his son succeeded him as **k**.
12: 1 had gone there to make him **k**.
12: 2 where he had fled from **K** Solomon),
12: 6 **K** Rehoboam consulted the elders who
12:12 as the **k** had said, "Come back to me
12:13 The **k** answered the people harshly.
12:15 the **k** did not listen to the people,
12:16 all Israel saw that the **k** refused to
12:16 they answered the **k**: "What share do
12:18 **K** Rehoboam sent out Adoniram, who
12:18 **K** Rehoboam, however, managed to get
12:20 and made him **k** over all Israel.
12:23 Rehoboam son of Solomon **k** of Judah
12:27 to their lord, Rehoboam **k** of Judah.
12:27 kill me and return to **K** Rehoboam."
12:28 the **k** made two golden calves.
13: 4 **K** Jeroboam heard what the man of God
13: 6 the **k** said to the man of God,
13: 7 The **k** said to the man of God, "Come
13: 8 the man of God answered the **k**, "Even
13:11 father what he had said to the **k**.
14: 2 me I would be **k** over this people.
14:14 up for himself a **k** over Israel
14:20 And Nadab his son succeeded him as **k**.
14:21 son of Solomon was **k** in Judah.
14:21 years old when he became **k**,
14:25 In the fifth year of **K** Rehoboam,
14:25 **k** of Egypt attacked Jerusalem.
14:27 **K** Rehoboam made bronze shields to
14:28 Whenever the **k** went to the LORD's
14:31 Abijah his son succeeded him as **k**.
15: 1 of Nebat, Abijah became **k** of Judah,

1Ki 15: 8 And Asa his son succeeded him as **k**.
15: 9 In the twentieth year of Jeroboam **k**
15: 9 of Israel, Asa became **k** of Judah,
15:16 **k** of Israel throughout their reigns.
15:17 Baasha **k** of Israel went up against
15:17 the territory of Asa **k** of Judah.
15:18 the son of Hezion, the **k** of Aram,
15:19 your treaty with Baasha **k** of Israel
15:20 Ben-Hadad agreed with **K** Asa and sent
15:22 **K** Asa issued an order to all
15:22 With them **K** Asa built up Geba in
15:24 his son succeeded him as **k**.
15:25 son of Jeroboam became **k** of Israel
15:25 the second year of Asa **k** of Judah,
15:28 **k** of Judah and succeeded him as **k**.
15:32 **k** of Israel throughout their reigns.
15:33 In the third year of Asa **k** of Judah,
15:33 Baasha son of Ahijah became **k** of all
16: 6 And Elah his son succeeded him as **k**.
16: 8 twenty-sixth year of Asa **k** of Judah
16: 8 Elah son of Baasha became **k** of
16:10 year of Asa **k** of Judah.
16:10 Then he succeeded him as **k**.
16:15 the twenty-seventh year of Asa **k** of
16:16 against the **k** and murdered him,
16:16 the commander of the army, **k** over
16:21 Tibni son of Ginath for **k**, and the
16:22 So Tibni died and Omri became **k**.
16:23 thirty-first year of Asa **k** of Judah
16:23 Omri became **k** of Israel, and he
16:28 And Ahab his son succeeded him as **k**.
16:29 In the thirty-eighth year of Asa **k**
16:29 Ahab son of Omri became **k** of Israel,
16:31 of Ethbaal **k** of the Sidonians,
19:15 there, anoint Hazael **k** over Aram.
19:16 Jehu son of Nimshi **k** over Israel
20: 1 Now Ben-Hadad **k** of Aram mustered his
20: 2 into the city to Ahab **k** of Israel,
20: 4 The **k** of Israel answered, "Just as
20: 7 The **k** of Israel summoned all the
20:11 The **k** of Israel answered, "Tell him:
20:13 a prophet came to Ahab **k** of Israel
20:20 But Ben-Hadad **k** of Aram escaped on
20:21 The **k** of Israel advanced and
20:22 Afterwards, the prophet came to the **k**
20:22 **k** of Aram will attack you again."
20:23 the officials of the **k** of Aram
20:28 The man of God came up and told the **k**
20:31 Let us go to the **k** of Israel with
20:32 they went to the **k** of Israel and
20:32 The **k** answered, "Is he still
20:33 "Go and get him," the **k** said.
20:38 stood by the road waiting for the **k**.
20:39 the **k** passed by, the prophet called
20:40 "That is your sentence," the **k** of
20:41 and the **k** of Israel recognised him
20:42 He said to the **k**, "This is what the
20:43 Sullen and angry, the **k** of Israel
21: 1 to the palace of Ahab **k** of Samaria.
21: 7 "Is this how you act as **k** over
21:10 he has cursed both God and the **k**.
21:13 Naboth has cursed both God and the **k**.
21:18 "Go down to meet Ahab **k** of Israel,
22: 2 third year Jehoshaphat **k** of Judah
22: 2 went down to see the **k** of Israel.
22: 3 The **k** of Israel had said to his
22: 3 to retake it from the **k** of Aram?"
22: 4 replied to the **k** of Israel,
22: 5 Jehoshaphat also said to the **k** of
22: 6 the **k** of Israel brought together the
22: 8 The **k** of Israel answered Jehoshaphat,
22: 8 "The **k** should not say that,"
22: 9 the **k** of Israel called one of his
22:10 the **k** of Israel and Jehoshaphat **k** of
22:13 are predicting success for the **k**.
22:15 he arrived, the **k** asked him,
22:16 The **k** said to him, "How many times
22:18 The **k** of Israel said to Jehoshaphat,
22:26 The **k** of Israel then ordered, "Take
22:27 say, 'This is what the **k** says: Put
22:29 the **k** of Israel and Jehoshaphat **k** of
22:30 The **k** of Israel said to Jehoshaphat,
22:30 So the **k** of Israel disguised
22:31 Now the **k** of Aram had ordered his
22:31 or great, except the **k** of Israel."
22:32 "Surely this is the **k** of Israel.

1Ki 22:33 **k** of Israel and stopped pursuing him.
22:34 hit the **k** of Israel between the
22:34 The **k** told his chariot driver,
22:35 and the **k** was propped up in his
22:37 the **k** died and was brought to
22:40 Ahaziah his son succeeded him as **k**.
22:41 Jehoshaphat son of Asa became **k** of
22:41 the fourth year of Ahab **k** of Israel.
22:42 years old when he became **k**,
22:44 also at peace with the **k** of Israel.
22:47 There was then no **k** in Edom;
22:51 Ahaziah son of Ahab became **k** of
22:51 year of Jehoshaphat **k** of Judah,
2Ki 1: 3 of the **k** of Samaria and ask them,
1: 5 the messengers returned to the **k**,
1: 6 'Go back to the **k** who sent you and
1: 7 The **k** asked them, "What kind of man
1: 8 The **k** said, "That was Elijah the
1: 9 of God, the **k** says, 'Come down!'
1:11 At this the **k** sent to Elijah another
1:11 the **k** says, 'Come down at once!'
1:13 the **k** sent a third captain with his
1:15 up and went down with him to the **k**.
1:16 He told the **k**, "This is what the
1:17 Joram succeeded him as **k** in the
1:17 son of Jehoshaphat **k** of Judah.
3: 1 Joram son of Ahab became **k** of Israel
3: 1 year of Jehoshaphat **k** of Judah,
3: 4 Now Mesha **k** of Moab raised sheep,
3: 4 and he had to supply the **k** of Israel
3: 5 died, the **k** of Moab rebelled
3: 5 rebelled against the **k** of Israel.
3: 6 at that time **K** Joram set out from
3: 7 message to Jehoshaphat **k** of Judah:
3: 7 **k** of Moab has rebelled against me.
3: 9 the **k** of Israel set out with the
3: 9 the **k** of Judah and the **k** of Edom.
3:10 "What!" exclaimed the **k** of Israel.
3:11 officer of the **k** of Israel answered,
3:12 So the **k** of Israel and Jehoshaphat
3:12 and the **k** of Edom went down to him.
3:13 Elisha said to the **k** of Israel,
3:13 "No," the **k** of Israel answered,
3:14 presence of Jehoshaphat **k** of Judah,
3:26 the **k** of Moab saw that the battle
3:26 to the **k** of Edom, but they failed.
3:27 who was to succeed him as **k**, and
4:13 the **k** or the commander of the army?'
5: 1 of the army of the **k** of Aram.
5: 5 "By all means, go," the **k** of Aram
5: 5 send a letter to the **k** of Israel
5: 6 The letter that he took to the **k**
5: 7 soon as the **k** of Israel read the
5: 8 the **k** of Israel had torn his robes,
6: 8 Now the **k** of Aram was at war with
6: 9 The man of God sent word to the **k**
6:10 the **k** of Israel checked on the place
6:10 Time and again Elisha warned the **k**,
6:11 This enraged the **k** of Aram.
6:11 is on the side of the **k** of Israel?"
6:12 tells the **k** of Israel the very words
6:13 where he is," the **k** ordered,
6:21 the **k** of Israel saw them, he asked
6:24 Some time later, Ben-Hadad **k** of Aram
6:26 the **k** of Israel was passing by on
6:27 The **k** replied, "If the LORD does not
6:30 the **k** heard the woman's words, he
6:32 The **k** sent a messenger ahead, but
6:33 the ⌊**k**⌋ said, "this disaster is
7: 2 The officer on whose arm the **k** was
7: 6 "Look, the **k** of Israel has hired the
7:12 The **k** got up in the night and said
7:14 **k** sent them after the Aramean army.
7:15 returned and reported to the **k**.
7:17 Now the **k** had put the officer on
7:17 when the **k** came down to his house.
7:18 said to the **k**: "About this time
8: 3 went to the **k** to beg for her house
8: 4 The **k** was talking to Gehazi, the
8: 5 Just as Gehazi was telling the **k** how
8: 5 came to beg the **k** for her house and
8: 6 The **k** asked the woman about it, and
8: 7 and Ben-Hadad **k** of Aram was ill.
8: 7 When the **k** was told, "The man of God
8: 9 "Your son Ben-Hadad **k** of Aram has
8:13 become **k** of Aram," answered Elisha.
2Ki 8:15 Then Hazael succeeded him as **k**.
8:16 of Joram son of Ahab **k** of Israel,
8:16 when Jehoshaphat was **k** of Judah,
8:16 began his reign as **k** of Judah.
8:17 years old when he became **k**,
8:20 against Judah and set up its own **k**.
8:24 Ahaziah his son succeeded him as **k**.
8:25 of Joram son of Ahab **k** of Israel,
8:25 Jehoram **k** of Judah began to reign.
8:26 years old when he became **k**,
8:26 a granddaughter of Omri **k** of Israel.
8:28 Hazael **k** of Aram at Ramoth Gilead.
8:29 **K** Joram returned to Jezreel to
8:29 in his battle with Hazael **k** of Aram.
8:29 Ahaziah son of Jehoram **k** of Judah
9: 3 says: I anoint you **k** over Israel.
9: 6 anoint you **k** over the LORD's people
9:12 says: I anoint you **k** over Israel.
9:13 and shouted, "Jehu is **k**!
9:14 Gilead against Hazael **k** of Aram,
9:15 **K** Joram had returned to Jezreel to
9:15 in the battle with Hazael **k** of Aram.
9:16 **k** of Judah had gone down to see him.
9:18 "This is what the **k** says: 'Do you
9:19 the **k** sent out a second horseman.
9:19 "This is what the **k** says: 'Do you
9:21 Joram **k** of Israel and Ahaziah **k** of
9:27 Ahaziah **k** of Judah saw what had
9:29 Ahab, Ahaziah had become **k** of Judah
10: 5 We will not appoint anyone as **k**;
10:13 he met some relatives of Ahaziah **k**
10:13 of the **k** and of the queen mother."
10:35 Jehoahaz his son succeeded him as **k**.
11: 2 Jehosheba, the daughter of **K** Jehoram
11: 7 all to guard the temple for the **k**.
11: 8 Station yourselves round the **k**, each
11: 8 close to the **k** wherever he goes."
11:10 shields that had belonged to **K** David
11:11 stationed themselves round the **k**
11:12 the covenant and proclaimed him **k**.
11:12 and shouted, "Long live the **k**!
11:14 She looked and there was the **k**,
11:14 the trumpeters were beside the **k**,
11:17 the **k** and people that they would be
11:17 between the **k** and the people.
11:19 and together they brought the **k** down
11:19 The **k** then took his place on the
12: 1 Joash became **k**, and he reigned in
12: 6 by the twenty-third year of **K** Joash
12: 7 Therefore **K** Joash summoned Jehoiada
12:17 About this time Hazael **k** of Aram
12:18 Joash **k** of Judah took all the sacred
12:18 he sent them to Hazael **k** of Aram,
12:21 Amaziah his son succeeded him as **k**.
13: 1 of Joash son of Ahaziah **k** of Judah,
13: 1 Jehoahaz son of Jehu became **k** of
13: 3 **k** of Aram and Ben-Hadad his son.
13: 4 the **k** of Aram was oppressing Israel.
13: 7 for the **k** of Aram had destroyed the
13: 9 Jehoash his son succeeded him as **k**.
13:10 In the thirty-seventh year of Joash **k**
13:10 Jehoash son of Jehoahaz became **k** of
13:12 his war against Amaziah **k** of Judah
13:14 Jehoash **k** of Israel went down to see
13:16 hands," he said to the **k** of Israel.
13:18 "Take the arrows," and the **k** took
13:22 Hazael **k** of Aram oppressed Israel
13:24 Hazael **k** of Aram died, and Ben-Hadad
13:24 Ben-Hadad his son succeeded him as **k**.
14: 1 Jehoash son of Jehoahaz **k** of Israel,
14: 1 of Joash **k** of Judah began to reign.
14: 2 years old when he became **k**,
14: 5 who had murdered his father the **k**.
14: 8 the son of Jehu, **k** of Israel, with
14: 9 Jehoash **k** of Israel replied to
14: 9 Israel replied to Amaziah **k** of Judah:
14:11 so Jehoash **k** of Israel attacked.
14:11 He and Amaziah **k** of Judah faced each
14:13 Jehoash **k** of Israel captured Amaziah
14:13 Israel captured Amaziah **k** of Judah,
14:15 including his war against Amaziah **k**
14:16 Jeroboam his son succeeded him as **k**.
14:17 Amaziah son of Joash **k** of Judah
14:17 Jehoash son of Jehoahaz **k** of Israel.
14:21 **k** in place of his father Amaziah.
14:23 of Amaziah son of Joash **k** of Judah,
2Ki 14:23 **k** of Israel became **k** in Samaria,
14:29 Zechariah his son succeeded him as **k**.
15: 1 year of Jeroboam **k** of Israel,
15: 1 Amaziah **k** of Judah began to reign.
15: 2 sixteen years old when he became **k**,
15: 5 The LORD afflicted the **k** with
15: 7 Jotham his son succeeded him as **k**.
15: 8 year of Azariah **k** of Judah,
15: 8 Zechariah son of Jeroboam became **k**
15:10 him and succeeded him as **k**.
15:13 Shallum son of Jabesh became **k** in
15:13 year of Uzziah **k** of Judah,
15:14 him and succeeded him as **k**.
15:17 the thirty-ninth year of Azariah **k**
15:17 son of Gadi became **k** of Israel
15:19 Pul **k** of Assyria invaded the land,
15:20 to be given to the **k** of Assyria.
15:20 So the **k** of Assyria withdrew and
15:22 Pekahiah his son succeeded him as **k**.
15:23 In the fiftieth year of Azariah **k** of
15:23 son of Menahem became **k** of Israel
15:25 Pekahiah and succeeded him as **k**.
15:27 the fifty-second year of Azariah **k**
15:27 son of Remaliah became **k** of Israel
15:29 In the time of Pekah **k** of Israel,
15:29 Tiglath-Pileser **k** of Assyria came
15:30 and then succeeded him as **k** in the
15:32 Pekah son of Remaliah **k** of Israel,
15:32 son of Uzziah **k** of Judah began to
15:33 years old when he became **k**,
15:37 LORD began to send Rezin **k** of Aram
15:38 And Ahaz his son succeeded him as **k**.
16: 1 son of Jotham **k** of Judah began to
16: 2 twenty years old when he became **k**,
16: 5 Rezin **k** of Aram and Pekah son of
16: 5 Pekah son of Remaliah **k** of Israel
16: 6 Rezin **k** of Aram recovered Elath
16: 7 say to Tiglath-Pileser **k** of Assyria,
16: 7 out of the hand of the **k** of Aram
16: 7 **k** of Israel who are attacking me."
16: 8 it as a gift to the **k** of Assyria.
16: 9 The **k** of Assyria complied by
16:10 **K** Ahaz went to Damascus to meet
16:10 meet Tiglath-Pileser **k** of Assyria.
16:11 that **K** Ahaz had sent from Damascus
16:11 finished it before **K** Ahaz returned.
16:12 the **k** came back from Damascus and
16:15 **K** Ahaz then gave these orders to
16:16 Uriah the priest did just as **K** Ahaz
16:17 **K** Ahaz took away the side panels and
16:18 in deference to the **k** of Assyria.
16:20 Hezekiah his son succeeded him as **k**.
17: 1 twelfth year of Ahaz **k** of Judah
17: 1 son of Elah became **k** of Israel
17: 3 Shalmaneser **k** of Assyria came up to
17: 4 the **k** of Assyria discovered that
17: 4 had sent envoys to So **k** of Egypt
17: 4 paid tribute to the **k** of Assyria,
17: 5 The **k** of Assyria invaded the entire
17: 6 the **k** of Assyria captured Samaria
17: 7 the power of Pharaoh **k** of Egypt.
17:21 made Jeroboam son of Nebat their **k**.
17:24 The **k** of Assyria brought people from
17:26 was reported to the **k** of Assyria:
17:27 the **k** of Assyria gave this order:
18: 1 of Hoshea son of Elah **k** of Israel,
18: 1 of Ahaz **k** of Judah began to reign.
18: 2 years old when he became **k**,
18: 7 **k** of Assyria and did not serve him.
18: 9 In **K** Hezekiah's fourth year, which
18: 9 of Hoshea son of Elah **k** of Israel,
18: 9 Shalmaneser **k** of Assyria marched
18:10 ninth year of Hoshea **k** of Israel.
18:11 The **k** of Assyria deported Israel to
18:13 fourteenth year of **K** Hezekiah's
18:13 Sennacherib **k** of Assyria attacked
18:14 Hezekiah **k** of Judah sent this
18:14 to the **k** of Assyria at Lachish:
18:14 **k** of Assyria exacted from Hezekiah
18:14 **k** of Judah three hundred talents of
18:16 At this time Hezekiah **k** of Judah
18:16 and gave it to the **k** of Assyria.
18:17 The **k** of Assyria sent his supreme
18:17 Lachish to **K** Hezekiah at Jerusalem.
18:18 They called for the **k**; and Eliakim
18:19 'This is what the great **k**, the **k** of

2Ki 18:21 **k** of Egypt to all who depend on him.
18:23 my master, the **k** of Assyria:
18:28 of the great **k**, the **k** of Assyria!
18:29 This is what the **k** says: Do not let
18:30 into the hand of the **k** of Assyria.'
18:31 This is what the **k** of Assyria says:
18:33 from the hand of the **k** of Assyria?
18:36 **k** had commanded, "Do not answer him.
19: 1 **K** Hezekiah heard this, he tore his
19: 4 whom his master, the **k** of Assyria,
19: 5 **K** Hezekiah's officials came to
19: 6 the **k** of Assyria have blasphemed me.
19: 8 the field commander heard that the **k**
19: 8 found the **k** fighting against Libnah.
19: 9 the Cushite **k** of Egypt, was marching
19:10 "Say to Hezekiah **k** of Judah: Do not
19:10 be handed over to the **k** of Assyria.'
19:13 Where is the **k** of Hamath, the **k** of
19:13 the **k** of the city of Sepharvaim,
19:20 concerning Sennacherib **k** of Assyria.
19:32 says concerning the **k** of Assyria:
19:36 Sennacherib **k** of Assyria broke camp
19:37 his son succeeded him as **k**.
20: 6 from the hand of the **k** of Assyria.
20:12 **k** of Babylon sent Hezekiah letters
20:14 prophet went to **K** Hezekiah
20:18 in the palace of the **k** of Babylon."
20:21 Manasseh his son succeeded him as **k**.
21: 1 twelve years old when he became **k**,
21: 3 pole, as Ahab **k** of Israel had done.
21:11 "Manasseh **k** of Judah has committed
21:18 Amon his son succeeded him as **k**.
21:19 years old when he became **k**,
21:23 assassinated the **k** in his palace.
21:24 all who had plotted against **K** Amon,
21:24 made Josiah his son **k** in his place.
21:26 Josiah his son succeeded him as **k**.
22: 1 eight years old when he became **k**,
22: 3 **K** Josiah sent the secretary, Shaphan
22: 9 Shaphan the secretary went to the **k**
22:10 Shaphan the secretary informed the **k**,
22:10 from it in the presence of the **k**.
22:11 the **k** heard the words of the Book of
22:16 in the book the **k** of Judah has read.
22:18 Tell the **k** of Judah, who sent you to
22:20 they took her answer back to the **k**.
23: 1 the **k** called together all the elders
23: 3 The **k** stood by the pillar and
23: 4 The **k** ordered Hilkiah the high
23:13 The **k** also desecrated the high
23:13 the ones Solomon **k** of Israel had
23:17 The **k** asked, "What is that tombstone
23:21 The **k** gave this order to all the
23:23 in the eighteenth year of **K** Josiah,
23:25 was there a **k** like him who turned
23:29 Josiah was **k**, Pharaoh Neco **k** of
23:29 River to help the **k** of Assyria.
23:29 **K** Josiah marched out to meet him in
23:30 made him **k** in place of his father.
23:31 years old when he became **k**,
23:34 **k** in place of his father Josiah
23:36 years old when he became **k**,
24: 1 Nebuchadnezzar **k** of Babylon invaded
24: 6 his son succeeded him as **k**.
24: 7 The **k** of Egypt did not march out
24: 7 because the **k** of Babylon had taken
24: 8 eighteen years old when he became **k**,
24:10 **k** of Babylon advanced on Jerusalem
24:12 Jehoiachin **k** of Judah, his mother,
24:12 of the reign of the **k** of Babylon,
24:13 Solomon **k** of Israel had made for
24:16 The **k** of Babylon also deported to
24:17 Jehoiachin's uncle, **k** in his place
24:18 years old when he became **k**,
24:20 rebelled against the **k** of Babylon.
25: 1 Nebuchadnezzar **k** of Babylon marched
25: 2 the eleventh year of **K** Zedekiah.
25: 5 the Babylonian army pursued the **k**
25: 6 He was taken to the **k** of Babylon at
25: 8 year of Nebuchadnezzar **k** of Babylon,
25: 8 the **k** of Babylon, came to Jerusalem.
25:11 had gone over to the **k** of Babylon.
25:20 them to the **k** of Babylon at Riblah.
25:21 of Hamath, the **k** had them executed.
25:22 Nebuchadnezzar **k** of Babylon
25:23 heard that the **k** of Babylon

2Ki 25:24 the land and serve the **k** of Babylon,
25:27 the exile of Jehoiachin **k** of Judah,
25:27 in the year Evil-Merodach became **k**
25:30 Day by day the **k** gave Jehoiachin a
1Ch 1:43 before any Israelite **k** reigned:
1:44 Zerah from Bozrah succeeded him as **k**.
1:45 of the Temanites succeeded him as **k**.
1:46 country of Moab, succeeded him as **k**.
1:47 from Masrekah succeeded him as **k**.
1:48 on the river succeeded him as **k**.
1:49 son of Acbor succeeded him as **k**.
1:50 Hanan died, Hadad succeeded him as **k**.
3: 2 daughter of Talmai **k** of Geshur;
4:23 stayed there and worked for the **k**.
4:41 in the days of Hezekiah **k** of Judah.
5: 6 Pileser **k** of Assyria took into exile.
5:17 **k** of Judah and Jeroboam **k** of Israel.
5:26 spirit of Pul **k** of Assyria (that is,
5:26 Tiglath-Pileser **k** of Assyria), who
11: 2 In the past, even while Saul was **k**,
11: 3 Israel had come to **K** David at Hebron,
11: 3 and they anointed David **k** over
12:31 to come and make David **k**—18,000;
12:38 to make David **k** over all Israel.
12:38 also of one mind to make David **k**.
14: 1 Now Hiram **k** of Tyre sent messengers
14: 2 established him as **k** over Israel
14: 8 had been anointed **k** over all Israel,
15:29 And when she saw **K** David dancing and
17:16 **K** David went in and sat before the
18: 3 David fought Hadadezer **k** of Zobah
18: 5 came to help Hadadezer **k** of Zobah,
18: 9 Tou **k** of Hamath heard that David had
18: 9 entire army of Hadadezer **k** of Zobah,
18:10 he sent his son Hadoram to **K** David
18:11 **K** David dedicated these articles to
19: 1 Nahash **k** of the Ammonites died,
19: 1 and his son succeeded him as **k**.
19: 5 The **k** said, "Stay at Jericho till
19: 7 as well as the **k** of Maacah with his
20: 2 the crown from the head of their **k**
21:24 **K** David replied to Araunah, "No, I
23: 1 made his son Solomon **k** over Israel.
24: 6 of the **k** and of the officials:
24:31 in the presence of **K** David and of
25: 6 were under the supervision of the **k**.
26:26 for the things dedicated by **K** David,
26:32 and **K** David put them in charge of
26:32 to God and for the affairs of the **k**.
27: 1 who served the **k** in all that
27:24 the book of the annals of **K** David.
27:31 in charge of **K** David's property.
28: 1 divisions in the service of the **k**,
28: 1 belonging to the **k** and his sons,
28: 2 **K** David rose to his feet and said:
28: 4 family to be **k** over Israel for ever.
28: 4 to make me **k** over all Israel.
29: 1 **K** David said to the whole assembly:
29: 9 David the **k** also rejoiced greatly.
29:20 prostrate before the LORD and the **k**.
29:22 son of David as **k** a second time,
29:23 as **k** in place of his father David.
29:24 as well as all of **K** David's sons,
29:24 their submission to **K** Solomon.
29:25 as no **k** over Israel ever had before.
29:26 David son of Jesse was **k** over all
29:28 His son Solomon succeeded him as **k**.
29:29 for the events of **K** David's reign,
2Ch 1: 8 and have made me **k** in his place.
1: 9 for you have made me **k** over a people
1:11 people over whom I have made you **k**,
1:12 riches and honour, such as no **k** who
1:15 The **k** made silver and gold as common
2: 3 sent this message to Hiram **k** of Tyre
2:11 Hiram **k** of Tyre replied by letter to
2:11 people, he has made you their **k**."
2:12 He has given **K** David a wise son,
4:11 for **K** Solomon in the temple of God:
4:16 made for **K** Solomon for the temple
4:17 The **k** had them cast in clay moulds
5: 3 came together to the **k** at the time
5: 6 **K** Solomon and the entire assembly of
6: 3 the **k** turned round and blessed them.
7: 4 the **k** and all the people offered
7: 5 **K** Solomon offered a sacrifice of
7: 5 So the **k** and all the people

2Ch 7: 6 which **K** David had made for praising
8:10 They were also **K** Solomon's chief
8:11 in the palace of David **k** of Israel,
8:18 which they delivered to **K** Solomon.
9: 5 She said to the **k**, "The report I
9: 8 as **k** to rule for the LORD your God.
9: 8 he has made you **k** over them, to
9: 9 she gave the **k** 120 talents of gold,
9: 9 queen of Sheba gave to **K** Solomon.
9:11 The **k** used the algum-wood to make
9:12 **K** Solomon gave the queen of Sheba
9:15 **K** Solomon made two hundred large
9:16 The **k** put them in the Palace of the
9:17 the **k** made a great throne inlaid
9:20 All **K** Solomon's goblets were gold,
9:21 The **k** had a fleet of trading ships
9:22 **K** Solomon was greater in riches and
9:27 The **k** made silver as common in
9:31 Rehoboam his son succeeded him as **k**.
10: 1 had gone there to make him **k**.
10: 2 **K** Solomon), he returned from Egypt.
10: 6 **K** Rehoboam consulted the elders who
10:12 as the **k** had said, "Come back to me
10:13 The **k** answered them harshly.
10:15 the **k** did not listen to the people,
10:16 all Israel saw that the **k** refused to
10:16 they answered the **k**: "What share do
10:18 **K** Rehoboam sent out Adoniram, who
10:18 **K** Rehoboam, however, managed to get
11: 3 Rehoboam son of Solomon **k** of Judah
11:22 brothers, in order to make him **k**.
12: 1 After Rehoboam's position as **k** was
12: 2 Shishak **k** of Egypt attacked
12: 2 in the fifth year of **K** Rehoboam.
12: 6 The leaders of Israel and the **k**
12: 9 Shishak **k** of Egypt attacked
12:10 **K** Rehoboam made bronze shields to
12:11 the **k** went to the LORD's temple
12:13 **K** Rehoboam established himself
12:13 in Jerusalem and continued as **k**.
12:13 years old when he became **k**,
12:16 Abijah his son succeeded him as **k**.
13: 1 Jeroboam, Abijah became **k** of Judah,
14: 1 Asa his son succeeded him as **k**, and
15:16 **K** Asa also deposed his grandmother
16: 1 **k** of Israel went up against Judah
16: 1 the territory of Asa **k** of Judah.
16: 2 and sent it to Ben-Hadad **k** of Aram,
16: 3 your treaty with Baasha **k** of Israel
16: 4 Ben-Hadad agreed with **K** Asa and sent
16: 6 **K** Asa brought all the men of Judah,
16: 7 to Asa **k** of Judah and said to him:
16: 7 "Because you relied on the **k** of Aram
16: 7 **k** of Aram has escaped from your hand.
17: 1 his son succeeded him as **k**
17:19 These were the men who served the **k**,
18: 3 Ahab **k** of Israel asked Jehoshaphat **k**
18: 4 Jehoshaphat also said to the **k** of
18: 5 the **k** of Israel brought together the
18: 7 The **k** of Israel answered Jehoshaphat,
18: 7 "The **k** should not say that,"
18: 8 the **k** of Israel called one of his
18: 9 the **k** of Israel and Jehoshaphat **k** of
18:12 are predicting success for the **k**.
18:14 he arrived, the **k** asked him,
18:15 The **k** said to him, "How many times
18:17 The **k** of Israel said to Jehoshaphat,
18:19 'Who will entice Ahab **k** of Israel
18:25 The **k** of Israel then ordered, "Take
18:26 say, 'This is what the **k** says: Put
18:28 the **k** of Israel and Jehoshaphat **k** of
18:29 The **k** of Israel said to Jehoshaphat,
18:29 So the **k** of Israel disguised
18:30 Now the **k** of Aram had ordered his
18:30 or great, except the **k** of Israel."
18:31 thought, "This is the **k** of Israel.
18:32 saw that he was not the **k** of Israel,
18:33 hit the **k** of Israel between the
18:33 The **k** told the chariot driver,
18:34 and the **k** of Israel propped himself
19: 1 Jehoshaphat **k** of Judah returned
19: 2 out to meet him and said to the **k**,
19:11 you in any matter concerning the **k**,
20:15 He said: "Listen, **K** Jehoshaphat and
20:31 years old when he became **k** of Judah,
20:35 Later, Jehoshaphat **k** of Judah made

2Ch 20:35 alliance with Ahaziah **k** of Israel,
21: 1 Jehoram his son succeeded him as **k**.
21: 2 sons of Jehoshaphat **k** of Israel.
21: 5 years old when he became **k**,
21: 8 against Judah and set up its own **k**.
21:12 Jehoshaphat or of Asa **k** of Judah.
21:20 years old when he became **k**,
22: 1 Jehoram's youngest son, **k** in his
22: 1 Jehoram **k** of Judah began to reign.
22: 2 years old when he became **k**,
22: 5 with Joram son of Ahab **k** of Israel
22: 5 Hazael **k** of Aram at Ramoth Gilead.
22: 6 in his battle with Hazael **k** of Aram.
22: 6 Then Ahaziah son of Jehoram **k** of
22:11 Jehosheba, the daughter of **K** Jehoram,
22:11 Jehosheba, the daughter of **K** Jehoram
23: 3 with the **k** at the temple of God.
23: 7 to station themselves round the **k**,
23: 7 close to the **k** wherever he goes."
23: 9 shields that had belonged to **K** David
23:10 round the **k**—near the altar and the
23:11 the covenant and proclaimed him **k**.
23:11 and shouted, "Long live the **k**!
23:12 people running and cheering the **k**,
23:13 She looked, and there was the **k**,
23:13 the trumpeters were beside the **k**,
23:16 and the **k** would be the LORD's
23:20 brought the **k** down from the temple
23:20 seated the **k** on the royal throne,
24: 1 seven years old when he became **k**,
24: 6 Therefore the **k** summoned Jehoiada
24:12 The **k** and Jehoiada gave it to the
24:14 of the money to the **k** and Jehoiada,
24:17 came and paid homage to the **k**,
24:21 and by order of the **k** they stoned
24:22 **K** Joash did not remember the
24:23 the plunder to their **k** in Damascus.
24:27 Amaziah his son succeeded him as **k**.
25: 1 years old when he became **k**,
25: 3 who had murdered his father the **k**.
25: 7 "O **k**, these troops from Israel must
25:16 still speaking, the **k** said to him,
25:16 appointed you an adviser to the **k**?
25:17 After Amaziah **k** of Judah consulted
25:17 the son of Jehu, **k** of Israel: "Come,
25:18 Jehoash **k** of Israel replied to
25:18 Israel replied to Amaziah **k** of Judah,
25:21 Jehoash **k** of Israel attacked. He and
25:21 He and Amaziah **k** of Judah faced each
25:23 Jehoash **k** of Israel captured Amaziah
25:23 Israel captured Amaziah **k** of Judah,
25:25 Amaziah son of Joash **k** of Judah
25:25 Jehoash son of Jehoahaz **k** of Israel.
26: 1 **k** in place of his father Amaziah.
26: 3 sixteen years old when he became **k**,
26:13 support the **k** against his enemies.
26:21 **K** Uzziah had leprosy until the day
26:23 Jotham his son succeeded him as **k**.
27: 1 years old when he became **k**,
27: 5 Jotham made war on the **k** of the
27: 8 years old when he became **k**,
27: 9 And Ahaz his son succeeded him as **k**.
28: 1 twenty years old when he became **k**,
28: 5 God handed him over to the **k** of Aram.
28: 5 into the hands of the **k** of Israel,
28: 7 and Elkanah, second to the **k**.
28:16 **K** Ahaz sent to the **k** of Assyria
28:19 because of Ahaz **k** of Israel,
28:20 Tiglath-Pileser **k** of Assyria came to
28:21 presented them to the **k** of Assyria,
28:22 In his time of trouble **K** Ahaz became
28:27 Hezekiah his son succeeded him as **k**.
29: 1 years old when he became **k**,
29:15 as the **k** had ordered, following the
29:18 they went in to **K** Hezekiah and
29:19 the articles that **K** Ahaz removed
29:19 his unfaithfulness while he was **k**.
29:20 Early the next morning **K** Hezekiah
29:21 The **k** commanded the priests, the
29:23 before the **k** and the assembly,
29:24 **k** had ordered the burnt offerings
29:27 instruments of David **k** of Israel.
29:29 the **k** and everyone present with him
29:30 **K** Hezekiah and his officials ordered
30: 2 The **k** and his officials and the
30: 4 plan seemed right both to the **k** and

2Ch 30: 6 from the **k** and from his officials,
30:12 the **k** and his officials had ordered,
30:24 Hezekiah **k** of Judah provided a
30:26 Solomon son of David **k** of Israel
31: 3 The **k** contributed from his own
31:13 by appointment of **K** Hezekiah and
32: 1 **k** of Assyria came and invaded Judah.
32: 7 because of the **k** of Assyria
32: 8 what Hezekiah the **k** of Judah said.
32: 9 Later, when Sennacherib **k** of Assyria
32: 9 message for Hezekiah **k** of Judah
32:10 what Sennacherib **k** of Assyria says
32:11 from the hand of the **k** of Assyria,'
32:17 The **k** also wrote letters insulting
32:20 **K** Hezekiah and the prophet Isaiah
32:21 in the camp of the Assyrian **k**.
32:22 hand of Sennacherib **k** of Assyria
32:23 gifts for Hezekiah **k** of Judah.
32:33 Manasseh his son succeeded him as **k**.
33: 1 twelve years old when he became **k**,
33:11 army commanders of the **k** of Assyria,
33:20 And Amon his son succeeded him as **k**.
33:21 years old when he became **k**,
33:25 all who had plotted against **K** Amon,
33:25 made Josiah his son **k** in his place.
34: 1 eight years old when he became **k**,
34:16 Shaphan took the book to the **k** and
34:18 Shaphan the secretary informed the **k**,
34:18 from it in the presence of the **k**.
34:19 the **k** heard the words of the Law, he
34:22 Hilkiah and those the **k** had sent
34:24 in the presence of the **k** of Judah.
34:26 Tell the **k** of Judah, who sent you to
34:28 they took her answer back to the **k**.
34:29 the **k** called together all the elders
34:31 The **k** stood by his pillar and
35: 3 son of David **k** of Israel built.
35: 4 **k** of Israel and by his son Solomon.
35:10 divisions as the **k** had ordered.
35:16 the LORD, as **K** Josiah had ordered.
35:20 Neco **k** of Egypt went up to fight at
35:21 between you and me, O **k** of Judah?
35:23 Archers shot **K** Josiah, and he told
36: 1 made him **k** in Jerusalem in place of
36: 2 years old when he became **k**,
36: 3 The **k** of Egypt dethroned him in
36: 4 The **k** of Egypt made Eliakim, a
36: 4 a brother of Jehoahaz, **k** over Judah
36: 5 years old when he became **k**,
36: 6 Nebuchadnezzar **k** of Babylon attacked
36: 8 his son succeeded him as **k**.
36: 9 eighteen years old when he became **k**,
36:10 In the spring, **K** Nebuchadnezzar sent
36:10 Zedekiah, **k** over Judah and Jerusalem.
36:11 years old when he became **k**,
36:13 rebelled against **K** Nebuchadnezzar
36:17 He brought up against them the **k** of
36:18 of the **k** and his officials.
36:22 first year of Cyrus **k** of Persia
36:22 moved the heart of Cyrus **k** of Persia
36:23 "This is what Cyrus **k** of Persia says:
Ezr 1: 1 first year of Cyrus **k** of Persia
1: 1 the LORD moved the heart of Cyrus **k**
1: 2 "This is what Cyrus **k** of Persia says:
1: 7 Moreover, **K** Cyrus brought out the
1: 8 Cyrus **k** of Persia had them brought
2: 1 whom Nebuchadnezzar **k** of Babylon had
3: 7 as authorised by Cyrus **k** of Persia.
3:10 as prescribed by David **k** of Israel.
4: 2 **k** of Assyria, who brought us here."
4: 3 as **K** Cyrus, the **k** of Persia,
4: 5 entire reign of Cyrus **k** of Persia
4: 5 to the reign of Darius **k** of Persia.
4: 7 days of Artaxerxes **k** of Persia,
4: 8 to Artaxerxes the **k** as follows:
4:11 To **K** Artaxerxes, From your servants,
4:12 The **k** should know that the Jews who
4:13 the **k** should know that if this city
4:14 for us to see the **k** dishonoured,
4:14 this message to inform the **k**,
4:16 We inform the **k** that if this city is
4:17 The **k** sent this reply: To Rehum the
4:23 copy of the letter of **K** Artaxerxes
4:24 of the reign of Darius **k** of Persia.
5: 6 Trans-Euphrates, sent to **K** Darius.
5: 7 To **K** Darius: Cordial greetings.

Ezr 5: 8 The **k** should know that we went to
5:11 **k** of Israel built and finished.
5:12 **k** of Babylon, who destroyed this
5:13 first year of Cyrus **k** of Babylon
5:13 **K** Cyrus issued a decree to rebuild
5:14 "Then **K** Cyrus gave them to a man
5:17 Now if it pleases the **k**, let a
5:17 to see if **K** Cyrus did in fact issue
5:17 Then let the **k** send us his decision
6: 1 **K** Darius then issued an order, and
6: 3 first year of **K** Cyrus, the **k** issued
6:10 well-being of the **k** and his sons.
6:12 overthrow any **k** or people who lifts
6:13 Then, because of the decree **K** Darius
6:15 sixth year of the reign of **K** Darius.
6:22 the attitude of the **k** of Assyria,
7: 1 the reign of Artaxerxes **k** of Persia
7: 6 The **k** had granted him everything he
7: 7 in the seventh year of **K** Artaxerxes.
7: 8 month of the seventh year of the **k**.
7:11 a copy of the letter **K** Artaxerxes
7:14 You are sent by the **k** and his seven
7:15 gold that the **k** and his advisers
7:21 Now I, **K** Artaxerxes, order all the
7:23 the realm of the **k** and of his sons?
7:26 **k** must surely be punished by death,
7:28 his good favour to me before the **k**
8: 1 during the reign of **K** Artaxerxes:
8:22 I was ashamed to ask the **k** for
8:22 because we had told the **k**, "The
8:25 gold and the articles that the **k**,
Ne 1:11 I was cupbearer to the **k**.
2: 1 the twentieth year of **K** Artaxerxes,
2: 1 took the wine and gave it to the **k**.
2: 2 the **k** asked me, "Why does your face
2: 3 I said to the **k**, "May the **k** live for
2: 4 The **k** said to me, "What is it you
2: 5 I answered the **k**, "If it pleases the
2: 5 "If it pleases the **k** and if your
2: 6 the **k**, with the queen sitting beside
2: 6 It pleased the **k** to send me;
2: 7 "If it pleases the **k**, may I have
2: 8 the **k** granted my requests.
2: 9 The **k** had also sent army officers
2:18 and what the **k** had said to me.
2:19 "Are you rebelling against the **k**?"
5:14 from the twentieth year of **K**
6: 6 you are about to become their **k**
6: 7 'There is a **k** in Judah!' Now this
6: 7 report will get back to the **k**;
7: 6 whom Nebuchadnezzar **k** of Babylon
9:22 the country of Sihon **k** of Heshbon
9:22 and the country of Og **k** of Bashan.
13: 6 Artaxerxes **k** of Babylon
13: 6 I had returned to the **k**.
13:26 that Solomon **k** of Israel sinned?
13:26 nations there was no **k** like him.
13:26 and God made him **k** over all Israel,
Est 1: 2 At that time **K** Xerxes reigned from
1: 5 the **k** gave a banquet, lasting seven
1: 8 for the **k** instructed all the wine
1: 9 in the royal palace of **K** Xerxes.
1:10 On the seventh day, when **K** Xerxes
1:12 Then the **k** became furious and burned
1:13 Since it was customary for the **k** to
1:14 were closest to the **k**—Carshena,
1:14 who had special access to the **k**
1:15 not obeyed the command of **K** Xerxes
1:16 presence of the **k** and the nobles,
1:16 not only against the **k** but also
1:16 of all the provinces of **K** Xerxes.
1:17 '**K** Xerxes commanded Queen Vashti to
1:19 "Therefore, if it pleases the **k**,
1:19 to enter the presence of **K** Xerxes.
1:19 Also let the **k** give her royal
1:21 The **k** and his nobles were pleased
1:21 so the **k** did as Memucan proposed.
2: 1 Later when the anger of **K** Xerxes
2: 2 beautiful young virgins for the **k**.
2: 3 Let the **k** appoint commissioners in
2: 4 let the girl who pleases the **k** be
2: 4 This advice appealed to the **k**, and
2: 6 by Nebuchadnezzar **k** of Babylon,
2: 6 captive with Jehoiachin **k** of Judah.
2:12 turn came to go in to **K** Xerxes,
2:13 this is how she would go to the **k**:

Est 2:14 She would not return to the **k** unless
2:15 his uncle Abihail) to go to the **k**,
2:16 She was taken to **K** Xerxes in the
2:17 Now the **k** was attracted to Esther
2:18 the **k** gave a great banquet, Esther's
2:21 to assassinate **K** Xerxes.
2:22 reported it to the **k**, giving credit
2:23 the annals in the presence of the **k**.
3: 1 After these events, **K** Xerxes
3: 2 **k** had commanded this concerning him.
3: 7 In the twelfth year of **K** Xerxes, in
3: 8 Haman said to **K** Xerxes, "There is a
3: 9 If it pleases the **k**, let a decree be
3:10 the **k** took his signet ring from his
3:11 "Keep the money," the **k** said to
3:12 written in the name of **K** Xerxes
3:15 The **k** and Haman sat down to drink,
4: 3 the edict and order of the **k** came,
4:11 approaches the **k** in the inner court
4:11 summoned the **k** has but one law:
4:11 **k** to extend the gold sceptre to him
4:11 since I was called to go to the **k**."
4:16 I will go to the **k**, even though it
5: 1 **k** was sitting on his royal throne
5: 3 the **k** asked, "What is it, Queen
5: 4 "If it pleases the **k**," replied
5: 4 "let the **k**, together with Haman,
5: 5 "Bring Haman at once," the **k** said,
5: 5 So the **k** and Haman went to the
5: 6 the **k** again asked Esther, "Now what
5: 8 If the **k** regards me with favour and
5: 8 if it pleases the **k** to grant my
5: 8 let the **k** and Haman come tomorrow to
5:11 and all the ways the **k** had honoured
5:12 the **k** to the banquet she gave.
5:12 me along with the **k** tomorrow.
5:14 and ask the **k** in the morning to have
5:14 Then go with the **k** to the dinner and
6: 1 That night the **k** could not sleep;
6: 2 to assassinate **K** Xerxes.
6: 3 received for this?" the **k** asked.
6: 4 The **k** said, "Who is in the court?"
6: 4 to speak to the **k** about hanging
6: 5 "Bring him in," the **k** ordered.
6: 6 Haman entered, the **k** asked him,
6: 6 the man the **k** delights to honour?"
6: 6 the **k** would rather honour than me?"
6: 7 answered the **k**, "For the man the **k**
6: 8 bring a royal robe the **k** has worn
6: 8 worn and a horse the **k** has ridden,
6: 9 Let them robe the man the **k** delights
6: 9 the man the **k** delights to honour!'
6:10 "Go at once," the **k** commanded Haman.
6:11 the man the **k** delights to honour!"
7: 1 the **k** and Haman went to dine with
7: 2 the **k** again asked, "Queen Esther,
7: 3 have found favour with you, O **k**,
7: 4 would justify disturbing the **k**."
7: 5 **K** Xerxes asked Queen Esther, "Who
7: 6 terrified before the **k** and queen.
7: 7 The **k** got up in a rage, left his
7: 7 But Haman, realising that the **k** had
7: 8 Just as the **k** returned from the
7: 8 The **k** exclaimed, "Will he even
7: 9 one of the eunuchs attending the **k**,
7: 9 Mordecai, who spoke up to help the **k**.
7: 9 The **k** said, "Hang him on it!"
8: 1 That same day **K** Xerxes gave Queen
8: 1 came into the presence of the **k**,
8: 2 The **k** took off his signet ring,
8: 3 Esther again pleaded with the **k**,
8: 4 the **k** extended the gold sceptre to
8: 5 "If it pleases the **k**," she said,
8: 7 **K** Xerxes replied to Queen Esther
8:10 wrote in the name of **K** Xerxes
8:10 horses especially bred for the **k**
8:12 in all the provinces of **K** Xerxes
8:17 wherever the edict of the **k** went,
9: 1 by the **k** was to be carried out.
9: 2 in all the provinces of **K** Xerxes
9:11 reported to the **k** that same day.
9:12 The **k** said to Queen Esther, "The
9:13 "If it pleases the **k**," Esther
9:14 the **k** commanded that this be done.
9:20 provinces of **K** Xerxes, near and far,
10: 1 **K** Xerxes imposed tribute throughout

Est 10: 2 to which the **k** had raised him,
10: 3 Jew was second in rank to **K** Xerxes,
Job 15:24 like a **k** poised to attack,
18:14 and marched off to the **k** of terrors.
29:25 I dwelt as a **k** among his troops;
41:34 he is **k** over all that are proud."
Ps 2: 6 "I have installed my **K** on Zion, my
5: 2 Listen to my cry for help, my **K** and
10:16 The LORD is **K** for ever and ever;
18:50 He gives his **k** great victories;
20: 9 O LORD, save the **k**! Answer us when
21: 1 O LORD, the **k** rejoices in your
21: 7 For the **k** trusts in the LORD;
24: 7 that the **K** of glory may come in.
24: 8 Who is this **K** of glory? The LORD
24: 9 that the **K** of glory may come in.
24:10 Who is he, this **K** of glory? The LORD
24:10 LORD Almighty—he is the **K** of glory.
29:10 the LORD is enthroned as **K** for ever.
33:16 No **k** is saved by the size of his
44: 4 You are my **K** and my God, who decrees
45: 1 as I recite my verses for the **k**;
45:11 The **k** is enthralled by your beauty;
45:14 garments she is led to the **k**;
45:15 they enter the palace of the **k**.
47: 2 the great **K** over all the earth!
47: 6 sing praises to our **K**, sing praises.
47: 7 For God is the **K** of all the earth;
48: 2 Zion, the city of the Great **K**.
63:11 the **k** will rejoice in God; all who
68:24 of my God and **K** into the sanctuary.
72: 1 Endow the **k** with your justice,
74:12 you, O God, are my **k** from of old;
84: 3 O LORD Almighty, my **K** and my God.
89:18 our **k** to the Holy One of Israel.
95: 3 God, the great **K** above all gods.
98: 6 for joy before the LORD, the **K**.
99: 4 The **K** is mighty, he loves justice
105:20 The **k** sent and released him, the
135:11 Sihon **k** of the Amorites, Og **k** of
136:19 Sihon **k** of the Amorites
136:20 Og **k** of Bashan—His love endures
145: 1 I will exalt you, my God the **K**;
149: 2 people of Zion be glad in their **K**.
Pr 1: 1 Solomon son of David, **k** of Israel:
14:35 A **k** delights in a wise servant, but
16:10 The lips of a **k** speak as an oracle,
20: 8 a **k** sits on his throne to judge,
20:26 A wise **k** winnows out the wicked;
20:28 Love and faithfulness keep a **k** safe
22:11 will have the **k** for his friend.
24:21 Fear the LORD and the **k**, my son,
25: 1 by the men of Hezekiah **k** of Judah:
29: 4 By justice a **k** gives a country
29:14 If a **k** judges the poor with fairness,
30:22 a servant who becomes **k**, a fool who
30:27 locusts have no **k**, yet they advance
30:31 and a **k** with his army around him
31: 1 The sayings of **K** Lemuel—an oracle
Ecc 1: 1 son of David, **k** of Jerusalem:
1:12 I, the Teacher, was **k** over Israel
4:13 wise youth than an old but foolish **k**
5: 9 **k** himself profits from the fields.
9:14 And a powerful **k** came against it,
10:16 O land whose **k** was a servant
10:17 O land whose **k** is of noble birth
10:20 Do not revile the **k** even in your
SS 1: 4 Let the **k** bring me into his chambers.
1:12 While the **k** was at his table, my
3: 9 **K** Solomon made for himself the
3:11 and look at **K** Solomon wearing the
7: 5 **k** is held captive by its tresses.
Isa 6: 1 In the year that **K** Uzziah died,
6: 5 have seen the **K**, the LORD Almighty."
7: 1 son of Uzziah, was **k** of Judah, **K**
7: 1 Pekah son of Remaliah **k** of Israel
7: 6 make the son of Tabeel **k** over it."
7:17 will bring the **k** of Assyria."
7:20 beyond the River—the **k** of Assyria
8: 4 carried off by the **k** of Assyria."
8: 7 the **k** of Assyria with all his pomp.
8:21 will curse their **k** and their God.
10:12 "I will punish the **k** of Assyria for
14: 4 this taunt against the **k** of Babylon:
14:28 oracle came in the year **K** Ahaz died
19: 4 and a fierce **k** will rule over them,"

Isa 20: 1 sent by Sargon **k** of Assyria, came to
20: 4 the **k** of Assyria will lead away
20: 6 deliverance from the **k** of Assyria!
30:33 it has been made ready for the **k**.
32: 1 a **k** will reign in righteousness
33:17 Your eyes will see the **k** in his
33:22 the LORD is our **k**; it is he who
36: 1 fourteenth year of **K** Hezekiah's
36: 1 Sennacherib **k** of Assyria attacked
36: 2 the **k** of Assyria sent his field
36: 2 Lachish to **K** Hezekiah at Jerusalem.
36: 4 'This is what the great **k**, the **k** of
36: 6 **k** of Egypt to all who depend on him.
36: 8 the **k** of Assyria: I will give you
36:13 of the great **k**, the **k** of Assyria!
36:14 This is what the **k** says: Do not let
36:15 into the hand of the **k** of Assyria.'
36:16 This is what the **k** of Assyria says:
36:18 from the hand of the **k** of Assyria?
36:21 **k** had commanded, "Do not answer him.
37: 1 **K** Hezekiah heard this, he tore his
37: 4 whom his master, the **k** of Assyria,
37: 5 **K** Hezekiah's officials came to
37: 6 the **k** of Assyria have blasphemed me.
37: 8 the field commander heard that the **k**
37: 8 found the **k** fighting against Libnah.
37: 9 the Cushite **k** of Egypt, was marching
37:10 "Say to Hezekiah **k** of Judah: Do not
37:10 be handed over to the **k** of Assyria.'
37:13 Where is the **k** of Hamath, the **k** of
37:13 the **k** of the city of Sepharvaim
37:21 concerning Sennacherib **k** of Assyria,
37:33 says concerning the **k** of Assyria:
37:37 Sennacherib **k** of Assyria broke camp
37:38 his son succeeded him as **k**.
38: 6 from the hand of the **k** of Assyria.
38: 9 A writing of Hezekiah **k** of Judah
39: 1 **k** of Babylon sent Hezekiah letters
39: 3 prophet went to **K** Hezekiah
39: 7 in the palace of the **k** of Babylon."
41:21 your arguments," says Jacob's **K**.
43:15 Holy One, Israel's Creator, your **K**."
44: 6 LORD says—Israel's **K** and Redeemer,
Jer 1: 2 of Josiah son of Amon **k** of Judah,
1: 3 Jehoiakim son of Josiah **k** of Judah,
1: 3 Zedekiah son of Josiah **k** of Judah,
3: 6 During the reign of **K** Josiah, the
4: 9 "the **k** and the officials will lose
8:19 in Zion? Is her **K** no longer there?"
10: 7 not revere you, O **K** of the nations?
10:10 he is the living God, the eternal **K**.
13:18 Say to the **k** and to the queen mother,
15: 4 Hezekiah **k** of Judah did in Jerusalem.
20: 4 I will hand all Judah over to the **k**
21: 1 **K** Zedekiah sent to him Pashhur
21: 2 **k** of Babylon is attacking us.
21: 4 which you are using to fight the **k**
21: 7 I will hand over Zedekiah **k** of Judah,
21: 7 to Nebuchadnezzar **k** of Babylon and
21:10 into the hands of the **k** of Babylon,
22: 1 to the palace of the **k** of Judah
22: 2 'Hear the word of the LORD, O **k** of
22: 6 about the palace of the **k** of Judah:
22:10 Do not weep for the dead **k** or mourn
22:11 succeeded his father as **k** of Judah
22:15 "Does it make you a **k** to have more
22:18 Jehoiakim son of Josiah **k** of Judah:
22:24 Jehoiachin son of Jehoiakim **k** of
22:25 **k** of Babylon and to the Babylonians.
23: 5 a **K** who will reign wisely and do
24: 1 After Jehoiachin son of Jehoiakim **k**
24: 1 by Nebuchadnezzar **k** of Babylon,
24: 8 I deal with Zedekiah **k** of Judah
25: 1 Jehoiakim son of Josiah **k** of Judah,
25: 1 year of Nebuchadnezzar **k** of Babylon.
25: 3 Amon **k** of Judah until this very day
25: 9 Nebuchadnezzar **k** of Babylon,"
25:11 the **k** of Babylon for seventy years.
25:12 I will punish the **k** of Babylon and
25:19 Pharaoh **k** of Egypt, his attendants,
25:26 the **k** of Sheshach will drink it too.
26: 1 Jehoiakim son of Josiah **k** of Judah,
26:18 in the days of Hezekiah **k** of Judah.
26:19 "Did Hezekiah **k** of Judah or anyone
26:21 **K** Jehoiakim and all his officers and
26:21 the **k** sought to put him to death.

Jer 26:22 **K** Jehoiakim, however, sent Elnathan
26:23 Egypt and took him to **K** Jehoiakim,
27: 1 Zedekiah son of Josiah **k** of Judah,
27: 3 to Jerusalem to Zedekiah **k** of Judah.
27: 6 servant Nebuchadnezzar **k** of Babylon;
27: 8 serve Nebuchadnezzar **k** of Babylon
27: 9 You will not serve the **k** of Babylon
27:11 of the **k** of Babylon and serve him,
27:12 same message to Zedekiah **k** of Judah
27:12 under the yoke of the **k** of Babylon;
27:13 will not serve the **k** of Babylon?
27:14 You will not serve the **k** of Babylon
27:17 Serve the **k** of Babylon, and you
27:18 in the palace of the **k** of Judah and
27:20 which Nebuchadnezzar **k** of Babylon
27:20 son of Jehoiakim **k** of Judah into
27:21 in the palace of the **k** of Judah
28: 1 in the reign of Zedekiah **k** of Judah
28: 2 break the yoke of the **k** of Babylon.
28: 3 **k** of Babylon removed from here
28: 4 son of Jehoiakim **k** of Judah
28: 4 break the yoke of the **k** of Babylon.
28:11 yoke of Nebuchadnezzar **k** of Babylon
28:14 serve Nebuchadnezzar **k** of Babylon,
29: 2 (This was after **K** Jehoiachin and the
29: 3 whom Zedekiah **k** of Judah sent to **K**
29:16 the **k** who sits on David's throne
29:21 over to Nebuchadnezzar **k** of Babylon,
29:22 **k** of Babylon burned in the fire.'
30: 9 David their **k**, whom I will raise
32: 1 tenth year of Zedekiah **k** of Judah,
32: 2 The army of the **k** of Babylon was
32: 3 Now Zedekiah **k** of Judah had
32: 3 to the **k** of Babylon, and he will
32: 4 Zedekiah **k** of Judah will not escape
32: 4 be handed over to the **k** of Babylon,
32:28 **k** of Babylon, who will capture it.
32:36 be handed over to the **k** of Babylon
34: 1 While Nebuchadnezzar **k** of Babylon
34: 2 says: Go to Zedekiah **k** of Judah and
34: 2 this city over to the **k** of Babylon,
34: 3 You will see the **k** of Babylon with
34: 4 of the LORD, O Zedekiah **k** of Judah.
34: 6 Zedekiah **k** of Judah, in Jerusalem,
34: 7 while the army of the **k** of Babylon
34: 8 **K** Zedekiah had made a covenant with
34:21 I will hand Zedekiah **k** of Judah and
34:21 to the army of the **k** of Babylon,
35: 1 Jehoiakim son of Josiah **k** of Judah:
35:11 when Nebuchadnezzar **k** of Babylon
36: 1 Jehoiakim son of Josiah **k** of Judah,
36: 9 Jehoiakim son of Josiah **k** of Judah,
36:16 report all these words to the **k**."
36:20 they went to the **k** in the courtyard
36:21 The **k** sent Jehudi to get the scroll,
36:21 read it to the **k** and all the
36:22 was the ninth month and the **k** was
36:23 the **k** cut them off with a scribe's
36:24 The **k** and all his attendants who
36:25 Delaiah and Gemariah urged the **k** not
36:26 Instead, the **k** commanded Jerahmeel,
36:26 a son of the **k**, Seraiah son of
36:27 After the **k** burned the scroll
36:28 Jehoiakim **k** of Judah burned up.
36:29 Also tell Jehoiakim **k** of Judah,
36:29 Why did you write on it that the **k**
36:30 LORD says about Jehoiakim **k** of Judah:
36:32 **k** of Judah had burned in the fire.
37: 1 son of Josiah was made **k** of Judah
37: 1 by Nebuchadnezzar **k** of Babylon;
37: 3 **K** Zedekiah, however, sent Jehucal
37: 7 the God of Israel, says: Tell the **k**
37:17 **K** Zedekiah sent for him and had him
37:17 be handed over to the **k** of Babylon."
37:18 Jeremiah said to **K** Zedekiah, "What
37:19 'The **k** of Babylon will not attack
37:21 **K** Zedekiah then gave orders for
38: 3 **k** of Babylon, who will capture it.
38: 4 the officials said to the **k**, "This
38: 5 "He is in your hands," **K** Zedekiah
38: 5 "The **k** can do nothing to oppose you."
38: 7 **k** was sitting in the Benjamin Gate,
38:10 the **k** commanded Ebed-Melech the
38:14 **K** Zedekiah sent for Jeremiah the
38:14 something," the **k** said to Jeremiah.
38:16 **K** Zedekiah swore this oath secretly

Jer 38:17 to the officers of the **k** of Babylon,
38:18 to the officers of the **k** of Babylon,
38:19 **K** Zedekiah said to Jeremiah, "I am
38:22 in the palace of the **k** of Judah
38:22 the officials of the **k** of Babylon.
38:23 be captured by the **k** of Babylon;
38:25 to the **k** and what the **k** said to you;
38:26 tell them, 'I was pleading with the **k**
38:27 the **k** had ordered him to say.
38:27 heard his conversation with the **k**.
39: 1 ninth year of Zedekiah **k** of Judah
39: 1 Nebuchadnezzar **k** of Babylon marched
39: 3 officials of the **k** of Babylon
39: 3 other officials of the **k** of Babylon.
39: 4 Zedekiah **k** of Judah and all the
39: 5 to Nebuchadnezzar **k** of Babylon
39: 6 There at Riblah the **k** of Babylon
39:11 Now Nebuchadnezzar **k** of Babylon
39:13 officers of the **k** of Babylon
40: 5 the **k** of Babylon has appointed
40: 7 the **k** of Babylon had appointed
40: 9 the land and serve the **k** of Babylon,
40:11 heard that the **k** of Babylon had
40:14 that Baalis **k** of the Ammonites
41: 2 the one whom the **k** of Babylon
41: 9 was the one **K** Asa had made as part
41: 9 defence against Baasha **k** of Israel.
41:18 whom the **k** of Babylon had appointed
42:11 Do not be afraid of the **k** of Babylon,
43:10 servant Nebuchadnezzar **k** of Babylon,
44:30 to hand Pharaoh Hophra **k** of Egypt
44:30 just as I handed Zedekiah **k** of Judah
44:30 over to Nebuchadnezzar **k** of Babylon,
45: 1 Jehoiakim son of Josiah **k** of Judah,
46: 2 the army of Pharaoh Neco **k** of Egypt,
46: 2 by Nebuchadnezzar **k** of Babylon
46: 2 Jehoiakim son of Josiah **k** of Judah
46:13 **k** of Babylon to attack Egypt:
46:17 will exclaim, 'Pharaoh **k** of Egypt
46:18 surely as I live," declares the **K**
46:26 **k** of Babylon and his officers.
48:15 **K**, whose name is the LORD Almighty.
49:28 which Nebuchadnezzar **k** of Babylon
49:30 "Nebuchadnezzar **k** of Babylon has
49:34 in the reign of Zedekiah **k** of Judah:
49:38 and destroy her **k** and officials,"
50:17 to devour him was the **k** of Assyria
50:17 was Nebuchadnezzar **k** of Babylon."
50:18 "I will punish the **k** of Babylon and
50:18 land as I punished the **k** of Assyria.
50:43 The **k** of Babylon has heard reports
51:31 to announce to the **k** of Babylon
51:34 "Nebuchadnezzar **k** of Babylon has
51:57 **K**, whose name is the LORD Almighty.
51:59 with Zedekiah **k** of Judah in the
52: 1 years old when he became **k**,
52: 3 rebelled against the **k** of Babylon.
52: 4 Nebuchadnezzar **k** of Babylon marched
52: 5 the eleventh year of **K** Zedekiah.
52: 8 army pursued **K** Zedekiah and
52: 9 He was taken to the **k** of Babylon at
52:10 There at Riblah the **k** of Babylon
52:12 year of Nebuchadnezzar **k** of Babylon,
52:12 the **k** of Babylon, came to Jerusalem.
52:15 had gone over to the **k** of Babylon.
52:20 which **K** Soloman had made for the
52:26 them to the **k** of Babylon at Riblah.
52:27 of Hamath, the **k** had them executed.
52:31 the exile of Jehoiachin **k** of Judah,
52:31 in the year Evil-Merodach became **k**
52:31 he released Jehoiachin **k** of Judah
52:34 Day by day the **k** of Babylon gave
Lam 2: 6 he has spurned both **k** and priest.
2: 9 Her **k** and her princes are exiled
Eze 1: 2 year of the exile of **K** Jehoiachin—
7:27 The **k** will mourn, the prince will be
17:12 'The **k** of Babylon went to Jerusalem
17:12 carried off her **k** and her nobles,
17:15 the **k** rebelled against him by
17:16 in the land of the **k** who put him on
19: 9 and brought him to the **k** of Babylon.
21:19 sword of the **k** of Babylon to take,
21:21 For the **k** of Babylon will stop at
24: 2 the **k** of Babylon has laid seige
26: 7 Nebuchadnezzar **k** of Babylon,
28:12 a lament concerning the **k** of Tyre

Eze 29: 2 face against Pharaoh **k** of Egypt
29: 3 against you, Pharaoh **k** of Egypt
29:18 Nebuchadnezzar **k** of Babylon drove
29:19 Egypt to Nebuchadnezzar **k** of Babylon,
30:10 hand of Nebuchadnezzar **k** of Babylon.
30:21 the arm of Pharaoh **k** of Egypt.
30:22 I am against Pharaoh **k** of Egypt.
30:24 I will strengthen the arms of the **k**
30:25 I will strengthen the arms of the **k**
30:25 into the hand of the **k** of Babylon
31: 2 say to Pharaoh **k** of Egypt and to his
32: 2 Pharaoh **k** of Egypt and say to him:
32:11 **k** of Babylon will come against you.
37:22 There will be one **k** over all of them
37:24 servant David will be **k** over them
Da 1: 1 the reign of Jehoiakim **k** of Judah,
1: 1 Nebuchadnezzar **k** of Babylon came to
1: 2 delivered Jehoiakim **k** of Judah
1: 3 the **k** ordered Ashpenaz, chief of his
1: 5 The **k** assigned them a daily amount
1:10 The **k** would then have my head
1:18 At the end of the time set by the **k**
1:19 The **k** talked with them, and he found
1:20 about which the **k** questioned them,
1:21 until the first year of **K** Cyrus.
2: 2 the **k** summoned the magicians,
2: 2 they came in and stood before the **k**,
2: 4 the astrologers answered the **k** in
2: 4 "O **k**, live for ever! Tell your
2: 5 The **k** replied to the astrologers,
2: 7 Once more they replied, "Let the **k**
2: 8 the **k** answered, "I am certain that
2:10 The astrologers answered the **k**,
2:10 who can do what the **k** asks! No **k**,
2:11 What the **k** asks is too difficult.
2:11 No-one can reveal it to the **k** except
2:12 This made the **k** so angry and furious
2:15 "Why did the **k** issue such a harsh
2:16 Daniel went in to the **k** and asked
2:23 known to us the dream of the **k**."
2:24 Arioch, whom the **k** had appointed
2:24 Take me to the **k**, and I will
2:25 Arioch took Daniel to the **k** at once
2:25 tell the **k** what his dream means."
2:26 The **k** asked Daniel (also called
2:27 can explain to the **k** the mystery
2:28 He has shown **K** Nebuchadnezzar what
2:29 "As you were lying there, O **k**, your
2:30 but so that you, O **k**, may know the
2:31 "You looked, O **k**, and there before
2:36 now we will interpret it to the **k**.
2:37 You, O **k**, are the **k** of kings. The
2:45 "The great God has shown the **k** what
2:46 **K** Nebuchadnezzar fell prostrate
2:47 The **k** said to Daniel, "Surely your
2:48 the **k** placed Daniel in a high
2:49 at Daniel's request the **k** appointed
3: 1 **K** Nebuchadnezzar made an image of
3: 3 that **K** Nebuchadnezzar had set up,
3: 5 that **K** Nebuchadnezzar has set up.
3: 7 that **K** Nebuchadnezzar had set up.
3: 9 said to **K** Nebuchadnezzar, "O **k**,
3:10 You have issued a decree, O **k**, that
3:12 pay no attention to you, O **k**.
3:13 these men were brought before the **k**
3:16 and Abednego replied to the **k**,
3:17 will rescue us from your hand, O **k**.
3:18 we want you to know, O **k**, that we
3:24 **K** Nebuchadnezzar leaped to his feet
3:24 They replied, "Certainly, O **k**.
3:30 the **k** promoted Shadrach, Meshach
4: 1 **K** Nebuchadnezzar, To the peoples,
4:18 dream that I, **K** Nebuchadnezzar, had
4:19 So the **k** said, "Belteshazzar, do not
4:22 you, O **k**, are that tree! You have
4:23 "You, O **k**, saw a messenger, a holy
4:24 "This is the interpretation, O **k**,
4:27 Therefore, O **k**, be pleased to accept
4:28 this happened to **K** Nebuchadnezzar
4:29 as the **k** was walking on the roof
4:31 decreed for you, **K** Nebuchadnezzar
4:37 praise and exalt and glorify the **K**
5: 1 **K** Belshazzar gave a great banquet
5: 2 so that the **k** and his nobles, his
5: 3 and the **k** and his nobles, his wives
5: 5 The **k** watched the hand as it wrote.

Da 5: 7 The **k** called out for the enchanters,
5: 8 writing or tell the **k** what it meant.
5: 9 **K** Belshazzar became even more
5:10 hearing the voices of the **k** and his
5:10 "O **k**, live for ever!" she said.
5:11 **K** Nebuchadnezzar your father
5:11 your father the **K**, I say—
5:12 This man Daniel, whom the **k** called
5:13 Daniel was brought before the **k**,
5:13 and the **k** said to him, "Are you
5:13 my father the **k** brought from Judah?
5:17 Daniel answered the **k**, "You may keep
5:17 the **k** and tell him what it means.
5:18 "O **k**, the Most High God gave your
5:19 Those the **k** wanted to put to death,
5:30 Belshazzar, **k** of the Babylonians
6: 2 so that the **k** might not suffer loss.
6: 3 the **k** planned to set him over the
6: 6 to the **k** and said: "O **K** Darius,
6: 7 have all agreed that the **k** should
6: 7 you, O **k**, shall be thrown into the
6: 8 Now, O **k**, issue the decree and put
6: 9 **K** Darius put the decree in writing.
6:12 they went to the **k** and spoke to him
6:12 you, O **k**, would be thrown into the
6:12 The **k** answered, "The decree stands
6:13 they said to the **k**, "Daniel, who is
6:13 pays no attention to you, O **k**, or to
6:14 the **k** heard this, he was greatly
6:15 the men went as a group to the **k** and
6:15 "Remember, O **k**, that according to
6:15 that the **k** issues can be changed."
6:16 the **k** gave the order, and they
6:16 The **k** said to Daniel, "May your God,
6:17 and the **k** sealed it with his own
6:18 the **k** returned to his palace and
6:19 the **k** got up and hurried to the
6:21 Daniel answered, "O **k**, live for ever!
6:22 ever done any wrong before you, O **k**
6:23 The **k** was overjoyed and gave orders
6:25 **K** Darius wrote to all the peoples,
7: 1 In the first year of Belshazzar **k** of
7:24 After them another **k** will arise,
8: 1 third year of **K** Belshazzar's reign
8:21 The shaggy goat is the **k** of Greece,
8:21 between his eyes is the first **k**.
8:23 **k**, a master of intrigue, will arise.
10: 1 third year of Cyrus **k** of Persia
10:13 detained there with the **k** of Persia.
11: 3 a mighty **k** will appear, who will
11: 5 "The **k** of the South will become
11: 6 The daughter of the **k** of the South
11: 6 **k** of the North to make an alliance,
11: 7 He will attack the forces of the **k**
11: 8 will leave the **k** of the North alone.
11: 9 the **k** of the North will invade the
11: 9 realm of the **k** of the South but
11:11 "Then the **k** of the South will march
11:11 fight against the **k** of the North,
11:12 the army is carried off, the **k** of
11:13 For the **k** of the North will muster
11:14 rise against the **k** of the South.
11:15 the **k** of the North will come and
11:17 an alliance with the **k** of the South.
11:25 courage against the **k** of the South.
11:25 The **k** of the South will wage war
11:28 The **k** of the North will return to
11:36 "The **k** will do as he pleases. He
11:40 the **k** of the South will engage
11:40 and the **k** of the North will storm
Hos 1: 1 Jeroboam son of Joash **k** of Israel:
3: 4 for many days without **k** or prince,
3: 5 LORD their God and David their **k**.
5:13 and sent to the great **k** for help.
7: 3 "They delight the **k** with their
7: 5 On the day of the festival of our **k**
8:10 the oppression of the mighty **k**.
10: 3 they will say, "We have no **k** because
10: 3 even if we had a **k**, what could he
10: 6 Assyria as tribute for the great **k**.
10: 7 Samaria and its **k** will float away
10:15 When that day dawns, the **k** of Israel
13:10 Where is your **k**, that he may save
13:10 you said, 'Give me a **k** and princes'
13:11 in my anger I gave you a **k**, and in
Am 1: 1 when Uzziah was **k** of Judah and
Am 1: 1 son of Jehoash was **k** of Israel.
1: 5 I will destroy the **k** who is in the
1: 8 I will destroy the **k** of Ashdod and
1:15 Her **k** will go into exile, he and his
2: 1 if to lime, the bones of Edom's **k**,
5:26 have lifted up the shrine of your **k**,
7:10 a message to Jeroboam **k** of Israel:
Jnh 3: 6 the news reached the **k** of Nineveh,
3: 7 "By the decree of the **k** and his
Mic 2:13 Their **k** will pass through before
4: 9 have you no **k**? Has your counsellor
6: 5 remember what Balak **k** of Moab
Na 3:18 O **k** of Assyria, your shepherds
Zep 1: 1 of Josiah son of Amon **k** of Judah:
3:15 The LORD, the **K** of Israel, is with
Hag 1: 1 In the second year of **K** Darius,
1:15 in the second year of **K** Darius.
Zec 7: 1 In the fourth year of **K** Darius,
9: 5 Gaza will lose her **k** and Ashkelon
9: 9 See, your **k** comes to you, righteous
11: 6 over to his neighbour and his **k**.
14: 5 in the days of Uzziah **k** of Judah.
14: 9 The LORD will be **k** over the whole
14:16 year after year to worship the **K**,
14:17 go up to Jerusalem to worship the **K**
Mal 1:14 For I am a great **k**," says the LORD
Mt 1: 6 Jesse the father of **K** David. David
2: 1 during the time of **K** Herod, Magi
2: 3 **K** Herod heard this he was disturbed,
2: 9 After they had heard the **k**, they
5:35 for it is the city of the Great **K**.
14: 9 The **k** was distressed, but because
18:23 the kingdom of heaven is like a **k**
21: 5 'See, your **k** comes to you, gentle
22: 2 "The kingdom of heaven is like a **k**
22: 7 The **k** was enraged. He sent his army
22:11 "But when the **k** came in to see the
22:13 "Then the **k** told the attendants,
25:34 "Then the **K** will say to those on his
25:40 "The **K** will reply, 'I tell you the
27:42 He's the **K** of Israel! Let him come
Mk 6:14 **K** Herod heard about this, for
6:22 The **k** said to the girl, "Ask me for
6:25 At once the girl hurried in to the **k**
6:26 The **k** was greatly distressed, but
15:32 Let this Christ, this **K** of Israel,
Lk 1: 5 In the time of Herod **k** of Judea
14:31 "Or suppose a **k** is about to go to
14:31 to go to war against another **k**.
19:12 appointed **k** and then to return.
19:14 don't want this man to be our **k**.'
19:15 "He was made **k**, however, and
19:27 be a **k** over them—bring them here
19:38 "Blessed is the **k** who comes in the
23: 2 Caesar and claims to be Christ, a **k**
Jn 1:49 Son of God; you are the **K** of Israel
6:15 to come and make him **k** by force,
12:13 "Blessed is the **K** of Israel!
12:15 see, your **k** is coming seated on a
18:37 "You are a **k**, then!" said Pilate.
18:37 "You are right in saying I am a **k**.
19:12 claims to be a **k** opposes Caesar."
19:14 "Here is your **k**," Pilate said to
19:15 I crucify your **k**?" Pilate asked.
19:15 "We have no **k** but Caesar," the chief
Ac 7:10 the goodwill of Pharaoh **k** of Egypt;
7:18 another **k**, who knew nothing about
12: 1 was about this time that **K** Herod
12:20 trusted personal servant of the **k**,
13:21 the people asked for a **k**, and he
13:22 Saul, he made David their **k**.
17: 7 is another **k**, one called Jesus."
25:13 A few days later **K** Agrippa and
25:14 discussed Paul's case with the **k**.
25:24 Festus said: "**K** Agrippa, and all
25:26 and especially before you, **K** Agrippa,
26: 2 "**K** Agrippa, I consider myself
26: 7 O **K**, it is because of this hope that
26:13 About noon, O **K**, as I was on the
26:19 "So then, **K** Agrippa, I was not
26:26 **k** is familiar with these things,
26:27 **K** Agrippa, do you believe the
26:30 The **k** rose, and with him the
2Co 11:32 the governor under **K** Aretas had
1Ti 1:17 Now to the **K** eternal, immortal,
Heb 7: 1 This Melchizedek was **k** of Salem and
Heb 7: 2 his name means "**k** of righteousness
7: 2 "**k** of Salem" means "**k** of peace".
1Pe 2:13 to the **k**, as the supreme authority,
2:17 believers, fear God, honour the **k**.
Rev 9:11 They had as **k** over them the angel
15: 3 true are your ways, **K** of the ages.
17:11 was, and now is not, is an eighth **k**.

King of kings

Ezr 7:12 Artaxerxes, **k**, To Ezra the priest, a
Eze 26: 7 **k**, with horses and chariots, with
Da 2:37 You, O king, are the **k**. The God of
1Ti 6:15 only Ruler, the **K** and Lord of lords,
Rev 17:14 he is Lord of lords and **K**
19:16 written: K AND LORD OF LORDS.

King of the Jews

Mt 2: 2 is the one who has been born **k**?
27:11 governor asked him, "Are you the **k**?
27:29 mocked him. "Hail, **k**!" they said.
27:37 against him: THIS IS JESUS, THE K.
Mk 15: 2 "Are you the **k**?" asked Pilate.
15: 9 want me to release to you the **k**?"
15:12 with the one you call the **k**?"
15:18 began to call out to him, "Hail, **k**!
15:26 charge against him read: THE K.
Lk 23: 3 Pilate asked Jesus, "Are you the **k**?"
23:37 "If you are the **k**, save yourself."
23:38 him, which read: THIS IS THE K.
Jn 18:33 and asked him, "Are you the **k**?
18: 39 Do you want me to release 'the **k**'?
19: 3 "Hail, **k**!" And they struck him
19:19 It read: JESUS OF NAZARETH, THE K.
19:21 "Do not write 'The **K**', but that
19: 21 this man claimed to be **k**.

King's (King)

Ge 14:17 of Shaveh (that is, the **K** Valley).
39:20 where the **k** prisoners were confined.
Nu 20:17 We will travel along the **k** highway
21:22 We will travel along the **k** highway
Jdg 3:21 and plunged it into the **k** belly.
1Sa 18:18 I should become the **k** son-in-law?"
18:23 matter to become the **k** son-in-law?
18:26 pleased to become the **k** son-in-law.
18:27 he might become the **k** son-in-law.
20:29 why he has not come to the **k** table."
21: 8 because the **k** business was urgent."
22:14 the **k** son-in-law, captain of your
22:17 But the **k** officials were not
26:16 Where are the **k** spear and water
26:22 "Here is the **k** spear," David
2Sa 9:11 David's table like one of the **k** sons.
9:13 because he always ate at the **k** table,
11: 1 **k** men and the whole Israelite army.
11:20 the **k** anger may flare up, and he may
11:24 wall, and some of the **k** men died.
13: 4 "Why do you, the **k** son, look so
13:23 all the **k** sons to come there.
13:27 Amnon and the rest of the **k** sons.
13:29 Then all the **k** sons got up, mounted
13:30 has struck down all the **k** sons;
13:33 report that all the **k** sons are dead.
13:35 the king, "See, the **k** sons are here
13:36 the **k** sons came in, wailing
14: 1 knew that the **k** heart longed for
14:28 Jerusalem without seeing the **k** face.
14:32 Now then, I want to see the **k** face,
15:15 The **k** officials answered him, "Your
15:35 anything you hear in the **k** palace.
16: 2 "The donkeys are for the **k** household
16: 6 pelted David and all the **k** officials
18:12 not lift my hand against the **k** son.
18:18 **K** Valley as a monument to himself,
18:20 today, because the **k** son is dead."
18:29 about to send the **k** servant and me,
19:18 ford to take the **k** household over
19:42 eaten any of the **k** provisions?
24: 4 The **k** word, however, overruled Joab
1Ki 1: 9 all his brothers, the **k** sons, and
1:19 and has invited all the **k** sons,
1:25 He has invited all the **k** sons, the
1:28 the **k** presence and stood before him.
1:44 and they have put him on the **k** mule,
2:19 throne brought for the **k** mother

1Ki 4:27 and all who came to the **k** table.
5:17 At the **k** command they removed from
13: 6 and the **k** hand was restored and
22: 6 Lord will give it into the **k** hand.
22:12 LORD will give it into the **k** hand.
22:15 LORD will give it into the **k** hand.
22:26 the city and to Joash the **k** son
2Ki 8:15 it over the **k** face, so that he died.
9:34 bury her, for she was a **k** daughter."
11: 4 Then he showed them the **k** son.
11:12 Jehoiada brought out the **k** son and
13:16 Elisha put his hands on the **k** hands.
15: 5 Jotham the **k** son had charge of the
16:15 the **k** burnt offering and his grain
22:12 and Asaiah the **k** attendant:
24:15 Jerusalem to Babylon the **k** mother,
25: 4 the two walls near the **k** garden,
25:29 ate regularly at the **k** table.
1Ch 9:18 being stationed at the **K** Gate on the
18:17 were chief officials at the **k** side.
21: 4 The **k** word, however, overruled Joab;
21: 6 the **k** command was repulsive to him.
25: 2 prophesied under the **k** supervision.
25: 5 were sons of Heman the **k** seer.
26:30 of the LORD and for the **k** service.
27:32 of Hacmoni took care of the **k** sons.
27:33 Ahithophel was the **k** counsellor.
27:33 Hushai the Arkite was the **k** friend.
29: 6 charge of the **k** work gave willingly.
2Ch 8:15 not deviate from the **k** commands
18: 5 God will give it into the **k** hand."
18:11 LORD will give it into the **k** hand."
18:25 of the city and to Joash the **k** son,
21:17 all the goods found in the **k** palace,
23: 3 Jehoiada said to them, "The **k** son
23:11 the **k** son and put the crown on him;
24: 8 At the **k** command, a chest was made
24:11 by the Levites to the **k** officials
28: 7 killed Maaseiah the **k** son, Azrikam
29:25 the **k** seer and Nathan the prophet;
30: 6 At the **k** command, couriers went
34:20 and Asaiah the **k** attendant:
35: 7 from the **k** own possessions.
35:15 Heman and Jeduthun the **k** seer.
Ezr 7:27 who has put it into the **k** heart to
7:28 and all the **k** powerful officials.
8:36 They also delivered the **k** orders to
Ne 2: 8 keeper of the **k** forest, so he will
2: 9 and gave them the **k** letters.
2:14 the Fountain Gate and the **K** Pool,
3:15 by the **K** Garden, as far as the steps
5: 4 **k** tax on our fields and vineyards.
11:23 The singers were under the **k** orders,
11:24 was the **k** agent in all affairs
Est 1: 5 enclosed garden of the **k** palace
1: 7 in keeping with the **k** liberality.
1: 8 By the **k** command each guest was
1:12 attendants delivered the **k** command
1:18 to all the **k** nobles in the same way.
1:20 the **k** edict is proclaimed throughout
2: 2 the **k** personal attendants proposed,
2: 3 the **k** eunuch, who is in charge of
2: 8 the **k** order and edict had been
2: 8 also was taken to the **k** palace
2: 9 maids selected from the **k** palace
2:13 her from the harem to the **k** palace.
2:14 the **k** eunuch who was in charge of
2:15 the **k** eunuch who was in charge of
2:19 Mordecai was sitting at the **k** gate.
2:21 Mordecai was sitting at the **k** gate,
2:21 and Teresh, two of the **k** officers
3: 2 royal officials at the **k** gate
3: 3 the royal officials at the **k** gate
3: 3 "Why do you disobey the **k** command?
3: 8 and who do not obey the **k** laws;
3: 8 **k** best interest to tolerate them.
3:12 all Haman's orders to the **k** satraps,
3:13 by couriers to all the **k** provinces
3:15 Spurred on by the **k** command, the
4: 2 he went only as far as the **k** gate,
4: 5 Hathach, one of the **k** eunuchs
4: 6 of the city in front of the **k** gate.
4: 8 the **k** presence to beg for mercy
4:11 "All the **k** officials and the people
4:13 because you are in the **k** house you
5: 1 the palace, in front of the **k** hall.
Est 5: 8 Then I will answer the **k** question."
5: 9 But when he saw Mordecai at the **k**
5:13 Jew Mordecai sitting at the **k** gate."
6: 2 two of the **k** officers who guarded
6: 9 to one of the **k** most noble princes.
6:10 the Jew, who sits at the **k** gate.
6:12 Mordecai returned to the **k** gate
6:14 the **k** eunuchs arrived and hurried
7: 8 soon as the word left the **k** mouth,
7:10 Then the **k** fury subsided.
8: 5 the Jews in all the **k** provinces.
8: 8 write another decree in the **k** name
8: 8 and seal it with the **k** signet
8: 8 no document written in the **k** name
8:10 dispatches with the **k** signet ring
8:11 The **k** edict granted the Jews in
8:14 out, spurred on by the **k** command.
8:15 Mordecai left the **k** presence wearing
9: 3 governors and the **k** administrators
9:12 done in the rest of the **k** provinces?
9:16 who were in the **k** provinces also
9:25 the plot came to the **k** attention
Ps 45: 5 pierce the hearts of the **k** enemies;
61: 6 Increase the days of the **k** life,
Pr 14:28 A large population is a **k** glory,
16:14 A **k** wrath is a messenger of death,
16:15 a **k** face brightens, it means life;
19:12 A **k** rage is like the roar of a lion,
20: 2 A **k** wrath is like the roar of a lion;
21: 1 The **k** heart is in the hand of the
25: 5 the wicked from the **k** presence
25: 6 exalt yourself in the **k** presence
Ecc 2:12 What more can the **k** successor do
4:15 followed the youth, the **k** successor.
8: 2 Obey the **k** command, I say, because
8: 3 in a hurry to leave the **k** presence
8: 4 Since a **k** word is supreme, who can
Isa 23:15 seventy years, the span of a **k** life.
Jer 38: 6 cistern of Malkijah, the **k** son,
39: 4 at night by way of the **k** garden,
41: 1 and had been one of the **k** officers,
41:10 the **k** daughters along with all the
43: 6 and children and the **k** daughters
52: 7 the two walls near the **k** garden,
52:33 life ate regularly at the **k** table.
Da 1: 4 qualified to serve in the **k** palace.
1: 5 of food and wine from the **k** table.
1: 5 they were to enter the **k** service.
1:19 so they entered the **k** service.
2:14 Arioch, the commander of the **k** guard,
2:15 He asked the **k** officer, "Why did the
3:22 The **k** command was so urgent and the
3:28 defied the **k** command and were
5: 8 all the **k** wise men came in, but they
6:24 At the **k** command, the men who had
8:27 and went about the **k** business
11:26 Those who eat from the **k** provisions
Am 7: 1 the **k** share had been harvested
7:13 because this is the **k** sanctuary and
Zep 1: 8 the **k** sons and all those clad in
Ac 12:20 the **k** country for their food supply.
Heb 11:23 they were not afraid of the **k** edict.
11:27 left Egypt, not fearing the **k** anger

Kingdom (King, *Kingdom of God, Kingdom of heaven*)

Ge 10:10 centres of his **k** were Babylon
20: 9 such great guilt upon me and my **k**?
Ex 19: 6 you will be for me a **k** of priests
Nu 24: 7 than Agag; their **k** will be exalted.
32:33 the **k** of Sihon king of the Amorites
32:33 the **k** of Og king of Bashan—the
Dt 3: 4 region of Argob, Og's **k** in Bashan.
3:10 Edrei, towns of Og's **k** in Bashan.
3:13 the **k** of Og, I gave to the
17:18 he takes the throne of his **k**, he is
17:20 a long time over his **k** in Israel.
Jos 13:12 that is, the whole **k** of Og in Bashan,
1Sa 13:13 your **k** over Israel for all time.
13:14 now your **k** will not endure; the LORD
15:28 "The LORD has torn the **k** of Israel
18: 8 What more can he get but the **k**?"
20:31 you nor your **k** will be established.
24:20 that the **k** of Israel will be
28:17 The LORD has torn the **k** out of your
2Sa 3:10 transfer the **k** from the house of
3:28 "I and my **k** are for ever innocent
5:12 had exalted his **k** for the sake of
7:12 body, and I will establish his **k**.
7:13 the throne of his **k** for ever.
7:16 Your house and your **k** shall endure
8: 6 in the Aramean **k** of Damascus,
16: 3 give me back my grandfather's **k**.
16: 8 The LORD has handed the **k** over to
1Ki 2:15 know," he said, "the **k** was mine.
2:15 and the **k** has gone to my brother;
2:22 request the **k** for him—after all,
2:46 The **k** was now firmly established in
10:20 had ever been made for any other **k**.
11:11 certainly tear the **k** away from you
11:13 I will not tear the whole **k** from him
11:31 to tear the **k** out of Solomon's hand
11:34 "'But I will not take the whole **k**
11:35 take the **k** from his son's hands
12:21 the **k** for Rehoboam son of Solomon.
12:26 "The **k** is now likely to revert to
14: 8 I tore the **k** away from the house of
18:10 there is not a nation or **k** where my
18:10 or **k** claimed you were not there
2Ki 14: 5 After the **k** was firmly in his grasp,
15:19 strengthen his own hold on the **k**.
20:13 **k** that Hezekiah did not show them.
1Ch 10:14 turned the **k** over to David son of
12:23 to turn Saul's **k** over to him, as the
14: 2 that his **k** had been highly exalted
16:20 to nation, from one **k** to another.
17:11 sons, and I will establish his **k**.
17:14 will set him over my house and my **k**
18: 6 in the Aramean **k** of Damascus,
22:10 of his **k** over Israel for ever.'
28: 5 of the **k** of the LORD over Israel.
28: 7 I will establish his **k** for ever if
29:11 Yours, O LORD, is the **k**; you are
2Ch 1: 1 himself firmly over his **k**,
9:19 had ever been made for any other **k**.
11: 1 and to regain the **k** for Rehoboam.
11:17 They strengthened the **k** of Judah and
13: 8 you plan to resist the **k** of the LORD
14: 5 and the **k** was at peace under him.
17: 5 established the **k** under his control
20:30 the **k** of Jehoshaphat was at peace,
21: 3 but he had given the **k** to Jehoram
21: 4 himself firmly over his father's **k**,
22: 9 powerful enough to retain the **k**.
25: 3 the **k** was firmly in his control
29:21 as a sin offering for the **k**, for
32:15 for no god of any nation or **k** has
33:13 him back to Jerusalem and to his **k**.
36:20 until the **k** of Persia came to power.
Ezr 7:13 that any of the Israelites in my **k**,
Ne 9:35 Even while they were in their **k**,
Est 1: 4 displayed the vast wealth of his **k**
1:14 the king and were highest in the **k**.
1:22 dispatches to all parts of the **k**,
3: 6 throughout the whole **k** of Xerxes.
3: 8 in all the provinces of your **k**
5: 3 up to half the **k**, it will be given
5: 6 to half the **k**, it will be granted."
7: 2 to half the **k**, it will be granted."
9:30 127 provinces of the **k** of Xerxes
Ps 45: 6 will be the sceptre of your **k**.
103:19 in heaven, and his **k** rules over all.
105:13 to nation, from one **k** to another.
145:11 will tell of the glory of your **k**
145:12 the glorious splendour of your **k**.
145:13 Your **k** is an everlasting **k**, and your
Ecc 4:14 been born in poverty within his **k**.
Isa 9: 7 on David's throne and over his **k**,
19: 2 city against city, **k** against **k**.
34:12 nothing there to be called a **k**,
39: 2 **k** that Hezekiah did not show them.
60:12 For the nation or **k** that will not
Jer 18: 7 a nation or **k** is to be uprooted,
18: 9 or **k** is to be built up and planted,
27: 8 any nation or **k** will not serve
Lam 2: 2 has brought her **k** and its princes
Eze 17:14 that the **k** would be brought low,
29:14 There they will be a lowly **k**.
Da 1:20 and enchanters in his whole **k**.
2:39 "After you, another **k** will rise,
2:39 a third **k**, one of bronze, will

Da 2:40 Finally, there will be a fourth **k**,
2:41 so this will be a divided **k**; yet it
2:42 so this **k** will be partly strong and
2:44 the God of heaven will set up a **k**
4: 3 his wonders! His **k** is an eternal **k**;
4:18 men in my **k** can interpret it for me.
4:26 means that your **k** will be restored
4:34 his **k** endures from generation to
4:36 to me for the glory of my **k**.
5: 7 the third highest ruler in the **k**."
5:11 There is a man in your **k** who has
5:16 the third highest ruler in the **k**."
5:28 Peres: Your **k** is divided and given
5:29 the third highest ruler in the **k**.
5:31 Darius the Mede took over the **k**,
6: 1 satraps to rule throughout the **k**,
6: 3 planned to set him over the whole **k**.
6:26 every part of my **k** people must fear
6:26 his **k** will not be destroyed,
7:14 and his **k** is one that will never be
7:18 receive the **k** and will possess it
7:22 time came when they possessed the **k**.
7:23 fourth **k** that will appear on earth.
7:24 ten kings who will come from this **k**.
7:27 His **k** will be an everlasting **k**, and
9: 1 made ruler over the Babylonian **k**—
10:13 the prince of the Persian **k** resisted
11: 2 up everyone against the **k** of Greece.
11: 5 rule his own **k** with great power.
11:17 come with the might of his entire **k**
11:17 in order to overthrow the **k**,
11:21 He will invade the **k** when its people
Hos 1: 4 I will put an end to the **k** of Israel.
Am 7:13 sanctuary and the temple of the **k**."
9: 8 Sovereign LORD are on the sinful **k**.
Ob :21 And the **k** will be the LORD's.
Mt 4:23 preaching the good news of the **k**,
6:10 your **k** come, your will be done on
6:33 seek first his **k** and his
8:12 the subjects of the **k** will be thrown
9:35 preaching the good news of the **k** and
12:25 "Every **k** divided against itself will
12:26 How then can his **k** stand?
13:19 anyone hears the message about the **k**
13:38 seed stands for the sons of the **k**.
13:41 and they will weed out of his **k**
13:43 the sun in the **k** of their Father.
16:28 see the Son of Man coming in his **k**."
20:21 the other at your left in your **k**."
24: 7 against nation, and **k** against **k**.
24:14 this gospel of the **k** will be
25:34 the **k** prepared for you since the
26:29 it anew with you in my Father's **k**."
Mk 3:24 If a **k** is divided against itself,
3:24 against itself, that **k** cannot stand.
6:23 I will give you, up to half my **k**."
11:10 "Blessed is the coming **k** of our
13: 8 against nation, and **k** against **k**.
Lk 1:33 for ever; his **k** will never end."
11: 2 hallowed be your name, your **k** come.
11:17 "Any **k** divided against itself will
11:18 himself, how can his **k** stand?
12:31 seek his **k**, and these things will be
12:32 has been pleased to give you the **k**.
21:10 against nation, and **k** against **k**.
22:29 I confer on you a **k**, just as my
22:30 my table in my **k** and sit on thrones,
23:42 me when you come into your **k**."
Jn 18:36 said, "My **k** is not of this world
18:36 But now my **k** is from another place."
Ac 1: 6 going to restore the **k** to Israel?"
20:25 the **k** will ever see me again.
1Co 15:24 when he hands over the **k** to God the
Eph 2: 2 of the ruler of the **k** of the air,
5: 5 in the **k** of Christ and of God.
Col 1:12 of the saints in the **k** of light.
1:13 us into the **k** of the Son he loves,
1Th 2:12 who calls you into his **k** and glory.
2Ti 4: 1 and his **k**, I give you this charge:
4:18 bring me safely to his heavenly **k**.
Heb 1: 8 will be the sceptre of your **k**.
12:28 receiving a **k** that cannot be
Jas 2: 5 inherit the **k** he promised those
2Pe 1:11 into the eternal **k** of our Lord
Rev 1: 6 has made us to be a **k** and priests
1: 9 companion in the suffering and **k**
Rev 5:10 You have made them to be a **k** and
11:15 The **k** of the world has become the **k**
12:10 and the power and the **k** of our God,
16:10 and his **k** was plunged into darkness
17:12 kings who have not yet received a **k**

Kingdom of God

Mt 12:28 then the **k** has come upon you.
19:24 than for a rich man to enter the **k**.
21:31 are entering the **k** ahead of you.
21:43 the **k** will be taken away from you
Mk 1:15 "The **k** is near. Repent and believe
4:11 The secret of the **k** has been given
4:26 said, "This is what the **k** is like.
4:30 "What shall we say the **k** is like,
9: 1 they see the **k** come with power."
9:47 It is better for you to enter the **k**
10:14 for the **k** belongs to such as these.
10:15 anyone who will not receive the **k**
10:23 it is for the rich to enter the **k**!"
10:24 how hard it is to enter the **k**!
10:25 than for a rich man to enter the **k**.
12:34 to him, "You are not far from the **k**.
14:25 day when I drink it anew in the **k**."
15:43 who was himself waiting for the **k**,
Lk 4:43 must preach the good news of the **k**
6:20 who are poor, for yours is the **k**.
7:28 least in the **k** is greater than he.
8: 1 proclaiming the good news of the **k**.
8:10 of the **k** has been given to you,
9: 2 he sent them out to preach the **k**
9:11 them and spoke to them about the **k**,
9:27 taste death before they see the **k**."
9:60 but you go and proclaim the **k**."
9:62 is fit for service in the **k**."
10: 9 and tell them, 'The **k** is near you.'
10:11 Yet be sure of this: The **k** is near.
11:20 then the **k** has come to you.
13:18 Jesus asked, "What is the **k** like?
13:20 "What shall I compare the **k** to?
13:28 and all the prophets in the **k**,
13:29 their places at the feast in the **k**.
14:15 who will eat at the feast in the **k**.
16:16 the good news of the **k** is being
17:20 the Pharisees when the **k** would come,
17:20 "The **k** does not come with your
17:21 because the **k** is within you."
18:16 for the **k** belongs to such as these.
18:17 anyone who will not receive the **k**
18:24 it is for the rich to enter the **k**!
18:25 than for a rich man to enter the **k**.
18:29 or children for the sake of the **k**
19:11 the **k** was going to appear at once.
21:31 you know that the **k** is near.
22:16 until it finds fulfilment in the **k**."
22:18 of the vine until the **k** comes."
23:51 and he was waiting for the **k**.
Jn 3: 3 no-one can see the **k** unless he is
3: 5 no-one can enter the **k** unless he is
Ac 1: 3 forty days and spoke about the **k**.
8:12 he preached the good news of the **k**
14:22 to enter the **k**," they said.
19: 8 arguing persuasively about the **k**.
28:23 declared to them the **k** and tried to
28:31 without hindrance he preached the **k**
Ro 14:17 For the **k** is not a matter of eating
1Co 4:20 For the **k** is not a matter of talk
6: 9 wicked will not inherit the **k**?
6:10 nor swindlers will inherit the **k**.
15:50 and blood cannot inherit the **k**,
Gal 5:21 like this will not inherit the **k**.
Col 4:11 among my fellow-workers for the **k**,
2Th 1: 5 will be counted worthy of the **k**,

Kingdom of Heaven

Mt 3: 2 saying, "Repent, for the **k** is near.
4:17 preach, "Repent, for the **k** is near.
5: 3 poor in spirit, for theirs is the **k**
5:10 righteousness, for theirs is the **k**.
5:19 same will be called least in the **k**,
5:19 will be called great in the **k**.
5:20 you will certainly not enter the **k**.
7:21 'Lord, Lord,' will enter the **k**, but
8:11 Abraham, Isaac and Jacob in the **k**.
10: 7 preach this message: 'The **k** is near
Mt 11:11 least in the **k** is greater than he.
11:12 the **k** has been forcefully advancing,
13:11 of the **k** has been given to you,
13:24 "The **k** is like a man who sowed good
13:31 "The **k** is like a mustard seed,
13:33 "The **k** is like yeast that a woman
13:44 "The **k** is like treasure hidden in a
13:45 "Again, the **k** is like a merchant
13:47 "Once again, the **k** is like a net
13:52 has been instructed about the **k**
16:19 I will give you the keys of the **k**;
18: 1 "Who is the greatest in the **k**?
18: 3 you will never enter the **k**.
18: 4 this child is the greatest in the **k**.
18:23 "Therefore, the **k** is like a king who
19:12 renounced marriage because of the **k**.
19:14 for the **k** belongs to such as these."
19:23 hard for a rich man to enter the **k**.
20: 1 "For the **k** is like a landowner who
22: 2 "The **k** is like a king who prepared
23:13 You shut the **k** in men's faces.
25: 1 At that time the **k** will be like ten

Kingdoms (King, *Kingdoms of the earth*)

Dt 3:21 LORD will do the same to all the **k**
28:25 of horror to all the **k** on earth.
Jos 11:10 had been the head of all these **k**.)
1Sa 10:18 and all the **k** that oppressed you.'
1Ki 4:21 Solomon ruled over all the **k** from
4:24 over all the **k** west of the River
2Ki 19:19 so that all **k** on earth may know
1Ch 29:30 and the **k** of all the other lands.
2Ch 17:10 **k** of the lands surrounding Judah,
20: 6 rule over all the **k** of the nations
20:29 The fear of God came upon all the **k**
Ne 9:22 "You gave them **k** and nations,
Ps 46: 6 Nations are in uproar, **k** fall;
79: 6 the **k** that do not call on your name;
102:22 the peoples and the **k** assemble to
Isa 10:10 seized the **k** of the idols, **k** whose
13: 4 an uproar among the **k**, like nations
13:19 Babylon, the jewel of **k**, the glory
14:16 shook the earth and made **k** tremble,
23:11 over the sea and made its **k** tremble.
23:17 all the **k** on the face of the earth.
37:20 so that all **k** on earth may know
47: 5 more will you be called queen of **k**.
Jer 1:10 and **k** to uproot and tear down,
1:15 all the peoples of the northern **k**,"
10: 7 in all their **k**, there is no-one
25:26 the **k** on the face of the earth.
28: 8 against many countries and great **k**.
33:24 'The LORD has rejected the two **k** he
34: 1 all his army and all the **k** and
49:28 Concerning Kedar and the **k** of Hazor,
51:20 nations, with you I destroy **k**,
51:27 these **k**: Ararat, Minni and Ashkenaz.
Eze 29:15 will be the lowliest of **k** and will
37:22 nations or be divided into two **k**.
Da 2:44 It will crush all those **k** and bring
4:17 is sovereign over the **k** of men
4:25 is sovereign over the **k** of men
4:32 is sovereign over the **k** of men
5:21 God is sovereign over the **k** of men
7:17 'The four great beasts are four **k**
7:23 be different from all the other **k**
7:27 power and greatness of the **k** under
8:22 represent four **k** that will emerge
Am 6: 2 they better off than your two **k**?
Na 3: 5 your nakedness and the **k** your shame.
Zep 3: 8 to gather the **k** and to pour out my
Hag 2:22 shatter the power of the foreign **k**.
Mt 4: 8 **k** of the world and their splendour.
Lk 4: 5 an instant all the **k** of the world.
Heb 11:33 who through faith conquered **k**,

Kingdoms of the earth

2Ki 19:15 you alone are God over all the **k**.
2Ch 36:23 has given me all the **k** and he has
Ezr 1: 2 has given me all the **k** and he has
Ps 68:32 Sing to God, O **k**, sing praise to the
Isa 37:16 you alone are God over all the **k**.
Jer 15: 4 abhorrent to all the **k** because
24: 9 and an offence to all the **k**,

Jer 29:18 make them abhorrent to all the **k**
34:17 make you abhorrent to all the **k**.

Kings (*Book of the kings*, King, *King of kings*, *Kings of Israel*)

Ge 14: 3 All these latter **k** joined forces in
14: 5 Kedorlaomer and the **k** allied with
14: 9 of Ellasar—four **k** against five.
14:10 and when the **k** of Sodom and Gomorrah
14:11 The four **k** seized all the goods of
14:17 and the **k** allied with him,
17: 6 of you, and **k** will come from you.
17:16 **k** of peoples will come from her."
35:11 and **k** will come from your body.
36:31 These were the **k** who reigned in Edom
Nu 31: 8 Hur and Reba—the five **k** of Midian.
Dt 3: 8 that time we took from these two **k**
3:21 your God has done to these two **k**.
4:47 two Amorite **k** east of the Jordan.
7:24 He will give their **k** into your hand,
31: 4 the **k** of the Amorites, whom he
Jos 2:10 the two **k** of the Amorites east of
5: 1 the Amorite **k** west of the Jordan
5: 1 all the Canaanite **k** along the coast
9: 1 all the **k** west of the Jordan
9: 1 as Lebanon (the **k** of the Hittites,
9:10 did to the two **k** of the Amorites
10: 5 the five **k** of the Amorites—the **k** of
10: 6 because all the Amorite **k** from the
10:16 Now the five **k** had fled and hidden
10:17 Joshua was told that the five **k** had
10:22 and bring those five **k** out to me."
10:23 they brought the five **k** out of the
10:23 out of the cave—the **k** of Jerusalem,
10:24 they had brought these **k** to Joshua,
10:24 your feet on the necks of these **k**.
10:26 Joshua struck and killed the **k** and
10:40 slopes, together with all their **k**.
10:42 All these **k** and their lands Joshua
11: 1 to the **k** of Shimron and Acshaph,
11: 2 to the northern **k** who were in the
11: 5 All these **k** joined forces and made
11:12 their **k** and put them to the sword.
11:17 He captured all their **k** and struck
11:18 Joshua waged war against all these **k**
12: 1 These are the **k** of the land whom the
12: 7 These are the **k** of the land that
12:24 thirty-one **k** in all.
24:12 before you—also the two Amorite **k**.
Jdg 1: 7 "Seventy **k** with their thumbs and
5: 3 "Hear this, you **k**! Listen, you
5:19 "**K** came, they fought; the **k** of
8: 5 Zebah and Zalmunna, the **k** of Midian.
8:12 and Zalmunna, the two **k** of Midian
8:26 garments worn by the **k** of Midian
1Sa 14:47 the **k** of Zobah, and the Philistines.
27: 6 to the **k** of Judah ever since.
2Sa 10:19 all the **k** who were vassals of
11: 1 at the time when **k** go off to war,
1Ki 3:13 you will have no equal among **k**.
4:34 sent by all the **k** of the world,
10:15 **k** and the governors of the land.
10:23 than all the other **k** of the earth.
10:29 to all the **k** of the Hittites and of
14:29 of the annals of the **k** of Judah?
15: 7 of the annals of the **k** of Judah?
15:23 of the annals of the **k** of Judah?
20: 1 Accompanied by thirty-two **k** with
20:12 the **k** were drinking in their tents,
20:16 the 32 **k** allied with him were in
20:24 Remove all the **k** from their commands
20:31 that the **k** of the houses of Israel
22:45 of the annals of the **k** of Judah?
2Ki 3:10 "Has the LORD called us three **k**
3:13 three **k** together to hand us over
3:21 **k** had come to fight against them;
3:23 "Those **k** must have fought and
7: 6 Hittite and Egyptian **k** to attack us!
8:23 of the annals of the **k** of Judah?
10: 4 **k** could not resist him, how can we?
12:18 Jehoram and Ahaziah, the **k** of Judah
12:19 of the annals of the **k** of Judah?
14:18 of the annals of the **k** of Judah?
15: 6 of the annals of the **k** of Judah?
15:36 of the annals of the **k** of Judah?
2Ki 16:19 of the annals of the **k** of Judah?
18: 5 like him among all the **k** of Judah,
19:11 have heard what the **k** of Assyria
19:17 that the Assyrian **k** have laid waste
20:20 of the annals of the **k** of Judah?
21:17 of the annals of the **k** of Judah?
21:25 of the annals of the **k** of Judah?
23: 5 appointed by the **k** of Judah
23:11 **k** of Judah had dedicated to the sun.
23:12 He pulled down the altars the **k** of
23:22 the **k** of Israel and the **k** of Judah,
23:28 of the annals of the **k** of Judah?
24: 5 of the annals of the **k** of Judah?
25:28 **k** who were with him in Babylon.
1Ch 1:43 These were the **k** who reigned in Edom
16:21 for their sake he rebuked **k**:
19: 9 **k** who had come were by themselves
20: 1 at the time when **k** go off to war,
2Ch 1:17 to all the **k** of the Hittites and
9:14 Also all the **k** of Arabia and the
9:22 than all the other **k** of the earth.
9:23 All the **k** of the earth sought
9:26 over all the **k** from the River
12: 8 and serving the **k** of other lands."
21:20 but not in the tombs of the **k**.
24:16 He was buried with the **k** in the City
24:25 but not in the tombs of the **k**.
26:23 for burial that belonged to the **k**,
28:23 "Since the gods of the **k** of Aram
30: 6 from the hand of the **k** of Assyria.
32: 4 "Why should the **k** of Assyria come
34:11 beams for the buildings that the **k**
Ezr 4:15 troublesome to **k** and provinces,
4:19 a long history of revolt against **k**
4:20 Jerusalem has had powerful **k** ruling
6:14 Darius and Artaxerxes, **k** of Persia.
9: 7 we and our **k** and our priests have
9: 7 at the hand of foreign **k**, as it is
9: 9 in the sight of the **k** of Persia:
Ne 9:24 along with their **k** and the peoples
9:32 upon our **k** and leaders, upon our
9:32 of the **k** of Assyria until today.
9:34 Our **k**, our leaders, our priests and
9:37 to the **k** you have placed over us.
Est 10: 2 annals of the **k** of Media and Persia?
Job 3:14 with **k** and counsellors of the earth,
12:18 takes off the shackles put on by **k**
34:18 Is he not the One who says to **k**,
36: 7 enthrones them with **k** and exalts
Ps 2: 2 The **k** of the earth take their stand
2:10 Therefore, you **k**, be wise; be warned,
45: 9 Daughters of **k** are among your
47: 9 the **k** of the earth belong to God;
48: 4 the **k** joined forces, when they
68:12 "**K** and armies flee in haste; in the
68:14 scattered the **k** in the land
68:29 at Jerusalem **k** will bring you gifts
72:10 The **k** of Tarshish and of distant
72:10 the **k** of Sheba and Seba will present
72:11 All **k** will bow down to him and all
76:12 he is feared by the **k** of the earth.
89:27 most exalted of the **k** of the earth.
102:15 all the **k** of the earth will revere
105:14 for their sake he rebuked **k**:
110: 5 crush **k** on the day of his wrath.
119:46 speak of your statutes before **k**
135:10 many nations and killed mighty **k**
135:11 of Bashan and all the **k** of Canaan
136:17 who struck down great **k**, His love
136:18 killed mighty **k**—His love endures
138: 4 May all the **k** of the earth praise
144:10 to the One who gives victory to **k**,
148:11 **k** of the earth and all nations, you
149: 8 to bind their **k** with fetters, their
Pr 8:15 By me **k** reign and rulers make laws
16:12 **K** detest wrongdoing, for a throne is
16:13 **K** take pleasure in honest lips;
22:29 He will serve before **k**; he will not
25: 2 out a matter is the glory of **k**.
25: 3 so the hearts of **k** are unsearchable.
31: 3 your vigour on those who ruin **k**.
31: 4 not for **k**, O Lemuel—not for **k** to
Ecc 2: 8 and the treasure of **k** and provinces.
Isa 1: 1 Ahaz and Hezekiah, **k** of Judah.
7:16 two **k** you dread will be laid waste.
10: 8 'Are not my commanders all **k**?' he
Isa 10:13 like a mighty one I subdued their **k**.
14: 9 those who were **k** over the nations.
14:18 All the **k** of the nations lie in
19:11 a disciple of the ancient **k**"?
24:21 above and the **k** on the earth below.
37:11 have heard what the **k** of Assyria
37:18 that the Assyrian **k** have laid waste
41: 2 to him and subdues **k** before him.
45: 1 him and to strip **k** of their armour,
49: 7 "**K** will see you and rise up, princes
49:23 **K** will be your foster fathers, and
52:15 and **k** will shut their mouths
60: 3 **k** to the brightness of your dawn.
60:10 walls, and their **k** will serve you.
60:11 their **k** led in triumphal procession.
62: 2 righteousness, and all **k** your glory
Jer 1:15 "Their **k** will come and set up their
1:18 whole land—against the **k** of Judah,
2:26 their **k** and their officials, their
8: 1 the bones of the **k** and officials of
13:13 including the **k** who sit on David's
17:19 through which the **k** of Judah go in
17:20 O **k** of Judah and all people of
17:25 **k** who sit on David's throne will
19: 3 'Hear the word of the LORD, O **k**
19: 4 nor the **k** of Judah ever knew,
19:13 those of the **k** of Judah will be
20: 5 all the treasures of the **k** of Judah.
22: 4 then **k** who sit on David's throne
25:14 by many nations and great **k**;
25:18 its **k** and officials, to make them a
25:20 all the **k** of Uz; all the **k** of the
25:22 all the **k** of Tyre and Sidon; the **k**
25:24 all the **k** of Arabia and all the **k** of
25:25 all the **k** of Zimri, Elam and Media;
25:26 all the **k** of the north, near and far,
27: 3 send word to the **k** of Edom, Moab,
27: 7 and great **k** will subjugate him.
32:32 their **k** and officials, their priests
34: 5 the former **k** who preceded you, so
44: 9 by the **k** and queens of Judah and the
44:17 our **k** and our officials did in the
44:21 your **k** and your officials and the
46:25 her gods and her **k**, and on those who
50:41 a great nation and many **k** are being
51:11 has stirred up the **k** of the Medes,
51:28 against her—the **k** of the Medes,
52:32 **k** who were with him in Babylon.
Lam 4:12 The **k** of the earth did not believe,
Eze 27:33 you enriched the **k** of the earth.
27:35 their **k** shudder with horror and
28:17 I made a spectacle of you before **k**.
32:10 and their **k** will shudder with horror
32:29 "Edom is there, her **k** and all her
43: 7 nor their **k**—by their prostitution
43: 7 of their **k** at their high places.
43: 9 and the lifeless idols of their **k**,
Da 2:21 he sets up **k** and deposes them.
2:44 "In the time of those **k**, the God of
2:47 God of gods and the Lord of **k** and
7:24 The ten horns are ten **k** who will
7:24 he will subdue three **k**.
8:20 the **k** of Media and Persia.
9: 6 who spoke in your name to our **k**,
9: 8 O LORD, we and our **k**, our princes
11: 2 Three more **k** will appear in Persia
11:27 The two **k**, with their hearts bent on
Hos 1: 1 Ahaz and Hezekiah, **k** of Judah
7: 7 **k** fall, and none of them calls on me.
8: 4 They set up **k** without my consent;
Mic 1: 1 Ahaz and Hezekiah, **k** of Judah—the
Hab 1:10 They deride **k** and scoff at rulers.
Mt 10:18 **k** as witnesses to them and to the
17:25 "From whom do the **k** of the earth
Mk 13: 9 and **k** as witnesses to them.
Lk 10:24 **k** wanted to see what you see but did
21:12 and you will be brought before **k** and
22:25 "The **k** of the Gentiles lord it over
Ac 4:26 The **k** of the earth take their stand
9:15 before the Gentiles and their **k**
1Co 4: 8 You have become **k**—and that without
4: 8 **k** so that we might be **k** with you!
1Ti 2: 2 for **k** and all those in authority,
Heb 7: 1 the defeat of the **k** and blessed him
Rev 1: 5 and the ruler of the **k** of the earth
6:15 the **k** of the earth, the princes,

Rev 10:11 peoples, nations, languages and **k**."
16:12 the way for the **k** from the East.
16:14 go out to the **k** of the whole world
16:16 they gathered the **k** together to the
17: 2 With her the **k** of the earth
17:10 They are also seven **k**. Five have
17:12 The ten horns you saw are ten **k** who
17:12 authority as **k** along with the beast.
17:18 that rules over the **k** of the earth.
18: 3 The **k** of the earth committed
18: 9 "When the **k** of the earth who
19:18 that you may eat the flesh of **k**,
19:19 I saw the beast and the **k** of the
21:24 and the **k** of the earth will bring

Kings of Israel
1Ki 14:19 in the book of the annals of the **k**.
15:31 in the book of the annals of the **k**?
16: 5 in the book of the annals of the **k**?
16:14 in the book of the annals of the **k**?
16:20 in the book of the annals of the **k**?
16:27 in the book of the annals of the **k**?
16:33 anger than did all the **k** before him
22:39 in the book of the annals of the **k**?
2Ki 1:18 in the book of the annals of the **k**?
8:18 He walked in the ways of the **k**,
10:34 in the book of the annals of the **k**?
13: 8 in the book of the annals of the **k**?
13:12 in the book of the annals of the **k**?
13:13 was buried in Samaria with the **k**.
14:15 in the book of the annals of the **k**?
14:16 was buried in Samaria with the **k**.
14:28 in the book of the annals of the **k**?
14:29 rested with his fathers, the **k**.
15:11 in the book of the annals of the **k**.
15:15 in the book of the annals of the **k**.
15:21 in the book of the annals of the **k**?
15:26 in the book of the annals of the **k**.
15:31 in the book of the annals of the **k**?
16: 3 He walked in the ways of the **k** and
17: 2 but not like the **k** who preceded him
17: 8 practices that the **k** had introduced
23:19 that the **k** had built in the towns
23:22 nor throughout the days of the **k**
1Ch 9: 1 genealogies in the book of the **k**.
2Ch 20:34 are recorded in the book of the **k**.
21: 6 He walked in the ways of the **k**,
21:13 have walked in the ways of the **k**
27: 7 in the book of the **k** and Judah.
28: 2 He walked in the ways of the **k** and
28:27 not placed in the tombs of the **k**.
33:18 are written in the annals of the **k**.
35:18 none of the **k** had ever celebrated
35:27 in the book of the **k** and Judah.
36: 8 in the book of the **k** and Judah.
Mic 1:14 Aczib will prove deceptive to the **k**

Kings' (King)
Pr 30:28 yet it is found in **k** palaces.
Mt 11: 8 wear fine clothes are in **k** palaces.

Kingship (King)
1Sa 10:16 what Samuel had said about the **k**.
10:25 the people the regulations of the **k**.
11:14 to Gilgal and there reaffirm the **k**.
1Ch 11:10 gave his **k** strong support to extend
2Ch 13: 5 the God of Israel, has given the **k**
Ecc 4:14 may have come from prison to the **k**,
Mic 4: 8 **k** will come to the Daughter of

Kinnereth
Nu 34:11 the slopes east of the Sea of **K**.
Dt 3:17 from **K** to the Sea of the Arabah
Jos 11: 2 in the Arabah south of **K**, in the
12: 3 from the Sea of **K** to the Sea of the
13:27 up to the end of the Sea of **K**).
19:35 Ziddim, Zer, Hammath, Rakkath, **K**,
1Ki 15:20 and all **K** in addition to Naphtali.

Kinsman (Kin)
Ru 3: 2 a **k** of ours? Tonight he will be
Pr 7: 4 and call understanding your **k**;

Kinsman-redeemer (Redeem)
Ru 3: 9 garment over me, since you are a **k**."
3:12 of kin, there is a **k** nearer than I.
4: 1 When the **k** he had mentioned came
4: 3 he said to the **k**, "Naomi, who has
4: 6 At this, the **k** said, "Then I cannot
4: 8 the **k** said to Boaz, "Buy it yourself
4:14 day has not left you without a **k**.

Kinsman-redeemers (Redeem)
Ru 2:20 close relative; he is one of our **k**.

Kinsmen (Kin)
1Ch 12: 2 they were **k** of Saul from the tribe
12:29 men of Benjamin, Saul's **k**—3,000,
2Ch 28: 8 their **k** two hundred thousand wives,
29:34 so their **k** the Levites helped them
Ezr 8:17 them what to say to Iddo and his **k**,
Job 19:14 My **k** have gone away; my friends

Kios
Ac 20:15 sail from there and arrived off **K**.

Kir
1. Region of Mesopotamia to which Tiglath-Pileser deported the Aramaeans (2Ki 16:9) and from which God later rescued them (Am 9:7). Appears in prophecy about Jerusalem (Isa 22:6). **2.** Walled city of Moab that withstood Israelite attack (2Ki 3:25) but would be destroyed (Isa 15:1; 16:7, 11; Jer 48:31, 36). Also known as Kir Hareseth.

2Ki 16: 9 to **K** and put Rezin to death.
Isa 15: 1 **K** in Moab is ruined, destroyed in a
22: 6 and horses; **K** uncovers the shield.
Am 1: 5 go into exile to **K**," says the LORD.
9: 7 Caphtor and the Arameans from **K**?

Kir Hareseth
2Ki 3:25 Only **K** was left with its stones in
Isa 16: 7 Lament and grieve for the men of **K**.
16:11 like a harp, my inmost being for **K**.
Jer 48:31 I cry out, I moan for the men of **K**.
48:36 like a flute for the men of **K**.

Kiriath
Jos 18:28 Gibeah and **K**—fourteen towns and

Kiriath Arba
Ge 23: 2 She died at **K** (that is, Hebron) in
35:27 near **K** (that is, Hebron), where
Jos 14:15 (Hebron used to be called **K** after
15:13 in Judah—**K**, that is, Hebron.
15:54 Humtah, **K** (that is, Hebron) and Zior
20: 7 and **K** (that is, Hebron) in the hill
21:11 They gave them **K** (that is, Hebron),
Jdg 1:10 in Hebron (formerly called **K**)
Ne 11:25 **K** and its surrounding settlements,

Kiriath Baal
Jos 15:60 **K** (that is, Kiriath Jearim) and
18:14 side and came out at **K** (that is,

Kiriath Huzoth
Nu 22:39 Balaam went with Balak to **K**.

Kiriath Jearim
One of 4 Gibeonite fortress cities (Jos 9:17), also known as Baalah (Jos 15:9), Kiriath Baal (Jos 15:60) and Kiriath (Jos 18:28). First allotted to Judah (Jos 15:60) then to Benjamin (Jos 18:28). 600 Danites camped here on their way to attack Laish (Jdg 18:12). After the Philistines returned the ark of the covenant it was kept here in Abinadab's house for 20 years (1Sa 6:21–7:2). Home of Uriah the prophet (Jer 26:20).

Jos 9:17 Gibeon, Kephirah, Beeroth and **K**.
15: 9 down towards Baalah (that is, **K**).
15:60 Kiriath Baal (that is, **K**) and Rabbah
18:14 Kiriath Baal (that is, **K**), a town
18:15 at the outskirts of **K** on the west,
Jdg 18:12 On their way they set up camp near **K**
18:12 **K** is called Mahaneh Dan to this day.
1Sa 6:21 sent messengers to the people of **K**,
1Sa 7: 1 the men of **K** came and took up the
7: 2 that the ark remained at **K**, and all
1Ch 2:50 Ephrathah: Shobal the father of **K**,
2:52 Shobal the father of **K** were: Haroeh,
2:53 the clans of **K**: the Ithrites,
13: 5 to bring the ark of God from **K**.
13: 6 went to Baalah of Judah (**K**) to
2Ch 1: 4 brought up the ark of God from **K** to
Ezr 2:25 of **K**, Kephirah and Beeroth 743
Ne 7:29 of **K**, Kephirah and Beeroth 743
Jer 26:20 (Now Uriah son of Shemaiah from **K**

Kiriath Sannah
Jos 15:49 Dannah, **K** (that is, Debir),

Kiriath Sepher
Jos 15:15 living in Debir (formerly called **K**)
15:16 the man who attacks and captures **K**.
Jdg 1:11 living in Debir (formerly called **K**)
1:12 the man who attacks and captures **K**.

Kiriathaim
1. City of refuge in territory of Naphtali, assigned to the Levites (1Ch 6:76). Also known as Kartan (Jos 21:32). **2.** Town east of Dead Sea, in hill country of Moab. The Emites were expelled from here (Ge 14:5). Taken by the Israelites and allotted to Reuben (Jos 13:19), who fortified it (Nu 32:37). Became Moabite territory, sharing in its downfall (Jer 48:1, 23; Eze 25:9).

Nu 32:37 rebuilt Heshbon, Elealeh and **K**,
Jos 13:19 **K**, Sibmah, Zereth Shahar on the hill
1Ch 6:76 **K**, together with their pasture-lands
Jer 48: 1 **K** will be disgraced and captured;
48:23 to **K**, Beth Gamul and Beth Meon,
Eze 25: 9 Meon and **K**—the glory of that land.

Kish
1Sa 9: 1 man of standing, whose name was **K**
9: 3 to Saul's father **K** were lost,
9: 3 and **K** said to his son Saul, "Take
10:11 that has happened to the son of **K**?
10:21 Finally Saul son of **K** was chosen.
14:51 Saul's father **K** and Abner's father
2Sa 21:14 in the tomb of Saul's father **K**,
1Ch 8:30 by Zur, **K**, Baal, Ner, Nadab,
8:33 Ner was the father of **K**, **K** the
9:36 by Zur, **K**, Baal, Ner, Nadab,
9:39 Ner was the father of **K**, **K** the
12: 1 from the presence of Saul son of **K**
23:21 The sons of Mahli: Eleazar and **K**.
23:22 the sons of **K**, married them.
24:29 From **K**: the son of **K**: Jerahmeel.
26:28 Samuel the seer and by Saul son of **K**
2Ch 29:12 **K** son of Abdi and Azariah son of
Est 2: 5 the son of Shimei, the son of **K**,
Ac 13:21 and he gave them Saul son of **K**,

Kishi
1Ch 6:44 at his left hand: Ethan son of **K**,

Kishion
Jos 19:20 Rabbith, **K**, Ebez,
21:28 from the tribe of Issachar, **K**,

Kishon
River flowing north-east from Mount Gilboa, past Mount Carmel to the Mediterranean Sea. Scene of Deborah's victory over Sisera (Jdg 4:7, 13; Ps 83:9), when the Canaanite chariots became bogged down by the flooded river (Jdg 5:21). Elijah brought the prophets of Baal here to be slaughtered (1Ki 18:40).

Jdg 4: 7 to the **K** River and give him into your
4:13 Harosheth Haggoyim to the **K** River.
5:21 The river **K** swept them away,
5:21 the age-old river, the river **K**.
1Ki 18:40 the **K** Valley and slaughtered there.
Ps 83: 9 to Sisera and Jabin at the river **K**,

Kislev
Ne 1: 1 month of **K** in the twentieth year,
Zec 7: 1 of the ninth month, the month of **K**.

Kislon
Nu 34:21 Elidad son of **K**, from the tribe of

Kisloth Tabor
Jos 19:12 the sunrise to the territory of **K**

Kiss (Kissed, Kisses, Kissing)
Ge 27:26 him, "Come here, my son, and **k** me.
31:28 You didn't even let me **k** my
2Sa 15: 5 hand, take hold of him and **k** him.
20: 9 beard with his right hand to **k** him.
1Ki 19:20 "Let me **k** my father and mother
Job 31:27 my hand offered them a **k** of homage,
Ps 2:12 **K** the Son, lest he be angry and you
85:10 and peace **k** each other.
Pr 24:26 An honest answer is like a **k** on the
SS 1: 2 Let him **k** me with the kisses of his
8: 1 found you outside, I would **k** you,
Hos 13: 2 sacrifice and **k** the calf-idols."
Mt 26:48 The one I **k** is the man; arrest him
Mk 14:44 The one I **k** is the man; arrest him
Lk 7:45 You did not give me a **k**, but this
22:47 He approached Jesus to **k** him,
22:48 betraying the Son of Man with a **k**?"
Ro 16:16 Greet one another with a holy **k**.
1Co 16:20 Greet one another with a holy **k**.
2Co 13:12 Greet one another with a holy **k**.
1Th 5:26 Greet all the brothers with a holy **k**
1Pe 5:14 Greet one another with a **k** of love.

Kissed (Kiss)
Ge 27:27 he went to him and **k** him. When Isaac
29:11 Jacob **k** Rachel and began to weep
29:13 He embraced him and **k** him and
31:55 Laban **k** his grandchildren and his
33: 4 his arms around his neck and **k** him.
45:15 he **k** all his brothers and wept over
48:10 his father **k** them and embraced them.
50: 1 father and wept over him and **k** him.
Ex 4:27 at the mountain of God and **k** him.
18: 7 and bowed down and **k** him.
Ru 1: 9 Then she **k** them and they wept
1:14 Then Orpah **k** her mother-in-law
1Sa 10: 1 poured it on Saul's head and **k** him,
20:41 they **k** each other and wept together
2Sa 14:33 And the king **k** Absalom.
19:39 The king **k** Barzillai and gave him
1Ki 19:18 all whose mouths have not **k** him."
Pr 7:13 She took hold of him and **k** him and
Mt 26:49 said, "Greetings, Rabbi!" and **k** him
Mk 14:45 Judas said, "Rabbi!" and **k** him.
Lk 7:38 **k** them and poured perfume on them.
15:20 threw his arms around him and **k** him
Ac 20:37 wept as they embraced him and **k** him

Kisses (Kiss)
Pr 27: 6 trusted, but an enemy multiplies **k**
SS 1: 2 kiss me with the **k** of his mouth

Kissing (Kiss)
Lk 7:45 I entered, has not stopped **k** my feet

Kit
Eze 9: 2 who had a writing **k** at his side.
9: 3 who had the writing **k** at his
9:11 the man in linen with the writing **k**

Kitchens
Eze 46:24 He said to me, "These are the **k**

Kite
Lev 11:14 the red **k**, any kind of black **k**,
Dt 14:13 the red **k**, the black **k**, any kind of

Kitlish
Jos 15:40 Cabbon, Lahmas, **K**,

Kitron
Jdg 1:30 Canaanites living in **K** or Nahalol,

Kittim
Ge 10: 4 Tarshish, the **K** and the Rodanim.
Nu 24:24 Ships will come from the shores of **K**
1Ch 1: 7 Tarshish, the **K** and the Rodanim.
Jer 2:10 Cross over to the coasts of **K** and

Knead (Kneaded, Kneading, Well-kneaded)
Ge 18: 6 flour and **k** it and bake some bread."
Jer 7:18 and the women **k** the dough and make

Kneaded (Knead)
1Sa 28:24 **k** it and baked bread without yeast.
2Sa 13: 8 She took some dough, **k** it, made the

Kneading (Knead)
Ex 8: 3 and into your ovens and **k** troughs.
12:34 in **k** troughs wrapped in clothing.
Dt 28: 5 Your basket and your **k** trough will
28:17 Your basket and your **k** trough will
Hos 7: 4 the **k** of the dough till it rises.

Knee (Knee-deep, Knees)
Isa 45:23 Before me every **k** will bow; by me
Eze 7:17 every **k** will become as weak as
21: 7 and every **k** become as weak as water.
Ro 11: 4 who have not bowed the **k** to Baal."
14:11 'Every **k** will bow before me; every
Php 2:10 name of Jesus every **k** should bow

Knee-deep (Knee)
Eze 47: 4 led me through water that was **k**.

Kneel (Kneeling, Knelt)
Ge 24:11 He made the camels **k** down near the
Jdg 7: 5 from those who **k** down to drink."
Est 3: 2 would not **k** down or pay him honour.
3: 5 Haman saw that Mordecai would not **k**
Ps 22:29 all who go down to the dust will **k**
95: 6 let us **k** before the LORD our Maker;
Eph 3:14 this reason I **k** before the Father,

Kneeling (Kneel)
1Ki 1:31 **k** before the king, said, "May my
8:54 where he had been **k** with his hands
Mt 20:20 and, **k** down, asked a favour of him.

Knees (Knee)
Ge 48:12 Joseph removed them from Israel's **k**
50:23 were placed at birth on Joseph's **k**.
Dt 28:35 The LORD will afflict your **k** and
Jdg 7: 6 rest got down on their **k** to drink.
1Ki 18:42 and put his face between his **k**.
19:18 whose **k** have not bowed down to Baal
2Ki 1:13 up and fell on his **k** before Elijah.
Ezr 9: 5 and fell on my **k** with my hands
Job 3:12 Why were there **k** to receive me and
4: 4 you have strengthened faltering **k**.
Ps 20: 8 They are brought to their **k** and fall,
109:24 My **k** give way from fasting; my body
Isa 35: 3 hands, steady the **k** that give way;
66:12 on her arm and dandled on her **k**.
Da 5: 6 so frightened that his **k** knocked
6:10 day he got down on his **k** and prayed,
10:10 set me trembling on my hands and **k**.
Na 2:10 Hearts melt, **k** give way, bodies
Mt 18:26 "The servant fell on his **k** before
18:29 "His fellow-servant fell to his **k**
Mk 1:40 came to him and begged him on his **k**,
5: 6 and fell on his **k** in front of him.
10:17 to him and fell on his **k** before him.
15:19 on their **k**, they paid homage to him.
Lk 5: 8 he fell at Jesus' **k** and said, "Go
Ac 7:60 he fell on his **k** and cried out,
9:40 he got down on his **k** and prayed.
Heb 12:12 your feeble arms and weak **k**!

Knelt (Kneel)
1Ki 1:16 Bathsheba bowed low and **k** before the
2Ch 6:13 He stood on the platform and then **k**
7: 3 they **k** on the pavement with their
29:29 with him **k** down and worshipped.
Est 3: 2 **k** down and paid honour to Haman,
Mt 8: 2 with leprosy came and **k** before him
9:18 a ruler came and **k** before him and
15:25 The woman came and **k** before him.
17:14 approached Jesus and **k** before him.
27:29 **k** in front of him and mocked him.
Lk 22:41 beyond them, **k** down and prayed,
Ac 20:36 he **k** down with all of them and
21: 5 and there on the beach we **k** to pray.

Knew (Know)
Ge 8:11 Then Noah **k** that the water had
16: 4 When she **k** she was pregnant, she
38: 9 Onan **k** that the offspring would not
Dt 7:15 horrible diseases you **k** in Egypt,
34:10 Moses, whom the LORD **k** face to face,
Jdg 2:10 another generation grew up, who **k**
1Sa 3:13 because of the sin he **k** about;
20:33 Then Jonathan **k** that his father
20:39 (The boy **k** nothing of all this;
20:39 only Jonathan and David **k**.)
22:17 They **k** he was fleeing, yet they did
22:22 I **k** he would be sure to tell Saul.
26:12 No-one saw or **k** about it, nor did
28:14 Then Saul **k** it was Samuel, and he
2Sa 1:10 because I **k** that after he had fallen
3:37 all Israel **k** that the king had no
5:12 David **k** that the LORD had
11:16 he **k** the strongest defenders were.
14: 1 Joab son of Zeruiah **k** that the
17:19 No-one **k** anything about it.
1Ki 9:27 his men—sailors who **k** the sea—
2Ki 4:39 though no-one **k** what they were.
1Ch 12:32 who understood the times and **k** what
14: 2 David **k** that the LORD had
2Ch 8:18 his own officers, men who **k** the sea.
33:13 Then Manasseh **k** that the LORD is God
Ne 9:10 for you **k** how arrogantly the
Job 23: 3 If only I **k** where to find him;
Ps 31: 7 and **k** the anguish of my soul.
Pr 24:12 "But we **k** nothing about this,"
Ecc 6: 5 never saw the sun or **k** anything,
Isa 48: 4 For I **k** how stubborn you were;
48: 7 you cannot say, 'Yes, I **k** of them.'
Jer 1: 5 I formed you in the womb I **k** you,
11:18 I **k** it, for at that time he showed
19: 4 nor the kings of Judah ever **k**,
32: 8 **k** that this was the word of the LORD
41: 4 before anyone **k** about it,
44: 3 nor you nor your fathers ever **k**.
44:15 all the men who **k** that their wives
50:24 and you were caught before you **k** it
Eze 28:19 All the nations who **k** you are
Da 5:22 yourself, though you **k** all this.
Jnh 1:10 (They **k** he was running away from
4: 2 I **k** that you are a gracious and
Zec 11:11 **k** it was the word of the LORD.
Mt 7:23 tell them plainly, 'I never **k** you.
12:25 Jesus **k** their thoughts and said to
21:45 they **k** he was talking about them.
24:39 they **k** nothing about what would
25:24 'Master,' he said, 'I **k** that you
25:26 So you **k** that I harvest where I
27:18 For he **k** it was out of envy that
Mk 1:34 speak because they **k** who he was.
2: 8 Immediately Jesus **k** in his spirit
12:12 **k** he had spoken the parable against
12:15 But Jesus **k** their hypocrisy.
Lk 4:41 because they **k** he was the Christ.
5:22 Jesus **k** what they were thinking and
6: 8 Jesus **k** what they were thinking and
11:17 Jesus **k** their thoughts and said to
19:22 **k**, did you, that I am a hard man
20:19 because they **k** he had spoken this
23:49 all those who **k** him, including the
Jn 2: 9 servants who had drawn the water **k**.
2:24 himself to them, for he **k** all men.
2:25 man, for he **k** what was in a man.
4:10 "If you **k** the gift of God and who
8:19 **k** me, you would know my Father also
11:42 I **k** that you always hear me, but I
13: 1 Jesus **k** that the time had come for
13: 3 Jesus **k** that the Father had put all
13:11 For he **k** who was going to betray him
14: 7 If you really **k** me, you would know
17: 8 They **k** with certainty that I came

Jn 18: 2 Now Judas, who betrayed him, **k** the
21:12 Who are you?" They **k** it was the Lord
Ac 2:30 prophet and **k** that God had promised
7:18 king, who **k** nothing about Joseph,
16: 3 all **k** that his father was a Greek.
18:25 he **k** only the baptism of John.
Ro 1:21 For although they **k** God, they
Heb 10:34 **k** that you yourselves had better

Knife (Knives)

Ge 22: 6 himself carried the fire and the **k**.
22:10 hand and took the **k** to slay his son.
Ex 4:25 Zipporah took a flint **k**, cut off her
Jdg 19:29 he reached home, he took a **k** and cut
Pr 23: 2 put a **k** to your throat if you are
Jer 36:23 cut them off with a scribe's **k** and

Knit (Close-knit, Knitted)

Job 10:11 skin and flesh and **k** me together
Ps 139:13 **k** me together in my mother's womb.

Knitted (Knit)

Lev 13:48 any woven or **k** material of linen or
13:49 or leather, or woven or **k** material,
13:51 or the woven or **k** material, or the
13:52 or the woven or **k** material of wool
13:53 **k** material, or the leather article,
13:56 leather, or the woven or **k** material.
13:57 or in the woven or **k** material, or in
13:58 or the woven or **k** material, or any
13:59 woven or **k** material, or any leather

Knives (Knife)

Jos 5: 2 "Make flint **k** and circumcise the
5: 3 Joshua made flint **k** and circumcised
Pr 30:14 **k** to devour the poor from the earth,
Isa 18: 5 cut off the shoots with pruning **k**,

Knock (Knocked, Knocking, Knocks)

Mt 7: 7 **k** and the door will be opened to you
Lk 11: 9 **k** and the door will be opened to you
Rev 3:20 Here I am! I stand at the door and **k**

Knocked (Knock)

Da 5: 6 **k** together and his legs gave way.
8: 7 the goat **k** him to the ground and
Ac 12:13 Peter **k** at the outer entrance, and

Knocking (Knock)

SS 5: 2 Listen! My lover is **k**: "Open to me,
Lk 13:25 you will stand outside **k** and
Ac 12:16 Peter kept on **k**, and when they

Knocks (Knock)

Ex 21:27 if he **k** out the tooth of a
Mt 7: 8 him who **k**, the door will be opened.
Lk 11:10 him who **k**, the door will be opened.
12:36 so that when he comes and **k** they

Knotted

Eze 27:24 with cords twisted and tightly **k**.

Know (Foreknew, Foreknowledge, Knew, *Know that I am the Lord*, *Know that the Lord*, Knowing, Knowledge, Known, Knows, Well-known)

Ge 4: 9 "I don't **k**," he replied.
12:11 "I **k** what a beautiful woman you are.
15: 8 "O Sovereign LORD, how can I **k** that
15:13 the LORD said to him, "**K** for certain
18:21 If not, I will **k**."
20: 6 "Yes, I **k** you did this with a clear
21:26 said, "I don't **k** who has done this.
22:12 Now I **k** that you fear God,
24:14 By this I will **k** that you have shown
24:49 so I may **k** which way to turn."
27: 2 and don't **k** the day of my death.
27:21 to **k** whether you really are my son
29: 5 He said to them, "Do you **k** Laban,
29: 5 "Yes, we **k** him," they answered.
30:26 **k** how much work I've done for you."
30:29 "You **k** how I have worked for you
Ge 31: 6 You **k** that I've worked for your
31:32 **k** that Rachel had stolen the gods.
37:13 Israel said to Joseph, "As you **k**,
42:33 'This is how I will **k** whether you
42:34 so I will **k** that you are not spies
43: 7 How were we to **k** he would say,
43:22 **k** who put our silver in our sacks."
44:15 Don't you **k** that a man like me can
44:27 **k** that my wife bore me two sons.
47: 6 And if you **k** of any among them with
48:19 refused and said, "I **k**, my son, I **k**.
Ex 1: 8 a new king, who did not **k** about
3:19 I **k** that the king of Egypt will not
4:14 the Levite? I **k** he can speak well.
5: 2 I do not **k** the LORD and I will not
8:10 so that you may **k** there is no-one
8:22 **k** that I, the LORD, am in this land.
9:14 so you may **k** that there is no-one
9:29 may **k** that the earth is the LORD's.
9:30 I **k** that you and your officials
10:26 until we get there we will not **k**
16: 6 you will **k** that it was the LORD
16: 8 "You will **k** that it was the LORD
16:15 For they did not **k** what it was.
23: 9 **k** how it feels to be aliens,
32: 1 don't **k** what has happened to him."
32:22 **k** how prone these people are to evil.
32:23 don't **k** what has happened to him.'
33:12 let me **k** whom you will send with me.
33:12 You have said, 'I **k** you by name and
33:13 teach me your ways so I may **k** you
33:16 How will anyone **k** that you are
33:17 with you and I **k** you by name."
36: 1 ability to **k** how to carry out all
Lev 5:17 even though he does not **k** it, he is
23:43 your descendants will **k** that I made
Nu 10:31 You **k** where we should camp in the
14:34 **k** what it is like to have me against
16:30 then you will **k** that these men have
20:14 You **k** about all the hardships that
22: 6 For I **k** that those you bless are
Dt 1:39 who do not yet **k** good from bad—
3:19 (I **k** you have much livestock)
7: 9 **K** therefore that the LORD your God
8: 2 order to **k** what was in your heart,
8: 5 **K** then in your heart that as a man
9: 2 **k** about them and have heard it said:
11:30 you **k**, these mountains are across
18:21 "How can we **k** when a message has not
20:20 you may cut down trees that you **k**
22: 2 you or if you do not **k** who he is,
28:33 A people that you do not **k** will eat
29:16 You yourselves **k** how we lived in
29:26 gods they did not **k**, gods he had
31:13 children, who do not **k** this law,
31:21 I **k** what they are disposed to do,
31:27 For I **k** how rebellious and
31:29 For I **k** that after my death you are
Jos 2: 4 I did not **k** where they had come from.
2: 5 I don't **k** which way they went. Go
3: 4 you will **k** which way to go, since
3: 7 that they may **k** that I am with you
3:10 you will **k** that the living God
4:24 might **k** that the hand of the LORD
8:14 But he did not **k** that an ambush had
14: 6 "You **k** what the LORD said to Moses
22:22 He knows! And let Israel **k**! If this
23:14 You **k** with all your heart and soul
Jdg 6:37 then I will **k** that you will save
14: 4 His parents did not **k** that this was
18:14 "Do you **k** that one of these houses
18:14 a cast idol? Now you **k** what to do."
Ru 2:11 with a people you did not **k** before.
3: 3 but don't let him **k** you are there
3:11 All my fellow townsmen **k** that you
4: 4 you will not, tell me, so I will **k**.
1Sa 3: 7 Now Samuel did not yet **k** the LORD:
6: 3 and you will **k** why his hand has not
6: 9 we shall **k** that it was not his hand
8: 9 let them **k** what the king who will
17:28 I **k** how conceited you are and how
17:46 **k** that there is a God in Israel.
17:47 All those gathered here will **k** that
17:55 as you live, O king, I don't **k**."
20: 3 Jonathan must not **k** this or he will
20:12 I not send you word and let you **k**?
1Sa 20:13 let you **k** and send you away safely.
20:30 Don't I **k** that you have sided with
21: 2 'No-one is to **k** anything about your
24:20 I **k** that you will surely be king and
28: 9 the woman said to him, "Surely you **k**
29: 9 Achish answered, "I **k** that you have
2Sa 1: 5 "How do you **k** that Saul and his son
3:25 You **k** Abner son of Ner; he came to
3:26 But David did not **k** it.
7:20 **k** your servant, O Sovereign LORD.
11:20 Didn't you **k** they would shoot arrows
15:20 when I do not **k** where I am going?
17: 8 You **k** your father and his men;
18:29 servant, but I don't **k** what it was."
19:20 I your servant **k** that I have sinned
19:22 **k** that today I am king over Israel?"
22:44 People I did not **k** are subject to me,
24: 2 so that I may **k** how many there are."
1Ki 1:18 my lord the king, do not **k** about it.
1:27 without letting his servants **k** who
2: 5 "Now you yourself **k** what Joab son of
2: 9 you will **k** what to do to him.
2:15 "As you **k**," he said, "the kingdom
2:44 "You **k** in your heart all the wrong
3: 7 do not **k** how to carry out my duties
5: 3 "You **k** that because of the wars
5: 6 You **k** that we have no-one so skilled
8:39 since you **k** his heart (for you alone
8:39 you alone **k** the hearts of all men),
8:43 may **k** your name and fear you, as do
8:43 and may **k** that this house I have
17:24 "Now I **k** that you are a man of God
18:12 I don't **k** where the Spirit of the
18:37 will **k** that you, O LORD, are God
20:13 you will **k** that I am the LORD.
20:28 you will **k** that I am the LORD.
22: 3 "Don't you **k** that Ramoth Gilead
2Ki 2: 3 "Yes, I **k**," Elisha replied, "but do
2: 5 "Yes, I **k**," he replied, "but do not
4: 1 and you **k** that he revered the LORD.
4: 9 She said to her husband, "I **k** that
5: 8 **k** that there is a prophet in Israel."
5:15 "Now I **k** that there is no God in all
7:12 They **k** we are starving; so they have
8:12 "Because I **k** the harm you will do to
9:11 "You **k** the man and the sort of
10:10 **K** then, that not a word the LORD has
17:26 do not **k** what the god of that
17:26 people do not **k** what he requires."
19:19 all kingdoms on earth may **k** that you
19:27 "'But I **k** where you stay and when
1Ch 17:18 For you **k** your servant,
21: 2 so that I may **k** how many there are."
29:17 I **k**, my God, that you test the heart
2Ch 2: 8 for I **k** that your men are skilled in
6:30 you **k** his heart (for you alone **k** the
6:33 earth may **k** your name and fear you,
6:33 and may **k** that this house that I
20:12 We do not **k** what to do, but our eyes
25:16 "I **k** that God has determined to
32:13 "Do you not **k** what I and my fathers
32:31 **k** everything that was in his heart.
Ezr 4:12 The king should **k** that the Jews who
4:13 the king should **k** that if this city
5: 8 The king should **k** that we went to
7:24 You are also to **k** that you have no
7:25 all who **k** the laws of your God.
7:25 are to teach any who do not **k** them.
Ne 2:16 The officials did not **k** where I had
4:11 "Before they **k** it or see us,
13:24 **k** how to speak the language of Judah.
Est 4:11 the people of the royal provinces **k**
Job 5:24 You will **k** that your tent is secure;
5:25 You will **k** that your children will
7:10 his place will **k** him no more.
8: 9 for we were born only yesterday and **k**
9: 2 "Indeed, I **k** that this is true.
9:28 I **k** you will not hold me innocent.
10: 7 though you **k** that I am not guilty
10:13 and I **k** that this was in your mind:
11: 6 **K** this: God has even forgotten some
11: 8 depths of the grave—what can you **k**?
12: 3 Who does not **k** all these things?
12: 9 Which of all these does not **k** that
13: 2 What you **k**, I also **k**; I am not
13:18 my case, I **k** I will be vindicated.

Job 14:21 are honoured, he does not **k** it;
15: 9 What do you **k** that we do not **k**?
19: 6 **k** that God has wronged me and drawn
19:25 I **k** that my Redeemer lives, and that
19:29 you will **k** that there is judgment."
20: 4 "Surely you **k** how it has been from
21:14 We have no desire to **k** your ways.
21:19 man himself, so that he will **k** it!
21:27 "I **k** full well what you are thinking,
22:13 Yet you say, 'What does God **k**? Does
24: 1 Why must those who **k** him look in
24:13 not **k** its ways or stay in its paths.
30:23 I **k** you will bring me down to death,
31: 6 and he will **k** that I am blameless—
32: 6 not daring to tell you what I **k**.
32:10 to me; I too will tell you what I **k**.
32:17 I too will tell what I **k**.
33: 3 my lips sincerely speak what I **k**.
34:33 so tell me what you **k**.
37: 7 all men he has made may **k** his work
37:15 Do you **k** how God controls the clouds
37:16 Do you **k** how the clouds hang poised,
38: 5 Surely you **k**! Who stretched a
38:18 Tell me, if you **k** all this.
38:20 you **k** the paths to their dwellings?
38:21 Surely you **k**, for you were already
38:33 Do you **k** the laws of the heavens?
39: 1 "Do you **k** when the mountain goats
39: 2 Do you **k** the time they give birth?
42: 2 "I **k** that you can do all things;
42: 3 things too wonderful for me to **k**.
Ps 9:10 Those who **k** your name will trust in
9:20 let the nations **k** they are but men.
18:43 people I did not **k** are subject to me
35:11 me on things I **k** nothing about.
36:10 Continue your love to those who **k**
39: 4 let me **k** how fleeting is my life.
40: 9 not seal my lips, as you **k**, O LORD.
41:11 I **k** that you are pleased with me,
46:10 "Be still, and **k** that I am God;
50:11 I **k** every bird in the mountains,
51: 3 For I **k** my transgressions, and my
56: 9 By this I will **k** that God is for me.
69: 5 You **k** my folly, O God; my guilt is
69:19 You **k** how I am scorned, disgraced
71:15 long, though I **k** not its measure.
73: 7 conceits of their minds **k** no limits.
73:11 They say, "How can God **k**? Does the
78: 6 that the next generation would **k**
82: 5 "They **k** nothing, they understand
83:18 Let them **k** that you, whose name is
92: 6 The senseless man does not **k**, fools
109:27 Let them **k** that it is your hand,
119:75 I **k**, O LORD, that your laws are
139: 1 you have searched me and you **k** me.
139: 2 You **k** when I sit and when I rise;
139: 4 a word is on my tongue you **k** it
139:14 are wonderful, I **k** that full well.
139:23 Search me, O God, and **k** my heart;
139:23 test me and **k** my anxious thoughts.
142: 3 within me, it is you who **k** my way.
145:12 that all men may **k** of your mighty
147:20 they do not **k** his laws.
Pr 4:19 do not **k** what makes them stumble.
9:18 little do they **k** that the dead are
10:32 The lips of the righteous **k** what is
24:12 not he who guards your life **k** it?
24:14 **K** also that wisdom is sweet to your
27: 1 do not **k** what a day may bring forth.
27:23 Be sure you **k** the condition of your
30: 4 name of his son? Tell me if you **k**!
Ecc 3:12 I **k** that there is nothing better for
3:14 I **k** that everything God does will
5: 1 who do not **k** that they do wrong.
7:22 for you **k** in your heart that many
8: 5 **k** the proper time and procedure.
8:12 I **k** that it will go better with
8:16 I applied my mind to **k** wisdom and to
9: 5 For the living **k** that they will die,
9: 5 but the dead **k** nothing; they have no
10:15 he does not **k** the way to town.
11: 2 you do not **k** what disaster may come
11: 5 you do not **k** the path of the wind,
11: 6 for you do not **k** which will succeed,
11: 9 but **k** that for all these things God
SS 1: 8 If you do not **k**, most beautiful of

Isa 1: 3 Israel does not **k**, my people do
5:19 Israel come, so that we may **k** it."
9: 9 All the people will **k** it—Ephraim
29:12 will answer, "I don't **k** how to read.
29:15 "Who sees us? Who will **k**?
32: 4 The mind of the rash will **k** and
37:20 **k** that you alone, O LORD, are God
37:28 "But I **k** where you stay and when you
40:21 Do you not **k**? Have you not heard?
40:28 Do you not **k**? Have you not heard?
41:20 that people may see and **k**, may
41:22 them and **k** their final outcome.
41:23 so that we may **k** you are gods.
41:26 so that we could **k**, or beforehand,
43:10 so that you may **k** and believe me and
44: 8 is no other Rock; I **k** not one."
44:18 They **k** nothing, they understand
45: 6 men may **k** there is none besides me.
47:11 will not **k** how to conjure it away.
48: 8 Well do I **k** how treacherous you are;
49:26 Then all mankind will **k** that I, the
50: 4 **k** the word that sustains the weary.
50: 7 and I **k** I will not be put to shame.
51: 7 "Hear me, you who **k** what is right,
52: 6 Therefore my people will **k** my name;
52: 6 will **k** that it is I who foretold it.
55: 5 **k** not, and nations that do not **k**
58: 2 they seem eager to **k** my ways,
59: 8 The way of peace they do not **k**;
59: 8 who walks in them will **k** peace.
60:16 Then you will **k** that I, the LORD,
63:16 though Abraham does not **k** us or
Jer 1: 6 I do not **k** how to speak; I am only
2: 8 who deal with the law did not **k** me;
4:22 people are fools; they do not **k** me.
4:22 they **k** not how to do good."
5: 4 they do not **k** the way of the LORD
5: 5 surely they **k** the way of the LORD,
5:15 people whose language you do not **k**,
6:15 they do not even **k** how to blush.
8: 7 not **k** the requirements of the LORD.
8:12 they do not even **k** how to blush.
10:23 I **k**, O LORD, that a man's life is
12: 3 Yet you **k** me, O LORD; you see me and
13:12 And if they say to you, 'Don't we **k**
14:18 have gone to a land they **k** not.
15:14 your enemies in a land you do not **k**,
16:21 will **k** that my name is the LORD.
17: 4 your enemies in a land you do not **k**,
17:16 you **k** I have not desired the day of
18:23 you **k**, O LORD, all their plots to
22:16 Is that not what it means to **k** me?"
22:28 out, cast into a land they do not **k**?
24: 7 I will give them a heart to **k** me,
29:11 For I **k** the plans I have for you,"
29:23 I **k** it and am a witness to it,"
31:34 **K** the LORD,' because they will all **k**
33: 3 unsearchable things you do not **k**.'
36:19 Don't let anyone **k** where you are."
38:24 "Do not let anyone **k** about this
40:14 said to him, "Don't you **k** that
40:15 of Nethaniah, and no-one will **k** it.
44:19 did not our husbands **k** that we were
44:28 Egypt will **k** whose word will stand
44:29 'so that you will **k** that my threats
48:17 around her, all who **k** her fame;
48:30 I **k** her insolence but it is futile,"
Eze 2: 5 **k** that a prophet has been among them.
5:13 they will **k** that I the LORD have
7: 9 you will **k** that it is I the LORD
11: 5 I **k** what is going through your mind.
13: 9 will **k** that I am the Sovereign LORD.
14:23 for you will **k** that I have done
17:12 Do you not **k** what these things mean?
17:21 will **k** that I the LORD have spoken.
17:24 All the trees of the field will **k**
20:12 **k** that I the LORD made them holy.
21: 5 all people will **k** that I the LORD
22:22 and you will **k** that I the LORD have
23:49 **k** that I am the Sovereign LORD."
24:24 **k** that I am the Sovereign LORD.'
25:14 they will **k** my vengeance, declares
28:24 will **k** that I am the Sovereign LORD.
29:16 will **k** that I am the Sovereign LORD
33:33 **k** that a prophet has been among them.
34:30 they will **k** that I, the LORD their

Eze 35:12 you will **k** that I the LORD have
36:32 I want you to **k** that I am not doing
36:36 will **k** that I the LORD have
37: 3 "O Sovereign LORD, you alone **k**.
37:14 Then you will **k** that I the LORD have
37:28 the nations will **k** that I the LORD
38:16 so that the nations may **k** me when I
39: 7 nations will **k** that I the LORD
39:23 the nations will **k** that the people
Da 2: 3 me and I want to **k** what it means."
2: 9 **k** that you can interpret it for me."
2:30 but so that you, O king, may **k** the
3:18 we want you to **k**, O king, that we
4: 9 **k** that the spirit of the holy gods
4:17 so that the living may **k** that the
7:19 "Then I wanted to **k** the true meaning
7:20 I also wanted to **k** about the ten
9:25 "**K** and understand this: From the
10:20 he said, "Do you **k** why I have come
11:32 **k** their God will firmly resist him.
Hos 5: 3 I **k** all about Ephraim; Israel is not
9: 7 Let Israel **k** this. Because your sins
Joel 2:27 you will **k** that I am in Israel, that
3:17 "Then you will **k** that I, the LORD
Am 3:10 "They do not **k** how to do right,"
5:12 For I **k** how many are your offences
Jnh 1:12 I **k** that it is my fault that this
Mic 3: 1 Should you not **k** justice,
4:12 they do not **k** the thoughts of the
6: 5 **k** the righteous acts of the LORD."
Zep 3: 5 yet the unrighteous **k** no shame.
Zec 4: 5 "Do you not **k** what these are?"
4:13 "Do you not **k** what these are?"
Mal 2: 4 you will **k** that I have sent you this
Mt 6: 3 **k** what your right hand is doing,
7:11 are evil, **k** how to give good gifts
9: 6 you may **k** that the Son of Man
15:12 "Do you **k** that the Pharisees were
16: 3 You **k** how to interpret the
20:22 "You don't **k** what you are asking,"
20:25 "You **k** that the rulers of the
21:27 they answered Jesus, "We don't **k**."
22:16 "we **k** you are a man of integrity
22:29 you do not **k** the Scriptures or the
24:32 come out, you **k** that summer is near.
24:33 **k** that it is near, right at the door.
24:42 you do not **k** on what day your Lord
25:12 I tell you the truth, I don't **k** you.
25:13 you do not **k** the day or the hour.
26: 2 "As you **k**, the Passover is two days
26:70 "I don't **k** what you're talking about
26:72 with an oath: "I don't **k** the man!
26:74 swore to them, "I don't **k** the man!
27:65 the tomb as secure as you **k** how."
28: 5 I **k** that you are looking for Jesus
Mk 1:24 **k** who you are—the Holy One of God!
2:10 that you may **k** that the Son of Man
4:27 and grows, though he does not **k** how.
5:43 not to let anyone **k** about this,
7:24 and did not want anyone to **k** it;
9: 6 He did not **k** what to say, they were
9:30 want anyone to **k** where they were,
10:19 You **k** the commandments: 'Do not
10:38 "You don't **k** what you are asking,"
10:42 "You **k** that those who are regarded
11:33 they answered Jesus, "We don't **k**."
12:14 we **k** you are a man of integrity.
12:24 **k** the Scriptures or the power of God?
13:28 come out, you **k** that summer is near.
13:29 **k** that it is near, right at the door.
13:33 do not **k** when that time will come.
13:35 you do not **k** when the owner of the
14:40 They did not **k** what to say to him.
14:68 he denied it. "I don't **k** or
14:71 swore to them, "I don't **k** this man
Lk 1: 4 that you may **k** the certainty of the
2:49 "Didn't you **k** I had to be in my
4:34 **k** who you are—the Holy One of God!"
5:24 that you may **k** that the Son of Man
7:39 he would **k** who is touching him and
8:46 I **k** that power has gone out from me
9:33 (He did not **k** what he was saying.)
11:13 are evil, **k** how to give good gifts
12:48 the one who does not **k** and does
12:56 Hypocrites! You **k** how to interpret
12:56 **k** how to interpret this present time?

Lk 13:25 don't **k** you or where you come from.'
13:27 "But he will reply, 'I don't **k** you
16: 4 I **k** what I'll do so that, when I
18:20 You **k** the commandments: 'Do not
18:34 did not **k** what he was talking about.
20: 7 they answered, "We don't **k** where it
20:21 "Teacher, we **k** that you speak and
21:20 will **k** that its desolation is near.
21:30 and **k** that summer is near.
21:31 **k** that the kingdom of God is near.
22:34 deny three times that you **k** me."
22:57 he denied it. "Woman, I don't **k** him,
22:60 Man, I don't **k** what you're talking
23:34 they do not **k** what they are doing.
24:18 do not **k** the things that have
Jn 1:26 among you stands one you do not **k**.
1:31 I myself did not **k** him, but the
1:48 "How do you **k** me?" Nathanael asked.
3: 2 "Rabbi, we **k** you are a teacher who
3:11 we speak of what we **k**, and we
4:22 do not **k**; we worship what we do **k**,
4:25 The woman said, "I **k** that Messiah"
4:32 to eat that you **k** nothing about."
4:42 and we **k** that this man really is the
5:32 and I **k** that his testimony about me
5:42 I **k** you. I **k** that you do not have
6:42 whose father and mother we **k**?
6:69 We believe and **k** that you are the
7:27 we **k** where this man is from;
7:27 no-one will **k** where he is from."
7:28 you **k** me, and you **k** where I am from.
7:28 You do not **k** him,
7:29 I **k** him because I am from him and he
8:14 I **k** where I came from and where I
8:19 You do not **k** me or my Father,"
8:19 me, you would **k** my Father also."
8:28 then you will **k** that I am ⌊the one I
8:32 you will **k** the truth, and the truth
8:37 I **k** you are Abraham's descendants.
8:52 we **k** that you are demon possessed!
8:55 Though you do not **k** him, I **k** him.
8:55 but I do **k** him and keep his word.
9:12 "I don't **k**," he said.
9:20 "We **k** he is our son," the parents
9:20 "and we **k** he was born blind.
9:21 or who opened his eyes, we don't **k**.
9:24 "We **k** this man is a sinner."
9:25 he is a sinner or not, I don't **k**.
9:25 One thing I do **k**. I was blind but
9:29 We **k** that God spoke to Moses, but
9:29 don't even **k** where he comes from."
9:30 You don't **k** where he comes from,
9:31 We **k** that God does not listen to
10: 4 follow him because they **k** his voice.
10:14 I **k** my sheep and my sheep **k** me—
10:15 Father knows me and I **k** the Father
10:27 I **k** them and they follow me.
10:38 that you may **k** and understand that
11:22 I **k** that even now God will give you
11:24 Martha answered, "I **k** he will rise
11:49 spoke up, "You **k** nothing at all!
12:35 dark does not **k** where he is going.
12:50 I **k** that his command leads to
13:17 Now that you **k** these things, you
13:18 I **k** those I have chosen. But this is
13:22 a loss to **k** which of them he meant.
13:35 By this all men will **k** that you are
14: 4 You **k** the way to the place where I
14: 5 "Lord, we don't **k** where you
14: 5 are going, so how can we **k** the way?"
14: 7 you would **k** my Father as well.
14: 7 you do **k** him and have seen him."
14: 9 Jesus answered: "Don't you **k** me,
14:17 But you **k** him, for he lives with you
15:15 does not **k** his master's business.
15:21 they do not **k** the One who sent me.
16:30 Now we can see that you **k** all things
17: 3 they may **k** you, the only true God,
17: 7 Now they **k** that everything you have
17:23 to let the world **k** that you sent me
17:25 the world does not **k** you, I **k** you,
17:25 and they **k** that you have sent me.
18:21 Surely they **k** what I said."
19: 4 to let you **k** that I find no basis
20: 2 we don't **k** where they have put him!"
20:13 I don't **k** where they have put him."
Jn 21:15 he said, "you **k** that I love you.
21:16 "Yes, Lord, you **k** that I love you.
21:17 **k** all things; you **k** that I love you.
21:24 We **k** that his testimony is true.
Ac 1: 7 "It is not for you to **k** the times or
1:24 "Lord, you **k** everyone's heart.
2:22 through him, as you yourselves **k**.
3:16 whom you see and **k** was made strong.
3:17 I **k** that you acted in ignorance,
4:10 **k** this, you and all the people of
7:40 don't **k** what has happened to him!'
10:36 You **k** the message God sent to the
10:37 You **k** what has happened throughout
12:11 "Now I **k** without a doubt that the
13:38 want you to **k** that through Jesus
15: 7 "Brothers, you **k** that some time ago
17:19 "May we **k** what this new teaching is
17:20 and we want to **k** what they mean."
19:15 Jesus I **k**, and I **k** about Paul, but
19:25 "Men, you **k** we receive a good income
19:32 did not even **k** why they were there.
19:35 doesn't all the world **k** that the
20:18 "You **k** how I lived the whole time
20:20 You **k** that I have not hesitated to
20:23 I only **k** that in every city the Holy
20:25 "Now I **k** that none of you among whom
20:29 I **k** that after I leave, savage
20:34 You yourselves **k** that these hands of
21:24 Then everybody will **k** there is no
22:14 has chosen you to **k** his will
22:19 'Lord,' I replied, 'these men **k**
23:28 I wanted to **k** why they were accusing
24:10 "I **k** that for a number of years you
25:10 Jews, as you yourself **k** very well.
26: 4 "The Jews all **k** the way I have lived
26:27 believe the prophets? I **k** you do."
28:22 for we **k** that people everywhere are
28:28 "Therefore I want you to **k** that
Ro 1:32 Although they **k** God's righteous
2: 2 Now we **k** that God's judgment against
2:18 if you **k** his will and approve of
3:17 the way of peace they do not **k**."
3:19 Now we **k** that whatever the law says,
5: 3 because we **k** that suffering produces
6: 3 Or don't you **k** that all of us who
6: 6 For we **k** that our old self was
6: 9 For we **k** that since Christ was
6:16 Don't you **k** that when you offer
7: 1 Do you not **k**, brothers—for I am
7: 1 I am speaking to men who **k** the law
7:14 We **k** that the law is spiritual; but
7:18 I **k** that nothing good lives in me,
8:22 We **k** that the whole creation has
8:26 We do not **k** what we ought to pray
8:28 we **k** that in all things God works
10: 3 they did not **k** the righteousness
11: 2 Don't you **k** what the Scripture says
15:29 I **k** that when I come to you, I will
1Co 1:21 through its wisdom did not **k** him,
2: 2 For I resolved to **k** nothing while I
3:16 Don't you **k** that you yourselves are
5: 6 Don't you **k** that a little yeast
6: 2 Do you not **k** that the saints will
6: 3 Do you not **k** that we will judge
6: 9 Do you not **k** that the wicked will
6:15 Do you not **k** that your bodies are
6:16 Do you not **k** that he who unites
6:19 Do you not **k** that your body is a
7:16 How do you **k**, wife, whether you will
7:16 how do you **k**, husband, whether you
8: 1 We **k** that we all possess knowledge.
8: 2 does not yet **k** as he ought to **k**.
8: 4 We **k** that an idol is nothing at all
9:13 Don't you **k** that those who work in
9:24 Do you not **k** that in a race all the
12: 2 You **k** that when you were pagans,
13: 9 For we **k** in part and we prophesy in
13:12 Now I **k** in part; then I shall **k**
14: 7 how will anyone **k** what tune is being
14: 9 how will anyone **k** what you are
14:16 he does not **k** what you are saying?
15:58 because you **k** that your labour in
16:15 You **k** that the household of
2Co 1: 7 because we **k** that just as you share
2: 4 you **k** the depth of my love for you.
4:14 we **k** that the one who raised the
2Co 5: 1 Now we **k** that if the earthly tent we
5: 6 **k** that as long as we are at home in
5:11 Since, then, we **k** what it is to fear
8: 1 now, brothers, we want you to **k**
8: 9 For you **k** the grace of our Lord
9: 2 For I **k** your eagerness to help, and
12: 2 I **k** a man in Christ who fourteen
12: 2 of the body I do not **k**—God knows.
12: 3 I **k** that this man—whether in the
12: 3 the body I do not **k**, but God knows—
Gal 1:11 I want you to **k**, brothers, that the
2:16 **k** that a man is not justified by
4: 8 Formerly, when you did not **k** God,
4: 9 now that you **k** God—or rather are
4:13 you **k**, it was because of an illness
Eph 1:17 so that you may **k** him better.
1:18 in order that you may **k** the hope to
3:19 to **k** this love that surpasses
4:20 did not come to **k** Christ that way
6: 9 Do not threaten them, since you **k**
6:21 may **k** how I am and what I am doing.
6:22 that you may **k** how we are, and that
Php 1:12 Now I want you to **k**, brothers, that
1:19 for I **k** that through your prayers
1:22 Yet what shall I choose? I do not **k**!
1:25 I **k** that I will remain, and I will
1:27 I will **k** that you stand firm in one
2:22 you **k** that Timothy has proved
3:10 I want to **k** Christ and the power of
4:12 I **k** what it is to be in need, and I **k**
4:15 Moreover, as you Philippians **k**, in
Col 2: 1 I want you to **k** how much I am
2: 2 **k** the mystery of God, namely, Christ,
3:24 since you **k** that you will receive an
4: 1 because you **k** that you also have a
4: 6 you may **k** how to answer everyone.
4: 8 you may **k** about our circumstances
1Th 1: 4 For we **k**, brothers loved by God,
1: 5 You **k** how we lived among you for
2: 1 You **k**, brothers, that our visit to
2: 2 as you **k**, but with the help of our
2: 5 You **k** we never used flattery, nor
2:11 For you **k** that we dealt with each
3: 3 You **k** quite well that we were
3: 4 turned out that way, as you well **k**.
4: 2 For you **k** what instructions we gave
4: 5 like the heathen, who do not **k** God;
5: 2 for you **k** very well that the day of
2Th 1: 8 He will punish those who do not **k**
2: 6 now you **k** what is holding him back,
3: 7 For you yourselves **k** how you ought
1Ti 1: 7 but they do not **k** what they are
1: 8 We **k** that the law is good if one
1: 9 We also **k** that law is made not for
3: 5 If anyone does not **k** how to manage
3:15 you will **k** how people ought to
4: 3 who believe and who **k** the truth.
2Ti 1:12 because I **k** whom I have believed,
1:15 You **k** that everyone in the province
1:18 You **k** very well in how many ways he
2:23 because you **k** they produce quarrels.
3:10 **k** all about my teaching, my way of
3:14 **k** those from whom you learned it,
Tit 1:16 They claim to **k** God, but by their
Heb 8:11 **K** the Lord,' because they will all **k**
10:30 For we **k** him who said, "It is mine
11: 8 he did not **k** where he was going.
12:17 Afterwards, as you **k**, when he wanted
13:23 I want you to **k** that our brother
Jas 1: 3 you **k** that the testing of your faith
3: 1 my brothers, because you **k** that we
4: 4 You adulterous people, don't you **k**
4:14 Why, you do not even **k** what will
5:11 As you **k**, we consider blessed those
1Pe 1:18 For you **k** that it was not with
5: 9 because you **k** that your brothers
2Pe 1:12 even though you **k** them and are
1:14 I **k** that I will soon put it aside,
3:17 friends, since you already **k** this,
1Jn 2: 3 We **k** that we have come to **k** him if
2: 4 The man who says, "I **k** him," but
2: 5 This is how we **k** we are in him:
2:11 he does not **k** where he is going,
2:18 This is how we **k** it is the last hour.
2:20 Holy One, and all of you **k** the truth.
2:21 you because you do not **k** the truth,

1Jn 2:21 but because you do **k** it and because
2:29 If you **k** that he is righteous, you **k**
3: 1 not **k** us is that it did not **k** him.
3: 2 But we **k** that when he appears, we
3: 5 you **k** that he appeared so that he
3:10 This is how we **k** who the children of
3:14 We **k** that we have passed from death
3:15 and you **k** that no murderer has
3:16 This is how we **k** what love is: Jesus
3:19 we **k** that we belong to the truth,
3:24 And this is how we **k** that he lives
3:24 We **k** it by the Spirit he gave us.
4: 8 Whoever does not love does not **k** God,
4:13 We **k** that we live in him and he in
4:16 we **k** and rely on the love God has
5: 2 This is how we **k** that we love the
5:13 may **k** that you have eternal life.
5:15 if we **k** that he hears us—whatever
5:15 **k** that we have what we asked of him.
5:18 We **k** that anyone born of God does
5:19 We **k** that we are children of God,
5:20 We **k** also that the Son of God has
5:20 so that we may **k** him who is true.
2Jn : 1 but also all who **k** the truth—
3Jn :12 you **k** that our testimony is true.
Jude : 5 Though you already **k** all this, I
Rev 2: 2 I **k** your deeds, your hard work and
2: 2 I **k** that you cannot tolerate wicked
2: 9 I **k** your afflictions and your
2: 9 I **k** the slander of those who say
2:13 I **k** where you live—where Satan has
2:19 I **k** your deeds, your love and faith,
2:23 the churches will **k** that I am he
3: 1 I **k** your deeds; you have a
3: 3 **k** at what time I will come to you.
3: 8 I **k** your deeds. See, I have placed
3: 8 I **k** that you have little strength,
3:15 I **k** your deeds, that you are neither
7:14 I answered, "Sir, you **k**." And he

Know that I am the Lord

Ex 6: 7 Then you will **k** your God, who
7: 5 the Egyptians will **k** when I stretch
7:17 By this you will **k**: With the staff
10: 2 among them, and that you may **k**."
14: 4 his army, and the Egyptians will **k**.
14:18 The Egyptians will **k** when I gain
16:12 Then you will **k** your God.'
29:46 They will **k** their God, who brought
31:13 that you may **k**, who makes you holy.
Dt 29: 6 this so that you might **k** your God.
Isa 45: 3 so that you may **k**, the God of Israel
49:23 Then you will **k**; those who hope in
Eze 6: 7 slain among you, and you will **k**.
6:10 they will **k**; I did not threaten
6:13 they will **k**, when their people lie
6: 14 Then they will **k**.'"
7: 4 Then you will **k**.
7:27 will judge them. Then they will **k**."
11:10 Then you will **k**.
11:12 you will **k**, for you have not
12:15 "They will **k**, when I disperse them
12:16 Then they will **k**."
12: 20 will be desolate. Then you will **k**.
13:14 be destroyed in it; and you will **k**.
13:21 Then you will **k**.
13: 23 And then you will **k**.'"
14: 8 Then you will **k**.
15: 7 my face against them, you will **k**.
16:62 covenant with you, and you will **k**.
20:20 Then you will **k** your God."
20:26 with horror so that they would **k**.'
20:38 Then you will **k**.
20:42 you will **k**, when I bring you into
20:44 You will **k**, when I deal with you for
22: 16 eyes of the nations, you will **k**.
24:27 be a sign to them, and they will **k**."
25: 5 Then you will **k**.
25: 7 I will destroy you, and you will **k**
25: 11 on Moab. Then they will **k**.'"
25:17 Then they will **k**, when I take
26: 6 Then they will **k**.
28:22 They will **k**, when I inflict
28:23 Then they will **k**.
28:26 Then they will **k** their God.'
Eze 29: 6 all who live in Egypt will **k**.
29: 9 Then they will **k**.
29:21 Then they will **k**."
30: 8 they will **k**, when I set fire to
30: 19 or Egypt, and they will **k**.'"
30:25 Then they will **k**, when I put my
30:26 Then they will **k**."
32:15 who live there, then they will **k**.'
33:29 they will **k**, when I have made the
34:27 They will **k**, when I break the bars
35: 4 will be desolate. Then you will **k**.
35: 9 not be inhabited. Then you will **k**.
35: 15 all of Edom. Then they will **k**.'"
36:11 Then you will **k**.
36:23 Then the nations will **k**, declares
36:38 Then they will **k**."
37: 6 come to life. Then you will **k**.'"
37:13 you, my people, will **k**, when I open
38:23 Then they will **k**.'
39: 6 in the coastlands, and they will **k**.
39:22 house of Israel will **k** their God.
39:28 they will **k** their God, for though I

Know that the Lord/Lord

Ex 11: 7 Then you will **k** makes a distinction
18:11 Now I **k** is greater than all other
Nu 16:28 "This is how you will **k** has sent me
Dt 4:35 things so that you might **k** is God;
Jos 2: 9 "I **k** has given this land to you
22:31 "Today we **k** is with us, because you
Jdg 16:20 But he did not **k** had left him.
17:13 said, "Now I **k** will be good to me,
1Ki 8:60 **k** is God and that there is no other.
2Ki 2: 3 "Do you **k** is going to take your
2: 5 "Do you **k** is going to take your
2Ch 13: 5 Don't you **k**, the God of Israel, has
Ps 4: 3 **K** has set apart the godly for
20: 6 Now I **k** saves his anointed; he
100: 3 **K** is God. It is he who made us, and
135: 5 I **k** is great, that our Lord is
140:12 I **k** secures justice for the poor and
Zec 2: 9 Then you will **k** Almighty has sent me.
2:11 will **k** Almighty has sent me to you.
4: 9 will **k** Almighty has sent me to you.
6:15 will **k** Almighty has sent me to you.
Eph 6: 8 you **k** will reward everyone for

Knowing (Know)

Ge 3: 5 will be like God, **k** good and evil."
3:22 like one of us, **k** good and evil.
2Sa 15:11 **k** nothing about the matter.
1Ki 1:11 king without our lord David's **k** it?
Job 9: 5 He moves mountains without their **k**
31:21 **k** that I had influence in court,
Ps 39: 6 up wealth, not **k** who will get it.
Pr 7:23 little **k** it will cost him his life.
Ecc 6: 8 What does a poor man gain by **k** how
Mt 9: 4 **K** their thoughts, Jesus said, "Why
22:18 Jesus, **k** their evil intent, said,
Mk 5:33 the woman, **k** what had happened to
6:20 **k** him to be a righteous and holy man.
15:10 **k** it was out of envy that the chief
Lk 8:53 laughed at him, **k** that she was dead
9:47 Jesus, **k** their thoughts, took a
11:44 which men walk over without **k** it."
Jn 6:15 Jesus, **k** that they intended to come
18: 4 Jesus, **k** all that was going to
19:28 Later, **k** that all was now completed,
Ac 5: 7 came in, not **k** what had happened.
20:22 not **k** what will happen to me there.
23: 6 Paul, **k** that some of them were
Php 1:16 do so in love, **k** that I am put here
3: 8 greatness of **k** Christ Jesus my Lord,
Phm :21 I write to you, **k** that you will do
Heb 13: 2 entertained angels without **k** it.
2Pe 2:20 of the world by **k** our Lord

Knowledge (Know)

Ge 2: 9 the tree of the **k** of good and evil.
2:17 the tree of the **k** of good and evil,
Ex 31: 3 and **k** in all kinds of crafts—
35:31 and **k** in all kinds of crafts—
Nu 24:16 who has **k** from the Most High, who
1Ki 2:32 because without the **k** of my father
2Ch 1:10 Give me wisdom and **k**, that I may
2Ch 1:11 **k** to govern my people over whom I
1:12 therefore wisdom and **k** will be given
Job 21:22 "Can anyone teach **k** to God, since he
34:35 'Job speaks without **k**; his words
35:16 without **k** he multiplies words."
36: 3 I get my **k** from afar; I will ascribe
36: 4 one perfect in **k** is with you.
36:12 by the sword and die without **k**.
37:16 wonders of him who is perfect in **k**?
38: 2 my counsel with words without **k**?
42: 3 that obscures my counsel without **k**?'
Ps 19: 2 night after night they display **k**.
73:11 Does the Most High have **k**?"
94:10 Does he who teaches man lack **k**?
119:66 Teach me **k** and good judgment, for I
139: 6 Such **k** is too wonderful for me, too
Pr 1: 4 **k** and discretion to the young
1: 7 of the Lord is the beginning of **k**,
1:22 delight in mockery and fools hate **k**?
1:29 Since they hated **k** and did not
2: 5 of the Lord and find the **k** of God.
2: 6 his mouth come **k** and understanding.
2:10 and **k** will be pleasant to your soul.
3:20 by his **k** the deeps were divided,
5: 2 and your lips may preserve **k**.
8: 9 are faultless to those who have **k**.
8:10 silver, **k** rather than choice gold,
8:12 I possess **k** and discretion.
9:10 **k** of the Holy One is understanding.
9:13 she is undisciplined and without **k**.
10:14 Wise men store up **k**, but the mouth
11: 9 but through **k** the righteous escape.
12: 1 Whoever loves discipline loves **k**,
12:23 A prudent man keeps his **k** to himself,
13:16 Every prudent man acts out of **k**, but
14: 6 **k** comes easily to the discerning.
14: 7 for you will not find **k** on his lips.
14:18 but the prudent are crowned with **k**.
15: 2 The tongue of the wise commends **k**,
15: 7 The lips of the wise spread **k**;
15:14 The discerning heart seeks **k**, but
17:27 A man of **k** uses words with restraint,
18:15 of the discerning acquires **k**;
19: 2 is not good to have zeal without **k**,
19:25 discerning man, and he will gain **k**.
19:27 you will stray from the words of **k**.
20:15 lips that speak **k** are a rare jewel.
21:11 wise man is instructed, he gets **k**.
22:12 eyes of the Lord keep watch over **k**,
22:20 for you, sayings of counsel and **k**,
23:12 and your ears to words of **k**.
24: 4 through **k** its rooms are filled with
24: 5 and a man of **k** increases strength;
28: 2 understanding and **k** maintains order.
30: 3 nor have I **k** of the Holy One.
Ecc 1:16 experienced much of wisdom and **k**."
1:18 the more **k**, the more grief.
2:21 **k** and skill, and then he must leave
2:26 God gives wisdom, **k** and happiness,
7:12 but the advantage of **k** is this:
9:10 nor planning nor **k** nor wisdom.
12: 9 also he imparted **k** to the people.
Isa 11: 2 the Spirit of **k** and of the fear of
11: 9 will be full of the **k** of the Lord
33: 6 store of salvation and wisdom and **k**;
40:14 Who was it that taught him **k** or
44:19 no-one has the **k** or understanding to
47:10 Your wisdom and **k** mislead you when
53:11 by his **k** my righteous servant will
56:10 they all lack **k**; they are all mute
Jer 3:15 lead you with **k** and understanding.
10:14 Everyone is senseless and without **k**;
51:17 Every man is senseless and without **k**
Da 1:17 To these four young men God gave **k**
2:21 to the wise and **k** to the discerning.
5:12 was found to have a keen mind and **k**
12: 4 go here and there to increase **k**."
Hos 4: 6 people are destroyed from lack of **k**.
4: 6 "Because you have rejected **k**, I also
Hab 2:14 with the **k** of the glory of the Lord,
Mal 2: 7 of a priest ought to preserve **k**,
Mt 13:11 "The **k** of the secrets of the kingdom
Lk 1:77 give his people the **k** of salvation
8:10 He said, "The **k** of the secrets of
11:52 you have taken away the key to **k**.
Ac 5: 2 With his wife's full **k** he kept back

Ac 18:24 with a thorough **k** of the Scriptures.
Ro 1:28 worth while to retain the **k** of God,
2:20 law the embodiment of **k** and truth—
10: 2 but their zeal is not based on **k**.
11:33 riches of the wisdom and **k** of God!
15:14 complete in **k** and competent to
1Co 1: 5 your speaking and in all your **k**—
8: 1 We know that we all possess **k**.
8: 1 **K** puffs up, but love builds up.
8:10 sees you who have this **k** eating
8:11 Christ died, is destroyed by your **k**.
12: 8 to another the message of **k** by
13: 2 can fathom all mysteries and all **k**,
13: 8 where there is **k**, it will pass away.
14: 6 **k** or prophecy or word of instruction?
2Co 2:14 the fragrance of the **k** of him.
4: 6 light of the **k** of the glory of God
8: 7 in speech, in **k**, in complete
10: 5 sets itself up against the **k** of God,
11: 6 a trained speaker, but I do have **k**.
Eph 3:19 to know this love that surpasses **k**
4:13 in the **k** of the Son of God and
Php 1: 9 and more in **k** and depth of insight,
Col 1: 9 asking God to fill you with the **k** of
1:10 good work, growing in the **k** of God,
2: 3 all the treasures of wisdom and **k**.
3:10 in **k** in the image of its Creator.
1Ti 2: 4 and to come to a **k** of the truth.
6:20 ideas of what is falsely called **k**,
2Ti 2:25 leading them to a **k** of the truth,
Tit 1: 1 the **k** of the truth that leads to
1: 2 a faith and **k** resting on the hope of
Heb 10:26 we have received the **k** of the truth,
2Pe 1: 2 the **k** of God and of Jesus our Lord.
1: 3 godliness through our **k** of him who
1: 5 faith goodness; and to goodness, **k**;
1: 6 to **k**, self-control; and to
1: 8 in your **k** of our Lord Jesus Christ.
3:18 grow in the grace and **k** of our Lord

Known (Know)

Ge 41:39 "Since God has made all this **k** to
45: 1 he made himself **k** to his brothers.
Ex 2:14 "What I did must have become **k**.
6: 3 LORD I did not make myself **k** to them.
21:36 However, if it was **k** that the bull
Nu 11:16 elders who are **k** to you as leaders
Dt 3:13 to be **k** as a land of the Rephaites.
8: 3 neither you nor your fathers had **k**,
8:16 something your fathers had never **k**,
9:24 the LORD ever since I have **k** you.
11:28 other gods, which you have not **k**.
13: 2 other gods" (gods you have not **k**)
13: 6 neither you nor your fathers have **k**,
13:13 other gods" (gods you have not **k**),
21: 1 and it is not **k** who killed him,
25:10 That man's line shall be **k** in Israel
28:64 neither you nor your fathers have **k**.
32:17 are not God—gods they had not **k**,
Ru 3:14 "Don't let it be **k** that a woman came
1Sa 10:11 all those who had formerly **k** him saw
18:23 I'm only a poor man and little **k**."
18:30 and his name became well **k**.
2Sa 7:21 thing and made it **k** to your servant.
1Ki 18:36 let it be **k** today that you are God
1Ch 16: 8 **k** among the nations what he has done.
17:19 and made **k** all these great promises
Ne 8:12 words that had been made **k** to them.
9:14 You made **k** to them your holy Sabbath
Est 1:17 For the queen's conduct will become **k**
2: 7 This girl, who was also **k** as Esther,
3:14 made **k** to the people of every
8:13 made **k** to the people of every
Job 36:33 even the cattle make **k** its approach.
42:11 sisters and everyone who had **k** him
Ps 9:16 The LORD is **k** by his justice; the
16:11 You have made **k** to me the path of
25:14 he makes his covenant **k** to them.
37:18 The days of the blameless are **k** to
59:13 Then it will be **k** to the ends of the
67: 2 that your ways may be **k** on earth,
76: 1 In Judah God is **k**; his name is great
78: 3 what we have heard and **k**, what our
79:10 make **k** among the nations that you
88:12 Are your wonders **k** in the place of
Ps 89: 1 **k** through all generations.
95:10 and they have not **k** my ways."
98: 2 The LORD has made his salvation **k**
103: 7 He made **k** his ways to Moses, his
105: 1 **k** among the nations what he has done.
106: 8 sake, to make his mighty power **k**.
119:168 for all my ways are **k** to you.
Pr 1:23 you and made my thoughts **k** to you.
14:33 among fools she lets herself be **k**.
20:11 Even a child is **k** by his actions, by
24: 8 He who plots evil will be **k** as a
Ecc 6:10 named, and what man is has been **k**;
Isa 12: 4 make **k** among the nations what he
12: 5 let this be **k** to all the world.
19:12 Let them show you and make **k** what
19:21 the LORD will make himself **k** to the
42:16 the blind by ways they have not **k**,
46:10 I make **k** the end from the beginning,
48: 3 announced them and I made them **k**;
61: 9 Their descendants will be **k** among
64: 2 come down to make your name **k** to
66:14 LORD will be made **k** to his servants,
Jer 7: 9 follow other gods you have not **k**,
9:16 they nor their fathers have **k**,
16:13 neither you nor your fathers have **k**,
Eze 20:11 decrees and made **k** to them my laws,
32: 9 nations, among lands you have not **k**.
35:11 **k** among them when I judge you.
38:23 **k** in the sight of many nations.
39: 7 "'I will make **k** my holy name among
43:11 make **k** to them the design of the
Da 2:23 you have made **k** to me what we asked
2:23 made **k** to us the dream of the king."
Hab 3: 2 in our time make them **k**;
Zec 14: 7 or night-time—a day **k** to the LORD.
Mt 10:26 or hidden that will not be made **k**.
12: 7 If you had **k** what these words mean,
24:43 If the owner of the house had **k** at
26: 6 home of a man **k** as Simon the Leper,
Mk 6:14 for Jesus' name had become well **k**.
14: 3 home of a man **k** as Simon the Leper,
Lk 8:17 be **k** or brought out into the open.
12: 2 or hidden that will not be made **k**.
12:39 **k** at what hour the thief was coming,
19:42 said, "If you, even you, had only **k**
Jn 1:18 the Father's side, has made him **k**.
1:33 I would not have **k** him, except that
6:64 For Jesus had **k** from the beginning
15:15 from my Father I have made **k** to you.
16: 3 they have not **k** the Father or me.
16:14 what is mine and making it **k** to you.
16:15 what is mine and make it **k** to you.
17:26 I have made you **k** to them, and will
17:26 and will continue to make you **k** in
18:15 Because this disciple was **k** to the
18:16 The other disciple, who was **k** to the
19:13 at a place **k** as the Stone Pavement
Ac 1:23 (also **k** as Justus) and Matthias.
2:28 You have made **k** to me the paths of
6: 3 who are **k** to be full of the Spirit
8:10 divine power **k** as the Great Power."
9:42 This became **k** all over Joppa, and
10: 1 what was **k** as the Italian Regiment.
10:18 Simon who was **k** as Peter was staying
15:18 that have been **k** for ages.
19:17 this became **k** to the Jews and Greeks
26: 5 They have **k** me for a long time and
Ro 1:19 since what may be **k** about God is
3:21 apart from law, has been made **k**,
7: 7 I would not have **k** what sin was
7: 7 For I would not have **k** what coveting
9:22 show his wrath and make his power **k**,
9:23 glory **k** to the objects of his mercy,
11:34 "Who has **k** the mind of the Lord?
15:20 the gospel where Christ was not **k**,
16:26 now revealed and made **k** through the
1Co 2:16 "For who has **k** the mind of the Lord
8: 3 the man who loves God is **k** by God.
13:12 know fully, even as I am fully **k**.
2Co 3: 2 our hearts, **k** and read by everybody.
6: 9 **k**, yet regarded as unknown; dying,
11:27 I have **k** hunger and thirst and have
Gal 4: 9 or rather are **k** by God—how is it
Eph 1: 9 he made **k** to us the mystery of his
3: 3 the mystery made **k** to me by revelation,
3: 5 which was not made **k** to men in other
Eph 3:10 God should be made **k** to the rulers
6:19 make **k** the mystery of the gospel,
Col 1:27 To them God has chosen to make **k**
1Th 1: 8 in God has become **k** everywhere.
1Ti 5:10 is well **k** for her good deeds,
2Ti 3:15 how from infancy you have **k** the holy
Heb 3:10 and they have not **k** my ways.'
11:24 **k** as the son of Pharaoh's daughter.
2Pe 2:21 not to have **k** the way of
2:21 than to have **k** it and then to turn
1Jn 2:13 **k** him who is from the beginning.
2:13 because you have **k** the Father.
2:14 **k** him who is from the beginning.
3: 2 we will be has not yet been made **k**.
3: 6 to sin has either seen him or **k** him.
Rev 1: 1 He made it **k** by sending his angel to
2:17 **k** only to him who receives it.

Knows (Know)

Ge 3: 5 "For God **k** that when you eat of it
16: 5 **k** she is pregnant, she despises me.
33:13 **k** that the children are tender
Dt 34: 6 day no-one **k** where his grave is.
Jos 22:22 Mighty one, God, the LORD! He **k**!
1Sa 2: 3 the LORD is a God who **k**, and by
16:18 Bethlehem who **k** how to play the harp.
20: 3 "Your father **k** very well that I have
22:15 for your servant **k** nothing at all
23:17 Even my father Saul **k** this."
25:11 to men coming from who **k** where?"
2Sa 12:22 I thought, 'Who **k**? The LORD may be
14:20 he **k** everything that happens in the
14:22 Joab said, "Today your servant **k**
17:10 for all Israel **k** that your father is
Est 4:14 And who **k** but that you have come to
Job 15:23 he **k** the day of darkness is at hand.
18:21 is the place of one who **k** not God."
23:10 he **k** the way that I take; when he
28: 7 No bird of prey **k** that hidden path,
28:23 it and he alone **k** where it dwells,
Ps 37:13 for he **k** their day is coming.
44:21 since he **k** the secrets of the heart?
74: 9 none of us **k** how long this will be.
90:11 Who **k** the power of your anger?
94:11 The LORD **k** the thoughts of man; he **k**
103:14 for he **k** how we are formed, he
104:19 and the sun **k** when to go down.
138: 6 lowly, but the proud he **k** from afar
Pr 5: 6 paths are crooked, but she **k** it not
14:10 Each heart **k** its own bitterness,
24:22 **k** what calamities they can bring?
Ecc 2:19 who **k** whether he will be a wise man
3:21 Who **k** if the spirit of man rises
4:13 who no longer **k** how to take warning
6:12 For who **k** what is good for a man in
8: 1 Who **k** the explanation of things?
8: 7 Since no man **k** the future, who can
8:17 Even if a wise man claims he **k**,
9: 1 **k** whether love or hate awaits him.
9:12 no man **k** when his hour will come
10:14 No-one **k** what is coming—who can
Isa 1: 3 The ox **k** his master, the donkey his
7:15 will eat curds and honey when he **k**
7:16 before the boy **k** enough to reject
8: 4 Before the boy **k** how to say 'My
29:16 say of the potter, "He **k** nothing"?
Jer 8: 7 Even the stork in the sky **k** her
9:24 that he understands and **k** me,
Da 2:22 he **k** what lies in darkness,
Joel 2:14 Who **k**? He may turn and have pity and
Jnh 3: 9 Who **k**? God may yet relent and with
Na 3:17 they fly away, and no-one **k** where.
Mt 6: 8 **k** what you need before you ask him.
6:32 Father **k** that you need them.
9:30 "See that no-one **k** about this.
11:27 No-one **k** the Son except the Father,
11:27 and no-one **k** the Father except the
24:36 "No-one **k** about that day or hour,
Mk 13:32 "No-one **k** about that day or hour,
Lk 10:22 No-one **k** who the Son is except the
10:22 and no-one **k** who the Father is
12:30 your Father **k** that you need them.
12:47 servant who **k** his master's will
16:15 eyes of men, but God **k** your hearts.
Jn 7:49 this mob that **k** nothing of the law

Jn 10:15 Father **k** me and I know the Father
14:17 it neither sees him nor **k** him.
19:35 He **k** that he tells the truth, and he
Ac 4:16 "Everybody living in Jerusalem **k**
15: 8 God, who **k** the heart, showed that he
Ro 8:27 he who searches our hearts **k** the
1Co 2:11 For who among men **k** the thoughts of
2:11 In the same way no-one **k** the
3:20 again, "The Lord **k** that the thoughts
8: 2 The man who thinks he **k** something
8: 7 not everyone **k** this. Some people are
2Co 7: 4 all our troubles my joy **k** no bounds.
11:11 I do not love you? God **k** I do!
11:31 for ever, **k** that I am not lying.
12: 2 of the body I do not know—God **k**.
12: 3 the body I do not know, but God **k**—
2Ti 2:19 "The Lord **k** those who are his," and,
Jas 4:17 Anyone, then, who **k** the good he
2Pe 2: 9 the Lord **k** how to rescue godly men
1Jn 3:20 our hearts, and he **k** everything.
4: 6 and whoever **k** God listens to us;
4: 7 has been born of God and **k** God.
Rev 12:12 he **k** that his time is short."
19:12 on him that no-one **k** but he himself.

Koa
Eze 23:23 the men of Pekod and Shoa and **K**,

Kohath (Kohath's, Kohathite, Kohathites)
Ge 46:11 The sons of Levi: Gershon, **K** and
Ex 6:16 records: Gershon, **K** and Merari.
6:18 The sons of **K** were Amram, Izhar,
6:18 **K** lived 133 years.
Nu 3:17 sons of Levi: Gershon, **K** and Merari.
3:27 To **K** belonged the clans of the
16: 1 Korah son of Izhar, the son of **K**,
26:57 through **K**, the Kohathite clan;
26:58 (**K** was the forefather of Amram;
1Ch 6: 1 The sons of Levi: Gershon, **K** and
6: 2 The sons of **K**: Amram, Izhar, Hebron
6:16 The sons of Levi: Gershon, **K** and
6:18 The sons of **K**: Amram, Izhar, Hebron
6:22 The descendants of **K**: Amminadab his
6:38 the son of Izhar, the son of **K**, the
15: 5 From the descendants of **K**, Uriel the
23: 6 sons of Levi: Gershon, **K** and Merari.
23:12 The sons of **K**: Amram, Izhar, Hebron
2Ch 34:12 and Meshullam, descended from **K**.

Kohath's (Kohath)
Jos 21: 5 The rest of **K** descendants were
1Ch 6:61 The rest of **K** descendants were

Kohathite (Kohath)
Nu 3:19 The **K** clans: Amram, Izhar, Hebron
3:27 Uzzielites; these were the **K** clans.
3:29 The **K** clans were to camp on the
3:30 The leader of the families of the **K**
4: 2 "Take a census of the **K** branch of
4:18 "See that the **K** tribal clans are not
4:37 all those in the **K** clans who served
26:57 through Kohath, the **K** clan;
Jos 21:10 from the **K** clans of the Levites,
21:20 The rest of the **K** clans of the
21:26 given to the rest of the **K** clans.
1Ch 6:54 of Aaron who were from the **K** clan,
6:60 the **K** clans, were thirteen in all.
6:66 Some of the **K** clans were given as
6:70 to the rest of the **K** clans.
9:32 Some of their **K** brothers were in

Kohathites (Kohath)
Nu 3:28 The **K** were responsible for the care
4: 4 "This is the work of the **K** in the
4:15 **K** are to come to do the carrying.
4:15 The **K** are to carry those things that
4:20 the **K** must not go in to look at the
4:34 the **K** by their clans and families.
7: 9 Moses did not give any to the **K**,
10:21 the **K** set out, carrying the holy
Jos 21: 4 The first lot came out for the **K**,
1Ch 6:33 From the **K**: Heman, the musician,
2Ch 20:19 some Levites from the **K** and
29:12 from the **K**, Mahath son of Amasai

Kolaiah
Ne 11: 7 the son of Pedaiah, the son of **K**,
Jer 29:21 says about Ahab son of **K** and

Korah (Korah's, Korahite, Korahites)
1. Son of Esau; Edomite chief (Ge 36:5,14,18).
2. Grandson of Kohath (1Ch 6:22); ancestor of group of musicians (Ps 42; 44–49; 84; 85; 87; 88) and temple gatekeepers (1Ch 9:19; 26:1,19); led rebellion against Moses; killed by God (Nu 16; 26:9–11; Jude 11).
3. Son of Hebron (1Ch 2:43).

Ge 36: 5 Oholibamah bore Jeush, Jalam and **K**.
36:14 bore to Esau: Jeush, Jalam and **K**.
36:16 **K**, Gatam and Amalek. These were the
36:18 Chiefs Jeush, Jalam and **K**.
Ex 6:21 The sons of Izhar were **K**, Nepheg and
6:24 The sons of **K** were Assir, Elkanah
Nu 16: 1 **K** son of Izhar, the son of Kohath,
16: 5 he said to **K** and all his followers:
16: 6 You, **K**, and all your followers are
16: 8 Moses also said to **K**, "Now listen,
16:16 Moses said to **K**, "You and all your
16:19 **K** had gathered all his followers in
16:24 the tents of **K**, Dathan and Abiram.
16:27 they moved away from the tents of **K**,
16:40 become like **K** and his followers.
16:49 to those who had died because of **K**.
26:10 and swallowed them along with **K**,
26:11 The line of **K**, however, did not die
1Ch 1:35 Eliphaz, Reuel, Jeush, Jalam and **K**.
2:43 The sons of Hebron: **K**, Tappuah,
6:22 his son, **K** his son, Assir his son,
6:37 the son of Ebiasaph, the son of **K**,
9:19 the son of Ebiasaph, the son of **K**,
26:19 were descendants of **K** and Merari.
Ps 42: T A maskil of the Sons of **K**.
44: T Of the Sons of **K**. A maskil.
45: T Of the Sons of **K**. A maskil.
46: T director of music. Of the Sons of **K**.
47: T director of music. Of the Sons of **K**.
48: T A song. A psalm of the Sons of **K**.
49: T director of music. Of the Sons of **K**.
84: T Of the Sons of **K**. A psalm.
85: T director of music. Of the Sons of **K**.
87: T Of the Sons of **K**. A psalm. A song.
88: T A song. A psalm of the Sons of **K**.

Korah's (Korah)
Nu 16:32 all **K** men and all their possessions.
26: 9 were among **K** followers when they
27: 3 He was not among **K** followers, who
Jude :11 have been destroyed in **K** rebellion.

Korahite (Korah)
Ex 6:24 These were the **K** clans.
Nu 26:58 the Mushite clan, the **K** clan.
1Ch 9:31 the firstborn son of Shallum the **K**,

Korahites (Korah)
1Ch 9:19 gatekeepers from his family (the **K**)
12: 6 Azarel, Joezer and Jashobeam the **K**;
26: 1 From the **K**: Meshelemiah son of Kore,
2Ch 20:19 and **K** stood up and praised the LORD,

Korazin
Mt 11:21 "Woe to you, **K**! Woe to you,
Lk 10:13 "Woe to you, **K**! Woe to you,

Kore
1Ch 9:19 Shallum son of **K**, the son of
26: 1 son of **K**, one of the sons of Asaph.
2Ch 31:14 **K** son of Imnah the Levite, keeper of

Koum
Mk 5:41 "Talitha **k**!" (which means, "Little

Koz
1Ch 4: 8 **K**, who was the father of Anub and

Kue
1Ki 10:28 from **K**—the royal merchants
10:28 merchants purchased them from **K**.
2Ch 1:16 from **K**—the royal merchants
1:16 merchants purchased them from **K**.

Kushaiah
1Ch 15:17 the Merarites, Ethan son of **K**;

Laadah
1Ch 4:21 **L** the father of Mareshah and the

Laban (Laban's)
Brother of Rebekah (Ge 24:29); gave permission for sister to marry Isaac (Ge 24:50–51). Received Jacob (Ge 29:13–14); gave daughters, Leah and Rachel, in exchange for service (Ge 29:15–30). Deceived by Jacob (Ge 30:25–31:21); pursued and made covenant with him (Ge 31:22–55).

Ge 24:29 Now Rebekah had a brother named **L**,
24:33 "Then tell us," ⌊**L**⌋ said.
24:50 **L** and Bethuel answered, "This is
25:20 and sister of **L** the Aramean.
27:43 at once to my brother **L** in Haran.
28: 2 from among the daughters of **L**,
28: 5 to **L** son of Bethuel the Aramean,
29: 5 He said to them, "Do you know **L**,
29:10 Jacob saw Rachel daughter of **L**, his
29:13 soon as **L** heard the news about Jacob,
29:14 **L** said to him, "You are my own flesh
29:15 **L** said to him, "Just because you are
29:16 Now **L** had two daughters; the name of
29:19 **L** said, "It's better that I give her
29:21 Jacob said to **L**, "Give me my wife.
29:22 **L** brought together all the people of
29:24 **L** gave his servant girl Zilpah to
29:25 So Jacob said to **L**, "What is this
29:26 **L** replied, "It is not our custom
29:28 and then **L** gave him his daughter
29:29 **L** gave his servant girl Bilhah to
29:30 he worked for **L** another seven years.
30:25 Jacob said to **L**, "Send me on my way
30:27 **L** said to him, "If I have found
30:34 "Agreed," said **L**. "Let it be as you
30:40 animals that belonged to **L**.
30:42 the weak animals went to **L** and the
31:12 all that **L** has been doing to you.
31:19 **L** had gone to shear his sheep,
31:20 Jacob deceived **L** the Aramean
31:22 On the third day **L** was told that
31:24 God came to **L** the Aramean in a dream
31:25 of Gilead when **L** overtook him,
31:25 **L** and his relatives camped there too.
31:26 **L** said to Jacob, "What have you done?
31:31 Jacob answered **L**, "I was afraid,
31:33 **L** went into Jacob's tent and into
31:34 **L** searched through everything in the
31:36 Jacob was angry and took **L** to task.
31:36 "What is my crime?" he asked **L**.
31:43 **L** answered Jacob, "The women are my
31:47 **L** called it Jegar Sahadutha, and
31:48 **L** said, "This heap is a witness
31:51 **L** also said to Jacob, "Here is this
31:55 **L** kissed his grandchildren and his
32: 4 I have been staying with **L** and have
46:18 whom **L** had given to his daughter
46:25 whom **L** had given to his daughter
Dt 1: 1 and Tophel, **L**, Hazeroth and Dizahab.

Laban's (Laban)
Ge 29:10 his mother's brother, and **L** sheep,
30:36 to tend the rest of **L** flocks.
30:40 and did not put them with **L** animals.
31: 1 Jacob heard that **L** sons were saying,
31: 2 Jacob noticed that **L** attitude

Labour (Laboured, Labourer, Labourer's, Labourers, Labouring, Labours)
Ge 5:29 "He will comfort us in the **l** and
49:15 the burden and submit to forced **l**.
Ex 1:11 them to oppress them with forced **l**,
1:14 made their lives bitter with hard **l**

Ex 1:14 in all their hard l the Egyptians
2:11 and watched them at their hard l.
5: 4 the people away from their l?
20: 9 Six days you shall l and do all your
34:21 "Six days you shall l, but on the
Dt 5:13 Six days you shall l and do all your
20:11 to forced l and shall work for you.
26: 6 us suffer, putting us to hard l.
28:33 eat what your land and l produce,
Jos 16:10 but are required to do forced l.
17:13 subjected the Canaanites to forced l
Jdg 1:28 the Canaanites into forced l but
1:30 they did subject them to forced l.
1:35 they too were pressed into forced l.
1Sa 4:19 she went into l and gave birth, but
4:19 but was overcome by her l pains.
2Sa 12:31 consigning them to l with saws and
20:24 Adoniram was in charge of forced l;
1Ki 4: 6 son of Abda—in charge of forced l.
5:14 was in charge of the forced l.
9:15 Here is the account of the forced l
9:21 slave l force, as it is to this day.
11:28 l force of the house of Joseph.
12: 4 but now lighten the harsh l and the
12:18 who was in charge of forced l, but
1Ch 20: 3 consigning them to l with saws and
2Ch 8: 8 slave l force, as it is to this day.
10: 4 but now lighten the harsh l and the
10:18 who was in charge of forced l, but
Job 24: 5 the poor go about their l of
37: 7 work, he stops every man from his l.
39: 3 young; their l pains are ended.
39:16 cares not that her l was in vain,
Ps 48: 6 pain like that of a woman in l.
104:23 man goes out to his work, to his l
107:12 he subjected them to bitter l; they
109:11 plunder the fruits of his l.
127: 1 the house, its builders l in vain.
128: 2 You will eat the fruit of your l;
Pr 12:24 rule, but laziness ends in slave l.
Ecc 1: 3 What does man gain from all his l at
2:10 this was the reward for all my l.
2:20 all my toilsome l under the sun.
4: 4 I saw that all l and all achievement
5:15 nothing from his l that he can carry
5:18 find satisfaction in his toilsome l
8:16 to observe man's l on earth—his
9: 9 in your toilsome l under the sun.
SS 8: 5 she who was in l gave you birth.
Isa 13: 8 they will writhe like a woman in l.
21: 3 like those of a woman in l;
23: 4 "I have neither been in l nor given
31: 8 young men will be put to forced l.
54: 1 you who were never in l;
55: 2 and your l on what does not satisfy?
66: 7 "Before she goes into l, she gives
66: 8 Yet no sooner is Zion in l than she
Jer 3:24 fruits of our fathers' l—their
4:31 I hear a cry as of a woman in l, a
6:24 pain like that of a woman in l.
13:21 grip you like that of a woman in l?
22:13 not paying them for their l.
22:23 pain like that of a woman in l!
30: 6 on his stomach like a woman in l,
31: 8 expectant mothers and women in l;
48:41 be like the heart of a woman in l.
49:22 be like the heart of a woman in l.
49:24 pain like that of a woman in l.
50:43 pain like that of a woman in l.
51:58 nations' l is only fuel for the
Lam 1: 3 After affliction and harsh l, Judah
Mic 4: 9 you like that of a woman in l?
4:10 like a woman in l, for now you must
5: 3 when she who is in l gives birth
Hab 2:13 peoples' l is only fuel for the fire
Hag 1:11 and on the l of your hands."
Mt 6:28 They do not l or spin.
Lk 12:27 They do not l or spin. Yet I tell
Jn 4:38 reaped the benefits of their l."
1Co 3: 8 be rewarded according to his own l.
15:58 your l in the Lord is not in vain.
Gal 4:27 you who have no l pains;
Php 1:22 this will mean fruitful l for me.
2:16 that I did not run or l for nothing.
Col 1:29 To this end I l, struggling with all
1Th 1: 3 your l prompted by love, and your
1Th 5: 3 as l pains on a pregnant woman, and
1Ti 4:10 (and for this we l and strive), that
Rev 14:13 they will rest from their l, for

Laboured (Labour)

Isa 47:12 which you have l at since childhood.
47:15 do for you—these you have l with
49: 4 I said, "I have l to no purpose; I
2Co 11:27 I have l and toiled and have often

Labourer (Labour)

Ecc 5:12 The sleep of a l is sweet, whether

Labourer's (Labour)

Pr 16:26 The l appetite works for him; his

Labourers (Labour)

Jdg 1:33 Beth Anath became forced l for them.
1Ki 5:13 King Solomon conscripted l from all
2Ch 34:13 had charge of the l and supervised
Ne 4:10 "The strength of the l is giving out,
Mal 3: 5 those who defraud l of their wages,

Labouring (Labour)

2Th 3: 8 worked night and day, l and toiling

Labours (Labour)

Ecc 2:22 with which he l under the sun?
1Co 16:16 who joins in the work, and l at it.

Lachish

Canaanite royal city in the lowlands of Judah near Libnah. Its king joined the alliance against Joshua but the alliance was defeated and the city was taken (Jos 10:1–35). Allotted to Judah (Jos 15:39). Fortified by Rehoboam (2Ch 11:5–9). Amaziah fled here from Jerusalem (2Ki 14:19; 2Ch 25:27). Captured by Sennacherib, it became base for negotiations with Hezekiah (2Ki 18:13–17; 2Ch 32:9; Isa 36:1–2). It was 1 of 2 fortified cities left in Judah during the Babylonian invasion (Jer 34:7). Denounced by Micah for its sin (Mic 1:13).

Jos 10: 3 king of L and Debir king of Eglon.
10: 5 Jarmuth, L and Eglon—joined forces.
10:23 Hebron, Jarmuth, L and Eglon.
10:31 with him moved on from Libnah to L;
10:32 The LORD handed L over to Israel,
10:33 king of Gezer had come up to help L,
10:34 with him moved on from L to Eglon;
10:35 in it, just as they had done to L.
12:11 the king of L one
15:39 L, Bozkath, Eglon,
2Ki 14:19 and he fled to L, but they sent men
14:19 after him to L and killed him there.
18:14 of Assyria at L: "I have done wrong.
18:17 from L to King Hezekiah at Jerusalem
19: 8 that the king of Assyria had left L,
2Ch 11: 9 Adoraim, L, Azekah,
25:27 him in Jerusalem and he fled to L,
25:27 after him to L and killed him there.
32: 9 his forces were laying siege to L,
Ne 11:30 Adullam and their villages, in L and
Isa 36: 2 from L to King Hezekiah at Jerusalem
37: 8 that the king of Assyria had left L,
Jer 34: 7 still holding out—L and Azekah.
Mic 1:13 You who live in L, harness the team

Lack (Lacked, Lacking, Lacks)

Dt 8: 9 be scarce and you will l nothing;
Job 4:11 The lion perishes for l of prey, and
24: 8 and hug the rocks for l of shelter.
31:19 anyone perishing for l of clothing
34:35 knowledge; his words l insight.'
38:41 God and wander about for l of food?
Ps 34: 9 for those who fear him l nothing.
34:10 who seek the LORD l no good thing.
94:10 Does he who teaches man l knowledge?
Pr 5:23 He will die for l of discipline, led
9: 4 she says to those who l judgment.
9:16 she says to those who l judgment.
10:21 but fools die for l of judgment.
11:14 For l of guidance a nation falls,
15:22 Plans fail for l of counsel, but
Pr 22:27 if you l the means to pay, your very
28:27 gives to the poor will l nothing
Isa 5:13 into exile for l of understanding;
34:16 be missing, not one will l her mate.
50: 2 Do I l the strength to rescue you?
50: 2 for l of water and die of thirst.
51:14 dungeon, nor will they l bread.
56:10 they all l knowledge; they are all
56:11 are shepherds who l understanding
Jer 14: 6 eyesight fails for l of pasture."
Lam 4: 9 waste away for l of food from the
Hos 4: 6 are destroyed from l of knowledge
Am 4: 6 and l of bread in every town,
Zec 10: 2 sheep oppressed for l of a shepherd.
Mt 13:58 there because of their l of faith.
19:20 "What do I still l?"
Mk 6: 6 he was amazed at their l of faith.
10:21 "One thing you l," he said. "Go,
16:14 he rebuked them for their l of faith
Lk 18:22 said to him, "You still l one thing.
22:35 bag or sandals, did you l anything?"
Ro 3: 3 Will their l of faith nullify God's
1Co 1: 7 you do not l any spiritual gift as
7: 5 because of your l of self-control.
Col 2:23 but they l any value in restraining

Lacked (Lack)

Dt 2: 7 you, and you have not l anything.
Jdg 18: 7 And since their land l nothing, they
1Ki 11:22 "What have you l here that you want
Ne 9:21 them in the desert; they l nothing,
Pr 7: 7 young men, a youth who l judgment.
1Co 12:24 honour to the parts that l it,

Lacking (Lack)

1Ki 4:27 They saw to it that nothing was l.
Job 24: 7 L clothes, they spend the night
24:10 L clothes, they go about naked;
Pr 17:18 A man l in judgment strikes hands in
Ecc 1:15 what is l cannot be counted.
Ro 12:11 Never be l in zeal, but keep your
1Co 16:17 have supplied what was l from you.
Col 1:24 l in regard to Christ's afflictions,
1Th 3:10 and supply what is l in your faith.
Jas 1: 4 mature and complete, not l anything.

Lacks (Lack)

Jdg 18:10 a land that l nothing whatever."
2Sa 3:29 falls by the sword or who l food."
Pr 6:32 a man who commits adultery l
10:13 for the back of him who l judgment.
11:12 A man who l judgment derides his
12:11 he who chases fantasies l judgment.
15:21 Folly delights a man who l judgment,
24:30 vineyard of the man who l judgment;
25:28 is a man who l self-control.
28:16 A tyrannical ruler l judgment, but
31:11 in her and l nothing of value.
Ecc 6: 2 so that he l nothing his heart
10: 3 the fool l sense and shows everyone
SS 7: 2 goblet that never l blended wine.
Eze 34: 8 because my flock l a shepherd and so
Jas 1: 5 If any of you l wisdom, he should

Ladan

1Ch 7:26 L his son, Ammihud his son, Elishama
23: 7 Belonging to the Gershonites: L and
23: 8 The sons of L: Jehiel the first,
23: 9 were the heads of the families of L.
26:21 The descendants of L, who were
26:21 who were Gershonites through L and
26:21 to L the Gershonite, were Jehieli,

Laden (Load)

Job 36:16 of your table l with choice food.
36:17 now you are l with the judgment due
Ps 105:37 He brought out Israel, l with silver

Ladies (Lady)

Jdg 5:29 The wisest of her l answer her;

Lady (Ladies)

2Jn : 1 The elder, To the chosen l and her
: 5 now, dear l, I am not writing you a

Lael
Nu 3:24 Gershonites was Eliasaph son of **L.**

Lagging
Dt 25:18 cut off all who were **l** behind;

Lahad
1Ch 4: 2 Jahath the father of Ahumai and **L.**

Lahmas
Jos 15:40 Cabbon, **L**, Kitlish,

Lahmi
1Ch 20: 5 killed **L** the brother of Goliath

Laid (Lay[1])
Ge 9:23 Shem and Japheth took a garment and **l**
22: 9 son Isaac and **l** him on the altar,
Ex 19:13 not a hand is to be **l** on him.
22: 8 to determine whether he has **l** his
Lev 8:14 his sons **l** their hands on its head.
8:18 his sons **l** their hands on its head.
8:22 his sons **l** their hands on its head.
9:20 these they **l** on the breasts, and
26:33 Your land will be **l** waste, and your
Nu 27:23 he **l** his hands on him and
Dt 24: 5 or have any other duty **l** on him.
34: 9 Moses had **l** his hands on him.
Jos 2: 6 of flax she had **l** out on the roof.)
2:19 on our head if a hand is **l** on him.
Jdg 2:20 that I **l** down for their forefathers
16:24 the one who **l** waste our land and
Ru 4:16 Naomi took the child, **l** him in her
1Sa 19:13 Michal took an idol and **l** it on the
2Sa 22:16 **l** bare at the rebuke of the LORD,
1Ki 1:21 my lord the king is **l** to rest with
6:37 was **l** in the fourth year, in the
7:10 The foundations were **l** with large
12:11 My father **l** on you a heavy yoke;
13:29 **l** it on the donkey, and brought it
13:30 he **l** the body in his own tomb, and
16:17 Gibbethon and **l** siege to Tirzah.
16:34 He **l** its foundations at the cost of
17:19 was staying, and **l** him on his bed.
18:33 into pieces and **l** it on the wood.
2Ki 4:21 She went up and **l** him on the bed of
4:31 Gehazi went on ahead and **l** the staff
6:24 marched up and **l** siege to Samaria.
17: 5 and **l** siege to it for three years.
18: 9 against Samaria and **l** siege to it.
19:17 Assyrian kings have **l** waste these
22:19 would become accursed and **l** waste,
24:10 on Jerusalem and **l** siege to it,
1Ch 6:32 to the regulations **l** down for them.
20: 1 He **l** waste the land of the Ammonites
2Ch 3: 3 The foundation Solomon **l** for
8:16 the LORD was **l** until its completion.
10:11 My father **l** on you a heavy yoke;
16:14 They **l** him on a bier covered with
29:23 and they **l** their hands on them.
32: 1 He **l** siege to the fortified cities,
Ezr 3: 6 LORD's temple had not yet been **l**.
3:10 the builders **l** the foundation of the
3:11 of the house of the LORD was **l**.
3:12 foundation of his temple being **l**,
5:16 this Sheshbazzar came and **l** the
6: 3 and let its foundations be **l**.
Ne 3: 3 They **l** its beams and put its doors
3: 6 They **l** its beams and put its doors
Job 14:10 man dies and is **l** low; he breathes
16:18 may my cry never be **l** to rest!
38: 4 "Where were you when I **l** the earth's
38: 6 set, or who **l** its cornerstone—
Ps 18:15 of the earth **l** bare at your rebuke,
66:11 prison and **l** burdens on our backs.
102:25 In the beginning you **l** the
119: 4 You have **l** down precepts that are to
119:25 I am **l** low in the dust; preserve my
119:138 The statutes you have **l** down are
139: 5 you have **l** your hand upon me.
141: 9 Keep me from the snares they have **l**
Pr 3:19 the LORD **l** the earth's foundations
Ecc 1:13 What a heavy burden God has **l** on men!
3:10 seen the burden God has **l** on men.
Isa 1: 7 **l** waste as when overthrown by
6:13 the land, it will again be **l** waste.
7:16 two kings you dread will be **l** waste.
14: 8 "Now that you have been **l** low, no
14:12 you who once **l** low the nations!
24: 3 The earth will be completely **l** waste
28: 1 the pride of those **l** low by wine!
37:18 Assyrian kings have **l** waste all
44:28 temple, "Let its foundations be **l**.
47: 6 on the aged you **l** a very heavy yoke.
48:13 My own hand **l** the foundations of the
49:17 who **l** you waste depart from you.
49:19 made desolate and your land **l** waste,
51:13 and **l** the foundations of the earth,
51:16 who **l** the foundations of the earth,
53: 6 has **l** on him the iniquity of us all.
Jer 2:15 They have **l** waste his land; his
9:12 the land been ruined and **l** waste
12:11 the whole land will be **l** waste
18:16 Their land will be **l** waste, an
25:37 The peaceful meadows will be **l** waste
39: 1 his whole army and **l** siege to it.
46:15 Why will your warriors be **l** low?
46:19 for Memphis will be **l** waste and lie
48: 9 salt on Moab, for she will be **l** waste
Lam 1:10 The enemy **l** hands on all her
2: 6 He has **l** waste his dwelling like a
3:28 for the LORD has **l** it on him.
Eze 6: 6 the towns will be **l** waste and the
6: 6 so that your altars will be **l** waste
12:20 The inhabited towns will be **l** waste
13:14 that its foundation will be **l** bare.
21:29 it will be **l** on the necks of the
24: 2 **l** siege to Jerusalem this very day.
25: 3 land of Israel when it was **l** waste
32:19 and be **l** among the uncircumcised.'
32:25 they are **l** among the slain.
32:29 **l** with those killed by the sword.
32:32 will be **l** among the uncircumcised,
35:12 You said, "They have been **l** waste
36:35 "This land that was **l** waste has
Hos 5: 9 Ephraim will be **l** waste on the day
Joel 1: 7 has **l** waste my vines and ruined my
Mic 5: 1 troops, for a siege is **l** against us.
Na 2: 2 though destroyers have **l** them waste
Hag 2:15 **l** on another in the LORD's temple.
2:18 of the LORD's temple was **l**.
Zec 4: 9 "The hands of Zerubbabel have **l** the
8: 9 **l** for the house of the LORD Almighty,
Mt 15:30 the mute and many others, and **l** them
22:15 the Pharisees went out and **l** plans
Mk 6:29 took his body and **l** it in a tomb.
15:47 mother of Joses saw where he was **l**.
16: 6 See the place where they **l** him.
Lk 6:48 deep and **l** the foundation on rock.
12:19 of good things **l** up for many years.
16:20 At his gate was **l** a beggar named
19:20 kept it **l** away in a piece of cloth.
23:53 one in which no-one had yet been **l**.
23:55 tomb and how his body was **l** in it.
Jn 7:30 but no-one **l** a hand on him, because
7:44 him, but no-one **l** a hand on him.
11:34 "Where have you **l** him?" he asked.
11:38 with a stone **l** across the entrance.
19:41 in which no-one had ever been **l**.
19:42 was near by, they **l** Jesus there.
Ac 5:15 **l** them on beds and mats so that at
6: 6 prayed and **l** their hands on them.
7:58 the witnesses **l** their clothes at
13:29 from the tree and **l** him in a tomb.
1Co 3:10 **l** a foundation as an expert builder
3:11 already **l**, which is Jesus Christ.
14:25 the secrets of his heart will be **l**
1Ti 4:14 body of elders **l** their hands on you.
Heb 1:10 "In the beginning, O Lord, you **l** the
4:13 Everything is uncovered and **l** bare
2Pe 3:10 and everything in it will be **l** bare.
1Jn 3:16 Jesus Christ **l** down his life for us.
Rev 21:16 The city was **l** out like a square, as

Lain (Lie[1])
Ge 24:16 virgin; no man had ever **l** with her.
1Sa 26: 5 commander of the army, had **l** down.

Lair (Lairs)
Jer 4: 7 A lion has come out of his **l**;
25:38 Like a lion he will leave his **l**, and
Zep 2:15 she has become, a **l** for wild beasts!

Lairs (Lair)
Na 2:12 filling his **l** with the kill and his

Laish
Jdg 18: 7 the five men left and came to **L**,
18:14 land of **L** said to their brothers,
18:27 and his priest, and went on to **L**,
18:29 the city used to be called **L**.
1Sa 25:44 son of **L**, who was from Gallim.
2Sa 3:15 from her husband Paltiel son of **L**.

Laishah
Isa 10:30 Listen, O **L**! Poor Anathoth!

Lake
Dt 33:23 he will inherit southward to the **l**."
Mt 4:13 which was by the **l** in the area of
4:18 into the **l**, for they were fishermen.
8:18 to cross to the other side of the **l**.
8:24 a furious storm came up on the **l**, so
8:32 into the **l** and died in the water.
13: 1 out of the house and sat by the **l**.
13:47 the **l** and caught all kinds of fish.
14:25 went out to them, walking on the **l**.
14:26 on the **l**, they were terrified.
16: 5 they went across the **l**, the
17:27 go to the **l** and throw out your line.
Mk 1:16 into the **l**, for they were fishermen.
2:13 again Jesus went out beside the **l**.
3: 7 with his disciples to the **l**,
4: 1 Again Jesus began to teach by the **l**.
4: 1 a boat and sat in it out on the **l**,
5: 1 They went across the **l** to the region
5:13 bank into the **l** and were drowned.
5:21 by boat to the other side of the **l**,
5:21 round him while he was by the **l**.
6:47 of the **l**, and he was alone on land.
6:48 went out to them, walking on the **l**.
6:49 when they saw him walking on the **l**,
Lk 5: 1 was standing by the **L** of Gennesaret,
8:22 go over to the other side of the **l**.
8:23 A squall came down on the **l**, so that
8:26 which is across the **l** from Galilee.
8:33 bank into the **l** and was drowned.
Jn 6:16 his disciples went down to the **l**,
6:17 set off across the **l** for Capernaum.
6:22 stayed on the opposite shore of the **l**
6:25 him on the other side of the **l**,
Rev 19:20 into the fiery **l** of burning sulphur.
20:10 thrown into the **l** of burning sulphur
20:14 Hades were thrown into the **l** of fire.
20:14 The **l** of fire is the second death.
20:15 he was thrown into the **l** of fire.
21: 8 in the fiery **l** of burning sulphur.

Lakkum
Jos 19:33 to **L** and ending at the Jordan.

Lama
Mt 27:46 "Eloi, Eloi, **l** sabachthani?"
Mk 15:34 "Eloi, Eloi, **l** sabachthani?"

Lamb (*Lamb of God*, Lamb's, Lambs)
Ge 22: 7 is the **l** for the burnt offering?"
22: 8 **l** for the burnt offering, my son.
30:32 **l** and every spotted or speckled goat.
30:33 or any **l** that is not dark-coloured,
Ex 12: 3 man is to take a **l** for his family,
12: 4 is too small for a whole **l**,
12: 4 You are to determine the amount of **l**
12:21 and slaughter the Passover **l**.
13:13 Redeem with a **l** every firstborn
29:40 With the first **l** offer a tenth of an
29:41 Sacrifice the other **l** at twilight
34:20 Redeem the firstborn donkey with a **l**,
Lev 3: 7 If he offers a **l**, he is to present
4:32 "If he brings a **l** as his sin
4:35 the **l** of the fellowship offering,

Lev 5: 6 must bring to the LORD a female l or
5: 7 "'If he cannot afford a l, he is to
9: 3 a calf and a l—both a year old and
12: 6 a year-old l for a burnt offering
12: 8 If she cannot afford a l, she is to
14:10 male lambs and one ewe l a year old,
14:13 He is to slaughter the l in the holy
14:21 he must take one male l as a guilt
14:24 The priest is to take the l for the
14:25 He shall slaughter the l for the
17: 3 a l or a goat in the camp or outside
22:27 "When a calf, a l or a goat is born,
23:12 LORD a l a year old without defect,
Nu 6:12 year-old male l as a guilt offering.
6:14 a year-old male l without defect for
6:14 a year-old ewe l without defect for
7:15 one male l a year old, for a burnt
7:21 one male l a year old, for a burnt
7:27 one male l a year old, for a burnt
7:33 one male l a year old, for a burnt
7:39 one male l a year old, for a burnt
7:45 one male l a year old, for a burnt
7:51 one male l a year old, for a burnt
7:57 one male l a year old, for a burnt
7:63 one male l a year old, for a burnt
7:69 one male l a year old, for a burnt
7:75 one male l a year old, for a burnt
7:81 one male l a year old, for a burnt
9:11 They are to eat the l, together with
15: 5 With each l for the burnt offering
15:11 Each bull or ram, each l or young
28: 4 Prepare one l in the morning and the
28: 7 hin of fermented drink with each l.
28: 8 Prepare the second l at twilight,
28:13 with each l, a grain offering of a
28:14 and with each l, a quarter of a hin.
1Sa 7: 9 Samuel took a suckling l and offered
2Sa 12: 3 one little ewe l that he had bought.
12: 4 Instead, he took the ewe l that
12: 6 He must pay for that l four times
2Ch 30:15 They slaughtered the Passover l on
35: 1 and the Passover l was slaughtered
Ezr 6:20 the Passover l for all the exiles,
Isa 11: 6 The wolf will live with the l, the
53: 7 was led like a l to the slaughter,
65:25 The wolf and the l will feed
66: 3 and whoever offers a l, like one who
Jer 11:19 I had been like a gentle l led to
Eze 46:13 you are to provide a year-old l
46:15 the l and the grain offering and the
Mk 14:12 to sacrifice the Passover l, Jesus'
Lk 22: 7 the Passover l had to be sacrificed.
Ac 8:32 and as a l before the shearer is
1Co 5: 7 For Christ, our Passover l, has been
1Pe 1:19 a l without blemish or defect.
Rev 5: 6 I saw a L, looking as if it had been
5: 8 elders fell down before the L.
5:12 "Worthy is the L, who was slain, to
5:13 to the L be praise and honour and
6: 1 I watched as the L opened the first
6: 3 the L opened the second seal, I
6: 5 the L opened the third seal, I heard
6: 7 the L opened the fourth seal, I
6:16 throne and from the wrath of the L!
7: 9 the throne and in front of the L.
7:10 sits on the throne, and to the L."
7:14 them white in the blood of the L.
7:17 For the L at the centre of the
12:11 L and by the word of their testimony;
13: 8 book of life belonging to the L that
13:11 two horns like a l, but he spoke like
14: 1 and there before me was the L,
14: 4 They follow the L wherever he goes.
14: 4 as firstfruits to God and the L.
14:10 of the holy angels and of the L.
15: 3 of God and the song of the L:
17:14 They will make war against the L,
17:14 but the L will overcome them because
19: 7 For the wedding of the L has come,
19: 9 to the wedding supper of the L!'
21: 9 you the bride, the wife of the L."
21:14 of the twelve apostles of the L.
21:22 Almighty and the L are its temple.
21:23 it light, and the L is its lamp.
22: 1 from the throne of God and of the L
22: 3 The throne of God and of the L will

Lamb of God

Jn 1:29 "Look, the L, who takes away the sin
1:36 passing by, he said, "Look, the L!

Lamb's (Lamb)

Rev 21:27 are written in the L book of life.

Lambs (Lamb)

Ge 21:28 Abraham set apart seven ewe l from
21:29 l you have set apart by themselves?"
21:30 He replied, "Accept these seven l
30:35 them) and all the dark-coloured l,
Ex 12: 7 of the houses where they eat the l.
29:38 each day: two l a year old.
Lev 14:10 male l and one ewe lamb a year old,
14:12 l and offer it as a guilt offering,
23:18 Present with this bread seven male l,
23:19 goat for a sin offering and two l,
23:20 The priest is to wave the two l
Nu 7:17 five male goats and five male l a
7:23 five male goats and five male l a
7:29 five male goats and five male l a
7:35 five male goats and five male l a
7:41 five male goats and five male l a
7:47 five male goats and five male l a
7:53 five male goats and five male l a
7:59 five male goats and five male l a
7:65 five male goats and five male l a
7:71 five male goats and five male l a
7:77 five male goats and five male l a
7:83 five male goats and five male l a
7:87 rams and twelve male l a year old
7:88 goats and sixty male l a year old.
28: 3 two l a year old without defect,
28: 9 make an offering of two l a year old
28:11 seven male l a year old, all without
28:19 seven male l a year old, all without
28:21 with each of the seven l, one-tenth.
28:27 one ram and seven male l a year old
28:29 with each of the seven l, one-tenth.
29: 2 seven male l a year old, all without
29: 4 with each of the seven l, one-tenth.
29: 8 seven male l a year old, all without
29:10 with each of the seven l, one-tenth.
29:13 fourteen male l a year old, all
29:15 with each of the fourteen l,
29:17 fourteen male l a year old, all
29:18 With the bulls, rams and l, prepare
29:20 fourteen male l a year old, all
29:21 With the bulls, rams and l, prepare
29:23 fourteen male l a year old, all
29:24 With the bulls, rams and l, prepare
29:26 fourteen male l a year old, all
29:27 With the bulls, rams and l, prepare
29:29 fourteen male l a year old, all
29:30 With the bulls, rams and l, prepare
29:32 fourteen male l a year old, all
29:33 With the bulls, rams and l, prepare
29:36 seven male l a year old, all without
29:37 With the bull, the ram and the l,
Dt 7:13 the l of your flocks in the land
28: 4 your herds and the l of your flocks.
28:18 your herds and the l of your flocks.
28:51 of your herds or l of your flocks
32:14 flock and with fattened l and goats,
1Sa 15: 9 and l—everything that was good.
2Ki 3: 4 of Israel with a hundred thousand l
1Ch 29:21 thousand rams and a thousand male l,
2Ch 29:21 seven rams, seven male l and seven
29:22 then they slaughtered the l and
29:32 two hundred male l—all of them for
30:17 Levites had to kill the Passover l
30:17 not consecrate their l to the LORD.
35: 6 Slaughter the Passover l, consecrate
35: 6 the l for your fellow countrymen,
35:11 The Passover l were slaughtered, and
Ezr 6: 9 rams, male l for burnt offerings to
6:17 four hundred male l and, as a sin
7:17 rams and male l, together with their
8:35 seventy-seven male l and, as a sin
Ps 114: 4 skipped like rams, the hills like l.
114: 6 like rams, you hills, like l?
Pr 27:26 the l will provide you with clothing,
Isa 1:11 the blood of bulls and l and goats.
5:17 l will feed among the ruins of the
Isa 16: 1 Send l as tribute to the ruler of
34: 6 the blood of l and goats, fat from
40:11 He gathers the l in his arms and
Jer 51:40 them down like l to the slaughter,
Eze 27:21 with you in l, rams and goats.
39:18 earth as if they were rams and l,
46: 4 six male l and a ram, all without
46: 5 and the grain offering with the l is
46: 6 six l and a ram, all without defect.
46: 7 and with the l as much as he wants
46:11 with the l as much as one pleases
Hos 4:16 LORD pasture them like l in a meadow?
Am 6: 4 on choice l and fattened calves.
Lk 10: 3 I am sending you out like l among
Jn 21:15 Jesus said, "Feed my l."

Lame

Lev 21:18 blind or l, disfigured or deformed;
Dt 15:21 If an animal has a defect, is l or
2Sa 4: 4 had a son who was l in both feet.
5: 6 blind and the l can ward you off.
5: 8 l and blind' who are David's enemies.
5: 8 and l' will not enter the palace."
19:26 since I your servant am l, I said,
Job 29:15 eyes to the blind and feet to the l.
Pr 25:19 Like a bad tooth or a l foot is
26: 7 Like a l man's legs that hang limp
Isa 33:23 even the l will carry off plunder.
35: 6 will the l leap like a deer, and the
Jer 31: 8 them will be the blind and the l,
Mic 4: 6 "I will gather the l; I will
4: 7 I will make the l a remnant, those
Zep 3:19 I will rescue the l and gather those
Mt 11: 5 The blind receive sight, the l walk,
15:30 bringing the l, the blind, the
15:31 the l walking and the blind seeing.
21:14 The blind and the l came to him at
Lk 7:22 the l walk, those who have leprosy
14:13 the crippled, the l, the blind,
14:21 the crippled, the blind and the l.'
Jn 5: 3 blind, the l, the paralysed.
Ac 14: 8 l from birth and had never walked.
Heb 12:13 so that the l may not be disabled,

Lamech

Ge 4:18 and Methushael was the father of L.
4:19 L married two women, one named Adah
4:23 L said to his wives, "Adah and
4:23 wives of L, hear my words.
4:24 times, then L seventy-seven times."
5:25 years, he became the father of L.
5:26 after he became the father of L,
5:28 L had lived 182 years, he had a son.
5:30 After Noah was born, L lived 595
5:31 Altogether, L lived 777 years, and
1Ch 1: 3 Enoch, Methuselah, L, Noah.
Lk 3:36 Shem, the son of Noah, the son of L,

Lament (Lamentation, Lamented, Laments)

2Sa 1:17 David took up this l concerning Saul
1:18 men of Judah be taught this l of the
3:33 The king sang this l for Abner:
Ps 56: 8 Record my l; list my tears on your
102: T and pours out his l before the LORD
Isa 3:26 The gates of Zion will l and mourn;
15: 5 Horonaim they l their destruction.
16: 7 L and grieve for the men of Kir
19: 8 The fishermen will groan and l, all
29: 2 besiege Ariel; she will mourn and l,
Jer 4: 8 put on sackcloth, l and wail, for
7:29 take up a l on the barren heights,
9:10 a l concerning the desert pastures.
9:20 how to wail; teach one another a l.
34: 5 your honour and l, "Alas, O master!"
Lam 2: 8 He made ramparts and walls l;
Eze 2:10 words of l and mourning and woe.
9: 4 l over all the detestable things
19: 1 "Take up a l concerning the princes
19:14 is a l and is to be used as a l."
24:16 do not l or weep or shed any tears.
26:17 they will take up a l concerning you
27: 2 "Son of man, take up a l concerning
27:32 they will take up a l concerning you:
28:12 "Son of man, take up a l concerning

Eze 32: 2 “Son of man, take up a l concerning
32:16 “This is the l they will chant for
Am 5: 1 this l I take up concerning you:

Lamentation (Lament)
Est 9:31 to their times of fasting and l.
Isa 15: 8 Eglaim, their l as far as Beer Elim.
Lam 2: 5 and l for the Daughter of Judah.

Lamented (Lament)
Ge 50:10 near the Jordan, they l loudly and

Laments (Lament)
2Ch 35:25 Jeremiah composed l for Josiah, and
35:25 singers commemorate Josiah in the l.
35:25 in Israel and are written in the L.
Isa 16:11 My heart l for Moab like a harp, my
Jer 48:36 “So my heart l for Moab like a flute;
48:36 it l like a flute for the men of Kir

Lamp (Lamps, Lampstand, Lampstands)
1Sa 3: 3 The l of God had not yet gone out,
2Sa 21:17 l of Israel will not be extinguished.
22:29 You are my l, O LORD; the LORD turns
1Ki 11:36 have a l before me in Jerusalem,
15: 4 the LORD his God gave him a l in
2Ki 4:10 a table, a chair and a l for him.
8:19 promised to maintain a l for David
2Ch 21: 7 had promised to maintain a l for him
Job 18: 5 “The l of the wicked is snuffed out;
18: 6 dark; the l beside him goes out.
21:17 l of the wicked snuffed out?
29: 3 his l shone upon my head and by his
Ps 18:28 You, O LORD, keep my l burning;
119:105 Your word is a l to my feet and a
132:17 and set up a l for my anointed one.
Pr 6:23 For these commands are a l, this
13: 9 the l of the wicked is snuffed out.
20:20 his l will be snuffed out in pitch
20:27 The l of the LORD searches the
21: 4 the l of the wicked, are sin!
24:20 l of the wicked will be snuffed out.
31:18 and her l does not go out at night.
Jer 25:10 millstones and the light of the l.
Mt 5:15 Neither do people light a l and put
6:22 “The eye is the l of the body. If
Mk 4:21 He said to them, “Do you bring in a l
Lk 8:16 “No-one lights a l and hides it in a
11:33 “No-one lights a l and puts it in a
11:34 Your eye is the l of your body. When
11:36 the light of a l shines on you.”
15: 8 Does she not light a l, sweep the
Jn 5:35 John was a l that burned and gave
Rev 18:23 The light of a l will never shine in
21:23 it light, and the Lamb is its l.
22: 5 They will not need the light of a l

Lamps (Lamp)
Ex 25:37 “Then make its seven l and set them
27:20 so that the l may be kept burning.
27:21 his sons are to keep the l burning
30: 7 every morning when he tends the l.
30: 8 when he lights the l at twilight
35:14 l and oil for the light;
37:23 They made its seven l, as well as
39:37 row of l and all its accessories,
40: 4 in the lampstand and set up its l.
40:25 set up the l before the LORD, as the
Lev 24: 2 l may be kept burning continually.
24: 3 Aaron is to tend the l before the
24: 4 The l on the pure gold lampstand
Nu 4: 9 together with its l, its wick
8: 2 ‘When you set up the seven l, they
8: 3 Aaron did so; he set up the l so
1Ki 7:49 gold floral work and l and tongs;
1Ch 28:15 for the gold lampstands and their l,
28:15 weight for each lampstand and its l
28:15 for each silver lampstand and its l
2Ch 4:20 of pure gold with their l,
4:21 the gold floral work and l and tongs
13:11 light the l on the gold lampstand
29: 7 of the portico and put out the l.
Zep 1:12 time I will search Jerusalem with l

Mt 25: 1 like ten virgins who took their l
25: 3 The foolish ones took their l but
25: 4 took oil in jars along with their l.
25: 7 virgins woke up and trimmed their l.
25: 8 of your oil; our l are going out.’
Lk 12:35 for service and keep your l burning,
Ac 20: 8 There were many l in the upstairs
Rev 4: 5 Before the throne, seven l were

Lampstand (Lamp)
Ex 25:31 “Make a l of pure gold and hammer it
25:32 sides of the l—three on one side
25:33 six branches extending from the l.
25:34 on the l there are to be four cups
25:35 of branches extending from the l,
25:36 the l, hammered out of pure gold.
25:39 for the l and all these accessories.
26:35 the l opposite it on the south side.
30:27 the table and all its articles, the l
31: 8 the pure gold l and all its
35:14 the l that is for light with its
37:17 They made the l of pure gold and
37:18 sides of the l—three on one side
37:19 six branches extending from the l.
37:20 on the l were four cups shaped like
37:21 of branches extending from the l,
37:22 the l, hammered out of pure gold.
37:24 They made the l and all its
39:37 the pure gold l with its row of
40: 4 bring in the l and set up its lamps.
40:24 He placed the l in the Tent of
Lev 24: 4 The lamps on the pure gold l before
Nu 3:31 the table, the l, the altars, the
4: 9 and cover the l that is for light,
8: 2 to light the area in front of the l.
8: 3 so that they faced forward on the l
8: 4 This is how the l was made: It was
8: 4 The l was made exactly like the
1Ch 28:15 with the weight for each l and its
28:15 for each silver l and its lamps,
28:15 according to the use of each l;
2Ch 13:11 lamps on the gold l every evening.
Da 5: 5 near the l in the royal palace.
Zec 4: 2 “I see a solid gold l with a bowl at
4:11 on the right and the left of the l?”
Heb 9: 2 In its first room were the l, the
Rev 2: 5 and remove your l from its place.

Lampstands (Lamp)
1Ki 7:49 the l of pure gold (five on the
1Ch 28:15 the weight of gold for the gold l
2Ch 4: 7 He made ten gold l according to the
4:20 the l of pure gold with their lamps,
Jer 52:19 censers, sprinkling bowls, pots, l,
Rev 1:12 when I turned I saw seven golden l,
1:13 among the l was someone “like a son
1:20 and of the seven golden l is this:
1:20 the seven l are the seven churches.
2: 1 and walks among the seven golden l:
11: 4 the two l that stand before the Lord

Lance
Job 39:23 along with the flashing spear and l.
41:29 he laughs at the rattling of the l.

Land (Borderland, *Good land*, Grasslands, *Land flowing with milk and honey*, *Land of Canaan*, *Land of the living*, Land's, Landed, Landowner, Lands, *Live in the land*, Mainland, *People of the land*, *Peoples of the land*, Shorelands, Swampland, Wasteland, Wastelands)
Ge 1:10 God called the dry ground “l”, and
1:11 God said, “Let the l produce
1:11 trees on the l that bear fruit with
1:12 The l produced vegetation: plants
1:24 God said, “Let the l produce living
2:11 l of Havilah, where there is gold.
2:12 (The gold of that l is good;
2:13 winds through the entire l of Cush.
4:14 Today you are driving me from the l,
4:16 lived in the l of Nod, east of Eden.
7:22 Everything on dry l that had the

Ge 10:11 From that l he went to Assyria,
11:28 Chaldeans, in the l of his birth.
12: 1 and go to the l I will show you.
12: 6 Abram travelled through the l as far
12: 6 time the Canaanites were in the l.
12: 7 To your offspring I will give this l.
12:10 Now there was a famine in the l, and
13: 6 the l could not support them while
13: 7 also living in the l at that time.
13: 9 Is not the whole l before you? Let's
13:10 like the l of Egypt, towards Zoar.
13:15 All the l that you see I will give
13:17 the l, for I am giving it to you.”
15: 7 this l to take possession of it.”
15:18 “To your descendants I give this l,
15:19 the l of the Kenites, Kenizzites,
19:23 Zoar, the sun had risen over the l.
19:25 also the vegetation in the l.
19:28 towards all the l of the plain, and
19:28 he saw dense smoke rising from the l
20:15 Abimelech said, “My l is before you;
21:32 to the l of the Philistines.
21:34 Abraham stayed in the l of the
23:15 “Listen to me, my lord; the l is
24: 5 to come back with me to this l?
24: 7 my native l and who spoke to me and
24: 7 your offspring I will give this l’
24:37 the Canaanites, in whose l I live,
25: 6 his son Isaac to the l of the east.
26: 1 Now there was a famine in the l
26: 3 Stay in this l for a while, and I
26:12 Isaac planted crops in that l and
26:22 room and we will flourish in the l.”
27:46 wife from among the women of this l,
28: 4 l where you now live as an alien,
28: 4 alien, the l God gave to Abraham.”
28:13 the l on which you are lying.
28:15 and I will bring you back to this l.
29: 1 to the l of the eastern peoples.
31: 3 “Go back to the l of your fathers
31:13 Now leave this l at once and go back
31:13 once and go back to your native l.
32: 3 the l of Seir, the country of Edom.
34: 1 out to visit the women of the l.
34:10 the l is open to you. Live in it,
34:21 “Let them live in our l and trade in
34:21 the l has plenty of room for them.
34:30 the people living in this l.
35:12 The l I gave to Abraham and Isaac I
35:12 l to your descendants after you.”
36: 6 and moved to a l some distance from
36: 7 the l where they were staying could
36:30 their divisions, in the l of Seir.
36:34 Husham from the l of the Temanites
36:43 settlements in the l they occupied.
37: 1 Jacob lived in the l where his
40:15 off from the l of the Hebrews,
41:19 ugly cows in all the l of Egypt.
41:29 coming throughout the l of Egypt,
41:30 and the famine will ravage the l.
41:31 The abundance in the l will not be
41:33 put him in charge of the l of Egypt.
41:34 commissioners over the l to take
41:41 in charge of the whole l of Egypt.”
41:43 in charge of the whole l of Egypt.
41:45 went throughout the l of Egypt.
41:47 the l produced plentifully.
41:52 fruitful in the l of my suffering.”
41:54 the whole l of Egypt there was food.
42: 6 Now Joseph was the governor of the l,
42: 9 to see where our l is unprotected.”
42:12 to see where our l is unprotected.”
42:30 “The man who is lord over the l
42:30 as though we were spying on the l.
42:33 “Then the man who is lord over the l
42:34 to you, and you can trade in the l.
43: 1 famine was still severe in the l.
43:11 best products of the l in your bags
45: 6 now there has been famine in the l,
45:18 give you the best of the l of Egypt
45:18 and you can enjoy the fat of the l.’
47: 6 the l of Egypt is before you; settle
47: 6 brothers in the best part of the l.
47:11 property in the best part of the l,
47:18 lord except our bodies and our l.
47:19 your eyes—we and our l as well?

Ge 47:19 us and our **l** in exchange for food,
47:19 our **l** will be in bondage to Pharaoh.
47:19 that the **l** may not become desolate."
47:20 Joseph bought all the **l** in Egypt for
47:20 The **l** became Pharaoh's,
47:22 he did not buy the **l** of the priests
47:22 is why they did not sell their **l**.
47:23 you and your **l** today for Pharaoh,
47:26 it as a law concerning **l** in Egypt
47:26 It was only the **l** of the priests
48: 4 and I will give this **l** as an
48:21 you back to the **l** of your fathers.
48:22 I give the ridge of **l** I took from
49:15 place and how pleasant is his **l**,
50:24 take you up out of this **l** to the **l**
Ex 1: 7 so that the **l** was filled with them.
2:22 become an alien in a foreign **l**."
3: 8 that **l** into a good and spacious **l**,
3:17 Egypt into the **l** of the Canaanites,
6: 8 I will bring you to the **l** I swore
8: 5 frogs come up on the **l** of Egypt.
8: 6 the frogs came up and covered the **l**.
8: 7 frogs come up on the **l** of Egypt.
8:14 into heaps, and the **l** reeked of them
8:16 throughout the **l** of Egypt the dust
8:17 dust throughout the **l** of Egypt
8:22 differently with the **l** of Goshen,
8:22 know that I, the LORD, am in this **l**.
8:24 Egypt the **l** was ruined by the flies.
8:25 to your God here in the **l**."
9: 5 the LORD will do this in the **l**."
9: 9 fine dust over the whole **l** of Egypt,
9: 9 men and animals throughout the **l**."
9:23 LORD rained hail on the **l** of Egypt;
9:24 It was the worst storm in all the **l**
9:26 it did not hail was the **l** of Goshen,
9:33 rain no longer poured down on the **l**.
10: 6 day they settled in this **l** till now.
10:12 that locusts will swarm over the **l**
10:13 made an east wind blow across the **l**
10:15 tree or plant in all the **l** of Egypt.
12:23 the LORD goes through the **l** to
12:25 you enter the **l** that the LORD will
12:48 take part like one born in the **l**.
13: 3 out of the **l** of slavery, because the
13: 5 the LORD brings you into the **l** of
13: 5 the **l** he swore to your forefathers
13:11 After the LORD brings you into the **l**
13:14 of Egypt, out of the **l** of slavery.
14: 3 wandering around the **l** in confusion,
14:21 east wind and turned it into dry **l**.
16:35 until they came to a **l** that was
18: 3 become an alien in a foreign **l**";
20: 2 of Egypt, out of the **l** of slavery.
20:12 **l** the LORD your God is giving you.
23:11 let the **l** lie unploughed and unused
23:23 you into the **l** of the Amorites,
23:26 miscarry or be barren in your **l**.
23:29 because the **l** would become desolate
23:30 enough to take possession of the **l**.
23:33 Do not let them live in your **l**, or
32:13 all this **l** I promised them,
33: 1 and go up to the **l** I promised on
34:24 and no-one will covet your **l** when
Lev 11: 2 all the animals that live on the **l**,
14:34 mildew in a house in that **l**,
18:25 Even the **l** was defiled; so I
18:25 the **l** vomited out its inhabitants.
18:27 who lived in the **l** before you,
18:27 you, and the **l** became defiled.
18:28 if you defile the **l**, it will vomit
19: 9 'When you reap the harvest of your **l**,
19:23 "'When you enter the **l** and plant
19:29 or the **l** will turn to prostitution
19:33 you in your **l**, do not ill-treat him.
20:22 so that the **l** where I am bringing
20:24 "You will possess their **l**; I will
22:24 You must not do this in your own **l**,
23:10 'When you enter the **l** I am going to
23:22 'When you reap the harvest of your **l**,
23:39 have gathered the crops of the **l**,
25: 2 'When you enter the **l** I am going to
25: 2 the **l** itself must observe a sabbath
25: 4 in the seventh year the **l** is to have
25: 5 The **l** is to have a year of rest.
25: 6 Whatever the **l** yields during the
Lev 25: 7 and the wild animals in your **l**.
25: 7 Whatever the **l** produces may be eaten.
25: 9 sound the trumpet throughout your **l**.
25:10 proclaim liberty throughout the **l** to
25:14 "'If you sell **l** to one of your
25:18 and you will live safely in the **l**.
25:19 the **l** will yield its fruit, and you
25:21 **l** will yield enough for three years.
25:23 "'The **l** must not be sold
25:23 because the **l** is mine and you are
25:24 provide for the redemption of the **l**.
26: 1 in your **l** to bow down before it.
26: 5 want and live in safety in your **l**.
26: 6 "'I will grant peace in the **l**, and
26: 6 remove savage beasts from the **l**,
26:20 trees of the **l** yield their fruit.
26:32 I will lay waste the **l**, so that your
26:33 Your **l** will be laid waste, and your
26:34 the **l** will enjoy its sabbath years
26:34 **l** will rest and enjoy its sabbaths.
26:35 the **l** will have the rest it did not
26:38 **l** of your enemies will devour you.
26:41 them into the **l** of their enemies
26:42 Abraham, and I will remember the **l**.
26:43 For the **l** will be deserted by them
26:44 when they are in the **l** of their
27:16 to the LORD part of his family **l**,
27:22 which is not part of his family **l**,
27:24 bought it, the one whose **l** it was.
27:28 family **l**—may be sold or redeemed;
27:30 "'A tithe of everything from the **l**,
Nu 10: 9 you go into battle in your own **l**
10:30 back to my own **l** and my own people."
11:12 to the **l** you promised on oath to
13:16 the men Moses sent to explore the **l**.
13:18 See what the **l** is like and whether
13:19 What kind of **l** do they live in? Is
13:20 back some of the fruit of the **l**.
13:21 they went up and explored the **l** from
13:25 they returned from exploring the **l**.
13:26 and showed them the fruit of the **l**.
13:27 "We went into the **l** to which you
13:30 go up and take possession of the **l**,
13:32 about the **l** they had explored.
13:32 They said, "The **l** we explored
14: 3 Why is the LORD bringing us to this **l**
14: 6 explored the **l**, tore their
14: 7 "The **l** we passed through and
14: 8 he will lead us into that **l**,
14:14 the inhabitants of this **l** about it.
14:16 into the **l** he promised them on oath;
14:23 not one of them will ever see the **l**
14:24 I will bring him into the **l** he went
14:30 Not one of you will enter the **l** I
14:31 in to enjoy the **l** you have rejected.
14:34 the forty days you explored the **l**
14:36 men Moses had sent to explore the **l**,
14:37 report about the **l** were struck down
14:38 Of the men who went to explore the **l**,
15: 2 the **l** I am giving you as a
15:18 enter the **l** to which I am taking
15:19 you eat the food of the **l**, present a
18:20 will have no inheritance in their **l**,
20:12 community into the **l** I give them."
20:24 He will not enter the **l** I give the
21:24 his **l** from the Arnon to the Jabbok,
21:26 him all his **l** as far as the Arnon.
21:31 Israel settled in the **l** of the
21:34 you, with his whole army and his **l**.
21:35 And they took possession of his **l**.
22: 5 near the River, in his native **l**.
22: 5 the **l** and have settled next to me.
22:11 of Egypt covers the face of the **l**.
26:53 "The **l** is to be allotted to them as
26:55 Be sure that the **l** is distributed by
27:12 the **l** I have given the Israelites.
32: 4 the **l** the LORD subdued before the
32: 5 "let this **l** be given to your
32: 7 into the **l** the LORD has given them?
32: 8 Kadesh Barnea to look over the **l**.
32: 9 Valley of Eshcol and viewed the **l**,
32: 9 the **l** the LORD had given them.
32:11 the **l** I promised on oath to Abraham,
32:17 from the inhabitants of the **l**.
32:22 the **l** is subdued before the LORD,
32:22 And this **l** will be your possession
Nu 32:29 then when the **l** is subdued before
32:29 the **l** of Gilead as their possession.
32:33 the whole **l** with its cities and the
33:52 the inhabitants of the **l** before you.
33:53 Take possession of the **l** and settle
33:53 I have given you the **l** to possess.
33:54 Distribute the **l** by lot, according
33:55 drive out the inhabitants of the **l**,
33:55 in the **l** where you will live.
34: 2 'When you enter Canaan, the **l** that
34:12 "'This will be your **l**, with its
34:13 this **l** by lot as an inheritance.
34:17 the **l** for you as an inheritance:
34:18 each tribe to help assign the **l**.
35: 8 you give the Levites from the **l** the
35:32 live on his own **l** before the death
35:33 "'Do not pollute the **l** where you
35:33 Bloodshed pollutes the **l**, and
35:33 the **l** on which blood has been shed,
35:34 Do not defile the **l** where you live
36: 2 to give the **l** as an inheritance to
36: 7 **l** inherited from his forefathers.
36: 8 Every daughter who inherits **l** in any
36: 9 tribe is to keep the **l** it inherits."
Dt 1: 7 to the **l** of the Canaanites and to
1: 8 See, I have given you this **l**.
1: 8 Go in and take possession of the **l**
1:21 LORD your God has given you the **l**.
1:22 men ahead to spy out the **l** for us
1:25 them some of the fruit of the **l**,
1:36 the **l** he set his feet on,
1:39 from bad—they will enter the **l**.
2: 5 I will not give you any of their **l**,
2: 9 not give you any part of their **l**.
2:12 just as Israel did in the **l** the LORD
2:19 of any **l** belonging to the Ammonites.
2:20 was considered a **l** of the Rephaites
2:29 **l** the LORD our God is giving us."
2:31 begin to conquer and possess his **l**."
2:37 on any of the **l** of the Ammonites,
2:37 neither the **l** along the course of
3: 2 you with his whole army and his **l**.
3:12 Of the **l** that we took over at that
3:13 to be known as a **l** of the Rephaites.
3:18 you this **l** to take possession of it.
3:20 and they too have taken over the **l**
3:27 Look at the **l** with your own eyes,
3:28 to inherit the **l** that you will see."
4: 1 possession of the **l** that the LORD,
4: 5 you may follow them in the **l** you are
4:14 laws you are to follow in the **l** that
4:22 I will die in this **l**; I will not
4:25 have lived in the **l** a long time—
4:26 you will quickly perish from the **l**
4:38 to bring you into their **l** to give it
4:40 that you may live long in the **l** the
4:46 in the **l** of Sihon king of the
4:47 of his **l** and the **l** of Og king of
4:48 This **l** extended from Aroer on the
5: 6 of Egypt, out of the **l** of slavery.
5:16 **l** the LORD your God is giving you.
5:21 on your neighbour's house or **l**,
5:31 the **l** I am giving them to possess."
5:33 days in the **l** that you will possess.
6: 1 to observe in the **l** that you are
6:10 into the **l** he swore to your fathers,
6:10 a **l** with large, flourishing cities
6:12 of Egypt, out of the **l** of slavery.
6:15 destroy you from the face of the **l**.
6:23 give us the **l** that he promised on
7: 1 the **l** you are entering to possess
7: 8 redeemed you from the **l** of slavery,
7:13 the crops of your **l**—your grain, new
7:13 the lambs of your flocks in the **l**
8: 1 may enter and possess the **l** that the
8: 7 **l** with streams and pools of water
8: 8 a **l** with wheat and barley, vines and
8: 9 a **l** where bread will not be scarce
8: 9 a **l** where the rocks are iron and you
8:14 of Egypt, out of the **l** of slavery.
8:15 that thirsty and waterless **l**, with
9: 4 this **l** because of my righteousness.
9: 5 in to take possession of their **l**;
9:23 of the **l** I have given you.
9:28 into the **l** he had promised them,
10: 7 Jotbathah, a **l** with streams of water.

Dt 10:11 possess the l that I swore to their
11: 8 take over the l that you are
11: 9 that you may live long in the l that
11:10 The l you are entering to take over
11:10 over is not like the l of Egypt,
11:11 the l you are crossing the Jordan to
11:11 possession of is a l of mountains
11:12 is a l the LORD your God cares for;
11:14 I will send rain on your l in its
11:21 may be many in the l that the LORD
11:25 you on the whole l, wherever you go.
11:29 the l you are entering to possess,
11:31 l the LORD your God is giving you.
12: 1 to follow in the l that the LORD,
12:10 settle in the l the LORD your God is
12:19 as long as you live in your l.
12:29 them out and settled in their l,
13: 5 redeemed you from the l of slavery;
13: 7 from one end of the l to the other),
13:10 of Egypt, out of the l of slavery.
15: 4 for in the l the LORD your God is
15: 7 in any of the towns of the l that
15:11 will always be poor people in the l.
15:11 the poor and needy in your l.
16: 4 in all your l for seven days.
16:20 l the LORD your God is giving you.
17:14 you enter the l the LORD your God is
18: 9 you enter the l the LORD your God is
19: 1 nations whose l he is giving you,
19: 2 the l the LORD your God is giving
19: 3 divide into three parts the l the
19: 8 you the whole l he promised them,
19:10 blood will not be shed in your l,
19:14 inheritance you receive in the l
21: 1 lying in a field in the l the LORD
21:23 You must not desecrate the l the
23:20 the l you are entering to possess.
24: 4 Do not bring sin upon the l the LORD
25:15 l the LORD your God is giving you.
25:19 the l he is giving you to possess
26: 1 you have entered the l that the LORD
26: 2 from the soil of the l that the LORD
26: 3 I have come to the l that the LORD
26: 9 to this place and gave us this l,
26:15 bless your people Israel and the l
27: 2 l the LORD your God is giving you,
27: 3 l the LORD your God is giving you,
28: 4 and the crops of your l and the
28: 8 bless you in the l he is giving you.
28:11 the l he swore to your forefathers
28:12 to send rain on your l in season and
28:18 and the crops of your l, and the
28:21 the l you are entering to possess.
28:33 eat what your l and labour produce,
28:42 your trees and the crops of your l.
28:51 of your l until you are destroyed.
28:52 to all the cities throughout your l
28:52 l the LORD your God is giving you.
28:63 the l you are entering to possess.
29: 2 all his officials and to all his l.
29: 8 We took their l and gave it as an
29:19 on the watered l as well as the dry.
29:22 that have fallen on the l
29:23 The whole l will be a burning waste
29:24 has the LORD done this to the l
29:27 LORD's anger burned against this l,
29:28 the LORD uprooted them from their l
29:28 and thrust them into another l,
30: 4 most distant l under the heavens,
30: 5 He will bring you to the l that
30: 9 livestock and the crops of your l.
30:16 the l you are entering to possess.
30:18 You will not live long in the l you
30:20 l he swore to give to your fathers,
31: 3 you will take possession of their l.
31: 4 he destroyed along with their l.
31: 7 must go with this people into the l
31:16 gods of the l they are entering.
31:20 the l I promised on oath to their
31:21 into the l I promised them on oath."
31:23 into the l I promised them on oath,
32:10 In a desert l he found him, in a
32:13 him ride on the heights of the l
32:43 make atonement for his l and people.
32:47 By them you will live long in the l
32:49 and view Canaan, the l I am giving

Dt 32:52 will see the l only from a distance
32:52 you will not enter the l I am giving
33:13 "May the LORD bless his l with the
33:21 He chose the best l for himself; the
33:28 secure in a l of grain and new wine,
34: 1 him the whole l—from Gilead to Dan,
34: 2 l of Judah as far as the western sea,
34: 4 the LORD said to him, "This is the l
34:11 his officials and to his whole l.
Jos 1: 2 the l I am about to give to them
1: 6 lead these people to inherit the l
1:11 take possession of the l the LORD
1:13 rest and has granted you this l.'
1:14 your livestock may stay in the l
1:15 taken possession of the l that the
1:15 may go back and occupy your own l,
2: 1 "Go, look over the l," he said,
2: 2 come here tonight to spy out the l."
2: 3 have come to spy out the whole l."
2: 9 the LORD has given this l to you
2:14 when the LORD gives us the l."
2:18 unless, when we enter the l, you
2:24 given the whole l into our hands;
5: 6 they would not see the l that he had
5:11 ate some of the produce of the l:
5:12 after they ate this food from the l
6:22 the two men who had spied out the l
6:27 his fame spread throughout the l.
8: 1 his people, his city and his l.
9:24 Moses to give you the whole l
11:16 Joshua took this entire l: the hill
11:23 Joshua took the entire l, just as
11:23 Then the l had rest from war.
12: 1 These are the kings of the l whom
12: 6 LORD gave their l to the Reubenites,
12: 7 These are the kings of the l that
13: 1 large areas of l to be taken over.
13: 2 "This is the l that remains: all the
13: 4 from the south, all the l of the
13: 6 Be sure to allocate this l to Israel
13:12 them and taken over their l.
14: 4 Levites received no share of the l
14: 5 the Israelites divided the l, just
14: 7 from Kadesh Barnea to explore the l.
14: 9 on that day Moses swore to me, 'The l
14:15 Then the l had rest from war.
15:19 you have given me l in the Negev
17: 5 of ten tracts of l besides Gilead
17: 6 The l of Gilead belonged to the rest
17: 8 (Manasseh had the l of Tappuah, but
17:10 On the south the l belonged to
17:15 go up into the forest and clear l
17:15 l of the Perizzites and Rephaites."
18: 3 possession of the l that the LORD,
18: 4 to make a survey of the l and to
18: 5 You are to divide the l into seven
18: 6 of the seven parts of the l,
18: 8 on their way to map out the l,
18: 8 make a survey of the l and write a
18: 9 the men left and went through the l.
18:10 and there he distributed the l to
19:49 they had finished dividing the l
19:51 And so they finished dividing the l.
21:43 gave Israel all the l he had sworn
22: 4 return to your homes in the l that
22: 7 Manasseh Moses had given l in Bashan,
22: 7 Joshua gave l on the west side of
22: 9 their own l, which they had acquired
22:13 the priest, to the l of Gilead—
22:19 If the l you possess is defiled,
22:19 come over to the LORD's l, where the
22:19 stands, and share the l with us.
23: 4 the l of the nations that remain
23: 5 you will take possession of their l
24: 3 took your father Abraham from the l
24: 8 brought you to the l of the Amorites
24: 8 and you took possession of their l.
24:13 I gave you a l on which you did not
24:15 Amorites, in whose l you are living.
24:17 from that l of slavery, and
24:18 the Amorites, who lived in the l.
24:30 they buried him in the l of his
24:32 at Shechem in the tract of l that
Jdg 1: 2 I have given the l into their hands."
1:15 Since you have given me l in the
1:26 He then went to the l of the

Jdg 1:27 were determined to live in that l.
1:32 the Canaanite inhabitants of the l.
1:33 the Canaanite inhabitants of the l,
2: 1 led you into the l that I swore to
2: 2 covenant with the people of this l,
2: 6 the l, each to his own inheritance.
2: 9 they buried him in the l of his
3:11 the l had peace for forty years,
3:30 the l had peace for eighty years.
5: 4 when you marched from the l of Edom,
5:31 Then the l had peace for forty years.
6: 4 They camped on the l and ruined the
6: 5 they invaded the l to ravage it.
6: 8 of Egypt, out of the l of slavery.
6: 9 before you and gave you their l.
6:10 the Amorites, in whose l you live.
8:28 the l enjoyed peace for forty years.
9:37 down from the centre of the l,
10: 8 in Gilead, the l of the Amorites.
11: 3 and settled in the l of Tob,
11: 5 to get Jephthah from the l of Tob.
11:13 they took away my l from the Arnon
11:15 l of Moab or the l of the Ammonites.
11:21 Israel took over all the l of the
12:12 in Aijalon in the l of Zebulun.
16:24 our l and multiplied our slain."
18: 2 to spy out the l and explore it.
18: 2 They told them, "Go, explore the l."
18: 7 And since their l lacked nothing,
18: 9 We have seen that the l is very good.
18:10 l that God has put into your hands,
18:10 a l that lacks nothing whatever."
18:14 the five men who had spied out the l
18:17 The five men who had spied out the l
18:30 the time of the captivity of the l.
20: 1 from the l of Gilead came out as one
21:21 Shiloh and go to the l of Benjamin.
Ru 1: 1 there was a famine in the l, and a
1: 7 take them back to the l of Judah.
4: 3 is selling the piece of l that
4: 5 Boaz said, "On the day you buy the l
1Sa 6: 5 from you and your gods and your l.
9:16 you a man from the l of Benjamin.
13: 3 blown throughout the l and said,
13: 7 Jordan to the l of Gad and Gilead.
13:19 be found in the whole l of Israel,
14:46 and they withdrew to their own l.
21:11 Isn't this David, the king of the l?
22: 5 Go into the l of Judah." So David
23:27 The Philistines are raiding the l."
27: 1 escape to the l of the Philistines.
27: 8 these peoples has lived in the l
28: 3 mediums and spiritists from the l.
28: 9 mediums and spiritists from the l.
29:11 go back to the l of the Philistines,
30:16 l of the Philistines and from Judah.
31: 9 throughout the l of the Philistines
2Sa 3:12 "Whose l is it? Make an agreement
9: 7 I will restore to you all the l that
9:10 farm the l for him and bring in the
10: 2 men came to the l of the Ammonites,
14:20 everything that happens in the l."
15: 4 I were appointed judge in the l!
17:26 Absalom camped in the l of Gilead.
21:14 answered prayer on behalf of the l.
24: 8 they had gone through the entire l,
24:13 you three years of famine in your l?
24:13 Or three days of plague in your l?
24:25 answered prayer on behalf of the l,
1Ki 2:34 buried on his own l in the desert.
4:10 and all the l of Hepher were his);
4:21 River to the l of the Philistines,
8:34 to the l you gave to their fathers.
8:36 and send rain on the l you gave your
8:37 When famine or plague comes to the l
8:41 a distant l because of your name—
8:46 to his own l, far away or near;
8:47 the l where they are held captive,
8:47 the l of their conquerors and say,
8:48 soul in the l of their enemies who
8:48 and pray to you towards the l you
9: 7 I will cut off Israel from the l I
9: 8 the LORD done such a thing to this l
9:13 And he called them the L of Cabul,
9:18 Tadmor in the desert, within his l,
9:21 descendants remaining in the l,

1Ki 10:15 kings and the governors of the l.
11:18 gave Hadad a house and l and
14:24 male shrine-prostitutes in the l;
15:12 male shrine-prostitutes from the l
17: 7 there had been no rain in the l.
17:14 day the LORD gives rain on the l.
18: 1 and I will send rain on the l."
18: 5 Go through the l to all the springs
18: 6 they divided the l they were to
20: 7 elders of the l and said to them,
22:36 man to his town; everyone to his l!
22:46 rid the l of the rest of the male
2Ki 2:19 is bad and the l is unproductive."
2:21 death or make the l unproductive.
3:20 And the l was filled with water.
3:24 invaded the l and slaughtered the
3:27 and returned to their own l.
8: 1 the l that will last seven years."
8: 2 stayed in the l of the Philistines
8: 3 back from the l of the Philistines
8: 3 the king to beg for her house and l.
8: 5 to beg the king for her house and l.
8: 6 including all the income from her l
10:33 the Jordan in all the l of Gilead
11: 3 years while Athaliah ruled the l.
15:19 Pul king of Assyria invaded the l,
15:20 and stayed in the l no longer.
15:29 including all the l of Naphtali,
17: 5 of Assyria invaded the entire l,
17:27 what the god of the l requires."
18:32 take you to a l like your own,
18:32 a l of grain and new wine, a l of
18:33 ever delivered his l from the hand
18:35 has been able to save his l from me?
19:37 and they escaped to the l of Ararat.
20:14 a distant l," Hezekiah replied.
21: 8 from the l I gave their forefathers,
23:33 at Riblah in the l of Hamath
23:35 In order to do so, he taxed the l
24: 1 king of Babylon invaded the l,
24:15 and the leading men of the l.
25:21 There at Riblah, in the l of Hamath,
25:21 into captivity, away from her l.
25:24 "Settle down in the l and serve the
1Ch 1:45 Husham from the l of the Temanites
4:40 l was spacious, peaceful and quiet.
5: 9 To the east they occupied the l up
5:22 they occupied the l until the exile.
5:23 in the l from Bashan to Baal Hermon,
10: 9 throughout the l of the Philistines
11:10 whole l, as the LORD had promised—
14:17 fame spread throughout every l,
19: 2 Hanun in the l of the Ammonites to
20: 1 He laid waste the l of the Ammonites
21:12 days of plague in the l, with the
22:18 the inhabitants of the l over to me,
22:18 and the l is subject to the LORD and
27:26 the field workers who farmed the l.
2Ch 6:25 l you gave to them and their fathers.
6:27 and send rain on the l that you gave
6:28 When famine or plague comes to the l
6:32 has come from a distant l because of
6:36 captive to a l far away or near;
6:37 the l where they are held captive,
6:37 in the l of their captivity and say,
6:38 soul in the l of their captivity
6:38 and pray towards the l that you gave
7:13 or command locusts to devour the l
7:14 their sin and will heal their l.
7:20 I will uproot Israel from my l,
7:21 thing to this l and to this temple?'
8: 8 descendants remaining in the l,
9:14 governors of the l brought gold and
9:26 River to the l of the Philistines,
14: 6 of Judah, since the l was at peace.
14: 7 The l is still ours, because we have
15: 8 idols from the whole l of Judah
19: 3 for you have rid the l of the
19: 5 He appointed judges in the l, in
20: 7 of this l before your people Israel
22:12 years while Athaliah ruled the l.
30: 9 and will come back to this l,
32: 4 stream that flowed through the l.
32:13 to deliver their l from my hand?
32:21 So he withdrew to his own l in
32:31 sign that had occurred in the l,
2Ch 33: 8 l I assigned to your forefathers,
34: 8 to purify the l and the temple, he
36:21 The l enjoyed its sabbath rests;
Ezr 9:11 'The l you are entering to possess
9:11 is a l polluted by the corruption of
9:12 eat the good things of the l and
Ne 4: 4 over as plunder in a l of captivity.
5:14 be their governor in the l of Judah,
5:16 the work; we did not acquire any l.
9: 8 descendants the l of the Canaanites,
9:10 and all the people of his l,
9:15 take possession of the l you had
9:23 and you brought them into the l that
9:24 in and took possession of the l.
9:24 Canaanites, who lived in the l;
9:25 fortified cities and fertile l;
9:35 and fertile l you gave them,
9:36 slaves in the l you gave our
10:31 year we will forgo working the l
Job 1: 1 In the l of Uz there lived a man
1:10 herds are spread throughout the l.
9:24 a l falls into the hands of the
10:21 to the l of gloom and deep shadow,
10:22 to the l of deepest night, of deep
12:15 them loose, they devastate the l.
15:19 (to whom alone the l was given when
15:29 his possessions spread over the l.
18:17 the earth; he has no name in the l.
22: 8 were a powerful man, owning l
24: 4 all the poor of the l into hiding.
24:18 their portion of the l is cursed,
30: 3 they roamed the parched l in
30: 8 they were driven out of the l.
31:38 "if my l cries out against me and
37:17 l lies hushed under the south wind,
38:26 to water a l where no man lives,
42:15 Nowhere in all the l were there
Ps 10:16 the nations will perish from his l.
16: 3 for the saints who are in the l,
25:13 his descendants will inherit the l.
35:20 those who live quietly in the l.
37: 3 dwell in the l and enjoy safe
37: 9 hope in the LORD will inherit the l.
37:11 the meek will inherit the l and
37:22 the LORD blesses will inherit the l,
37:27 you will dwell in the l for ever.
37:29 the righteous will inherit the l
37:34 He will exalt you to inherit the l;
41: 2 he will bless him in the l and not
42: 6 you from the l of the Jordan,
44: 3 by their sword that they won the l,
45:16 make them princes throughout the l.
60: 2 You have shaken the l and torn it
63: 1 and weary l where there is no water.
65: 9 You care for the l and water it;
66: 6 He turned the sea into dry l, they
67: 6 the l will yield its harvest, and
68: 6 rebellious live in a sun-scorched l.
68:14 scattered the kings in the l,
72:16 Let corn abound throughout the l;
74: 8 where God was worshipped in the l.
74:20 fill the dark places of the l.
76: 8 and the l feared and was quiet—
76: 9 to save all the afflicted of the l.
78:12 l of Egypt, in the region of Zoan.
78:54 them to the border of his holy l,
80: 9 and it took root and filled the l.
85: 1 You showed favour to your l, O LORD;
85: 9 that his glory may dwell in our l.
85:12 and our l will yield its harvest.
88:12 deeds in the l of oblivion?
95: 5 and his hands formed the dry l.
101: 6 will be on the faithful in the l,
101: 8 to silence all the wicked in the l;
105:16 He called down famine on the l and
105:23 lived as an alien in the l of Ham.
105:27 them, his wonders in the l of Ham.
105:28 He sent darkness and made the l dark
105:30 Their l teemed with frogs, which
105:32 with lightning throughout their l;
105:35 ate up every green thing in their l,
105:36 down all the firstborn in their l,
106:22 miracles in the l of Ham and awesome
106:24 they despised the pleasant l;
106:38 the l was desecrated by their blood.
107:34 fruitful l into a salt waste,
Ps 112: 2 His children will be mighty in the l
125: 3 the l allotted to the righteous,
135:12 he gave their l as an inheritance,
136:21 gave their l as an inheritance,
137: 4 of the LORD while in a foreign l?
140:11 not be established in the l;
143: 6 thirsts for you like a parched l.
Pr 2:22 the wicked will be cut off from the l
10:30 the wicked will not remain in the l.
12:11 He who works his l will have
25:25 is good news from a distant l.
28:19 He who works his l will have
30:16 the grave, the barren womb, l, which
31:23 his seat among the elders of the l.
Ecc 5: 9 The increase from the l is taken by
10:16 Woe to you, O l whose king was a
10:17 Blessed are you, O l whose king is
11: 2 what disaster may come upon the l.
SS 2:12 cooing of doves is heard in our l.
Isa 1:19 you will eat the best from the l;
2: 7 Their l is full of silver and gold;
2: 7 Their l is full of horses; there is
2: 8 Their l is full of idols; they bow
4: 2 and the fruit of the l will be the
5: 8 is left and you live alone in the l.
5:30 And if one looks at the l, he will
6:12 away and the l is utterly forsaken.
6:13 though a tenth remains in the l, it
6:13 seed will be the stump in the l."
7:16 the l of the two kings you dread
7:18 and for bees from the l of Assyria.
7:22 in the l will eat curds and honey.
7:24 for the l will be covered with
8: 8 the breadth of your l, O Immanuel!"
8:21 they will roam through the l;
9: 1 l of Zebulun and the l of Naphtali,
9: 2 on those living in the l of the
9:19 the l will be scorched and the people
10:23 decreed upon the whole l.
13: 9 to make the l desolate and destroy
13:14 each will flee to his native l.
14: 1 will settle them in their own l.
14: 2 and maidservants in the LORD's l.
14:20 destroyed your l and killed your
14:21 are not to rise to inherit the l
14:25 I will crush the Assyrian in my l;
15: 9 and upon those who remain in the l.
16: 1 as tribute to the ruler of the l,
16: 4 aggressor will vanish from the l.
18: 1 Woe to the l of whirring wings along
18: 2 whose l is divided by rivers.
18: 7 whose l is divided by rivers—
19:17 the l of Judah will bring terror to
19:20 the LORD Almighty in the l of Egypt.
21: 1 from the desert, from a l of terror.
23: 1 From the l of Cyprus word has come
23:10 Till your l as along the Nile,
23:13 Look at the l of the Babylonians,
26: 1 song will be sung in the l of Judah:
26:10 even in a l of uprightness they go
26:15 extended all the borders of the l.
28:22 decreed against the whole l.
30: 6 Through a l of hardship and distress,
30:23 the l will be rich and plentiful.
32: 2 of a great rock in a thirsty l.
32:13 the l of my people, a l overgrown
33: 9 The l mourns and wastes away,
33:17 and view a l that stretches afar.
34: 7 Their l will be drenched with blood,
34: 9 her l will become blazing pitch!
35: 1 The desert and the parched l will be
36:10 and destroy this l without the LORD?
36:17 take you to a l like your own—
36:17 a l of corn and new wine, a l of
36:18 ever delivered his l from the hand
36:20 has been able to save his l from me?
37:38 and they escaped to the l of Ararat.
39: 3 From a distant l," Hezekiah replied
44: 3 I will pour water on the thirsty l,
45:19 from somewhere in a l of darkness;
46:11 from a far-off l, a man to fulfil my
49: 8 to restore the l and to reassign its
49:19 made desolate and your l laid waste,
57:13 me his refuge will inherit the l
58:11 in a sun-scorched l and will
58:14 you to ride on the heights of the l

Isa 60: 6 Herds of camels will cover your l,
60:18 will violence be heard in your l,
60:21 they will possess the l for ever.
61: 7 inherit a double portion in their l,
62: 4 Deserted, or name your l Desolate.
62: 4 and your l Beulah; for the LORD will
62: 4 in you, and your l will be married.
65:16 Whoever invokes a blessing in the l
65:16 he who takes an oath in the l will
Jer 1:18 to stand against the whole l—
2: 2 the desert, through a l not sown.
2: 6 through a l of deserts and rifts,
2: 6 a l of drought and darkness, a l
2: 7 I brought you into a fertile l to
2: 7 you came and defiled my l and made
2:15 They have laid waste his l;
2:31 to Israel or a l of great darkness?
3: 1 Would not the l be completely
3: 2 You have defiled the l with your
3: 9 she defiled the l and committed
3:16 have increased greatly in the l,"
3:18 come from a northern l to the l I
3:19 sons and give you a desirable l,
4: 5 Sound the trumpet throughout the l!
4: 7 left his place to lay waste your l.
4:16 army is coming from a distant l,
4:20 disaster; the whole l lies in ruins.
4:26 and the fruitful l was a desert;
4:27 "The whole l will be ruined, though
5:19 served foreign gods in your own l,
5:19 foreigners in a l not your own.'
5:30 thing has happened in the l:
6: 8 make your l desolate so that no-one
6:20 or sweet calamus from a distant l?
6:22 "Look, an army is coming from the l
7: 7 in the l I gave to your forefathers
7:34 for the l will become desolate.
8:16 stallions the whole l trembles.
8:16 They have come to devour the l and
8:19 cry of my people from a l far away:
9: 3 by truth that they triumph in the l.
9:12 Why has the l been ruined and laid
9:19 We must leave our l because our
10:17 to leave the l, you who live under
10:18 hurl out those who live in this l;
10:22 commotion from the l of the north!
11: 5 and honey'—the l you possess today.
12: 4 How long will the l lie parched and
12:11 the whole l will be laid waste
12:12 from one end of the l to the other;
13:13 drunkenness all who live in this l,
14: 2 they wail for the l, and a cry goes
14: 4 because there is no rain in the l;
14: 8 are you like a stranger in the l,
14:15 No sword or famine will touch this l
14:18 have gone to a l they know not.
15: 7 fork at the city gates of the l.
15:10 a man with whom the whole l strives
15:14 your enemies in a l you do not know,
16: 3 daughters born in this l and about
16: 6 Both high and low will die in this l
16:13 throw you out of this l into a l
16:15 up out of the l of the north
16:15 the l I gave to their forefathers.
16:18 because they have defiled my l with
17: 3 My mountain in the l and your wealth
17: 4 your enemies in a l you do not know,
17: 6 in a salt l where no-one lives.
18:16 Their l will be laid waste, an
22:10 return nor see his native l again.
22:12 he will not see this l again."
22:27 You will never come back to the l
22:28 cast into a l they do not know?
22:29 O l, l, l, hear the word of the LORD
23: 5 do what is just and right in the l.
23: 8 Israel up out of the l of the north
23: 8 Then they will live in their own l."
23:10 The l is full of adulterers;
23:10 because of the curse the l lies
23:15 has spread throughout the l."
24: 5 place to the l of the Babylonians.
24: 6 I will bring them back to this l.
24: 8 remain in this l or live in Egypt.
24:10 l I gave to them and their fathers.
25: 5 and you can stay in the l the LORD
25: 9 I will bring them against this l
Jer 25:12 the l of the Babylonians, for their
25:13 I will bring upon that l all the
25:30 and roar mightily against his l.
25:38 and their l will become desolate
26:17 Some of the elders of the l stepped
26:20 against this city and this l as
27: 7 until the time for his l comes;
27:11 own l to till it and to live there,
30: 3 restore them to the l I gave to
30:10 from the l of their exile.
31: 8 See, I will bring them from the l of
31:16 will return from the l of the enemy.
31:17 children will return to their own l.
31:23 the people in the l of Judah and in
32:15 will again be bought in this l.'
32:22 You gave them this l you had sworn
32:41 plant them in this l with all my
32:43 bought in this l of which you say,
33:11 I will restore the fortunes of the l
33:15 do what is just and right in the l.
34:13 of Egypt, out of the l of slavery.
35: 7 time in the l where you are nomads.'
35:11 king of Babylon invaded this l,
36:29 destroy this l and cut off both men
37: 7 will go back to its own l, to Egypt.
37:19 will not attack you or this l'?
39: 5 at Riblah in the l of Hamath, where
39:10 left behind in the l of Judah some
40: 6 who were left behind in the l.
40: 7 as governor over the l and had put
40: 7 who were the poorest in the l
40: 9 "Settle down in the l and serve the
40:12 they all came back to the l of Judah,
41: 2 appointed as governor over the l.
41:18 appointed as governor over the l.
42:10 'If you stay in this l, I will build
42:12 on you and restore you to your l.'
42:13 say, 'We will not stay in this l,'
43: 4 command to stay in the l of Judah.
44: 9 your wives in the l of Judah and the
44:14 survive to return to the l of Judah,
44:22 your l became an object of cursing
44:28 return to the l of Judah from Egypt
45: 4 I have planted throughout the l
46:10 will offer sacrifice in the l of the
46:27 from the l of their exile.
47: 2 They will overflow the l and
47: 2 all who dwell in the l will wail
49:19 chase Edom from its l in an instant.
50: 1 Babylon and the l of the Babylonians:
50: 3 will attack her and lay waste her l.
50: 8 "Flee out of Babylon; leave the l of
50: 9 nations from the l of the north.
50:12 a wilderness, a dry l, a desert.
50:16 let everyone flee to his own l.
50:18 punish the king of Babylon and his l
50:21 "Attack the l of Merathaim and those
50:22 The noise of battle is in the l, the
50:25 to do in the l of the Babylonians.
50:34 that he may bring rest to their l,
50:38 For it is a l of idols, idols that
50:44 Babylon from its l in an instant.
50:45 what he has purposed against the l
51: 2 winnow her and to devastate her l;
51: 5 though their l is full of guilt
51: 9 leave her and each go to his own l,
51:27 "Lift up a banner in the l! Blow the
51:29 The l trembles and writhes, for the
51:29 to lay waste the l of Babylon so
51:43 a dry and desert l, a l where no-one
51:46 rumours are heard in the l;
51:46 rumours of violence in the l and of
51:47 her whole l will be disgraced and
51:50 Remember the LORD in a distant l,
51:52 her l the wounded will groan.
51:54 from the l of the Babylonians.
52: 9 at Riblah in the l of Hamath, where
52:27 There at Riblah, in the l of Hamath,
52:27 into captivity, away from her l.
Lam 3:34 underfoot all prisoners in the l,
Eze 1: 3 River in the l of the Babylonians.
6:14 make the l a desolate waste from the
7: 2 LORD says to the l of Israel:
7: 2 come upon the four corners of the l.
7: 7 upon you—you who dwell in the l.
7:13 The seller will not recover the l he
Eze 7:23 "Prepare chains, because the l is
8:12 the LORD has forsaken the l.
8:17 Must they also fill the l with
9: 9 the l is full of bloodshed and the
9: 9 The LORD has forsaken the l;
11:15 l was given to us as our possession.
11:17 give you back the l of Israel
12: 6 so that you cannot see the l,
12:12 so that he cannot see the l.
12:13 the l of the Chaldeans, but he will
12:19 in Jerusalem and in the l of Israel:
12:19 for their l will be stripped of
12:20 waste and the l will be desolate.
12:22 proverb you have in the l of Israel:
13: 9 nor will they enter the l of Israel.
14:16 saved, but the l would be desolate.
14:17 'Let the sword pass throughout the l,
14:19 "Or if I send a plague into that l
15: 8 I will make the l desolate because
16: 3 were in the l of the Canaanites;
16:29 a l of merchants, but even with this
17: 4 carried it away to a l of merchants,
17: 5 "'He took some of the seed of your l
17:13 away the leading men of the l,
17:16 he shall die in Babylon, in the l of
18: 2 proverb about the l of Israel:
19: 4 him with hooks to the l of Egypt.
19: 7 The l and all who were in it were
19:13 the desert, in a dry and thirsty l.
20: 6 a l I had searched out for them,
20:15 them into the l I had given them
20:28 I brought them into the l I had
20:36 in the desert of the l of Egypt,
20:38 out of the l where they are living,
20:38 they will not enter the l of Israel.
20:40 there in the l the entire house of
20:42 I bring you into the l of Israel
20:42 the l I had sworn with uplifted hand
21: 2 Prophesy against the l of Israel
21:30 l of your ancestry, I will judge you.
21:32 your blood will be shed in your l,
22:24 "Son of man, say to the l, 'You are
22:24 'You are a l that has had no rain or
22:30 on behalf of the l so that I would
23: 3 In that l their breasts were fondled
23:48 put an end to lewdness in the l,
25: 3 over the l of Israel when it was
25: 6 your heart against the l of Israel,
25: 9 and Kiriathaim—the glory of that l.
28:25 they will live in their own l,
29:10 and I will make the l of Egypt a
29:12 I will make the l of Egypt desolate
29:14 Upper Egypt, the l of their ancestry.
29:19 plunder the l as pay for his army.
30: 5 the people of the covenant l will
30:11 will be brought in to destroy the l.
30:11 Egypt and fill the l with the slain.
30:12 the Nile and sell the l to evil men;
30:12 waste the l and everything in it.
30:13 I will spread fear throughout the l.
31:12 broken in all the ravines of the l.
32: 4 I will throw you on the l and hurl
32: 6 I will drench the l with your
32: 8 I will bring darkness over your l,
32:15 I make Egypt desolate and strip the l
33: 2 'When I bring the sword against a l,
33: 3 sees the sword coming against the l
33:24 ruins in the l of Israel are saying,
33:24 one man, yet he possessed the l.
33:24 surely the l has been given to us as
33:25 should you then possess the l?
33:26 Should you then possess the l?'
33:28 I will make the l a desolate waste,
33:29 when I have made the l a desolate
34:13 I will bring them into their own l.
34:13 and in all the settlements in the l.
34:14 of Israel will be their grazing l.
34:14 will lie down in good grazing l,
34:25 rid the l of wild beasts so that
34:27 people will be secure in their l.
34:29 I will provide for them a l renowned
34:29 victims of famine in the l or bear
36: 5 they made my l their own possession
36: 6 Therefore prophesy concerning the l
36:17 Israel were living in their own l,
36:18 they had shed blood in the l

Eze 36:20 and yet they had to leave his **l**.'
36:24 and bring you back into your own **l**.
36:34 The desolate **l** will be cultivated
36:35 say, "This **l** that was laid waste
37:12 bring you back to the **l** of Israel.
37:14 and I will settle you in your own **l**.
37:21 bring them back into their own **l**.
37:22 I will make them one nation in the **l**,
37:25 the **l** where your fathers lived.
38: 2 against Gog, of the **l** of Magog, the
38: 8 In future years you will invade a **l**
38: 9 will be like a cloud covering the **l**.
38:11 You will say, "I will invade a **l** of
38:12 living at the centre of the **l**."
38:16 like a cloud that covers the **l**.
38:16 I will bring you against my **l**, so
38:18 When Gog attacks the **l** of Israel,
38:19 great earthquake in the **l** of Israel.
39:12 them in order to cleanse the **l**.
39:14 regularly employed to cleanse the **l**.
39:14 Some will go throughout the **l** and,
39:15 they go through the **l** and one of
39:16 And so they will cleanse the **l**.'
39:26 they lived in safety in their **l**
39:28 I will gather them to their own **l**,
40: 2 took me to the **l** of Israel and set
43: 2 the **l** was radiant with his glory.
45: 1 you allot the **l** as an inheritance
45: 1 of the **l** as a sacred district,
45: 2 with 50 cubits around it for open **l**.
45: 4 will be the sacred portion of the **l**
45: 7 "'The prince will have the **l**
45: 8 This **l** will be his possession in
45: 8 the **l** according to their tribes.
47:13 by which you are to divide the **l** for
47:14 this **l** will become your inheritance.
47:15 "This is to be the boundary of the **l**:
47:18 between Gilead and the **l** of Israel,
47:21 distribute this **l** among yourselves
48:12 from the sacred portion of the **l**,
48:14 This is the best of the **l** and must
48:29 "This is the **l** you are to allot as
Da 4:10 stood a tree in the middle of the **l**.
6:25 of every language throughout the **l**:
8: 9 east and towards the Beautiful **L**.
11:16 himself in the Beautiful **L**
11:39 will distribute the **l** at a price.
11:41 He will also invade the Beautiful **L**.
Hos 1: 2 because the **l** is guilty of the
1:11 and will come up out of the **l**,
2: 3 parched **l**, and slay her with thirst.
2:18 battle I will abolish from the **l**,
2:23 I will plant her for myself in the **l**;
4: 1 no acknowledgment of God in the **l**.
4: 3 the **l** mourns, and all who live in
7:16 will be ridiculed in the **l** of Egypt.
9: 3 They will not remain in the LORD's **l**
10: 1 as his **l** prospered, he adorned his
13: 5 desert, in the **l** of burning heat.
Joel 1: 6 A nation has invaded my **l**, powerful
2: 3 the **l** is like the garden of Eden,
2:18 the LORD will be jealous for his **l**
2:20 it into a parched and barren **l**,
2:21 Be not afraid, O **l**; be glad and
3: 2 the nations and divided up my **l**.
3:19 in whose **l** they shed innocent blood.
Am 2:10 to give you the **l** of the Amorites.
3:11 "An enemy will overrun the **l**; he
5: 2 deserted in her own **l**, with no-one
5: 8 out over the face of the **l**—
6: 2 Is their **l** larger than yours?
7: 2 they had stripped the **l** clean,
7: 4 the great deep and devoured the **l**.
7:10 The **l** cannot bear all his words.
7:11 exile, away from their native **l**.
7:12 you seer! Go back to the **l** of Judah.
7:17 Your **l** will be measured and divided
7:17 exile, away from their native **l**.
8: 4 and do away with the poor of the **l**,
8: 8 "Will not the **l** tremble for this,
8: 8 The whole **l** will rise like the Nile;
8:11 I will send a famine through the **l**
9: 5 the whole **l** rises like the Nile,
9: 6 out over the face of the **l**—
9:15 I will plant Israel in their own **l**,
9:15 from the **l** I have given them,"
Ob :19 possess the **l** of the Philistines.
:20 possess the **l** as far as Zarephath;
Jnh 1: 9 who made the sea and the **l**."
1:13 men did their best to row back to **l**.
2:10 and it vomited Jonah onto dry **l**.
Mic 2: 5 of the LORD to divide the **l** by lot.
5: 5 When the Assyrian invades our **l** and
5: 6 They will rule the **l** of Assyria with
5: 6 the **l** of Nimrod with drawn sword.
5: 6 he invades our **l** and marches into
5:11 I will destroy the cities of your **l**
6: 4 redeemed you from the **l** of slavery.
7: 2 The godly have been swept from the **l**;
Na 3:13 gates of your **l** are wide open to
3:16 they strip the **l** and then fly away.
Hab 3:13 You crushed the leader of the **l** of
Zep 2: 3 all you humble of the **l**, you who
2: 5 you, O Canaan, **l** of the Philistines.
2: 6 The **l** by the sea, where the
2: 8 and made threats against their **l**.
2: 9 of my nation will inherit their **l**."
2:11 he destroys all the gods of the **l**.
2:11 worship him, every one in its own **l**.
3:19 **l** where they were put to shame.
Hag 2: 6 the earth, the sea and the dry **l**.
Zec 1:21 **l** of Judah to scatter its people."
2: 6 Come! Flee from the **l** of the north
2:12 Judah as his portion in the holy **l**
3: 9 the sin of this **l** in a single day.
5: 3 that is going out over the whole **l**;
5: 6 of the people throughout the **l**."
6: 8 Spirit rest in the **l** of the north."
7:14 The **l** was left so desolate behind
7:14 This is how they made the pleasant **l**
9: 1 The word of the LORD is against the **l**
9:16 in his **l** like jewels in a crown.
11: 6 They will oppress the **l**, and I will
11:16 to raise up a shepherd over the **l**
12:12 The **l** will mourn, each clan by
13: 2 the names of the idols from the **l**,
13: 2 the spirit of impurity from the **l**.
13: 5 the **l** has been my livelihood
13: 8 In the whole **l**," declares the LORD,
14:10 The whole **l**, from Geba to Rimmon,
Mal 1: 4 They will be called the Wicked **L**, a
3:12 yours will be a delightful **l**,"
4: 6 come and strike the **l** with a curse."
Mt 2: 6 you, Bethlehem, in the **l** of Judah
2:20 mother and go to the **l** of Israel,
2:21 mother and went to the **l** of Israel.
4:15 "**L** of Zebulun and **l** of Naphtali, the
4:16 on those living in the **l** of the
14:24 a considerable distance from **l**,
23:15 You travel over **l** and sea to win a
27:45 darkness came over all the **l**.
Mk 6:47 of the lake, and he was alone on **l**.
15:33 the whole **l** until the ninth hour.
Lk 4:25 a severe famine throughout the **l**.
21:23 will be great distress in the **l**
23:44 the whole **l** until the ninth hour,
Ac 5: 3 the money you received for the **l**?
5: 8 you and Ananias got for the **l**?"
7: 3 'and go to the **l** I will show you.'
7: 4 "So he left the **l** of the Chaldeans
7: 4 to this **l** where you are now living.
7: 5 after him would possess the **l**,
7:45 when they took the **l** from the
7:45 in the **l** until the time of David,
13:19 **l** to his people as their inheritance.
27:27 sensed they were approaching **l**.
27:39 they did not recognise the **l**, but
27:43 jump overboard first and get to **l**.
27:44 way everyone reached **l** in safety.
Heb 6: 7 **L** that drinks in the rain often
6: 8 **l** that produces thorns and thistles
11: 9 he made his home in the promised **l**
11:29 through the Red Sea as on dry **l**;
Jas 5: 7 See how the farmer waits for the **l**
5:17 it did not rain on the **l** for
Rev 7: 1 on the **l** or on the sea or on any
7: 2 power to harm the **l** and the sea:
7: 3 "Do not harm the **l** or the sea or the
10: 2 the sea and his left foot on the **l**,
10: 5 standing on the sea and on the **l**
10: 8 standing on the sea and on the **l**."
16: 2 and poured out his bowl on the **l**,

Land flowing with milk and honey

Ex 3: 8 into a good and spacious land, a **l**
3:17 Hivites and Jebusites—a **l**.'
13: 5 your forefathers to give you, a **l**
33: 3 Go up to the **l**. But I will not go
Lev 20:24 it to you as an inheritance, a **l**.
Nu 14: 8 land, a **l**, and will give it to us.
16:13 out of a **l** to kill us in the desert?
16:14 you haven't brought us into a **l** or
Dt 6: 3 you may increase greatly in a **l**,
11: 9 to them and their descendants, a **l**.
26: 9 place and gave us this land, a **l**;
26:15 on oath to our forefathers, a **l**."
27: 3 a **l**, just as the LORD, the God of
31:20 I have brought them into the **l**, the
Jos 5: 6 their fathers to give us, a **l**.
Jer 11: 5 a **l**'—the land you possess today.
32:22 to give to their forefathers, a **l**.
Eze 20: 6 **l**, the most beautiful of all lands.
20:15 **l**, most beautiful of all lands—

Land of Canaan

Ge 12: 5 they set out for the **l**, and they
13:12 Abram lived in the **l**, while Lot
17: 8 The whole **l**, where you are now an
23: 2 Hebron) in the **l**, and Abraham went
23:19 Mamre (which is at Hebron) in the **l**.
31:18 to go to his father Isaac in the **l**.
35: 6 to Luz (that is, Bethel) in the **l**.
37: 1 where his father had stayed, the **l**.
42: 5 for the famine was in the **l** also.
42: 7 "From the **l**," they replied, "to buy
42:13 sons of one man, who lives in the **l**.
42:29 came to their father Jacob in the **l**,
44: 8 brought back to you from the **l** the
45:17 your animals and return to the **l**,
45:25 came to their father Jacob in the **l**.
46:12 (but Er and Onan had died in the **l**).
46:31 were living in the **l**, have come
47: 1 from the **l** and are now in Goshen."
48: 3 appeared to me at Luz in the **l**,
48: 7 to my sorrow Rachel died in the **l**
50: 5 the tomb I dug for myself in the **l**.
50:13 They carried him to the **l** and buried
Ex 6: 4 the **l**, where they lived as aliens.
Lev 14:34 "When you enter the **l**, which I am
18: 3 in the **l**, where I am bringing you.
25:38 give you the **l** and to be your God.
Nu 13: 2 "Send some men to explore the **l**,
34:29 to the Israelites in the **l**.
Jos 14: 1 received as an inheritance in the **l**,
22:10 Geliloth near the Jordan in the **l**,
1Ch 16:18 "To you I will give the **l** as the
Ps 105:11 "To you I will give the **l** as the

Land of the living

Job 28:13 it cannot be found in the **l**.
Ps 27:13 the goodness of the LORD in the **l**.
52: 5 he will uproot you from the **l**.
116: 9 I may walk before the LORD in the **l**.
142: 5 are my refuge, my portion in the **l**."
Isa 38:11 see the LORD, the LORD, in the **l**;
53: 8 For he was cut off from the **l**;
Jer 11:19 let us cut him off from the **l**,
Eze 26:20 return or take your place in the **l**.
32:23 spread terror in the **l** are slain,
32:24 All who had spread terror in the **l**
32:25 their terror had spread in the **l**,
32:26 they spread their terror in the **l**.
32:27 warriors had stalked through the **l**.
32:32 I had him spread terror in the **l**,

Land's (Land)

Nu 18:13 All the **l** firstfruits that they

Landed (Land)

Mt 14:14 Jesus **l** and saw a large crowd, he
14:34 crossed over, they **l** at Gennesaret.
Mk 6:34 Jesus **l** and saw a large crowd, he
6:53 crossed over, they **l** at Gennesaret.
Jn 6:23 boats from Tiberias **l** near the place
21: 9 they **l**, they saw a fire of burning
Ac 18:22 he **l** at Caesarea, he went up and
21: 3 We **l** at Tyre, where our ship was to

Ac 21: 7 voyage from Tyre and l at Ptolemais,
27: 3 The next day we l at Sidon; and
27: 5 Pamphylia, we l at Myra in Lycia.

Landowner (Land)
Mt 20: 1 kingdom of heaven is like a l who
20:11 they began to grumble against the l.
21:33 There was a l who planted a vineyard.

Lands (Land)
Ge 26: 3 descendants I will give all these l
26: 4 sky and will give them all these l,
41:54 There was famine in all the other l,
Lev 26:36 hearts so fearful in the l of their
26:39 will waste away in the l of their
Nu 32: 1 saw that the l of Jazer and Gilead
Dt 29:22 foreigners who come from distant l
Jos 10:42 All these kings and their l Joshua
12: 7 (their l Joshua gave as an
12: 8 the l of the Hittites, Amorites,
Jdg 11:18 skirted the l of Edom and Moab,
2Ki 19:17 laid waste these nations and their l
19:24 I have dug wells in foreign l and
1Ch 7:28 Their l and settlements included
29:30 and the kingdoms of all the other l.
2Ch 12: 8 and serving the kings of other l."
13: 9 own as the peoples of other l do?
15: 5 the inhabitants of the l were
17:10 kingdoms of the l surrounding Judah,
26:10 fertile l, for he loved the soil.
31:19 who lived on the farm l around their
32:13 to all the peoples of the other l?
32:17 gods of the peoples of the other l
Ps 49:11 they had named l after themselves.
76:11 let all the neighbouring l bring
78:55 their l to them as an inheritance;
105:44 he gave them the l of the nations,
106:27 and scatter them throughout the l.
107: 3 those he gathered from the l, from
111: 6 giving them the l of other nations.
Isa 8: 9 Listen, all you distant l.
13: 5 They come from faraway l, from the
14: 7 All the l are at rest and at peace;
23: 7 taken her to settle in far-off l?
37:18 waste all these peoples and their l
37:25 I have dug wells in foreign l and
Jer 12:14 I will uproot them from their l and
27:10 serve to remove you far from your l;
32:37 surely gather them from all the l
46:16 to our own people and our native l,
Eze 6: 8 scattered among the l and nations.
20: 6 honey, the most beautiful of all l.
20:15 and honey, most beautiful of all l—
29:12 Egypt desolate among devastated l,
30: 7 will be desolate among desolate l,
32: 9 nations, among l you have not known.
Hab 2: 8 destroyed l and cities and everyone
2:17 destroyed l and cities and everyone
Zec 10: 9 in distant l they will remember me.
Ac 4:34 who owned l or houses sold them,

Lanes
Lk 14:23 'Go out to the roads and country l

Language (Languages)
Ge 10: 5 their nations, each with its own l.)
11: 1 Now the whole world had one l and a
11: 6 same l they have begun to do this,
11: 7 let us go down and confuse their l
11: 9 confused the l of the whole world.
Dt 28:49 whose l you will not understand,
Ezr 4: 7 Aramaic script and in the Aramaic l
Ne 13:24 spoke the l of Ashdod or the l of
13:24 know how to speak the l of Judah.
Est 1:22 and to each people in its own l,
3:12 in the l of each people all Haman's
8: 9 the l of each people and also to the
8: 9 the Jews in their own script and l.
Ps 19: 3 There is no speech or l where their
81: 5 we heard a l we did not understand.
Isa 19:18 in Egypt will speak the l of Canaan
Jer 5:15 a people whose l you do not know,
Eze 3: 5 difficult l, but to the house of
3: 6 difficult l, whose words you cannot
Da 1: 4 l and literature of the Babylonians.
3: 4 peoples, nations and men of every l:
3: 7 nations and men of every l fell down
3:29 the people of any nation or l who
4: 1 nations and men of every l, who live
5:19 men of every l dreaded and feared
6:25 peoples, nations and men of every l
7:14 and men of every l worshipped him.
Jn 8:43 Why is my l not clear to you?
8:44 When he lies, he speaks his native l,
16:25 I will no longer use this kind of l
Ac 1:19 in their l Akeldama, that is, Field
2: 6 heard them speaking in his own l.
2: 8 us hears them in his own native l?
14:11 they shouted in the Lycaonian l,
Col 3: 8 slander and filthy l from your lips.
Rev 5: 9 tribe and l and people and nation.
7: 9 tribe, people and l, standing before
11: 9 tribe, l and nation will gaze on
13: 7 every tribe, people, l and nation.
14: 6 every nation, tribe, l and people.

Languages (Language)
Ge 10:20 sons of Ham by their clans and l,
10:31 sons of Shem by their clans and l,
Zec 8:23 "In those days ten men from all l
1Co 14:10 Undoubtedly there are all sorts of l
Rev 10:11 many peoples, nations, l and kings."
17:15 peoples, multitudes, nations and l.

Languish (Languishes)
Isa 24: 4 withers, the exalted of the earth l.
Jer 14: 2 "Judah mourns, her cities l; they

Languishes (Languish)
Isa 24: 4 the world l and withers, the exalted

Lanterns
Jn 18: 3 carrying torches, l and weapons.

Laodicea (Laodiceans)
City in Phrygia, in the Lycus Valley, about 12 miles west of Colosse. Its church was probably not established by Paul (Col 2:1; 4:12–13), but he addressed a letter to them (Col 4:16). Accused of being lukewarm in one of the 7 letters of Revelation (Rev 3:14–22).

Col 2: 1 for you and for those at L,
4:13 and for those at L and Hierapolis.
4:15 my greetings to the brothers at L,
4:16 you in turn read the letter from L.
Rev 1:11 Sardis, Philadelphia and L."
3:14 "To the angel of the church in L

Laodiceans (Laodicea)
Col 4:16 is also read in the church of the L

Lap[1] (Laps)
Jdg 16:19 Having put him to sleep on her l,
Ru 4:16 laid him in her l and cared for him.
2Ki 4:20 the boy sat on her l until noon,
Pr 6:27 Can a man scoop fire into his l
16:33 The lot is cast into the l, but its
Ecc 7: 9 for anger resides in the l of fools.
Lk 6:38 over, will be poured into your l.

Lap[2] (Lapped)
Jdg 7: 5 "Separate those who l the water with

Lapped (Lap[2])
Jdg 7: 6 Three hundred men l with their hands
7: 7 "With the three hundred men that l I

Lappidoth
Jdg 4: 4 Deborah, a prophetess, the wife of L

Laps (Lap[1])
Ps 79:12 Pay back into the l of our
Isa 65: 6 I will pay it back into their l—
65: 7 I will measure into their l the full
Jer 32:18 the l of their children after them.

Lasea
Ac 27: 8 Fair Havens, near the town of L.

Lash (Lashed, Lashes)
Job 5:21 protected from the l of the tongue
Isa 10:26 LORD Almighty will l them with a whip

Lasha
Ge 10:19 Admah and Zeboiim, as far as L.

Lasharon
Jos 12:18 the king of L one

Lashed (Lash)
Isa 54:11 "O afflicted city, l by storms and

Lashes (Lash)
Dt 25: 2 the number of l his crime deserves,
25: 3 must not give him more than forty l.
Pr 17:10 more than a hundred l a fool.
2Co 11:24 from the Jews the forty l minus one.

Last[1] (*First and the last, Last day, Last days*)
Ge 19:34 "L night I lay with my father.
25: 8 Abraham breathed his l and died at a
25:17 He breathed his l and died, and he
29:34 "Now at l my husband will become
31:29 but l night the God of your father
31:42 hands, and l night he rebuked you."
33: 7 L of all came Joseph and Rachel, and
35:18 she breathed her l—for she was
35:29 he breathed his l and died and was
49:33 breathed his l and was gathered to
Ex 14:24 During the l watch of the night the
Lev 26:10 still be eating l year's harvest
Nu 2:31 set out l, under their standards.
14:33 l of your bodies lies in the desert.
24:20 but he will come to ruin at l."
Dt 2:16 Now when the l of these fighting men
Jos 12: 4 one of the l of the Rephaites, who
13:12 as one of the l of the Rephaites.
1Sa 11:11 during the l watch of the night they
15:16 what the LORD said to me l night.
2Sa 19:11 'Why should you be the l to bring
19:12 be the l to bring back the king?'
23: 1 These are the l words of David: "The
1Ki 14:10 cut off from Jeroboam every l male
21:21 cut off from Ahab every l male in
2Ki 8: 1 the land that will l seven years."
9: 8 cut off from Ahab every l male in
1Ch 23:27 According to the l instructions of
Ezr 8:13 descendants of Adonikam, the l ones,
Ne 8:18 from the first day to the l, Ezra
Job 14:10 he breathes his l and is no more.
Ps 76: 5 they sleep their l sleep; not one of
Isa 41: 4 with the first of them and with the l
44: 6 I am the first and I am the l;
48:12 I am the first and I am the l.
Jer 15: 9 will grow faint and breathe her l.
50:17 the l to crush his bones was
Am 1: 8 the l of the Philistines is dead,"
4: 2 the l of you with fish-hooks.
Mt 5:26 out until you have paid the l penny.
19:30 be l, and many who are l will be
20: 8 beginning with the l ones hired and
20:12 'These men who were hired l worked
20:14 was hired l the same as I gave you.
20:16 "So the l will be first, and the
20:16 be first, and the first will be l."
21:37 L of all, he sent his son to them.
27:64 This l deception will be worse than
Mk 9:35 the very l, and the servant of all."
10:31 first will be l, and the l first."
12: 6 He sent him l of all, saying, 'They
12:22 L of all, the woman died too.
15:37 With a loud cry, Jesus breathed his l
Lk 12:59 until you have paid the l penny."
13:30 there are those who are l who will
13:30 be first, and first who will be l."
23:46 he had said this, he breathed his l.
Jn 7:37 On the l and greatest day of the
16:31 "You believe at l!" Jesus answered.
Ac 27:23 L night an angel of the God whose I

Ac 27:33 "For the l fourteen days," he said,
Ro 1:10 I pray that now at l by God's will
1:17 that is by faith from first to l,
1Co 15: 8 l of all he appeared to me also, as
15:26 The l enemy to be destroyed is death.
15:45 the l Adam, a life-giving spirit.
15:52 of an eye, at the l trumpet.
2Co 8:10 L year you were the first not only
9: 2 telling them that since l year you
Php 4:10 at l you have renewed your concern
1Th 2:16 of God has come upon them at l.
1Pe 1: 5 ready to be revealed in the l time.
1:20 in these l times for your sake.
1Jn 2:18 Dear children, this is the l hour;
2:18 This is how we know it is the l hour.
Jude :18 They said to you, "In the l times
Rev 15: 1 angels with the seven l plagues—l,
21: 9 seven l plagues came and said to me,

Last[2] (Lasted, Lasting, Lasts)
Lev 8:33 your ordination will l seven days.
15:19 monthly period will l seven days,
Ps 45: 6 Your throne, O God, will l for ever
81:15 their punishment would l for ever.
119:152 you established them to l for ever.
Isa 51: 6 But my salvation will l for ever, my
51: 8 But my righteousness will l for ever,
Jer 32:14 jar so that they will l a long time.
Da 9: 2 of Jerusalem would l seventy years.
11: 6 and he and his power will not l.
Mk 4:17 no root, they l only a short time.
Jn 15:16 and bear fruit—fruit that will l.
1Co 9:25 it to get a crown that will not l;
9:25 to get a crown that will l for ever.
Heb 1: 8 "Your throne, O God, will l for ever

Last day
Jn 6:39 me, but raise them up at the l.
6:40 and I will raise him up at the l."
6:44 and I will raise him up at the l.
6:54 and I will raise him up at the l.
11:24 again in the resurrection at the l."
12:48 I spoke will condemn him at the l.

Last days
Isa 2: 2 In the l the mountain of the LORD's
Hos 3: 5 LORD and to his blessings in the l.
Mic 4: 1 In the l the mountain of the LORD's
Ac 2:17 "'In the l, God says, I will pour
2Ti 3: 1 will be terrible times in the l.
Heb 1: 2 in these l he has spoken to us by
Jas 5: 3 You have hoarded wealth in the l.
2Pe 3: 3 you must understand that in the l

Lasted (Last[2])
2Sa 3: 1 the house of David l a long time.
2Ki 6:25 the siege l so long that a donkey's

Lasting (Last[2])
Ex 12:14 festival to the LORD—a l ordinance.
12:17 Celebrate this day as a l ordinance
12:24 these instructions as a l ordinance
27:21 This is to be a l ordinance among
28:43 "This is to be a l ordinance for
29: 9 The priesthood is theirs by a l
30:21 This is to be a l ordinance for
31:16 generations to come as a l covenant.
Lev 3:17 "'This is a l ordinance for the
10: 9 This is a l ordinance for the
16:29 "This is to be a l ordinance for you:
16:31 yourselves; it is a l ordinance.
16:34 "This is to be a l ordinance for you:
17: 7 This is to be a l ordinance for them
23:14 This is to be a l ordinance for the
23:21 This is to be a l ordinance for the
23:31 This is to be a l ordinance for the
23:41 This is to be a l ordinance for the
24: 3 This is to be a l ordinance for the
24: 8 of the Israelites, as a l covenant.
Nu 10: 8 This is to be a l ordinance for you
15:15 this is a l ordinance for the
18:23 This is a l ordinance for the
19:10 This will be a l ordinance both for
19:21 This is a l ordinance for them. "The
25:13 have a covenant of a l priesthood,
Dt 11: 4 how the LORD brought l ruin on them.
1Sa 25:28 make a l dynasty for my master,
2Ch 2: 4 This is a l ordinance for Israel.
Est 1: 5 king gave a banquet, l seven days
Jer 14:13 Indeed, I will give you l peace in
18:16 laid waste, an object of l scorn;
Eze 45:21 a feast l seven days, during which
46:14 to the LORD is a l ordinance.
Heb 10:34 had better and l possessions.

Lasts (Last[2])
Lev 23:34 begins, and it l for seven days.
Job 20: 5 joy of the godless l but a moment.
Ps 30: 5 For his anger l only a moment, but
30: 5 but his favour l a lifetime;
Pr 12:19 but a lying tongue l only a moment.
Mt 13:21 no root, he l only a short time.
2Co 3:11 is the glory of that which l!

Latch-opening
SS 5: 4 lover thrust his hand through the l

Late
Ps 127: 2 In vain you rise early and stay up l,
Isa 5:11 who stay up l at night till they are
Mt 14:15 place, and it's already getting l.
Mk 6:35 By this time it was l in the day, so
6:35 they said, "and it's already very l.
11:11 but since it was already l, he went
Lk 9:12 L in the afternoon the Twelve came
Rev 6:13 as l figs drop from a fig-tree when

Latin
Jn 19:20 was written in Aramaic, L and Greek.

Latrine
2Ki 10:27 have used it for a l to this day.

Lattice
Jdg 5:28 behind the l she cried out,
2Ki 1: 2 Now Ahaziah had fallen through the l
Pr 7: 6 my house I looked out through the l.
SS 2: 9 the windows, peering through the l.

Laugh (Laughed, Laughing-stock, Laughs, Laughter)
Ge 18:13 "Why did Sarah l and say, 'Will I
18:15 so she lied and said, "I did not l.
18:15 But he said, "Yes, you did l."
21: 6 hears about this will l with me."
Job 5:22 You will l at destruction and famine,
Ps 52: 6 they will l at him, saying,
59: 8 you, O LORD, l at them; you scoff at
Pr 1:26 I in turn will l at your disaster;
31:25 she can l at the days to come.
Ecc 3: 4 a time to weep and a time to l, a
Hab 1:10 They l at all fortified cities; they
Lk 6:21 you who weep now, for you will l.
6:25 l now, for you will mourn and weep.

Laughed (Laugh)
Ge 17:17 he l and said to himself, "Will a
18:12 Sarah l to herself as she thought,
Lam 1: 7 at her and l at her destruction.
Mt 9:24 dead, but asleep." But they l at him
Mk 5:40 they l at him. After he put them all
Lk 8:53 They l at him, knowing that she was

Laughing-stock (Laugh)
Ge 38:23 what she has, or we will become a l.
Ex 32:25 and so become a l to their enemies.
Job 12: 4 "I have become a l to my friends,
12: 4 a mere l, though righteous and
Lam 3:14 I became the l of all my people;
Eze 22: 4 and a l to all the countries.

Laughs (Laugh)
Job 39: 7 He l at the commotion in the town;
39:18 to run, she l at horse and rider.
39:22 He l at fear, afraid of nothing;
41:29 he l at the rattling of the lance.
Ps 2: 4 The One enthroned in heaven l;
37:13 the Lord l at the wicked, for he

Laughter (Laugh)
Ge 21: 6 Sarah said, "God has brought me l,
Job 8:21 He will yet fill your mouth with l
Ps 126: 2 Our mouths were filled with l, our
Pr 14:13 Even in l the heart may ache, and
Ecc 2: 2 "L," I said, "is foolish. And what
7: 3 Sorrow is better than l, because a
7: 6 under the pot, so is the l of fools.
10:19 A feast is made for l, and wine
Jer 51:39 so that they shout with l—then
Jas 4: 9 Change your l to mourning and your

Launch
Jdg 10:18 "Whoever will l the attack against

Launderer's
Mal 3: 2 like a refiner's fire or a l soap.

Lavished
Isa 43:24 l on me the fat of your sacrifices.
Eze 16:15 You l your favours on anyone who
Da 2:48 position and l many gifts on him.
Hos 2: 8 who l on her the silver and gold
Eph 1: 8 that he l on us with all wisdom and
1Jn 3: 1 the love the Father has l on us,

Law (*Book of the Law, Law of God, Law of Moses, Law of the LORD, Law of the Lord*, Law's, Law-breaker, Lawbreakers, Law-breakers, Lawful, Lawgiver, Laws, Lawyer, *Teachers of the law*)
Ge 47:26 Joseph established it as a l
Ex 12:49 same l applies to the native-born
15:25 LORD made a decree and a l for them
21:31 This l also applies if the bull
24:12 with the l and commands I have
Lev 7: 7 "'The same l applies to both the
24:22 You are to have the same l for the
Nu 5:29 "'This, then, is the l of jealousy
5:30 is to apply this entire l to her.
6:13 "'Now this is the l for the
6:21 "'This is the l of the Nazirite who
6:21 according to the l of the Nazirite.
15:29 One and the same l applies to
19: 2 "This is a requirement of the l that
19:14 "This is the l that applies when a
31:21 of the l that the LORD gave Moses:
Dt 1: 5 began to expound this l, saying:
4:44 This is the l Moses set before the
6:25 if we are careful to obey all this l
17:11 Act according to the l they teach
17:18 on a scroll a copy of this l,
17:19 all the words of this l and these
17:20 turn from the l to the right or to
27: 3 Write on them all the words of this l
27: 8 very clearly all the words of this l
27:26 of this l by carrying them out.
28:58 follow all the words of this l,
29:29 may follow all the words of this l.
31: 9 Moses wrote down this l and gave it
31:11 this l before them in their hearing.
31:12 carefully all the words of this l.
31:13 who do not know this l, must hear it
31:24 of this l from beginning to end,
32:46 carefully all the words of this l.
33: 4 the l that Moses gave us, the
33:10 to Jacob and your l to Israel.
Jos 1: 7 Be careful to obey all the l my
8:34 Joshua read all the words of the l
22: 5 the l that Moses the servant of the
2Ki 17:13 in accordance with the entire L that
21: 8 L that my servant Moses gave them."
23:24 to fulfil the requirements of the l
2Ch 6:16 to walk before me according to my l,
15: 3 a priest to teach and without the l.
19:10 or other concerns of the l,
25: 4 with what is written in the L,
31:21 obedience to the l and the commands,
34:19 the king heard the words of the L,
Ezr 7:12 a teacher of the L of the God of

Ezr 7:14 L of your God, which is in your hand.
7:21 a teacher of the L of the God of
7:26 Whoever does not obey the l of your
7:26 the l of the king must surely be
10: 3 Let it be done according to the L.
Ne 8: 2 Ezra the priest brought the L before
8: 7 instructed the people in the L while
8: 9 they listened to the words of the L.
8:13 attention to the words of the L.
8:14 They found written in the L, which
9:26 they put your l behind their backs.
9:29 You warned them to return to your l
9:34 our fathers did not follow your l;
10:34 our God, as it is written in the L.
10:36 "As it is also written in the L, we
12:44 required by the L for the priests
13: 3 the people heard this l, they
Est 1:13 experts in matters of l and justice,
1:15 "According to l, what must be done
3:14 to be issued as l in every province
4:11 but one l: that he be put to death.
4:16 even though it is against the l.
8:13 to be issued as l in every province
Ps 1: 2 on his l he meditates day and night.
37:31 The l of his God is in his heart;
40: 8 O my God; your l is within my heart."
78: 5 and established the l in Israel,
78:10 and refused to live by his l.
89:30 "If his sons forsake my l and do not
94:12 LORD, the man you teach from your l;
119:18 I may see wonderful things in your l.
119:29 be gracious to me through your l.
119:34 I will keep your l and obey it with
119:44 I will always obey your l, for ever
119:51 but I do not turn from your l.
119:53 wicked, who have forsaken your l.
119:55 O LORD, and I will keep your l.
119:61 ropes, I will not forget your l.
119:70 unfeeling, but I delight in your l.
119:72 The l from your mouth is more
119:77 I may live, for your l is my delight.
119:85 pitfalls for me, contrary to your l.
119:92 If your l had not been my delight, I
119:97 Oh, how I love your l! I meditate on
119:109 my hands, I will not forget your l.
119:113 men, but I love your l.
119:126 act, O LORD; your l is being broken.
119:136 my eyes, for your l is not obeyed.
119:142 is everlasting and your l is true.
119:150 near, but they are far from your l.
119:153 me, for I have not forgotten your l.
119:163 abhor falsehood but I love your l.
119:165 Great peace have they who love your l
119:174 O LORD, and your l is my delight.
Pr 28: 4 Those who forsake the l praise the
28: 4 those who keep the l resist them.
28: 7 He who keeps the l is a discerning
28: 9 If anyone turns a deaf ear to the l,
29:18 but blessed is he who keeps the l.
31: 5 drink and forget what the l decrees
Isa 1:10 listed to the l of our God, you
2: 3 The l will go out from Zion, the
8:16 seal up the l among my disciples.
8:20 To the l and to the testimony!
42: 4 In his l the islands will put their
42:21 to make his l great and glorious.
42:24 his ways; they did not obey his l.
51: 4 my nation: The l will go out from me;
51: 7 you people who have my l in your
Jer 2: 8 Those who deal with the l did not
6:19 to my words and have rejected my l.
9:13 is because they have forsaken my l,
9:13 have not obeyed me or followed my l.
16:11 forsook me and did not keep my l.
18:18 teaching of the l by the priest will
26: 4 my l, which I have set before you,
31:33 "I will put my l in their minds and
32:23 did not obey you or follow your l;
44:10 nor have they followed my l and the
44:23 not obeyed him or followed his l or
Lam 2: 9 the l is no more, and her prophets
Eze 7:26 teaching of the l by the priest will
22:26 Her priests do violence to my l and
43:12 "This is the l of the temple: All
43:12 Such is the l of the temple.
Da 6: 5 to do with the l of his God."
Da 6:15 according to the l of the Medes and
9:11 All Israel has transgressed your l
Hos 4: 6 you have ignored the l of your God,
8: 1 covenant and rebelled against my l.
8:12 for them the many things of my l,
Mic 4: 2 The l will go out from Zion, the
Hab 1: 4 Therefore the l is paralysed, and
1: 7 they are a l to themselves and
Zep 3: 4 sanctuary and do violence to the l.
Hag 2:11 'Ask the priests what the l says:
Zec 7:12 would not listen to the l or to the
Mal 2: 9 partiality in matters of the l."
4: 4 "Remember the l of my servant Moses,
Mt 5:17 to abolish the L or the Prophets;
5:18 disappear from the L until everything
7:12 this sums up the L and the Prophets.
8:19 a teacher of the l came to him and
11:13 For all the Prophets and the L
12: 5 Or haven't you read in the L that on
13:52 "Therefore every teacher of the l
22:35 One of them, an expert in the l,
22:36 the greatest commandment in the L?"
22:40 All the L and the Prophets hang on
23:23 l—justice, mercy and faithfulness.
27: 6 "It is against the l to put this
Mk 10: 5 wrote you this l," Jesus replied.
Lk 2:27 what the custom of the L required,
7:30 the Pharisees and experts in the l
10:25 On one occasion an expert in the l
10:26 "What is written in the L?" he
10:37 The expert in the l replied, "The
11:45 One of the experts in the l answered
11:46 "And you experts in the l, woe to
11:52 "Woe to you experts in the l,
14: 3 the Pharisees and experts in the l,
16:16 "The L and the Prophets were
16:17 of a pen to drop out of the L.
Jn 1:17 For the l was given through Moses;
1:45 the one Moses wrote about in the L,
5:10 l forbids you to carry your mat."
7:19 Has not Moses given you the l? Yet
7:19 Yet not one of you keeps the l.
7:49 this mob that knows nothing of the l
7:51 "Does our l condemn a man without
8: 5 In the L Moses commanded us to stone
8:17 In your own L it is written that the
10:34 Is it not written in your L, 'I have
12:34 "We have heard from the L that the
15:25 to fulfil what is written in their L
18:31 and judge him by your own l.
19: 7 have a l, and according to that l he
Ac 5:34 a teacher of the l, who was honoured
6:13 this holy place and against the l.
7:53 you who have received the l that was
10:28 it is against our l for a Jew to
13:15 After the reading from the L and the
18:13 God in ways contrary to the l."
18:15 own l—settle the matter yourselves.
21:20 all of them are zealous for the l.
21:24 are living in obedience to the l.
21:28 our people and our l and this place.
22: 3 trained in the l of our fathers
22:12 He was a devout observer of the l
23: 3 to judge me according to the l,
23: 3 yourself violate the l by commanding
23:29 to do with questions about their l,
24:14 everything that agrees with the L
25: 8 done nothing wrong against the l of
Ro 2:12 All who sin apart from the l will
2:12 will also perish apart from the l,
2:12 under the l will be judged by the l.
2:13 For it is not those who hear the l
2:13 those who obey the l who will be
2:14 Gentiles, who do not have the l, do
2:14 by nature things required by the l,
2:14 they are a l for themselves, even
2:14 even though they do not have the l,
2:15 requirements of the l are written
2:17 if you rely on the l and brag about
2:18 because you are instructed by the l;
2:20 because you have in the l the
2:23 You who brag about the l, do you
2:23 dishonour God by breaking the l?
2:25 has value if you observe the l,
2:25 but if you break the l, you have
2:27 obeys the l will condemn you who,
Ro 3:19 we know that whatever the l says,
3:19 says to those who are under the l,
3:20 in his sight by observing the l;
3:20 the l we become conscious of sin.
3:21 apart from l, has been made known,
3:21 the L and the Prophets testify.
3:27 On that of observing the l? No, but
3:28 by faith apart from observing the l.
3:31 Do we, then, nullify the l by this
3:31 Not at all! Rather, we uphold the l.
4:13 was not through l that Abraham and
4:14 For if those who live by l are heirs,
4:15 l brings wrath. And where there is
4:15 is no l there is no transgression.
4:16 not only to those who are of the l
5:13 for before the l was given, sin was
5:13 into account when there is no l.
5:20 The l was added so that the trespass
6:14 are not under l, but under grace.
6:15 sin because we are not under l
7: 1 I am speaking to men who know the l
7: 1 that the l has authority over a man
7: 2 by l a married woman is bound to her
7: 2 is released from the l of marriage.
7: 3 she is released from that l and is
7: 4 my brothers, you also died to the l
7: 5 aroused by the l were at work in our
7: 6 we have been released from the l so
7: 7 shall we say, then? Is the l sin?
7: 7 what sin was except through the l.
7: 7 the l had not said, "Do not covet.
7: 8 For apart from l, sin is dead.
7: 9 Once I was alive apart from l;
7:12 then, the l is holy, and the
7:14 We know that the l is spiritual;
7:16 to do, I agree that the l is good.
7:21 I find this l at work: When I want
7:22 my inner being I delight in God's l;
7:23 I see another l at work in the
7:23 waging war against the l of my mind
7:23 l of sin at work within my members.
7:25 in my mind am a slave to God's l,
7:25 nature a slave to the l of sin.
8: 2 the l of the Spirit of life set me
8: 2 free from the l of sin and death.
8: 3 For what the l was powerless to do
8: 4 of the l might be fully met in us,
8: 7 submit to God's l, nor can it do so.
9: 4 the receiving of the l, the temple
9:31 who pursued a l of righteousness
10: 4 Christ is the end of the l so that
10: 5 the righteousness that is by the l:
13: 8 his fellow-man has fulfilled the l.
13:10 love is the fulfilment of the l.
1Co 6: 6 instead, one brother goes to l
9: 8 Doesn't the L say the same thing?
9:20 the l I became like one under the l
9:20 I myself am not under the l),
9:20 so as to win those under the l.
9:21 To those not having the l I became
9:21 like one not having the l (though
9:21 God's l but am under Christ's l),
9:21 so as to win those not having the l.
14:21 In the L it is written: "Through men
14:34 be in submission, as the L says.
15:56 sin, and the power of sin is the l.
Gal 2:16 not justified by observing the l,
2:16 Christ and not by observing the l,
2:16 by observing the l no-one will be
2:19 For through the l I died to the l so
2:21 the l, Christ died for nothing!"
3: 2 by observing the l, or by believing
3: 5 among you because you observe the l,
3:10 All who rely on observing the l are
3:11 is justified before God by the l,
3:12 The l is not based on faith; on the
3:13 of the l by becoming a curse for us,
3:17 What I mean is this: The l,
3:18 if the inheritance depends on the l,
3:19 What, then, was the purpose of the l?
3:19 The l was put into effect through
3:21 Is the l, therefore, opposed to the
3:21 if a l had been given that could
3:21 would certainly have come by the l.
3:23 we were held prisoners by the l,
3:24 the l was put in charge to lead us

Gal 3:25 under the supervision of the l.
4: 4 Son, born of a woman, born under l,
4: 5 to redeem those under l, that we
4:21 you who want to be under the l, are
4:21 you not aware of what the l says?
5: 3 he is required to obey the whole l.
5: 4 who are trying to be justified by l
5:14 The entire l is summed up in a
5:18 by the Spirit, you are not under l.
5:23 Against such things there is no l.
6: 2 way you will fulfil the l of Christ.
6:13 who are circumcised obey the l,
Eph 2:15 by abolishing in his flesh the l
Php 3: 5 in regard to the l, a Pharisee;
3: 9 of my own that comes from the l,
1Ti 1: 8 We know that the l is good if one
1: 9 We also know that l is made not for
Tit 3: 9 arguments and quarrels about the l,
Heb 7: 5 Now the l requires the descendants
7:11 on the basis of it the l was given
7:12 must also be a change of the l.
7:19 (for the l made nothing perfect),
7:28 For the l appoints as high priests
7:28 the oath, which came after the l,
8: 4 offer the gifts prescribed by the l.
9:19 every commandment of the l to
9:22 In fact, the l requires that nearly
10: 1 The l is only a shadow of the good
10: 8 the l required them to be made).
Jas 1:25 the perfect l that gives freedom,
2: 8 If you really keep the royal l found
2: 9 convicted by the l as law-breakers.
2:10 For whoever keeps the whole l and
2:12 judged by the l that gives freedom,
4:11 speaks against the l and judges it.
4:11 When you judge the l, you are not
1Jn 3: 4 Everyone who sins breaks the l;

Law of God

Jos 24:26 these things in the Book of the L.
Ne 8: 8 They read from the Book of the L,
8:18 Ezra read from the Book of the L.
10:28 peoples for the sake of the L,
10:29 an oath to follow the L given

Law of Moses

Jos 8:31 is written in the Book of the L—
8:32 Joshua copied on stones the l,
23: 6 is written in the Book of the L,
1Ki 2: 3 as written in the L, so that you may
2Ki 14: 6 of the L where the LORD commanded:
23:25 in accordance with all the L.
2Ch 23:18 of the LORD as written in the L,
30:16 prescribed in the L the man of God.
Ezr 3: 2 is written in the L the man of God.
7: 6 was a teacher well versed in the L,
Ne 8: 1 to bring out the Book of the L,
Da 9:11 sworn judgments written in the L,
9:13 Just as it is written in the L, all
Lk 2:22 to the L had been completed,
24:44 the L, the Prophets and the Psalms."
Jn 7:23 so that the l may not be broken,
Ac 13:39 not be justified from by the l.
15: 5 and required to obey the l."
28:23 from the L and from the Prophets.
1Co 9: 9 For it is written in the L: "Do not
Heb 10:28 Anyone who rejected the l died

Law of the LORD

Ex 13: 9 that the l is to be on your lips.
2Ki 10:31 Jehu was not careful to keep the l,
1Ch 16:40 in the L, which he had given Israel.
22:12 so that you may keep the l your God.
2Ch 12: 1 all Israel with him abandoned the l.
17: 9 taking with them the Book of the L;
19: 8 to administer the l and to settle
31: 3 feasts as written in the L.
31: 4 could devote themselves to the L.
34:14 L that had been given through Moses.
35:26 to what is written in the L—
Ezr 7:10 the study and observance of the L,
Ne 9: 3 L their God for a quarter of the day,
Ps 1: 2 his delight is in the l, and on his
19: 7 The l is perfect, reviving the soul.
119: 1 who walk according to the l.
Isa 5:24 for they have rejected the l
Jer 8: 8 "We are wise, for we have the l,"
Am 2: 4 Because they have rejected the l and

Law of the Lord

Lk 2:23 (as it is written in the L, "Every
2:24 keeping with what is said in the L:
2:39 done everything required by the L,

Law's (Law)

Ro 2:26 circumcised keep the l requirements,

Law-breaker (Law)

Ro 2:27 code and circumcision, are a l.
Gal 2:18 I destroyed, I prove that I am a l.
Jas 2:11 commit murder, you have become a l.

Lawbreakers (Law)

1Ti 1: 9 the righteous but for l and rebels,

Law-breakers (Law)

Jas 2: 9 and are convicted by the law as l.

Lawful (Law)

Mt 12: 4 was not l for them to do,
12:10 "Is it l to heal on the Sabbath?
12:12 it is l to do good on the Sabbath."
14: 4 "It is not l for you to have her.
19: 3 "Is it l for a man to divorce his
Mk 2:26 which is l only for priests to eat.
3: 4 Jesus asked them, "Which is l on the
6:18 "It is not l for you to have your
10: 2 it l for a man to divorce his wife?"
Lk 6: 4 what is l only for priests to eat.
6: 9 "I ask you, which is l on the
14: 3 it l to heal on the Sabbath or not?"

Lawgiver (Law)

Isa 33:22 the LORD is our l, the LORD is our
Jas 4:12 There is only one L and Judge, the

Lawless (Lawlessness)

2Sa 3:33 Should Abner have died as the l die?
2Th 2: 8 the l one will be revealed, whom the
2: 9 The coming of the l one will be in
Heb 10:17 he adds: "Their sins and l acts I
2Pe 2: 7 by the filthy lives of l men
2: 8 by the l deeds he saw and heard)—
3:17 carried away by the error of l men

Lawlessness (Lawless)

2Th 2: 3 and the man of l is revealed
2: 7 secret power of l is already at work
1Jn 3: 4 breaks the law; in fact, sin is l.

Laws (Law)

Ge 26: 5 my commands, my decrees and my l."
Ex 18:16 inform them of God's decrees and l."
18:20 Teach them the decrees and l, and
21: 1 "These are the l you are to set
24: 3 people all the LORD's words and l,
Lev 18: 4 You must obey my l and be careful to
18: 5 Keep my decrees and l, for the man
18:26 you must keep my decrees and my l.
19:37 "'Keep all my decrees and all my l
20:22 "'Keep all my decrees and l and
25:18 decrees and be careful to obey my l,
26:15 abhor my l and fail to carry out all
26:43 they rejected my l and abhorred my
26:46 These are the decrees, the l and the
Nu 15:16 The same l and regulations will
Dt 4: 1 Hear now, O Israel, the decrees and l
4: 5 See, I have taught you decrees and l
4: 8 l as this body of l I am setting
4:14 l you are to follow in the land that
4:45 decrees and l Moses gave them when
5: 1 l I declare in your hearing today.
5:31 decrees and l that you are to teach
6: 1 These are the commands, decrees and l
6:20 decrees and l the LORD our God has
7:11 decrees and l I give you today.
7:12 If you pay attention to these l and
8:11 his l and his decrees that I am
11: 1 his l and his commands always.
11:32 and l I am setting before you today.
12: 1 These are the decrees and l you must
19: 9 you carefully follow all these l I
26:16 to follow these decrees and l;
26:17 keep his decrees, commands and l,
30:16 to keep his commands, decrees and l;
Jos 24:25 he drew up for them decrees and l.
2Sa 22:23 All his l are before me; I have not
1Ki 2: 3 his l and requirements, as written
9: 4 and observe my decrees and l,
11:33 nor kept my statutes and l as David,
2Ki 17:34 the l and commands that the LORD
17:37 the l and commands he wrote for you.
1Ch 22:13 l that the LORD gave to Moses for
28: 7 in carrying out my commands and l,
2Ch 7:17 and observe my decrees and l,
14: 4 and to obey his l and commands.
33: 8 commanded them concerning all the l,
Ezr 7:10 its decrees and l in Israel.
7:25 who know the l of your God.
Ne 1: 7 and l you gave your servant Moses.
9:13 You gave them regulations and l that
9:14 and l through your servant Moses.
Est 1:19 in the l of Persia and Media,
3: 8 and who do not obey the king's l;
Job 38:33 Do you know the l of the heavens?
Ps 10: 5 haughty and your l are far from him
18:22 All his l are before me; I have not
50:16 What right have you to recite my l
105:45 keep his precepts and observe his l.
119: 7 heart as I learn your righteous l.
119:13 With my lips I recount all the l
119:20 longing for your l at all times.
119:30 I have set my heart on your l.
119:39 I dread, for your l are good.
119:43 for I have put my hope in your l.
119:52 I remember your ancient l, O LORD,
119:62 you thanks for your righteous l.
119:75 I know, O LORD, that your l are
119:91 Your l endure to this day, for all
119:102 I have not departed from your l, for
119:106 that I will follow your righteous l.
119:108 of my mouth, and teach me your l.
119:120 of you; I stand in awe of your l.
119:137 are you, O LORD, and your l are right.
119:149 life, O LORD, according to you l.
119:156 my life according to your l.
119:160 all your righteous l are eternal.
119:164 I praise you for your righteous l.
119:175 you, and may your l sustain me.
147:19 Jacob, his l and decrees to Israel.
147:20 nation; they do not know his l.
Pr 8:15 By me kings reign and rulers make l
Isa 10: 1 Woe to those who make unjust l, to
24: 5 people; they have disobeyed the l,
26: 8 LORD, walking in the way of your l,
Jer 33:25 and the fixed l of heaven and earth,
Eze 5: 6 she has rebelled against my l
5: 6 rejected my l and has not followed
5: 7 followed my decrees or kept my l.
11:12 not followed my decrees or kept my l
11:20 decrees and be careful to keep my l
18: 9 decrees and faithfully keeps my l.
18:17 He keeps my l and follows my decrees
20:11 decrees and made known to them my l,
20:13 follow my decrees but rejected my l
20:16 they rejected my l and did not
20:18 or keep their l or defile yourselves
20:19 decrees and be careful to keep my l.
20:21 they were not careful to keep my l
20:24 they had not obeyed my l but had
20:25 good and l they could not live by;
36:27 decrees and be careful to keep my l.
37:24 follow my l and be careful to keep
43:11 and all its regulations and l.
44:24 They are to keep my l and my decrees
Da 6: 8 the l of the Medes and Persians,
6:12 the l of the Medes and Persians,
7:25 to change the set times and the l.
9: 5 away from your commands and l.
9:10 or kept the l he gave us through
Mal 4: 4 l I gave him at Horeb for all Israel.
Heb 8:10 I will put my l in their minds and
10:16 I will put my l in their hearts, and

Lawsuit (Lawsuits)

Ex 23: 2 When you give testimony in a l, do
23: 3 favouritism to a poor man in his l.

Lawsuits (Lawsuit)

Ex 23: 6 to your poor people in their l.
Dt 17: 8 whether bloodshed, l or assaults
Hos 10: 4 therefore l spring up like poisonous
1Co 6: 7 very fact that you have l among you

Lawyer (Law)

Ac 24: 1 the elders and a l named Tertullus,
Tit 3:13 you can to help Zenas the l

Lax

Jer 48:10 "A curse on him who is l in doing

Lay[1] (Laid, Layer, Laying, Lays, Lie)

Ge 4: 1 Adam l with his wife Eve, and she
4:17 Cain l with his wife, and she became
4:25 Adam l with his wife again, and she
9:21 and l uncovered inside his tent.
19:33 daughter went in and l with him.
19:33 when she l down or when she got up.
19:34 "Last night I l with my father.
19:35 daughter went and l with him.
19:35 when she l down or when she got up.
22:12 "Do not l a hand on the boy," he
28:11 under his head and l down to sleep.
29:23 her to Jacob, and Jacob l with her.
29:30 Jacob l with Rachel also, and he
37:22 desert, but don't l a hand on him.
37:27 not l our hands on him; after all,
38: 2 He married her and l with her;
38: 9 he l with his brother's wife,
Ex 7: 4 Then I will l my hand on Egypt and
22:11 the neighbour did not l hands on
29:10 shall l their hands on its head.
29:15 shall l their hands on its head.
29:19 shall l their hands on its head.
Lev 1: 4 He is to l his hand on the head of
3: 2 He is to l his hand on the head of
3: 8 He is to l his hand on the head of
3:13 He is to l his hand on its head and
4: 4 He is to l his hand on its head and
4:15 The elders of the community are to l
4:24 He is to l his hand on the goat's
4:29 He is to l his hand on the head of
4:33 He is to l his hand on its head and
16:21 He is to l both hands on the head of
24:14 All those who heard him are to l
26:31 ruins and l waste your sanctuaries,
26:32 I will l waste the land, so that
Nu 8:10 are to l their hands on them.
8:12 "After the Levites l their hands on
22:27 she l down under Balaam, and he was
27:18 the spirit, and l your hand on him.
Dt 9:25 I l prostrate before the LORD those
20:12 you in battle, l siege to that city.
20:19 you l siege to a city for a long
28:52 They will l siege to all the cities
Jos 2: 8 Before the spies l down for the
6:26 son will he l its foundations;
8: 9 and l in wait between Bethel and Ai,
18:11 Their allotted territory l between
19: 1 l within the territory of Judah.
Jdg 4:21 while he l fast asleep, exhausted.
4:22 and there l Sisera with the tent peg
5:27 feet he sank, he fell; there he l.
7: 8 camp of Midian l below him in the
16: 2 l in wait for him all night at the
16: 3 Samson l there only until the middle
19:26 the door and l there until daylight.
19:27 there l his concubine, fallen in the
Ru 3: 7 uncovered his feet and l down.
3:14 she l at his feet until morning, but
1Sa 1:19 Elkanah l with Hannah his wife, and
3: 5 So he went and l down.
3: 9 Samuel went and l down in his place.
3:15 Samuel l down until morning and then
9:23 you, the one I told you to l aside."
19:24 He l that way all that day and night.
23:17 "My father Saul will not l a hand on
26: 9 Who can l a hand on the LORD's
1Sa 26:11 LORD forbid that I should l a hand on
26:23 not l a hand on the LORD's anointed.
2Sa 12:24 and he went to her and l with her.
13: 6 Amnon l down and pretended to be ill.
13:31 tore his clothes and l down on the
16:22 and he l with his father's
20:12 Amasa l wallowing in his blood in
1Ki 3:19 son died because she l on him.
13:31 buried; l my bones beside his bones.
19: 5 he l down under the tree and fell
19: 6 ate and drank and then l down again.
21: 4 He l on his bed sulking and refused
21:27 He l in sackcloth and went around
2Ki 4:11 up to his room and l down there.
4:29 L my staff on the boy's face."
4:34 he got on the bed and l upon the boy,
1Ch 2:21 Later, Hezron l with the daughter of
7:23 he l with his wife again, and she
2Ch 24:22 who said as he l dying, "May the
Ne 13:21 this again, I will l hands on you.
Est 4: 3 Many l in sackcloth and ashes.
9:10 not l their hands on the plunder.
9:15 not l their hands on the plunder.
9:16 not l their hands on the plunder.
Job 1:12 the man himself do not l a finger.
5: 8 God; I would l my cause before him.
9:33 us, to l his hand upon us both,
22:22 and l up his words in your heart.
30:12 they l snares for my feet, they
41: 8 If you l a hand on him, you will
Ps 5: 3 in the morning I l my requests
21: 8 Your hand will l hold on all your
22:15 you l me in the dust of death.
73: 9 Their mouths l claim to heaven, and
Pr 3:18 who l hold of her will be blessed.
4: 4 L hold of my words with all your
Ecc 10: 4 calmness can l great errors to rest.
Isa 11:14 They will l hands on Edom and Moab,
21: 2 Elam, attack! Media, l siege! I will
24: 1 See, the LORD is going to l waste
25:12 high fortified walls and l them low;
28:16 "See, I l a stone in Zion, a tested
34:15 The owl will nest there and l eggs,
35: 7 In the haunts where jackals once l,
42:15 I will l waste the mountains and
43:17 and they l there, never to rise
44: 7 Let him declare and l out before me
52:10 The LORD will l bare his holy arm in
64: 7 name or strives to l hold of you;
Jer 2:20 tree you l down as a prostitute.
4: 7 He has left his place to l waste
4:26 towns l in ruins before the LORD,
9:11 I will l waste the towns of Judah
15: 6 will l hands on you and destroy you
17:11 that hatches eggs it did not l is
34:22 And I will l waste the towns of
50: 3 attack her and l waste her land.
51:29 to l waste the land of Babylon so
Lam 4:19 and l in wait for us in the desert.
Eze 4: 2 l siege to it: Erect siege works
6: 5 I will l the dead bodies of the
16: 6 and as you l there in your blood I
19: 2 She l down among the young lions and
25:13 I will l it waste, and from Teman to
26:16 l aside their robes and take off
30:12 hand of foreigners I will l waste
30:14 I will l waste Upper Egypt, set fire
31:12 its branches l broken in all the
39:21 I inflict and the hand I l upon them.
Da 2:28 mind as you l on your bed are these:
8:27 I, Daniel, was exhausted and l ill
Jnh 1: 5 l down and fell into a deep sleep.
Mic 1: 6 valley and l bare her foundations.
7:16 will l their hands on their mouths
Mt 8:20 of Man has nowhere to l his head."
11:12 and forceful men l hold of it.
28: 6 Come and see the place where he l.
Mk 6: 5 except l his hands on a few sick
Lk 5:18 the house to l him before Jesus.
9:58 of Man has nowhere to l his head."
21:12 will l hands on you and persecute
22:53 and you did not l a hand on me.
Jn 4:46 whose son l sick at Capernaum.
10:15 I l down my life for the sheep.
10:17 loves me is that I l down my life
10:18 No-one takes it from me, but I l it
Jn 10:18 I have authority to l it down and
11: 2 whose brother Lazarus now l sick,
13:37 now? I will l down my life for you."
13:38 Jesus answered, "Will you really l
15:13 he l down his life for his friends.
Ac 8:19 everyone on whom I l my hands may
Ro 9:33 is written: "See, I l in Zion a
1Co 3:11 For no-one can l any foundation
7:17 rule I l down in all the churches.
1Ti 6:19 In this way they will l up treasure
1Pe 2: 6 it says: "See, I l a stone in Zion,
1Jn 3:16 l down our lives for our brothers.
Rev 4:10 They l their crowns before the
10: 2 scroll, which l open in his hand.

Lay[2]

2Ch 35: 5 fellow countrymen, the l people.
35: 7 Josiah provided for all the l people

Layer (Lay[1])

Ex 16:13 was a l of dew around the camp.
Lev 9:19 the l of fat, the kidneys and the

Laying (Lay[1])

2Ch 32: 9 his forces were l siege to Lachish,
Job 34:30 from l snares for the people.
Lk 4:40 and l his hands on each one, he
Ac 8:18 as given at the l on of the apostles'
1Ti 5:22 Do not be hasty in the l on of hands,
2Ti 1: 6 in you through the l on of my hands.
Heb 6: 1 not l again the foundation of
6: 2 about baptisms, the l on of hands, the

Lays (Lay[1])

Job 27:17 what he l up the righteous will wear,
28: 9 l bare the roots of the mountains.
30:24 "Surely no-one l a hand on a broken
39:14 She l her eggs on the ground and
Ps 104: 3 l the beams of his upper chambers on
Isa 26: 5 he l the lofty city low; he levels
30:32 Every stroke the LORD l on them with
Zec 12: 1 who l the foundation of the earth,
Lk 14:29 For if he l the foundation and is
Jn 10:11 l down his life for the sheep.

Lazarus

1. Beggar in Jesus' parable (Lk 16:19–31).
2. Brother of Mary and Martha; raised to life by Jesus (Jn 11:1–12:11).

Lk 16:20 At his gate was laid a beggar named L
16:23 Abraham far away, with L by his side.
16:24 have pity on me and send L to dip
16:25 while L received bad things, but now
16:27 father, send L to my father's house,
Jn 11: 1 Now a man named L was sick. He was
11: 2 Mary, whose brother L now lay sick
11: 5 loved Martha and her sister and L.
11: 6 Yet when he heard that L was sick,
11:11 "Our friend L has fallen asleep; but
11:14 he told them plainly, "L is dead,
11:17 Jesus found that L had already been
11:43 in a loud voice, "L, come out!
12: 1 arrived at Bethany, where L lived,
12: 2 L was among those reclining at the
12: 9 L, whom he had raised from the dead.
12:10 made plans to kill L as well,
12:17 him when he called L from the tomb

Laziness (Lazy)

Pr 12:24 rule, but l ends in slave labour
19:15 L brings on deep sleep, and the

Lazy (Laziness)

Ex 5: 8 They are l; that is why they are
5:17 "L, that's what you are—l! That is
Pr 10: 4 L hands make a man poor, but
12:27 The l man does not roast his game,
26:15 too l to bring it back to his mouth.
Ecc 10:18 If a man is l, the rafters sag; if
Mt 25:26 replied, 'You wicked, l servant!
Tit 1:12 liars, evil brutes, l gluttons."
Heb 6:12 We do not want you to become l, but

Lead[1] (Leader, Leader's, Leaders, Leaders', Leadership, Leading, Leads, Led, Ringleader)

Ge 32:17 He instructed the one in the l:
Ex 13:17 God did not l them on the road
15:13 "In your unfailing love you will l
32:34 Now go, l the people to the place I
33:12 'L these people,' but you have not
34:16 will l your sons to do the same.
Nu 14: 8 he will l us into that land, a land
21:15 the ravines that l to the site of Ar
27:17 one who will l them out and bring
Dt 1:38 he will l Israel to inherit it.
3:28 for he will l this people across and
10:11 LORD said to me, "and l the people
21: 4 l her down to a valley that has not
31: 2 and I am no longer able to l you.
Jos 1: 6 because you will l these people to
Jdg 4: 6 Zebulun and l the way to Mount Tabor.
5: 2 the princes in Israel take the l,
7:17 "Follow my l. When I get to the edge
1Sa 8: 5 now appoint a king to l us, such as
8: 6 they said, "Give us a king to l us,"
8:20 with a king to l us and to go out
30:15 David asked him, "Can you l me down
2Ki 4:24 "L on; don't slow down for me unless
6:19 Follow me, and I will l you to the
2Ch 1:10 that I may l this people, for who is
8:14 the Levites to l the praise and to
Est 6: 9 and l him on the horse through the
Job 38:32 or l out the Bear with its cubs?
Ps 5: 8 L me, O LORD, in your righteousness
26:11 I l a blameless life; redeem me and
27:11 O LORD; l me in a straight path
31: 3 sake of your name l and guide me.
60: 9 city? Who will l me to Edom?
61: 2 l me to the rock that is higher than
80: 1 you who l Joseph like a flock;
101: 2 I will be careful to l a blameless
108:10 city? Who will l me to Edom?
139:24 and l me in the way everlasting.
143:10 good Spirit l me on level ground.
Pr 4:11 and l you along straight paths.
5: 5 her steps l straight to the grave.
21: 5 plans of the diligent l to profit
Ecc 5: 6 Do not let your mouth l you into sin
SS 8: 2 I would l you and bring you to my
Isa 3:12 O my people, your guides l you
11: 6 and a little child will l them.
20: 4 the king of Assyria will l away
42:16 I will l the blind by ways they have
43: 8 L out those who have eyes but are
49:10 and l them beside springs of water.
60: 9 in the l are the ships of Tarshish,
Jer 3:15 who will l you with knowledge and
23:32 "They tell them and l my people
31: 9 I will l them beside streams of
31:32 by the hand to l them out of Egypt,
50: 8 be like the goats that l the flock.
Eze 13:10 "'Because they l my people astray,
Da 12: 3 those who l many to righteousness
Hos 2:14 I will l her into the desert and
5: 8 cry in Beth Aven; l on, O Benjamin.
Mic 3: 5 As for the prophets who l my people
6: 4 I sent Moses to l you, also Aaron
Mt 6:13 l us not into temptation, but
Mk 14:44 him and l him away under guard."
Lk 6:39 "Can a blind man l a blind man?
11: 4 And l us not into temptation.'
13:15 stall and l it out to give it water?
Jn 21:18 l you where you do not want to go."
Ac 13:11 someone to l him by the hand.
Gal 3:24 was put in charge to l us to Christ
1Th 4:11 it your ambition to l a quiet life
Heb 6: 1 repentance from acts that l to death
8: 9 by the hand to l them out of Egypt,
9:14 from acts that l to death, so that
1Jn 2:26 who are trying to l you astray.
3: 7 do not let anyone l you astray.
5:16 a sin that does not l to death,
5:16 those whose sin does not l to death.
5:17 is sin that does not l to death.
Rev 7:17 l them to springs of living water.

Lead[2]

Nu 31:22 Gold, silver, bronze, iron, tin, l
Job 19:24 inscribed with an iron tool on l,
Jer 6:29 to burn away the l with fire,
Eze 22:18 iron and l left inside a furnace.
22:20 men gather silver, copper, iron, l
27:12 tin and l for your merchandise.
Zec 5: 7 the cover of l was raised, and there
5: 8 the l cover down over its mouth.

Leader (Lead[1])

Lev 4:22 When a l sins unintentionally and
Nu 2: 3 The l of the people of Judah is
2: 5 The l of the people of Issachar is
2: 7 The l of the people of Zebulun is
2:10 The l of the people of Reuben is
2:12 The l of the people of Simeon is
2:14 The l of the people of Gad is
2:18 The l of the people of Ephraim is
2:20 The l of the people of Manasseh is
2:22 The l of the people of Benjamin is
2:25 The l of the people of Dan is
2:27 The l of the people of Asher is
2:29 The l of the people of Naphtali is
3:24 The l of the families of the
3:30 The l of the families of the
3:32 The chief l of the Levites was
3:35 The l of the families of the
7: 3 an ox from each l and a cart from
7:11 one l is to bring his offering
7:18 l of Issachar, brought his offering.
7:24 Eliab son of Helon, the l of the
7:30 the l of the people of Reuben,
7:36 the l of the people of Simeon,
7:42 the l of the people of Gad, brought
7:48 the l of the people of Ephraim,
7:54 the l of the people of Manasseh,
7:60 the l of the people of Benjamin,
7:66 the l of the people of Dan, brought
7:72 the l of the people of Asher,
7:78 the l of the people of Naphtali,
14: 4 choose a l and go back to Egypt."
17: 2 l of each of their ancestral tribes.
17: 6 one for the l of each of their
25:14 Salu, the l of a Simeonite family.
25:18 the daughter of a Midianite l, the
34:18 appoint one l from each tribe to
34:22 Bukki son of Jogli, the l from the
34:23 Hanniel son of Ephod, the l from the
34:24 Kemuel son of Shiphtan, the l from
34:25 Elizaphan son of Parnach, the l from
34:26 Paltiel son of Azzan, the l from the
34:27 Ahihud son of Shelomi, the l from
34:28 Pedahel son of Ammihud, the l from
1Sa 7: 6 And Samuel was l of Israel at Mizpah.
9:16 Anoint him l over my people Israel;
10: 1 anointed you l over his inheritance?
12: 2 Now you have a king as your l. As
12: 2 your l from my youth until this day.
13:14 and appointed him l of his people,
19:20 Samuel standing there as their l,
22: 2 round him, and he became their l.
25:30 and has appointed him l over Israel,
1Ki 11:24 became the l of a band of rebels
14: 7 made you a l over my people Israel.
16: 2 and made you l of my people Israel,
2Ki 20: 5 tell Hezekiah, the l of my people,
1Ch 2:10 the l of the people of Judah.
5: 6 Beerah was a l of the Reubenites.
12: 4 who was a l of the Thirty;
12:27 Jehoiada, l of the family of Aaron
15: 5 Uriel the l and 120 relatives;
15: 6 Asaiah the l and 220 relatives;
15: 7 Joel the l and 130 relatives;
15: 8 Shemaiah the l and 200 relatives;
15: 9 Hebron, Eliel the l and 80 relatives
15:10 Amminadab the l and 112 relatives.
27: 4 Mikloth was the l of his division.
28: 4 He chose Judah as l, and from the
2Ch 6: 5 to be the l over my people Israel.
13:12 God is with us; he is our l. His
19:11 the l of the tribe of Judah,
Ezr 8:17 them to Iddo, the l in Casiphia
Ne 9:17 in their rebellion appointed a l in
Isa 3: 6 "You have a cloak, you be our l;
3: 7 do not make me the l of the people."
55: 4 a l and commander of the peoples.
Jer 30:21 Their l will be one of their own;
Hos 1:11 they will appoint one l and will
Hab 3:13 You crushed the l of the land of

Leader's (Lead[1])

Dt 33:21 the l portion was kept for him.

Leaders (Lead[1])

Ex 15:15 the l of Moab will be seized with
16:22 the l of the community came and
18:25 and made them l of the people,
24:11 against these l of the Israelites;
34:31 l of the community came back to him,
35:27 The l brought onyx stones and other
Nu 1:16 the l of their ancestral tribes.
1:44 Aaron and the twelve l of Israel,
4:34 Aaron and the l of the community
4:46 Moses, Aaron and the l of Israel
7: 2 the l of Israel, the heads of
7: 2 the tribal l in charge of those
7:10 the l brought their offerings
7:84 the offerings of the Israelite l
10: 4 l—the heads of the clans of Israel
11:16 as l and officials among the people
13: 2 ancestral tribe send one of its l."
13: 3 All of them were l of the Israelites
16: 2 community l who had been appointed
17: 6 and their l gave him twelve staffs,
25: 4 "Take all the l of these people,
27: 2 l and the whole assembly, and said,
31:13 all the l of the community went
32: 2 to the l of the community, and said,
36: 1 and spoke before Moses and the l,
Dt 29:10 your l and chief men, your elders
32:42 captives, the heads of the enemy l.
33: 5 when the l of the people assembled
Jos 8:10 and he and the l of Israel marched
9:15 the l of the assembly ratified it
9:18 the l of the assembly had sworn
9:18 assembly grumbled against the l,
9:19 all the l answered, "We have given
17: 4 Joshua son of Nun, and the l and
22:30 Phinehas the priest and the l of the
22:32 the l returned to Canaan from their
23: 2 summoned all Israel—their elders, l,
24: 1 He summoned the elders, l, judges
Jdg 7:25 of the Midianite l, Oreb and Zeeb.
8: 3 the Midianite l, into your hands.
10:18 The l of the people of Gilead said
20: 2 The l of all the people of the
1Sa 14:38 here, all you who are l of the army
2Sa 4: 2 two men who were l of raiding bands
7:11 I appointed l over my people Israel.
1Ch 4:38 The men listed above by name were l
7:40 brave warriors and outstanding l.
12:18 made them l of his raiding bands.
12:20 l of units of a thousand in Manasseh
15:16 David told the l of the Levites to
17: 6 did I ever say to any of their l
17:10 I appointed l over my people Israel.
22:17 David ordered all the l of Israel to
23: 2 He also gathered together all the l
24: 4 A larger number of l were found
26: 6 who were l in their father's family
29: 6 the l of families, the officers of
29: 9 at the willing response of their l,
2Ch 1: 2 l in Israel, the heads of families—
12: 5 to the l of Judah who had assembled
12: 6 The l of Israel and the king humbled
24:23 and killed all the l of the people.
26:12 The total number of family l over
28:12 some of the l in Ephraim—Azariah
32:21 the l and officers in the camp of
35: 9 and Jozabad, the l of the Levites,
36:14 all the l of the priests and the
Ezr 5:10 write down the names of their l
8:16 Zechariah and Meshullam, who were l
9: 1 the l came to me and said, "The
9: 2 And the l and officials have led the
Ne 9:32 upon our kings and l, upon our
9:34 Our kings, our l, our priests and
9:38 putting it in writing, and our l,
10:14 The l of the people: Parosh,

Ne 11: 1 Now the l of the people settled in
11: 3 These are the provincial l who
12: 7 These were the l of the priests and
12:24 the l of the Levites were Hashabiah,
12:31 I had the l of Judah go up on top of
12:32 Hoshaiah and half the l of Judah
Est 1: 3 The military l of Persia and Media,
Job 12:24 He deprives the l of the earth of
Isa 3:14 the elders and l of his people:
14: 9 all those who were l in the world;
19:13 the l of Memphis are deceived;
22: 3 All your l have fled together;
Jer 2: 8 know me; the l rebelled against me.
5: 5 I will go to the l and speak to them
25:34 in the dust, you l of the flock.
25:35 l of the flock no place to escape.
25:36 the wailing of the l of the flock,
29: 2 and the l of Judah and Jerusalem,
34:19 The l of Judah and Jerusalem, the
Eze 11: 1 son of Benaiah, l of the people.
32:21 mighty l will say of Egypt and her
Da 11:41 but Edom, Moab and the l of Ammon
Hos 5:10 Judah's l are like those who move
7:16 Their l will fall by the sword
9:15 all their l are rebellious.
Mic 3: 1 I said, "Listen, you l of Jacob, you
3: 9 Hear this, you l of the house of
3:11 Her l judge for a bribe, her priests
5: 5 shepherds, even eight l of men.
Zec 9: 7 to our God and become l in Judah,
10: 3 and I will punish the l; for the
12: 5 the l of Judah will say in their
12: 6 I will make the l of Judah like a
Lk 19:47 the teachers of the law and the l
Jn 12:42 even among the l believed in him.
Ac 3:17 acted in ignorance, as did your l.
14: 5 together with their l, to ill-treat
15:22 men who were l among the brothers.
25: 2 where the chief priests and Jewish l
25: 5 Let some of your l come with me and
28:17 called together the l of the Jews.
Gal 2: 2 to those who seemed to be l,
Heb 13: 7 Remember your l, who spoke the word
13:17 Obey your l and submit to their
13:24 Greet all your l and all God's

Leaders' (Lead[1])

Jos 9:21 So the l promise to them was kept.

Leadership (Lead[1])

Nu 33: 1 under the l of Moses and Aaron.
Ps 109: 8 may another take his place of l.
Ac 1:20 "'May another take his place of l.
Ro 12: 8 if it is l, let him govern

Leading (Lead[1])

Dt 1:15 I took the l men of your tribes,
5:23 all the l men of your tribes and
Jdg 3:27 him from the hills, with him l them.
4: 4 Lappidoth, was l Israel at that time.
12: 5 fords of the Jordan l to Ephraim,
20:31 l to Bethel and the other to Gibeah.
2Sa 10:16 of Hadadezer's army l them.
15: 2 side of the road l to the city gate.
17:11 you yourself l them into battle.
2Ki 10: 6 seventy of them, were with the l men
19: 2 the secretary and the l priests,
24:15 officials and the l men of the land.
1Ch 19:16 of Hadadezer's army l them.
2Ch 23:13 instruments were l the praises.
Ezr 7:28 l men from Israel to go up with me.
8:24 I set apart twelve of the l priests,
8:29 in Jerusalem before the l priests
10: 5 Ezra rose up and put the l priests
Ps 42: 4 l the procession to the house of God
68:27 little tribe of Benjamin l them,
Pr 7:27 l down to the chambers of death.
8: 3 beside the gates l into the city,
Isa 37: 2 the secretary, and the l priests,
Eze 17:13 carried away the l men of the land,
40:20 north, l into the outer court.
Mt 26:55 "Am I l a rebellion, that you have
Mk 6:21 commanders and the l men of Galilee.
10:32 with Jesus l the way, and the
14:48 "Am I l a rebellion," said Jesus,
Lk 22:47 Judas, one of the Twelve, was l them.
22:52 "Am I l a rebellion, that you have
Ac 12:10 came to the iron gate l to the city.
13:50 standing and the l men of the city.
16:12 l city of that district of Macedonia.
25:23 officers and the l men of the city.
Ro 6:19 to righteousness l to holiness.
15:18 in l the Gentiles to obey God by
2Ti 2:25 l them to a knowledge of the truth,

Leads (Lead[1])

Dt 27:18 "Cursed is the man who l the blind
Jos 2: 7 that l to the fords of the Jordan,
1Ch 11: 6 had said, "Whoever l the attack
Job 12:17 He l counsellors away stripped and
12:19 He l priests away stripped and
Ps 23: 2 he l me beside quiet waters,
37: 8 do not fret—it l only to evil.
68: 6 he l forth the prisoners with
Pr 2:18 For her house l down to death and
10:17 ignores correction l others astray.
12:26 the way of the wicked l them astray.
14:12 a man, but in the end it l to death.
14:23 but mere talk l only to poverty.
15:24 The path of life l upward for the
16:25 a man, but in the end it l to death.
16:29 l him down a path that is not good.
19:23 The fear of the LORD l to life:
20: 7 The righteous man l a blameless life
21: 5 as surely as haste l to poverty.
28:10 He who l the upright along an evil
Isa 30:28 peoples a bit that l them astray.
40:11 he gently l those that have young.
Hos 4:12 A spirit of prostitution l them
Mt 7:13 is the road that l to destruction,
7:14 l to life, and only a few find it.
12:20 out, till he l justice to victory.
15:14 If a blind man l a blind man, both
Jn 10: 3 own sheep by name and l them out.
12:50 that his command l to eternal life.
Ro 2: 4 kindness l you towards repentance?
6:16 which l to death, or to obedience,
6:16 obedience, which l to righteousness?
6:22 the benefit you reap l to holiness,
14:19 l to peace and to mutual edification.
2Co 2:14 thanks be to God, who always l us in
7:10 brings repentance that l to salvation
Eph 5:18 drunk on wine, which l to debauchery
Tit 1: 1 of the truth that l to godliness—
1Jn 5:16 There is a sin that l to death. I am
Rev 12: 9 Satan, who l the whole world astray.

Leaf (Leafy, Leaves)

Ge 8:11 beak was a freshly plucked olive l!
Lev 26:36 the sound of a wind-blown l will
Job 13:25 Will you torment a wind-blown l?
Ps 1: 3 season and whose l does not wither.
Pr 11:28 will thrive like a green l.
Isa 64: 6 we all shrivel up like a l, and
Mk 11:13 in the distance a fig-tree in l,

Leafy (Leaf)

Lev 23:40 and palm fronds, l branches and
Eze 6:13 every spreading tree and every l oak
17: 6 branches and put out l boughs.
20:28 saw any high hill or any l tree,

Leah (Leah's)

Daughter of Laban; wife of Jacob (Ge 29:16–23); bore six sons and one daughter (Ge 29:31–35; 30:16–21; 34:1; 35:23).

Ge 29:16 the name of the older was L,
29:17 L had weak eyes, but Rachel was
29:23 he took his daughter L and gave her
29:25 morning came, there was L! So Jacob
29:28 He finished the week with L, and
29:30 and he loved Rachel more than L.
29:31 the LORD saw that L was not loved,
29:32 L became pregnant and gave birth to
30: 9 L saw that she had stopped having
30:11 L said, "What good fortune!" So she
30:13 L said, "How happy I am! The women
30:14 which he brought to his mother L.
Ge 30:14 Rachel said to L, "Please give me
30:16 evening, L went out to meet him.
30:17 God listened to L, and she became
30:18 L said, "God has rewarded me for
30:19 L conceived again and bore Jacob a
30:20 L said, "God has presented me with a
31: 4 Jacob sent word to Rachel and L to
31:14 Rachel and L replied, "Do we still
33: 1 L, Rachel and the two maidservants.
33: 2 L and her children next, and Rachel
33: 7 Next, L and her children came and
34: 1 Now Dinah, the daughter L had borne
35:23 The sons of L: Reuben the firstborn
46:15 These were the sons L bore to Jacob
46:18 to his daughter L—sixteen in all.
49:31 were buried, and there I buried L.
Ru 4:11 into your home like Rachel and L,

Leah's (Leah)

Ge 30:10 L servant Zilpah bore Jacob a son.
30:12 L servant Zilpah bore Jacob a second
31:33 into L tent and into the tent of the
31:33 out of L tent, he entered Rachel's
35:26 The sons of L maidservant Zilpah:

Leaks

Ecc 10:18 if his hands are idle, the house l.

Lean (Leaned, Leaning, Leans)

Ge 41:19 scrawny and very ugly and l.
41:20 The l, ugly cows ate up the seven
41:27 The seven l, ugly cows that came up
Jdg 16:26 so that I may l against them."
Pr 3: 5 and l not on your own understanding;
Eze 34:20 the fat sheep and the l sheep.
Mic 3:11 Yet they l upon the LORD and say,

Leaned (Lean)

Ge 47:31 as he l on the top of his staff.
2Ki 7:17 on whose arm he l in charge of the
Eze 29: 7 when they l on you, you broke and
Jn 21:20 (This was the one who had l back
Heb 11:21 as he l on the top of his staff.

Leaning (Lean)

2Sa 1: 6 "and there was Saul, l on his spear,
2Ki 5:18 he is l on my arm and I bow there
7: 2 on whose arm the king was l said to
Ps 62: 3 this l wall, this tottering fence?
SS 8: 5 up from the desert l on her lover?
Jn 13:25 L back against Jesus, he asked him,

Leannoth

Ps 88: T According to mahalath l. A maskil

Leans (Lean)

2Sa 3:29 or who l on a crutch or who falls
2Ki 18:21 hand and wounds him if he l on it!
Job 8:15 He l on his web, but it gives way;
Isa 36: 6 hand and wounds him if he l on it!

Leap (Leaped, Leaping, Leaps)

Job 39:20 Do you make him l like a locust,
Isa 13:21 there the wild goats will l about.
35: 6 will the lame l like a deer, and the
Joel 2: 5 they l over the mountaintops,
Mal 4: 2 you will go out and l like calves
Lk 6:23 "Rejoice in that day and l for joy,

Leaped (Leap)

Da 3:24 King Nebuchadnezzar l to his feet in
Lk 1:41 the baby l in her womb, and
1:44 ears, the baby in my womb l for joy.

Leaping (Leap)

2Sa 6:16 And when she saw King David l and
SS 2: 8 l across the mountains, bounding

Leaps (Leap)

Job 37: 1 "At this my heart pounds and l from
Ps 28: 7 My heart l for joy and I will give

Learn (Learned, Learning, Learns)

Ge 24:21 the man watched her closely to **l**
Dt 4:10 so that they may **l** to revere me
5: 1 **L** them and be sure to follow them.
14:23 **l** to revere the LORD your God always.
17:19 he may **l** to revere the LORD his God
18: 9 do not **l** to imitate the detestable
31:12 **l** to fear the LORD your God and
31:13 must hear it and **l** to fear the LORD
Jdg 18: 5 "Please enquire of God to **l** whether
1Sa 22: 3 until I **l** what God will do for me?"
1Ki 1:20 to **l** from you who will sit on the
2Ch 12: 8 so that they may **l** the difference
Job 34: 4 let us **l** together what is good.
Ps 14: 4 Will evildoers never **l**—those who
53: 4 Will the evildoers never **l**—those
119: 7 heart as I **l** your righteous laws.
119:71 so that I might **l** your decrees.
119:73 me understanding to **l** your commands.
141: 6 **l** that my words were well spoken.
Pr 19:25 Flog a mocker, and the simple will **l**
22:25 or you may **l** his ways and get
Isa 1:17 **l** to do right! Seek justice,
26: 9 people of the world **l** righteousness.
26:10 they do not **l** righteousness; even in
Jer 2:33 worst of women can **l** from your ways.
10: 2 This is what the LORD says: "Do not **l**
12:16 if they **l** well the ways of my people
35:13 'Will you not **l** a lesson and obey my
Mt 9:13 go and **l** what this means: 'I desire
11:29 Take my yoke upon you and **l** from me,
24:32 "Now **l** this lesson from the fig-tree:
Mk 13:28 "Now **l** this lesson from the fig-tree:
Jn 14:31 the world must **l** that I love the
Ac 24: 8 you will be able to **l** the truth
1Co 4: 6 so that you may **l** from us the
Gal 3: 2 I would like to **l** just one thing
1Th 4: 4 should **l** to control his own body in
1Ti 2:11 A woman should **l** in quietness and
5: 4 these should **l** first of all to put
Tit 3:14 Our people must **l** to devote
Heb 5:11 explain because you are slow to **l**.
Rev 14: 3 No-one could **l** the song except the

Learned (Learn)

Ge 28: 6 Now Esau **l** that Isaac had blessed
30:27 I have **l** by divination that the LORD
42: 1 Jacob **l** that there was grain in
Lev 5: 1 something he has seen or **l** about,
Nu 20:29 the whole community **l** that Aaron had
1Sa 4: 6 they **l** that the ark of the LORD had
23: 9 David **l** that Saul was plotting
23:15 he **l** that Saul had come out to take
26: 4 he sent out scouts and **l** that Saul
Ezr 7:11 a man **l** in matters concerning the
Ne 13: 7 Here I **l** about the evil thing
13:10 I also **l** that the portions assigned
Est 3: 6 Yet having **l** who Mordecai's people
4: 1 Mordecai **l** of all that had been done,
Job 8: 8 and find out what their fathers **l**,
Ps 89:15 Blessed are those who have **l** to
119:152 Long ago I **l** from your statutes that
Pr 24:32 and **l** a lesson from what I saw:
30: 3 I have not **l** wisdom, nor have I
Ecc 1:17 but I **l** that this, too, is a chasing
9:11 to the brilliant or favour to the **l**;
Eze 19: 3 He **l** to tear the prey and he
19: 6 He **l** to tear the prey and he
Da 6:10 Now when Daniel **l** that the decree
Mt 2:16 the time he had **l** from the Magi.
11:25 these things from the wise and **l**,
Mk 15:45 he **l** from the centurion that it was
Lk 7:37 **l** that Jesus was eating at the
9:11 the crowds **l** about it and followed
10:21 these things from the wise and **l**,
23: 7 he **l** that Jesus was under Herod's
Jn 4: 3 the Lord **l** of this, he left Judea
5: 6 Jesus saw him lying there and **l** that
15:15 for everything that I **l** from my
Ac 7:13 and Pharaoh **l** about Joseph's family.
9:24 Saul **l** of their plan. Day and night
9:30 the brothers **l** of this, they took
17:13 the Jews in Thessalonica **l** that Paul
18:24 He was a **l** man, with a thorough
23:27 I had **l** that he is a Roman citizen.
Ro 16:17 contrary to the teaching you have **l**.
Php 4: 9 Whatever you have **l** or received or
4:11 for I have **l** to be content whatever
4:12 I have **l** the secret of being content
Col 1: 7 You **l** it from Epaphras, our dear
2Ti 3:14 continue in what you have **l** and have
3:14 you know those from whom you **l** it,
Heb 5: 8 he was a son, he **l** obedience from
Rev 2:24 have not **l** Satan's so-called deep

Learning (Learn)

Ezr 8:16 and Elnathan, who were men of **l**,
Job 34: 2 listen to me, you men of **l**.
Pr 1: 5 the wise listen and add to their **l**,
4: 2 I give you sound **l**, so do not
9: 9 man and he will add to his **l**.
Isa 44:25 who overthrows the **l** of the wise and
Da 1: 4 aptitude for every kind of **l**,
1:17 of all kinds of literature and **l**.
Jn 7:15 get such **l** without having studied?"
Ac 23:34 **L** that he was from Cilicia,
26:24 "Your great **l** is driving you insane."
2Ti 3: 7 always **l** but never able to

Learns (Learn)

Lev 5: 3 when he **l** of it he will be guilty.
5: 4 when he **l** of it he will be guilty.
Jn 6:45 Father and **l** from him comes to me.

Leash

Job 41: 5 or put him on a **l** for your girls?

Leather

Lev 13:48 wool, any **l** or anything made of **l**—
13:49 or **l**, or woven or knitted material,
13:49 or any **l** article, is greenish or
13:51 or the **l**, whatever its use, it is a
13:52 or any **l** article that has the
13:53 knitted material, or the **l** article,
13:56 **l**, or the woven or knitted material.
13:57 or in the **l** article, it is spreading,
13:58 or any **l** article that has been
13:59 knitted material, or any **l** article,
15:17 Any clothing or **l** that has semen on
Nu 31:20 made of **l**, goat hair or wood."
2Ki 1: 8 and with a **l** belt round his waist.
Eze 16:10 dress and put **l** sandals on you.
Mt 3: 4 and he had a **l** belt round his waist.
Mk 1: 6 with a **l** belt round his waist, and

Leave (Leaves[1], Leaving, Leftover)

Ge 2:24 a man will **l** his father and mother
12: 1 said to Abram, "**L** your country,
18:16 the men got up to **l**, they looked
28:15 I will not **l** you until I have done
31:13 Now **l** this land at once and go back
33:15 Esau said, "Then let me **l** some of my
42:15 you will not **l** this place unless
42:33 **L** one of your brothers here with me,
44:22 we said to my lord, 'The boy cannot **l**
45: 1 "Make everyone **l** my presence!" So
Ex 1:10 fight against us and **l** the country."
2:20 "Why did you **l** him? Invite him to
3:21 you **l** you will not go empty-handed.
8: 9 Moses said to Pharaoh, "I **l** to you
8:11 The frogs will **l** you and your houses,
8:29 Moses answered, "As soon as I **l** you,
8:29 and tomorrow the flies will **l**
10:23 No-one could see anyone else or **l**
10:24 **l** your flocks and herds behind."
11: 8 follow you!' After that I will **l**.
12:10 Do not **l** any of it till morning; if
12:31 "Up! **L** my people, you and the
12:33 people to hurry and **l** the country.
14:12 Didn't we say to you in Egypt, '**L** us
23: 5 under its load, do not **l** it there;
23:11 wild animals may eat what they **l**.
32:10 Now **l** me alone so that my anger may
33: 1 the LORD said to Moses, "**L** this
33:11 Joshua son of Nun did not **l** the tent.
34: 7 Yet he does not **l** the guilty
Lev 2:13 Do not **l** the salt of the covenant of
7:15 he must **l** none of it till morning.
8:33 Do not **l** the entrance to the Tent of
Lev 10: 7 Do not **l** the entrance to the Tent of
16:23 Place, and he is to **l** them there.
19:10 **L** them for the poor and the alien.
21:12 nor **l** the sanctuary of his God or
22:30 **l** none of it till morning.
23:22 **L** them for the poor and the alien.
Nu 9:12 They must not **l** any of it till
10:31 Moses said, "Please do not **l** us.
11:20 "Why did we ever **l** Egypt?" '
14:18 Yet he does not **l** the guilty
24:11 Now **l** at once and go home! I said I
32:15 he will again **l** all this people in
Dt 15:16 "I do not want to **l** you," because he
20:16 not **l** alive anything that breathes.
21:23 you must not **l** his body on the tree
24:19 **L** it for the alien, the fatherless
24:20 **L** what remains for the alien, the
24:21 **L** what remains for the alien, the
28:51 They will **l** you no grain, new wine
31: 6 will never **l** you nor forsake you."
31: 8 he will never **l** you nor forsake you.
Jos 1: 5 I will never **l** you nor forsake you.
Jdg 7: 3 may turn back and **l** Mount Gilead.
16:17 my strength would **l** me, and I would
19: 5 got up early and he prepared to **l**,
19: 9 got up to **l**, his father-in-law, the
Ru 1:16 Ruth replied, "Don't urge me to **l**
2:16 and **l** them for her to pick up,
1Sa 10: 2 you **l** me today, you will meet two
10: 9 Saul turned to **l** Samuel, God changed
14:36 and let us not **l** one of them alive.
15: 6 Kenites, "Go away, **l** the Amalekites
15:27 Samuel turned to **l**, Saul caught hold
16:23 and the evil spirit would **l** him.
17:28 And with whom did you **l** those few
25:22 if by morning I **l** alive one male of
27: 9 he did not **l** a man or woman alive,
27:11 He did not **l** a man or woman alive to
29:10 and **l** in the morning as soon as it
2Sa 4: 4 she hurried to **l**, he fell and became
15:14 We must **l** immediately, or he will
16:11 **L** him alone; let his curse, for the
1Ki 2:37 The day you **l** and cross the Kidron
2:42 'On the day you **l** to go anywhere
8:57 may he never **l** us nor forsake us.
15:29 He did not **l** Jeroboam anyone that
17: 3 "**L** here, turn eastward and hide in
18:12 the LORD may carry you when I **l** you.
20:36 as you **l** me a lion will kill you.
2Ki 1: 4 will not **l** the bed you are lying on.
1: 6 will not **l** the bed you are lying on.
1:16 never **l** the bed you are lying on.
2: 2 and as you live, I will not **l** you.
2: 4 and as you live, I will not **l** you.
2: 6 and as you live, I will not **l** you.
4:27 "**L** her alone! She is in bitter
4:30 and as you live, I will not **l** you.
23:18 "**L** it alone," he said. "Don't let
2Ch 26:18 **L** the sanctuary, for you have been
26:20 Indeed, he himself was eager to **l**,
33: 8 make the feet of the Israelites **l**
35:15 gate did not need to **l** their posts,
Ezr 9:12 **l** it to your children as an
Ne 6: 3 while I **l** it and go down to you?"
Job 21:14 Yet they say to God, '**L** us alone! We
22:17 They said to God, '**L** us alone! What
39: 4 the wilds; they **l** and do not return.
39:11 Will you **l** your heavy work to him?
Ps 35:12 evil for good and **l** my soul forlorn.
37:33 LORD will not **l** them in their power
49:10 perish and **l** their wealth to others.
55:11 and lies never **l** its streets.
119:121 do not **l** me to my oppressors.
Pr 2:13 who **l** the straight paths to walk in
3: 3 Let love and faithfulness never **l**
9: 6 **L** your simple ways and you will live;
17:13 good, evil will never **l** his house.
Ecc 2:18 **l** them to the one who comes after me.
2:21 and then he must **l** all he owns to
8: 3 in a hurry to **l** the king's presence
10: 4 rises against you, do not **l** your post;
Isa 6:13 as the terebinth and oak **l** stumps
10: 3 Where will you **l** your riches?
30:11 **L** this way, get off this path, and
48:20 **L** Babylon, flee from the Babylonians!
52:12 you will not **l** in haste or go in

Isa 65:15 You will l your name to my chosen
Jer 2:37 You will also l that place with your
9: 2 so that I might l my people and go
9:19 We must l our land because our
10:17 up your belongings to l the land,
25:38 Like a lion he will l his lair, and
37: 9 'The Babylonians will surely l us.
37:12 Jeremiah started to l the city to go
44: 7 so l yourselves without a remnant?
49: 9 would they not l a few grapes? If
49:11 L your orphans; I will protect their
50: 8 l the land of the Babylonians,
50:26 destroy her and l her no remnant.
51: 9 let us l her and each go to his own
51:50 the sword, l and do not linger!
Eze 5:17 you, and they will l you childless.
10:16 the wheels did not l their side.
12:12 on his shoulder at dusk and l,
14:15 they l it childless and it becomes
16:39 jewellery and l you naked and bare.
23:29 They will l you naked and bare, and
29: 5 I will l you in the desert, you and
36:20 and yet they had to l his land.'
42:14 until they l behind the garments in
44:19 in and l them in the sacred rooms,
Da 4:23 but l the stump, bound with iron and
4:26 The command to l the stump of the
11: 8 will l the king of the North alone.
Hos 4:17 is joined to idols; l him alone!
12:14 his Lord will l upon him the guilt
Joel 2:14 have pity and l behind a blessing
2:16 l his room and the bride her chamber.
Ob : 5 you, would they not l a few grapes?
Mic 4:10 l the city to camp in the open field.
Na 1: 3 will not l the guilty unpunished.
2:13 I will l you no prey on the earth.
Zep 3: 3 who l nothing for the morning.
3:12 I will l within you the meek and
Mt 5:24 l your gift there in front of the
8:34 pleaded with him to l their region.
10:11 and stay at his house until you l.
10:14 feet when you l that home or town.
15:14 L them; they are blind guides. If a
18:12 will he not l the ninety-nine on the
19: 5 'For this reason a man will l his
27:49 The rest said, "Now l him alone.
Mk 5:17 plead with Jesus to l their region.
6:10 stay there until you l that town.
6:11 the dust off your feet when you l,
10: 7 'For this reason a man will l his
14: 6 "L her alone," said Jesus. "Why are
15:36 "Now l him alone. Let's see if
Lk 8:37 the Gerasenes asked Jesus to l them,
9: 4 stay there until you l that town.
9: 5 off your feet when you l their town,
13: 8 'l it alone for one more year, and
13:31 "L this place and go somewhere else.
15: 4 Does he not l the ninety-nine in the
19:44 They will not l one stone on another,
Jn 1:43 Jesus decided to l for Galilee.
6:67 "You do not want to l too, do you?"
7: 3 "You ought to l here and go to Judea,
8:11 "Go now and l your life of sin."
12: 7 "L her alone," Jesus replied. "It
13: 1 l this world and go to the Father.
14:18 I will not l you as orphans; I will
14:27 Peace I l with you; my peace I give
14:31 "Come now; let us l.
16:32 You will l me all alone. Yet I am
Ac 1: 4 "Do not l Jerusalem, but wait for
5:38 I advise you: L these men alone!
7: 3 'L your country and your people,'
16:10 ready at once to l for Macedonia
16:36 Now you can l. Go in peace."
16:39 requesting them to l the city.
18: 2 had ordered all the Jews to l Rome.
20: 7 because he intended to l the next
20:29 I know that after I l, savage wolves
22:18 'Quick!' he said to me. 'L Jerusalem
24:25 "That's enough for now! You may l.
28:25 began to l after Paul had made this
Ro 12:19 my friends, but l room for God's
1Co 5:10 case you would have to l this world.
Eph 5:31 "For this reason a man will l his
Heb 6: 1 Therefore let us l the elementary
13: 5 Never will I l you; never will I
Rev 3:12 Never again will he l it. I will
17:16 bring her to ruin and l her naked;

Leavened

Am 4: 5 Burn l bread as a thank-offering and

Leaves[1] (Leave)

Ge 44:22 if he l him, his father will die.'
Nu 27: 8 'If a man dies and l no son, give
Dt 24: 2 if after she l his house she becomes
Job 21:21 he care about the family he l behind
41:32 Behind him he l a glistening wake;
Pr 13:22 A good man l an inheritance for his
15:10 discipline awaits him who l the path
28: 3 like a driving rain that l no crops.
Isa 32: 6 the hungry he l empty and from the
Jer 3: 1 man divorces his wife and she l him
Mk 12:19 dies and l a wife but no children,
13:34 a man going away: He l his house
Lk 9:39 ever l him and is destroying him.
20:28 dies and l a wife but no children,
1Co 7:15 if the unbeliever l, let him do so.
2Co 7:10 leads to salvation and l no regret,

Leaves[2] (Leaf)

Ge 3: 7 so they sewed fig l together and
1Ki 6:34 having two l that turned in sockets.
Isa 1:30 You will be like an oak with fading l
33: 9 and Bashan and Carmel drop their l.
34: 4 fall like withered l from the vine,
Jer 8:13 the tree, and their l will wither.
17: 8 heat comes; its l are always green.
Eze 41:24 Each door had two l—two hinged l
47:12 Their l will not wither, nor will
47:12 for food and their l for healing."
Da 4:12 Its l were beautiful, its fruit
4:14 off its l and scatter its fruit.
4:21 with beautiful l and abundant fruit,
Mt 21:19 it but found nothing on it except l.
24:32 twigs get tender and its l come out,
Mk 11:13 he found nothing but l, because it
13:28 twigs get tender and its l come out,
Lk 21:30 they sprout l, you can see for
Rev 22: 2 And the l of the tree are for the

Leaving (Leave)

Ge 45:24 and as they were l he said to them,
Ex 13: 4 in the month of Abib, you are l.
13:20 After l Succoth they camped at Etham
Nu 21:35 his whole army, l them no survivors.
Dt 3: 3 We struck them down, l no survivors.
Jos 5: 4 the desert on the way after l Egypt.
8:22 them down, l them neither survivors
2Sa 14: 7 l my husband neither name nor
15:24 the people had finished l the city.
1Ki 15:17 to prevent anyone from l or entering
2Ki 10:11 and his priests, l him no survivor.
2Ch 16: 1 to prevent anyone from l or entering
Ezr 9: 8 has been gracious in l us a remnant
9:14 us, l us no remnant or survivor?
Job 22: 6 men of their clothing, l them naked.
41:30 l a trail in the mud like a
Isa 17: 6 l two or three olives on the
Eze 39:28 to their own land, not l any behind.
Da 2:35 swept them away without l a trace
Joel 1: 7 it away, l their branches white.
Zep 2:13 l Nineveh utterly desolate and dry
Mt 4:13 L Nazareth, he went and lived in
11: 7 John's disciples were l, Jesus began
15:21 L that place, Jesus withdrew to the
20:29 Jesus and his disciples were l
Mk 4:36 L the crowd behind, they took him
6:33 many who saw them l recognised them
6:46 After l them, he went up on a
10:46 with a large crowd, were l the city
11:12 The next day as they were l Bethany,
12:20 and died without l any children.
12:21 widow, but he also died, l no child.
13: 1 he was l the temple, one of his
14:52 he fled naked, l his garment behind.
Lk 4:42 they tried to keep him from l them.
9:33 the men were l Jesus, Peter said to
10:30 him and went away, l him half-dead.
11:42 latter without l the former undone.
20:31 way the seven died, l no children.
Jn 4:28 Then, l her water jar, the woman
16:28 now I am l the world and going back
Ac 13:42 Paul and Barnabas were l the
21: 8 L the next day, we reached Caesarea
1Pe 2:21 suffered for you, l you an example

Leb Kamai

Jer 51: 1 against Babylon and the people of L.

Lebana

Ne 7:48 L, Hagaba, Shalmai,

Lebanah

Ezr 2:45 L, Hagabah, Akkub,

Lebanon

Mountainous region to the north of Palestine, along the Mediterranean coast. Regarded as part of the promised land (Dt 1:7; 3:25; 11:24; Jos 1:4; 13:5–6; 1Ki 9:19; Zec 10:10), but occupied by the Hivites (Jdg 3:3–5; 1Ki 9:20–21; 2Ch 8:7–8). Renowned for its forests of cedar and cypress (Jdg 9:15; 1Ki 4:33; 2Ki 14:9; 19:23; 2Ch 25:18), which were used by Solomon (1Ki 5; 7:2; 2Ch 2:8, 16), and Zerubbabel (Ezr 3:7). Used figuratively to speak of righteousness (Ps 92:12), pride (Isa 2:13), glory (Isa 60:13), security (Hos 14:5), etc.

Dt 1: 7 the land of the Canaanites and to L,
3:25 fine hill country and L."
11:24 will extend from the desert to L,
Jos 1: 4 will extend from the desert to L,
9: 1 far as L (the kings of the Hittites,
11:17 the Valley of L below Mount Hermon.
12: 7 from Baal Gad in the Valley of L to
13: 5 the area of the Gebalites; and all L
13: 6 regions from L to Misrephoth Maim,
Jdg 3: 3 and the Hivites living in the L
9:15 and consume the cedars of L!'
1Ki 4:33 from the cedar of L to the hyssop
5: 6 give orders that cedars of L be cut
5: 9 My men will haul them down from L to
5:14 He sent them off to L in shifts of
5:14 month in L and two months at home.
7: 2 Forest of L a hundred cubits long,
9:19 in L and throughout all the
10:17 in the Palace of the Forest of L.
10:21 of the Forest of L were pure gold.
2Ki 14: 9 "A thistle in L sent a message to a
14: 9 in L sent a message to a cedar in L,
19:23 mountains, the utmost heights of L.
2Ch 2: 8 pine and algum logs from L, for I
2:16 we will cut all the logs from L that
8: 6 in L and throughout all the
9:16 in the Palace of the Forest of L.
9:20 of the Forest of L were pure gold.
25:18 "A thistle in L sent a message to a
25:18 in L sent a message to a cedar in L,
Ezr 3: 7 cedar logs by sea from L to Joppa,
Ps 29: 5 breaks in pieces the cedars of L.
29: 6 He makes L skip like a calf, Sirion
72:16 Let its fruit flourish like L;
92:12 they will grow like a cedar of L;
104:16 the cedars of L that he planted.
SS 3: 9 carriage; he made it of wood from L.
4: 8 L, my bride, come with me from L.
4:11 of your garments is like that of L.
4:15 flowing water streaming down from L.
5:15 is like L, choice as its cedars.
7: 4 tower of L looking towards Damascus.
Isa 2:13 for all the cedars of L, tall and
10:34 L will fall before the Mighty One.
14: 8 cedars of L exult over you and say,
29:17 will not L be turned into a fertile
33: 9 away, L is ashamed and withers,
35: 2 The glory of L will be given to it,
37:24 mountains, the utmost heights of L.
40:16 L is not sufficient for altar fires,
60:13 "The glory of L will come to you,
Jer 18:14 Does the snow of L ever vanish from
22: 6 like the summit of L, I will surely
22:20 "Go up to L and cry out, let your
22:23 You who live in 'L', who are nestled
Eze 17: 3 plumage of varied colours came to L.

Eze 27: 5 cedar from L to make a mast for you.
31: 3 Consider Assyria, once a cedar in L,
31:15 Because of it I clothed L with gloom,
31:16 the choicest and best of L, all the
Hos 14: 5 Like a cedar of L he will send down
14: 6 his fragrance like a cedar of L.
14: 7 fame will be like the wine from L.
Na 1: 4 wither and the blossoms of L fade.
Hab 2:17 The violence you have done to L will
Zec 10:10 I will bring them to Gilead and L,
11: 1 Open your doors, O L, so that fire

Lebaoth

Jos 15:32 L, Shilhim, Ain and Rimmon—a total

Lebo Hamath

Nu 13:21 of Zin as far as Rehob, towards L.
34: 8 from Mount Hor to L. Then the
Jos 13: 5 Baal Gad below Mount Hermon to L.
Jdg 3: 3 from Mount Baal Hermon to L.
1Ki 8:65 people from L to the Wadi of Egypt.
2Ki 14:25 from L to the Sea of the Arabah,
1Ch 13: 5 from the Shihor River in Egypt to L,
2Ch 7: 8 people from L to the Wadi of Egypt.
Eze 47:15 by the Hethlon road past L to Zedad,
47:20 the boundary to a point opposite L.
48: 1 will follow the Hethlon road to L;
Am 6:14 from L to the valley of the Arabah."

Lebonah

Jdg 21:19 to Shechem, and to the south of L."

Lecah

1Ch 4:21 son of Judah: Er the father of L,

Lecture

Jn 9:34 you l us!" And they threw him out.
Ac 19: 9 daily in the l hall of Tyrannus.

Led (Lead[1])

Ge 19:16 and l them safely out of the city,
24:27 the LORD has l me on the journey to
24:48 who had l me on the right road to
Ex 3: 1 he l the flock to the far side of
13:18 God l the people around by the
15:22 Moses l Israel from the Red Sea and
19:17 Moses l the people out of the camp
32:21 you l them into such great sin?"
Dt 8: 2 Remember how the LORD your God l you
8:15 He l you through the vast and
13:13 l the people of their town astray,
17:17 or his heart will be l astray.
29: 5 During the forty years that I l you
32:12 The LORD alone l him; no foreign god
Jos 24: 3 l him throughout Canaan and gave him
Jdg 2: 1 out of Egypt and l you into the land
3:28 fords of the Jordan that l to Moab,
9:39 Gaal l out the citizens of Shechem
10: 2 He l Israel for twenty-three years;
10: 3 who l Israel for twenty-two years.
12: 7 Jephthah l Israel for six years.
12: 8 Ibzan of Bethlehem l Israel.
12: 9 Ibzan l Israel for seven years.
12:11 Elon the Zebulunite l Israel for
12:13 of Hillel, from Pirathon, l Israel.
12:14 He l Israel for eight years.
15:13 ropes and l him up from the rock.
15:20 Samson l Israel for twenty years in
16:31 He had l Israel for twenty years.
1Sa 4:18 He had l Israel for forty years.
18:13 l the troops in their campaigns.
18:16 he l them in their campaigns.
30:16 He l David down, and there they were,
2Sa 5: 2 l Israel on their military campaigns.
1Ki 6: 8 a stairway l up to the middle level
11: 3 and his wives l him astray.
13:34 of Jeroboam that l to its downfall
2Ki 6:19 And he l them to Samaria.
15:15 and the conspiracy he l, are written
21: 9 Manasseh l them astray, so that
21:11 has l Judah into sin with his idols.
23:22 the days of the judges who l Israel,
1Ch 4:42 of these Simeonites, l by Pelatiah,
11: 2 l Israel on their military campaigns.
1Ch 20: 1 to war, Joab l out the armed forces.
2Ch 20:27 Then, l by Jehoshaphat, all the men
21:11 themselves and had l Judah astray.
21:13 and you have l Judah and the people
25:11 l his army to the Valley of Salt,
26:16 his pride l to his downfall.
33: 9 Manasseh l Judah and the people of
Ezr 9: 2 l the way in this unfaithfulness."
Ne 9:12 By day you l them with a pillar of
11:17 the director who l in thanksgiving
12:36 Ezra the scribe l the procession.
13:26 he was l into sin by foreign women.
Est 6:11 He robed Mordecai, and l him on
Job 31: 7 if my heart has been l by my eyes,
Ps 26: 1 for I have l a blameless life;
45:14 garments she is l to the king; her
45:15 They are l in with joy and gladness;
68:18 you ascended on high, you l captives
77:19 Your path l through the sea, your
77:20 You l your people like a flock by
78:13 He divided the sea and l them
78:26 l forth the south wind by his power.
78:52 l them like sheep through the desert.
78:72 with skilful hands he l them.
106: 9 he l them through the depths as
107: 7 He l them by a straight way to a
136:16 to him who l his people through the
Pr 5:23 l astray by his own great folly.
7:21 With persuasive words she l him
20: 1 is l astray by them is not wise.
24:11 Rescue those being l away to death;
Isa 9:16 those who are guided are l astray.
19:13 of her peoples have l Egypt astray.
48:21 They did not thirst when he l them
53: 7 was l like a lamb to the slaughter,
55:12 out in joy and be l forth in peace;
60:11 kings l in triumphal procession.
63:13 who l them through the depths? Like
Jer 2: 6 l us through the barren wilderness,
2:17 your God when he l you in the way?
11:19 a gentle lamb l to the slaughter
22:12 place where they have l him captive;
23:13 Baal and l my people Israel astray.
29:31 him, and has l you to believe a lie,
41:16 l away all the survivors from Mizpah
43: 5 all the army officers l away all the
43: 6 They also l away all the men, women
50: 6 their shepherds have l them astray
Eze 19: 4 They l him with hooks to the land of
20:10 Therefore I l them out of Egypt and
29:18 from the campaign he l against Tyre.
37: 2 He l me to and fro among them, and I
40:22 Seven steps l up to it, with its
40:24 he l me to the south side and I saw
40:26 Seven steps l up to it, with its
40:31 jambs, and eight steps l up to it.
40:34 side, and eight steps l up to it.
40:37 side, and eight steps l up to it.
42: 1 the man l me northward into the
42:15 he l me out by the east gate and
46:21 and l me round to its four corners,
47: 2 l me round the outside to the outer
47: 3 then l me through water that was
47: 4 l me through water that was
47: 4 l me through water that was up to
47: 6 l me back to the bank of the river.
Da 7:13 of Days and was l into his presence.
Hos 11: 4 I l them with cords of human
Am 2: 4 have been l astray by false gods,
2:10 and I l you for forty years in the
Mt 4: 1 Jesus was l by the Spirit into the
17: 1 and l them up a high mountain by
27: 2 They bound him, l him away and
27:31 Then they l him away to crucify him.
Mk 8:23 hand and l him outside the village.
9: 2 James and John with him and l them
15: 1 They bound Jesus, l him away and
15:16 The soldiers l Jesus away into the
15:20 Then they l him out to crucify him.
Lk 4: 1 was l by the Spirit in the desert,
4: 5 The devil l him up to a high place
4: 9 The devil l him to Jerusalem and had
18:39 Those who l the way rebuked him and
22:54 seizing him, they l him away and
22:66 and Jesus was l before them.
23: 1 the whole assembly rose and l him
Lk 23:26 they l him away, they seized Simon
23:32 also l out with him to be executed.
24:50 he had l them out to the vicinity of
Jn 18:28 the Jews l Jesus from Caiaphas to
Ac 5:37 and l a band of people in revolt.
7:36 He l them out of Egypt and did
7:40 As for this fellow Moses who l us
8:32 "He was l like a sheep to the
9: 8 l him by the hand into Damascus.
13:17 power he l them out of that country,
19:26 l astray large numbers of people
21:38 l four thousand terrorists out into
22:11 My companions l me by the hand into
Ro 8:14 those who are l by the Spirit of God
1Co 12: 2 and l astray to mute idols.
2Co 7: 9 your sorrow l you to repentance.
11: 3 your minds may somehow be l astray
11:29 Who is l into sin, and I do not
Gal 2:13 even Barnabas was l astray.
5:18 if you are l by the Spirit, you are
Eph 4: 8 on high, he l captives in his train
Heb 3:16 not all those Moses l out of Egypt?
Rev 18:23 spell all the nations were l astray.

Ledge (Ledges)

Ex 27: 5 Put it under the l of the altar so
38: 4 under its l, halfway up the altar.
Eze 43:14 the lower l it is two cubits high
43:14 and from the smaller l up to the
43:14 the larger l it is four cubits high
43:17 The upper l also is square, fourteen
43:20 the upper l and all round the rim,
45:19 on the four corners of the upper l
46:23 of the four courts was a l of stone,
46:23 fire built all round under the l.

Ledges (Ledge)

1Ki 6: 6 He made offset l around the outside
Eze 41: 6 There were l all round the wall of

Lee

Ac 27: 4 passed to the l of Cyprus because
27: 7 to the l of Crete, opposite Salmone.
27:16 we passed to the l of a small island

Leech

Pr 30:15 "The l has two daughters. 'Give!

Leeks

Nu 11: 5 melons, l, onions and garlic.

Left[1]

Ge 7:23 Only Noah was l, and those with him
12: 4 Abram l, as the LORD had told him;
18:33 he l, and Abraham returned home.
19:30 Lot and his two daughters l Zoar and
24:10 ten of his master's camels and l,
24:61 So the servant took Rebekah and l.
25: 5 Abraham l everything he owned to
25:34 and drank, and then got up and l.
26:31 their way, and they l him in peace.
27: 5 When Esau l for the open country to
27:30 scarcely l his father's presence,
28:10 Jacob l Beersheba and set out for
31:55 Then he l and returned home.
32: 8 the group that is l may escape."
32:24 Jacob was l alone, and a man
34:26 Dinah from Shechem's house and l.
38: 1 At that time, Judah l his brothers
38:19 After she l, she took off her veil
39: 6 he l in Joseph's care everything he
39:12 he l his cloak in her hand and ran
39:13 she saw that he had l his cloak in
39:15 he l his cloak beside me and ran
39:18 as soon as I screamed for help, he l
42:26 their grain on their donkeys and l.
42:38 is dead and he is the only one l.
44:20 the only one of his mother's sons l
46: 5 Jacob l Beersheba, and Israel's sons
47:18 there is nothing l for our lord
50: 8 flocks and herds were l in Goshen.
50:16 l these instructions before he died:
Ex 5:20 they l Pharaoh, they found Moses and
8:12 After Moses and Aaron l Pharaoh,

Ex 8:30 Moses l Pharaoh and prayed to the
8:31 The flies l Pharaoh and his
9:21 the word of the LORD l their slaves
9:33 Moses l Pharaoh and went out of the
10: 5 little you have l after the hail,
10: 6 Then Moses turned and l Pharaoh.
10:12 fields, everything l by the hail."
10:15 They devoured all that was l after
10:18 Moses then l Pharaoh and prayed to
10:19 Not a locust was l anywhere in Egypt.
10:26 not a hoof is to be l behind.
11: 8 Moses, hot with anger, l Pharaoh.
12:10 is l till morning, you must burn it.
12:41 all the LORD's divisions l Egypt.
13:22 l its place in front of the people.
16:23 Save whatever is l and keep it until
19: 1 month after the Israelites l Egypt
26:12 the half curtain that is l over is
26:13 what is l will hang over the sides
29:34 is l over till morning, burn it up.
36: 4 work on the sanctuary l their work
Lev 6: 2 to him or l in his care or stolen,
7:16 l over may be eaten on the next day.
7:17 Any meat of the sacrifice l over
10:12 "Take the grain offering l over from
19: 6 anything l over until the third day
25:15 of years l for harvesting crops.
26:36 "'As for those of you who are l,
26:39 Those of you who are l will waste
Nu 12: 9 burned against them, and he l them.
12:16 After that, the people l Hazeroth
14:19 the time they l Egypt until now."
22: 7 The elders of Moab and Midian l,
25: 7 the priest, saw this, he l the
26:65 and not one of them was l except
27: 3 died for his own sin and l no sons.
33: 5 The Israelites l Rameses and camped
33: 6 They l Succoth and camped at Etham,
33: 7 l Etham, turned back to Pi Hahiroth
33: 8 They l Pi Hahiroth and passed
33: 9 They l Marah and went to Elim, where
33:10 l Elim and camped by the Red Sea.
33:11 They l the Red Sea and camped in the
33:12 They l the Desert of Sin and camped
33:13 They l Dophkah and camped at Alush.
33:14 They l Alush and camped at Rephidim,
33:15 They l Rephidim and camped in the
33:16 They l the Desert of Sinai and
33:17 They l Kibroth Hattaavah and camped
33:18 They l Hazeroth and camped at
33:19 They l Rithmah and camped at
33:20 They l Rimmon Perez and camped at
33:21 They l Libnah and camped at Rissah.
33:22 They l Rissah and camped at
33:23 They l Kehelathah and camped at
33:24 They l Mount Shepher and camped at
33:25 They l Haradah and camped at
33:26 They l Makheloth and camped at
33:27 They l Tahath and camped at Terah.
33:28 They l Terah and camped at Mithcah.
33:29 They l Mithcah and camped at
33:30 They l Hashmonah and camped at
33:31 They l Moseroth and camped at
33:32 They l Bene Jaakan and camped at
33:33 They l Hor Haggidgad and camped at
33:34 They l Jotbathah and camped at
33:35 l Abronah and camped at Ezion Geber
33:36 They l Ezion Geber and camped at
33:37 l Kadesh and camped at Mount Hor
33:41 They l Mount Hor and camped at
33:42 They l Zalmonah and camped at Punon.
33:43 They l Punon and camped at Oboth.
33:44 l Oboth and camped at Iye Abarim
33:45 They l Iyim and camped at Dibon Gad.
33:46 They l Dibon Gad and camped at
33:47 They l Almon Diblathaim and camped
33:48 They l the mountains of Abarim and
Dt 1:24 They l and went up into the hill
2:14 from the time we l Kadesh Barnea
2:34 and children. We l no survivors.
3:11 (Only Og king of Bashan was l of the
9: 7 From the day you l Egypt until you
16: 3 because you l Egypt in haste—so
28:55 It will be all he has l because of
28:62 the sky will be l but few in number,
32:36 gone and no-one is l, slave or free.
Jos 2: 5 to close the city gate, the men l.
2:22 they l, they went into the hills and
5: 6 age when they l Egypt had died,
8:17 They l the city open and went in
8:29 tree and l him there until evening.
9:12 home on the day we l to come to you.
10:20 the few who were l reached their
10:26 l hanging on the trees until evening.
10:28 every one in it. He l no survivors.
10:30 the sword. He l no survivors there.
10:33 his army—until no survivors were l.
10:37 They l no survivors. Just as at
10:39 destroyed. They l no survivors.
10:40 He l no survivors. He totally
11: 8 the east, until no survivors were l.
11:15 he l nothing undone of all that the
11:22 No Anakites were l in Israelite
18: 9 the men l and went through the land.
22: 9 the half-tribe of Manasseh l the
Jdg 2:21 the nations Joshua l when he died.
3: 1 These are the nations the LORD l to
3: 4 They were l to test the Israelites
3:19 Quiet!" And all his attendants l him.
4:11 Now Heber the Kenite had l the other
4:16 fell by the sword; not a man was l.
5:13 "Then the men who were l came down
7: 3 men l, while ten thousand remained.
8:10 all that were l of the armies of the
16:19 subdue him. And his strength l him.
16:20 not know that the LORD had l him.
17: 8 l that town in search of some other
18: 7 the five men l and came to Laish,
18:21 of them, they turned away and l.
19: 2 She l him and went back to her
19:10 the man l and went towards Jebus
21: 7 provide wives for those who are l,
21:16 provide wives for the men who are l?
21:24 At that time the Israelites l that
Ru 1: 3 and she was l with her two sons.
1: 5 and Naomi was l without her two sons
1: 7 With her two daughters-in-law she l
2:11 how you l your father and mother
2:14 all she wanted and had some l over.
2:18 l over after she had eaten enough.
4:14 l you without a kinsman-redeemer.
1Sa 2:36 everyone l in your family line will
11:11 that no two of them were l together.
13:15 Samuel l Gilgal and went up to
14: 3 No-one was aware that Jonathan had l.
14:17 the forces and see who has l us.
15:34 Samuel l for Ramah, but Saul went up
17:20 Early in the morning David l the
17:22 David l his things with the keeper
18:12 LORD was with David but had l Saul.
19:22 Finally, he himself l for Ramah and
20:42 Then David l, and Jonathan went
22: 1 David l Gath and escaped to the cave
22: 4 he l them with the king of Moab, and
22: 5 l and went to the forest of Hereth.
23:13 six hundred in number, l Keilah
24: 7 And Saul l the cave and went his way.
25:34 have been l alive by daybreak."
26:12 jug near Saul's head, and they l.
27: 2 the six hundred men with him l and
28:25 That same night they got up and l.
29: 3 and from the day he l Saul until now,
30: 4 they had no strength l to weep.
30:21 were l behind at the Besor Ravine.
2Sa 2:12 Saul, l Mahanaim and went to Gibeon.
3:26 Joab then l David and sent
5:13 After he l Hebron, David took more
9: 1 David asked, "Is there anyone still l
9: 3 "Is there no-one still l of the
11: 8 So Uriah l the palace, and a gift
13: 9 Amnon said. So everyone l him.
13:30 king's sons; not one of them is l."
14: 7 out the only burning coal I have l,
15:16 but he l ten concubines to take care
16:21 he l to take care of the palace.
17:12 nor any of his men will be l alive.
17:18 So the two of them l quickly and
17:22 no-one was l who had not crossed
18: 9 He was l hanging in mid-air, while
19: 7 not a man will be l with you by
19:19 day my lord the king l Jerusalem.
19:24 l until the day he returned safely.
2Sa 20: 3 he took the ten concubines he had l
24: 4 so they l the presence of the king
1Ki 7:47 Solomon l all these things unweighed,
9:20 All the people l from the Amorites,
10:13 Then she l and returned with her
14:17 Jeroboam's wife got up and l and
15:18 gold that was l in the treasuries of
18:22 only one of the LORD's prophets l,
19: 3 in Judah, he l his servant there,
19:10 I am the only one l, and now they
19:14 I am the only one l, and now they
19:20 Elisha then l his oxen and ran after
19:21 Elisha l him and went back. He took
20: 9 They l and took the answer back
2Ki 3:25 Only Kir Hareseth was l with its
4: 5 She l him and afterwards shut the
4: 6 he replied, "There is not a jar l.
4: 7 your sons can live on what is l."
4:43 'They will eat and have some l over.
4:44 and they ate and had some l over,
5: 5 So Naaman l, taking with him ten
5:24 He sent the men away and they l.
7: 7 They l the camp as it was and ran
7:10 and the tents l just as they were."
7:12 so they have l the camp to hide in
7:13 the horses that are l in the city.
7:13 of all the Israelites l here—yes,
8: 6 day she l the country until now."
8:14 Hazael l Elisha and returned to his
10:14 forty-two men. He l no survivor.
10:15 After he l there, he came upon
10:17 he killed all who were l there of
13: 7 Nothing had been l of the army of
17:18 Only the tribe of Judah was l,
19: 8 the king of Assyria had l Lachish,
20: 4 Before Isaiah had l the middle court,
20:17 Nothing will be l, says the LORD.
24:14 poorest people of the land were l.
25:12 the commander l behind some of the
25:22 the people he had l behind in Judah.
1Ch 6:44 the Merarites, at his l hand: Ethan
16:37 David l Asaph and his associates
16:38 He also l Obed-Edom and his
16:39 David l Zadok the priest and his
16:43 all the people l, each for his own
20: 1 attacked Rabbah and l it in ruins.
21: 4 so Joab l and went throughout Israel
21:21 he l the threshing-floor and bowed
2Ch 8: 7 All the people l from the Hittites,
9:12 Then she l and returned with her
20:20 Early in the morning they l for the
21:17 Not a son was l to him except
24:25 they l Joash severely wounded.
25:10 Judah and l for home in a great rage.
30: 6 that he may return to you who are l,
31:10 and this great amount is l over."
32:31 God l him to test him and to know
Ezr 4:16 l with nothing in Trans-Euphrates.
9:15 We are l this day as a remnant.
Ne 6: 1 the wall and not a gap was l in it
Est 7: 7 king got up in a rage, l his wine
7: 8 soon as the word l the king's mouth,
8:15 Mordecai l the king's presence
Job 20:19 the poor and l them destitute;
20:21 Nothing is l for him to devour;
20:26 and devour what is l in his tent.
21:34 Nothing is l of your answers but
Ps 34: T who drove him away, and he l.
69:20 my heart and has l me helpless;
74: 9 no prophets are l, and none of us
105:38 Egypt was glad when they l, because
Pr 2:17 who has l the partner of her youth
29:15 a child l to himself disgraces his
Ecc 5:14 a son there is nothing l for him.
SS 5: 6 but my lover had l; he was gone.
Isa 1: 8 The Daughter of Zion is l like a
1: 9 Unless the LORD Almighty had l us
4: 3 Those who are l in Zion, who remain
5: 8 no space is l and you live alone in
5: 9 fine mansions l without occupants.
6:11 until the houses are l deserted and
11:11 the remnant that is l of his people
11:16 remnant of his people that is l
15: 6 is gone and nothing green is l.
17: 2 will be deserted and l to flocks,
17: 9 which they l because of the

Isa 18: 6 They will all be **l** to the mountain
21:11 "Watchman, what is **l** of the night?
21:11 Watchman, what is **l** of the night?"
23: 1 and **l** without house or harbour.
24: 6 are burned up, and very few are **l**.
24:12 The city is **l** in ruins, its gate is
24:13 are **l** after the grape harvest.
27: 9 incense altars will be **l** standing.
30:17 till you are **l** like a flagstaff on a
37: 8 the king of Assyria had **l** Lachish,
39: 6 Nothing will be **l**, says the LORD.
44:19 a detestable thing from what is **l**?
49:21 I was **l** all alone, but these—
Jer 4: 7 He has **l** his place to lay waste your
7:25 From the time your forefathers **l**
10:20 no-one is **l** now to pitch my tent or
11:23 Not even a remnant will be **l** to them,
25:20 Ekron, and the people **l** at Ashdod);
27:19 furnishings that are **l** in this city,
27:21 says about the things that are **l** in
29:32 He will have no-one **l** among this
34: 7 only fortified cities **l** in Judah.
37:10 wounded men were **l** in their tents,
38: 4 the soldiers who are **l** in this city,
38:22 All the women **l** in the palace of the
39: 4 they **l** the city at night by way of
39:10 **l** behind in the land of Judah some
40: 6 who were **l** behind in the land.
40:11 of Babylon had **l** a remnant in Judah
41:10 all the others who were **l** there,
42: 2 once many, now only a few are **l**.
43: 6 had **l** with Gedaliah son of Ahikam,
48:11 like wine **l** on its dregs, not poured
52: 7 They **l** the city at night through the
52:16 Nebuzaradan **l** behind the rest of the
Lam 3:11 mangled me and **l** me without help.
Eze 7:11 none of the people will be **l**,
9: 8 they were killing and I was **l** alone
19:14 No strong branch is **l** on it fit for
22:18 iron and lead **l** inside a furnace.
23:25 who are **l** will fall by the sword.
23:25 who are **l** will be consumed by fire.
24:21 you **l** behind will fall by the sword.
31:12 nations cut it down and **l** it.
31:12 out from under its shade and **l** it.
33:27 those who are **l** in the ruins will
47:11 fresh; they will be **l** for salt.
Da 2:44 nor will it be **l** to another people.
7: 7 trampled underfoot whatever was **l**.
7:19 trampled underfoot whatever was **l**.
10: 8 I was **l** alone, gazing at this great
10: 8 I had no strength **l**, my face turned
Joel 1: 4 What the locust swarm has **l** the
1: 4 what the great locusts have **l** the
1: 4 young locusts have **l** other locusts
Am 5: 3 Israel will have only a hundred **l**;
5: 3 strong will have only ten **l**."
6: 9 If ten men are **l** in one house, they
9: 1 are **l** I will kill with the sword.
Hab 2: 8 peoples who are **l** will plunder you.
Zep 1:12 who are like wine **l** on its dregs,
2: 4 Gaza will be abandoned and Ashkelon **l**
2: 5 destroy you, and none will be **l**."
3: 6 I have **l** their streets deserted,
3: 6 no-one will be **l**—no-one at all.
Hag 2: 3 'Who of you is **l** who saw this house
2:19 Is there yet any seed **l** in the barn?
Zec 2: 3 the angel who was speaking to me **l**,
7:14 The land was **l** so desolate behind
9: 7 Those who are **l** will belong to our
11: 9 who are **l** eat one another's flesh."
13: 8 yet one-third will be **l** in it.
Mal 1: 3 **l** his inheritance to the desert
4: 1 root or a branch will be **l** to them.
Mt 2:14 during the night and **l** for Egypt,
4:11 the devil **l** him, and angels came and
4:20 At once they **l** their nets and
4:22 immediately they **l** the boat and
8:15 He touched her hand and the fever **l**
12:44 says, 'I will return to the house I **l**
13:36 he **l** the crowd and went into the
14:20 of broken pieces that were **l** over.
15:29 Jesus **l** there and went along the Sea
15:37 of broken pieces that were **l** over.
16: 4 Jesus then **l** them and went away.
19: 1 he **l** Galilee and went into the
Mt 19:27 Peter answered him, "We have **l**
19:29 everyone who has **l** houses or
21:17 he **l** them and went out of the city
22:22 So they **l** him and went away.
22:25 he **l** his wife to his brother.
23:38 Look, your house is **l** to you
24: 1 Jesus **l** the temple and was walking
24: 2 not one stone here will be **l** on
24:40 one will be taken and the other **l**.
24:41 one will be taken and the other **l**.
26:44 he **l** them and went away once more
27: 5 the money into the temple and **l**.
Mk 1:18 At once they **l** their nets and
1:20 and they **l** their father Zebedee in
1:29 soon as they **l** the synagogue, they
1:31 fever **l** her and she began to wait on
1:35 Jesus got up, **l** the house and went
1:42 Immediately the leprosy **l** him and he
2: 2 gathered that there was no room **l**,
6: 1 Jesus **l** there and went to his home
7:17 After he had **l** the crowd and entered
7:24 Jesus **l** that place and went to the
7:29 go; the demon has **l** your daughter."
7:31 Jesus **l** the vicinity of Tyre and
8: 8 of broken pieces that were **l** over.
8:13 he **l** them, got back into the boat
9:30 They **l** that place and passed through
10: 1 Jesus then **l** that place and went
10:28 Peter said to him, "We have **l**
10:29 "no-one who has **l** home or brothers
12: 6 "He had one **l** to send, a son, whom
12:12 so they **l** him and went away.
12:22 none of the seven **l** any children
13: 2 "Not one stone here will be **l** on
14:16 The disciples **l**, went into the city
Lk 1:38 Then the angel **l** her.
2:15 the angels had **l** them and gone into
2:37 She never **l** the temple but
4:13 he **l** him until an opportune time.
4:38 Jesus **l** the synagogue and went to
4:39 and rebuked the fever, and it **l** her.
5: 2 two boats, **l** there by the fishermen,
5:11 **l** everything and followed him.
5:13 And immediately the leprosy **l** him.
5:28 Levi got up, **l** everything and
7:24 After John's messengers **l**, Jesus
8:37 So he got into the boat and **l**.
9:17 of broken pieces that were **l** over.
10:40 don't you care that my sister has **l**
11:14 When the demon **l**, the man who had
11:24 'I will return to the house I **l**.'
11:53 Jesus **l** there, the Pharisees and the
13:35 Look, your house is **l** to you
17:29 the day Lot **l** Sodom, fire and
17:34 one will be taken and the other **l**.
17:35 one will be taken and the other **l**."
18:28 Peter said to him, "We have **l** all we
18:29 "no-one who has **l** home or wife or
21: 6 not one stone will be **l** on another;
22:13 They **l** and found things just as
24:51 While he was blessing them, he **l**
Jn 4: 3 the Lord learned of this, he **l** Judea
4:43 After the two days he **l** for Galilee.
4:52 **l** him yesterday at the seventh hour."
6:12 "Gather the pieces that are **l** over.
6:13 **l** over by those who had eaten.
7:10 However, after his brothers had **l**
8: 9 until only Jesus was **l**, with the
8:29 is with me; he has not **l** me alone,
12:36 Jesus **l** and hid himself from them.
18: 1 he had finished praying, Jesus **l**
19:31 **l** on the crosses during the Sabbath,
Ac 1:25 Judas **l** to go where he belongs."
5:41 The apostles **l** the Sanhedrin,
7: 4 "So he **l** the land of the Chaldeans
12:10 street, suddenly the angel **l** him.
12:17 and then he **l** for another place.
13:13 John **l** them to return to Jerusalem.
14:17 Yet he has not **l** himself without
14:20 day he and Barnabas **l** for Derbe.
15:40 Paul chose Silas and **l**, commended by
16:18 At that moment the spirit **l** her.
16:40 and encouraged them. Then they **l**.
17:15 then **l** with instructions for Silas
17:33 At that, Paul **l** the Council.
18: 1 After this, Paul **l** Athens and went
Ac 18: 7 Paul **l** the synagogue and went next
18:18 Then he **l** the brothers and sailed
18:19 Ephesus, where Paul **l** Priscilla and
18:21 as he **l**, he promised, "I will come
19: 9 So Paul **l** them. He took the
19:12 cured and the evil spirits **l** them.
20:11 After talking until daylight, he **l**.
21: 5 when our time was up, we **l** and
24:27 to the Jews, he **l** Paul in prison.
25:14 man here whom Felix **l** as a prisoner.
26:31 They **l** the room, and while talking
27:40 Cutting loose the anchors, they **l**
Ro 3:25 because in his forbearance he had **l**
9:29 "Unless the Lord Almighty had **l** us
11: 3 only one **l**, and they are trying to
2Co 2: 2 For if I grieve you, who is **l** to
1Th 3: 1 best to be **l** by ourselves in Athens.
4:15 who are **l** till the coming of the
4:17 we who are still alive and are **l**
1Ti 5: 5 who is really in need and **l** all alone
2Ti 4:13 you come, bring the cloak that I **l**
4:20 Erastus stayed in Corinth, and I **l**
Tit 1: 5 The reason I **l** you in Crete was that
1: 5 straighten out what was **l** unfinished
Heb 2: 8 **l** nothing that is not subject to him.
10:26 truth, no sacrifice for sins is **l**,
11:15 thinking of the country they had **l**,
11:27 By faith he **l** Egypt, not fearing the
2Pe 2:15 They have **l** the straight way and
Rev 10: 2 the sea and his **l** foot on the land,

Left² (Left-handed)

Ge 13: 9 If you go to the **l**, I'll go to the
13: 9 go to the right, I'll go to the **l**."
48:13 his right towards Israel's **l** hand
48:13 his **l** towards Israel's right hand,
48:14 crossing his arms, he put his **l** hand
Ex 14:22 water on their right and on their **l**.
14:29 water on their right and on their **l**.
Lev 14:15 it in the palm of his own **l** hand,
14:26 oil into the palm of his own **l** hand,
Nu 20:17 not turn to the right or to the **l**
22:26 either to the right or to the **l**.
Dt 2:27 turn aside to the right or to the **l**.
5:32 turn aside to the right or to the **l**.
17:11 tell you, to the right or to the **l**.
17:20 the law to the right or to the **l**.
28:14 to the right or to the **l**, following
Jos 1: 7 from it to the right or to the **l**,
19:27 and Neiel, passing Cabul on the **l**.
23: 6 aside to the right or to the **l**.
Jdg 3:21 Ehud reached with his **l** hand, drew
7:20 the torches in their **l** hands and
16:29 the one and his **l** hand on the other,
1Sa 6:12 not turn to the right or to the **l**.
2Sa 2:19 nor to the **l** as he pursued him.
2:21 Turn aside to the right or to the **l**
14:19 turn to the right or to the **l** from
16: 6 guard were on David's right and **l**.
1Ki 7:49 five on the right and five on the **l**
22:19 round him on his right and on his **l**
2Ki 2: 8 divided to the right and to the **l**,
2:14 divided to the right and to the **l**,
22: 2 aside to the right or to the **l**.
23: 8 which is on the **l** of the city gate.
2Ch 18:18 standing on his right and on his **l**.
34: 2 aside to the right or to the **l**.
Ne 8: 4 on his **l** were Pedaiah, Mishael,
Pr 3:16 in her **l** hand are riches and honour.
4:27 Do not swerve to the right or the **l**;
Ecc 10: 2 but the heart of the fool to the **l**.
SS 2: 6 His **l** arm is under my head, and his
8: 3 His **l** arm is under my head and his
Isa 9:20 on the **l** they will eat, but not be
30:21 you turn to the right or to the **l**,
54: 3 out to the right and to the **l**;
Eze 1:10 and on the **l** the face of an ox; each
4: 4 "Then lie on your **l** side and put the
21:16 slash to the right, then to the **l**,
39: 3 strike your bow from your **l** hand
Da 12: 7 lifted his right hand and his **l** hand
Jnh 4:11 tell their right hand from their **l**,
Zec 4: 3 of the bowl and the other on its **l**
4:11 right and the **l** of the lampstand?"
12: 6 They will consume right and **l** all

Mt 6: 3 do not let your **l** hand know what
20:21 other at your **l** in your kingdom."
20:23 right or **l** is not for me to grant.
25:33 on his right and the goats on his **l**
25:41 Then he will say to those on his **l**,
27:38 one on his right and one on his **l**.
Mk 10:37 the other at your **l** in your glory."
10:40 to sit at my right or **l** is not for
15:27 one on his right and one on his **l**.
Lk 23:33 on his right, the other on his **l**.
2Co 6: 7 in the right hand and in the **l**;

Left-handed (Hand, Left[2])
Jdg 3:15 Ehud, a **l** man, the son of Gera the
20:16 seven hundred chosen men who were **l**,
1Ch 12: 2 to sling stones right-handed or **l**;

Leftover (Leave)
Ru 2: 2 pick up the **l** grain behind anyone in

Leg (Legs)
1Sa 9:24 the cook took up the **l** with what was
Eze 24: 4 pieces—the **l** and the shoulder.
Am 3:12 two **l** bones or a piece of an ear,

Legal (Legalising, Legalistic, Legally)
Nu 27:11 This is to be a **l** requirement for
35:29 "'These are to be **l** requirements
Ac 19:39 it must be settled in a **l** assembly.
22:25 "Is it **l** for you to flog a Roman

Legalising (Legal)
Ru 4: 7 method of **l** transactions in Israel.)

Legalistic (Legal)
Php 3: 6 as for **l** righteousness, faultless.

Legally (Legal)
Ge 23:17 of the field—was **l** made over
23:20 and the cave in it were **l** made over

Legion (Legions)
Mk 5: 9 "My name is **L**," he replied, "for we
5:15 been possessed by the **l** of demons,
Lk 8:30 "What is your name?" "**L**," he replied,

Legions (Legion)
Mt 26:53 more than twelve **l** of angels?

Legs (Leg)
Ex 12: 9 the fire—head, **l** and inner parts.
25:26 four corners, where the four **l** are.
29:17 and wash the inner parts and the **l**,
37:13 four corners, where the four **l** were.
Lev 1: 9 inner parts and the **l** with water,
1:13 inner parts and the **l** with water,
4:11 and **l**, the inner parts and offal—
8:21 He washed the inner parts and the **l**
9:14 He washed the inner parts and the **l**
11:21 jointed **l** for hopping on the ground.
11:23 that have four **l** you are to detest.
Dt 28:35 **l** with painful boils that cannot be
1Sa 17: 6 on his **l** he wore bronze greaves, and
Ps 147:10 nor his delight in the **l** of a man;
Pr 26: 7 Like a lame man's **l** that hang limp
SS 5:15 His **l** are pillars of marble set on
7: 1 Your graceful **l** are like jewels,
Isa 7:20 your head and the hair of your **l**,
47: 2 Lift up your skirts, bear your **l**,
Eze 1: 7 Their **l** were straight; their feet
Da 2:33 its **l** of iron, its feet partly of
5: 6 knocked together and his **l** gave way.
10: 6 his arms and **l** like the gleam of
Hab 3:16 into my bones, and my **l** trembled.
Jn 19:31 **l** broken and the bodies taken down.
19:32 broke the **l** of the first man who had
19:33 dead, they did not break his **l**.
Rev 10: 1 and his **l** were like fiery pillars.

Lehabites
Ge 10:13 Ludites, Anamites, **L**, Naphtuhites,
1Ch 1:11 Ludites, Anamites, **L**, Naphtuhites,

Lehi
Jdg 15: 9 in Judah, spreading out near **L**.
15:14 he approached **L**, the Philistines
15:19 God opened up the hollow place in **L**,
15:19 Hakkore, and it is still there in **L**.

Lemuel
Pr 31: 1 The sayings of King **L**—an oracle his
31: 4 "It is not for kings, O **L**—not for

Lend (Lender, Lending, Lends, Lent, Money-lender)
Ex 22:25 "If you **l** money to one of my people
Lev 25:37 You must not **l** him money at interest
Dt 15: 6 and you will **l** to many nations but
15: 8 Rather be open-handed and freely **l**
28:12 You will **l** to many nations but will
28:44 He will **l** to you, but you will not **l**
Ps 37:26 are always generous and **l** freely
83: 8 has joined them to **l** strength to
Eze 18: 8 He does not **l** at usury or take
Lk 6:34 if you **l** to those from whom you
6:34 'sinners' **l** to 'sinners', expecting
6:35 do good to them, and **l** to them
11: 5 'Friend, **l** me three loaves of bread,

Lender (Lend)
Pr 22: 7 the borrower is servant to the **l**.
Isa 24: 2 for borrower as for **l**, for debtor

Lending (Lend)
Ne 5:10 also **l** the people money and grain.

Lends (Lend)
Ps 15: 5 who **l** his money without usury and
112: 5 to him who is generous and **l** freely,
Pr 19:17 He who is kind to the poor **l** to the
Eze 18:13 He **l** at usury and takes excessive

Length (Long[1])
Ge 13:17 Go, walk through the **l** and breadth
Ex 12:40 Now the **l** of time the Israelite
26:12 for the additional **l** of the tent
Lev 19:35 measuring **l**, weight or quantity.
1Sa 28:20 Immediately Saul fell full **l** on the
2Sa 2:11 The **l** of time David was king in
8: 2 measured them off with a **l** of cord.
8: 2 the third **l** was allowed to live
2Ch 3: 8 its **l** corresponding to the width of
Ps 21: 4 him—**l** of days, for ever and ever.
90:10 The **l** of our days is seventy years—
Pr 10:27 The fear of the LORD adds **l** to life,
Eze 40: 5 The **l** of the measuring rod in the
40:11 and its **l** was thirteen cubits.
40:20 he measured the **l** and width of the
41: 4 he measured the **l** of the inner
41: 8 the **l** of the rod, six long cubits.
41:12 round, and its **l** was ninety cubits.
41:15 he measured the **l** of the building
42:10 south side along the **l** of the wall
42:11 they had the same **l** and width,
48: 8 and its **l** from east to west will
48:13 Its total **l** will be 25,000 cubits
48:18 portion and running the **l** of it,
48:21 Both these areas running the **l** of
Ac 12:10 When they had walked the **l** of one
Rev 21:16 found it to be 12,000 stadia in **l**,

Lengthen (Long[1])
Ecc 8:13 their days will not **l** like a shadow.
Isa 54: 2 **l** your cords, strengthen your stakes.

Lengths (Long[1])
2Sa 8: 2 Every two **l** of them were put to
Eze 13:18 make veils of various **l** for their

Lengthwise (Long[1])
Eze 45: 7 running **l** from the western to the

Lengthy (Long[1])
Mk 12:40 and for a show make **l** prayers.
Lk 20:47 and for a show make **l** prayers.

Lent (Lend)
Jer 15:10 I have neither **l** nor borrowed,

Lentil (Lentils)
Ge 25:34 gave Esau some bread and some **l** stew

Lentils (Lentil)
2Sa 17:28 and roasted grain, beans and **l**,
23:11 where there was a field full of **l**,
Eze 4: 9 "Take wheat and barley, beans and **l**,

Leopard (Leopards)
Isa 11: 6 the **l** will lie down with the goat,
Jer 5: 6 a **l** will lie in wait near their
13:23 change his skin or the **l** its spots?
Da 7: 6 beast, one that looked like a **l**.
Hos 13: 7 like a **l** I will lurk by the path.
Rev 13: 2 The beast I saw resembled a **l**, but

Leopards (Leopard)
SS 4: 8 and the mountain haunts of the **l**.
Hab 1: 8 Their horses are swifter than **l**,

Leper (Leprosy)
Mt 26: 6 home of a man known as Simon the **L**,
Mk 14: 3 home of a man known as Simon the **L**,

Leprosy (Leper, Leprous)
Nu 12:10 towards her and saw that she had **l**;
2Sa 3:29 someone who has a running sore or **l**
2Ki 5: 1 was a valiant soldier, but he had **l**.
5: 3 Samaria! He would cure him of his **l**."
5: 6 so that you may cure him of his **l**."
5: 7 someone to me to be cured of his **l**?
5:11 over the spot and cure me of my **l**.
5:27 Naaman's **l** will cling to you and to
7: 3 Now there were four men with **l** at
7: 8 The men who had **l** reached the edge
15: 5 The LORD afflicted the king with **l**
2Ch 26:19 temple, **l** broke out on his forehead.
26:20 they saw that he had **l** on his
26:21 King Uzziah had **l** until the day he
26:23 kings, for people said, "He had **l**.
Mt 8: 2 A man with **l** came and knelt before
8: 3 Immediately he was cured of his **l**.
10: 8 those who have **l**, drive out demons.
11: 5 walk, those who have **l** are cured,
Mk 1:40 A man with **l** came to him and begged
1:42 Immediately the **l** left him and he
Lk 4:27 there were many in Israel with **l** in
5:12 came along who was covered with **l**.
5:13 And immediately the **l** left him.
7:22 walk, those who have **l** are cured,
17:12 village, ten men who had **l** met him.

Leprous (Leprosy)
Ex 4: 6 he took it out, it was **l**, like snow.
Nu 12:10 there stood Miriam—**l**, like snow.
Dt 24: 8 In cases of **l** diseases be very
2Ki 5:27 and he was **l**, as white as snow.
2Ch 26:21 **l**, and excluded from the temple of the

Leshem
Jos 19:47 so they went up and attacked **L**,
19:47 They settled in **L** and named it Dan

Lesson
Jdg 8:16 taught the men of Succoth a **l** by
1Sa 14:12 up to us and we'll teach you a **l**.
Pr 24:32 and learned a **l** from what I saw:
Jer 35:13 'Will you not learn a **l** and obey my
Mt 24:32 "Now learn this **l** from the fig-tree:
Mk 13:28 "Now learn this **l** from the fig-tree:

Let
Ge 1: 3 God said, "**L** there be light," and
1: 6 God said, "**L** there be an expanse
1: 9 God said, "**L** the water under the sky

Ge 1: 9 one place, and l dry ground appear.
1:11 God said, "L the land produce
1:14 God said, "L there be lights in the
1:14 and l them serve as signs to mark
1:15 l them be lights in the expanse of
1:20 God said, "L the water teem with
1:20 and l birds fly above the earth
1:22 l the birds increase on the earth."
1:24 God said, "L the land produce living
1:26 "L us make man in our likeness,
1:26 and l them rule over the fish of
11: 4 they said, "Come, l us build
11: 7 Come, l us go down and confuse their
12:12 will kill me but will l you live.
14:24 L them have their share."
18: 4 L a little water be brought, and
18: 5 L me get you something to eat, so
18:30 Lord not be angry, but l me speak.
18:32 but l me speak just once more.
19: 8 L me bring them out to you, and you
19:20 L me flee to it—it is very small,
20: 6 is why I did not l you touch her.
23: 8 "If you are willing to l me bury my
24:14 'Please l down your jar that I may
24:14 l her be the one you have chosen
24:43 "Please l me drink a little water
24:44 l her be the one the LORD has chosen
24:51 and l her become the wife of your
24:55 "L the girl remain with us ten days
25:30 He said to Jacob, "Quick, l me have
26:28 L us make a treaty with you.
27:13 "My son, l the curse fall on me.
30:32 L me go through all your flocks
30:34 Laban. "L it be as you have said
31:28 You didn't even l me kiss my
31:37 l them judge between the two of us.
31:44 l it serve as a witness between us."
32:26 the man said, "L me go, for it is
32:26 not l you go unless you bless me."
33:12 Esau said, "L us be on our way; I'll
33:14 l my lord go on ahead of his servant,
33:15 Esau said, "Then l me leave some of
33:15 "Just l me find favour in the eyes
34:11 "L me find favour in your eyes, and
34:21 "L them live in our land and trade
34:23 So l us give our consent to them,
35: 3 come, l us go up to Bethel, where I
38:16 "Come now, l me sleep with you.
38:23 Judah said, "L her keep what she has,
41:33 "And now l Pharaoh look for a
41:34 L Pharaoh appoint commissioners over
42:19 If you are honest men, l one of your
43:14 that he will l your other brother
44:10 he said, "l it be as you say.
44:18 lord, l your servant speak a word.
44:33 please l your servant remain here
44:33 l the boy return with his brothers.
44:34 No! Do not l me see the misery that
47: 4 l your servants settle in Goshen."
47: 6 L them live in Goshen. And if you
49: 6 L me not enter their council, l me
49:26 L all these rest on the head of
50: 5 Now l me go up and bury my father;
Ex 1:16 but if it is a girl, l her live."
1:17 them to do; they l the boys live.
1:18 this? Why have you l the boys live?"
1:22 the Nile, but l every girl live."
3:18 L us take a three-day journey into
3:19 the king of Egypt will not l you go
3:20 After that, he will l you go.
4:18 "L me go back to my own people in
4:21 so that he will not l the people go.
4:23 I told you, "L my son go, so that he
4:23 But you refused to l him go; so I
4:26 the LORD l him alone. (At that time
5: 1 'L my people go, so that they may
5: 2 that I should obey him and l Israel
5: 2 LORD and I will not l Israel go."
5: 3 Now l us take a three-day journey
5: 7 l them go and gather their own straw.
5: 8 'L us go and sacrifice to our God.'
5:17 'L us go and sacrifice to the LORD.'
6: 1 of my mighty hand he will l them go
6:11 king of Egypt to l the Israelites go
7: 2 tell Pharaoh to l the Israelites go
7:14 he refuses to l the people go.

Ex 7:16 me to say to you: L my people go,
8: 1 the LORD says: L my people go,
8: 2 If you refuse to l them go, I will
8: 8 and I will l your people go to offer
8:20 the LORD says: L my people go,
8:21 If you do not l my people go, I will
8:28 Pharaoh said, "I will l you go to
8:32 heart and would not l the people go.
9: 1 "L my people go, so that they may
9: 2 If you refuse to l them go and
9: 7 and he would not l the people go.
9:13 the Hebrews, says: L my people go,
9:17 my people and will not l them go.
9:28 I will l you go; you don't have to
9:35 he would not l the Israelites go,
10: 3 L my people go, so that they may
10: 4 If you refuse to l them go, I will
10: 7 L the people go, so that they may
10:10 The LORD be with you—if I l you go,
10:11 No! L only the men go; and worship
10:20 he would not l the Israelites go.
10:27 and he was not willing to l them go.
11: 1 After that, he will l you go from
11:10 and he would not l the Israelites go
13:15 Pharaoh stubbornly refused to l us
13:17 Pharaoh l the people go, God did not
14: 5 We have l the Israelites go and have
14:12 us alone; l us serve the Egyptians
21: 8 himself, he must l her be redeemed.
21:26 he must l the servant go free to
21:27 he must l the servant go free to
22:30 L them stay with their mothers for
23:11 during the seventh year l the land
23:13 do not l them be heard on your lips.
23:33 Do not l them live in your land, or
32:25 that Aaron had l them get out of
33:12 l me know whom you will send with me.
34: 9 said, "then l the Lord go with us.
34:25 and do not l any of the sacrifice
Lev 10: 6 "Do not l your hair become unkempt,
13:45 l his hair be unkempt, cover the
21:10 must not l his hair become unkempt
Nu 6: 5 l the hair of his head grow long.
11:15 do not l me face my own ruin."
12:12 Do not l her be like a stillborn
14: 3 land only to l us fall by the sword?
16:38 L them be a sign to the Israelites."
20:17 Please l us pass through your
20:21 Since Edom refused to l them go
21:22 "L us pass through your country. We
21:23 Sihon would not l Israel pass
21:27 and l it be rebuilt; l Sihon's city
22:13 has refused to l me go with you."
22:16 Do not l anything keep you from
23:10 L me die the death of the righteous,
23:27 said to Balaam, "Come, l me take you
23:27 to l you curse them for me from there
24:14 but come, l me warn you of what this
32: 5 "l this land be given to your
Dt 1:22 "L us send men ahead to spy out the
2:27 "L us pass through your country.
2:28 Only l us pass through on foot—
2:30 king of Heshbon refused to l us pass
3:25 L me go over and see the good land
4: 9 or l them slip from your heart as
9:14 L me alone, so that I may destroy
13: 2 "L us follow other gods" (gods you
13: 2 not known) "and l us worship them,"
13: 6 "L us go and worship other gods"
13:13 "L us go and worship other gods"
15:12 seventh year you must l him go free.
16: 4 L no yeast be found in your
16: 4 Do not l any of the meat you
17:14 "L us set a king over us like all
18:10 L no-one be found among you who
18:16 "L us not hear the voice of the LORD
20: 5 L him go home, or he may die in
20: 6 L him go home, or he may die in
20: 7 L him go home, or he may die in
20: 8 L him go home so that his brothers
21:14 l her go wherever she wishes.
22: 7 but be sure to l the mother go, so
23:16 L him live among you wherever he
24:11 Stay outside and l the man to whom
32: 2 L my teaching fall like rain and my
32:38 L them rise up to help you! L them

Dt 33: 6 "L Reuben live and not die, nor his
33:12 L the beloved of the LORD rest
33:16 L all these rest on the head of
33:24 l him be favoured by his brothers,
33:24 and l him bathe his feet in oil.
34: 4 I have l you see it with your eyes,
Jos 1: 8 Do not l this Book of the Law depart
2:15 she l them down by a rope through
2:18 window through which you l us down,
2:21 she replied. "L it be as you say."
8:15 Israel l themselves be driven back
9:15 of peace with them to l them live,
9:20 do to them: We will l them live,
9:21 continued, "L them live, but l them
10:19 and don't l them reach their cities,
22:22 LORD! He knows! And l Israel know!
22:26 we said, 'L us get ready and build
Jdg 6:32 "L Baal contend with him,"
6:39 L me make just one more request.
7: 7 L all the other men go, each to his
9:15 then l fire come out of the
9:20 if you have not, l fire come out
9:20 and l fire come out from you,
10:14 L them save you when you are in
11:19 'L us pass through your country to
11:27 L the LORD, the Judge, decide the
11:38 may go," he said. And he l her go
12: 5 "L me cross over," the men of Gilead
13: 8 "O Lord, I beg you, l the man of God
14:12 "L me tell you a riddle," Samson
15: 1 But her father would not l him go in.
15: 5 lit the torches and l the foxes
16:28 and l me with one blow get revenge
16:30 Samson said, "L me die with the
19:20 "L me supply whatever you need. Only
19:25 night, and at dawn they l her go.
Ru 2: 2 to Naomi, "L me go to the fields
2: 7 She said, 'Please l me glean and
3: 3 but don't l him know you are there
3:13 wants to redeem, good; l him redeem.
3:14 "Don't l it be known that a woman
1Sa 2: 3 or l your mouth speak such arrogance
2:16 "L the fat be burned up first, and
3:18 l him do what is good in his eyes."
3:19 and he l none of his words fall to
4: 3 L us bring the ark of the LORD's
5:11 l it go back to its own place,
8: 9 but warn them solemnly and l them
9: 9 "Come, l us go to the seer," because
9:19 and in the morning I will l you go
11:14 said to the people, "Come, l us go
13: 3 and said, "L the Hebrews hear!
14: 8 towards the men and l them see us.
14:36 Saul said, "L us go down after the
14:36 l us not leave one of them alive.
14:36 But the priest said, "L us enquire
14:38 and l us find out what sin has been
15:16 Samuel said to Saul. "L me tell you
16:16 L our lord command his servants here
17:10 me a man and l us fight each other."
17:32 David said to Saul, "L no-one lose
18: 2 l him return to his father's house.
18:17 L the Philistines do that!"
19: 4 "L not the king do wrong to his
19:12 Michal l David down through a window,
19:17 him, "He said to me, 'L me get away.
20: 5 but l me go and hide in the field
20:12 not send you word and l you know?
20:13 l you know and send you away safely.
20:29 He said, 'L me go, because our
20:29 eyes, l me go to see my brothers.
22: 3 "Would you l my father and mother
22:15 L not the king accuse your servant
24:19 his enemy, does he l him get away
25:24 lord, l the blame be on me alone.
25:24 Please l your servant speak to you;
25:27 l this gift, which your servant has
25:28 L no wrongdoing be found in you as
26: 8 Now l me pin him to the ground with
26:19 Now l my lord the king listen to his
26:20 Now do not l my blood fall to the
26:22 "L one of your young men come over
27: 5 l a place be assigned to me in one
28:22 l me give you some food so that you
2Sa 2:14 "All right, let them do it," Joab
3:21 Abner said to David, "L me go at

2Sa 3:24 Why did you l him go? Now he is gone!
10:12 Be strong and l us fight bravely for
11:25 'Don't l this upset you; the sword
12:22 to me and l the child live.'
13: 5 L her prepare the food in my sight
13:26 "If not, please l my brother Amnon
14: 9 "My lord the king, l the blame rest
14: 9 and l the king and his throne be
14:11 "Then l the king invoke the LORD
14:12 said, "L your servant speak a word
14:18 "L my lord the king speak," the
14:32 of anything, l him put me to death."
15: 7 "L me go to Hebron and fulfil a vow
15:25 he will bring me back and l me see
15:26 l him do to me whatever seems good
16: 9 L me go over and cut off his head."
16:11 l him curse, for the LORD has told
17:11 "So I advise you: L all Israel, from
18:19 Ahimaaz son of Zadok said, "L me run
18:22 please l me run behind the Cushite.
19:30 "L him take everything, now that my
19:37 L your servant return, that I may
19:37 L him cross over with my lord the
20:11 is for David, l him follow Joab!"
21: 6 l seven of his male descendants be
21:10 she did not l the birds of the air
24:14 L us fall into the hands of the LORD
24:14 l me fall into the hands of men."
24:17 L your hand fall upon me and my
24:22 Araunah said to David, "L my lord
1Ki 1: 2 his servants said to him, "L us look
1:12 Now then, l me advise you how you
1:51 He says, 'L King Solomon swear to me
2: 6 but do not l his grey head go down
2: 7 l them be among those who eat at
2:21 she said, "L Abishag the Shunammite
8:26 now, O God of Israel, l your word
11:21 Then Hadad said to Pharaoh, "L me go,
11:22 Hadad replied, "but do l me go!"
15:19 "L there be a treaty between me and
17:21 l this boy's life return to him!"
18:23 L them choose one for themselves,
18:23 and l them cut it into pieces and
18:36 l it be known today that you are God
18:40 Don't l anyone get away!" They
19:20 "L me kiss my father and mother
20:31 L us go to the king of Israel with
20:32 Ben-Hadad says: 'Please l me live.
20:34 a treaty with him, and l him go.
21: 2 Ahab said to Naboth, "L me have your
22:13 L your word agree with theirs, and
22:17 L each one go home in peace.'
22:49 "L my men sail with your men," but
2Ki 2: 9 "L me inherit a double portion of
2:16 L them go and look for your master.
5:17 "please l me, your servant, be given
6: 2 L us go to the Jordan, where each of
6: 2 and l us build a place there for us
7:13 So l us send them to find out what
9:15 don't l anyone slip out of the city
10:25 Go in and kill them; l no-one escape.
12: 5 L every priest receive the money
12: 5 and l it be used to repair whatever
18:29 Do not l Hezekiah deceive you.
18:30 Do not l Hezekiah persuade you to
19:10 Do not l the god you depend on
23:18 "Don't l anyone disturb his bones.
1Ch 4:10 territory! L your hand be with me,
13: 2 l us send word far and wide to the
13: 3 L us bring the ark of our God back
16:10 Glory in his holy name; l the hearts
16:31 L the heavens rejoice, l the earth
16:31 l them say among the nations, "The
16:32 L the sea resound, and all that is
16:32 l the fields be jubilant, and
17:23 LORD, l the promise you have made
19:13 Be strong and l us fight bravely for
21:13 L me fall into the hands of the LORD,
21:13 l me fall into the hands of men."
21:17 l your hand fall upon me and my
21:17 l this plague remain on your people."
21:22 David said to him, "L me have the
21:23 "Take it! L my lord the king do
2Ch 1: 9 Now, LORD God, l your promise to my
2:15 "Now l my lord send his servants the
6:17 O LORD, God of Israel, l your word
2Ch 14: 7 "L us build up these towns," he said
14:11 do not l man prevail against you.
16: 3 "L there be a treaty between me and
18:12 L your word agree with theirs, and
18:16 L each one go home in peace.'
19: 7 Now l the fear of the LORD be upon
32:11 to l you die of hunger and thirst.
32:15 Now do not l Hezekiah deceive you
36:23 God be with him, and l him go up.
Ezr 1: 3 and l him go up to Jerusalem in
4: 2 "L us help you build because, like
4:22 Why l this threat grow, to the
5:17 l a search be made in the royal
5:17 Then l the king send us his decision
6: 3 L the temple be rebuilt as a place
6: 3 and l its foundations be laid.
6: 7 L the governor of the Jews and the
6:12 L it be carried out with diligence.
7:23 l it be done with diligence for the
10: 3 Now l us make a covenant before our
10: 3 L it be done according to the Law.
10:14 L our officials act for the whole
10:14 Then l everyone in our towns who has
Ne 1: 6 l your ear be attentive and your
1:11 O Lord, l your ear be attentive to
2: 5 l him send me to the city in Judah
2:17 Come, l us rebuild the wall of
2:18 They replied, "L us start rebuilding.
5:10 But l the exacting of usury stop!
6: 2 "Come, l us meet together in one of
6: 7 so come, l us confer together."
6:10 said, "L us meet in the house of God
6:10 and l us close the temple doors
9:32 do not l all this hardship seem
Est 1:19 l him issue a royal decree and l it
2: 2 "L a search be made for beautiful
2: 3 L the king appoint commissioners in
2: 3 L them be placed under the care of
2: 3 l beauty treatments be given to them.
2: 4 l the girl who pleases the king be
3: 9 l a decree be issued to destroy
5: 4 "l the king, together with Haman,
5: 8 l the king and Haman come tomorrow
6: 9 l the robe and horse be entrusted to
6: 9 L them robe the man the king
8: 5 with me, l an order be written
9:13 and l Haman's ten sons be hanged on
Job 6: 9 to l loose his hand and cut me off!
7:16 L me alone; my days have no meaning.
7:19 or l me alone even for an instant?
9:18 He would not l me regain my breath
10:14 not l my offence go unpunished.
12: 8 or l the fish of the sea inform you.
13:13 "Keep silent and l me speak; then l
13:17 l your ears take in what I say.
13:22 or l me speak, and you reply.
14: 6 look away from him and l him alone,
15:17 l me tell you what I have seen,
15:31 L him not deceive himself by
17: 4 you will not l them triumph.
20:13 though he cannot bear to l it go and
21: 2 l this be the consolation you give
21:19 L him repay the man himself, so
21:20 L his own eyes see his destruction;
21:20 l him drink of the wrath of the
24:23 He may l them rest in a feeling of
27: 6 righteousness and never l go of it;
31: 6 l God weigh me in honest scales and
31:16 l the eyes of the widow grow weary,
31:22 l my arm fall from the shoulder,
31:22 l it be broken off at the joint.
31:35 defence—l the Almighty answer me;
31:35 l my accuser put his indictment in
31:40 l briers come up instead of wheat
32:13 l God refute him, not man.
34: 4 L us discern for ourselves what is
34: 4 l us learn together what is good.
36:18 not l a large bribe turn you aside.
Job 39: 5 "Who l the wild donkey go free? Who
40: 2 L him who accuses God answer him!"
Ps 2: 3 "L us break their chains," they say,
4: 6 L the light of your face shine upon
5:10 L their intrigues be their downfall
5:11 l all who take refuge in you be glad
5:11 l them ever sing for joy.
7: 5 l my enemy pursue and overtake me;
Ps 7: 5 l him trample my life to the ground
7: 7 L the assembled peoples gather round
7: 8 l the LORD judge the peoples. Judge
9:19 l not man triumph; l the nations
9:20 l the nations know they are but men
14: 7 l Jacob rejoice and Israel be glad!
16:10 will you l your Holy One see decay.
22: 8 l the LORD rescue him. L him deliver
25: 2 not l me be put to shame, nor l my
25:20 l me not be put to shame, for I
30: 1 did not l my enemies gloat over me.
31: 1 l me never be put to shame;
31:16 L your face shine on your servant;
31:17 L me not be put to shame, O LORD,
31:17 but l the wicked be put to shame
31:18 L their lying lips be silenced, for
32: 6 Therefore l everyone who is godly
33: 8 L all the earth fear the LORD; l all
34: 2 l the afflicted hear and rejoice.
34: 3 Glorify the LORD with me: l us exalt
35:19 L not those gloat over me who are my
35:19 l not those who hate me without
35:24 my God; do not l them gloat over me.
35:25 Do not l them think, "Aha, just what
37:33 or l them be condemned when brought
38:16 For I said, "Do not l them gloat or
39: 4 l me know how fleeting is my life.
43: 3 l them guide me; l them bring me to
45: 4 l your right hand display awesome
45: 5 L your sharp arrows pierce the
45: 5 l the nations fall beneath your feet.
51: 8 L me hear joy and gladness; l the
53: 6 l Jacob rejoice and Israel be glad!
54: 5 L evil recoil on those who slander
55:15 L death take my enemies by surprise;
55:15 l them go down alive to the grave,
55:22 he will never l the righteous fall.
56: 7 On no account l them escape; in your
57: 5 l your glory be over all the earth.
57:11 l your glory be over all the earth.
58: 7 L them vanish like water that flows
58: 7 the bow, l their arrows be blunted.
59:10 l me gloat over those who slander me.
59:12 l them be caught in their pride.
64:10 L the righteous rejoice in the LORD
64:10 l all the upright in heart praise
66: 6 on foot—come, l us rejoice in him.
66: 7 l not the rebellious rise up
66: 8 l the sound of his promise be heard
66:12 You l men ride over our heads;
66:16 l me tell you what he has done for
69:14 me from the mire, do not l me sink;
69:15 Do not l the floodwaters engulf me
69:24 l your fierce anger overtake
69:25 l there be no-one to dwell in their
69:27 not l them share in your salvation.
69:34 L heaven and earth praise him, the
70: 4 always say, "L God be exalted!
71: 1 refuge; l me never be put to shame.
72:16 L corn abound throughout the land;
72:16 L its fruit flourish like Lebanon;
72:16 l it thrive like the grass of the
74:21 Do not l the oppressed retreat in
76:11 l all the neighbouring lands bring
78:26 He l loose the east wind from the
80:17 L your hand rest on the man at your
83: 4 "Come," they say, "l us destroy them
83:12 who said, "L us take possession of
83:18 L them know that you, whose name is
85: 8 but l them not return to folly.
95: 1 Come, l us sing for joy to the LORD;
95: 1 l us sing for joy to the LORD; l us
95: 2 L us come before him with
95: 6 Come, l us bow down in worship, l us
96:11 L the heavens rejoice, l the earth
96:11 l the sea resound, and all that is
96:12 l the fields be jubilant, and
97: 1 l the earth be glad; l the distant
97:10 L those who love the LORD hate evil,
98: 7 L the sea resound, and everything in
98: 8 L the rivers clap their hands, l the
98: 9 l them sing before the LORD, for he
99: 1 The LORD reigns, l the nations
99: 1 the cherubim, l the earth shake.
99: 3 L them praise your great and awesome
102: 1 l my cry for help come to you.

Ps 102:18 **L** this be written for a future
105: 3 **l** the hearts of those who seek the
106:48 **L** all the people say, "Amen!" Praise
107: 2 **L** the redeemed of the LORD say this—
107: 8 **L** them give thanks to the LORD for
107:15 **L** them give thanks to the LORD for
107:21 **L** them give thanks to the LORD for
107:22 **L** them sacrifice thank-offerings and
107:31 **L** them give thanks to the LORD for
107:32 **L** them exalt him in the assembly of
107:38 he did not **l** their herds diminish.
107:43 Whoever is wise, **l** him heed these
108: 5 **l** your glory be over all the earth.
109: 6 **l** an accuser stand at his right
109: 7 he is tried, **l** him be found guilty,
109:27 **L** them know that it is your hand,
113: 2 **L** the name of the LORD be praised,
118: 2 **L** Israel say: "His love endures for
118: 3 **L** the house of Aaron say: "His love
118: 4 **L** those who fear the LORD say: "His
118:24 **l** us rejoice and be glad in it.
119:10 not **l** me stray from your commands.
119:27 **L** me understand the teaching of your
119:31 O LORD; do not **l** me be put to shame.
119:77 **L** your compassion come to me that I
119:116 live; do not **l** my hopes be dashed.
119:122 **l** not the arrogant oppress me.
119:133 to your word; **l** no sin rule over me.
119:175 **L** me live that I may praise you,
121: 3 He will not **l** your foot slip—he
122: 1 "**L** us go to the house of the LORD.
124: 1 been on our side—**l** Israel say—
124: 6 the LORD, who has not **l** us be torn
129: 1 me from my youth—**l** Israel say—
130: 2 O Lord, hear my voice. **L** your ears
132: 7 "**L** us go to his dwelling-place; **l** us
140: 8 O LORD; do not **l** their plans succeed,
140: 9 **L** the heads of those who surround me
140:10 **L** burning coals fall upon them; may
140:11 **L** slanderers not be established in
141: 4 **L** not my heart be drawn to what is
141: 4 **l** me not eat of their delicacies.
141: 5 **L** a righteous man strike me—it is a
141: 5 **l** him rebuke me—it is oil on my
141:10 **L** the wicked fall into their own
143: 8 **L** the morning bring me word of your
145:21 **L** every creature praise his holy
148: 5 **L** them praise the name of the LORD,
148:13 **L** them praise the name of the LORD,
149: 2 **L** Israel rejoice in their Maker;
149: 2 **l** the people of Zion be glad in
149: 3 **L** them praise his name with dancing
149: 5 **L** the saints rejoice in this honour
150: 6 **L** everything that has breath praise
Pr 1: 5 **l** the wise listen and add to their
1: 5 and **l** the discerning get guidance—
3: 3 **L** love and faithfulness never leave
3:20 and the clouds **l** drop the dew.
3:21 do not **l** them out of your sight;
4:13 on to instruction, do not **l** it go;
4:21 Do not **l** them out of your sight,
4:25 **L** your eyes look straight ahead, fix
5:17 **L** them be yours alone, never to be
6:25 **l** her captivate you with her eyes,
7:25 Do not **l** your heart turn to her ways
9: 4 "**L** all who are simple come in here!"
9:16 "**L** all who are simple come in here!"
10: 3 The LORD does not **l** the righteous go
23:17 Do not **l** your heart envy sinners,
23:26 and **l** your eyes keep to my ways,
24:17 do not **l** your heart rejoice,
27: 2 **L** another praise you, and not your
28:17 till death; **l** no-one support him.
31: 7 **l** them drink and forget their
31:31 and **l** her works bring her praise at
Ecc 5: 2 on earth, so **l** your words be few.
5: 6 Do not **l** your mouth lead you into
7:18 the one and not **l** go of the other.
11: 6 at evening **l** not your hands be idle
11: 8 man may live, **l** him enjoy them all
11: 8 But **l** him remember the days of
11: 9 **l** your heart give you joy in the
SS 1: 2 **L** him kiss me with the kisses of his
1: 4 **l** us hurry! **L** the king bring me
2:14 me your face, **l** me hear your voice;
3: 4 I held him and would not **l** him go
SS 4:16 **L** my lover come into his garden and
7:11 **l** us go to the countryside, let us
7:12 **L** us go early to the vineyards to
8:11 he **l** out his vineyard to tenants.
8:13 in attendance, **l** me hear your voice!
Isa 1:18 "Come now, **l** us reason together,"
2: 3 "Come, **l** us go up to the mountain of
2: 5 **l** us walk in the light of the LORD
4: 1 only **l** us be called by your name.
5:19 "**L** God hurry, **l** him hasten his work
5:19 **L** it approach, **l** the plan of the
7: 6 "**L** us invade Judah; **l** us tear it
12: 5 **l** this be known to all the world.
14:17 would not **l** his captives go home?"
16: 4 **L** the Moabite fugitives stay with
19:12 **L** them show you and make known what
21: 7 **l** him be alert, fully alert."
22: 4 away from me; **l** me weep bitterly.
22:13 "**L** us eat and drink," you say, "for
25: 9 **l** us rejoice and be glad in his
26:11 **L** them see your zeal for your people
26:11 **l** the fire reserved for your enemies
27: 5 Or else **l** them come to me for refuge;
27: 5 **l** them make peace with me, yes **l**
28:12 the resting-place, **l** the weary rest
29: 1 and **l** your cycle of festivals go on.
34: 1 you peoples! **L** the earth hear, and
36:14 says: Do not **l** Hezekiah deceive you
36:15 Do not **l** Hezekiah persuade you to
36:18 "Do not **l** Hezekiah mislead you when
37:10 Do not **l** the god you depend on
38:16 restored me to health and **l** me live.
41: 1 **L** the nations renew their strength!
41: 1 **L** them come forward and speak;
41: 1 **l** us meet together at the place of
42:11 **L** the desert and its towns raise
42:11 **l** the settlements where Kedar lives
42:11 **L** the people of Sela sing for joy;
42:11 **l** them shout from the mountaintops.
42:12 **L** them give glory to the LORD and
43: 9 **L** them bring in their witnesses to
43:26 Review the past for me, **l** us argue
44: 7 Who then is like me? **L** him proclaim
44: 7 **L** him declare and lay out before me
44: 7 yes, **l** him foretell what will come.
44:11 **L** them all come together and take
44:14 He **l** it grow among the trees of the
44:28 "**L** it be rebuilt," and of the temple,
44:28 temple, "**L** its foundations be laid.
45: 8 **l** the clouds shower it down. **L** the
45: 8 **l** salvation spring up,
45: 8 **l** righteousness grow with it;
45:21 **l** them take counsel together.
47:13 **L** your astrologers come forward,
47:13 **l** them save you from what is coming
48:11 How can I **l** myself be defamed? I
50: 8 **L** us face each other! Who is my
50: 8 Who is my accuser? **L** him confront me!
50:10 **L** him who walks in the dark,
55: 7 **L** the wicked forsake his way and the
55: 7 **L** him turn to the LORD, and he will
56: 3 **L** no foreigner who has bound himself
56: 3 And **l** not any eunuch complain, "I
56:12 "**L** me get wine! **L** us drink our fill
57:13 **l** your collection ⌊of idols⌋ save
66: 5 '**L** the LORD be glorified, that we
Jer 2:28 **L** them come if they can save you
3:25 **L** us lie down in our shame, and **l**
4: 5 **L** us flee to the fortified cities!'
5:13 so **l** what they say be done to them."
5:24 '**L** us fear the LORD our God, who
6: 4 Arise, **l** us attack at noon! But,
6: 5 arise, **l** us attack at night and
6: 9 "**L** them glean the remnant of Israel
7: 3 and I will **l** you live in this place.
7: 7 I will **l** you live in this place, in
8:14 **L** us flee to the fortified cities
9:18 **L** them come quickly and wail over us
9:23 "**L** not the wise man boast of his
9:24 **l** him who boasts boast about this:
11:19 "**L** us destroy the tree and its fruit;
11:19 **l** us cut him off from the land of
11:20 **l** me see your vengeance upon them,
13: 1 waist, but do not **l** it touch water."
14:17 **L** my eyes overflow with tears
15: 1 away from my presence! **L** them go!
Jer 15:19 **L** this people turn to you, but you
17:15 of the LORD? **L** it now be fulfilled!"
17:18 **L** my persecutors be put to shame,
17:18 **l** them be terrified, but keep me
18:21 **L** their wives be made childless and
18:21 **l** their men be put to death, their
18:22 **L** a cry be heard from their houses
18:23 **L** them be overthrown before you;
20:12 **l** me see your vengeance upon them,
22:20 **l** your voice be heard in Bashan,
23:28 **L** the prophet who has a dream tell
23:28 but **l** the one who has my word speak
27:11 I will **l** that nation remain in its
27:18 **l** them plead with the LORD Almighty
29: 8 "Do not **l** the prophets and diviners
30:11 not **l** you go entirely unpunished.'
31: 6 'Come, **l** us go up to Zion, to the
32:37 place and **l** them live in safety.
33: 6 will **l** them enjoy abundant peace
34:14 six years, you must **l** him go free.
36:19 Don't **l** anyone know where you are."
37:20 **L** me bring my petition before you:
38:11 and **l** them down with ropes to
38:24 "Do not **l** anyone know about this
40: 5 and a present and **l** him go.
40:15 "**L** me go and kill Ishmael son of
41: 8 So he **l** them alone and did not kill
45: 5 I will **l** you escape with your life.
46:16 They will say, 'Get up, **l** us go back
46:28 not **l** you go entirely unpunished."
48: 2 Come, **l** us put an end to that nation.
48:26 **L** Moab wallow in her vomit; **l** her be
50:16 **l** everyone return to his own people,
50:16 **l** everyone flee to his own land.
50:27 Kill all her young bulls; **l** them go
50:29 all round her; **l** no-one escape
50:33 them fast, refusing to **l** them go.
51: 3 **L** not the archer string his bow,
51: 3 bow, nor **l** him put on his armour.
51: 9 **l** us leave her and each go to his
51:10 **l** us tell in Zion what the LORD
Lam 1:22 "**L** all their wickedness come before
2:17 he has **l** the enemy gloat over you,
2:18 **l** your tears flow like a river
3:28 **L** him sit alone in silence, for the
3:29 **L** him bury his face in the dust—
3:30 **L** him offer his cheek to one who
3:30 and **l** him be filled with disgrace.
3:40 **L** us examine our ways and test them,
3:40 them, and **l** us return to the LORD.
3:41 **L** us lift up our hearts and our
Eze 3:27 Whoever will listen **l** him listen,
3:27 and whoever will refuse **l** him refuse;
4:15 "I will **l** you bake your bread
7:12 **L** not the buyer rejoice nor the
14: 3 Should I **l** them enquire of me at all?
14:17 '**L** the sword pass throughout the
20: 3 I will not **l** you enquire of me,
20:26 I **l** them become defiled through
20:31 Am I to **l** you enquire of me, O house
20:31 LORD, I will not **l** you enquire of me.
21:14 **L** the sword strike twice, even three
23:43 'Now **l** them use her as a prostitute,
24:10 spices; and **l** the bones be charred.
32: 4 I will **l** all the birds of the air
32:14 I will **l** her waters settle and make
32:20 sword is drawn; **l** her be dragged off
39: 7 I will no longer **l** my holy name be
43: 9 Now **l** them put away from me their
43:10 **L** them consider the plan,
44:20 heads or **l** their hair grow long,
Da 2: 7 "**L** the king tell his servants the
4:14 **L** the animals flee from under it and
4:15 **l** the stump and its roots, bound
4:15 "'**L** him be drenched with the dew of
4:15 and **l** him live with the animals
4:16 **L** his mind be changed from that of a
4:16 **l** him be given the mind of an animal,
4:19 **l** the dream or its meaning alarm you.
4:23 **L** him be drenched with the dew of
4:23 **l** him live like the wild animals,
Hos 2: 2 **L** her remove the adulterous look
4: 4 **l** no man bring a charge, **l** no man
4:15 O Israel, **l** not Judah become guilty.
6: 1 "Come, **l** us return to the LORD. He
6: 3 **L** us acknowledge the LORD; **l** us

Hos 9: 7 L Israel know this. Because your
Joel 1: 3 l your children tell it to their
2: 1 L all who live in the land tremble,
2:16 L the bridegroom leave his room and
2:17 L the priests, who minister before
2:17 L them say, "Spare your people,
3: 9 L all the fighting men draw near
3:10 L the weakling say, "I am strong!"
3:12 "L the nations be roused; l them
Am 5:24 l justice roll on like a river,
Ob : 1 l us go against her for battle"—
Jnh 1: 7 "Come, l us cast lots to find out
1:14 "O LORD, please do not us l die for
3: 7 nobles: Do not l any man or beast,
3: 7 do not l them eat or drink.
3: 8 l man and beast be covered with
3: 8 L everyone call urgently on God.
3: 8 L them give up their evil ways and
Mic 4: 2 "Come, l us go up to the mountain of
4:11 "L her be defiled, l our eyes gloat
6: 1 l the hills hear what you have to
7:14 L them feed in Bashan and Gilead as
Hab 2:20 l all the earth be silent before
Zep 3:16 Zion; do not l your hands hang limp.
Zec 8: 9 l your hands be strong so that the
8:13 afraid, but l your hands be strong."
8:21 'L us go at once to entreat the LORD
8:23 'L us go with you, because we have
11: 9 L the dying die, and the perishing
11: 9 L those who are left eat one
Mt 3:15 Jesus replied, "L it be so now; it
5:16 In the same way, l your light shine
5:37 Simply l your 'Yes' be 'Yes', and
5:40 l him have your cloak as well.
6: 3 do not l your left hand know what
7: 4 L me take the speck out of your eye
8:21 first l me go and bury my father."
8:22 l the dead bury their own dead.
10:13 l your peace rest on it; if it
10:13 is not, l your peace return to you.
11:15 He who has ears, l him hear.
13: 9 He who has ears, l him hear."
13:30 L both grow together until the
13:43 He who has ears, l him hear.
13:47 a net that was l down into the lake
14:36 begged him to l the sick just touch
18:27 cancelled the debt and l him go.
19: 6 together, l man not separate."
19:14 Jesus said, "L the little children
23:13 you l those enter who are trying to.
24:15 Daniel—l the reader understand—
24:16 l those who are in Judea flee to the
24:17 L no-one on the roof of his house go
24:18 L no-one in the field go back to get
24:43 not have l his house be broken into.
26:46 Rise, l us go! Here comes my
27:25 answered, "L his blood be on us
27:42 L him come down now from the cross,
27:43 He trusts in God. L God rescue him
Mk 1:34 but he would not l the demons speak
1:38 Jesus replied, "L us go somewhere
4: 9 He who has ears to hear, l him hear
4:23 anyone has ears to hear, l him hear
4:35 "L us go over to the other side.
5:19 Jesus did not l him, but said, "Go
5:37 He did not l anyone follow him
5:43 strict orders not to l anyone know
6:56 They begged him to l them touch even
7: 8 You have l go of the commands of God
7:12 you no longer l him do anything for
7:27 "First l the children eat all they
9: 5 L us put up three shelters—one for
10: 9 together, l man not separate."
10:14 "L the little children come to me,
10:37 "L one of us sit at your right and
11: 6 them to, and the people l them go.
12:15 me a denarius and l me look at it."
13:14 l the reader understand—then l
13:15 L no-one on the roof of his house go
13:16 L no-one in the field go back to get
13:36 do not l him find you sleeping.
14:42 Rise! L us go! Here comes my
15:32 L this Christ, this King of Israel,
Lk 5: 4 and l down the nets for a catch."
5: 5 you say so, I will l down the nets."
6:42 'Brother, l me take the speck out of
Lk 8: 8 He who has ears to hear, l him hear
8:32 The demons begged Jesus to l them go
8:51 he did not l anyone go in with him
9:33 L us put up three shelters—one for
9:59 first l me go and bury my father."
9:60 "L the dead bury their own dead,
9:61 Lord; but first l me go back and say
12:39 not have l his house be broken into.
14:35 He who has ears to hear, l him hear."
16:28 have five brothers. L him warn them
16:29 Prophets; l them listen to them.'
18:16 "L the little children come to me,
21:21 l those who are in Judea flee to the
21:21 l those in the city get out, and l
23:35 said, "He saved others; l him save
Jn 6:12 are left over. L nothing be wasted."
7:37 thirsty, l him come to me and drink.
8: 7 l him be the first to throw a stone
11: 7 he said to his disciples, "L us go
11:15 But l us go to him."
11:16 "L us also go, that we may die with
11:44 off the grave clothes and l him go."
11:48 If we l him go on like this,
14: 1 "Do not l your hearts be troubled.
14:27 Do not l your hearts be troubled and
14:31 "Come now; l us leave.
17:23 l the world know that you sent me
18: 8 for me, then l these men go."
19: 4 him out to you to l you know that
19:12 "If you l this man go, you are no
Ac 1:20 l there be no-one to dwell in it,'
2:14 l me explain this to you; listen
2:27 will you l your Holy One see decay.
2:36 "Therefore l all Israel be assured
3:13 though he had decided to l him go.
4:21 After further threats they l them go.
5:38 Leave these men alone! L them go!
5:40 in the name of Jesus, and l them go.
10:11 l down to earth by its four corners.
11: 5 like a large sheet being l down from
13:35 will not l your Holy One see decay.'
14:16 In the past, he l all nations go
15:36 "L us go back and visit the brothers
16:37 No! L them come themselves and
17: 9 the others on bail and l them go.
19:30 but the disciples would not l him.
21:39 Please l me speak to the people."
23:32 The next day they l the cavalry go
25: 5 L some of your leaders come with me
27:17 and l the ship be driven along.
27:30 the sailors l the lifeboat down into
27:32 the lifeboat and l it fall away.
Ro 3: 4 Not at all! L God be true, and every
3: 8 us do evil that good may result"?
6:12 not l sin reign in your mortal body
12: 6 l him use it in proportion to his
12: 7 If it is serving, l him serve;
12: 7 if it is teaching, l him teach;
12: 8 it is encouraging, l him encourage;
12: 8 l him give generously; if it is
12: 8 l him govern diligently; if it is
12: 8 mercy, l him do it cheerfully.
13: 8 L no debt remain outstanding, except
13:12 So l us put aside the deeds of
13:13 L us behave decently, as in the
14:13 Therefore l us stop passing judgment
14:19 L us therefore make every effort to
1Co 1:31 "L him who boasts boast in the
5: 8 Therefore l us keep the Festival,
7:15 the unbeliever leaves, l him do so
7:21 Don't l it trouble you—although if
10:13 he will not l you be tempted beyond
14:37 l him acknowledge that what I am
15:32 "L us eat and drink, for tomorrow we
15:58 L nothing move you. Always give
2Co 2: 4 not to grieve you but to l you know
4: 6 For God, who said, "L light shine
7: 1 dear friends, l us purify ourselves
10:17 L him who boasts boast in the Lord
11:16 L no-one take me for a fool.
Gal 1: 8 you, l him be eternally condemned!
1: 9 l him be eternally condemned!
3:15 Brothers, l me take an example from
5: 1 and do not l yourselves be burdened
5: 2 if you l yourselves be circumcised
5:25 l us keep in step with the Spirit.
Gal 5:26 L us not become conceited, provoking
6: 9 L us not become weary in doing good,
6:10 l us do good to all people,
6:17 Finally, l no-one cause me trouble,
Eph 4:26 Do not l the sun go down
4:29 Do not l any unwholesome talk come
5: 6 L no-one deceive you with empty
Php 3:16 Only l us live up to what we have
4: 5 L your gentleness be evident to all.
Col 2:16 Therefore do not l anyone judge you
2:18 Do not l anyone who delights in
3:15 L the peace of Christ rule in your
3:16 L the word of Christ dwell in you
4: 6 L your conversation be always full
1Th 5: 6 then, l us not be like others, who
5: 6 l us be alert and self-controlled.
5: 8 l us be self-controlled, putting
2Th 2: 3 Don't l anyone deceive you in any
1Ti 3:10 them, l them serve as deacons.
4:12 Don't l anyone look down on you
5:16 and not l the church be burdened
Tit 2:15 Do not l anyone despise you.
Heb 1: 6 "L all God's angels worship him.
4: 1 l us be careful that none of you be
4:11 L us, therefore, make every effort
4:14 l us hold firmly to the faith we
4:16 L us then approach the throne of
6: 1 l us leave the elementary teachings
10:22 l us draw near to God with a sincere
10:23 L us hold unswervingly to the hope
10:24 l us consider how we may spur one
10:25 L us not give up meeting together,
10:25 but l us encourage one another—and
12: 1 l us throw off everything that
12: 1 and l us run with perseverance the
12: 2 L us fix our eyes on Jesus, the
12:28 l us be thankful, and so worship God
13:13 L us, then, go to him outside the
13:15 l us continually offer to God a
Jas 3:13 L him show it by his good life,
5:12 L your "Yes" be yes, and your "No",
5:13 happy? L him sing songs of praise.
1Jn 3: 7 do not l anyone lead you astray.
3:18 l us not love with words or tongue
4: 7 Dear friends, l us love one another,
Rev 2: 7 He who has an ear, l him hear what
2:11 He who has an ear, l him hear what
2:17 He who has an ear, l him hear what
2:29 He who has an ear, l him hear what
3: 6 He who has an ear, l him hear what
3:13 He who has an ear, l him hear what
3:22 He who has an ear, l him hear what
13: 9 He who has an ear, l him hear.
13:18 l him calculate the number of the
19: 7 L us rejoice and be glad and give
22:11 L him who does wrong continue to do
22:11 l him who is vile continue to be
22:11 l him who does right continue to do
22:11 and l him who is holy continue to be
22:17 And l him who hears say, "Come!"
22:17 Whoever is thirsty, l him come
22:17 and whoever wishes, l him take

Lethek

Hos 3: 2 and about a homer and a l of barley.

Letter (Letters)

2Sa 11:14 In the morning David wrote a l to
2Ki 5: 5 "I will send a l to the king of
5: 6 The l that he took to the king of
5: 6 "With this l I am sending my servant
5: 7 soon as the king of Israel read the l
10: 2 "As soon as this l reaches you,
10: 6 Jehu wrote them a second l, saying,
10: 7 the l arrived, these men took the
19:14 Hezekiah received the l from the
2Ch 2:11 Hiram king of Tyre replied by l to
21:12 Jehoram received a l from Elijah the
Ezr 4: 7 associates wrote a l to Artaxerxes.
4: 7 The l was written in Aramaic script
4: 8 Shimshai the secretary wrote a l
4:11 (This is a copy of the l they sent
4:18 The l you sent us has been read and
4:23 soon as the copy of the l of King
5: 6 This is a copy of the l that

Ezr 7:11 This is a copy of the **l** King
Ne 2: 8 may I have a **l** to Asaph, keeper of
6: 5 and in his hand was an unsealed **l**
Est 9:26 of everything written in this **l**
9:29 this second **l** concerning Purim.
Isa 37:14 Hezekiah received the **l** from the
Jer 29: 1 This is the text of the **l** that the
29: 3 He entrusted the **l** to Elasah son of
29:29 read the **l** to Jeremiah the prophet.
Mt 5:18 not the smallest **l**, not the least
Ac 15:23 With them they sent the following **l**:
15:30 church together and delivered the **l**.
23:25 He wrote a **l** as follows:
23:33 they delivered the **l** to the governor
23:34 The governor read the **l** and asked
Ro 16:22 I, Tertius, who wrote down this **l**,
1Co 5: 9 I have written to you in my **l** not to
2Co 3: 2 You yourselves are our **l**, written on
3: 3 You show that you are a **l** from
3: 6 not of the **l** but of the Spirit;
3: 6 for the **l** kills, but the Spirit
7: 8 Even if I caused you sorrow by my **l**,
7: 8 regret it—I see that my **l** hurt you,
Col 4:16 After this **l** has been read to you,
4:16 in turn read the **l** from Laodicea.
1Th 5:27 this **l** read to all the brothers.
2Th 2: 2 report or **l** supposed to have come
2:15 whether by word of mouth or by **l**.
3:14 in this **l**, take special note of him.
Heb 13:22 I have written you only a short **l**.
2Pe 3: 1 Dear friends, this is now my second **l**

Letters (Letter)
1Ki 21: 8 she wrote **l** in Ahab's name, placed
21: 9 In those **l** she wrote: "Proclaim a
21:11 in the **l** she had written to them.
2Ki 10: 1 So Jehu wrote **l** and sent them to
20:12 Babylon sent Hezekiah **l** and a gift,
2Ch 30: 1 wrote **l** to Ephraim and Manasseh,
30: 6 Judah with **l** from the king and from
32:17 The king also wrote **l** insulting the
Ne 2: 7 may I have **l** to the governors of
2: 9 Euphrates and gave them the king's **l**.
6:17 Judah were sending many **l** to Tobiah,
6:19 And Tobiah sent **l** to intimidate me.
Est 9:20 and he sent **l** to all the Jews
9:30 Mordecai sent **l** to all the Jews in
Isa 39: 1 Babylon sent Hezekiah **l** and a gift,
Jer 29:25 the God of Israel, says: You sent **l**
Ac 9: 2 asked him for **l** to the synagogues in
22: 5 I even obtained **l** from them to their
28:21 "We have not received any **l** from
1Co 16: 3 Then, when I arrive, I will give **l**
2Co 3: 1 **l** of recommendation to you or from
3: 7 which was engraved in **l** on stone,
10: 9 be trying to frighten you with my **l**.
10:10 For some say, "His **l** are weighty and
10:11 we are in our **l** when we are absent,
Gal 6:11 See what large **l** I use as I write to
2Th 3:17 the distinguishing mark in all my **l**.
2Pe 3:16 He writes the same way in all his **l**,
3:16 His **l** contain some things that are

Letushites
Ge 25: 3 Asshurites, the **L** and the Leummites.

Leummites
Ge 25: 3 Asshurites, the Letushites and the **L**

Level (Levelled, Levels)
1Ki 6: 8 a stairway led up to the middle **l**
Ps 26:12 My feet stand on **l** ground; in the
65:10 You drench its furrows and **l** its ridges
143:10 good Spirit lead me on **l** ground.
Pr 4:26 Make **l** paths for your feet and take
Isa 26: 7 The path of the righteous is **l**;
40: 4 become **l**, the rugged places a plain.
45: 2 before you and will **l** the mountains
Jer 31: 9 **l** path where they will not stumble,
Eze 13:14 will **l** it to the ground so that its
41: 6 one above another, thirty on each **l**.
41: 7 were wider at each successive **l**.
Zec 4: 7 Zerubbabel you will become **l** ground.
Lk 6:17 with them and stood on a **l** place.
Heb 12:13 "Make **l** paths for your feet," so

Levelled (Level)
Isa 28:25 he has **l** the surface, does he not
32:19 forest and the city is **l** completely,
Jer 51:58 "Babylon's thick wall will be **l** and

Levels (Level)
Isa 26: 5 he lays the lofty city low; he **l** it
Eze 41: 6 The side rooms were on three **l**, one
42: 3 faced gallery at the three **l**.

Levi (Levi's, Levite, Levites, Levitical)
1. Son of Jacob by Leah (Ge 29:34; 35:23); with Simeon killed Shechemites to avenge rape of sister Dinah (Ge 34); blessed by Jacob (Ge 49:5–7). **2.** Tribe descended from Levi. Blessed by Moses (Dt 33:8–11). Numbered separately (Nu 1:47–49; 3:14–39; 26:57–62); responsible for tabernacle (Nu 1:50–53; 3:14–37; 4; 8; 18:2–4); dedicated to God in place of firstborn (Nu 3:11–13,40–41). Given towns (Nu 35; Jos 21) but not land (Nu 18:20–24; 26:62; Dt 10:9; Jos 13:14); allocated land in new division (Eze 48:13–14). **3.** See *Matthew*.

Ge 29:34 So he was named **L**.
34:25 two of Jacob's sons, Simeon and **L**,
34:30 Jacob said to Simeon and **L**, "You
35:23 **L**, Judah, Issachar and Zebulun.
46:11 The sons of **L**: Gershon, Kohath and
49: 5 "Simeon and **L** are brothers—their
Ex 1: 2 Reuben, Simeon, **L** and Judah;
2: 1 Now a man of the house of **L** married
6:16 These were the names of the sons of **L**
6:16 **L** lived 137 years.
6:19 clans of **L** according to their
Nu 1:47 The families of the tribe of **L**,
1:49 "You must not count the tribe of **L**
3: 6 "Bring the tribe of **L** and present
3:17 These were the names of the sons of **L**
16: 1 the son of Kohath, the son of **L**, and
17: 3 On the staff of **L** write Aaron's name,
17: 8 which represented the house of **L**,
26:59 a descendant of **L**, who was born to
Dt 10: 8 the LORD set apart the tribe of **L**
18: 1 indeed the whole tribe of **L**—are to
21: 5 The priests, the sons of **L**, shall
27:12 **L**, Judah, Issachar, Joseph and
31: 9 the sons of **L**, who carried the ark
33: 8 About **L** he said: "Your Thummim and
Jos 13:14 to the tribe of **L** he gave no
13:33 to the tribe of **L**, Moses had given
1Ch 2: 1 Simeon, **L**, Judah, Issachar, Zebulun,
6: 1 The sons of **L**: Gershon, Kohath and
6:16 The sons of **L**: Gershon, Kohath and
6:38 the son of **L**, the son of Israel;
6:43 the son of Gershon, the son of **L**;
6:47 the son of Merari, the son of **L**.
12:26 men of **L**—4,600,
21: 6 Joab did not include **L** and Benjamin
23: 6 sons of **L**: Gershon, Kohath and
23:14 counted as part of the tribe of **L**.
23:24 These were the descendants of **L** by
24:20 for the rest of the descendants of **L**:
27:17 over **L**: Hashabiah son of Kemuel;
Ezr 8:18 the descendants of Mahli son of **L**,
Ne 12:23 among the descendants of **L** up to
Ps 135:20 O house of **L**, praise the LORD; you
Eze 48:31 the gate of Judah and the gate of **L**.
Zec 12:13 the clan of the house of **L** and their
Mal 2: 4 my covenant with **L** may continue,"
2: 8 have violated the covenant with **L**,
Mk 2:14 along, he saw **L** son of Alphaeus
2:14 him, and **L** got up and followed him.
Lk 3:24 the son of Matthat, the son of **L**,
3:29 the son of Matthat, the son of **L**,
5:27 name of **L** sitting at his tax booth.
5:28 **L** got up, left everything and
5:29 **L** held a great banquet for Jesus at
Heb 7: 5 law requires the descendants of **L**
7: 6 did not trace his descent from **L**,
7: 9 One might even say that **L**, who
Heb 7:10 **L** was still in the body of his
Rev 7: 7 from the tribe of **L** 12,000, from the

Levi's (Levi)
Mk 2:15 While Jesus was having dinner at **L**

Leviathan
Job 3: 8 those who are ready to rouse **L**.
41: 1 "Can you pull in the **l** with a
Ps 74:14 was you who crushed the heads of **L**
104:26 **l**, which you formed to frolic there.
Isa 27: 1 **L** the gliding serpent, **L** the coiling

Levite (Levi)
Ex 2: 1 the house of Levi married a **L** woman,
4:14 Aaron the **L**? I know he can speak
6:25 of the **L** families, clan by clan.
Nu 3:20 **L** clans, according to their families.
26:58 These also were **L** clans: the Libnite
Dt 18: 6 If a **L** moves from one of your towns
26:12 you shall give it to the **L**, the
26:13 portion and have given it to the **L**,
Jos 21:27 The **L** clans of the Gershonites were
Jdg 17: 7 A young **L** from Bethlehem in Judah,
17: 9 "I'm a **L** from Bethlehem in Judah
17:11 the **L** agreed to live with him, and
17:12 Micah installed the **L**, and the young
17:13 since this **L** has become my priest."
18: 3 recognised the voice of the young **L**;
18:15 house of the young **L** at Micah's
19: 1 Now a **L** who lived in a remote area
20: 4 the **L**, the husband of the murdered
1Ch 9:31 A **L** named Mattithiah, the firstborn
9:33 were musicians, heads of **L** families
9:34 All these were heads of **L** families,
15:22 Kenaniah the head **L** was in charge of
24: 6 Shemaiah son of Nethanel, a **L**,
2Ch 20:14 the son of Mattaniah, a **L** and
31:12 Conaniah, a **L**, was in charge of
31:14 Kore son of Imnah the **L**, keeper of
Ezr 10:15 and Shabbethai the **L**, opposed this.
Ne 13:13 the scribe, and a **L** named Pedaiah
Lk 10:32 too, a **L**, when he came to the place
Ac 4:36 Joseph, a **L** from Cyprus, whom the

Levites (Levi, *Priests and Levites, Priests and the Levites*)
Ex 32:26 And all the **L** rallied to him.
32:28 The **L** did as Moses commanded, and
38:21 recorded at Moses' command by the **L**
Lev 25:32 "'The **L** always have the right to
25:33 the property of the **L** is redeemable—
25:33 houses in the towns of the **L** are
Nu 1:50 Instead, appoint the **L** to be in
1:51 the **L** are to take it down, and
1:51 is to be set up, the **L** shall do it.
1:53 The **L**, however, are to set up their
1:53 The **L** are to be responsible for the
2:17 the camp of the **L** will set out in
2:33 The **L**, however, were not counted
3: 9 Give the **L** to Aaron and his sons;
3:12 "I have taken the **L** from among the
3:12 The **L** are mine,
3:15 "Count the **L** by their families and
3:32 The chief leader of the **L** was
3:39 The total number of **L** counted at the
3:41 Take the **L** for me in place of all
3:41 and the livestock of the **L** in place
3:45 "Take the **L** in place of all the
3:45 livestock of the **L** in place of their
3:45 The **L** are to be mine. I am the LORD.
3:46 who exceed the number of the **L**,
3:49 the number redeemed by the **L**.
4: 2 the **L** by their clans and families.
4:18 clans are not cut off from the **L**.
4:46 the **L** by their clans and families.
7: 5 the **L** as each man's work requires."
7: 6 and oxen and gave them to the **L**.
8: 6 "Take the **L** from among the other
8: 9 Bring the **L** to the front of the Tent
8:10 You are to bring the **L** before the
8:11 Aaron is to present the **L** before the
8:12 "After the **L** lay their hands on the
8:12 to make atonement for the **L**.

Nu 8:13 Make the **L** stand in front of Aaron
8:14 In this way you are to set the **L**
8:14 Israelites, and the **L** will be mine.
8:15 "After you have purified the **L** and
8:18 I have taken the **L** in place of all
8:19 I have given the **L** as gifts to Aaron
8:20 **L** just as the LORD commanded Moses.
8:21 The **L** purified themselves and washed
8:22 the **L** came to do their work at the
8:22 **L** just as the LORD commanded Moses.
8:24 "This applies to the **L**: Men
8:26 the responsibilities of the **L**."
16: 7 You **L** have gone too far!"
16: 8 said to Korah, "Now listen, you **L**
16:10 and all your fellow **L** near himself,
18: 2 Bring your fellow **L** from your
18: 6 I myself have selected your fellow **L**
18:21 "I give to the **L** all the tithes in
18:23 is the **L** who are to do the work at
18:24 Instead, I give to the **L** as their
18:26 "Speak to the **L** and say to them:
18:30 "Say to the **L**: 'When you present the
26:57 These were the **L** who were counted by
26:59 Levi, who was born to the **L** in Egypt.
26:62 All the male **L** a month old or more
31:30 Give them to the **L**, who are
31:47 and gave them to the **L**, who were
35: 2 Command the Israelites to give the **L**
35: 4 the towns that you give the **L** will
35: 6 "Six of the towns you give the **L**
35: 7 In all you must give the **L**
35: 8 The towns you give the **L** from the
Dt 10: 9 That is why the **L** have no share or
12:12 and the **L** from your towns, who have
12:18 and the **L** from your towns—and you
12:19 Be careful not to neglect the **L** as
14:27 do not neglect the **L** living in your
14:29 that the **L** (who have no allotment or
16:11 the **L** in your towns, and the aliens,
16:14 and the **L**, the aliens, the
17: 9 Go to the priests, who are **L**, and to
17:18 from that of the priests, who are **L**.
18: 1 The priests, who are **L**—indeed the
18: 7 like all his fellow **L** who serve
24: 8 priests, who are **L**, instruct you.
26:11 you and the **L** and the aliens among
27: 9 Moses and the priests, who are **L**,
27:14 The **L** shall recite to all the people
31:25 he gave this command to the **L** who
Jos 3: 3 and the priests, who are **L**, carrying
8:33 carried it—the priests, who were **L**.
14: 3 the **L** an inheritance among the rest,
14: 4 The **L** received no share of the land
18: 7 The **L**, however, do not get a portion
21: 1 Now the family heads of the **L**
21: 3 the Israelites gave the **L** the
21: 4 The **L** who were descendants of Aaron
21: 8 the Israelites allotted to the **L**
21:10 from the Kohathite clans of the **L**,
21:20 the Kohathite clans of the **L** were
21:34 Merarite clans (the rest of the **L**)
21:40 were the rest of the **L**, were twelve.
21:41 The towns of the **L** in the territory
1Sa 6:15 The **L** took down the ark of the LORD,
2Sa 15:24 Zadok was there, too, and all the **L**
1Ki 12:31 people, even though they were not **L**.
1Ch 6:19 **L** listed according to their fathers:
6:48 Their fellow **L** were assigned to all
6:64 the Israelites gave the **L** these
6:77 The Merarites (the rest of the **L**)
9: 2 priests, **L** and temple servants.
9:14 Of the **L**: Shemaiah son of Hasshub,
9:18 belonging to the camp of the **L**.
9:26 who were **L**, were entrusted with the
15: 2 "No-one but the **L** may carry the ark
15: 4 the descendants of Aaron and the **L**:
15:11 Shemaiah, Eliel and Amminadab the **L**
15:12 you and your fellow **L** are to
15:13 was because you, the **L**, did not
15:14 the priests and **L** consecrated
15:15 the **L** carried the ark of God with
15:16 David told the leaders of the **L** to
15:17 the **L** appointed Heman son of Joel;
15:26 God had helped the **L** who were
15:27 as were all the **L** who were carrying
16: 4 He appointed some of the **L** to
1Ch 23: 3 The **L** thirty years old or more were
23: 6 David divided the **L** into groups
23:26 the **L** no longer need to carry the
23:27 the **L** were counted from those twenty
23:28 The duty of the **L** was to help
23:32 the **L** carried out their
24: 6 of the priests and of the **L**—
24:30 the **L**, according to their families.
24:31 of the priests and of the **L**.
26:17 There were six **L** a day on the east,
26:20 Their fellow **L** were in charge of the
2Ch 5: 4 had arrived, the **L** took up the ark,
5: 5 who were **L**, carried them up;
5:12 All the **L** who were musicians—Asaph,
7: 6 as did the **L** with the LORD's musical
7: 6 Opposite the **L**, the priests blew
8:14 the **L** to lead the praise and to
8:15 priests or to the **L** in any matter,
11:14 The **L** even abandoned their
11:16 the God of Israel, followed the **L** to
13: 9 the sons of Aaron, and the **L**, and
13:10 of Aaron, and the **L** assist them.
17: 8 With them were certain **L**—Shemaiah,
19: 8 Jehoshaphat appointed some of the **L**,
19:11 **L** will serve as officials before you.
20:19 some **L** from the Kohathites and
23: 2 gathered the **L** and the heads of
23: 7 The **L** are to station themselves
23: 8 The **L** and all the men of Judah did
23:18 who were **L**, to whom David had made
24: 5 Do it now." But the **L** did not act at
24: 6 "Why haven't you required the **L** to
24:11 brought in by the **L** to the king's
29: 5 said, "Listen to me, **L**! Consecrate
29:12 these **L** set to work: from the
29:16 The **L** took it and carried it out to
29:25 He stationed the **L** in the temple of
29:26 the **L** stood ready with David's
29:30 his officials ordered the **L** to
29:34 so their kinsmen the **L** helped them
29:34 for the **L** had been more
30:16 the blood handed to them by the **L**.
30:17 the **L** had to kill the Passover lambs
30:21 while the **L** and priests sang to the
30:22 spoke encouragingly to all the **L**,
31: 2 to their duties as priests or **L**—
31:17 to the **L** twenty years old or more,
31:19 in the genealogies of the **L**.
34: 9 the **L** who were the doorkeepers
34:12 **L** descended from Merari, and
34:12 The **L**—all who were skilled in
34:13 Some of the **L** were secretaries,
35: 3 He said to the **L**, who instructed all
35: 5 in the holy place with a group of **L**
35: 9 the leaders of the **L**, provided five
35: 9 hundred head of cattle for the **L**.
35:10 stood in their places with the **L**
35:11 while the **L** skinned the animals.
35:14 So the **L** made preparations for
35:15 **L** made the preparations for them.
35:18 with the priests, the **L** and all
Ezr 2:40 The **L**: the descendants of Jeshua and
2:70 The priests, the **L**, the singers, the
3: 8 appointing **L** twenty years of age and
3: 9 their sons and brothers—all **L**—
3:10 and the **L** (the sons of Asaph) with
6:16 the **L** and the rest of the
6:18 the **L** in their groups for the
6:20 The **L** slaughtered the Passover lamb
7: 7 including priests, **L**, singers,
7:24 **L**, singers, gatekeepers, temple
8:15 and the priests, I found no **L** there.
8:20 had established to assist the **L**.
8:33 and so were the **L** Jozabad son of
10:23 Among the **L**: Jozabad, Shimei,
Ne 3:17 by the **L** under Rehum son of Bani.
7: 1 singers and the **L** were appointed.
7:43 The **L**: the descendants of Jeshua
7:73 The priests, the **L**, the gatekeepers
8: 7 The **L**—Jeshua, Bani, Sherebiah,
8: 9 and the **L** who were instructing the
8:11 The **L** calmed all the people, saying,
9: 4 Standing on the stairs were the
9: 5 the **L**—Jeshua, Kadmiel, Bani,
9:38 and our leaders, our **L** and our
10: 9 The **L**: Jeshua son of Azaniah, Binnui
Ne 10:28 The rest of the people—priests, **L**,
10:34 "We—the priests, the **L** and the
10:37 to the **L**, for it is the **L** who
10:38 accompany the **L** when they receive
10:38 and the **L** are to bring a tenth of
10:39 The people of Israel, including the **L**
11: 3 priests, **L**, temple servants and
11:15 From the **L**: Shemaiah son of Hasshub,
11:16 two of the heads of the **L**, who had
11:18 The **L** in the holy city totalled 284.
11:22 chief officer of the **L** in Jerusalem
11:36 Some of the divisions of the **L** of
12: 8 The **L** were Jeshua, Binnui, Kadmiel,
12:22 The family heads of the **L** in the
12:24 the leaders of the **L** were Hashabiah,
12:27 the **L** were sought out from where
12:47 aside the portion for the other **L**,
12:47 and the **L** set aside the portion for
13: 5 wine and oil prescribed for the **L**,
13:10 portions assigned to the **L** had not
13:10 and that all the **L** and singers
13:22 I commanded the **L** to purify
13:29 of the priesthood and of the **L**.
Jer 33:18 nor will the priests, who are **L**,
33:21 my covenant with the **L** who are
33:22 the **L** who minister before me as
Eze 40:46 who are the only **L** who may draw near
43:19 who are **L**, of the family of Zadok,
44:10 "'The **L** who went far from me when
44:15 "'But the priests, who are **L** and
45: 5 cubits wide will belong to the **L**,
48:11 did not go astray as the **L** did when
48:12 bordering the territory of the **L**.
48:13 the **L** will have an allotment 25,000
48:22 the property of the **L** and the
Mal 3: 3 he will purify the **L** and refine them

Levitical (Levi)

Lev 25:32 in the **L** towns, which they possess.
1Ch 15:12 "You are the heads of the **L** families;
Heb 7:11 attained through the **L** priesthood

Levy

2Ki 23:33 and he imposed on Judah a **l** of a
2Ch 36: 3 imposed on Judah a **l** of a hundred

Lewd (Lewdness)

Jdg 20: 6 **l** and disgraceful act in Israel.
Eze 16:27 who were shocked by your **l** conduct.
22: 9 mountain shrines and commit **l** acts.
23:44 those **l** women, Oholah and Oholibah.

Lewdness (Lewd)

Eze 16:43 Did you not add **l** to all your other
16:58 bear the consequences of your **l**
23:21 you longed for the **l** of your youth,
23:27 I will put a stop to the **l** and
23:29 Your **l** and promiscuity
23:35 bear the consequences of your **l**
23:48 "So I will put an end to **l** in the
23:49 will suffer the penalty for your **l**
24:13 "'Now your impurity is **l**. Because I
Hos 2:10 now I will expose her **l** before the
Mk 7:22 greed, malice, deceit, **l**, envy,

Liable

Jos 6:18 the camp of Israel **l** to destruction
7:12 have been made **l** to destruction.

Liar (Lie[2])

Dt 19:18 and if the witness proves to be a **l**,
Job 34: 6 I am considered a **l**; although I am
Pr 17: 4 a **l** pays attention to a malicious
19:22 better to be poor than a **l**.
30: 6 will rebuke you and prove you a **l**.
Mic 2:11 If a **l** and deceiver comes and says,
Jn 8:44 he is a **l** and the father of lies.
8:55 If I said I did not, I would be a **l**
Ro 3: 4 Let God be true, and every man a **l**.
1Jn 1:10 we make him out to be a **l** and his
2: 4 is a **l**, and the truth is not in him.
2:22 Who is the **l**? It is the man who
4:20 yet hates his brother, he is a **l**.
5:10 God has made him out to be a **l**,

Liars (Lie[2])
Ps 63:11 the mouths of l will be silenced.
116:11 in my dismay I said, "All men are l."
Isa 57: 4 brood of rebels, the offspring of l?
Mic 6:12 her people are l and their tongues
1Ti 1:10 for slave traders and l and
4: 2 come through hypocritical l,
Tit 1:12 l, evil brutes, lazy gluttons."
Rev 3: 9 but are l—I will make them come and
21: 8 the idolaters and all l—their place

Libations
Ps 16: 4 I will not pour out their l of blood

Liberal (Liberality)
2Co 8:20 the way we administer this l gift.

Liberality (Liberal)
Est 1: 7 in keeping with the king's l.
2:18 and distributed gifts with royal l.

Liberated (Liberty)
Ro 8:21 that the creation itself will be l

Liberty (Liberated)
Lev 25:10 proclaim l throughout the land to

Libnah (Libnite, Libnites)
1. A place where the Israelites camped during the exodus from Egypt (Nu 33:20–21). **2.** Canaanite town in lowlands of Judah, near Lachish. Captured by Joshua (Jos 10:29–32, 39), allotted to Judah (Jos 15:42) and designated a Levitical city (Jos 21:13; 1Ch 6:57). Participated in revolt against Jehoram (2Ki 8:22; 2Ch 21:10) and attacked by Sennacherib (2Ki 19:8; Isa 37:8). Home of Hamutal, the mother of Jehoahaz and Zedekiah (2Ki 23:31; 24:18; Jer 52:1).

Nu 33:20 left Rimmon Perez and camped at L.
33:21 They left L and camped at Rissah.
Jos 10:29 from Makkedah to L and attacked it.
10:31 with him moved on from L to Lachish;
10:32 the sword, just as he had done to L.
10:39 to L and its king and to Hebron.
12:15 the king of L one the king of
15:42 L, Ether, Ashan,
21:13 for one accused of murder), L,
2Ki 8:22 L revolted at the same time.
19: 8 found the king fighting against L.
23:31 of Jeremiah; she was from L.
24:18 of Jeremiah; she was from L.
1Ch 6:57 of refuge), and L, Jattir, Eshtemoa,
2Ch 21:10 L revolted at the same time, because
Isa 37: 8 found the king fighting against L.
Jer 52: 1 of Jeremiah; she was from L.

Libni
Ex 6:17 sons of Gershon, by clans, were L
Nu 3:18 the Gershonite clans: L and Shimei.
1Ch 6:17 the sons of Gershon: L and Shimei.
6:20 Of Gershon: L his son, Jehath his
6:29 The descendants of Merari: Mahli, L

Libnite (Libnah)
Nu 26:58 also were Levite clans: the L clan,

Libnites (Libnah)
Nu 3:21 the clans of the L and Shimeites;

Libya (Libyans)
Eze 30: 5 and Put, Lydia and all Arabia, L
Na 3: 9 Put and L were among her allies.
Ac 2:10 and the parts of L near Cyrene;

Libyans (Libya)
2Ch 12: 3 and the innumerable troops of L,
16: 8 Were not the Cushites and L a mighty
Isa 66:19 to the L and Lydians (famous as
Da 11:43 the L and Nubians in submission.

Licence
Jude : 4 of our God into a l for immorality

Lick (Licked, Licks)
Nu 22: 4 "This horde is going to l up
1Ki 21:19 will l up your blood—yes, yours!'
Ps 72: 9 him and his enemies will l the dust.
Isa 5:24 as tongues of fire l up straw
49:23 they will l the dust at your feet.
Mic 7:17 They will l dust like a snake, like

Licked (Lick)
1Ki 18:38 also l up the water in the trench.
21:19 where dogs l up Naboth's blood,
22:38 and the dogs l up his blood, as the
Lk 16:21 Even the dogs came and l his sores.

Licks (Lick)
Nu 22: 4 an ox l up the grass of the field.

Lid
Nu 19:15 every open container without a l
2Ki 12: 9 a chest and bored a hole in its l.

Lie[1] (Lain, Lay, Lies, Lying)
Ge 19:31 is no man around here to l with us,
19:32 then l with him and preserve our
19:34 and you go in and l with him so we
29:21 and I want to l with her."
38: 8 Judah said to Onan, "L with your
Ex 23:11 the land l unploughed and unused.
Lev 18:22 "'Do not l with a man as one lies
26: 6 and you will l down and no-one will
26:33 and your cities will l in ruins.
Nu 21:15 Ar and l along the border of Moab."
24: 9 Like a lion they crouch and l down,
Dt 6: 7 when you l down and when you get up.
11:19 when you l down and when you get up.
25: 2 the judge shall make him l down and
33:13 with the deep waters that l below;
Jdg 9:32 come and l in wait in the fields.
Ru 3: 4 go and uncover his feet and l down
3: 7 he went over to l down at the far
3:13 L here until morning."
1Sa 3: 5 "I did not call; go back and l down.
3: 6 "I did not call; go back and l down.
3: 9 Eli told Samuel, "Go and l down, and
22: 8 l in wait for me, as he does today."
2Sa 8: 2 He made them l down on the ground
11:11 to eat and drink and l with my wife?
12:11 l with your wives in broad daylight.
16:21 Ahithophel answered, "L with your
20: 3 for them, but did not l with them.
23: 7 they are burned up where they l."
1Ki 1: 2 She can l beside him so that our
Job 7: 4 I l down I think, 'How long before I
7:21 For I shall soon l down in the dust;
11:19 You will l down, with no-one to make
20:11 bones will l with him in the dust.
21:26 Side by side they l in the dust, and
29:19 dew will l all night on my branches.
38:40 crouch in their dens or l in wait
Ps 3: 5 I l down and sleep; I wake again,
4: 8 I will l down and sleep in peace,
23: 2 He makes me l down in green pastures,
31:17 to shame and l silent in the grave.
36:12 See how the evildoers l fallen—
37:32 The wicked l in wait for the
38: 9 All my longings l open before you,
57: 4 I l among ravenous beasts—
59: 3 See how they l in wait for me!
76: 5 Valiant men l plundered, they sleep
76: 6 both horse and chariot l still.
88: 5 like the slain who l in the grave,
102: 7 I l awake; I have become like a bird
104:22 return and l down in their dens.
Pr 1:11 "Come along with us; let's l in wait
1:18 These men l in wait for their own
3:24 you l down, you will not be afraid;
3:24 l down, your sleep will be sweet.
6: 9 How long will you l there, you
12: 6 The words of the wicked l in wait
15:11 Death and Destruction l open before
22: 5 In the paths of the wicked l thorns
24:15 Do not l in wait like an outlaw
Ecc 4:11 Also, if two l down together, they
11: 3 where it falls, there will it l.
Isa 6:11 "Until the cities l ruined and
11: 6 the leopard will l down with the
11: 7 their young will l down together,
13:21 desert creatures will l there,
14:18 kings of the nations l in state
14:30 and the needy will l down in safety.
17: 2 which will l down, with no-one to
21: 9 gods l shattered on the ground!'
27:10 the calves graze there they l down;
34:10 to generation it will l desolate;
50:11 my hand: You will l down in torment.
51:20 they l at the head of every street
56:10 they cannot bark; they l around and
57: 2 they find rest as they l in death.
Jer 3:25 Let us l down in our shame, and let
4: 7 will l in ruins without inhabitant.
5: 6 a leopard will l in wait near their
5:26 people are wicked men who l in wait
9:22 bodies of men will l like refuse
12: 4 How long will the land l parched and
44: 2 Today they l deserted and in
46:19 and l in ruins without inhabitant.
51:47 slain will all l fallen within her.
Lam 2:21 "Young and old l together in the
4: 5 in purple now l on ash heaps.
Eze 4: 4 "Then l on your left side and put
4: 4 number of days you l on your side.
4: 6 have finished this, l down again,
4: 9 the 390 days you l on your side.
6:13 when their people l slain among
18: 6 or l with a woman during her period.
29:12 and her cities will l desolate for
30: 7 cities will l among ruined cities.
31:18 you will l among the uncircumcised,
32:21 and they l with the uncircumcised
32:27 Do they not l with the other
32:28 will be broken and will l among the
32:29 They l with the uncircumcised, with
32:30 They l uncircumcised with those
34:14 will l down in good grazing land
34:15 l down, declares the Sovereign LORD.
48:22 the property of the city will l in
48:22 will l between the border of Judah
Hos 2:18 so that all may l down in safety.
6: 9 marauders l in ambush for a man,
Am 2: 8 They l down beside every altar on
6: 4 You l on beds inlaid with ivory and
Mic 7: 2 All men l in wait to shed blood;
Na 3:18 slumber; your nobles l down to rest.
Zep 2: 7 In the evening they will l down in
2:14 Flocks and herds will l down there,
3:13 They will eat and l down and no-one
Jn 5: 3 disabled people used to l—the blind
Rev 11: 8 Their bodies will l in the street of

Lie[2] (Liar, Liars, Lied, Lies, Lying)
Lev 19:11 "'Do not steal. "'Do not l. "'Do
Nu 23:19 God is not a man, that he should l,
1Sa 15:29 Israel does not l or change his mind;
Job 6:28 Would I l to your face?
Ps 62: 9 a breath, the highborn are but a l;
89:35 and I will not l to David—
Isa 28:15 for we have made a l our refuge and
28:17 will sweep away your refuge, the l,
44:20 this thing in my right hand a l?"
Jer 9: 5 They have taught their tongues to l;
23:14 They commit adultery and live a l.
29:31 and has led you to believe a l,
Eze 13: 6 are false and their divinations a l.
Da 11:27 the same table and l to each other
Zec 10: 2 diviners see visions that l; they
Ro 1:25 exchanged the truth of God for a l,
Gal 1:20 what I am writing to you is no l.
Col 3: 9 Do not l to each other, since you
2Th 2:11 so that they will believe the l
Tit 1: 2 which God, who does not l, promised
Heb 6:18 which it is impossible for God to l,
1Jn 1: 6 we l and do not live by the truth.
2:21 because no l comes from the truth.
Rev 14: 5 No l was found in their mouths; they

Lied (Lie[2])
Ge 18:15 Sarah was afraid, so she l and said,
Jos 7:11 they have l, they have put them with
Jdg 16:10 have made a fool of me; you l to me.

Jer 5:12 They have l about the LORD; they
Ac 5: 3 that you have l to the Holy Spirit
5: 4 You have not l to men but to God."

Lies[1] (Lie[1])

Ge 21:17 heard the boy crying as he l there.
49: 9 Like a lion he crouches and l down,
49:25 blessings of the deep that l below,
Lev 15: 4 Any bed the man with a discharge l on
15:18 a man l with a woman and there is an
15:20 Anything she l on during her period
15:24 "'If a man l with her and her
15:24 any bed he l on will be unclean.
15:26 Any bed she l on while her discharge
15:33 and for a man who l with a woman who
18:22 with a man as one l with a woman
20:13 l with a man as one l with a woman
20:18 "'If a man l with a woman during
26:34 all the time that it l desolate
26:35 All the time that it l desolate, the
26:43 while it l desolate without them.
Nu 14:33 last of your bodies l in the desert.
Dt 19:11 hates his neighbour and l in wait
Ru 3: 4 he l down, note the place where he
1Sa 14:39 l with my son Jonathan, he must die.
22:13 l in wait for me, as he does today?"
2Sa 1:19 "Your glory, O Israel, l slain on
1:25 Jonathan l slain on your heights.
Ne 2: 3 my fathers are buried l in ruins,
2:17 we are in: Jerusalem l in ruins,
Job 14:12 man l down and does not rise; till
18:10 on the ground; a trap l in his path.
19:28 the root of the trouble l in him,'
20:26 total darkness l in wait for his
26: 6 before God; Destruction l uncovered.
27:19 He l down wealthy, but will do so no
37:17 land l hushed under the south wind,
40:21 Under the lotus plant he l, hidden
Ps 10: 8 He l in wait near the villages; from
10: 9 He l in wait like a lion in cover;
10: 9 he l in wait to catch the helpless;
41: 8 get up from the place where he l."
88: 7 Your wrath l heavily upon me; you
Pr 23:28 Like a bandit she l in wait, and
Isa 24:10 The ruined city l desolate; the
64:11 all that we treasured l in ruins.
Jer 4:20 disaster; the whole land l in ruins.
23:10 of the curse the land l parched
40: 4 Look, the whole country l before you
Lam 1: 1 How deserted l the city, once so
5:18 for Mount Zion, which l desolate,
Eze 26: 2 that she l in ruins I will prosper,
32:23 pit and her army l around her grave.
47:16 and Sibraim (which l on the border
Da 2:22 he knows what l in darkness, and
Mic 7: 5 Even with her who l in your embrace
Mt 8: 6 "my servant l at home paralysed
Rev 10: 8 "Go, take the scroll that l open in

Lies[2] (Lie[2])

Ex 5: 9 working and pay no attention to l."
Lev 6: 3 finds lost property and l about it
Job 13: 4 You, however, smear me with l; you
Ps 5: 6 You destroy those who tell l;
10: 7 His mouth is full of curses and l
12: 2 Everyone l to his neighbour; their
34:13 evil and your lips from speaking l.
55:11 and l never leave its streets.
58: 3 womb they are wayward and speak l.
59:12 For the curses and l they utter,
62: 4 lofty place; they take delight in l.
119:69 the arrogant have smeared me with l,
144: 8 whose mouths are full of l, whose
144:11 whose mouths are full of l, whose
Pr 6:19 a false witness who pours out l and
12:17 but a false witness tells l.
14: 5 but a false witness pours out l.
19: 5 he who pours out l will not go free.
19: 9 and he who pours out l will perish.
29:12 If a ruler listens to l, all his
30: 8 Keep falsehood and l far from me;
Isa 9:15 prophets who teach l are the tail.
32: 7 schemes to destroy the poor with l,
59: 3 Your lips have spoken l, and your
59: 4 rely on empty arguments and speak l;
Isa 59:13 l our hearts have conceived.
Jer 5:31 The prophets prophesy l, the priests
9: 3 their tongue like a bow, to shoot l
14:14 are prophesying l in my name.
20: 6 to whom you have prophesied l.
23:25 say who prophesy l in my name.
23:32 people astray with their reckless l
27:10 They prophesy l to you that will
27:14 for they are prophesying l to you.
27:15 'They are prophesying l in my name.
27:16 They are prophesying l to you.
28:15 persuaded this nation to trust in l
29: 9 They are prophesying l to you in my
29:21 who are prophesying l to you in my
29:23 in my name have spoken l, which I
Eze 13:19 my people, who listen to l, you have
13:22 the righteous with your l,
Hos 7: 3 the princes with their l.
7:13 them but they speak l against me.
11:12 Ephraim has surrounded me with l,
12: 1 day and multiplies l and violence.
Na 3: 1 Woe to the city of blood, full of l,
Hab 2:18 Or an image that teaches l? For he
Zep 3:13 do no wrong; they will speak no l,
Zec 13: 3 you have told l in the LORD's name.
Jn 8:44 When he l, he speaks his native
8:44 he is a liar and the father of l.

Life (Alive, *Book of life, Bread of life, Breath of life, Eternal life, Fountain of life, Life and death*, Life's, Lifetime, Life-time, Lives, *Tree of life*)

Ge 3:14 eat dust all the days of your l.
3:17 eat of it all the days of your l.
6:17 to destroy all l under the heavens,
7:11 the six hundredth year of Noah's l
9: 5 for the l of his fellow man.
9:11 Never again will all l be cut off by
9:15 become a flood to destroy all l.
9:17 between me and all l on the earth."
12:13 my l will be spared because of you."
19:19 kindness to me in sparing my l.
19:20 isn't it? Then my l will be spared."
26: 9 I might lose my l on account of her."
27:46 my l will not be worth living."
32:30 to face, and yet my l was spared."
37:21 "Let's not take his l," he said.
42:21 when he pleaded with us for his l,
43: 9 bear the blame before you all my l.
44:30 whose l is closely bound up with the
44:30 closely bound up with the boy's l,
44:32 before you, my father, all my l!'
47:28 years, and the years of his l were
48:15 my shepherd all my l to this day,
Ex 21: 6 Then he will be his servant for l.
21:23 injury, you are to take l for l,
21:30 may redeem his l by paying whatever
23:26 I will give you a full l span.
30:12 for his l at the time he is counted.
Lev 17:11 For the l of a creature is in the
17:11 that makes atonement for one's l.
17:14 the l of every creature is its blood
17:14 because the l of every creature is
19:16 that endangers your neighbour's l.
24:17 anyone takes the l of a human being
24:18 who takes the l of someone's animal
24:18 must make restitution—l for l.
25:46 and can make them slaves for l,
26:16 your sight and drain away your l.
Nu 35:31 not accept a ransom for the l of a
Dt 4:42 one of these cities and save his l.
6: 2 and so that you may enjoy long l.
12:23 because the blood is the l, and you
12:23 must not eat the l with the meat.
15:17 he will become your servant for l.
16: 3 so that all the days of your l you
17:19 to read it all the days of his l
19: 4 flees there to save his l—one who
19: 5 one of these cities and save his l.
19:21 Show no pity: l for l, eye for eye,
22: 7 with you and you may have a long l.
28:66 night and day, never sure of your l.
30:15 See, I set before you today l and
30:19 Now choose l, so that you and your
30:20 For the LORD is your l, and he will
Dt 32:39 I put to death and I bring to l, I
32:47 idle words for you—they are your l.
Jos 1: 5 against you all the days of your l.
4:14 revered him all the days of his l,
Jdg 5: 7 Village l in Israel ceased, ceased
9:17 risked his l to rescue you from the
12: 3 I took my l in my hands and crossed
13:12 the rule for the boy's l and work?"
Ru 1:20 Almighty has made my l very bitter.
4:15 He will renew your l and sustain you
1Sa 1:11 the LORD for all the day of his l
1:28 For his whole l he shall be given
2:33 will die in the prime of l.
7:15 over Israel all the days of his l.
19: 5 He took his l in his hands when he
19:11 If you don't run for your l tonight
20: 1 that he is trying to take my l?"
22:23 seeking your l is seeking mine also.
23:15 Saul had come out to take his l.
24:11 are hunting me down to take my l.
25: 6 Say to him: 'Long l to you! Good
25:29 is pursuing you to take your l,
25:29 the l of my master will be bound
26:21 Because you considered my l precious
26:24 surely as I valued your l today, so
26:24 may the LORD value my l and deliver
28: 2 I will make you my bodyguard for l."
28: 9 Why have you set a trap for my l to
28:21 I took my l in my hands and did what
2Sa 1:23 "Saul and Jonathan—in l they were
4: 8 enemy, who tried to take your l.
14: 7 the l of his brother whom he killed;
14:14 But God does not take away l;
15:21 whether it means l or death, there
16:11 own flesh, is trying to take my l.
18:13 if I had put my l in jeopardy—and
19: 5 who have just saved your l and the
1Ki 1:12 own l and the l of your son Solomon.
2:23 not pay with his l for this request!
3:11 for long l or wealth for yourself,
3:14 did, I will give you a long l."
4:21 were Solomon's subjects all his l.
4:33 He described plant l, from the cedar
11:34 him ruler all the days of his l
15: 5 commands all the days of his l—
15:14 committed to the LORD all his l.
17:21 let this boy's l return to him!"
17:22 l returned to him, and he lived.
19: 2 make your l like that of one of
19: 3 Elijah was afraid and ran for his l.
19: 4 "Take my l; I am no better than my
20:31 Perhaps he will spare your l."
20:39 it will be your l for his l, or you
20:42 Therefore it is your l for his l,
2Ki 1:13 "please have respect for my l and
1:14 But now have respect for my l!"
5: 7 Can I kill and bring back to l? Why
8: 1 whose son he had restored to l,
8: 5 Elisha had restored the dead to l,
8: 5 son Elisha had brought back to l
8: 5 her son whom Elisha restored to l."
10:24 it will be your l for his l."
13:21 came to l and stood up on his feet.
18:32 Choose l and not death! "Do not
20: 6 I will add fifteen years to your l.
25:29 for the rest of his l ate regularly
1Ch 29:28 enjoyed long l, wealth and honour.
2Ch 1:11 asked for a long l but for wisdom
15:17 committed ⌊to the LORD⌋ all his l
Ezr 9: 9 He has granted us new l to rebuild
Ne 4: 2 Can they bring the stones back to l
6:11 to save his l? I will not go!"
9: 6 You give l to everything, and the
Est 4:11 gold sceptre to him and spare his l.
7: 3 grant me my l—this is my petition.
7: 7 to beg Queen Esther for his l.
Job 2: 4 will give all he has for his own l.
2: 6 hands; but you must spare his l."
3:20 misery, and l to the bitter of soul,
3:23 Why is l given to a man whose way is
7: 7 O God, that my l is but a breath;
7:16 I despise my l; I would not live for
8:19 Surely its l withers away, and from
9:21 for myself; I despise my own l.
10: 1 "I loathe my very l; therefore I
10:12 You gave me l and showed me kindness,

Job 11:17 **L** will be brighter than noonday, and
12:10 In his hand is the **l** of every
12:12 Does not long **l** bring understanding?
13:14 jeopardy and take my **l** in my hands?
24:22 they have no assurance of **l**.
27: 3 long as I have **l** within me, the
27: 8 cut off, when God takes away his **l**?
30:16 "And now my **l** ebbs away; days of
31:30 by invoking a curse against his **l**—
33: 4 breath of the Almighty gives me **l**.
33:18 his **l** from perishing by the sword.
33:22 his **l** to the messengers of death.
33:30 the light of **l** may shine on him.
41: 4 to take him as your slave for **l**?
42:12 part of Job's **l** more than the first.
Ps 7: 5 let him trample my **l** to the ground
16:11 have made known to me the path of **l**;
17:14 world whose reward is in this **l**.
21: 4 He asked you for **l**, and you gave it
22:20 my **l** from the sword, my precious **l**
23: 6 will follow me all the days of my **l**,
25:20 Guard my **l** and rescue me; let me not
26: 1 for I have led a blameless **l**; I have
26: 9 sinners, my **l** with bloodthirsty men,
26:11 I lead a blameless **l**; redeem me and
27: 1 The LORD is the stronghold of my **l**
27: 4 of the LORD all the days of my **l**,
31:10 My **l** is consumed by anguish and my
31:13 against me and plot to take my **l**.
34:12 Whoever of you loves **l** and desires
35: 4 May those who seek my **l** be disgraced
35:17 Rescue my **l** from their ravages,
35:17 my precious **l** from these lions.
38:12 Those who seek my **l** set their traps,
39: 4 let me know how fleeting is my **l**.
39: 5 Each man's **l** is but a breath.
40:14 May all who seek to take my **l** be put
41: 2 will protect him and preserve his **l**;
42: 8 a prayer to the God of my **l**.
49: 7 No man can redeem the **l** of another
49: 8 the ransom for a **l** is costly, no
49:15 God will redeem my **l** from the grave;
49:19 who will never see the light of **l**.
54: 3 ruthless men seek my **l**—men
56: 6 watch my steps, eager to take my **l**.
56:13 walk before God in the light of **l**.
61: 6 Increase the days of the king's **l**,
63: 3 your love is better than **l**, my lips
63: 9 They who seek my **l** will be destroyed;
64: 1 protect my **l** from the threat of the
70: 2 May those who seek my **l** be put to
71:20 you will restore my **l** again; from
74:19 Do not hand over the **l** of your dove
86: 2 Guard my **l**, for I am devoted to you.
86:14 ruthless men seek my **l**—men without
88: 3 and my **l** draws near the grave.
89:47 Remember how fleeting is my **l**. For
91:16 With long **l** will I satisfy him and
101: 2 be careful to lead a blameless **l**
102:23 In the course of my **l** he broke my
103: 4 who redeems your **l** from the pit and
104:33 I will sing to the LORD all my **l**;
109:31 to save his **l** from those who
119:25 preserve my **l** according to your
119:37 preserve my **l** according to your
119:40 Preserve my **l** in your righteousness
119:50 this: Your promise preserves my **l**.
119:88 Preserve my **l** according to your love,
119:93 for by them you have preserved my **l**.
119:107 I have suffered much; preserve my **l**,
119:109 I constantly take my **l** in my hands,
119:149 preserve my **l**, O LORD, according to
119:154 preserve my **l** according to your
119:156 preserve my **l** according to your
119:159 preserve my **l**, O LORD, according to
121: 7 harm—he will watch over your **l**;
128: 5 from Zion all the days of your **l**;
133: 3 his blessing, even **l** for evermore.
138: 7 you preserve my **l**; you stretch out
142: 4 no refuge; no-one cares for my **l**.
143:11 O LORD, preserve my **l**; in your
146: 2 I will praise the LORD all my **l**;
Pr 1: 3 a disciplined and prudent **l**,
2:19 her return or attain the paths of **l**.
3: 2 for they will prolong your **l** many
3:16 Long **l** is in her right hand; in her

Pr 3:22 they will be **l** for you, an ornament
4:10 the years of your **l** will be many.
4:13 guard it well, for it is your **l**.
4:22 for they are **l** to those who find
4:23 for it is the wellspring of **l**.
5: 6 She gives no thought to the way of **l**
5:11 At the end of your **l** you will groan,
6:23 of discipline are the way to **l**,
6:26 adulteress preys upon your very **l**.
7:23 knowing it will cost him his **l**.
8:35 For whoever finds me finds **l** and
9:11 and years will be added to your **l**.
10:16 wages of the righteous bring them **l**,
10:17 heeds discipline shows the way to **l**,
10:27 The fear of the LORD adds length to **l**
11:19 The truly righteous man attains **l**,
12:28 way of righteousness there is **l**;
13: 3 He who guards his lips guards his **l**,
13: 8 A man's riches may ransom his **l**, but
14:30 A heart at peace gives **l** to the body,
15:24 The path of **l** leads upward for the
16:15 a king's face brightens, it means **l**;
16:17 he who guards his way guards his **l**.
16:31 it is attained by a righteous **l**.
18:21 The tongue has the power of **l** and
19: 3 A man's own folly ruins his **l**, yet
19:16 who obeys instructions guards his **l**,
19:23 The fear of the LORD leads to **l**:
20: 2 he who angers him forfeits his **l**.
20: 7 The righteous man leads a blameless **l**
21:21 love finds **l**, prosperity and honour.
22: 4 LORD bring wealth and honour and **l**.
23:22 Listen to your father, who gave you **l**
24:12 Does not he who guards your **l** know
28:16 ill-gotten gain will enjoy a long **l**.
31:12 not harm, all the days of her **l**.
Ecc 2:17 I hated **l**, because the work that is
5:18 the few days of **l** God has given him
5:20 reflects on the days of his **l**,
6:12 knows what is good for a man in **l**,
7:12 preserves the **l** of its possessor.
7:15 In this meaningless **l** of mine I have
8:15 I commend the enjoyment of **l**,
8:15 all the days of the **l** God has given
9: 9 Enjoy **l** with your wife, whom you
9: 9 all the days of this meaningless **l**
9: 9 For this is your lot in **l** and in
10:19 and wine makes **l** merry, but money is
Isa 23:15 years, the span of a king's **l**.
38: 5 I will add fifteen years to your **l**.
38:10 I said, "In the prime of my **l** must I
38:12 Like a weaver I have rolled up my **l**,
38:16 and my spirit finds **l** in them too.
42: 5 and **l** to those who walk on it:
43: 4 and people in exchange for your **l**.
53:10 and though the LORD makes his **l** a
53:11 he will see the light of **l** and be
53:12 he poured out his **l** unto death
Jer 4:30 despise you; they seek your **l**.
4:31 my **l** is given over to murderers."
8: 3 will prefer death to **l**, declares
10:23 that a man's **l** is not his own'
11:21 who are seeking your **l** and saying,
17:11 When his **l** is half gone, they will
20:13 He rescues the **l** of the needy from
21: 8 the way of **l** and the way of death.
21: 9 he will escape with his **l**.
22:25 you over to those who seek your **l**,
38: 2 escape with his **l**; he will live.'
38:16 to those who are seeking your **l**."
38:17 your **l** will be spared and this city
38:20 with you, and your **l** will be spared.
39:18 sword but will escape with your **l**,
40:14 son of Nethaniah to take your **l**?"
40:15 Why should he take your **l** and cause
44:30 over to his enemies who seek his **l**,
44:30 the enemy who was seeking his **l**.
45: 5 I will let you escape with your **l**.
52:33 for the rest of his **l** ate regularly
Lam 3:53 They tried to end my **l** in a pit and
3:58 took up my case; you redeemed my **l**.
4:20 LORD's anointed, our very **l** breath
Eze 3:18 evil ways in order to save his **l**,
7:13 not one of them will preserve his **l**.
18:27 just and right, he will save his **l**.
32:10 will tremble every moment for his **l**.

Eze 33: 4 the sword comes and takes his **l**,
33: 6 and takes the **l** of one of them,
33:15 follows the decrees that give **l**,
37: 5 enter you, and you will come to **l**.
37: 6 in you, and you will come to **l**.
37:10 they came to **l** and stood up on their
Da 5:23 God who holds in his hand your **l**
12: 2 will awake: some to everlasting **l**,
Am 2:14 and the warrior will not save his **l**
2:15 the horseman will not save his **l**.
Jnh 1:14 us die for taking this man's **l**.
2: 6 you brought my **l** up from the pit,
2: 7 "When my **l** was ebbing away, I
4: 3 Now, O LORD, take away my **l** for it
Hab 2:10 own house and forfeiting your **l**.
2:19 who says to wood, 'Come to **l**!' Or
Mal 2: 5 a covenant of **l** and peace, and I
Mt 2:20 to take the child's **l** are dead."
6:25 do not worry about your **l**, what you
6:25 Is not **l** more important than food,
6:27 can add a single hour to his **l**?
7:14 narrow the road that leads to **l**,
10:39 Whoever finds his **l** will lose it,
10:39 whoever loses his **l** for my sake
13:22 but the worries of this **l** and the
16:21 and on the third day be raised to **l**.
16:25 wants to save his **l** will lose it,
16:25 loses his **l** for me will find it.
17:23 third day he will be raised to **l**.
18: 8 It is better for you to enter **l**
18: 9 It is better for you to enter **l** with
19:17 If you want to enter **l**, obey the
20:19 third day he will be raised to **l**!"
20:28 to give his **l** as a ransom for many."
27:52 who had died were raised to **l**.
Mk 3: 4 to do evil, to save **l** or to kill?"
4:19 the worries of this **l**, the
8:35 wants to save his **l** will lose it,
8:35 but whoever loses his **l** for me and
9:43 It is better for you to enter **l**
9:45 It is better for you to enter **l**
10:45 to give his **l** as a ransom for many."
Lk 6: 9 evil, to save **l** or to destroy it?"
7:37 a woman who had lived a sinful **l** in
9: 8 of long ago had come back to **l**.
9:19 of long ago has come back to **l**."
9:22 on the third day be raised to **l**."
9:24 For whoever wants to save his **l** will
9:24 loses his **l** for me will save it.
12:15 a man's **l** does not consist in the
12:19 Take **l** easy; eat, drink and be merry.
12:20 your **l** will be demanded from you.
12:22 do not worry about your **l**, what you
12:23 **L** is more than food, and the body
12:25 can add a single hour to his **l**?
14:26 yea, even his own **l**—he cannot be
17:33 tries to keep his **l** will lose it
17:33 loses his **l** will preserve it.
21:19 By standing firm you will gain **l**.
21:34 drunkenness and the anxieties of **l**,
Jn 1: 4 In him was **l**, and that **l** was the
3:36 rejects the Son will not see **l**,
5:21 raises the dead and gives them **l**,
5:21 even so the Son give **l** to whom he
5:24 he has crossed over from death to **l**.
5:26 For as the Father has **l** in himself,
5:26 the Son to have **l** in himself.
5:40 you refuse to come to me to have **l**.
6:33 heaven and gives **l** to the world."
6:47 he who believes has everlasting **l**.
6:51 I will give for the **l** of the world."
6:53 his blood, you have no **l** in you.
6:63 The Spirit gives **l**; the flesh counts
6:63 to you are spirit and they are **l**.
7: 1 there were waiting to take his **l**.
8:11 "Go now and leave your **l** of sin."
8:12 but will have the light of **l**."
9: 3 of God might be displayed in his **l**.
10:10 may have **l**, and have it to the full.
10:11 lays down his **l** for the sheep.
10:15 I lay down my **l** for the sheep.
10:17 lay down my **l**—only to take it up
11:25 "I am the resurrection and the **l**.
11:53 day on they plotted to take his **l**.
12:25 The man who loves his **l** will lose it,
12:25 while the man who hates his **l** in

Jn 13:37 I will lay down my l for you."
13:38 "Will you really lay down your l for
14: 6 I am the way and the truth and the l.
15:13 he lay down his l for his friends.
20:31 you may have l in his name.
Ac 2:28 made known to me the paths of l;
2:32 God has raised this Jesus to l, and
3:15 You killed the author of l, but God
5:20 the full message of this new l."
8:33 For his l was taken from the earth."
11:18 the Gentiles repentance unto l."
17:25 l and breath and everything else.
20:24 I consider my l worth nothing to me
26: 4 from the beginning of my l in my own
27:43 centurion wanted to spare Paul's l
Ro 4:17 God who gives l to the dead
4:25 raised to l for our justification.
5:10 shall we be saved through his l!
5:17 l through the one man, Jesus Christ.
5:18 that brings l for all men.
6: 4 the Father, we too may live a new l
6:10 but the l he lives, he lives to God
6:13 have been brought from death to l;
7: 9 came, sin sprang to l and I died.
7:10 to bring l actually brought death.
8: 2 law of the Spirit of l set me free
8: 6 by the Spirit is l and peace;
8:11 will also give l to your mortal
8:34 who was raised to l—is at the right
8:38 convinced that neither death nor l,
11:15 acceptance be but l from the dead?
14: 9 Christ died and returned to l so
1Co 3:22 or the world or l or death or the
4:17 He will remind you of my way of l in
6: 3 How much more the things of this l!
7:17 place in l that the Lord assigned
7:28 will face many troubles in this l,
15:19 If only for this l we have hope in
15:36 does not come to l unless it dies.
2Co 1: 8 so that we despaired even of l.
2:16 to the other, the fragrance of l.
3: 6 kills, but the Spirit gives l.
4:10 so that the l of Jesus may also be
4:11 l may be revealed in our mortal body.
4:12 at work in us, but l is at work in
5: 4 is mortal may be swallowed up by l.
Gal 1:13 of my previous way of l in Judaism,
2:20 The l I live in the body, I live by
3:15 me take an example from everyday l.
3:21 had been given that could impart l,
Eph 4: 1 then, I urge you to live a l worthy
4:18 separated from the l of God because
4:22 with regard to your former way of l,
5: 2 live a l of love, just as Christ
6: 3 you may enjoy long l on the earth."
Php 1:20 my body, whether by l or by death.
2:16 you hold out the word of l—in order
2:30 risking his l to make up for the
Col 1:10 you may live a l worthy of the Lord
3: 3 For you died, and your l is now
3: 4 Christ, who is your l, appears, then
3: 7 these ways, in the l you once lived.
1Th 4: 7 to be impure, but to live a holy l.
4:11 it your ambition to lead a quiet l,
4:12 that your daily l may win the
1Ti 4: 8 the present l and the l to come.
4:12 in l, in love, in faith and in
4:16 Watch your l and doctrine closely.
6:13 of God, who gives l to everything
6:19 take hold of the l that is truly l.
2Ti 1: 1 according to the promise of l that
1: 9 called us to a holy l—not because
1:10 has brought l and immortality to
3:10 my way of l, my purpose, faith,
3:12 to live a godly l in Christ Jesus
Heb 5: 7 During the days of Jesus' l on earth,
7: 3 beginning of days or end of l,
7:16 of the power of an indestructible l.
11: 5 By faith Enoch was taken from this l
11:35 back their dead, raised to l again.
13: 7 way of l and imitate their faith.
Jas 1:12 he will receive the crown of l that
1:20 the righteous l that God desires.
3: 6 sets the whole course of his l on
3:13 you? Let him show it by his good l,
4:14 What is your l? You are a mist that
1Pe 1:18 redeemed from the empty way of l
3: 7 with you of the gracious gift of l,
3:10 would love l and see good days
4: 2 earthly l for evil human desires,
2Pe 1: 3 given us everything we need for l
1Jn 1: 1 proclaim concerning the Word of l.
1: 2 The l appeared; we have seen it and
3:14 that we have passed from death to l
3:16 Jesus Christ laid down his l for us
5:11 and this l is in his Son.
5:12 He who has the Son has l; he who
5:12 have the Son of God does not have l
5:16 should pray and God will give him l
Rev 2: 8 Last, who died and came to l again.
2:10 and I will give you the crown of l.
20: 4 They came to l and reigned with
20: 5 rest of the dead did not come to l
21: 6 from the spring of the water of l.
22: 1 me the river of the water of l,
22:17 the free gift of the water of l.

Life and death
Dt 30:19 I have set before you l, blessings
Pr 18:21 The tongue has the power of l, and

Life's (Life)
Ps 39: 4 "Show me, O LORD, my l end and the
Lk 8:14 way they are choked by l worries,

Lifeblood (Blood)
Ge 9: 4 eat meat that has its l still in it.
9: 5 for your l I will surely demand an
Jer 2:34 On your clothes men find the l of

Lifeboat (Boat)
Ac 27:16 hardly able to make the l secure.
27:30 the sailors let the l down into the
27:32 held the l and let it fall away.

Life-giving (Give)
Pr 15:31 He who listens to a l rebuke will be
1Co 15:45 being"; the last Adam, a l spirit.

Lifeless
Lev 26:30 bodies on the l forms of your idols,
Ps 106:28 ate sacrifices offered to l gods;
Jer 16:18 the l forms of their vile images
Eze 43: 7 the l idols of their kings at their
43: 9 and the l idols of their kings,
Hab 2:19 to life!' Or to l stone, 'Wake up!'
1Co 14: 7 Even in the case of l things that

Lifetime (Life)
Nu 3: 4 during the l of their father Aaron.
Jos 24:31 the LORD throughout the l of Joshua
Jdg 2: 7 the LORD throughout the l of Joshua
8:28 During Gideon's l, the land enjoyed
1Sa 7:13 Throughout Samuel's l, the hand of
1Ki 3:13 in your l you will have no equal
4:25 During Solomon's l Judah and Israel,
11:12 I will not do it during your l.
12: 6 his father Solomon during his l.
15: 6 Jeroboam throughout ⌊Abijah's⌋ l
2Ki 20:19 not be peace and security in my l?"
2Ch 10: 6 his father Solomon during his l.
Ps 30: 5 but his favour lasts a l; weeping
Isa 39: 8 will be peace and security in my l."
Jer 22:30 a man who will not prosper in his l,
Lk 16:25 'Son, remember that in your l you

Life-time (Life)
2Sa 18:18 During his l Absalom had taken a

Lift (Lifted, Lifting, Lifts, Uplifted)
Ge 13:14 "L up your eyes from where you are
21:18 L the boy up and take him by the
40:13 Within three days Pharaoh will l up
40:19 Within three days Pharaoh will l off
41:44 will l hand or foot in all Egypt."
Ex 40:37 if the cloud did not l, they did not
Dt 28:32 after day, powerless to l a hand.
32:40 I l my hand to heaven and declare:
1Sa 6: 5 Perhaps he will l his hand from you
1Sa 24: 6 the LORD's anointed, or l my hand
24:10 'I will not l my hand against my
2Sa 1:14 "Why were you not afraid to l your
18:12 not l my hand against the king's
2Ki 6: 7 "L it out," he said. Then the man
Ezr 9: 6 disgraced to l up my face to you
Job 10:15 I cannot l my head, for I am full of
11:15 you will l up your face without
22:26 and will l up your face to God.
22:29 brought low and you say, 'L them up
Ps 3: 3 bestow glory on me and l up my head.
9:13 and l me up from the gates of death,
10:12 Arise, LORD! L up your hand, O God.
20: 5 will l up our banners in the name of
24: 4 who does not l up his soul to an
24: 7 L up your heads, O you gates; be
24: 9 L up your heads, O you gates; l them
25: 1 To you, O LORD, I l up my soul;
28: 2 as I l up my hands towards your Most
63: 4 in your name I will l up my hands.
75: 4 the wicked, 'Do not l up your horns.
75: 5 Do not l your horns against heaven;
76: 5 one of the warriors can l his hands.
86: 4 for to you, O Lord, I l up my soul.
91:12 they will l you up in their hands,
110: 7 therefore he will l up his head.
116:13 I will l up the cup of salvation and
119:48 I l up my hands to your commands,
121: 1 I l up my eyes to the hills—where
123: 1 I l up my eyes to you, to you whose
134: 2 L up your hands in the sanctuary and
142: 1 I l up my voice to the LORD for
143: 8 go, for to you I l up my soul.
Isa 10:24 beat you with a rod and l up a club
40: 9 l up your voice with a shout, l it
40:26 L your eyes and look to the heavens:
46: 7 They l it to their shoulders and
47: 2 L up your skirts, bare your legs,
49:18 L up your eyes and look around; all
49:22 I will l up my banner to the peoples;
51: 6 L up your eyes to the heavens, look
52: 8 Your watchmen l up their voices
60: 4 "L up your eyes and look about you:
Jer 13:20 L up your eyes and see those who are
38:10 l Jeremiah the prophet out of the
50: 2 l up a banner and proclaim it; keep
51:12 L up a banner against the walls of
51:27 "L up a banner in the land! Blow the
Lam 2:19 L up your hands to him for the lives
3:41 Let us l up our hearts and our hands
Da 6:23 orders to l Daniel out of the den.
Am 5: 2 own land, with no-one to l her up."
Na 3: 5 "I will l your skirts over your face.
Mt 4: 6 and they will l you up in their
12:11 not take hold of it and l it out?
23: 4 willing to l a finger to move them.
Lk 4:11 they will l you up in their hands,
11:46 will not l one finger to help them.
21:28 stand up and l up your heads,
1Ti 2: 8 men everywhere to l up holy hands
Jas 4:10 the Lord, and he will l you up.
1Pe 5: 6 that he may l you up in due time.

Lifted (Lift)
Ge 7:17 they l the ark high above the earth.
40:20 He l up the heads of the chief
Ex 17:16 He said, "For hands were l up to the
40:36 whenever the cloud l from above the
40:37 did not set out—until the day it l.
Lev 9:22 Aaron l his hands towards the people
Nu 9:17 Whenever the cloud l from above the
9:21 it l in the morning, they set out.
9:21 whenever the cloud l, they set out.
9:22 but when it l, they would set out.
10:11 the cloud l from above the
12:10 the cloud l from above the Tent,
Jdg 9:48 which he l to his shoulders.
16: 3 He l them to his shoulders and
1Sa 2: 1 in the LORD my horn is l high.
6: 3 his hand has not been l from you."
2Sa 18:28 the men who l their hands against
20:21 has l up his hand against the king,
1Ki 16: 2 "I l you up from the dust and made
2Ki 4:20 After the servant had l him up and
19:22 your voice and l your eyes in pride?

Ezr 6:11 he is to be l up and impaled on it.
Ne 8: 6 and all the people l their hands
Job 5:11 and those who mourn are l to safety.
Ps 24: 7 gates; be l up you ancient doors,
30: 1 LORD, for you l me out of the depths
40: 2 He l me out of the slimy pit, out of
41: 9 bread, has l up his heel against me.
75:10 of the righteous shall be l up.
93: 3 l up, O LORD, the seas have l up
93: 3 seas have l up their pounding waves.
107:25 up a tempest that l high the waves.
107:41 he l the needy out of their
112: 9 his horn will be l high in honour.
118:16 The LORD's right hand is l high;
Isa 10:27 In that day their burden will be l
26:11 O LORD, your hand is l high, but
33:10 I be exalted; now will I be l up.
37:23 your voice and l your eyes in pride?
52:13 raised and l up and highly exalted.
63: 9 he l them up and carried them all
Jer 38:13 ropes and l him out of the cistern.
Eze 3:12 the Spirit l me up, and I heard
3:14 The Spirit then l me up and took me
8: 3 The Spirit l me up between earth and
11: 1 the Spirit l me up and brought me to
11:24 The Spirit l me up and brought me to
43: 5 the Spirit l me up and brought me
Da 6:23 And when Daniel was l from the den,
7: 4 it was l from the ground so that it
12: 7 l his right hand and his left hand
Hos 11: 4 I l the yoke from their neck and
Am 5:26 You have l up the shrine of your
Mic 5: 9 Your hand will be l up in triumph
Hab 3:10 deep roared and l its waves on high.
Zec 1:21 of the nations who l up their horns
5: 9 and they l up the basket between
Mt 11:23 will you be l up to the skies? No,
Mk 9:27 Jesus took him by the hand and l him
Lk 1:52 thrones but has l up the humble.
10:15 will you be l up to the skies? No,
24:50 he l up his hands and blessed them.
Jn 3:14 Just as Moses l up the snake in the
3:14 so the Son of Man must be l up,
8:28 "When you have l up the Son of Man
12:32 I, when I am l up from the earth,
12:34 say, 'The son of Man must be l up'?
13:18 bread has l up his heel against me.'
19:29 plant, and l it to Jesus' lips.
Ac 7:43 You have l up the shrine of Molech

Lifting (Lift)

Ps 141: 2 may the l up of my hands be like the
Eze 31:10 l its top above the thick foliage,
31:14 l their tops above the thick foliage.

Lifts (Lift)

1Sa 2: 8 and l the needy from the ash heap;
Ezr 6:12 any king or people who l a hand to
Ps 46: 6 he l his voice, the earth melts.
113: 7 and l the needy from the ash heap;
145:14 and l up all who are bowed down.
146: 8 the LORD l up those who are bowed
Isa 5:26 He l up a banner for the distant
10:15 a rod were to wield him who l it up,

Ligament (Ligaments)

Eph 4:16 held together by every supporting l

Ligaments (Ligament)

Col 2:19 held together by its l and sinews,

Light[1] (Daylight, Lighted, Lights, Lit, Sunlight, Twilight)

Ge 1: 3 "Let there be l," and there was l.
1: 4 l was good, and he separated the l
1: 5 God called the l "day", and the
1:15 of the sky to give l on the earth.
1:16 greater l to govern the day
1:16 the lesser l to govern the night.
1:17 of the sky to give l on the earth,
1:18 and to separate l from darkness.
Ex 10:23 l in the places where they lived.
13:21 in a pillar of fire to give them l,
14:20 to the one side and l to the other;
Ex 25: 6 olive oil for the l; spices for the
25:37 they l the space in front of it.
27:20 oil of pressed olives for the l
35: 3 Do not l a fire in any of your
35: 8 olive oil for the l; spices for the
35:14 the lampstand that is for l with its
35:14 lamps and oil for the l;
35:28 olive oil for the l and for the
39:37 accessories, and the oil for the l;
Lev 24: 2 oil of pressed olives for the l
Nu 4: 9 cover the lampstand that is for l,
4:16 to have charge of the oil for the l,
8: 2 l the area in front of the lampstand.
1Sa 29:10 in the morning as soon as it is l."
2Sa 22:29 the LORD turns my darkness into l.
23: 4 he is like the l of morning at
1Ki 3:21 at him closely in the morning l,
18:25 of your god, but do not l the fire."
2Ch 13:11 l the lamps on the gold lampstand
Ezr 9: 8 and so our God gives l to our eyes
Ne 4:21 l of dawn till the stars came out.
9:12 give them l on the way they were to
Job 3: 4 about it; may no l shine upon it.
3: 5 may blackness overwhelm its l.
3:16 infant who never saw the l of day?
3:20 "Why is l given to those in misery,
9: 7 he seals off the l of the stars.
10:22 where even the l is like darkness."
12:22 and brings deep shadows into the l.
12:25 They grope in darkness with no l;
17:12 of darkness they say, 'L is near.'
18: 6 The l in his tent becomes dark; the
18:18 He is driven from l into darkness
22:28 done, and l will shine on your ways.
24:13 are those who rebel against the l,
24:16 they want nothing to do with the l.
25: 3 Upon whom does his l not rise?
26:10 a boundary between l and darkness.
28:11 and brings hidden things to l.
29: 3 by his l I walked through darkness!
29:24 l of my face was precious to them.
30:26 I looked for l, then came darkness.
33:28 and I shall live to enjoy the l.'
33:30 that the l of life may shine on him.
38:15 The wicked are denied their l, and
38:19 "What is the way to the abode of l?
41:18 His snorting throws out flashes of l
Ps 4: 6 l of your face shine upon us, O LORD.
13: 3 Give l to my eyes, or I will sleep
18:28 my God turns my darkness into l.
19: 8 are radiant, giving l to the eyes.
27: 1 The LORD is my l and my salvation—
36: 9 of life; in your l we see l.
38:10 even the l has gone from my eyes.
43: 3 Send forth your l and your truth,
44: 3 l of your face, for you loved them.
49:19 who will never see the l of life.
56:13 walk before God in the l of life.
76: 4 You are resplendent with l, more
78:14 and with l from the fire all night.
89:15 in the l of your presence, O LORD.
90: 8 sins in the l of your presence.
97:11 L is shed upon the righteous and joy
104: 2 He wraps himself in l as with a
105:39 and a fire to give l at night.
112: 4 Even in darkness l dawns for the
118:27 and he has made his l shine upon us
119:105 lamp to my feet and a l for my path
119:130 The unfolding of your words gives l
139:11 and the l become night around me,"
139:12 day, for darkness is as l to you.
Pr 4:18 brighter till the full l of day.
6:23 this teaching is a l, and the
13: 9 The l of the righteous shines
Ecc 2:13 just as l is better than darkness.
11: 7 L is sweet, and it pleases the eyes
12: 2 before the sun and the l and the
Isa 2: 5 let us walk in the l of the LORD.
5:20 who put darkness for l and l for
5:30 l will be darkened by the clouds.
8:20 this word, they have no l of dawn.
9: 2 in darkness have seen a great l;
9: 2 the shadow of death a l has dawned.
10:17 The L of Israel will become a fire,
13:10 will not show their l.
13:10 and the moon will not give its l.
Isa 30:26 like the l of seven full days, when
42: 6 the people and a l for the Gentiles,
42:16 I will turn the darkness into l
45: 7 I form the l and create darkness, I
49: 6 I will also make you a l for the
50:10 who has no l, trust in the name of
50:11 all you who l fires and provide
50:11 go, walk in the l of your fires and
51: 4 will become a l to the nations.
53:11 he will see the l of life and be
57: 6 In the l of these things, should I
58: 8 your l will break forth like the
58:10 then your l will rise in the
59: 9 We look for l, but all is darkness;
60: 1 "Arise, shine, for your l has come,
60: 3 Nations will come to your l, and
60:19 sun will no more be your l by day
60:19 LORD will be your everlasting l,
60:20 LORD will be your everlasting l,
Jer 4:23 the heavens, and their l was gone.
7:18 the fathers l the fire, and the
13:16 You hope for l, but he will turn it
25:10 of millstones and the l of the lamp.
Lam 3: 2 me walk in darkness rather than l;
Eze 1: 4 and surrounded by brilliant l.
1:27 and brilliant l surrounded him.
32: 7 and the moon will not give its l.
Da 2:22 in darkness, and l dwells with him.
6:19 At the first l of dawn, the king got
Am 5:18 That day will be darkness, not l.
5:20 not l—pitch-dark, without a ray of
Mic 2: 1 At morning's l they carry it out
7: 8 in darkness, the LORD will be my l.
7: 9 He will bring me out into the l;
Zec 14: 6 On that day there will be no l, no
14: 7 When evening comes, there will be l.
Mal 1:10 that you would not l useless fires
Mt 4:16 in darkness have seen a great l;
4:16 the shadow of death a l has dawned."
5:14 "You are the l of the world. A city
5:15 Neither do people l a lamp and put
5:15 it gives l to everyone in the house.
5:16 In the same way, let your l shine
6:22 your whole body will be full of l.
6:23 If then the l within you is darkness,
11:30 my yoke is easy and my burden is l."
17: 2 clothes became as white as the l.
24:29 and the moon will not give its l;
Mk 13:24 and the moon will not give its l;
Lk 2:32 a l for revelation to the Gentiles
8:16 those who come in can see the l.
11:33 those who come in may see the l.
11:34 your whole body also is full of l.
11:35 See to it, then, that the l within
11:36 if your whole body is full of l, and
11:36 as when the l of a lamp shines on
15: 8 Does she not l a lamp, sweep the
16: 8 kind than are the people of the l.
Jn 1: 4 and that life was the l of men.
1: 5 The l shines in the darkness, but
1: 7 to testify concerning that l,
1: 8 He himself was not the l; he came
1: 8 he came only as a witness to the l.
1: 9 The true l that gives l to every man
3:19 verdict: L has come into the world,
3:19 instead of l because their deeds were
3:20 Everyone who does evil hates the l,
3:20 and will not come into the l for
3:21 lives by the truth comes into the l,
5:35 was a lamp that burned and gave l,
5:35 you chose for a time to enjoy his l.
8:12 he said, "I am the l of the world.
8:12 but will have the l of life."
9: 5 world, I am the l of the world."
11: 9 for he sees by this world's l.
11:10 that he stumbles, for he has no l."
12:35 to have the l just a little while
12:35 Walk while you have the l, before
12:36 Put your trust in the l while you
12:36 so that you may become sons of l.
12:46 I have come into the world as a l,
Ac 9: 3 a l from heaven flashed around him.
12: 7 appeared and a l shone in the cell.
13:11 be unable to see the l of the sun.
13:47 have made you a l for the Gentiles
22: 6 l from heaven flashed around me.

Ac 22: 9 My companions saw the l, but they
22:11 brilliance of the l had blinded me.
26:13 on the road, I saw a l from heaven
26:18 and turn them from darkness to l,
26:23 would proclaim l to his own people
Ro 2:19 a l for those who are in the dark,
13:12 darkness and put on the armour of l.
1Co 3:13 because the Day will bring it to l.
4: 5 He will bring to l what is hidden in
2Co 4: 4 they cannot see the l of the gospel
4: 6 For God, who said, "Let l shine out
4: 6 made his l shine in our hearts to
4: 6 give us the l of the knowledge of
6:14 fellowship can l have with darkness?
11:14 masquerades as an angel of l.
Eph 5: 8 but now you are l in the Lord.
5: 8 Live as children of l
5: 9 (for the fruit of the l consists in
5:13 everything exposed by the l becomes
5:14 for it is l that makes everything
Col 1:12 of the saints in the kingdom of l.
1Th 5: 5 You are all sons of the l and sons
1Ti 6:16 l, whom no-one has seen or can see.
2Ti 1:10 immortality to l through the gospel.
Tit 1: 3 he brought his word to l through
Heb 10:32 days after you had received the l,
1Pe 2: 9 of darkness into his wonderful l.
2Pe 1:19 as to a l shining in a dark place,
1Jn 1: 5 God is l; in him there is no
1: 7 we walk in the l, as he is in the l
2: 8 and the true l is already shining.
2: 9 Anyone who claims to be in the l but
2:10 loves his brother lives in the l,
Rev 8:12 A third of the day was without l,
18:23 The l of a lamp will never shine in
21:23 the glory of God gives it l, and
21:24 The nations will walk by its l, and
22: 5 the l of a lamp or the l of the sun,
22: 5 for the Lord God will give them l.

Light[2] (Lighten, Lightened, Lighter)
Dt 25:13 in your bag—one heavy, one l.
Heb 12: 5 "My son, do not make l of the Lord's

Lighted (Light[1])
Lk 11:36 it will be completely l, as when the

Lighten (Light[2])
1Ki 12: 4 but now l the harsh labour and the
12: 9 'L the yoke your father put on us'?"
2Ch 10: 4 but now l the harsh labour and the
10: 9 'L the yoke your father put on us'?"
Jnh 1: 5 cargo into the sea to l the ship.

Lightened (Light[2])
Ac 27:38 they l the ship by throwing the

Lighter (Light[2])
Ex 18:22 That will make your load l, because
1Ki 12:10 but make our yoke l'—tell them, 'My
2Ch 10:10 but make our yoke l'—tell them, 'My

Lighting
Mt 3:16 descending like a dove and l on him.

Lightning
Ex 9:23 and l flashed down to the ground.
9:24 hail fell and l flashed back and
19:16 third day there was thunder and l,
20:18 the people saw the thunder and l and
2Sa 22:13 presence bolts of l blazed forth.
22:15 enemies, bolts of l and routed them.
Job 36:30 See how he scatters his l about him,
36:32 He fills his hands with l and
37: 3 He unleashes his l beneath the whole
37:11 he scatters his l through them.
37:15 the clouds and makes his l flash?
38:24 the place where the l is dispersed,
38:35 Do you send the l bolts on their way?
Ps 18:12 with hailstones and bolts of l.
18:14 great bolts of l and routed them.
29: 7 the LORD strikes with flashes of l.
77:18 your l lit up the world; the earth
78:48 hail, their livestock to bolts of l.
Ps 97: 4 His l lights up the world; the earth
105:32 hail, with l throughout their land;
135: 7 he sends l with the rain and brings
144: 6 Send forth l and scatter the enemies;
148: 8 l and hail, snow and clouds, stormy
Jer 10:13 He sends l with the rain and brings
51:16 He sends l with the rain and brings
Eze 1: 4 an immense cloud with flashing l
1:13 was bright, and l flashed out of it.
1:14 back and forth like flashes of l.
21:10 polished to flash like l!
21:15 It is made to flash like l, it is
21:28 to consume and to flash like l!
Da 10: 6 his face like l, his eyes like
Hos 6: 5 judgments flashed like l upon you.
Na 2: 4 torches; they dart about like l.
Hab 3:11 at the l of your flashing spear.
Zec 9:14 his arrow will flash like l.
Mt 24:27 For as l that comes from the east is
28: 3 His appearance was like l, and his
Lk 9:29 became as bright as a flash of l.
10:18 He replied, "I saw Satan fall like l
17:24 Man in his day will be like the l,
24: 4 gleamed like l stood beside them.
Rev 4: 5 From the throne came flashes of l,
8: 5 flashes of l and an earthquake.
11:19 And there came flashes of l,
16:18 there came flashes of l, rumblings,

Lights (Light[1])
Ge 1:14 God said, "Let there be l in the
1:15 let them be l in the expanse of the
1:16 God made two great l—the greater
Ex 30: 8 incense again when he l the lamps
Ps 97: 4 His lightning l up the world; the
136: 7 who made the great l—His love
Eze 32: 8 All the shining l in the heavens
Zec 4: 2 a bowl at the top and seven l on it,
4: 2 on it, with seven channels to the l.
Lk 8:16 "No-one l a lamp and hides it in a
11:33 "No-one l a lamp and puts it in a
17:24 which flashes and l up the sky from
Ac 16:29 The jailer called for l, rushed in
Jas 1:17 from the Father of the heavenly l,

Like-minded (Mind)
Php 2: 2 make my joy complete by being l,

Likeness
Ge 1:26 in our l, and let them rule over the
5: 1 man, he made him in the l of God.
5: 3 he had a son in his own l, in his
Ps 17:15 be satisfied with seeing your l.
Isa 52:14 and his form marred beyond human l—
Eze 1:28 of the l of the glory of the LORD.
10: 1 looked, and I saw the l of a throne
Ro 8: 3 l of sinful man to be a sin offering.
8:29 to be conformed to the l of his Son,
1Co 15:49 have borne the l of the earthly man
15:49 bear the l of the man from heaven.
2Co 3:18 are being transformed into his l
Php 2: 7 of a servant, being made in human l
Jas 3: 9 men, who have been made in God's l.

Likhi
1Ch 7:19 were: Ahian, Shechem, L and Aniam.

Lilies (Lily)
1Ki 7:19 in the shape of l, four cubits high.
7:22 on top were in the shape of l.
Ps 45: T of music. To ⌊the tune of⌋ "L".
69: T of music. To ⌊the tune of⌋ "L".
80: T tune of⌋ "The L of the Covenant".
SS 2:16 I am his; he browses among the l.
4: 5 a gazelle that browse among the l.
5:13 lips are like l dripping with myrrh.
6: 2 in the gardens and to gather l.
6: 3 is mine; he browses among the l.
7: 2 is a mound of wheat encircled by l.
Mt 6:28 See how the l of the field grow.
Lk 12:27 "Consider how the l grow. They do

Lily (Lilies)
1Ki 7:26 the rim of a cup, like a l blossom.
2Ch 4: 5 the rim of a cup, like a l blossom.
Ps 60: T the tune of⌋ "The L of the Covenant"
SS 2: 1 rose of Sharon, a l of the valleys
2: 2 Like a l among thorns is my darling
Hos 14: 5 to Israel; he will blossom like a l.

Limb (Limbs)
Jdg 19:29 l by l, into twelve parts and sent

Limbs (Limb)
Job 18:13 death's firstborn devours his l.
40:18 of bronze, his l like rods of iron.
41:12 "I will not fail to speak of his l,

Lime
Isa 33:12 peoples will be burned as if to l
Am 2: 1 he burned, as if to l, the bones of

Limit (Limits)
Ezr 7:22 of olive oil, and salt without l.
Job 15: 8 Do you l wisdom to yourself?
Ps 119:96 To all perfection I see a l; but
147: 5 his understanding has no l.
Isa 5:14 and opens its mouth without l;
Jer 5:28 Their evil deeds have no l; they do
Jn 3:34 for God gives the Spirit without l.
1Th 2:16 always heap up their sins to the l.

Limits (Limit)
Ex 19:12 Put l for the people around the
19:23 'Put l around the mountain and set
Nu 35:26 ever goes outside the l of the city
Jos 17:18 and its farthest l will be yours;
Job 11: 7 Can you probe the l of the Almighty?
14: 5 and have set l he cannot exceed.
38:10 I fixed l for it and set its doors
Ps 73: 7 conceits of their minds know no l.
2Co 10:13 will not boast beyond proper l, but
10:15 Neither do we go beyond our l by

Limp (Limping)
Pr 26: 7 Like a lame man's legs that hang l
Isa 13: 7 of this, all hands will go l, every
Jer 6:24 about them, and our hands hang l.
47: 3 children; their hands will hang l.
50:43 about them, and his hands hang l.
Eze 7:17 Every hand will go l, and every knee
21: 7 heart will melt and every hand go l;
30:25 but the arms of Pharaoh will fall l.
Zep 3:16 O Zion; do not let your hands hang l.

Limping (Limp)
Ge 32:31 and he was l because of his hip.

Line (Lined, Lines)
Ge 5: 1 is the written account of Adam's l.
19:32 our family l through our father."
19:34 our family l through our father."
Nu 26:11 l of Korah, however, did not die out
34: 7 a l from the Great Sea to Mount
34:10 For your eastern boundary, run a l
Dt 25: 9 build up his brother's family l."
25:10 man's l shall be known in Israel
Ru 4: 4 it except you, and I am next in l.
4:18 This, then, is the family l of Perez:
1Sa 2:31 not be an old man in your family l
2:32 in your family l there will never
2:36 everyone left in your family l will
4:12 the battle l and went to Shiloh,
4:16 I have just come from the battle l
17: 2 battle l to meet the Philistines.
17: 8 "Why do you come out and l up for
17:48 towards the battle l to meet him.
2Sa 11:15 front l where the fighting is
1Ki 7:15 high and twelve cubits round, by l.
7:23 It took a l of thirty cubits to
11:14 Edomite, from the royal l of Edom.
2Ki 21:13 measuring l used against Samaria
2Ch 4: 2 It took a l of thirty cubits to
13: 3 and Jeroboam drew up a battle l
Ezr 2: 6 through the l of Jeshua and Joab

Ezr 2:40 (through the l of Hodaviah) 74
Ne 7:11 through the l of Jeshua and Joab
7:43 Kadmiel through the l of Hodaviah)
Job 38: 5 stretched a measuring l across it?
Ps 89: 4 'I will establish your l for ever
89:29 I will establish his l for ever, his
89:36 that his l will continue for ever
Isa 28:17 I will make justice the measuring l
34:11 over Edom the measuring l of chaos
44:13 The carpenter measures with a l and
48: 1 Israel and come from the l of Judah,
Jer 31:39 The measuring l will stretch from
33:15 Branch sprout from David's l;
Lam 2: 8 He stretched out a measuring l and
Eze 47: 3 with a measuring l in his hand,
Da 11: 7 "One from her family l will arise to
Joel 2: 7 They all march in l, not swerving
Zec 1:16 And the measuring l will be
2: 1 man with a measuring l in his hand!
Mt 17:27 go to the lake and throw out your l.
Lk 2: 4 to the house and l of David.
Gal 2:14 were not acting in l with the truth

Lined (Line)

1Ki 6:15 He l its interior walls with cedar

Linen (Linens)

Ge 41:42 He dressed him in robes of fine l
Ex 25: 4 scarlet yarn and fine l; goat hair;
26: 1 of finely twisted l and blue,
26:31 scarlet yarn and finely twisted l,
26:36 l—the work of an embroiderer.
27: 9 have curtains of finely twisted l,
27:16 scarlet yarn and finely twisted l
27:18 with curtains of finely twisted l
28: 5 purple and scarlet yarn, and fine l.
28: 6 l—the work of a skilled craftsman.
28: 8 yarn, and with finely twisted l.
28:15 yarn, and of finely twisted l.
28:39 fine l and make the turban of fine l
28:42 "Make l undergarments as a covering
35: 6 scarlet yarn and fine l; goat hair;
35:23 purple or scarlet yarn or fine l,
35:25 purple or scarlet yarn or fine l.
35:35 purple and scarlet yarn and fine l,
36: 8 of finely twisted l and blue,
36:35 scarlet yarn and finely twisted l,
36:37 l—the work of an embroiderer;
38: 9 had curtains of finely twisted l,
38:16 courtyard were of finely twisted l.
38:18 l—the work of an embroiderer.
38:23 purple and scarlet yarn and fine l.
39: 2 yarn, and of finely twisted l.
39: 3 l—the work of a skilled craftsman.
39: 5 yarn, and with finely twisted l,
39: 8 yarn, and of finely twisted l.
39:24 l around the hem of the robe.
39:27 of fine l—the work of a weaver—
39:28 the turban of fine l, the l
39:28 undergarments of finely twisted l.
39:29 The sash was of finely twisted l
Lev 6:10 shall then put on his l clothes,
6:10 with l undergarments next to his
13:47 mildew—any woollen or l clothing,
13:48 any woven or knitted material of l
13:52 or knitted material of wool or l,
13:59 by mildew in woollen or l clothing,
16: 4 He is to put on the sacred l tunic,
16: 4 with l undergarments next to his
16: 4 he is to tie the l sash around him
16: 4 around him and put on the l turban.
16:23 take off the l garments he put on
16:32 to put on the sacred l garments
Dt 22:11 Do not wear clothes of wool and l
Jdg 14:12 I will give you thirty l garments
14:13 you must give me thirty l garments
1Sa 2:18 the LORD—a boy wearing a l ephod.
22:18 men who wore the l ephod.
2Sa 6:14 David, wearing a l ephod, danced
1Ch 4:21 of the l workers at Beth Ashbea,
15:27 was clothed in a robe of fine l,
15:27 David also wore a l ephod.
2Ch 2:14 blue and crimson yarn and fine l.
3:14 l, with cherubim worked into it.
5:12 dressed in fine l and playing
Est 1: 6 had hangings of white and blue l,
1: 6 fastened with cords of white l and
8:15 of gold and a purple robe of fine l
Pr 31:22 she is clothed in fine l and purple
31:24 She makes l garments and sells them
Isa 3:23 mirrors, and the l garments and
19: 9 weavers of fine l will lose hope.
Jer 13: 1 "Go and buy a l belt and put it
Eze 9: 2 With them was a man clothed in l who
9: 3 man clothed in l who had the
9:11 the man in l with the writing kit at
10: 2 LORD said to the man clothed in l
10: 6 the LORD commanded the man in l,
10: 7 into the hands of the man in l,
16:10 I dressed you in fine l and covered
16:13 your clothes were of fine l and
27: 7 Fine embroidered l from Egypt was
27:16 embroidered work, fine l, coral and
40: 3 in the gateway with a l cord
44:17 they are to wear l clothes; they
44:18 They are to wear l turbans on their
44:18 l undergarments round their waists.
Da 10: 5 before me was a man dressed in l,
12: 6 them said to the man clothed in l,
12: 7 The man clothed in l, who was above
Hos 2: 5 wool and my l, my oil and my drink.
2: 9 I will take back my wool and my l,
Mt 27:59 body, wrapped it in a clean l cloth,
Mk 14:51 wearing nothing but a l garment
15:46 Joseph bought some l cloth, took
15:46 wrapped it in the l, and placed it
Lk 16:19 was dressed in purple and fine l
23:53 he took it down, wrapped it in l
24:12 Bending over, he saw the strips of l
Jn 11:44 wrapped with strips of l, and a
19:40 with the spices, in strips of l.
20: 5 looked in at the strips of l lying
20: 6 He saw the strips of l lying there,
20: 7 up by itself, separate from the l.
Rev 15: 6 shining l and wore golden sashes
18:12 precious stones and pearls; fine l,
18:16 O great city, dressed in fine l,
19: 8 Fine l, bright and clean, was given
19: 8 (Fine l stands for the righteous
19:14 dressed in fine l, white and clean.

Linens (Linen)

Pr 7:16 have covered my bed with coloured l

Lines (Line)

Ge 10:32 l of descent, within their nations.
14: 8 battle l in the Valley of
1Sa 17:21 up their l facing each other.
17:22 battle l and greeted his brothers.
17:23 stepped out from his l and shouted
2Sa 10: 9 Joab saw that there were battle l in
10:17 The Arameans formed their battle l
23:16 men broke through the Philistine l,
1Ch 11:18 Three broke through the Philistine l,
19:10 Joab saw that there were battle l in
19:17 formed his battle l opposite them.
19:17 David formed his l to meet the
Ps 16: 6 The boundary l have fallen for me in

Linger (Lingering)

Jdg 5:17 And Dan, why did he l by the ships?
Pr 23:30 Those who l over wine, who go to
Jer 51:50 leave and do not l! Remember the
Mic 5: 7 not wait for man or l for mankind.
Hab 2: 3 Though it l, wait for it; it will

Lingering (Linger)

Dt 28:59 and severe and l illnesses.
2Ch 21:15 ill with a l disease of the bowels,

Linus

2Ti 4:21 L, Claudia and all the brothers.

Lion (Lion's, Lioness, Lionesses, Lions, Lions')

Ge 49: 9 Like a l he crouches and lies down,
Nu 23:24 they rouse themselves like a l that
24: 9 Like a l they crouch and lie down,
Dt 33:20 like a l, tearing at arm or head.
Jdg 14: 5 a young l came roaring towards him.
14: 6 tore the l apart with his bare hands
14:18 honey? What is stronger than a l?"
1Sa 17:34 When a l or a bear came and carried
17:36 Your servant has killed both the l
17:37 delivered me from the paw of the l
2Sa 17:10 heart is like the heart of a l,
23:20 a pit on a snowy day and killed a l.
1Ki 10:19 a l standing beside each of them.
13:24 he went on his way, a l met him on
13:24 donkey and the l standing beside it.
13:25 with the l standing beside the body,
13:26 The LORD has given him over to the l,
13:28 donkey and the l standing beside it.
13:28 The l had neither eaten the body nor
20:36 as you leave me a l will kill you.
20:36 away, a l found him and killed him.
1Ch 11:22 a pit on a snowy day and killed a l.
2Ch 9:18 a l standing beside each of them.
Job 4:11 The l perishes for lack of prey,
10:16 you stalk me like a l and again
28: 8 foot on it, and no l prowls there.
Ps 7: 2 or they will tear me like a l and
10: 9 He lies in wait like a l in cover;
17:12 They are like a l hungry for prey,
17:12 like a great l crouching in cover.
91:13 You will tread upon the l and the
91:13 trample the great l and the serpent.
Pr 19:12 king's rage is like the roar of a l
20: 2 wrath is like the roar of a l;
22:13 The sluggard says, "There is a l
26:13 is a l in the road, a fierce l
28: 1 the righteous are as bold as a l.
28:15 Like a roaring l or a charging bear
30:30 a l, mighty among beasts, who
Ecc 9: 4 dog is better off than a dead l!
Isa 5:29 Their roar is like that of the l,
11: 6 the calf and the l and the yearling
11: 7 the l will eat straw like the ox.
15: 9 a l upon the fugitives of Moab
31: 4 "As a l growls, a great l over his
35: 9 No l will be there, nor will any
38:13 but like a l he broke all my bones;
65:25 the l will eat straw like the ox,
Jer 2:30 your prophets like a ravening l.
4: 7 A l has come out of his lair;
5: 6 Therefore a l from the forest will
12: 8 become to me like a l in the forest.
25:38 Like a l he will leave his lair,
49:19 "Like a l coming up from Jordan's
50:44 Like a l coming up from Jordan's
51:38 young lions, they growl like l cubs
Lam 3:10 lying in wait, like a l in hiding
Eze 1:10 right side each had the face of a l
10:14 the third the face of a l, and the
19: 3 her cubs, and he became a strong l.
19: 5 her cubs and made him a strong l.
19: 6 lions, for he was now a strong l.
22:25 like a roaring l tearing its prey;
32: 2 'You are like a l among the nations;
41:19 face of a l towards the palm tree
Da 7: 4 "The first was like a l, and it had
Hos 5:14 For I will be like a l to Ephraim,
5:14 to Ephraim, like a great l to Judah.
11:10 the LORD; he will roar like a l.
13: 7 I will come upon them like a l, like
13: 8 Like a l I will devour them; a wild
Joel 1: 6 the teeth of a l, the fangs of a
Am 3: 4 Does a l roar in the thicket when he
3: 8 The l has roared—who will not fear?
5:19 will be as though a man fled from a l
Mic 5: 8 like a l among the beasts of the
5: 8 like a young l among flocks of sheep,
Na 2:11 where the l and lioness went, and
2:12 The l killed enough for his cubs and
1Pe 5: 8 l looking for someone to devour.
Rev 4: 7 first living creature was like a l,
5: 5 See, the L of the tribe of Judah,
10: 3 a loud shout like the roar of a l.
13: 2 a bear and a mouth like that of a l

Lion's (Lion)

Ge 49: 9 You are a l cub, O Judah; you return
Dt 33:22 About Dan he said: "Dan is a l cub,
Jdg 14: 8 aside to look at the l carcass.

Jdg 14: 9 taken the honey from the l carcass.
Am 3:12 a shepherd saves from the l mouth
2Ti 4:17 And I was delivered from the l mouth.

Lioness (Lion)

Ge 49: 9 like a l—who dares to rouse him?
Nu 23:24 The people rise like a l; they rouse
24: 9 like a l—who dares to rouse them?
Job 4:11 and the cubs of the l are scattered.
38:39 "Do you hunt the prey for the l and
Eze 19: 2 say: " 'What a l was your mother
Joel 1: 6 teeth of a lion, the fangs of a l.
Na 2:11 where the lion and l went, and the

Lionesses (Lion)

Isa 30: 6 of lions and l, of adders and

Lions (Lion)

2Sa 1:23 eagles, they were stronger than l.
1Ki 7:29 panels between the uprights were l,
7:29 Above and below the l and bulls were
7:36 He engraved cherubim, l and palm
10:20 Twelve l stood on the six steps, one
2Ki 17:25 so he sent l among them and they
17:26 He has sent l among them, which are
1Ch 12: 8 Their faces were the faces of l, and
2Ch 9:19 Twelve l stood on the six steps, one
Job 4:10 The l may roar and growl, yet the
4:10 the teeth of the great l are broken.
38:39 and satisfy the hunger of the l
Ps 22:13 Roaring l tearing their prey open
22:21 Rescue me from the mouth of the l;
34:10 The l may grow weak and hungry, but
35:17 my precious life from these l.
57: 4 I am in the midst of l; I lie among
58: 6 tear out, O LORD, the fangs of the l
104:21 The l roar for their prey and seek
Isa 5:29 they roar like young l; they growl
30: 6 of l and lionesses, of adders and
Jer 2:15 L have roared; they have growled at
50:17 flock that l have chased away.
51:38 Her people all roar like young l,
Eze 19: 2 lioness was your mother among the l!
19: 2 the young l and reared her cubs.
19: 6 He prowled among the l, for he was
Da 6:20 been able to rescue you from the l?"
6:22 and he shut the mouths of the l.
6:24 the l overpowered them and crushed
6:27 Daniel from the power of the l."
Na 2:13 the sword will devour your young l.
Zep 3: 3 Her officials are roaring l, her
Zec 11: 3 Listen to the roar of the l;
Heb 11:33 who shut the mouths of l,
Rev 9:17 the horses resembled the heads of l

Lions' (Lion)

SS 4: 8 summit of Hermon, from the l dens
Da 6: 7 shall be thrown into the l den.
6:12 would be thrown into the l den?"
6:16 Daniel and threw him into the l den
6:19 got up and hurried to the l den.
6:24 in and thrown into the l den,
Na 2:11 Where now is the l den, the place
Rev 9: 8 and their teeth were like l teeth.

Lips

Ex 6:12 since I speak with faltering l?"
6:30 Since I speak with faltering l,
13: 9 law of the LORD is to be on your l.
23:13 do not let them be heard on your l.
Nu 30: 6 makes a vow or after her l utter a
30:12 that came from her l will stand.
Dt 23:23 Whatever your l utter you must be
1Sa 1:13 and her l were moving but her voice
Job 6:30 Is there any wickedness on my l?
8:21 and your l with shouts of joy.
11: 5 that he would open his l against
12:20 He silences the l of trusted
13: 6 listen to the plea of my l.
15: 6 your own l testify against you.
16: 5 from my l would bring you relief.
23:12 departed from the commands of his l;
27: 4 my l will not speak wickedness, and
32:20 I must open my l and reply.
Job 33: 3 my l sincerely speak what I know.
Ps 8: 2 From the l of children and infants
12: 2 flattering l speak with deception.
12: 3 the LORD cut off all flattering l
12: 4 we own our l—who is our master?"
16: 4 or take up their names on my l.
17: 1 it does not rise from deceitful l.
17: 4 by the word of your l I have kept
21: 2 not withheld the request of his l.
31:18 Let their lying l be silenced, for
34: 1 his praise will always be on my l.
34:13 evil and your l from speaking lies
40: 9 not seal my l, as you know, O LORD.
45: 2 your l have been anointed with grace
50:16 laws or take my covenant on your l?
51:15 O Lord, open my l, and my mouth will
59: 7 they spew out swords from their l,
59:12 for the words of their l, let them
63: 3 than life, my l will glorify you.
63: 5 with singing l my mouth will praise
66:14 vows my l promised and my mouth
71:23 My l will shout for joy when I sing
89:34 or alter what my l have uttered.
106:33 and rash words came from Moses' l.
119:13 With my l I recount all the laws
119:171 May my l overflow with praise, for
120: 2 Save me, O LORD, from lying l and
140: 3 the poison of vipers is on their l.
140: 9 the trouble their l have caused.
141: 3 keep watch over the door of my l.
Pr 4:24 keep corrupt talk far from your l.
5: 2 and your l may preserve knowledge.
5: 3 For the l of an adulteress drip
8: 6 I open my l to speak what is right.
8: 7 is true, for my l detest wickedness.
10:13 Wisdom is found on the l of the
10:18 who conceals his hatred has lying l,
10:21 The l of the righteous nourish many,
10:32 The l of the righteous know what is
12:14 From the fruit of his l a man is
12:19 Truthful l endure for ever, but a
12:22 The LORD detests lying l, but he
13: 2 From the fruit of his l a man enjoys
13: 3 He who guards his l guards his life,
14: 3 but the l of the wise protect them.
14: 7 will not find knowledge on his l.
15: 7 The l of the wise spread knowledge;
16:10 The l of a king speak as an oracle,
16:13 Kings take pleasure in honest l;
16:23 and his l promote instruction.
16:30 who purses his l is bent on evil.
17: 4 A wicked man listens to evil l; a
17: 7 Arrogant l are unsuited to a fool
17: 7 how much worse lying l to a ruler!
18: 6 A fool's l bring him strife, and
18: 7 and his l are a snare to his soul.
18:20 harvest from his l he is satisfied.
19: 1 than a fool whose l are perverse.
20:15 l that speak knowledge are a rare
22:18 have all of them ready on your l.
23:16 when your l speak what is right.
24: 2 their l talk about making trouble.
24:26 answer is like a kiss on the l.
24:28 cause, or use your l to deceive.
26:23 are fervent l with an evil heart.
26:24 man disguises himself with his l,
27: 2 someone else, and not your own l.
Ecc 10:12 a fool is consumed by his own l.
SS 4: 3 Your l are like a scarlet ribbon;
4:11 Your l drop sweetness as the
5:13 His l are like lilies dripping with
7: 9 flowing gently over l and teeth.
Isa 6: 5 ruined! For I am a man of unclean l
6: 5 I live among a people of unclean l,
6: 7 "See, this has touched your l;
11: 4 breath of his l he will slay the
28:11 Very well then, with foreign l and
29:13 honour me with their l, but their
30:27 of smoke; his l are full of wrath,
57:19 creating praise on the l of the
59: 3 Your l have spoken lies, and your
Jer 7:28 it has vanished from their l.
12: 2 You are always on their l but far
17:16 What passes my l is open before you.
Da 4:31 The words were still on his l when
10: 3 no meat or wine touched my l; and I
Da 10:16 who looked like a man touched my l,
Hos 2:17 the names of the Baals from her l;
8: 1 Put the trumpet to your l! An eagle
14: 2 we may offer the fruit of our l.
Joel 1: 5 it has been snatched from your l.
Hab 3:16 my l quivered at the sound;
Zep 3: 9 will I purify the l of the peoples
Mal 2: 6 nothing false was found on his l.
2: 7 "For the l of a priest ought to
Mt 15: 8 people honour me with their l,
21:16 'From the l of children and infants
Mk 7: 6 people honour me with their l,
Lk 4:22 gracious words that came from his l.
22:71 We have heard it from his own l."
Jn 19:29 plant, and lifted it to Jesus' l.
Ac 15: 7 from my l the message of the gospel
Ro 3:13 "The poison of vipers is on their l.
1Co 14:21 through the l of foreigners I will
Col 3: 8 and filthy language from your l.
Heb 13:15 fruit of l that confess his name.
1Pe 3:10 and his l from deceitful speech.

Liquid

Ex 30:23 fine spices: 500 shekels of l myrrh,
Lev 11:34 and any l that could be drunk from

List (Listed, Listing)

Nu 3:40 or more and make a l of their names.
Jos 17:11 (the third in the l is Naphoth).
1Ch 11:11 this is the l of David's mighty men:
25: 1 Here is the l of the men who
27: 1 This is the l of the Israelites—
Ezr 2: 2 l of the men of the people of Israel:
Ne 7: 7 Baanah): The l of the men of Israel:
Ps 56: 8 Record my lament; l my tears on your
1Ti 5: 9 No widow may be put on the l of
5:11 widows, do not put them on such a l.

Listed (List)

Ge 25:13 l in the order of their birth:
Nu 1:18 or more were l by name, one by one,
1:20 to serve in the army were l by name,
1:22 the army were counted and l by name,
1:24 to serve in the army were l by name,
1:26 to serve in the army were l by name,
1:28 to serve in the army were l by name,
1:30 to serve in the army were l by name,
1:32 to serve in the army were l by name,
1:34 to serve in the army were l by name,
1:36 to serve in the army were l by name,
1:38 to serve in the army were l by name,
1:40 to serve in the army were l by name,
1:42 to serve in the army were l by name,
3:43 old or more, l by name, was 22,273.
11:26 They were l among the elders, but
26:54 according to the number of those l.
1Ch 4:38 The men l above by name were leaders
4:41 The men whose names were l came in
5: 1 so he could not be l in the
5: 7 l according to their genealogical
6:19 Levites l according to their fathers
7: 2 descendants of Tola l as fighting men
7: 5 as l in their genealogy, were 87,000
7: 7 record l 22,034 fighting men.
7: 9 Their genealogical record l the
7:40 as l in their genealogy, was 26,000.
8:28 chiefs as l in their genealogy, and
9: 1 All Israel was l in the genealogies
9: 9 The people from Benjamin, as l in
9:34 chiefs as l in their genealogy, and
2Ch 31:18 l in these genealogical records.
Ps 69:28 and not be l with the righteous.
Eze 13: 9 or be l in the records of the
48: 1 "These are the tribes, l by name:

Listen (Listened, Listening, Listens)

Ge 4:10 L! your brother's blood cries out to
4:23 "Adah and Zillah, l to me; wives of
21:12 L to whatever Sarah tells you,
23: 6 "Sir, l to us. You are a mighty
23: 8 then l to me and intercede with
23:11 "No, my lord," he said. "L to me;
23:13 hearing, "L to me, if you will.
23:15 "L to me, my lord; the land is worth

Ge 27: 8 Now, my son, **l** carefully and do what
37: 6 He said to them, "**L** to this dream I
37: 9 "**L**," he said, "I had another dream,
42:21 but we would not **l**; that's why this
42:22 But you wouldn't **l**! Now we must give
49: 2 Assemble and **l**, sons of Jacob; **l** to
Ex 3:18 The elders of Israel will **l** to you.
4: 1 What if they do not believe me or **l**
4: 9 believe these two signs or **l** to you
6: 9 but they did not **l** to him because of
6:12 If the Israelites will not **l** to me,
6:12 why would Pharaoh **l** to me, since I
6:30 lips, why would Pharaoh **l** to me?"
7: 4 he will not **l** to you. Then I will
7:13 **l** to them, just as the LORD had said.
7:22 he would not **l** to Moses and Aaron,
8:15 and would not **l** to Moses and Aaron,
8:19 not **l**, just as the LORD had said.
9:12 he would not **l** to Moses and Aaron,
11: 9 "Pharaoh will refuse to **l** to you—
15:26 He said, "If you **l** carefully to the
18:19 **L** now to me and I will give you some
20:19 "Speak to us yourself and we will **l**
23:21 Pay attention to him and **l** to what
23:22 If you **l** carefully to what he says
Lev 26:14 "'But if you will not **l** to me and
26:18 If after all this you will not **l**
26:21 towards me and refuse to **l** to me,
26:27 in spite of this you still do not **l**
Nu 12: 6 he said, "**L** to my words: "When a
16: 8 Moses also said to Korah, "Now **l**,
20:10 "**L**, you rebels, must we bring you
23:18 Arise, Balak, and **l**; hear me, son of
Dt 1:43 I told you, but you would not **l**.
3:26 angry with me and would not **l** to me
5:27 Go near and **l** to all that the LORD
5:27 We will **l** and obey."
13: 3 you must not **l** to the words of that
13: 8 do not yield to him or **l** to him.
18:14 The nations you will dispossess **l**
18:15 You must **l** to him.
18:19 If anyone does not **l** to my words
21:18 **l** to them when they discipline him,
23: 5 LORD your God would not **l** to Balaam
27: 9 "Be silent, O Israel, and **l**! You
30:20 **l** to his voice, and hold fast to him
31:12 in your towns—so that they can **l**
32: 1 **L**, O heavens, and I will speak;
Jos 3: 9 **l** to the words of the LORD your God.
8: 4 with these orders: "**L** carefully. You
24:10 I would not **l** to Balaam, so he
Jdg 2:17 Yet they would not **l** to their judges
5: 3 "Hear this, you kings! **L**, you rulers!
7:11 **l** to what they are saying.
9: 7 "**L** to me, citizens of Shechem,
9: 7 so that God may **l** to you.
11:17 but the king of Edom would not **l**.
19:25 the men would not **l** to him. So the
20:13 not **l** to their fellow Israelites.
Ru 2: 8 Boaz said to Ruth, "My daughter, **l**
1Sa 2:25 did not **l** to their father's rebuke
8: 7 the LORD told him: "**L** to all that
8: 9 Now **l** to them; but warn them
8:19 the people refused to **l** to Samuel.
8:22 The LORD answered, "**L** to them and
15: 1 **l** now to the message from the LORD.
22: 7 said to them, "**L**, men of Benjamin
22:12 Saul said, "**L** now, son of Ahitub."
24: 9 He said to Saul, "Why do you **l** when
26:19 Now let my lord the king **l** to his
28:22 Now please **l** to your servant and let
30:24 Who will **l** to what you say? The
2Sa 12:18 to David but he would not **l** to us.
13:14 he refused to **l** to her, and since he
13:16 But he refused to **l** to her.
13:28 Absalom ordered his men, "**L**! When
20:16 "**L**! **L**! Tell Joab to come here so
20:17 She said, "**L** to what your servant
1Ki 4:34 Men of all nations came to **l** to
8:52 and may you **l** to them whenever they
12:15 the king did not **l** to the people,
12:16 that the king refused to **l** to them,
20: 8 **l** to him or agree to his demands."
2Ki 14:11 Amaziah, however, would not **l**, so
17:14 they would not **l** and were as
17:40 They would not **l**, however, but
2Ki 18:31 "Do not **l** to Hezekiah. This is what
18:32 not death! "Do not **l** to Hezekiah
19: 7 **L**! I am going to put such a spirit
19:16 **l** to the words Sennacherib has
21: 9 the people did not **l**. Manasseh led
1Ch 28: 2 "**L** to me, my brothers and my people.
2Ch 10:15 the king did not **l** to the people,
10:16 that the king refused to **l** to them,
13: 4 "Jeroboam and all Israel, **l** to me!
15: 2 "**L** to me, Asa and all Judah and
20:15 He said: "**L**, King Jehoshaphat and
20:20 "**L** to me, Judah and people of
24:19 against them, they would not **l**.
25:20 Amaziah, however, would not **l**, for
28:11 Now **l** to me! Send back your fellow
29: 5 said, "**L** to me, Levites! Consecrate
35:22 He would not **l** to what Neco had said
Ne 9:17 They refused to **l** and failed to
9:29 stiff-necked and refused to **l**.
Job 13: 6 **l** to the plea of my lips.
13:17 **L** carefully to my words; let your
15: 8 Do you **l** in on God's council? Do you
15:17 "**L** to me and I will explain to you;
21: 2 "**L** carefully to my words; let this
27: 9 Does God **l** to his cry when distress
32:10 "Therefore I say: **L** to me; I too
33: 1 "But now, Job, **l** to my words; pay
33:31 "Pay attention, Job, and **l** to me;
33:33 if not, then **l** to me; be silent,
34: 2 **l** to me, you men of learning.
34:10 **l** to me, you men of understanding
34:16 hear this; **l** to what I say.
35:13 God does not **l** to their empty plea
35:14 How much less, then, will he **l** when
36:10 He makes them **l** to correction and
36:12 if they do not **l**, they will perish
37: 2 **L**! **L** to the roar of his voice, to
37:14 "**L** to this, Job; stop and consider
42: 4 "You said, '**L** now, and I will speak;
Ps 5: 2 **L** to my cry for help, my King and my
10:17 them, and you **l** to their cry,
17: 1 my righteous plea; **l** to my cry.
34:11 Come, my children, **l** to me; I will
39:12 "Hear my prayer, O LORD, **l** to my cry
45:10 **L**, O daughter, consider and give ear
49: 1 **l**, all who live in this world,
54: 2 O God; **l** to the words of my mouth.
55: 1 **L** to my prayer, O God, do not ignore
61: 1 Hear my cry, O God; **l** to my prayer.
66:16 Come and **l**, all you who fear God;
78: 1 **l** to the words of my mouth.
81: 8 if you would but **l** to me, O Israel!
81:11 "But my people would not **l** to me;
81:13 "If my people would but **l** to me, if
84: 8 Almighty; **l** to me, O God of Jacob.
85: 8 I will **l** to what God the LORD will
86: 6 Hear my prayer, O LORD; **l** to my cry
142: 6 **L** to my cry, for I am in desperate
143: 1 O LORD, hear my prayer, **l** to my cry
Pr 1: 5 let the wise **l** and add to their
1: 8 **L**, my son, to your father's
4: 1 **L**, my sons, to a father's
4:10 **L**, my son, accept what I say, and
4:20 what I say; **l** closely to my words.
5: 1 **l** well to my words of insight,
5: 7 Now then, my sons, **l** to me; do not
5:13 would not obey my teachers or **l** to
7:24 Now then, my sons, **l** to me; pay
8: 6 **L**, for I have worthy things to say;
8:32 "Now then, my sons, **l** to me;
8:33 **L** to my instruction and be wise;
13: 1 but a mocker does not **l** to rebuke.
19:20 **L** to advice and accept instruction,
22:17 Pay attention and **l** to the sayings
23:19 **L**, my son, and be wise, and keep
23:22 **L** to your father, who gave you life,
Ecc 5: 1 Go near to **l** rather than to offer
7: 5 than to **l** to the song of fools.
SS 2: 8 **L**! My lover! Look! Here he comes,
5: 2 I slept but my heart was awake. **L**!
Isa 1: 2 Hear, O heavens! **L**, O earth! For the
1:10 **l** to the law of our God, your people
1:15 offer many prayers, I will not **l**.
8: 9 shattered! **L**, all you distant lands.
10:30 O Daughter of Gallim! **L**, O Laishah!
13: 4 **L**, a noise on the mountains, like
Isa 13: 4 **L**, an uproar among the kingdoms,
28:12 of repose"— but they would not **l**.
28:23 **L** and hear my voice; pay attention
30: 9 to **l** to the LORD's instruction.
32: 3 the ears of those who hear will **l**.
32: 9 rise up and **l** to me; you daughters
34: 1 Come near, you nations, and **l**; pay
36:16 "Do not **l** to Hezekiah. This is what
37: 7 **L**! I am going to put a spirit in him
37:17 **l** to all the words Sennacherib has
42:23 Which of you will **l** to this or pay
44: 1 "But now **l**, O Jacob, my servant,
46: 3 "**L** to me, O house of Jacob, all you
46:12 **L** to me, you stubborn-hearted, you
47: 8 "Now then, **l**, you wanton creature,
48: 1 "**L** to this, O house of Jacob, you
48:12 "**L** to me, O Jacob, Israel, whom I
48:14 "Come together, all of you, and **l**:
48:16 "Come near me and **l** to this: "From
49: 1 **L** to me, you islands; hear this,
50: 4 my ear to **l** like one being taught.
51: 1 "**L** to me, you who pursue
51: 4 "**L** to me, my people; hear me, my
52: 8 **L**! Your watchmen lift up their
55: 2 labour on what does not satisfy? **L**,
55: 2 **l** to me, and eat what is good, and
65:12 answer, I spoke but you did not **l**.
Jer 6:10 Who will **l** to me? Their ears are
6:17 '**L** to the sound of the trumpet!'
6:17 But you said, 'We will not **l**.'
7:13 but you did not **l**; I called you,
7:16 with me, for I will not **l** to you.
7:24 they did not **l** or pay attention;
7:26 they did not **l** to me or pay
7:27 they will not **l** to you; when you
8:19 **L** to the cry of my people from a
10:22 **L**! The report is coming—a great
11: 2 "**L** to the terms of this covenant
11: 6 '**L** to the terms of this covenant
11: 8 they did not **l** or pay attention;
11:10 who refused to **l** to my words.
11:11 cry out to me, I will not **l** to them
11:14 because I will not **l** when they call
12:17 if any nation does not **l**, I will
13:10 These wicked people, who refuse to **l**
13:17 if you do not **l**, I will weep in
14:12 they fast, I will not **l** to their cry
17:23 Yet they did not **l** or pay attention
17:23 not **l** or respond to discipline.
18:19 **L** to me, O LORD; hear what my
19: 3 the God of Israel, says: **L**! I am
19:15 '**L**! I am going to bring on this city
19:15 and would not **l** to my words.
22:21 'I will not **l**!' This has been your
23:16 "Do not **l** to what the prophets are
25: 7 "But you did not **l** to me," declares
26: 3 Perhaps they will **l** and each will
26: 4 do not **l** to me and follow my law,
26: 5 if you do not **l** to the words of my
27: 9 do not **l** to your prophets, your
27:14 Do not **l** to the words of the
27:16 Do not **l** to the prophets who say,
27:17 Do not **l** to them. Serve the king of
28: 7 Nevertheless, **l** to what I have to
28:15 "**L**, Hananiah! The LORD has not sent
29: 8 Do not **l** to the dreams you encourage
29:12 and pray to me, and I will **l** to you.
32:33 not **l** or respond to discipline.
34:14 not **l** to me or pay attention to me.
35:17 **L**! I am going to bring on Judah and
35:17 I spoke to them, but they did not **l**;
36:25 the scroll, he would not **l** to them.
37:14 But Irijah would not **l** to him;
37:20 now, my lord the king, please **l**.
38:15 you counsel, you would not **l** to me.
44: 5 they did not **l** or pay attention;
44:16 "We will not **l** to the message you
48: 3 **L** to the cries from Horonaim, cries
50:28 **L** to the fugitives and refugees from
Lam 1:18 **L**, all you peoples; look upon my
Eze 2: 5 whether they **l** or fail to **l**—for
2: 7 whether they **l** or fail to **l**, for
2: 8 son of man, **l** to what I say to you
3: 7 is not willing to **l** to you because
3: 7 they are not willing to **l** to me,
3:10 "Son of man, **l** carefully and take

Eze 3:11 whether they l or fail to l."
3:27 Whoever will l let him l, and
8:18 in my ears, I will not l to them."
13:19 lying to my people, who l to lies,
20: 8 against me and would not l to me;
20:39 afterwards you will surely l to me
33:31 sit before you to l to your words
44: 5 "Son of man, look carefully, l
Da 9:19 O Lord, l! O Lord, forgive! O Lord,
Hos 5: 1 you Israelites! L, O royal house!
Joel 1: 2 l, all who live in the land.
Am 5:23 not l to the music of your harps.
Mic 1: 2 O peoples, all of you, l, O earth
3: 1 I said, "L, you leaders of Jacob,
6: 1 L to what the LORD says: "Stand up,
6: 2 l, you everlasting foundation of
6: 9 L! The LORD is calling to the city—
Hab 1: 2 but you do not l? Or cry out to
Zep 1:14 L! The cry on the day of the LORD
Zec 1: 4 But they would not l or pay
3: 8 "'L, O high priest Joshua and your
7:12 would not l to the law or to the
7:13 "'When I called, they did not l; so
7:13 not l,' says the LORD Almighty.
11: 3 L to the wail of the shepherds:
11: 3 L to the roar of the lions;
Mal 2: 2 If you do not l, and if you do not
Mt 10:14 If anyone will not welcome you or l
12:42 the earth to l to Solomon's wisdom,
13:18 "L then to what the parable of the
15:10 to him and said, "L and understand.
17: 5 him I am well pleased. L to him!"
18:16 if he will not l, take one or two
18:17 If he refuses to l to them, tell it
18:17 he refuses to l even to the church,
21:33 "L to another parable: There was a
Mk 4: 3 "L! A farmer went out to sow his
6:11 will not welcome you or l to you,
6:20 puzzled; yet he liked to l to him.
7:14 "L to me, everyone, and understand
9: 7 my Son, whom I love. L to him!"
15:35 they said, "L, he's calling Elijah.
Lk 8:18 consider carefully how you l.
9:35 Son, whom I have chosen; l to him."
9:44 "L carefully to what I am about to
11:31 the earth to l to Solomon's wisdom,
16:29 the Prophets; let them l to them.'
16:31 "He said to him, 'If they do not l
18: 6 Lord said, "L to what the unjust
Jn 9:27 told you already and you did not l.
9:31 We know that God does not l to
10: 3 him, and the sheep l to his voice.
10: 8 but the sheep did not l to them.
10:16 They too will l to my voice, and
10:20 and raving mad. Why l to him?"
10:27 My sheep l to my voice; I know them
Ac 2:14 to you; l carefully to what I say.
2:22 "Men of Israel, l to this: Jesus of
3:22 must l to everything he tells you.
3:23 Anyone who does not l to him will be
7: 2 "Brothers and fathers, l to me! The
10:33 here in the presence of God to l to
13:16 Gentiles who worship God, l to me!
15:13 James spoke up: "Brothers, l to me.
18:14 be reasonable for me to l to you.
22: 1 and fathers, l now to my defence."
26: 3 I beg you to l to me patiently.
28:28 to the Gentiles, and they will l!"
1Co 14:21 will not l to me," says the Lord.
15:51 L, I tell you a mystery: We will not
2Co 13:11 Aim for perfection, l to my appeal,
Eph 4:29 that it may benefit those who l.
2Ti 2:14 value, and only ruins those who l.
Jas 1:19 this: Everyone should be quick to l,
1:22 Do not merely l to the word, and so
2: 5 L, my dear brothers: Has not God
4:13 Now l, you who say, "Today or
5: 1 Now l, you rich people, weep and
1Jn 4: 6 is not from God does not l to us.

Listened (Listen)

Ge 3:17 he said, "Because you l to your wife
30: 6 has l to my plea and given me a son.
30:17 God l to Leah, and she became
30:22 God remembered Rachel; he l to her
Ex 7:16 But until now you have not l.
18:24 Moses l to his father-in-law and did
Nu 21: 3 The LORD l to Israel's plea and gave
Dt 9:19 But again the LORD l to me.
10:10 the LORD l to me at this time also.
34: 9 So the Israelites l to him and did
Jos 10:14 a day when the LORD l to a man.
Jdg 2:20 forefathers and has not l to me,
6:10 But you have not l to me."
1Sa 12: 1 Samuel said to all Israel, "I have l
19: 6 Saul l to Jonathan and took this
28:23 in urging him, and he l to them.
2Ki 13: 4 and the LORD l to him, for he saw
18:12 They neither l to the commands nor
2Ch 24:17 to the king, and he l to them.
25:16 this and have not l to my counsel."
33:13 by his entreaty and l to his plea;
Ne 8: 3 l attentively to the Book of the Law
8: 9 as they l to the words of the Law.
Job 29:21 "Men l to me expectantly, waiting in
32:11 you spoke, I l to your reasoning;
Ps 22:24 him but has l to his cry for help.
66:18 my heart, the Lord would not have l
66:19 God has surely l and heard my voice
Isa 66: 4 answered, when I spoke, no-one l.
Jer 6:19 because they have not l to my words
8: 6 I have l attentively, but they do
13:11 But they have not l.'
23:18 Who has l and heard his word?
25: 3 again and again, but you have not l.
25: 4 have not l or paid any attention.
25: 8 you have not l to my words
26: 5 and again (though you have not l),
29:19 For they have not l to my words,"
29:19 And you exiles have not l either,"
35:15 have not paid attention or l to me.
36:31 them, because they have not l.
Eze 3: 6 to them, they would have l to you.
9: 5 I l, he said to the others, "Follow
Da 9: 6 We have not l to your servants the
10: 9 him speaking, and as I l to him,
Jnh 2: 2 for help, and you l to my cry.
Mal 3:16 other, and the LORD l and heard.
Mk 12:37 large crowd l to him with delight.
Ac 14: 9 He l to Paul as he was speaking.
15:12 became silent as they l to Barnabas
22:22 The crowd l to Paul until he said
24:24 He sent for Paul and l to him as he

Listening (Listen)

Ge 18:10 Now Sarah was l at the entrance to
27: 5 Now Rebekah was l as Isaac spoke to
1Sa 3: 9 'Speak, LORD, for your servant is l.
3:10 said, "Speak, for your servant is l.
2Sa 20:17 "I'm l," he said.
Pr 18:13 He who answers before l—that is
19:27 Stop l to instruction, my son, and
25:12 is a wise man's rebuke to a l ear.
Lk 2:46 l to them and asking them questions.
5: 1 round him and l to the word of God,
10:39 the Lord's feet l to what he said.
19:11 While they were l to this, he went
20:45 While all the people were l, Jesus
Ac 16:14 One of those l was a woman named
16:25 the other prisoners were l to them.
17:21 about and l to the latest ideas.)
26:29 l to me today may become what I am,
27:11 the centurion, instead of l to what

Listens (Listen)

Pr 1:33 whoever l to me will live in safety
8:34 Blessed is the man who l to me,
12:15 to him, but a wise man l to advice.
15:31 He who l to a life-giving rebuke
17: 4 A wicked man l to evil lips; a liar
21:28 l to him will be destroyed for ever.
29:12 If a ruler l to lies, all his
Mt 18:15 If he l to you, you have won your
Lk 10:16 "He who l to you l to me; he who
Jn 3:29 the bridegroom waits and l for him,
6:45 Everyone who l to the Father and
9:31 He l to the godly man who does his
18:37 on the side of truth l to me."
Jas 1:23 Anyone who l to the word but does
1Jn 4: 5 the world, and the world l to them.
4: 6 and whoever knows God l to us;

Listing (List)

Nu 1: 2 l every man by name, one by one.

Lit (Light[1])

Jdg 15: 5 l the torches and let the foxes
Ps 77:18 your lightning l up the world;

Literature

Da 1: 4 language and l of the Babylonians.
1:17 of all kinds of l and learning.

Little faith

Mt 6:30; 8:26; 14:31; 16:8; 17:20; Lk 12:28

Live[1] (*Live by faith, Live in the land,* Lived, Lives, Living, Outlived)

Ge 3:22 of life and eat, and l for ever."
4:20 who l in tents and raise livestock.
9:27 may Japheth l in the tents of Shem,
12:10 and Abram went down to Egypt to l
12:12 will kill me but will let you l.
13:18 went to l near the great trees of
16:12 he will l in hostility towards all
17:18 Ishmael might l under your blessing!"
20: 7 he will pray for you and you will l.
20:15 is before you; l wherever you like."
24:37 the Canaanites, in whose land I l,
26: 2 in the land where I tell you to l.
27:40 You will l by the sword and you will
28: 4 land where you now l as an alien,
31:32 who has your gods, he shall not l.
34:10 L in it, trade in it, and acquire
34:21 "Let them l in our land and trade in
34:22 the men will consent to l with us as
38:11 "L as a widow in your father's house
38:11 went to l in her father's house.
42: 2 us, so that we may l and not die."
42:18 this and you will l, for I fear God
43: 8 and our children may l and not die.
45:10 You shall l in the region of Goshen
47: 4 "We have come to l here awhile,
47: 6 Let them l in Goshen. And if you
47:19 Give us seed so that we may l and
49:13 "Zebulun will l by the seashore and
Ex 1:16 but if it is a girl, let her l."
1:17 them to do; they let the boys l.
1:18 Why have you let the boys l?"
1:22 the Nile, but let every girl l."
2:15 Pharaoh and went to l in Midian,
8:22 land of Goshen, where my people l
12:20 Wherever you l, you must eat
18:20 l and the duties they are to perform
19:13 he shall not be permitted to l.
20:12 so that you may l long in the land
22:18 "Do not allow a sorceress to l.
23:33 Do not let them l in your land,
33:20 for no-one may see me and l."
34:10 The people you l among will see how
Lev 3:17 wherever you l: You must not eat any
7:26 wherever you l, you must not eat the
11: 2 'Of all the animals that l on land,
13:46 l alone; he must l outside the camp.
18: 3 where you used to l, and you must
18: 5 man who obeys them will l by them.
20:22 to l may not vomit you out.
20:23 You must not l according to the
22:13 and she returns to l in her father's
23: 3 wherever you l, it is a Sabbath
23:14 generations to come, wherever you l.
23:17 From wherever you l, bring two
23:21 generations to come, wherever you l.
23:31 generations to come, wherever you l.
23:42 L in booths for seven days: All
23:42 Israelites are to l in booths
23:43 I made the Israelites l in booths
25: 6 temporary resident who l among you,
25:18 and you will l safely in the land.
25:19 eat your fill and l there in safety.
25:35 that he can continue to l among you.
25:36 may continue to l among you.
26: 5 want and l in safety in your land.

Lev 26:32 who l there will be appalled.
Nu 4:19 that they may l and not die when
13:18 who l there are strong or weak,
13:19 What kind of land do they l in? Is
13:19 What kind of towns do they l in?
13:28 the people who l there are powerful,
13:29 The Amalekites l in the Negev; the
13:29 Jebusites and Amorites l in the hill
13:29 l near the sea and along the Jordan.
14:21 Nevertheless, as surely as I l and
14:28 tell them, 'As surely as I l,
21: 8 who is bitten can look at it and l."
23: 9 I see people who l apart and do not
24:23 "Ah, who can l when God does this?
31:15 Have you allowed all the women to l?
32:17 children will l in fortified cities,
33:55 in the land where you will l.
35: 2 to give the Levites towns to l in
35: 3 they will have towns to l in and
35:29 generations to come, wherever you l.
35:32 him to go back and l on his own land
35:34 Do not defile the land where you l
Dt 2: 4 descendants of Esau, who l in Seir.
2: 8 descendants of Esau, who l in Seir.
2:10 (The Emites used to l there—a
2:12 Horites used to l in Seir, but the
2:20 who used to l there; but the
2:29 descendants of Esau, who l in Seir
2:29 and the Moabites, who l in Ar, did
4: 1 Follow them so that you may l and
4: 9 from your heart as long as you l.
4:26 You will not l there long but will
4:40 that you may l long in the land the
5:16 so that you may l long and that it
5:24 can l even if God speaks with him.
5:33 so that you may l and prosper and
6: 2 as you l by keeping all his decrees
8: 1 so that you may l and increase and
8: 3 to teach you that man does not l on
11: 9 that you may l long in the land that
12:10 you so that you will l in safety.
12:19 as long as you l in your land.
13:12 LORD your God is giving you to l
13:15 to the sword all who l in that town.
14:29 and the widows who l in your towns
16:14 and the widows who l in your towns.
16:20 so that you may l and possess the
18: 1 They shall l on the offerings made
22: 2 If the brother does not l near you
23: 6 with them as long as you l.
23:16 Let him l among you wherever he
25:15 so that you may l long in the land
28:30 a house, but you will not l in it.
28:66 You will l in constant suspense,
30: 6 heart and with all your soul, and l.
30:16 decrees and laws; then you will l
30:18 You will not l long in the land you
30:19 so that you and your children may l
32:40 declare: As surely as I l for ever,
32:47 By them you will l long in the land
33: 6 "Let Reuben l and not die, nor his
33:28 Israel will l in safety alone;
Jos 2: 9 so that all who l in this country
9: 7 Hivites, "But perhaps you l near us.
9:15 of peace with them to let them l,
9:20 will do to them: We will let them l,
9:21 They continued, "Let them l, but let
9:22 'We l a long way from you,' while
9:22 you,' while actually you l near us?
13:13 l among the Israelites to this day.
14: 4 of the land but only towns to l in,
15:63 l there with the people of Judah.
16:10 to this day the Canaanites l among
17:12 were determined to l in that region.
17:16 and all the Canaanites who l in the
20: 4 and give him a place to l with them.
21: 2 Moses that you give us towns to l in,
24:13 and you l in them and eat from
Jdg 1:16 to l among the people of the Desert
1:21 l there with the Benjamites.
1:27 were determined to l in that land.
1:29 continued to l there among them.
6:10 the Amorites, in whose land you l.
8:29 son of Joash went back home to l.
11: 8 our head over all who l in Gilead."
17:10 Micah said to him, "L with me and be
Jdg 17:11 the Levite agreed to l with him, and
19:18 hill country of Ephraim where I l.
Ru 1: 1 l for a while in the country of Moab.
2:11 to l with a people you did not know
1Sa 1:22 LORD, and he will l there always."
1:26 said to him, "As surely as you l,
10:24 people shouted, "Long l the king
17:55 as you l, O king, I don't know."
20: 3 as the LORD lives and as you l,
20:14 as long as I l, so that I may not
25:26 as the LORD lives and as you l,
25:28 be found in you as long as you l.
27: 5 country towns, that I may l there.
27: 5 l in the royal city with you?"
2Sa 8: 2 the third length was allowed to l.
11:11 As surely as you l, I will not do
12:22 gracious to me and let the child l.'
14:19 "As surely as you l, my lord the
16:16 "Long l the king! Long l the king!
19:34 "How many more years shall I l,
1Ki 1:25 and saying, 'Long l King Adonijah!'
1:31 "May my lord King David l for ever!
1:34 and shout, 'Long l King Solomon!'
1:39 shouted, "Long l King Solomon!
2: 4 If your descendants watch how they l
2:36 l there, but do not go anywhere else
3:17 woman and I l in the same house.
6:13 I will l among the Israelites and
7: 8 the palace in which he was to l,
8:36 Teach them the right way to l, and
8:61 to l by his decrees and obey his
20:32 Ben-Hadad says: 'Please let me l.
2Ki 2: 2 and as you l, I will not leave you.
2: 4 and as you l, I will not leave you.
2: 6 and as you l, I will not leave you.
4: 7 your sons can l on what is left."
4:30 and as you l, I will not leave you.
6: 2 us build a place there for us to l.
7: 4 If they spare us, we l; if they kill
10:19 who fails to come will no longer l.
11:12 and shouted, "Long l the king!
17:27 from Samaria go back to l there
17:28 from Samaria came to l in Bethel
2Ch 2: 3 him cedar to build a palace to l in.
6:27 Teach them the right way to l, and
8:11 "My wife must not l in the palace of
19:10 countrymen who l in the cities—
20:15 Jehoshaphat and all who l in Judah
23:11 and shouted, "Long l the king!
34:28 this place and on those who l here.
Ne 2: 3 the king, "May the king l for ever!
8:14 the Israelites were to l in booths
9:29 which a man will l if he obeys them.
11: 1 out of every ten to l in Jerusalem,
11: 2 who volunteered to l in Jerusalem.
Job 4:19 how much more those who l in houses
7:16 I despise my life; I would not l for
14:14 If a man dies, will he l again? All
21: 7 Why do the wicked l on, growing old
26: 5 the waters and all that l in them.
27: 6 will not reproach me as long as I l.
30: 6 They were forced to l in the dry
33:28 and I shall l to enjoy the light.'
Ps 15: 1 Who may l on your holy hill?
22:26 may your hearts l for ever!
24: 1 it, the world, and all who l in it;
26: 8 I love the house where you l, O LORD
33:14 he watches all who l on earth—
35:20 those who l quietly in the land.
49: 1 listen, all who l in this world,
49: 9 that he should l on for ever and not
55:23 men will not l out half their days.
63: 4 I will praise you as long as I l,
65: 4 and bring near to l in your courts!
68: 6 rebellious l in a sun-scorched land.
69:32 you who seek God, may your hearts l!
72:15 Long may he l! May gold from Sheba
78:10 and refused to l by his law.
89:48 What man can l and not see death,
98: 7 it, the world, and all who l in it.
102:28 The children of your servants will l
104:33 praise to my God as long as I l.
107:36 there he brought the hungry to l,
116: 2 I will call on him as long as I l.
118:17 I will not die but l, and will
119:17 good to your servant, and I will l
Ps 119:77 compassion come to me that I may l
119:116 and I shall l; do not let my hopes
119:144 give me understanding that I may l.
119:175 Let me l that I may praise you, and
120: 5 that I l among the tents of Kedar!
128: 6 may you l to see your children's
133: 1 when brothers l together in unity!
140:13 and the upright will l before you.
146: 2 praise to my God as long as I l.
Pr 1:33 listens to me will l in safety
4: 4 keep my commands and you will l.
7: 2 Keep my commands and you will l;
9: 6 your simple ways and you will l;
15:27 but he who hates bribes will l.
16: 7 his enemies l at peace with him.
19:10 is not fitting for a fool to l in
21: 9 Better to l on a corner of the roof
21:19 Better to l in a desert than with a
25:24 Better to l on a corner of the roof
Ecc 3:12 be happy and do good while they l.
6: 3 a hundred children and l many years;
9: 3 in their hearts while they l,
11: 8 However many years a man may l, let
Isa 5: 8 is left and you l alone in the land.
6: 5 I l among a people of unclean lips
10:24 "O my people who l in Zion, do not
11: 6 The wolf will l with the lamb, the
18: 3 you who l on the earth, when a
20: 6 In that day the people who l on this
21:14 for the thirsty; you who l in Tema,
22:21 He will be a father to those who l
23:18 Her profits will go to those who l
26:14 They are now dead, they l no more;
26:19 your dead will l; their bodies will
30:19 O people of Zion, who l in Jerusalem,
32:16 l in the fertile field.
32:18 will l in peaceful dwelling-places
38:16 Lord, by such things men l; and my
38:16 restored me to health and let me l.
40:22 them out like a tent to l in.
42:10 you islands, and all who l in them.
49:18 As surely as I l," declares the LORD,
49:20 give us more space to l in.'
51:13 that you l in constant terror every
52: 4 went down to Egypt to l; lately,
55: 3 hear me, that your soul may l.
57:15 "I l in a high and holy place, but
65: 9 them, and there will my servants l.
65:20 old man who does not l out his years
65:22 build houses and others l in them
Jer 6: 8 so that no-one can l in it."
7: 3 and I will let you l in this place.
7: 7 I will let you l in this place, in
8:16 it, the city and all who l there."
9: 6 You l in the midst of deception;
9:11 Judah so that no-one can l there."
9:26 l in the desert in distant places.
10:17 the land, you who l under siege.
10:18 hurl out those who l in this land;
11: 2 and to those who l in Jerusalem.
11: 9 Judah and those who l in Jerusalem.
12: 1 Why do all the faithless l at ease?
12: 4 those who l in it are wicked,
13:13 drunkenness all who l in this land,
19:12 to those who l here, declares the
20: 6 you, Pashhur, and all who l in your
21: 6 I will strike down those who l in
21: 9 will l; he will escape with his life
21:13 you who l above this valley on
22:23 You who l in 'Lebanon', who are
22:24 "As surely as I l," declares the
23: 6 saved and Israel will l in safety.
23: 8 they will l in their own land."
23:14 They commit adultery and l a lie.
24: 8 remain in this land or l in Egypt.
25:24 foreign people who l in the desert;
25:29 a sword upon all who l on the earth,
25:30 against all who l on the earth.
26:15 this city and on those who l in it,
27:11 and to l there, declares the LORD.
27:12 him and his people, and you will l.
27:17 the king of Babylon, and you will l.
31:24 People will l together in Judah and
32:37 this place and let them l in safety.
33:16 and Jerusalem will l in safety.
34:22 Judah so that no-one can l there."

Jer 35: 7 things, but must always l in tents.
35: 7 Then you will l a long time in the
35: 9 or built houses to l in or had
38: 2 goes over to the Babylonians will l.
38: 2 escape with his life; he will l.'
38:17 you and your family will l.
40: 5 and l with him among the people, or
40:10 l in the towns you have taken over."
42:14 say, 'No, we will go and l in Egypt
44: 8 where you have come to l? You will
44:13 I will punish those who l in Egypt
44:14 who have gone to l in Egypt will
44:14 to which they long to return and l;
44:28 who came to l in Egypt will know
46:18 "As surely as I l," declares the
46:19 you who l in Egypt, for Memphis will
47: 2 the towns and those who l in them.
48: 9 desolate, with no-one to l in them.
48:17 Mourn for her, all who l around her,
48:19 road and watch, you who l in Aroer.
48:28 among the rocks, you who l in Moab.
49: 1 Why do his people l in its towns?
49: 8 in deep caves, you who l in Dedan
49:16 you who l in the clefts of the rocks
49:18 no-one will l there; no man will
49:20 against those who l in Teman:
49:30 who l in Hazor," declares the LORD.
49:31 gates nor bars; its people l alone.
49:33 No-one will l there; no man will
50: 3 No-one will l in it; both men and
50:21 Merathaim and those who l in Pekod.
50:34 unrest to those who l in Babylon.
50:35 "against those who l in Babylon and
50:39 creatures and hyenas will l there,
50:40 no-one will l there; no man will
51:13 You who l by many waters and are
51:24 all who l in Babylonia for all the
51:29 Babylon so that no-one will l there.
51:35 "May our blood be on those who l in
51:62 neither man nor animal will l in it;
Lam 4:20 shadow we would l among the nations.
Eze 2: 6 around you and you l among scorpions
3:21 he will surely l because he took
5:11 Therefore as surely as I l, declares
6: 6 Wherever you l, the towns will be
6:14 desert to Diblah—wherever they l.
7:13 has sold as long as both of them l,
12:19 of the violence of all who l there.
13:19 have spared those who should not l.
14:16 as surely as I l, declares the
14:18 as surely as I l, declares the
14:20 as surely as I l, declares the
16: 6 in your blood I said to you, "L!
16:48 As surely as I l, declares the
17:16 "'As surely as I l, declares the
17:19 LORD says: As surely as I l,
18: 3 "As surely as I l, declares the
18: 9 he will surely l, declares the
18:13 Will such a man l? He will not!
18:17 his father's sin; he will surely l
18:19 all my decrees, he will surely l.
18:21 he will surely l; he will not die.
18:22 things he has done, he will l.
18:23 they turn from their ways and l?
18:24 will he l? None of the righteous
18:28 he will surely l; he will not die.
18:32 Repent and l!
20: 3 to enquire of me? As surely as I l,
20:11 man who obeys them will l by them.
20:13 man who obeys them will l by them
20:21 man who obeys them will l by them
20:25 good and laws they could not l by;
20:31 O house of Israel? As surely as I l,
20:33 surely as I l, declares the
27:35 All who l in the coastlands are
28:25 Then they will l in their own land,
28:26 They will l there in safety and will
28:26 they will l in safety when I inflict
29: 6 all who l in Egypt will know that I
29:11 no-one will l there for forty years.
32:15 when I strike down all who l there,
33:10 How then can we l?" '
33:11 Say to them, 'As surely as I l,
33:11 they turn from their ways and l.
33:12 will not be allowed to l because of
33:13 righteous man that he will surely l,
Eze 33:15 he will surely l; he will not die.
33:16 is just and right; he will surely l.
33:19 and right, he will l by doing so.
33:27 LORD says: As surely as I l,
34: 8 surely as I l, declares the
34:25 so that they may l in the desert
34:28 They will l in safety, and no-one
35: 6 therefore as surely as I l, declares
35:11 therefore as surely as I l, declares
37: 3 "Son of man, can these bones l?"
37: 9 into these slain, that they may l.
37:14 put my Spirit in you and you will l,
37:25 children will l here for ever,
38: 8 and now all of them l in safety.
39: 6 who l in safety in the coastlands,
39: 9 Then those who l in the towns of
43: 7 This is where I will l among the
43: 9 and I will l among them for ever.
44: 9 who l among the Israelites.
45: 5 their possession for towns to l in.
47: 9 Swarms of living creatures will l
47: 9 the river flows everything will l.
Da 2: 4 "O king, l for ever! Tell your
2:11 gods, and they do not l among men."
2:38 Wherever they l, he has made you
3: 9 "O king, l for ever!
4: 1 who l in all the world: May you
4:15 and let him l with the animals among
4:23 let him l like the wild animals,
4:25 and will l with the wild animals;
4:32 and will l with the wild animals;
5:10 "O king, l for ever!" she said.
6: 6 "O King Darius, l for ever!
6:21 Daniel answered, "O king, l for ever!
7:12 allowed to l for a period of time.)
Hos 3: 3 I told her, "You are to l with me
3: 3 any man, and I will l with you."
3: 4 Israelites will l for many days
4: 3 and all who l in it waste away;
6: 2 us, that we may l in his presence.
10: 5 The people who l in Samaria fear for
12: 9 I will make you l in tents again,
Am 5: 4 the house of Israel: "Seek me and l
5: 6 Seek the LORD and l, or he will
5:11 you will not l in them; though you
5:14 Seek good, not evil, that you may l.
8: 8 and all who l in it mourn? The whole
9: 5 and all who l in it mourn—the whole
9:14 the ruined cities and l in them.
Ob : 3 you who l in the clefts of the rocks
Jnh 4: 3 is better for me to die than to l."
4: 8 be better for me to die than to l."
Mic 1:11 and shame, you who l in Shaphir.
1:11 Those who l in Zaanan will not come
1:12 Those who l in Maroth writhe in pain
1:13 You who l in Lachish, harness the
1:15 against you who l in Mareshah.
5: 4 And they will l securely, for then
Na 1: 5 the world and all who l in it.
Hab 2: 4 the righteous will l by his faith—
Zep 1: 4 and against all who l in Jerusalem.
1:11 Wail, you who l in the market
1:13 will build houses but not l in them
1:18 end of all who l in the earth."
2: 5 Woe to you who l by the sea,
2: 9 Therefore, as surely as I l,"
Zec 1: 5 the prophets, do they l for ever?
2: 7 "Come, O Zion! Escape, you who l in
2:10 I am coming, and I will l among you
2:11 I will l among you and you will know
8: 8 I will bring them back to l in
12: 8 shield those who l in Jerusalem,
Mt 4: 4 'Man does not l on bread alone, but
9:18 your hand on her, and she will l."
12:45 itself, and they go in and l there.
Mk 5:23 so that she will be healed and l."
7: 5 "Why don't your disciples l
12:44 in everything—all she had to l on.
Lk 4: 4 'Man does not l on bread alone.'"
10:28 "Do this and you will l."
11:26 itself, and they go in and l there.
21: 4 poverty put in all she had to l on."
21:35 it will come upon all those who l
Jn 4:50 "You may go. Your son will l."
4:53 had said to him, "Your son will l.
5:25 Son of God and those who hear will l
Jn 5:29 who have done good will rise to l,
6:51 of this bread, he will l for ever.
6:57 me and I l because of the Father,
6:57 feeds on me will l because of me.
6:58 on this bread will l for ever."
7:35 people l scattered among the Greeks,
11:25 in me will l, even though he dies;
14:19 Because I l, you also will l.
Ac 2:14 Fellow Jews and all of you who l in
2:26 my body also will l in hope,
7:48 the Most High does not l in houses
17:24 not l in temples built by hands.
17:26 exact places where they should l.
17:28 'For in him we l and move and have
21:21 the Jews who l among the Gentiles
21:21 or l according to our customs.
22:22 earth of him! He's not fit to l!"
25:24 that he ought not to l any longer.
28: 4 Justice has not allowed him to l."
28:16 Paul was allowed to l by himself,
Ro 4:14 For if those who l by law are heirs,
6: 2 sin; how can we l in it any longer?
6: 4 the Father, we too may l a new life.
6: 8 that we will also l with him.
8: 4 who do not l according to the sinful
8: 5 Those who l according to the sinful
8: 5 but those who l in accordance with
8:12 sinful nature, to l according to it.
8:13 For if you l according to the sinful
8:13 misdeeds of the body, you will l,
10: 5 does these things will l by them."
12:16 L in harmony with one another. Do
12:18 on you, l at peace with everyone.
14: 8 If we l, we l to the Lord; and if we
14: 8 we l or die, we belong to the Lord.
14:11 is written: "'As surely as I l,'
1Co 7:12 l with him, he must not divorce her.
7:13 l with her, she must not divorce him
7:15 God has called us to l in peace.
7:29 wives should l as if they had none;
7:35 but that you may l in a right way in
8: 6 through whom we l; and there is but
8: 6 things came and through whom we l.
2Co 5: 1 earthly tent we l in is destroyed,
5:15 that those who l should no longer l
6: 9 we l on; beaten, and yet not killed;
6:16 As God has said: "I will l with them
7: 3 that we would l or die with you.
10: 2 we l by the standards of this world.
10: 3 For though we l in the world, we do
13: 4 we will l with him to serve you.
13:11 appeal, be of one mind, l in peace.
Gal 2:14 l like a Gentile and not like a Jew.
2:19 the law so that I might l for God.
2:20 I no longer l, but Christ lives in
2:20 The life I l in the body, I live by
3:12 does these things will l by them."
5:16 I say, l by the Spirit, and you will
5:21 those who l like this will not
5:25 Since we l by the Spirit, let us
Eph 2: 2 in which you used to l when you
4: 1 then, I urge you to l a life worthy
4:17 that you must no longer l as the
5: 2 l a life of love, just as Christ
5: 8 L as children of light
5:15 Be very careful, then, how you l
Php 1:21 For to me, to l is Christ and to die
3:16 Only let us l up to what we have
3:17 and take note of those who l
3:18 l as enemies of the cross of Christ.
Col 1:10 we pray this in order that you may l
2: 6 Jesus as Lord, continue to l in him,
1Th 2:12 comforting and urging you to l lives
3: 8 For now we really l, since you are
4: 1 we instructed you how to l in order
4: 7 to be impure, but to l a holy life.
5:10 asleep, we may l together with him.
5:13 L in peace with each other.
2Th 3: 6 does not l according to the teaching
1Ti 2: 2 that we may l peaceful and quiet
2Ti 2:11 with him, we will also l with him;
3:12 who wants to l a godly life in
Tit 2: 3 to be reverent in the way they l,
2:12 and to l self-controlled, upright
3:14 and not l unproductive lives.
Heb 12: 9 the Father of our spirits and l!

Heb 12:14 Make every effort to l in peace with
13:18 desire to l honourably in every way.
Jas 4: 5 caused to l in us envies intensely?
4:15 we will l and do this or that."
1Pe 1:17 l your lives as strangers here in
2:12 L such good lives among the pagans
2:16 L as free men, but do not use your
2:16 for evil; l as servants of God.
2:24 die to sins and l for righteousness
3: 7 as you l with your wives,
3: 8 Finally, all of you, l in harmony
4: 2 not l the rest of his earthly life
4: 6 but l according to God in regard to
2Pe 1:13 as I l in the tent of this body,
2:18 escaping from those who l in error.
3:11 You ought to l holy and godly
1Jn 1: 6 we lie and do not l by the truth.
2: 6 Whoever claims to l in him must walk
3:24 Those who obey his commands l in him,
4: 9 world that we might l through him.
4:13 know that we l in him and he in us
Rev 2:13 I know where you l—where Satan has
3:10 to test those who l on the earth.
11:10 had tormented those who l on earth.
13: 6 and those who l in heaven.
14: 6 who l on the earth—to every nation,
21: 3 with men, and he will l with them.

Live[2]

Ex 21:35 they are to sell the l one and
Lev 14: 4 shall order that two l clean birds
14: 6 He is then to take the l bird and
14: 7 release the l bird in the open fields
14:51 the scarlet yarn and the l bird,
14:52 the fresh water, the l bird, the
14:53 he is to release the l bird in the
16:20 he shall bring forward the l goat.
16:21 hands on the head of the l goat
Ecc 9: 4 l dog is better off than a dead lion
Isa 6: 6 to me with a l coal in his hand,

Live by faith

Ro 1:17 is written: "The righteous will l.
2Co 5: 7 We l, not by sight.
Gal 2:20 in the body, I l in the Son of God,
3:11 law, because, "The righteous will l.
Heb 10:38 my righteous one will l. And if he

Live in the land

Ge 26: 2 l where I tell you to live.
Ex 23:31 hand over to you the people who l
34:12 those who l where you are going,
34:15 to make a treaty with those who l;
Dt 4:10 to revere me as long as they l
12: 1 you to possess—as long as you l.
31:13 as long as you l you are crossing
1Ki 8:40 time they l you gave our fathers.
2Ch 6:31 they l that you gave our fathers.
Pr 2:21 For the upright will l, and the
Jer 1:14 will be poured out on all who l.
6:12 those who l," declares the LORD.
35:15 Then you shall l I have given to you
43: 5 who had come back to l of Judah from
Lam 4:21 O Daughter of Edom, you who l of Uz.
Eze 36:28 You will l I gave your forefathers;
37:25 They will l I gave to my servant
Hos 4: 1 against you who l: "There is no
Joel 1: 2 you elders; listen, all who l.
1:14 Summon the elders and all who l to
2: 1 Let all who l tremble, for the day

Lived (Live)

Ge 4:16 l in the land of Nod, east of Eden.
5: 3 Adam had l 130 years, he had a son
5: 4 Seth was born, Adam l 800 years
5: 5 Altogether, Adam l 930 years, and
5: 6 Seth had l 105 years, he became the
5: 7 Seth l 807 years and had other sons
5: 8 Altogether, Seth l 912 years, and
5: 9 Enosh had l 90 years, he became the
5:10 Enosh l 815 years and had other sons
5:11 Altogether, Enosh l 905 years, and
5:12 Kenan had l 70 years, he became the
5:13 Kenan l 840 years and had other sons
Ge 5:14 Altogether, Kenan l 910 years, and
5:15 Mahalalel had l 65 years, he became
5:16 Mahalalel l 830 years and had other
5:17 Altogether, Mahalalel l 895 years,
5:18 Jared had l 162 years, he became the
5:19 Jared l 800 years and had other sons
5:20 Altogether, Jared l 962 years, and
5:21 Enoch had l 65 years, he became the
5:23 Altogether, Enoch l 365 years.
5:25 Methuselah had l 187 years, he
5:26 Methuselah l 782 years and had other
5:27 Altogether, Methuselah l 969 years,
5:28 Lamech had l 182 years, he had a son.
5:30 Noah was born, Lamech l 595 years
5:31 Altogether, Lamech l 777 years, and
9:28 After the flood Noah l 350 years.
9:29 Altogether, Noah l 950 years, and
10:30 The region where they l stretched
11:11 Shem l 500 years and had other sons
11:12 Arphaxad had l 35 years, he became
11:13 Arphaxad l 403 years and had other
11:14 Shelah had l 30 years, he became the
11:15 Shelah l 403 years and had other
11:16 Eber had l 34 years, he became the
11:17 Eber l 430 years and had other sons
11:18 Peleg had l 30 years, he became the
11:19 Peleg l 209 years and had other sons
11:20 Reu had l 32 years, he became the
11:21 Reu l 207 years and had other sons
11:22 Serug had l 30 years, he became the
11:23 Serug l 200 years and had other sons
11:24 Nahor had l 29 years, he became the
11:25 Nahor l 119 years and had other sons
11:26 After Terah had l 70 years, he
11:32 Terah l 205 years, and he died in
13:12 Abram l in the land of Canaan, while
13:12 while Lot l among the cities of the
19:29 the cities where Lot had l.
19:30 He and his two daughters l in a cave.
20: 1 Negev and l between Kadesh and Shur.
21:20 l in the desert and became an archer.
23: 1 Sarah l to be a hundred and
25: 7 Altogether, Abraham l a hundred and
25:11 who then l near Beer Lahai Roi.
25:17 Altogether, Ishmael l a hundred and
25:18 And they l in hostility towards all
35:28 Isaac l a hundred and eighty years.
37: 1 Jacob l in the land where his father
38:21 He asked the men who l there, "Where
38:22 Besides, the men who l there said,
39: 2 and he l in the house of his
47:28 Jacob l in Egypt seventeen years,
50:11 the Canaanites who l there saw the
50:22 He l a hundred and ten years
Ex 6: 4 of Canaan, where they l as aliens.
6:16 Levi l 137 years.
6:18 Kohath l 133 years.
6:20 Amram l 137 years.
10:23 light in the places where they l.
12:40 people l in Egypt was 430 years.
Lev 18:27 people who l in the land before you,
26:35 during the sabbaths you l in it.
Nu 13:22 Talmai, the descendants of Anak, l.
14:45 and Canaanites who l in that hill
20:15 Egypt, and we l there many years.
21: 1 king of Arad, who l in the Negev
21: 9 looked at the bronze snake, he l.
33:40 king of Arad, who l in the Negev
Dt 1:44 The Amorites who l in those hills
2:22 who l in Seir, when he destroyed the
2:22 have l in their place to this day.
2:23 for the Avvites who l in villages as
4:25 grandchildren and have l in the land
4:33 out of fire, as you have, and l?
21:13 After she has l in your house and
23: 7 you l as an alien in his country.
26: 5 l there and became a great nation,
29:16 You yourselves know how we l in
Jos 2:15 she l in was part of the city wall.
8:26 he had destroyed all who l in Ai.
8:35 and the aliens who l among them.
13:21 with Sihon—who l in that country.
22:33 the Reubenites and the Gadites l.
24: 2 l beyond the River and worshipped
24: 7 you l in the desert for a long time.
24: 8 Amorites who l east of the Jordan.
Jos 24:18 the Amorites, who l in the land.
Jdg 1:32 of this the people of Asher l among
1:33 but the Naphtalites too l among the
2:18 enemies as long as the judge l;
3: 5 The Israelites l among the
4: 2 Sisera, who l in Harosheth Haggoyim.
8:31 His concubine, who l in Shechem,
9:21 escaping to Beer, and he l there
10: 1 He l in Shamir, in the hill country
11:21 the Amorites who l in that country,
16:30 more when he died than while he l.
17:12 his priest and l in his house.
18: 7 Also, they l a long way from the
18:22 the men who l near Micah were called
18:28 they l a long way from Sidon and
19: 1 Now a Levite who l in a remote area
Ru 1: 2 And they went to Moab and l there.
1: 4 they had l there about ten years,
2:23 And she l with her mother-in-law.
1Sa 10:12 man who l there answered, "And who
12:11 every side, so that you l securely.
23:29 David went up from there and l in
27: 7 David l in Philistine territory for
27: 8 had l in the land extending to Shur
27:11 as he l in Philistine territory.
2Sa 4: 3 have l there as aliens to this day.
5: 6 attack the Jebusites, who l there.
9:13 Mephibosheth l in Jerusalem, because
13:20 l in her brother Absalom's house
14:28 Absalom l for two years in Jerusalem
1Ki 4:25 from Dan to Beersheba, l in safety,
11:20 l with Pharaoh's own children.
11:25 adversary as long as Solomon l,
12:25 hill country of Ephraim and l there.
13:25 in the city where the old prophet l.
14: 9 more evil than all who l before you.
17:22 life returned to him, and he l.
21: 8 who l in Naboth's city with him.
21:11 the elders and nobles who l in
2Ki 13: 5 Israelites l in their own homes
14:17 Amaziah son of Joash king of Judah l
15: 5 died, and he l in a separate house.
16: 6 Elath and have l there to this day.
17:24 over Samaria and l in its towns.
17:25 they first l there, they did not
22:14 She l in Jerusalem, in the Second
25:30 a regular allowance as long as he l
1Ch 2:55 the clans of scribes who l at Jabez
4:23 were the potters who l at Netaim
4:28 They l in Beersheba, Moladah, Hazar
4:40 Some Hamites had l there formerly.
4:43 and they have l there to this day.
5:11 The Gadites l next to them in Bashan,
5:16 The Gadites l in Gilead, in Bashan
7:29 son of Israel l in these towns.
8:28 genealogy, and they l in Jerusalem.
8:29 Jeiel the father of Gibeon l in
8:32 l near their relatives in Jerusalem.
9: 3 Manasseh who l in Jerusalem were:
9:16 the son of Elkanah, who l in the
9:34 genealogy, and they l in Jerusalem.
9:35 Jeiel the father of Gibeon l in
9:38 l near their relatives in Jerusalem.
11: 4 The Jebusites who l there
2Ch 11: 5 Rehoboam l in Jerusalem and built up
19: 4 Jehoshaphat l in Jerusalem, and he
19: 8 And they l in Jerusalem.
20: 8 They have l in it and have built in
21:16 the Arabs who l near the Cushites.
24:14 As long as Jehoiada l, burnt
25:25 Amaziah son of Joash king of Judah l
26: 7 against the Arabs who l in Gur Baal
26:21 He l in a separate house—leprous,
30:25 Israel and those who l in Judah.
31: 6 The men of Israel and Judah who l
31:19 the descendants of Aaron, who l on
34:22 She l in Jerusalem, in the Second
34:33 As long as he l, they did not fail
Ne 4:12 the Jews who l near them came and
8:17 exile built booths and l in them.
9:24 who l in the land; you handed the
11: 3 servants l in the towns of Judah,
11: 4 Judah and Benjamin l in Jerusalem):
11: 6 The descendants of Perez who l in
11:21 temple servants l on the hill of
11:25 some of the people of Judah l in

Ne 11:31 Benjamites from Geba l in Michmash,
12:27 were sought out from where they l
13:16 Men from Tyre who l in Jerusalem
Job 1: 1 In the land of Uz there l a man
18:19 people, no survivor where once he l.
21:28 the tents where wicked men l?'
38:21 born! You have l so many years!
42:16 Job l a hundred and forty years;
Ps 49:18 Though while he l he counted himself
105:23 Jacob l as an alien in the land of
107:34 the wickedness of those who l there.
120: 6 Too long have I l among those who
Ecc 4:15 I saw that all who l and walked
9:15 Now there l in that city a man poor
Isa 13:20 She will never be inhabited or l in
Jer 3: 1 But you have l as a prostitute with
35:10 We have l in tents and have fully
42:18 out on those who l in Jerusalem,
50:39 l in from generation to generation.
52:34 as he l, till the day of his death.
Lam 2:16 waited for; we have l to see it."
Eze 3:15 to the exiles who l at Tel Abib
16:46 Samaria, who l to the north of you
16:46 who l to the south of you with her
20: 9 eyes of the nations they l among
26:17 put your terror on all who l there.
31: 6 the great nations l in its shade.
31:17 Those who l in its shade, its allies
37:25 Jacob, the land where your fathers l.
39:26 when they l in safety in their land
Da 4:12 birds of the air l in its branches
5:21 he l with the wild donkeys and ate
Zep 2:15 the carefree city that l in safety
Mt 2:23 he went and l in a town called
4:13 Leaving Nazareth, he went and l in
23:30 you say, 'If we had l in the days of
Mk 5: 3 This man l in the tombs, and no-one
Lk 1:80 and he l in the desert until he
2:36 had l with her husband seven years
7:37 a woman who had l a sinful life in
8:27 l in a house, but had l in the tombs
16:19 linen and l in luxury every day.
Jn 7:42 Bethlehem, the town where David l?"
12: 1 Lazarus l, whom Jesus had raised
Ac 7: 2 Mesopotamia, before he l in Haran.
9:35 All those who l in Lydda and Sharon
16: 1 where a disciple named Timothy l,
16: 3 of the Jews who l in that area,
17:21 the foreigners who l there spent
19:10 Greeks who l in the province of Asia
20:18 "You know how I l the whole time I
26: 4 "The Jews all know the way I have l
26: 5 of our religion, I l as a Pharisee.
Eph 2: 3 All of us also l among them at one
Col 3: 7 these ways, in the life you once l.
1Th 1: 5 how we l among you for your sake.
2Ti 1: 5 which first l in your grandmother
Tit 3: 3 We l in malice and envy, being hated
Heb 11: 9 in a foreign country; he l in tents,
Jas 5: 5 You have l on earth in luxury and
1Pe 1:14 you had when you l in ignorance.
Rev 13:14 was wounded by the sword and yet l.

Livelihood
Dt 24: 6 be taking a man's l as security.
Zec 13: 5 land has been my l since my youth.'

Liver
Ex 29:13 the covering of the l, and both
29:22 the covering of the l, both kidneys
Lev 3: 4 and the covering of the l, which he
3:10 and the covering of the l, which he
3:15 and the covering of the l, which he
4: 9 and the covering of the l, which he
7: 4 and the covering of the l, which is
8:16 the covering of the l, and both
8:25 the covering of the l, both kidneys
9:10 of the l from the sin offering,
9:19 kidneys and the covering of the l—
Job 20:25 the gleaming point out of his l.
Pr 7:23 till an arrow pierces his l, like a
Eze 21:21 his idols, he will examine the l.

Lives[1] (*As surely as the* Lord *lives,* Live[1])
Ge 9: 3 Everything that l and moves will be
42:13 man, who l in the land of Canaan.
42:15 be tested: As surely as Pharaoh l,
42:16 surely as Pharaoh l, you are spies!"
Lev 19:33 "'When an alien l with you in your
Dt 22:19 not divorce her as long as he l.
22:29 never divorce her as long as he l.
28:43 The alien who l among you will rise
33:20 domain! Gad l there like a lion,
Jos 6:25 l among the Israelites to this day.
1Sa 14:39 as the Lord who rescues Israel l,
20:31 long as the son of Jesse l on this
25:34 the God of Israel, l, who has kept
2Sa 2:27 Joab answered, "As surely as God l,
15:21 and as my lord the king l, wherever
22:47 "The Lord l! Praise be to my Rock!
1Ki 17: 1 "As the Lord, the God of Israel, l,
17:12 "As surely as the Lord your God l,"
18:10 surely as the Lord your God l, there
18:15 Elijah said, "As the Lord Almighty l,
2Ki 3:14 "As surely as the Lord Almighty l,
Job 15:28 house where no-one l, houses
19:25 I know that my Redeemer l, and that
27: 2 "As surely as God l, who has denied
38:26 to water a land where no man l, a
Ps 18:46 The Lord l! Praise be to my Rock!
Pr 3:29 who l trustfully near you.
Ecc 6: 3 years; yet no matter how long he l,
6: 6 even if he l a thousand years twice
8:12 crimes and still l a long time,
Isa 42:11 settlements where Kedar l rejoice.
57:15 he who l for ever, whose name is
65:20 it an infant who l but a few days,
Jer 2: 6 where no-one travels and no-one l?'
4:29 are deserted; no-one l in them.
17: 6 in a salt land where no-one l.
44:26 "As surely as the Sovereign Lord l.
49:31 at ease, which l in confidence,"
51:37 and scorn, a place where no-one l.
51:43 a land where no-one l, through
Da 4:34 and glorified him who l for ever.
12: 7 and I heard him swear by him who l
Am 8:14 'As surely as your god l, O Dan',
8:14 surely as the god of Beersheba l'
Mic 7:14 which l by itself in a forest, in
Hab 1:16 for by his net he l in luxury and
Jn 3:21 whoever l by the truth comes into
11:26 whoever l and believes in me will
14:17 he l with you and will be in you.
Ac 10:32 Simon the tanner, who l by the sea.
Ro 6:10 but the life he l, he l to God.
7: 1 over a man only as long as he l?
7:18 I know that nothing good l in me,
8: 9 if the Spirit of God l in you.
8:11 through his Spirit, who l in you.
14: 7 For none of us l to himself alone
1Co 3:16 and that God's Spirit l in you?
7:39 to her husband as long as he l.
2Co 13: 4 weakness, yet he l by God's power.
Gal 2:20 I no longer live, but Christ l in me
Eph 2:22 in which God l by his Spirit.
Col 2: 9 of the Deity l in bodily form,
1Ti 5: 6 the widow who l for pleasure is dead
5: 6 pleasure is dead even while she l.
6:16 who alone is immortal and who l in
2Ti 1: 5 I am persuaded, now l in you also.
1:14 help of the Holy Spirit who l in us.
Heb 5:13 Anyone who l on milk, being still an
7:24 Jesus l for ever, he has a permanent
7:25 he always l to intercede for them.
1Jn 2:10 loves his brother l in the light,
2:14 and the word of God l in you, and
2:17 who does the will of God l for ever.
3: 6 No-one who l in him keeps on sinning.
3:24 this is how we know that he l in us:
4:12 God l in us and his love is made
4:15 of God, God l in him and he in God.
4:16 l in love l in God, and God in him.
2Jn : 2 of the truth, which l in us and will
Rev 2:13 death in your city—where Satan l.
4: 9 throne and who l for ever and ever,
4:10 worship him who l for ever and ever.
10: 6 he swore by him who l for ever and
15: 7 of God, who l for ever and ever.

Lives[2] (Life)
Ge 19:17 "Flee for your l! Don't look back,
45: 5 it was to save l that God sent me
45: 7 save your l by a great deliverance.
47:25 "You have saved our l," they said.
50:20 being done, the saving of many l.
Ex 1:14 They made their l bitter with hard
30:15 to the Lord to atone for your l.
30:16 Lord, making atonement for your l."
Nu 16:38 who sinned at the cost of their l.
Jos 2:13 that you will spare the l of my
2:14 "Our l for your l!" the men assured
9:24 So we feared for our l because of
Jdg 5:18 of Zebulun risked their very l;
8:19 if you had spared their l, I would
18:25 and your family will lose your l."
1Sa 25:29 l of your enemies he will hurl away
2Sa 18: 8 claimed more l that day than the
19: 5 the l of your sons and daughters and
19: 5 the l of your wives and concubines.
23:17 who went at the risk of their l?"
2Ki 1:13 l of these fifty men, your servants
7: 7 camp as it was and ran for their l.
1Ch 11:19 who went at the risk of their l?"
11:19 risked their l to bring it back,
Ps 37:32 the righteous, seeking their very l
66: 9 he has preserved our l and kept our
74:19 not forget the l of your afflicted
97:10 for he guards the l of his faithful
107: 5 and thirsty, and their l ebbed away.
Pr 1:19 takes away the l of those who get
14:25 A truthful witness saves l, but a
Ecc 2: 3 during the few days of their l.
Isa 38:20 all the days of our l in the temple
Jer 19: 7 the hands of those who seek their l
19: 9 by the enemies who seek their l.'
21: 7 to their enemies who seek their l.
34:20 to their enemies who seek their l.
34:21 to their enemies who seek their l,
46:26 them over to those who seek their l
48: 6 Flee! Run for your l; become like a
49:11 orphans; I will protect their l.
49:37 before those who seek their l;
51: 6 Flee from Babylon! Run for your l!
51:45 my people! Run for your l! Run from
Lam 2:12 l ebb away in their mothers' arms.
2:19 for the l of your children, who
5: 9 get our bread at the risk of our l
Eze 13:18 Will you ensnare the l of my people
13:22 their evil ways and so save their l,
17:17 works erected to destroy many l.
Da 3:28 were willing to give up their l
Ac 15:26 men who have risked their l for the
27:10 and cargo, and to our own l also."
27:24 you the l of all who sail with you.'
Ro 16: 4 They risked their l for me. Not only
2Co 1: 5 of Christ flow over into our l,
1Th 2: 8 the gospel of God but our l as well,
2:12 urging you to live l worthy of God,
1Ti 2: 2 we may live peaceful and quiet l
Tit 2:12 and godly l in this present age,
3:14 and not live unproductive l.
Heb 2:15 free those who all their l were held
13: 5 Keep your l free from the love of
1Pe 1:17 live your l as strangers here in
2:12 Live such good l among the pagans
3: 2 the purity and reverence of your l.
2Pe 2: 7 by the filthy l of lawless men
3:11 You ought to live holy and godly l
1Jn 1:10 and his word has no place in our l.
3:16 to lay down our l for our brothers.
Rev 12:11 they did not love their l so much

Livestock
Ge 1:24 according to their kinds: l,
1:25 the l according to their kinds, and
1:26 over the l, over all the earth, and
2:20 the man gave names to all the l, the
3:14 "Cursed are you above all the l and
4:20 those who live in tents and raise l.
7:14 all l according to their kinds,
7:21 l, wild animals, all the creatures

Ge 8: 1 the l that were with him in the ark,
9:10 the l and all the wild animals, all
13: 2 Abram had become very wealthy in l
30:29 how your l has fared under my care.
31: 9 God has taken away your father's l
31:18 he drove all his l ahead of him,
33:17 himself and made shelters for his l.
34: 5 sons were in the fields with his l;
34:23 Won't their l, their property and
36: 6 as well as his l and all his other
36: 7 them both because of their l.
46: 6 They also took with them their l and
46:32 The men are shepherds; they tend l,
46:34 'Your servants have tended l from
47: 6 put them in charge of my own l."
47:16 "Then bring your l," said Joseph.
47:16 in exchange for your l, since your
47:17 they brought their l to Joseph, and
47:17 food in exchange for all their l.
47:18 is gone and our l belongs to you,
Ex 9: 3 your l in the field—on your horses
9: 4 the l of Israel and that of Egypt,
9: 6 All the l of the Egyptians died,
9:19 Give an order now to bring your l
9:20 their slaves and their l inside.
9:21 their slaves and l in the field.
10:26 Our l too must go with us; not a
12:29 the firstborn of all the l as well.
12:38 droves of l, both flocks and herds.
13:12 males of your l belong to the LORD.
17: 3 our children and l die of thirst?"
22: 5 "If a man grazes his l in a field or
34:19 your l, whether from herd or flock.
Lev 5: 2 or of unclean l or of unclean
25: 7 well as for your l and the wild
Nu 3:41 and the l of the Levites in place of
3:41 of the l of the Israelites.
3:45 l of the Levites in place of their l
20: 4 that we and our l should die here?
20: 8 so that they and their l can drink."
20:11 and the community and their l drank.
20:19 and if we or our l drink any of your
32: 1 Jazer and Gilead were suitable for l
32: 4 for l, and your servants have l.
32:16 like to build pens here for our l
35: 3 flocks and all their other l.
Dt 2:35 the l and the plunder from the towns
3: 7 all the l and the plunder from their
3:19 your l (I know you have much l) may
7:14 nor any of your l without young.
13:15 both its people and its l.
20:14 for the women, the children, the l
28: 4 the young of your l—the calves of
28:11 the young of your l and the crops of
28:51 They will devour the young of your l
30: 9 your l and the crops of your land.
Jos 1:14 Your wives, your children and your l
8: 2 their plunder and l for yourselves.
8:27 the l and plunder of this city,
11:14 the plunder and l of these cities,
21: 2 in, with pasture-lands for our l."
22: 8 great wealth—with large herds of l,
Jdg 6: 5 They came up with their l and their
18:21 their l and their possessions in
1Sa 23: 5 Philistines and carried off their l.
30:20 men drove them ahead of the other l
1Ch 5: 9 their l had increased in Gilead.
5:21 They seized the l of the Hagrites
7:21 they went down to seize their l.
28: 1 l belonging to the king and his sons,
2Ch 26:10 l in the foothills and in the plain.
Ezr 1: 4 with goods and l, and with freewill
1: 6 with goods and l, and with valuable
Ps 78:48 hail, their l to bolts of lightning.
Eze 38:12 rich in l and goods, living at the
38:13 to take away l and goods and to
Zec 2: 4 the great number of men and l in it.

Living (Live, *Land of the living, Living creatures, Living God, Living water*)

Ge 1:21 every l and moving thing with which
1:28 l creature that moves on the ground."
2: 7 life, and the man became a l being.
2:19 each l creature, that was its name.
3:20 become the mother of all the l.
7: 4 earth every l creature I have made."
7:16 l thing, as God had commanded Noah.
7:21 Every l thing that moved on the
7:23 Every l thing on the face of the
8:17 Bring out every kind of l creature
9:10 with every l creature that was with
9:10 with you—every l creature on earth.
9:12 you and every l creature with you,
13: 7 also l in the land at that time.
14: 7 Amorites who were l in Hazezon Tamar
14:12 since he was l in Sodom.
14:13 Now Abram was l near the great trees
16: 3 Abram had been l in Canaan ten years
19:25 including all those l in the cities—
21:21 he was l in the Desert of Paran
21:23 country where you are l as an alien
24: 3 the Canaanites, among whom I am l,
24:62 for he was l in the Negev.
25: 6 while he was still l, he gave gifts
27:46 "I'm disgusted with l because of
27:46 these, my life will not be worth l."
34:30 the people l in this land.
35:22 While Israel was l in that region,
36:20 who were l in the region: Lotan,
43: 7 'Is your father still l?' he asked
43:27 you told me about? Is he still l?"
45: 3 I am Joseph! Is my father still l?"
46:31 who were l in the land of Canaan,
Ex 3:22 any woman l in her house for
12:48 "An alien l among you who wants to
12:49 and to the alien l among you."
Lev 11: 9 "'Of all the creatures l in the
11:12 Anything l in the water that does
11:46 birds, every l thing that moves in
16:29 or an alien l among you—
17: 8 Israelite or any alien l among them
17:10 Israelite or any alien l among them
17:12 may an alien l among you eat blood."
17:13 Israelite or any alien l among you
18:18 with her while your wife is l.
18:26 The native-born and the aliens l
19:34 The alien l with you must be treated
20: 2 Israelite or any alien l in Israel
22:18 an Israelite or an alien l in Israel
25:45 the temporary residents l among you
25:47 sells himself to the alien l among
Nu 9:14 "'An alien l among you who wants to
13:32 we explored devours those l in it.
14:25 and Canaanites are l in the valleys,
15:14 an alien or anyone else l among you
15:15 you and for the alien l among you;
15:16 to you and to the alien l among you.
15:26 aliens l among them will be forgiven
16:48 He stood between the l and the dead,
19:10 and for the aliens l among them.
30: 3 "When a young woman still l in her
30:10 "If a woman l with her husband makes
30:16 young daughter still l in his house.
35:15 aliens and any other people l among
Dt 11: 6 every l thing that belonged to them.
11:30 of those Canaanites l in the Arabah
11:31 have taken it over and are l there,
14: 9 Of all the creatures l in the water,
14:21 You may give it to an alien l in any
14:27 do not neglect the Levites l in your
16:11 and the widows l among you.
17: 2 If a man or woman l among you in one
18: 6 anywhere in Israel where he is l,
24:14 or an alien l in one of your towns.
25: 5 If brothers are l together and one
29:11 and the aliens l in your camps who
31:12 and the aliens l in your towns—so
Jos 6:21 every l thing in it—men and women,
9:11 and all those l in our country said
9:16 they were neighbours, l near them.
10: 1 with Israel and were l near them.
11:19 Except for the Hivites l in Gibeon,
15:15 against the people l in Debir
15:63 Jebusites, who were l in Jerusalem;
16:10 dislodge the Canaanites l in Gezer;
17: 7 include the people l at En Tappuah.
20: 9 Israelites or any alien l among them
24:15 Amorites, in whose land you are l.
Jdg 1: 9 Canaanites l in the hill country,
1:10 against the Canaanites l in Hebron
1:11 against the people l in Debir
1:17 the Canaanites l in Zephath,
1:21 Jebusites, who were l in Jerusalem;
1:29 drive out the Canaanites l in Gezer,
1:30 Canaanites l in Kitron or Nahalol,
1:31 Nor did Asher drive out those l in
1:33 l in Beth Shemesh or Beth Anath;
1:33 l in Beth Shemesh and Beth Anath
3: 3 the Sidonians, and the Hivites l in
6: 4 did not spare a l thing for Israel,
10:18 the head of all those l in Gilead."
17: 7 had been l within the clan of Judah,
18: 7 that the people were l in safety,
19:16 who was l in Gibeah (the men of the
20:15 chosen men from those l in Gibeah.
21:10 and put to the sword those l there,
21:12 among the people l in Jabesh Gilead
Ru 1: 7 left the place where she had been l
2:20 his kindness to the l and the dead.
4:17 The women l there said, "Naomi has
1Sa 25:29 of the l by the LORD your God.
2Sa 7: 2 "Here I am, l in a palace of cedar,
12:18 "While the child was still l, we
15: 8 While your servant was l at Geshur
20: 3 the day of their death, l as widows.
1Ki 3:22 The other woman said, "No! The l one
3:22 one is yours; the l one is mine.
3:25 an order: "Cut the l child in two
3:26 my lord, give her the l baby!
3:27 "Give the l baby to the first woman
12:17 as for the Israelites who were l in
13:11 a certain old prophet l in Bethel
1Ch 8: 6 of families of those l in Geba
8:13 of families of those l in Aijalon
12:15 and they put to flight everyone l in
17: 1 "Here I am, l in a palace of cedar,
22: 2 to assemble the aliens l in Israel,
2Ch 10:17 as for the Israelites who were l in
31: 4 He ordered the people l in Jerusalem
Ezr 1: 4 place where survivors may now be l
4:17 the rest of their associates l in
Ne 3:26 the temple servants l on the hill of
3:30 repairs opposite his l quarters.
11:30 So they were l all the way from
Est 9:19 why rural Jews—those l in villages
Job 22: 8 land—an honoured man, l on it.
28:21 is hidden from the eyes of every l
30:23 the place appointed for all the l.
Ps 65: 8 Those l far away fear your wonders;
104:25 l things both large and small.
119: 9 pure? By l according to your word.
143: 2 no-one l is righteous before you.
145:16 the desires of every l thing.
Ecc 4: 2 are happier than the l, who are
7: 2 the l should take this to heart.
7:15 wicked man l long in his wickedness.
9: 4 Anyone who is among the l has
9: 5 For the l know that they will die,
Isa 4: 3 recorded among the l in Jerusalem.
8:19 consult the dead on behalf of the l?
9: 2 on those l in the land of the shadow
33:24 No-one l in Zion will say, "I am ill
38:19 The l, the l—they praise you, as I
Jer 13:13 and all those l in Jerusalem.
17:20 all people of Judah and everyone l
17:25 of Judah and those l in Jerusalem,
18:11 of Judah and those l in Jerusalem,
25: 2 and to all those l in Jerusalem:
35:17 on everyone l in Jerusalem every
36:31 on them and those l in Jerusalem
44: 1 Jews l in Lower Egypt—in Migdol,
44:15 people l in Lower and Upper Egypt,
44:26 of the LORD, all Jews l in Egypt
44:26 'that no-one from Judah l anywhere
Lam 3:39 Why should any l man complain when
Eze 3:15 And there, where they were l, I sat
12: 2 "Son of man, you are l among a
12:19 LORD says about those l in Jerusalem
14: 7 Israelite or any alien l in Israel
15: 6 I treat the people l in Jerusalem.
18: 4 For every l soul belongs to me, the
20:38 out of the land where they are l,
33:24 "Son of man, the people l in those
36:17 when the people of Israel were l in
38:11 all of them l without walls and
38:12 l at the centre of the land."

Eze 38:14 my people Israel are l in safety
Da 2:30 greater wisdom than other l men,
4:17 so that the l may know that the Most
Hag 1: 4 to be l in your panelled houses,
Mt 4:16 the people l in darkness have seen a
4:16 on those l in the land of the shadow
22:32 the God of the dead but of the l."
Mk 12:27 the God of the dead, but of the l.
Lk 1:79 to shine on those l in darkness and
2: 8 were shepherds l out in the fields
13: 4 than all the others l in Jerusalem?
15:13 squandered his wealth in wild l.
20:38 the God of the dead, but of the l,
24: 5 you look for the l among the dead?
Jn 4:51 with the news that his boy was l.
6:51 I am the l bread that came down from
6:57 Just as the l Father sent me and I
14:10 l in me, who is doing his work.
Ac 4:16 "Everybody l in Jerusalem knows they
7: 4 to this land where you are now l.
7:38 received l words to pass on to us.
9:22 and baffled the Jews l in Damascus
9:31 numbers, l in the fear of the Lord.
10:42 as judge of the l and the dead.
11:29 help for the brothers l in Judea.
19:17 to the Jews and Greeks l in Ephesus,
21:24 are l in obedience to the law.
22:12 respected by all the Jews l there.
Ro 7:17 who do it, but it is sin l in me.
7:20 but it is sin l in me that does it.
8:11 Jesus from the dead is l in you,
12: 1 to offer your bodies as l sacrifices
14: 9 the Lord of both the dead and the l.
1Co 9: 6 and Barnabas who must work for a l?
9:14 receive their l from the gospel.
15: 6 most of whom are still l, though
15:45 The first man Adam became a l being
Php 1:22 If I am to go on l in the body, this
4:12 whether l in plenty or in want.
1Th 1: 9 idols to serve the l and true God,
4: 1 please God, as in fact you are l.
2Ti 4: 1 who will judge the l and the dead,
Heb 4:12 For the word of God is l and active
7: 8 by him who is declared to be l.
9:17 while the one who made it is l.
10:20 by a new and l way opened for us
11:13 these people were still l by faith
1Pe 1: 3 given us new birth into a l hope
1:23 the l and enduring word of God.
2: 4 you come to him, the l stone—
2: 5 you also, like l stones, are being
4: 3 choose to do—l in debauchery,
4: 5 ready to judge the l and the dead.
2Pe 2: 8 (for that righteous man, l among
Rev 1:18 I am the L One; I was dead, and
4: 7 The first l creature was like a lion,
6: 3 I heard the second l creature say,
6: 5 the third l creature say, "Come!"
6: 7 I heard the voice of the fourth l
16: 3 and every l thing in the sea died.
18:17 who earn their l from the sea, will

Living creatures
Ge 1:20 said, "Let the water teem with l,
1:24 God said, "Let the land produce l
6:19 to bring into the ark two of all l,
8:21 I destroy all l, as I have done.
9:15 me and you and all l of every kind.
9:16 all l of every kind on the earth."
Lev 11:10 l in the water—you are to detest.
11:47 between l that may be eaten and
Eze 1: 5 fire was what looked like four l.
1:13 The appearance of the l was like
1:15 I looked at the l, I saw a wheel on
1:19 the l moved, the wheels beside them
1:19 and when the l rose from the ground,
1:20 spirit of the l was in the wheels.
1:21 spirit of the l was in the wheels.
1:22 Spread out above the heads of the l
3:13 the sound of the wings of the l
10:15 the l I had seen by the Kebar River
10:17 the spirit of the l was in them.
10:20 These were the l I had seen beneath
47: 9 Swarms of l will live wherever the
Rev 4: 6 around the throne, were four l, and
4: 8 Each of the four l had six wings
4: 9 Whenever the l give glory, honour
5: 6 by the four l and the elders.
5: 8 he had taken it, the four l and the
5:11 the throne and the l and the elders
5:14 The four l said, "Amen", and the
6: 1 Then I heard one of the four l say
6: 6 like a voice among the four l,
7:11 around the elders and the four l.
8: 9 a third of the l in the sea died,
14: 3 before the four l and the elders.
15: 7 one of the four l gave to the seven
19: 4 twenty-four elders and the four l

Living God
Dt 5:26 voice of the l speaking out of fire,
Jos 3:10 This is how you will know that the l
1Sa 17:26 he should defy the armies of the l?"
17:36 he has defied the armies of the l.
2Ki 19: 4 has sent to ridicule the l, and that
19:16 Sennacherib has sent to insult the l
Ps 42: 2 My soul thirsts for God, for the l.
84: 2 and my flesh cry out for the l.
Isa 37: 4 has sent to ridicule the l, and that
37:17 Sennacherib has sent to insult the l
Jer 10:10 LORD is the true God; he is the l
23:36 the l, the LORD Almighty, our God.
Da 6:20 "Daniel, servant of the l, has your
6:26 "For he is the l and he endures for
Hos 1:10 they will be called 'sons of the l'
Mt 16:16 are the Christ, the Son of the l."
26:63 "I charge you under oath by the l:
Ac 14:15 these worthless things to the l,
Ro 9:26 will be called 'sons of the l'."
2Co 3: 3 ink but with the Spirit of the l,
6:16 For we are the temple of the l.
1Ti 3:15 which is the church of the l, the
4:10 that we have put our hope in the l,
Heb 3:12 heart that turns away from the l.
9:14 death, so that we may serve the l!
10:31 to fall into the hands of the l.
12:22 Jerusalem, the city of the l.
Rev 7: 2 the east, having the seal of the l

Living water
Jer 2:13 the spring of l, and have dug their
17:13 forsaken the LORD, the spring of l.
Zec 14: 8 On that day l will flow out from
Jn 4:10 him and he would have given you l.
4:11 Where can you get this l?
7:38 of l will flow from within him."
Rev 7:17 he will lead them to springs of l.

Lizard
Lev 11:29 the rat, any kind of great l,
11:30 gecko, the monitor l, the wall l,
Pr 30:28 a l can be caught with the hand, yet

Lo Debar
2Sa 9: 4 house of Makir son of Ammiel in L."
9: 5 King David had him brought from L,
17:27 and Makir son of Ammiel from L,
Am 6:13 who rejoice in the conquest of L

Load (Camel-loads, Laden, Loaded, Loading, Loads, Spice-laden)
Ge 45:17 'Do this: L your animals and return
Ex 18:22 That will make your l lighter,
23: 5 hates you fallen down under its l,
Ne 13:19 so that no l could be brought in on
Job 35: 9 "Men cry out under a l of oppression
Isa 22:25 l hanging on it will be cut down.
Jer 17:21 Be careful not to carry a l on the
17:22 Do not bring a l out of your houses
17:24 declares the LORD, and bring no l
17:27 day holy by not carrying any l
Lk 11:46 woe to you, because you l people
Gal 6: 5 for each one should carry his own l.

Loaded (Load)
Ge 37:25 Their camels were l with spices,
42:26 they l their grain on their donkeys
44:13 Then they all l their donkeys and
45:23 l with the best things of Egypt,
45:23 and ten female donkeys l with grain
Jos 9: 4 donkeys were l with worn-out sacks
1Sa 16:20 Jesse took a donkey l with bread, a
17:20 l up and set out, as Jesse had
25:18 pressed figs, and l them on donkeys.
2Sa 16: 1 l with two hundred loaves of bread,
Isa 1: 4 Ah, sinful nation, a people l with
Am 2:13 as a cart crushes when l with grain.
2Ti 3: 6 who are l down with sins and are

Loading (Load)
Ne 13:15 in grain and l it on donkeys,

Loads (Load)
Ne 13:15 figs and all other kinds of l.
Job 37:11 He l the clouds with moisture; he
Ps 144:14 our oxen will draw heavy l. There
Lam 5:13 boys stagger under l of wood.
Mt 23: 4 They tie up heavy l and put them on

Loaf (Loaves)
Ex 29:23 which is before the LORD, take a l,
Lev 24: 5 two-tenths of an ephah for each l.
Jdg 7:13 "A round l of barley bread came
2Sa 6:19 he gave a l of bread, a cake of
1Ch 16: 3 he gave a l of bread, a cake of
Pr 6:26 prostitute reduces you to a l of
Mk 8:14 l they had with them in the boat.
1Co 10:17 there is one l, we, who are many,
10:17 for we all partake of the one l.

Lo-Ammi
Hos 1: 9 the LORD said, "Call him L, for you

Loan
Dt 15: 2 Every creditor shall cancel the l
24:10 you make a l of any kind to your
24:11 making the l bring the pledge out to
Eze 18: 7 what he took in pledge for a l.
18:16 anyone or require a pledge for a l.
33:15 back what he took in pledge for a l

Loathe (Loathed, Loathes, Loathing, Loathsome)
Nu 11:20 you l it—because you have rejected
Job 10: 1 "I l my very life; therefore I will
Eze 6: 9 They will l themselves for the evil
20:43 and you will l yourselves for all
36:31 and you will l yourselves for your

Loathed (Loathe)
Ps 107:18 They l all food and drew near the

Loathes (Loathe)
Job 33:20 and his soul l the choicest meal.
Pr 27: 7 He who is full l honey, but to the

Loathing (Loathe)
Ps 119:158 I look on the faithless with l, for

Loathsome (Loathe)
Job 19:17 I am l to my own brothers.
Ps 38: 5 My wounds fester and are l because
Isa 66:24 and they will be l to all mankind."
Jer 6:15 Are they ashamed of their l conduct?
8:12 Are they ashamed of their l conduct?

Loaves (Loaf)
Lev 23:17 From wherever you live, bring two l
24: 5 "Take fine flour and bake twelve l
1Sa 10: 3 another three l of bread, and
10: 4 you and offer you two l of bread,
17:17 these ten l of bread for your
21: 3 l of bread, or whatever you can find
25:18 She took two hundred l of bread, two
2Sa 16: 1 loaded with two hundred l of bread,
1Ki 14: 3 Take ten l of bread with you, some
2Ki 4:42 bringing the man of God twenty l of
Mt 14:17 "We have here only five l of bread
14:19 Taking the five l and the two fish
14:19 he gave thanks and broke the l.
15:34 "How many l do you have?" Jesus

Mt 15:36 he took the seven l and the fish,
16: 9 the five l for the five thousand,
16:10 the seven l for the four thousand,
Mk 6:38 "How many l do you have?" he asked.
6:41 Taking the five l and the two fish
6:41 he gave thanks and broke the l.
6:52 had not understood about the l;
8: 5 "How many l do you have?" Jesus
8: 6 When he had taken the seven l and
8:19 I broke the five l for the five
8:20 "And when I broke the seven l for
Lk 9:13 They answered, "We have only five l
9:16 Taking the five l and the two fish
11: 5 'Friend, lend me three l of bread,
Jn 6: 9 five small barley l and two small
6:11 Jesus then took the l, gave thanks,
6:13 l left over by those who had eaten.
6:26 you ate the l and had your fill.

Lobe (Lobes)
Lev 8:23 it on the l of Aaron's right ear,
14:14 put it on the l of the right ear of
14:17 on the l of the right ear of the
14:25 put it on the l of the right ear of
14:28 on the l of the right ear of the one
Dt 15:17 it through his ear l into the door,

Lobes (Lobe)
Ex 29:20 put it on the l of the right ears of
Lev 8:24 blood on the l of their right ears,

Local
Mt 10:17 will hand you over to the l councils
Mk 13: 9 will be handed over to the l councils

Located (Locations)
Dt 19: 2 three cities centrally l in the land

Locations (Located)
1Ch 6:54 were the l of their settlements

Lock (Locked)
SS 5: 5 myrrh, on the handles of the l.

Locked (Lock)
Jdg 3:23 upper room behind him and l them.
3:24 found the doors of the upper room l.
9:51 They l themselves in and climbed up
SS 4:12 You are a garden l up, my sister, my
Lk 3:20 them all: He l John up in prison.
11: 7 The door is already l, and my
Jn 20:19 with the doors l for fear of the
20:26 Though the doors were l, Jesus came
Ac 5:23 "We found the jail securely l, with
Gal 3:23 l up until faith should be revealed.
Rev 20: 3 and l and sealed it over him,

Locust (Locusts)
Ex 10:19 Not a l was left anywhere in Egypt.
Lev 11:22 Of these you may eat any kind of l,
Job 39:20 Do you make him leap like a l,
Ps 78:46 grasshopper, their produce to the l.
109:23 I am shaken off like a l.
Joel 1: 4 What the l swarm has left the great
2:25 eaten—the great l and the young l,
2:25 the other locusts and the l swarm—

Locusts (Locust)
Ex 10: 4 bring l into your country tomorrow.
10:12 so that l will swarm over the land
10:13 morning the wind had brought the l;
10:14 had there been such a plague of l,
10:19 which caught up the l and carried
Dt 28:38 little, because l will devour it.
28:42 Swarms of l will take over all your
Jdg 6: 5 and their tents like swarms of l.
7:12 settled in the valley, thick as l.
1Ki 8:37 or blight or mildew, l or
2Ch 6:28 or blight or mildew, l or
7:13 or command l to devour the land or
Ps 105:34 He spoke, and the l came,
Pr 30:27 l have no king, yet they advance
Isa 33: 4 is harvested as by young l; like a
Isa 33: 4 like a swarm of l men pounce on it.
Jer 46:23 more numerous than l, they cannot
51:14 as with a swarm of l, and they will
51:27 send up horses like a swarm of l.
Joel 1: 4 has left the great l have eaten;
1: 4 great l have left the young l have
1: 4 young l have left other l have
2:25 for the years the l have eaten—
2:25 the other l and the locust swarm—
Am 4: 9 L devoured your fig and olive trees,
7: 1 He was preparing swarms of l after
Na 3:15 like grasshoppers, multiply like l!
3:16 but like l they strip the land and
3:17 Your guards are like l, your
3:17 your officials like swarms of l that
Mt 3: 4 His food was l and wild honey.
Mk 1: 6 waist, and he ate l and wild honey.
Rev 9: 3 out of the smoke l came down upon
9: 7 The l looked like horses prepared

Lod
City in Plain of Sharon, 11 miles south-east of Joppa. Built by the sons of Elpaal (1Ch 8:12) and occupied after the exile by the Benjamites (Ne 11:35). Known later as Lydda, Peter healed Aeneas here (Ac 9:32–35).

1Ch 8:12 L with its surrounding villages),
Ezr 2:33 of L, Hadid and Ono 725
Ne 7:37 of L, Hadid and Ono 721
11:35 in L and Ono, and in the Valley of

Lodge (Lodged, Lodging)
Ps 119:54 the theme of my song wherever I l.

Lodged (Lodge)
Ezr 4: 6 they l an accusation against the

Lodging (Lodge)
Ex 4:24 At a l place on the way, the LORD
Ps 55:15 grave, for evil finds l among them.
Jer 9: 2 Oh, that I had in the desert a l
Mic 6: 2 he is l a charge against Israel.
Lk 9:12 and countryside and find food and l,
Jas 2:25 did when she gave l to the spies

Loftiness (Lofty)
Ps 48: 2 is beautiful in its l, the joy of

Lofty (Loftiness)
Job 22:12 And see how l are the highest stars!
Ps 62: 4 to topple him from his l place;
139: 6 for me, too l for me to attain.
Isa 2:12 in store for all the proud and l,
2:13 the cedars of Lebanon, tall and l,
2:15 for every l tower and every
10:33 The l trees will be felled, the tall
26: 5 he lays the l city low; he levels it
30:25 high mountain and every l hill.
57: 7 made your bed on a high and l hill;
57:15 is what the high and l One says—
63:15 your l throne, holy and glorious.
Jer 51:53 sky and fortifies her l stronghold,
Eze 16:24 a l shrine in every public square.
16:25 built your l shrines and degraded
16:31 l shrines in every public square,
16:39 mounds and destroy your l shrines.
17:22 plant it on a high and l mountain.
Am 9: 6 he who builds his l palace in the

Log (Logs)
Lev 14:10 a grain offering, and one l of oil.
14:12 along with the l of oil; he shall
14:15 then take some of the l of oil,
14:21 for a grain offering, a l of oil,
14:24 together with the l of oil, and wave

Logs (Log)
2Sa 5:11 along with cedar l and carpenters
1Ki 5: 8 in providing the cedar and pine l.
5:10 all the cedar and pine l he wanted,
1Ch 14: 1 along with cedar l, stonemasons and
22: 4 He also provided more cedar l than
2Ch 2: 3 "Send me cedar l as you did for my
2Ch 2: 8 Send me also cedar, pine and algum l
2:16 we will cut all the l from Lebanon
Ezr 3: 7 they would bring cedar l by sea
Ecc 10: 9 whoever splits l may be endangered

Loincloth
Job 12:18 and ties a l round their waist.

Loins
Lev 3: 4 with the fat on them near the l,
3:10 with the fat on them near the l,
3:15 with the fat on them near the l,
4: 9 with the fat on them near the l,
7: 4 with the fat on them near the l,
Dt 33:11 Smite the l of those who rise up
Job 40:16 What strength he has in his l,

Lois
2Ti 1: 5 in your grandmother L and in your

Lonely (Alone)
Ps 25:16 to me, for I am l and afflicted.
68: 6 God sets the l in families, he leads
Mk 1:45 but stayed outside in l places.
Lk 5:16 Jesus often withdrew to l places and

Long[1] (Length, Lengthen, Lengths, Lengthwise, Lengthy)
Ge 6:15 450 feet l, 75 feet wide and 45 feet
8:22 As l as the earth endures, seedtime
21:34 of the Philistines for a l time.
26: 8 Isaac had been there a l time,
38:12 After a l time Judah's wife, the
46:29 his father and wept for a l time.
Ex 2:23 During that l period, the king of
10: 3 'How l will you refuse to humble
10: 7 "How l will this man be a snare to
14:20 went near the other all night l.
16:28 the LORD said to Moses, "How l will
17:11 As l as Moses held up his hands,
19:13 the ram's horn sounds a l blast
20:12 so that you may live l in the land
25:10 wood—two and a half cubits l,
25:17 two and a half cubits l and a
25:23 table of acacia wood—two cubits l,
26: 2 twenty-eight cubits l and four
26: 8 thirty cubits l and four cubits
26:16 Each frame is to be ten cubits l
27: 1 five cubits l and five cubits wide.
27: 9 side shall be a hundred cubits l
27:11 a hundred cubits l and is to have
27:14 Curtains fifteen cubits l are to be
27:15 curtains fifteen cubits l are to be
27:16 provide a curtain twenty cubits l,
27:18 a hundred cubits l and fifty
28:16 to be square—a span l and a span
30: 2 is to be square, a cubit l and a
32: 1 Moses was so l in coming down from
36: 9 twenty-eight cubits l and four
36:15 thirty cubits l and four cubits
36:21 Each frame was ten cubits l and
37: 1 wood—two and a half cubits l,
37: 6 two and a half cubits l and a
37:10 table of acacia wood—two cubits l,
37:25 It was square, a cubit l and a cubit
38: 1 five cubits l and five cubits wide.
38: 9 south side was a hundred cubits l
38:11 side was also a hundred cubits l
38:14 Curtains fifteen cubits l were on
38:15 curtains fifteen cubits l were on
38:18 It was twenty cubits l and, like the
39: 9 was square—a span l and a span wide
Lev 13:46 l as he has the infection he remains
15:25 she will be unclean as l as she has
Nu 6: 4 l as he is a Nazirite, he must not
6: 5 let the hair of his head grow l.
9:18 As l as the cloud stayed over the
9:19 over the tabernacle a l time,
14:11 The LORD said to Moses, "How l will
14:11 How l will they refuse to believe in
14:27 "How l will this wicked community
36: 6 as l as they marry within the
Dt 1: 6 stayed l enough at this mountain.
2: 1 For a l time we made our way around

Dt 2: 3 around this hill country l enough;
3:11 thirteen feet l and six feet wide.
4: 9 from your heart as l as you live.
4:10 me as l as they live in the land
4:25 have lived in the land a l time—
4:26 You will not live there l but will
4:32 former days, l before your time,
4:40 that you may live l in the land the
5:16 so that you may live l and that it
6: 2 as l as you live by keeping all his
6: 2 and so that you may enjoy l life.
11: 9 that you may live l in the land that
12: 1 l as you live in the land.
12:19 as l as you live in your land.
17:20 a l time over his kingdom in Israel.
20:19 you lay siege to a city for a l time,
22: 7 with you and you may have a l life.
22:19 not divorce her as l as he lives.
22:29 never divorce her as l as he lives.
23: 6 with them as l as you live.
25:15 so that you may live l in the land
30:18 You will not live l in the land you
31:13 as l as you live in the land you
32: 7 consider the generations l past.
32:47 By them you will live l in the land
33:12 for he shields him all day l, and
Jos 6: 5 you hear them sound a l blast on the
9:13 are worn out by the very l journey."
9:22 'We live a l way from you,' while
11:18 all these kings for a l time.
18: 3 "How l will you wait before you
22: 3 For a l time now—to this very
23: 1 After a l time had passed and the
24: 2 'L ago your forefathers, including
24: 7 lived in the desert for a l time.
Jdg 2:18 enemies as l as the judge lived;
3:16 sword about a foot and a half l,
5:28 'Why is his chariot so l in coming?
18: 7 Also, they lived a l way from the
18:28 they lived a l way from Sidon
1Sa 1:14 said to her, "How l will you keep on
7: 2 was a l time, twenty years in all,
10:24 people shouted, "L live the king!"
16: 1 The Lord said to Samuel, "How l will
20:14 that of the Lord as l as I live,
20:31 l as the son of Jesse lives on this
22: 4 as l as David was in the stronghold.
25: 6 Say to him: 'L life to you! Good
25:28 be found in you as l as you live.
27:11 was his practice as l as he lived
2Sa 2:26 How l before you order your men to
3: 1 the house of David lasted a l time.
16:16 "L live the king! L live the king!
20:18 She continued, "L ago they used to
1Ki 1:25 and saying, 'L live King Adonijah!'
1:34 and shout, 'L live King Solomon!'
1:39 shouted, "L live King Solomon!
2:38 stayed in Jerusalem for a l time.
3:11 for l life or wealth for yourself,
3:14 did, I will give you a l life."
6: 2 sixty cubits l, twenty wide and
6:17 of this room was forty cubits l.
6:20 twenty cubits l, twenty wide and
6:24 the first cherub was five cubits l,
7: 2 Forest of Lebanon a hundred cubits l
7: 6 He made a colonnade fifty cubits l
7:27 four cubits l, four wide and three
8: 8 These poles were so l that their
11:25 Israel's adversary as l as Solomon
18: 1 After a l time, in the third year,
18:21 "How l will you waver between two
22:35 All day l the battle raged, and the
2Ki 6:25 the siege lasted so l that a
9:22 "as l as all the idolatry and
11:12 shouted, "L live the king!
13: 3 and for a l time he kept them under
14:13 section about six hundred feet l.
19:25 "'Have you not heard? L ago I
25:30 regular allowance as l as he lived.
1Ch 29:28 enjoyed l life, wealth and honour.
2Ch 1:11 you have not asked for a l life
3: 3 temple of God was sixty cubits l
3: 4 twenty cubits l across the width
3: 8 twenty cubits l and twenty cubits
3:11 five cubits l and touched the
3:11 also five cubits l, touched the wing
2Ch 3:12 five cubits l and touched the other
3:12 also five cubits l, touched the wing
3:15 were thirty-five cubits l, each
4: 1 made a bronze altar twenty cubits l,
5: 9 These poles were so l that their
6:13 five cubits l, five cubits wide and
15: 3 For a l time Israel was without the
18:34 All day l the battle raged, and the
23:11 him and shouted, "L live the king! l
24:14 As l as Jehoiada lived, burnt
25:23 section about six hundred feet l.
26: 5 As l as he sought the Lord, God gave
34:33 As l as he lived, they did not fail
Ezr 4:19 this city has a l history of revolt
Ne 2: 6 "How l will your journey take, and
12:46 For l ago, in the days of David and
Est 5:13 as l as I see that Jew Mordecai
Job 7: 4 I lie down I think, 'How l before I
8: 2 "How l will you say such things?
12:12 Does not l life bring understanding?
12:19 and overthrows men l established.
19: 2 "How l will you torment me and crush
27: 3 l as I have life within me, the
27: 6 will not reproach me as l as I live.
Ps 4: 2 How l, O men, will you turn my glory
4: 2 How l will you love delusions and
6: 3 in anguish. How l, O Lord, how l?
6: 6 all night l I flood my bed with
13: 1 How l, O Lord? Will you forget me
13: 1 How l will you hide your face from
13: 2 How l must I wrestle with my
13: 2 How l will my enemy triumph over me?
25: 5 and my hope is in you all day l.
32: 3 away through my groaning all day l.
35:17 O Lord, how l will you look on?
35:28 and of your praises all day l.
38: 6 all day l I go about mourning.
38:12 all day l they plot deception.
39: 1 l as the wicked are in my presence."
42: 3 while men say to me all day l,
42:10 saying to me all day l, "Where is
44: 1 did in their days, in days l ago.
44: 8 In God we make our boast all day l,
44:15 My disgrace is before me all day l,
44:22 your sake we face death all day l;
52: 1 Why do you boast all day l, you
56: 1 all day l they press their attack.
56: 2 My slanderers pursue me all day l;
56: 5 All day l they twist my words; they
62: 3 How l will you assault a man? Would
63: 4 I will praise you as l as I live,
71: 8 declaring your splendour all day l.
71:15 of your salvation all day l, though
71:24 of your righteous acts all day l,
72: 5 will endure as l as the sun, as l
72:15 L may he live! May gold from Sheba
72:15 for him and bless him all day l.
72:17 may it continue as l as the sun.
73:14 All day l I have been plagued;
74: 9 none of us knows how l this will be.
74:10 How l will the enemy mock you, O God
74:22 how fools mock you all day l.
77: 5 the former days, the years of l ago;
77:11 remember your miracles of l ago.
79: 5 How l, O Lord? Will you be angry for
79: 5 How l will your jealousy burn
80: 4 O Lord God Almighty, how l will your
82: 2 "How l will you defend the unjust
86: 3 O Lord, for I call to you all day l.
88:17 All day l they surround me like a
89:16 They rejoice in your name all day l;
89:29 throne as l as the heavens endure.
89:46 How l, O Lord? Will you hide
89:46 How l will your wrath burn like fire?
90:13 Relent, O Lord! How l will it be?
91:16 With l life will I satisfy him and
93: 2 Your throne was established l ago;
94: 3 How l will the wicked, O Lord, how l
102: 8 All day l my enemies taunt me;
104:33 praise to my God as l as I live.
116: 2 I will call on him as l as I live.
119:84 How l must your servant wait? When
119:97 law! I meditate on it all day l.
119:152 L ago I learned from your statutes
120: 6 Too l have I lived among those who
129: 3 my back and made their furrows l.
Ps 143: 3 dwell in darkness like those l dead.
143: 5 I remember the days of l ago;
146: 2 praise to my God as l as I live.
Pr 1:22 "How l will you simple ones love
1:22 How l will mockers delight in
3:16 L life is in her right hand; in her
6: 9 How l will you lie there, you
7:19 at home; he has gone on a l journey.
21:26 All day l he craves for more, but
28:16 ill-gotten gain will enjoy a l life.
Ecc 1:10 l ago; it was here before our time.
2:16 like the fool, will not be l
6: 3 yet no matter how l he lives,
7:15 man living l in his wickedness.
8:12 crimes and still lives a l time,
9: 6 jealousy have l since vanished;
SS 3: 1 All night l on my bed I looked for
Isa 6:11 I said, "For how l, O Lord?" And he
22:11 for the One who planned it l ago.
25: 1 things, things planned l ago.
30:33 Topheth has l been prepared; it has
37:26 you not heard? L ago I ordained it.
42:14 "For a l time I have kept silent,
44: 8 foretell it l ago? You are my
45:21 Who foretold this l ago, who
46: 9 the former things, those of l ago;
48: 3 I foretold the former things l ago,
48: 5 I told you these things l ago;
48: 7 They are created now, and not l ago;
52: 5 all day l my name is constantly
57:11 it not because I have l been silent
61: 4 and restore the places l devastated;
65: 2 All day l I have held out my hands
65:22 l enjoy the works of their hands.
Jer 2:20 "L ago you broke off your yoke and
4:14 l will you harbour wicked thoughts?
4:21 How l must I see the battle standard
6: 4 and the shadows of evening grow l.
12: 4 How l will the land lie parched and
13:27 How l will you be unclean?"
20: 7 all day l; everyone mocks me.
20: 8 me insult and reproach all day l.
23:26 How l will this continue in the
29:28 us in Babylon: It will be a l time.
31:22 How l will you wander, O unfaithful
32:14 jar so that they will last a l time.
35: 7 Then you will live a l time in the
37:16 dungeon, where he remained a l time.
47: 5 how l will you cut yourselves?
47: 6 'how l till you rest? Return to your
52:34 regular allowance as l as he lived,
Lam 1:13 me desolate, faint all the day l.
2:17 his word, which he decreed l ago.
3: 3 me again and again, all day l.
3: 6 dwell in darkness like those l dead.
3:14 they mock me in song all day l.
3:62 and mutter against me all day l.
5:20 us? Why do you forsake us so l?
Eze 7:13 has sold as l as both of them live,
17: 3 l feathers and full plumage of
26:20 to the pit, to the people of l ago.
31: 5 increased and its branches grew l,
38: 8 Israel, which had l been desolate.
40: 5 in the man's hand was six l cubits,
40: 7 were one rod l and one rod wide,
40:18 as they were l; this was the lower
40:21 fifty cubits l and twenty-five
40:25 fifty cubits l and twenty-five
40:29 fifty cubits l and twenty-five
40:33 fifty cubits l and twenty-five
40:36 fifty cubits l and twenty-five
40:42 each a cubit and a half l, a cubit
40:43 each a handbreadth l, were attached
40:47 a hundred cubits l and a hundred
41: 2 forty cubits l and twenty cubits
41: 8 the length of the rod, six l cubits.
41:13 it was a hundred cubits l, and
41:13 walls were also a hundred cubits l.
42: 2 a hundred cubits l and fifty cubits
42: 4 cubits wide and a hundred cubits l.
42: 8 the outer court was fifty cubits l,
42: 8 sanctuary was a hundred cubits l.
42:20 five hundred cubits l and five
43:13 of the altar in l cubits,
43:16 twelve cubits l and twelve cubits
43:17 fourteen cubits l and fourteen

Eze 44:20 heads or let their hair grow l,
45: 1 25,000 cubits l and 20,000 cubits
45: 3 25,000 cubits l and 10,000 cubits
45: 5 An area 25,000 cubits l and 10,000
45: 6 cubits wide and 25,000 cubits l,
46:22 forty cubits l and thirty cubits
48: 9 25,000 cubits l and 10,000 cubits
48:10 It will be 25,000 cubits l on the
48:10 25,000 cubits l on the south side.
48:13 25,000 cubits l and 10,000 cubits
48:15 cubits wide and 25,000 cubits l,
48:30 north side, which is 4,500 cubits l,
48:32 east side, which is 4,500 cubits l,
48:34 which is 4,500 cubits l, will be
Da 8: 3 the canal, and the horns were l.
8:13 "How l will it take for the vision
12: 6 "How l will it be before these
Hos 8: 5 l will they be incapable of purity?
Mic 7:14 Bashan and Gilead as in days l ago.
7:20 oath to our fathers in days l ago.
Hab 1: 2 How l, O LORD, must I call for help,
2: 6 extortion! How l must this go on?'
Zec 1:12 "LORD Almighty, how l will you
2: 2 find out how wide and how l it is."
5: 2 thirty feet l and fifteen feet wide.
Mt 5:21 it was said to the people l ago,
5:33 it was said to the people l ago,
11:21 l ago in sackcloth and ashes.
17:17 how l shall I stay with you? How l
20: 6 here all day l doing nothing?'
23: 5 the tassels on their garments l;
24:48 master is staying away a l time,'
25: 5 The bridegroom was a l time in
25:19 "After a l time the master of those
Mk 2:19 so l as they have him with them.
6:15 like one of the prophets of l ago."
8: 3 of them have come a l distance."
9:19 how l shall I stay with you? How l
9:21 Jesus asked the boy's father, "How l
Lk 1:21 why he stayed so l in the temple.
1:70 through his holy prophets of l ago),
8:27 For a l time this man had not worn
9: 8 of l ago had come back to life.
9:19 of l ago has come back to life."
9:41 how l shall I stay with you and put
10:13 they would have repented l ago,
12:45 'My master is taking a l time in
13:16 has kept bound for eighteen l years,
14:32 the other is still a l way off
15:13 "Not l after that, the younger son
15:20 "But while he was still a l way off,
20: 9 farmers and went away for a l time.
23: 8 because for a l time he had been
Jn 5: 6 been in this condition for a l time,
9: 4 l as it is day, we must do the work
10:24 "How l will you keep us in suspense?
14: 9 I have been among you such a l time?
14:19 Before l, the world will not see me
Ac 1:16 Holy Spirit spoke l ago through
3:21 as he promised l ago through his
8:11 them for a l time with his magic.
14:28 they stayed there a l time with the
24: 2 "We have enjoyed a l period of peace
26: 5 They have known me for a l time and
26:29 Paul replied, "Short time or l—I
27:14 Before very l, a wind of hurricane
27:21 After the men had gone a l time
28: 6 but after waiting a l time and
Ro 7: 1 over a man only as l as he lives?
7: 2 to her husband as l as he is alive,
8:36 your sake we face death all day l;
10:21 he says, "All day l I have held out
16:25 the mystery hidden for l ages past,
1Co 7:39 bound to her husband as l as he lives
11:14 has l hair, it is a disgrace to him,
11:15 that if a woman has l hair, it is
11:15 l hair is given to her as a covering.
2Co 5: 6 know that as l as we are at home in
Gal 4: 1 What I am saying is that as l as the
Eph 3:18 to grasp how wide and l and high and
6: 3 you may enjoy l life on the earth."
Heb 3:13 encourage one another daily, as l as
4: 7 calling it Today, when a l time
9: 8 as l as the first tabernacle was
1Pe 3:20 who disobeyed l ago when God waited
2Pe 1:13 l as I live in the tent of this body,
2Pe 2: 3 condemnation has l been hanging over
3: 5 they deliberately forget that l ago
Jude : 4 condemnation was written about l ago
Rev 6:10 "How l, Sovereign Lord, holy and
21:16 like a square, as l as it was wide.
21:16 and as wide and high as it is l.

Long² (Longed, Longing, Longings, Longs)

Job 3:21 to those who l for death that does
14:15 you will l for the creature your
29: 2 "How I l for the months gone by, for
36:20 Do not l for the night, to drag
Ps 61: 4 I l to dwell in your tent for ever
119:40 How I l for your precepts! Preserve
119:174 I l for your salvation, O LORD, and
Jer 22:27 to the land you l to return to."
44:14 to which they l to return and live;
Hos 7:13 I l to redeem them but they speak
Am 5:18 Woe to you who l for the day of the
5:18 Why do you l for the day of the LORD?
Lk 17:22 is coming when you will l to see
Ro 1:11 I l to see you so that I may impart
Php 1: 8 God can testify how I l for all of
4: 1 brothers, you whom I love and l for
1Th 3: 6 of us and that you l to see us,
3: 6 us, just as we also l to see you.
2Ti 1: 4 Recalling your tears, I l to see you,
1Pe 1:12 angels l to look into these things.
Rev 9: 6 l to die, but death will elude them.

Longed (Long²)

Ge 31:30 gone off because you l to return
2Sa 13:39 the spirit of the king l to go to
14: 1 that the king's heart l for Absalom.
23:15 David l for water and said, "Oh,
1Ch 11:17 David l for water and said, "Oh,
Isa 21: 4 I l for has become a horror to me.
Eze 23:21 you l for the lewdness of your youth,
Mt 13:17 prophets and righteous men l to see
23:37 how often I have l to gather your
Lk 13:34 how often I have l to gather your
15:16 He l to fill his stomach with the
2Ti 4: 8 to all who have l for his appearing.
Rev 18:14 "They will say, 'The fruit you l for

Longing (Long²)

Dt 28:65 with l, and a despairing heart.
Job 7: 2 Like a slave l for the evening
Ps 119:20 My soul is consumed with l for your
119:81 My soul faints with l for your
119:131 I open my mouth and pant, l for your
Pr 13:12 but a l fulfilled is a tree of life.
13:19 A l fulfilled is sweet to the soul,
Eze 23:27 with l or remember Egypt any more.
Lk 16:21 l to eat what fell from the rich
Ro 15:23 been l for many years to see you,
2Co 5: 2 Meanwhile we groan, l to be clothed
7: 7 He told us about your l for me,
7:11 what alarm, what l, what concern,
1Th 2:17 intense l we made every effort to
Heb 11:16 they were l for a better country

Longings (Long²)

Ps 38: 9 All my l lie open before you, O Lord:
112:10 l of the wicked will come to nothing.

Longs (Long²)

Ps 63: 1 my body l for you, in a dry and
Isa 26: 9 in the morning my spirit l for you.
30:18 Yet the LORD l to be gracious to you;
Php 2:26 For he l for all of you and is

Long-suffering (Suffer)

Jer 15:15 You are l—do not take me away;

Long-winded

Job 16: 3 Will your l speeches never end? What

Look (Fine-looking, Looked, Looking, Lookout, Lookouts, Looks)

Ge 4: 5 on Cain and his offering he did not l
13:14 l north and south, east and west.
15: 5 He took him outside and said, "L up
19: 8 L, I have two daughters who have
19:17 "Flee for your lives! Don't l back,
19:20 L, here is a town near enough to run
25:32 "L, I am about to die," Esau said.
27: 6 Rebekah said to her son Jacob, "L, I
29: 7 "L," he said, "the sun is still high;
31:12 he said, 'L up and see that all the
39:14 "L," she said to them, "this Hebrew
41:33 "And now let Pharaoh l for a
49:18 "I l for your deliverance, O LORD.
Ex 1: 9 "L," he said to his people, "the
3: 4 LORD saw that he had gone over to l,
3: 6 because he was afraid to l at God.
5: 5 Pharaoh said, "L, the people of the
5:21 they said, "May the LORD l upon you
Lev 13:36 the priest does not need to l for
26: 9 "'I will l on you with favour and
Nu 4:20 the Kohathites must not go in to l
15:39 You will have these tassels to l at
21: 8 who is bitten can l at it and live."
32: 8 Kadesh Barnea to l over the land.
Dt 3:27 Go up to the top of Pisgah and l
3:27 L at the land with your own eyes,
4:19 you l up to the sky and see the sun,
4:29 you will find him if you l for him
7:16 Do not l on them with pity and do
26:15 L down from heaven, your holy
Jos 2: 1 "Go, l over the land," he said,
2: 2 The king of Jericho was told, "L!
22:28 we will answer: L at the replica of
Jdg 6:37 l, I will place a wool fleece on the
9:36 Gaal saw them, he said to Zebul, "L,
9:37 Gaal spoke up again: "L, people are
14: 8 aside to l at the lion's carcass.
19: 9 said, "Now l, it's almost evening.
19:24 L, here is my virgin daughter, and
21:19 l, there is the annual festival of
Ru 1:15 "L," said Naomi, "your sister-in-law
1Sa 1:11 if you will only l upon your
9: 3 you and go and l for the donkeys."
9: 6 the servant replied, "L, in this
9: 8 The servant answered him again. "L,"
10: 2 set out to l for have been found.
14:11 "L!" said the Philistines. "The
14:33 someone said to Saul, "L, the men
16: 7 The LORD does not l at the things
18:22 'L, the king is pleased with you,
20: 2 L, my father doesn't do anything,
20: 5 David said, "L, tomorrow is the
20:21 If I say to him, 'L, the arrows are
20:22 if I say to the boy, 'L, the arrows
21:14 Achish said to his servants, "L at
23: 1 David was told, "L, the Philistines
24: 2 set out to l for David and his men
24:11 See, my father, l at this piece of
26:16 L around you. Where are the king's
26:20 The king of Israel has come out to l
28:14 "What does he l like?" he asked. "An
28:21 "L, your maidservant has obeyed you.
2Sa 2:22 I l your brother Joab in the face?"
3:24 have you done? L, Abner came to you.
13: 4 "Why do you, the king's son, l so
14:30 he said to his servants, "L, Joab's
14:32 Absalom said to Joab, "L, I sent
15: 3 Absalom would say to him, "L, your
18:26 "L, another man running alone!" The
1Ki 1: 2 his servants said to him, "Let us l
12:16 L after your own house, O David!"
17:23 "L, your son is alive!"
18:10 has not sent someone to l for you.
18:43 "Go and l towards the sea," he told
20:31 His officials said to him, "L, we
22:13 "L, as one man the other prophets
2Ki 2:16 "L," they said, "we your servants
2:16 Let them go and l for your master.
2:19 "L, our lord, this town is well
3:14 not l at you or even notice you.
4:25 "L! There's the Shunammite!
6: 1 "L, the place where we meet with you
6:32 L, when the messenger comes, shut
7: 2 "L, even if the LORD should open the
7: 6 "L, the king of Israel has hired the
7:19 "L, even if the LORD should open the
9: 2 you get there, l for Jehu son of
10:23 "L around and see that no servants

2Ki 18:21 L now, you are depending on Egypt,
1Ch 16:11 L to the LORD and his strength; seek
21:23 L, I will give the oxen for the
2Ch 10:16 L after your own house, O David!"
18:12 "L, as one man the other prophets
Ne 2: 2 "Why does your face l so sad when
2: 3 Why should my face not l sad when
Est 1:11 nobles, for she was lovely to l at.
Job 6:19 The caravans of Tema l for water,
6:19 merchants of Sheba l in hope.
6:28 "But now be so kind as to l at me.
7: 8 l for me, but I will be no more.
7:19 Will you never l away from me, or
8: 5 if you will l to God and plead with
11:18 you will l about you and take your
14: 6 l away from him and let him alone,
19:15 they l upon me as an alien.
20: 9 his place will l on him no more.
21: 5 L at me and be astonished; clap your
24: 1 know him l in vain for such days?
30:20 I stand up, but you merely l at me.
31: 1 eyes not to l lustfully at a girl.
35: 5 L up at the heavens and see; gaze at
37:21 Now no-one can l at the sun, bright
40:11 Unleash the fury of your wrath, l at
40:12 l at every proud man and humble him,
40:15 "L at the behemoth, which I made
Ps 11: 2 For l, the wicked bend their bows;
13: 3 L on me and answer, O LORD my God.
25:18 L upon my affliction and my distress
34: 5 Those who l to him are radiant;
35:17 O Lord, how long will you l on?
37:10 l for them, they will not be found.
39: 7 "But now, Lord, what do I l for?
39:13 L away from me, that I may rejoice
40: 4 who does not l to the proud, to
59: 4 Arise to help me; l on my plight!
80:14 L down from heaven and see! Watch
84: 9 L upon our shield, O God; l with
104:27 These all l to you to give them
105: 4 L to the LORD and his strength; seek
112: 8 he will l in triumph on his foes.
113: 6 who stoops down to l on the heavens
118: 7 I will l in triumph on my enemies.
119:153 L upon my suffering and deliver me,
119:158 I l on the faithless with loathing,
123: 2 the eyes of slaves l to the hand of
123: 2 as the eyes of a maid l to the hand
123: 2 so our eyes l to the LORD our God,
142: 4 L to my right and see; no-one is
145:15 The eyes of all l to you, and you
Pr 1:28 will l for me but will not find me.
2: 4 if you l for it as for silver and
4:25 Let your eyes l straight ahead, fix
15:30 A cheerful l brings joy to the heart,
Ecc 1:10 "L! This is something new"? It was
1:16 I thought to myself, "L, I have
7:27 "L," says the Teacher, "this is what
SS 2: 8 Listen! My lover! L! Here he comes,
2: 9 L! There he stands behind our wall,
3: 7 L! It is Solomon's carriage,
3:11 l at King Solomon wearing the crown
6: 1 that we may l for him with you?
6:11 l at the new growth in the valley,
Isa 3: 9 The l on their faces testifies
8:22 they will l towards the earth and
10:12 heart and the haughty l in his eyes.
13: 8 They will l aghast at each other,
13:18 they l with compassion on children.
17: 7 In that day men will l to their
17: 8 They will not l to the altars, the
18: 4 "I will remain quiet and will l on
21: 9 L, here comes a man in a chariot
22:11 but you did not l to the One who
23:13 L at the land of the Babylonians,
30: 2 l for help to Pharaoh's protection,
31: 1 do not l to the Holy One of Israel
33: 7 L, their brave men cry aloud in the
33:20 L upon Zion, the city of our
34:16 L in the scroll of the LORD and read
36: 6 L now, you are depending on Egypt,
38:11 no longer will I l on mankind,
40:26 Lift your eyes and l to the heavens
41:27 I was the first to tell Zion, 'L,
41:28 I l but there is no-one—no-one
42:18 "Hear, you deaf; l, you blind, and

Isa 48: 6 heard these things; l at them all
49:18 Lift up your eyes and l around;
51: 1 L to the rock from which you were
51: 2 l to Abraham, your father, and to
51: 3 l with compassion on all her ruins;
51: 5 l to me and wait in hope for my arm.
51: 6 eyes to the heavens, l at the earth
59: 9 We l for light, but all is darkness
59:11 We l for justice, but find none;
60: 4 "Lift up your eyes and l about you:
60: 5 you will l and be radiant, your
60: 9 Surely the islands l to me; in the
63:15 L down from heaven and see from your
64: 9 Oh, l upon us we pray, for we are
66:24 "And they will go out and l upon the
Jer 2:10 over to the coasts of Kittim and l,
3: 2 "L up to the barren heights and see.
3: 3 have the brazen l of a prostitute
4:13 L! He advances like the clouds, his
5: 1 l around and consider, search
5: 3 O LORD, do not your eyes l for truth?
6:16 "Stand at the crossroads and l; ask
6:22 LORD says: "L, an army is coming
7: 8 l, you are trusting in deceptive
18:11 'This is what the LORD says: L! I am
25:32 "L! Disaster is spreading from
39:12 "Take him and l after him; don't
40: 4 if you like, and I will l after you;
40: 4 L, the whole country lies before you;
48:40 what the LORD says: "L! An eagle is
49:22 L! An eagle will soar and swoop down,
50:41 "L! An army is coming from the north;
Lam 1: 9 "L, O LORD, on my affliction, for
1:11 "L, O LORD, and consider, for I am
1:12 you who pass by? L around and see.
1:18 you peoples; l upon my suffering.
2:20 "L, O LORD, and consider: Whom have
3:63 L at them! Sitting or standing, they
5: 1 to us; l, and see our disgrace.
Eze 5:11 not l on you with pity or spare you.
7: 4 I will not l on you with pity or
7: 9 I will not l on you with pity or
8: 5 "Son of man, l towards the north
8:17 L at them putting the branch to
8:18 l on them with pity or spare them.
9:10 I will not l on them with pity or
18: 6 or l to the idols of the house of
18:15 or l to the idols of the house of
23:27 You will not l on these things with
25: 8 'Because Moab and Seir said, "L, the
33:25 and l to your idols and shed blood,
34:11 for my sheep and l after them.
34:12 them, so will I l after my sheep.
36: 9 am concerned for you and will l on
40: 4 The man said to me, "Son of man, l
44: 5 The LORD said to me, "Son of man, l
Da 2:13 and men were sent to l for Daniel
3:25 He said, "L! I see four men walking
5:10 "Don't be alarmed! Don't l so pale!
9:17 For your sake, O Lord, l with favour
Hos 2: 2 the adulterous l from her face
2: 7 will l for them but not find them.
Am 6: 2 Go to Calneh and l at it; go from
7: 8 said, "L, I am setting a plumb-line
Ob :12 You should not l down on your
:13 nor l down on them in their calamity
Jnh 2: 4 l again towards your holy temple.'
Mic 1: 3 L! The LORD is coming from his
Na 1:15 L, there on the mountains, the feet
2: 4 They l like flaming torches; they
3:13 L at your troops—they are all
Hab 1: 3 Why do you make me l at injustice?
1: 5 "L at the nations and watch—and be
1:13 Your eyes are too pure to l on evil
2: 1 l to see what he will say to me,
Hag 2: 3 How does it l to you now? Does it
Zec 5: 5 "L up and see what this is that is
6: 8 he called to me, "L, those going
12:10 They will l on me, the one they have
Mt 6:16 "When you fast, do not l sombre as
6:26 L at the birds of the air; they do
7: 3 "Why do you l at the speck of
12: 2 "L! Your disciples are doing what is
18:10 "See that you do not l down on one
18:12 to l for the one that wandered off?
23:27 which l beautiful on the outside but

Mt 23:38 L, your house is left to you
24:23 'L, here is the Christ!' or, 'There
25:43 prison and you did not l after me.'
26:45 L, the hour is near, and the Son of
26:65 L, now you have heard the blasphemy.
28: 1 other Mary went to l at the tomb.
Mk 1:36 Simon and his companions went to l
2:24 The Pharisees said to him, "L, why
8:24 they l like trees walking around."
11:21 "Rabbi, l! The fig-tree you cursed
12:15 me a denarius and let me l at it."
13: 1 "L, Teacher! What massive stones!
13:21 'L, here is the Christ!' or, 'L,
14:41 L, the Son of Man is betrayed into
Lk 2:45 went back to Jerusalem to l for him.
6:41 "Why do you l at the speck of
9:38 l at my son, for he is my only child
10:35 'L after him,' he said, 'and when I
13: 6 and he went to l for fruit on it,
13: 7 to l for fruit on this fig-tree
13:35 L, your house is left to you
15:29 he answered his father, 'L! All
18:13 He would not even l up to heaven,
19: 8 "L, Lord! Here and now I give half
21:29 He told them this parable: "L at the
24: 5 you l for the living among the dead?
24:39 L at my hands and my feet. It is I
Jn 1:29 "L, the Lamb of God, who takes away
1:36 saw Jesus passing by, he said, "L,
4:35 open your eyes and l at the fields!
7:34 You will l for me, but you will not
7:36 'You will l for me, but you will not
7:52 you from Galilee, too? L into it
8:21 am going away, and you will l for me
12:19 L how the whole world has gone after
13:33 You will l for me, and just as I
19: 4 "L, I am bringing him out to you to
19:37 l on the one they have pierced."
20:11 she bent over to l into the tomb
Ac 3: 4 Then Peter said, "L at us!"
5: 9 L! The feet of the men who buried
5:25 someone came and said, "L! The men
7:31 As he went over to l more closely,
7:32 with fear and did not dare to l.
7:56 "L," he said, "I see heaven open and
8:36 the eunuch said, "L, here is water.
11:25 Barnabas went to Tarsus to l for
13:41 "'L, you scoffers, wonder and
Ro 1:23 images made to l like mortal man
14: 3 must not l down on him who does not,
14:10 why do you l down on your brother?
1Co 1:22 signs and Greeks l for wisdom,
7:27 you unmarried? Do not l for a wife.
2Co 3: 7 so that the Israelites could not l
Php 2: 4 Each of you should l not only to
1Ti 4:12 Don't let anyone l down on you
Jas 1:27 to l after orphans and widows in
5: 4 L! The wages you failed to pay the
1Pe 1:12 angels long to l into these things.
2Pe 3:12 you l forward to the day of God and
Rev 1: 7 L, he is coming with the clouds, and
5: 3 open the scroll or even l inside it.
5: 4 to open the scroll or l inside.

Looked (Look)

Ge 4: 4 The LORD l with favour on Abel and
13:10 Lot l up and saw that the whole
18: 2 Abraham l up and saw three men
18:16 the men got up to leave, they l down
19:26 Lot's wife l back, and she became a
19:28 He l down towards Sodom and Gomorrah,
22: 4 On the third day Abraham l up and
22:13 Abraham l up and there in a thicket
24:63 he l up, he saw camels approaching.
24:64 Rebekah also l up and saw Isaac. She
26: 8 king of the Philistines l down from
31:10 I once had a dream in which I l up
33: 1 Jacob l up and there was Esau,
33: 5 Esau l up and saw the women and
37:25 they l up and saw a caravan of
41:21 they l just as ugly as before.
43:29 he l about and saw his brother
43:30 out and l for a place to weep.
43:33 l at each other in astonishment.
Ex 2:25 God l on the Israelites and was

Ex 14:10 the Israelites l up, and there were
14:24 LORD l down from the pillar of fire
16:10 they l towards the desert, and there
24:17 the glory of the LORD l like a
Nu 9:15 above the tabernacle l like fire.
9:16 it, and at night it l like fire.
11: 7 coriander seed and l like resin.
13:33 eyes, and we l the same to them."
17: 9 They l at them, and each man took
21: 9 and l at the bronze snake, he lived.
24: 2 Balaam l out and saw Israel encamped
Dt 9:16 I l, I saw that you had sinned
Jos 5:13 he l up and saw a man standing in
8:20 The men of Ai l back and saw the
Jdg 13: 6 He l like an angel of God, very
19:17 he l and saw the traveller in the
1Sa 6:13 and when they l up and saw the ark,
6:19 they had l into the ark of the LORD.
9:16 I have l upon my people, for their
10:21 l for him, he was not to be found.
17:42 He l David over and saw that he was
24: 8 When Saul l behind him, David
2Sa 2:20 Abner l behind him and asked, "Is
13:34 Now the man standing watch l up and
18:24 l out, he saw a man running alone.
24:20 Araunah l and saw the king and his
1Ki 2:15 All Israel l to me as their king.
3:21 But when I l at him closely in the
18:43 And he went up and l. "There is
19: 6 He l around, and there by his head
2Ki 2:24 He turned round, l at them and
3:22 the water l red—like blood.
6:17 he l and saw the hills full of
6:20 LORD opened their eyes and they l,
6:30 the people l, and there, underneath,
9:30 her hair and l out of a window.
9:32 He l up at the window and called out
9:32 Two or three eunuchs l down at him.
11:14 She l and there was the king,
23:16 Josiah l around, and when he saw the
1Ch 17:17 You have l on me as though I were
21:16 David l up and saw the angel of the
21:21 and when Araunah l and saw him, he
2Ch 20:24 desert and l towards the vast army,
23:13 She l, and there was the king,
26:20 and all the other priests l at him,
Ne 4:14 After I l things over, I stood up
Est 3: 6 Instead Haman l for a way to destroy
Job 28:27 he l at wisdom and appraised it; he
30:26 I l for light, then came darkness.
Ps 37:36 I l for him, he could not be found.
54: 7 eyes have l in triumph on my foes.
69:20 left me helpless; I l for sympathy,
102:19 "The LORD l down from his sanctuary
114: 3 The sea l and fled, the Jordan
Pr 7: 6 At the window of my house I l out
7:15 I came out to meet you; I l for you
Ecc 4: 1 Again I l and saw all the oppression
SS 3: 1 All night long on my bed I l for the
3: 1 I l for him but did not find him.
3: 2 So I l for him but did not find him.
5: 6 I l for him but did not find him.
Isa 5: 2 Then he l for a crop of good grapes,
5: 4 for it? When I l for good grapes,
5: 7 And he l for justice, but saw
22: 8 you l in that day to the weapons
38:14 My eyes grew weak as I l to the
57: 8 love, and you l on their nakedness.
59:15 The LORD l and was displeased that
63: 5 I l, but there was no-one to help,
Jer 4:23 I l at the earth, and it was
4:24 I l at the mountains, and they were
4:25 I l, and there were no people;
4:26 I l, and the fruitful land was a
31:26 At this I awoke and l around. My
36:16 they l at each other in fear and
Lam 1: 7 Her enemies l at her and laughed at
Eze 1: 4 I l, and I saw a windstorm coming
1: 4 of the fire l like glowing metal,
1: 5 in the fire was what l like four
1:10 Their faces l like this: Each of
1:15 I l at the living creatures, I saw
1:16 chrysolite, and all four l alike.
1:22 was what l like an expanse,
1:26 what l like a throne of sapphire,
1:27 waist up he l like glowing metal,
Eze 1:27 and that from there down he l like
2: 9 I l, and I saw a hand stretched out
8: 2 I l, and I saw a figure like that of
8: 3 He stretched out what l like a hand
8: 5 So I l, and in the entrance north
8: 7 I l, and I saw a hole in the wall.
8:10 went in and l, and I saw portrayed
10: 1 I l, and I saw the likeness of a
10: 8 what l like the hands of a man.)
10: 9 I l, and I saw beside the cherubim
10:10 the four of them l alike; each was
10:21 was what l like the hands of a man.
16: 5 No-one l on you with pity or had
16: 8 "'Later I passed by, and when I l
20:17 Yet I l on them with pity and did
22:30 "I l for a man among them who would
23:15 l like Babylonian chariot officers,
34: 6 and no-one searched or l for them.
37: 8 I l, and tendons and flesh appeared
40: 2 some buildings that l like a city.
44: 4 I l and saw the glory of the LORD
Da 1:15 At the end of the ten days they l
2:31 "You l, O king, and there before you
4:10 I l, and there before me stood a
4:13 I l, and there before me was a
7: 2 "In my vision at night I l, and
7: 5 a second beast, which l like a bear.
7: 6 "After that, I l, and there before
7: 6 beast, one that l like a leopard.
7: 7 in my vision at night I l, and there
7: 9 "As I l, "thrones were set in place,
7:13 "In my vision at night I l, and
7:20 l more imposing than the others
8: 3 I l up, and there before me was a
8:15 me stood one who l like a man.
10: 5 I l up and there before me was a man
10:16 one who l like a man touched my lips
10:18 Again the one who l like a man
12: 5 I, Daniel, l, and there before me
Hab 3: 6 He stood, and shook the earth; he l
Zec 1:18 I l up—and there before me were
2: 1 I l up—and there before me was a
5: 1 I l again—and there before me was a
5: 9 I l up—and there before me were two
6: 1 I l up again—and there before me
Mt 17: 8 they l up, they saw no-one except
19:26 Jesus l at them and said, "With man
21:46 They l for a way to arrest him, but
25:36 I was sick and you l after me, I was
Mk 3: 5 He l round at them in anger and,
3:34 he l at those seated in a circle
7:34 He l up to heaven and with a deep
8:24 He l up and said, "I see people;
8:33 when Jesus turned and l at his
9: 8 Suddenly, when they l round, they no
9:26 The boy l so much like a corpse that
10:21 Jesus l at him and loved him. "One
10:23 Jesus l around and said to his
10:27 Jesus l at them and said, "With man
11:11 He l around at everything, but since
12:12 they l for a way to arrest him
14:67 Peter warming himself, she l closely
16: 4 when they l up, they saw that the
Lk 6:10 He l round at them all, and then
16:23 where he was in torment, he l up and
18: 9 and l down on everybody else,
18:24 Jesus l at him and said, "How hard
19: 5 Jesus reached the spot, he l up and
20:17 Jesus l directly at them and asked,
20:19 the chief priests l for a way to
21: 1 he l up, Jesus saw the rich putting
22:56 She l closely at him and said, "This
22:61 The Lord turned and l straight at
Jn 1:42 Jesus l at him and said, "You are
6: 5 Jesus l up and saw a great crowd
11:41 Then Jesus l up and said, "Father, I
17: 1 After Jesus said this, he l towards
20: 5 He bent over and l in at the strips
Ac 3: 4 Peter l straight at him, as did John
6:15 the Sanhedrin l intently at Stephen,
7:55 Stephen, full of the Holy Spirit, l
11: 6 I l into it and saw four-footed
13: 9 l straight at Elymas and said,
14: 9 Paul l directly at him, saw that he
17:23 For as I walked around and l
23: 1 Paul l straight at the Sanhedrin
1Jn 1: 1 which we have l at and our hands
Rev 4: 1 After this I l, and there before me
4: 6 was what l like a sea of glass,
5:11 I l and heard the voice of many
6: 2 I l, and there before me was a white
6: 5 "Come!" I l, and there before me was
6: 8 I l, and there before me was a pale
7: 9 After this I l and there before me
9: 7 The locusts l like horses prepared
9:17 I saw in my vision l like this:
11:12 a cloud, while their enemies l on.
14: 1 I l, and there before me was the
14:14 I l, and there before me was a white
15: 2 I saw what l like a sea of glass
15: 5 After this I l and in heaven the
16:13 I saw three evil spirits that l like

Looking (Look)

Ge 37:15 asked him, "What are you l for?"
37:16 He replied, "I'm l for my brothers.
42: 1 do you just keep l at each other?"
Ex 22:10 or is taken away while no-one is l,
25:20 each other, l towards the cover.
37: 9 each other, l towards the cover.
Dt 22: 2 and keep it until he comes l for it.
Jdg 4:22 I will show you the man you're l for
17: 9 "and I'm l for a place to stay.
1Sa 10:14 been?" "L for the donkeys," he said.
19: 2 warned him, "My father Saul is l for
1Ki 20: 7 "See how this man is l for trouble!
2Ki 6:19 lead you to the man you are l for.
Ps 69: 3 My eyes fail, l for my God.
119:82 My eyes fail, l for your promise;
119:123 l for your salvation, l for your
Ecc 12: 3 l through the windows grow dim;
SS 7: 4 tower of Lebanon l towards Damascus.
Isa 8:21 will become enraged and, l upward,
Jer 46: 5 They flee in haste without l back,
Lam 4:17 Moreover, our eyes failed, l in vain
Da 1:10 Why should he see you l worse than
7:11 I kept l until the beast was slain
Mt 12:10 L for a reason to accuse Jesus, they
13:45 like a merchant l for fine pearls.
14:19 and the two fish and l up to heaven,
26:59 the whole Sanhedrin were l for false
28: 5 are l for Jesus, who was crucified.
Mk 1:37 exclaimed: "Everyone is l for you!"
3: 2 Some of them were l for a reason to
3:32 and brothers are outside l for you."
5:32 Jesus kept l around to see who had
6:41 and the two fish and l up to heaven,
11:18 and began l for a way to kill him,
14: 1 the teachers of the law were l for
14:55 the whole Sanhedrin were l for
16: 6 "You are l for Jesus the Nazarene,
Lk 2:38 to all who were l forward to the
2:44 Then they began l for him among
4:42 The people were l for him and when
6: 7 were l for a reason to accuse Jesus,
6:20 L at his disciples, he said:
9:16 and the two fish and l up to heaven,
17: 7 ploughing or l after the sheep.
22: 2 l for some way to get rid of Jesus,
Jn 6:26 "I tell you the truth, you are l for
11:56 They kept l for Jesus, and as they
18: 8 l for me, then let these men go."
20:15 crying? Who is it you are l for?"
Ac 1:10 They were l intently up into the sky
1:11 "why do you stand here l into the
10:19 "Simon, three men are l for you.
10:21 the men, "I'm the one you're l for.
2Co 10: 7 You are l only on the surface of
Php 4:17 I am l for a gift, but I am l for
1Th 2: 6 We were not l for praise from men,
Heb 11:10 For he was l forward to the city
11:14 are l for a country of their own.
11:26 he was l ahead to his reward.
13:14 are l for the city that is to come.
Jas 1:24 and, after l at himself, goes away
1Pe 5: 8 lion l for someone to devour.
2Pe 3:13 we are l forward to a new heaven
3:14 since you are l forward to this,
Rev 5: 6 I saw a Lamb, l as if it had been

Lookout (Look)
2Ki 9:17 the **l** standing on the tower in
9:18 The **l** reported, "The messenger has
9:20 The **l** reported, "He has reached them,
Isa 21: 6 post a **l** and have him report what
21: 8 the **l** shouted, "Day after day, my

Lookouts (Look)
1Sa 14:16 Saul's **l** at Gibeah in Benjamin saw

Looks (Look)
Lev 14:35 that **l** like mildew in my house.'
1Sa 16: 7 not look at the things man **l** at.
16: 7 Man **l** at the outward appearance,
16: 7 but the LORD **l** at the heart."
Ezr 8:22 our God is on everyone who **l** to him,
Job 8:17 and **l** for a place among the stones.
41:34 He **l** down on all that are haughty;
Ps 14: 2 The LORD **l** down from heaven on the
33:13 From heaven the LORD **l** down and sees
53: 2 God **l** down from heaven on the sons
85:11 righteousness **l** down from heaven.
104:32 he who **l** at the earth, and it
138: 6 is on high, he **l** upon the lowly
Pr 20: 4 harvest time he **l** but finds nothing.
25:23 so a sly tongue brings angry **l**.
27:18 **l** after his master will be honoured.
Ecc 11: 4 **l** at the clouds will not reap.
Isa 5:30 And if one **l** at the land, he will
40:20 He **l** for a skilled craftsman to set
Lam 3:50 until the LORD **l** down from heaven
Eze 18:12 He **l** to the idols. He does
34:12 a shepherd **l** after his scattered
Da 3:25 fourth **l** like a son of the gods."
Mt 5:28 I tell you that anyone who **l** at a
16: 4 wicked and adulterous generation **l**
Lk 9:62 "No-one who **l** back is fit for
Jn 6:40 is that everyone who **l** to the Son
9: 9 Others said, "No, he only **l** like him
12:45 he **l** at me, he sees the one who sent
Php 2:21 For everyone **l** out for his own
Jas 1:23 a man who **l** at his face in a
1:24 immediately forgets what he **l** like.
1:25 the man who **l** intently into the

Loom (Looms)
Jdg 16:13 into the fabric ⌊on the **l**⌋ and
16:14 the pin and the **l**, with the fabric.
Isa 38:12 and he has cut me off from the **l**;

Looms (Loom)
Jer 6: 1 For disaster **l** out of the north,

Loops
Ex 26: 4 Make **l** of blue material along the
26: 5 Make fifty **l** on one curtain and
26: 5 fifty **l** on the end curtain of the
26: 5 set, with the **l** opposite each other.
26:10 Make fifty **l** along the edge of the
26:11 put them in the **l** to fasten the tent
36:11 they made **l** of blue material along
36:12 They also made fifty **l** on one
36:12 fifty **l** on the end curtain of the
36:12 set, with the **l** opposite each other.
36:17 they made fifty **l** along the edge of

Loose (Loosed, Loosen, Loosened)
Jdg 15: 5 lit the torches and let the foxes **l**
16: 3 posts, and tore them **l**, bar and all.
Job 6: 9 to let **l** his hand and cut me off!
12:15 them **l**, they devastate the land.
38:31 Can you **l** the cords of Orion?
Ps 78:26 He let **l** the east wind from the
Isa 7:25 are turned **l** and where sheep run.
33:23 Your rigging hangs **l**: The mast is
58: 6 to **l** the chains of injustice and
Mt 16:19 **l** on earth will be loosed in heaven.
18:18 **l** on earth will be loosed in heaven.
Ac 16:26 open, and everybody's chains came **l**.
27:40 Cutting **l** the anchors, they left

Loosed (Loose)
Mt 16:19 loose on earth will be **l** in heaven.
18:18 loose on earth will be **l** in heaven.
Lk 1:64 was opened and his tongue was **l**,

Loosen (Loose)
Nu 5:18 he shall **l** her hair and place in her

Loosened (Loose)
Isa 5:27 not a belt is **l** at the waist,
Mk 7:35 was **l** and he began to speak plainly.

Loot (Looted, Looter, Looting)
Isa 10: 6 to seize **l** and snatch plunder, and
17:14 is the portion of those who **l** us,
21: 2 traitor betrays, the looter takes **l**
42:22 rescue them; they have been made **l**,
42:24 Who handed Jacob over to become **l**,
Eze 7:21 and as **l** to the wicked of the earth
26:12 your wealth and **l** your merchandise;
29:19 He will **l** and plunder the land as
38:12 I will plunder and **l** and turn my
38:13 Have you gathered your hordes to **l**,
39:10 them and **l** those who looted them,
Da 11:24 He will distribute plunder, **l** and
Am 3:10 plunder and **l** in their fortresses."

Looted (Loot)
Ge 34:27 **l** the city where their sister had
2Ki 21:14 **l** and plundered by all their foes,
Isa 13:16 will be **l** and their wives ravished.
42:22 this is a people plundered and **l**,
Eze 39:10 **l** them, declares the Sovereign LORD.

Looter (Loot)
Isa 21: 2 traitor betrays, the **l** takes loot.

Looting (Loot)
1Sa 23: 1 and are **l** the threshing-floors,"

Lop
Isa 10:33 **l** off the boughs with great power.

LORD (*Angel of the LORD, Anger of the LORD, Ark of the LORD, Arm of the LORD, As surely as the LORD lives, As the LORD commanded, Before the LORD, Covenant of the LORD, Day of the LORD, Declares the LORD, Evil in the eyes of the LORD, Fear of the LORD, Fear the LORD, Glory of the LORD, Hand of the LORD, Holy to the LORD, House of the LORD, I am the LORD, Know that I am the LORD, Know that the LORD, Law of the LORD, LORD Almighty, LORD God, LORD God Almighty, LORD is my rock, LORD your God, LORD's, Love the LORD, Moses the servant of the LORD, Mountain of the LORD, Name of the LORD, Praise be to the LORD, Praise the LORD, Presence of the LORD, Return to the LORD, Right in the eyes of the LORD, Servant of the LORD, Sing to the LORD, Sovereign LORD, Spirit of the LORD, Temple of the LORD, Voice of the LORD, Way of the LORD, Word of the LORD, Zeal of the LORD*)
Ge 4: 1 "With the help of the **L** I have
4: 3 of the soil as an offering to the **L**.
4: 4 The **L** looked with favour on Abel and
4: 6 the **L** said to Cain, "Why are you
4: 9 the **L** said to Cain, "Where is your
4:10 The **L** said, "What have you done?
4:13 Cain said to the **L**, "My punishment
4:15 the **L** said to him, "Not so; if
4:15 Then the **L** put a mark on Cain so
5:29 by the ground the **L** has cursed."
6: 3 the **L** said, "My Spirit will not
6: 5 The **L** saw how great man's wickedness
6: 6 The **L** was grieved that he had made
6: 7 the **L** said, "I will wipe mankind,
6: 8 found favour in the eyes of the **L**.
7: 1 The **L** then said to Noah, "Go into
7: 5 Noah did all that the **L** commanded
Ge 7:16 Then the **L** shut him in.
8:20 Noah built an altar to the **L** and,
8:21 The **L** smelled the pleasing aroma and
9:26 He also said, "Blessed be the **L**, the
11: 5 the **L** came down to see the city and
11: 6 The **L** said, "If as one people
11: 8 the **L** scattered them from there over
11: 9 because there the **L** confused the
11: 9 From there the **L** scattered them over
12: 1 The **L** had said to Abram, "Leave your
12: 4 Abram left, as the **L** had told him;
12: 7 The **L** appeared to Abram and said,
12: 7 he built an altar there to the **L**,
12: 8 There he built an altar to the **L**
12:17 the **L** inflicted serious diseases on
13:10 like the garden of the **L**, like the
13:13 were sinning greatly against the **L**.
13:14 The **L** said to Abram after Lot had
13:18 where he built an altar to the **L**.
14:22 "I have raised my hand to the **L**,
15: 6 Abram believed the **L**, and he
15: 9 the **L** said to him, "Bring me a
15:13 the **L** said to him, "Know for certain
15:18 On that day the **L** made a covenant
16: 2 she said to Abram, "The **L** has kept
16: 5 May the **L** judge between you and me."
16:11 for the **L** has heard of your misery.
16:13 She gave this name to the **L** who
17: 1 the **L** appeared to him and said,
18: 1 The **L** appeared to Abraham near the
18:10 the **L** said, "I will surely return to
18:13 the **L** said to Abraham, "Why did
18:14 Is anything too hard for the **L**?
18:17 the **L** said, "Shall I hide from
18:19 the **L** will bring about for Abraham
18:20 the **L** said, "The outcry against
18:26 The **L** said, "If I find fifty
18:33 the **L** had finished speaking with
19:13 The outcry to the **L** against its
19:14 the **L** is about to destroy the city!"
19:16 for the **L** was merciful to them.
19:24 the **L** rained down burning sulphur on
19:24 from the **L** out of the heavens.
20:18 for the **L** had closed up every womb
21: 1 Now the **L** was gracious to Sarah as
21: 1 **L** did for Sarah what he had promised
22:14 called that place The **L** Will Provide
24: 1 the **L** had blessed him in every way.
24: 3 I want you to swear by the **L**, the
24: 7 "The **L**, the God of heaven, who
24:12 he prayed, "O **L**, God of my master
24:21 **L** had made his journey successful.
24:26 man bowed down and worshipped the **L**,
24:27 As for me, the **L** has led me on the
24:31 "Come, you who are blessed by the **L**,"
24:35 The **L** has blessed my master
24:40 "He replied, 'The **L**, before whom I
24:42 'O **L**, God of my master Abraham, if
24:44 **L** has chosen for my master's son.'
24:48 I bowed down and worshipped the **L**.
24:48 I praised the **L**, the God of my
24:50 answered, "This is from the **L**;
24:51 as the **L** has directed."
24:56 **L** has granted success to my journey.
25:21 Isaac prayed to the **L** on behalf of
25:21 The **L** answered his prayer, and his
25:22 So she went to enquire of the **L**.
25:23 The **L** said to her, "Two nations are
26: 2 The **L** appeared to Isaac and said,
26:12 because the **L** blessed him.
26:22 "Now the **L** has given us room and we
26:24 That night the **L** appeared to him and
26:28 saw clearly that the **L** was with you
26:29 And now you are blessed by the **L**."
27:27 of a field that the **L** has blessed.
28:13 There above it stood the **L**, and he
28:16 "Surely the **L** is in this place, and
28:21 then the **L** will be my God
29:31 the **L** saw that Leah was not loved,
29:32 because the **L** has seen my misery.
29:33 the **L** heard that I am not loved,
30:24 "May the **L** add to me another son.
30:27 **L** has blessed me because of you."
30:30 and the **L** has blessed you wherever I
31: 3 the **L** said to Jacob, "Go back to the
31:49 "May the **L** keep watch between you

Ge 32: 9 Jacob prayed, "O God of my father
38: 7 so the **L** put him to death.
39: 2 The **L** was with Joseph and he
39: 3 his master saw that the **L** was with
39: 3 that the **L** gave him success in
39: 5 the **L** blessed the household of the
39: 5 The blessing of the **L** was on
39:21 the **L** was with him; he showed him
39:23 because the **L** was with Joseph and
49:18 "I look for your deliverance, O **L**.
Ex 3: 4 the **L** saw that he had gone over to
3: 7 The **L** said, "I have indeed seen the
3:15 'The **L**, the God of your fathers—the
3:16 'The **L**, the God of your fathers—the
3:18 'The **L**, the God of the Hebrews, has
3:18 offer sacrifices to the **L** our God.'
4: 1 say, 'The **L** did not appear to you'?"
4: 2 the **L** said to him, "What is that in
4: 3 The **L** said, "Throw it on the ground."
4: 4 the **L** said to him, "Reach out your
4: 5 "This," said the **L**, "is so that they
4: 5 so that they may believe that the **L**,
4: 6 the **L** said, "Put your hand inside
4: 8 the **L** said, "If they do not believe
4:10 Moses said to the **L**, "O Lord, I have
4:11 The **L** said to him, "Who gave man his
4:11 makes him blind? Is it not I, the **L**?
4:19 the **L** had said to Moses in Midian,
4:21 The **L** said to Moses, "When you
4:22 say to Pharaoh, 'This is what the **L**
4:24 the **L** met ⌊Moses⌋ and was about to
4:26 So the **L** let him alone.
4:27 The **L** said to Aaron, "Go into the
4:28 everything the **L** had sent him to
4:30 Aaron told them everything the **L** had
4:31 they heard that the **L** was concerned
5: 1 what the **L**, the God of Israel
5: 2 Pharaoh said, "Who is the **L**, that I
5: 2 I do not know the **L** and I will not
5: 3 offer sacrifices to the **L** our God,
5:17 'Let us go and sacrifice to the **L**.'
5:21 they said, "May the **L** look upon you
5:22 Moses returned to the **L** and said,
6: 1 the **L** said to Moses, "Now you will
6: 3 but by my name the **L** I did not make
6:10 Then the **L** said to Moses,
6:12 Moses said to the **L**, "If the
6:13 Now the **L** spoke to Moses and Aaron
6:26 Aaron and Moses to whom the **L** said,
6:28 the **L** spoke to Moses in Egypt,
6:30 Moses said to the **L**, "Since I speak
7: 1 the **L** said to Moses, "See, I have
7: 8 The **L** said to Moses and Aaron,
7:13 to them, just as the **L** had said.
7:14 the **L** said to Moses, "Pharaoh's
7:16 say to him, 'The **L**, the God of the
7:17 This is what the **L** says: By this you
7:19 The **L** said to Moses, "Tell Aaron,
7:20 did just as the **L** had commanded.
7:22 and Aaron, just as the **L** had said.
7:25 passed after the **L** struck the Nile.
8: 1 the **L** said to Moses, "Go to Pharaoh
8: 1 'This is what the **L** says: Let my
8: 5 the **L** said to Moses, "Tell Aaron,
8: 8 "Pray to the **L** to take the frogs
8: 8 go to offer sacrifices to the **L**."
8:10 there is no-one like the **L** our God.
8:12 Moses cried out to the **L** about the
8:13 And the **L** did what Moses asked.
8:15 and Aaron, just as the **L** had said.
8:16 the **L** said to Moses, "Tell Aaron,
8:19 not listen, just as the **L** had said.
8:20 the **L** said to Moses, "Get up early
8:20 'This is what the **L** says: Let my
8:22 know that I, the **L**, am in this land.
8:24 the **L** did this. Dense swarms of
8:26 sacrifices we offer the **L** our God
8:27 offer sacrifices to the **L** our God
8:29 I will pray to the **L**, and tomorrow
8:29 go to offer sacrifices to the **L**."
8:30 left Pharaoh and prayed to the **L**,
8:31 the **L** did what Moses asked: The
9: 1 the **L** said to Moses, "Go to Pharaoh
9: 1 what the **L**, the God of the Hebrews
9: 4 the **L** will make a distinction
9: 5 The **L** set a time and said, "Tomorrow

Ex 9: 5 the **L** will do this in the land."
9: 6 the next day the **L** did it: All the
9: 8 the **L** said to Moses and Aaron, "Take
9:12 the **L** hardened Pharaoh's heart and
9:12 just as the **L** had said to Moses.
9:13 the **L** said to Moses, "Get up early
9:13 what the **L**, the God of the Hebrews
9:22 the **L** said to Moses, "Stretch out
9:23 the **L** sent thunder and hail, and
9:23 **L** rained hail on the land of Egypt;
9:27 The **L** is in the right, and I and my
9:28 Pray to the **L**, for we have had
9:29 out my hands in prayer to the **L**.
9:33 spread out his hand towards the **L**
9:35 as the **L** had said through Moses.
10: 1 the **L** said to Moses, "Go to Pharaoh,
10: 3 what the **L**, the God of the Hebrews
10: 7 they may worship the **L** their God.
10: 9 to celebrate a festival to the **L**."
10:10 Pharaoh said, "The **L** be with you—if
10:11 worship the **L**, since that's what you
10:12 the **L** said to Moses, "Stretch out
10:13 and the **L** made an east wind blow
10:18 left Pharaoh and prayed to the **L**.
10:19 the **L** changed the wind to a very
10:20 the **L** hardened Pharaoh's heart, and
10:21 the **L** said to Moses, "Stretch out
10:24 Moses and said, "Go, worship the **L**.
10:25 to present to the **L** our God.
10:26 them in worshipping the **L** our God,
10:26 we are to use to worship the **L**."
10:27 the **L** hardened Pharaoh's heart, and
11: 1 Now the **L** said to Moses, "I will
11: 3 (The **L** made the Egyptians favourably
11: 4 Moses said, "This is what the **L** says
11: 9 The **L** had said to Moses, "Pharaoh
11:10 but the **L** hardened Pharaoh's heart,
12: 1 The **L** said to Moses and Aaron in
12:14 celebrate it as a festival to the **L**
12:23 the **L** goes through the land to
12:25 the land that the **L** will give you
12:27 is the Passover sacrifice to the **L**,
12:28 did just what the **L** commanded Moses
12:29 At midnight the **L** struck down all
12:31 worship the **L** as you have requested
12:36 The **L** had made the Egyptians
12:42 the **L** kept vigil that night to bring
12:42 are to keep vigil to honour the **L**
12:43 The **L** said to Moses and Aaron,
12:50 did just what the **L** had commanded
12:51 on that very day the **L** brought the
13: 1 The **L** said to Moses,
13: 3 because the **L** brought you out of it
13: 5 the **L** brings you into the land of
13: 6 hold a festival to the **L**.
13: 8 'I do this because of what the **L** did
13: 9 For the **L** brought you out of Egypt
13:11 "After the **L** brings you into the
13:12 you are to give over to the **L** the
13:12 of your livestock belong to the **L**.
13:14 'With a mighty hand the **L** brought us
13:15 the **L** killed every firstborn in
13:15 This is why I sacrifice to the **L** the
13:16 that the **L** brought us out of Egypt
13:21 By day the **L** went ahead of them in a
14: 1 Then the **L** said to Moses,
14: 8 The **L** hardened the heart of Pharaoh
14:10 terrified and cried out to the **L**.
14:13 the **L** will bring you today.
14:14 The **L** will fight for you; you need
14:15 the **L** said to Moses, "Why are you
14:21 all that night the **L** drove the sea
14:24 the **L** looked down from the pillar of
14:25 **L** is fighting for them against Egypt
14:26 the **L** said to Moses, "Stretch out
14:27 and the **L** swept them into the sea.
14:30 That day the **L** saved Israel from the
14:31 great power the **L** displayed against
14:31 the people feared the **L** and put
15: 1 Israelites sang this song to the **L**
15: 2 The **L** is my strength and my song;
15: 3 **L** is a warrior; the **L** is his name
15: 6 "Your right hand, O **L**, was majestic
15: 6 hand, O **L**, shattered the enemy.
15:11 Who among the gods is like you, O **L**?
15:16 until your people pass by, O **L**,

Ex 15:17 the place, O **L**, you made for your
15:18 The **L** will reign for ever and ever."
15:19 the **L** brought the waters of the sea
15:25 Moses cried out to the **L**, and the **L**
15:25 There the **L** made a decree and a law
16: 4 the **L** said to Moses, "I will rain
16: 6 the **L** who brought you out of Egypt,
16: 8 "You will know that it was the **L**
16: 8 against us, but against the **L**."
16:11 The **L** said to Moses,
16:15 bread the **L** has given you to eat.
16:16 This is what the **L** has commanded:
16:23 "This is what the **L** commanded:
16:23 of rest, a holy Sabbath to the **L**.
16:25 today is a Sabbath to the **L**.
16:28 the **L** said to Moses, "How long will
16:29 the **L** has given you the Sabbath;
16:32 "This is what the **L** has commanded:
17: 2 Why do you put the **L** to the test?"
17: 4 Moses cried out to the **L**, "What am I
17: 5 The **L** answered Moses, "Walk on ahead
17: 7 tested the **L** saying, "Is the **L** among us
17:14 the **L** said to Moses, "Write this on
17:15 and called it The **L** is my Banner.
17:16 lifted up to the throne of the **L**.
17:16 The **L** will be at war against the
18: 1 **L** had brought Israel out of Egypt.
18: 8 the **L** had done to Pharaoh
18: 8 and how the **L** had saved them.
18: 9 all the good things the **L** had done
19: 3 **L** called to him from the mountain
19: 7 the **L** had commanded him to speak.
19: 8 We will do everything the **L** has said
19: 8 brought their answer back to the **L**.
19: 9 The **L** said to Moses, "I am going to
19: 9 told the **L** what the people had said.
19:10 the **L** said to Moses, "Go to the
19:11 on that day the **L** will come down on
19:18 the **L** descended on it in fire.
19:20 The **L** descended to the top of Mount
19:21 the **L** said to him, "Go down and warn
19:21 to see the **L** and many of them perish
19:22 Even the priests, who approach the **L**
19:22 the **L** will break out against them."
19:23 Moses said to the **L**, "The people
19:24 The **L** replied, "Go down and bring
19:24 way through to come up to the **L**,
20: 7 the **L** will not hold anyone guiltless
20:11 in six days the **L** made the heavens
20:11 Therefore the **L** blessed the Sabbath
20:22 the **L** said to Moses, "Tell the
22:20 other than the **L** must be destroyed.
24: 1 he said to Moses, "Come up to the **L**
24: 2 Moses alone is to approach the **L**;
24: 3 the **L** has said we will do."
24: 4 down everything the **L** had said.
24: 5 as fellowship offerings to the **L**.
24: 7 will do everything the **L** has said;
24: 8 blood of the covenant that the **L** has
24:12 The **L** said to Moses, "Come up to me
24:16 and on the seventh day the **L** called
25: 1 The **L** said to Moses,
28:38 they will be acceptable to the **L**.
29:18 It is a burnt offering to the **L**,
29:18 an offering made to the **L** by fire.
29:25 for a pleasing aroma to the **L**,
29:25 an offering made to the **L** by fire.
29:28 the Israelites are to make to the **L**
29:41 an offering made to the **L** by fire.
30:11 Then the **L** said to Moses,
30:12 each one must pay the **L** a ransom for
30:13 half shekel is an offering to the **L**.
30:14 are to give an offering to the **L**.
30:15 the offering to the **L** to atone for
30:17 Then the **L** said to Moses,
30:20 an offering made to the **L** by fire,
30:22 Then the **L** said to Moses,
30:34 the **L** said to Moses, "Take fragrant
31: 1 Then the **L** said to Moses,
31:12 Then the **L** said to Moses,
31:17 in six days the **L** made the heavens
31:18 the **L** finished speaking to Moses on
32: 5 there will be a festival to the **L**."
32: 7 the **L** said to Moses, "Go down,
32 : 9 have seen these people," the **L** said
32:11 sought the favour of the **L** his God

Ex 32:11 "O **L**," he said, "why should your
32:14 the **L** relented and did not bring on
32:26 "Whoever is for the **L**, come to me.
32:27 he said to them, "This is what the **L**,
32:29 "You have been set apart to the **L**
32:30 But now I will go up to the **L**;
32:31 Moses went back to the **L** and said,
32:33 The **L** replied to Moses, "Whoever has
32:35 **L** struck the people with a plague
33: 1 the **L** said to Moses, "Leave this
33: 5 For the **L** had said to Moses, "Tell
33: 7 Anyone enquiring of the **L** would go
33: 9 while the **L** spoke with Moses.
33:11 The **L** would speak to Moses face to
33:12 Moses said to the **L**, "You have been
33:14 The **L** replied, "My Presence will go
33:17 the **L** said to Moses, "I will do the
33:19 the **L** said, "I will cause all my
33:19 I will proclaim my name, the **L**,
33:21 the **L** said, "There is a place near
34: 1 The **L** said to Moses, "Chisel out two
34: 4 as the **L** had commanded him; and he
34: 5 the **L** came down in the cloud and
34: 5 and proclaimed his name, the **L**.
34: 6 "The **L**, the **L**, the compassionate and
34:10 the **L** said: "I am making a covenant
34:10 work that I, the **L**, will do for you.
34:14 for the **L**, whose name is Jealous, is
34:27 the **L** said to Moses, "Write down
34:28 was there with the **L** forty days
34:29 because he had spoken with the **L**.
34:32 the commands the **L** had given him
34:35 he went in to speak with the **L**.
35: 1 the **L** has commanded you to do:
35: 2 a Sabbath of rest to the **L**.
35: 4 "This is what the **L** has commanded:
35: 5 take an offering for the **L**.
35: 5 bring to the **L** an offering of gold,
35:10 make everything the **L** has commanded:
35:21 brought an offering to the **L** for the
35:22 gold as a wave offering to the **L**.
35:24 brought it as an offering to the **L**,
35:29 brought to the **L** freewill offerings
35:29 for all the work the **L** through Moses
35:30 "See, the **L** has chosen Bezalel
36: 1 every skilled person to whom the **L**
36: 1 work just as the **L** has commanded."
36: 2 person to whom the **L** has given skill
36: 5 work the **L** commanded to be done."
38:22 everything the **L** commanded Moses;
39:42 just as the **L** had commanded Moses.
39:43 done it just as the **L** had commanded.
40: 1 Then the **L** said to Moses:
40:38 the cloud of the **L** was over the
Lev 1: 1 The **L** called to Moses and spoke to
1: 2 of you brings an offering to the **L**,
1: 3 that it will be acceptable to the **L**.
1: 9 by fire, an aroma pleasing to the **L**.
1:13 by fire, an aroma pleasing to the **L**.
1:14 "'If the offering to the **L** is a
1:17 by fire, an aroma pleasing to the **L**.
2: 1 brings a grain offering to the **L**,
2: 2 by fire, an aroma pleasing to the **L**.
2: 3 the offerings made to the **L** by fire.
2: 8 made of these things to the **L**;
2: 9 by fire, an aroma pleasing to the **L**.
2:10 the offerings made to the **L** by fire.
2:11 grain offering you bring to the **L**
2:11 an offering made to the **L** by fire.
2:12 You may bring them to the **L** as an
2:14 offering of firstfruits to the **L**,
2:16 an offering made to the **L** by fire.
3: 3 a sacrifice made to the **L** by fire:
3: 5 by fire, an aroma pleasing to the **L**.
3: 6 as a fellowship offering to the **L**,
3: 9 a sacrifice made to the **L** by fire:
3:11 an offering made to the **L** by fire.
3:14 make this offering to the **L** by fire:
4: 1 The **L** said to Moses,
4: 3 he must bring to the **L** a young bull
4:22 of the commands of the **L** his God,
4:31 altar as an aroma pleasing to the **L**.
4:35 the offerings made to the **L** by fire.
5: 6 he must bring to the **L** a female lamb
5: 7 to the **L** as a penalty for his sin
5:12 the offerings made to the **L** by fire.
Lev 5:14 The **L** said to Moses:
5:15 he is to bring to the **L** as a penalty
5:19 guilty of wrongdoing against the **L**."
6: 1 The **L** said to Moses:
6: 2 is unfaithful to the **L** by deceiving
6: 6 to the priest, that is, to the **L**,
6: 8 The **L** said to Moses:
6:15 altar as an aroma pleasing to the **L**.
6:18 share of the offerings made to the **L**
6:19 The **L** also said to Moses,
6:20 to the **L** on the day he is anointed:
6:21 as an aroma pleasing to the **L**.
6:24 The **L** said to Moses,
7: 5 an offering made to the **L** by fire.
7:11 a person may present to the **L**:
7:14 offering, a contribution to the **L**;
7:20 offering belonging to the **L**,
7:21 offering belonging to the **L**,
7:22 The **L** said to Moses,
7:25 may be made to the **L** must be cut off
7:28 The **L** said to Moses,
7:29 a fellowship offering to the **L** is to
7:29 of it as his sacrifice to the **L**.
7:30 the offering made to the **L** by fire;
7:35 the offerings made to the **L** by fire
7:35 presented to serve the **L** as priests.
7:36 the **L** commanded that the Israelites
7:38 the **L** gave Moses on Mount Sinai
7:38 to bring their offerings to the **L**,
8: 1 The **L** said to Moses,
8: 5 this is what the **L** has commanded
8:28 an offering made to the **L** by fire.
8:34 commanded by the **L** to make atonement
8:35 and do what the **L** requires, so that
8:36 the **L** commanded through Moses.
9: 4 For today the **L** will appear to you.'
9: 6 "This is what the **L** has commanded
9: 7 for them, as the **L** has commanded."
10: 3 "This is what the **L** spoke of when he
10: 6 you will die and the **L** will be angry
10: 6 those the **L** has destroyed by fire.
10: 8 Then the **L** said to Aaron,
10:11 the **L** has given them through Moses."
10:12 the offerings made to the **L** by fire
10:13 the offerings made to the **L** by fire;
10:15 children, as the **L** has commanded."
10:19 Would the **L** have been pleased if I
11: 1 The **L** said to Moses and Aaron,
12: 1 The **L** said to Moses,
13: 1 The **L** said to Moses and Aaron,
14: 1 The **L** said to Moses,
14:33 The **L** said to Moses and Aaron,
15: 1 The **L** said to Moses and Aaron,
16: 1 The **L** spoke to Moses after the death
16: 1 who died when they approached the **L**.
16: 2 The **L** said to Moses: "Tell your
16: 8 one lot for the **L** and the other for
16: 9 the goat whose lot falls to the **L**
17: 1 The **L** said to Moses,
17: 2 'This is what the **L** has commanded:
17: 4 present it as an offering to the **L**
17: 4 in front of the tabernacle of the **L**
17: 5 the Israelites will bring to the **L**
17: 5 to the priest, that is, to the **L**,
17: 6 the blood against the altar of the **L**
17: 6 fat as an aroma pleasing to the **L**.
17: 9 to sacrifice it to the **L**—
18: 1 The **L** said to Moses,
19: 1 The **L** said to Moses,
19: 5 a fellowship offering to the **L**,
19:21 for a guilt offering to the **L**.
19:24 an offering of praise to the **L**.
20: 1 The **L** said to Moses,
20:26 I, the **L**, am holy, and I have set
21: 1 The **L** said to Moses, "Speak to the
21: 6 the offerings made to the **L** by fire,
21: 8 I the **L** am holy—I who make you holy.
21:16 The **L** said to Moses,
21:21 the offerings made to the **L** by fire.
22: 1 The **L** said to Moses,
22: 3 the Israelites consecrate to the **L**,
22:15 the Israelites present to the **L**
22:17 The **L** said to Moses,
22:18 gift for a burnt offering to the **L**,
22:21 a fellowship offering to the **L**
22:22 Do not offer to the **L** the blind,
Lev 22:22 an offering made to the **L** by fire.
22:24 You must not offer to the **L** an
22:26 The **L** said to Moses,
22:27 an offering made to the **L** by fire.
22:29 sacrifice a thank-offering to the **L**,
23: 1 The **L** said to Moses,
23: 2 the appointed feasts of the **L**, which
23: 3 you live, it is a Sabbath to the **L**.
23: 8 an offering made to the **L** by fire.
23: 9 The **L** said to Moses,
23:12 as a burnt offering to the **L** a lamb
23:13 offering made to the **L** by fire,
23:16 an offering of new grain to the **L**.
23:17 offering of firstfruits to the **L**.
23:18 will be a burnt offering to the **L**,
23:18 by fire, an aroma pleasing to the **L**.
23:20 offering to the **L** for the priest.
23:23 The **L** said to Moses,
23:25 an offering made to the **L** by fire.
23:26 The **L** said to Moses,
23:27 an offering made to the **L** by fire.
23:33 The **L** said to Moses,
23:36 offerings made to the **L** by fire,
23:36 an offering made to the **L** by fire.
23:37 bringing offerings made to the **L**
23:38 offerings you give to the **L**.)
23:39 celebrate the festival to the **L** for
23:41 Celebrate this as a festival to the **L**
23:44 the appointed feasts of the **L**.
24: 1 The **L** said to Moses,
24: 7 an offering made to the **L** by fire.
24: 9 offerings made to the **L** by fire."
24:12 will of the **L** should be made clear
24:13 Then the **L** said to Moses:
25: 1 The **L** said to Moses on Mount Sinai,
25: 2 must observe a sabbath to the **L**.
25: 4 sabbath of rest, a sabbath to the **L**.
26:46 regulations that the **L** established
27: 1 The **L** said to Moses,
27: 2 vow to dedicate persons to the **L**
27: 9 acceptable as an offering to the **L**,
27: 9 animal given to the **L** becomes holy.
27:11 acceptable as an offering to the **L**
27:16 "'If a man dedicates to the **L** part
27:21 like a field devoted to the **L**;
27:22 "'If a man dedicates to the **L** a
27:26 firstborn already belongs to the **L**;
27:28 devotes to the **L**—whether man or
27:34 These are the commands the **L** gave
Nu 1: 1 The **L** spoke to Moses in the Tent of
1:19 as the **L** commanded Moses. And so he
1:48 The **L** had said to Moses:
2: 1 The **L** said to Moses and Aaron:
2:34 the Israelites did everything the **L**
3: 1 **L** talked with Moses on Mount Sinai.
3: 5 The **L** said to Moses,
3:11 The **L** also said to Moses,
3:14 The **L** said to Moses in the Desert of
3:40 The **L** said to Moses, "Count all the
3:44 The **L** also said to Moses,
4: 1 The **L** said to Moses and Aaron:
4:17 The **L** said to Moses and Aaron,
4:21 The **L** said to Moses,
5: 1 The **L** said to Moses,
5: 4 just as the **L** had instructed Moses.
5: 5 The **L** said to Moses,
5: 6 and so is unfaithful to the **L**,
5: 8 the restitution belongs to the **L** and
5:11 Then the **L** said to Moses,
5:21 the **L** cause your people to curse
6: 1 The **L** said to Moses,
6: 2 separation to the **L** as a Nazirite,
6: 5 his separation to the **L** is over;
6: 6 period of his separation to the **L**
6: 8 he is consecrated to the **L**.
6:12 He must dedicate himself to the **L**
6:14 to present his offerings to the **L**:
6:17 as a fellowship offering to the **L**,
6:21 who vows his offering to the **L**
6:22 The **L** said to Moses,
6:24 "'The **L** bless you and keep you;
6:25 the **L** make his face shine upon you
6:26 the **L** turn his face towards you and
7: 4 The **L** said to Moses,
7:11 For the **L** had said to Moses, "Each
7:89 Tent of Meeting to speak with the **L**

Nu 8: 1 The L said to Moses,
8: 4 the pattern the L had shown Moses.
8: 5 The L said to Moses:
8:11 be ready to do the work of the L.
8:12 the one for a sin offering to the L
8:13 them as a wave offering to the L.
8:23 The L said to Moses,
9: 1 The L spoke to Moses in the Desert
9: 8 what the L commands concerning you."
9: 9 Then the L said to Moses,
10: 1 The L said to Moses:
10:29 the L said, 'I will give it to you.
10:29 L has promised good things to Israel.
10:32 good things the L gives us."
10:34 The cloud of the L was over them by
10:35 "Rise up, O L! May your enemies be
10:36 "Return, O L, to the countless
11: 1 hardships in the hearing of the L,
11: 1 fire from the L burned among them
11: 2 he prayed to the L and the fire died
11: 3 fire from the L had burned among
11:10 The L became exceedingly angry, and
11:11 He asked the L, "Why have you
11:16 The L said to Moses: "Bring me
11:18 The L heard you when you wailed, "If
11:18 Now the L will give you meat,
11:20 because you have rejected the L,
11:23 The L answered Moses, "Is the LORD's
11:24 told the people what the L had said.
11:25 the L came down in the cloud and
11:29 the L would put his Spirit on them!"
11:31 Now a wind went out from the L and
12: 2 Has the L spoken only through Moses?
12: 2 through us?" And the L heard this.
12: 4 At once the L said to Moses, Aaron
12: 5 the L came down in a pillar of cloud;
12: 6 a prophet of the L is among you,
12: 8 he sees the form of the L.
12:13 Moses cried out to the L, "O God,
12:14 The L replied to Moses, "If her
13: 1 The L said to Moses,
14: 3 Why is the L bringing us to this
14: 8 If the L is pleased with us, he will
14: 9 Only do not rebel against the L.
14: 9 is gone, but the L is with us.
14:11 The L said to Moses, "How long will
14:13 Moses said to the L, "Then the
14:14 you, O L, are with these people and
14:14 that you, O L, have been seen face
14:16 'The L was not able to bring these
14:18 'The L is slow to anger, abounding
14:20 The L replied, "I have forgiven them,
14:26 The L said to Moses and Aaron:
14:35 I, the L, have spoken, and I will
14:40 go up to the place the L promised."
14:42 Do not go up, because the L is not
14:43 you have turned away from the L,
15: 1 The L said to Moses,
15: 3 you present to the L offerings made
15: 3 as an aroma pleasing to the L
15: 4 present to the L a grain offering
15: 7 it as an aroma pleasing to the L.
15: 8 or a fellowship offering to the L,
15:10 by fire, an aroma pleasing to the L.
15:13 fire as an aroma pleasing to the L.
15:14 fire as an aroma pleasing to the L,
15:17 The L said to Moses,
15:19 a portion as an offering to the L.
15:21 are to give this offering to the L
15:22 of these commands the L gave Moses
15:23 from the day the L gave them and
15:24 as an aroma pleasing to the L,
15:25 they have brought to the L for their
15:30 blasphemes the L, and that person
15:35 the L said to Moses, "The man must
15:37 The L said to Moses,
15:39 remember all the commands of the L,
16: 3 one of them, and the L is with them.
16: 5 "In the morning the L will show who
16: 7 The man the L chooses will be the
16:11 It is against the L that you and all
16:15 said to the L, "Do not accept their
16:20 The L said to Moses and Aaron,
16:23 Then the L said to Moses,
16:29 to men, then the L has not sent me.
16:30 if the L brings about something

Nu 16:30 have treated the L with contempt."
16:35 fire came out from the L and
16:36 The L said to Moses,
16:40 the L directed him through Moses.
16:44 and the L said to Moses,
16:46 Wrath has come out from the L;
17: 1 The L said to Moses,
17:10 The L said to Moses, "Put back
17:13 the tabernacle of the L will die.
18: 1 The L said to Aaron, "You, your sons
18: 6 dedicated to the L to do the work at
18: 8 the L said to Aaron, "I myself have
18:12 grain they give to the L as the
18:13 they bring to the L will be yours.
18:14 that is devoted to the L is yours.
18:15 that is offered to the L is yours.
18:17 by fire, an aroma pleasing to the L.
18:19 Israelites present to the L I give
18:20 The L said to Aaron, "You will have
18:24 present as an offering to the L.
18:25 The L said to Moses,
18:28 will present an offering to the L
19: 1 The L said to Moses and Aaron:
19: 2 of the law that the L has commanded:
19:20 has defiled the sanctuary of the L.
20: 7 The L said to Moses,
20:12 But the L said to Moses and Aaron,
20:13 Israelites quarrelled with the L
20:16 we cried out to the L, he heard our
20:23 the L said to Moses and Aaron,
21: 2 Israel made this vow to the L: "If
21: 3 The L listened to Israel's plea and
21: 6 the L sent venomous snakes among
21: 7 spoke against the L and against you.
21: 7 Pray that the L will take the snakes
21: 8 The L said to Moses, "Make a snake
21:14 Book of the Wars of the L says:
21:16 the well where the L said to Moses,
21:34 The L said to Moses, "Do not be
22: 8 you back the answer the L gives me.
22:13 L has refused to let me go with you.
22:18 beyond the command of the L my God.
22:19 out what else the L will tell me."
22:28 the L opened the donkey's mouth,
22:31 the L opened Balaam's eyes, and he
23: 3 Perhaps the L will come to meet with
23: 5 L put a message in Balaam's mouth
23: 8 those whom the L has not denounced?
23:12 speak what the L puts in my mouth?"
23:16 The L met with Balaam and put a
23:17 asked him, "What did the L say?
23:21 The L their God is with them;
23:26 I must do whatever the L says?"
24: 1 it pleased the L to bless Israel,
24: 6 like aloes planted by the L, like
24:11 L has kept you from being rewarded.
24:13 to go beyond the command of the L
24:13 I must say only what the L says'?
25: 4 The L said to Moses, "Take all the
25:10 The L said to Moses,
25:16 The L said to Moses,
26: 1 After the plague the L said to Moses
26: 9 when they rebelled against the L.
26:52 The L said to Moses,
26:65 For the L had told those Israelites
27: 3 who banded together against the L,
27: 6 and the L said to him,
27:12 the L said to Moses, "Go up this
27:15 Moses said to the L,
27:16 "May the L, the God of the spirits
27:18 the L said to Moses, "Take Joshua
27:23 as the L instructed through Moses.
28: 1 The L said to Moses,
28: 3 that you are to present to the L:
28: 6 an offering made to the L by fire.
28: 7 offering to the L at the sanctuary.
28: 8 by fire, an aroma pleasing to the L.
28:11 present to the L a burnt offering of
28:13 an offering made to the L by fire.
28:15 to the L as a sin offering.
28:19 Present to the L an offering made by
28:24 as an aroma pleasing to the L;
28:26 when you present to the L an
28:27 as an aroma pleasing to the L.
29: 2 an aroma pleasing to the L, prepare
29: 6 to the L by fire—a pleasing aroma.

Nu 29: 8 as an aroma pleasing to the L
29:12 a festival to the L for seven days.
29:13 fire as an aroma pleasing to the L,
29:36 fire as an aroma pleasing to the L,
29:39 prepare these for the L at your
29:40 all that the L commanded him.
30: 1 "This is what the L commands:
30: 2 a man makes a vow to the L or takes
30: 3 makes a vow to the L or binds
30: 5 the L will release her because her
30: 8 herself, and the L will release her.
30:12 them, and the L will release her.
30:16 These are the regulations the L gave
31: 1 The L said to Moses,
31:16 the Israelites away from the L
31:21 of the law that the L gave Moses:
31:25 The L said to Moses,
31:28 set apart as tribute for the L one
31:37 which the tribute for the L was 675
31:38 which the tribute for the L was 72;
31:39 which the tribute for the L was 61;
31:40 which the tribute for the L was 32.
31:50 have brought as an offering to the L
31:52 to the L weighed 16,750 shekels.
32: 4 the land the L subdued before the
32: 7 into the land the L has given them?
32: 9 the land the L had given them.
32:12 they followed the L wholeheartedly.'
32:14 making the L even more angry with
32:22 the land is subdued before the L,
32:22 obligation to the L and to Israel.
32:22 be your possession before the L.
32:23 you will be sinning against the L;
32:31 will do what the L has said.
33: 4 firstborn, whom the L had struck
33: 4 L had brought judgment on their gods.
33:50 from Jericho the L said to Moses,
34: 1 The L said to Moses,
34:13 The L has ordered that it be given
34:16 The L said to Moses,
34:29 These are the men the L commanded to
35: 1 from Jericho, the L said to Moses,
35: 9 Then the L said to Moses:
35:34 I, the L, dwell among the Israelites
36: 2 They said, "When the L commanded my
36: 6 This is what the L commands for
36:13 regulations the L gave through Moses
Dt 1: 3 L had commanded him concerning them.
1: 6 The L our God said to us at Horeb,
1: 8 land that the L swore he would give
1:11 May the L, the God of your fathers,
1:19 Then, as the L our God commanded us,
1:20 which the L our God is giving us.
1:21 L, the God of your fathers, told you
1:25 that the L our God is giving us."
1:27 "The L hates us; so he brought us
1:34 When the L heard what you said,
1:36 he followed the L wholeheartedly."
1:37 the L became angry with me also
1:41 "We have sinned against the L.
1:41 fight, as the L our God commanded
1:42 the L said to me, "Tell them, 'Do
2: 1 Red Sea, as the L had directed me.
2: 2 Then the L said to me,
2: 9 the L said to me, "Do not harass the
2:12 L gave them as their possession.)
2:13 the L said, "Now get up and cross
2:14 camp, as the L had sworn to them.
2:17 the L said to me,
2:21 The L destroyed them from before the
2:22 The L had done the same for the
2:29 land the L our God is giving us."
2:31 The L said to me, "See, I have begun
2:33 the L our God delivered him over to
2:36 The L our God gave us all of them.
2:37 with the command of the L our God,
3: 2 The L said to me, "Do not be afraid
3: 3 the L our God also gave into our
3:20 until the L gives rest to your
3:21 The L will do the same to all the
3:23 At that time I pleaded with the L:
3:26 the L was angry with me and would
3:26 "That is enough," the L said. "Do
4: 1 that the L, the God of your fathers
4: 3 with your own eyes what the L did
4: 5 laws as the L my God commanded me,

Dt 4: 7 the way the **L** our God is near us
4:12 the **L** spoke to you out of the fire.
4:14 the **L** directed me at that time to
4:15 the day the **L** spoke to you at Horeb
4:20 as for you, the **L** took you and
4:21 **L** was angry with me because of you
4:27 The **L** will scatter you among the
4:27 to which the **L** will drive you.
4:39 the **L** is God in heaven above and on
5: 2 The **L** our God made a covenant with
5: 3 **L** made this covenant, but with us
5: 4 The **L** spoke to you face to face out
5: 5 I stood between the **L** and you to
5:11 **L** will not hold anyone guiltless
5:22 the commandments the **L** proclaimed
5:24 you said, "The **L** our God has shown
5:27 listen to all that the **L** our God
5:27 Then tell us whatever the **L** our God
5:28 The **L** heard you when you spoke to me
5:28 spoke to me and the **L** said to me,
6: 3 as the **L**, the God of your fathers,
6: 4 The **L** our God, the **L** is one.
6:12 that you do not forget the **L**,
6:18 the good land that the **L** promised
6:19 enemies before you, as the **L** said.
6:20 the **L** our God has commanded you?"
6:21 but the **L** brought us out of Egypt
6:22 Before our eyes the **L** sent
6:24 The **L** commanded us to obey all these
7: 7 **L** did not set his affection on you
7: 8 the **L** loved you and kept the oath
7:15 The **L** will keep you free from every
8: 1 possess the land that the **L** promised
8: 3 that comes from the mouth of the **L**.
8:20 Like the nations the **L** destroyed
9: 3 quickly, as the **L** has promised you.
9: 4 "The **L** has brought me here to take
9:4 the **L** is going to drive them out
9: 7 have been rebellious against the **L**.
9: 9 that the **L** had made with you,
9:10 The **L** gave me two stone tablets
9:10 the commandments the **L** proclaimed
9:11 the **L** gave me the two stone tablets,
9:12 the **L** told me, "Go down from here at
9:13 the **L** said to me, "I have seen this
9:16 way that the **L** had commanded you.
9:19 feared the anger and wrath of the **L**
9:19 But again the **L** listened to me.
9:20 the **L** was angry enough with Aaron to
9:22 You also made the **L** angry at Taberah
9:23 the **L** sent you out from Kadesh
9:24 have been rebellious against the **L**
9:25 the **L** had said he would destroy you.
9:26 I prayed to the **L** and said,
9:28 the **L** was not able to take them
10: 1 At that time the **L** said to me,
10: 4 The **L** wrote on these tablets what he
10: 4 And the **L** gave them to me.
10: 8 At that time the **L** set apart the
10: 9 the **L** is their inheritance,
10:10 **L** listened to me at this time also.
10:11 "Go," the **L** said to me, "and lead
10:15 Yet the **L** set his affection on your
11: 4 the **L** brought lasting ruin on them.
11: 7 these great things the **L** has done.
11: 9 in the land that the **L** swore to
11:17 the good land the **L** is giving you.
11:21 **L** swore to give your forefathers,
11:23 the **L** will drive out all these
12: 1 the **L**, the God of your fathers
12:11 possessions you have vowed to the **L**.
12:14 only at the place the **L** will choose
12:21 and flocks the **L** has given you,
12:26 go to the place the **L** will choose.
12:31 of detestable things the **L** hates.
13:17 so that the **L** will turn from his
14: 2 the **L** has chosen you to be his
14:24 the **L** will choose to put his Name
15: 9 may then appeal to the **L** against you
16: 2 the place the **L** will choose as a
16:15 at the place the **L** will choose.
17: 2 in one of the towns the **L** gives you
17:10 at the place the **L** will choose.
17:16 for the **L** has told you, "You are not
17:19 may learn to revere the **L** his God
18: 1 the offerings made to the **L** by fire,

Dt 18: 2 the **L** is their inheritance,
18: 6 to the place the **L** will choose,
18:12 these things is detestable to the **L**,
18:17 The **L** said to me: "What they say is
18:22 is a message the **L** has not spoken.
19: 8 If the **L** your God enlarges your
21: 8 Israel, whom you have redeemed, O **L**
23: 1 may enter the assembly of the **L**.
23: 2 may enter the assembly of the **L**,
23: 3 may enter the assembly of the **L**,
23: 8 may enter the assembly of the **L**.
24: 4 be detestable in the eyes of the **L**.
24:15 Otherwise he may cry to the **L**
26: 3 that the **L** swore to our forefathers
26: 7 we cried out to the **L**, the God of
26: 7 and the **L** heard our voice and saw
26: 8 the **L** brought us out of Egypt with a
26:10 that you, O **L**, have given me."
26:14 I have obeyed the **L** my God; I have
26:17 the **L** is your God and that you will
26:18 the **L** has declared this day that you
27: 3 the **L**, the God of your fathers
27:15 idol—a thing detestable to the **L**,
28: 7 The **L** will grant that the enemies
28: 8 The **L** will send a blessing on your
28: 9 The **L** will establish you as his holy
28:11 The **L** will grant you abundant
28:12 The **L** will open the heavens, the
28:13 The **L** will make you the head, not
28:20 The **L** will send on you curses,
28:21 The **L** will plague you with diseases
28:22 The **L** will strike you with wasting
28:24 The **L** will turn the rain of your
28:25 The **L** will cause you to be defeated
28:27 The **L** will afflict you with the
28:28 The **L** will afflict you with madness,
28:35 The **L** will afflict your knees and
28:36 The **L** will drive you and the king
28:37 nations where the **L** will drive you.
28:48 the enemies the **L** sends against you.
28:49 **L** will bring a nation against you
28:59 **L** will send fearful plagues on you
28:61 The **L** will also bring on you every
28:63 it pleased the **L** to make you prosper
28:64 the **L** will scatter you among all
28:65 the **L** will give you an anxious mind
28:68 The **L** will send you back in ships to
29: 1 the covenant the **L** commanded Moses
29: 2 that the **L** did in Egypt to Pharaoh,
29: 4 to this day the **L** has not given you
29:12 a covenant the **L** is making with you
29:18 turns away from the **L** our God to go
29:20 The **L** will never be willing to
29:20 and the **L** will blot out his name
29:21 The **L** will single him out from all
29:22 with which the **L** has afflicted it.
29:23 the **L** overthrew in fierce anger.
29:24 "Why has the **L** done this to this
29:28 in great wrath the **L** uprooted them
29:29 The secret things belong to the **L**
30: 8 You will again obey the **L** and follow
30: 9 The **L** will again delight in you and
30:20 For the **L** is your life, and he will
31: 2 The **L** has said to me, 'You shall not
31: 3 over ahead of you, as the **L** said.
31: 4 the **L** will do to them what he did to
31: 5 The **L** will deliver them to you, and
31: 7 into the land that the **L** swore to
31: 8 The **L** himself goes before you and
31:14 The **L** said to Moses, "Now the day of
31:15 the **L** appeared at the Tent in a
31:16 the **L** said to Moses: "You are going
31:23 The **L** gave this command to Joshua
31:27 have been rebellious against the **L**
31:29 will do evil in the sight of the **L**
32: 6 Is this the way you repay the **L**, O
32:12 The **L** alone led him; no foreign god
32:19 The **L** saw this and rejected them
32:27 the **L** has not done all this.
32:30 unless the **L** had given them up?
32:36 **L** will judge his people and have
32:48 On that same day the **L** told Moses,
33: 2 He said: "The **L** came from Sinai and
33: 7 he said about Judah: "Hear, O **L**,
33:11 Bless all his skills, O **L**, and be
33:12 "Let the beloved of the **L** rest

Dt 33:12 and the one the **L** loves rests
33:13 "May the **L** bless his land with
33:23 abounding with the favour of the **L**
33:29 a people saved by the **L**? He is your
34: 1 the **L** showed him the whole land
34: 4 the **L** said to him, "This is the land
34: 5 there in Moab, as the **L** had said.
34: 9 did what the **L** had commanded Moses.
34:10 Moses, whom the **L** knew face to face,
34:11 wonders the **L** sent him to do in
Jos 1: 1 the **L** said to Joshua son of Nun,
1:15 until the **L** gives them rest, as he
2:10 heard how the **L** dried up the water
2:12 please swear to me by the **L** that
2:14 when the **L** gives us the land."
2:24 They said to Joshua, "The **L** has
3: 5 **L** will do amazing things among you."
3: 7 the **L** said to Joshua, "Today I will
3:13 priests who carry the ark of the **L**
4: 1 the Jordan, the **L** said to Joshua,
4: 8 as the **L** had told Joshua; and they
4:10 until everything the **L** had commanded
4:14 That day the **L** exalted Joshua in the
4:15 Then the **L** said to Joshua,
5: 1 how the **L** had dried up the Jordan
5: 2 At that time the **L** said to Joshua,
5: 6 since they had not obeyed the **L**.
5: 6 For the **L** had sworn to them that
5: 9 the **L** said to Joshua, "Today I have
5:14 as commander of the army of the **L**
6: 2 the **L** said to Joshua, "See, I have
6:16 For the **L** has given you the city!
6:17 is in it are to be devoted to the **L**
6:19 are sacred to the **L** and must go into
6:21 They devoted the city to the **L** and
6:27 the **L** was with Joshua, and his fame
7:10 The **L** said to Joshua, "Stand up!
7:13 what the **L**, the God of Israel, says
7:14 The tribe that the **L** takes shall
7:14 the clan that the **L** takes shall
7:14 and the family that the **L** takes
7:19 "My son, give glory to the **L**, the
7:20 against the **L**, the God of Israel.
7:25 **L** will bring trouble on you today.
7:26 the **L** turned from his fierce anger
8: 1 the **L** said to Joshua, "Do not be
8: 8 Do what the **L** has commanded. See to
8:18 the **L** said to Joshua, "Hold out
8:27 as the **L** had instructed Joshua.
8:30 altar to the **L**, the God of Israel,
8:31 offered to the **L** burnt offerings
9:14 but did not enquire of the **L**.
9:18 to them by the **L**, the God of Israel.
9:19 We have given them our oath by the **L**
9:27 community and for the altar of the **L**
9:27 at the place the **L** would choose.
10: 8 The **L** said to Joshua, "Do not be
10:10 The **L** threw them into confusion
10:11 the **L** hurled large hailstones down
10:12 On the day the **L** gave the Amorites
10:12 Joshua said to the **L** in the presence
10:14 a day when the **L** listened to a man.
10:14 Surely the **L** was fighting for Israel
10:25 This is what the **L** will do to all
10:30 The **L** also gave that city and its
10:32 The **L** handed Lachish over to Israel,
10:40 **L**, the God of Israel, had commanded.
10:42 because the **L**, the God of Israel,
11: 6 The **L** said to Joshua, "Do not be
11: 8 the **L** gave them into the hand of
11: 9 did to them as the **L** had directed
11:15 of all that the **L** commanded Moses.
11:20 For it was the **L** himself who
11:20 mercy, as the **L** had commanded Moses.
11:23 just as the **L** had directed Moses,
13: 1 the **L** said to him, "You are very old
13:14 the offerings made by fire to the **L**,
13:33 the **L**, the God of Israel, is their
14: 2 the **L** had commanded through Moses.
14: 5 just as the **L** had commanded Moses.
14: 6 "You know what the **L** said to Moses
14: 8 followed the **L** my God wholeheartedly
14: 9 followed the **L** my God wholeheartedly
14:10 "Now then, just as the **L** promised,
14:12 that the **L** promised me that day.
14:12 but, the **L** helping me, I will drive

Jos 14:14 followed the **L**, the God of Israel,
17: 4 The **L** commanded Moses to give us an
17:14 the **L** has blessed us abundantly."
18: 3 that the **L**, the God of your fathers
18: 7 of the **L** is their inheritance.
19:50 as the **L** had commanded. They gave
20: 1 Then the **L** said to Joshua:
21: 2 "The **L** commanded through Moses that
21: 3 So, as the **L** had commanded, the
21: 8 the **L** had commanded through Moses.
21:43 the **L** gave Israel all the land he
21:44 The **L** gave them rest on every side,
21:44 the **L** handed all their enemies over
22: 9 the command of the **L** through Moses.
22:16 "The whole assembly of the **L** says:
22:16 How could you turn away from the **L**
22:17 fell on the community of the **L**!
22:18 are you now turning away from the **L**?
22:18 "If you rebel against the **L** today,
22:19 But do not rebel against the **L** or
22:19 than the altar of the **L** our God.
22:22 the **L**! The Mighty One, God, the **L**!
22:23 own altar to turn away from the **L**
22:23 the **L** himself call us to account.
22:24 to do with the **L**, the God of Israel?
22:25 The **L** has made the Jordan a boundary
22:25 Gadites! You have no share in the **L**.
22:25 cause ours to stop fearing the **L**.
22:27 that we will worship the **L** at his
22:27 ours, 'You have no share in the **L**.'
22:29 it from us to rebel against the **L**
22:29 altar of the **L** our God that stands
22:31 towards the **L** in this matter.
22:34 Witness Between Us that the **L** is God
23: 1 the **L** had given Israel rest from all
23: 9 "The **L** has driven out before you
23:15 so the **L** will bring on you all the
24: 2 what the **L**, the God of Israel, says
24: 7 they cried to the **L** for help, and he
24:14 River and in Egypt, and serve the **L**.
24:15 if serving the **L** seems undesirable
24:15 my household, we will serve the **L**."
24:16 forsake the **L** to serve other gods!
24:17 was the **L** our God himself who
24:18 the **L** drove out before us all the
24:18 serve the **L**, because he is our God."
24:19 "You are not able to serve the **L**.
24:20 If you forsake the **L** and serve
24:21 to Joshua, "No! We will serve the **L**.
24:22 that you have chosen to serve the **L**.
24:23 hearts to the **L**, the God of Israel."
24:24 serve the **L** our God and obey him."
24:26 oak near the holy place of the **L**.
24:27 heard all the words the **L** has said
24:31 Israel served the **L** throughout the
24:31 the **L** had done for Israel.
Jdg 1: 1 the Israelites asked the **L**, "Who
1: 2 The **L** answered, "Judah is to go;
1: 4 Judah attacked, the **L** gave the
1:19 The **L** was with the men of Judah.
1:22 Bethel, and the **L** was with them.
2: 5 they offered sacrifices to the **L**.
2: 7 The people served the **L** throughout
2: 7 things the **L** had done for Israel.
2:10 who knew neither the **L** nor what he
2:12 They forsook the **L**, the God of their
2:12 They provoked the **L** to anger
2:14 In his anger against Israel the **L**
2:16 **L** raised up judges, who saved them
2:18 Whenever the **L** raised up a judge for
2:18 for the **L** had compassion on them as
2:20 Therefore the **L** was very angry with
2:23 The **L** had allowed those nations to
3: 1 These are the nations the **L** left to
3: 7 they forgot the **L** their God and
3: 9 when they cried out to the **L**, he
3:10 The **L** gave Cushan-Rishathaim king of
3:12 because they did this evil the **L**
3:15 the Israelites cried out to the **L**,
3:28 the **L** has given Moab, your enemy,
4: 2 the **L** sold them into the hands of
4: 3 years, they cried to the **L** for help.
4: 6 "The **L**, the God of Israel, commands
4: 9 **L** will hand Sisera over to a woman.
4:14 **L** has given Sisera into your hands.
4:14 Has not the **L** gone ahead of you?"
Jdg 4:15 the **L** routed Sisera and all his
5: 3 music to the **L**, the God of Israel.
5: 4 "O **L**, when you went out from Seir,
5:11 recite the righteous acts of the **L**,
5:11 the **L** went down to the city gates.
5:13 the people of the **L** came to me with
5:23 to help the **L**, to help the **L** against
5:31 So may all your enemies perish, O **L**!
6: 6 they cried out to the **L** for help.
6: 7 the Israelites cried to the **L**
6: 8 what the **L**, the God of Israel, says
6:12 "The **L** is with you, mighty warrior.
6:13 replied, "if the **L** is with us,
6:13 'Did not the **L** bring us up out of
6:13 But now the **L** has abandoned us
6:14 The **L** turned to him and said, "Go in
6:16 The **L** answered, "I will be with you,
6:18 And the **L** said, "I will wait until
6:23 the **L** said to him, "Peace! Do not be
6:24 Gideon built an altar to the **L** there
6:24 and called it The **L** is Peace.
6:25 That same night the **L** said to him,
6:27 servants and did as the **L** told him.
7: 2 The **L** said to Gideon, "You have too
7: 4 the **L** said to Gideon, "There are
7: 5 There the **L** told him, "Separate
7: 7 The **L** said to Gideon, "With the
7: 9 During that night the **L** said to
7:15 "Get up! The **L** has given the
7:18 shout, 'For the **L** and for Gideon.
7:20 "A sword for the **L** and for Gideon!
7:22 the **L** caused the men throughout the
8: 7 "Just for that, when the **L** has given
8:23 The **L** will rule over you."
8:34 did not remember the **L** their God,
10: 6 the Israelites forsook the **L** and
10:10 the Israelites cried out to the **L**,
10:11 The **L** replied, "When the Egyptians,
10:15 the Israelites said to the **L**, "We
10:16 gods among them and served the **L**.
11: 9 and the **L** gives them to me—will I
11:10 replied, "The **L** is our witness;
11:21 "Then the **L**, the God of Israel, gave
11:23 "Now since the **L**, the God of Israel,
11:24 whatever the **L** our God has given us,
11:27 Let the **L**, the Judge, decide the
11:30 Jephthah made a vow to the **L**: "If
11:32 and the **L** gave them into his hands.
11:35 a vow to the **L** that I cannot break."
11:36 "you have given your word to the **L**.
11:36 now that the **L** has avenged you of
12: 3 the **L** gave me the victory over them.
13: 1 so the **L** delivered them into the
13: 8 Manoah prayed to the **L**: "O Lord, I
13:16 a burnt offering, offer it to the **L**.
13:19 sacrificed it on a rock to the **L**.
13:19 And the **L** did an amazing thing while
13:23 "If the **L** had meant to kill us, he
13:24 He grew and the **L** blessed him,
14: 4 not know that this was from the **L**,
15:18 he cried out to the **L**, "You have
16:28 Samson prayed to the **L**, "O Sovereign
17: 2 his mother said, "The **L** bless you,
17: 3 consecrate my silver to the **L** for
20:18 The **L** replied, "Judah shall go first.
20:23 evening, and they enquired of the **L**.
20:23 The **L** answered, "Go up against them.
20:26 and fellowship offerings to the **L**.
20:27 the Israelites enquired of the **L**.
20:28 The **L** responded, "Go, for tomorrow
20:35 The **L** defeated Benjamin before
21: 3 "O **L**, the God of Israel," they cried
21: 7 we have taken an oath by the **L** not
21:15 the **L** had made a gap in the tribes
21:19 annual festival of the **L** in Shiloh,
Ru 1: 6 the **L** had come to the aid of his
1: 8 May the **L** show kindness to you, as
1: 9 May the **L** grant that each of you
1:17 May the **L** deal with me, be it ever
1:21 the **L** has brought me back empty.
1:21 The **L** has afflicted me; the Almighty
2: 4 "The **L** be with you!" "The **L** bless
2:12 May the **L** repay you for what you
2:12 May you be richly rewarded by the **L**,
2:20 "The **L** bless him!" Naomi said to her
3:10 "The **L** bless you, my daughter," he
Ru 4:11 May the **L** make the woman who is
4:12 Through the offspring the **L** gives
4:13 and the **L** enabled her to conceive
1Sa 1: 3 sons of Eli, were priests of the **L**.
1: 5 her, and the **L** had closed her womb.
1: 6 the **L** had closed her womb, her rival
1:10 Hannah wept much and prayed to the **L**.
1:11 then I will give him to the **L** for
1:12 As she kept on praying to the **L**,
1:15 I was pouring out my soul to the **L**.
1:19 his wife, and the **L** remembered her.
1:20 "Because I asked the **L** for him.
1:21 offer the annual sacrifice to the **L**
1:23 only may the **L** make good his word.
1:26 here beside you praying to the **L**.
1:27 the **L** has granted me what I asked
1:28 So now I give him to the **L**.
1:28 he shall be given over to the **L**.
1:28 And he worshipped the **L** there.
2: 1 heart rejoices in the **L**; in the **L** my
2: 2 "There is no-one holy like the **L**;
2: 3 for the **L** is a God who knows, and by
2: 6 "The **L** brings death and makes alive;
2: 7 The **L** sends poverty and wealth;
2:10 those who oppose the **L** will be
2:10 **L** will judge the ends of the earth.
2:12 they had no regard for the **L**.
2:20 "May the **L** give you children by this
2:20 she prayed for and gave to the **L**.
2:21 And the **L** was gracious to Hannah;
2:25 if a man sins against the **L**, who
2:26 in favour with the **L** and with men.
2:27 "This is what the **L** says: 'Did I not
2:30 "Therefore the **L**, the God of Israel,
2:30 But now the **L** declares: 'Far be it
3: 4 the **L** called Samuel. Samuel answered,
3: 6 Again the **L** called, "Samuel!" And
3: 7 Now Samuel did not yet know the **L**:
3: 8 The **L** called Samuel a third time,
3: 8 that the **L** was calling the boy.
3: 9 say, 'Speak, **L**, for your servant is
3:10 The **L** came and stood there, calling
3:11 the **L** said to Samuel: "See, I am
3:18 Then Eli said, "He is the **L**; let him
3:19 The **L** was with Samuel as he grew up,
3:20 was attested as a prophet of the **L**.
3:21 The **L** continued to appear at Shiloh,
4: 3 "Why did the **L** bring defeat upon us
6: 9 **L** has brought this great disaster
6:14 cows as a burnt offering to the **L**.
6:15 and made sacrifices to the **L**.
6:17 sent as a guilt offering to the **L**
6:19 the heavy blow the **L** had dealt them,
7: 2 mourned and sought after the **L**.
7: 3 "If you are returning to the **L** with
7: 3 commit yourselves to the **L** and serve
7: 4 Ashtoreths, and served the **L** only.
7: 5 I will intercede with the **L** for you.
7: 6 "We have sinned against the **L**.
7: 8 "Do not stop crying out to the **L** our
7: 9 as a whole burnt offering to the **L**.
7: 9 the **L** on Israel's behalf, and the **L**
7:10 But that day the **L** thundered with
7:12 "Thus far has the **L** helped us.
7:17 And he built an altar there to the **L**
8: 6 so he prayed to the **L**.
8: 7 the **L** told him: "Listen to all that
8:10 Samuel told all the words of the **L**
8:18 **L** will not answer you in that day."
8:22 The **L** answered, "Listen to them and
9:15 the **L** had revealed this to Samuel:
9:17 sight of Saul, the **L** said to him,
10: 1 "Has not the **L** anointed you leader
10:17 people of Israel to the **L** at Mizpah
10:18 what the **L**, the God of Israel, says
10:22 they enquired further of the **L**, "Has
10:22 **L** said, "Yes, he has hidden himself
10:24 "Do you see the man the **L** has chosen?
11: 7 Then the terror of the **L** fell on
11:13 this day the **L** has rescued Israel."
12: 5 Samuel said to them, "The **L** is
12: 6 "It is the **L** who appointed Moses and
12: 7 righteous acts performed by the **L**
12: 8 they cried to the **L** for help, and
12: 8 and the **L** sent Moses and Aaron, who
12: 9 "But they forgot the **L** their God;

1Sa 12:10 They cried out to the L and said,
12:10 we have forsaken the L and served
12:11 the L sent Jerub-Baal, Barak,
12:13 see, the L has set a king over you.
12:15 if you do not obey the L, and if you
12:16 L is about to do before your eyes!
12:17 call upon the L to send thunder and
12:17 of the L when you asked for a king."
12:18 Samuel called upon the L, and that
12:18 day the L sent thunder and rain.
12:18 stood in awe of the L and of Samuel.
12:20 yet do not turn away from the L,
12:20 but serve the L with all your heart.
12:22 the L will not reject his people
12:22 L was pleased to make you his own.
12:23 sin against the L by failing to pray
13:14 the L has sought out a man after his
14: 6 Perhaps the L will act on our behalf.
14: 6 Nothing can hinder the L from saving,
14:10 L has given them into our hands."
14:12 L has given them into the hand of
14:23 the L rescued Israel that day, and
14:33 the men are sinning against the L by
14:34 Do not sin against the L by eating
14:35 Saul built an altar to the L; it was
14:39 surely as the L who rescues Israel
14:41 Saul prayed to the L, the God of
15: 1 "I am the one the L sent to anoint
15: 1 now to the message from the L.
15:11 cried out to the L all that night.
15:13 Saul said, "The L bless you! I have
15:16 "Let me tell you what the L said to
15:17 The L anointed you king over Israel.
15:19 Why did you not obey the L? Why did
15:20 "But I did obey the L," Saul said.
15:20 went on the mission the L assigned
15:22 Samuel replied: "Does the L delight
15:25 me, so that I may worship the L."
15:26 and the L has rejected you as king
15:28 Samuel said to him, "The L has torn
15:31 Saul, and Saul worshipped the L.
15:35 And the L was grieved that he had
16: 1 The L said to Samuel, "How long will
16: 2 The L said, "Take a heifer with you
16: 2 'I have come to sacrifice to the L.'
16: 4 Samuel did what the L said. When he
16: 5 I have come to sacrifice to the L.
16: 7 the L said to Samuel, "Do not
16: 7 The L does not look at the things
16: 7 but the L looks at the heart."
16: 8 L has not chosen this one either."
16: 9 "Nor has the L chosen this one.
16:10 to him, "The L has not chosen these.
16:12 Then the L said, "Rise and anoint
16:14 spirit from the L tormented him.
16:18 And the L is with him."
17:37 The L who delivered me from the paw
17:37 "Go, and the L be with you."
17:46 This day the L will hand you over
17:47 by sword or spear that the L saves;
18:12 L was with David but had left Saul.
18:14 success, because the L was with him.
18:17 and fight the battles of the L.
18:28 realised that the L was with David
19: 5 The L won a great victory for all
19: 9 an evil spirit from the L came upon
20:12 Jonathan said to David: "By the L,
20:13 may the L deal with me, be it ever
20:13 May the L be with you as he has been
20:14 that of the L as long as I live,
20:15 not even when the L has cut off
20:16 L call David's enemies to account."
20:22 go, because the L has sent you away.
20:23 the L is witness between you and me
20:42 'The L is witness between you and me,
22:10 Ahimelech enquired of the L for him;
22:17 "Turn and kill the priests of the L,
22:17 hand to strike the priests of the L.
22:21 Saul had killed the priests of the L.
23: 2 he enquired of the L, saying, "Shall
23: 2 The L answered him, "Go, attack the
23: 4 Once again David enquired of the L,
23: 4 and the L answered him, "Go down to
23:10 David said, "O L, God of Israel,
23:11 L, God of Israel, tell your servant.
23:11 And the L said, "He will."

1Sa 23:12 And the L said, "They will.
23:21 Saul replied, "The L bless you for
24: 4 "This is the day the L spoke of
24: 6 He said to his men, "The L forbid
24: 6 for he is the anointed of the L."
24:10 L gave you into my hands in the cave
24:12 May the L judge between you and me.
24:12 And may the L avenge the wrongs you
24:15 May the L be our judge and decide
24:18 the L gave me into your hands,
24:19 May the L reward you well for the
24:21 Now swear to me by the L that you
25:26 "Now since the L has kept you, my
25:28 for the L will certainly make a
25:30 the L has done for my master every
25:31 And when the L has brought my master
25:34 Otherwise, as surely as the L, the
25:38 About ten days later, the L struck
26:10 "the L himself will strike him;
26:11 the L forbid that I should lay a
26:12 L had put them into a deep sleep.
26:19 If the L has incited you against me,
26:23 The L rewards every man for his
26:23 The L gave you into my hands today,
26:24 so may the L value my life and
28: 6 He enquired of the L, but the L did
28:10 Saul swore to her by the L, "As
28:16 now that the L has turned away from
28:17 The L has done what he predicted
28:17 The L has torn the kingdom out of
28:18 you did not obey the L or carry out
28:18 the L has done this to you today.
28:19 The L will hand over both Israel and
28:19 The L will also hand over the army
30: 6 found strength in the L his God.
30: 8 David enquired of the L, "Shall I
30:23 that with what the L has given us.
2Sa 1:12 and for the army of the L and the
2: 1 of time, David enquired of the L.
2: 1 The L said, "Go up." David asked,
2: 1 I go?" "To Hebron," the L answered.
2: 5 "The L bless you for showing this
2: 6 May the L now show you kindness and
3: 9 what the L promised him on oath
3:18 Now do it! For the L promised David,
3:39 May the L repay the evildoer
4: 8 This day the L has avenged my lord
5: 2 And the L said to you, 'You shall
5:12 David knew that the L had
5:19 David enquired of the L, "Shall I go
5:19 The L answered him, "Go, for I will
5:20 the L has broken out against my
5:23 David enquired of the L, and he
5:24 mean the L has gone out in front
6: 9 David was afraid of the L that day
6:11 and the L blessed him and his entire
6:12 David was told, "The L has blessed
7: 1 the L had given him rest from all
7: 3 and do it, for the L is with you."
7: 5 'This is what the L says: Are you
7:11 "'The L declares to you that the L
7:24 you, O L, have become their God.
8: 6 The L gave David victory wherever he
8:11 dedicated these articles to the L,
8:14 The L gave David victory wherever he
10:12 L will do what is good in his sight."
11:27 David had done displeased the L.
12: 1 The L sent Nathan to David. When he
12: 7 what the L, the God of Israel, says
12:11 "This is what the L says: 'Out of
12:13 "I have sinned against the L.
12:13 "The L has taken away your sin.
12:14 enemies of the L show utter contempt
12:15 L struck the child that Uriah's wife
12:22 The L may be gracious to me and let
12:24 named him Solomon. The L loved him;
12:25 the L loved him, he sent word
14:11 "Then let the king invoke the L his
15: 7 and fulfil a vow I made to the L.
15: 8 'If the L takes me back to Jerusalem,
15: 8 I will worship the L in Hebron.
15:31 So David prayed, "O L, turn
16: 8 The L has repaid you for all the
16: 8 The L has handed the kingdom over to
16:10 the L said to him, 'Curse David,'
16:11 curse, for the L has told him to.

2Sa 16:12 the L will see my distress and
16:18 "No, the one chosen by the L, by
17:14 the L had determined to frustrate
18:19 the L has delivered him from the
18:31 The L has delivered you today from
19: 7 I swear by the L that if you don't
21: 1 so David sought the face of the L.
21: 1 The L said, "It is on account of
22: 1 David sang to the L the words of
22: 1 when the L delivered him from the
22: 4 I call to the L, who is worthy of
22: 7 In my distress I called to the L;
22:14 The L thundered from heaven;
22:16 laid bare at the rebuke of the L,
22:19 disaster, but the L was my support.
22:21 "The L has dealt with me according
22:22 For I have kept the ways of the L;
22:25 The L has rewarded me according to
22:29 You are my lamp, O L; the L turns my
22:32 For who is God besides the L?
22:42 to the L, but he did not answer.
22:47 "The L lives! Praise be to my Rock!
22:50 Therefore I will praise you, O L,
23:10 The L brought about a great victory
23:12 the L brought about a great victory.
23:17 "Far be it from me, O L, to do this!"
24:10 and he said to the L, "I have sinned
24:10 Now, O L, I beg you, take away the
24:12 'This is what the L says: I am
24:14 Let us fall into the hands of the L,
24:15 the L sent a plague on Israel from
24:16 the L was grieved because of the
24:17 he said to the L, "I am the one who
24:18 "Go up and build an altar to the L
24:19 David went up, as the L had
24:21 that I can build an altar to the L,
24:24 I will not sacrifice to the L my God
24:25 David built an altar to the L there
24:25 Then the L answered prayer on behalf
1Ki 1:30 today what I swore to you by the L,
1:36 "Amen! May the L, the God of my lord
1:37 the L was with my lord the king, so
2: 4 that the L may keep his promise to
2: 8 I swore to him by the L: 'I will not
2:15 for it has come to him from the L.
2:23 King Solomon swore by the L: "May
2:27 from the priesthood of the L,
2:27 fulfilling the word the L had spoken
2:28 he fled to the tent of the L and
2:29 had fled to the tent of the L and
2:30 Benaiah entered the tent of the L
2:32 The L will repay him for the blood
2:42 "Did I not make you swear by the L
2:43 did you not keep your oath to the L
2:44 L will repay you for your wrongdoing.
3: 3 Solomon showed his love for the L by
3: 5 At Gibeon the L appeared to Solomon
3: 7 "Now, O L my God, you have made
5: 3 L put his enemies under his feet.
5: 4 now the L my God has given me rest
5: 5 as the L told my father David, when
5:12 The L gave Solomon wisdom, just as
6: 2 that King Solomon built for the L
8: 9 where the L made a covenant with the
8:12 Solomon said, "The L has said that
8:18 the L said to my father David,
8:20 "The L has kept the promise he made:
8:20 just as the L promised, and I have
8:22 stood before the altar of the L
8:23 said: "O L, God of Israel, there is
8:25 "Now L, God of Israel, keep for your
8:28 and his plea for mercy, O L my God.
8:44 and when they pray to the L towards
8:54 prayers and supplications to the L,
8:54 rose from before the altar of the L,
8:57 May the L our God be with us as he
8:59 near to the L our God day and night
8:61 be fully committed to the L our God,
8:63 of fellowship offerings to the L:
8:66 L had done for his servant David
9: 2 the L appeared to him a second time,
9: 3 The L said to him: "I have heard the
9: 8 'Why has the L done such a thing to
9: 9 'Because they have forsaken the L
9: 9 L brought all this disaster on them.
9:25 on the altar he had built for the L,

1Ki 11: 2 which the **L** had told the Israelites,
11: 4 not fully devoted to the **L** his God,
11: 6 he did not follow the **L** completely,
11: 9 The **L** became angry with Solomon
11: 9 heart had turned away from the **L**,
11:11 the **L** said to Solomon, "Since this
11:14 the **L** raised up against Solomon an
11:31 for this is what the **L**, the God of
12:15 this turn of events was from the **L**,
12:15 to fulfil the word the **L** had spoken
12:24 'This is what the **L** says: Do not go
12:24 home again, as the **L** had ordered.
13: 2 altar! This is what the **L** says:
13: 3 "This is the sign the **L** has declared:
13: 6 man of God interceded with the **L**,
13:21 "This is what the **L** says: 'You have
13:26 **L** has given him over to the lion,
14: 5 the **L** had told Ahijah, "Jeroboam's
14: 7 what the **L**, the God of Israel, says
14:11 The **L** has spoken!'
14:13 in whom the **L**, the God of Israel,
14:14 "The **L** will raise up for himself a
14:15 the **L** will strike Israel, so that it
14:15 provoked the **L** to anger by making
14:18 the **L** had said through his servant
14:21 the city the **L** had chosen out of all
14:24 practices of the nations the **L** had
15: 3 not fully devoted to the **L** his God,
15: 4 for David's sake the **L** his God gave
15:14 committed to the **L** all his life.
15:30 the **L**, the God of Israel, to anger.
16: 7 he had done in the eyes of the **L**,
16:13 provoked the **L**, the God of Israel,
16:26 provoked the **L**, the God of Israel,
16:33 and did more to provoke the **L**,
17: 1 As the **L**, the God of Israel, lives,
17: 5 he did what the **L** had told him.
17:14 what the **L**, the God of Israel, says
17:14 day the **L** gives rain on the land.
17:20 he cried out to the **L**, "O **L** my God,
17:21 boy three times and cried to the **L**,
17:21 "O **L** my God, let this boy's life
17:22 The **L** heard Elijah's cry, and the
18: 3 was a devout believer in the **L**.
18:12 worshipped the **L** since my youth.
18:13 was killing the prophets of the **L**?
18:21 If the **L** is God, follow him; but if
18:30 altar of the **L**, which was in ruins.
18:36 prayed, "O **L**, God of Abraham, Isaac
18:37 Answer me, O **L**, answer me, so
18:37 you, O **L**, are God, and that you are
18:38 the fire of the **L** fell and burned up
18:39 "The **L**—he is God! The **L**—he is God!
18:46 The power of the **L** came upon Elijah
19: 4 "I have had enough, **L**," he said.
19:11 The **L** said, "Go out and stand on the
19:11 for the **L** is about to pass by.
19:11 but the **L** was not in the wind.
19:11 but the **L** was not in the earthquake.
19:12 fire, but the **L** was not in the fire.
19:15 The **L** said to him, "Go back the way
20:13 "This is what the **L** says: 'Do you
20:14 This is what the **L** says: 'The young
20:28 "This is what the **L** says: 'Because
20:28 the Arameans think the **L** is a god
20:36 "Because you have not obeyed the **L**,
20:42 "This is what the **L** says: 'You have
21: 3 Naboth replied, "The **L** forbid that I
21:19 Say to him, 'This is what the **L** says:
21:19 'This is what the **L** says: In the
21:23 also concerning Jezebel the **L** says
21:26 the **L** drove out before Israel.)
22: 5 "First seek the counsel of the **L**.
22: 7 "Is there not a prophet of the **L**
22: 8 whom we can enquire of the **L**,
22:11 "This is what the **L** says: 'With
22:12 **L** will give it into the king's hand
22:14 tell him only what the **L** tells me."
22:15 **L** will give it into the king's hand
22:17 **L** said, 'These people have no master
22:19 I saw the **L** sitting on his throne
22:20 the **L** said, 'Who will entice Ahab
22:22 "'By what means?' the **L** asked.
22:22 in enticing him,' said the **L**.
22:23 "So now the **L** has put a lying spirit
22:23 The **L** has decreed disaster for you."
1Ki 22:24 "Which way did the spirit from the **L**
22:28 the **L** has not spoken through me.
22:53 worshipped Baal and provoked the **L**,
2Ki 1: 4 Therefore this is what the **L** says:
1: 6 "This is what the **L** says: Is it
1:16 the king, "This is what the **L** says
2: 1 the **L** was about to take Elijah up to
2: 2 the **L** has sent me to Bethel.
2: 4 the **L** has sent me to Jericho.
2: 6 the **L** has sent me to the Jordan.
2:14 "Where now is the **L**, the God of
2:21 **L** says: 'I have healed this water.
3:10 "Has the **L** called us three kings
3:11 "Is there no prophet of the **L** here,
3:11 may enquire of the **L** through him?"
3:13 "because it was the **L** who called us
3:16 he said, "This is what the **L** says:
3:17 For this is what the **L** says: You
3:18 an easy thing in the eyes of the **L**;
4: 1 and you know that he revered the **L**.
4:27 but the **L** has hidden it from me and
4:33 the two of them and prayed to the **L**.
4:43 For this is what the **L** says: 'They
5: 1 through him the **L** had given victory
5:17 to any other god but the **L**.
5:18 may the **L** forgive your servant for
5:18 **L** forgive your servant for this."
6:17 Elisha prayed, "O **L**, open his eyes
6:17 the **L** opened the servant's eyes,
6:18 Elisha prayed to the **L**, "Strike
6:20 "**L**, open the eyes of these men so
6:20 Then the **L** opened their eyes and
6:27 The king replied, "If the **L** does not
6:33 said, "This disaster is from the **L**.
6:33 should I wait for the **L** any longer?"
7: 1 This is what the **L** says: About this
7: 2 "Look, even if the **L** should open the
7:16 for a shekel, as the **L** had said.
7:19 "Look, even if the **L** should open the
8: 1 because the **L** has decreed a famine
8: 8 Consult the **L** through him; ask him,
8:10 but the **L** has revealed to me that he
8:13 "The **L** has shown me that you will
8:19 **L** was not willing to destroy Judah.
9: 3 'This is what the **L** says: I anoint
9: 6 what the **L**, the God of Israel, says
9:12 'This is what the **L** says: I anoint
9:25 the **L** made this prophecy about him:
10:10 that not a word the **L** has spoken
10:10 The **L** has done what he promised
10:16 with me and see my zeal for the **L**.
10:23 see that no servants of the **L** are
10:30 The **L** said to Jehu, "Because you
10:32 In those days the **L** began to reduce
11:17 then made a covenant between the **L**
13: 4 and the **L** listened to him, for he
13: 5 The **L** provided a deliverer for
13:23 the **L** was gracious to them and had
14: 6 Law of Moses where the **L** commanded:
14:26 The **L** had seen how bitterly everyone
14:27 since the **L** had not said he would
15: 5 The **L** afflicted the king with
15:37 (In those days the **L** began to send
16: 3 of the nations the **L** had driven out
17: 7 had sinned against the **L** their God,
17: 8 the **L** had driven out before them,
17: 9 did things against the **L** their God
17:11 nations whom the **L** had driven out
17:11 things that provoked the **L** to anger.
17:12 **L** had said, "You shall not do this.
17:13 The **L** warned Israel and Judah
17:14 did not trust in the **L** their God.
17:15 although the **L** had ordered them,
17:15 the **L** had forbidden them to do.
17:16 all the commands of the **L** their God
17:18 the **L** was very angry with Israel and
17:19 the commands of the **L** their God.
17:20 **L** rejected all the people of Israel
17:21 Israel away from following the **L**
17:23 until the **L** removed them from his
17:25 they did not worship the **L**; so he
17:28 taught them how to worship the **L**.
17:32 They worshipped the **L**, but they also
17:33 They worshipped the **L**, but they also
17:34 They neither worship the **L** nor
17:34 laws and commands that the **L** gave
2Ki 17:35 the **L** made a covenant with the
17:36 **L**, who brought you up out of Egypt
17:41 these people were worshipping the **L**
18: 5 Hezekiah trusted in the **L**, the God
18: 6 He held fast to the **L** and did not
18: 6 the commands the **L** had given Moses.
18: 7 And the **L** was with him; he was
18:12 they had not obeyed the **L** their God,
18:22 "We are depending on the **L** our God"
18:25 this place without word from the **L**?
18:25 The **L** himself told me to march
18:30 you to trust in the **L** when he says,
18:30 'The **L** will surely deliver us;
18:32 he says, 'The **L** will deliver us.'
18:35 **L** deliver Jerusalem from my hand?"
19: 6 'This is what the **L** says: Do not be
19:15 Hezekiah prayed to the **L**: "O **L**, God
19:16 Give ear, O **L**, and hear;
19:16 open your eyes, O **L**, and see;
19:17 "It is true, O **L**, that the
19:19 Now, O **L** our God, deliver us from
19:19 know that you alone, O **L**, are God."
19:20 what the **L**, the God of Israel, says
19:21 is the word that the **L** has spoken
19:32 "Therefore this is what the **L** says
20: 1 "This is what the **L** says: Put your
20: 2 to the wall and prayed to the **L**,
20: 3 "Remember, O **L**, how I have walked
20: 5 'This is what the **L**, the God of your
20: 8 the sign that the **L** will heal me
20: 9 the **L** will do what he has promised:
20:11 the prophet Isaiah called upon the **L**
20:11 and the **L** made the shadow go back
20:17 Nothing will be left, says the **L**.
21: 2 the nations the **L** had driven out
21: 4 of which the **L** had said, "In
21: 7 of which the **L** had said to David and
21: 9 than the nations the **L** had destroyed
21:10 The **L** said through his servants the
21:12 what the **L**, the God of Israel, says
21:22 He forsook the **L**, the God of his
22:13 "Go and enquire of the **L** for me and
22:15 what the **L**, the God of Israel, says
22:16 'This is what the **L** says: I am going
22:18 who sent you to enquire of the **L**,
22:18 what the **L**, the God of Israel, says
23: 3 to follow the **L** and keep his
23: 9 at the altar of the **L** in Jerusalem,
23:19 that had provoked the **L** to anger.
23:23 celebrated to the **L** in Jerusalem.
23:25 who turned to the **L** as he did—
23:26 the **L** did not turn away from the
23:27 the **L** said, "I will remove Judah
24: 2 The **L** sent Babylonian, Aramean,
24: 4 the **L** was not willing to forgive.
24:13 the **L** had declared, Nebuchadnezzar
1Ch 2: 3 so the **L** put him to death.
6:15 was deported when the **L** sent Judah
9:19 entrance to the dwelling of the **L**.
9:20 gatekeepers, and the **L** was with him.
10:14 did not enquire of the **L**. So the **L**
11: 3 the **L** had promised through Samuel.
11:10 whole land, as the **L** had promised—
11:14 the **L** brought about a great victory.
12:23 over to him, as the **L** had said:
13: 2 if it is the will of the **L** our God,
13: 6 up from there the ark of God the **L**,
13:14 and the **L** blessed his household and
14: 2 David knew that the **L** had
14:10 The **L** answered him, "Go, I will
14:17 the **L** made all the nations fear him.
15: 2 the **L** chose them to carry the ark
15:13 the **L** our God broke out in anger
16: 7 this psalm of thanks to the **L**:
16: 8 Give thanks to the **L**, call on his
16:10 of those who seek the **L** rejoice.
16:11 Look to the **L** and his strength;
16:14 He is the **L** our God; his judgments
16:25 For great is the **L** and most worthy
16:26 but the **L** made the heavens.
16:28 Ascribe to the **L**, O families of
16:28 ascribe to the **L** glory and strength,
16:29 ascribe to the **L** the glory due to
16:29 **L** in the splendour of his holiness.
16:31 say among the nations, "The **L** reigns
16:34 Give thanks to the **L**, for he is good

1Ch 16:39 before the tabernacle of the **L**
16:40 to present burnt offerings to the **L**
16:41 by name to give thanks to the **L**,
17: 4 'This is what the **L** says: You are
17:10 the **L** will build a house for you:
17:19 O **L**. For the sake of your servant
17:20 "There is no-one like you, O **L**,
17:22 you, O **L**, have become their God
17:23 "And now, **L**, let the promise you
17:26 O **L**, you are God! You have promised
17:27 you, O **L**, have blessed it, and it
18: 6 The **L** gave David victory everywhere
18:11 dedicated these articles to the **L**,
18:13 The **L** gave David victory everywhere
19:13 **L** will do what is good in his sight.
21: 3 Joab replied, "May the **L** multiply
21: 9 The **L** said to Gad, David's seer,
21:10 'This is what the **L** says: I am
21:11 what the **L** says: 'Take your choice:
21:12 or three days of the sword of the **L**
21:13 Let me fall into the hands of the **L**,
21:14 the **L** sent a plague on Israel, and
21:15 the **L** saw it and was grieved
21:17 O **L** my God, let your hand fall upon
21:18 build an altar to the **L** on the
21:22 that I can build an altar to the **L**,
21:24 I will not take for the **L** what is
21:26 David built an altar to the **L** there
21:26 He called on the **L**, and the **L**
21:27 the **L** spoke to the angel, and he put
21:28 David saw that the **L** had answered
21:29 The tabernacle of the **L**, which Moses
22: 5 and the house to be built for the **L**
22: 6 house for the **L**, the God of Israel.
22:11 "Now, my son, the **L** be with you, and
22:12 May the **L** give you discretion and
22:13 that the **L** gave to Moses for Israel.
22:16 the work, and the **L** be with you."
22:18 subject to the **L** and to his people.
23:25 For David had said, "Since the **L**,
23:31 were presented to the **L** on Sabbaths
24:19 as the **L**, the God of Israel, had
25: 3 harp in thanking and praising the **L**.
25: 7 music for the **L**—they numbered 288.
26:30 for all the work of the **L** and for
27:23 because the **L** had promised to make
28: 4 "Yet the **L**, the God of Israel, chose
28: 5 sons—and the **L** has given me many—
28: 5 of the kingdom of the **L** over Israel.
28: 8 Israel and of the assembly of the **L**,
28: 9 for the **L** searches every heart and
28:10 for the **L** has chosen you to build
29: 5 consecrate himself today to the **L**?
29: 9 freely and wholeheartedly to the **L**.
29:10 David praised the **L** in the presence
29:10 "Praise be to you, O **L**, God of our
29:11 Yours, O **L**, is the greatness and the
29:11 Yours, O **L**, is the kingdom; you are
29:16 O **L** our God, as for all this
29:18 O **L**, God of our fathers Abraham,
29:20 So they all praised the **L**, the God
29:21 day they made sacrifices to the **L**
29:23 Solomon sat on the throne of the **L**
29:25 The **L** highly exalted Solomon in the
2Ch 1: 1 for the **L** his God was with him and
1: 5 in front of the tabernacle of the **L**;
2: 4 appointed feasts of the **L** our God.
2:11 "Because the **L** loves his people, he
2:12 a temple for the **L** and a palace for
3: 1 **L** had appeared to his father David.
5:10 where the **L** made a covenant with the
5:13 to give praise and thanks to the **L**.
5:13 voices in praise to the **L** and sang:
6: 1 Solomon said, "The **L** has said that
6: 8 the **L** said to my father David,
6:10 "The **L** has kept the promise he made.
6:10 just as the **L** promised, and I have
6:12 stood before the altar of the **L**
6:14 He said: "O **L**, God of Israel,
6:16 "Now **L**, God of Israel, keep for your
6:17 now, O **L**, God of Israel, let your
6:19 and his plea for mercy, O **L** my God.
7: 3 worshipped and gave thanks to the **L**,
7: 6 David had made for praising the **L**
7:10 things the **L** had done for David
7:12 the **L** appeared to him at night and

2Ch 7:21 'Why has the **L** done such a thing to
7:22 'Because they have forsaken the **L**,
8:12 On the altar of the **L** that he had
8:12 sacrificed burnt offerings to the **L**,
10:15 to fulfil the word that the **L** had
11: 4 'This is what the **L** says: Do not go
11: 4 So they obeyed the words of the **L**
11:14 rejected them as priests of the **L**.
11:16 set their hearts on seeking the **L**,
11:16 to the **L**, the God of their fathers.
12: 2 they had been unfaithful to the **L**,
12: 5 "This is what the **L** says: 'You have
12: 6 themselves and said, "The **L** is just.
12: 7 **L** saw that they humbled themselves
12:13 the city the **L** had chosen out of all
12:14 not set his heart on seeking the **L**.
13: 8 plan to resist the kingdom of the **L**,
13: 9 you drive out the priests of the **L**,
13:10 "As for us, the **L** is our God, and we
13:10 The priests who serve the **L** are sons
13:11 and fragrant incense to the **L**.
13:11 the requirements of the **L** our God.
13:12 do not fight against the **L**, the God
13:14 Then they cried out to the **L**.
13:18 relied on the **L**, the God of their
13:20 the **L** struck him down and he died.
14: 4 He commanded Judah to seek the **L**,
14: 6 years, for the **L** gave him rest.
14: 7 because we have sought the **L** our God
14:11 Asa called to the **L** his God and said
14:11 **L**, there is no-one like you to help
14:11 Help us, O **L** our God, for we rely on
14:11 O **L**, you are our God; do not let man
14:12 The **L** struck down the Cushites
14:14 terror of the **L** had fallen upon them
15: 2 **L** is with you when you are with him
15: 4 their distress they turned to the **L**,
15: 8 He repaired the altar of the **L** that
15: 9 saw that the **L** his God was with him.
15:11 that time they sacrificed to the **L**
15:12 into a covenant to seek the **L**,
15:13 All who would not seek the **L**, the
15:14 They took an oath to the **L** with loud
15:15 the **L** gave them rest on every side.
15:17 heart was fully committed ⌊to the **L**
16: 8 Yet when you relied on the **L**, he
16: 9 For the eyes of the **L** range
16:12 he did not seek help from the **L**,
17: 3 The **L** was with Jehoshaphat because
17: 5 The **L** established the kingdom under
17: 6 devoted to the ways of the **L**;
17:16 himself for the service of the **L**,
18: 4 "First seek the counsel of the **L**.
18: 6 Is there not a prophet of the **L** here
18: 7 whom we can enquire of the **L**,
18:10 "This is what the **L** says: 'With
18:11 **L** will give it into the king's hand."
18:16 **L** said, 'These people have no master.
18:18 I saw the **L** sitting on his throne
18:19 the **L** said, 'Who will entice Ahab
18:20 "'By what means?' the **L** asked.
18:21 in enticing him,' said the **L**.
18:22 "So now the **L** has put a lying spirit
18:22 The **L** has decreed disaster for you."
18:23 "Which way did the spirit from the **L**
18:27 the **L** has not spoken through me.
18:31 cried out, and the **L** helped him.
19: 2 and love those who hate the **L**?
19: 2 the wrath of the **L** is upon you.
19: 4 to the **L**, the God of their fathers.
19: 6 not judging for man but for the **L**,
19: 7 for with the **L** our God there is no
19:10 warn them not to sin against the **L**;
19:11 you in any matter concerning the **L**,
19:11 the **L** be with those who do well."
20: 3 resolved to enquire of the **L**,
20: 4 together to seek help from the **L**;
20: 6 said: "O **L**, God of our fathers,
20:15 This is what the **L** says to you:
20:17 the deliverance the **L** will give you
20:17 and the **L** will be with you.
20:19 Korahites stood up and praised the **L**
20:21 "Give thanks to the **L**, for his love
20:22 the **L** set ambushes against the men
20:26 Beracah, where they praised the **L**.
20:27 for the **L** had given them cause to

2Ch 20:29 heard how the **L** had fought against
20:37 **L** will destroy what you have made.
21: 7 covenant the **L** had made with David
21: 7 the **L** was not willing to destroy the
21:10 the **L**, the God of his fathers.
21:12 This is what the **L**, the God of your
21:14 now the **L** is about to strike your
21:16 The **L** aroused against Jehoram the
21:18 the **L** afflicted Jehoram with an
22: 7 whom the **L** had anointed to destroy
22: 9 who sought the **L** with all his heart.
23: 3 as the **L** promised concerning the
23: 6 what the **L** has assigned to them.
23:18 the burnt offerings of the **L**
24: 9 should bring to the **L** the tax that
24:19 Although the **L** sent prophets to the
24:20 Because you have forsaken the **L**, he
24:22 May the **L** see this and call you to
24:24 the **L** delivered into their hands a
24:24 Because Judah had forsaken the **L**,
25: 4 where the **L** commanded: "Fathers
25: 7 for the **L** is not with Israel—not
25: 9 **L** can give you much more than that."
25:27 turned away from following the **L**,
26: 5 sought the **L**, God gave him success.
26:16 He was unfaithful to the **L** his God,
26:17 priests of the **L** followed him in.
26:18 Uzziah, to burn incense to the **L**.
26:20 because the **L** had afflicted him.
28: 3 nations that the **L** had driven out
28: 5 the **L** his God handed him over to
28: 6 the **L**, the God of their fathers.
28: 9 a prophet of the **L** named Oded was
28: 9 He said to them, "Because the **L**,
28:19 The **L** had humbled Judah because of
28:19 had been most unfaithful to the **L**.
28:22 even more unfaithful to the **L**.
28:25 provoked the **L**, the God of his
29:10 to make a covenant with the **L**,
29:11 **L** has chosen you to stand before
29:16 into the sanctuary of the **L** to
29:17 they reached the portico of the **L**.
29:21 offer these on the altar of the **L**.
29:25 by the **L** through his prophets
29:27 singing to the **L** began also,
29:31 now dedicated yourselves to the **L**.
29:32 them for burnt offerings to the **L**.
30: 1 Passover to the **L**, the God of Israel
30: 5 Passover to the **L**, the God of Israel
30: 7 who were unfaithful to the **L**, the
30: 8 your fathers were; submit to the **L**.
30: 9 for the **L** your God is gracious and
30:17 consecrate ⌊their lambs⌋ to the **L**
30:18 the **L**, who is good, pardon
30:19 —the **L**, the God of his fathers—
30:20 the **L** heard Hezekiah and healed the
30:21 and priests sang to the **L** every day,
30:22 of the service of the **L**.
30:22 the **L**, the God of their fathers.
31: 6 things dedicated to the **L** their God,
31: 8 they praised the **L** and blessed his
31:10 because the **L** has blessed his people
31:14 the contributions made to the **L** and
32: 8 but with us is the **L** our God to help
32:11 Hezekiah says, 'The **L** our God will
32:17 also wrote letters insulting the **L**,
32:21 the **L** sent an angel, who annihilated
32:22 the **L** saved Hezekiah and the people
32:23 offerings to Jerusalem for the **L**
32:24 He prayed to the **L**, who answered him
33: 2 of the nations the **L** had driven out
33: 4 of which the **L** had said, "My Name
33: 9 than the nations the **L** had destroyed
33:10 The **L** spoke to Manasseh and his
33:11 the **L** brought against them the army
33:12 sought the favour of the **L** his God
33:13 he prayed to him, the **L** was moved by
33:13 Then Manasseh knew that the **L** is God.
33:16 he restored the altar of the **L** and
33:16 to serve the **L**, the God of Israel.
33:17 places, but only to the **L** their God.
34:21 Go and enquire of the **L** for me and
34:23 what the **L**, the God of Israel, says
34:24 'This is what the **L** says: I am going
34:26 who sent you to enquire of the **L**,
34:26 what the **L**, the God of Israel, says

2Ch 34:31 to follow the **L** and keep his
34:33 in Israel serve the **L** their God.
34:33 the **L**, the God of their fathers.
35: 1 the Passover to the **L** in Jerusalem,
35: 3 who had been consecrated to the **L**:
35: 6 what the **L** commanded through Moses
35:12 of the people to offer to the **L**,
35:16 the entire service of the **L** was
35:16 offerings on the altar of the **L**,
36:13 turn to the **L**, the God of Israel.
36:15 The **L**, the God of their fathers,
36:16 **L** was aroused against his people
36:22 **L** moved the heart of Cyrus king of
36:23 'The **L**, the God of heaven, has given
36:23 may the **L** his God be with him, and
Ezr 1: 1 **L** moved the heart of Cyrus king of
1: 2 'The **L**, the God of heaven, has given
3: 3 burnt offerings on it to the **L**,
3: 5 appointed sacred feasts of the **L**,
3: 5 as freewill offerings to the **L**.
3: 6 to offer burnt offerings to the **L**,
3:11 thanksgiving they sang to the **L**:
3:11 a great shout of praise to the **L**,
4: 1 temple for the **L**, the God of Israel
4: 3 We alone will build it for the **L**,
6:21 to seek the **L**, the God of Israel.
6:22 because the **L** had filled them with
7: 6 the **L**, the God of Israel, had given
7:11 and decrees of the **L** for Israel:
8:28 articles are consecrated to the **L**.
8:28 to the **L**, the God of your fathers.
8:35 this was a burnt offering to the **L**.
9: 5 my hands spread out to the **L** my
9: 8 the **L** our God has been gracious
9:15 O **L**, God of Israel, you are
10:11 Now make confession to the **L**, the
Ne 1: 5 I said: "O **L**, God of heaven, the
5:13 said, "Amen," and praised the **L**.
8: 1 the **L** had commanded for Israel.
8: 6 Ezra praised the **L**, the great God;
8: 6 bowed down and worshipped the **L**
8:10 the joy of the **L** is your strength."
8:14 which the **L** had commanded through
9: 3 and in worshipping the **L** their God.
9: 4 with loud voices to the **L** their God.
9: 6 You alone are the **L**. You made the
10:29 and decrees of the **L** our Lord.
10:34 burn on the altar of the **L** our God,
Job 1: 7 The **L** said to Satan, "Where have you
1: 7 Satan answered the **L**, "From roaming
1: 8 the **L** said to Satan, "Have you
1:12 The **L** said to Satan, "Very well,
1:21 The **L** gave and the **L** has taken away;
2: 2 the **L** said to Satan, "Where have you
2: 2 Satan answered the **L**, "From roaming
2: 3 the **L** said to Satan, "Have you
2: 6 The **L** said to Satan, "Very well,
38: 1 the **L** answered Job out of the storm.
40: 1 The **L** said to Job:
40: 3 Then Job answered the **L**:
40: 6 the **L** spoke to Job out of the storm:
42: 1 Then Job replied to the **L**:
42: 7 After the **L** had said these things to
42: 9 Naamathite did what the **L** told them;
42: 9 and the **L** accepted Job's prayer.
42:10 the **L** made him prosperous again and
42:11 trouble the **L** had brought upon him,
42:12 The **L** blessed the latter part of
Ps 1: 6 For the **L** watches over the way of
2: 2 the **L** and against his Anointed One.
2: 7 I will proclaim the decree of the **L**
2:11 Serve the **L** with fear and rejoice
3: 1 O **L**, how many are my foes! How many
3: 3 you are a shield around me, O **L**;
3: 4 To the **L** I cry aloud, and he answers
3: 5 again, because the **L** sustains me.
3: 7 Arise, O **L**! Deliver me, O my God!
3: 8 From the **L** comes deliverance. May
4: 3 the **L** will hear when I call to him.
4: 5 right sacrifices and trust in the **L**.
4: 6 your face shine upon us, O **L**
4: 8 alone, O **L**, make me dwell in safety.
5: 1 Give ear to my words, O **L**, consider
5: 3 In the morning, O **L**, you hear my
5: 6 and deceitful men the **L** abhors.
5: 8 Lead me, O **L**, in your righteousness

Ps 5:12 For surely, O **L**, you bless the
6: 1 O **L**, do not rebuke me in your anger
6: 2 Be merciful to me, **L**, for I am faint
6: 2 O **L**, heal me, for my bones are in
6: 3 in anguish. How long, O **L**, how long?
6: 4 Turn, O **L**, and deliver me; save me
6: 8 for the **L** has heard my weeping.
6: 9 The **L** has heard my cry for mercy;
6: 9 the **L** accepts my prayer.
7: T he sang to the **L** concerning Cush
7: 1 O **L** my God, I take refuge in you;
7: 3 O **L** my God, if I have done this and
7: 6 Arise, O **L**, in your anger; rise up
7: 8 let the **L** judge the peoples.
7: 8 Judge me, O **L**, according to my
7:17 I will give thanks to the **L** because
8: 1 O **L**, our Lord, how majestic is your
8: 9 O **L**, our Lord, how majestic is your
9: 1 I will praise you, O **L**, with all my
9: 7 The **L** reigns for ever; he has
9: 9 The **L** is a refuge for the oppressed,
9:10 for you, **L**, have never forsaken
9:11 Sing praises to the **L**, enthroned in
9:13 O **L**, see how my enemies persecute me
9:16 The **L** is known by his justice;
9:19 Arise, O **L**, let not man triumph;
9:20 Strike them with terror, O **L**;
10: 1 Why, O **L**, do you stand far off?
10: 3 the greedy and reviles the **L**.
10:12 Arise, **L**! Lift up your hand, O God.
10:16 The **L** is King for ever and ever;
10:17 You hear, O **L**, the desire of the
11: 1 In the **L** I take refuge. How then can
11: 4 **L** is in his holy temple; the **L** is on
11: 5 The **L** examines the righteous, but
11: 7 For the **L** is righteous, he loves
12: 1 Help, **L**, for the godly are no more;
12: 3 May the **L** cut off all flattering
12: 5 I will now arise," says the **L**.
12: 6 the words of the **L** are flawless,
12: 7 O **L**, you will keep us safe and
13: 1 How long, O **L**? Will you forget me
13: 3 Look on me and answer, O **L** my God.
14: 2 The **L** looks down from heaven on the
14: 4 and who do not call on the **L**?
14: 6 the poor, but the **L** is their refuge.
14: 7 When the **L** restores the fortunes of
15: 1 **L**, who may dwell in your sanctuary?
16: 2 I said to the **L**, "You are my Lord;
16: 5 **L**, you have assigned me my portion
16: 8 I have set the **L** always before me.
17: 1 Hear, O **L**, my righteous plea; listen
17:13 Rise up, O **L**, confront them, bring
17:14 O **L**, by your hand save me from such
18: T sang to the **L** the words of this song
18: T when the **L** delivered him from the
18: 1 I love you, O **L**, my strength.
18: 3 I call to the **L**, who is worthy of
18: 6 In my distress I called to the **L**;
18:13 The **L** thundered from heaven;
18:15 O **L**, at the blast of breath from
18:18 disaster, but the **L** was my support.
18:20 The **L** has dealt with me according to
18:21 For I have kept the ways of the **L**;
18:24 The **L** has rewarded me according to
18:28 You, O **L**, keep my lamp burning;
18:31 For who is God besides the **L**?
18:41 to the **L**, but he did not answer.
18:46 The **L** lives! Praise be to my Rock!
18:49 praise you among the nations, O **L**;
19: 7 The statutes of the **L** are
19: 8 The precepts of the **L** are right,
19: 8 The commands of the **L** are radiant,
19: 9 The ordinances of the **L** are sure
19:14 be pleasing in your sight, or **L**,
20: 1 May the **L** answer you when you are in
20: 5 May the **L** grant all your requests.
20: 9 O **L**, save the king! Answer us when
21: 1 O **L**, the king rejoices in your
21: 7 For the king trusts in the **L**;
21: 9 In his wrath the **L** will swallow them
21:13 Be exalted, O **L**, in your strength;
22: 8 He trusts in the **L**; let the **L** rescue
22:19 But you, O **L**, be not far off;
22:26 they who seek the **L** will praise him
22:27 will remember and turn to the **L**,

Ps 22:28 for dominion belongs to the **L** and he
23: 1 The **L** is my shepherd, I shall not be
24: 3 Who may ascend the hill of the **L**?
24: 5 He will receive blessing from the **L**
24: 8 **L** strong and mighty, the **L** mighty in
25: 1 To you, O **L**, I lift up my soul;
25: 4 Show me your ways, O **L**, teach me
25: 6 Remember, O **L**, your great mercy and
25: 7 Remember not the sins of my youth
25: 8 Good and upright is the **L**; therefore
25:10 All the ways of the **L** are loving and
25:11 For the sake of your name, O **L**,
25:12 then, is the man that fears the **L**?
25:14 The **L** confides in those who fear him;
25:15 My eyes are ever on the **L**, for only
26: 1 Vindicate me, O **L**, for I have led a
26: 1 trusted in the **L** without wavering.
26: 2 Test me, O **L**, and try me, examine my
26: 6 and go about your altar, O **L**,
26: 8 I love the house where you live, O **L**
27: 1 The **L** is my light and my salvation—
27: 1 The **L** is the stronghold of my life—
27: 4 One thing I ask of the **L**, this is
27: 4 to gaze upon the beauty of the **L**
27: 6 I will sing and make music to the **L**
27: 7 Hear my voice when I call, O **L**;
27: 8 Your face, **L**, I will seek.
27:10 forsake me, the **L** will receive me.
27:11 Teach me your way, O **L**; lead me in
27:13 I will see the goodness of the **L** in
27:14 Wait for the **L**; be strong and take
27:14 and take heart and wait for the **L**.
28: 1 To you I call, O **L** my Rock; do not
28: 5 no regard for the works of the **L**
28: 7 The **L** is my strength and my shield;
28: 8 The **L** is the strength of his people
29: 1 Ascribe to the **L**, O mighty ones,
29: 1 ascribe to the **L** glory and strength
29: 2 Ascribe to the **L** the glory due to
29: 2 worship the **L** in the splendour of
29: 3 **L** thunders over the mighty waters.
29: 5 the **L** breaks in pieces the cedars of
29: 8 the **L** shakes the Desert of Kadesh.
29:10 The **L** sits enthroned over the flood;
29:10 the **L** is enthroned as King for ever.
29:11 The **L** gives strength to his people;
29:11 the **L** blesses his people with peace.
30: 1 I will exalt you, O **L**, for you
30: 2 O **L** my God, I called to you for help
30: 3 O **L**, you brought me up from the
30: 7 O **L**, when you favoured me, you made
30: 8 To you, O **L**, I called; to the Lord I
30:10 Hear, O **L**, and be merciful to me;
30:10 O **L**, be my help."
30:12 O **L** my God, I will give you thanks
31: 1 In you, O **L**, I have taken refuge;
31: 5 redeem me, O **L**, the God of truth.
31: 6 worthless idols; I trust in the **L**.
31: 9 Be merciful to me, O **L**, for I am in
31:14 I trust in you, O **L**; I say, "You are
31:17 Let me not be put to shame, O **L**, for
31:23 Love the **L**, all his saints!
31:23 The **L** preserves the faithful, but
31:24 heart, all you who hope in the **L**.
32: 2 whose sin the **L** does not count
32: 5 my transgressions to the **L**"—
32:11 Rejoice in the **L** and be glad, you
33: 1 Sing joyfully to the **L**, you
33: 5 The **L** loves righteousness and
33:10 The **L** foils the plans of the nations;
33:11 the plans of the **L** stand firm for
33:12 is the nation whose God is the **L**,
33:13 From heaven the **L** looks down and
33:18 the eyes of the **L** are on those who
33:20 We wait in hope for the **L**; he is our
33:22 unfailing love rest upon us, O **L**,
34: 1 I will extol the **L** at all times;
34: 2 My soul will boast in the **L**; let the
34: 3 Glorify the **L** with me: let us exalt
34: 4 I sought the **L**, and he answered me;
34: 6 poor man called, and the **L** heard
34: 8 Taste and see that the **L** is good;
34:10 who seek the **L** lack no good thing.
34:15 The eyes of the **L** are on the
34:16 the face of the **L** is against those
34:17 righteous cry out, and the **L** hears

Ps 34:18 The **L** is close to the broken-hearted
34:19 the **L** delivers him from them all;
34:22 The **L** redeems his servants; no-one
35: 1 Contend, O **L**, with those who contend
35: 9 my soul will rejoice in the **L** and
35:10 "Who is like you, O **L**? You rescue
35:22 O **L**, you have seen this; be not
35:24 in your righteousness, O **L** my God;
35:27 "The **L** be exalted, who delights in
36: 5 Your love, O **L**, reaches to the
36: 6 O **L**, you preserve both man and beast
37: 3 Trust in the **L** and do good; dwell in
37: 4 Delight yourself in the **L** and he
37: 5 Commit your way to the **L**; trust in
37: 9 those who hope in the **L** will inherit
37:17 but the **L** upholds the righteous.
37:18 of the blameless are known to the **L**,
37:22 those the **L** blesses will inherit the
37:23 If the **L** delights in a man's way, he
37:24 for the **L** upholds him with his hand.
37:28 For the **L** loves the just and will
37:33 the **L** will not leave them in their
37:34 Wait for the **L** and keep his way.
37:39 of the righteous comes from the **L**;
37:40 The **L** helps them and delivers them;
38: 1 O **L**, do not rebuke me in your anger
38:15 I wait for you, O **L**; you will answer
38:21 O **L**, do not forsake me; be not far
39: 4 Show me, O **L**, my life's end and the
39:12 "Hear my prayer, O **L**, listen to my
40: 1 I waited patiently for the **L**; he
40: 3 fear and put their trust in the **L**.
40: 4 Blessed is the man who makes the **L**
40: 5 Many, O **L** my God, are the wonders
40: 9 not seal my lips, as you know, O **L**.
40:11 not withhold your mercy from me, O **L**
40:13 pleased, O **L**, to save me; O **L**, come
40:16 always say, "The **L** be exalted!
41: 1 **L** delivers him in times of trouble.
41: 2 The **L** will protect him and preserve
41: 3 The **L** will sustain him on his
41: 4 I said, "O **L**, have mercy on me;
41:10 But you, O **L**, have mercy on me;
42: 8 By day the **L** directs his love, at
46: 8 Come and see the works of the **L**, the
47: 2 How awesome is the **L** Most High, the
47: 5 the **L** amid the sounding of trumpets.
48: 1 Great is the **L**, and most worthy of
50: 1 The Mighty One, God, the **L**, speaks
54: 6 I will praise your name, O **L**, for
55:16 I call to God, and the **L** saves me.
55:22 Cast your cares on the **L** and he will
56:10 in the **L**, whose word I praise
58: 6 tear out, O **L**, the tongues of the
59: 3 for no offence or sin of mine, O **L**
59: 8 you, O **L**, laugh at them; you scoff
64:10 Let the righteous rejoice in the **L**
68: 4 —his name is the **L**—
68:16 the **L** himself will dwell for ever?
69:13 I pray to you, O **L**, in the time of
69:16 Answer me, O **L**, out of the goodness
69:31 This will please the **L** more than an
69:33 The **L** hears the needy and does not
70: 1 O **L**, come quickly to help me.
70: 5 my deliverer; O **L**, do not delay.
71: 1 In you, O **L**, I have taken refuge;
74:18 O **L**, how foolish people have reviled
77:11 I will remember the deeds of the **L**;
78: 4 the praiseworthy deeds of the **L**,
78:21 the **L** heard them, he was very angry;
79: 5 How long, O **L**? Will you be angry for
81:15 Those who hate the **L** would cringe
83:16 Cover their faces with shame so that
83:18 know that you, whose name is the **L**—
84: 2 even faints, for the courts of the **L**
84:11 the **L** bestows favour and honour;
85: 1 You showed favour to your land, O **L**
85: 7 Show us your unfailing love, O **L**,
85: 8 listen to what God the **L** will say
85:12 The **L** will indeed give what is good,
86: 1 Hear, O **L**, and answer me, for I am
86: 6 Hear my prayer, O **L**; listen to my
86:11 Teach me your way, O **L**, and I will
86:17 for you, O **L**, have helped me
87: 2 the **L** loves the gates of Zion more
87: 6 The **L** will write in the register of

Ps 88: 1 O **L**, the God who saves me, day and
88: 9 I call to you, O **L**, every day;
88:13 I cry to you for help, O **L**; in the
88:14 Why, O **L**, do you reject me and hide
89: 5 The heavens praise your wonders, O **L**,
89: 6 skies above can compare with the **L**?
89: 6 the **L** among the heavenly beings?
89: 8 You are mighty, O **L**, and your
89:15 in the light of your presence, O **L**
89:18 Indeed, our shield belongs to the **L**,
89:46 How long, O **L**? Will you hide
89:51 which your enemies have mocked O **L**,
90:13 Relent, O **L**! How long will it be?
91: 2 I will say of the **L**, "He is my
91: 9 even the **L**, who is my refuge—
91:14 "Because he loves me," says the **L**,
92: 4 you make me glad by your deeds, O **L**;
92: 5 How great are your works, O **L**, how
92: 8 you, O **L**, are exalted for ever.
92: 9 For surely your enemies, O **L**, surely
92:15 proclaiming, "The **L** is upright;
93: 1 The **L** reigns, he is robed in majesty;
93: 1 the **L** is robed in majesty and
93: 3 The seas have lifted up, O **L**, the
93: 4 the **L** on high is mighty.
93: 5 your house for endless days, O **L**.
94: 1 O **L**, the God who avenges, O God who
94: 3 How long will the wicked, O **L**, how
94: 5 They crush your people, O **L**; they
94: 7 They say, "The **L** does not see; the
94:11 The **L** knows the thoughts of man; he
94:12 O **L**, the man you teach from your law
94:14 For the **L** will not reject his people
94:17 Unless the **L** had given me help, I
94:18 your love, O **L**, supported me.
94:22 the **L** has become my fortress, and my
94:23 the **L** our God will destroy them.
95: 1 Come, let us sing for joy to the **L**;
95: 3 For the **L** is the great God, the
96: 4 For great is the **L** and most worthy
96: 5 but the **L** made the heavens.
96: 7 Ascribe to the **L**, O families of
96: 7 ascribe to the **L** glory and strength.
96: 8 Ascribe to the **L** the glory due to
96: 9 Worship the **L** in the splendour of
96:10 Say among the nations, "The **L** reigns
97: 1 The **L** reigns, let the earth be glad;
97: 8 because of your judgments, O **L**.
97: 9 For you, O **L**, are the Most High over
97:10 Let those who love the **L** hate evil,
97:12 Rejoice in the **L**, you who are
98: 2 The **L** has made his salvation known
98: 4 Shout for joy to the **L**, all the
98: 5 make music to the **L** with the harp,
99: 1 The **L** reigns, let the nations
99: 2 Great is the **L** in Zion; he is
99: 5 Exalt the **L** our God and worship at
99: 6 called on the **L** and he answered
99: 8 O **L** our God, you answered them;
99: 9 Exalt the **L** our God and worship at
99: 9 mountain, for the **L** our God is holy.
100: 1 Shout for joy to the **L**, all the
100: 2 Worship the **L** with gladness; come
100: 5 For the **L** is good and his love
101: 1 to you, O **L**, I will sing praise.
101: 8 evildoer from the city of the **L**.
102: 1 Hear my prayer, O **L**; let my cry for
102:12 you, O **L**, sit enthroned for ever;
102:16 For the **L** will rebuild Zion and
102:19 "The **L** looked down from his
102:22 kingdoms assemble to worship the **L**.
103: 6 The **L** works righteousness and
103: 8 The **L** is compassionate and gracious,
103:13 so the **L** has compassion on those who
103:19 The **L** has established his throne in
104:16 The trees of the **L** are well watered,
104:24 How many are your works, O **L**!
104:31 may the **L** rejoice in his works—
104:34 to him, as I rejoice in the **L**.
105: 1 Give thanks to the **L**, call on his
105: 3 of those who seek the **L** rejoice.
105: 4 Look to the **L** and his strength;
105: 7 He is the **L** our God; his judgments
105:24 The **L** made his people very fruitful;
106: 1 Give thanks to the **L**, for he is
106: 2 proclaim the mighty acts of the **L**

Ps 106: 4 Remember me, O **L**, when you show
106:16 Aaron, who was consecrated to the **L**.
106:25 their tents and did not obey the **L**.
106:29 they provoked the **L** to anger by
106:32 waters of Meribah they angered the **L**
106:34 peoples as the **L** had commanded them,
106:40 Therefore the **L** was angry with his
106:47 Save us, O **L** our God, and gather us
107: 1 Give thanks to the **L**, for he is good
107: 2 Let the redeemed of the **L** say this—
107: 6 they cried out to the **L** in their
107: 8 Let them give thanks to the **L** for
107:13 they cried to the **L** in their trouble
107:15 Let them give thanks to the **L** for
107:19 they cried to the **L** in their trouble
107:21 Let them give thanks to the **L** for
107:24 They saw the works of the **L**, his
107:28 they cried out to the **L** in their
107:31 Let them give thanks to the **L** for
107:43 consider the great love of the **L**.
108: 3 I will praise you, O **L**, among the
109:26 Help me, O **L** my God; save me in
109:27 that you, O **L**, have done it.
109:30 my mouth I will greatly extol the **L**;
110: 1 The **L** says to my Lord: "Sit at my
110: 2 **L** will extend your mighty sceptre
110: 4 The **L** has sworn and will not change
111: 1 I will extol the **L** with all my
111: 2 Great are the works of the **L**; they
111: 4 the **L** is gracious and compassionate.
112: 1 Blessed is the man who fears the **L**,
112: 7 is steadfast, trusting in the **L**.
113: 1 Praise, O servants of the **L**,
113: 4 The **L** is exalted over all the
113: 5 Who is like the **L** our God, the One
115: 1 Not to us, O **L**, not to us but to
115: 9 O house of Israel, trust in the **L**—
115:10 O house of Aaron, trust in the **L**—
115:11 You who fear him, trust in the **L**—
115:12 The **L** remembers us and will bless us:
115:14 May the **L** make you increase, both
115:15 May you be blessed by the **L**, the
115:16 The highest heavens belong to the **L**,
115:18 It is we who extol the **L**, both now
116: 1 I love the **L**, for he heard my voice;
116: 4 "O **L**, save me!"
116: 5 The **L** is gracious and righteous;
116: 6 The **L** protects the simple-hearted;
116: 7 for the **L** has been good to you.
116: 8 For you, O **L**, have delivered my soul
116:12 How can I repay the **L** for all his
116:14 I will fulfil my vows to the **L** in
116:15 Precious in the sight of the **L** is
116:16 O **L**, truly I am your servant; I am
116:18 I will fulfil my vows to the **L** in
117: 2 the faithfulness of the **L** endures
118: 1 Give thanks to the **L**, for he is good;
118: 5 In my anguish I cried to the **L**, and
118: 6 The **L** is with me; I will not be
118: 7 The **L** is with me; he is my helper.
118: 8 is better to take refuge in the **L**
118: 9 is better to take refuge in the **L**
118:13 about to fall, but the **L** helped me.
118:14 The **L** is my strength and my song; he
118:17 will proclaim what the **L** has done.
118:18 The **L** has chastened me severely, but
118:19 will enter and give thanks to the **L**.
118:20 This is the gate of the **L** through
118:23 the **L** has done this, and it is
118:24 This is the day the **L** has made; let
118:25 O **L**, save us; O **L**, grant us success.
118:27 The **L** is God, and he has made his
118:29 Give thanks to the **L**, for he is good
119:12 Praise be to you, O **L**; teach me your
119:31 I hold fast to your statutes, O **L**;
119:33 Teach me, O **L**, to follow your
119:41 your unfailing love come to me, O **L**
119:52 I remember your ancient laws, O **L**,
119:55 the night I remember your name, O **L**
119:57 You are my portion, O **L**; I have
119:64 earth is filled with your love, O **L**
119:65 according to your word, O **L**
119:75 I know, O **L**, that your laws are
119:89 Your word, O **L**, is eternal; it
119:107 preserve my life, O **L**,
119:108 Accept, O **L**, the willing praise of

Ps 119:126 is time for you to act, O **L**;
119:137 Righteous are you, O **L**, and your
119:145 answer me, O **L**, and I will obey
119:149 preserve my life, O **L**,
119:151 Yet you are near, O **L**, and all your
119:156 Your compassion is great, O **L**;
119:159 preserve my life, O **L**,
119:166 I wait for your salvation, O **L**, and
119:169 May my cry come before you, O **L**;
119:174 I long for your salvation, O **L**, and
120: 1 I call on the **L** in my distress, and
120: 2 Save me, O **L**, from lying lips and
121: 2 My help comes from the **L**, the Maker
121: 5 The **L** watches over you—the **L** is
121: 7 The **L** will keep you from all harm—
121: 8 the **L** will watch over your coming
122: 4 the tribes of the **L**, to praise the
123: 2 so our eyes look to the **L** our God,
123: 3 Have mercy on us, O **L**, have mercy on
124: 1 If the **L** had not been on our side—
124: 2 if the **L** had not been on our side
125: 1 Those who trust in the **L** are like
125: 2 so the **L** surrounds his people both
125: 4 Do good, O **L**, to those who are good,
125: 5 the **L** will banish with the evildoers
126: 1 the **L** brought back the captives to
126: 2 **L** has done great things for them."
126: 3 The **L** has done great things for us,
126: 4 Restore our fortunes, O **L**, like
127: 1 Unless the **L** builds the house, its
127: 1 Unless the **L** watches over the city,
127: 3 Sons are a heritage from the **L**,
128: 4 is the man blessed who fears the **L**.
128: 5 May the **L** bless you from Zion all
129: 4 the **L** is righteous; he has cut me
129: 8 "The blessing of the **L** be upon you;
130: 1 Out of the depths I cry to you, O **L**
130: 3 If you, O **L**, kept a record of sins,
130: 5 I wait for the **L**, my soul waits, and
130: 7 O Israel, put your hope in the **L**,
130: 7 for with the **L** is unfailing love and
131: 1 My heart is not proud, O **L**, my eyes
131: 3 O Israel, put your hope in the **L**
132: 1 O **L**, remember David and all the
132: 2 He swore an oath to the **L** and made a
132: 5 till I find a place for the **L**, a
132: 8 arise, O **L**, and come to your resting
132:11 The **L** swore an oath to David, a sure
132:13 For the **L** has chosen Zion, he has
133: 3 For there the **L** bestows his blessing,
134: 1 all you servants of the **L** who
134: 3 May the **L**, the Maker of heaven and
135: 1 praise him, you servants of the **L**,
135: 3 for the **L** is good; sing praise to his
135: 4 For the **L** has chosen Jacob to be his
135: 6 The **L** does whatever pleases him, in
135:13 Your name, O **L**, endures for ever,
135:13 your renown, O **L**, through all
135:14 For the **L** will vindicate his people
136: 1 Give thanks to the **L**, for he is good
137: 4 How can we sing the songs of the **L**
137: 7 Remember, O **L**, what the Edomites did
138: 1 I will praise you, O **L**, with all my
138: 4 kings of the earth praise you, O **L**,
138: 5 May they sing of the ways of the **L**,
138: 6 Though the **L** is on high, he looks
138: 8 The **L** will fulfil his purpose for me
138: 8 your love, O **L**, endures for ever—
139: 1 O **L**, you have searched me and you
139: 4 tongue you know it completely, O **L**.
139:21 I not hate those who hate you, O **L**
140: 1 Rescue me, O **L**, from evil men;
140: 4 Keep me, O **L**, from the hands of the
140: 6 O **L**, I say to you, "You are my God."
140: 6 Hear, O **L**, my cry for mercy.
140: 8 the wicked their desires, O **L**;
141: 1 O **L**, I call to you; come quickly to
141: 3 Set a guard over my mouth, O **L**;
142: 1 I cry aloud to the **L**; I lift up my
142: 1 lift up my voice to the **L** for mercy.
142: 5 I cry to you, O **L**; I say, "You are
143: 1 O **L**, hear my prayer, listen to my
143: 7 Answer me quickly, O **L**; my spirit
143: 9 Rescue me from my enemies, O **L**, for
143:11 For your name's sake, O **L**, preserve
144: 3 O **L**, what is man that you care for

Ps 144: 5 Part your heavens, O **L**, and come
144:15 are the people whose God is the **L**.
145: 3 Great is the **L** and most worthy of
145: 8 The **L** is gracious and compassionate,
145: 9 The **L** is good to all; he has
145:10 you have made will praise you, O **L**
145:13 The **L** is faithful to all his
145:14 The **L** upholds all those who fall and
145:17 The **L** is righteous in all his ways
145:18 The **L** is near to all who call on him
145:20 The **L** watches over all who love him,
145:21 mouth will speak in praise of the **L**.
146: 5 whose hope is in the **L** his God,
146: 6 **L**, who remains faithful for ever.
146: 7 The **L** sets prisoners free,
146: 8 the **L** gives sight to the blind,
146: 8 **L** lifts up those who are bowed down
146: 8 down, the **L** loves the righteous.
146: 9 The **L** watches over the alien and
146:10 The **L** reigns for ever, your God,
147: 2 The **L** builds up Jerusalem; he
147: 6 The **L** sustains the humble but casts
147:11 the **L** delights in those who fear him,
147:12 Extol the **L**, O Jerusalem; praise
149: 4 For the **L** takes delight in his
Pr 2: 6 For the **L** gives wisdom, and from his
3: 5 Trust in the **L** with all your heart
3: 9 Honour the **L** with your wealth, with
3:12 the **L** disciplines those he loves,
3:19 **L** laid the earth's foundations,
3:26 for the **L** will be your confidence
3:32 for the **L** detests a perverse man but
5:21 man's ways are in full view of the **L**
6:16 There are six things the **L** hates,
8:22 The **L** brought me forth as the first
8:35 and receives favour from the **L**.
10: 3 The **L** does not let the righteous go
10:22 The blessing of the **L** brings wealth,
11: 1 The **L** abhors dishonest scales, but
11:20 The **L** detests men of perverse heart
12: 2 A good man obtains favour from the **L**
12: 2 but the **L** condemns a crafty man.
12:22 The **L** detests lying lips, but he
14: 2 He whose walk is upright fears the **L**
14:16 A wise man fears the **L** and shuns
14:26 He who fears the **L** has a secure
15: 3 The eyes of the **L** are everywhere,
15: 8 The **L** detests the sacrifice of the
15: 9 The **L** detests the way of the wicked
15:25 **L** tears down the proud man's house
15:26 The **L** detests the thoughts of the
15:29 The **L** is far from the wicked but he
16: 1 from the **L** comes the reply of the
16: 2 but motives are weighed by the **L**.
16: 3 Commit to the **L** whatever you do,
16: 4 The **L** works out everything for his
16: 5 The **L** detests all the proud of heart
16: 7 a man's ways are pleasing to the **L**,
16: 9 but the **L** determines his steps.
16:11 scales and balances are from the **L**;
16:20 blessed is he who trusts in the **L**.
16:33 its every decision is from the **L**.
17: 3 for gold, but the **L** tests the heart.
17:15 innocent—the **L** detests them both.
18:22 good and receives favour from the **L**.
19: 3 yet his heart rages against the **L**.
19:14 but a prudent wife is from the **L**.
19:17 is kind to the poor lends to the **L**,
20:10 measures—the **L** detests them both.
20:12 that see—the **L** has made them both.
20:22 Wait for the **L**, and he will deliver
20:23 The **L** detests differing weights,
20:24 A man's steps are directed by the **L**.
20:27 The lamp of the **L** searches the
21: 2 to him, but the **L** weighs the heart.
21: 3 acceptable to the **L** than sacrifice.
21:30 plan that can succeed against the **L**.
21:31 but victory rests with the **L**.
22: 2 The **L** is the Maker of them all.
22:12 The eyes of the **L** keep watch over
22:19 that your trust may be in the **L**,
22:23 for the **L** will take up their case
24:18 or the **L** will see and disapprove
25:22 his head, and the **L** will reward you.
28: 5 who seek the **L** understand it fully.
28:14 is the man who always fears the **L**,

Pr 28:25 he who trusts in the **L** will prosper.
29:13 **L** gives sight to the eyes of both.
29:25 trusts in the **L** is kept safe.
29:26 is from the **L** that man gets justice.
30: 7 "Two things I ask of you, O **L**;
30: 9 disown you and say, 'Who is the **L**?'
31:30 who fears the **L** is to be praised.
Isa 1: 2 For the **L** has spoken: "I reared
1: 4 They have forsaken the **L**;
1:11 what are they to me?" says the **L**.
1:18 let us reason together," says the **L**.
1:20 For the mouth of the **L** has spoken.
1:28 those who forsake the **L** will perish.
2: 5 let us walk in the light of the **L**.
2:10 from dread of the **L** and the
2:11 **L** alone will be exalted in that day.
2:17 **L** alone will be exalted in that day,
2:19 from the dread of the **L** and the
2:21 from dread of the **L** and the
3: 8 words and deeds are against the **L**,
3:13 The **L** takes his place in court; he
3:14 The **L** enters into judgment against
3:16 The **L** says, "The women of Zion are
3:17 the **L** will make their scalps bald."
4: 2 In that day the Branch of the **L** will
4: 5 **L** will create over all of Mount Zion
5:12 no regard for the deeds of the **L**,
6:12 the **L** has sent everyone far away
7: 3 the **L** said to Isaiah, "Go out, you
7:10 Again the **L** spoke to Ahaz,
7:12 I will not put the **L** to the test."
7:17 The **L** will bring on you and on your
7:18 In that day the **L** will whistle for
8: 1 The **L** said to me, "Take a large
8: 3 And the **L** said to me, "Name him
8: 5 The **L** spoke to me again:
8:11 The **L** spoke to me with his strong
8:17 I will wait for the **L**, who is hiding
8:18 and the children the **L** has given me
9:11 the **L** has strengthened Rezin's foes
9:14 the **L** will cut off from Israel both
10:20 on the **L**, the Holy One of Israel.
11: 2 knowledge and of the fear of the **L**—
11: 3 he will delight in the fear of the **L**
11: 9 be full of the knowledge of the **L**
11:15 The **L** will dry up the gulf of the
12: 1 will say: "I will praise you, O **L**.
12: 2 The **L**, the **L**, is my strength and my
12: 4 "Give thanks to the **L**, call on his
13: 5 the **L** and the weapons of his wrath
14: 1 The **L** will have compassion on Jacob
14: 3 On the day the **L** gives you relief
14: 5 The **L** has broken the rod of the
14:32 "The **L** has established Zion, and in
16:13 the word the **L** has already spoken
16:14 now the **L** says: "Within three years
18: 4 This is what the **L** says to me: "I
19: 1 the **L** rides on a swift cloud and is
19:14 The **L** has poured into them a spirit
19:19 an altar to the **L** in the heart of
19:19 a monument to the **L** at its border.
19:20 When they cry out to the **L** because
19:21 the **L** will make himself known to the
19:21 day they will acknowledge the **L**.
19:21 make vows to the **L** and keep them.
19:22 The **L** will strike Egypt with a
19:22 They will turn to the **L**, and he will
20: 2 at that time the **L** spoke through
20: 3 the **L** said, "Just as my servant
21:17 The **L**, the God of Israel, has spoken.
22:17 "Beware, the **L** is about to take firm
22:25 be cut down." The **L** has spoken.
23:11 The **L** has stretched out his hand
23:17 the **L** will deal with Tyre.
23:18 will be set apart for the **L**;
24: 1 See, the **L** is going to lay waste the
24: 3 The **L** has spoken this word.
24:21 In that day the **L** will punish the
25: 1 O **L**, you are my God; I will exalt
25: 8 The **L** has spoken.
25: 9 This is the **L**, we trusted in him;
26: 4 Trust in the **L** for ever, for the
26: 4 the **L**, the **L**, is the Rock eternal.
26: 8 Yes, **L**, walking in the way of your
26:10 and regard not the majesty of the **L**.
26:11 O **L**, your hand is lifted high, but

Isa 26:12 **L**, you establish peace for us;
26:13 O **L**, our God, other lords besides
26:15 You have enlarged the nation, O **L**;
26:16 **L**, they came to you in their
26:17 so were we in your presence, O **L**
26:21 the **L** is coming out of his dwelling
27: 1 In that day, the **L** will punish with
27: 3 I, the **L**, watch over it; I water it
27: 7 Has the **L** struck her as he struck
27:12 In that day the **L** will thresh from
27:13 will come and worship the **L** on the
28:21 The **L** will rise up as he did at
29:10 The **L** has brought over you a deep
29:15 to hide their plans from the **L**,
29:19 the humble will rejoice in the **L**;
29:22 Therefore this is what the **L**, who
30:18 Yet the **L** longs to be gracious to
30:18 For the **L** is a God of justice.
30:26 when the **L** binds up the bruises of
30:30 The **L** will cause men to hear his
30:32 Every stroke the **L** lays on them with
30:33 the breath of the **L**, like a stream
31: 1 of Israel, or seek help from the **L**.
31: 3 When the **L** stretches out his hand,
31: 4 This is what the **L** says to me: "As
32: 6 and spreads error concerning the **L**;
33: 2 O **L**, be gracious to us; we long for
33: 5 The **L** is exalted, for he dwells on
33: 6 the **L** is the key to this treasure.
33:10 "Now will I arise," says the **L**.
33:21 There the **L** will be our Mighty One.
33:22 For the **L** is our judge, the **L** is our
33:22 lawgiver, the **L** is our king;
34: 2 The **L** is angry with all nations;
34: 6 The sword of the **L** is bathed in
34: 6 For the **L** has a sacrifice in Bozrah
34: 8 For the **L** has a day of vengeance, a
34:16 Look in the scroll of the **L** and read
35:10 the ransomed of the **L** will return.
36: 7 "We are depending on the **L** our God"
36:10 and destroy this land without the **L**?
36:10 The **L** himself told me to march
36:15 you to trust in the **L** when he says,
36:15 'The **L** will surely deliver us;
36:18 he says, 'The **L** will deliver us.
36:20 **L** deliver Jerusalem from my hand?"
37: 6 'This is what the **L** says: Do not be
37:15 Hezekiah prayed to the **L**:
37:17 Give ear, O **L**, and hear;
37:17 open your eyes, O **L**, and see;
37:18 "It is true, O **L**, that the
37:20 Now, O **L** our God, deliver us from
37:20 know that you alone, O **L**, are God."
37:21 what the **L**, the God of Israel, says
37:22 this is the word the **L** has spoken
37:33 "Therefore this is what the **L** says
38: 1 "This is what the **L** says: Put your
38: 2 to the wall and prayed to the **L**,
38: 3 "Remember, O **L**, how I have walked
38: 5 the **L**, the God of your father David
38: 7 the **L** will do what he has promised:
38:11 I said, "I will not again see the **L**,
38:11 the **L**, in the land of the living;
38:20 The **L** will save me, and we will sing
39: 6 Nothing will be left, says the **L**.
40: 3 desert prepare the way for the **L**;
40: 5 For the mouth of the **L** has spoken."
40: 7 the breath of the **L** blows on them.
40:13 Who has understood the mind of the **L**
40:14 Whom did the **L** consult to enlighten
40:27 "My way is hidden from the **L**; my
40:28 The **L** is the everlasting God,
40:31 those who hope in the **L** will renew
41: 4 I, the **L**—with the first of them
41:16 But you will rejoice in the **L** and
41:17 But I the **L** will answer them; I, the
41:21 "Present your case," says the **L**.
42: 5 This is what God the **L** says—he who
42: 6 "I, the **L**, have called you in
42:12 Let them give glory to the **L** and
42:13 **L** will march out like a mighty man
42:21 pleased the **L** for the sake of his
42:24 Was it not the **L**, against whom we
43: 1 But now, this is what the **L** says—
43:11 I, even I, am the **L**, and apart from
43:14 This is what the **L** says—your

Isa 43:16 This is what the **L** says—he who
44: 2 This is what the **L** says—he who
44: 5 One will say, 'I belong to the **L**';
44: 6 "This is what the **L** says—Israel's
44:23 O heavens, for the **L** has done this;
44:23 for the **L** has redeemed Jacob, he
44:24 "This is what the **L** says—your
45: 1 "This is what the **L** says to his
45: 7 I, the **L**, do all these things.
45: 8 I, the **L**, have created it.
45:11 "This is what the **L** says—the Holy
45:14 This is what the **L** says: "The
45:17 Israel will be saved by the **L** with
45:18 For this is what the **L** says—he who
45:19 I, the **L**, speak the truth;
45:21 Was it not I, the **L**? And there is no
45:24 'In the **L** alone are righteousness
45:25 in the **L** all the descendants of
48:17 This is what the **L** says— your
48:20 **L** has redeemed his servant Jacob."
48:22 "There is no peace," says the **L**,
49: 1 Before I was born the **L** called me;
49: 5 now the **L** says—he who formed me in
49: 5 I am honoured in the eyes of the **L**
49: 7 This is what the **L** says— the
49: 7 because of the **L**, who is faithful,
49: 8 This is what the **L** says: "In the
49:13 For the **L** comforts his people and
49:14 Zion said, "The **L** has forsaken me,
49:25 this is what the **L** says: "Yes,
49:26 I, the **L**, am your Saviour, your
50: 1 This is what the **L** says: "Where is
50:10 Who among you fears the **L** and obeys
51: 1 righteousness and who seek the **L**:
51: 3 The **L** will surely comfort Zion and
51: 3 wastelands like the garden of the **L**.
51:11 The ransomed of the **L** will return.
51:13 that you forget the **L** your Maker,
51:20 are filled with the wrath of the **L**
52: 3 For this is what the **L** says: "You
52: 8 When the **L** returns to Zion, they
52: 9 for the **L** has comforted his people,
52:10 The **L** will lay bare his holy arm in
52:11 you who carry the vessels of the **L**.
52:12 for the **L** will go before you,
53: 6 and the **L** has laid on him the
53:10 and though the **L** makes his life a
53:10 the will of the **L** will prosper
54: 1 her who has a husband," says the **L**
54: 6 The **L** will call you back as if you
54: 8 on you," says the **L** your Redeemer.
54:10 the **L**, who has compassion on you.
54:13 your sons will be taught by the **L**
54:17 heritage of the servants of the **L**,
55: 6 Seek the **L** while he may be found;
55: 7 Let him turn to the **L**, and he will
56: 1 This is what the **L** says: "Maintain
56: 3 who has bound himself to the **L** say,
56: 3 "The **L** will surely exclude me from
56: 4 For this is what the **L** says: "To the
56: 6 themselves to the **L** to serve him,
57:19 to those far and near," says the **L**.
58: 5 a fast, a day acceptable to the **L**?
58: 9 you will call, and the **L** will answer
58:11 The **L** will guide you always; he will
58:14 you will find your joy in the **L**, and
58:14 The mouth of the **L** has spoken.
59:13 and treachery against the **L**,
59:15 The **L** looked and was displeased that
59:19 the breath of the **L** drives along.
59:21 my covenant with them," says the **L**.
59:21 and for ever," says the **L**.
60: 2 but the **L** rises upon you and his
60: 6 and proclaiming the praise of the **L**.
60:14 call you the City of the **L**, Zion
60:16 Then you will know that I, the **L**,
60:19 **L** will be your everlasting light
60:20 **L** will be your everlasting light,
61: 1 the **L** has anointed me to preach
61: 3 a planting of the **L** for the
61: 6 you will be called priests of the **L**,
61: 8 "For I, the **L**, love justice; I hate
61: 9 are a people the **L** has blessed."
61:10 I delight greatly in the **L**; my soul
62: 2 that the mouth of the **L** will bestow.
62: 4 for the **L** will take delight in you,

Isa 62: 6 You who call on the **L**, give
62: 8 The **L** has sworn by his right hand
62:11 The **L** has made proclamation to the
62:12 Holy People, the Redeemed of the **L**;
63: 7 tell of the kindnesses of the **L**,
63: 7 according to all the **L** has done for
63:16 you, O **L**, are our Father, our
63:17 Why, O **L**, do you make us wander from
64: 8 Yet, O **L**, you are our Father. We are
64: 9 Do not be angry beyond measure, O **L**;
64:12 After all this, O **L**, will you hold
65: 7 sins of your fathers," says the **L**.
65: 8 This is what the **L** says: "As when
65:11 "But as for you who forsake the **L**
65:23 will be a people blessed by the **L**,
65:25 on all my holy mountain," says the **L**
66: 1 This is what the **L** says: "Heaven is
66: 5 Let the **L** be glorified, that we may
66: 6 It is the sound of the **L** repaying
66: 9 and not give delivery?" says the **L**.
66:12 For this is what the **L** says: "I will
66:15 See, the **L** is coming with fire, and
66:16 **L** will execute judgment upon all men,
66:16 many will be those slain by the **L**.
66:20 as an offering to the **L**—on horses,
66:20 on mules and camels," says the **L**.
66:21 be priests and Levites," says the **L**.
66:23 and bow down before me," says the **L**.
Jer 1: 7 the **L** said to me, "Do not say, 'I am
1: 9 the **L** reached out his hand and
1:12 The **L** said to me, "You have seen
1:14 The **L** said to me, "From the north
2: 5 This is what the **L** says: "What fault
2: 6 They did not ask, 'Where is the **L**,
2: 8 did not ask, 'Where is the **L**?'
2:37 for the **L** has rejected those you
3: 6 the **L** said to me, "Have you seen
3:11 The **L** said to me, "Faithless Israel
3:17 call Jerusalem The Throne of the **L**,
3:21 and have forgotten the **L** their God.
3:22 to you, for you are the **L** our God.
3:23 **L** our God is the salvation of Israel
3:25 We have sinned against the **L** our God
3:25 we have not obeyed the **L** our God."
4: 3 This is what the **L** says to the men
4: 4 Circumcise yourselves to the **L**,
4:27 This is what the **L** says: "The whole
5: 3 O **L**, do not your eyes look for truth
5:10 these people do not belong to the **L**.
5:12 They have lied about the **L**; they
5:19 people ask, 'Why has the **L** our God
6:11 I am full of the wrath of the **L**, and
6:15 when I punish them," says the **L**
6:16 This is what the **L** says: "Stand at
6:21 Therefore this is what the **L** says:
6:22 This is what the **L** says: "Look, an
6:30 because the **L** has rejected them."
7: 1 that came to Jeremiah from the **L**:
7: 2 these gates to worship the **L**.
7:28 that has not obeyed the **L** its God
7:29 for the **L** has rejected and abandoned
8: 4 to them, 'This is what the **L** says:
8: 7 not know the requirements of the **L**.
8:12 when they are punished, says the **L**.
8:14 For the **L** our God has doomed us to
8:19 "Is the **L** not in Zion? Is her King
9:12 Who has been instructed by the **L** and
9:13 The **L** said, "It is because they have
9:22 Say, "This is what the **L** declares:
9:23 This is what the **L** says: "Let not
10: 1 Hear what the **L** says to you, O house
10: 2 This is what the **L** says: "Do not
10: 6 No-one is like you, O **L**; you are
10:10 the **L** is the true God; he is the
10:18 For this is what the **L** says: "At
10:21 and do not enquire of the **L**;
10:23 I know, O **L**, that a man's life is
10:24 Correct me, **L**, but only with justice
11: 1 that came to Jeremiah from the **L**:
11: 3 what the **L**, the God of Israel, says
11: 5 I answered, "Amen, **L**."
11: 6 The **L** said to me, "Proclaim all
11: 9 the **L** said to me, "There is a
11:11 Therefore this is what the **L** says:
11:16 **L** called you a thriving olive tree
11:18 the **L** revealed their plot to me, I

Jer 11:21 "Therefore this is what the **L** says
12: 1 You are always righteous, O **L**, when
12: 3 Yet you know me, O **L**; you see me and
12:12 for the sword of the **L** will devour
12:14 This is what the **L** says: "As for all
13: 1 This is what the **L** said to me: "Go
13: 2 I bought a belt, as the **L** directed,
13: 5 at Perath, as the **L** had told me
13: 6 Many days later the **L** said to me,
13: 9 "This is what the **L** says: 'In the
13:12 what the **L**, the God of Israel, says
13:13 tell them, 'This is what the **L** says:
13:15 be arrogant, for the **L** has spoken.
13:21 What will you say when ⌊the **L**⌋ sets
14: 7 O **L**, do something for the sake of
14: 9 You are among us, O **L**, and we bear
14:10 This is what the **L** says about this
14:10 So the **L** does not accept them;
14:11 the **L** said to me, "Do not pray for
14:14 the **L** said to me, "The prophets are
14:15 Therefore, this is what the **L** says
14:20 O **L**, we acknowledge our wickedness
14:22 No, it is you, O **L** our God.
15: 1 the **L** said to me: "Even if Moses and
15: 2 'This is what the **L** says: "'Those
15:11 The **L** said, "Surely I will deliver
15:15 You understand, O **L**; remember me and
15:19 Therefore this is what the **L** says:
16: 3 For this is what the **L** says about
16: 5 For this is what the **L** says: "Do not
16:10 'Why has the **L** decreed such a great
16:10 we committed against the **L** our God?'
16:19 O **L**, my strength and my fortress, my
16:21 will know that my name is the **L**.
17: 5 This is what the **L** says: "Cursed is
17: 5 whose heart turns away from the **L**.
17: 7 the **L**, whose confidence is in him.
17:10 "I the **L** search the heart and
17:13 O **L**, the hope of Israel, all who
17:13 they have forsaken the **L**, the spring
17:14 Heal me, O **L**, and I shall be healed;
17:19 This is what the **L** said to me: "Go
17:21 This is what the **L** says: Be careful
18: 1 that came to Jeremiah from the **L**:
18:11 This is what the **L** says: Look! I am
18:13 Therefore this is what the **L** says:
18:19 Listen to me, O **L**; hear what my
18:23 you know, O **L**, all their plots to
19: 1 This is what the **L** says: "Go and buy
19:14 where the **L** had sent him to prophesy,
20: 4 For this is what the **L** says: 'I will
20: 7 O **L**, you deceived me, and I was
20:11 the **L** is with me like a mighty
20:13 Give praise to the **L**! He rescues
20:16 be like the towns the **L** overthrew
21: 1 The word came to Jeremiah from the **L**
21: 2 "Enquire now of the **L** for us because
21: 2 Perhaps the **L** will perform wonders
21: 4 what the **L**, the God of Israel, says
21: 8 'This is what the **L** says: See, I am
21:12 of David, this is what the **L** says:
22: 1 This is what the **L** says: "Go down to
22: 3 This is what the **L** says: Do what is
22: 6 For this is what the **L** says about
22: 8 'Why has the **L** done such a thing to
22:11 For this is what the **L** says about
22:18 Therefore this is what the **L** says
22:30 This is what the **L** says: "Record
23: 2 what the **L**, the God of Israel, says
23: 6 be called: The **L** Our Righteousness.
23: 9 because of the **L** and his holy words.
23:16 not from the mouth of the **L**.
23:17 'The **L** says: You will have peace.
23:18 has stood in the council of the **L**
23:19 See, the storm of the **L** will burst
23:31 and yet declare, 'The **L** declares.'
23:33 'What is the oracle of the **L**?'
23:34 'This is the oracle of the **L**,'
23:35 or 'What has the **L** spoken?'
23:36 'the oracle of the **L**' again, because
23:37 or 'What has the **L** spoken?'
23:38 'This is the oracle of the **L**,' this
23:38 what the **L** says: You used the words,
23:38 'This is the oracle of the **L**,' even
23:38 'This is the oracle of the **L**.'
24: 1 the **L** showed me two baskets of figs

Jer 24: 3 the **L** asked me, "What do you see,
24: 5 what the **L**, the God of Israel, says
24: 8 they cannot be eaten,' says the **L**,
25: 4 the **L** has sent all his servants
25: 5 can stay in the land the **L** gave
25:15 what the **L**, the God of Israel, said
25:30 'The **L** will roar from on high; he
25:31 for the **L** will bring charges against
25:33 At that time those slain by the **L**
25:36 the **L** is destroying their pasture.
26: 1 of Judah, this word came from the **L**:
26: 4 to them, 'This is what the **L** says
26: 8 the **L** had commanded him to say,
26:12 "The **L** sent me to prophesy against
26:13 Then the **L** will relent and not bring
26:15 in truth the **L** has sent me to you
26:19 And did not the **L** relent, so that
27: 1 word came to Jeremiah from the **L**:
27: 2 This is what the **L** said to me: "Make
27:13 with which the **L** has threatened
27:16 "This is what the **L** says: Do not
28: 6 "Amen! May the **L** do so! May the **L**
28: 9 one truly sent by the **L** only if his
28:11 "This is what the **L** says: 'In the
28:13 'This is what the **L** says: You have
28:15 The **L** has not sent you, yet you
28:16 Therefore, this is what the **L** says:
28:16 preached rebellion against the **L**.
29: 7 Pray to the **L** for it, because if it
29:10 This is what the **L** says: "When
29:15 You may say, "The **L** has raised up
29:16 this is what the **L** says about the
29:22 'The **L** treat you like Zedekiah and
29:26 'The **L** has appointed you priest in
29:31 'This is what the **L** says about
29:32 this is what the **L** says: I will
30: 1 that came to Jeremiah from the **L**:
30: 2 what the **L**, the God of Israel, says
30: 3 to possess,' says the **L**."
30: 4 These are the words the **L** spoke
30: 5 "This is what the **L** says: "'Cries
30: 9 they will serve the **L** their God and
30:12 "This is what the **L** says: "'Your
30:18 "This is what the **L** says: "'I will
30:23 See, the storm of the **L** will burst
31: 2 This is what the **L** says: "The people
31: 3 The **L** appeared to us in the past,
31: 6 us go up to Zion, to the **L** our God.
31: 7 This is what the **L** says: "Sing with
31: 7 'O **L**, save your people, the remnant
31:11 For the **L** will ransom Jacob and
31:12 will rejoice in the bounty of the **L**
31:15 This is what the **L** says: "A voice is
31:16 This is what the **L** says: "Restrain
31:18 because you are the **L** my God.
31:22 **L** will create a new thing on earth
31:23 **L** bless you, O righteous dwelling
31:34 saying, 'Know the **L**,' because they
31:35 This is what the **L** says, he who
31:37 This is what the **L** says: "Only if
32: 1 that came to Jeremiah from the **L**
32: 3 This is what the **L** says: I am about
32: 8 "Then, just as the **L** had said, my
32:16 son of Neriah, I prayed to the **L**:
32:28 Therefore, this is what the **L** says:
32:36 what the **L**, the God of Israel, says:
32:42 "This is what the **L** says: As I have
33: 2 "This is what the **L** says, he who
33: 2 the earth, the **L** who formed it
33: 2 established it—the **L** is his name:
33: 4 what the **L**, the God of Israel, says
33:10 "This is what the **L** says: 'You say
33:11 **L** is good; his love endures for ever.
33:11 as they were before,' says the **L**.
33:13 one who counts them,' says the **L**.
33:16 be called: The **L** Our Righteousness.'
33:17 For this is what the **L** says: 'David
33:20 "This is what the **L** says: 'If you
33:24 'The **L** has rejected the two kingdoms
33:25 This is what the **L** says: 'If I have
34: 1 word came to Jeremiah from the **L**:
34: 2 what the **L**, the God of Israel, says
34: 2 'This is what the **L** says: I am about
34: 4 "'Yet hear the promise of the **L**,
34: 4 This is what the **L** says concerning
34: 8 The word came to Jeremiah from the **L**

Jer 34:13 what the **L**, the God of Israel, says
34:17 Therefore, this is what the **L** says:
35: 1 that came to Jeremiah from the **L**
36: 1 word came to Jeremiah from the **L**:
36: 4 the words the **L** had spoken to him,
36: 6 the words of the **L** that you wrote
36: 7 this people by the **L** are great."
36: 8 the words of the **L** from the scroll.
36:11 the words of the **L** from the scroll,
36:26 But the **L** had hidden them.
36:29 This is what the **L** says: You burned
36:30 Therefore, this is what the **L** says
37: 2 to the words the **L** had spoken
37: 3 Please pray to the **L** our God for us.
37: 7 what the **L**, the God of Israel, says
37: 9 "This is what the **L** says: Do not
37:17 "Is there any word from the **L**?"
38: 2 "This is what the **L** says: 'Whoever
38: 3 this is what the **L** says: 'This city
38:20 Obey the **L** by doing what I tell you.
38:21 is what the **L** has revealed to me:
40: 1 The word came to Jeremiah from the **L**
40: 3 now the **L** has brought it about; he
40: 3 against the **L** and did not obey him.
42: 4 tell you everything the **L** says and
42: 5 they said to Jeremiah, "May the **L** be
42: 6 we will obey the **L** our God, to whom
42: 6 for we will obey the **L** our God."
42: 9 He said to them, "This is what the **L**,
42:19 "O remnant of Judah, the **L** has told
42:20 'Pray to the **L** our God for us; tell
43: 1 all the words of the **L** their God
43: 1 the **L** had sent him to tell them—
43: 2 The **L** our God has not sent you to
43: 7 in disobedience to the **L** and went
44:21 "Did not the **L** remember and think
44:22 the **L** could no longer endure your
44:23 have sinned against the **L** and have
44:26 swear by my great name,' says the **L**,
44:30 This is what the **L** says: 'I am going
45: 2 what the **L**, the God of Israel, says
45: 3 'Woe to me! The **L** has added sorrow
45: 4 ⌊The **L** said,⌋ "Say this to him:
45: 4 'This is what the **L** says: I will
46:13 This is the message the **L** spoke to
46:15 for the **L** will push them down.
47: 2 This is what the **L** says: "See how
47: 4 The **L** is about to destroy the
47: 6 "'Ah, sword of the **L**,' you cry,
47: 7 when the **L** has commanded it,
48: 8 destroyed, because the **L** has spoken.
48:26 her drunk, for she has defied the **L**.
48:40 This is what the **L** says: "Look! An
48:42 a nation because she defied the **L**.
49: 1 This is what the **L** says: "Has Israel
49: 2 who drove her out," says the **L**.
49:12 This is what the **L** says: "If those
49:14 I have heard a message from the **L**:
49:18 neighbouring towns," says the **L**,
49:20 hear what the **L** has planned against
49:28 This is what the **L** says: "Arise,
50: 1 This is the word the **L** spoke through
50: 4 go in tears to seek the **L** their God.
50: 5 bind themselves to the **L** in an
50: 7 for they sinned against the **L**, their
50: 7 the **L**, the hope of their fathers.'
50:14 for she has sinned against the **L**.
50:15 Since this is the vengeance of the **L**
50:24 captured because you opposed the **L**.
50:25 The **L** has opened his arsenal and
50:28 the **L** our God has taken vengeance,
50:29 the **L**, the Holy One of Israel.
50:45 hear what the **L** has planned against
51: 1 This is what the **L** says: "See, I
51:10 "'The **L** has vindicated us; come,
51:10 what the **L** our God has done.'
51:11 The **L** has stirred up the kings of
51:11 The **L** will take vengeance, vengeance
51:12 The **L** will carry out his purpose,
51:36 Therefore, this is what the **L** says:
51:50 Remember the **L** in a distant land,
51:55 The **L** will destroy Babylon; he will
51:56 For the **L** is a God of retribution;
51:62 say, 'O **L**, you have said you will
Lam 1: 5 The **L** has brought her grief because
1: 9 "Look, O **L**, on my affliction, for

Lam 1:11 "Look, O **L**, and consider, for I am
1:12 that the **L** brought on me in the day
1:17 The **L** has decreed for Jacob that his
1:18 "The **L** is righteous, yet I rebelled
1:20 "See, O **L**, how distressed I am! I am
2: 6 The **L** has made Zion forget her
2: 8 The **L** determined to tear down the
2: 9 no longer find visions from the **L**.
2:17 The **L** has done what he planned; he
2:20 "Look, O **L**, and consider: Whom have
3:18 all that I had hoped from the **L**."
3:24 say to myself, "The **L** is my portion
3:25 The **L** is good to those whose hope is
3:26 quietly for the salvation of the **L**.
3:28 for the **L** has laid it on him.
3:50 until the **L** looks down from heaven
3:55 I called on your name, O **L**, from the
3:59 You have seen, O **L**, the wrong done
3:61 O **L**, you have heard their insults,
3:64 Pay them back what they deserve, O **L**
3:66 from under the heavens of the **L**.
4:11 The **L** has given full vent to his
4:16 The **L** himself has scattered them;
5: 1 Remember, O **L**, what has happened to
5:19 You, O **L**, reign for ever; your
5:21 Restore us to yourself, O **L**, that we
Eze 4:13 The **L** said, "In this way the people
5:13 that I the **L** have spoken in my zeal.
5:15 I the **L** have spoken.
5:17 I the **L** have spoken."
7: 9 it is I the **L** who strikes the blow.
8:12 'The **L** does not see us; the **L** has
9: 3 **L** called to the man clothed in linen
9: 9 **L** has forsaken the land; the **L** does
10: 2 **L** said to the man clothed in linen
10: 6 the **L** commanded the man in linen,
11: 2 The **L** said to me, "Son of man, these
11: 5 "This is what the **L** says: That is
11:15 'They are far away from the **L**;
11:25 everything the **L** had shown me.
12:25 I the **L** will speak what I will, and
13: 6 "The **L** declares", when the **L** has not
13: 7 "The **L** declares", though I have not
14: 4 I the **L** will answer him myself in
14: 7 I the **L** will answer him myself.
14: 9 I the **L** have enticed that prophet,
17:21 will know that I the **L** have spoken.
17:24 I the **L** bring down the tall tree
17:24 "'I the **L** have spoken, and I will
20: 1 came to enquire of the **L**, and
20:12 know that I the **L** made them holy.
20:48 see that I the **L** have kindled it;
21: 3 say to her: 'This is what the **L** says:
21: 5 I the **L** have drawn my sword from its
21:17 I the **L** have spoken."
21:32 no more; for I the **L** have spoken.
22:14 I the **L** have spoken, and I will do
22:22 **L** have poured out my wrath upon you.
22:28 says'-when the **L** has not spoken
23:36 The **L** said to me: "Son of man, will
24:14 "'I the **L** have spoken. The time has
26:14 rebuilt, for I the **L** have spoken,
30: 6 "'This is what the **L** says: "'The
30:12 I the **L** have spoken.
33:30 message that has come from the **L**.'
34:24 I the **L** will be their God, and my
34:24 I the **L** have spoken.
34:30 will know that I, the **L** their God
35:10 even though I the **L** was there,
35:12 will know that I the **L** have heard
36:36 **L** have rebuilt what was destroyed
36:36 I the **L** have spoken, and I will do
37:14 will know that I the **L** have spoken
37:28 know that I the **L** make Israel holy,
39: 7 I the **L** am the Holy One in Israel.
40:46 to the **L** to minister before him."
42:13 **L** will eat the most holy offerings.
43:24 them as a burnt offering to the **L**.
44: 2 The **L** said to me, "This gate is to
44: 2 It is to remain shut because the **L**,
44: 5 The **L** said to me, "Son of man, look
44:29 devoted to the **L** will belong to them
45: 1 are to present to the **L** a portion
45:23 defect as a burnt offering to the **L**,
46: 4 offering the prince brings to the **L**
46:12 a freewill offering to the **L**—
Eze 46:13 for a burnt offering to the **L**;
46:14 to the **L** is a lasting ordinance.
48: 9 you are to offer to the **L** will be
48:10 it will be the sanctuary of the **L**.
48:35 will be: THE **L** IS THERE.*
Da 9: 4 I prayed to the **L** my God and
9: 8 O **L**, we and our kings, our princes
9:10 we have not obeyed the **L** our God or
9:13 the favour of the **L** our God by
9:14 The **L** did not hesitate to bring the
9:14 for the **L** our God is righteous in
9:20 making my request to the **L** my God
Hos 1: 2 the **L** began to speak through Hosea,
1: 2 the **L** said to him, "Go, take to
1: 2 adultery in departing from the **L**."
1: 4 the **L** said to Hosea, "Call him
1: 6 Then the **L** said to Hosea, "Call her
1: 7 horsemen, but by the **L** their God."
1: 9 the **L** said, "Call him Lo-Ammi, for
2:20 and you will acknowledge the **L**.
3: 1 The **L** said to me, "Go, show your
3: 1 Love her as the **L** loves the
3: 5 **L** their God and David their king.
3: 5 They will come trembling to the **L**
4: 1 because the **L** has a charge to bring
4:10 they have deserted the **L** to give
4:16 How then can the **L** pasture them like
5: 4 they do not acknowledge the **L**.
5: 6 flocks and herds to seek the **L**,
5: 7 They are unfaithful to the **L**; they
6: 3 Let us acknowledge the **L**; let us
8:13 but the **L** is not pleased with them.
9: 4 pour out wine offerings to the **L**,
9: 5 on the festival days of the **L**?
9:14 Give them, O **L**—what will you give
10: 2 The **L** will demolish their altars and
10: 3 because we did not revere the **L**.
10:12 for it is time to seek the **L**,
11:10 They will follow the **L**; he will roar
12: 2 The **L** has a charge to bring against
12:13 The **L** used a prophet to bring Israel
13:15 An east wind from the **L** will come,
14: 9 The ways of the **L** are right; the
Joel 1:19 To you, O **L**, I call, for fire has
2:11 The **L** thunders at the head of his
2:11 The day of the **L** is great; it is
2:17 them say, "Spare your people, O **L**.
2:18 the **L** will be jealous for his land
2:19 The **L** will reply to them: "I am
2:21 Surely the **L** has done great things.
2:32 as the **L** has said, among the
2:32 the survivors whom the **L** calls.
3: 8 The **L** has spoken.
3:11 Bring down your warriors, O **L**!
3:16 The **L** will roar from Zion and
3:16 But the **L** will be a refuge for his
3:21 The **L** dwells in Zion!
Am 1: 2 He said: "The **L** roars from Zion and
1: 3 This is what the **L** says: "For three
1: 5 go into exile to Kir," says the **L**
1: 6 This is what the **L** says: "For three
1: 9 This is what the **L** says: "For three
1:11 This is what the **L** says: "For three
1:13 This is what the **L** says: "For three
1:15 his officials together," says the **L**
2: 1 This is what the **L** says: "For three
2: 3 officials with him," says the **L**
2: 4 This is what the **L** says: "For three
2: 6 This is what the **L** says: "For three
3: 1 Hear this word the **L** has spoken
3: 6 to a city, has not the **L** caused it?
3:12 This is what the **L** says: "As a
5: 4 This is what the **L** says to the house
5: 6 Seek the **L** and live, or he will
5: 8 of the land—the **L** is his name—
5:17 through your midst," says the **L**.
5:27 the **L**, whose name is God Almighty.
6:11 For the **L** has given the command, and
7: 3 So the **L** relented.
7: 3 "This will not happen," the **L** said.
7: 8 the **L** asked me, "What do you see,
7:15 the **L** took me from tending the flock
7:17 "Therefore this is what the **L** says:
8: 2 Then the **L** said to me, "The time is
8: 7 **L** has sworn by the Pride of Jacob
8:11 of hearing the words of the **L**.
Am 9: 6 of the land—the **L** is his name.
Ob : 1 We have heard a message from the **L**:
:18 The **L** has spoken.
Jnh 1: 3 Jonah ran away from the **L** and headed
1: 3 for Tarshish to flee from the **L**.
1: 4 the **L** sent a great wind on the sea,
1: 9 "I am a Hebrew and I worship the **L**,
1:10 knew he was running away from the **L**,
1:14 they cried to the **L**, "O **L**, please do
1:14 you, O **L**, have done as you pleased."
1:16 At this the men greatly feared the **L**,
1:16 offered a sacrifice to the **L** and
1:17 the **L** provided a great fish to
2: 1 Jonah prayed to the **L** his God.
2: 2 called to the **L**, and he answered me.
2: 6 my life up from the pit, O **L** my God
2: 7 I remembered you, **L**, and my prayer
2: 9 Salvation comes from the **L**."
2:10 the **L** commanded the fish, and it
4: 2 He prayed to the **L**, "O **L**, is this
4: 3 Now, O **L**, take away my life, for
4: 4 the **L** replied, "Have you any right
4:10 the **L** said, "You have been concerned
Mic 1: 3 Look! The **L** is coming from his
1:12 disaster has come from the **L**, even
2: 3 Therefore, the **L** says: "I am
2: 5 no-one in the assembly of the **L** to
2:13 before them, the **L** at their head."
3: 4 they will cry out to the **L**, but he
3: 5 This is what the **L** says: "As for the
3:11 Yet they lean upon the **L** and say,
3:11 "Is not the **L** among us? No disaster
4: 7 The **L** will rule over them in Mount
4:10 There the **L** will redeem you out of
4:12 do not know the thoughts of the **L**;
4:13 their ill-gotten gains to the **L**,
5: 4 his flock in the strength of the **L**,
5: 7 of many peoples like dew from the **L**,
6: 1 Listen to what the **L** says: "Stand up
6: 2 the **L** has a case against his people
6: 5 know the righteous acts of the **L**."
6: 7 Will the **L** be pleased with thousands
6: 8 And what does the **L** require of you?
6: 9 Listen! The **L** is calling to the city
7: 7 I watch in hope for the **L**, I wait
7: 8 in darkness, the **L** will be my light.
7:17 will turn in fear to the **L** our God
Na 1: 2 The **L** is a jealous and avenging God;
1: 2 the **L** takes vengeance and is filled
1: 2 The **L** takes vengeance on his foes
1: 3 The **L** is slow to anger and great in
1: 3 the **L** will not leave the guilty
1: 7 The **L** is good, a refuge in times of
1: 9 Whatever they plot against the **L** he
1:11 who plots evil against the **L** and
1:12 This is what the **L** says: "Although
1:14 The **L** has given a command concerning
2: 2 The **L** will restore the splendour of
Hab 1: 2 How long, O **L**, must I call for help,
1:12 O **L**, are you not from everlasting?
1:12 O **L**, you have appointed them to
2: 2 the **L** replied: "Write down the
2:20 the **L** is in his holy temple; let all
3: 2 **L**, I have heard of your fame;
3: 2 I stand in awe of your deeds, O **L**.
3: 8 Were you angry with the rivers, O **L**?
3:18 yet I will rejoice in the **L**, I will
Zep 1: 5 who bow down and swear by the **L**
1: 6 who turn back from following the **L**
1: 6 seek the **L** nor enquire of him.
1: 7 the **L** has prepared a sacrifice;
1:12 The **L** will do nothing, either good
1:17 they have sinned against the **L**.
2: 3 Seek the **L**, all you humble of the
2: 7 The **L** their God will care for them;
2:11 The **L** will be awesome to them when
3: 2 She does not trust in the **L**, she
3: 5 The **L** within her is righteous; he
3:15 The **L** has taken away your punishment
3:15 The **L**, the King of Israel, is with
3:20 before your very eyes," says the **L**
Hag 1: 8 and be honoured," says the **L**.
1:12 the **L** their God had sent him.
1:12 And the people feared the **L**.
1:13 gave this message of the **L** to the
1:14 the **L** stirred up the spirit of

Zec 1: 2 "The **L** was very angry with your
1:10 They are the ones the **L** has sent to
1:13 **L** spoke kind and comforting words
1:16 "Therefore, this is what the **L** says:
1:17 and the **L** will again comfort Zion
1:20 the **L** showed me four craftsmen.
2:11 be joined with the **L** in that day
2:12 The **L** will inherit Judah as his
3: 2 **L** said to Satan, "The **L** rebuke you
3: 2 The **L**, who has chosen Jerusalem,
4:10 (These seven are the eyes of the **L**,
7: 2 with their men, to entreat the **L**
7: 7 these not the words the **L** proclaimed
8: 3 This is what the **L** says: "I will
8:21 'Let us go at once to entreat the **L**
9: 1 the tribes of Israel are on the **L**
9:14 the **L** will appear over them; his
9:16 The **L** their God will save them on
10: 1 Ask the **L** for rain in the springtime
10: 1 is the **L** who makes the storm clouds.
10: 5 Because the **L** is with them, they
10: 7 their hearts will rejoice in the **L**.
10:12 I will strengthen them in the **L** and
11: 4 This is what the **L** my God says:
11:13 the **L** said to me, "Throw it to the
11:15 the **L** said to me, "Take again the
12: 1 The **L**, who stretches out the heavens
12: 7 "The **L** will save the dwellings of
12: 8 On that day the **L** will shield those
13: 9 they will say, 'The **L** is our God.
14: 3 the **L** will go out and fight against
14: 5 the **L** my God will come, and all
14: 7 or night-time—a day known to the **L**.
14: 9 The **L** will be king over the whole
14: 9 one **L**, and his name the only name.
14:12 plague with which the **L** will strike
14:13 stricken by the **L** with great panic.
14:18 The **L** will bring on them the plague
Mal 1: 2 "I have loved you," says the **L**.
1: 2 Esau Jacob's brother?" the **L** says.
1: 4 always under the wrath of the **L**.
1: 5 'Great is the **L**—even beyond the
1:13 them from your hands?" says the **L**.
2:11 the sanctuary the **L** loves,
2:12 may the **L** cut him off from the tents
2:14 the **L** is acting as the witness
2:15 Has not ⌊the **L**⌋ made them one?
2:17 have wearied the **L** with your words
2:17 are good in the eyes of the **L**,
3: 3 Then the **L** will have men who will
3: 4 will be acceptable to the **L**,
3: 6 "I the **L** do not change. So you, O
3:13 things against me," says the **L**.
3:16 those who feared the **L** talked with
3:16 other, and the **L** listened and heard.
3:16 feared the **L** and honoured his name.

Lord Almighty

1Sa 1: 3 and sacrifice to the **L** at Shiloh,
1:11 made a vow, saying, "O **L**, if you
4: 4 the ark of the covenant of the **L**,
15: 2 This is what the **L** says: 'I will
17:45 against you in the name of the **L**,
2Sa 6: 2 the name of the **L**, who is enthroned
6:18 the people in the name of the **L**.
7: 8 'This is what the **L** says: I took you
7:26 Then men will say, 'The **L** is God
7:27 "O **L**, God of Israel, you have
1Ki 18:15 Elijah said, "As the **L** lives, whom
2Ki 3:14 said, "As surely as the **L** lives,
19:31 zeal of the **L** will accomplish this.
1Ch 11: 9 because the **L** was with him.
17: 7 'This is what the **L** says: I took you
17:24 Then men will say, 'The **L**, the God
Ps 24:10 The **L**—he is the King of glory.
46: 7 The **L** is with us; the God of Jacob
46:11 The **L** is with us; the God of Jacob
48: 8 have we seen in the city of the **L**,
69: 6 because of me, O Lord, the **L**;
84: 1 lovely is your dwelling-place, O **L**!
84: 3 your altar, O **L**, my King and my God
84:12 O **L**, blessed is the man who trusts
Isa 1: 9 Unless the **L** had left us some
1:24 Therefore the Lord, the **L**, the
2:12 The **L** has a day in store for all
Isa 3: 1 See now, the Lord, the **L**, is about
5: 7 The vineyard of the **L** is the house
5: 9 The **L** has declared in my hearing:
5:16 **L** will be exalted by his justice,
5:24 they have rejected the law of the **L**
6: 3 "Holy, holy, holy is the **L**; the
6: 5 my eyes have seen the King, the **L**."
8:13 The **L** is the one you are to regard
8:18 the **L**, who dwells on Mount Zion.
9: 7 zeal of the **L** will accomplish this.
9:13 them, nor have they sought the **L**.
9:19 By the wrath of the **L** the land will
10:16 Therefore, the Lord, the **L**, will
10:23 The Lord, the **L**, will carry out the
10:24 this is what the Lord, the **L**, says:
10:26 The **L** will lash them with a whip,
10:33 See, the Lord, the **L**, will lop off
13: 4 The **L** is mustering an army for war.
13:13 at the wrath of the **L**, in the day
14:22 up against them," declares the **L**.
14:23 of destruction," declares the **L**.
14:24 The **L** has sworn, "Surely, as I have
14:27 For the **L** has purposed, and who can
17: 3 of the Israelites," declares the **L**.
18: 7 brought to the **L** from a people tall
18: 7 Zion, the place of the Name of the **L**
19: 4 them," declares the Lord, the **L**.
19:12 the **L** has planned against Egypt.
19:16 hand that the **L** raises against them.
19:17 what the **L** is planning against them.
19:18 Canaan and swear allegiance to the **L**
19:20 will be a sign and witness to the **L**
19:25 The **L** will bless them, saying,
21:10 from the **L**, from the God of Israel.
22: 5 The Lord, the **L**, has a day of tumult
22:12 The Lord, the **L**, called you on that
22:14 The **L** has revealed this in my
22:14 atoned for," says the Lord, the **L**.
22:15 This is what the Lord, the **L**, says:
22:25 "In that day," declares the **L**, "the
23: 9 The **L** planned it, to bring low the
24:23 for the **L** will reign on Mount Zion
25: 6 On this mountain the **L** will prepare
28: 5 In that day the **L** will be a glorious
28:22 the **L**, has told me of the
28:29 All this also comes from the **L**,
29: 6 the **L** will come with thunder and
31: 4 so the **L** will come down to do
31: 5 the **L** will shield Jerusalem;
37:16 "O **L**, God of Israel, enthroned
37:32 zeal of the **L** will accomplish this.
39: 5 "Hear the word of the **L**:
44: 6 the **L**: I am the first and I am the
45:13 for a price or reward, says the **L**."
47: 4 Our Redeemer—the **L** is his name—
48: 2 God of Israel—the **L** is his name:
51:15 its waves roar—the **L** is his name.
54: 5 the **L** is his name—the Holy One of
Jer 2:19 of me," declares the Lord, the **L**.
6: 6 This is what the **L** says: "Cut down
6: 9 This is what the **L** says: "Let them
7: 3 This is what the **L**, the God of
7:21 "'This is what the **L**, the God of
8: 3 death to life, declares the **L**.'
9: 7 Therefore this is what the **L** says:
9:15 Therefore, this is what the **L**, the
9:17 This is what the **L** says: "Consider
10:16 his inheritance—the **L** is his name.
11:17 The **L**, who planted you, has decreed
11:20 But, O **L**, you who judge righteously
11:22 therefore this is what the **L** says:
16: 9 For this is what the **L**, the God of
19: 3 This is what the **L**, the God of
19:11 to them, 'This is what the **L** says
19:15 "This is what the **L**, the God of
20:12 O **L**, you who examine the righteous
23:15 Therefore, this is what the **L** says
23:16 This is what the **L** says: "Do not
23:36 of the living God, the **L**, our God.
25: 8 Therefore the **L** says this: "Because
25:27 Then tell them, 'This is what the **L**
25:28 what the **L** says: You must drink it!
25:29 live on the earth, declares the **L**.'
25:32 This is what the **L** says: "Look!
26:18 'This is what the **L** says: " 'Zion
27: 4 the **L**, the God of Israel says:
Jer 27:18 let them plead with the **L** that the
27:19 For this is what the **L** says about
27:21 yes, this is what the **L**, the God of
28: 2 "This is what the **L**, the God of
28:14 This is what the **L**, the God of
29: 4 This is what the **L**, the God of
29: 8 Yes, this is what the **L**, the God of
29:17 yes, this is what the **L** says: "I
29:21 This is what the **L**, the God of
29:25 "This is what the **L**, the God of
30: 8 "'In that day,' declares the **L**,
31:23 This is what the **L**, the God of
31:35 its waves roar—the **L** is his name:
32:14 'This is what the **L**, the God of
32:15 For this is what the **L**, the God of
32:18 powerful God, whose name is the **L**,
33:11 "Give thanks to the **L**, for the LORD
33:12 "This is what the **L** says: 'In this
35:13 "This is what the **L**, the God of
35:18 "This is what the **L**, the God of
35:19 Therefore, this is what the **L**, the
39:16 'This is what the **L**, the God of
42:15 This is what the **L**, the God of
42:18 This is what the **L**, the God of
43:10 say to them, 'This is what the **L**,
44: 2 "This is what the **L**, the God of
44:11 "Therefore, this is what the **L**, the
44:25 This is what the **L**, the God of
46:10 that day belongs to the Lord, the **L**
46:10 For the Lord, the **L**, will offer
46:18 whose name is the **L**, "one will come
46:25 The **L**, the God of Israel, says: "I
48: 1 This is what the **L**, says: "Is there
48:15 the King, whose name is the **L**.
49: 5 you," declares the Lord, the **L**.
49: 7 Concerning Edom: This is what the **L**
49:26 in that day," declares the **L**.
49:35 This is what the **L** says: "See, I
50:18 Therefore this is what the **L**, the
50:25 for the Sovereign **L** has work to do
50:31 declares the Lord, the **L**, "for your
50:33 This is what the **L** says: "The people
50:34 is strong; the **L** is his name.
51: 5 by their God, the **L**, though their
51:14 The **L** has sworn by himself: I will
51:19 his inheritance—the **L** is his name.
51:33 This is what the **L**, the God of
51:57 the King, whose name is the **L**.
51:58 This is what the **L** says: "Babylon's
Am 9: 5 The Lord, the **L**, he who touches the
Mic 4: 4 them afraid, for the **L** has spoken.
Na 2:13 "I am against you," declares the **L**.
3: 5 "I am against you," declares the **L**.
Hab 2:13 Has not the **L** determined that the
Zep 2: 9 surely as I live," declares the **L**,
2:10 and mocking the people of the **L**.
Hag 1: 2 This is what the **L** says: "These
1: 5 Now this is what the **L** says: "Give
1: 7 This is what the **L** says: "Give
1: 9 Why?" declares the **L**. "Because of my
1:14 on the house of the **L**, their God,
2: 4 For I am with you,' declares the **L**.
2: 6 "This is what the **L** says: 'In a
2: 7 this house with glory,' says the **L**.
2: 8 the gold is mine,' declares the **L**.
2: 9 of the former house,' says the **L**.
2: 9 I will grant peace,' declares the **L**
2:11 "This is what the **L** says: 'Ask the
2:23 "'On that day,' declares the **L**, 'I
2:23 I have chosen you,' declares the **L**.
Zec 1: 3 is what the **L** says: 'Return to me
1: 3 'Return to me,' declares the **L**,
1: 3 I will return to you,' says the **L**.
1: 4 This is what the **L** says: 'Turn from
1: 6 'The **L** has done to us what our ways
1:12 the angel of the LORD said, "**L**, how
1:14 This is what the **L** says: 'I am very
1:16 out over Jerusalem,' declares the **L**.
1:17 further: This is what the **L** says:
2: 8 For this is what the **L** says: "After
2: 9 will know that the **L** has sent me.
2:11 know that the **L** has sent me to you.
3: 7 "This is what the **L** says: 'If you
3: 9 an inscription on it,' says the **L**,
3:10 vine and fig-tree,' declares the **L**."
4: 6 but by my Spirit,' says the **L**.

Zec 4: 9 know that the **L** has sent me to you.
5: 4 The **L** declares, 'I will send it out,
6:12 Tell him this is what the **L** says:
6:15 know that the **L** has sent me to you.
7: 3 the house of the **L** and the prophets,
7: 4 the word of the **L** came to me:
7: 9 "This is what the **L** says:
7:12 or to the words that the **L** had sent
7:12 So the **L** was very angry.
7:13 I would not listen,' says the **L**.
8: 1 Again the word of the **L** came to me.
8: 2 This is what the **L** says: "I am very
8: 3 **L** will be called the Holy Mountain."
8: 4 This is what the **L** says: "Once again
8: 6 This is what the **L** says: "It may
8: 6 marvellous to me?" declares the **L**.
8: 7 This is what the **L** says: "I will
8: 9 This is what the **L** says: "You who
8: 9 was laid for the house of the **L**,
8:11 I did in the past," declares the **L**.
8:14 This is what the **L** says: "Just as I
8:14 fathers angered me," says the **L**,
8:18 Again the word of the **L** came to me.
8:19 This is what the **L** says: "The fasts
8:20 This is what the **L** says: "Many
8:21 to entreat the LORD and seek the **L**.
8:22 to seek the **L** and to entreat him."
8:23 This is what the **L** says: "In those
9:15 the **L** will shield them. They will
10: 3 for the **L** will care for his flock,
12: 5 strong, because the **L** is their God.'
13: 2 remembered no more," declares the **L**.
13: 7 who is close to me!" declares the **L**.
14:16 to worship the King, the **L**, and to
14:17 to worship the King, the **L**, they
14:21 and Judah will be holy to the **L**,
14:21 a Canaanite in the house of the **L**.
Mal 1: 4 But this is what the **L** says: "They
1: 6 the respect due to me?" says the **L**.
1: 8 Would he accept you?" says the **L**.
1: 9 will he accept you?"—says the **L**.
1:10 not pleased with you," says the **L**,
1:11 among the nations," says the **L**.
1:13 at it contemptuously," says the **L**.
1:14 For I am a great king," says the **L**,
2: 2 to honour my name," says the **L**,
2: 4 with Levi may continue," says the **L**.
2: 7 he is the messenger of the **L**.
2: 8 the covenant with Levi," says the **L**.
2:12 though he brings offerings to the **L**.
2:16 as with his garment," says the **L**.
3: 1 you desire, will come," says the **L**.
3: 5 but do not fear me," says the **L**.
3: 7 I will return to you," says the **L**.
3:10 Test me in this," says the **L**, "and
3:11 not cast their fruit," says the **L**.
3:12 be a delightful land," says the **L**.
3:14 about like mourners before the **L**?
3:17 "They will be mine," says the **L**,
4: 1 will set them on fire," says the **L**.
4: 3 when I do these things," says the **L**.

LORD God (*LORD God Almighty*)

Ge 2: 4 **L** made the earth and the heavens—
2: 5 for the **L** had not sent rain on the
2: 7 the **L** formed the man from the dust
2: 8 Now the **L** had planted a garden in
2: 9 the **L** made all kinds of trees grow
2:15 The **L** took the man and put him in
2:16 the **L** commanded the man, "You are
2:18 The **L** said, "It is not good for the
2:19 Now the **L** had formed out of the
2:21 the **L** caused the man to fall into a
2:22 the **L** made a woman from the rib he
3: 1 of the wild animals the **L** had made.
3: 8 his wife heard the sound of the **L**
3: 8 the **L** among the trees of the garden.
3: 9 the **L** called to the man, "Where are
3:13 the **L** said to the woman, "What is
3:14 the **L** said to the serpent, "Because
3:21 The **L** made garments of skin for Adam
3:22 the **L** said, "The man has now become
3:23 the **L** banished him from the Garden
Ex 9:30 officials still do not fear the **L**."
2Sa 7:25 "And now, **L**, keep for ever the
1Ch 17:16 "Who am I, O **L**, and what is my
17:17 I were the most exalted of men, O **L**.
22: 1 David said, "The house of the **L** is
22:19 to build the sanctuary of the **L**,
28:20 for the **L**, my God, is with you.
29: 1 is not for man but for the **L**.
2Ch 1: 9 Now, **L**, let your promise to my
6:41 "Now arise, O **L**, and come to your
6:41 May your priests, O **L**, be clothed
6:42 **L**, do not reject your anointed one.
26:18 you will not be honoured by the **L**."
32:16 spoke further against the **L** and
Ne 9: 7 "You are the **L**, who chose Abram and
Ps 68:18 that you, O **L**, might dwell there.
72:18 Praise be to the **L**, the God of
84:11 For the **L** is a sun and shield; the
Jnh 4: 6 the **L** provided a vine and made it
Mal 2:16 hate divorce," says the **L** of Israel

LORD God Almighty

2Sa 5:10 because the **L** was with him.
1Ki 19:10 I have been very zealous for the **L**.
19:14 I have been very zealous for the **L**.
Ps 59: 5 O **L**, the God of Israel, rouse
80: 4 O **L**, how long will your anger
80:19 Restore us, O **L**; make your face
84: 8 Hear my prayer, O **L**; listen to me,
89: 8 O **L**, who is like you? You are mighty,
Jer 5:14 Therefore this is what the **L** says:
15:16 delight, for I bear your name, O **L**.
35:17 "Therefore, this is what the **L**, the
38:17 "This is what the **L**, the God of
44: 7 "Now this is what the **L**, the God of
Hos 12: 5 the **L**, the LORD is his name of
Am 3:13 of Jacob," declares the Lord, the **L**
4:13 of the earth— the **L** is his name.
5:14 Then the **L** will be with you, just as
5:15 Perhaps the **L** will have mercy on the
5:16 the **L**, says: "There will be wailing
6: 8 sworn by himself—the **L** declares:
6:14 For the **L** declares, "I will stir up

LORD is my rock

2Sa 22: 2 He said: "The **L**, my fortress and my
Ps 18: 2 The **L**, my fortress and my deliverer;

LORD your God

Ge 27:20 The **L** gave me success," he replied.
Ex 6: 7 Then you will know that I am the **L**,
8:28 sacrifices to the **L** in the desert,
10: 8 "Go, worship the **L**," he said. "But
10:16 against the **L** and against you.
10:17 pray to the **L** to take this deadly
15:26 to the voice of the **L** and do what
16:12 Then you will know that I am the **L**.'
20: 2 "I am the **L**, who brought you out of
20: 5 for I, the **L**, am a jealous God,
20: 7 shall not misuse the name of the **L**,
20:10 seventh day is a Sabbath to the **L**
20:12 in the land the **L** is giving you.
23:19 of your soil to the house of the **L**.
23:25 Worship the **L**, and his blessing will
34:24 each year to appear before the **L**.
34:26 of your soil to the house of the **L**.
Lev 11:44 I am the **L**; consecrate yourselves
18: 2 and say to them: 'I am the **L**.
18: 4 to follow my decrees. I am the **L**.
18:30 with them. I am the **L**.
19: 2 'Be holy because I, the **L**, am holy.
19: 3 observe my Sabbaths. I am the **L**.
19: 4 metal for yourselves. I am the **L**.
19:10 the poor and the alien. I am the **L**.
19:25 will be increased. I am the **L**.
19:31 defiled by them. I am the **L**.
19:34 aliens in Egypt. I am the **L**.
19:36 the **L**, who brought you out of Egypt.
20: 7 and be holy, because I am the **L**.
20:24 I am the **L**, who has set you apart
23:22 the poor and the alien. I am the **L**.
23:28 is made for you before the **L**.
23:40 rejoice before the **L** for seven days.
Lev 23:43 out of Egypt. I am the **L**.
24:22 and the native-born. I am the **L**.
25:17 fear your God. I am the **L**.
25:38 I am the **L**, who brought you out of
25:55 out of Egypt. I am the **L**.
26: 1 to bow down before it. I am the **L**.
26:13 I am the **L**, who brought you out of
Nu 10: 9 the **L** and rescued from your enemies.
10:10 before your God. I am the **L**."
15:41 I am the **L**, who brought you out of
15:41 to be your God. I am the **L**.'
Dt 1:10 The **L** has increased your numbers so
1:21 See, the **L** has given you the land.
1:26 against the command of the **L**.
1:30 The **L**, who is going before you, will
1:31 There you saw how the **L** carried you,
1:32 of this, you did not trust in the **L**,
2: 7 The **L** has blessed you in all the
2: 7 These forty years the **L** has been
2:30 For the **L** had made his spirit
3:18 "The **L** has given you this land
3:20 **L** is giving them, across the Jordan.
3:21 the **L** has done to these two kings.
3:22 the **L** himself will fight for you."
4: 2 commands of the **L** that I give you.
4: 3 The **L** destroyed from among you
4: 4 all of you who held fast to the **L**
4:10 day you stood before the **L** at Horeb
4:19 worshipping things the **L** has
4:21 **L** is giving you as your inheritance
4:23 not to forget the covenant of the **L**
4:23 of anything the **L** has forbidden.
4:24 For the **L** is a consuming fire, a
4:25 of the **L** and provoking him to anger,
4:29 if from there you seek the **L**, you
4:30 will return to the **L** and obey him.
4:31 For the **L** is a merciful God; he will
4:34 all the things the **L** did for you
4:40 land the **L** gives you for all time.
5: 6 "I am the **L**, who brought you out of
5: 9 for I, the **L**, am a jealous God,
5:11 shall not misuse the name of the **L**,
5:12 it holy, as the **L** has commanded you.
5:14 seventh day is a Sabbath to the **L**
5:15 that the **L** brought you out of there
5:15 Therefore the **L** has commanded you to
5:16 as the **L** has commanded you, so that
5:16 you in the land the **L** is giving you.
5:32 to do what the **L** has commanded
5:33 Walk in all the way that the **L** has
6: 1 decrees and laws the **L** directed me
6: 2 may fear the **L** as long as you live
6: 5 Love the **L** with all your heart and
6:10 the **L** brings you into the land he
6:13 Fear the **L**, serve him only and take
6:15 for the **L**, who is among you, is a
6:16 Do not test the **L** as you did at
6:17 sure to keep the commands of the **L**
7: 1 the **L** brings you into the land you
7: 2 the **L** has delivered them over to you
7: 6 For you are a people holy to the **L**.
7: 6 The **L** has chosen you out of all the
7: 9 Know therefore that the **L** is God;
7:12 then the **L** will keep his covenant of
7:16 the peoples the **L** gives over to you.
7:18 remember well what the **L** did to
7:19 with which the **L** brought you out.
7:19 The **L** will do the same to all the
7:20 Moreover, the **L** will send the hornet
7:21 for the **L**, who is among you, is a
7:22 The **L** will drive out those nations
7:23 the **L** will deliver them over to you,
7:25 for it is detestable to the **L**.
8: 2 Remember how the **L** led you all the
8: 5 his son, so the **L** disciplines you.
8: 6 Observe the commands of the **L**,
8: 7 For the **L** is bringing you into a
8:10 praise the **L** for the good land he
8:11 that you do not forget the **L**,
8:14 proud and you will forget the **L**,
8:18 remember the **L**, for it is he who
8:19 If you ever forget the **L** and follow
8:20 be destroyed for not obeying the **L**.
9: 3 be assured today that the **L** is the
9: 4 After the **L** has driven them out
9: 5 the **L** will drive them out before you,

Dt 9: 6 the **L** is giving you this good land
9: 7 provoked the **L** to anger in the
9:16 that you had sinned against the **L**;
9:23 against the command of the **L**.
10: 9 inheritance, as the **L** told them.)
10:12 the **L** ask of you but to fear the **L**,
10:14 To the **L** belong the heavens, even
10:17 the **L** is God of gods and Lord of
10:20 Fear the **L** and serve him. Hold fast
10:22 and now the **L** has made you as
11: 1 Love the **L** and keep his requirements
11: 2 discipline of the **L**: his majesty,
11:12 **L** cares for; the eyes of the **L** are
11:13 I am giving you today—to love the **L**
11:22 giving you to follow—to love the **L**,
11:25 The **L**, as he promised you, will put
11:27 of the **L** that I am giving you today;
11:28 you disobey the commands of the **L**
11:29 the **L** has brought you into the land
11:31 of the land the **L** is giving you.
12: 4 You must not worship the **L** in their
12: 5 to seek the place the **L** will choose
12: 7 There, in the presence of the **L**, you
12: 7 because the **L** has blessed you.
12: 9 the inheritance the **L** is giving you.
12:10 **L** is giving you as an inheritance,
12:11 to the place the **L** will choose as a
12:12 there rejoice before the **L**, you,
12:15 to the blessing the **L** gives you.
12:18 **L** at the place the **L** will choose
12:18 **L** in everything you put your hand to
12:20 the **L** has enlarged your territory as
12:21 If the place where the **L** chooses to
12:27 on the altar of the **L**, both the
12:27 beside the altar of the **L**, but
12:28 good and right in the eyes of the **L**.
12:29 The **L** will cut off before you the
12:31 You must not worship the **L** in their
13: 3 The **L** is testing you to find out
13: 4 is the **L** you must follow, and him
13: 5 he preached rebellion against the **L**,
13: 5 way the **L** commanded you to follow.
13:10 tried to turn you away from the **L**,
13:12 towns the **L** is giving you to live
13:16 as a whole burnt offering to the **L**.
13:18 you obey the **L**, keeping all his
14: 1 You are the children of the **L**. Do
14: 2 for you are a people holy to the **L**.
14:21 But you are a people holy to the **L**.
14:23 flocks in the presence of the **L** at
14:23 may learn to revere the **L** always.
14:24 you have been blessed by the **L** and
14:25 go to the place the **L** will choose.
14:26 the presence of the **L** and rejoice.
14:29 and so that the **L** may bless you in
15: 4 for in the land the **L** is giving you
15: 5 if only you fully obey the **L** and are
15: 6 For the **L** will bless you as he has
15: 7 the land that the **L** is giving you,
15:10 **L** will bless you in all your work
15:14 Give to him as the **L** has blessed you
15:15 in Egypt and the **L** redeemed you.
15:18 And the **L** will bless you in
15:19 Set apart for the **L** every firstborn
15:20 in the presence of the **L** at the
15:21 you must not sacrifice it to the **L**.
16: 1 and celebrate the Passover of the **L**,
16: 2 Sacrifice as the Passover to the **L**
16: 5 Passover in any town the **L** gives
16: 7 it at the place the **L** will choose.
16: 8 an assembly to the **L** and do no work.
16:10 the Feast of Weeks to the **L** by
16:10 to the blessings the **L** has given you
16:11 rejoice before the **L** at the place he
16:15 to the **L** at the place the LORD will
16:15 For the **L** will bless you in all your
16:16 before the **L** at the place he will
16:17 to the way the **L** has blessed you.
16:18 in every town the **L** is giving you,
16:20 the land the **L** is giving you.
16:21 beside the altar you build to the **L**,
16:22 sacred stone, for these the **L** hates.
17: 1 Do not sacrifice to the **L** an ox or a
17: 2 doing evil in the eyes of the **L** in
17: 8 them to the place the **L** will choose.
17:12 there to the **L** must be put to death.

Dt 17:14 enter the land the **L** is giving you
17:15 over you the king the **L** chooses.
18: 5 for the **L** has chosen them and their
18: 9 enter the land the **L** is giving you
18:12 the **L** will drive out those nations
18:13 You must be blameless before the **L**.
18:14 **L** has not permitted you to do so.
18:15 The **L** will raise up for you a
18:16 For this is what you asked of the **L**
19: 1 the **L** has destroyed the nations
19: 2 land the **L** is giving you to possess.
19: 3 **L** is giving you as an inheritance,
19: 8 If the **L** enlarges your territory,
19: 9 I command you today—to love the **L**
19:10 which the **L** is giving you as your
19:14 land the **L** is giving you to possess.
20: 1 because the **L**, who brought you up
20: 4 For the **L** is the one who goes with
20:13 the **L** delivers it into your hand,
20:14 the **L** gives you from your enemies.
20:16 in the cities of the nations the **L**
20:17 the **L** has commanded you.
20:18 and you will sin against the **L**.
21: 1 lying in a field in the land the **L**
21: 5 shall step forward, for the **L** has
21:10 the **L** delivers them into your hands
21:23 **L** is giving you as an inheritance.
22: 5 the **L** detests anyone who does this.
23: 5 However, the **L** would not listen to
23: 5 for you, because the **L** loves you.
23:14 For the **L** moves about in your camp
23:18 the house of the **L** to pay any vow,
23:18 because the **L** detests them both.
23:20 so that the **L** may bless you in
23:21 If you make a vow to the **L**, do not
23:21 the **L** will certainly demand it of
23:23 made your vow freely to the **L** with
24: 4 **L** is giving you as an inheritance.
24: 9 Remember what the **L** did to Miriam
24:13 righteous act in the sight of the **L**.
24:18 and the **L** redeemed you from there.
24:19 so that the **L** may bless you in all
25:15 in the land the **L** is giving you.
25:16 For the **L** detests anyone who does
25:19 the **L** gives you rest from all the
26: 1 the land that the **L** is giving you
26: 2 the land that the **L** is giving you
26: 2 to the place that the **L** will choose
26: 3 "I declare today to the **L** that I
26: 4 down in front of the altar of the **L**.
26: 5 you shall declare before the **L**: "My
26:10 before the **L** and bow down before
26:11 good things the **L** has given to you
26:13 say to the **L**: "I have removed from
26:16 The **L** commands you this day to
26:19 holy to the **L**, as he promised.
27: 2 into the land the **L** is giving you,
27: 3 enter the land the **L** is giving you,
27: 5 Build there an altar to the **L**, an
27: 6 Build the altar of the **L** with stones
27: 6 burnt offerings on it to the **L**.
27: 7 rejoicing in the presence of the **L**.
27: 9 have now become the people of the **L**.
27:10 Obey the **L** and follow his commands
28: 1 If you fully obey the **L** and
28: 1 the **L** will set you high above all
28: 2 and accompany you if you obey the **L**
28: 8 The **L** will bless you in the land he
28: 9 commands of the **L** and walk in his
28:13 commands of the **L** that I give you
28:15 However, if you do not obey the **L**
28:45 because you did not obey the **L** and
28:47 you did not serve the **L** joyfully and
28:52 the land the **L** is giving you.
28:53 and daughters the **L** has given you.
28:58 glorious and awesome name—the **L**—
28:62 because you did not obey the **L**.
29: 6 that you might know that I am the **L**.
29:10 in the presence of the **L**—your
29:12 to enter into a covenant with the **L**,
30: 1 **L** disperses you among the nations,
30: 2 you and your children return to the **L**
30: 3 the **L** will restore your fortunes and
30: 4 **L** will gather you and bring you back.
30: 6 The **L** will circumcise your hearts
30: 7 The **L** will put all these curses on

Dt 30: 9 the **L** will make you most prosperous
30:10 if you obey the **L** and keep his
30:10 turn to the **L** with all your heart
30:16 I command you today to love the **L**
30:16 and the **L** will bless you in the land
30:20 that you may love the **L**, listen to
31: 3 The **L** himself will cross over ahead
31: 6 for the **L** goes with you; he will
31:11 before the **L** at the place he will
31:12 learn to fear the **L** and follow
31:13 learn to fear the **L** as long as you
31:26 the ark of the covenant of the **L**.
Jos 1: 9 **L** will be with you wherever you go."
1:11 land the **L** is giving you for your
1:13 'The **L** is giving you rest and has
1:15 the land that the **L** is giving them.
1:17 **L** be with you as he was with Moses.
2:11 for the **L** is God in heaven above
3: 3 the ark of the covenant of the **L**,
3: 9 and listen to the words of the **L**.
4: 5 before the ark of the **L** into the
4:23 For the **L** dried up the Jordan before
4:23 The **L** did to the Jordan just what he
4:24 that you might always fear the **L**."
8: 7 The **L** will give it into your hand.
9: 9 because of the fame of the **L**.
9:24 told how the **L** had commanded his
10:19 **L** has given them into your hand."
22: 3 out the mission the **L** gave you.
22: 4 Now that the **L** has given your
22: 5 the LORD gave you: to love the **L**,
23: 3 have seen everything the **L** has done
23: 3 it was the **L** who fought for you.
23: 5 The **L** himself will drive them out
23: 5 their land, as the **L** promised you.
23: 8 you are to hold fast to the **L**, as
23:10 because the **L** fights for you, just
23:11 be very careful to love the **L**.
23:13 you may be sure that the **L** will no
23:13 land, which the **L** has given you.
23:14 promises the **L** gave you has failed.
23:15 just as every good promise of the **L**
23:16 If you violate the covenant of the **L**
Jdg 6:10 I said to you, 'I am the **L**; do not
6:26 a proper kind of altar to the **L**
1Sa 12:12 though the **L** was your king.
12:14 reigns over you follow the **L**—good!
12:19 "Pray to the **L** for your servants so
13:13 "You have not kept the command the **L**
15:15 to sacrifice to the **L**, but we
15:21 sacrifice them to the **L** at Gilgal."
15:30 me, so that I may worship the **L**."
25:29 the bundle of the living by the **L**.
2Sa 14:17 May the **L** be with you.'
18:28 "Praise be to the **L**! He has
24: 3 Joab replied to the king, "May the **L**
24:23 said to him, "May the **L** accept you.
1Ki 1:17 swore to me your servant by the **L**:
2: 3 observe what the **L** requires: Walk in
10: 9 Praise be to the **L**, who has
13: 6 "Intercede with the **L** and pray for
13:21 not kept the command the **L** gave you.
17:12 "As surely as the **L** lives," she
18:10 surely as the **L** lives, there is not
2Ki 17:39 Rather, worship the **L**; it is he who
19: 4 may be that the **L** will hear all the
19: 4 him for the words the **L** has heard.
23:21 "Celebrate the Passover to the **L**,
1Ch 11: 2 And the **L** said to you, 'You will
22:11 build the house of the **L**, as he
22:12 that you may keep the law of the **L**.
22:18 He said to them, "Is not the **L** with
22:19 heart and soul to seeking the **L**.
28: 8 to follow all the commands of the **L**
29:20 the whole assembly, "Praise the **L**.
2Ch 9: 8 Praise be to the **L**, who has
9: 8 throne as king to rule for the **L**.
16: 7 the king of Aram and not on the **L**,
20:20 in the **L** and you will be upheld;
28:10 also guilty of sins against the **L**?
30: 8 Serve the **L**, so that his fierce
30: 9 the **L** is gracious and compassionate.
35: 3 serve the **L** and his people Israel.
Ne 8: 9 all, "This day is sacred to the **L**.
9: 5 "Stand up and praise the **L**, who is
Ps 76:11 Make vows to the **L** and fulfil them;

Ps 81:10 I am the **L**, who brought you up out
Isa 7:11 "Ask the **L** for a sign, whether in
37: 4 may be that the **L** will hear the
37: 4 him for the words the **L** has heard.
48:17 "I am the **L**, who teaches you what
51:15 For I am the **L**, who churns up the
55: 5 because of the **L**, the Holy One of
60: 9 the honour of the **L**, the Holy One
Jer 2:17 by forsaking the **L** when he led you
2:19 you forsake the **L** and have no awe
3:13 you have rebelled against the **L**,
13:16 Give glory to the **L** before he
26:13 and your actions and obey the **L**.
40: 2 "The **L** decreed this disaster for
42: 2 pray to the **L** for this entire
42: 3 Pray that the **L** will tell us where
42: 4 "I will certainly pray to the **L** as
42: 5 the **L** sends you to tell us.
42:13 in this land,' and so disobey the **L**
42:20 when you sent me to the **L** and said,
42:21 not obeyed the **L** in all he sent me
Eze 20: 5 hand I said to them, "I am the **L**.
20: 7 the idols of Egypt. I am the **L**."
20:19 I am the **L**; follow my decrees and
20:20 Then you will know that I am the **L**.
Hos 12: 9 "I am the **L**, who brought you out of
13: 4 "But I am the **L**, who brought you out
14: 1 Return, O Israel, to the **L**. Your
Joel 1:14 to the house of the **L**, and cry out
2:13 Return to the **L**, for he is gracious
2:14 and drink offerings for the **L**.
2:23 O people of Zion, rejoice in the **L**,
2:26 you will praise the name of the **L**,
2:27 that I am the **L**, and that there is
3:17 "Then you will know that I, the **L**,
Am 9:15 I have given them," says the **L**.
Mic 7:10 "Where is the **L**?" My eyes will see
Zep 3:17 The **L** is with you, he is mighty to
Zec 6:15 if you diligently obey the **L**."

LORD'S (LORD, *LORD'S anointed*)

Ge 4:16 Cain went out from the **L** presence
38: 7 was wicked in the **L** sight; so the
38:10 he did was wicked in the **L** sight
Ex 4:14 the **L** anger burned against Moses and
9:29 you may know that the earth is the **L**
12:11 it in haste; it is the **L** Passover.
12:41 day, all the **L** divisions left Egypt.
12:48 wants to celebrate the **L** Passover
16: 3 "If only we had died by the **L** hand
24: 3 the people all the **L** words and laws,
29:11 Slaughter it in the **L** presence at
34:34 whenever he entered the **L** presence
Lev 3:16 All the fat is the **L**.
4: 2 forbidden in any of the **L** commands
4:13 forbidden in any of the **L** commands,
4:27 any of the **L** commands, he is guilty.
5:15 regard to any of the **L** holy things,
5:17 forbidden in any of the **L** commands,
6:22 It is the **L** regular share and is to
10: 7 the **L** anointing oil is on you.
23: 4 "'These are the **L** appointed feasts,
23: 5 The **L** Passover begins at twilight on
23: 6 **L** Feast of Unleavened Bread begins;
23:34 the **L** Feast of Tabernacles begins,
23:37 'These are the **L** appointed feasts,
23:38 to those for the **L** Sabbaths
27:26 an ox or a sheep, it is the **L**
Nu 3:39 counted at the **L** command by Moses
4:37 to the **L** command through Moses.
4:41 them according to the **L** command.
4:45 to the **L** command through Moses.
4:49 At the **L** command through Moses, each
9: 7 kept from presenting the **L** offering
9:10 may still celebrate the **L** Passover.
9:13 he did not present the **L** offering
9:14 wants to celebrate the **L** Passover
9:18 At the **L** command the Israelites set
9:19 the **L** order and did not set out.
9:20 at the **L** command they would encamp,
9:23 At the **L** command they encamped, and
9:23 and at the **L** command they set out.
9:23 They obeyed the **L** order, in
10:13 at the **L** command through Moses.
Nu 11:23 "Is the **L** arm too short?
11:29 I wish that all the **L** people were
13: 3 at the **L** command Moses sent them out
14:41 are you disobeying the **L** command?
14:44 the **L** covenant moved from the camp.
15:23 any of the **L** commands to you through
15:31 he has despised the **L** word and
16: 3 yourselves above the **L** assembly?"
16: 9 to do the work at the **L** tabernacle
16:41 "You have killed the **L** people," they
17: 9 **L** presence to all the Israelites.
18:26 of that tithe as the **L** offering.
18:28 the **L** portion to Aaron the priest.
18:29 You must present as the **L** portion
19:13 himself defiles the **L** tabernacle.
20: 4 Why did you bring the **L** community
20: 9 took the staff from the **L** presence
25: 3 And the **L** anger burned against them.
25: 4 so that the **L** fierce anger may turn
27:17 so that the **L** people will not be
28:16 month the **L** Passover is to be held.
31: 3 carry out the **L** vengeance on them.
31:16 that a plague struck the **L** people.
31:29 to Eleazar the priest as the **L** part.
31:30 for the care of the **L** tabernacle."
31:41 as the **L** part, as the LORD commanded
31:47 for the care of the **L** tabernacle.
32:10 The **L** anger was aroused that day and
32:13 The **L** anger burned against Israel
33: 2 At the **L** command Moses recorded the
33:38 At the **L** command Aaron the priest
36: 5 at the **L** command Moses gave this
Dt 1:43 You rebelled against the **L** command
2:15 The **L** hand was against them until he
6:18 is right and good in the **L** sight
7: 4 and the **L** anger will burn against
9: 8 At Horeb you aroused the **L** wrath so
9:18 doing what was evil in the **L** sight
10:13 to observe the **L** commands and
11:17 the **L** anger will burn against you,
15: 2 because the **L** time for cancelling
18: 5 and minister in the **L** name always.
29:27 Therefore the **L** anger burned against
32: 9 For the **L** portion is his people,
33:21 he carried out the **L** righteous will,
Jos 5:15 The commander of the **L** army replied,
6: 8 ark of the **L** covenant followed them.
6:24 into the treasury of the **L** house.
7: 1 So the **L** anger burned against Israel
15:13 In accordance with the **L** command to
17: 4 father, according to the **L** command.
21:45 Not one of all the **L** good promises
22:19 the **L** land, where the **L** tabernacle
22:28 Look at the replica of the **L** altar,
22:31 the Israelites from the **L** hand."
23:16 the **L** anger will burn against you,
Jdg 2:17 way of obedience to the **L** commands.
3: 4 they would obey the **L** commands,
11:31 be the **L**, and I will sacrifice it
18: 6 Your journey has the **L** approval."
Ru 1:13 the **L** hand has gone out against me!"
1Sa 1: 9 by the doorpost of the **L** temple.
2: 8 foundations of the earth are the **L**
2:17 men was very great in the **L** sight,
2:17 the **L** offering with contempt.
2:24 I hear spreading among the **L** people.
2:25 was the **L** will to put them to death.
4: 3 ark of the **L** covenant from Shiloh,
4: 5 the ark of the **L** covenant came into
5: 6 The **L** hand was heavy upon the people
5: 9 the **L** hand was against that city
13:12 and I have not sought the **L** favour.
13:14 you have not kept the **L** command."
14: 3 son of Eli, the **L** priest in Shiloh.
15:13 carried out the **L** instructions."
15:24 I violated the **L** command and your
17:47 the battle is the **L**, and he will
25:28 because he fights the **L** battles.
26:19 my share in the **L** inheritance and
30:26 from the plunder of the **L** enemies."
2Sa 6: 7 The **L** anger burned against Uzzah
6: 8 because the **L** wrath had broken out
6:21 me ruler over the **L** people Israel
15:25 If I find favour in the **L** eyes, he
20:19 to swallow up the **L** inheritance?"
21: 3 you will bless the **L** inheritance?"
2Sa 21: 6 at Gibeah of Saul—the **L** chosen one
1Ki 2:33 may there be the **L** peace for ever."
7:48 that were in the **L** temple:
7:51 in the treasuries of the **L** temple.
8: 1 to bring up the ark of the **L**
8: 6 brought the ark of the **L** covenant
9:15 conscripted to build the **L** temple,
10: 9 Because of the **L** eternal love for
11:10 Solomon did not keep the **L** command.
14:28 the king went to the **L** temple, the
15: 5 any of the **L** commands all the days
15:18 the **L** temple and of his own palace.
18: 4 was killing off the **L** prophets,
18:13 of the **L** prophets in two caves,
18:18 You have abandoned the **L** commands
18:22 I am the only one of the **L** prophets
2Ki 9: 6 you king over the **L** people Israel.
9: 7 all the **L** servants shed by Jezebel.
11:17 that they would be the **L** people.
13: 3 the **L** anger burned against Israel,
13: 4 Jehoahaz sought the **L** favour, and
13:17 "The **L** arrow of victory, the arrow
20: 9 Isaiah answered, "This is the **L** sign
22:13 Great is the **L** anger that burns
24: 3 to Judah according to the **L** command,
24:20 was because of the **L** anger that all
1Ch 2: 3 was wicked in the **L** sight; so the
13:10 The **L** anger burned against Uzzah,
13:11 David was angry because the **L** wrath
2Ch 1: 3 **L** servant had made in the desert.
5: 2 bring up the ark of the **L** covenant
5: 7 brought the ark of the **L** covenant
7: 6 with the **L** musical instruments
12:11 the king went to the **L** temple,
12:12 the **L** anger turned from him, and he
15: 8 of the portico of the **L** temple.
16: 2 of the treasuries of the **L** temple
23:16 and the king would be the **L** people.
23:19 at the gates of the **L** temple
24:12 carpenters to restore the **L** temple,
24:14 were made articles for the **L** temple:
24:20 Why do you disobey the **L** commands?
24:21 in the courtyard of the **L** temple.
26:19 the incense altar in the **L** temple,
28:11 the **L** fierce anger rests on you."
28:24 He shut the doors of the **L** temple
29: 6 away from the **L** dwelling-place
29:16 out to the courtyard of the **L** temple
29:19 are now in front of the **L** altar."
30:21 by the **L** instruments of praise.
31: 2 at the gates of the **L** dwelling.
32:25 therefore the **L** wrath was on him and
32:26 therefore the **L** wrath did not come
34:10 supervise the work on the **L** temple.
34:21 Great is the **L** anger that is poured
35: 2 them in the service of the **L** temple.
36:18 and the treasures of the **L** temple
Ezr 3: 6 the **L** temple had not yet been laid.
Ps 24: 1 The earth is the **L**, and everything
32:10 but the **L** unfailing love surrounds
37:20 The **L** enemies will be like the
89: 1 I will sing of the **L** great love for
103:17 **L** love is with those who fear him
109:20 May this be the **L** payment to my
118:15 **L** right hand has done mighty things!
118:16 The **L** right hand is lifted high;
118:16 **L** right hand has done mighty things!
Pr 3:11 son, do not despise the **L** disciple
3:33 The **L** curse is on the house of the
19:21 it is the **L** purpose that prevails.
22:14 under the **L** wrath will fall into it.
Isa 2: 2 the mountain of the **L** temple will
5:25 Therefore the **L** anger burns against
14: 2 and maidservants in the **L** land.
24:14 the west they acclaim the **L** majesty.
30: 9 to listen to the **L** instruction.
38: 7 "'This is the **L** sign to you that
40: 2 received from the **L** hand double for
44: 5 will write on his hand, 'The **L**',
48:14 The **L** chosen ally will carry out his
49: 4 what is due to me is in the **L** hand
53:10 Yet it was the **L** will to crush him
55:13 This will be for the **L** renown, for
58:13 and the **L** holy day honourable,
61: 2 to proclaim the year of the **L** favour
62: 3 a crown of splendour in the **L** hand,

Jer 7: 2 “Stand at the gate of the **L** house
12:13 because of the **L** fierce anger.”
13:17 the **L** flock will be taken captive.
19:14 **L** temple and said to all the people,
20: 2 Gate of Benjamin at the **L** temple.
20: 3 “The **L** name for you is not Pashhur,
23:35 ‘What is the **L** answer?’ or ‘What has
23:37 ‘What is the **L** answer to you?’ or
25:17 I took the cup from the **L** hand and
25:38 and because of the **L** fierce anger.
26: 2 in the courtyard of the **L** house
26: 9 Why do you prophesy in the **L** name
26:10 of the New Gate of the **L** house.
27:16 the articles from the **L** house will
28: 3 all the articles of the **L** house
28: 6 the articles of the **L** house
36: 5 I cannot go to the **L** temple.
36: 8 at the **L** temple he read the words of
36:10 to all the people at the **L** temple
43: 4 people disobeyed the **L** command to
48:10 him who is lax in doing the **L** work!
50:13 of the **L** anger she will not be
51: 6 It is time for the **L** vengeance; he
51: 7 Babylon was a gold cup in the **L** hand
51:29 for the **L** purposes against Babylon
51:51 the holy places of the **L** house.”
52: 3 was because of the **L** anger that all
Lam 2:22 In the day of the **L** anger no-one
3:22 of the **L** great love we are not
Eze 7:19 save them in the day of the **L** wrath.
10:19 to the east gate of the **L** house,
36:20 ‘These are the **L** people, and yet
Hos 9: 3 They will not remain in the **L** land;
Joel 3:18 will flow out of the **L** house and
Ob :21 And the kingdom will be the **L**.
Mic 4: 1 the mountain of the **L** temple will
6: 2 Hear, O mountains, the **L** accusation;
7: 9 I will bear the **L** wrath, until he
Hab 2:16 **L** right hand is coming round to you,
Zep 1: 8 On the day of the **L** sacrifice I will
1:18 save them on the day of the **L** wrath.
2: 2 day of the **L** wrath comes upon you.
2: 3 sheltered on the day of the **L** anger.
Hag 1: 2 come for the **L** house to be built.
1:13 Haggai, the **L** messenger, gave this
2:15 was laid on another in the **L** temple.
2:18 foundation of the **L** temple was laid.
Zec 13: 3 you have told lies in the **L** name.
14:20 and the cooking pots in the **L** house
Mal 1: 7 that the **L** table is contemptible.
2:13 You flood the **L** altar with tears.

LORD's anointed

1Sa 16: 6 the **L** stands here before the LORD.”
24: 6 the **L**, or lift my hand against him;
24:10 my master, because he is the **L**.’
26: 9 a hand on the **L** and be guiltless?
26:11 that I should lay a hand on the **L**.
26:16 did not guard your master, the **L**.
26:23 but I would not lay a hand on the **L**.
2Sa 1:14 to lift your hand to destroy the **L**?”
1:16 you when you said, ‘I killed the **L**.
19:21 to death for this? He cursed the **L**.”
Lam 4:20 The **L**, our very life breath, was

Lord[1] ***(Angel of the Lord, Arm of the LORD, As the LORD commanded, Before the Lord, Covenant of the LORD, Day of the Lord, Declares the Lord, Fear of the LORD, Fear the LORD, Glory of the LORD, Hand of the LORD, I am the Lord, Know that the LORD, Law of the Lord, Lord Almighty, Lord God, Lord God Almighty, Lord Jesus, Lord Jesus Christ, Lord the king, Lord your God, Lord's, Lords[1], Love the Lord, Name of the Lord, Praise be to the LORD, Praise the LORD, Presence of the Lord, Sovereign Lord, Spirit of the Lord, Temple of the LORD, Voice of the LORD, Way of the Lord, Word of the Lord)***

Ge 18: 3 my **l**, do not pass your servant by.
18:27 been so bold as to speak to the **L**,
18:30 he said, “May the **L** not be angry,
18:31 been so bold as to speak to the **L**,
18:32 he said, “May the **L** not be angry,
20: 4 “**L**, will you destroy an innocent
23:11 “No, my **l**,” he said. “Listen to me;
23:15 “Listen to me, my **l**; the land is
24:18 “Drink, my **l**,” she said, and quickly
27:29 Be **l** over your brothers, and may the
27:37 “I have made him **l** over you and have
31:35 “Don't be angry, my **l**, that I cannot
32: 5 I am sending this message to my **l**,
32:18 They are a gift sent to my **l** Esau,
33: 8 favour in your eyes, my **l**,” he said.
33:13 Jacob said to him, “My **l** knows that
33:14 let my **l** go on ahead of his servant,
33:14 until I come to my **l** in Seir.”
33:15 me find favour in the eyes of my **l**.”
42:10 “No, my **l**,” they answered. “Your
42:30 “The man who is **l** over the land
42:33 “Then the man who is **l** over the land
44: 7 they said to him, “Why does my **l** say
44:16 “What can we say to my **l**?” Judah
44:18 “Please, my **l**, let your servant
44:18 your servant speak a word to my **l**.
44:19 My **l** asked his servants, ‘Do you
44:22 we said to my **l**, ‘The boy cannot
44:24 we told him what my **l** had said.
45: 8 **l** of his entire household and ruler
45: 9 God has made me **l** of all Egypt.
47:18 “We cannot hide from our **l** the fact
47:18 there is nothing left for our **l**
47:25 we find favour in the eyes of our **l**
Ex 4:10 Moses said to the LORD, “O **L**, I have
4:13 Moses said, “O **L**, please send
5:22 “O **L**, why have you brought trouble
15:17 the sanctuary, O **L**, your hands
32:22 “Do not be angry, my **l**,” Aaron
34: 9 “O **L**, if I have found favour in your
34: 9 he said, “then let the **L** go with us.
Nu 11:28 “Moses, my **l**, stop them!
12:11 he said to Moses, “Please, my **l**, do
32:25 servants will do as our **l** commands.
32:27 the LORD, just as our **l** says.”
36: 2 “When the LORD commanded my **l** to
Dt 10:17 God is God of gods and **L** of lords,
Jos 3:13 the **L** of all the earth—set foot in
5:14 does my **L** have for his servant?”
7: 8 O **L**, what can I say, now that Israel
Jdg 3:25 their **l** fallen to the floor, dead.
4:18 to him, “Come, my **l**, come right in.
6:15 “But **L**,” Gideon asked, “how can I
13: 8 Manoah prayed to the LORD: “O **L**, I
Ru 2:13 in your eyes, my **l**,” she said.
1Sa 1:15 “Not so, my **l**,” Hannah replied, “I
1:26 “As surely as you live, my **l**, I am
16:16 Let our **l** command his servants here
22:12 “Yes, my **l**,” he answered.
25:24 fell at his feet and said: “My **l**,
25:25 May my **l** pay no attention to that
26:18 he added, “Why is my **l** pursuing his
2Sa 1:10 and have brought them here to my **l**.
10: 3 nobles said to Hanun their **l**,
13:32 “My **l** should not think that they
14:20 My **l** has wisdom like that of an
19:19 said to him, “May my **l** not hold me
1Ki 1:11 without our **l** David's knowing it?
1:17 She said to him, “My **l**, you yourself
1:31 “May my **l** King David live for ever!
1:37 than the throne of my **l** King David!”
1:43 **l** King David has made Solomon king.
1:47 to congratulate our **l** King David,
3:10 The **L** was pleased that Solomon had
3:17 One of them said, “My **l**, this woman
3:26 “Please, my **l**, give her the living
12:27 to their **l**, Rehoboam king of Judah.
18: 7 “Is it really you, my **l** Elijah?
18:13 Haven't you heard, my **l**, what I did
22: 6 **L** will give it into the king's hand.
2Ki 2:19 “Look, our **l**, this town is well
4:16 “No, my **l**,” she objected. “Don't
4:28 “Did I ask you for a son, my **l**?” she
6: 5 “Oh, my **l**,” he cried out, “it was
6:15 “Oh, my **l**, what shall we do?” the
7: 6 for the **L** had caused the Arameans to
8:12 “Why is my **l** weeping?” asked Hazael.
19:23 you have heaped insults on the **L**.
1Ch 21: 3 Why does my **l** want to do this?
2Ch 2:14 those of my **l**, David your father.
2:15 “Now let my **l** send his servants the
Ezr 10: 3 accordance with the counsel of my **l**
Ne 1:11 O **L**, let your ear be attentive to
4:14 Remember the **L**, who is great and
8:10 This day is sacred to our **L**. Do not
10:29 and decrees of the LORD our **L**.
Ps 2: 4 heaven laughs; the **L** scoffs at them.
8: 1 O LORD, our **L**, how majestic is your
8: 9 O LORD, our **L**, how majestic is your
16: 2 I said to the LORD, “You are my **L**;
22:30 will be told about the **L**.
30: 8 to the **L** I cried for mercy:
35:17 O **L**, how long will you look on?
35:22 Do not be far from me, O **L**.
35:23 Contend for me, my God and **L**.
37:13 the **L** laughs at the wicked, for he
38: 9 my longings lie open before you, O **L**
38:15 O LORD; you will answer, O **L** my God.
38:22 quickly to help me, O **L** my Saviour
39: 7 “But now, **L**, what do I look for? My
40:17 and needy; may the **L** think of me.
44:23 Awake, O **L**! Why do you sleep? Rouse
45:11 honour him, for he is your **l**.
51:15 O **L**, open my lips, and my mouth will
54: 4 the **L** is the one who sustains me.
55: 9 Confuse the wicked, O **L**, confound
57: 9 I will praise you, O **L**, among the
59:11 do not kill them, O **L** our shield,
62:12 that you, O **L**, are loving. Surely
66:18 the **L** would not have listened;
68:11 The **L** announced the word, and great
68:17 the **L** has come from Sinai into his
68:22 The **L** says, “I will bring them from
68:32 earth, sing praise to the **L**,
69: 6 O **L**, the LORD Almighty; may those
73:20 so when you arise, O **L**, you will
77: 2 I was in distress, I sought the **L**;
77: 7 Will the **L** reject for ever? Will he
78:65 the **L** awoke as from sleep, as a man
79:12 they have hurled at you, O **L**.
86: 3 Have mercy on me, O **L**, for I call
86: 4 for to you, O **L**, I lift up my soul.
86: 5 You are forgiving and good, O **L**,
86: 8 gods there is none like you, O **L**;
86: 9 come and worship before you, O **L**;
86:12 I will praise you, O **L** my God, with
86:15 you, O **L**, are a compassionate and
89:49 O **L**, where is your former great love
89:50 Remember, **L**, how your servant has
90: 1 **L**, you have been our dwelling-place
90:17 favour of the **L** our God rest upon us
110: 1 The LORD says to my **L**: “Sit at my
110: 5 The **L** is at your right hand; he will
130: 2 O **L**, hear my voice. Let your ears be
130: 3 of sins, O **L**, who could stand?
130: 6 My soul waits for the **L** more than
135: 5 that our **L** is greater than all gods.
136: 3 Give thanks to the **L** of lords: His
147: 5 Great is our **L** and mighty in power;
Isa 1:24 Therefore the **L**, the LORD Almighty,
3: 1 See now, the **L**, the LORD Almighty,
3:17 Therefore the **L** will bring sores on
3:18 In that day the **L** will snatch away
4: 4 The **L** will wash away the filth of
6: 1 saw the **L** seated on a throne, high
6:11 I said, “For how long, O **L**?” And he
7:14 Therefore the **L** himself will give
7:20 In that day the **L** will use a razor
8: 7 therefore the **L** is about to bring
9: 8 The **L** has sent a message against
9:17 Therefore the **L** will take no
10:12 the **L** has finished all his work
10:16 Therefore, the **L**, the LORD Almighty
10:23 The **L**, the LORD Almighty, will carry
10:24 Therefore, this is what the **L**, the
10:33 See, the **L**, the LORD Almighty, will
11:11 In that day the **L** will reach out his
21: 6 This is what the **L** says to me: “Go,
21: 8 Day after day, my **l**, I stand on the
21:16 This is what the **L** says to me:
22: 5 The **L**, the LORD Almighty, has a day
22:12 The **L**, the LORD Almighty, called you
22:14 for,” says the **L**, the LORD Almighty.
22:15 This is what the **L**, the LORD
28: 2 See, the **L** has one who is powerful

Isa 28:22 **L**, the LORD Almighty, has told me
29:13 The **L** says: "These people come near
30:20 Although the **L** gives you the bread
37:24 you have heaped insults on the **L**.
38:14 I am troubled; O **L**, come to my aid!
38:16 **L**, by such things men live; and my
49:14 me, the **L** has forgotten me."
Jer 46:10 that day belongs to the **L**, the LORD
46:10 For the **L**, the LORD Almighty, will
Lam 1:14 and the **L** has sapped my strength.
1:15 "The **L** has rejected all the warriors
1:15 In his winepress the **L** has trampled
2: 1 How the **L** has covered the Daughter
2: 2 Without pity the **L** has swallowed up
2: 5 The **L** is like an enemy; he has
2: 7 The **L** has rejected his altar and
2:18 of the people cry out to the **L**.
2:20 be killed in the sanctuary of the **L**?
3:31 For men are not cast off by the **L**
3:36 would not the **L** see such things?
3:37 happen if the **L** has not decreed it?
3:58 O **L**, you took up my case; you
Eze 21: 9 'This is what the **L** says: "'A sword,
Da 1: 2 the **L** delivered Jehoiakim king of
2:47 the **L** of kings and a revealer of
4:19 Belteshazzar answered, "My **l**, if
5:23 yourself up against the **L** of heaven.
9: 4 O **L**, the great and awesome God, who
9: 7 "**L**, you are righteous, but this day
9: 9 The **L** our God is merciful and
9:15 Now, O **L** our God, who brought your
9:16 O **L**, in keeping with all your
9:17 For your sake, O **L**, look with favour
9:19 O **L**, listen! O **L**, forgive! O **L**, hear
10:16 the vision, my **l**, and I am helpless.
10:17 your servant, talk with you, my **l**?
10:19 "Speak, my **l**, since you have given
12: 8 So I asked, "My **l**, what will the
Hos 12:14 his **L** will leave upon him the guilt
Am 5:16 Therefore this is what the **L**, the
7: 7 the **L** was standing by a wall that
7: 8 the **L** said, "Look, I am setting
9: 1 I saw the **L** standing by the altar,
9: 5 The **L**, the LORD Almighty, he who
Mic 1: 2 you, the **L** from his holy temple.
4:13 wealth to the **L** of all the earth.
Zec 1: 9 I asked, "What are these, my **l**?"
4: 4 "What are these, my **l**?
4: 5 "No, my **l**," I replied.
4:13 "No, my **l**," I said.
4:14 to serve the **L** of all the earth."
6: 4 "What are these, my **l**?
9: 4 the **L** will take away her possessions
Mal 1:14 a blemished animal to the **L**.
3: 1 Then suddenly the **L** you are seeking
Mt 1:22 the **L** had said through the prophet:
2:15 so was fulfilled what the **L** had said
3: 3 'Prepare the way for the **L**, make
5:33 the oaths you have made to the **L**.'
7:21 Not everyone who says to me, '**L**, **L**,
7:22 '**L**, **L**, did we not prophesy in your
8: 2 "**L**, if you are willing, you can make
8: 6 "**L**," he said, "my servant lies at
8: 8 The centurion replied, "**L**, I do not
8:21 Another disciple said to him, "**L**,
8:25 "**L**, save us! We're going to drown!
9:28 "Yes, **L**," they replied.
9:38 Ask the **L** of the harvest, therefore,
11:25 "I praise you, Father, **L** of heaven
12: 8 Son of Man is **L** of the Sabbath
14:28 "**L**, if it's you," Peter replied,
14:30 to sink, cried out, "**L**, save me!"
15:22 "**L**, Son of David, have mercy on me!
15:25 "**L**, help me!" she said.
15:27 "Yes, **L**," she said, "but even the
16:22 "Never, **L**!" he said. "This shall
17: 4 Peter said to Jesus, "**L**, it is good
17:15 "**L**, have mercy on my son," he said.
18:21 Peter came to Jesus and asked, "**L**,
20:30 "**L**, Son of David, have mercy on us!
20:31 "**L**, Son of David, have mercy on us!
20:33 "**L**," they answered, "we want our
21: 3 tell him that the **L** needs them, and
21:42 the **L** has done this, and it is
22:43 Spirit, calls him '**L**'? For he says,
22:44 "'The **L** said to my **L**: "Sit at my
Mt 22:45 If then David calls him '**L**', how can
24:42 know on what day your **L** will come.
25:37 '**L**, when did we see you hungry and
25:44 "They also will answer, '**L**, when did
26:22 after the other, "Surely not I, **L**?
Mk 1: 3 'Prepare the way for the **L**, make
2:28 the Son of Man is **L** even of the
5:19 how much the **L** has done for you,
7:28 "Yes, **L**," she replied, "but even the
11: 3 'The **L** needs it and will send it
12:11 the **L** has done this, and it is
12:29 Israel, the **L** our God, the **L** is one.
12:36 'The **L** said to my **L**: "Sit at my
12:37 David himself calls him '**L**'. How
13:20 If the **L** had not cut short those
16:20 and the **L** worked with them and
Lk 1:15 will be great in the sight of the **L**
1:16 he bring back to the **L** their God.
1:17 ready a people prepared for the **L**."
1:25 "The **L** has done this for me," she
1:28 highly favoured! The **L** is with you."
1:43 mother of my **L** should come to me?
1:45 believed that what the **L** has said to
1:46 Mary said: "My soul glorifies the **L**
1:58 the **L** had shown her great mercy,
2:11 born to you; he is Christ the **L**.
2:15 which the **L** has told us about."
2:22 to Jerusalem to present him to the **L**
2:23 is to be consecrated to the **L**"),
3: 4 'Prepare the way for the **L**, make
5: 8 away from me, **L**; I am a sinful man!
5:12 "**L**, if you are willing, you can make
5:17 And the power of the **L** was present
6: 5 "The Son of Man is **L** of the Sabbath.
6:46 "Why do you call me, '**L**, **L**,' and do
7: 6 "**L**, don't trouble yourself, for I do
7:13 the **L** saw her, his heart went out to
7:19 he sent them to the **L** to ask, "Are
9:54 "**L**, do you want us to call fire down
9:59 But the man replied, "**L**, first let
9:61 "I will follow you, **L**; but first let
10: 1 the **L** appointed seventy-two others
10: 2 Ask the **L** of the harvest, therefore,
10:17 "**L**, even the demons submit to us in
10:21 "I praise you, Father, **L** of heaven
10:40 to him and asked, "**L**, don't you care
10:41 "Martha, Martha," the **L** answered,
11: 1 "**L**, teach us to pray, just as John
11:39 the **L** said to him, "Now then, you
12:41 Peter asked, "**L**, are you telling
12:42 The **L** answered, "Who then is the
13:15 The **L** answered him, "You hypocrites!
13:23 Someone asked him, "**L**, are only a
17: 5 The apostles said to the **L**,
17:37 "Where, **L**?" they asked. He replied,
18: 6 the **L** said, "Listen to what the
18:41 "**L**, I want to see," he replied.
19: 8 Zacchaeus stood up and said to the **L**
19: 8 "Look, **L**! Here and now I give half
19:31 tell him, 'The **L** needs it.
19:34 They replied, "The **L** needs it."
20:37 he calls the **L** 'the God of Abraham,
20:42 'The **L** said to my **L**: "Sit at my
20:44 David calls him '**L**'. How then can he
22:33 he replied, "**L**, I am ready to go
22:38 The disciples said, "See, **L**, here
22:49 **L**, should we strike with our swords?"
22:61 The **L** turned and looked straight at
22:61 remembered the word the **L** had spoken
24:34 saying, "It is true! The **L** has risen
Jn 1:23 'Make straight the way for the **L**.
4: 3 the **L** learned of this, he left Judea
6:23 bread after the **L** had given thanks.
6:68 Simon Peter answered him, "**L**, to
9:38 the man said, "**L**, I believe," and he
11: 2 poured perfume on the **L** and wiped
11: 3 the sisters sent word to Jesus, "**L**,
11:12 His disciples replied, "**L**, if he
11:21 "**L**," Martha said to Jesus, "if you
11:27 "Yes, **L**," she told him, "I believe
11:32 "**L**, if you had been here, my brother
11:34 "Come and see, **L**," they replied.
11:39 "But, **L**," said Martha, the sister of
12:38 "**L**, who has believed our message and
13: 6 "**L**, are you going to wash my feet?
13: 9 "Then, **L**," Simon Peter replied, "not
Jn 13:13 "You call me 'Teacher' and '**L**', and
13:14 Now that I, your **L** and Teacher, have
13:25 he asked him, "**L**, who is it?
13:36 Simon Peter asked him, "**L**, where are
13:37 Peter asked, "**L**, why can't I follow
14: 5 Thomas said to him, "**L**, we don't
14: 8 Philip said, "**L**, show us the Father
14:22 "But, **L**, why do you intend to show
20: 2 "They have taken the **L** out of the
20:13 "They have taken my **L** away," she
20:18 "I have seen the **L**!" And she told
20:20 were overjoyed when they saw the **L**.
20:25 "We have seen the **L**!" But he said to
20:28 Thomas said to him, "My **L** and my God!
21: 7 "It is the **L**!" As soon as Simon
21: 7 "It is the **L**," he wrapped his outer
21:12 Who are you?" They knew it was the **L**.
21:15 "Yes, **L**," he said, "you know that I
21:16 "Yes, **L**, you know that I love you.
21:17 "Do you love me?" He said, "**L**, you
21:20 "**L**, who is going to betray you?"
21:21 Peter saw him, he asked, "**L**, what
Ac 1: 6 "**L**, are you at this time going to
1:24 they prayed, "**L**, you know everyone's
2:25 David said about him: "'I saw the **L**
2:34 'The **L** said to my **L**: "Sit at my
2:36 you crucified, both **L** and Christ."
2:39 all whom the **L** our God will call."
2:47 And the **L** added to their number
3:19 of refreshing may come from the **L**,
4:26 **L** and against his Anointed One.',
4:29 Now, **L**, consider their threats and
5:14 believed in the **L** and were added to
7:33 "Then the **L** said to him, 'Take off
7:49 will you build for me? says the **L**.
7:60 **L**, do not hold this sin against them
8:22 this wickedness and pray to the **L**.
8:24 Simon answered, "Pray to the **L** for
9: 5 "Who are you, **L**?" Saul asked.
9:10 The **L** called to him in a vision,
9:10 "Ananias!" "Yes, **L**," he answered.
9:11 The **L** told him, "Go to the house of
9:13 "**L**," Ananias answered, "I have heard
9:15 the **L** said to Ananias, "Go! This man
9:27 seen the **L** and that the **L** had spoken
9:31 living in the fear of the **L**.
9:35 Sharon saw him and turned to the **L**.
9:42 and many people believed in the **L**.
10: 4 What is it, **L**?" he asked. The angel
10:14 "Surely not, **L**!" Peter replied. "I
10:33 the **L** has commanded you to tell us.
10:36 Jesus Christ, who is **L** of all.
11: 8 "I replied, 'Surely not, **L**! Nothing
11:16 I remembered what the **L** had said:
11:21 people believed and turned to the **L**.
11:23 true to the **L** with all their hearts.
11:24 of people were brought to the **L**.
12:11 a doubt that the **L** sent his angel
12:17 the **L** had brought him out of prison.
13: 2 While they were worshipping the **L**
13:10 perverting the right ways of the **L**?
13:12 amazed at the teaching about the **L**.
13:47 For this is what the **L** has commanded
14: 3 speaking boldly for the **L**, who
14:23 committed them to the **L**, in whom
15:17 the remnant of men may seek the **L**,
15:17 says the **L**, who does these things'
15:40 the brothers to the grace of the **L**.
16:14 The **L** opened her heart to respond to
16:15 consider me a believer in the **L**,"
17:24 everything in it is the **L** of heaven
18: 8 entire household believed in the **L**;
18: 9 One night the **L** spoke to Paul in a
20:19 I served the **L** with great humility
22: 8 "'Who are you, **L**?' I asked.
22:10 "'What shall I do, **L**?' I asked.
22:10 "'Get up,' the **L** said, 'and go into
22:18 saw the **L** speaking. 'Quick!' he said
22:19 "'**L**,' I replied, 'these men know
22:21 "Then the **L** said to me, 'Go; I will
23:11 The following night the **L** stood near
26:15 "Then I asked, 'Who are you, **L**?'
26:15 you are persecuting,' the **L** replied.
Ro 1: 4 from the dead: Jesus Christ our **L**.
4: 8 whose sin the **L** will never count
4:24 raised Jesus our **L** from the dead.

Ro 5:21 life through Jesus Christ our **L.**
6:23 eternal life in Christ Jesus our **L.**
7:25 Jesus Christ our **L**! So then,
8:39 God that is in Christ Jesus our **L.**
9:28 For the **L** will carry out his
10: 9 "Jesus is **L**," and believe in your
10:12 the same **L** is **L** of all and richly
10:16 Isaiah says, "**L**, who has believed
11: 3 "**L**, they have killed your prophets
11:34 "Who has known the mind of the **L**?
12:11 spiritual fervour, serving the **L.**
12:19 avenge; I will repay," says the **L.**
14: 4 for the **L** is able to make him stand.
14: 6 day as special, does so to the **L.**
14: 6 He who eats meat, eats to the **L**, for
14: 6 so to the **L** and gives thanks to God.
14: 8 If we live, we live to the **L**;
14: 8 and if we die, we die to the **L.**
14: 9 **L** of both the dead and the living.
14:11 'As surely as I live,' says the **L**,
16: 2 I ask you to receive her in the **L** in
16: 8 Ampliatus, whom I love in the **L.**
16:11 of Narcissus who are in the **L.**
16:12 those women who work hard in the **L.**
16:12 who has worked very hard in the **L.**
16:13 Greet Rufus, chosen in the **L**, and
16:18 such people are not serving our **L**
16:22 this letter, greet you in the **L.**
1Co 1: 2 Jesus Christ—their **L** and ours:
1: 9 Son Jesus Christ our **L**, is faithful.
1:31 "Let him who boasts boast in the **L.**
2: 8 not have crucified the **L** of glory.
2:16 For who has known the mind of the **L**
3: 5 the **L** has assigned to each his task.
3:20 "The **L** knows that the thoughts of
4: 4 It is the **L** who judges me.
4: 5 wait till the **L** comes. He will bring
4:17 I love, who is faithful in the **L.**
4:19 if the **L** is willing, and then I will
6:13 for the **L**, and the **L** for the body.
6:14 God raised the **L** from the dead,
6:17 he who unites himself with the **L** is
7:10 (not I, but the **L**): A wife must not
7:12 To the rest I say this (I, not the **L**
7:17 in life that the **L** assigned to him
7:22 by the **L** is the Lord's freedman;
7:25 I have no command from the **L**,
7:32 affairs—how he can please the **L.**
7:34 to the **L** in both body and spirit.
7:35 way in undivided devotion to the **L.**
7:39 wishes, but he must belong to the **L.**
8: 6 there is but one **L**, Jesus Christ,
9: 1 Have I not seen Jesus our **L**? Are you
9: 1 not the result of my work in the **L**?
9: 2 the seal of my apostleship in the **L.**
9:14 In the same way, the **L** has commanded
10: 9 We should not test the **L**, as some of
10:21 You cannot drink the cup of the **L**
11:11 In the **L**, however, woman is not
11:23 For I received from the **L** what I
11:27 or drinks the cup of the **L** in an
11:27 against the body and blood of the **L**
11:29 recognising the body of the **L** eats
11:32 we are judged by the **L**, we are being
12: 3 no-one can say "Jesus is **L**," except
12: 5 kinds of service, but the same **L.**
14:21 will not listen to me," says the **L.**
15:31 over you in Christ Jesus our **L.**
15:58 fully to the work of the **L**,
15:58 your labour in the **L** is not in vain.
16: 7 time with you, if the **L** permits.
16:10 on the work of the **L**, just as I am.
16:19 Priscilla greet you warmly in the **L**,
16:22 If anyone does not love the **L**—
16:22 a curse be on him. Come, O **L**!
2Co 2:12 that the **L** had opened a door for me,
3:16 whenever anyone turns to the **L**, the
3:17 Now the **L** is the Spirit, and where
3:18 comes from the **L**, who is the Spirit.
4: 5 but Jesus Christ as **L**, and ourselves
5: 6 in the body we are away from the **L.**
5: 8 the body and at home with the **L.**
6:17 them and be separate, says the **L.**
8: 5 they gave themselves first to the **L**
8:19 in order to honour the **L** himself
8:21 not only in they eyes of the **L** but
2Co 10: 8 about the authority the **L** gave us
10:17 "Let him who boasts boast in the **L.**
10:18 but the one whom the **L** commends.
11:17 as the **L** would, but as a fool.
12: 1 visions and revelations from the **L.**
12: 8 Three times I pleaded with the **L** to
13:10 the **L** gave me for building you up,
Gal 5:10 I am confident in the **L** that you
Eph 2:21 to become a holy temple in the **L.**
3:11 accomplished in Christ Jesus our **L.**
4: 1 a prisoner for the **L**, then, I urge
4: 5 one **L**, one faith, one baptism;
4:17 and insist on it in the **L**, that you
5: 8 but now you are light in the **L.**
5:10 find out what pleases the **L.**
5:19 make music in your heart to the **L**,
5:22 submit to your husbands as to the **L.**
6: 1 Children, obey your parents in the **L**
6: 4 training and instruction of the **L.**
6: 7 if you were serving the **L**, not men,
6:10 Finally, be strong in the **L** and in
6:21 and faithful servant in the **L**,
Php 1:14 most of the brothers in the **L** have
2:11 confess that Jesus Christ is **L**, to
2:24 I am confident in the **L** that I
2:29 Welcome him in the **L** with great joy,
3: 1 my brothers, rejoice in the **L**! It is
3: 8 of knowing Christ Jesus my **L**,
4: 1 stand firm in the **L**, dear friends!
4: 2 to agree with each other in the **L.**
4: 4 Rejoice in the **L** always. I will say
4: 5 The **L** is near.
4:10 I rejoice greatly in the **L** that at
Col 1:10 you may live a life worthy of the **L**
2: 6 as you received Christ Jesus as **L**
3:13 Forgive as the **L** forgave you.
3:18 husbands, as is fitting in the **L.**
3:20 everything, for this pleases the **L.**
3:22 of heart and reverence for the **L.**
3:23 as working for the **L**, not for men,
3:24 inheritance from the **L** as a reward.
3:24 It is the **L** Christ you are serving.
4: 7 and fellow-servant in the **L.**
4:17 work you have received in the **L.**"
1Th 1: 6 become imitators of us and of the **L**
3: 8 you are standing firm in the **L.**
3:12 May the **L** make your love increase
4: 6 The **L** will punish men for all such
4:15 are left till the coming of the **L**,
4:16 For the **L** himself will come down
4:17 the clouds to meet the **L** in the air
4:17 so we will be with the **L** for ever.
5:12 you in the **L** and who admonish you.
2Th 2:13 brothers loved by the **L**, because
3: 1 that the message of the **L** may spread
3: 3 the **L** is faithful, and he will
3: 4 We have confidence in the **L** that you
3: 5 May the **L** direct your hearts into
3:16 Now may the **L** of peace himself give
3:16 The **L** be with all of you.
1Ti 1: 2 the Father and Christ Jesus our **L.**
1:12 I thank Christ Jesus our **L**, who has
1:14 The grace of our **L** was poured out on
6:15 the King of kings and **L** of lords,
2Ti 1: 2 the Father and Christ Jesus our **L.**
1: 8 ashamed to testify about our **L**, or
1:16 May the **L** show mercy to the
1:18 May the **L** grant that he will find
1:18 find mercy from the **L** on that day!
2: 7 for the **L** will give you insight into
2:19 **L** must turn away from wickedness."
2:22 call on the **L** out of a pure heart.
3:11 the **L** rescued me from all of them.
4: 8 which the **L**, the righteous Judge,
4:14 The **L** will repay him for what he has
4:17 the **L** stood at my side and gave me
4:18 The **L** will rescue me from every evil
4:22 The **L** be with your spirit. Grace be
Phm :16 as a man and as a brother in the **L.**
:20 have some benefit from you in the **L**;
Heb 1:10 also says, "In the beginning, O **L**,
2: 3 which was first announced by the **L**,
7:14 For it is clear that our **L** descended
7:21 "The **L** has sworn and will not change
8: 2 set up by the **L**, not by man.
8:11 'Know the **L**,' because they will all
Heb 10:16 them after that time, says the **L.**
10:30 again, "The **L** will judge his people.
12: 6 the **L** disciplines those he loves,
12:14 holiness no-one will see the **L.**
13: 6 we say with confidence, "The **L** is my
Jas 1: 7 he will receive anything from the **L**;
3: 9 With the tongue we praise our **L** and
5:11 what the **L** finally brought about.
5:11 **L** is full of compassion and mercy.
5:15 the **L** will raise him up.
1Pe 2: 3 you have tasted that the **L** is good.
3:12 For the eyes of the **L** are on the
3:12 the **L** is against those who do evil."
3:15 in your hearts set apart Christ as **L**
2Pe 1: 2 knowledge of God and of Jesus our **L.**
1:11 of our **L** and Saviour Jesus Christ.
2: 9 if this is so, then the **L** knows how
2:20 of the world by knowing our **L**
3: 2 command given by your **L** and Saviour
3: 8 dear friends: With the **L** a day is
3: 9 The **L** is not slow in keeping his
3:18 of our **L** and Saviour Jesus Christ.
Jude : 4 Christ our only Sovereign and **L.**
: 5 I want to remind you that the **L**
: 9 but said, "The **L** rebuke you!"
:14 See, the **L** is coming with thousands
:25 through Jesus Christ our **L**, before
Rev 4:11 "You are worthy, our **L** and God, to
11: 8 where also their **L** was crucified.
11:15 kingdom of our **L** and of his Christ,
14:13 dead who die in the **L** from now on.
15: 4 Who will not fear you, O **L**, and
17:14 them because he is **L** of lords
19:16 KING OF KINGS AND **L** OF LORDS.
22: 6 The **L**, the God of the spirits of the

Lord Almighty

Ro 9:29 "Unless the **L** had left us
2Co 6:18 my sons and daughters, says the **L.**"
Jas 5: 4 have reached the ears of the **L.**

Lord God (*Lord God Almighty*)

Da 9: 3 I turned to the **L** and pleaded with
Lk 1:32 The **L** will give him the throne of
Rev 1: 8 Alpha and the Omega," says the **L**,
18: 8 for mighty is the **L** who judges her.
22: 5 for the **L** will give them light.

Lord God Almighty

Rev 4: 8 **L**, who was, and is, and is to come."
11:17 saying: "We give thanks to you, **L**,
15: 3 and marvellous are your deeds, **L.**
16: 7 I heard the altar respond: "Yes, **L**,
19: 6 "Hallelujah! For our **L** reigns.
21:22 the **L** and the Lamb are its temple.

Lord Jesus (*Lord Jesus Christ*)

Mk 16:19 After the **L** had spoken to them, he
Lk 24: 3 they did not find the body of the **L.**
Ac 1:21 time the **L** went in and out among us,
4:33 to the resurrection of the **L**,
7:59 prayed, "**L**, receive my spirit.
8:16 baptised into the name of the **L.**
11:20 them the good news about the **L.**
15:11 grace of our **L** that we are saved,
16:31 They replied, "Believe in the **L**,
19: 5 baptised into the name of the **L.**
19:13 tried to invoke the name of the **L**
19:17 name of the **L** was held in high
20:21 repentance and have faith in our **L.**
20:24 complete the task the **L** has given me
20:35 the words the **L** himself said: it is
21:13 in Jerusalem for the name of the **L.**
Ro 14:14 one who is in the **L**, I am fully
16:20 The grace of our **L** be with you.
1Co 5: 4 assembled in the name of our **L**
5: 4 and the power of our **L** is present,
11:23 The **L**, on the night he was betrayed
16:23 The grace of the **L** be with you.
2Co 1:14 boast of you in the day of the **L.**
4:14 know that the one who raised the **L**
11:31 The God and Father of the **L**, who is
Eph 1:15 your faith in the **L** and your love
Php 2:19 I hope in the **L** to send Timothy to

Col 3:17 do it all in the name of the **L**,
1Th 2:15 who killed the **L** and the prophets
2:19 presence of our **L** when he comes?
3:11 Father himself and our **L** clear the
3:13 our **L** comes with all his holy ones.
4: 1 urge you in the **L** to do this more
4: 2 gave you by the authority of the **L**.
2Th 1: 7 will happen when the **L** is revealed
1: 8 and do not obey the gospel of our **L**.
1:12 of our **L** may be glorified in you,
2: 8 whom the **L** will overthrow with the
Phm : 5 I hear about your faith in the **L** and
Heb 13:20 **L**, that great Shepherd of the sheep,
Rev 22:20 Amen. Come, **L**.
22:21 The grace of the **L** be with God's

Lord Jesus Christ

Ac 11:17 who believed in the **L**, who was I to
15:26 their lives for the name of our **L**.
28:31 of God and taught about the **L**.
Ro 1: 7 from God our Father and from the **L**.
5: 1 have peace with God through our **L**,
5:11 also rejoice in God through our **L**,
13:14 Rather, clothe yourselves with the **L**
15: 6 glorify the God and Father of our **L**.
15:30 I urge you, brothers, by our **L** and
1Co 1: 2 justified in the name of our **L**—
1: 3 you from God our Father and the **L**.
1: 7 wait for our **L** to be revealed.
1: 8 be blameless on the day of our **L**.
1:10 brothers, in the name of our **L**, that
6:11 justified in the name of the **L**
15:57 gives us the victory through our **L**.
2Co 1: 2 you from God our Father and the **L**.
1: 3 be to the God and Father of our **L**,
8: 9 For you know the grace of our **L**,
13:14 May the grace of the **L**, and the
Gal 1: 3 you from God our Father and the **L**,
6:14 boast except in the cross of our **L**,
6:18 The grace of our **L** be with your
Eph 1: 2 you from God our Father and the **L**.
1: 3 be to the God and Father of our **L**,
1:17 keep asking that the God of our **L**,
5:20 everything, in the name of our **L**.
6:23 faith from God the Father and the **L**
6:24 who love our **L** with an undying love
Php 1: 2 you from God our Father and the **L**.
3:20 await a Saviour from there, the **L**,
4:23 The grace of the **L** be with your
Col 1: 3 thank God, the Father of our **L**,
1Th 1: 1 in God the Father and the **L**: Grace
1: 3 endurance inspired by hope in our **L**
5: 9 to receive salvation through our **L**.
5:23 blameless at the coming of our **L**.
5:28 The grace of our **L** be with you.
2Th 1: 1 in God our Father and the **L**:
1: 2 you from God the Father and the **L**.
1:12 to the grace of our God and the **L**.
2: 1 Concerning the coming of our **L** and
2:14 might share in the glory of our **L**.
2:16 May our **L** himself and God our Father
3: 6 In the name of the **L**, we command you
3:12 urge in the **L** to settle down and
3:18 The grace of our **L** be with you all.
1Ti 6: 3 to the sound instruction of our **L**
6:14 blame until the appearing of our **L**,
Phm : 3 peace from God our Father and the **L**.
:25 The grace of the **L** be with your
Jas 1: 1 James, a servant of God and of the **L**
2: 1 as believers in our glorious **L**,
1Pe 1: 3 be to the God and Father of our **L**!
2Pe 1: 8 in your knowledge of our **L**.
1:14 as our **L** has made clear to me.
1:16 about the power and coming of our **L**,
Jude :17 what the apostles of our **L** foretold.
:21 for the mercy of our **L** to bring you

Lord the king

1Sa 24: 8 came and called out to Saul, "My **l**
26:15 Why didn't you guard your **l**?
26:15 Someone came to destroy your **l**.
26:17 David replied, "Yes it is, my **l**.
26:19 Now let my **l** listen to his servant's
29: 8 fight against the enemies of my **l**?"
2Sa 3:21 and assemble all Israel for my **l**,
4: 8 This day the LORD has avenged my **l**
9:11 "Your servant will do whatever my **l**
13:33 My **l** should not be concerned about
14: 9 "My **l**, let the blame rest on me and
14:12 your servant speak a word to my **l**
14:15 I have come to say this to my **l**
14:17 May the word of my **l** bring me rest,
14:17 for my **l** is like an angel of God.
14:18 "Let my **l** speak," the woman said.
14:19 "As surely as you live, my **l**,
14:19 to the left from anything my **l** says
14:22 has found favour in your eyes, my **l**
15:15 ready to do whatever our **l** chooses."
15:21 as my **l** lives, wherever my **l** may be
16: 4 May I find favour in your eyes, my **l**
16: 9 "Why should this dead dog curse my **l**
18:28 who lifted their hands against my **l**
18:31 the Cushite arrived and said, "My **l**
18:32 "May the enemies of my **l** and all
19:19 on the day my **l** left Jerusalem.
19:20 to come down and meet my **l**."
19:26 He said, "My **l**, since I your servant
19:27 has slandered your servant to my **l**
19:27 My **l** is like an angel of God;
19:28 deserved nothing but death from my **l**
19:30 **l** the king has arrived home safely."
19:35 servant be an added burden to my **l**?
19:37 Let him cross over with my **l**.
24: 3 and may the eyes of my **l** see it.
24: 3 does my **l** want to do such a thing?"
24:21 Araunah said, "Why has my **l** come to
24:22 Araunah said to David, "Let my **l**
1Ki 1: 2 So that our **l** may keep warm."
1:13 'My **l**, did you not swear to me your
1:18 and you, my **l**, do not know about it.
1:20 My **l**, the eyes of all Israel are on
1:20 sit on the throne of my **l** after him
1:21 as soon as my **l** is laid to rest
1:24 Nathan said, "Have you, my **l**,
1:27 Is this something my **l** has done
1:27 on the throne of my **l** after him?"
1:36 LORD, the God of my **l**, so declare it.
1:37 the LORD was with my **l**, so may he be
2:38 servant will do as my **l** has said
20: 4 answered, "Just as you say, my **l**
20: 9 "Tell my **l**, 'Your servant will do
2Ki 6:12 "None of us, my **l**," said one of his
6:26 cried to him, "Help me, my **l**!
8: 5 "This is the woman, my **l**, and this
1Ch 21: 3 My **l**, are they not all my lord's
21:23 Let my **l** do whatever pleases him.
Jer 37:20 now, my **l**, please listen. Let me
38: 9 "My **l**, these men have acted wickedly
Da 1:10 "I am afraid of my **l**, who has
4:24 Most High has issued against my **l**

Lord your God

Mt 4: 7 'Do not put the **L** to the test.'"
4:10 the **L**, and serve him only.'"
22:37 Jesus replied: "'Love the **L** with
Mk 12:30 Love the **L** with all your heart and
Lk 4: 8 'Worship the **L** and serve him only.'"
4:12 'Do not put the **L** to the test.'"
10:27 He answered: "'Love the **L** with all
Ac 3:22 For Moses said, 'The **L** will raise up

Lord's (Lord)

Ge 44: 9 rest of us will become my **l** slaves."
44:16 We are now my **l** slaves—we ourselves
44:33 as my **l** slave in place of the boy,
Nu 14:17 "Now may the **L** strength be displayed,
2Sa 11:11 **l** men are camped in the open fields.
1Ki 1:33 to them: "Take your **l** servants with
3:15 before the ark of the **L** covenant
1Ch 21: 3 are they not all my **l** subjects? Why
Mal 1:12 profane it by saying of the **L** table,
Lk 1: 6 observing all the **L** commandments and
1:38 "I am the **L** servant," Mary answered.
1:66 to be?" For the **L** hand was with him.
2:26 die before he had seen the **L** Christ.
4:19 to proclaim the year of the **L** favour.
10:39 sat at the **L** feet listening to what
Ac 7:31 more closely, he heard the **L** voice:
9: 1 threats against the **L** disciples.
11:21 The **L** hand was with them, and a
21:14 up and said, "The **L** will be done.
1Co 7:22 by the Lord is the **L** freedman;
7:25 who by the **L** mercy is trustworthy.
7:32 is concerned about the **L** affairs
7:34 is concerned about the **L** affairs:
9: 5 and the **L** brothers and Cephas?
10:21 the **L** table and the table of demons.
10:22 we trying to arouse the **L** jealousy?
10:26 "The earth is the **L**, and
11:20 it is not the **L** Supper you eat,
11:26 proclaim the **L** death until he comes.
14:37 I am writing to you is the **L** command.
2Co 3:18 faces all reflect the **L** glory,
Gal 1:19 apostles—only James, the **L** brother.
Eph 5:17 but understand what the **L** will is.
1Th 1: 8 The **L** message rang out from you not
4:15 According to the **L** own word, we tell
2Ti 2:24 the **L** servant must not quarrel;
Heb 12: 5 not make light of the **L** discipline
Jas 4:15 "If it is the **L** will, we will live
5: 7 then, brothers, until the **L** coming.
5: 8 firm, because the **L** coming is near.
1Pe 2:13 Submit yourselves for the **L** sake to
2Pe 3:15 Bear in mind that our **L** patience
Rev 1:10 On the **L** Day I was in the Spirit,

Lord[2] (Lorded, Lording, Lords[2])

Nu 16:13 now you also want to **l** it over us?
Mt 20:25 rulers of the Gentiles **l** it over them
Mk 10:42 as rulers of the Gentiles **l** it over
Lk 22:25 kings of the Gentiles **l** it over them
2Co 1:24 Not that we **l** it over your faith,

Lorded (Lord[2])

Ne 5:15 Their assistants also **l** it over the

Lording (Lord[2])

1Pe 5: 3 not **l** it over those entrusted to you,

Lords[1] (Lord[1])

Ge 19: 2 "My **l**," he said, "please turn aside
19:18 Lot said to them, "No, my **l**, please!
Dt 10:17 God is God of gods and Lord of **l**,
Ps 136: 3 Give thanks to the Lord of **l**: His
Isa 26:13 O LORD, our God, other **l** besides you
1Co 8: 5 there are many "gods" and many "**l**")
1Ti 6:15 the King of kings and Lord of **l**,
Rev 17:14 them because he is Lord of **l**
19:16 KING OF KINGS AND LORD OF **L**.

Lords[2] (Lord[2])

Ecc 8: 9 a man **l** it over others to his own

Lo-Ruhamah

Hos 1: 6 "Call her **L**, for I will no longer
1: 8 After she had weaned **L**, Gomer had

Lose (Loses, Loss, Losses, Lost)

Ge 26: 9 I might **l** my life on account of her."
27:45 should I **l** both of you in one day?"
Dt 1:28 Our brothers have made us **l** heart.
Jdg 18:25 and your family will **l** your lives."
1Sa 17:32 said to Saul, "Let no-one **l** heart
2Sa 22:46 They all **l** heart; they come
Ps 18:45 They all **l** heart; they come
Pr 25:10 will never **l** your bad reputation.
Isa 7: 4 Do not **l** heart because of these two
19: 3 The Egyptians will **l** heart, and I
19: 9 weavers of fine linen will **l** hope.
Jer 4: 9 king and the officials will **l** heart
17: 4 own fault you will **l** the inheritance
51:46 Do not **l** heart or be afraid when
Da 11:30 oppose him, and he will **l** heart.
Zec 9: 5 Gaza will **l** her king and Ashkelon
Mt 5:29 It is better for you to **l** one part
5:30 It is better for you to **l** one part
10:39 Whoever finds his life will **l** it,
10:42 he will certainly not **l** his reward."
16:25 wants to save his life will **l** it,
Mk 8:35 wants to save his life will **l** it,
9:41 will certainly not **l** his reward.
Lk 9:24 wants to save his life will **l** it,
9:25 and yet **l** or forfeit his very self?
16: 4 what I'll do so that, when I **l** my job

Lk 17:33 tries to keep his life will l it,
Jn 6:39 that I shall l none of all that he
12:25 The man who loves his life will l it,
Ac 19:27 that our trade will l its good name,
27:34 will l a single hair from his head."
2Co 4: 1 this ministry, we do not l heart.
4:16 Therefore we do not l heart. Though
Heb 12: 3 you will not grow weary and l heart.
12: 5 do not l heart when he rebukes you,
2Jn : 8 Watch out that you do not l what you

Loses (Lose)
Dt 22: 3 or his cloak or anything he l.
1Sa 20: 7 But if he l his temper, you can be
Isa 44:12 He gets hungry and l his strength;
Mt 5:13 But if the salt l its saltiness, how
10:39 l his life for my sake will find it.
16:25 l his life for me will find it.
Mk 8:35 but whoever l his life for me and
9:50 "Salt is good, but if it l its
Lk 9:24 l his life for me will save it.
14:34 "Salt is good, but if it l its
15: 4 a hundred sheep and l one of them.
15: 8 has ten silver coins and l one.
17:33 whoever l his life will preserve it.

Loss (Lose)
Ge 31:39 by wild beasts; I bore the l myself
Ex 21:19 injured man for the l of his time
21:34 of the pit must pay for the l;
22:15 paid for the hire covers the l.
Isa 47: 8 widow or suffer the l of children.'
47: 9 l of children and widowhood.
Jer 22:10 for the dead ⌊king⌋ or mourn his l;
Da 6: 2 that the king might not suffer l.
Jn 11:19 them in the l of their brother.
13:22 a l to know which of them he meant.
Ac 25:20 I was at a l how to investigate such
27:10 and bring great l to ship and cargo,
27:21 spared yourselves this damage and l.
Ro 11:12 and their l means riches for the
1Co 3:15 it is burned up, he will suffer l;
Php 3: 7 consider l for the sake of Christ.
3: 8 I consider everything a l compared
Heb 6: 6 because to their l they are

Losses (Lose)
1Sa 4:17 and the army has suffered heavy l.
23: 5 He inflicted heavy l on the
1Ki 20:21 inflicted heavy l on the Arameans.
2Ch 13:17 his men inflicted heavy l on them,

Lost (Lose)
Ge 34:19 l no time in doing what they said,
Ex 14: 5 go and have l their services!"
22: 9 a garment, or any other l property
Lev 6: 3 or if he finds l property and lies
6: 4 to him, or the l property he found,
13:40 "When a man has l his hair and is
13:41 If he has l his hair from the front
Nu 11: 6 now we have l our appetite; we never
17:12 We shall die! We are l, we are all l!
1Sa 4:10 l thirty thousand foot soldiers.
9: 3 to Saul's father Kish were l,
9:20 for the donkeys you l three days ago
25:18 Abigail l no time. She took two
2Sa 4: 1 he l courage, and all Israel became
1Ki 20:25 like the one you l—horse for horse
Ne 6:16 afraid and l their self-confidence,
Ps 73: 2 slipped; I had nearly l my foothold
119:176 I have strayed like a l sheep.
Ecc 5:14 or wealth l through some misfortune
Jer 18:18 the law by the priest will not be l
50: 6 "My people have been l sheep; their
Lam 4: 1 How the gold has l its lustre, the
Eze 7:26 of the law by the priest will be l,
34: 4 the strays or searched for the l.
34:16 I will search for the l and bring
Zec 11:16 land who will not care for the l,
Mt 10: 6 Go rather to the l sheep of Israel.
15:24 sent only to the l sheep of Israel.
18:14 of these little ones should be l.
Lk 15: 4 after the l sheep until he finds it
15: 6 with me; I have found my l sheep.'
Lk 15: 9 with me; I have found my l coin.'
15:24 alive again; he was l and is found
15:32 alive again; he was l and is found
19:10 to seek and to save what was l."
Jn 17:12 None has been l except the one
18: 9 not l one of those you gave me."
Ac 27: 9 Much time had been l, and sailing
27:22 because not one of you will be l;
1Co 15:18 have fallen asleep in Christ are l.
Eph 4:19 Having l all sensitivity, they have
Php 3: 8 for whose sake I have l all things.
Col 2:19 He has l connection with the Head,
Rev 12: 8 and they l their place in heaven.

Lot[1] (Lot's)
Nephew of Abraham (Ge 11:27); accompanied him from Haran (Ge 12:4–5; 13:1). Settled in Sodom (Ge 13:5–13); rescued by Abraham (Ge 14), and by two angels (Ge 19; 2Pe 2:7–8). Wife became pillar of salt (Ge 19:26). Fathered Ammon and Moab by his two daughters (Ge 19:30–38).

Ge 11:27 And Haran became the father of L.
11:31 his grandson L son of Haran, and his
12: 4 had told him; and L went with him.
12: 5 He took his wife Sarai, his nephew L,
13: 1 he had, and L went with him.
13: 5 Now L, who was moving about with
13: 7 herdsmen and the herdsmen of L.
13: 8 Abram said to L, "Let's not have any
13:10 L looked up and saw that the whole
13:11 L chose for himself the whole plain
13:12 while L lived among the cities of
13:14 The LORD said to Abram after L had
14:12 Abram's nephew L and his possessions,
14:16 his relative L and his possessions,
19: 1 and L was sitting in the gateway of
19: 5 They called to L, "Where are the men
19: 6 L went outside to meet them and shut
19: 9 They kept bringing pressure on L
19:10 pulled L back into the house and
19:12 The two men said to L, "Do you have
19:14 L went out and spoke to his
19:15 the angels urged L, saying, "Hurry!
19:18 L said to them, "No, my lords,
19:23 By the time L reached Zoar, the sun
19:29 and he brought L out of the
19:29 the cities where L had lived.
19:30 L and his two daughters left Zoar
Dt 2: 9 descendants of L as a possession."
2:19 possession to the descendants of L."
Ps 83: 8 strength to the descendants of L.
Lk 17:28 "It was the same in the days of L.
17:29 the day L left Sodom, fire and
2Pe 2: 7 if he rescued L, a righteous man,

Lot's (Lot[1])
Ge 19:26 L wife looked back, and she became
19:36 both of L daughters became pregnant
Lk 17:32 Remember L wife!

Lot[2] (Lots)
Lev 16: 8 the two goats—one l for the LORD
16: 9 the goat whose l falls to the LORD
16:10 the goat chosen by l as the
Nu 26:55 that the land is distributed by l.
26:56 distributed by l among the larger
33:54 Distribute the land by l, according
33:54 Whatever falls to them by l will be
34:13 this land by l as an inheritance.
36: 2 inheritance to the Israelites by l,
Jos 14: 2 inheritances were assigned by l
18:11 The l came up for the tribe of
19: 1 The second l came out for the tribe
19:10 The third l came up for Zebulun,
19:17 The fourth l came out for Issachar,
19:24 The fifth l came out for the tribe
19:32 The sixth l came out for Naphtali,
19:40 The seventh l came out for the tribe
19:51 assigned by l at Shiloh in the
21: 4 The first l came out for the
21:10 because the first l fell to them):
Jdg 20: 9 go up against it as the l directs.
1Sa 14:41 Jonathan and Saul were taken by l,
1Sa 14:42 Saul said, "Cast the l between me
1Ch 6:54 because the first l was for them):
24: 7 The first l fell to Jehoiarib, the
25: 9 The first l, which was for Asaph,
26:14 The l for the East Gate fell to
26:14 l for the North Gate fell to him.
26:15 The l for the South Gate fell to
26:15 the l for the storehouse fell to
Est 3: 7 they cast the pur (that is, the l)
3: 7 And the l fell on the twelfth month,
9:24 had cast the pur (that is, the l)
Job 31: 2 For what is man's l from God above,
Ps 11: 6 a scorching wind will be their l.
16: 5 you have made my l secure.
50:18 you throw in your l with adulterers.
Pr 1:14 throw in your l with us, and we will
6:33 Blows and disgrace are his l, and
16:33 The l is cast into the lap, but its
18:18 Casting the l settles disputes and
Ecc 3:22 his work, because that is his l.
5:18 has given him—for this is his l.
5:19 to accept his l and be happy in his
9: 9 For this is your l in life and in
Isa 17:14 us, the l of those who plunder us.
57: 6 your portion; they, they are your l.
Jer 13:25 This is your l, the portion I have
Eze 21:22 Into his right hand will come the l
Jnh 1: 7 cast lots and the l fell on Jonah.
Mic 2: 5 of the LORD to divide the land by l.
Lk 1: 9 he was chosen by l, according to the
Jn 19:24 "Let's decide by l who will get it."
Ac 1:26 they cast lots, and the l fell to

Lotan (Lotan's)
Ge 36:20 the region: L, Shobal, Zibeon, Anah,
36:22 The sons of L: Hori and Homam. Timna
36:29 These were the Horite chiefs: L,
1Ch 1:38 The sons of Seir: L, Shobal, Zibeon,
1:39 The sons of L: Hori and Homam. Timna

Lotan's (Lotan)
Ge 36:22 Timna was L sister.
1Ch 1:39 Timna was L sister.

Lotions
2Sa 12:20 After he had washed, put on l and
14: 2 and don't use any cosmetic l.
Da 10: 3 and I used no l at all until the
Am 6: 6 by the bowlful and use the finest l,

Lots (Lot[2])
Lev 16: 8 He is to cast l for the two
Jos 18: 6 I will cast l for you in the
18: 8 Then return to me, and I will cast l
18:10 Joshua then cast l for them in
1Ch 24: 5 them impartially by drawing l,
24:31 They also cast l, just as their
25: 8 as student, cast l for their duties.
26:13 L were cast for each gate, according
26:14 Then l were cast for his son
26:16 The l for the West Gate and the
Ne 10:34 the people—have cast l to determine
11: 1 and the rest of the people cast l to
Job 6:27 You would even cast l for the
Ps 22:18 them and cast l for my clothing.
Eze 21:21 He will cast l with arrows, he will
24: 6 by piece without casting l for them.
Joel 3: 3 They cast l for my people and traded
Ob :11 his gates and cast l for Jerusalem,
Jnh 1: 7 "Come, let us cast l to find out who
1: 7 cast l and the lot fell on Jonah.
Na 3:10 L were cast for her nobles, and all
Mt 27:35 divided up his clothes by casting l.
Mk 15:24 cast l to see what each would get.
Lk 23:34 divided up his clothes by casting l.
Jn 19:24 them and cast l for my clothing.
Ac 1:26 they cast l, and the lot fell to

Lotus (Lotuses)
Job 40:21 Under the l plant he lies, hidden

Lotuses (Lotus)
Job 40:22 The l conceal him in their shadow;

Loud (Aloud)
Ge 27:34 he burst out with a l and bitter cry
Ex 11: 6 There will be l wailing throughout
12:30 and there was l wailing in Egypt,
19:16 and a very l trumpet blast.
Dt 5:22 proclaimed in a l voice to your
27:14 the people of Israel in a l voice:
Jos 6: 5 make all the people give a l shout;
6:20 when the people gave a l shout, the
1Sa 7:10 l thunder against the Philistines
1Ki 8:55 of Israel in a l voice, saying:
2Ch 15:14 oath to the LORD with l acclamation
20:19 God of Israel, with a very l voice.
Ezr 10:12 assembly responded with a l voice:
Ne 9: 4 with l voices to the LORD their God.
Ps 102: 5 of my l groaning I am reduced to
Pr 7:11 (She is l and defiant, her feet
9:13 The woman Folly is l; she is
Jer 12: 6 have raised a l cry against you.
46:17 king of Egypt is only a l noise;
Eze 3:12 and I heard behind me a l rumbling
3:13 beside them, a l rumbling sound.
9: 1 I heard him call out in a l voice,
11:13 down and cried out in a l voice,
Da 4:14 He called in a l voice: 'Cut down
Zep 1:10 and a l crash from the hills.
Mt 24:31 his angels with a l trumpet call
27:46 hour Jesus cried out in a l voice,
27:50 had cried out again in a l voice
Mk 15:34 hour Jesus cried out in a l voice,
15:37 With a l cry, Jesus breathed his
Lk 1:42 In a l voice she exclaimed: "Blessed
17:13 called out in a l voice, "Jesus,
17:15 back, praising God in a l voice.
19:37 joyfully to praise God in l voices
23:23 with l shouts they insistently
23:46 Jesus called out with a l voice,
Jn 7:37 Jesus stood and said in a l voice,
11:43 said this, Jesus called in a l voice
1Th 4:16 with a l command, with the voice of
Heb 5: 7 petitions with l cries and tears to
Rev 1:10 behind me a l voice like a trumpet,
5: 2 angel proclaiming in a l voice,
5:12 In a l voice they sang: "Worthy is
6:10 They called out in a l voice, "How
7: 2 He called out in a l voice to the
7:10 they cried out in a l voice:
8:13 in mid-air call out in a l voice:
10: 3 he gave a l shout like the roar of
11:12 they heard a l voice from heaven
11:15 and there were l voices in heaven,
12:10 I heard a l voice in heaven say:
14: 2 waters and like a l peal of thunder.
14: 7 He said in a l voice, "Fear God and
14: 9 followed them and said in a l voice:
14:15 called in a l voice to him who was
14:18 called in a l voice to him who had
16: 1 I heard a l voice from the temple
16:17 out of the temple came a l voice
19: 6 waters and like l peals of thunder,
19:17 who cried in a l voice to all the
21: 3 I heard a l voice from the throne

Lounge (Lounging)
Am 6: 4 with ivory and l on your couches.

Lounging (Lounge)
Isa 47: 8 wanton creature, l in your security
Am 6: 7 your feasting and l will end.

Love (Beloved, *Love endures for ever, Love of God, Love one another, Love the LORD, Love the Lord, Love your neighbour*, Loved, Lovely, Lover, Lover's, Lovers, Loves, Loving, Loving-kindness, Peace-loving, *Unfailing love*)
Ge 20:13 'This is how you can show your l to
22: 2 your only son, Isaac, whom you l,
29:18 Jacob was in l with Rachel and said,
29:20 to him because of his l for her.
29:32 Surely my husband will l me now."
Ex 20: 6 showing l to a thousand generations
20: 6 who l me and keep my commandments.
21: 5 'I l my master and my wife and
Ex 34: 6 abounding in l and faithfulness,
34: 7 maintaining l to thousands, and
Lev 19:34 L him as yourself, for you were
Nu 14:18 slow to anger, abounding in l
14:19 In accordance with your great l,
Dt 5:10 showing l to a thousand generations
5:10 who l me and keep my commandments.
7: 9 keeping his covenant of l to a
7: 9 who l him and keep his commands.
7:12 keep his covenant of l with you,
7:13 He will l you and bless you and
10:12 to walk in all his ways, to l him,
10:19 you are to l those who are aliens,
13: 3 you l him with all your heart
13: 6 or the wife you l, or your closest
21:15 the son of the wife he does not l,
21:16 the son of the wife he does not l.
30: 6 so that you may l him with all your
33: 3 Surely it is you who l the people;
Jdg 5:31 may they who l you be like the sun
14:16 "You hate me! You don't really l me.
16: 4 Some time later, he fell in l with a
16:15 'I l you,' when you won't confide in
1Sa 18:20 Now Saul's daughter Michal was in l
20:17 reaffirm his oath out of l for him,
2Sa 1:26 Your l for me was wonderful, more
7:15 my l will never be taken away from
13: 1 Amnon son of David fell in l with
13: 4 "I'm in l with Tamar, my brother
16:17 Is this the l you show your friend?
19: 6 You l those who hate you and hate
19: 6 and hate those who l you.
1Ki 3: 3 Solomon showed his l for the LORD by
8:23 you who keep your covenant of l with
10: 9 Because of the LORD's eternal l for
11: 2 Solomon held fast to them in l.
1Ch 17:13 I will never take my l away from him
2Ch 6:14 you who keep your covenant of l with
6:42 the great l promised to David your
9: 8 Because of the l of your God for
19: 2 and l those who hate the LORD?
Ezr 3:11 his l to Israel endures for ever.
Ne 1: 5 who keeps his covenant of l with
1: 5 who l him and obey his commands,
9:17 slow to anger and abounding in l.
9:32 who keeps his covenant of l, do not
13:22 to me according to your great l.
Job 15:34 the tents of those who l bribes.
19:19 those I l have turned against me.
37:13 to water his earth and show his l.
Ps 4: 2 How long will you l delusions and
5:11 who l your name may rejoice in you.
11: 5 those who l violence his soul hates.
17: 7 Show the wonder of your great l,
18: 1 I l you, O LORD, my strength.
23: 6 Surely goodness and l will follow me
25: 6 your great mercy and l, for they
25: 7 according to your l remember me,
26: 3 for your l is ever before me, and I
26: 8 I l the house where you live, O LORD,
31: 7 will be glad and rejoice in your l,
31:21 for he showed his wonderful l to me
36: 5 Your l, O LORD, reaches to the
36:10 your l to those who know you,
40:10 I do not conceal your l and your
40:11 l and your truth always protect me.
40:16 who l your salvation always say,
42: 8 By day the LORD directs his l, at
45: 7 You l righteousness and hate
52: 3 You l evil rather than good,
52: 4 You l every harmful word, O you
57: 3 God sends his l and his faithfulness
57:10 For great is your l, reaching to the
59:16 the morning I will sing of your l;
60: 5 that those you l may be delivered.
61: 7 l and faithfulness to protect him.
63: 3 your l is better than life, my lips
66:20 my prayer or withheld his l from me!
69:13 of your favour; in your great l,
69:16 out of the goodness of your l;
69:36 who l his name will dwell there.
70: 4 who l your salvation always say,
85:10 L and faithfulness meet together;
86: 5 abounding in l to all who call to
86:13 For great is your l towards me;
86:15 abounding in l and faithfulness.
Ps 88:11 Is your l declared in the grave,
89: 1 I will sing of the LORD's great l
89: 2 I will declare that your l stands
89:14 l and faithfulness go before you.
89:24 My faithful l will be with him, and
89:28 will maintain my l to him for ever,
89:33 will not take my l from him, nor
89:49 Lord, where is your former great l,
92: 2 to proclaim your l in the morning
94:18 your l, O LORD, supported me.
98: 3 He has remembered his l and his
101: 1 I will sing of your l and justice;
103: 4 crowns you with l and compassion,
103: 8 slow to anger, abounding in l.
103:11 is his l for those who fear him;
103:17 LORD's l is with those who fear him,
106:45 and out of his great l he relented.
107:43 consider the great l of the LORD.
108: 4 For great is your l, higher than
108: 6 that those you l may be delivered.
109:21 the goodness of your l, deliver me.
109:26 save me in accordance with your l.
115: 1 because of your l and faithfulness.
117: 2 For great is his l towards us, and
119:47 in your commands because I l them.
119:48 your commands, which I l, and I
119:64 The earth is filled with your l,
119:88 Preserve my life according to your l,
119:97 Oh, how I l your law! I meditate on
119:113 double-minded men, but I l your law
119:119 therefore I l your statutes.
119:124 according to your l and teach me
119:127 I l your commands more than gold,
119:132 always do to those who l your name.
119:149 voice in accordance with your l;
119:159 See how I l your precepts; preserve
119:159 life, O LORD, according to your l.
119:163 abhor falsehood but I l your law.
119:165 Great peace have they who l your law
119:167 I obey your statutes, for I l them
122: 6 "May those who l you be secure.
138: 2 for your l and your faithfulness,
138: 8 your l, O LORD, endures for ever
145: 8 slow to anger and rich in l.
145:20 The LORD watches over all who l him
Pr 1:22 you simple ones l your simple ways?
3: 3 Let l and faithfulness never leave
4: 6 l her, and she will watch over you.
5:19 may you ever be captivated by her l
7:18 Come, let's drink deep of l till
7:18 let's enjoy ourselves with l!
8:17 I l those who l me, and those who
8:21 bestowing wealth on those who l me
8:36 all who hate me l death."
9: 8 rebuke a wise man and he will l you
10:12 but l covers over all wrongs.
14:22 is good find l and faithfulness.
15:17 meal of vegetables where there is l
16: 6 Through l and faithfulness sin is
17: 9 covers over an offence promotes l,
18:21 those who l it will eat its fruit.
20:13 Do not l sleep or you will grow poor;
20:28 L and faithfulness keep a king safe;
20:28 through l his throne is made secure.
21:21 He who pursues righteousness and l
27: 5 Better is open rebuke than hidden l.
Ecc 3: 8 a time to l and a time to hate, a
9: 1 knows whether l or hate awaits him.
9: 6 Their l, their hate and their
9: 9 life with your wife, whom you l
SS 1: 2 your l is more delightful than wine.
1: 3 No wonder the maidens l you!
1: 4 will praise your l more than wine.
1: 7 Tell me, you whom I l, where you
2: 4 hall, and his banner over me is l.
2: 5 with apples, for I am faint with l.
2: 7 or awaken l until it so desires.
3: 5 or awaken l until it so desires.
4:10 How delightful is your l, my sister,
4:10 more pleasing is your l than wine,
5: 8 Tell him I am faint with l.
7: 6 pleasing, O l, with your delights!
7:12 bloom—there I will give you my l.
8: 4 or awaken l until it so desires.
8: 6 for l is as strong as death, its
8: 7 Many waters cannot quench l; rivers

SS 8: 7 al the wealth of his house for **l**,
Isa 1:23 all **l** bribes and chase after gifts.
5: 1 I will sing for the one I **l** a song
16: 5 In **l** a throne will be established;
38:17 In your **l** you kept me from the pit
43: 4 and because I **l** you, I will give men
55: 3 my faithful **l** promised to David.
56: 6 to **l** the name of the LORD, and to
56:10 around and dream, they **l** to sleep.
57: 8 a pact with those whose beds you **l**,
61: 8 "For I, the LORD, **l** justice; I hate
63: 9 In his **l** and mercy he redeemed them
66:10 all you who **l** her; rejoice greatly
Jer 2:25 'It's no use! I **l** foreign gods,
2:33 How skilled you are at pursuing **l**!
5:31 and my people **l** it this way.
12: 7 give the one I **l** into the hands of
14:10 "They greatly **l** to wander; they do
16: 5 my **l** and my pity from this people,"
31: 3 loved you with an everlasting **l**;
32:18 You show **l** to thousands but bring
Lam 3:22 of the LORD's great **l** we are not
Eze 16: 8 saw that you were old enough for **l**,
23:17 to the bed of **l**, and in their lust
33:32 who sings **l** songs with a beautiful
Da 9: 4 who keeps his covenant of **l** with all
9: 4 all who **l** him and obey his commands,
Hos 1: 6 for I will no longer show **l** to the
1: 7 Yet I will show **l** to the house of
2: 4 I will not show my **l** to her children
2:19 and justice, in **l** and compassion.
2:23 I will show my **l** to the one I called
3: 1 LORD said to me, "Go, show your **l**
3: 1 **L** her as the LORD loves the
3: 1 and **l** the sacred raisin cakes."
4: 1 "There is no faithfulness, no **l**, no
4:18 their rulers dearly **l** shameful ways.
6: 4 Your **l** is like the morning mist,
9: 1 you **l** the wages of a prostitute at
9:15 I will no longer **l** them; all their
11: 4 of human kindness, with ties of **l**;
12: 6 maintain **l** and justice, and wait
14: 4 their waywardness and **l** them freely
Joel 2:13 slow to anger and abounding in **l**,
Am 4: 5 for this is what you **l** to do,"
5:15 Hate evil, **l** good; maintain justice
Jnh 4: 2 slow to anger and abounding in **l**,
Mic 3: 2 you who hate good and **l** evil;
6: 8 To act justly and to **l** mercy and
Zep 3:17 he will quiet you with his **l**, he
Zec 8:17 and do not **l** to swear falsely.
8:19 Therefore **l** truth and peace."
Mt 3:17 "This is my Son, whom I **l**;
5:44 I tell you: **L** your enemies and pray
5:46 If you **l** those who **l** you, what
6: 5 for they **l** to pray standing in the
6:24 will hate the one and **l** the other
12:18 the one I **l**, in whom I delight;
17: 5 said, "This is my Son, whom I **l**;
23: 6 they **l** the place of honour at
23: 7 they **l** to be greeted in the
24:12 the **l** of most will grow cold
Mk 1:11 "You are my Son, whom I **l**;
9: 7 cloud: "This is my Son, whom I **l**.
12:33 To **l** him with all your heart, with
Lk 3:22 "You are my Son, whom I **l**;
6:27 **L** your enemies, do good to those
6:32 "If you **l** those who **l** you, what
6:32 Even 'sinners' **l** those who **l** them.
6:35 **l** your enemies, do good to them,
7:42 Now which of them will **l** him more?"
11:43 you **l** the most important seats in
16:13 will hate the one and **l** the other
20:13 I will send my son, whom I **l**;
20:46 **l** to be greeted in the market-places
Jn 8:42 you would **l** me, for I came from God
11: 3 Jesus, "Lord, the one you **l** is sick.
13: 1 them the full extent of his **l**.
14:15 "If you **l** me, you will obey what I
14:21 will **l** him and show myself to him."
14:23 My Father will **l** him, and we will
14:24 He who does not **l** me will not obey
14:31 the world must learn that I **l** the
15: 9 I loved you. Now remain in my **l**.
15:10 you will remain in my **l**, just as I
15:10 commands and remain in his **l**.
Jn 15:12 My command is this: **L** each other as
15:13 Greater **l** has no-one than this, that
15:17 This is my command: **L** each other.
15:19 world, it would **l** you as its own.
17:26 **l** you have for me may be in them
21:15 Simon son of John, do you truly **l** me
21:15 he said, "you know that I **l** you.
21:16 Simon son of John, do you truly **l** me
21:16 "Yes, Lord, you know that I **l** you.
21:17 "Simon son of John, do you **l** me?"
21:17 "Do you **l** me?" He said, "Lord, you
21:17 all things; you know that I **l** you.
Ro 5: 5 because God has poured out his **l**
5: 8 God demonstrates his own **l** for us
8:28 for the good of those who **l** him,
8:35 Who shall separate us from the **l** of
12: 9 **L** must be sincere. Hate what is evil;
12:10 to one another in brotherly **l**.
13:10 **L** does no harm to its neighbour.
13:10 **l** is the fulfilment of the law.
14:15 you are no longer acting in **l**.
15:30 Christ and by the **l** of the Spirit,
16: 8 Greet Ampliatus, whom I **l** in the
1Co 2: 9 has prepared for those who **l** him"
4:17 to you, Timothy, my son whom I **l**,
4:21 or in **l** and with a gentle spirit?
8: 1 Knowledge puffs up, but **l** builds up
13: 1 but have not **l**, I am only a
13: 2 but have not **l**, I am nothing.
13: 3 but have not **l**, I gain nothing.
13: 4 **L** is patient, **l** is kind. It does not
13: 6 **L** does not delight in evil but
13: 8 **L** never fails. But where there are
13:13 three remain: faith, hope and **l**.
13:13 But the greatest of these is **l**.
14: 1 Follow the way of **l** and eagerly
16:14 Do everything in **l**.
16:24 My **l** to all of you in Christ Jesus.
2Co 2: 4 you know the depth of my **l** for you.
2: 8 to reaffirm your **l** for him.
5:14 For Christ's **l** compels us, because
6: 6 in the Holy Spirit and in sincere **l**
8: 7 in your **l** for us—see that you also
8: 8 to test the sincerity of your **l**
8:24 show these men the proof of your **l**
11:11 Why? Because I do not **l** you? God
12:15 If I **l** you more, will you **l** me less?
13:11 God of **l** and peace will be with you.
Gal 5: 6 faith expressing itself through **l**.
5:13 rather, serve one another in **l**.
5:22 the fruit of the Spirit is **l**, joy,
Eph 1: 4 and blameless in his sight. In **l**
1:15 Jesus and your **l** for all the saints,
2: 4 of his great **l** for us, God, who is
3:17 being rooted and established in **l**,
3:18 high and deep is the **l** of Christ,
3:19 to know this **l** that surpasses
4: 2 bearing with one another in **l**.
4:15 Instead, speaking the truth in **l**, we
4:16 builds itself up in **l**, as each part
5: 2 live a life of **l**, just as Christ
5:25 Husbands, **l** your wives, just as
5:28 husbands ought to **l** their wives as
5:33 each one of you also must **l** his wife
6:23 **l** with faith from God the Father
6:24 Grace to all who **l** our Lord Jesus
6:24 Lord Jesus Christ with an undying **l**.
Php 1: 9 your **l** may abound more and more
1:16 The latter do so in **l**, knowing that
2: 1 if any comfort from his **l**, if any
2: 2 having the same **l**, being one in
4: 1 brothers, you whom I **l** and long for
Col 1: 4 the **l** you have for all the saints—
1: 5 the faith and **l** that spring from the
1: 8 who also told us of your **l** in the
2: 2 encouraged in heart and united in **l**,
3:14 over all these virtues put on **l**,
3:19 Husbands, **l** your wives and do not be
1Th 1: 3 your labour prompted by **l**, and your
3: 6 good news about your faith and **l**.
3:12 May the Lord make your **l** increase
4: 9 Now about brotherly **l** we do not need
4: 9 been taught by God to **l** each other.
4:10 in fact, you do **l** all the brothers
5: 8 on faith and **l** as a breastplate,
5:13 Hold them in the highest regard in **l**
2Th 1: 3 and the **l** every one of you has for
2:10 to **l** the truth and so be saved.
3: 5 God's **l** and Christ's perseverance.
1Ti 1: 5 The goal of this command is **l**,
1:14 and **l** that are in Christ Jesus.
2:15 **l** and holiness with propriety.
4:12 life, in **l**, in faith and in purity.
6:10 For the **l** of money is a root of all
6:11 faith, **l**, endurance and gentleness.
2Ti 1: 7 power, of **l** and of self-discipline.
1:13 with faith and **l** in Christ Jesus.
2:22 and pursue righteousness, faith, **l**
3: 3 without **l**, unforgiving, slanderous,
3:10 faith, patience, **l**, endurance,
Tit 2: 2 in faith, in **l** and in endurance.
2: 4 they can train the younger women to **l**
3:15 Greet those who **l** us in the faith.
Phm : 5 Jesus and your **l** for all the saints.
: 7 Your **l** has given me great joy and
: 9 I appeal to you on the basis of **l**
Heb 6:10 the **l** you have shown him as you have
10:24 another on towards **l** and good deeds.
13: 5 your lives free from the **l** of money
Jas 1:12 God has promised to those who **l** him.
2: 5 kingdom he promised those who **l** him?
1Pe 1: 8 you have not seen him, you **l** him;
1:22 **l** one another deeply, from the heart.
2:17 **L** the brotherhood of believers,
3: 8 **l** as brothers, be compassionate and
3:10 For, "Whoever would **l** life and see
4: 8 Above all, **l** each other deeply,
4: 8 **l** covers over a multitude of sins.
5:14 Greet one another with a kiss of **l**.
2Pe 1: 7 and to brotherly kindness, **l**.
1:17 saying, "This is my Son, whom I **l**;
1Jn 2: 5 God's **l** is truly made complete
2:15 Do not **l** the world or anything in
2:15 love of the Father is not in him.
3: 1 How great is the **l** the Father has
3:10 anyone who does not **l** his brother.
3:14 to life, because we **l** our brothers.
3:14 who does not **l** remains in death.
3:16 This is how we know what **l** is: Jesus
3:18 Dear children, let us not **l** with
4: 7 **l** one another, for **l** comes from God.
4: 8 Whoever does not **l** does not know God,
4: 8 does not know God, because God is **l**.
4: 9 is how God showed his **l** among us;
4:10 This is **l**: not that we loved God,
4:12 us and his **l** is made complete in us.
4:16 and rely on the **l** God has for us.
4:16 God is **l**. Whoever lives in **l** lives
4:17 In this way, **l** is made complete
4:18 There is no fear in **l**. But perfect **l**
4:18 who fears is not made perfect in **l**.
4:19 We **l** because he first loved us.
4:20 If anyone says, "I **l** God," yet hates
4:20 For anyone who does not **l** his
4:20 cannot **l** God, whom he has not seen.
4:21 loves God must also **l** his brother.
5: 2 This is how we know that we **l** the
5: 3 This is **l** for God: to obey his
2Jn : 1 whom I **l** in the truth—and not I
: 3 Son, will be with us in truth and **l**.
: 6 this is **l**: that we walk in obedience
: 6 his command is that you walk in **l**.
3Jn : 1 friend Gaius, whom I **l** in the truth.
: 6 have told the church about your **l**.
Jude : 2 Mercy, peace and **l** be yours in
:12 These men are blemishes at your **l**
:21 Keep yourselves in God's **l** as you
Rev 2: 4 You have forsaken your first **l**.
2:19 I know your deeds, your **l** and faith,
3:19 Those whom I **l** I rebuke and
12:11 they did not **l** their lives so much

Love endures for ever

1Ch 16:34 to the LORD, for he is good; his **l**.
16:41 give thanks to the LORD, "for his **l**.
2Ch 5:13 LORD and sang: "He is good; his **l**.
7: 3 LORD, saying, "He is good; his **l**.
7: 6 when he gave thanks, saying, "His **l**.
20:21 "Give thanks to the LORD, for his **l**.
Ps 100: 5 For the LORD is good and his **l**;
106: 1 to the LORD, for he is good; his **l**.

Ps 107: 1 to the LORD, for he is good; his l.
118: 1 to the LORD, for he is good; his l.
118: 2 Let Israel say: "His l."
118: 3 Let the house of Aaron say: "His l."
118: 4 those who fear the LORD say: "His l.
118:29 to the LORD, for he is good; his l.
136: 1 to the LORD, for he is good. His l.
136: 2 thanks to the God of Gods. His l.
136: 3 thanks to the Lord of lords: His l.
136: 4 alone does great wonders, His l.
136: 5 made the heavens, His l.
136: 6 the earth upon the waters, His l.
136: 7 who made the great lights—His l.
136: 8 the sun to govern the day, His l.
136: 9 stars to govern the night; His l.
136:10 down the firstborn of Egypt His l.
136:11 Israel out from among them His l.
136:12 hand and outstretched arm; His l.
136:13 divided the Red Sea asunder His l.
136:14 through the midst of it, His l.
136:15 his army into the Red Sea; His l.
136:16 people through the desert, His l.
136:17 who struck down great kings, His l.
136:18 killed mighty kings—His l.
136:19 Sihon king of the Amorites His l.
136:20 Og king of Bashan—His l.
136:21 land as an inheritance, His l.
136:22 to his servant Israel; His l.
136:23 us in our low estate His l.
136:24 freed us from our enemies, His l.
136:25 gives food to every creature. His l
136:26 thanks to the God of heaven. His l.
Jer 33:11 for the LORD is good; his l.

Love of God

Lk 11:42 but you neglect justice and the l.
Jn 5:42 do not have the l in your hearts.
Ro 8:39 l that is in Christ Jesus our Lord.
2Co 13:14 and the l, and the fellowship of the
Tit 3: 4 when the kindness and l our Saviour
1Jn 3:17 on him, how can the l be in him?

Love one another

Jn 13:34 "A new command I give you: L. As I
13:34 As I have loved you, so you must l.
13:35 you are my disciples, if you l."
Ro 13: 8 except the continuing debt to l, for
1Pe 1:22 brothers, l deeply, from the heart.
1Jn 3:11 from the beginning: We should l.
3:23 Christ, and to l as he commanded us.
4: 7 Dear friends, let us l, for love
4:11 God so loved us, we also ought to l.
4:12 but if we l, god lives in us and
2Jn : 5 from the beginning. I ask that we l.

Love the LORD

Dt 6: 5 L your God with all your heart and
11: 1 L your God and keep his requirements,
11:13 I am giving you today—to l your God
11:22 giving you to follow—to l your God,
19: 9 I command you today—to l your God
30:16 I command you today to l your God
30:20 that you may l your God, listen to
Jos 22: 5 to l your God, to walk in all his
23:11 be very careful to l your God.
Ps 31:23 L, all his saints! The LORD
97:10 Let those who l hate evil, for he
116: 1 I l, for he heard my voice; he heard

Love the Lord

Mt 22:37 Jesus replied: "'L your God with
Mk 12:30 L your God with all your heart and
Lk 10:27 He answered: "'L your God with all
1Co 16:22 If anyone does not l—a curse be on

Love your neighbour

Lev 19:18 of your people, but l as yourself.
Mt 5:43 it was said, 'L and hate your enemy
19:19 and mother,' and 'l as yourself.'"
22:39 second is like it: 'L as yourself
Mk 12:31 The second is this: 'L as yourself.'
12:33 to l as yourself is more important
Lk 10:27 your mind'; and, 'L as yourself.'"
Ro 13: 9 up in this one rule: "L as yourself.
Gal 5:14 in a single command: "L as yourself.
Jas 2: 8 L as yourself," you are doing right

Loved (Love)

Ge 24:67 she became his wife, and he l her;
25:28 l Esau, but Rebekah l Jacob.
29:30 with Rachel also, and he l Rachel
29:31 the LORD saw that Leah was not l, he
29:33 I am not l, he gave me this one too.
34: 3 l the girl and spoke tenderly to her.
37: 3 Now Israel l Joseph more than any of
37: 4 brothers saw that their father l him
Dt 4:37 he l your forefathers and chose
7: 8 was because the LORD l you and kept
10:15 on your forefathers and l them,
1Sa 1: 5 a double portion because he l her,
18: 1 with David, and he l him as himself.
18: 3 David because he l him as himself.
18:16 all Israel and Judah l David,
18:28 that his daughter Michal l David,
20:17 because he l him as he l himself.
2Sa 1:23 in life they were l and gracious,
12:24 named him Solomon. The LORD l him
12:25 the LORD l him, he sent word through
13:15 he hated her more than he had l her.
1Ki 11: 1 King Solomon, however, l many
2Ch 11:21 Rehoboam l Maacah daughter of
26:10 fertile lands, for he l the soil.
Ne 13:26 He was l by his God, and God made
Ps 44: 3 light of your face, for you l them.
47: 4 us, the pride of Jacob, whom he l.
78:68 of Judah, Mount Zion, which he l.
88:18 have taken my companions and l ones
109:17 He l to pronounce a curse—may it
Isa 5: 1 My l one had a vineyard on a fertile
Jer 2: 2 as a bride you l me and followed me
8: 2 which they have l and served and
31: 3 "I have l you with an everlasting
Eze 16:37 you l as well as those you hated.
Hos 2: 1 and of your sisters, 'My l one'.
2:23 the one I called 'Not my l one'.
3: 1 l by another and is an adulteress.
9:10 became as vile as the thing they l.
11: 1 "When Israel was a child, I l him,
Mal 1: 2 "I have l you," says the LORD. "But
1: 2 "But you ask, 'How have you l us?'
1: 2 "Yet I have l Jacob,
Mk 10:21 Jesus looked at him and l him. "One
12: 6 one left to send, a son, whom he l.
Lk 7:47 have been forgiven—for she l much.
16:14 The Pharisees, who l money, heard
Jn 3:16 "For God so l the world that he gave
3:19 but men l darkness instead of light
11: 5 Jesus l Martha and her sister and
11:36 the Jews said, "See how he l him!"
12:43 they l praise from men more than
13: 1 Having l his own who were in the
13:23 Jesus l, was reclining next to him.
13:34 l you, so you must love one another
14:21 who loves me will be l by my Father
14:28 If you l me, you would be glad that
15: 9 Father has l me, so have I l you.
15:12 Love each other as I have l you.
16:27 loves you because you have l me
17:23 have l them even as you have l me.
17:24 you l me before the creation of the
19:26 and the disciple whom he l standing
20: 2 the one Jesus l, and said, "They
21: 7 the disciple whom Jesus l said to
21:20 whom Jesus l was following them.
Ro 1: 7 To all in Rome who are l by God and
8:37 conquerors through him who l us.
9:13 Just as it is written: "Jacob I l,
9:25 her 'my l one' who is not my l one,"
11:28 are l on account of the patriarchs,
Gal 2:20 who l me and gave himself for me.
Eph 5: 1 therefore, as dearly l children
5: 2 a life of love, just as Christ l us
5:25 just as Christ l the church and
Col 3:12 holy and dearly l, clothe yourselves
1Th 1: 4 For we know, brothers l by God, that
2: 8 We l you so much that we were
2Th 2:13 brothers l by the Lord, because from
2:16 who l us and by his grace gave us
2Ti 4:10 for Demas, because he l this world,
Heb 1: 9 You have l righteousness and hated
2Pe 2:15 Beor, who l the wages of wickedness.
1Jn 4:10 not that we l God, but that he l us
4:11 Dear friends, since God so l us, we
4:19 We love because he first l us.
Jude : 1 who are l by God the Father and kept
Rev 3: 9 and acknowledge that I have l you.

Lovely (Love)

Ge 29:17 Leah had weak eyes, but Rachel was l
Est 1:11 nobles, for she was l to look at.
2: 7 who was also known as Esther, was l
Ps 84: 1 How l is your dwelling-place, O LORD
SS 1: 5 Dark am I, yet l, O daughters of
2:14 voice is sweet, and your face is l.
4: 3 a scarlet ribbon; your mouth is l.
5:16 he is altogether l.
6: 4 as Tirzah, l as Jerusalem,
Am 8:13 "In that day "the l young women and
Php 4: 8 whatever is pure, whatever is l,

Lover (Love)

SS 1:13 My l is to me a sachet of myrrh
1:14 My l is to me a cluster of henna
1:16 How handsome you are, my l! Oh, how
2: 3 forest is my l among the young men.
2: 8 Listen! My l! Look! Here he comes,
2: 9 My l is like a gazelle or a young
2:10 My l spoke and said to me, "Arise,
2:16 My l is mine and I am his;
2:17 turn, my l, and be like a gazelle or
4:16 Let my l come into his garden and
5: 2 Listen! My l is knocking: "Open to
5: 4 My l thrust his hand through the
5: 5 I arose to open for my l, and my
5: 6 I opened for my l, but my l had left
5: 8 I charge you—if you find my l,
5:10 My l is radiant and ruddy,
5:16 This is my l, this my friend,
6: 1 has your l gone, most beautiful
6: 1 of women? Which way did your l turn,
6: 2 My l has gone down to his garden, to
6: 3 I am my lover's and my l is mine;
7: 9 May the wine go straight to my l,
7:10 I belong to my l, and his desire is
7:11 Come, my l, let us go to the
7:13 that I have stored up for you, my l.
8: 5 from the desert leaning on her l?
8:14 Come away, my l, and be like a
1Ti 3: 3 not quarrelsome, not a l of money.

Lover's (Love)

SS 6: 3 I am my l and my lover is mine;

Lovers (Love)

SS 5: 1 and drink; drink your fill, O l.
Jer 3: 1 lived as a prostitute with many l—
3: 2 the roadside you sat waiting for l,
4:30 l despise you; they seek your life.
Lam 1: 2 Among all her l there is none to
Eze 16:33 but you give gifts to all your l,
16:36 in your promiscuity with your l,
16:37 I am going to gather all your l,
16:39 I will hand you over to your l,
16:41 and you will no longer pay your l.
23: 5 and she lusted after her l, the
23: 9 Therefore I handed her over to her l
23:20 There she lusted after her l, whose
23:22 I will stir up your l against you,
Hos 2: 5 She said, 'I will go after my l, who
2: 7 She will chase after her l but not
2:10 lewdness before the eyes of her l;
2:12 she said were her pay from her l;
2:13 after her l, but me she forgot,"
8: 9 Ephraim has sold herself to l.
2Ti 3: 2 will be l of themselves, l of money
3: 3 brutal, not l of the good,
3: 4 l of pleasure rather than l of God—

Loves (Love)

Ge 44:20 sons left, and his father l him.'
Dt 10:18 and l the alien, giving him food and
15:16 to leave you," because he l you
21:15 If a man has two wives, and he l one

Dt 21:16 to the son of the wife he l in
23: 5 because the LORD your God l you.
28:54 wife he l or his surviving children,
28:56 husband she l and her own son or
33:12 the one the LORD l rests between his
Ru 4:15 For your daughter-in-law, who l you
2Ch 2:11 "Because the LORD l his people, he
Ps 11: 7 the LORD is righteous, he l justice
33: 5 The LORD l righteousness and justice;
34:12 Whoever of you l life and desires to
37:28 For the LORD l the just and will not
87: 2 the LORD l the gates of Zion more
91:14 "Because he l me," says the LORD,
99: 4 The King is mighty, he l justice—
119:140 tested, and your servant l them.
127: 2 for he grants sleep to those he l.
146: 8 down, the LORD l the righteous.
Pr 3:12 the LORD disciplines those he l, as
12: 1 Whoever l discipline l knowledge,
13:24 l him is careful to discipline him.
15: 9 he l those who pursue righteousness.
17:17 A friend l at all times, and a
17:19 He who l a quarrel l sin; he who
19: 8 He who gets wisdom l his own soul;
21:17 He who l pleasure will become poor;
21:17 l wine and oil will never be rich.
22:11 He who l a pure heart and whose
29: 3 A man who l wisdom brings joy to his
Ecc 5:10 Whoever l money never has money
5:10 whoever l wealth is never satisfied
SS 3: 1 I looked for the one my heart l;
3: 2 will search for the one my heart l.
3: 3 "Have you seen the one my heart l?"
3: 4 when I found the one my heart l.
Hos 3: 1 Love her as the LORD l the
10:11 a trained heifer that l to thresh;
12: 7 dishonest scales; he l to defraud.
Mal 2:11 desecrated the sanctuary the LORD l,
Mt 10:37 "Anyone who l his father or mother
10:37 anyone who l his son or daughter
Lk 7: 5 he l our nation and has built our
7:47 has been forgiven little l little."
Jn 3:35 The Father l the Son and has placed
5:20 For the Father l the Son and shows
10:17 The reason my Father l me is that I
12:25 The man who l his life will lose it,
14:21 obeys them, he is the one who l me.
14:21 He who l me will be loved by my
14:23 Jesus replied, "If anyone l me, he
16:27 No, the Father himself l you because
Ro 13: 8 for he who l his fellow-man has
1Co 8: 3 the man who l God is known by God.
2Co 9: 7 for God l a cheerful giver.
Eph 1: 6 has freely given us in the One he l.
5:28 He who l his wife l himself.
5:33 must love his wife as he l himself,
Col 1:13 us into the kingdom of the Son he l,
Tit 1: 8 one who l what is good, who is
Heb 12: 6 the Lord disciplines those he l, and
1Jn 2:10 Whoever l his brother lives in the
2:15 If anyone l the world, the love of
4: 7 l has been born of God and knows God
4:21 l God must also love his brother.
5: 1 l the father l his child as well.
3Jn : 9 but Diotrephes, who l to be first,
Rev 1: 5 To him who l us and has freed us
20: 9 camp of God's people, the city he l.
22:15 who l and practises falsehood.

Loving (Love)
Ps 25:10 All the ways of the LORD are l and
59:10 my l God. God will go before me and
59:17 O God, are my fortress, my l God.
62:12 that you, O Lord, are l. Surely you
144: 2 He is my l God and my fortress, my
145:13 and l towards all he has made.
145:17 ways and l towards all he has made.
Pr 5:19 A l doe, a graceful deer—may her
Heb 13: 1 Keep on l each other as brothers.
1Jn 5: 2 l God and carrying out his commands.

Loving-kindness (Love)
Jer 31: 3 love; I have drawn you with l.

Low (Lowborn, Lower, Lowered, Lowest, Lowliest, Lowly)
Ge 18: 2 meet them and bowed l to the ground.
43:28 And they bowed l to pay him honour.
Nu 22:31 So he bowed l and fell face down.
2Sa 22:28 are on the haughty to bring them l.
1Ki 1:16 Bathsheba bowed l and knelt before
1:31 Bathsheba bowed l with her face to
1Ch 29:20 they bowed l and fell prostrate
Job 14:10 man dies and is laid l; he breathes
14:21 are brought l, he does not see it.
22:29 men are brought l and you say, 'Lift
24:24 they are brought l and gathered up
40:11 at every proud man and bring him l,
Ps 18:27 You save the humble but bring l
36: 7 Both high and l among men find
38: 6 I am bowed down and brought very l;
49: 2 l and high, rich and poor alike:
119:25 I am laid l in the dust; preserve my
136:23 who remembered us in our l estate
Pr 29:23 A man's pride brings him l, but a
Ecc 10: 6 while the rich occupy the l ones.
Isa 2: 9 man will be brought l and mankind
2:11 and the pride of men brought l;
2:17 arrogance of man will be brought l
5:15 man will be brought l and mankind
10:33 the tall ones will be brought l.
14: 8 "Now that you have been laid l,
14:12 you who once laid l the nations!
23: 9 to bring l the pride of all glory
25:12 high fortified walls and lay them l
26: 5 he lays the lofty city l; he levels
28: 1 the pride of those laid l by wine!
29: 4 Brought l, you will speak from the
40: 4 every mountain and hill made l;
46: 1 Bel bows down, Nebo stoops l;
Jer 16: 6 "Both high and l will die in this
46:15 Why will your warriors be laid l?
Eze 17: 6 and became a l, spreading vine.
17:14 that the kingdom would be brought l
17:24 tree and make the l tree grow tall.
21:26 and the exalted will be brought l.
Da 8:11 of his sanctuary was brought l.
Lk 3: 5 every mountain and hill made l.
Ac 8:10 all the people, both high and l,
Ro 12:16 associate with people of l position.
Jas 1:10 should take pride in his l position,

Lowborn (Bear[1], Low)
Ps 62: 9 L men are but a breath, the highborn

Lower (Low)
Ge 6:16 and make l, middle and upper decks.
Lev 13:45 cover the l part of his face and cry
Dt 28:43 higher, but you will sink l and l.
Jos 15:19 gave her the upper and l springs.
16: 3 of L Beth Horon and on to Gezer,
18:13 on the hill south of L Beth Horon.
Jdg 1:15 gave her the upper and l springs.
1Ki 9:17 He built up L Beth Horon,
1Ch 7:24 who built L and Upper Beth Horon
2Ch 8: 5 Upper Beth Horon and L Beth Horon
Job 41:24 hard as rock, hard as a l millstone.
Ps 8: 5 You made him a little l than the
Isa 11:11 from L Egypt, from Upper Egypt, from
22: 9 you stored up water in the L Pool.
Jer 44: 1 Jews living in L Egypt—in Migdol,
44:15 people living in L and Upper Egypt,
Eze 24:17 do not cover the l part of your face
24:22 You will not cover the l part of
40:18 were long; this was the l pavement.
40:19 from the inside of the l gateway
42: 5 l and middle floors of the building.
42: 6 those on the l and middle floors.
42: 9 The l rooms had an entrance on the
43:14 the l ledge it is two cubits high
Ac 27:30 to l some anchors from the bow.
2Co 11: 7 Was it a sin for me to l myself in
Eph 4: 9 descended to the l, earthly regions?
Heb 2: 7 You made him a little l than the
2: 9 made a little l than the angels,

Lowered (Low)
Ge 24:18 she said, and quickly l the jar
24:46 "She quickly l her jar from her
44:11 Each of them quickly l his sack to
Ex 17:11 but whenever he l his hands, the
Jer 38: 6 They l Jeremiah by ropes into the
Eze 1:24 stood still, they l their wings.
1:25 heads as they stood with l wings.
Mk 2: 4 after digging through it, l the mat
Lk 5:19 they went up on the roof and l him
Ac 9:25 him by night and l him in a basket
27:17 they l the sea anchor and let the
2Co 11:33 I was l in a basket from a window in

Lowest (Low)
Ge 9:25 "Cursed be Canaan! The l of slaves
1Ki 6: 6 The l floor was five cubits wide,
6: 8 The entrance to the l floor was on
Ne 4:13 behind the l points of the wall at
Ps 88: 6 You have put me in the l pit, in the
Eze 41: 7 A stairway went up from the l floor
Lk 14:10 you are invited, take the l place

Lowing
1Sa 6:12 on the road and l all the way;
15:14 is this l of cattle that I hear?"
Jer 9:10 and the l of cattle is not heard.

Lowliest (Low)
Eze 29:15 will be the l of kingdoms and will
Da 4:17 and sets over them the l of men.'

Lowly (Low)
Job 5:11 The l he sets on high, and those who
Ps 119:141 Though I am l and despised, I do not
138: 6 he looks upon the l, but the proud
Pr 16:19 Better to be l in spirit and among
29:23 but a man of l spirit gains honour.
Isa 57:15 him who is contrite and l in spirit,
57:15 to revive the spirit of the l and to
Eze 21:26 It will not be as it was: The l will
29:14 There they will be a l kingdom.
1Co 1:28 He chose the l things of this world
Php 3:21 will transform our l bodies so that

Loyal (Loyalty)
1Sa 22:14 "Who of all your servants is as l as
2Sa 3: 8 This very day I am l to the house of
1Ki 12:20 remained l to the house of David.
1Ch 12:29 l to Saul's house until then;
29:18 and keep their hearts l to you.
Ps 78: 8 whose hearts were not l to God,
78:37 their hearts were not l to him,
Php 4: 3 Yes, and I ask you, l yokefellow,

Loyalty (Loyal)
1Ch 12:33 help David with undivided l—50,000;

Lucius
Ac 13: 1 Simeon called Niger, L of Cyrene,
Ro 16:21 L, Jason and Sosipater, my relatives.

Lud (Ludites)
Ge 10:22 Elam, Asshur, Arphaxad, L and Aram.
1Ch 1:17 Elam, Asshur, Arphaxad, L and Aram.

Ludites (Lud)
Ge 10:13 Mizraim was the father of the L,
1Ch 1:11 Mizraim was the father of the L,

Luhith
Isa 15: 5 They go up the way to L, weeping as
Jer 48: 5 They go up the way to L, weeping

Luke
Doctor; co-worker and close companion of Paul (Col 4:14; 2Ti 4:11; Phm 24). Writer of third Gospel and Acts.

Col 4:14 Our dear friend L, the doctor, and
2Ti 4:11 Only L is with me. Get Mark and
Phm :24 do Mark, Aristarchus, Demas and L,

Lukewarm (Warm)
Rev 3:16 So, because you are l—neither hot

Lump
Ro 9:21 out of the same l of clay some

Luncheon
Lk 14:12 When you give a l or dinner, do not

Lure (Lured)
Jdg 4: 7 I will l Sisera, the commander of
16: 5 "See if you can l him into showing

Lured (Lure)
Jos 8: 6 pursue us until we have l them away
8:16 Joshua and were l away from the city.

Lurk (Lurked, Lurks)
Ps 56: 6 They conspire, they l, they watch my
Hos 13: 7 like a leopard I will l by the path.

Lurked (Lurk)
Job 31: 9 if I have l at my neighbour's door,

Lurks (Lurk)
Pr 7:12 the squares, at every corner she l.)

Lush
Am 5:11 though you have planted l vineyards,
Zec 11: 3 l thicket of the Jordan is ruined!

Lust (Lusted, Lustful, Lustfully, Lusts, Lusty)
Pr 6:25 Do not l in your heart after her
Isa 57: 5 You burn with l among the oaks and
Eze 20:30 did and l after their vile images?
23: 8 and poured out their l upon her.
23:11 yet in her l and prostitution she
23:17 and in their l they defiled her.
Na 3: 4 all because of the wanton l of a
Ro 1:27 inflamed with l for one another.
Eph 4:19 with a continual l for more.
Col 3: 5 impurity, l, evil desires and greed,
1Th 4: 5 not in passionate l like the heathen,
1Pe 4: 3 l, drunkenness, orgies, carousing
1Jn 2:16 the l of his eyes and the boasting

Lusted (Lust)
Eze 6: 9 which have l after their idols.
20:24 eyes ⌊l⌋ after their Fathers' idols
23: 5 and she l after her lovers,
23: 7 the idols of everyone she l after.
23: 9 the Assyrians, for whom she l.
23:12 She too l after the Assyrians
23:16 as she saw them, she l after them
23:20 There she l after her lovers, whose
23:30 because you l after the nations and

Lustful (Lust)
Jer 13:27 your adulteries and l neighings,
Eze 16:26 your l neighbours, and provoked me
2Pe 2:18 by appealing to the l desires of

Lustfully (Lust)
Job 31: 1 my eyes not to look l at a girl.
Mt 5:28 anyone who looks at a woman l has

Lustre
Lam 4: 1 How the gold has lost its l, the

Lusts (Lust)
Nu 15:39 the l of your own hearts and eyes.
Ro 1:26 God gave them over to shameful l.

Lusty (Lust)
Jer 5: 8 They are well-fed, l stallions, each

Lutes
1Sa 18: 6 songs and with tambourines and l.
2Ch 20:28 LORD with harps and l and trumpets.

Luxuries (Luxury)
Rev 18: 3 grew rich from her excessive l."

Luxurious (Luxury)
Isa 13:22 jackals in her l palaces.

Luxury (Luxuries, Luxurious)
Pr 19:10 not fitting for a fool to live in l
Hab 1:16 in l and enjoys the choicest food.
Lk 7:25 and indulge in l are in palaces.
16:19 fine linen and lived in l every day.
Jas 5: 5 You have lived on earth in l and
Rev 18: 7 as the glory and l she gave herself.
18: 9 her l see the smoke of her burning,

Luz See **Bethel 1.**
Ge 28:19 though the city used to be called **L**.
35: 6 people with him came to **L** (that is,
48: 3 "God Almighty appeared to me at **L** in
Jos 16: 2 went on from Bethel (that is, **L**),
18:13 to the south slope of **L** (that is,
Jdg 1:23 spy out Bethel (formerly called **L**),
1:26 **L**, which is its name to this day.

Lycaonian
Ac 14: 6 fled to the **L** cities of Lystra and
14:11 they shouted in the **L** language, "The

Lycia
Ac 27: 5 Pamphylia, we landed at Myra in **L**.

Lydda See **Lod**
Ac 9:32 he went to visit the saints in **L**.
9:35 All those who lived in **L** and Sharon
9:38 **L** was near Joppa; so when the
9:38 disciples heard that Peter was in **L**

Lydia (Lydia's, Lydians)
God-fearing woman living in Philippi; accepted Paul's message; baptised; offered hospitality (Ac 16:14–15, 40).
Jer 46: 9 shields, men of **L** who draw the bow.
Eze 27:10 " 'Men of Persia, **L** and Put served
30: 5 Cush and Put, **L** and all Arabia,
Ac 16:14 those listening was a woman named **L**

Lydia's (Lydia)
Ac 16:40 they went to **L** house, where they met

Lydians (Lydia)
Isa 66:19 to the Libyans and **L** (famous as

Lying[1] (Lie[1])
Ge 28:13 the land on which you are l.
29: 2 with three flocks of sheep l near it
34: 7 Israel by l with Jacob's daughter
49:14 "Issachar is a scrawny donkey l down
Ex 14:30 the Egyptians l dead on the shore.
Dt 21: 1 If a man is found slain, l in a
22:13 takes a wife and, after l with her
Jos 17: 9 l among the towns of Manasseh,
Ru 3: 4 down, note the place where he is l.
3: 8 discovered a woman l at his feet.
1Sa 3: 2 see, was l down in his usual place.
3: 3 and Samuel was l down in the temple
5: 4 off and were l on the threshold;
26: 5 Saul was l inside the camp, with the
26: 7 and there was Saul, l asleep inside
26: 7 and the soldiers were l round him.
2Sa 4: 7 he was l on the bed in his bedroom.
12:16 spent the nights l on the ground.
13: 8 her brother Amnon, who was l down.
2Ki 1: 4 will not leave the bed you are l on
1: 6 will not leave the bed you are l on
1:16 never leave the bed you are l on.
4:32 was the boy l dead on his couch.
2Ch 20:24 l on the ground; no-one had escaped.
Job 3:13 For now I would be l down in peace;
3:14 themselves places now l in ruins,
Ps 139: 3 discern my going out and my l down
Pr 23:34 high seas, l on top of the rigging.
Isa 58: 5 and for l on sackcloth and ashes?
Jer 8: 2 will be like refuse l on the ground
16: 4 will be like refuse l on the ground
25:33 will be like refuse l on the ground
Lam 3:10 Like a bear l in wait, like a lion
Eze 29: 3 great monster l among your streams.
36:34 be cultivated instead of l desolate
36:35 the cities that were l in ruins,
Da 2:29 "As you were l there, O king, your
4: 5 As I was l in my bed, the images
4:10 These are the visions I saw while l
4:13 the visions I saw while l in my bed
7: 1 his mind as he was l on his bed.
Mt 8:14 mother-in-law l in bed with a fever.
9: 2 to him a paralytic, l on a mat.
Mk 2: 4 the mat the paralysed man was l on.
7:30 and found her child l on the bed,
Lk 2:12 in cloths and l in a manger."
2:16 the baby, who was l in the manger.
5:25 took what he had been l on and went
24:12 strips of linen l by themselves
Jn 5: 6 Jesus saw him l there and learned
20: 5 of linen l there but did not go in.
20: 6 He saw the strips of linen l there,

Lying[2] (Lie[2])
Jdg 16:13 making a fool of me and l to me.
1Ki 13:18 (But he was l to him.)
22:22 "'I will go out and be a l spirit
22:23 now the LORD has put a l spirit in
2Ch 18:21 "'I will go and be a l spirit in
18:22 now the LORD has put a l spirit in
Ps 31:18 Let their l lips be silenced, for
78:36 mouths, l to him with their tongues
109: 2 spoken against me with l tongues.
120: 2 Save me, O LORD, from l lips and
Pr 6:17 haughty eyes, a l tongue, hands that
10:18 who conceals his hatred has l lips
12:19 but a l tongue lasts only a moment.
12:22 The LORD detests l lips, but he
17: 7 how much worse l lips to a ruler!
21: 6 A fortune made by a l tongue is a
26:28 A l tongue hates those it hurts, and
Jer 8: 8 l pen of the scribes has handled it
23:26 in the hearts of these l prophets,
43: 2 "You are l! The LORD our God has not
Eze 13: 7 uttered l divinations when you say,
13: 8 of your false words and l visions,
13: 9 visions and utter l divinations.
13:19 By l to my people, who listen to
21:29 you and l divinations about you,
22:28 false visions and l divinations.
Hos 4: 2 There is only cursing, l and murder,
Ro 9: 1 the truth in Christ—I am not l,
2Co 11:31 for ever, knows that I am not l.
1Ti 2: 7 I am not l—and a teacher of the

Lyre (Lyres)
Ps 33: 2 music to him on the ten-stringed l.
57: 8 Awake, my soul! Awake, harp and l!
71:22 with the l, O Holy One of Israel.
81: 2 play the melodious harp and l.
92: 3 to the music of the ten-stringed l
108: 2 Awake, harp and l! I will awaken the
144: 9 on the ten-stringed l I will make
150: 3 praise him with the harp and l,
Da 3: 5 flute, zither, l, harp, pipes and
3: 7 flute, zither, l, harp and all kinds
3:10 flute, zither, l, harp, pipes and
3:15 flute, zither, l, harp, pipes and

Lyres (Lyre)
1Sa 10: 5 down from the high place with l,
2Sa 6: 5 l, tambourines, sistrums and cymbals
1Ki 10:12 make harps and l for the musicians.
1Ch 13: 8 l, tambourines, cymbals and trumpets
15:16 instruments: l, harps and cymbals.
15:20 play the l according to alamoth,
15:28 and the playing of l and harps.
16: 5 They were to play the l and harps,
25: 1 accompanied by harps, l and cymbals.
25: 6 with cymbals, l and harps, for the
2Ch 5:12 and playing cymbals, harps and l.
9:11 make harps and l for the musicians.
29:25 harps and l in the way prescribed
Ne 12:27 the music of cymbals, harps and l.
Isa 5:12 They have harps and l at their

Lysanias
Lk 3: 1 and **L** tetrarch of Abilene—

Lysias
Ac 23:26 Claudius **L**, To His Excellency,
24:22 "When **L** the commander comes," he

Lystra
City in Lycaonia 18 miles from Iconium. Paul and Barnabas fled here (Ac 14:6) and healed a crippled man (Ac 14:8–10). Jews from Pisidian Antioch and Iconium arrived to stone Paul, but he survived and left for Derbe (Ac 14:19–20), returning later (Ac 14:21–22). Timothy lived here (Ac 16:1). Paul reminded Timothy of the persecution here (2Ti 3:11).

Ac 14: 6 fled to the Lycaonian cities of **L**
14: 8 In **L** there sat a man crippled in his
14:21 returned to **L**, Iconium and Antioch,
16: 1 He came to Derbe and then to **L**,
16: 2 The brothers at **L** and Iconium spoke
2Ti 3:11 in Antioch, Iconium and **L**, the

Maacah (Maacathite, Maacathites)
Ge 22:24 sons: Tebah, Gaham, Tahash and **M**.
Jos 12: 5 of the people of Geshur and **M**,
13:11 of the people of Geshur and **M**,
13:13 out the people of Geshur and **M**,
2Sa 3: 3 **M** daughter of Talmai king of Geshur;
10: 6 as well as the king of **M** with a
10: 8 Rehob and the men of Tob and **M** were
1Ki 2:39 slaves ran off to Achish son of **M**,
15: 2 name was **M** daughter of Abishalom.
15:10 name was **M** daughter of Abishalom.
15:13 He even deposed his grandmother **M**
1Ch 2:48 Caleb's concubine **M** was the mother
3: 2 the third, Absalom the son of **M**
7:15 His sister's name was **M**. Another
7:16 Makir's wife **M** gave birth to a
8:29 His wife's name was **M**,
9:35 His wife's name was **M**,
11:43 Hanan son of **M**, Joshaphat the
19: 7 as well as the king of **M** with his
27:16 the Simeonites: Shephatiah son of **M**;
2Ch 11:20 he married **M** daughter of Absalom,
11:21 Rehoboam loved **M** daughter of Absalom
11:22 Rehoboam appointed Abijah son of **M**
13: 2 His mother's name was **M**, a daughter
15:16 Asa also deposed his grandmother **M**

Maacathite (Maacah)
2Sa 23:34 Eliphelet son of Ahasbai the **M**,
2Ki 25:23 the son of the **M**, and their men.
1Ch 4:19 the Garmite, and Eshtemoa the **M**.
Jer 40: 8 the son of the **M**, and their men.

Maacathites (Maacah)
Dt 3:14 and the **M**; it was named after him,

Maadai
Ezr 10:34 From the descendants of Bani: **M**,

Maai
Ne 12:36 Azarel, Milalai, Gilalai, **M**,

Maarath
Jos 15:59 **M**, Beth Anoth and Eltekon—six towns

Maasai
1Ch 9:12 and **M** son of Adiel, the son of

Maaseiah
1Ch 15:18 Jehiel, Unni, Eliab, Benaiah, **M**,
15:20 Shemiramoth, Jehiel, Unni, Eliab, **M**
2Ch 23: 1 Azariah son of Obed, **M** son of Adaiah,
26:11 **M** the officer under the direction of
28: 7 an Ephraimite warrior, killed **M** the
34: 8 Azaliah and **M** the ruler of the city,
Ezr 10:18 **M**, Eliezer, Jarib and Gedaliah.
10:21 From the descendants of Harim: **M**,
10:22 **M**, Ishmael, Nethanel, Jozabad and
10:30 Kelal, Benaiah, **M**, Mattaniah,
Ne 3:23 Azariah son of **M**, the son of Ananiah,
8: 4 Shema, Anaiah, Uriah, Hilkiah and **M**;
8: 7 Jamin, Akkub, Shabbethai, Hodiah, **M**,
10:25 Rehum, Hashabnah, **M**,
11: 5 **M** son of Baruch, the son of
11: 7 the son of Kolaiah, the son of **M**,
12:41 well as the priests—Eliakim, **M**,
12:42 also **M**, Shemaiah, Eleazar, Uzzi,
Jer 21: 1 and the priest Zephaniah son of **M**.
29:21 of Kolaiah and Zedekiah son of **M**,
29:25 to Zephaniah son of **M** the priest,
35: 4 of **M** son of Shallum the door-keeper.
37: 3 with the priest Zephaniah son of **M**

Maath
Lk 3:26 the son of **M**, the son of Mattathias,

Maaz
1Ch 2:27 of Jerahmeel: **M**, Jamin and Eker.

Maaziah
1Ch 24:18 Delaiah and the twenty-fourth to **M**.
Ne 10: 8 **M**, Bilgai and Shemaiah. These were

Macbannai
1Ch 12:13 Jeremiah the tenth and **M** the

Macbenah
1Ch 2:49 to Sheva the father of **M** and Gibea.

Macedonia (Macedonian, Macedonians)
Country north of Greece, with capital Philippi. Paul visited here after being invited in a vision (Ac 16:9–10); also Silas and Timothy (Ac 18:5) and Erastus (Ac 19:22). Home of Paul's companions Gaius and Aristarchus (Ac 19:29). Paul returned during his third journey (Ac 19:21; 20:1–6; 1Co 16:5; 2Co 1:16; 2:13; 7:5) and may have returned again later (1Ti 1:3). The church here was generous in supporting Jerusalem (Ro 15:26; 2Co 8:1–5; Php 4:15–18) and Paul himself (2Co 11:9).

Ac 16: 9 a man of **M** standing and begging him,
16: 9 him, "Come over to **M** and help us.
16:10 we got ready at once to leave for **M**,
16:12 leading city of that district of **M**.
18: 5 Silas and Timothy came from **M**, Paul
19:21 passing through **M** and Achaia.
19:22 Timothy and Erastus, to **M**, while he
19:29 Paul's travelling companions from **M**,
20: 1 said good-bye and set out for **M**.
20: 3 he decided to go back through **M**.
Ro 15:26 For **M** and Achaia were pleased to
1Co 16: 5 After I go through **M**, I will come to
16: 5 you—for I will be going through **M**.
2Co 1:16 to **M** and to come back to you from **M**,
2:13 good-bye to them and went on to **M**.
7: 5 For when we came into **M**, this body
11: 9 came from **M** supplied what I needed.
Php 4:15 when I set out from **M**, not one
1Th 1: 7 all the believers in **M** and Achaia.
1: 8 rang out from you not only in **M**
4:10 love all the brothers throughout **M**.
1Ti 1: 3 I urged you when I went into **M**, stay

Macedonian (Macedonia)
Ac 27: 2 a **M** from Thessalonica, was with us.
2Co 8: 1 that God has given the **M** churches.

Macedonians (Macedonia)
2Co 9: 2 been boasting about it to the **M**,
9: 4 For if any **M** come with me and find

Machines
2Ch 26:15 In Jerusalem he made **m** designed by

Machpelah
Ge 23: 9 that he will sell me the cave of **M**,
23:17 Ephron's field in **M** near Mamre—both
23:19 Sarah in the cave in the field of **M**
25: 9 him in the cave of **M** near Mamre,
49:30 the cave in the field of **M**, near
50:13 him in the cave in the field of **M**,

Macnadebai
Ezr 10:40 **M**, Shashai, Sharai,

Mad (Madman, Madmen, Madness)
Dt 28:34 The sights you see will drive you **m**.
Jer 25:16 they will stagger and go **m** because
50:38 idols that will go **m** with terror.
51: 7 therefore they have now gone **m**.
Jn 10:20 "He is demon-possessed and raving **m**.

Madai
Ge 10: 2 The sons of Japheth: Gomer, Magog, **M**,
1Ch 1: 5 The sons of Japheth: Gomer, Magog, **M**,

Maddening
Rev 14: 8 drink the **m** wine of her adulteries."
18: 3 the nations have drunk the **m** wine

Madman (Mad)
1Sa 21:13 in their hands he acted like a **m**,
2Ki 9:11 right? Why did this **m** come to you?"
9:20 son of Nimshi—he drives like a **m**."
Pr 26:18 Like a **m** shooting firebrands or
Jer 29:26 you should put any **m** who acts like a

Madmannah
Jos 15:31 Ziklag, **M**, Sansannah,
1Ch 2:49 birth to Shaaph the father of **M**

Madmen (Mad)
1Sa 21:15 Am I so short of **m** that you have to
Jer 48: 2 You too, O **M**, will be silenced; the

Madmenah
Isa 10:31 **M** is in flight; the people of Gebim

Madness (Mad)
Dt 28:28 The LORD will afflict you with **m**,
Ecc 1:17 and also of **m** and folly, but I
2:12 wisdom, and also **m** and folly.
7:25 of wickedness and the **m** of folly.
9: 3 are full of evil and there is **m** in
10:13 at the end they are wicked **m**—
Zec 12: 4 with panic and its rider with **m**,"
2Pe 2:16 and restrained the prophet's **m**.

Madon
Jos 11: 1 he sent word to Jobab king of **M**, to
12:19 the king of **M** one the king of Hazor

Magadan
Mt 15:39 boat and went to the vicinity of **M**.

Magbish
Ezr 2:30 of **M** 156

Magdalene, Mary
Mt 27:56 Among them were Mary **M**, Mary the
27:61 Mary **M** and the other Mary were
28: 1 Mary **M** and the other Mary went to
Mk 15:40 Among them were Mary **M**, Mary the
15:47 Mary **M** and Mary the mother of Joses
16: 1 the Sabbath was over, Mary **M**, Mary
16: 9 he appeared first to Mary **M**, out of
Lk 8: 2 Mary (called **M**) from whom seven
24:10 was Mary **M**, Joanna, Mary the mother
Jn 19:25 Mary the wife of Clopas, and Mary **M**.
20: 1 while it was still dark, Mary **M** went
20:18 Mary **M** went to the disciples with

Magdiel
Ge 36:43 **M** and Iram. These were the chiefs of
1Ch 1:54 **M** and Iram. These were the chiefs of

Maggot (Maggots)
Job 25: 6 how much less man, who is but a **m**—

Maggots (Maggot)
Ex 16:20 it was full of **m** and began to smell.
16:24 and it did not stink or get **m** in it.
Isa 14:11 **m** are spread out beneath you and

Magi
Mt 2: 1 **M** from the east came to Jerusalem
2: 7 Herod called the **M** secretly and
2:16 that he had been outwitted by the **M**,
2:16 the time he had learned from the **M**.

Magic (Magician, Magicians)
Isa 47:12 "Keep on, then, with your **m** spells
Eze 13:18 Woe to the women who sew **m** charms on
13:20 I am against your **m** charms with
Ac 8:11 them for a long time with his **m**.
Rev 9:21 murders, their **m** arts, their sexual
18:23 By your **m** spell all the nations were
21: 8 those who practise **m** arts, the
22:15 those who practise **m** arts, the

Magician (Magic)
Da 2:10 of any **m** or enchanter or astrologer.
2:27 "No wise man, enchanter, **m** or

Magicians (Magic)
Ge 41: 8 for all the **m** and wise men of Egypt.
41:24 told this to the **m**, but none could
Ex 7:11 and the Egyptian **m** also did the same
7:22 the Egyptian **m** did the same things
8: 7 the **m** did the same things by their
8:18 when the **m** tried to produce gnats by
8:19 The **m** said to Pharaoh, "This is the
9:11 The **m** could not stand before Moses
Da 1:20 ten times better than all the **m**
2: 2 the king summoned the **m**, enchanters,
4: 7 the **m**, enchanters, astrologers and
4: 9 I said, "Belteshazzar, chief of the **m**
5:11 I say—appointed him chief of the **m**,

Magistrate (Magistrates)
Lk 12:58 going with your adversary to the **m**,

Magistrates (Magistrate)
Ezr 7:25 which you possess, appoint **m** and
Da 3: 2 advisers, treasurers, judges, **m** and
3: 3 advisers, treasurers, judges, **m** and
Ac 16:20 They brought them before the **m** and
16:22 and the **m** ordered them to be
16:35 was daylight, the **m** sent their
16:36 The jailer told Paul, "The **m** have
16:38 The officers reported this to the **m**,

Magnificence (Magnify)
1Ch 22: 5 for the LORD should be of great **m**

Magnificent (Magnify)
1Ki 8:13 I have indeed built a **m** temple for
2Ch 2: 9 temple I build must be large and **m**.
6: 2 I have built a **m** temple for you, a
Isa 28:29 in counsel and **m** in wisdom.
Mk 13: 1 massive stones! What **m** buildings!"

Magnify (Magnificence, Magnificent)
Da 11:36 He will exalt and **m** himself above

Magog
Ge 10: 2 The sons of Japheth: Gomer, **M**, Madai,
1Ch 1: 5 The sons of Japheth: Gomer, **M**, Madai,
Eze 38: 2 of the land of **M**, the chief prince
39: 6 I will send fire on **M** and on those
Rev 20: 8 Gog and **M**—to gather them for battle.

Magor-Missabib
Jer 20: 3 name for you is not Pashhur, but **M**.

Magpiash
Ne 10:20 **M**, Meshullam, Hezir,

Mahalalel
Ge 5:12 70 years, he became the father of **M**.
5:13 after he became the father of **M**,
5:15 **M** had lived 65 years, he became the
5:16 **M** lived 830 years and had other sons
5:17 Altogether, **M** lived 895 years, and
1Ch 1: 2 Kenan, **M**, Jared,
Ne 11: 4 the son of **M**, a descendant of Perez;
Lk 3:37 the son of **M**, the son of Kenan,

Mahalath
Ge 28: 9 he went to Ishmael and married **M**,
2Ch 11:18 Rehoboam married **M**, who was the
Ps 53: T director of music. According to **m**.
88: T of music. According to **m** leannoth.

Mahanaim
Town in Gilead, east of the Jordan, on the south bank of the Jabbok. Named by Jacob when he saw the angels of God (Ge 32:1–2). On border between Manasseh and Gad (Jos 13:26,30); assigned to the Levites (Jos 21:38; 1Ch 6:80). Here Ish-Bosheth reigned (2Sa 2:8, 12, 29) and David found refuge from Absalom (2Sa 17:24, 27; 19:32; 1Ki 2:8). Became capital of one of Solomon's districts (1Ki 4:14).

Ge 32: 2 of God!" So he named that place **M**.
Jos 13:26 from **M** to the territory of Debir;
13:30 The territory extending from **M** and
21:38 for one accused of murder), **M**,
2Sa 2: 8 of Saul and brought him over to **M**.
2:12 of Saul, left **M** and went to Gibeon.
2:29 the whole Bithron and came to **M**.
17:24 David went to **M**, and Absalom crossed
17:27 David came to **M**, Shobi son of Nahash
19:32 in **M**, for he was a very wealthy man.
1Ki 2: 8 curses on me the day I went to **M**.
4:14 Ahinadab son of Iddo—in **M**;
1Ch 6:80 they received Ramoth in Gilead, **M**,
SS 6:13 the Shulammite as on the dance of **M**?

Mahaneh Dan
Jdg 13:25 was in **M**, between Zorah and Eshtaol.
18:12 Jearim is called **M** to this day.

Maharai
2Sa 23:28 Zalmon the Ahohite, **M** the
1Ch 11:30 **M** the Netophathite, Heled son of
27:13 The tenth, for the tenth month, was **M**

Mahath
1Ch 6:35 the son of **M**, the son of Amasai,
2Ch 29:12 **M** son of Amasai and Joel son of
31:13 Jozabad, Eliel, Ismakiah, **M** and

Mahavite
1Ch 11:46 Eliel the **M**, Jeribai and Joshaviah

Mahazioth
1Ch 25: 4 Joshbekashah, Mallothi, Hothir and **M**.
25:30 the twenty-third to **M**, his sons and

Maher-Shalal-Hash-Baz
Isa 8: 1 write on it with an ordinary pen: **M**.
8: 3 And the LORD said to me, "Name him **M**.

Mahlah (Mahlite, Mahlites)
Nu 26:33 **M**, Noah, Hoglah, Milcah and Tirzah.)
27: 1 The names of the daughters were **M**,
36:11 Zelophehad's daughters—**M**, Tirzah,
Jos 17: 3 **M**, Noah, Hoglah, Milcah and Tirzah.
1Ch 7:18 gave birth to Ishhod, Abiezer and **M**.

Mahli
Ex 6:19 The sons of Merari were **M** and Mushi.
Nu 3:20 The Merarite clans: **M** and Mushi.
1Ch 6:19 The sons of Merari: **M** and Mushi.
6:29 The descendants of Merari: **M**, Libni
6:47 the son of **M**, the son of Mushi, the
23:21 The sons of Merari: **M** and Mushi. The
23:21 The sons of **M**: Eleazar and Kish.
23:23 The sons of Mushi: **M**, Eder and
24:26 The sons of Merari: **M** and Mushi. The
24:28 From **M**: Eleazar, who had no sons.
24:30 the sons of Mushi: **M**, Eder and
Ezr 8:18 from the descendants of **M** son of

Mahlite (Mahlah)
Nu 26:58 the Hebronite clan, the **M** clan, the

Mahlites (Mahlah)
Nu 3:33 To Merari belonged the clans of the **M**

Mahlon (Mahlon's)
Ru 1: 2 of his two sons were **M** and Kilion.
1: 5 both **M** and Kilion also died, and
4: 9 property of Elimelech, Kilion and **M**.

Mahlon's (Mahlon)
Ru 4:10 **M** widow, as my wife, in order to

Mahol
1Ki 4:31 Calcol and Darda, the sons of **M**.

Mahseiah
Jer 32:12 the son of **M**, in the presence of my
51:59 the son of **M**, when he went to

Maid (Maiden, Maidens, Maids)
Ps 123: 2 as the eyes of a **m** look to the hand
Isa 24: 2 for mistress as for **m**, for seller as

Maiden (Maid)
Ge 24:43 if a **m** comes out to draw water and I
Pr 30:19 seas, and the way of a man with a **m**.
Isa 62: 5 a young man marries a **m**, so will
Jer 2:32 Does a **m** forget her jewellery, a
51:22 with you I shatter young man and **m**,

Maidens (Maid)
Ps 68:25 them are the **m** playing tambourines.
78:63 and their **m** had no wedding songs;
148:12 young men and **m**, old men and
SS 1: 3 No wonder the **m** love you!
2: 2 thorns is my darling among the **m**.
6: 9 The **m** saw her and called her blessed;
Jer 31:13 **m** will dance and be glad, young men
Lam 1: 4 her priests groan, her **m** grieve, and
1:18 men and **m** have gone into exile.
2:21 men and **m** have fallen by the sword.
Eze 9: 6 Slaughter old men, young men and **m**,

Maids (Maid)
Ge 24:61 Rebekah and her **m** got ready and
1Sa 25:42 attended by her five **m**, went with
Est 2: 9 He assigned to her seven **m** selected
2: 9 **m** into the best place in the harem.
4: 4 Esther's **m** and eunuchs came and told
4:16 I and my **m** will fast as you do. When
Pr 9: 3 She has sent out her **m**, and she

Maidservant (Servant)
Ge 16: 1 she had an Egyptian **m** named Hagar;
16: 2 Go, sleep with my **m**; perhaps I can
16: 3 Sarai his wife took her Egyptian **m**
21:12 distressed about the boy and your **m**.
21:13 I will make the son of the **m** into a
25:12 whom Sarah's **m**, Hagar the Egyptian,
29:24 Zilpah to his daughter as her **m**.
29:29 to his daughter Rachel as her **m**.
30: 3 she said, "Here is Bilhah, my **m**.
30: 9 she took her **m** Zilpah and gave her
30:18 me for giving my **m** to my husband.
35:25 The sons of Rachel's **m** Bilhah: Dan
35:26 The sons of Leah's **m** Zilpah: Gad and
Ex 20:10 nor your manservant or **m**, nor your
20:17 or his manservant or **m**, his ox or
21:26 "If a man hits a manservant or **m** in
21:27 out the tooth of a manservant or **m**,
Lev 25: 6 your manservant and **m**, and the hired
Dt 5:14 nor your manservant or **m**, nor your
5:14 and **m** may rest, as you do.
5:21 his manservant or **m**, his ox or
15:17 Do the same for your **m**.
Jdg 19:19 your **m**, and the young man with us.
1Sa 25:41 "Here is your **m**, ready to serve you
28:21 said, "Look, your **m** has obeyed you.
Ps 86:16 servant and save the son of your **m**.
116:16 your servant, the son of you **m**;
Pr 30:23 and a **m** who displaces her mistress.

Maidservants (Servant)
Ge 12:16 menservants and **m**, and camels.
24:35 and **m**, and camels and donkeys.
30:43 and **m** and menservants, and camels
31:33 of the two **m**, but he found nothing.
32: 5 sheep and goats, menservants and **m**.
32:22 his two **m** and his eleven sons and
33: 1 among Leah, Rachel and the two **m**.
33: 2 He put the **m** and their children in
33: 6 the **m** and their children approached
Dt 12:12 your menservants and **m**, and the
12:18 your menservants and **m**, and the
16:11 your menservants and **m**, the Levites
16:14 your menservants and **m**, and the
1Sa 8:16 Your menservants and **m** and the best
2Ki 5:26 flocks, herds, or menservants and **m**?
Ezr 2:65 their 7,337 menservants and **m**;
Ne 7:67 their 7,337 menservants and **m**;
Job 19:15 My guests and my **m** count me a
31:13 justice to my menservants and **m**
Isa 14: 2 and **m** in the LORD's land.
Lk 12:45 to beat the menservants and **m** and

Maimed
Lev 22:22 the injured or the **m**, or anything
Mt 18: 8 It is better for you to enter life **m**
Mk 9:43 It is better for you to enter life **m**

Main
Nu 20:19 "We will go along the **m** road, and if
Dt 2:27 We will stay on the **m** road; we will
1Ki 6: 3 portico at the front of the **m** hall
6: 5 Against the walls of the **m** hall and
6:17 The **m** hall in front of this room was
6:33 wood for the entrance to the **m** hall.
7:50 doors of the **m** hall of the temple.
2Ch 3: 5 He panelled the **m** hall with pine and
3:13 on their feet, facing the **m** hall.
4:22 Place and the doors of the **m** hall.
Eze 19:14 spread from one of its **m** branches

Mainland (Land)
Eze 26: 6 her settlements on the **m** will be
26: 8 settlements on the **m** with the sword;

Mainstay
Jer 49:35 bow of Elam, the **m** of their might.

Maintain (Maintained, Maintaining, Maintains)
Ru 4: 5 in order to **m** the name of the dead
4:10 as my wife, in order to **m** the name
1Ki 10: 9 to **m** justice and righteousness."
2Ki 8:19 He had promised to **m** a lamp for
2Ch 9: 8 to **m** justice and righteousness."
21: 7 He had promised to **m** a lamp for him
Job 27: 6 I will **m** my righteousness and never
Ps 82: 3 **m** the rights of the poor and
89:28 I will **m** my love to him for ever,
106: 3 Blessed are they who **m** justice, who
Pr 5: 2 that you may **m** discretion and your
Isa 56: 1 "**M** justice and do what is right,
Da 11:20 collector to **m** the royal splendour.
Hos 12: 6 you must return to your God; **m** love
Am 5:15 Hate evil, love good; **m** justice in
Ro 3:28 For we **m** that a man is justified by

Maintained (Maintain)
Rev 6: 9 of God and the testimony they had **m**.

Maintaining (Maintain)
Ex 34: 7 **m** love to thousands, and forgiving

Maintains (Maintain)
Job 2: 3 And he still **m** his integrity, though
Pr 28: 2 understanding and knowledge **m** order.
Na 1: 2 and **m** his wrath against his enemies.

Majestic (Majesty)
Ex 15: 6 "Your right hand, O LORD, was **m** in
15:11 Who is like you—**m** in holiness,
Job 37: 4 roar; he thunders with his **m** voice.
Ps 8: 1 O LORD, our Lord, how **m** is your name
8: 9 O LORD, our Lord, how **m** is your name
29: 4 the voice of the LORD is **m**.
68:15 The mountains of Bashan are **m**
76: 4 more **m** than mountains rich with
111: 3 Glorious and **m** are his deeds, and
SS 6: 4 Jerusalem, **m** as troops with banners.
6:10 sun, **m** as the stars in procession?
Isa 30:30 will cause men to hear his **m** voice
Eze 31: 7 was **m** in beauty, with its spreading
2Pe 1:17 voice came to him from the **M** Glory,

Majesty (Majestic)
Ex 15: 7 In the greatness of your **m** you threw
Dt 5:24 God has shown us his glory and his **m**,
11: 2 of the LORD your God: his **m**, his
33:17 In **m** he is like a firstborn bull;
33:26 help you and on the clouds in his **m**.
1Ch 16:27 Splendour and **m** are before him;
29:11 glory and the **m** and the splendour,
Est 1: 4 the splendour and glory of his **m**.
7: 3 O king, and if it pleases your **m**,
Job 37:22 splendour; God comes in awesome **m**.
40:10 and clothe yourself in honour and **m**.
Ps 21: 5 bestowed on him splendour and **m**.
45: 3 yourself with splendour and **m**.
45: 4 In your **m** ride forth victoriously on
68:34 Proclaim the power of God, whose **m**
93: 1 The LORD reigns, he is robed in **m**;
93: 1 in **m** and is armed with strength.
96: 6 Splendour and **m** are before him;
104: 1 are clothed with splendour and **m**.
110: 3 Arrayed in holy **m**, from the womb of
145: 5 of the glorious splendour of your **m**,
Isa 2:10 the LORD and the splendour of his **m**!
2:19 the splendour of his **m**, when he
2:21 the splendour of his **m**, when he
24:14 the west they acclaim the LORD's **m**.
26:10 and regard not the **m** of the LORD.
53: 2 He had no beauty or **m** to attract us
Eze 31: 2 'Who can be compared with you in **m**
31:18 you in splendour and **m**? Yet you,
Da 4:30 power and for the glory of my **m**?"
Mic 5: 4 in the **m** of the name of the LORD
Zec 6:13 and he will be clothed with **m** and
Ac 19:27 will be robbed of her divine **m**."
25:26 to write to His **M** about him.
2Th 1: 9 the Lord and from the **m** of his
Heb 1: 3 the right hand of the **M** in heaven.
8: 1 of the throne of the **M** in heaven,
2Pe 1:16 but we were eye-witnesses of his **m**.
Jude :25 be glory, **m**, power and authority,

Major (Majority)
2Ki 3:19 fortified city and every **m** town.

Majority (Major)
Ac 27:12 the **m** decided that we should sail on,
2Co 2: 6 him by the **m** is sufficient for him.

Makaz
1Ki 4: 9 Ben-Deker—in **M**, Shaalbim, Beth

Maker (Makers)
Job 4:17 Can a man be more pure than his **M**?
9: 9 He is the **M** of the Bear and Orion,
32:22 my **M** would soon take me away.
35:10 no-one says, 'Where is God my **M**, who
36: 3 I will ascribe justice to my **M**.
40:19 yet his **M** can approach him with his
Ps 95: 6 let us kneel before the LORD our **M**;
115:15 May you be blessed by the LORD, the **M**
121: 2 My help comes from the LORD, the **M**
124: 8 the LORD, the **M** of heaven and earth.
134: 3 May the LORD, the **M** of heaven and
146: 6 the **M** of heaven and earth, the sea,
149: 2 Let Israel rejoice in their **M**; let
Pr 14:31 the poor shows contempt for their **M**,
17: 5 the poor shows contempt for their **M**;
22: 2 The LORD is the **M** of them all.
Ecc 11: 5 work of God, the **M** of all things.
Isa 17: 7 In that day men will look to their **M**
27:11 their **M** has no compassion on them,
45: 9 "Woe to him who quarrels with his **M**,
45:11 and its **M**: Concerning things to come,
51:13 that you forget the LORD your **M**, who
54: 5 For your **M** is your husband—the
Jer 10:16 for he is the **M** of all things,
51:19 for he is the **M** of all things,
Hos 8:14 Israel has forgotten his **M** and built

Makers (Maker)
Isa 45:16 All the **m** of idols will be put to

Makheloth
Nu 33:25 They left Haradah and camped at **M**.
33:26 They left **M** and camped at Tahath.

Maki
Nu 13:15 from the tribe of Gad, Geuel son of **M**

Makir (Makir's, Makirite, Makirites)
Ge 50:23 Also the children of **M** son of
Nu 26:29 descendants of Manasseh: through **M**,
26:29 (**M** was the father of Gilead);
27: 1 the son of Gilead, the son of **M**, the
32:39 The descendants of **M** son of Manasseh
36: 1 of the clan of Gilead son of **M**,
Dt 3:15 I gave Gilead to **M**.
Jos 13:31 This was for the descendants of **M**
13:31 half of the sons of **M**, clan by clan.
17: 1 is, for **M**, Manasseh's firstborn.
17: 1 **M** was the ancestor of the Gileadites,
17: 3 the son of Gilead, the son of **M**, the
Jdg 5:14 From **M** captains came down, from
2Sa 9: 4 at the house of **M** son of Ammiel
9: 5 from the house of **M** son of Ammiel.
17:27 and **M** son of Ammiel from Lo Debar,
1Ch 2:21 Hezron lay with the daughter of **M**
2:23 All these were descendants of **M**
7:14 birth to **M** the father of Gilead.
7:15 **M** took a wife from among the
7:17 Gilead son of **M**, the son of Manasseh.

Makir's (Makir)
1Ch 7:16 **M** wife Maacah gave birth to a son

Makirite (Makir)
Nu 26:29 the **M** clan (Makir was the father of

Makirites (Makir)
Nu 32:40 Moses gave Gilead to the **M**, the
Jos 17: 1 because the **M** were great soldiers.

Makkedah
Canaanite royal town (Jos 12:16) in the lowlands of Judah. Joshua captured the city and its inhabitants. The 5 Amorite kings were executed after hiding in a cave nearby (Jos 10:16–27). Allotted to Judah (Jos 15:41).
Jos 10:10 down all the way to Azekah and **M**.
10:16 fled and hidden in the cave at **M**.
10:17 been found hiding in the cave at **M**,
10:21 safely to Joshua in the camp at **M**,
10:28 That day Joshua took **M**. He put the
10:28 And he did to the king of **M** as he
10:29 on from **M** to Libnah and attacked it.
12:16 the king of **M** one the king of Bethel
15:41 Gederoth, Beth Dagon, Naamah and **M**

Malachi
Prophet; name means "my messenger" (Mal 1:1).
Mal 1: 1 of the LORD to Israel through **M**.

Malcam
1Ch 8: 9 Hodesh he had Jobab, Zibia, Mesha, **M**,

Malchus
Jn 18:10 (The servant's name was **M**.)

Male (Males)
Ge 1:27 him; **m** and female he created them.
5: 2 He created them **m** and female and
6:19 **m** and female, to keep them alive
7: 2 a **m** and its mate, and two of every
7: 2 of unclean animal, a **m** and its mate,
7: 3 also seven of every kind of bird, **m**

Ge 7: 9 **m** and female, came to Noah and
7:16 The animals going in were **m** and
12:16 **m** and female donkeys, menservants
17:10 **m** among you shall be circumcised.
17:12 For the generations to come every **m**
17:14 Any uncircumcised **m**, who has not
17:23 every **m** in his household, and
17:27 every **m** in Abraham's household,
20:14 cattle and **m** and female slaves and
30:35 same day he removed all the **m** goats
31:10 saw that the **m** goats mating with the
31:12 see that all the **m** goats mating
32:14 two hundred female goats and twenty **m**
32:15 female donkeys and ten **m** donkeys.
34:24 every **m** in the city was circumcised.
34:25 unsuspecting city, killing every **m**.
Ex 12:48 No uncircumcised **m** may eat of it.
13: 2 "Consecrate to me every firstborn **m**.
13:15 the first **m** offspring of every womb
21:20 "If a man beats his **m** or female
21:32 If the bull gores a **m** or female
Lev 1: 3 he is to offer a **m** without defect.
1:10 he is to offer a **m** without defect.
3: 1 whether **m** or female, he is to
3: 6 offer a **m** or female without defect.
4:23 offering a **m** goat without defect.
6:18 Any **m** descendant of Aaron may eat it.
6:29 Any **m** in a priest's family may eat
7: 6 Any **m** in a priest's family may eat
9: 3 say to the Israelites: 'Take a **m**
14:10 **m** lambs and one ewe lamb a year old,
14:12 is to take one of the **m** lambs
14:21 he must take one **m** lamb as a guilt
16: 5 take two **m** goats for a sin offering
22:19 you must present a **m** without defect
23:18 with this bread seven **m** lambs
23:19 sacrifice one **m** goat for a sin
25:44 "'Your **m** and female slaves are to
27: 3 set the value of a **m** between the
27: 5 set the value of a **m** at twenty
27: 6 set the value of a **m** at five shekels
27: 7 set the value of a **m** at fifteen
Nu 3:12 **m** offspring of every Israelite woman.
3:15 Count every **m** a month old or more."
3:39 **m** a month old or more, was 22,000.
5: 3 Send away **m** and female alike; send
6:12 year-old **m** lamb as a guilt offering.
6:14 a year-old **m** lamb without defect for
7:15 young bull, one ram and one **m** lamb
7:16 one **m** goat for a sin offering;
7:17 five **m** goats and five **m** lambs
7:21 young bull, one ram and one **m** lamb
7:22 one **m** goat for a sin offering;
7:23 five **m** goats and five **m** lambs
7:27 young bull, one ram and one **m** lamb
7:28 one **m** goat for a sin offering;
7:29 five **m** goats and five **m** lambs
7:33 young bull, one ram and one **m** lamb
7:34 one **m** goat for a sin offering;
7:35 five **m** goats and five **m** lambs
7:39 young bull, one ram and one **m** lamb
7:40 one **m** goat for a sin offering;
7:41 five **m** goats and five **m** lambs
7:45 young bull, one ram and one **m** lamb
7:46 one **m** goat for a sin offering;
7:47 five **m** goats and five **m** lambs
7:51 young bull, one ram and one **m** lamb
7:52 one **m** goat for a sin offering;
7:53 five **m** goats and five **m** lambs
7:57 young bull, one ram and one **m** lamb
7:58 one **m** goat for a sin offering;
7:59 five **m** goats and five **m** lambs
7:63 young bull, one ram and one **m** lamb
7:64 one **m** goat for a sin offering;
7:65 five **m** goats and five **m** lambs
7:69 young bull, one ram and one **m** lamb
7:70 one **m** goat for a sin offering;
7:71 five **m** goats and five **m** lambs
7:75 young bull, one ram and one **m** lamb
7:76 one **m** goat for a sin offering;
7:77 five **m** goats and five **m** lambs
7:81 young bull, one ram and one **m** lamb
7:82 one **m** goat for a sin offering;
7:83 five **m** goats and five **m** lambs
7:87 twelve rams and twelve **m** lambs a
7:87 Twelve **m** goats were used for the sin
Nu 7:88 **m** goats and sixty **m** lambs a year old.
8:16 the first **m** offspring from every
8:17 Every firstborn **m** in Israel, whether
15:24 and a **m** goat for a sin offering.
18:10 most holy; every **m** shall eat it.
18:15 firstborn **m** of unclean animals.
26:62 All the **m** Levites a month old or
28:11 one ram and seven **m** lambs a year old,
28:15 one **m** goat is to be presented to the
28:19 one ram and seven **m** lambs a year old,
28:22 Include one **m** goat as a sin offering
28:27 one ram and seven **m** lambs a year old
28:30 Include one **m** goat to make atonement
29: 2 one ram and seven **m** lambs a year old,
29: 5 Include one **m** goat as a sin offering
29: 8 one ram and seven **m** lambs a year old,
29:11 Include one **m** goat as a sin offering,
29:13 two rams and fourteen **m** lambs a year
29:16 Include one **m** goat as a sin offering,
29:17 two rams and fourteen **m** lambs a year
29:19 Include one **m** goat as a sin offering,
29:20 two rams and fourteen **m** lambs a year
29:22 Include one **m** goat as a sin offering,
29:23 two rams and fourteen **m** lambs a year
29:25 Include one **m** goat as a sin offering,
29:26 two rams and fourteen **m** lambs a year
29:28 Include one **m** goat as a sin offering,
29:29 two rams and fourteen **m** lambs a year
29:31 Include one **m** goat as a sin offering,
29:32 two rams and fourteen **m** lambs a year
29:34 Include one **m** goat as a sin offering,
29:36 one ram and seven **m** lambs a year old,
29:38 Include one **m** goat as a sin offering,
Dt 15:19 every firstborn **m** of your herds and
23:18 or of a **m** prostitute into the house
28:68 your enemies as **m** and female slaves,
Jos 17: 2 These are the other **m** descendants of
Jdg 21:11 "Kill every **m** and every woman who is
1Sa 25:22 one **m** of all who belong to him!"
25:34 not one **m** belonging to Nabal would
2Sa 21: 6 let seven of his **m** descendants be
1Ki 14:10 last **m** in Israel—slave or free.
14:24 There were even **m** shrine-prostitutes
15:12 He expelled the **m** shrine-prostitutes
16:11 He did not spare a single **m**,
21:21 last **m** in Israel—slave or free.
22:46 He rid the land of the rest of the **m**
2Ki 9: 8 last **m** in Israel—slave or free.
23: 7 of the **m** shrine-prostitutes,
1Ch 29:21 rams and a thousand **m** lambs,
2Ch 29:21 seven **m** lambs and seven **m** goats as
29:32 rams and two hundred **m** lambs—
31:19 portions to every **m** among them
Ezr 6: 9 rams, **m** lambs for burnt offerings to
6:17 rams, four hundred **m** lambs
6:17 twelve **m** goats, one for each of the
7:17 rams and **m** lambs, together with
8:35 rams, seventy-seven **m** lambs and
8:35 as a sin offering, twelve **m** goats.
Est 7: 4 If we had merely been sold as **m** and
Job 36:14 among **m** prostitutes of the shrines.
Ecc 2: 7 I bought **m** and female slaves and had
Jer 34: 9 both **m** and female; no-one was to
34:10 agreed that they would free their **m**
34:16 each of you has taken back the **m** and
Eze 16:17 and you made for yourself **m** idols
43:22 offer a **m** goat without defect for
43:25 a **m** goat daily for a sin offering;
45:23 and a **m** goat for a sin offering.
46: 4 day is to be six **m** lambs and a ram,
Mal 1:14 **m** in his flock and vows to give it,
Mt 19: 4 Creator 'made them **m** and female',
Mk 10: 6 God 'made them **m** and female'.
Lk 2:23 **m** is to be consecrated to the Lord"),
1Co 6: 9 nor adulterers nor **m** prostitutes
Gal 3:28 slave nor free, **m** nor female, for
Rev 12: 5 She gave birth to a son, a **m** child,
12:13 who had given birth to the **m** child.

Males (Male)

Ge 34:15 like us by circumcising all your **m**.
34:22 condition that our **m** be circumcised,
Ex 12: 5 must be year-old **m** without defect,
12:48 the **m** in his household circumcised;
13:12 All the firstborn **m** of your
Ex 34:19 including all the firstborn **m** of
Nu 3:22 The number of all the **m** a month old
3:28 The number of all the **m** a month old
3:34 The number of all the **m** a month old
3:40 "Count all the firstborn Israelite **m**
3:43 The total number of firstborn **m** a
2Ch 31:16 distributed to the **m** three years
Jer 2:24 Any **m** that pursue her need not tire

Malice (Malicious, Maliciously)

Nu 35:20 If anyone with **m** aforethought pushes
Dt 4:42 neighbour without **m** aforethought.
19: 4 without **m** aforethought.
19: 6 neighbour without **m** aforethought.
Jos 20: 5 and without **m** aforethought.
Job 6:30 my lips? Can my mouth not discern **m**?
Ps 28: 3 but harbour **m** in their hearts.
41: 5 My enemies say of me in **m**, "When
55:10 walls; **m** and abuse are within it.
73: 8 They scoff, and speak with **m**; in
Pr 26:26 His **m** may be concealed by deception,
Eze 25: 6 rejoicing with all the **m** of your
25:15 took revenge with **m** in their hearts,
36: 5 for with glee and with **m** in their
Mk 7:22 greed, **m**, deceit, lewdness, envy,
Ro 1:29 envy, murder, strife, deceit and **m**.
1Co 5: 8 the yeast of **m** and wickedness, but
Eph 4:31 slander, along with every form of **m**.
Col 3: 8 rage, **m**, slander and filthy language
Tit 3: 3 We lived in **m** and envy, being hated
1Pe 2: 1 Therefore, rid yourselves of all **m**

Malicious (Malice)

Ex 23: 1 a wicked man by being a **m** witness.
Dt 19:16 If a **m** witness takes the stand to
Pr 17: 4 a liar pays attention to a **m** tongue.
26:24 A **m** man disguises himself with his
Isa 58: 9 with the pointing finger and **m** talk,
Eze 28:24 **m** neighbours who are painful briers
36: 3 of people's **m** talk and slander,
1Ti 3:11 not **m** talkers but temperate and
6: 4 strife, **m** talk, evil suspicions

Maliciously (Malice)

Ps 35:16 Like the ungodly they **m** mocked; they
35:19 me without reason **m** wink the eye.
Pr 10:10 He who winks **m** causes grief, and a
1Pe 3:16 so that those who speak **m** against
3Jn :10 he is doing, gossiping **m** about us.

Malign (Maligned)

Ps 12: 5 protect them from those who **m** them."
Tit 2: 5 that no-one will **m** the word of God.

Maligned (Malign)

Eze 28:26 on all their neighbours who **m** them.
Ac 19: 9 to believe and publicly **m** the Way.

Malkiel (Malkielite)

Ge 46:17 The sons of Beriah: Heber and **M**.
Nu 26:45 through **M**, the Malkielite clan.
1Ch 7:31 The sons of Beriah: Heber and **M**, who

Malkielite (Malkiel)

Nu 26:45 clan; through Malkiel, the **M** clan.

Malkijah

1Ch 6:40 the son of Baaseiah, the son of **M**,
9:12 the son of Pashhur, the son of **M**;
24: 9 the fifth to **M**, the sixth to Mijamin,
Ezr 10:25 **M**, Mijamin, Eleazar, **M** and Benaiah.
10:31 Ishijah, **M**, Shemaiah, Shimeon,
Ne 3:11 **M** son of Harim and Hasshub son of
3:14 The Dung Gate was repaired by **M** son
3:31 Next to him, **M**, one of the
8: 4 Mishael, **M**, Hashum, Hashbaddanah,
10: 3 Pashhur, Amariah, **M**,
11:12 the son of Pashhur, the son of **M**,
12:42 Uzzi, Jehohanan, **M**, Elam and Ezer.
Jer 21: 1 sent to him Pashhur son of **M**
38: 1 and Pashhur son of **M** heard what
38: 6 and put him into the cistern of **M**,

Malkiram
1Ch 3:18 **M**, Pedaiah, Shenazzar, Jekamiah,

Malki-Shua
1Sa 14:49 sons were Jonathan, Ishvi and **M**.
31: 2 his sons Jonathan, Abinadab and **M**.
1Ch 8:33 Jonathan, **M**, Abinadab and Esh-Baal.
9:39 Jonathan, **M**, Abinadab and Esh-Baal.
10: 2 his sons Jonathan, Abinadab and **M**.

Mallothi
1Ch 25: 4 **M**, Hothir and Mahazioth.
25:26 the nineteenth to **M**, his sons and

Malluch (Malluch's)
1Ch 6:44 Kishi, the son of Abdi, the son of **M**,
Ezr 10:29 **M**, Adaiah, Jashub, Sheal and
10:32 Benjamin, **M** and Shemariah.
Ne 10: 4 Hattush, Shebaniah, **M**,
10:27 **M**, Harim and Baanah.
12: 2 Amariah, **M**, Hattush,

Malluch's (Malluch)
Ne 12:14 of **M**, Jonathan; of Shecaniah's,

Malta
Island in Mediterranean, between Sicily and Africa where Paul was shipwrecked (Ac 28:1). He stayed for three months surviving a snake attack, healing the sick and receiving hospitality (Ac 28:1–11).

Ac 28: 1 out that the island was called **M**.

Mamre
Wooded area north of Hebron where Abram set up camp and built an altar (Ge 13:18). Here Abram heard of Lot's capture (Ge 14:13) and received promise of a son (Ge 18:1, 10). He bought a field and cave here (Ge 23:17): the burial site for Sarah (Ge 23:19), Abraham (Ge 25:8–9), Isaac (Ge 35:27–29), Rebekah, Leah and Jacob (Ge 49:29–33; 50:12–13).

Ge 13:18 near the great trees of **M** at Hebron,
14:13 the great trees of **M** the Amorite,
14:24 went with me—to Aner, Eshcol and **M**.
18: 1 to Abraham near the great trees of **M**
23:17 Ephron's field in Machpelah near **M**
23:19 in the field of Machpelah near **M**
25: 9 him in the cave of Machpelah near **M**,
35:27 came home to his father Isaac in **M**,
49:30 near **M** in Canaan, which Abraham
50:13 near **M**, which Abraham had bought as

Man (Countryman, Countrymen, Fellow-man, Fellow-men, Horseman, Horsemen, *Man of God*, Man's, Manhood, Mankind, Man-made, Manned, Men, Men's, *Righteous man, Son of man*, Spokesman, Spokesmen, Woodsman, Woodsmen, Workman, Workman's, Workmen)
Ge 1:26 God said, "Let us make **m** in our
1:27 God created **m** in his own image, in
2: 5 there was no **m** to work the ground,
2: 7 the LORD God formed the **m** from the
2: 7 and the **m** became a living being.
2: 8 there he put the **m** he had formed.
2:15 The LORD God took the **m** and put him
2:16 the LORD God commanded the **m**, "You
2:18 It is not good for the **m** to be alone.
2:19 He brought them to the **m** to see what
2:19 the **m** called each living creature,
2:20 the **m** gave names to all the
2:21 the LORD God caused the **m** to fall
2:22 the **m**, and he brought her to the **m**.
2:23 The **m** said, "This is now bone of my
2:23 for she was taken out of **m**."
2:24 For this reason a **m** will leave his
2:25 The **m** and his wife were both naked,
3: 8 the **m** and his wife heard the sound
3: 9 the LORD God called to the **m**, "Where
3:12 The **m** said, "The woman you put here
3:22 the LORD God said, "The **m** has now
Ge 3:24 After he drove the **m** out, he placed
4: 1 the LORD I have brought forth a **m**."
4:23 a **m** for wounding me, a young **m** for
5: 1 When God created **m**, he made him in
5: 2 were created, he called them "**m**".
6: 3 "My Spirit will not contend with **m**
6: 6 that he had made **m** on the earth,
8:21 I curse the ground because of **m**,
9: 5 And from each **m**, too, I will demand
9: 5 for the life of his fellow **m**.
9: 6 "Whoever sheds the blood of **m**, by **m**
9: 6 in the image of God has God made **m**.
9:20 Noah, a **m** of the soil, proceeded to
15: 4 "This **m** will not be your heir, but a
16:12 He will be a wild donkey of a **m**; his
17:17 "Will a son be born to a **m** a hundred
19: 8 who have never slept with a **m**.
19:31 and there is no **m** around here to lie
24:16 virgin; no **m** had ever lain with her.
24:21 Without saying a word, the **m** watched
24:22 the **m** took out a gold nose ring
24:26 the **m** bowed down and worshipped the
24:29 hurried out to the **m** at the spring.
24:30 Rebekah tell what the **m** said to her,
24:30 he went out to the **m** and found him
24:32 the **m** went to the house, and the
24:58 with this **m**?" "I will go," she said.
24:61 camels and went back with the **m**.
24:65 asked the servant, "Who is that **m** in
25: 8 an old **m** and full of years; and he
25:27 a **m** of the open country, while Jacob
25:27 a quiet **m**, staying among the tents.
26:11 "Anyone who molests this **m** or his
26:13 The **m** became rich, and his wealth
27: 2 Isaac said, "I am now an old **m** and
27:11 Esau is a hairy **m**, and I'm a **m**
29:19 her to you than to some other **m**.
30:43 In this way the **m** grew exceedingly
32:24 Jacob was left alone, and a **m**
32:25 the **m** saw that he could not
32:25 wrenched as he wrestled with the **m**.
32:26 the **m** said, "Let me go, for it is
32:27 The **m** asked him, "What is your name?"
32:28 the **m** said, "Your name will no
34:14 to a **m** who is not circumcised.
34:19 The young **m**, who was the most
37: 2 Joseph, a young **m** of seventeen, was
37:15 a **m** found him wandering around in
37:17 "They have moved on from here," the **m**
38: 1 with a **m** of Adullam named Hirah.
38: 2 of a Canaanite **m** named Shua.
38:25 "I am pregnant by the **m** who owns
41:12 giving each **m** the interpretation
41:13 and the other **m** was hanged."
41:33 wise **m** and put him in charge of the
41:38 twelve brothers, the sons of one **m**,
42:11 We are all the sons of one **m**. Your
42:13 twelve brothers, the sons of one **m**,
42:30 "The **m** who is lord over the land
42:33 "Then the **m** who is lord over the
43: 3 Judah said to him, "The **m** warned us
43: 5 we will not go down, because the **m**
43: 6 the **m** you had another brother?"
43: 7 They replied, "The **m** questioned us
43:11 take them down to the **m** as a gift—a
43:13 also and go back to the **m** at once.
43:14 grant you mercy before the **m** so
43:17 The **m** did as Joseph told him and
44:15 Don't you know that a **m** like me can
44:17 Only the **m** who was found to have the
Ex 2: 1 Now a **m** of the house of Levi married
2:14 The **m** said, "Who made you ruler and
2:21 Moses agreed to stay with the **m**, who
4:11 said to him, "Who gave **m** his mouth?
9:19 the hail will fall on every **m**
10: 7 "How long will this **m** be a snare to
11: 7 a dog will bark at any **m** or animal.
12: 3 each **m** is to take a lamb for his
13: 2 belongs to me, whether **m** or animal."
13:15 in Egypt, both **m** and animal.
19:13 Whether **m** or animal, he shall not be
21: 4 and only the **m** shall go free.
21: 7 "If a **m** sells his daughter as a
21:12 "Anyone who strikes a **m** and kills
21:14 if a **m** schemes and kills another **m**
21:19 he must pay the injured **m** for the
Ex 21:20 "If a **m** beats his male or female
21:26 "If a **m** hits a manservant or
21:28 "If a bull gores a **m** or a woman to
21:29 penned up and it kills a **m** or woman,
21:33 "If a **m** uncovers a pit or digs one
22: 1 "If a **m** steals an ox or a sheep and
22: 5 "If a **m** grazes his livestock in a
22: 7 "If a **m** gives his neighbour silver
22:10 "If a **m** gives a donkey, an ox, a
22:14 "If a **m** borrows an animal from his
22:16 "If a **m** seduces a virgin who is not
23: 1 Do not help a wicked **m** by being
23: 3 do not show favouritism to a poor **m**
25: 2 each **m** whose heart prompts him to
32:27 'Each **m** strap a sword to his side.
33:11 face, as a **m** speaks with his friend.
36: 6 "No **m** or woman is to make anything
Lev 13: 6 The **m** must wash his clothes, and he
13:29 "If a **m** or woman has a sore on the
13:38 "When a **m** or woman has white spots
13:40 "When a **m** has lost his hair and is
13:44 the **m** is diseased and is unclean.
15: 2 'When any **m** has a bodily discharge,
15: 4 "'Any bed the **m** with a discharge
15: 6 Whoever sits on anything that the **m**
15: 7 "'Whoever touches the **m** who has a
15: 8 "'If the **m** with the discharge spits
15: 9 "'Everything the **m** sits on when
15:11 "'Anyone the **m** with a discharge
15:12 "'A clay pot that the **m** touches
15:13 "'When a **m** is cleansed from his
15:15 for the **m** because of his discharge.
15:16 "'When a **m** has an emission of semen,
15:18 a **m** lies with a woman and there is
15:24 "'If a **m** lies with her and her
15:32 These are the regulations for a **m**
15:33 a **m** or a woman with a discharge,
15:33 for a **m** who lies with a woman who
16:21 care of a **m** appointed for the task.
16:22 **m** shall release it in the desert.
16:26 "The **m** who releases the goat as a
16:28 The **m** who burns them must wash his
17: 4 that **m** shall be considered guilty of
17: 9 **m** must be cut off from his people.
18: 5 the **m** who obeys them will live
18:22 "'Do not lie with a **m** as one lies
19:13 the wages of a hired **m** overnight.
19:20 "'If a **m** sleeps with a woman who
19:20 a slave girl promised to another **m**
19:21 The **m**, however, must bring a ram to
20: 3 I will set my face against that **m**
20: 4 close their eyes when that **m** gives
20: 5 I will set my face against that **m**
20:10 "'If a **m** commits adultery with
20:11 "'If a **m** sleeps with his father's
20:11 Both the **m** and the woman must be put
20:12 "'If a **m** sleeps with his
20:13 "'If a **m** lies with a **m** as one lies
20:14 "'If a **m** marries both a woman and
20:15 "'If a **m** has sexual relations with
20:17 "'If a **m** marries his sister, the
20:18 "'If a **m** lies with a woman during
20:20 "'If a **m** sleeps with his aunt, he
20:21 "'If a **m** marries his brother's wife,
20:27 "'A **m** or woman who is a medium or
21:18 No **m** who has any defect may come
21:18 no **m** who is blind or lame,
21:19 no **m** with a crippled foot or hand,
24:21 kills a **m** must be put to death.
25:26 If, however, a **m** has no-one to
25:27 balance to the **m** to whom he sold it;
25:29 "'If a **m** sells a house in a walled
25:50 a hired **m** for that number of years.
25:53 He is to be treated as a **m** hired
27: 8 the **m** making the vow can afford.
27:14 "'If a **m** dedicates his house as
27:15 If the **m** who dedicates his house
27:16 "'If a **m** dedicates to the LORD part
27:19 If the **m** who dedicates the field
27:22 "'If a **m** dedicates to the LORD a
27:23 and the **m** must pay its value on that
27:28 "'But nothing that a **m** owns and
27:28 devotes to the LORD—whether **m** or
27:31 If a **m** redeems any of his tithe, he
Nu 1: 2 listing every **m** by name, one by one.
1: 4 One **m** from each tribe, each the head

Nu 1:52 each **m** in his own camp under his own
2: 2 each **m** under his standard with the
3:13 in Israel, whether **m** or animal.
4:19 assign each **m** his work and what
4:32 Assign to each **m** the specific
5: 6 "Say to the Israelites: 'When a **m** or
5:13 by sleeping with another **m**, and this
5:19 "If no other **m** has slept with you
5:20 with a **m** other than your husband"—
5:30 a **m** because he suspects his wife.
6: 2 'If a **m** or woman wants to make a
8:17 Israel, whether **m** or animal, is mine.
9:13 if a **m** who is ceremonially clean and
9:13 That **m** will bear the consequences of
11:27 A young **m** ran and told Moses, "Eldad
12: 3 (Now Moses was a very humble **m**, more
15:32 a **m** was found gathering wood on the
15:35 the LORD said to Moses, "The **m** must
16: 5 The **m** he chooses he will cause to
16: 7 The **m** the LORD chooses will be the
16:17 Each **m** is to take his censer and put
16:18 each **m** took his censer, put fire and
16:22 assembly when only one **m** sins?"
17: 2 the name of each **m** on his staff.
17: 5 The staff belonging to the **m** I
17: 9 them, and each **m** took his own staff.
18:15 both **m** and animal, that is offered
19: 8 The **m** who burns it must also wash
19: 9 "A **m** who is clean shall gather up
19:10 The **m** who gathers up the ashes of
19:18 a **m** who is ceremonially clean is to
19:19 The **m** who is clean is to sprinkle
19:21 "The **m** who sprinkles the water of
23:19 God is not a **m**, that he should lie,
25: 6 an Israelite **m** brought to his family
27: 8 "Say to the Israelites, 'If a **m** dies
27:16 appoint a **m** over this community
27:18 "Take Joshua son of Nun, a **m** in whom
30: 2 a **m** makes a vow to the LORD or takes
30:16 between a **m** and his wife,
31: 7 commanded Moses, and killed every **m**.
31:17 every woman who has slept with a **m**,
31:18 girl who has never slept with a **m**.
31:35 women who had never slept with a **m**.
32:27 your servants, every **m** armed for
32:29 every **m** armed for battle, cross over
35:16 "'If a **m** strikes someone with an
Dt 1:17 Do not be afraid of any **m**, for
1:23 of you, one **m** from each tribe.
1:35 "Not a **m** of this evil generation
4:16 whether formed like a **m** or a woman,
4:32 from the day God created **m** on the
5:24 Today we have seen that a **m** can live
5:26 For what mortal **m** has ever heard the
8: 3 to teach you that **m** does not live on
8: 5 Know then in your heart that as a **m**
11:25 No **m** will be able to stand against
15: 7 If there is a poor **m** among your
15:12 If a fellow Hebrew, a **m** or woman,
16:16 No **m** should appear before the LORD
17: 2 If a **m** or woman living among you in
17: 5 take the **m** or woman who has done
17: 6 witnesses a **m** shall be put to death,
17:12 The **m** who shows contempt for the
19: 3 anyone who kills a **m** may flee there.
19: 4 This is the rule concerning the **m**
19: 5 For instance, a **m** may go into the
19: 5 That **m** may flee to one of these
19:11 if a **m** hates his neighbour and lies
19:15 to convict a **m** accused of any crime
19:16 the stand to accuse a **m** of a crime,
20: 8 the officers shall add, "Is any **m**
21: 1 If a **m** is found slain, lying in a
21: 8 of the blood of an innocent **m**."
21:15 If a **m** has two wives, and he loves
21:18 If a **m** has a stubborn and rebellious
21:22 If a **m** guilty of a capital offence
22: 5 nor a **m** wear women's clothing, for
22:13 If a **m** takes a wife and, after lying
22:16 to this **m**, but he dislikes her.
22:18 the elders shall take the **m** and
22:19 because this **m** has given an
22:22 If a **m** is found sleeping with
22:22 both the **M** who slept with her and
22:23 If a **m** happens to meet in a town a
22:24 and the **m** because he violated
Dt 22:25 if out in the country a **m** happens to
22:25 the **m** who has done this shall die.
22:27 for the **m** found the girl out in the
22:28 If a **m** happens to meet a virgin who
22:30 A **m** is not to marry his father's
23:17 No Israelite **m** or woman is to become
24: 1 If a **m** marries a woman who becomes
24: 2 she becomes the wife of another **m**,
24: 5 If a **m** has recently married, he must
24: 7 If a **m** is caught kidnapping one of
24:11 Stay outside and let the **m** to whom
24:12 If the **m** is poor, do not go to sleep
24:14 Do not take advantage of a hired **m**
25: 2 If the guilty **m** deserves to be
25: 7 However, if a **m** does not want to
25: 9 "This is what is done to the **m** who
27:15 "Cursed is the **m** who carves an image
27:16 "Cursed is the **m** who dishonours his
27:17 "Cursed is the **m** who moves his
27:18 "Cursed is the **m** who leads the blind
27:19 "Cursed is the **m** who withholds
27:20 "Cursed is the **m** who sleeps with his
27:21 "Cursed is the **m** who has sexual
27:22 "Cursed is the **m** who sleeps with his
27:23 "Cursed is the **m** who sleeps with his
27:24 "Cursed is the **m** who kills his
27:25 "Cursed is the **m** who accepts a bribe
27:26 "Cursed is the **m** who does not uphold
28:29 about like a blind **m** in the dark.
28:54 Even the most gentle and sensitive **m**
29:18 Make sure there is no **m** or woman,
29:20 and zeal will burn against that **m**.
32:30 How could one **m** chase a thousand, or
33: 8 Urim belong to the **m** you favoured.
Jos 5:13 he looked up and saw a **m** standing in
6: 5 will go up, every **m** straight in."
6:20 the wall collapsed; so every **m**
6:26 "Cursed before the LORD is the **m** who
7:14 LORD takes shall come forward **m** by **m**.
7:18 had his family come forward **m** by **m**,
8:17 Not a **m** remained in Ai or Bethel who
10:14 a day when the LORD listened to a **m**.
10:20 almost to a **m**—but the few who were
14:15 the greatest **m** among the Anakites.
15:16 in marriage to the **m** who attacks
Jdg 1:12 in marriage to the **m** who attacks
1:24 the spies saw a **m** coming out of the
1:25 spared the **m** and his whole family.
3:15 Ehud, a left-handed **m**, the son
3:17 king of Moab, who was a very fat **m**.
3:29 and strong; not a **m** escaped.
4:16 fell by the sword; not a **m** was left.
4:22 show you the **m** you're looking for.
5:30 spoils: a girl or two for each **m**,
7:13 Gideon arrived just as a **m** was
7:21 While each **m** held his position
8:14 He caught a young **m** of Succoth and
8:14 and the young **m** wrote down for him
8:21 'As is the **m**, so is his strength.'"
8:25 and each **m** threw a ring from his
9: 2 s sons rule over you, or just one **m**?'
10: 1 time of Abimelech a **m** of Issachar
13: 2 A certain **m** of Zorah, named Manoah,
13:10 He's here! The **m** who appeared to me
13:11 When he came to the **m**, he said,
16: 7 I'll become as weak as any other **m**."
16:11 I'll become as weak as any other **m**."
16:13 I'll become as weak as any other **m**."
16:17 become as weak as any other **m**."
16:19 she called a **m** to shave off the
17: 1 Now a **m** named Micah from the hill
17: 5 Now this **m** Micah had a shrine, and
17:11 **m** was to him like one of his sons.
17:12 and the young **m** became his priest
19: 7 the **m** got up to go, his
19: 9 the **m**, with his concubine and his
19:10 the **m** left and went towards Jebus
19:16 That evening an old **m** from the hill
19:17 the old **m** asked, "Where are you
19:19 and the young **m** with us.
19:20 at my house," the old **m** said.
19:22 they shouted to the old **m** who owned
19:22 "Bring out the **m** who came to your
19:23 Since this **m** is my guest, don't do
19:24 But to this **m**, don't do such a
19:25 So the **m** took his concubine and sent
Jdg 19:28 Then the **m** put her on his donkey
20: 1 land of Gilead came out as one **m**
20: 8 All the people rose as one **m**, saying,
20:11 united as one **m** against the city.
21:12 women who had never slept with a **m**,
21:23 While the girls were dancing, each **m**
Ru 1: 1 and a **m** from Bethlehem in Judah,
2: 1 **m** of standing, whose name was Boaz.
2:19 be the **m** who took notice of you!"
2:19 "The name of the **m** I worked with
2:20 She added, "That **m** is our close
3: 8 the night something startled the **m**,
3:18 For the **m** will not rest until the
1Sa 1: 1 There was a certain **m** from Ramathaim,
1: 3 Year after year this **m** went up from
1:21 the **m** Elkanah went up with all his
2:15 say to the **m** who was sacrificing,
2:16 If the **m** said to him, "Let the fat
2:25 If a **m** sins against another **m**, God
2:25 but if a **m** sins against the LORD,
2:31 not be an old **m** in your family
2:32 line there will never be an old **m**.
4:10 and every **m** fled to his tent.
4:13 When the **m** entered the town and told
4:14 uproar?" The **m** hurried over to Eli,
4:17 The **m** who brought the news replied,
4:18 died, for he was an old **m** and heavy.
9: 1 There was a Benjamite, a **m** of
9: 2 an impressive young **m** without equal
9: 7 what can we give the **m**? The food
9: 9 (Formerly in Israel, if a **m** went to
9:16 you a **m** from the land of Benjamin.
9:17 "This is the **m** I spoke to you about;
10:12 A **m** who lived there answered, "And
10:22 "Has the **m** come here yet?" And the
10:24 "Do you see the **m** the LORD has
11: 7 and they turned out as one **m**.
13:14 the LORD has sought out a **m** after
14: 1 to the young **m** bearing his armour,
14:24 "Cursed be any **m** who eats food
14:28 'Cursed be any **m** who eats food today!
14:52 Saul saw a mighty or brave **m**, he
15:29 is not a **m**, that he should change
16: 7 not look at the things **m** looks at.
16: 7 **M** looks at the outward appearance,
16:18 He is a brave **m** and a warrior. He
16:18 speaks well and is a fine-looking **m**.
17: 8 a **m** and have him come down to me.
17:10 me a **m** and let us fight each other."
17:24 the Israelites saw the **m**, they all
17:25 "Do you see how this **m** keeps coming
17:25 great wealth to the **m** who kills him.
17:26 "What will be done for the **m** who
17:27 be done for the **m** who kills him."
17:33 been a fighting **m** from his youth."
17:55 "Abner, whose son is that young **m**?"
17:56 "Find out whose son this young **m** is.
17:58 "Whose son are you, young **m**?" Saul
18:23 I'm only a poor **m** and little known."
19: 5 wrong to an innocent **m** like David
21:14 "Look at the **m**! He is insane!
21:15 me? Must this **m** come into my house?"
22:23 the **m** who is seeking your life is
24:19 a **m** finds his enemy, does he let him
25: 2 A certain **m** in Maon, who had
25:17 such a wicked **m** that no-one can
25:25 no attention to that wicked **m** Nabal.
26:15 David said, "You're a **m**, aren't you?
26:23 The LORD rewards every **m** for his
27: 3 Each **m** had his family with him, and
27: 9 he did not leave a **m** or woman alive,
27:11 He did not leave a **m** or woman alive
28:14 "An old **m** wearing a robe is coming
29: 4 "Send the **m** back, that he may return
30:22 However, each **m** may take his wife
30:24 The share of the **m** who stayed with
2Sa 1: 2 On the third day a **m** arrived from
1: 5 David said to the young **m** who
1: 6 on Mount Gilboa," the young **m** said,
1:13 David said to the young **m** who
2:16 each **m** grabbed his opponent by the
2:23 And every **m** stopped when he came to
3:38 a great **m** has fallen in Israel this day?
4:10 a **m** told me, 'Saul is dead,' and
4:11 an innocent **m** in his own house
7:19 of dealing with **m**, O Sovereign LORD?

2Sa 11: 3 The **m** said, "Isn't this Bathsheba,
12: 2 The rich **m** had a very large number
12: 3 the poor **m** had nothing except one
12: 4 "Now a traveller came to the rich **m**,
12: 4 but the rich **m** refrained from taking
12: 4 lamb that belonged to the poor **m**
12: 5 David burned with anger against the **m**
12: 5 the **m** who did this deserves to die!
12: 7 Nathan said to David, "You are the **m**!
13: 3 Jonadab was a very shrewd **m**.
13:34 Now the **m** standing watch looked up
14:16 from the hand of the **m** who is
14:21 Go, bring back the young **m** Absalom."
14:25 In all Israel there was not a **m** so
16: 5 King David approached Bahurim, a **m**
16: 7 out, you **m** of blood, you scoundrel!
16: 8 ruin because you are a **m** of blood!"
17: 3 The death of the **m** you seek will
17:18 a young **m** saw them and told Absalom.
17:18 went to the house of a **m** in Bahurim.
17:25 Amasa was the son of a **m** named
18: 5 the young **m** Absalom for my sake.
18:11 Joab said to the **m** who had told him
18:12 the **m** replied, "Even if a thousand
18:12 'Protect the young **m** Absalom for my
18:24 out, he saw a **m** running alone.
18:25 And the **m** came closer and closer.
18:26 the watchman saw another **m** running,
18:26 "Look, another **m** running alone!" The
18:27 "He's a good **m**," the king said. "He
18:29 The king asked, "Is the young **m**
18:32 "Is the young **m** Absalom safe?" The
18:32 to harm you be like that young **m**."
19: 7 if you don't go out, not a **m** will
19:14 of Judah as though they were one **m**.
19:32 Now Barzillai was a very old **m**,
19:32 for he was a very wealthy **m**.
20: 1 son! Every **m** to his tent, O Israel!"
20:12 and the **m** saw that all the troops
20:21 A **m** named Sheba son of Bicri,
20:21 Hand over this one **m**, and I'll
21: 5 They answered the king, "As for the **m**
21:20 there was a huge **m** with six fingers
23: 1 the oracle of the **m** exalted by the
23: 1 the **m** anointed by the God of Jacob,
1Ki 1:42 Adonijah said, "Come in. A worthy **m**
1:52 If he shows himself to be a worthy **m**,
2: 2 "So be strong, show yourself a **m**,
2: 4 have a **m** on the throne of Israel.'
2: 9 You are a **m** of wisdom; you will know
4:25 safety, each **m** under his own vine
4:31 He was wiser than any other **m**,
7:14 **m** of Tyre and a craftsman in bronze.
8:25 'You shall never fail to have a **m** to
8:31 "When a **m** wrongs his neighbour and
8:39 Forgive and act; deal with each **m**
9: 5 have a **m** on the throne of Israel.'
11:28 Now Jeroboam was a **m** of standing,
11:28 how well the young **m** did his work,
13: 4 out towards the **m** shrivelled up,
16: 9 **m** in charge of the palace at Tirzah.
20: 7 "See how this **m** is looking for
20:35 your weapon," but the **m** refused.
20:36 And after the **m** went away, a lion
20:37 The prophet found another **m** and said,
20:37 So the **m** struck him and wounded him.
20:39 a captive and said, 'Guard this **m**.
20:40 here and there, the **m** disappeared.
20:42 a **m** I had determined should die.
21:19 murdered a **m** and seized his property
21:25 (There was never a **m** like Ahab, who
22: 8 "There is still one **m** through whom
22:13 "Look, as one **m** the other prophets
22:36 "Every **m** to his town; everyone to his
2Ki 1: 6 "A **m** came to meet us," they replied.
1: 7 The king asked them, "What kind of **m**
1: 8 They replied, "He was a **m** with a
3:21 to fight against them; so every **m**,
3:25 They destroyed the towns, and each **m**
4: 1 The wife of a **m** from the company of
4: 9 "I know that this **m** who often comes
4:42 A **m** came from Baal Shalishah,
5: 1 He was a great **m** in the sight of his
5: 8 Make the **m** come to me and he will
5:26 the **m** got down from his chariot
6: 7 "Lift it out," he said. Then the **m**

2Ki 6:19 you to the **m** you are looking for.
7: 5 edge of the camp, not a **m** was there,
7:10 not a **m** was there—not a sound of
9: 1 The prophet Elisha summoned a **m** from
9: 4 the young **m**, the prophet, went to
9:11 "You know the **m** and the sort of
11: 8 each **m** with his weapon in his hand.
13:21 some Israelites were burying a **m**,
13:21 the **m**'s body into Elisha's tomb.
14:12 Israel, and every **m** fled to his home.
15:20 Every wealthy **m** had to contribute
22:15 says: Tell the **m** who sent you to me,
1Ch 12: 4 Ishmaiah the Gibeonite, a mighty **m**
16: 3 to each Israelite **m** and woman.
16:21 He allowed no **m** to oppress them; for
20: 6 there was a huge **m** with six fingers
22: 9 you will have a son who will be a **m**
27: 6 who was a mighty **m** among the Thirty
27:32 a **m** of insight and a scribe.
28:21 and every willing **m** skilled in any
29: 1 is not for **m** but for the LORD God.
2Ch 2: 7 "Send me, therefore, a **m** skilled to
2:13 you Huram-Abi, a **m** of great skill,
6:16 'You shall never fail to have a **m** to
6:22 "When a **m** wrongs his neighbour and
6:30 Forgive, and deal with each **m**
7:18 to have a **m** to rule over Israel.'
14:11 do not let **m** prevail against you."
15:13 whether small or great, **m** or woman.
18: 7 "There is still one **m** through whom
18:12 "Look, as one **m** the other prophets
19: 6 because you are not judging for **m**
23: 7 each **m** with his weapons in his hand.
25:22 Israel, and every **m** fled to his home.
34:23 says: Tell the **m** who sent you to me,
36:17 spared neither young **m** nor young
Ezr 2:61 Hakkoz and Barzillai (a **m** who had
3: 1 assembled as one **m** in Jerusalem.
5:14 "Then King Cyrus gave them to a **m**
7:11 a **m** learned in matters concerning
8:18 a capable **m**, from the descendants of
Ne 1:11 favour in the presence of this **m**.
4:18 But the **m** who sounded the trumpet
4:22 "Have every **m** and his helper stay
5:13 every **m** who does not keep this
5:13 So may such a **m** be shaken out and
6:11 I said, "Should a **m** like me run away?
7: 2 because he was a **m** of integrity and
7:63 Hakkoz and Barzillai (a **m** who had
8: 1 all the people assembled as one **m** in
9:29 a **m** will live if he obeys them.
Est 1: 8 to serve each **m** what he wished.
1:22 every **m** should be ruler over his
4:11 any **m** or woman who approaches the
6: 6 "What should be done for the **m** the
6: 7 he answered the king, "For the **m** the
6: 9 robe the **m** the king delights to
6: 9 the **m** the king delights to honour!'
6:11 the **m** the king delights to honour!"
7: 5 **m** who has dared to do such a thing?"
Job 1: 1 In the land of Uz there lived a **m**
1: 1 This **m** was blameless and upright; he
1: 3 the greatest **m** among all the people
1: 8 a **m** who fears God and shuns evil."
1:12 the **m** himself do not lay a finger.
2: 3 a **m** who fears God and shuns evil.
2: 4 Satan replied. "A **m** will give all
3:23 Why is life given to a **m** whose way
4:17 Can a **m** be more pure than his Maker?
5: 7 Yet **m** is born to trouble as surely
5:17 "Blessed is the **m** whom God corrects;
6:14 "A despairing **m** should have the
6:26 the words of a despairing **m** as wind?
7: 1 "Does not **m** have hard service on
7: 1 his days like those of a hired **m**?
7: 2 **m** waiting eagerly for his wages,
7:17 "What is **m** that you make so much of
8:20 God does not reject a blameless **m**
9:32 "He is not a **m** like me that I might
10: 5 or your years like those of a **m**,
11:12 a witless **m** can no more become wise
11:12 wild donkey's colt can be born a **m**.
12:14 **m** he imprisons cannot be released.
13:16 no godless **m** would dare come before
13:28 "So **m** wastes away like something
14: 1 "**M** born of woman is of few days and

Job 14: 6 has put in his time like a hired **m**.
14:10 **m** dies and is laid low; he breathes
14:12 **m** lies down and does not rise; till
14:14 If a **m** dies, will he live again? All
15: 2 "Would a wise **m** answer with empty
15: 7 "Are you the first **m** ever born? Were
15:14 "What is **m**, that he could be pure,
15:16 how much less **m**, who is vile and
15:20 All his days the wicked **m** suffers
16:21 on behalf of a **m** he pleads with God
16:21 God as a **m** pleads for his friend.
17: 5 If a **m** denounces his friends for
17: 6 a **m** in whose face people spit.
17:10 I will not find a wise **m** among you.
18:21 such is the dwelling of an evil **m**;
20: 4 since **m** was placed on the earth,
21: 4 "Is my complaint directed to **m**? Why
21:19 Let him repay the **m** himself, so
21:23 One **m** dies in full vigour,
21:25 Another **m** dies in bitterness of soul,
21:30 that the evil **m** is spared from the
22: 2 "Can a **m** be of benefit to God? Can
22: 2 God? Can even a wise **m** benefit him?
22: 8 though you were a powerful **m**, owning
22: 8 land—an honoured **m**, living on it.
23: 7 There an upright **m** could present his
25: 4 How then can a **m** be righteous before
25: 6 how much less **m**, who is but a maggot
27:13 the heritage a ruthless **m** receives
28: 3 **M** puts an end to the darkness; he
28: 4 places forgotten by the foot of **m**;
28:13 **M** does not comprehend its worth; it
28:28 he said to **m**, 'The fear of the Lord—
29:13 The **m** who was dying blessed me; I
30:24 no-one lays a hand on a broken **m**
31:19 or a needy **m** without a garment,
32: 8 is the spirit in a **m**, the breath of
32:13 wisdom; let God refute him, not **m**.'
32:21 to no-one, nor will I flatter any **m**;
33:12 right, for God is greater than **m**.
33:14 though **m** may not perceive it.
33:17 to turn **m** from wrongdoing and keep
33:19 Or a **m** may be chastened on a bed of
33:23 to tell a **m** what is right for him,
33:29 "God does all these things to a **m**—
34: 7 What **m** is like Job, who drinks scorn
34: 9 For he says, 'It profits a **m** nothing
34:11 He repays a **m** for what he has done;
34:15 and **m** would return to the dust.
34:29 Yet he is over **m** and nation alike,
34:30 to keep a godless **m** from ruling,
34:31 "Suppose a **m** says to God, 'I am
34:36 for answering like a wicked **m**!
35: 8 Your wickedness affects only a **m**
37: 7 he stops every **m** from his labour.
37:20 Would any **m** ask to be swallowed up?
38: 3 Brace yourself like a **m**; I will
38:26 to water a land where no **m** lives, a
40: 7 "Brace yourself like a **m**; I will
40:11 at every proud **m** and bring him low,
40:12 look at every proud **m** and humble him,
Ps 1: 1 Blessed is the **m** who does not walk
8: 4 what is **m** that you are mindful of
9:19 Arise, O LORD, let not **m** triumph;
10: 2 In his arrogance the wicked **m** hunts
10:13 Why does the wicked **m** revile God?
10:15 the arm of the wicked and evil **m**;
10:18 in order that **m**, who is of the earth,
15: 4 who despises a vile **m** but honours
22: 6 I am a worm and not a **m**, scorned by
25:12 Who, then, is the **m** that fears the
32: 2 Blessed is the **m** whose sin the LORD
32:10 unfailing love surrounds the **m** who
34: 6 This poor **m** called, and the LORD
34: 8 is the **m** who takes refuge in him.
36: 6 you preserve both **m** and beast.
37:35 I have seen a wicked and ruthless **m**
37:37 is a future for the **m** of peace.
38:13 I am like a deaf **m**, who cannot hear,
38:14 I have become like a **m** who does not
39: 6 **M** is a mere phantom as he goes to
39:11 a moth—each **m** is but a breath.
40: 4 Blessed is the **m** who makes the LORD
49: 7 No **m** can redeem the life of another
49:12 **m**, despite his riches, does not
49:16 Do not be overawed when a **m** grows

Ps 49:20 A **m** who has riches without
52: 1 you mighty **m**? Why do you boast all
52: 7 "Here now is the **m** who did not make
55:13 is you, a **m** like myself, my
56: 4 What can mortal **m** do to me?
56:11 not be afraid. What can **m** do to me?
60:11 for the help of **m** is worthless.
62: 3 How long will you assault a **m**? Would
64: 4 from ambush at the innocent **m**;
64: 6 the mind and heart of **m** are cunning.
73: 5 free from the burdens common to **m**;
75: 6 or from the desert can exalt a **m**.
78:65 the Lord awoke as from sleep, as a **m**
80:17 Let your hand rest on the **m** at your
84:12 O LORD Almighty, blessed is the **m**
88: 4 pit; I am like a **m** without strength.
89:19 a young **m** from among the people.
89:22 no wicked **m** will oppress him.
89:48 What **m** can live and not see death,
90: T A prayer of Moses the **m** of God.
92: 6 The senseless **m** does not know, fools
94:10 Does he who teaches **m** lack knowledge?
94:11 The LORD knows the thoughts of **m**; he
94:12 Blessed is the **m** you discipline, O
94:12 LORD, the **m** you teach from your law;
102: T A prayer of an afflicted **m**. When he
103:15 for **m**, his days are like grass, he
104:14 and plants for **m** to cultivate—
104:15 wine that gladdens the heart of **m**,
104:23 **m** goes out to his work, to his
105:17 he sent a **m** before them—Joseph,
108:12 for the help of **m** is worthless.
109: 4 accuse me, but I am a **m** of prayer.
109: 6 Appoint an evil **m** to oppose him; let
112: 1 Praise the LORD. Blessed is the **m**
112:10 The wicked **m** will see and be vexed,
115:16 but the earth he has given to **m**.
118: 6 be afraid. What can **m** do to me?
118: 8 in the LORD than to trust in **m**.
119: 9 How can a young **m** keep his way pure?
120: 7 I am a **m** of peace; but when I speak,
127: 5 Blessed is the **m** whose quiver is
128: 4 Thus is the **m** blessed who fears the
144: 3 O LORD, what is **m** that you care for
144: 4 **M** is like a breath; his days are
147:10 nor his delight in the legs of a **m**;
Pr 3: 4 good name in the sight of God and **m**.
3:13 Blessed is the **m** who finds wisdom,
3:13 the **m** who gains understanding,
3:30 Do not accuse a **m** for no reason—
3:31 Do not envy a violent **m** or choose
3:32 for the LORD detests a perverse **m**
5:22 The evil deeds of a wicked **m** ensnare
6:11 bandit and scarcity like an armed **m**.
6:19 a **m** who stirs up dissension among
6:27 Can a **m** scoop fire into his lap
6:28 Can a **m** walk on hot coals without
6:32 a **m** who commits adultery lacks
8:34 Blessed is the **m** who listens to me,
9: 7 rebukes a wicked **m** incurs abuse.
9: 8 a wise **m** and he will love you.
9: 9 Instruct a wise **m** and he will be
10: 4 Lazy hands make a **m** poor, but
10: 9 The **m** of integrity walks securely,
10:23 but a **m** of understanding delights in
11: 7 a wicked **m** dies, his hope perishes;
11:12 A **m** who lacks judgment derides his
11:12 **m** of understanding holds his tongue.
11:13 but a trustworthy **m** keeps a secret.
11:17 A kind **m** benefits himself, but a
11:17 a cruel **m** brings trouble on himself.
11:18 The wicked **m** earns deceptive wages,
11:24 One **m** gives freely, yet gains even
11:25 A generous **m** will prosper; he who
11:26 People curse the **m** who hoards grain,
12: 2 A good **m** obtains favour from the
12: 2 but the LORD condemns a crafty **m**.
12: 3 A **m** cannot be established through
12: 8 A **m** is praised according to his
12:13 An evil **m** is trapped by his sinful
12:14 From the fruit of his lips a **m** is
12:15 him, but a wise **m** listens to advice.
12:16 but a prudent **m** overlooks an insult.
12:23 A prudent **m** keeps his knowledge to
12:25 An anxious heart weighs a **m** down,
12:27 The lazy **m** does not roast his game,

Pr 12:27 diligent **m** prizes his possessions.
13: 2 From the fruit of his lips a **m**
13: 6 Righteousness guards the **m** of
13: 7 One **m** pretends to be rich, yet has
13: 8 life, but a poor **m** hears no threat.
13:14 a **m** from the snares of death.
13:16 Every prudent **m** acts out of
13:22 A good **m** leaves an inheritance for
14: 7 Stay away from a foolish **m**, for you
14:12 a way that seems right to a **m**, but
14:14 and the good **m** rewarded for his.
14:15 A simple **m** believes anything, but a
14:15 a prudent **m** gives thought to his
14:16 A wise **m** fears the LORD and shuns
14:17 A quick-tempered **m** does foolish
14:17 things, and a crafty **m** is hated.
14:27 a **m** from the snares of death.
14:29 A patient **m** has great understanding,
14:29 a quick-tempered **m** displays folly.
15:18 A hot-tempered **m** stirs up dissension,
15:18 but a patient **m** calms a quarrel.
15:20 but a foolish **m** despises his mother.
15:21 Folly delights a **m** who lacks
15:21 but a **m** of understanding keeps a
15:23 A **m** finds joy in giving an apt reply
15:27 A greedy **m** brings trouble to his
15:33 The fear of the LORD teaches a **m**
16: 1 To **m** belong the plans of the heart,
16: 6 fear of the LORD a **m** avoids evil.
16: 9 In his heart a **m** plans his course,
16:13 they value a **m** who speaks the truth.
16:14 death, but a wise **m** will appease it.
16:25 a way that seems right to a **m**, but
16:28 A perverse **m** stirs up dissension,
16:29 A violent **m** entices his neighbour
16:32 Better a patient **m** than a warrior, a
16:32 a **m** who controls his temper than one
17: 4 A wicked **m** listens to evil lips; a
17:10 rebuke impresses a **m** of discernment
17:11 An evil **m** is bent only on rebellion;
17:13 If a **m** pays back evil for good, evil
17:18 A **m** lacking in judgment strikes
17:20 A **m** of perverse heart does not
17:23 A wicked **m** accepts a bribe in secret
17:24 A discerning **m** keeps wisdom in view,
17:26 is not good to punish an innocent **m**,
17:27 A **m** of knowledge uses words with
17:27 **m** of understanding is even-tempered.
18: 1 An unfriendly **m** pursues selfish ends;
18:23 A poor **m** pleads for mercy, but a
18:23 mercy, but a rich **m** answers harshly.
18:24 A **m** of many companions may come to
19: 1 Better a poor **m** whose walk is
19: 6 the friend of a **m** who gives gifts.
19: 7 A poor **m** is shunned by all his
19:15 and the shiftless **m** goes hungry.
19:19 A hot-tempered **m** must pay the
19:22 What a **m** desires is unfailing love;
19:25 rebuke a discerning **m**, and he will
20: 5 a **m** of understanding draws them out.
20: 6 Many a **m** claims to have unfailing
20: 6 love, but a faithful **m** who can find?
20:17 gained by fraud tastes sweet to a **m**,
20:19 so avoid a **m** who talks too much.
20:20 If a **m** curses his father or mother,
20:25 is a trap for a **m** to dedicate
20:27 searches the spirit of a **m**; it
21:10 The wicked **m** craves evil; his
21:11 **m** is instructed, he gets knowledge.
21:13 If a **m** shuts his ears to the cry of
21:16 A **m** who strays from the path of
21:20 but a foolish **m** devours all he has.
21:22 A wise **m** attacks the city of the
21:24 The proud and arrogant **m**—"Mocker"
21:29 A wicked **m** puts up a bold front, but
21:29 upright **m** gives thought to his ways.
22: 3 A prudent **m** sees danger and takes
22: 9 A generous **m** will himself be blessed,
22:24 with a hot-tempered **m**, do not
22:26 Do not be a **m** who strikes hands in
22:29 Do you see a **m** skilled in his work?
23: 6 Do not eat the food of a stingy **m**,
23: 7 for he is the kind of **m** who is
24: 5 A wise **m** has great power, and a **m** of
24:20 for the evil **m** has no future hope,
24:29 pay that **m** back for what he did."

Pr 24:30 of the **m** who lacks judgment;
24:34 bandit and scarcity like an armed **m**.
25:14 wind without rain is a **m** who boasts
25:18 is the **m** who gives false testimony
25:28 down is a **m** who lacks self-control.
26:12 Do you see a **m** wise in his own eyes?
26:19 is a **m** who deceives his neighbour
26:21 a quarrelsome **m** for kindling strife.
26:24 A malicious **m** disguises himself with
26:27 If a **m** digs a pit, he will fall into
26:27 if a **m** rolls a stone, it will roll
27: 8 is a **m** who strays from his home.
27:14 If a **m** loudly blesses his neighbour
27:17 iron sharpens iron, so one **m**
27:19 so a man's heart reflects the **m**.
27:20 and neither are the eyes of **m**.
27:21 but **m** is tested by the praise he
28: 1 The wicked **m** flees though no-one
28: 2 it has many rulers, but a **m** of
28: 6 Better a poor **m** whose walk is
28: 6 a rich **m** whose ways are perverse.
28:11 A rich **m** may be wise in his own eyes,
28:11 but a poor **m** who has discernment
28:14 Blessed is the **m** who always fears
28:15 charging bear is a wicked **m** ruling
28:17 A **m** tormented by the guilt of murder
28:20 A faithful **m** will be richly blessed,
28:21 **m** will do wrong for a piece of bread.
28:22 A stingy **m** is eager to get rich and
28:23 He who rebukes a **m** will in the end
28:25 A greedy **m** stirs up dissension, but
29: 1 A **m** who remains stiff-necked after
29: 3 A **m** who loves wisdom brings joy to
29: 6 An evil **m** is snared by his own sin,
29: 9 If a wise **m** goes to court with a
29:10 Bloodthirsty men hate a **m** of
29:11 wise **m** keeps himself under control.
29:13 The poor **m** and the oppressor have
29:20 Do you see a **m** who speaks in haste?
29:21 If a **m** pampers his servant from
29:22 An angry **m** stirs up dissension, and
29:23 a **m** of lowly spirit gains honour.
29:25 Fear of **m** will prove to be a snare,
29:26 from the LORD that **m** gets justice
30: 1 oracle: This **m** declared to Ithiel,
30:19 and the way of a **m** with a maiden.
Ecc 1: 3 What does **m** gain from all his labour
2: 8 delights of the heart of **m**.
2:14 The wise **m** has eyes in his head,
2:16 For the wise **m**, like the fool, will
2:16 the fool, the wise **m** too must die!
2:19 who knows whether he will be a wise **m**
2:21 For a **m** may do his work with wisdom,
2:22 What does a **m** get for all the toil
2:24 A **m** can do nothing better than to
2:26 To the **m** who pleases him, God gives
3:19 **m** has no advantage over the animal.
3:21 Who knows if the spirit of **m** rises
3:22 for a **m** than to enjoy his work,
4: 8 There was a **m** all alone; he had
4:10 But pity the **m** who falls and has
5:12 of a rich **m** permits him no sleep.
5:15 Naked a **m** comes from his mother's
5:16 As a **m** comes, so he departs, and
5:18 and proper for a **m** to eat and drink,
5:19 Moreover, when God gives any **m**
6: 2 God gives a **m** wealth, possessions
6: 3 A **m** may have a hundred children and
6: 5 it has more rest than does that **m**—
6: 8 What advantage has a wise **m** over a
6: 8 What does a poor **m** gain by knowing
6:10 and what **m** is has been known; no **m**
6:12 For who knows what is good for a **m**
7: 2 for death is the destiny of every **m**;
7: 7 Extortion turns a wise **m** into a fool,
7:14 Therefore, a **m** cannot discover
7:15 a wicked **m** living long in his
7:18 The **m** who fears God will avoid all
7:19 Wisdom makes one wise **m** more
7:26 The **m** who pleases God will escape
7:28 one upright **m** among a thousand,
8: 1 Who is like the wise **m**? Who knows
8: 7 Since no **m** knows the future, who can
8: 8 No **m** has power over the wind to
8: 9 There is a time when a **m** lords it
8:12 Although a wicked **m** commits a

Ecc 8:15 because nothing is better for a **m**
8:17 out, **m** cannot discover its meaning.
8:17 Even if a wise **m** claims he knows, he
9: 1 but no **m** knows whether love or hate
9: 2 As it is with the good **m**, so with
9:12 Moreover, no **m** knows when his hour
9:15 Now there lived in that city a **m**
9:15 But nobody remembered that poor **m**.
10:18 If a **m** is lazy, the rafters sag; if
11: 8 However many years a **m** may live, let
11: 9 Be happy, young **m**, while you are
12: 5 Then **m** goes to his eternal home and
12:13 for this is the whole ⌊duty⌋ of **m**.
Isa 1:31 The mighty **m** will become tinder and
2: 9 **m** will be brought low and mankind
2:11 The eyes of the arrogant **m** will be
2:17 The arrogance of **m** will be brought
2:22 Stop trusting in **m**, who has but a
3: 3 the captain of fifty and **m** of rank,
3: 5 oppress each other—**m** against **m**,
3: 6 A **m** will seize one of his brothers
4: 1 will take hold of one **m** and say,
5:15 **m** will be brought low and mankind
6: 5 For I am a **m** of unclean lips,
7:21 In that day, a **m** will keep alive a
10:18 as when a sick **m** wastes away.
13:12 I will make **m** scarcer than pure gold,
14:16 "Is this the **m** who shook the earth
14:17 the **m** who made the world a desert,
16: 5 in faithfulness a **m** will sit on it—
17: 5 as when a **m** gleans ears of corn in
21: 9 Look, here comes a **m** in a chariot
22:17 and hurl you away, O you mighty **m**.
29: 8 a hungry **m** dreams that he is eating,
29: 8 **m** dreams that he is drinking,
29:21 those who with a word make a **m** out
31: 8 a sword that is not of **m**; a sword,
32: 2 Each **m** will be like a shelter from
32: 8 the noble **m** makes noble plans, and
33:16 this is the **m** who will dwell on the
40:20 A **m** too poor to present such an
42:13 LORD will march out like a mighty **m**,
44:13 He shapes it in the form of **m**, of **m**
46:11 land, a **m** to fulfil my purpose.
52:14 so disfigured beyond that of any **m**
53: 3 a **m** of sorrows, and familiar with
55: 7 his way and the evil **m** his thoughts.
56: 2 Blessed is the **m** who does this, the **m**
57:13 But the **m** who makes me his refuge
57:16 for then the spirit of **m** would grow
57:16 the breath of **m** that I have created.
58: 5 only a day for a **m** to humble himself?
62: 5 a young **m** marries a maiden, so will
65:20 or an old **m** who does not live out
66: 3 a bull is like one who kills a **m**,
Jer 3: 1 "If a **m** divorces his wife and she
3: 1 leaves him and marries another **m**,
7:20 on **m** and beast, on the trees of the
8: 4 a **m** turns away, does he not return?
9:12 What **m** is wise enough to understand
9:23 "Let not the wise **m** boast of his
9:23 the strong **m** boast of his strength
9:23 or the rich **m** boast of his riches,
10:23 it is not for **m** to direct his steps.
11: 3 'Cursed is the **m** who does not obey
14: 9 Why are you like a **m** taken by
15:10 that you gave me birth, a **m** with
15:12 "Can a **m** break iron—iron from the
17: 5 "Cursed is the one who trusts in **m**,
17: 7 "But blessed is the **m** who trusts in
17:10 to reward a **m** according to his
17:11 **m** who gains riches by unjust means.
20:15 Cursed be the **m** who brought my
20:16 May that **m** be like the towns the
22: 7 each **m** with his weapons, and they
22:28 Is this **m** Jehoiachin a despised,
22:30 "Record this **m** as if childless, a **m**
23: 9 I am like a drunken **m**, like a **m**
23:34 punish that **m** and his household.
26:11 "This **m** should be sentenced to death
26:16 "This **m** should not be sentenced to
26:20 another **m** who prophesied in the
30: 6 Ask and see: Can a **m** bear children?
30: 6 Then why do I see every strong **m**
31:22 earth—a woman will surround a **m**."
31:34 No longer will a **m** teach his
Jer 31:34 or a **m** his brother, saying, 'Know
33:17 'David will never fail to have a **m**
33:18 ever fail to have a **m** to stand
35:19 never fail to have a **m** to serve me.
38: 4 "This **m** should be put to death.
38: 4 This **m** is not seeking the good of
48:19 Ask the **m** fleeing and the woman
49:18 live there; no **m** will dwell in it.
49:33 live there; no **m** will dwell in it."
50:40 live there; no **m** will dwell in it.
51:17 "Every **m** is senseless and without
51:22 with you I shatter **m** and woman,
51:22 with you I shatter old **m** and youth,
51:22 with you I shatter young **m** and
51:43 lives, through which no **m** travels.
51:62 so that neither **m** nor animal will
Lam 3: 1 I am the **m** who has seen affliction
3:27 is good for a **m** to bear the yoke
3:35 to deny a **m** his rights before the
3:36 to deprive a **m** of justice—would
3:39 Why should any living **m** complain
Eze 1: 5 their form was that of a **m**,
1: 8 sides they had the hands of a **m**.
1:10 Each of the four had the face of a **m**,
1:26 was a figure like that of a **m**.
3:18 I say to a wicked **m**, 'You will
3:18 that wicked **m** will die for his sin,
3:19 if you do warn the wicked **m** and he
8: 2 and I saw a figure like that of a **m**.
9: 2 With them was a **m** clothed in linen
9: 3 Then the LORD called to the **m**
9:11 the **m** in linen with the writing kit
10: 2 The LORD said to the **m** clothed in
10: 3 of the temple when the **m** went in,
10: 6 the LORD commanded the **m** in linen,
10: 6 **m** went in and stood beside a wheel.
10: 7 **m** in linen, who took it and went out.
10: 8 what looked like the hands of a **m**.)
10:14 the second the face of a **m**, the
10:21 what looked like the hands of a **m**.
14: 8 I will set my face against that **m**
18: 8 and judges fairly between **m** and **m**.
18: 9 That **m** is righteous; he will surely
18:13 Will such a **m** live? He will not!
18:21 "But if a wicked **m** turns away from
18:24 detestable things the wicked **m** does,
18:27 if a wicked **m** turns away from the
20:11 **m** who obeys them will live by them.
20:13 **m** who obeys them will live by them
20:21 **m** who obeys them will live by them
22:11 In you one **m** commits a detestable
22:30 "I looked for a **m** among them who
28: 2 But you are a **m** and not a god,
28: 9 who kill you? You will be but a **m**,
29:11 No foot of **m** or animal will pass
30:24 him like a mortally wounded **m**.
32:13 stirred by the foot of a **m** or
33: 6 that **m** will be taken away because of
33: 8 I say to the wicked, 'O wicked **m**,
33: 8 that wicked **m** will die for his sin,
33: 9 if you do warn the wicked **m** to turn
33:12 and the wickedness of the wicked **m**
33:14 if I say to the wicked **m**, 'You will
33:19 if a wicked **m** turns away from his
33:21 a **m** who had escaped from Jerusalem
33:22 Now the evening before the **m** arrived,
33:22 the **m** came to me in the morning.
33:24 Abraham was only one **m**, yet he
40: 3 He took me there, and I saw a **m**
40: 4 The **m** said to me, "Son of **m**, look
41: 1 the **m** brought me to the outer
41:19 the face of a **m** towards the palm
41:22 The **m** said to me, "This is the table
42: 1 the **m** led me northward into the
43: 1 the **m** brought me to the gate facing
43: 6 While the **m** was standing beside me,
44: 1 the **m** brought me back to the outer
44: 4 the **m** brought me by way of the north
46:19 the **m** brought me through the
47: 1 The **m** brought me back to the
47: 3 the **m** went eastward with a measuring
Da 2:10 "There is not a **m** on earth who can
2:25 "I have found a **m** among the exiles
2:27 Daniel replied, "No wise **m**,
4:16 mind be changed from that of a **m**
5:11 There is a **m** in your kingdom who has
Da 5:12 This **m** Daniel, whom the king called
6: 5 for charges against this **m** Daniel
6: 7 or **m** during the next thirty days,
6:12 prays to any god or **m** except to you,
7: 4 that it stood on two feet like a **m**,
7: 4 the heart of a **m** was given to it.
7: 8 eyes like the eyes of a **m** and a
8:15 me stood one who looked like a **m**.
8:16 this **m** the meaning of the vision."
9:21 Gabriel, the **m** I had seen in the
10: 5 before me was a **m** dressed in linen,
10:16 one who looked like a **m** touched my
10:18 Again the one who looked like a **m**
10:19 "Do not be afraid, O **m** highly
12: 6 One of them said to the **m** clothed in
12: 7 The **m** clothed in linen, who was
Hos 3: 3 any **m**, and I will live with you."
4: 4 "But let no **m** bring a charge, let no
4: 4 let no **m** accuse another, for your
6: 9 marauders lie in ambush for a **m**, so
9: 7 a fool, the inspired **m** a maniac.
11: 9 For I am God, and not **m**—the Holy
12: 3 heel; as a **m** he struggled with God.
Am 4:13 and reveals his thoughts to **m**, he
5:13 Therefore the prudent **m** keeps quiet
5:19 will be as though a **m** fled from a
Jnh 1:14 for killing an innocent **m**, for you,
3: 7 nobles: Do not let any **m** or beast,
3: 8 let **m** and beast be covered with
Mic 2: 2 They defraud a **m** of his home, a
4: 4 Every **m** will sit under his own vine
5: 7 wait for **m** or linger for mankind.
6: 8 He has showed you, O **m**, what is good.
6:11 Shall I acquit a **m** with dishonest
7: 2 the land; not one upright **m** remains.
Hab 2:18 "Of what value is an idol, since a **m**
Zep 1: 3 off **m** from the face of the earth,"
Zec 1: 8 me was a **m** riding a red horse!
1:10 the **m** standing among the myrtle
2: 1 **m** with a measuring line in his hand!
2: 4 said to him: "Run, tell that young **m**,
3: 2 rebuke you! Is not this **m** a burning
4: 1 as a **m** is wakened from his sleep.
6:12 'Here is the **m** whose name is the
8:10 there were no wages for **m** or beast.
8:10 every **m** against his neighbour.
12: 1 spirit of **m** within him, declares:
13: 7 against the **m** who is close to me!"
14:13 Each **m** will seize the hand of
Mal 2:12 for the **m** who does this, whoever he
3: 8 "Will a **m** rob God? Yet you rob me.
3:17 a **m** spares his son who serves him.
Mt 4: 4 '**M** does not live on bread alone,
7:24 **m** who built his house on the rock.
7:26 **m** who built his house on sand.
8: 2 A **m** with leprosy came and knelt
8: 3 out his hand and touched the **m**.
8: 9 For I myself am a **m** under authority,
8:27 "What kind of **m** is this? Even the
9: 7 the **m** got up and went home.
9: 9 he saw a **m** named Matthew sitting
9:32 a **m** who was demon-possessed and
9:33 the demon was driven out, the **m** who
10:35 I have come to turn "'a **m** against
11: 6 Blessed is the **m** who does not fall
11: 8 what did you go out to see? A **m**
12:10 a **m** with a shrivelled hand was there.
12:12 How much more valuable is a **m** than a
12:13 he said to the **m**, "Stretch out your
12:22 they brought him a demon-possessed **m**
12:29 strong **m**? Then he can rob his house.
12:35 The good **m** brings good things out of
12:35 and the evil **m** brings evil things
12:43 "When an evil spirit comes out of a **m**
12:45 And the final condition of that **m** is
13:20 places is the **m** who hears the word
13:22 thorns is the **m** who hears the word,
13:23 soil is the **m** who hears the word
13:24 **m** who sowed good seed in his field.
13:31 a **m** took and planted in his field.
13:44 When a **m** found it, he hid it again,
13:54 "Where did this **m** get this wisdom
13:56 did this **m** get all these things?"
15: 5 you say that if a **m** says to his
15:14 If a blind **m** leads a blind **m**, both
15:18 heart, and these make a **m** 'unclean'.

Mt 15:20 These are what make a **m** 'unclean';
16:17 not revealed to you by **m**, but by my
16:26 What good will it be for a **m** if he
16:26 a **m** give in exchange for his soul?
17:14 a **m** approached Jesus and knelt
18: 7 woe to the **m** through whom they come!
18:12 If a **m** owns a hundred sheep,
18:24 he began the settlement, a **m** who
18:30 went off and had the **m** thrown into
19: 3 "Is it lawful for a **m** to divorce
19: 5 'For this reason a **m** will leave his
19: 6 together, let **m** not separate."
19: 7 "did Moses command that a **m** give his
19:16 Now a **m** came up to Jesus and asked,
19:18 "Which ones?" the **m** enquired. Jesus
19:20 "All these I have kept," the young **m**
19:22 the young **m** heard this, he went away
19:23 is hard for a rich **m** to enter the
19:24 rich **m** to enter the kingdom of God."
19:26 "With **m** this is impossible, but with
20:14 I want to give the **m** who was hired
21:28 There was a **m** who had two sons.
22:11 he noticed a **m** there who was not
22:12 clothes?' The **m** was speechless.
22:16 "we know you are a **m** of integrity
22:24 "Moses told us that if a **m** dies
25:14 like a **m** going on a journey, who
25:16 The **m** who had received the five
25:18 the **m** who had received the one
25:20 The **m** who had received the five
25:22 "The **m** with the two talents also
25:24 "Then the **m** who had received the one
25:24 'I knew that you are a hard **m**,
26: 6 of a **m** known as Simon the Leper,
26:18 "Go into the city to a certain **m** and
26:24 But woe to that **m** who betrays the
26:48 The one I kiss is the **m**; arrest him."
26:72 with an oath: "I don't know the **m**!"
26:74 "I don't know the **m**!" Immediately
27:19 anything to do with that innocent **m**,
27:32 met a **m** from Cyrene, named Simon
27:57 there came a rich **m** from Arimathea,
Mk 1:23 Just then a **m** in their synagogue who
1:26 The evil spirit shook the **m**
1:40 A **m** with leprosy came to him and
1:41 out his hand and touched the **m**.
2: 4 mat the paralysed **m** was lying on.
2:27 made for **m**, not **m** for the Sabbath.
3: 1 **m** with a shrivelled hand was there.
3: 3 Jesus said to the **m** with the
3: 5 to the **m**, "Stretch out your hand.
3:27 he first ties up the strong **m**.
4:26 A **m** scatters seed on the ground.
5: 2 a **m** with an evil spirit came from
5: 3 This **m** lived in the tombs, and
5: 8 Come out of this **m**, you evil spirit!"
5:15 they came to Jesus, they saw the **m**
5:16 the demon-possessed **m**—and told
5:18 the **m** who had been demon-possessed
5:20 the **m** went away and began to tell in
6: 2 "Where did this **m** get these things?"
6:16 "John, the **m** I beheaded, has been
6:20 him to be a righteous and holy **m**.
6:27 **m** went, beheaded John in the prison,
7:11 you say that if a **m** says to his
7:15 Nothing outside a **m** can make him
7:15 of a **m** that makes him 'unclean'."
7:18 nothing that enters a **m** from the
7:20 He went on: "What comes out of a **m**
7:23 from inside and make a **m** 'unclean'."
7:32 There some people brought to him a **m**
7:32 him to place his hand on the **m**.
8:22 brought a blind **m** and begged Jesus
8:23 He took the blind **m** by the hand and
8:36 What good is it for a **m** to gain the
8:37 Or what can a **m** give in exchange for
9:17 A **m** in the crowd answered, "Teacher,
9:38 "Teacher," said John, "we saw a **m**
10: 2 lawful for a **m** to divorce his wife?"
10: 4 They said, "Moses permitted a **m** to
10: 7 'For this reason a **m** will leave his
10: 9 together, let **m** not separate."
10:12 another **m**, she commits adultery."
10:17 Jesus started on his way, a **m** ran up
10:25 rich **m** to enter the kingdom of God."
10:27 "With **m** this is impossible, but not
Mk 10:46 were leaving the city, a blind **m**,
10:49 So they called to the blind **m**,
10:51 The blind **m** said, "Rabbi, I want to
12: 1 parables: "A **m** planted a vineyard.
12: 4 they struck this **m** on the head and
12:14 we know you are a **m** of integrity.
12:19 the **m** must marry the widow and have
12:32 "Well said, teacher," the **m** replied.
13:34 It's like a **m** going away: He leaves
14: 3 of a **m** known as Simon the Leper,
14:13 "Go into the city, and a **m** carrying
14:21 But woe to that **m** who betrays the
14:44 "The one I kiss is the **m**; arrest him
14:51 A young **m**, wearing nothing but a
14:58 will build another, not made by **m**.
14:71 know this **m** you're talking about."
15: 7 A **m** called Barabbas was in prison
15:21 A certain **m** from Cyrene, Simon, the
15:36 One **m** ran, filled a sponge with wine
15:39 "Surely this **m** was the Son of God!
16: 5 they saw a young **m** dressed in a
Lk 1:18 am an old **m** and my wife is well on
1:27 to be married to a **m** named Joseph,
2:25 Now there was a **m** in Jerusalem
3:11 John answered, "The **m** with two
4: 4 **M** does not live on bread alone.
4:33 In the synagogue there was a **m**
4:35 threw the **m** down before them all
5: 8 from me, Lord; I am a sinful **m**!"
5:12 a **m** came along who was covered with
5:13 out his hand and touched the **m**.
5:24 to the paralysed **m**, "I tell you,
6: 6 and a **m** was there whose right hand
6: 8 to the **m** with the shrivelled hand,
6:10 to the **m**, "Stretch out your hand.
6:39 "Can a blind **m** lead a blind **m**? Will
6:45 The good **m** brings good things out of
6:45 and the evil **m** brings evil things
6:48 He is like a **m** building a house, who
6:49 is like a **m** who built a house on
7: 4 "This **m** deserves to have you do
7: 8 For I myself am a **m** under authority,
7:14 He said, "Young **m**, I say to you, get
7:15 The dead **m** sat up and began to talk,
7:23 Blessed is the **m** who does not fall
7:25 what did you go out to see? A **m**
7:39 "If this **m** were a prophet, he would
8:27 a demon-possessed **m** from the town.
8:27 For a long time this **m** had not worn
8:29 evil spirit to come out of the **m**.
8:33 the demons came out of the **m**, they
8:35 they found the **m** from whom the
8:36 demon-possessed **m** had been cured.
8:38 The **m** from whom the demons had gone
8:39 So the **m** went away and told all
8:41 a **m** named Jairus, a ruler of the
9:25 What good is it for a **m** to gain the
9:38 A **m** in the crowd called out,
9:49 "Master," said John, "we saw a **m**
9:57 a **m** said to him, "I will follow you
9:59 He said to another **m**, "Follow me."
9:59 But the **m** replied, "Lord, first let
10: 6 If a **m** of peace is there, your peace
10:30 In reply Jesus said: "A **m** was going
10:31 when he saw the **m**, he passed by
10:33 as he travelled, came where the **m**
10:34 Then he put the **m** on his own donkey,
10:36 **m** who fell into the hands of robbers?
11:14 When the demon left, the **m** who had
11:21 "When a strong **m**, fully armed,
11:22 the armour in which the **m** trusted
11:24 "When an evil spirit comes out of a **m**
11:26 of that **m** is worse than the first."
12:14 Jesus replied, "**M**, who appointed me
12:16 certain rich **m** produced a good crop.
13: 6 this parable: "A **m** had a fig-tree,
13: 7 he said to the **m** who took care of
13: 8 "'Sir,' the **m** replied, 'leave it
13:19 a mustard seed, which a **m** took
14: 2 was a **m** suffering from dropsy.
14: 4 taking hold of the **m**, he healed him
14: 9 say to you, 'Give this **m** your seat.
14:15 "Blessed is the **m** who will eat at
14:16 Jesus replied: "A certain **m** was
15: 2 "This **m** welcomes sinners, and eats
15:11 Jesus continued: "There was a **m** who
Lk 16: 1 "There was a rich **m** whose manager
16:18 and the **m** who marries a divorced
16:19 "There was a rich **m** who was dressed
16:22 The rich **m** also died and was buried.
18:14 "I tell you that this **m**, rather than
18:23 because he was a **m** of great wealth.
18:25 rich **m** to enter the kingdom of God."
18:35 Jesus approached Jericho, a blind **m**
18:40 Jesus stopped and ordered the **m** to
19: 2 A **m** was there by the name of
19: 3 but being a short **m** he could not,
19: 9 this **m**, too, is a son of Abraham.
19:12 He said: "A **m** of noble birth went to
19:14 We don't want this **m** to be our king.'
19:21 of you, because you are a hard **m**.
19:22 did you, that I am a hard **m**, taking
20: 9 "A **m** planted a vineyard, rented it
20:28 the **m** must marry the widow and have
22:10 "As you enter the city, a **m** carrying
22:22 but woe to that **m** who betrays him."
22:47 and the **m** who was called Judas, one
22:56 him and said, "This **m** was with him.
22:58 "**M**, I am not!" Peter replied.
22:60 Peter replied, "**M**, I don't know what
23: 2 found this **m** subverting our nation.
23: 4 basis for a charge against this **m**."
23: 6 Pilate asked if the **m** was a Galilean.
23:14 "You brought me this **m** as one who
23:18 this **m**! Release Barabbas to us!"
23:22 What crime has this **m** committed?
23:25 He released the **m** who had been
23:41 But this **m** has done nothing wrong."
23:50 Now there was a **m** named Joseph, a
23:50 the Council, a good and upright **m**,
Jn 1: 6 There came a **m** who was sent from God;
1: 9 every **m** was coming into the world.
1:30 'A **m** who comes after me has
1:33 'The **m** on whom you see the Spirit
2:25 **m**, for he knew what was in a **m**.
3: 1 Now there was a **m** of the Pharisees
3: 4 "How can a **m** be born when he is old?"
3:26 "Rabbi, that **m** who was with you on
3:27 To this John replied, "A **m** can
3:33 The **m** who has accepted it has
4:18 **m** you now have is not your husband.
4:29 "Come, see a **m** who told me
4:42 **m** really is the Saviour of the world.
4:47 this **m** heard that Jesus had arrived
4:50 Your son will live." The **m** took
5: 9 At once the **m** was cured; he picked
5:10 the Jews said to the **m** who had been
5:11 he replied, "The **m** who made me well
5:13 The **m** who was healed had no idea who
5:15 The **m** went away and told the Jews
6:50 which a **m** may eat and not die.
6:52 this **m** give us his flesh to eat?"
7:11 him and asking, "Where is that **m**?
7:12 Some said, "He is a good **m**." Others
7:15 "How did this **m** get such learning
7:18 one who sent him is a **m** of truth;
7:23 healing the whole **m** on the Sabbath?
7:25 this the **m** they are trying to kill?
7:27 we know where this **m** is from; when
7:31 more miraculous signs than this **m**?"
7:35 "Where does this **m** intend to go that
7:40 said, "Surely this **m** is the Prophet.
7:46 "No-one ever spoke the way this **m**
7:51 "Does our law condemn a **m** without
8:40 you are determined to kill me, a **m**
9: 1 he went along, he saw a **m** blind from
9: 2 "Rabbi, who sinned, this **m** or his
9: 3 "Neither this **m** nor his parents
9: 7 So the **m** went and washed, and came
9: 8 the same **m** who used to sit and beg?"
9: 9 But he himself insisted, "I am the **m**.
9:11 He replied, "The **m** they call Jesus
9:12 "Where is this **m**?" they asked him.
9:13 They brought to the Pharisees the **m**
9:15 "He put mud on my eyes," the **m**
9:16 Some of the Pharisees said, "This **m**
9:17 they turned again to the blind **m**,
9:17 The **m** replied, "He is a prophet."
9:24 A second time they summoned the **m**
9:24 "We know this **m** is a sinner."
9:30 The **m** answered, "Now that is
9:31 to the godly **m** who does his will.

Jn 9:32 opening the eyes of a **m** born blind.
9:33 If this **m** were not from God, he
9:36 "Who is he, sir?" the **m** asked. "Tell
9:38 the **m** said, "Lord, I believe," and
10: 1 the **m** who does not enter the sheep
10: 2 The **m** who enters by the gate is the
10:13 The **m** runs away because he is a
10:21 sayings of a **m** possessed by a demon.
10:33 you, a mere **m**, claim to be God."
10:41 John said about this **m** was true."
11: 1 Now a **m** named Lazarus was sick. He
11: 9 **m** who walks by day will not stumble,
11:37 **m** have kept this **m** from dying?"
11:39 Martha, the sister of the dead **m**,
11:44 The dead **m** came out, his hands and
11:47 **m** performing many miraculous signs.
11:50 it is better for you that one **m** die
12:25 The **m** who loves his life will lose
12:25 while the **m** who hates his life in
12:35 The **m** who walks in the dark does not
12:44 Jesus cried out, "When a **m** believes
15: 5 If a **m** remains in me and I in him,
18:14 good if one **m** died for the people.
18:26 a relative of the **m** whose ear Peter
18:29 are you bringing against this **m**?"
19: 5 said to them, "Here is the **m**!
19:12 "If you let this **m** go, you are no
19:21 **m** claimed to be king of the Jews."
19:32 **m** who had been crucified with Jesus,
19:35 The **m** who saw it has given testimony,
19:39 the **m** who earlier had visited Jesus
Ac 2:22 Jesus of Nazareth was a **m** accredited
2:23 This **m** was handed over to you by God'
3: 2 Now a **m** crippled from birth was
3: 5 the **m** gave them his attention,
3:10 they recognised him as the same **m**
3:12 godliness we had made this **m** walk?
3:16 By faith in the name of Jesus, this **m**
4:10 this **m** stands before you healed.
4:14 since they could see the **m** who had
4:22 For the **m** who was miraculously
5: 1 Now a **m** named Ananias, together with
6: 5 They chose Stephen, a **m** full of
6: 8 Now Stephen, a **m** full of God's grace
7:27 "But the **m** who was ill-treating the
7:58 at the feet of a young **m** named Saul.
8: 9 Now for some time a **m** named Simon
8:10 "This **m** is the divine power known as
8:27 **m** had gone to Jerusalem to worship,
8:30 the **m** reading Isaiah the prophet.
9:11 ask for a **m** from Tarsus named Saul,
9:12 In a vision he has seen a **m** named
9:13 heard many reports about this **m**
9:15 the Lord said to Ananias, "Go! This **m**
9:21 "Isn't he the **m** who caused havoc in
9:33 There he found a **m** named Aeneas, a
10: 1 At Caesarea there was a **m** named
10: 5 a **m** named Simon who is called Peter.
10:22 He is a righteous and God-fearing **m**,
10:26 "Stand up," he said, "I am only a **m**
10:28 not call any **m** impure or unclean.
10:30 **m** in shining clothes stood before
11:24 He was a good **m**, full of the Holy
12:22 is the voice of a god, not of a **m**."
13: 7 The proconsul, an intelligent **m**,
13:22 'I have found David son of Jesse a **m**
14: 8 In Lystra there sat a **m** crippled in
14:10 the **m** jumped up and began to walk.
16: 9 vision of a **m** of Macedonia standing
17:26 From one **m** he made every nation of
17:31 justice by the **m** he has appointed.
18:13 "This **m**," they charged, "is
18:24 He was a learned **m**, with a thorough
19:16 the **m** who had the evil spirit jumped
19:29 rushed as one **m** into the theatre.
20: 9 Seated in a window was a young **m**
20:10 young **m** and put his arms around him.
20:12 The people took the young **m** home
21:16 He was a **m** from Cyprus and one of
21:28 help us! This is the **m** who teaches
22:12 "A **m** named Ananias came to see me.
22:26 "This **m** is a Roman citizen."
23: 9 "We find nothing wrong with this **m**,"
23:17 "Take this young **m** to the commander;
23:18 asked me to bring this young **m** to
23:19 The commander took the young **m** by

Ac 23:22 The commander dismissed the young **m**
23:27 This **m** was seized by the Jews and
23:30 the **m**, I sent him to you at once.
24: 5 "We have found this **m** to be a
24:16 conscience clear before God and **m**.
25: 5 press charges against the **m** there,
25:14 **m** here whom Felix left as a prisoner.
25:16 **m** before he has faced his accusers
25:17 and ordered the **m** to be brought in.
25:19 about a dead **m** named Jesus whom Paul
25:22 "I would like to hear this **m** myself.
25:24 you see this **m**! The whole Jewish
26:31 "This **m** is not doing anything that
26:32 Agrippa said to Festus, "This **m**
28: 4 "This **m** must be a murderer; for
Ro 1:23 **m** and birds and animals and reptiles.
2: 3 when you, a mere **m**, pass judgment on
2:28 A **m** is not a Jew if he is only one
2:29 No, a **m** is a Jew if he is one
3: 4 Let God be true, and every **m** a liar.
3:28 **m** is justified by faith apart from
4: 4 Now when a **m** works, his wages are
4: 5 However, to the **m** who does not work
4: 6 **m** to whom God credits righteousness
4: 8 Blessed is the **m** whose sin the Lord
5: 7 for a good **m** someone might possibly
5:12 sin entered the world through one **m**,
5:15 died by the trespass of the one **m**,
5:15 that came by the grace of the one **m**,
5:17 For if, by the trespass of the one **m**,
5:17 death reigned through that one **m**,
5:17 through the one **m**, Jesus Christ.
5:19 the disobedience of the one **m**
5:19 through the obedience of the one **m**
7: 1 over a **m** only as long as he lives?
7: 3 then, if she marries another **m** while
7: 3 even though she marries another **m**.
7:24 What a wretched **m** I am! Who will
8: 3 of sinful **m** to be a sin offering.
8: 3 And so he condemned sin in sinful **m**,
8: 6 The mind of sinful **m** is death, but
9:20 who are you, O **m**, to talk back to
10: 5 "The **m** who does these things will
14: 2 but another **m**, whose faith is weak,
14: 3 The **m** who eats everything must not
14: 3 the **m** who does not eat everything
14: 3 must not condemn the **m** who does,
14: 5 One **m** considers one day more sacred
14: 5 another **m** considers every day alike.
14:20 but it is wrong for a **m** to eat
14:22 Blessed is the **m** who does not
14:23 the **m** who has doubts is condemned if
1Co 1:20 Where is the wise **m**? Where is the
2:11 **m** except the man's spirit within him?
2:14 The **m** without the Spirit does not
2:15 The spiritual **m** makes judgments
3: 8 The **m** who plants and the **m** who
3:12 If any **m** builds on this foundation
4: 6 pride in one **m** over against another.
5: 1 pagans: A **m** has his father's wife.
5: 2 your fellowship the **m** who did this?
5: 5 hand this **m** over to Satan, so that
5:11 With such a **m** do not even eat.
5:13 "Expel the wicked **m** from among you."
6:18 All other sins a **m** commits are
7: 1 It is good for a **m** not to marry.
7: 2 each **m** should have his own wife, and
7: 7 But each **m** has his own gift from God;
7:15 A believing **m** or woman is not bound
7:18 Was a **m** already circumcised when he
7:18 Was a **m** uncircumcised when he was
7:22 he who was a free **m** when he was
7:24 Brothers, each **m**, as responsible to
7:32 An unmarried **m** is concerned about
7:33 a married **m** is concerned about the
7:37 the **m** who has settled the matter in
7:37 this **m** also does the right thing.
8: 2 The **m** who thinks he knows something
8: 3 the **m** who loves God is known by God.
9:19 Though I am free and belong to no **m**,
9:26 Therefore I do not run like a **m**
9:26 not fight like a **m** beating the air.
10:13 you except what is common to **m**.
10:28 for the sake of the **m** who told you
11: 3 that the head of every **m** is Christ,
11: 3 and the head of the woman is **m**, and

1Co 11: 4 Every **m** who prays or prophesies with
11: 7 A **m** ought not to cover his head,
11: 7 but the woman is the glory of **m**.
11: 8 For **m** did not come from woman, but
11: 9 neither was **m** created for woman, but
11:11 of **m**, nor is **m** independent of woman.
11:12 For as woman came from **m**, so also **m**
11:14 teach you that if a **m** has long hair,
11:28 A **m** ought to examine himself before
13:11 a **m**, I put childish ways behind me.
14:17 but the other **m** is not edified.
15:21 For since death came through a **m**,
15:21 of the dead comes also through a **m**.
15:45 is written: "The first **m** Adam became
15:47 The first **m** was of the dust of the
15:47 the earth, the second **m** from heaven.
15:48 was the earthly **m**, so are those who
15:48 earth; and as is the **m** from heaven,
15:49 borne the likeness of the earthly **m**,
15:49 the likeness of the **m** from heaven.
2Co 9: 7 Each **m** should give what he has
12: 2 I know a **m** in Christ who fourteen
12: 3 I know that this **m**—whether in the
12: 4 that **m** is not permitted to tell.
12: 5 I will boast about a **m** like that,
Gal 1: 1 apostle—sent not from men nor by **m**,
1:11 is not something that **m** made up.
1:12 I did not receive it from any **m**, nor
1:16 Gentiles, I did not consult any **m**,
1:23 They only heard the report: "The **m**
2:16 know that a **m** is not justified by
3: 9 along with Abraham, the **m** of faith.
3:12 "The **m** who does these things will
5: 3 Again I declare to every **m** who lets
6: 7 A **m** reaps what he sows.
Eph 2:15 in himself one new **m** out of the two
5: 5 impure or greedy person—such a **m** is
5:31 "For this reason a **m** will leave his
Php 1:27 as one **m** for the faith of the
2: 8 being found in appearance as a **m**, he
1Th 4: 8 does not reject **m** but God, who gives
2Th 2: 3 the **m** doomed to destruction.
2: 3 and the **m** of lawlessness is
3:10 **m** will not work, he shall not eat."
1Ti 1:13 and a persecutor and a violent **m**,
2: 5 God and men, the **m** Christ Jesus,
2:12 over a **m**; she must be silent.
5: 1 Do not rebuke an older **m** harshly,
2Ti 2:21 If a **m** cleanses himself from the
Tit 1: 6 a **m** whose children believe and
3:11 You may be sure that such a **m** is
Phm : 9 I then, as Paul—an old **m** and now
:16 as a **m** and as a brother in the Lord.
Heb 2: 6 "What is **m** that you are mindful of
7: 6 This **m**, however, did not trace his
8: 2 set up by the Lord, not by **m**.
8:11 No longer will a **m** teach his
8:11 or a **m** his brother, saying, 'Know
9:27 Just as **m** is destined to die once,
10:29 think a **m** deserves to be punished
11:12 from this one **m**, and he as good as
13: 6 not be afraid. What can **m** do to me?"
Jas 1: 7 That **m** should not think he will
1: 8 he is a double-minded **m**, unstable in
1:11 In the same way, the rich **m** will
1:12 Blessed is the **m** who perseveres
1:23 **m** who looks at his face in a mirror
1:25 the **m** who looks intently into the
2: 2 Suppose a **m** comes into your meeting
2: 2 **m** in shabby clothes also comes in.
2: 3 the **m** wearing fine clothes and say,
2: 3 say to the poor **m**, "You stand there"
2:14 What good is it, my brothers, if a **m**
2:20 You foolish **m**, do you want evidence
3: 2 he is a perfect **m**, able to keep his
3: 7 tamed and have been tamed by **m**,
3: 8 no **m** can tame the tongue. It is a
5:17 Elijah was a **m** just like us. He
1Pe 2:19 For it is commendable if a **m** bears
2Pe 1:21 had its origin in the will of **m**,
2:19 for a **m** is a slave to whatever has
1Jn 2: 4 The **m** who says, "I know him," but
2:16 the world—the cravings of sinful **m**,
2:17 but the **m** who does the will of God
2:22 Who is the liar? It is the **m** who
2:22 Such a **m** is the antichrist—he

Rev 4: 7 the third had a face like a **m**, the
6:15 and every slave and every free **m** hid
9: 5 of a scorpion when it strikes a **m**.
16: 3 into blood like that of a dead **m**,
16:18 occurred since **m** has been on earth,

Man of God

Dt 33: 1 This is the blessing that Moses the **m**
Jos 14: 6 what the LORD said to Moses the **m**
Jdg 13: 6 and told him, "A **m** came to me.
13: 8 "O Lord, I beg you, let the **m** you
1Sa 2:27 Now a **m** came to Eli and said to him,
9: 6 "Look, in this town there is a **m**; he
9: 7 We have no gift to take to the **m**.
9: 8 I will give it to the **m** so that he
9:10 out for the town where the **m** was.
1Ki 12:22 word of God came to Shemaiah the **m**:
13: 1 By the word of the LORD a **m** came
13: 3 That same day the **m** gave a sign:
13: 4 King Jeroboam heard what the **m** cried
13: 5 by the **m** by the word of the LORD.
13: 6 the king said to the **m**, "Intercede
13: 6 So the **m** interceded with the LORD,
13: 7 The king said to the **m**, "Come home
13: 8 the **m** answered the king, "Even if
13:11 that the **m** had done there that day.
13:12 road the **m** from Judah had taken.
13:14 rode after the **m**. He found him
13:14 "Are you the **m** who came from Judah?"
13:16 The **m** said, "I cannot turn back and
13:19 the **m** returned with him and ate and
13:21 He cried out to the **m** who had come
13:23 the **m** had finished eating and
13:26 **m** who defied the word of the LORD.
13:29 prophet picked up the body of the **m**,
13:31 bury me in the grave where the **m** is
17:18 "What do you have against me, **m**? Did
17:24 "Now I know that you are a **m** and
20:28 The **m** came up and told the king of
2Ki 1: 9 "**M**, the king says, 'Come down!'
1:10 "If I am a **m**, may fire come down
1:11 The captain said to him, "**M**, this is
1:12 "If I am a **m**," Elijah replied, "may
1:13 "**M**," he begged, "please have respect
4: 7 She went and told the **m**, and he said,
4: 9 who often comes our way is a holy **m**.
4:16 "Don't mislead your servant, O **m**!"
4:21 laid him on the bed of the **m**, then
4:22 can go to the **m** quickly and return."
4:25 she set out and came to the **m** at
4:25 the **m** said to his servant Gehazi,
4:27 she reached the **m** at the mountain,
4:27 but the **m** said, "Leave her alone!
4:40 "O **m**, there is death in the pot!"
4:42 bringing the **m** twenty loaves of
5: 8 Elisha the **m** heard that the king of
5:14 as the **m** had told him, and his flesh
5:15 his attendants went back to the **m**.
5:20 Gehazi, the servant of Elisha the **m**,
6: 6 The **m** asked, "Where did it fall?"
6: 9 The **m** sent word to the king of
6:10 on the place indicated by the **m**.
6:15 the servant of the **m** got up and went
7: 2 the king was leaning said to the **m**,
7:17 and he died, just as the **m** had
7:18 happened as the **m** had said to the
7:19 The officer had said to the **m**, "Look,
7:19 The **m** had replied, "You will see it
8: 2 The woman proceeded to do as the **m**
8: 4 the servant of the **m**, and had said,
8: 7 When the king was told, "The **m** has
8: 8 gift with you and go to meet the **m**.
8:11 Then the **m** began to weep.
13:19 The **m** was angry with him and said,
23:16 by the **m** who foretold these things.
23:17 "It marks the tomb of the **m** who came
1Ch 23:14 The sons of Moses the **m** were counted
2Ch 8:14 was what David the **m** had ordered.
11: 2 of the LORD came to Shemaiah the **m**:
25: 7 a **m** came to him and said, "O king,
25: 9 Amaziah asked the **m**, "But what about
25: 9 The **m** replied, "The LORD can give
30:16 in the Law of Moses the **m**.
Ezr 3: 2 written in the Law of Moses the **m**.
Ne 12:24 other, as prescribed by David the **m**.
Ne 12:36 prescribed by David the **m**.
Jer 35: 4 sons of Hanan son of Igdaliah the **m**.
1Ti 6:11 you, **m**, flee from all this, and
2Ti 3:17 that the **m** may be thoroughly

Man's (Man)

Ge 2:21 he took one of the **m** ribs and closed
6: 5 The LORD saw how great **m** wickedness
20: 7 Now return the **m** wife, for he is a
42:25 to put each **m** silver back in his
42:35 there in each **m** sack was his pouch
44: 1 **m** silver in the mouth of his sack.
44:26 We cannot see the **m** face unless our
Ex 21:35 "If a **m** bull injures the bull of
22: 5 and they graze in another **m** field,
22: 8 his hands on the other **m** property.
Lev 4:26 the **m** sin, and he will be forgiven.
20:10 adultery with another **m** wife—
Nu 5:10 Each **m** sacred gifts are his own, but
5:12 'If a **m** wife goes astray and is
7: 5 Levites as each **m** work requires."
Dt 22:22 found sleeping with another **m** wife,
22:24 because he violated another **m** wife.
24: 6 taking a **m** livelihood as security.
25:10 That **m** line shall be known in Israel
Jdg 18:19 rather than just one **m** household?"
Ru 1: 2 The **m** name was Elimelech, his wife's
4: 5 you acquire the dead **m** widow, in
2Sa 10: 4 shaved off half of each **m** beard, cut
1Ki 18:44 as a **m** hand is rising from the sea.
2Ki 13:21 threw the **m** body into Elisha's tomb.
18:21 which pierces a **m** hand and wounds
Job 14: 5 **M** days are determined; you have
14:19 the soil, so you destroy **m** hope.
21:19 'God stores up a **m** punishment for
21:28 'Where now is the great **m** house,
28: 9 **M** hand assaults the flinty rock and
31: 2 For what is **m** lot from God above,
31:10 may my wife grind another **m** grain,
33:13 him that he answers none of **m** words?
Ps 37:23 If the LORD delights in a **m** way, he
39: 5 Each **m** life is but a breath.
66: 5 how awesome his works on **m** behalf!
Pr 4:22 them and health to a **m** whole body.
5:10 your toil enrich another **m** house.
5:20 embrace the bosom of another **m** wife?
5:21 For a **m** ways are in full view of the
6:29 is he who sleeps with another **m** wife;
13: 8 A **m** riches may ransom his life, but
13:23 A poor **m** field may produce abundant
15:25 LORD tears down the proud **m** house
16: 2 All a **m** ways seem innocent to him,
16: 7 a **m** ways are pleasing to the LORD,
16:23 A wise **m** heart guides his mouth, and
18: 4 The words of a **m** mouth are deep
18: 8 they go down to a **m** inmost parts.
18:12 Before his downfall a **m** heart is
18:14 A **m** spirit sustains him in sickness,
18:20 fruit of his mouth a **m** stomach
19: 3 A **m** own folly ruins his life, yet
19: 4 but a poor **m** friend deserts him.
19:11 A **m** wisdom gives him patience; it is
19:21 Many are the plans in a **m** heart, but
20: 3 is to a **m** honour to avoid strife,
20: 5 The purposes of a **m** heart are deep
20:24 A **m** steps are directed by the LORD.
21: 2 All a **m** ways seem right to him, but
24:15 outlaw against a righteous **m** house,
25: 9 do not betray another **m** confidence,
25:12 a wise **m** rebuke to a listening ear.
26: 7 Like a lame **m** legs that hang limp is
26:22 they go down to a **m** inmost parts.
27:19 water reflects a face, so a **m** heart
29:23 A **m** pride brings him low, but a man
30: 2 I do not have a **m** understanding.
Ecc 3:19 **M** fate is like that of the animals;
4: 4 spring from **m** envy of his neighbour.
6: 7 All **m** efforts are for his mouth, yet
7: 5 is better to heed a wise **m** rebuke
8: 1 Wisdom brightens a **m** face and
8: 6 a **m** misery weighs heavily upon him.
8:16 to observe **m** labour on earth–his
9:16 But the poor **m** wisdom is despised,
10:12 Words from a wise **m** mouth are
Isa 13: 7 go limp, every **m** heart will melt.
Isa 36: 6 which pierces a **m** hand and wounds
44:15 is **m** fuel for burning; some of it he
Jer 5: 8 each neighing for another **m** wife.
10:23 I know, O LORD, that a **m** life is not
13:11 as a belt is bound round a **m** waist
23:36 because every **m** own word becomes his
Eze 38:21 **m** sword will be against his brother.
40: 5 in the **m** hand was six long cubits,
Da 8:16 I heard a **m** voice from the Ulai
Jnh 1:14 taking this **m** life. Do not hold us
Mic 7: 6 a **m** enemies are the members of his
Hab 2: 8 For you have shed **m** blood; you have
2:17 For you have shed **m** blood; you have
Mal 2:16 "and I hate a **m** covering himself
Mt 10:36 a **m** enemies will be the members of
10:41 will receive a righteous **m** reward.
12:29 enter a strong **m** house and carry
15:11 What goes into a **m** mouth does not
27:24 "I am innocent of this **m** blood," he
Mk 3:27 no-one can enter a strong **m** house
6:37 would take eight months of a **m** wages
7:33 put his fingers into the **m** ears.
7:33 he spat and touched the **m** tongue.
7:35 At this, the **m** ears were opened, his
8:23 When he had spat on the **m** eyes and
8:25 Jesus put his hands on the **m** eyes.
10:22 At this the **m** face fell. He went
12:19 wrote for us that if a **m** brother
Lk 11: 8 yet because of the **m** boldness he
12:15 a **m** life does not consist in the
16:21 eat what fell from the rich **m** table.
20:28 wrote for us that if a **m** brother
22:51 he touched the **m** ear and healed him.
Jn 2:25 He did not need **m** testimony about
9: 6 saliva, and put it on the **m** eyes.
9:14 and opened the **m** eyes was a Sabbath.
9:18 until they sent for the **m** parents.
Ac 3: 7 the **m** feet and ankles became strong.
5:28 to make us guilty of this **m** blood."
11:12 with me, and we entered the **m** house.
13:23 "From this **m** descendants God has
17:29 image made by **m** design and skill.
Ro 2:29 Such a **m** praise is not from men, but
5:16 like the result of the one **m** sin:
9:16 not, therefore, depend on **m** desire
12: 6 If a **m** gift is prophesying, let him
14: 2 One **m** faith allows him to eat
1Co 1:25 of God is wiser than **m** wisdom,
1:25 of God is stronger than **m** strength.
2:11 man except the **m** spirit within him?
2:15 is not subject to any **m** judgment:
3:13 test the quality of each **m** work.
10:29 the other **m** conscience, I mean, not
2Co 4: 2 **m** conscience in the sight of God.
10:16 already done in another **m** territory.
Jas 1:20 for **m** anger does not bring about the
1Pe 1:17 who judges each **m** work impartially,
2Pe 2:16 speech—who spoke with a **m** voice
1Jn 5: 9 We accept **m** testimony, but God's
Rev 13:18 of the beast, for it is **m** number.
21:17 by **m** measurement, which the angel

Manaen

Ac 13: 1 Lucius of Cyrene, **M** (who had been

Manage (Managed, Management, Manager)

Jer 12: 5 you **m** in the thickets by the Jordan?
1Ti 3: 4 He must **m** his own family well and
3: 5 not know how to **m** his own family,
3:12 must **m** his children and his
5:14 to have children, to **m** their homes

Managed (Manage)

1Ki 12:18 King Rehoboam, however, **m** to get
2Ch 10:18 King Rehoboam, however, **m** to get

Management (Manage)

Lk 16: 2 you? Give an account of your **m**,

Manager (Manage)

Lk 8: 3 Chuza, the **m** of Herod's household
12:42 "Who then is the faithful and wise **m**,
16: 1 "There was a rich man whose **m** was

Lk 16: 2 because you cannot be **m** any longer.'
16: 3 "The **m** said to himself, 'What shall
16: 6 "The **m** told him, 'Take your bill,
16: 8 "The master commended the dishonest **m**

Manahath (Manahathites)

Ge 36:23 The sons of Shobal: Alvan, **M**, Ebal,
1Ch 1:40 The sons of Shobal: Alvan, **M**, Ebal,
8: 6 in Geba and were deported to **M**:

Manahathites (Manahath)

1Ch 2:52 Jearim were: Haroeh, half the **M**,
2:54 Beth Joab, half the **M**, the Zorites,

Manasseh (Manasseh's, Manassites)

1. Joseph's elder son (Ge 41:51; 46:20); blessed by Jacob but not as firstborn (Ge 48:13–20). **2.** Tribe descended from Manasseh. Blessed by Moses (Dt 33:13–17). Included in census (Nu 1:34–35; 26:29–34). Apportioned land on both sides of Jordan: east (Nu 32:33, 39–42; Jos 13:8, 29–31); west (Jos 17:1–11; Eze 48:4); failed to fully possess (Jos 17:12–13). **3.** Territory to the west and to the east of River Jordan south of the Sea of Galilee. Allotted to the descendants of Joseph's older son. Territories of Manasseh and Ephraim often treated together (Jos 16:1–17:1, 14). Its towns and borders were listed, to the east (Jos 13:8, 29–31), and to the west (Jos 17:7–11). Territory divided by the Jordan, so its inhabitants were treated as two half-tribes (Jos 13:6–8). The eastern half had good grazing (Nu 32:1). In the western half the Canaanites were not driven out but enslaved (Jos 17:12–13). **4.** King of Judah; son of Hezekiah (2Ki 20:21; 2Ch 32:33). Led Israel into idolatry (2Ki 21:2–9; 2Ch 33:2–9); sin held responsible for exile (2Ki 21:10–15; Jer 15:3–4). Deported to Babylon; repented; carried out limited reform (2Ch 33:10–19). Death (2Ki 21:18; 2Ch 33:20).

Ge 41:51 Joseph named his firstborn **M** and
46:20 In Egypt, **M** and Ephraim were born to
48: 1 sons **M** and Ephraim along with him.
48: 5 as mine; Ephraim and **M** will be mine,
48:13 **M** on his left towards Israel's right
48:14 even though **M** was the firstborn.
48:20 God make you like Ephraim and **M**.
48:20 So he put Ephraim ahead of **M**.
50:23 Also the children of Makir son of **M**
Nu 1:10 from **M**, Gamaliel son of Pedahzur;
1:34 From the descendants of **M**: All the
1:35 The number from the tribe of **M** was
2:20 The tribe of **M** will be next to them.
2:20 of **M** is Gamaliel son of Pedahzur.
7:54 people of **M**, brought his offering.
10:23 over the division of the tribe of **M**,
13:11 from the tribe of **M** (a tribe of
26:28 clans through **M** and Ephraim were:
26:29 The descendants of **M**: through Makir,
26:34 These were the clans of **M**; those
27: 1 the son of Makir, the son of **M**,
27: 1 to the clans of **M** son of Joseph.
32:33 the half-tribe of **M** son of Joseph
32:39 The descendants of Makir son of **M**
32:40 of **M**, and they settled there.
32:41 Jair, a descendant of **M**, captured
34:14 **M** have received their inheritance.
34:23 from the tribe of **M** son of Joseph;
36: 1 the son of **M**, who were from the
36:12 the descendants of **M** son of Joseph,
Dt 3:13 Og, I gave to the half-tribe of **M**.
3:14 Jair, a descendant of **M**, took the
29: 8 the Gadites and the half-tribe of **M**.
33:17 such are the thousands of **M**."
34: 2 the territory of Ephraim and **M**, all
Jos 1:12 the half-tribe of **M**, Joshua said,
4:12 Gad and the half-tribe of **M** crossed
12: 6 of **M** to be their possession.
13: 7 tribes and half of the tribe of **M**."
13: 8 The other half of **M**, the Reubenites
13:29 had given to the half-tribe of **M**,
13:29 the descendants of **M**, clan by clan:
13:31 of **M**—for half of the sons of Makir,
14: 4 become two tribes—**M** and Ephraim.
16: 4 **M** and Ephraim, the descendants of
Jos 17: 1 tribe of **M** as Joseph's firstborn,
17: 2 people of **M**—the clans of Abiezer,
17: 2 of **M** son of Joseph by their clans.
17: 3 the son of Makir, the son of **M**, had
17: 6 the daughters of the tribe of **M**
17: 6 to the rest of the descendants of **M**.
17: 7 The territory of **M** extended from
17: 8 (**M** had the land of Tappuah, but
17: 8 of **M**, belonged to the Ephraimites.)
17: 9 Ephraim lying among the towns of **M**,
17: 9 but the boundary of **M** was the
17:10 to Ephraim, on the north to **M**.
17:10 The territory of **M** reached the sea
17:11 Within Issachar and Asher, **M** also
17:17 **M**—"You are numerous and very
18: 7 Reuben and the half-tribe of **M** have
20: 8 Golan in Bashan in the tribe of **M**.
21: 5 of Ephraim, Dan and half of **M**.
21: 6 and the half-tribe of **M** in Bashan.
21:25 From half the tribe of **M** they
21:27 given: from the half-tribe of **M**,
22: 1 the Gadites and the half-tribe of **M**
22: 7 (To the half-tribe of **M** Moses had
22: 9 the Gadites and the half-tribe of **M**
22:10 the Gadites and the half-tribe of **M**
22:13 Reuben, Gad and the half-tribe of **M**.
22:15 half-tribe of **M**—they said to them:
22:21 Reuben, Gad and the half-tribe of **M**
22:30 and **M** had to say, they were pleased.
22:31 said to Reuben, Gad and **M**, "Today we
Jdg 1:27 **M** did not drive out the people of
6:15 My clan is the weakest in **M**, and I
6:35 He sent messengers throughout **M**,
7:23 Asher and all **M** were called out, and
11:29 He crossed Gilead and **M**, passed
12: 4 are renegades from Ephraim and **M**."
1Ki 4:13 of Jair son of **M** in Gilead were his,
2Ki 10:33 Reuben and **M**), from Aroer by the
20:21 And **M** his son succeeded him as king.
21: 1 **M** was twelve years old when he
21: 9 **M** led them astray, so that they did
21:11 "**M** king of Judah has committed these
21:16 Moreover, **M** also shed so much
21:18 **M** rested with his fathers and was
21:20 the LORD, as his father **M** had done.
23:12 and the altars **M** had built in the
23:26 **M** had done to provoke him to anger.
24: 3 the sins of **M** and all he had done,
1Ch 3:13 son, Hezekiah his son, **M** his son,
5:18 the Gadites and the half-tribe of **M**
5:23 The people of the half-tribe of **M**
5:26 and the half-tribe of **M** into exile.
6:61 the clans of half the tribe of **M**.
6:62 of the tribe of **M** that is in Bashan.
6:70 from half the tribe of **M** the
6:71 of **M** they received Golan in Bashan
7:14 The descendants of **M**: Asriel was his
7:17 Gilead son of Makir, the son of **M**.
7:29 Along the borders of **M** were Beth
9: 3 and **M** who lived in Jerusalem were:
12:19 Some of the men of **M** defected to
12:20 these were the men of **M** who defected
12:20 leaders of units of a thousand in **M**.
12:31 men of half the tribe of **M**,
12:37 Gad, and the half-tribe of **M**, armed
26:32 the Gadites and the half-tribe of **M**
27:20 the tribe of **M**: Joel son of Pedaiah;
27:21 over the half-tribe of **M** in Gilead:
2Ch 15: 9 **M** and Simeon who had settled among
30: 1 also wrote letters to Ephraim and **M**,
30:10 from town to town in Ephraim and **M**,
30:11 Nevertheless, some men of Asher, **M**
30:18 **M**, Issachar and Zebulun had not
31: 1 and Benjamin and in Ephraim and **M**.
32:33 And **M** his son succeeded him as king.
33: 1 **M** was twelve years old when he
33: 9 **M** led Judah and the people of
33:10 The LORD spoke to **M** and his people,
33:11 who took **M** prisoner, put a hook in
33:13 Then **M** knew that the LORD is God.
33:20 **M** rested with his fathers and was
33:22 the LORD, as his father **M** had done.
33:22 to all the idols **M** had made.
33:23 unlike his father **M**, he did not
34: 6 In the towns of **M**, Ephraim and
34: 9 had collected from the people of **M**,
Ezr 10:30 Mattaniah, Bezalel, Binnui and **M**.
10:33 Eliphelet, Jeremai, **M** and Shimei.
Ps 60: 7 Gilead is mine, and **M** is mine;
80: 2 before Ephraim, Benjamin and **M**.
108: 8 Gilead is mine, **M** is mine; Ephraim
Isa 9:21 **M** will feed on Ephraim, and Ephraim
9:21 and Ephraim on **M**; together they will
Jer 15: 4 because of what **M** son of Hezekiah
Eze 48: 4 "**M** will have one portion; it will
48: 5 territory of **M** from east to west.
Mt 1:10 Hezekiah the father of **M**, **M** the
Rev 7: 6 from the tribe of **M** 12,000,

Manasseh's (Manasseh)

Ge 48:14 he put his left hand on **M** head, even
48:17 it from Ephraim's head to **M** head.
Jos 17: 1 that is, for Makir, **M** firstborn.
17: 5 **M** share consisted of ten tracts of
2Ki 21:17 for the other events of **M** reign, and
2Ch 33:18 The other events of **M** reign,

Manassites (Manasseh)

Dt 4:43 and Golan in Bashan, for the **M**.
Jos 16: 9 within the inheritance of the **M**.
17:12 Yet the **M** were not able to occupy

Mandrake (Mandrakes)

Ge 30:14 the fields and found some **m** plants,

Mandrakes (Mandrake)

Ge 30:14 Please give me some of your son's **m**."
30:15 Will you take my son's **m** too?"
30:15 tonight in return for your son's **m**."
30:16 "I have hired you with my son's **m**."
SS 7:13 The **m** send out their fragrance, and

Mane

Job 39:19 or clothe his neck with a flowing **m**?

Manger

Job 39: 9 Will he stay by your **m** at night?
Pr 14: 4 Where there are no oxen, the **m** is
Isa 1: 3 the donkey his owner's **m**, but Israel
Lk 2: 7 him in cloths and placed him in a **m**,
2:12 wrapped in cloths and lying in a **m**."
2:16 the baby, who was lying in the **m**.

Mangled (Mangles)

Lam 3:11 he dragged me from the path and **m** me

Mangles (Mangled)

Mic 5: 8 **m** as it goes, and no-one can rescue.

Manhood (Man)

Ps 78:51 of **m** in the tents of Ham.
105:36 the firstfruits of all their **m**.

Maniac

Hos 9: 7 a fool, the inspired man a **m**.

Manifestation

1Co 12: 7 Now to each one the **m** of the Spirit

Mankind (Man)

Ge 6: 7 the LORD said, "I will wipe **m**, whom
7:21 swarm over the earth, and all **m**.
Nu 16:22 "O God, God of the spirits of all **m**,
27:16 of all **m**, appoint a man over this
Dt 32: 8 when he divided all **m**, he set up
32:26 and blot out their memory from **m**,
Job 12:10 creature and the breath of all **m**.
34:15 all **m** would perish together and man
36:25 All **m** has seen it; men gaze on it
36:28 and abundant showers fall on **m**.
Ps 21:10 the earth, their posterity from **m**.
33:13 the LORD looks down and sees all **m**;
64: 9 All **m** will fear; they will proclaim
Pr 8: 4 call out; I raise my voice to all **m**.
8:31 his whole world and delighting in **m**.
30:14 the earth, the needy from among **m**.
Ecc 7:29 This only have I found: God made **m**
Isa 2: 9 man will be brought low and **m**

Isa 5:15 man will be brought low and **m**
38:11 living; no longer will I look on **m**,
40: 5 and all **m** together will see it.
45:12 is I who made the earth and created **m**
49:26 Then all **m** will know that I, the
66:23 **m** will come and bow down before me,"
66:24 they will be loathsome to all **m**."
Jer 25:31 will bring judgment on all **m** and
32:20 both in Israel and among all **m**, and
32:27 "I am the LORD, the God of all **m**. Is
Da 2:38 in your hands he has placed **m** and
Joel 1:12 Surely the joy of **m** is withered away.
Mic 5: 7 do not wait for man or linger for **m**.
Zec 2:13 Be still before the LORD, all **m**,
Lk 3: 6 all **m** will see God's salvation.'
Rev 9:15 were released to kill a third of **m**.
9:18 A third of **m** was killed by the three
9:20 The rest of **m** that were not killed

Man-made (Man)
Dt 4:28 There you will worship **m** gods of
Mk 14:58 'I will destroy this **m** temple and in
Ac 19:26 says that **m** gods are no gods at all.
Heb 9:11 perfect tabernacle that is not **m**,
9:24 Christ did not enter a **m** sanctuary

Manna
Ex 16:31 people of Israel called the bread **m**.
16:32 'Take an omer of **m** and keep it for
16:33 a jar and put an omer of **m** in it.
16:34 Aaron put the **m** in front of the
16:35 The Israelites ate **m** for forty years,
16:35 they ate **m** until they reached the
Nu 11: 6 we never see anything but this **m**!"
11: 7 The **m** was like coriander seed and
11: 9 camp at night, the **m** also came down.
Dt 8: 3 hunger and then feeding you with **m**,
8:16 He gave you **m** to eat in the desert,
Jos 5:12 The **m** stopped the day after they ate
5:12 no longer any **m** for the Israelites,
Ne 9:20 You did not withhold your **m** from
Ps 78:24 he rained down **m** for the people to
Jn 6:31 Our forefathers ate the **m** in the
6:49 Your forefathers ate the **m** in the
6:58 Your forefathers ate **m** and died, but
Heb 9: 4 This ark contained the gold jar of **m**,
Rev 2:17 I will give some of the hidden **m**.

Manned (Man)
2Ch 9:21 of trading ships **m** by Hiram's men.
Eze 27:11 Men of Arvad and Helech **m** your walls

Manner
Nu 15:11 goat, is to be prepared in this **m**.
Jos 6:15 the city seven times in the same **m**,
1Ki 21:26 He behaved in the vilest **m** by going
1Co 11:27 the cup of the Lord in an unworthy **m**
2Co 1:17 do I make my plans in a worldly **m**
Php 1:27 a **m** worthy of the gospel of Christ.
3Jn :6 on their way in a **m** worthy of God.

Manoah
Jdg 13: 2 A certain man of Zorah, named **M**,
13: 8 **M** prayed to the LORD: "O Lord, I beg
13: 9 God heard **M**, and the angel of God
13: 9 but her husband **M** was not with her.
13:11 **M** got up and followed his wife. When
13:12 **M** asked him, "When your words are
13:15 **M** said to the angel of the LORD, "We
13:16 (**M** did not realise that it was the
13:17 **M** enquired of the angel of the LORD,
13:19 **M** took a young goat, together with
13:19 thing while **M** and his wife watched:
13:20 Seeing this, **M** and his wife fell
13:21 himself again to **M** and his wife,
13:21 **M** realised that it was the angel of
16:31 Eshtaol in the tomb of **M** his father.

Manservant (Servant)
Ex 20:10 nor your **m** or maidservant, nor your
20:17 or his **m** or maidservant, his ox or
21:26 "If a man hits a **m** or maidservant in
21:27 if he knocks out the tooth of a **m** or
Lev 25: 6 your **m** and maidservant, and the
Dt 5:14 nor your **m** or maidservant, nor your
5:14 so that your **m** and maidservant may
5:21 his **m** or maidservant, his ox or

Mansions
Ps 49:14 grave, far from their princely **m**.
Isa 5: 9 the fine **m** left without occupants.
Am 3:15 and the **m** will be demolished,"
5:11 though you have built stone **m**, you

Mantle (Mantled)
Ps 89:45 have covered him with a **m** of shame.

Mantled (Mantle)
Ps 65:13 and the valleys are **m** with corn;

Manure
Isa 25:10 as straw is trampled down in the **m**.
Eze 4:15 cow **m** instead of human excrement."
Lk 14:35 for the **m** heap; it is thrown out.

Maoch
1Sa 27: 2 to Achish son of **M** king of Gath.

Maon (Maonites)
Jos 15:55 **M**, Carmel, Ziph, Juttah,
1Sa 23:24 **M**, in the Arabah south of Jeshimon.
23:25 rock and stayed in the Desert of **M**.
23:25 the Desert of **M** in pursuit of David.
25: 1 moved down into the Desert of **M**.
25: 2 A certain man in **M**, who had property
1Ch 2:45 The son of Shammai was **M**, and **M** was

Maonites (Maon)
Jdg 10:12 the Amalekites and the **M** oppressed

Map
Jos 18: 8 on their way to **m** out the land

Mara
Ru 1:20 "Call me **M**, because the Almighty has

Marah
Ex 15:23 they came to **M**, they could not drink
15:23 (That is why the place is called **M**.)
Nu 33: 8 Desert of Etham, they camped at **M**.
33: 9 They left **M** and went to Elim, where

Maralah
Jos 19:11 Going west it ran to **M**, touched

Marauders (Marauding)
Job 12: 6 The tents of **m** are undisturbed, and
15:21 when all seems well, **m** attack him.
Hos 6: 9 **m** lie in ambush for a man, so do

Marauding (Marauders)
Zec 9: 8 I will defend my house against **m**

Marble
1Ch 29: 2 **m**—all of these in large quantities.
Est 1: 6 to silver rings on **m** pillars.
1: 6 **m**, mother-of-pearl and other costly
SS 5:15 His legs are pillars of **m** set on
Rev 18:12 costly wood, bronze, iron and **m**;

March (Marched, Marches, Marching)
Nu 10:28 This was the order of **m** for the
20:18 **m** out and attack you with the sword."
Dt 20:10 you **m** up to attack a city, make its
Jos 6: 3 **M** around the city once with all the
6: 4 On the seventh day, **m** around the
6: 7 "Advance! **M** around the city, with
10: 9 After an all-night **m** from Gilgal,
Jdg 5:21 **M** on, my soul; be strong!
2Sa 15:22 David said to Ittai, "Go ahead, **m** on.
18: 2 I myself will surely **m** out with you."
2Ki 3: 9 After a roundabout **m** of seven days,
18:25 The LORD himself told me to **m**
24: 7 The king of Egypt did not **m** out from
2Ch 20:16 Tomorrow **m** down against them. They
25: 7 these troops from Israel must not **m**
Isa 27: 4 I would **m** against them in battle;
36:10 The LORD himself told me to **m**
42:13 The LORD will **m** out like a mighty
Jer 46: 3 and small, and **m** out for battle!
46: 9 O charioteers! **M** on, O warriors—
Da 11:11 "Then the king of the South will **m**
Joel 2: 7 They all **m** in line, not swerving
Ob :13 You should not **m** through the gates
Zec 9:14 will **m** in the storms of the south,

Marched (March)
Ge 14: 8 **m** out and drew up their battle lines
Nu 21:23 He mustered his entire army and **m**
21:33 his whole army **m** out to meet them in
33: 3 They **m** out boldly in full view of
Dt 1:43 you **m** up into the hill country.
3: 1 **m** out to meet us in battle at Edrei.
Jos 6: 9 The armed guard **m** ahead of the
6:14 on the second day they **m** around the
6:15 they got up at daybreak and **m** around
8:10 of Israel **m** before them to Ai.
8:11 The entire force that was with him **m**
10: 7 Joshua **m** up from Gilgal with his
15:15 From there he **m** against the people
Jdg 5: 4 when you **m** from the land of Edom,
1Sa 29: 2 the Philistine rulers **m** with their
2Sa 2:29 All that night Abner and his men **m**
2:32 Then Joab and his men **m** all night
5: 6 The king and his men **m** to Jerusalem
15:18 All his men **m** past him, along with
15:18 him from Gath **m** before the king.
15:22 So Ittai the Gittite **m** on with all
18: 4 the men **m** out in units of hundreds
18: 6 The army **m** into the field to fight
20: 7 They **m** out from Jerusalem to pursue
1Ki 20:19 **m** out of the city with the army
20:27 provisions, they **m** out to meet them.
2Ki 6:24 and **m** up and laid siege to Samaria.
16: 5 **m** up to fight against Jerusalem
17: 5 **m** against Samaria and laid siege to
18: 9 Shalmaneser king of Assyria **m**
23:29 King Josiah **m** out to meet him in
25: 1 Nebuchadnezzar king of Babylon **m**
1Ch 11: 4 David and all the Israelites **m** to
2Ch 14: 9 Zerah the Cushite **m** out against them
24:23 the army of Aram **m** against Joash; it
35:20 Josiah **m** out to meet him in battle.
Job 18:14 and **m** off to the king of terrors.
Ps 68: 7 you **m** through the wasteland,
Isa 7: 1 **m** up to fight against Jerusalem,
Jer 37: 5 Pharaoh's army had **m** out of Egypt,
37: 7 'Pharaoh's army, which has **m** out to
39: 1 Nebuchadnezzar king of Babylon **m**
52: 4 Nebuchadnezzar king of Babylon **m**
Heb 11:30 had **m** around them for seven days.
Rev 20: 9 They **m** across the breadth of the

Marches (March)
Joel 2: 8 They do not jostle each other; each **m**
Am 5: 3 "The city that **m** out a thousand
5: 3 the town that **m** out a hundred strong
Mic 5: 5 land and **m** through our fortresses,
5: 6 our land and **m** into our borders.

Marching (March)
Ex 14: 8 Israelites, who were **m** out boldly.
14:10 were the Egyptians, **m** after them.
Jos 6:13 **m** before the ark of the LORD and
1Sa 29: 2 men were **m** at the rear with Achish.
2Sa 5:24 soon as you hear the sound of **m** in
2Ki 19: 9 was **m** out to fight against him.
1Ch 14:15 soon as you hear the sound of **m** in
2Ch 11: 4 turned back from **m** against Jeroboam.
Isa 37: 9 was **m** out to fight against him.

Marduk
Jer 50: 2 put to shame, **M** filled with terror.

Mare
SS 1: 9 I liken you, my darling, to a **m**

Mareshah
Jos 15:44 Keilah, Aczib and **M**—nine towns and
1Ch 2:42 son **M**, who was the father of Hebron.
4:21 Laadah the father of **M** and the clans
2Ch 11: 8 Gath, **M**, Ziph,
14: 9 chariots, and came as far as **M**.
14:10 in the Valley of Zephathah near **M**.
20:37 Eliezer son of Dodavahu of **M**
Mic 1:15 conqueror against you who live in **M**.

Mariners (Maritime)
Eze 27:27 merchandise and wares, your **m**,
27:29 the **m** and all the seamen will stand

Marital (Marry)
Ex 21:10 of her food, clothing and **m** rights.
Mt 5:32 except for **m** unfaithfulness, causes
19: 9 except for **m** unfaithfulness, and
1Co 7: 3 The husband should fulfil his **m** duty

Maritime (Mariners)
Ge 10: 5 (From these the **m** peoples spread out

Mark[1]
Also called John (Ac 12:12). Cousin of Barnabas (Col 4:10). Accompanied Paul and Barnabas (Ac 12:25) but later deserted them (Ac 13:13). Cause of disagreement (Ac 15:37–39). Reconciled to Paul (2Ti 4:11) and a fellow-worker (Phm 24); close to Peter (1Pe 5:13). Wrote second Gospel.

Ac 12:12 also called **M**, where many people had
12:25 with them John, also called **M**.
15:37 take John, also called **M**, with them,
15:39 took **M** and sailed for Cyprus,
Col 4:10 as does **M**, the cousin of Barnabas.
2Ti 4:11 Only Luke is with me. Get **M** and
Phm :24 do **M**, Aristarchus, Demas and Luke,
1Pe 5:13 her greetings, and so does my son **M**.

Mark[2] (Marked, Marker, Marks)
Ge 1:14 to **m** seasons and days and years,
4:15 Then the LORD put a **m** on Cain so
1Ki 22:28 Then he added, "**M** my words, all you
2Ch 18:27 Then he added, "**M** my words, all you
Job 36:32 and commands it to strike its **m**.
Isa 59: 7 ruin and destruction **m** their ways.
Eze 9: 4 put a **m** on the foreheads of those
9: 6 do not touch anyone who has the **m**.
21:19 "Son of man, **m** out two roads for the
21:20 **M** out one road for the sword to come
Ro 3:16 ruin and misery **m** their ways,
2Co 12:12 The things that **m** an apostle—signs,
Gal 5: 2 **M** my words! I, Paul, tell you that
2Th 3:17 distinguishing **m** in all my letters.
2Ti 3: 1 **m** this: There will be terrible times
Rev 13:16 free and slave, to receive a **m** on
13:17 buy or sell unless he had the **m**,
14: 9 **m** on the forehead or on the hand,
14:11 who receives the **m** of his name."
16: 2 people who had the **m** of the beast
19:20 who had received the **m** of the beast
20: 4 **m** on their foreheads or their hands.

Marked (Mark[2])
Jos 18:20 These were the boundaries that **m** out
Job 15:22 the darkness; he is **m** for the sword.
38: 5 Who **m** off its dimensions? Surely you
Pr 8:27 when he **m** out the horizon on the
8:29 **m** out the foundations of the earth.
Isa 40:12 or with the breadth of his hand **m**
Zec 11: 4 "Pasture the flock **m** for slaughter.
11: 7 I pastured the flock **m** for slaughter,
Eph 1:13 Having believed, you were **m** in him
Heb 12: 1 perseverance the race **m** out for us.

Marker (Mark[2])
Isa 44:13 line and makes an outline with a **m**;
Eze 39:15 he will set up a **m** beside it until

Market (Market-place, Market-places)
1Ki 20:34 "You may set up your own **m** areas in
Am 8: 5 that we may **m** wheat?"—skimping the
Zep 1:11 Wail, you who live in the **m** district;
Jn 2:16 turn my Father's house into a **m**!"
1Co 10:25 Eat anything sold in the meat **m**

Market-place (Market)
Isa 23: 3 and she became the **m** of the nations.
Eze 27:24 In your **m** they traded with you
Mt 20: 3 standing in the **m** doing nothing.
Mk 7: 4 they come from the **m** they do not eat
Lk 7:32 like children sitting in the **m**
Ac 16:19 into the **m** to face the authorities.
17: 5 up some bad characters from the **m**,
17:17 as well as in the **m** day by day with

Market-places (Market)
Mt 11:16 in the **m** and calling out to others:
23: 7 they love to be greeted in the **m** and
Mk 6:56 they placed the sick in the **m**.
12:38 robes and be greeted in the **m**,
Lk 11:43 synagogues and greetings in the **m**.
20:46 love to be greeted in the **m** and have

Marks (Mark[2])
Ge 35:20 day that pillar **m** Rachel's tomb.
Lev 19:28 dead or put tattoo **m** on yourselves.
1Sa 21:13 making **m** on the doors of the gate
2Ki 23:17 "It **m** the tomb of the man of God who
Job 13:27 putting **m** on the soles of my feet.
26:10 He **m** out the horizon on the face of
Ps 104:19 The moon **m** off the seasons, and the
Isa 44:13 chisels and **m** it with compasses.
Jn 20:25 "Unless I see the nail **m** in his
Gal 6:17 I bear on my body the **m** of Jesus.

Maroth
Mic 1:12 Those who live in **M** writhe in pain,

Marred
Isa 52:14 his form **m** beyond human likeness—
Jer 18: 4 from the clay was **m** in his hands;

Marriage (Marry)
Ge 29:26 daughter in **m** before the older one.
Ex 2:21 his daughter Zipporah to Moses in **m**.
Lev 21: 4 to him by **m**, and so defile himself.
Dt 22:16 **m** to this man, but he dislikes her.
23: 2 No-one born of a forbidden **m** nor any
Jos 15:16 "I will give my daughter Acsah in **m**
15:17 gave his daughter Acsah to him in **m**.
Jdg 1:12 "I will give my daughter Acsah in **m**
1:13 gave his daughter Acsah to him in **m**.
3: 6 They took their daughters in **m** and
12: 9 He gave his daughters away in **m** to
21: 1 his daughter in **m** to a Benjamite."
21: 7 them any of our daughters in **m**?"
1Sa 17:25 also give him his daughter in **m**
18:17 I will give her to you in **m**; only
18:19 was given in **m** to Adriel of Meholah.
18:27 gave him his daughter Michal in **m**.
1Ki 2:21 in **m** to your brother Adonijah."
11:19 his own wife, Queen Tahpenes, in **m**.
2Ki 8:27 was related by **m** to Ahab's family.
14: 9 'Give your daughter to my son in **m**.
1Ch 2:35 Sheshan gave his daughter in **m** to
5: 1 when he defiled his father's **m** bed
2Ch 18: 1 he allied himself with Ahab by **m**.
25:18 'Give your daughter to my son in **m**.
Ezr 9:12 do not give your daughters in **m** to
Ne 10:30 not to give our daughters in **m** to
13:25 your daughters in **m** to their sons,
13:25 **m** for your sons or for yourselves.
Jer 29: 6 sons and give your daughters in **m**,
Da 11:17 And he will give him a daughter in **m**
Mal 2:14 the wife of your **m** covenant.
Mt 19:12 renounced **m** because of the kingdom
22:30 neither marry nor be given in **m**;
24:38 marrying and giving in **m**, up to the
Mk 12:25 neither marry nor be given in **m**;
Lk 2:36 her husband seven years after her **m**,
17:27 **m** up to the day Noah entered the ark.
20:34 this age marry and are given in **m**.
20:35 neither marry nor be given in **m**,
Ro 7: 2 she is released from the law of **m**.
Heb 13: 4 **M** should be honoured by all, and the
13: 4 and the **m** bed kept pure, for God

Marriages (Marry)
Ne 13:26 Was it not because of **m** like these

Married (Marry)
Ge 4:19 Lamech **m** two women, one named Adah
6: 2 and they **m** any of them they chose.
11:29 Abram and Nahor both **m**. The name of
20: 3 you have taken; she is a **m** woman."
24:67 his mother Sarah, and he **m** Rebekah.
25:20 Isaac was forty years old when he **m**
26:34 Esau was forty years old, he **m**
28: 9 he went to Ishmael and **m** Mahalath,
38: 2 He **m** her and lay with her;
Ex 2: 1 Now a man of the house of Levi **m** a
6:20 Amram **m** his father's sister Jochebed,
6:23 Aaron **m** Elisheba, daughter of
6:25 Eleazar son of Aaron **m** one of the
22:16 pledged to be **m** and sleeps with her,
Nu 5:19 impure while **m** to your husband,
5:20 if you have gone astray while **m** to
5:29 herself while **m** to her husband,
12: 1 Cushite wife, for he had **m** a Cushite.
36:11 Milcah and Noah—**m** their cousins
36:12 They **m** within the clans of the
Dt 20: 7 and not **m** her? Let him go home,
22:14 "I **m** this woman, but when I
22:23 to be **m** and he sleeps with her,
22:25 girl pledged to be **m** and rapes her,
22:28 a virgin who is not pledged to be **m**
24: 5 If a man has recently **m**, he must not
24: 5 happiness to the wife he has **m**.
28:30 You will be pledged to be **m** to a
Ru 1: 4 They **m** Moabite women, one named
1Sa 25:43 David had also **m** Ahinoam of Jezreel,
2Sa 13:13 not keep me from being **m** to you."
17:25 an Israelite who had **m** Abigail, the
1Ki 3: 1 king of Egypt and **m** his daughter.
4:11 **m** to Taphath daughter of Solomon);
4:15 Ahimaaz—in Naphtali (he had **m**
7: 8 Pharaoh's daughter, whom he had **m**.
16:31 but he also **m** Jezebel daughter of
2Ki 8:18 done, for he **m** a daughter of Ahab.
1Ch 2:19 Azubah died, Caleb **m** Ephrath, who
2:21 **m** her when he was sixty years old),
4:18 daughter Bithiah, whom Mered had **m**.
23:22 cousins, the sons of Kish, **m** them.
2Ch 11:18 Rehoboam **m** Mahalath, who was the
11:20 he **m** Maacah daughter of Absalom, who
13:21 Abijah grew in strength. He **m**
21: 6 done, for he **m** a daughter of Ahab.
Ezr 2:61 Barzillai (a man who had **m** a
10:10 you have **m** foreign women,
10:14 **m** a foreign woman come at a set time,
10:17 all the men who had **m** foreign women.
10:18 the following had **m** foreign women:
10:44 All these had **m** foreign women, and
Ne 6:18 and his son Jehohanan had **m** the
7:63 Barzillai (a man who had **m** a
13:23 **m** women from Ashdod, Ammon and Moab.
Pr 30:23 an unloved woman who is **m**, and a
Isa 54: 6 who **m** young, only to be rejected,"
62: 4 in you, and your land will be **m**.
Hos 1: 3 he **m** Gomer daughter of Diblaim, and
Mt 1:18 Mary was pledged to be **m** to Joseph,
22:25 The first one **m** and died, and since
22:28 since all of them were **m** to her?"
Mk 6:17 Philip's wife, whom he had **m**.
12:20 The first one **m** and died without
12:21 The second one **m** the widow, but he
12:23 be, since the seven were **m** to her?"
Lk 1:27 to a virgin pledged to be **m** to a man
2: 5 **m** to him and was expecting a child.
14:20 have just got **m**, so I can't come.'
20:29 one **m** a woman and died childless.
20:31 the third **m** her, and in the same way
20:33 be, since the seven were **m** to her?"
Ro 7: 2 For example, by law a **m** woman is
1Co 7:10 To the **m** I give this command (not I,
7:27 Are you **m**? Do not seek a divorce.
7:33 a **m** man is concerned about the
7:34 But a **m** woman is concerned about the
7:36 He is not sinning. They should get **m**.

Marries (Marry)

Ex 21:10 If he **m** another woman, he must not
Lev 20:14 "'If a man **m** both a woman and her
20:17 "'If a man **m** his sister, the
20:21 "'If a man **m** his brother's wife, it
21:13 "'The woman he **m** must be a virgin.
22:12 If a priest's daughter **m** anyone
Nu 30: 6 "If she **m** after she makes a vow or
Dt 24: 1 If a man **m** a woman who becomes
Isa 62: 5 a young man **m** a maiden, so will your
Jer 3: 1 she leaves him and **m** another man,
Mt 5:32 and anyone who **m** the divorced woman
19: 9 **m** another woman commits adultery."
Mk 10:11 "Anyone who divorces his wife and **m**
10:12 if she divorces her husband and **m**
Lk 16:18 "Anyone who divorces his wife and **m**
16:18 **m** a divorced woman commits adultery.
Ro 7: 3 then, if she **m** another man while her
7: 3 even though she **m** another man.
1Co 7:28 if a virgin **m**, she has not sinned.
7:38 then, he who **m** the virgin does right,

Marrow

Job 21:24 nourished, his bones rich with **m**.
Heb 4:12 joints and **m**; it judges the thoughts

Marry (Intermarry, Marital, Marriage, Marriages, Married, Marries, Marrying)

Ge 19:14 who were pledged to **m** his daughters.
28: 1 him: "Do not **m** a Canaanite woman.
28: 6 "Do not **m** a Canaanite woman,
34:21 We can **m** their daughters and they
34:21 their daughters and they can **m** ours.
Lev 21: 7 "'They must not **m** women defiled by
21:14 He must not **m** a widow, a divorced
Nu 36: 3 Now suppose they **m** men from other
36: 3 to that of the tribe they **m** into.
36: 4 that of the tribe into which they **m**,
36: 6 They may **m** anyone they please as
36: 6 **m** within the tribal clan of their
36: 8 must **m** someone in her father's
Dt 20: 7 in battle and someone else **m** her."
22:29 He must **m** the girl, for he has
22:30 A man is not to **m** his father's wife;
24: 4 is not allowed to **m** her again after
25: 5 widow must not **m** outside the family.
25: 5 **m** her and fulfil the duty of a
25: 7 However, if a man does not want to **m**
25: 8 "I do not want to **m** her,
Jdg 11:37 my friends, because I will never **m**."
11:38 and wept because she would never **m**.
14: 8 when he went back to **m** her, he
Isa 62: 5 so will your sons **m** you; as a
Jer 16: 2 "You must not **m** and have sons or
29: 6 **M** and have sons and daughters; find
Eze 44:22 They must not **m** widows or divorced
44:22 they may **m** only virgins of Israelite
Mt 19:10 and wife, it is better not to **m**."
22:24 his brother must **m** the widow and
22:30 neither **m** nor be given in marriage;
Mk 12:19 the man must **m** the widow and have
12:25 the dead rise, they will neither **m**
Lk 20:28 the man must **m** the widow and have
20:34 age **m** and are given in marriage.
20:35 neither **m** nor be given in marriage,
1Co 7: 1 It is good for a man not to **m**.
7: 9 they should **m**, for it is better to **m**
7:28 if you do **m**, you have not sinned;
7:28 But those who **m** will face many
7:36 to **m**, he should do as he wants.
7:37 who has made up his mind not to **m**
7:38 who does not **m** her does even better.
7:39 she is free to **m** anyone she wishes,
1Ti 4: 3 They forbid people to **m** and order
5:11 to Christ, they want to **m**.
5:14 I counsel younger widows to **m**, to

Marrying (Marry)

Ezr 10: 2 **m** foreign women from the peoples
Ne 13:27 to our God by **m** foreign women?"
Mal 2:11 by **m** the daughter of a foreign god.
Mt 24:38 people were eating and drinking, **m**
Lk 17:27 People were eating, drinking, **m** and

Marsena

Est 1:14 Admatha, Tarshish, Meres, **M** and

Marsh (Marshes)

Job 8:11 grow tall where there is no **m**?
40:21 hidden among the reeds in the **m**.

Marshal (Marshalled)

Mic 5: 1 **M** your troops, O city of troops, for
Na 2: 1 yourselves, **m** all your strength!

Marshalled (Marshal)

2Ch 25:11 Amaziah then **m** his strength and led
Job 6: 4 God's terrors are **m** against me.
32:14 Job has not **m** his words against me,
Isa 45:12 the heavens; I **m** their starry hosts.

Marshes (Marsh)

Jer 51:32 crossings seized, the **m** set on fire
Eze 47:11 the swamps and **m** will not become

Martha

Sister of Mary and Lazarus (Lk 10:38–39; Jn 11). Concerned with practical things (Lk 10:40–41; Jn 12:2).

Lk 10:38 named **M** opened her home to him.
10:40 **M** was distracted by all the
10:41 "**M**, **M**," the Lord answered, "you are
Jn 11: 1 village of Mary and her sister **M**.
11: 5 Jesus loved **M** and her sister and
11:19 many Jews had come to **M** and Mary to
11:20 **M** heard that Jesus was coming, she
11:21 "Lord," **M** said to Jesus, "if you had
11:24 **M** answered, "I know he will rise
11:30 at the place where **M** had met him.
11:39 "But, Lord," said **M**, the sister of
12: 2 **M** served, while Lazarus was among

Martyr

Ac 22:20 the blood of your **m** Stephen was shed,

Marvelled (Marvellous)

Lk 2:33 The child's father and mother **m** at
2Th 1:10 to be **m** at among all those who have

Marvelling (Marvellous)

Lk 9:43 While everyone was **m** at all that

Marvellous (Marvelled, Marvelling)

1Ch 16:24 his **m** deeds among all peoples.
Job 37: 5 God's voice thunders in **m** ways; he
Ps 71:17 to this day I declare your **m** deeds.
72:18 of Israel, who alone does **m** deeds.
86:10 For you are great and do **m** deeds;
96: 3 his **m** deeds among all peoples.
98: 1 for he has done **m** things; his right
118:23 the LORD has done this, and it is **m**
Isa 25: 1 **m** things, things planned long ago.
Zec 8: 6 "It may seem **m** to the remnant of
8: 6 it seem **m** to me?" declares the LORD
Mt 21:42 done this, and it is **m** in our eyes'?
Mk 12:11 the Lord has done this, and it is **m**
Rev 15: 1 I saw in heaven another great and **m**
15: 3 **m** are your deeds, Lord God Almighty.

Mary (Mary's)

1. Mother of Jesus; husband of Joseph (Mt 1:16–25; Lk 1–2). Visited by Gabriel (Lk 1:26–38); praised God (Lk 1:46–55). With Jesus at wedding in Cana (Jn 2:1–11). Witnessed crucifixion (Jn 19:25); entrusted to John's care (Jn 19:26–27). With disciples after resurrection (Ac 1:14). **2.** See *Magdalene*. Demoniac delivered by Jesus (Lk 8:2; Mk 16:9). At crucifixion (Mt 27:55–56; Mk 15:40–41,47; Jn 19:25); visited tomb (Mt 28:1; Mk 16:1; Lk 24:1–10; Jn 20:1); met by risen Jesus (Jn 20:10–18). **3.** Sister of Martha and Lazarus (Lk 10:38–39; Jn 11); commended for devotion (Lk 10:39–42); anointed Jesus' feet (Jn 12:3; 11:2). **4.** Mother of James and Joses; wife of Clopas. At crucifixion (Mt 27:55–56; Mk 15:40–41,47; Jn 19:25); visited tomb (Mt 28:1; Mk 16:1; Lk 24:1–10). **5.** Mother of John Mark whose home used by one Jerusalem church (Ac 12:12–17). **6.** Believer in Rome (Ro 16:6).

Mt 1:16 the husband of **M**, of whom was born
1:18 His mother **M** was pledged to be
1:20 do not be afraid to take **M** home as
1:24 him and took **M** home as his wife.
2:11 saw the child with his mother **M**,
13:55 son? Isn't his mother's name **M**,
27:56 Among them were **M** Magdalene, **M** the
27:61 **M** Magdalene and the other **M** were
28: 1 **M** Magdalene and the other **M** went to
Mk 15:40 Among them were **M** Magdalene, **M** the
15:47 **M** Magdalene and **M** the mother of
16: 1 the Sabbath was over, **M** Magdalene, **M**
16: 9 he appeared first to **M** Magdalene,
Lk 1:27 The virgin's name was **M**.
1:29 **M** was greatly troubled at his words
1:30 **M**, you have found favour with God.
1:34 "How will this be," **M** asked the
1:38 "I am the Lord's servant," **M**
1:39 At that time **M** got ready and hurried
1:46 **M** said: "My soul glorifies the
1:56 **M** stayed with Elizabeth for about
2: 5 He went there to register with **M**,
2:16 they hurried off and found **M** and
2:19 **M** treasured up all these things and
2:22 Joseph and **M** took him to Jerusalem
2:34 Simeon blessed them and said to **M**,
2:39 Joseph and **M** had done everything
8: 2 **M** (called Magdalene) from whom seven
10:39 She had a sister called **M**, who sat
10:42 only one thing is needed. **M** has
24:10 **M** Magdalene, Joanna, **M** the mother
Jn 11: 1 village of **M** and her sister Martha.
11: 2 This **M**, whose brother Lazarus now
11:19 many Jews had come to Martha and **M**
11:20 to meet him, but **M** stayed at home.
11:28 back and called her sister **M** aside.
11:29 **M** heard this, she got up quickly and
11:31 the Jews who had been with **M** in the
11:32 **M** reached the place where Jesus was
11:45 of the Jews who had come to visit **M**,
12: 3 **M** took about a pint of pure nard, an
19:25 his mother's sister, **M** the wife of
19:25 the wife of Clopas, and **M** Magdalene.
20: 1 while it was still dark, **M** Magdalene
20:11 **M** stood outside the tomb crying. As
20:16 Jesus said to her, "**M**." She turned
20:18 **M** Magdalene went to the disciples
Ac 1:14 along with the women and **M** the
12:12 he went to the house of **M** the mother
Ro 16: 6 Greet **M**, who worked very hard for

Mary's (Mary)

Mk 6: 3 this **M** son and the brother of James,
Lk 1:41 Elizabeth heard **M** greeting, the baby

Mash

Isa 30:24 **m**, spread out with fork and shovel.

Mashal

1Ch 6:74 of Asher they received **M**, Abdon,

Mask

1Th 2: 5 nor did we put on a **m** to cover up

Maskil

Ps 32: T Of David. A **m**.
42: T A **m** of the Sons of Korah.
44: T Of the Sons of Korah. A **m**.
45: T A **m**. A wedding song.
52: T director of music. A **m** of David.
53: T A **m** of David.
54: T A **m** of David. When the Ziphites.
55: T instruments. A **m** of David.
74: T A **m** of Asaph.
78: T A **m** of Asaph.
88: T A **m** of Heman the Ezrahite.
89: T A **m** of Ethan the Ezrahite.
142: T **m** of David. When he was in the cave

Masons
2Ki 12:12 the **m** and stonecutters. They
22: 6 carpenters, the builders and the **m**.
1Ch 22:15 **m** and carpenters, as well as men
2Ch 24:12 They hired **m** and carpenters to
Ezr 3: 7 they gave money to the **m** and

Masquerade (Masquerades, Masquerading)
2Co 11:15 **m** as servants of righteousness.

Masquerades (Masquerade)
2Co 11:14 Satan himself **m** as an angel of

Masquerading (Masquerade)
2Co 11:13 workmen, **m** as apostles of Christ.

Masrekah
Ge 36:36 Hadad died, Samlah from **M** succeeded
1Ch 1:47 Hadad died, Samlah from **M** succeeded

Massa
Ge 25:14 Mishma, Dumah, **M**,
1Ch 1:30 Mishma, Dumah, **M**, Hadad, Tema,

Massacre
Hos 1: 4 house of Jehu for the **m** at Jezreel,

Massah See Meribah
Ex 17: 7 he called the place **M** and Meribah
Dt 6:16 the LORD your God as you did at **M**.
9:22 at **M** and at Kibroth Hattaavah.
33: 8 You tested him at **M**; you contended
Ps 95: 8 you did that day at **M** in the desert,

Masses (Massing)
Isa 5:13 their **m** will be parched with thirst.
5:14 **m** with all their brawlers and

Massing (Masses)
Isa 13: 4 like nations **m** together! The LORD

Massive
Mk 13: 1 "Look, Teacher! What **m** stones! What

Mast
Isa 33:23 Your rigging hangs loose: The **m** is
Eze 27: 5 from Lebanon to make a **m** for you.

Master (Master's, Mastered, Masters, Masters', Mastery)
Ge 4: 7 to have you, but you must **m** it."
18:12 "After I am worn out and my **m** is old,
24: 9 under the thigh of his **m** Abraham
24:10 all kinds of good things from his **m**.
24:12 and show kindness to my **m** Abraham.
24:12 he prayed, "O LORD, God of my **m**
24:14 you have shown kindness to my **m**."
24:27 the God of my **m** Abraham, who has not
24:27 kindness and faithfulness to my **m**.
24:35 The LORD has blessed my **m** abundantly,
24:37 my **m** made me swear an oath, and said,
24:39 "Then I asked my **m**, 'What if the
24:42 'O LORD, God of my **m** Abraham, if you
24:48 I praised the LORD, the God of my **m**
24:49 kindness and faithfulness to my **m**,
24:54 he said, "Send me on my way to my **m**.
24:56 me on my way so I may go to my **m**."
24:65 "He is my **m**," the servant answered.
32: 4 "This is what you are to say to my **m**
39: 2 in the house of his Egyptian **m**.
39: 3 his **m** saw that the LORD was with him
39: 8 "my **m** does not concern himself with
39: 9 My **m** has withheld nothing from me
39:16 beside her until his **m** came home.
39:19 his **m** heard the story his wife told
39:20 Joseph's **m** took him and put him in
40: 1 offended their **m**, the king of Egypt.
44: 5 Isn't this the cup my **m** drinks from
Ex 21: 4 If his **m** gives him a wife and she
21: 4 children shall belong to her **m**,
Ex 21: 5 'I love my **m** and my wife and
21: 6 his **m** must take him before the
21: 8 If she does not please the **m** who has
21:32 of silver to the **m** of the slave,
35:35 of them **m** craftsmen and designers.
Dt 23:15 you, do not hand him over to his **m**.
Jdg 19:11 the servant said to his **m**, "Come,
19:12 His **m** replied, "No. We won't go into
19:26 the house where her **m** was staying,
19:27 her **m** got up in the morning and
1Sa 20:38 up the arrow and returned to his **m**.
24: 6 I should do such a thing to my **m**,
24:10 will not lift my hand against my **m**,
25:14 desert to give our **m** his greetings,
25:17 over our **m** and his whole household.
25:25 I did not see the men my **m** sent.
25:26 my **m**, from bloodshed and from
25:26 intend to harm my **m** be like Nabal.
25:27 your servant has brought to my **m**,
25:28 make a lasting dynasty for my **m**,
25:29 the life of my **m** will be bound
25:30 the LORD has done for my **m** every
25:31 my **m** will not have on his conscience
25:31 the LORD has brought my **m** success,
26:16 guard your **m**, the LORD's anointed.
30:13 My **m** abandoned me when I became ill
30:15 or hand me over to my **m**, and I
2Sa 2: 5 to Saul your **m** by burying him.
2: 7 for Saul your **m** is dead, and the
9:10 And Mephibosheth, grandson of your **m**,
11:11 and my **m** Joab and my lord's men are
1Ki 11:23 from his **m**, Hadadezer king of Zobah.
18: 8 "Yes," he replied. "Go tell your **m**,
18:10 where my **m** has not sent someone to
18:11 now you tell me to go to my **m** and
18:14 now you tell me to go to my **m** and
22:17 LORD said, 'These people have no **m**.
2Ki 2: 3 to take your **m** from you today?"
2: 5 to take your **m** from you today?"
2:16 Let them go and look for your **m**.
5: 1 sight of his **m** and highly regarded,
5: 3 "If only my **m** would see the prophet
5: 4 Naaman went to his **m** and told him
5:18 When my **m** enters the temple of
5:20 "My **m** was too easy on Naaman, this
5:22 "My **m** sent me to say, 'Two young men
5:25 he went in and stood before his **m**
6:22 drink and then go back to their **m**."
6:23 away, and they returned to their **m**.
8:14 left Elisha and returned to his **m**.
9: 7 to destroy the house of Ahab your **m**,
9:31 Zimri, you murderer of your **m**?"
10: 9 It was I who conspired against my **m**
18:23 "'Come now, make a bargain with my **m**
18:27 "Was it only to your **m** and you that
18:27 my **m** sent me to say these things,
19: 4 whom his **m**, the king of Assyria, has
19: 6 Isaiah said to them, "Tell your **m**,
1Ch 12:19 heads if he deserts to his **m** Saul.")
2Ch 13: 6 of David, rebelled against his **m**.
18:16 LORD said, 'These people have no **m**.
Job 3:19 and the slave is freed from his **m**.
Ps 12: 4 we own our lips—who is our **m**?"
105:21 He made him **m** of his household,
123: 2 slaves look to the hand of their **m**,
Pr 27:18 looks after his **m** will be honoured.
30:10 "Do not slander a servant to his **m**,
Isa 1: 3 The ox knows his **m**, the donkey his
19: 4 over to the power of a cruel **m**,
24: 2 for **m** as for servant, for mistress
36: 8 "'Come now, make a bargain with my **m**
36:12 "Was it only to your **m** and you that
36:12 my **m** sent me to say these things,
37: 4 whom his **m**, the king of Assyria, has
37: 6 Isaiah said to them, "Tell your **m**,
Jer 22:18 'Alas, my **m**! Alas, his splendour!'
34: 5 "Alas, O **m**!" I myself make this
Da 8:23 king, a **m** of intrigue, will arise.
Hos 2:16 you will no longer call me 'my **m**'.
Mal 1: 6 his father, and a servant his **m**.
1: 6 If I am a **m**, where is the respect
Mt 10:24 teacher, nor a servant above his **m**.
10:25 teacher, and the servant like his **m**.
18:25 Since he was not able to pay, the **m**
18:27 The servant's **m** took pity on him,
18:31 went and told their **m** everything
Mt 18:32 "Then the **m** called the servant in.
18:34 In anger his **m** turned him over to
23: 8 only one **M** and you are all brothers.
24:45 whom the **m** has put in charge of the
24:46 will be good for that servant whose **m**
24:48 'My **m** is staying away a long time,'
24:50 The **m** of that servant will come on a
25:19 "After a long time the **m** of those
25:20 '**M**,' he said, 'you entrusted me with
25:21 "His **m** replied, 'Well done, good and
25:22 '**M**,' he said, 'you entrusted me with
25:23 "His **m** replied, 'Well done, good and
25:24 '**M**,' he said, 'I knew that you are a
25:26 "His **m** replied, 'You wicked, lazy
Lk 5: 5 Simon answered, "**M**, we've worked
7: 2 whom his **m** valued highly, was sick
8:24 "**M**, **M**, we're going to drown!" He got
8:45 "**M**, the people are crowding and
9:33 "**M**, it is good for us to be here.
9:49 "**M**," said John, "we saw a man
12:36 like men waiting for their **m** to
12:37 **m** finds them watching when he comes.
12:38 servants whose **m** finds them ready,
12:42 whom the **m** puts in charge of his
12:43 **m** finds doing so when he returns.
12:45 'My **m** is taking a long time in
12:46 The **m** of that servant will come on a
12:47 not do what his **m** wants will be
14:21 back and reported this to his **m**.
14:23 "Then the **m** told his servant, 'Go
16: 3 I do now? My **m** is taking away my job.
16: 5 first, 'How much do you owe my **m**?'
16: 8 "The **m** commended the dishonest
17:13 called out in a loud voice, "Jesus, **M**
19:17 my good servant!' his **m** replied.
19:19 "His **m** answered, 'You take charge of
19:22 "His **m** replied, 'I will judge you by
Jn 2: 8 and take it to the **m** of the banquet.
2: 9 the **m** of the banquet tasted the
13:16 no servant is greater than his **m**,
15:20 'No servant is greater than his **m**.
Ro 6:14 For sin shall not be your **m**, because
14: 4 To his own **m** he stands or falls.
Eph 6: 9 their **M** and yours is in heaven,
Col 4: 1 that you also have a **M** in heaven.
2Ti 2:21 made holy, useful to the **M**
1Pe 3: 6 obeyed Abraham and called him her **m**.

Master's (Master)
Ge 24:10 the servant took ten of his **m** camels
24:27 to the house of my **m** relatives."
24:36 My **m** wife Sarah has borne him a son
24:44 the LORD has chosen for my **m** son.'
24:48 of my **m** brother for his son.
24:51 **m** son, as the LORD has directed."
39: 7 after a while his **m** wife took notice
40: 7 in custody with him in his **m** house,
44: 8 silver or gold from your **m** house?
1Sa 25:41 and wash the feet of my **m** servants."
29: 4 could he regain his **m** favour
29:10 along with your **m** servants who
2Sa 9: 9 "I have given your **m** grandson
9:10 your **m** grandson may be provided for.
11: 9 the palace with all his **m** servants
11:13 his **m** servants; he did not go home.
12: 8 I gave your **m** house to you, and your
12: 8 and your **m** wives into your arms.
16: 3 asked, "Where is your **m** grandson?"
20: 6 Take your **m** men and pursue him, or
2Ki 6:32 of his **m** footsteps behind him?"
10: 2 since your **m** sons are with you and
10: 3 most worthy of your **m** sons and set
10: 3 Then fight for your **m** house."
10: 6 take the heads of your **m** sons and
18:24 of the least of my **m** officials,
Isa 22:18 you disgrace to your **m** house!
36: 9 of the least of my **m** officials,
Mt 25:18 in the ground and hid his **m** money.
25:21 Come and share your **m** happiness!'
25:23 Come and share your **m** happiness!'
Lk 12:47 "That servant who knows his **m** will
16: 5 in each one of his **m** debtors.
Jn 15:15 does not know his **m** business.

Mastered (Master)
1Co 6:12 I will not be **m** by anything.
2Pe 2:19 is a slave to whatever has **m** him.

Masters (Master)
Ex 1:11 they put slave **m** over them to
1Sa 25:10 away from their **m** these days.
Pr 25:13 he refreshes the spirit of his **m**.
Jer 27: 4 Give them a message for their **m** and
27: 4 says: "Tell this to your **m**
Lam 1: 5 Her foes have become her **m**; her
Mt 6:24 "No-one can serve two **m**. Either he
Lk 16:13 "No servant can serve two **m**. Either
Eph 6: 5 Slaves, obey your earthly **m** with
6: 9 **m**, treat your slaves in the same way.
Col 3:22 Slaves, obey your earthly **m** in
4: 1 **M**, provide your slaves with what is
1Ti 6: 1 their **m** worthy of full respect,
6: 2 Those who have believing **m** are not
Tit 2: 9 Teach slaves to be subject to their **m**
1Pe 2:18 Slaves, submit yourselves to your **m**

Masters' (Master)
Mt 15:27 that fall from their **m** table."

Mastery (Master)
Ro 6: 9 death no longer has **m** over him.

Mat (Mats)
2Sa 11:13 his **m** among his master's servants;
Mt 9: 2 to him a paralytic, lying on a **m**.
9: 6 "Get up, take your **m** and go home.
Mk 2: 4 **m** the paralysed man was lying on.
2: 9 say, 'Get up, take your **m** and walk'?
2:11 "I tell you, get up, take your **m** and
2:12 He got up, took his **m** and walked out
Lk 5:18 came carrying a paralytic on a **m**
5:19 lowered him on his **m** through the
5:24 get up, take your **m** and go home."
Jn 5: 8 "Get up! Pick up your **m** and walk.
5: 9 he picked up his **m** and walked.
5:10 law forbids you to carry your **m**."
5:11 to me, 'Pick up your **m** and walk.
Ac 9:34 Get up and tidy up your **m**."

Match (Matched, Matching)
1Ch 12:14 the least was a **m** for a hundred,
Eze 31: 8 garden of God could **m** its beauty.
Lk 5:36 from the new will not **m** the old.

Matched (Match)
2Co 8:11 may be **m** by your completion of it,

Matching (Match)
Ezr 1:10 gold bowls 30 **m** silver bowls 410

Mate (Mated, Mating)
Ge 7: 2 a male and its **m**, and two of every
7: 2 of unclean animal, a male and its **m**,
30:41 that they would **m** near the branches,
Lev 19:19 Do not **m** different kinds of animals
Isa 34:15 will gather, each with its **m**.
34:16 be missing, not one will lack her **m**.
Na 2:12 and strangled the prey for his **m**,

Mated (Mate)
Ge 30:39 they **m** in front of the branches. And

Mating (Mate)
Ge 31:10 **m** with the flock were streaked,
31:12 goats **m** with the flock are streaked,
Jer 2:24 at **m** time they will find her.

Matred
Ge 36:39 of **M**, the daughter of Me-Zahab.
1Ch 1:50 of **M**, the daughter of Me-Zahab.

Matri's
1Sa 10:21 clan by clan, and **M** clan was chosen.

Mats (Mat)
Mk 6:55 on **m** to wherever they heard he was.
Ac 5:15 laid them on beds and **m** so that at

Mattan
2Ki 11:18 pieces and killed **M** the priest
2Ch 23:17 idols and killed **M** the priest of
Jer 38: 1 Shephatiah son of **M**, Gedaliah son of

Mattanah
Nu 21:18 Then they went from the desert to **M**,
21:19 from **M** to Nahaliel, from Nahaliel to

Mattaniah
2Ki 24:17 He made **M**, Jehoiachin's uncle, king
1Ch 9:15 Bakbakkar, Heresh, Galal and **M** son
25: 4 for Heman, from his sons: Bukkiah, **M**,
25:16 the ninth to **M**, his sons and
2Ch 20:14 the son of Jeiel, the son of **M**, a
29:13 of Asaph, Zechariah and **M**;
Ezr 10:26 From the descendants of Elam: **M**,
10:27 **M**, Jeremoth, Zabad and Aziza.
10:30 **M**, Bezalel, Binnui and Manasseh.
10:37 **M**, Mattenai and Jaasu.
Ne 11:17 **M** son of Mica, the son of Zabdi, the
11:22 the son of **M**, the son of Mica.
12: 8 Sherebiah, Judah, and also **M**, who,
12:25 **M**, Bakbukiah, Obadiah, Meshullam,
12:35 the son of Shemaiah, the son of **M**,
13:13 the son of **M**, their assistant,

Mattatha
Lk 3:31 the son of Menna, the son of **M**, the

Mattathias
Lk 3:25 the son of **M**, the son of Amos, the
3:26 the son of Maath, the son of **M**, the

Mattattah
Ezr 10:33 **M**, Zabad, Eliphelet, Jeremai,

Mattenai
Ezr 10:33 From the descendants of Hashum: **M**,
10:37 Mattaniah, **M** and Jaasu.
Ne 12:19 of Joiarib's, **M**; of Jedaiah's, Uzzi;

Matthan
Mt 1:15 father of **M**, **M** the father of Jacob,

Matthat
Lk 3:24 the son of **M**, the son of Levi, the
3:29 Jorim, the son of **M**, the son of Levi,

Matthew (Matthew's)
Apostle; tax collector, also called Levi (Mt 9:9–13; Mk 2:14–17; Lk 5:27–32; Mt 10:3; Mk 3:18; Ac 1:13). Wrote first Gospel.

Mt 9: 9 he saw a man named **M** sitting at the
9: 9 him, and **M** got up and followed him.
10: 3 Philip and Bartholomew; Thomas and **M**
Mk 3:18 Andrew, Philip, Bartholomew, **M**,
Lk 6:15 **M**, Thomas, James son of Alphaeus,
Ac 1:13 Bartholomew and **M**; James son of

Matthew's (Matthew)
Mt 9:10 Jesus was having dinner at **M** house

Matthias
Ac 1:23 (also known as Justus) and **M**.
1:26 they cast lots, and the lot fell to **M**

Mattithiah
1Ch 9:31 A Levite named **M**, the firstborn son
15:18 Unni, Eliab, Benaiah, Maaseiah, **M**,
15:21 **M**, Eliphelehu, Mikneiah, Obed-Edom,
16: 5 then Jeiel, Shemiramoth, Jehiel, **M**,
25: 3 Jeshaiah, Shimei, Hashabiah and **M**,
25:21 the fourteenth to **M**, his sons and
Ezr 10:43 **M**, Zabad, Zebina, Jaddai, Joel and
Ne 8: 4 Beside him on his right stood **M**,

Mattocks
1Sa 13:20 **m**, axes and sickles sharpened.
13:21 for sharpening ploughshares and **m**,

Mature (Maturity)
Lk 8:14 and pleasures, and they do not **m**.
1Co 2: 6 a message of wisdom among the **m**,
Eph 4:13 of the Son of God and become **m**,
Php 3:15 All of us who are **m** should take such
Col 4:12 will of God, **m** and fully assured.
Heb 5:14 solid food is for the **m**, who by
Jas 1: 4 **m** and complete, not lacking anything.

Maturity (Mature)
Heb 6: 1 about Christ and go on to **m**,

Mauled (Mauls)
1Ki 13:26 which has **m** him and killed him, as
13:28 eaten the body nor **m** the donkey.
2Ki 2:24 woods and **m** forty-two of the youths.

Mauls (Mauled)
Mic 5: 8 which **m** and mangles as it goes, and

Maxims
Job 13:12 Your **m** are proverbs of ashes; your

Me Jarkon
Jos 19:46 **M** and Rakkon, with the area facing

Meadow (Meadows)
Isa 44: 4 They will spring up like grass in a **m**
Hos 4:16 LORD pasture them like lambs in a **m**?

Meadows (Meadow)
Ps 65:13 The **m** are covered with flocks and
Isa 30:23 your cattle will graze in broad **m**.
Jer 25:37 The peaceful **m** will be laid waste

Meal (Mealtime)
Ge 19: 3 He prepared a **m** for them, baking
31:54 and invited his relatives to a **m**.
37:25 they sat down to eat their **m**, they
Nu 15:20 from the first of your ground **m**
15:21 LORD from the first of your ground **m**.
1Sa 20:27 the son of Jesse come to the **m**,
2Sa 12: 4 to prepare a **m** for the traveller
1Ki 4:22 of fine flour and sixty cors of **m**,
17:12 and make a **m** for myself and my son,
2Ki 4: 8 who urged him to stay for a **m**.
Ne 10:37 the first of our ground **m**, of our
Job 33:20 and his soul loathes the choicest **m**.
Pr 15:17 Better a **m** of vegetables where there
Isa 44:16 the fire; over it he prepares his **m**,
Jer 16: 5 a house where there is a funeral **m**;
Eze 44:30 the first portion of your ground **m**
Lk 11:38 wash before the **m**, was surprised.
Jn 13: 2 The evening **m** was being served, and
13: 4 he got up from the **m**, took off his
13:28 no-one at the **m** understood why Jesus
Ac 10:10 and while the **m** was being prepared,
16:34 his house and set a **m** before them;
1Co 10:27 If some unbeliever invites you to a **m**
10:30 If I take part in the **m** with
Heb 12:16 who for a single **m** sold his

Mealtime (Meal)
Ru 2:14 At **m** Boaz said to her, "Come over

Mean[1] (Meaning, Means[1], Meant)
Ge 33: 8 Esau asked, "What do you **m** by all
Ex 12:26 'What does this ceremony **m** to you?'
13:14 'What does this **m**?' say to him,
Jos 4: 6 ask you, 'What do these stones **m**?'
4:21 fathers, 'What do these stones **m**?'
1Sa 1: 8 Don't I **m** more to you than ten sons?"
2Sa 5:24 move quickly, because that will **m**
17: 3 The death of the man you seek will **m**
19: 6 and their men **m** nothing to you.
1Ch 14:15 because that will **m** God has gone out
Job 6:26 Do you **m** to correct what I say, and
Isa 3:15 What do you **m** by crushing my people

Eze 17:12 ‘Do you not know what these things **m**?
18: 2 “What do you people **m** by quoting
37:18 you tell us what you **m** by this?’
Da 5:26 “This is what these words **m**: Mene:
Mt 12: 7 If you had known what these words **m**,
Jn 7:36 What did he **m** when he said, ‘You
7:47 “You **m** he has deceived you also?”
16:17 “What does he **m** by saying, ‘In a
16:18 They kept asking, “What does he **m** by
Ac 2:12 one another, “What does this **m**?
17:20 and we want to know what they **m**.”
1Co 1:12 What I **m** is this: One of you says,
7:29 What I **m**, brothers, is that the time
10:19 Do I **m** then that a sacrifice offered
10:29 the other man’s conscience, I **m**, not
15:31 I die every day—I **m** that, brothers—
Gal 2:17 does that **m** that Christ promotes sin?
3:17 What I **m** is this: The law,
Eph 4: 9 (What does “he ascended” **m** except
Php 1:22 this will **m** fruitful labour for me.

Mean[2]

1Sa 25: 3 was surly and **m** in his dealings.

Meaning (Mean[1])

Ge 21:29 “What is the **m** of these seven ewe
40: 5 and each dream had a **m** of its own.
41:11 and each dream had a **m** of its own.
Dt 6:20 “What is the **m** of the stipulations,
1Sa 4:14 “What is the **m** of this uproar?” The
1Ki 1:41 the **m** of all the noise in the city?”
Ne 8: 8 making it clear and giving the **m** so
Job 7:16 Let me alone; my days have no **m**.
Ecc 6: 4 comes without **m**, it departs in
6:11 The more the words, the less the **m**,
8:17 it out, man cannot discover its **m**.
Da 2:45 This is the **m** of the vision of the
4:19 let the dream or its **m** alarm you.
4:19 and its **m** to your adversaries!
7:16 asked him the true **m** of all this.
7:19 “Then I wanted to know the true **m** of
8:16 tell this man the **m** of the vision.”
Lk 8:11 “This is the **m** of the parable: The
18:34 Its **m** was hidden from them, and they
20:17 “Then what is the **m** of that which is
Ac 10:17 While Peter was wondering about the **m**
1Co 4: 6 so that you may learn from us the **m**
5:10 not at all **m** the people of this
14:10 yet none of them is without **m**.
14:11 If then I do not grasp the **m** of what
Gal 3:16 “and to seeds”, **m** many people, but
3:16 seed”, **m** one person, who is Christ.

Meaningless

Job 27:12 Why then this **m** talk?
Ecc 1: 2 “**M**! **m**!” says the Teacher.
1: 2 “Utterly **m**! Everything is **m**.”
1:14 are **m**, a chasing after the wind.
2: 1 But that also proved to be **m**.
2:11 everything was **m**, a chasing after
2:15 I said in my heart, “This too is **m**.
2:17 it is **m**, a chasing after the wind.
2:19 under the sun. This too is **m**.
2:21 This too is **m** and a great misfortune.
2:23 does not rest. This too is **m**.
2:26 too is **m**, a chasing after the wind.
3:19 over the animal. Everything is **m**.
4: 4 too is **m**, a chasing after the wind.
4: 7 Again I saw something **m** under the
4: 8 This too is **m**—a miserable business!
4:16 too is **m**, a chasing after the wind.
5: 7 Much dreaming and many words are **m**.
5:10 with his income. This too is **m**.
6: 2 This is **m**, a grievous evil.
6: 9 too is **m**, a chasing after the wind.
6:12 during the few and **m** days he passes
7: 6 of fools. This too is **m**.
7:15 In this **m** life of mine I have seen
8:10 they did this. This too is **m**.
8:14 There is something else **m** that
8:14 This too, I say, is **m**.
9: 9 all the days of this **m** life that God
9: 9 you under the sun—all your **m** days.
11: 8 Everything to come is **m**.
11:10 body, for youth and vigour are **m**.
Ecc 12: 8 “**M**! **M**!” says the Teacher.
12: 8 “Everything is **m**!”
Isa 1:13 Stop bringing **m** offerings! Your
1Ti 1: 6 from these and turned to **m** talk.

Means[1] (Mean[1])

Ge 40:12 “This is what it **m**,” Joseph said to
40:18 “This is what it **m**,” Joseph said.
2Sa 15:21 whether it **m** life or death, there
Pr 16:15 a king’s face brightens, it **m** life;
Jer 22:16 Is that not what it **m** to know me?”
Da 2: 3 me and I want to know what it **m**.”
2:25 can tell the king what his dream **m**.
4:18 Belteshazzar, tell me what it **m**,
4:26 **m** that your kingdom will be restored
5: 7 tells me what it **m** will be clothed
5:12 will tell you what the writing **m**.”
5:15 it **m**, but they could not explain it.
5:16 this writing and tell me what it **m**,
5:17 for the king and tell him what it **m**.
Mt 1:23 Immanuel”—which **m**, “God with us.
9:13 go and learn what this **m**: ‘I desire
13:18 to what the parable of the sower **m**:
23:16 it **m** nothing; but if anyone swears
23:18 If anyone swears by the altar, it **m**
27:33 (which **m** The Place of the Skull).
27:46 lama sabachthani?”—which **m**, “My
Mk 3:17 Boanerges, which **m** Sons of Thunder);
5:41 “Talitha koum!” (which **m**, “Little
7:34 Ephphatha!” (which **m**, “Be opened!”).
15:22 (which **m** The Place of the Skull).
15:34 Eloi, lama sabachthani?”—which **m**,
Jn 1:38 “Rabbi” (which **m** Teacher), “where
8:54 I glorify myself, my glory **m** nothing.
9: 7 Pool of Siloam” (this word **m** Sent).
13:24 and said, “Ask him which one he **m**.
20:16 “Rabboni!” (which **m** Teacher).
Ac 4:36 (which **m** Son of Encouragement),
13: 8 is what his name **m**) opposed them
Ro 11:12 if their transgression **m** riches for
11:12 and their loss **m** riches for the
1Co 6: 7 lawsuits among you **m** you have been
Gal 6:15 nor uncircumcision **m** anything;
Heb 7: 2 First, his name **m** “king of
7: 2 “king of Salem” **m** “king of peace”.
2Pe 3:15 our Lord’s patience **m** salvation,

Means[2]

Ex 28:30 Thus Aaron will always bear the **m** of
Lev 11:43 by **m** of them or be made unclean by
25:26 acquires sufficient **m** to redeem it,
25:28 if he does not acquire the **m** to
Nu 31:16 were the **m** of turning the Israelites
1Sa 6: 3 all **m** send a guilt offering to him.
1Ki 22:22 “‘By what **m**?’ the LORD asked. “I
2Ki 5: 5 “By all **m**, go,” the king of Aram
5:23 “By all **m**, take two talents,” said
2Ch 18:20 “‘By what **m**?’ the LORD asked.
Pr 22:27 if you lack the **m** to pay, your very
Jer 17:11 man who gains riches by unjust **m**.
Eze 44:19 the people by **m** of their garments.
Hos 11: 7 High, he will by no **m** exalt them.
Mt 2: 6 land of Judah, are by no **m** least
5:18 will by any **m** disappear from the Law
Lk 8: 3 to support them out of their own **m**.
Ro 6: 2 By no **m**! We died to sin; how can we
6:15 under law but under grace? By no **m**!
7:13 then, become death to me? By no **m**!
11: 1 By no **m**! I am an Israelite myself,
1Co 9:22 by all possible **m** I might save some.
12: 8 knowledge by **m** of the same Spirit,
2Co 8:11 of it, according to your **m**.
1Ti 6: 5 godliness is a **m** to financial gain.
Heb 9:12 He did not enter by **m** of the blood

Meant (Mean[1])

Jdg 13:23 his wife answered, “If the LORD had **m**
Da 5: 8 writing or tell the king what it **m**.
Mk 4:22 For whatever is hidden is **m** to be
4:22 **m** to be brought out into the open.
9:10 what “rising from the dead” **m**.
9:32 they did not understand what he **m**
Lk 8: 9 asked him what this parable **m**.
9:45 they did not understand what this **m**.
Jn 1:30 This is the one I **m** when I said, ‘A
Jn 6:71 (He **m** Judas, the son of Simon
7:39 By this he **m** the Spirit, whom those
11:13 thought he **m** natural sleep.
13:22 a loss to know which of them he **m**.
16:19 “Are you asking one another what I **m**
1Co 6:13 The body is not **m** for sexual

Measure (Measured, Measurement, Measurements, Measures, Measuring)

Ge 15:16 has not yet reached its full **m**.”
41:49 records because it was beyond **m**.
Nu 35: 5 Outside the town, **m** three thousand
Dt 21: 2 judges shall go out and **m** the
1Ki 7:23 line of thirty cubits to **m** round it.
2Ch 4: 2 line of thirty cubits to **m** round it.
Job 11: 9 Their **m** is longer than the earth and
Ps 60: 6 and **m** off the Valley of Succoth.
71:15 day long, though I know not its **m**.
108: 7 and **m** off the Valley of Succoth.
Isa 34:17 his hand distributes them by **m**.
47: 9 They will come upon you in full **m**,
64: 9 Do not be angry beyond **m**, O LORD; do
64:12 keep silent and punish us beyond **m**?
65: 7 I will **m** into their laps the full
Lam 5:22 us and are angry with us beyond **m**.
Eze 4:11 Also **m** out a sixth of a hin of water
45: 3 In the sacred district, **m** off a
45:11 is to be the standard **m** for both.
Am 8: 5 may market wheat?”—skimping the **m**,
Zec 2: 2 “To **m** Jerusalem, to find out how
Mt 7: 2 and with the **m** you use, it will be
23:32 Fill up, then, the **m** of the sin of
Mk 4:24 “With the **m** you use, it will be
Lk 6:38 A good **m**, pressed down, shaken
6:38 For with the **m** you use, it will be
Jn 17:13 the full **m** of my joy within them.
Ro 12: 3 the **m** of faith God has given you.
15:29 full **m** of the blessing of Christ.
2Co 10:12 When they **m** themselves by themselves
Eph 3:19 to the **m** of all the fulness of God.
4:13 whole **m** of the fulness of Christ.
2Pe 1: 8 these qualities in increasing **m**,
Rev 11: 1 “Go and **m** the temple of God and the
11: 2 exclude the outer court; do not **m** it,
21:15 **m** the city, its gates and its walls.

Measured (Measure)

Ex 16:18 they **m** it by the omer, he who
2Sa 8: 2 **m** them off with a length of cord.
1Ki 6:25 The second cherub also **m** ten cubits,
7:31 basework it **m** a cubit and a half.
Job 28:25 of the wind and **m** out the waters,
Isa 40:12 Who has **m** the waters in the hollow
Jer 31:37 “Only if the heavens above can be **m**
Eze 40: 5 He **m** the wall; it was one measuring
40: 6 He climbed its steps and **m** the
40: 8 he **m** the portico of the gateway;
40:11 he **m** the width of the entrance to
40:13 he **m** the gateway from the top of the
40:14 He **m** along the faces of the
40:19 he **m** the distance from the inside of
40:20 he **m** the length and width of the
40:23 He **m** from one gate to the opposite
40:24 He **m** its jambs and its portico, and
40:27 and he **m** from this gate to the outer
40:28 and he **m** the south gate; it had the
40:32 and he **m** the gateway; it had the
40:35 he brought me to the north gate and **m**
40:47 he **m** the court: It was square—a
40:48 and **m** the jambs of the portico;
41: 1 the outer sanctuary and **m** the jambs;
41: 2 He also **m** the outer sanctuary; it
41: 3 and **m** the jambs of the entrance;
41: 4 he **m** the length of the inner
41: 5 he **m** the wall of the temple; it was
41:13 he **m** the temple; it was a hundred
41:15 he **m** the length of the building
42:15 east gate and **m** the area all around:
42:16 He **m** the east side with the
42:17 He **m** the north side; it was five
42:18 He **m** the south side; it was five
42:19 he turned to the west side and **m**; it
42:20 he **m** the area on all four sides. It
45:14 The prescribed portion of oil, **m** by
47: 3 he **m** off a thousand cubits and then

Eze 47: 4 He **m** off another thousand cubits and
47: 4 He **m** off another thousand and led me
47: 5 He **m** off another thousand, but now
Hos 1:10 which cannot be **m** or counted.
Am 7:17 Your land will be **m** and divided up,
Mt 7: 2 you use, it will be **m** to you.
Mk 4:24 it will be **m** to you—and even more.
Lk 6:38 you use, it will be **m** to you."
Rev 21:16 He **m** the city with the rod and found
21:17 He **m** its wall and it was 144 cubits

Measureless
1Ki 4:29 as **m** as the sand on the seashore.
Jer 33:22 as **m** as the sand on the seashore.

Measurement (Measure)
Eze 40:14 The **m** was up to the portico facing
Rev 21:17 man's **m**, which the angel was using.

Measurements (Measure)
1Ch 23:29 and all **m** of quantity and size.
Eze 40:10 each side; the three had the same **m**,
40:10 walls on each side had the same **m**.
40:21 **m** as those of the first gateway.
40:22 **m** as those of the gate facing east.
40:24 they had the same **m** as the others.
40:28 it had the same **m** as the others.
40:29 had the same **m** as the others.
40:32 it had the same **m** as the others.
40:33 had the same **m** as the others.
40:35 It had the same **m** as the others,
43:13 "These are the **m** of the altar in
48:16 will have these **m**: the north side

Measures (Measure)
Dt 25:14 Do not have two differing **m** in your
25:15 accurate and honest weights and **m**,
Ru 3:15 six **m** of barley and put it on her.
3:17 added, "He gave me these six **m** of
Pr 20:10 Differing weights and differing **m**—
Isa 44:13 The carpenter **m** with a line and
Eze 48:33 "On the south side, which **m** 4,500
Hag 2:16 anyone came to a heap of twenty **m**,
2:16 fifty **m**, there were only twenty.

Measuring (Measure)
Lev 19:35 when **m** length, weight or quantity.
1Ki 7:10 some **m** ten cubits and some eight.
7:23 circular in shape, **m** ten cubits from
7:38 each holding forty baths and **m** four
2Ki 21:13 the **m** line used against Samaria
2Ch 3:15 a capital on top **m** five cubits.
4: 2 circular in shape, **m** ten cubits from
Job 38: 5 Who stretched a **m** line across it?
Isa 28:17 I will make justice the **m** line and
34:11 out over Edom the **m** line of chaos
Jer 31:39 The **m** line will stretch from there
Lam 2: 8 He stretched out a **m** line and did
Eze 40: 3 linen cord and a **m** rod in his hand.
40: 5 The length of the **m** rod in the man's
40: 5 one **m** rod thick and one rod high.
42:15 he had finished **m** what was inside
42:16 the east side with the **m** rod; it
42:17 five hundred cubits by the **m** rod.
42:18 five hundred cubits by the **m** rod.
42:19 five hundred cubits by the **m** rod.
47: 3 the man went eastward with a **m** line
Zec 1:16 And the **m** line will be stretched out
2: 1 was a man with a **m** line in his hand!
5: 6 it?" He replied, "It is a **m** basket.
Rev 11: 1 I was given a reed like a **m** rod and
21:15 talked with me had a **m** rod of gold

Meat (Meats)
Ge 9: 4 "But you must not eat **m** that has its
Ex 12: 8 That same night they are to eat the **m**
12: 9 Do not eat the **m** raw or cooked in
12:46 none of the **m** outside the house.
16: 3 of **m** and ate all the food we wanted,
16: 8 gives you **m** to eat in the evening
16:12 'At twilight you will eat **m**, and in
21:28 death, and its **m** must not be eaten.
Ex 22:31 So do not eat the **m** of an animal
27: 3 bowls, **m** forks and firepans.
29:31 and cook the **m** in a sacred place.
29:32 Aaron and his sons are to eat the **m**
29:34 if any of the **m** of the ordination
38: 3 bowls, **m** forks and firepans.
Lev 6:28 The clay pot that the **m** is cooked in
7:15 The **m** of his fellowship offering of
7:17 Any **m** of the sacrifice left over
7:18 If any **m** of the fellowship offering
7:19 "'**M** that touches anything
7:19 As for other **m**, anyone ceremonially
7:20 if anyone who is unclean eats any **m**
7:21 then eats any of the **m** of the
8:31 "Cook the **m** at the entrance to the
8:32 burn up the rest of the **m** and the
11: 8 You must not eat their **m** or touch
11:11 you must not eat their **m** and you
19:26 "'Do not eat any **m** with the blood
Nu 4:14 including the firepans, **m** forks,
11: 4 said, "If only we had **m** to eat!
11:13 Where can I get **m** for all these
11:13 wailing to me, 'Give us **m** to eat!'
11:18 for tomorrow, when you will eat **m**.
11:18 "If only we had **m** to eat! We were
11:18 give you **m**, and you will eat it.
11:21 them **m** to eat for a whole month!'
11:33 while the **m** was still between their
18:18 Their **m** is to be yours, just as the
Dt 12:15 eat as much of the **m** as you want,
12:20 **m** and say, "I would like some **m**,"
12:23 must not eat the life with the **m**.
12:27 your God, both the **m** and the blood.
12:27 LORD your God, but you may eat the **m**.
14: 8 their **m** or touch their carcasses.
16: 4 Do not let any of the **m** you
Jdg 6:19 Putting the **m** in a basket and its
6:20 "Take the **m** and the unleavened bread,
6:21 the **m** and the unleavened bread.
6:21 rock, consuming the **m** and the bread.
1Sa 1: 4 he would give portions of the **m** to
2:13 and while the **m** was being boiled,
2:15 "Give the priest some **m** to roast; he
2:15 boiled **m** from you, but only raw."
9:23 "Bring the piece of **m** I gave you,
14:33 by eating **m** that has blood in it.
14:34 by eating **m** with blood still in it.
25:11 and the **m** I have slaughtered for my
1Ki 17: 6 The ravens brought him bread and **m**
17: 6 and bread and **m** in the evening,
19:21 the **m** and gave it to the people,
2Ch 4:16 the pots, shovels, **m** forks and all
Job 31:31 has not had his fill of Job's **m**?'—
Ps 78:20 Can he supply **m** for his people?"
78:27 He rained **m** down on them like dust,
Pr 9: 2 She has prepared her **m** and mixed her
23:20 much wine or gorge themselves on **m**,
Isa 22:13 eating of **m** and drinking of wine!
44:16 he roasts his **m** and eats his fill.
44:19 its coals, I roasted **m** and I ate.
65: 4 whose pots hold broth of unclean **m**;
Jer 7:21 sacrifices and eat the **m** yourselves!
11:15 Can consecrated **m** avert your
Eze 4:14 unclean **m** has ever entered my mouth
11: 3 is a cooking pot, and we are the **m**.'
11: 7 are the **m** and this city is the pot,
11:11 nor will you be the **m** in it; I will
24: 4 Put into it the pieces of **m**, all the
24:10 Cook the **m** well, mixing in the
33:25 Since you eat **m** with the blood still
Da 10: 3 I ate no choice food; no **m** or wine
Hos 8:13 given to me and they eat the **m**,
Mic 3: 3 who chop them up like **m** for the pan,
Hag 2:12 If a person carries consecrated **m** in
Zec 11:16 but will eat the **m** of the choice
Ac 15:20 from the **m** of strangled animals
15:29 from blood, from the **m** of strangled
21:25 from blood, from the **m** of strangled
Ro 14: 6 He who eats **m**, eats to the Lord, for
14:21 is better not to eat **m** or drink wine
1Co 8:13 I will never eat **m** again, so that I
10:25 Eat anything sold in the **m** market

Meats (Meat)
Isa 25: 6 best of **m** and the finest of wines.

Mebunnai
2Sa 23:27 from Anathoth, **M** the Hushathite,

Meconah
Ne 11:28 in Ziklag, in **M** and its settlements,

Medad
Nu 11:26 and **M**, had remained in the camp.
11:27 and **M** are prophesying in the camp."

Medan
Ge 25: 2 She bore him Zimran, Jokshan, **M**,
1Ch 1:32 Jokshan, **M**, Midian, Ishbak and Shuah.

Meddler (Meddles)
1Pe 4:15 kind of criminal, or even as a **m**.

Meddles (Meddler)
Pr 26:17 who **m** in a quarrel not his own.

Mede (Media)
Da 5:31 Darius the **M** took over the kingdom,
9: 1 son of Xerxes (a **M** by descent),
11: 1 in the first year of Darius the **M**, I

Medeba
Nu 21:30 far as Nophah, which extends to **M**."
Jos 13: 9 whole plateau of **M** as far as Dibon,
13:16 gorge, and the whole plateau past **M**
1Ch 19: 7 who came and camped near **M**, while
Isa 15: 2 to weep; Moab wails over Nebo and **M**.

Medes (Media)
2Ki 17: 6 River and in the towns of the **M**.
18:11 Habor River, and in towns of the **M**.
Isa 13:17 I will stir up against them the **M**,
Jer 51:11 has stirred up the kings of the **M**,
51:28 against her—the kings of the **M**,
Da 5:28 and given to the **M** and Persians."
6: 8 with the laws of the **M** and Persians,
6:12 with the laws of the **M** and Persians,
6:15 that according to the law of the **M**
Ac 2: 9 Parthians, **M** and Elamites; residents

Media (Mede, Medes, Median)
Mountainous country south of Caspian Sea. Some people of Samaria deported here (2Ki 17:6; 18:11). Darius searched its city Ecbatana for Cyrus' decree to rebuild Jerusalem (Ezr 6:2). Absorbed into Persian Empire, its military leaders were invited to dine with King Xerxes (Est 1:3, 14). Mordecai's greatness was recorded in its annals (Est 10:2). Its defeat of Babylonian Empire was prophesied (Isa 13:17; 21:2; Jer 51:11, 28; Da 5:28) and its own eventual defeat by Greece (Jer 25:25; Da 8:20–21). Its people were in the crowd at Pentecost (Ac 2:9). See *Persia*.

Ezr 6: 2 of Ecbatana in the province of **M**,
Est 1: 3 The military leaders of Persia and **M**,
1:14 the seven nobles of Persia and **M** who
1:19 written in the laws of Persia and **M**,
10: 2 annals of the kings of **M** and Persia?
Isa 21: 2 Elam, attack! **M**, lay siege! I will
Jer 25:25 all the kings of Zimri, Elam and **M**;
Da 8:20 the kings of **M** and Persia.

Median (Media)
Est 1:18 very day the Persian and **M** women

Mediate (Mediator)
1Sa 2:25 God may **m** for him; but if a man sins

Mediator (Mediate)
Job 33:23 is an angel on his side as a **m**,
Gal 3:19 into effect through angels by a **m**.
3:20 A **m**, however, does not represent
1Ti 2: 5 For there is one God and one **m**
Heb 8: 6 he is **m** is superior to the old one,
9:15 For this reason Christ is the **m** of a
12:24 to Jesus the **m** of a new covenant,

Medicine
Pr 17:22 A cheerful heart is good **m**, but a

Meditate (Meditated, Meditates, Meditation)
Ge 24:63 out to the field one evening to **m**,
Jos 1: 8 your mouth; **m** on it day and night,
Ps 48: 9 Within your temple, O God, we **m** on
77:12 I will **m** on all your works and
119:15 I **m** on your precepts and consider
119:23 your servant will **m** on your decrees.
119:27 then I will **m** on your wonders.
119:48 I love, and I **m** on your decrees.
119:78 but I will **m** on your precepts.
119:97 Oh, how I love your law! I **m** on it
119:99 teachers, for I **m** on your statutes.
119:148 that I may **m** on your promises.
143: 5 I **m** on all your works and consider
145: 5 I will **m** on your wonderful works.

Meditated (Meditate)
Ps 39: 3 and as I **m**, the fire burned; then I

Meditates (Meditate)
Ps 1: 2 and on his law he **m** day and night.

Meditation (Meditate)
Ps 19:14 May the words of my mouth and the **m**
104:34 May my **m** be pleasing to him, as I

Mediterranean Sea See Great Sea

Medium (Mediums)
Lev 20:27 "'A man or woman who is a **m** or
Dt 18:11 or casts spells, or who is a **m** or
1Sa 28: 7 "Find me a woman who is a **m**, so that
1Ch 10:13 and even consulted a **m** for guidance,

Mediums (Medium)
Lev 19:31 "'Do not turn to **m** or seek out
20: 6 against the person who turns to **m**
1Sa 28: 3 the **m** and spiritists from the land.
28: 9 He has cut off the **m** and spiritists
2Ki 21: 6 and consulted **m** and spiritists.
23:24 Furthermore, Josiah got rid of the **m**
2Ch 33: 6 and consulted **m** and spiritists.
Isa 8:19 men tell you to consult **m** and
19: 3 the dead, the **m** and the spiritists.
Jer 27: 9 your interpreters of dreams, your **m**

Meek (Meekness)
Ps 37:11 the **m** will inherit the land and
Zep 3:12 I will leave within you the **m** and
Mt 5: 5 Blessed are the **m**, for they will

Meekness (Meek)
2Co 10: 1 By the **m** and gentleness of Christ, I

Meet (Meeting, Meetings, Meets, Met)
Ge 14:17 the king of Sodom came out to **m** him
18: 2 **m** them and bowed low to the ground.
19: 1 When he saw them, he got up to **m**
19: 6 Lot went outside to **m** them and shut
24:17 The servant hurried to **m** her and
24:65 man in the field coming to **m** us?"
29:13 sister's son, he hurried to **m** him.
30:16 evening, Leah went out to **m** him.
32: 6 and now he is coming to **m** you, and
32:19 same thing to Esau when you **m** him.
33: 4 Esau ran to **m** Jacob and embraced him;
46:29 to Goshen to **m** his father Israel.
Ex 4:14 He is already on his way to **m** you,
4:27 "Go into the desert to **m** Moses.
5:14 "Why didn't you **m** your quota of
5:20 Moses and Aaron waiting to **m** them,
7:15 Wait on the bank of the Nile to **m**
18: 7 went out to **m** his father-in-law
19:17 out of the camp to **m** with God,
25:22 I will **m** with you and give you all
29:42 There I will **m** you and speak to you
29:43 there also I will **m** with the
Ex 30: 6 Testimony—where I will **m** with you.
30:36 Meeting, where I will **m** with you.
Nu 14:35 They will **m** their end in this desert;
17: 4 Testimony, where I **m** with you.
21:33 out to **m** them in battle at Edrei.
22:36 he went out to **m** him at the Moabite
23: 3 Perhaps the LORD will come to **m** with
23:15 while I **m** with him over there."
31:13 went to **m** them outside the camp.
Dt 2:32 Sihon and all his army came out to **m**
3: 1 out to **m** us in battle at Edrei.
22:23 If a man happens to **m** in a town a
22:25 to **m** a girl pledged to be married
22:28 If a man happens to **m** a virgin who
23: 4 For they did not come to **m** you with
Jos 8:14 to **m** Israel in battle at a certain
9:11 go and **m** them and say to them,
Jdg 4:18 Jael went out to **m** Sisera and said
4:22 Sisera, and Jael went out to **m** him.
6:35 so that they too went up to **m** them.
11:31 of my house to **m** me when I return
11:34 who should come out to **m** him but his
20:31 The Benjamites came out to **m** them
1Sa 4: 2 deployed their forces to **m** Israel,
10: 2 you leave me today, you will **m** two
10: 3 to God at Bethel will **m** you there.
10: 5 As you approach the town, you will **m**
15:12 Samuel got up and went to **m** Saul,
17: 2 battle line to **m** the Philistines.
17:48 towards the battle line to **m** him.
17:55 Saul watched David going out to **m**
18: 6 **m** King Saul with singing and dancing,
21: 2 them to **m** me at a certain place.
23:28 David and went to **m** the Philistines.
25:32 who has sent you today to **m** me.
25:34 if you had not come quickly to **m** me,
30:21 They came out to **m** David and the
2Sa 6:20 of Saul came out to **m** him and said,
10: 5 he sent messengers to **m** the men, for
10:17 to **m** David and fought against him.
15:32 Hushai the Arkite was there to **m** him,
16: 1 of Mephibosheth, waiting to **m** him.
18: 9 Now Absalom happened to **m** David's
19:15 **m** the king and bring him across the
19:16 the men of Judah to **m** King David.
19:20 come down and **m** my lord the king."
19:24 also went down to **m** the king.
19:25 he came from Jerusalem to **m** the king,
20: 8 in Gibeon, Amasa came to **m** them.
1Ki 2: 8 When he came down to **m** me at the
2:19 the king stood up to **m** her, bowed
18:16 Obadiah went to **m** Ahab and told him,
18:16 told him, and Ahab went to **m** Elijah.
18:19 over Israel to **m** me on Mount Carmel.
20: 9 time, but this demand I cannot **m**.
20:27 they marched out to **m** them.
21:18 "Go down to **m** Ahab king of Israel,
2Ki 1: 3 "Go up and **m** the messengers of the
1: 6 "A man came to **m** us," they replied.
1: 7 came to **m** you and told you this?"
2:15 And they went to **m** him and bowed to
4:26 Run to **m** her and ask her, 'Are you
4:29 If you **m** anyone, do not greet him,
4:31 So Gehazi went back to **m** Elisha and
5:21 got down from the chariot to **m** him.
5:26 got down from his chariot to **m** you?
6: 1 we **m** with you is too small for us.
8: 8 with you and go to **m** the man of God.
8: 9 Hazael went to **m** Elisha, taking with
9:17 "Send him to **m** them and ask, 'Do you
9:18 The horseman rode off to **m** Jehu and
9:21 each in his own chariot, to **m** Jehu.
10:15 Recab, who was on his way to **m** him.
14: 8 challenge: "Come, **m** me face to face.
16:10 King Ahaz went to Damascus to **m**
23:29 King Josiah marched out to **m** him in
1Ch 12:17 David went out to **m** them and said to
14: 8 about it and went out to **m** them.
19: 5 he sent messengers to **m** them, for
19:17 David formed his lines to **m** the
2Ch 14:10 Asa went out to **m** him, and they took
15: 2 He went out to **m** Asa and said to him,
19: 2 the son of Hanani, went out to **m** him
22: 7 he went out with Joram to **m** Jehu son
25:17 of Israel: "Come, **m** me face to face.
28: 9 and he went out to **m** the army when
2Ch 35:20 marched out to **m** him in battle.
Ne 4: 9 day and night to **m** this threat.
6: 2 "Come, let us **m** together in one of
6:10 He said, "Let us **m** in the house of
Ps 42: 2 When can I go and **m** with God?
79: 8 **m** us, for we are in desperate need.
85:10 Love and faithfulness **m** together;
Pr 7:10 out came a woman to **m** him, dressed
7:15 I came out to **m** you; I looked for
8: 2 the paths **m**, she takes her stand;
17:12 Better to **m** a bear robbed of her
Isa 7: 3 **m** Ahaz at the end of the aqueduct
14: 9 The grave below is all astir to **m**
34:14 Desert creatures will **m** with hyenas,
41: 1 **m** together at the place of judgment.
66:17 they will **m** their end together,"
Jer 41: 6 Mizpah to **m** them, weeping as he went.
Am 4:12 prepare to **m** your God, O Israel."
5:19 fled from a lion only to **m** a bear,
9:10 will not overtake or **m** us.'
Zec 2: 3 and another angel came to **m** him
Mt 8:34 the whole town went out to **m** Jesus.
25: 1 and went out to **m** the bridegroom.
25: 6 the bridegroom! Come out to **m** him!'
Mk 5: 2 spirit came from the tombs to **m** him.
14:13 carrying a jar of water will **m** you.
Lk 22:10 carrying a jar of water will **m** you.
Jn 11:20 to **m** him, but Mary stayed at home.
12:13 out to **m** him, shouting, "Hosanna!"
12:18 miraculous sign, went out to **m** him.
Ac 2:46 Every day they continued to **m**
5:12 **m** together in Solomon's Colonnade.
28:15 Appius and the Three Taverns to **m** us.
28:23 They arranged to **m** Paul on a certain
1Co 11:34 so that when you **m** together it may
Php 4:19 my God will **m** all your needs
1Th 4:17 the clouds to **m** the Lord in the air.

Meeting (Meet, *Tent of Meeting*)
Jos 22:32 from their **m** with the Reubenites
1Sa 20:35 to the field for his **m** with David.
2Ki 4:38 of the prophets was **m** with him,
Ne 5: 7 together a large **m** to deal with
Lam 2: 6 he has destroyed his place of **m**.
Jn 11:47 called a **m** of the Sanhedrin.
Ac 4:31 place where they were **m** was shaken.
17:19 they took him and brought him to a **m**
17:22 Paul then stood up in the **m** of the
20: 8 the upstairs room where we were **m**.
Heb 10:25 Let us not give up **m** together, as
Jas 2: 2 Suppose a man comes into your **m**

Meetings (Meet)
1Co 11:17 for your **m** do more harm than good.

Meets (Meet)
Ge 32:17 "When my brother Esau **m** you and asks,
Nu 35:19 he **m** him, he shall put him to death.
35:21 the murderer to death when he **m** him.
Ro 16: 5 Greet also the church that **m** at
1Co 16:19 the church that **m** at their house.
Phm : 2 to the church that **m** in your home:
Heb 7:26 Such a high priest **m** our need—one

Megiddo
Canaanite royal town, south-east of Carmel, on trade route between Egypt and Syria. Conquered by Joshua (Jos 12:21), allotted to the tribe of Manasseh (Jos 17:11; 1Ch 7:29). Scene of Deborah's victory over Sisera (Jdg 5:19). One of Solomon's 12 districts (1Ki 4:12) and fortified by him (1Ki 9:15). Ahaziah fled here from Jehu (2Ki 9:27). Josiah was mortally wounded here (2Ki 23:29–30; 2Ch 35:20–24). Zechariah prophesies that a great battle would take place near here (Zec 12:11), often identified with the battle of Armageddon (Rev 16:16).

Jos 12:21 the king of Taanach one the king of **M**
17:11 Endor, Taanach and **M**, together with
Jdg 1:27 **M** and their surrounding settlements,
5:19 at Taanach by the waters of **M**,
1Ki 4:12 Baana son of Ahilud—in Taanach and **M**
9:15 Jerusalem, and Hazor, **M** and Gezer.
2Ki 9:27 but he escaped to **M** and died there.
23:29 Neco faced him and killed him at **M**.

2Ki 23:30 in a chariot from **M** to Jerusalem
1Ch 7:29 Taanach, **M** and Dor, together with
2Ch 35:22 went to fight him on the plain of **M**.
Zec 12:11 of Hadad Rimmon in the plain of **M**.

Mehetabel

Ge 36:39 and his wife's name was **M** daughter
1Ch 1:50 and his wife's name was **M** daughter
Ne 6:10 of **M**, who was shut in at his home.

Mehida

Ezr 2:52 Bazluth, **M**, Harsha,
Ne 7:54 Bazluth, **M**, Harsha,

Mehir

1Ch 4:11 of **M**, who was the father of Eshton.

Meholah

1Sa 18:19 given in marriage to Adriel of **M**.

Meholathite

2Sa 21: 8 to Adriel son of Barzillai the **M**.

Mehujael

Ge 4:18 and Irad was the father of **M**, and **M**

Mehuman

Est 1:10 the seven eunuchs who served him—**M**,

Mekerathite

1Ch 11:36 Hepher the **M**, Ahijah the Pelonite,

Melatiah

Ne 3: 7 Mizpah—**M** of Gibeon and Jadon of

Melchizedek

King of Salem and priest of God Most High who blessed Abraham and received tithe from him (Ge 14:18–20; Heb 7:1–10). Presented as a type of Christ (Ps 110:4; Heb 5:6, 10; 6:20; 7:11–17).

Ge 14:18 **M** king of Salem brought out bread
Ps 110: 4 priest for ever, in the order of **M**."
Heb 5: 6 priest for ever, in the order of **M**."
5:10 to be high priest in the order of **M**.
6:20 priest for ever, in the order of **M**.
7: 1 This **M** was king of Salem and priest
7:10 when **M** met Abraham, Levi was still
7:11 of **M**, not in the order of Aaron?
7:15 if another priest like **M** appears,
7:17 priest for ever, in the order of **M**."

Melea

Lk 3:31 the son of **M**, the son of Menna, the

Melech

1Ch 8:35 The sons of Micah: Pithon, **M**, Tarea
9:41 The sons of Micah: Pithon, **M**, Tahrea

Melki

Lk 3:24 the son of Levi, the son of **M**, the
3:28 the son of **M**, the son of Addi, the

Melodious (Melody)

Ps 81: 2 play the **m** harp and lyre.

Melody (Melodious)

Ps 92: 3 lyre and the **m** of the harp.

Melon (Melons)

Jer 10: 5 Like a scarecrow in a **m** patch, their

Melons (Melon)

Nu 11: 5 **m**, leeks, onions and garlic.
Isa 1: 8 field of **m**, like a city under siege.

Melt (Melted, Melting, Melts)

Ex 15:15 the people of Canaan will **m** away;
2Sa 17:10 will **m** with fear, for all Israel
Ps 97: 5 The mountains **m** like wax before the
Isa 13: 7 go limp, every man's heart will **m**.
Isa 14:31 Wail, O gate! Howl, O city! **M** away,
19: 1 of the Egyptians **m** within them.
Eze 21: 7 Every heart will **m** and every hand go
21:15 that hearts may **m** and the fallen be
22:20 lead and tin into a furnace to **m** it
22:20 put you inside the city and **m** you.
Mic 1: 4 The mountains **m** beneath him and the
Na 1: 5 before him and the hills **m** away.
2:10 plundered, stripped! Hearts **m**, knees
2Pe 3:12 and the elements will **m** in the heat.

Melted (Melt)

Ex 16:21 when the sun grew hot, it **m** away.
Jos 7: 5 the people **m** and became like water.
Job 24:19 and drought snatch away the **m** snow
Ps 22:14 to wax; it has **m** away within me.
107:26 in their peril their courage **m** away.
Eze 22:21 wrath, and you will be **m** inside her.
22:22 silver is **m** in a furnace, so you
22:22 so you will be **m** inside her, and you
24:11 be **m** and its deposit burned away.

Melting (Melt)

Jos 2: 9 are **m** in fear because of you.
2:24 people are **m** in fear because of us."
1Sa 14:16 the army **m** away in all directions.
Job 6:16 thawing ice and swollen with **m** snow,
Ps 58: 8 Like a slug **m** away as it moves along,

Melts (Melt)

Ps 46: 6 he lifts his voice, the earth **m**.
68: 2 may you blow them away; as wax **m**
147:18 He sends his word and **m** them; he
Am 9: 5 he who touches the earth and it **m**,

Member (Members)

Lev 4:27 "'If a **m** of the community sins
25:47 you or to a **m** of the alien's clan,
Eze 17:13 he took a **m** of the royal family and
Mk 15:43 Joseph of Arimathea, a prominent **m**
Lk 23:50 Now there was a man named Joseph, a **m**
Jn 3: 1 a **m** of the Jewish ruling council.
Ac 17:34 Among them was Dionysius, a **m** of the
Ro 12: 5 each **m** belongs to all the others.

Members (Member)

Ge 36: 6 and all the **m** of his household,
46:27 the **m** of Jacob's family, which went
50: 8 besides all the **m** of Joseph's
Lev 25:45 **m** of their clans born in your
Nu 16: 2 had been appointed **m** of the council.
2Sa 9:12 and all the **m** of Ziba's household
2Ch 21:13 **m** of your father's house, men who
Mic 7: 6 are the **m** of his own household.
Mt 10:25 much more the **m** of his household!
10:36 a man's enemies will be the **m** of his
Ac 5:17 who were **m** of the party of the
6: 9 Opposition arose, however, from **m** of
16:15 she and the **m** of her household were
Ro 7:23 I see another law at work in the **m**
7:23 the law of sin at work within my **m**.
12: 4 each of us has one body with many **m**,
12: 4 **m** do not all have the same function,
1Co 6:15 your bodies are **m** of Christ himself?
6:15 Shall I then take the **m** of Christ
12:24 But God has combined the **m** of the
Eph 2:19 people and **m** of God's household,
3: 6 **m** together of one body, and sharers
4:25 for we are all **m** of one body.
5:30 for we are **m** of his body.
Col 3:15 since as **m** of one body you were

Memorable (Memory)

Eze 39:13 glorified will be a **m** day for them,

Memorandum

Ezr 6: 2 Media, and this was written on it: **M**:

Memorial (Memory)

Ex 28:12 as **m** stones for the sons of Israel.
28:12 shoulders as a **m** before the LORD.
28:29 as a continuing **m** before the LORD.
30:16 It will be a **m** for the Israelites
Ex 39: 7 as **m** stones for the sons of Israel,
Lev 2: 2 and burn this as a **m** portion on the
2: 9 He shall take out the **m** portion from
2:16 The priest shall burn the **m** portion
5:12 take a handful of it as a **m** portion
6:15 and burn the **m** portion on the altar
24: 7 a **m** portion to represent the bread
Nu 5:26 **m** offering and burn it on the altar;
10:10 will be a **m** for you before your God.
31:54 **m** for the Israelites before the LORD.
Jos 4: 7 **m** to the people of Israel for ever."
Isa 56: 5 its walls a **m** and a name better than
66: 3 and whoever burns **m** incense, like
Zec 6:14 as a **m** in the temple of the LORD.
Ac 10: 4 come up as a **m** offering before God.

Memories (Memory)

1Th 3: 6 **m** of us and that you long to see us,

Memory (Memorable, Memorial, Memories)

Ex 17:14 the **m** of Amalek from under heaven."
Dt 25:19 the **m** of Amalek from under heaven.
32:26 and blot out their **m** from mankind,
2Sa 18:18 no son to carry on the **m** of my name.
Est 9:28 nor should the **m** of them die out
Job 18:17 The **m** of him perishes from the earth;
Ps 9: 6 even the **m** of them has perished.
34:16 off the **m** of them from the earth.
45:17 I will perpetuate your **m** through all
109:15 off the **m** of them from the earth.
Pr 10: 7 The **m** of the righteous will be a
Ecc 9: 5 and even the **m** of them is forgotten.
Isa 26:14 ruin; you wiped out all **m** of them.
Mt 26:13 will also be told, in **m** of her."
Mk 14: 9 will also be told, in **m** of her."
2Pe 1:13 I think it is right to refresh your **m**

Memphis

Egyptian royal city on west bank of the Nile, about 13 miles south of Cairo. Referred to by the prophets as a place of false hope (Isa 19:13; Jer 2:16; 44:1; 46:14, 19; Eze 30:13, 16; Hos 9:6).

Isa 19:13 the leaders of **M** are deceived; the
Jer 2:16 Also, the men of **M** and Tahpanhes
44: 1 Tahpanhes and **M**—and in Upper Egypt:
46:14 proclaim it also in **M** and Tahpanhes:
46:19 you who live in Egypt, for **M** will be
Eze 30:13 and put an end to the images in **M**.
30:16 **M** will be in constant distress.
Hos 9: 6 gather them, and **M** will bury them.

Memucan

Est 1:14 Tarshish, Meres, Marsena and **M**, the
1:16 **M** replied in the presence of the
1:21 so the king did as **M** proposed.

Men (Man, *Men of Israel, Wise men*)

Ge 4:26 At that time **m** began to call on the
6: 1 **m** began to increase in number on the
6: 2 the daughters of **m** were beautiful,
6: 4 daughters of **m** and had children
6: 4 were the heroes of old, **m** of renown.
6: 7 from the face of the earth—**m** and
7:23 **m** and animals and the creatures that
11: 2 **m** moved eastward, they found a plain
11: 5 the tower that the **m** were building.
12:20 gave orders about Abram to his **m**,
13:11 The two **m** parted company:
13:13 Now the **m** of Sodom were wicked and
14:10 some of the **m** fell into them and the
14:14 he called out the 318 trained **m** born
14:15 During the night Abram divided his **m**
14:24 I will accept nothing but what my **m**
14:24 to the **m** who went with me—to Aner,
18: 2 Abraham looked up and saw three **m**
18:16 the **m** got up to leave, they looked
18:22 The **m** turned away and went towards
19: 4 all the **m** from every part of the
19: 5 They called to Lot, "Where are the **m**
19: 8 But don't do anything to these **m**,
19:10 the **m** inside reached out and pulled
19:11 they struck the **m** who were at the

Ge 19:12 The two **m** said to Lot, "Do you have
19:16 he hesitated, the **m** grasped his hand
21:27 and the two **m** made a treaty.
21:31 the two **m** swore an oath there.
24:32 him and his **m** to wash their feet.
24:54 he and the **m** who were with him ate
24:59 and Abraham's servant and his **m**.
26: 7 the **m** of that place asked him about
26: 7 He thought, "The **m** of this place
26:10 One of the **m** might well have slept
26:31 Early the next morning the **m** swore
32: 6 and four hundred **m** are with him."
32:28 God and with **m** and have overcome."
33: 1 coming with his four hundred **m**; so
33:15 let me leave some of my **m** with you.
34:21 "These **m** are friendly towards us,"
34:22 the **m** will consent to live with us
34:24 All the **m** who went out of the city
38:12 he went up to Timnah, to the **m** who
38:21 He asked the **m** who lived there,
38:22 Besides, the **m** who lived there said,
40: 5 each of the two **m**—the cupbearer and
41:43 **m** shouted before him, "Make way!"
42:11 servants are honest **m**, not spies."
42:19 If you are honest **m**, let one of your
42:31 we said to him, 'We are honest **m**; we
42:33 I will know whether you are honest **m**:
42:34 that you are not spies but honest **m**.
43:15 the **m** took the gifts and double the
43:16 "Take these **m** to my house, slaughter
43:17 and took the **m** to Joseph's house.
43:18 Now the **m** were frightened when they
43:24 The steward took the **m** into Joseph's
43:33 The **m** had been seated before him in
44: 3 morning dawned, the **m** were sent on
44: 4 "Go after those **m** at once, and when
46:32 The **m** are shepherds; they tend
49: 6 for they have killed **m** in their
Ex 4:19 **m** who wanted to kill you are dead."
5: 9 Make the work harder for the **m** so
8:17 gnats came upon **m** and animals.
8:18 And the gnats were on **m** and animals.
9: 7 Pharaoh sent **m** to investigate and
9: 9 **m** and animals throughout the land."
9:10 boils broke out on **m** and animals.
9:22 hail will fall all over Egypt—on **m**
9:25 in the fields—both **m** and animals;
10:11 No! Let only the **m** go; and worship
11: 2 Tell the people that **m** and women
12:12 strike down every firstborn—both **m**
12:37 six hundred thousand **m** on foot,
17: 9 Choose some of our **m** and go out to
18:21 select capable **m** from all the people
18:21 from all the people—**m** who fear God,
18:21 trustworthy **m** who hate dishonest
18:25 He chose capable **m** from all Israel
21:18 "If **m** quarrel and one hits the other
21:22 "If **m** who are fighting hit a
23:17 "Three times a year all the **m** are to
24: 5 he sent young Israelite **m**, and they
28: 3 Tell all the skilled **m** to whom I
34:23 Three times a year all your **m** are to
35:22 All who were willing, **m** and women
35:29 All the Israelite **m** and women who
36: 8 All the skilled **m** among the workmen
38:26 old or more, a total of 603,550 **m**.
Nu 1: 3 the **m** in Israel twenty years old
1: 5 These are the names of the **m** who are
1:16 These were the **m** appointed from the
1:17 Moses and Aaron took these **m** whose
1:18 and the **m** twenty years old or more
1:20 All the **m** twenty years old or more
1:22 All the **m** twenty years old or more
1:24 All the **m** twenty years old or more
1:26 All the **m** twenty years old or more
1:28 All the **m** twenty years old or more
1:30 All the **m** twenty years old or more
1:32 All the **m** twenty years old or more
1:34 All the **m** twenty years old or more
1:36 All the **m** twenty years old or more
1:38 All the **m** twenty years old or more
1:40 All the **m** twenty years old or more
1:42 All the **m** twenty years old or more
1:44 These were the **m** counted by Moses
2: 9 All the **m** assigned to the camp of
2:16 All the **m** assigned to the camp of
Nu 2:24 All the **m** assigned to the camp of
2:31 All the **m** assigned to the camp of
4: 3 Count all the **m** from thirty to fifty
4:23 Count all the **m** from thirty to fifty
4:30 Count all the **m** from thirty to fifty
4:35 All the **m** from thirty to fifty years
4:39 All the **m** from thirty to fifty years
4:43 All the **m** from thirty to fifty years
4:47 All the **m** from thirty to fifty years
8:24 "This applies to the Levites: **M**
11:21 six hundred thousand **m** on foot,
11:26 However, two **m**, whose names were
13: 2 "Send some **m** to explore the land of
13:16 These are the names of the **m** Moses
13:31 the **m** who had gone up with him said,
14:22 not one of the **m** who saw my glory
14:36 the **m** Moses had sent to explore the
14:37 these **m** responsible for spreading
14:38 Of the **m** who went to explore the
16: 2 With them were 250 Israelite **m**,
16:14 of these **m**? No, we will not come!"
16:26 from the tents of these wicked **m**!
16:29 If these **m** die a natural death and
16:29 what usually happens to **m**, then the
16:30 then you will know that these **m** have
16:32 Korah's **m** and all their possessions.
16:35 250 **m** who were offering the incense.
16:38 the censers of the **m** who sinned at
22: 9 asked, "Who are these **m** with you?
22:20 "Since these **m** have come to summon
22:35 "Go with the **m**, but speak only what
25: 1 the **m** began to indulge in sexual
25: 5 put to death those of your **m** who
26: 4 "Take a census of **m** twenty years old
26:10 when the fire devoured the 250 **m**.
26:14 of Simeon; there were 22,200 **m**.
31: 3 "Arm some of your **m** to go to war
31: 4 Send into battle a thousand **m** from
31: 5 twelve thousand **m** armed for battle,
31:42 apart from that of the fighting **m**—
32:11 not one of the **m** twenty years old or
34:17 "These are the names of the **m** who
34:29 These are the **m** the LORD commanded
36: 3 Now suppose they marry **m** from other
Dt 1:13 understanding and respected **m** from
1:15 I took the leading **m** of your tribes,
1:15 wise and respected **m**, and appointed
1:22 "Let us send **m** ahead to spy out the
2:14 **m** had perished from the camp,
2:16 Now when the last of these fighting **m**
2:34 them—**m**, women and children.
3: 6 every city—**m**, women and children.
3:18 But all your able-bodied **m**, armed
5:23 all the leading **m** of your tribes and
7:14 your **m** or women will be childless,
13:13 that wicked **m** have arisen among you
16:16 Three times a year all your **m** must
19:17 the two **m** involved in the dispute
20:13 put to the sword all the **m** in it.
21:21 all the **m** of his town shall stone
22:21 there the **m** of her town shall stone
23:10 If one of your **m** is unclean because
25: 1 **m** have a dispute, they are to take
25:11 If two **m** are fighting and the wife
29:10 your God—your leaders and chief **m**,
31:12 Assemble the people—**m**, women and
32:25 Young **m** and young women will perish
32:25 infants and grey-haired **m**.
33: 6 live and not die, nor his **m** be few."
Jos 1:14 but all your fighting **m**, fully armed,
2: 3 "Bring out the **m** who came to you and
2: 4 the woman had taken the two **m** and
2: 4 She said, "Yes, the **m** came to me,
2: 5 to close the city gate, the **m** left.
2: 7 the **m** set out in pursuit of the
2:14 "Our lives for your lives!" the **m**
2:17 The **m** said to her, "This oath you
2:23 the two **m** started back. They went
3:12 Now then, choose twelve **m** from the
4: 2 "Choose twelve **m** from among the
4: 4 Joshua called together the twelve **m**
4:12 The **m** of Reuben, Gad and the
5: 4 all the **m** of military age—died in
5: 6 all the **m** who were of military age
6: 2 with its king and its fighting **m**.
6: 3 the city once with all the armed **m**.
Jos 6:13 The armed **m** went ahead of them and
6:21 living thing in it—**m** and women,
6:22 Joshua said to the two **m** who had
6:23 the young **m** who had done the spying
6:25 because she hid the **m** Joshua had
7: 2 Now Joshua sent **m** from Jericho to Ai,
7: 2 So the **m** went up and spied out Ai.
7: 3 Send two or three thousand **m** to take
7: 3 people, for only a few **m** are there."
7: 4 about three thousand **m** went up; but
7: 4 but they were routed by the **m** of Ai,
8: 3 best fighting **m** and sent them out
8: 5 and when the **m** come out against us,
8:10 next morning Joshua mustered his **m**,
8:12 had taken about five thousand **m**
8:14 he and all the **m** of the city hurried
8:16 All the **m** of Ai were called to
8:19 soon as he did this, the **m** in the
8:20 The **m** of Ai looked back and saw the
8:21 round and attacked the **m** of Ai.
8:22 The **m** of the ambush also came out of
8:24 Israel had finished killing all the **m**
8:25 Twelve thousand **m** and women fell
9: 5 The **m** put worn and patched sandals
10: 2 Ai, and all its **m** were good fighters.
10: 7 including all the best fighting **m**.
10:18 and post some **m** there to guard it.
14: 6 Now the **m** of Judah approached Joshua
18: 4 Appoint three **m** from each tribe.
18: 8 the **m** started on their way to map
18: 9 the **m** left and went through the land.
22:14 With him they sent ten of the chief **m**
Jdg 1: 3 the **m** of Judah said to the
1: 4 struck down ten thousand **m** at Bezek.
1: 8 The **m** of Judah attacked Jerusalem
1: 9 After that, the **m** of Judah went down
1:16 with the **m** of Judah to live among
1:17 the **m** of Judah went with the
1:18 The **m** of Judah also took Gaza,
1:19 The LORD was with the **m** of Judah.
1:23 they sent **m** to spy out Bethel
3:18 their way the **m** who had carried it.
4: 6 'Go, take with you ten thousand **m** of
4:10 Ten thousand **m** followed him, and
4:13 chariots and all the **m** with him,
4:14 Tabor, followed by ten thousand **m**.
5:13 "Then the **m** who were left came down
6: 5 It was impossible to count the **m** and
6:27 of his family and the **m** of the town,
6:28 In the morning when the **m** of the
6:30 The **m** of the town demanded of Joash,
7: 1 his **m** camped at the spring of Harod.
7: 2 "You have too many **m** for me to
7: 3 **m** left, while ten thousand remained.
7: 4 Gideon, "There are still too many **m**.
7: 5 Gideon took the **m** down to the water.
7: 6 Three hundred **m** lapped with their
7: 7 "With the three hundred **m** that
7: 7 other **m** go, each to his own place."
7:16 Dividing the three hundred **m** into
7:19 Gideon and the hundred **m** with him
7:22 the LORD caused the **m** throughout the
7:24 So all the **m** of Ephraim were called
8: 4 Gideon and his three hundred **m**,
8: 5 He said to the **m** of Succoth, "Give
8: 8 answered as the **m** of Succoth had.
8: 9 he said to the **m** of Peniel, "When I
8:10 a force of about fifteen thousand **m**,
8:15 Gideon came and said to the **m** of
8:15 give bread to your exhausted **m**?'
8:16 taught the **m** of Succoth a lesson by
8:17 Peniel and killed the **m** of the town.
8:18 "What kind of **m** did you kill at
8:18 "**M** like you," they answered, "each
9: 9 oil, by which both gods and **m** are
9:13 wine, which cheers both gods and **m**
9:25 set **m** on the hilltops to ambush
9:28 his deputy? Serve the **m** of Hamor,
9:32 during the night you and your **m**
9:33 When Gaal and his **m** come out against
9:36 the shadows of the mountains for **m**."
9:38 Aren't these the **m** you ridiculed?
9:43 he took his **m**, divided them into
9:48 all his **m** went up Mount Zalmon.
9:48 He ordered the **m** with him, "Quick!
9:49 all the **m** cut branches and followed

Jdg 9:49 a thousand **m** and women, also died.
9:51 to which all the **m** and women–all
9:57 God also made the **m** of Shechem pay
11:20 He mustered all his **m** and encamped
11:21 gave Sihon and all his **m** into Israel'
12: 1 The **m** of Ephraim called out their
12: 4 Jephthah then called together the **m**
12: 5 "Let me cross over," the **m** of Gilead
14:18 day the **m** of the town said to him,
14:19 struck down thirty of their **m**,
15:10 The **m** of Judah asked, "Why have you
15:11 three thousand **m** from Judah went
15:15 it and struck down a thousand **m**.
15:16 I have killed a thousand **m**."
16: 9 With **m** hidden in the room, she
16:12 Then, with **m** hidden in the room, she
16:27 Now the temple was crowded with **m**
16:27 **m** and women watching Samson perform
18: 2 These **m** represented all their clans.
18: 2 The **m** entered the hill country of
18: 7 the five **m** left and came to Laish,
18:11 six hundred **m** from the clan of the
18:14 the five **m** who had spied out the
18:17 The five **m** who had spied out the
18:17 **m** stood at the entrance to the gate.
18:18 these **m** went into Micah's house and
18:22 the **m** who lived near Micah were
18:23 you called out your **m** to fight?"
18:25 or some hot-tempered **m** will attack
19:16 who was living in Gibeah (the **m** of
19:22 **m** of the city surrounded the house.
19:25 the **m** would not listen to him. So
20: 5 During the night the **m** of Gibeah
20:10 We'll take ten **m** out of every
20:12 The tribes of Israel sent **m**
20:13 Now surrender those wicked **m** of
20:15 **m** from those living in Gibeah.
20:16 chosen **m** who were left-handed,
20:17 swordsmen, all of them fighting **m**.
20:31 so that about thirty **m** fell in the
20:34 ten thousand of Israel's finest **m**
20:37 The **m** who had been in ambush made a
20:41 and the **m** of Benjamin were terrified,
20:45 five thousand **m** along the roads.
20:47 six hundred **m** turned and fled into
21:10 sent twelve thousand fighting **m**
21:16 wives for the **m** who are left?
Ru 2: 9 Watch the field where the **m** are
2: 9 I have told the **m** not to touch you.
2: 9 the water jars the **m** have filled."
2:15 Boaz gave orders to his **m**, "Even if
3:10 the younger **m**, whether rich or poor.
1Sa 2:12 Eli's sons were wicked **m**; they had
2:17 This sin of the young **m** was very
2:26 in favour with the LORD and with **m**.
4: 4 the people sent **m** to Shiloh, and
4: 9 Be strong, Philistines! Be **m**, or you
4: 9 have been to you. Be **m**, and fight!"
5: 7 the **m** of Ashdod saw what was
6:19 God struck down some of the **m** of
6:20 the **m** of Beth Shemesh asked, "Who
7: 1 the **m** of Kiriath Jearim came and
10: 2 you will meet two **m** near Rachel's
10: 3 Three **m** going up to God at Bethel
10:26 **m** whose hearts God had touched.
11: 1 And all the **m** of Jabesh said to him,
11: 5 him what the **m** of Jabesh had said.
11: 8 and the **m** of Judah thirty thousand.
11: 9 "Say to the **m** of Jabesh Gilead, 'By
11: 9 the **m** of Jabesh, they were elated.
11:11 The next day Saul separated his **m**
11:12 reign over us?' Bring these **m** to us
13: 2 Saul chose three thousand **m** from
13: 2 the **m** he sent back to their homes.
13: 8 and Saul's **m** began to scatter.
13:11 Saul replied, "When I saw that the **m**
13:15 Saul counted the **m** who were with him.
13:16 Saul and his son Jonathan and the **m**
14: 2 With him were about six hundred **m**,
14: 8 towards the **m** and let them see us.
14:12 The **m** of the outpost shouted to
14:14 **m** in an area of about half an acre.
14:17 Saul said to the **m** who were with him,
14:20 Saul and all his **m** assembled and
14:28 That is why the **m** are faint."
14:30 if the **m** had eaten today some of
1Sa 14:33 someone said to Saul, "Look, the **m**
14:34 he said, "Go out among the **m** and
14:39 But not one of the **m** said a word.
14:40 "Do what seems best to you," the **m**
14:41 by lot, and the **m** were cleared.
14:45 the **m** said to Saul, "Should Jonathan
14:45 So the **m** rescued Jonathan, and he
15: 3 Do not spare them; put to death **m**
15: 4 Saul summoned the **m** and mustered
15: 4 and ten thousand **m** from Judah.
17:26 David asked the **m** standing near him,
17:28 heard him speaking with the **m**, he
17:30 and the **m** answered him as before.
18: 6 the **m** were returning home after
18:13 gave him command over a thousand **m**,
18:27 David and his **m** went out and killed
19:11 Saul sent **m** to David's house to
19:14 Saul sent the **m** to capture David,
19:15 Saul sent the **m** back to see David
19:16 when the **m** entered, there was the
19:20 he sent **m** to capture him. But when
19:20 Saul's **m** and they also prophesied.
19:21 more **m**, and they prophesied too.
19:21 Saul sent **m** a third time, and they
21: 2 As for my **m**, I have told them to
21: 4 **m** have kept themselves from women."
22: 2 About four hundred **m** were with him.
22: 6 Now Saul heard that David and his **m**
22: 7 to them, "Listen, **m** of Benjamin!
22:18 **m** who wore the linen ephod.
22:19 the town of the priests, with its **m**
23: 3 David's **m** said to him, "Here in
23: 5 David and his **m** went to Keilah,
23: 8 Keilah to besiege David and his **m**.
23:12 surrender me and my **m** to Saul?"
23:13 David and his **m**, about six hundred
23:24 Now David and his **m** were in the
23:25 Saul and his **m** began the search, and
23:26 and David and his **m** were on the
23:26 on David and his **m** to capture them,
24: 2 Saul took three thousand chosen **m**
24: 2 **m** near the Crags of the Wild Goats.
24: 3 and his **m** were far back in the cave.
24: 4 The **m** said, "This is the day the
24: 6 He said to his **m**, "The LORD forbid
24: 7 With these words David rebuked his **m**
24: 9 "Why do you listen when **m** say,
24:22 and his **m** went up to the stronghold.
25: 5 he sent ten young **m** and said to them,
25: 8 be favourable towards my young **m**,
25: 9 David's **m** arrived, they gave Nabal
25:11 to **m** coming from who knows where?"
25:12 David's **m** turned round and went back.
25:13 David said to his **m**, "Put on your
25:13 About four hundred **m** went up with
25:15 Yet these **m** were very good to us.
25:20 there were David and his **m**
25:25 I did not see the **m** my master sent.
25:27 be given to the **m** who follow you.
26:16 you and your **m** deserve to die,
26:19 If, however, **m** have done it, may
26:22 your young **m** come over and get it.
27: 2 David and the six hundred **m** with him
27: 3 David and his **m** settled in Gath with
27: 8 Now David and his **m** went up and
28: 1 **m** will accompany me in the army."
28: 8 he and two **m** went to the woman.
28:23 But his **m** joined the woman in
28:25 she set it before Saul and his **m**,
29: 2 David and his **m** were marching at the
29: 4 by taking the heads of our own **m**?
29:11 David and his **m** got up early in the
30: 1 David and his **m** reached Ziklag on
30: 3 David and his **m** came to Ziklag, they
30: 4 David and his **m** wept aloud until
30: 6 the **m** were talking of stoning him;
30: 9 David and the six hundred **m** with him
30:10 for two hundred **m** were too exhausted
30:10 hundred **m** continued the pursuit.
30:17 **m** who rode off on camels and fled.
30:20 and his **m** drove them ahead of the
30:21 David came to the two hundred **m** who
30:21 his **m** approached, he greeted them.
30:22 all the evil **m** and troublemakers
30:31 where David and his **m** had roamed.
31: 6 his **m** died together that same day.
1Sa 31:12 all their valiant **m** journeyed
2Sa 1: 4 He said, "The **m** fled from the battle
1:11 David and all the **m** with him took
1:15 David called one of his **m** and said,
1:18 ordered that the **m** of Judah be
2: 3 David also took the **m** who were with
2: 4 the **m** of Judah came to Hebron and
2: 4 the **m** of Jabesh Gilead who had
2: 5 he sent messengers to the **m** of
2:12 Abner son of Ner, together with the **m**
2:13 Joab son of Zeruiah and David's **m**
2:14 "Let's have some of the young **m** get
2:15 were counted off—twelve **m** for
2:17 Israel were defeated by David's **m**.
2:21 take on one of the young **m** and
2:25 the **m** of Benjamin rallied behind
2:26 **m** to stop pursuing their brothers?"
2:27 if you had not spoken, the **m** would
2:28 Joab blew the trumpet, and all the **m**
2:29 All that night Abner and his **m**
2:30 Abner and assembled all his **m**.
2:30 of David's **m** were found missing.
2:31 David's **m** had killed 360 Benjamites
2:32 Then Joab and his **m** marched all
3:20 Abner, who had twenty **m** with him,
3:20 prepared a feast for him and his **m**.
3:22 Just then David's **m** and Joab
3:34 fell as one falls before wicked **m**.
3:38 the king said to his **m**, "Do you not
4: 2 Now Saul's son had two **m** who were
4:11 How much more—when wicked **m** have
4:12 David gave an order to his **m**, and
5: 6 The king and his **m** marched to
5:21 David and his **m** carried them off.
6: 1 chosen **m**, thirty thousand in all.
6: 2 He and all his **m** set out from Baalah
6:19 of Israelites, both **m** and women.
7: 9 of the greatest **m** of the earth.
7:14 of **m**, with floggings inflicted by **m**.
7:26 Then **m** will say, 'The LORD Almighty
10: 2 **m** came to the land of the Ammonites,
10: 3 **m** to you to express sympathy?
10: 4 Hanun seized David's **m**, shaved off
10: 5 **m**, for they were greatly humiliated.
10: 6 king of Maacah with a thousand **m**,
10: 6 and also twelve thousand **m** from Tob.
10: 7 with the entire army of fighting **m**.
10: 8 Rehob and the **m** of Tob and Maacah
10:10 He put the rest of the **m** under the
11: 1 **m** and the whole Israelite army.
11:11 **m** are camped in the open fields.
11:17 the **m** of the city came out and
11:17 some of the **m** in David's army fell;
11:23 said to David, "The **m** overpowered
11:24 wall, and some of the king's **m** died.
12: 1 "There were two **m** in a certain town,
13:28 Absalom ordered his **m**, "Listen! When
13:29 Absalom's **m** did to Amnon what
13:34 "I see **m** in the direction of
15: 1 with fifty **m** to run ahead of him.
15:11 Two hundred **m** from Jerusalem had
15:18 All his **m** marched past him, along
15:22 Gittite marched on with all his **m**
16: 2 the bread and fruit are for the **m** to
16:13 David and his **m** continued along the
17: 1 "I would choose twelve thousand **m**
17: 8 You know your father and his **m**; they
17:12 nor any of his **m** will be left alive.
17:20 Absalom's **m** came to the woman at the
17:20 The **m** searched but found no-one, so
17:21 After the **m** had gone, the two
18: 1 David mustered the **m** who were with
18: 3 the **m** said, "You must not go out; if
18: 4 **m** marched out in units of hundreds
18: 7 of Israel was defeated by David's **m**,
18: 7 day were great—twenty thousand **m**.
18: 9 Absalom happened to meet David's **m**.
18:10 one of the **m** saw this, he told Joab,
18:28 He has delivered up the **m** who lifted
19: 3 The **m** stole into the city that day
19: 3 as **m** steal in who are ashamed when
19: 5 Today you have humiliated all your **m**,
19: 6 and their **m** mean nothing to you.
19: 7 Now go out and encourage your **m**. I
19: 8 When the **m** were told, "The king is
19:14 He won over the hearts of all the **m**

2Sa 19:14 king, "Return, you and all your **m**.
19:15 Now the **m** of Judah had come to
19:16 the **m** of Judah to meet King David.
19:35 Can I still hear the voices of **m** and
19:41 did our brothers, the **m** of Judah,
19:41 Jordan, together with all his **m**?"
19:42 All the **m** of Judah answered the
19:43 answered the **m** of Judah, "We have
19:43 But the **m** of Judah responded even
20: 2 But the **m** of Judah stayed by their
20: 4 the king said to Amasa, "Summon the **m**
20: 6 Take your master's **m** and pursue him,
20: 7 Joab's **m** and the Kerethites and
20:11 One of Joab's **m** stood beside Amasa
20:13 all the **m** went on with Joab to
20:22 So he sounded the trumpet, and his **m**
21:15 David went down with his **m** to fight
21:17 Then David's **m** swore to him, saying,
21:22 at the hands of David and his **m**.
22: 3 from violent **m** you save me.
22:49 from violent **m** you rescued me.
23: 3 to me: 'When one rules over **m** in
23: 6 evil **m** are all to be cast aside like
23: 8 David's mighty **m**: Josheb-Basshebeth,
23: 8 **m**, whom he killed in one encounter.
23: 9 As one of the three mighty **m**, he was
23:13 three of the thirty chief **m** came
23:16 the three mighty **m** broke through the
23:17 "Is it not the blood of **m** who went
23:17 the exploits of the three mighty **m**.
23:18 his spear against three hundred **m**,
23:20 He struck down two of Moab's best **m**.
23:22 was as famous as the three mighty **m**.
24: 2 Beersheba and enrol the fighting **m**,
24: 9 of the fighting **m** to the king:
24: 9 **m** who could handle a sword,
24:10 after he had counted the fighting **m**,
24:14 let me fall into the hands of **m**."
24:20 king and his **m** coming towards him,
1Ki 1: 5 with fifty **m** to run ahead of him.
1: 9 **m** of Judah who were royal officials,
1:53 King Solomon sent **m**, and they
2:32 **m** and killed them with the sword.
2:32 better **m** and more upright than he.
4:30 the wisdom of all the **m** of the East,
4:34 **M** of all nations came to listen to
5: 6 My **m** will work with yours, and I
5: 6 for your **m** whatever wages you set.
5: 9 My **m** will haul them down from
5:13 from all Israel—thirty thousand **m**.
5:18 Hiram and the **m** of Gebal cut and
8:39 you alone know the hearts of all **m**),
8:42 for **m** will hear of your great name
9:22 Israelites; they were his fighting **m**,
9:23 supervising the **m** who did the work.
9:27 Hiram sent his **m**—sailors who knew
9:27 serve in the fleet with Solomon's **m**.
10: 8 How happy your **m** must be! How happy
11:15 had struck down all the **m** in Edom.
11:16 had destroyed all the **m** in Edom.
11:18 Then taking **m** from Paran with them,
11:24 He gathered **m** around him and became
12: 8 consulted the young **m** who had grown
12:10 The young **m** who had grown up with
12:14 he followed the advice of the young **m**
12:21 eighty thousand fighting **m**—to make
20:10 to give each of my **m** a handful."
20:12 ordered his **m**: "Prepare to attack.
20:15 of the provincial commanders, 232 **m**.
20:17 "**M** are advancing from Samaria.
20:33 The **m** took this as a good sign and
22: 6 four hundred **m**—and asked them,
22:49 "Let my **m** sail with your **m**," but
2Ki 1: 6 are sending **m** to consult Baal-Zebub,
1: 9 captain with his company of fifty **m**.
1:10 and consume you and your fifty **m**!"
1:10 and consumed the captain and his **m**.
1:11 another captain with his fifty **m**.
1:12 and consume you and your fifty **m**!"
1:12 and consumed him and his fifty **m**.
1:13 a third captain with his fifty **m**.
1:13 of these fifty **m**, your servants!
1:14 first two captains and all their **m**.
2: 7 Fifty **m** of the company of the
2:16 "we your servants have fifty able **m**.
2:17 And they sent fifty **m**, who searched
2Ki 2:19 The **m** of the city said to Elisha,
3:25 but **m** armed with slings surrounded
4:38 pot and cook some stew for these **m**."
4:40 The stew was poured out for the **m**,
4:43 a hundred **m**?" his servant asked.
5:22 'Two young **m** from the company of the
5:24 He sent the **m** away and they left.
6:13 that I can send **m** and capture him.
6:20 of these **m** so that they can see.
6:22 "Would you kill **m** you have captured
7: 3 Now there were four **m** with leprosy
7: 8 The **m** who had leprosy reached the
7:13 "Make some **m** take five of the horses
8:12 kill their young **m** with the sword,
10: 6 were with the leading **m** of the city,
10: 7 the letter arrived, these **m** took the
10:11 as well as all his chief **m**, his
10:14 the well of Beth Eked—forty-two **m**.
10:24 Now Jehu had posted eighty **m** outside
10:24 "If one of you lets any of the **m** I
11: 9 Each one took his **m**—those who were
12:11 they gave the money to the **m**
14:19 but they sent **m** after him to Lachish
15:25 Taking fifty **m** of Gilead with him,
16: 6 Aram by driving out the **m** of Judah.
17:30 The **m** from Babylon made Succoth
17:30 the **m** from Cuthah made Nergal, and
17:30 and the **m** from Hamath made Ashima;
18:27 and not to the **m** sitting on the wall
19:35 thousand **m** in the Assyrian camp.
20:14 "What did those **m** say, and where did
22: 5 Make them entrust it to the **m**
22: 5 And make these **m** pay the workers who
23: 2 of the LORD with the **m** of Judah,
23:17 The **m** of the city said, "It marks
24:14 all the officers and fighting **m**,
24:15 and the leading **m** of the land.
24:16 force of seven thousand fighting **m**,
25:19 fighting **m** and five royal advisers.
25:19 of his **m** who were found in the city.
25:23 all the army officers and their **m**
25:23 son of the Maacathite, and their **m**.
25:24 oath to reassure them and their **m**.
25:25 came with ten **m** and assassinated
25:25 assassinated Gedaliah and also the **m**
1Ch 4:12 These were the **m** of Recah.
4:22 Jokim, the **m** of Cozeba, and Joash
4:38 The **m** listed above by name were
4:41 The **m** whose names were listed came
5:18 44,760 **m** ready for military service
5:18 **m** who could handle shield and sword
5:24 **m**, and heads of their families.
6:31 These are the **m** David put in charge
6:33 Here are the **m** who served, together
7: 2 **m** in their genealogy numbered 22,600
7: 4 they had 36,000 **m** ready for battle,
7: 5 The relatives who were fighting **m**
7: 7 record listed 22,034 fighting **m**.
7: 9 of families and 20,200 fighting **m**.
7:11 fighting **m** ready to go out to war.
7:21 killed by the native-born **m** of Gath,
7:40 choice **m**, brave warriors and
7:40 The number of **m** ready for battle, as
9: 9 **m** were heads of their families.
9:13 They were able **m**, responsible for
10:12 all their valiant **m** went and took
11:10 chiefs of David's mighty **m**—they,
11:11 this is the list of David's mighty **m**
11:11 **m**, whom he killed in one encounter.
11:12 Ahohite, one of the three mighty **m**.
11:19 "Should I drink the blood of these **m**
11:19 the exploits of the three mighty **m**.
11:20 his spear against three hundred **m**,
11:22 He struck down two of Moab's best **m**.
11:24 was as famous as the three mighty **m**.
11:26 The mighty **m** were: Asahel the
12: 1 These were the **m** who came to David
12:16 Other Benjamites and some **m** from
12:19 Some of the **m** of Manasseh defected
12:19 (He and his **m** did not help the
12:20 these were the **m** of Manasseh who
12:22 Day after day **m** came to help David,
12:23 These are the numbers of the **m** armed
12:24 **m** of Judah, carrying shield and
12:25 **m** of Simeon, warriors ready for
12:26 **m** of Levi—4,600,
1Ch 12:27 the family of Aaron with 3,700 **m**,
12:29 **m** of Benjamin, Saul's kinsmen—3,000
12:30 **m** of Ephraim, brave warriors, famous
12:31 **m** of half the tribe of Manasseh,
12:32 **m** of Issachar, who understood the
12:33 **m** of Zebulun, experienced soldiers
12:34 **m** of Naphtali—1,000 officers,
12:34 **m** carrying shields and spears;
12:35 **m** of Dan, ready for battle—28,600;
12:36 **m** of Asher, experienced soldiers
12:37 from east of the Jordan, **m** of Reuben,
12:38 All these were fighting **m** who
12:39 The **m** spent three days there with
14:11 David and his **m** went up to Baal
17: 8 of the greatest **m** of the earth.
17:17 the most exalted of **m**, O LORD God.
17:24 Then **m** will say, 'The LORD Almighty,
19: 2 When David's **m** came to Hanun in the
19: 3 **m** to you to express sympathy?
19: 3 Haven't his **m** come to you to explore
19: 4 Hanun seized David's **m**, shaved them,
19: 5 came and told David about the **m**,
19: 8 with the entire army of fighting **m**.
19:11 He put the rest of the **m** under the
20: 8 at the hands of David and his **m**.
21: 5 number of the fighting **m** to David:
21: 5 thousand **m** who could handle a sword,
21:13 let me fall into the hands of **m**."
21:17 the fighting **m** to be counted?
22:15 as **m** skilled in every kind of
23: 3 of **m** was thirty-eight thousand.
25: 1 of the **m** who performed this service:
25: 6 these **m** were under the supervision
26: 6 because they were very capable **m**.
26: 7 Elihu and Semakiah were also able **m**.
26: 8 their relatives were capable **m** with
26: 9 who were able **m**—18 in all.
26:12 through their chief **m**, had duties
26:30 seventeen hundred able **m**—were
26:31 and capable **m** among the Hebronites
26:32 who were able **m** and heads of
27: 1 Each division consisted of 24,000 **m**.
27: 2 There were 24,000 **m** in his division.
27: 4 There were 24,000 **m** in his division.
27: 5 there were 24,000 **m** in his division.
27: 7 There were 24,000 **m** in his division.
27: 8 There were 24,000 **m** in his division.
27: 9 There were 24,000 **m** in his division.
27:10 There were 24,000 **m** in his division.
27:11 There were 24,000 **m** in his division.
27:12 There were 24,000 **m** in his division.
27:13 There were 24,000 **m** in his division.
27:14 There were 24,000 **m** in his division.
27:15 There were 24,000 **m** in his division.
27:23 of the **m** twenty years old or less,
27:24 to count the **m** but did not finish.
28: 1 mighty **m** and all the brave warriors.
29:24 All the officers and mighty **m**, as
2Ch 2: 2 He conscripted seventy thousand **m** as
2: 8 for I know that your **m** are skilled
2: 8 My **m** shall work with yours
6:18 dwell on earth with **m**? The heavens,
6:30 (for you alone know the hearts of **m**),
8: 9 his work; they were his fighting **m**,
8:10 fifty officials supervising the **m**.
8:18 own officers, **m** who knew the sea.
8:18 These, with Solomon's **m**, sailed to
9: 7 How happy your **m** must be! How happy
9:10 (The **m** of Hiram and the **m** of Solomon
9:21 trading ships manned by Hiram's **m**.
10: 8 consulted the young **m** who had grown
10:10 The young **m** who had grown up with
10:14 he followed the advice of the young **m**
11: 1 eighty thousand fighting **m**—to make
13: 3 hundred thousand able fighting **m**,
13:15 the **m** of Judah raised the battle cry.
13:17 Abijah and his **m** inflicted heavy
13:17 casualties among Israel's able **m**.
13:18 and the **m** of Judah were victorious
14: 8 three hundred thousand **m** from Judah,
14: 8 All these were brave fighting **m**.
14:13 The **m** of Judah carried off a large
16: 6 King Asa brought all the **m** of Judah,
17:13 experienced fighting **m** in Jerusalem.
17:14 commander, with 300,000 fighting **m**;
17:17 **m** armed with bows and shields;

2Ch 17:18 next, Jehozabad, with 180,000 **m**
17:19 These were the **m** who served the king,
18: 5 the prophets—four hundred **m**—and
20: 2 Some **m** came and told Jehoshaphat, "A
20:10 "But now here are **m** from Ammon, Moab
20:13 All the **m** of Judah, with their wives
20:21 Jehoshaphat appointed **m** to sing to
20:22 the LORD set ambushes against the **m**
20:23 The **m** of Ammon and Moab rose up
20:23 Moab rose up against the **m** from
20:23 slaughtering the **m** from Seir,
20:24 the **m** of Judah came to the place
20:25 Jehoshaphat and his **m** went to carry
20:27 Then, led by Jehoshaphat, all the **m**
21:13 house, **m** who were better than you.
22: 9 and his **m** captured him while he was
23: 5 and all the other **m** are to be in the
23: 6 but all the other **m** are to guard
23: 8 The Levites and all the **m** of Judah
23: 8 Each one took his **m**—those who were
23:10 He stationed all the **m**, each with
24:12 Jehoiada gave it to the **m** who
24:13 The **m** in charge of the work were
24:24 army had come with only a few **m**,
25: 5 **m** ready for military service,
25: 6 a hundred thousand fighting **m** from
25:11 he killed ten thousand **m** of Seir.
25:12 also captured ten thousand **m** alive,
25:27 but they sent **m** after him to Lachish
26:12 over the fighting **m** was 2,600.
26:13 army of 307,500 **m** trained for war,
26:15 by skilful **m** for use on the towers
28:10 now you intend to make the **m** and
28:15 The **m** designated by name took the
30:11 Nevertheless, some **m** of Asher,
31:19 **m** were designated by name to
32: 4 A large force of **m** assembled, and
32:21 who annihilated all the fighting **m**
34:10 they entrusted it to the **m** appointed
34:10 These **m** paid the workers who
34:12 The **m** did the work faithfully. Over
34:30 of the LORD with the **m** of Judah,
35:25 and to this day all the **m** and women
36:17 who killed their young **m** with the
Ezr 2: 2 of the **m** of the people of Israel:
2:21 the **m** of Bethlehem 123
2:65 also had 200 **m** and women singers.
4: 9 officials over the **m** from Tripolis,
4:11 servants, the **m** of Trans-Euphrates:
4:21 Now issue an order to these **m** to
5: 4 the **m** constructing this building?"
6: 8 The expenses of these **m** are to be
7:28 **m** from Israel to go up with me.
8: 3 and with him were registered 150 **m**;
8: 4 son of Zerahiah, and with him 200 **m**;
8: 5 son of Jahaziel, and with him 300 **m**;
8: 6 son of Jonathan, and with him 50 **m**;
8: 7 son of Athaliah, and with him 70 **m**;
8: 8 son of Michael, and with him 80 **m**;
8: 9 son of Jehiel, and with him 218 **m**;
8:10 of Josiphiah, and with him 160 **m**;
8:11 son of Bebai, and with him 28 **m**;
8:12 son of Hakkatan, and with him 110 **m**;
8:13 and Shemaiah, and with them 60 **m**;
8:14 Uthai and Zaccur, and with them 70 **m**.
8:16 Elnathan, who were **m** of learning,
8:18 Sherebiah's sons and brothers, 18 **m**;
8:19 and his brothers and nephews, 20 **m**.
10: 1 a large crowd of Israelites—**m**,
10: 9 Within the three days, all the **m** of
10:16 Ezra the priest selected **m** who were
10:17 the **m** who had married foreign women.
Ne 1: 2 came from Judah with some other **m**,
2:12 out during the night with a few **m**.
3: 2 The **m** of Jericho built the adjoining
3: 5 was repaired by the **m** of Tekoa,
3: 7 Next to them, repairs were made by **m**
3:27 Next to them, the **m** of Tekoa
4: 7 the Ammonites and the **m** of Ashdod
4:16 From that day on, half of my **m** did
4:21 we continued the work with half the **m**
4:23 Neither I nor my brothers nor my **m**
5: 1 Now the **m** and their wives raised a
5:10 I and my brothers and my **m** are also
5:16 All my **m** were assembled there for
6:10 because **m** are coming to kill you—by
Ne 7: 2 and feared God more than most **m** do.
7:26 the **m** of Bethlehem and Netophah 188
7:67 also had 245 **m** and women singers.
8: 2 which was made up of **m** and women and
8: 3 Water Gate in the presence of the **m**,
11: 2 The people commended all the **m** who
11: 6 in Jerusalem totalled 468 able **m**.
11: 8 followers, Gabbai and Sallai—928 **m**.
11:12 on work for the temple—822 **m**;
11:13 who were heads of families—242 **m**;
11:14 associates, who were able **m**–128 **m**.
11:19 who kept watch at the gates—172 **m**.
12:44 At that time **m** were appointed to be
13:13 these **m** were considered trustworthy.
13:15 In those days I saw **m** in Judah
13:16 **M** from Tyre who lived in Jerusalem
13:19 I stationed some of my own **m** at the
13:23 Moreover, in those days I saw **m** of
13:25 I beat some of the **m** and pulled out
Est 3: 9 the **m** who carry out this business."
9: 6 killed and destroyed five hundred **m**.
9:12 destroyed five hundred **m** and the ten
9:15 to death in Susa three hundred **m**,
Job 4:13 night, when deep sleep falls on **m**,
7:20 O watcher of **m**? Why have you made me
11: 3 Will your idle talk reduce **m** to
11:11 Surely he recognises deceitful **m**;
12: 5 **M** at ease have contempt for
12:19 and overthrows **m** long established.
13: 9 deceive him as you might deceive **m**?
14:12 **m** will not awake or be roused from
15:10 side, **m** even older than your father.
16:10 **M** open their mouths to jeer at me;
16:11 God has turned me over to evil **m** and
17: 8 Upright **m** are appalled at this; the
17:12 These **m** turn night into day; in the
18:20 **M** of the west are appalled at his
18:20 **m** of the east are seized with horror.
21:28 the tents where wicked **m** lived?'
21:33 to him; all **m** follow after him,
22: 6 you stripped **m** of their clothing,
22:15 the old path that evil **m** have trod?
22:29 When **m** are brought low and you say,
24: 2 **M** move boundary stones; they pasture
24:16 In the dark, **m** break into houses,
24:20 evil **m** are no longer remembered
28: 4 far from **m** he dangles and sways.
29: 8 the young **m** saw me and stepped aside
29: 8 and the old **m** rose to their feet;
29: 9 the chief **m** refrained from speaking
29:21 "**M** listened to me expectantly,
30: 1 "But now they mock me, **m** younger
31:10 and may other **m** sleep with her.
31:31 if the **m** of my household have never
31:33 if I have concealed my sin as **m** do,
32: 1 these three **m** stopped answering Job,
32: 5 when he saw that the three **m** had
33:15 on **m** as they slumber in their beds,
33:27 he comes to **m** and says, 'I have
34: 2 listen to me, you **m** of learning.
34: 8 he associates with wicked **m**.
34:10 listen to me, you **m** of understanding
34:21 "His eyes are on the ways of **m**; he
34:23 God has no need to examine **m** further,
34:34 "**M** of understanding declare,
35: 8 righteousness only the sons of **m**.
35: 9 "**M** cry out under a load of
35:12 He does not answer when **m** cry out
36: 5 but does not despise **m**; he is mighty,
36: 8 if **m** are bound in chains, held fast
36:24 his work, which **m** have praised
36:25 All mankind has seen it; **m** gaze on
37: 7 that all **m** he has made may know his
37:13 He brings the clouds to punish **m**, or
37:24 Therefore, **m** revere him, for does he
Ps 4: 2 How long, O **m**, will you turn my
5: 6 and deceitful **m** the LORD abhors.
9:20 let the nations know they are but **m**.
11: 4 sons of **m**; his eyes examine them.
11: 7 upright **m** will see his face.
12: 1 faithful have vanished from among **m**.
12: 8 what is vile is honoured among **m**.
14: 2 on the sons of **m** to see if there
14: 4 who devour my people as **m** eat bread
17: 4 for the deeds of **m**—by the word of
17:14 by your hand save me from such **m**,
Ps 17:14 from **m** of this world whose reward is
18:48 foes; from violent **m** you rescued me.
22: 6 by **m** and despised by the people.
22:16 a band of evil **m** has encircled me,
26: 4 I do not sit with deceitful **m**, nor
26: 9 my life with bloodthirsty **m**,
27: 2 evil **m** advance against me to devour
31:19 you bestow in the sight of **m** on
31:20 hide them from the intrigues of **m**;
36: 7 Both high and low among **m** find
37: 1 Do not fret because of evil **m** or be
37: 7 fret when **m** succeed in their ways,
37: 9 For evil **m** will be cut off, but
39:11 You rebuke and discipline **m** for
42: 3 while **m** say to me all day long,
43: 1 me from deceitful and wicked **m**.
45: 2 You are the most excellent of **m** and
45:12 **m** of wealth will seek your favour.
49:18 and **m** praise you when you prosper—
53: 2 on the sons of **m** to see if there
53: 4 who devour my people as **m** eat bread
54: 3 ruthless **m** seek my life—**m** without
55:19 **m** who never change their ways and
55:23 **m** will not live out half their days.
56: 1 **m** hotly pursue me; all day long
57: 4 **m** whose teeth are spears and arrows,
58: 1 Do you judge uprightly among **m**?
58:11 **m** will say, "Surely the righteous
59: T Saul had sent **m** to watch David's
59: 2 and save me from bloodthirsty **m**.
59: 3 Fierce **m** conspire against me for no
62: 9 Lowborn **m** are but a breath, the
65: 2 hear prayer, to you all **m** will come.
66:12 You let **m** ride over our heads; we
68:12 in the camps **m** divide the plunder.
68:18 train; you received gifts from **m**,
71: 4 from the grasp of evil and cruel **m**.
74: 5 They behaved like **m** wielding axes to
75: 1 **m** tell of your wonderful deeds.
76: 5 Valiant **m** lie plundered, they sleep
76:10 Surely your wrath against **m** brings
78: 9 The **m** of Ephraim, though armed with
78:25 **M** ate the bread of angels; he sent
78:60 the tent he had set up among **m**.
78:63 Fire consumed their young **m**, and
82: 7 you will die like mere **m**; you will
83:16 that **m** will seek your name, O LORD.
86:14 O God; a band of ruthless **m** seeks my
86:14 my life—**m** without regard for you.
89:47 futility you have created all **m**!
90: 3 You turn **m** back to dust, saying,
90: 3 "Return to dust, O sons of **m**.
90: 5 You sweep **m** away in the sleep of
101: 3 **m** I hate; they shall not cling to me.
101: 4 **M** of perverse heart shall be far
107: 8 love and his wonderful deeds for **m**,
107:15 love and his wonderful deeds for **m**,
107:21 love and his wonderful deeds for **m**.
107:27 staggered like drunken **m**; they
107:31 love and his wonderful deeds for **m**.
109: 2 for wicked and deceitful **m** have
115: 4 and gold, made by the hands of **m**.
116:11 dismay I said, "All **m** are liars."
119:86 for **m** persecute me without cause.
119:113 I hate double-minded **m**, but I love
119:134 Redeem me from the oppression of **m**,
124: 2 been on our side when **m** attacked us,
126: 1 to Zion, we were like **m** who dreamed.
135: 8 the firstborn of **m** and animals.
135:15 and gold, made by the hands of **m**.
139:19 Away from me, you bloodthirsty **m**!
140: 1 from evil **m**; protect me from **m** of
140: 4 protect me from **m** of violence who
140: 5 Proud **m** have hidden a snare for me;
140:11 disaster hunt down **m** of violence.
141: 4 to take part in wicked deeds with **m**
142: 3 I walk **m** have hidden a snare for me.
145:12 that all **m** may know of your mighty
146: 3 in mortal **m**, who cannot save.
148:12 young **m** and maidens, old **m** and
Pr 1:18 These **m** lie in wait for their own
2:12 wicked **m**, from **m** whose words are
2:20 you will walk in the ways of good **m**
4:14 wicked or walk in the way of evil **m**.
6:30 **M** do not despise a thief if he
7: 7 among the young **m**, a youth who

Pr 8: 4 "To you, O **m**, I call out; I raise my
11:16 but ruthless **m** gain only wealth.
11:20 The LORD detests **m** of perverse heart
12: 7 Wicked **m** are overthrown and are no
12: 8 **m** with warped minds are despised.
12:12 wicked desire the plunder of evil **m**,
12:22 he delights in **m** who are truthful.
14:19 Evil **m** will bow down in the presence
15:11 LORD—how much more the hearts of **m**!
20:29 The glory of young **m** is their
22:29 he will not serve before obscure **m**.
23:28 multiplies the unfaithful among **m**.
24: 1 Do not envy wicked **m**, do not desire
24: 9 are sin, and **m** detest a mocker.
24:19 Do not fret because of evil **m** or be
25: 1 by the **m** of Hezekiah king of Judah:
25: 6 do not claim a place among great **m**;
26:16 than seven **m** who answer discreetly.
28: 5 Evil **m** do not understand justice,
28:12 rise to power, **m** go into hiding.
29:10 Bloodthirsty **m** hate a man of
30: 2 "I am the most ignorant of **m**; I do
Ecc 1:11 There is no remembrance of **m** of old,
1:13 a heavy burden God has laid on **m**!
2: 3 worth while for **m** to do under
2: 8 I acquired **m** and women singers, and
3:10 seen the burden God has laid on **m**.
3:11 set eternity in the hearts of **m**;
3:12 better for **m** than to be happy
3:14 does it so that **m** will revere him.
3:18 I also thought, "As for **m**, God tests
6: 1 the sun, and it weighs heavily on **m**:
7:29 but **m** have gone in search of many
8:12 **m**, who are reverent before God.
8:14 **m** who get what the wicked deserve,
8:14 **m** who get what the righteous deserve.
9: 3 The hearts of **m**, moreover, are full
9:12 so **m** are trapped by evil times
12: 3 and the strong **m** stoop, when the
12: 4 **m** rise up at the sound of birds,
12: 5 **m** are afraid of heights and of
SS 2: 3 is my lover among the young **m**.
Isa 2:11 and the pride of **m** brought low;
2:17 low and the pride of **m** humbled;
2:19 **M** will flee to caves in the rocks
2:20 In that day **m** will throw away to the
3:25 Your **m** will fall by the sword, your
5: 3 "Now you dwellers in Jerusalem and **m**
5: 7 and the **m** of Judah are the garden of
5:13 their **m** of rank will die of hunger
7:13 not enough to try the patience of **m**?
7:24 **M** will go there with bow and arrow,
8:14 be a stone that causes **m** to stumble
8:19 **m** tell you to consult mediums and
9: 3 **m** rejoice when dividing the plunder.
9:15 the elders and prominent **m** are the
9:17 take no pleasure in the young **m**,
10:14 nations; as **m** gather abandoned eggs,
11:15 so that **m** can cross over in sandals.
13:18 bows will strike down the young **m**;
15: 4 Therefore the armed **m** of Moab cry
16: 7 grieve for the **m** of Kir Hareseth.
17: 7 In that day **m** will look to their
29:13 made up only of rules taught by **m**.
30:30 The LORD will cause **m** to hear his
31: 3 the Egyptians are **m** and not God;
31: 8 **m** will be put to forced labour.
33: 4 a swarm of locusts **m** pounce on it.
33: 7 Look, their brave **m** cry aloud in the
36:12 and not to the **m** sitting on the wall
37:36 thousand **m** in the Assyrian camp.
38:16 Lord, by such things **m** live; and my
39: 3 "What did those **m** say, and where did
40: 6 shall I cry?" "All **m** are like grass
40:30 weary, and young **m** stumble and fall;
43: 4 I will give **m** in exchange for you,
44:11 shame; craftsmen are nothing but **m**.
45: 6 **m** may know there is none besides me.
51: 7 Do not fear the reproach of **m** or
51:12 **m**, the sons of **m**, who are but grass,
51:17 the goblet that makes **m** stagger.
53: 3 He was despised and rejected by **m**, a
53: 3 Like one from whom **m** hide their
57: 1 his heart; devout **m** are taken away,
59:10 feeling our way like **m** without eyes.
59:19 From the west, **m** will fear the name
Isa 60:11 day or night, so that **m** may bring
65: 8 in a cluster of grapes and **m** say,
66:16 will execute judgment upon all **m**,
Jer 2:16 Also, the **m** of Memphis and Tahpanhes
2:34 On your clothes **m** find the lifeblood
3:16 "**m** will no longer say, 'The ark of
4: 3 This is what the LORD says to the **m**
4: 4 circumcise your hearts, you **m** of
4:17 They surround her like **m** guarding a
5:26 "Among my people are wicked **m** who
5:26 lie in wait like **m** who snare birds
5:26 like those who set traps to catch **m**.
6:11 on the young **m** gathered together;
6:23 **m** in battle formation to attack you,
8: 4 'When **m** fall down, do they not get
8:10 I will give their wives to other **m**
9:21 the young **m** from the public squares.
9:22 'The dead bodies of **m** will lie like
11:21 the **m** of Anathoth who are seeking
11:22 Their young **m** will die by the sword,
11:23 bring disaster on the **m** of Anathoth
12: 5 "If you have raced with **m** on foot
15: 8 the mothers of their young **m**;
16: 3 and the **m** who are their fathers:
16:14 "when **m** will no longer say, 'As
16:20 Do **m** make their own gods? Yes, but
17:25 accompanied by the **m** of Judah and
18:21 widows; let their **m** be put to death,
18:21 **m** slain by the sword in battle.
21: 6 those who live in this city—both **m**
26:22 to Egypt, along with some other **m**.
31:13 be glad, young **m** and old as well.
31:27 the offspring of **m** and of animals.
32:19 eyes are open to all the ways of **m**;
32:32 priests and prophets, the **m** of Judah
32:43 'It is a desolate waste, without **m**
33: 5 **m** I will slay in my anger and wrath.
33:10 waste, without **m** or animals.
33:10 inhabited by neither **m** nor animals,
33:12 desolate and without **m** or animals
34:18 The **m** who have violated my covenant
35: 5 some cups before the **m** of the
35:13 says: Go and tell the **m** of Judah and
36:29 cut off both **m** and animals from it?"
37:10 wounded **m** were left in their tents,
38: 9 "My lord the king, these **m** have
38:10 "Take thirty **m** from here with you
38:11 Ebed-Melech took the **m** with him and
40: 7 all the army officers and their **m**
40: 7 and had put him in charge of the **m**,
40: 8 son of the Maacathite, and their **m**.
40: 9 oath to reassure them and their **m**.
41: 1 came with ten **m** to Gedaliah son of
41: 2 the ten **m** who were with him got up
41: 5 eighty **m** who had shaved off their
41: 7 Ishmael son of Nethaniah and the **m**
41: 9 the bodies of the **m** he had killed
41:12 they took all their **m** and went to
41:15 eight of his **m** escaped from Johanan
43: 2 all the arrogant **m** said to Jeremiah,
43: 6 They also led away all the **m**, women
44: 7 off from Judah the **m** and women,
44:15 all the **m** who knew that their wives
44:20 **m** and women, who were answering him,
46: 9 O warriors—**m** of Cush and Put who
46: 9 **m** of Lydia who draw the bow.
46:22 axes, like **m** who cut down trees.
48: 2 **m** will plot her downfall: 'Come,
48:12 "when I will send **m** who pour from
48:14 are warriors, **m** valiant in battle
48:15 **m** will go down in the slaughter,"
48:31 I moan for the **m** of Kir Hareseth.
48:36 a flute for the **m** of Kir Hareseth.
49:15 among the nations, despised among **m**.
49:26 Surely, her young **m** will fall in the
49:29 **M** will shout to them, 'Terror on
50: 3 both **m** and animals will flee away.
50:30 Therefore, her young **m** will fall in
50:42 **m** in battle formation to attack you,
51: 3 Do not spare her young **m**;
51:14 I will surely fill you with **m**,
52:25 officer in charge of the fighting **m**
52:25 of his **m** who were found in the city.
Lam 1:15 army against me to crush my young **m**.
1:18 **m** and maidens have gone into exile.
2:12 **m** in the streets of the city,
Lam 2:21 my young **m** and maidens have fallen
3:31 For **m** are not cast off by the Lord
3:33 or grief to the children of **m**.
4:14 the streets like **m** who are blind.
4:15 You are unclean!" **m** cry to them.
4:18 **M** stalked us at every step, so we
5:13 Young **m** toil at the millstones; boys
5:14 young **m** have stopped their music.
Eze 8:16 the altar, were about twenty-five **m**.
9: 2 I saw six **m** coming from the
9: 6 Slaughter old **m**, young **m** and maidens,
11: 1 to the gate were twenty-five **m**,
11: 2 "Son of man, these are the **m** who are
14: 3 "Son of man, these **m** have set up
14:13 it and kill its **m** and their animals,
14:14 even if these three **m**—Noah, Daniel
14:16 even if these three **m** were in it,
14:17 and I kill its **m** and their animals,
14:18 even if these three **m** were in it,
14:19 killing its **m** and their animals,
14:21 kill its **m** and their animals!
17:13 away the leading **m** of the land,
19: 3 to tear the prey and he devoured **m**.
19: 6 to tear the prey and he devoured **m**.
21:31 brutal **m**, **m** skilled in destruction.
22: 9 In you are slanderous **m** bent on
22:12 In you **m** accept bribes to shed blood;
22:20 **m** gather silver, copper, iron, lead
23: 6 young **m**, and mounted horsemen.
23: 8 during her youth **m** slept with her,
23:12 horsemen, all handsome young **m**.
23:14 She saw **m** portrayed on a wall,
23:23 the **m** of Pekod and Shoa and Koa, and
23:23 handsome young **m**, all of them
23:23 chariot officers and **m** of high rank,
23:40 "They even sent messengers for **m** who
23:42 desert along with **m** from the rabble,
23:44 they slept with her. As **m** sleep with
23:45 righteous **m** will sentence them to
25:13 and kill its **m** and their animals.
26:10 as **m** enter a city whose walls have
26:17 O city of renown, peopled by **m** of
27: 8 **M** of Sidon and Arvad were your
27: 8 your skilled **m**, O Tyre, were aboard
27:10 "'**M** of Persia, Lydia and Put served
27:11 **M** of Arvad and Helech manned your
27:11 **m** of Gammad were in your towers.
27:14 "'**M** of Beth Togarmah exchanged work
27:15 "'The **m** of Rhodes traded with you,
29: 8 and kill your **m** and their animals.
30:12 Nile and sell the land to evil **m**;
30:17 The young **m** of Heliopolis and
31:14 among mortal **m**, with those who go
32:12 fall by the swords of mighty **m**—
33: 2 their **m** and make him their watchman,
36:11 I will increase the number of **m** and
36:13 "You devour **m** and deprive your
36:14 therefore you will no longer devour **m**
39:14 "'**M** will be regularly employed to
39:18 You will eat the flesh of mighty **m**
39:20 mighty **m** and soldiers of every kind,'
Da 1: 4 young **m** without any physical defect,
1:10 than the other young **m** of your age?
1:13 the young **m** who eat the royal food,
1:15 the young **m** who ate the royal food.
1:17 To these four young **m** God gave
2:11 gods, and they do not live among **m**."
2:13 and **m** were sent to look for Daniel
2:30 greater wisdom than other living **m**,
3: 4 nations and **m** of every language:
3: 7 all the peoples, nations and **m** of
3:13 **m** were brought before the king,
3:21 these **m**, wearing their robes,
3:23 these three **m**, firmly tied, fell
3:24 "Weren't there three **m** that we tied
3:25 He said, "Look! I see four **m** walking
4: 1 To the peoples, nations and **m** of
4:17 is sovereign over the kingdoms of **m**
4:17 sets over them the lowliest of **m**.'
4:25 is sovereign over the kingdoms of **m**
4:32 is sovereign over the kingdoms of **m**
5:19 all the peoples and nations and **m** of
5:21 is sovereign over the kingdoms of **m**
6: 5 Finally these **m** said, "We will never
6:11 these **m** went as a group and found
6:15 the **m** went as a group to the king

Da 6:24 At the king's command, the **m** who had
6:25 nations and **m** of every language
7:14 **m** of every language worshipped him.
8:24 the mighty **m** and the holy people.
9: 7 covered with shame—the **m** of Judah
10: 7 the **m** with me did not see it,
11:14 The violent **m** among your own people
Hos 4:14 because the **m** themselves consort
6: 8 Gilead is a city of wicked **m**,
13: 1 Ephraim spoke, **m** trembled; he was
14: 7 **M** will dwell again in his shade. He
Joel 2:28 your old **m** will dream dreams, your
2:28 your young **m** will see visions.
2:29 Even on my servants, both **m** and
3: 9 the fighting **m** draw near and attack.
Am 2:11 Nazirites from among your young **m**.
4:10 I killed your young **m** with the sword,
6: 1 you notable **m** of the foremost nation,
6: 9 If ten **m** are left in one house, they
8:12 **M** will stagger from sea to sea and
8:13 **m** will faint because of thirst.
Ob : 8 **m** of understanding in the mountains
Jnh 1:13 Instead, the **m** did their best to row
1:16 At this the **m** greatly feared the
Mic 2: 4 In that day **m** will ridicule you;
2: 8 care, like **m** returning from battle.
5: 5 shepherds, even eight leaders of **m**.
6:12 Her rich **m** are violent; her people
7: 2 All **m** lie in wait to shed blood;
Na 3:10 all her great **m** were put in chains.
Hab 1:11 **m**, whose own strength is their god."
1:14 You have made **m** like fish in the sea,
Zep 1: 3 "I will sweep away both **m** and
1:17 and they will walk like blind **m**,
3: 4 arrogant; they are treacherous **m**.
Hag 1:11 on **m** and cattle, and on the labour
Zec 2: 4 number of **m** and livestock in it.
3: 8 who are **m** symbolic of things to come:
4:10 **M** will rejoice when they see the
7: 2 with their **m**, to entreat the
8: 4 "Once again **m** and women of ripe old
8:23 "In those days ten **m** from all
9: 1 upon Damascus—for the eyes of **m**
9:17 Grain will make the young **m** thrive,
10: 1 He gives showers of rain to **m**, and
10: 5 Together they will be like mighty **m**
10: 7 will become like mighty **m**,
14:13 On that day **m** will be stricken by
Mal 2: 7 and from his mouth **m** should seek
3: 3 Then the LORD will have **m** who will
Mt 4:19 "and I will make you fishers of **m**.
5:13 to be thrown out and trampled by **m**.
5:16 let your light shine before **m**, that
6: 1 before **m**, to be seen by them.
6: 2 on the streets, to be honoured by **m**.
6: 5 the street corners to be seen by **m**.
6:14 For if you forgive **m** when they sin
6:15 if you do not forgive **m** their sins,
6:16 faces to show **m** they are fasting.
6:18 that it will not be obvious to **m**
8:27 The **m** were amazed and asked, "What
8:28 **m** coming from the tombs met him.
8:33 happened to the demon-possessed **m**.
9: 2 Some **m** brought to him a paralytic,
9: 8 who had given such authority to **m**.
9:17 Neither do **m** pour new wine into old
9:27 Jesus went on from there, two blind **m**
9:28 he had gone indoors, the blind **m**
10:17 "Be on your guard against **m**; they
10:22 All **m** will hate you because of me,
10:32 "Whoever acknowledges me before **m**, I
10:33 whoever disowns me before **m**, I will
11:12 and forceful **m** lay hold of it.
12:31 and blasphemy will be forgiven **m**,
12:36 I tell you that **m** will have to give
12:41 The **m** of Nineveh will stand up at
13:17 many prophets and righteous **m** longed
14:21 **m**, besides women and children.
14:35 the **m** of that place recognised Jesus,
15: 9 are but rules taught by **m**.'"
16:23 things of God, but the things of **m**."
17:22 to be betrayed into the hands of **m**.
19:12 others were made that way by **m**; and
20: 1 to hire **m** to work in his vineyard.
20:12 'These **m** who were hired last worked
20:30 Two blind **m** were sitting by the
Mt 21:25 Was it from heaven, or from **m**?"
21:26 if we say, 'From **m**'—we are afraid
22:16 You aren't swayed by **m**, because you
23: 5 "Everything they do is done for **m** to
23: 7 and to have **m** call them 'Rabbi'.
23:19 You blind **m**! Which is greater: the
24:40 Two **m** will be in the field; one will
26:40 "Could you **m** not keep watch with me
26:50 Then the **m** stepped forward, seized
26:62 these **m** are bringing against you?"
28: 4 they shook and became like dead **m**.
Mk 1:17 "and I will make you fishers of **m**.
1:20 with the hired **m** and followed him.
2: 3 Some **m** came, bringing to him a
3:28 blasphemies of **m** will be forgiven
5:35 some **m** came from the house of Jairus,
6:21 and the leading **m** of Galilee.
6:44 The number of the **m** who had eaten
7: 7 are but rules taught by **m**.'
7: 8 holding on to the traditions of **m**."
8: 9 About four thousand **m** were present.
8:33 things of God, but the things of **m**."
9:31 to be betrayed into the hands of **m**.
11:30 it from heaven, or from **m**? Tell me!"
11:32 But if we say, 'From **m**' ...."
12:14 You aren't swayed by **m**, because you
12:40 **m** will be punished most severely."
13:13 All **m** will hate you because of me,
13:26 "At that time **m** will see the Son of
14:46 The **m** seized Jesus and arrested him.
14:60 these **m** are bringing against you?"
Lk 2:14 to **m** on whom his favour rests."
2:52 and in favour with God and **m**.
5:10 from now on you will catch **m**."
5:18 Some **m** came carrying a paralytic on
6:22 Blessed are you when **m** hate you,
6:26 Woe to you when all **m** speak well of
7:10 the **m** who had been sent returned to
7:20 the **m** came to Jesus, they said,
7:41 "Two **m** owed money to a certain
9:14 (About five thousand **m** were there.)
9:30 Two **m**, Moses and Elijah,
9:32 and the two **m** standing with him.
9:33 the **m** were leaving Jesus, Peter said
9:44 to be betrayed into the hands of **m**."
11:31 with the **m** of this generation
11:32 The **m** of Nineveh will stand up at
11:44 graves, which **m** walk over without
12: 8 whoever acknowledges me before **m**,
12: 9 he who disowns me before **m** will be
12:36 like **m** waiting for their master to
14:24 I tell you, not one of those **m** who
14:31 with ten thousand **m** to oppose the
15:17 'How many of my father's hired **m**
15:19 make me like one of your hired **m**.'
16:15 justify yourselves in the eyes of **m**
16:15 valued among **m** is detestable in
17:12 he was going into a village, ten **m**
17:23 **M** will tell you, 'There he is!' or
18: 2 feared God nor cared about **m**.
18: 4 I don't fear God or care about **m**,
18:10 "Two **m** went up to the temple to pray,
18:11 that I am not like other **m**—robbers,
18:27 with **m** is possible with God."
20: 4 it from heaven, or from **m**?"
20: 6 if we say, 'From **m**', all the people
20:47 **m** will be punished most severely."
21:17 All **m** will hate you because of me.
21:26 **M** will faint from terror,
22:63 The **m** who were guarding Jesus began
23:31 For if **m** do these things when the
23:32 Two other **m**, both criminals, were
24: 4 suddenly two **m** in clothes that
24: 5 but the **m** said to them, "Why do you
24: 7 into the hands of sinful **m**,
Jn 1: 4 and that life was the light of **m**.
1: 7 through him all **m** might believe.
2:14 In the temple courts he found **m**
2:24 himself to them, for he knew all **m**.
3:19 but **m** loved darkness instead of
5:41 "I do not accept praise from **m**,
6:10 and the **m** sat down, about five
8:17 the testimony of two **m** is valid.
12:32 earth, will draw all **m** to myself."
12:43 for they loved praise from **m** more
13:35 By this all **m** will know that you are
Jn 16: 9 in regard to sin, because **m** do not
18: 8 for me, then let these **m** go."
Ac 1: 3 he showed himself to these **m** and
1:10 **m** dressed in white stood beside them.
1:11 "**M** of Galilee," they said, "why do
1:21 choose one of the **m** who have been
1:23 they proposed two **m**: Joseph called
2: 7 these **m** who are speaking Galileans?
2:15 These **m** are not drunk, as you
2:17 your young **m** will see visions, your
2:17 your old **m** will dream dreams.
2:18 Even on my servants, both **m** and
2:23 with the help of wicked **m**, put him
4: 4 of **m** grew to about five thousand.
4: 6 other **m** of the high priest's family.
4:12 to **m** by which we must be saved."
4:13 ordinary **m**, they were astonished and
4:13 that these **m** had been with Jesus.
4:16 "What are we going to do with these **m**
4:17 we must warn these **m** to speak no
5: 4 You have not lied to **m** but to God."
5: 6 the young **m** came forward, wrapped up
5: 9 Look! The feet of the **m** who buried
5:10 Then the young **m** came in and,
5:14 Nevertheless, more and more **m** and
5:25 "Look! The **m** you put in jail are
5:29 "We must obey God rather than **m**
5:34 **m** be put outside for a little while.
5:35 what you intend to do to these **m**.
5:36 about four hundred **m** rallied to him.
5:38 Leave these **m** alone! Let them go!
5:39 will not be able to stop these **m**;
6: 3 Brothers, choose seven **m** from among
6: 6 They presented these **m** to the
6: 9 These **m** began to argue with Stephen,
6:11 they secretly persuaded some **m** to
7:26 '**M**, you are brothers; why do you
7:48 does not live in houses made by **m**.
8: 2 Godly **m** buried Stephen and mourned
8: 3 dragged of **m** and women and put
8:12 were baptised, both **m** and women.
9: 2 whether **m** or women, he might take
9: 7 The **m** travelling with Saul stood
9:38 they sent two **m** to him and urged him,
10: 5 Now send **m** to Joppa to bring back a
10:17 the **m** sent by Cornelius found out
10:19 "Simon, three **m** are looking for you.
10:21 Peter went down and said to the **m**,
10:22 The **m** replied, "We have come from
10:23 Peter invited the **m** into the house
10:35 accepts **m** from every nation who fear
11: 3 uncircumcised **m** and ate with them."
11:11 "Right then three **m** who had been
11:20 Some of them, however, **m** from Cyprus
13:50 and the leading **m** of the city.
14:15 "**M**, why are you doing this? We too
14:15 We too are only **m**, human like you.
15: 1 Some **m** came down from Judea to
15:17 that the remnant of **m** may seek the
15:22 to choose some of their own **m**
15:22 two **m** who were leaders among the
15:25 we all agreed to choose some **m** and
15:26 **m** who have risked their lives for
15:30 The **m** were sent off and went down to
16:17 "These **m** are servants of the Most
16:20 "These **m** are Jews, and are throwing
16:35 with the order: "Release those **m**.
17: 6 "These **m** who have caused trouble all
17:12 Greek women and many Greek **m**.
17:15 The **m** who escorted Paul brought him
17:22 "**M** of Athens! I see that in every
17:25 because he himself gives all **m** life
17:26 one man he made every nation of **m**,
17:27 God did this so that **m** would seek
17:31 all **m** by raising him from the dead."
17:34 A few **m** became followers of Paul and
19: 7 There were about twelve **m** in all.
19:25 said: "**M**, you know we receive a
19:35 "**M** of Ephesus, doesn't all the world
19:37 You have brought these **m** here,
20: 5 These **m** went on ahead and waited for
20:26 I am innocent of the blood of all **m**.
20:30 Even from your own number **m** will
21:23 There are four **m** with us who have
21:24 Take these **m**, join in their
21:26 The next day Paul took the **m** and

Ac 21:28 This is the man who teaches all **m**
22: 4 arresting both **m** and women and
22:15 You will be his witness to all **m** of
22:19 "'Lord,' I replied, 'these **m** know
23:13 More than forty **m** were involved in
24:15 the same hope in God as these **m**,
25:23 and the leading **m** of the city.
27:10 "**M**, I can see that our voyage is
27:17 the **m** had hoisted it aboard, they
27:21 After the **m** had gone a long time
27:21 "**M**, you should have taken my advice
27:25 keep up your courage, **m**, for I have
27:31 "Unless these **m** stay with the ship,
28:15 At the sight of these **m** Paul thanked
Ro 1:18 wickedness of **m** who suppress the
1:20 made, so that **m** are without excuse.
1:27 In the same way the **m** also abandoned
1:27 **M** committed indecent acts with other
1:27 with other **m**, and received in
2:29 praise is not from **m**, but from God.
5:12 came to all **m**, because all sinned—
5:18 trespass was condemnation for all **m**,
5:18 that brings life for all **m**.
7: 1 I am speaking to **m** who know the law
9:33 I lay in Zion a stone that causes **m**
11:32 For God has bound all **m** over to
14:18 pleasing to God and approved by **m**.
1Co 2:11 For who among **m** knows the thoughts
3: 3 Are you not acting like mere **m**?
3: 4 follow Apollos," are you not mere **m**?
3:21 then, no more boasting about **m**! All
4: 1 **m** ought to regard us as servants
4: 9 **m** condemned to die in the arena.
4: 9 universe, to angels as well as to **m**.
6: 4 **m** of little account in the church!
7: 7 I wish that all **m** were as I am. But
7:23 a price; do not become slaves of **m**.
9:22 I have become all things to all **m** so
12: 6 same God works all of them in all **m**.
13: 1 If I speak in the tongues of **m** and
14: 2 does not speak to **m** but to God.
14: 3 everyone who prophesies speaks to **m**
14:21 In the Law it is written: "Through **m**
15:19 we are to be pitied more than all **m**.
15:39 All flesh is not the same: **M** have
16: 3 introduction to the **m** you approve
16:13 faith; be **m** of courage; be strong.
16:18 Such **m** deserve recognition.
2Co 2:17 sincerity, like **m** sent from God.
3: 9 If the ministry that condemns **m** is
5:11 fear the Lord, we try to persuade **m**.
8:21 the Lord but also in the eyes of **m**.
8:24 Therefore show these **m** the proof of
9:13 **m** will praise God for the obedience
11:13 For such **m** are false apostles,
12:17 you through any of the **m** I sent you?
Gal 1: 1 Paul, an apostle—sent not from **m**
1:10 now trying to win the approval of **m**,
1:10 Or am I trying to please **m**? If I
1:10 If I were still trying to please **m**,
2: 6 **m** added nothing to my message.
2:12 Before certain **m** came from James, he
Eph 2:11 done in the body by the hands of **m**)
3: 5 which was not made known to **m** in
4: 8 in his train and gave gifts to **m**."
4:14 of **m** in their deceitful scheming.
6: 7 if you were serving the Lord, not **m**,
Php 2:29 great joy, and honour **m** like him,
3: 2 Watch out for those dogs, those **m**
Col 2:11 circumcision done by the hands of **m**,
3:23 as working for the Lord, not for **m**,
1Th 2: 4 On the contrary, we speak as **m**
2: 4 not trying to please **m** but God,
2: 6 We were not looking for praise from **m**
2:13 accepted it not as the word of **m**,
2:15 God and are hostile to all **m**
4: 6 The Lord will punish **m** for all such
4:13 the rest of **m**, who have no hope.
2Th 3: 2 evil **m**, for not everyone has faith.
1Ti 1: 3 command certain **m** not to teach
2: 4 who wants all **m** to be saved and to
2: 5 God and **m**, the man Christ Jesus,
2: 6 gave himself as a ransom for all **m**
2: 8 I want **m** everywhere to lift up holy
3: 8 Deacons, likewise, are to be **m**
4:10 who is the Saviour of all **m**, and
1Ti 5: 1 Treat younger **m** as brothers,
5:24 The sins of some **m** are obvious,
6: 5 constant friction between **m** of
6: 9 plunge **m** into ruin and destruction.
2Ti 2: 2 entrust to reliable **m** who will also
3: 8 so also these **m** oppose the truth—**m**
3: 9 as in the case of those **m**, their
3:13 while evil **m** and impostors will go
4: 3 For the time will come when **m** will
Tit 2: 2 Teach the older **m** to be temperate,
2: 6 Similarly, encourage the young **m** to
2:11 salvation has appeared to all **m**.
3: 2 to show true humility towards all **m**.
Heb 2:11 Both the one who makes **m** holy and
5: 1 priest is selected from among **m**
6:16 **M** swear by someone greater than
7: 8 the tenth is collected by **m** who die;
7:28 as high priests **m** who are weak;
8: 4 for there are already **m** who offer
12: 3 such opposition from sinful **m**,
12:14 in peace with all **m** and to be holy;
12:23 come to God, the judge of all **m**,
12:23 spirits of righteous **m** made perfect,
13:17 They keep watch over you as **m** who
Jas 3: 9 and with it we curse **m**, who have
5: 6 **m**, who were not opposing you.
1Pe 1:24 For, "All **m** are like grass, and all
2: 4 the living Stone—rejected by **m** but
2: 8 and, "A stone that causes **m** to
2:13 authority instituted among **m**:
2:15 the ignorant talk of foolish **m**.
2:16 Live as free **m**, but do not use your
4: 6 to **m** in regard to the body,
5: 5 Young **m**, in the same way be
2Pe 1:21 but **m** spoke from God as they were
2: 7 by the filthy lives of lawless **m**
2: 9 how to rescue godly **m** from trials
2:10 Bold and arrogant, these **m** are not
2:12 these **m** blaspheme in matters they do
2:17 These **m** are springs without water
3: 7 and destruction of ungodly **m**.
3:17 by the error of lawless **m** and fall
1Jn 2:13 I write to you, young **m**, because you
2:14 I write to you, young **m**, because you
3Jn : 8 show hospitality to such **m** so that
Jude : 4 For certain **m** whose condemnation was
: 4 They are godless **m**, who change the
:10 Yet these **m** speak abusively against
:12 These **m** are blemishes at your love
:14 prophesied about these **m**: "See, the
:16 These **m** are grumblers and
:19 These are the **m** who divide you, who
Rev 2: 2 that you cannot tolerate wicked **m**,
5: 9 and with your blood you purchased **m**
6: 4 earth and to make **m** slay each other.
9: 6 During those days **m** will seek death,
11: 6 These **m** have power to shut up the
11: 9 For three and a half days **m** from
13: 4 **M** worshipped the dragon because he
13:13 heaven to earth in full view of **m**.
14: 4 They were purchased from among **m** and
16:10 **M** gnawed their tongues in agony
16:21 a hundred pounds each fell upon **m**.
18:13 and bodies and souls of **m**.
18:23 merchants were the world's great **m**.
19:18 generals, and mighty **m**, of horses
21: 3 with **m**, and he will live with them.

Men of Israel

Nu 26:51 The total number of the **m** was 601,730
Dt 29:10 and officials, and all the other **m**,
Jos 9: 6 at Gilgal and said to him and the **m**,
9: 7 The **m** said to the Hivites, "But
9:14 The **m** sampled their provisions but
10:24 he summoned all the **m** and said to
Jdg 20:11 all the **m** got together and united as
20:20 The **m** went out to fight the
20:22 the **m** encouraged one another and
20:33 All the **m** moved from their places
20:36 Now the **m** had given way before
20:38 The **m** had arranged with the ambush
20:39 the **m** would turn in the battle. The
20:39 casualties on the **m** (about thirty),
20:41 the **m** turned on them, and the men of
20:42 And the **m** who came out of the towns
Jdg 20:48 The **m** went back to Benjamin and put
21: 1 The **m** had taken an oath at Mizpah:
1Sa 7:11 The **m** rushed out of Mizpah and
8:22 Then Samuel said to the **m**,
11: 8 Saul mustered them at Bezek, the **m**
13: 6 the **m** saw that their situation was
14:24 Now the **m** were in distress that day,
17:19 They are with Saul and all the **m** in
17:52 the **m** and Judah surged forward with
26: 2 chosen **m**, to search there for David.
2Sa 2:17 the **m** were defeated by David's men.
15: 6 and so he stole the hearts of the **m**.
15:13 hearts of the **m** are with Absalom."
16:15 Meanwhile, Absalom and all the **m**
16:18 by these people and by all the **m**—
17:14 Absalom and all the **m** said, "The
17:24 crossed the Jordan with all the **m**.
19:41 Soon all the **m** were coming to the
19:42 All the men of Judah answered the **m**,
19:43 the **m** answered the men of Judah, "We
19:43 even more harshly than the **m**.
20: 2 all the **m** deserted David to follow
23: 9 for battle. Then the **m** retreated,
24: 4 of the king to enrol the fighting **m**.
1Ki 8: 2 All the **m** came together to King
1Ch 21:14 and seventy thousand **m** fell dead.
2Ch 5: 3 all the **m** came together to the king
13:12 **M**, do not fight against the LORD,
13:18 The **m** were subdued on that occasion,
31: 6 The **m** and Judah who lived in the
Ne 7: 7 Nehum and Baanah): The list of the **m**:
Ps 78:31 them, cutting down the young **m**.
Ac 2:22 "**M**, listen to this: Jesus of
3:12 Peter saw this, he said to them: "**M**,
5:35 he addressed them: "**M**, consider
13:16 "**M** and you Gentiles who worship God,
21:28 shouting, "**M**, help us! This is the

Men's (Man)

Ge 44: 1 "Fill the **m** sacks with as much food
Ex 30:32 Do not pour it on **m** bodies and do
Dt 22: 5 A woman must not wear **m** clothing,
1Sa 21: 5 The **m** things are holy even on
2Ki 19:18 and stone, fashioned by **m** hands.
2Ch 32:19 of the world—the work of **m** hands.
Mt 23: 4 loads and put them on **m** shoulders,
23:13 the kingdom of heaven in **m** faces.
23:27 dead **m** bones and everything unclean.
Mk 7:21 For from within, out of **m** hearts,
Ro 2:16 **m** secrets through Jesus Christ,
1Co 2: 5 faith might not rest on **m** wisdom,
4: 5 will expose the motives of **m** hearts.
2Co 5:19 not counting **m** sins against them.

Menahem (Menahem's)

2Ki 15:14 **M** son of Gadi went from Tirzah up to
15:16 At that time **M**, starting out from
15:17 **M** son of Gadi became king of Israel,
15:19 and **M** gave him a thousand talents of
15:20 **M** exacted this money from Israel.
15:22 **M** rested with his fathers. And
15:23 Pekahiah son of **M** became king of

Menahem's (Menahem)

2Ki 15:21 for the other events of **M** reign, and

Mend (Mended)

Ps 60: 2 **m** its fractures, for it is quaking.
Ecc 3: 7 a time to tear and a time to **m**, a

Mended (Mend)

Jos 9: 4 and old wineskins, cracked and **m**.

Mene

Da 5:25 written: M, M, tekel, parsin
5:26 "This is what these words mean: **M**:

Menna

Lk 3:31 the son of Melea, the son of **M**, the

Menservants (Servant)

Ge 12:16 **m** and maidservants, and camels.
24:35 silver and gold, **m** and maidservants,

Ge 30:43 and **m**, and camels and donkeys.
32: 5 sheep and goats, **m** and maidservants.
Ex 21: 7 she is not to go free as **m** do.
Dt 12:12 your sons and daughters, your **m** and
12:18 your sons and daughters, your **m** and
16:11 your sons and daughters, your **m** and
16:14 your sons and daughters, your **m** and
1Sa 8:16 Your **m** and maidservants and the best
2Ki 5:26 herds, or **m** and maidservants?
Ezr 2:65 besides their 7,337 **m** and
Ne 7:67 besides their 7,337 **m** and
Job 31:13 "If I have denied justice to my **m**
Isa 14: 2 Israel will possess the nations as **m**
Lk 12:45 he then begins to beat the **m** and

Menstrual
Isa 30:22 away like a **m** cloth and say to them,

Mention (Mentioned, Mentioning)
Ge 40:14 show me kindness; **m** me to Pharoah
Job 28:18 Coral and jasper are not worthy of **m**;
Isa 49: 1 my birth he has made **m** of my name.
Jer 19: 5 or **m**, nor did it enter my mind.
20: 9 if I say, "I will not **m** him or speak
23:36 you must not **m** 'the oracle of the
Eze 16:56 You would not even **m** your sister
Am 6:10 We must not **m** the name of the LORD."
Jn 5:34 but I **m** it that you may be saved.
Eph 5:12 For it is shameful even to **m** what
Phm :19 to **m** that you owe me your very self.

Mentioned (Mention)
Ru 4: 1 When the kinsman-redeemer he had **m**
1Sa 4:18 he **m** the ark of God, Eli fell
Isa 14:20 of the wicked will never be **m** again.
19:17 whom Judah is **m** will be terrified,

Mentioning (Mention)
1Th 1: 2 We always thank God for all of you, **m**

Meonothai
1Ch 4:13 The sons of Othniel: Hathath and **M**.
4:14 **M** was the father of Ophrah. Seraiah

Mephaath
Jos 13:18 Jahaz, Kedemoth, **M**,
21:37 Kedemoth and **M**, together with their
1Ch 6:79 Kedemoth and **M**, together with their
Jer 48:21 plateau—to Holon, Jahzah and **M**,

Mephibosheth
1. Son of Jonathan; also called Merib-Baal (1Ch 8:34; 9:40). Crippled by a fall (2Sa 4:4); shown kindness by David (2Sa 9:1–13). Slandered by Ziba (2Sa 16:1–4); reconciled to David (2Sa 19:24–30). **2.** Son of Saul, executed by the Gibeonites (2Sa 21:8–9).

2Sa 4: 4 became crippled. His name was **M**.)
9: 6 **M** son of Jonathan, the son of Saul,
9: 6 David said, "**M**!" "Your servant," he
9: 8 **M** bowed down and said, "What is your
9:10 And **M**, grandson of your master, will
9:11 So **M** ate at David's table like one
9:12 **M** had a young son named Mica, and
9:12 Ziba's household were servants of **M**.
9:13 **M** lived in Jerusalem, because he
16: 1 steward of **M**, waiting to meet him.
16: 4 that belonged to **M** is now yours.
19:24 **M**, Saul's grandson, also went down
19:25 "Why didn't you go with me, **M**?
19:30 **M** said to the king, "Let him take
21: 7 The king spared **M** son of Jonathan,
21: 8 the king took Armoni and **M**, the two

Merab
1Sa 14:49 The name of his older daughter was **M**,
18:17 David, "Here is my older daughter **M**.
18:19 when the time came for **M**, Saul's
2Sa 21: 8 the five sons of Saul's daughter **M**,

Meraiah
Ne 12:12 family, **M**; of Jeremiah's, Hananiah;

Meraioth
1Ch 6: 6 Zerahiah, Zerahiah the father of **M**,
6: 7 **M** the father of Amariah, Amariah the
6:52 **M** his son, Amariah his son, Ahitub
9:11 the son of Zadok, the son of **M**, the
Ezr 7: 3 the son of Azariah, the son of **M**,
Ne 11:11 the son of Zadok, the son of **M**, the

Merari (Merarite, Merarites)
Ge 46:11 sons of Levi: Gershon, Kohath and **M**.
Ex 6:16 records: Gershon, Kohath and **M**.
6:19 The sons of **M** were Mahli and Mushi.
Nu 3:17 sons of Levi: Gershon, Kohath and **M**.
3:33 To **M** belonged the clans of the
26:57 clan; through **M**, the Merarite clan.
Jos 21: 7 The descendants of **M**, clan by clan,
1Ch 6: 1 sons of Levi: Gershon, Kohath and **M**.
6:16 sons of Levi: Gershon, Kohath and **M**.
6:19 The sons of **M**: Mahli and Mushi.
6:29 The descendants of **M**: Mahli, Libni
6:47 Mushi, the son of **M**, the son of Levi.
6:63 The descendants of **M**, clan by clan,
15: 6 from the descendants of **M**, Asaiah
23: 6 sons of Levi: Gershon, Kohath and **M**.
23:21 The sons of **M**: Mahli and Mushi. The
24:26 The sons of **M**: Mahli and Mushi. The
24:27 The sons of **M**: from Jaaziah: Beno,
26:19 who were descendants of Korah and **M**.
2Ch 34:12 Levites descended from **M**, and
Ezr 8:19 Jeshaiah from the descendants of **M**,

Merarite (Merari)
Nu 3:20 The **M** clans: Mahli and Mushi. These
3:33 Mushites; these were the **M** clans.
3:35 The leader of the families of the **M**
4:33 This is the service of the **M** clans
4:45 the total of those in the **M** clans.
26:57 clan; through Merari, the **M** clan.
Jos 21:34 The **M** clans (the rest of the Levites)
21:40 the towns allotted to the **M** clans,
1Ch 9:14 Azrikam, the son of Hashabiah, a **M**;
26:10 Hosah the **M** had sons: Shimri the

Merarites (Merari)
Nu 3:36 The **M** were appointed to take care of
4:29 "Count the **M** by their clans and
4:42 The **M** were counted by their clans
7: 8 to the **M**, as their work required.
10:17 and **M**, who carried it, set out.
1Ch 6:44 from their associates, the **M**, at his
6:77 The **M** (the rest of the Levites)
15:17 the **M**, Ethan son of Kushaiah;
2Ch 29:12 and Joel son of Azariah; from the **M**,

Merathaim
Jer 50:21 "Attack the land of **M** and those who

Mercenaries
Jer 46:21 The **m** in her ranks are like fattened

Merchandise
Ne 10:31 **m** or grain to sell on the Sabbath,
13:16 all kinds of **m** and selling them in
Isa 45:14 "The products of Egypt and the **m** of
Eze 26:12 plunder your wealth and loot your **m**;
27:12 iron, tin and lead for your **m**.
27:14 war horses and mules for your **m**.
27:16 linen, coral and rubies for your **m**.
27:19 your **m**; they exchanged wrought iron,
27:22 for your **m** they exchanged the finest
27:27 Your wealth, **m** and wares, your
27:33 your **m** went out on the seas, you
Mk 11:16 would not allow anyone to carry **m**

Merchant (Merchants)
Pr 31:14 She is like the **m** ships, bringing
SS 3: 6 made from all the spices of the **m**?
Eze 27: 3 **m** of peoples on many coasts, 'This
Hos 12: 7 The **m** uses dishonest scales; he
Mt 13:45 is like a **m** looking for fine pearls.

Merchants (Merchant)
Ge 23:16 to the weight current among the **m**.
37:28 when the Midianite **m** came by, his
1Ki 10:15 not including the revenues from **m**
10:28 royal **m** purchased them from Kue.
2Ch 1:16 royal **m** purchased them from Kue.
9:14 brought in by **m** and traders.
Ne 3:31 of the temple servants and the **m**,
3:32 the goldsmiths and **m** made repairs.
13:20 Once or twice the **m** and sellers of
Job 6:19 travelling **m** of Sheba look in hope.
41: 6 Will they divide him up among the **m**?
Ps 107:23 they were **m** on the mighty waters.
Pr 31:24 and supplies the **m** with sashes.
Isa 23: 2 you people of the island and you **m**
23: 8 the bestower of crowns, whose **m** are
Eze 16:29 a land of **m**, but even with this you
17: 4 and carried it away to a land of **m**,
27:22 "'The **m** of Sheba and Raamah traded
27:23 "'Haran, Canneh and Eden and **m** of
27:27 seamen and shipwrights, your **m** and
27:36 The **m** among the nations hiss at you;
38:13 and Dedan and the **m** of Tarshish
Na 3:16 have increased the number of your **m**
Zep 1:11 all your **m** will be wiped out,
Rev 18: 3 and the **m** of the earth grew rich
18:11 "The **m** of the earth will weep and
18:15 The **m** who sold these things and
18:23 Your **m** were the world's great men.

Merciful (Mercy)
Ge 19:16 city, for the LORD was **m** to them.
Dt 4:31 For the LORD your God is a **m** God; he
1Ki 20:31 kings of the house of Israel are **m**.
Ne 9:31 for you are a gracious and **m** God.
Ps 4: 1 be **m** to me and hear my prayer.
6: 2 Be **m** to me, LORD, for I am faint;
26:11 life; redeem me and be **m** to me.
27: 7 O LORD; be **m** to me and answer me.
30:10 Hear, O LORD, and be **m** to me; O LORD,
31: 9 Be **m** to me, O LORD, for I am in
56: 1 Be **m** to me, O God, for men hotly
77: 9 Has God forgotten to be **m**? Has he in
78:38 Yet he was **m**; he forgave their
Jer 3:12 frown on you no longer, for I am **m**,'
Da 9: 9 The Lord our God is **m** and forgiving,
Mt 5: 7 Blessed are the **m**, for they will be
Lk 1:54 servant Israel, remembering to be **m**
6:36 Be **m**, just as your Father is **m**.
Heb 2:17 in order that he might become a **m**
Jas 2:13 shown to anyone who has not been **m**.
Jude :22 Be **m** to those who doubt;

Merciless
Pr 17:11 **m** official will be sent against him.

Mercy (Merciful)
Ge 43:14 may God Almighty grant you **m** before
Ex 33:19 I will have **m** on whom I will have **m**,
Dt 7: 2 with them, and show them no **m**.
13:17 fierce anger; he will show you **m**,
Jos 11:20 exterminating them without **m**, as
2Sa 24:14 for his **m** is great; but do not let
1Ki 8:28 and his plea for **m**, O LORD my God.
8:50 their conquerors to show them **m**;
1Ch 21:13 for his **m** is very great; but do not
2Ch 6:19 and his plea for **m**, O LORD my God.
Ne 9:31 in your great **m** you did not put an
13:22 show **m** to me according to your great
Est 4: 8 beg for **m** and plead with him for her
Job 9:15 only plead with my Judge for **m**.
27:22 hurls itself against him without **m**
41: 3 Will he keep begging you for **m**? Will
Ps 5: 7 I, by your great **m**, will come into
6: 9 The LORD has heard my cry for **m**; the
9:13 Have **m** and lift me up from the gates
25: 6 Remember, O LORD, your great **m** and
28: 2 Hear my cry for **m** as I call to you
28: 6 LORD, for he has heard my cry for **m**.
30: 8 I called; to the Lord I cried for **m**:
31:22 for **m** when I called to you for help.
40:11 Do not withhold your **m** from me,
41: 4 I said, "O LORD, have **m** on me; heal
41:10 you, O LORD, have **m** on me; raise me
51: 1 Have **m** on me, O God, according to

Ps 57: 1 Have **m** on me, O God, have **m** on me,
59: 5 show no **m** to wicked traitors.
69:16 love; in your great **m** turn to me.
79: 8 may your **m** come quickly to meet us,
86: 3 Have **m** on me, O Lord, for I call to
86: 6 O LORD; listen to my cry for **m**.
86:16 Turn to me and have **m** on me; grant
116: 1 my voice; he heard my cry for **m**.
119:132 Turn to me and have **m** on me, as you
123: 2 LORD our God, till he shows us his **m**.
123: 3 Have **m** on us, O LORD, have **m** on us,
130: 2 ears be attentive to my cry for **m**.
140: 6 Hear, O LORD, my cry for **m**.
142: 1 I lift up my voice to the LORD for **m**.
143: 1 listen to my cry for **m**; in your
Pr 6:34 show no **m** when he takes revenge.
18:23 A poor man pleads for **m**, but a rich
21:10 his neighbour gets no **m** from him.
28:13 and renounces them finds **m**.
Isa 13:18 they will have no **m** on infants nor
47: 6 your hand, and you showed them no **m**.
55: 7 and he will have **m** on him, and to
63: 9 In his love and **m** he redeemed them;
Jer 6:23 spear; they are cruel and show no **m**.
13:14 I will allow no pity or **m** or
21: 7 them no **m** or pity or compassion.'
50:42 they are cruel and without **m**.
Da 2:18 He urged them to plead for **m** from
9:18 but because of your great **m**.
Hos 6: 6 For I desire **m**, not sacrifice, and
Am 5:15 have **m** on the remnant of Joseph.
Mic 6: 8 To act justly and to love **m** and to
7:18 for ever but delight to show **m**.
7:20 will be true to Jacob, and show **m**
Hab 1:17 net, destroying nations without **m**?
3: 2 them known; in wrath remember **m**.
Zec 1:12 how long will you withhold **m** from
1:16 'I will return to Jerusalem with **m**,
7: 9 **m** and compassion to one another.
Mt 5: 7 merciful, for they will be shown **m**.
9:13 means: 'I desire **m**, not sacrifice.
9:27 "Have **m** on us, Son of David!
12: 7 'I desire **m**, not sacrifice,' you
15:22 "Lord, Son of David, have **m** on me!
17:15 "Lord, have **m** on my son," he said.
18:33 Shouldn't you have had **m** on your
20:30 "Lord, Son of David, have **m** on us!
20:31 "Lord, Son of David, have **m** on us!
23:23 law—justice, **m** and faithfulness.
Mk 5:19 you, and how he has had **m** on you."
10:47 "Jesus, Son of David, have **m** on me!
10:48 "Son of David, have **m** on me!
Lk 1:50 His **m** extends to those who fear him,
1:58 great **m**, and they shared her joy.
1:72 to show **m** to our fathers and to
1:78 of the tender **m** of our God, by which
10:37 replied, "The one who had **m** on him.
18:13 said, 'God, have **m** on me, a sinner.'
18:38 "Jesus, Son of David, have **m** on me!
18:39 "Son of David, have **m** on me!
Ro 9:15 "I will have **m** on whom I have **m**, and
9:16 desire or effort, but on God's **m**.
9:18 Therefore God has **m** on whom he wants
9:18 God has **m** on whom he wants to have **m**,
9:23 glory known to the objects of his **m**,
11:30 **m** as a result of their disobedience,
11:31 **m** as a result of God's **m** to you.
11:32 so that he may have **m** on them all.
12: 1 brothers, in view of God's **m**, to
12: 8 showing **m**, let him do it cheerfully.
15: 9 Gentiles may glorify God for his **m**,
1Co 7:25 who by the Lord's **m** is trustworthy.
2Co 4: 1 Therefore, since through God's **m** we
Gal 6:16 Peace and **m** to all who follow this
Eph 2: 4 love for us, God, who is rich in **m**,
Php 2:27 But God had **m** on him, and not on him
1Ti 1: 2 **m** and peace from God the Father and
1:13 I was shown **m** because I acted in
1:16 for that very reason I was shown **m**
2Ti 1: 2 To Timothy, my dear son: Grace, **m**
1:16 May the Lord show **m** to the household
1:18 find **m** from the Lord on that day!
Tit 3: 5 we had done, but because of his **m**.
Heb 4:16 so that we may receive **m** and find
10:28 died without **m** on the testimony of
Jas 2:13 judgment without **m** will be shown to
2:13 **M** triumphs over judgment!
3:17 considerate, submissive, full of **m**
5:11 The Lord is full of compassion and **m**.
1Pe 1: 3 In his great **m** he has given us new
2:10 **m**, but now you have received **m**.
2Jn : 3 Grace, **m** and peace from God the
Jude : 2 **M**, peace and love be yours in
:21 as you wait for the **m** of our Lord
:23 and save them; to others show **m**,

Mered (Mered's)

1Ch 4:17 The sons of Ezrah: Jether, **M**, Epher
4:18 Bithiah, whom **M** had married.

Mered's (Mered)

1Ch 4:17 One of **M** wives gave birth to Miriam,

Meremoth (Meremoth's)

Ezr 8:33 hands of **M** son of Uriah, the priest.
10:36 Vaniah, **M**, Eliashib,
Ne 3: 4 **M** son of Uriah, the son of Hakkoz,
3:21 Next to him, **M** son of Uriah, the son
10: 5 Harim, **M**, Obadiah,
12: 3 Shecaniah, Rehum, **M**,

Meremoth's (Meremoth)

Ne 12:15 of Harim's, Adna; of **M**, Helkai;

Meres

Est 1:14 Shethar, Admatha, Tarshish, **M**,

Meribah

1. Place of a spring near Rephidim, in the Desert of Sin. Means "strife". Here the Israelites grumbled against Moses because of lack of water and God provided water when Moses struck a rock (Ex 17:1–7). Also known as Massah (Ex 17:7; Dt 6:16; 9:22; 33:8; Ps 95:8). **2.** Place of a spring near Kadesh, in the Desert of Zin. Once again the Israelites grumbled about lack of water, and water was provided despite Moses' rebellion (Nu 20:1–13). Also known as Meribah Kadesh (Nu 27:14; Dt 32:51).

Ex 17: 7 he called the place Massah and **M**
Nu 20:13 These were the waters of **M**, where
20:24 my command at the waters of **M**.
Dt 33: 8 with him at the waters of **M**.
Ps 81: 7 I tested you at the waters of **M**.
95: 8 harden your hearts as you did at **M**,
106:32 By the waters of **M** they angered the

Meribah Kadesh

Nu 27:14 waters of **M**, in the Desert of Zin.)
Dt 32:51 waters of **M** in the Desert of Zin
Eze 47:19 Tamar as far as the waters of **M**,
48:28 south from Tamar to the waters of **M**,

Merib-Baal

1Ch 8:34 The son of Jonathan: **M**, who was the
9:40 The son of Jonathan: **M**, who was the

Merodach-Baladan

2Ki 20:12 At that time **M** son of Baladan king
Isa 39: 1 At that time **M** son of Baladan king

Merom

Jos 11: 5 Waters of **M**, to fight against Israel.
11: 7 the Waters of **M** and attacked them,

Meronoth (Meronothite)

Ne 3: 7 Jadon of **M**—places under the

Meronothite (Meronoth)

1Ch 27:30 the **M** was in charge of the donkeys.

Meroz

Jdg 5:23 'Curse **M**,' said the angel of the

Merriment (Merry)

Isa 32:13 of **m** and for this city of revelry.

Merry (Merriment, Merrymakers)

Job 21:12 make **m** to the sound of the flute.
Ecc 10:19 and wine makes life **m**, but money is
Jer 15:17 never made **m** with them; I sat alone
Lk 12:19 Take life easy; eat, drink and be **m**."

Merrymakers (Merry)

Isa 24: 7 the vine withers; all the **m** groan.

Mesh

Job 18: 8 a net and he wanders into its **m**.

Mesha

Ge 10:30 stretched from **M** towards Sephar,
2Ki 3: 4 Now **M** king of Moab raised sheep, and
1Ch 2:42 of Jerahmeel: **M** his firstborn,
8: 9 he had Jobab, Zibia, **M**, Malcam,

Meshach

Formerly Mishael; member of Jewish nobility taken to Babylon with Daniel, Shadrach and Abednego (Da 1:3–7). Refused unclean food (Da 1:8–16); appointed as administrator (Da 2:49). Refused to worship golden image; kept safe in fiery furnace (Da 3).

Da 1: 7 Mishael, **M**; and to Azariah, Abednego.
2:49 **M** and Abednego administrators over
3:12 **M** and Abednego—who pay no attention
3:13 summoned Shadrach, **M** and Abednego.
3:14 "Is it true, Shadrach, **M** and
3:16 Shadrach, **M** and Abednego replied to
3:19 **M** and Abednego, and his attitude
3:20 **M** and Abednego and throw them into
3:22 took up Shadrach, **M** and Abednego,
3:26 "Shadrach, **M** and Abednego, servants
3:26 **M** and Abednego came out of the fire,
3:28 "Praise be to the God of Shadrach, **M**
3:29 **M** and Abednego be cut into pieces
3:30 the king promoted Shadrach, **M** and

Meshech

Ge 10: 2 Madai, Javan, Tubal, **M** and Tiras.
10:23 sons of Aram: Uz, Hul, Gether and **M**.
1Ch 1: 5 Madai, Javan, Tubal, **M** and Tiras.
1:17 sons of Aram: Uz, Hul, Gether and **M**.
Ps 120: 5 Woe to me that I dwell in **M**, that I
Eze 27:13 "'Greece, Tubal and **M** traded with
32:26 "**M** and Tubal are there, with all
38: 2 of **M** and Tubal; prophesy against
38: 3 O Gog, chief prince of **M** and Tubal.
39: 1 O Gog, chief prince of **M** and Tubal.

Meshelemiah

1Ch 9:21 Zechariah son of **M** was the
26: 1 From the Korahites: **M** son of Kore,
26: 2 **M** had sons: Zechariah the firstborn,
26: 9 **M** had sons and relatives, who were

Meshezabel

Ne 3: 4 the son of **M**, made repairs, and next
10:21 **M**, Zadok, Jaddua,
11:24 Pethahiah son of **M**, one of the

Meshillemith

1Ch 9:12 the son of **M**, the son of Immer.

Meshillemoth

2Ch 28:12 Berekiah son of **M**, Jehizkiah son of
Ne 11:13 the son of **M**, the son of Immer,

Meshobab

1Ch 4:34 **M**, Jamlech, Joshah son of Amaziah,

Meshullam

2Ki 22: 3 son of **M**, to the temple of the LORD.
1Ch 3:19 The sons of Zerubbabel: **M** and
5:13 by families, were: Michael, **M**, Sheba,
8:17 Zebadiah, **M**, Hizki, Heber,
9: 7 Of the Benjamites: Sallu son of **M**,
9: 8 the son of Micri; and **M** son of
9:11 Azariah son of Hilkiah, the son of **M**,
9:12 the son of Jahzerah, the son of **M**,
2Ch 34:12 and **M**, descended from Kohath.

Ezr 8:16 Elnathan, Nathan, Zechariah and **M**,
10:15 supported by **M** and Shabbethai the
10:29 From the descendants of Bani: **M**,
Ne 3: 4 Next to him **M** son of Berekiah, the
3: 6 of Paseah and **M** son of Besodeiah.
3:30 Next to them, **M** son of Berekiah made
6:18 the daughter of **M** son of Berekiah.
8: 4 Hashbaddanah, Zechariah and **M**.
10: 7 **M**, Abijah, Mijamin,
10:20 Magpiash, **M**, Hezir,
11: 7 of Benjamin: Sallu son of **M**,
11:11 Seraiah son of Hilkiah, the son of **M**,
12:13 of Ezra's, **M**; of Amariah's,
12:16 Iddo's, Zechariah; of Ginnethon's, **M**;
12:25 Mattaniah, Bakbukiah, Obadiah, **M**,
12:33 along with Azariah, Ezra, **M**,

Meshullemeth

2Ki 21:19 His mother's name was **M** daughter of

Mesopotamia

Means "between the rivers", used in the NT to refer to the region around the Euphrates and Tigris. In the OT it was known as Aram Naharaim, Paddan Aram or simply as "beyond the river". Original home of Abraham, where he worshipped other gods (Jos 24:14–15) and where God first appeared to him (Ac 7:2; Jos 24:2–3). Home of Rebekah (Ge 24:10; 25:20), Leah and Rachel (Ge 28:2, 5–7; 29:1–28) and several sons of Jacob (Ge 35:26; 46:15). Jacob lived here for a time (Ge 27:43–44; 28:2) but left to return to Canaan (Ge 31:17–18; 33:18). Home of Balaam (Dt 23:4). Its armies fought with Aram (Jdg 3:8; 2Sa 10:16; 1Ch 19:16), defeating the Israelites (Isa 7:20), and scattering them across this region (1Ki 14:15). Its people were in the crowd at Pentecost (Ac 2:9).

Ac 2: 9 Medes and Elamites; residents of **M**,
7: 2 in **M**, before he lived in Haran.

Message (Messenger, Messengers)

Ge 32: 5 Now I am sending this **m** to my lord,
38:25 she sent a **m** to her father-in-law.
50:17 their **m** came to him, Joseph wept.
Nu 22:10 Zippor, king of Moab, sent me this **m**:
23: 5 The LORD put a **m** in Balaam's mouth
23: 5 back to Balak and give him this **m**."
23:16 The LORD met with Balaam and put a **m**
23:16 back to Balak and give him this **m**."
Dt 18:21 "How can we know when a **m** has not
18:22 that is a **m** the LORD has not spoken.
Jos 2: 3 the king of Jericho sent this **m** to
5:14 **m** does my Lord have for his servant?"
Jdg 3:19 "I have a secret **m** for you, O king.
3:20 said, "I have a **m** from God for you.
11:28 to the **m** Jephthah sent him.
1Sa 9:27 that I may give you a **m** from God."
15: 1 listen now to the **m** from the LORD.
25: 9 gave Nabal this **m** in David's name.
2Sa 17:16 Now send a **m** immediately and tell
19:11 King David sent this **m** to Zadok and
1Ki 5: 2 Solomon sent back this **m** to Hiram:
5: 7 Hiram heard Solomon's **m**, he was
5: 8 "I have received the **m** you sent me
13:32 For the **m** he declared by the word of
20:10 Ben-Hadad sent another **m** to Ahab:
20:12 Ben-Hadad heard this **m** while he and
2Ki 3: 7 He also sent this **m** to Jehoshaphat
5: 8 he sent him this **m**: "Why have you
9: 5 "I have a **m** for you, commander," he
10: 5 the guardians sent this **m** to Jehu:
14: 9 "A thistle in Lebanon sent a **m** to a
18:14 Hezekiah king of Judah sent this **m**
19:20 Isaiah son of Amoz sent a **m** to
2Ch 2: 3 Solomon sent this **m** to Hiram king of
25:18 "A thistle in Lebanon sent a **m** to a
32: 9 this **m** for Hezekiah king of Judah
Ezr 4:14 sending this **m** to inform the king,
Ne 6: 2 Sanballat and Geshem sent me this **m**:
6: 4 Four times they sent me the same **m**,
6: 5 his assistant to me with the same **m**,
Pr 26: 6 of a **m** by the hand of a fool.
Isa 9: 8 The Lord has sent a **m** against Jacob;
28: 9 To whom is he explaining his **m**? To
28:19 of this **m** will bring sheer terror.
Isa 30:12 "Because you have rejected this **m**,
37:21 Isaiah son of Amoz sent a **m** to
53: 1 Who has believed our **m** and to whom
Jer 3:12 Go, proclaim this **m** towards the
7: 2 house and there proclaim this **m**:
18: 2 and there I will give you my **m**."
22: 1 of Judah and proclaim this **m** there:
23:21 yet they have run with their **m**; I
27: 4 Give them a **m** for their masters and
27:12 I gave the same **m** to Zedekiah king
29:28 He has sent this **m** to us in Babylon:
29:31 "Send this **m** to all the exiles:
37: 3 to Jeremiah the prophet with this **m**:
44:16 "We will not listen to the **m** you
46: 2 Concerning Egypt: This is the **m**
46:13 This is the **m** the LORD spoke to
49:14 I have heard a **m** from the LORD: An
51:59 This is the **m** Jeremiah gave to the
Eze 33:30 the **m** that has come from the LORD.'
Da 9:23 the **m** and understand the vision:
10: 1 Its **m** was true and it concerned a
10: 1 of the **m** came to him in a vision.
Am 7:10 Amaziah the priest of Bethel sent a **m**
Ob : 1 We have heard a **m** from the LORD:
Jnh 3: 2 proclaim to it the **m** I give you.
Hag 1:12 God and the **m** of the prophet Haggai,
1:13 the LORD's messenger, gave this **m** of
Mt 10: 7 you go, preach this **m**: 'The kingdom
13:19 anyone hears the **m** about the kingdom
27:19 his wife sent him this **m**: "Don't
Mk 1: 7 this was his **m**: "After me will come
Lk 4:32 because his **m** had authority.
Jn 12:38 "Lord, who has believed our **m** and to
17:20 will believe in me through their **m**,
Ac 2:41 Those who accepted his **m** were
4: 4 many who heard the **m** believed, and
5:20 people the full **m** of this new life."
10:36 You know the **m** God sent to the
10:44 Spirit came on all who heard the **m**.
11:14 He will bring you a **m** through which
11:19 Antioch, telling the **m** only to Jews.
13:15 if you have a **m** of encouragement
13:26 this **m** of salvation has been sent.
14: 3 who confirmed the **m** of his grace by
15: 7 the **m** of the gospel and believe.
15:31 and were glad for its encouraging **m**.
16:14 her heart to respond to Paul's **m**.
17:11 for they received the **m** with great
19:31 friends of Paul, sent him a **m**
Ro 10:16 "Lord, who has believed our **m**?
10:17 faith comes from hearing the **m**, and
10:17 and the **m** is heard through the word
1Co 1:18 the **m** of the cross is foolishness
2: 4 My **m** and my preaching were not with
2: 6 We do, however, speak a **m** of wisdom
12: 8 through the Spirit the **m** of wisdom,
12: 8 to another the **m** of knowledge by
2Co 1:18 as surely as God is faithful, our **m**
5:19 to us the **m** of reconciliation.
Gal 2: 6 men added nothing to my **m**.
Col 4: 3 that God may open a door for our **m**,
1Th 1: 6 you welcomed the **m** with the joy
1: 8 The Lord's **m** rang out from you not
2Th 3: 1 brothers, pray for us that the **m** of
1Ti 4:14 given you through a prophetic **m**
2Ti 4:15 because he strongly opposed our **m**.
4:17 so that through me the **m** might be
Tit 1: 9 trustworthy **m** as it has been taught,
Heb 2: 2 For if the **m** spoken by angels was
4: 2 just as they did; but the **m** they
1Pe 2: 8 stumble because they disobey the **m**
1Jn 1: 5 This is the **m** we have heard from him
2: 7 old command is the **m** you have heard.
3:11 This is the **m** you heard from the

Messenger (Message)

1Sa 23:27 a **m** came to Saul, saying, "Come
2Sa 11:19 He instructed the **m**: "When you have
11:22 The **m** set out, and when he arrived
11:23 The **m** said to David, "The men
11:25 David told the **m**, "Say this to Joab:
15:13 A **m** came and told David, "The hearts
1Ki 19: 2 Jezebel sent a **m** to Elijah to say,
22:13 The **m** who had gone to summon Micaiah
2Ki 5:10 Elisha sent a **m** to say to him, "Go,
2Ki 6:32 The king sent a **m** ahead, but before
6:32 when the **m** comes, shut the door and
6:33 to them, the **m** came down to him.
9:18 The lookout reported, "The **m** has
10: 8 the **m** arrived, he told Jehu, "They
2Ch 18:12 The **m** who had gone to summon Micaiah
Job 1:14 a **m** came to Job and said, "The oxen
1:16 another **m** came and said, "The fire
1:17 another **m** came and said, "The
1:18 yet another **m** came and said, "Your
Pr 13:17 A wicked **m** falls into trouble, but a
16:14 A king's wrath is a **m** of death, but
25:13 trustworthy **m** to those who send him;
Ecc 5: 6 do not protest to the ⌊temple⌋ **m**,
Isa 41:27 to Jerusalem a **m** of good tidings.
42:19 and deaf like the **m** I send? Who is
Jer 51:31 **m** follows **m** to announce to the king
Da 4:13 and there before me was a **m**, a holy
4:23 "You, O king, saw a **m**, a holy one,
Hag 1:13 Haggai, the LORD's **m**, gave this
Mal 2: 7 he is the **m** of the LORD Almighty.
3: 1 "See, I will send my **m**, who will
3: 1 his temple; the **m** of the covenant,
Mt 11:10 'I will send my **m** ahead of you, who
Mk 1: 2 "I will send my **m** ahead of you, who
Lk 7:27 'I will send my **m** ahead of you, who
Jn 13:16 **m** greater than the one who sent him.
2Co 12: 7 flesh, a **m** of Satan, to torment me.
Php 2:25 who is also your **m**, whom you sent to

Messengers (Message)

Ge 32: 3 Jacob sent **m** ahead of him to his
32: 6 the **m** returned to Jacob, they said,
Nu 20:14 Moses sent **m** from Kadesh to the king
21:21 Israel sent **m** to say to Sihon king
22: 5 sent **m** to summon Balaam son of Beor,
24:12 "Did I not tell the **m** you sent
Dt 2:26 From the desert of Kedemoth I sent **m**
Jos 7:22 Joshua sent **m**, and they ran to the
Jdg 6:35 He sent **m** throughout Manasseh,
7:24 Gideon sent **m** throughout the hill
9:31 Under cover he sent **m** to Abimelech,
11:12 Jephthah sent **m** to the Ammonite king
11:13 the Ammonites answered Jephthah's **m**,
11:14 Jephthah sent back **m** to the Ammonite
11:17 Israel sent **m** to the king of Edom,
11:19 "Then Israel sent **m** to Sihon king of
1Sa 6:21 they sent **m** to the people of Kiriath
11: 3 we can send **m** throughout Israel;
11: 4 the **m** came to Gibeah of Saul and
11: 7 and sent the pieces by **m** throughout
11: 9 They told the **m** who had come, "Say
11: 9 When the **m** went and reported this
16:19 Saul sent **m** to Jesse and said, "Send
25:14 "David sent **m** from the desert to
25:42 with David's **m** and became his wife.
31: 9 and they sent **m** throughout the land
2Sa 2: 5 he sent **m** to the men of Jabesh
3:12 Abner sent **m** on his behalf to say to
3:14 David sent **m** to Ish-Bosheth son of
3:26 Joab then left David and sent **m**
5:11 Now Hiram king of Tyre sent **m** to
10: 5 David was told about this, he sent **m**
11: 4 David sent **m** to get her. She came to
12:27 Joab then sent **m** to David, saying,
15:10 Absalom sent secret **m** throughout the
1Ki 20: 2 He sent **m** into the city to Ahab king
20: 5 The **m** came again and said, "This is
20: 9 he replied to Ben-Hadad's **m**, "Tell
2Ki 1: 2 So he sent **m**, saying to them, "Go
1: 3 "Go up and meet the **m** of the king of
1: 5 the **m** returned to the king, he asked
1:16 have sent **m** to consult Baal-Zebub,
7:15 **m** returned and reported to the king.
14: 8 Amaziah sent **m** to Jehoash son of
16: 7 Ahaz sent **m** to say to
19: 9 he again sent **m** to Hezekiah with
19:14 the letter from the **m** and read it.
19:23 By your **m** you have heaped insults on
20:13 Hezekiah received the **m** and showed
1Ch 10: 9 and sent **m** throughout the land of
14: 1 Now Hiram king of Tyre sent **m** to
19: 5 he sent **m** to meet them, for they
19:16 they sent **m** and had Arameans brought
2Ch 35:21 Neco sent **m** to him saying, "What

2Ch 36:15 sent word to them through his **m**
36:16 they mocked God's **m**, despised his
Ne 6: 3 I sent **m** to them with this reply: "I
Job 33:22 pit, and his life to the **m** of death.
Ps 104: 4 He makes winds his **m**, flames of fire
Isa 18: 2 Go, swift **m**, to a people tall and
37: 9 heard it, he sent **m** to Hezekiah
37:14 the letter from the **m** and read it.
37:24 By your **m** you have heaped insults on
44:26 fulfils the predictions of his **m**,
Eze 23:16 them and sent **m** to them in Chaldea.
23:40 "They even sent **m** for men who came
30: 9 "'On that day **m** will go out from me
Da 4:17 "'The decision is announced by **m**,
Na 2:13 of your **m** will no longer be heard."
Lk 7:22 he replied to the **m**, "Go back and
7:24 After John's **m** left, Jesus began to
9:52 he sent **m** on ahead, who went into a

Messiah (Christ)
Jn 1:41 found the **M**" (that is, the Christ).
4:25 The woman said, "I know that **M**"

Met (Meet)
Ge 32: 1 way, and the angels of God **m** him.
33: 8 you mean by all these droves I **m**?"
38: 2 There Judah **m** the daughter of a
Ex 3:18 God of the Hebrews, has **m** with us.
4:24 **m** Moses and was about to kill him.
4:27 So he **m** Moses at the mountain of
5: 3 The God of the Hebrews has **m** with us.
18: 8 about all the hardships they had **m**
Nu 23: 4 God **m** with him, and Balaam said, "I
23:16 The LORD **m** with Balaam and put a
Dt 25:18 were weary and worn out, they **m** you
1Sa 9:11 they **m** some girls coming out to draw
10:10 a procession of prophets **m** him; the
16: 4 the town trembled when they **m** him.
18:30 David **m** with more success than
21: 1 Ahimelech trembled when he **m** him,
25:20 towards her, and she **m** them.
2Sa 2:13 and **m** them at the pool of Gibeon.
1Ki 11:29 and Ahijah the prophet of Shiloh **m**
13:24 he went on his way, a lion **m** him on
18: 7 Obadiah was walking along, Elijah **m**
2Ki 9:21 They **m** him at the plot of ground
10:13 he **m** some relatives of Ahaziah king
12:12 and **m** all the other expenses of
Ne 13: 2 they had not **m** the Israelites with
Job 2:11 they set out from their homes and **m**
Ps 74: 4 in the place where you **m** with us;
Jer 41: 6 When he **m** them, he said, "Come to
Mt 8:28 men coming from the tombs **m** him.
27:32 they were going out, they **m** a man
28: 9 Suddenly Jesus **m** them. "Greetings,"
28:12 the chief priests had **m** with the
Lk 8:27 Jesus stepped ashore, he was **m** by a
9:37 the mountain, a large crowd **m** him.
17:12 ten men who had leprosy **m** him.
22:66 **m** together, and Jesus was led before
Jn 4:51 his servants **m** him with the news
11:30 at the place where Martha had **m** him.
18: 2 often **m** there with his disciples.
Ac 1: 6 when they **m** together, they asked him,
4: 5 teachers of the law **m** in Jerusalem.
4:27 Indeed Herod and Pontius Pilate **m**
8:27 he started out, and on his way he **m**
10:25 Peter entered the house, Cornelius **m**
11:26 Saul **m** with the church and taught
13: 6 There they **m** a Jewish sorcerer and
15: 6 The apostles and elders **m** to
16:16 we were **m** by a slave girl who had a
16:40 where they **m** with the brothers and
18: 2 There he **m** a Jew named Aquila, a
20:14 he **m** us at Assos, we took him aboard
Ro 8: 4 of the law might be fully **m** in us,
Col 2: 1 all who have not **m** me personally.
Heb 7: 1 He **m** Abraham returning from the
7:10 when Melchizedek **m** Abraham, Levi was

Metal (Metals, Metalworker)
Lev 19: 4 make gods of cast **m** for yourselves.
1Ki 7:23 He made the Sea of cast **m**, circular
7:33 spokes and hubs were all of cast **m**.
14: 9 idols made of **m**; you have provoked
2Ch 4: 2 He made the Sea of cast **m**, circular
Ps 106:19 and worshipped an idol cast from **m**.
Isa 48: 5 image and **m** god ordained them.'
Eze 1: 4 of the fire looked like glowing **m**,
1:27 waist up he looked like glowing **m**,
8: 2 was as bright as glowing **m**.
Da 11: 8 their **m** images and their valuable
Na 2: 3 The **m** on the chariots flashes on the

Metals (Metal)
Jer 6:27 "I have made you a tester of **m** and

Metalworker (Metal, Work)
2Ti 4:14 Alexander the **m** did me a great deal

Mete
Ps 58: 2 hands **m** out violence on the earth.

Metheg Ammah
2Sa 8: 1 and he took **M** from the control of

Method (Methods)
Ru 4: 7 This was the **m** of legalising

Methods (Method)
Isa 32: 7 The scoundrel's **m** are wicked, he

Methuselah
Son of Enoch; grandfather of Noah; lived to be 969 (Ge 5:21–27; 1Ch 1:3; Lk 3:36–37).

Ge 5:21 65 years, he became the father of **M**.
5:22 after he became the father of **M**,
5:25 **M** had lived 187 years, he became the
5:26 **M** lived 782 years and had other sons
5:27 Altogether, **M** lived 969 years, and
1Ch 1: 3 Enoch, **M**, Lamech, Noah.
Lk 3:37 the son of **M**, the son of Enoch, the

Methushael
Ge 4:18 **M**, and **M** was the father of Lamech.

Meunim
Ezr 2:50 Asnah, **M**, Nephussim,
Ne 7:52 Besai, **M**, Nephussim,

Meunites
1Ch 4:41 also the **M** who were there and
2Ch 20: 1 **M** came to make war on Jehoshaphat.
26: 7 lived in Gur Baal and against the **M**.

Me-Zahab
Ge 36:39 of Matred, the daughter of **M**.
1Ch 1:50 of Matred, the daughter of **M**.

Mezobaite
1Ch 11:47 Eliel, Obed and Jaasiel the **M**.

Mibhar
1Ch 11:38 of Nathan, **M** son of Hagri,

Mibsam
Ge 25:13 of Ishmael, Kedar, Adbeel, **M**,
1Ch 1:29 of Ishmael, Kedar, Adbeel, **M**,
4:25 Shallum was Shaul's son, **M** his son

Mibzar
Ge 36:42 Kenaz, Teman, **M**,
1Ch 1:53 Kenaz, Teman, **M**,

Mica
2Sa 9:12 Mephibosheth had a young son named **M**,
1Ch 9:15 Galal and Mattaniah son of **M**, the
Ne 10:11 **M**, Rehob, Hashabiah,
11:17 Mattaniah son of **M**, the son of Zabdi,
11:22 the son of Mattaniah, the son of **M**.

Micah (Micah's)
1. Prophet from Moresheth (Jer 26:18–19; Mic 1:1) **2.** Ephraimite whose idols and priest were taken by migrating Danites (Jdg 17–18). **3.** Micaiah. Prophet (1Ki 22:4–28; 2Ch 18:1–27).

Jdg 17: 1 Now a man named **M** from the hill
17: 5 Now this man **M** had a shrine, and he
17: 9 **M** asked him, "Where are you from?"
17:10 **M** said to him, "Live with me and be
17:12 **M** installed the Levite, and the
17:13 **M** said, "Now I know that the LORD
18: 2 came to the house of **M**, where they
18: 4 He told them what **M** had done for him,
18:22 the men who lived near **M** were called
18:23 the Danites turned and said to **M**,
18:26 the Danites went their way, and **M**,
18:27 they took what **M** had made, and his
18:31 They continued to use the idols **M**
1Ch 5: 5 **M** his son, Reaiah his son, Baal his
8:34 Merib-Baal, who was the father of **M**.
8:35 The sons of **M**: Pithon, Melech, Tarea
9:40 Merib-Baal, who was the father of **M**.
9:41 The sons of **M**: Pithon, Melech,
23:20 The sons of Uzziel: **M** the first and
24:24 The son of Uzziel: **M**; from the sons
24:24 **M**; from the sons of **M**: Shamir.
24:25 The brother of **M**: Isshiah; from the
2Ch 34:20 Abdon son of **M**, Shaphan the
Jer 26:18 "**M** of Moresheth prophesied in the
Mic 1: 1 The word of the LORD that came to **M**

Micah's (Micah)
Jdg 17: 4 And they were put in **M** house.
17: 8 On his way he came to **M** house in the
18: 3 they were near **M** house, they
18:13 of Ephraim and came to **M** house.
18:15 Levite at **M** place and greeted him.
18:18 these men went into **M** house and took
18:22 gone some distance from **M** house,

Micaiah
1Ki 22: 8 always bad. He is **M** son of Imlah."
22: 9 said, "Bring **M** son of Imlah at once.
22:13 had gone to summon **M** said to him,
22:14 **M** said, "As surely as the LORD lives,
22:15 he arrived, the king asked him, "**M**,
22:17 **M** answered, "I saw all Israel
22:19 **M** continued, "Therefore hear the
22:24 went up and slapped **M** in the face.
22:25 **M** replied, "You will find out on the
22:26 "Take **M** and send him back to Amon
22:28 **M** declared, "If you ever return
2Ki 22:12 Acbor son of **M**, Shaphan the
2Ch 17: 7 **M** to teach in the towns of Judah.
18: 7 always bad. He is **M** son of Imlah."
18: 8 said, "Bring **M** son of Imlah at once.
18:12 had gone to summon **M** said to him,
18:13 **M** said, "As surely as the LORD lives,
18:14 he arrived, the king asked him, "**M**,
18:16 **M** answered, "I saw all Israel
18:18 **M** continued, "Therefore hear the
18:23 went up and slapped **M** in the face.
18:24 **M** replied, "You will find out on the
18:25 "Take **M** and send him back to Amon
18:27 **M** declared, "If you ever return
Ne 12:35 the son of Mattaniah, the son of **M**,
12:41 Maaseiah, Miniamin, **M**, Elioenai,
Jer 36:11 **M** son of Gemariah, the son of
36:13 After **M** told them everything he had

Michael
Archangel (Jude 9). Heavenly guardian of Israel against power of Greece and Persia (Da 10:13,21; 12:1). Defeated Satan and cast him from heaven (Rev 12:7–9).

Nu 13:13 the tribe of Asher, Sethur son of **M**;
1Ch 5:13 Their relatives, by families, were: **M**
5:14 the son of Gilead, the son of **M**, the
6:40 the son of **M**, the son of Baaseiah,
7: 3 The sons of Izrahiah: **M**, Obadiah,
8:16 **M**, Ishpah and Joha were the sons of
12:20 Jozabad, Jediael, **M**, Jozabad, Elihu
27:18 David; over Issachar: Omri son of **M**;
2Ch 21: 2 Azariahu, **M** and Shephatiah.
Ezr 8: 8 son of **M**, and with him 80 men;
Da 10:13 Then **M**, one of the chief princes,
10:21 against them except **M**, your prince.

Da 12: 1 "At that time **M**, the great prince
Jude : 9 even the archangel **M**, when he was
Rev 12: 7 there was war in heaven. **M** and his

Michal
Daughter of Saul (1Sa 14:49). Became David's wife (1Sa 18:20–29); warned him of Saul's plot (1Sa 19:11–17). Given to Paltiel (1Sa 25:44); returned to David (2Sa 3:13–16). Despised David (2Sa 6:16–23; 1Ch 15:29).

1Sa 14:49 Merab, and that of the younger was **M**.
18:20 Now Saul's daughter **M** was in love
18:27 gave him his daughter **M** in marriage.
18:28 and that his daughter **M** loved David,
19:11 But **M**, David's wife, warned him, "If
19:12 **M** let David down through a window,
19:13 **M** took an idol and laid it on the
19:14 capture David, **M** said: "He is ill."
19:17 Saul said to **M**, "Why did you deceive
19:17 **M** told him, "He said to me, 'Let me
25:44 Saul had given his daughter **M**,
2Sa 3:13 bring **M** daughter of Saul when you
3:14 "Give me my wife **M**, whom I betrothed
6:16 **M** daughter of Saul watched from a
6:20 **M** daughter of Saul came out to meet
6:21 David said to **M**, "It was before the
6:23 **M** daughter of Saul had no children
1Ch 15:29 **M** daughter of Saul watched from a

Michmash
A town of Benjamin north of Jerusalem. Scene of battle between Israel and the Philistines where Jonathan's men won a great victory (1Sa 13:2, 5–7; 14:4–15, 31). The Assyrians stored supplies here (Isa 10:28).

1Sa 13: 2 **M** and in the hill country of Bethel,
13: 5 and camped at **M**, east of Beth Aven.
13:11 Philistines were assembling at **M**,
13:16 while the Philistines camped at **M**.
13:23 had gone out to the pass at **M**.
14: 5 cliff stood to the north towards **M**,
14:31 **M** to Aijalon, they were exhausted.
Ezr 2:27 of **M** 122
Ne 7:31 of **M** 122
11:31 **M**, Aija, Bethel and its settlements,
Isa 10:28 Migron; they store supplies at **M**.

Micmethath
Jos 16: 6 continued to the sea. From **M** on the
17: 7 from Asher to **M** east of Shechem.

Micri
1Ch 9: 8 the son of **M**; and Meshullam son of

Mid-air (Air)
2Sa 18: 9 He was left hanging in **m**, while the
Rev 8:13 in **m** call out in a loud voice:
14: 6 I saw another angel flying in **m**, and
19:17 voice to all the birds flying in **m**,

Midday (Day)
Dt 28:29 At **m** you will grope about like a
1Ki 18:29 **M** passed, and they continued their
Ps 91: 6 nor the plague that destroys at **m**.
SS 1: 7 and where you rest your sheep at **m**.
Isa 59:10 At **m** we stumble as if it were
Jer 15: 8 At **m** I will bring a destroyer
Zep 2: 4 At **m** Ashdod will be emptied and

Middin
Jos 15:61 In the desert: Beth Arabah, **M**,

Midian (Midian's, Midianite, Midianites)
Land inhabited by Midian's descendants (Ge 25:1–2; 1Ch 1:32–33), on eastern side of Gulf of Aqaba. Moses fled here (Ex 2:15; Ac 7:29) and married Zipporah (Ex 2:16–21). Here God spoke to Moses from a burning bush (Ex 3:1–10; 4:19). Its elders were consulted by the Moabites about the approaching Israelites (Nu 22:4). Israel defeated its army (Nu 31:7–12) but its people soon recovered and oppressed Israel (Jdg 6:2, 6–7). God used Gideon to save the Israelites (Jdg 6:11–8:28) and the victory was remembered in later poetry (Ps 83:9; Isa 9:4; 10:26; Hab 3:7).

Ge 25: 2 Jokshan, Medan, **M**, Ishbak and Shuah.
25: 4 The sons of **M** were Ephah, Epher,
36:35 Hadad son of Bedad, who defeated **M**
Ex 2:15 in **M**, where he sat down by a well.
2:16 Now a priest of **M** had seven
3: 1 the priest of **M**, and he led the
4:19 Now the LORD had said to Moses in **M**,
18: 1 Now Jethro, the priest of **M** and
Nu 22: 4 The Moabites said to the elders of **M**,
22: 7 The elders of Moab and **M** left,
31: 7 They fought against **M**, as the LORD
31: 8 Hur and Reba—the five kings of **M**.
Jdg 6: 2 the power of **M** was so oppressive,
6: 6 **M** so impoverished the Israelites
6: 7 cried to the LORD because of **M**,
6:13 us and put us into the hand of **M**."
7: 1 The camp of **M** was north of them in
7: 2 me to deliver **M** into their hands.
7: 8 of **M** lay below him in the valley.
8: 1 call us when you went to fight **M**?"
8: 5 Zebah and Zalmunna, the kings of **M**."
8:12 the two kings of **M**, fled, but he
8:22 have saved us out of the hand of **M**."
8:26 garments worn by the kings of **M**
8:28 Thus **M** was subdued before the
9:17 to rescue you from the hand of **M**
1Ki 11:18 They set out from **M** and went to
1Ch 1:32 Jokshan, Medan, **M**, Ishbak and Shuah.
1:33 The sons of **M**: Ephah, Epher, Hanoch,
1:46 Hadad son of Bedad, who defeated **M**
Ps 83: 9 Do to them as you did to **M**, as you
Isa 10:26 as when he struck down **M** at the rock
60: 6 land, young camels of **M** and Ephah.
Hab 3: 7 the dwellings of **M** in anguish.
Ac 7:29 Moses heard this, he fled to **M**,

Midian's (Midian)
Jdg 6:14 have and save Israel out of **M** hand.
Isa 9: 4 For as in the day of **M** defeat, you

Midianite (Midian)
Ge 37:28 when the **M** merchants came by, his
Nu 10:29 said to Hobab son of Reuel the **M**,
25: 6 brought to his family a **M** woman
25:14 the **M** woman was Zimri son of Salu,
25:15 the name of the **M** woman who was put
25:15 Zur, a tribal chief of a **M** family.
25:18 the daughter of a **M** leader, the
31: 9 The Israelites captured the **M** women
31: 9 **M** herds, flocks and goods as plunder.
Jos 13:21 had defeated him and the **M** chiefs
Jdg 7:13 bread came tumbling into the **M** camp.
7:15 given the **M** camp into your hands."
7:25 captured two of the **M** leaders,
8: 3 Oreb and Zeeb, the **M** leaders

Midianites (Midian)
Ge 37:36 Meanwhile, the **M** sold Joseph in
Nu 25:17 "Treat the **M** as enemies and kill
31: 2 "Take vengeance on the **M** for the
31: 3 your men to go to war against the **M**
31:10 They burned all the towns where the **M**
Jdg 6: 1 gave them into the hands of the **M**.
6: 3 the **M**, Amalekites and other eastern
6:11 a winepress to keep it from the **M**.
6:16 strike down all the **M** together."
6:33 Now all the **M**, Amalekites and other
7: 7 you and give the **M** into your hands.
7:12 The **M**, the Amalekites and all the
7:14 **M** and the whole camp into his hands."
7:21 the **M** ran, crying out as they fled.
7:23 called out, and they pursued the **M**.
7:24 "Come down against the **M** and seize
7:25 They pursued the **M** and brought the

Midnight (Night)
Ex 11: 4 'About **m** I will go throughout Egypt.
12:29 At **m** the LORD struck down all the
Ps 119:62 At **m** I rise to give you thanks for
Mt 25: 6 "At **m** the cry rang out: 'Here's the
Mk 13:35 or at **m**, or when the cock crows, or
Lk 11: 5 and he goes to him at **m** and says,
Ac 16:25 About **m** Paul and Silas were praying
20: 7 next day, kept on talking until **m**.
27:27 when about **m** the sailors sensed they

Midwife (Midwives)
Ge 35:17 the **m** said to her, "Don't be afraid,
38:28 so the **m** took a scarlet thread and

Midwives (Midwife)
Ex 1:15 king of Egypt said to the Hebrew **m**,
1:17 The **m**, however, feared God and did
1:18 the king of Egypt summoned the **m** and
1:19 The **m** answered Pharaoh, "Hebrew
1:19 and give birth before the **m** arrive."
1:20 God was kind to the **m** and the people
1:21 the **m** feared God, he gave them

Migdal Eder
Ge 35:21 again and pitched his tent beyond **M**.

Migdal El
Jos 19:38 Iron, **M**, Horem, Beth Anath and Beth

Migdal Gad
Jos 15:37 Zenan, Hadashah, **M**,

Migdol
Fortified town in the north-east of Egypt, where the Israelites camped after leaving Egypt (Ge 14:2; Nu 33:7) and Jewish refugees moved after Jerusalem was destroyed (Jer 44:1). Its downfall was foretold (Jer 46:14).

Ex 14: 2 Pi Hahiroth, between **M** and the sea.
Nu 33: 7 of Baal Zephon, and camped near **M**.
Jer 44: 1 Jews living in Lower Egypt—in **M**,
46:14 and proclaim it in **M**; proclaim it
Eze 29:10 a desolate waste from **M** to Aswan,
30: 6 From **M** to Aswan they will fall by

Might (Almighty, Mightier, Mightiest, Mightily, Mighty)
Ge 49: 3 "Reuben, you are my firstborn, my **m**,
Jdg 16:30 Then he pushed with all his **m**,
2Sa 6: 5 with all their **m** before the LORD,
6:14 before the LORD with all his **m**,
1Ch 13: 8 with all their **m** before God,
2Ch 6:41 place, you and the ark of your **m**.
20: 6 Power and **m** are in your hand,
Est 10: 2 all his acts of power and **m**,
Job 30:21 with the **m** of your hand you attack
Ps 21:13 we will sing and praise your **m**.
54: 1 your name; vindicate me by your **m**.
59:11 In your **m** make them wander about,
71:18 your **m** to all who are to come.
78:61 He sent the ark of his **m** into
80: 2 Awaken your **m**; come and save us.
132: 8 place, you and the ark of your **m**.
145:11 of your kingdom and speak of your **m**,
Ecc 9:10 do it with all your **m**, for in the
Isa 44:12 he forges it with the **m** of his arm.
63:15 Where are your zeal and your **m**? Your
Jer 16:21 I will teach them my power and **m**.
49:35 of Elam, the mainstay of their **m**.
Da 2:37 dominion and power and **m** and glory;
11:17 with the **m** of his entire kingdom
Mic 3: 8 and with justice and **m**, to declare
Zec 4: 6 'Not by **m** nor by power, but by me
Col 1:11 power according to his glorious **m**
1Ti 6:16 To him be honour and **m** for ever.

Mightier (Might)
Ps 93: 4 **M** than the thunder of the great
93: 4 **m** than the breakers of the sea—the

Mightiest (Might)
Da 11:39 He will attack the **m** fortresses with

Mightily (Might)
Jer 25:30 and roar **m** against his land.

Mighty (Might, *Mighty hand, Mighty one*)

Ge 10: 8 grew to be a **m** warrior on the earth.
10: 9 He was a **m** hunter before the LORD;
10: 9 Nimrod, a **m** hunter before the LORD."
23: 6 listen to us. You are a **m** prince
Ex 6: 6 arm and with **m** acts of judgment.
7: 4 with **m** acts of judgment I will bring
15:10 They sank like lead in the **m** waters.
Dt 3:24 can do the deeds and **m** works you do?
10:17 the great God, **m** and awesome, who
34:12 no-one has ever shown the **m** power
Jdg 5:13 of the LORD came to me with the **m**.
5:22 galloping go his **m** steeds.
5:23 to help the LORD against the **m**.'
6:12 "The LORD is with you, **m** warrior.
11: 1 the Gileadite was a **m** warrior.
1Sa 4: 8 us from the hand of these **m** gods?
14:52 and whenever Saul saw a **m** or brave
2Sa 1:19 How the **m** have fallen!
1:21 For there the shield of the **m** was
1:22 from the flesh of the **m**, the bow of
1:25 "How the **m** have fallen in battle!
1:27 "How the **m** have fallen! The weapons
20: 7 Pelethites and all the **m** warriors
23: 8 These are the names of David's **m** men:
23: 9 As one of the three **m** men, he was
23:16 the three **m** men broke through the
23:17 the exploits of the three **m** men.
23:22 was as famous as the three **m** men.
2Ki 17:36 with **m** power and outstretched arm,
1Ch 1:10 who grew to be a **m** warrior on earth.
11:10 were the chiefs of David's **m** men
11:11 this is the list of David's **m** men:
11:12 the Ahohite, one of the three **m** men.
11:19 the exploits of the three **m** men.
11:24 was as famous as the three **m** men.
11:26 The **m** men were: Asahel the brother
12: 4 Ishmaiah the Gibeonite, a **m** man
27: 6 This was the Benaiah who was a **m** man
28: 1 **m** men and all the brave warriors.
29:24 All the officers and **m** men, as well
2Ch 14:11 to help the powerless against the **m**.
16: 8 the Cushites and Libyans a **m** army
Ne 9:11 depths, like a stone into **m** waters.
9:32 O our God, the great, **m** and awesome
Job 1:19 suddenly a **m** wind swept in from the
9:19 he is **m**! And if it is a matter of
12:21 on nobles and disarms the **m**.
24:22 God drags away the **m** by his power;
34:20 **m** are removed without human hand.
34:24 Without enquiry he shatters the **m**
36: 5 "God is **m**, but does not despise men;
36: 5 he is **m**, and firm in his purpose.
36:19 wealth or even all your **m** efforts
37: 6 the rain shower, 'Be a **m** downpour.'
41:25 he rises up, the **m** are terrified;
Ps 24: 8 strong and **m**, the LORD **m** in battle.
29: 1 Ascribe to the LORD, O **m** ones,
29: 3 the LORD thunders over the **m** waters.
32: 6 surely when the **m** waters rise,
36: 6 Your righteousness is like the **m**
52: 1 Why do you boast of evil, you **m** man?
62: 7 on God; he is my **m** rock, my refuge.
68:33 above, who thunders with **m** voice.
71:16 I will come and proclaim your **m** acts,
77:12 works and consider all your **m** deeds.
77:15 With your **m** arm you redeemed your
77:19 your way through the **m** waters,
80:10 the **m** cedars with its branches.
89: 8 who is like you? You are **m**, O LORD,
93: 4 of the sea—the LORD on high is **m**.
99: 4 The King is **m**, he loves justice—
103:20 you his angels, you **m** ones who do
106: 2 Who can proclaim the **m** acts of the
106: 8 sake, to make his **m** power known.
107:23 they were merchants on the **m** waters.
110: 2 The LORD will extend your **m** sceptre
112: 2 His children will be **m** in the land;
118:15 LORD's right hand has done **m** things!
118:16 LORD's right hand has done **m** things!"
135:10 many nations and killed **m** kings—
136:18 killed **m** kings—His love endures
144: 7 me and rescue me from the **m** waters,
145: 4 they will tell of your **m** acts.
Ps 145:12 that all men may know of your **m** acts
147: 5 Great is our Lord and **m** in power;
150: 1 praise him in his **m** heavens.
Pr 7:26 down; her slain are a **m** throng.
21:22 A wise man attacks the city of the **m**
30:30 a lion, **m** among beasts, who retreats
SS 8: 6 like blazing fire, like a **m** flame.
Isa 1:31 The **m** man will become tinder and his
8: 7 them the **m** floodwaters of the River
9: 6 **M** God, Everlasting Father, Prince of
10:21 of Jacob will return to the **M** God.
22:17 you and hurl you away, O you **m** man.
33:21 ride them, no **m** ship will sail them.
40:26 Because of his great power and **m**
42:13 The LORD will march out like a **m** man,
43:16 sea, a path through the **m** waters,
56:11 They are dogs with **m** appetites; they
60:22 a thousand, the smallest a **m** nation.
62: 8 by his right hand and by his **m** arm:
63: 1 in righteousness, **m** to save."
Jer 5:16 grave; all of them are **m** warriors.
10: 6 great, and your name is **m** in power.
11:16 But with the roar of a **m** storm he
20:11 the LORD is with me like a **m** warrior;
21: 5 a **m** arm in anger and fury and great
25:32 a **m** storm is rising from the ends of
32:19 great are your purposes and **m** are
48:17 'How broken is the **m** sceptre, how
Eze 7:24 put an end to the pride of the **m**,
17:17 Pharaoh with his **m** army and great
32:12 to fall by the swords of **m** men
32:18 her and the daughters of **m** nations,
32:21 From within the grave the **m** leaders
38:15 on horses, a great horde, a **m** army.
39:18 You will eat the flesh of **m** men and
39:20 **m** men and soldiers of every kind,'
Da 2:10 however great and **m**, has ever asked
4: 3 How great are his signs, how **m** his
4:30 by my **m** power and for the glory of
8:24 the **m** men and the holy people.
11: 3 a **m** king will appear, who will rule
Hos 8:10 under the oppression of the **m** king.
Joel 2: 2 mountains a large and **m** army comes,
2: 5 like a **m** army drawn up for battle.
2:11 **m** are those who obey his command.
Zep 3:17 God is with you, he is **m** to save.
Zec 4: 7 "What are you, O **m** mountain? Before
10: 5 Together they will be like **m** men
10: 7 Ephraimites will become like **m** men
Lk 1:51 He has performed **m** deeds with his
22:69 at the right hand of the **m** God."
Ac 13:17 with **m** power he led them out of that
Eph 1:19 like the working of his **m** strength,
6:10 in the Lord and in his **m** power.
Rev 5: 2 I saw a **m** angel proclaiming in a
6:15 the generals, the rich, the **m**, and
10: 1 I saw another **m** angel coming down
18: 2 With a **m** voice he shouted: "Fallen!
18: 8 **m** is the Lord God who judges her.
18:21 a **m** angel picked up a boulder the
19:18 generals, and **m** men, of horses and

Mighty hand

Ex 3:19 let you go unless a **m** compels him.
6: 1 Because of my **m** he will let them go;
6: 1 because of my **m** he will drive them
13: 3 LORD brought you out of it with a **m**.
13: 9 brought you out of Egypt with his **m**.
13:14 'With a **m** the LORD brought us out of
13:16 brought us out of Egypt with his **m**."
32:11 of Egypt with great power and a **m**?
Dt 4:34 by war, by a **m** and an outstretched
5:15 with a **m** and an outstretched arm.
6:21 brought us out of Egypt with a **m**.
7: 8 that he brought you out with a **m**
7:19 the **m** and outstretched arm, with
9:26 and brought out of Egypt with a **m**.
11: 2 his **m**, his outstretched arm;
26: 8 with a **m** and an outstretched arm,
1Ki 8:42 your **m** and your outstretched arm
2Ch 6:32 your **m** and your outstretched arm
Ne 1:10 by your great strength and your **m**.
Ps 136:12 with a **m** and outstretched arm; His
Jer 32:21 by a **m** and an outstretched arm and
Eze 20:33 I will rule over you with a **m** and an
Eze 20:34 you have been scattered—with a **m**
Da 9:15 your people out of Egypt with a **m**
1Pe 5: 6 therefore, under God's **m**, that he

Mighty one

Ge 49:24 because of the hand of the **M** of
Jos 22:22 "The **M**, God, the LORD! The **M**, God,
Job 34:17 Will you condemn the just and **m**?
Ps 45: 3 Gird your sword upon your side, O **m**;
50: 1 The **M**, God, the LORD, speaks and
132: 2 and made a vow to the **M** of Jacob:
132: 5 LORD, a dwelling for the **M** of Jacob."
Isa 1:24 the LORD Almighty, the **M** of Israel,
10:13 like a **m** I subdued their kings.
10:34 axe; Lebanon will fall before the **M**.
33:21 There the LORD will be our **M**. It
49:26 your Redeemer, the **M** of Jacob."
60:16 your Redeemer, the **M** of Jacob.
Mt 26:64 at the right hand of the **M** and
Mk 14:62 at the right hand of the **M** and
Lk 1:49 for the **M** has done great things for

Migration

Jer 8: 7 thrush observe the time of their **m**.

Migron

1Sa 14: 2 Gibeah under a pomegranate tree in **M**.
Isa 10:28 They enter Aiath; they pass through **M**

Mijamin

1Ch 24: 9 the fifth to Malkijah, the sixth to **M**
Ezr 10:25 **M**, Eleazar, Malkijah and Benaiah.
Ne 10: 7 Meshullam, Abijah, **M**,
12: 5 **M**, Moadiah, Bilgah,

Mikloth

1Ch 8:32 **M**, who was the father of Shimeah.
9:37 Gedor, Ahio, Zechariah and **M**.
9:38 **M** was the father of Shimeam. They
27: 4 **M** was the leader of his division.

Mikneiah

1Ch 15:18 Maaseiah, Mattithiah, Eliphelehu, **M**,
15:21 Mattithiah, Eliphelehu, **M**, Obed-Edom,

Miktam

Ps 16: T A **m** of David.
56: T Of David. A **m**. When the Philistines
57: T Of David. A **m**. When he had fled
58: T Of David. A **m**.
59: T Of David. A **m**. When Saul had sent
60: T A **m** of David. For teaching.

Milalai

Ne 12:36 his associates—Shemaiah, Azarel, **M**,

Milcah

Ge 11:29 and the name of Nahor's wife was **M**;
11:29 the father of both **M** and Iscah.
22:20 later Abraham was told, "**M** is also
22:23 **M** bore these eight sons to Abraham's
24:15 the daughter of Bethuel son of **M**,
24:24 the son that **M** bore to Nahor."
24:47 son of Nahor, whom **M** bore to him.
Nu 26:33 Mahlah, Noah, Hoglah, **M** and Tirzah.
27: 1 Mahlah, Noah, Hoglah, **M** and Tirzah.
36:11 Tirzah, Hoglah, **M** and Noah—married
Jos 17: 3 Mahlah, Noah, Hoglah, **M** and Tirzah.

Mildew

Lev 13:47 is contaminated with **m**—any woollen
13:49 **m** and must be shown to the priest.
13:50 The priest is to examine the **m** and
13:51 and if the **m** has spread in the
13:51 destructive **m**; the article is
13:52 because the **m** is destructive; the
13:53 when the priest examines it, the **m**
13:55 and if the **m** has not changed its
13:55 **m** has affected one side or the other.
13:56 when the priest examines it, the **m**
13:57 has the **m** must be burned with fire.
13:58 has been washed and is rid of the **m**,
13:59 by **m** in woollen or linen clothing,

Lev 14:34 spreading **m** in a house in that land,
14:35 that looks like **m** in my house.'
14:36 before he goes in to examine the **m**,
14:37 He is to examine the **m** on the walls,
14:39 If the **m** has spread on the walls,
14:43 "If the **m** reappears in the house
14:44 if the **m** has spread in the house, it
14:44 destructive **m**; the house is unclean.
14:48 the **m** has not spread after the house
14:48 house clean, because the **m** is gone.
14:55 for **m** in clothing or in a house,
14:57 for infectious skin diseases and **m**.
Dt 28:22 with blight and **m**, which will plague
1Ki 8:37 or blight or **m**, locusts or
2Ch 6:28 or blight or **m**, locusts or
Am 4: 9 I struck them with blight and **m**.
Hag 2:17 **m** and hail, yet you did not turn to

Mile (Miles)

Mt 5:41 If someone forces you to go one **m**,

Miles (Mile)

Mt 5:41 to go one mile, go with him two **m**.
Lk 24:13 Emmaus, about seven **m** from Jerusalem.
Jn 6:19 rowed three or three and a half **m**,
11:18 Bethany was less than two **m** from

Miletus

Seaport on eastern coast of Asia Minor, about 37 miles south of Ephesus. Paul visited here (Ac 20:15). He summoned Ephesian elders and addressed them here (Ac 20:16–38). Possibly Paul revisited it leaving Trophimus sick here (2Ti 4:20).

Ac 20:15 on the following day arrived at **M**.
20:17 From **M**, Paul sent to Ephesus for the
2Ti 4:20 and I left Trophimus sick in **M**.

Military

Jos 5: 4 all the men of **m** age—died in the
5: 6 **m** age when they left Egypt had died,
2Sa 5: 2 who led Israel on their **m** campaigns.
20: 8 Joab was wearing his **m** tunic, and
1Ki 22:45 he achieved and his **m** exploits
2Ki 14:28 all he did, and his **m** achievements,
18:20 you have strategy and **m** strength
1Ch 5:18 had 44,760 men ready for **m** service
11: 2 who led Israel on their **m** campaigns.
2Ch 25: 5 thousand men ready for **m** service,
32: 3 he consulted with his officials and **m**
32: 6 He appointed **m** officers over the
33:14 He stationed **m** commanders in all the
Est 1: 3 The **m** leaders of Persia and Media,
Isa 36: 5 you have strategy and **m** strength
Mk 6:21 **m** commanders and the leading men of

Milk (*Land flowing with milk and honey*)

Ge 18: 8 He then brought some curds and **m** and
49:12 than wine, his teeth whiter than **m**.
Ex 23:19 cook a young goat in its mother's **m**.
34:26 a young goat in its mother's **m**."
Nu 13:27 with **m** and honey! Here is its fruit.
Dt 14:21 cook a young goat in its mother's **m**.
32:14 with curds and **m** from herd and flock
Jdg 4:19 She opened a skin of **m**, gave him a
5:25 and she gave him **m**; in a bowl fit
5:25 nobles she brought him curdled **m**.
2Sa 17:29 **m** for David and his people to eat.
Job 10:10 Did you not pour me out like **m** and
Pr 27:27 You will have plenty of goats' **m** to
30:33 For as churning the **m** produces
SS 4:11 **m** and honey are under your tongue.
5: 1 I have drunk my wine and my **m**.
5:12 washed in **m**, mounted like jewels.
Isa 7:22 of the abundance of the **m** they give,
28: 9 To children weaned from their **m**,
55: 1 **m** without money and without cost.
60:16 You will drink the **m** of nations and
Lam 4: 7 than snow and whiter than **m**,
Eze 25: 4 eat your fruit and drink your **m**.
Joel 3:18 and the hills will flow with **m**; all
1Co 3: 2 I gave you **m**, not solid food, for
9: 7 a flock and does not drink of the **m**?
Heb 5:12 You need **m**, not solid food!
5:13 Anyone who lives on **m**, being still
1Pe 2: 2 crave pure spiritual **m**, so that by

Mill

Ex 11: 5 who is at her hand **m**, and all the
Nu 11: 8 a hand **m** or crushed it in a mortar.
Joel 1:18 How the cattle moan! The herds **m**
Mt 24:41 will be grinding with a hand **m**;

Millet

Eze 4: 9 beans and lentils, **m** and spelt; put

Million

1Ch 21: 5 one **m** one hundred thousand men who
22:14 a **m** talents of silver, quantities of
Rev 9:16 mounted troops was two hundred **m**.

Millstone (Stone)

Jdg 9:53 a woman dropped an upper **m** on his
2Sa 11:21 an upper **m** on him from the wall,
Job 41:24 is hard as rock, hard as a lower **m**.
Mt 18: 6 have a large **m** hung around his neck
Mk 9:42 with a large **m** tied around his neck.
Lk 17: 2 with a **m** tied round his neck than
Rev 18:21 a large **m** and threw it into the sea,
18:22 The sound of a **m** will never be

Millstones (Stone)

Dt 24: 6 Do not take a pair of **m**—not even
Isa 47: 2 Take **m** and grind flour; take off
Jer 25:10 the sound of **m** and the light of
Lam 5:13 Young men toil at the **m**; boys

Mina (Minas)

Eze 45:12 plus fifteen shekels equal one **m**.
Lk 19:16 'Sir, your **m** has earned ten more.'
19:18 'Sir, your **m** has earned five more.'
19:20 'Sir, here is your **m**; I have kept it
19:24 'Take his **m** away from him and give

Minas (Mina)

1Ki 10:17 with three **m** of gold in each shield.
Ezr 2:69 5,000 **m** of silver and 100 priestly
Ne 7:71 of gold and 2,200 **m** of silver.
7:72 2,000 **m** of silver and 67 garments
Lk 19:13 of his servants and gave them ten **m**.
19:24 give it to the one who has ten **m**.'

Mincing

Isa 3:16 tripping along with **m** steps, with

Mind (Double-minded, Like-minded, Minded, Mindful, Minds)

Ge 37:11 but his father kept the matter in **m**.
41: 8 In the morning his **m** was troubled,
45:20 Never **m** about your belongings,
Ex 16:29 Bear in **m** that the LORD has given
Nu 23:19 of man, that he should change his **m**.
Dt 28:28 blindness and confusion of **m**.
28:65 the LORD will give you an anxious **m**,
29: 4 the LORD has not given you a **m** that
1Sa 2:35 to what is in my heart and **m**.
14: 7 "Do all that you have in **m**," his
15:29 change his **m**; for he is not a man,
15:29 a man, that he should change his **m**."
2Sa 7: 3 "Whatever you have in **m**, go ahead
19:19 May the king put it out of his **m**.
1Ki 10: 2 him about all that she had on her **m**.
2Ki 10:30 house of Ahab all I had in **m** to do,
24: 1 But then he changed his **m** and
1Ch 12:38 also of one **m** to make David king.
17: 2 in **m**, do it, for God is with you."
28: 9 devotion and with a willing **m**,
28:12 that the Spirit had put in his **m**
2Ch 7:11 all he had in **m** to do in the temple
9: 1 with him about all she had on her **m**.
30:12 unity of **m** to carry out what the
Ne 5: 7 I pondered them in my **m** and then
Job 10:13 and I know that this was in your **m**:
12: 3 I have a **m** as well as you; I am not
38:36 or gave understanding to the **m**?
Ps 26: 2 try me, examine my heart and my **m**;
64: 6 the **m** and heart of man are cunning.
83: 5 With one **m** they plot together; they
110: 4 sworn and will not change his **m**:
Pr 23:33 and your **m** imagine confusing things.
Ecc 2: 3 **m** still guiding me with wisdom.
2:23 even at night his **m** does not rest.
7:25 I turned my **m** to understand, to
8: 9 All this I saw, as I applied my **m** to
8:16 I applied my **m** to know wisdom and to
Isa 10: 7 this is not what he has in **m**; his
26: 3 peace him whose **m** is steadfast,
32: 4 The **m** of the rash will know and
32: 6 For the fool speaks folly, his **m** is
40:13 Who has understood the **m** of the LORD,
46: 8 "Remember this, fix it in **m**, take it
65:17 remembered, nor will they come to **m**.
Jer 7:31 not command, nor did it enter my **m**.
11:20 and test the heart and **m**, let me
17:10 search the heart and examine the **m**,
19: 5 or mention, nor did it enter my **m**.
20:12 righteous and probe the heart and **m**,
32:35 nor did it enter my **m**, that they
Lam 3:21 Yet this I call to **m** and therefore I
Eze 11: 5 I know what is going through your **m**.
20:32 you have in **m** will never happen.
21:24 have brought to **m** your guilt by
38:10 thoughts will come into your **m** and
Da 2: 1 Nebuchadnezzar had dreams; his **m** was
2:28 through your **m** as you lay on your
2:29 O king, your **m** turned to things to
2:30 understand what went through your **m**.
4: 5 passed through my **m** terrified me.
4:16 Let his **m** be changed from that of a
4:16 let him be given the **m** of an animal,
5:12 was found to have a keen **m** and
5:21 people and given the **m** of an animal;
7: 1 his **m** as he was lying on his bed.
7:15 passed through my **m** disturbed me.
10:12 set your **m** to gain understanding
Mt 1:19 he had in **m** to divorce her quietly.
16:23 do not have in **m** the things of God,
21:29 but later he changed his **m** and went.
22:37 all your soul and with all your **m**.'
Mk 3:21 for they said, "He is out of his **m**.
5:15 his right **m**; and they were afraid.
8:33 "You do not have in **m** the things of
12:30 your **m** and with all your strength.'
Lk 8:35 his right **m**; and they were afraid.
10:27 strength and with all your **m**'; and,
21:14 make up your **m** not to worry
Jn 6: 6 had in **m** what he was going to do.
15:18 "If the world hates you, keep in **m**
Ac 4:32 believers were one in heart and **m**.
12:15 "You're out of your **m**," they told
26:24 "You are out of your **m**, Paul!" he
Ro 1:28 gave them over to a depraved **m**, to
7:23 waging war against the law of my **m**
7:25 I myself in my **m** am a slave to God's
8: 6 The **m** of sinful man is death, but
8: 6 but the **m** controlled by the Spirit
8: 7 the sinful **m** is hostile to God. It
8:27 hearts knows the **m** of the Spirit,
11:34 "Who has known the **m** of the Lord? Or
12: 2 by the renewing of your **m**.
14: 5 be fully convinced in his own **m**.
14:13 Instead, make up your **m** not to put
1Co 1:10 perfectly united in **m** and thought.
2: 9 no ear has heard, no **m** has conceived
2:16 "For who has known the **m** of the Lord
2:16 him?" But we have the **m** of Christ.
7:37 has settled the matter in his own **m**,
7:37 and who has made up his **m** not to
14:14 prays, but my **m** is unfruitful.
14:15 but I will also pray with my **m**; I
14:15 but I will also sing with my **m**.
14:23 not say that you are out of your **m**?
2Co 2: 1 I made up my **m** that I would not make
2:13 I still had no peace of **m**, because I
5:13 If we are out of our **m**, it is for
5:13 are in our right **m**, it is for you.
11:23 (I am out of my **m** to talk like this.
13:11 appeal, be of one **m**, live in peace.
Eph 6:18 With this in **m**, be alert and always
Php 3:19 Their **m** is on earthly things.
Col 2:18 **m** puffs him up with idle notions.
1Th 4:11 to **m** your own business and to work

2Th 1:11 With this in **m**, we constantly pray
1Ti 6: 5 friction between men of corrupt **m**,
Heb 7:21 his **m**: 'You are a priest for ever.
12:17 He could bring about no change of **m**,
2Pe 3:15 Bear in **m** that our Lord's patience
Rev 17: 9 "This calls for a **m** with wisdom. The

Minded (Mind)

1Pe 4: 7 be clear **m** and self-controlled so

Mindful (Mind)

Ps 8: 4 what is man that you are **m** of him,
Lk 1:48 for he has been **m** of the humble
Heb 2: 6 "What is man that you are **m** of him,

Minds (Mind)

Ex 13:17 change their **m** and return to Egypt."
14: 5 changed their **m** about them and said,
Dt 11:18 words of mine in your hearts and **m**;
Job 17: 4 You have closed their **m** to
Ps 7: 9 O righteous God, who searches **m** and
73: 7 conceits of their **m** know no limits.
Pr 12: 8 but men with warped **m** are despised.
Isa 44:18 and their **m** closed so that they
Jer 3:16 It will never enter their **m** or be
14:14 and the delusions of their own **m**.
23:16 visions from their own **m**, not from
23:26 the delusions of their own **m**?
31:33 "I will put my law in their **m** and
34:11 afterwards they changed their **m** and
Lk 24:38 and why do doubts rise in your **m**?
24:45 he opened their **m** so they could
Ac 14: 2 their **m** against the brothers.
15:24 troubling your **m** by what they said.
28: 6 their **m** and said he was a god.
Ro 8: 5 **m** set on what that nature desires;
8: 5 **m** set on what the Spirit desires.
16:18 deceive the **m** of naïve people.
2Co 3:14 their **m** were made dull, for to this
4: 4 The god of this age has blinded the **m**
11: 3 your **m** may somehow be led astray
Eph 4:23 made new in the attitude of your **m**;
Php 4: 7 hearts and your **m** in Christ Jesus.
Col 1:21 enemies in your **m** because of your
3: 2 Set your **m** on things above, not on
2Ti 3: 8 oppose the truth—men of depraved **m**,
Tit 1:15 **m** and consciences are corrupted.
Heb 8:10 I will put my laws in their **m** and
10:16 and I will write them on their **m**."
1Pe 1:13 Therefore, prepare your **m** for action;
Rev 2:23 I am he who searches hearts and **m**,

Mine

Job 28: 1 There is a **m** for silver and a place

Mingle (Mingled)

Ps 102: 9 my food and **m** my drink with tears

Mingled (Mingle)

Ezr 9: 2 and have **m** the holy race with the
Ps 106:35 they **m** with the nations and adopted

Miniamin (Miniamin's)

2Ch 31:15 Eden, **M**, Jeshua, Shemaiah, Amariah
Ne 12:41 Maaseiah, **M**, Micaiah, Elioenai,

Miniamin's (Miniamin)

Ne 12:17 of Abijah's, Zicri; of **M** and of

Minister (Ministered, Ministering, Ministers, Ministry)

Ex 28:43 the altar to **m** in the Holy Place,
29:30 comes to the Tent of Meeting to **m** in
30:20 when they approach the altar to **m** by
Nu 16: 9 before the community and **m** to them?
18: 2 **m** before the Tent of the Testimony.
Dt 10: 8 to stand before the LORD to **m** and to
18: 5 and **m** in the LORD's name always.
18: 7 he may **m** in the name of the LORD his
21: 5 LORD your God has chosen them to **m**
1Sa 2:30 house would **m** before me for ever.
2:35 **m** before my anointed one always.
1Ch 15: 2 LORD and to **m** before him for ever."
1Ch 16: 4 He appointed some of the Levites to **m**
16:37 of the LORD to **m** there regularly,
16:38 associates to **m** with them.
23:13 to **m** before him and to pronounce
2Ch 29:11 **m** before him and to burn incense."
31: 2 to **m**, to give thanks and to sing
Ps 101: 6 walk is blameless will **m** to me.
134: 1 **m** by night in the house of the LORD.
135: 2 you who **m** in the house of the LORD,
Jer 33:22 the Levites who **m** before me as
Eze 40:46 near to the LORD to **m** before him."
42:14 in which they **m**, for these are holy.
43:19 who come near to **m** before me,
44:15 are to come near to **m** before me;
44:16 **m** before me and perform my service.
44:27 the sanctuary to **m** in the sanctuary,
45: 4 who **m** in the sanctuary and who draw
45: 4 who draw near to **m** before the LORD.
46:24 kitchens where those who **m** at the
Joel 1: 9 those who **m** before the LORD.
1:13 wail, you who **m** before the altar.
1:13 you who **m** before my God; for the
2:17 Let the priests, who **m** before the
Ro 15:16 to be a **m** of Christ Jesus to the
Col 1: 7 faithful **m** of Christ on our behalf,
4: 7 a faithful **m** and fellow-servant in
1Ti 4: 6 you will be a good **m** of Christ Jesus,
Heb 13:10 who **m** at the tabernacle have no

Ministered (Minister)

1Sa 2:11 but the boy **m** before the LORD under
3: 1 The boy Samuel **m** before the LORD
1Ch 6:32 They **m** with music before the

Ministering (Minister)

Ex 35:19 the woven garments worn for **m** in the
39: 1 garments for **m** in the sanctuary.
39:26 for **m**, as the LORD commanded Moses.
39:41 the woven garments worn for **m** in the
Nu 3:31 articles of the sanctuary used in **m**,
4:12 used for **m** in the sanctuary,
4:14 utensils used for **m** at the altar,
Dt 17:12 stands **m** there to the LORD your God
Jdg 20:28 the son of Aaron, **m** before it.
1Sa 2:18 Samuel was **m** before the LORD—a boy
1Ch 9:13 for **m** in the house of God.
24: 3 for their appointed order of **m**.
24:19 This was their appointed order of **m**
26:12 had duties for **m** in the temple of
Ezr 2:63 priest **m** with the Urim and Thummim.
Ne 7:65 priest **m** with the Urim and Thummim.
10:36 of our God, to the priests **m** there.
10:39 are kept and where the **m** priests,
12:44 with the **m** priests and Levites.
Jer 33:21 priests **m** before me—can be broken
Eze 44:17 wear any woollen garment while **m**
44:19 off the clothes they have been **m** in
Heb 1:14 Are not all angels **m** spirits sent to

Ministers (Minister)

Ex 28:35 Aaron must wear it when he **m**. The
2Ki 10:19 Baal, all his **m** and all his priests.
10:19 in order to destroy the **m** of Baal.
10:21 **m** of Baal came; not one stayed away.
10:22 "Bring robes for all the **m** of Baal.
10:23 Jehu said to the **m** of Baal, "Look
10:23 are here with you—only **m** of Baal."
Isa 61: 6 LORD, you will be named **m** of our God.
2Co 3: 6 He has made us competent as **m** of a

Ministry (Minister)

1Ch 25: 1 Heman and Jeduthun for the **m** of
25: 6 for the **m** at the house of God.
Lk 3:23 years old when he began his **m**.
Ac 1:17 of our number and shared in this **m**."
1:25 to take over this apostolic **m**, which
6: 2 to neglect the **m** of the word of God
6: 4 to prayer and the **m** of the word."
8:21 You have no part or share in this **m**,
21:19 among the Gentiles through his **m**.
Ro 11:13 to the Gentiles, I make much of my **m**
2Co 3: 3 the result of our **m**, written not
3: 7 Now if the **m** that brought death,
3: 8 will not the **m** of the Spirit be even
2Co 3: 9 If the **m** that condemns men is
3: 9 is the **m** that brings righteousness!
4: 1 have this **m**, we do not lose heart.
5:18 and gave us the **m** of reconciliation:
6: 3 that our **m** will not be discredited.
Gal 2: 8 For God, who was at work in the **m** of
2: 8 my **m** as an apostle to the Gentiles.
2Ti 4: 5 discharge all the duties of your **m**.
4:11 because he is helpful to me in my **m**.
Heb 8: 6 the **m** Jesus has received is as
9: 6 the outer room to carry on their **m**.

Minni

Jer 51:27 kingdoms: Ararat, **M** and Ashkenaz.

Minnith

Jdg 11:33 of **M**, as far as Abel Keramim.
Eze 27:17 wheat from **M** and confections,

Mint

Mt 23:23 of your spices—**m**, dill and cummin.
Lk 11:42 you give God a tenth of your **m**,

Miracle (Miracles, Miraculous, Miraculously)

Ex 7: 9 'Perform a **m**,' then say to Aaron,
Mk 9:39 "No-one who does a **m** in my name can
Lk 23: 8 he hoped to see him perform some **m**.
Jn 7:21 Jesus said to them, "I did one **m**,
Ac 4:16 they have done an outstanding **m**,

Miracles (Miracle)

1Ch 16:12 **m**, and the judgments he pronounced,
Ne 9:17 the **m** you performed among them.
Job 5: 9 fathomed, **m** that cannot be counted.
9:10 fathomed, **m** that cannot be counted.
Ps 77:11 I will remember your **m** of long ago.
77:14 You are the God who performs **m**; you
78:12 He did **m** in the sight of their
105: 5 **m**, and the judgments he pronounced,
106: 7 they gave no thought to your **m**; they
106:22 **m** in the land of Ham and awesome
Mt 7:22 out demons and perform many **m**?'
11:20 most of his **m** had been performed,
11:21 Bethsaida! If the **m** that were
11:23 If the **m** that were performed in you
13:58 he did not do many **m** there because
24:24 perform great signs and **m** to deceive
Mk 6: 2 been given him, that he even does **m**!
6: 5 He could not do any **m** there, except
13:22 perform signs and **m** to deceive the
Lk 10:13 Bethsaida! For if the **m** that were
19:37 voices for all the **m** they had seen:
Jn 7: 3 your disciples may see the **m** you do.
10:25 The **m** I do in my Father's name speak
10:32 you many great **m** from the Father.
10:38 believe the **m**, that you may know and
14:11 on the evidence of the **m** themselves.
15:24 But now they have seen these **m**, and
Ac 2:22 a man accredited by God to you by **m**,
8:13 by the great signs and **m** he saw.
19:11 God did extraordinary **m** through Paul,
Ro 15:19 by the power of signs and **m**, through
1Co 12:28 third teachers, then workers of **m**,
12:29 Are all teachers? Do all work **m**?
2Co 12:12 wonders and **m**—were done among you
Gal 3: 5 work **m** among you because you observe
2Th 2: 9 of counterfeit **m**, signs and wonders,
Heb 2: 4 wonders and various **m**, and gifts of

Miraculous (Miracle, *Miraculous signs, Miraculous signs and wonders*)

Ex 4: 8 the first **m** sign, they may believe
8:23 This **m** sign will occur tomorrow.'
Dt 13: 1 announces to you a **m** sign or wonder,
2Ch 32:24 answered him and gave him a **m** sign.
32:31 **m** sign that had occurred in the land,
Mt 12:38 we want to see a **m** sign from you."
12:39 generation asks for a **m** sign!
13:54 and these **m** powers?" they asked.
14: 2 is why **m** powers are at work in him."
16: 4 generation looks for a **m** sign,
Mk 6:14 is why **m** powers are at work in him."
8:12 for a **m** sign? I tell you the truth,

Lk 11:29 It asks for a **m** sign, but none will
Jn 2:18 Jews demanded of him, "What **m** sign
4:54 This was the second **m** sign that
6:14 After the people saw the **m** sign that
6:30 they asked him, "What **m** sign then
10:41 John never performed a **m** sign
12:18 this **m** sign, went out to meet him.
1Co 12:10 to another **m** powers, to another

Miraculous signs (*Miraculous signs and wonders*)
Ex 4:17 so that you can perform **m** with it."
4:28 **m** he had commanded him to perform.
10: 1 perform these **m** of mine among
Nu 14:11 the **m** I have performed among them?
14:22 the **m** I performed in Egypt and in
Dt 29: 3 trials, those **m** and great wonders.
Ps 74: 9 We are given no **m**; no prophets are
78:43 the day he displayed his **m** in Egypt,
105:27 They performed his **m** among them, his
Jn 2:11 This, the first of his **m**, Jesus
2:23 many people saw the **m** he was doing
3: 2 For no-one could perform the **m** you
6: 2 the **m** he had performed on the sick.
6:26 not because you saw **m** but because
7:31 will he do more **m** than this man?"
9:16 do such **m**?" they were divided.
11:47 "Here is this man performing many **m**.
12:37 Even after Jesus had done all these **m**
20:30 Jesus did many other **m** in the
Ac 2:43 and **m** were done by the apostles.
6: 8 wonders and **m** among the people.
7:36 Egypt and did wonders and **m** in Egypt,
8: 6 the crowds heard Philip and saw the **m**
1Co 1:22 Jews demand **m** and Greeks look for
Rev 13:13 he performed great and **m**, even
16:14 are spirits of demons performing **m**,
19:20 had performed the **m** on his behalf.

Miraculous signs and wonders
Ex 7: 3 and though I multiply my **m** in Egypt,
Dt 4:34 by testings, by **m**, by war, by a
6:22 Before our eyes the LORD sent **m**
7:19 great trials, the **m**, the mighty hand
26: 8 with great terror and with **m**.
34:11 did all those **m** the LORD sent him
Ne 9:10 You sent **m** against Pharaoh, against
Jer 32:20 You performed **m** in Egypt and have
Da 4: 2 my pleasure to tell you about the **m**
Jn 4:48 "Unless you people see **m**, Jesus told
Ac 4:30 perform **m** through the name of your
5:12 The apostles performed many **m** among
14: 3 by enabling them to do **m**.
15:12 telling about the **m** God had done

Miraculously (Miracle)
Ac 4:22 For the man who was **m** healed was

Mire (Miry)
Ps 40: 2 out of the mud and **m**; he set my feet
69:14 Rescue me from the **m**, do not let me
Isa 57:20 rest, whose waves cast up **m** and mud.
Mic 7:10 underfoot like **m** in the streets.

Miriam
Sister of Moses and Aaron (Nu 25:59; 1Ch 6:3). Watched Moses in bulrushes; suggested mother as nurse (Ex 2:4–8). Prophetess; led dancing and sang at Red Sea (Ex 15:20–21); criticised Moses, became leprous (Nu 12:1–15; Dt 24:9). Death (Nu 20:1).

Ex 15:20 **M** the prophetess, Aaron's sister,
15:21 **M** sang to them: "Sing to the LORD,
Nu 12: 1 **M** and Aaron began to talk against
12: 4 Aaron and **M**, "Come out to the Tent
12: 5 the Tent and summoned Aaron and **M**.
12:10 there stood **M**—leprous, like snow.
12:15 **M** was confined outside the camp for
20: 1 There **M** died and was buried.
26:59 Aaron, Moses and their sister **M**.
Dt 24: 9 what the LORD your God did to **M**
1Ch 4:17 One of Mered's wives gave birth to **M**,
6: 3 of Amram: Aaron, Moses and **M**.
Mic 6: 4 Moses to lead you, also Aaron and **M**.

Mirmah
1Ch 8:10 Jeuz, Sakia and **M**. These were his

Mirror (Mirrors)
Job 37:18 skies, hard as a **m** of cast bronze?
1Co 13:12 a **m**; then we shall see face to face.
Jas 1:23 a man who looks at his face in a **m**

Mirrors (Mirror)
Ex 38: 8 its bronze stand from the **m** of the
Isa 3:23 **m**, and the linen garments and tiaras

Mirth
Job 20: 5 that the **m** of the wicked is brief,

Miry (Mire)
Ps 69: 2 I sink in the **m** depths, where there
140:10 fire, into **m** pits, never to rise.

Miscarried (Miscarry)
Ge 31:38 Your sheep and goats have not **m**, nor

Miscarry (Miscarried)
Ex 23:26 none will **m** or be barren in your
Job 21:10 their cows calve and do not **m**.
Hos 9:14 that **m** and breasts that are dry.

Misdeeds
Ps 99: 8 God, though you punished their **m**.
Ro 8:13 the **m** of the body, you will live,

Misdemeanour
Ac 18:14 about some **m** or serious crime,

Miserable (Misery)
Nu 21: 5 water! And we detest this **m** food!"
Jdg 11:35 "Oh! My daughter! You have made me **m**
Job 16: 2 these; **m** comforters are you all!
Ecc 4: 8 too is meaningless—a **m** business!
Gal 4: 9 back to those weak and **m** principles?

Misery (Miserable)
Ge 16:11 for the LORD has heard of your **m**.
29:32 It is because the LORD has seen my **m**.
44:29 grey head down to the grave in **m**.'
44:34 **m** that would come upon my father."
Ex 3: 7 seen the **m** of my people in Egypt.
3:17 out of your **m** in Egypt into the
4:31 had seen their **m**, they bowed down
Nu 23:21 "No misfortune is seen in Jacob, no **m**
Dt 26: 7 and saw our **m**, toil and oppression.
Jdg 10:16 he could bear Israel's **m** no longer.
1Sa 1:11 look upon your servants **m** and
Job 3:20 "Why is light given to those in **m**,
6: 2 all my **m** be placed on the scales!
7: 3 nights of **m** have been assigned to
9:18 but would overwhelm me with **m**.
20:22 full force of **m** will come upon him.
Ps 44:24 and forget our **m** and oppression?
94:20 one that brings on **m** by its decrees?
Pr 31: 7 and remember their **m** no more.
Ecc 8: 6 a man's **m** weighs heavily upon him.
Hos 5:15 will seek my face; in their **m** they
Mic 7: 1 What **m** is mine! I am like one who
Ro 3:16 ruin and **m** mark their ways,
Jas 5: 1 of the **m** that is coming upon you.

Misfortune
Nu 23:21 "No **m** is seen in Jacob, no misery
Ru 1:21 the Almighty has brought **m** upon me."
1Ch 7:23 there had been **m** in his family.
Job 12: 5 Men at ease have contempt for **m** as
31:29 "If I have rejoiced at my enemy's **m**
Pr 13:21 **M** pursues the sinner, but prosperity
Ecc 2:21 too is meaningless and a great **m**.
5:14 or wealth lost through some **m**, so
Isa 65:23 vain or bear children doomed to **m**;
Ob :12 on your brother in the day of his **m**,

Mishael
Ex 6:22 The sons of Uzziel were **M**, Elzaphan
Lev 10: 4 Moses summoned **M** and Elzaphan, sons
Ne 8: 4 **M**, Malkijah, Hashum, Hashbaddanah,
Da 1: 6 Daniel, Hananiah, **M** and Azariah.
1: 7 **M**, Meshach; and to Azariah, Abednego.
1:11 Daniel, Hananiah, **M** and Azariah,
1:19 Hananiah, **M** and Azariah; so they
2:17 his friends Hananiah, **M** and Azariah.

Mishal
Jos 19:26 Allammelech, Amad and **M**. On the west
21:30 from the tribe of Asher, **M**, Abdon,

Misham
1Ch 8:12 The sons of Elpaal: Eber, **M**, Shemed

Mishma
Ge 25:14 **M**, Dumah, Massa,
1Ch 1:30 **M**, Dumah, Massa, Hadad, Tema,
4:25 son, Mibsam his son and **M** his son.
4:26 The descendants of **M**: Hammuel his

Mishmannah
1Ch 12:10 **M** the fourth, Jeremiah the fifth,

Mishraites
1Ch 2:53 Puthites, Shumathites and **M**.

Mislead (Misleading, Misleads, Misled)
2Ki 4:16 "Don't **m** your servant, O man of God!"
2Ch 32:15 deceive you and **m** you like this.
Isa 9:16 Those who guide this people **m** them,
36:18 "Do not let Hezekiah **m** you when he
47:10 Your wisdom and knowledge **m** you

Misleading (Mislead)
2Ki 18:32 for he is **m** you when he says, 'The
2Ch 32:11 the king of Assyria,' he is **m** you,
Lam 2:14 they gave you were false and **m**.
Da 2: 9 You have conspired to tell me **m** and

Misleads (Mislead)
Isa 44:20 He feeds on ashes, a deluded heart **m**
Rev 2:20 By her teaching she **m** my servants

Misled (Mislead)
Jer 38:22 'They **m** you and overcame you—those
1Co 15:33 Do not be **m**: "Bad company corrupts

Mispar
Ezr 2: 2 Reelaiah, Mordecai, Bilshan, **M**,

Mispereth
Ne 7: 7 Nahamani, Mordecai, Bilshan, **M**,

Misrephoth Maim
Jos 11: 8 to **M**, and to the Valley of Mizpah on
13: 6 mountain regions from Lebanon to **M**,

Miss (Missed, Misses, Missing)
Jdg 20:16 sling a stone at a hair and not **m**.
Pr 19: 2 nor to be hasty and **m** the way.

Missed (Miss)
1Sa 20:18 **m**, because your seat will be empty.
Jer 3:16 be **m**, nor will another one be made.
46:17 noise; he has **m** his opportunity.'

Misses (Miss)
1Sa 20: 6 If your father **m** me at all, tell him,
Heb 12:15 See to it that no-one **m** the grace of

Missing (Miss)
Nu 31:49 under our command, and not one is **m**.
Jdg 21: 3 one tribe be **m** from Israel today?
1Sa 25: 7 at Carmel nothing of theirs was **m**.
25:15 the fields near them nothing was **m**.
25:21 desert so that nothing of his was **m**.
30:19 Nothing was **m**: young or old, boy or
2Sa 2:30 of David's men were found **m**.
1Ki 20:39 If he is **m**, it will be your life for
2Ki 10:19 See that no-one is **m**, because I am

Job 5:24 of your property and find nothing **m**.
Isa 34:16 be **m**, not one will lack her mate.
40:26 strength, not one of them is **m**.
Jer 23: 4 will any be **m**," declares the LORD.

Mission (Missions)
Jos 22: 3 the **m** the LORD your God gave you.
1Sa 15:18 he sent you on a **m**, saying, 'Go and
15:20 "I went on the **m** the LORD assigned
21: 2 about your **m** and your instructions.
Isa 48:15 him, and he will succeed in his **m**.
Ac 12:25 and Saul had finished their **m**,

Missions (Mission)
1Sa 21: 5 The men's things are holy even on **m**

Mist (Mists)
Isa 44:22 cloud, your sins like the morning **m**.
Hos 6: 4 Your love is like the morning **m**,
13: 3 they will be like the morning **m**,
Ac 13:11 Immediately **m** and darkness came
Jas 4:14 What is your life? You are a **m** that

Mistake (Mistaken)
Ge 43:12 your sacks. Perhaps it was a **m**.
Lev 22:14 anyone eats a sacred offering by **m**,
Jdg 9:36 "You **m** the shadows of the mountains
Ecc 5: 6 messenger, "My vow was a **m**."
Jer 42:20 that you made a fatal **m** when you

Mistaken (Mistake)
Mk 12:27 of the living. You are badly **m**!"

Mistress
Ge 16: 4 she began to despise her **m**.
16: 8 away from my **m** Sarai," she answered.
16: 9 Go back to your **m** and submit to her."
2Ki 5: 3 She said to her **m**, "If only my
Ps 123: 2 of a maid look to the hand of her **m**,
Pr 30:23 a maidservant who displaces her **m**.
Isa 24: 2 for master as for servant, for **m** as
Na 3: 4 alluring, the **m** of sorceries, who

Mists (Mist)
2Pe 2:17 water and **m** driven by a storm.

Misunderstand
Dt 32:27 lest the adversary **m** and say, 'Our

Misuse (Misuses)
Ex 20: 7 "You shall not **m** the name of the
Dt 5:11 "You shall not **m** the name of the
Ps 139:20 your adversaries **m** your name.

Misuses (Misuse)
Ex 20: 7 anyone guiltless who **m** his name.
Dt 5:11 anyone guiltless who **m** his name.

Mithcah
Nu 33:28 They left Terah and camped at **M**.
33:29 They left **M** and camped at Hashmonah.

Mithnite
1Ch 11:43 Hanan son of Maacah, Joshaphat the **M**,

Mithredath
Ezr 1: 8 had them brought by **M** the treasurer,
4: 7 Bishlam, **M**, Tabeel and the rest of

Mitylene
Ac 20:14 we took him aboard and went on to **M**.

Mix (Mixed, Mixes, Mixing, Mixture, Well-mixed)
Rev 18: 6 **M** her a double portion from her own

Mixed (Mix)
Ex 29: 2 make bread, and cakes **m** with oil,
29:40 **m** with a quarter of a hin of oil
Lev 2: 4 made without yeast and **m** with oil,
2: 5 flour **m** with oil, and without yeast.
Lev 7:10 every grain offering, whether **m** with
7:12 made without yeast and **m** with oil,
7:12 flour well-kneaded and **m** with oil.
9: 4 with a grain offering **m** with oil.
14:10 **m** with oil for a grain offering,
14:21 **m** with oil for a grain offering,
23:13 an ephah of fine flour **m** with oil
Nu 6:15 made of fine flour **m** with oil,
7:13 **m** with oil as a grain offering;
7:19 **m** with oil as a grain offering;
7:25 **m** with oil as a grain offering;
7:31 **m** with oil as a grain offering;
7:37 **m** with oil as a grain offering;
7:43 **m** with oil as a grain offering;
7:49 **m** with oil as a grain offering;
7:55 **m** with oil as a grain offering;
7:61 **m** with oil as a grain offering;
7:67 **m** with oil as a grain offering;
7:73 **m** with oil as a grain offering;
7:79 **m** with oil as a grain offering;
8: 8 offering of fine flour **m** with oil;
15: 4 **m** with a quarter of a hin of oil.
15: 6 **m** with a third of a hin of oil,
15: 9 fine flour **m** with half a hin of oil.
28: 5 **m** with a quarter of a hin of oil
28: 9 an ephah of fine flour **m** with oil.
28:12 fine flour **m** with oil; with the ram,
28:12 an ephah of fine flour **m** with oil;
28:13 an ephah of fine flour **m** with oil.
28:20 **m** with oil; with the ram, two-tenths;
28:28 **m** with oil; with the ram, two-tenths;
29: 3 **m** with oil; with the ram, two-tenths;
29: 9 **m** with oil; with the ram, two-tenths;
29:14 an ephah of fine flour **m** with oil;
Ps 75: 8 wine **m** with spices; he pours it out,
Pr 9: 2 She has prepared her meat and **m** her
9: 5 my food and drink the wine I have **m**.
23:30 who go to sample bowls of **m** wine.
Isa 65:11 fill bowls of **m** wine for Destiny,
Da 2:41 even as you saw iron **m** with clay.
2:43 just as you saw the iron **m** with
Mt 13:33 **m** into a large amount of flour until
27:34 **m** with gall; but after tasting it,
Mk 15:23 they offered him wine **m** with myrrh,
Lk 13: 1 Pilate had **m** with their sacrifices.
13:21 like yeast that a woman took and **m**
Jude :23 **m** with fear—hating even the
Rev 8: 7 and there came hail and fire **m** with
15: 2 like a sea of glass **m** with fire and,

Mixes (Mix)
Da 2:43 any more than iron **m** with clay.
Hos 7: 8 "Ephraim **m** with the nations; Ephraim

Mixing (Mix)
1Ch 9:30 some of the priests took care of **m**
23:29 the baking and the **m**, and all
Isa 5:22 wine and champions at **m** drinks,
Eze 24:10 Cook the meat well, **m** in the spices;

Mixture (Mix)
Da 2:43 so the people will be a **m** and will
Jn 19:39 Nicodemus brought a **m** of myrrh and

Mizar
Ps 42: 6 the heights of Hermon—from Mount **M**.

Mizpah
1. A town of Benjamin (Jos 18:26), where the Israelites assembled before the LORD (Jdg 20:1, 3; 21:1, 5, 8). Here Samuel and the Israelites defeated the Philistines (1Sa 7:5, 7, 11) and Saul was proclaimed king (1Sa 10:17–25). Fortified by Asa (1Ki 15:22; 2Ch 16:6) who built a cistern which was used by Ishmael for Gedaliah and others whom he slaughtered (Jer 41:1-9). **2.** Town in Gilead, east of Jordan, where Jacob set up a memorial to his covenant with Laban (Ge 31:48–49). Probably an Israelite camp (Jdg 10:17) and home of Jephthah (Jdg 11:11, 34). Also known as Ramath Mizpah (Jos 13:26). **3.** Region near foot of Mount Hermon, where Jabin's allies the Hivites lived (Jos 11:1–3) whom Joshua defeated (Jos 11:8). **4.** Town in Moab, where David took his parents for safety from Saul (1Sa 22:3). **5.** Town in the lowlands of Judah (Jos 15:38).

Ge 31:49 was also called **M**, because he said,
Jos 11: 3 below Hermon in the region of **M**.
11: 8 and to the Valley of **M** on the east,
15:38 Dilean, **M**, Joktheel,
18:26 **M**, Kephirah, Mozah,
Jdg 10:17 Israelites assembled and camped at **M**.
11:11 all his words before the LORD in **M**.
11:29 passed through **M** of Gilead, and from
11:34 Jephthah returned to his home in **M**,
20: 1 and assembled before the LORD in **M**.
20: 3 the Israelites had gone up to **M**.
21: 1 of Israel had taken an oath at **M**:
21: 5 **M** should certainly be put to death.
21: 8 to assemble before the LORD at **M**?"
1Sa 7: 5 "Assemble all Israel at **M** and I will
7: 6 they had assembled at **M**, they drew
7: 6 And Samuel was leader of Israel at **M**.
7: 7 that Israel had assembled at **M**,
7:11 The men of Israel rushed out of **M**
7:12 and set it up between **M** and Shen.
7:16 circuit from Bethel to Gilgal to **M**,
10:17 people of Israel to the LORD at **M**
22: 3 From there David went to **M** in Moab
1Ki 15:22 up Geba in Benjamin, and also **M**.
2Ki 25:23 they came to Gedaliah at **M**—Ishmael
25:25 Babylonians who were with him at **M**.
2Ch 16: 6 With them he built up Geba and **M**.
Ne 3: 7 **M**—Melatiah of Gibeon and Jadon of
3:15 ruler of the district of **M**.
3:19 Ezer son of Jeshua, ruler of **M**,
Jer 40: 6 went to Gedaliah son of Ahikam at **M**
40: 8 they came to Gedaliah at **M**—Ishmael
40:10 I myself will stay in **M** to represent
40:12 to Gedaliah at **M**, from all the
40:13 open country came to Gedaliah at **M**
40:15 said privately to Gedaliah in **M**,
41: 1 men to Gedaliah son of Ahikam at **M**.
41: 3 Jews who were with Gedaliah at **M**,
41: 6 went out from **M** to meet them,
41:10 rest of the people who were in **M**
41:14 had taken captive at **M** turned
41:16 led away all the survivors from **M**
Hos 5: 1 at **M**, a net spread out on Tabor.

Mizraim
Ge 10: 6 The sons of Ham: Cush, **M**, Put and
10:13 **M** was the father of the Ludites,
1Ch 1: 8 The sons of Ham: Cush, **M**, Put and
1:11 **M** was the father of the Ludites,

Mizzah
Ge 36:13 Reuel: Nahath, Zerah, Shammah and **M**.
36:17 Chiefs Nahath, Zerah, Shammah and **M**.
1Ch 1:37 Reuel: Nahath, Zerah, Shammah and **M**.

Mnason
Ac 21:16 home of **M**, where we were to stay.

Moab (Moab's, Moabite, Moabites, Moabitess)
Country east of the Dead Sea, inhabited by descendants of Lot's son (Ge 19:36–37). Also called the plains of Moab; captured by the Amorites before the Israelites conquered it (Nu 21:17–31). Here God instructed Moses how to allot the promised land (Nu 33:50–36:12), Moses expounded the commandments (Nu 36:13; Dt 1:5) and made the covenant with God (Dt 29:1). Moses viewed promised land from Moab's Mount Nebo before he died here (Nu 27:12–23; Dt 34:1–6). Birthplace of Ruth (Ru 2:6). Its people were defeated by Israelites under Ehud (Jdg 3:29–30), Saul (1Sa 14:47) and David (2Sa 8:2). The tension continued under Jehoshaphat (2Ch 20:1–23), Jehoram (2Ki 3:4–27) and Jehoiakim (2Ki 24:2). The prophets announced its destruction (Isa 15–16; Jer 48).

Ge 19:37 and she named him **M**; he is the
36:35 country of **M**, succeeded him as king.
Ex 15:15 the leaders of **M** will be seized with
Nu 21:11 that faces **M** towards the sunrise.
21:13 of **M**, between **M** and the Amorites.
21:15 Ar and lie along the border of **M**."
21:20 from Bamoth to the valley in **M** where
21:26 fought against the former king of **M**
21:28 **M**, the citizens of Arnon's heights.

Nu 21:29 Woe to you, O **M**! You are destroyed,
22: 1 travelled to the plains of **M**
22: 3 **M** was terrified because there were
22: 3 Indeed, **M** was filled with dread
22: 4 who was king of **M** at that time,
22: 7 The elders of **M** and Midian left,
22:10 king of **M**, sent me this message:
22:21 and went with the princes of **M**.
23: 6 offering, with all the princes of **M**.
23: 7 of **M** from the eastern mountains.
23:17 his offering, with the princes of **M**.
24:17 He will crush the foreheads of **M**,
26: 3 on the plains of **M** by the Jordan
26:63 **M** by the Jordan across from Jericho.
31:12 **M**, by the Jordan across from Jericho.
33:44 at Iye Abarim, on the border of **M**.
33:48 **M** by the Jordan across from Jericho.
33:49 There on the plains of **M** they camped
33:50 On the plains of **M** by the Jordan
35: 1 On the plains of **M** by the Jordan
36:13 **M** by the Jordan across from Jericho.
Dt 1: 5 of the Jordan in the territory of **M**,
2: 8 along the desert road of **M**.
2:18 to pass by the region of **M** at Ar.
29: 1 to make with the Israelites in **M**,
32:49 the Abarim Range to Mount Nebo in **M**,
34: 1 plains of **M** to the top of Pisgah,
34: 5 there in **M**, as the LORD had said.
34: 6 He buried him in **M**, in the valley
34: 8 Moses in the plains of **M** thirty days,
Jos 13:32 **M** across the Jordan east of Jericho.
24: 9 Balak son of Zippor, the king of **M**,
Jdg 3:12 Eglon king of **M** power over Israel.
3:14 Eglon king of **M** for eighteen years.
3:15 him with tribute to Eglon king of **M**.
3:17 king of **M**, who was a very fat man.
3:28 **M**, your enemy, into your hands.
3:28 fords of the Jordan that led to **M**,
3:30 That day **M** was made subject to
10: 6 the gods of Sidon, the gods of **M**,
11:15 of **M** or the land of the Ammonites.
11:17 They sent also to the king of **M**, and
11:18 skirted the lands of Edom and **M**,
11:18 eastern side of the country of **M**,
11:18 of **M**, for the Arnon was its border.
11:25 king of **M**? Did he ever quarrel with
Ru 1: 1 for a while in the country of **M**.
1: 2 And they went to **M** and lived there.
1: 6 she heard in **M** that the LORD had
1:22 Naomi returned from **M** accompanied by
2: 6 who came back from **M** with Naomi.
4: 3 "Naomi, who has come back from **M**, is
1Sa 12: 9 king of **M**, who fought against them.
14:47 their enemies on every side: **M**,
22: 3 in **M** and said to the king of **M**,
22: 4 he left them with the king of **M**, and
2Sa 8:12 Edom and **M**, the Ammonites and the
1Ki 11: 7 for Chemosh the detestable god of **M**,
2Ki 1: 1 After Ahab's death, **M** rebelled
3: 4 Now Mesha king of **M** raised sheep,
3: 5 after Ahab died, the king of **M**
3: 7 king of **M** has rebelled against me.
3: 7 go with me to fight against **M**?"
3:10 together only to hand us over to **M**?"
3:13 together to hand us over to **M**."
3:18 he will also hand **M** over to you.
3:23 Now to the plunder, **M**!"
3:26 the king of **M** saw that the battle
23:13 for Chemosh the vile god of **M**, and
1Ch 1:46 country of **M**, succeeded him as king.
4:22 who ruled in **M** and Jashubi Lehem.
8: 8 Sons were born to Shaharaim in **M**
18:11 from all these nations: Edom and **M**,
2Ch 20:10 "But now here are men from Ammon, **M**
20:22 **M** and Mount Seir who were invading
20:23 The men of Ammon and **M** rose up
Ne 13:23 women from Ashdod, Ammon and **M**.
Ps 60: 8 **M** is my washbasin, upon Edom I toss
83: 6 Ishmaelites, of **M** and the Hagrites,
108: 9 **M** is my washbasin, upon Edom I toss
Isa 11:14 They will lay hands on Edom and **M**,
15: 1 concerning **M**: Ar in **M** is ruined,
15: 1 **M** is ruined, destroyed in a night!
15: 2 weep; **M** wails over Nebo and Medeba.
15: 4 Therefore the armed men of **M** cry out,
15: 5 My heart cries out over **M**; her
Isa 15: 8 outcry echoes along the border of **M**;
15: 9 a lion upon the fugitives of **M**
16: 2 of **M** at the fords of the Arnon.
16: 7 wail, they wail together for **M**.
16:11 My heart laments for **M** like a harp,
16:12 **M** appears at her high place, she
16:13 LORD has already spoken concerning **M**.
25:10 but **M** will be trampled under him as
Jer 9:26 Egypt, Judah, Edom, Ammon, **M** and all
25:21 Edom, **M** and Ammon;
27: 3 send word to the kings of Edom, **M**,
40:11 all the Jews in **M**, Ammon, Edom and
48: 1 Concerning **M**: This is what the LORD
48: 2 **M** will be praised no more; in
48: 4 **M** will be broken; her little ones
48: 9 Put salt on **M**, for she will be laid
48:11 "**M** has been at rest from youth, like
48:13 **M** will be ashamed of Chemosh, as the
48:15 **M** will be destroyed and her towns
48:16 "The fall of **M** is at hand; her
48:18 for he who destroys **M** will come up
48:20 **M** is disgraced, for she is shattered.
48:20 by the Arnon that **M** is destroyed.
48:24 to all the towns of **M**, far and near.
48:26 Let **M** wallow in her vomit; let her
48:28 among the rocks, you who live in **M**.
48:31 I wail over **M**, for all **M** I cry out,
48:33 from the orchards and fields of **M**.
48:35 In **M** I will put an end to those who
48:36 "So my heart laments for **M** like a
48:38 On all the roofs in **M** and in the
48:38 **M** like a jar that no-one wants,"
48:39 How they wail! How **M** turns her back
48:39 **M** has become an object of ridicule,
48:40 down, spreading its wings over **M**.
48:42 **M** will be destroyed as a nation
48:43 O people of **M**," declares the LORD.
48:44 upon **M** the year of her punishment,"
48:45 it burns the foreheads of **M**,
48:46 Woe to you, O **M**! The people of
48:47 "Yet I will restore the fortunes of **M**
48:47 Here ends the judgment on **M**.
Eze 25: 8 'Because **M** and Seir said, "Look, the
25: 9 I will expose the flank of **M**,
25:10 I will give **M** along with the
25:11 I will inflict punishment on **M**. Then
Da 11:41 but Edom, **M** and the leaders of Ammon
Am 2: 1 "For three sins of **M**, even for four,
2: 2 I will send fire upon **M** that will
2: 2 **M** will go down in great tumult amid
Mic 6: 5 remember what Balak king of **M**
Zep 2: 8 "I have heard the insults of **M** and
2: 9 "surely **M** will become like Sodom,

Moab's (Moab)

2Sa 23:20 He struck down two of **M** best men. He
1Ch 11:22 He struck down two of **M** best men. He
Isa 16: 6 We have heard of **M** pride—her
16:14 **M** splendour and all her many people
Jer 48:25 **M** horn is cut off; her arm is broken,
48:29 "We have heard of **M** pride—her
48:41 In that day the hearts of **M** warriors

Moabite (Moab)

Nu 22: 8 So the **M** princes stayed with him.
22:14 the **M** princes returned to Balak and
22:36 went out to meet him at the **M** town
25: 1 in sexual immorality with **M** women,
Dt 23: 3 No Ammonite or **M** or any of his
Ru 1: 4 They married **M** women, one named
2Ki 13:20 Now **M** raiders used to enter the
24: 2 The LORD sent Babylonian, Aramean, **M**
1Ch 11:46 the sons of Elnaam, Ithmah the **M**,
2Ch 24:26 Jehozabad, son of Shimrith a **M** woman.
Ne 13: 1 found written that no Ammonite or **M**
Isa 16: 4 Let the **M** fugitives stay with you;

Moabites (Moab)

Ge 19:37 he is the father of the **M** of today.
Nu 22: 4 The **M** said to the elders of Midian,
Dt 2: 9 "Do not harass the **M** or provoke them
2:11 but the **M** called them Emites.
2:29 who live in Seir, and the **M**, who
Jdg 3:29 struck down about ten thousand **M**,
2Sa 8: 2 David also defeated the **M**. He made
2Sa 8: 2 So the **M** became subject to David and
1Ki 11: 1 women besides Pharaoh's daughter—**M**,
11:33 Chemosh the god of the **M**, and Molech
2Ki 3:21 Now all the **M** had heard that the
3:22 To the **M** across the way, the water
3:24 when the **M** came to the camp of
3:24 the land and slaughtered the **M**.
1Ch 18: 2 David also defeated the **M**, and they
2Ch 20: 1 After this, the **M** and Ammonites with
Ezr 9: 1 Ammonites, **M**, Egyptians and Amorites.
Isa 16: 7 Therefore the **M** wail, they wail

Moabitess (Moab)

Ru 1:22 from Moab accompanied by Ruth the **M**,
2: 2 Ruth the **M** said to Naomi, "Let me go
2: 6 The foreman replied, "She is the **M**
2:21 Ruth the **M** said, "He even said to me,
4: 5 land from Naomi and from Ruth the **M**,
4:10 I have also acquired Ruth the **M**,

Moadiah (Moadiah's)

Ne 12: 5 Mijamin, **M**, Bilgah,

Moadiah's (Moadiah)

Ne 12:17 of Miniamin's and of **M**, Piltai;

Moan (Moaned, Moaning)

Ps 90: 9 wrath; we finish our years with a **m**.
Isa 59:11 We all growl like bears; we **m**
Jer 48:31 I **m** for the men of Kir Hareseth.
Joel 1:18 How the cattle **m**! The herds mill
Mic 1: 8 like a jackal and **m** like an owl.
Na 2: 7 Its slave girls **m** like doves and

Moaned (Moan)

Isa 38:14 I **m** like a mourning dove.

Moaning (Moan)

Jer 31:18 "I have surely heard Ephraim's **m**:
Eze 7:16 **m** like doves of the valleys, each

Mob

Eze 16:40 They will bring a **m** against you, who
23:46 Bring a **m** against them and give them
23:47 The **m** will stone them and cut them
Jn 7:49 No! But this **m** that knows nothing of
Ac 17: 5 a **m** and started a riot in the city.
21:35 the violence of the **m** was so great

Mobilised

Jdg 20:15 At once the Benjamites **m** twenty-six
2Ki 3: 6 out from Samaria and **m** all Israel.
6:24 Ben-Hadad king of Aram **m** his entire

Mock (Mocked, Mocker, Mockers, Mockery, Mocking, Mocks)

Job 11: 3 Will no-one rebuke you when you **m**?
21: 3 and after I have spoken, **m** on.
22:19 the innocent **m** them, saying,
30: 1 "But now they **m** me, men younger than
30: 9 "And now their sons **m** me in song; I
Ps 22: 7 All who see me **m** me; they hurl
69:12 Those who sit at the gate **m** me, and
74:10 How long will the enemy **m** you, O God?
74:22 how fools **m** you all day long.
80: 6 neighbours, and our enemies **m** us.
119:51 The arrogant **m** me without restraint,
Pr 1:26 will **m** when calamity overtakes you—
14: 9 Fools **m** at making amends for sin,
Isa 52: 5 who rule them **m**," declares the LORD.
Lam 3:14 they **m** me in song all day long.
3:63 standing, they **m** me in their songs.
Eze 22: 5 those who are far away will **m** you,
Mk 10:34 who will **m** him and spit on him, flog
Lk 18:32 They will **m** him, insult him, spit on

Mocked (Mock)

2Ch 36:16 they **m** God's messengers, despised
Ne 2:19 about it, they **m** and ridiculed us.
Ps 35:16 Like the ungodly they maliciously **m**;
74:18 Remember how the enemy has **m** you,
89:50 Lord, how your servant has been **m**,
89:51 with which your enemies have **m**,

Ps 89:51 **m** every step of your anointed one.
Mt 20:19 to be **m** and flogged and crucified.
27:29 and knelt in front of him and **m** him.
27:31 After they had **m** him, they took off
27:41 of the law and the elders **m** him.
Mk 15:20 they had **m** him, they took off the
15:31 of the law **m** him among themselves.
Lk 23:11 his soldiers ridiculed and **m** him.
23:36 The soldiers also came up and **m** him.
Gal 6: 7 Do not be deceived: God cannot be **m**.

Mocker (Mock)
Pr 9: 7 "Whoever corrects a **m** invites insult;
9: 8 Do not rebuke a **m** or he will hate
9:12 you are a **m**, you alone will suffer."
13: 1 but a **m** does not listen to rebuke.
14: 6 The **m** seeks wisdom and finds none,
15:12 A **m** resents correction; he will not
19:25 Flog a **m**, and the simple will learn
20: 1 Wine is a **m** and beer a brawler;
21:11 a **m** is punished, the simple gain
21:24 The proud and arrogant man—"**M**" is
22:10 Drive out the **m**, and out goes strife;
24: 9 folly are sin, and men detest a **m**.

Mockers (Mock)
Job 17: 2 Surely **m** surround me; my eyes must
Ps 1: 1 of sinners or sit in the seat of **m**.
Pr 1:22 How long will **m** delight in mockery
3:34 He mocks proud **m** but gives grace to
19:29 Penalties are prepared for **m**, and
29: 8 **M** stir up a city, but wise men turn
Isa 29:20 The ruthless will vanish, the **m** will
Hos 7: 5 wine, and he joins hands with the **m**.

Mockery (Mock)
Pr 1:22 How long will mockers delight in **m**
Jer 10:15 They are worthless, the objects of **m**;
51:18 They are worthless, the objects of **m**;

Mocking (Mock)
Ge 21: 9 Egyptian had borne to Abraham was **m**,
Isa 28:22 Now stop your **m**, or your chains will
50: 6 hide my face from **m** and spitting.
57: 4 Whom are you **m**? At whom do you sneer
Zep 2:10 **m** the people of the LORD Almighty.
Lk 22:63 began **m** and beating him.

Mocks (Mock)
2Ki 19:21 of Zion despises you and **m** you.
Job 9:23 he **m** the despair of the innocent.
Pr 3:34 He **m** proud mockers but gives grace
17: 5 He who **m** the poor shows contempt for
19:28 A corrupt witness **m** at justice, and
30:17 "The eye that **m** a father, that
Isa 37:22 Daughter of Zion despises and **m** you.
Jer 20: 7 all day long; everyone **m** me.

Model (Models)
Eze 28:12 'You were the **m** of perfection, full
1Th 1: 7 you became a **m** to all the believers
2Th 3: 9 ourselves a **m** for you to follow.

Models (Model)
1Sa 6: 5 Make **m** of the tumours and of the
6:11 gold rats and the **m** of the tumours.

Modestly (Modesty)
1Ti 2: 9 I also want women to dress **m**, with

Modesty (Modestly)
1Co 12:23 are treated with special **m**,

Moisten (Moisture)
Eze 46:14 of a hin of oil to **m** the flour.

Moisture (Moisten)
Job 36:28 the clouds pour down their **m** and
37:11 He loads the clouds with **m**; he
Lk 8: 6 withered because they had no **m**.

Moladah
Jos 15:26 Amam, Shema, **M**,
19: 2 included: Beersheba (or Sheba), **M**,
1Ch 4:28 They lived in Beersheba, **M**, Hazar
Ne 11:26 in Jeshua, in **M**, in Beth Pelet,

Molech
Lev 18:21 your children to be sacrificed to **M**,
20: 2 children to **M** must be put to death.
20: 3 for by giving his children to **M**,
20: 4 man gives one of his children to **M**
20: 5 him in prostituting themselves to **M**.
1Ki 11: 5 and **M** the detestable god of the
11: 7 and for **M** the detestable god of the
11:33 and **M** the god of the Ammonites, and
2Ki 23:10 son or daughter in the fire to **M**.
23:13 and for **M** the detestable god of the
Isa 57: 9 You went to **M** with olive oil and
Jer 32:35 their sons and daughters to **M**,
49: 1 Has she no heirs? Why then has **M**
49: 3 for **M** will go into exile, together
Zep 1: 5 by the LORD and who also swear by **M**,
Ac 7:43 You have lifted up the shrine of **M**

Molest (Molests)
Ge 26:29 just as we did not **m** you but always
Est 7: 8 The king exclaimed, "Will he even **m**

Molests (Molest)
Ge 26:11 "Anyone who **m** this man or his wife

Molid
1Ch 2:29 Abihail, who bore him Ahban and **M**.

Moment (Moment's, Momentary)
Ex 33: 5 even for a **m**, I might destroy you.
Nu 4:20 even for a **m**, or they will die."
1Ki 1:25 At this very **m** they are eating and
Ezr 9: 8 "But now, for a brief **m**, the LORD
Job 7:18 every morning and test him every **m**?
20: 5 joy of the godless lasts but a **m**.
Ps 2:12 for his wrath can flare up in a **m**.
30: 5 For his anger lasts only a **m**, but
Pr 12:19 but a lying tongue lasts only a **m**.
Isa 47: 9 of these will overtake you in a **m**,
54: 7 "For a brief **m** I abandoned you, but
54: 8 I hid my face from you for a **m**,
66: 8 or a nation be brought forth in a **m**?
66: 9 Do I bring to the **m** of birth and not
Jer 4:20 are destroyed, my shelter in a **m**.
Lam 4: 6 Sodom, which was overthrown in a **m**
Eze 26:16 trembling every **m**, appalled at you.
32:10 will tremble every **m** for his life.
Mt 3:16 At that **m** heaven was opened, and he
9:22 And the woman was healed from that **m**.
17:18 boy, and he was healed from that **m**.
27:51 At that **m** the curtain of the temple
Mk 9:39 next **m** say anything bad about me,
Lk 2:38 Coming up to them at that very **m**,
6:49 The **m** the torrent struck that house,
Jn 18:27 Again Peter denied it, and at that **m**
Ac 5:10 At that **m** she fell down at his feet
16:18 her!" At that **m** the spirit left her.
22:13 that very **m** I was able to see him.
1Co 4:13 Up to this **m** we have become the scum
Gal 2: 5 We did not give in to them for a **m**,
Rev 12: 4 devour her child the **m** it was born.

Moment's (Moment)
Job 10:20 from me so that I can have a **m** joy

Momentary (Moment)
2Co 4:17 For our light and **m** troubles are

Money
Ge 17:12 or bought with **m** from a foreigner
17:13 your **m**, they must be circumcised.
17:23 his household or bought with his **m**,
42:35 the **m** pouches, they were frightened.
47:14 Joseph collected all the **m** that was
47:15 the **m** of the people of Egypt and
47:15 before your eyes? Our **m** is used up."
47:16 livestock, since your **m** is gone."
Ge 47:18 the fact that since our **m** is gone
Ex 21:11 go free, without any payment of **m**.
21:35 the **m** and the dead animal equally.
22:15 **m** paid for the hire covers the loss.
22:25 "If you lend **m** to one of my people
30:16 Receive the atonement **m** from the
Lev 22:11 if a priest buys a slave with **m**, or
25:37 You must not lend him **m** at interest
Nu 3:48 Give the **m** for the redemption of the
3:49 Moses collected the redemption **m**
3:51 Moses gave the redemption **m** to Aaron
Dt 18: 8 received **m** from the sale of family
23:19 whether on **m** or food or anything
2Ki 5:26 Is this the time to take **m**,
12: 4 "Collect all the **m** that is brought
12: 4 LORD—the **m** collected in the census,
12: 4 the **m** received from personal vows
12: 4 **m** brought voluntarily to the temple.
12: 5 Let every priest receive the **m** from
12: 7 Take no more **m** from your treasurers,
12: 8 collect any more **m** from the people
12: 9 put into the chest all the **m** that
12:10 a large amount of **m** in the chest,
12:10 counted the **m** that had been brought
12:11 they gave the **m** to the men appointed
12:13 The **m** brought into the temple was
12:15 they gave the **m** to pay the workers,
12:16 The **m** from the guilt offerings and
15:20 Menahem exacted this **m** from Israel.
22: 4 make him get ready the **m** that has
22: 7 they need not account for the **m**
22: 9 "Your officials have paid out the **m**
2Ch 24: 5 the **m** due annually from all Israel,
24:11 that there was a large amount of **m**,
24:11 and collected a great amount of **m**.
24:14 they brought the rest of the **m** to
34: 9 gave him the **m** that had been brought
34:11 They also gave **m** to the carpenters
34:14 While they were bringing out the **m**
34:17 They have paid out the **m** that was in
Ezr 3: 7 they gave **m** to the masons and
7:17 With this **m** be sure to buy bulls,
Ne 5: 4 "We have had to borrow **m** to pay the
5:10 also lending the people **m** and grain.
5:11 of the **m**, grain, new wine and oil."
Est 3:11 "Keep the **m**," the king said to Haman,
4: 7 including the exact amount of **m**
Ps 15: 5 who lends his **m** without usury and
Pr 7:20 He took his purse filled with **m** and
13:11 Dishonest **m** dwindles away, but he
13:11 **m** little by little makes it grow.
17:16 Of what use is **m** in the hand of a
Ecc 5:10 Whoever loves **m** never has **m** enough;
7:12 Wisdom is a shelter as **m** is a
10:19 but **m** is the answer for everything.
Isa 52: 3 and without **m** you will be redeemed."
55: 1 the waters; and you who have no **m**,
55: 1 and milk without **m** and without cost.
55: 2 Why spend **m** on what is not bread,
Mic 3:11 her prophets tell fortunes for **m**.
Mt 6:24 You cannot serve both God and **M**.
20:15 to do what I want with my own **m**?
25:15 To one he gave five talents of **m**, to
25:16 his **m** to work and gained five more.
25:18 the ground and hid his master's **m**.
25:27 Well then, you should have put my **m**
26: 9 price and the **m** given to the poor."
27: 5 Judas threw the **m** into the temple
27: 6 the treasury, since it is blood **m**."
27: 7 they decided to use the **m** to buy the
28:12 gave the soldiers a large sum of **m**,
28:15 the soldiers took the **m** and did as
Mk 6: 8 bread, no bag, no **m** in your belts.
12:41 their **m** into the temple treasury.
14: 5 wages and the **m** given to the poor.
14:11 this and promised to give him **m**.
Lk 3:14 "Don't extort **m** and don't accuse
7:41 "Two men owed **m** to a certain
7:42 Neither of them had the **m** to pay him
9: 3 bag, no bread, no **m**, no extra tunic.
14:28 if he has enough **m** to complete it?
16:13 You cannot serve both God and **M**."
16:14 The Pharisees, who loved **m**, heard
19:13 'Put this **m** to work,' he said,
19:15 servants to whom he had given the **m**,
19:23 Why then didn't you put my **m** on

Lk 22: 5 delighted and agreed to give him **m**.
Jn 2:14 sitting at tables exchanging **m**.
12: 5 sold and the **m** given to the poor?
12: 6 was a thief; as keeper of the **m** bag,
13:29 Since Judas had charge of the **m**,
Ac 3: 3 about to enter, he asked them for **m**.
4:34 them, brought the **m** from the
4:37 **m** and put it at the apostles' feet.
5: 2 kept back part of the **m** for himself,
5: 3 of the **m** you received for the land?
5: 4 wasn't the **m** at your disposal? What
7:16 at Shechem for a certain sum of **m**.
8:18 apostles' hands, he offered them **m**
8:20 Peter answered: "May your **m** perish
8:20 could buy the gift of God with **m**!
16:16 **m** for her owners by fortune-telling.
16:19 their hope of making **m** was gone,
1Co 16: 2 sum of **m** in keeping with his income,
1Ti 3: 3 not quarrelsome, not a lover of **m**.
6:10 For the love of **m** is a root of all
6:10 Some people, eager for **m**, have
2Ti 3: 2 lovers of **m**, boastful, proud,
Heb 13: 5 free from the love of **m** and be
Jas 4:13 carry on business and make **m**."
1Pe 5: 2 greedy for **m**, but eager to serve;

Money-changers (Change)

Mt 21:12 He overturned the tables of the **m**
Mk 11:15 He overturned the tables of the **m**
Jn 2:15 the **m** and overturned their tables.

Money-lender (Lend)

Ex 22:25 be like a **m**; charge him no interest.
Lk 7:41 "Two men owed money to a certain **m**.

Monitor

Lev 11:30 the gecko, the **m** lizard, the wall

Monster

Job 7:12 Am I the sea, or the **m** of the deep,
Ps 74:13 the heads of the **m** in the waters.
Isa 27: 1 he will slay the **m** of the sea.
51: 9 pieces, who pierced that **m** through?
Eze 29: 3 great **m** lying among your streams.
32: 2 you are like a **m** in the seas

Month (Monthly, Months, Months')

Ge 7:11 the seventeenth day of the second **m**
8: 4 the seventh **m** the ark came to rest
8: 5 to recede until the tenth **m**,
8: 5 and on the first day of the tenth **m**
8:13 By the first day of the first **m** of
8:14 **m** the earth was completely dry.
29:14 had stayed with him for a whole **m**,
Ex 12: 2 "This **m** is to be for you the first
12: 2 first **m**, the first **m** of your year.
12: 3 the tenth day of this **m** each man is
12: 6 until the fourteenth day of the **m**,
12:18 In the first **m** you are to eat bread
13: 4 Today, in the **m** of Abib, you are
13: 5 to observe this ceremony in this **m**:
16: 1 **m** after they had come out of Egypt.
19: 1 In the third **m** after the Israelites
23:15 the appointed time in the **m** of Abib,
23:15 for in that **m** you came out of Egypt.
34:18 the appointed time in the **m** of Abib,
34:18 for in that **m** you came out of Egypt.
40: 2 on the first day of the first **m**.
40:17 of the first **m** in the second year.
Lev 16:29 On the tenth day of the seventh **m**
23: 5 the fourteenth day of the first **m**.
23: 6 On the fifteenth day of that **m** the
23:24 'On the first day of the seventh **m**
23:27 "The tenth day of this seventh **m** is
23:32 the ninth day of the **m** until the
23:34 the fifteenth day of the seventh **m**
23:39 the fifteenth day of the seventh **m**,
23:41 come; celebrate it in the seventh **m**.
25: 9 on the tenth day of the seventh **m**;
27: 6 If it is a person between one **m** and
Nu 1: 1 on the first day of the second **m**
1:18 on the first day of the second **m**.
3:15 Count every male a **m** old or more."
3:22 The number of all the males a **m** old
Nu 3:28 The number of all the males a **m** old
3:34 The number of all the males a **m** old
3:39 male a **m** old or more, was 22,000.
3:40 males who are a **m** old or more
3:43 of firstborn males a **m** old or more,
9: 1 in the first **m** of the second year
9: 3 on the fourteenth day of this **m**,
9: 5 the fourteenth day of the first **m**.
9:11 day of the second **m** at twilight.
9:22 for two days or a **m** or a year,
10:11 On the twentieth day of the second **m**
11:20 for a whole **m**—until it comes out of
11:21 them meat to eat for a whole **m**!'
18:16 they are a **m** old, you must redeem
20: 1 In the first **m** the whole Israelite
26:62 All the male Levites a **m** old or more
28:11 "'On the first of every **m**, present
28:16 **m** the LORD's Passover is to be held.
28:17 On the fifteenth day of this **m** there
29: 1 "'On the first day of the seventh **m**
29: 7 "'On the tenth day of this seventh **m**
29:12 the fifteenth day of the seventh **m**,
33: 3 first **m**, the day after the Passover.
33:38 the fifth **m** of the fortieth year
Dt 1: 3 on the first day of the eleventh **m**,
16: 1 Observe the **m** of Abib and celebrate
16: 1 because in the **m** of Abib he brought
21:13 her father and mother for a full **m**,
Jos 4:19 On the tenth day of the first **m** the
5:10 of the fourteenth day of the **m**,
1Sa 20:27 the next day, the second day of the **m**
20:34 second day of the **m** he did not eat,
1Ki 4: 7 supplies for one **m** in the year.
4:27 The district officers, each in his **m**,
5:14 in shifts of ten thousand a **m**,
5:14 **m** in Lebanon and two months at home.
6: 1 in the **m** of Ziv, the second **m**, he
6:37 in the fourth year, in the **m** of Ziv.
6:38 In the eleventh year in the **m** of Bul,
6:38 the eighth **m**, the temple was
8: 2 in the **m** of Ethanim, the seventh **m**.
12:32 the fifteenth day of the eighth **m**,
12:33 On the fifteenth day of the eighth **m**,
12:33 a **m** of his own choosing, he offered
2Ki 15:13 and he reigned in Samaria for one **m**.
25: 1 on the tenth day of the tenth **m**,
25: 3 By the ninth day of the ⌊fourth⌋ **m**
25: 8 On the seventh day of the fifth **m**,
25:25 In the seventh **m**, however, Ishmael
25:27 twenty-seventh day of the twelfth **m**.
1Ch 12:15 crossed the Jordan in the first **m**
27: 1 on duty **m** by **m** throughout the year.
27: 2 the first division, for the first **m**
27: 3 the army officers for the first **m**.
27: 4 the second **m** was Dodai the Ahohite;
27: 5 for the third **m**, was Benaiah son of
27: 7 The fourth, for the fourth **m**, was
27: 8 The fifth, for the fifth **m**, was the
27: 9 The sixth, for the sixth **m**, was Ira
27:10 The seventh, for the seventh **m**, was
27:11 The eighth, for the eighth **m**, was
27:12 The ninth, for the ninth **m**, was
27:13 The tenth, for the tenth **m**, was
27:14 The eleventh, for the eleventh **m**,
27:15 The twelfth, for the twelfth **m**, was
2Ch 3: 2 second **m** in the fourth year of his
5: 3 of the festival in the seventh **m**.
7:10 **m** he sent the people to their homes,
15:10 at Jerusalem in the third **m** of the
29: 3 In the first **m** of the first year of
29:17 on the first day of the first **m**,
29:17 and by the eighth day of the **m** they
29:17 in the sixteenth day of the first **m**.
30: 2 the Passover in the second **m**.
30:13 of Unleavened Bread in the second **m**.
30:15 the fourteenth day of the second **m**.
31: 7 They began doing this in the third **m**
31: 7 and finished in the seventh **m**.
35: 1 the fourteenth day of the first **m**.
Ezr 3: 1 the seventh **m** came and the
3: 6 On the first day of the seventh **m**
3: 8 In the second **m** of the second year
6:15 on the third day of the **m** Adar,
6:19 On the fourteenth day of the first **m**,
7: 8 **m** of the seventh year of the king.
7: 9 on the first day of the first **m**,
Ezr 7: 9 on the first day of the fifth **m**,
8:31 On the twelfth day of the first **m** we
10: 9 on the twentieth day of the ninth **m**,
10:16 On the first day of the tenth **m** they
10:17 by the first day of the first **m** they
Ne 1: 1 **m** of Kislev in the twentieth year,
2: 1 In the **m** of Nisan in the twentieth
7:73 When the seventh **m** came and the
8: 2 on the first day of the seventh **m**,
8:13 On the second day of the **m**, the
8:14 during the feast of the seventh **m**
9: 1 the twenty-fourth day of the same **m**,
Est 2:16 the royal residence in the tenth **m**,
2:16 the **m** of Tebeth, in the seventh year
3: 7 in the first **m**, the **m** of Nisan, they
3: 7 of Haman to select a day and **m**.
3: 7 on the twelfth **m**, the **m** of Adar.
3:12 on the thirteenth day of the first **m**
3:13 the twelfth **m**, the **m** of Adar,
8: 9 day of the third **m**, the **m** of Sivan.
8:12 day of the twelfth **m**, the **m** of Adar.
9: 1 of the twelfth **m**, the **m** of Adar,
9:15 the fourteenth day of the **m** of Adar,
9:17 the thirteenth day of the **m** of Adar,
9:19 of the **m** of Adar as a day of joy
9:21 and fifteenth days of the **m** of
9:22 and as the **m** when their sorrow was
Isa 47:13 who make predictions **m** by **m**,
Jer 1: 3 down to the fifth **m** of the eleventh
28: 1 In the fifth **m** of that same year,
28:17 In the seventh **m** of that same year,
36: 9 In the ninth **m** of the fifth year of
36:22 was the ninth **m** and the king was
39: 1 in the tenth **m**, Nebuchadnezzar king
39: 2 on the ninth day of the fourth **m** of
41: 1 In the seventh **m** Ishmael son of
52: 4 on the tenth day of the tenth **m**,
52: 6 By the ninth day of the fourth **m** the
52:12 On the tenth day of the fifth **m**, in
52:31 twenty-fifth day of the twelfth **m**.
Eze 1: 1 in the fourth **m** on the fifth day,
1: 2 On the fifth of the **m**—it was the
8: 1 In the sixth year, in the sixth **m** on
20: 1 In the seventh year, in the fifth **m**
24: 1 In the ninth year, in the tenth **m** on
26: 1 first day of the **m**, the word of the
29: 1 In the tenth year, in the tenth **m** on
29:17 in the first **m** on the first day, the
30:20 In the eleventh year, in the first **m**
31: 1 In the eleventh year, in the third **m**
32: 1 In the twelfth year, in the twelfth **m**
32:17 day of the **m**, the word of the LORD
33:21 in the tenth **m** on the fifth day, a
40: 1 on the tenth of the **m**, in the
45:18 In the first **m** on the first day you
45:20 same on the seventh day of the **m**
45:21 "'In the first **m** on the fourteenth
45:25 which begins in the seventh **m** on the
47:12 Every **m** they will bear, because the
Da 10: 4 twenty-fourth day of the first **m**,
Hag 1: 1 on the first day of the sixth **m**, the
1:15 **m** in the second year of King Darius.
2: 1 twenty-first day of the seventh **m**,
2:10 twenty-fourth day of the ninth **m**,
2:18 twenty-fourth day of the ninth **m**,
2:20 on the twenty-fourth day of the **m**:
Zec 1: 1 In the eighth **m** of the second year
1: 7 twenty-fourth day of the eleventh **m**,
1: 7 the **m** of Shebat, in the second year
7: 1 day of the ninth **m**, the **m** of Kislev.
7: 3 mourn and fast in the fifth **m**,
11: 8 In one **m** I got rid of the three
Lk 1:26 In the sixth **m**, God sent the angel
1:36 said to be barren is in her sixth **m**.
Rev 9:15 day and **m** and year were released to
22: 2 fruit, yielding its fruit every **m**.

Monthly (Month)

Lev 12: 2 she is unclean during her **m** period.
15:19 the impurity of her **m** period will
15:24 "'If a man lies with her and her **m**
15:25 at a time other than her **m** period
15:26 as is her bed during her **m** period,
15:33 for a woman in her **m** period, for a
18:19 the uncleanness of her **m** period.

Lev 20:18 with a woman during her **m** period
Nu 28:14 This is the **m** burnt offering to be
29: 6 in addition to the **m** and daily
Eze 36:17 a woman's **m** uncleanness in my sight.

Months (Month)

Ge 38:24 About three **m** later Judah was told,
Ex 2: 2 fine child, she hid him for three **m**.
Jdg 11:37 "Give me two **m** to roam the hills and
11:38 And he let her go for two **m**. She and
11:39 After the two **m**, she returned to her
19: 2 After she had been there for four **m**,
20:47 Rimmon, where they stayed for four **m**.
1Sa 6: 1 in Philistine territory for seven **m**,
27: 7 territory for a year and four **m**.
2Sa 2:11 of Judah was seven years and six **m**.
5: 5 Judah for seven years and six **m**,
6:11 Obed-Edom the Gittite for three **m**,
24: 8 the end of nine **m** and twenty days.
24:13 Or three **m** of fleeing from your
1Ki 5:14 month in Lebanon and two **m** at home.
11:16 Israelites stayed there for six **m**,
2Ki 15: 8 Samaria, and he reigned for six **m**.
23:31 he reigned in Jerusalem for three **m**.
24: 8 he reigned in Jerusalem for three **m**.
1Ch 3: 4 reigned for seven years and six **m**.
13:14 Obed-Edom in his house for three **m**,
21:12 three years of famine, three **m** of
2Ch 36: 2 he reigned in Jerusalem for three **m**.
36: 9 Jerusalem for three **m** and ten days.
Est 2:12 she had to complete twelve **m** of
2:12 six **m** with oil of myrrh and six with
Job 3: 6 year nor be entered in any of the **m**.
7: 3 I have been allotted **m** of futility,
14: 5 have decreed the number of his **m**
21:21 when his allotted **m** come to an end?
29: 2 "How I long for the **m** gone by, for
39: 2 Do you count the **m** till they bear?
Eze 39:12 "'For seven **m** the house of Israel
39:14 At the end of the seven **m** they will
Da 4:29 Twelve **m** later, as the king was
Am 4: 7 the harvest was still three **m** away.
Zec 7: 5 mourned in the fifth and seventh **m**
8:19 fifth, seventh and tenth **m** will
Mk 6:37 "That would take eight **m** of a man's
Lk 1:24 for five **m** remained in seclusion.
1:56 three **m** and then returned home.
Jn 4:35 Do you not say, 'Four **m** more and
Ac 7:20 For three **m** he was cared for in his
19: 8 and spoke boldly there for three **m**,
20: 3 where he stayed three **m**. Because the
28:11 After three **m** we put out to sea in a
Gal 4:10 You are observing special days and **m**
Heb 11:23 him for three **m** after he was born,
Rev 9: 5 but only to torture them for five **m**.
9:10 power to torment people for five **m**.
11: 2 trample on the holy city for 42 **m**.
13: 5 his authority for forty-two **m**.

Months' (Month)

Jn 6: 7 Philip answered him, "Eight **m** wages

Monument

1Sa 15:12 There he has set up a **m** in his own
2Sa 18:18 the King's Valley as a **m** to himself,
18:18 is called Absalom's **M** to this day.
Isa 19:19 and a **m** to the LORD at its border.

Moon (Moons, *New Moon*)

Ge 37: 9 and this time the sun and **m** and
Dt 4:19 the **m** and the stars—all the
17: 3 or the **m** or the stars of the sky,
33:14 and the finest the **m** can yield;
Jos 10:12 O **m**, over the Valley of Aijalon."
10:13 the sun stood still, and the **m**
2Ki 23: 5 incense to Baal, to the sun and **m**,
Job 25: 5 If even the **m** is not bright and the
26: 9 He covers the face of the full **m**,
31:26 or the **m** moving in splendour,
Ps 8: 3 the work of your fingers, the **m** and
72: 5 as the **m**, through all generations.
72: 7 will abound till the **m** is no more.
74:16 you established the sun and **m**.
81: 3 when the **m** is full, on the day of
Ps 89:37 **m**, the faithful witness in the sky.
104:19 The **m** marks off the seasons, and the
121: 6 harm you by day, nor the **m** by night.
136: 9 the **m** and stars to govern the night;
148: 3 Praise him, sun and **m**, praise him,
Pr 7:20 and will not be home till full **m**."
Ecc 12: 2 and the **m** and the stars grow dark,
SS 6:10 fair as the **m**, bright as the sun,
Isa 13:10 and the **m** will not give its light.
24:23 The **m** will be abashed, the sun
30:26 The **m** will shine like the sun, and
60:19 nor will the brightness of the **m**
60:20 and your **m** will wane no more; the
Jer 8: 2 be exposed to the sun and the **m**
31:35 who decrees the **m** and stars to shine
Eze 32: 7 and the **m** will not give its light.
Joel 2:10 the sky trembles, the sun and **m** are
2:31 the **m** to blood before the coming of
3:15 The sun and **m** will be darkened, and
Hab 3:11 Sun and **m** stood still in the heavens
Mt 24:29 'the sun will be darkened, and the **m**
Mk 13:24 and the **m** will not give its light;
Lk 21:25 "There will be signs in the sun, **m**
Ac 2:20 the **m** to blood before the coming of
1Co 15:41 the **m** another and the stars another;
Rev 6:12 hair, the whole **m** turned blood red,
8:12 a third of the **m**, and a third of the
12: 1 with the **m** under her feet and a
21:23 the sun or the **m** to shine on it,

Moons (Moon)

2Ch 2: 4 evening and on Sabbaths and New **M**
8:13 New **M** and the three annual feasts
31: 3 New **M** and appointed feasts as
Isa 1:13 New **M**, Sabbaths and convocations—
Eze 45:17 the New **M** and the Sabbaths—at all
46: 3 On the Sabbaths and New **M** the people
Hos 2:11 her New **M**, her Sabbath days—all her

Moral

Jas 1:21 Therefore, get rid of all **m** filth

Mordecai (Mordecai's)

1. Benjamite exile; brought up cousin, Esther, as own daughter (Est 2:5–7,15,20). Reported plot to kill Xerxes (Est 2:21–23). Refused to bow to Haman resulting in plot against Jews (Est 3:1–6); mourned; persuaded Esther to help (Est 4). Honoured (Est 6); given Haman's position as next in rank to king (Est 8:1–2; 10). Saved Jews; instituted feast of Purim (Est 8–9). **2.** Jewish exile who returned with Zerubbabel (Ezr 2:2; Ne 7:7).

Ezr 2: 2 Nehemiah, Seraiah, Reelaiah, **M**,
Ne 7: 7 Azariah, Raamiah, Nahamani, **M**,
Est 2: 5 named **M** son of Jair, the son of
2: 7 **M** had a cousin named Hadassah, whom
2: 7 and **M** had taken her as his own
2:10 **M** had forbidden her to do so.
2:15 the turn came for Esther (the girl **M**
2:19 **M** was sitting at the king's gate.
2:20 just as **M** had told her to do,
2:21 During the time **M** was sitting at the
2:22 **M** found out about the plot and told
2:22 it to the king, giving credit to **M**.
3: 2 But **M** would not kneel down or pay
3: 3 at the king's gate asked **M**,
3: 5 Haman saw that **M** would not kneel
3: 6 scorned the idea of killing only **M**.
4: 1 **M** learned of all that had been done,
4: 4 about **M**, she was in great distress.
4: 5 out what was troubling **M** and why.
4: 6 Hathach went out to **M** in the open
4: 7 **M** told him everything that had
4: 9 reported to Esther what **M** had said.
4:10 she instructed him to say to **M**,
4:12 Esther's words were reported to **M**,
4:15 Esther sent this reply to **M**:
4:17 **M** went away and carried out all of
5: 9 But when he saw **M** at the king's gate
5: 9 he was filled with rage against **M**.
5:13 Jew **M** sitting at the king's gate."
5:14 the morning to have **M** hanged on it.
6: 2 was found recorded there that **M** had
6: 3 "What honour and recognition has **M**
Est 6: 4 about hanging **M** on the gallows he
6:10 as you have suggested for **M** the Jew,
6:11 He robed **M**, and led him on horseback
6:12 Afterwards **M** returned to the king's
6:13 "Since **M**, before whom your downfall
7: 9 He had it made for **M**, who spoke up
7:10 the gallows he had prepared for **M**.
8: 1 And **M** came into the presence of the
8: 2 from Haman, and presented it to **M**.
8: 7 to Queen Esther and to **M** the Jew,
8:10 **M** wrote in the name of King Xerxes,
8:15 **M** left the king's presence wearing
9: 3 because fear of **M** had seized them.
9: 4 **M** was prominent in the palace; his
9:20 **M** recorded these events, and he sent
9:23 doing what **M** had written to them.
9:29 daughter of Abihail, along with **M**
9:30 **M** sent letters to all the Jews in
9:31 as **M** the Jew and Queen Esther had
10: 2 full account of the greatness of **M**
10: 3 **M** the Jew was second in rank to King

Mordecai's (Mordecai)

Est 2:20 continued to follow **M** instructions
3: 4 **M** behaviour would be tolerated,
3: 6 Yet having learned who **M** people were,
3: 6 for a way to destroy all **M** people,
8: 9 They wrote out all **M** orders to the

Moreh

Ge 12: 6 of the great tree of **M** at Shechem.
Dt 11:30 near the great trees of **M**, in the
Jdg 7: 1 in the valley near the hill of **M**.

Moresheth

Jer 26:18 "Micah of **M** prophesied in the days
Mic 1: 1 of **M** during the reigns of Jotham,

Moresheth Gath

Mic 1:14 you will give parting gifts to **M**.

Moriah, Mount

Abraham was instructed by God to sacrifice Isaac here (Ge 22:2). Exact location unknown, but visible after a 3 day journey from Beersheba (Ge 22:4). Probably also the site of Solomon's temple at Jerusalem (2Ch 3:1).

Ge 22: 2 you love, and go to the region of **M**.
2Ch 3: 1 of the LORD in Jerusalem on Mount **M**,

Morning (Morning's, Mornings)

Ge 1: 5 and there was **m**—the first day.
1: 8 and there was **m**—the second day.
1:13 there was evening, and there was **m**
1:19 there was evening, and there was **m**
1:23 there was evening, and there was **m**
1:31 and there was **m**—the sixth day.
19: 2 then go on your way early in the **m**.
19:27 Early the next **m** Abraham got up and
20: 8 Early the next **m** Abimelech summoned
21:14 Early the next **m** Abraham took some
22: 3 Early the next **m** Abraham got up and
24:54 When they got up the next **m**, he said,
26:31 Early the next **m** the men swore an
28:18 Early the next **m** Jacob took the
29:25 **m** came, there was Leah! So Jacob
31:55 Early the next **m** Laban kissed his
40: 6 Joseph came to them the next **m**, he
41: 8 In the **m** his mind was troubled, so
44: 3 **m** dawned, the men were sent on their
49:27 wolf; in the **m** he devours the prey,
Ex 7:15 Go to Pharaoh in the **m** as he goes
8:20 "Get up early in the **m** and confront
9:13 "Get up early in the **m**, confront
10:13 **m** the wind had brought the locusts;
12:10 Do not leave any of it till **m**; if
12:10 is left till **m**, you must burn it.
12:22 of the door of his house until **m**.
16: 7 in the **m** you will see the glory of
16: 8 and all the bread you want in the **m**,
16:12 the **m** you will be filled with bread.
16:13 and in the **m** there was a layer of
16:19 No-one is to keep any of it until **m**."

Ex 16:20 they kept part of it until **m**,
16:21 Each **m** everyone gathered as much as
16:23 is left and keep it until **m**.
16:24 they saved it until **m**, as Moses
18:13 stood round him from **m** till evening.
18:14 round you from **m** till evening?"
19:16 On the **m** of the third day there was
23:18 offerings must not be kept until **m**.
24: 4 He got up early the next **m** and built
27:21 before the LORD from evening till **m**.
29:34 is left over till **m**, burn it up.
29:39 Offer one in the **m** and the other at
29:41 as in the **m**—a pleasing aroma,
30: 7 every **m** when he tends the lamps.
34: 2 Be ready in the **m**, and then come up
34: 4 went up Mount Sinai early in the **m**,
34:25 the Passover Feast remain until **m**.
36: 3 bring freewill offerings **m** after **m**.
Lev 6: 9 till **m**, and the fire must be kept
6:12 Every **m** the priest is to add
6:20 it in the **m** and half in the evening.
7:15 he must leave none of it till **m**.
22:30 same day; leave none of it till **m**.
24: 3 from evening till **m**, continually.
Nu 9:12 They must not leave any of it till **m**
9:15 From evening till **m** the cloud above
9:21 stayed only from evening till **m**,
9:21 it lifted in the **m**, they set out.
14:40 Early the next **m** they went up
16: 5 "In the **m** the LORD will show who
22:13 The next **m** Balaam got up and said to
22:21 Balaam got up in the **m**, saddled his
22:41 The next **m** Balak took Balaam up to
28: 4 Prepare one lamb in the **m** and the
28: 8 offering that you prepare in the **m**.
28:23 to the regular **m** burnt offering.
Dt 16: 4 of the first day remain until **m**.
16: 7 Then in the **m** return to your tents.
28:67 In the **m** you will say, "If only it
28:67 in the evening, "If only it were **m**!"
Jos 3: 1 Early in the **m** Joshua and all the
6:12 Joshua got up early the next **m** and
7:14 "'In the **m**, present yourselves
7:16 Early the next **m** Joshua had Israel
8:10 Early the next **m** Joshua mustered his
8:14 in the **m** to meet Israel in battle
Jdg 6:28 In the **m** when the men of the town
6:31 death by **m**! If Baal really is a god,
7: 1 Early in the **m**, Jerub-Baal (that is,
9:33 In the **m** at sunrise, advance against
19: 8 On the **m** of the fifth day, when he
19: 9 Early tomorrow **m** you can get up and
19:27 her master got up in the **m** and
20:19 The next **m** the Israelites got up and
Ru 2: 7 has worked steadily from **m** till now,
3:13 Stay here for the night, and in the **m**
3:13 I will do it. Lie here until **m**."
3:14 she lay at his feet until **m**, but got
1Sa 1:19 Early the next **m** they arose and
3:15 Samuel lay down until **m** and then
5: 4 the following **m** when they rose,
9:19 and in the **m** I will let you go and
15:12 Early in the **m** Samuel got up and
17:16 **m** and evening and took his stand.
17:20 Early in the **m** David left the flock
19: 2 tomorrow **m**; go into hiding and
19:11 watch it and to kill him in the **m**.
20:35 In the **m** Jonathan went out to the
25:22 be it ever so severely, if by **m** I
25:37 in the **m**, when Nabal was sober, his
29:10 in the **m** as soon as it is light."
29:11 his men got up early in the **m** to go
2Sa 2:27 pursuit of their brothers until **m**."
11:14 In the **m** David wrote a letter to
13: 4 look so haggard **m** after **m**?
23: 4 he is like the light of **m** at sunrise
23: 4 a cloudless **m**, like the brightness
24:11 Before David got up the next **m**, the
24:15 sent a plague on Israel from that **m**
1Ki 3:21 The next **m**, I got up to nurse my son
3:21 at him closely in the **m** light,
17: 6 brought him bread and meat in the **m**
18:26 the name of Baal from **m** till noon.
2Ki 3:20 The next **m**, about the time for
3:22 they got up early in the **m**, the sun
6:15 up and went out early the next **m**,
2Ki 10: 8 entrance of the city gate until **m**."
10: 9 The next **m** Jehu went out. He stood
16:15 On the large new altar, offer the **m**
19:35 **m**—there were all the dead bodies!
1Ch 9:27 of the key for opening it each **m**.
16:40 **m** and evening, in accordance with
23:30 They were also to stand every **m** to
2Ch 2: 4 for making burnt offerings every **m**
13:11 Every **m** and evening they present
20:20 Early in the **m** they left for the
29:20 Early the next **m** King Hezekiah
31: 3 from his own possessions for the **m**
Ezr 3: 3 both the **m** and evening sacrifices.
Est 2:14 in the **m** return to another part of
5:14 the **m** to have Mordecai hanged on it.
Job 1: 5 Early in the **m** he would sacrifice a
3: 9 May its **m** stars become dark; may it
7:18 that you examine him every **m** and
11:17 and darkness will become like **m**.
24:17 deep darkness is their **m**; they make
38: 7 while the **m** stars sang together and
38:12 Have you ever given orders to the **m**,
Ps 5: 3 In the **m**, O LORD, you hear my voice;
5: 3 O LORD, you hear my voice; in the *m*
22: T To ⌊the tune of⌋ "The Doe of the **M**"
30: 5 night, but rejoicing comes in the **m**.
49:14 will rule over them in the **m**;
55:17 Evening, **m** and noon I cry out in
59:16 in the **m** I will sing of your love;
65: 8 where **m** dawns and evening fades you
73:14 I have been punished every **m**.
88:13 in the **m** my prayer comes before you.
90: 5 are like the new grass of the **m**—
90: 6 though in the **m** it springs up new,
90:14 Satisfy us in the **m** with your
92: 2 to proclaim your love in the **m** and
101: 8 Every **m** I will put to silence all
130: 6 **m**, more than watchmen wait for the **m**
143: 8 Let the **m** bring me word of your
Pr 7:18 Come, let's drink deep of love till **m**
27:14 his neighbour early in the **m**,
Ecc 10:16 and whose princes feast in the **m**.
11: 6 Sow your seed in the **m**, and at
Isa 5:11 Woe to those who rise early in the **m**
14:12 have fallen from heaven, O **m** star,
17:11 you make them grow, and on the **m**
17:14 sudden terror! Before the **m**, they
21:12 The watchman replies, "**M** is coming,
26: 9 in the **m** my spirit longs for you.
26:19 Your dew is like the dew of the **m**;
28:19 it will carry you away; **m** after **m**,
33: 2 Be our strength every **m**, our
37:36 **m**—there were all the dead bodies!
44:22 a cloud, your sins like the **m** mist.
50: 4 He wakens me **m** by **m**, wakens my ear
Jer 20:16 in the **m**, a battle cry at noon.
21:12 'Administer justice every **m**; rescue
Lam 3:23 They are new every **m**; great is your
Eze 12: 8 In the **m** the word of the LORD came
24:18 I spoke to the people in the **m**, and
24:18 **m** I did as I had been commanded.
33:22 before the man came to me in the **m**.
46:13 LORD; **m** by **m** you shall provide it.
46:14 with it **m** by **m** a grain offering,
46:15 **m** by **m** for a regular burnt offering.
Hos 6: 4 Judah? Your love is like the **m** mist,
7: 6 the **m** it blazes like a flaming fire.
13: 3 they will be like the **m** mist,
Am 4: 4 Bring your sacrifices every **m**, your
Zep 3: 3 wolves, who leave nothing for the **m**.
3: 5 **M** by **m** he dispenses his justice, and
Mt 16: 3 in the **m**, 'Today it will be stormy,
20: 1 in the **m** to hire men to work in his
21:18 Early in the **m**, as he was on his way
27: 1 Early in the **m**, all the chief
Mk 1:35 Very early in the **m**, while it was
11:20 In the **m**, as they went along, they
15: 1 Very early in the **m**, the chief
Lk 6:13 **m** came, he called his disciples to
21:38 all the people came early in the **m**
24: 1 very early in the **m**, the women took
24:22 They went to the tomb early this **m**
Jn 18:28 By now it was early **m**, and to avoid
21: 4 Early in the **m**, Jesus stood on the
Ac 2:15 It's only nine in the **m**!
12:18 In the **m**, there was no small
Ac 23:12 The next **m** the Jews formed a
28:23 From **m** till evening he explained and
2Pe 1:19 and the **m** star rises in your hearts.
Rev 2:28 I will also give him the **m** star.
22:16 of David, and the bright **M** Star."

Morning's (Morning)

Lev 9:17 in addition to the **m** burnt offering.
Mic 2: 1 At **m** light they carry it out because

Mornings (Morning)

Da 8:14 "It will take 2,300 evenings and **m**;
8:26 "The vision of the evenings and **m**

Morsels

Pr 18: 8 words of a gossip are like choice **m**;
26:22 words of a gossip are like choice **m**;

Mortal (Mortally, Mortals)

Ge 6: 3 for he is **m**; his days will be a
Dt 5:26 For what **m** man has ever heard the
Job 4:17 'Can a **m** be more righteous than God?
9: 2 how can a **m** be righteous before God?
10: 4 of flesh? Do you see as a **m** sees?
10: 5 Are your days like those of a **m** or
Ps 17: 9 from my **m** enemies who surround me.
42:10 My bones suffer **m** agony as my foes
56: 4 What can **m** man do to me?
146: 3 princes, in **m** men, who cannot save.
Isa 51:12 Who are you that you fear **m** men, the
Eze 31:14 for the earth below, among **m** men,
Ro 1:23 for images made to look like **m** man
6:12 do not let sin reign in your **m** body
8:11 to your **m** bodies through his Spirit,
1Co 15:53 and the **m** with immortality.
15:54 and the **m** with immortality, then the
2Co 4:11 life may be revealed in our **m** body.
5: 4 is **m** may be swallowed up by life.

Mortally (Mortal)

Eze 30:24 before him like a **m** wounded man.

Mortals (Mortal)

Isa 31: 8 a sword, not of **m**, will devour them.

Mortar

Ge 11: 3 instead of stone, and bitumen for **m**.
Ex 1:14 with hard labour in brick and **m**
Nu 11: 8 in a hand mill or crushed it in a **m**.
Pr 27:22 Though you grind a fool in a **m**,
Isa 41:25 treads on rulers as if they were **m**,
Na 3:14 tread the **m**, repair the brickwork!

Mortgaging

Ne 5: 3 were saying, "We are **m** our fields

Mosaic

Est 1: 6 silver on a **m** pavement of porphyry,

Moserah

Dt 10: 6 the wells of the Jaakanites to **M**.

Moseroth

Nu 33:30 They left Hashmonah and camped at **M**.
33:31 They left **M** and camped at Bene

Moses (*Law of Moses*, Moses', *Moses the servant of the LORD*, *My servant Moses*)

Levite; brother of Aaron (Ex 6:20; 1Ch 6:3). Put into Nile in basket; found and raised by Pharaoh's daughter; killed Egyptian; fled to Midian; married Zipporah (Ex 2; Ac 7:20–29). Called by God at burning bush (Ex 3–4; Ac 7:30–36); confronted Pharaoh (Ex 5:1–4; 7:1–13); plagues (Ex 7–11; Ps 105:26–36). Led people out of Egypt (Ex 12–13), through Red Sea (Ex 14). Brought water from rock (Ex 17:1–7); raised hands to enable victory over Amalekites (Ex 17:8–16); appointed judges (Ex 18; Dt 1:9–18). Given Law on Mt Sinai (Ex 19–23); spoke to people; confirmed covenant (Ex 19:7–8; 24:1–11; Heb 9:19); returned to mountain to receive stone tablets (Ex 24:12–18; 31:18). Broke

tablets over golden calf (Ex 32:15–19; Dt 9:7–17); interceded for people (Ex 32:10–14; Dt 9:25–29). Saw God's glory (Ex 33:18–23); given new tablets (Ex 34; Dt 10:1–5); face shone (Ex 34:29–35). Supervised building of tabernacle (Ex 35–40; Heb 8:5); consecrated Aaron and sons as priests (Ex 28–29; Lev 8–9). Took census (Nu 1–4; 26). Opposed by Aaron and Miriam (Nu 12), Korah (Nu 16; Jude 11). Sent spies into Canaan (Nu 13; Dt 1:19–25). Forbidden to enter Canaan for striking rock (Nu 20:12; 27:12–14; Dt 3:27; 32:48–52). Lifted up bronze snake (Nu 21:4–9). Allocated land east of Jordan (Nu 32). Last words to Israel (Dt 31–33); death (Dt 34); succeeded by Joshua (Dt 3:28; 34:9; Jos 1:1–9). Faithfulness as God's servant commended (Heb 3:3–5). Prayer of Moses (Ps 90); songs of Moses (Ex 15:1–18; Dt 32; Rev 15:3–4).

Ex 2:10 She named him **M**, saying, "I drew him
2:11 One day, after **M** had grown up, he
2:14 Then **M** was afraid and thought,
2:15 he tried to kill **M**, but **M** fled from
2:17 but **M** got up and came to their
2:21 **M** agreed to stay with the man, who
2:21 daughter Zipporah to **M** in marriage.
2:22 Zipporah gave birth to a son, and **M**
3: 1 Now **M** was tending the flock of
3: 2 **M** saw that though the bush was on
3: 3 **M** thought, "I will go over and see
3: 4 "**M**! **M**!" And **M** said, "Here I am.
3: 6 At this, **M** hid his face, because he
3:11 **M** said to God, "Who am I, that I
3:13 **M** said to God, "Suppose I go to the
3:14 God said to **M**, "I AM WHO I AM.
3:15 God also said to **M**, "Say to the
4: 1 **M** answered, "What if they do not
4: 3 **M** threw it on the ground and it
4: 4 So **M** reached out and took hold of
4: 6 So **M** put his hand into his cloak,
4: 7 So **M** put his hand back into his
4:10 **M** said to the LORD, "O Lord, I have
4:13 **M** said, "O Lord, please send someone
4:14 the LORD's anger burned against **M**
4:18 **M** went back to Jethro his
4:19 Now the LORD had said to **M** in Midian,
4:20 **M** took his wife and sons, put them
4:21 The LORD said to **M**, "When you return
4:24 met ⌊**M**⌋ and was about to kill
4:27 Aaron, "Go into the desert to meet **M**.
4:27 So he met **M** at the mountain of God
4:28 **M** told Aaron everything the LORD had
4:29 **M** and Aaron brought together all the
4:30 everything the LORD had said to **M**.
5: 1 Afterwards **M** and Aaron went to
5: 4 the king of Egypt said, "**M** and Aaron,
5:20 they left Pharaoh, they found **M** and
5:22 **M** returned to the LORD and said,
6: 1 the LORD said to **M**, "Now you will
6: 2 God also said to **M**, "I am the LORD.
6: 9 **M** reported this to the Israelites,
6:10 Then the LORD said to **M**,
6:12 **M** said to the LORD, "If the
6:13 Now the LORD spoke to **M** and Aaron
6:20 Jochebed, who bore him Aaron and **M**.
6:26 was this same Aaron and **M** to whom
6:27 It was the same **M** and Aaron.
6:28 Now when the LORD spoke to **M** in
6:30 **M** said to the LORD, "Since I speak
7: 1 the LORD said to **M**, "See, I have
7: 6 **M** and Aaron did just as the LORD
7: 7 **M** was eighty years old and Aaron
7: 8 The LORD said to **M** and Aaron,
7:10 **M** and Aaron went to Pharaoh and did
7:14 the LORD said to **M**, "Pharaoh's heart
7:19 The LORD said to **M**, "Tell Aaron,
7:20 **M** and Aaron did just as the LORD had
7:22 he would not listen to **M** and Aaron,
8: 1 the LORD said to **M**, "Go to Pharaoh
8: 5 the LORD said to **M**, "Tell Aaron,
8: 8 Pharaoh summoned **M** and Aaron and
8: 9 **M** said to Pharaoh, "I leave to you
8:10 "Tomorrow," Pharaoh said. **M** replied,
8:12 After **M** and Aaron left Pharaoh, **M**
8:13 the LORD did what **M** asked. The frogs
8:15 and would not listen to **M** and Aaron,
8:16 the LORD said to **M**, "Tell Aaron,

Ex 8:20 the LORD said to **M**, "Get up early in
8:25 Pharaoh summoned **M** and Aaron and
8:26 **M** said, "That would not be right.
8:29 **M** answered, "As soon as I leave you,
8:30 **M** left Pharaoh and prayed to the
8:31 the LORD did what **M** asked: The flies
9: 1 the LORD said to **M**, "Go to Pharaoh
9: 8 the LORD said to **M** and Aaron, "Take
9: 8 have **M** toss it into the air in the
9:10 **M** tossed it into the air, and
9:11 magicians could not stand before **M**
9:12 he would not listen to **M** and Aaron,
9:12 just as the LORD had said to **M**.
9:13 the LORD said to **M**, "Get up early in
9:22 the LORD said to **M**, "Stretch out
9:23 **M** stretched out his staff towards
9:27 Pharaoh summoned **M** and Aaron. "This
9:29 **M** replied, "When I have gone out of
9:33 **M** left Pharaoh and went out of the
9:35 just as the LORD had said through **M**.
10: 1 the LORD said to **M**, "Go to Pharaoh,
10: 3 **M** and Aaron went to Pharaoh and said
10: 6 Then **M** turned and left Pharaoh.
10: 8 **M** and Aaron were brought back to
10: 9 **M** answered, "We will go with our
10:11 Then **M** and Aaron were driven out of
10:12 the LORD said to **M**, "Stretch out
10:13 **M** stretched out his staff over Egypt,
10:16 Pharaoh quickly summoned **M** and Aaron
10:18 **M** then left Pharaoh and prayed to
10:21 the LORD said to **M**, "Stretch out
10:22 **M** stretched out his hand towards the
10:24 Pharaoh summoned **M** and said, "Go,
10:25 **M** said, "You must allow us to have
10:28 Pharaoh said to **M**, "Get out of my
10:29 "Just as you say," **M** replied, "I
11: 1 Now the LORD said to **M**, "I will
11: 3 and **M** himself was highly regarded in
11: 4 **M** said, "This is what the LORD says:
11: 8 Then **M**, hot with anger, left Pharaoh.
11: 9 The LORD had said to **M**, "Pharaoh
11:10 **M** and Aaron performed all these
12: 1 The LORD said to **M** and Aaron in
12:21 **M** summoned all the elders of Israel
12:28 what the LORD commanded **M** and Aaron.
12:31 During the night Pharaoh summoned **M**
12:35 The Israelites did as **M** instructed
12:43 The LORD said to **M** and Aaron, "These
12:50 the LORD had commanded **M** and Aaron.
13: 1 The LORD said to **M**,
13: 3 **M** said to the people, "Commemorate
13:19 **M** took the bones of Joseph with him
14: 1 Then the LORD said to **M**,
14:11 They said to **M**, "Was it because
14:13 **M** answered the people, "Do not be
14:15 the LORD said to **M**, "Why are you
14:21 **M** stretched out his hand over the
14:26 the LORD said to **M**, "Stretch out
14:27 **M** stretched out his hand over the
14:31 trust in him and in **M** his servant.
15: 1 **M** and the Israelites sang this song
15:22 **M** led Israel from the Red Sea and
15:24 the people grumbled against **M**,
15:25 **M** cried out to the LORD, and the
16: 2 grumbled against **M** and Aaron.
16: 4 the LORD said to **M**, "I will rain
16: 6 **M** and Aaron said to all the
16: 8 **M** also said, "You will know that it
16: 9 **M** told Aaron, "Say to the entire
16:11 The LORD said to **M**,
16:15 **M** said to them, "It is the bread the
16:19 **M** said to them, "No-one is to keep
16:20 some of them paid no attention to **M**;
16:20 So **M** was angry with them.
16:22 came and reported this to **M**.
16:24 they saved it until morning, as **M**
16:25 "Eat it today," **M** said, "because
16:28 the LORD said to **M**, "How long will
16:32 **M** said, "This is what the LORD has
16:33 **M** said to Aaron, "Take a jar and put
16:34 the LORD commanded **M**, Aaron put the
17: 2 they quarrelled with **M** and said,
17: 2 **M** replied, "Why do you quarrel with
17: 3 there, and they grumbled against **M**.
17: 4 **M** cried out to the LORD, "What am I
17: 5 The LORD answered **M**, "Walk on ahead

Ex 17: 6 So **M** did this in the sight of the
17: 9 **M** said to Joshua, "Choose some of
17:10 Joshua fought the Amalekites as **M**
17:10 and **M**, Aaron and Hur went to the top
17:11 long as **M** held up his hands, the
17:14 the LORD said to **M**, "Write this on a
17:15 **M** built an altar and called it The
18: 1 of Midian and father-in-law of **M**,
18: 1 for **M** and for his people Israel,
18: 2 After **M** had sent away his wife
18: 3 One son was named Gershom, for **M**
18: 7 **M** went out to meet his father-in-law
18: 8 **M** told his father-in-law about
18:13 The next day **M** took his seat to
18:14 his father-in-law saw all that **M** was
18:15 **M** answered him, "Because the people
18:24 **M** listened to his father-in-law and
18:26 difficult cases they brought to **M**,
18:27 **M** sent his father-in-law on his way,
19: 3 **M** went up to God, and the LORD
19: 7 **M** went back and summoned the elders
19: 8 So **M** brought their answer back to
19: 9 The LORD said to **M**, "I am going to
19: 9 Then **M** told the LORD what the
19:10 the LORD said to **M**, "Go to the
19:14 After **M** had gone down the mountain
19:17 **M** led the people out of the camp to
19:19 Then **M** spoke and the voice of God
19:20 the top of Mount Sinai and called **M**
19:20 top of the mountain. So **M** went up
19:23 **M** said to the LORD, "The people
19:25 **M** went down to the people and told
20:19 said to **M**, "Speak to us yourself and
20:20 **M** said to the people, "Do not be
20:21 while **M** approached the thick
20:22 the LORD said to **M**, "Tell the
24: 1 he said to **M**, "Come up to the LORD,
24: 2 **M** alone is to approach the LORD; the
24: 3 **M** went and told the people all the
24: 4 **M** then wrote down everything the
24: 6 **M** took half of the blood and put it
24: 8 **M** then took the blood, sprinkled it
24: 9 **M** and Aaron, Nadab and Abihu, and
24:12 The LORD said to **M**, "Come up to me
24:13 **M** set out with Joshua his assistant,
24:13 **M** went up on the mountain of God.
24:15 **M** went up on the mountain, the cloud
24:16 called to **M** from within the cloud.
24:18 **M** entered the cloud as he went on up
25: 1 The LORD said to **M**,
30:11 Then the LORD said to **M**,
30:17 Then the LORD said to **M**,
30:22 Then the LORD said to **M**,
30:34 the LORD said to **M**, "Take fragrant
31: 1 Then the LORD said to **M**,
31:12 Then the LORD said to **M**,
31:18 the LORD finished speaking to **M** on
32: 1 the people saw that **M** was so long in
32: 1 As for this fellow **M** who brought us
32: 7 the LORD said to **M**, "Go down,
32: 9 these people," the LORD said to **M**,
32:11 **M** sought the favour of the LORD his
32:15 **M** turned and went down the mountain
32:17 he said to **M**, "There is the sound of
32:18 **M** replied: "It is not the sound of
32:19 **M** approached the camp and saw the
32:23 As for this fellow **M** who brought us
32:25 **M** saw that the people were running
32:28 The Levites did as **M** commanded, and
32:29 **M** said, "You have been set apart to
32:30 The next day **M** said to the people,
32:31 **M** went back to the LORD and said,
32:33 The LORD replied to **M**, "Whoever has
33: 1 the LORD said to **M**, "Leave this
33: 5 For the LORD had said to **M**, "Tell
33: 7 Now **M** used to take a tent and pitch
33: 8 whenever **M** went out to the tent, all
33: 8 **M** until he entered the tent.
33: 9 **M** went into the tent, the pillar of
33: 9 while the LORD spoke with **M**.
33:11 The LORD would speak to **M** face to
33:11 Then **M** would return to the camp, but
33:12 **M** said to the LORD, "You have been
33:15 **M** said to him, "If your Presence
33:17 the LORD said to **M**, "I will do the
33:18 **M** said, "Now show me your glory."

Ex 34: 1 The LORD said to **M**, "Chisel out two
34: 4 **M** chiselled out two stone tablets
34: 6 he passed in front of **M**, proclaiming,
34: 8 **M** bowed to the ground at once and
34:27 the LORD said to **M**, "Write down
34:28 **M** was there with the LORD forty days
34:29 **M** came down from Mount Sinai with
34:30 Aaron and all the Israelites saw **M**,
34:31 **M** called to them; so Aaron and all
34:33 **M** finished speaking to them, he put
34:35 Then **M** would put the veil back over
35: 1 **M** assembled the whole Israelite
35: 4 **M** said to the whole Israelite
35:29 through **M** had commanded them to do.
35:30 **M** said to the Israelites, "See, the
36: 2 **M** summoned Bezalel and Oholiab and
36: 3 They received from **M** all the
36: 5 said to **M**, "The people are bringing
36: 6 **M** gave an order and they sent this
38:22 everything the LORD commanded **M**;
39: 1 for Aaron, as the LORD commanded **M**.
39: 5 linen, as the LORD commanded **M**.
39: 7 of Israel, as the LORD commanded **M**.
39:21 the ephod—as the LORD commanded **M**.
39:26 as the LORD commanded **M**.
39:29 as the LORD commanded **M**.
39:31 the turban, as the LORD commanded **M**.
39:32 just as the LORD commanded **M**.
39:33 they brought the tabernacle to **M**:
39:42 just as the LORD had commanded **M**.
39:43 **M** inspected the work and saw that
39:43 So **M** blessed them.
40: 1 Then the LORD said to **M**:
40:16 **M** did everything just as the LORD
40:18 **M** set up the tabernacle, he put the
40:22 **M** placed the table in the Tent of
40:26 **M** placed the gold altar in the Tent
40:31 **M** and Aaron and his sons used it to
40:32 the altar, as the LORD commanded **M**.
40:33 **M** set up the courtyard around the
40:33 And so **M** finished the work.
40:35 **M** could not enter the Tent of
Lev 1: 1 The LORD called to **M** and spoke to
4: 1 The LORD said to **M**,
5:14 The LORD said to **M**:
6: 1 The LORD said to **M**:
6: 8 The LORD said to **M**:
6:19 The LORD also said to **M**,
6:24 The LORD said to **M**,
7:22 The LORD said to **M**,
7:28 The LORD said to **M**,
7:38 which the LORD gave **M** on Mount Sinai
8: 1 The LORD said to **M**,
8: 4 **M** did as the LORD commanded him, and
8: 5 **M** said to the assembly, "This is
8: 6 **M** brought Aaron and his sons forward
8: 9 of it, as the LORD commanded **M**.
8:10 **M** took the anointing oil and
8:13 on them, as the LORD commanded **M**.
8:15 **M** slaughtered the bull and took some
8:16 **M** also took all the fat around the
8:17 the camp, as the LORD commanded **M**.
8:19 **M** slaughtered the ram and sprinkled
8:21 by fire, as the LORD commanded **M**.
8:23 **M** slaughtered the ram and took some
8:24 **M** also brought Aaron's sons forward
8:28 **M** took them from their hands and
8:29 offering, as the LORD commanded **M**.
8:30 **M** took some of the anointing oil and
8:31 **M** then said to Aaron and his sons,
8:36 the LORD commanded through **M**.
9: 1 On the eighth day **M** summoned Aaron
9: 5 They took the things **M** commanded to
9: 6 **M** said, "This is what the LORD has
9: 7 **M** said to Aaron, "Come to the altar
9:10 offering, as the LORD commanded **M**;
9:21 as a wave offering, as **M** commanded.
9:23 **M** and Aaron then went into the Tent
10: 3 **M** then said to Aaron, "This is what
10: 4 **M** summoned Mishael and Elzaphan,
10: 5 outside the camp, as **M** ordered.
10: 6 **M** said to Aaron and his sons Eleazar
10: 7 So they did as **M** said.
10:11 the LORD has given them through **M**."
10:12 **M** said to Aaron and his remaining
10:16 **M** enquired about the goat of the sin
Lev 10:19 Aaron replied to **M**, "Today they
10:20 **M** heard this, he was satisfied.
11: 1 The LORD said to **M** and Aaron,
12: 1 The LORD said to **M**,
13: 1 The LORD said to **M** and Aaron,
14: 1 The LORD said to **M**,
14:33 The LORD said to **M** and Aaron,
15: 1 The LORD said to **M** and Aaron,
16: 1 The LORD spoke to **M** after the death
16: 2 The LORD said to **M**: "Tell your
16:34 was done, as the LORD commanded **M**.
17: 1 The LORD said to **M**,
18: 1 The LORD said to **M**,
19: 1 The LORD said to **M**,
20: 1 The LORD said to **M**,
21: 1 The LORD said to **M**, "Speak to the
21:16 The LORD said to **M**,
21:24 **M** told this to Aaron and his sons
22: 1 The LORD said to **M**,
22:17 The LORD said to **M**,
22:26 The LORD said to **M**,
23: 1 The LORD said to **M**,
23: 9 The LORD said to **M**,
23:23 The LORD said to **M**,
23:26 The LORD said to **M**,
23:33 The LORD said to **M**,
23:44 **M** announced to the Israelites the
24: 1 The LORD said to **M**,
24:11 a curse; so they brought him to **M**.
24:13 the LORD said to **M**:
24:23 **M** spoke to the Israelites, and they
24:23 did as the LORD commanded **M**.
25: 1 The LORD said to **M** on Mount Sinai,
26:46 and the Israelites through **M**.
27: 1 The LORD said to **M**,
27:34 **M** on Mount Sinai for the Israelites.
Nu 1: 1 The LORD spoke to **M** in the Tent of
1:17 **M** and Aaron took these men whose
1:19 the LORD commanded **M**. And so he
1:44 These were the men counted by **M** and
1:48 The LORD had said to **M**:
1:54 this just as the LORD commanded **M**.
2: 1 The LORD said to **M** and Aaron:
2:33 Israelites, as the LORD commanded **M**.
2:34 did everything the LORD commanded **M**;
3: 1 **M** at the time the LORD talked with **M**
3: 5 The LORD said to **M**,
3:11 The LORD also said to **M**,
3:14 The LORD said to **M** in the Desert of
3:16 **M** counted them, as he was commanded
3:38 **M** and Aaron and his sons were to
3:39 **M** and Aaron according to their clans,
3:40 The LORD said to **M**, "Count all the
3:42 **M** counted all the firstborn of the
3:44 The LORD also said to **M**,
3:49 **M** collected the redemption money
3:51 **M** gave the redemption money to Aaron
4: 1 The LORD said to **M** and Aaron:
4:17 The LORD said to **M** and Aaron,
4:21 The LORD said to **M**,
4:34 **M**, Aaron and the leaders of the
4:37 **M** and Aaron counted them according
4:37 to the LORD's command through **M**.
4:41 **M** and Aaron counted them according
4:45 **M** and Aaron counted them according
4:45 to the LORD's command through **M**.
4:46 **M**, Aaron and the leaders of Israel
4:49 At the LORD's command through **M**,
4:49 counted, as the LORD commanded **M**.
5: 1 The LORD said to **M**,
5: 4 just as the LORD had instructed **M**.
5: 5 The LORD said to **M**,
5:11 Then the LORD said to **M**,
6: 1 The LORD said to **M**,
6:22 The LORD said to **M**,
7: 1 **M** finished setting up the tabernacle,
7: 4 The LORD said to **M**,
7: 6 **M** took the carts and oxen and gave
7: 9 **M** did not give any to the Kohathites,
7:11 For the LORD had said to **M**, "Each
7:89 **M** entered the Tent of Meeting to
8: 1 The LORD said to **M**,
8: 3 just as the LORD commanded **M**.
8: 4 the pattern the LORD had shown **M**.
8: 5 The LORD said to **M**:
8:20 **M**, Aaron and the whole Israelite
Nu 8:20 Levites just as the LORD commanded **M**.
8:22 Levites just as the LORD commanded **M**.
8:23 The LORD said to **M**,
9: 1 The LORD spoke to **M** in the Desert of
9: 4 **M** told the Israelites to celebrate
9: 5 just as the LORD commanded **M**.
9: 6 came to **M** and Aaron that same
9: 7 said to **M**, "We have become unclean
9: 8 **M** answered them, "Wait until I find
9: 9 Then the LORD said to **M**,
9:23 with his command through **M**.
10: 1 The LORD said to **M**:
10:13 at the LORD's command through **M**.
10:29 Now **M** said to Hobab son of Reuel the
10:31 **M** said, "Please do not leave us. You
10:35 Whenever the ark set out, **M** said,
11: 2 the people cried out to **M**, he prayed
11:10 **M** heard the people of every family
11:10 angry, and **M** was troubled.
11:16 The LORD said to **M**: "Bring me
11:21 **M** said, "Here I am among six hundred
11:23 The LORD answered **M**, "Is the LORD's
11:24 **M** went out and told the people what
11:27 A young man ran and told **M**, "Eldad
11:28 "**M**, my lord, stop them!
11:29 **M** replied, "Are you jealous for my
11:30 **M** and the elders of Israel returned
12: 1 **M** because of his Cushite wife,
12: 2 "Has the LORD spoken only through **M**?"
12: 3 (Now **M** was a very humble man, more
12: 4 At once the LORD said to **M**, Aaron
12:11 he said to **M**, "Please, my lord, do
12:13 **M** cried out to the LORD, "O God,
12:14 The LORD replied to **M**, "If her
13: 1 The LORD said to **M**,
13: 3 at the LORD's command **M** sent them
13:16 These are the names of the men **M**
13:16 (**M** gave Hoshea son of Nun the name
13:17 **M** sent them to explore Canaan, he
13:26 They came back to **M** and Aaron and
13:27 They gave **M** this account: "We went
13:30 Caleb silenced the people before **M**
14: 2 All the Israelites grumbled against **M**
14: 5 **M** and Aaron fell face down in front
14:11 The LORD said to **M**, "How long will
14:13 **M** said to the LORD, "Then the
14:26 The LORD said to **M** and Aaron:
14:36 the men **M** had sent to explore the
14:39 **M** reported this to all the
14:41 **M** said, "Why are you disobeying the
14:44 though neither **M** nor the ark of the
15: 1 The LORD said to **M**,
15:17 The LORD said to **M**,
15:22 of these commands the LORD gave **M**—
15:33 **M** and Aaron and the whole assembly,
15:35 the LORD said to **M**, "The man must
15:36 to death, as the LORD commanded **M**.
15:37 The LORD said to **M**,
16: 2 rose up against **M**. With them were 250
16: 3 They came as a group to oppose **M** and
16: 4 **M** heard this, he fell face down.
16: 8 **M** also said to Korah, "Now listen,
16:12 **M** summoned Dathan and Abiram, the
16:15 **M** became very angry and said to the
16:16 **M** said to Korah, "You and all your
16:18 and stood with **M** and Aaron at the
16:20 The LORD said to **M** and Aaron,
16:22 **M** and Aaron fell face down and cried
16:23 Then the LORD said to **M**,
16:25 **M** got up and went to Dathan and
16:28 **M** said, "This is how you will know
16:36 The LORD said to **M**,
16:40 the LORD directed him through **M**.
16:41 grumbled against **M** and Aaron.
16:42 gathered in opposition to **M** and
16:43 **M** and Aaron went to the front of the
16:44 the LORD said to **M**,
16:46 **M** said to Aaron, "Take your censer
16:47 Aaron did as **M** said, and ran into
16:50 Aaron returned to **M** at the entrance
17: 1 The LORD said to **M**,
17: 6 **M** spoke to the Israelites, and their
17: 7 **M** placed the staffs before the LORD
17: 8 The next day **M** entered the Tent of
17: 9 **M** brought out all the staffs from
17:10 The LORD said to **M**, "Put back

Nu 17:11 **M** did just as the LORD commanded him.
17:12 The Israelites said to **M**, "We shall
18:25 The LORD said to **M**,
19: 1 The LORD said to **M** and Aaron:
20: 2 in opposition to **M** and Aaron.
20: 3 They quarrelled with **M** and said, "If
20: 6 **M** and Aaron went from the assembly
20: 7 The LORD said to **M**,
20: 9 **M** took the staff from the LORD's
20:10 of the rock and **M** said to them,
20:11 **M** raised his arm and struck the rock
20:12 the LORD said to **M** and Aaron,
20:14 **M** sent messengers from Kadesh to the
20:23 Edom, the LORD said to **M** and Aaron,
20:27 **M** did as the LORD commanded: They
20:28 **M** removed Aaron's garments and put
20:28 Then **M** and Eleazar came down from
21: 5 they spoke against God and against **M**,
21: 7 The people came to **M** and said, "We
21: 7 So **M** prayed for the people.
21: 8 The LORD said to **M**, "Make a snake
21: 9 **M** made a bronze snake and put it up
21:16 the well where the LORD said to **M**,
21:32 After **M** had sent spies to Jazer, the
21:34 The LORD said to **M**, "Do not be
25: 4 The LORD said to **M**, "Take all the
25: 5 **M** said to Israel's judges, "Each of
25: 6 woman right before the eyes of **M**
25:10 The LORD said to **M**,
25:16 The LORD said to **M**,
26: 1 After the plague the LORD said to **M**
26: 3 **M** and Eleazar the priest spoke with
26: 4 or more, as the LORD commanded **M**.
26: 9 officials who rebelled against **M**
26:52 The LORD said to **M**,
26:59 Aaron, **M** and their sister Miriam.
26:63 These are the ones counted by **M** and
26:64 them was among those counted by **M**
27: 2 Tent of Meeting and stood before **M**,
27: 5 **M** brought their case before the
27:11 Israelites, as the LORD commanded **M**.
27:12 the LORD said to **M**, "Go up this
27:15 **M** said to the LORD,
27:18 the LORD said to **M**, "Take Joshua son
27:22 **M** did as the LORD commanded him. He
27:23 as the LORD instructed through **M**.
28: 1 The LORD said to **M**,
29:40 **M** told the Israelites all that the
30: 1 **M** said to the heads of the tribes of
30:16 the regulations the LORD gave **M**
31: 1 The LORD said to **M**,
31: 3 **M** said to the people, "Arm some of
31: 6 **M** sent them into battle, a thousand
31: 7 commanded **M**, and killed every man.
31:12 spoils and plunder to **M** and Eleazar
31:13 **M**, Eleazar the priest and all the
31:14 **M** was angry with the officers of the
31:21 of the law that the LORD gave **M**:
31:25 The LORD said to **M**,
31:31 **M** and Eleazar the priest did as the
31:31 priest did as the LORD commanded **M**.
31:41 **M** gave the tribute to Eleazar the
31:41 LORD's part, as the LORD commanded **M**.
31:42 which **M** set apart from that of the
31:47 **M** selected one out of every fifty
31:48 commanders of hundreds—went to **M**
31:51 **M** and Eleazar the priest accepted
31:52 commanders of hundreds that **M** and
31:54 **M** and Eleazar the priest accepted
32: 2 they came to **M** and Eleazar the
32: 6 **M** said to the Gadites and Reubenites,
32:20 **M** said to them, "If you will do this
32:25 The Gadites and Reubenites said to **M**,
32:28 **M** gave orders about them to Eleazar
32:33 Then **M** gave to the Gadites, the
32:40 **M** gave Gilead to the Makirites, the
33: 1 under the leadership of **M** and Aaron.
33: 2 At the LORD's command **M** recorded the
33:50 from Jericho the LORD said to **M**,
34: 1 The LORD said to **M**,
34:13 **M** commanded the Israelites: "Assign
34:16 The LORD said to **M**,
35: 1 from Jericho, the LORD said to **M**,
35: 9 the LORD said to **M**:
36: 1 came and spoke before **M** and the
36: 5 at the LORD's command **M** gave this
Nu 36:10 did as the LORD commanded **M**.
36:13 regulations the LORD gave through **M**
Dt 1: 1 These are the words **M** spoke to all
1: 3 **M** proclaimed to the Israelites all
1: 5 **M** began to expound this law, saying:
4:41 **M** set aside three cities east of the
4:44 This is the law **M** set before the
4:45 decrees and laws **M** gave them when
4:46 was defeated by **M** and the Israelites
5: 1 **M** summoned all Israel and said: Hear,
27: 1 **M** and the elders of Israel commanded
27: 9 **M** and the priests, who are Levites,
27:11 On the same day **M** commanded the
29: 1 the covenant the LORD commanded **M**
29: 2 **M** summoned all the Israelites and
31: 1 **M** went out and spoke these words to
31: 7 **M** summoned Joshua and said to him in
31: 9 **M** wrote down this law and gave it to
31:10 **M** commanded them: "At the end of
31:14 The LORD said to **M**, "Now the day of
31:14 So **M** and Joshua came and presented
31:16 the LORD said to **M**: "You are going
31:22 **M** wrote down this song that day and
31:24 After **M** finished writing in a book
31:30 **M** recited the words of this song
32:44 **M** came with Joshua son of Nun and
32:45 **M** finished reciting all these words
32:48 On that same day the LORD told **M**,
33: 1 This is the blessing that **M** the man
33: 4 the law that **M** gave us, the
34: 1 **M** climbed Mount Nebo from the plains
34: 7 **M** was a hundred and twenty years old
34: 8 The Israelites grieved for **M** in the
34: 9 because **M** had laid his hands on him.
34: 9 did what the LORD had commanded **M**.
34:10 **M**, whom the LORD knew face to face,
34:12 **M** did in the sight of all Israel.
Jos 1: 2 "**M** my servant is dead. Now then, you
1: 3 you set your foot, as I promised **M**.
1: 5 As I was with **M**, so I will be with
1:14 that **M** gave you east of the Jordan,
1:17 Just as we fully obeyed **M**, so we
1:17 God be with you as he was with **M**.
3: 7 that I am with you as I was with **M**.
4:10 just as **M** had directed Joshua.
4:12 Israelites, as **M** had directed them.
4:14 life, just as they had revered **M**.
8:35 There was not a word of all that **M**
9:24 **M** to give you the whole land
11:15 the LORD commanded his servant **M**, so
11:15 so **M** commanded Joshua, and Joshua
11:15 of all that the LORD commanded **M**.
11:20 mercy, as the LORD had commanded **M**.
11:23 just as the LORD had directed **M**, and
13: 8 **M** had given them east of the Jordan,
13:12 **M** had defeated them and taken over
13:15 This is what **M** had given to the
13:21 **M** had defeated him and the Midianite
13:24 This is what **M** had given to the
13:29 This is what **M** had given to the
13:32 This is the inheritance **M** had given
13:33 to the tribe of Levi, **M** had given no
14: 2 as the LORD had commanded through **M**.
14: 3 **M** had granted the two-and-a-half
14: 5 just as the LORD had commanded **M**.
14: 6 "You know what the LORD said to **M**
14: 9 on that day **M** swore to me, 'The land
14:10 since the time he said this to **M**,
14:11 today as the day **M** sent me out;
17: 4 "The LORD commanded **M** to give us an
20: 2 as I instructed you through **M**,
21: 2 "The LORD commanded through **M** that
21: 8 as the LORD had commanded through **M**.
22: 7 (To the half-tribe of Manasseh **M** had
22: 9 the command of the LORD through **M**.
24: 5 "'Then I sent **M** and Aaron, and I
Jdg 1:20 **M** had promised, Hebron was given to
3: 4 given their forefathers through **M**.
18:30 the son of **M**, and his sons were
1Sa 12: 6 "It is the LORD who appointed **M** and
12: 8 and the LORD sent **M** and Aaron, who
1Ki 8: 9 that **M** had placed in it at Horeb,
8:53 through your servant **M** when you,
8:56 he gave through his servant **M**.
2Ki 18: 4 pieces the bronze snake **M** had made,
18: 6 the commands the LORD had given **M**.
1Ch 6: 3 The children of Amram: Aaron, **M** and
6:49 **M** the servant of God had commanded.
15:15 as **M** had commanded in accordance
21:29 The tabernacle of the LORD, which **M**
22:13 that the LORD gave to **M** for Israel.
23:13 The sons of Amram: Aaron and **M**.
23:14 The sons of **M** the man of God were
23:15 The sons of **M**: Gershom and Eliezer.
26:24 a descendant of Gershom son of **M**,
2Ch 1: 3 which **M** the LORD's servant had made
5:10 that **M** had placed in it at Horeb,
8:13 commanded by **M** for Sabbaths,
24: 9 bring to the LORD the tax that **M**
25: 4 in the Book of **M**, where the LORD
33: 8 and ordinances given through **M**."
34:14 LORD that had been given through **M**.
35: 6 what the LORD commanded through **M**.
35:12 LORD, as is written in the Book of **M**.
Ezr 6:18 to what is written in the Book of **M**.
Ne 1: 7 and laws you gave your servant **M**.
1: 8 instruction you gave your servant **M**,
8:14 the LORD had commanded through **M**,
9:14 and laws through your servant **M**.
10:29 given through **M** the servant of God
13: 1 On that day the Book of **M** was read
Ps 77:20 a flock by the hand of **M** and Aaron.
90: T A prayer of **M** the man of God.
99: 6 **M** and Aaron were among his priests,
103: 7 He made known his ways to **M**, his
105:26 He sent **M** his servant, and Aaron,
106:16 In the camp they grew envious of **M**
106:23 he would destroy them—had not **M**,
106:32 trouble came to **M** because of them;
Isa 63:11 the days of **M** and his people—where
Jer 15: 1 the LORD said to me: "Even if **M** and
Mic 6: 4 **M** to lead you, also Aaron and Miriam.
Mt 8: 4 **M** commanded, as a testimony to them."
17: 3 **M** and Elijah, talking with Jesus.
17: 4 you, one for **M** and one for Elijah."
19: 7 "Why then," they asked, "did **M**
19: 8 Jesus replied, "**M** permitted you to
22:24 "Teacher," they said, "**M** told us
Mk 1:44 that **M** commanded for your cleansing,
7:10 For **M** said, 'Honour your father and
9: 4 and **M**, who were talking with Jesus.
9: 5 you, one for **M** and one for Elijah."
10: 3 "What did **M** command you?" he replied.
10: 4 They said, "**M** permitted a man to
10: 5 **M** wrote you this law," Jesus replied.
12:19 "Teacher," they said, "**M** wrote for
12:26 you not read in the book of **M**,
Lk 5:14 that **M** commanded for your cleansing,
9:30 Two men, **M** and Elijah,
9:33 you, one for **M** and one for Elijah.
16:29 "Abraham replied, 'They have **M** and
16:31 'If they do not listen to **M** and the
20:28 "Teacher," they said, "**M** wrote for
20:37 in the account of the bush, even **M**
24:27 beginning with **M** and all the
Jn 1:17 For the law was given through **M**;
1:45 "We have found the one **M** wrote about
3:14 Just as **M** lifted up the snake in the
5:45 is **M**, on whom your hopes are set.
5:46 If you believed **M**, you would believe
6:32 "I tell you the truth, it is not **M**
7:19 Has not **M** given you the law? Yet not
7:22 Yet, because **M** gave you circumcision
7:22 actually it did not come from **M**,
8: 5 In the Law **M** commanded us to stone
9:28 disciple! We are disciples of **M**!
9:29 We know that God spoke to **M**, but as
Ac 3:22 For **M** said, 'The Lord your God will
6:11 against **M** and against God."
6:14 the customs **M** handed down to us."
7:20 "At that time **M** was born, and he was
7:22 **M** was educated in all the wisdom of
7:23 "When **M** was forty years old, he
7:25 **M** thought that his own people would
7:26 The next day **M** came upon two
7:27 the other pushed **M** aside and said,
7:29 **M** heard this, he fled to Midian,
7:30 an angel appeared to **M** in the flames
7:32 **M** trembled with fear and did not
7:35 "This is the same **M** whom they had
7:37 "This is that **M** who told the
7:40 As for this fellow **M** who led us out

Ac 7:44 It had been made as God directed **M**,
15: 1 taught by **M**, you cannot be saved."
15:21 For **M** has been preached in every
21:21 the Gentiles to turn away from **M**,
26:22 prophets and **M** said would happen—
Ro 5:14 the time of Adam to the time of **M**,
9:15 For he says to **M**, "I will have mercy
10: 5 **M** describes in this way the
10:19 **M** says, "I will make you envious by
1Co 10: 2 They were all baptised into **M** in the
2Co 3: 7 the face of **M** because of its glory,
3:13 We are not like **M**, who would put a
3:15 Even to this day when **M** is read, a
2Ti 3: 8 Just as Jannes and Jambres opposed **M**,
Heb 3: 2 **M** was faithful in all God's house.
3: 3 worthy of greater honour than **M**,
3: 5 **M** was faithful as a servant in all
3:16 not all those **M** led out of Egypt?
7:14 tribe **M** said nothing about priests.
8: 5 This is why **M** was warned when he was
9:19 **M** had proclaimed every commandment
11:24 By faith **M**, when he had grown up,
12:21 The sight was so terrifying that **M**
Jude : 9 with the devil about the body of **M**,
Rev 15: 3 sang the song of **M** the servant of

Moses' (Moses)

Ex 4:25 foreskin and touched ⌊**M**⌋ feet with
17:12 **M** hands grew tired, they took a
18: 5 **M** father-in-law, together with **M**
18:12 Jethro, **M** father-in-law, brought a
18:12 to eat bread with **M** father-in-law
18:17 **M** father-in-law replied, "What you
35:20 community withdrew from **M** presence,
38:21 which were recorded at **M** command by
Lev 8:29 He also took the breast—**M** share of
Nu 10:29 the Midianite, **M** father-in-law,
11:28 of Nun, who had been **M** assistant
Jos 1: 1 to Joshua son of Nun, **M** assistant:
Jdg 1:16 The descendants of **M** father-in-law,
4:11 of Hobab, **M** brother-in-law,
Ps 106:33 God, and rash words came from **M** lips.
Isa 63:12 arm of power to be at **M** right hand,
Mt 23: 2 law and the Pharisees sit in **M** seat.
Heb 11:23 By faith **M** parents hid him for three

Moses the servant of the LORD

Dt 34: 5 **M** died there in Moab, as the LORD
Jos 1: 1 After the death of **M**, the LORD said
1:13 "Remember the command that **M** gave
1:15 which **M** gave you east of the Jordan
8:31 **M** had commanded the Israelites. He
8:33 as **M** had formerly commanded when he
11:12 destroyed them, as **M** had commanded.
12: 6 And **M** gave their land to the
14: 7 I was forty years old when **M** sent me
18: 7 **M** gave it to them."
22: 2 "You have done all that **M** commanded,
22: 4 land that **M** gave you on the other side
22: 5 and the law that **M** gave you:
2Ki 18:12 his covenant—all that **M** commanded.
2Ch 24: 6 Jerusalem the tax imposed by **M** and

Most High (*God Most High*)

Nu 24:16; Dt 32:8; 2Sa 22:14; 23:1; Ps 7:8, 17; 9:2; 18:13; 21:7; 46:4; 47:2; 50:14; 73:11; 77:10; 78:17, 56; 82:6; 83:18; 87:5; 91:1, 9; 92:1; 97:9; 107:11; Isa 14:14; Lam 3:35, 38; Da 3:26; 4:2, 17, 24, 25, 32, 34; 5:18, 21; 7:18, 22, 25, 27; Hos 7:16; 11:7; Mk 5:7; Lk 1:32, 35, 76; 6:35; 8:28; Ac 7:48; 16:17

Most holy (*Most holy place*)

Ex 29:37; 30:10, 29, 36; 40:10; Lev 2:3, 10; 6:17, 25, 29; 7:1, 6; 10:12, 17; 14:13; 21:22; 24:9; 27:28; Nu 4:4, 19; 18:9, 10; 1Ch 23:13; Eze 42:13; 43:12; 44:13; 48:12; Da 9:24; Jude 20

Most holy place

Ex 26:33, 34; Lev 16:2, 16, 17, 20, 23, 27, 33; 1Ki 6:16; 7:50; 8:6; 1Ch 6:49; 2Ch 3:8, 10 ; 4:22; 5:7; Ps 28:2; Eze 41:4, 21, 23; 45:3; Heb 9:3, 8, 12, 25; 10:19; 13:11

Moth (Moth's, Moths)

Job 4:19 are crushed more readily than a **m**!
Ps 39:11 like a **m**—each man is but a breath.
Isa 51: 8 For the **m** will eat them up like a
Hos 5:12 I am like a **m** to Ephraim, like rot
Mt 6:19 where **m** and rust destroy, and where
6:20 where **m** and rust do not destroy, and
Lk 12:33 thief comes near and no **m** destroys.

Moth's (Moth)

Job 27:18 The house he builds is like a **m**

Mother (Grandmother, Grandmother's, Mother's, Mother-in-law, Mothers, Mothers')

Ge 2:24 and **m** and be united to his wife,
3:20 become the **m** of all the living.
17:16 that she will be the **m** of nations;
20:12 not of my **m**; and she became my wife.
21:21 his **m** got a wife for him from Egypt.
22:20 "Milcah is also a **m**; she has borne
24:53 gifts to her brother and to her **m**.
24:55 her brother and her **m** replied, "Let
24:67 his **m** Sarah, and he married Rebekah.
27:11 Jacob said to Rebekah his **m**, "But my
27:13 His **m** said to him, "My son, let the
27:14 got them and brought them to his **m**,
27:29 the sons of your **m** bow down to you.
28: 5 who was the **m** of Jacob and Esau.
28: 7 and **m** and had gone to Paddan Aram.
30:14 which he brought to his **m** Leah.
37:10 Will your **m** and I and your brothers
Ex 2: 8 the girl went and got the baby's **m**.
20:12 "Honour your father and your **m**, so
21:15 or his **m** must be put to death.
21:17 "Anyone who curses his father or **m**
Lev 18: 7 having sexual relations with your **m**.
18: 7 **m**; do not have relations with her.
19: 3 "'Each of you must respect his **m**
20: 9 "'If anyone curses his father or **m**,
20: 9 He has cursed his father or his **m**,
20:14 a woman and her **m**, it is wicked.
20:17 of either his father or his **m**,
20:19 of either your **m** or your father,
21: 2 such as his **m** or father, his son or
21:11 unclean, even for his father or **m**,
22:27 to remain with its **m** for seven days.
24:10 Now the son of an Israelite **m** and an
Nu 6: 7 Even if his own father or **m** or
Dt 5:16 "Honour your father and your **m**, as
21:13 her father and **m** for a full month,
21:18 does not obey his father and **m**
21:19 his father and **m** shall take hold of
22: 6 and the **m** is sitting on the young or
22: 6 do not take the **m** with the young.
22: 7 but be sure to let the **m** go, so that
22:15 the girl's father and **m** shall bring
27:16 who dishonours his father or his **m**.
27:22 his father or the daughter of his **m**.
33: 9 He said of his father and **m**, 'I have
Jos 2:13 spare the lives of my father and **m**,
2:18 you have brought your father and **m**,
6:23 her father and **m** and brothers and
Jdg 5: 7 Deborah, arose, arose a **m** in Israel.
5:28 "Through the window peered Sisera's **m**
8:19 my brothers, the sons of my own **m**.
11: 1 was Gilead; his **m** was a prostitute.
14: 2 he said to his father and **m**, "I have
14: 3 His father and **m** replied, "Isn't
14: 5 together with his father and **m**.
14: 6 father nor his **m** what he had done.
14:16 explained it to my father or **m**,"
17: 2 said to his **m**, "The eleven hundred
17: 2 Then his **m** said, "The LORD bless
17: 3 hundred shekels of silver to his **m**,
17: 4 he returned the silver to his **m**, and
Ru 2:11 how you left your father and **m** and
1Sa 2:19 Each year his **m** made him a little
15:33 your **m** be childless among women.
20:30 to the shame of the **m** who bore you?
22: 3 "Would you let my father and **m** come
2Sa 17:25 and sister of Zeruiah the **m** of Joab.
19:37 near the tomb of my father and **m**.
20:19 a city that is a **m** in Israel.
1Ki 1: 5 Now Adonijah, whose **m** was Haggith,
1Ki 1:11 Nathan asked Bathsheba, Solomon's **m**,
2:13 went to Bathsheba, Solomon's **m**.
2:19 a throne brought for the king's **m**,
2:20 it, my **m**; I will not refuse you."
2:22 King Solomon answered his **m**, "Why do
3:27 Do not kill him; she is his **m**."
7:14 whose **m** was a widow from the tribe
11:26 and his **m** was a widow named Zeruah.
15:13 Maacah from her position as queen **m**,
17:23 He gave him to his **m** and said, "Look,
19:20 "Let me kiss my father and **m**
22:52 in the ways of his father and **m**
2Ki 3: 2 not as his father and **m** had done.
3:13 father and the prophets of your **m**.
4:19 told a servant, "Carry him to his **m**.
4:20 him up and carried him to his **m**,
4:30 the child's **m** said, "As surely as
9:22 of your **m** Jezebel abound?"
10:13 of the king and of the queen **m**."
11: 1 Athaliah the **m** of Ahaziah saw that
24:12 Jehoiachin king of Judah, his **m**, his
24:15 Jerusalem to Babylon the king's **m**,
1Ch 2:17 Abigail was the **m** of Amasa, whose
2:26 was Atarah; she was the **m** of Onam.
2:46 Caleb's concubine Ephah was the **m** of
2:48 Caleb's concubine Maacah was the **m**
4: 9 His **m** had named him Jabez, saying,
2Ch 2:14 whose **m** was from Dan and whose
15:16 Maacah from her position as queen **m**,
22: 3 his **m** encouraged him in doing wrong.
22:10 Athaliah the **m** of Ahaziah saw that
Est 2: 7 she had neither father nor **m**.
2: 7 daughter when her father and **m** died.
Job 17:14 to the worm, 'My **m**' or 'My sister',
Ps 27:10 Though my father and **m** forsake me,
35:14 in grief as though weeping for my **m**.
51: 5 from the time my **m** conceived me.
109:14 sin of his **m** never be blotted out.
113: 9 her home as a happy **m** of children.
131: 2 like a weaned child with its **m**,
Pr 4: 3 tender, and an only child of my **m**,
10: 1 but a foolish son grief to his **m**.
15:20 but a foolish man despises his **m**.
19:26 drives out his **m** is a son who brings
20:20 If a man curses his father or **m**, his
23:22 not despise your **m** when she is old.
23:25 May your father and **m** be glad; may
28:24 He who robs his father or **m** and says,
29:15 left to himself disgraces his **m**.
30:17 that scorns obedience to a **m**, will
31: 1 Lemuel—an oracle his **m** taught him:
SS 3:11 the crown with which his **m** crowned
6: 9 the only daughter of her **m**, the
8: 5 you; there your **m** conceived you,
Isa 8: 4 'My father' or 'My **m**', the wealth of
45:10 **m**, 'What have you brought to birth?'
49:15 "Can a **m** forget the baby at her
50: 1 transgressions your **m** was sent away.
66:13 a **m** comforts her child, so will I
Jer 13:18 Say to the king and to the queen **m**,
15: 9 The **m** of seven will grow faint and
15:10 Alas, my **m**, that you gave me birth,
16: 7 not even for a father or a **m**–nor
20:14 the day my **m** bore me not be blessed!
20:17 with my **m** as my grave, her womb
22:26 I will hurl you and the **m** who gave
29: 2 King Jehoiachin and the queen **m**,
50:12 your **m** will be greatly ashamed; she
Eze 16: 3 was an Amorite and your **m** a Hittite.
16:44 about you: "Like **m**, like daughter.
16:45 You are a true daughter of your **m**,
16:45 Your **m** was a Hittite and your father
19: 2 say: "'What a lioness was your **m**
19:10 "'Your **m** was like a vine in your
22: 7 In you they have treated father and **m**
23: 2 two women, daughters of the same **m**.
44:25 the dead person was his father or **m**,
Hos 2: 2 "Rebuke your **m**, rebuke her, for she
2: 5 Their **m** has been unfaithful and has
4: 5 So I will destroy your **m**—
Mic 7: 6 a daughter rises up against her **m**, a
Zec 13: 3 his father and **m**, to whom he was
Mt 1: 3 whose **m** was Tamar, Perez the father
1: 5 father of Boaz, whose **m** was Rahab
1: 5 **m** was Ruth, Obed the father of Jesse,
1: 6 whose **m** had been Uriah's wife,

Mt 1:18 His **m** Mary was pledged to be married
2:11 they saw the child with his **m** Mary,
2:13 child and his **m** and escape to Egypt.
2:14 he got up, took the child and his **m**
2:20 "Get up, take the child and his **m**
2:21 he got up, took the child and his **m**
10:35 a daughter against her **m**, a
10:37 "Anyone who loves his father or **m**
12:46 his **m** and brothers stood outside,
12:47 Someone told him, "Your **m** and
12:48 He replied to him, "Who is my **m**, and
12:49 "Here are my **m** and my brothers.
12:50 is my brother and sister and **m**."
14: 8 Prompted by her **m**, she said, "Give
14:11 the girl, who carried it to her **m**.
15: 4 'Honour your father and **m**' and
15: 4 father or **m** must be put to death.'
15: 5 if a man says to his father or **m**,
19: 5 and **m** and be united to his wife,
19:19 honour your father and **m**,' and 'love
19:29 **m** or children or fields for my sake
20:20 the **m** of Zebedee's sons came to
27:56 Mary the **m** of James and Joses, and
27:56 Joses, and the **m** of Zebedee's sons.
Mk 3:31 Jesus' **m** and brothers arrived.
3:32 "Your **m** and brothers are outside
3:33 "Who are my **m** and my brothers?" he
3:34 "Here are my **m** and my brothers!
3:35 is my brother and sister and **m**."
5:40 he took the child's father and **m** and
6:24 She went out and said to her **m**,
6:28 the girl, and she gave it to her **m**.
7:10 'Honour your father and your **m**,' and,
7:10 father or **m** must be put to death.'
7:11 if a man says to his father or **m**:
7:12 him do anything for his father or **m**.
10: 7 and **m** and be united to his wife,
10:19 defraud, honour your father and **m**.'"
10:29 home or brothers or sisters or **m**
15:40 Mary the **m** of James the younger and
15:47 Mary Magdalene and Mary the **m** of
16: 1 Mary Magdalene, Mary the **m** of James,
Lk 1:43 why am I so favoured, that the **m** of
1:60 his **m** spoke up and said, "No! He is
2:33 The child's father and **m** marvelled
2:34 said to Mary, his **m**: "This child is
2:48 His **m** said to him, "Son, why have
2:51 But his **m** treasured all these things
7:12 son of his **m**, and she was a widow.
7:15 and Jesus gave him back to his **m**.
8:19 Now Jesus' **m** and brothers came to
8:20 Someone told him, "Your **m** and
8:21 He replied, "My **m** and brothers are
8:51 James, and the child's father and **m**.
11:27 "Blessed is the **m** who gave you birth
12:53 **m** against daughter and daughter
12:53 daughter and daughter against **m**,
14:26 and does not hate his father and **m**,
18:20 honour your father and **m**.'"
24:10 Joanna, Mary the **m** of James, and the
Jn 2: 1 Cana in Galilee. Jesus' **m** was there
2: 3 the wine was gone, Jesus' **m** said to
2: 5 His **m** said to the servants, "Do
2:12 **m** and brothers and his disciples.
6:42 whose father and **m** we know? How can
19:25 Near the cross of Jesus stood his **m**,
19:26 Jesus saw his **m** there, and the
19:26 he said to his **m**, "Dear woman, here
19:27 to the disciple, "Here is your **m**."
Ac 1:14 **m** of Jesus, and with his brothers.
12:12 to the house of Mary the **m** of John
16: 1 whose **m** was a Jewess and a believer,
Ro 16:13 his **m**, who has been a **m** to me, too.
Gal 4:26 is above is free, and she is our **m**.
Eph 5:31 and **m** and be united to his wife,
6: 2 "Honour your father and **m**"—which is
1Th 2: 7 we were gentle among you, like a **m**
2Ti 1: 5 Lois and in your **m** Eunice and,
Heb 7: 3 Without father or **m**, without
Rev 17: 5 BABYLON THE GREAT THE **M** OF

Mother's (Mother)

Ge 24:28 ran and told her **m** household
24:67 was comforted after his **m** death.
28: 2 the house of your **m** father Bethuel.
28: 2 daughters of Laban, your **m** brother.
29:10 his **m** brother, and Laban's sheep, he
43:29 his own **m** son, he asked, "Is this
44:20 and he is the only one of his **m** sons
Ex 23:19 not cook a young goat in its **m** milk.
34:26 cook a young goat in its **m** milk."
Lev 18: 9 daughter or your **m** daughter,
18:13 sexual relations with your **m** sister,
18:13 she is your **m** close relative.
24:11 (His **m** name was Shelomith, the
Nu 12:12 infant coming from its **m** womb
Dt 14:21 not cook a young goat in its **m** milk.
Jdg 9: 1 went to his **m** brothers in Shechem
9: 1 said to them and to all his **m** clan,
Ru 1: 8 Go back, each of you, to your **m** home.
1Ki 14:21 His **m** name was Naamah; she was an
14:31 His **m** name was Naamah; she was an
15: 2 His **m** name was Maacah daughter of
22:42 **m** name was Azubah daughter of Shilhi.
2Ki 8:26 His **m** name was Athaliah, a
12: 1 His **m** name was Zibiah; she was from
14: 2 His **m** name was Jehoaddin; she was
15: 2 His **m** name was Jecoliah; she was
15:33 **m** name was Jerusha daughter of Zadok.
18: 2 His **m** name was Abijah daughter of
21: 1 His **m** name was Hephzibah.
21:19 His **m** name was Meshullemeth daughter
22: 1 His **m** name was Jedidah daughter of
23:31 His **m** name was Hamutal daughter of
23:36 His **m** name was Zebidah daughter of
24: 8 His **m** name was Nehushta daughter of
24:18 His **m** name was Hamutal daughter of
2Ch 12:13 His **m** name was Naamah; she was an
13: 2 His **m** name was Maacah, a daughter of
20:31 **m** name was Azubah daughter of Shilhi.
22: 2 His **m** name was Athaliah, a
24: 1 His **m** name was Zibiah; she was from
25: 1 His **m** name was Jehoaddin; she was
26: 3 His **m** name was Jecoliah; she was
27: 1 **m** name was Jerusha daughter of Zadok.
29: 1 His **m** name was Abijah daughter of
Job 1:21 said: "Naked I came from my **m** womb,
Ps 22: 9 me trust in you even at my **m** breast.
22:10 from my **m** womb you have been my God.
50:20 brother and slander your own **m** son.
69: 8 brothers, an alien to my own **m** sons;
71: 6 you brought me forth from my **m** womb.
139:13 you knit me together in my **m** womb.
Pr 1: 8 and do not forsake your **m** teaching.
6:20 and do not forsake your **m** teaching.
Ecc 5:15 Naked a man comes from his **m** womb,
11: 5 the body is formed in a **m** womb,
SS 1: 6 My **m** sons were angry with me and
3: 4 I had brought him to my **m** house,
8: 1 who was nursed at my **m** breasts! Then,
8: 2 my **m** house—she who has taught me.
Isa 50: 1 "Where is your **m** certificate of
Jer 52: 1 His **m** name was Hamutal daughter of
Mt 13:55 son? Isn't his **m** name Mary,
Jn 3: 4 time into his **m** womb to be born!"
19:25 his **m** sister, Mary the wife of

Mother-in-law (Mother)

Dt 27:23 is the man who sleeps with his **m**.
Ru 1:14 Orpah kissed her **m** good-bye, but
2:11 done for your **m** since the death of
2:18 her **m** saw how much she had gathered.
2:19 Her **m** asked her, "Where did you
2:19 Ruth told her **m** about the one at
2:23 And she lived with her **m**.
3: 1 One day Naomi her **m** said to her, "My
3: 6 did everything her **m** told her to do.
3:16 Ruth came to her **m**, Naomi asked,
3:17 Don't go back to your **m** empty-handed.
Mic 7: 6 a daughter-in-law against her **m**—a
Mt 8:14 Peter's **m** lying in bed with a fever.
10:35 a daughter-in-law against her **m**—
Mk 1:30 Simon's **m** was in bed with a fever,
Lk 4:38 Now Simon's **m** was suffering from a
12:53 **m** against daughter-in-law and
12:53 and daughter-in-law against **m**."

Mother-of-pearl (Pearl)

Est 1: 6 marble, **m** and other costly stones.

Mothers (Mother)

Ge 32:11 and also the **m** with their children.
Ex 22:30 Let them stay with their **m** for seven
Job 31:15 same one form us both within our **m**?
Pr 30:11 fathers and do not bless their **m**;
Isa 49:23 and their queens your nursing **m**.
Jer 15: 8 against the **m** of their young men;
16: 3 **m** and the men who are their fathers:
31: 8 expectant **m** and women in labour; a
Lam 2:12 They say to their **m**, "Where is bread
5: 3 and fatherless, our **m** like widows.
Hos 10:14 when **m** were dashed to the ground
Mt 24:19 for pregnant women and nursing **m**!
Mk 10:30 brothers, sisters, **m**, children and
13:17 for pregnant women and nursing **m**!
Lk 21:23 for pregnant women and nursing **m**!
1Ti 1: 9 their fathers or **m**, for murderers,
5: 2 older women as **m**, and younger women

Mothers' (Mother)

Lam 2:12 lives ebb away in their **m** arms.

Moths (Moth)

Job 13:28 rotten, like a garment eaten by **m**.
Isa 50: 9 a garment; the **m** will eat them up.
Jas 5: 2 Your wealth has rotted, and **m** have

Motioned (Motions)

Jn 13:24 Simon Peter **m** to this disciple and
Ac 12:17 Peter **m** with his hand for them to be
13:16 Standing up, Paul **m** with his hand
19:33 He **m** for silence in order to make a
21:40 on the steps and **m** to the crowd.
24:10 the governor **m** for him to speak,
26: 1 So Paul **m** with his hand and began

Motions (Motioned)

Pr 6:13 his feet and **m** with his fingers,

Motive (Motives)

1Ch 28: 9 every **m** behind the thoughts.

Motives (Motive)

Pr 16: 2 him, but **m** are weighed by the LORD.
1Co 4: 5 will expose the **m** of men's hearts.
Php 1:18 false **m** or true, Christ is preached.
1Th 2: 3 from error or impure **m**, nor are we
Jas 4: 3 because you ask with wrong **m**, that

Moulded (Moulds)

Job 10: 9 Remember that you **m** me like clay.

Moulding (Moulds)

Ex 25:11 out, and make a gold **m** around it.
25:24 gold and make a gold **m** around it.
25:25 wide and put a gold **m** on the rim.
30: 3 gold, and make a gold **m** around it.
30: 4 rings for the altar below the **m**
37: 2 out, and made a gold **m** around it.
37:11 gold and made a gold **m** around it.
37:12 wide and put a gold **m** on the rim.
37:26 gold, and made a gold **m** around it.
37:27 They made two gold rings below the **m**

Moulds (Moulded, Moulding)

1Ki 7:37 They were all cast in the same **m** and
7:46 The king had them cast in clay **m** in
2Ch 4:17 The king had them cast in clay **m** in

Mouldy

Jos 9: 5 of their food supply was dry and **m**.
9:12 But now see how dry and **m** it is.

Mound (Mounds)

SS 7: 2 is a **m** of wheat encircled by lilies.
Jer 26:18 hill a **m** overgrown with thickets.'
49: 2 it will become a **m** of ruins,
Eze 16:24 you built a **m** for yourself and made
Mic 3:12 hill a **m** overgrown with thickets.

Mounds (Mound)
Jos 11:13 cities built on their **m**—except
Eze 16:31 you built your **m** at the head of
16:39 tear down your **m** and destroy

Mount[1] (*Mount of Olives, Mount Sinai, Mount Zion*, Mountain, Mountains, Mountainside, Mountaintop, Mountaintops)
Ex 33: 6 off their ornaments at **M** Horeb.
Nu 20:22 out from Kadesh and came to **M** Hor.
20:23 At **M** Hor, near the border of Edom,
20:25 son Eleazar and take them up **M** Hor.
20:27 They went up **M** Hor in the sight of
21: 4 They travelled from **M** Hor along the
33:23 Kehelathah and camped at **M** Shepher.
33:24 They left **M** Shepher and camped at
33:37 They left Kadesh and camped at **M** Hor,
33:38 Aaron the priest went up **M** Hor,
33:39 years old when he died on **M** Hor.
33:41 They left **M** Hor and camped at
34: 7 a line from the Great Sea to **M** Hor
34: 8 from **M** Hor to Lebo Hamath. Then the
Dt 1: 2 Kadesh Barnea by the **M** Seir road.)
3: 8 the Arnon Gorge as far as **M** Hermon.
4:48 Gorge to **M** Siyon (that is, Hermon),
11:29 you are to proclaim on **M** Gerizim the
11:29 blessings, and on **M** Ebal the curses.
27: 4 set up these stones on **M** Ebal, as I
27:12 tribes shall stand on **M** Gerizim
27:13 these tribes shall stand on **M** Ebal
32:49 into the Abarim Range to **M** Nebo
32:50 Aaron died on **M** Hor and was
33: 2 Seir; he shone forth from **M** Paran.
34: 1 Moses climbed **M** Nebo from the plains
Jos 8:30 Joshua built on **M** Ebal an altar to
8:33 people stood in front of **M** Gerizim
8:33 and half of them in front of **M** Ebal,
11:17 from **M** Halak, which rises towards
11:17 Valley of Lebanon below **M** Hermon.
12: 1 from the Arnon Gorge to **M** Hermon,
12: 5 He ruled over **M** Hermon, Salecah, all
12: 7 in the Valley of Lebanon to **M** Halak,
13: 5 Gad below **M** Hermon to Lebo Hamath.
13:11 all of **M** Hermon and all Bashan as
15: 9 came out at the towns of **M** Ephron
15:10 westward from Baalah to **M** Seir
15:10 the northern slope of **M** Jearim
15:11 to **M** Baalah and reached Jabneel.
24:30 of Ephraim, north of **M** Gaash.
Jdg 1:35 also to hold out in **M** Heres,
2: 9 of Ephraim, north of **M** Gaash.
3: 3 mountains from **M** Baal Hermon to
4: 6 Zebulun and lead the way to **M** Tabor.
4:12 of Abinoam had gone up to **M** Tabor,
4:14 of you?" So Barak went down **M** Tabor,
7: 3 may turn back and leave **M** Gilead.
9: 7 climbed up on the top of **M** Gerizim
9:48 he and all his men went up **M** Zalmon.
1Sa 31: 1 and many fell slain on **M** Gilboa.
31: 8 his three sons fallen on **M** Gilboa.
2Sa 1: 6 "I happened to be on **M** Gilboa," the
1Ki 18:19 over Israel to meet me on **M** Carmel.
18:20 assembled the prophets on **M** Carmel.
2Ki 2:25 he went on to **M** Carmel and from
4:25 came to the man of God at **M** Carmel.
1Ch 5:23 Hermon, that is, to Senir (**M** Hermon).
10: 1 and many fell slain on **M** Gilboa.
10: 8 Saul and his sons fallen on **M** Gilboa.
2Ch 3: 1 the LORD in Jerusalem on **M** Moriah,
13: 4 Abijah stood on **M** Zemaraim, in the
20:10 Moab and **M** Seir, whose territory you
20:22 and **M** Seir who were invading Judah,
20:23 rose up against the men from **M** Seir
Ps 42: 6 the heights of Hermon—from **M** Mizar.
SS 4: 1 of goats descending from **M** Gilead.
7: 5 Your head crowns you like **M** Carmel.
Isa 10:32 at the **m** of the Daughter of Zion,
14:13 sit enthroned on the **m** of assembly,
16: 1 to the **m** of the Daughter of Zion.
28:21 will rise up as he did at **M** Perazim
Eze 28:14 You were on the holy **m** of God; you
28:16 you in disgrace from the **m** of God,
35: 2 man, set your face against **M** Seir;
35: 3 I am against you, **M** Seir, and I
Eze 35: 7 I will make **M** Seir a desolate waste
35:15 You will be desolate, O **M** Seir, you
Am 4: 1 you cows of Bashan on **M** Samaria, you
6: 1 you who feel secure on **M** Samaria
Hab 3: 3 Teman, the Holy One from **M** Paran.

Mount[2] (Mounted, Mountings, Mounts)
Ex 28:11 Then **m** the stones in gold filigree
28:17 **m** four rows of precious stones on it.
28:20 **M** them in gold filigree settings.
Ne 2:14 enough room for my **m** to get through;
Ps 89: 9 when its waves **m** up, you still them.
Jer 46: 4 Harness the horses, **m** the steeds!
Hos 14: 3 we will not **m** war-horses. We will

Mount of Olives
2Sa 15:30 David continued up the **M**, weeping as
Zec 14: 4 day his feet will stand on the **M**,
14: 4 east of Jerusalem, and the **M** will be
Mt 21: 1 on the **M**, Jesus sent two disciples,
24: 3 Jesus was sitting on the **M**, the
26:30 sung a hymn, they went out to the **M**.
Mk 11: 1 to Bethphage and Bethany at the **M**,
13: 3 Jesus was sitting on the **M** opposite
14:26 sung a hymn, they went out to the **M**.
Lk 19:29 Bethany at the hill called the **M**,
19:37 where the road goes down the **M**,
21:37 the night on the hill called the **M**,
22:39 Jesus went out as usual to the **M**,
Jn 8: 1 Jesus went to the **M**.
Ac 1:12 Jerusalem from the hill called the **M**,

Mount Sinai
Ex 19:11 on **M** in the sight of all the people.
19:18 **M** was covered with smoke, because
19:20 The LORD descended to the top of **M**
19:23 "The people cannot come up **M**,
24:16 the glory of the LORD settled on **M**.
31:18 LORD finished speaking to Moses on **M**,
34: 2 the morning, and then come up on **M**.
34: 4 and went up **M** early in the morning,
34:29 Moses came down from **M** with the two
34:32 the LORD had given him on **M**.
Lev 7:38 which the LORD gave Moses on **M** on
25: 1 The LORD said to Moses on **M**,
26:46 established on **M** between himself
27:34 gave Moses on **M** for the Israelites.
Nu 3: 1 the LORD talked with Moses on **M**.
28: 6 instituted at **M** as a pleasing aroma,
Ne 9:13 "You came down on **M**; you spoke to
Ac 7:30 a burning bush in the desert near **M**.
7:38 the angel who spoke to him on **M**,
Gal 4:24 One covenant is from **M** and bears
4:25 Now Hagar stands for **M** in Arabia and

Mount Zion
2Ki 19:31 and out of **M** a band of survivors.
Ps 48: 2 is **M**, the city of the Great King.
48:11 **M** rejoices, the villages of Judah
74: 2 you redeemed—**M**, where you dwelt.
78:68 he chose the tribe of Judah, **M**,
125: 1 who trust in the LORD are like **M**,
133: 3 the dew of Hermon were falling on **M**.
Isa 4: 5 the LORD will create over all of **M**
8:18 the LORD Almighty, who dwells on **M**.
10:12 his work against **M** and Jerusalem,
18: 7 the gifts will be brought to **M**,
24:23 will reign on **M** and in Jerusalem,
29: 8 the nations that fight against **M**.
31: 4 do battle on **M** and on its heights.
37:32 and out of **M** a band of survivors.
Lam 5:18 for **M**, which lies desolate, with
Joel 2:32 for on **M** and in Jerusalem there will
Ob :17 on **M** will be deliverance; it will be
:21 Deliverers will go up on **M** to govern
Mic 4: 7 in **M** from that day and for ever.
Heb 12:22 you have come to **M**, to the heavenly
Rev 14: 1 standing on **M**, and with him 144,000

Mountain (Mount[1], *Mountain of God, Mountain of the LORD*)
Ex 3:12 you will worship God on this **m**."
15:17 **m** of your inheritance—the place,
Ex 19: 2 in the desert in front of the **m**.
19: 3 called to him from the **m** and said,
19:12 people around the **m** and tell them,
19:12 go up the **m** or touch the foot of it.
19:12 Whoever touches the **m** shall surely
19:13 long blast may they go up to the **m**."
19:14 After Moses had gone down the **m** to
19:16 thick cloud over the **m**, and a very
19:17 and they stood at the foot of the **m**.
19:18 the whole **m** trembled violently,
19:20 called Moses to the top of the **m**.
19:23 the **m** and set it apart as holy.
20:18 **m** in smoke, they trembled with fear.
24: 4 built an altar at the foot of the **m**
24:12 "Come up to me on the **m** and stay
24:15 Moses went up on the **m**, the cloud
24:16 For six days the cloud covered the **m**,
24:17 a consuming fire on top of the **m**.
24:18 the cloud as he went on up the **m**.
24:18 the **m** forty days and forty nights.
25:40 to the pattern shown you on the **m**.
26:30 to the plan shown you on the **m**.
27: 8 just as you were shown on the **m**.
32: 1 so long in coming down from the **m**,
32:15 Moses turned and went down the **m**
32:19 them to pieces at the foot of the **m**.
34: 2 to me there on top of the **m**.
34: 3 you or be seen anywhere on the **m**;
34: 3 herds may graze in front of the **m**."
Nu 20:28 And Aaron died there on top of the **m**.
20:28 and Eleazar came down from the **m**,
27:12 the LORD said to Moses, "Go up this **m**
Dt 1: 6 have stayed long enough at this **m**.
4:11 stood at the foot of the **m** while it
5: 4 to face out of the fire on the **m**.
5: 5 of the fire and did not go up the **m**.
5:22 there on the **m** from out of the fire,
5:23 while the **m** was ablaze with fire,
9: 9 I went up on the **m** to receive the
9: 9 I stayed on the **m** forty days and
9:10 to you on the **m** out of the fire,
9:15 I turned and went down from the **m**
9:21 a stream that flowed down the **m**.
10: 1 ones and come up to me on the **m**.
10: 3 up on the **m** with the two tablets
10: 4 he had proclaimed to you on the **m**,
10: 5 I came back down the **m** and put the
10:10 Now I had stayed on the **m** forty days
14: 5 ibex, the antelope and the **m** sheep.
32:50 There on the **m** that you have climbed
33: 2 from the south, from his **m** slopes.
33:19 They will summon peoples to the **m**
Jos 10:40 the western foothills and the **m**
12: 8 the Arabah, the **m** slopes, the desert
13: 6 "As for all the inhabitants of the **m**
Jdg 6: 2 in **m** clefts, caves and strongholds.
1Sa 23:26 was going along one side of the **m**,
25:20 riding her donkey into a **m** ravine
1Ki 19:11 "Go out and stand on the **m** in the
2Ki 2:16 down on some **m** or in some valley.
4:27 she reached the man of God at the **m**,
Job 14:18 "But as a **m** erodes and crumbles and
24: 8 They are drenched by **m** rains and hug
39: 1 "Do you know when the **m** goats give
Ps 11: 1 to me: "Flee like a bird to your **m**.
30: 7 favoured me, you made my **m** stand
43: 3 bring me to your holy **m**, to the
48: 1 in the city of our God, his holy **m**.
68:16 O rugged mountains, at the **m** where
87: 1 set his foundation on the holy **m**;
95: 4 and the **m** peaks belong to him.
99: 9 worship at his holy **m**, for the LORD
SS 4: 6 I will go to the **m** of myrrh and to
4: 8 and the **m** haunts of the leopards.
Isa 2: 2 In the last days the **m** of the LORD's
11: 9 harm nor destroy on all my holy **m**,
14:13 the utmost heights of the sacred **m**.
18: 6 They will all be left to the **m** birds
25: 6 On this **m** the LORD Almighty will
25: 7 On this **m** he will destroy the shroud
25:10 of the LORD will rest on this **m**;
27:13 the LORD on the holy **m** in Jerusalem.
30:25 every high **m** and every lofty hill.
33:16 whose refuge will be the **m** fortress.
40: 4 every **m** and hill made low; the rough
40: 9 tidings to Zion, go up on a high **m**.

Isa 56: 7 these I will bring to my holy **m** and
57:13 the land and possess my holy **m**."
65:11 the LORD and forget my holy **m**,
65:25 on all my holy **m**," says the LORD.
66:20 from all the nations, to my holy **m**
Jer 16:16 they will hunt them down on every **m**
17: 3 My **m** in the land and your wealth and
31:23 O righteous dwelling, O sacred **m**.'
50: 6 They wandered over **m** and hill and
51:25 "I am against you, O destroying **m**,
51:25 cliffs, and make you a burnt-out **m**.
Eze 11:23 and stopped above the **m** east of it.
17:22 and plant it on a high and lofty **m**.
17:23 On the **m** heights of Israel I will
18: 6 He does not eat at the **m** shrines or
18:11 of them): "He eats at the **m** shrines.
18:15 "He does not eat at the **m** shrines or
20:40 on my holy **m**, the high **m** of Israel
22: 9 the **m** shrines and commit lewd acts.
34:14 and the **m** heights of Israel will be
40: 2 Israel and set me on a very high **m**,
43:12 on top of the **m** will be most holy.
Da 2:35 a huge **m** and filled the whole earth.
2:45 vision of the rock cut out of a **m**,
11:45 the seas at the beautiful holy **m**.
Mic 4: 1 In the last days the **m** of the LORD's
7:12 and from sea to sea and from **m** to **m**.
Zec 4: 7 "What are you, O mighty **m**? Before
8: 3 Almighty will be called the Holy **M**."
14: 4 **m** moving north and half moving south.
14: 5 You will flee by my **m** valley, for it
Mt 4: 8 the devil took him to a very high **m**
17: 1 led them up a high **m** by themselves.
17: 9 they were coming down the **m**, Jesus
17:20 to this **m**, 'Move from here to there'
21:21 **m**, 'Go, throw yourself into the sea,'
28:16 **m** where Jesus had told them to go.
Mk 9: 2 a high **m**, where they were all alone.
9: 9 they were coming down the **m**, Jesus
11:23 **m**, 'Go, throw yourself into the sea,'
Lk 3: 5 in, every **m** and hill made low.
9:28 him and went up onto a **m** to pray.
9:37 from the **m**, a large crowd met him.
Jn 4:20 Our fathers worshipped on this **m**,
4:21 neither on this **m** nor in Jerusalem.
6:15 withdrew again to a **m** by himself.
Heb 8: 5 to the pattern shown you on the **m**."
12:18 You have not come to a **m** that can be
12:20 touches the **m**, it must be stoned."
2Pe 1:18 we were with him on the sacred **m**.
Rev 6:14 rolling up, and every **m** and island
8: 8 and something like a huge **m**, all
21:10 in the Spirit to a **m** great and high,

Mountain of God

Ex 3: 1 the desert and came to Horeb, the **m**.
4:27 met Moses at the **m** and kissed him.
18: 5 where he was camped near the **m**.
24:13 and Moses went up on the **m**.
1Ki 19: 8 until he reached Horeb, the **m**.

Mountain of the LORD

Ge 22:14 said, "On the **m** it will be provided.
Nu 10:33 they set out from the **m** and
Isa 2: 3 "Come, let us go up to the **m**, to
30:29 to the **m**, to the Rock of Israel.
Mic 4: 2 "Come, let us go up to the **m**, to
Zec 8: 3 and the **m** Almighty will be called

Mountains (Mount[1])

Ge 7:19 and all the high **m** under the entire
7:20 The waters rose and covered the **m** to
8: 4 ark came to rest on the **m** of Ararat.
8: 5 the tops of the **m** became visible.
19:17 to the **m** or you will be swept away!"
19:19 But I can't flee to the **m**; this
19:30 left Zoar and settled in the **m**, for
22: 2 one of the **m** I will tell you about."
49:26 than the blessings of the ancient **m**,
Ex 32:12 to kill them in the **m** and to wipe
Nu 23: 7 the king of Moab from the eastern **m**.
33:47 in the **m** of Abarim, near Nebo.
33:48 They left the **m** of Abarim and camped
Dt 1: 7 in the **m**, in the western foothills,
11:11 take possession of is a land of **m**
Dt 11:30 you know, these **m** are across the
12: 2 all the places on the high **m**
32:22 on fire the foundations of the **m**.
33:15 the choicest gifts of the ancient **m**
Jos 11: 2 northern kings who were in the **m**,
11:16 **m** of Israel with their foothills,
Jdg 3: 3 the Hivites living in the Lebanon **m**
5: 5 The **m** quaked before the LORD, the
9:36 coming down from the tops of the **m**!"
9:36 the shadows of the **m** for men."
1Sa 26:20 one hunts a partridge in the **m**."
2Sa 1:21 "O **m** of Gilboa, may you have neither
1Ki 19:11 powerful wind tore the **m** apart and
2Ki 19:23 **m**, the utmost heights of Lebanon.
1Ch 12: 8 were as swift as gazelles in the **m**.
Job 9: 5 He moves **m** without their knowing it
28: 9 and lays bare the roots of the **m**.
Ps 18: 7 and the foundations of the **m** shook;
36: 6 righteousness is like the mighty **m**,
46: 2 **m** fall into the heart of the sea,
46: 3 and the **m** quake with their surging.
50:11 I know every bird in the **m**, and the
65: 6 who formed the **m** by your power,
68:15 The **m** of Bashan are majestic **m**;
68:15 rugged are the **m** of Bashan.
68:16 Why gaze in envy, O rugged **m**, at the
72: 3 The **m** will bring prosperity to the
76: 4 more majestic than **m** rich with game.
80:10 The **m** were covered with its shade,
83:14 forest or a flame sets the **m** ablaze,
90: 2 Before the **m** were born or you
97: 5 The **m** melt like wax before the LORD,
98: 8 let the **m** sing together for joy;
104: 6 the waters stood above the **m**.
104: 8 they flowed over the **m**, they went
104:10 the ravines; it flows between the **m**.
104:13 He waters the **m** from his upper
104:18 The high **m** belong to the wild goats;
104:32 who touches the **m**, and they smoke.
114: 4 the **m** skipped like rams, the hills
114: 6 you **m**, that you skipped like rams,
125: 2 the **m** surround Jerusalem, so the
144: 5 touch the **m**, so that they smoke.
148: 9 you **m** and all hills, fruit trees and
Pr 8:25 before the **m** were settled in place,
SS 2: 8 the **m**, bounding over the hills.
8:14 a young stag on the spice-laden **m**.
Isa 2: 2 established as chief among the **m**;
2:14 for all the towering **m** and all the
5:25 The **m** shake, and the dead bodies are
13: 4 Listen, a noise on the **m**, like that
14:25 on my **m** I will trample him down.
18: 3 when a banner is raised on the **m**,
22: 5 walls and of crying out to the **m**.
34: 3 **m** will be soaked with their blood.
37:24 **m**, the utmost heights of Lebanon.
40:12 or weighed the **m** on the scales and
41:15 You will thresh the **m** and crush them,
42:15 I will lay waste the **m** and hills and
44:23 Burst into song, you **m**, you forests
45: 2 go before you and will level the **m**;
49:11 I will turn all my **m** into roads, and
49:13 O earth; burst into song, O **m**! For
52: 7 How beautiful on the **m** are the feet
54:10 Though the **m** be shaken and the hills
55:12 the **m** and hills will burst into song
64: 1 that the **m** would tremble before you!
64: 3 down, and the **m** trembled before you.
65: 7 on the **m** and defied me on the hills,
65: 9 Judah those who will possess my **m**;
Jer 3:23 on the hills and **m** is a deception;
4:24 I looked at the **m**, and they were
9:10 I will weep and wail for the **m** and
46:18 among the **m**, like Carmel by the sea.
50: 6 and caused them to roam on the **m**.
Lam 4:19 they chased us over the **m** and lay in
Eze 6: 2 against the **m** of Israel; prophesy
6: 3 say: 'O **m** of Israel, hear the word
6: 3 LORD says to the **m** and hills,
7: 7 there is panic, not joy, upon the **m**.
7:16 survive and escape will be in the **m**,
19: 9 heard no longer on the **m** of Israel.
31:12 Its boughs fell on the **m** and in all
32: 5 I will spread your flesh on the **m**
32: 6 flowing blood all the way to the **m**,
33:28 and the **m** of Israel will become
Eze 34: 6 My sheep wandered over all the **m** and
34:13 I will pasture them on the **m** of
34:14 a rich pasture on the **m** of Israel.
35: 8 I will fill your **m** with the slain;
35:12 have said against the **m** of Israel.
36: 1 "Son of man, prophesy to the **m** of
36: 1 'O **m** of Israel, hear the word of the
36: 4 therefore, O **m** of Israel, hear the
36: 4 LORD says to the **m** and hills,
36: 6 Israel and say to the **m** and hills,
36: 8 "'But you, O **m** of Israel, will
37:22 in the land, on the **m** of Israel.
38: 8 many nations to the **m** of Israel,
38:20 The **m** will be overturned, the cliffs
38:21 a sword against Gog on all my **m**,
39: 2 send you against the **m** of Israel.
39: 4 On the **m** of Israel you will fall,
39:17 great sacrifice on the **m** of Israel.
Hos 10: 8 Then they will say to the **m**, "Cover
Joel 2: 2 Like dawn spreading across the **m** a
3:18 "In that day the **m** will drip new
Am 3: 9 "Assemble yourselves on the **m** of
4:13 He who forms the **m**, creates the wind,
9:13 the **m** and flow from all the hills.
Ob : 8 of understanding in the **m** of Esau?
: 9 **m** will be cut down in the slaughter.
:19 the Negev will occupy the **m** of Esau,
:21 Mount Zion to govern the **m** of Esau.
Jnh 2: 6 To the roots of the **m** I sank down;
Mic 1: 4 The **m** melt beneath him and the
4: 1 established as chief among the **m**;
6: 1 plead your case before the **m**; let
6: 2 Hear, O **m**, the LORD's accusation;
Na 1: 5 The **m** quake before him and the hills
1:15 Look, there on the **m**, the feet of
3:18 on the **m** with no-one to gather them.
Hab 3: 6 The ancient **m** crumbled and the
3:10 the **m** saw you and writhed. Torrents
Hag 1: 8 Go up into the **m** and bring down
1:11 a drought on the fields and the **m**,
Zec 6: 1 out from between two **m**—**m** of bronze!
Mal 1: 3 have turned his **m** into a wasteland
Mt 24:16 who are in Judea flee to the **m**.
Mk 13:14 who are in Judea flee to the **m**.
Lk 21:21 who are in Judea flee to the **m**,
23:30 "'they will say to the **m**, "Fall on
1Co 13: 2 if I have a faith that can move **m**,
Heb 11:38 They wandered in deserts and **m**, and
Rev 6:15 caves and among the rocks of the **m**.
6:16 They called to the **m** and the rocks,
16:20 Every island fled away and the **m**

Mountainside (Mount[1])

SS 2:14 in the hiding-places on the **m**, show
Mt 5: 1 he went up on a **m** and sat down.
8: 1 he came down from the **m**, large
14:23 went up on a **m** by himself to pray.
15:29 Then he went up on a **m** and sat down.
Mk 3:13 Jesus went up on a **m** and called to
6:46 After leaving them, he went up on a **m**
Lk 6:12 days Jesus went out to a **m** to pray,
Jn 6: 3 Jesus went up on a **m** and sat down

Mountaintop (Mount[1])

Isa 30:17 on a **m**, like a banner on a hill."

Mountaintops (Mount[1])

Isa 42:11 for joy; let them shout from the **m**.
Eze 6:13 on every high hill and on all the **m**,
Hos 4:13 They sacrifice on the **m** and burn
Joel 2: 5 of chariots they leap over the **m**,

Mounted (Mount[2])

Ge 24:61 Rebekah and her maids got ready and **m**
Ex 25: 7 onyx stones and other gems to be **m**
35: 9 onyx stones and other gems to be **m**
35:27 be **m** on the ephod and breastpiece.
39: 6 They **m** the onyx stones in gold
39:10 they **m** four rows of precious stones
39:13 were **m** in gold filigree settings.
2Sa 13:29 sons got up, **m** their mules and fled.
22:11 He **m** the cherubim and flew; he
1Ki 13:13 saddled the donkey for him, he **m**
Est 8:10 and sent them by **m** couriers, who

Ps 18:10 He **m** the cherubim and flew; he
107:26 They **m** up to the heavens and went
SS 5:12 washed in milk, **m** like jewels.
Eze 23: 6 handsome young men, and **m** horsemen.
23:12 **m** horsemen, all handsome young men.
23:23 men of high rank, all **m** on horses.
Rev 9:16 The number of the **m** troops was two

Mountings (Mount²)
Eze 28:13 Your settings and **m** were made of

Mounts (Mount²)
Ne 2:12 There were no **m** with me except the
Ac 23:24 Provide **m** for Paul so that he may be

Mourn (Mourned, Mourners, Mournful, Mournfully, Mourning, Mourns)
Ge 23: 2 to **m** for Sarah and to weep over her.
Ex 33: 4 **m** and no-one put on any ornaments.
Lev 10: 6 all the house of Israel, may **m** for
1Sa 16: 1 "How long will you **m** for Saul, since
1Ki 13:29 own city to **m** for him and bury him.
14:13 All Israel will **m** for him and bury
Ezr 10: 6 because he continued to **m** over the
Ne 8: 9 Do not **m** or weep." For all the
Job 5:11 those who **m** are lifted to safety.
Ecc 3: 4 a time to **m** and a time to dance,
Isa 3:26 The gates of Zion will lament and **m**;
29: 2 Yet I will besiege Ariel; she will **m**
32:13 **m** for all houses of merriment and
61: 2 of our God, to comfort all who **m**,
66:10 with her, all you who **m** over her.
Jer 4:28 Therefore the earth will **m** and the
6:26 **m** with bitter wailing as for an only
8:21 crushed; I **m**, and horror grips me.
15: 5 O Jerusalem? Who will **m** for you? Who
16: 5 do not go to **m** or show sympathy,
16: 7 to comfort those who **m** for the dead
22:10 Do not weep for the dead king or **m**
22:18 "They will not **m** for him: 'Alas, my
22:18 my sister!' They will not **m** for him:
48:17 **M** for her, all who live around her,
49: 3 of Rabbah! Put on sackcloth and **m**;
Lam 1: 4 The roads to Zion **m**, for no-one
Eze 7:27 The king will **m**, the prince will be
24:17 Groan quietly; do not **m** for the dead.
24:23 You will not **m** or weep but will
27:32 they wail and **m** over you, they will
Hos 10: 5 Its people will **m** over it, and so
Joel 1: 8 **M** like a virgin in sackcloth
1:13 Put on sackcloth, O priests, and **m**;
Am 8: 8 and all who live in it **m**? The whole
9: 5 and all who live in it **m**—the whole
Na 3: 7 'Nineveh is in ruins—who will **m** for
Zec 7: 3 "Should I **m** and fast in the fifth
12:10 and they will **m** for him as one
12:12 The land will **m**, each clan by itself,
Mt 5: 4 Blessed are those who **m**, for they
9:15 bridegroom **m** while he is with them?
11:17 we sang a dirge, and you did not **m**.'
24:30 all the nations of the earth will **m**.
Lk 6:25 laugh now, for you will **m** and weep.
Jn 11:31 was going to the tomb to **m** there.
16:20 weep and **m** while the world rejoices.
Ro 12:15 who rejoice; **m** with those who **m**.
1Co 7:30 those who **m**, as if they did not;
Jas 4: 9 Grieve, **m** and wail. Change your
Rev 1: 7 of the earth will **m** because of him.
18: 7 am not a widow, and I will never **m**.'
18: 9 they will weep and **m** over her.
18:11 **m** over her because no-one buys their
18:15 her torment. They will weep and **m**

Mourned (Mourn)
Ge 37:34 and **m** for his son many days.
50: 3 Egyptians **m** for him seventy days.
Nu 14:39 all the Israelites, they **m** bitterly.
20:29 of Israel **m** for him thirty days.
Dt 21:13 **m** her father and mother for a full
1Sa 6:19 The people **m** because of the heavy
7: 2 Israel **m** and sought after the LORD.
15:35 Saul again, though Samuel **m** for him.
25: 1 and all Israel assembled and **m** for
28: 3 and all Israel had **m** for him and
2Sa 1:12 They **m** and wept and fasted till
11:26 her husband was dead, she **m** for him.
13:37 King David **m** for his son every day.
1Ki 13:30 and they **m** over him and said, "Oh,
14:18 They buried him, and all Israel **m**
1Ch 7:22 Their father Ephraim **m** for them many
2Ch 35:24 all Judah and Jerusalem **m** for him.
Ne 1: 4 For some days I **m** and fasted and
Jer 16: 4 They will not be **m** or buried but
16: 6 They will not be buried or **m**, and
25:33 They will not be **m** or gathered up or
Da 10: 2 I, Daniel, **m** for three weeks.
Zec 7: 5 'When you fasted and **m** in the fifth
Lk 23:27 women who **m** and wailed for him.
Ac 8: 2 Godly men buried Stephen and **m**

Mourners (Mourn)
Job 29:25 I was like one who comforts **m**.
Ecc 12: 5 home and **m** go about the streets.
Isa 57:19 creating praise on the lips of the **m**
Eze 24:17 or eat the customary food ⌊of **m**⌋.
24:22 or eat the customary food ⌊of **m**⌋.
Hos 9: 4 will be to them like the bread of **m**
Am 5:16 summoned to weep and the **m** to wail.
Mal 3:14 like **m** before the LORD Almighty?

Mournful (Mourn)
Mic 2: 4 will taunt you with this **m** song:

Mournfully (Mourn)
Isa 59:11 We all growl like bears; we moan **m**

Mourning (Mourn)
Ge 27:41 He said to himself, "The days of **m**
37:35 "No," he said, "in **m** will I go down
50: 4 the days of **m** had passed, Joseph
50:10 period of **m** for his father.
50:11 **m** at the threshing-floor of Atad,
50:11 are holding a solemn ceremony of **m**.
Dt 26:14 the sacred portion while I was in **m**,
34: 8 the time of weeping and **m** was over.
2Sa 3:31 and walk in **m** in front of Abner.
11:27 After the time of **m** was over, David
14: 2 said to her, "Pretend you are in **m**.
14: 2 Dress in **m** clothes, and don't use
19: 1 king is weeping and **m** for Absalom."
19: 2 victory that day was turned into **m**,
Est 4: 3 there was great **m** among the Jews,
9:22 their **m** into a day of celebration.
Job 30:31 My harp is tuned to **m**, and my flute
Ps 35:14 I went about **m** as though for my
38: 6 very low; all day long I go about **m**.
42: 9 go about **m**, oppressed by the enemy?"
43: 2 I go about **m**, oppressed by the enemy?
Ecc 7: 2 is better to go to a house of **m** than
7: 4 of the wise is in the house of **m**,
Isa 38:14 or thrush, I moaned like a **m** dove.
61: 3 the oil of gladness instead of **m**,
Jer 31:13 I will turn their **m** into gladness; I
31:15 "A voice is heard in Ramah, **m** and
47: 5 Gaza will shave her head in **m**;
48:38 squares there is nothing but **m**,
Lam 2: 5 He has multiplied **m** and lamentation
5:15 hearts; our dancing has turned to **m**.
Eze 2:10 words of lament and **m** and woe.
8:14 women sitting there, **m** for Tammuz.
27:31 anguish of soul and with bitter **m**.
31:15 **m** for it; I held back its streams,
Joel 1: 9 The priests are in **m**, those who
2:12 with fasting and weeping and **m**."
Am 8:10 turn your religious feasts into **m**
8:10 I will make that time like **m** for an
Mic 1:11 is in **m**; its protection is taken
1:16 Shave your heads in **m** for the
Mt 2:18 weeping and great **m**, Rachel weeping
Mk 16:10 with him and who were **m** and weeping.
Lk 8:52 people were wailing and **m** for her.
Jas 4: 9 laughter to **m** and your joy to gloom.
Rev 18: 8 overtake her: death, **m** and famine.
18:19 and with weeping and **m** cry out:
21: 4 There will be no more death or **m** or

Mourns (Mourn)
Job 14:22 own body and **m** only for himself."
Isa 33: 9 The land **m** and wastes away, Lebanon
Jer 14: 2 "Judah **m**, her cities languish; they
Hos 4: 3 of this the land **m**, and all who live
Zec 12:10 for him as one **m** for an only child,

Moustache
2Sa 19:24 or trimmed his **m** or washed his

Mouth (Mouths)
Ge 4:11 which opened its **m** to receive your
29: 2 over the **m** of the well was large.
29: 3 the well's **m** and water the sheep.
29: 3 to its place over the **m** of the well.
29: 8 rolled away from the **m** of the well.
29:10 rolled the stone away from the **m** of
42:27 saw his silver in the **m** of his sack.
43:21 exact weight—in the **m** of his sack.
44: 1 man's silver in the **m** of his sack.
44: 2 cup, the silver one, in the **m** of the
Ex 4:11 "Who gave man his **m**? Who makes him
4:15 speak to him and put words in his **m**;
4:16 as if he were your **m** and as if you
Nu 16:30 and the earth opens its **m** and
16:32 the earth opened its **m** and swallowed
22:28 the LORD opened the donkey's **m**, and
22:38 speak only what God puts in my **m**."
23: 5 The LORD put a message in Balaam's **m**
23:12 speak what the LORD puts in my **m**?"
23:16 and put a message in his **m** and said,
26:10 The earth opened its **m** and swallowed
Dt 8: 3 that comes from the **m** of the LORD.
11: 6 when the earth opened its **m** right in
18:18 I will put my words in his **m**,
23:23 the LORD your God with your own **m**.
30:14 it is in your **m** and in your heart so
32: 1 hear, O earth, the words of my **m**.
Jos 1: 8 Book of the Law depart from your **m**;
10:18 "Roll large rocks up to the **m** of the
10:22 Joshua said, "Open the **m** of the cave
10:27 At the **m** of the cave they placed
15: 5 Sea as far as the **m** of the Jordan.
15: 5 of the sea at the **m** of the Jordan,
18:19 at the **m** of the Jordan in the south.
1Sa 1:12 to the LORD, Eli observed her **m**.
2: 1 My **m** boasts over my enemies, for I
2: 3 or let your **m** speak such arrogance,
14:26 no-one put his hand to his **m**,
14:27 to his **m**, and his eyes brightened.
17:35 it and rescued the sheep from its **m**.
2Sa 1:16 Your own **m** testified against you
14: 3 And Joab put the words in her **m**.
14:19 words into the **m** of your servant.
22: 9 consuming fire came from his **m**,
1Ki 8:15 with his own **m** to my father David.
8:24 with your **m** you have promised and
17:24 the LORD from your **m** is the truth."
19:13 out and stood at the **m** of the cave.
2Ki 4:34 **m** to **m**, eyes to eyes, hands to hands.
19:28 in your nose and my bit in your **m**,
2Ch 6: 4 with his **m** to my father David.
6:15 with your **m** you have promised and
Est 7: 8 soon as the word left the king's **m**,
Job 3: 1 After this, Job opened his **m** and
5:15 the needy from the sword in their **m**;
5:16 hope, and injustice shuts its **m**.
6:30 lips? Can my **m** not discern malice?
8:21 He will yet fill your **m** with
9:20 Even if I were innocent, my **m** would
15: 5 Your sin prompts your **m**; you adopt
15: 6 Your own **m** condemns you, not mine;
15:13 and pour out such words from your **m**?
15:30 of God's **m** will carry him away.
16: 5 my **m** would encourage you; comfort
19:16 though I beg him with my own **m**.
20:12 "Though evil is sweet in his **m** and
20:13 to let it go and keeps it in his **m**,
21: 5 clap your hand over your **m**.
22:22 Accept instruction from his **m** and
23: 4 him and fill my **m** with arguments.
23:12 of his **m** more than my daily bread.
26: 4 And whose spirit spoke from your **m**?
31:30 I have not allowed my **m** to sin by
33: 2 I am about to open my **m**; my words

Job 35:16 Job opens his **m** with empty talk;
37: 2 the rumbling that comes from his **m**.
40: 4 to you? I put my hand over my **m**.
40:23 Jordan should surge against his **m**.
41:14 Who dares open the doors of his **m**,
41:19 Firebrands stream from his **m**; sparks
41:21 ablaze, and flames dart from his **m**.
Ps 5: 9 Not a word from their **m** can be
10: 7 His **m** is full of curses and lies and
17: 3 resolved that my **m** will not sin.
18: 8 consuming fire came from his **m**,
19:14 May the words of my **m** and the
22:15 tongue sticks to the roof of my **m**;
22:21 Rescue me from the **m** of the lions;
33: 6 starry host by the breath of his **m**.
36: 3 The words of his **m** are wicked and
37:30 The **m** of the righteous man utters
38:13 like a mute, who cannot open his **m**;
38:14 hear, whose **m** can offer no reply.
39: 1 I will put a muzzle on my **m** as long
39: 9 I was silent; I would not open my **m**,
40: 3 He put a new song in my **m**, a hymn of
49: 3 My **m** will speak words of wisdom; the
50:19 You use your **m** for evil and harness
51:15 O Lord, open my lips, and my **m** will
54: 2 O God; listen to the words of my **m**.
63: 5 singing lips my **m** will praise you.
66:14 vows my lips promised and my **m** spoke
66:17 I cried out to him with my **m**; his
69:15 up or the pit close its **m** over me.
71: 8 My **m** is filled with your praise,
71:15 My **m** will tell of your righteousness,
78: 1 listen to the words of my **m**.
78: 2 I will open my **m** in parables, I will
81:10 Open wide your **m** and I will fill it.
89: 1 with my **m** I will make your
109:30 With my **m** I will greatly extol the
119:13 all the laws that come from your **m**.
119:43 snatch the word of truth from my **m**,
119:72 The law from your **m** is more precious
119:88 I will obey the statutes of your **m**.
119:103 taste, sweeter than honey to my **m**!
119:108 of my **m**, and teach me your laws.
119:131 I open my **m** and pant, longing for
137: 6 of my **m** if I do not remember you,
138: 4 when they hear the words of your **m**.
141: 3 Set a guard over my **m**, O LORD; keep
141: 7 scattered at the **m** of the grave."
145:21 My **m** will speak in praise of the
Pr 2: 6 from his **m** come knowledge and
4:24 Put away perversity from your **m**;
6: 2 ensnared by the words of your **m**,
6:12 who goes about with a corrupt **m**,
8: 7 My **m** speaks what is true, for my
8: 8 All the words of my **m** are just; none
10: 6 overwhelms the **m** of the wicked.
10:11 The **m** of the righteous is a fountain
10:11 overwhelms the **m** of the wicked.
10:14 but the **m** of a fool invites ruin.
10:31 The **m** of the righteous brings forth
10:32 but the **m** of the wicked only what is
11: 9 With his **m** the godless destroys his
11:11 the **m** of the wicked it is destroyed.
15: 2 but the **m** of the fool gushes folly.
15:14 but the **m** of a fool feeds on folly.
15:28 but the **m** of the wicked gushes evil.
16:10 and his **m** should not betray justice.
16:23 A wise man's heart guides his **m**, and
18: 4 The words of a man's **m** are deep
18: 6 strife, and his **m** invites a beating.
18: 7 A fool's **m** is his undoing, and his
18:20 From the fruit of his **m** a man's
19:24 not even bring it back to his **m**!
19:28 the **m** of the wicked gulps down evil.
20:17 he ends up with a **m** full of gravel.
21:23 He who guards his **m** and his tongue
22:14 The **m** of an adulteress is a deep pit;
26: 7 is a proverb in the **m** of a fool.
26: 9 is a proverb in the **m** of a fool.
26:15 too lazy to bring it back to his **m**.
26:28 and a flattering **m** works ruin.
27: 2 and not your own **m**; someone else,
30:20 wipes her **m** and says, 'I've done
30:32 evil, clap your hand over your **m**!
Ecc 5: 2 Do not be quick with your **m**, do not
5: 6 Do not let your **m** lead you into sin.
Ecc 6: 7 All man's efforts are for his **m**, yet
10:12 Words from a wise man's **m** are
SS 1: 2 kiss me with the kisses of his **m**
4: 3 a scarlet ribbon; your **m** is lovely.
5:16 His **m** is sweetness itself; he is
7: 9 your **m** like the best wine. May the
Isa 1:20 For the **m** of the LORD has spoken.
5:14 and opens its **m** without limit;
6: 7 With it he touched my **m** and said,
9:12 have devoured Israel with open **m**.
9:17 and wicked, every **m** speaks vileness.
10:14 a wing, or opened its **m** to chirp.
11: 4 the earth with the rod of his **m**;
19: 7 the Nile, at the **m** of the river.
29:13 come near to me with their **m** and
34:16 For it is his **m** that has given the
37:29 in your nose and my bit in your **m**,
40: 5 For the **m** of the LORD has spoken."
45:23 By myself I have sworn, my **m** has
48: 3 my **m** announced them and I made them
49: 2 He made my **m** like a sharpened sword,
51:16 I have put my words in your **m** and
53: 7 yet he did not open his **m**; he was
53: 7 is silent, so he did not open his **m**.
53: 9 nor was any deceit in his **m**.
55:11 is my word that goes out from my **m**:
58:14 The **m** of the LORD has spoken.
59:21 your **m** will not depart from your **m**,
62: 2 that the **m** of the LORD will bestow.
Jer 1: 9 and touched my **m** and said to me,
1: 9 "Now, I have put my words in your **m**.
5:14 I will make my words in your **m** a
9: 8 With his **m** each speaks cordially to
9:20 your ears to the words of his **m**.
23:16 minds, not from the **m** of the LORD.
48:28 makes its nest at the **m** of a cave.
Lam 3:38 Is it not from the **m** of the Most
4: 4 sticks to the roof of its **m**;
Eze 2: 8 your **m** and eat what I give you."
3: 2 I opened my **m**, and he gave me the
3: 3 it tasted as sweet as honey in my **m**.
3:26 your **m** so that you will be silent
3:27 I will open your **m** and you shall say
4:14 unclean meat has ever entered my **m**."
16:63 your **m** because of your humiliation,
24:27 At that time your **m** will be opened;
29:21 and I will open your **m** among them.
33:22 and he opened my **m** before the man
33:22 So my **m** was opened and I was no
Da 6:17 and placed over the **m** of the den,
7: 5 ribs in its **m** between its teeth.
7: 8 a man and a **m** that spoke boastfully.
7:20 eyes and a **m** that spoke boastfully.
10:16 I opened my **m** and began to speak.
Hos 6: 5 I killed you with the words of my **m**;
Am 3:12 saves from the lion's **m** only two
Na 3:12 figs fall into the **m** of the eater.
Zec 5: 8 the lead cover down over its **m**.
Mal 2: 6 True instruction was in his **m** and
2: 7 and from his **m** men should seek
Mt 4: 4 word that comes from the **m** of God.'"
12:34 overflow of the heart the **m** speaks.
13:35 "I will open my **m** in parables, I
15:11 What goes into a man's **m** does not
15:11 what comes out of his **m**, that is
15:17 enters the **m** goes into the stomach
15:18 the things that come out of the **m**
17:27 open its **m** and you will find a
Mk 9:18 He foams at the **m**, gnashes his teeth
9:20 and rolled around, foaming at the **m**.
Lk 1:64 Immediately his **m** was opened and his
6:45 overflow of his heart his **m** speaks.
9:39 so that he foams at the **m**.
Ac 1:16 the **m** of David concerning Judas,
4:25 Spirit through the **m** of your servant,
8:32 is silent, so he did not open his **m**.
11: 8 or unclean has ever entered my **m**.'
15:27 by word of **m** what we are writing.
22:14 One and to hear words from his **m**.
23: 2 near Paul to strike him on the **m**.
Ro 3:19 so that every **m** may be silenced and
10: 8 it is in your **m** and in your heart,"
10: 9 That if you confess with your **m**,
10:10 **m** that you confess and are saved.
15: 6 that with one heart and **m** you may
Eph 6:19 that whenever I open my **m**, words may
2Th 2: 8 overthrow with the breath of his **m**
2:15 whether by word of **m** or by letter.
2Ti 4:17 I was delivered from the lion's **m**.
Jas 3:10 Out of the same **m** come praise and
1Pe 2:22 and no deceit was found in his **m**."
2Pe 2:18 For they **m** empty, boastful words and,
Rev 1:16 **m** came a sharp double-edged sword.
2:16 against them with the sword of my **m**.
3:16 am about to spit you out of my **m**.
10: 9 in your **m** it will be as sweet as
10:10 It tasted as sweet as honey in my **m**,
12:15 from his **m** the serpent spewed water
12:16 helped the woman by opening its **m**
12:16 the dragon had spewed out of his **m**.
13: 2 a bear and a **m** like that of a lion.
13: 5 The beast was given a **m** to utter
13: 6 He opened his **m** to blaspheme God,
16:13 came out of the **m** of the dragon,
16:13 out of the **m** of the beast and out of
16:13 out of the **m** of the false prophet.
19:15 Out of his **m** comes a sharp sword
19:21 of the **m** of the rider on the horse,

Mouths (Mouth)

Ge 43:12 put back into the **m** of your sacks.
44: 8 we found inside the **m** of our sacks.
Jdg 7: 6 lapped with their hands to their **m**.
1Ki 19:18 all whose **m** have not kissed him."
22:22 the **m** of all his prophets,' he said.
22:23 **m** of all these prophets of yours.
2Ch 18:21 the **m** of all his prophets,' he said.
18:22 in the **m** of these prophets of yours.
Ne 9:20 withhold your manna from their **m**,
Job 16:10 Men open their **m** to jeer at me; they
29: 9 covered their **m** with their hands;
29:10 stuck to the roof of their **m**.
Ps 17:10 and their **m** speak with arrogance.
22:13 prey open their **m** wide against me.
58: 6 Break the teeth in their **m**, O God;
59: 7 See what they spew from their **m**—
59:12 For the sins of their **m**, for the
62: 4 With their **m** they bless, but in
63:11 the **m** of liars will be silenced.
73: 9 Their **m** lay claim to heaven, and
78:30 even while it was still in their **m**,
78:36 they would flatter him with their **m**,
107:42 but all the wicked shut their **m**.
109: 2 men have opened their **m** against me;
115: 5 They have **m**, but cannot speak, eyes,
126: 2 Our **m** were filled with laughter, our
135:16 They have **m**, but cannot speak, eyes,
135:17 nor is there breath in their **m**.
144: 8 whose **m** are full of lies, whose
144:11 foreigners whose **m** are full of lies,
149: 6 May the praise of God be in their **m**
Isa 52:15 will shut their **m** because of him.
59:21 or from the **m** of your children, or
59:21 or from the **m** of their descendants
Lam 2:16 All your enemies open their **m** wide
3:46 "All our enemies have opened their **m**
Eze 33:31 With their **m** they express devotion,
34:10 I will rescue my flock from their **m**,
Da 6:22 and he shut the **m** of the lions.
Mic 7:16 will lay their hands on their **m**
Zep 3:13 nor will deceit be found in their **m**.
Zec 9: 7 I will take the blood from their **m**,
14:12 their tongues will rot in their **m**.
Ro 3:14 "Their **m** are full of cursing and
Eph 4:29 unwholesome talk come out of your **m**,
Heb 11:33 promised; who shut the **m** of lions,
Jas 3: 3 we put bits into the **m** of horses to
Rev 9:17 out of their **m** came fire, smoke
9:18 sulphur that came out of their **m**.
9:19 was in their **m** and in their tails;
11: 5 their **m** and devours their enemies.
14: 5 No lie was found in their **m**; they

Movable (Move)

1Ki 7:27 He also made ten **m** stands of bronze;
2Ki 16:17 the basins from the **m** stands.
25:13 the **m** stands and the bronze Sea that
25:16 the Sea and the **m** stands, which
Jer 27:19 the Sea, the **m** stands and the other
52:17 the **m** stands and the bronze Sea that
52:20 and the **m** stands, which King Solomon

Move (Movable, Moved, Movements, Moves, Moving)

Ge 1:24 creatures that **m** along the ground,
1:25 and all the creatures that **m** along
1:26 creatures that **m** along the ground."
1:30 all the creatures that **m** on the
6: 7 and creatures that **m** along the
7: 8 creatures that **m** along the ground,
7:23 animals and the creatures that **m**
8:17 and all the creatures that **m** along
8:19 all the creatures that **m** along the
26:16 Abimelech said to Isaac, "**M** away
33:14 while I **m** along slowly at the pace
48:17 hand to **m** it from Ephraim's head
Ex 14:15 to me? Tell the Israelites to **m** on.
Lev 5: 2 creatures that **m** along the ground
11:29 "'Of the animals that **m** about on
11:31 Of all those that **m** along the ground,
26:10 **m** it out to make room for the new.
Nu 1:51 Whenever the tabernacle is to **m**, the
4: 5 the camp is to **m**, Aaron and his sons
4:15 and when the camp is ready to **m**, the
12:15 not **m** on till she was brought back.
16:24 "Say to the assembly, '**M** away from
16:26 He warned the assembly, "**M** back from
Dt 19:14 Do not **m** your neighbour's boundary
Jos 3: 3 carrying it, you are to **m** out from
Jdg 16: 2 They made no **m** during the night,
2Sa 5:24 **m** quickly, because that will mean
15:14 or he will **m** quickly to overtake us
1Ch 14:15 **m** out to battle, because that will
Job 24: 2 Men **m** boundary stones; they pasture
Ps 69:34 the seas and all that **m** in them,
Pr 22:28 Do not **m** an ancient boundary stone
23:10 Do not **m** an ancient boundary stone
30:29 four that **m** with stately bearing:
Isa 46: 7 From that spot it cannot **m**. Though
Jer 31:24 those who **m** about with their flocks.
Eze 36:27 I will put my Spirit in you and **m**
Hos 2:18 creatures that **m** along the ground.
5:10 Judah's leaders are like those who **m**
Zec 12: 3 try to **m** it will injure themselves.
Mt 17:20 can say to this mountain, '**M** from
17:20 from here to there' and it will **m**.
23: 4 willing to lift a finger to **m** them.
Lk 10: 7 Do not **m** around from house to house.
14:10 'Friend, **m** up to a better place.
Ac 17:28 'For in him we live and **m** and have
27:41 The bow stuck fast and would not **m**,
1Co 13: 2 and if I have a faith that can **m**
15:58 Let nothing **m** you. Always give
2Co 11:26 I have been constantly on the **m**. I

Moved (Move)

Ge 7:21 Every living thing that **m** on the
11: 2 men **m** eastward, they found a plain
13:18 Abram **m** his tents and went to live
19: 9 **m** forward to break down the door.
20: 1 Now Abraham **m** on from there into the
26:17 Isaac **m** away from there and encamped
26:22 He **m** on from there and dug another
35:16 they **m** on from Bethel. While they
35:21 Israel **m** on again and pitched his
36: 6 and **m** to a land some distance from
37:17 "They have **m** on from here," the man
43:30 Deeply **m** at the sight of his brother,
Ex 14:19 The pillar of cloud also **m** from in
35:21 whose heart **m** him came and brought
Nu 14:44 the LORD's covenant **m** from the camp.
16:27 they **m** away from the tents of Korah,
21:10 The Israelites **m** on and camped at
21:12 From there they **m** on and camped in
22:26 the angel of the LORD **m** on ahead and
Jos 5: 6 The Israelites had **m** about in the
8: 3 Joshua and the whole army **m** out to
10: 5 They **m** up with all their troops and
10:29 Joshua and all Israel with him **m** on
10:31 Joshua and all Israel with him **m** on
10:34 Joshua and all Israel with him **m** on
14:10 while Israel **m** about in the desert.
Jdg 9:26 Now Gaal son of Ebed **m** with his
20:33 All the men of Israel **m** from their
1Sa 5: 8 ark of the god of Israel **m** to Gath.
5: 8 they **m** the ark of the God of Israel.
5: 9 after they had **m** it, the LORD's hand
1Sa 14:23 the battle **m** on beyond Beth Aven.
15: 6 Kenites **m** away from the Amalekites.
17:48 the Philistine **m** closer to attack
25: 1 David **m** down into the Desert of Maon.
2Sa 7: 7 Wherever I have **m** with all the
15:23 the people **m** on towards the desert.
2Ki 16: 6 Edomites then **m** into Elath and have
1Ch 13: 7 They **m** the ark of God from
16:30 firmly established; it cannot be **m**.
17: 5 I have **m** from one tent site to
17: 6 Wherever I have **m** with all the
19: 7 their towns and **m** out for battle.
2Ch 33:13 he prayed to him, the LORD was **m** by
33:19 His prayer and how God was **m** by his
36:22 the LORD **m** the heart of Cyrus king
Ezr 1: 1 the LORD **m** the heart of Cyrus king
1: 5 heart God had **m**—prepared to go up
Ne 2:14 I **m** on towards the Fountain Gate and
Est 2: 9 **m** her and her maids into the best
Job 14:18 and as a rock is **m** from its place,
18: 4 the rocks be **m** from their place?
Ps 93: 1 firmly established; it cannot be **m**.
96:10 it cannot be **m**; he will judge the
104: 5 its foundations; it can never be **m**.
Isa 33:20 a tent that will not be **m**; its
Eze 1: 9 ahead; they did not turn as they **m**.
1:13 Fire **m** back and forth among the
1:17 they **m**, they would go in any one of
1:19 the living creatures **m**, the wheels
1:19 the wheels beside them **m**; and when
1:21 the creatures **m**, they also **m**; when
1:24 the creatures **m**, I heard the sound
9: 3 **m** to the threshold of the temple.
10: 4 **m** to the threshold of the temple.
10:11 they **m**, they would go in any one of
10:16 the cherubim **m**, the wheels beside
10:16 the wheels beside them **m**; and when
Mt 13:53 these parables, he **m** on from there.
Lk 2:27 **M** by the Spirit, he went into the
Jn 11:33 was deeply **m** in spirit and troubled.
11:38 Jesus, once more deeply **m**, came to
11:54 Therefore Jesus no longer **m** about
Ac 9:28 Saul stayed with them and **m** about
27: 8 We **m** along the coast with difficulty
Col 1:23 established and firm, not **m** from the

Movements (Move)

2Sa 3:25 observe your **m** and find out

Moves (Move)

Ge 1:28 creature that **m** on the ground."
6:20 of every kind of creature that **m**
7:14 every creature that **m** along the
8:19 **m** on the earth—came out of the ark,
9: 2 upon every creature that **m** along the
9: 3 Everything that lives and **m** will be
Lev 11:41 "'Every creature that **m** about on
11:42 creature that **m** about on the ground,
11:42 whether it **m** on its belly or walks
11:44 creature that **m** about on the ground.
11:46 birds, every living thing that **m** in
11:46 creature that **m** about on the ground.
20:25 or anything that **m** along the ground
Dt 4:18 or like any creature that **m** along
18: 6 If a Levite **m** from one of your towns
23:14 For the LORD your God **m** about in
27:17 "Cursed is the man who **m** his
Job 9: 5 He **m** mountains without their knowing
Ps 58: 8 Like a slug melting away as it **m**
102:14 her very dust **m** them to pity.
Isa 41: 3 He pursues them and **m** on unscathed,
Eze 38:20 every creature that **m** along the

Moving (Move)

Ge 1:21 **m** thing with which the water teems,
13: 5 Now Lot, who was **m** about with Abram,
1Sa 1:13 were **m** but her voice was not heard.
12:12 of the Ammonites was **m** against you,
23:13 and kept **m** from place to place.
2Sa 7: 6 I have been **m** from place to place
Job 31:26 radiance or the moon **m** in splendour,
Zec 14: 4 mountain **m** north and half **m** south.

Mowed (Mown)

Jas 5: 4 the workmen who **m** your fields are

Mown (Mowed)

Ps 72: 6 be like rain falling on a **m** field

Moza

1Ch 2:46 the mother of Haran, **M** and Gazez.
8:36 Zimri, and Zimri was the father of **M**.
8:37 **M** was the father of Binea; Raphah
9:42 Zimri, and Zimri was the father of **M**.
9:43 **M** was the father of Binea; Rephaiah

Mozah

Jos 18:26 Mizpah, Kephirah, **M**,

Mud (Muddied, Muddy, Muddying)

2Sa 22:43 trampled them like **m** in the streets.
Job 30:19 He throws me into the **m**, and I am
41:30 in the **m** like a threshing-sledge.
Ps 18:42 them out like **m** in the streets.
40: 2 out of the **m** and mire; he set my
Isa 10: 6 them down like **m** in the streets.
57:20 whose waves cast up mire and **m**.
Jer 38: 6 **m**, and Jeremiah sank down into the **m**.
38:22 Your feet are sunk in the **m**; your
Jn 9: 6 he spat on the ground, made some **m**
9:11 made some **m** and put it on my eyes.
9:14 day on which Jesus had made the **m**
9:15 "He put **m** on my eyes," the man
2Pe 2:22 back to her wallowing in the **m**."

Muddied (Mud)

Pr 25:26 Like a **m** spring or a polluted well
Eze 32:13 of man or **m** by the hoofs of cattle.
34:19 what you have **m** with your feet?

Muddy (Mud)

Eze 34:18 you also **m** the rest with your feet?
Zec 10: 5 trampling the **m** streets in battle.

Muddying (Mud)

Eze 32: 2 with your feet and **m** the streams.

Mulberry

Lk 17: 6 you can say to this **m** tree, 'Be

Mule (Mules)

2Sa 18: 9 He was riding his **m**, and as the **m**
18: 9 the **m** he was riding kept on going.
1Ki 1:33 my own **m** and take him down to Gihon.
1:38 David's **m** and escorted him to Gihon.
1:44 they have put him on the king's **m**,
Ps 32: 9 Do not be like the horse or the **m**,

Mules (Mule)

2Sa 13:29 got up, mounted their **m** and fled.
1Ki 10:25 and spices, and horses and **m**.
18: 5 **m** alive so we will not have to kill
2Ki 5:17 much earth as a pair of **m** can carry,
1Ch 12:40 food on donkeys, camels, **m** and oxen.
2Ch 9:24 and spices, and horses and **m**.
Ezr 2:66 They had 736 horses, 245 **m**,
Ne 7:68 There were 736 horses, 245 **m**,
Isa 66:20 and on **m** and camels," says the LORD.
Eze 27:14 horses and **m** for your merchandise.
Zec 14:15 plague will strike the horses and **m**,

Multicoloured (Coloured)

Eze 27:24 fabric, embroidered work and **m** rugs

Multiplied (Multiply)

Ex 1: 7 the Israelites were fruitful and **m**
1:12 the more they **m** and spread; so the
11: 9 that my wonders may be **m** in Egypt."
Dt 8:13 gold increase and all you have is **m**,
Jdg 16:24 waste our land and **m** our slain."
Ps 25:17 The troubles of my heart have **m**;
Lam 2: 5 He has **m** mourning and lamentation

Multiplies (Multiply)
Job 34:37 us and **m** his words against God.”
35:16 talk; without knowledge he **m** words.”
Pr 23:28 lies in wait, and **m** the unfaithful
27: 6 be trusted, but an enemy **m** kisses.
Ecc 10:14 the fool **m** words. No-one knows what
Hos 12: 1 all day and **m** lies and violence.

Multiply (Multiplied, Multiplies, Multiplying)
Ge 8:17 ground—so they can **m** on the earth
9: 7 **m** on the earth and increase upon it.”
Ex 7: 3 and though I **m** my miraculous signs
Lev 26:21 I will **m** your afflictions seven
Dt 7:22 the wild animals will **m** around you.
2Sa 24: 3 “May the LORD your God **m** the troops
1Ch 21: 3 Joab replied, “May the LORD **m** his
Job 9:17 me with a storm and **m** my wounds
Jer 46:11 But you **m** remedies in vain; there is
Eze 36:10 I will **m** the number of people upon
Na 3:15 **M** like grasshoppers, **m** like locusts!

Multiplying (Multiply)
Mk 4: 8 grew and produced a crop, **m** thirty,

Multitude (Multitudes)
Ps 42: 4 soul: how I used to go with the **m**,
Isa 1:11 “The **m** of your sacrifices—what are
13: 4 like that of a great **m**! Listen, an
31: 1 who trust in the **m** of their chariots
Da 10: 6 and his voice like the sound of a **m**.
Jas 5:20 death and cover over a **m** of sins.
1Pe 4: 8 love covers over a **m** of sins.
Rev 7: 9 a great **m** that no-one could count,
19: 1 of a great **m** in heaven shouting:
19: 6 I heard what sounded like a great **m**,

Multitudes (Multitude)
Ne 9: 6 and the **m** of heaven worship you.
Da 12: 2 **M** who sleep in the dust of the earth
Joel 3:14 **M**, **m** in the valley of decision! For
Rev 17:15 peoples, **m**, nations and languages.

Mumble
Isa 29: 4 your speech will **m** out of the dust.

Muppim
Ge 46:21 Naaman, Ehi, Rosh, **M**, Huppim and Ard.

Murder (Murdered, Murderer, Murderers, Murdering, Murderous, Murders)
Ex 20:13 “You shall not **m**.
Nu 35:12 so that a person accused of **m** may
35:25 of **m** from the avenger of blood
35:27 accused without being guilty of **m**.
Dt 5:17 “You shall not **m**.
Jos 21:13 for one accused of **m**), Libnah,
21:21 for one accused of **m**) and Gezer,
21:27 one accused of **m**) and Be Eshtarah,
21:32 of refuge for one accused of **m**),
21:38 for one accused of **m**), Mahanaim,
Jdg 9:24 who had helped him **m** his brothers.
2Sa 3:37 part in the **m** of Abner son of Ner.
Ps 94: 6 the alien; they **m** the fatherless.
Pr 28:17 A man tormented by the guilt of **m**
Isa 33:15 stops his ears against plots of **m**
Jer 7: 9 “‘Will you steal and **m**, commit
Hos 4: 2 There is only cursing, lying and **m**,
6: 9 so do bands of priests; they **m** on
Mt 5:21 ‘Do not **m**, and anyone who murders
15:19 **m**, adultery, sexual immorality,
19:18 Jesus replied, “‘Do not **m**, do not
Mk 7:21 immorality, theft, **m**, adultery,
10:19 You know the commandments: ‘Do not **m**,
15: 7 who had committed **m** in the uprising.
Lk 18:20 ‘Do not commit adultery, do not **m**,
23:19 in the city, and for **m**.)
23:25 into prison for insurrection and **m**,
Ro 1:29 They are full of envy, **m**, strife,
13: 9 “Do not commit adultery,” “Do not **m**,”
Jas 2:11 adultery,” also said, “Do not **m**.
2:11 commit **m**, you have become a
1Jn 3:12 And why did he **m** him? Because his

Murdered (Murder)
Jdg 9: 5 on one stone **m** his seventy brothers,
9:18 **m** his seventy sons on a single stone,
20: 4 the husband of the **m** woman, said
2Sa 3:30 (Joab and his brother Abishai **m**
1Ki 16:16 plotted against the king and **m** him,
21:19 not **m** a man and seized his property?’
2Ki 11: 2 princes, who were about to be **m**.
12:21 The officials who **m** him were Jozabad
14: 5 who had **m** his father the king.
2Ch 21:13 You have also **m** your own brothers,
22:11 princes who were about to be **m**
25: 3 who had **m** his father the king.
Pr 22:13 “I will be **m** in the streets!
Mt 23:31 of those who **m** the prophets.
23:35 **m** between the temple and the altar.
Ac 7:52 now you have betrayed and **m** him—
Jas 5: 6 You have condemned and **m** innocent
1Jn 3:12 to the evil one and **m** his brother.

Murderer (Murder)
Nu 35:16 is a **m**; the **m** shall be put to death.
35:17 is a **m**; the **m** shall be put to death.
35:18 is a **m**; the **m** shall be put to death.
35:19 The avenger of blood shall put the **m**
35:21 shall be put to death; he is a **m**.
35:21 the **m** to death when he meets him.
35:30 **m** only on the testimony of witnesses.
35:31 life of a **m**, who deserves to die.
2Ki 6:32 “Don’t you see how this **m** is sending
9:31 peace, Zimri, you **m** of your master?”
Job 24:14 daylight is gone, the **m** rises up and
Jn 8:44 He was a **m** from the beginning, not
Ac 3:14 asked that a **m** be released to you.
28: 4 “This man must be a **m**; for though he
1Pe 4:15 it should not be as a **m** or thief or
1Jn 3:15 Anyone who hates his brother is a **m**,
3:15 that no **m** has eternal life in him.

Murderers (Murder)
Isa 1:21 used to dwell in her—but now **m**!
Jer 4:31 my life is given over to **m**.”
Mt 22: 7 those **m** and burned their city.
1Ti 1: 9 their fathers or mothers, for **m**,
Rev 21: 8 the unbelieving, the vile, the **m**,
22:15 the sexually immoral, the **m**, the

Murdering (Murder)
Jdg 9:56 father by **m** his seventy brothers.
2Ch 24:25 **m** the son of Jehoiada the priest,

Murderous (Murder)
Ac 9: 1 breathing out **m** threats against the

Murders (Murder)
Dt 22:26 who attacks and **m** his neighbour,
Ps 10: 8 from ambush he **m** the innocent,
Mt 5:21 who **m** will be subject to judgment.’
Rev 9:21 Nor did they repent of their **m**,

Muscles
Job 40:16 what power in the **m** of his belly!

Mused
Ps 77: 3 I **m**, and my spirit grew faint.
77: 6 My heart **m** and my spirit enquired:

Mushi (Mushite, Mushites)
Ex 6:19 The sons of Merari were Mahli and **M**.
Nu 3:20 The Merarite clans: Mahli and **M**.
1Ch 6:19 The sons of Merari: Mahli and **M**.
6:47 the son of Mahli, the son of **M**, the
23:21 The sons of Merari: Mahli and **M**. The
23:23 The sons of **M**: Mahli, Eder and
24:26 The sons of Merari: Mahli and **M**. The
24:30 the sons of **M**: Mahli, Eder and

Mushite (Mushi)
Nu 26:58 clan, the **M** clan, the Korahite clan.

Mushites (Mushi)
Nu 3:33 **M**; these were the Merarite clans.

Music (Musical, Musician, Musicians)
Ge 31:27 to the **m** of tambourines and harps?
Jdg 5: 3 **m** to the LORD, the God of Israel.
1Ch 6:31 men David put in charge of the **m** in
6:32 They ministered with **m** before the
25: 6 for the **m** of the temple of the LORD,
25: 7 **m** for the LORD—they numbered 288.
Ne 12:27 the **m** of cymbals, harps and lyres.
Job 21:12 They sing to the **m** of tambourine and
Ps 4: T For the director of **m**. With stringed
5: T For the director of **m**. For flutes.
6: T For the director of **m**. With stringed
8: T For the director of **m**. According to
9: T For the director of **m**. To ⌊the tune
11: T For the director of **m**. Of David.
12: T For the director of **m**. According to
13: T For the director of **m**. A psalm of
14: T For the director of **m**. Of David.
18: T For the director of **m**. Of David the
19: T For the director of **m**. A psalm of
20: T For the director of **m**. A psalm of
21: T For the director of **m**. A psalm of
22: T For the director of **m**. To ⌊the tune
27: 6 I will sing and make **m** to the LORD.
31: T For the director of **m**. A psalm of
33: 2 Praise the LORD with the harp; make **m**
36: T For the director of **m**. Of David
39: T For the director of **m**. For Jeduthun
40: T For the director of **m**. Of David.
41: T For the director of **m**. A psalm
42: T For the director of **m**. A maskil
44: T For the director of **m**. Of the Sons
45: T For the director of **m**. To ⌊the tune
45: 8 the **m** of the strings makes you glad.
46: T For the director of **m**. Of the Sons
47: T For the director of **m**. Of the Sons
49: T For the director of **m**. Of the Sons
51: T For the director of **m**. A psalm of
52: T For the director of **m**. A maskil
53: T For the director of **m**. According to
54: T For the director of **m**. With stringed
55: T For the director of **m**. With stringed
56: T For the director of **m**. To ⌊the tune
57: T For the director of **m**. ⌊To the tune
57: 7 steadfast; I will sing and make **m**.
58: T For the director of **m**. ⌊To the tune
59: T For the director of **m**. ⌊To the tune
60: T For the director of **m**. To ⌊the tune
61: T For the director of **m**. With stringed
62: T For the director of **m**. For Jeduthun
64: T For the director of **m**. A psalm of
65: T For the director of **m**. A psalm of
66: T For the director of **m**. A song.
67: T For the director of **m**. With stringed
68: T For the director of **m**. Of David.
69: T For the director of **m**. To ⌊the tune
70: T For the director of **m**. Of David.
75: T For the director of **m**. ⌊To the tune
76: T For the director of **m**. With stringed
77: T For the director of **m**. For Jeduthun
80: T For the director of **m**. To ⌊the tune
81: T For the director of **m**. According to
81: 2 Begin the **m**, strike the tambourine,
84: T For the director of **m**. According to
85: T For the director of **m**. Of the Sons
87: 7 they make **m** they will sing, “All my
88: T of Korah. For the director of **m**.
92: 1 is good to praise the LORD and make **m**
92: 3 to the **m** of the ten-stringed lyre
95: 2 and extol him with **m** and song.
98: 4 burst into jubilant song with **m**;
98: 5 make **m** to the LORD with the harp,
108: 1 sing and make **m** with all my soul.
109: T For the director of **m**. Of David.
139: T For the director of **m**. Of David.
140: T For the director of **m**. A psalm of
144: 9 lyre I will make **m** to you,
147: 7 make **m** to our God on the harp.
149: 3 **m** to him with tambourine and harp.
Isa 30:32 to the **m** of tambourines and harps,
Lam 5:14 the young men have stopped their **m**.
Eze 26:13 and the **m** of your harps will be
Da 3: 5 harp, pipes and all kinds of **m**, you
3: 7 lyre, harp and all kinds of **m**, all

Da 3:10 harp, pipes and all kinds of **m** must
3:15 harp, pipes and all kinds of **m**, if
Am 5:23 not listen to the **m** of your harps.
Hab 3:19 For the director of **m**. On my
Lk 15:25 the house, he heard **m** and dancing.
Eph 5:19 make **m** in your heart to the Lord,
Rev 18:22 The **m** of harpists and musicians,

Musical (Music)
1Ch 15:16 accompanied by **m** instruments: lyres,
23: 5 the LORD with the **m** instruments
2Ch 7: 6 with the LORD's **m** instruments,
23:13 and singers with **m** instruments were
34:12 skilled in playing **m** instruments—
Ne 12:36 and Hanani—with **m** instruments
Am 6: 5 David and improvise on **m** instruments.

Musician (Music)
1Ch 6:33 the **m**, the son of Joel, the son of

Musicians (Music)
1Ki 10:12 to make harps and lyres for the **m**.
1Ch 9:33 Those who were **m**, heads of Levite
15:19 The **m** Heman, Asaph and Ethan were to
2Ch 5:12 All the Levites who were **m**—Asaph,
9:11 to make harps and lyres for the **m**.
35:15 The **m**, the descendants of Asaph,
Ps 68:25 after them the **m**; with them are the
Rev 18:22 The music of harpists and **m**, flute

Mustard
Mt 13:31 kingdom of heaven is like a **m** seed
17:20 have faith as small as a **m** seed
Mk 4:31 is like a **m** seed, which is the
Lk 13:19 is like a **m** seed, which a man took
17: 6 have faith as small as a **m** seed

Muster (Mustered, Mustering)
1Sa 14:17 **M** the forces and see who has left us.
2Sa 12:28 Now **m** the rest of the troops and
Da 11:13 For the king of the North will **m**
Am 2:14 the strong will not **m** their strength,

Mustered (Muster)
Nu 21:23 He **m** his entire army and marched out
Jos 8:10 Early the next morning Joshua **m** his
Jdg 11:20 He **m** all his men and encamped at
20:17 Israel, apart from Benjamin, **m** four
1Sa 11: 8 Saul **m** them at Bezek, the men of
15: 4 Saul summoned the men and **m** them at
2Sa 12:29 David **m** the entire army and went to
18: 1 David **m** the men who were with him
1Ki 12:21 Rehoboam arrived in Jerusalem, he **m**
20: 1 Now Ben-Hadad king of Aram **m** his
20:26 The next spring Ben-Hadad **m** the
20:27 the Israelites were also **m** and given
1Ch 19: 7 while the Ammonites were **m** from
2Ch 11: 1 Rehoboam arrived in Jerusalem, he **m**
25: 5 He then **m** those twenty years old or
26:11 numbers as **m** by Jeiel the secretary

Mustering (Muster)
Isa 13: 4 LORD Almighty is **m** an army for war.

Mute
Ex 4:11 Who makes him deaf or **m**? Who gives
Ps 38:13 like a **m**, who cannot open his mouth;
Isa 35: 6 and the **m** tongue shout for joy.
56:10 lack knowledge; they are all **m** dogs,
Mt 9:33 out, the man who had been **m** spoke.
12:22 man who was blind and **m**, and Jesus
15:30 the blind, the crippled, the **m** and
15:31 amazed when they saw the **m** speaking,
Mk 7:37 the deaf hear and the **m** speak."
9:25 "You deaf and **m** spirit," he said, "I
Lk 11:14 was driving out a demon that was **m**.
11:14 **m** spoke, and the crowd was amazed.
1Co 12: 2 and led astray to **m** idols.

Mutilators
Php 3: 2 who do evil, those **m** of the flesh.

Mutter (Muttered, Mutters)
Isa 8:19 who whisper and **m**, should not a
Lam 3:62 what my enemies whisper and **m**
Lk 19: 7 the people saw this and began to **m**,

Muttered (Mutter)
Lk 15: 2 and the teachers of the law **m**,

Mutters (Mutter)
Isa 59: 3 and your tongue **m** wicked things.

Mutual (Mutually)
Ro 14:19 leads to peace and to **m** edification.
1Co 7: 5 each other except by **m** consent and

Mutually (Mutual)
Ro 1:12 that you and I may be **m** encouraged

Muzzle
Dt 25: 4 Do not **m** an ox while it is treading
Ps 39: 1 I will put a **m** on my mouth as long
1Co 9: 9 "Do not **m** an ox while it is treading
1Ti 5:18 Scripture says, "Do not **m** the ox

My covenant
Ge 6:18; 9:9, 11, 15; 17:2, 4, 7, 9, 10, 13, 14, 19, 21; Ex 6:4, 5; 19:5; Lev 26:9, 15, 42, 44; Nu 25:12; Dt 31:20; Jos 7:11; Jdg 2:1; 1Ki 11:11; Ps 50:16; 89:28, 34; 132:12; Isa 54:10; 56:4, 6; 59:21; Jer 31:32; 33:20, 21, 25; 34:18; Eze 16:61, 62; 17:19; 44:7; Hos 8:1; Zec 9:11; Mal 2:4, 5; Ro 11:27; Heb 8:9

My people Israel
1Sa 2:29; 9:16; 2Sa 3:18; 5:2; 7:7, 8, 10, 11; 1Ki 6:13; 8:16; 14:7; 16:2; 1Ch 11:2; 17:7, 9, 10; 2Ch 6:5, 6; Jer 7:12; 12:14; 23:13; 30:3; Eze 14:9; 25:14; 36:8, 12; 38:14, 16; 39:7; Da 9:20; Joel 3:2; Am 7:8, 15; 8:2; Mt 2:6

My servant Moses
Nu 12:7, 8; Jos 1:7; 2Ki 21:8; Mal 4:4

My son
Ge 21:10; 22:7, 8; 24:3, 4, 6, 7, 8, 37, 38, 40; 27:1, 8, 13, 18, 20, 21, 24, 25, 26, 27, 37, 43; 34:8; 37:35; 38:11, 26; 42:38; 43:29; 45:28; 48:19; 49:9; Ex 4:23; Jos 7:19; Jdg 8:23; 17:2, 3; 1Sa 3:6, 16; 4:16; 10:2; 14:39, 40, 42; 22:8; 24:16; 26:17, 21, 25; 2Sa 7:14; 13:25; 14:11, 16; 16:11; 18:22, 33; 19:4; 1Ki 1:21, 33; 3:20, 21, 22, 23; 17:12, 18; 2Ki 6:28, 29; 14:9; 1Ch 17:13; 22:5, 7, 10, 11; 28:5, 6, 9; 29:1, 19; 2Ch 25:18; Ps 2:7; Pr 1:8, 10, 15; 2:1; 3:1, 11, 21; 4:10, 20; 5:1, 20; 6:1, 3, 20; 7:1; 19:27; 23:15, 19, 26; 24:13, 21; 27:11; 31:2; Ecc 12:12; Eze 21:10; Hos 11:1; Mt 2:15; 3:17; 17:5, 15; 21:37; Mk 1:11; 9:7, 17; 12:6; Lk 3:22; 9:35, 38; 15:31; 20:13; Ac 13:33; 1Co 4:17; 1Ti 1:18; 2Ti 2:1; Phm 10; Heb 1:5; 5:5; 12:5; 1Pe 5:13; 2Pe 1:17; Rev 21:7

My spirit
Ge 6:3; 2Ki 5:26; Job 6:4; 7:11; 10:12; 17:1; Ps 31:5; 73:21; 77:3, 6; 142:3; 143:4, 7; Isa 26:9; 30:1; 38:16; 42:1; 44:3; 59:21; Lam 1:16; Eze 3:14; 36:27; 37:14; 39:29; Joel 2:28, 29; Hag 2:5; Zec 4:6; 6:8; Mt 12:18; Lk 1:47; 23:46; Ac 2:17, 18; 7:59; 1Co 14:14, 15; 16:18

Myra
Ac 27: 5 Pamphylia, we landed at **M** in Lycia.

Myriads
Dt 33: 2 He came with **m** of holy ones from the

Myrrh
Ge 37:25 balm and **m**, and they were on their
43:11 **m**, some pistachio nuts and almonds.
Ex 30:23 spices: 500 shekels of liquid **m**,
Est 2:12 six months with oil of **m** and six
Ps 45: 8 All your robes are fragrant with **m**
Pr 7:17 I have perfumed my bed with **m**, aloes
SS 1:13 My lover is to me a sachet of **m**
3: 6 perfumed with **m** and incense made
SS 4: 6 of **m** and to the hill of incense.
4:14 with **m** and aloes and all the finest
5: 1 I have gathered my **m** with my spice.
5: 5 and my hands dripped with **m**, my
5: 5 **m**, on the handles of the lock.
5:13 are like lilies dripping with **m**.
Mt 2:11 of gold and of incense and of **m**.
Mk 15:23 they offered him wine mixed with **m**,
Jn 19:39 Nicodemus brought a mixture of **m** and
Rev 18:13 of incense, **m** and frankincense, of

Myrtle (Myrtles)
Isa 41:19 and the acacia, the **m** and the olive.
55:13 instead of briers the **m** will grow.
Zec 1: 8 among the **m** trees in a ravine.
1:10 the man standing among the **m** trees
1:11 who was standing among the **m** trees,

Myrtles (Myrtle)
Ne 8:15 and from **m**, palms and shade trees,

Mysia
Ac 16: 7 they came to the border of **M**, they
16: 8 they passed by **M** and went down to

Mysteries (Mystery)
Job 11: 7 "Can you fathom the **m** of God? Can
Da 2:28 is a God in heaven who reveals **m**.
2:29 the revealer of **m** showed you what
2:47 Lord of kings and a revealer of **m**,
1Co 13: 2 can fathom all **m** and all knowledge,
14: 2 him; he utters **m** with his spirit.

Mystery (Mysteries)
Da 2:18 the God of heaven concerning this **m**,
2:19 During the night the **m** was revealed
2:27 the king the **m** he has asked about,
2:30 for me, this **m** has been revealed to
2:47 for you were able to reveal this **m**."
4: 9 and no **m** is too difficult for you.
Ro 11:25 want you to be ignorant of this **m**,
16:25 of the **m** hidden for long ages past,
1Co 15:51 Listen, I tell you a **m**: We will not
Eph 1: 9 he made known to us the **m** of his
3: 3 that is, the **m** made known to me by
3: 4 my insight into the **m** of Christ,
3: 6 This **m** is that through the gospel
3: 9 the administration of this **m**,
5:32 This is a profound **m**—but I am
6:19 make known the **m** of the gospel,
Col 1:26 the **m** that has been kept hidden for
1:27 the glorious riches of this **m**,
2: 2 know the **m** of God, namely, Christ,
4: 3 so that we may proclaim the **m** of
1Ti 3:16 Beyond all question, the **m** of
Rev 1:20 The **m** of the seven stars that you
10: 7 the **m** of God will be accomplished,
17: 5 **M** BABYLON THE GREAT
17: 7 I will explain to you the **m** of the

Myths
1Ti 1: 4 nor to devote themselves to **m** and
4: 7 Have nothing to do with godless **m**
2Ti 4: 4 from the truth and turn aside to **m**.
Tit 1:14 will pay no attention to Jewish **m** or

Naam
1Ch 4:15 son of Jephunneh: Iru, Elah and **N**.

Naamah
Ge 4:22 Tubal-Cain's sister was **N**.
Jos 15:41 Gederoth, Beth Dagon, **N** and Makkedah
1Ki 14:21 name was **N**; she was an Ammonite.
14:31 His mother's name was **N**; she was an
2Ch 12:13 name was **N**; she was an Ammonite.

Naaman (Naaman's, Naamite)
Commander-in-chief of Aramaean army; leprosy healed by Elisha (2Ki 5).

Ge 46:21 **N**, Ehi, Rosh, Muppim, Huppim and Ard.
Nu 26:40 through Ard and **N** were: through Ard,
26:40 clan; through **N**, the Naamite clan.

2Ki 5: 1 Now **N** was commander of the army of
5: 4 **N** went to his master and told him
5: 5 So **N** left, taking with him ten
5: 6 I am sending my servant **N** to you so
5: 9 **N** went with his horses and chariots
5:11 **N** went away angry and said, "I
5:15 **N** and all his attendants went back
5:16 even though **N** urged him, he refused.
5:17 "If you will not," said **N**, "please
5:19 After **N** had travelled some distance
5:20 "My master was too easy on **N**, this
5:21 Gehazi hurried after **N**. When **N** saw
5:23 means, take two talents," said **N**.
1Ch 8: 4 Abishua, **N**, Ahoah,
8: 7 **N**, Ahijah and Gera, who deported
Lk 4:27 was cleansed—only **N** the Syrian."

Naaman's (Naaman)

2Ki 5: 2 from Israel, and she served **N** wife.
5:13 **N** servants went to him and said, "My
5:27 **N** leprosy will cling to you and to

Naamathite

Job 2:11 Bildad the Shuhite and Zophar the **N**,
11: 1 Zophar the **N** replied:
20: 1 Zophar the **N** replied:
42: 9 Bildad the Shuhite and Zophar the **N**

Naamite (Naaman)

Nu 26:40 clan; through Naaman, the **N** clan.

Naarah

Jos 16: 7 down from Janoah to Ataroth and **N**,
1Ch 4: 5 of Tekoa had two wives, Helah and **N**.
4: 6 **N** bore him Ahuzzam, Hepher, Temeni
4: 6 These were the descendants of **N**.

Naarai

1Ch 11:37 Hezro the Carmelite, **N** son of Ezbai,

Naaran

1Ch 7:28 **N** to the east, Gezer and its

Nabal (Nabal's)

1Sa 25: 3 His name was **N** and his wife's name
25: 4 he heard that **N** was shearing sheep.
25: 5 "Go up to **N** at Carmel and greet him
25: 9 gave **N** this message in David's name
25:10 **N** answered David's servants, "Who is
25:19 But she did not tell her husband **N**.
25:25 no attention to that wicked man **N**.
25:26 intend to harm my master be like **N**.
25:34 not one male belonging to **N** would
25:36 Abigail went to **N**, he was in the
25:37 in the morning, when **N** was sober,
25:38 the LORD struck **N** and he died.
25:39 David heard that **N** was dead, he said,
25:39 upheld my cause against **N** for
27: 3 Abigail of Carmel, the widow of **N**.
30: 5 Abigail, the widow of **N** of Carmel.
2Sa 2: 2 Abigail, the widow of **N** of Carmel.
3: 3 the widow of **N** of Carmel; the third,

Nabal's (Nabal)

1Sa 25:14 One of the servants told **N** wife
25:39 brought **N** wrongdoing down on his

Naboth (Naboth's)

Jezreelite, killed by Jezebel so Ahab could take possession of his vineyard (1Ki 21:1–16).

1Ki 21: 1 belonging to **N** the Jezreelite.
21: 2 Ahab said to **N**, "Let me have your
21: 3 **N** replied, "The LORD forbid that I
21: 4 sullen and angry because **N** the
21: 6 I said to **N** the Jezreelite, 'Sell
21: 7 the vineyard of **N** the Jezreelite."
21: 9 seat **N** in a prominent place among
21:12 They proclaimed a fast and seated **N**
21:13 charges against **N** before the people,
21:13 "**N** has cursed both God and the king.
21:14 to Jezebel: "**N** has been stoned
21:15 soon as Jezebel heard that **N** had
1Ki 21:15 take possession of the vineyard of **N**
21:16 Ahab heard that **N** was dead, he got
2Ki 9:21 had belonged to **N** the Jezreelite.
9:25 that belonged to **N** the Jezreelite.
9:26 'Yesterday I saw the blood of **N** and

Naboth's (Naboth)

1Ki 21: 8 nobles who lived in **N** city with him.
21:11 nobles who lived in **N** city did as
21:16 to take possession of **N** vineyard.
21:18 He is now in **N** vineyard, where he
21:19 place where dogs licked up **N** blood,

Nacon

2Sa 6: 6 they came to the threshing-floor of **N**

Nadab (Nadab's)

Ex 6:23 she bore him **N** and Abihu, Eleazar
24: 1 you and Aaron, **N** and Abihu, and
24: 9 Moses and Aaron, **N** and Abihu, and
28: 1 with his sons **N** and Abihu, Eleazar
Lev 10: 1 Aaron's sons **N** and Abihu took their
Nu 3: 2 The names of the sons of Aaron were **N**
3: 4 **N** and Abihu, however, fell dead
26:60 Aaron was the father of **N** and Abihu,
26:61 **N** and Abihu died when they made an
1Ki 14:20 And **N** his son succeeded him as king.
15:25 **N** son of Jeroboam became king of
15:27 **N** and all Israel were besieging it.
15:28 Baasha killed **N** in the third year of
1Ch 2:28 The sons of Shammai: **N** and Abishur.
2:30 The sons of **N**: Seled and Appaim.
6: 3 Aaron: **N**, Abihu, Eleazar and Ithamar.
8:30 followed by Zur, Kish, Baal, Ner, **N**,
9:36 followed by Zur, Kish, Baal, Ner, **N**,
24: 1 were **N**, Abihu, Eleazar and Ithamar.
24: 2 **N** and Abihu died before their father

Nadab's (Nadab)

1Ki 15:31 for the other events of **N** reign, and

Naggai

Lk 3:25 Nahum, the son of Esli, the son of **N**,

Nagging

Jdg 16:16 With such **n** she prodded him day

Nahalal

Jos 19:15 Included were Kattath, **N**, Shimron,
21:35 Dimnah and **N**, together with their

Nahaliel

Nu 21:19 from Mattanah to **N**, from **N** to Bamoth,

Nahalol

Jdg 1:30 Canaanites living in Kitron or **N**,

Naham

1Ch 4:19 the sister of **N**: the father of

Nahamani

Ne 7: 7 Nehemiah, Azariah, Raamiah, **N**,

Naharai

2Sa 23:37 Zelek the Ammonite, **N** the Beerothite,
1Ch 11:39 Zelek the Ammonite, **N** the Berothite,

Nahash

1Sa 11: 1 **N** the Ammonite went up and besieged
11: 2 **N** the Ammonite replied, "I will make
12:12 "But when you saw that **N** king of the
2Sa 10: 2 show kindness to Hanun son of **N**,
17:25 the daughter of **N** and sister of
17:27 Shobi son of **N** from Rabbah of the
1Ch 19: 1 In the course of time, **N** king of the
19: 2 show kindness to Hanun son of **N**,

Nahath

Ge 36:13 The sons of Reuel: **N**, Zerah, Shammah
36:17 Chiefs **N**, Zerah, Shammah and Mizzah.
1Ch 1:37 The sons of Reuel: **N**, Zerah, Shammah
1Ch 6:26 Elkanah his son, Zophai his son, **N**
2Ch 31:13 Jehiel, Azaziah, **N**, Asahel, Jerimoth,

Nahbi

Nu 13:14 from the tribe of Naphtali, **N** son of

Nahor (Nahor's)

Ge 11:22 30 years, he became the father of **N**.
11:23 after he became the father of **N**,
11:24 **N** had lived 29 years, he became the
11:25 **N** lived 119 years and had other sons
11:26 the father of Abram, **N** and Haran.
11:27 Terah became the father of Abram, **N**
11:29 Abram and **N** both married. The name
22:20 has borne sons to your brother **N**:
22:23 eight sons to Abraham's brother **N**.
24:10 and made his way to the town of **N**.
24:15 was the wife of Abraham's brother **N**.
24:24 the son that Milcah bore to **N**."
24:47 son of **N**, whom Milcah bore to him.
31:53 the God of Abraham and the God of **N**,
Jos 24: 2 Terah the father of Abraham and **N**,
1Ch 1:26 Serug, **N**, Terah
Lk 3:34 the son of Terah, the son of **N**,

Nahor's (Nahor)

Ge 11:29 and the name of **N** wife was Milcah;
29: 5 "Do you know Laban, **N** grandson?"

Nahshon

Ex 6:23 of Amminadab and sister of **N**,
Nu 1: 7 from Judah, **N** son of Amminadab;
2: 3 of Judah is **N** son of Amminadab.
7:12 his offering on the first day was **N**
7:17 the offering of **N** son of Amminadab.
10:14 **N** son of Amminadab was in command.
Ru 4:20 Amminadab the father of **N**, **N** the
1Ch 2:10 **N**, the leader of the people of Judah.
2:11 **N** was the father of Salmon, Salmon
Mt 1: 4 father of **N**, **N** the father of Salmon,
Lk 3:32 the son of Salmon, the son of **N**,

Nahum

Prophet; spoke against Nineveh (Na 1:1).

Na 1: 1 of the vision of **N** the Elkoshite.
Lk 3:25 the son of Amos, the son of **N**, the

Nail (Nailing, Nails)

Jn 20:25 "Unless I see the **n** marks in his

Nailing (Nail)

Ac 2:23 him to death by **n** him to the cross.
Col 2:14 he took it away, **n** it to the cross.

Nails (Nail)

Dt 21:12 make her shave her head, trim her **n**
1Ch 22: 3 **n** for the doors of the gateways
2Ch 3: 9 The gold **n** weighed fifty shekels. He
Ecc 12:11 embedded **n**—given by one Shepherd.
Isa 41: 7 He **n** down the idol so that it will
Jer 10: 4 and **n** so that it will not totter.
Da 4:33 and his **n** like the claws of a bird.
Jn 20:25 and put my finger where the **n** were,

Nain

Town in south-west Galilee where Jesus raised to life a widow's son (Lk 7:11–15).

Lk 7:11 Jesus went to a town called **N**, and

Naioth

1Sa 19:18 Samuel went to **N** and stayed there.
19:19 Word came to Saul: "David is in **N** at
19:22 "Over in **N** at Ramah," they said.
19:23 Saul went to **N** at Ramah. But the
19:23 prophesying until he came to **N**.
20: 1 David fled from **N** at Ramah and went

Naïve

Ro 16:18 they deceive the minds of **n** people.

Naked (Nakedness)

Ge 2:25 The man and his wife were both **n**,
3: 7 and they realised that they were **n**;
3:10 afraid because I was **n**; so I hid."
3:11 "Who told you that you were **n**? Have
2Ch 28:15 plunder they clothed all who were **n**.
Job 1:21 said: "**N** I came from my mother's
1:21 mother's womb, and **n** I shall depart.
22: 6 of their clothing, leaving them **n**.
24: 7 they spend the night **n**; they have
24:10 Lacking clothes, they go about **n**;
26: 6 Death is **n** before God; Destruction
Ecc 5:15 **N** a man comes from his mother's womb,
Isa 58: 7 with shelter—when you see the **n**,
Lam 4:21 you will be drunk and stripped **n**.
Eze 16: 7 hair grew, you who were **n** and bare.
16:22 when you were **n** and bare, kicking
16:39 jewellery and leave you **n** and bare.
18: 7 and provides clothing for the **n**.
18:16 and provides clothing for the **n**.
23:10 They stripped her **n**, took away her
23:29 They will leave you **n** and bare, and
Hos 2: 3 Otherwise I will strip her **n** and
Am 2:16 Even the bravest warriors will flee **n**
Mic 1: 8 I will go about barefoot and **n**.
Hab 2:15 that he can gaze on their **n** bodies.
Mk 14:52 he fled **n**, leaving his garment
Ac 19:16 ran out of the house **n** and bleeding.
2Co 5: 3 are clothed, we will not be found **n**.
11:27 food; I have been cold and **n**.
Rev 3:17 pitiful, poor, blind and **n**.
16:15 not go **n** and be shamefully exposed."
17:16 bring her to ruin and leave her **n**;

Nakedness (Naked)

Ge 9:22 saw his father's **n** and told his two
9:23 and covered their father's **n**.
9:23 they would not see their father's **n**.
Ex 20:26 lest your **n** be exposed on it.'
Dt 28:48 and thirst, in **n** and dire poverty
Isa 47: 3 Your **n** will be exposed and your
57: 8 you love, and you looked on their **n**.
Lam 1: 8 have seen her **n**; she herself groans
Eze 16: 8 garment over you and covered your **n**.
16:36 exposed your **n** in your promiscuity
16:37 them, and they will see all your **n**.
23:18 openly and exposed her **n**,
Hos 2: 9 my linen, intended to cover her **n**.
Mic 1:11 Pass on in **n** and shame, you who live
Na 3: 5 I will show the nations your **n** and the
Ro 8:35 or famine or **n** or danger or sword?
Rev 3:18 cover your shameful **n**; and salve to

Name (*Holy name, Name of Jesus, Name of the Lord, Name of the Lord, Name's, Named, Names*)

Ge 2:11 The **n** of the first is the Pishon; it
2:13 The **n** of the second river is the
2:14 The **n** of the third river is the
2:19 the man to see what he would **n** them;
2:19 living creature, that was its **n**.
4:21 His brother's **n** was Jubal; he was
11: 4 that we may make a **n** for ourselves
11:29 The **n** of Abram's wife was Sarai,
11:29 and the **n** of Nahor's wife was Milcah;
12: 2 I will make your **n** great, and you
16:11 You shall **n** him Ishmael, for the
16:13 She gave this **n** to the Lord who
16:15 Abram gave the **n** Ishmael to the son
17: 5 Abram; your **n** will be Abraham,
17:15 call her Sarai; her **n** will be Sarah.
21: 3 Abraham gave the **n** Isaac to the son
22:24 His concubine, whose **n** was Reumah,
25: 1 Abraham took another wife, whose **n**
26:33 **n** of the town has been Beersheba.
29:16 the **n** of the older was Leah,
29:16 and the **n** of the younger was Rachel.
30:28 He added, "**N** your wages, and I will
31:53 in the **n** of the Fear of his father
32:27 The man asked him, "What is your **n**?"
32:28 the man said, "Your **n** will no longer
32:29 Jacob said, "Please tell me your **n**."
32:29 "Why do you ask my **n**?" Then
35:10 God said to him, "Your **n** is Jacob,
35:10 called Jacob; your **n** will be Israel.
Ge 36:39 and his wife's **n** was Mehetabel
36:40 by **n**, according to their clans and
38: 6 his firstborn, and her **n** was Tamar.
38:30 out and he was given the **n** Zerah.
41:45 Pharaoh gave Joseph the **n**
48:16 May they be called by my **n** and the
48:20 "In your **n** will Israel pronounce
Ex 3:13 ask me, 'What is his **n**?' Then what
3:15 This is my **n** for ever, the **n** by
5:23 I went to Pharaoh to speak in your **n**,
6: 3 but by my **n** the Lord I did not make
9:16 that my **n** might be proclaimed in all
15: 3 Lord is a warrior; the Lord is his **n**.
20: 7 anyone guiltless who misuses his **n**.
20:24 Wherever I cause my **n** to be honoured,
23:21 rebellion, since my **N** is in him.
28:21 the **n** of one of the twelve tribes.
33:12 'I know you by **n** and you have
33:17 with you and I know you by **n**."
33:19 my **n**, the Lord, in your presence.
34: 5 him and proclaimed his **n**, the Lord.
34:14 the Lord, whose **n** is Jealous,
39:14 the **n** of one of the twelve tribes.
Lev 18:21 must not profane the **n** of your God.
19:12 "'Do not swear falsely by my **n** and
19:12 and so profane the **n** of your God.
21: 6 must not profane the **n** of their God.
24:11 woman blasphemed the **N** with a curse;
24:11 (His mother's **n** was Shelomith, the
24:16 blasphemes the **N**, he must be put to death.
Nu 1: 2 listing every man by **n**, one by one.
1:18 more were listed by **n**, one by one,
1:20 serve in the army were listed by **n**,
1:22 army were counted and listed by **n**,
1:24 serve in the army were listed by **n**,
1:26 serve in the army were listed by **n**,
1:28 serve in the army were listed by **n**,
1:30 serve in the army were listed by **n**,
1:32 serve in the army were listed by **n**,
1:34 serve in the army were listed by **n**,
1:36 serve in the army were listed by **n**,
1:38 serve in the army were listed by **n**,
1:40 serve in the army were listed by **n**,
1:42 serve in the army were listed by **n**,
3:43 or more, listed by **n**, was 22,273.
6:27 "So they will put my **n** on the
13:16 Hoshea son of Nun the **n** Joshua.)
17: 2 Write the **n** of each man on his staff.
17: 3 On the staff of Levi write Aaron's **n**,
25:14 The **n** of the Israelite who was
25:15 the **n** of the Midianite woman who was
26:59 the **n** of Amram's wife was Jochebed,
27: 4 Why should our father's **n** disappear
Dt 5:11 anyone guiltless who misuses his **n**.
6:13 only and take your oaths in his **n**.
9:14 blot out their **n** from under heaven.
10: 8 in his **n**, as they still do today.
10:20 to him and take your oaths in his **n**.
12: 5 to put his **N** there for his dwelling.
12:11 will choose as a dwelling for his **N**
12:21 put his **N** is too far away from you,
14:23 will choose as a dwelling for his **N**,
14:24 choose to put his **N** is so far away),
16: 2 will choose as a dwelling for his **N**.
16: 6 will choose as a dwelling for his **N**.
16:11 choose as a dwelling for his **N**—you,
18: 5 and minister in the Lord's **n** always.
18:19 that the prophet speaks in my **n**,
18:20 who presumes to speak in my **n**
18:20 who speaks in the **n** of other gods
22:14 slanders her and gives her a bad **n**,
22:19 given an Israelite virgin a bad **n**.
25: 6 carry on the **n** of the dead brother
25: 6 that his **n** will not be blotted out
25: 7 carry on his brother's **n** in Israel.
26: 2 will choose as a dwelling for his **N**
28:58 and awesome **n**—the Lord your God—
29:20 blot out his **n** from under heaven.
Jos 7: 9 and wipe out our **n** from the earth.
7: 9 will you do for your own great **n**?"
21: 9 allotted the following towns by **n**
22:34 the Gadites gave the altar this **n**:
Jdg 1:26 it Luz, which is its **n** to this day.
13: 6 from, and he didn't tell me his **n**.
13:17 "What is your **n**, so that we may
13:18 He replied, "Why do you ask my **n**? It
Jdg 16: 4 Valley of Sorek whose **n** was Delilah.
Ru 1: 2 The man's **n** was Elimelech, his
1: 2 his wife's **n** Naomi, and the names of
2: 1 a man of standing, whose **n** was Boaz.
2:19 "The **n** of the man I worked with
4: 5 maintain the **n** of the dead with his
4:10 to maintain the **n** of the dead
4:10 so that his **n** will not disappear
1Sa 1: 1 whose **n** was Elkanah son of Jeroham,
8: 2 The **n** of his firstborn was Joel and
8: 2 and the **n** of his second was Abijah,
9: 1 a man of standing, whose **n** was Kish
12:22 For the sake of his great **n** the Lord
14:49 The **n** of his older daughter was
14:50 His wife's **n** was Ahinoam daughter of
14:50 The **n** of the commander of Saul's
18:30 and his **n** became well known.
24:21 out my **n** from my father's family."
25: 3 His **n** was Nabal and his wife's **n** was
25: 5 at Carmel and greet him in my **n**.
25: 9 Nabal this message in David's **n**.
25:25 He is just like his **n**—his **n** is Fool,
28: 8 "and bring up for me the one I **n**.
2Sa 4: 4 His **n** was Mephibosheth.)
6: 2 ark of God which is called by the **N**
7: 9 Now I will make your **n** great, like
7:13 one who will build a house for my **N**,
7:23 and to make a **n** for himself, and to
7:26 that your **n** will be great for ever.
12:25 Nathan the prophet to **n** him Jedidiah.
14: 7 leaving my husband neither **n** nor
14:27 The daughter's **n** was Tamar, and she
16: 5 His **n** was Shimei son of Gera, and he
18:18 son to carry on the memory of my **n**.
22:50 I will sing praises to your **n**.
1Ki 1:47 'May your God make Solomon's **n** more
5: 5 will build the temple for my **N**.'
8:16 a temple built for my **N** to be there,
8:18 heart to build a temple for my **N**,
8:19 who will build the temple for my **N**.'
8:29 'My **N** shall be there,' so that you
8:33 turn back to you and confess your **n**,
8:35 confess your **n** and turn from their
8:41 a distant land because of your **n**—
8:42 for men will hear of your great **n**
8:43 earth may know your **n** and fear you,
8:43 house I have built bears your **N**.
8:44 the temple I have built for your **N**,
8:48 the temple I have built for your **N**;
9: 3 by putting my **N** there for ever.
9: 7 temple I have consecrated for my **N**.
9:13 of Cabul, a **n** they have to this day.
11:36 the city where I chose to put my **N**.
14:21 of Israel in which to put his **N**.
14:21 His mother's **n** was Naamah; she was
14:31 His mother's **n** was Naamah; she was
15: 2 His mother's **n** was Maacah daughter
15:10 His grandmother's **n** was Maacah
16:24 Shemer, the **n** of the former owner
18:24 you call on the **n** of your god, and I
18:25 Call on the **n** of your god, but do
18:26 Then they called on the **n** of Baal
18:31 saying, "Your **n** shall be Israel.
21: 8 she wrote letters in Ahab's **n**,
22:42 His mother's **n** was Azubah daughter
2Ki 8:26 His mother's **n** was Athaliah, a
12: 1 His mother's **n** was Zibiah; she was
14: 2 His mother's **n** was Jehoaddin; she
14: 7 Joktheel, the **n** it has to this day.
14:27 the **n** of Israel from under heaven,
15: 2 His mother's **n** was Jecoliah; she was
15:33 His mother's **n** was Jerusha daughter
18: 2 His mother's **n** was Abijah daughter
21: 1 His mother's **n** was Hephzibah.
21: 4 said, "In Jerusalem I will put my **N**.
21: 7 of Israel, I will put my **N** for ever.
21:19 His mother's **n** was Meshullemeth
22: 1 His mother's **n** was Jedidah daughter
23:27 I said, 'There shall my **N** be.'"
23:31 His mother's **n** was Hamutal daughter
23:34 changed Eliakim's **n** to Jehoiakim.
23:36 His mother's **n** was Zebidah daughter
24: 8 His mother's **n** was Nehushta daughter
24:17 place and changed his **n** to Zedekiah.
24:18 His mother's **n** was Hamutal daughter
1Ch 1:50 and his wife's **n** was Mehetabel

1Ch 2:26 another wife, whose **n** was Atarah;
4:38 The men listed above by **n** were
7:15 His sister's **n** was Maacah. Another
8:29 His wife's **n** was Maacah,
9:35 His wife's **n** was Maacah,
12:31 designated by **n** to come and make
13: 6 ark that is called by the **N**.
16: 8 call on his **n**; make known among the
16:29 to the LORD the glory due to his **n**.
16:41 by **n** to give thanks to the LORD,
17: 8 Now I will make your **n** like the
17:21 and to make a **n** for yourself, and to
17:24 that your **n** will be great for ever.
22: 8 are not to build a house for my **N**,
22: 9 His **n** will be Solomon, and I will
22:10 one who will build a house for my **N**.
23:13 blessings in his **n** for ever.
28: 3 are not to build a house for my **N**,
29:13 thanks, and praise your glorious **n**.
2Ch 6: 5 a temple built for my **N** to be there,
6: 6 now I have chosen Jerusalem for my **N**
6: 8 heart to build a temple for my **N**,
6: 9 who will build the temple for my **N**.'
6:20 you said you would put your **N** there.
6:24 they turn back and confess your **n**,
6:26 confess your **n** and turn from their
6:32 land because of your great **n**
6:33 earth may know your **n** and fear you,
6:33 that I have built bears your **N**.
6:34 the temple I have built for your **N**,
6:38 temple that I have built for your **N**;
7:14 if my people, who are called by my **n**,
7:16 so that my **N** may be there for ever.
7:20 which I have consecrated for my **N**.
12:13 of Israel in which to put his **N**.
12:13 His mother's **n** was Naamah; she was
13: 2 His mother's **n** was Maacah, a
14:11 in your **n** we have come against this
20: 8 it a sanctuary for your **N**, saying,
20: 9 this temple that bears your **N**
20:31 His mother's **n** was Azubah daughter
22: 2 His mother's **n** was Athaliah, a
24: 1 His mother's **n** was Zibiah; she was
25: 1 His mother's **n** was Jehoaddin; she
26: 3 His mother's **n** was Jecoliah; she was
27: 1 His mother's **n** was Jerusha daughter
28:15 The men designated by **n** took the
29: 1 His mother's **n** was Abijah daughter
31:19 men were designated by **n** to
33: 4 "My **N** will remain in Jerusalem for
33: 7 of Israel, I will put my **N** for ever.
36: 4 changed Eliakim's **n** to Jehoiakim.
36:13 made him take an oath in God's **n**.
Ezr 2:61 Gileadite and was called by that **n**).
5: 1 in the **n** of the God of Israel,
6:12 May God, who has caused his **N** to
8:20 All were registered by **n**.
10:16 and all of them designated by **n**.
Ne 1: 9 have chosen as a dwelling for my **N**.'
1:11 who delight in revering your **n**.
6:13 give me a bad **n** to discredit me.
7:63 Gileadite and was called by that **n**).
9: 5 "Blessed be your glorious **n**, and
9:10 You made a **n** for yourself, which
13:25 I made them take an oath in God's **n**
Est 2:14 with her and summoned her by **n**.
3:12 These were written in the **n** of King
8: 8 another decree in the king's **n**
8: 8 no document written in the king's **n**
8:10 Mordecai wrote in the **n** of King
Job 1: 1 Uz there lived a man whose **n** was Job.
18:17 the earth; he has no **n** in the land.
Ps 5:11 who love your **n** may rejoice in you.
8: 1 our Lord, how majestic is your **n** in
8: 9 majestic is your **n** in all the earth!
9: 2 sing praise to your **n**, O Most High.
9: 5 blotted out their **n** for ever and
9:10 Those who know your **n** will trust in
18:49 LORD; I will sing praises to your **n**.
20: 1 the **n** of the God of Jacob protect
20: 5 up our banners in the **n** of our God.
22:22 I will declare your **n** to my brothers;
25:11 For the sake of your **n**, O LORD,
29: 2 to the LORD the glory due to his **n**;
31: 3 sake of your **n** lead and guide me.
34: 3 me: let us exalt his **n** together.
Ps 41: 5 "When will he die and his **n** perish?
44: 5 through your **n** we trample our foes.
44: 8 and we will praise your **n** for ever.
44:20 If we had forgotten the **n** of our God
48:10 Like your **n**, O God, your praise
52: 9 in you **n** I will hope, for your **n**
54: 1 Save me, O God, by your **n**; vindicate
54: 6 your **n**, O LORD, for it is good.
61: 5 heritage of those who fear your **n**.
61: 8 will I ever sing praise to your **n**
63: 4 in your **n** I will lift up my hands.
63:11 swear by God's **n** will praise him,
66: 2 Sing the glory of his **n**; make his
66: 4 to you, they sing praise to your **n**.
68: 4 Sing to God, sing praise to his **n**,
68: 4 on the clouds—his **n** is the LORD—
69:30 I will praise God's **n** in song and
69:36 who love his **n** will dwell there.
72:17 May his **n** endure for ever; may it
72:19 Praise be to his glorious **n** for ever;
74: 7 the dwelling-place of your **N**.
74:10 Will the foe revile your **n** for ever?
74:18 foolish people have reviled your **n**.
74:21 the poor and needy praise your **n**.
75: 1 O God, we give thanks, for your **N** is
76: 1 is known; his **n** is great in Israel.
79: 6 kingdoms that do not call on your **n**;
79: 9 for the glory of your **n**; deliver us
80:18 us, and we will call on your **n**.
83: 4 the **n** of Israel be remembered no
83:16 that men will seek your **n**, O LORD.
83:18 know that you, whose **n** is the LORD
86: 9 they will bring glory to your **n**.
86:11 heart, that I may fear your **n**.
86:12 I will glorify your **n** for ever.
89:12 and Hermon sing for joy at your **n**.
89:16 They rejoice in your **n** all day long;
89:24 my **n** his horn will be exalted.
91:14 him, for he acknowledges my **n**.
92: 1 make music to your **n**, O Most High,
96: 2 Sing to the LORD, praise his **n**;
96: 8 to the LORD the glory due to his **n**;
99: 3 great and awesome **n**—he is holy.
99: 6 was among those who called on his **n**;
100: 4 give thanks to him and praise his **n**.
102: 8 rail against me use my **n** as a curse.
105: 1 call on his **n**; make known among the
111: 9 ever—holy and awesome is his **n**.
115: 1 O LORD, not to us but to your **n** be
119:55 In the night I remember your **n**, O
119:132 always do to those who love your **n**.
135: 3 to his **n**, for that is pleasant.
135:13 Your **n**, O LORD, endures for ever,
138: 2 will praise your **n** for your love and
138: 2 all things your **n** and your word.
139:20 your adversaries misuse your **n**.
140:13 the righteous will praise your **n**
142: 7 my prison, that I may praise your **n**.
145: 1 praise your **n** for ever and ever.
145: 2 and extol your **n** for ever and ever.
147: 4 the stars and calls them each by **n**.
148:13 for his **n** alone is exalted; his
149: 3 Let them praise his **n** with dancing
Pr 3: 4 you will win favour and a good **n** in
10: 7 but the **n** of the wicked will rot.
21:24 arrogant man—"Mocker" is his **n**;
22: 1 A good **n** is more desirable than
30: 4 What is his **n**, and the **n** of his son?
30: 9 and so dishonour the **n** of my God.
Ecc 6: 4 and in darkness its **n** is shrouded.
7: 1 A good **n** is better than fine perfume,
SS 1: 3 your **n** is like perfume poured out.
Isa 4: 1 only let us be called by your **n**.
8: 3 And the LORD said to me, "**N** him
12: 4 call on his **n**; make known among the
12: 4 and proclaim that his **n** is exalted.
14:22 "I will cut off from Babylon her **n**
25: 1 I will exalt you and praise your **n**,
26: 8 we wait for you; your **n** and renown
26:13 us, but your **n** alone do we honour.
29:23 they will keep my **n** holy; they will
40:26 by one, and calls them each by **n**.
41:25 the rising sun who calls on my **n**.
42: 8 "I am the LORD; that is my **n**! I will
43: 1 summoned you by **n**; you are mine.
43: 7 everyone who is called by my **n**, whom
Isa 44: 5 will call himself by the **n** of Jacob
44: 5 LORD's', and will take the **n** Israel.
45: 3 God of Israel, who summons you by **n**.
45: 4 I summon you by **n** and bestow on you
47: 4 his **n**—is the Holy One of Israel.
48: 1 you who take oaths in the **n** of the
48: 2 Israel—the LORD Almighty is his **n**:
48:19 their **n** would never be cut off nor
49: 1 birth he has made mention of my **n**.
51:15 roar—the LORD Almighty is his **n**.
52: 5 long my **n** is constantly blasphemed.
52: 6 Therefore my people will know my **n**;
54: 5 the LORD Almighty is his **n**—the
56: 5 a **n** better than sons and daughters;
56: 5 an everlasting **n** that will not be
57:15 whose **n** is holy: "I live in a high
62: 2 you will be called by a new **n** that
62: 4 Deserted, or **n** your land Desolate.
63:14 to make for yourself a glorious **n**.
63:16 our Redeemer from of old is your **n**.
63:19 they have not been called by your **n**.
64: 2 come down to make your **n** known to
64: 7 No-one calls on your **n** or strives to
65: 1 a nation that did not call on my **n**,
65:15 You will leave your **n** to my chosen
65:15 his servants he will give another **n**.
66: 5 and exclude you because of my **n**,
66:22 will your **n** and descendants endure.
Jer 7:10 which bears my **N**, and say, "We are
7:11 Has this house, which bears my **N**,
7:12 I first made a dwelling for my **N**,
7:14 now do to the house that bears my **N**,
7:30 that bears my **N** and have defiled it.
10: 6 and your **n** is mighty in power.
10:16 the LORD Almighty is his **n**.
10:25 peoples who do not call on your **n**.
11:19 that his **n** be remembered no more."
12:16 ways of my people and swear by my **n**,
14: 7 do something for the sake of your **n**.
14: 9 we bear your **n**; do not forsake us!
14:14 are prophesying lies in my **n**.
14:15 in my **n**: I did not send them,
14:21 For the sake of your **n** do not
15:16 I bear your **n**, O LORD God Almighty.
16:21 will know that my **n** is the LORD.
20: 3 "The LORD's **n** for you is not Pashhur,
20: 9 him or speak any more in his **n**,"
23: 6 This is the **n** by which he will be
23:25 say who prophesy lies in my **n**.
23:27 will make my people forget my **n**,
23:27 forgot my **n** through Baal worship.
25:29 on the city that bears my **N**,
26: 9 Why do you prophesy in the LORD's **n**
27:15 'They are prophesying lies in my **n**.
29: 9 are prophesying lies to you in my **n**.
29:21 are prophesying lies to you in my **n**:
29:23 wives and in my **n** have spoken lies,
29:25 sent letters in your own **n** to all
31:35 roar—the LORD Almighty is his **n**:
32:18 God, whose **n** is the LORD Almighty,
32:34 that bears my **N** and defiled it.
33: 2 established it—the LORD is his **n**:
33:16 This is the **n** by which it will be
34:15 me in the house that bears my **N**.
34:16 have turned round and profaned my **n**;
37:13 the captain of the guard, whose **n**
44:26 'I swear by my great **n**,' says the
44:26 ever again invoke my **n** or swear,
46:18 whose **n** is the LORD Almighty, "one
48:15 King, whose **n** is the LORD Almighty.
50:34 strong; the LORD Almighty is his **n**.
51:19 the LORD Almighty is his **n**.
51:57 King, whose **n** is the LORD Almighty.
52: 1 His mother's **n** was Hamutal daughter
Lam 3:55 I called on your **n**, O LORD, from the
Eze 20: 9 for the sake of my **n** I did what
20:14 for the sake of my **n** I did what
20:22 and for the sake of my **n** I did what
36:23 show the holiness of my great **n**,
36:23 the **n** you have profaned among them.
48: 1 "These are the tribes, listed by **n**:
48:35 "And the **n** of the city from that
Da 1: 7 the **n** Belteshazzar; to Hananiah,
2:20 said: "Praise be to the **n** of God for
4: 8 after the **n** of my god, and the
9: 6 who spoke in your **n** to our kings,

Da 9:15 a **n** that endures to this day,
9:18 of the city that bears your **N**.
9:19 city and your people bear your **N**."
12: 1 everyone whose **n** is found written in
Hos 12: 5 the LORD is his **n** of renown!
Am 4:13 the LORD God Almighty is his **n**.
5: 8 of the land—the LORD is his **n**—
5:27 the LORD, whose **n** is God Almighty.
9: 6 of the land—the LORD is his **n**.
9:12 and all the nations that bear my **n**,"
Mic 4: 5 All the nations may walk in the **n** of
6: 9 to fear your **n** is wisdom—"Heed the
Na 1:14 have no descendants to bear your **n**.
Zec 5: 4 of him who swears falsely by my **n**.
6:12 the man whose **n** is the Branch,
10:12 in his **n** they will walk," declares
13: 3 you have told lies in the LORD's **n**.
13: 9 They will call on my **n** and I will
14: 9 be one LORD, and his **n** the only **n**.
Mal 1: 6 priests, who show contempt for my **n**.
1: 6 have we shown contempt for your **n**?'
1:11 My **n** will be great among the nations,
1:11 offerings will be brought to my **n**,
1:11 My **n** will be great among the nations
1:14 my **n** is to be feared among the
2: 2 not set your heart to honour my **n**,"
2: 5 revered me and stood in awe of my **n**.
3:16 feared the LORD and honoured his **n**.
4: 2 for you who revere my **n**, the sun of
Mt 1:21 and you are to give him the **n** Jesus,
1:25 And he gave him the **n** Jesus.
6: 9 Father in heaven, hallowed be your **n**,
7:22 Lord, did we not prophesy in your **n**,
7:22 and in your **n** drive out demons and
12:21 In his **n** the nations will put their
13:55 son? Isn't his mother's **n** Mary,
18: 5 child like this in my **n** welcomes me.
18:20 in my **n**, there am I with them."
24: 5 For many will come in my **n**, claiming,
26: 3 high priest, whose **n** was Caiaphas,
28:19 baptising them in the **n** of the
Mk 3:16 Simon (to whom he gave the **n** Peter);
3:17 (to them he gave the **n** Boanerges,
5: 9 "What is your **n**?" "My **n** is Legion,"
6:14 for Jesus' **n** had become well known.
9:37 little children in my **n** welcomes me;
9:38 in your **n** and we told him to stop,
9:39 "No-one who does a miracle in my **n**
9:41 gives you a cup of water in my **n**
11: 9 he who comes in the **n** of the Lord!"
13: 6 Many will come in my **n**, claiming, 'I
16:17 In my **n** they will drive out demons;
Lk 1:13 and you are to give him the **n** John.
1:27 The virgin's **n** was Mary.
1:31 and you are to give him the **n** Jesus.
1:49 great things for me—holy is his **n**.
1:59 to **n** him after his father Zechariah,
1:61 your relatives who has that **n**."
1:62 what he would like to **n** the child.
1:63 he wrote, "His **n** is John.
2:21 he was named Jesus, the **n** the angel
5:27 a tax collector by the **n** of Levi
6:22 insult you and reject your **n** as evil
8:30 Jesus asked him, "What is your **n**?"
9:48 little child in my **n** welcomes me;
9:49 in your **n** and we tried to stop him,
10:17 the demons submit to us in your **n**."
11: 2 hallowed be your **n**, your kingdom
19: 2 man was there by the **n** of Zacchaeus
21: 8 For many will come in my **n**, claiming,
21:12 and all on account of my **n**.
24:47 be preached in his **n** to all nations,
Jn 1: 6 was sent from God; his **n** was John.
1:12 to those who believed in his **n**, he
2:23 he was doing and believed in his **n**.
3:18 in the **n** of God's one and only Son.
5:43 I have come in my Father's **n**, and
5:43 in his own **n**, you will accept him.
10: 3 own sheep by **n** and leads them out.
10:25 I do in my Father's **n** speak for me,
12:28 Father, glorify your **n**!" Then a
14:13 I will do whatever you ask in my **n**,
14:14 You may ask me for anything in my **n**,
14:26 whom the Father will send in my **n**,
15:16 give you whatever you ask in my **n**.
15:21 treat you this way because of my **n**,
Jn 16:23 give you whatever you ask in my **n**.
16:24 have not asked for anything in my **n**.
16:26 In that day you will ask in my **n**. I
17:11 the power of your **n**—the **n** you gave
17:12 them safe by that **n** you gave me.
18:10 (The servant's **n** was Malchus.)
20:31 you may have life in his **n**.
Ac 3:16 It is Jesus' **n** and the faith that
4: 7 power or what **n** did you do this?"
4:12 for there is no other **n** under heaven
4:17 no longer to anyone in this **n**."
4:30 the **n** of your holy servant Jesus."
5:28 not to teach in this **n**," he said.
5:41 of suffering disgrace for the **N**.
9:14 to arrest all who call on your **n**."
9:15 to carry my **n** before the Gentiles
9:16 how much he must suffer for my **n**."
9:21 among those who call on this **n**?
10:43 forgiveness of sins through his **n**."
13: 8 sorceror (for that is what his **n**
15:17 and all the Gentiles who bear my **n**,
15:26 for the **n** of our Lord Jesus Christ.
19:27 that our trade will lose its good **n**,
22:16 your sins away, calling on his **n**.'
Ro 2:24 is written: "God's **n** is blasphemed
9:17 that my **n** might be proclaimed in all
15: 9 I will sing hymns to your **n**."
1Co 1: 2 on the **n** of our Lord Jesus Christ
1:10 I appeal to you, brothers, in the **n**
1:13 Were you baptised into the **n** of Paul?
1:15 that you were baptised into my **n**.
5: 4 are assembled in the **n** of our Lord
Eph 3:15 heaven and on earth derives its **n**.
5:20 in the **n** of our Lord Jesus Christ.
Php 2: 9 him the **n** that is above every **n**,
2Th 1:12 We pray this so that the **n** of our
1Ti 6: 1 so that God's **n** and our teaching may
Heb 1: 4 the **n** he has inherited is superior
2:12 He says, "I will declare your **n** to
7: 2 First, his **n** means "king of
13:15 fruit of lips that confess his **n**.
Jas 2: 7 noble **n** of him to whom you belong?
1Pe 4:14 If you are insulted because of the **n**
4:16 but praise God that you bear that **n**.
1Jn 2:12 been forgiven on account of his **n**.
3:23 to believe in the **n** of his Son,
5:13 who believe in the **n** of the Son
3Jn : 7 was for the sake of the **N** that they
:14 Greet the friends there by **n**.
Rev 2: 3 for my **n**, and have not grown weary.
2:13 Yet you remain true to my **n**. You did
2:17 stone with a new **n** written on it,
3: 5 I will never blot out his **n** from the
3: 5 acknowledge his **n** before my Father
3: 8 my word and have not denied my **n**.
3:12 I will write on him the **n** of my God
3:12 God and the **n** of the city of my God,
3:12 I will also write on him my new **n**.
8:11 the **n** of the star is Wormwood. A
9:11 whose **n** in Hebrew is Abaddon, and in
11:18 and those who reverence your **n**,
13: 1 and on each head a blasphemous **n**.
13: 6 and to slander his **n** and his
13:17 which is the **n** of the beast or the
13:17 of the beast or the number of his **n**.
14: 1 and with him 144,000 who had his **n**
14: 1 his Father's **n** written on their
14:11 who receives the mark of his **n**."
15: 2 image and over the number of his **n**.
15: 4 and bring glory to your **n**? For you
16: 9 heat and they cursed the **n** of God,
19:12 He has a **n** written on him that
19:13 blood, and his **n** is the Word of God.
19:16 on his thigh he has this **n** written:
20:15 If anyone's **n** was not found written
22: 4 his **n** will be on their foreheads.

Name of Jesus

Ac 2:38 every one of you, in the **n** Christ
3: 6 In the **n** Christ of Nazareth, walk."
3:16 By faith in the **n**, this man whom you
4:10 It is by the **n** Christ of Nazareth,
4:18 to speak or teach at all in the **n**.
5:40 to speak in the **n**, and let them go.
8:12 the kingdom of God and the **n** Christ,
Ac 9:27 he had preached fearlessly in the **n**.
10:48 they be baptised in the **n** Christ.
16:18 "In the **n** Christ I command you to
19:13 They would say, "In the **n**, whom Paul
26: 9 to oppose the **n** of Nazareth.
Php 2:10 that at the **n** every knee should bow,

Name of the LORD

Ge 4:26 time men began to call on the **n**.
12: 8 to the LORD and called on the **n**.
13: 4 There Abram called on the **n**.
21:33 called upon the **n**, the Eternal God.
26:25 an altar there and called on the **n**.
Ex 20: 7 "You shall not misuse the **n** your God,
Lev 24:16 anyone who blasphemes the **n** must be
Dt 5:11 "You shall not misuse the **n** your God,
18: 7 he may minister in the **n** his God
18:22 If what a prophet proclaims in the **n**
21: 5 to pronounce blessings in the **n** and
28:10 by the **n**, and they will fear you.
32: 3 I will proclaim the **n**. Oh, praise
1Sa 17:45 but I come against you in the **n**
20:42 friendship with each other in the **n**,
2Sa 6: 2 which is called by the Name, the **n**
6:18 the people in the **n** Almighty.
1Ki 3: 2 had not yet been built for the **N**.
5: 3 could not build a temple for the **N**
5: 5 to build a temple for the **N** my God,
8:17 temple for the **N**, the God of Israel.
8:20 temple for the **N**, the God of Israel.
10: 1 Solomon and his relation to the **n**,
18:24 your god, and I will call on the **n**.
18:32 stones he built an altar in the **n**,
2Ki 2:24 down a curse on them in the **n**.
5:11 and stand and call on the **n** his God,
1Ch 16: 2 he blessed the people in the **n**.
21:19 word that Gad had spoken in the **n**.
22: 7 to build a house for the **N** my God.
22:19 that will be built for the **N**."
2Ch 2: 1 to build a temple for the **N** and a
2: 4 to build a temple for the **N** my God
6: 7 temple for the **N**, the God of Israel.
6:10 temple for the **N**, the God of Israel.
33:18 the seers spoke to him in the **n**,
Job 1:21 taken away; may the **n** be praised."
Ps 7:17 will sing praise to the **n** Most High.
20: 7 but we trust in the **n** our God.
102:15 The nations will fear the **n**, all the
102:21 the **n** will be declared in Zion and
113: 1 O servants of the LORD, praise the **n**.
113: 2 Let the **n** be praised, both now and
113: 3 it sets, the **n** is to be praised.
116: 4 I called on the **n**: "O LORD, save me!"
116:13 cup of salvation and call on the **n**.
116:17 to you and call on the **n**.
118:10 me, but in the **n** I cut them off.
118:11 side, but in the **n** I cut them off.
118:12 thorns; in the **n** I cut them off.
118:26 Blessed is he who comes in the **n**.
122: 4 to praise the **n** according to the
124: 8 Our help is in the **n**, the Maker of
129: 8 be upon you; we bless you in the **n**."
135: 1 Praise the LORD. Praise the **n**;
148: 5 Let them praise the **n**, for he
148:13 Let them praise the **n**, for his name
Pr 18:10 The **n** is a strong tower; the
Isa 18: 7 Zion, the place of the **N** Almighty.
24:15 give glory to the LORD; exalt the **n**,
30:27 See, the **N** comes from afar, with
48: 1 you who take oaths in the **n** and
50:10 trust in the **n** and rely on his God.
56: 6 to love the **n**, and to worship him,
59:19 From the west, men will fear the **n**,
Jer 3:17 gather in Jerusalem to honour the **n**.
11:21 'Do not prophesy in the **n** or you
26:16 has spoken to us in the **n** our God."
26:20 another man who prophesied in the **n**;
44:16 you have spoken to us in the **n**!
Joel 2:26 and you will praise the **n** your God,
2:32 everyone who calls on the **n** will be
Am 6:10 "Hush! We must not mention the **n**.
Mic 4: 5 in the **n** our God for ever and ever.
5: 4 in the majesty of the **n** his God.
Zep 3: 9 may call on the **n** and serve him
3:12 meek and humble, who trust in the **n**.

Name of the Lord

1Ki 22:16 me nothing but the truth in the **n**?"
2Ch 18:15 me nothing but the truth in the **n**?"
Mt 21: 9 "Blessed is he who comes in the **n**!"
23:39 'Blessed is he who comes in the **n**.'"
Mk 11: 9 "Blessed is he who comes in the **n**!
Lk 13:35 'Blessed is he who comes in the **n**.'"
19:38 is the king who comes in the **n**!"
Jn 12:13 "Blessed is he who comes in the **n**!"
Ac 2:21 everyone who calls on the **n** will be
8:16 been baptised into the **n** Jesus.
9:28 Jerusalem, speaking boldly in the **n**.
19: 5 they were baptised into the **n** Jesus.
19:13 tried to invoke the **n** Jesus over
19:17 the **n** Jesus was held in high honour.
21:13 die in Jerusalem for the **n** Jesus."
Ro 10:13 for, "Everyone who calls on the **n**
1Co 6:11 you were justified in the **n** Jesus
Col 3:17 do it all in the **n** Jesus, giving
2Th 3: 6 In the **n** Jesus Christ, we command
2Ti 2:19 "Everyone who confesses the **n** must
Jas 5:10 the prophets who spoke in the **n**.
5:14 and anoint him with oil in the **n**.

Name's (Name)

Ps 23: 3 of righteousness for his **n** sake.
79: 9 forgive our sins for your **n** sake.
106: 8 Yet he saved them for his **n** sake, to
109:21 deal well with me for your **n** sake;
143:11 For your **n** sake, O LORD, preserve my
Isa 48: 9 For my own **n** sake I delay my wrath;
Eze 20:44 when I deal with you for my **n** sake
Ro 1: 5 Through him and for his **n** sake, we

Named (Name)

Ge 3:20 Adam **n** his wife Eve, because she
4:17 and he **n** it after his son Enoch.
4:19 Lamech married two women, one **n** Adah
4:25 gave birth to a son and **n** him Seth
4:26 Seth also had a son, and he **n** him
5: 3 in his own image; and he **n** him Seth.
5:29 He **n** him Noah and said, "He will
10:25 were born to Eber: One was **n** Peleg
10:25 divided; his brother was **n** Joktan.
16: 1 had an Egyptian maidservant **n** Hagar;
19:37 and she **n** him Moab; he is the father
19:38 and she **n** him Ben-Ammi; he is the
23:16 **n** in the hearing of the Hittites:
24:29 Now Rebekah had a brother **n** Laban,
25:25 a hairy garment; so they **n** him Esau.
25:26 Esau's heel; so he was **n** Jacob.
26:20 So he **n** the well Esek, because
26:21 that one also; so he **n** it Sitnah.
26:22 He **n** it Rehoboth, saying, "Now the
27:36 Esau said, "Isn't he rightly **n** Jacob?
29:32 She **n** him Reuben, for she said, "It
29:33 this one too." So she **n** him Simeon.
29:34 three sons." So he was **n** Levi.
29:35 So she **n** him Judah. Then she
30: 6 Because of this she **n** him Dan.
30: 8 I have won." So she **n** him Naphtali.
30:11 What good fortune!" So she **n** him Gad.
30:13 call me happy." So she **n** him Asher.
30:18 So she **n** him Issachar.
30:20 six sons." So she **n** him Zebulun.
30:21 birth to a daughter and **n** her Dinah.
30:24 She **n** him Joseph, and said, "May the
32: 2 God!" So he **n** that place Mahanaim.
35: 8 So it was **n** Allon Bacuth.
35:10 So he **n** him Israel.
35:18 was dying—she **n** her son Ben-Oni.
35:18 But his father **n** him Benjamin.
36:12 concubine **n** Timna, who bore him
36:32 His city was **n** Dinhabah.
36:35 His city was **n** Avith.
36:39 His city was **n** Pau, and his wife's
38: 1 stay with a man of Adullam **n** Hirah.
38: 2 daughter of a Canaanite man **n** Shua.
38: 3 gave birth to a son, who was **n** Er.
38: 4 gave birth to a son and **n** him Onan.
38: 5 still another son and **n** him Shelah.
38:29 broken out!" And he was **n** Perez.
41:51 Joseph **n** his firstborn Manasseh and
41:52 The second son he **n** Ephraim and said,
Ex 2:10 She **n** him Moses, saying, "I drew him
2:22 and Moses **n** him Gershom, saying, "I
18: 3 her two sons. One son was **n** Gershom,
18: 4 the other was **n** Eliezer, for he said,
Nu 11:34 Therefore the place was **n** Kibroth
21: 3 towns; so the place was **n** Hormah.
26:46 (Asher had a daughter **n** Serah.)
Dt 3:14 the Maacathites; it was **n** after him,
Jos 2: 1 prostitute **n** Rahab and stayed there.
19:47 **n** it Dan after their forefather.)
Jdg 8:31 bore him a son, whom he **n** Abimelech.
13: 2 A certain man of Zorah, **n** Manoah,
13:24 birth to a boy and **n** him Samson.
17: 1 Now a man **n** Micah from the hill
18:29 They **n** it Dan after their forefather
Ru 1: 4 married Moabite women, one **n** Orpah
4:17 And they **n** him Obed. He was the
1Sa 1:20 She **n** him Samuel, saying, "Because I
4:21 She **n** the boy Ichabod, saying, "The
7:12 He **n** it Ebenezer, saying, "Thus far
9: 2 He had a son **n** Saul, an impressive
17: 4 A champion **n** Goliath, who was from
17:12 the son of an Ephrathite **n** Jesse,
2Sa 3: 7 Saul had had a concubine **n** Rizpah
4: 2 One was **n** Baanah and the other Recab;
9: 2 servant of Saul's household **n** Ziba.
9:12 Mephibosheth had a young son **n** Mica,
12:24 a son, and they **n** him Solomon.
12:28 city, and it will be **n** after me."
13: 3 Now Amnon had a friend **n** Jonadab son
17:25 Amasa was the son of a man **n** Jether,
18:18 He **n** the pillar after himself, and
20: 1 Now a troublemaker **n** Sheba son of
20:21 A man **n** Sheba son of Bicri, from
1Ki 7:21 The pillar to the south he **n** Jakin
11:20 Tahpenes bore him a son **n** Genubath,
11:26 and his mother was a widow **n** Zeruah.
13: 2 'A son **n** Josiah will be born to the
2Ki 17:34 of Jacob, whom he **n** Israel.
23:11 room of an official **n** Nathan-Melech.
1Ch 1:19 were born to Eber: One was **n** Peleg
1:19 divided; his brother was **n** Joktan.
1:43 of Beor, whose city was **n** Dinhabah.
1:46 His city was **n** Avith.
1:50 His city was **n** Pau, and his wife's
2:29 Abishur's wife was **n** Abihail, who
2:34 He had an Egyptian servant **n** Jarha.
4: 3 Their sister was **n** Hazzelelponi.
4: 9 His mother had **n** him Jabez, saying,
6:65 allotted the previously **n** towns.
7:15 Another descendant was **n** Zelophehad,
7:15 birth to a son and **n** him Peresh.
7:15 His brother was **n** Sheresh, and his
7:23 He **n** him Beriah, because there had
9:31 A Levite **n** Mattithiah, the firstborn
2Ch 3:17 The one to the south he **n** Jakin and
28: 9 a prophet of the LORD **n** Oded was
Ezr 5:14 gave them to a man **n** Sheshbazzar,
Ne 9: 7 of the Chaldeans and **n** him Abraham.
13:13 a Levite **n** Pedaiah in charge
Est 2: 5 **n** Mordecai son of Jair, the son of
2: 7 Mordecai had a cousin **n** Hadassah,
Job 42:14 The first daughter he **n** Jemimah, the
Ps 49:11 they had **n** lands after themselves.
Ecc 6:10 Whatever exists has already been **n**,
Isa 61: 6 you will be **n** ministers of our God.
Eze 23: 4 The older was **n** Oholah, and her
48:31 the gates of the city will be **n**
Mt 9: 9 he saw a man **n** Matthew sitting at
27:32 they met a man from Cyrene, **n** Simon,
27:57 a rich man from Arimathea, **n** Joseph
Mk 5:22 of the synagogue rulers, **n** Jairus
Lk 1: 5 Judea there was a priest **n** Zechariah,
1:27 man **n** Joseph, a descendant of David.
2:21 he was **n** Jesus, the name the angel
6:14 Simon (whom he **n** Peter), his brother
8:41 a man **n** Jairus, a ruler of the
10:38 **n** Martha opened her home to him.
16:20 a beggar **n** Lazarus, covered with
23:50 Now there was a man **n** Joseph, a
24:18 One of them, **n** Cleopas, asked him,
Jn 3: 1 a man of the Pharisees **n** Nicodemus,
11: 1 Now a man **n** Lazarus was sick. He was
11:49 one of them, **n** Caiaphas, who was
Ac 5: 1 Now a man **n** Ananias, together with
5:34 a Pharisee **n** Gamaliel, a teacher of
7:58 at the feet of a young man **n** Saul.
8: 9 Now for some time a man **n** Simon had
9:10 there was a disciple **n** Ananias.
9:11 a man from Tarsus **n** Saul,
9:12 In a vision he has seen a man **n**
9:33 There he found a man **n** Aeneas, a
9:36 there was a disciple **n** Tabitha
9:43 for some time with a tanner **n** Simon.
10: 1 there was a man **n** Cornelius
10: 5 a man **n** Simon who is called Peter.
11:28 One of them, **n** Agabus, stood up and
12:13 **n** Rhoda came to answer the door.
13: 6 and false prophet **n** Bar-Jesus,
16: 1 where a disciple **n** Timothy lived,
16:14 listening was a woman **n** Lydia,
17:34 a woman **n** Damaris, and a number of
18: 2 There he met a Jew **n** Aquila, a
18:24 Meanwhile a Jew **n** Apollos, a native
19:24 A silversmith **n** Demetrius, who made
20: 9 window was a young man **n** Eutychus,
21:10 a prophet **n** Agabus came down from
22:12 "A man **n** Ananias came to see me. He
24: 1 the elders and a lawyer **n** Tertullus,
25:19 a dead man **n** Jesus whom Paul
27: 1 handed over to a centurion **n** Julius,
Rev 6: 8 a pale horse! Its rider was **n** Death,

Nameless

Job 30: 8 A base and **n** brood, they were driven

Names (Name)

Ge 2:20 the man gave **n** to all the livestock,
25:13 These are the **n** of the sons of
25:16 and these are the **n** of the twelve
26:18 same **n** his father had given them.
36:10 These are the **n** of Esau's sons:
46: 8 These are the **n** of the sons of
48: 6 under the **n** of their brothers.
48:16 **n** of my fathers Abraham and Isaac,
Ex 1: 1 These are the **n** of the sons of
1:15 whose **n** were Shiphrah and Puah,
6:16 These were the **n** of the sons of Levi
23:13 Do not invoke the **n** of other gods;
28: 9 engrave on them the **n** of the sons
28:10 in the order of their birth—six **n**
28:11 Engrave the **n** of the sons of Israel
28:12 Aaron is to bear the **n** on his
28:21 one for each of the **n** of the sons of
28:29 he will bear the **n** of the sons of
39: 6 with the **n** of the sons of Israel.
39:14 one for each of the **n** of the sons of
Nu 1: 5 These are the **n** of the men who are
1:17 these men whose **n** had been given,
3: 2 The **n** of the sons of Aaron were
3: 3 Those were the **n** of Aaron's sons,
3:17 These were the **n** of the sons of Levi:
3:18 These were the **n** of the Gershonite
3:40 or more and make a list of their **n**.
11:26 However, two men, whose **n** were Eldad
13: 4 These are their **n**: from the tribe of
13:16 These are the **n** of the men Moses
26:33 whose **n** were Mahlah, Noah, Hoglah,
26:53 based on the number of **n**.
26:55 to the **n** for its ancestral tribe.
27: 1 The **n** of the daughters were Mahlah,
32:38 Baal Meon (these **n** were changed)
32:38 gave **n** to the cities they rebuilt.
34:17 "These are the **n** of the men who are
34:19 These are their **n**: Caleb son of
Dt 7:24 wipe out their **n** from under heaven.
12: 3 wipe out their **n** from those places.
Jos 17: 3 whose **n** were Mahlah, Noah, Hoglah,
23: 7 do not invoke the **n** of their gods
Jdg 8:14 wrote down for him the **n** of the
Ru 1: 2 his wife's name Naomi, and the **n** of
2Sa 5:14 These are the **n** of the children born
7: 9 **n** of the greatest men of the earth.
23: 8 These are the **n** of David's mighty
1Ki 4: 8 These are their **n**: Ben-Hur—in the
1Ch 4:41 The men whose **n** were listed came in
6:17 These are the **n** of the sons of
8:38 and these were their **n**: Azrikam,
9:44 and these were their **n**: Azrikam,
14: 4 These are the **n** of the children born
17: 8 **n** of the greatest men of the earth.
23:24 their **n** and counted individually,

1Ch 24: 6 a Levite, recorded their **n** in the
2Ch 31:16 **n** were in the genealogical records-
Ezr 5: 4 asked, "What are the **n** of the men
5:10 We also asked them their **n**, so that
5:10 so that we could write down the **n** of
8:13 the last ones, whose **n** were
Ps 16: 4 blood or take up their **n** on my lips.
109:13 their **n** blotted out from the next
Da 1: 7 The chief official gave them new **n**:
Hos 2:17 I will remove the **n** of the Baals
2:17 no longer will their **n** be invoked.
Zep 1: 4 the **n** of the pagan and the
Zec 13: 2 I will banish the **n** of the idols
Mt 10: 2 These are the **n** of the twelve
Lk 10:20 that your **n** are written in heaven."
Ac 18:15 about words and **n** and your own law
Php 4: 3 whose **n** are in the book of life.
Heb 12:23 whose **n** are written in heaven.
Rev 13: 8 all whose **n** have not been written in
17: 3 was covered with blasphemous **n**
17: 8 The inhabitants of the earth whose **n**
21:12 **n** of the twelve tribes of Israel.
21:14 **n** of the twelve apostles of the Lamb.
21:27 but only those whose **n** are written

Naomi (Naomi's)

Mother-in-law of Ruth. With husband Elimelech, moved from Bethlehem to Moab during famine; returned with Ruth after death of husband and sons (Ru 1). Encouraged Ruth's marriage to Boaz (Ru 2:19–3:6); nursed Ruth's son (Ru 4:16–17).

Ru 1: 2 his wife's name **N**, and the names of
1: 5 and **N** was left without her two sons
1: 6 **N** and her daughters-in-law prepared
1: 8 **N** said to her two daughters-in-law,
1:11 **N** said, "Return home, my daughters.
1:15 "Look," said **N**, "your sister-in-law
1:18 **N** realised that Ruth was determined
1:19 exclaimed, "Can this be **N**?
1:20 "Don't call me **N**," she told them.
1:21 Why call me **N**? The LORD has
1:22 **N** returned from Moab accompanied by
2: 1 Now **N** had a relative on her
2: 2 Ruth the Moabitess said to **N**, "Let
2: 2 **N** said to her, "Go ahead, my
2: 6 who came back from Moab with **N**.
2:20 "The LORD bless him!" **N** said to her
2:22 **N** said to Ruth her daughter-in-law,
3: 1 One day **N** her mother-in-law said to
3:16 Ruth came to her mother-in-law, **N**
3:18 **N** said, "Wait, my daughter, until
4: 3 to the kinsman-redeemer, "**N**, who has
4: 5 "On the day you buy the land from **N**
4: 9 bought from **N** all the property
4:14 The women said to **N**: "Praise be to
4:16 **N** took the child, laid him in her
4:17 The women living there said, "**N** has

Naomi's (Naomi)

Ru 1: 3 Now Elimelech, **N** husband, died, and

Naphish

Ge 25:15 Hadad, Tema, Jetur, **N** and Kedemah.
1Ch 1:31 Jetur, **N** and Kedemah. These were the
5:19 the Hagrites, Jetur, **N** and Nodab.

Naphoth Dor

Jos 11: 2 foothills and in **N** on the west;
12:23 the king of Dor (in **N**) one the king
1Ki 4:11 Ben-Abinadab—in **N** (he was married

Naphtali (Naphtalites)

1. Son of Jacob by Bilhah (Ge 30:8; 35:25; 1Ch 2:2). Blessed by Jacob (Ge 49:21). **2.** Tribe descended from Naphtali. Blessed by Moses (Dt 33:23). Included in census (Nu 1:42–43; 26:48–50). Apportioned land (Jos 19:32–39; Eze 48:3); unable to take full possession (Jdg 1:33). **3.** Territory to the west of Sea of Galilee, with Zebulun and Asher to the west, and Issachar to the south. Allotted to the descendants of Jacob's fifth son. Its towns and borders were clearly listed (Jos 19:32–39). Canaanite inhabitants not driven out but enslaved (Jdg 1:33). Conquered by Assyria before fall of Samaria and its people deported (2Ki 15:29). Isaiah predicted great honour for this land (Isa 9:1), fulfilled in Jesus' ministry there (Mt 4:13–16).

Ge 30: 8 So she named him **N**.
35:25 maidservant Bilhah: Dan and **N**.
46:24 The sons of **N**: Jahziel, Guni, Jezer
49:21 "**N** is a doe set free that bears
Ex 1: 4 Dan and **N**; Gad and Asher.
Nu 1:15 from **N**, Ahira son of Enan."
1:42 From the descendants of **N**: All the
1:43 The number from the tribe of **N** was
2:29 The tribe of **N** will be next. The
2:29 people of **N** is Ahira son of Enan.
7:78 people of **N**, brought his offering.
10:27 over the division of the tribe of **N**.
13:14 from the tribe of **N**, Nahbi son of
26:48 The descendants of **N** by their clans
26:50 These were the clans of **N**; those
34:28 the leader from the tribe of **N**."
Dt 27:13 Gad, Asher, Zebulun, Dan and **N**.
33:23 About **N** he said: "**N** is abounding
34: 2 all of **N**, the territory of Ephraim
Jos 19:32 The sixth lot came out for **N**, clan
19:39 of the tribe of **N**, clan by clan.
20: 7 in Galilee in the hill country of **N**,
21: 6 Asher, **N** and the half-tribe of
21:32 from the tribe of **N**, Kedesh in
Jdg 1:33 Neither did **N** drive out those living
4: 6 from Kedesh in **N** and said to him,
4: 6 take with you ten thousand men of **N**
4:10 where he summoned Zebulun and **N**. Ten
5:18 did **N** on the heights of the field.
6:35 and also into Asher, Zebulun and **N**,
7:23 Israelites from **N**, Asher and all
1Ki 4:15 Ahimaaz—in **N** (he had married
7:14 was a widow from the tribe of **N**
15:20 and all Kinnereth in addition to **N**.
2Ki 15:29 including all the land of **N**, and
1Ch 2: 2 Dan, Joseph, Benjamin, **N**, Gad and
6:62 Asher and **N**, and from the part of
6:76 from the tribe of **N** they received
7:13 The sons of **N**: Jahziel, Guni, Jezer
12:34 men of **N**—1,000 officers, together
12:40 Zebulun and **N** came bringing food on
27:19 over **N**: Jerimoth son of Azriel;
2Ch 16: 4 Maim and all the store cities of **N**.
34: 6 as **N**, and in the ruins around them,
Ps 68:27 the princes of Zebulun and of **N**.
Isa 9: 1 land of Zebulun and the land of **N**,
Eze 48: 3 "**N** will have one portion; it will
48: 4 territory of **N** from east to west.
48:34 the gate of Asher and the gate of **N**.
Mt 4:13 lake in the area of Zebulun and **N**—
4:15 "Land of Zebulun and land of **N**, the
Rev 7: 6 from the tribe of **N** 12,000, from the

Naphtalites (Naphtali)

Jdg 1:33 but the **N** too lived among the

Naphtuhites

Ge 10:13 the Ludites, Anamites, Lehabites, **N**,
1Ch 1:11 the Ludites, Anamites, Lehabites, **N**,

Narcissus

Ro 16:11 household of **N** who are in the Lord.

Nard

SS 4:13 choice fruits, with henna and **n**,
4:14 **n** and saffron, calamus and cinnamon,
Mk 14: 3 expensive perfume, made of pure **n**.
Jn 12: 3 Mary took about a pint of pure **n**, an

Narrow (Narrower)

Nu 22:24 the angel of the LORD stood in a **n**
22:26 stood in a **n** place where there was
1Ki 6: 4 He made **n** clerestory windows in the
Pr 23:27 pit and a wayward wife is a **n** well.
Isa 28:20 blanket too **n** to wrap around you.
Eze 40:16 by **n** parapet openings all round,
40:25 and its portico had **n** openings
41:16 the thresholds and the **n** windows
41:26 **n** windows with palm trees carved on
Mt 7:13 "Enter through the **n** gate. For wide
7:14 small is the gate and **n** the road
Lk 13:24 effort to enter through the **n** door,

Narrower (Narrow)

Eze 42: 5 Now the upper rooms were **n**, for the

Nathan

1. Prophet; announced God's promise to David of lasting dynasty (2Sa 7:1–17; 1Ch 17:1–15); rebuked David's sin with Bathsheba (2Sa 12:1–14). Supported Solomon's succession (1Ki 1:8–40). Chronicled reigns of David and Solomon (1Ch 29:29; 2Ch 9:29) **2.** Son of David (2Sa 5:14; Zec 12:12); included in Jesus' genealogy (Lk 3:31).

2Sa 5:14 there: Shammua, Shobab, **N**, Solomon,
7: 2 he said to **N** the prophet, "Here I am,
7: 3 **N** replied to the king, "Whatever you
7: 4 word of the LORD came to **N**, saying:
7:17 **N** reported to David all the words of
12: 1 The LORD sent **N** to David. When he
12: 5 anger against the man and said to **N**,
12: 7 **N** said to David, "You are the man!
12:13 David said to **N**, "I have sinned
12:13 **N** replied, "The LORD has taken away
12:15 After **N** had gone home, the LORD
12:25 **N** the prophet to name him Jedidiah.
23:36 Igal son of **N** from Zobah, the son of
1Ki 1: 8 son of Jehoiada, **N** the prophet
1:10 he did not invite **N** the prophet or
1:11 **N** asked Bathsheba, Solomon's mother,
1:22 the king, **N** the prophet arrived.
1:23 they told the king, "**N** the prophet
1:24 **N** said, "Have you, my lord the king,
1:32 Zadok the priest, **N** the prophet
1:34 the priest and **N** the prophet anoint
1:38 Zadok the priest, **N** the prophet,
1:44 **N** the prophet, Benaiah son of
1:45 Zadok the priest and **N** the prophet
4: 5 Azariah son of **N**—in charge of the
4: 5 Zabud son of **N**—a priest and
1Ch 2:36 Attai was the father of **N**, **N** the
3: 5 Shammua, Shobab, **N** and Solomon.
11:38 Joel the brother of **N**, Mibhar son of
14: 4 there: Shammua, Shobab, **N**, Solomon,
17: 1 he said to **N** the prophet, "Here I am,
17: 2 **N** replied to David, "Whatever you
17: 3 That night the word of God came to **N**,
17:15 **N** reported to David all the words of
29:29 the records of **N** the prophet and the
2Ch 9:29 in the records of **N** the prophet,
29:25 the king's seer and **N** the prophet;
Ezr 8:16 Elnathan, **N**, Zechariah and
10:39 Shelemiah, **N**, Adaiah,
Ps 51: T prophet **N** came to him after David
Zec 12:12 of the house of **N** and their wives,
Lk 3:31 the son of **N**, the son of David,

Nathanael

Apostle from Cana in Galilee; brought to Jesus by Philip (Jn 1:45–51; 21:2). Possibly to be identified with Bartholomew, who is also linked with Philip (Mt 10:3).

Jn 1:45 Philip found **N** and told him, "We
1:46 good come from there?" **N** asked.
1:47 Jesus saw **N** approaching, he said of
1:48 "How do you know me?" **N** asked. Jesus
1:49 **N** declared, "Rabbi, you are the Son
21: 2 Thomas (called Didymus), **N** from Cana

Nathan-Melech

2Ki 23:11 the room of an official named **N**.

Nation (National, Nationalities, Nationality, Nations, Nations', *Whole nation*)

Ge 12: 2 "I will make you into a great **n** and
15:14 I will punish the **n** they serve as
17:20 and I will make him into a great **n**.
18:18 become a great and powerful **n**,
20: 4 Lord, will you destroy an innocent **n**?
21:13 into a **n** also, because he is your
21:18 for I will make him into a great **n**."
35:11 A **n** and a community of nations will
46: 3 I will make you into a great **n** there.
Ex 9:24 of Egypt since it had become a **n**.
19: 6 a kingdom of priests and a holy **n**.
23:27 confusion every **n** you encounter.

Ex 32:10 Then I will make you into a great **n**."
33:13 Remember that this **n** is your people."
34:10 done in any **n** in all the world.
Nu 14:12 a **n** greater and stronger than they."
Dt 4: 6 "Surely this great **n** is a wise and
4: 7 What other **n** is so great as to have
4: 8 what other **n** is so great as to have
4:34 for himself one **n** out of another **n**,
9:14 And I will make you into a **n**
26: 5 a great **n**, powerful and numerous.
28:32 will be given to another **n**,
28:36 a **n** unknown to you or your fathers.
28:49 The LORD will bring a **n** against you
28:49 a **n** whose language you will not
28:50 a fierce-looking **n** without respect
32:21 by a **n** that has no understanding.
32:28 They are a **n** without sense, there is
Jos 10:13 and the moon stopped, till the **n**
Jdg 2:20 "Because this **n** has violated the
2Sa 7:23 the one **n** on earth that God went out
1Ki 5: 7 wise son to rule over this great **n**."
18:10 there is not a **n** or kingdom where my
18:10 And whenever a **n** or kingdom claimed
2Ki 18:33 Has the god of any **n** ever delivered
1Ch 16:20 they wandered from **n** to **n**, from one
17:21 the one **n** on earth whose God went
2Ch 15: 6 One **n** was being crushed by another
32:15 for no god of any **n** or kingdom has
Job 34:29 him? Yet he is over man and **n** alike,
Ps 33:12 Blessed is the **n** whose God is the
43: 1 plead my cause against an ungodly **n**;
83: 4 "let us destroy them as a **n**, that
105:13 they wandered from **n** to **n**, from one
106: 5 I may share in the joy of your **n**
147:20 He has done this for no other **n**;
Pr 11:14 For lack of guidance a **n** falls, but
14:34 Righteousness exalts a **n**, but sin is
Isa 1: 4 Ah, sinful **n**, a people loaded with
2: 4 **N** will not take up sword against **n**
9: 3 You have enlarged the **n** and
10: 6 I send him against a godless **n**, I
14:32 to the envoys of that **n**?
18: 2 an aggressive **n** of strange speech,
18: 7 an aggressive **n** of strange speech,
26: 2 righteous **n** may enter, the **n** that
26:15 You have enlarged the **n**, O LORD; you
26:15 **n**, O LORD; you have enlarged the **n**.
30: 6 of camels, to that unprofitable **n**,
36:18 Has the god of any **n** ever delivered
49: 7 was despised and abhorred by the **n**,
51: 4 my people; hear me, my **n**: The law
58: 2 as if they were a **n** that does what
60:12 For the **n** or kingdom that will not
60:22 a thousand, the smallest a mighty **n**.
65: 1 To a **n** that did not call on my name,
66: 8 or a **n** be brought forth in a moment?
Jer 2:11 Has a **n** ever changed its gods? (Yet
3:19 most beautiful inheritance of any **n**.
5: 9 avenge myself on such a **n** as this?
5:15 "I am bringing a distant **n** against
5:15 you—an ancient and enduring **n**,
5:29 avenge myself on such a **n** as this?
6:22 a great **n** is being stirred up from
7:28 'This is the **n** that has not obeyed
8: 3 all the survivors of this evil **n**
9: 9 avenge myself on such a **n** as this?"
12:17 if any **n** does not listen, I will
18: 7 If at any time I announce that a **n**
18: 8 if that **n** I warned repents of its
18: 9 a **n** or kingdom is to be built up
19:11 I will smash this **n** and this city
25:12 the king of Babylon and his **n**,
25:32 Disaster is spreading from **n** to **n**;
27: 8 If, however, any **n** or kingdom will
27: 8 I will punish that **n** with the sword,
27:11 if any **n** will bow its neck under the
27:11 I will let that **n** remain in its own
27:13 LORD has threatened any **n** that
28:15 persuaded this **n** to trust in lies.
31:36 ever cease to be a **n** before me."
33:24 and no longer regard them as a **n**.
48: 2 'Come, let us put an end to that **n**.
48:42 Moab will be destroyed as a **n**
49:31 "Arise and attack a **n** at ease, which
49:31 "a **n** that has neither gates nor bars;
49:36 a **n** where Elam's exiles do not go.
Jer 50: 3 A **n** from the north will attack her
50:41 a great **n** and many kings are being
Lam 4:17 for a **n** that could not save us.
Eze 2: 3 to a rebellious **n** that has rebelled
36:13 and deprive your **n** of its children,"
36:14 devour men or make your **n** childless,
36:15 the peoples or cause your **n** to fall,
37:22 I will make them one **n** in the land,
Da 3:29 I decree that the people of any **n**
8:22 will emerge from his **n** but will
Joel 1: 6 A **n** has invaded my land, powerful
3: 8 them to the Sabeans, a **n** far away.
Am 6: 1 men of the foremost **n**, to whom
6:14 "I will stir up a **n** against you,
Mic 4: 3 **N** will not take up sword against **n**
4: 7 those driven away a strong **n**.
Hab 3:16 to come on the **n** invading us.
Zep 2: 1 gather together, O shameful **n**,
2: 9 survivors of my **n** will inherit
Hag 2:14 this **n** in my sight,' declares the
Mt 24: 7 **N** will rise against **n**, and kingdom
Mk 13: 8 **N** will rise against **n**, and kingdom
Lk 7: 5 he loves our **n** and has built our
21:10 **N** will rise against **n**, and kingdom
23: 2 found this man subverting our **n**.
Jn 11:48 take away both our place and our **n**."
11:51 Jesus would die for the Jewish **n**,
11:52 not only for that **n** but also for the
Ac 2: 5 Jews from every **n** under heaven.
7: 7 I will punish the **n** they serve as
10:35 accepts men from every **n** who fear
17:26 From one man he made every **n** of men,
24: 2 has brought about reforms in this **n**.
24:10 you have been a judge over this **n**;
Ro 10:19 envious by those who are not a **n**;
10:19 by a **n** that has no understanding."
1Pe 2: 9 a royal priesthood, a holy **n**, a
Rev 5: 9 tribe and language and people and **n**.
7: 9 from every **n**, tribe, people and
11: 9 tribe, language and **n** will gaze on
13: 7 every tribe, people, language and **n**.
14: 6 every **n**, tribe, language and people.

National (Nation)

2Ki 17:29 Nevertheless, each **n** group made its

Nationalities (Nation)

Est 8:17 And many people of other **n** became
9: 2 all the other **n** were afraid of them.

Nationality (Nation)

Est 2:10 Esther had not revealed her **n** and
2:20 **n** just as Mordecai had told her to
3:14 made known to the people of every **n**
8:11 annihilate any armed force of any **n**
8:13 made known to the people of every **n**

Nations (*All nations*, Nation)

Ge 10: 5 by their clans within their **n**,
10:20 in their territories and **n**.
10:31 in their territories and **n**.
10:32 lines of descent, within their **n**.
10:32 From these the **n** spread out over the
17: 4 You will be the father of many **n**.
17: 5 I have made you a father of many **n**.
17: 6 very fruitful; I will make **n** of you,
17:16 so that she will be the mother of **n**;
25:23 to her, "Two **n** are in in your womb
27:29 May **n** serve you and peoples bow down
35:11 A nation and a community of **n** will
48:19 will become a group of **n**."
49:10 and the obedience of the **n** is his.
Ex 15:14 The **n** will hear and tremble; anguish
34:24 I will drive out **n** before you and
Lev 18:24 because this is how the **n** that I am
18:28 out the **n** that were before you.
20:23 **n** I am going to drive out before you.
20:24 who has set you apart from the **n**.
20:26 you apart from the **n** to be my own.
25:44 are to come from the **n** around you;
26:33 I will scatter you among the **n** and
26:38 You will perish among the **n**; the
26:45 the sight of the **n** to be their God.
Nu 14:15 the **n** who have heard this report
Nu 23: 9 consider themselves one of the **n**.
24: 8 They devour hostile **n** and break
24:20 "Amalek was first among the **n**, but
Dt 2:25 of you on all the **n** under heaven.
4: 6 wisdom and understanding to the **n**,
4:19 to all the **n** under heaven.
4:27 **n** to which the LORD will drive you.
4:38 to drive out before you **n** greater
7: 1 out before you many **n**—the Hittites,
7: 1 seven **n** larger and stronger than
7:17 You may say to yourselves, "These **n**
7:22 **n** before you, little by little.
8:20 Like the **n** the LORD destroyed before
9: 1 dispossess **n** greater and stronger
9: 4 the wickedness of these **n**
9: 5 of the wickedness of these **n**,
10:15 above all the **n**, as it is today.
11:23 the LORD will drive out all these **n**
11:23 **n** larger and stronger than you.
12: 2 the **n** you are dispossessing worship
12:29 you the **n** you are about to invade
12:30 "How do these **n** serve their gods? We
15: 6 to many **n** but will borrow from none.
15: 6 many **n** but none will rule over you.
17:14 over us like all the **n** around us,"
18: 9 the detestable ways of the **n** there.
18:12 will drive out those **n** before you.
18:14 The **n** you will dispossess listen to
19: 1 the LORD your God has destroyed the **n**
20:15 and do not belong to the **n** nearby.
20:16 However, in the cities of the **n** the
26:19 honour high above all the **n** he has
28: 1 you high above all the **n** on earth.
28:12 to many **n** but will borrow from none.
28:37 the **n** where the LORD will drive you.
28:65 Among those **n** you will find no
29:18 go and worship the gods of those **n**;
29:24 All the **n** will ask: "Why has the
30: 1 your God disperses you among the **n**,
30: 3 all the **n** where he scattered you.
31: 3 He will destroy these **n** before you,
32: 8 the Most High gave the **n** their
32:43 Rejoice, O **n**, with his people, for
33:17 With them he will gore the **n**, even
Jos 23: 3 done to all these **n** for your sake;
23: 4 all the land of the **n** that remain
23: 4 **n** I conquered—between the Jordan
23: 7 Do not associate with these **n** that
23: 9 out before you great and powerful **n**;
23:12 of these **n** that remain among you
23:13 longer drive out these **n** before you.
24:17 the **n** through which we travelled.
24:18 LORD drove out before us all the **n**,
Jdg 2:21 of the **n** Joshua left when he died.
2:23 The LORD had allowed those **n** to
3: 1 These are the **n** the LORD left to
1Sa 8: 5 us, such as all the other **n** have."
8:20 we shall be like all the other **n**,
2Sa 7:23 awesome wonders by driving out **n** and
8:11 gold from all the **n** he had subdued:
22:44 have preserved me as the head of **n**.
22:48 avenges me, who puts the **n** under me,
22:50 among the **n**; I will sing praises to
1Ki 4:31 spread to all the surrounding **n**.
8:53 singled them out from all the **n** of
11: 2 They were from **n** about which the
14:24 the detestable practices of the **n**
2Ki 16: 3 the detestable ways of the **n** the
17: 8 followed the practices of the **n** the
17:11 as the **n** whom the LORD had driven
17:15 They imitated the **n** around them
17:33 the customs of the **n** from which
19:12 Did the gods of the **n** that were
19:17 laid waste these **n** and their lands.
21: 2 the detestable practices of the **n**
21: 9 more evil than the **n** the LORD had
1Ch 14:17 the LORD made all the **n** fear him.
16: 8 known among the **n** what he has done.
16:24 Declare his glory among the **n**, his
16:26 For all the gods of the **n** are idols,
16:28 Ascribe to the LORD, O families of **n**,
16:31 be glad; let them say among the **n**,
16:35 gather us and deliver us from the **n**,
17:21 driving out **n** from before your
18:11 from all these **n**: Edom and Moab,
22: 5 splendour in the sight of all the **n**.

2Ch 20: 6 rule over all the kingdoms of the **n**
28: 3 the detestable ways of the **n** that
32:13 Were the gods of those **n** ever able
32:14 Who of all the gods of these **n** that
32:23 he was highly regarded by all the **n**.
33: 2 detestable practices of the **n** the
33: 9 did more evil than the **n** the LORD
36:14 the detestable practices of the **n**
Ne 1: 8 I will scatter you among the **n**,
5:17 came to us from the surrounding **n**.
6: 6 "It is reported among the **n**—and
6:16 all the surrounding **n** were afraid
9:22 "You gave them kingdoms and **n**,
13:26 many **n** there was no king like him.
Job 12:23 He makes **n** great, and destroys them;
12:23 he enlarges **n**, and disperses them.
36:31 This is the way he governs the **n** and
Ps 2: 1 Why do the **n** conspire and the
2: 8 Ask of me, and I will make the **n**
9: 5 You have rebuked the **n** and destroyed
9:11 among the **n** what he has done.
9:15 The **n** have fallen into the pit they
9:17 grave, all the **n** that forget God.
9:19 the **n** be judged in your presence.
9:20 let the **n** know they are but men.
10:16 the **n** will perish from his land.
18:43 you have made me the head of **n**;
18:47 avenges me, who subdues **n** under me,
18:49 I will praise you among the **n**,
22:27 families of the **n** will bow down
22:28 to the LORD and he rules over the **n**.
33:10 The LORD foils the plans of the **n**;
44: 2 With your hand you drove out the **n**
44:11 and have scattered us among the **n**.
44:14 You have made us a byword among the **n**
45: 5 let the **n** fall beneath your feet.
45:17 **n** will praise you for ever and ever.
46: 6 **N** are in uproar, kingdoms fall; he
46:10 I will be exalted among the **n**,
47: 1 Clap your hands, all you **n**; shout to
47: 3 He subdued **n** under us, peoples under
47: 8 God reigns over the **n**; God is seated
47: 9 The nobles of the **n** assemble as the
56: 7 your anger, O God, bring down the **n**.
57: 9 O Lord, among the **n**; I will sing of
59: 5 punish all the **n**; show no mercy
59: 8 at them; you scoff at all those **n**.
65: 7 waves, and the turmoil of the **n**.
66: 7 his eyes watch the **n**—let not the
67: 4 May the **n** be glad and sing for joy,
67: 4 justly and guide the **n** of the earth.
68:30 of bulls among the calves of the **n**.
68:30 Scatter the **n** who delight in war.
78:55 He drove out **n** before them and
79: 1 O God, the **n** have invaded your
79: 6 Pour out your wrath on the **n** that do
79:10 Why should the **n** say, "Where is
79:10 make known among the **n** that you
80: 8 you drove out the **n** and planted it.
82: 8 for all the **n** are your inheritance.
86: 9 All the **n** you have made will come
89:50 in my heart the taunts of all the **n**,
94:10 Does he who disciplines **n** not punish?
96: 3 Declare his glory among the **n**, his
96: 5 For all the gods of the **n** are idols,
96: 7 Ascribe to the LORD, O families of **n**,
96:10 Say among the **n**, "The LORD reigns."
98: 2 revealed his righteousness to the **n**.
99: 1 The LORD reigns, let the **n** tremble;
99: 2 Zion; he is exalted over all the **n**.
102:15 The **n** will fear the name of the LORD,
105: 1 known among the **n** what he has done.
105:44 he gave them the lands of the **n**, and
106:27 their descendants fall among the **n**
106:35 they mingled with the **n** and adopted
106:41 He handed them over to the **n**, and
106:47 and gather us from the **n**, that we
108: 3 O LORD, among the **n**; I will sing of
110: 6 He will judge **n**, heaping up the dead
111: 6 giving them the lands of other **n**.
113: 4 The LORD is exalted over all the **n**,
115: 2 Why do the **n** say, "Where is their
117: 1 Praise the LORD, all you **n**; extol
118:10 All the **n** surrounded me, but in the
126: 2 Then it was said among the **n**, "The
135:10 He struck down many **n** and killed
Ps 135:15 The idols of the **n** are silver and
149: 7 to inflict vengeance on the **n** and
Pr 24:24 will curse him and **n** denounce him.
Isa 2: 4 He will judge between the **n** and will
5:26 lifts up a banner for the distant **n**,
8: 9 Raise the war cry, you **n**, and be
10: 7 to destroy, to put an end to many **n**.
10:13 I removed the boundaries of **n**, I
10:14 reached for the wealth of the **n**;
11:10 peoples; the **n** will rally to him,
11:12 He will raise a banner for the **n** and
12: 4 known among the **n** what he has done,
13: 4 like **n** massing together! The LORD
14: 2 **N** will take them and bring them to
14: 2 will possess the **n** as menservants
14: 6 in fury subdued **n** with relentless
14: 9 all those who were kings over the **n**.
14:12 earth, you who once laid low the **n**!
14:18 All the kings of the **n** lie in state,
16: 8 The rulers of the **n** have trampled
17:12 Oh, the raging of many **n**—they rage
23: 3 became the market-place of the **n**.
24:13 it be on the earth and among the **n**,
25: 3 of ruthless **n** will revere you.
29: 7 the hordes of all the **n** that fight
29: 8 the **n** that fight against Mount Zion.
30:28 He shakes the **n** in the sieve of
33: 3 when you rise up, the **n** scatter.
33: 4 Your plunder, O **n**, is harvested as
34: 1 Come near, you **n**, and listen; pay
37:12 Did the gods of the **n** that were
40:15 Surely the **n** are like a drop in a
40:17 Before him all the **n** are as nothing;
41: 1 Let the **n** renew their strength!
41: 2 He hands **n** over to him and subdues
42: 1 and he will bring justice to the **n**.
43: 9 All the **n** gather together and the
45: 1 take hold of to subdue **n** before him
45:20 assemble, you fugitives from the **n**.
49: 1 hear this, you distant **n**: Before I
51: 4 will become a light to the **n**.
51: 5 my arm will bring justice to the **n**.
52:10 holy arm in the sight of all the **n**,
52:15 will he sprinkle many **n**, and kings
54: 3 your descendants will dispossess **n**
55: 5 Surely you will summon **n** you know
55: 5 and **n** that do not know you will
60: 3 **N** will come to your light, and kings
60: 5 you the riches of the **n** will come.
60:11 may bring you the wealth of the **n**
60:16 You will drink the milk of **n** and be
61: 6 You will feed on the wealth of **n**,
61: 9 will be known among the **n**
62: 2 The **n** will see your righteousness,
62:10 Raise a banner for the **n**.
63: 3 from the **n** no-one was with me.
63: 6 I trampled the **n** in my anger; in my
64: 2 and cause the **n** to quake before you!
66:12 and the wealth of **n** like a flooding
66:19 who survive to the **n**—to Tarshish,
66:19 will proclaim my glory among the **n**.
66:20 from all the **n**, to my holy mountain
Jer 1: 5 you as a prophet to the **n**."
1:10 See, today I appoint you over **n** and
4: 2 then the **n** will be blessed by him
4: 7 lair; a destroyer of **n** has set out.
4:16 "Tell this to the **n**, proclaim it to
6:18 Therefore hear, O **n**; observe, O
9:16 I will scatter them among **n** that
9:26 For all these **n** are really
10: 2 "Do not learn the ways of the **n** or
10: 2 though the **n** are terrified by them.
10: 7 O King of the **n**? This is your due.
10: 7 Among all the wise men of the **n** and
10:10 the **n** cannot endure his wrath.
10:25 Pour out your wrath on the **n** that do
14:22 worthless idols of the **n** bring rain?
16:19 to you the **n** will come from the ends
18:13 "Enquire among the **n**: Who has ever
22: 8 "People from many **n** will pass by
25: 9 and against all the surrounding **n**.
25:11 and these **n** will serve the king of
25:13 by Jeremiah against all the **n**.
25:14 enslaved by many **n** and great kings;
25:15 the **n** to whom I send you drink it.
25:17 the **n** to whom he sent me drink it:
Jer 25:31 will bring charges against the **n**;
26: 6 among all the **n** of the earth.
27: 7 **n** and great kings will subjugate him.
28:11 neck of all the **n** within two years.
28:14 yoke on the necks of all these **n**
29:14 I will gather you from all the **n** and
29:18 among all the **n** where I drive them.
30:11 all the **n** among which I scatter you,
31: 7 shout for the foremost of the **n**.
31:10 "Hear the word of the LORD, O **n**;
36: 2 Judah and all the other **n** from the
43: 5 the **n** where they had been scattered.
44: 8 reproach among all the **n** on earth.
46: 1 the prophet concerning the **n**:
46:12 The **n** will hear of your shame; your
46:28 all the **n** among which I scatter you,
49:14 An envoy was sent to the **n** to say,
49:15 among the **n**, despised among men.
50: 2 "Announce and proclaim among the **n**,
50: 9 great **n** from the land of the north.
50:12 She will be the least of the **n**—a
50:23 How desolate is Babylon among the **n**!
50:46 its cry will resound among the **n**.
51: 7 The **n** drank her wine; therefore they
51:20 with you I shatter **n**, with you I
51:27 Blow the trumpet among the **n**!
51:27 Prepare the **n** for battle against her;
51:28 Prepare the **n** for battle against her
51:41 horror Babylon will be among the **n**!
51:44 The **n** will no longer stream to him.
Lam 1: 1 who once was great among the **n**! She
1: 3 She dwells among the **n**; she finds no
1:10 she saw pagan **n** enter her sanctuary—
2: 9 her princes are exiled among the **n**,
3:45 made us scum and refuse among the **n**.
4:15 **n** say, "They can stay here no longer.
4:20 shadow we would live among the **n**.
Eze 4:13 the **n** where I will drive them."
5: 5 set in the centre of the **n**, with
5: 6 than the **n** and countries around her.
5: 7 more unruly than the **n** around you
5: 7 the standards of the **n** around you.
5: 8 on you in the sight of the **n**.
5:14 a reproach among the **n** around you,
5:15 an object of horror to the **n** around
6: 8 are scattered among the lands and **n**.
6: 9 in the **n** where they have been
7:24 I will bring the most wicked of the **n**
11:12 the standards of the **n** around you."
11:16 I sent them far away among the **n**
11:17 I will gather you from the **n** and
12:15 when I disperse them among the **n** and
12:16 famine and plague, so that in the **n**
16:14 your fame spread among the **n** on
19: 4 The **n** heard about him, and he was
19: 8 the **n** came against him, those from
20: 9 the eyes of the **n** they lived among
20:14 profaned in the eyes of the **n** in
20:22 profaned in the eyes of the **n** in
20:23 I would disperse them among the **n**
20:32 You say, "We want to be like the **n**
20:34 I will bring you from the **n** and
20:35 into the desert of the **n** and there,
20:41 when I bring you out from the **n**
20:41 among you in the sight of the **n**.
22: 4 you an object of scorn to the **n**
22:15 I will disperse you among the **n** and
22:16 been defiled in the eyes of the **n**,
23:30 because you lusted after the **n** and
25: 7 and give you as plunder to the **n**.
25: 7 I will cut you off from the **n** and
25: 8 has become like all the other **n**,"
25:10 will not be remembered among the **n**;
26: 2 'Aha! The gate to the **n** is broken,
26: 3 I will bring many **n** against you,
26: 5 She will become plunder for the **n**,
27:33 you satisfied many **n**; with your
27:36 The merchants among the **n** hiss at
28: 7 the most ruthless of **n**; they will
28:19 All the **n** who knew you are appalled
28:25 **n** where they have been scattered,
28:25 among them in the sight of the **n**.
29:12 disperse the Egyptians among the **n**
29:13 the **n** where they were scattered.
29:15 exalt itself above the other **n**.
29:15 it will never again rule over the **n**.

Eze 30: 3 of clouds, a time of doom for the **n**.
30:11 his army—the most ruthless of **n**—
30:23 disperse the Egyptians among the **n**
30:26 disperse the Egyptians among the **n**
31: 6 all the great **n** lived in its shade.
31:11 it over to the ruler of the **n**,
31:12 the most ruthless of foreign **n** cut
31:12 All the **n** of the earth came out from
31:16 I made the **n** tremble at the sound of
31:17 its allies among the **n**, had also
32: 2 'You are like a lion among the **n**;
32: 9 your destruction among the **n**, among
32:16 The daughters of the **n** will chant it;
32:18 mighty **n**, with those who go down to
34:13 I will bring them out from the **n** and
34:28 no longer be plundered by the **n**,
34:29 the land or bear the scorn of the **n**.
35:10 'Because you have said, "These two **n**
36: 3 the possession of the rest of the **n**
36: 4 by the rest of the **n** around you—
36: 5 spoken against the rest of the **n**,
36: 6 have suffered the scorn of the **n**.
36: 7 **n** around you will also suffer scorn.
36:15 I make you hear the taunts of the **n**,
36:19 I dispersed them among the **n**, and
36:20 wherever they went among the **n** they
36:21 among the **n** where they had gone.
36:22 among the **n** where you have gone.
36:23 which has been profaned among the **n**,
36:23 Then the **n** will know that I am the
36:24 For I will take you out of the **n**;
36:30 among the **n** because of famine.
36:36 the **n** around you that remain will
37:21 out of the **n** where they have gone.
37:22 never again be two **n** or be divided
37:28 the **n** will know that I the LORD make
38: 6 all its troops—the many **n** with you.
38: 8 many **n** to the mountains of Israel,
38: 8 They had been brought out from the **n**,
38: 9 and the many **n** with you will go up,
38:12 and the people gathered from the **n**,
38:15 you and many **n** with you, all of them
38:16 so that the **n** may know me when I
38:22 troops and on the many **n** with him.
38:23 myself known in the sight of many **n**.
39: 4 all your troops and the **n** with you.
39: 7 and the **n** will know that I the LORD
39:21 "I will display my glory among the **n**,
39:21 and all the **n** will see the
39:23 the **n** will know that the people of
39:27 I have brought them back from the **n**
39:27 through them in the sight of many **n**.
39:28 I sent them into exile among the **n**,
Da 3: 4 **n** and men of every language:
3: 7 all the peoples, **n** and men of every
4: 1 To the peoples, **n** and men of every
5:19 all the peoples and **n** and men of
6:25 **n** and men of every language
7:14 **n** and men of every language
12: 1 from the beginning of **n** until then.
Hos 7: 8 "Ephraim mixes with the **n**; Ephraim
8: 8 among the **n** like a worthless thing.
8:10 have sold themselves among the **n**, I
9: 1 do not be jubilant like the other **n**.
9:17 they will be wanderers among the **n**.
10:10 punish them; **n** will be gathered
Joel 2: 6 the sight of them, **n** are in anguish
2:17 of scorn, a byword among the **n**.
2:19 you an object of scorn to the **n**.
3: 2 among the **n** and divided up my land.
3: 9 Proclaim this among the **n**: Prepare
3:11 Come quickly, all you **n** from every
3:12 "Let the **n** be roused; let them
3:12 to judge all the **n** on every side.
Am 9: 9 the **n** as grain is shaken in a sieve,
9:12 and all the **n** that bear my name,"
Ob :1 An envoy was sent to the **n** to say,
:2 make you small among the **n**; you
:16 so all the **n** will drink continually;
Mic 4: 2 Many **n** will come and say, "Come, let
4: 3 disputes for strong **n** far and wide.
4: 5 All the **n** may walk in the name of
4:11 now many **n** are gathered against you.
4:13 and you will break to pieces many **n**.
5: 8 of Jacob will be among the **n**,
5:15 upon the **n** that have not obeyed me."
Mic 6:16 you will bear the scorn of the **n**."
7:16 **N** will see and be ashamed, deprived
Na 3: 4 who enslaved **n** by her prostitution
3: 5 I will show the **n** your nakedness and
Hab 1: 5 "Look at the **n** and watch—and be
1:17 his net, destroying **n** without mercy?
2: 5 he gathers to himself all the **n**
2: 8 you have plundered many **n**, the
2:13 **n** exhaust themselves for nothing?
3: 6 he looked, and made the **n** tremble.
3:12 and in anger you threshed the **n**.
Zep 2:11 The **n** on every shore will worship
3: 6 "I have cut off **n**; their strongholds
3: 8 I have decided to assemble the **n**, to
Zec 1:15 I am very angry with the **n** that feel
1:21 throw down these horns of the **n** who
2: 8 has sent me against the **n** that have
2:11 "Many **n** will be joined with the LORD
7:14 the **n**, where they were strangers.
8:13 an object of cursing among the **n**,
8:22 many peoples and powerful **n** will
8:23 **n** will take firm hold of one Jew by
9:10 He will proclaim peace to the **n**. His
11:10 covenant I had made with all the **n**.
12: 3 On that day, when all the **n** of the
12: 3 an immovable rock for all the **n**.
12: 4 I will blind all the horses of the **n**.
12: 9 all the **n** that attack Jerusalem.
14: 2 I will gather all the **n** to Jerusalem
14: 3 against those **n**, as he fights in
14:12 the **n** that fought against Jerusalem:
14:14 The wealth of all the surrounding **n**
14:16 the survivors from all the **n** that
14:18 the plague he inflicts on the **n**
14:19 the punishment of all the **n** that do
Mal 1:11 My name will be great among the **n**,
1:11 will be great among the **n**," says
1:14 my name is to be feared among the **n**.
3:12 "Then all the **n** will call you
Mt 12:18 he will proclaim justice to the **n**.
12:21 In his name the **n** will put their
24:30 all the **n** of the earth will mourn.
25:32 All the **n** will be gathered before
Lk 21:24 be taken as prisoners to all the **n**.
21:25 On the earth, **n** will be in anguish
Ac 4:25 **n** rage and the peoples plot in vain?
7:45 the **n** God drove out before them.
13:19 he overthrew seven **n** in Canaan and
Ro 4:17 "I have made you a father of many **n**.
4:18 and so became the father of many **n**,
15:12 who will arise to rule over the **n**;
1Ti 3:16 was preached among the **n**, was
Jas 1: 1 scattered among the **n**: Greetings.
Rev 2:26 I will give authority over the **n**—
10:11 peoples, **n**, languages and kings."
11:18 The **n** were angry; and your wrath has
12: 5 rule all the **n** with an iron sceptre.
14: 8 which made all the **n** drink the
16:19 and the cities of the **n** collapsed.
17:15 multitudes, **n** and languages.
18: 3 For all the **n** have drunk the
18:23 spell all the **n** were led astray.
19:15 with which to strike down the **n**.
20: 3 to keep him from deceiving the **n** any
20: 8 will go out to deceive the **n** in the
21:24 The **n** will walk by its light, and
21:26 The glory and honour of the **n** will
22: 2 tree are for the healing of the **n**.

Nations' (Nation)

Jer 51:58 the **n** labour is only fuel for the

Native (Natives)

Ge 24: 7 my **n** land and who spoke to me and
31:13 at once and go back to your **n** land.
Nu 22: 5 near the River, in his **n** land.
Ps 37:35 like a green tree in its **n** soil,
Isa 13:14 each will flee to his **n** land.
Jer 22:10 return nor see his **n** land again.
46:16 to our own people and our **n** lands,
Am 7:11 into exile, away from their **n** land.
7:17 into exile, away from their **n** land.
Jn 8:44 he lies, he speaks his **n** language,
Ac 2: 8 us hears them in his own **n** language?
Ac 18: 2 a Jew named Aquila, a **n** of Pontus
18:24 named Apollos, a **n** of Alexandria

Native-born (Bear[1])

Ex 12:19 Israel, whether he is an alien or **n**.
12:49 The same law applies to the **n** and to
Lev 16:29 **n** or an alien living among you—
17:15 "'Anyone, whether **n** or alien, who
18:26 The **n** and the aliens living among
19:34 must be treated as one of your **n**.
23:42 Live in booths for seven days: All **n**
24:16 Whether an alien or **n**, when he
24:22 same law for the alien and the **n**.
Nu 9:14 regulations for the alien and the **n**.
15:13 "'Everyone who is **n** must do these
15:29 he is a **n** Israelite or an alien.
15:30 whether **n** or alien, blasphemes the
1Ch 7:21 were killed by the **n** men of Gath,
Eze 47:22 You are to consider them as **n**

Natives (Native)

Eze 23:15 chariot officers, **n** of Chaldea.

Natural (Nature)

Nu 16:29 If these men die a **n** death and
19:16 or someone who has died a **n** death,
19:18 or someone who has died a **n** death.
Jn 1:13 children born not of **n** descent, nor
11:13 disciples thought he meant **n** sleep.
Ro 1:26 **n** relations for unnatural ones.
1:27 abandoned **n** relations with women
6:19 you are weak in your **n** selves.
9: 8 it is not the **n** children who are
11:21 God did not spare the **n** branches
11:24 the **n** branches, be grafted into
1Co 15:44 is sown a **n** body, it is raised a
15:44 If there is a **n** body, there is also
15:46 the **n**, and after that the spiritual.
Jude :19 who follow mere **n** instincts and do

Nature (Natural, *Sinful nature*)

Ro 1: 3 human **n** was a descendant of David,
1:20 divine **n**—have been clearly seen,
2:14 who do not have the law, do by **n**
8: 5 minds set on what that **n** desires;
11:24 of an olive tree that is wild by **n**,
11:24 and contrary to **n** were grafted into
1Co 11:14 Does not the very **n** of things teach
Gal 4: 8 to those who by **n** are not gods.
5:24 **n** with its passions and desires.
6: 8 from that **n** will reap destruction;
Eph 2: 3 rest, we were by **n** objects of wrath.
Php 2: 6 Who, being in very **n** God, did not
2: 7 taking the very **n** of a servant,
Col 3: 5 whatever belongs to your earthly **n**:
Heb 6:17 God wanted to make the unchanging **n**
2Pe 1: 4 you may participate in the divine **n**
2:18 lustful desires of sinful human **n**,

Navel

SS 7: 2 Your **n** is a rounded goblet that

Nazarene (Nazareth)

Mt 2:23 prophets: "He will be called a **N**.
Mk 14:67 "You also were with that **N**, Jesus,"
16: 6 "You are looking for Jesus the **N**,
Ac 24: 5 He is a ringleader of the **N** sect

Nazareth (*Jesus of Nazareth*, Nazarene)

Town in Galilee between Sea of Galilee and Mediterranean. Home of Mary and Joseph (Lk 1:26; 2:4, 39); home of Jesus (Mt 2:23; 21:11; Lk 2:51), which he left to begin his preaching (Mt 4:13–17; Mk 1:9). Jesus returned here (Lk 4:16) but was rejected (Lk 4:29). He was often called Jesus of Nazareth (Mt 26:71; Mk 1:24; 10:47; Lk 4:34; 18:37; 24:19; Jn 1:45; 18:5, 7; 19:19; Ac 2:22; 3:6; 4:10; 6:14; 10:38; 22:8; 26:9) or the Nazarene (Mt 2:23; Mk 14:67; 16:6). The town had a poor reputation (Jn 1:46).

Mt 2:23 he went and lived in a town called **N**.
4:13 Leaving **N**, he went and lived in

Mt 21:11 the prophet from N in Galilee."
Mk 1: 9 At that time Jesus came from N in
Lk 1:26 Gabriel to N, a town in Galilee,
2: 4 the town of N in Galilee to Judea,
2:39 to Galilee to their own town of N.
2:51 he went down to N with them and was
4:16 He went to N, where he had been
Jn 1:46 "N! Can anything good come from
Ac 3: 6 name of Jesus Christ of N, walk."
4:10 is by the name of Jesus Christ of N,

Nazirite (Nazirites)

Nu 6: 2 of separation to the LORD as a N,
6: 4 long as he is a N, he must not eat
6:13 "'Now this is the law for the N
6:18 the N must shave off the hair that
6:19 "'After the N has shaved off the
6:20 After that, the N may drink wine.
6:21 "'This is the law of the N who vows
6:21 made, according to the law of the N.
Jdg 13: 5 because the boy is to be a N, set
13: 7 because the boy will be a N of God
16:17 a N set apart to God since birth.

Nazirites (Nazirite)

Am 2:11 and N from among your young men.
2:12 "But you made the N drink wine and

Neah

Jos 19:13 out at Rimmon and turned towards N.

Neapolis

Ac 16:11 Samothrace, and the next day on to N.

Neariah

1Ch 3:22 Bariah, N and Shaphat–six in all.
3:23 The sons of N: Elioenai, Hizkiah and
4:42 led by Pelatiah, N, Rephaiah and

Nebai

Ne 10:19 Hariph, Anathoth, N,

Nebaioth

Ge 25:13 birth: N the firstborn of Ishmael,
28: 9 the sister of N and daughter of
36: 3 daughter of Ishmael and sister of N.
1Ch 1:29 their descendants: N the firstborn
Isa 60: 7 the rams of N will serve you; they

Neballat

Ne 11:34 in Hadid, Zeboim and N,

Nebat

1Ki 11:26 Also, Jeroboam son of N rebelled
12: 2 Jeroboam son of N heard this (he was
12:15 spoken to Jeroboam son of N through
15: 1 the reign of Jeroboam son of N,
16: 3 like that of Jeroboam son of N.
16:26 of Jeroboam son of N and in his sin,
16:31 the sins of Jeroboam son of N,
21:22 like that of Jeroboam son of N and
22:52 son of N, who caused Israel to sin.
2Ki 3: 3 to the sins of Jeroboam son of N,
9: 9 like the house of Jeroboam son of N
10:29 from the sins of Jeroboam son of N,
13: 2 the sins of Jeroboam son of N,
13:11 of the sins of Jeroboam son of N,
14:24 of the sins of Jeroboam son of N,
15: 9 from the sins of Jeroboam son of N,
15:18 from the sins of Jeroboam son of N,
15:24 from the sins of Jeroboam son of N,
15:28 from the sins of Jeroboam son of N,
17:21 made Jeroboam son of N their king.
23:15 place made by Jeroboam son of N,
2Ch 9:29 seer concerning Jeroboam son of N?
10: 2 Jeroboam son of N heard this (he was
10:15 spoken to Jeroboam son of N through
13: 6 Yet Jeroboam son of N, an official

Nebo

1. Mountain of the Abarim Range in Moab (Nu 33:47). Here Moses viewed the promised land then died (Dt 32:49–50; 34:1–6). **2.** Town in Moab allotted to and rebuilt by tribe of Reuben (Nu 32:3, 37–38; 1Ch 5:8). Named by the prophets in their laments (Isa 15:2; 46:1; Jer 48:1,22). **3.** Possibly a town in Judah whose inhabitants returned from exile (Ezr 2:29). Called by Nehemiah "the other Nebo" (Ne 7:33).

Nu 32: 3 Heshbon, Elealeh, Sebam, N and Beon—
32:38 well as N and Baal Meon (these names
33:47 in the mountains of Abarim, near N.
Dt 32:49 the Abarim Range to Mount N in Moab,
34: 1 Moses climbed Mount N from the
1Ch 5: 8 area from Aroer to N and Baal Meon.
Ezr 2:29 of N 52
10:43 From the descendants of N: Jeiel,
Ne 7:33 of the other N 52
Isa 15: 2 weep; Moab wails over N and Medeba.
46: 1 Bel bows down, N stoops low; their
Jer 48: 1 "Woe to N, for it will be ruined.
48:22 to Dibon, N and Beth Diblathaim,

Nebo-Sarsekim

Jer 39: 3 N a chief officer, Nergal-Sharezer a

Nebuchadnezzar (Nebuchadnezzar's)

King of Babylon. Defeated Egyptians at Carchemish (Jer 46:2); invaded and subdued Judah; took exiles to Babylon; destroyed Jerusalem (2Ki 24–25; 2Ch 36; Jer 39; Da 1:1–5). Dreams interpreted by Daniel (Da 2; 4); fiery furnace (Da 3); madness and restoration; worshipped God (Da 3:28–29; 4:34–35).

2Ki 24: 1 During Jehoiakim's reign, N king of
24: 1 his mind and rebelled against N.
24:10 At that time the officers of N king
24:11 N himself came up to the city while
24:13 N removed all the treasures from
24:15 N took Jehoiachin captive to Babylon.
25: 1 N king of Babylon marched against
25: 8 in the nineteenth year of N king of
25:22 N king of Babylon appointed Gedaliah
1Ch 6:15 into exile by the hand of N.
2Ch 36: 6 N king of Babylon attacked him and
36: 7 N also took to Babylon articles from
36:10 In the spring, King N sent for him
36:13 He also rebelled against King N, who
36:17 God handed all of them over to N.
Ezr 1: 7 which N had carried away from
2: 1 whom N king of Babylon had taken
5:12 he handed them over to N the
5:14 which N had taken from the temple in
6: 5 which N took from the temple in
Ne 7: 6 exiles whom N king of Babylon had
Est 2: 6 from Jerusalem by N king of Babylon,
Jer 21: 2 N king of Babylon is attacking us.
21: 7 sword and famine, to N king of
22:25 those you fear—to N king of Babylon
24: 1 to Babylon by N king of Babylon,
25: 1 the first year of N king of Babylon.
25: 9 and my servant N king of Babylon,"
27: 6 to my servant N king of Babylon;
27: 8 nation or kingdom will not serve N
27:20 which N king of Babylon did not take
28: 3 N king of Babylon removed from here
28:11 same way will I break the yoke of N
28:14 make them serve N king of Babylon,
29: 1 all the other people N had carried
29: 3 of Judah sent to King N in Babylon.
29:21 "I will hand them over to N king of
32: 1 which was the eighteenth year of N.
32:28 Babylonians and to N king of Babylon,
34: 1 While N king of Babylon and all his
35:11 when N king of Babylon invaded this
37: 1 king of Judah by N king of Babylon;
39: 1 in the tenth month, N king of
39: 5 They captured him and took him to N
39:11 Now N king of Babylon had given
43:10 says: I will send for my servant N
44:30 of Judah over to N king of Babylon,
46: 2 on the Euphrates River by N king of
46:13 N king of Babylon to attack Egypt:
46:26 N king of Babylon and his officers.
49:28 which N king of Babylon attacked:
49:30 "N king of Babylon has plotted
50:17 his bones was N king of Babylon."
51:34 "N king of Babylon has devoured us,
Jer 52: 4 N king of Babylon marched against
52:12 in the nineteenth year of N king of
52:28 This is the number of the people N
Eze 26: 7 against Tyre N king of Babylon,
29:18 "Son of man, N king of Babylon drove
29:19 to give Egypt to N king of Babylon,
30:10 by the hand of N king of Babylon.
Da 1: 1 N king of Babylon came to Jerusalem
1:18 chief official presented them to N.
2: 1 In the second year of his reign, N
2:28 He has shown King N what will happen
2:46 King N fell prostrate before Daniel
3: 1 King N made an image of gold, ninety
3: 3 of the image that King N had set up,
3: 5 of gold that King N has set up.
3: 7 of gold that King N had set up.
3: 9 They said to King N, "O king, live
3:13 Furious with rage, N summoned
3:14 N said to them, "Is it true,
3:16 "O N, we do not need to defend
3:19 N was furious with Shadrach, Meshach
3:24 King N leaped to his feet in
3:26 N then approached the opening of the
3:28 N said, "Praise be to the God of
4: 1 King N, To the peoples, nations and
4: 4 I, N, was at home in my palace,
4:18 "This is the dream that I, King N,
4:28 All this happened to King N.
4:31 King N: Your royal authority has
4:33 had been said about N was fulfilled.
4:34 At the end of that time, I, N,
4:37 Now I, N, praise and exalt and
5: 2 silver goblets that N his father had
5:11 King N your father—your father the
5:18 God gave your father N sovereignty

Nebuchadnezzar's (Nebuchadnezzar)

Jer 52:29 in N eighteenth year, 832 people

Nebushazban

Jer 39:13 N a chief officer, Nergal-Sharezer a

Nebuzaradan

2Ki 25: 8 N commander of the imperial guard,
25:11 N the commander of the guard carried
25:20 N the commander took them all and
Jer 39: 9 N commander of the imperial guard
39:10 N the commander of the guard left
39:11 N commander of the imperial guard:
39:13 N the commander of the guard,
40: 1 to Jeremiah from the LORD after N
40: 5 before Jeremiah turned to go, N
41:10 over whom N commander of the
43: 6 the king's daughters whom N
52:12 N commander of the imperial guard,
52:15 N the commander of the guard carried
52:16 N left behind the rest of the
52:26 N the commander took them all and
52:30 745 Jews taken into exile by N the

Necessary (Necessities)

Ac 1:21 Therefore it is **n** to choose one of
Ro 13: 5 Therefore, it is **n** to submit to the
2Co 9: 5 I thought it **n** to urge the brothers
Php 1:24 is more **n** for you that I remain in
2:25 I think it is **n** to send back to you
Heb 8: 3 and so it was **n** for this one also to
9:16 In the case of a will, it is **n** to
9:23 was **n**, then, for the copies of the

Necessities (Necessary)

Tit 3:14 provide for daily **n** and not live

Neck (Necks, Stiff-necked)

Ge 27:16 part of his **n** with the goatskins.
27:40 throw his yoke from off your **n**."
33: 4 arms around his **n** and kissed him.
41:42 and put a gold chain around his **n**.
49: 8 your hand will be on the **n** of your
Ex 13:13 you do not redeem it, break its **n**.
34:20 you do not redeem it, break its **n**.
Lev 5: 8 its **n**, not severing it completely,
Dt 21: 4 they are to break the heifer's **n**.

Dt 21: 6 whose **n** was broken in the valley,
28:48 an iron yoke on your **n** until he has
Jdg 5:30 embroidered garments for my **n**
1Sa 4:18 His **n** was broken and he died, for he
Job 16:12 seized me by the **n** and crushed me.
30:18 binds me like the **n** of my garment.
39:19 or clothe his **n** with a flowing mane?
41:22 Strength resides in his **n**; dismay
Ps 69: 1 for the waters have come up to my **n**.
75: 5 do not speak with outstretched **n**.
105:18 shackles, his **n** was put in irons,
Pr 1: 9 head and a chain to adorn your **n**.
3: 3 leave you; bind them around your **n**,
3:22 you, an ornament to grace your **n**.
6:21 for ever; fasten them around your **n**.
SS 1:10 your **n** with strings of jewels.
4: 4 Your **n** is like the tower of David,
7: 4 Your **n** is like an ivory tower. Your
Isa 8: 8 through it and reaching up to the **n**.
10:27 their yoke from your **n**; the yoke
30:28 rushing torrent, rising up to the **n**.
48: 4 the sinews of your **n** were iron,
52: 2 from the chains on your **n**,
66: 3 like one who breaks a dog's **n**;
Jer 27: 2 and crossbars and put it on your **n**.
27: 8 Babylon or bow its **n** under his yoke,
27:11 if any nation will bow its **n** under
27:12 I said, "Bow your **n** under the yoke
28:10 off the **n** of the prophet Jeremiah
28:11 off the **n** of all the nations within
28:12 off the **n** of the prophet Jeremiah,
Lam 1:14 They have come upon my **n** and the
Eze 16:11 arms and a necklace around your **n**,
Da 5: 7 a gold chain placed around his **n**,
5:16 a gold chain placed around your **n**,
5:29 gold chain was placed around his **n**,
Hos 10:11 so I will put a yoke on her fair **n**.
11: 4 I lifted the yoke from their **n** and
Na 1:13 your **n** and tear your shackles away."
Mt 18: 6 a large millstone hung around his **n**
Mk 9:42 a large millstone tied around his **n**.
Lk 17: 2 with a millstone tied round his **n**

Neck-irons (Iron)

Jer 29:26 a prophet into the stocks and **n**.

Necklace (Necklaces)

Ps 73: 6 Therefore pride is their **n**; they
SS 4: 9 your eyes, with one jewel of your **n**.
Eze 16:11 your arms and a **n** around your neck,

Necklaces (Necklace)

Nu 31:50 signet rings, ear-rings and **n**—to
Isa 3:18 and headbands and crescent **n**,

Necks (Neck)

Jos 10:24 your feet on the **n** of these kings.
10:24 and placed their feet on their **n**.
Jdg 8:21 the ornaments off their camels' **n**.
8:26 chains that were on their camels' **n**.
Isa 3:16 walking along with outstretched **n**,
Jer 28:14 I will put an iron yoke on the **n** of
30: 8 'I will break the yoke off their **n**
Eze 21:29 it will be laid on the **n** of the
Ac 15:10 on the **n** of the disciples a yoke

Neco

Pharaoh. Reluctantly fought and killed Josiah, who opposed support for Assyria (2Ki 23:29–30; 2Ch 35:20–25). Deposed Jehoahaz, appointed Jehoiakim as vassal (2Ki 23:31–35; 2Ch 36:2–4). Defeated by Nebuchadnezzar at Carchemish (Jer 46:2).

2Ki 23:29 While Josiah was king, Pharaoh **N**
23:29 but **N** faced him and killed him at
23:33 Pharaoh **N** put him in chains at
23:34 Pharaoh **N** made Eliakim son of Josiah
23:35 Jehoiakim paid Pharaoh **N** the silver
2Ch 35:20 **N** king of Egypt went up to fight at
35:21 **N** sent messengers to him saying,
35:22 He would not listen to what **N** had
36: 4 But **N** took Eliakim's brother
Jer 46: 2 the army of Pharaoh **N** king of Egypt,

Nectar

SS 8: 2 to drink, the **n** of my pomegranates.

Nedabiah

1Ch 3:18 Shenazzar, Jekamiah, Hoshama and **N**.

Need (Needed, Needing, Needs, Needy)

Ge 33:11 gracious to me and I have all I **n**.
Ex 14:14 for you; you **n** only to be still."
Lev 13:36 the priest does not **n** to look for
Jdg 19:19 with us. We don't **n** anything."
19:20 "Let me supply whatever you **n**. Only
1Ki 8:59 Israel according to each day's **n**,
2Ki 22: 7 they **n** not account for the money
1Ch 23:26 the Levites no longer **n** to carry the
2Ch 2:16 the logs from Lebanon that you **n**
35:15 gate did not **n** to leave their posts,
Job 5:21 **n** not fear when destruction comes.
5:22 **n** not fear the beasts of the earth.
34:23 God has no **n** to examine men further,
Ps 50: 9 I have no **n** of a bull from your
79: 8 meet us, for we are in desperate **n**.
116: 6 when I was in great **n**, he saved me.
142: 6 for I am in desperate **n**; rescue me
Pr 24: 6 for waging war you **n** guidance, and
Jer 2:24 pursue her **n** not tire themselves;
Eze 39:10 They will not **n** to gather wood from
Da 3:16 we do not **n** to defend ourselves
Hos 7: 4 whose fire the baker **n** not stir
Mt 3:14 saying, "I **n** to be baptised by you,
6: 8 knows what you **n** before you ask him.
6:32 Father knows that you **n** them.
9:12 who **n** a doctor, but the sick.
14:16 Jesus replied, "They do not **n** to go
26:65 Why do we **n** any more witnesses? Look,
Mk 2:17 who **n** a doctor, but the sick.
2:25 his companions were hungry and in **n**?
14:63 "Why do we **n** any more witnesses?" he
Lk 5:31 who **n** a doctor, but the sick.
12:30 your Father knows that you **n** them.
15: 7 persons who do not **n** to repent.
15:14 country, and he began to be in **n**.
22:71 they said, "Why do we **n** any more
Jn 2:25 He did not **n** man's testimony about
16:30 **n** to have anyone ask you questions.
Ac 2:45 they gave to anyone as he had **n**.
4:35 distributed to anyone as he had **n**.
10: 2 in **n** and prayed to God regularly.
27:34 You **n** it to survive. Not one of you
Ro 12:13 Share with God's people who are in **n**.
16: 2 her any help she may **n** from you,
1Co 12:21 "I don't **n** you!" And the head cannot
12:21 say to the feet, "I don't **n** you!
12:24 while our presentable parts **n** no
2Co 3: 1 commend ourselves again? Or do we **n**,
8:14 your plenty will supply what they **n**,
8:14 their plenty will supply what you **n**.
9: 1 There is no **n** for me to write to you
9: 8 having all that you **n**, you will
Eph 4:28 something to share with those in **n**.
Php 4:11 not saying this because I am in **n**,
4:12 I know what it is to be in **n**, and I
4:16 aid again and again when I was in **n**.
1Th 1: 8 do not **n** to say anything about it,
4: 9 Now about brotherly love we do not **n**
5: 1 dates we do not **n** to write to you,
1Ti 5: 3 to those widows who are really in **n**.
5: 5 The widow who is really in **n** and
5:16 those widows who are really in **n**.
2Ti 2:15 a workman who does not **n** to be
Tit 3:13 that they have everything they **n**.
Heb 4:16 grace to help us in our time of **n**.
5:12 you **n** someone to teach you the
5:12 You **n** milk, not solid food!
7:11 why was there still **n** for another
7:26 Such a high priest meets our **n**—one
7:27 he does not **n** to offer sacrifices
10:36 You **n** to persevere so that when you
2Pe 1: 3 given us everything we **n** for life
1Jn 2:27 you do not **n** anyone to teach you.
3:17 brother in **n** but has no pity on him,
Rev 3:17 wealth and do not **n** a thing.
21:23 The city does not **n** the sun or the
22: 5 They will not **n** the light of a lamp

Needed (Need)

Ex 12: 4 determine the amount of lamb **n** in
16:18 Each one gathered as much as he **n**.
16:21 everyone gathered as much as he **n**,
Jos 19: 9 Judah's portion was more than they **n**.
Ezr 6: 9 Whatever is **n**—young bulls, rams,
7:20 anything else **n** for the temple of
Ecc 10:10 is **n** but skill will bring success.
Mt 25:36 I **n** clothes and you clothed me, I
25:43 I **n** clothes and you did not clothe
Lk 9:11 God, and healed those who **n** healing.
10:42 only one thing is **n**. Mary has chosen
Jn 13:29 him to buy what was **n** for the Feast,
Ac 17:25 as if he **n** anything, because he
28:10 furnished us with the supplies we **n**.
2Co 11: 9 I was with you and **n** something, I
11: 9 from Macedonia supplied what I **n**.

Needing (Need)

Mt 25:38 you in, or **n** clothes and clothe you?
25:44 or **n** clothes or sick or in prison,

Needle

Mt 19:24 camel to go through the eye of a **n**
Mk 10:25 camel to go through the eye of a **n**
Lk 18:25 camel to go through the eye of a **n**

Needless

1Sa 25:31 staggering burden of **n** bloodshed
Pr 23:29 Who has **n** bruises? Who has

Needs (Need)

Ex 16:16 one is to gather as much as he **n**.
Nu 4:26 that **n** to be done with these things.
Dt 15: 8 and freely lend him whatever he **n**.
Pr 12:10 A righteous man cares for the **n** of
Isa 58:10 and satisfy the **n** of the oppressed,
58:11 he will satisfy your **n** in a
Jer 5: 7 I supplied all their **n**, yet they
Mt 21: 3 tell him that the Lord **n** them, and
27:55 Jesus from Galilee to care for his **n**.
Mk 11: 3 'The Lord **n** it and will send it back
15:41 followed him and cared for his **n**.
Lk 11: 8 get up and give him as much as he **n**.
19:31 it?' tell him, 'The Lord **n** it.
19:34 They replied, "The Lord **n** it."
Jn 13:10 "A person who has had a bath **n** only
Ac 20:34 my own **n** and the **n** of my companions.
24:23 his friends to take care of his **n**.
27: 3 so they might provide for his **n**.
Ro 12: 8 is contributing to the **n** of others,
2Co 9:12 supplying the **n** of God's people
Eph 4:29 others up according to their **n**,
Php 2:25 whom you sent to take care of my **n**.
4:19 my God will meet all your **n**
Jas 2:16 his physical **n**, what good is it?

Needy (Need)

Ex 22:25 one of my people among you who is **n**,
Dt 15: 9 your **n** brother and give him nothing.
15:11 towards the poor and **n** in your land.
24:14 of a hired man who is poor and **n**,
1Sa 2: 8 and lifts the **n** from the ash heap;
Job 5:15 He saves the **n** from the sword in
24: 4 They thrust the **n** from the path and
24:14 rises up and kills the poor and **n**;
29:16 I was a father to the **n**; I took up
31:19 or a **n** man without a garment,
34:28 so that he heard the cry of the **n**.
Ps 9:18 the **n** will not always be forgotten,
12: 5 the groaning of the **n**, I will now
35:10 poor and **n** from those who rob them."
37:14 bow to bring down the poor and **n**,
40:17 Yet I am poor and **n**; may the Lord
69:33 The LORD hears the **n** and does not
70: 5 Yet I am poor and **n**; come quickly to
72: 4 save the children of the **n**; he will
72:12 For he will deliver the **n** who cry
72:13 and the **n** and save the **n** from death.
74:21 may the poor and **n** praise your name.
82: 4 Rescue the weak and **n**; deliver them
86: 1 and answer me, for I am poor and **n**.

Ps 107:41 he lifted the **n** out of their
109:16 and the **n** and the broken-hearted.
109:22 For I am poor and **n**, and my heart is
109:31 at the right hand of the **n** one,
113: 7 and lifts the **n** from the ash heap;
140:12 poor and upholds the cause of the **n**.
Pr 14:21 blessed is he who is kind to the **n**.
14:31 is kind to the **n** honours God.
22:22 and do not crush the **n** in court,
30:14 the earth, the **n** from among mankind.
31: 9 the rights of the poor and **n**."
31:20 poor and extends her hands to the **n**.
Isa 11: 4 righteousness he will judge the **n**,
14:30 and the **n** will lie down in safety.
25: 4 a refuge for the **n** in his distress,
29:19 the **n** will rejoice in the Holy One
32: 7 even when the plea of the **n** is just.
41:17 "The poor and **n** search for water,
Jer 20:13 the **n** from the hands of the wicked.
22:16 poor and **n**, and so all went well.
Eze 16:49 they did not help the poor and **n**.
18:12 He oppresses the poor and **n**. He
22:29 poor and **n** and ill-treat the alien,
Am 2: 6 and the **n** for a pair of sandals.
4: 1 oppress the poor and crush the **n**
8: 4 Hear this, you who trample the **n** and
8: 6 buying the poor with silver and the **n**
Mt 6: 2 "So when you give to the **n**, do not
6: 3 when you give to the **n**, do not let
Ac 4:34 There were no **n** persons among them.

Negev

The southern desert region of Judah (Jos 15:21). Abraham (Ge 12:9; 13:1, 3; 20:1) and Isaac (Ge 24:62) camped here. 12 spies approached Canaan from this direction (Nu 13:17, 22). The home of the Canaanite King Arad (Nu 21:1; 33:40). Part of the promised land (Dt 1:7; 34:3) which Joshua conquered (Jos 10:40; 11:16; 12:8). Land here given by Caleb to his daughter (Jos 15:19; Jdg 1:15), and some land was re-allocated to the tribe of Simeon (Jos 19:8). It was prone to attack from Amalekites (1Sa 30:1, 14), and Philistines (2Ch 28:18). Included in David's census (2Sa 24:7). Used poetically to portray difficulty and hardship (Ps 126:4; Isa 30:6) and referred to by the prophets (Jer 13:19; 17:26; 32:44; 33:13; Ob 19–20; Zec 7:7).

Ge 12: 9 set out and continued towards the **N**.
13: 1 Abram went up from Egypt to the **N**,
13: 3 From the **N** he went from place to
20: 1 into the region of the **N** and lived
24:62 Roi, for he was living in the **N**.
Nu 13:17 the **N** and on into the hill country.
13:22 They went up through the **N** and came
13:29 The Amalekites live in the **N**; the
21: 1 who lived in the **N**, heard that
33:40 who lived in the **N** of Canaan, heard
Dt 1: 7 in the western foothills, in the **N**
34: 3 the **N** and the whole region from the
Jos 10:40 including the hill country, the **N**,
11:16 all the **N**, the whole region of
12: 8 the desert and the **N**—the lands of
15:19 land in the **N**, give me also
15:21 the **N** towards the boundary of Edom
19: 8 as Baalath Beer (Ramah in the **N**).
Jdg 1: 9 the **N** and the western foothills.
1:15 land in the **N**, give me also
1:16 Desert of Judah in the **N** near Arad.
1Sa 27:10 "Against the **N** of Judah" or "Against
27:10 "Against the **N** of Jerahmeel" or
27:10 or "Against the **N** of the Kenites.
30: 1 Now the Amalekites had raided the **N**
30:14 We raided the **N** of the Kerethites
30:14 to Judah and the **N** of Caleb.
2Sa 24: 7 on to Beersheba in the **N** of Judah.
2Ch 28:18 the foothills and in the **N** of Judah.
Ps 126: 4 O LORD, like streams in the **N**.
Isa 30: 6 concerning the animals of the **N**:
Jer 13:19 The cities in the **N** will be shut up,
17:26 from the hill country and the **N**,
32:44 the western foothills and of the **N**,
33:13 the western foothills and of the **N**,
Ob :19 People from the **N** will occupy the
:20 will possess the towns of the **N**.
Zec 7: 7 and the **N** and the western foothills

Neglect (Neglected, Neglecting, Negligent)

Dt 12:19 Be careful not to **n** the Levites as
14:27 do not **n** the Levites living in your
Ezr 4:22 Be careful not to **n** this matter. Why
Ne 10:39 "We will not **n** the house of our God."
Est 6:10 not **n** anything you have recommended.
Ps 119:16 decrees; I will not **n** your word.
Lk 11:42 you **n** justice and the love of God.
Ac 6: 2 "It would not be right for us to **n**
1Ti 4:14 Do not **n** your gift, which was given

Neglected (Neglect)

Ne 13:11 "Why is the house of God **n**?" Then I
SS 1: 6 vineyards; my own vineyard I have **n**.
Mt 23:23 But you have **n** the more important

Neglecting (Neglect)

Mt 23:23 the latter, without **n** the former.

Negligent (Neglect)

2Ch 29:11 My sons, do not be **n** now, for the
Da 6: 4 and neither corrupt nor **n**.

Nehelamite

Jer 29:24 Tell Shemaiah the **N**,
29:31 the LORD says about Shemaiah the **N**:
29:32 Shemaiah the **N** and his descendants.

Nehemiah

Cupbearer to Artaxerxes (Ne 1:10). Prayed over state of Jerusalem (Ne 1); allowed to return to rebuild city walls (Ne 2–6); appointed governor (Ne 5:14; 8:9). Called Ezra to read Law (Ne 8); confessed nation's sin (Ne 9); dedicated wall (12:27–47); made other reforms (Ne 13).

Ezr 2: 2 in company with Zerubbabel, Jeshua, **N**
Ne 1: 1 The words of **N** son of Hacaliah: In
3:16 Beyond him, **N** son of Azbuk, ruler of
7: 7 in company with Zerubbabel, Jeshua, **N**
8: 9 **N** the governor, Ezra the priest and
8:10 **N** said, "Go and enjoy choice food
10: 1 Those who sealed it were: **N** the
12:26 and in the days of **N** the governor
12:47 in the days of Zerubbabel and of **N**,

Nehum

Ne 7: 7 Bilshan, Mispereth, Bigvai, **N** and

Nehushta

2Ki 24: 8 His mother's name was **N** daughter of

Nehushtan

2Ki 18: 4 (It was called **N**.)

Neiel

Jos 19:27 and **N**, passing Cabul on the left.

Neigh (Neighing, Neighings)

Jer 50:11 threshing corn and **n** like stallions,

Neighbour (*Love your neighbour*, Neighbour's, Neighbouring, Neighbours, Neighbours')

Ex 3:22 Every woman is to ask her **n** and any
12: 4 must share one with their nearest **n**,
20:16 give false testimony against your **n**.
20:17 or anything that belongs to your **n**."
22: 7 "If a man gives his **n** silver or
22: 9 must pay back double to his **n**.
22:10 animal to his **n** for safekeeping
22:11 that the **n** did not lay hands on the
22:12 if the animal was stolen from the **n**,
22:14 a man borrows an animal from his **n**
32:27 his brother and friend and **n**.
Lev 6: 2 deceiving his **n** about something
19:13 "'Do not defraud your **n** or rob him.
19:15 the great, but judge your **n** fairly.
19:17 Rebuke your **n** frankly so that you
20:10 wife of his **n**—both the adulterer
24:19 If anyone injures his **n**, whatever he
Dt 4:42 his **n** without malice aforethought.
5:20 give false testimony against your **n**.
5:21 or anything that belongs to your **n**."
19: 4 who kills his **n** unintentionally,
19: 5 the forest with his **n** to cut wood,
19: 5 fly off and hit his **n** and kill him.
19: 6 his **n** without malice aforethought.
19:11 if a man hates his **n** and lies in
22:26 who attacks and murders his **n**,
24:10 you make a loan of any kind to your **n**
27:24 "Cursed is the man who kills his **n**
Jos 20: 5 because he killed his **n**
1Ki 8:31 "When a man wrongs his **n** and is
2Ch 6:22 "When a man wrongs his **n** and is
Ps 12: 2 Everyone lies to his **n**; their
15: 3 who does his **n** no wrong and casts no
101: 5 Whoever slanders his **n** in secret,
Pr 3:28 Do not say to your **n**, "Come back
3:29 Do not plot harm against your **n**, who
6: 1 you have put up security for your **n**,
6: 3 press your plea with your **n**!
11: 9 mouth the godless destroys his **n**,
11:12 who lacks judgment derides his **n**,
14:21 He who despises his **n** sins, but
16:29 A violent man entices his **n** and
17:18 and puts up security for his **n**.
21:10 craves evil; his **n** gets no mercy
24:28 Do not testify against your **n**
25: 8 the end if your **n** puts you to shame?
25: 9 If you argue your case with a **n**, do
25:18 gives false testimony against his **n**.
26:19 is a man who deceives his **n** and says,
27:10 a **n** nearby than a brother far away.
27:14 If a man loudly blesses his **n** early
29: 5 Whoever flatters his **n** is spreading
Ecc 4: 4 spring from man's envy of his **n**.
Isa 3: 5 man against man, **n** against **n**.
19: 2 **n** against **n**, city against city,
Jer 9: 8 each speaks cordially to his **n**,
31:34 No longer will a man teach his **n**, or
Mic 7: 5 Do not trust a **n**; put no confidence
Zec 3:10 invite his **n** to sit under his vine
8:10 I had turned every man against his **n**.
8:17 do not plot evil against your **n**, and
11: 6 "I will hand everyone over to his **n**
Lk 10:29 "And who is my **n**?"
10:36 of these three do you think was a **n**
Ro 13:10 Love does no harm to its **n**.
15: 2 Each of us should please his **n** for
Eph 4:25 and speak truthfully to his **n**,
Heb 8:11 No longer will a man teach his **n**, or
Jas 4:12 But you—who are you to judge your **n**?

Neighbour's (Neighbour)

Ex 20:17 "You shall not covet your **n** house.
20:17 You shall not covet your **n** wife, or
22: 7 they are stolen from the **n** house,
22:26 If you take your **n** cloak as a pledge,
Lev 18:20 **n** wife and defile yourself with her.
19:16 anything that endangers your **n** life.
Dt 5:21 "You shall not covet your **n** wife.
5:21 your desire on your **n** house or land,
19:14 Do not move your **n** boundary stone
23:24 If you enter your **n** vineyard, you
23:25 If you enter your **n** cornfield, you
27:17 who moves his **n** boundary stone.
Job 31: 9 or if I have lurked at my **n** door,
Pr 6: 3 you have fallen into your **n** hands
25:17 Seldom set foot in your **n** house—
Eze 18: 6 He does not defile his **n** wife or lie
18:11 He defiles his **n** wife.
18:15 He does not defile his **n** wife.
22:11 detestable offence with his **n** wife,
33:26 and each of you defiles his **n** wife.

Neighbouring (Neighbour)

Dt 1: 7 to all the **n** peoples in the Arabah,
21: 2 from the body to the **n** towns.
1Sa 7:14 and Israel delivered the **n** territory
Ezr 9: 1 the **n** peoples with their detestable
Ne 9:30 handed them over to the **n** peoples.
10:28 themselves from the **n** peoples for
10:31 "When the **n** peoples bring
Ps 76:11 let all the **n** lands bring gifts to
Jer 49:18 along with their **n** towns,"
50:40 Gomorrah along with their **n** towns,"

Neighbours (Neighbour)
Ex 11: 2 ask their **n** for articles of silver
Jos 9:16 that they were **n**, living near them.
1Sa 15:28 given it to one of your **n**—to one
28:17 given it to one of your **n**—to David.
2Ki 4: 3 and ask all your **n** for empty jars.
1Ch 12:40 Also, their **n** from as far away as
Ezr 1: 6 All their **n** assisted them with
6:21 Gentile **n** in order to seek the LORD,
Ps 28: 3 speak cordially with their **n** but
31:11 I am the utter contempt of my **n**;
38:11 of my wounds; my **n** stay far away.
44:13 You have made us a reproach to our **n**,
79: 4 We are objects of reproach to our **n**,
79:12 Pay back into the laps of our **n**
80: 6 to our **n**, and our enemies mock us.
89:41 he has become the scorn of his **n**.
Pr 14:20 The poor are shunned even by their **n**,
Jer 6:21 them; **n** and friends will perish."
12:14 "As for all my wicked **n** who seize
49:10 His children, relatives and **n** will
Lam 1:17 Jacob that his **n** become his foes;
Eze 16:26 your lustful **n**, and provoked me to
16:57 all her **n** and the daughters of the
22:12 gain from your **n** by extortion.
28:24 malicious **n** who are painful briers
28:26 on all their **n** who maligned them.
Hab 2:15 "Woe to him who gives drink to his **n**,
Lk 1:58 Her **n** and relatives heard that the
1:65 The **n** were all filled with awe, and
14:12 or your rich **n**; if you do, they may
15: 6 Then he calls his friends and **n**
15: 9 she calls her friends and **n** together
Jn 9: 8 His **n** and those who had formerly

Neighbours' (Neighbour)
Jer 29:23 adultery with their **n** wives

Neighing (Neigh)
Jer 5: 8 each **n** for another man's wife.
8:16 at the **n** of their stallions the

Neighings (Neigh)
Jer 13:27 your adulteries and lustful **n**, your

Nekoda
Ezr 2:48 Rezin, **N**, Gazzam,
2:60 of Delaiah, Tobiah and **N** 652
Ne 7:50 Reaiah, Rezin, **N**,
7:62 of Delaiah, Tobiah and **N** 642

Nemuel (Nemuelite)
Nu 26: 9 the sons of Eliab were **N**, Dathan and
26:12 by their clans were: through **N**,
1Ch 4:24 The descendants of Simeon: **N**, Jamin,

Nemuelite (Nemuel)
Nu 26:12 the **N** clan; through Jamin, the

Nepheg
Ex 6:21 The sons of Izhar were Korah, **N** and
2Sa 5:15 Ibhar, Elishua, **N**, Japhia,
1Ch 3: 7 Nogah, **N**, Japhia,
14: 6 Nogah, **N**, Japhia,

Nephew (Nephews)
Ge 12: 5 He took his wife Sarai, his **n** Lot,
14:12 They also carried off Abram's **n** Lot

Nephews (Nephew)
Ezr 8:19 and his brothers and **n**, 20 men.

Nephilim
Ge 6: 4 The **N** were on the earth in those
Nu 13:33 We saw the **N** there (the descendants
13:33 of Anak come from the **N**).

Nephtoah
Jos 15: 9 the spring of the waters of **N**,
18:15 at the spring of the waters of **N**.

Nephussim
Ezr 2:50 Asnah, Meunim, **N**,
Ne 7:52 Besai, Meunim, **N**,

Ner
1Sa 14:50 son of **N**, and **N** was Saul's uncle.
14:51 and Abner's father **N** were sons of
26: 5 saw where Saul and Abner son of **N**,
26:14 to the army and to Abner son of **N**,
2Sa 2: 8 Meanwhile, Abner son of **N**, the
2:12 Abner son of **N**, together with the
3:23 Abner son of **N** had come to the king
3:25 You know Abner son of **N**; he came
3:28 the blood of Abner son of **N**.
3:37 the murder of Abner son of **N**.
1Ki 2: 5 Abner son of **N** and Amasa son of
2:32 Abner son of **N**, commander of
1Ch 8:30 by Zur, Kish, Baal, **N**, Nadab,
8:33 **N** was the father of Kish, Kish the
9:36 by Zur, Kish, Baal, **N**, Nadab,
9:39 **N** was the father of Kish, Kish the
26:28 Abner son of **N** and Joab son of

Nereus
Ro 16:15 Greet Philologus, Julia, **N** and his

Nergal
2Ki 17:30 the men from Cuthah made **N**, and the

Nergal-Sharezer
Jer 39: 3 in the Middle Gate: **N** of Samgar,
39: 3 a chief officer, **N** a high official
39:13 a chief officer, **N** a high official

Neri
Lk 3:27 the son of Shealtiel, the son of **N**,

Neriah
Jer 32:12 I gave this deed to Baruch son of **N**,
32:16 son of **N**, I prayed to the LORD:
36: 4 Jeremiah called Baruch son of **N**, and
36: 8 Baruch son of **N** did everything
36:14 So Baruch son of **N** went to them
36:32 it to the scribe Baruch son of **N**,
43: 3 Baruch son of **N** is inciting you
43: 6 the prophet and Baruch son of **N**.
45: 1 the prophet told Baruch son of **N**
51:59 the staff officer Seraiah son of **N**,

Nest (Nested, Nesting, Nests)
Nu 24:21 is secure, your **n** is set in a rock;
Dt 22: 6 If you come across a bird's **n** beside
32:11 like an eagle that stirs up its **n**
Job 39:27 command and build his **n** on high?
Ps 84: 3 and the swallow a **n** for herself,
104:12 The birds of the air **n** by the waters;
Pr 27: 8 Like a bird that strays from its **n**
Isa 10:14 one reaches into a **n**, so my hand
11: 8 put his hand into the viper's **n**.
16: 2 fluttering birds pushed from the **n**,
34:11 owl and the raven will **n** there.
34:15 The owl will **n** there and lay eggs,
Jer 48:28 makes its **n** at the mouth of a cave.
49:16 Though you build your **n** as high as
Eze 17:23 Birds of every kind will **n** in it;
Ob : 4 and make your **n** among the stars,
Hab 2: 9 by unjust gain to set his **n** on high,

Nested (Nest)
Eze 31: 6 All the birds of the air **n** in its

Nesting (Nest)
Da 4:21 and having **n** places in its branches

Nestled
Jer 22:23 You who live in 'Lebanon', who are **n**

Nests (Nest)
Ps 104:17 There the birds make their **n**; the
Isa 60: 8 like clouds, like doves to their **n**?
Mt 8:20 holes and birds of the air have **n**,
Lk 9:58 holes and birds of the air have **n**,

Net (Drag-net, Nets)
Job 18: 8 His feet thrust him into a **n** and he
19: 6 me and drawn his **n** around me.
Ps 9:15 caught in the **n** they have hidden.
10: 9 and drags them off in his **n**.
35: 7 Since they hid their **n** for me
35: 8 may the **n** they hid entangle them,
57: 6 They spread a **n** for my feet—I was
140: 5 spread out the cords of their **n**
Pr 1:17 How useless to spread a **n** in full
29: 5 is spreading a **n** for his feet.
Ecc 9:12 As fish are caught in a cruel **n**,
Isa 51:20 street, like antelope caught in a **n**.
Lam 1:13 He spread a **n** for my feet and turned
Eze 12:13 I will spread my **n** for him, and he
17:20 I will spread my **n** for him, and he
19: 8 They spread their **n** for him, and he
32: 3 of people I will cast my **n** over you,
32: 3 and they will haul you up in my **n**.
Hos 5: 1 at Mizpah, a **n** spread out on Tabor.
7:12 they go, I will throw my **n** over them;
Mic 7: 2 each hunts his brother with a **n**.
Hab 1:15 he catches them in his **n**, he gathers
1:16 Therefore he sacrifices to his **n** and
1:16 by his **n** he lives in luxury and
1:17 Is he to keep on emptying his **n**,
Mt 4:18 They were casting a **n** into the lake,
13:47 the kingdom of heaven is like a **n**
Mk 1:16 Andrew casting a **n** into the lake,
Jn 21: 6 He said, "Throw your **n** on the right
21: 6 they were unable to haul the **n** in
21: 8 towing the **n** full of fish, for they
21:11 aboard and dragged the **n** ashore.
21:11 with so many the **n** was not torn.

Netaim
1Ch 4:23 They were the potters who lived at **N**

Nethanel
Nu 1: 8 from Issachar, **N** son of Zuar;
2: 5 people of Issachar is **N** son of Zuar.
7:18 On the second day **N** son of Zuar, the
7:23 was the offering of **N** son of Zuar.
10:15 **N** son of Zuar was over the division
1Ch 2:14 the fourth **N**, the fifth Raddai,
15:24 Shebaniah, Joshaphat, **N**, Amasai,
24: 6 The scribe Shemaiah son of **N**, a
26: 4 Sacar the fourth, **N** the fifth,
2Ch 17: 7 Obadiah, Zechariah, **N** and Micaiah to
35: 9 Conaniah along with Shemaiah and **N**,
Ezr 10:22 Ishmael, **N**, Jozabad and Elasah.
Ne 12:21 Hashabiah; of Jedaiah's, **N**.
12:36 Azarel, Milalai, Gilalai, Maai, **N**,

Nethaniah
2Ki 25:23 Gedaliah at Mizpah—Ishmael son of **N**,
25:25 however, Ishmael son of **N**, the son
1Ch 25: 2 Zaccur, Joseph, **N** and Asarelah.
25:12 the fifth to **N**, his sons and
2Ch 17: 8 **N**, Zebadiah, Asahel, Shemiramoth,
Jer 36:14 the officials sent Jehudi son of **N**,
40: 8 Gedaliah at Mizpah—Ishmael son of **N**,
40:14 Ishmael son of **N** to take your life?"
40:15 son of **N**, and no-one will know it.
41: 1 In the seventh month Ishmael son of **N**
41: 2 Ishmael son of **N** and the ten men who
41: 6 Ishmael son of **N** went out from
41: 7 Ishmael son of **N** and the men who
41: 9 son of **N** filled it with the dead.
41:10 Ishmael son of **N** took them captive
41:11 Ishmael son of **N** had committed,
41:12 and went to fight Ishmael son of **N**.
41:15 Ishmael son of **N** and eight of his
41:16 recovered from Ishmael son of **N**
41:18 **N** had killed Gedaliah son of Ahikam,

Netophah
Ezr 2:22 of **N** 56
Ne 7:26 the men of Bethlehem and **N** 188

Netophathite (Netophathites)
2Sa 23:28 Zalmon the Ahohite, Maharai the **N**,
23:29 Heled son of Baanah the **N**, Ithai son
2Ki 25:23 Seraiah son of Tanhumeth the **N**,

1Ch 11:30 the **N**, Heled son of Baanah the **N**,
27:13 was Maharai the **N**, a Zerahite.
27:15 the **N**, from the family of Othniel.
Jer 40: 8 the sons of Ephai the **N**, and

Netophathites (Netophathite)

1Ch 2:54 the **N**, Atroth Beth Joab, half the
9:16 who lived in the villages of the **N**.
Ne 12:28 the villages of the **N**,

Nets (Net)

Ps 141:10 Let the wicked fall into their own **n**,
Isa 19: 8 throw **n** on the water will pine away.
Eze 26: 5 become a place to spread fishing **n**,
26:14 become a place to spread fishing **n**.
47:10 will be places for spreading **n**.
Mt 4:20 At once they left their **n** and
4:21 father Zebedee, preparing their **n**.
Mk 1:18 At once they left their **n** and
1:19 John in a boat, preparing their **n**.
Lk 5: 2 fishermen, who were washing their **n**.
5: 4 and let down the **n** for a catch."
5: 5 you say so, I will let down the **n**."
5: 6 of fish that their **n** began to break.

Nettles

Isa 34:13 Thorns will overrun her citadels, **n**

Network

Ex 27: 4 Make a grating for it, a bronze **n**,
27: 4 each of the four corners of the **n**.
38: 4 a bronze **n**, to be under its ledge,
1Ki 7:17 A **n** of interwoven chains festooned
7:18 in two rows encircling each **n** to
7:20 the bowl-shaped part next to the **n**,
7:41 the two sets of **n** decorating the two
7:42 pomegranates for the two sets of **n**
7:42 (two rows of pomegranates for each **n**,
2Ki 25:17 was decorated with a **n** and
25:17 pillar, with its **n**, was similar.
2Ch 4:12 the two sets of **n** decorating the two
4:13 pomegranates for the two sets of **n**
4:13 (two rows of pomegranates for each **n**,
Jer 52:22 was decorated with a **n** and
52:23 the surrounding **n** was a hundred.

Never

Ge 8:21 "**N** again will I curse the ground
8:21 And **n** again will I destroy all
8:22 winter, day and night will **n** cease."
9:11 my covenant with you: **N** again will
9:11 **n** again will there be a flood to
9:15 **N** again will the waters become a
14:23 **n** be able to say, 'I made Abram rich.
19: 8 daughters who have **n** slept with a
21:10 that slave woman's son will **n** share
41:19 I had **n** seen such ugly cows in all
45:20 **N** mind about your belongings,
48:11 Israel said to Joseph, "I **n** expected
Ex 4:10 "O Lord, I have **n** been eloquent,
10:14 **N** before had there been such a
10:29 "I will **n** appear before you again.
14:13 you see today you will **n** see again.
34:10 I will do wonders **n** before done in
Lev 27:20 someone else, it can **n** be redeemed.
Nu 11: 6 we **n** see anything but this manna!"
19: 2 and that has **n** been under a yoke.
31:18 girl who has **n** slept with a man.
31:35 32,000 women who had **n** slept with a
Dt 8:16 something your fathers had **n** known,
9: 7 Remember this and **n** forget how you
13:16 a ruin for ever, **n** to be rebuilt.
19:20 and **n** again will such an evil thing
21: 3 **n** been worked and has **n** worn a
22:29 **n** divorce her as long as he lives.
28:13 be at the top, **n** at the bottom.
28:66 night and day, **n** sure of your life.
28:68 I said you should **n** make again.
29:20 The LORD will **n** be willing to
31: 6 will **n** leave you nor forsake you."
31: 8 he will **n** leave you nor forsake you.
Jos 1: 5 I will **n** leave you nor forsake you.
3: 4 you have **n** been this way before.
9:23 a curse: You will **n** cease to serve
Jos 10:14 There has **n** been a day like it
Jdg 1:28 but **n** drove them out completely.
2: 1 will **n** break my covenant with you,
11:37 my friends, because I will **n** marry."
11:38 and wept because she would **n** marry.
16:11 new ropes that have **n** been used,
19:30 "Such a thing has **n** been seen or
21:12 women who had **n** slept with a man,
1Sa 2:32 line there will **n** be an old man.
3:14 'The guilt of Eli's house will **n** be
6: 7 have calved and have **n** been yoked.
14:45 **N**! As surely as the LORD lives,
20: 2 "**N**!" Jonathan replied. "You are not
20: 9 "**N**!" Jonathan said. "If I had the
2Sa 3:29 May Joab's house **n** be without
7:15 my love will **n** be taken away from
12:10 the sword shall **n** depart from
13:22 Absalom **n** said a word to Amnon,
21:17 "**N** again will you go out with us to
1Ki 1: 6 (His father had **n** interfered with
2: 4 you will **n** fail to have a man on the
3:12 so that there will **n** have been
8:25 'You shall **n** fail to have a man to
8:57 may he **n** leave us nor forsake us.
9: 5 'You shall **n** fail to have a man on
10:10 **N** again were so many spices brought
10:12 So much almug-wood has **n** been
21:25 (There was **n** a man like Ahab, who
22: 8 I hate him because he **n** prophesies
22:18 "Didn't I tell you that he **n**
22:48 but they **n** set sail—they were
2Ki 1:16 **n** leave the bed you are lying on.
2:21 **N** again will it cause death or make
5:17 for your servant will **n** again make
1Ch 17:13 I will **n** take my love away from him,
2Ch 6:16 'You shall **n** fail to have a man to
7:18 'You shall **n** fail to have a man to
9: 9 There had **n** been such spices as
18: 7 I hate him because he **n** prophesies
18:17 "Didn't I tell you that he **n**
Ne 5:18 In spite of all this, I **n** demanded
Est 1:19 that Vashti is **n** again to enter the
9:28 these days of Purim should **n** cease
Job 3:16 infant who **n** saw the light of day?
7: 7 my eyes will **n** see happiness again.
7:10 He will **n** come to his house again;
7:19 Will you **n** look away from me, or let
8:18 disowns it and says, 'I **n** saw you.'
10:19 If only I had **n** come into being, or
16: 3 Will your long-winded speeches **n** end?
16:18 blood; may my cry **n** be laid to rest!
19:22 Will you **n** get enough of my flesh?
21:10 Their bulls **n** fail to breed; their
21:25 **n** having enjoyed anything good.
21:29 Have you **n** questioned those who
27: 5 I will **n** admit you are in the right;
27: 6 my righteousness and **n** let go of it;
27:14 offspring will **n** have enough to eat.
30:17 my bones; my gnawing pains **n** rest.
30:27 The churning inside me **n** stops; days
31:31 the men of my household have **n** said
35:15 further, that his anger **n** punishes
41: 8 the struggle and **n** do it again!
Ps 9:10 have **n** forsaken those who seek you.
10: 6 always be happy and **n** have trouble."
10:11 he covers his face and **n** sees."
14: 4 Will evildoers **n** learn—those who
15: 5 does these things will **n** be shaken.
28: 5 them down and **n** build them up again.
30: 6 I said, "I shall **n** be shaken."
31: 1 refuge; let me **n** be put to shame;
34: 5 faces are **n** covered with shame.
37:25 yet I have **n** seen the righteous
41: 8 he will **n** get up from the place
49:19 who will **n** see the light of life.
53: 4 Will the evildoers **n** learn—those
55:11 and lies **n** leave its streets.
55:19 men who **n** change their ways and
55:22 he will **n** let the righteous fall.
62: 2 is my fortress, I shall **n** be shaken.
71: 1 refuge; let me **n** be put to shame.
77: 7 Will he **n** show his favour again?
89:28 my covenant with him will **n** fail.
94:14 he will **n** forsake his inheritance.
95:11 anger, "They shall **n** enter my rest.
102:27 the same, and your years will **n** end.
Ps 104: 5 its foundations; it can **n** be moved.
104: 9 **n** again will they cover the earth.
109:14 sin of his mother **n** be blotted out.
109:16 For he **n** thought of doing a kindness,
112: 6 Surely he will **n** be shaken; a
119:93 I will **n** forget your precepts, for
140:10 the fire, into miry pits, **n** to rise.
148: 6 gave a decree that will **n** pass away.
Pr 3: 3 Let love and faithfulness **n** leave
5:17 be yours alone, **n** to be shared
6:33 and his shame will **n** be wiped away;
7:11 and defiant, her feet **n** stay at home
10:30 The righteous will **n** be uprooted,
17:13 good, evil will **n** leave his house.
21:17 loves wine and oil will **n** be rich.
25:10 you will **n** lose your bad reputation.
27:20 and Destruction are **n** satisfied
30:15 "There are three things that are **n**
30:15 four that **n** say, 'Enough!':
30:16 land, which is **n** satisfied with
30:16 and fire, which **n** says, 'Enough!'
Ecc 1: 7 into the sea, yet the sea is **n** full.
1: 8 The eye **n** has enough of seeing, nor
5:10 Whoever loves money **n** has money
5:10 is **n** satisfied with his income.
6: 5 Though it **n** saw the sun or knew
6: 7 yet his appetite is **n** satisfied.
7:20 who does what is right and **n** sins.
9: 6 **n** again will they have a part in
SS 7: 2 Your navel is a rounded goblet that **n**
Isa 6: 9 'Be ever hearing, but **n**
6: 9 be ever seeing, but **n** perceiving.'
13:20 She will **n** be inhabited or lived in
14:20 wicked will **n** be mentioned again.
24:20 that it falls—**n** to rise again.
25: 2 city no more; it will **n** be rebuilt.
28:16 one who trusts will **n** be dismayed.
33:20 its stakes will **n** be pulled up,
43:17 and they lay there, **n** to rise again,
45:17 will **n** be put to shame or disgraced,
47: 8 I will **n** be a widow or suffer the
48:19 their name would **n** be cut off nor
51: 6 ever, my righteousness will **n** fail.
51:22 of my wrath, you will **n** drink again.
54: 1 woman, you who **n** bore a child
54: 1 shout for joy, you who were **n** in
54: 9 Noah would **n** again cover the earth.
54: 9 with you, **n** to rebuke you again.
56:11 appetites; they **n** have enough.
58:11 like a spring whose waters **n** fail.
60:11 they will **n** be shut, day or night,
60:20 Your sun will **n** set again, and your
62: 6 they will **n** be silent day or night.
62: 8 "**N** again will I give your grain as
62: 8 and **n** again will foreigners drink
65:20 "**N** again will there be in it an
Jer 3:16 It will **n** enter their minds or be
5:12 us; we will **n** see sword or famine.
15:17 I **n** sat in the company of revellers,
15:17 **n** made merry with them; I sat alone
17: 8 drought and **n** fails to bear fruit."
20:11 their dishonour will **n** be forgotten.
22:10 because he will **n** return nor see his
22:11 from this place: "He will **n** return.
22:27 You will **n** come back to the land you
31:40 **n** again be uprooted or demolished."
32:35 though I **n** commanded, nor did it
32:40 I will **n** stop doing good to them,
32:40 that they will **n** turn away from me.
33:17 'David will **n** fail to have a man to
35: 7 Also you must **n** build houses, sow
35: 7 you must **n** have any of these things,
35:19 **n** fail to have a man to serve me.
42:18 you will **n** see this place again.'
50:39 It will **n** again be inhabited or
Lam 3:22 for his compassions **n** fail.
Eze 4:14 LORD! I have **n** defiled myself.
4:14 I have **n** eaten anything found dead
5: 9 **n** done before and will **n** do again.
16:48 her daughters **n** did what you and
16:63 be ashamed and **n** again open your
20:32 what you have in mind will **n** happen.
26:14 You will **n** be rebuilt, for I the
26:21 but you will **n** again be found,
29:15 will **n** again exalt itself above the
29:15 will **n** again rule over the nations.

Eze 36:12 you will **n** again deprive them of
37:22 they will **n** again be two nations or
43: 7 The house of Israel will **n** again
Da 2:44 a kingdom that will **n** be destroyed,
6: 5 said, "We will **n** find any basis for
6:26 destroyed, his dominion will **n** end.
7:14 is one that will **n** be destroyed.
Hos 14: 3 We will **n** again say 'Our gods' to
Joel 2: 2 such as **n** was of old nor ever will
2:19 **n** again will I make you an object
2:26 **n** again will my people be shamed.
2:27 **n** again will my people be shamed.
3:17 **n** again will foreigners invade her.
Am 5: 2 "Fallen is Virgin Israel, **n** to rise
8: 7 **n** forget anything they have done.
8:14 they will fall, **n** to rise again."
9:15 **n** again to be uprooted from the land
Ob :16 drink and be as if they had **n** been.
Na 3: 1 full of plunder, **n** without victims!
Hab 1: 4 paralysed, and justice **n** prevails.
2: 5 him; he is arrogant and **n** at rest.
2: 5 grave and like death is **n** satisfied,
Zep 3:11 **N** again will you be haughty on my
3:15 you; **n** again will you fear any harm.
Hag 1: 6 You eat, but **n** have enough. You
1: 6 You drink, but **n** have your fill. You
Zec 9: 8 **N** again will an oppressor overrun my
14:11 will be inhabited; **n** again will it
Mt 7:23 I will tell them plainly, 'I **n** knew
13:14 ever hearing but **n** understanding
13:14 be ever seeing but **n** perceiving.
16:22 "**N**, Lord!" he said. "This shall **n**
18: 3 will **n** enter the kingdom of heaven.
21:16 replied Jesus, "have you **n** read,
21:19 Then he said to it, "May you **n** bear
21:42 Jesus said to them, "Have you **n** read
24:21 now—and **n** to be equalled again.
24:35 away, but my words will **n** pass away.
26:33 away on account of you, I **n** will."
26:35 die with you, I will **n** disown you.
Mk 2:12 "We have **n** seen anything like this!
2:25 He answered, "Have you **n** read what
3:29 the Holy Spirit will **n** be forgiven;
4:12 ever seeing but **n** understanding
4:12 and ever hearing but **n** understanding;
9:25 out of him and **n** enter him again."
9:43 hell, where the fire **n** goes out.
10:15 a little child will **n** enter it."
13:19 now—and **n** to be equalled again.
13:31 away, but my words will **n** pass away.
14:31 die with you, I will **n** disown you.
Lk 1:15 He is **n** to take wine or other
1:33 for ever; his kingdom will **n** end."
2:37 She **n** left the temple but worshipped
6: 3 "Have you **n** read what David did
15:29 for you and **n** disobeyed your orders.
15:29 Yet you **n** gave me even a young goat
18:17 a little child will **n** enter it."
20:16 they said, "May this **n** be!"
21:33 away, but my words will **n** pass away.
23:29 the wombs that **n** bore and the
23:29 bore and the breasts that **n** nursed!'
Jn 4:14 the water I give him will **n** thirst.
4:48 Jesus told him, "you will **n** believe.
5:37 **n** heard his voice nor seen his form,
6:35 He who comes to me will **n** go hungry,
6:35 believes in me will **n** be thirsty.
6:37 comes to me I will **n** drive away.
8:12 Whoever follows me will **n** walk in
8:33 and have **n** been slaves of anyone.
8:51 keeps my word, he will **n** see death."
8:52 your word, he will **n** taste death.
10: 5 they will **n** follow a stranger; in
10:28 and they shall **n** perish; no-one can
10:41 They said, "Though John **n** performed
11:26 lives and believes in me will **n** die.
13: 8 "No," said Peter, "you shall **n** wash
Ac 5:42 they **n** stopped teaching and
6:13 "This fellow **n** stops speaking
10:14 **n** eaten anything impure or unclean."
13:10 Will you **n** stop perverting the right
13:34 him from the dead, **n** to decay
13:41 **n** believe, even if someone told you.
14: 8 lame from birth and had **n** walked.
20:31 three years I **n** stopped warning
20:38 they would **n** see his face again.
Ac 28:26 ever hearing but **n** understanding
28:26 be ever seeing but **n** perceiving."
Ro 4: 8 the Lord will **n** count against him."
9:33 in him will **n** be put to shame."
10:11 in him will **n** be put to shame."
12:11 **N** be lacking in zeal, but keep your
1Co 6:15 and unite them with a prostitute? **N**!
8:13 I will **n** eat meat again, so that I
13: 8 Love **n** fails. But where there are
2Co 12:13 except that I was **n** a burden to you?
Gal 4:30 the slave woman's son will **n** share
6:14 May I **n** boast except in the cross of
1Th 2: 5 You know we **n** used flattery, nor did
2Th 3:13 for you, brothers, **n** tire of doing
2Ti 3: 7 always learning but **n** able to
Heb 1:12 same, and your years will **n** end."
3:11 anger, 'They shall **n** enter my rest.
3:18 swear that they would **n** enter his
4: 3 anger, 'They shall **n** enter my rest.
4: 5 says, "They shall **n** enter my rest.
9: 7 once a year, and **n** without blood,
9:17 it **n** takes effect while the one who
10: 1 For this reason it can **n**, by the
10:11 which can **n** take away sins.
13: 5 "**N** will I leave you; **n** will I
Jas 3: 2 If anyone is **n** at fault in what he
1Pe 1: 4 an inheritance that can **n** perish
2: 6 in him will **n** be put to shame."
5: 4 of glory that will **n** fade away.
2Pe 1:10 do these things, you will **n** fall,
1:21 For prophecy **n** had its origin in the
2:14 of adultery, they **n** stop sinning,
Rev 3: 5 I will **n** blot out his name from the
3:12 **N** again will he leave it. I will
4: 8 Day and night they **n** stop saying:
7:16 **N** again will they hunger; **n** again
18: 7 am not a widow, and I will **n** mourn.'
18:14 have vanished, **n** to be recovered.'
18:21 be thrown down, **n** to be found again.
18:22 will **n** be heard in you again.
18:22 will **n** be heard in you again.
18:23 The light of a lamp will **n** shine in
18:23 bride will **n** be heard in you again.

Never-failing

Am 5:24 righteousness like a **n** stream!

New (Anew, *New covenant, New earth, New heart, New heaven, New heavens, New Jerusalem, New Moon, New song, New wine,* Newly-built)

Ge 45:22 To each of them he gave **n** clothing,
Ex 1: 8 a **n** king, who did not know about
Lev 2:14 of **n** grain roasted in the fire.
14:42 take **n** clay and plaster the house.
23:14 or roasted or **n** grain, until the
23:16 an offering of **n** grain to the LORD.
26:10 move it out to make room for the **n**.
Nu 16:30 brings about something totally **n**,
28:26 **n** grain during the Feast of Weeks,
Dt 20: 5 "Has anyone built a **n** house and not
22: 8 you build a **n** house, make a parapet
32: 2 like showers on **n** grass, like
Jos 9:13 these wineskins that we filled were **n**
Jdg 5: 8 they chose **n** gods, war came to the
15:13 they bound him with two **n** ropes
16:11 ties me securely with **n** ropes
16:12 Delilah took **n** ropes and tied him
1Sa 6: 7 "Now then, get a **n** cart ready, with
2Sa 6: 3 They set the ark of God on a **n** cart
6: 3 were guiding the **n** cart
21:16 a **n** sword, said he would kill David.
1Ki 11:29 him on the way, wearing a **n** cloak.
11:30 Ahijah took hold of the **n** cloak he
2Ki 2:20 "Bring me a **n** bowl," he said, "and
4:42 along with some ears of **n** corn.
16:14 temple—from between the **n** altar
16:14 it on the north side of the **n** altar.
16:15 "On the large **n** altar, offer the
1Ch 13: 7 from Abinadab's house on a **n** cart,
2Ch 2: 4 evening and on Sabbaths and **N** Moons
8:13 **N** Moons and the three annual feasts—
20: 5 in the front of the **n** courtyard
31: 3 **N** Moons and appointed feasts as
Ezr 9: 9 He has granted us **n** life to rebuild
Job 10:17 You bring **n** witnesses against me and
14: 7 and its **n** shoots will not fail.
29:20 in me, the bow ever **n** in my hand.'
32:19 like **n** wineskins ready to burst.
Ps 90: 5 like the **n** grass of the morning—
90: 6 though in the morning it springs up **n**
Pr 27:25 the hay is removed and **n** growth
Ecc 1: 9 there is nothing **n** under the sun.
1:10 "Look! This is something **n**"? It was
SS 6:11 look at the **n** growth in the valley,
7:13 both **n** and old, that I have stored
Isa 1:13 **N** Moons, Sabbaths and convocations—
41:15 **n** and sharp, with many teeth.
42: 9 and **n** things I declare; before they
43:19 See, I am doing a **n** thing! Now it
48: 6 "From now on I will tell you of **n**
62: 2 you will be called by a **n** name that
Jer 8:10 men and their fields to **n** owners.
26:10 of the **N** Gate of the LORD's house.
31:22 The LORD will create a **n** thing on
36:10 of the **N** Gate of the temple,
Lam 3:23 They are **n** every morning; great is
Eze 11:19 heart and put a **n** spirit in them;
17: 9 All its **n** growth will wither.
18:31 and get a **n** heart and a **n** spirit.
36:26 put a **n** spirit in you; I will
45:17 the **N** Moons and the Sabbaths—at all
46: 3 On the Sabbaths and **N** Moons the
Da 1: 7 The chief official gave them **n** names:
Hos 2:11 her **N** Moons, her Sabbath days—all
4:11 to prostitution, to old wine and **n**,
Zep 1:10 wailing from the **N** Quarter, and a
3: 5 and every **n** day he does not fail,
Mt 9:17 into **n** wineskins, and both are
13:52 **n** treasures as well as old."
27:60 placed it in his own **n** tomb that he
Mk 1:27 "What is this? A **n** teaching—and
2:21 If he does, the **n** piece will pull
2:22 he pours **n** wine into **n** wineskins."
16:17 they will speak in **n** tongues;
Lk 5:36 **n** garment and sews it on an old one.
5:36 torn the **n** garment, and the patch
5:36 from the **n** will not match the old.
5:38 must be poured into **n** wineskins
5:39 **n**, for he says, 'The old is better.
Jn 13:34 "A **n** command I give you: Love one
19:41 and in the garden a **n** tomb, in which
Ac 5:20 the full message of this **n** life."
17:19 "May we know what this **n** teaching is
Ro 6: 4 Father, we too may live a **n** life.
7: 6 we serve in the **n** way of the Spirit,
1Co 5: 7 you may be a **n** batch without yeast
2Co 5:17 is in Christ, he is a **n** creation;
5:17 the old has gone, the **n** has come!
Gal 6:15 what counts is a **n** creation.
Eph 2:15 in himself one **n** man out of the two,
4:23 to be made **n** in the attitude of your
4:24 to put on the **n** self, created to be
Col 3:10 have put on the **n** self, which is
Heb 8:13 By calling this covenant "**n**", he has
9:10 until the time of the **n** order.
10:20 by a **n** and living way opened for us
1Pe 1: 3 given us **n** birth into a living hope
1Jn 2: 7 I am not writing you a **n** command but
2: 8 Yet I am writing you a **n** command;
2Jn :5 I am not writing you a **n** command
Rev 2:17 stone with a **n** name written on it,
3:12 I will also write on him my **n** name.
21: 5 "I am making everything **n**!" Then he

New covenant

Jer 31:31 "when I will make a **n** with the house
Lk 22:20 "This cup is the **n** in my blood,
1Co 11:25 "This cup is the **n** in my blood; do
2Co 3: 6 us competent as ministers of a **n**
Heb 8: 8 when I will make a **n** with the house
9:15 Christ is the mediator of a **n**,
12:24 to Jesus the mediator of a **n**, and to

New earth

Isa 65:17 I will create new heavens and a **n**.
66:22 "As the new heavens and the **n** that I
2Pe 3:13 and a **n**, the home of righteousness.
Rev 21: 1 I saw a new heaven and a **n**, for the

New heart
Eze 18:31 and get a **n** and a new spirit.
36:26 I will give you a **n** and put a new

New heaven
2Pe 3:13 forward to a **n** and a new earth,
Rev 21: 1 I saw a **n** and a new earth, for the

New heavens
Isa 65:17 "Behold, I will create **n** and a new
66:22 "As the **n** and the new earth that I

New Jerusalem
Rev 3:12 the **n**, which is coming down out of
21: 2 I saw the Holy City, the **n**, coming

New Moon
Nu 10:10 **N** festivals—you are to sound the
28:14 be made at each **n** during the year.
1Sa 20: 5 David said, "Look, tomorrow is the **N**
20:18 David: "Tomorrow is the **N** festival.
20:24 and when the **N** festival came, the
2Ki 4:23 "It's not the **N** or the Sabbath."
1Ch 23:31 **N** festivals and at appointed feasts.
Ezr 3: 5 the **N** sacrifices and the sacrifices
Ne 10:33 **N** festivals and appointed feasts;
Ps 81: 3 Sound the ram's horn at the **N**, and
Isa 1:14 Your **N** festivals and your appointed
66:23 From one **N** to another and from one
Eze 46: 1 the day of the **N** it is to be opened.
46: 6 On the day of the **N** he is to offer a
Hos 5: 7 Now their **N** festivals will devour
Am 8: 5 saying, "When will the **N** be over
Col 2:16 a **N** celebration or a Sabbath day.

New song
Ps 33: 3 Sing to him a **n**; play skilfully, and
40: 3 He put a **n** in my mouth, a hymn of
96: 1 Sing to the LORD a **n**; sing to the
98: 1 Sing to the LORD a **n**, for he has
144: 9 I will sing a **n** to you, O God; on
149: 1 Praise the LORD. Sing to the LORD a **n**
Isa 42:10 Sing to the LORD a **n**, his praise
Rev 5: 9 they sang a **n**: "You are worthy to
14: 3 they sang a **n** before the throne and

New wine
Ge 27:28 an abundance of grain and **n**.
27:37 have sustained him with grain and **n**.
Nu 18:12 all the finest **n** and grain they give
Dt 7:13 **n** and oil—the calves of your herds
11:14 may gather in your grain, **n** and oil.
12:17 tithe of your grain and **n** and oil,
14:23 Eat the tithe of your grain, **n** and
18: 4 **n** and oil, and the first wool from
28:51 They will leave you no grain, **n** or
33:28 and **n**, where the heavens drop dew.
2Ki 18:32 a land of grain and **n**, a land of
2Ch 31: 5 **n**, oil and honey and all that the
32:28 **n** and oil; and he made stalls for
Ne 5:11 of the money, grain, **n** and oil."
10:37 all our trees and of our **n** and oil.
10:39 **n** and oil to the storerooms where
13: 5 and also the tithes of grain, **n** and
13:12 **n** and oil into the storerooms.
Ps 4: 7 than when their grain and **n** abound.
Pr 3:10 and your vats will brim over with **n**.
Isa 24: 7 The **n** dries up and the vine withers;
36:17 a land of corn and **n**, a land of
62: 8 the **n** for which you have toiled;
Jer 31:12 the **n** and the oil, the young of the
Hos 2: 8 the **n** and oil, who lavished on her
2: 9 ripens, and my **n** when it is ready.
2:22 the **n** and oil, and they will respond
7:14 grain and **n** but turn away from me.
9: 2 the people; the **n** will fail them.
Joel 1: 5 of wine; wail because of the **n**,
1:10 the **n** is dried up, the oil fails.
2:19 "I am sending you grain, **n** and oil,
2:24 vats will overflow with **n** and oil.
3:18 that day the mountains will drip **n**,
Am 9:13 **N** will drip from the mountains and
Hag 1:11 on the grain, the **n**, the oil and
Zec 9:17 men thrive, and **n** the young women.

Mt 9:17 Neither do men pour **n** into old
9:17 No, they pour **n** into new wineskins,
Mk 2:22 no-one pours **n** into old wineskins.
2:22 No, he pours **n** into new wineskins."
Lk 5:37 no-one pours **n** into old wineskins.
5:37 If he does, the **n** will burst the
5:38 No, **n** must be poured into new

Newborn (Bear[1])
Jer 14: 5 deserts her **n** fawn because there is
Ac 7:19 **n** babies so that they would die.
1Pe 2: 2 Like **n** babies, crave pure spiritual

Newly-built (New)
Jdg 6:28 bull sacrificed on the **n** altar!

News (*Good news*)
Ge 29:13 soon as Laban heard the **n** about
45:16 the **n** reached Pharaoh's palace that
1Sa 4:17 The man who brought the **n** replied,
4:19 When she heard the **n** that the ark of
13: 4 all Israel heard the **n**: "Saul has
31: 9 the **n** in the temple of their idols
2Sa 4: 4 He was five years old when the **n**
4:10 was the reward I gave him for his **n**!
18:19 "Let me run and take the **n** to the
18:20 "You are not the one to take the **n**
18:20 "You may take the **n** another time,
18:22 any **n** that will bring you a reward."
1Ki 2:28 the **n** reached Joab, who had
14: 6 I have been sent to you with bad **n**.
2Ki 7:11 The gatekeepers shouted the **n**, and
9:15 to go and tell the **n** in Jezreel."
1Ch 10: 9 proclaim the **n** among their idols and
Ps 112: 7 He will have no fear of bad **n**; his
Jer 20:15 the man who brought my father the **n**,
49:23 dismayed, for they have heard bad **n**.
Eze 21: 7 'Because of the **n** that is coming.
24:26 will come to tell you the **n**.
Jnh 3: 6 the **n** reached the king of Nineveh,
Na 3:19 Everyone who hears the **n** about you
Mt 4:24 **N** about him spread all over Syria,
9:26 **N** of this spread through all that
9:31 they went out and spread the **n** about
Mk 1:28 **N** about him spread quickly over the
1:45 to talk freely, spreading the **n**.
Lk 4:14 and **n** about him spread through the
4:37 the **n** about him spread throughout
5:15 Yet the **n** about him spread all the
7:17 This **n** about Jesus spread throughout
Jn 4:51 with the **n** that his boy was living.
20:18 with the **n**: "I have seen the Lord!"
Ac 11:22 **N** of this reached the ears of the
15: 3 **n** made all the brothers very glad.
21:31 While they were trying to kill him, **n**
Php 2:19 cheered when I receive **n** about you.
Col 4: 7 Tychicus will tell you all the **n**

Neziah
Ezr 2:54 **N** and Hatipha
Ne 7:56 **N** and Hatipha

Nezib
Jos 15:43 Iphtah, Ashnah, **N**,

Nibhaz
2Ki 17:31 the Avvites made **N** and Tartak, and

Nibshan
Jos 15:62 **N**, the City of Salt and En Gedi—six

Nicanor
Ac 6: 5 Procorus, **N**, Timon, Parmenas, and

Nicodemus
Pharisee, member of Sanhedrin who visited Jesus at night (Jn 3:1–15). Argued against condemning Jesus without a hearing (Jn 7:50–51). With Joseph anointed and buried Jesus (Jn 19:38–42).

Jn 3: 1 was a man of the Pharisees named **N**,
3: 4 be born when he is old?" **N** asked.
3: 9 "How can this be?" **N** asked.
7:50 **N**, who had gone to Jesus earlier and
19:39 He was accompanied by **N**, the man who
19:39 **N** brought a mixture of myrrh and

Nicolaitans
Rev 2: 6 of the **N**, which I also hate.
2:15 who hold to the teaching of the **N**.

Nicolas
Ac 6: 5 **N** from Antioch, a convert to Judaism.

Nicopolis
Tit 3:12 do your best to come to me at **N**,

Niger
Ac 13: 1 Simeon called **N**, Lucius of Cyrene,

Night (All-night, Midnight, Nightfall, Nights, Night-time, Overnight)
Ge 1: 5 and the darkness he called "**n**".
1:14 sky to separate the day from the **n**,
1:16 the lesser light to govern the **n**.
1:18 to govern the day and the **n**, and to
8:22 winter, day and **n** will never cease."
14:15 During the **n** Abram divided his men
19: 2 spend the **n** and then go on your way
19: 2 "we will spend the **n** in the square.
19:33 That **n** they got their father to
19:34 "Last **n** I lay with my father.
19:35 father to drink wine that **n** also,
20: 3 in a dream one **n** and said to him,
24:23 house for us to spend the **n**?"
24:25 as room for you to spend the **n**."
24:54 ate and drank and spent the **n** there.
26:24 That **n** the LORD appeared to him and
28:11 for the **n** because the sun had set.
30:16 So he slept with her that **n**.
31:24 in a dream at **n** and said to him,
31:29 last **n** the God of your father said
31:39 for whatever was stolen by day or **n**.
31:40 at **n**, and sleep fled from my eyes.
31:42 hands, and last **n** he rebuked you."
31:54 had eaten, they spent the **n** there.
32:13 He spent the **n** there, and from what
32:21 he himself spent the **n** in the camp.
32:22 That **n** Jacob got up and took his two
40: 5 in prison—had a dream the same **n**,
41:11 Each of us had a dream the same **n**,
42:27 place where they stopped for the **n**
43:21 for the **n** we opened our sacks
46: 2 God spoke to Israel in a vision at **n**
Ex 10:13 land all that day and all that **n**.
12: 8 That same **n** they are to eat the meat
12:12 "On that same **n** I will pass through
12:30 the Egyptians got up during the **n**,
12:31 During the **n** Pharaoh summoned Moses
12:42 the LORD kept vigil that **n** to bring
12:42 on this **n** all the Israelites are to
13:21 by **n** in a pillar of fire to give
13:21 that they could travel by day or **n**.
13:22 nor the pillar of fire by **n** left
14:20 Throughout the **n** the cloud brought
14:20 went near the other all **n** long.
14:21 and all that **n** the LORD drove the
14:24 During the last watch of the **n** the
40:38 and fire was in the cloud by **n**, in
Lev 6: 9 the altar hearth throughout the **n**,
8:35 day and **n** for seven days and do
Nu 9:16 it, and at **n** it looked like fire.
9:21 Whether by day or by **n**, whenever the
11: 9 the dew settled on the camp at **n**,
11:32 All that day and **n** and all the next
14: 1 That **n** all the people of the
14:14 by day and a pillar of fire by **n**.
22: 8 "Spend the **n** here," Balaam said to
22:20 That **n** God came to Balaam and said,
Dt 1:33 in fire by **n** and in a cloud by day,
16: 1 he brought you out of Egypt by **n**.
28:66 **n** and day, never sure of your life.
Jos 1: 8 mouth; meditate on it day and **n**,
2: 8 Before the spies lay down for the **n**,
6:11 to camp and spent the **n** there.
8: 3 fighting men and sent them out at **n**
8: 9 Joshua spent that **n** with the people.

Jos 8:13 That **n** Joshua went into the valley.
Jdg 6:25 That same **n** the LORD said to him,
6:27 it at **n** rather than in the daytime.
6:40 That **n** God did so. Only the fleece
7: 9 During that **n** the LORD said to
9:32 Now then, during the **n** you and your
9:34 all his troops set out by **n** and took
16: 1 He went in to spend the **n** with her.
16: 2 wait for him all **n** at the city gate.
16: 2 They made no move during the **n**,
16: 3 only until the middle of the **n**.
18: 2 of Micah, where they spent the **n**.
19: 7 him, so he stayed there that **n**.
19: 9 Spend the **n** here; the day is nearly
19:10 But, unwilling to stay another **n**,
19:11 of the Jebusites and spend the **n**."
19:13 spend the **n** in one of those places."
19:15 There they stopped to spend the **n**.
19:15 took them into his home for the **n**.
19:20 don't spend the **n** in the square."
19:25 the **n**, and at dawn they let her go.
20: 4 Gibeah in Benjamin to spend the **n**.
20: 5 During the **n** the men of Gibeah came
Ru 3: 8 In the middle of the **n** something
3:13 Stay here for the **n**, and in the
1Sa 3: 2 One **n** Eli, whose eyes were becoming
11:11 during the last watch of the **n** they
14:34 ox that **n** and slaughtered it there.
14:36 by **n** and plunder them till dawn,
15:11 he cried out to the LORD all that **n**.
15:16 you what the LORD said to me last **n**.
19:10 That **n** David made good his escape.
19:24 He lay that way all that day and **n**.
25:16 **N** and day they were a wall around us
26: 7 and Abishai went to the army by **n**,
28: 8 at **n** he and two men went to the
28:20 eaten nothing all that day and **n**.
28:25 That same **n** they got up and left.
31:12 through the **n** to Beth Shan.
2Sa 2:29 All that **n** Abner and his men marched
2:32 marched all **n** and arrived at Hebron
4: 7 all **n** by way of the Arabah.
7: 4 That **n** the word of the LORD came to
17: 8 not spend the **n** with the troops.
17:16 'Do not spend the **n** at the fords in
21:10 by day or the wild animals by **n**.
1Ki 3: 5 to Solomon during the **n** in a dream,
3:19 "During the **n** this woman's son died
3:20 she got up in the middle of the **n**
8:29 open towards this temple **n** and day,
8:59 near to the LORD our God day and **n**,
19: 9 he went into a cave and spent the **n**.
2Ki 6:14 went by **n** and surrounded the city.
7:12 The king got up in the **n** and said to
8:21 he rose up and broke through by **n**;
19:35 That **n** the angel of the LORD went
25: 4 and the whole army fled at **n** through
1Ch 9:27 They would spend the **n** stationed
9:33 responsible for the work day and **n**.
17: 3 That **n** the word of God came to
2Ch 1: 7 That **n** God appeared to Solomon and
6:20 open towards this temple day and **n**,
7:12 the LORD appeared to him at **n** and
21: 9 he rose up and broke through by **n**.
Ne 1: 6 you day and **n** for your servants,
2:12 I set out during the **n** with a few
2:13 By **n** I went out through the Valley
2:15 I went up the valley by **n**, examining
4: 9 guard day and **n** to meet this threat.
4:22 helper stay inside Jerusalem at **n**,
4:22 as guards by **n** and workmen by day."
6:10 by **n** they are coming to kill you.
9:12 and by **n** with a pillar of fire to
9:19 nor the pillar of fire by **n** to shine
13:20 goods spent the **n** outside Jerusalem.
13:21 "Why do you spend the **n** by the wall?
Est 4:16 or drink for three days, **n** or day.
6: 1 That **n** the king could not sleep; so
Job 3: 3 the **n** it was said, 'A boy is born!'
3: 6 That **n**—may thick darkness seize it;
3: 7 May that **n** be barren; may no shout
4:13 Amid disquieting dreams in the **n**,
5:14 at noon they grope as in the **n**.
7: 4 The **n** drags on, and I toss till dawn.
10:22 to the land of deepest **n**, of deep
17:12 These men turn **n** into day; in the
Job 20: 8 banished like a vision of the **n**.
24: 7 Lacking clothes, they spend the **n**
24:14 the **n** he steals forth like a thief.
27:20 tempest snatches him away in the **n**.
29:19 dew will lie all **n** on my branches.
30: 3 land in desolate wastelands at **n**.
30:17 **N** pierces my bones; my gnawing pains
31:32 no stranger had to spend the **n** in
33:15 In a dream, in a vision of the **n**,
34:20 in the middle of the **n**; the people
34:25 them in the **n** and they are crushed.
35:10 my Maker, who gives songs in the **n**,
36:20 Do not long for the **n**, to drag
39: 9 Will he stay by your manger at **n**?
39:28 on a cliff and stays there at **n**;
Ps 1: 2 on his law he meditates day and **n**.
6: 6 I am worn out from groaning; all **n**
16: 7 me; even at **n** my heart instructs me.
17: 3 probe my heart and examine me at **n**,
19: 2 **n** after **n** they display knowledge.
22: 2 not answer, by **n**, and am not silent.
30: 5 weeping may remain for a **n**,
32: 4 For day and **n** your hand was heavy
42: 3 My tears have been my food day and **n**,
42: 8 at **n** his song is with me—a prayer
55:10 Day and **n** they prowl about on its
63: 6 of you through the watches of the **n**.
74:16 day is yours, and yours also the **n**;
77: 2 I sought the Lord; at **n** I stretched
77: 6 I remembered my songs in the **n**. My
78:14 and with light from the fire all **n**.
88: 1 me, day and **n** I cry out before you.
90: 4 gone by, or like a watch in the **n**.
91: 5 You will not fear the terror of **n**,
92: 2 morning and your faithfulness at **n**,
104:20 You bring darkness, it becomes **n**,
105:39 and a fire to give light at **n**.
119:55 In the **n** I remember your name, O
119:148 open through the watches of the **n**,
121: 6 harm you by day, nor the moon by **n**.
134: 1 by **n** in the house of the LORD.
136: 9 the moon and stars to govern the **n**;
139:11 and the light become **n** around me,"
139:12 you; the **n** will shine like the day,
Pr 7: 9 was fading, as the dark of **n** set in.
31:18 and her lamp does not go out at **n**.
Ecc 2:23 even at **n** his mind does not rest.
8:16 eyes not seeing sleep day or **n**—
SS 3: 1 All **n** long on my bed I looked for
3: 8 prepared for the terrors of the **n**.
5: 2 my hair with the dampness of the **n**."
7:11 let us spend the **n** in the villages.
Isa 4: 5 day and a glow of flaming fire by **n**;
5:11 who stay up late at **n** till they are
15: 1 destroyed in a **n**! Kir in Moab is
15: 1 in Moab is ruined, destroyed in a **n**!
16: 3 Make your shadow like **n**—at high
21: 8 every **n** I stay at my post.
21:11 **n**? Watchman, what is left of the **n**?"
21:12 "Morning is coming, but also the **n**.
26: 9 My soul yearns for you in the **n**; in
27: 3 and **n** so that no-one may harm it.
28:19 day and by **n**, it will sweep through.
29: 7 a dream, with a vision in the **n**—
30:29 you will sing as on the **n** you
34:10 will not be quenched **n** and day; its
34:14 there the **n** creatures will also
38:12 day and **n** you made an end of me.
38:13 day and **n** you made an end of me.
58:10 your **n** will become like the noonday.
60:11 they will never be shut, day or **n**,
62: 6 they will never be silent day or **n**.
Jer 6: 5 arise, let us attack at **n** and
9: 1 and **n** for the slain of my people.
14: 8 like a traveller who stays only a **n**?
14:17 'Let my eyes overflow with tears **n**
16:13 you will serve other gods day and **n**
31:35 the moon and stars to shine by **n**,
33:20 the day and my covenant with the **n**,
33:20 so that day and **n** no longer come at
33:25 my covenant with day and **n** and the
36:30 the heat by day and the frost by **n**.
39: 4 they fled; they left the city at **n**
49: 9 If thieves came during the **n**,
52: 7 They left the city at **n** through the
Lam 1: 2 Bitterly she weeps at **n**, tears are
Lam 2:18 day and **n**; give yourself no relief,
2:19 Arise, cry out in the **n**, as the
2:19 as the watches of the **n** begin; pour
Da 2:19 During the **n** the mystery was
5:30 That very **n** Belshazzar, king of the
6:18 spent the **n** without eating and
7: 2 Daniel said: "In my vision at **n** I
7: 7 "After that, in my vision at **n** I
7:13 "In my vision at **n** I looked, and
Hos 4: 5 You stumble day and **n**, and the
7: 6 Their passion smoulders all **n**; in
Joel 1:13 Come, spend the **n** in sackcloth, you
Am 5: 8 into dawn and darkens day into **n**,
Ob : 5 if robbers in the **n**—Oh, what a
Mic 3: 6 Therefore **n** will come over you,
Zec 1: 8 During the **n** I had a vision—and
Mt 2:14 during the **n** and left for Egypt,
14:25 During the fourth watch of the **n**
21:17 to Bethany, where he spent the **n**.
24:43 what time of **n** the thief was coming,
26:31 Jesus told them, "This very **n** you
26:34 "this very **n**, before the cock crows,
28:13 'His disciples came during the **n** and
Mk 4:27 **N** and day, whether he sleeps or gets
5: 5 **N** and day among the tombs and in the
6:48 About the fourth watch of the **n** he
Lk 2: 8 watch over their flocks at **n**.
2:37 **n** and day, fasting and praying.
5: 5 all **n** and haven't caught anything.
6:12 and spent the **n** praying to God.
12:20 'You fool! This very **n** your life
12:38 the second or third watch of the **n**.
17:34 I tell you, on that **n** two people
18: 7 who cry out to him day and **n**?
21:37 went out to spend the **n** on the hill
Jn 3: 2 He came to Jesus at **n** and said,
9: 4 **N** is coming, when no-one can work.
11:10 is when he walks by **n** that he
13:30 he went out. And it was **n**.
19:39 who earlier had visited Jesus at **n**.
21: 3 but that **n** they caught nothing.
Ac 5:19 during the **n** an angel of the Lord
9:24 Saul learned of their plan. Day and **n**
9:25 his followers took him by **n** and
12: 6 The **n** before Herod was to bring him
16: 9 During the **n** Paul had a vision of a
16:33 At that hour of the **n** the jailer
17:10 soon as it was **n**, the brothers sent
18: 9 One **n** the Lord spoke to Paul in a
20:31 each of you **n** and day with tears.
23:11 The following **n** the Lord stood near
23:31 took Paul with them during the **n** and
26: 7 they earnestly serve God day and **n**.
27:23 Last **n** an angel of the God whose I
27:27 On the fourteenth **n** we were still
Ro 13:12 The **n** is nearly over; the day is
1Co 11:23 the **n** he was betrayed, took bread,
2Co 11:25 spent a **n** and a day in the open sea,
1Th 2: 9 our toil and hardship; we worked **n**
3:10 **N** and day we pray most earnestly
5: 2 Lord will come like a thief in the **n**.
5: 5 belong to the **n** or to the darkness.
5: 7 For those who sleep, sleep at **n**, and
5: 7 those who get drunk, get drunk at **n**.
2Th 3: 8 On the contrary, we worked **n** and day,
1Ti 5: 5 continues **n** and day to pray and to
2Ti 1: 3 with a clear conscience, as **n** and
Rev 4: 8 Day and **n** they never stop saying:
7:15 serve him day and **n** in his temple;
8:12 light, and also a third of the **n**.
12:10 God day and **n**, has been hurled down.
14:11 There is no rest day or **n** for those
20:10 day and **n** for ever and ever.
21:25 shut, for there will be no **n** there.
22: 5 There will be no more **n**. They will

Nightfall (Night)

2Sa 19: 7 a man will be left with you by **n**.
2Ch 35:14 and the fat portions until **n**.

Nights (Forty nights, Night)

Dt 10:10 on the mountain forty days and **n**,
1Sa 30:12 water for three days and three **n**.
2Sa 12:16 and spent the **n** lying on the ground.
Job 2:13 with him for seven days and seven **n**.

Job 7: 3 **n** of misery have been assigned to me.
Isa 65: 4 spend their **n** keeping secret vigil;
Jnh 1:17 the fish three days and three **n**.
Mt 12:40 three **n** in the belly of a huge fish,
12:40 three **n** in the heart of the earth.
2Co 6: 5 hard work, sleepless **n** and hunger;

Night-time (Night)
Zec 14: 7 or **n**—a day known to the LORD.

Nile, River
Running about 3,500 miles from central Africa, northwards to the Egyptian delta on the Mediterranean coast. Appears in Pharaoh's dream that Joseph interpreted (Ge 41:1, 3, 17). All Hebrew baby boys were to be drowned here (Ex 1:22); Moses escaped and was discovered by Pharaoh's daughter (Ex 2:5-10). During the plagues its water was turned to blood (Ex 4:9; 7:17–25; Ps 78:4), and its frogs invaded the land (Ex 8:3, 9, 11). Used symbolically by the prophets because of its importance and regular flooding (Isa 19:7–8; 23:3, 10; Jer 46:7–8; Eze 29:3, 9; 30:12; Am 8:8; 9:5; Na 3:8; Zec 10:11).

Ge 41: 1 a dream: He was standing by the **N**,
41: 3 came up out of the **N** and stood
41:17 I was standing on the bank of the **N**,
Ex 1:22 the **N**, but let every girl live."
2: 3 the reeds along the bank of the **N**.
2: 5 Pharaoh's daughter went down to the **N**
4: 9 the **N** and pour it on the dry ground.
7:15 Wait on the bank of the **N** to meet
7:17 I will strike the water of the **N**,
7:18 The fish in the **N** will die, and the
7:20 and struck the water of the **N**,
7:21 The fish in the **N** died, and the
7:24 all the Egyptians dug along the **N** to
7:25 passed after the LORD struck the **N**.
8: 3 The **N** will teem with frogs. They
8: 9 for those that remain in the **N**."
8:11 they will remain only in the **N**."
17: 5 with which you struck the **N**, and go.
Isa 19: 7 also the plants along the **N**, at the
19: 7 Every sown field along the **N** will
19: 8 all who cast hooks into the **N**; those
23: 3 of the **N** was the revenue of Tyre,
23:10 Till your land as along the **N**, O
Jer 46: 7 "Who is this that rises like the **N**,
46: 8 Egypt rises like the **N**, like rivers
Eze 29: 3 The **N** is mine; I made it for myself."
29: 9 "'Because you said, "The **N** is mine;
30:12 I will dry up the streams of the **N**
Am 8: 8 The whole land will rise like the **N**;
9: 5 the whole land rises like the **N**,
Na 3: 8 situated on the **N**, with water around
Zec 10:11 all the depths of the **N** will dry up.

Nimrah
Nu 32: 3 "Ataroth, Dibon, Jazer, **N**, Heshbon,

Nimrim
Isa 15: 6 The waters of **N** are dried up and the
Jer 48:34 even the waters of **N** are dried up.

Nimrod
Ge 10: 8 Cush was the father of **N**, who grew
10: 9 **N**, a mighty hunter before the LORD."
1Ch 1:10 Cush was the father of **N**, who grew
Mic 5: 6 the land of **N** with drawn sword.

Nimshi
1Ki 19:16 Also, anoint Jehu son of **N** king over
2Ki 9: 2 son of Jehoshaphat, the son of **N**.
9:14 Jehu son of Jehoshaphat, the son of **N**
9:20 son of **N**—he drives like a madman."
2Ch 22: 7 with Joram to meet Jehu son of **N**,

Nineveh (Ninevites)
City on bank of River Tigris, built by Nimrod, in Assyria (Ge 10:11-12). Sennacherib's capital city, where he was murdered by his sons (2Ki 19:36; Isa 37:37–38). God instructed Jonah to preach here; its people repented and turned to God (Jnh 1:2; 3:2–10; 4:11). Nahum pronounced God's judgment upon it (Na 1:1, 8, 11, 14; 2:1, 8; 3:7); Zephaniah foretold its destruction (Zep 2:13). Jesus compared its people in Jonah's time with his own stubborn generation (Mt 12:41; Lk 11:32).

Ge 10:11 where he built **N**, Rehoboth Ir,
10:12 Resen, which is between **N** and Calah;
2Ki 19:36 He returned to **N** and stayed there.
Isa 37:37 He returned to **N** and stayed there.
Jnh 1: 2 "Go to the great city of **N** and
3: 2 "Go to the great city of **N** and
3: 3 the word of the LORD and went to **N**.
3: 3 Now **N** was a very important city—a
3: 4 more days and **N** will be overturned."
3: 6 the news reached the king of **N**, he
3: 7 he issued a proclamation in **N**: "By
4:11 **N** has more than a hundred and twenty
Na 1: 1 An oracle concerning **N**. The book of
1: 8 flood he will make an end of **N**;
1:11 From you, O **N**, has one come forth
1:14 **N**: "You will have no descendants to
2: 1 An attacker advances against you, **N**.
2: 8 **N** is like a pool, and its water is
3: 7 '**N** is in ruins—who will mourn for
Zep 2:13 leaving **N** utterly desolate and dry
Mt 12:41 The men of **N** will stand up at the
Lk 11:32 The men of **N** will stand up at the

Ninevites (Nineveh)
Jnh 3: 5 The **N** believed God. They declared a
Lk 11:30 For as Jonah was a sign to the **N**, so

Nisan
Ne 2: 1 In the month of **N** in the twentieth
Est 3: 7 in the first month, the month of **N**,

Nisroch
2Ki 19:37 in the temple of his god **N**,
Isa 37:38 in the temple of his god **N**,

Noadiah
Ezr 8:33 son of Jeshua and **N** son of Binnui.
Ne 6:14 remember also the prophetess **N** and

Noah (Noah's)
Righteous man (Ge 6:8–9; 7:1; Eze 14:14,20; Heb 11:7). Obeyed God's command to build ark (Ge 6:11–22). God's covenant with (Ge 6:18; 9:8–17). Planted vineyard; became drunk, dishonoured by Ham (Ge 9:20–23); cursed Canaan; blessed Shem and Japheth (Ge 9:24–27). Death (Ge 9:28–29).

Ge 5:29 He named him **N** and said, "He will
5:30 After **N** was born, Lamech lived 595
5:32 After **N** was 500 years old, he became
6: 8 **N** found favour in the eyes of the
6: 9 This is the account of **N**. **N** was a
6:10 **N** had three sons: Shem, Ham and
6:13 God said to **N**, "I am going to put an
6:22 **N** did everything just as God
7: 1 The LORD then said to **N**, "Go into
7: 5 **N** did all that the LORD commanded
7: 6 **N** was six hundred years old when the
7: 7 **N** and his sons and his wife and his
7: 9 male and female, came to **N** and
7: 9 the ark, as God had commanded **N**.
7:13 On that very day **N** and his sons,
7:15 them came to **N** and entered the ark.
7:16 thing, as God had commanded **N**.
7:23 Only **N** was left, and those with him
8: 1 God remembered **N** and all the wild
8: 6 After forty days **N** opened the window
8: 9 so it returned to **N** in the ark.
8:11 Then **N** knew that the water had
8:13 **N** then removed the covering from the
8:15 Then God said to **N**,
8:18 **N** came out, together with his sons
8:20 **N** built an altar to the LORD and,
9: 1 God blessed **N** and his sons, saying
9: 8 God said to **N** and to his sons with
9:17 God said to **N**, "This is the sign of
9:18 The sons of **N** who came out of the
9:19 These were the three sons of **N**, and
9:20 **N**, a man of the soil, proceeded to
9:24 **N** awoke from his wine and found out
Ge 9:28 After the flood **N** lived 350 years.
9:29 Altogether, **N** lived 950 years, and
Nu 26:33 **N**, Hoglah, Milcah and Tirzah.)
27: 1 Mahlah, **N**, Hoglah, Milcah and Tirzah.
36:11 Tirzah, Hoglah, Milcah and **N**
Jos 17: 3 Mahlah, **N**, Hoglah, Milcah and Tirzah.
1Ch 1: 3 Enoch, Methuselah, Lamech, **N**.
1: 4 The sons of **N**: Shem, Ham and Japheth.
Isa 54: 9 "To me this is like the days of **N**,
54: 9 **N** would never again cover the earth.
Eze 14:14 even if these three men—**N**, Daniel
14:20 even if **N**, Daniel and Job were in it,
Mt 24:37 was in the days of **N**, so it will be
24:38 up to the day **N** entered the ark;
Lk 3:36 the son of **N**, the son of Lamech,
17:26 "Just as it was in the days of **N**, so
17:27 up to the day **N** entered the ark.
Heb 11: 7 By faith **N**, when warned about things
1Pe 3:20 of **N** while the ark was being built.
2Pe 2: 5 but protected **N**, a preacher of

Noah's (Noah)
Ge 7:11 In the six hundredth year of **N** life,
8:13 of **N** six hundred and first year,
10: 1 Ham and Japheth, **N** sons, who
10:32 These are the clans of **N** sons,

Nob
Priestly town (1Sa 22:19) in territory of Benjamin (Ne 11:32), about 2 miles east of Jerusalem. David fled here from Saul (1Sa 21:1) and was given consecrated bread and Goliath's sword (1Sa 21:1–9). All of its priests were then executed by Saul (1Sa 22:11–19). The Assyrian army camped here before assaulting Jerusalem (Isa 10:32).

1Sa 21: 1 David went to **N**, to Ahimelech the
22: 9 to Ahimelech son of Ahitub at **N**.
22:11 at **N**, and they all came to the king.
22:19 He also put to the sword **N**, the town
Ne 11:32 in Anathoth, **N** and Ananiah,
Isa 10:32 This day they will halt at **N**; they

Nobah
Nu 32:42 **N** captured Kenath and its
32:42 and called it **N** after himself.
Jdg 8:11 the route of the nomads east of **N**

Nobility (Noble)
Est 1:18 Median women of the **n** who have heard
Da 1: 3 from the royal family and the **n**—

Noble (Nobility, Nobleman, Nobles, Noblest)
Ru 3:11 that you are a woman of **n** character.
Est 6: 9 to one of the king's most **n** princes.
Ps 45: 1 My heart is stirred by a **n** theme as
Pr 12: 4 A wife of **n** character is her
31:10 A wife of **n** character who can find?
31:29 "Many women do **n** things, but you
Ecc 10:17 O land whose king is of **n** birth and
Isa 32: 5 No longer will the fool be called **n**
32: 8 the **n** man makes **n** plans, and by **n**
Lk 8:15 for those with a **n** and good heart,
19:12 He said: "A man of **n** birth went to a
Ac 17:11 Now the Bereans were of more **n**
Ro 9:21 **n** purposes and some for common use?
1Co 1:26 not many were of **n** birth.
Php 4: 8 whatever is true, whatever is **n**,
1Ti 3: 1 an overseer, he desires a **n** task.
2Ti 2:20 for **n** purposes and some for ignoble.
2:21 he will be an instrument for **n**
Jas 2: 7 **n** name of him to whom you belong?

Nobleman (Noble)
Pr 25: 7 for him to humiliate you before a **n**.

Nobles (Noble)
Nu 21:18 that the **n** of the people sank—the **n**
Jdg 5:13 who were left came down to the **n**;
5:25 for **n** she brought him curdled milk.
2Sa 10: 3 the Ammonite **n** said to Hanun their
1Ki 21: 8 and sent them to the elders and **n**
21:11 the elders and **n** who lived in

2Ki 24:12 his mother, his attendants, his **n**
1Ch 19: 3 the Ammonite **n** said to Hanun, "Do
2Ch 23:20 the **n**, the rulers of the people and
Ne 2:16 to the Jews or the priests or **n** or
3: 5 but their **n** would not put their
4:14 I stood up and said to the **n**, the
4:19 I said to the **n**, the officials and
5: 7 then accused the **n** and officials.
5:12 made the **n** and officials take an
6:17 Also, in those days the **n** of Judah
7: 5 it into my heart to assemble the **n**,
10:29 these now join their brothers the **n**,
13:17 I rebuked the **n** of Judah and said to
Est 1: 3 banquet for all his **n** and officials.
1: 3 the **n** of the provinces were present.
1:11 her beauty to the people and **n**
1:14 Marsena and Memucan, the seven **n** of
1:16 the presence of the king and the **n**,
1:16 the king but also against all the **n**
1:18 to all the king's **n** in the same way.
1:21 The king and his **n** were pleased with
2:18 for all his **n** and officials.
3: 1 higher than that of all the other **n**.
3:12 and the **n** of the various peoples.
5:11 him above the other **n** and officials.
8: 9 and to the satraps, governors and **n**
9: 3 all the **n** of the provinces, the
Job 12:21 He pours contempt on **n** and disarms
29:10 the voices of the **n** were hushed, and
34:18 and to **n**, 'You are wicked,'
Ps 47: 9 The **n** of the nations assemble as the
83:11 Make their **n** like Oreb and Zeeb, all
107:40 he who pours contempt on **n** made them
149: 8 their **n** with shackles of iron,
Pr 8:16 by me princes govern, and all **n** who
Isa 5:14 into it will descend their **n** and
13: 2 to them to enter the gates of the **n**.
34:12 Her **n** will have nothing there to be
Jer 14: 3 The **n** send their servants for water;
27:20 all the **n** of Judah and Jerusalem—
39: 6 and also killed all the **n** of Judah.
Eze 17:12 and carried off her king and her **n**,
Da 4:36 My advisers and **n** sought me out, and
5: 1 of his **n** and drank wine with them.
5: 2 so that the king and his **n**, his
5: 3 and the king and his **n**, his wives
5: 9 grew more pale. His **n** were baffled.
5:10 his **n**, came into the banquet hall.
5:23 and you and your **n**, your wives and
6:17 ring and with the rings of his **n**,
Jnh 3: 7 "By the decree of the king and his **n**:
Na 3:10 Lots were cast for her **n**, and all
3:18 slumber; your **n** lie down to rest.

Noblest (Noble)

SS 3: 7 by sixty warriors, the **n** of Israel,

Nocturnal

Dt 23:10 is unclean because of a **n** emission,

Nod

Ge 4:16 in the land of **N**, east of Eden.

Nodab

1Ch 5:19 the Hagrites, Jetur, Naphish and **N**.

Nogah

1Ch 3: 7 **N**, Nepheg, Japhia,
14: 6 **N**, Nepheg, Japhia,

Nohah

1Ch 8: 2 **N** the fourth and Rapha the fifth.

Noise (Noisy)

Ex 32:17 Joshua heard the **n** of the people
1Ki 1:41 meaning of all the **n** in the city?"
1:45 That's the **n** you hear.
2Ki 11:13 Athaliah heard the **n** made by the
2Ch 23:12 Athaliah heard the **n** of the people
Ezr 3:13 because the people made so much **n**.
Isa 13: 4 Listen, a **n** on the mountains, like
14:11 along with the **n** of your harps;
24: 8 the **n** of the revellers has stopped,
29: 6 thunder and earthquake and great **n**,
Isa 66: 6 hear that **n** from the temple! It is
Jer 46:17 king of Egypt is only a loud **n**;
47: 3 at the **n** of enemy chariots and the
50:22 The **n** of battle is in the land, the **n**
Eze 23:42 "The **n** of a carefree crowd was
26:10 Your walls will tremble at the **n** of
37: 7 there was a **n**, a rattling sound, and
Joel 2: 5 With a **n** like that of chariots they
Am 5:23 Away with the **n** of your songs! I

Noisy (Noise)

Ps 64: 2 from that **n** crowd of evildoers.
Pr 1:21 at the head of the **n** streets she
Isa 32:14 be abandoned, the **n** city deserted
Jer 48:45 Moab, the skulls of the **n** boasters.
51:55 Babylon; he will silence her **n** din.
Eze 26:13 I will put an end to your **n** songs,
Mt 9:23 the flute players and the **n** crowd,

Nomad (Nomads)

Jer 3: 2 lovers, sat like a **n** in the desert.

Nomads (Nomad)

Jdg 8:11 Gideon went up by the route of the **n**
Jer 35: 7 time in the land where you are **n**.'

Non-Greeks

Ro 1:14 I am bound both to Greeks and **n**,

Nonsense

Job 21:34 how can you console me with your **n**?
Isa 44:25 of the wise and turns it into **n**,
Lk 24:11 their words seemed to them like **n**.

Noon (Afternoon, Noonday)

Ge 43:16 they are to eat with me at **n**."
43:25 gifts for Joseph's arrival at **n**,
1Ki 18:26 name of Baal from morning till **n**.
18:27 At **n** Elijah began to taunt them.
20:16 They set out at **n** while Ben-Hadad
2Ki 4:20 her lap until **n**, and then he died.
Ne 8: 3 He read it aloud from daybreak till **n**
Job 5:14 at **n** they grope as in the night.
Ps 55:17 Evening, morning and **n** I cry out in
Isa 16: 3 your shadow like night—at high **n**.
Jer 6: 4 let us attack at **n**! But, alas, the
20:16 in the morning, a battle cry at **n**.
Am 8: 9 "I will make the sun go down at **n**
Ac 10: 9 About **n** the following day as they
22: 6 "About **n** as I came near Damascus,
26:13 About **n**, O King, as I was on the

Noonday (Noon)

2Sa 4: 5 day while he was taking his **n** rest.
Job 11:17 Life will be brighter than **n**, and
Ps 37: 6 of your cause like the **n** sun.
Isa 58:10 your night will become like the **n**.

Noose

Job 18:10 A **n** is hidden for him on the ground;
Pr 7:22 like a deer stepping into a **n**

Nophah

Nu 21:30 far as **N**, which extends to Medeba."

North (North-easter, Northern, Northward, North-west)

Ge 13:14 and look **n** and south, east and west.
14:15 them as far as Hobah, **n** of Damascus.
28:14 the east, to the **n** and to the south.
Ex 26:20 For the other side, the **n** side of
26:35 on the **n** side of the tabernacle
27:11 The **n** side shall also be a hundred
36:25 For the other side, the **n** side of
38:11 The **n** side was also a hundred cubits
40:22 on the **n** side of the tabernacle
Lev 1:11 He is to slaughter it at the **n** side
Nu 2:25 On the **n** will be the divisions of
3:35 on the **n** side of the tabernacle.
34: 9 This will be your boundary on the **n**.
35: 5 the **n**, with the town in the centre.
Dt 2: 3 country long enough; now turn **n**.
3:12 **n** of Aroer by the Arnon Gorge,
Dt 3:27 look west and **n** and south and east.
Jos 8:11 They set up camp **n** of Ai, with the
8:13 in the camp to the **n** of the city
13: 3 to the territory of Ekron on the **n**,
15: 6 continued **n** of Beth Arabah to the
15: 7 of Achor and turned **n** to Gilgal,
16: 6 From Micmethath on the **n** it curved
17:10 to Ephraim, on the **n** to Manasseh.
17:10 on the **n** and Issachar on the east.
18: 5 of Joseph in its territory on the **n**.
18:12 On the **n** side their boundary began
18:16 Hinnom, **n** of the Valley of Rephaim.
18:17 then curved **n**, went to En Shemesh,
19:14 went round on the **n** to Hannathon
19:27 and went **n** to Beth Emek and Neiel,
24:30 of Ephraim, **n** of Mount Gaash.
Jdg 2: 9 of Ephraim, **n** of Mount Gaash.
7: 1 The camp of Midian was **n** of them in
21:19 to the **n** of Bethel, and east of the
1Sa 14: 5 One cliff stood to the **n** towards
1Ki 7:21 Jakin and the one to the **n** Boaz.
7:25 three facing **n**, three facing west,
7:39 of the temple and five on the **n**.
2Ki 11:11 side to the **n** side of the temple.
16:14 it on the **n** side of the new altar.
1Ch 9:24 four sides: east, west, **n** and south.
26:14 the lot for the **N** Gate fell to him.
26:17 four a day on the **n**, four a day on
2Ch 3:17 one to the south and one to the **n**.
3:17 Jakin and the one to the **n** Boaz.
4: 4 three facing **n**, three facing west,
4: 6 on the south side and five on the **n**.
4: 7 on the south side and five on the **n**.
4: 8 on the south side and five on the **n**.
23:10 side to the **n** side of the temple.
Job 23: 9 he is at work in the **n**, I do not see
37:22 Out of the **n** he comes in golden
Ps 89:12 You created the **n** and the south;
107: 3 east and west, from **n** and south.
Pr 25:23 a **n** wind brings rain, so a sly
Ecc 1: 6 to the **n**; round and round it goes,
11: 3 tree falls to the south or to the **n**,
SS 4:16 Awake, **n** wind, and come, south wind!
Isa 14:31 A cloud of smoke comes from the **n**,
41:25 "I have stirred up one from the **n**,
43: 6 I will say to the **n**, 'Give them up!'
49:12 come from afar—some from the **n**,
Jer 1:13 away from the **n**," I answered.
1:14 The LORD said to me, "From the **n**
3:12 the **n**: "'Return, faithless Israel,'
4: 6 the **n**, even terrible destruction."
6: 1 of the **n**, even terrible destruction.
6:22 is coming from the land of the **n**;
10:22 commotion from the land of the **n**!
13:20 see those who are coming from the **n**.
15:12 iron—iron from the **n**—or bronze?
16:15 up out of the land of the **n**
23: 8 Israel up out of the land of the **n**
25: 9 summon all the peoples of the **n**
25:26 all the kings of the **n**, near and far,
31: 8 bring them from the land of the **n**
46: 6 In the **n** by the River Euphrates they
46:10 of the **n** by the River Euphrates.
46:20 is coming against her from the **n**.
46:24 handed over to the people of the **n**."
47: 2 how the waters are rising in the **n**;
50: 3 A nation from the **n** will attack her
50: 9 nations from the land of the **n**.
50: 9 and from the **n** she will be captured.
50:41 "Look! An army is coming from the **n**;
51:48 the **n** destroyers will attack her,"
Eze 1: 4 saw a windstorm coming out of the **n**
8: 3 to the entrance to the **n** gate of the
8: 5 me, "Son of man, look towards the **n**.
8: 5 So I looked, and in the entrance **n**
8:14 the **n** gate of the house of the LORD,
9: 2 which faces **n**, each with a deadly
16:46 who lived to the **n** of you with her
20:47 south to **n** will be scorched by it.
21: 4 against everyone from south to **n**.
26: 7 From the **n** I am going to bring
32:30 "All the princes of the **n** and all
38: 6 and Beth Togarmah from the far **n**
38:15 come from your place in the far **n**,
39: 2 I will bring you from the far **n** and
40:19 the east side as well as on the **n**.

Eze 40:20 and width of the gate facing **n**,
40:23 the inner court facing the **n** gate,
40:35 he brought me to the **n** gate and
40:40 to the **n** gateway were two tables,
40:44 one at the side of the **n** gate and
40:44 side of the south gate and facing **n**.
40:46 the room facing **n** is for the priests
41:11 one on the **n** and another on the
42: 1 the outer wall on the **n** side.
42: 2 The building whose door faced **n** was
42: 4 Their doors were on the **n**.
42:11 These were like the rooms on the **n**;
42:11 Similar to the doorways on the **n**
42:13 he said to me, "The **n** and south
42:17 He measured the **n** side; it was five
44: 4 brought me by way of the **n** gate
46: 9 whoever enters by the **n** gate to
46: 9 gate is to go out by the **n** gate.
46:19 gate to the sacred rooms facing **n**,
47: 2 He then brought me out through the **n**
47:15 "On the **n** side it will run from the
47:17 with the border of Hamath to the **n**.
47:17 This will be the **n** boundary.
48:10 be 25,000 cubits long on the **n** side,
48:16 will have these measurements: the **n**
48:17 city will be 250 cubits on the **n**,
48:30 **n** side, which is 4,500 cubits long,
48:31 The three gates on the **n** side will
Da 8: 4 the west and the **n** and the south.
11: 6 king of the **N** to make an alliance,
11: 7 of the **N** and enter his fortress;
11: 8 will leave the king of the **N** alone.
11: 9 the king of the **N** will invade the
11:11 and fight against the king of the **N**,
11:13 For the king of the **N** will muster
11:15 the king of the **N** will come and
11:28 The king of the **N** will return to his
11:40 and the king of the **N** will storm out
11:44 reports from the east and the **n** will
Am 8:12 to sea and wander from **n** to east,
Zep 2:13 against the **n** and destroy Assyria,
Zec 2: 6 Come! Flee from the land of the **n**,"
6: 6 is going towards the **n** country,
6: 8 "Look, those going towards the **n**
6: 8 Spirit rest in the land of the **n**."
14: 4 moving **n** and half moving south.
Lk 13:29 from east and west and **n** and south,
Rev 21:13 three on the **n**, three on the south

North-easter (East, North)
Ac 27:14 the "**n**", swept down from the island.

Northern (North)
Nu 34: 7 "For your **n** boundary, run a line
Jos 11: 2 to the **n** kings who were in the
15: 5 The **n** boundary started from the bay
15: 8 the **n** end of the Valley of Rephaim.
15:10 ran along the **n** slope of Mount
15:11 went to the **n** slope of Ekron, turned
17: 9 was the **n** side of the ravine
18:12 passed the **n** slope of Jericho and
18:18 continued to the **n** slope of Beth
18:19 then went to the **n** slope of Beth
18:19 out at the **n** bay of the Salt Sea,
Job 26: 7 He spreads out the **n** skies over
Jer 1:15 the **n** kingdoms," declares the LORD.
3:18 they will come from a **n** land to
Eze 47:17 along the **n** border of Damascus, with
48: 1 listed by name: At the **n** frontier,
48: 1 Hazar Enan and the **n** border of
Joel 2:20 "I will drive the **n** army far from

Northward (North)
Eze 42: 1 the man led me **n** into the outer

North-west (West, North)
Ac 27:12 Crete, facing both south-west and **n**.

Nose (Noses)
Ge 24:22 the man took out a gold **n** ring
24:30 soon as he had seen the **n** ring, and
24:47 her **n** and the bracelets on her arms,
2Ki 19:28 I will put my hook in your **n** and my
2Ch 33:11 put a hook in his **n**, bound him with
Job 40:24 eyes, or trap him and pierce his **n**?
41: 2 Can you put a cord through his **n** or
Pr 30:33 and as twisting the **n** produces blood,
SS 7: 4 Your **n** is like the tower of Lebanon
Isa 3:21 the signet rings and **n** rings,
37:29 I will put my hook in your **n** and my
Eze 8:17 them putting the branch to their **n**!
16:12 I put a ring on your **n**, ear-rings on

Noses (Nose)
Ps 115: 6 they have ears, but cannot hear, **n**,
Eze 23:25 They will cut off your **n** and your

Nostrils
Ge 2: 7 into his **n** the breath of life,
7:22 the breath of life in its **n** died.
Ex 15: 8 By the blast of your **n** the waters
Nu 11:20 month—until it comes out of your **n**
2Sa 10: 6 had become an offence to David's **n**,
16:21 an offence to your father's **n**,
22: 9 Smoke rose from his **n**; consuming
22:16 at the blast of breath from his **n**.
1Ch 19: 6 had become an offence to David's **n**,
Job 27: 3 me, the breath of God in my **n**,
41:20 Smoke pours from his **n** as from a
Ps 18: 8 Smoke rose from his **n**; consuming
18:15 at the blast of breath from your **n**.
Isa 2:22 man, who has but a breath in his **n**.
65: 5 Such people are smoke in my **n**,
Am 4:10 I filled your **n** with the stench of

Notable (Note)
Am 6: 1 you **n** men of the foremost nation, to

Note (Annotations, Notable, Notes)
Ru 3: 4 he lies down, **n** the place where he
2Sa 3:36 All the people took **n** and were
Job 11:11 he sees evil, does he not take **n**?
34:25 he takes **n** of their deeds, he
Ps 106:44 he took **n** of their distress when he
Pr 21:12 The Righteous One takes **n** of the
23: 1 you sit to dine with a ruler, **n** well
Jer 31:21 Take **n** of the highway, the road that
Eze 20:37 I will take **n** of you as you pass
Ac 4:13 **n** that these men had been with Jesus.
Php 3:17 brothers, and take **n** of those who
2Th 3:14 this letter, take special **n** of him.
Jas 1:19 My dear brothers, take **n** of this:

Notes (Note)
1Co 14: 7 there is a distinction in the **n**?

Notice (Noticed, Noticing)
Ge 39: 7 wife took **n** of Joseph and said,
Dt 21:11 if you **n** among the captives a
Ru 2:10 eyes that you **n** me—a foreigner?"
2:19 be the man who took **n** of you!"
2Sa 9: 8 you should **n** a dead dog like me?"
2Ki 3:14 would not look at you or even **n** you.
Job 35:15 not take the least **n** of wickedness.
Eze 38:14 safety, will you not take **n** of it?
Hos 7: 9 with grey, but he does not **n**.
Jnh 1: 6 your god! Maybe he will take **n** of
Mk 15:26 The written **n** of the charge against
Lk 23:38 There was a written **n** above him,
Jn 19:19 Pilate had a **n** prepared and fastened
Ac 21:26 Then he went to the temple to give **n**
26:26 that none of this has escaped his **n**,

Noticed (Notice)
Ge 31: 2 Jacob **n** that Laban's attitude
2Sa 12:19 David **n** that his servants were
1Ki 21:29 "Have you **n** how Ahab has humbled
Pr 7: 7 I saw among the simple, I **n** among
Isa 58: 3 ourselves, and you have not **n**?'
Jer 33:24 "Have you not **n** that these people
Mt 22:11 he **n** a man there who was not wearing
Lk 14: 7 he **n** how the guests picked the
Jn 11:31 comforting her, **n** how quickly she

Noticing (Notice)
Mk 12:28 **N** that Jesus had given them a good
Lk 11:38 the Pharisee, **n** that Jesus did not

Notions
Job 15: 2 "Would a wise man answer with empty **n**
Col 2:18 mind puffs him up with idle **n**.

Notorious
Mt 27:16 At that time they had a **n** prisoner,

Nourish (Nourished, Nourishing, Nourishment, Well-nourished)
Pr 10:21 The lips of the righteous **n** many,
27:27 family and to **n** your servant girls.

Nourished (Nourish)
Dt 32:13 He **n** him with honey from the rock,
Job 21:24 his body well **n**, his bones rich with
Eze 31: 4 The waters **n** it, deep springs made
Da 1:15 better **n** than any of the young men

Nourishing (Nourish)
Ro 11:17 in the **n** sap from the olive root,

Nourishment (Nourish)
Pr 3: 8 to your body and **n** to your bones.

Nubians
Da 11:43 the Libyans and **N** in submission.

Nuggets
Job 22:24 assign your **n** to the dust, your gold
28: 6 and its dust contains **n** of gold.

Nullified (Nullify)
Nu 30:12 Her husband has **n** them, and the LORD

Nullifies (Nullify)
Nu 30: 8 he **n** the vow that binds her or the
30:12 if her husband **n** them when he hears
30:15 If, however, he **n** them some time

Nullify (Annulled, Nullified, Nullifies)
Nu 30:13 Her husband may confirm or **n** any vow
Mt 15: 6 Thus you **n** the word of God for the
Mk 7:13 Thus you **n** the word of God by your
Ro 3: 3 lack of faith **n** God's faithfulness?
3:31 Do we, then, **n** the law by this faith?
1Co 1:28 are not—to **n** the things that are,

Number (Numbered, Numbering, Numbers, Numerous, Outnumber)
Ge 1:22 "Be fruitful and increase in **n** and
1:28 in **n**; fill the earth and subdue it.
6: 1 men began to increase in **n** on the
8:17 fruitful and increase in **n** upon it."
9: 1 increase in **n** and fill the earth.
9: 7 be fruitful and increase in **n**;
18:28 what if the **n** of the righteous is
26:24 will increase the **n** of your
34:30 We are few in **n**, and if they join
35:11 be fruitful and increase in **n**.
42:16 Send one of your **n** to get your
47:12 to the **n** of their children.
47:27 fruitful and increased greatly in **n**.
Ex 5: 8 require them to make the same **n** of
5:19 "You are not to reduce the **n** of
12: 4 account the **n** of people there are.
30:12 will come on them when you **n** them.
Lev 25:15 of the **n** of years since the Jubilee.
25:15 **n** of years left for harvesting crops.
25:16 selling you is the **n** of crops.
25:50 to a hired man for that **n** of years.
26:22 make you so few in **n** that your
27:18 value according to the **n** of years
Nu 1: 3 You and Aaron are to **n** by their
1:21 The **n** from the tribe of Reuben was
1:23 The **n** from the tribe of Simeon was
1:25 The **n** from the tribe of Gad was
1:27 The **n** from the tribe of Judah was
1:29 The **n** from the tribe of Issachar was
1:31 The **n** from the tribe of Zebulun was
1:33 The **n** from the tribe of Ephraim was
1:35 The **n** from the tribe of Manasseh was

Nu 1:37 The **n** from the tribe of Benjamin was
1:39 The **n** from the tribe of Dan was
1:41 The **n** from the tribe of Asher was
1:43 The **n** from the tribe of Naphtali was
1:46 The total **n** was 603,550.
2: 9 to their divisions, **n** 186,400.
2:16 to their divisions, **n** 151,450.
2:24 to their divisions, **n** 108,100.
2:31 to the camp of Dan **n** 157,600.
2:32 by their divisions, **n** 603,550.
3:22 The **n** of all the males a month old
3:28 The **n** of all the males a month old
3:34 The **n** of all the males a month old
3:39 The total **n** of Levites counted at
3:43 The total **n** of firstborn males a
3:46 who exceed the **n** of the Levites,
3:49 the **n** redeemed by the Levites.
7:87 The total **n** of animals for the burnt
7:88 The total **n** of animals for the
23:10 Who can count the dust of Jacob or **n**
26:51 The total **n** of the men of Israel was
26:53 inheritance based on the **n** of names.
26:54 according to the **n** of those listed.
29:18 according to the **n** specified.
29:21 according to the **n** specified.
29:24 according to the **n** specified.
29:27 according to the **n** specified.
29:30 according to the **n** specified.
29:33 according to the **n** specified.
29:37 according to the **n** specified.
Dt 25: 2 the **n** of lashes his crime deserves,
28:62 the sky will be left but few in **n**,
28:63 make you prosper and increase in **n**,
32: 8 to the **n** of the sons of Israel.
Jos 4: 5 **n** of the tribes of the Israelites,
4: 8 according to the **n** of the tribes of
11: 4 a large **n** of horses and chariots—a
1Sa 6: 4 according to the **n** of the Philistine
6:18 the **n** of the gold rats was according
6:18 according to the **n** of Philistine
9:22 who were invited—about thirty in **n**.
18:27 presented the full **n** to the king so
23:13 about six hundred in **n**, left Keilah
2Sa 12: 2 The rich man had a very large **n** of
24: 9 Joab reported the **n** of the fighting
1Ki 3: 8 people, too numerous to count or **n**.
1Ch 7:40 The **n** of men ready for battle, as
16:19 they were but few in **n**, few indeed,
21: 5 Joab reported the **n** of the fighting
22:16 bronze and iron—craftsmen beyond **n**.
23: 3 **n** of men was thirty-eight thousand.
23:31 proper **n** and in the way prescribed
24: 4 A larger **n** of leaders were found
27:23 David did not take the **n** of the men
27:24 and the **n** was not entered in the
2Ch 14:13 Such a great **n** of Cushites fell that
26:12 The total **n** of family leaders over
29:32 The **n** of burnt offerings the
30:24 **n** of priests consecrated themselves.
Ezr 3: 4 the required **n** of burnt offerings
8:34 Everything was accounted for by **n**
Est 9:11 The **n** of those slain in the citadel
Job 1: 3 and had a large **n** of servants.
14: 5 you have decreed the **n** of his months
36:26 **n** of his years is past finding out.
Ps 39: 4 my life's end and the **n** of my days
40:12 For troubles without **n** surround me;
90:12 Teach us to **n** our days aright, that
104:25 teeming with creatures beyond **n**—
105:12 they were but few in **n**, few indeed,
105:34 came, grasshoppers without **n**;
147: 4 He determines the **n** of the stars and
SS 6: 8 concubines, and virgins beyond **n**;
Jer 2:32 have forgotten me, days without **n**.
23: 3 will be fruitful and increase in **n**.
29: 6 Increase in **n** there; do not decrease.
52:23 the total **n** of pomegranates above
52:28 This is the **n** of the people
Eze 4: 4 the **n** of days you lie on your side.
4: 5 I have assigned you the same **n** of
36:10 I will multiply the **n** of people upon
36:11 I will increase the **n** of men and
47: 7 I arrived there, I saw a great **n** of
Joel 1: 6 powerful and without **n**; it has the
2:11 his army; his forces are beyond **n**,
Na 3: 3 piles of dead, bodies without **n**,
Na 3:16 You have increased the **n** of your
Zec 2: 4 great **n** of men and livestock in it.
Mt 14:21 The **n** of those who ate was about
15:38 The **n** of those who ate was four
Mk 5:13 The herd, about two thousand in **n**,
6:44 The **n** of the men who had eaten was
Lk 5: 6 they caught such a large **n** of fish
6:17 **n** of people from all over Judea,
23:27 A large **n** of people followed him,
Jn 5: 3 Here a great **n** of disabled people
7:50 who was one of their own **n**, asked,
21: 6 in because of the large **n** of fish.
Ac 1:17 he was one of our **n** and shared in
2:41 were added to their **n** that day.
2:47 the Lord added to their **n** daily
4: 4 **n** of men grew to about five thousand.
5:14 the Lord and were added to their **n**.
6: 1 those days when the **n** of disciples
6: 7 the word of God spread. The **n** of
6: 7 and a large **n** of priests became
7:17 the **n** of our people in Egypt greatly
11:21 and a great **n** of people believed and
11:24 **n** of people were brought to the Lord.
14: 1 **n** of Jews and Gentiles believed.
14:21 city and won a large **n** of disciples.
17: 4 as did a large **n** of God-fearing
17:12 as did also a **n** of prominent Greek
17:34 named Damaris, and a **n** of others.
19:19 A **n** who had practised sorcery
20:30 Even from your own **n** men will arise
21:10 After we had been there a **n** of days,
24:10 "I know that for a **n** of years you
Ro 9:27 "Though the **n** of the Israelites be
11:25 full **n** of the Gentiles has come in.
1Co 11:30 and a **n** of you have fallen asleep.
2Ti 4: 3 around them a great **n** of teachers
Rev 6:11 until the **n** of their fellow-servants
7: 4 I heard the **n** of those who were
9:16 The **n** of the mounted troops was two
9:16 I heard their **n**.
13:17 of the beast or the **n** of his name.
13:18 **n** of the beast, for it is man's **n**.
13:18 His **n** is 666.
15: 2 image and over the **n** of his name.
20: 8 In **n** they are like the sand on the

Numbered (Number)

Ge 46:26 sons' wives—**n** sixty-six persons.
Ex 1: 5 The descendants of Jacob **n** seventy
Nu 25: 9 those who died in the plague **n** 24,000
26: 7 of Reuben; those **n** were 43,730.
26:18 clans of Gad; those **n** were 40,500.
26:22 clans of Judah; those **n** were 76,500.
26:25 of Issachar; those **n** were 64,300.
26:27 of Zebulun; those **n** were 60,500.
26:34 of Manasseh; those **n** were 52,700.
26:37 of Ephraim; those **n** were 32,500.
26:41 of Benjamin; those **n** were 45,600.
26:43 clans; and those **n** were 64,400.
26:47 clans of Asher; those **n** were 53,400.
26:50 of Naphtali; those **n** were 45,400.
26:62 Levites a month old or more **n** 23,000.
1Sa 11: 8 the men of Israel **n** three hundred
13:15 They **n** about six hundred.
1Ki 4:32 and his songs **n** a thousand and five.
1Ch 7: 2 men in their genealogy **n** 22,600.
9: 6 The people from Judah **n** 690.
9: 9 as listed in their genealogy, **n** 956.
9:13 were heads of families, **n** 1,760.
9:22 gatekeepers at the thresholds **n** 212.
25: 7 in music for the LORD—they **n** 288.
Ezr 2:64 The whole company **n** 42,360,
Ne 7:66 The whole company **n** 42,360,
Job 25: 3 Can his forces be **n**? Upon whom does
Isa 53:12 and was **n** with the transgressors.
Lam 4:18 days were **n**, for our end had come.
Da 5:26 Mene: God has **n** the days of your
Mt 10:30 very hairs of your head are all **n**.
Lk 12: 7 very hairs of your head are all **n**.
22:37 he was **n** with the transgressors

Numbering (Number)

1Ch 21: 6 include Levi and Benjamin in the **n**,
27:24 came on Israel on account of this **n**,

Ac 1:15 group **n** about a hundred and twenty)
Rev 5:11 **n** thousands upon thousands, and ten

Numberless

Isa 48:19 your children like its **n** grains;

Numbers (Number)

Ge 17: 2 and will greatly increase your **n**."
17:20 and will greatly increase his **n**.
28: 3 increase your **n** until you become a
48: 4 fruitful and will increase your **n**.
Ex 10:14 area of the country in great **n**.
Lev 26: 9 you fruitful and increase your **n**,
Nu 2: 4 His division **n** 74,600.
2: 6 His division **n** 54,400.
2: 8 His division **n** 57,400.
2:11 His division **n** 46,500.
2:13 His division **n** 59,300.
2:15 His division **n** 45,650.
2:19 His division **n** 40,500.
2:21 His division **n** 32,200.
2:23 His division **n** 35,400.
2:26 His division **n** 62,700.
2:28 His division **n** 41,500.
2:30 His division **n** 53,400.
Dt 1:10 God has increased your **n** so that
7:13 and bless you and increase your **n**.
13:17 and increase your **n**, as he promised
17:16 must not acquire great **n** of horses
1Ki 1:19 He has sacrificed great **n** of cattle,
1:25 and sacrificed great **n** of cattle,
1Ch 12:23 These are the **n** of the men armed for
22: 4 brought large **n** of them to David.
2Ch 15: 9 for large **n** had come over to him
16: 8 great **n** of chariots and horsemen?
26:11 **n** as mustered by Jeiel the secretary
30: 5 **n** according to what was written.
32: 5 made large **n** of weapons and shields.
32:29 great **n** of flocks and herds,
Ps 107:38 he blessed them, and their **n** greatly
107:39 their **n** decreased, and they were
Jer 3:16 In those days, when your **n** have
30:19 I will add to their **n**, and they will
Eze 37:26 establish them and increase their **n**,
47: 9 There will be large **n** of fish,
Ac 9:31 it grew in **n**, living in the fear
11:26 church and taught great **n** of people.
16: 5 in the faith and grew daily in **n**.
19:26 led astray large **n** of people here in
28:23 came in even larger **n** to the place

Numerous (Number)

Ge 16:10 that they will be too **n** to count."
22:17 your descendants as **n** as the stars
26: 4 I will make your descendants as **n** as
Ex 1: 7 greatly and became exceedingly **n**,
1: 9 have become much too **n** for us.
1:10 or they will become even more **n** and,
1:20 increased and became even more **n**.
5: 5 the people of the land are now **n**,
23:29 and the wild animals too **n** for you.
32:13 'I will make your descendants as **n**
Nu 22:15 Balak sent other princes, more **n** and
Dt 2:10 and **n**, and as tall as the Anakites.
2:21 They were a people strong and **n**, and
7: 7 you were more **n** than other peoples,
9:14 stronger and more **n** than they."
10:22 you as **n** as the stars in the sky.
26: 5 a great nation, powerful and **n**.
28:62 You who were as **n** as the stars in
30: 5 prosperous and **n** than your fathers.
Jos 11: 4 as **n** as the sand on the seashore.
17:14 We are a **n** people and the LORD has
17:15 "If you are so **n**," Joshua answered,
17:17 "You are **n** and very powerful.
1Sa 13: 5 as **n** as the sand on the seashore.
2Sa 17:11 from Dan to Beersheba—as **n** as the
1Ki 3: 8 people, too **n** to count or number.
4:20 as **n** as the sand on the seashore;
1Ch 4:27 become as **n** as the people of Judah.
5:23 the half-tribe of Manasseh were **n**;
23:17 the sons of Rehabiah were very **n**.
27:23 Israel as **n** as the stars in the sky.
2Ch 1: 9 are as **n** as the dust of the earth.
Ne 5: 2 "We and our sons and daughters are **n**;

Ne 9:23 You made their sons as **n** as the
Job 29:18 my days as **n** as the grains of sand.
Ps 38:19 who hate me without reason are **n**.
105:24 he made them too **n** for their foes,
Jer 15: 8 I will make their widows more **n** than
46:23 They are more **n** than locusts, they
Eze 36:11 they will be fruitful and become **n**.
36:37 make their people as **n** as sheep,
36:38 as **n** as the flocks for offerings at
Na 1:12 "Although they have allies and are **n**,
Zec 10: 8 them; they will be as **n** as before.
Heb 11:12 came descendants as **n** as the stars

Nun

Ex 33:11 son of **N** did not leave the tent.
Nu 11:28 Joshua son of **N**, who had been Moses'
13: 8 tribe of Ephraim, Hoshea son of **N**;
13:16 Hoshea son of **N** the name Joshua.)
14: 6 Joshua son of **N** and Caleb son of
14:30 of Jephunneh and Joshua son of **N**.
14:38 only Joshua son of **N** and Caleb son
26:65 of Jephunneh and Joshua son of **N**.
27:18 "Take Joshua son of **N**, a man in whom
32:12 the Kenizzite and Joshua son of **N**,
32:28 Joshua son of **N** and to the family
34:17 the priest and Joshua son of **N**.
Dt 1:38 your assistant, Joshua son of **N**,
31:23 son of **N**: "Be strong and courageous,
32:44 Moses came with Joshua son of **N** and
34: 9 Now Joshua son of **N** was filled with
Jos 1: 1 Joshua son of **N**, Moses' assistant:
2: 1 Joshua son of **N** secretly sent two
2:23 came to Joshua son of **N** and told him
6: 6 Joshua son of **N** called the priests
14: 1 Joshua son of **N** and the heads of the
17: 4 Joshua son of **N**, and the leaders and
19:49 son of **N** an inheritance among them,
19:51 Joshua son of **N** and the heads of the
21: 1 Joshua son of **N**, and the heads of
24:29 After these things, Joshua son of **N**,
Jdg 2: 8 Joshua son of **N**, the servant of the
1Ki 16:34 the LORD spoken by Joshua son of **N**.
1Ch 7:27 **N** his son and Joshua his son.
Ne 8:17 From the days of Joshua son of **N**

Nurse (Nursed, Nursing)

Ge 21: 7 Abraham that Sarah would **n** children?
24:59 with her **n** and Abraham's servant and
35: 8 Now Deborah, Rebekah's **n**, died and
Ex 2: 7 Hebrew women to **n** the baby for you?"
2: 9 **n** him for me, and I will pay you.
Nu 11:12 as a **n** carries an infant, to the
2Sa 4: 4 His **n** picked him up and fled, but as
1Ki 3:21 next morning, I got up to **n** my son
2Ki 11: 2 She put him and his **n** in a bedroom
11: 3 He remained hidden with his **n** at the
2Ch 22:11 and put him and his **n** in a bedroom.
Isa 66:11 For you will **n** and be satisfied at
66:12 you will **n** and be carried on her arm
Lam 4: 3 Even jackals offer their breasts to **n**

Nursed (Nurse)

Ex 2: 9 So the woman took the baby and **n** him.
1Sa 1:23 **n** her son until she had weaned him.
Job 3:12 me and breasts that I might be **n**?
SS 8: 1 who was **n** at my mother's breasts!
Isa 60:16 nations and be **n** at royal breasts.
Mk 6:19 Herodias **n** a grudge against John and
Lk 11:27 who gave you birth and **n** you."
23:29 bore and the breasts that never **n**!'

Nursing (Nurse)

Ge 33:13 and cows that are **n** their young.
Isa 49:23 and their queens your **n** mothers.
Joel 2:16 the children, those **n** at the breast.
Mt 24:19 for pregnant women and **n** mothers!
Mk 13:17 for pregnant women and **n** mothers!
Lk 21:23 for pregnant women and **n** mothers!

Nurtured (Well-nurtured)

Lam 4: 5 **n** in purple now lie on ash heaps.

Nut (Nuts)

SS 6:11 I went down to the grove of **n** trees

Nuts (Nut)

Ge 43:11 myrrh, some pistachio **n** and almonds.

Nympha

Col 4:15 to **N** and the church in her house.

Oak (Oaks)

Ge 35: 4 buried them under the **o** at Shechem.
35: 8 was buried under the **o** below Bethel.
Jos 24:26 under the **o** near the holy place of
Jdg 6:11 sat down under the **o** in Ophrah that
6:19 and offered them to him under the **o**.
2Sa 18: 9 the thick branches of a large **o**,
18:10 seen Absalom hanging in an **o** tree."
18:14 was still alive in the **o** tree.
1Ki 13:14 He found him sitting under an **o** tree
Ps 56: T the tune of⌋ "A Dove on Distant **O**."
Isa 1:30 You will be like an **o** with fading
6:13 But as the terebinth and **o** leave
44:14 or perhaps took a cypress or **o**.
Eze 6:13 every leafy **o**—places where they
Hos 4:13 under **o**, poplar and terebinth, where

Oaks (Oak)

Ps 29: 9 The voice of the LORD twists the **o**
Isa 1:29 **o** in which you have delighted;
2:13 and lofty, and all the **o** of Bashan,
57: 5 You burn with lust among the **o** and
61: 3 will be called **o** of righteousness
Eze 27: 6 Of **o** from Bashan they made your oars;
Am 2: 9 as the cedars and strong as the **o**.
Zec 11: 2 Wail, **o** of Bashan; the dense forest

Oars (Oarsmen)

Isa 33:21 No galley with **o** will ride them, no
Eze 27: 6 Of oaks from Bashan they made your **o**;
27:29 All who handle the **o** will abandon
Mk 6:48 straining at the **o**, because the

Oarsmen (Oars)

Eze 27: 8 Men of Sidon and Arvad were your **o**;
27:26 Your **o** take you out to the high seas.

Oath (Oaths)

Ge 14:22 and earth, and have taken an **o**
21:31 the two men swore an **o** there.
24: 7 spoke to me and promised me on **o**,
24: 8 be released from this **o** of mine.
24: 9 an **o** to him concerning this matter.
24:37 my master made me swear an **o**, and
24:41 you will be released from my **o** even
24:41 will be released from my **o**.'
25:33 So he swore an **o** to him, selling
26: 3 **o** I swore to your father Abraham.
26:31 the men swore an **o** to each other.
31:53 So Jacob took an **o** in the name of
50: 5 'My father made me swear an **o** and
50:24 on **o** to Abraham, Isaac and Jacob."
50:25 sons of Israel swear an **o** and said,
Ex 13:11 on **o** to you and your forefathers,
13:19 made the sons of Israel swear an **o**.
22:11 be settled by the taking of an **o**
33: 1 the land I promised on **o** to Abraham,
Lev 5: 4 takes an **o** to do anything,
Nu 5:19 the woman under **o** and say to her,
5:21 the woman under this curse of the **o**
11:12 promised on **o** to their forefathers?
14:16 into the land he promised them on **o**;
14:23 I promised on **o** to their forefathers.
30: 2 an **o** to bind himself by a pledge,
30:10 or binds herself by a pledge under **o**
32:10 that day and he swore this **o**:
32:11 on **o** to Abraham, Isaac and Jacob—
Dt 4:31 which he confirmed to them by **o**.
6:18 promised on **o** to your forefathers,
6:23 he promised on **o** to our forefathers.
7: 8 kept the **o** he swore to your
8: 1 promised on **o** to your forefathers.
13:17 promised on **o** to your forefathers,
19: 8 as he promised on **o** to your
26:15 promised on **o** to our forefathers,
28: 9 as he promised you on **o**, if you keep
29:12 you this day and sealing with an **o**,
29:14 I am making this covenant, with its **o**
29:19 a person hears the words of this **o**,
31:20 the land I promised on **o** to their
31:21 into the land I promised them on **o**."
31:23 the land I promised them on **o**,
34: 4 "This is the land I promised on **o** to
Jos 2:17 The men said to her, "This **o** you
2:20 from the **o** you made us swear."
6:22 in accordance with your **o** to her."
6:26 Joshua pronounced this solemn **o**:
9:15 of the assembly ratified it by **o**.
9:18 had sworn an **o** to them by the LORD,
9:19 "We have given them our **o** by the
9:20 breaking the **o** we swore to them."
Jdg 21: 1 The men of Israel had taken an **o** at
21: 5 For they had taken a solemn **o** that
21: 7 since we have taken an **o** by the LORD
21:18 we Israelites have taken this **o**:
1Sa 14:24 Saul had bound the people under an **o**,
14:26 mouth, because they feared the **o**.
14:27 had bound the people with the **o**,
14:28 bound the army under a strict **o**,
19: 6 took this **o**: "As surely as the LORD
20: 3 David took an **o** and said, "Your
20:17 Jonathan made David reaffirm his **o**
24:22 David gave his **o** to Saul. Then Saul
2Sa 3: 9 David what the LORD promised him on **o**
3:35 was still day; but David took an **o**,
19:23 And the king promised him on **o**.
21: 7 the son of Saul, because of the **o**
1Ki 1:29 The king then took an **o**: "As surely
2:43 Why then did you not keep your **o** to
8:31 is required to take an **o** and he
8:31 and swears the **o** before your altar
2Ki 11: 4 under **o** at the temple of the LORD.
25:24 Gedaliah took an **o** to reassure them
1Ch 16:16 Abraham, the **o** he swore to Isaac.
2Ch 6:22 is required to take an **o** and he
6:22 and swears the **o** before your altar
15:14 They took an **o** to the LORD with loud
15:15 All Judah rejoiced about the **o**
36:13 made him take an **o** in God's name.
Ezr 10: 5 all Israel under **o** to do what had
10: 5 And they took the **o**.
Ne 5:12 an **o** to do what they had promised.
6:18 For many in Judah were under **o** to
10:29 an **o** to follow the Law of God given
13:25 I made them take an **o** in God's name
Ps 15: 4 who keeps his **o** even when it hurts,
95:11 I declared on **o** in my anger, "They
105: 9 Abraham, the **o** he swore to Isaac.
119:106 I have taken an **o** and confirmed it,
132: 2 He swore an **o** to the LORD and made a
132:11 The LORD swore an **o** to David, a sure
132:11 a sure **o** that he will not revoke:
Pr 29:24 is put under **o** and dare not testify.
Ecc 8: 2 because you took an **o** before God.
Isa 65:16 he who takes an **o** in the land will
Jer 11: 5 I will fulfil the **o** I swore to your
38:16 King Zedekiah swore this **o** secretly
40: 9 an **o** to reassure them and their men.
Eze 16: 8 I gave you my solemn **o** and entered
16:59 my **o** by breaking the covenant.
17:13 with him, putting him under **o**.
17:16 whose **o** he despised and whose treaty
17:18 He despised the **o** by breaking the
17:19 I will bring down on his head my **o**
Mic 7:20 as you pledged on **o** to our fathers
Mt 5:33 'Do not break your **o**, but keep the
14: 7 that he promised with an **o** to give
23:16 the temple, he is bound by his **o**.'
23:18 gift on it, he is bound by his **o**.'
26:63 "I charge you under **o** by the living
26:72 He denied it again, with an **o**: "I
Mk 6:23 he promised her with an **o**, "Whatever
Lk 1:73 the **o** he swore to our father Abraham:
Ac 2:30 knew that God had promised him on **o**
23:12 bound themselves with an **o** not to
23:14 "We have taken a solemn **o** not to eat
23:21 They have taken an **o** not to eat or
Heb 3:11 I declared on **o** in my anger, 'They
4: 3 "So I declared on **o** in my anger,
6:16 and the **o** confirms what is said and
6:17 promised, he confirmed it with an **o**.
7:20 was not without an **o**! Others became
7:20 Others became priests without any **o**,
7:21 he became a priest with an **o** when

Heb 7:22 of this **o**, Jesus has become the
7:28 priests men who are weak; but the **o**,

Oaths (Oath)

Dt 6:13 only and take your **o** in his name.
10:20 to him and take your **o** in his name.
Ecc 9: 2 as it is with those who take **o**,
Isa 48: 1 you who take **o** in the name of the
Hos 10: 4 They make many promises, take false **o**
Mt 5:33 the **o** you have made to the Lord.'
14: 9 but because of his **o** and his dinner
Mk 6:26 but because of his **o** and his dinner

Obadiah

1. Official in charge of Ahab's palace; believer; hid 100 prophets from Jezebel (1Ki 18:1–16).
2. Prophet; spoke against Edom (Ob 1).

1Ki 18: 3 Ahab had summoned **O**, who was in
18: 3 (**O** was a devout believer in the LORD.
18: 4 **O** had taken a hundred prophets and
18: 5 Ahab had said to **O**, "Go through the
18: 6 in one direction and **O** in another.
18: 7 **O** was walking along, Elijah met him.
18: 7 **O** recognised him, bowed down to the
18: 9 "What have I done wrong," asked **O**,
18:16 **O** went to meet Ahab and told him,
1Ch 3:21 of Aman, of **O** and of Shecaniah.
7: 3 The sons of Izrahiah: Michael, **O**,
8:38 Ishmael, Sheariah, **O** and Hanan.
9:16 **O** son of Shemaiah, the son of Galal,
9:44 Ishmael, Sheariah, **O** and Hanan.
12: 9 Ezer was the chief, **O** the second in
27:19 over Zebulun: Ishmaiah son of **O**;
2Ch 17: 7 **O**, Zechariah, Nethanel and Micaiah
34:12 to direct them were Jahath and **O**,
Ezr 8: 9 of the descendants of Joab, **O** son of
Ne 10: 5 Harim, Meremoth, **O**,
12:25 Mattaniah, Bakbukiah, **O**, Meshullam,
Ob : 1 The vision of **O**. This is what the

Obal

Ge 10:28 **O**, Abimael, Sheba,
1Ch 1:22 **O**, Abimael, Sheba,

Obed

Ru 4:17 And they named him **O**. He was the
4:21 of Boaz, Boaz the father of **O**,
4:22 **O** the father of Jesse, and Jesse the
1Ch 2:12 Boaz the father of **O** and **O** the
2:37 of Ephlal, Ephlal the father of **O**,
2:38 **O** the father of Jehu, Jehu the
11:47 Eliel, **O** and Jaasiel the Mezobaite.
26: 7 Rephael, **O** and Elzabad; his
2Ch 23: 1 Azariah son of **O**, Maaseiah son of
Mt 1: 5 Boaz the father of **O**, whose mother
1: 5 was Ruth, **O** the father of Jesse,
Lk 3:32 the son of Jesse, the son of **O**, the

Obed-Edom

2Sa 6:10 aside to the house of **O** the Gittite.
6:11 of **O** the Gittite for three months,
6:12 of **O** and everything he has,
6:12 the ark of God from the house of **O**
1Ch 13:13 aside to the house of **O** the Gittite.
13:14 of **O** in his house for three months,
15:18 **O** and Jeiel, the gatekeepers.
15:21 Mattithiah, Eliphelehu, Mikneiah, **O**,
15:24 **O** and Jehiah were also to be
15:25 from the house of **O**, with rejoicing.
16: 5 Eliab, Benaiah, **O** and Jeiel.
16:38 He also left **O** and his sixty-eight
16:38 **O** son of Jeduthun, and also Hosah,
26: 4 **O** also had sons: Shemaiah the
26: 5 (For God had blessed **O**.)
26: 8 All these were descendants of **O**;
26: 8 work—descendants of **O**, 62 in all.
26:15 The lot for the South Gate fell to **O**,
2Ch 25:24 God that had been in the care of **O**,

Obedience (Obey)

Ge 49:10 and the **o** of the nations is his.
Jdg 2:17 the way of **o** to the LORD's commands.
1Ch 21:19 David went up in **o** to the word that
2Ch 31:21 in **o** to the law and the commands,
Pr 30:17 that scorns **o** to a mother, will be
Lk 23:56 the Sabbath in **o** to the commandment.
Ac 21:24 yourself are living in **o** to the law.
Ro 1: 5 to the **o** that comes from faith.
5:19 so also through the **o** of the one man
6:16 to **o**, which leads to righteousness?
16:19 Everyone has heard about your **o**, so
2Co 9:13 men will praise God for the **o** that
10: 6 once your **o** is complete.
Phm :21 Confident of your **o**, I write to you,
Heb 5: 8 Although he was a son, he learned **o**
1Pe 1: 2 for **o** to Jesus Christ and sprinkling
2Jn : 6 this is love: that we walk in **o** to

Obedient (Obey)

Dt 30:17 heart turns away and you are not **o**,
Isa 1:19 If you are willing and **o**, you will
Lk 2:51 Nazareth with them and was **o** to them.
Ac 6: 7 of priests became **o** to the faith.
2Co 2: 9 the test and be **o** in everything.
7:15 he remembers that you were all **o**,
10: 5 thought to make it **o** to Christ.
Php 2: 8 **o** to death—even death on a cross!
Tit 3: 1 to be **o**, to be ready to do whatever
1Pe 1:14 **o** children, do not conform to the

Obey (Obedience, Obedient, Obeyed, Obeying, Obeys)

Ex 5: 2 "Who is the LORD, that I should **o**
12:24 "**O** these instructions as a lasting
19: 5 Now if you **o** me fully and keep my
24: 7 the LORD has said; we will **o**."
34:11 **O** what I command you today. I will
Lev 18: 4 You must **o** my laws and be careful to
25:18 decrees and be careful to **o** my laws,
26: 3 and are careful to **o** my commands,
Nu 15:39 that you may **o** them and not
15:40 you will remember to **o** all my
27:20 Israelite community will **o** him.
Dt 4:30 to the LORD your God and **o** him.
5:27 We will listen and **o**."
6: 3 Hear, O Israel, and be careful to **o**
6:24 The LORD commanded us to **o** all these
6:25 if we are careful to **o** all this law
9:23 You did not trust him or **o** him.
11:13 if you faithfully **o** the commands I
11:27 the blessing if you **o** the commands
11:32 be sure that you **o** all the decrees
12:28 Be careful to **o** all these
13: 4 Keep his commands and **o** him; serve
13:18 you **o** the LORD your God, keeping all
15: 5 if only you fully **o** the LORD your
21:18 rebellious son who does not **o** his
21:20 He will not **o** us. He is a profligate
26:17 and laws, and that you will **o** him.
27:10 **O** the LORD your God and follow his
28: 1 If you fully **o** the LORD your God and
28: 2 you if you **o** the LORD your God:
28:15 However, if you do not **o** the LORD
28:45 because you did not **o** the LORD your
28:62 you did not **o** the LORD your God.
30: 2 **o** him with all your heart and with
30: 8 You will again **o** the LORD and follow
30:10 if you **o** the LORD your God and keep
30:12 it to us so that we may **o** it?
30:13 it to us so that we may **o** it?"
30:14 in your heart so that you may **o** it.
32:46 command your children to **o**
Jos 1: 7 Be careful to **o** all the law my
1:17 obeyed Moses, so we will **o** you.
1:18 your word and does not **o** your words,
22: 5 to walk in all his ways, to **o** his
23: 6 "Be very strong; be careful to **o** all
24:24 serve the LORD our God and **o** him."
Jdg 3: 4 they would **o** the LORD's commands,
1Sa 12:14 If you fear the LORD and serve and **o**
12:15 if you do not **o** the LORD, and if you
15:19 Why did you not **o** the LORD? Why did
15:20 "But I did **o** the LORD," Saul said.
15:22 LORD? To **o** is better than sacrifice,
28:18 you did not **o** the LORD or carry out
2Sa 22:45 as soon as they hear me, they **o** me.
1Ki 2:42 'What you say is good. I will **o**.'
2:43 LORD and **o** the command I gave you?"
1Ki 3:14 if you walk in my ways and **o** my
6:12 and keep all my commands and **o** them,
8:61 **o** his commands, as at this time."
2Ki 10: 6 "If you are on my side and will **o** me,
17:13 that I commanded your fathers to **o**
1Ch 28:21 people will **o** your every command."
2Ch 14: 4 and to **o** his laws and commands.
34:31 and to **o** the words of the covenant
Ezr 7:26 Whoever does not **o** the law of your
Ne 1: 5 who love him and **o** his commands
1: 9 if you return to me and **o** my
9:16 and did not **o** your commands.
10:29 and to **o** carefully all the commands,
Est 3: 8 and who do not **o** the king's laws;
Job 36:11 If they **o** and serve him, they will
Ps 18:44 soon as they hear me, they **o** me;
103:18 and remember to **o** his precepts.
103:20 who do his bidding, who **o** his word.
106:25 their tents and did not **o** the LORD.
119: 8 I will **o** your decrees; do not
119:17 and I will live; I will **o** your word.
119:34 your law and **o** it with all my heart.
119:44 I will always **o** your law, for ever
119:56 This has been my practice: I **o** your
119:57 I have promised to **o** your words.
119:60 I will hasten and not delay to **o**
119:67 I went astray, but now I **o** your word.
119:88 I will **o** the statutes of your mouth.
119:100 the elders, for I **o** your precepts.
119:101 path so that I might **o** your word.
119:129 are wonderful; therefore I **o** them.
119:134 of men, that I may **o** your precepts.
119:145 O LORD, and I will **o** your decrees.
119:158 for they do not **o** your word.
119:167 I **o** your statutes, for I love them
119:168 I **o** your precepts and your statutes,
Pr 5:13 I would not **o** my teachers or listen
Ecc 8: 2 **O** the king's command, I say, because
Isa 42:24 his ways; they did not **o** his law.
Jer 7:23 I gave them this command: **O** me, and
11: 3 not **o** the terms of this covenant—
11: 4 I said, '**O** me and do everything I
11: 7 them again and again, saying, "**O** me.
17:24 if you are careful to **o** me, declares
17:27 if you do not **o** me to keep the
18:10 evil in my sight and does not **o** me,
22: 5 if you do not **o** these commands,
26:13 actions and **o** the LORD your God.
32:23 but they did not **o** you or follow
35:13 and **o** my words?' declares the LORD.
35:14 they **o** their forefather's command.
38:20 "**O** the LORD by doing what I tell you.
40: 3 against the LORD and did not **o** him.
42: 6 we will **o** the LORD our God, to whom
42: 6 us, for we will **o** the LORD our God."
Da 7:27 all rulers will worship and **o** him.'
9: 4 all who love him and **o** his commands,
9:11 and turned away, refusing to **o** you.
Joel 2:11 mighty are those who **o** his command.
Zec 6:15 you diligently **o** the LORD your God."
Mt 8:27 Even the winds and the waves **o** him!"
19:17 to enter life, **o** the commandments."
23: 3 you must **o** them and do everything
28:20 teaching them to **o** everything I have
Mk 1:27 to evil spirits and they **o** him."
4:41 Even the wind and the waves **o** him!"
Lk 8:25 and the water, and they **o** him."
11:28 who hear the word of God and **o** it."
17: 6 in the sea,' and it will **o** you.
Jn 14:15 "If you love me, you will **o** what I
14:23 loves me, he will **o** my teaching.
14:24 He who does not love me will not **o**
15:10 If you **o** my commands, you will
15:20 my teaching, they will **o** yours also.
Ac 4:19 God's sight to **o** you rather than God.
5:29 "We must **o** God rather than men!
5:32 God has given to those who **o** him."
7:39 "But our fathers refused to **o** him.
15: 5 and required to **o** the law of Moses."
16: 4 in Jerusalem for the people to **o**.
Ro 2:13 but it is those who **o** the law who
6:12 body so that you **o** its evil desires.
6:16 to someone to **o** him as slaves,
6:16 are slaves to the one whom you **o**
15:18 **o** God by what I have said and done—
16:26 nations might believe and **o** him—

Gal 5: 3 he is required to **o** the whole law.
6:13 Not even those who are circumcised **o**
Eph 6: 1 Children, **o** your parents in the Lord,
6: 5 Slaves, **o** your earthly masters with
6: 5 heart, just as you would **o** Christ.
6: 6 **O** them not only to win their favour
Col 3:20 Children, **o** your parents in
3:22 Slaves, **o** your earthly masters in
2Th 1: 8 not **o** the gospel of our Lord Jesus.
3:14 If anyone does not **o** our instruction
1Ti 3: 4 children **o** him with proper respect.
Heb 5: 9 eternal salvation for all who **o**
13:17 **O** your leaders and submit to their
13:17 **O** them so that their work will be a
Jas 3: 3 horses to make them **o** us, we can
1Pe 4:17 who do not **o** the gospel of God?
1Jn 2: 3 to know him if we **o** his commands.
3:22 because we **o** his commands and do
3:24 Those who **o** his commands live in him,
5: 3 This is love for God: to **o** his
Rev 3: 3 and heard; **o** it, and repent.
12:17 who **o** God's commandments
14:12 the saints who **o** God's commandments

Obeyed (Obey)

Ge 22:18 be blessed, because you have **o** me."
26: 5 Abraham **o** me and kept my
28: 7 that Jacob had **o** his father and
Nu 9:19 the Israelites **o** the LORD's order
9:23 They **o** the LORD's order, in
Dt 26:14 I have **o** the LORD my God; I have
Jos 1:17 Just as we fully **o** Moses, so we will
5: 6 died, since they had not **o** the LORD.
22: 2 have **o** me in everything I commanded.
1Sa 28:21 "Look, your maidservant has **o** you.
1Ki 12:24 So they **o** the word of the LORD
20:36 "Because you have not **o** the LORD, as
2Ki 18:12 This happened because they had not **o**
22:13 have not **o** the words of this book;
1Ch 29:23 He prospered and all Israel **o** him.
2Ch 11: 4 So they **o** the words of the LORD
Ne 1: 7 We have not **o** the commands, decrees
Est 1:15 "She has not **o** the command of King
Ps 119: 4 precepts that are to be fully **o**.
119:136 from my eyes, for your law is not **o**.
Jer 3:13 have not **o** me,'" declares the LORD.
3:25 day we have not **o** the LORD our God."
7:28 'This is the nation that has not **o**
9:13 have not **o** me or followed my law.
22:21 from your youth; you have not **o** me.
34:17 You have not **o** me; you have not
35: 8 We have **o** everything our forefather
35:10 have fully **o** everything our
35:14 and again, yet you have not **o** me.
35:16 but these people have not **o** me.'
35:18 'You have **o** the command of your
42:21 but you still have not **o** the LORD
44:23 have not **o** him or followed his law
Eze 20:24 they had not **o** my laws but had
Da 9:10 we have not **o** the LORD our God or
9:14 he does; yet we have not **o** him.
Hos 9:17 them because they have not **o** him;
Jnh 3: 3 Jonah **o** the word of the LORD and
Mic 5:15 the nations that have not **o** me."
Hag 1:12 the whole remnant of the people **o**
Jn 15:10 just as I have **o** my Father's
15:20 If they **o** my teaching, they will
17: 6 to me and they have **o** your word.
Ac 7:53 through angels but have not **o** it."
Ro 6:17 you wholeheartedly **o** the form of
Php 2:12 as you have always **o**—not only in my
Heb 11: 8 **o** and went, even though he did not
1Pe 3: 6 like Sarah, who **o** Abraham and called

Obeying (Obey)

Dt 8:20 for not **o** the LORD your God.
1Sa 15:22 much as in **o** the voice of the LORD?
Ps 119: 5 Oh, that my ways were steadfast in **o**
Jer 16:12 of his evil heart instead of **o** me.
Gal 5: 7 you and kept you from **o** the truth?
1Pe 1:22 purified yourselves by **o** the truth

Obeys (Obey)

Lev 18: 5 man who **o** them will live by them.
Ne 9:29 which a man will live if he **o** them.
Pr 19:16 He who **o** instructions guards his
Ecc 8: 5 Whoever **o** his command will come to
Isa 50:10 Who among you fears the LORD and **o**
Eze 20:11 man who **o** them will live by them.
20:13 man who **o** them will live by them
20:21 man who **o** them will live by them
Zep 3: 2 She **o** no-one, she accepts no
Jn 14:21 Whoever has my commands and **o** them,
Ro 2:27 yet **o** the law will condemn you who,
1Jn 2: 5 if anyone **o** his word, God's love is

Obil

1Ch 27:30 **O** the Ishmaelite was in charge of

Object (Objects)

Nu 35:16 with an iron **o** so that he dies,
35:18 Or if anyone has a wooden **o** in his
Dt 28:37 an **o** of scorn and ridicule to all
1Ki 9: 7 an **o** of ridicule among all peoples.
2Ch 7:20 an **o** of ridicule among all peoples.
29: 8 an **o** of dread and horror and scorn,
30: 7 them an **o** of horror, as you see.
Ps 109:25 I am an **o** of scorn to my accusers;
Jer 18:16 laid waste, an **o** of lasting scorn;
19: 8 this city and make it an **o** of scorn;
22:28 broken pot, an **o** no-one wants? Why
24: 9 and a byword, an **o** of ridicule
25: 9 make them an **o** of horror and scorn,
25:18 make them a ruin and an **o** of horror
26: 6 this city an **o** of cursing among all
29:18 and an **o** of cursing and horror,
42:18 You will be an **o** of cursing and
44: 8 make yourselves an **o** of cursing and
44:12 They will become an **o** of cursing and
44:22 your land became an **o** of cursing and
48:26 vomit; let her be an **o** of ridicule.
48:27 Was not Israel the **o** of your
48:39 Moab has become an **o** of ridicule,
48:39 **o** of horror to all those around her."
49:13 become a ruin and an **o** of horror,
49:17 "Edom will become an **o** of horror;
51:37 a haunt of jackals, an **o** of horror
Eze 5:15 a warning and an **o** of horror to the
22: 4 I will make you an **o** of scorn
24:21 your eyes, the **o** of your affection.
36: 3 the **o** of people's malicious talk and
Da 9:16 **o** of scorn to all those around us.
Joel 2:17 Do not make your inheritance an **o** of
2:19 you an **o** of scorn to the nations.
Zec 8:13 you have been an **o** of cursing among

Objected (Objection)

2Ki 4:16 "No, my lord," she **o**. "Don't
Jn 12: 4 who was later to betray him, **o**,
18:31 to execute anyone," the Jews **o**.
Ac 28:19 when the Jews **o**, I was compelled to

Objection (Objected, Objections)

Ac 10:29 for, I came without raising any **o**.

Objections (Objection)

Ac 11:18 they had no further **o** and praised

Objects (Object)

1Sa 6: 8 in a chest beside it put the gold **o**
6:15 the chest containing the gold **o**,
1Ki 7:45 All these **o** that Huram made for King
2Ki 12:18 sacred **o** dedicated by his fathers
2Ch 4:16 All the **o** that Huram-Abi made for
24: 7 even its sacred **o** for the Baals.
24:14 and other **o** of gold and silver.
Ps 79: 4 We are **o** of reproach to our
Jer 10:15 They are worthless, the **o** of mockery;
51:18 They are worthless, the **o** of mockery;
Ac 17:23 carefully at your **o** of worship,
Ro 9:22 bore with great patience the **o** of
9:23 glory known to the **o** of his mercy,
Eph 2: 3 rest, we were by nature **o** of wrath.

Obligation (Obligations)

Nu 30: 9 "Any vow or **o** taken by a widow or
32:22 your **o** to the LORD and to Israel.
Ezr 4:14 Now since we are under **o** to the
Ro 4: 4 to him as a gift, but as an **o**.
8:12 Therefore, brothers, we have an **o**

Obligations (Obligation)

Nu 3: 8 fulfilling the **o** of the Israelites
1Ki 9:25 them, and so fulfilled the temple **o**.

Oblivion

Ps 88:12 righteous deeds in the land of **o**?

Oboth

Nu 21:10 Israelites moved on and camped at **O**.
21:11 they set out from **O** and camped in
33:43 They left Punon and camped at **O**.
33:44 They left **O** and camped at Iye Abarim,

Obscenity

Eph 5: 4 Nor should there be **o**, foolish talk

Obscure (Obscures)

Pr 22:29 he will not serve before **o** men.
Isa 33:19 those people of an **o** speech, with
Eze 3: 5 of **o** speech and difficult language,
3: 6 not to many peoples of **o** speech and

Obscures (Obscure)

Job 42: 3 'Who is this that **o** my counsel

Observance (Observe)

Ex 13: 9 This **o** will be for you like a sign
Ezr 7:10 study and **o** of the Law of the LORD,

Observation (Observe)

Lk 17:20 does not come with your careful **o**,

Observe (Observance, Observation, Observed, Observer, Observes, Observing)

Ex 1:16 and **o** them on the delivery stool,
12:25 you as he promised, **o** this ceremony.
13: 5 to **o** this ceremony in this month:
31:13 "Say to the Israelites, 'You must **o**
31:14 "'**O** the Sabbath, because it is holy
31:16 The Israelites are to **o** the Sabbath,
Lev 19: 3 father, and you must **o** my Sabbaths.
19:30 "'**O** my Sabbaths and have reverence
23:32 evening you are to **o** your sabbath."
25: 2 itself must **o** a sabbath to the LORD.
26: 2 "'**O** my Sabbaths and have reverence
Dt 4: 6 **O** them carefully, for this will show
5:12 "**O** the Sabbath day by keeping it
5:15 commanded you to **o** the Sabbath day.
6: 1 to teach you to **o** in the land that
8: 6 **O** the commands of the LORD your God,
8:11 failing to **o** his commands, his laws
10:13 to **o** the LORD's commands and decrees
11: 8 **O** therefore all the commands I am
11:22 If you carefully **o** all these
12:14 there **o** everything I command you.
16: 1 **O** the month of Abib and celebrate
26:16 carefully **o** them with all your heart
28:45 **o** the commands and decrees he gave
2Sa 3:25 he came to deceive you and **o** your
1Ki 2: 3 **o** what the LORD your God requires:
9: 4 I command and **o** my decrees and laws,
9: 6 do not **o** the commands and decrees I
2Ki 17:13 **O** my commands and decrees, in
1Ch 22:13 if you are careful to **o** the decrees
2Ch 7:17 I command, and **o** my decrees and laws,
Est 9:19 those living in villages—**o** the
9:22 He wrote to them to **o** the days as
9:27 **o** these two days every year, in the
Ps 37:37 the blameless, **o** the upright;
91: 8 You will only **o** with your eyes and
105:45 keep his precepts and **o** his laws.
Ecc 8:16 to **o** man's labour on earth—his eyes
Jer 2:10 send to Kedar and **o** closely; see if
6:18 hear, O nations; **o**, O witnesses,
6:27 that you may **o** and test their ways.
8: 7 **o** the time of their migration.
Eze 45:21 day you are to **o** the Passover,
Mk 7: 4 And they **o** many other traditions,
7: 9 in order to **o** your own traditions!

Ro 2:25 Circumcision has value if you **o** the
Gal 3: 5 among you because you **o** the law,

Observed (Observe)

Ge 50:10 and there Joseph **o** a seven-day
Nu 23:21 in Jacob, no misery **o** in Israel.
1Sa 1:12 to the LORD, Eli **o** her mouth.
1Ki 8:65 Solomon **o** the festival at that time,
11:34 and who **o** my commands and statutes.
2Ki 23:22 Judah, had any such Passover been **o**.
2Ch 7: 8 Solomon **o** the festival at that time
35:17 **o** the Feast of Unleavened Bread for
35:18 The Passover had not been **o** like
Est 5: 9 **o** that he neither rose nor showed
9:28 These days should be remembered and **o**
Job 4: 8 I have **o**, those who plough evil and
Pr 24:32 I applied my heart to what I **o** and
Mic 6:16 You have **o** the statutes of Omri and

Observer (Observe)

Ac 22:12 He was a devout **o** of the law and

Observes (Observe)

Ps 11: 4 He **o** the sons of men; his eyes

Observing (Observe)

1Sa 20:29 'Let me go, because our family is **o**
2Ch 13:11 We are **o** the requirements of the
Lk 1: 6 **o** all the Lord's commandments and
Ro 3:20 in his sight by **o** the law; rather,
3:27 **o** the law? No, but on that of faith.
3:28 by faith apart from **o** the law.
Gal 2:16 a man is not justified by **o** the law,
2:16 in Christ and not by **o** the law,
2:16 **o** the law no-one will be justified.
3: 2 you receive the Spirit by **o** the law,
3:10 All who rely on **o** the law are under
4:10 You are **o** special days and months

Obsession

Ac 26:11 In my **o** against them, I even went to

Obsolete

Heb 8:13 "new", he has made the first one **o**;
8:13 is **o** and ageing will soon disappear.

Obstacle (Obstacles)

Ro 14:13 or **o** in your brother's way.

Obstacles (Obstacle)

Isa 57:14 the **o** out of the way of my people."
Jer 6:21 "I will put **o** before this people.
Ro 16:17 put **o** in your way that are contrary

Obstinate

Dt 2:30 his heart **o** in order to give him
Isa 30: 1 "Woe to the **o** children," declares
65: 2 held out my hands to an **o** people,
Eze 2: 4 I am sending you are **o** and stubborn.
3: 7 house of Israel is hardened and **o**.
Ac 19: 9 some of them became **o**; they refused
Ro 10:21 to a disobedient and **o** people."

Obtain (Obtained, Obtains)

Nu 27:21 who will **o** decisions for him by
Ezr 7:16 may **o** from the province of Babylon,
Pr 20:18 advice; if you wage war, **o** guidance.
Jn 5:44 yet make no effort to **o** the praise
Ro 11: 7 it did not **o**, but the elect did.
2Ti 2:10 that they too may **o** the salvation

Obtained (Obtain)

Ex 38:25 The silver **o** from those of the
Ac 22: 5 I even **o** letters from them to their
27:13 they thought they had **o** what they
Ro 9:30 have **o** it, a righteousness that is
Php 3:12 Not that I have already **o** all this,
Heb 9:12 blood, having **o** eternal redemption.

Obtains (Obtain)

Pr 12: 2 A good man **o** favour from the LORD,

Obvious

Mt 6:18 that it will not be **o** to men that
Gal 5:19 The acts of the sinful nature are **o**:
1Ti 5:24 The sins of some men are **o**, reaching
5:25 In the same way, good deeds are **o**,

Occasion (Occasions)

Jdg 14: 4 who was seeking an **o** to confront the
1Sa 9:24 it was set aside for you for this **o**,
2Ch 13:18 of Israel were subdued on that **o**,
Ezr 7:20 God that you may have **o** to supply,
10: 9 by the **o** and because of the rain.
Ne 8: 4 wooden platform built for the **o**.
Lk 10:25 On one **o** an expert in the law stood
Ac 1: 4 On one **o**, while he was eating with
2Co 9:11 that you can be generous on every **o**,

Occasions (Occasion)

Zec 8:19 **o** and happy festivals for Judah.
Eph 6:18 pray in the Spirit on all **o** with all

Occupants (Occupy)

Isa 5: 9 the fine mansions left without **o**.

Occupation (Occupy)

Ge 46:33 you in and asks, 'What is your **o**?'
47: 3 "What is your **o**?" "Your servants are

Occupied (Occupy)

Ge 36:43 settlements in the land they **o**.
Nu 21:25 cities of the Amorites and **o** them,
Jos 19:47 it, put it to the sword and **o** it.
Jdg 11:26 For three hundred years Israel **o**
1Sa 17: 3 The Philistines **o** one hill and the
31: 7 And the Philistines came and **o** them.
1Ch 5: 9 To the east they **o** the land up to
5:10 they **o** the dwellings of the Hagrites
5:22 And they **o** the land until the exile.
10: 7 And the Philistines came and **o** them.
2Ch 28:18 They captured and **o** Beth Shemesh,
Ecc 5:20 keeps him **o** with gladness of heart.

Occupy (Occupants, Occupation, Occupied)

Jos 1:15 After that, you may go back and **o**
17:12 Yet the Manassites were not able to **o**
Ne 2: 8 and for the residence I will **o**?"
Ecc 10: 6 while the rich **o** the low ones.
Jer 49:16 who **o** the heights of the hill.
Ob :19 People from the Negev will **o** the
:19 They will **o** the fields of Ephraim
Zec 9: 6 Foreigners will **o** Ashdod, and I will

Occur (Occurred, Occurs)

Ex 8:23 This miraculous sign will **o** tomorrow.
Eze 16:16 not happen, nor should they ever **o**.
1Co 5: 1 and of a kind that does not **o** even

Occurred (Occur)

2Ch 32:31 sign that had **o** in the land,
1Co 10: 6 Now these things **o** as examples to
Rev 16:18 No earthquake like it has ever **o**

Occurs (Occur)

Ecc 8:14 else meaningless that **o** on earth:
2Th 2: 3 until the rebellion **o** and the man of

Ocean (Oceans)

Ps 148: 7 sea creatures and all **o** depths,
Eze 26:19 and when I bring the **o** depths over

Oceans (Ocean)

Pr 8:24 there were no **o**, I was given birth,

Ocran

Nu 1:13 from Asher, Pagiel son of **O**;
2:27 people of Asher is Pagiel son of **O**.
7:72 On the eleventh day Pagiel son of **O**,
7:77 was the offering of Pagiel son of **O**.
10:26 Pagiel son of **O** was over the

Oded

2Ch 15: 1 of God came upon Azariah son of **O**.
15: 8 Azariah son of **O** the prophet,
28: 9 a prophet of the LORD named **O** was

Odious

1Sa 27:12 "He has become so **o** to his people,

Odour

Jn 11:39 "by this time there is a bad **o**,

Offal

Ex 29:14 its hide and its **o** outside the camp.
Lev 4:11 and legs, the inner parts and **o**—
8:17 its **o** he burned up outside the camp,
16:27 flesh and **o** are to be burned up.
Nu 19: 5 hide, flesh, blood and **o**.
Mal 2: 3 the **o** from your festival sacrifices,

Offence (Offend)

Ge 20:16 This is to cover the **o** against you
Dt 19:15 crime or **o** he may have committed.
21:22 If a man guilty of a capital **o** is
1Sa 13: 4 has become an **o** to the Philistines.
25:28 Please forgive your servant's **o**, for
2Sa 3: 8 me of an **o** involving this woman!
10: 6 had become an **o** to David's nostrils,
16:21 an **o** to your father's nostrils,
1Ch 19: 6 had become an **o** to David's nostrils,
Job 10:14 would not let my **o** go unpunished.
13:23 I committed? Show me my **o** and my sin.
Ps 59: 3 me for no **o** or sin of mine, O LORD.
Pr 17: 9 He who covers over an **o** promotes
19:11 it is to his glory to overlook an **o**.
Jer 24: 9 I will make them abhorrent and an **o**
Eze 22:11 In you one man commits a detestable **o**
Mt 13:57 they took **o** at him. But Jesus said
Mk 6: 3 with us?" And they took **o** at him.
Gal 5:11 **o** of the cross has been abolished.

Offences (Offend)

Nu 18: 1 for **o** against the sanctuary,
18: 1 for **o** against the priesthood.
18:23 the responsibility for **o** against it.
1Ki 8:50 **o** they have committed against you,
Job 7:21 Why do you not pardon my **o** and
14:17 My **o** will be sealed up in a bag; you
Isa 43:24 sins and wearied me with your **o**.
44:22 I have swept away your **o** like a
59:12 For our **o** are many in your sight,
59:12 Our **o** are ever with us, and we
Eze 18:22 None of the **o** he has committed will
18:28 he considers all the **o** he has
18:30 Repent! Turn away from all your **o**;
18:31 Rid yourselves of all the **o** you have
33:10 "Our **o** and sins weigh us down,
37:23 vile images or with any of their **o**,
39:24 their uncleanness and their **o**, and
Am 5:12 For I know how many are your **o** and

Offend (Offence, Offences, Offended, Offender, Offenders, Offensive)

Job 34:31 God, 'I am guilty but will **o** no more.
Mt 17:27 "But so that we may not **o** them, go
Jn 6:61 said to them, "Does this **o** you?

Offended (Offend)

Ge 40: 1 **o** their master, the king of Egypt.
Pr 18:19 An **o** brother is more unyielding than
Mt 15:12 were **o** when they heard this?"

Offender (Offend)

Ex 21:22 the **o** must be fined whatever the

Offenders (Offend)

1Co 6: 9 male prostitutes nor homosexual **o**

Offensive (Offend)

Job 19:17 My breath is **o** to my wife; I am
Ps 139:24 See if there is any **o** way in me, and
Jer 6:10 The word of the LORD is **o** to them;

Offer (Offered, Offering, Offerings, Offers)

Ex 3:18 **o** sacrifices to the LORD our God.'
5: 3 to **o** sacrifices to the LORD our God,
8: 8 go to **o** sacrifices to the LORD."
8:26 The sacrifices we **o** the LORD our God
8:26 And if we **o** sacrifices that are
8:27 to **o** sacrifices to the LORD our God,
8:28 Pharaoh said, "I will let you go to **o**
8:29 go to **o** sacrifices to the LORD."
23:18 "Do not **o** the blood of a sacrifice
29:38 "This is what you are to **o** on the
29:39 **O** one in the morning and the other
29:40 With the first lamb **o** a tenth of an
30: 9 Do not **o** on this altar any other
34:25 "Do not **o** the blood of a sacrifice
Lev 1: 3 he is to **o** a male without defect.
1:10 he is to **o** a male without defect.
1:14 he is to **o** a dove or a young pigeon.
2:14 **o** crushed heads of new grain roasted
3: 6 **o** a male or female without defect.
5: 8 **o** the one for the sin offering.
5:10 The priest shall then **o** the other as
7:12 **o** cakes of bread made without yeast
12: 7 He shall **o** them before the LORD to
14:12 lambs and **o** it as a guilt offering,
14:20 **o** it on the altar, together with the
16: 6 "Aaron is to **o** the bull for his own
17: 7 They must no longer **o** any of their
21: 8 Regard them as holy, because they **o**
21:17 come near to **o** the food of his God.
21:21 come near to **o** the food of his God.
22:22 Do not **o** to the LORD the blind, the
22:24 You must not **o** to the LORD an animal
22:25 and **o** them as the food of your God.
Nu 6:11 The priest is to **o** one as a sin
15: 7 **O** it as an aroma pleasing to the
15:24 then the whole community is to **o** a
Dt 12:14 **O** them only at the place the LORD
20:10 city, make its people an **o** of peace.
27: 6 **o** burnt offerings on it to the LORD
28:68 There you will **o** yourselves for sale
33:19 there **o** sacrifices of righteousness;
Jos 22:23 to **o** burnt offerings and grain
Jdg 5: 2 **o** themselves—praise the LORD!
6:26 **o** the second bull as a burnt
13:16 a burnt offering, **o** it to the LORD.
16:23 to **o** a great sacrifice to Dagon
21:13 whole assembly sent an **o** of peace
1Sa 1:21 **o** the annual sacrifice to the LORD
2:19 husband to **o** the annual sacrifice.
10: 4 They will greet you and **o** you two
13:12 compelled to **o** the burnt offering."
2Sa 7:27 found courage to **o** you this prayer.
24:22 whatever pleases him and **o** it up.
1Ki 3: 4 The king went to Gibeon to **o**
12:27 If these people go up to **o**
22:43 **o** sacrifices and burn incense there.
2Ki 12: 3 **o** sacrifices and burn incense there.
14: 4 **o** sacrifices and burn incense there.
15: 4 **o** sacrifices and burn incense there.
15:35 **o** sacrifices and burn incense there.
16:15 "On the large new altar, **o** the
17:36 bow down and to him **o** sacrifices.
1Ch 23:13 to **o** sacrifices before the LORD, to
2Ch 11:16 to **o** sacrifices to the LORD,
29:21 to **o** these on the altar of the LORD.
31: 2 or Levites—to **o** burnt offerings
35:12 of the people to **o** to the LORD,
Ezr 3: 6 to **o** burnt offerings to the LORD,
6:10 that they may **o** sacrifices pleasing
Ne 4: 2 Will they **o** sacrifices? Will they
Ps 4: 5 **O** right sacrifices and trust in the
38:14 hear, whose mouth can **o** no reply.
66:15 of rams; I will **o** bulls and goats.
Ecc 5: 1 Go near to listen rather than to **o**
9: 2 **o** sacrifices and those who do not.
Isa 1:15 **o** many prayers, I will not listen.
57: 7 you went up to **o** your sacrifices.
Jer 7:16 pray for this people nor **o** any plea
11:14 "Do not pray for this people nor **o**
14:12 though they **o** burnt offerings and
16: 7 No-one will **o** food to comfort those
33:18 me continually to **o** burnt offerings,
46:10 the LORD Almighty, will **o** sacrifice
Lam 3:30 Let him **o** his cheek to one who would
4: 3 Even jackals **o** their breasts to
Eze 20:31 you **o** your gifts—the sacrifice of
43:22 "On the second day you are to **o** a
43:23 you are to **o** a young bull and a ram
43:24 You are to **o** them before the LORD,
44:15 me to **o** sacrifices of fat and blood,
44:27 he is to **o** a sin offering for
45:13 is the special gift you are to **o**:
46: 6 On the day of the New Moon he is to **o**
46:12 He shall **o** his burnt offering or his
48: 9 "The special portion you are to **o** to
Hos 8:13 They **o** sacrifices given to me and
13: 2 "They **o** human sacrifice and
14: 2 that we may **o** the fruit of our lips.
Mic 6: 7 **o** my firstborn for my transgression,
Hag 2:14 whatever they **o** there is defiled.
Mal 1:13 crippled or diseased animals and **o**
Mt 5:24 brother; then come and **o** your gift.
8: 4 show yourself to the priest and **o**
Mk 1:44 show yourself to the priest and **o**
Lk 2:24 to **o** a sacrifice in keeping with
5:14 show yourself to the priest and **o**
Ac 14:13 wanted to **o** sacrifices to them.
24:26 that Paul would **o** him a bribe,
Ro 6:13 Do not **o** the parts of your body to
6:13 but rather **o** yourselves to God, as
6:13 and **o** the parts of your body to him
6:16 Don't you know that when you **o**
6:19 Just as you used to **o** the parts of
6:19 so now **o** them in slavery to
12: 1 **o** your bodies as living sacrifices
1Co 9:18 gospel I may **o** it free of charge,
Heb 5: 1 to **o** gifts and sacrifices for sins.
5: 3 This is why he has to **o** sacrifices
7:27 he does not need to **o** sacrifices day
8: 3 Every high priest is appointed to **o**
8: 3 one also to have something to **o**.
8: 4 **o** the gifts prescribed by the law.
9:25 Nor did he enter heaven to **o** himself
13:15 let us continually **o** to God a
1Pe 4: 9 **O** hospitality to one another without
Rev 8: 3 He was given much incense to **o**, with

Offered (Offer)

Ge 31:54 He **o** a sacrifice there in the hill
46: 1 and when he reached Beersheba, he **o**
Ex 24: 5 and they **o** burnt offerings and
40:29 the Tent of Meeting, and **o** on it
Lev 2:12 **o** on the altar as a pleasing aroma.
7: 3 All its fat shall be **o**: the fat tail
7:15 must be eaten on the day it is **o**;
7:18 not be credited to the one who **o** it,
9:15 slaughtered it and **o** it for a sin
9:16 He brought the burnt offering and **o**
10: 1 **o** unauthorised fire before the LORD,
Nu 16:47 but Aaron **o** the incense and made
18:15 that is **o** to the LORD is yours.
23: 2 **o** a bull and a ram on each altar.
23: 4 altar I have **o** a bull and a ram."
23:14 **o** a bull and a ram on each altar.
23:30 as Balaam had said, and **o** a bull
Dt 26:14 nor have I **o** any of it to the dead.
Jos 8:31 On it they **o** to the LORD burnt
Jdg 2: 5 There they **o** sacrifices to the LORD.
6:19 out and **o** them to him under the oak.
Ru 2:14 he **o** her some roasted grain.
1Sa 2:13 that whenever anyone **o** a sacrifice
6:15 of Beth Shemesh **o** burnt offerings
7: 9 Samuel took a suckling lamb and **o** it
13: 9 And Saul **o** up the burnt offering.
2Sa 15:24 and Abiathar **o** sacrifices until all
1Ki 3: 3 except that he **o** sacrifices and
3: 4 and Solomon **o** a thousand burnt
8:62 the king and all Israel with him **o**
8:63 Solomon **o** a sacrifice of fellowship
8:64 and there he **o** burnt offerings,
1Ki 11: 8 and **o** sacrifices to their gods.
12:32 Judah, and **o** sacrifices on the altar.
12:33 **o** sacrifices on the altar he had
20:34 took from your father," Ben-Hadad **o**.
2Ki 3:27 and **o** him as a sacrifice on the city
16: 4 He **o** sacrifices and burned incense
16:13 He **o** up his burnt offering and grain
1Ch 21:28 the Jebusite, he **o** sacrifices there.
2Ch 1: 6 **o** a thousand burnt offerings on it.
6:40 to the prayers **o** in this place.
7: 4 the king and all the people **o**
7: 5 King Solomon **o** a sacrifice of
7: 7 and there he **o** burnt offerings and
7:15 to the prayers **o** in this place.
28: 4 He **o** sacrifices and burned incense
28:23 He **o** sacrifices to the gods of
30:22 **o** fellowship offerings and praised
33:22 Amon worshipped and **o** sacrifices to
Ezr 6:17 house of God they **o** a hundred bulls,
Ne 12:43 on that day they **o** great sacrifices,
Job 26: 3 What advice you have **o** to one
31:27 and my hand **o** them a kiss of homage,
Ps 51:19 then bulls will be **o** on your altar.
106:28 ate sacrifices **o** to lifeless gods;
Isa 50: 6 I **o** my back to those who beat me, my
57: 6 offerings and **o** grain offerings.
Eze 6:13 every leafy oak—places where they **o**
16:18 **o** my oil and incense before them.
16:19 **o** as fragrant incense before them.
20:28 there they **o** their sacrifices, made
44: 7 desecrating my temple while you **o** me
Jnh 1:16 and they **o** a sacrifice to the LORD
Mt 26:27 he took the cup, gave thanks and **o**
27:34 There they **o** Jesus wine to drink,
27:48 a stick, and **o** it to Jesus to drink.
Mk 14:23 he took the cup, gave thanks and **o**
15:23 they **o** him wine mixed with myrrh,
15:36 a stick, and **o** it to Jesus to drink.
Lk 23:36 They **o** him wine vinegar
Ac 8:18 apostles' hands, he **o** them money
Ro 11:16 If the part of the dough **o** as
1Co 9:13 share in what is **o** on the altar?
10:19 Do I mean then that a sacrifice **o** to
10:20 but the sacrifices of pagans are **o**
10:28 "This has been **o** in sacrifice," then
Heb 5: 7 he **o** up prayers and petitions with
6:18 to take hold of the hope **o** to us
7:27 sins once for all when he **o** himself.
9: 7 and never without blood, which he **o**
9: 9 sacrifices being **o** were not able to
9:14 who through the eternal Spirit **o**
10: 2 would they not have stopped being **o**?
10:12 when this priest had **o** for all time
11: 4 By faith Abel **o** God a better
11:17 tested him, **o** Isaac as a sacrifice.
Jas 2:21 he **o** his son Isaac on the altar?
5:15 the prayer **o** in faith will make the
Rev 14: 4 **o** as firstfruits to God and the Lamb.

Offering (*Burnt offering, Drink offering, Fellowship offering, Freewill offering, Grain offering, Guilt offering,* Offer, *Sin offering, Thank-offering, Wave offering*)

Ge 4: 3 of the soil as an **o** to the LORD.
4: 4 with favour on Abel and his **o**,
4: 5 on Cain and his **o** he did not look
Ex 25: 2 "Tell the Israelites to bring me an **o**
25: 2 You are to receive the **o** for me from
29:18 an **o** made to the LORD by fire.
29:25 LORD, an **o** made to the LORD by fire.
29:41 an **o** made to the LORD by fire.
30:13 This half shekel is an **o** to the LORD.
30:14 more, are to give an **o** to the LORD.
30:15 when you make the **o** to the LORD
30:20 an **o** made to the LORD by fire,
35: 5 From what you have, take an **o** for
35: 5 LORD an **o** of gold, silver and bronze;
35:21 brought an **o** to the LORD for the
35:24 Those presenting an **o** of silver or
35:24 brought it as an **o** to the LORD,
36: 6 else as an **o** for the sanctuary.
Lev 1: 2 'When any of you brings an **o** to the
1: 2 bring as your **o** an animal from
1: 3 "'If the **o** is a burnt **o** from the

Lev 1: 9 an **o** made by fire, an aroma pleasing
1:10 "'If the **o** is a burnt **o** from the
1:13 an **o** made by fire, an aroma pleasing
1:14 "'If the **o** to the LORD is a burnt
1:17 an **o** made by fire, an aroma pleasing
2: 1 LORD, his **o** is to be of fine flour.
2: 2 an **o** made by fire, an aroma pleasing
2: 9 on the altar as an **o** made by fire,
2:11 in an **o** made to the LORD by fire.
2:12 the LORD as an **o** of the firstfruits,
2:16 as an **o** made to the LORD by fire.
3: 1 "'If someone's **o** is a fellowship
3: 2 lay his hand on the head of his **o**
3: 5 as an **o** made by fire, an aroma
3: 8 lay his hand on the head of his **o**
3:11 food, an **o** made to the LORD by fire.
3:12 "'If his **o** is a goat, he is to
3:14 to make this **o** to the LORD by fire:
3:16 an **o** made by fire, a pleasing aroma.
4:23 as his **o** a male goat without defect.
4:28 he must bring as his **o** for the sin
5:11 he is to bring as an **o** for his sin a
5:13 The rest of the **o** will belong to the
6:20 "This is the **o** Aaron and his sons
7: 5 as an **o** made to the LORD by fire.
7:13 he is to present an **o** with cakes
7:14 to bring one of each kind as an **o**,
7:16 "'If, however, his **o** is the result
7:25 from which an **o** by fire may be made
7:30 the **o** made to the LORD by fire;
7:37 the ordination **o** and the fellowship
8:21 a pleasing aroma, an **o** made to the
8:28 as an ordination **o**, a pleasing
8:28 an **o** made to the LORD by fire.
9: 7 sacrifice the **o** that is for the
9:15 Aaron then brought the **o** that was
17: 4 present it as an **o** to the LORD in
19:24 be holy, an **o** of praise to the LORD.
22:10 family may eat the sacred **o**,
22:14 "'If anyone eats a sacred **o** by
22:14 restitution to the priest for the **o**
22:22 as an **o** made to the LORD by fire.
22:27 as an **o** made to the LORD by fire.
23: 8 For seven days present an **o** made to
23:13 oil—an **o** made to the LORD by fire,
23:14 day you bring this **o** to your God.
23:16 an **o** of new grain to the LORD.
23:18 an **o** made by fire, an aroma
23:20 sacred **o** to the LORD for the priest.
23:25 Do no regular work, but present an **o**
23:27 an **o** made to the LORD by fire.
23:36 an **o** made to the LORD by fire.
24: 7 to be an **o** made to the LORD by fire.
27: 9 is acceptable as an **o** to the LORD,
27:11 one that is not acceptable as an **o**
Nu 3: 4 made an **o** with unauthorised fire
5:15 He must also take an **o** of a tenth of
5:15 a reminder **o** to draw attention to
5:18 place in her hands the reminder **o**,
5:26 as a memorial **o** and burn it on
6:21 the Nazirite who vows his **o**
7:11 **o** for the dedication of the altar."
7:12 The one who brought his **o** on the
7:13 His **o** was one silver plate weighing
7:17 the **o** of Nahshon son of Amminadab.
7:18 leader of Issachar, brought his **o**.
7:19 The **o** he brought was one silver
7:23 was the **o** of Nethanel son of Zuar.
7:24 people of Zebulun, brought his **o**.
7:25 His **o** was one silver plate weighing
7:29 This was the **o** of Eliab son of Helon.
7:30 the people of Reuben, brought his **o**.
7:31 His **o** was one silver plate weighing
7:35 was the **o** of Elizur son of Shedeur.
7:36 the people of Simeon, brought his **o**.
7:37 His **o** was one silver plate weighing
7:41 **o** of Shelumiel son of Zurishaddai.
7:42 of the people of Gad, brought his **o**.
7:43 His **o** was one silver plate weighing
7:47 was the **o** of Eliasaph son of Deuel.
7:48 people of Ephraim, brought his **o**.
7:49 His **o** was one silver plate weighing
7:53 the **o** of Elishama son of Ammihud.
7:54 people of Manasseh, brought his **o**.
7:55 His **o** was one silver plate weighing
7:59 the **o** of Gamaliel son of Pedahzur.
Nu 7:60 people of Benjamin, brought his **o**.
7:61 His **o** was one silver plate weighing
7:65 was the **o** of Abidan son of Gideoni.
7:66 of the people of Dan, brought his **o**.
7:67 His **o** was one silver plate weighing
7:71 the **o** of Ahiezer son of Ammishaddai.
7:72 the people of Asher, brought his **o**.
7:73 His **o** was one silver plate weighing
7:77 was the **o** of Pagiel son of Ocran.
7:78 people of Naphtali, brought his **o**.
7:79 His **o** was one silver plate weighing
7:83 This was the **o** of Ahira son of Enan.
9: 7 kept from presenting the LORD's **o**
9:13 the LORD's **o** at the appointed time.
15: 4 the one who brings his **o** shall
15: 4 one who brings his **o** shall present
15:10 It will be an **o** made by fire, an
15:13 when he brings an **o** made by fire
15:14 presents an **o** made by fire as an
15:19 a portion as an **o** to the LORD.
15:20 it as an **o** from the threshing-floor.
15:21 you are to give this **o** to the LORD
15:25 for their wrong an **o** made by fire
16:15 to the LORD, "Do not accept their **o**.
16:35 the 250 men who were **o** the incense.
18:17 burn their fat as an **o** made by fire,
18:24 present as an **o** to the LORD.
18:26 tenth of that tithe as the LORD's **o**.
18:27 Your **o** will be reckoned to you as
18:28 present an **o** to the LORD from all
19:17 burned purification **o** into a jar
23: 3 here beside your **o** while I go aside.
23: 6 his **o**, with all the princes of Moab.
23:15 "Stay here beside your **o** while I
23:17 his **o**, with the princes of Moab.
26:61 Abihu died when they made an **o**
28: 3 Say to them: 'This is the **o** made by
28: 6 an **o** made to the LORD by fire.
28: 8 This is an **o** made by fire, an aroma
28: 9 "'On the Sabbath day, make an **o** of
28:13 an **o** made to the LORD by fire.
28:19 Present to the LORD an **o** made by
28:24 prepare the food for the **o** made by
28:26 when you present to the LORD an **o** of
29:13 Present an **o** made by fire as an
29:36 Present an **o** made by fire as an
31:50 we have brought as an **o** to the LORD
Dt 2:26 king of Heshbon **o** peace and saying,
24:10 to get what he is **o** as a pledge.
Jdg 6:18 bring my **o** and set it before you.
1Sa 2:17 treating the LORD's **o** with contempt.
2:29 Why do you scorn my sacrifice and **o**
2:29 every **o** made by my people Israel?'
3:14 be atoned for by sacrifice or **o**.
13:10 Just as he finished making the **o**,
26:19 against me, then may he accept an **o**.
2Sa 15:12 While Absalom was **o** sacrifices, he
1Ki 13: 1 standing by the altar to make an **o**.
18:33 pour it on the **o** and on the wood."
2Ki 3:20 about the time for **o** the sacrifice,
1Ch 9:31 for baking the **o** bread.
16:29 Bring an **o** and come before him;
2Ch 29:27 As the **o** began, singing to the LORD
35:16 the **o** of burnt offerings on the
Ezr 8:25 I weighed out to them the **o** of
Ps 40: 6 Sacrifice and **o** you did not desire,
66:15 fat animals to you and an **o** of rams;
96: 8 bring an **o** and come into his courts.
Isa 40:20 A man too poor to present such an **o**
65: 3 **o** sacrifices in gardens and burning
66:20 as an **o** to the LORD—on horses,
Eze 16:25 degraded your beauty, **o** your body
Da 2:46 **o** and incense be presented to him.
9:27 will put an end to sacrifice and **o**.
Mal 1: 8 is that not wrong? Try **o** them to
1:10 I will accept no **o** from your hands.
Mt 5:23 "Therefore, if you are **o** your gift
Jn 16: 2 will think he is **o** a service to God.
Ac 10: 4 come up as a memorial **o** before God.
21:26 **o** would be made for each of them.
Ro 15:16 might become an **o** acceptable to God,
2Co 8:19 to accompany us as we carry the **o**,
Eph 5: 2 a fragrant **o** and sacrifice to God.
Php 4:18 They are a fragrant **o**, an acceptable
Heb 10: 5 "Sacrifice and **o** you did not desire,
1Pe 2: 5 **o** spiritual sacrifices acceptable to

Offerings (*Burnt offerings, Drink offerings, Fellowship offerings, Freewill offerings, Grain offerings, Guilt offerings,* Offer, *Sin offerings, Thank-offerings, Wave offerings*)

Ex 22:29 "Do not hold back **o** from your
23:18 **o** must not be kept until morning.
25: 3 These are the **o** you are to receive
25:29 and bowls for the pouring out of **o**.
29:33 They are to eat these **o** by which
36: 3 They received from Moses all the **o**
Lev 2: 3 of the **o** made to the LORD by fire.
2:10 of the **o** made to the LORD by fire.
2:13 add salt to all your **o**.
4:35 of the **o** made to the LORD by fire.
5:12 of the **o** made to the LORD by fire.
6:17 share of the **o** made to me by fire.
6:18 It is his regular share of the **o**
7:35 This is the portion of the **o** made to
7:38 to bring their **o** to the LORD,
8:31 from the basket of ordination **o**,
10:12 from the **o** made to the LORD by fire
10:13 of the **o** made to the LORD by fire;
10:15 fat portions of the **o** made by fire,
14:11 his **o** before the LORD at the
14:32 the regular **o** for his cleansing.
21: 6 Because they present the **o** made to
21:21 the **o** made to the LORD by fire.
22: 2 **o** the Israelites consecrate to me,
22: 3 yet comes near the sacred **o** that the
22: 4 the sacred **o** until he is cleansed.
22: 6 He must not eat any of the sacred **o**
22: 7 the sacred **o**, for they are his food.
22:15 **o** the Israelites present to the
22:16 by allowing them to eat the sacred **o**
23:36 For seven days present **o** made to the
23:37 bringing **o** made to the LORD by fire
23:38 These **o** are in addition to those for
24: 9 of the **o** made to the LORD by fire."
26:31 in the pleasing aroma of your **o**.
Nu 6:14 There he is to present his **o** to the
7: 2 of those who were counted, made **o**.
7:10 the leaders brought their **o** for its
7:84 These were the **o** of the Israelite
7:88 These were the **o** for the dedication
15: 3 you present to the LORD **o** made by
15: 3 vows or freewill **o** or festival **o**—
18: 8 in charge of the **o** presented to me;
18: 8 all the holy **o** the Israelites give
18: 9 holy **o** that is kept from the fire.
18: 9 gifts they bring me as most holy **o**,
18:19 Whatever is set aside from the holy **o**
18:32 defile the holy **o** of the Israelites,
28: 2 time the food for my **o** made by fire,
Dt 18: 1 They shall live on the **o** made to the
Jos 13:14 since the **o** made by fire to the LORD,
1Sa 2:28 **o** made with fire by the Israelites.
2Sa 1:21 nor fields that yield **o** of grain.
1Ki 12:33 and went up to the altar to make **o**.
13: 2 the high places who now make **o** here,
2Ki 12: 4 sacred **o** to the temple of the LORD
16:12 approached it and presented **o** on it.
1Ch 6:49 **o** on the altar of burnt offering
2Ch 8:13 **o** commanded by Moses for Sabbaths,
29:29 the **o** were finished, the king and
32:23 Many brought **o** to Jerusalem for the
35: 7 sheep and goats for the Passover **o**,
35: 8 Passover **o** and three hundred cattle.
35: 9 provided five thousand Passover **o**
35:13 and boiled the holy **o** in pots,
Ne 10:33 for the **o** on the Sabbaths, New Moon
10:33 appointed feasts; for the holy **o**;
Isa 1:13 Stop bringing meaningless **o**! Your
60: 7 will be accepted as **o** on my altar,
Jer 19: 5 their sons in the fire as **o** to Baal—
48:35 those who make **o** on the high places
Eze 20:28 made **o** that provoked me to anger,
20:40 There I will require your **o** and your
36:38 numerous as the flocks for **o** at
40:43 tables were for the flesh of the **o**.
42:13 the LORD will eat the most holy **o**.
42:13 There they will put the most holy **o**—
44:13 of my holy things or my most holy **o**;
Hos 4:13 and burn **o** on the hills,
9: 4 They will not pour out wine **o** to the

Am 5:25 "Did you bring me sacrifices and **o**
Zep 3:10 scattered people, will bring me **o**.
Mal 1: 9 With such **o** from your hands, will he
1:11 In every place incense and pure **o**
2:12 he brings **o** to the LORD Almighty.
2:13 no longer pays attention to your **o**
3: 3 who will bring **o** in righteousness,
3: 4 the **o** of Judah and Jerusalem will be
3: 8 How do we rob you?' "In tithes and **o**.
Mk 12:41 the place where the **o** were put
Jn 8:20 near the place where the **o** were put.
Ac 7:42 'Did you bring me sacrifices and **o**
24:17 gifts for the poor and to present **o**.
Heb 10: 8 First he said, "Sacrifices and **o**,
11: 4 man, when God spoke well of his **o**.

Offers (Offer)

Lev 3: 1 and he **o** an animal from the herd,
3: 6 "'If he **o** an animal from the flock
3: 7 If he **o** a lamb, he is to present it
3:14 From what he **o** he is to make this
6:26 The priest who **o** it shall eat it; it
7: 8 The priest who **o** a burnt offering
7: 9 belongs to the priest who **o** it,
7:12 "'If he **o** it as an expression of
7:16 shall be eaten on the day he **o** it,
7:33 The son of Aaron who **o** the blood and
17: 8 who **o** a burnt offering or
Dt 33:10 He **o** incense before you and whole
Isa 66: 3 and whoever **o** a lamb, like one who
Heb 10:11 and again he **o** the same sacrifices,

Office (Officer, Officers, Official, Officials, Officiate)

Dt 17: 9 the judge who is in **o** at that time.
19:17 the judges who are in **o** at the time.
26: 3 say to the priest in **o** at the time,
1Sa 2:36 "Appoint me to some priestly **o** so
Ne 13:29 because they defiled the priestly **o**
Isa 22:19 I will depose you from your **o**, and
Heb 7:23 prevented them from continuing in **o**;

Officer (Office)

1Sa 29: 3 "Is this not David, who was an **o** of
2Ki 3:11 An **o** of the king of Israel answered,
7: 2 The **o** on whose arm the king was
7:17 Now the king had put the **o** on whose
7:19 The **o** had said to the man of God,
9:25 Jehu said to Bidkar, his chariot **o**,
18:17 his chief **o** and his field commander
18:24 How can you repulse one **o** of the
25:19 he took the **o** in charge of the
25:19 chief **o** in charge of conscripting
1Ch 26:24 the **o** in charge of the treasuries.
2Ch 24:11 the royal secretary and the **o** of the
26:11 **o** under the direction of Hananiah,
28: 7 Azrikam the **o** in charge of the
Ezr 4: 8 Rehum the commanding **o** and Shimshai
4: 9 Rehum the commanding **o** and Shimshai
4:17 reply: To Rehum the commanding **o**,
Ne 11: 9 Joel son of Zicri was their chief **o**,
11:14 **o** was Zabdiel son of Haggedolim.
11:22 The chief **o** of the Levites in
Isa 33:18 "Where is that chief **o**? Where is the
33:18 is the **o** in charge of the towers?"
36: 9 How then can you repulse one **o** of
Jer 20: 1 the chief **o** in the temple of the
39: 3 Nebo-Sarsekim a chief **o**,
39:13 Nebushazban a chief **o**,
51:59 the staff **o** Seraiah son of Neriah,
52:25 he took the **o** in charge of the
52:25 chief **o** in charge of conscripting
Da 2:15 He asked the king's **o**, "Why did the
Mt 5:25 judge may hand you over to the **o**,
Lk 12:58 **o**, and the **o** throw you into prison.
2Ti 2: 4 wants to please his commanding **o**.

Officers (Office)

Ex 14: 7 of Egypt, with **o** over all of them.
15: 4 **o** are drowned in the Red Sea.
Nu 31:14 Moses was angry with the **o** of the
31:48 the **o** who were over the units of the
Dt 20: 5 The **o** shall say to the army: "Has
20: 8 the **o** shall add, "Is any man afraid
20: 9 the **o** have finished speaking to the
Jos 1:10 Joshua ordered the **o** of the people:
3: 2 After three days the **o** went
1Sa 18: 5 the people, and Saul's **o** as well.
18:30 success than the rest of Saul's **o**,
2Sa 8: 7 that belonged to the **o** of Hadadezer
1Ki 4: 5 Nathan—in charge of the district **o**;
4:27 The district **o**, each in his month,
9:22 his government officials, his **o**, his
20:14 'The young **o** of the provincial
20:15 Ahab summoned the young **o** of the
20:17 The young **o** of the provincial
20:19 The young **o** of the provincial
20:24 and replace them with other **o**.
2Ki 6: 8 After conferring with his **o**, he said,
6:11 He summoned his **o** and demanded of
6:12 lord the king," said one of his **o**,
7:12 up in the night and said to his **o**,
7:13 One of his **o** answered, "Make some
9: 5 he arrived, he found the army **o**
9:11 Jehu went out to his fellow **o**, one
10:25 he ordered the guards and **o**: "Go in
10:25 The guards and **o** threw the bodies
11:14 The **o** and the trumpeters were beside
15:25 One of his chief **o**, Pekah son of
24:10 At that time the **o** of Nebuchadnezzar
24:11 city while his **o** were besieging it.
24:14 all the **o** and fighting men,
25:23 all the army **o** and their men heard
25:26 together with the army **o**, fled to
1Ch 11:11 a Hacmonite, was chief of the **o**; he
12:28 warrior, with 22 **o** from his family;
12:34 men of Naphtali—1,000 **o**, together
13: 1 David conferred with each of his **o**,
18: 7 carried by the **o** of Hadadezer
27: 1 and their **o**, who served the king in
27: 3 all the army **o** for the first month.
27:16 The **o** over the tribes of Israel:
27:22 the **o** over the tribes of Israel.
28: 1 at Jerusalem: the **o** over the tribes,
29: 6 the leaders of families, the **o** of
29:24 All the **o** and mighty men, as well as
2Ch 8:18 by his own **o**, men who knew the sea.
21: 9 Jehoram went there with his **o** and
23:13 The **o** and the trumpeters were beside
32: 6 He appointed military **o** over the
32: 9 he sent his **o** to Jerusalem with this
32:16 Sennacherib's **o** spoke further
32:21 **o** in the camp of the Assyrian king.
35:23 shot King Josiah, and he told his **o**,
Ne 2: 9 sent army **o** and cavalry with me.
4:16 The **o** posted themselves behind all
Est 2:21 two of the king's **o** who guarded the
6: 2 two of the king's **o** who guarded the
Isa 21: 5 Get up, you **o**, oil the shields!
Jer 26:21 King Jehoiakim and all his **o** and
38:17 'If you surrender to the **o** of the
38:18 if you will not surrender to the **o**
39:13 the other **o** of the king of
40: 7 all the army **o** and their men who
40:13 all the army **o** still in the open
41: 1 and had been one of the king's **o**,
41:11 all the army **o** who were with him
41:13 **o** who were with him, they were glad.
41:16 all the army **o** who were with him led
42: 1 all the army **o**, including Johanan
42: 8 all the army **o** who were with him and
43: 4 all the army **o** and all the people
43: 5 all the army **o** led away all the
46:26 king of Babylon and his **o**.
51:57 her governors, **o** and warriors as
Eze 23:15 chariot **o**, natives of Chaldea.
23:23 chariot **o** and men of high rank, all
Lk 22: 4 the **o** of the temple guard and
22:52 the **o** of the temple guard, and the
Ac 5:22 on arriving at the jail, the **o** did
5:26 At that, the captain went with his **o**
16:35 the magistrates sent their **o** to the
16:37 Paul said to the **o**: "They beat us
16:38 The **o** reported this to the
21:32 He at once took some **o** and soldiers
25:23 **o** and the leading men of the city.

Official (Office)

2Ki 8: 6 Then he assigned an **o** to her case
23:11 room of an **o** named Nathan-Melech.
25: 8 an **o** of the king of Babylon, came to
1Ch 9:11 the **o** in charge of the house of God;
2Ch 13: 6 Yet Jeroboam son of Nebat, an **o** of
31:13 **o** in charge of the temple of God.
Ne 2:10 the Ammonite **o** heard about this,
2:19 Tobiah the Ammonite **o** and Geshem the
Pr 17:11 a merciless **o** will be sent against
Ecc 5: 8 for one **o** is eyed by a higher one,
Jer 38: 7 Ebed-Melech, a Cushite, an **o** in the
39: 3 Nergal-Sharezer a high **o** and all the
39:13 Nergal-Sharezer a high **o** and all the
Da 1: 7 The chief **o** gave them new names: to
1: 8 and he asked the chief **o** for
1: 9 Now God had caused the **o** to show
1:10 the **o** told Daniel, "I am afraid of
1:11 chief **o** had appointed over Daniel,
1:18 **o** presented them to Nebuchadnezzar.
Jn 4:46 **o** whose son lay sick at Capernaum.
4:49 The royal **o** said, "Sir, come down
Ac 8:27 an important **o** in charge of all the
28: 7 Publius, the chief **o** of the island.

Officials (Office)

Ge 12:15 Pharaoh's **o** saw her, they praised
20: 8 Abimelech summoned all his **o**,
37:36 Potiphar, one of Pharaoh's **o**,
39: 1 Egyptian who was one of Pharaoh's **o**,
40: 2 Pharaoh was angry with his two **o**,
40: 7 he asked Pharaoh's **o** who were in
40:20 and he gave a feast for all his **o**.
40:20 baker in the presence of his **o**:
41:37 good to Pharaoh and to all his **o**.
45:16 Pharaoh and all his **o** were pleased.
50: 7 All Pharaoh's **o** accompanied him—the
Ex 5:21 his **o** and have put a sword in their
7:10 and his **o**, and it became a snake.
7:20 in the presence of Pharoah and his **o**
8: 3 into the houses of your **o** and on
8: 4 you and your people and all your **o**.
8: 9 your **o** and your people that you and
8:11 your **o** and your people; they will
8:21 swarms of flies on you and your **o**,
8:24 palace and into the houses of his **o**,
8:29 Pharaoh and his **o** and his people.
8:31 **o** and his people; not a fly remained.
9:14 and against your **o** and your people,
9:20 Those **o** of Pharaoh who feared the
9:30 I know that you and your **o** still do
9:34 He and his **o** hardened their hearts.
10: 1 the hearts of his **o** so that I may
10: 6 those of all your **o** and all the
10: 7 Pharaoh's **o** said to him, "How long
11: 3 by Pharaoh's **o** and by the people.)
11: 8 All these **o** of yours will come to me,
12:30 Pharaoh and all his **o** and all the
14: 5 Pharaoh and his **o** changed their
18:21 appoint them as **o** over thousands,
18:25 **o** over thousands, hundreds, fifties
Nu 11:16 as leaders and **o** among the people.
26: 9 Abiram were the community **o** who
Dt 1:15 fifties and of tens and as tribal **o**.
16:18 Appoint judges and **o** for each of
29: 2 to all his **o** and to all his land.
29:10 **o**, and all the other men of Israel,
31:28 of your tribes and all your **o**,
34:11 to all his **o** and to his whole land.
Jos 8:33 with their elders, **o** and judges,
23: 2 leaders, judges and **o**—and said to
24: 1 leaders, judges and **o** of Israel, and
Jdg 8: 6 the **o** of Succoth said, "Do you
8:14 **o** of Succoth, the elders of the town.
1Sa 8:15 and give it to his **o** and attendants.
22: 6 with all his **o** standing round him.
22: 9 who was standing with Saul's **o**, said,
22:17 But the king's **o** were not willing
2Sa 13:24 the king and his **o** please join me?"
15:14 David said to all his **o** who were
15:15 The king's **o** answered him, "Your
16: 6 He pelted David and all the king's **o**
16:11 then said to Abishai and all his **o**,
1Ki 1: 9 the men of Judah who were royal **o**,
1:47 Also, the royal **o** have come to

1Ki 4: 2 these were his chief **o**: Azariah son
9:22 his government **o**, his officers, his
9:23 They were also the chief **o** in charge
9:23 550 **o** supervising the men who did
10: 5 the seating of his **o**, the attending
10: 8 your men must be! How happy your **o**,
11:17 Edomite **o** who had served his father.
11:26 He was one of Solomon's **o**, an
15:18 He entrusted it to his **o** and sent
16: 9 Zimri, one of his **o**, who had command
20: 6 to send my **o** to search your palace
20: 6 palace and the houses of your **o**.
20:23 Meanwhile, the **o** of the king of Aram
20:31 His **o** said to him, "Look, we have
22: 3 The king of Israel had said to his **o**,
22: 9 Israel called one of his **o** and said,
2Ki 10: 1 to Samaria: to the **o** of Jezreel,
12:20 His **o** conspired against him and
12:21 The **o** who murdered him were Jozabad
14: 5 he executed the **o** who had murdered
18:24 of the least of my master's **o**,
19: 5 King Hezekiah's **o** came to Isaiah,
21:23 Amon's **o** conspired against him and
22: 9 "Your **o** have paid out the money that
24:12 and his **o** all surrendered to him.
24:15 **o** and the leading men of the land.
25:24 of the Babylonian **o**," he said.
1Ch 18:17 were chief **o** at the king's side.
23: 4 six thousand are to be **o** and judges.
24: 5 for there were **o** of the sanctuary
24: 5 **o** of God among the descendants of
24: 6 king and of the **o**: Zadok the priest,
26:29 temple, as **o** and judges over Israel.
27:31 **o** in charge of King David's property.
28: 1 David summoned all the **o** of Israel
28: 1 and the **o** in charge of all the
28: 1 together with the palace **o**, the
28:21 The **o** and all the people will obey
29: 6 and the **o** in charge of the king's
2Ch 8:10 They were also King Solomon's chief **o**
8:10 and fifty **o** supervising the men.
9: 4 the seating of his **o**, the attending
9: 7 your men must be! How happy your **o**,
17: 7 of his reign he sent his **o** Ben-Hail,
18: 8 Israel called one of his **o** and said,
19:11 Levites will serve as **o** before you.
24:10 All the **o** and all the people brought
24:11 in by the Levites to the king's **o**
24:17 After the death of Jehoiada, the **o**
24:25 His **o** conspired against him for
25: 3 he executed the **o** who had murdered
26:11 of Hananiah, one of the royal **o**.
28:14 of the **o** and all the assembly.
29:20 gathered the city **o** together
29:30 King Hezekiah and his **o** ordered the
30: 2 The king and his **o** and the whole
30: 6 from the king and from his **o**,
30:12 what the king and his **o** had ordered,
30:24 and the **o** provided them with a
31: 8 Hezekiah and his **o** came and saw the
32: 3 he consulted with his **o** and military
33:24 Amon's **o** conspired against him and
34:16 "Your **o** are doing everything that
35: 8 His **o** also contributed voluntarily
36:18 the treasures of the king and his **o**.
Ezr 4: 9 and **o** over the men from Tripolis,
5: 6 the **o** of Trans-Euphrates, sent to
6: 6 their fellow **o** of that province,
7:28 and all the king's powerful **o**.
8:20 the **o** had established to assist the
8:25 his advisers, his **o** and all Israel
9: 2 And the leaders and **o** have led the
10: 8 the decision of the **o** and elders,
10:14 Let our **o** act for the whole assembly.
Ne 2:16 The **o** did not know where I had gone
2:16 nobles or **o** or any others who would
4:14 the **o** and the rest of the people,
4:19 I said to the nobles, the **o** and the
5: 7 and then accused the nobles and **o**.
5:12 made the nobles and **o** take an oath
5:17 a hundred and fifty Jews and **o** ate
7: 5 the **o** and the common people for
9:10 against all his **o** and all the people
12:40 so did I, together with half the **o**,
13:11 I rebuked the **o** and asked them, "Why
Est 1: 3 a banquet for all his nobles and **o**.
Est 2:18 banquet, for all his nobles and **o**.
2:23 the two **o** were hanged on a gallows.
3: 2 All the royal **o** at the king's gate
3: 3 the royal **o** at the king's gate asked
4:11 "All the king's **o** and the people of
5:11 him above the other nobles and **o**.
Pr 17:26 or to flog **o** for their integrity.
29:12 If a ruler listens to lies, all his **o**
Isa 3: 4 I will make boys their **o**; mere
19:11 The **o** of Zoan are nothing but fools;
19:13 The **o** of Zoan have become fools, the
30: 4 Though they have **o** in Zoan and their
36: 9 of the least of my master's **o**,
37: 5 King Hezekiah's **o** came to Isaiah,
Jer 1:18 its **o**, its priests and the people of
2:26 **o**, their priests and their prophets.
4: 9 "the king and the **o** will lose heart,
8: 1 the bones of the kings and **o** of
17:25 the gates of this city with their **o**.
17:25 They and their **o** will come riding in
21: 7 his **o** and the people in this city
22: 2 your **o** and your people who come
22: 4 by their **o** and their people.
24: 1 Jehoiakim king of Judah and the **o**,
24: 8 his **o** and the survivors from
25:18 its kings and **o**, to make them a ruin
25:19 his **o** and all his people,
26:10 the **o** of Judah heard about these
26:11 said to the **o** and all the people,
26:12 Jeremiah said to all the **o** and all
26:16 the **o** and all the people said to the
26:21 his officers and **o** heard his words,
29: 2 the court **o** and the leaders of Judah
32:32 their kings and **o**, their priests and
34:10 all the **o** and people who entered
34:19 the court **o**, the priests and all the
34:21 his **o** over to their enemies who seek
35: 4 It was next to the room of the **o**,
36:12 where all the **o** were sitting:
36:12 of Hananiah, and all the other **o**.
36:14 all the **o** sent Jehudi son of
36:19 the **o** said to Baruch, "You and
36:21 and all the **o** standing beside him.
37:14 Jeremiah and brought him to the **o**.
37:18 you or your **o** or this people,
38: 4 the **o** said to the king, "This man
38:22 out to the **o** of the king of Babylon.
38:25 If the **o** hear that I talked with you,
38:27 All the **o** did come to Jeremiah and
39: 3 all the **o** of the king of Babylon
39: 3 the other **o** of the king of Babylon.
41:16 court **o** he had brought from Gibeon.
44:17 our kings and our **o** did in the towns
44:21 your **o** and the people of the land?
48: 7 together with his priests and **o**.
49: 3 together with his priests and **o**.
49:38 her king and **o**," declares the LORD.
50:35 and against her **o** and wise men!
51:23 with you I shatter governors and **o**.
51:28 **o**, and all the countries they rule.
51:57 I will make her **o** and wise men drunk,
52:10 he also killed all the **o** of Judah.
Eze 22:27 Her **o** within her are like wolves
Da 1: 3 chief of his court **o**, to bring in
3: 2 all the other provincial **o** to come
3: 3 all the other provincial **o** assembled
Am 1:15 and his **o** together," says the LORD.
2: 3 all her **o** with him," says the LORD.
Na 3:17 like locusts, your **o** like swarms of
Zep 3: 3 Her **o** are roaring lions, her rulers
Mt 20:25 high **o** exercise authority over them.
Mk 6:21 Herod gave a banquet for his high **o**
10:42 high **o** exercise authority over them.
Jn 18: 3 some **o** from the chief priests and
18:12 and the Jewish **o** arrested Jesus.
18:18 servants and **o** stood round a fire
18:22 Jesus said this, one of the **o** near
19: 6 soon as the chief priests and their **o**
Ac 17: 6 other brothers before the city **o**,
17: 8 the city **o** were thrown into turmoil.
19:31 Even some of the **o** of the province,

Officiate (Office)
2Ki 17:32 people to **o** for them as priests in

Offset
1Ki 6: 6 He made **o** ledges around the outside

Offshoots (Shoot)
Isa 22:24 and **o**—all its lesser vessels,

Offspring
Ge 3:15 and between your **o** and hers; he will
12: 7 "To your **o** I will give this land.
13:15 give to you and your **o** for ever.
13:16 I will make your **o** like the dust of
13:16 dust, then your **o** could be counted.
15: 5 he said to him, "So shall your **o** be.
17:12 foreigner—those who are not your **o**.
21:12 Isaac that your **o** will be reckoned.
21:13 nation also, because he is your **o**."
22:18 through your **o** all nations on earth
24: 7 'To your **o** I will give this
24:60 **o** possess the gates of their enemies.
26: 4 and through your **o** all nations on
28:14 be blessed through you and your **o**.
38: 8 to produce **o** for your brother."
38: 9 Onan knew that the **o** would not be
38: 9 from producing **o** for his brother.
46: 6 Jacob and all his **o** went to Egypt.
46: 7 and granddaughters—all his **o**.
Ex 13: 2 The first **o** of every womb among the
13:12 the LORD the first **o** of every womb.
13:15 LORD the first male **o** of every womb
34:19 "The first **o** of every womb belongs
Lev 21:15 that he will not defile his **o** among
Nu 3:12 male **o** of every Israelite woman.
8:16 male **o** from every Israelite woman.
18:15 The first **o** of every womb, both man
18:19 the LORD for both you and your **o**."
Ru 4:12 Through the **o** the LORD gives you by
2Sa 4: 8 the king against Saul and his **o**."
7:12 I will raise up your **o** to succeed
1Ch 17:11 I will raise up your **o** to succeed
Job 18:19 He has no **o** or descendants among his
21: 8 them, their **o** before their eyes.
27:14 his **o** will never have enough to eat.
Ps 37:28 the **o** of the wicked will be cut off;
Isa 9:20 will feed on the flesh of his own **o**:
14:20 The **o** of the wicked will never be
14:22 survivors, her **o** and descendants,"
22:24 its **o** and offshoots—all its lesser
44: 3 I will pour out my Spirit on your **o**,
53:10 he will see his **o** and prolong his
57: 3 you **o** of adulterers and prostitutes!
57: 4 a brood of rebels, the **o** of liars?
61: 9 and their **o** among the peoples.
Jer 22:30 for none of his **o** will prosper, none
31:27 with the **o** of men and of animals.
Lam 2:20 like this? Should women eat their **o**,
Hos 9:16 I will slay their cherished **o**."
Mal 2:15 Because he was seeking godly **o**.
Ac 3:25 He said to Abraham, 'Through your **o**
17:28 own poets have said, 'We are his **o**.'
17:29 "Therefore since we are God's **o**, we
Ro 4:13 his **o** received the promise that he
4:16 may be guaranteed to all Abraham's **o**
4:18 said to him, "So shall your **o** be.
9: 7 Isaac that your **o** will be reckoned."
9: 8 who are regarded as Abraham's **o**.
Heb 11:18 Isaac that your **o** will be reckoned."
Rev 12:17 **o**—those who obey God's commandments
22:16 I am the Root and the **O** of David,

Og (Og's)
Nu 21:33 and **O** king of Bashan and his whole
32:33 the kingdom of **O** king of Bashan—the
Dt 1: 4 and at Edrei had defeated **O** king of
3: 1 and **O** king of Bashan with his whole
3: 3 **O** king of Bashan and all his army.
3:11 (Only **O** king of Bashan was left of
3:13 the kingdom of **O**, I gave to the
4:47 and the land of **O** king of Bashan,
29: 7 Sihon king of Heshbon and **O** king of
31: 4 to them what he did to Sihon and **O**,
Jos 2:10 and what you did to Sihon and **O**, the
9:10 and **O** king of Bashan, who reigned in
12: 4 the territory of **O** king of Bashan,
13:12 that is, the whole kingdom of **O** in
13:30 the entire realm of **O** king of Bashan

Jos 13:31 (the royal cities of **O** in Bashan).
1Ki 4:19 the country of **O** king of Bashan).
Ne 9:22 and the country of **O** king of Bashan.
Ps 135:11 Sihon king of the Amorites, **O** king
136:20 **O** king of Bashan—His love endures

Og's (Og)

Dt 3: 4 of Argob, **O** kingdom in Bashan.
3:10 Edrei, towns of **O** kingdom in Bashan.

Ohad

Ge 46:10 The sons of Simeon: Jemuel, Jamin, **O**,
Ex 6:15 Jamin, **O**, Jakin, Zohar and Shaul the

Ohel

1Ch 3:20 **O**, Berekiah, Hasadiah and

Oholah

Eze 23: 4 The older was named **O**, and her
23: 4 **O** is Samaria, and Oholibah is
23: 5 "**O** engaged in prostitution while she
23:36 "Son of man, will you judge **O** and
23:44 those lewd women, **O** and Oholibah.

Oholiab See Bezalel

Ex 31: 6 I have appointed **O** son of Ahisamach
35:34 he has given both him and **O** son of
36: 1 Bezalel, **O** and every skilled person
36: 2 Moses summoned Bezalel and **O** and
38:23 with him was **O** son of Ahisamach, of

Oholibah

Eze 23: 4 named Oholah, and her sister was **O**.
23: 4 is Samaria, and **O** is Jerusalem.
23:11 "Her sister **O** saw this, yet in her
23:22 "Therefore, **O**, this is what the
23:36 will you judge Oholah and **O**? Then
23:44 with those lewd women, Oholah and **O**.

Oholibamah

Ge 36: 2 and **O** daughter of Anah and
36: 5 **O** bore Jeush, Jalam and Korah. These
36:14 The sons of Esau's wife **O** daughter
36:18 The sons of Esau's wife **O**: Chiefs
36:18 from Esau's wife **O** daughter of Anah.
36:25 The children of Anah: Dishon and **O**
36:41 **O**, Elah, Pinon,
1Ch 1:52 **O**, Elah, Pinon,

Oil (*Anointing oil*, Oils)

Ge 28:18 a pillar and poured **o** on top of it.
35:14 on it; he also poured **o** on it.
Ex 25: 6 olive **o** for the light; spices for
27:20 **o** of pressed olives for the light
29: 2 with **o**, and wafers spread with **o**.
29:23 and a cake made with **o**, and a wafer.
29:40 of a hin of **o** from pressed olives,
30:24 shekel—and a hin of olive **o**.
30:32 make any **o** with the same formula.
35: 8 olive **o** for the light; spices for
35:14 lamps and **o** for the light;
35:28 They also brought spices and olive **o**
39:37 and the **o** for the light;
Lev 2: 1 to pour **o** on it, put incense on
2: 2 a handful of the fine flour and **o**,
2: 4 made without yeast and mixed with **o**,
2: 4 without yeast and spread with **o**.
2: 5 mixed with **o**, and without yeast.
2: 6 Crumble it and pour **o** on it; it is a
2: 7 is to be made of fine flour and **o**.
2:15 Put **o** and incense on it; it is a
2:16 of the crushed grain and the **o**,
5:11 He must not put **o** or incense on it,
6:15 take a handful of fine flour and **o**,
6:21 Prepare it with **o** on a griddle;
7:10 whether mixed with **o** or dry, belongs
7:12 made without yeast and mixed with **o**,
7:12 without yeast and spread with **o**,
7:12 flour well-kneaded and mixed with **o**.
8:11 He sprinkled some of the **o** on the
8:26 and one made with **o**, and a wafer; he
9: 4 with a grain offering mixed with **o**.
14:10 mixed with **o** for a grain offering,
Lev 14:10 a grain offering, and one log of **o**.
14:12 along with the log of **o**; he shall
14:15 then take some of the log of **o**,
14:16 dip his right forefinger into the **o**
14:17 The priest is to put some of the **o**
14:18 The rest of the **o** in his palm the
14:21 **o** for a grain offering, a log of **o**,
14:24 together with the log of **o**, and wave
14:26 The priest is to pour some of the **o**
14:27 sprinkle some of the **o** from his
14:28 Some of the **o** in his palm he is to
14:29 The rest of the **o** in his palm the
23:13 an ephah of fine flour mixed with **o**
24: 2 **o** of pressed olives for the light
Nu 4: 9 jars for the **o** used to supply it.
4:16 is to have charge of the **o** for the
5:15 He must not pour **o** on it or put
6:15 with **o**, and wafers spread with **o**.
7:13 mixed with **o** as a grain offering;
7:19 mixed with **o** as a grain offering;
7:25 mixed with **o** as a grain offering;
7:31 mixed with **o** as a grain offering;
7:37 mixed with **o** as a grain offering;
7:43 mixed with **o** as a grain offering;
7:49 mixed with **o** as a grain offering;
7:55 mixed with **o** as a grain offering;
7:61 mixed with **o** as a grain offering;
7:67 mixed with **o** as a grain offering;
7:73 mixed with **o** as a grain offering;
7:79 mixed with **o** as a grain offering;
8: 8 offering of fine flour mixed with **o**;
11: 8 like something made with olive **o**.
15: 4 mixed with a quarter of a hin of **o**.
15: 6 mixed with a third of a hin of **o**,
15: 9 flour mixed with half a hin of **o**.
18:12 "I give you all the finest olive **o**
28: 5 of a hin of **o** from pressed olives.
28: 9 an ephah of fine flour mixed with **o**.
28:12 flour mixed with **o**; with the ram,
28:12 an ephah of fine flour mixed with **o**;
28:13 an ephah of fine flour mixed with **o**.
28:20 with **o**; with the ram, two-tenths;
28:28 with **o**; with the ram, two-tenths;
29: 3 with **o**; with the ram, two-tenths;
29: 9 with **o**; with the ram, two-tenths;
29:14 with **o**; with each of the two rams,
35:25 who was anointed with holy **o**.
Dt 7:13 new wine and **o**—the calves of your
8: 8 pomegranates, olive **o** and honey;
11:14 in your grain, new wine and **o**.
12:17 of your grain and new wine and **o**,
14:23 new wine and **o**, and the firstborn of
18: 4 new wine and **o**, and the first wool
28:40 not use the **o**, because the olives
28:51 new wine or **o**, nor any calves of
32:13 and with **o** from the flinty crag,
33:24 and let him bathe his feet in **o**.
Jdg 9: 9 'Should I give up my **o**, by which
1Sa 10: 1 Samuel took a flask of **o** and poured
16: 1 your horn with **o** and be on your way;
16:13 Samuel took the horn of **o** and
2Sa 1:21 of Saul—no longer rubbed with **o**.
1Ki 1:39 Zadok the priest took the horn of **o**
5:11 thousand baths, of pressed olive **o**.
17:12 in a jar and a little **o** in a jug.
17:14 the jug of **o** will not run dry until
17:16 up and the jug of **o** did not run dry,
2Ki 4: 2 all," she said, "except a little **o**.
4: 4 Pour **o** into all the jars, and as
4: 6 Then the **o** stopped flowing.
4: 7 "Go, sell the **o** and pay your debts.
9: 1 take this flask of **o** with you and
9: 3 take the flask and pour the **o** on his
9: 6 Then the prophet poured the **o** on
20:13 the gold, the spices and the fine **o**—
1Ch 9:29 wine, and the **o**, incense and spices.
12:40 fig cakes, raisin cakes, wine, **o**,
27:28 charge of the supplies of olive **o**.
2Ch 2:10 twenty thousand baths of olive **o**."
2:15 the olive **o** and wine he promised,
11:11 supplies of food, olive **o** and wine.
31: 5 new wine, **o** and honey and all that
32:28 new wine and **o**; and he made stalls
Ezr 3: 7 and gave food and drink and **o** to the
6: 9 and wheat, salt, wine and **o**, as
7:22 of olive **o**, and salt without limit.
Ne 5:11 the money, grain, new wine and **o**."
10:37 wine and **o**. And we will bring a
10:39 new wine and **o** to the storerooms
13: 5 new wine and **o** prescribed for the
13:12 new wine and **o** into the storerooms.
Est 2:12 six months with **o** of myrrh and six
Job 29: 6 out for me streams of olive **o**.
Ps 23: 5 my head with **o**; my cup overflows.
45: 7 by anointing you with the **o** of joy.
55:21 words are more soothing than **o**, yet
89:20 my sacred **o** I have anointed him.
104:15 **o** to make his face shine, and bread
109:18 like water, into his bones like **o**.
133: 2 is like precious **o** poured on the
141: 5 him rebuke me—it is **o** on my head.
Pr 5: 3 and her speech is smoother than **o**;
21:17 loves wine and **o** will never be rich.
21:20 are stores of choice food and **o**,
27:16 wind or grasping **o** with the hand.
Ecc 9: 8 and always anoint your head with **o**.
Isa 1: 6 or bandaged or soothed with **o**.
21: 5 Get up, you officers, **o** the shields!
39: 2 the gold, the spices, the fine **o**,
57: 9 You went to Molech with olive **o** and
61: 3 the **o** of gladness instead of
Jer 31:12 **o**, the young of the flocks and herds.
40:10 summer fruit and **o**, and put them in
41: 8 **o** and honey, hidden in a field.
Eze 16:13 was fine flour, honey and olive **o**.
16:18 my **o** and incense before them.
16:19 olive **o** and honey I gave you to eat—
23:41 incense and **o** that belonged to me.
27:17 honey, **o** and balm for your wares.
32:14 and make her streams flow like **o**,
45:14 The prescribed portion of **o**,
45:24 with a hin of **o** for each ephah.
45:25 offerings, grain offerings and **o**.
46: 5 with a hin of **o** for each ephah.
46: 7 with a hin of **o** with each ephah.
46:11 with a hin of **o** for each ephah.
46:14 of a hin of **o** to moisten the flour.
46:15 the grain offering and the **o** shall
Hos 2: 5 and my linen, my **o** and my drink.'
2: 8 the new wine and **o**, who lavished on
2:22 wine and **o**, and they will respond
12: 1 Assyria and sends olive **o** to Egypt.
Joel 1:10 new wine is dried up, the **o** fails.
2:19 new wine and **o**, enough to satisfy
2:24 will overflow with new wine and **o**.
Mic 6: 7 with ten thousand rivers of **o**? Shall
6:15 but not use the **o** on yourselves,
Hag 1:11 on the grain, the new wine, the **o**
2:12 some wine, **o** or other food, does it
Zec 4:12 gold pipes that pour out golden **o**?"
Mt 6:17 when you fast, put **o** on your head
25: 3 but did not take any **o** with them.
25: 4 The wise, however, took **o** in jars
25: 8 of your **o**; our lamps are going out.'
25: 9 sell **o** and buy some for yourselves.'
25:10 buy the **o**, the bridegroom arrived.
Mk 6:13 sick people with **o** and healed them.
Lk 7:46 You did not put **o** on my head, but
10:34 his wounds, pouring on **o** and wine.
16: 6 "'Eight hundred gallons of olive **o**,'
Heb 1: 9 by anointing you with the **o** of joy."
Jas 5:14 him with **o** in the name of the Lord.
Rev 6: 6 do not damage the **o** and the wine!"
18:13 of wine and olive **o**, of fine flour

Oils (Oil)

Ps 92:10 ox; fine **o** have been poured upon me.

Ointment (Ointments)

Job 41:31 stirs up the sea like a pot of **o**.

Ointments (Ointment)

Eze 16: 9 the blood from you and put **o** on you.

Old (*Old age*, Older, Oldest)

Ge 5:32 After Noah was 500 years **o**, he
6: 4 were the heroes of **o**, men of renown.
7: 6 Noah was six hundred years **o** when
11:10 when Shem was 100 years **o**, he
12: 4 years **o** when he set out from Haran.

Ge 15: 9 each three years **o**, along with a
16:16 Abram was eighty-six years **o** when
17: 1 Abram was ninety-nine years **o**, the
17:12 is eight days **o** must be circumcised,
17:17 be born to a man a hundred years **o**?
17:24 Abraham was ninety-nine years **o** when
18:11 Abraham and Sarah were already **o** and
18:12 I am worn out and my master is **o**,
18:13 have a child, now that I am **o**?'
19: 4 young and **o**—surrounded the house.
19:11 young and **o**, with blindness so that
19:31 "Our father is **o**, and there is no
21: 4 his son Isaac was eight days **o**,
21: 5 Abraham was a hundred years **o** when
23: 1 a hundred and twenty-seven years **o**.
24: 1 Abraham was now **o** and well advanced
25: 8 an **o** man and full of years; and he
25:20 Isaac was forty years **o** when he
25:26 Isaac was sixty years **o** when
26:34 Esau was forty years **o**, he married
27: 1 Isaac was **o** and his eyes were so
27: 2 Isaac said, "I am now an **o** man and
35:29 to his people, **o** and full of years.
41:46 Joseph was thirty years **o** when he
47: 8 Pharaoh asked him, "How **o** are you?"
Ex 7: 7 Moses was eighty years **o** and Aaron
10: 9 "We will go with our young and **o**,
29:38 each day: two lambs a year **o**.
30:14 those twenty years **o** or more, are to
38:26 **o** or more, a total of 603,550 men.
Lev 9: 3 a calf and a lamb—both a year **o** and
14:10 lambs and one ewe lamb a year **o**,
23:12 LORD a lamb a year **o** without defect,
23:18 each a year **o** and without defect,
23:19 a year **o**, for a fellowship offering.
25:22 you will eat from the **o** crop and
27: 7 If it is a person sixty years **o** or
Nu 1: 3 men in Israel twenty years **o** or
1:18 and the men twenty years **o** or more
1:20 All the men twenty years **o** or more
1:22 All the men twenty years **o** or more
1:24 All the men twenty years **o** or more
1:26 All the men twenty years **o** or more
1:28 All the men twenty years **o** or more
1:30 All the men twenty years **o** or more
1:32 All the men twenty years **o** or more
1:34 All the men twenty years **o** or more
1:36 All the men twenty years **o** or more
1:38 All the men twenty years **o** or more
1:40 All the men twenty years **o** or more
1:42 All the men twenty years **o** or more
1:45 All the Israelites twenty years **o** or
3:15 Count every male a month **o** or more."
3:22 The number of all the males a month **o**
3:28 The number of all the males a month **o**
3:34 The number of all the males a month **o**
3:39 male a month **o** or more, was 22,000.
3:40 males who are a month **o** or more
3:43 firstborn males a month **o** or more,
7:15 lamb a year **o**, for a burnt offering;
7:17 goats and five male lambs a year **o**,
7:21 lamb a year **o**, for a burnt offering;
7:23 goats and five male lambs a year **o**,
7:27 lamb a year **o**, for a burnt offering;
7:29 goats and five male lambs a year **o**,
7:33 lamb a year **o**, for a burnt offering;
7:35 goats and five male lambs a year **o**,
7:39 lamb a year **o**, for a burnt offering;
7:41 goats and five male lambs a year **o**,
7:45 lamb a year **o**, for a burnt offering;
7:47 goats and five male lambs a year **o**,
7:51 lamb a year **o**, for a burnt offering;
7:53 goats and five male lambs a year **o**,
7:57 lamb a year **o**, for a burnt offering;
7:59 goats and five male lambs a year **o**,
7:63 lamb a year **o**, for a burnt offering;
7:65 goats and five male lambs a year **o**,
7:69 lamb a year **o**, for a burnt offering;
7:71 goats and five male lambs a year **o**,
7:75 lamb a year **o**, for a burnt offering;
7:77 goats and five male lambs a year **o**,
7:81 lamb a year **o**, for a burnt offering;
7:83 goats and five male lambs a year **o**,
7:87 rams and twelve male lambs a year **o**,
7:88 goats and sixty male lambs a year **o**.
8:24 Men twenty-five years **o** or more
Nu 14:29 every one of you twenty years **o** or
18:16 they are a month **o**, you must redeem
26: 2 all those twenty years **o** or more who
26: 4 "Take a census of men twenty years **o**
26:62 All the male Levites a month **o** or
28: 3 two lambs a year **o** without defect,
28: 9 two lambs a year **o** without defect,
28:11 lambs a year **o**, all without defect.
28:19 lambs a year **o**, all without defect.
28:27 seven male lambs a year **o** as an
29: 2 lambs a year **o**, all without defect.
29: 8 lambs a year **o**, all without defect.
29:13 lambs a year **o**, all without defect.
29:17 lambs a year **o**, all without defect.
29:20 lambs a year **o**, all without defect.
29:23 lambs a year **o**, all without defect.
29:26 lambs a year **o**, all without defect.
29:29 lambs a year **o**, all without defect.
29:32 lambs a year **o**, all without defect.
29:36 lambs a year **o**, all without defect.
32:11 not one of the men twenty years **o** or
33:39 years **o** when he died on Mount Hor.
Dt 28:50 for the **o** or pity for the young.
31: 2 twenty years **o** and I am no longer
32: 7 Remember the days of **o**; consider the
34: 7 and twenty years **o** when he died,
Jos 6:21 young and **o**, cattle, sheep and
9: 4 and **o** wineskins, cracked and mended.
9: 5 on their feet and wore **o** clothes.
13: 1 Joshua was **o** and well advanced in
13: 1 "You are very **o**, and there are still
14: 7 I was forty years **o** when Moses the
14:10 I am today, eighty-five years **o**!
23: 1 then **o** and well advanced in years,
23: 2 "I am **o** and well advanced in years.
Jdg 6:25 herd, the one seven years **o**.
19:16 That evening an **o** man from the hill
19:17 the **o** man asked, "Where are you
19:20 welcome at my house," the **o** man said
19:22 they shouted to the **o** man who owned
Ru 1:12 Return home, my daughters; I am too **o**
1Sa 2:22 Now Eli, who was very **o**, heard about
2:31 not be an **o** man in your family
2:32 line there will never be an **o** man.
4:15 who was ninety-eight years **o** and
4:18 died, for he was an **o** man and heavy.
5: 9 and **o**, with an outbreak of tumours.
8: 1 Samuel grew **o**, he appointed his sons
8: 5 They said to him, "You are **o**, and
12: 2 As for me, I am **o** and grey, and my
13: 1 Saul was thirty years **o** when he
17:12 he was **o** and well advanced in years.
24:13 the **o** saying goes, 'From evildoers
28:14 "An **o** man wearing a robe is coming
30: 2 who were in it, both young and **o**.
30:19 Nothing was missing: young or **o**, boy
2Sa 2:10 forty years **o** when he became king
4: 4 He was five years **o** when the news
5: 4 David was thirty years **o** when he
19:32 Now Barzillai was a very **o** man,
19:35 I am now eighty years **o**. Can I tell
1Ki 1: 1 King David was **o** and well advanced
11: 4 Solomon grew **o**, his wives turned his
13:11 Now there was a certain **o** prophet
13:18 The **o** prophet answered, "I too am a
13:20 **o** prophet who had brought him back.
13:25 the city where the **o** prophet lived.
14:21 He was forty-one years **o** when he
22:42 Jehoshaphat was thirty-five years **o**
2Ki 3:21 young and **o**, who could bear arms was
4:14 has no son and her husband is **o**."
8:17 He was thirty-two years **o** when he
8:26 Ahaziah was twenty-two years **o** when
11:21 Joash was seven years **o** when he
14: 2 He was twenty-five years **o** when he
14:21 who was sixteen years **o**, and made
15: 2 He was sixteen years **o** when he
15:33 He was twenty-five years **o** when he
16: 2 Ahaz was twenty years **o** when he
18: 2 He was twenty-five years **o** when he
19:25 In days of **o** I planned it; now I
21: 1 Manasseh was twelve years **o** when he
21:19 Amon was twenty-two years **o** when he
22: 1 Josiah was eight years **o** when he
23:31 Jehoahaz was twenty-three years **o**
23:36 Jehoiakim was twenty-five years **o**
2Ki 24: 8 Jehoiachin was eighteen years **o** when
24:18 Zedekiah was twenty-one years **o** when
1Ch 2:21 when he was sixty years **o**), and she
23: 1 David was **o** and full of years, he
23: 3 The Levites thirty years **o** or more
23:24 that is, the workers twenty years **o**
23:27 from those twenty years **o** or more.
25: 8 Young and **o** alike, teacher as well
26:13 their families, young and **o** alike.
27:23 of the men twenty years **o** or less,
2Ch 3: 3 (using the cubit of the **o** standard).
12:13 He was forty-one years **o** when he
20:31 He was thirty-five years **o** when he
21: 5 Jehoram was thirty-two years **o** when
21:20 Jehoram was thirty-two years **o** when
22: 2 Ahaziah was twenty-two years **o** when
24: 1 Joash was seven years **o** when he
24:15 Now Jehoiada was **o** and full of years,
25: 1 Amaziah was twenty-five years **o** when
25: 5 those twenty years **o** or more
26: 1 who was sixteen years **o**, and made
26: 3 Uzziah was sixteen years **o** when he
27: 1 Jotham was twenty-five years **o** when
27: 8 He was twenty-five years **o** when he
28: 1 Ahaz was twenty years **o** when he
29: 1 Hezekiah was twenty-five years **o**
31:15 their divisions, **o** and young alike.
31:16 the males three years **o** or more
31:17 the Levites twenty years **o** or more,
33: 1 Manasseh was twelve years **o** when he
33:21 Amon was twenty-two years **o** when he
34: 1 Josiah was eight years **o** when he
36: 2 Jehoahaz was twenty-three years **o**
36: 5 Jehoiakim was twenty-five years **o**
36: 9 Jehoiachin was eighteen years **o** when
36:11 Zedekiah was twenty-one years **o** when
36:17 man nor young woman, **o** man or aged.
Est 3:13 all the Jews—young and **o**,
Job 14: 8 Its roots may grow **o** in the ground
20: 4 you know how it has been from of **o**,
21: 7 Why do the wicked live on, growing **o**
22:15 Will you keep to the **o** path that
29: 8 and the **o** men rose to their feet;
32: 6 "I am young in years, and you are **o**;
32: 9 is not only the **o** who are wise, not
42:17 he died, **o** and full of years.
Ps 25: 6 and love, for they are from of **o**.
37:25 I was young and now I am **o**, yet I
71: 9 Do not cast me away when I am **o**; do
71:18 Even when I am **o** and grey, do not
74: 2 the people you purchased of **o**,
74:12 you, O God, are my king from of **o**;
78: 2 hidden things, things from of **o**—
148:12 young men and maidens, **o** men and
Pr 8:22 his works, before his deeds of **o**;
20:29 grey hair the splendour of the **o**.
22: 6 he is **o** he will not turn from it.
23:22 despise your mother when she is **o**.
Ecc 1:11 There is no remembrance of men of **o**,
4:13 youth than an **o** but foolish king
7:10 Do not say, "Why were the **o** days
SS 7:13 both new and **o**, that I have stored
Isa 1:26 restore your judges as in days of **o**,
3: 5 young will rise up against the **o**,
20: 4 young and **o**, with buttocks bared—to
22:11 walls for the water of the **O** Pool,
23: 7 the **o**, **o** city, whose feet have taken
37:26 In days of **o** I planned it; now I
48: 8 from of **o** your ear has not been open
51: 9 gone by, as in generations of **o**.
63: 9 and carried them all the days of **o**.
63:11 his people recalled the days of **o**,
63:16 our Redeemer from of **o** is your name.
63:19 We are yours from of **o**; but you have
65:20 or an **o** man who does not live out
Jer 6:11 **o**, those weighed down with years.
30:20 children will be as in days of **o**,
31:13 be glad, young men and **o** as well.
38:11 He took some **o** rags and worn-out
38:12 "Put these **o** rags and worn-out
51:22 with you I shatter **o** man and youth,
52: 1 Zedekiah was twenty-one years **o** when
Lam 1: 7 that were hers in days of **o**.
2:21 "Young and **o** lie together in the
3: 4 grow **o** and has broken my bones.
5:21 may return; renew our days as of **o**

Eze 9: 6 Slaughter **o** men, young men and
16: 8 saw that you were **o** enough for love,
Hos 4:11 to prostitution, to **o** wine and new,
Joel 2: 2 as never was of **o** nor ever will be
2:28 your **o** men will dream dreams, your
Mic 5: 2 are from of **o**, from ancient times."
6: 6 offerings, with calves a year **o**?
Mt 2:16 who were two years **o** and under,
9:16 of unshrunk cloth on an **o** garment,
9:17 Neither do men pour new wine into **o**
13:52 new treasures as well as **o**."
Mk 2:21 of unshrunk cloth on an **o** garment.
2:21 from the **o**, making the tear worse.
2:22 no-one pours new wine into **o**
5:42 around (she was twelve years **o**).
Lk 1:18 I am an **o** man and my wife is well on
2:36 She was very **o**; she had lived with
2:42 he was twelve years **o**, they went up
3:23 years **o** when he began his ministry.
5:36 new garment and sews it on an **o** one.
5:36 from the new will not match the **o**.
5:37 no-one pours new wine into **o**
5:39 no-one after drinking **o** wine wants
5:39 new, for he says, 'The **o** is better.
Jn 3: 4 "How can a man be born when he is **o**?"
8:57 "You are not yet fifty years **o**," the
21:18 when you are **o** you will stretch out
Ac 2:17 your **o** men will dream dreams.
4:22 healed was over forty years **o**.
7:23 "When Moses was forty years **o**, he
Ro 4:19 he was about a hundred years **o**
6: 6 For we know that our **o** self was
7: 6 in the **o** way of the written code.
1Co 5: 7 Get rid of the **o** yeast that you may
5: 8 not with the **o** yeast, the yeast of
2Co 3:14 remains when the **o** covenant is read.
5:17 the **o** has gone, the new has come!
Eph 4:22 to put off your **o** self, which is
Col 3: 9 have taken off your **o** self with its
1Ti 4: 7 with godless myths and **o** wives' tales
Phm : 9 I then, as Paul—an **o** man and now
Heb 8: 6 mediator is superior to the **o** one,
1Jn 2: 7 you a new command but an **o** one,
2: 7 This **o** command is the message you
Rev 21: 4 **o** order of things has passed away."

Old age

Ge 15:15 in peace and be buried at a good **o**.
21: 2 and bore a son to Abraham in his **o**,
21: 7 Yet I have borne him a son in his **o**."
24:36 Sarah has borne him a son in her **o**,
25: 8 his last and died at a good **o**,
37: 3 he had been born to him in his **o**;
44:20 is a young son born to him in his **o**.
48:10 of **o**, and he could hardly see.
Jdg 8:32 Gideon son of Joash died at a good **o**
Ru 4:15 your life and sustain you in your **o**.
1Ki 15:23 **o**, however, his feet became diseased.
1Ch 29:28 He died at a good **o**, having enjoyed
Ps 92:14 They will still bear fruit in **o**,
Isa 46: 4 Even to your **o** and grey hairs I am
Zec 8: 4 "Once again men and women of ripe **o**
Lk 1:36 is going to have a child in her **o**,

Older (Old)

Ge 10:21 Shem, whose **o** brother was Japheth;
19:31 One day the **o** daughter said to the
19:33 **o** daughter went in and lay with him.
19:34 The next day the **o** daughter said to
19:37 The **o** daughter had a son, and she
25:23 and the **o** will serve the younger."
27: 1 his **o** son and said to him, "My son.
27:15 the best clothes of Esau her **o** son,
27:42 Rebekah was told what her **o** son Esau
29:16 the name of the **o** was Leah,
29:26 in marriage before the **o** one.
Ex 2:10 the child grew **o**, she took him to
1Sa 14:49 The name of his **o** daughter was Merab,
18:17 Saul said to David, "Here is my **o**
1Ki 2:22 he is my **o** brother—yes, for him and
2Ch 22: 1 the camp, had killed all the **o** sons.
Ezr 3: 8 Levites twenty years of age and **o**
3:12 many of the **o** priests and Levites
Job 15:10 side, men even **o** than your father.
32: 4 to Job because they were **o** than he.
Eze 16:46 Your **o** sister was Samaria, who lived
16:61 **o** than you and those who are younger.
23: 4 The **o** was named Oholah, and her
Lk 15:25 "Meanwhile, the **o** son was in the
15:28 "The **o** brother became angry and
Jn 8: 9 the **o** ones first, until only Jesus
Ro 9:12 told, "The **o** will serve the younger.
1Ti 5: 1 Do not rebuke an **o** man harshly, but
5: 2 **o** women as mothers, and younger
Tit 2: 2 Teach the **o** men to be temperate,
2: 3 Likewise, teach the **o** women to be
1Pe 5: 5 be submissive to those who are **o**.

Oldest (Old)

Ge 44:12 the **o** and ending with the youngest.
Jdg 8:20 Turning to Jether, his **o** son, he
1Sa 17:13 Jesse's three **o** sons had followed
17:14 David was the youngest. The three **o**
17:28 Eliab, David's **o** brother, heard him
1Ch 24:31 The families of the **o** brother were
Job 1:13 wine at the **o** brother's house,
1:18 wine at the **o** brother's house,
Heb 12:16 his inheritance rights as the **o** son.

Olive (Olives)

Ge 8:11 beak was a freshly plucked **o** leaf!
Ex 23:11 with your vineyard and your **o** grove.
25: 6 **o** oil for the light; spices for the
30:24 shekel—and a hin of **o** oil.
35: 8 **o** oil for the light; spices for the
35:28 They also brought spices and **o** oil
Nu 11: 8 like something made with **o** oil.
18:12 "I give you all the finest **o** oil and
Dt 6:11 and vineyards and **o** groves you did
8: 8 pomegranates, **o** oil and honey;
28:40 You will have **o** trees throughout
Jos 24:13 **o** groves that you did not plant.'
Jdg 9: 8 said to the **o** tree, 'Be our king.'
9: 9 "But the **o** tree answered, 'Should I
15: 5 with the vineyards and **o** groves.
1Sa 8:14 vineyards and **o** groves and give them
1Ki 5:11 thousand baths, of pressed **o** oil.
6:23 of **o** wood, each ten cubits high.
6:31 of **o** wood with five-sided jambs.
6:32 on the two **o** wood doors he carved
6:33 he made four-sided jambs of **o** wood
2Ki 5:26 or to accept clothes, **o** groves,
18:32 a land of **o** trees and honey.
1Ch 27:28 in charge of the **o** and sycamore-fig
27:28 in charge of the supplies of **o** oil.
2Ch 2:10 and twenty thousand baths of **o** oil."
2:15 and the **o** oil and wine he promised,
11:11 supplies of food, **o** oil and wine.
Ezr 7:22 of **o** oil, and salt without limit.
Ne 5:11 vineyards, **o** groves and houses, and
8:15 branches from **o** and wild **o** trees,
9:25 vineyards, **o** groves and fruit
Job 15:33 an **o** tree shedding its blossoms.
29: 6 poured out for me streams of **o** oil.
Ps 52: 8 I am like an **o** tree flourishing in
128: 3 be like **o** shoots round your table.
Isa 17: 6 as when an **o** tree is beaten, leaving
24:13 as when an **o** tree is beaten, or as
41:19 the acacia, the myrtle and the **o**.
57: 9 You went to Molech with **o** oil and
Jer 11:16 The LORD called you a thriving **o**
Eze 16:13 was fine flour, honey and **o** oil.
16:19 **o** oil and honey I gave you to
Hos 12: 1 Assyria and sends **o** oil to Egypt.
14: 6 His splendour will be like an **o** tree,
Am 4: 9 devoured your fig and **o** trees,
Hab 3:17 though the **o** crop fails and the
Hag 2:19 and the **o** tree have not borne fruit.
Zec 4: 3 Also there are two **o** trees by it,
4:11 "What are these two **o** trees on the
4:12 "What are these two **o** branches
Lk 16: 6 "'Eight hundred gallons of **o** oil,'
Jn 18: 1 other side there was an **o** grove
18:26 I see you with him in the **o** grove?"
Ro 11:17 and you, though a wild **o** shoot, have
11:17 the nourishing sap from the **o** root,
11:24 if you were cut out of an **o** tree
11:24 grafted into a cultivated **o** tree,
11:24 be grafted into their own **o** tree!
Rev 11: 4 These are the two **o** trees and the
18:13 of wine and **o** oil, of fine flour and

Olives (Olive)

Ex 27:20 oil of pressed **o** for the light
29:40 of a hin of oil from pressed **o**,
Lev 24: 2 oil of pressed **o** for the light
Nu 28: 5 of a hin of oil from pressed **o**.
Dt 24:20 you beat the **o** from your trees, do
28:40 oil, because the **o** will drop off.
Job 24:11 They crush **o** among the terraces;
Isa 17: 6 leaving two or three **o** on the
Mic 6:15 you will press **o** but not use the
Jas 3:12 My brothers, can a fig-tree bear **o**,

Olives, Mount of

East of Jerusalem, across the Kidron Valley. David climbed it on hearing of Absalom's revolt (2Sa 15:30). In the end times the LORD will stand here, and it will split in two from east to west (Zec 14:4). In Jesus' time Bethany and Bethphage were located here (Mt 21:1; Mk 11:1; Lk 19:29). Jesus talked with his disciples here (Mt 24:3; 26:30; Mk 13:3; 14:26; Lk 19:37; 21:37; Jn 8:1), and prayed here on the night of his arrest (Lk 22:39). Probably the site of Jesus' ascension (Ac 1:12). See *Mount of Olives*.

Olympas

Ro 16:15 and **O** and all the saints with them.

Omar

Ge 36:11 The sons of Eliphaz: Teman, **O**, Zepho,
36:15 Esau: Chiefs Teman, **O**, Zepho, Kenaz,
1Ch 1:36 The sons of Eliphaz: Teman, **O**, Zepho,

Omega

Rev 1: 8 "I am the Alpha and the **O**," says the
21: 6 I am the Alpha and the **O**, the
22:13 I am the Alpha and the **O**, the First

Omen (Omens)

Eze 21:21 to seek an **o**: He will cast lots with
21:23 will seem like a false **o** to those

Omens (Omen)

Dt 18:10 interprets **o**, engages in witchcraft,

Omer (Omers)

Ex 16:16 Take an **o** for each person you have
16:18 they measured it by the **o**, he who
16:32 'Take an **o** of manna and keep it for
16:33 a jar and put an **o** of manna in it.
16:36 (An **o** is one tenth of an ephah.)

Omers (Omer)

Ex 16:22 they gathered twice as much—two **o**

Omit

Jer 26: 2 I command you; do not **o** a word.

Omri (Omri's)

King of Israel; father of Ahab (1Ki 16:30). Army commander, appointed king after Zimri assassinated Baasha (1Ki 16:15–28). Sinned against God (1Ki 16:25–26).

1Ki 16:16 they proclaimed **O**, the commander of
16:17 **O** and all the Israelites with him
16:21 and the other half supported **O**.
16:22 So Tibni died and **O** became king.
16:23 **O** became king of Israel, and he
16:25 **O** did evil in the eyes of the LORD
16:28 **O** rested with his fathers and was
16:29 Ahab son of **O** became king of Israel,
16:30 Ahab son of **O** did more evil in the
2Ki 8:26 a granddaughter of **O** king of Israel.
1Ch 7: 8 Joash, Eliezer, Elioenai, **O**,
9: 4 Uthai son of Ammihud, the son of **O**,
27:18 over Issachar: **O** son of Michael;
2Ch 22: 2 was Athaliah, a granddaughter of **O**.
Mic 6:16 You have observed the statutes of **O**

Omri's (Omri)
1Ki 16:22 O followers proved stronger than
16:27 for the other events of O reign,

On
Town in Egypt about 20 miles north-east of Memphis, east of River Nile. Home of Joseph's wife Asenath (Ge 41:45, 50; 46:20). Later known by its Greek name Heliopolis (Eze 30:17), when its capture by Nebuchadnezzar was foretold.

Ge 41:45 daughter of Potiphera, priest of O,
41:50 daughter of Potiphera, priest of O.
46:20 daughter of Potiphera, priest of O.

Onam
Ge 36:23 Alvan, Manahath, Ebal, Shepho and O.
1Ch 1:40 Alvan, Manahath, Ebal, Shepho and O.
2:26 was Atarah; she was the mother of O.
2:28 The sons of O: Shammai and Jada. The

Onan
Ge 38: 4 gave birth to a son and named him O.
38: 8 Judah said to O, "Lie with your
38: 9 O knew that the offspring would not
46:12 The sons of Judah: Er, O, Shelah,
46:12 O had died in the land of Canaan).
Nu 26:19 Er and O were sons of Judah, but
1Ch 2: 3 The sons of Judah: Er, O and Shelah.

One another See Love one another
Ge 42:21; Lev 19:11; 26:37; Jdg 20:22; 2Ki 7:6; 2Ch 20:23; Est 9:22; Job 41:17; Isa 6:3; Jer 9:20; 22:8; 23:27, 30; Eze 1:9; Zec 7:9; Mal 2:10; Mk 8:16; 12:7; 14:4; Lk 2:15; 6:11; 8:25; 12:1; Jn 5:44; 7:35; 11:56; 12:19; 13:22, 34, 35; 16:17, 19; 19:24; Ac 2:12; 26:31; Ro 1:24, 27; 12:10, 16; 13:8; 14:13; 15:7, 14; 16:16; 1Co 1:10; 16:20; 2Co 13:12; Gal 5:13; Eph 4:2, 32; 5:19, 21; Col 3:13, 16; 1Th 5:11; Tit 3:3; Heb 3:13; 10:24, 25; Jas 4:11; 1Pe 1:22; 3:8; 4:9; 5:5, 14; 1Jn 1:7; 3:11, 23; 4:7, 11, 12; 2Jn 5

One body
Ro 12: 4 Just as each of us has o with many
12: 5 in Christ we who are many form o,
1Co 10:17 we, who are many, are o, for we all
12:12 all its parts are many, they form o.
12:13 into o—whether Jews or Greeks,
12:20 is, there are many parts, but o.
Eph 2:16 in this o to reconcile both of them
3: 6 members together of o, and sharers
4: 4 There is o and one Spirit—just as
4:25 for we are all members of o.
Col 3:15 as members of o you were called to

One God
Mal 2:10 Have we not all one Father? Did not o
Ro 3:30 since there is only o, who will
1Co 8: 6 yet for us there is but o, the
Eph 4: 6 o and Father of all, who is over all
1Ti 2: 5 For there is o and one mediator
Jas 2:19 You believe that there is o. Good!

Onesimus
Runaway slave belonging to Philemon; converted by Paul and dear to him (Col 4:9; Phm 10-16).

Col 4: 9 He is coming with O, our faithful
Phm :10 I appeal to you for my son O, who

Onesiphorus
2Ti 1:16 show mercy to the household of O,
4:19 and Aquila and the household of O.

Onions
Nu 11: 5 melons, leeks, o and garlic.

Only Son
Ge 22:2, 12, 16; Jer 6:26; Am 8:10; Lk 7:12; Jn 3:16, 18; Heb 11:17; 1Jn 4:9

Ono
1Ch 8:12 Misham, Shemed (who built O and Lod
Ezr 2:33 of Lod, Hadid and O 725
Ne 6: 2 of the villages on the plain of O.
7:37 of Lod, Hadid and O 721
11:35 in Lod and O, and in the Valley of

Onycha
Ex 30:34 "Take fragrant spices—gum resin, o

Onyx
Ge 2:12 resin and o are also there.)
Ex 25: 7 o stones and other gems to be
28: 9 "Take two o stones and engrave on
28:20 in the fourth row a chrysolite, an o
35: 9 o stones and other gems to be
35:27 The leaders brought o stones and
39: 6 They mounted the o stones in gold
39:13 in the fourth row a chrysolite, an o
1Ch 29: 2 as well as o for the settings,
Job 28:16 Ophir, with precious o or sapphires.
Eze 28:13 topaz and emerald, chrysolite, o and

Oozing
1Sa 14:26 they saw the honey o out, yet no-one

Open-handed (Hand)
Dt 15: 8 Rather be o and freely lend him
15:11 Therefore I command you to be o

Ophel
2Ch 27: 3 work on the wall at the hill of O.
33:14 encircling the hill of O; he also
Ne 3:26 on the hill of O made repairs up to
3:27 projecting tower to the wall of O.
11:21 servants lived on the hill of O,

Ophir
Region famous for gold and precious stones; location is uncertain. Reached by sea (1Ki 9:28; 10:11; 22:48; 2Ch 8:18), its gold was brought to Solomon for his building projects (1Ki 9:28; 10:10–21; 1Ch 29:4; 2Ch 8:18; 9:10). Used figuratively on account of its great wealth (Job 22:24; 28:16; Ps 45:9; Isa 13:12).

Ge 10:29 O, Havilah and Jobab. All these were
1Ki 9:28 They sailed to O and brought back
10:11 (Hiram's ships brought gold from O;
22:48 trading ships to go to O for gold,
1Ch 1:23 O, Havilah and Jobab. All these were
29: 4 talents of gold (gold of O)
2Ch 8:18 with Solomon's men, sailed to O and
9:10 men of Solomon brought gold from O;
Job 22:24 of O to the rocks in the ravines,
28:16 cannot be bought with the gold of O,
Ps 45: 9 is the royal bride in gold of O.
Isa 13:12 gold, more rare than the gold of O.

Ophni
Jos 18:24 Kephar Ammoni, O and Geba—twelve

Ophrah
1. City of Benjamin (Jos 18:23), attacked by Philistines (1Sa 13:17). Probably also known as Ephraim (Jn 11:54) and Ephron (2Ch 13:19). Exact location unknown. **2.** City of Manasseh, occupied by Abiezrites (Jdg 6:11). Here Gideon built an altar (Jdg 6:24), placed the golden ephod (Jdg 8:27) and was buried (Jdg 8:32). Abimelech came to his father's home here and murdered 70 sons of Jerub-Baal to take the throne (Jdg 9:5). Exact location unknown.

Jos 18:23 Avvim, Parah, O,
Jdg 6:11 sat down under the oak in O that
6:24 it stands in O of the Abiezrites.
8:27 which he placed in O, his town.
8:32 father Joash in O of the Abiezrites.
9: 5 He went to his father's home in O
1Sa 13:17 towards O in the vicinity of Shual,
1Ch 4:14 Meonothai was the father of O.

Opinion (Opinions)
2Sa 17: 6 he says? If not, give us your o."
Mt 22:17 Tell us then, what is your o? Is it

Opinions (Opinion)
1Ki 18:21 between two o? If the LORD is God,
Pr 18: 2 but delights in airing his own o.

Opponent (Oppose)
2Sa 2:16 each man grabbed his o by the head
1Ki 20:20 each one struck down his o. At that,
Job 16: 9 o fastens on me his piercing eyes.

Opponent's (Oppose)
2Sa 2:16 thrust his dagger into his o side,

Opponents (Oppose)
Pr 18:18 disputes and keeps strong o apart.
Lk 13:17 this, all his o were humiliated

Opportune (Opportunity)
Mk 6:21 Finally the o time came. On his
Lk 4:13 he left him until an o time.

Opportunity (Opportune)
1Sa 18:21 a second o to become my son-in-law."
Jer 46:17 a loud noise; he has missed his o.'
Mt 26:16 From then on Judas watched for an o
Mk 14:11 watched for an o to hand him over.
Lk 22: 6 He consented, and watched for an o
Ac 25:16 has had an o to defend himself
Ro 7: 8 sin, seizing the o afforded by the
7:11 For sin, seizing the o afforded by
1Co 16:12 but he will go when he has the o.
2Co 5:12 but are giving you an o to take
11:12 want an o to be considered equal
Gal 6:10 Therefore, as we have o, let us do
Eph 5:16 making the most of every o, because
Php 4:10 but you had no o to show it.
Col 4: 5 outsiders; make the most of every o.
1Ti 5:14 to give the enemy no o for slander.
Heb 11:15 they would have had o to return.

Oppose (Opponent, Opponent's, Opponents, Opposed, Opposes, Opposing, Opposition)
Ex 23:22 enemies and will o those who o you.
Nu 16: 3 They came as a group to o Moses and
22:22 the LORD stood in the road to o him.
22:32 I have come here to o you because
22:34 were standing in the road to o me.
Jdg 20:25 came out from Gibeah to o them,
1Sa 2:10 those who o the LORD will be
Job 11:10 and convenes a court, who can o him?
23: 6 Would he o me with great power? No,
23:13 he stands alone, and who can o him?
Ps 55:18 against me, even though many o me.
109: 6 Appoint an evil man to o him; let an
Isa 41:11 those who o you will be as nothing
Jer 38: 5 "The king can do nothing to o you."
51: 2 they will o her on every side in the
Da 11:30 will o him, and he will lose heart.
Lk 11:53 the teachers of the law began to o
14:31 with ten thousand men to o the one
Ac 11:17 was I to think that I could o God?"
26: 9 to o the name of Jesus of Nazareth.
1Co 16: 9 to me, and there are many who o me.
Php 1:28 in any way by those who o you.
2Th 2: 4 He will o and will exalt himself
2Ti 2:25 Those who o him he must gently
3: 8 so also these men o the truth—men
Tit 1: 9 doctrine and refute those who o it.
2: 8 that those who o you may be ashamed

Opposed (Oppose)
Ex 15: 7 you threw down those who o you.
2Ch 13: 7 o Rehoboam son of Solomon when he
Ezr 10:15 and Shabbethai the Levite, o this.
Jer 50:24 and captured because you o the LORD.
Ac 13: 8 that is what his name means) o them
18: 6 when the Jews o Paul and became
Gal 2:11 Peter came to Antioch, I o him to
3:21 Is the law, therefore, o to the
Col 2:14 that stood o to us; he took it away,
2Ti 3: 8 Just as Jannes and Jambres o Moses,
4:15 because he strongly o our message.

Opposes (Oppose)
Mk 3:26 if Satan **o** himself and is divided,
Lk 23: 2 He **o** payment of taxes to Caesar and
Jn 19:12 who claims to be a king **o** Caesar."
Jas 4: 6 Scripture says: "God **o** the proud
1Pe 5: 5 "God **o** the proud but gives grace to

Opposing (Oppose)
2Ch 35:21 God has told me to hurry; so stop **o**
1Ti 6:20 the **o** ideas of what is falsely
Jas 5: 6 innocent men, who were not **o** you.

Opposition (Oppose)
Nu 16:19 gathered all his followers in **o** to
16:42 when the assembly gathered in **o** to
20: 2 gathered in **o** to Moses and Aaron.
Jdg 9:25 In **o** to him these citizens of
Ac 6: 9 **O** arose, however, from members of
1Th 2: 2 you his gospel in spite of strong **o**.
Heb 12: 3 Consider him who endured such **o** from

Oppress (Oppressed, Oppresses, Oppressing, Oppression, Oppressive, Oppressor, Oppressors)
Ex 1:11 they put slave masters over them to **o**
22:21 "Do not ill-treat an alien or **o** him,
23: 9 "Do not **o** an alien; you yourselves
Dt 23:16 town he chooses. Do not **o** him.
2Sa 7:10 Wicked people shall not **o** them any
1Ch 16:21 He allowed no man to **o** them; for
17: 9 Wicked people will not **o** them any
Job 10: 3 Does it please you to **o** me, to spurn
37:23 great righteousness, he does not **o**.
Ps 89:22 tribute; no wicked man will **o** him.
94: 5 O LORD; they **o** your inheritance.
105:14 He allowed no-one to **o** them; for
119:122 let not the arrogant **o** me.
Isa 3: 5 People will **o** each other—man
3:12 Youths **o** my people, women rule over
Jer 7: 6 if you do not **o** the alien, the
30:20 me; I will punish all who **o** them.
Eze 18: 7 He does not **o** anyone, but returns
18:16 He does not **o** anyone or require a
22:29 they **o** the poor and needy and
45: 8 And my princes will no longer **o** my
Da 7:25 **o** his saints and try to change the
Am 4: 1 you women who **o** the poor and crush
5:12 You **o** the righteous and take bribes
6:14 O house of Israel, that will **o** you
Zec 7:10 Do not **o** the widow or the fatherless,
11: 6 They will **o** the land, and I will not
Mal 3: 5 who **o** the widows and the fatherless,

Oppressed (Oppress)
Ex 1:12 the more they were **o**, the more they
Dt 28:29 after day you will be **o** and robbed,
Jdg 2:18 those who **o** and afflicted them.
4: 3 **o** the Israelites for twenty years,
10: 8 For eighteen years they **o** all the
10:12 Amalekites and the Maonites **o** you
1Sa 10:18 and all the kingdoms that **o** you.'
12: 3 Whom have I cheated? Whom have I **o**?
12: 4 "You have not cheated or **o** us," they
2Ki 13:22 Hazael king of Aram **o** Israel
2Ch 16:10 Asa brutally **o** some of the people.
Ne 9:27 over to their enemies, who **o** them.
9:27 But when they were **o** they cried out
Job 20:19 For he has **o** the poor and left them
Ps 9: 9 The LORD is a refuge for the **o**, a
10:18 defending the fatherless and the **o**,
42: 9 I go about mourning, **o** by the enemy?"
43: 2 I go about mourning, **o** by the enemy?
74:21 Do not let the **o** retreat in disgrace;
82: 3 the rights of the poor and **o**.
103: 6 and justice for all the **o**.
106:42 Their enemies **o** them and subjected
129: 1 They have greatly **o** me from my youth
129: 2 they have greatly **o** me from my youth,
146: 7 He upholds the cause of the **o** and
Pr 15:15 All the days of the **o** are wretched,
16:19 among the **o** than to share plunder
31: 5 deprive all the **o** of their rights.
Ecc 4: 1 I saw the tears of the **o**—and they
5: 8 If you see the poor **o** in a district,
Isa 1:17 Seek justice, encourage the **o**.
10: 2 justice from the **o** of my people,
26: 6 of the **o**, the footsteps of the poor.
52: 4 to live; lately, Assyria has **o** them.
53: 7 He was **o** and afflicted, yet he did
58: 6 set the **o** free and break every yoke?
58:10 and satisfy the needs of the **o**,
Jer 50:33 The people of Israel are **o**, and the
Eze 22: 7 in you they have **o** the alien and
Da 4:27 wickedness by being kind to the **o**.
Hos 5:11 Ephraim is **o**, trampled in judgment,
Am 2: 7 ground and deny justice to the **o**.
Zep 3:19 time I will deal with all who **o** you;
Zec 10: 2 like sheep **o** for lack of a shepherd.
11: 7 particularly the **o** of the flock.
Lk 4:18 for the blind, to release the **o**,
Ac 7:19 **o** our forefathers by forcing them to

Oppresses (Oppress)
Pr 14:31 He who **o** the poor shows contempt for
22:16 He who **o** the poor to increase his
28: 3 A ruler who **o** the poor is like a
Eze 18:12 He **o** the poor and needy. He commits

Oppressing (Oppress)
Ex 3: 9 the way the Egyptians are **o** them.
Nu 10: 9 an enemy who is **o** you, sound a
2Ki 13: 4 the king of Aram was **o** Israel.

Oppression (Oppress)
Dt 26: 7 and saw our misery, toil and **o**.
28:33 nothing but cruel **o** all your days.
Job 35: 9 "Men cry out under a load of **o**; they
Ps 12: 5 "Because of the **o** of the weak and
44:24 face and forget our misery and **o**?
72:14 He will rescue them from **o** and
73: 8 in their arrogance they threaten **o**.
107:39 humbled by **o**, calamity and sorrow;
119:134 Redeem me from the **o** of men, that I
Ecc 4: 1 Again I looked and saw all the **o**
Isa 30:12 relied on **o** and depended on deceit,
53: 8 By **o** and judgment he was taken away.
58: 9 "If you do away with the yoke of **o**,
59:13 fomenting **o** and revolt, uttering
Jer 6: 6 be punished; it is filled with **o**.
22:17 blood and on **o** and extortion."
Eze 45: 9 and **o** and do what is just and right.
Hos 8:10 away under the **o** of the mighty king.
Am 3: 9 her and the **o** among her people."
Ac 7:34 I have indeed seen the **o** of my

Oppressive (Oppress)
Jdg 6: 2 the power of Midian was so **o**, the
Ps 73:16 understand all this, it was **o** to
Isa 10: 1 laws, to those who issue **o** decrees,

Oppressor (Oppress)
Ps 72: 4 of the needy; he will crush the **o**.
78:42 the day he redeemed them from the **o**,
Pr 29:13 The poor man and the **o** have this in
Isa 9: 4 their shoulders, the rod of their **o**.
14: 4 How the **o** has come to an end! How
16: 4 The **o** will come to an end, and
51:13 day because of the wrath of the **o**,
51:13 For where is the wrath of the **o**?
Jer 21:12 his **o** the one who has been robbed,
22: 3 Rescue from the hand of his **o** the
25:38 because of the sword of the **o**
46:16 away from the sword of the **o**.'
50:16 Because of the sword of the **o** let
Zec 9: 8 Never again will an **o** overrun my

Oppressors (Oppress)
Jdg 6: 9 and from the hand of all your **o**.
Ps 27:11 in a straight path because of my **o**.
119:121 and just; do not leave me to my **o**.
Ecc 4: 1 power was on the side of their **o**—
Isa 14: 2 their captors and rule over their **o**.
19:20 out to the LORD because of their **o**,
49:26 I will make your **o** eat their own
60:14 The sons of your **o** will come bowing
Zep 3: 1 Woe to the city of **o**, rebellious and

Options
2Sa 24:12 LORD says: I am giving you three **o**.
1Ch 21:10 LORD says: I am giving you three **o**.

Oracle (Oracles)
Nu 23: 7 Balaam uttered his **o**: "Balak brought
23:18 he uttered his **o**: "Arise, Balak, and
24: 3 he uttered his **o**: "The **o** of Balaam
24: 3 the **o** of one whose eye sees clearly,
24: 4 the **o** of one who hears the words of
24:15 he uttered his **o**: "The **o** of Balaam
24:15 the **o** of one whose eye sees clearly,
24:16 the **o** of one who hears the words of
24:20 Balaam saw Amalek and uttered his **o**:
24:21 he saw the Kenites and uttered his **o**:
24:23 he uttered his **o**: "Ah, who can live
2Sa 23: 1 "The **o** of David son of Jesse, the **o**
Ps 36: 1 An **o** is within my heart concerning
Pr 16:10 The lips of a king speak as an **o**,
30: 1 sayings of Agur son of Jakeh—an **o**:
31: 1 The sayings of King Lemuel—an **o** his
Isa 13: 1 An **o** concerning Babylon that Isaiah
14:28 This **o** came in the year King Ahaz
15: 1 An **o** concerning Moab: Ar in Moab is
17: 1 An **o** concerning Damascus: "See,
19: 1 An **o** concerning Egypt: See, the LORD
21: 1 An **o** concerning the Desert by the
21:11 An **o** concerning Dumah: Someone calls
21:13 An **o** concerning Arabia: You caravans
22: 1 An **o** concerning the Valley of Vision:
23: 1 An **o** concerning Tyre: Wail, O ships
30: 6 An **o** concerning the animals of the
Jer 23:33 'What is the **o** of the LORD?' say
23:33 'What **o**? I will forsake you,
23:34 'This is the **o** of the LORD,' I will
23:36 you must not mention 'the **o** of the
23:36 every man's own word becomes his **o**
23:38 Although you claim, 'This is the **o**
23:38 'This is the **o** of the LORD,' even
23:38 claim, 'This is the **o** of the LORD.'
Eze 12:10 This **o** concerns the prince in
Na 1: 1 An **o** concerning Nineveh. The book of
Hab 1: 1 The **o** that Habakkuk the prophet
Zec 9: 1 An **O** The word of the LORD is against
12: 1 An **O** This is the word of the LORD
Mal 1: 1 An **o**: The word of the LORD to Israel

Oracles (Oracle)
Lam 2:14 The **o** they gave you were false and

Orchard (Orchards)
SS 4:13 Your plants are an **o** of pomegranates

Orchards (Orchard)
Isa 16:10 gladness are taken away from the **o**;
Jer 48:33 Joy and gladness are gone from the **o**

Ordain (Ordained, Ordination)
Ex 28:41 and his sons, anoint and **o** them.
29: 9 way you shall **o** Aaron and his sons.
29:35 you, taking seven days to **o** them.

Ordained (Ordain)
Ex 29:29 they can be anointed and **o** in them.
Lev 16:32 The priest who is anointed and **o** to
21:10 **o** to wear the priestly garments,
Nu 3: 3 who were **o** to serve as priests.
2Ki 19:25 Have you not heard? Long ago I **o** it
Ps 8: 2 **o** praise because of your enemies,
65: 9 with corn, for so you have **o** it.
111: 9 he **o** his covenant for ever—holy
139:16 All the days **o** for me were written
Isa 37:26 "Have you not heard? Long ago I **o** it.
48: 5 wooden image and metal god **o** them.'
Eze 28:14 a guardian cherub, for so I **o** you.
Hab 1:12 O Rock, you have **o** them to punish.
Mt 21:16 and infants you have **o** praise'?"

Order (Ordered, Orderly, Orders)
Ge 25:13 listed in the **o** of their birth:
38:20 in **o** to get his pledge back from
43:33 before him in the **o** of their ages,
Ex 1:22 Pharaoh gave this **o** to all his

Ex 5: 6 That same day Pharaoh gave this **o** to
9:19 Give an **o** now to bring your
28:10 in the **o** of their birth—six names
36: 6 Moses gave an **o** and they sent this
Lev 13:54 he shall **o** that the contaminated
14: 4 the priest shall **o** that two live
14: 5 the priest shall **o** that one of the
14:36 The priest is to **o** the house to be
14:40 he is to **o** that the contaminated
22:19 sheep or goats in **o** that it may be
Nu 2:17 They will set out in the same **o** as
9:19 the LORD's **o** and did not set out.
9:23 They obeyed the LORD's **o**, in
10:28 This was the **o** of march for the
36: 5 Moses gave this **o** to the Israelites:
Dt 2:30 in **o** to give him into your hands,
8: 2 to humble you and to test you in **o**
29:12 You are standing here in **o** to enter
Jos 10:27 At sunset Joshua gave the **o** and they
Jdg 7: 2 In **o** that Israel may not boast
9:24 God did this in **o** that the crime
Ru 4: 5 in **o** to maintain the name of the
4:10 Mahlon's widow, as my wife, in **o** to
1Sa 1: 6 provoking her in **o** to irritate her.
15:21 in **o** to sacrifice them to the LORD
2Sa 2:26 How long before you **o** your men to
4:12 David gave an **o** to his men, and they
13:28 you this **o**? Be strong and brave."
14: 8 I will issue an **o** on your behalf."
14:29 Absalom sent for Joab in **o** to send
17:14 in **o** to bring disaster on Absalom.
17:23 He put his house in **o** and then
19:29 **o** you and Ziba to divide the fields."
1Ki 2:46 the king gave the **o** to Benaiah son
3:25 He then gave an **o**: "Cut the living
15:22 King Asa issued an **o** to all
2Ki 10:19 **o** to destroy the ministers of Baal.
17:27 the king of Assyria gave this **o**:
20: 1 the LORD says: Put your house in **o**,
23:21 The king gave this **o** to all the
23:35 In **o** to do so, he taxed the land and
24: 3 in **o** to remove them from his
1Ch 15:14 in **o** to bring up the ark of the
24: 3 their appointed **o** of ministering.
24:19 This was their appointed **o** of
2Ch 11:22 his brothers, in **o** to make him king.
24:21 they plotted against him, and by **o**
29:27 Hezekiah gave the **o** to sacrifice the
31: 5 soon as the **o** went out, the
32:18 afraid in **o** to capture the city.
35:20 when Josiah had set the temple in **o**,
36:22 in **o** to fulfil the word of the LORD
Ezr 1: 1 in **o** to fulfil the word of the LORD
4:19 I issued an **o** and a search was made,
4:21 Now issue an **o** to these men to stop
4:21 will not be rebuilt until I so **o**.
6: 1 King Darius then issued an **o**, and
6:21 neighbours in **o** to seek the LORD,
7:21 Now I, King Artaxerxes, **o** all the
Ne 5: 2 in **o** for us to eat and stay alive,
9:17 in **o** to return to their slavery.
9:26 who had admonished them in **o** to turn
13:22 in **o** to keep the Sabbath day holy.
Est 1:11 wearing her royal crown, in **o** to
2: 8 the king's **o** and edict had been
3:13 provinces with the **o** to destroy,
4: 3 the edict and **o** of the king came,
8: 5 let an **o** be written overruling the
Job 25: 2 **o** in the heights of heaven.
Ps 10:18 in **o** that man, who is of the earth,
59: T watch David's house in **o** to kill him
110: 4 for ever, in the **o** of Melchizedek."
Pr 28: 2 and knowledge maintains **o**.
Ecc 12: 9 out and set in **o** many proverbs.
Isa 23:11 He has given an **o** concerning
34:16 is his mouth that has given the **o**,
38: 1 the LORD says: Put your house in **o**,
Jer 34:22 I am going to give the **o**, declares
Eze 3:18 his evil ways in **o** to save his life,
13:18 their heads in **o** to ensnare people.
39:12 them in **o** to cleanse the land.
Da 6:16 the king gave the **o**, and they
11:17 in **o** to overthrow the kingdom,
Am 1:13 Gilead in **o** to extend his borders,
Zec 13: 4 garment of hair in **o** to deceive.
Mt 12:44 swept clean and put in **o**.
Mt 27:64 give the **o** for the tomb to be made
Mk 7: 9 in **o** to observe your own traditions!
Lk 4:29 in **o** to throw him down the cliff.
8:31 they begged him repeatedly not to **o**
11:25 the house swept clean and put in **o**.
19:15 in **o** to find out what they had
Jn 8: 6 **o** to have a basis for accusing him.
17:26 will continue to make you known in **o**
Ac 6: 2 word of God in **o** to wait on tables.
9:24 on the city gates in **o** to kill him.
16:35 with the **o**: "Release those men.
17: 5 in **o** to bring them out to the crowd.
19:33 He motioned for silence in **o** to make
20:30 **o** to draw away disciples after them.
22:24 questioned in **o** to find out why the
24: 4 in **o** not to weary you further, I
Ro 1:13 in **o** that I might have a harvest
4:11 in **o** that righteousness might be
6: 4 baptism into death in **o** that,
7: 4 **o** that we might bear fruit to God.
7:13 By no means! But in **o** that sin might
8: 4 in **o** that the righteous requirements
8:17 in **o** that we may also share in his
9:11 in **o** that God's purpose in election
11:31 in **o** that they too may now receive
15: 7 you, in **o** to bring praise to God.
2Co 1:23 it was in **o** to spare you that I did
2:11 in **o** that Satan might not outwit us.
8:19 which we administer in **o** to honour
9: 3 I am sending the brothers in **o** that
11: 7 lower myself in **o** to elevate you
11:12 in **o** to cut the ground from under
11:32 Damascenes guarded in **o** to arrest me.
Gal 3:14 He redeemed us in **o** that the
Eph 1:12 in **o** that we, who were the first to
1:18 in **o** that you may know the hope to
2: 7 in **o** that in the coming ages he
4:10 in **o** to fill the whole universe.)
Php 2:16 you hold out the word of life—in **o**
Col 1:10 we pray this in **o** that you may live
2: 2 in **o** that they may know the mystery
1Th 2: 9 we worked night and day in **o** not to
4: 1 we instructed you how to live in **o**
2Th 3: 9 but in **o** to make ourselves a model
3:14 him, in **o** that he may feel ashamed.
1Ti 4: 3 They forbid people to marry and **o**
Tit 3:14 in **o** that they may provide for daily
Phm : 8 **o** you to do what you ought to do,
Heb 2:17 in **o** that he might become a merciful
5: 6 for ever, in the **o** of Melchizedek."
5:10 high priest in the **o** of Melchizedek.
6:11 end, in **o** to make your hope sure.
6:20 for ever, in the **o** of Melchizedek.
7:11 come—one in the **o** of Melchizedek,
7:11 Melchizedek, not in the **o** of Aaron?
7:17 for ever, in the **o** of Melchizedek."
9:10 until the time of the new **o**.
Rev 21: 4 old **o** of things has passed away."

Ordered (Order)

Ex 17:10 the Amalekites as Moses had **o**,
Lev 10: 5 outside the camp, as Moses **o**.
Nu 34:13 The LORD has **o** that it be given to
36: 2 he **o** you to give the inheritance of
Jos 1:10 Joshua **o** the officers of the people:
6: 7 he **o** the people, "Advance! March
8:29 At sunset, Joshua **o** them to take his
Jdg 3:28 "Follow me," he **o**, "for the LORD has
9:48 He **o** the men with him, "Quick! Do
1Sa 18:22 Saul **o** his attendants: "Speak to
20:29 and my brother has **o** me to be there.
22:17 the king **o** the guards at his side:
22:18 The king then **o** Doeg, "You turn and
2Sa 1:18 **o** that the men of Judah be taught
13:28 Absalom **o** his men, "Listen! When
13:29 men did to Amnon what Absalom had **o**.
1Ki 2:29 Then Solomon **o** Benaiah son of
12:24 went home again, as the LORD had **o**.
17: 4 **o** the ravens to feed you there."
18:34 "Do it a third time," he **o**, and
20:12 he **o** his men: "Prepare to attack.
22:26 The king of Israel then **o**, "Take
22:31 Now the king of Aram had **o** his
2Ki 6:13 find out where he is," the king **o**,
9:17 "Get a horseman," Joram **o**. "Send
2Ki 9:21 "Hitch up my chariot," Joram **o**. And
10: 8 Then Jehu **o**, "Put them in two piles
10:14 "Take them alive!" he **o**. So they
10:25 he **o** the guards and officers: "Go in
11: 9 did just as Jehoiada the priest **o**.
11:15 Jehoiada the priest **o** the commanders
16:16 priest did just as King Ahaz had **o**.
17:15 had **o** them, "Do not do as they do,"
23: 4 The king **o** Hilkiah the high priest,
1Ch 21:17 "Was it not I who **o** the fighting men
21:18 the angel of the LORD **o** Gad to tell
22:17 David **o** all the leaders of Israel to
2Ch 8:14 was what David the man of God had **o**.
18:25 The king of Israel then **o**, "Take
18:30 Now the king of Aram had **o** his
23: 8 did just as Jehoiada the priest **o**.
23:18 and singing, as David had **o**.
29:15 **o**, following the word of the LORD.
29:24 because the king had **o** the burnt
29:30 King Hezekiah and his officials **o**
30:12 **o**, following the word of the LORD.
31: 4 He **o** the people living in Jerusalem
35:10 their divisions as the king had **o**.
35:16 of the LORD, as King Josiah had **o**.
Ezr 2:63 The governor **o** them not to eat any
Ne 7:65 The governor, therefore, **o** them not
13:19 I **o** the doors to be shut and not
Est 4: 5 and **o** him to find out what was
6: 1 so he **o** the book of the chronicles,
6: 5 "Bring him in," the king **o**.
Jer 35:14 'Jonadab son of Recab **o** his sons not
35:18 and have done everything he **o**.'
38:27 the king had **o** him to say.
47: 7 when he has **o** it to attack Ashkelon
Da 1: 3 the king **o** Ashpenaz, chief of his
2:12 furious that he **o** the execution of
2:46 paid him honour and **o** that an
3:19 He **o** the furnace to be heated seven
Mt 14: 9 he **o** that her request be granted
18:25 the master **o** that he and his wife
27:58 Pilate **o** that it be given to him.
Lk 5:14 Jesus **o** him, "Don't tell anyone, but
8:56 Her parents were astonished, but he **o**
14:21 became angry and **o** his servant,
14:22 'Sir,' the servant said, 'what you **o**
18:40 Jesus stopped and **o** the man to be
Ac 4:15 they **o** them to withdraw from the
5:34 stood up in the Sanhedrin and **o** that
5:40 Then they **o** them not to speak in the
10:48 he **o** that they be baptised in the
12:19 guards and **o** that they be executed.
16:22 **o** them to be stripped and beaten.
16:36 **o** that you and Silas be released.
18: 2 had **o** all the Jews to leave Rome.
21:33 **o** him to be bound with two chains.
21:34 he **o** that Paul be taken into the
22:24 the commander **o** Paul to be taken
22:30 he released him and **o** the chief
23: 2 At this the high priest Ananias **o**
23:10 He **o** the troops to go down and take
23:23 he called two of his centurions and **o**
23:30 I also **o** his accusers to present to
23:35 Then he **o** that Paul be kept under
24:23 He **o** the centurion to keep Paul
25: 6 **o** that Paul be brought before him.
25:17 day and **o** the man to be brought in.
25:21 I **o** him to be held until I could
27:43 He **o** those who could swim to jump
Rev 13:14 He **o** them to set up an image in

Orderly (Order)

Lk 1: 3 to me to write an **o** account for you,
1Co 14:40 be done in a fitting and **o** way.
Col 2: 5 delight to see how **o** you are and how

Orders (Order)

Ge 12:20 Pharaoh gave **o** about Abram to his
26:11 Abimelech gave **o** to all the people:
41:40 my people are to submit to your **o**.
42:25 Joseph gave **o** to fill their bags
Nu 32:28 Moses gave **o** about them to Eleazar
Dt 2: 4 Give the people these **o**: 'You are
Jos 3: 3 giving **o** to the people: "When you
8: 4 with these **o**: "Listen carefully. You
8: 8 See to it; you have my **o**."

Ru 2:15 she got up to glean, Boaz gave **o** to
2Sa 3:15 Ish-Bosheth gave **o** and had her taken
18: 5 king giving **o** concerning Absalom
1Ki 2:25 King Solomon gave **o** to Benaiah son
5: 6 "So give **o** that cedars of Lebanon be
2Ki 16:15 King Ahaz then gave these **o** to Uriah
22:12 He gave these **o** to Hilkiah the
1Ch 14:12 gave **o** to burn them in the fire.
22: 2 David gave **o** to assemble the aliens
2Ch 2: 1 Solomon gave **o** to build a temple for
19: 9 He gave them these **o**: "You must
31:11 Hezekiah gave **o** to prepare
34:20 He gave these **o** to Hilkiah, Ahikam
Ezr 8:36 They also delivered the king's **o** to
Ne 11:23 The singers were under the king's **o**,
13: 9 I gave **o** to purify the rooms, and
Est 3:12 all Haman's **o** to the king's satraps,
8: 9 They wrote out all Mordecai's **o** to
8: 9 These **o** were written in the script
9:25 he issued written **o** that the evil
Job 38:12 "Have you ever given **o** to the
Isa 45:11 me **o** about the work of my hands?
Jer 37:21 King Zedekiah then gave **o** for
39:11 had given these **o** about Jeremiah
Da 5: 2 he gave **o** to bring in the gold and
6:23 The king was overjoyed and gave **o** to
Mt 2:16 he was furious, and he gave **o** to
8:18 he gave **o** to cross to the other side
Mk 1:27 **o** to evil spirits and they obey him."
3:12 he gave them strict **o** not to tell
5:43 He gave strict **o** not to let anyone
6:17 For Herod himself had given **o** to
6:27 with **o** to bring John's head.
9: 9 Jesus gave them **o** not to tell anyone
Lk 4:36 **o** to evil spirits and they come out!"
15:29 for you and never disobeyed your **o**.
Jn 11:57 Pharisees had given **o** that if anyone
Ac 5:28 "We gave you strict **o** not to teach
8:38 he gave **o** to stop the chariot. Then
16:24 Upon receiving such **o**, he put them
23:31 the soldiers, carrying out their **o**,

Ordinance (Ordinances)
Ex 12:14 a festival to the LORD—a lasting **o**.
12:17 **o** for the generations to come.
12:24 **o** for you and your descendants.
13:10 You must keep this **o** at the
27:21 This is to be a lasting **o** among the
28:43 **o** for Aaron and his descendants.
29: 9 priesthood is theirs by a lasting **o**.
30:21 This is to be a lasting **o** for Aaron
Lev 3:17 "'This is a lasting **o** for the
10: 9 **o** for the generations to come.
16:29 "This is to be a lasting **o** for you:
16:31 deny yourselves; it is a lasting **o**.
16:34 "This is to be a lasting **o** for you:
17: 7 This is to be a lasting **o** for them
23:14 This is to be a lasting **o** for the
23:21 This is to be a lasting **o** for the
23:31 This is to be a lasting **o** for the
23:41 This is to be a lasting **o** for the
24: 3 **o** for the generations to come.
Nu 10: 8 This is to be a lasting **o** for you
15:15 **o** for the generations to come.
18:23 This is a lasting **o** for the
19:10 This will be a lasting **o** both for
19:21 This is a lasting **o** for them. "The
1Sa 30:25 David made this a statute and **o** for
2Ch 2: 4 This is a lasting **o** for Israel.
8:14 In keeping with the **o** of his father
Ps 81: 4 this is a decree for Israel, an **o** of
Eze 46:14 offering to the LORD is a lasting **o**.

Ordinances (Ordinance)
2Ki 17:34 LORD nor adhere to the decrees and **o**,
17:37 careful to keep the decrees and **o**,
2Ch 19:10 commands, decrees or **o**—you are to
33: 8 decrees and **o** given through Moses."
Ne 9:29 They sinned against your **o**, by which
Ps 19: 9 The **o** of the LORD are sure and
Eze 44:24 and decide it according to my **o**.

Ordinary
1Sa 21: 4 "I don't have any **o** bread to hand;
Isa 8: 1 and write on it with an **o** pen:
Ac 4:13 **o** men, they were astonished and they
7:20 was born, and he was no **o** child.
21:39 in Cilicia, a citizen of no **o** city.
Gal 4:23 slave woman was born in the **o** way;
4:29 At that time the son born in the **o**
Heb 11:23 because they saw he was no **o** child,

Ordination (Ordain)
Ex 29:22 (This is the ram for the **o**.)
29:26 the breast of the ram for Aaron's **o**,
29:27 "Consecrate those parts of the **o** ram
29:31 "Take the ram for the **o** and cook the
29:33 made for their **o** and consecration.
29:34 if any of the meat of the **o** ram or
Lev 7:37 the guilt offering, the **o** offering
8:22 the ram for the **o**, and Aaron and his
8:28 the burnt offering as an **o** offering,
8:29 breast—Moses' share of the **o** ram
8:31 from the basket of **o** offerings,
8:33 until the days of your **o** are
8:33 for your **o** will last seven days.

Ore
Job 28: 2 earth, and copper is smelted from **o**.
28: 3 for **o** in the blackest darkness.
Jer 6:27 of metals and my people the **o**,

Oreb
Jdg 7:25 the Midianite leaders, **O** and Zeeb.
7:25 They killed **O** at the rock of **O**, and
7:25 the heads of **O** and Zeeb to Gideon,
8: 3 God gave **O** and Zeeb, the Midianite
Ps 83:11 Make their nobles like **O** and Zeeb,
Isa 10:26 struck down Midian at the rock of **O**;

Oren
1Ch 2:25 Bunah, **O**, Ozem and Ahijah.

Orgies
Ro 13:13 as in the daytime, not in **o** and
Gal 5:21 envy; drunkenness, **o**, and the like.
1Pe 4: 3 **o**, carousing and detestable idolatry.

Origin (Original, Originate, Origins)
Est 6:13 is of Jewish **o**, you cannot stand
Ac 5:38 is of human **o**, it will fail.
2Pe 1:21 For prophecy never had its **o** in the

Original (Origin)
2Ch 24:13 to its **o** design and reinforced it.

Originate (Origin)
1Co 14:36 Did the word of God **o** with you? Or

Origins (Origin)
Mic 5: 2 whose **o** are from of old, from

Orion
Job 9: 9 He is the Maker of the Bear and **O**,
38:31 Can you loose the cords of **O**?
Am 5: 8 (he who made the Pleiades and **O**, who

Ornament (Ornamented, Ornaments)
Pr 3:22 they will be life for you, an **o** to
25:12 Like an ear-ring of gold or an **o** of

Ornamented (Ornament)
Ge 37: 3 and he made a richly **o** robe for him.
37:23 richly **o** robe he was wearing—
37:32 They took the **o** robe back to their
2Sa 13:18 She was wearing a richly **o** robe, for
13:19 and tore the **o** robe she was wearing.

Ornaments (Ornament)
Ex 33: 4 to mourn and no-one put on any **o**.
33: 5 Now take off your **o** and I will
33: 6 the Israelites stripped off their **o**
35:22 brooches, ear-rings, rings and **o**.
Jdg 8:21 took the **o** off their camels' necks.
8:26 not counting the **o**, the pendants and
2Sa 1:24 your garments with **o** of gold.
Isa 3:16 with **o** jingling on their ankles.
49:18 "you will wear them all as **o**; you
Jer 2:32 a bride her wedding **o**? Yet my people

Orpah
Ru 1: 4 one named **O** and the other Ruth.
1:14 Then **O** kissed her mother-in-law

Orphan (Orphan's, Orphans)
Ex 22:22 take advantage of a widow or an **o**.

Orphan's (Orphan)
Job 24: 3 They drive away the **o** donkey and

Orphans (Orphan)
Jer 49:11 Leave your **o**; I will protect their
Lam 5: 3 We have become **o** and fatherless, our
Jn 14:18 I will not leave you as **o**; I will
Jas 1:27 to look after **o** and widows in their

Osprey
Lev 11:18 the white owl, the desert owl, the **o**,
Dt 14:17 the desert owl, the **o**, the cormorant,

Ostrich (Ostriches)
Job 39:13 "The wings of the **o** flap joyfully,

Ostriches (Ostrich)
Lam 4: 3 heartless like **o** in the desert.

Other gods
Ex 18:11; 20:3; 23:13; Dt 5:7; 6:14; 7:4; 8:19; 11:16, 28; 13:2, 6, 13; 17:3; 18:20; 28:14, 36, 64; 29:26; 30:17; 31:18, 20; Jos 23:16; 24:2, 16; Jdg 2:17, 19; 10:13; 1Sa 8:8; 26:19; 1Ki 9:6, 9; 11:4,10; 14:9; 2Ki 17:7, 35, 37, 38; 22:17; 2Ch 2:5; 7:19, 22; 28:25; 34:25; Ps 16:4; Jer 1:16; 7:6, 9, 18; 11:10; 13:10; 16:11, 13; 19:13; 22:9; 25:6; 32:29; 35:15; 44:3, 5, 8, 15; Hos 3:1

Othni
1Ch 26: 7 The sons of Shemaiah: **O**, Rephael,

Othniel
Jos 15:17 **O** son of Kenaz, Caleb's brother,
15:18 One day when she came to **O**, she
Jdg 1:13 **O** son of Kenaz, Caleb's younger
1:14 One day when she came to **O**, she
3: 9 **O** son of Kenaz, Caleb's younger
3:10 the hands of **O**, who overpowered him.
3:11 years, until **O** son of Kenaz died.
1Ch 4:13 The sons of Kenaz: **O** and Seraiah.
4:13 The sons of **O**: Hathath and Meonothai.
27:15 Netophathite, from the family of **O**.

Ousted
Isa 22:19 you will be **o** from your position.

Outbreak
1Sa 5: 9 young and old, with an **o** of tumours.

Outbursts
2Co 12:20 jealousy, **o** of anger, factions,

Outcast (Cast)
Jer 30:17 an **o**, Zion for whom no-one cares.'

Outcome
Isa 41:22 them and know their final **o**.
Da 11:29 this time the **o** will be different
12: 8 what will the **o** of all this be?"
Mt 26:58 down with the guards to see the **o**.
Heb 13: 7 Consider the **o** of their way of life
1Pe 4:17 what will the **o** be for those who do

Outcry
Ge 18:20 the LORD said, "The **o** against Sodom
18:21 as bad as the **o** that has reached me.
19:13 The **o** to the LORD against its people
1Sa 4:14 Eli heard the **o** and asked, "What is
5:12 the **o** of the city went up to heaven.

Ne 5: 1 o against their Jewish brothers.
5: 6 I heard their o and these charges, I
Isa 15: 8 Their o echoes along the border of

Outer
Nu 4:25 its covering and the o covering of
2Sa 18:24 between the inner and o gates,
20:15 stood against the o fortifications.
1Ki 6:29 in both the inner and o rooms, he
6:30 and o rooms of the temple with gold.
7: 9 a saw on their inner and o faces.
2Ch 6:13 it in the centre of the o court.
33:14 Afterwards he rebuilt the o wall of
Est 6: 4 Haman had just entered the o court
Job 26:14 these are but the o fringe of his
41:13 Who can strip off his o coat? Who
Eze 10: 5 be heard as far away as the o court,
40:17 he brought me into the o court.
40:20 north, leading into the o court.
40:27 to the o gate on the south side;
40:31 Its portico faced the o court; palm
40:34 Its portico faced the o court; palm
40:37 Its portico faced the o court; palm
41: 1 man brought me to the o sanctuary
41: 2 He also measured the o sanctuary; it
41: 4 across the end of the o sanctuary.
41: 9 The o wall of the side rooms was
41:15 The o sanctuary, the inner sanctuary
41:17 all round the inner and o sanctuary
41:20 on the wall of the o sanctuary.
41:21 The o sanctuary had a rectangular
41:23 Both the o sanctuary and the Most
41:25 on the doors of the o sanctuary were
42: 1 led me northward into the o court
42: 1 the o wall on the north side.
42: 3 the pavement of the o court,
42: 7 There was an o wall parallel to the
42: 7 to the rooms and the o court;
42: 8 the o court was fifty cubits long,
42: 9 as one enters them from the o court.
42:10 length of the wall of the o court,
42:10 and opposite the o wall, were
42:14 they are not to go into the o court
44: 1 man brought me back to the o gate
44:19 they go out into the o court where
46:20 o court and consecrating the people."
46:21 He then brought me to the o court
46:22 In the four corners of the o court
47: 2 outside to the o gate facing east,
Jn 13: 4 took off his o clothing, and wrapped
21: 7 "It is the Lord," he wrapped his o
Ac 12:13 Peter knocked at the o entrance, and
Heb 9: 6 o room to carry on their ministry.
Rev 11: 2 exclude the o court; do not measure

Outlaw
Pr 24:15 Do not lie in wait like an o against

Outlet
2Ch 32:30 was Hezekiah who blocked the upper o

Outline
Isa 44:13 a line and makes an o with a marker;

Outlived (Live)
Jos 24:31 of the elders who o him and who had
Jdg 2: 7 of the elders who o him and who had

Outlying
1Ch 5:16 in Bashan and its o villages, and on
27:25 the storehouses in the o districts,

Outnumber (Number)
Ps 69: 4 Those who hate me without reason o
139:18 they would o the grains of sand.

Outpost (Outposts)
1Sa 10: 5 God, where there is a Philistine o.
13: 3 Jonathan attacked the Philistine o
13: 4 "Saul has attacked the Philistine o,
14: 1 the Philistine o on the other side.
14: 4 cross to reach the Philistine o
14: 6 o of those uncircumcised fellows.
1Sa 14:11 themselves to the Philistine o.
14:12 The men of the o shouted to Jonathan

Outposts (Outpost)
Jdg 7:11 went down to the o of the camp.
1Sa 14:15 and those in the o and raiding

Outpoured (Pour)
Ps 79:10 avenge the o blood of your servants.
Eze 20:33 outstretched arm and with o wrath.
20:34 outstretched arm and with o wrath.

Outpouring (Pour)
Eze 9: 8 this o of your wrath on Jerusalem?"

Outrageous (Rage)
Jer 29:23 For they have done o things in

Outran (Run)
2Sa 18:23 way of the plain and o the Cushite.
Jn 20: 4 o Peter and reached the tomb first.

Outsiders
Col 4: 5 Be wise in the way you act towards o;
1Th 4:12 daily life may win the respect of o
1Ti 3: 7 also have a good reputation with o,

Outskirts
Nu 11: 1 consumed some of the o of the camp.
Jos 18:15 The southern side began at the o of
1Sa 14: 2 Saul was staying on the o of Gibeah
1Ch 4:39 they went to the o of Gedor to the

Outspread (Spread)
Isa 8: 8 Its o wings will cover the breadth

Outstanding
1Ch 7:40 men, brave warriors and o leaders.
SS 5:10 My lover is radiant and ruddy, o
Da 5:14 insight, intelligence and o wisdom.
Ac 4:16 an o miracle, and we cannot deny it.
Ro 13: 8 Let no debt remain o, except the
16: 7 They are o among the apostles, and

Outstretched (*Outstretched arm*, Stretch)
Ps 75: 5 heaven; do not speak with o neck.
Isa 3:16 walking along with o necks, flirting
Jer 21: 5 fight against you with an o hand

Outstretched arm
Ex 6: 6 o and with mighty acts of judgment.
Dt 4:34 by war, by a mighty hand and an o,
5:15 there with a mighty hand and an o.
7:19 the mighty hand and o, with which
9:29 out by your great power and your o."
11: 2 his majesty, his mighty hand, his o;
26: 8 Egypt with a mighty hand and an o,
1Ki 8:42 your mighty hand and your o—when he
2Ki 17:36 and o, is the one you must worship.
2Ch 6:32 your mighty hand and your o—when he
Ps 136:12 with a mighty hand and o; His love
Jer 27: 5 With my great power and o I made the
32:17 the earth by your great power and o.
32:21 hand and an o and with great terror.
Eze 20:33 and an o and with outpoured wrath.
20:34 and an o and with outpoured wrath.

Outward (Outwardly)
1Sa 16: 7 Man looks at the o appearance, but
Ro 2:28 circumcision merely o and physical.
1Pe 3: 3 Your beauty should not come from o

Outwardly (Outward)
Ro 2:28 is not a Jew if he is only one o,
2Co 4:16 Though o we are wasting away, yet
Gal 6:12 want to make a good impression o
Heb 9:13 them so that they are o clean.

Outweigh (Weigh)
Job 6: 3 would surely o the sand of the seas—

Outweighs (Weigh)
Ecc 10: 1 a little folly o wisdom and honour.
2Co 4:17 eternal glory that far o them all.

Outwit (Outwitted)
2Co 2:11 in order that Satan might not o us.

Outwitted (Outwit)
Mt 2:16 Herod realised that he had been o by

Oven (Ovens)
Lev 2: 4 a grain offering baked in an o,
7: 9 Every grain offering baked in an o
11:35 o or cooking pot must be broken up.
26:26 be able to bake your bread in one o,
Lam 5:10 Our skin is hot as an o, feverish
Hos 7: 4 burning like an o whose fire the
7: 6 Their hearts are like an o; they
7: 7 All of them are hot as an o; they

Ovens (Oven)
Ex 8: 3 into your o and kneading troughs.
Ne 3:11 section and the Tower of the O.
12:38 Tower of the O to the Broad Wall,

Overawed (Awe)
Ps 49:16 Do not be o when a man grows rich,

Overbearing
Tit 1: 7 he must be blameless—not o, not

Overboard
Jnh 1:15 they took Jonah and threw him o, and
Ac 27:18 day they began to throw the cargo o.
27:19 tackle o with their own hands.
27:43 to jump o first and get to land.

Overcame (Overcome)
Ex 17:13 Joshua o the Amalekite army with the
Jer 38:22 'They misled you and o you—those
Hos 12: 4 He struggled with the angel and o
Rev 3:21 just as I o and sat down with my
12:11 They o him by the blood of the Lamb

Overcast
Mt 16: 3 be stormy, for the sky is red and o.

Overcome (Overcame, Overcomes)
Ge 32:28 with God and with men and have o."
1Sa 4:19 but was o by her labour pains.
17: 9 but if I o him and kill him,
Ps 13: 4 my enemy will say, "I have o him,"
39:10 Remove your scourge from me; I am o
116: 3 me; I was o by trouble and sorrow.
Jer 1:19 against you but will not o you,
15:20 against you but will not o you,
23: 9 like a man o by wine, because of the
Da 10:16 "I am o with anguish because of the
Zec 9:15 They will destroy and o with
Mt 16:18 the gates of Hades will not o it.
Mk 9:24 I do believe; help me o my unbelief!"
Lk 8:37 them, because they were o with fear.
10:19 and to o all the power of the enemy;
Jn 16:33 But take heart! I have o the world."
Ro 12:21 Do not be o by evil, but o evil with
1Ti 5:11 when their sensual desires o their
2Pe 2:20 and are again entangled in it and o,
1Jn 2:13 because you have o the evil one.
2:14 in you, and you have o the evil one.
4: 4 are from God and have o them,
5: 4 has o the world, even our faith.
Rev 17:14 but the Lamb will o them because he

Overcomes (Overcome)
1Jn 5: 4 for everyone born of God o the world.
5: 5 Who is it that o the world? Only he
Rev 2: 7 To him who o, I will give the right
2:11 He who o will not be hurt at all by
2:17 To him who o, I will give some of
2:26 To him who o and does my will to the
3: 5 He who o will, like them, be dressed
3:12 Him who o I will make a pillar in

Rev 3:21 To him who o, I will give the right
21: 7 He who o will inherit all this, and

Overfed (Feed)
Eze 16:49 o and unconcerned; they did not help

Overflow (Overflowing, Overflows)
Job 6:15 streams, as the streams that o
Ps 65:11 and your carts o with abundance.
65:12 The grasslands of the desert o; the
119:171 May my lips o with praise, for you
Pr 5:16 Should your springs o in the streets,
Isa 8: 7 It will o all its channels, run over
28:17 and water will o your hiding-place.
Jer 9:18 wail over us till our eyes o with
14:17 'Let my eyes o with tears night and
47: 2 They will o the land and everything
Lam 1:16 "This is why I weep and my eyes o
Joel 2:24 vats will o with new wine and oil.
3:13 is full and the vats o—so great is
Zec 1:17 towns will again o with prosperity
Mt 12:34 the o of the heart the mouth speaks.
Lk 6:45 the o of his heart his mouth speaks.
Ro 5:15 man, Jesus Christ, o to the many!
15:13 so that you may o with hope by the
2Co 4:15 may cause thanksgiving to o
Php 1:26 Christ Jesus will o on account of me.
1Th 3:12 love increase and o for each other

Overflowing (Overflow)
1Ch 12:15 month when it was o all its banks,
Pr 3:10 your barns will be filled to o, and
Isa 66:11 and delight in her o abundance."
Jer 13:17 o with tears, because the LORD's
47: 2 they will become an o torrent.
2Co 8: 2 the most severe trial, their o joy
9:12 o in many expressions of thanks
Col 2: 7 taught, and o with thankfulness.

Overflows (Overflow)
Ps 23: 5 anoint my head with oil; my cup o.
2Co 1: 5 also through Christ our comfort o.

Overgrown (Grow)
Isa 32:13 a land o with thorns and briers—
Jer 26:18 hill a mound o with thickets.'
Mic 3:12 temple hill a mound o with thickets.

Overhang (Hang)
Eze 41:25 a wooden o on the front of the

Overhanging (Hang)
1Ki 7: 6 of that were pillars and an o roof.
Isa 2:21 to the o crags from dread of the
57: 5 the ravines and under the o crags.

Overhangs (Hang)
Eze 41:26 side rooms of the temple also had o.

Overhead
Isa 31: 5 Like birds hovering o, the LORD

Overheard (Hear)
Ge 27: 6 "Look, I o your father say to your
1Sa 17:31 What David said was o and reported

Overjoyed (Joy)
Da 6:23 The king was o and gave orders to
Mt 2:10 they saw the star, they were o.
Jn 20:20 were o when they saw the Lord.
Ac 12:14 she was so o she ran back without
1Pe 4:13 may be o when his glory is revealed.

Overlaid (Overlay)
Ex 26:32 posts of acacia wood o with gold
26:37 posts of acacia wood o with gold.
36:34 They o the frames with gold and made
36:34 They also o the crossbars with gold.
36:36 wood for it and o them with gold.
36:38 They o the tops of the posts and
37: 2 He o it with pure gold, both inside
37: 4 of acacia wood and o them with gold.
Ex 37:11 they o it with pure gold and made a
37:15 of acacia wood and were o with gold.
37:26 They o the top and all the sides and
37:28 of acacia wood and o them with gold.
38: 2 and they o the altar with bronze.
38: 6 acacia wood and o them with bronze.
38:17 and their tops were o with silver;
38:19 and their tops were o with silver.
1Ki 6:20 He o the inside with pure gold, and
6:20 and he also o the altar of cedar.
6:21 sanctuary, which was o with gold.
6:22 he o the whole interior with gold.
6:22 He also o with gold the altar that
6:28 He o the cherubim with gold.
6:32 o the cherubim and palm trees with
6:35 open flowers on them and o them with
10:18 with ivory and o with fine gold.
2Ch 3: 4 He o the inside with pure gold.
3: 7 He o the ceiling beams, door-frames,
3: 8 He o the inside with six hundred
3: 9 He also o the upper parts with gold.
3:10 cherubim and o them with gold.
4: 9 court, and o the doors with bronze.
9:17 with ivory and o with pure gold.
Isa 30:22 defile your idols o with silver

Overlay (Overlaid, Overlaying, Overlays)
Ex 25:11 O it with pure gold, both inside and
25:13 make poles of acacia wood and o them
25:24 O it with pure gold and make a gold
25:28 poles of acacia wood, o them with
26:29 O the frames with gold and make gold
26:29 Also o the crossbars with gold.
27: 2 piece, and o the altar with bronze.
27: 6 the altar and o them with bronze.
30: 3 O the top and all the sides and the
30: 5 poles of acacia wood and o them with
38:28 to o the tops of the posts, and to
Nu 16:38 Hammer the censers into sheets to o
16:39 them hammered out to o the altar,

Overlaying (Overlay)
1Ch 29: 4 the o of the walls of the buildings,

Overlays (Overlay)
Isa 40:19 and a goldsmith o it with gold and

Overlook (Overlooked, Overlooking, Overlooks)
Dt 9:27 O the stubbornness of this people,
24:19 o a sheaf, do not go back to get it.
Pr 19:11 it is to his glory to o an offence.

Overlooked (Overlook)
Ac 6: 1 o in the daily distribution of food.
17:30 In the past God o such ignorance,

Overlooking (Overlook)
Nu 23:28 to the top of Peor, o the wasteland.
Jos 8:14 at a certain place o the Arabah.
1Sa 13:18 towards the borderland o the Valley

Overlooks (Overlook)
Nu 21:20 the top of Pisgah o the wasteland.
2Ch 20:24 came to the place that o the desert
Pr 12:16 once, but a prudent man o an insult.

Overnight (Night)
Lev 19:13 back the wages of a hired man o.
Dt 21:23 not leave his body on the tree o.
Isa 10:29 and say, "We will camp o at Geba.
Jnh 4:10 It sprang up o and died o.

Overpower (Overpowered, Overpowering, Overpowers)
Ge 32:25 the man saw that he could not o him,
43:18 He wants to attack us and o us and
Jdg 16: 5 how we can o him so that we may tie
2Ki 16: 5 Ahaz, but they could not o him.
Est 9: 1 of the Jews had hoped to o them,
Job 14:20 You o him once for all, and he is
Isa 7: 1 Jerusalem, but they could not o it.
Ob : 7 your friends will deceive and o you;
Rev 11: 7 attack them, and o and kill them.

Overpowered (Overpower)
Jdg 3:10 the hands of Othniel, who o him.
2Sa 11:23 "The men o us and came out against
1Ki 20:21 The king of Israel advanced and o
2Ki 10:32 Hazael o the Israelites throughout
Ecc 4:12 Though one may be o, two can defend
Jer 20: 7 deceived; you o me and prevailed.
Da 6:24 o them and crushed all their bones.
Ac 19:16 jumped on them and o them all.

Overpowering (Overpower)
Job 41: 9 false; the mere sight of him is o.

Overpowers (Overpower)
Lk 11:22 when someone stronger attacks and o

Overran (Run)
Jdg 20:43 chased them and easily o them in the

Over-righteous (Righteous)
Ecc 7:16 Do not be o, neither be overwise—

Overruled (Overruling)
2Sa 24: 4 The king's word, however, o Joab and
1Ch 21: 4 The king's word, however, o Joab; so

Overruling (Overruled)
Est 8: 5 let an order be written o the

Overrun (Run)
Isa 34:13 Thorns will o her citadels, nettles
Hos 9: 6 and thorns will o their tents.
Am 3:11 "An enemy will o the land; he will
Zec 9: 8 Never again will an oppressor o my

Overseer (Overseers, Oversight)
Pr 6: 7 has no commander, no o or ruler,
1Ti 3: 1 being an o, he desires a noble task.
3: 2 Now the o must be above reproach,
Tit 1: 7 Since an o is entrusted with God's
1Pe 2:25 to the Shepherd and O of your souls.

Overseers (Overseer)
Ac 20:28 the Holy Spirit has made you o.
Php 1: 1 together with the o and deacons:
1Pe 5: 2 serving as o—not because you must,

Overshadow (Overshadowed, Overshadowing)
Lk 1:35 power of the Most High will o you.

Overshadowed (Overshadow)
1Ki 8: 7 o the ark and its carrying poles.

Overshadowing (Overshadow)
Ex 25:20 upwards, o the cover with them.
37: 9 upwards, o the cover with them.
Eze 31: 3 with beautiful branches o the forest;
Heb 9: 5 of the Glory, o the atonement cover.

Oversight (Overseer)
2Ch 23:18 Jehoiada placed the o of the temple

Overstep (Step)
Pr 8:29 the waters would not o his command,

Overtake (Overtaken, Overtakes, Overtaking, Overtook)
Ge 19:19 disaster will o me, and I'll die.
Ex 15: 9 'I will pursue, I will o them.
Dt 19: 6 o him if the distance is too great,
28:15 curses will come upon you and o you:
28:45 They will pursue you and o you until
1Sa 30: 8 this raiding party? Will I o them?"
30: 8 o them and succeed in the rescue."
2Sa 15:14 or he will move quickly to o us and
2Ki 7: 9 daylight, punishment will o us.
Job 20:22 distress will o him; the full force

Job 27:20 Terrors **o** him like a flood; a
Ps 7: 5 let my enemy pursue and **o** me; let
35: 8 may ruin **o** them by surprise—may
69:24 them; let your fierce anger **o** them.
Pr 6:15 Therefore disaster will **o** him in an
10:24 What the wicked dreads will **o** him;
Ecc 2:15 fate of the fool will **o** me also.
Isa 35:10 Gladness and joy will **o** them, and
47: 9 Both of these will **o** you in a moment,
51:11 Gladness and joy will **o** them, and
Jer 42:16 the sword you fear will **o** you there,
Hos 10: 9 not war **o** the evildoers in Gibeah?
Am 9:10 'Disaster will not **o** or meet us.'
Mic 2: 6 things; disgrace will not **o** us."
Zec 1: 6 the prophets, **o** your forefathers?
Rev 12:15 to **o** the woman and sweep her away
18: 8 plagues will **o** her: death, mourning

Overtaken (Overtake)
Ps 9: 6 Endless ruin has **o** the enemy, you
40:12 my sins have **o** me, and I cannot see.
Lam 1: 3 All who pursue her have **o** her in
Am 9:13 reaper will be **o** by the ploughman

Overtakes (Overtake)
Pr 1:26 I will mock when calamity **o** you—
1:27 calamity **o** you like a storm, when
3:25 or of the ruin that **o** the wicked,
Ecc 2:14 that the same fate **o** them both.
9: 3 the sun: The same destiny **o** all.
Jn 12:35 the light, before darkness **o** you.

Overtaking (Overtake)
1Ch 21:12 with their swords **o** you, or three

Overthrew (Overthrow)
Ge 19:25 Thus he **o** those cities and the
19:29 **o** the cities where Lot had lived.
Dt 29:23 which the LORD **o** in fierce anger.
Isa 14:17 who **o** its cities and would not let
Jer 20:16 the towns the LORD **o** without pity.
50:40 God **o** Sodom and Gomorrah along with
Am 4:11 "I **o** some of you as I **o** Sodom and
Ac 13:19 he **o** seven nations in Canaan and

Overthrow (Overthrew, Overthrown, Overthrows)
Ge 19:21 I will not **o** the town you speak of.
2Sa 10: 3 the city and spy it out and **o** it?"
2Ki 3:19 You will **o** every fortified city and
1Ch 19: 3 and spy out the country and **o** it?"
2Ch 25: 8 God will **o** you before the enemy, for
25: 8 God has the power to help or to **o**."
Ezr 6:12 **o** any king or people who lifts a
Jer 1:10 to destroy and **o**, to build and
31:28 to **o**, destroy and bring disaster,
45: 4 I will **o** what I have built and
Da 11:17 marriage in order to **o** the kingdom,
11:24 He will plot the **o** of fortresses—
Hag 2:22 I will **o** chariots and their drivers;
Zec 10: 5 they will fight and **o** the horsemen.
2Th 2: 8 whom the Lord Jesus will **o** with the

Overthrown (Overthrow)
Nu 21:30 "But we have **o** them; Heshbon is
Pr 12: 7 Wicked men are **o** and are no more,
Isa 1: 7 laid waste as when **o** by strangers.
13:19 be **o** by God like Sodom and Gomorrah.
Jer 18:23 Let them be **o** before you; deal with
49:18 Sodom and Gomorrah were **o**, along
Lam 2:17 He has **o** you without pity, he has
4: 6 which was **o** in a moment without a
Eze 32:12 Egypt, and all her hordes will be **o**.

Overthrows (Overthrow)
Job 12:19 and **o** men long established.
34:25 their deeds, he **o** them in the night
Pr 13: 6 but wickedness **o** the sinner.
Isa 44:25 who **o** the learning of the wise and

Overtook (Overtake)
Ge 31:25 country of Gilead when Laban **o** him,
Ex 14: 9 pursued the Israelites and **o** them
Jdg 18:22 called together and **o** the Danites.
1Sa 31: 3 **o** him, they wounded him critically.
2Ki 25: 5 and **o** him in the plains of Jericho.
1Ch 10: 3 the archers **o** him, they wounded him.
Ps 18:37 I pursued my enemies and **o** them; I
Jer 2: 3 guilty, and disaster **o** them,
39: 5 **o** Zedekiah in the plains of Jericho.
52: 8 and **o** him in the plains of Jericho.

Overturn (Overturned, Overturns)
Hag 2:22 I will **o** royal thrones and shatter

Overturned (Overturn)
Jdg 7:13 that the tent **o** and collapsed."
Eze 38:20 The mountains will be **o**, the cliffs
Jnh 3: 4 more days and Nineveh will be **o**."
Mt 21:12 **o** the tables of the money-changers
Mk 11:15 **o** the tables of the money-changers
Jn 2:15 money-changers and **o** their tables.

Overturns (Overturn)
Job 9: 5 knowing it and **o** them in his anger.

Overweening
Pr 21:24 his name; he behaves with **o** pride.
Isa 16: 6 heard of Moab's pride—her **o** pride
Jer 48:29 pride—her **o** pride and conceit,

Overwhelm (Overwhelmed, Overwhelming, Overwhelms)
Job 3: 5 over it; may blackness **o** its light.
9:18 breath but would **o** me with misery.
15:24 **o** him, like a king poised to attack,
30:15 Terrors **o** me; my dignity is driven
Pr 1:27 when distress and trouble **o** you.
SS 6: 5 Turn your eyes from me; they **o** me.
Hab 2:17 you have done to Lebanon will **o** you,

Overwhelmed (Overwhelm)
Dt 11: 4 how he **o** them with the waters of the
2Sa 22: 5 the torrents of destruction **o** me.
1Ki 10: 5 the temple of the LORD, she was **o**.
2Ch 9: 4 the temple of the LORD, she was **o**.
Ps 14: 5 There they are, **o** with dread, for
18: 4 the torrents of destruction **o** me.
38: 4 My guilt has **o** me like a burden too
53: 5 There they were, **o** with dread, where
55: 5 have beset me; horror has **o** me.
65: 3 we were **o** by sins, you forgave our
88: 7 you have **o** me with all your waves.
Eze 3:15 I sat among them for seven days—**o**.
Da 10: 7 but such terror **o** them that they
Mt 26:38 to them, "My soul is **o** with sorrow
Mk 7:37 People were **o** with amazement. "He
9:15 **o** with wonder and ran to greet him.
14:34 "My soul is **o** with sorrow to the
2Co 2: 7 will not be **o** by excessive sorrow.

Overwhelming (Overwhelm)
Pr 27: 4 Anger is cruel and fury **o**, but who
Isa 10:22 has been decreed, **o** and righteous.
28:15 When an **o** scourge sweeps by, it
28:18 When the **o** scourge sweeps by, you
Da 11:22 an **o** army will be swept away before
Na 1: 8 with an **o** flood he will make an end

Overwhelms (Overwhelm)
Pr 10: 6 violence **o** the mouth of the wicked.
10:11 violence **o** the mouth of the wicked.

Overwicked (Wicked)
Ecc 7:17 Do not be **o**, and do not be a fool—

Overwise (Wise)
Ecc 7:16 neither be **o**—why destroy yourself?

Owe (Owed, Owes)
Mt 18:28 Pay back what you **o** me!' he demanded.
Lk 16: 5 'How much do you **o** my master?'
16: 7 the second, 'And how much do you **o**?'
Ro 13: 7 Give everyone what you **o** him: If you
13: 7 what you **o** him: If you **o** taxes,
Ro 15:27 do it, and indeed they **o** it to them.
15:27 they **o** it to the Jews to share with
Phm :19 that you **o** me your very self.

Owed (Owe)
Mt 18:24 he began the settlement, a man who **o**
18:28 who **o** him a hundred denarii.
18:34 until he should pay back all he **o**.
Lk 7:41 "Two men **o** money to a certain
7:41 One **o** him five hundred denarii, and

Owes (Owe)
Dt 15: 3 cancel any debt your brother **o** you.
Phm :18 If he has done you any wrong or **o**

Owl (Owls)
Lev 11:16 the horned **o**, the screech **o**, the
11:17 **o**, the cormorant, the great **o**,
11:18 the white **o**, the desert **o**, the
Dt 14:15 the horned **o**, the screech **o**, the
14:16 little **o**, the great **o**, the white **o**,
14:17 the desert **o**, the osprey, the
Ps 102: 6 I am like a desert **o**, like an **o**
Isa 34:11 The desert **o** and screech **o** will
34:11 **o** and the raven will nest there.
34:15 The **o** will nest there and lay eggs,
Jer 50:39 there, and there the **o** will dwell.
Mic 1: 8 like a jackal and moan like an **o**.
Zep 2:14 The desert **o** and the screech **o** will

Owls (Owl)
Job 30:29 of jackals, a companion of **o**.
Isa 13:21 her houses; there the **o** will dwell,
14:23 "I will turn her into a place for **o**
34:13 a haunt for jackals, a home for **o**.
43:20 the jackals and the **o**, because I

Own (Owned, Owner, Owner's, Owners, Ownership, Owning, Owns)
Ge 30:43 and came to **o** large flocks,
46:32 and herds and everything they **o**.'
47: 1 and herds and everything they **o**,
Ps 12: 4 we **o** our lips—who is our master?"

Owned (Own)
Ge 25: 5 Abraham left everything he **o** to
31: 1 has taken everything our father **o**
39: 4 to his care everything he **o**.
39: 5 his household and of all that he **o**,
Nu 16:33 with everything they **o**; the earth
Jdg 19:22 to the old man who **o** the house
1Ki 17:17 woman who **o** the house became ill.
Job 1: 3 he **o** seven thousand sheep, three
Ecc 2: 7 I also **o** more herds and flocks than
Jer 39:10 the poor people, who **o** nothing;
Ac 4:34 those who **o** lands or houses sold
4:37 sold a field he **o** and brought the

Owner (Own)
Ex 21:28 But the **o** of the bull will not be
21:29 the **o** has been warned but has not
21:29 and the **o** also must be put to death.
21:32 the **o** must pay thirty shekels of
21:34 the **o** of the pit must pay for the
21:34 he must pay its **o**, and the
21:36 yet the **o** did not keep it penned up,
21:36 the **o** must pay, animal for animal,
22: 8 if the thief is not found, the **o** of
22:11 The **o** is to accept this, and no
22:12 he must make restitution to the **o**.
22:14 or dies while the **o** is not present,
22:15 if the **o** is with the animal, the
Lev 6: 5 give it all to the **o** on the day he
14:35 the **o** of the house must go and tell
25:53 see to it that his **o** does not rule
27:13 If the **o** wishes to redeem the animal,
Jdg 19:23 The **o** of the house went outside and
1Ki 16:24 name of the former **o** of the hill.
Ecc 5:11 what benefit are they to the **o**
5:13 wealth hoarded to the harm of its **o**,
Mt 13:52 like the **o** of a house who brings
20: 8 the **o** of the vineyard said to
21:40 when the **o** of the vineyard comes,

Mt 24:43 understand this: If the **o** of the
Mk 12: 9 "What then will the **o** of the
13:35 the **o** of the house will come back
14:14 Say to the **o** of the house he enters,
Lk 12:39 understand this: If the **o** of the
13:25 Once the **o** of the house gets up and
14:21 Then the **o** of the house became angry
20:13 "Then the **o** of the vineyard said,
20:15 the **o** of the vineyard do to them?
22:11 say to the **o** of the house, 'The
Ac 21:11 will bind the **o** of this belt
27:11 the pilot and of the **o** of the ship.

Owner's (Own)

Isa 1: 3 the donkey his **o** manger, but Israel
Mt 13:27 "The **o** servants came to him and said,

Owners (Own)

Jer 8:10 other men and their fields to new **o**.
Lk 19:33 they were untying the colt, its **o**
Ac 16:16 money for her **o** by fortune-telling.
16:19 the **o** of the slave girl realised

Ownership (Own)

2Co 1:22 set his seal of **o** on us, and put his

Owning (Own)

Job 22: 8 you were a powerful man, **o** land—

Owns (Own)

Ge 24:36 he has given him everything he **o**.
32:17 **o** all these animals in front of you?
38:25 "I am pregnant by the man who **o**
39: 8 he **o** he has entrusted to my care.
Lev 27:28 "'But nothing that a man **o** and
Ecc 2:21 and then he must leave all he **o** to
Mt 18:12 If a man **o** a hundred sheep, and one
Jn 10:12 is not the shepherd who **o** the sheep.
Gal 4: 1 although he **o** the whole estate.

Ox (Oxen)

Ex 20:17 his **o** or donkey, or anything that
21:33 and an **o** or a donkey falls into it,
22: 1 "If a man steals an **o** or a sheep and
22: 1 the **o** and four sheep for the sheep.
22: 4 whether **o** or donkey or sheep—he
22: 9 cases of illegal possession of an **o**,
22:10 "If a man gives a donkey, an **o**, a
23: 4 "If you come across your enemy's **o**
23:12 so that your **o** and your donkey may
Lev 4:10 just as the fat is removed from the **o**
9: 4 an **o** and a ram for a fellowship
9:18 He slaughtered the **o** and the ram as
9:19 the fat portions of the **o** and the
17: 3 Any Israelite who sacrifices an **o**, a
22:23 present as a freewill offering an **o**
27:26 an **o** or a sheep, it is the LORD's.
Nu 7: 3 twelve oxen—an **o** from each leader
18:17 **o**, a sheep or a goat; they are holy.
22: 4 **o** licks up the grass of the field.
23:22 they have the strength of a wild **o**.
24: 8 they have the strength of a wild **o**.
Dt 5:14 nor your **o**, your donkey or any of
5:21 his **o** or donkey, or anything that
14: 4 may eat: the **o**, the sheep, the goat,
17: 1 an **o** or a sheep that has any defect
22: 1 If you see your brother's **o** or sheep
22: 4 donkey or his **o** fallen on the road,
22:10 Do not plough with an **o** and a donkey
25: 4 Do not muzzle an **o** while it is
28:31 Your **o** will be slaughtered before
33:17 his horns are the horns of a wild **o**.
1Sa 12: 3 Whose **o** have I taken? Whose donkey
14:34 So everyone brought his **o** that
2Sa 24:22 and **o** yokes for the wood.
Ne 5:18 Each day one **o**, six choice sheep and
Job 6: 5 or an **o** bellow when it has fodder?
24: 3 and take the widow's **o** in pledge.
39: 9 "Will the wild **o** consent to serve
40:15 and which feeds on grass like an **o**.
Ps 29: 6 a calf, Sirion like a young wild **o**.
69:31 will please the LORD more than an **o**,
92:10 my horn like that of a wild **o**;
Pr 7:22 All at once he followed her like an **o**
Pr 14: 4 from the strength of an **o** comes an
Isa 1: 3 The **o** knows his master, the donkey
11: 7 the lion will eat straw like the **o**.
65:25 the lion will eat straw like the **o**,
Eze 1:10 and on the left the face of an **o**;
Lk 13:15 his **o** or donkey from the stall
14: 5 "If one of you has a son or an **o**
1Co 9: 9 **o** while it is treading out the grain.
1Ti 5:18 "Do not muzzle the **o** while it is
Rev 4: 7 the second was like an **o**, the third

Oxen (Ox)

Ge 49: 6 and hamstrung **o** as they pleased.
Nu 7: 3 twelve **o**—an ox from each leader and
7: 6 Moses took the carts and **o** and gave
7: 7 He gave two carts and four **o** to the
7: 8 he gave four carts and eight **o** to
7:17 two **o**, five rams, five male goats
7:23 two **o**, five rams, five male goats
7:29 two **o**, five rams, five male goats
7:35 two **o**, five rams, five male goats
7:41 two **o**, five rams, five male goats
7:47 two **o**, five rams, five male goats
7:53 two **o**, five rams, five male goats
7:59 two **o**, five rams, five male goats
7:65 two **o**, five rams, five male goats
7:71 two **o**, five rams, five male goats
7:77 two **o**, five rams, five male goats
7:83 two **o**, five rams, five male goats
7:88 offering came to twenty-four **o**,
Dt 15:19 Do not put the firstborn of your **o**
1Sa 11: 5 from the fields, behind his **o**, and
11: 7 He took a pair of **o**, cut them into
11: 7 "This is what will be done to the **o**
2Sa 6: 6 ark of God, because the **o** stumbled.
24:22 Here are **o** for the burnt offering,
24:24 the **o** and paid fifty shekels of
1Ki 19:19 was ploughing with twelve yoke of **o**,
19:20 Elisha then left his **o** and ran after
19:21 He took his yoke of **o** and
1Ch 12:40 on donkeys, camels, mules and **o**.
13: 9 the ark, because the **o** stumbled.
21:23 I will give the **o** for the burnt
Job 1: 3 five hundred yoke of **o** and five
1:14 "The **o** were ploughing and the
42:12 yoke of **o** and a thousand donkeys.
Ps 22:21 me from the horns of the wild **o**.
144:14 our **o** will draw heavy loads. There
Pr 14: 4 Where there are no **o**, the manger is
Isa 30:24 The **o** and donkeys that work the soil
34: 7 the wild **o** will fall with them, the
Jer 51:23 with you I shatter farmer and **o**,
Am 6:12 Does one plough there with **o**? But
Mt 22: 4 My **o** and fattened cattle have been
Lk 14:19 'I have just bought five yoke of **o**,
1Co 9: 9 Is it about **o** that God is concerned?

Ox-goad

Jdg 3:31 six hundred Philistines with an **o**.

Ozem

1Ch 2:15 the sixth **O** and the seventh David.
2:25 Bunah, Oren, **O** and Ahijah.

Ozni (Oznite)

Nu 26:16 through **O**, the Oznite clan; through

Oznite (Ozni)

Nu 26:16 through Ozni, the **O** clan; through

Paarai

2Sa 23:35 Hezro the Carmelite, **P** the Arbite,

Pace

Ge 33:14 along slowly at the **p** of the droves

Pacifies (Peace)

Pr 21:14 in the cloak **p** great wrath.

Pacify (Peace)

Ge 32:20 "I will **p** him with these gifts I am

Pack (Packed)

Jer 46:19 **P** your belongings for exile, you who
Eze 12: 3 son of man, **p** your belongings for

Packed (Pack)

Jos 9:12 This bread of ours was warm when we **p**
Eze 12: 4 out your belongings **p** for exile.
12: 7 I brought out my things **p** for exile.

Pact

Isa 57: 8 a **p** with those whose beds you love,

Pad

Jer 38:12 under your arms to **p** the ropes.

Paddan

Ge 48: 7 I was returning from **P**, to my sorrow

Paddan Aram See Aram; Mesopotamia

Ge 25:20 of Bethuel the Aramean from **P**
28: 2 Go at once to **P**, to the house of
28: 5 and he went to **P**, to Laban son of
28: 6 had sent him to **P** to take a wife
28: 7 father and mother and had gone to **P**.
31:18 the goods he had accumulated in **P**,
33:18 After Jacob came from **P**, he arrived
35: 9 After Jacob returned from **P**, God
35:26 of Jacob, who were born to him in **P**.
46:15 the sons Leah bore to Jacob in **P**,

Padon

Ezr 2:44 Keros, Siaha, **P**,
Ne 7:47 Keros, Sia, **P**,

Pagan (Pagans)

2Ki 23: 5 He did away with the **p** priests
Isa 57: 8 you have put your **p** symbols.
Lam 1:10 she saw **p** nations enter her
Am 7:17 yourself will die in a **p** country.
Zep 1: 4 the **p** and the idolatrous priests—
Mt 18:17 as you would a **p** or a tax collector.
Lk 12:30 For the **p** world runs after all such
1Co 10: 7 and got up to indulge in **p** revelry."

Pagans (Pagan)

Isa 2: 6 Philistines and clasp hands with **p**.
Mt 5:47 than others? Do not even **p** do that?
6: 7 do not keep on babbling like **p**, for
6:32 For the **p** run after all these things,
1Co 5: 1 that does not occur even among **p**:
10:20 the sacrifices of **p** are offered to
12: 2 You know that when you were **p**,
1Pe 2:12 Live such good lives among the **p**
4: 3 the past doing what **p** choose to do
3Jn : 7 out, receiving no help from the **p**.

Pagiel

Nu 1:13 from Asher, **P** son of Ocran;
2:27 people of Asher is **P** son of Ocran.
7:72 On the eleventh day **P** son of Ocran,
7:77 was the offering of **P** son of Ocran.
10:26 **P** son of Ocran was over the division

Pahath-Moab

Ezr 2: 6 of **P** (through the line of Jeshua and
8: 4 of the descendants of **P**, Eliehoenai
10:30 From the descendants of **P**: Adna,
Ne 3:11 Hasshub son of **P** repaired another
7:11 of **P** (through the line of Jeshua and
10:14 The leaders of the people: Parosh, **P**,

Paid (Pay)

Ge 30:33 check on the wages you have **p** me.
31:15 he has used up what was **p** for us.
39:23 The warder **p** no attention to
Ex 16:20 However, some of them **p** no attention
22:15 **p** for the hire covers the loss.
Lev 25:50 on the rate **p** to a hired man for that
25:51 larger share of the price **p** for him.
Dt 1:45 but he **p** no attention to your
Jdg 1: 7 Now God has **p** me back for what I did

Jdg 11:28 **p** no attention to the message
1Sa 25:21 He has **p** me back evil for good.
2Sa 24:24 **p** fifty shekels of silver for them.
1Ki 18:29 no-one answered, no-one **p** attention.
2Ki 12:11 With it they **p** those who worked on
12:14 was **p** to the workmen, who used it to
17: 3 vassal and had **p** him tribute.
17: 4 and he no longer **p** tribute to the
22: 9 "Your officials have **p** out the money
23:35 Jehoiakim **p** Pharaoh Neco the silver
1Ch 21:25 David **p** Araunah six hundred shekels
2Ch 24:17 came and **p** homage to the king, and
25: 9 I **p** for these Israelite troops?"
27: 5 That year the Ammonites **p** him a
33:10 his people, but they **p** no attention.
34:10 These men **p** the workers who repaired
34:17 They have **p** out the money that was
Ezr 4:13 tribute or duty will be **p**, and the
4:20 tribute and duty were **p** to them.
6: 4 are to be **p** by the royal treasury.
6: 8 fully **p** out of the royal treasury,
Ne 9:30 Yet they **p** no attention, so you
Est 3: 2 knelt down and **p** honour to Haman,
Job 15:32 Before his time he will be **p** in full,
21:29 you **p** no regard to their accounts—
Isa 3:11 They will be **p** back for what their
40: 2 that her sin has been **p** for, that
42:20 things, but have **p** no attention;
48:18 If only you had **p** attention to my
Jer 25: 4 not listened or **p** any attention.
35:15 not **p** attention or listened to me.
37: 2 **p** any attention to the words the
Eze 27:15 **p** you with ivory tusks and ebony.
Da 2:46 **p** him honour and ordered that an
Zec 11:12 So they **p** me thirty pieces of silver.
Mt 5:26 out until you have **p** the last penny.
22: 5 "But they **p** no attention and went
Mk 15:19 their knees, they **p** homage to him.
Lk 12:59 until you have **p** the last penny."
Ac 8: 6 **p** close attention to what he said.
Heb 7: 9 tenth, **p** the tenth through Abraham,
2Pe 2:13 They will be **p** back with harm for

Pain (Painful, Pains)

Ge 3:16 with **p** you will give birth to
6: 6 and his heart was filled with **p**.
34:25 while all of them were still in **p**,
1Ch 4: 9 saying, "I gave birth to him in **p**.
4:10 harm so that I will be free from **p**.
2Ch 21:19 the disease, and he died in great **p**.
Job 6:10 my joy in unrelenting **p**—that I
14:22 He feels but the **p** of his own body
16: 6 "Yet if I speak, my **p** is not
33:19 may be chastened on a bed of **p** with
Ps 38: 7 My back is filled with searing **p**;
38:17 and my **p** is ever with me.
48: 6 **p** like that of a woman in labour.
69:26 talk about the **p** of those you hurt.
69:29 I am in **p** and distress; may your
Ecc 2:23 All his days his work is **p** and grief;
Isa 13: 8 **p** and anguish will grip them;
17:11 the day of disease and incurable **p**.
21: 3 At this my body is racked with **p**,
26:17 writhes and cries out in her **p**,
26:18 We were with child, we writhed in **p**,
Jer 4:19 anguish, my anguish! I writhe in **p**.
5: 3 but they felt no **p**; you crushed them
6:24 **p** like that of a woman in labour.
13:21 Will not **p** grip you like that of a
15:18 Why is my **p** unending and my wound
22:23 **p** like that of a woman in labour!
30:15 your **p** that has no cure? Because of
45: 3 The LORD has added sorrow to my **p**;
49:24 anguish and **p** have seized her,
49:24 **p** like that of a woman in labour.
50:43 **p** like that of a woman in labour.
51: 8 Get balm for her **p**; perhaps she can
Mic 1:12 Those who live in Maroth writhe in **p**,
4: 9 that **p** seizes you like that of a
Mt 4:24 those suffering severe **p**, the
Jn 16:21 A woman giving birth to a child has **p**
1Pe 2:19 man bears up under the **p** of unjust
Rev 12: 2 She was pregnant and cried out in **p**
21: 4 death or mourning or crying or **p**,

Painful (Pain)

Ge 3:17 through **p** toil you will eat of it
5:29 **p** toil of our hands caused by the
Dt 28:35 with **p** boils that cannot be cured,
Job 2: 7 afflicted Job with **p** sores from the
6:25 How **p** are honest words! But what do
Eze 28:24 who are **p** briers and sharp thorns.
2Co 2: 1 not make another **p** visit to you.
Heb 12:11 seems pleasant at the time, but **p**.
1Pe 4:12 do not be surprised at the **p** trial
Rev 16: 2 and ugly and **p** sores broke out on

Pains (Pain)

Ge 3:16 "I will greatly increase your **p** in
1Sa 4:19 but was overcome by her labour **p**.
1Ch 22:14 "I have taken great **p** to provide for
2Ch 6:29 one aware of his afflictions and **p**,
Job 30:17 my gnawing **p** never rest.
39: 3 their labour **p** are ended.
Isa 66: 7 **p** come upon her, she delivers a son.
Hos 13:13 **P** as of a woman in childbirth come
Ro 8:22 groaning as in the **p** of childbirth
2Co 8:21 For we are taking **p** to do what is
Gal 4:19 for whom I am again in the **p** of
4:27 you who have no labour **p**; because
1Th 5: 3 as labour **p** on a pregnant woman, and
Rev 16:11 because of their **p** and their sores,

Paint (Painted)

Jer 4:30 Why shade your eyes with **p**?

Painted (Paint)

2Ki 9:30 she **p** her eyes, arranged her hair
Eze 23:40 **p** your eyes and put on your

Pair (Pairs)

Ex 25:35 One bud shall be under the first **p**
25:35 a second bud under the second **p**, and
25:35 a third bud under the third **p**—
37:21 One bud was under the first **p** of
37:21 a second bud under the second **p**, and
37:21 a third bud under the third **p**—
Dt 24: 6 Do not take a **p** of millstones—not
Jdg 15: 4 a torch to every **p** of tails,
1Sa 11: 7 He took a **p** of oxen, cut them into
1Ki 6:23 made a **p** of cherubim of olive wood,
19:19 himself was driving the twelfth **p**.
2Ki 5:17 as much earth as a **p** of mules can
2Ch 3:10 he made a **p** of sculptured cherubim
Am 2: 6 and the needy for a **p** of sandals.
8: 6 and the needy for a **p** of sandals,
Lk 2:24 "a **p** of doves or two young pigeons".
Rev 6: 5 holding a **p** of scales in his hand.

Pairs (Pair)

Ge 7: 8 **P** of clean and unclean animals, of
7:15 **P** of all creatures that have the
Jdg 15: 4 and tied them tail to tail in **p**.

Palace (Palaces, Palatial)

Ge 12:15 and she was taken into his **p**.
41:40 You shall be in charge of my **p**, and
45:16 the news reached Pharaoh's **p** that
47:14 and he brought it to Pharaoh's **p**.
Ex 7:23 he turned and went into his **p**, and
8: 3 They will come up into your **p** and
8:24 of flies poured into Pharaoh's **p**
Nu 22:18 "Even if Balak gave me his **p** filled
24:13 'Even if Balak gave me his **p** filled
Jdg 3:20 upper room of his summer **p** and said,
2Sa 5: 8 and lame' will not enter the **p**."
5:11 and they built a **p** for David.
7: 1 After the king was settled in his **p**
7: 2 "Here I am, living in a **p** of cedar,
11: 2 walked around on the roof of the **p**.
11: 8 So Uriah left the **p**, and a gift
11: 9 Uriah slept at the entrance to the **p**
13: 7 David sent word to Tamar at the **p**:
15:16 concubines to take care of the **p**.
15:35 anything you hear in the king's **p**.
16:21 whom he left to take care of the **p**.
19:11 to bring the king back to his **p**,
20: 3 David returned to his **p** in Jerusalem,
20: 3 he had left to take care of the **p**

1Ki 3: 1 his **p** and the temple of the LORD,
4: 6 Ahishar—in charge of the **p**;
7: 1 complete the construction of his **p**.
7: 2 He built the **P** of the Forest of
7: 8 the **p** in which he was to live, set
7: 8 Solomon also made a **p** like this hall
9: 1 temple of the LORD and the royal **p**,
9:10 temple of the LORD and the royal **p**—
9:15 his own **p**, the supporting terraces,
9:24 to the **p** Solomon had built for her,
10: 4 of Solomon and the **p** he had built,
10:12 of the LORD and for the royal **p**,
10:17 in the **P** of the Forest of Lebanon.
10:21 all the household articles in the **P**
11:20 Tahpenes brought up in the royal **p**.
14:26 and the treasures of the royal **p**.
14:27 duty at the entrance to the royal **p**.
15:18 the LORD's temple and of his own **p**.
16: 9 man in charge of the **p** at Tirzah.
16:18 into the citadel of the royal **p**
16:18 and set the **p** on fire around him.
18: 3 Obadiah, who was in charge of his **p**.
20: 6 search your **p** and the houses of
20:43 of Israel went to his **p** in Samaria.
21: 1 to the **p** of Ahab king of Samaria.
21: 2 garden, since it is close to my **p**.
22:39 including all he did, the **p** he built
2Ki 7: 9 and report this to the royal **p**."
7:11 and it was reported within the **p**.
10: 5 the **p** administrator, the city
11: 5 third of you guarding the royal **p**,
11:16 the horses enter the **p** grounds,
11:19 of the LORD and went into the **p**,
11:20 been slain with the sword at the **p**.
12:18 of the LORD and of the royal **p**,
14:14 in the treasuries of the royal **p**.
15: 5 the king's son had charge of the **p**
15:25 citadel of the royal **p** at Samaria.
16: 8 in the treasuries of the royal **p** and
18:15 in the treasuries of the royal **p**.
18:18 son of Hilkiah the **p** administrator,
18:37 son of Hilkiah the **p** administrator,
19: 2 He sent Eliakim the **p** administrator,
20:13 There was nothing in his **p** or in all
20:15 "What did they see in your **p**?"
20:15 everything in my **p**," Hezekiah said.
20:17 come when everything in your **p**,
20:18 in the **p** of the king of Babylon."
21:18 in his **p** garden, the garden of Uzza.
21:23 and assassinated the king in his **p**.
24:13 of the LORD and from the royal **p**,
25: 9 the royal **p** and all the houses of
1Ch 14: 1 and carpenters to build a **p** for him.
17: 1 After David was settled in his **p**, he
17: 1 "Here I am, living in a **p** of cedar,
28: 1 together with the **p** officials, the
2Ch 2: 1 the LORD and a royal **p** for himself.
2: 3 him cedar to build a **p** to live in.
2:12 for the LORD and a **p** for himself.
7:11 temple of the LORD and the royal **p**,
7:11 temple of the LORD and in his own **p**,
8: 1 temple of the LORD and his own **p**,
8:11 David to the **p** he had built for her,
8:11 "My wife must not live in the **p** of
9: 3 as well as the **p** he had built,
9:11 of the LORD and for the royal **p**,
9:16 in the **P** of the Forest of Lebanon.
9:20 all the household articles in the **P**
12: 9 and the treasures of the royal **p**.
12:10 duty at the entrance to the royal **p**.
16: 2 of his own **p** and sent it to
19: 1 safely to his **p** in Jerusalem,
21:17 goods found in the king's **p**,
23: 5 a third of you at the royal **p** and a
23:15 of the Horse Gate on the **p** grounds,
23:20 They went into the **p** through the
25:24 together with the **p** treasures and
26:21 Jotham his son had charge of the **p**
28: 7 the officer in charge of the **p**,
28:21 from the royal **p** and from the
33:20 his fathers and was buried in his **p**.
33:24 him and assassinated him in his **p**.
Ezr 4:14 we are under obligation to the **p**
Ne 3:25 upper **p** near the court of the guard.
Est 1: 5 the enclosed garden of the king's **p**,
1: 9 women in the royal **p** of King Xerxes.

Est 2: 8 taken to the king's **p** and entrusted
2: 9 maids selected from the king's **p**
2:13 her from the harem to the king's **p**.
5: 1 stood in the inner court of the **p**,
6: 4 entered the outer court of the **p**
7: 7 wine and went out into the **p** garden.
7: 8 Just as the king returned from the **p**
9: 4 Mordecai was prominent in the **p**;
Ps 45:15 they enter the **p** of the king.
144:12 be like pillars carved to adorn a **p**.
Isa 22: 8 the weapons in the **P** of the Forest;
22:15 Shebna, who is in charge of the **p**:
36: 3 son of Hilkiah the **p** administrator
36:22 son of Hilkiah the **p** administrator
37: 2 He sent Eliakim the **p** administrator,
39: 2 There was nothing in his **p** or in all
39: 4 "What did they see in your **p**?"
39: 4 everything in my **p**," Hezekiah said.
39: 6 come when everything in your **p**,
39: 7 in the **p** of the king of Babylon."
Jer 22: 1 "Go down to the **p** of the king of
22: 4 come through the gates of this **p**,
22: 5 that this **p** will become a ruin.
22: 6 about the **p** of the king of Judah:
22:13 "Woe to him who builds his **p** by
22:14 a great **p** with spacious upper rooms.
26:10 they went up from the royal **p** to the
27:18 in the **p** of the king of Judah and in
27:21 in the **p** of the king of Judah and in
30:18 **p** will stand in its proper place.
32: 2 the guard in the royal **p** of Judah.
36:12 the secretary's room in the royal **p**,
37:17 him and had him brought to the **p**,
38: 7 an official in the royal **p**, heard
38: 8 Ebed-Melech went out of the **p** and
38:11 a room under the treasury in the **p**.
38:22 All the women left in the **p** of the
39: 8 Babylonians set fire to the royal **p**
43: 9 to Pharaoh's **p** in Tahpanhes.
52:13 the royal **p** and all the houses of
Da 1: 4 qualified to serve in the king's **p**.
4: 4 in my **p**, contented and prosperous.
4:29 the roof of the royal **p** of Babylon,
5: 5 near the lampstand in the royal **p**.
6:18 the king returned to his **p** and spent
Am 9: 6 he who builds his lofty **p** in the
Na 2: 6 are thrown open and the **p** collapses.
Mt 26: 3 in the **p** of the high priest,
Mk 15:16 led Jesus away into the **p** (that is,
Jn 18:28 to the **p** of the Roman governor.
18:28 the Jews did not enter the **p**;
18:33 Pilate then went back inside the **p**,
19: 9 he went back inside the **p**. "Where do
Ac 7:10 him ruler over Egypt and all his **p**.
23:35 be kept under guard in Herod's **p**.
Php 1:13 clear throughout the whole **p** guard

Palaces (Palace)
2Ch 36:19 they burned all the **p** and destroyed
Ps 45: 8 from **p** adorned with ivory the music
Pr 30:28 hand, yet it is found in kings' **p**.
Isa 13:22 jackals in her luxurious **p**.
Jer 33: 4 the royal **p** of Judah that have been
Lam 2: 5 He has swallowed up all her **p** and
2: 7 to the enemy the walls of her **p**;
Hos 8:14 forgotten his Maker and built **p**;
Mt 11: 8 wear fine clothes are in kings' **p**.
Lk 7:25 and indulge in luxury are in **p**.

Palal
Ne 3:25 **P** son of Uzai worked opposite the

Palatial (Palace)
1Ch 29: 1 because this **p** structure is not for
29:19 to build the **p** structure for which

Pale
Isa 29:22 no longer will their faces grow **p**.
Jer 30: 6 labour, every face turned deathly **p**?
Da 5: 6 His face turned **p** and he was so
5: 9 terrified and his face grew more **p**.
5:10 "Don't be alarmed! Don't look so **p**!
7:28 and my face turned **p**, but I kept
10: 8 turned deathly **p** and I was helpless.

Joel 2: 6 are in anguish; every face turns **p**.
Na 2:10 bodies tremble, every face grows **p**.
Rev 6: 8 and there before me was a **p** horse!

Pallu (Palluite)
Ge 46: 9 The sons of Reuben: Hanoch, **P**,
Ex 6:14 were Hanoch and **P**, Hezron and Carmi.
Nu 26: 5 through **P**, the Palluite clan;
26: 8 The son of **P** was Eliab,
1Ch 5: 3 Israel: Hanoch, **P**, Hezron and Carmi.

Palluite (Pallu)
Nu 26: 5 through Pallu, the **P** clan;

Palm (Palms)
Ex 15:27 twelve springs and seventy **p** trees,
Lev 14:15 it in the **p** of his own left hand,
14:16 forefinger into the oil in his **p**,
14:17 some of the oil remaining in his **p**
14:18 The rest of the oil in his **p** the
14:26 oil into the **p** of his own left hand,
14:27 some of the oil from his **p**
14:28 Some of the oil in his **p** he is to
14:29 The rest of the oil in his **p** the
23:40 and **p** fronds, leafy branches and
Nu 33: 9 twelve springs and seventy **p** trees,
Jdg 4: 5 held court under the **P** of Deborah
1Ki 6:29 cherubim, **p** trees and open flowers.
6:32 **p** trees and open flowers, and
6:32 and **p** trees with beaten gold.
6:35 He carved cherubim, **p** trees and open
7:36 cherubim, lions and **p** trees on the
2Ch 3: 5 it with **p** tree and chain designs.
Ps 92:12 will flourish like a **p** tree,
SS 7: 7 Your stature is like that of the **p**,
7: 8 I said, "I will climb the **p** tree;
Isa 9:14 **p** branch and reed in a single day;
19:15 do—head or tail, **p** branch or reed.
Eze 40:16 walls were decorated with **p** trees.
40:22 its portico and its **p** tree
40:26 it had **p** tree decorations on the
40:31 **p** trees decorated its jambs,
40:34 **p** trees decorated the jambs on
40:37 **p** trees decorated the jambs on
41:18 were carved cherubim and **p** trees.
41:18 **P** trees alternated with cherubim.
41:19 the face of a man towards the **p** tree
41:19 towards the **p** tree on the other.
41:20 cherubim and **p** trees were carved on
41:25 **p** trees like those carved on the
41:26 with **p** trees carved on each side.
Joel 1:12 the **p** and the apple tree—all the
Jn 12:13 They took **p** branches and went out to
Rev 7: 9 holding **p** branches in their hands.

Palms (Palm)
Dt 34: 3 the City of **P**, as far as Zoar.
Jdg 1:16 went up from the City of **P** with the
3:13 took possession of the City of **P**.
2Ch 28:15 at Jericho, the City of **P**, and
Ne 8:15 and from myrtles, **p** and shade trees,
Isa 49:16 engraved you on the **p** of my hands;

Palti
Nu 13: 9 from the tribe of Benjamin, **P** son of

Paltiel
Nu 34:26 **P** son of Azzan, the leader from the
1Sa 25:44 **P** son of Laish, who was from Gallim.
2Sa 3:15 from her husband **P** son of Laish.

Paltite
2Sa 23:26 Helez the **P**, Ira son of Ikkesh from

Pampers
Pr 29:21 If a man **p** his servant from youth,

Pamphylia
Province along southern coast of Asia Minor, between Lycia and Cilicia. Capital city was Perga (Ac 13:13). Its people were represented in Jerusalem at Pentecost (Ac 2:10). Paul's point of entry into Asia Minor on his first journey (Ac 13:13–14); he returned on his way back to Jerusalem (Ac 14:24–26). Paul sailed near here on his way to Rome (Ac 27:5).

Ac 2:10 Phrygia and **P**, Egypt and the parts
13:13 his companions sailed to Perga in **P**,
14:24 through Pisidia, they came into **P**,
15:38 because he had deserted them in **P**
27: 5 off the coast of Cilicia and **P**,

Pan (Pans)
Lev 2: 7 grain offering is cooked in a **p**,
7: 9 baked in an oven or cooked in a **p**
1Sa 2:14 He would plunge it into the **p** or
2Sa 13: 9 she took the **p** and served him the
Eze 4: 3 take an iron **p**, place it as an iron
Mic 3: 3 for the **p**, like flesh for the pot."

Panelled (Panels)
2Ch 3: 5 He **p** the main hall with pine and
Hag 1: 4 to be living in your **p** houses,

Panelling (Panels)
1Ki 6:15 **p** them from the floor of the temple
Ps 74: 6 They smashed all the carved **p** with

Panels (Panelled, Panelling)
1Ki 7:28 They had side **p** attached to uprights.
7:29 On the **p** between the uprights were
7:31 The **p** of the stands were square, not
7:32 The four wheels were under the **p**,
7:35 The supports and **p** were attached to
7:36 of the supports and on the **p**,
2Ki 16:17 King Ahaz took away the side **p** and
SS 8: 9 we will enclose her with **p** of cedar.
Jer 22:14 **p** it with cedar and decorates it in

Pangs
Isa 21: 3 **p** seize me, like those of a woman in
Jer 22:23 how you will groan when **p** come upon

Panic
Dt 20: 3 or give way to **p** before them.
1Sa 5: 9 city, throwing it into a great **p**.
5:11 death had filled the city with **p**;
7:10 threw them into such a **p** that they
14:15 **p** struck the whole army—those in
14:15 It was a **p** sent by God.
Isa 31: 9 standard their commanders will **p**,"
Jer 49:24 to flee and **p** has gripped her;
Eze 7: 7 is **p**, not joy, upon the mountains.
Zec 12: 4 strike every horse with **p** and its
14:13 stricken by the LORD with great **p**.

Pans (Pan)
2Ch 35:13 cauldrons and **p** and served them
Ezr 1: 9 30 silver dishes 1,000 silver **p**

Pant (Pants)
Job 5: 5 and the thirsty **p** after his wealth.
Ps 119:131 I open my mouth and **p**, longing for
Isa 42:14 childbirth, I cry out, I gasp and **p**.
Jer 14: 6 barren heights and **p** like jackals;
Joel 1:20 Even the wild animals **p** for you;

Pants (Pant)
Ps 42: 1 the deer **p** for streams of water, so
42: 1 water, so my soul **p** for you, O God.

Paper
2Jn :12 but I do not want to use **p** and ink.

Paphos
Port on south-western coast of Cyprus. Paul and Barnabas visited here, and its governor was converted (Ac 13:6–13). From here they sailed to Perga in Pamphylia (Ac 13:6–13).

Ac 13: 6 whole island until they came to **P**.
13:13 From **P**, Paul and his companions

Papyrus
Ex 2: 3 she got a **p** basket for him and
Job 8:11 Can **p** grow tall where there is no

Job 9:26 They skim past like boats of **p**, like
Isa 18: 2 which sends envoys by sea in **p** boats
35: 7 grass and reeds and **p** will grow.

Parable (Parables)

Eze 17: 2 and tell the house of Israel a **p**.
24: 3 Tell this rebellious house a **p** and
Mt 13:18 "Listen then to what the **p** of the
13:24 Jesus told them another **p**: "The
13:31 He told them another **p**: "The kingdom
13:33 He told them still another **p**: "The
13:34 anything to them without using a **p**.
13:36 us the **p** of the weeds in the field."
15:15 Peter said, "Explain the **p** to us."
21:33 "Listen to another **p**: There was a
Mk 4:13 "Don't you understand this **p**?
4:13 How then will you understand any **p**?
4:30 what **p** shall we use to describe it?
4:34 anything to them without using a **p**.
7:17 disciples asked him about this **p**.
12:12 he had spoken the **p** against them.
Lk 5:36 He told them this **p**: "No-one tears a
6:39 He also told them this **p**: "Can a
8: 4 town after town, he told this **p**:
8: 9 His disciples asked him what this **p**
8:11 "This is the meaning of the **p**: The
12:16 he told them this **p**: "The ground of
12:41 "Lord, are you telling this **p** to us
13: 6 he told this **p**: "A man had a
14: 7 at the table, he told them this **p**:
15: 3 Jesus told them this **p**:
18: 1 Jesus told his disciples a **p** to show
18: 9 everybody else, Jesus told this **p**:
19:11 he went on to tell them a **p**, because
20: 9 He went on to tell the people this **p**:
20:19 he had spoken this **p** against them.
21:29 He told them this **p**: "Look at the

Parables (Parable)

Ps 78: 2 I will open my mouth in **p**, I will
Pr 1: 6 for understanding proverbs and **p**,
Eze 20:49 of me, 'Isn't he just telling **p**?'
Hos 12:10 visions and told **p** through them."
Mt 13: 3 he told them many things in **p**,
13:10 Why do you speak to the people in **p**?"
13:13 This is why I speak to them in **p**:
13:34 all these things to the crowd in **p**;
13:35 "I will open my mouth in **p**, I will
13:53 Jesus had finished these **p**, he moved
21:45 and the Pharisees heard Jesus' **p**,
22: 1 Jesus spoke to them again in **p**,
Mk 3:23 called them and spoke to them in **p**:
4: 2 He taught them many things by **p**, and
4:10 around him asked him about the **p**.
4:11 the outside everything is said in **p**
4:33 With many similar **p** Jesus spoke the
12: 1 He then began to speak to them in **p**:
Lk 8:10 to others I speak in **p**, so that,

Parade

Isa 3: 9 they **p** their sin like Sodom; they do

Paradise

Lk 23:43 today you will be with me in **p**."
2Co 12: 4 was caught up to **p**. He heard
Rev 2: 7 of life, which is in the **p** of God.

Parah

Jos 18:23 Avvim, **P**, Ophrah,

Parallel

Ex 26:17 with two projections set **p** to each
36:22 with two projections set **p** to each
Eze 42: 7 There was an outer wall **p** to the
42:12 was **p** to the corresponding wall
45: 7 **p** to one of the tribal portions.

Paralysed (Paralytic, Paralytics)

Hab 1: 4 Therefore the law is **p**, and justice
Mt 4:24 and the **p**, and he healed them.
8: 6 home **p** and in terrible suffering."
Mk 2: 4 the mat the **p** man was lying on.
Lk 5:24 He said to the **p** man, "I tell you,
Jn 5: 3 to lie—the blind, the lame, the **p**.

Paralytic (Paralysed)

Mt 9: 2 Some men brought to him a **p**, lying
9: 2 he said to the **p**, "Take heart, son;
9: 6 Then he said to the **p**, "Get up,
Mk 2: 3 Some men came, bringing to him a **p**,
2: 5 said to the **p**, "Son, your sins are
2: 9 Which is easier: to say to the **p**,
2:10 He said to the **p**,
Lk 5:18 Some men came carrying a **p** on a mat
Ac 9:33 a **p** who had been bedridden for eight

Paralytics (Paralysed)

Ac 8: 7 and many **p** and cripples were healed.

Paran

1. Wilderness region in Sinai Peninsula, known also as El-Paran (Ge 14:6). Here Hagar fled with Ishmael (Ge 21:21) and the Israelites stayed after leaving Egypt (Nu 10:12; 12:16). From here the spies were sent into Canaan (Nu 13:3, 26). **2.** Mountain in Seir (Edom), associated with God coming to help his people (Dt 33:2; Hab 3:3). Hadad passed through here on his way to Egypt (1Ki 11:18).

Ge 21:21 he was living in the Desert of **P**,
Nu 10:12 came to rest in the Desert of **P**.
12:16 and encamped in the Desert of **P**.
13: 3 sent them out from the Desert of **P**.
13:26 at Kadesh in the Desert of **P**.
Dt 1: 1 between **P** and Tophel, Laban,
33: 2 he shone forth from Mount **P**.
1Ki 11:18 set out from Midian and went to **P**.
11:18 Then taking men from **P** with them,
Hab 3: 3 Teman, the Holy One from Mount **P**.

Parapet

Dt 22: 8 you build a new house, make a **p**
Eze 40:13 one **p** opening to the opposite one.
40:16 by narrow **p** openings all round,

Parcel (Parcelled)

Ps 60: 6 "In triumph I will **p** out Shechem and
108: 7 "In triumph I will **p** out Shechem and

Parcelled (Parcel)

Da 11: 4 his empire will be broken up and **p**

Parched

Job 14:11 or a river bed becomes **p** and dry,
30: 3 they roamed the **p** land in desolate
Ps 69: 3 calling for help; my throat is **p**.
107:35 the **p** ground into flowing springs;
143: 6 soul thirsts for you like a **p** land.
Isa 5:13 their masses will be **p** with thirst.
19: 5 and the river bed will be **p** and dry.
19: 7 field along the Nile will become **p**,
35: 1 The desert and the **p** land will be
41:17 their tongues are **p** with thirst.
41:18 and the **p** ground into springs.
Jer 12: 4 How long will the land lie **p** and the
12:11 will be made a wasteland, **p** and
17: 6 He will dwell in the **p** places of the
23:10 of the curse the land lies **p**
48:18 your glory and sit on the **p** ground,
Hos 2: 3 turn her into a **p** land, and slay
Joel 2:20 pushing it into a **p** and barren land,

Parchments

2Ti 4:13 and my scrolls, especially the **p**.

Pardon (Pardoned, Pardons)

2Ch 30:18 May the LORD, who is good, **p**
Job 7:21 Why do you not **p** my offences and
Isa 55: 7 to our God, for he will freely **p**.
Joel 3:21 which I have not pardoned, I will **p**.

Pardoned (Pardon)

Nu 14:19 just as you have **p** them from the
Joel 3:21 Their bloodguilt, which I have not **p**,

Pardons (Pardon)

Mic 7:18 Who is a God like you, who **p** sin and

Parents (Grandparents)

Dt 22:17 Then her **p** shall display the cloth
Jdg 14: 4 (His **p** did not know that this was
14: 9 When he rejoined his **p**, he gave them
Pr 17: 6 **p** are the pride of their children.
19:14 and wealth are inherited from **p**,
Zec 13: 3 prophesies, his own **p** will stab him.
Mt 10:21 children will rebel against their **p**
Mk 13:12 Children will rebel against their **p**
Lk 2:27 When the **p** brought in the child
2:41 Every year his **p** went to Jerusalem
2:43 while his **p** were returning home,
2:48 his **p** saw him, they were astonished.
8:56 Her **p** were astonished, but he
18:29 left home or wife or brothers or **p**
21:16 You will be betrayed even by **p**,
Jn 9: 2 who sinned, this man or his **p**,
9: 3 "Neither this man nor his **p** sinned,"
9:18 until they sent for the man's **p**.
9:20 he is our son," the **p** answered,
9:22 His **p** said this because they were
9:23 That was why his **p** said, "He is of
Ro 1:30 of doing evil; they disobey their **p**;
2Co 12:14 their **p**, but **p** for their children.
Eph 6: 1 Children, obey your **p** in the Lord,
Col 3:20 Children, obey your **p** in everything,
1Ti 5: 4 repaying their **p** and grandparents,
2Ti 3: 2 to their **p**, ungrateful, unholy,
Heb 11:23 By faith Moses' **p** hid him for three

Parks

Ecc 2: 5 I made gardens and **p** and planted all

Parmashta

Est 9: 9 **P**, Arisai, Aridai and Vaizatha,

Parmenas

Ac 6: 5 Procorus, Nicanor, Timon, **P**, and

Parnach

Nu 34:25 Elizaphan son of **P**, the leader from

Parosh

Ezr 2: 3 the descendants of **P** 2,172
8: 3 of the descendants of **P**, Zechariah,
10:25 From the descendants of **P**: Ramiah,
Ne 3:25 Next to him, Pedaiah son of **P**
7: 8 the descendants of **P** 2,172
10:14 The leaders of the people: **P**,

Parshandatha

Est 9: 7 They also killed **P**, Dalphon, Aspatha,

Parsin

Da 5:25 MENE, MENE, TEKEL, **P**

Part (Parted, Parting, Parts)

Ge 13: 9 land before you? Let's **p** company.
19: 4 all the men from every **p** of the city
27:16 **p** of his neck with the goatskins.
47: 6 brothers in the best **p** of the land.
47:11 property in the best **p** of the land,
Ex 12:48 take **p** like one born in the land.
16:20 they kept **p** of it until morning,
35:24 for any **p** of the work brought it.
Lev 2: 3 it is a most holy **p** of the offerings
2:10 it is a most holy **p** of the offerings
7:29 **p** of it as his sacrifice to the LORD.
13:45 cover the lower **p** of his face and
13:56 he is to tear the contaminated **p** out
24: 9 because it is a most holy **p** of their
27:16 to the LORD **p** of his family land,
27:22 which is not **p** of his family land,
Nu 8:24 come to take **p** in the work at the
18: 9 You are to have the **p** of the most
18: 9 that **p** belongs to you and your sons.
18:29 **p** of everything given to you.'
18:30 'When you present the best **p**, it
18:32 By presenting the best **p** of it you
22:41 from there he saw **p** of the people.
23:10 or number the fourth **p** of Israel?
23:13 see only a **p** but not all of them.
31:27 soldiers who took **p** in the battle

Nu 31:29 Eleazar the priest as the LORD's **p**.
31:41 Eleazar the priest as the LORD's **p**,
36: 3 And so **p** of the inheritance allotted
Dt 2: 9 not give you any **p** of their land.
23:13 **p** of your equipment have something
Jos 2:15 she lived in was **p** of the city wall.
1Sa 30:12 **p** of a cake of pressed figs and two
2Sa 3:37 **p** in the murder of Abner son of Ner.
4: 2 is considered **p** of Benjamin,
4: 6 They went into the inner **p** of the
20: 1 "We have no share in David, no **p** in
21: 2 (Now the Gibeonites were not a **p** of
23: 5 arranged and secured in every **p**?
1Ki 7: 5 in the front **p** in sets of three,
7:20 above the bowl-shaped **p** next to the
8:64 the middle **p** of the courtyard in
12:16 in David, what **p** in Jesse's son?
1Ch 6:62 and from the **p** of the tribe of
21:12 the LORD ravaging every **p** of Israel.
23:14 counted as **p** of the tribe of Levi.
2Ch 7: 7 Solomon consecrated the middle **p** of
10:16 in David, what **p** in Jesse's son?
25:13 had not allowed to take **p** in the war
Ezr 4: 3 "You have no **p** with us in building a
Ne 5:11 them—the hundredth **p** of the money,
Est 2:14 in the morning return to another **p**
Job 42:12 blessed the latter **p** of Job's life
Ps 141: 4 to take **p** in wicked deeds with men
144: 5 **P** your heavens, O LORD, and come
Ecc 9: 6 never again will they have a **p** in
Jer 41: 9 made as **p** of his defence against
Eze 24:17 do not cover the lower **p** of your
24:22 You will not cover the lower **p** of
43:21 burn it in the designated **p** of the
48: 1 will be **p** of its border from the
Da 6:26 "I issue a decree that in every **p** of
8:23 "In the latter **p** of their reign,
Zec 14:18 and take **p**, they will have no rain.
Mt 5:29 It is better for you to lose one **p**
5:30 It is better for you to lose one **p**
23:30 we would not have taken **p** with them
Lk 11:36 and no **p** of it dark, it will be
20:35 worthy of taking **p** in that age
Jn 13: 8 I wash you, you have no **p** with me."
18:40 Barabbas had taken **p** in a rebellion.
Ac 5: 2 back **p** of the money for himself,
8:21 You have no **p** or share in this
Ro 11:16 If the **p** of the dough offered as
11:25 a hardening in **p** until the full
1Co 10:21 have a **p** in both the Lord's table
10:30 If I take **p** in the meal with
12:14 Now the body is not made up of one **p**
12:15 reason cease to be **p** of the body.
12:16 reason cease to be **p** of the body.
12:19 If they were all one **p**, where would
12:26 If one **p** suffers, every **p** suffers
12:26 if one **p** is honoured, every **p**
12:27 and each one of you is a **p** of it.
13: 9 For we know in **p** and we prophesy in **p**
13:12 Now I know in **p**; then I shall know
2Co 1:14 you have understood us in **p**, you
8: 6 this act of grace on your **p**.
Eph 4:16 up in love, as each **p** does its work.
Heb 9:11 is to say, not a **p** of this creation.
Jas 3: 5 Likewise the tongue is a small **p** of
Rev 13:10 faithfulness on the **p** of the saints.
14:12 endurance on the **p** of the saints
20: 6 have **p** in the first resurrection.

Partake
1Co 10:17 body, for we all **p** of the one loaf.

Parted (Part)
Ge 13:11 The two men **p** company:
13:14 to Abram after Lot had **p** from him,
2Sa 1:23 and in death they were not **p**.
22:10 He **p** the heavens and came down;
Job 41:17 they cling together and cannot be **p**.
Ps 18: 9 He **p** the heavens and came down;
Ac 15:39 disagreement that they **p** company.

Parthians
Ac 2: 9 **P**, Medes and Elamites; residents of

Partial (Partiality)
Pr 18: 5 is not good to be **p** to the wicked or

Partiality (Partial)
Lev 19:15 do not show **p** to the poor or
Dt 1:17 Do not show **p** in judging; hear both
10:17 shows no **p** and accepts no bribes.
16:19 Do not pervert justice or show **p**.
2Ch 19: 7 is no injustice or **p** or bribery."
Job 13: 8 Will you show him **p**? Will you argue
13:10 rebuke you if you secretly showed **p**.
32:21 I will show **p** to no-one, nor will I
34:19 who shows no **p** to princes and does
Ps 82: 2 and show **p** to the wicked?
Pr 24:23 To show **p** in judging is not good:
28:21 To show **p** is not good—yet a man
Mal 2: 9 have shown **p** in matters of the law."
Lk 20:21 and that you do not show **p** but teach
1Ti 5:21 keep these instructions without **p**,

Participants (Participate)
1Co 10:20 do not want you to be **p** with demons.

Participate (Participants, Participation)
Eze 45:16 All the people of the land will **p** in
1Co 10:18 eat the sacrifices **p** in the altar?
1Pe 4:13 rejoice that you **p** in the sufferings
2Pe 1: 4 so that through them you may **p** in

Participation (Participate)
1Co 10:16 thanks a **p** in the blood of Christ?
10:16 we break a **p** in the body of Christ?

Parties (Party)
Ex 18:16 and I decide between the **p** and
22: 9 'This is mine,' both **p** are to bring
1Sa 13:17 Raiding **p** went out from the
14:15 those in the outposts and raiding **p**
Job 1:17 The Chaldeans formed three raiding **p**

Parting (Part)
Mic 1:14 Therefore you will give **p** gifts to

Partitioned
1Ki 6:16 He **p** off twenty cubits at the rear

Partner (Partners, Partnership)
Pr 2:17 who has left the **p** of her youth and
28:24 he is **p** to him who destroys.
Mal 2:14 though she is your **p**, the wife of
2Co 8:23 for Titus, he is my **p** and
Phm :17 if you consider me a **p**, welcome him
1Pe 3: 7 them with respect as the weaker **p**

Partners (Partner)
Lk 5: 7 they signalled to their **p** in the
5:10 John, the sons of Zebedee, Simon's **p**.
Eph 5: 7 Therefore do not be **p** with them.

Partnership (Partner)
Php 1: 5 of your **p** in the gospel from the

Partridge
1Sa 26:20 one hunts a **p** in the mountains."
Jer 17:11 Like a **p** that hatches eggs it did

Parts (Part)
Ex 12: 9 the fire—head, legs and inner **p**.
29:13 take all the fat around the inner **p**,
29:17 and wash the inner **p** and the legs,
29:22 the fat around the inner **p**, the
29:27 "Consecrate those **p** of the
Lev 1: 9 He is to wash the inner **p** and the
1:13 He is to wash the inner **p** and the
3: 3 the inner **p** or is connected to them,
3: 9 the inner **p** or is connected to them,
3:14 the inner **p** or is connected to them,
4: 8 the inner **p** or is connected to them,
4:11 and legs, the inner **p** and offal—
7: 3 and the fat that covers the inner **p**,
8:16 took all the fat around the inner **p**,
Lev 8:21 He washed the inner **p** and the legs
8:25 all the fat around the inner **p**, the
9:14 He washed the inner **p** and the legs
Dt 18: 3 shoulder, the jowls and the inner **p**.
19: 3 divide into three **p** the land the
25:11 out and seizes him by his private **p**,
Jos 18: 5 are to divide the land into seven **p**.
18: 6 of the seven **p** of the land,
18: 9 town by town, in seven **p**, and
Jdg 19:29 limb by limb, into twelve **p** and sent
1Sa 2:29 the choice **p** of every offering made
2Ki 19:23 I have reached its remotest **p**,
1Ch 28:11 its storerooms, its upper **p**, its
2Ch 3: 9 also overlaid the upper **p** with gold.
Est 1:22 He sent dispatches to all **p** of the
Job 18:13 It eats away **p** of his skin;
Ps 51: 6 you desire truth in the inner **p**;
Pr 18: 8 they go down to a man's inmost **p**.
26:22 they go down to a man's inmost **p**.
Da 4:22 extends to distant **p** of the earth.
Ac 2:10 Egypt and the **p** of Libya near Cyrene;
Ro 6:13 Do not offer the **p** of your body to
6:13 and offer the **p** of your body to him
6:19 Just as you used to offer the **p** of
1Co 12:12 though it is made up of many **p**;
12:12 its **p** are many, they form one body.
12:18 in fact God has arranged the **p** in
12:20 is, there are many **p**, but one body.
12:22 On the contrary, those **p** of the body
12:23 the **p** that we think are less
12:23 And the **p** that are unpresentable are
12:24 while our presentable **p** need no
12:24 honour to the **p** that lacked it,
12:25 but that its **p** should have equal
Jas 3: 6 of evil among the **p** of the body.
Rev 16:19 The great city split into three **p**,

Party (Parties)
Ru 4: 7 one **p** took off his sandal and gave
1Sa 30: 8 "Shall I pursue this raiding **p**?
30:15 you lead me down to this raiding **p**?"
Pr 19:18 do not be a willing **p** to his death.
Ac 5:17 who were members of the **p** of the
15: 5 **p** of the Pharisees stood up and said,
2Co 7:12 did the wrong or of the injured **p**,
Gal 3:20 does not represent just one **p**;

Paruah
1Ki 4:17 Jehoshaphat son of **P**—in Issachar;

Parvaim
2Ch 3: 6 And the gold he used was gold of **P**.

Pas Dammim
2Sa 23: 9 Philistines gathered at **P** for battle.
1Ch 11:13 He was with David at **P** when the

Pasach
1Ch 7:33 The sons of Japhlet: **P**, Bimhal and

Paseah
1Ch 4:12 **P** and Tehinnah the father of Ir
Ezr 2:49 Uzza, **P**, Besai,
Ne 3: 6 repaired by Joiada son of **P** and
7:51 Gazzam, Uzza, **P**,

Pashhur
1Ch 9:12 Adaiah son of Jeroham, the son of **P**,
Ezr 2:38 of **P** 1,247
10:22 From the descendants of **P**: Elioenai,
Ne 7:41 of **P** 1,247
10: 3 **P**, Amariah, Malkijah,
11:12 the son of **P**, the son of Malkijah,
Jer 20: 1 the priest **P** son of Immer, the chief
20: 3 The next day, when **P** released him
20: 3 you is not **P**, but Magor-Missabib.
20: 6 you, **P**, and all who live in your
21: 1 sent to him **P** son of Malkijah
38: 1 Gedaliah son of **P**, Jehucal son of
38: 1 and **P** son of Malkijah heard what

Pass[1] (Passed, Passer-by, Passes, Passing)

Ge 18: 3 my lord, do not **p** your servant by.
Ex 12:12 "On that same night I will **p** through
12:13 I see the blood, I will **p** over you.
12:23 and will **p** over that doorway,
15:16 as a stone—until your people **p** by,
15:16 until the people you bought **p** by.
33:19 "I will cause all my goodness to **p**
Lev 26: 6 will not **p** through your country.
Nu 20:17 Please let us **p** through your country.
20:18 Edom answered: "You may not **p**
20:19 to **p** through on foot—nothing else."
20:20 Again they answered: "You may not **p**
21:22 "Let us **p** through your country.
21:23 Sihon would not let Israel **p** through
36: 7 No inheritance in Israel is to **p**
36: 9 No inheritance may **p** from tribe to
Dt 2: 4 'You are about to **p** through the
2:18 "Today you are to **p** by the region of
2:27 "Let us **p** through your country.
2:28 Only let us **p** through on foot—
2:30 Heshbon refused to let us **p** through.
Jos 3: 6 and **p** on ahead of the people.
Jdg 11:19 'Let us **p** through your country to
11:20 Israel to **p** through his territory.
1Sa 16: 8 and made him **p** in front of Samuel.
16: 9 Jesse then made Shammah **p** by, but
16:10 made seven of his sons **p** before
1Ki 9: 8 all who **p** by will be appalled and
19:11 LORD, for the LORD is about to **p** by.
2Ki 19:25 now I have brought it to **p**,
1Ch 28: 8 **p** it on as an inheritance to your
2Ch 7:21 all who **p** by will be appalled and
Job 16:22 "Only a few years will **p** before I go
19: 8 blocked my way so that I cannot **p**;
34:20 people are shaken and they **p** away;
41:16 the next that no air can **p** between.
Ps 80:12 that all who **p** by pick its grapes?
84: 6 they **p** through the Valley of Baca,
89:41 All who **p** by have plundered him;
90: 9 All our days **p** away under your wrath;
90:10 for they quickly **p**, and we fly away.
105:19 till what he foretold came to **p**,
129: 8 May those who **p** by not say, "The
141:10 own nets, while I **p** by in safety.
148: 6 a decree that will never **p** away.
Pr 9:15 calling out to those who **p** by, who
Isa 10:28 enter Aiath; they **p** through Migron;
31: 5 '**p** over' it and will rescue it."
34:10 no-one will ever **p** through it again.
37:26 now I have brought it to **p**,
43: 2 you **p** through the waters, I will be
43: 2 and when you **p** through the rivers,
48: 3 I acted, and they came to **p**.
62:10 **P** through, **p** through the gates!
Jer 2:35 But I will **p** judgment on you
6: 9 **p** your hand over the branches again,
18:16 all who **p** by will be appalled and
19: 8 all who **p** by will be appalled and
22: 8 "People from many nations will **p** by
33:13 flocks will again **p** under the hand
49:17 all who **p** by will be appalled and
50:13 All who **p** Babylon will be horrified
Lam 1:12 nothing to you, all you who **p** by?
2:15 All who **p** your way clap their hands
Eze 5:14 you, in the sight of all who **p** by.
14:15 **p** through it because of the beasts,
14:17 'Let the sword **p** throughout the land,
20:37 I will take note of you as you **p**
29:11 No foot of man or animal will **p**
36:34 the sight of all who **p** through it.
48:14 and must not **p** into other hands,
Da 4:16 till seven times **p** by for him.
4:23 until seven times **p** by for him.'
4:25 Seven times will **p** by for you until
4:32 Seven times will **p** by for you until
7:14 dominion that will not **p** away,
Am 5:17 **p** through your midst," says the LORD.
Mic 1:11 **P** on in nakedness and shame, you who
2: 8 from those who **p** by without a care,
2:13 Their king will **p** through before
Na 1:12 they will be cut off and **p** away.
Zep 2:15 **p** by her scoff and shake their fists.
Zec 10:11 They will **p** through the sea of
Zec 10:11 and Egypt's sceptre will **p** away.
Mt 8:28 that no-one could **p** that way.
24:34 certainly not **p** away until all
24:35 Heaven and earth will **p** away, but my
24:35 but my words will never **p** away.
Mk 6:48 He was about to **p** by them,
13:30 certainly not **p** away until all
13:31 Heaven and earth will **p** away, but my
13:31 but my words will never **p** away.
14:35 possible the hour might **p** from him.
Lk 21:32 certainly not **p** away until all
21:33 Heaven and earth will **p** away, but my
21:33 but my words will never **p** away.
Jn 8:15 I **p** judgment on no-one.
Ac 7:38 received living words to **p** on to us.
Ro 2: 1 have no excuse, you who **p** judgment
2: 1 who **p** judgment do the same things.
2: 3 when you, a mere man, **p** judgment on
1Co 13: 8 there is knowledge, it will **p** away.
Jas 1:10 he will **p** away like a wild flower.
1Jn 2:17 The world and its desires **p** away,

Pass[2]

Nu 34: 4 cross south of Scorpion **P**, continue
Jos 15: 3 crossed south of Scorpion **P**,
15: 7 the **P** of Adummim south of the gorge.
18:17 which faces the **P** of Adummim, and
Jdg 1:36 from Scorpion **P** to Sela and beyond.
8:13 from the battle by the **P** of Heres.
1Sa 13:23 had gone out to the **p** at Michmash.
14: 4 On each side of the **p** that Jonathan
2Ch 20:16 will be climbing up by the **P** of Ziz
Isa 10:29 They go over the **p**, and say, "We

Passage (Passageway)

Ac 8:32 The eunuch was reading this **p** of
8:35 Philip began with that very **p** of
Ro 11: 2 Scripture says in the **p** about Elijah
Heb 4: 5 again in the **p** above he says, "They

Passageway (Passage)

Eze 42: 4 In front of the rooms was an inner **p**
42:11 with a **p** in front of them.
42:12 doorway at the beginning of the **p**

Passed (Pass[1])

Ge 15:17 appeared and **p** between the pieces.
32:31 The sun rose above him as he **p**
41: 1 two full years had **p**, Pharaoh had a
50: 4 the days of mourning had **p**, Joseph
Ex 7:25 Seven days **p** after the LORD struck
12:27 who **p** over the houses of the
33:22 you with my hand until I have **p** by.
34: 6 he **p** in front of Moses, proclaiming,
Lev 25:30 redeemed before a full year has **p**,
Nu 14: 7 "The land we **p** through and explored
20:17 we have **p** through your territory."
21:22 we have **p** through your territory."
33: 8 They left Pi Hahiroth and **p** through
Dt 2:14 Thirty-eight years **p** from the time
29:16 how we **p** through the countries on
Jos 3:17 while all Israel **p** by until the
15: 4 then **p** along to Azmon and joined the
15:11 **p** along to Mount Baalah and reached
18:12 **p** the northern slope of Jericho and
23: 1 After a long time had **p** and the LORD
Jdg 3:26 **p** by the idols and escaped to Seirah.
9:25 to ambush and rob everyone who **p** by,
11:18 **p** along the eastern side of the
11:29 **p** through Mizpah of Gilead, and
1Sa 9: 4 he **p** through the hill country of
9: 4 Then he **p** through the territory of
2Sa 15:23 wept aloud as all the people **p** by.
20:14 Sheba **p** through all the tribes of
1Ki 13:25 Some people who **p** by saw the body
18:29 Midday **p**, and they continued their
20:39 the king **p** by, the prophet called
2Ch 21:20 He **p** away, to no-one's regret, and
Ne 9:11 so that they **p** through it on dry
12:37 **p** above the house of David to the
Est 4:11 But thirty days have **p** since I was
Job 14:13 conceal me till your anger has **p**!
15:19 given when no alien **p** among them):
17:11 My days have **p**, my plans are
Ps 37:36 he soon **p** away and was no more;
57: 1 your wings until the disaster has **p**.
66: 6 they **p** through the waters on foot—
SS 3: 4 Scarcely had I **p** them when I found
Isa 26:20 while until his wrath has **p** by.
Lam 4:21 But to you also the cup will be **p**;
Eze 16: 6 "'Then I **p** by and saw you kicking
16: 8 "'Later I **p** by, and when I looked
16:15 who **p** by and your beauty became his.
16:25 promiscuity to anyone who **p** by.
Da 2:28 Your dream and the visions that **p**
4: 5 that **p** through my mind terrified me.
7: 1 and visions **p** through his mind as
7:15 that **p** through my mind disturbed me.
Mt 27:39 Those who **p** by hurled insults at him,
Mk 9:30 They left that place and **p** through
15:29 Those who **p** by hurled insults at him,
Lk 10:31 the man, he **p** by on the other side.
10:32 and saw him, **p** by on the other side.
Ac 5:15 fall on some of them as he **p** by.
7:30 "After forty years had **p**, an angel
12:10 They **p** the first and second guards
16: 8 they **p** by Mysia and went down to
17: 1 they had **p** through Amphipolis and
24:27 two years had **p**, Felix was succeeded
27: 4 **p** to the lee of Cyprus because the
27:16 we **p** to the lee of a small island
27:17 they **p** ropes under the ship itself
1Co 5: 3 And I have already **p** judgment on the
10: 1 and that they all **p** through the sea.
11: 2 just as I **p** them on to you.
11:23 I also **p** on to you: The Lord Jesus,
15: 3 For what I received I **p** on to you as
2Th 2:15 to the teachings we **p** on to you,
Heb 11:29 By faith the people **p** through the
2Pe 2:21 command that was **p** on to them.
1Jn 3:14 We know that we have **p** from death to
Rev 11:14 The second woe has **p**; the third woe
21: 1 and the first earth had **p** away,
21: 4 the old order of things has **p** away."

Passer-by (Pass[1])

Pr 26:10 is he who hires a fool or any **p**.
26:17 is a **p** who meddles in a quarrel not

Passes (Pass[1])

Ex 33:22 my glory **p** by, I will put you in a
Lev 27:32 —every tenth animal that **p** under
Job 9:11 he **p** me, I cannot see him; when he
Ecc 6:12 days he **p** through like a shadow?
Jer 17:16 What **p** my lips is open before you.

Passing (Pass[1])

Jos 16: 6 **p** by it to Janoah on the east.
19:27 Emek and Neiel, **p** Cabul on the left.
19:33 **p** Adami Nekeb and Jabneel to Lakkum
2Ki 6: 9 "Beware of **p** that place, because the
6:26 the king of Israel was **p** by on the
Ps 78:39 a **p** breeze that does not return.
Isa 8: 8 swirling over it, **p** through it and
Zep 3: 6 deserted, with no-one **p** through.
Mk 15:21 was **p** by on his way in from the
Lk 18:37 him, "Jesus of Nazareth is **p** by.
19: 1 Jesus entered Jericho and was **p**
Jn 1:36 he saw Jesus **p** by, he said, "Look,
Ac 19:21 **p** through Macedonia and Achaia.
21: 3 After sighting Cyprus and **p** to the
Ro 14: 1 **p** judgment on disputable matters.
14:13 Therefore let us stop **p** judgment on
15:24 I hope to visit you while **p** through
1Co 7:31 world in its present form is **p** away.
16: 7 see you now and make only a **p** visit;
1Jn 2: 8 because the darkness is **p** and the

Passion (Passionate, Passions)

Hos 7: 6 Their **p** smoulders all night; in the
1Co 7: 9 better to marry than to burn with **p**.

Passionate (Passion)

1Th 4: 5 not in **p** lust like the heathen, who

Passions (Passion)

Ro 7: 5 the sinful **p** aroused by the law were
Gal 5:24 nature with its **p** and desires.

Tit 2:12 "No" to ungodliness and worldly **p**,
3: 3 by all kinds of **p** and pleasures.

Passover (*Passover feast*)
Ex 12:11 Eat it in haste; it is the LORD's **P**.
12:21 families and slaughter the **P** lamb.
12:27 tell them, 'It is the **P** sacrifice to
12:43 These are the regulations for the **P**:
12:48 who wants to celebrate the LORD's **P**
Lev 23: 5 The LORD's **P** begins at twilight on
Nu 9: 2 "Make the Israelites celebrate the **P**
9: 4 the Israelites to celebrate the **P**,
9: 6 could not celebrate the **P** on that day
9:10 may still celebrate the LORD's **P**.
9:12 When they celebrate the **P**, they must
9:13 a journey fails to celebrate the **P**,
9:14 who wants to celebrate the LORD's **P**
28:16 month the LORD's **P** is to be held.
33: 3 first month, the day after the **P**.
Dt 16: 1 the **P** of the LORD your God,
16: 2 Sacrifice as the **P** to the LORD your
16: 5 You must not sacrifice the **P** in any
16: 6 There you must sacrifice the **P** in
Jos 5:10 the Israelites celebrated the **P**.
5:11 The day after the **P**, that very day,
2Ki 23:21 "Celebrate the **P** to the LORD your
23:22 Judah, had any such **P** been observed.
23:23 this **P** was celebrated to the LORD in
2Ch 30: 1 **P** to the LORD, the God of Israel.
30: 2 celebrate the **P** in the second month.
30: 5 **P** to the LORD, the God of Israel.
30:15 They slaughtered the **P** lamb on the
30:17 the Levites had to kill the **P** lambs
30:18 yet they ate the **P**, contrary to
35: 1 Josiah celebrated the **P** to the LORD
35: 1 and the **P** lamb was slaughtered on
35: 6 Slaughter the **P** lambs, consecrate
35: 7 sheep and goats for the **P** offerings,
35: 8 **P** offerings and three hundred cattle.
35: 9 provided five thousand **P** offerings
35:11 The **P** lambs were slaughtered, and
35:13 They roasted the **P** animals over the
35:16 out for the celebration of the **P**
35:17 celebrated the **P** at that time
35:18 The **P** had not been observed like
35:18 celebrated such a **P** as did Josiah,
35:19 This **P** was celebrated in the
Ezr 6:19 month, the exiles celebrated the **P**.
6:20 The Levites slaughtered the **P** lamb
Eze 45:21 day you are to observe the **P**,
Mt 26: 2 "As you know, the **P** is two days away
26:17 preparations for you to eat the **P**?"
26:18 I am going to celebrate the **P** with
26:19 directed them and prepared the **P**.
Mk 14: 1 Now the **P** and the Feast of
14:12 customary to sacrifice the **P** lamb,
14:12 preparations for you to eat the **P**?"
14:14 I may eat the **P** with my disciples?'
14:16 So they prepared the **P**.
Lk 2:41 to Jerusalem for the Feast of the **P**.
22: 1 Bread, called the **P**, was approaching,
22: 7 the **P** lamb had to be sacrificed.
22: 8 preparations for us to eat the **P**."
22:11 I may eat the **P** with my disciples?'
22:13 So they prepared the **P**.
22:15 eat this **P** with you before I suffer.
Jn 2:13 was almost time for the Jewish **P**,
11:55 was almost time for the Jewish **P**,
11:55 ceremonial cleansing before the **P**.
12: 1 Six days before the **P**, Jesus arrived
18:28 they wanted to be able to eat the **P**.
18:39 one prisoner at the time of the **P**.
19:14 was the day of Preparation of **P** Week,
Ac 12: 4 out for public trial after the **P**.
1Co 5: 7 our **P** lamb, has been sacrificed.
Heb 11:28 By faith he kept the **P** and the

Passover feast
Ex 34:25 sacrifice from the **P** remain until
Jn 2:23 while he was in Jerusalem at the **P**,
4:45 he had done in Jerusalem at the **P**,
6: 4 The Jewish **P** was near.
13: 1 was just before the **P**. Jesus knew

Past
Ge 18:11 Sarah was **p** the age of childbearing.
31:52 that I will not go **p** this heap to
31:52 that you will not go **p** this heap and
Ex 4:10 neither in the **p** nor since you have
Dt 2: 8 we went on **p** our brothers the
32: 7 consider the generations long **p**.
Jos 13:16 and the whole plateau **p** Medeba
15: 3 Then it ran **p** Hezron up to Addar and
1Sa 15:32 Surely the bitterness of death is **p**."
2Sa 5: 2 In the **p**, while Saul was king over
15:18 All his men marched **p** him, along
15:34 was your father's servant in the **p**,
1Ch 11: 2 In the **p**, even while Saul was king,
Ne 12:38 —**p** the Tower of the Ovens to the
Job 4:15 A spirit glided **p** my face, and the
9:26 They skim **p** like boats of papyrus,
36:26 of his years is **p** finding out.
Pr 24:30 I went **p** the field of the sluggard,
24:30 **p** the vineyard of the man who lacks
Ecc 3:15 and God will call the **p** to account.
SS 2:11 See! The winter is **p**; the rains are
Isa 9: 1 In the **p** he humbled the land of
43:18 do not dwell on the **p**.
43:26 Review the **p** for me, let us argue
45:21 who declared it from the distant **p**?
65:16 For the **p** troubles will be forgotten
Jer 8:20 "The harvest is **p**, the summer has
21: 2 wonders for us as in times **p**
31: 3 The LORD appeared to us in the **p**,
46:26 as in times **p**," declares the LORD.
Eze 36:11 settle people on you as in the **p**
47:15 Hethlon road **p** Lebo Hamath to Zedad,
Hab 1:11 they sweep **p** like the wind and go on
Zec 7: 5 months for the **p** seventy years,
8:11 as I did in the **p**," declares the
Ac 14:16 In the **p**, he let all nations go
17:30 In the **p** God overlooked such
20:16 Paul had decided to sail **p** Ephesus
Ro 15: 4 in the **p** was written to teach us,
16:25 the mystery hidden for long ages **p**,
Eph 3: 9 which for ages **p** was kept hidden in
Heb 1: 1 In the **p** God spoke to our
11:11 even though he was **p** age—and Sarah
1Pe 3: 5 the way the holy women of the **p** who put
4: 3 spent enough time in the **p** doing
2Pe 1: 9 has been cleansed from his **p** sins.
3: 2 in the **p** by the holy prophets
Rev 9:12 The first woe is **p**; two other woes

Pastors
Eph 4:11 and some to be **p** and teachers,

Pasture (Pastured, Pasture-land, Pasture-lands, Pastures)
Ge 29: 7 the sheep and take them back to **p**."
47: 4 and your servants' flocks have no **p**.
2Sa 7: 8 I took you from the **p** and from
1Ch 4:39 in search of **p** for their flocks.
4:40 They found rich, good **p**, and the
4:41 there was **p** for their flocks.
17: 7 I took you from the **p** and from
Job 24: 2 they **p** flocks they have stolen.
39: 8 He ranges the hills for his **p** and
Ps 37: 3 dwell in the land and enjoy safe **p**.
74: 1 against the sheep of your **p**?
79:13 we your people, the sheep of your **p**,
95: 7 and we are the people of his **p**,
100: 3 are his people, the sheep of his **p**.
Isa 5:17 sheep will graze as in their own **p**;
14:30 The poorest of the poor will find **p**,
32:14 delight of donkeys, a **p** for flocks,
49: 9 and find **p** on every barren hill.
65:10 Sharon will become a **p** for flocks,
Jer 14: 6 their eyesight fails for lack of **p**."
23: 1 and scattering the sheep of my **p**!"
23: 3 and will bring them back to their **p**,
25:36 for the LORD is destroying their **p**.
49:20 destroy their **p** because of them.
50: 7 against the LORD, their true **p**,
50:19 I will bring Israel back to his own **p**
50:45 destroy their **p** because of them.
Lam 1: 6 are like deer that find no **p**;
Eze 25: 5 I will turn Rabbah into a **p** for
34:13 I will **p** them on the mountains of
Eze 34:14 I will tend them in a good **p**, and
34:14 a rich **p** on the mountains of Israel.
34:18 for you to feed on the good **p**?
34:18 the rest of your **p** with your feet?
34:31 You my sheep, the sheep of my **p**, are
Hos 4:16 LORD **p** them like lambs in a meadow?
Joel 1:18 mill about because they have no **p**;
Mic 2:12 in a pen, like a flock in its **p**;
Zep 2: 7 of Judah; there they will find **p**.
Zec 11: 4 "**P** the flock marked for slaughter.
Jn 10: 9 will come in and go out, and find **p**.

Pastured (Pasture)
Zec 11: 7 I **p** the flock marked for slaughter,
11: 7 the other Union, and I **p** the flock.

Pasture-fed (Feed)
1Ki 4:23 twenty of **p** cattle and a hundred

Pasture-land (Pasture)
Lev 25:34 the **p** belonging to their towns must
Nu 35: 5 have this area as **p** for the towns.
Jos 21:11 with its surrounding **p**, in the hill
Jer 49:19 from Jordan's thickets to a rich **p**,
50:44 from Jordan's thickets to a rich **p**,
Eze 36: 5 so that they might plunder its **p**.'
48:15 of the city, for houses and for **p**.
48:17 **p** for the city will be 250 cubits

Pasture-lands (Pasture)
Nu 35: 2 And give them **p** around the towns.
35: 3 they will have towns to live in and **p**
35: 4 "The **p** around the towns that you
35: 7 towns, together with their **p**.
Jos 14: 4 with **p** for their flocks and herds.
21: 2 live in, with **p** for our livestock."
21: 3 and **p** out of their own inheritance:
21: 8 the Levites these towns and their **p**,
21:16 together with their **p**—nine towns
21:18 together with their **p**—four towns.
21:19 thirteen, together with their **p**.
21:22 together with their **p**—four towns.
21:24 together with their **p**—four towns.
21:25 together with their **p**—two towns.
21:26 All these ten towns and their **p** were
21:27 together with their **p**—two towns;
21:29 together with their **p**—four towns;
21:31 together with their **p**—four towns;
21:32 together with their **p**—three towns.
21:33 thirteen, together with their **p**.
21:35 together with their **p**—four towns;
21:37 together with their **p**—four towns;
21:39 with their **p**—four towns in all.
21:41 in all, together with their **p**.
21:42 Each of these towns had **p**
1Ch 5:16 **p** of Sharon as far as they extended.
6:55 in Judah with its surrounding **p**.
6:59 Beth Shemesh, together with their **p**.
6:60 and Anathoth, together with their **p**.
6:64 the Levites these towns and their **p**.
6:69 Gath Rimmon, together with their **p**.
6:70 together with their **p**, to the rest
6:71 Ashtaroth, together with their **p**;
6:73 and Anem, together with their **p**;
6:75 and Rehob, together with their **p**;
6:76 Kiriathaim, together with their **p**.
6:77 and Tabor, together with their **p**;
6:79 and Mephaath, together with their **p**;
6:81 and Jazer, together with their **p**.
13: 2 are with them in their towns and **p**,
2Ch 11:14 The Levites even abandoned their **p**
Ps 83:12 us take possession of the **p** of God."
Mic 7:14 by itself in a forest, in fertile **p**.

Pastures (Pasture)
Ps 23: 2 He makes me lie down in green **p**, he
Jer 9:10 up a lament concerning the desert **p**.
23:10 the **p** in the desert are withered.
33:12 **p** for shepherds to rest their flocks.
Eze 45:15 from the well-watered **p** of Israel.
Joel 1:19 for fire has devoured the open **p** and
1:20 up and fire has devoured the open **p**.
2:22 for the open **p** are becoming green.

Am 1: 2 the **p** of the shepherds dry up,
Zec 11: 3 their rich **p** are destroyed! Listen

Patara
Ac 21: 1 went to Rhodes and from there to **P**.

Patch (Patched)
Jer 10: 5 Like a scarecrow in a melon **p**, their
Mt 9:16 "No-one sews a **p** of unshrunk cloth
9:16 for the **p** will pull away from the
Mk 2:21 "No-one sews a **p** of unshrunk cloth
Lk 5:36 "No-one tears a **p** from a new garment
5:36 and the **p** from the new will not

Patched (Patch)
Jos 9: 5 The men put worn and **p** sandals on

Path (Bypaths, Paths)
Ge 49:17 a viper along the **p**, that bites the
Nu 22:24 in a narrow **p** between two vineyards,
22:32 your **p** is a reckless one before me.
2Sa 22:37 You broaden the **p** beneath me, so
Ne 9:19 not cease to guide them on their **p**,
Job 18:10 on the ground; a trap lies in his **p**.
22:15 Will you keep to the old **p** that evil
24: 4 They thrust the needy from the **p** and
28: 7 No bird of prey knows that hidden **p**,
28:26 rain and a **p** for the thunderstorm,
29: 6 my **p** was drenched with cream and the
31: 7 if my steps have turned from the **p**,
38:25 rain, and a **p** for the thunderstorm,
Ps 16:11 You have made known to me the **p** of
18:36 You broaden the **p** beneath me, so
27:11 straight **p** because of my oppressors.
35: 6 may their **p** be dark and slippery,
44:18 feet had not strayed from your **p**.
57: 6 They dug a pit in my **p**—but they
77:19 Your **p** led through the sea, your way
78:50 He prepared a **p** for his anger;
119:32 I run in the **p** of your commands, for
119:35 Direct me in the **p** of your commands,
119:101 I have kept my feet from every evil **p**
119:104 therefore I hate every wrong **p**.
119:105 to my feet and a light for my **p**.
119:128 right, I hate every wrong **p**.
140: 5 have set traps for me along my **p**.
142: 3 In the **p** where I walk men have
Pr 2: 9 and just and fair—every good **p**.
4:14 Do not set foot on the **p** of the
4:18 The **p** of the righteous is like the
5: 8 Keep to a **p** far from her, do not go
12:28 along that **p** is immortality.
15:10 awaits him who leaves the **p**;
15:19 the **p** of the upright is a highway.
15:24 The **p** of life leads upward for the
16:29 leads him down a **p** that is not good.
21:16 A man who strays from the **p** of
23:19 and keep your heart on the right **p**.
28:10 evil **p** will fall into his own trap,
Ecc 11: 5 you do not know the **p** of the wind,
Isa 3:12 they turn you from the **p**.
26: 7 The **p** of the righteous is level;
30:11 Leave this way, get off this **p**, and
40:14 showed him the **p** of understanding?
41: 3 **p** his feet have not travelled before.
43:16 sea, a **p** through the mighty waters,
Jer 23:12 "Therefore their **p** will become
31: 9 level **p** where they will not stumble,
Lam 3:11 he dragged me from the **p** and mangled
Hos 2: 6 Therefore I will block her **p** with
13: 7 like a leopard I will lurk by the **p**.
Mt 13: 4 some fell along the **p**, and the birds
13:19 This is the seed sown along the **p**.
Mk 4: 4 some fell along the **p**, and the birds
4:15 Some people are like seed along the **p**
Lk 1:79 guide our feet into the **p** of peace."
8: 5 some fell along the **p**; it was
8:12 Those along the **p** are the ones who
2Co 6: 3 no stumbling-block in anyone's **p**,

Pathrusites
Ge 10:14 **P**, Casluhites (from whom the
1Ch 1:12 **P**, Casluhites (from whom the

Paths (Path)
Jdg 5: 6 travellers took to winding **p**.
Job 13:27 you keep close watch on all my **p** by
19: 8 he has shrouded my **p** in darkness.
24:13 not know its ways or stay in its **p**.
33:11 he keeps close watch on all my **p**.'
38:20 Do you know the **p** to their dwellings?
Ps 8: 8 all that swim the **p** of the seas.
17: 5 My steps have held to your **p**;
23: 3 He guides me in **p** of righteousness
25: 4 your ways, O LORD, teach me your **p**;
Pr 1:15 them, do not set foot on their **p**;
2:13 who leave the straight **p** to walk in
2:15 whose **p** are crooked and who are
2:18 her **p** to the spirits of the dead.
2:19 her return or attain the **p** of life.
2:20 and keep to the **p** of the righteous.
3: 6 and he will make your **p** straight.
3:17 ways, and all her **p** are peace.
4:11 and lead you along straight **p**.
4:26 Make level **p** for your feet and take
5: 6 **p** are crooked, but she knows it not.
5:21 the LORD, and he examines all his **p**.
7:25 to her ways or stray into her **p**.
8: 2 the **p** meet, she takes her stand;
8:20 along the **p** of justice,
10: 9 takes crooked **p** will be found out.
22: 5 In the **p** of the wicked lie thorns
Isa 2: 3 ways, so that we may walk in his **p**.
42:16 along unfamiliar **p** I will guide them;
59: 8 there is no justice in their **p**.
Jer 6:16 ask for the ancient **p**, ask where the
18:15 in their ways and in the ancient **p**.
Lam 3: 9 of stone; he has made my **p** crooked.
Hos 9: 8 yet snares await him on all his **p**,
Mic 4: 2 ways, so that we may walk in his **p**.
Mt 3: 3 the Lord, make straight **p** for him.
Mk 1: 3 the Lord, make straight **p** for him.
Lk 3: 4 the Lord, make straight **p** for him.
Ac 2:28 You have made known to me the **p** of
Ro 11:33 and his **p** beyond tracing out!
Heb 12:13 "Make level **p** for your feet," so

Patience (Patient)
Pr 19:11 A man's wisdom gives him **p**; it is to
25:15 Through **p** a ruler can be persuaded,
Ecc 7: 8 and **p** is better than pride.
Isa 7:13 Is it not enough to try the **p** of men?
7:13 Will you try the **p** of my God also?
Ro 2: 4 tolerance and **p**, not realising that
9:22 bore with great **p** the objects of his
2Co 6: 6 in purity, understanding, **p** and
Gal 5:22 **p**, kindness, goodness, faithfulness,
Col 1:11 great endurance and **p**, and
3:12 humility, gentleness and **p**.
1Ti 1:16 might display his unlimited **p** as an
2Ti 3:10 purpose, faith, **p**, love, endurance,
4: 2 great **p** and careful instruction.
Heb 6:12 those who through faith and **p**
Jas 5:10 Brothers, as an example of **p** in the
2Pe 3:15 Bear in mind that our Lord's **p** means

Patient (Patience, Patiently)
Ne 9:30 For many years you were **p** with them.
Job 6:11 What prospects, that I should be **p**?
Pr 14:29 A **p** man has great understanding, but
15:18 but a **p** man calms a quarrel.
16:32 Better a **p** man than a warrior, a man
Mt 18:26 'Be **p** with me,' he begged, 'and I
18:29 **p** with me, and I will pay you back.'
Ro 12:12 Be joyful in hope, **p** in affliction,
1Co 13: 4 Love is **p**, love is kind. It does not
2Co 1: 6 which produces in you **p** endurance of
Eph 4: 2 be **p**, bearing with one another in
1Th 5:14 help the weak, be **p** with everyone.
Jas 5: 7 Be **p**, then, brothers, until the
5: 7 how **p** he is for the autumn and
5: 8 You too, be **p** and stand firm,
2Pe 3: 9 He is **p** with you, not wanting anyone
Rev 1: 9 **p** endurance that are ours in Jesus,
13:10 This calls for **p** endurance and
14:12 This calls for **p** endurance on the

Patiently (Patient)
Ps 37: 7 Be still before the LORD and wait **p**
40: 1 I waited **p** for the LORD; he turned
Isa 38:13 I waited **p** till dawn, but like a
Hab 3:16 Yet I will wait **p** for the day of
Ac 26: 3 I beg you to listen to me **p**.
Ro 8:25 do not yet have, we wait for it **p**.
Heb 6:15 after waiting **p**, Abraham received
1Pe 3:20 when God waited **p** in the days of
Rev 3:10 have kept my command to endure **p**,

Patmos
Island in the Aegean where the Romans banished criminals. Here John wrote the book of Revelation (Rev 1:9).
Rev 1: 9 was on the island of **P** because of

Patriarch (Patriarchs)
Ac 2:29 the **p** David died and was buried,
Heb 7: 4 Even the **p** Abraham gave him a tenth

Patriarchs (Patriarch)
Jn 7:22 come from Moses, but from the **p**),
Ac 7: 8 became the father of the twelve **p**.
7: 9 "Because the **p** were jealous of
Ro 9: 5 Theirs are the **p**, and from them is
11:28 they are loved on account of the **p**,
15: 8 confirm the promises made to the **p**

Patrobas
Ro 16:14 Greet Asyncritus, Phlegon, Hermes, **P**,

Pattern
Ex 25: 9 exactly like the **p** I will show you.
25:40 to the **p** shown you on the mountain.
Nu 8: 4 like the **p** the LORD had shown Moses.
Ac 7:44 according to the **p** he had seen.
Ro 5:14 Adam, who was a **p** of the one to come.
12: 2 Do not conform any longer to the **p**
Php 3:17 live according to the **p** we gave you.
2Ti 1:13 What you heard from me, keep as the **p**
Heb 8: 5 to the **p** shown you on the mountain."

Pau
Ge 36:39 His city was named **P**, and his wife's
1Ch 1:50 His city was named **P**, and his wife's

Paul (Paul's, Saul)
Apostle (Gal 1:1); also called Saul (Ac 13:9). From Tarsus (Ac 9:11; 21:39; 22:3; Php 3:5); Pharisee (Ac 23:6; 26:5; Php 3:5); taught by Gamaliel (Ac 22:3).
Approved of Stephen's death (Ac 7:58; 8:1); persecuted church (Ac 8:3; 9:1–2; 1Co 15:9; Gal 1:13). Saw Jesus on Damascus road (Ac 9:3–9; 22:6–11; 26:12–18); healed and baptised by Ananias (Ac 9:17–19; 22:12–16). Into Arabia (Gal 1:17); escaped from Damascus in a basket (Ac 9:23–25; 2Co 11:32–33). Introduced to apostles in Jerusalem by Barnabas; sent to Tarsus (Ac 9:26–30; Gal 1:18–21). Brought to Antioch by Barnabas (Ac 11:22–26).
Visited Jerusalem; message and commission confirmed by apostles (Ac 11:30; Gal 2:1–10). First missionary journey, with Barnabas, (Ac 13–14). Stoned at Lystra (Ac 14:19–20). At Council of Jerusalem (Ac 15). Disagreed with Barnabas over Mark (Ac 15:36–39). Second missionary journey, with Silas (Ac 15:40–18:22). Called to Macedonia (Ac 16:9–10); miraculously released from prison in Philippi (Ac 16:16–40); in Athens (Ac 17:16–34); in Corinth (Ac 18). Third missionary journey (Ac 18:23). In Ephesus (Ac 19); raised Eutychus to life (Ac 20:7–12); farewell to Ephesian elders (Ac 20:13–37). Travelled to Jerusalem (Ac 21); arrested (Ac 21:27–36); appealed as Roman citizen (Ac 22:25–29); before Sanhedrin (Ac 22:30–23:10). Taken to Caesarea (Ac 23:12–35); before Felix, Festus and Agrippa (Ac 24–26). Journeyed to Rome (Ac 27–28); shipwrecked on Malta (Ac 27:27–28:10); under house arrest in Rome; preached gospel (Ac 28:16–31).
Letters: Romans, 1 & 2 Corinthians, Galatians, Ephesians, Philippians, Colossians, 1 & 2 Thessalonians, 1 & 2 Timothy, Titus, Philemon.

Ac 13: 9 Saul, who was also called **P**, filled
13:13 From Paphos, **P** and his companions
13:16 Standing up, **P** motioned with his
13:42 **P** and Barnabas were leaving the
13:43 to Judaism followed **P** and Barnabas,
13:45 abusively against what **P** was saying.
13:46 **P** and Barnabas answered them boldly:
13:50 persecution against **P** and Barnabas,
14: 1 At Iconium **P** and Barnabas went as
14: 3 **P** and Barnabas spent considerable
14: 9 He listened to **P** as he was speaking.
14: 9 **P** looked directly at him, saw that
14:11 the crowd saw what **P** had done, they
14:12 and **P** they called Hermes because he
14:14 when the apostles Barnabas and **P**
14:19 They stoned **P** and dragged him
14:23 **P** and Barnabas appointed elders for
15: 2 This brought **P** and Barnabas into
15: 2 So **P** and Barnabas were appointed,
15:12 **P** telling about the miraculous signs
15:22 them to Antioch with **P** and Barnabas.
15:25 our dear friends Barnabas and **P**—
15:35 **P** and Barnabas remained in Antioch,
15:36 Some time later **P** said to Barnabas,
15:38 **P** did not think it wise to take him,
15:40 **P** chose Silas and left, commended by
16: 3 **P** wanted to take him along on the
16: 6 **P** and his companions travelled
16: 9 During the night **P** had a vision of a
16:10 After **P** had seen the vision, we got
16:17 This girl followed **P** and the rest of
16:18 Finally **P** became so troubled that he
16:19 they seized **P** and Silas and dragged
16:22 in the attack against **P** and Silas,
16:25 About midnight **P** and Silas were
16:28 **P** shouted, "Don't harm yourself!
16:29 fell trembling before **P** and Silas.
16:36 The jailer told **P**, "The magistrates
16:37 **P** said to the officers: "They beat
16:38 and when they heard that **P** and Silas
16:40 After **P** and Silas came out of the
17: 2 **P** went into the synagogue, and on
17: 4 persuaded and joined **P** and Silas,
17: 5 to Jason's house in search of **P**
17:10 sent **P** and Silas away to Berea.
17:11 day to see if what **P** said was true.
17:13 **P** was preaching the word of God
17:14 The brothers immediately sent **P** to
17:15 The men who escorted **P** brought him
17:16 While **P** was waiting for them in
17:18 They said this because **P** was
17:22 **P** then stood up in the meeting of
17:33 At that, **P** left the Council.
17:34 A few men became followers of **P** and
18: 1 After this, **P** left Athens and went
18: 2 **P** went to see them,
18: 5 **P** devoted himself exclusively to
18: 6 when the Jews opposed **P** and became
18: 7 **P** left the synagogue and went next
18: 9 One night the Lord spoke to **P** in a
18:11 **P** stayed for a year and a half,
18:12 on **P** and brought him into court.
18:14 Just as **P** was about to speak, Gallio
18:18 **P** stayed on in Corinth for some time.
18:19 They arrived at Ephesus, where **P**
18:23 **P** set out from there and travelled
19: 1 **P** took the road through the
19: 3 **P** asked, "Then what baptism did you
19: 4 **P** said, "John's baptism was a
19: 6 **P** placed his hands on them, the Holy
19: 8 **P** entered the synagogue and spoke
19: 9 So **P** left them. He took the
19:11 extraordinary miracles through **P**,
19:13 the name of Jesus, whom **P** preaches,
19:15 I know about **P**, but who are you?"
19:21 **P** decided to go to Jerusalem,
19:26 you see and hear how this fellow **P**
19:30 **P** wanted to appear before the crowd,
19:31 friends of **P**, sent him a message
20: 1 the uproar had ended, **P** sent for the
20: 7 **P** spoke to the people and, because
20: 9 a deep sleep as **P** talked on and on.
20:10 **P** went down, threw himself on the
20:13 we were going to take **P** aboard.
20:16 **P** had decided to sail past Ephesus
20:17 From Miletus, **P** sent to Ephesus for

Ac 21: 4 urged **P** not to go on to Jerusalem.
21:12 with **P** not to go up to Jerusalem.
21:13 **P** answered, "Why are you weeping and
21:18 The next day **P** and the rest of us
21:19 **P** greeted them and reported in
21:20 Then they said to **P**: "You see,
21:26 The next day **P** took the men and
21:27 of Asia saw **P** at the temple.
21:29 the Ephesian in the city with **P**
21:29 assumed that **P** had brought him into
21:30 Seizing **P**, they dragged him from the
21:32 soldiers, they stopped beating **P**.
21:34 that **P** be taken into the barracks.
21:35 **P** reached the steps, the violence of
21:37 the soldiers were about to take **P**
21:39 **P** answered, "I am a Jew, from Tarsus
21:40 **P** stood on the steps and motioned to
22: 2 Then **P** said:
22:22 The crowd listened to **P** until he
22:24 the commander ordered **P** to be taken
22:25 **P** said to the centurion standing
22:27 The commander went to **P** and asked,
22:28 I was born a citizen," **P** replied.
22:29 put **P**, a Roman citizen, in chains.
22:30 why **P** was being accused by the Jews,
22:30 he brought **P** and had him stand
23: 1 **P** looked straight at the Sanhedrin
23: 2 near **P** to strike him on the mouth.
23: 3 **P** said to him, "God will strike you,
23: 4 Those who were standing near **P** said,
23: 5 **P** replied, "Brothers, I did not
23: 6 **P**, knowing that some of them were
23:10 **P** would be torn to pieces by them.
23:11 the Lord stood near **P** and said,
23:12 or drink until they had killed **P**.
23:14 eat anything until we have killed **P**.
23:16 went into the barracks and told **P**.
23:17 **P** called one of the centurions and
23:18 The centurion said, "**P**, the prisoner,
23:20 to bring **P** before the Sanhedrin
23:24 Provide mounts for **P** so that he may
23:31 took **P** with them during the night
23:33 governor and handed **P** over to him.
23:35 Then he ordered that **P** be kept
24: 1 against **P** before the governor.
24: 2 **P** was called in, Tertullus presented
24:10 **P** replied: "I know that for a number
24:23 He ordered the centurion to keep **P**
24:24 He sent for **P** and listened to him as
24:25 **P** discoursed on righteousness,
24:26 he was hoping that **P** would offer
24:27 to the Jews, he left **P** in prison.
25: 2 and presented the charges against **P**.
25: 3 to have **P** transferred to Jerusalem,
25: 4 Festus answered, "**P** is being held at
25: 6 that **P** be brought before him.
25: 7 **P** appeared, the Jews who had come
25: 8 **P** made his defence: "I have done
25: 9 said to **P**, "Are you willing to go up
25:10 **P** answered: "I am now standing
25:19 Jesus whom **P** claimed was alive.
25:21 **P** made his appeal to be held over
25:23 command of Festus, **P** was brought in.
26: 1 Agrippa said to **P**, "You have
26: 1 So **P** motioned with his hand and
26:24 "You are out of your mind, **P**!" he
26:25 most excellent Festus," **P** replied.
26:28 Agrippa said to **P**, "Do you think
26:29 **P** replied, "Short time or long—I
27: 1 **P** and some other prisoners were
27: 3 in kindness to **P**, allowed him to go
27: 9 after the Fast. So **P** warned them,
27:11 instead of listening to what **P** said,
27:21 **P** stood up before them and said:
27:24 said, 'Do not be afraid, **P**. You must
27:31 **P** said to the centurion and the
27:33 Just before dawn **P** urged them all to
28: 3 **P** gathered a pile of brushwood and,
28: 5 **P** shook the snake off into the fire
28: 8 **P** went in to see him and, after
28:15 **P** thanked God and was encouraged.
28:16 we got to Rome, **P** was allowed to
28:17 When they had assembled, **P** said to
28:23 They arranged to meet **P** on a certain
28:25 **P** had made this final statement:
28:30 For two whole years **P** stayed there

Ro 1: 1 **P**, a servant of Christ Jesus, called
1Co 1: 1 **P**, called to be an apostle of Christ
1:12 "I follow **P**"; another, "I follow
1:13 Is Christ divided? Was **P** crucified
1:13 Were you baptised into the name of **P**?
3: 4 For when one says, "I follow **P**," and
3: 5 And what is **P**? Only servants,
3:22 whether **P** or Apollos or Cephas or
16:21 I, **P**, write this greeting in my own
2Co 1: 1 **P**, an apostle of Christ Jesus by the
10: 1 I appeal to you—I, **P**, who am "timid"
Gal 1: 1 **P**, an apostle—sent not from men nor
5: 2 Mark my words! I, **P**, tell you that
Eph 1: 1 **P**, an apostle of Christ Jesus by the
3: 1 For this reason I, **P**, the prisoner
Php 1: 1 **P** and Timothy, servants of Christ
Col 1: 1 **P**, an apostle of Christ Jesus by the
1:23 which I, **P**, have become a servant.
4:18 I, **P**, write this greeting in my own
1Th 1: 1 **P**, Silas and Timothy, To the church
2:18 certainly, I **P**, did, again and
2Th 1: 1 **P**, Silas and Timothy,
3:17 I, **P**, write this greeting in my own
1Ti 1: 1 **P**, an apostle of Christ Jesus by the
2Ti 1: 1 **P**, an apostle of Christ Jesus by the
Tit 1: 1 **P**, a servant of God and an apostle
Phm : 1 **P**, a prisoner of Christ Jesus, and
: 9 I then, as **P**—an old man and now
:19 I, **P**, am writing this with my own
2Pe 3:15 just as our dear brother **P** also

Paul's (Paul)

Ac 16:14 her heart to respond to **P** message.
19:29 **P** travelling companions from
21:11 Coming over to us, he took **P** belt,
23:16 when the son of **P** sister heard of
25:14 discussed **P** case with the king.
26:24 Festus interrupted **P**'s defence.
27:43 the centurion wanted to spare **P** life

Paulus (Sergius)

Ac 13: 7 of the proconsul, Sergius **P**.

Pavement

Ex 24:10 something like a **p** made of sapphire,
2Ch 7: 3 they knelt on the **p** with their faces
Est 1: 6 silver on a mosaic **p** of porphyry,
Jer 43: 9 bury them in clay in the brick **p** at
Eze 40:17 There I saw some rooms and a **p** that
40:17 there were thirty rooms along the **p**.
40:18 were long; this was the lower **p**.
42: 3 opposite the **p** of the outer court,
Jn 19:13 seat at a place known as the Stone **P**

Pavilion

Job 36:29 clouds, how he thunders from his **p**?
Ps 19: 5 bridegroom coming forth from his **p**,

Paw (Paws)

1Sa 17:37 delivered me from the **p** of the lion
17:37 the **p** of the bear will deliver me

Paws (Paw)

Lev 11:27 those that walk on their **p** are
Job 39:21 He **p** fiercely, rejoicing in his

Pay (Paid, Paying, Payment, Pays, Repay)

Ge 23:13 I will **p** the price of the field.
30:28 "Name your wages, and I will **p** them.
34:12 and I'll **p** whatever you ask me.
43:28 And they bowed low to **p** him honour.
Ex 2: 9 nurse him for me, and I will **p** you.
4: 8 do not believe you or **p** attention
5: 9 working and **p** no attention to lies."
15:26 if you **p** attention to his commands
21:19 he must **p** the injured man for the
21:32 the owner must **p** thirty shekels of
21:34 the owner of the pit must **p** for the
21:34 he must **p** its owner, and the dead
21:36 the owner must **p**, animal for animal,
22: 1 he must **p** back five head of cattle
22: 3 he must be sold to **p** for his theft.

Ex 22: 4 or sheep—he must **p** back double.
22: 7 if he is caught, must **p** back double.
22: 9 must **p** back double to his neighbour.
22:13 required to **p** for the torn animal.
22:15 the borrower will not have to **p**.
22:16 he must **p** the bride-price, and she
22:17 still **p** the bride-price for virgins.
23:21 **P** attention to him and listen to
30:12 each one must **p** the LORD a ransom
Lev 25:51 If many years remain, he must **p** for
25:52 **p** for his redemption accordingly.
26:41 humbled and they **p** for their sin,
26:43 They will **p** for their sins because
27: 8 too poor to **p** the specified amount,
27:23 and the man must **p** its value on that
Nu 20:19 any of your water, we will **p** for it.
Dt 2: 6 You are to **p** them in silver for the
7:12 If you **p** attention to these laws and
22:29 **p** the girl's father fifty shekels
23:18 of the LORD your God to **p** any vow,
23:21 do not be slow to **p** it, for the LORD
24:15 **P** him his wages each day before
28:13 If you **p** attention to the commands
Jdg 9:57 God also made the men of Shechem **p**
1Sa 4:20 did not respond or **p** any attention.
6: 5 and **p** honour to Israel's god.
25:25 May my lord **p** no attention to that
2Sa 1: 2 fell to the ground to **p** him honour.
9: 6 David, he bowed down to **p** him honour.
12: 6 He must **p** for that lamb four times
14: 4 face to the ground to **p** him honour,
14:22 face to the ground to **p** him honour,
1Ki 2:23 **p** with his life for this request!
5: 6 and I will **p** you for your men
20:39 or you must **p** a talent of silver.'
21: 2 I will **p** you whatever it is worth."
2Ki 4: 7 "Go, sell the oil and **p** your debts.
9:26 and I will surely make you **p** for it
12:15 gave the money to **p** the workers,
18:14 I will **p** whatever you demand of me.
22: 5 And make these men **p** the workers who
Ne 5: 4 to borrow money to **p** the king's tax
9:34 they did not **p** attention to your
Est 3: 2 not kneel down or **p** him honour.
3: 5 or **p** him honour, he was enraged.
4: 7 Haman had promised to **p** into the
Job 6:22 **p** a ransom for me from your wealth,
33: 1 **p** attention to everything I say
33:31 "**P** attention, Job, and listen to me;
41:11 a claim against me that I must **p**?
Ps 79:12 **P** back into the laps of our
94: 2 **p** back to the proud what they
Pr 4: 1 **p** attention and gain understanding.
4:20 My son, **p** attention to what I say;
5: 1 My son, **p** attention to my wisdom,
6:31 he is caught, he must **p** sevenfold
7:24 **p** attention to what I say.
13:13 He who scorns instruction will **p** for
19:19 A hot-tempered man must **p** the
20:22 Do not say, "I'll **p** you back for
22:17 **P** attention and listen to the
22:27 if you lack the means to **p**, your
24:29 **p** that man back for what he did."
30:10 curse you, and you will **p** for it.
Ecc 7:21 Do not **p** attention to every word
Isa 28:23 **p** attention and hear what I say.
34: 1 **p** attention, you peoples!
42:23 or **p** close attention in time to
65: 6 keep silent but will **p** back in full
65: 6 I will **p** it back into their laps—
Jer 7:24 they did not listen or **p** attention;
7:26 did not listen to me or **p** attention
11: 8 they did not listen or **p** attention;
13:15 Hear and **p** attention, do not be
17:23 they did not listen or **p** attention;
18:18 **p** no attention to anything he says."
34:14 listen to me or **p** attention to me.
44: 5 they did not listen or **p** attention;
51: 6 he will **p** her what she deserves.
Lam 3:64 **P** them back what they deserve,
Eze 16:41 you will no longer **p** your lovers.
29:19 plunder the land as **p** for his army.
40: 4 hear with your ears and **p** attention
Da 3:12 **p** no attention to you, O king.
Hos 2:12 which she said were her **p** from her
5: 1 "Hear this, you priests! **P** attention,
12:12 and to **p** for her he tended sheep.
Zec 1: 4 **p** attention to me, declares the LORD.
7:11 "But they refused to **p** attention;
11:12 give me my **p**; but if not, keep it.
Mt 7: 3 **p** no attention to the plank in your
17:24 your teacher **p** the temple tax?"
18:25 Since he was not able to **p**, the
18:26 'and I will **p** back everything.'
18:28 **P** back what you owe me!' he demanded.
18:29 with me, and I will **p** you back.'
18:30 prison until he could **p** the debt.
18:34 until he should **p** back all he owed.
20: 2 He agreed to **p** them a denarius for
20: 4 and I will **p** you whatever is right.'
20: 8 'Call the workers and **p** them their
20:14 Take your **p** and go. I want to give
22:16 you **p** no attention to who they are.
22:17 right to **p** taxes to Caesar or not?"
Mk 12:14 because you **p** no attention to who
12:14 right to **p** taxes to Caesar or not?
12:15 Should we **p** or shouldn't we?"
Lk 3:14 falsely—be content with your **p**."
6:41 **p** no attention to the plank in your
7:42 Neither of them had the money to **p**
19: 8 I will **p** back four times the amount."
20:22 Is it right for us to **p** taxes to
Ac 21:24 rites and **p** their expenses,
22:28 "I had to **p** a big price for my
25:13 to **p** their respects to Festus.
Ro 13: 6 This is also why you **p** taxes, for
13: 7 If you owe taxes, **p** taxes;
Gal 5:10 **p** the penalty, whoever he may be.
2Th 1: 6 God is just: He will **p** back trouble
Tit 1:14 will **p** no attention to Jewish myths
Phm :19 I will **p** it back—not to mention
Heb 2: 1 We must **p** more careful attention,
Jas 5: 4 wages you failed to **p** the workmen
2Pe 1:19 and you will do well to **p** attention
Rev 18: 6 **p** her back double for what she has

Paying (Pay)

Ex 21: 2 shall go free, without **p** anything.
21:30 his life by **p** whatever is demanded.
2Sa 24:24 "No, I insist on **p** you for it.
1Ch 21:24 "No, I insist on **p** the full price.
Jer 22:13 not **p** them for their labour.
Joel 3: 4 I have done? If you are **p** me back,
Jnh 1: 3 After **p** the fare, he went aboard and
Mt 22:19 Show me the coin used for **p** the tax."
2Th 3: 8 eat anyone's food without **p** for it.

Payment (Pay)

Ge 31:39 And you demanded **p** from me for
47:14 in **p** for the grain they were buying,
Ex 21:11 to go free, without any **p** of money.
21:30 However, if **p** is demanded of him, he
Lev 22:16 bring upon them guilt requiring **p**.
Dt 15: 2 He shall not require **p** from his
15: 3 You may require **p** from a foreigner,
Job 31:39 I have devoured its yield without **p**
Ps 49: 8 is costly, no **p** is ever enough—
109:20 May this be the LORD's **p** to my
Isa 65: 7 the full **p** for their former deeds."
Eze 16:31 a prostitute, because you scorned **p**.
16:34 you give **p** and none is given to you.
Lk 23: 2 He opposes **p** of taxes to Caesar and
Php 4:18 I have received full **p** and even more;

Pays (Pay)

Ge 50:15 **p** us back for all the wrongs we did
Job 35:13 the Almighty **p** no attention to it.
Ps 31:23 but the proud he **p** back in full.
94: 7 the God of Jacob **p** no heed."
Pr 17: 4 **p** attention to a malicious tongue.
17:13 If a man **p** back evil for good, evil
Da 6:13 **p** no attention to you, O king, or to
Mal 2:13 because he no longer **p** attention
1Th 5:15 Make sure that nobody **p** back wrong

Peace (*Grace and peace, In peace,* Pacifies, Pacify, *Peace with God,* Peaceable, Peaceably, Peaceful, Peacefully, Peace-loving, Peacemakers, Peacetime)

Lev 26: 6 "'I will grant **p** in the land, and
Nu 6:26 his face towards you and give you **p**.
25:12 am making my covenant of **p** with him.
Dt 2:26 of Heshbon offering **p** and saying,
20:10 city, make its people an offer of **p**.
20:12 If they refuse to make **p** and they
Jos 9:15 Joshua made a treaty of **p** with them
10: 1 had made a treaty of **p** with Israel
10: 4 **p** with Joshua and the Israelites."
11:19 not one city made a treaty of **p** with
Jdg 3:11 the land had **p** for forty years,
3:30 and the land had **p** for eighty years.
5:31 Then the land had **p** for forty years.
6:23 the LORD said to him, "**P**! Do not be
6:24 there and called it The LORD is **P**.
8:28 the land enjoyed **p** for forty years.
21:13 the whole assembly sent an offer of **p**
1Sa 7:14 **p** between Israel and the Amorites.
2Sa 10:19 they made **p** with the Israelites and
1Ki 2:33 may there be the LORD's **p** for ever."
4:24 to Gaza, and had **p** on all sides.
20:18 He said, "If they have come out for **p**
22:44 Jehoshaphat was also at **p** with the
2Ki 9:18 "What do you have to do with **p**?"
9:19 "What do you have to do with **p**?
9:22 "How can there be **p**," Jehu replied,
18:31 Make **p** with me and come out to me.
20:19 be **p** and security in my lifetime?"
1Ch 19:19 they made **p** with David and became
22: 9 son who will be a man of **p** and rest,
22: 9 Israel **p** and quiet during his reign.
2Ch 13:23 the country was at **p** for ten years.
14: 1 and the kingdom was at **p** under him.
14: 5 and the kingdom was at **p** under him.
14: 6 of Judah, since the land was at **p**.
20:30 the kingdom of Jehoshaphat was at **p**,
Job 3:26 I have no **p**, no quietness; I have no
5:23 wild animals will be at **p** with you.
22:21 "Submit to God and be at **p** with him;
Ps 7: 4 done evil to him who is at **p** with me
29:11 the LORD blesses his people with **p**.
34:14 and do good; seek **p** and pursue it.
37:11 inherit the land and enjoy great **p**.
37:37 there is a future for the man of **p**.
85: 8 he promises **p** to his people,
85:10 righteousness and **p** kiss each other.
119:165 Great **p** have they who love your law,
120: 6 have I lived among those who hate **p**.
120: 7 I am a man of **p**; but when I speak,
122: 6 Pray for the **p** of Jerusalem: "May
122: 7 May there be **p** within your walls and
122: 8 I will say, "**P** be within you.
125: 5 **P** be upon Israel.
128: 6 **P** be upon Israel.
147:14 He grants **p** to your borders and
Pr 3:17 ways, and all her paths are **p**.
12:20 but joy for those who promote **p**.
14:30 A heart at **p** gives life to the body,
16: 7 even his enemies live at **p** with him.
17: 1 Better a dry crust with **p** and quiet
29: 9 rages and scoffs, and there is no **p**.
29:17 and he will give you **p**; he will
Ecc 3: 8 a time for war and a time for **p**.
Isa 9: 6 God, Everlasting Father, Prince of **P**.
9: 7 and **p** there will be no end.
14: 7 All the lands are at rest and at **p**;
26: 3 You will keep in perfect **p** him whose
26:12 LORD, you establish **p** for us;
27: 5 for refuge; let them make **p** with me,
27: 5 me, yes, let them make **p** with me."
32:17 The fruit of righteousness will be **p**;
33: 7 the envoys of **p** weep bitterly.
36:16 Make **p** with me and come out to me.
39: 8 be **p** and security in my lifetime."
48:18 your **p** would have been like a river,
48:22 "There is no **p**," says the LORD, "for
52: 7 who proclaim **p**, who bring good
53: 5 that brought us **p** was upon him,
54:10 nor my covenant of **p** be removed,"
54:13 and great will be your children's **p**.
57: 2 Those who walk uprightly enter into **p**

Isa 57:19 **P**, **p**, to those far and near," says
57:21 "There is no **p**," says my God, "for
59: 8 The way of **p** they do not know;
59: 8 who walks in them will know **p**.
60:17 I will make **p** your governor and
66:12 "I will extend **p** to her like a river,
Jer 4:10 'You will have **p**,' when the sword
6:14 '**P**, **p**' they say, when there is no **p**.
8:11 "**P**, **p**," they say, when there is no **p**.
8:15 We hoped for **p** but no good has come,
14:13 Indeed, I will give you lasting **p** in
14:19 We hoped for **p** but no good has come,
23:17 me, 'The LORD says: You will have **p**.
28: 9 the prophet who prophesies **p** will be
29: 7 Also, seek the **p** and prosperity of
30: 5 of fear are heard—terror, not **p**.
30:10 Jacob will again have **p** and security,
33: 6 them enjoy abundant **p** and security.
33: 9 prosperity and **p** I provide for it.'
46:27 Jacob will again have **p** and security,
Lam 3:17 I have been deprived of **p**; I have
Eze 7:25 terror comes, they will seek **p**, but
13:10 "**P**", when there is no **p**, and because,
13:16 of **p** for her when there was no **p**,
34:25 "'I will make a covenant of **p** with
37:26 I will make a covenant of **p** with
Da 10:19 "**P**! Be strong now; be strong."
Mic 3: 5 one feeds them, they proclaim '**p**';
5: 5 he will be their **p**. When the
Na 1:15 brings good news, who proclaims **p**!
Hag 2: 9 in this place I will grant **p**,'
Zec 8:19 Therefore love truth and **p**."
9:10 He will proclaim **p** to the nations.
Mal 2: 5 a covenant of life and **p**, and I gave
Mt 10:13 deserving, let your **p** rest on it;
10:13 it is not, let your **p** return to you.
10:34 I have come to bring **p** to the earth.
10:34 not come to bring **p**, but a sword.
Mk 9:50 and be at **p** with each other."
Lk 1:79 guide our feet into the path of **p**."
2:14 **p** to men on whom his favour rests."
10: 5 house, first say, '**P** to this house.'
10: 6 If a man of **p** is there, your **p** will
12:51 Do you think I came to bring **p** on
14:32 way off and will ask for terms of **p**.
19:38 "**P** in heaven and glory in the
19:42 on this day what would bring you **p**
24:36 and said to them, "**P** be with you.
Jn 14:27 **P** I leave with you; my **p** I give you.
16:33 so that in me you may have **p**.
20:19 them and said, "**P** be with you!"
20:21 Again Jesus said, "**P** be with you!
20:26 them and said, "**P** be with you!"
Ac 9:31 and Samaria enjoyed a time of **p**.
10:36 telling the good news of **p** through
12:20 they asked for **p**, because they
15:33 with the blessing of **p** to return to
24: 2 "We have enjoyed a long period of **p**
Ro 2:10 glory, honour and **p** for everyone who
3:17 the way of **p** they do not know."
8: 6 by the Spirit is life and **p**;
12:18 on you, live at **p** with everyone.
14:17 **p** and joy in the Holy Spirit,
14:19 to **p** and to mutual edification.
15:13 all joy and **p** as you trust in him,
15:33 The God of **p** be with you all. Amen.
16:20 The God of **p** will soon crush Satan
1Co 14:33 is not a God of disorder but of **p**.
2Co 2:13 I still had no **p** of mind, because I
13:11 God of love and **p** will be with you.
Gal 5:22 joy, **p**, patience, kindness, goodness,
6:16 **P** and mercy to all who follow this
Eph 2:14 For he himself is our **p**, who has
2:15 man out of the two, thus making **p**,
2:17 He came and preached **p** to you who
2:17 away and **p** to those who were near.
4: 3 of the Spirit through the bond of **p**.
6:15 that comes from the gospel of **p**.
6:23 **P** to the brothers, and love with
Php 4: 7 the **p** of God, which transcends all
4: 9 And the God of **p** will be with you.
Col 1:20 by making **p** through his blood, shed
3:15 Let the **p** of Christ rule in your
3:15 of one body you were called to **p**.
1Th 5: 3 people are saying, "**P** and safety"
5:23 May God himself, the God of **p**,
2Th 3:16 Now may the Lord of **p** himself
3:16 give you **p** at all times and in
1Ti 1: 2 mercy and **p** from God the Father and
2Ti 1: 2 Grace, mercy and **p** from God the
2:22 faith, love and **p**, along with those
Phm : 3 Grace to you and **p** from God our
Heb 7: 2 "king of Salem" means "king of **p**".
12:11 **p** for those who have been trained by
13:20 May the God of **p**, who through the
1Pe 3:11 he must seek **p** and pursue it.
5:14 **P** to all of you who are in Christ.
2Pe 3:14 blameless and at **p** with him.
2Jn : 3 Grace, mercy and **p** from God the
3Jn :14 **P** to you. The friends here send
Jude : 2 Mercy, **p** and love be yours in
Rev 6: 4 power to take **p** from the earth

Peace with God
Ro 5: 1 **p** through our Lord Jesus Christ,

Peaceable (Peace)
Tit 3: 2 to slander no-one, to be **p** and

Peaceably (Peace)
Jdg 11:13 Now give it back **p**."
Ps 35:20 They do not speak **p**, but devise

Peaceful (Peace)
Jdg 18:27 against a **p** and unsuspecting people.
2Sa 20:19 We are the **p** and faithful in Israel.
1Ki 5:12 There were **p** relations between Hiram
1Ch 4:40 the land was spacious, **p** and quiet.
Isa 32:18 will live in **p** dwelling-places,
33:20 a **p** abode, a tent that will not be
Jer 25:37 The **p** meadows will be laid waste
Eze 38:11 I will attack a **p** and unsuspecting
1Ti 2: 2 that we may live **p** and quiet lives

Peacefully (Peace)
1Ki 2:13 Bathsheba asked him, "Do you come **p**?"
2:13 He answered, "Yes, **p**."
Jer 34: 5 you will die **p**. As people made a

Peace-loving (Peace, Love)
Jas 3:17 then **p**, considerate, submissive,

Peacemakers (Peace)
Mt 5: 9 Blessed are the **p**, for they will be
Jas 3:18 **P** who sow in peace raise a harvest

Peacetime (Peace)
1Ki 2: 5 shedding their blood in **p** as if in

Peaks
Nu 23: 9 From the rocky **p** I see them, from
Ps 95: 4 and the mountain **p** belong to him.

Peal (Peals)
Rev 14: 2 waters and like a loud **p** of thunder.

Peals (Peal)
Rev 4: 5 rumblings and **p** of thunder.
8: 5 and there came **p** of thunder,
11:19 rumblings, **p** of thunder, an
16:18 **p** of thunder and a severe earthquake.
19: 6 waters and like loud **p** of thunder,

Pearl (Mother-of-pearl, Pearls)
Rev 21:21 each gate made of a single **p**.

Pearls (Pearl)
Mt 7: 6 do not throw your **p** to pigs.
13:45 like a merchant looking for fine **p**.
1Ti 2: 9 or gold or **p** or expensive clothes,
Rev 17: 4 with gold, precious stones and **p**.
18:12 silver, precious stones and **p**;
18:16 with gold, precious stones and **p**!
21:21 The twelve gates were twelve **p**, each

Pebble (Pebbles)
Am 9: 9 and not a **p** will reach the ground.

Pebbles (Pebble)
Ps 147:17 He hurls down hail like **p**. Who can

Pecked
Pr 30:17 will be **p** out by the ravens of the

Pedahel
Nu 34:28 **P** son of Ammihud, the leader from

Pedahzur
Nu 1:10 from Manasseh, Gamaliel son of **P**;
2:20 of Manasseh is Gamaliel son of **P**.
7:54 On the eighth day Gamaliel son of **P**,
7:59 the offering of Gamaliel son of **P**.
10:23 Gamaliel son of **P** was over the

Pedaiah
2Ki 23:36 name was Zebidah daughter of **P**;
1Ch 3:18 Malkiram, **P**, Shenazzar, Jekamiah,
3:19 The sons of **P**: Zerubbabel and Shimei.
27:20 tribe of Manasseh: Joel son of **P**;
Ne 3:25 Next to him, **P** son of Parosh
8: 4 and on his left were **P**, Mishael,
11: 7 the son of Joed, the son of **P**, the
13:13 and a Levite named **P** in charge of

Peddle
2Co 2:17 Unlike so many, we do not **p** the word

Pedestal
Am 5:26 the **p** of your idols, the star of

Peeled (Peeling, Peels)
Ge 30:38 he placed the **p** branches in all the

Peeling (Peeled)
Ge 30:37 made white stripes on them by **p** the

Peels (Peeled)
Job 30:30 My skin grows black and **p**; my body

Peered (Peering)
Jdg 5:28 "Through the window **p** Sisera's

Peering (Peered)
SS 2: 9 the windows, **p** through the lattice.

Peg (Pegs)
Jdg 4:21 Heber's wife, picked up a tent **p** and
4:21 She drove the **p** through his temple
4:22 the tent **p** through his temple—dead.
5:26 Her hand reached for the tent **p**, her
Isa 22:23 I will drive him like a **p** into a
22:25 "the **p** driven into the firm place
Zec 10: 4 from him the tent **p**, from him the

Pegs (Peg)
Ex 27:19 including all the tent **p** for it and
35:18 the tent **p** for the tabernacle and
38:20 All the tent **p** of the tabernacle and
38:31 all the tent **p** for the tabernacle
39:40 the ropes and tent **p** for the
Nu 3:37 with their bases, tent **p** and ropes.
4:32 tent **p**, ropes, all their equipment
Eze 15: 3 make **p** from it to hang things on?

Pekah (Pekah's)
2Ki 15:25 chief officers, **P** son of Remaliah,
15:25 So **P** killed Pekahiah and
15:27 **P** son of Remaliah became king of
15:29 In the time of **P** king of Israel,
15:30 conspired against **P** son of Remaliah.
15:32 In the second year of **P** son of
15:37 **P** son of Remaliah against Judah.)
16: 1 In the seventeenth year of **P** son of
16: 5 **P** son of Remaliah king of Israel
2Ch 28: 6 In one day **P** son of Remaliah killed
Isa 7: 1 **P** son of Remaliah king of Israel

Pekah's (Pekah)
2Ki 15:31 for the other events of **P** reign, and

Pekahiah (Pekahiah's)
2Ki 15:22 And **P** his son succeeded him as king.
15:23 **P** son of Menahem became king of
15:24 **P** did evil in the eyes of the LORD.
15:25 he assassinated **P**, along with Argob
15:25 killed **P** and succeeded him as king.

Pekahiah's (Pekahiah)
2Ki 15:26 The other events of **P** reign, and all

Pekod
Jer 50:21 Merathaim and those who live in **P**.
Eze 23:23 the men of **P** and Shoa and Koa, and

Pelaiah
1Ch 3:24 Eliashib, **P**, Akkub, Johanan, Delaiah
Ne 8: 7 Azariah, Jozabad, Hanan and **P**—
10:10 Shebaniah, Hodiah, Kelita, **P**, Hanan,

Pelaliah
Ne 11:12 the son of **P**, the son of Amzi, the

Pelatiah
1Ch 3:21 The descendants of Hananiah: **P** and
4:42 led by **P**, Neariah, Rephaiah and
Ne 10:22 **P**, Hanan, Anaiah,
Eze 11: 1 son of Azzur and **P** son of Benaiah,
11:13 prophesying, **P** son of Benaiah died.

Peleg
Ge 10:25 One was named **P**, because in his
11:16 34 years, he became the father of **P**.
11:17 after he became the father of **P**,
11:18 **P** had lived 30 years, he became the
11:19 **P** lived 209 years and had other
1Ch 1:19 One was named **P**, because in his
1:25 Eber, **P**, Reu,
Lk 3:35 the son of Reu, the son of **P**, the

Pelet
1Ch 2:47 Jotham, Geshan, **P**, Ephah and Shaaph.
12: 3 Jeziel and **P** the sons of Azmaveth;

Peleth (Pelethites)
Nu 16: 1 and On son of **P**—became insolent
1Ch 2:33 The sons of Jonathan: **P** and Zaza.

Pelethites (Peleth)
2Sa 8:18 was over the Kerethites and **P**;
15:18 along with all the Kerethites and **P**;
20: 7 Joab's men and the Kerethites and **P**
20:23 was over the Kerethites and **P**;
1Ki 1:38 the Kerethites and the **P** went down
1:44 the Kerethites and the **P**, and they
1Ch 18:17 was over the Kerethites and **P**;

Pelonite
1Ch 11:27 Shammoth the Harorite, Helez the **P**,
11:36 Hepher the Mekerathite, Ahijah the **P**,
27:10 was Helez the **P**, an Ephraimite.

Pelt (Pelted)
Na 3: 6 I will **p** you with filth, I will

Pelted (Pelt)
2Sa 16: 6 He **p** David and all the king's

Pelusium
Eze 30:15 I will pour out my wrath on **P**, the
30:16 **P** will writhe in agony.

Pen[1]
Ps 45: 1 tongue is the **p** of a skilful writer.
Isa 8: 1 write on it with an ordinary **p**:
Jer 8: 8 the lying **p** of the scribes has
Mt 5:18 not the least stroke of a **p**, will by
Lk 16:17 the least stroke of a **p** to drop out
3Jn :13 do not want to do so with **p** and ink.

Pen[2] (Penned, Pens, Pent-up)
1Sa 6: 7 their calves away and **p** them up.
Mic 2:12 them together like sheep in a **p**,
Hab 3:17 there are no sheep in the **p** and no
Jn 10: 1 not enter the sheep **p** by the gate,
10:16 sheep that are not of this sheep **p**.

Penalties (Penalty)
Pr 19:29 **P** are prepared for mockers, and

Penalty (Penalties)
Lev 5: 6 as a **p** for the sin he has committed
5: 7 to the LORD as a **p** for his sin
5:15 he is to bring to the LORD as a **p**
6: 6 a **p** he must bring to the priest,
Job 8: 4 them over to the **p** of their sin.
Pr 19:19 A hot-tempered man must pay the **p**;
Eze 23:49 You will suffer the **p** for your
Da 2: 9 dream, there is just one **p** for you.
Lk 23:22 in him no grounds for the death **p**.
Ro 1:27 the due **p** for their perversion.
Gal 5:10 will pay the **p**, whoever he may be.

Pendants
Jdg 8:26 not counting the ornaments, the **p**

Penetrates
Heb 4:12 it **p** even to dividing soul and

Peniel
Place along the Jabbok where Jacob wrestled with God (Ge 32:22–32; Hos 12:4); means "the face of God". Its inhabitants refused to give Gideon bread for his men, so he destroyed the city and its tower (Jdg 8:8–9, 17). Later fortified by King Jeroboam (1Ki 12:25).
Ge 32:30 Jacob called the place **P**, saying,
32:31 The sun rose above him as he passed **P**
Jdg 8: 8 From there he went up to **P** and made
8: 9 he said to the men of **P**, "When I
8:17 He also pulled down the tower of **P**
1Ki 12:25 there he went out and built up **P**.

Peninnah
1Sa 1: 2 was called Hannah and the other **P**.
1: 2 **P** had children, but Hannah had none.
1: 4 give portions of meat to his wife **P**

Penitent (Repent)
Isa 1:27 her **p** ones with righteousness.

Penned (Pen[2])
Ex 21:29 has not kept it **p** up and it kills a
21:36 yet the owner did not keep it **p** up,
1Sa 6:10 to the cart and **p** up their calves.

Pennies (Penny)
Lk 12: 6 Are not five sparrows sold for two **p**?

Penny (Pennies)
Mt 5:26 out until you have paid the last **p**.
10:29 Are not two sparrows sold for a **p**?
Mk 12:42 coins, worth only a fraction of a **p**.
Lk 12:59 out until you have paid the last **p**."

Pens (Pen[2])
Nu 32:16 "We would like to build **p** here for
32:24 and **p** for your flocks, but do what
32:36 and built **p** for their flocks.
1Sa 24: 3 He came to the sheep **p** along the way;
2Ch 32:28 of cattle, and **p** for the flocks.
Ps 50: 9 your stall or of goats from your **p**,
78:70 and took him from the sheep **p**;
Zep 2: 6 a place for shepherds and sheep **p**.

Pentecost
Ac 2: 1 the day of **P** came, they were all
20:16 if possible, by the day of **P**.
1Co 16: 8 I will stay on at Ephesus until **P**,

Pent-up (Pen[2])
Isa 59:19 For he will come like a **p** flood that

Penuel
1Ch 4: 4 **P** was the father of Gedor, and Ezer
8:25 Iphdeiah and **P** were the sons of

People (*All people, All the people, Holy people, My people Israel, People of God, People of Israel, People of the land*, People's, Peopled, Peoples)
Ge 6: 9 blameless among the **p** of his time,
9:19 **p** who were scattered over the earth.
11: 6 The LORD said, "If as one **p** speaking
12: 1 "Leave your country, your **p** and your
12: 5 the **p** they had acquired in Haran,
14:16 with the women and the other **p**.
14:21 "Give me the **p** and keep the goods
17:14 will be cut off from his **p**; he has
18:24 What if there are fifty righteous **p**
18:24 sake of the fifty righteous **p** in it?
18:26 "If I find fifty righteous **p** in the
18:28 the whole city because of five **p**?"
19:13 The outcry to the LORD against its **p**
23:10 the Hittite was sitting among his **p**
23:11 it to you in the presence of my **p**.
25: 8 and he was gathered to his **p**.
25:17 died, and he was gathered to his **p**.
25:23 one **p** will be stronger than the
32: 7 divided the **p** who were with him
34:16 among you and become one **p** with you.
34:22 consent to live with us as one **p**
34:30 the **p** living in this land.
35:29 died and was gathered to his **p**,
41:40 my **p** are to submit to your orders.
41:55 the **p** cried to Pharaoh for food.
42: 6 the one who sold grain to all its **p**.
47:15 the money of the **p** of Egypt and
47:21 Joseph reduced the **p** to servitude,
47:23 Joseph said to the **p**, "Now that I
48:19 He too will become a **p**, and he too
49:16 "Dan will provide justice for his **p**
49:29 "I am about to be gathered to my **p**.
49:33 his last and was gathered to his **p**.
Ex 1: 9 "Look," he said to his **p**, "the
1:20 the **p** increased and became even more
1:22 Pharaoh gave this order to all his **p**:
2:11 he went out to where his own **p** were
2:11 beating a Hebrew, one of his own **p**.
3: 7 seen the misery of my **p** in Egypt.
3:10 my **p** the Israelites out of Egypt."
3:12 you have brought the **p** out of Egypt,
3:21 favourably disposed towards this **p**,
4:16 He will speak to the **p** for you, and
4:18 "Let me go back to my own **p** in Egypt
4:21 so that he will not let the **p** go.
4:30 performed the signs before the **p**,
5: 1 'Let my **p** go, so that they may hold
5: 4 why are you taking the **p** away from
5: 6 and foremen in charge of the **p**:
5: 7 "You are no longer to supply the **p**
5:10 foremen went out and said to the **p**,
5:12 the **p** scattered all over Egypt to
5:16 but the fault is with your own **p**."
5:22 you brought trouble upon this **p**?
5:23 he has brought trouble upon this **p**,
5:23 you have not rescued your **p** at all."
6: 7 I will take you as my own **p**, and I
7: 4 my divisions, my **p** the Israelites.
7:14 he refuses to let the **p** go.
7:16 Let my **p** go, so that they may
8: 1 Let my **p** go, so that they may
8: 3 of your officials and on your **p**,
8: 4 and your **p** and all your officials.
8: 8 the frogs away from me and my **p**,
8: 8 and I will let your **p** go to offer
8: 9 your officials and your **p** that you
8:11 houses, your officials and your **p**;
8:20 Let my **p** go, so that they may
8:21 If you do not let my **p** go, I will
8:21 on your **p** and into your houses.
8:22 land of Goshen, where my **p** live;
8:23 distinction between my **p** and your **p**.
8:29 Pharaoh and his officials and his **p**.
8:29 by not letting the **p** go to offer
8:31 Pharaoh and his officials and his **p**
8:32 heart and would not let the **p** go.
9: 1 Let my **p** go, so that they may

Ex 9: 7 and he would not let the **p** go.
9:13 Let my **p** go, so that they may
9:14 against your officials and your **p**,
9:15 struck you and your **p** with a plague
9:17 You still set yourself against my **p**
9:27 and I and my **p** are in the wrong.
10: 3 Let my **p** go, so that they may
10: 7 man be a snare to us? Let the **p** go,
11: 2 Tell the **p** that men and women alike
11: 3 favourably disposed towards the **p**,
11: 3 Pharaoh's officials and by the **p**.)
12: 4 account the number of **p** there are.
12:27 Then the **p** bowed down and worshipped.
12:31 "Up! Leave my **p**, you and the
12:33 The Egyptians urged the **p** to hurry
12:34 the **p** took their dough before the
12:36 favourably disposed towards the **p**,
12:38 Many other **p** went up with them, as
12:40 **p** lived in Egypt was 430 years.
13: 3 Moses said to the **p**, "Commemorate
13:17 Pharaoh let the **p** go, God did not
13:18 God led the **p** around by the desert
13:22 left its place in front of the **p**.
14: 5 the king of Egypt was told that the **p**
14:13 Moses answered the **p**, "Do not be
14:31 the **p** feared the LORD and put their
15:13 will lead the **p** you have redeemed.
15:14 will grip the **p** of Philistia.
15:15 the **p** of Canaan will melt away;
15:16 as a stone—until your **p** pass by,
15:16 LORD, until the **p** you bought pass by.
15:24 the **p** grumbled against Moses, saying,
16: 4 The **p** are to go out each day and
16:27 Nevertheless, some of the **p** went out
16:30 the **p** rested on the seventh day.
17: 1 was no water for the **p** to drink.
17: 3 the **p** were thirsty for water there,
17: 4 "What am I to do with these **p**?
17: 5 Moses, "Walk on ahead of the **p**.
17: 6 come out of it for the **p** to drink.
18: 1 done for Moses and for his **p** Israel,
18:10 rescued the **p** from the hand of the
18:13 seat to serve as judge for the **p**,
18:14 all that Moses was doing for the **p**,
18:14 is this you are doing for the **p**?
18:14 while all these **p** stand round you
18:15 "Because the **p** come to me to seek
18:18 You and these **p** who come to you will
18:22 Have them serve as judges for the **p**
18:23 all these **p** will go home satisfied."
18:25 and made them leaders of the **p**,
18:26 They served as judges for the **p** at
19: 7 summoned the elders of the **p** and set
19: 8 The **p** all responded together, "We
19: 9 so that the **p** will hear me speaking
19: 9 told the LORD what the **p** had said.
19:10 the LORD said to Moses, "Go to the **p**
19:12 Put limits for the **p** around the
19:14 had gone down the mountain to the **p**,
19:15 he said to the **p**, "Prepare
19:17 Moses led the **p** out of the camp to
19:21 "Go down and warn the **p** so they do
19:23 "The **p** cannot come up Mount Sinai,
19:24 But the priests and the **p** must not
19:25 Moses went down to the **p** and told
20:18 the **p** saw the thunder and lightning
20:20 Moses said to the **p**, "Do not be
20:21 The **p** remained at a distance, while
22:25 "If you lend money to one of my **p**
22:28 God or curse the ruler of your **p**.
23: 6 "Do not deny justice to your poor **p**
23:11 Then the poor among your **p** may get
23:31 I will hand over to you the **p** who
24: 2 And the **p** may not come up with him."
24: 3 Moses went and told the **p** all the
24: 7 the Covenant and read it to the **p**.
24: 8 sprinkled it on the **p** and said,
30:33 a priest must be cut off from his **p**.
30:38 must be cut off from his **p**."
31:14 that day must be cut off from his **p**.
32: 1 the **p** saw that Moses was so long in
32: 6 the next day the **p** rose early and
32: 7 "Go down, because your **p**, whom you
32: 9 "I have seen these **p**," the LORD said
32: 9 "and they are a stiff-necked **p**.
32:11 your anger burn against your **p**,

Ex 32:12 and do not bring disaster on your **p**.
32:14 did not bring on his **p** the disaster
32:17 Joshua heard the noise of the **p**
32:21 He said to Aaron, "What did these **p**
32:22 know how prone these **p** are to evil.
32:25 Moses saw that the **p** were running
32:28 about three thousand of the **p** died.
32:30 The next day Moses said to the **p**,
32:31 "Oh, what a great sin these **p** have
32:34 Now go, lead the **p** to the place I
32:35 the LORD struck the **p** with a plague
33: 1 "Leave this place, you and the **p** you
33: 3 you are a stiff-necked **p** and I
33: 4 the **p** heard these distressing words,
33: 5 'You are a stiff-necked **p**.
33:10 Whenever the **p** saw the pillar of
33:12 'Lead these **p**,' but you have not let
33:13 Remember that this nation is your **p**."
33:16 with your **p** unless you go with us?
33:16 your **p** from all the other **p** on the
34: 9 Although this is a stiff-necked **p**,
34:10 The **p** you live among will see how
36: 3 And the **p** continued to bring
36: 5 said to Moses, "The **p** are bringing
36: 6 the **p** were restrained from bringing
Lev 4: 3 bringing guilt on the **p**, he must
6: 3 commits any such sin that **p** may do—
7:20 person must be cut off from his **p**.
7:21 person must be cut off from his **p**.
7:25 the LORD must be cut off from his **p**.
7:27 person must be cut off from his **p**.
9: 7 atonement for yourself and the **p**;
9: 7 the offering that is for the **p** and
9:15 the offering that was for the **p**.
9:18 the fellowship offering for the **p**.
9:22 Aaron lifted his hands towards the **p**
9:23 they came out, they blessed the **p**;
16:15 goat for the sin offering for the **p**
16:24 and the burnt offering for the **p**,
16:24 atonement for himself and for the **p**.
17: 4 and must be cut off from his **p**.
17: 9 man must be cut off from his **p**.
17:10 and will cut him off from his **p**.
18:27 **p** who lived in the land before you,
18:29 must be cut off from their **p**.
19: 8 person must be cut off from his **p**.
19:16 spreading slander among your **p**.
19:18 bear a grudge against one of your **p**,
20: 2 **p** of the community are to stone him.
20: 3 and I will cut him off from his **p**;
20: 4 If the **p** of the community close
20: 5 will cut off from their **p** both him
20: 6 and I will cut him off from his **p**.
20:17 cut off before the eyes of their **p**.
20:18 them must be cut off from their **p**.
21: 1 unclean for any of his **p** who die,
21: 4 for **p** related to him by marriage,
21:14 but only a virgin from his own **p**,
21:15 defile his offspring among his **p**.
23:29 that day must be cut off from his **p**.
23:30 I will destroy from among his **p**
26:12 be your God, and you will be my **p**.
Nu 1:18 The **p** indicated their ancestry by
2: 3 The leader of the **p** of Judah is
2: 5 The leader of the **p** of Issachar is
2: 7 The leader of the **p** of Zebulun is
2:10 The leader of the **p** of Reuben is
2:12 The leader of the **p** of Simeon is
2:14 The leader of the **p** of Gad is
2:18 The leader of the **p** of Ephraim is
2:20 The leader of the **p** of Manasseh is
2:22 The leader of the **p** of Benjamin is
2:25 The leader of the **p** of Dan is
2:27 The leader of the **p** of Asher is
2:29 The leader of the **p** of Naphtali is
5:21 the LORD cause your **p** to curse
5:27 will become accursed among her **p**.
7:24 the leader of the **p** of Zebulun,
7:30 the leader of the **p** of Reuben,
7:36 the leader of the **p** of Simeon,
7:42 the leader of the **p** of Gad, brought
7:48 the leader of the **p** of Ephraim,
7:54 the leader of the **p** of Manasseh,
7:60 the leader of the **p** of Benjamin,
7:66 the leader of the **p** of Dan, brought
7:72 the leader of the **p** of Asher,

Nu 7:78 the leader of the **p** of Naphtali,
9:13 person must be cut off from his **p**
10:30 back to my own land and my own **p**."
11: 1 Now the **p** complained about their
11: 2 the **p** cried out to Moses, he prayed
11: 8 The **p** went around gathering it, and
11:10 Moses heard the **p** of every family
11:11 put the burden of all these **p** on me?
11:12 Did I conceive all these **p**? Did I
11:13 Where can I get meat for all these **p**?
11:14 I cannot carry all these **p** by myself;
11:16 leaders and officials among the **p**.
11:17 help you carry the burden of the **p**
11:18 "Tell the **p**: 'Consecrate yourselves
11:24 Moses went out and told the **p** what
11:29 I wish that all the LORD's **p** were
11:32 the **p** went out and gathered quail.
11:33 of the LORD burned against the **p**,
11:34 the **p** who had craved other food.
11:35 the **p** travelled to Hazeroth and
12:15 and the **p** did not move on till she
12:16 After that, the **p** left Hazeroth and
13:18 **p** who live there are strong or weak,
13:28 the **p** who live there are powerful,
13:30 Caleb silenced the **p** before Moses
13:31 "We can't attack those **p**;
14:11 "How long will these **p** treat me with
14:13 brought these **p** up from among them.
14:14 you, O LORD, are with these **p**
14:15 If you put these **p** to death all at
14:16 able to bring these **p** into the land
14:19 forgive the sin of these **p**, just as
15:30 person must be cut off from his **p**.
16:41 "You have killed the LORD's **p**," they
16:47 had already started among the **p**,
16:49 14,700 **p** died from the plague, in
19:18 and the **p** who were there.
20: 2 and the **p** gathered in opposition to
20:24 "Aaron will be gathered to his **p**.
20:26 Aaron will be gathered to his **p**;
21: 2 "If you will deliver these **p** into
21: 4 But the **p** grew impatient on the way;
21: 6 bit the **p** and many Israelites died.
21: 7 The **p** came to Moses and said, "We
21: 7 So Moses prayed for the **p**.
21:16 "Gather the **p** together and I will
21:18 that the nobles of the **p** sank—the
21:29 You are destroyed, O **p** of Chemosh!
22: 3 because there were so many **p**.
22: 5 Balak said: "A **p** has come out of
22: 6 Now come and put a curse on these **p**,
22:11 'A **p** that has come out of Egypt
22:12 must not put a curse on those **p**,
22:17 and put a curse on these **p** for me."
22:41 and from there he saw part of the **p**.
23: 9 I see **p** who live apart and do not
23:24 The **p** rise like a lioness;
24:14 Now I am going back to my **p**, but
24:14 **p** will do to your **p** in days to come."
25: 2 The **p** ate and bowed down before
25: 4 "Take all the leaders of these **p**,
27:13 you too will be gathered to your **p**,
27:17 so that the LORD's **p** will not be
31: 2 you will be gathered to your **p**."
31: 3 Moses said to the **p**, "Arm some of
31:11 spoils, including the **p** and animals,
31:16 that a plague struck the LORD's **p**.
31:40 16,000 **p**, of which the tribute for
31:46 16,000 **p**.
32:15 he will again leave all this **p** in
33:14 was no water for the **p** to drink.
35:15 aliens and any other **p** living among
Dt 1:28 They say, 'The **p** are stronger and
2: 4 Give the **p** these orders: 'You are
2:10 a **p** strong and numerous, and as
2:16 fighting men among the **p** had died,
2:21 They were a **p** strong and numerous,
3:28 for he will lead this **p** across and
4: 6 is a wise and understanding **p**."
4:10 "Assemble the **p** before me to hear my
4:20 to be the **p** of his inheritance,
4:33 Has any other **p** heard the voice of
5:28 I have heard what this **p** said to you.
7: 6 For you are a **p** holy to the LORD
7: 6 be his **p**, his treasured possession.
7:14 be blessed more than any other **p**;

Dt 9: 2 The **p** are strong and tall—Anakites!
9: 6 for you are a stiff-necked **p**.
9:12 because your **p** whom you brought out
9:13 "I have seen this **p**, and they are a
9:13 they are a stiff-necked **p** indeed!
9:26 do not destroy your **p**, your own
9:27 Overlook the stubbornness of this **p**
9:29 they are your **p**, your inheritance
10:11 "and lead the **p** on their way, so
13:13 led the **p** of their town astray,
13:15 both its **p** and its livestock.
14: 2 for you are a **p** holy to the LORD
14:21 But you are a **p** holy to the LORD
15:11 There will always be poor **p** in the
16:18 and they shall judge the **p** fairly.
17:16 or make the **p** return to Egypt to
18: 3 **p** who sacrifice a bull or a sheep:
19:20 The rest of the **p** will hear of this
20:10 city, make its **p** an offer of peace.
20:19 Are the trees of the field **p**,
21: 8 Accept this atonement for your **p**
21: 8 and do not hold your **p** guilty of
26: 5 he went down into Egypt with a few **p**
26:15 and bless your **p** Israel and the land
26:18 this day that you are his **p**,
26:19 be a **p** holy to the LORD your God,
27: 1 elders of Israel commanded the **p**:
27: 9 become the **p** of the LORD your God.
27:11 On the same day Moses commanded the **p**
27:12 on Mount Gerizim to bless the **p**:
28:33 A **p** that you do not know will eat
29:13 to confirm you this day as his **p**,
29:25 "It is because this **p** abandoned the
31: 7 for you must go with this **p** into the
31:12 Assemble the **p**—men, women and
31:16 and these **p** will soon prostitute
32: 6 O foolish and unwise **p**? Is he not
32: 9 For the LORD's portion is his **p**,
32:21 envious by those who are not a **p**;
32:36 The LORD will judge his **p** and have
32:43 Rejoice, O nations, with his **p**,
32:43 make atonement for his land and **p**.
32:44 this song in the hearing of the **p**.
32:50 will die and be gathered to your **p**,
32:50 Mount Hor and was gathered to his **p**.
33: 3 Surely it is you who love the **p**;
33: 5 when the leaders of the **p** assembled,
33: 7 cry of Judah; bring him to his **p**.
33:21 When the heads of the **p** assembled,
33:29 is like you, a **p** saved by the LORD?
Jos 1: 2 Now then, you and all these **p**, get
1: 6 because you will lead these **p** to
1:10 Joshua ordered the officers of the **p**:
1:11 "Go through the camp and tell the **p**,
3: 3 giving orders to the **p**: "When you
3: 5 Joshua told the **p**, "Consecrate
3: 6 covenant and pass on ahead of the **p**.
3:14 when the **p** broke camp to cross the
3:16 the **p** crossed over opposite Jericho.
4: 2 "Choose twelve men from among the **p**,
4:10 was done by the **p**, just as Moses
4:10 directed Joshua. The **p** hurried over,
4:11 the other side while the **p** watched.
4:19 month the **p** went up from the Jordan
6: 5 **p** will go up, every man straight in."
6: 7 he ordered the **p**, "Advance! March
6: 8 Joshua had spoken to the **p**, the
6:10 Joshua had commanded the **p**, "Do not
6:11 Then the **p** returned to camp and
6:16 Joshua commanded the **p**, "Shout! For
6:20 the trumpets sounded, the **p** shouted,
6:20 when the **p** gave a loud shout, the
7: 5 the hearts of the **p** melted and
7: 7 why did you ever bring this **p** across
7: 9 The Canaanites and the other **p** of
7:13 "Go, consecrate the **p**. Tell them,
8: 1 of Ai, his **p**, his city and his land.
8: 9 Joshua spent that night with the **p**.
8:33 Half of the **p** stood in front of
9: 3 However, when the **p** of Gibeon heard
10: 1 and that the **p** of Gibeon had made a
10: 2 He and his **p** were very much alarmed
12: 5 of the **p** of Geshur and Maacah,
13:11 the territory of the **p** of Geshur and
13:13 out the **p** of Geshur and Maacah,
14: 8 me made the hearts of the **p** sink.
Jos 15:12 the **p** of Judah by their clans.
15:15 From there he marched against the **p**
15:63 live there with the **p** of Judah.
16:10 the Canaanites live among the **p** of
17: 2 for the rest of the **p** of Manasseh—
17: 7 include the **p** living at En Tappuah.
17:11 Ibleam and the **p** of Dor, Endor,
17:14 The **p** of Joseph said to Joshua, "Why
17:14 We are a numerous **p** and the LORD has
17:16 The **p** of Joseph replied, "The hill
18:14 Jearim), a town of the **p** of Judah.
24:16 the **p** answered, "Far be it from us
24:19 Joshua said to the **p**, "You are not
24:21 the **p** said to Joshua, "No! We will
24:24 the **p** said to Joshua, "We will serve
24:25 Joshua made a covenant for the **p**,
24:28 Joshua sent the **p** away, each to his
Jdg 1:11 against the **p** living in Debir
1:16 live among the **p** of the Desert of
1:19 but they were unable to drive the **p**
1:27 Manasseh did not drive out the **p** of
1:32 of this the **p** of Asher lived among
2: 2 a covenant with the **p** of this land,
2: 4 the Israelites, the **p** wept aloud,
2: 7 The **p** served the LORD throughout the
2:19 when the judge died, the **p** returned
5: 2 the **p** willingly offer themselves—
5: 9 the willing volunteers among the **p**.
5:11 "Then the **p** of the LORD went down to
5:13 the **p** of the LORD came to me with
5:14 was with the **p** who followed you.
5:18 The **p** of Zebulun risked their very
5:23 'Curse its **p** bitterly, because they
7: 3 announce now to the **p**, 'Anyone who
9:29 If only this **p** were under my command!
9:36 "Look, **p** are coming down from the
9:37 Gaal spoke up again: "Look, **p** are
9:42 The next day the **p** of Shechem went
9:43 When he saw the **p** coming out of the
9:45 he had captured it and killed its **p**.
9:49 set it on fire over the **p** inside.
10:18 The leaders of the **p** of Gilead said
11:11 and the **p** made him head and
11:23 Amorites out before his **p** Israel,
12: 2 Jephthah answered, "I and my **p** were
14: 3 your relatives or among all our **p**?
14:16 You've given my **p** a riddle, but you
14:17 turn explained the riddle to her **p**.
16: 2 The **p** of Gaza were told, "Samson is
16:24 the **p** saw him, they praised their
18: 7 where they saw that the **p** were
18:10 you will find an unsuspecting **p** and
18:20 image and went along with the **p**.
18:27 a peaceful and unsuspecting **p**.
19:12 city, whose **p** are not Israelites.
21: 2 The **p** went to Bethel, where they sat
21: 4 Early the next day the **p** built an
21: 9 For when they counted the **p**, they
21: 9 the **p** of Jabesh Gilead were there.
21:12 They found among the **p** living in
21:15 The **p** grieved for Benjamin, because
Ru 1: 6 of his **p** by providing food for them,
1:10 "We will go back with you to your **p**.
1:15 is going back to her **p** and her gods.
1:16 **p** will be my **p** and your God my God.
2:11 with a **p** you did not know before.
4: 4 the presence of the elders of my **p**.
1Sa 2:13 practice of the priests with the **p**
2:24 I hear spreading among the LORD's **p**.
4: 4 the **p** sent men to Shiloh, and they
5: 3 the **p** of Ashdod rose early the next
5: 6 The LORD's hand was heavy upon the **p**
5: 9 He afflicted the **p** of the city, both
5:10 the **p** of Ekron cried out, "They have
5:10 round to us to kill us and our **p**."
5:11 place, or it will kill us and our **p**.
6:13 Now the **p** of Beth Shemesh were
6:14 The **p** chopped up the wood of the
6:15 On that day the **p** of Beth Shemesh
6:19 The **p** mourned because of the heavy
6:21 they sent messengers to the **p** of
8: 7 "Listen to all that the **p** are saying
8:10 **p** who were asking him for a king.
8:19 the **p** refused to listen to Samuel.
8:21 Samuel heard all that the **p** said, he
9:12 for the **p** have a sacrifice at the
1Sa 9:13 The **p** will not begin eating until he
9:16 he will deliver my **p** from the hand
9:16 I have looked upon my **p**, for their
9:17 to you about; he will govern my **p**."
10:23 and as he stood among the **p** he was a
10:24 Then the **p** shouted, "Long live the
10:25 Samuel explained to the **p** the
10:25 Samuel dismissed the **p**, each to his
11: 4 terms to the **p**, they all wept aloud.
11: 5 "What is wrong with the **p**? Why are
11: 7 terror of the LORD fell on the **p**,
11:12 The **p** then said to Samuel, "Who was
11:14 Samuel said to the **p**, "Come, let us
12: 6 Samuel said to the **p**, "It is the
12:19 The **p** all said to Samuel, "Pray to
12:22 name the LORD will not reject his **p**,
13: 4 And the **p** were summoned to join
13:14 and appointed him leader of his **p**,
14:24 because Saul had bound the **p** under
14:27 had bound the **p** with the oath,
15: 1 anoint you king over his **p** Israel;
15:18 completely destroy those wicked **p**,
15:24 I was afraid of the **p** and so I gave
19:24 This is why **p** say, "Is Saul also
23: 5 and saved the **p** of Keilah.
27:12 "He has become so odious to his **p**,
30:21 to meet David and the **p** with him.
31: 9 of their idols and among their **p**.
31:11 the **p** of Jabesh Gilead heard of what
2Sa 4: 3 the **p** of Beeroth fled to Gittaim and
5:12 for the sake of his **p** Israel.
6:18 he blessed the **p** in the name of the
6:21 me ruler over the LORD's **p** Israel
7:10 Wicked **p** shall not oppress them any
7:23 who is like your **p** Israel—the one
7:23 out to redeem as a **p** for himself,
7:23 your **p**, whom you redeemed from
7:24 You have established your **p** Israel
10:12 for our **p** and the cities of our God.
12:31 brought out the **p** who were there,
13:34 saw many **p** on the road west of him,
14:15 because the **p** have made me afraid.
15:32 summit, where **p** used to worship God
16:18 by these **p** and by all the men of
17:29 milk for David and his **p** to eat.
17:29 For they said, "The **p** have become
19: 9 the **p** were all arguing with each
22:44 me from the attacks of my **p**;
22:44 **P** I did not know are subject to me,
24:15 of the **p** from Dan to Beersheba died.
24:16 the angel who was afflicting the **p**,
24:17 angel who was striking down the **p**,
24:21 the plague on the **p** may be stopped."
1Ki 3: 2 The **p**, however, were still
3: 8 Your servant is here among the **p** you
3: 8 a great **p**, too numerous to count or
3: 9 a discerning heart to govern your **p**
3: 9 to govern this great **p** of yours?"
4:20 The **p** of Judah and Israel were as
8:30 of your **p** Israel when they pray
8:33 "When your **p** Israel have been
8:34 forgive the sin of your **p** Israel and
8:35 your **p** have sinned against you,
8:36 sin of your servants, your **p** Israel.
8:36 you gave your **p** for an inheritance.
8:38 is made by any of your **p** Israel—
8:41 does not belong to your **p** Israel
8:43 as do your own **p** Israel, and may
8:44 "When your **p** go to war against their
8:50 forgive your **p**, who have sinned
8:51 for they are your **p** and your
8:52 and to the plea of your **p** Israel,
8:56 to his **p** Israel just as he promised.
8:59 the cause of his **p** Israel according
8:65 **p** from Lebo Hamath to the Wadi of
8:66 On the following day he sent the **p**
8:66 his servant David and his **p** Israel.
9: 9 **P** will answer, 'Because they have
12: 5 So the **p** went away.
12: 6 you advise me to answer these **p**?"
12: 7 you will be a servant to these **p**
12: 9 we answer these **p** who say to me,
12:10 "Tell these **p** who have said to you,
12:13 The king answered the **p** harshly.
12:15 the king did not listen to the **p**,
12:23 Benjamin, and to the rest of the **p**,

1Ki 12:27 If these **p** go up to offer sacrifices
12:28 He said to the **p**, "It is too much
12:30 the **p** went even as far as Dan to
12:31 priests from all sorts of **p**, even
13:25 Some **p** who passed by saw the body
13:33 the high places from all sorts of **p**.
14: 2 told me I would be king over this **p**.
14: 7 'I raised you up from among the **p**
14:24 the **p** engaged in all the detestable
18:19 Now summon the **p** from all over
18:21 Elijah went before the **p** and said,
18:21 But the **p** said nothing.
18:37 so these **p** will know that you
19:21 and gave it to the **p**, and they ate.
20: 8 The elders and the **p** all answered,
20:42 life for his life, your **p** for his **p**.
21: 9 in a prominent place among the **p**.
21:12 in a prominent place among the **p**.
21:13 charges against Naboth before the **p**,
22: 4 "I am as you are, my **p** as your **p**, my
22:17 LORD said, 'These **p** have no master.
22:28 "Mark my words, all you **p**!
22:43 the **p** continued to offer sacrifices
2Ki 3: 7 "I am as you are, my **p** as your **p**, my
4:13 "I have a home among my own **p**.
4:41 and said, "Serve it to the **p** to eat.
4:42 "Give it to the **p** to eat," Elisha
4:43 answered, "Give it to the **p** to eat.
6:18 LORD, "Strike these **p** with blindness.
6:30 went along the wall, the **p** looked,
7:16 the **p** went out and plundered the
7:17 and the **p** trampled him in the
7:20 for the **p** trampled him in the
9: 6 you king over the LORD's **p** Israel.
10:27 and **p** have used it for a latrine to
11:12 They anointed him, and the **p** clapped
11:13 noise made by the guards and the **p**,
11:13 to the **p** at the temple of the LORD.
11:17 between the LORD and the king and **p**
11:17 that they would be the LORD's **p**.
11:17 covenant between the king and the **p**.
12: 3 the **p** continued to offer sacrifices
12: 8 collect any more money from the **p**
14: 4 the **p** continued to offer sacrifices
15: 4 the **p** continued to offer sacrifices
15:10 He attacked him in front of the **p**,
15:29 and deported the **p** to Assyria.
15:35 the **p** continued to offer sacrifices
17:24 The king of Assyria brought **p** from
17:25 them and they killed some of the **p**.
17:26 "The **p** you deported and resettled in
17:26 the **p** do not know what he requires."
17:27 teach the **p** what the god of the
17:29 shrines the **p** of Samaria had made
17:32 appointed all sorts of their own **p**
17:41 Even while these **p** were worshipping
18:26 the hearing of the **p** on the wall."
18:36 the **p** remained silent and said
19:12 the **p** of Eden who were in Tel Assar?
19:26 Their **p**, drained of power, are
19:35 When the **p** got up the next morning
20: 5 tell Hezekiah, the leader of my **p**,
21: 9 the **p** did not listen. Manasseh led
22: 4 have collected from the **p**.
22:13 for the **p** and for all Judah about
22:16 disaster on this place and its **p**,
22:19 spoken against this place and its **p**,
23: 2 the **p** of Jerusalem, the priests and
23: 6 over the graves of the common **p**.
23:13 detestable god of the **p** of Ammon.
25: 3 there was no food for the **p** to eat.
25:11 the **p** who remained in the city,
25:22 the **p** he had left behind in Judah.
1Ch 2:10 the leader of the **p** of Judah.
4:14 this because its **p** were craftsmen.
4:27 as numerous as the **p** of Judah.
5:21 took one hundred thousand **p** captive,
5:23 The **p** of the half-tribe of Manasseh
9: 1 The **p** of Judah were taken captive to
9: 6 The **p** from Judah numbered 690.
9: 9 The **p** from Benjamin, as listed in
10: 9 news among their idols and their **p**.
14: 2 for the sake of his **p** Israel.
16: 2 he blessed the **p** in the name of the
17: 6 whom I commanded to shepherd my **p**,
17: 9 Wicked **p** will not oppress them any
1Ch 17:21 who is like your **p** Israel—the one
17:21 went out to redeem a **p** for himself,
17:21 out nations from before your **p**,
17:22 You made your **p** Israel your very own
19:13 for our **p** and the cities of our God.
20: 3 brought out the **p** who were there,
21:15 the angel who was destroying the **p**,
21:17 not let this plague remain on your **p**
21:22 the plague on the **p** may be stopped.
22:18 is subject to the LORD and to his **p**.
23:25 has granted rest to his **p** and has
28: 2 "Listen to me, my brothers and my **p**.
29: 9 The **p** rejoiced at the willing
29:14 "But who am I, and who are my **p**,
29:17 your **p** who are here have given to
29:18 this desire in the hearts of your **p**
2Ch 1: 9 for you have made me king over a **p**
1:10 that I may lead this **p**, for who is
1:10 to govern this great **p** of yours?"
1:11 my **p** over whom I have made you king,
2:11 The LORD loves his **p**, he has made
2:18 over them to keep the **p** working.
6: 5 'since the day I brought my **p** out of
6:21 of your **p** Israel when they pray
6:24 "When your **p** Israel have been
6:25 forgive the sin of your **p** Israel and
6:26 your **p** have sinned against you,
6:27 sin of your servants, your **p** Israel.
6:27 you gave your **p** for an inheritance.
6:29 is made by any of your **p** Israel—
6:32 does not belong to your **p** Israel
6:33 as do your own **p** Israel, and may
6:34 "When your **p** go to war against their
6:39 forgive your **p**, who have sinned
7: 8 **p** from Lebo Hamath to the Wadi of
7:10 month he sent the **p** to their homes,
7:10 and Solomon and for his **p** Israel.
7:13 land or send a plague among my **p**,
7:14 if my **p**, who are called by my name,
7:22 **P** will answer, 'Because they have
10: 5 in three days." So the **p** went away.
10: 6 you advise me to answer these **p**?"
10: 7 "If you will be kind to these **p** and
10: 9 we answer these **p** who say to me,
10:10 "Tell the **p** who have said to you,
10:15 the king did not listen to the **p**,
15: 9 and Benjamin and the **p** from Ephraim,
16:10 Asa brutally oppressed some of the **p**.
17: 9 the towns of Judah and taught the **p**.
18: 2 cattle for him and the **p** with him
18: 3 "I am as you are, and my **p** as your **p**;
18:16 LORD said, 'These **p** have no master.
18:27 "Mark my words, all you **p**!
19: 4 and he went out again among the **p**
20: 4 The **p** of Judah came together to seek
20: 7 of this land before your **p** Israel
20:20 to me, Judah and **p** of Jerusalem!
20:21 After consulting the **p**, Jehoshaphat
20:33 were not removed, and the **p** still
21:11 had caused the **p** of Jerusalem to
21:13 led Judah and the **p** of Jerusalem
21:14 the LORD is about to strike your **p**,
21:19 His **p** made no fire in his honour, as
22: 1 The **p** of Jerusalem made Ahaziah,
23:12 Athaliah heard the noise of the **p**
23:16 **p** and the king would be the LORD's **p**.
23:20 the nobles, the rulers of the **p** and
24:19 to the **p** to bring them back to him,
24:20 He stood before the **p** and said,
24:23 and killed all the leaders of the **p**.
25: 5 Amaziah called the **p** of Judah
25: 7 with any of the **p** of Ephraim.
25:13 They killed three thousand **p** and
25:14 back the gods of the **p** of Seir.
25:15 save their own **p** from your hand?"
26:10 He had **p** working his fields and
26:23 kings, for **p** said, "He had leprosy.
27: 2 The **p**, however, continued their
28: 5 took many of his **p** as prisoners and
29:36 God had brought about for his **p**,
30: 3 **p** had not assembled in Jerusalem.
30: 5 calling the **p** to come to Jerusalem
30:10 the **p** scorned and ridiculed them.
30:12 the hand of God was on the **p** to
30:13 A very large crowd of **p** assembled in
30:18 Although most of the many **p** who came
2Ch 30:20 LORD heard Hezekiah and healed the **p**.
30:27 the Levites stood to bless the **p**,
31: 4 He ordered the **p** living in Jerusalem
31: 8 the LORD and blessed his **p** Israel.
31:10 "Since the **p** began to bring their
31:10 because the LORD has blessed his **p**,
32: 6 military officers over the **p** and
32: 8 And the **p** gained confidence from
32:14 has been able to save his **p** from me?
32:15 able to deliver his **p** from my hand
32:17 did not rescue their **p** from my hand,
32:17 will not rescue his **p** from my hand."
32:18 they called out in Hebrew to the **p**
32:22 the LORD saved Hezekiah and the **p** of
32:26 his heart, as did the **p** of Jerusalem;
32:33 All Judah and the **p** of Jerusalem
33: 9 Manasseh led Judah and the **p** of
33:10 The LORD spoke to Manasseh and his **p**,
33:17 The **p**, however, continued to
34: 9 collected from the **p** of Manasseh,
34: 9 from all the **p** of Judah and Benjamin
34:24 disaster on this place and its **p**—
34:27 spoke against this place and its **p**,
34:30 the **p** of Jerusalem, the priests and
34:32 the **p** of Jerusalem did this in
35: 3 the LORD your God and his **p** Israel.
35: 5 your fellow countrymen, the lay **p**.
35: 7 Josiah provided for all the lay **p**
35: 8 the **p** and the priests and Levites.
35:12 of the **p** to offer to the LORD,
35:18 were there with the **p** of Jerusalem.
36:14 leaders of the priests and the **p**
36:15 on his **p** and on his dwelling-place.
36:16 aroused against his **p** and there was
36:23 Anyone of his **p** among you—may the
Ezr 1: 3 Anyone of his **p** among you—may his
1: 4 the **p** of any place where survivors
2: 1 Now these are the **p** of the province
2:70 along with some of the other **p**, and
3: 1 **p** assembled as one man in Jerusalem.
3: 7 and oil to the **p** of Sidon and Tyre,
3:13 because the **p** made so much noise.
4: 4 out to discourage the **p** of Judah
4: 6 the **p** of Judah and Jerusalem.
4:10 the other **p** whom the great and
5: 8 The **p** are building it with large
5:12 and deported the **p** to Babylon.
6:12 overthrow any king or **p** who lifts a
7:16 as the freewill offerings of the **p**
8:15 When I checked among the **p** and the
8:36 to the **p** and to the house of God.
10:13 there are many **p** here and it is the
Ne 1: 9 then even if your exiled **p** are at
1:10 "They are your servants and your **p**,
4: 6 the **p** worked with all their heart.
4:10 Meanwhile, the **p** in Judah said, "The
4:13 Therefore I stationed some of the **p**
4:14 officials and the rest of the **p**,
4:19 the officials and the rest of the **p**,
4:22 At that time I also said to the **p**,
5:10 also lending the **p** money and grain.
5:13 And the **p** did as they had promised.
5:15 me—placed a heavy burden on the **p**
5:15 also lorded it over the **p**.
5:18 the demands were heavy on these **p**.
5:19 God, for all I have done for these **p**.
7: 4 but there were few **p** in it, and the
7: 5 and the common **p** for registration
7: 6 These are the **p** of the province who
7:72 The total given by the rest of the **p**
7:73 along with certain of the **p** and the
8: 5 as he opened it, the **p** all stood up.
8: 7 instructed the **p** in the Law
8: 7 while the **p** were standing there.
8: 8 so that the **p** could understand what
8: 9 instructing the **p** said to them all,
8:16 the **p** went out and brought back
9:32 upon our fathers and all your **p**,
10:14 The leaders of the **p**: Parosh,
10:28 "The rest of the **p**—priests, Levites,
10:34 the Levites and the **p**—have cast
11: 1 Now the leaders of the **p** settled in
11: 1 and the rest of the **p** cast lots to
11: 2 The **p** commended all the men who
11: 4 while other **p** from both Judah and
11:24 in all affairs relating to the **p**.

Ne 11:25 some of the **p** of Judah lived in
12:30 they purified the **p**, the gates and
12:38 together with half the **p**—past the
13: 1 read aloud in the hearing of the **p**
13: 3 the **p** heard this law, they excluded
13:16 on the Sabbath to the **p** of Judah.
Est 1:11 her beauty to the **p** and nobles,
1:22 and to each **p** in its own language,
3: 6 learned who Mordecai's **p** were,
3: 6 a way to destroy all Mordecai's **p**,
3: 8 "There is a certain **p** dispersed and
3: 8 different from those of all other **p**
3:11 "and do with the **p** as you please.
3:12 in the language of each **p** all
3:14 made known to the **p** of every
4: 8 mercy and plead with him for her **p**.
4:11 the **p** of the royal provinces know
7: 3 And spare my **p**—this is my request.
7: 4 For I and my **p** have been sold for
8: 6 I bear to see disaster fall on my **p**?
8: 9 the language of each **p** and also to
8:13 made known to the **p** of every
8:17 And many **p** of other nationalities
9: 2 because the **p** of all the other
10: 3 he worked for the good of his **p**
Job 12: 2 "Doubtless you are the **p**, and wisdom
17: 6 a man in whose face **p** spit.
18:19 or descendants among his **p**,
28: 4 Far from where **p** dwell he cuts a
34:20 the **p** are shaken and they pass away
34:30 from laying snares for the **p**.
36:20 to drag **p** away from their homes.
Ps 3: 8 May your blessing be on your **p**.
12: 7 and protect us from such **p** for ever.
14: 4 who devour my **p** as men eat bread
14: 7 LORD restores the fortunes of his **p**,
18:43 me from the attacks of the **p**;
18:43 **p** I did not know are subject to me.
22: 6 by men and despised by the **p**.
22:17 **p** stare and gloat over me.
22:31 righteousness to a **p** yet unborn—
28: 8 The LORD is the strength of his **p**, a
28: 9 Save your **p** and bless your
29:11 The LORD gives strength to his **p**;
29:11 the LORD blesses his **p** with peace.
33:12 the **p** he chose for his inheritance.
35:18 throngs of **p** I will praise you.
44:12 You sold your **p** for a pittance,
45:10 your **p** and your father's house.
47: 9 as the **p** of the God of Abraham,
50: 4 the earth, that he may judge his **p**:
50: 7 "Hear, O my **p**, and I will speak,
53: 4 who devour my **p** as men eat bread
53: 6 God restores the fortunes of his **p**,
59:11 Lord our shield, or my **p** will forget.
60: 3 You have shown your **p** desperate
62: 8 Trust in him at all times, O **p**;
65: 9 water to provide the **p** with corn,
68: 7 you went out before your **p**, O God,
68:10 Your **p** settled in it, and from your
68:35 gives power and strength to his **p**.
69:11 I put on sackcloth, **p** make sport of
69:33 and does not despise his captive **p**.
69:35 **p** will settle there and possess it;
72: 2 will judge your **p** in righteousness,
72: 3 will bring prosperity to the **p**,
72: 4 defend the afflicted among the **p**
72:15 May **p** ever pray for him and bless
73:10 Therefore their **p** turn to them and
74: 2 Remember the **p** you purchased of old,
74:18 foolish **p** have reviled your name.
74:19 lives of your afflicted **p** for ever.
75: 3 the earth and all its **p** quake, it is
77:15 your mighty arm you redeemed your **p**,
77:20 You led your **p** like a flock by the
78: 1 O my **p**, hear my teaching; listen to
78:20 Can he supply meat for his **p**?"
78:24 rained down manna for the **p** to eat,
78:52 he brought his **p** out like a flock;
78:62 He gave his **p** over to the sword;
78:71 to be the shepherd of his **p** Jacob,
79:13 we your **p**, the sheep of your pasture,
80: 4 against the prayers of your **p**?
80:16 at your rebuke your **p** perish.
81: 8 "Hear, O my **p**, and I will warn you—
81:11 "But my **p** would not listen to me;
Ps 81:13 "If my **p** would but listen to me, if
83: 3 they conspire against your **p**;
83: 7 Philistia, with the **p** of Tyre.
85: 2 You forgave the iniquity of your **p**
85: 6 that your **p** may rejoice in you?
85: 8 he promises peace to his **p**,
89:19 to your faithful **p** you said: "I have
89:19 a young man from among the **p**.
94: 5 They crush your **p**, O LORD;
94: 8 you senseless ones among the **p**;
94:14 For the LORD will not reject his **p**;
95: 7 and we are the **p** of his pasture,
95:10 "They are a **p** whose hearts go astray,
100: 3 are his **p**, the sheep of his pasture.
102:18 that a **p** not yet created may praise
105:24 The LORD made his **p** very fruitful;
105:25 whose hearts he turned to hate his **p**,
105:43 He brought out his **p** with rejoicing,
106: 4 when you show favour to your **p**,
106:40 the LORD was angry with his **p**
107:32 exalt him in the assembly of the **p**
111: 6 He has shown his **p** the power of his
111: 9 He provided redemption for his **p**;
113: 8 with the princes of their **p**.
114: 1 of Jacob from a **p** of foreign tongue,
125: 2 so the LORD surrounds his **p** both
135:12 an inheritance to his **p** Israel.
135:14 For the LORD will vindicate his **p**
136:16 to him who led his **p** through the
144:15 Blessed are the **p** of whom this is
144:15 are the **p** whose God is the LORD.
147:13 gates and blesses your **p** within you.
148:14 He has raised up for his **p** a horn,
148:14 of Israel, the **p** close to his heart.
149: 2 the **p** of Zion be glad in their King.
149: 4 For the LORD takes delight in his **p**;
Pr 11:26 **P** curse the man who hoards grain,
14:34 but sin is a disgrace to any **p**.
28:15 wicked man ruling over a helpless **p**.
28:28 rise to power, **p** go into hiding;
29: 2 the righteous thrive, the **p** rejoice;
29: 2 when the wicked rule, the **p** groan.
29:18 the **p** cast off restraint;
Ecc 7:21 pay attention to every word **p** say,
8:11 the hearts of the **p** are filled with
9:14 small city with only a few **p** in it.
12: 9 also he imparted knowledge to the **p**.
SS 6:12 me among the royal chariots of my **p**.
Isa 1: 3 not know, my **p** do not understand."
1: 4 Ah, sinful nation, a **p** loaded with
1:10 law of our God, you **p** of Gomorrah!
2: 6 You have abandoned your **p**, the house
3: 5 **P** will oppress each other—man
3: 7 do not make me the leader of the **p**."
3:12 Youths oppress my **p**, women rule over
3:12 O my **p**, your guides lead you astray;
3:13 in court; he rises to judge the **p**.
3:14 the elders and leaders of his **p**:
3:15 What do you mean by crushing my **p**
5:13 Therefore my **p** will go into exile
5:25 LORD's anger burns against his **p**;
6: 5 and I live among a **p** of unclean lips,
6: 9 He said, "Go and tell this **p**:
6:10 Make the heart of this **p** calloused;
7: 2 of Ahaz and his **p** were shaken,
7: 8 will be too shattered to be a **p**.
7:17 on your **p** and on the house of your
8: 6 "Because this **p** has rejected the
8:11 me not to follow the way of this **p**.
8:12 that these **p** call conspiracy;
8:14 And for the **p** of Jerusalem he will
8:19 should not a **p** enquire of their God?
9: 2 The **p** walking in darkness have seen
9: 3 you as **p** rejoice at the harvest,
9:13 the **p** have not returned to him who
9:16 Those who guide this **p** mislead them,
9:19 and the **p** will be fuel for the fire;
10: 2 justice from the oppressed of my **p**,
10: 6 I dispatch him against a **p** who anger
10:22 Though your **p**, O Israel, be like the
10:24 "O my **p** who live in Zion, do not be
10:31 the **p** of Gebim take cover.
11:11 that is left of his **p** from Assyria,
11:12 assemble the scattered **p** of Judah
11:14 they will plunder the **p** to the east.
11:16 of his **p** that is left from Assyria,
Isa 12: 6 aloud and sing for joy, **p** of Zion,
13:14 each will return to his own **p**,
14:20 your land and killed your **p**.
14:25 His yoke will be taken from my **p**,
14:32 his afflicted **p** will find refuge."
16:14 Moab's splendour and all her many **p**
18: 2 Go, swift messengers, to a **p** tall
18: 2 to a **p** feared far and wide, an
18: 7 from a **p** tall and smooth-skinned,
18: 7 from a **p** feared far and wide, an
19:25 "Blessed be Egypt my **p**, Assyria my
20: 6 In that day the **p** who live on this
21:10 O my **p**, crushed on the
22: 4 me over the destruction of my **p**."
23: 2 Be silent, you **p** of the island and
23: 6 wail, you **p** of the island.
23:13 this **p** that is now of no account!
24: 2 will be the same for priest as for **p**,
24: 5 The earth is defiled by its **p**;
24: 6 its **p** must bear their guilt.
24:17 snare await you, O **p** of the earth.
25: 8 of his **p** from all the earth.
26: 9 **p** of the world learn righteousness.
26:11 Let them see your zeal for your **p**
26:18 not given birth to **p** of the world.
26:20 Go, my **p**, enter your rooms and shut
26:21 the **p** of the earth for their sins.
27:11 this is a **p** without understanding;
28: 5 wreath for the remnant of his **p**.
28:11 tongues God will speak to this **p**,
28:14 who rule this **p** in Jerusalem.
29:13 The Lord says: "These **p** come near to
29:14 these **p** with wonder upon wonder;
30: 5 because of a **p** useless to them,
30: 9 These are rebellious **p**, deceitful
30:19 O **p** of Zion, who live in Jerusalem,
30:26 binds up the bruises of his **p** and
30:29 rejoice as when **p** go up with flutes
32:18 My **p** will live in peaceful
33:19 You will see those arrogant **p** no
33:19 those **p** of an obscure speech, with
34: 5 Edom, the **p** I have totally destroyed.
36:11 the hearing of the **p** on the wall."
36:21 the **p** remained silent and said
37:12 the **p** of Eden who were in Tel Assar?
37:27 Their **p**, drained of power, are
37:36 When the **p** got up the next morning
40: 1 Comfort, comfort my **p**, says your God.
40: 7 Surely the **p** are grass.
40:22 and its **p** are like grasshoppers.
41:20 that **p** may see and know, may
42: 5 who gives breath to its **p**, and life
42: 6 a covenant for the **p** and a
42:11 Let the **p** of Sela sing for joy;
42:22 this is a **p** plundered and looted,
43: 4 and **p** in exchange for your life.
43:20 to give drink to my **p**, my chosen,
43:21 the **p** I formed for myself that they
44: 7 since I established my ancient **p**,
47: 6 I was angry with my **p** and desecrated
49: 8 make you to be a covenant for the **p**,
49:13 For the LORD comforts his **p** and will
49:19 you will be too small for your **p**,
51: 4 "Listen to me, my **p**; hear me, my
51: 7 you **p** who have my law in your
51:16 and who say to Zion, 'You are my **p**.
51:22 your God, who defends his **p**: "See, I
52: 4 "At first my **p** went down to Egypt to
52: 5 "For my **p** have been taken away for
52: 6 Therefore my **p** will know my name;
52: 9 for the LORD has comforted his **p**,
53: 8 of my **p** he was stricken.
56: 3 will surely exclude me from his **p**.
57:14 obstacles out of the way of my **p**."
58: 1 Declare to my **p** their rebellion and
58:12 Your **p** will rebuild the ancient
60:21 will all your **p** be righteous and
61: 7 Instead of their shame my **p** will
61: 9 they are a **p** the LORD has blessed."
62:10 Prepare the way for the **p**.
63: 8 He said, "Surely they are my **p**, sons
63:11 his **p** recalled the days of old, the
63:11 the days of Moses and his **p**—where
63:14 This is how you guided your **p** to
63:18 For a little while your **p** possessed
64: 9 us we pray, for we are all your **p**.

Isa 65: 2 held out my hands to an obstinate **p**,
65: 3 a **p** who continually provoke me to my
65: 5 Such **p** are smoke in my nostrils,
65: 9 my chosen **p** will inherit them,
65:10 for herds, for my **p** who seek me.
65:18 to be a delight and its **p** a joy.
65:19 Jerusalem and take delight in my **p**;
65:22 so will be the days of my **p**;
65:23 will be a **p** blessed by the LORD,
Jer 1: 3 the **p** of Jerusalem went into exile.
1:16 I will pronounce my judgments on my **p**
2:11 But my **p** have exchanged their Glory
2:13 "My **p** have committed two sins: They
2:30 "In vain I punished your **p**; they did
2:31 Why do my **p** say, 'We are free to
2:32 Yet my **p** have forgotten me,
3:14 "Return, faithless **p**," declares the
3:22 "Return, faithless **p**; I will cure
4: 4 you men of Judah and **p** of Jerusalem,
4:10 this **p** and Jerusalem by saying,
4:11 At that time this **p** and Jerusalem
4:11 in the desert blows towards my **p**,
4:22 "My **p** are fools; they do not know me.
4:25 I looked, and there were no **p**;
5:10 these **p** do not belong to the LORD.
5:14 "Because the **p** have spoken these
5:14 and these **p** the wood it consumes.
5:15 a **p** whose language you do not know,
5:19 the **p** ask, 'Why has the LORD our God
5:21 you foolish and senseless **p**, who
5:23 these **p** have stubborn and rebellious
5:26 "Among my **p** are wicked men who lie
5:31 and my **p** love it this way.
6: 1 "Flee for safety, **p** of Benjamin!
6:14 They dress the wound of my **p** as
6:19 I am bringing disaster on this **p**,
6:21 "I will put obstacles before this **p**.
6:26 O my **p**, put on sackcloth and roll in
6:27 a tester of metals and my **p** the ore,
7:15 your brothers, the **p** of Ephraim.'
7:16 "So do not pray for this **p** nor offer
7:23 be your God and you will be my **p**.
7:30 "'The **p** of Judah have done evil in
7:32 **p** will no longer call it Topheth
7:33 the carcasses of this **p** will become
8: 1 and the bones of the **p** of Jerusalem
8: 5 Why then have these **p** turned away?
8: 7 But my **p** do not know the
8:11 They dress the wound of my **p** as
8:19 Listen to the cry of my **p** from a
8:21 Since my **p** are crushed, I am crushed;
8:22 no healing for the wound of my **p**?
9: 1 day and night for the slain of my **p**.
9: 2 so that I might leave my **p** and go
9: 2 adulterers, a crowd of unfaithful **p**.
9: 7 can I do because of the sin of my **p**?
9:15 "See, I will make this **p** eat bitter
11: 2 tell them to the **p** of Judah and to
11: 4 be my **p**, and I will be your God.
11: 9 "There is a conspiracy among the **p**
11:12 The towns of Judah and the **p** of
11:14 "Do not pray for this **p** nor offer
12: 4 Moreover, the **p** are saying, "He will
12:16 if they learn well the ways of my **p**
12:16 even as they once taught my **p** to
12:16 they will be established among my **p**.
13:10 These wicked **p**, who refuse to listen
13:11 'to be my **p** for my renown and praise
14:10 is what the LORD says about this **p**:
14:11 pray for the well-being of this **p**.
14:16 the **p** they are prophesying to will
14:17 my virgin daughter—my **p**—has suffered
15: 1 my heart would not go out to this **p**.
15: 7 bereavement and destruction on my **p**,
15:19 Let this **p** turn to you, but you must
15:20 I will make you a wall to this **p**, a
16: 5 my love and my pity from this **p**,"
16:10 "When you tell these **p** all this and
17:19 "Go and stand at the gate of the **p**,
17:26 **P** will come from the towns of Judah
18:11 "Now therefore say to the **p** of Judah
18:15 Yet my **p** have forgotten me;
19: 1 some of the elders of the **p** and of
19: 3 O kings of Judah and **p** of Jerusalem.
19: 6 **p** will no longer call this place
21: 7 his officials and the **p** in this city

Jer 21: 8 "Furthermore, tell the **p**, 'This is
22: 2 your **p** who come through these gates.
22: 4 by their officials and their **p**.
22: 8 "**P** from many nations will pass by
23: 2 says to the shepherds who tend my **p**:
23: 7 "when **p** will no longer say, 'As
23:14 **p** of Jerusalem are like Gomorrah."
23:22 have proclaimed my words to my **p**
23:27 will make my **p** forget my name,
23:32 "They tell them and lead my **p** astray
23:32 They do not benefit these **p** in the
23:33 "When these **p**, or a prophet or a
24: 7 They will be my **p**, and I will be
25:19 his officials and all his **p**,
25:20 all the foreign **p** there; all the
25:20 Ekron, and the **p** left at Ashdod);
25:24 foreign **p** who live in the desert;
26:17 said to the entire assembly of **p**,
26:23 the burial place of the common **p**.)
26:24 over to the **p** to be put to death.
27: 5 I made the earth and its **p** and the
27:12 serve him and his **p**, and you will
27:13 Why will you and your **p** die by the
27:16 I said to the priests and all these **p**
29: 1 the prophets and all the other **p**
29:32 will have no-one left among this **p**,
29:32 the good things I will do for my **p**,
30:22 "'so you will be my **p**, and I will
31: 1 of Israel, and they will be my **p**."
31: 2 "The **p** who survive the sword will
31: 7 save your **p**, the remnant of Israel.'
31:14 my **p** will be filled with my bounty,"
31:23 the **p** in the land of Judah and in
31:24 **P** will live together in Judah and
31:29 "In those days **p** will no longer say,
31:33 be their God, and they will be my **p**.
32:21 You brought your **p** Israel out of
32:29 houses where the **p** provoked me to
32:32 men of Judah and the **p** of Jerusalem.
32:38 They will be my **p**, and I will be
32:42 all this great calamity on this **p**,
33: 6 I will heal my **p** and will let them
33:24 "Have you not noticed that these **p**
33:24 So they despise my **p** and no longer
34: 5 As **p** made a funeral fire in honour
34:10 all the officials and **p** who entered
35:13 men of Judah and the **p** of Jerusalem,
35:16 but these **p** have not obeyed me.'
36: 3 Perhaps when the **p** of Judah hear
36: 6 Read them to all the **p** of Judah who
36: 7 this **p** by the LORD are great."
36:13 Baruch read to the **p** from the scroll,
36:14 you have read to the **p** and come.
36:31 in Jerusalem and the **p** of Judah
37: 4 was free to come and go among the **p**,
37:12 of the property among the **p** there.
37:18 you or your officials or this **p**,
38: 4 the good of these **p** but their ruin."
39: 8 the houses of the **p** and broke down
39: 9 the **p** who remained in the city,
39: 9 over to him, and the rest of the **p**.
39:10 land of Judah some of the poor **p**,
39:14 So he remained among his own **p**.
40: 3 happened because you **p** sinned
40: 5 and live with him among the **p**,
40: 6 **p** who were left behind in the land.
41:10 rest of the **p** who were in Mizpah—
43: 1 Jeremiah finished telling the **p** all
44:24 LORD, all you **p** of Judah in Egypt.
45: 5 For I will bring disaster on all **p**,
46: 8 I will destroy cities and their **p**.'
46:16 'Get up, let us go back to our own **p**
46:24 handed over to the **p** of the north."
47: 2 The **p** will cry out; all who dwell in
48:43 and snare await you, O **p** of Moab,"
48:46 The **p** of Chemosh are destroyed;
49: 1 Why do his **p** live in its towns?
49:28 Kedar and destroy the **p** of the East.
49:31 gates nor bars; its **p** live alone.
50: 4 "the **p** of Israel and the **p** of Judah
50: 6 "My **p** have been lost sheep;
50:16 let everyone return to his own **p**,
50:33 and the **p** of Judah as well.
51: 1 Babylon and the **p** of Leb Kamai.
51:12 his decree against the **p** of Babylon.
51:38 Her **p** all roar like young lions,

Jer 51:45 "Come out of her, my **p**! Run for your
51:64 And her **p** will fall.'"
52: 6 there was no food for the **p** to eat.
52:15 into exile some of the poorest **p**
52:28 This is the number of the **p**
52:29 year, 832 **p** from Jerusalem;
52:30 There were 4,600 **p** in all.
Lam 1: 1 lies the city, once so full of **p**!
1: 7 When her **p** fell into enemy hands,
1:11 All her **p** groan as they search for
1:21 "**P** have heard my groaning, but there
2:11 ground because my **p** are destroyed,
2:18 The hearts of the **p** cry out to the
3:14 the laughing-stock of all my **p**;
3:48 my eyes because my **p** are destroyed.
4: 3 but my **p** have become heartless like
4: 6 The punishment of my **p** is greater
4:10 their food when my **p** were destroyed.
4:12 nor did any of the world's **p**, that
4:15 **p** among the nations say, "They can
Eze 2: 4 The **p** to whom I am sending you are
3: 5 You are not being sent to a **p** of
3:25 that you cannot go out among the **p**.
4:12 bake it in the sight of the **p**,
4:16 The **p** will eat rationed food in
5:12 A third of your **p** will die of the
6: 4 slay your **p** in front of your idols.
6: 7 Your **p** will fall slain among you,
6:13 when their **p** lie slain among their
7:11 none of the **p** will be left,
11: 1 son of Benaiah, leaders of the **p**.
11: 6 You have killed many **p** in this city
11:15 whom the **p** of Jerusalem have said,
11:20 be my **p**, and I will be their God.
12: 2 you are living among a rebellious **p**.
12: 2 hear, for they are a rebellious **p**.
13: 9 not belong to the council of my **p**
13:10 "'Because they lead my **p** astray,
13:12 the wall collapses, will **p** not ask
13:17 the daughters of your **p** who
13:18 their heads in order to ensnare **p**.
13:18 lives of my **p** but preserve your own?
13:19 You have profaned me among my **p** for
13:19 By lying to my **p**, who listen to lies,
13:20 with which you ensnare **p** like birds
13:20 the **p** that you ensnare like birds.
13:21 veils and save my **p** from your hands,
13:23 I will save my **p** from your hands.
14: 8 I will cut him off from my **p**.
14:11 They will be my **p**, and I will be
15: 6 I treat the **p** living in Jerusalem.
17: 9 many **p** to pull it up by the roots.
18: 2 "What do you **p** mean by quoting this
18:18 and did what was wrong among his **p**.
21:12 son of man, for it is against my **p**;
21:12 thrown to the sword along with my **p**.
21:24 'Because you **p** have brought to mind
22:25 they devour **p**, take treasures and
22:27 and kill **p** to make unjust gain.
23:24 and wagons and with a throng of **p**;
24:18 I spoke to the **p** in the morning, and
24:19 the **p** asked me, "Won't you tell us
25: 3 **p** of Judah when they went into exile,
25: 4 give you to the **p** of the East as a
25:10 the **p** of the East as a possession,
26:11 he will kill your **p** with the sword,
26:20 to the pit, to the **p** of long ago.
30: 5 Libya and the **p** of the covenant land
32: 3 'With a great throng of **p** I will
33: 3 and blows the trumpet to warn the **p**,
33: 6 not blow the trumpet to warn the **p**
33:24 "Son of man, the **p** living in those
33:31 My **p** come to you, as they usually do,
34:27 the **p** will be secure in their land.
34:30 they, the house of Israel, are my **p**
34:31 the sheep of my pasture, are **p**, and
36:10 I will multiply the number of **p** upon
36:11 I will settle **p** on you as in the
36:12 I will cause **p**, my **p** Israel, to walk
36:13 LORD says: Because **p** say to you,
36:20 'These are the LORD's **p**, and yet
36:28 be my **p**, and I will be your God.
36:37 make their **p** as numerous as sheep,
36:38 cities be filled with flocks of **p**.
37:12 O my **p**, I am going to open your
37:13 you, my **p**, will know that I am the

Eze 37:23 be my **p**, and I will be their God.
37:27 be their God, and they will be my **p**.
38: 8 whose **p** were gathered from many
38:11 unsuspecting **p**—all of them living
38:12 and the **p** gathered from the nations,
42:14 near the places that are for the **p**."
44:11 sacrifices for the **p** and stand
44:11 stand before the **p** and serve them.
44:19 the outer court where the **p** are,
44:19 do not consecrate the **p** by means of
44:23 They are to teach my **p** the
45: 8 princes will no longer oppress my **p**
45: 9 Stop dispossessing my **p**, declares
45:15 to make atonement for the **p**,
46:18 any of the inheritance of the **p**,
46:18 so that none of my **p** will be
46:20 outer court and consecrating the **p**."
46:24 will cook the sacrifices of the **p**."
Da 2:43 so the **p** will be a mixture and will
2:44 nor will it be left to another **p**.
3:29 the **p** of any nation or language who
4:25 You will be driven away from **p** and
4:32 You will be driven away from **p** and
4:33 He was driven away from **p** and ate
5:21 He was driven away from **p** and given
6:26 part of my kingdom **p** must fear
7:27 the saints, the **p** of the Most High.
9: 7 and **p** of Jerusalem and all Israel,
9:15 O Lord our God, who brought your **p**
9:16 your **p** an object of scorn to all
9:19 city and your **p** bear your Name."
9:24 'sevens' are decreed for your **p** and
9:26 The **p** of the ruler who will come
10:14 will happen to your **p** in the future,
11:14 The violent men among your own **p**
11:21 the kingdom when its **p** feel secure,
11:23 only a few **p** he will rise to power.
11:32 but the **p** who know their God will
11:39 He will make them rulers over many **p**
12: 1 who protects your **p**, will arise.
12: 1 But at that time your **p**—everyone
Hos 1: 9 are not my **p**, and I am not your God.
1:10 'You are not my **p**', they will be
1:11 The **p** of Judah and the **p** of Israel
2: 1 "Say of your brothers, 'My **p**', and
2:23 I will say to those called 'Not my **p**'
2:23 'You are my **p**'; and they will say,
4: 4 for your **p** are like those who bring
4: 6 my **p** are destroyed from lack of
4: 8 They feed on the sins of my **p** and
4: 9 it will be: Like **p**, like priests.
4:12 of my **p**. They consult a wooden idol
4:14 a **p** without understanding will come
5:12 Ephraim, like rot to the **p** of Judah.
6:11 I would restore the fortunes of my **p**,
8: 1 the **p** have broken my covenant
9: 2 winepresses will not feed the **p**;
10: 5 The **p** who live in Samaria fear for
10: 5 Its **p** will mourn over it, and so
10:14 of battle will rise against your **p**,
11: 7 My **p** are determined to turn from me.
12:11 Gilead wicked? Its **p** are worthless!
13: 2 It is said of these **p**, "They offer
13:16 The **p** of Samaria must bear their
Joel 2:16 Gather the **p**, consecrate the
2:17 Let them say, "Spare your **p**, O LORD.
2:18 for his land and take pity on his **p**.
2:23 Be glad, O **p** of Zion, rejoice in the
2:26 never again will my **p** be shamed.
2:27 never again will my **p** be shamed.
3: 2 for they scattered my **p** among the
3: 3 They cast lots for my **p** and traded
3: 6 You sold the **p** of Judah and
3: 8 and daughters to the **p** of Judah,
3:16 LORD will be a refuge for his **p**,
3:19 of violence done to the **p** of Judah,
Am 1: 5 The **p** of Aram will go into exile to
3: 6 in a city, do not the **p** tremble?
3: 9 her and the oppression among her **p**."
4: 8 **P** staggered from town to town for
9:10 All the sinners among my **p** will die
9:14 I will bring back my exiled **p** Israel;
Ob :12 nor rejoice over the **p** of Judah in
:13 not march through the gates of my **p**
:19 **P** from the Negev will occupy the
:19 **p** from the foothills will possess
Jnh 1: 8 your country? From what **p** are you?"
4:11 twenty thousand **p** who cannot tell
Mic 1: 9 has reached the very gate of my **p**,
2: 3 am planning disaster against this **p**,
2: 8 Lately my **p** have risen up like an
2: 9 You drive the women of my **p** from
2:11 be just the prophet for this **p**!
2:12 the place will throng with **p**.
3: 2 who tear the skin from my **p** and the
3: 5 "As for the prophets who lead my **p**
6: 2 the LORD has a case against his **p**;
6: 3 "My **p**, what have I done to you?
6: 5 My **p**, remember what Balak king of
6:12 her **p** are liars and their tongues
6:16 over to ruin and your **p** to derision;
7:12 In that day **p** will come to you from
7:14 Shepherd your **p** with your staff, the
Na 3: 3 **p** stumbling over the corpses—
3:18 Your **p** are scattered on the
Hab 1: 6 that ruthless and impetuous **p**, who
1: 7 They are a feared and dreaded **p**;
3:13 You came out to deliver your **p**, to
Zep 1:17 I will bring distress on the **p** and
2: 5 O Kerethite **p**; the word of the LORD
2: 8 who insulted my **p** and made threats
2: 9 The remnant of my **p** will plunder
2:10 mocking the **p** of the LORD Almighty.
3:10 my worshippers, my scattered **p**,
Hag 1: 2 "These **p** say, 'The time has not yet
1:12 and the whole remnant of the **p**
1:12 And the **p** feared the LORD.
1:13 this message of the LORD to the **p**:
1:14 of the whole remnant of the **p**.
2: 2 priest, and to the remnant of the **p**.
2:14 Haggai said, "'so it is with this **p**
Zec 1: 3 Therefore tell the **p**: This is what
1:21 the land of Judah to scatter its **p**."
2:11 in that day and will become my **p**.
5: 6 of the **p** throughout the land."
7: 2 The **p** of Bethel had sent Sharezer
8: 6 the remnant of this **p** at that time,
8: 7 "I will save my **p** from the countries
8: 8 they will be my **p**, and I will be
8:11 of this **p** as I did in the past,"
8:12 to the remnant of this **p**.
9: 8 will an oppressor overrun my **p**,
9:16 on that day as the flock of his **p**.
10: 2 Therefore the **p** wander like sheep
12: 5 'The **p** of Jerusalem are strong,
13: 9 'They are my **p**,' and they will say,
14: 2 **p** will not be taken from the city.
14:18 If the Egyptian **p** do not go up and
Mal 1: 4 **p** always under the wrath of the LORD.
Mt 1:21 he will save his **p** from their sins."
3: 5 **P** went out to him from Jerusalem and
4:16 the **p** living in darkness have seen a
4:23 disease and sickness among the **p**.
4:24 and **p** brought to him all who were
5:11 "Blessed are you when **p** insult you,
5:15 Neither do **p** light a lamp and put it
5:21 that it was said to the **p** long ago,
5:33 that it was said to the **p** long ago,
7:16 Do **p** pick grapes from thornbushes,
12:27 by whom do your **p** drive them out?
13:10 do you speak to the **p** in parables?"
13:54 he began teaching the **p** in their
14: 5 but he was afraid of the **p**, because
14:19 he directed the **p** to sit down on the
14:19 the disciples gave them to the **p**.
14:35 **P** brought all their sick to
15: 8 "'These **p** honour me with their lips,
15:31 The **p** were amazed when they saw the
15:32 "I have compassion for these **p**;
15:36 and they in turn to the **p**.
16:13 "Who do **p** say the Son of Man is?
18: 7 The things that cause **p** to sin!
21:23 and the elders of the **p** came to him.
21:26 'From men'—we are afraid of the **p**,
21:43 to a **p** who will produce its fruit.
21:46 the **p** held that he was a prophet.
22:30 At the resurrection **p** will neither
23:28 on the outside you appear to **p** as
24:11 will appear and deceive many **p**.
24:38 flood, **p** were eating and drinking,
25:32 and he will separate the **p** one from
26: 3 the elders of the **p** assembled in the
Mt 26: 5 "or there may be a riot among the **p**.
26:47 priests and the elders of the **p**.
26:71 saw him and said to the **p** there,
27: 1 the elders of the **p** came to the
27:53 holy city and appeared to many **p**.
27:64 steal the body and tell the **p** that
Mk 1: 5 the **p** of Jerusalem went out to him.
1:22 The **p** were amazed at his teaching,
1:27 The **p** were all so amazed that they
1:32 after sunset the **p** brought to Jesus
1:45 **p** still came to him from everywhere.
2: 1 the **p** heard that he had come home.
2:18 Some **p** came and asked Jesus, "How is
3: 8 many **p** came to him from Judea,
3: 9 to keep the **p** from crowding him.
4:15 Some **p** are like seed along the path,
5:14 **p** went out to see what had happened.
5:16 Those who had seen it told the **p**
5:17 the **p** began to plead with Jesus to
5:31 "You see the **p** crowding against you,"
5:38 with **p** crying and wailing loudly.
6: 5 hands on a few sick **p** and heal them.
6:12 and preached that **p** should repent.
6:13 sick **p** with oil and healed them.
6:31 Then, because so many **p** were coming
6:36 Send the **p** away so that they can go
6:41 his disciples to set before the **p**.
6:54 of the boat, **p** recognised Jesus,
7: 6 'These **p** honour me with their lips,
7:32 There some **p** brought to him a man
7:37 **P** were overwhelmed with amazement.
8: 2 "I have compassion for these **p**;
8: 6 set before the **p**, and they did so.
8: 8 The **p** ate and were satisfied.
8:22 and some **p** brought a blind man and
8:24 He looked up and said, "I see **p**;
8:27 he asked them, "Who do **p** say I am?"
10: 1 Again crowds of **p** came to him, and
10:13 **P** were bringing little children to
11: 5 some **p** standing there asked, "What
11: 6 told them to, and the **p** let them go.
11: 8 Many **p** spread their cloaks on the
11:32 (They feared the **p**, for everyone
12:41 Many rich **p** threw in large amounts.
14: 2 they said, "or the **p** may riot.
15: 6 a prisoner whom the **p** requested.
16:18 will place their hands on sick **p**,
Lk 1:17 ready a **p** prepared for the Lord."
1:21 Meanwhile, the **p** were waiting for
1:25 taken away my disgrace among the **p**."
1:65 **p** were talking about all these things
1:68 he has come and has redeemed his **p**.
1:77 to give his **p** the knowledge of
2:32 and for glory to your **p** Israel."
3:14 don't accuse **p** falsely—be content
3:15 The **p** were waiting expectantly and
3:18 John exhorted the **p** and preached
4:31 on the Sabbath began to teach the **p**.
4:40 the **p** brought to Jesus all who had
4:41 Moreover, demons came out of many **p**,
4:42 The **p** were looking for him and when
5: 1 with the **p** crowding round him and
5: 3 down and taught the **p** from the boat.
5:15 so that crowds of **p** came to hear him
6:17 number of **p** from all over Judea,
6:19 the **p** all tried to touch him,
6:44 **P** do not pick figs from thorn-bushes,
7: 1 all this in the hearing of the **p**,
7:16 "God has come to help his **p**."
7:31 "To what, then, can I compare the **p**
8: 4 **p** were coming to Jesus from town
8:35 the **p** went out to see what had
8:36 Those who had seen it told the **p** how
8:45 "Master, the **p** are crowding and
9: 5 If **p** do not welcome you, shake the
9: 6 the gospel and healing **p** everywhere.
9:16 the disciples to set before the **p**.
9:53 the **p** there did not welcome him,
11:40 You foolish **p**! Did not the one who
11:46 woe to you, because you load **p** down
13:14 the synagogue ruler said to the **p**,
13:17 but the **p** were delighted with all
13:23 "Lord, are only a few **p** going to be
13:29 **P** will come from east and west and
13:32 'I will drive out demons and heal **p**
16: 4 **p** will welcome me into their houses.'

Lk 16: 8 For the **p** of this world are more
16: 8 kind than are the **p** of the light.
17: 1 "Things that cause **p** to sin are
17:21 nor will **p** say, 'Here it is,' or
17:27 **P** were eating, drinking, marrying
17:28 **P** were eating and drinking, buying
17:34 I tell you, on that night two **p** will
18:15 **P** were also bringing babies to Jesus
18:43 the **p** saw it, they also praised God.
19:11 the **p** thought that the kingdom of
19:36 he went along, **p** spread their cloaks
19:47 among the **p** were trying to kill him.
20: 1 One day as he was teaching the **p** in
20: 9 He went on to tell the **p** this
20:16 When the **p** heard this, they said,
20:19 But they were afraid of the **p**.
20:34 Jesus replied, "The **p** of this age
21: 4 All these **p** gave their gifts out of
21:23 the land and wrath against this **p**.
22: 2 Jesus, for they were afraid of the **p**.
22:66 the council of the elders of the **p**,
23: 5 they insisted, "He stirs up the **p**
23:13 chief priests, the rulers and the **p**,
23:14 who was inciting the **p** to rebellion.
23:27 A large number of **p** followed him,
23:35 The **p** stood watching, and the rulers
Jn 2:23 many **p** saw the miraculous signs he
3:11 you **p** do not accept our testimony.
3:23 and **p** were constantly coming to be
4:28 back to the town and said to the **p**,
4:48 "Unless you **p** see miraculous signs
5: 3 Here a great number of disabled **p**
6: 2 a great crowd of **p** followed him
6: 5 we buy bread for these **p** to eat?"
6:10 Jesus said, "Make the **p** sit down."
6:14 After the **p** saw the miraculous sign
6:23 where the **p** had eaten the bread
7:12 replied, "No, he deceives the **p**.
7:25 At that point some of the **p** of
7:35 **p** live scattered among the Greeks,
7:40 On hearing his words, some of the **p**
7:43 Thus the **p** were divided because of
8:12 Jesus spoke again to the **p**, he said,
10:41 many **p** came to him. They said,
11:42 the benefit of the **p** standing here,
11:50 that one man die for the **p** than
12:18 Many **p**, because they had heard that
18:14 be good if one man died for the **p**.
18:35 "It was your **p** and your chief
Ac 2:37 the **p** heard this, they were cut to
3:22 like me from among your own **p**;
3:23 cut off from among his **p**.'
4: 1 while they were speaking to the **p**.
4: 2 the apostles were teaching the **p**
4: 8 "Rulers and elders of the **p**!
4:17 spreading any further among the **p**,
4:23 John went back to their own **p** and
5:12 signs and wonders among the **p**.
5:13 they were highly regarded by the **p**.
5:15 **p** brought the sick into the streets
5:20 tell the **p** the full message of this
5:21 been told, and began to teach the **p**.
5:25 the temple courts teaching the **p**."
5:26 feared that the **p** would stone them.
5:37 and led a band of **p** in revolt.
6: 8 and miraculous signs among the **p**.
6:12 they stirred up the **p** and the elders
7: 3 'Leave your country and your **p**,' God
7:17 of our **p** in Egypt greatly increased.
7:19 He dealt treacherously with our **p**
7:25 Moses thought that his own **p** would
7:34 the oppression of my **p** in Egypt.
7:37 a prophet like me from your own **p**.'
7:51 "You stiff-necked **p**, with
9:42 and many **p** believed in the Lord.
10:22 is respected by all the Jewish **p**.
10:27 and found a large gathering of **p**.
10:42 He commanded us to preach to the **p**
10:47 "Can anyone keep these **p** from being
11:21 **p** believed and turned to the Lord.
11:24 of **p** were brought to the Lord.
11:26 and taught great numbers of **p**.
12:11 the Jewish **p** were anticipating."
12:12 **p** had gathered and were praying.
12:20 He had been quarrelling with the **p**
12:21 delivered a public address to the **p**.

Ac 13:15 message of encouragement for the **p**,
13:17 he made the **p** prosper during their
13:19 land to his **p** as their inheritance.
13:21 the **p** asked for a king, and he gave
13:27 The **p** of Jerusalem and their rulers
13:31 They are now his witnesses to our **p**.
13:42 the **p** invited them to speak further
14: 4 The **p** of the city were divided;
15:14 from the Gentiles a **p** for himself.
15:31 The **p** read it and were glad for its
16: 4 in Jerusalem for the **p** to obey.
18:10 because I have many **p** in this city."
18:13 "is persuading the **p** to worship God
19: 4 He told the **p** to believe in the one
19:26 led astray large numbers of **p** here
19:29 The **p** seized Gaius and Aristarchus,
19:32 Most of the **p** did not even know why
19:33 to make a defence before the **p**.
20: 2 words of encouragement to the **p**,
20: 7 Paul spoke to the **p** and, because he
20:12 The **p** took the young man home alive
21:12 we heard this, we and the **p** there
21:28 our **p** and our law and this place.
21:30 and the **p** came running from all
21:39 Please let me speak to the **p**."
22: 5 and went there to bring these **p** as
22:24 why the **p** were shouting at him
23: 5 evil about the ruler of your **p**.'"
24:17 I came to Jerusalem to bring my **p**
26:17 I will rescue you from your own **p**
26:23 to his own **p** and to the Gentiles."
28: 6 The **p** expected him to swell up or
28:17 I have done nothing against our **p**
28:19 charge to bring against my own **p**.
28:22 for we know that **p** everywhere are
28:26 "'Go to this **p** and say, "You will
Ro 1: 5 apostleship to call **p** from among all
2:22 You who say that **p** should not commit
9:25 call them 'my **p**' who are not my **p**;
9:26 'You are not my **p**,' they will be
10:21 to a disobedient and obstinate **p**."
11: 1 I ask then: Did God reject his **p**?
11: 2 God did not reject his **p**, whom he
11:14 own **p** to envy and save some of them.
12:13 Share with God's **p** who are in need.
12:16 to associate with **p** of low position.
15:10 "Rejoice, O Gentiles, with his **p**.
16: 2 great help to many **p**, including me.
16:18 For such **p** are not serving our Lord
16:18 they deceive the minds of naïve **p**.
1Co 4:19 how these arrogant **p** are talking,
5: 9 associate with sexually immoral **p**—
5:10 not at all meaning the **p** of this
8: 7 Some **p** are still so accustomed to
10: 7 "The **p** sat down to eat and drink and
10:15 I speak to sensible **p**; judge for
14:21 foreigners I will speak to this **p**,
14:36 Or are you the only **p** it has reached?
15:29 at all, why are **p** baptised for them?
16: 1 Now about the collection for God's **p**:
2Co 3: 1 Or do we need, like some **p**, letters
4:15 more **p** may cause thanksgiving to
6:16 their God, and they will be my **p**."
9:12 only supplying the needs of God's **p**
10: 2 as I expect to be towards some **p**
10:11 Such **p** should realise that what we
13: 7 Not that **p** will see that we have
Gal 1: 7 Evidently some **p** are throwing you
3:16 "and to seeds", meaning many **p**,
4:17 Those **p** are zealous to win you over,
Eph 2:19 fellow-citizens with God's **p** and
3: 8 less than the least of all God's **p**,
4:12 to prepare God's **p** for works of
Col 3:12 Therefore, as God's chosen **p**, holy
1Th 5: 3 While **p** are saying, "Peace and
2Th 3:12 Such **p** we command and urge in the
1Ti 3:15 if I am delayed, you will know how **p**
4: 3 They forbid **p** to marry and order
5: 7 Give the **p** these instructions, too,
6: 9 **P** who want to get rich fall into
6:10 Some **p**, eager for money, have
2Ti 3: 2 **P** will be lovers of themselves,
Tit 1:10 For there are many rebellious **p**,
2:14 himself a **p** that are his very own,
3: 1 Remind the **p** to be subject to rulers
3:14 Our **p** must learn to devote

Heb 2:17 atonement for the sins of the **p**.
5: 3 as well as for the sins of the **p**.
6:10 his **p** and continue to help them.
7: 5 collect a tenth from the **p**—that is,
7:11 of it the law was given to the **p**),
7:27 and then for the sins of the **p**.
8: 8 God found fault with the **p** and said:
8:10 be their God, and they will be my **p**.
9: 7 the **p** had committed in ignorance.
9:28 to take away the sins of many **p**;
10:30 again, "The Lord will judge his **p**.
11:13 All these **p** were still living by
11:14 **P** who say such things show that they
11:29 By faith the **p** passed through the
11:30 after the **p** had marched around them
13: 2 some **p** have entertained angels
13:12 the **p** holy through his own blood.
13:24 all your leaders and all God's **p**.
Jas 4: 4 You adulterous **p**, don't you know
5: 1 Now listen, you rich **p**, weep and
1Pe 2: 9 you are a chosen **p**, a royal
2: 9 a holy nation, a **p** belonging to God,
2:10 Once you were not a **p**, but now you
3:20 In it only a few **p**, eight in all,
2Pe 2: 1 also false prophets among the **p**,
2: 5 brought the flood on its ungodly **p**,
2:18 they entice **p** who are just escaping
3:11 what kind of **p** ought you to be?
3:16 which ignorant and unstable **p**
Jude : 5 Lord delivered his **p** out of Egypt,
Rev 2:14 You have **p** there who hold to the
3: 4 Yet you have a few **p** in Sardis who
5: 9 tribe and language and **p** and nation.
7: 9 from every nation, tribe, **p** and
8:11 and many **p** died from the waters that
9: 4 but only those **p** who did not have
9:10 power to torment **p** for five months.
11: 9 men from every **p**, tribe, language
11:13 Seven thousand **p** were killed in the
13: 7 every tribe, **p**, language and nation.
14: 6 every nation, tribe, language and **p**.
16: 2 painful sores broke out on the **p** who
16: 8 given power to scorch **p** with fire.
18: 4 "Come out of her, my **p**, so that you
20: 9 camp of God's **p**, the city he loves.
21: 3 They will be his **p**, and God himself
22:21 of the Lord Jesus be with God's **p**.

People of God

Jdg 20: 2 places in the assembly of the **p**,
2Sa 14:13 a thing like this against the **p**?
Heb 4: 9 then, a Sabbath-rest for the **p**;
11:25 to be ill-treated along with the **p**
1Pe 2:10 but now you are the **p**; once you had

People of Israel

Ex 16:31 The **p** called the bread manna. It was
19: 3 Jacob and what you are to tell the **p**:
Nu 32: 4 land the LORD subdued before the **p**
Dt 27:14 The Levites shall recite to all the **p**
32:52 the land I am giving to the **p**."
Jos 4: 7 to be a memorial to the **p** for ever."
8:33 he gave instructions to bless the **p**.
1Sa 7: 2 **p** mourned and sought after the LORD.
10:17 Samuel summoned the **p** to the LORD at
1Ki 16:21 the **p** were split into two factions;
2Ki 17:20 Therefore the LORD rejected all the **p**
17:23 So the **p** were taken from their
2Ch 6:11 the LORD that he made with the **p**."
30: 6 "**P**, return to the LORD, the God of
Ezr 2: 2 The list of the men of the **p**:
6:16 the **p**—the priests, the Levites and
9: 1 "The **p**, including the priests and
Ne 1: 6 and night for your servants, the **p**.
10:39 The **p**, including the Levites, are to
Ps 103: 7 ways to Moses, his deeds to the **p**:
Jer 3:21 the weeping and pleading of the **p**,
32:30 "The **p** and Judah have done nothing
32:30 the **p** have done nothing but provoke
32:32 The **p** and Judah have provoked me by
50: 4 "the **p** and the people of Judah
50:33 "The **p** are oppressed, and the people
Eze 4:13 "In this way the **p** will eat defiled
12:24 flattering divinations among the **p**.
14: 5 to recapture the hearts of the **p**,

Eze 14:11 the **p** will no longer stray from me,
20:13 "'Yet the **p** rebelled against me in
20:27 son of man, speak to the **p** and say
28:24 "'No longer will the **p** have
28:25 When I gather the **p** from the nations
29:16 be a source of confidence for the **p**
36:17 "Son of man, when the **p** were living
39:23 the nations will know that the **p**
39:25 will have compassion on all the **p**,
43:10 describe the temple to the **p**, that
Hos 1:11 The people of Judah and the **p** will
Joel 3:16 his people, a stronghold for the **p**.
Am 2:11 Is this not true, **p**?" declares the
3: 1 LORD has spoken against you, O **p**
6: 1 foremost nation, to whom the **p** come!
Mt 27: 9 the price set on him by the **p**,
Lk 1:16 Many of the **p** will he bring back to
Ac 4:10 know this, you and all the **p**: It is
4:27 the **p** in this city to conspire
9:15 and their kings and before the **p**.
10:36 know the message God sent to the **p**,
13:17 The God of the **p** chose our fathers;
13:24 repentance and baptism to all the **p**.
Ro 9: 4 the **p**. Theirs is the adoption as
1Co 10:18 Consider the **p**: Do not those who eat
Php 3: 5 of the **p**, of the tribe of Benjamin,

People of the land

Ge 23: 7 down before the **p**, the Hittites.
23:12 Again Abraham bowed down before the **p**
Ex 5: 5 Pharaoh said, "Look, the **p** are now
Nu 14: 9 And do not be afraid of the **p**,
2Ki 11:14 and all the **p** were rejoicing and
11:18 All the **p** went to the temple of Baal
11:19 the guards and all the **p**, and
11:20 all the **p** rejoiced. And the city was
15: 5 of the palace and governed the **p**.
16:15 and the burnt offering of all the **p**,
21:24 the **p** killed all who had plotted
23:30 And the **p** took Jehoahaz son of
23:35 the silver and gold from the **p**
24:14 Only the poorest **p** were left.
25:12 **p** to work the vineyards and fields.
25:19 in charge of conscripting the **p**
2Ch 23:13 and all the **p** were rejoicing and
23:20 rulers of the people and all the **p**
23:21 all the **p** rejoiced. And the city was
26:21 of the palace and governed the **p**.
33:25 the **p** killed all who had plotted
36: 1 the **p** took Jehoahaz son of Josiah
Jer 1:18 officials, its priests and the **p**.
34:19 the priests and all the **p** who walked
37: 2 nor his attendants nor the **p** paid
44:21 kings and your officials and the **p**?
52:16 **p** to work the vineyards and fields.
52:25 in charge of conscripting the **p**
Eze 7:27 and the hands of the **p** will tremble.
12:19 Say to the **p**: 'This is what the
22:29 The **p** practise extortion and commit
33: 2 and the **p** choose one of their men
39:13 All the **p** will bury them, and the
45:16 All the **p** will participate in this
45:22 for himself and for all the **p**.
46: 3 **p** are to worship in the presence
46: 9 "'When the **p** come before the LORD
Da 9: 6 and our fathers, and to all the **p**.
Hag 2: 4 Be strong, all you **p**,' declares the
Zec 7: 5 "Ask all the **p** and the priests,
11: 6 pity on the **p**," declares the LORD.

People's (People)

Ex 18:19 You must be the **p** representative
Lev 9:15 He took the goat for the **p** sin
2Ch 25:15 "Why do you consult this **p** gods,
Est 1:22 proclaiming in each **p** tongue that
Eze 36: 3 of **p** malicious talk and slander,
Mic 2: 4 my **p** possession is divided up.
3: 3 who eat my **p** flesh, strip off their
Hab 2:13 **p** labour is only fuel for the fire,
Mt 2: 4 together all the **p** chief priests
13:15 For this **p** heart has become
Ac 28:27 For this **p** heart has become

Peopled (People)

Eze 26:17 O city of renown, **p** by men of the

Peoples (*All peoples, All the peoples, People, Peoples of the land*)

Ge 10: 5 (From these the maritime **p** spread
17:16 kings of **p** will come from her."
25:23 and two **p** from within you will be
27:29 May nations serve you and **p** bow down
28: 3 until you become a community of **p**.
29: 1 came to the land of the eastern **p**.
48: 4 I will make you a community of **p**,
Dt 1: 7 the neighbouring **p** in the Arabah,
4:27 The LORD will scatter you among the **p**
6:14 gods, the gods of the **p** around you;
7: 7 were more numerous than other **p**,
13: 7 gods of the **p** around you, whether
32: 8 he set up boundaries for the **p**
33:19 They will summon **p** to the mountain
Jdg 2:12 various gods of the **p** around them.
6: 3 other eastern **p** invaded the country.
6:33 Amalekites and other eastern **p**
7:12 eastern **p** had settled in the valley,
8:10 left of the armies of the eastern **p**;
1Sa 27: 8 (From ancient times these **p** had
1Ki 9:20 (these **p** were not Israelites),
2Ch 8: 7 (these **p** were not Israelites),
13: 9 your own as the **p** of other lands do?
32:17 gods of the **p** of the other lands
32:19 gods of the other **p** of the world
Ezr 3: 3 Despite their fear of the **p** around
4: 4 the **p** around them set out to
9: 1 separate from the neighbouring **p**
9: 2 holy race with the **p** around them.
9:11 polluted by the corruption of its **p**.
9:14 intermarry with the **p** who commit
10: 2 foreign women from the **p** around us.
10:11 Separate yourselves from the **p**
Ne 9:24 along with their kings and the **p** of
9:30 them over to the neighbouring **p**.
10:28 from the neighbouring **p** for the
10:30 in marriage to the **p** around us or
10:31 "When the neighbouring **p** bring
13:24 the language of one of the other **p**,
Est 1:16 the **p** of all the provinces of King
3: 8 scattered among the **p** in all the
3:12 and the nobles of the various **p**.
Ps 2: 1 conspire and the **p** plot in vain?
7: 7 Let the assembled **p** gather round you.
7: 8 let the LORD judge the **p**.
9: 8 he will govern the **p** with justice.
33:10 he thwarts the purposes of the **p**.
44: 2 you crushed the **p** and made our
44:14 the **p** shake their heads at us.
47: 3 nations under us, **p** under our feet.
57: 9 I will sing of you among the **p**.
66: 8 Praise our God, O **p**, let the sound
67: 3 May the **p** praise you, O God; may all
67: 4 for you rule the **p** justly and guide
67: 5 May the **p** praise you, O God; may all
77:14 you display your power among the **p**.
87: 6 write in the register of the **p**:
96:10 he will judge the **p** with equity.
96:13 and the **p** in his truth.
98: 9 righteousness and the **p** with equity.
102:22 the **p** and the kingdoms assemble to
105:20 him, the ruler of **p** set him free.
106:34 They did not destroy the **p** as the
108: 3 I will sing of you among the **p**.
117: 1 you nations; extol him, all you **p**.
144: 2 take refuge, who subdues **p** under me.
149: 7 the nations and punishment on the **p**,
Pr 24:24 **p** will curse him and nations
Isa 2: 3 Many **p** will come and say, "Come, let
2: 4 and will settle disputes for many **p**.
11:10 will stand as a banner for the **p**;
14: 6 which in anger struck down **p** with
17:12 the uproar of the **p**—they roar like
17:13 Although the **p** roar like the roar of
19:13 of her **p** have led Egypt astray.
25: 3 Therefore strong **p** will honour you;
30:28 he places in the jaws of the **p** a
33: 3 thunder of your voice, the **p** flee;
33:12 The **p** will be burned as if to lime;
34: 1 and listen; pay attention, you **p**!
37:18 kings have laid waste all these **p**
43: 9 gather together and the **p** assemble.
49:22 I will lift up my banner to the **p**;
Isa 55: 4 I have made him a witness to the **p**,
55: 4 a leader and commander of the **p**.
60: 2 and thick darkness is over the **p**,
61: 9 and their offspring among the **p**.
Jer 10: 3 For the customs of the **p** are
10:25 the **p** who do not call on your name.
34: 1 all the kingdoms and **p** in the empire
51:58 **p** exhaust themselves for nothing,
Eze 3: 6 not to many **p** of obscure speech and
20:32 like the **p** of the world, who serve
27: 3 merchant of **p** on many coasts, 'This
32: 9 I will trouble the hearts of many **p**
32:10 I will cause many **p** to be appalled
36:15 suffer the scorn of the **p** or cause
Da 3: 4 **p**, nations and men of every language:
4: 1 To the **p**, nations and men of every
4:35 of heaven and the **p** of the earth.
Joel 2:17 Why should they say among the **p**,
Mic 1: 2 Hear, O **p**, all of you, listen, O
4: 1 the hills, and **p** will stream to it.
4: 3 He will judge between many **p** and
5: 7 of many **p** like dew from the LORD,
5: 8 in the midst of many **p**, like a lion
Na 3: 4 and **p** by her witchcraft.
Hab 2: 8 the **p** who are left will plunder you.
2:10 You have plotted the ruin of many **p**,
Zep 3: 9 "Then will I purify the lips of the **p**
Zec 8:20 "Many **p** and the inhabitants of many
8:22 many **p** and powerful nations will
10: 9 Though I scatter them among the **p**,
12: 2 sends all the surrounding **p** reeling.
12: 6 and left all the surrounding **p**,
14:17 If any of the **p** of the earth do not
Ac 4:25 nations rage and the **p** plot in vain?
Ro 15:11 and sing praises to him, all you **p**."
Rev 10:11 **p**, nations, languages and kings."
17:15 **p**, multitudes, nations and languages.

Peoples of the land

1Ch 5:25 themselves to the gods of the **p**,
Ne 9:24 along with their kings and the **p**,

Peor

Nu 23:28 Balak took Balaam to the top of **P**,
25: 3 joined in worshipping the Baal of **P**.
25: 5 in worshipping the Baal of **P**."
25:18 affair of **P** and their sister Cozbi,
25:18 the plague came as a result of **P**."
31:16 from the LORD in what happened at **P**,
Dt 4: 3 everyone who followed the Baal of **P**,
Jos 22:17 Was not the sin of **P** enough for us?
Ps 106:28 yoked themselves to the Baal of **P**

Perath

Jer 13: 4 and go now to **P** and hide it there in
13: 5 I went and hid it at **P**, as the LORD
13: 6 "Go now to **P** and get the belt I told
13: 7 I went to **P** and dug up the belt and

Perazim

Isa 28:21 will rise up as he did at Mount **P**,

Perceive (Perceived, Perceiving)

Job 9:11 when he goes by, I cannot **p** him.
33:14 another—though man may not **p** it.
Ps 139: 2 you **p** my thoughts from afar.
Pr 24:12 not he who weighs the heart **p** it?
Isa 43:19 Now it springs up; do you not **p** it?

Perceived (Perceive)

Isa 64: 4 no ear has **p**, no eye has seen any

Perceiving (Perceive)

Isa 6: 9 be ever seeing, but never **p**.'
Mt 13:14 you will be ever seeing but never **p**.
Mk 4:12 'they may be ever seeing but never **p**,
Ac 28:26 will be ever seeing but never **p**."

Perch (Perched)

Mt 13:32 the air come and **p** in its branches."
Mk 4:32 of the air can **p** in its shade."

Perched (Perch)
Lk 13:19 birds of the air **p** in its branches."

Peres
Da 5:28 **P**: Your kingdom is divided and

Peresh
1Ch 7:15 gave birth to a son and named him **P**.

Perez (Perezite)
Ge 38:29 broken out!" And he was named **P**.
46:12 Er, Onan, Shelah, **P** and Zerah
46:12 The sons of **P**: Hezron and Hamul.
Nu 26:20 through **P**, the Perezite clan;
26:21 The descendants of **P** were: through
Ru 4:12 of **P**, whom Tamar bore to Judah."
4:18 This, then, is the family line of **P**:
4:18 **P** was the father of Hezron,
1Ch 2: 4 bore him **P** and Zerah. Judah had
2: 5 The sons of **P**: Hezron and Hamul.
4: 1 The descendants of Judah: **P**, Hezron,
9: 4 Bani, a descendant of **P** son of Judah.
27: 3 He was a descendant of **P** and chief
Ne 11: 4 son of Mahalalel, a descendant of **P**;
11: 6 The descendants of **P** who lived in
Mt 1: 3 Judah the father of **P** and Zerah,
1: 3 was Tamar, **P** the father of Hezron,
Lk 3:33 the son of **P**, the son of Judah,

Perez Uzzah
2Sa 6: 8 to this day that place is called **P**.
1Ch 13:11 to this day that place is called **P**.

Perezite (Perez)
Nu 26:20 through Perez, the **P** clan;

Perfect (Perfecter, Perfecting, Perfection)
Dt 32: 4 He is the Rock, his works are **p**, and
2Sa 22:31 "As for God, his way is **p**; the word
22:33 me with strength and makes my way **p**.
Job 36: 4 one **p** in knowledge is with you.
37:16 of him who is **p** in knowledge?
Ps 18:30 for God, his way is **p**; the word of
18:32 me with strength and makes my way **p**.
19: 7 The law of the LORD is **p**, reviving
50: 2 From Zion, **p** in beauty, God shines
64: 6 "We have devised a **p** plan!"
SS 6: 9 my dove, my **p** one, is unique, the
Isa 25: 1 for in **p** faithfulness you have done
26: 3 You will keep in **p** peace him whose
Eze 16:14 I had given you made your beauty **p**,
27: 3 'You say, O Tyre, "I am **p** in beauty.
28:12 full of wisdom and **p** in beauty.
Mt 5:48 Be **p**, therefore, as your heavenly
5:48 as your heavenly Father is **p**.
19:21 Jesus answered, "If you want to be **p**,
Ro 12: 2 is—his good, pleasing and **p** will.
2Co 12: 9 for my power is made **p** in weakness.
Php 3:12 or have already been made **p**, but I
Col 1:28 we may present everyone **p** in Christ.
3:14 binds them all together in **p** unity.
Heb 2:10 their salvation **p** through suffering.
5: 9 and, once made **p**, he became the
7:19 (for the law made nothing **p**), and a
7:28 Son, who has been made **p** for ever.
9:11 **p** tabernacle that is not man-made,
10: 1 make **p** those who draw near to
10:14 by one sacrifice he has made **p** for
11:40 with us would they be made **p**.
12:23 the spirits of righteous men made **p**,
Jas 1:17 Every good and **p** gift is from above,
1:25 who looks intently into the **p** law
3: 2 he is a **p** man, able to keep his
1Jn 4:18 But **p** love drives out fear, because
4:18 one who fears is not made **p** in love.

Perfecter (Perfect)
Heb 12: 2 the author and **p** of our faith, who

Perfecting (Perfect)
2Co 7: 1 **p** holiness out of reverence for God.

Perfection (Perfect)
Ps 119:96 To all **p** I see a limit; but your
Lam 2:15 that was called the **p** of beauty,
Eze 27: 4 builders brought your beauty to **p**.
27:11 they brought your beauty to **p**.
28:12 'You were the model of **p**, full of
1Co 13:10 when **p** comes, the imperfect
2Co 13: 9 and our prayer is for your **p**.
13:11 Aim for **p**, listen to my appeal, be
Heb 7:11 If **p** could have been attained

Perform (Performance, Performed, Performing, Performs)
Ex 3:20 wonders that I will **p** among them.
4:17 you can **p** miraculous signs with it."
4:21 see that you **p** before Pharaoh all
4:28 signs he had commanded him to **p**.
7: 9 Pharaoh says to you, '**P** a miracle,'
10: 1 that I may **p** these miraculous signs
18:20 live and the duties they are to **p**.
Nu 3: 7 They are to **p** duties for him and for
4:31 This is their duty as they **p** service
18: 3 are to **p** all the duties of the Tent,
Jdg 16:27 men and women watching Samson **p**.
2Sa 7:23 and to **p** great and awesome wonders
1Ki 8:11 the priests could not **p** their
1Ch 17:21 and to **p** great and awesome wonders
2Ch 5:14 the priests could not **p** their
31:16 to **p** the daily duties of their
Isa 28:21 and **p** his task, his alien task.
Jer 21: 2 Perhaps the LORD will **p** wonders for
Eze 44:16 minister before me and **p** my service.
Mt 7:22 out demons and **p** many miracles?'
24:24 will appear and **p** great signs
Mk 13:22 will appear and **p** signs and
Lk 23: 8 he hoped to see him **p** some miracle.
Jn 3: 2 For no-one could **p** the miraculous
Ac 4:30 to heal and **p** miraculous signs and
2Co 9:12 This service that you **p** is not only

Performance (Perform)
1Ch 23:28 the **p** of other duties at the house

Performed (Perform)
Ex 4:30 also **p** the signs before the people,
10: 2 and how I **p** my signs among them,
11:10 Moses and Aaron **p** all these wonders
Nu 14:11 signs I have **p** among them?
14:22 the miraculous signs I **p** in Egypt
Dt 10:21 who **p** for you those great and
11: 3 the signs he **p** and the things he did
34:12 or **p** the awesome deeds that Moses
Jos 24:17 **p** those great signs before our eyes.
Jdg 16:25 of the prison, and he **p** for them.
1Sa 12: 7 acts **p** by the LORD for you
2Sa 23:20 from Kabzeel, who **p** great exploits.
1Ch 6:32 They **p** their duties according to the
11:22 from Kabzeel, who **p** great exploits.
25: 1 list of the men who **p** this service:
Ne 9:17 the miracles you **p** among them.
12:45 They **p** the service of their God and
Ps 105:27 They **p** his miraculous signs among
Jer 32:20 You **p** miraculous signs and wonders
Da 4: 2 that the Most High God has **p** for me.
Mt 11:20 most of his miracles had been **p**,
11:21 If the miracles that were **p** in you
11:21 in you had been **p** in Tyre and Sidon,
11:23 were **p** in you had been **p** in Sodom,
Lk 1:51 He has **p** mighty deeds with his arm;
10:13 For if the miracles that were **p** in
10:13 in you had been **p** in Tyre and Sidon,
Jn 2:11 signs, Jesus **p** at Cana in Galilee.
4:54 second miraculous sign that Jesus **p**
6: 2 signs he had **p** on the sick.
10:41 John never **p** a miraculous sign
Ac 5:12 The apostles **p** many miraculous signs
Rev 13:13 he **p** great and miraculous signs,
19:20 **p** the miraculous signs on his behalf.

Performing (Perform)
Nu 8:26 assist their brothers in **p** their
Jn 11:47 is this man **p** many miraculous signs.
Rev 16:14 They are spirits of demons **p**

Performs (Perform)
Job 5: 9 He **p** wonders that cannot be fathomed,
9:10 He **p** wonders that cannot be fathomed,
Ps 77:14 You are the God who **p** miracles;
Da 6:27 he **p** signs and wonders in the
Heb 10:11 stands and **p** his religious duties;

Perfume (Perfumed, Perfume-makers, Perfumer, Perfumers, Perfumes)
Ex 30:33 Whoever makes **p** like it and whoever
Ru 3: 3 Wash and **p** yourself, and put on your
Pr 27: 9 **P** and incense bring joy to the heart,
Ecc 7: 1 A good name is better than fine **p**,
10: 1 dead flies give **p** a bad smell, so a
SS 1: 3 your name is like **p** poured out.
1:12 my **p** spread its fragrance.
4:10 fragrance of your **p** than any spice!
5:13 are like beds of spice yielding **p**.
Isa 3:20 sashes, the **p** bottles and charms,
Mt 26: 7 alabaster jar of very expensive **p**,
26: 9 "This **p** could have been sold at a
26:12 she poured this **p** on my body, she
Mk 14: 3 very expensive **p**, made of pure nard.
14: 3 jar and poured the **p** on his head.
14: 4 one another, "Why this waste of **p**
14: 8 She poured **p** on my body beforehand
Lk 7:37 she brought an alabaster jar of **p**,
7:38 kissed them and poured **p** on them.
7:46 but she has poured **p** on my feet.
Jn 11: 2 was the same one who poured **p** on the
12: 3 pint of pure nard, expensive **p**;
12: 3 filled with the fragrance of the **p**.
12: 5 "Why wasn't this **p** sold and the
12: 7 she should save this **p** for the day

Perfumed (Perfume)
Pr 7:17 I have **p** my bed with myrrh, aloes
SS 3: 6 **p** with myrrh and incense made from

Perfume-makers (Perfume)
Ne 3: 8 Hananiah, one of the **p**, made

Perfumer (Perfume)
Ex 30:25 a fragrant blend, the work of a **p**.
30:35 blend of incense, the work of a **p**.
37:29 fragrant incense—the work of a **p**.

Perfumers (Perfume)
1Sa 8:13 He will take your daughters to be **p**

Perfumes (Perfume)
2Ch 16:14 with spices and various blended **p**,
Est 2:12 myrrh and six with **p** and cosmetics.
SS 1: 3 Pleasing is the fragrance of your **p**;
Isa 57: 9 with olive oil and increased your **p**.
Lk 23:56 went home and prepared spices and **p**.

Perga
Capital city of Pamphylia, on southern coast of Asia Minor. Paul and Barnabas passed through here twice. John Mark left them during the first visit (Ac 13:13–14); they returned later to preach (Ac 14:25).

Ac 13:13 Paul and his companions sailed to **P**
13:14 From **P** they went on to Pisidian
14:25 they had preached the word in **P**,

Pergamum
Capital city of Asia Minor where Antipas was martyred (Rev 2:13). One of the 7 letters of Revelation was addressed to the church here which was praised for its faithfulness and warned about false teaching (Rev 2:12–15).

Rev 1:11 Smyrna, **P**, Thyatira, Sardis,
2:12 "To the angel of the church in **P**

Perida
Ne 7:57 descendants of Sotai, Sophereth, **P**,

Peril

Job 22:10 you, why sudden **p** terrifies you,
Ps 107:26 their **p** their courage melted away.
2Co 1:10 delivered us from such a deadly **p**,

Period (Periods)

Ge 31:35 in your presence; I'm having my **p**.
50:10 **p** of mourning for his father.
Ex 2:23 During that long **p**, the king of
Lev 12: 2 she is unclean during her monthly **p**.
12: 5 will be unclean, as during her **p**.
15:19 the impurity of her monthly **p** will
15:20 "'Anything she lies on during her **p**
15:25 other than her monthly **p** or has a
15:25 that continues beyond her **p**, she
15:25 just as in the days of her **p**.
15:26 as is her bed during her monthly **p**,
15:26 on will be unclean, as during her **p**.
15:33 for a woman in her monthly **p**, for a
18:19 the uncleanness of her monthly **p**.
20:18 with a woman during her monthly **p**
25: 8 amount to a **p** of forty-nine years.
Nu 6: 5 "'During the entire **p** of his vow of
6: 5 He must be holy until the **p** of his
6: 6 Throughout the **p** of his separation
6: 8 Throughout the **p** of his separation
6:12 LORD for the **p** of his separation
6:13 the **p** of his separation is over.
Job 1: 5 a **p** of feasting had run its course,
Eze 18: 6 or lie with a woman during her **p**.
22:10 who violate women during their **p**,
Da 7:12 allowed to live for a **p** of time.)
Ac 1: 3 He appeared to them over a **p** of
24: 2 "We have enjoyed a long **p** of peace

Periods (Period)

1Ch 9:25 share their duties for seven-day **p**.

Perish (Perishable, Perished, Perishes, Perishing)

Ge 6:17 Everything on earth will **p**.
47:19 Why should we **p** before your eyes—we
Ex 19:21 to see the LORD and many of them **p**.
Lev 26:38 You will **p** among the nations;
Dt 4:26 you will quickly **p** from the land
11:17 and you will soon **p** from the good
28:22 which will plague you until you **p**.
32:25 Young men and young women will **p**,
Jos 23:13 until you **p** from this good land,
23:16 and you will quickly **p** from the good
Jdg 5:31 "So may all your enemies **p**, O LORD!
1Sa 26:10 or he will go into battle and **p**.
2Ki 9: 8 The whole house of Ahab will **p**.
Est 4:14 you and your father's family will **p**.
4:16 against the law. And if I **p**, I **p**."
Job 3: 3 "May the day of my birth **p**, and the
3:11 "Why did I not **p** at birth, and die
4: 9 at the blast of his anger they **p**.
4:20 unnoticed, they **p** for ever.
6:18 they go up into the wasteland and **p**.
20: 7 he will **p** for ever, like his own
34:15 all mankind would **p** together and man
36:12 if they do not listen, they will **p**
Ps 1: 6 but the way of the wicked will **p**.
9: 3 they stumble and **p** before you.
9:18 the hope of the afflicted ever **p**.
10:16 the nations will **p** from his land.
37:20 the wicked will **p**: The LORD's
41: 5 "When will he die and his name **p**?
49:10 foolish and the senseless alike **p**
49:12 he is like the beasts that **p**.
49:20 is like the beasts that **p**.
68: 2 fire, may the wicked **p** before God.
71:13 May my accusers **p** in shame;
73:27 Those who are far from you will **p**;
80:16 at your rebuke your people **p**.
83:17 may they **p** in disgrace.
92: 9 O LORD, surely your enemies will **p**;
102:26 They will **p**, but you remain; they
Pr 11:10 wicked **p**, there are shouts of joy.
19: 9 and he who pours out lies will **p**.
21:28 A false witness will **p**, and whoever
28:28 the wicked **p**, the righteous thrive.
Isa 1:28 those who forsake the LORD will **p**.
29:14 the wisdom of the wise will **p**,
Isa 31: 3 will fall; both will **p** together.
41:11 oppose you will be as nothing and **p**.
57: 1 The righteous **p**, and no-one ponders
60:12 that will not serve you will **p**;
Jer 6:21 neighbours and friends will **p**."
8:14 to the fortified cities and **p** there!
8:14 the LORD our God has doomed us to **p**
10:11 will **p** from the earth and from under
10:15 their judgment comes, they will **p**.
14:15 prophets will **p** by sword and famine.
16: 4 They will **p** by sword and famine, and
27:10 I will banish you and you will **p**.
27:15 I will banish you and you will **p**,
40:15 and the remnant of Judah to **p**?"
44:12 They will all **p** in Egypt; they will
44:27 the Jews in Egypt will **p** by sword
49:10 relatives and neighbours will **p**,
51:18 their judgment comes, they will **p**.
Eze 5:12 plague or **p** by famine inside you;
Jnh 1: 6 notice of us, and we will not **p**."
3: 9 fierce anger so that we will not **p**."
Zec 11: 9 the dying die, and the perishing **p**.
13: 8 will be struck down and **p**;
Lk 13: 3 you repent, you too will all **p**.
13: 5 you repent, you too will all **p**."
21:18 not a hair of your head will **p**.
Jn 3:16 shall not **p** but have eternal life.
10:28 and they shall never **p**; no-one can
11:50 than that the whole nation **p**."
Ac 8:20 Peter answered: "May your money **p**
13:41 "'Look, you scoffers, wonder and **p**,
Ro 2:12 law will also **p** apart from the law,
Col 2:22 These are all destined to **p** with use,
2Th 2:10 They **p** because they refused to love
Heb 1:11 They will **p**, but you remain;
1Pe 1: 4 into an inheritance that can never **p**,
2Pe 2:12 and like beasts they too will **p**.
3: 9 not wanting anyone to **p**, but

Perishable (Perish)

1Co 15:42 The body that is sown is **p**, it is
15:50 does the **p** inherit the imperishable.
15:53 For the **p** must clothe itself with
15:54 the **p** has been clothed with the
1Pe 1:18 it was not with **p** things such as
1:23 not of **p** seed, but of imperishable,

Perished (Perish)

Ge 7:21 that moved on the earth **p**—birds,
Nu 16:33 **p** and were gone from the community.
Dt 2:14 of fighting men had **p** from the camp,
7:20 survivors who hide from you have **p**.
2Sa 1:27 The weapons of war have **p**!"
Job 4: 7 Who, being innocent, has ever **p**?
Ps 9: 6 even the memory of them has **p**.
83:10 who **p** at Endor and became like
119:92 I would have **p** in my affliction.
Jer 7:28 Truth has **p**; it has vanished from
12: 4 the animals and birds have **p**.
49: 7 Has counsel **p** from the prudent?
Lam 1:19 My priests and my elders **p** in the
Mic 4: 9 you no king? Has your counsellor **p**,

Perishes (Perish)

Job 4:11 The lion **p** for lack of prey, and the
8:13 so **p** the hope of the godless.
18:17 The memory of him **p** from the earth;
Pr 11: 7 a wicked man dies, his hope **p**;
1Pe 1: 7 which **p** even though refined by fire—

Perishing (Perish)

Job 31:19 if I have seen anyone **p** for lack of
33:18 pit, his life from **p** by the sword.
Pr 31: 6 Give beer to those who are **p**, wine
Ecc 7:15 man **p** in his righteousness,
Isa 27:13 Those who were **p** in Assyria and
Jer 44:18 have been **p** by sword and famine."
Zec 11: 9 Let the dying die, and the **p** perish.
1Co 1:18 is foolishness to those who are **p**,
2Co 2:15 are being saved and those who are **p**.
4: 3 it is veiled to those who are **p**.
2Th 2:10 evil that deceives those who are **p**.

Perizzites

Ge 13: 7 The Canaanites and **P** were also
15:20 Hittites, **P**, Rephaites,
34:30 **P**, the people living in this land.
Ex 3: 8 Amorites, **P**, Hivites and Jebusites.
3:17 Hittites, Amorites, **P**, Hivites and
23:23 Hittites, **P**, Canaanites, Hivites and
33: 2 Hittites, **P**, Hivites and Jebusites.
34:11 Hittites, **P**, Hivites and Jebusites.
Dt 7: 1 Amorites, Canaanites, **P**, Hivites and
20:17 Amorites, Canaanites, **P**, Hivites and
Jos 3:10 Hittites, Hivites, **P**, Girgashites,
9: 1 **P**, Hivites and Jebusites)—
11: 3 Hittites, **P** and Jebusites in the
12: 8 **P**, Hivites and Jebusites):
17:15 in the land of the **P** and Rephaites."
24:11 as did also the Amorites, **P**,
Jdg 1: 4 the LORD gave the Canaanites and **P**
1: 5 to rout the Canaanites and **P**.
3: 5 Amorites, **P**, Hivites and Jebusites.
1Ki 9:20 Hittites, **P**, Hivites and Jebusites
2Ch 8: 7 Amorites, **P**, Hivites and Jebusites
Ezr 9: 1 Hittites, **P**, Jebusites, Ammonites,
Ne 9: 8 **P**, Jebusites and Girgashites.

Perjurers (Perjury)

Mal 3: 5 adulterers and **p**, against those who
1Ti 1:10 for slave traders and liars and **p**

Perjury (Perjurers)

Jer 7: 9 commit adultery and **p**, burn incense

Permanent (Permanently)

Lev 25:34 be sold; it is their **p** possession.
Jos 8:28 Ai and made it a **p** heap of ruins,
Jn 8:35 Now a slave has no **p** place in the
Heb 7:24 for ever, he has a **p** priesthood.

Permanently (Permanent)

Lev 25:23 "'The land must not be sold **p**,
25:30 shall belong **p** to the buyer and his

Permissible (Permit)

1Co 6:12 "Everything is **p** for me"—but not
6:12 "Everything is **p** for me"—but I will
10:23 "Everything is **p**"—but not
10:23 "Everything is **p**"—but not

Permission (Permit)

Jdg 11:17 'Give us **p** to go through your
1Sa 20: 6 'David earnestly asked my **p** to hurry
20:28 asked me for **p** to go to Bethlehem.
Ne 13: 6 Some time later I asked his **p**
Est 9:13 "give the Jews in Susa **p** to carry
Isa 22:16 who gave you **p** to cut out a grave
Da 1: 8 **p** not to defile himself in this way.
Mk 5:13 He gave them **p**, and the evil spirits
Lk 8:32 go into them, and he gave them **p**.
Jn 19:38 With Pilate's **p**, he came and took
Ac 21:40 Having received the commander's **p**,
26: 1 Agrippa said to Paul, "You have **p** to

Permit (Permissible, Permission, Permits, Permitted, Permitting)

Ex 12:23 and he will not **p** the destroyer to
Hos 5: 4 "Their deeds do not **p** them to return
Ac 24:23 **p** his friends to take care of his
1Ti 2:12 I do not **p** a woman to teach or to

Permits (Permit)

Ecc 5:12 of a rich man **p** him no sleep.
1Co 16: 7 some time with you, if the Lord **p**.

Permitted (Permit)

Ex 19:13 animal, he shall not be **p** to live.
Dt 18:14 LORD your God has not **p** you to do so.
Mt 19: 8 Jesus replied, "Moses **p** you to
Mk 10: 4 They said, "Moses **p** a man to write a
2Co 12: 4 things that man is not **p** to tell.

Permitting (Permit)

Heb 6: 3 God **p**, we will do so.

Perpetuate
Ps 45:17 I will **p** your memory through all

Perplexed (Perplexity)
Da 4:19 was greatly **p** for a time, and his
Lk 9: 7 And he was **p**, because some were
Ac 2:12 Amazed and **p**, they asked one another,
2Co 4: 8 not crushed; **p**, but not in despair;
Gal 4:20 my tone, because I am **p** about you!

Perplexity (Perplexed)
Lk 21:25 nations will be in anguish and **p** at

Persecute (Persecuted, Persecuting, Persecution, Persecutions, Persecutor, Persecutors)
Dt 30: 7 on your enemies who hate and **p** you.
Ps 9:13 O LORD, see how my enemies **p** me!
69:26 For they **p** those you wound and talk
119:86 help me, for men **p** me without cause.
119:157 Many are the foes who **p** me, but I
119:161 Rulers **p** me without cause, but my
Mt 5:11 **p** you and falsely say all kinds of
5:44 and pray for those who **p** you,
Lk 11:49 will kill and others they will **p**.'
21:12 will lay hands on you and **p** you.
Jn 15:20 persecuted me, they will **p** you also
Ac 7:52 a prophet your fathers did not **p**?
9: 4 "Saul, Saul, why do you **p** me?
12: 1 to the church, intending to **p** them.
22: 7 me, 'saul! Saul! Why do you **p** me?'
26:11 went to foreign cities to **p** them.
26:14 'saul, Saul, why do you **p** me? It is
Ro 12:14 Bless those who **p** you; bless and do

Persecuted (Persecute)
Mt 5:10 Blessed are those who are **p** because
5:12 **p** the prophets who were before you.
10:23 you are **p** in one place, flee to
24: 9 "Then you will be handed over to be **p**
Jn 5:16 on the Sabbath, the Jews **p** him.
15:20 If they **p** me, they will persecute
Ac 22: 4 I **p** the followers of this Way to
1Co 4:12 when we are **p**, we endure it;
15: 9 because I **p** the church of God.
2Co 4: 9 **p**, but not abandoned; struck down,
Gal 1:13 how intensely I **p** the church of God
1:23 "The man who formerly **p** us is now
4:29 ordinary way **p** the son born by the
5:11 why am I still being **p**? In that case
6:12 being **p** for the cross of Christ.
1Th 3: 4 kept telling you that we would be **p**.
2Ti 3:12 life in Christ Jesus will be **p**,
Heb 11:37 destitute, **p** and ill-treated—

Persecuting (Persecute)
Ac 9: 5 "I am Jesus, whom you are **p**," he
22: 8 Jesus of Nazareth, whom you are **p**,'
26:15 "'I am Jesus, whom you are **p**,'
Php 3: 6 for zeal, **p** the church; as for

Persecution (Persecute)
Mt 13:21 When trouble or **p** comes because of
Mk 4:17 When trouble or **p** comes because of
Ac 8: 1 On that day a great **p** broke out
11:19 by the **p** in connection with Stephen
13:50 They stirred up **p** against Paul and
Ro 8:35 Shall trouble or hardship or **p** or
1Th 3: 7 brothers, in all our distress and **p**
Heb 10:33 publicly exposed to insult and **p**;
Rev 2:10 and you will suffer **p** for ten days.

Persecutions (Persecute)
Mk 10:30 and fields—and with them, **p**)
2Co 12:10 in hardships, in **p**, in difficulties.
2Th 1: 4 the **p** and trials you are enduring.
2Ti 3:11 **p**, sufferings—what kinds of things
3:11 Iconium and Lystra, the **p** I endured.

Persecutor (Persecute)
1Ti 1:13 and a **p** and a violent man,

Persecutors (Persecute)
Ps 119:84 When will you punish my **p**?
Jer 15:15 Avenge me on my **p**. You are
17:18 Let my **p** be put to shame, but keep
20:11 my **p** will stumble and not prevail.

Perseverance (Persevere)
Ro 5: 3 we know that suffering produces **p**;
5: 4 **p**, character; and character, hope.
2Co 12:12 done among you with great **p**.
2Th 1: 4 God's churches we boast about your **p**
3: 5 into God's love and Christ's **p**.
Heb 12: 1 with **p** the race marked out for us.
Jas 1: 3 testing of your faith develops **p**.
1: 4 **P** must finish its work so that you
5:11 You have heard of Job's **p** and have
2Pe 1: 6 to self-control, **p**; and to **p**,
Rev 2: 2 deeds, your hard work and your **p**.
2:19 your service and **p**, and that you are

Persevere (Perseverance, Persevered, Perseveres, Persevering)
1Ti 4:16 **P** in them, because if you do, you
Heb 10:36 You need to **p** so that when you have

Persevered (Persevere)
Heb 11:27 he **p** because he saw him who is
Jas 5:11 consider blessed those who have **p**.
Rev 2: 3 You have **p** and have endured

Perseveres (Persevere)
1Co 13: 7 trusts, always hopes, always **p**.
Jas 1:12 Blessed is the man who **p** under trial,

Persevering (Persevere)
Lk 8:15 retain it, and by **p** produce a crop.

Persia (Persian, Persians)
Ancient empire that began east of Persian Gulf, but under Cyrus absorbed Media and Babylonia (2Ch 36:20). Its kings allowed the exiled Jews to return to Jerusalem to rebuild the temple (2Ch 36:22–23; Ezr 1:1–11; 7:1–28; 9:9). Its military leaders were guests of King Xerxes (Est 1:3, 14). Mordecai's greatness was recorded in their Kings' annals (Est 10:2). Persians served in the armies of Tyre (Eze 27:10) and Magog (Eze 38:5). Its defeat of the Babylonian Empire was prophesied (Da 5:28), as was its own eventual defeat by Greece (Da 10–11). See *Media*

2Ch 36:20 the kingdom of **P** came to power.
36:22 In the first year of Cyrus king of **P**,
36:22 moved the heart of Cyrus king of **P**
36:23 "This is what Cyrus king of **P** says:
Ezr 1: 1 In the first year of Cyrus king of **P**,
1: 1 moved the heart of Cyrus king of **P**
1: 2 "This is what Cyrus king of **P** says:
1: 8 Cyrus king of **P** had them brought by
3: 7 as authorised by Cyrus king of **P**.
4: 3 Cyrus, the king of **P**, commanded us."
4: 5 the entire reign of Cyrus king of **P**
4: 5 to the reign of Darius king of **P**.
4: 7 in the days of Artaxerxes king of **P**,
4: 9 **P**, Erech and Babylon, the Elamites
4:24 of the reign of Darius king of **P**.
6:14 Darius and Artaxerxes, kings of **P**.
7: 1 the reign of Artaxerxes king of **P**,
9: 9 in the sight of the kings of **P**:
Est 1: 3 The military leaders of **P** and Media,
1:14 the seven nobles of **P** and Media who
1:19 written in the laws of **P** and Media,
10: 2 annals of the kings of Media and **P**?
Eze 27:10 "'Men of **P**, Lydia and Put served as
38: 5 **P**, Cush and Put will be with them,
Da 8:20 represents the kings of Media and **P**.
10: 1 In the third year of Cyrus king of **P**,
10:13 detained there with the king of **P**.
10:20 to fight against the prince of **P**,
11: 2 Three more kings will appear in **P**,

Persian (Persia)
Ne 12:22 in the reign of Darius the **P**.
Est 1:18 This very day the **P** and Median women
Da 6:28 Darius and the reign of Cyrus the **P**.
10:13 the prince of the **P** kingdom resisted

Persians (Persia)
Da 5:28 and given to the Medes and **P**."
6: 8 with the laws of the Medes and **P**,
6:12 with the laws of the Medes and **P**,
6:15 law of the Medes and **P** no decree

Persis
Ro 16:12 Greet my dear friend **P**, another

Persist (Persisted, Persistence, Persists)
Dt 29:19 even though I **p** in going my own way.
1Sa 12:25 Yet if you **p** in doing evil, both you
2Ki 17:34 To this day they **p** in their former
Isa 1: 5 Why do you **p** in rebellion?
Ro 11:23 if they do not **p** in unbelief, they

Persisted (Persist)
2Ki 2:17 they **p** until he was too ashamed to
17:22 The Israelites **p** in all the sins of
17:40 but **p** in their former practices.

Persistence (Persist)
Ro 2: 7 To those who by **p** in doing good seek

Persists (Persist)
Dt 25: 8 If he **p** in saying, "I do not want to

Person (Person's, Persons)
Ex 12: 4 with what each **p** will eat.
16:16 Take an omer for each **p** you have in
16:22 twice as much—two omers for each **p**
23: 7 an innocent or honest **p** to death,
36: 1 Bezalel, Oholiab and every skilled **p**
36: 2 Oholiab and every skilled **p** to whom
38:26 one beka per **p**, that is, half a
Lev 5: 1 "'If a **p** sins because he does not
5: 2 "'Or if a **p** touches anything
5: 4 "'Or if a **p** thoughtlessly takes an
5:15 "When a **p** commits a violation and
5:17 "If a **p** sins and does what is
7:11 a **p** may present to the LORD:
7:18 the **p** who eats any of it will be
7:20 **p** must be cut off from his people.
7:21 **p** must be cut off from his people.
7:27 If anyone eats blood, that **p** must be
13: 4 put the infected **p** in isolation for
13:12 of the infected **p** from head to foot,
13:13 he shall pronounce that **p** clean.
13:17 pronounce the infected **p** clean;
13:30 the priest shall pronounce that **p**
13:31 put the infected **p** in isolation for
13:36 for yellow hair; the **p** is unclean.
13:39 out on the skin; that **p** is clean.
13:45 "The **p** with such an infectious
14: 2 the regulations for the diseased **p**
14: 3 If the **p** has been healed of his
14: 8 "The **p** to be cleansed must wash his
14:30 pigeons, which the **p** can afford,
15: 8 that **p** must wash his clothes and
17:10 face against that **p** who eats blood
19: 8 **p** must be cut off from his people.
20: 6 "'I will set my face against the **p**
22: 3 **p** must be cut off from my presence.
22: 5 or any **p** who makes him unclean,
22:13 No authorised **p**, however, may eat
27: 5 If it is a **p** between the ages of
27: 6 If it is a **p** between one month and
27: 7 If it is a **p** sixty years old or more,
27: 8 he is to present the **p** to the priest,
27:24 to the **p** from whom he bought it,
27:29 "'No **p** devoted to destruction may
Nu 5: 6 to the LORD, that **p** is guilty
5: 7 give it all to the **p** he has wronged.
5: 8 if that **p** has no close relative to
9:13 that **p** must be cut off from his
15:27 "'But if just one **p** sins
15:30 **p** must be cut off from his people.
15:31 that **p** must surely be cut off;
16: 5 he will make that **p** come near him.

Nu 19:13 That **p** must be cut off from Israel.
19:14 applies when a **p** dies in a tent:
19:17 "For the unclean **p**, put some ashes
19:19 sprinkle the unclean **p** on the third
19:19 The **p** being cleansed must wash his
19:20 if a **p** who is unclean does not
19:22 Anything that an unclean **p** touches
35: 6 a **p** who has killed someone may flee.
35:11 to which a **p** who has killed someone
35:12 so that a **p** accused of murder may
35:21 that **p** shall be put to death; he is
35:30 "'Anyone who kills a **p** is to be put
Dt 4:42 to which anyone who had killed a **p**
17: 5 city gate and stone that **p** to death.
27:25 a bribe to kill an innocent **p**.
29:19 such a **p** hears the words of this
Jos 20: 3 anyone who kills a **p** accidentally
1Sa 10: 6 will be changed into a different **p**.
2Sa 3:19 also spoke to the Benjamites in **p**.
6:19 to each **p** in the whole crowd of
14:14 a banished **p** may not remain
Est 5:12 "I'm the only **p** Queen Esther invited
Ps 62:12 Surely you will reward each **p**
Pr 24:12 Will he not repay each **p**
Jer 5: 1 If you can find but one **p** who deals
Eze 44:25 himself by going near a dead **p**;
44:25 if the dead **p** was his father or
Da 11:21 be succeeded by a contemptible **p**
Hag 2:12 If a **p** carries consecrated meat in
2:13 Haggai said, "If a **p** defiled by
Mt 5:39 I tell you, Do not resist an evil **p**.
10:11 search for some worthy **p** there and
16:27 he will reward each **p** according to
Lk 7:12 a dead **p** was being carried out—
14: 8 for a **p** more distinguished than you
17: 1 to that **p** through whom they come.
Jn 12:47 "As for the **p** who hears my words but
13:10 Jesus answered, "A **p** who has had a
Ro 2: 6 God "will give to each **p** according
2Co 10:10 but in **p** he is unimpressive and his
Gal 3:16 seed", meaning one **p**, who is Christ.
Eph 5: 5 impure or greedy **p**—such a man is an
Col 2:18 Such a **p** goes into great detail
1Th 2:17 a short time (in **p**, not in thought)
Tit 3:10 Warn a divisive **p** once, and then
Heb 7: 7 without doubt the lesser **p** is
Jas 2:24 You see that a **p** is justified by
3: 6 It corrupts the whole **p**, sets the
5:15 in faith will make the sick **p** well;
2Jn : 7 Any such **p** is the deceiver and the
Rev 20:13 and each **p** was judged according to

Person's (Person)
Ex 22:11 lay hands on the other **p** property.

Persons (Person)
Ge 46:26 sons' wives—numbered sixty-six **p**.
Lev 18:29 such **p** must be cut off from their
27: 2 special vow to dedicate **p** to the
Nu 31:28 whether **p**, cattle, donkeys, sheep
31:30 whether **p**, cattle, donkeys, sheep,
31:47 out of every fifty **p** and animals,
Lk 15: 7 righteous **p** who do not need to
Ac 4:34 There were no needy **p** among them.

Perspire
Eze 44:18 not wear anything that makes them **p**.

Persuade (Persuaded, Persuading, Persuasion, Persuasive)
Jdg 19: 3 her husband went to her to **p** her to
2Ki 18:30 Do not let Hezekiah **p** you to trust
Isa 36:15 Do not let Hezekiah **p** you to trust
Ac 18: 4 trying to **p** Jews and Greeks.
26:28 you can **p** me to be a Christian?"
2Co 5:11 to fear the Lord, we try to **p** men.

Persuaded (Persuade)
Jdg 19: 7 his father-in-law **p** him, so he
Pr 25:15 Through patience a ruler can be **p**,
Jer 28:15 have **p** this nation to trust in lies.
Mt 27:20 priests and the elders **p** the crowd
Lk 20: 6 they are **p** that John was a prophet."
Ac 5:40 His speech **p** them. They called the
6:11 they secretly **p** some men to say, "We
16:15 stay at my house." And she **p** us.
17: 4 Some of the Jews were **p** and joined
Ro 4:21 being fully **p** that God had power to
2Ti 1: 5 and, I am **p**, now lives in you also.

Persuading (Persuade)
Ac 18:13 "This man," they charged, "is **p** the

Persuasion (Persuade)
Gal 5: 8 That kind of **p** does not come from

Persuasive (Persuade)
Pr 7:21 With **p** words she led him astray;
1Co 2: 4 were not with wise and **p** words,

Peruda
Ezr 2:55 of Sotai, Hassophereth, **P**,

Perverse (Pervert)
Dt 32:20 for they are a **p** generation,
1Sa 20:30 "You son of a **p** and rebellious woman!
Ps 101: 4 Men of **p** heart shall be far from me;
Pr 2:12 men, from men whose words are **p**,
3:32 for the LORD detests a **p** man but
8: 8 none of them is crooked or **p**.
8:13 evil behaviour and **p** speech.
10:31 but a **p** tongue will be cut out.
10:32 mouth of the wicked only what is **p**.
11:20 The LORD detests men of **p** heart but
16:28 A **p** man stirs up dissension, and a
17:20 A man of **p** heart does not prosper;
19: 1 than a fool whose lips are **p**.
28: 6 than a rich man whose ways are **p**.
28:18 whose ways are **p** will suddenly fall.
Mt 17:17 "O unbelieving and **p** generation,"
Lk 9:41 "O unbelieving and **p** generation,"

Perverseness (Pervert)
Pr 2:14 wrong and rejoice in the **p** of evil,

Perversion (Pervert)
Lev 18:23 relations with it; that is a **p**.
20:12 What they have done is a **p**;
Ro 1:27 the due penalty for their **p**.
Jude : 7 up to sexual immorality and **p**.

Perversity (Pervert)
Pr 4:24 Put away **p** from your mouth;
16:30 winks with his eye is plotting **p**;

Pervert (Perverse, Perverseness, Perversion, Perversity, Perverted, Perverting, Perverts)
Ex 23: 2 **p** justice by siding with the crowd,
Lev 19:15 "'Do not **p** justice; do not show
Dt 16:19 Do not **p** justice or show partiality.
Job 8: 3 Does God **p** justice? Does the
8: 3 Does the Almighty **p** what is right?
34:12 that the Almighty would **p** justice.
Pr 17:23 secret to **p** the course of justice.
Gal 1: 7 trying to **p** the gospel of Christ.

Perverted (Pervert)
1Sa 8: 3 and accepted bribes and **p** justice.
Job 33:27 'I have sinned, and **p** what was right,
Jer 3:21 because they have **p** their ways and
Hab 1: 4 the righteous, so that justice is **p**.

Perverting (Pervert)
Ac 13:10 stop **p** the right ways of the Lord?

Perverts (Pervert)
1Ti 1:10 for adulterers and **p**, for slave

Pestilence (Pestilences)
Dt 32:24 consuming **p** and deadly plague;
Ps 91: 3 snare and from the deadly **p**.
91: 6 nor the **p** that stalks in the
Hab 3: 5 before him; **p** followed his steps.

Pestilences (Pestilence)
Lk 21:11 famines and **p** in various places, and

Pestle
Pr 27:22 grinding him like grain with a **p**,

Pests
Mal 3:11 I will prevent **p** from devouring your

Pet
Job 41: 5 Can you make a **p** of him like a bird

Peter (Cephas, Peter's, Simon, Simon's)
Name means "rock"; in Aramaic, Cephas (Jn 1:42). Apostle; brother of Andrew, also called Simon (Mt 4:18; Mk 1:16–18; Lk 5:3–11; Jn 1:40–42; Mt 10:2; Mk 3:16; Lk 6:14; Ac 1:13). With James and John, especially close to Jesus at raising of Jairus' daughter (Mk 5:37; Lk 8:51); transfiguration (Mt 17:1–2; Mk 9:2; Lk 9:28–29); in Gethsemane (Mt 26:36–38; Mk 14:32–34). Confessed Jesus as Christ (Mt 16:13–20; Mk 8:27–30; Lk 9:18–21). Caught fish with coin (Mt 17:24–27). Denial predicted (Mt 26:33–35; Mk 14:29–31; Lk 22:31–34; Jn 13:37–38). Followed Jesus after arrest (Mt 26:58; Mk 14:54; Jn 18:15); denied Jesus (Mt 26:69–75; Mk 14:66–72; Lk 22:54–62; Jn 18:17–27). Commissioned by Jesus after resurrection (Jn 21). Exercised leadership in early church (Ac 1:15; 2:14; 5:3–11). Preached on day of Pentecost (Ac 2). Healed lame man at temple gate (Ac 3); before Sanhedrin (Ac 4). In Samaria (Ac 8:14–25). Received vision; went to Cornelius (Ac 10); supported Gentile mission (Ac 11; 15:7–11); lapsed and rebuked by Paul at Antioch (Gal 2:11–21). Miraculously released from prison (Ac 12). Wrote 1 & 2 Peter.

Mt 4:18 called **P** and his brother Andrew.
10: 2 Simon (who is called **P**) and his
14:28 "Lord, if it's you," **P** replied,
14:29 "Come," he said. Then **P** got down out
15:15 **P** said, "Explain the parable to us."
16:16 Simon **P** answered, "You are the
16:18 I tell you that you are **P**, and on
16:22 **P** took him aside and began to rebuke
16:23 Jesus turned and said to **P**, "Get
17: 1 After six days Jesus took with him **P**,
17: 4 **P** said to Jesus, "Lord, it is good
17:24 two-drachma tax came to **P** and asked,
17:25 When **P** came into the house, Jesus
17:26 "From others," **P** answered. "Then the
18:21 **P** came to Jesus and asked, "Lord,
19:27 **P** answered him, "We have left
26:33 **P** replied, "Even if all fall away on
26:35 **P** declared, "Even if I have to die
26:37 He took **P** and the two sons of
26:40 with me for one hour?" he asked **P**.
26:58 **P** followed him at a distance, right
26:69 Now **P** was sitting out in the
26:73 those standing there went up to **P**
26:75 **P** remembered the word Jesus had
Mk 3:16 Simon (to whom he gave the name **P**);
5:37 not let anyone follow him except **P**,
8:29 **P** answered, "You are the Christ."
8:32 and **P** took him aside and began to
8:33 at his disciples, he rebuked **P**.
9: 2 After six days Jesus took **P**, James
9: 5 **P** said to Jesus, "Rabbi, it is good
10:28 **P** said to him, "We have left
11:21 **P** remembered and said to Jesus,
13: 3 **P**, James, John and Andrew asked him
14:29 **P** declared, "Even if all fall away,
14:31 **P** insisted emphatically, "Even if I
14:33 He took **P**, James and John along with
14:37 "Simon," he said to **P**, "are you
14:54 **P** followed him at a distance, right
14:66 While **P** was below in the courtyard,
14:67 she saw **P** warming himself, she
14:70 those standing near said to **P**,
14:72 Then **P** remembered the word Jesus had
16: 7 go, tell his disciples and **P**, 'He is
Lk 5: 8 Simon **P** saw this, he fell at Jesus' knees
6:14 Simon (whom he named **P**), his brother
8:45 When they all denied it, **P** said,
8:51 let anyone go in with him except **P**,

Lk 9:20 **P** answered, "The Christ of God."
9:28 he took **P**, John and James with him
9:32 **P** and his companions were very
9:33 **P** said to him, "Master, it is good
12:41 **P** asked, "Lord, are you telling this
18:28 **P** said to him, "We have left all we
22: 8 Jesus sent **P** and John, saying, "Go
22:34 Jesus answered, "I tell you, **P**,
22:54 **P** followed at a distance.
22:55 down together, **P** sat down with them.
22:58 "Man, I am not!" **P** replied.
22:60 **P** replied, "Man, I don't know what
22:61 Lord turned and looked straight at **P**.
22:61 Then **P** remembered the word the Lord
24:12 **P**, however, got up and ran to the
Jn 1:42 (which, when translated, is **P**).
1:44 Philip, like Andrew and **P**, was from
6:68 Simon **P** answered him, "Lord, to whom
13: 6 He came to Simon **P**, who said to him,
13: 8 "No," said **P**, "you shall never wash
13: 9 "Then, Lord," Simon **P** replied, "not
13:24 Simon **P** motioned to this disciple
13:36 Simon **P** asked him, "Lord, where are
13:37 **P** asked, "Lord, why can't I follow
18:10 Simon **P**, who had a sword, drew it
18:11 Jesus commanded **P**, "Put your sword
18:15 Simon **P** and another disciple were
18:16 **P** had to wait outside at the door.
18:16 girl on duty there and brought **P** in.
18:17 you?" the girl at the door asked **P**.
18:18 **P** also was standing with them,
18:25 Simon **P** stood warming himself, he
18:26 of the man whose ear **P** had cut off,
18:27 Again **P** denied it, and at that
20: 2 she came running to Simon **P** and the
20: 3 **P** and the other disciple started for
20: 4 outran **P** and reached the tomb first.
20: 6 Simon **P**, who was behind him, arrived
21: 2 Simon **P**, Thomas (called Didymus),
21: 3 going out to fish," Simon **P** told
21: 7 disciple whom Jesus loved said to **P**
21: 7 As soon as Simon **P** heard him say
21:11 Simon **P** climbed aboard and dragged
21:15 Jesus said to Simon **P**, "Simon son of
21:17 **P** was hurt because Jesus asked him
21:19 death by which **P** would glorify God.
21:20 **P** turned and saw that the disciple
21:21 **P** saw him, he asked, "Lord, what
Ac 1:13 Those present were **P**, John, James
1:15 In those days **P** stood up among the
1:20 "For," said **P**, "it is written in the
2:14 **P** stood up with the Eleven, raised
2:37 said to **P** and the other apostles,
2:38 **P** replied, "Repent and be baptised,
3: 1 One day **P** and John were going up to
3: 3 he saw **P** and John about to enter, he
3: 4 **P** looked straight at him, as did
3: 4 Then **P** said, "Look at us!"
3: 6 **P** said, "Silver or gold I do not
3:11 While the beggar held on to **P** and
3:12 **P** saw this, he said to them: "Men of
4: 1 the Sadducees came up to **P** and John
4: 3 They seized **P** and John, and because
4: 7 They had **P** and John brought before
4: 8 **P**, filled with the Holy Spirit, said
4:13 they saw the courage of **P** and John
4:19 **P** and John replied, "Judge for
4:23 On their release, **P** and John went
5: 3 **P** said, "Ananias, how is it that
5: 8 **P** asked her, "Tell me, is this the
5: 9 **P** said to her, "How could you agree
5:29 **P** and the other apostles replied:
8:14 God, they sent **P** and John to them.
8:17 **P** and John placed their hands on
8:20 **P** answered: "May your money perish
8:25 **P** and John returned to Jerusalem,
9:32 **P** travelled about the country, he
9:34 "Aeneas," **P** said to him, "Jesus
9:38 disciples heard that **P** was in Lydda,
9:39 **P** went with them, and when he
9:40 **P** sent them all out of the room;
9:40 her eyes, and seeing **P** she sat up.
9:43 **P** stayed in Joppa for some time with
10: 5 a man named Simon who is called **P**.
10: 9 city, **P** went up on the roof to pray.
10:13 a voice told him, "Get up, **P**. Kill
Ac 10:14 "Surely not, Lord!" **P** replied.
10:17 While **P** was wondering about the
10:18 was known as **P** was staying there.
10:19 While **P** was still thinking about the
10:21 **P** went down and said to the men,
10:23 **P** invited the men into the house to
10:23 The next day **P** started out with them,
10:25 **P** entered the house, Cornelius met
10:26 **P** made him get up. "Stand up," he
10:27 Talking with him, **P** went inside and
10:32 to Joppa for Simon who is called **P**.
10:34 **P** began to speak: "I now realise how
10:44 While **P** was still speaking these
10:45 believers who had come with **P** were
10:46 Then **P** said,
10:48 they asked **P** to stay with them for
11: 2 when **P** went up to Jerusalem, the
11: 4 **P** began and explained everything to
11: 7 a voice telling me, 'Get up, **P**.
11:13 to Joppa for Simon who is called **P**.
12: 3 Jews, he proceeded to seize **P** also.
12: 5 **P** was kept in prison, but the church
12: 6 **P** was sleeping between two soldiers,
12: 7 He struck **P** on the side and woke him
12: 8 And **P** did so. "Wrap your cloak
12: 9 **P** followed him out of the prison,
12:11 **P** came to himself and said, "Now I
12:13 **P** knocked at the outer entrance, and
12:14 "**P** is at the door!"
12:16 **P** kept on knocking, and when they
12:17 **P** motioned with his hand for them to
12:18 soldiers as to what had become of **P**.
15: 7 After much discussion, **P** got up and
1Co 15: 5 that he appeared to **P**, and then to
Gal 1:18 get acquainted with **P** and stayed
2: 7 just as **P** had been to the Jews.
2: 8 of **P** as an apostle to the Jews,
2: 9 James, **P** and John, those reputed to
2:11 **P** came to Antioch, I opposed him to
2:14 I said to **P** in front of them all,
1Pe 1: 1 **P**, an apostle of Jesus Christ, To
2Pe 1: 1 Simon **P**, a servant and apostle of

Peter's (Peter)

Mt 8:14 Jesus came into **P** house,
8:14 he saw **P** mother-in-law lying in bed
Jn 1:40 Andrew, Simon **P** brother, was one of
6: 8 Andrew, Simon **P** brother, spoke up,
Ac 5:15 mats so that at least **P** shadow might
12: 7 and the chains fell off **P** wrists.
12:14 she recognised **P** voice, she was so

Pethahiah

1Ch 24:16 the nineteenth to **P**, the twentieth
Ezr 10:23 is Kelita), **P**, Judah and Eliezer.
Ne 9: 5 Sherebiah, Hodiah, Shebaniah and **P**
11:24 **P** son of Meshezabel, one of the

Pethor

Nu 22: 5 who was at **P**, near the River, in his
Dt 23: 4 they hired Balaam son of Beor from **P**

Pethuel

Joel 1: 1 the LORD that came to Joel son of **P**.

Petition (Petitioned, Petitions)

1Ch 16: 4 to make **p**, to give thanks, and to
Est 5: 6 asked Esther, "Now what is your **p**?
5: 7 Esther replied, "My **p** and my request
5: 8 to grant my **p** and fulfil my request,
7: 2 "Queen Esther, what is your **p**?
7: 3 grant me my life—this is my **p**.
9:12 Now what is your **p**? It will be
Ps 38: T A psalm of David. A **p**.
70: T director of music. Of David. A **p**.
Jer 7:16 nor offer any plea or **p** for them;
11:14 nor offer any plea or **p** for them,
36: 7 Perhaps they will bring their **p**
37:20 Let me bring my **p** before you: Do not
42: 2 "Please hear our **p** and pray to the
42: 9 you sent me to present your **p**, says:
Da 9: 3 pleaded with him in prayer and **p**,
Ac 23:15 Now then, you and the Sanhedrin **p**
Php 4: 6 but in everything, by prayer and **p**,

Petitioned (Petition)

Ezr 8:23 we fasted and **p** our God about this,
Ac 25:24 The whole Jewish community has **p** me

Petitions (Petition)

Da 9:17 "Now, our God, hear the prayers and **p**
Heb 5: 7 he offered up prayers and **p** with

Peullethai

1Ch 26: 5 the seventh and **P** the eighth.

Phantom

Ps 39: 6 Man is a mere **p** as he goes to and

Phanuel

Lk 2:36 Anna, the daughter of **P**, of the

Pharaoh (Pharaoh's)

Ge 12:15 they praised her to **P**, and she was
12:17 LORD inflicted serious diseases on **P**
12:18 **P** summoned Abram. "What have you
12:20 **P** gave orders about Abram to his men,
40: 2 **P** was angry with his two officials,
40:13 Within three days **P** will lift up
40:14 mention me to **P** and get me out of
40:17 were all kinds of baked goods for **P**,
40:19 Within three days **P** will lift off
41: 1 **P** had a dream: He was standing by
41: 4 sleek, fat cows. Then **P** woke up.
41: 7 Then **P** woke up; it had been a dream.
41: 8 **P** told them his dreams, but no-one
41: 9 the chief cupbearer said to **P**,
41:10 **P** was once angry with his servants,
41:14 **P** sent for Joseph, and he was
41:14 his clothes, he came before **P**.
41:15 **P** said to Joseph, "I had a dream,
41:16 "I cannot do it," Joseph replied to **P**
41:16 will give **P** the answer he desires."
41:17 **P** said to Joseph, "In my dream I was
41:25 Joseph said to **P**, "The dreams of **P**
41:25 God has revealed to **P** what he is
41:28 "It is just as I said to **P**: God has
41:28 has shown **P** what he is about to do.
41:32 The reason the dream was given to **P**
41:33 "And now let **P** look for a discerning
41:34 Let **P** appoint commissioners over the
41:35 under the authority of **P**, to be
41:37 The plan seemed good to **P** and to all
41:38 **P** asked them, "Can we find anyone
41:39 **P** said to Joseph, "Since God has
41:41 **P** said to Joseph, "I hereby put you
41:42 **P** took his signet ring from his
41:44 **P** said to Joseph, "I am **P**, but
41:45 **P** gave Joseph the name
41:46 the service of **P** king of Egypt.
41:55 the people cried to **P** for food.
41:55 Then **P** told all the Egyptians, "Go
42:15 As surely as **P** lives, you will not
42:16 surely as **P** lives, you are spies!"
44:18 though you are equal to **P** himself.
45: 8 He made me father to **P**, lord of his
45:16 **P** and all his officials were pleased.
45:17 **P** said to Joseph, "Tell your
45:21 gave them carts, as **P** had commanded
46: 5 that **P** had sent to transport him.
46:31 "I will go up and speak to **P** and
46:33 **P** calls you in and asks, 'What is
47: 1 Joseph went and told **P**, "My father
47: 2 and presented them before **P**.
47: 3 **P** asked the brothers, "What is your
47: 3 they replied to **P**, "just as our
47: 5 **P** said to Joseph, "Your father and
47: 7 Jacob in and presented him before **P**.
47: 7 After Jacob blessed **P**,
47: 8 **P** asked him, "How old are you?"
47: 9 Jacob said to **P**, "The years of my
47:10 Jacob blessed **P** and went out from
47:11 district of Rameses, as **P** directed.
47:19 our land will be in bondage to **P**.
47:20 bought all the land in Egypt for **P**.
47:22 received a regular allotment from **P**
47:22 from the allotment **P** gave them.
47:23 you and your land today for **P**,
47:24 comes in, give a fifth of it to **P**.

Ge 47:25 we will be in bondage to **P**."
47:26 of the produce belongs to **P**.
50: 4 in your eyes, speak to **P** for me.
50: 6 **P** said, "Go up and bury your father,
Ex 1:11 and Rameses as store cities for **P**.
1:19 The midwives answered **P**, "Hebrew
1:22 **P** gave this order to all his people:
2:15 **P** heard of this, he tried to kill
2:15 but Moses fled from **P** and went to
3:10 I am sending you to **P** to bring my
3:11 "Who am I, that I should go to **P** and
4:21 see that you perform before **P** all
4:22 say to **P**, 'This is what the LORD
5: 1 Afterwards Moses and Aaron went to **P**
5: 2 **P** said, "Who is the LORD, that I
5: 5 **P** said, "Look, the people of the
5: 6 That same day **P** gave this order to
5:10 "This is what **P** says: 'I will not
5:15 foremen went and appealed to **P**:
5:17 **P** said, "Lazy, that's what you
5:20 they left **P**, they found Moses and
5:21 You have made us a stench to **P** and
5:23 Ever since I went to **P** to speak in
6: 1 Now you will see what I will do to **P**:
6:11 "Go, tell **P** king of Egypt to let the
6:12 why would **P** listen to me, since I
6:13 the Israelites and **P** king of Egypt,
6:27 They were the ones who spoke to **P**
6:29 Tell **P** king of Egypt everything I
6:30 lips, why would **P** listen to me?"
7: 1 "See, I have made you like God to **P**,
7: 2 and your brother Aaron is to tell **P**
7: 7 eighty-three when they spoke to **P**.
7: 9 "When **P** says to you, 'Perform a
7: 9 staff and throw it down before **P**,'
7:10 Moses and Aaron went to **P** and did
7:10 in front of **P** and his officials,
7:11 **P** then summoned the wise men and
7:15 Go to **P** in the morning as he goes
7:20 his staff in the presence of **P**
8: 1 the LORD said to Moses, "Go to **P** and
8: 8 **P** summoned Moses and Aaron and said,
8: 9 Moses said to **P**, "I leave to you the
8:10 "Tomorrow," **P** said. Moses replied,
8:12 After Moses and Aaron left **P**, Moses
8:12 about the frogs he had brought on **P**.
8:15 when **P** saw that there was relief, he
8:19 The magicians said to **P**, "This is
8:20 confront **P** as he goes to the water
8:25 **P** summoned Moses and Aaron and said,
8:28 **P** said, "I will let you go to offer
8:29 **P** and his officials and his people.
8:29 Only be sure that **P** does not act
8:30 Moses left **P** and prayed to the LORD,
8:31 The flies left **P** and his officials
8:32 this time also **P** hardened his heart
9: 1 the LORD said to Moses, "Go to **P** and
9: 7 **P** sent men to investigate and found
9: 8 into the air in the presence of **P**.
9:10 from a furnace and stood before **P**.
9:13 confront **P** and say to him, 'This is
9:20 Those officials of **P** who feared the
9:27 **P** summoned Moses and Aaron.
9:33 Moses left **P** and went out of the
9:34 **P** saw that the rain and hail and
10: 1 the LORD said to Moses, "Go to **P**,
10: 3 Moses and Aaron went to **P** and said
10: 6 Then Moses turned and left **P**.
10: 8 and Aaron were brought back to **P**.
10:10 **P** said, "The LORD be with you—if I
10:16 **P** quickly summoned Moses and Aaron
10:18 Moses then left **P** and prayed to the
10:24 **P** summoned Moses and said, "Go,
10:28 **P** said to Moses, "Get out of my
11: 1 one more plague on **P** and on Egypt.
11: 5 from the firstborn son of **P**, who
11: 8 Then Moses, hot with anger, left **P**.
11: 9 The LORD had said to Moses, "**P** will
11:10 all these wonders before **P**,
12:29 from the firstborn of **P**, who sat on
12:30 **P** and all his officials and all the
12:31 During the night **P** summoned Moses
13:15 **P** stubbornly refused to let us go,
13:17 **P** let the people go, God did not
14: 3 **P** will think, 'The Israelites are
14: 4 myself through **P** and all his army,
Ex 14: 5 **P** and his officials changed their
14: 8 The LORD hardened the heart of **P**
14:10 **P** approached, the Israelites looked
14:17 And I will gain glory through **P** and
14:18 gain glory through **P**, his chariots
14:28 the entire army of **P** that followed
18: 4 he saved me from the sword of **P**."
18: 8 everything the LORD had done to **P**
18:10 the hand of the Egyptians and of **P**,
Dt 6:21 tell him: "We were slaves of **P** in
6:22 Egypt and **P** and his whole household.
7: 8 from the power of **P** king of Egypt.
7:18 your God did to **P** and to all Egypt.
11: 3 both to **P** king of Egypt and to his
29: 2 all that the LORD did in Egypt to **P**,
34:11 to **P** and to all his officials and
1Sa 2:27 when they were in Egypt under **P**?
6: 6 hearts as the Egyptians and **P** did?
1Ki 3: 1 Solomon made an alliance with **P** king
9:16 (**P** king of Egypt had attacked and
11:18 they went to Egypt, to **P** king of
11:19 **P** was so pleased with Hadad that he
11:21 Then Hadad said to **P**, "Let me go, so
11:22 back to your own country?" **P** asked.
2Ki 17: 7 under the power of **P** king of Egypt.
18:21 Such is **P** king of Egypt to all who
23:29 **P** Neco king of Egypt went up to the
23:33 **P** Neco put him in chains at Riblah
23:34 **P** Neco made Eliakim son of Josiah
23:35 Jehoiakim paid **P** Neco the silver and
Ne 9:10 signs and wonders against **P**,
Ps 135: 9 against **P** and all his servants.
136:15 swept **P** and his army into the Red
SS 1: 9 to one of the chariots of **P**.
Isa 19:11 the wise counsellors of **P** give
19:11 How can you say to **P**, "I am one of
36: 6 Such is **P** king of Egypt to all who
Jer 25:19 **P** king of Egypt, his attendants, his
44:30 'I am going to hand **P** Hophra king of
46: 2 the army of **P** Neco king of Egypt,
46:17 '**P** king of Egypt is only a loud
46:25 on **P**, on Egypt and her gods and her
46:25 kings, and on those who rely on **P**.
47: 1 Philistines before **P** attacked Gaza:
Eze 17:17 **P** with his mighty army and great
29: 2 "Son of man, set your face against **P**
29: 3 'I am against you, **P** king of Egypt,
30:21 broken the arm of **P** king of Egypt.
30:22 says: I am against **P** king of Egypt.
30:24 but I will break the arms of **P**, and
30:25 but the arms of **P** will fall limp.
31: 2 "Son of man, say to **P** king of Egypt
31:18 "'This is **P** and all his hordes,
32: 2 a lament concerning **P** king of Egypt
32:28 "You too, O **P**, will be broken and
32:31 "**P**—he and all his army—will see
32:32 **P** and all his hordes will be laid
Ac 7:10 the goodwill of **P** king of Egypt;
7:13 and **P** learned about Joseph's family.
Ro 9:17 For the Scripture says to **P**: "I

Pharaoh's (Pharaoh)

Ge 12:15 **P** officials saw her, they praised
37:36 one of **P** officials, the captain of
39: 1 Egyptian who was one of **P** officials
40: 7 he asked **P** officials who were in
40:11 **P** cup was in my hand, and I took the
40:11 squeezed them into **P** cup and put
40:13 and you will put **P** cup in his hand,
40:20 Now the third day was **P** birthday,
40:21 once again put the cup into **P** hand,
41:46 And Joseph went out from **P** presence
45: 2 him, and **P** household heard about it.
45:16 the news reached **P** palace that
47:14 and he brought it to **P** palace.
50: 4 Joseph said to **P** court, "If I have
50: 7 All **P** officials accompanied him—the
Ex 2: 5 **P** daughter went down to the Nile to
2: 7 his sister asked **P** daughter, "Shall
2: 9 **P** daughter said to her, "Take this
2:10 she took him to **P** daughter and he
5:14 foremen appointed by **P** slave drivers
7: 3 I will harden **P** heart, and though I
7:13 Yet **P** heart became hard and he would
7:14 the LORD said to Moses, "**P** heart is
Ex 7:22 and **P** heart became hard; he would
8:19 But **P** heart was hard and he would
8:24 of flies poured into **P** palace and
9:12 the LORD hardened **P** heart and he
9:35 **P** heart was hard and he would not
10: 7 **P** officials said to him, "How long
10:11 Aaron were driven out of **P** presence.
10:20 the LORD hardened **P** heart, and he
10:27 the LORD hardened **P** heart, and he
11: 3 by **P** officials and by the people.)
11:10 but the LORD hardened **P** heart, and
14: 4 I will harden **P** heart, and he will
14: 9 The Egyptians—all **P** horses and
14:23 and all **P** horses and chariots and
15: 4 **P** chariots and his army he has
15: 4 The best of **P** officers are drowned
15:19 **P** horses, chariots and horsemen went
1Ki 7: 8 for **P** daughter, whom he had married.
9:24 After **P** daughter had come up from
11: 1 foreign women besides **P** daughter
11:20 Genubath lived with **P** own children.
1Ch 4:18 the children of **P** daughter Bithiah,
2Ch 8:11 Solomon brought **P** daughter up from
Isa 30: 2 who look for help to **P** protection,
30: 3 **P** protection will be to your shame,
Jer 37: 5 **P** army had marched out of Egypt, and
37: 7 '**P** army, which has marched out to
37:11 from Jerusalem because of **P** army,
43: 9 entrance to **P** palace in Tahpanhes.
Ac 7:21 **P** daughter took him and brought him
Heb 11:24 be known as the son of **P** daughter.

Pharisee (Pharisee's, Pharisees)

Mt 23:26 Blind **P**! First clean the inside of
Lk 7:39 the **P** who had invited him saw this,
11:37 a **P** invited him to eat with him;
11:38 the **P**, noticing that Jesus did not
14: 1 eat in the house of a prominent **P**,
18:10 a **P** and the other a tax collector.
18:11 The **P** stood up and prayed about
Ac 5:34 a **P** named Gamaliel, a teacher of the
23: 6 brothers, I am a **P**, the son of a **P**.
26: 5 of our religion, I lived as a **P**.
Php 3: 5 in regard to the law, a **P**;

Pharisee's (Pharisee)

Lk 7:36 so he went to the **P** house and
7:37 Jesus was eating at the **P** house,

Pharisees (Pharisee)

Mt 3: 7 when he saw many of the **P** and
5:20 the **P** and the teachers of the law,
9:11 the **P** saw this, they asked his
9:14 "How is it that we and the **P** fast,
9:34 the **P** said, "It is by the prince of
12: 2 the **P** saw this, they said to him,
12:14 the **P** went out and plotted how they
12:24 when the **P** heard this, they said,
12:38 some of the **P** and teachers of the
15: 1 some **P** and teachers of the law came
15:12 "Do you know that the **P** were
16: 1 The **P** and Sadducees came to Jesus
16: 6 the yeast of the **P** and Sadducees."
16:11 the yeast of the **P** and Sadducees."
16:12 the teaching of the **P** and Sadducees.
19: 3 Some **P** came to him to test him.
21:45 the chief priests and the **P** heard
22:15 the **P** went out and laid plans to
22:34 the Sadducees, the **P** got together.
22:41 While the **P** were gathered together,
23: 2 "The teachers of the law and the **P**
23:13 teachers of the law and **P**, you
23:15 teachers of the law and **P**, you
23:23 teachers of the law and **P**, you
23:25 teachers of the law and **P**, you
23:27 teachers of the law and **P**, you
23:29 teachers of the law and **P**, you
27:62 priests and the **P** went to Pilate.
Mk 2:16 the teachers of the law who were **P**
2:18 Now John's disciples and the **P** were
2:18 **P** are fasting, but yours are not?"
2:24 The **P** said to him, "Look, why are
3: 6 the **P** went out and began to plot
7: 1 The **P** and some of the teachers of
7: 3 (The **P** and all the Jews do not eat

Mk 7: 5 the **P** and teachers of the law asked
8:11 The **P** came and began to question
8:15 yeast of the **P** and that of Herod."
10: 2 Some **P** came and tested him by asking,
12:13 Later they sent some of the **P** and
Lk 5:17 **P** and teachers of the law, who had
5:21 The **P** and the teachers of the law
5:30 the **P** and the teachers of the law
5:33 and so do the disciples of the **P**,
6: 2 Some of the **P** asked, "Why are you
6: 7 The **P** and the teachers of the law
7:30 the **P** and experts in the law
7:36 Now one of the **P** invited Jesus to
11:39 "Now then, you **P** clean the outside
11:42 "Woe to you **P**, because you give God
11:43 "Woe to you **P**, because you love the
11:53 the **P** and the teachers of the law
12: 1 yeast of the **P**, which is hypocrisy.
13:31 At that time some **P** came to Jesus
14: 3 Jesus asked the **P** and experts in the
15: 2 the **P** and the teachers of the law
16:14 The **P**, who loved money, heard all
17:20 Once, having been asked by the **P**
19:39 Some of the **P** in the crowd said to
Jn 1:24 Now some **P** who had been sent
3: 1 Now there was a man of the **P** named
4: 1 The **P** heard that Jesus was gaining
7:32 The **P** heard the crowd whispering
7:32 **P** sent temple guards to arrest him.
7:45 back to the chief priests and **P**,
7:47 deceived you also?" the **P** retorted.
7:48 "Has any of the rulers or of the **P**
8: 3 The teachers of the law and the **P**
8:13 The **P** challenged him, "Here you are,
9:13 They brought to the **P** the man who
9:15 Therefore the **P** also asked him how
9:16 Some of the **P** said, "This man is not
9:40 Some **P** who were with him heard him
11:46 some of them went to the **P** and told
11:47 the chief priests and the **P** called a
11:57 the chief priests and **P** had given
12:19 the **P** said to one another, "See,
12:42 But because of the **P** they would not
18: 3 from the chief priests and **P**.
Ac 15: 5 party of the **P** stood up and said,
23: 6 were Sadducees and the others **P**,
23: 7 a dispute broke out between the **P**
23: 8 but the **P** acknowledge them all.)
23: 9 **P** stood up and argued vigorously.

Pharpar

2Ki 5:12 Are not Abana and **P**, the rivers of

Phicol

Ge 21:22 Abimelech and **P** the commander of
21:32 Abimelech and **P** the commander of his
26:26 and **P** the commander of his forces.

Philadelphia

City of the province of Lydia in western Asia Minor. One of the 7 letters of Revelation was addressed to its church which was praised for its endurance (Rev 3:7–13).

Rev 1:11 Thyatira, Sardis, **P** and Laodicea."
3: 7 "To the angel of the church in **P**

Philemon

Co-worker with Paul (Phm 1); owner of runaway slave, Onesimus (Phm 8–11).

Phm : 1 **P** our dear friend and fellow-worker,

Philetus

2Ti 2:17 Among them are Hymenaeus and **P**,

Philip (Philip's)

1. Apostle (Mt 10:3; Mk 3:18; Lk 6:14; Ac 1:13); from Bethsaida; brought Nathaniel to Jesus (Jn 1:43–45). **2.** Deacon (Ac 6:1–7). Evangelist (Ac 21:8); in Samaria (Ac 8:4–13); spoke to Ethiopian official (Ac 8:26–40).

Mt 10: 3 **P** and Bartholomew; Thomas and
Mk 3:18 Andrew, **P**, Bartholomew, Matthew,
Lk 3: 1 his brother **P** tetrarch of Iturea and
6:14 Andrew, James, John, **P**, Bartholomew,
Jn 1:43 Finding **P**, he said to him, "Follow
1:44 **P**, like Andrew and Peter, was from
1:45 **P** found Nathanael and told him, "We
1:46 "Come and see," said **P**.
1:48 the fig-tree before **P** called you."
6: 5 he said to **P**, "Where shall we buy
6: 7 **P** answered him, "Eight months' wages
12:21 They came to **P**, who was from
12:22 **P** went to tell Andrew; Andrew and **P**
14: 8 **P** said, "Lord, show us the Father
14: 9 Jesus answered: "Don't you know me, **P**
Ac 1:13 John, James and Andrew; **P** and Thomas,
6: 5 also **P**, Procorus, Nicanor, Timon,
8: 5 **P** went down to a city in Samaria and
8: 6 the crowds heard **P** and saw the
8:12 when they believed **P** as he preached
8:13 And he followed **P** everywhere,
8:26 Now an angel of the Lord said to **P**,
8:29 The Spirit told **P**, "Go to that
8:30 **P** ran up to the chariot and heard
8:30 what you are reading?" **P** asked.
8:31 invited **P** to come up and sit with
8:34 The eunuch asked **P**, "Tell me, please,
8:35 **P** began with that very passage of
8:38 Then both **P** and the eunuch went down
8:38 into the water and **P** baptised him.
8:39 of the Lord suddenly took **P** away,
8:40 **P**, however, appeared at Azotus and
21: 8 **P** the evangelist, one of the Seven.

Philip's (Philip)

Mt 14: 3 of Herodias, his brother **P** wife,
Mk 6:17 brother **P** wife, whom he had married.

Philippi (Philippians)

City in eastern Macedonia, near northern shore of the Aegean. Paul stayed here several days and preached to the women including Lydia, who believed and was baptised (Ac 16:12–15). A fortune-teller was released from spirit possession by Paul resulting in his own imprisonment and the jailer's conversion (Ac 16:16–34). Paul wrote to the Christians here expressing fondness for them (Php 1:1–8).

Ac 16:12 From there we travelled to **P**, a
20: 6 we sailed from **P** after the Feast of
Php 1: 1 all the saints in Christ Jesus at **P**,
1Th 2: 2 suffered and been insulted in **P**,

Philippians (Philippi)

Php 4:15 Moreover, as you **P** know, in the

Philistia (Philistine)

Also known as "the land of the Philistines" or "the region of the Philistines". It extended from the River Shihor (Brook of Egypt) northwards to Ekron (Jos 13:2–3). The term "Philistia" is common in poetry (Ex 15:14; Ps 60:8; 87:4; 108:9; Isa 11:14).

Ex 15:14 anguish will grip the people of **P**.
Ps 60: 8 over **P** I shout in triumph."
83: 7 Gebal, Ammon and Amalek, **P**, with the
87: 4 those who acknowledge me—**P** too,
108: 9 over **P** I shout in triumph."
Isa 11:14 down on the slopes of **P** to the west;
Joel 3: 4 and Sidon and all you regions of **P**?
Am 6: 2 and then go down to Gath in **P**.

Philistine (Philistia, Philistine's, Philistines)

Ex 13:17 on the road through the **P** country,
Jos 13: 3 of the five **P** rulers in Gaza,
Jdg 14: 1 Timnah and saw there a young **P** woman.
14: 2 "I have seen a **P** woman in Timnah;
1Sa 6: 1 the ark of the LORD had been in **P**
6: 4 to the number of the **P** rulers,
6:18 **P** towns belonging to the five rulers
10: 5 of God, where there is a **P** outpost.
13: 3 Jonathan attacked the **P** outpost at
13: 4 "Saul has attacked the **P** outpost,
13:17 parties went out from the **P** camp
14: 1 to the **P** outpost on the other side.
14: 4 to reach the **P** outpost was a cliff;
1Sa 14:11 showed themselves to the **P** outpost.
14:19 the **P** camp increased more and more.
17: 4 from Gath, came out of the **P** camp.
17: 8 Am I not a **P**, and are you not the
17:10 the **P** said, "This day I defy the
17:16 For forty days the **P** came forward
17:23 Goliath, the **P** champion from Gath,
17:26 done for the man who kills this **P**
17:26 Who is this uncircumcised **P** that he
17:32 lose heart on account of this **P**;
17:33 go out against this **P** and fight him
17:36 **P** will be like one of them,
17:37 deliver me from the hand of this **P**.
17:40 sling in his hand, approached the **P**.
17:41 the **P**, with his shield-bearer in
17:43 And the **P** cursed David by his gods.
17:45 David said to the **P**, "You come
17:46 the **P** army to the birds of the air
17:48 the **P** moved closer to attack him,
17:49 it and struck the **P** on the forehead.
17:50 David triumphed over the **P** with a
17:50 he struck down the **P** and killed him.
17:55 David going out to meet the **P**,
17:57 David returned from killing the **P**,
18: 6 home after David had killed the **P**,
18:25 bride than a hundred **P** foreskins,
18:30 The **P** commanders continued to go out
19: 5 in his hands when he killed the **P**.
21: 9 "The sword of Goliath the **P**, whom
22:10 and the sword of Goliath the **P**."
23: 3 go to Keilah against the **P** forces!"
27: 7 David lived in **P** territory for a
27:11 as long as he lived in **P** territory.
28: 5 Saul saw the **P** army, he was afraid;
29: 2 the **P** rulers marched with their
29: 4 the **P** commanders were angry with him
29: 7 nothing to displease the **P** rulers."
29: 9 the **P** commanders have said, 'He must
2Sa 3:14 the price of a hundred **P** foreskins."
5:24 front of you to strike the **P** army."
21:17 he struck the **P** down and killed him.
23:14 and the **P** garrison was at Bethlehem.
23:16 men broke through the **P** lines,
1Ki 15:27 at Gibbethon, a **P** town, while Nadab
16:15 encamped near Gibbethon, a **P** town.
1Ch 11:16 and the **P** garrison was at Bethlehem.
11:18 the Three broke through the **P** lines,
14:15 front of you to strike the **P** army."
14:16 and they struck down the **P** army, all

Philistine's (Philistine)

1Sa 17:11 On hearing the **P** words, Saul and all
17:51 He took hold of the **P** sword and drew
17:54 David took the **P** head and brought it
17:54 put the **P** weapons in his own tent.
17:57 with David still holding the **P** head.

Philistines (Philistine)

Ge 10:14 Casluhites (from whom the **P** came)
21:32 returned to the land of the **P**.
21:34 Abraham stayed in the land of the **P**
26: 1 to Abimelech king of the **P** in Gerar.
26: 8 Abimelech king of the **P** looked down
26:14 and servants that the **P** envied him.
26:15 the **P** stopped up, filling them with
26:18 which the **P** had stopped up after
Ex 23:31 to the Sea of the **P**, and from the
Jos 13: 2 the regions of the **P** and Geshurites:
Jdg 3: 3 the five rulers of the **P**, all the
3:31 down six hundred **P** with an ox-goad.
10: 6 the Ammonites and the gods of the **P**.
10: 7 hands of the **P** and the Ammonites,
10:11 the Amorites, the Ammonites, the **P**,
13: 1 the hands of the **P** for forty years.
13: 5 of Israel from the hands of the **P**."
14: 3 the uncircumcised **P** to get a wife?"
14: 4 an occasion to confront the **P**;
15: 3 a right to get even with the **P**;
15: 5 loose in the standing corn of the **P**.
15: 6 the **P** asked, "Who did this?" they
15: 6 So the **P** went up and burned her and
15: 9 The **P** went up and camped in Judah,
15:11 "Don't you realise that the **P** are
15:12 you up and hand you over to the **P**.
15:14 the **P** came towards him shouting.

Jdg 15:20 twenty years in the days of the **P**.
16: 5 The rulers of the **P** went to her and
16: 8 the rulers of the **P** brought her
16: 9 "Samson, the **P** are upon you!" But he
16:12 "Samson, the **P** are upon you!" But he
16:14 "Samson, the **P** are upon you!"
16:18 sent word to the rulers of the **P**,
16:18 So the rulers of the **P** returned
16:20 "Samson, the **P** are upon you!"
16:21 the **P** seized him, gouged out his
16:23 Now the rulers of the **P** assembled to
16:27 all the rulers of the **P** were there,
16:28 revenge on the **P** for my two eyes."
16:30 Samson said, "Let me die with the **P**!"
1Sa 4: 1 went out to fight against the **P**.
4: 1 at Ebenezer, and the **P** at Aphek.
4: 2 The **P** deployed their forces to meet
4: 2 Israel was defeated by the **P**, who
4: 3 defeat upon us today before the **P**?
4: 6 Hearing the uproar, the **P** asked,
4: 7 the **P** were afraid. "A god has come
4: 9 Be strong, **P**! Be men, or you will be
4:10 the **P** fought, and the Israelites
4:17 "Israel fled before the **P**, and the
5: 1 After the **P** had captured the ark of
5: 8 the rulers of the **P** and asked them,
5:11 all the rulers of the **P** and said,
6: 2 the **P** called for the priests and the
6: 4 The **P** asked, "What guilt offering
6:12 The rulers of the **P** followed them as
6:16 The five rulers of the **P** saw all
6:17 are the gold tumours the **P** sent
6:21 **P** have returned the ark of the LORD.
7: 3 you out of the hand of the **P**."
7: 7 the **P** heard that Israel had
7: 7 rulers of the **P** came up to attack
7: 7 they were afraid because of the **P**.
7: 8 rescue us from the hand of the **P**."
7:10 the **P** drew near to engage Israel in
7:10 with loud thunder against the **P**
7:11 out of Mizpah and pursued the **P**,
7:13 the **P** were subdued and did not
7:13 hand of the LORD was against the **P**.
7:14 that the **P** had captured from Israel
7:14 territory from the power of the **P**.
9:16 my people from the hand of the **P**.
12: 9 and into the hands of the **P** and the
13: 3 at Geba, and the **P** heard about it.
13: 4 has become an offence to the **P**.
13: 5 The **P** assembled to fight Israel,
13:11 the **P** were assembling at Michmash,
13:12 I thought, 'Now the **P** will come down
13:16 while the **P** camped at Michmash.
13:19 because the **P** had said, "Otherwise
13:20 all Israel went down to the **P** to
13:23 Now a detachment of **P** had gone out
14:11 "Look!" said the **P**. "The Hebrews are
14:13 The **P** fell before Jonathan, and his
14:20 They found the **P** in total confusion,
14:21 who had previously been with the **P**
14:22 heard that the **P** were on the run,
14:30 slaughter of the **P** have been even
14:31 struck down the **P** from Michmash to
14:36 "Let us go down after the **P** by night
14:37 "Shall I go down after the **P**?
14:46 Saul stopped pursuing the **P**, and
14:47 Edom, the kings of Zobah, and the **P**.
14:52 Saul there was bitter war with the **P**,
17: 1 Now the **P** gathered their forces for
17: 2 up their battle line to meet the **P**.
17: 3 The **P** occupied one hill and the
17:19 of Elah, fighting against the **P**."
17:21 Israel and the **P** were drawing up
17:51 When the **P** saw that their hero was
17:52 pursued the **P** to the entrance of
17:53 returned from chasing the **P**, they
18:17 against him. Let the **P** do that!"
18:21 hand of the **P** may be against him.
18:25 David fall by the hands of the **P**.
18:27 went out and killed two hundred **P**.
19: 8 and David went out and fought the **P**.
23: 1 David was told, "Look, the **P** are
23: 2 "Shall I go and attack these **P**?"
23: 2 "Go, attack the **P** and save Keilah.
23: 4 going to give the **P** into your hand."
23: 5 fought the **P** and carried off their
1Sa 23: 5 inflicted heavy losses on the **P**
23:27 The **P** are raiding the land."
23:28 of David and went to meet the **P**.
24: 1 Saul returned from pursuing the **P**,
27: 1 is to escape to the land of the **P**.
28: 1 In those days the **P** gathered their
28: 4 The **P** assembled and came and set up
28:15 "The **P** are fighting against me, and
28:19 over both Israel and you to the **P**,
28:19 over the army of Israel to the **P**."
29: 1 The **P** gathered all their forces at
29: 3 The commanders of the **P** asked, "What
29:11 to go back to the land of the **P**,
29:11 and the **P** went up to Jezreel.
30:16 the land of the **P** and from Judah.
31: 1 Now the **P** fought against Israel;
31: 2 The **P** pressed hard after Saul and
31: 7 And the **P** came and occupied them.
31: 8 The next day, when the **P** came to
31: 9 throughout the land of the **P** to
31:11 of what the **P** had done to Saul,
2Sa 1:20 lest the daughters of the **P** be glad,
3:18 Israel from the hand of the **P**
5:17 the **P** heard that David had been
5:18 Now the **P** had come and spread out in
5:19 "Shall I go and attack the **P**? Will
5:19 will surely hand the **P** over to you."
5:21 The **P** abandoned their idols there,
5:22 Once more the **P** came up and spread
5:25 he struck down the **P** all the way
8: 1 David defeated the **P** and subdued
8: 1 Ammah from the control of the **P**.
8:12 the Ammonites and the **P**, and Amalek.
19: 9 rescued us from the hand of the **P**.
21:12 where the **P** had hung them after they
21:15 a battle between the **P** and Israel.
21:15 to fight against the **P**, and he
21:18 another battle with the **P**, at Gob.
21:19 In another battle with the **P** at Gob,
23: 9 **P** gathered at Pas Dammim for battle.
23:10 struck down the **P** till his hand grew
23:11 When the **P** banded together at a
23:12 He defended it and struck the **P** down,
23:13 while a band of **P** was encamped in
1Ki 4:21 from the River to the land of the **P**
2Ki 8: 2 the land of the **P** for seven years.
8: 3 came back from the land of the **P**
18: 8 he defeated the **P**, as far as Gaza
1Ch 1:12 Casluhites (from whom the **P** came)
10: 1 Now the **P** fought against Israel;
10: 2 The **P** pressed hard after Saul and
10: 7 And the **P** came and occupied them.
10: 8 The next day, when the **P** came to
10: 9 throughout the land of the **P** to
10:11 everything the **P** had done to Saul,
11:13 the **P** gathered there for battle.
11:13 barley, the troops fled from the **P**.
11:14 They defended it and struck the **P**
11:15 while a band of **P** was encamped in
12:19 with the **P** to fight against Saul.
12:19 (He and his men did not help the **P**
14: 8 the **P** heard that David had been
14: 9 Now the **P** had come and raided the
14:10 "Shall I go and attack the **P**?
14:12 The **P** had abandoned their gods there,
14:13 Once more the **P** raided the valley;
18: 1 David defeated the **P** and subdued
18: 1 villages from the control of the **P**.
18:11 the Ammonites and the **P**, and Amalek.
20: 4 war broke out with the **P**, at Gezer.
20: 4 Rephaites, and the **P** were subjugated.
20: 5 In another battle with the **P**,
2Ch 9:26 from the River to the land of the **P**,
17:11 Some **P** brought Jehoshaphat gifts and
21:16 Jehoram the hostility of the **P**
26: 6 He went to war against the **P** and
26: 6 Ashdod and elsewhere among the **P**.
26: 7 God helped him against the **P** and
28:18 while the **P** had raided towns in the
Ps 56: T When the **P** had seized him in Gath.
Isa 2: 6 they practise divination like the **P**
9:12 from the east and **P** from the west
14:29 Do not rejoice, all you **P**, that the
14:31 O city! Melt away, all you **P**!
Jer 25:20 kings of the **P** (those of Ashkelon,
47: 1 the **P** before Pharaoh attacked Gaza:
Jer 47: 4 day has come to destroy all the **P**
47: 4 The LORD is about to destroy the **P**,
Eze 16:27 the daughters of the **P**, who were
16:57 the daughters of the **P**—all those
25:15 'Because the **P** acted in vengeance
25:16 stretch out my hand against the **P**,
Am 1: 8 till the last of the **P** is dead,"
9: 7 the **P** from Caphtor and the Arameans
Ob :19 will possess the land of the **P**.
Zep 2: 5 you, O Canaan, land of the **P**.
Zec 9: 6 I will cut off the pride of the **P**.

Philologus

Ro 16:15 Greet **P**, Julia, Nereus and his

Philosopher (Philosophy)

1Co 1:20 Where is the **p** of this age? Has not

Philosophers (Philosophy)

Ac 17:18 A group of Epicurean and Stoic **p**

Philosophy (Philosopher, Philosophers)

Col 2: 8 through hollow and deceptive **p**,

Phinehas

1. Son of Eleazar; grandson of Aaron (Ex 6:25). Priest (Nu 31:6; Jdg 20:28). Held back God's judgment by killing Israelite and pagan Midianite woman (Nu 25:6–11; Ps 106:28–31); zeal rewarded by everlasting covenant of priesthood (Nu 26:12–13). In charge of temple gatekeepers (1Ch 9:20). **2.** Disreputable son of Eli (1Sa 1:3; 2:12–17). Condemned with his brother (1Sa 2:34). Both died in battle (1Sa 4:11).

Ex 6:25 of Putiel, and she bore him **P**.
Nu 25: 7 **P** son of Eleazar, the son of Aaron,
25:11 "**P** son of Eleazar, the son of Aaron,
31: 6 along with **P** son of Eleazar, the
Jos 22:13 the Israelites sent **P** son of Eleazar,
22:30 **P** the priest and the leaders of the
22:31 **P** son of Eleazar, the priest, said
22:32 **P** son of Eleazar, the priest, and
24:33 had been allotted to his son **P** in
Jdg 20:28 with **P** son of Eleazar, the son of
1Sa 1: 3 where Hophni and **P**, the two sons of
2:34 to your two sons, Hophni and **P**,
4: 4 And Eli's two sons, Hophni and **P**,
4:11 Eli's two sons, Hophni and **P**, died.
4:17 Also your two sons, Hophni and **P**,
4:19 His daughter-in-law, the wife of **P**,
14: 3 Ichabod's brother Ahitub son of **P**,
1Ch 6: 4 Eleazar was the father of **P**,
6: 4 **P** the father of Abishua,
6:50 his son, **P** his son, Abishua his son,
9:20 In earlier times **P** son of Eleazar
Ezr 7: 5 the son of Abishua, the son of **P**,
8: 2 of the descendants of **P**, Gershom;
8:33 Eleazar son of **P** was with him, and
Ps 106:30 **P** stood up and intervened, and the

Phlegon

Ro 16:14 Greet Asyncritus, **P**, Hermes,

Phoebe

Ro 16: 1 I commend to you our sister **P**, a

Phoenicia

Isa 23:11 He has given an order concerning **P**
Ac 11:19 with Stephen travelled as far as **P**,
15: 3 and as they travelled through **P** and
21: 2 We found a ship crossing over to **P**,

Phoenix

Ac 27:12 hoping to reach **P** and winter there.

Phrygia

Mountainous region of Asia Minor, between Asia and Galatia. Its people were represented in Jerusalem on the Day of Pentecost (Ac 2:10). Paul travelled through this province on his journeys (Ac 16:6; 18:23), but does not appear to have founded the churches here (Col 2:1).

Ac 2:10 **P** and Pamphylia, Egypt and the parts
16: 6 the region of **P** and Galatia,
18:23 the region of Galatia and **P**,

Phygelus

2Ti 1:15 me, including **P** and Hermogenes.

Phylacteries

Mt 23: 5 They make their **p** wide and the

Physical (Physically)

Da 1: 4 young men without any **p** defect,
Ro 2:28 circumcision merely outward and **p**.
Col 1:22 reconciled you by Christ's **p** body
1Ti 4: 8 For **p** training is of some value, but
Jas 2:16 about his **p** needs, what good is it?

Physically (Physical)

Ro 2:27 The one who is not circumcised **p** and
1Co 5: 3 Even though I am not **p** present, I am

Physician (Physicians)

Jer 8:22 Is there no **p** there? Why then is
Lk 4:23 '**P**, heal yourself! Do here in your

Physicians (Physician)

Ge 50: 2 Joseph directed the **p** in his service
50: 2 So the **p** embalmed him,
2Ch 16:12 from the LORD, but only from the **p**.
Job 13: 4 you are worthless **p**, all of you!

Pi Hahiroth

Ex 14: 2 near **P**, between Migdol and the sea.
14: 9 sea near **P**, opposite Baal Zephon.
Nu 33: 7 They left Etham, turned back to **P**,
33: 8 They left **P** and passed through the

Pick (Picked, Pickers, Picks)

Lev 19:10 or **p** up the grapes that have fallen.
27:33 He must not **p** out the good from the
Dt 23:25 you may **p** the ears with your hands,
Ru 2: 2 "Let me go to the fields and **p** up
2:16 leave them for her to **p** up, and
1Ki 20:33 and were quick to **p** up his word.
2Ki 5: 7 is trying to **p** a quarrel with me!"
9:25 "**P** him up and throw him on the field
9:26 Now then, **p** him up and throw him on
Ps 80:12 that all who pass by **p** its grapes?
Isa 41:16 the wind will **p** them up, and a gale
Eze 24: 5 take the **p** of the flock. Pile wood
Jnh 1:12 "**P** me up and throw me into the sea,"
Mt 7:16 Do people **p** grapes from thornbushes,
12: 1 to **p** some ears of corn and eat them.
Mk 2:23 they began to **p** some ears of corn.
8:19 basketfuls of pieces did you **p** up?"
8:20 basketfuls of pieces did you **p** up?"
16:18 they will **p** up snakes with their
Lk 6: 1 and his disciples began to **p** some
6:44 People do not **p** figs from
Jn 5: 8 **P** up your mat and walk."
5:11 said to me, '**P** up your mat and walk.'
5:12 who told you to **p** it up and walk?"

Picked (Pick)

Jdg 1: 7 off have **p** up scraps under my table.
4:21 Jael, Heber's wife, **p** up a tent peg
1Sa 20:38 The boy **p** up the arrow and returned
2Sa 4: 4 His nurse **p** him up and fled, but as
1Ki 13:29 the prophet **p** up the body of the man
17:23 Elijah **p** up the child and carried
2Ki 2:13 He **p** up the cloak that had fallen
2:16 the Spirit of the LORD has **p** him up
Eze 29: 5 field and not be gathered or **p** up.
Na 2: 5 He summons his **p** troops, yet they
Mt 14:20 the disciples **p** up twelve basketfuls
15:37 the disciples **p** up seven basketfuls
27: 6 The chief priests **p** up the coins and
Mk 6:43 the disciples **p** up twelve basketfuls
8: 8 the disciples **p** up seven basketfuls
Lk 9:17 the disciples **p** up twelve basketfuls
14: 7 he noticed how the guests **p** the
Jn 5: 9 he **p** up his mat and walked.
8:59 At this, they **p** up stones to stone
10:31 Again the Jews **p** up stones to stone
15: 6 and withers; such branches are **p** up,
Ac 20: 9 the third storey and was **p** up dead.
Rev 18:21 a mighty angel **p** up a boulder the

Pickers (Pick)

Ob : 5 If grape **p** came to you, would they

Picks (Pick)

Lev 11:25 Whoever **p** up one of their carcasses
11:28 Anyone who **p** up their carcasses must
11:40 Anyone who **p** up the carcass must
15:10 whoever **p** up those things must wash
2Sa 12:31 with saws and with iron **p** and axes,
1Ch 20: 3 with saws and with iron **p** and axes.

Piece (Pieces)

Ex 15:25 and the LORD showed him a **p** of wood.
25:19 cherubim of one **p** with the cover,
25:31 blossoms shall be of one **p** with it.
25:36 all be of one **p** with the lampstand,
27: 2 horns and the altar are of one **p**,
28: 8 of one **p** with the ephod and made
30: 2 high—its horns of one **p** with it.
37: 8 made them of one **p** with the cover.
37:17 and blossoms were of one **p** with it.
37:22 all of one **p** with the lampstand,
37:25 high—its horns of one **p** with it.
38: 2 horns and the altar were of one **p**,
39: 5 of one **p** with the ephod and made
Lev 9:13 him the burnt offering **p** by **p**,
Jdg 16: 9 as easily as a **p** of string snaps
20: 6 cut her into pieces and sent one **p**
Ru 4: 3 is selling the **p** of land that
1Sa 2:36 bow down before him for a **p** of
9:23 "Bring the **p** of meat I gave you,
24:11 look at this **p** of your robe in my
2Sa 17:13 not even a **p** of it can be found."
1Ki 7:24 in two rows in one **p** with the Sea.
17:11 "And bring me, please, a **p** of bread.
2Ch 4: 3 in two rows in one **p** with the Sea.
Job 2: 8 Job took a **p** of broken pottery and
41:29 A club seems to him but a **p** of straw;
42:11 him a **p** of silver and a gold ring.
Pr 28:21 man will do wrong for a **p** of bread.
Eze 24: 6 **p** by **p** without casting lots for them.
Am 3:12 only two leg bones or a **p** of an ear,
Mk 2:21 If he does, the new **p** will pull away
Lk 19:20 kept it laid away in a **p** of cloth.
24:42 They gave him a **p** of broiled fish,
Jn 13:26 to whom I will give this **p** of bread
13:26 Then, dipping the **p** of bread, he
19:23 woven in one **p** from top to bottom.
Ac 5: 1 Sapphira, also sold a **p** of property.

Pieces (Piece)

Ge 15:17 appeared and passed between the **p**.
33:19 For a hundred **p** of silver, he bought
37:33 Joseph has surely been torn to **p**."
44:28 said, "He has surely been torn to **p**.
Ex 22:13 If it was torn to **p** by a wild animal,
23:24 and break their sacred stones to **p**.
28: 7 is to have two shoulder **p** attached
28:12 fasten them on the shoulder **p** of the
28:25 shoulder **p** of the ephod at the
28:27 shoulder **p** on the front of the
29:17 Cut the ram into **p** and wash the
29:17 them with the head and the other **p**.
32:19 breaking them to **p** at the foot of
39: 4 They made shoulder **p** for the ephod,
39: 7 they fastened them on the shoulder **p**
39:18 shoulder **p** of the ephod at the
39:20 shoulder **p** on the front of the
Lev 1: 6 burnt offering and cut it into **p**.
1: 8 the priests shall arrange the **p**,
1:12 He is to cut it into **p**, and the
6:21 broken in **p** as an aroma pleasing to
8:20 He cut the ram into **p** and burned the
8:20 burned the head, the **p** and the fat.
Nu 24: 8 nations and break their bones in **p**;
Dt 9:17 breaking them to **p** before your eyes.
Jos 24:32 **p** of silver from the sons of Hamor,
Jdg 20: 6 I took my concubine, cut her into **p**
1Sa 11: 7 cut them into **p**, and sent the **p** by
1Ki 11:30 wearing and tore it into twelve **p**.
11:31 he said to Jeroboam, "Take ten **p** for
18:23 and let them cut it into **p** and put
18:33 bull into **p** and laid it on the wood.
2Ki 11:18 smashed the altars and idols to **p**
18: 4 He broke into **p** the bronze snake
23:12 smashed them to **p** and threw the
2Ch 25:12 down so that all were dashed to **p**.
34: 4 he cut to **p** the incense altars that
34: 4 These he broke to **p** and scattered
34: 7 cut to **p** all the incense altars
Job 4:20 dawn and dusk they are broken to **p**;
18: 4 You who tear yourself to **p** in your
26:12 by his wisdom he cut Rahab to **p**.
Ps 2: 9 will dash them to **p** like pottery."
7: 2 me to **p** with no-one to rescue me.
29: 5 breaks in **p** the cedars of Lebanon.
50:22 tear you to **p**, with none to rescue:
119:72 thousands of **p** of silver and gold.
Isa 13:16 Their infants will be dashed to **p**
24:12 in ruins, its gate is battered to **p**.
27: 9 be like chalk stones crushed to **p**,
30:14 will break in **p** like pottery,
30:14 among its **p** not a fragment will be
51: 9 Was it not you who cut Rahab to **p**,
Jer 5: 6 to tear to **p** any who venture out,
23:29 a hammer that breaks a rock in **p**?
34:18 two and then walked between its **p**.
34:19 walked between the **p** of the calf,
Eze 16:40 and hack you to **p** with their swords.
23:34 dash it to **p** and tear your breasts.
24: 4 Put into it the **p** of meat, all the
24: 4 choice **p**—the leg and the shoulder.
27:26 you to **p** in the heart of the sea.
Da 2: 5 I will have you cut into **p** and your
2:35 the gold were broken to **p** at the
2:40 as iron breaks things to **p**,
2:45 clay, the silver and the gold to **p**.
3:29 Meshach and Abednego be cut into **p**
Hos 5:14 I will tear them to **p** and go away;
6: 1 He has torn us to **p** but he will heal
6: 5 Therefore I cut you in **p** with my
8: 6 broken in **p**, that calf of Samaria.
Am 6:11 will smash the great house into **p**
Mic 1: 7 All her idols will be broken to **p**;
3: 3 skin and break their bones in **p**;
4:13 you will break to **p** many nations.
Na 3:10 Her infants were dashed to **p** at the
Zec 11:12 So they paid me thirty **p** of silver.
11:13 So I took the thirty **p** of silver and
Mt 7: 6 and then turn and tear you to **p**.
14:20 of broken **p** that were left over.
15:37 of broken **p** that were left over.
21:44 on this stone will be broken to **p**,
24:51 He will cut him to **p** and assign him
Mk 6:43 of broken **p** of bread and fish.
8: 8 of broken **p** that were left over.
8:19 basketfuls of **p** did you pick up?"
8:20 basketfuls of **p** did you pick up?"
Lk 9:17 of broken **p** that were left over.
12:46 He will cut him to **p** and assign him
20:18 on that stone will be broken to **p**,
Jn 6:12 "Gather the **p** that are left over.
6:13 filled twelve baskets with the **p** of
Ac 23:10 Paul would be torn to **p** by them.
27:41 to **p** by the pounding of the surf.
27:44 there on planks or on **p** of the ship.
Rev 2:27 he will dash them to **p** like pottery'

Pierce (Pierced, Pierces, Piercing)

Ex 21: 6 door-post and **p** his ear with an awl.
Nu 24: 8 with their arrows they **p** them.
Job 40:24 eyes, or trap him and **p** his nose?
41: 2 his nose or **p** his jaw with a hook?
Ps 37:15 their swords will **p** their own hearts,
45: 5 Let your sharp arrows **p** the hearts
Pr 12:18 Reckless words **p** like a sword, but
Eze 28: 7 wisdom and **p** your shining splendour.
Lk 2:35 a sword will **p** your own soul too."

Pierced (Pierce)

Jdg 5:26 she shattered and **p** his temple.
2Ki 9:24 The arrow **p** his heart and he slumped
Job 26:13 his hand **p** the gliding serpent.
Ps 22:16 they have **p** my hands and my feet.

Ps 38: 2 For your arrows have **p** me, and your
40: 6 not desire, but my ears you have **p**;
Isa 14:19 with those **p** by the sword, those who
51: 9 pieces, who **p** that monster through?
53: 5 he was **p** for our transgressions, he
Lam 3:13 He **p** my heart with arrows from his
Hab 3:14 With his own spear you **p** his head
Zec 12:10 the one they have **p**, and they will
Jn 19:34 one of the soldiers **p** Jesus' side
19:37 will look on the one they have **p**."
1Ti 6:10 and **p** themselves with many griefs.
Rev 1: 7 even those who **p** him; and all the

Pierces (Pierce)

2Ki 18:21 which **p** a man's hand and wounds him
Job 16:13 Without pity, he **p** my kidneys and
20:24 weapon, a bronze-tipped arrow **p** him.
30:17 Night **p** my bones; my gnawing pains
Pr 7:23 till an arrow **p** his liver, like a
Isa 36: 6 which **p** a man's hand and wounds him
Jer 4:18 it is! How it **p** to the heart!"

Piercing (Pierce)

Job 16: 9 opponent fastens on me his **p** eyes.

Piety

Job 4: 6 Should not your **p** be your confidence
15: 4 you even undermine **p** and hinder
22: 4 "Is it for your **p** that he rebukes

Pig (Pig's, Pigs)

Lev 11: 7 the **p**, though it has a split hoof
Dt 14: 8 The **p** is also unclean; although it

Pig's (Pig)

Pr 11:22 Like a gold ring in a **p** snout is a
Isa 66: 3 is like one who presents **p** blood,

Pigeon (Pigeons)

Ge 15: 9 along with a dove and a young **p**."
Lev 1:14 he is to offer a dove or a young **p**.
12: 6 **p** or a dove for a sin offering.

Pigeons (Pigeon)

Lev 5: 7 to bring two doves or two young **p**
5:11 afford two doves or two young **p**,
12: 8 to bring two doves or two young **p**,
14:22 two doves or two young **p**, which he
14:30 the doves or the young **p**, which the
15:14 must take two doves or two young **p**
15:29 must take two doves or two young **p**
Nu 6:10 bring two doves or two young **p** to
Lk 2:24 "a pair of doves or two young **p**".

Pigs (Pig)

Isa 65: 4 who eat the flesh of **p**,
66:17 of those who eat the flesh of **p**
Mt 7: 6 do not throw your pearls to **p**.
8:30 them a large herd of **p** was feeding.
8:31 us out, send us into the herd of **p**."
8:32 So they came out and went into the **p**,
8:33 Those tending the **p** ran off, went
Mk 5:11 A large herd of **p** was feeding on the
5:12 begged Jesus, "Send us among the **p**;
5:13 came out and went into the **p**.
5:14 Those tending the **p** ran off and
5:16 man—and told about the **p** as well.
Lk 8:32 A large herd of **p** was feeding there
8:33 they went into the **p**, and the herd
8:34 those tending the **p** saw what had
15:15 sent him to his fields to feed **p**.
15:16 the pods that the **p** were eating,

Pilate (Pilate's)

Roman governor of Judea (Lk 3:1). Questioned Jesus (Mt 27:11–14; Mk 15:2–5; Lk 23:2–5; Jn 18:33–38); gave way to crowds: freed Barabbas; washed hands and gave Jesus up to be crucified (Mt 27:15–26; Mk 15:6–15; Lk 23:13–25; Jn 19). Released Jesus' body to Joseph (Mt 27:57–58; Mk 15:43–46; Lk 23:50–54); allowed guard on tomb (Mt 27:62–66).

Mt 27: 2 handed him over to **P**, the governor.
27:13 **P** asked him, "Don't you hear the
27:17 when the crowd had gathered, **P** asked
27:19 While **P** was sitting on the judge's
27:22 Jesus who is called Christ?" **P** asked.
27:23 crime has he committed?" asked **P**.
27:24 **P** saw that he was getting nowhere,
27:58 Going to **P**, he asked for Jesus' body,
27:58 **P** ordered that it be given to him.
27:62 priests and the Pharisees went to **P**.
27:65 "Take a guard," **P** answered. "Go,
Mk 15: 1 him away and turned him over to **P**.
15: 2 you the king of the Jews?" asked **P**.
15: 4 again **P** asked him, "Aren't you going
15: 5 made no reply, and **P** was amazed.
15: 8 The crowd came up and asked **P** to do
15: 9 you the king of the Jews?" asked **P**,
15:11 to have **P** release Barabbas instead.
15:12 the king of the Jews?" **P** asked them.
15:14 crime has he committed?" asked **P**.
15:15 **P** released Barabbas to them.
15:43 to **P** and asked for Jesus' body.
15:44 **P** was surprised to hear that he was
Lk 3: 1 Pontius **P** was governor of Judea,
13: 1 **P** had mixed with their sacrifices.
23: 1 assembly rose and led him off to **P**.
23: 3 **P** asked Jesus, "Are you the king of
23: 4 **P** announced to the chief priests and
23: 6 On hearing this, **P** asked if the man
23:11 robe, they sent him back to **P**.
23:12 That day Herod and **P** became friends—
23:13 **P** called together the chief priests,
23:20 Wanting to release Jesus, **P** appealed
23:24 **P** decided to grant their demand.
23:52 Going to **P**, he asked for Jesus' body.
Jn 18:29 **P** came out to them and asked, "What
18:31 **P** said, "Take him yourselves and
18:33 **P** then went back inside the palace,
18:35 "Am I a Jew?" **P** replied. "It was
18:37 "You are a king, then!" said **P**.
18:38 "What is truth?" **P** asked. With this
19: 1 **P** took Jesus and had him flogged.
19: 4 Once more **P** came out and said to the
19: 5 **P** said to them, "Here is the man!"
19: 6 "Crucify! Crucify!" But **P** answered,
19: 8 **P** heard this, he was even more
19:10 you refuse to speak to me?" **P** said.
19:12 From then on, **P** tried to set Jesus
19:13 **P** heard this, he brought Jesus out
19:14 "Here is your king," **P** said to the
19:15 I crucify your king?" **P** asked.
19:16 Finally **P** handed him over to them to
19:19 **P** had a notice prepared and fastened
19:21 priests of the Jews protested to **P**,
19:22 **P** answered, "What I have written, I
19:31 they asked **P** to have the legs broken
19:38 Later, Joseph of Arimathea asked **P**
Ac 3:13 and you disowned him before **P**,
4:27 Indeed Herod and Pontius **P** met
13:28 they asked **P** to have him executed.
1Ti 6:13 Pontius **P** made the good confession,

Pilate's (Pilate)

Jn 19:38 With **P** permission, he came and took

Pildash

Ge 22:22 Kesed, Hazo, **P**, Jidlaph and Bethuel."

Pile (Piled, Piles)

Lev 26:30 and **p** your dead bodies on the
Jos 7:26 they heaped up a large **p** of rocks,
8:29 And they raised a large **p** of rocks
Ru 3: 7 down at the far end of the grain **p**.
Ezr 6:11 house is to be made a **p** of rubble.
Job 8:17 entwines its roots around a **p** of
Jer 50:26 **p** her up like heaps of grain.
Eze 24: 5 **P** wood beneath it for the bones;
24: 9 I, too, will **p** the wood high.
Ac 28: 3 Paul gathered a **p** of brushwood and,

Piled (Pile)

Ge 31:46 So they took stones and **p** them in a
Ex 8:14 They were **p** into heaps, and the land
15: 8 of your nostrils the waters **p** up.
Jos 3:16 It **p** up in a heap a great distance
Jdg 9:49 They **p** them against the stronghold
2Sa 18:17 **p** up a large heap of rocks over him.
2Ch 31: 6 their God, and they **p** them in heaps.
Rev 18: 5 for her sins are **p** up to heaven, and

Piles (Pile)

2Ki 10: 8 "Put them in two **p** at the entrance
19:25 fortified cities into **p** of stone.
Job 27:16 dust and clothes like **p** of clay,
Isa 37:26 fortified cities into **p** of stone.
Da 2: 5 your houses turned into **p** of rubble.
3:29 houses be turned into **p** of rubble,
Hos 12:11 **p** of stones on a ploughed field.
Na 3: 3 **p** of dead, bodies without number,
Hab 2: 6 'Woe to him who **p** up stolen goods

Pilgrimage

Ge 47: 9 of my **p** are a hundred and thirty.
47: 9 the years of the **p** of my fathers."
Ps 84: 5 you, who have set their hearts on **p**.

Pilha

Ne 10:24 Hallohesh, **P**, Shobek,

Pillage (Pillaged)

Ezr 9: 7 to **p** and humiliation at the hand of
Jer 50:11 you who **p** my inheritance, because

Pillaged (Pillage)

Ob : 6 ransacked, his hidden treasures **p**!
Na 2:10 She is **p**, plundered, stripped!

Pillar (*Pillar of cloud, Pillar of fire,* Pillars)

Ge 19:26 back, and she became a **p** of salt.
28:18 as a **p** and poured oil on top of it.
28:22 this stone that I have set up as a **p**
31:13 where you annointed a **p** and where
31:45 took a stone and set it up as a **p**.
31:51 here is this **p** I have set up
31:52 and this **p** is a witness, that I
31:52 heap and **p** to my side to harm me.
35:14 Jacob set up a stone **p** at the place
35:20 Over her tomb Jacob set up a **p**, and
35:20 this day that **p** marks Rachel's tomb.
Jdg 9: 6 the great tree at the **p** in Shechem
2Sa 18:18 Absalom had taken a **p** and erected
18:18 He named the **p** after himself, and
1Ki 7:21 The **p** to the south he named Jakin
2Ki 11:14 the king, standing by the **p**, as the
23: 3 The king stood by the **p** and renewed
25:17 Each **p** was twenty-seven feet high.
25:17 The bronze capital on top of one **p**
25:17 The other **p**, with its network, was
2Ch 23:13 standing by his **p** at the entrance.
34:31 The king stood by his **p** and renewed
Jer 1:18 an iron **p** and a bronze wall to stand
52:22 of the one **p** was five cubits high
52:22 The other **p**, with its pomegranates,
1Ti 3:15 the **p** and foundation of the truth.
Rev 3:12 Him who overcomes I will make a **p** in

Pillar of cloud

Ex 13:21 in a **p** to guide them on their way
13:22 Neither the **p** by day nor the pillar
14:19 The **p** also moved from in front and
33: 9 the **p** would come down and stay at
33:10 Whenever the people saw the **p**
Nu 12: 5 the LORD came down in a **p**; he stood
14:14 and that you go before them in a **p**
Dt 31:15 the LORD appeared at the Tent in a **p**,
Ne 9:12 By day you led them with a **p**, and by
9:19 By day the **p** did not cease to guide
Ps 99: 7 He spoke to them from the **p**;

Pillar of fire

Ex 13:21 by night in a **p** to give them light,
13:22 nor the **p** by night left its place
14:24 the LORD looked down from the **p**
Nu 14:14 of cloud by day and a **p** by night.
Ne 9:12 and by night with a **p** to give them
9:19 nor the **p** by night to shine on the

Pillars (Pillar)

Ex 24: 4 set up twelve stone **p** representing
Jdg 16:25 When they stood him among the **p**,
16:26 "Put me where I can feel the **p** that
16:29 central **p** on which the temple stood.
1Ki 7: 6 in front of that were **p** and an
7:15 He cast two bronze **p**, each eighteen
7:16 bronze to set on the tops of the **p**;
7:17 capitals on top of the **p**, seven for
7:18 the capitals on top of the **p**.
7:19 The capitals on top of the **p** in the
7:20 On the capitals of both **p**, above the
7:21 He erected the **p** at the portico of
7:22 so the work on the **p** was completed.
7:41 the two **p**; the two bowl-shaped
7:41 capitals on top of the **p**;
7:41 capitals on top of the **p**;
7:42 capitals on top of the **p**);
2Ki 25:13 The Babylonians broke up the bronze **p**
25:16 The bronze from the two **p**, the Sea
1Ch 18: 8 the **p** and various bronze articles.
2Ch 3:15 front of the temple he made two **p**,
3:16 chains and put them on top of the **p**.
3:17 He erected the **p** in the front of the
4:12 the two **p**; the two bowl-shaped
4:12 capitals on top of the **p**;
4:12 capitals on top of the **p**;
4:13 capitals on top of the **p**);
Est 1: 6 to silver rings on marble **p**.
Job 9: 6 its place and makes its **p** tremble.
26:11 The **p** of the heavens quake, aghast
Ps 75: 3 quake, it is I who hold its **p** firm.
144:12 be like **p** carved to adorn a palace.
Pr 9: 1 she has hewn out its seven **p**.
SS 5:15 His legs are **p** of marble set on
Jer 27:19 the LORD Almighty says about the **p**,
43:13 Egypt he will demolish the sacred **p**
52:17 The Babylonians broke up the bronze **p**
52:20 The bronze from the two **p**, the Sea
52:21 Each of the **p** was eighteen cubits
Eze 26:11 strong **p** will fall to the ground.
40:49 were **p** on each side of the jambs.
42: 6 The rooms on the third floor had no **p**
Am 9: 1 "Strike the tops of the **p** so that
Gal 2: 9 those reputed to be **p**, gave me and
Rev 10: 1 sun, and his legs were like fiery **p**.

Pilot

Ac 27:11 followed the advice of the **p** and of
Jas 3: 4 rudder wherever the **p** wants to go.

Piltai

Ne 12:17 of Miniamin's and of Moadiah's, **P**;

Pin

Jdg 16:13 and tighten it with the **p**, I'll
16:14 tightened it with the **p**. Again she
16:14 pulled up the **p** and the loom, with
1Sa 18:11 himself, "I'll **p** David to the wall.
19:10 Saul tried to **p** him to the wall with
26: 8 Now let me **p** him to the ground with

Pine (Pines)

1Ki 5: 8 in providing the cedar and **p** logs.
5:10 all the cedar and **p** logs he wanted,
6:15 of the temple with planks of **p**.
6:34 He also made two **p** doors, each
9:11 the cedar and **p** and gold he wanted.
2Ch 2: 8 "Send me also cedar, **p** and algum
3: 5 He panelled the main hall with **p** and
Ps 104:17 stork has its home in the **p** trees.
Isa 14: 8 Even the **p** trees and the cedars of
19: 8 throw nets on the water will **p** away.
44:14 or planted a **p**, and the rain made
55:13 the thornbush will grow the **p** tree,
60:13 the **p**, the fir and the cypress
Eze 27: 5 They made all your timbers of **p**
31: 8 nor could the **p** trees equal its
Hos 14: 8 I am like a green **p** tree;
Na 2: 3 the spears of **p** are brandished.
Zec 11: 2 Wail, O **p** tree, for the cedar has

Pines (Pine)

1Sa 2: 5 she who has had many sons **p** away.
2Ki 19:23 cedars, the choicest of its **p**.
Isa 37:24 cedars, the choicest of its **p**.
41:19 I will set **p** in the wasteland, the

Pinions

Dt 32:11 them and carries them on its **p**.
Job 39:13 the **p** and feathers of the stork.

Pinon

Ge 36:41 Oholibamah, Elah, **P**,
1Ch 1:52 Oholibamah, Elah, **P**,

Pint

Jn 12: 3 Mary took about a **p** of pure nard, an

Pipes

Da 3: 5 flute, zither, lyre, harp, **p** and all
3:10 flute, zither, lyre, harp, **p** and all
3:15 flute, zither, lyre, harp, **p** and all
Zec 4:12 gold **p** that pour out golden oil?"

Piram

Jos 10: 3 **P** king of Jarmuth, Japhia king of

Pirathon (Pirathonite)

Jdg 12:13 son of Hillel, from **P**, led Israel.
12:15 and was buried at **P** in Ephraim, in

Pirathonite (Pirathon)

2Sa 23:30 Benaiah the **P**, Hiddai from the
1Ch 11:31 Gibeah in Benjamin, Benaiah the **P**,
27:14 was Benaiah the **P**, an Ephraimite.

Pisgah

Headland near Mount Nebo in the Abarim range, where Moses viewed the promised land (Nu 21:20; Dt 3:17, 27; 4:49; 34:1). Probably a sacred "high place"; Balaam built 7 altars here (Nu 23:14). Originally ruled by King Sihon (Jos 12:3), but eventually allotted to tribe of Reuben (Jos 13:20).

Nu 21:20 top of **P** overlooks the wasteland.
23:14 the field of Zophim on the top of **P**,
Dt 3:17 Salt Sea), below the slopes of **P**.
3:27 Go up to the top of **P** and look west
4:49 the Arabah, below the slopes of **P**.
34: 1 the top of **P**, across from Jericho.
Jos 12: 3 southward below the slopes of **P**.
13:20 Beth Peor, the slopes of **P**, and

Pishon

Ge 2:11 The name of the first is the **P**;

Pisidia

Ac 14:24 After going through **P**, they came

Pisidian

Ac 13:14 From Perga they went on to **P** Antioch.

Pispah

1Ch 7:38 The sons of Jether: Jephunneh, **P** and

Pistachio

Ge 43:11 and myrrh, some **p** nuts and almonds.

Pit (*Go down to the pit*, Pits)

Ex 21:33 "If a man uncovers a **p** or digs one
21:34 the owner of the **p** must pay for the
2Sa 18:17 threw him into a big **p** in the forest
23:20 went down into a **p** on a snowy day
1Ch 11:22 went down into a **p** on a snowy day
Job 9:31 you would plunge me into a slime **p**
33:18 to preserve his soul from the **p**, his
33:22 His soul draws near to the **p**, and
33:24 'Spare him from going down to the **p**
33:28 my soul from going down to the **p**,
33:30 to turn back his soul from the **p**,
Ps 7:15 it out falls into the **p** he has made.
9:15 The nations have fallen into the **p**
28: 1 those who have gone down to the **p**.
30: 3 me from going down into the **p**.
30: 9 in my going down into the **p**?
35: 7 and without cause dug a **p** for me,
35: 8 they fall into the **p**, to their ruin.
40: 2 He lifted me out of the slimy **p**, out
55:23 the wicked into the **p** of corruption;
57: 6 They dug a **p** in my path—but they
69:15 up or the **p** close its mouth over me.
88: 6 You have put me in the lowest **p**, in
94:13 till a **p** is dug for the wicked.
103: 4 who redeems your life from the **p** and
Pr 22:14 mouth of an adulteress is a deep **p**;
23:27 for a prostitute is a deep **p** and a
26:27 If a man digs a **p**, he will fall into
Ecc 10: 8 Whoever digs a **p** may fall into it;
Isa 14:15 the grave, to the depths of the **p**.
14:19 who descend to the stones of the **p**.
24:17 Terror and **p** and snare await you,
24:18 sound of terror will fall into a **p**;
24:18 whoever climbs out of the **p** will be
30:33 Its fire **p** has been made deep and
38:17 In your love you kept me from the **p**
Jer 18:20 Yet they have dug a **p** for me.
18:22 for they have dug a **p** to capture me
48:43 Terror and **p** and snare await you,
48:44 from the terror will fall into a **p**,
48:44 whoever climbs out of the **p** will be
Lam 3:53 They tried to end my life in a **p** and
3:55 O LORD, from the depths of the **p**.
Eze 19: 4 him, and he was trapped in their **p**.
19: 8 him, and he was trapped in their **p**.
28: 8 They will bring you down to the **p**,
32:23 graves are in the depths of the **p**
Jnh 2: 6 you brought my life up from the **p**,
Zec 9:11 your prisoners from the waterless **p**.
Mt 12:11 it falls into a **p** on the Sabbath,
15:14 blind man, both will fall into a **p**."
Mk 12: 1 dug a **p** for the winepress and built
Lk 6:39 Will they not both fall into a **p**?

Pitch (Pitched)

Ge 6:14 and coat it with **p** inside and out.
Ex 2: 3 him and coated it with tar and **p**.
33: 7 a tent and **p** it outside the camp
Pr 20:20 will be snuffed out in **p** darkness.
Isa 13:20 no Arab will **p** his tent there,
34: 9 Edom's streams will be turned into **p**,
34: 9 her land will become blazing **p**!
Jer 6: 3 they will **p** their tents round her,
10:20 **p** my tent or to set up my shelter.
Eze 25: 4 camps and **p** their tents among you;
Da 11:45 He will **p** his royal tents between

Pitch-dark (Dark)

Am 5:20 **p**, without a ray of brightness?

Pitched (Pitch)

Ge 12: 8 hills east of Bethel and **p** his tent,
13:12 plain and **p** his tents near Sodom.
26:25 There he **p** his tent, and there his
31:25 Jacob had **p** his tent in the hill
33:19 plot of ground where he **p** his tent.
35:21 Israel moved on again and **p** his tent
Jdg 4:11 and **p** his tent by the great tree
20:19 got up and **p** camp near Gibeah.
1Sa 17: 1 They **p** camp at Ephes Dammim, between
2Sa 6:17 the tent that David had **p** for it,
16:22 they **p** a tent for Absalom on the
1Ch 15: 1 the ark of God and **p** a tent for it.
16: 1 the tent that David had **p** for it,
2Ch 1: 4 he had **p** a tent for it in Jerusalem.
Ps 19: 4 heavens he has **p** a tent for the sun,

Pitcher (Pitchers)

Ecc 12: 6 the **p** is shattered at the spring,

Pitchers (Pitcher)

Ex 25:29 as well as its **p** and bowls for the
37:16 dishes and bowls and its **p** for the
1Ch 28:17 forks, sprinkling bowls and **p**;
Mk 7: 4 the washing of cups, **p** and kettles.)

Pitfalls
Ps 119:85 The arrogant dig **p** for me, contrary
Lam 3:47 We have suffered terror and **p**, ruin

Pithom
Ex 1:11 and they built **P** and Rameses as

Pithon
1Ch 8:35 The sons of Micah: **P**, Melech, Tarea
9:41 The sons of Micah: **P**, Melech, Tahrea

Pitied (Pity)
Ps 106:46 He caused them to be **p** by all who
1Co 15:19 we are to be **p** more than all men.

Pitiful (Pity)
Rev 3:17 wretched, **p**, poor, blind and naked.

Pits (Pit)
Ge 14:10 Valley of Siddim was full of tar **p**,
1Sa 13: 6 the rocks, and in **p** and cisterns.
Ps 140:10 fire, into miry **p**, never to rise.
Isa 42:22 in **p** or hidden away in prisons.
Zep 2: 9 a place of weeds and salt **p**,

Pittance
Ps 44:12 You sold your people for a **p**,

Pity (Pitied, Pitiful)
Dt 7:16 Do not look on them with **p** and do
13: 8 Show him no **p**. Do not spare him or
19:13 Show him no **p**. You must purge from
19:21 Show no **p**: life for life, eye for
25:12 cut off her hand. Show her no **p**.
28:50 for the old or **p** for the young.
2Sa 12: 6 he did such a thing and had no **p**."
2Ch 36:15 because he had **p** on his people and
Job 16:13 Without **p**, he pierces my kidneys
19:21 "Have **p** on me, my friends, have **p**,
Ps 72:13 He will take **p** on the weak and the
102:14 her very dust moves them to **p**.
109:12 take **p** on his fatherless children.
Ecc 4:10 But **p** the man who falls and has
Isa 9:17 nor will he **p** the fatherless and
Jer 13:14 I will allow no **p** or mercy or
15: 5 "Who will have **p** on you, O Jerusalem?
16: 5 my love and my **p** from this people,"
20:16 towns the LORD overthrew without **p**.
21: 7 them no mercy or **p** or compassion.'
Lam 2: 2 Without **p** the Lord has swallowed up
2:17 He has overthrown you without **p**, he
2:21 you have slaughtered them without **p**.
3:43 you have slain without **p**.
Eze 5:11 not look on you with **p** or spare you.
7: 4 I will not look on you with **p** or
7: 9 I will not look on you with **p** or
8:18 look on them with **p** or spare them.
9: 5 without showing **p** or compassion.
9:10 I will not look on them with **p** or
16: 5 No-one looked on you with **p** or had
20:17 Yet I looked on them with **p** and did
24:14 I will not have **p**, nor will I relent.
Joel 2:14 Who knows? He may turn and have **p**
2:18 his land and take **p** on his people.
Zec 8:14 no **p** when your fathers angered me,"
11: 6 For I will no longer have **p** on the
Mt 18:27 The servant's master took **p** on him,
Mk 9:22 anything, take **p** on us and help us."
Lk 10:33 when he saw him, he took **p** on him.
16:24 'Father Abraham, have **p** on me and
17:13 "Jesus, Master, have **p** on us!
1Jn 3:17 brother in need but has no **p** on him,

Placed (Placing)
Ge 3:24 he **p** on the east side of the Garden
22: 6 offering and **p** it on his son Isaac,
28:18 the stone he had **p** under his head
30:35 he **p** them in the care of his sons.
30:38 he **p** the peeled branches in all the
50:23 were **p** at birth on Joseph's knees.
Ge 50:26 him, he was **p** in a coffin in Egypt.
Ex 2: 3 Then she **p** the child in it and put
40:20 He took the Testimony and **p** it in
40:22 Moses **p** the table in the Tent of
40:24 He **p** the lampstand in the Tent of
40:26 Moses **p** the gold altar in the Tent
40:30 He **p** the basin between the Tent of
Lev 8: 8 He **p** the breastpiece on him and put
8: 9 he **p** the turban on Aaron's head and
Nu 17: 7 Moses **p** the staffs before the LORD
Jos 10:24 and **p** their feet on their necks.
10:27 of the cave they **p** large rocks,
Jdg 7:16 he **p** trumpets and empty jars in the
8:27 which he **p** in Ophrah, his town.
1Sa 6:11 They **p** the ark of the LORD on the
6:15 and **p** them on the large rock.
2Sa 12:30 it was **p** on David's head.
15: 2 be **p** before the king for a decision,
1Ki 6:27 He **p** the cherubim inside the
7: 4 Its windows were **p** high in sets of
7:39 He **p** five of the stands on the south
7:39 He **p** the Sea on the south side, at
7:51 and he **p** them in the treasuries of
8: 9 that Moses had **p** in it at Horeb,
10: 9 and **p** you on the throne of Israel.
21: 8 in Ahab's name, **p** his seal on them,
2Ki 12: 9 He **p** it beside the altar, on the
1Ch 20: 2 it was **p** on David's head.
2Ch 4: 6 **p** five on the south side and five on
4: 7 for them and **p** them in the temple,
4: 8 He made ten tables and **p** them in the
4:10 He **p** the Sea on the south side, at
5: 1 all the furnishings—and he **p** them
5:10 that Moses had **p** in it at Horeb,
6:11 There I have **p** the ark, in which is
6:13 and had **p** it in the centre of the
9: 8 and **p** you on his throne as king to
23:18 Jehoiada **p** the oversight of the
24: 8 a chest was made and **p** outside, at
28:27 but he was not **p** in the tombs of the
Ezr 1: 7 and had **p** in the temple of his god.
Ne 5:15 me—**p** a heavy burden on the people
9:37 to the kings you have **p** over us.
Est 2: 3 Let them be **p** under the care of
6: 8 with a royal crest **p** on its head.
Job 6: 2 all my misery be **p** on the scales!
20: 4 ever since man was **p** on the earth,
Ps 21: 3 **p** a crown of pure gold on his head.
Jer 24: 1 **p** in front of the temple of the LORD.
37:21 be **p** in the courtyard of the guard
Eze 23:41 it on which you had **p** the incense
32:27 whose swords were **p** under their
40:42 On them were **p** the utensils for
43: 8 they **p** their threshold next to my
Da 2:38 in your hands he has **p** mankind and
2:48 the king **p** Daniel in a high position
2:48 **p** him in charge of all its wise men.
5: 7 have a gold chain **p** around his neck,
5:16 a gold chain **p** around your neck,
5:29 a gold chain was **p** around his neck,
6:17 A stone was brought and **p** over the
Mt 19:15 he had **p** his hands on them, he went
21: 7 **p** their cloaks on them, and Jesus
27:37 Above his head they **p** the written
27:60 **p** it in his own new tomb that he had
Mk 6:56 **p** the sick in the market-places.
15:46 and **p** it in a tomb cut out of rock.
Lk 2: 7 in cloths and **p** him in a manger,
23:53 and **p** it in a tomb cut in the rock,
Jn 3:35 and has **p** everything in his hands.
6:27 Father has **p** his seal of approval."
Ac 7:16 **p** in the tomb that Abraham had
7:21 he was **p** outside, Pharaoh's daughter
8:17 Peter and John **p** their hands on them,
9:37 washed and **p** in an upstairs room.
13: 3 they **p** their hands on them and sent
19: 6 Paul **p** his hands on them, the Holy
28: 8 **p** his hands on him and healed him.
Eph 1:22 God **p** all things under his feet and
Rev 1:17 Then he **p** his right hand on me and
3: 8 I have **p** before you an open door

Placing (Placed)
Ge 48:17 Joseph saw his father **p** his right
2Ki 10:24 the men I am **p** in your hands escape,
Ezr 5: 8 and **p** the timbers in the walls.
Ac 9:17 **P** his hands on Saul, he said,

Plague (Plagued, Plagues)
Ex 8: 2 **p** your whole country with frogs.
9: 3 **p** on your livestock in the field
9:15 struck you and your people with a **p**
10:14 Never before had there been such a **p**
10:17 to take this deadly **p** away from me."
11: 1 one more **p** on Pharaoh and on Egypt.
12:13 **p** will touch you when I strike Egypt.
30:12 Then no **p** will come on them when you
32:35 the LORD struck the people with a **p**
Lev 26:25 I will send a **p** among you, and you
Nu 8:19 so that no **p** will strike the
11:33 and he struck them with a severe **p**.
14:12 I will strike them down with a **p** and
14:37 and died of a **p** before the LORD.
16:46 from the LORD; the **p** has started."
16:47 The **p** had already started among the
16:48 and the dead, and the **p** stopped.
16:49 14,700 people died from the **p**, in
16:50 of Meeting, for the **p** had stopped.
25: 8 **p** against the Israelites was stopped;
25: 9 those who died in the **p** numbered
25:18 the **p** came as a result of Peor."
26: 1 After the **p** the LORD said to Moses
31:16 that a **p** struck the LORD's people.
Dt 28:21 The LORD will **p** you with diseases
28:22 which will **p** you until you perish.
32:24 consuming pestilence and deadly **p**;
Jos 22:17 **p** fell on the community of the LORD!
1Sa 6: 4 because the same **p** has struck both
2Sa 24:13 or three days of **p** in your land?
24:15 the LORD sent a **p** on Israel from
24:21 the **p** on the people may be stopped."
24:25 and the **p** on Israel was stopped.
1Ki 8:37 "When famine or **p** comes to the land,
1Ch 21:12 of the LORD—days of **p** in the land,
21:14 the LORD sent a **p** on Israel, and
21:17 do not let this **p** remain on your
21:22 the **p** on the people may be stopped."
2Ch 6:28 "When famine or **p** comes to the land,
7:13 land or send a **p** among my people,
20: 9 whether the sword of judgment, or **p**
Job 27:15 The **p** will bury those who survive
Ps 78:50 death but gave them over to the **p**.
91: 6 nor the **p** that destroys at midday.
106:29 deeds, and a **p** broke out among them.
106:30 intervened, and the **p** was checked.
Isa 19:22 The LORD will strike Egypt with a **p**;
Jer 14:12 them with the sword, famine and **p**."
21: 6 they will die of a terrible **p**.
21: 7 in this city who survive the **p**,
21: 9 will die by the sword, famine or **p**.
24:10 I will send the sword, famine and **p**
27: 8 famine and **p**, declares the LORD,
27:13 famine and **p** with which the LORD has
28: 8 disaster and **p** against many
29:17 "I will send the sword, famine and **p**
29:18 famine and **p** and will make them
32:24 Because of the sword, famine and **p**,
32:36 'By the sword, famine and **p** it will
34:17 to fall by the sword, **p** and famine.
38: 2 will die by the sword, famine or **p**,
42:17 will die by the sword, famine and **p**;
42:22 famine and **p** in the place where you
44:13 with the sword, famine and **p**,
Eze 5:12 will die of the **p** or perish by
5:17 **P** and bloodshed will sweep through
6:11 fall by the sword, famine and **p**.
6:12 He that is far away will die of the **p**
7:15 "Outside is the sword, inside are **p**
7:15 will be devoured by famine and **p**.
12:16 from the sword, famine and **p**, so
14:19 "Or if I send a **p** into that land and
14:21 and famine and wild beasts and **p**
28:23 I will send a **p** upon her and make
33:27 and caves will die of a **p**.
38:22 upon him with **p** and bloodshed;
Hab 3: 5 **P** went before him; pestilence
Zec 14:12 This is the **p** with which the LORD
14:15 A similar **p** will strike the horses
14:18 The LORD will bring on them the **p** he
Rev 6: 8 famine and **p**, and by the wild beasts

Rev 11: 6 kind of **p** as often as they want.
16:21 God on account of the **p** of hail,
16:21 because the **p** was so terrible.

Plagued (Plague)

Ps 73: 5 they are not **p** by human ills.
73:14 All day long I have been **p**; I have

Plagues (Plague)

Ex 5: 3 strike us with **p** or with the sword."
9:14 the full force of my **p** against you
Dt 28:59 the LORD will send fearful **p** on you
1Sa 4: 8 with all kinds of **p** in the desert.
Hos 13:14 Where, O death, are your **p**?
Am 4:10 "I sent **p** among you as I did to
Rev 9:18 was killed by the three **p** of fire,
9:20 that were not killed by these **p**
15: 1 angels with the seven last **p**—last,
15: 6 the seven angels with the seven **p**.
15: 8 **p** of the seven angels were completed.
16: 9 who had control over these **p**, but
18: 4 you will not receive any of her **p**;
18: 8 Therefore in one day her **p** will
21: 9 seven last **p** came and said to me,
22:18 to him the **p** described in this book.

Plain[1] (Plains)

Ge 11: 2 they found a **p** in Shinar and
13:10 **p** of the Jordan was well watered,
13:11 Lot chose for himself the whole **p** of
13:12 lived among the cities of the **p**
19:17 and don't stop anywhere in the **p**!
19:25 those cities and the entire **p**,
19:28 towards all the land of the **p**, and
19:29 God destroyed the cities of the **p**,
Jos 17:16 live in the **p** have iron chariots,
Jdg 1:34 them to come down into the **p**.
2Sa 18:23 way of the **p** and outran the Cushite.
1Ki 7:46 the **p** of the Jordan between Succoth
2Ch 4:17 the **p** of the Jordan between Succoth
26:10 in the foothills and in the **p**.
35:22 to fight him on the **p** of Megiddo.
Ne 6: 2 one of the villages on the **p** of Ono.
Isa 40: 4 become level, the rugged places a **p**.
63:14 like cattle that go down to the **p**,
Jer 47: 5 O remnant on the **p**, how long will
Eze 3:22 go out to the **p**, and there I will
3:23 I got up and went out to the **p**.
8: 4 in the vision I had seen in the **p**.
Da 3: 1 **p** of Dura in the province of Babylon.
Zec 12:11 of Hadad Rimmon in the **p** of Megiddo.

Plain[2] (Plainly)

Hab 2: 2 make it **p** on tablets so that a
Ro 1:19 may be known about God is **p** to them,
1:19 because God has made it **p** to them.
2Co 5:11 What we are is **p** to God, and I hope
5:11 it is also **p** to your conscience.
Eph 3: 9 to make **p** to everyone the

Plainly (Plain[2])

Mt 7:23 I will tell them **p**, 'I never knew
Mk 7:35 loosened and he began to speak **p**.
8:32 He spoke **p** about this, and Peter
Jn 3:21 so that it may be seen **p** that what
10:24 If you are the Christ, tell us **p**."
11:14 then he told them **p**, "Lazarus is
16:25 but will tell you **p** about my Father.
2Co 4: 2 by setting forth the truth **p** we

Plains (Plain[1])

Nu 22: 1 travelled to the **p** of Moab and
26: 3 on the **p** of Moab by the Jordan
26:63 on the **p** of Moab by the Jordan
31:12 at their camp on the **p** of Moab,
33:48 camped on the **p** of Moab by the
33:49 There on the **p** of Moab they camped
33:50 On the **p** of Moab by the Jordan
35: 1 On the **p** of Moab by the Jordan
36:13 on the **p** of Moab by the Jordan
Dt 34: 1 Moses climbed Mount Nebo from the **p**
34: 8 Moses in the **p** of Moab thirty days,
Jos 4:13 LORD to the **p** of Jericho for war.
5:10 at Gilgal on the **p** of Jericho,
13:32 the **p** of Moab across the Jordan
Jdg 1:19 to drive the people from the **p**,
1Ki 20:23 But if we fight them on the **p**,
20:25 we can fight Israel on the **p**.
2Ki 25: 5 overtook him in the **p** of Jericho.
Jer 39: 5 Zedekiah in the **p** of Jericho.
52: 8 overtook him in the **p** of Jericho.

Plan (Planned, Planning, Plans)

Ge 11: 6 nothing they **p** to do will be
41:37 The **p** seemed good to Pharaoh and to
Ex 26:30 to the **p** shown you on the mountain.
Nu 33:56 I will do to you what I **p** to do to
1Sa 18:25 Saul's **p** was to have David fall
2Sa 17: 4 This **p** seemed good to Absalom and to
1Ch 28:18 He also gave him the **p** for the
28:19 in all the details of the **p**."
2Ch 13: 8 "And now you **p** to resist the kingdom
30: 4 The **p** seemed right both to the king
Est 8: 3 to the evil **p** of Haman the Agagite,
Job 42: 2 no **p** of yours can be thwarted.
Ps 64: 6 "We have devised a perfect **p**!"
140: 4 of violence who **p** to trip my feet.
Pr 14:22 But those who **p** what is good find
21:30 There is no wisdom, no insight, no **p**
Isa 5:19 let the **p** of the Holy One of Israel
8:10 propose your **p**, but it will not
14:26 This is the **p** determined for the
Jer 18:11 you and devising a **p** against you.
36: 3 disaster I **p** to inflict on them,
49:30 he has devised a **p** against you.
Eze 43:10 Let them consider the **p**,
Am 3: 7 his **p** to his servants the prophets.
Mic 2: 1 Woe to those who **p** iniquity, to
4:12 they do not understand his **p**,
Mt 28:12 met with the elders and devised a **p**,
Ac 9:24 Saul learned of their **p**. Day and
27:43 kept them from carrying out their **p**.
Ro 15:24 I **p** to do so when I go to Spain.
Eph 1:11 according to the **p** of him who works

Plane

Ge 30:37 almond and **p** trees and made white
Eze 31: 8 nor could the **p** trees compare with

Plank (Planks)

Mt 7: 3 attention to the **p** in your own eye?
7: 4 time there is a **p** in your own eye?
7: 5 You hypocrite, first take the **p** out
Lk 6:41 attention to the **p** in your own eye?
6:42 fail to see the **p** in your own eye?
6:42 first take the **p** out of your eye,

Planks (Plank)

1Ki 6: 9 roofing it with beams and cedar **p**.
6:15 floor of the temple with **p** of pine.
Ac 27:44 The rest were to get there on **p** or

Planned (Plan)

2Ki 19:25 In days of old I **p** it; now I have
Ps 40: 5 The things you **p** for us no-one can
Pr 30:32 or if you have **p** evil, clap your
Isa 14:24 "Surely, as I have **p**, so it will be,
19:12 LORD Almighty has **p** against Egypt.
22:11 for the One who **p** it long ago.
23: 8 Who **p** this against Tyre, the
23: 9 The LORD Almighty **p** it, to bring low
25: 1 things, things **p** long ago.
37:26 In days of old I **p** it; now I have
46:11 what I have **p**, that will I do.
Jer 18: 8 inflict on it the disaster I had **p**.
49:20 Therefore, hear what the LORD has **p**
50:45 Therefore, hear what the LORD has **p**
Lam 2:17 The LORD has done what he **p**; he has
Da 6: 3 the king **p** to set him over the
Ac 27:42 The soldiers **p** to kill the prisoners
Ro 1:13 that I **p** many times to come to you
2Co 1:15 I **p** to visit you first so that you
1:16 I **p** to visit you on my way to
1:17 I **p** this, did I do it lightly? Or do
Heb 11:40 God had **p** something better for us so

Planning (Plan)

Ecc 9:10 nor **p** nor knowledge nor wisdom.
Isa 19:17 the LORD Almighty is **p** against them.
Jer 26: 3 the disaster I was **p** because of the
Mic 2: 3 "I am **p** disaster against this

Plans (Plan)

1Sa 23:10 Saul **p** to come to Keilah and
2Ki 16:10 detailed **p** for its construction.
16:11 all the **p** that King Ahaz had
1Ch 28: 2 our God, and I made **p** to build it.
28:11 David gave his son Solomon the **p** for
28:12 He gave him the **p** of all that the
Ezr 4: 5 frustrate their **p** during the entire
Job 5:12 He thwarts the **p** of the crafty, so
17:11 have passed, my **p** are shattered,
23:14 many such **p** he still has in store.
Ps 14: 6 You evildoers frustrate the **p** of the
20: 4 heart and make all your **p** succeed.
33:10 The LORD foils the **p** of the nations;
33:11 the **p** of the LORD stand firm for
64: 5 They encourage each other in evil **p**,
140: 2 who devise evil **p** in their hearts
140: 8 do not let their **p** succeed, or they
146: 4 very day their **p** come to nothing.
Pr 12: 5 The **p** of the righteous are just, but
15:22 **P** fail for lack of counsel, but with
16: 1 To man belong the **p** of the heart,
16: 3 you do, and your **p** will succeed.
16: 9 In his heart a man **p** his course, but
19:21 Many are the **p** in a man's heart, but
20:18 Make **p** by seeking advice; if you
21: 5 The **p** of the diligent lead to profit
Isa 19: 3 and I will bring their **p** to nothing;
29:15 to hide their **p** from the LORD,
30: 1 "to those who carry out **p** that are
32: 8 the noble man makes noble **p**, and by
Jer 18:12 We will continue with our own **p**;
18:18 They said, "Come, let's make **p**
19: 7 "'In this place I will ruin the **p**
29:11 For I know the **p** I have for you,"
29:11 "**p** to prosper you and not to harm
29:11 **p** to give you hope and a future.
Da 11:17 his **p** will not succeed or help him.
Hos 11: 6 gates and put an end to their **p**.
Mt 22:15 the Pharisees went out and laid **p** to
Jn 12:10 the chief priests made **p** to kill
2Co 1:17 Or do I make my **p** in a worldly

Plant (Planted, Planter, Planting, Plants, Replanted, Transplanted)

Ge 1:29 "I give you every seed-bearing **p** on
1:30 it—I give every green **p** for food.
2: 5 no **p** of the field had yet sprung up,
9:20 the soil, proceeded to **p** a vineyard.
47:23 for you so you can **p** the ground.
Ex 10:15 tree or **p** in all the land of Egypt.
15:17 You will bring them in and **p** them on
Lev 19:19 "'Do not **p** your field with two
19:23 "'When you enter the land and **p** any
25:20 we do not **p** or harvest our crops?"
25:22 While you **p** during the eighth year,
26:16 You will **p** seed in vain, because
Dt 6:11 olive groves you did not **p**—then
22: 9 Do not **p** two kinds of seed in your
22: 9 not only the crops you **p** but also
28:30 You will **p** a vineyard, but you will
28:39 You will **p** vineyards and cultivate
Jos 24:13 olive groves that you did not **p**.'
2Sa 7:10 will **p** them so that they can have a
1Ki 4:33 He described **p** life, from the cedar
2Ki 19:29 **p** vineyards and eat their fruit.
1Ch 17: 9 will **p** them so that they can have a
Job 8:16 He is like a well-watered **p** in the
14: 9 bud and put forth shoots like a **p**.
40:21 Under the lotus **p** he lies, hidden
Ecc 3: 2 a time to **p** and a time to uproot,
11: 4 Whoever watches the wind will not **p**;
Isa 17:10 finest plants and **p** imported vines,
17:11 and on the morning when you **p** them,
28:25 Does he not **p** wheat in its place,
37:30 **p** vineyards and eat their fruit.
61:11 the soil makes the young **p** come up
65:21 **p** vineyards and eat their fruit.
65:22 live in them, or **p** and others eat.

Jer 1:10 and overthrow, to build and to **p**."
24: 6 I will **p** them and not uproot them.
29: 5 **p** gardens and eat what they produce
29:28 **p** gardens and eat what they produce.
31: 5 Again you will **p** vineyards on the
31: 5 will **p** them and enjoy their fruit.
31:27 "when I will **p** the house of Israel
31:28 watch over them to build and to **p**,"
32:41 will assuredly **p** them in this land
35: 7 sow seed or **p** vineyards; you must
42:10 I will **p** you and not uproot you,
Eze 16: 7 I made you grow like a **p** of the
17:22 the very top of a cedar and **p** it;
17:22 **p** it on a high and lofty mountain.
17:23 heights of Israel I will **p** it;
28:26 will build houses and **p** vineyards;
Hos 2:23 I will **p** her for myself in the land;
Am 9:14 They will **p** vineyards and drink
9:15 I will **p** Israel in their own land,
Mic 6:15 You will **p** but not harvest; you will
Zep 1:13 **p** vineyards but not drink the wine.
Mt 15:13 He replied, "Every **p** that my
Mk 4:31 smallest seed you **p** in the ground.
Jn 19:29 sponge on a stalk of the hyssop **p**,
1Co 15:37 you sow, you do not **p** the body that
Jas 1:11 scorching heat and withers the **p**;
Rev 9: 4 grass of the earth or any **p** or tree,

Planted (Plant)

Ge 2: 8 Now the LORD God had **p** a garden in
21:33 Abraham **p** a tamarisk tree in
26:12 Isaac **p** crops in that land and the
Lev 11:37 that are to be **p**, they remain clean.
Nu 24: 6 like aloes **p** by the LORD, like
Dt 11:10 where you **p** your seed and irrigated
20: 6 Has anyone **p** a vineyard and not
21: 4 that has not been ploughed or **p**
29:23 nothing **p**, nothing sprouting, no
Jdg 6: 3 Whenever the Israelites **p** their
Ps 1: 3 He is like a tree **p** by streams of
44: 2 out the nations and **p** our fathers;
80: 8 you drove out the nations and **p** it.
80:15 the root your right hand has **p**, the
92:13 **p** in the house of the LORD, they
104:16 the cedars of Lebanon that he **p**.
107:37 They sowed fields and **p** vineyards
Ecc 2: 4 houses for myself and **p** vineyards.
2: 5 **p** all kinds of fruit trees in
Isa 5: 2 and **p** it with the choicest vines.
40:24 No sooner are they **p**, no sooner are
44:14 **p** a pine, and the rain made it grow.
60:21 They are the shoot I have **p**, the
Jer 2:21 I had **p** you like a choice vine of
11:17 The LORD Almighty, who **p** you, has
12: 2 You have **p** them, and they have taken
17: 8 He will be like a tree **p** by the
18: 9 or kingdom is to be built up and **p**,
45: 4 and uproot what I have **p**,
Eze 17: 4 where he **p** it in a city of traders.
17: 5 **p** it like a willow by abundant water,
17: 7 him from the plot where it was **p**
17: 8 had been **p** in good soil by abundant
19:10 in your vineyard **p** by the water;
19:13 Now it is **p** in the desert, in a dry
Hos 9:13 like Tyre, **p** in a pleasant place.
10:13 you have **p** wickedness, you have
Am 5:11 though you have **p** lush vineyards,
Hag 1: 6 You have **p** much, but have harvested
Mt 13:31 which a man took and **p** in his field.
15:13 has not **p** will be pulled up by the
21:33 was a landowner who **p** a vineyard.
Mk 4:32 Yet when **p**, it grows and becomes the
12: 1 in parables: "A man **p** a vineyard.
Lk 13: 6 "A man had a fig-tree, **p** in his
13:19 a man took and **p** in his garden.
17: 6 'Be uprooted and **p** in the sea,'
20: 9 "A man **p** a vineyard, rented it to
1Co 3: 6 I **p** the seed, Apollos watered it,
Jas 1:21 word **p** in you, which can save you.
Rev 10: 2 He **p** his right foot on the sea and

Planter (Plant)

Am 9:13 the **p** by the one treading grapes.

Planting (Plant)

Lev 26: 5 grape harvest will continue until **p**,
Isa 28:24 a farmer ploughs for **p**, does he
61: 3 a **p** of the LORD for the display of
Mic 1: 6 of rubble, a place for **p** vineyards.
Lk 17:28 buying and selling, **p** and building.

Plants (Plant)

Ge 1:11 seed-bearing **p** and trees on the land
1:12 **p** bearing seed according to their
3:18 and you will eat the **p** of the field.
9: 3 Just as I gave you green **p**, I now
30:14 fields and found some mandrake **p**,
Dt 32: 2 like abundant rain on tender **p**.
2Ki 19:26 They are like **p** in the field, like
Job 8:19 and from the soil other **p** grow.
Ps 37: 2 green **p** they will soon die away.
104:14 and **p** for man to cultivate—
144:12 youth will be like well-nurtured **p**,
Pr 31:16 of her earnings she **p** a vineyard.
SS 4:13 Your **p** are an orchard of
Isa 17:10 finest **p** and plant imported vines,
19: 7 also the **p** along the Nile, at the
37:27 They are like **p** in the field, like
Da 4:15 animals among the **p** of the earth.
Zec 10: 1 men, and **p** of the field to everyone.
Mt 13: 6 when the sun came up, the **p** were
13: 7 which grew up and choked the **p**.
13:32 it is the largest of garden **p** and
Mk 4: 6 when the sun came up, the **p** were
4: 7 grew up and choked the **p**, so that
4:32 becomes the largest of all garden **p**,
Lk 8: 6 and when it came up, the **p** withered
8: 7 grew up with it and choked the **p**.
1Co 3: 7 neither he who **p** nor he who waters
3: 8 The man who **p** and the man who waters
9: 7 Who **p** a vineyard and does not eat of

Plaster (Plastered)

Lev 14:42 and take new clay and **p** the house.
14:45 timbers and all the **p**—and taken out
Dt 27: 2 large stones and coat them with **p**.
27: 4 you today, and coat them with **p**.
Da 5: 5 and wrote on the **p** of the wall,

Plastered (Plaster)

Lev 14:43 out and the house scraped and **p**,
14:48 spread after the house has been **p**,
Isa 44:18 are **p** over so that they cannot see,

Plate (Plates, Platter)

Ex 28:36 "Make a **p** of pure gold and engrave
39:30 They made the **p**, the sacred diadem,
Lev 8: 9 on Aaron's head and set the gold **p**,
Nu 7:13 His offering was one silver **p**
7:19 brought was one silver **p** weighing a
7:25 His offering was one silver **p**
7:31 His offering was one silver **p**
7:37 His offering was one silver **p**
7:43 His offering was one silver **p**
7:49 His offering was one silver **p**
7:55 His offering was one silver **p**
7:61 His offering was one silver **p**
7:67 His offering was one silver **p**
7:73 His offering was one silver **p**
7:79 His offering was one silver **p**
7:85 Each silver **p** weighed a hundred and

Plateau

Dt 3:10 We took all the towns on the **p**, and
4:43 were these: Bezer in the desert **p**,
Jos 13: 9 whole **p** of Medeba as far as Dibon,
13:16 gorge, and the whole **p** past Medeba
13:17 to Heshbon and all its towns on the **p**
13:21 —all the towns on the **p** and the
20: 8 on the **p** in the tribe of Reuben,
Jer 21:13 above this valley on the rocky **p**,
48: 8 will be ruined and the **p** destroyed,
48:21 Judgment has come to the **p**—to

Plates (Plate)

Ex 25:29 make its **p** and dishes of pure gold,
37:16 its **p** and dishes and bowls and its
Nu 4: 7 a blue cloth and put on it the **p**,
7:84 it was anointed: twelve silver **p**,

Platform

2Ch 6:13 Now he had made a bronze **p**, five
6:13 He stood on the **p** and then knelt
Ne 8: 4 wooden **p** built for the occasion.

Platter (Plate)

Mt 14: 8 "Give me here on a **p** the head of
14:11 His head was brought in on a **p** and
Mk 6:25 head of John the Baptist on a **p**."
6:28 brought back his head on a **p**.

Play (Played, Players, Playing, Plays)

Ge 4:21 of all who **p** the harp and flute.
19: 9 and now he wants to **p** the judge!
1Sa 16:16 for someone who can **p** the harp.
16:16 He will **p** when the evil spirit from
16:18 who knows how to **p** the harp.
16:23 David would take his harp and **p**.
1Ch 15:20 **p** the lyres according to alamoth,
15:21 Jeiel and Azaziah were to **p** the
16: 5 They were to **p** the lyres and harps,
Job 40:20 and all the wild animals **p** nearby.
Ps 33: 3 **p** skilfully, and shout for joy.
81: 2 **p** the melodious harp and lyre.
Isa 11: 8 The infant will **p** near the hole of
23:16 **p** the harp well, sing many a song,

Played (Play)

1Sa 10: 5 flutes and harps being **p** before them,
2Ch 29:28 singers sang and the trumpeters **p**.
Pr 30:32 "If you have **p** the fool and exalted
Mt 11:17 "'We **p** the flute for you, and you
Lk 7:32 'We **p** the flute for you, and you did
1Co 14: 7 anyone know what tune is being **p**

Players (Play)

Mt 9:23 saw the flute **p** and the noisy crowd,
Rev 18:22 flute **p** and trumpeters, will never

Playing (Play)

1Sa 18:10 was **p** the harp, as he usually did.
19: 9 While David was **p** the harp,
1Ki 1:40 **p** flutes and rejoicing greatly,
2Ki 3:15 While the harpist was **p**, the hand
1Ch 15:28 and the **p** of lyres and harps.
16:42 cymbals and for the **p** of the other
2Ch 5:12 and **p** cymbals, harps and lyres.
34:12 skilled in **p** musical instruments—
Ps 68:25 them are the maidens **p** tambourines.
Zec 8: 5 filled with boys and girls **p** there."
Rev 14: 2 like that of harpists **p** their harps.

Plays (Play)

1Sa 16:17 "Find someone who **p** well and bring
Eze 33:32 voice and **p** an instrument well,

Plea (Plead, Pleaded, Pleading, Pleads, Pleas)

Ge 30: 6 listened to my **p** and given me a son.
Nu 21: 3 The LORD listened to Israel's **p** and
1Ki 8:28 and his **p** for mercy, O LORD my God.
8:38 a prayer or **p** is made by any of your
8:45 heaven their prayer and their **p**,
8:49 hear their prayer and their **p**, and
8:52 your servant's **p** and to the **p** of
9: 3 "I have heard the prayer and **p** you
2Ch 6:19 and his **p** for mercy, O LORD my God.
6:29 a prayer or **p** is made by any of your
6:35 heaven their prayer and their **p**,
33:13 his entreaty and listened to his **p**;
Job 13: 6 listen to the **p** of my lips.
35:13 God does not listen to their empty **p**;
Ps 17: 1 Hear, O LORD, my righteous **p**; listen
55: 1 prayer, O God, do not ignore my **p**;
102:17 he will not despise their **p**.
Pr 6: 3 press your **p** with your neighbour!
Isa 32: 7 when the **p** of the needy is just.
Jer 7:16 offer any **p** or petition for them;
11:14 offer any **p** or petition for them,

Lam 3:56 You heard my **p**: "Do not close your
Eze 36:37 Once again I will yield to the **p** of
Lk 18: 3 who kept coming to him with the **p**,

Plead (Plea)

Jdg 6:31 "Are you going to **p** Baal's cause?
1Sa 2:36 silver and a crust of bread and **p**,
1Ki 8:47 and repent and **p** with you in the
2Ch 6:37 and repent and **p** with you in the
Est 4: 8 mercy and **p** with him for her people.
Job 8: 5 if you will look to God and **p** with
9:15 only **p** with my Judge for mercy.
35: 9 they **p** for relief from the arm of
Ps 43: 1 Vindicate me, O God, and **p** my cause
Isa 1:17 fatherless, **p** the case of the widow.
45:14 They will bow down before you and **p**
Jer 5:28 they do not **p** the case of the
7:16 do not **p** with me, for I will not
15:11 I will make your enemies **p** with you
27:18 let them **p** with the LORD Almighty
30:13 There is no-one to **p** your cause, no
Da 2:18 He urged them to **p** for mercy from
Mic 6: 1 "Stand up, **p** your case before the
Mk 5:17 the people began to **p** with Jesus to
Gal 4:12 I **p** with you, brothers, become like
Php 4: 2 I **p** with Euodia and I **p** with

Pleaded (Plea)

Ge 42:21 was when he **p** with us for his life,
Dt 3:23 At that time I **p** with the LORD:
2Sa 12:16 David **p** with God for the child.
Est 8: 3 Esther again **p** with the king,
Da 9: 3 I turned to the Lord God and **p** with
Mt 8:34 **p** with him to leave their region.
Mk 5:23 **p** earnestly with him, "My little
Lk 7: 4 they came to Jesus, they **p** earnestly
15:28 his father went out and **p** with him.
Ac 2:40 he warned them; and he **p** with them,
21:12 we and the people there **p** with Paul
2Co 8: 4 they urgently **p** with us for the
12: 8 Three times I **p** with the Lord to

Pleading (Plea)

Pr 19: 7 Though he pursues them with **p**, they
Jer 3:21 the weeping and **p** of the people of
38:26 tell them, 'I was **p** with the king
Lk 8:41 **p** with him to come to his house
13:25 and **p**, 'sir, open the door for us.

Pleads (Plea)

Job 16:21 **p** with God as a man **p** for his friend.
Pr 18:23 A poor man **p** for mercy, but a rich
Isa 59: 4 no-one **p** his case with integrity.
Mic 7: 9 **p** my case and establishes my right.

Pleas (Plea)

2Ch 6:39 hear their prayer and their **p**, and
Isa 19:22 respond to their **p** and heal them.

Pleasant (Pleasantness)

Ge 49:15 resting place and how **p** is his land,
Ps 16: 6 have fallen for me in **p** places;
106:24 they despised the **p** land; they did
133: 1 How good and **p** it is when brothers
135: 3 praise to his name, for that is **p**.
147: 1 God, how **p** and fitting to praise him!
Pr 2:10 knowledge will be **p** to your soul.
3:17 Her ways are **p** ways, and all her
16:21 and **p** words promote instruction.
16:24 **P** words are a honeycomb, sweet to
Isa 30:10 Tell us **p** things, prophesy illusions.
32:12 Beat your breasts for the **p** fields,
Jer 12:10 they will turn my **p** field into a
31:26 My sleep had been **p** to me.
Hos 4:13 and terebinth, where the shade is **p**.
9:13 like Tyre, planted in a **p** place.
Mic 2: 9 of my people from their **p** homes.
Zec 7:14 This is how they made the **p** land
1Th 3: 6 you always have **p** memories of us
Heb 12:11 No discipline seems **p** at the time,

Pleasantness (Pleasant)

Pr 27: 9 and the **p** of one's friend springs

Please (Pleased, Pleases, Pleasing)

Ge 19: 2 "My lords," he said, "**p** turn aside
19:18 Lot said to them, "No, my lords, **p**!
24:14 '**P** let down your jar that I may have
24:17 "**P** give me a little water from your
24:23 **P** tell me, is there room in your
24:42 if you will, **p** grant success to the
24:43 "**P** let me drink a little water from
24:45 I said to her, '**P** give me a drink.'
27:19 **P** sit up and eat some of my game so
30:14 Rachel said to Leah, "**P** give me some
30:27 found favour in your eyes, **p** stay.
32:29 Jacob said, "**P** tell me your name."
33:10 "No, **p**!" said Jacob. "If I have
33:11 **P** accept the present that was
34: 8 **P** give her to him as his wife.
43:20 "**P**, sir," they said, "we came down
44:18 "**P**, my lord, let your servant speak
44:33 "Now then, **p** let your servant remain
47: 4 So now, **p** let your servants settle
50:17 Now **p** forgive the sins of the
Ex 4:13 Moses said, "O Lord, **p** send someone
21: 8 If she does not **p** the master who has
32:32 now, **p** forgive their sin—but if not,
Nu 10:31 Moses said, "**P** do not leave us.
12:11 he said to Moses, "**P**, my lord, do
12:13 to the LORD, "O God, **p** heal her!
20:17 **P** let us pass through your country.
23:27 Perhaps it will **p** God to let you
36: 6 They may marry anyone they **p** as long
Dt 12:13 your burnt offerings anywhere you **p**.
28:63 will **p** him to ruin and destroy you.
Jos 2:12 Now then, **p** swear to me by the LORD
Jdg 4:19 "**P** give me some water."
6:18 **P** do not go away until I come back
10:15 think best, but **p** rescue us now."
16:28 O God, **p** strengthen me just once
18: 5 they said to him, "**P** enquire of God
19: 6 "**P** stay tonight and enjoy yourself.
Ru 2: 7 She said, '**P** let me glean and gather
1Sa 9:18 **p** tell me where the seer's house is?"
15:30 But **p** honour me before the elders
25: 8 **P** give your servants and your son
25:24 **P** let your servant speak to you;
25:28 **P** forgive your servant's offence,
28:22 Now **p** listen to your servant and let
2Sa 13:13 **P** speak to the king; he will not
13:24 king and his officials **p** join me?"
13:26 Absalom said, "If not, **p** let my
18:22 **p** let me run behind the Cushite.
1Ki 2:17 he continued, "**P** ask King Solomon
3:26 "**P**, my lord, give her the living
17:11 "And bring me, **p**, a piece of bread.
20:32 Ben-Hadad says: '**P** let me live.
20:37 another man and said, "Strike me, **p**.
2Ki 1:13 begged, "**p** have respect for my life
4:22 "**P** send me one of the servants and
5:15 **P** accept now a gift from your
5:17 "**p** let me, your servant, be given
5:22 **P** give them a talent of silver and
6: 3 one of them said, "Won't you **p** come
18:26 "**P** speak to your servants in Aramaic,
2Ch 10: 7 **p** them and give them a favourable
Ne 9:37 our bodies and our cattle as they **p**.
Est 3:11 "and do with the people as you **p**.
Job 10: 3 Does it **p** you to oppress me, to
34: 9 man nothing when he tries to **p** God.'
Ps 69:31 This will **p** the LORD more than an ox,
Pr 20:23 and dishonest scales do not **p** him.
Isa 29:11 "Read this, **p**," he will answer, "I
29:12 "Read this, **p**," he will answer, "I
36:11 "**P** speak to your servants in Aramaic,
44:28 and will accomplish all that I **p**;
46:10 stand, and I will do all that I **p**.
58: 3 you do as you **p** and exploit all
58:13 from doing as you **p** on my holy day,
58:13 as you **p** or speaking idle words,
Jer 6:20 your sacrifices do not **p** me."
27: 5 on it, and I give it to anyone I **p**.
36:15 They said to him, "Sit down, **p**, and
37: 3 "**P** pray to the LORD our God for us.
37:20 now, my lord the king, **p** listen.
40: 4 lies before you; go wherever you **p**."
40: 5 people, or go anywhere else you **p**.
42: 2 "**P** hear our petition and pray to the
Da 1:12 "**P** test your servants for ten days:
Hos 9: 4 nor will their sacrifices **p** him.
10:10 I **p**, I will punish them; nations
Jnh 1:14 "O LORD, **p** do not let us die for
Mk 5:23 **P** come and put your hands on her so
Lk 14:18 I must go and see it. **P** excuse me.'
14:19 way to try them out. **P** excuse me.'
Jn 5:30 not to **p** myself but him who sent me.
Ac 8:34 The eunuch asked Philip, "Tell me, **p**,
9:38 and urged him, "**P** come at once!"
13:15 for the people, **p** speak."
21:39 **P** let me speak to the people."
Ro 8: 8 by the sinful nature cannot **p** God.
15: 1 of the weak and not to **p** ourselves.
15: 2 Each of us should **p** his neighbour
15: 3 For even Christ did not **p** himself
1Co 7:32 affairs—how he can **p** the Lord.
7:33 this world—how he can **p** his wife—
7:34 world—how she can **p** her husband.
10:33 even as I try to **p** everybody in
2Co 5: 9 we make it our goal to **p** him,
Gal 1:10 or of God? Or am I trying to **p** men?
1:10 If I were still trying to **p** men,
6: 8 The one who sows to **p** his sinful
6: 8 the one who sows to **p** the Spirit,
Col 1:10 the Lord and may **p** him in every way:
1Th 2: 4 We are not trying to **p** men but God,
4: 1 you how to live in order to **p** God,
2Ti 2: 4 wants to **p** his commanding officer.
Tit 2: 9 to **p** them, not to talk back to them,
Heb 11: 6 without faith it is impossible to **p**

Pleased (Please)

Ge 45:16 Pharaoh and all his officials were **p**.
49: 6 anger and hamstrung oxen as they **p**.
Ex 33:13 If you are **p** with me, teach me your
33:16 How will anyone know that you are **p**
33:17 because I am **p** with you and I know
Lev 10:19 Would the LORD have been **p** if I had
Nu 14: 8 If the LORD is **p** with us, he will
24: 1 Now when Balaam saw that it **p** the
Dt 21:14 If you are not **p** with her, let her
28:63 Just as it **p** the LORD to make you
33:11 and be **p** with the work of his hands.
Jos 22:30 Manasseh had to say, they were **p**.
1Sa 12:22 the LORD was **p** to make you his own.
16:22 in my service, for I am **p** with him."
18: 5 This **p** all the people, and Saul's
18:20 they told Saul about it, he was **p**.
18:22 'Look, the king is **p** with you, and
18:26 **p** to become the king's son-in-law.
29: 6 and I would be **p** to have you serve
2Sa 3:36 All the people took note and were **p**;
3:36 everything the king did **p** them.
7:29 Now be **p** to bless the house of your
15:26 if he says, 'I am not **p** with you,'
19: 6 I see that you would be **p** if Absalom
1Ki 3:10 The Lord was **p** that Solomon had
5: 7 he was greatly **p** and said, "Praise
9:12 given him, he was not **p** with them.
11:19 Pharaoh was so **p** with Hadad that he
1Ch 17:27 Now you have been **p** to bless the
28: 4 he was **p** to make me king over all
29:17 the heart and are **p** with integrity.
Ne 2: 6 It **p** the king to send me
9:24 land, to deal with them as they **p**.
12:44 for Judah was **p** with the ministering
Est 1:21 The king and his nobles were **p** with
2: 9 The girl **p** him and won his favour.
2:14 king unless he was **p** with her and
5: 2 he was **p** with her and held out to
8: 5 and if he is **p** with me, let an order
9: 5 what they **p** to those who hated them.
Ps 40:13 Be **p**, O LORD, to save me;
41:11 I know that you are **p** with me, for
105:22 to instruct his princes as he **p** and
Ecc 4:16 But those who came later were not **p**
Isa 42:21 **p** the LORD for the sake of his
Eze 18:23 Rather, am I not **p** when they turn
Da 4:27 Therefore, O king, be **p** to accept my
6: 1 **p** Darius to appoint 120 satraps to
8: 4 He did as he **p** and became great.
Hos 8:13 but the LORD is not **p** with them.
Jnh 1:14 you, O LORD, have done as you **p**."
Mic 6: 7 Will the LORD be **p** with thousands of

Mal 1: 8 Would he be **p** with you? Would he
1:10 on my altar! I am not **p** with you,"
2:17 of the LORD, and he is **p** with them"
Mt 3:17 whom I love; with him I am well **p**."
14: 6 danced for them and **p** Herod so
17: 5 whom I love; with him I am well **p**.
Mk 1:11 whom I love; with you I am well **p**."
6:22 she **p** Herod and his dinner guests.
Lk 3:22 whom I love; with you I am well **p**."
12:32 has been **p** to give you the kingdom.
23: 8 Herod saw Jesus, he was greatly **p**,
Jn 5:21 life to whom he is **p** to give it.
Ac 6: 5 This proposal **p** the whole group.
12: 3 he saw that this **p** the Jews, he
Ro 15:26 For Macedonia and Achaia were **p** to
15:27 They were **p** to do it, and indeed
1Co 1:21 God was **p** through the foolishness of
10: 5 Nevertheless, God was not **p** with
Gal 1:15 and called me by his grace, was **p**
Col 1:19 For God was **p** to have all his
Heb 10: 6 and sin offerings you were not **p**.
10: 8 desire, nor were you **p** with them"
10:38 back, I will not be **p** with him."
11: 5 he was commended as one who **p** God.
13:16 for with such sacrifices God is **p**.
2Pe 1:17 whom I love; with him I am well **p**."

Pleases (Please)

1Sa 23:20 Now, O king, come down whenever it **p**
2Sa 19:27 angel of God; so do whatever **p** you.
19:37 Do for him whatever **p** you."
19:38 I will do for him whatever **p** you.
24:22 take whatever **p** him and offer it up.
1Ch 21:23 my lord the king do whatever **p** him.
Ezr 5:17 Now if it **p** the king, let a search
Ne 2: 5 "If it **p** the king and if your
2: 7 "If it **p** the king, may I have
Est 1:19 "Therefore, if it **p** the king, let
2: 4 let the girl who **p** the king be queen
3: 9 If it **p** the king, let a decree be
5: 4 "If it **p** the king," replied Esther,
5: 8 if it **p** the king to grant my
7: 3 O king, and if it **p** your majesty,
8: 5 "If it **p** the king," she said, "and
9:13 "If it **p** the king," Esther answered,
Job 23:13 oppose him? He does whatever he **p**.
Ps 115: 3 in heaven; he does whatever **p** him.
135: 6 The LORD does whatever **p** him, in the
Pr 15: 8 but the prayer of the upright **p** him.
21: 1 it like a watercourse wherever he **p**.
Ecc 2:26 To the man who **p** him, God gives
2:26 hand it over to the one who **p** God.
7:26 The man who **p** God will escape her,
8: 3 cause, for he will do whatever he **p**.
11: 7 Light is sweet, and it **p** the eyes to
Isa 56: 4 who choose what **p** me and hold fast
Eze 46: 5 the lambs is to be as much as he **p**,
46:11 and with the lambs as much as one **p**,
Da 4:35 He does as he **p** with the powers of
11: 3 with great power and do as he **p**.
11:16 The invader will do as he **p**;
11:36 "The king will do as he **p**. He will
Jn 3: 8 The wind blows wherever it **p**.
8:29 alone, for I always do what **p** him."
Eph 5:10 find out what **p** the Lord.
Col 3:20 in everything, for this **p** the Lord.
1Ti 2: 3 This is good, and **p** God our Saviour,
1Jn 3:22 obey his commands and do what **p** him.

Pleasing (Please)

Ge 2: 9 were **p** to the eye and good for food.
3: 6 was good for food and **p** to the eye,
8:21 The LORD smelled the **p** aroma and
Ex 29:18 a **p** aroma, an offering made to the
29:25 offering for a **p** aroma to the LORD,
29:41 as in the morning—a **p** aroma,
Lev 1: 9 by fire, an aroma **p** to the LORD.
1:13 by fire, an aroma **p** to the LORD.
1:17 by fire, an aroma **p** to the LORD.
2: 2 by fire, an aroma **p** to the LORD.
2: 9 by fire, an aroma **p** to the LORD.
2:12 offered on the altar as a **p** aroma.
3: 5 by fire, an aroma **p** to the LORD.
3:16 an offering made by fire, a **p** aroma.
4:31 the altar as an aroma **p** to the LORD.
Lev 6:15 the altar as an aroma **p** to the LORD.
6:21 in pieces as an aroma **p** to the LORD.
8:21 a **p** aroma, an offering made to the
8:28 a **p** aroma, an offering made to the
17: 6 the fat as an aroma **p** to the LORD.
23:13 made to the LORD by fire, a **p** aroma
23:18 by fire, an aroma **p** to the LORD.
26:31 in the **p** aroma of your offerings.
Nu 15: 3 as an aroma **p** to the LORD—whether
15: 7 Offer it as an aroma **p** to the LORD.
15:10 by fire, an aroma **p** to the LORD.
15:13 by fire as an aroma **p** to the LORD.
15:14 by fire as an aroma **p** to the LORD,
15:24 offering as an aroma **p** to the LORD,
18:17 by fire, an aroma **p** to the LORD.
28: 2 made by fire, as an aroma **p** to me.'
28: 6 at Mount Sinai as a **p** aroma,
28: 8 by fire, an aroma **p** to the LORD.
28:13 is for a burnt offering, a **p** aroma,
28:24 days as an aroma **p** to the LORD;
28:27 year old as an aroma **p** to the LORD.
29: 2 an aroma **p** to the LORD, prepare a
29: 6 made to the LORD by fire—a **p** aroma.
29: 8 Present as an aroma **p** to the LORD a
29:13 by fire as an aroma **p** to the LORD,
29:36 by fire as an aroma **p** to the LORD,
1Sa 29: 9 as **p** in my eyes as an angel of God;
Ezr 6:10 that they may offer sacrifices **p** to
Ps 19:14 of my heart be **p** in your sight,
104:34 May my meditation be **p** to him, as I
Pr 15:26 but those of the pure are **p** to him.
16: 7 a man's ways are **p** to the LORD, he
22:18 for it is **p** when you keep them in
SS 1: 3 **P** is the fragrance of your perfumes;
4:10 How much more **p** is your love than
7: 6 How beautiful you are and how **p**, O
Lam 2: 4 has slain all who were **p** to the eye;
Ro 12: 1 holy and **p** to God—this is your
12: 2 is—his good, **p** and perfect will.
14:18 way is **p** to God and approved by men.
Php 4:18 an acceptable sacrifice, **p** to God.
1Ti 5: 4 grandparents, for this is **p** to God.
Heb 13:21 may he work in us what is **p** to him

Pleasure (Pleasures)

Ge 18:12 is old, will I now have this **p**?"
Job 22: 3 What **p** would it give the Almighty if
Ps 5: 4 You are not a God who takes **p** in
51:16 do not take **p** in burnt offerings.
51:18 In your good **p** make Zion prosper;
109:17 he found no **p** in blessing—may it
147:10 His **p** is not in the strength of the
Pr 10:23 A fool finds **p** in evil conduct, but
16:13 Kings take **p** in honest lips;
18: 2 A fool finds no **p** in understanding
21:17 He who loves **p** will become poor;
Ecc 2: 1 you with **p** to find out what is good.
2: 2 And what does **p** accomplish?"
2:10 I refused my heart no **p**.
5: 4 He has no **p** in fools; fulfil your
7: 4 heart of fools is in the house of **p**.
12: 1 you will say, "I find no **p** in them"
Isa 1:11 I have no **p** in the blood of bulls
9:17 Therefore the Lord will take no **p** in
Jer 6:10 to them; they find no **p** in it.
Eze 16:37 with whom you found **p**, those you
18:23 Do I take any **p** in the death of the
18:32 For I take no **p** in the death of
33:11 I take no **p** in the death of the
Da 4: 2 is my **p** to tell you about the
Hag 1: 8 I may take **p** in it and be honoured,"
Mal 2:13 accepts them with **p** from your hands.
Mt 11:26 Yes, Father, for this was your good **p**
Lk 10:21 Father, for this was your good **p**.
Eph 1: 5 in accordance with his **p** and will—
1: 9 according to his good **p**, which he
1Ti 5: 6 the widow who lives for **p** is dead
2Ti 3: 4 lovers of **p** rather than lovers of
2Pe 2:13 Their idea of **p** is to carouse in

Pleasures (Pleasure)

Ps 16:11 with eternal **p** at your right hand.
Lk 8:14 by life's worries, riches and **p**,
Tit 3: 3 by all kinds of passions and **p**.
Heb 11:25 enjoy the **p** of sin for a short time.
Jas 4: 3 may spend what you get on your **p**.
2Pe 2:13 their **p** while they feast with you.

Pledge (Pledged, Pledges)

Ge 38:17 "Will you give me something as a **p**
38:18 He said, "What **p** should I give you?"
38:20 to get his **p** back from the woman,
Ex 22:26 take your neighbour's cloak as a **p**,
Nu 30: 2 an oath to bind himself by a **p**,
30: 3 to the LORD or binds herself by a **p**
30: 4 her father hears about her vow or **p**
30: 4 then all her vows and every **p** by
30:10 or binds herself by a **p** under
30:13 or any sworn **p** to deny herself.
Dt 24:10 to get what he is offering as a **p**.
24:11 the loan bring the **p** out to you.
24:12 sleep with his **p** in your possession.
24:17 take the cloak of the widow as a **p**.
2Ch 34:32 and Benjamin **p** themselves to it;
Ezr 10:19 (They all gave their hands in **p** to
Job 17: 3 "Give me, O God, the **p** you demand.
24: 3 donkey and take the widow's ox in **p**.
Pr 6: 1 have struck hands in **p** for another,
11:15 to strike hands in **p** is safe.
17:18 in judgment strikes hands in **p** and
20:16 hold it in **p** if he does it for a
22:26 a man who strikes hands in **p** or
27:13 hold it in **p** if he does it for a
Eze 17:18 Because he had given his hand in **p**
18: 7 what he took in **p** for a loan.
18:12 He does not return what he took in **p**.
18:16 anyone or require a **p** for a loan.
33:15 if he gives back what he took in **p**
Am 2: 8 every altar on garments taken in **p**.
1Ti 5:12 they have broken their first **p**.
1Pe 3:21 **p** of a good conscience towards God.

Pledged (Pledge)

Ge 19:14 who were **p** to marry his daughters.
Ex 22:16 **p** to be married and sleeps with her,
Dt 20: 7 Has anyone become **p** to a woman and
22:23 in a town a virgin **p** to be married
22:25 girl **p** to be married and rapes her,
22:28 a virgin who is not **p** to be married
28:30 You will be **p** to be married to a
2Ki 23: 3 people **p** themselves to the covenant.
1Ch 29:24 **p** their submission to King Solomon.
Mic 7:20 as you **p** an oath to our fathers in
Mt 1:18 Mary was **p** to be married to Joseph,
Lk 1:27 to a virgin **p** to be married to a man
2: 5 who was **p** to be married to him and

Pledges (Pledge)

Nu 30: 5 none of her vows or the **p** by which
30: 7 then her vows or the **p** by which she
30:11 then all her vows or the **p** by which
30:12 **p** that came from her lips will stand.
30:14 her vows or the **p** binding on her.

Pleiades

Job 9: 9 the **P** and the constellations of the
38:31 "Can you bind the beautiful **P**?
Am 5: 8 (he who made the **P** and Orion, who

Plentiful (Plenty)

1Ki 10:27 and cedar as **p** as sycamore-fig trees
1Ch 12:40 There were **p** supplies of flour, fig
2Ch 1:15 and cedar as **p** as sycamore-fig trees
9:27 and cedar as **p** as sycamore-fig trees
Isa 30:23 from the land will be rich and **p**.
Eze 36:29 make it **p** and will not bring famine
Mt 9:37 "The harvest is **p** but the workers
Lk 10: 2 He told them, "The harvest is **p**, but

Plentifully (Plenty)

Ge 41:47 of abundance the land produced **p**.

Plenty (Plentiful, Plentifully)

Ge 24:25 she added, "We have **p** of straw and
33: 9 Esau said, "I already have **p**, my
34:21 the land has **p** of room for them.
2Ch 2: 9 to provide me with **p** of timber,
31:10 we have had enough to eat and **p** to
32: 4 and find **p** of water?" they said.

Job 20:22 In the midst of his **p**, distress will
Ps 17:14 their sons have **p**, and they store
37:19 in days of famine they will enjoy **p**.
Pr 27:27 You will have **p** of goats' milk to
Jer 44:17 At that time we had **p** of food and
Joel 2:26 You will have **p** to eat, until you
Mic 2:11 'I will prophesy for you **p** of wine
Lk 12:19 "You have **p** of good things laid up
Jn 3:23 because there was **p** of water, and
6:10 There was **p** of grass in that place,
Ac 14:17 he provides you with **p** of food and
2Co 8:14 At the present time your **p** will
8:14 their **p** will supply what you need.
Php 4:12 and I know what it is to have **p**.
4:12 whether living in **p** or in want.

Plied (Ply)

Lk 23: 9 He **p** him with many questions, but

Plight

2Ki 7:13 Their **p** will be like that of all the
Ps 59: 4 Arise to help me; look on my **p**!

Plot (Plots, Plotted, Plotting)

Ge 33:19 the **p** of ground where he pitched
2Ki 9:10 devour her on the **p** of ground at
9:21 They met him at the **p** of ground that
9:26 this **p** of ground, declares the LORD.
9:26 pick him up and throw him on that **p**,
9:36 On the **p** of ground at Jezreel dogs
9:37 on the ground in the **p** at Jezreel,
Ne 4:15 we were aware of their **p** and that
Est 2:22 Mordecai found out about the **p** and
9:25 when the **p** came to the king's
Ps 2: 1 conspire and the peoples **p** in vain?
21:11 Though they **p** evil against you and
31:13 against me and **p** to take my life.
35: 4 may those who **p** my ruin be turned
37:12 The wicked **p** against the righteous
38:12 all day long they **p** deception.
64: 6 They **p** injustice and say, "We have
83: 3 they **p** against those you cherish.
83: 5 With one mind they **p** together;
Pr 3:29 Do not **p** harm against your neighbour,
12:20 in the hearts of those who **p** evil,
14:22 Do not those who **p** evil go astray?
24: 2 for their hearts **p** violence, and
Isa 28:25 barley in its **p**, and spelt in its
Jer 11:18 the LORD revealed their **p** to me, I
48: 2 men will **p** her downfall: 'Come,
Eze 17: 7 him from the **p** where it was planted
17:10 away in the **p** where it grew?'
Da 11:24 He will **p** the overthrow of
Hos 7:15 them, but they **p** evil against me.
Mic 2: 1 to those who **p** evil on their beds!
Na 1: 9 Whatever they **p** against the LORD he
Zec 8:17 do not **p** evil against your neighbour,
Mk 3: 6 the Pharisees went out and began to **p**
Jn 4: 5 near the **p** of ground Jacob had given
Ac 4:25 rage and the peoples **p** in vain?
14: 5 There was a **p** afoot among the
20: 3 Because the Jews made a **p** against
23:13 forty men were involved in this **p**.
23:16 of Paul's sister heard of this **p**,
23:30 I was informed of a **p** to be carried

Plots (Plot)

Ps 36: 4 Even on his bed he **p** evil;
52: 2 Your tongue **p** destruction; it is
Pr 6:14 who **p** evil with deceit in his heart—
16:27 A scoundrel **p** evil, and his speech
24: 8 He who **p** evil will be known as a
Isa 33:15 who stops his ears against **p** of
Jer 18:23 you know, O LORD, all their **p** to
Lam 3:60 vengeance, all their **p** against me.
3:61 insults, all their **p** against me—
Da 11:25 of the **p** devised against him.
Na 1:11 who **p** evil against the LORD
Ac 20:19 tested by the **p** of the Jews.

Plotted (Plot)

Ge 37:18 he reached them, they **p** to kill him.
2Sa 21: 5 **p** against us so that we have been
1Ki 15:27 the house of Issachar **p** against him,
1Ki 16: 9 of half his chariots, **p** against him.
16:16 **p** against the king and murdered him,
2Ki 21:24 all who had **p** against King Amon,
2Ch 24:21 they **p** against him, and by order of
33:25 all who had **p** against King Amon,
Ne 4: 8 They all **p** together to come and
Est 9:24 had **p** against the Jews to destroy
Isa 7: 5 son have **p** your ruin, saying,
Jer 11:19 realise that they had **p** against me,
49:30 king of Babylon has **p** against you;
Hab 2:10 You have **p** the ruin of many peoples,
Mt 12:14 the Pharisees went out and **p** how
26: 4 they **p** to arrest Jesus in some sly
Jn 11:53 from that day on they **p** to take his

Plotting (Plot)

1Sa 23: 9 David learned that Saul was **p**
Ne 6: 6 you and the Jews are **p** to revolt,
Ps 56: 5 they are always **p** to harm me.
Pr 16:30 winks with his eye is **p** perversity;
Eze 11: 2 these are the men who are **p** evil and

Plough (Ploughed, Ploughing, Ploughman, Ploughmen, Ploughs, Ploughshares)

Dt 22:10 Do not **p** with an ox and a donkey
1Sa 8:12 and others to **p** his ground and reap
Job 4: 8 I have observed, those who **p** evil
Pr 20: 4 A sluggard does not **p** in season;
Isa 28:24 planting, does he **p** continually?
Hos 10:11 I will drive Ephraim, Judah must **p**,
Am 6:12 Does one **p** there with oxen? But you
Lk 9:62 "No-one who puts his hand to the **p**

Ploughed (Plough)

Dt 21: 4 that has not been **p** or planted
Jdg 14:18 "If you had not **p** with my heifer,
Ps 129: 3 Ploughmen have **p** my back and made
Jer 26:18 'Zion will be **p** like a field,
Eze 36: 9 with favour; you will be **p** and sown,
Hos 10: 4 like poisonous weeds in a **p** field.
12:11 like piles of stones on a **p** field.
Mic 3:12 Zion will be **p** like a field,

Ploughing (Plough)

Ge 45: 6 there will not be **p** and reaping.
Ex 34:21 during the **p** season and harvest you
1Ki 19:19 He was **p** with twelve yoke of oxen,
19:21 He burned the **p** equipment to cook
Job 1:14 "The oxen were **p** and the donkeys
Lk 17: 7 "Suppose one of you had a servant **p**

Ploughman (Plough)

Am 9:13 reaper will be overtaken by the **p**
1Co 9:10 because when the **p** ploughs and the

Ploughmen (Plough)

Ps 129: 3 **P** have ploughed my back and made

Ploughs (Plough)

Ps 141: 7 They will say, "As one **p** and breaks
Isa 28:24 a farmer **p** for planting, does he
1Co 9:10 because when the ploughman **p** and the

Ploughshares (Plough)

1Sa 13:20 to the Philistines to have their **p**,
13:21 for sharpening **p** and mattocks,
Isa 2: 4 They will beat their swords into **p**
Joel 3:10 Beat your **p** into swords and your
Mic 4: 3 They will beat their swords into **p**

Pluck (Plucked)

Mk 9:47 eye causes you to sin, **p** it out.

Plucked (Pluck)

Ge 8:11 its beak was a freshly **p** olive leaf

Plumage

Eze 17: 3 and full **p** of varied colours came
17: 7 with powerful wings and full **p**.

Plumb (Plumb-line)

Am 7: 7 wall that had been built true to **p**,

Plumb-line (Plumb)

2Ki 21:13 **p** used against the house of Ahab.
Isa 28:17 and righteousness the **p**;
34:11 of chaos and the **p** of desolation.
Am 7: 7 true to plumb, with a **p** in his hand.
7: 8 do you see, Amos?" "A **p**," I replied.
7: 8 "Look, I am setting a **p** among my
Zec 4:10 see the **p** in the hand of Zerubbabel.

Plunder (Plundered, Plunderers)

Ge 34:29 as **p** everything in the houses.
49:27 in the evening he divides the **p**."
Ex 3:22 And so you will **p** the Egyptians."
Nu 14: 3 and children will be taken as **p**.
14:31 that you said would be taken as **p**,
31: 9 herds, flocks and goods as **p**.
31:11 They took all the **p** and spoils,
31:12 brought the captives, spoils and **p**
31:32 The **p** remaining from the spoils that
31:53 Each soldier had taken **p** for himself.
Dt 2:35 the livestock and the **p** from the
3: 7 all the livestock and the **p** from
13:16 Gather all the **p** of the town into
13:16 all its **p** as a whole burnt offering
20:14 may take these as **p** for yourselves.
20:14 And you may use the **p** the LORD your
Jos 7:21 I saw in the **p** a beautiful robe from
8: 2 **p** and livestock for yourselves.
8:27 the livestock and **p** of this city,
11:14 the **p** and livestock of these cities,
22: 8 brothers the **p** from your enemies."
Jdg 5:19 they carried off no silver, no **p**.
5:30 colourful garments as **p** for Sisera,
5:30 for my neck—all this as **p**?'
8:24 ear-ring from your share of the **p**.
8:25 man threw a ring from his **p** onto it.
1Sa 14:30 the **p** they took from their enemies.
14:32 They pounced on the **p** and, taking
14:36 by night and **p** them till dawn,
15:19 Why did you pounce on the **p** and do
15:21 took sheep and cattle from the **p**,
30:16 because of the great amount of **p**
30:19 **p** or anything else they had taken.
30:20 saying, "This is David's **p**."
30:22 share with them the **p** we recovered.
30:26 he sent some of the **p** to the elders
30:26 from the **p** of the LORD's enemies."
2Sa 3:22 brought with them a great deal of **p**.
8:12 He also dedicated the **p** taken from
12:30 a great quantity of **p** from the
2Ki 3:23 Now to the **p**, Moab!"
1Ch 20: 2 a great quantity of **p** from the
26:27 Some of the **p** taken in battle they
2Ch 14:13 carried off a large amount of **p**.
15:11 from the **p** they had brought back.
20:25 his men went to carry off their **p**,
20:25 There was so much **p** that it took
24:23 all the **p** to their king in Damascus.
25:13 carried off great quantities of **p**.
28: 8 They also took a great deal of **p**,
28:14 gave up the prisoners and **p** in the
28:15 from the **p** they clothed all who
Ne 4: 4 over as **p** in a land of captivity.
Est 3:13 month of Adar, and to **p** their goods.
8:11 to **p** the property of their enemies.
9:10 did not lay their hands on the **p**.
9:15 did not lay their hands on the **p**.
9:16 did not lay their hands on the **p**.
Ps 68:12 in the camps men divide the **p**.
109:11 **p** the fruits of his labour.
Pr 1:13 things and fill our houses with **p**;
12:12 The wicked desire the **p** of evil men,
16:19 than to share **p** with the proud.
22:23 case and will **p** those who **p** them.
Isa 3:14 **p** from the poor is in your houses.
8: 4 of Damascus and the **p** of Samaria
9: 3 as men rejoice when dividing the **p**.
10: 6 to seize loot and snatch **p**, and to
11:14 they will **p** the people to the east.
17:14 loot us, the lot of those who **p** us.
33: 4 Your **p**, O nations, is harvested as
33:23 and even the lame will carry off **p**.

Isa 42:22 They have become **p**, with no-one to
49:24 Can **p** be taken from warriors, or
49:25 and **p** retrieved from the fierce;
Jer 2:14 by birth? Why then has he become **p**?
15:13 and your treasures I will give as **p**,
17: 3 treasures I will give away as **p**,
20: 5 They will take it away as **p** and
30:16 Those who **p** you will be plundered;
49:32 Their camels will become **p**, and
50:10 all who **p** her will have their fill,"
Eze 7:21 I will hand it all over as **p** to
23:46 and give them over to terror and **p**.
25: 7 and give you as **p** to the nations.
26: 5 She will become **p** for the nations,
26:12 They will **p** your wealth and loot
29:19 and **p** the land as pay for his army.
36: 5 that they might **p** its pasture-land.'
38:12 I will **p** and loot and turn my hand
38:13 "Have you come to **p**? Have you
38:13 and goods and to seize much **p**?"'
39:10 And they will **p** those who plundered
Da 11:24 He will distribute **p**, loot and
Am 3:10 **p** and loot in their fortresses."
3:11 strongholds and **p** your fortresses."
Na 2: 9 **P** the silver! **P** the gold! The supply
3: 1 full of **p**, never without victims!
Hab 2: 8 the peoples who are left will **p** you.
Zep 2: 9 The remnant of my people will **p** them;
Zec 2: 9 so that their slaves will **p** them.
14: 1 your **p** will be divided among you.
Heb 7: 4 Abraham gave him a tenth of the **p**!

Plundered (Plunder)

Ex 12:36 asked for; so they **p** the Egyptians.
Jdg 2:14 them over to raiders who **p** them.
1Sa 14:48 the hands of those who had **p** them.
17:53 the Philistines, they **p** their camp.
2Ki 7:16 the people went out and **p** the camp
21:14 be looted and **p** by all their foes,
2Ch 14:14 They **p** all these villages, since
Ps 44:10 and our adversaries have **p** us.
76: 5 Valiant men lie **p**, they sleep their
89:41 All who pass by have **p** him; he has
Isa 10:13 I **p** their treasures; like a mighty
24: 3 completely laid waste and totally **p**.
42:22 this is a people **p** and looted, all
Jer 30:16 Those who plunder you will be **p**;
50:10 Babylonia will be **p**; all who plunder
50:37 her treasures! They will be **p**.
Eze 34: 8 so has been **p** and has become food
34:22 flock, and they will no longer be **p**.
34:28 They will no longer be **p** by the
36: 4 the deserted towns that have been **p**
39:10 And they will plunder those who **p**
Da 11:33 sword or be burned or captured or **p**.
Hos 13:15 will be **p** of all its treasures.
Na 2:10 She is pillaged, **p**, stripped!
Hab 2: 8 you have **p** many nations, the peoples
Zep 1:13 Their wealth will be **p**, their houses
Zec 2: 8 against the nations that have **p** you

Plunderers (Plunder)

2Ki 17:20 and gave them into the hands of **p**,
Isa 42:24 become loot, and Israel to the **p**?

Plunge (Plunged)

1Sa 2:14 He would **p** it into the pan or kettle
Job 9:31 you would **p** me into a slime pit so
Ps 68:23 that you may **p** your feet in the
Joel 2: 8 They **p** through defences without
1Ti 6: 9 **p** men into ruin and destruction.
1Pe 4: 4 strange that you do not **p** with them

Plunged (Plunge)

Jdg 3:21 and **p** it into the king's belly.
2Sa 18:14 **p** them into Absalom's heart while
20:10 and Joab **p** it into his belly, and
Rev 16:10 and his kingdom was **p** into darkness.

Ply (Plied)

Isa 23:17 will **p** her trade with all the

Pocket

1Sa 25:29 hurl away as from the **p** of a sling.

Pods

2Ki 6:25 of a cab of seed **p** for five shekels.
Lk 15:16 the **p** that the pigs were eating,

Poets

Nu 21:27 That is why the **p** say: "Come to
Ac 17:28 **p** have said, 'We are his offspring.'

Point (Pointed, Pointing, Points)

Jdg 3:25 waited to the **p** of embarrassment,
1Sa 7:11 along the way to a **p** below Beth Car.
17: 7 iron **p** weighed six hundred shekels.
2Sa 13: 2 Amnon became frustrated to the **p** of
2Ki 19: 3 children come to the **p** of birth
20: 1 ill and was at the **p** of death.
2Ch 32:24 ill and was at the **p** of death.
Ne 3:16 made repairs up to a **p** opposite the
3:19 from a **p** facing the ascent to the
3:26 made repairs up to a **p** opposite
Job 20:25 the gleaming **p** out of his liver.
Pr 9: 3 from the highest **p** of the city.
9:14 a seat at the highest **p** of the city,
Isa 37: 3 children come to the **p** of birth
38: 1 ill and was at the **p** of death.
Jer 17: 1 inscribed with a flint **p**, on the
Eze 47:20 to a **p** opposite Lebo Hamath.
Mt 4: 5 on the highest **p** of the temple.
26:38 with sorrow to the **p** of death.
Mk 14:34 to the **p** of death," he said to them.
Lk 4: 9 on the highest **p** of the temple.
Jn 7:25 At that **p** some of the people of
Ac 26:24 At this **p** Festus interrupted Paul's
Ro 2: 1 for at whatever **p** you judge the
1Co 9: 8 this merely from a human **p** of view?
2Co 5:16 no-one from a worldly **p** of view.
7:11 At every **p** you have proved
Php 3:15 if on some **p** you think differently,
1Ti 4: 6 If you **p** these things out to the
2Ti 2: 9 even to the **p** of being chained like
Heb 8: 1 The **p** of what we are saying is this:
12: 4 to the **p** of shedding your blood.
Jas 2:10 yet stumbles at just one **p** is
Rev 2:10 Be faithful, even to the **p** of death,

Pointed (Point)

Jn 4:44 (Now Jesus himself had **p** out that a

Pointing (Point)

Isa 58: 9 the **p** finger and malicious talk,
Mt 12:49 **P** to his disciples, he said, "Here
1Pe 1:11 the Spirit of Christ in them was **p**

Points (Point)

Ne 4:13 **p** of the wall at the exposed places,
Ac 25:19 Instead, they had some **p** of dispute
Ro 15:15 to you quite boldly on some **p**,

Poised

Job 15:24 him, like a king **p** to attack,
37:16 Do you know how the clouds hang **p**,

Poison (Poisoned, Poisonous, Poisons)

Dt 29:18 you that produces such bitter **p**.
32:32 Their grapes are filled with **p**, and
32:33 of serpents, the deadly **p** of cobras.
Job 6: 4 my spirit drinks in their **p**;
20:16 He will suck the **p** of serpents;
Ps 140: 3 the **p** of vipers is on their lips.
Am 6:12 But you have turned justice into **p**
Mk 16:18 and when they drink deadly **p**,
Ro 3:13 "The **p** of vipers is on their lips."
Jas 3: 8 a restless evil, full of deadly **p**.

Poisoned (Poison)

Jer 8:14 and given us **p** water to drink,
9:15 eat bitter food and drink **p** water.
23:15 eat bitter food and drink **p** water,
Ac 14: 2 **p** their minds against the brothers.

Poisonous (Poison)

Hos 10: 4 up like **p** weeds in a ploughed field.

Poisons (Poison)

Pr 23:32 like a snake and **p** like a viper.

Pokereth-hazzebaim

Ezr 2:57 Shephatiah, Hattil, **P** and
Ne 7:59 Shephatiah, Hattil, **P** and

Pole (Poles)

Nu 13:23 Two of them carried it on a **p**
21: 8 "Make a snake and put it up on a **p**;
21: 9 a bronze snake and put it up on a **p**.
Dt 16:21 Do not set up any wooden Asherah **p**
Jdg 6:25 cut down the Asherah **p** beside it.
6:26 Using the wood of the Asherah **p** that
6:28 demolished, with the Asherah **p**
6:30 cut down the Asherah **p** beside it."
1Ki 15:13 she had made a repulsive Asherah **p**.
15:13 Asa cut the **p** down and burned it in
16:33 Ahab also made an Asherah **p** and did
2Ki 6: 2 where each of us can get a **p**;
13: 6 the Asherah **p** remained standing in
17:16 shape of calves, and an Asherah **p**.
21: 3 made an Asherah **p**, as Ahab king of
21: 7 He took the carved Asherah **p** he had
23: 6 He took the Asherah **p** from the
23:15 and burned the Asherah **p** also.
2Ch 15:16 she had made a repulsive Asherah **p**.
15:16 Asa cut the **p** down, broke it up and

Poles (Pole)

Ex 25:13 make **p** of acacia wood and overlay
25:14 Insert the **p** into the rings on the
25:15 The **p** are to remain in the rings of
25:27 the **p** used in carrying the table.
25:28 Make the **p** of acacia wood, overlay
27: 6 Make **p** of acacia wood for the altar
27: 7 The **p** are to be inserted into the
30: 4 hold the **p** used to carry it.
30: 5 Make the **p** of acacia wood and
34:13 stones and cut down their Asherah **p**.
35:12 the ark with its **p** and the atonement
35:13 the table with its **p** and all its
35:15 the altar of incense with its **p**, the
35:16 its **p** and all its utensils;
37: 4 he made **p** of acacia wood and
37: 5 he inserted the **p** into the rings on
37:14 the **p** used in carrying the table.
37:15 The **p** for carrying the table were
37:27 hold the **p** used to carry it.
37:28 They made the **p** of acacia wood and
38: 5 They cast bronze rings to hold the **p**
38: 6 They made the **p** of acacia wood and
38: 7 They inserted the **p** into the rings
39:35 the ark of the Testimony with its **p**
39:39 its **p** and all its utensils;
40:20 attached the **p** to the ark and put
Nu 4: 6 over that and put the **p** in place.
4: 8 of sea cows and put its **p** in place.
4:11 of sea cows and put its **p** in place.
4:14 of sea cows and put its **p** in place.
Dt 7: 5 cut down their Asherah **p** and burn
12: 3 burn their Asherah **p** in the fire;
1Ki 8: 7 the ark and its carrying **p**.
8: 8 These **p** were so long that their ends
14:15 LORD to anger by making Asherah **p**.
14:23 sacred stones and Asherah **p** on every
2Ki 17:10 Asherah **p** on every high hill and
18: 4 stones and cut down the Asherah **p**.
23:14 cut down the Asherah **p** and covered
1Ch 15:15 God with the **p** on their shoulders,
2Ch 5: 8 covered the ark and its carrying **p**.
5: 9 These **p** were so long that their ends,
14: 3 stones and cut down the Asherah **p**.
17: 6 places and the Asherah **p** from Judah.
19: 3 have rid the land of the Asherah **p**
24:18 and worshipped Asherah **p** and idols.
31: 1 stones and cut down the Asherah **p**.
33: 3 to the Baals and made Asherah **p**.
33:19 set up Asherah **p** and idols before he
34: 3 Asherah **p**, carved idols and cast
34: 4 Asherah **p**, the idols and the images.
34: 7 the Asherah **p** and crushed the idols
Isa 17: 8 have no regard for the Asherah **p**
27: 9 no Asherah **p** or incense altars will

Jer 17: 2 Asherah **p** beside the spreading trees
Mic 5:14 from among you your Asherah **p**

Polish (Polished)
Jer 46: 4 **P** your spears, put on your armour!

Polished (Polish)
2Ch 4:16 temple of the LORD were of **p** bronze.
Ezr 8:27 two fine articles of **p** bronze,
SS 5:14 **p** ivory decorated with sapphires.
Isa 49: 2 he made me into a **p** arrow and
Eze 21: 9 'A sword, a sword, sharpened and **p**—
21:10 **p** to flash like lightning!
21:11 "'The sword is appointed to be **p**,
21:11 it is sharpened and **p**, made ready
21:28 **p** to consume and to flash like

Pollute (Polluted, Pollutes)
Nu 35:33 "'Do not **p** the land where you are.
Jude : 8 these dreamers **p** their own bodies,

Polluted (Pollute)
Ezr 9:11 **p** by the corruption of its peoples.
Pr 25:26 Like a muddied spring or a **p** well is
Ac 15:20 to abstain from food **p** by idols
Jas 1:27 oneself from being **p** by the world.

Pollutes (Pollute)
Nu 35:33 Bloodshed **p** the land, and atonement

Pollux
Ac 28:11 of the twin gods Castor and **P**.

Pomegranate (Pomegranates)
1Sa 14: 2 of Gibeah under a **p** tree in Migron.
SS 4: 3 veil are like the halves of a **p**.
6: 7 veil are like the halves of a **p**.
Joel 1:12 the **p**, the palm and the apple tree
Hag 2:19 the vine and the fig-tree, the **p** and

Pomegranates (Pomegranate)
Ex 28:33 Make **p** of blue, purple and scarlet
28:34 The gold bells and the **p** are to
39:24 They made **p** of blue, purple and
39:25 them around the hem between the **p**.
39:26 The bells and **p** alternated around
Nu 13:23 them, along with some **p** and figs.
20: 5 no grain or figs, grapevines or **p**.
Dt 8: 8 fig-trees, **p**, olive oil and honey;
1Ki 7:18 He made **p** in two rows encircling
7:20 two hundred **p** in rows all around.
7:42 the four hundred **p** for the two sets
7:42 (two rows of **p** for each network,
2Ki 25:17 network and **p** of bronze all around.
2Ch 3:16 He also made a hundred **p** and
4:13 the four hundred **p** for the two sets
4:13 (two rows of **p** for each network,
SS 4:13 Your plants are an orchard of **p** with
6:11 had budded or the **p** were in bloom.
7:12 and if the **p** are in bloom—there I
8: 2 wine to drink, the nectar of my **p**.
Jer 52:22 network and **p** of bronze all around.
52:22 pillar, with its **p**, was similar.
52:23 There were ninety-six **p** on the sides;
52:23 the total number of **p** above the

Pomp
Isa 8: 7 the king of Assyria with all his **p**.
10:16 under his **p** a fire will be kindled
14:11 All your **p** has been brought down to
21:16 the **p** of Kedar will come to an end.
Ac 25:23 Bernice came with great **p** and

Ponder (Pondered, Ponders)
Ps 64: 9 works of God and **p** what he has done.
119:95 me, but I will **p** your statutes.
Isa 14:16 they **p** your fate: "Is this the man
33:18 In your thoughts you will **p** the

Pondered (Ponder)
Ne 5: 7 I **p** them in my mind and then accused
Ps 111: 2 are **p** by all who delight in them.
Ecc 12: 9 He **p** and searched out and set in
Isa 57:11 me nor **p** this in your hearts?
Lk 2:19 things and **p** them in her heart.

Ponders (Ponder)
Isa 57: 1 and no-one **p** it in his heart;

Ponds
Ex 7:19 over the **p** and all the reservoirs'
8: 5 over the streams and canals and **p**,

Pontius See Pilate
Lk 3: 1 **P** Pilate was governor of Judea,
Ac 4:27 Indeed Herod and **P** Pilate met
1Ti 6:13 who while testifying before **P** Pilate

Pontus
Ac 2: 9 Judea and Cappadocia, **P** and Asia,
18: 2 a native of **P**, who had recently come
1Pe 1: 1 scattered throughout **P**, Galatia,

Pool (Pools)
2Sa 2:13 out and met them at the **p** of Gibeon.
2:13 sat down on one side of the **p**
4:12 hung the bodies by the **p** in Hebron.
1Ki 22:38 They washed the chariot at a **p** in
2Ki 18:17 at the aqueduct of the Upper **P**,
20:20 how he made the **p** and the tunnel by
Ne 2:14 the Fountain Gate and the King's **P**,
3:15 the wall of the **P** of Siloam,
3:16 as far as the artificial **p** and the
Ps 114: 8 who turned the rock into a **p**, the
Isa 7: 3 end of the aqueduct of the Upper **P**,
22: 9 you stored up water in the Lower **P**.
22:11 walls for the water of the Old **P**,
35: 7 The burning sand will become a **p**,
36: 2 at the aqueduct of the Upper **P**,
Jer 41:12 with him near the great **p** in Gibeon.
Na 2: 8 Nineveh is like a **p**, and its water
Jn 5: 2 Jerusalem near the Sheep Gate a **p**,
5: 7 the **p** when the water is stirred.
9: 7 told him, "wash in the **P** of Siloam"

Pools (Pool)
Dt 8: 7 land with streams and **p** of water,
Ps 84: 6 autumn rains also cover it with **p**.
107:35 He turned the desert into **p** of water
SS 7: 4 Your eyes are the **p** of Heshbon by
Isa 41:18 I will turn the desert into **p** of
42:15 into islands and dry up the **p**.

Poor (Impoverished, Poorest, Poverty)
Ex 23: 3 do not show favouritism to a **p** man
23: 6 "Do not deny justice to your **p**
23:11 Then the **p** among your people may get
30:15 the **p** are not to give less when you
Lev 14:21 "If, however, he is **p** and cannot
19:10 Leave them for the **p** and the alien.
19:15 do not show partiality to the **p** or
23:22 Leave them for the **p** and the alien.
25:25 'If one of your countrymen becomes **p**
25:35 'If one of your countrymen becomes **p**
25:39 'If one of your countrymen becomes **p**
25:47 one of your countrymen becomes **p** and
27: 8 If anyone making the vow is too **p** to
Nu 13:20 How is the soil? Is it fertile or **p**?
Dt 15: 4 However, there should be no **p** among
15: 7 If there is a **p** man among your
15: 7 tight-fisted towards your **p** brother.
15:11 There will always be **p** people in the
15:11 the **p** and needy in your land.
24:12 If the man is **p**, do not go to sleep
24:14 of a hired man who is **p** and needy,
24:15 he is **p** and is counting on it.
Ru 3:10 the younger men, whether rich or **p**.
1Sa 2: 8 He raises the **p** from the dust and
18:23 I'm only a **p** man and little known."
2Sa 12: 1 town, one rich and the other **p**.
12: 3 the **p** man had nothing except one
12: 4 ewe lamb that belonged to the **p** man
Est 9:22 to one another and gifts to the **p**.
Job 5:16 the **p** have hope, and injustice shuts
Job 20:10 children must make amends to the **p**;
20:19 For he has oppressed the **p** and left
24: 4 all the **p** of the land into hiding.
24: 5 the **p** go about their labour of
24: 9 the infant of the **p** is seized for a
24:14 rises up and kills the **p** and needy;
29:12 I rescued the **p** who cried for help,
30:25 Has not my soul grieved for the **p**?
31:16 I have denied the desires of the **p**
34:19 does not favour the rich over the **p**,
34:28 They caused the cry of the **p** to come
Ps 14: 6 frustrate the plans of the **p**, but
22:26 The **p** will eat and be satisfied;
34: 6 This **p** man called, and the LORD
35:10 You rescue the **p** from those too
35:10 **p** and needy from those who rob them."
37:14 bow to bring down the **p** and needy,
40:17 Yet I am **p** and needy; may the Lord
49: 2 both low and high, rich and **p** alike:
68:10 O God, you provided for the **p**.
69:32 The **p** will see and be glad—you who
70: 5 Yet I am **p** and needy; come quickly
74:21 the **p** and needy praise your name.
82: 3 the rights of the **p** and oppressed.
86: 1 and answer me, for I am **p** and needy.
109:16 but hounded to death the **p** and the
109:22 For I am **p** and needy, and my heart
112: 9 scattered abroad his gifts to the **p**,
113: 7 He raises the **p** from the dust and
132:15 her **p** will I satisfy with food.
140:12 the LORD secures justice for the **p**
Pr 10: 4 Lazy hands make a man **p**, but
10:15 but poverty is the ruin of the **p**.
13: 7 another pretends to be **p**, yet has
13: 8 life, but a **p** man hears no threat.
13:23 A **p** man's field may produce abundant
14:20 The **p** are shunned even by their
14:31 He who oppresses the **p** shows
17: 5 He who mocks the **p** shows contempt
18:23 A **p** man pleads for mercy, but a rich
19: 1 Better a **p** man whose walk is
19: 4 but a **p** man's friend deserts him.
19: 7 A **p** man is shunned by all his
19:17 He who is kind to the **p** lends to the
19:22 better to be **p** than a liar.
20:13 Do not love sleep or you will grow **p**;
21:13 shuts his ears to the cry of the **p**,
21:17 He who loves pleasure will become **p**;
22: 2 Rich and **p** have this in common: The
22: 7 The rich rule over the **p**, and the
22: 9 for he shares his food with the **p**.
22:16 He who oppresses the **p** to increase
22:22 exploit the **p** because they are **p**
23:21 for drunkards and gluttons become **p**,
28: 3 A ruler who oppresses the **p** is like
28: 6 Better a **p** man whose walk is
28: 8 another, who will be kind to the **p**.
28:11 but a **p** man who has discernment sees
28:27 He who gives to the **p** will lack
29: 7 care about justice for the **p**,
29:13 The **p** man and the oppressor have
29:14 If a king judges the **p** with fairness,
30: 9 Or I may become **p** and steal,
30:14 to devour the **p** from the earth,
31: 9 the rights of the **p** and needy."
31:20 She opens her arms to the **p** and
Ecc 4:13 Better a **p** but wise youth than an
5: 8 If you see the **p** oppressed in a
6: 8 What does a **p** man gain by knowing
9:15 in that city a man **p** but wise,
9:15 But nobody remembered that **p** man.
9:16 But the **p** man's wisdom is despised,
Isa 3:14 from the **p** is in your houses.
3:15 and grinding the faces of the **p**?"
10: 2 to deprive the **p** of their rights and
10:30 Listen, O Laishah! **P** Anathoth!
11: 4 decisions for the **p** of the earth.
14:30 The poorest of the **p** will find
25: 4 You have been a refuge for the **p**, a
26: 6 oppressed, the footsteps of the **p**.
32: 7 schemes to destroy the **p** with lies,
40:20 A man too **p** to present such an
41:17 "The **p** and needy search for water,
58: 7 to provide the **p** wanderer with
61: 1 me to preach good news to the **p**.
Jer 2:34 the lifeblood of the innocent **p**,

Jer 5: 4 I thought, "These are only the **p**;
5:28 do not defend the rights of the **p**.
22:16 He defended the cause of the **p** and
24: 2 the other basket had very **p** figs,
24: 3 but the **p** ones are so bad that they
24: 8 "'But like the **p** figs, which are so
29:17 I will make them like **p** figs that
39:10 land of Judah some of the **p** people,
Eze 16:49 they did not help the **p** and needy.
18:12 He oppresses the **p** and needy.
22:29 they oppress the **p** and needy and
Am 2: 7 They trample on the heads of the **p**
4: 1 you women who oppress the **p** and
5:11 You trample on the **p** and force him
5:12 you deprive the **p** of justice in
8: 4 and do away with the **p** of the land,
8: 6 buying the **p** with silver and the
Zec 7:10 the fatherless, the alien or the **p**.
Mt 5: 3 "Blessed are the **p** in spirit, for
11: 5 the good news is preached to the **p**.
19:21 your possessions and give to the **p**,
26: 9 price and the money given to the **p**."
26:11 The **p** you will always have with you,
Mk 10:21 you have and give to the **p**,
12:42 a **p** widow came and put in two very
12:43 "I tell you the truth, this **p** widow
14: 5 wages and the money given to the **p**.
14: 7 The **p** you will always have with you,
Lk 4:18 me to preach good news to the **p**.
6:20 "Blessed are you who are **p**,
7:22 the good news is preached to the **p**.
11:41 what is inside ⌞the dish⌟ to the **p**,
12:33 your possessions and give to the **p**.
14:13 when you give a banquet, invite the **p**
14:21 of the town and bring in the **p**,
18:22 you have and give to the **p**,
19: 8 half of my possessions to the **p**,
21: 2 He also saw a **p** widow put in two
21: 3 "this **p** widow has put in more than
Jn 12: 5 and the money given to the **p**?
12: 6 cared about the **p** but because he
12: 8 You will always have the **p** among you,
13:29 Feast, or to give something to the **p**.
Ac 9:36 always doing good and helping the **p**.
10: 4 "Your prayers and gifts to the **p**
10:31 and remembered your gifts to the **p**.
24:17 for the **p** and to present offerings.
Ro 15:26 the **p** among the saints in Jerusalem.
1Co 13: 3 If I give all I possess to the **p** and
13:12 Now we see but a **p** reflection as in
2Co 6:10 **p**, yet making many rich;
8: 9 yet for your sakes he became **p**, so
9: 9 scattered abroad his gifts to the **p**;
Gal 2:10 should continue to remember the **p**,
Jas 2: 2 and a **p** man in shabby clothes also
2: 3 say to the **p** man, "You stand there"
2: 5 Has not God chosen those who are **p**
2: 6 you have insulted the **p**. Is it not
Rev 3:17 pitiful, **p**, blind and naked.
13:16 small and great, rich and **p**, free

Poorest (Poor)
2Ki 24:14 the **p** people of the land were left.
25:12 some of the **p** people of the land
Isa 14:30 The **p** of the poor will find pasture,
Jer 40: 7 women and children who were the **p** in
52:15 into exile some of the **p** people
52:16 rest of the **p** people of the land

Poplar (Poplars)
Ge 30:37 took fresh-cut branches from **p**,
Isa 44: 4 like **p** trees by flowing streams.
Hos 4:13 under oak, **p** and terebinth, where

Poplars (Poplar)
Lev 23:40 leafy branches and **p**, and rejoice
Job 40:22 the **p** by the stream surround him.
Ps 137: 2 There on the **p** we hung our harps,
Isa 15: 7 carry away over the Ravine of the **P**.

Populace (Population)
2Ki 25:11 along with the rest of the **p** and

Population (Populace)
Pr 14:28 A large **p** is a king's glory, but

Poratha
Est 9: 8 **P**, Adalia, Aridatha,

Porch (Portico, Porticoes)
Jdg 3:23 Ehud went out to the **p**; he shut the
Joel 2:17 between the temple **p** and the altar.

Porcius
Ac 24:27 Felix was succeeded by **P** Festus, but

Porphyry
Est 1: 6 silver on a mosaic pavement of **p**,

Port
Jnh 1: 3 he found a ship bound for that **p**.

Portent
Ps 71: 7 I have become like a **p** to many, but
Isa 20: 3 a sign and **p** against Egypt and Cush,

Portico (Porch)
1Ki 6: 3 The **p** at the front of the main hall
7: 6 In front of it was a **p**, and in front
7:12 the temple of the LORD with its **p**.
7:19 on top of the pillars in the **p**
7:21 He erected the pillars at the **p** of
1Ch 28:11 the plans for the **p** of the temple,
2Ch 3: 4 The **p** at the front of the temple was
8:12 that he had built in front of the **p**,
15: 8 front of the **p** of the LORD's temple.
29: 7 They also shut the doors of the **p**
29:17 they reached the **p** of the LORD.
Eze 8:16 between the **p** and the altar, were
40: 7 **p** facing the temple was one rod deep.
40: 8 he measured the **p** of the gateway;
40: 9 **p** of the gateway faced the temple.
40:14 up to the **p** facing the courtyard.
40:15 far end of its **p** was fifty cubits.
40:16 openings all round, as was the **p**;
40:21 its **p** had the same measurements as
40:22 Its openings, its **p** and its palm
40:22 up to it, with its **p** opposite them.
40:24 He measured its jambs and its **p**, and
40:25 The gateway and its **p** had narrow
40:26 Seven steps led up to it, with its **p**
40:29 its projecting walls and its **p** had
40:29 The gateway and its **p** had openings
40:31 Its **p** faced the outer court;
40:33 its projecting walls and its **p** had
40:33 The gateway and its **p** had openings
40:34 Its **p** faced the outer court;
40:36 its projecting walls and its **p**,
40:37 Its **p** faced the outer court; palm
40:38 A room with a doorway was by the **p**
40:39 In the **p** of the gateway were two
40:40 By the outside wall of the **p** of the
40:48 He brought me to the **p** of the temple
40:48 and measured the jambs of the **p**;
40:49 The **p** was twenty cubits wide, and
41:15 and the **p** facing the court,
41:25 overhang on the front of the **p**.
41:26 On the side walls of the **p** were
44: 3 He is to enter by way of the **p** of
46: 2 through the **p** of the gateway
46: 8 he is to go in through the **p** of the

Porticoes (Porch)
Eze 40:30 (The **p** of the gateways around the

Portion (Apportioned, Portions)
Ge 43:34 Benjamin's **p** was five times as much
Lev 2: 2 and burn this as a memorial **p** on the
2: 9 He shall take out the memorial **p**
2:16 The priest shall burn the memorial **p**
5:12 a handful of it as a memorial **p**
6:15 and burn the memorial **p** on the altar
7:35 This is the **p** of the offerings made
24: 7 a memorial **p** to represent the bread
Nu 15:19 a **p** as an offering to the LORD.
18: 8 sons as your **p** and regular share.
18:28 the LORD's **p** to Aaron the priest.
18:29 You must present as the LORD's **p** the
Dt 26:13 removed from my house the sacred **p**
26:14 I have not eaten any of the sacred **p**
32: 9 For the LORD's **p** is his people,
33:21 the leader's **p** was kept for him.
Jos 15:13 Jephunneh a **p** in Judah—Kiriath Arba,
17:14 and one **p** for an inheritance?
18: 7 The Levites, however, do not get a **p**
19: 9 Judah's **p** was more than they needed.
1Sa 1: 5 to Hannah he gave a double **p** because
2Ki 2: 9 inherit a double **p** of your spirit,"
1Ch 16:18 Canaan as the **p** you will inherit."
2Ch 30:22 days they ate their assigned **p**
31: 4 to give the **p** due to the priests
Ne 12:47 They also set aside the **p** for the
12:47 the **p** for the descendants of Aaron.
Job 24:18 their **p** of the land is cursed,
Ps 16: 5 LORD, you have assigned me my **p** and
73:26 of my heart and my **p** for ever.
105:11 Canaan as the **p** you will inherit."
119:57 You are my **p**, O LORD; I have
142: 5 my **p** in the land of the living."
Isa 17:14 This is the **p** of those who loot us,
53:12 Therefore I will give him a **p** among
57: 6 stones of the ravines are your **p**;
61: 7 my people will receive a double **p**,
61: 7 inherit a double **p** in their land,
Jer 6: 3 round her, each tending his own **p**."
10:16 He who is the **P** of Jacob is not like
13:25 This is your lot, the **p** I have
51:19 He who is the **P** of Jacob is not like
Lam 3:24 I say to myself, "The LORD is my **p**;
Eze 44:30 You are to give them the first **p** of
45: 1 present to the LORD a **p** of the land
45: 4 will be the sacred **p** of the land for
45: 6 adjoining the sacred **p**; it will
45:14 The prescribed **p** of oil, measured by
48: 1 Dan will have one **p**; it will follow
48: 2 "Asher will have one **p**; it will
48: 3 "Naphtali will have one **p**; it will
48: 4 "Manasseh will have one **p**; it will
48: 5 "Ephraim will have one **p**; it will
48: 6 "Reuben will have one **p**; it will
48: 7 "Judah will have one **p**; it will
48: 8 the **p** you are to present as a
48: 9 "The special **p** you are to offer to
48:10 This will be the sacred **p** for the
48:12 them from the sacred **p** of the land,
48:12 a most holy **p**, bordering the
48:18 bordering on the sacred **p** and
48:20 The entire **p** will be a square, 25,000
48:20 you will set aside the sacred **p**,
48:21 of the area formed by the sacred **p**
48:21 the sacred **p** to the eastern border,
48:21 sacred **p** with the temple sanctuary
48:23 Benjamin will have one **p**; it will
48:24 "Simeon will have one **p**; it will
48:25 "Issachar will have one **p**; it will
48:26 "Zebulun will have one **p**; it will
48:27 "Gad will have one **p**; it will border
Zec 2:12 The LORD will inherit Judah as his **p**
Rev 18: 6 Mix her a double **p** from her own cup.

Portions (Portion)
Ge 4: 4 Abel brought fat **p** from some of the
43:34 **p** were served to them from Joseph's
Lev 8:26 on the fat **p** and on the right thigh.
9:19 the fat **p** of the ox and the ram—the
9:24 offering and the fat **p** on the altar.
10:15 fat **p** of the offerings made by fire,
Jos 19:49 the land into its allotted **p**,
1Sa 1: 4 he would give **p** of the meat to his
2Ch 7: 7 the grain offerings and the fat **p**.
31:19 distribute **p** to every male among
35:14 and the fat **p** until nightfall.
Ne 8:12 to send **p** of food and to celebrate
12:44 the **p** required by the Law for the
12:47 **p** for the singers and gatekeepers.
13:10 I also learned that the **p** assigned
Pr 31:15 family and **p** for her servant girls.
Ecc 11: 2 Give **p** to seven, yes to eight, for
Isa 34:17 He allots their **p**; his hand
Eze 45: 7 parallel to one of the tribal **p**.
47:13 of Israel, with two **p** for Joseph.

Eze 48: 8 west will equal one of the tribal **p**;
48:21 tribal **p** will belong to the prince,
48:29 and these will be their **p**,"

Portrait
Mt 22:20 he asked them, "Whose **p** is this?
Mk 12:16 he asked them, "Whose **p** is this?
Lk 20:24 Whose **p** and inscription are on it?"

Portrayed
Eze 8:10 and I saw **p** all over the walls all
23:14 She saw men **p** on a wall, figures of
23:14 wall, figures of Chaldeans **p** in red,
Gal 3: 1 Christ was clearly **p** as crucified.

Ports
Ac 27: 2 about to sail for **p** along the coast

Poses
Jer 29:27 who **p** as a prophet among you?

Position (Positions)
Ge 40:13 your head and restore you to your **p**,
40:21 the chief cupbearer to his **p**,
41:13 I was restored to my **p**, and the
Jos 8:19 from their **p** and rushed forward.
Jdg 7:21 While each man held his **p** around the
9:44 **p** at the entrance to the city gate.
2Sa 3: 6 his own **p** in the house of Saul.
1Ki 2:35 Jehoiada over the army in Joab's **p**
15:13 Maacah from her **p** as queen mother,
20:22 "Strengthen your **p** and see what must
2Ch 12: 1 After Rehoboam's **p** as king was
15:16 Maacah from her **p** as queen mother,
Est 1:19 give her royal **p** to someone else
4:14 you have come to royal **p** for such a
Isa 22:19 and you will be ousted from your **p**.
Da 2:48 the king placed Daniel in a high **p**
5:19 of the high **p** he gave him, all the
Ro 12:16 to associate with people of low **p**.
Jas 1: 9 ought to take pride in his high **p**.
1:10 rich should take pride in his low **p**,
2Pe 3:17 men and fall from your secure **p**.

Positions (Position)
Jos 3: 3 move out from your **p** and follow it.
8:13 They had the soldiers take up their **p**
10: 5 took up **p** against Gibeon and
10:31 he took up **p** against it and attacked
10:34 they took up **p** against it and
Jdg 9:34 took up concealed **p** near Shechem in
20:20 took up battle **p** against them at
20:22 again took up their **p** where they had
20:30 took up **p** against Gibeah as they had
20:33 places and took up **p** at Baal Tamar,
1Sa 17:20 going out to its battle **p**, shouting
1Ch 9:22 to their **p** of trust by David
2Ch 7: 6 The priests took their **p**, as did the
14:10 and they took up battle **p** in the
20:17 Take up your **p**; stand firm and see
30:16 they took up their regular **p** as
Ecc 10: 6 Fools are put in many high **p**, while
Jer 46: 4 Take your **p** with helmets on!
46:14 'Take your **p** and get ready, for the
50: 9 They will take up their **p** against
50:14 "Take up your **p** round Babylon, all
Eze 23:24 they will take up **p** against you on
Jude : 6 the angels who did not keep their **p**

Possess (Possessed, Possessing, Possession, Possessions, Possessor)
Ge 24:60 **p** the gates of their enemies."
Lev 20:24 I said to you, "You will **p** their
25:32 the Levitical towns, which they **p**.
Nu 27:11 in his clan, that he may **p** it.
33:53 for I have given you the land to **p**.
35: 2 inheritance the Israelites will **p**.
35: 8 from the land the Israelites **p** are
36: 8 **p** the inheritance of his fathers.
Dt 2:31 Now begin to conquer and **p** his land."
4:14 you are crossing the Jordan to **p**.
4:26 you are crossing the Jordan to **p**.
5:31 in the land I am giving them to **p**."
Dt 5:33 days in the land that you will **p**.
6: 1 you are crossing the Jordan to **p**,
7: 1 into the land you are entering to **p**
8: 1 increase and may enter and **p** the
9: 6 is giving you this good land to **p**,
10:11 so that they may enter and **p** the
11: 8 you are crossing the Jordan to **p**,
11:29 into the land you are entering to **p**,
12: 1 has given you to **p**—as long as you
15: 4 giving you to **p** as your inheritance,
16:20 so that you may live and **p** the land
19: 2 LORD your God is giving you to **p**.
19:14 LORD your God is giving you to **p**.
21: 1 LORD your God is giving you to **p**,
23:20 in the land you are entering to **p**.
25:19 giving you to **p** as an inheritance,
28:21 from the land you are entering to **p**.
28:63 from the land you are entering to **p**.
30:16 in the land you are entering to **p**.
30:18 crossing the Jordan to enter and **p**.
31:13 you are crossing the Jordan to **p**."
32:47 you are crossing the Jordan to **p**."
Jos 22:19 If the land you **p** is defiled, come
Jdg 11:24 LORD our God has given us, we will **p**.
1Ch 28: 8 that you may **p** this good land and
Ezr 7:25 wisdom of your God, which you **p**,
9:11 'The land you are entering to **p** is a
Ne 9:23 told their fathers to enter and **p**.
Ps 69:35 people will settle there and **p** it;
Pr 8:12 I **p** knowledge and discretion.
Isa 14: 2 And the house of Israel will **p** the
34:11 desert owl and screech owl will **p** it;
34:17 They will **p** it for ever and dwell
57:13 the land and **p** my holy mountain."
60:21 and they will **p** the land for ever.
65: 9 those who will **p** my mountains;
Jer 11: 5 and honey'—the land you **p** today.
30: 3 forefathers to **p**,' says the LORD."
32: 8 it and **p** it, buy it for yourself.
Eze 33:25 blood, should you then **p** the land?
33:26 Should you then **p** the land?'
36:12 They will **p** you, and you will be
45: 8 **p** the land according to their tribes.
Da 7:18 kingdom and will **p** it for ever—yes,
Am 9:12 that they may **p** the remnant of Edom
Ob :17 of Jacob will **p** its inheritance.
:19 will **p** the land of the Philistines.
:19 Samaria, and Benjamin will **p** Gilead.
:20 will **p** the land as far as Zarephath;
:20 will **p** the towns of the Negev.
Jn 5:39 that by them you **p** eternal life.
Ac 7: 5 after him would **p** the land,
1Co 8: 1 We know that we all **p** knowledge.
13: 3 If I give all I **p** to the poor and
2Pe 1: 8 For if you **p** these qualities in

Possessed (Possess)
Ps 105:21 his household, ruler over all he **p**,
Isa 63:18 your people **p** your holy place,
Jer 16:19 "Our fathers **p** nothing but false
Eze 33:24 was only one man, yet he **p** the land.
Da 7:22 time came when they **p** the kingdom.
Mk 1:23 was **p** by an evil spirit cried out,
3:22 "He is **p** by Beelzebub! By the prince
5:15 they saw the man who had been **p** by
7:25 a woman whose little daughter was **p**
9:17 I brought you my son, who is **p** by a
Lk 4:33 In the synagogue there was a man **p**
Jn 8:49 "I am not **p** by a demon," said Jesus,
10:21 the sayings of a man **p** by a demon.

Possessing (Possess)
2Co 6:10 nothing, and yet **p** everything.

Possession (Possess)
Ge 15: 7 give you this land to take **p** of it."
15: 8 I know that I shall gain **p** of it?"
17: 8 I will give as an everlasting **p** to
22:17 take **p** of the cities of their
28: 4 so that you may take **p** of the land
30:33 Any goat in my **p** that is not
48: 4 as an everlasting **p** to your
Ex 6: 8 I will give it to you as a **p**. I am
19: 5 nations you will be my treasured **p**.
22: 4 animal is found alive in his **p**—
Ex 22: 9 In all cases of illegal **p** of an ox,
23:30 enough to take **p** of the land.
Lev 14:34 which I am giving you as your **p**, and
25:24 the country that you hold as a **p**,
25:28 what he sold will remain in the **p** of
25:34 be sold; it is their permanent **p**.
Nu 13:30 "We should go up and take **p** of the
21:35 And they took **p** of his land.
32: 5 be given to your servants as our **p**.
32:22 land will be your **p** before the LORD.
32:29 them the land of Gilead as their **p**.
32:30 accept their **p** with you in Canaan."
33:53 Take **p** of the land and settle in it,
Dt 1: 8 Go in and take **p** of the land that
1:21 Go up and take **p** of it as the LORD,
1:39 to them and they will take **p** of it.
2: 9 Ar to the descendants of Lot as a **p**."
2:12 land the LORD gave them as their **p**.)
2:19 for I will not give you **p** of any
2:19 as a **p** to the descendants of Lot."
2:24 Begin to take **p** of it and engage
3:18 given you this land to take **p** of it.
3:20 go back to the **p** I have given you."
4: 1 take **p** of the land that the LORD,
4: 5 you are entering to take **p** of it.
4:22 over and take **p** of that good land.
4:47 They took **p** of his land and the land
7: 6 to be his people, his treasured **p**.
9: 4 to take **p** of this land because of my
9: 5 going in to take **p** of their land;
9:23 take **p** of the land I have given you.
11:11 to take **p** of is a land of mountains
11:31 take **p** of the land the LORD your God
14: 2 chosen you to be his treasured **p**.
16: 4 Let no yeast be found in your **p** in
17:14 taken **p** of it and settled in it,
24:12 to sleep with his pledge in your **p**.
26: 1 taken **p** of it and settled in it,
26:18 his treasured **p** as he promised, and
30: 5 fathers, and you will take **p** of it.
31: 3 and you will take **p** of their land.
32:49 the Israelites as their own **p**.
33: 4 the **p** of the assembly of Jacob.
Jos 1:11 take **p** of the land the LORD your God
1:15 and until they too have taken **p** of
12: 6 of Manasseh to be their **p**.
18: 3 to take **p** of the land that the LORD,
19:47 taking **p** of their territory,
21:12 to Caleb son of Jephunneh as his **p**.
21:43 they took **p** of it and settled there.
23: 5 and you will take **p** of their land,
24: 8 you, and you took **p** of their land.
Jdg 1:19 They took **p** of the hill country, but
2: 6 they went to take **p** of the land,
3:13 they took **p** of the City of Palms.
3:28 taking **p** of the fords of the Jordan
8: 6 of Zebah and Zalmunna in your **p**?
8:15 of Zebah and Zalmunna in your **p**?
1Ki 21:15 "Get up and take **p** of the vineyard
21:16 down to take **p** of Naboth's vineyard.
21:18 where he has gone to take **p** of it.
2Ch 20:11 the **p** you gave us as an inheritance.
Ne 9:15 you told them to go in and take **p** of
9:24 Their sons went in and took **p** of the
9:25 they took **p** of houses filled with
Ps 2: 8 the ends of the earth your **p**.
73: 9 their tongues take **p** of the earth.
83:12 who said, "Let us take **p** of the
135: 4 own, Israel to be his treasured **p**.
Jer 32:23 They came in and took **p** of it, but
49: 1 Why then has Molech taken **p** of Gad?
Eze 7:24 nations to take **p** of their houses;
11:15 this land was given to us as our **p**.'
25: 4 to the people of the East as a **p**.
25:10 to the people of the East as a **p**,
33:24 land has been given to us as our **p**.'
35:10 be ours and we will take **p** of them,"
36: 2 ancient heights have become our **p**.
36: 3 the **p** of the rest of the nations
36: 5 they made my land their own **p** so
44:28 no **p** in Israel; I will be their **p**.
45: 5 as their **p** for towns to live in.
45: 8 This land will be his **p** in Israel.
Mic 2: 4 my people's **p** is divided up.
Mal 3:17 day when I make up my treasured **p**.
Eph 1:14 redemption of those who are God's **p**

Possessions (Possess)

Ge 12: 5 his nephew Lot, all the **p** they had
13: 6 for their **p** were so great that they
14:12 off Abram's nephew Lot and his **p**,
14:16 back his relative Lot and his **p**,
15:14 they will come out with great **p**.
32:23 the stream, he sent over all his **p**.
36: 7 Their **p** were too great for them to
46: 6 the **p** they had acquired in Canaan,
Nu 16:32 and all Korah's men and all their **p**.
Dt 12:11 choice **p** you have vowed to the LORD.
18: 8 money from the sale of family **p**.
Jos 7:11 they have put them with their own **p**.
Jdg 18:21 their livestock and their **p** in front
1Ki 13: 8 if you were to give me half your **p**,
2Ch 31: 3 The king contributed from his own **p**
35: 7 cattle—all from the king's own **p**.
Ezr 8:21 us and our children, with all our **p**.
Ne 5:13 God shake out of his house and **p**
Job 15:29 nor will his **p** spread over the land.
Pr 12:27 but the diligent man prizes his **p**.
Ecc 5:19 when God gives any man wealth and **p**,
6: 2 God gives a man wealth, **p** and honour,
Zec 9: 4 the Lord will take away her **p** and
Mt 12:29 carry off his **p** unless he first ties
19:21 go, sell your **p** and give to the poor,
24:47 will put him in charge of all his **p**.
Mk 3:27 carry off his **p** unless he first ties
Lk 11:21 his own house, his **p** are safe.
12:15 consist in the abundance of his **p**."
12:33 Sell your **p** and give to the poor.
12:44 will put him in charge of all his **p**.
16: 1 was accused of wasting his **p**.
19: 8 now I give half of my **p** to the poor,
Ac 2:45 Selling their **p** and goods, they gave
4:32 No-one claimed that any of his **p** was
2Co 12:14 what I want is not your **p** but you.
Heb 10:34 yourselves had better and lasting **p**.
1Jn 3:17 If anyone has material **p** and sees

Possessor (Possess)

Ecc 7:12 wisdom preserves the life of its **p**.

Possible

Ne 5: 8 said: "As far as **p**, we have bought
Mt 19:26 but with God all things are **p**."
24:24 even the elect—if that were **p**.
26:39 "My Father, if it is **p**, may this
26:42 "My Father, if it is not **p** for this
Mk 9:23 is **p** for him who believes."
10:27 all things are **p** with God."
13:22 deceive the elect—if that were **p**.
14:35 if **p** the hour might pass from him.
14:36 he said, "everything is **p** for you.
Lk 18:27 impossible with men is **p** with God."
Ac 17:15 Timothy to join him as soon as **p**.
20:16 if **p**, by the day of Pentecost.
26: 9 do all that was **p** to oppose the
Ro 12:18 If it is **p**, as far as it depends on
13: 5 not only because of **p** punishment but
1Co 6: 5 Is it **p** that there is nobody among
9:19 to everyone, to win as many as **p**.
9:22 by all **p** means I might save some.

Post (Posted, Posting, Posts)

Jos 10:18 and **p** some men there to guard it.
Ecc 10: 4 against you, do not leave your **p**;
Isa 21: 6 "Go, **p** a lookout and have him report
21: 8 every night I stay at my **p**.

Posted (Post)

2Ki 10:24 Now Jehu had **p** eighty men outside
11:18 **p** guards at the temple of the LORD.
Ne 4: 9 we prayed to our God and **p** a guard
4:16 The officers **p** themselves behind all
Isa 22: 7 horsemen are **p** at the city gates;
62: 6 I have **p** watchmen on your walls,

Posterity

Ps 21:10 the earth, their **p** from mankind.
22:30 **P** will serve him; future generations

Posting (Post)

Ne 4:13 **p** them by families, with their
Mt 27:66 a seal on the stone and **p** the guard.

Posts[1] (Post)

2Ch 35:15 gate did not need to leave their **p**,
Ne 7: 3 some at their **p** and some near their
13:11 and stationed them at their **p**.

Posts[2] (Gatepost, Gateposts)

Ex 26:32 Hang it with gold hooks on four **p** of
26:37 **p** of acacia wood overlaid with gold.
27:10 with twenty **p** and twenty bronze
27:10 silver hooks and bands on the **p**.
27:11 with twenty **p** and twenty bronze
27:11 silver hooks and bands on the **p**.
27:12 curtains, with ten **p** and ten bases.
27:14 with three **p** and three bases,
27:15 side, with three **p** and three bases.
27:16 with four **p** and four bases.
27:17 All the **p** around the courtyard are
35:11 frames, crossbars, **p** and bases;
35:17 the courtyard with its **p** and bases,
36:36 They made four **p** of acacia wood for
36:38 they made five **p** with hooks for them.
36:38 They overlaid the tops of the **p** and
38:10 with twenty **p** and twenty bronze
38:10 silver hooks and bands on the **p**.
38:11 twenty **p** and twenty bronze bases,
38:11 silver hooks and bands on the **p**.
38:12 with ten **p** and ten bases, with
38:12 silver hooks and bands on the **p**.
38:14 with three **p** and three bases,
38:15 with three **p** and three bases.
38:17 The bases for the **p** were bronze.
38:17 The hooks and bands on the **p** were
38:17 **p** of the courtyard had silver bands.
38:19 with four **p** and four bronze bases.
38:28 shekels to make the hooks for the **p**,
38:28 to overlay the tops of the **p**, and
39:33 frames, crossbars, **p** and bases;
39:40 the courtyard with its **p** and bases,
40:18 the crossbars and set up the **p**.
Nu 3:36 its crossbars, **p**, bases, all its
3:37 as well as the **p** of the surrounding
4:31 its crossbars, **p** and bases,
4:32 as well as the **p** of the surrounding
Jdg 16: 3 together with the two **p**, and tore
SS 3:10 Its **p** he made of silver, its base of

Pot (Pots, Potsherd, Potsherds, Potter, Potter's, Potters, Pottery)

Lev 6:28 The clay **p** that the meat is cooked
6:28 but if it is cooked in a bronze **p**,
6:28 the **p** is to be scoured and rinsed
11:33 If one of them falls into a clay **p**,
11:33 unclean, and you must break the **p**.
11:34 on it from such a **p** is unclean,
11:35 oven or cooking **p** must be broken up.
14: 5 killed over fresh water in a clay **p**.
14:50 birds over fresh water in a clay **p**.
15:12 "'A clay **p** that the man touches
Nu 11: 8 They cooked it in a **p** or made it
Jdg 6:19 in a basket and its broth in a **p**,
1Sa 2:14 the pan or kettle or cauldron or **p**,
2Ki 4:38 "Put on the large **p** and cook some
4:39 he cut them up into the **p** of stew,
4:40 of God, there is death in the **p**!"
4:41 He put it into the **p** and said,
4:41 there was nothing harmful in the **p**.
Job 41:20 a boiling **p** over a fire of reeds.
41:31 up the sea like a **p** of ointment.
Ecc 7: 6 crackling of thorns under the **p**,
Isa 29:16 Can the **p** say of the potter, "He
Jer 1:13 "I see a boiling **p**, tilting away
18: 4 the **p** he was shaping from the clay
18: 4 the potter formed it into another **p**,
22:28 broken **p**, an object no-one wants?
Eze 11: 3 a cooking **p**, and we are the meat.'
11: 7 this city is the **p**, but I will
11:11 This city will not be a **p** for you,
24: 3 "'Put on the cooking **p**; put it on
24: 6 to the **p** now encrusted, whose
24:11 set the empty **p** on the coals till it
Mic 3: 3 for the pan, like flesh for the **p**."
Zec 14:21 Every **p** in Jerusalem and Judah will

Potent

Isa 47: 9 sorceries and all your **p** spells.

Potiphar

Egyptian official who bought Joseph (Ge 37:36; 39:1) and made him chief steward (Ge 39:2–6). Sent him to prison (Ge 39:7–20).

Ge 37:36 Midianites sold Joseph in Egypt to **P**,
39: 1 **P**, an Egyptian who was one of
39: 4 **P** put him in charge of his household,
39: 5 of the LORD was on everything **P** had,

Potiphera

Ge 41:45 Asenath daughter of **P**, priest of On,
41:50 Asenath daughter of **P**, priest of On.
46:20 Asenath daughter of **P**, priest of On.

Pots (Pot)

Ex 16: 3 There we sat round **p** of meat and ate
27: 3 bronze—its **p** to remove the ashes,
38: 3 all its utensils of bronze—its **p**,
1Ki 7:45 the **p**, shovels and sprinkling bowls.
2Ki 25:14 They also took away the **p**, shovels,
2Ch 4:11 He also made the **p** and shovels and
4:16 the **p**, shovels, meat forks and all
35:13 and boiled the holy offerings in **p**,
Ps 58: 9 Before your **p** can feel the heat of
Isa 65: 4 whose **p** hold broth of unclean meat;
Jer 52:18 They also took away the **p**, shovels,
52:19 censers, sprinkling bowls, **p**,
Lam 4: 2 are now considered as **p** of clay, the
Zec 14:20 and the cooking **p** in the LORD's
14:21 take some of the **p** and cook in them.

Potsherd (Pot)

Ps 22:15 My strength is dried up like a **p**,
Isa 45: 9 to him who is but a **p** among the
Jer 19: 2 near the entrance of the **P** Gate.

Potsherds (Pot)

Job 41:30 His undersides are jagged **p**, leaving
Isa 45: 9 potsherd among the **p** on the ground.

Potter (Pot)

Isa 29:16 as if the **p** were thought to be like
29:16 Can the pot say of the **p**, "He knows
41:25 as if he were a **p** treading the clay.
45: 9 Does the clay say to the **p**, 'What
64: 8 We are the clay, you are the **p**;
Jer 18: 4 so the **p** formed it into another pot,
18: 6 as this **p** does?" declares the LORD.
18: 6 "Like clay in the hand of the **p**, so
19: 1 "Go and buy a clay jar from a **p**.
Zec 11:13 "Throw it to the **p**"—the handsome
11:13 into the house of the LORD to the **p**.
Ro 9:21 Does not the **p** have the right to

Potter's (Pot)

Jer 18: 2 "Go down to the **p** house, and there I
18: 3 I went down to the **p** house, and I
19:11 this city just as this **p** jar is
Lam 4: 2 pots of clay, the work of a **p** hands!
Mt 27: 7 to use the money to buy the **p** field
27:10 they used them to buy the **p** field,

Potters (Pot)

1Ch 4:23 They were the **p** who lived at Netaim

Pottery (Pot)

2Sa 17:28 bedding and bowls and articles of **p**.
Job 2: 8 Job took a piece of broken **p** and
Ps 2: 9 will dash them to pieces like **p**."
31:12 I have become like broken **p**.
Isa 30:14 will break in pieces like **p**,
Jer 25:34 fall and be shattered like fine **p**.
Ro 9:21 of clay some **p** for noble purposes
Rev 2:27 he will dash them to pieces like **p**'—

Pouch (Pouches)
Ge 42:35 there in each man's sack was his **p**
1Sa 17:40 put them in the **p** of his shepherd's

Pouches (Pouch)
Ge 42:35 the money **p**, they were frightened.

Poultice
2Ki 20: 7 Isaiah said, "Prepare a **p** of figs."
Isa 38:21 Isaiah had said, "Prepare a **p** of

Poultry
Ne 5:18 six choice sheep and some **p** were

Pounce (Pounced)
1Sa 15:19 Why did you **p** on the plunder and do
Isa 33: 4 like a swarm of locusts men **p** on it.

Pounced (Pounce)
1Sa 14:32 They **p** on the plunder and, taking

Pound (Pounded, Pounding, Pounds)
SS 5: 4 my heart began to **p** for him.

Pounded (Pound)
2Sa 22:43 I **p** and trampled them like mud in
Hab 3:16 I heard and my heart **p**, my lips

Pounding (Pound)
Jdg 19:22 **P** on the door, they shouted to the
Ps 93: 3 seas have lifted up their **p** waves.
Ac 27:41 to pieces by the **p** of the surf.

Pounds[1] (Pound)
Job 37: 1 "At this my heart **p** and leaps from
Ps 38:10 My heart **p**, my strength fails me;
Jer 4:19 My heart **p** within me, I cannot keep

Pounds[2]
Jn 19:39 and aloes, about seventy-five **p**.
Rev 16:21 a hundred **p** each fell upon men.

Pour (Downpour, Outpoured, Outpouring, Poured, Pouring, Pours)
Ex 4: 9 the Nile and **p** it on the dry ground.
29:12 and **p** out the rest of it at the base
30: 9 and do not **p** a drink offering on it.
30:32 Do not **p** it on men's bodies and do
Lev 2: 1 is to **p** oil on it, put incense on
2: 6 Crumble it and **p** oil on it; it is a
4: 7 he shall **p** out at the base of the
4:18 The rest of the blood he shall **p** out
4:25 **p** out the rest of the blood at the
4:30 **p** out the rest of the blood at the
4:34 **p** out the rest of the blood at the
14:15 **p** it in the palm of his own left
14:26 The priest is to **p** some of the oil
Nu 5:15 He must not **p** oil on it or put
19:17 a jar and **p** fresh water over them.
20: 8 eyes and it will **p** out its water.
28: 7 **P** out the drink offering to the LORD
Dt 12:16 **p** it out on the ground like water.
12:24 **p** it out on the ground like water.
15:23 **p** it out on the ground like water.
Jdg 6:20 on this rock, and **p** out the broth.
1Ki 18:33 **p** it on the offering and on the wood.
2Ki 3:11 to **p** water on the hands of Elijah."
4: 4 **P** oil into all the jars, and as each
9: 3 take the flask and **p** the oil on his
Job 3:24 of food; my groans **p** out like water.
10:10 Did you not **p** me out like milk and
15:13 **p** out such words from your mouth?
16:20 as my eyes **p** out tears to God;
36:28 the clouds **p** down their moisture and
Ps 16: 4 I will not **p** out their libations of
19: 2 Day after day they **p** forth speech;
42: 4 These things I remember as I **p** out
62: 8 O people; **p** out your hearts to him,
69:24 **P** out your wrath on them; let your
79: 6 **P** out your wrath on the nations that
94: 4 They **p** out arrogant words; all the
104:10 He makes springs **p** water into the
Ps 142: 2 I **p** out my complaint before him;
Ecc 11: 3 water, they **p** rain upon the earth.
Isa 44: 3 For I will **p** water on the thirsty
44: 3 **p** out my Spirit on your offspring,
46: 6 Some **p** out gold from their bags and
Jer 6:11 "**P** it out on the children in the
7:18 They **p** out drink offerings to other
10:25 **P** out your wrath on the nations that
14:16 I will **p** out on them the calamity
44:17 will **p** out drink offerings to her
44:25 **p** out drink offerings to the Queen
48:12 "when I will send men who **p** from
48:12 and they will **p** her out; they will
Lam 2:19 **p** out your heart like water in the
Eze 7: 8 I am about to **p** out my wrath on you
14:19 **p** out my wrath upon it through
20: 8 So I said I would **p** out my wrath on
20:13 So I said I would **p** out my wrath on
20:21 So I said I would **p** out my wrath on
21:31 I will **p** out my wrath upon you and
22:31 I will **p** out my wrath on them and
24: 3 put it on and **p** water into it.
24: 7 she did not **p** it on the ground,
30:15 I will **p** out my wrath on Pelusium,
38:22 I will **p** down torrents of rain,
39:29 for I will **p** out my Spirit on the
Hos 5:10 I will **p** out my wrath on them like a
9: 4 They will not **p** out wine offerings
Joel 2:28 "And afterwards, I will **p** out my
2:29 I will **p** out my Spirit in those days.
Mic 1: 6 I will **p** her stones into the valley
Zep 3: 8 to gather the kingdoms and to **p** out
Zec 4:12 gold pipes that **p** out golden oil?"
12:10 "And I will **p** out on the house of
Mal 3:10 **p** out so much blessing that you will
Mt 9:17 Neither do men **p** new wine into old
9:17 No, they **p** new wine into new
Ac 2:17 I will **p** out my Spirit on all people.
2:18 I will **p** out my Spirit in those
Rev 16: 1 "Go, **p** out the seven bowls of God's

Poured (Pour)
Ge 28:18 as a pillar and **p** oil on top of it.
35:14 and he **p** out a drink offering on it;
35:14 offering on it; he also **p** oil on it.
Ex 8:24 of flies **p** into Pharaoh's palace
9:33 rain no longer **p** down on the land.
Lev 8:12 He **p** some of the anointing oil on
8:15 He **p** out the rest of the blood at
9: 9 he **p** out at the base of the altar.
21:10 had the anointing oil **p** on his head
Dt 12:27 must be **p** beside the altar of the
Jdg 5: 4 heavens **p**, the clouds **p** down water.
Ru 3:15 When she did so, he **p** into it six
1Sa 7: 6 water and **p** it out before the LORD.
10: 1 Samuel took a flask of oil and **p** it
2Sa 21:10 till the rain **p** down from the
23:16 he **p** it out before the LORD.
1Ki 13: 3 and the ashes on it will be **p** out."
13: 5 its ashes **p** out according to the
2Ki 4:40 The stew was **p** out for the men, but
9: 6 Then the prophet **p** the oil on Jehu's
16:13 **p** out his drink offering, and
1Ch 11:18 he **p** it out before the LORD.
2Ch 12: 7 My wrath will not be **p** out on
34:21 LORD's anger that is **p** out on us
34:25 my anger will be **p** out on this place
Job 29: 6 **p** out for me streams of olive oil.
Ps 18:42 I **p** them out like mud in the streets.
22:14 I am **p** out like water, and all my
68: 8 the earth shook, the heavens **p** down
77:17 The clouds **p** down water, the skies
79: 3 They have **p** out blood like water all
92:10 fine oils have been **p** upon me.
133: 2 is like precious oil **p** on the head,
Pr 1:23 I would have **p** out my heart to you
25:20 or like vinegar **p** on soda, is one
Ecc 2:19 into which I have **p** my effort and
SS 1: 3 your name is like perfume **p** out.
Isa 19:14 The LORD has **p** into them a spirit of
32:15 till the Spirit is **p** upon us from on
42:25 he **p** out on them his burning anger,
53:12 because he **p** out his life unto death,
57: 6 Yes, to them you have **p** out drink
63: 6 and **p** their blood on the ground."
Jer 1:14 **p** out on all who live in the land.
7:20 wrath will be **p** out on this place,
19:13 **p** out drink offerings to other gods.
42:18 and wrath have been **p** out on those
42:18 so will my wrath be **p** out on you
44: 6 Therefore, my fierce anger was **p** out;
44:19 and **p** out drink offerings to her,
48:11 not **p** from one jar to another—
Lam 2: 4 he has **p** out his wrath like fire on
2:11 my heart is **p** out on the ground
4:11 he has **p** out his fierce anger.
Eze 16:36 Because you **p** out your wealth and
20:28 and **p** out their drink offerings.
22:22 LORD have **p** out my wrath upon you.
23: 8 bosom and **p** out their lust upon her.
24: 7 She **p** it on the bare rock; she did
36:18 I **p** out my wrath on them because
Da 9:11 the servant of God, have been **p** out
9:27 that is decreed is **p** out on him."
Na 1: 6 His wrath is **p** out like fire;
Zep 1:17 Their blood will be **p** out like dust
Mt 26: 7 which she **p** on his head as he was
26:12 she **p** this perfume on my body, she
26:28 which is **p** out for many for the
Mk 14: 3 jar and **p** the perfume on his head.
14: 8 She **p** perfume on my body beforehand
14:24 is **p** out for many," he said to them.
Lk 5:38 No, new wine must be **p** into new
6:38 over, will be **p** into your lap.
7:38 kissed them and **p** perfume on them.
7:46 but she has **p** perfume on my feet.
22:20 in my blood, which is **p** out for you.
Jn 11: 2 was the same one who **p** perfume on
12: 3 she **p** it on Jesus's feet and wiped
13: 5 After that, he **p** water into a basin
Ac 2:33 has **p** out what you now see and hear.
10:45 had been **p** out even on the Gentiles.
Ro 5: 5 because God has **p** out his love into
Php 2:17 even if I am being **p** out like a
1Ti 1:14 The grace of our Lord was **p** out on
2Ti 4: 6 For I am already being **p** out like a
Tit 3: 6 whom he **p** out on us generously
Rev 14:10 which has been **p** full strength into
16: 2 The first angel went and **p** out his
16: 3 The second angel **p** out his bowl on
16: 4 The third angel **p** out his bowl on
16: 8 The fourth angel **p** out his bowl on
16:10 The fifth angel **p** out his bowl on
16:12 The sixth angel **p** out his bowl on
16:17 The seventh angel **p** out his bowl

Pouring (Pour)
Ex 25:29 bowls for the **p** out of offerings.
29: 7 and anoint him by **p** it on his head.
37:16 for the **p** out of drink offerings.
1Sa 1:15 I was **p** out my soul to the LORD.
2Ki 4: 5 the jars to her and she kept **p**.
Jer 32:29 **p** out drink offerings to other gods.
44:18 and **p** out drink offerings to her,
44:19 and **p** out drink offerings to her?"
Hab 2:15 **p** it from the wineskin till they are
Lk 10:34 his wounds, **p** on oil and wine.

Pours (Pour)
Job 12:21 He **p** contempt on nobles and disarms
41:20 Smoke **p** from his nostrils as from a
Ps 75: 8 he **p** it out, and all the wicked of
102: T he is faint and **p** out his lament
107:40 he who **p** contempt on nobles made
Pr 6:19 a false witness who **p** out lies and a
14: 5 but a false witness **p** out lies.
19: 5 he who **p** out lies will not go free.
19: 9 and he who **p** out lies will perish.
Jer 6: 7 a well **p** out its water, so she **p** out
Am 5: 8 **p** them out over the face of the land
9: 6 **p** them out over the face of the land
Mk 2:22 no-one **p** new wine into old wineskins.
2:22 he **p** new wine into new wineskins."
Lk 5:37 no-one **p** new wine into old wineskins.

Poverty (Poor)
Dt 28:48 in nakedness and dire **p**, you will
1Sa 2: 7 The LORD sends **p** and wealth;
Pr 6:11 **p** will come on you like a bandit and
10:15 city, but **p** is the ruin of the poor.

Pr 11:24 withholds unduly, but comes to **p**.
13:18 He who ignores discipline comes to **p**
14:23 but mere talk leads only to **p**.
21: 5 as surely as haste leads to **p**.
22:16 gifts to the rich—both come to **p**.
24:34 **p** will come on you like a bandit and
28:19 fantasies will have his fill of **p**.
28:22 and is unaware that **p** awaits him.
30: 8 give me neither **p** nor riches,
31: 7 let them drink and forget their **p**
Ecc 4:14 been born in **p** within his kingdom.
Mk 12:44 out of her **p**, put in everything—all
Lk 21: 4 out of her **p** put in all she had to
2Co 8: 2 **p** welled up in rich generosity.
8: 9 you through his **p** might become rich.
Rev 2: 9 I know your afflictions and your **p**

Powder

Ex 30:36 Grind some of it to **p** and place it
32:20 in the fire; then he ground it to **p**,
Dt 9:21 Then I crushed it and ground it to **p**
28:24 of your country into dust and **p**;
2Ki 23: 6 He ground it to **p** and scattered the
23:15 the high place and ground it to **p**,
2Ch 34: 7 crushed the idols to **p** and cut to

Power (*Power of God*, Powerful, Powerfully, Powers)

Ge 31:29 I have the **p** to harm you; but last
49: 3 excelling in honour, excelling in **p**.
Ex 1: 8 about Joseph, came to **p** in Egypt.
4:21 I have given you the **p** to do.
9:16 that I might show you my **p** and that
14:31 the Israelites saw the great **p** the
15: 6 hand, O LORD, was majestic in **p**.
15:16 By the **p** of your arm they will be as
32:11 with great **p** and a mighty hand?
Nu 14:13 By your **p** you brought these people
Dt 7: 8 from the **p** of Pharaoh king of Egypt.
8:17 "My **p** and the strength of my hands
9:26 that you redeemed by your great **p**
9:29 great **p** and your outstretched arm."
34:12 no-one has ever shown the mighty **p**
Jdg 1:35 but when the **p** of the house of
3:12 Eglon king of Moab **p** over Israel.
6: 2 the **p** of Midian was so oppressive,
6: 9 I snatched you from the **p** of Egypt
14: 6 came upon him in **p** so that he tore
14:19 of the LORD came upon him in **p**.
15:14 of the LORD came upon him in **p**.
1Sa 7:14 from the **p** of the Philistines.
10: 6 of the LORD will come upon you in **p**,
10:10 Spirit of God came upon him in **p**,
10:18 and I delivered you from the **p** of
11: 6 him in **p**, and he burned with anger.
16:13 of the LORD came upon David in **p**.
1Ki 18:46 The **p** of the LORD came upon Elijah
2Ki 13: 3 under the **p** of Hazael king of Aram
13: 5 and they escaped from the **p** of Aram.
17: 7 the **p** of Pharaoh king of Egypt.
17:36 with mighty **p** and outstretched arm,
19:26 Their people, drained of **p**, are
1Ch 29:11 O LORD, is the greatness and the **p**
29:12 **p** to exalt and give strength to all.
29:30 with the details of his reign and **p**,
2Ch 13:20 Jeroboam did not regain **p** during the
20: 6 **P** and might are in your hand,
20:12 For we have no **p** to face this vast
25: 8 has the **p** to help or to overthrow."
32: 7 a greater **p** with us than with him.
36:20 the kingdom of Persia came to **p**.
Est 10: 2 all his acts of **p** and might,
Job 6:13 Do I have any **p** to help myself, now
9: 4 wisdom is profound, his **p** is vast.
10:16 display your awesome **p** against me.
12:13 "To God belong wisdom and **p**;
21: 7 on, growing old and increasing in **p**?
23: 6 Would he oppose me with great **p**?
24:22 God drags away the mighty by his **p**;
26:12 By his **p** he churned up the sea;
26:14 understand the thunder of his **p**?"
27:22 as he flees headlong from its **p**.
30:18 In his great **p** God becomes like
36:22 "God is exalted in his **p**. Who is a
37:23 beyond our reach and exalted in **p**;
Job 40:16 what **p** in the muscles of his belly!
Ps 20: 6 with the saving **p** of his right hand.
22:20 life from the **p** of the dogs.
37:17 for the **p** of the wicked will be
37:33 LORD will not leave them in their **p**
63: 2 and beheld your **p** and your glory.
65: 6 who formed the mountains by your **p**,
66: 3 So great is your **p** that your enemies
66: 7 He rules for ever by his **p**, his eyes
68:28 Summon your **p**, O God; show us your
68:34 Israel, whose **p** is in the skies.
68:35 gives **p** and strength to his people.
71:18 O God, till I declare your **p** to the
74:13 who split open the sea by your **p**;
77:14 display your **p** among the peoples.
78: 4 his **p**, and the wonders he has done.
78:26 led forth the south wind by his **p**.
78:42 They did not remember his **p**—the
89:13 Your arm is endued with **p**; your hand
89:48 himself from the **p** of the grave?
90:11 Who knows the **p** of your anger?
106: 8 sake, to make his mighty **p** known.
106:42 them and subjected them to their **p**.
111: 6 He has shown his people the **p** of his
145: 6 They will tell of the **p** of your
147: 5 Great is our Lord and mighty in **p**;
150: 2 Praise him for his acts of **p**; praise
Pr 3:27 it, when it is in your **p** to act.
8:14 I have understanding and **p**.
11: 7 from his **p** comes to nothing.
18:21 The tongue has the **p** of life and
24: 5 A wise man has great **p**, and a man of
28:12 when the wicked rise to **p**, men go
28:28 the wicked rise to **p**, people go into
30:26 conies are creatures of little **p**,
Ecc 4: 1 **p** was on the side of their
8: 8 No man has **p** over the wind to
8: 8 has **p** over the day of his death.
Isa 10:33 lop off the boughs with great **p**.
11: 2 the Spirit of counsel and of **p**, the
17: 3 and royal **p** from Damascus;
19: 4 over to the **p** of a cruel master,
33:13 you who are near, acknowledge my **p**!
37:27 Their people, drained of **p**, are
40:10 See, the Sovereign LORD comes with **p**,
40:26 Because of his great **p** and mighty
40:29 and increases the **p** of the weak.
47:14 themselves from the **p** of the flame.
63:12 who sent his glorious arm of **p** to be
Jer 10: 6 great, and your name is mighty in **p**.
10:12 God made the earth by his **p**;
16:21 I will teach them my **p** and might.
18:21 them over to the **p** of the sword.
23:10 course and use their **p** unjustly.
27: 5 With my great **p** and outstretched arm
32:17 your great **p** and outstretched arm.
51:15 "He made the earth by his **p**;
Eze 13:21 will no longer fall prey to your **p**.
22: 6 are in you uses his **p** to shed blood.
26:17 You were a **p** on the seas, you and
32:29 despite their **p**, they are laid with
32:30 the terror caused by their **p**.
Da 2:20 ever and ever; wisdom and **p** are his.
2:23 You have given me wisdom and **p**,
2:37 dominion and **p** and might and glory;
4:30 by my mighty **p** and for the glory of
6:27 Daniel from the **p** of the lions."
7:14 authority, glory and sovereign **p**;
7:26 and his **p** will be taken away and
7:27 the sovereignty, **p** and greatness of
8: 4 and none could rescue from his **p**.
8: 7 could rescue the ram from his **p**.
8: 8 but at the height of his **p** his large
8: 9 which started small but grew in **p** to
8:22 nation but will not have the same **p**.
8:24 very strong, but not by his own **p**.
8:25 be destroyed, but not by human **p**.
11: 2 When he has gained **p** by his wealth,
11: 3 with great **p** and do as he pleases.
11: 4 nor will it have the **p** he exercised,
11: 5 rule his own kingdom with great **p**.
11: 6 but she will not retain her **p**,
11: 6 and he and his **p** will not last.
11:16 and will have the **p** to destroy it.
11:23 only a few people he will rise to **p**.
11:42 He will extend his **p** over many
Da 12: 7 When the **p** of the holy people has
Hos 13:14 "I will ransom them from the **p** of
Mic 2: 1 because it is in their **p** to do it.
3: 8 for me, I am filled with **p**, with the
7:16 be ashamed, deprived of all their **p**.
Na 1: 3 LORD is slow to anger and great in **p**;
Hab 3: 4 his hand, where his **p** was hidden.
Hag 2:22 the **p** of the foreign kingdoms.
Zec 4: 6 'Not by might nor by **p**, but by my
9: 4 and destroy her **p** on the sea,
Mt 24:30 of the sky, with **p** and great glory.
Mk 5:30 Jesus realised that **p** had gone out
9: 1 see the kingdom of God come with **p**."
13:26 in clouds with great **p** and glory.
Lk 1:17 in the spirit and **p** of Elijah, to
1:35 and the **p** of the Most High will
4:14 to Galilee in the **p** of the Spirit,
4:36 With authority and **p** he gives orders
5:17 And the **p** of the Lord was present
6:19 because **p** was coming from him and
8:46 I know that **p** has gone out from me."
9: 1 he gave them **p** and authority to
10:19 to overcome all the **p** of the enemy;
12: 5 body, has **p** to throw you into hell.
20:20 the **p** and authority of the governor.
21:27 in a cloud with **p** and great glory.
24:49 been clothed with **p** from on high."
Jn 13: 3 had put all things under his **p**,
17:11 protect them by the **p** of your name
19:10 "Don't you realise I have **p** either
19:11 Jesus answered, "You would have no **p**
Ac 1: 8 you will receive **p** when the Holy
3:12 as if by our own **p** or godliness we
4: 7 "By what **p** or what name did you do
4:28 They did what your **p** and will had
4:33 With great **p** the apostles continued
6: 8 a man full of God's grace and **p**, did
8:10 the divine **p** known as the Great **P**."
10:38 Nazareth with the Holy Spirit and **p**,
10:38 who were under the **p** of the devil,
13:17 with mighty **p** he led them out of
19:20 Lord spread widely and grew in **p**.
26:18 and from the **p** of Satan to God, so
Ro 1: 4 with **p** to be the Son of God,
1:20 invisible qualities—his eternal **p**
4:21 being fully persuaded that God had **p**
9:17 that I might display my **p** in you and
9:22 show his wrath and make his **p** known,
15:13 hope by the **p** of the Holy Spirit.
15:19 by the **p** of signs and miracles,
15:19 through the **p** of the Spirit.
1Co 1:17 cross of Christ be emptied of its **p**.
2: 4 a demonstration of the Spirit's **p**,
2: 5 on men's wisdom, but on God's **p**.
4:19 are talking, but what **p** they have.
4:20 God is not a matter of talk but of **p**.
5: 4 the **p** of our Lord Jesus is present,
6:14 By his **p** God raised the Lord from
15:24 all dominion, authority and **p**.
15:43 sown in weakness, it is raised in **p**;
15:56 and the **p** of sin is the law.
2Co 4: 7 **p** is from God and not from us.
10: 4 divine **p** to demolish strongholds.
12: 9 my **p** is made perfect in weakness.
12: 9 so that Christ's **p** may rest on me.
13: 4 weakness, yet he lives by God's **p**.
13: 4 yet by God's **p** we will live with
Gal 4:29 the son born by the **p** of the Spirit.
Eph 1:19 his incomparably great **p** for us who
1:19 That **p** is like the working of his
1:21 rule and authority, **p** and dominion,
3: 7 me through the working of his **p**.
3:16 strengthen you with **p** through his
3:18 may have **p**, together with all the
3:20 to his **p** that is at work within us,
6:10 in the Lord and in his mighty **p**.
Php 3:10 and the **p** of his resurrection
3:21 who, by the **p** that enables him to
Col 1:11 being strengthened with all **p**
2:10 the Head over every **p** and authority.
1Th 1: 5 but also with **p**, with the Holy
2Th 1: 9 Lord and from the majesty of his **p**
1:11 and that by his **p** he may fulfil
2: 7 For the secret **p** of lawlessness is
2Ti 1: 7 a spirit of **p**, of love and of
3: 5 form of godliness but denying its **p**.

Heb 2:14 the **p** of death—that is, the devil—
7:16 of the **p** of an indestructible life.
1Pe 1: 5 are shielded by God's **p** until the
4:11 To him be the glory and the **p** for
5:11 To him be the **p** for ever and ever.
2Pe 1: 3 His divine **p** has given us everything
1:16 when we told you about the **p** and
Jude :25 majesty, **p** and authority, through
Rev 1: 6 glory and **p** for ever and ever! Amen.
4:11 to receive glory and honour and **p**,
5:12 who was slain, to receive **p** and
5:13 and glory and **p**, for ever and ever!"
6: 4 Its rider was given **p** to take peace
6: 8 They were given **p** over a fourth of
7: 2 **p** to harm the land and the sea:
7:12 wisdom and thanks and honour and **p**
9: 3 were given **p** like that of scorpions
9: 5 They were not given **p** to kill them,
9:10 **p** to torment people for five months.
9:19 The **p** of the horses was in their
11: 3 I will give **p** to my two witnesses,
11: 6 These men have **p** to shut up the sky
11: 6 and they have **p** to turn the waters
11:17 you have taken your great **p** and
12:10 the **p** and the kingdom of our God,
13: 2 The dragon gave the beast his **p**
13: 7 He was given **p** to make war against
13:14 of the signs he was given **p** to do on
13:15 He was given **p** to give breath to the
15: 8 the glory of God and from his **p**,
16: 8 given **p** to scorch people with fire.
17:13 their **p** and authority to the beast.
17:17 to give the beast their **p** to rule,
18:10 O great city, O Babylon, city of **p**!
19: 1 and glory and **p** belong to our God,
20: 6 The second death has no **p** over them,

Power of God

Job 27:11 "I will teach you about the **p**;
Ps 68:34 Proclaim the **p**, whose majesty is
Mt 22:29 do not know the Scriptures or the **p**.
Mk 12:24 do not know the Scriptures or the **p**?
Ro 1:16 because it is the **p** for the
1Co 1:18 us who are being saved it is the **p**.
1:24 Christ the **p** and the wisdom of God.
2Co 6: 7 in truthful speech and in the **p**;
Col 2:12 the **p**, who raised him from the dead.
2Ti 1: 8 suffering for the gospel, by the **p**,

Powerful (Power)

Ge 18:18 surely become a great and **p** nation,
26:16 you have become too **p** for us."
Nu 13:28 the people who live there are **p**, and
20:20 them with a large and **p** army.
22: 6 because they are too **p** for me.
Dt 26: 5 a great nation, **p** and numerous.
Jos 4:24 know that the hand of the LORD is **p**
17:17 "You are numerous and very **p**.
23: 9 out before you great and **p** nations;
2Sa 5:10 he became more and more **p**, because
22:18 He rescued me from my **p** enemy, from
1Ki 19:11 Then a great and **p** wind tore the
1Ch 11: 9 David became more and more **p**,
2Ch 17:12 Jehoshaphat became more and more **p**;
22: 9 **p** enough to retain the kingdom.
26: 8 Egypt, because he had become very **p**.
26:13 a **p** force to support the king
26:15 greatly helped until he became **p**.
26:16 after Uzziah became **p**, his pride led
27: 6 Jotham grew **p** because he walked
Ezr 4:20 Jerusalem has had **p** kings ruling
7:28 and all the king's **p** officials.
Est 9: 4 and he became more and more **p**.
Job 5:15 them from the clutches of the **p**.
22: 8 though you were a **p** man, owning land
35: 9 for relief from the arm of the **p**.
Ps 18:17 He rescued me from my **p** enemy, from
29: 4 The voice of the LORD is **p**;
Ecc 7:19 Wisdom makes one wise man more **p**
9:14 And a **p** king came against it,
Isa 27: 1 his fierce, great and **p** sword,
28: 2 See, the Lord has one who is **p** and
Jer 5:27 they have become rich and **p**
32:18 O great and **p** God, whose name is the
Eze 17: 3 says: A great eagle with **p** wings,
Eze 17: 7 eagle with **p** wings and full plumage.
Da 7: 7 and frightening and very **p**. It had
11:25 war with a large and very **p** army,
Joel 1: 6 my land, **p** and without number;
Mic 7: 3 the **p** dictate what they desire—
Zec 6: 3 the fourth dappled—all of them **p**.
6: 7 the **p** horses went out, they were
8:22 many peoples and **p** nations will come
Mt 3:11 will come one who is more **p** than I,
Mk 1: 7 "After me will come one more **p** than
Lk 3:16 But one more **p** than I will come, the
24:19 "He was a prophet, **p** in word and
Ac 7:22 and was **p** in speech and action.
9:22 Yet Saul grew more and more **p** and
2Co 13: 3 with you, but is **p** among you.
2Th 1: 7 in blazing fire with his **p** angels.
2:11 God sends them a **p** delusion so that
Heb 1: 3 sustaining all things by his **p** word.
11:34 and who became **p** in battle and
Jas 5:16 a righteous man is **p** and effective.
2Pe 2:11 they are stronger and more **p**,

Powerfully (Power)

Col 1:29 his energy, which so **p** works in me.

Powerless

Dt 28:32 day after day, **p** to lift a hand.
2Ch 14:11 to help the **p** against the mighty.
Ne 5: 5 but we are **p**, because our fields and
Job 26: 2 "How you have helped the **p**! How you
Jer 14: 9 like a warrior **p** to save? You are
Da 8: 7 The ram was **p** to stand against him;
11:15 The forces of the South will be **p** to
Ro 5: 6 when we were still **p**, Christ died
8: 3 For what the law was **p** to do in that

Powers (Power)

Isa 24:21 punish the **p** in the heavens above
Da 4:35 He does as he pleases with the **p** of
Mt 13:54 and these miraculous **p**?" they asked.
14: 2 miraculous **p** are at work in him."
Mk 6:14 miraculous **p** are at work in him."
Ro 8:38 present nor the future, nor any **p**,
1Co 12:10 to another miraculous **p**, to another
Eph 6:12 against the **p** of this dark world and
Col 1:16 whether thrones or **p** or rulers or
2:15 disarmed the **p** and authorities
Heb 6: 5 of God and the **p** of the coming age,
1Pe 3:22 with angels, authorities and **p** in

Practice (Practices)

1Sa 2:13 Now it was the **p** of the priests with
27:11 And such was his **p** as long as he
Ps 119:56 This has been my **p**: I obey your
Eze 33:31 but they do not put them into **p**.
33:32 words but do not put them into **p**.
Mt 7:24 puts them into **p** is like a wise man
7:26 does not put them into **p** is like a
Lk 6:47 hears my words and puts them into **p**.
6:49 does not put them into **p** is like a
8:21 hear God's word and put it into **p**."
1Co 11:16 we have no other **p**—nor do the
Php 4: 9 me, or seen in me—put it into **p**.
1Ti 5: 4 put their religion into **p** by caring
Jas 3:16 you find disorder and every evil **p**.

Practices (Practice)

Ex 23:24 or worship them or follow their **p**.
Lev 18: 3 Do not follow their **p**.
Dt 18:12 and because of these detestable **p**
Jdg 2:19 up their evil **p** and stubborn ways.
1Ki 14:24 all the detestable **p** of the nations
2Ki 17: 8 followed the **p** of the nations the
17: 8 as well as the **p** that the kings of
17:19 the **p** Israel had introduced.
17:34 day they persist in their former **p**.
17:40 but persisted in their former **p**.
21: 2 following the detestable **p** of the
2Ch 17: 4 rather than the **p** of Israel.
27: 2 however, continued their corrupt **p**.
33: 2 following the detestable **p** of the
36:14 following all the detestable **p** of
Ezr 6:21 the unclean **p** of their Gentile
9: 1 peoples with their detestable **p**,
Ezr 9:11 By their detestable **p** they have
9:14 who commit such detestable **p**?
Jer 25: 5 from your evil ways and your evil **p**,
Eze 5:11 your vile images and detestable **p**,
6: 9 done and for all their detestable **p**.
6:11 detestable **p** of the house of Israel,
7: 3 repay you for all your detestable **p**.
7: 4 and the detestable **p** among you.
7: 8 repay you for all your detestable **p**.
7: 9 and the detestable **p** among you.
12:16 acknowledge all their detestable **p**.
14: 6 and renounce all your detestable **p**!
16: 2 Jerusalem with her detestable **p**
16:22 In all your detestable **p** and your
16:43 to all your other detestable **p**?
16:47 ways and copied their detestable **p**,
16:58 lewdness and your detestable **p**,
20: 4 the detestable **p** of their fathers
20:44 your evil ways and your corrupt **p**,
22: 2 her with all her detestable **p**
23:36 them with their detestable **p**,
36:31 for your sins and detestable **p**.
43: 8 my holy name by their detestable **p**.
44: 6 detestable **p**, O house of Israel!
44: 7 to all your other detestable **p**,
44:13 the shame of their detestable **p**.
Mic 6:16 Omri and all the **p** of Ahab's house,
Zec 1: 4 from your evil ways and your evil **p**.
1: 6 to us what our ways and **p** deserve,
Col 3: 9 taken off your old self with its **p**
Rev 2: 6 You hate the **p** of the Nicolaitans,

Practise (Practised, Practises)

Lev 19:26 "'Do not **p** divination or sorcery.
Dt 18:14 those who **p** sorcery or divination.
Ps 52: 2 a sharpened razor, you who **p** deceit.
Ecc 8: 8 will not release those who **p** it.
Isa 2: 6 they **p** divination like the
Jer 6:13 and priests alike, all **p** deceit.
8:10 and priests alike, all **p** deceit.
Eze 13:23 see false visions or **p** divination.
22:29 The people of the land **p** extortion
Hos 7: 1 They **p** deceit, thieves break into
Mt 23: 3 for they do not **p** what they preach.
Ac 16:21 for us Romans to accept or **p**."
Ro 1:32 also approve of those who **p** them.
3:13 open graves; their tongues **p** deceit.
12:13 who are in need. **P** hospitality.
Rev 21: 8 immoral, those who **p** magic arts,
22:15 the dogs, those who **p** magic arts,

Practised (Practise)

Lev 18:30 customs that were **p** before you came
Jos 13:22 Balaam son of Beor, who **p** divination.
2Ki 17:17 They **p** divination and sorcery and
21: 6 **p** sorcery and divination, and
2Ch 33: 6 **p** sorcery, divination and witchcraft,
Eze 18:18 because he **p** extortion, robbed his
Mt 23:23 You should have **p** the latter,
Lk 11:42 You should have **p** the latter without
Ac 8: 9 Simon had **p** sorcery in the city
19:19 A number who had **p** sorcery brought

Practises (Practise)

Dt 18:10 who **p** divination or sorcery,
Ps 101: 7 No-one who **p** deceit will dwell in my
Isa 32: 6 He **p** ungodliness and spreads error
Mt 5:19 but whoever **p** and teaches these
Rev 22:15 everyone who loves and **p** falsehood.

Praetorium

Mt 27:27 soldiers took Jesus into the **P**
Mk 15:16 into the palace (that is, the **P**)

Praise (*Praise be to the LORD, Praise the LORD, Praised, Praises, Praiseworthy, Praising, Sing praise)*

Ge 49: 8 "Judah, your brothers will **p** you;
Ex 15: 2 He is my God, and I will **p** him, my
Lev 19:24 holy, an offering of **p** to the LORD.
Dt 10:21 He is your **p**; he is your God, who
26:19 declared that he will set you in **p**,
32: 3 Oh, **p** the greatness of our God!
Jos 7:19 God of Israel, and give him the **p**.

2Sa 22: 4 to the LORD, who is worthy of **p**,
22:47 "The LORD lives! **P** be to my Rock!
22:50 Therefore I will **p** you, O LORD,
1Ch 16:25 is the LORD and most worthy of **p**;
16:35 name, that we may glory in your **p**."
29:10 "**P** be to you, O LORD,
29:13 thanks, and **p** your glorious name.
2Ch 5:13 to give **p** and thanks to the LORD.
5:13 they raised their voices in **p** to the
8:14 the Levites to lead the **p** and to
20:21 to **p** him for the splendour of his
20:22 they began to sing and **p**, the LORD
30:21 by the LORD's instruments of **p**.
Ezr 3:11 With **p** and thanksgiving they sang to
3:11 gave a great shout of **p** to the LORD,
Ne 9: 5 be exalted above all blessing and **p**.
12:24 who stood opposite them to give **p**
12:46 songs of **p** and thanksgiving to God.
Ps 8: 2 ordained **p** because of your enemies,
9: 1 I will **p** you, O LORD, with all my
18: 3 to the LORD, who is worthy of **p**,
18:46 The LORD lives! **P** be to my Rock!
18:49 Therefore I will **p** you among the
21:13 we will sing and **p** your might.
22: 3 Holy One; you are the **p** of Israel.
22:22 in the congregation I will **p** you.
22:23 You who fear the LORD, **p** him!
22:25 From you comes the theme of my **p** in
22:26 they who seek the LORD will **p** him—
26: 7 proclaiming aloud your **p** and telling
30: 4 you saints of his; **p** his holy name.
30: 9 Will the dust **p** you? Will it
33: 1 is fitting for the upright to **p** him.
34: 1 his **p** will always be on my lips.
35:18 throngs of people I will **p** you.
40: 3 in my mouth, a hymn of **p** to our God.
42: 5 for I will yet **p** him, my Saviour
42:11 yet **p** him, my Saviour and my God.
43: 4 **p** you with the harp, O God, my God.
43: 5 for I will yet **p** him, my Saviour
44: 8 and we will **p** your name for ever.
45:17 the nations will **p** you for ever and
47: 7 the earth; sing to him a psalm of **p**.
48: 1 and most worthy of **p**, in the city of
48:10 your **p** reaches to the ends of the
49:18 and men **p** you when you prosper—
51:15 and my mouth will declare your **p**.
52: 9 I will **p** you for ever for what you
52: 9 I will **p** you in the presence of
54: 6 I will **p** your name, O LORD, for it
56: 4 In God, whose word I **p**, in God I
56:10 In God, whose word I **p**, in the LORD,
56:10 in the LORD, whose word I **p**—
57: 9 I will **p** you, O Lord, among the
63: 4 I will **p** you as long as I live, and
63: 5 singing lips my mouth will **p** you.
63:11 who swear by God's name will **p** him,
64:10 let all the upright in heart **p** him!
65: 1 **P** awaits you, O God, in Zion; to you
66: 2 of his name; make his **p** glorious!
66: 8 **P** our God, O peoples, let the sound
66: 8 let the sound of his **p** be heard;
66:17 my mouth; his **p** was on my tongue.
66:20 **P** be to God, who has not rejected my
67: 3 May the peoples **p** you, O God;
67: 3 may all the peoples **p** you.
67: 5 May the peoples **p** you, O God;
67: 5 may all the peoples **p** you.
68:26 **P** God in the great congregation;
68:35 **P** be to God!
69:30 I will **p** God's name in song and
69:34 Let heaven and earth **p** him, the seas
71: 6 I will ever **p** you.
71: 8 My mouth is filled with your **p**,
71:14 I will **p** you more and more.
71:22 I will **p** you with the harp for your
72:19 **P** be to his glorious name for ever;
74:21 may the poor and needy **p** your name.
76:10 your wrath against men brings you **p**,
79:13 your pasture, will **p** you for ever;
79:13 generation we will recount your **p**.
86:12 I will **p** you, O Lord my God, with
88:10 are dead rise up and **p** you?
89: 5 The heavens **p** your wonders, O LORD,
96: 2 Sing to the LORD, **p** his name;
96: 4 is the LORD and most worthy of **p**;
Ps 97:12 are righteous, and **p** his holy name.
99: 3 Let them **p** your great and awesome
100: 4 thanksgiving and his courts with **p**;
100: 4 give thanks to him and **p** his name.
102:21 in Zion and his **p** in Jerusalem
103: 1 my inmost being, **p** his holy name.
106: 2 of the LORD or fully declare his **p**?
106: 5 join your inheritance in giving **p**.
106:12 his promises and sang his **p**.
106:47 your holy name and glory in your **p**.
107:32 **p** him in the council of the elders.
108: 3 I will **p** you, O LORD, among the
109: 1 O God, whom I **p**, do not remain
109:30 in the great throng I will **p** him.
111:10 To him belongs eternal **p**.
113: 1 **P**, O servants of the LORD,
113: 1 **p** the name of the LORD.
119: 7 I will **p** you with an upright heart
119:12 **P** be to you, O LORD; teach me your
119:108 Accept, O LORD, the willing **p** of my
119:164 Seven times a day I **p** you for your
119:171 May my lips overflow with **p**, for you
119:175 Let me live that I may **p** you, and
122: 4 to **p** the name of the LORD according
135: 1 **P** the name of the LORD;
135: 1 **p** him, you servants of the LORD,
138: 1 I will **p** you, O LORD, with all my
138: 1 the "gods" I will sing your **p**.
138: 2 will **p** your name for your love and
138: 4 May all the kings of the earth **p** you,
139:14 I **p** you because I am fearfully and
140:13 Surely the righteous will **p** your
142: 7 my prison, that I may **p** your name.
145: T A psalm of **p**. Of David.
145: 1 I will **p** your name for ever and ever.
145: 2 Every day I will **p** you and extol
145: 3 is the LORD and most worthy of **p**;
145:10 All you have made will **p** you, O LORD;
145:21 My mouth will speak in **p** of the LORD.
145:21 Let every creature **p** his holy name
147:12 O Jerusalem; **p** your God, O Zion,
148: 1 heavens, **p** him in the heights above.
148: 2 **P** him, all his angels, **p** him, all
148: 3 **P** him, sun and moon, **p** him, all you
148: 4 **P** him, you highest heavens and you
148: 5 Let them **p** the name of the LORD, for
148:13 Let them **p** the name of the LORD, for
148:14 the **p** of all his saints, of Israel,
149: 1 his **p** in the assembly of the saints.
149: 3 Let them **p** his name with dancing and
149: 6 May the **p** of God be in their mouths
150: 1 **P** God in his sanctuary;
150: 1 **p** him in his mighty heavens
150: 2 **P** him for his acts of power;
150: 2 **p** him for his surpassing greatness.
150: 3 **P** him with the sounding of the
150: 3 **p** him with the harp and lyre,
150: 4 **p** him with tambourine and dancing,
150: 4 **p** him with the strings and flute,
150: 5 **p** him with the clash of cymbals,
150: 5 **p** him with resounding cymbals.
Pr 27: 2 Let another **p** you, and not your own
27:21 man is tested by the **p** he receives.
28: 4 who forsake the law **p** the wicked,
31:31 works bring her **p** at the city gate.
Ecc 8:10 receive **p** in the city where they
SS 1: 4 we will **p** your love more than wine.
Isa 12: 1 "I will **p** you, O LORD.
25: 1 I will exalt you and **p** your name,
38:18 For the grave cannot **p** you, death
38:18 death cannot sing your **p**; those who
38:19 The living, the living—they **p** you,
42: 8 glory to another or my **p** to idols.
42:10 his **p** from the ends of the earth,
42:12 and proclaim his **p** in the islands.
43:21 myself that they may proclaim my **p**.
48: 9 of my **p** I hold it back from you,
57:19 creating **p** on the lips of the
60: 6 and proclaiming the **p** of the LORD.
60:18 walls Salvation and your gates **P**.
61: 3 a garment of **p** instead of a spirit
61:11 righteousness and **p** spring up
62: 7 and makes her the **p** of the earth.
Jer 13:11 for my renown and **p** and honour.
17:14 be saved, for you are the one I **p**.
20:13 Sing to the LORD! Give **p** to the LORD!
Jer 33: 9 joy, **p** and honour before all nations
Da 2:20 "**P** be to the name of God for ever
2:23 I thank and **p** you, O God of my
3:28 "**P** be to the God of Shadrach,
4:37 Now I, Nebuchadnezzar, **p** and exalt
Joel 2:26 and you will **p** the name of the LORD
Hab 3: 3 heavens and his **p** filled the earth.
Zep 3:19 I will give them **p** and honour in
3:20 I will give you honour and **p** among
Mt 5:16 deeds and **p** your Father in heaven.
11:25 At that time Jesus said, "I **p** you,
21:16 and infants you have ordained **p**'?"
Lk 5:26 Everyone was amazed and gave **p** to
10:21 "I **p** you, Father, Lord of heaven and
17:18 Was no-one found to return and give **p**
19:37 joyfully to **p** God in loud voices
Jn 5:41 "I do not accept **p** from men,
5:44 How can you believe if you accept **p**
5:44 the **p** that comes from the only God?
12:43 loved **p** from men more than **p** from
Ac 12:23 because Herod did not give **p** to God,
Ro 2:29 **p** is not from men, but from God.
15: 7 you, in order to bring **p** to God.
15: 9 "Therefore I will **p** you among the
1Co 4: 5 each will receive his **p** from God.
11: 2 I **p** you for remembering me in
11:17 directives I have no **p** for you,
11:22 I **p** you for this? Certainly not!
2Co 1: 3 **P** be to the God and Father of our
9:13 men will **p** God for the obedience
Eph 1: 3 **P** be to the God and Father of our
1: 6 to the **p** of his glorious grace,
1:12 might be for the **p** of his glory.
1:14 possession—to the **p** of his glory.
Php 1:11 Christ—to the glory and **p** of God.
1Th 2: 6 We were not looking for **p** from men,
Heb 13:15 offer to God a sacrifice of **p**—
Jas 3: 9 With the tongue we **p** our Lord and
3:10 Out of the same mouth come **p** and
5:13 Let him sing songs of **p**.
1Pe 1: 3 **P** be to the God and Father of our
1: 7 proved genuine and may result in **p**,
4:16 but **p** God that you bear that name.
Rev 5:12 and honour and glory and **p**!"
5:13 be **p** and honour and glory and power,
7:12 saying: "Amen! **P** and glory and
19: 5 "**P** our God, all you his servants,

Praise be to the LORD/Lord

Ge 24:27 saying, "**P**, the God of my master
Ex 18:10 He said, "**P**, who rescued you from
Ru 4:14 "**P**, who this day has not left you
1Sa 25:32 "**P**, the God of Israel, who has sent
25:39 "**P**, who has upheld my cause against
2Sa 18:28 "**P** your God! He has delivered up the
1Ki 1:48 said, '**P**, the God of Israel, who has
5: 7 "**P** today, for he has given David a
8:15 he said: "**P**, the God of Israel, who
8:56 "**P**, who has given rest to his people
10: 9 **P** your God, who has delighted in you
1Ch 16:36 **P**, the God of Israel, from
2Ch 2:12 Hiram added: "**P**, the God of Israel,
6: 4 he said: "**P**, the God of Israel, who
9: 8 **P** your God, who has delighted in you
Ezr 7:27 **P**, the God of our fathers, who has
Ps 28: 6 **P**, for he has heard my cry for mercy.
31:21 **P**, for he showed his wonderful love
41:13 **P**, the God of Israel, from
68:19 **P**, to God our Saviour, who daily
72:18 **P** God, the God of Israel, who alone
89:52 **P** for ever! Amen and Amen.
106:48 **P**, the God of Israel, from
124: 6 **P**, who has not let us be torn by
135:21 **P** from Zion, to him who dwells in
144: 1 **P** my Rock, who trains my hands for
Lk 1:68 "**P**, the God of Israel, because he

Praise the LORD/Lord

Ge 29:35 a son she said, "This time I will **p**.
Dt 8:10 **p** your God for the good land he has
Jdg 5: 2 willingly offer themselves—**p**!
5: 9 volunteers among the people. **P**!
1Ch 16: 4 thanks, and to **p**, the God of Israel:

1Ch 16:36 all the people said "Amen" and "P."
23: 5 four thousand are to p with the
23:30 stand every morning to thank and p.
29:20 David said to the whole assembly, "P
2Ch 29:30 Levites to p with the words of David
Ezr 3:10 took their places to p, as
Ne 9: 5 "Stand up and p your God, who is
Ps 16: 7 I will p, who counsels me; even at
26:12 in the great assembly I will p.
33: 2 P with the harp; make music to him
68:26 p in the assembly of Israel.
92: 1 is good to p and make music to your
102:18 that a people not yet created may p:
103: 1 P, O my soul; all my inmost being,
103: 2 P, O my soul, and forget not all his
103:20 P, you his angels, you mighty ones
103:21 P, all his heavenly hosts, you his
103:22 P, all his works everywhere in his
103:22 P, O my soul.
104: 1 P, O my soul. O LORD my God, you are
104:35 P, O my soul. P.
105:45 P.
106: 1 P. Give thanks to the LORD, for he
106:48 Let all the people say, "Amen!" P.
111: 1 P. I will extol the LORD with all my
112: 1 P. Blessed is the man who fears the
113: 1 P. Praise, O servants of the LORD,
113: 9 P.
115:17 is not the dead who p, those who go
115:18 P.
116:19 P.
117: 1 P, all you nations; extol him, all
117: 2 P.
134: 1 P, all you servants of the LORD who
134: 2 your hands in the sanctuary and p.
135: 1 P. Praise the name of the LORD;
135: 3 P, for the LORD is good; sing praise
135:19 O house of Israel, p;
135:19 O house of Aaron, p;
135:20 O house of Levi, p;
135:20 you who fear him, p.
135:21 P.
146: 1 P. P, O my soul.
146: 2 I will p all my life; I will sing
146:10 P.
147: 1 P. How good it is to sing praises to
147:20 P.
148: 1 P. P from the heavens, praise him in
148: 7 P from the earth, you great sea
148:14 P.
149: 1 P. Sing to the LORD a new song, his
149: 9 P.
150: 1 P. Praise God in his sanctuary;
150: 6 Let everything that has breath p.
150: 6 P.
Isa 62: 9 who harvest it will eat it and p,
Zec 11: 5 who sell them say, 'P, I am rich!'
Ro 15:11 again, "P, all you Gentiles, and

Praised (Praise)

Ge 12:15 they p her to Pharoah, and she was
24:48 I p the LORD, the God of my master
Jos 22:33 glad to hear the report and p God.
Jdg 16:24 the people saw him, they p their god,
2Sa 14:25 there was not a man so highly p for
1Ch 29:10 David p the LORD in the presence of
29:20 So they all p the LORD, the God of
2Ch 20:19 Korahites stood up and p the LORD,
20:26 of Beracah, where they p the LORD.
30:22 p the LORD, the God of their fathers.
31: 8 they p the LORD and blessed his
Ne 5:13 said, "Amen," and p the LORD.
8: 6 Ezra p the LORD, the great God;
Job 1:21 may the name of the LORD be p."
36:24 his work, which men have p in song.
Ps 113: 2 Let the name of the LORD be p, both
113: 3 the name of the LORD is to be p.
Pr 12: 8 A man is p according to his wisdom,
31:30 woman who fears the LORD is to be p.
SS 6: 9 the queens and concubines p her.
Isa 63: 7 the deeds for which he is to be p,
64:11 where our fathers p you, has been
Jer 48: 2 Moab will be p no more; in Heshbon
Eze 3:12 LORD be p in his dwelling-place!—
Da 2:19 Then Daniel p the God of heaven
4:34 Then I p the Most High; I honoured
5: 4 they p the gods of gold and silver,
5:23 You p the gods of silver and gold,
Mt 9: 8 and they p God, who had given such
15:31 And they p the God of Israel.
Mk 2:12 This amazed everyone and they p God,
Lk 2:28 took him in his arms and p God,
4:15 synagogues, and everyone p him.
7:16 were all filled with awe and p God.
13:13 she straightened up and p God.
18:43 the people saw it, they also p God.
23:47 seeing what had happened, p God and
Ac 11:18 had no further objections and p God,
21:20 they heard this, they p God.
Ro 1:25 than the Creator—who is for ever p.
9: 5 is God over all, for ever p! Amen.
2Co 8:18 the brother who is p by all the
11:31 who is to be p for ever, knows that
Gal 1:24 they p God because of me.
1Pe 4:11 God may be p through Jesus Christ.

Praises (Praise, *Sing praises*)

2Ch 23:13 instruments were leading the p.
29:30 So they sang p with gladness and
Ps 6: 5 Who p you from his grave?
9:14 that I may declare your p in the
35:28 and of your p all day long.
Pr 31:28 her husband also, and he p her:
Jer 31: 7 Make your p heard, and say, 'O LORD,
Heb 2:12 congregation I will sing your p."
1Pe 2: 9 that you may declare the p of him

Praiseworthy (Praise)

Ps 78: 4 generation the p deeds of the LORD,
Php 4: 8 if anything is excellent or p—

Praising (Praise)

1Ch 25: 3 the harp in thanking and p the LORD.
2Ch 7: 6 King David had made for p the LORD
Ps 84: 4 in your house; they are ever p you.
Lk 1:64 and he began to speak, p God.
2:13 with the angel, p God and saying,
2:20 glorifying and p God for all the
5:25 been lying on and went home p God.
17:15 came back, p God in a loud voice.
18:43 his sight and followed Jesus, p God.
24:53 continually at the temple, p God.
Ac 2:47 p God and enjoying the favour of all
3: 8 walking and jumping, and p God.
3: 9 the people saw him walking and p God
4:21 all the people were p God for what
10:46 them speaking in tongues and p God.
1Co 14:16 If you are p God with your spirit,

Pray (Prayed, Prayer, Prayers, Praying, Prays)

Ge 20: 7 he will p for you and you will live.
32:11 Save me, I p, from the hand of my
Ex 8: 8 "P to the LORD to take the frogs
8: 9 the time for me to p for you
8:28 not go very far. Now p for me."
8:29 I leave you, I will p to the LORD,
9:28 P to the LORD, for we have had
10:17 and p to the LORD your God to take
Nu 21: 7 P that the LORD will take the snakes
Dt 4: 7 God is near us whenever we p to him?
1Sa 12:19 "P to the LORD your God for your
12:23 the LORD by failing to p for you.
1Ki 8:30 when they p towards this place.
8:35 and when they p towards this place
8:44 and when they p to the LORD towards
8:48 and p to you towards the land you
13: 6 p for me that my hand may be
2Ki 19: 4 Therefore p for the remnant that
1Ch 17:25 has found courage to p to you.
2Ch 6:21 when they p towards this place.
6:26 and when they p towards this place
6:34 and when they p to you towards this
6:38 and p towards the land that you gave
7:14 will humble themselves and p and
Ezr 6:10 p for the well-being of the king and
Job 22:27 You will p to him, and he will hear
42: 8 My servant Job will p for you, and I
Ps 5: 2 my King and my God, for to you I p.
32: 6 let everyone who is godly p to you
69:13 I p to you, O LORD, in the time of
72:15 p for him and bless him all day long.
122: 6 P for the peace of Jerusalem: "May
Isa 16:12 her shrine to p, it is to no avail.
37: 4 Therefore p for the remnant that
45:20 who p to gods that cannot save.
64: 9 Oh, look upon us we p, for we are
Jer 7:16 "So do not p for this people nor
11:14 "Do not p for this people nor offer
14:11 the LORD said to me, "Do not p for
29: 7 P to the LORD for it, because if it
29:12 you will call upon me and come and p
31: 9 they will p as I bring them back.
37: 3 Please p to the LORD our God for us."
42: 2 and p to the LORD your God for this
42: 3 P that the LORD your God will tell
42: 4 "I will certainly p to the LORD your
42:20 'P to the LORD our God for us;
Da 9:23 soon as you began to p, an answer
Mt 5:44 and p for those who persecute you,
6: 5 "And when you p, do not be like the
6: 5 for they love to p standing in the
6: 6 when you p, go into your room, close
6: 6 and p to your Father, who is unseen.
6: 7 And when you p, do not keep on
6: 9 "This, then, is how you should p:
14:23 on a mountainside by himself to p.
19:13 his hands on them and p for them.
24:20 P that your flight will not take
26:36 here while I go over there and p."
26:41 "Watch and p so that you will not
Mk 6:46 he went up on a mountainside to p.
13:18 P that this will not take place in
14:32 his disciples, "Sit here while I p.
14:38 Watch and p so that you will not
Lk 5:33 "John's disciples often fast and p,
6:12 went out to a mountainside to p,
6:28 p for those who ill-treat you.
9:28 and went up onto a mountain to p.
11: 1 "Lord, teach us to p, just as John
11: 2 He said to them, "When you p, say:
18: 1 should always p and not give up.
18:10 "Two men went up to the temple to p,
21:36 and p that you may be able to
22:40 "P that you will not fall into
22:46 "Get up and p so that you will not
Jn 17: 9 I p for them. I am not praying for
17:20 I p also for those who will believe
Ac 8:22 Repent of this wickedness and p to
8:24 Simon answered, "P to the Lord for
10: 9 Peter went up on the roof to p.
21: 5 there on the beach we knelt to p.
26:29 "Short time or long—I p God that
Ro 1:10 and I p that now at last by God's
8:26 We do not know what we ought to p
15:31 P that I may be rescued from the
1Co 11:13 to p to God with her head uncovered?
14:13 p that he may interpret what he says.
14:14 For if I p in a tongue, my spirit
14:15 I will p with my spirit,
14:15 but I will also p with my mind;
2Co 13: 7 Now we p to God that you will not do
Eph 1:18 I p also that the eyes of your heart
3:16 I p that out of his glorious riches
3:17 And I p that you, being rooted and
6:18 p in the Spirit on all occasions
6:19 P also for me, that whenever I open
6:20 P that I may declare it fearlessly,
Php 1: 4 for all of you, I always p with
Col 1: 3 Lord Jesus Christ, when we p for you,
1:10 we p this in order that you may live
4: 3 p for us, too, that God may open a
4: 4 P that I may proclaim it clearly, as
1Th 3:10 Night and day we p most earnestly
5:17 p continually;
5:25 Brothers, p for us.
2Th 1:11 we constantly p for you, that our
1:12 We p this so that the name of our
3: 1 Finally, brothers, p for us that the
3: 2 p that we may be delivered from
1Ti 5: 5 continues night and day to p and to
Phm : 6 I p that you may be active in

Heb 13:18 **P** for us. We are sure that we have a
13:19 I particularly urge you to **p** so that
Jas 5:13 one of you in trouble? He should **p**.
5:14 elders of the church to **p** over him
5:16 **p** for each other so that you may be
1Pe 4: 7 self-controlled so that you can **p**.
1Jn 5:16 should **p** and God will give him life.
5:16 saying that he should **p** about that.
3Jn : 2 Dear friend, I **p** that you may enjoy
Jude :20 holy faith and **p** in the Holy Spirit.

Prayed (Pray)

Ge 20:17 Abraham **p** to God, and God healed
24:12 he **p**, "O LORD, God of my master
25:21 Isaac **p** to the LORD on behalf of his
32: 9 Jacob **p**, "O God of my father Abraham,
Ex 8:30 Moses left Pharaoh and **p** to the LORD,
10:18 Moses then left Pharaoh and **p** to the
Nu 11: 2 he **p** to the LORD and the fire died
21: 7 So Moses **p** for the people.
Dt 9:20 but at that time I **p** for Aaron too.
9:26 I **p** to the LORD and said, "O
Jdg 13: 8 Manoah **p** to the LORD: "O Lord, I beg
16:28 Samson **p** to the LORD, "O Sovereign
1Sa 1:10 Hannah wept much and **p** to the LORD.
1:27 I **p** for this child, and the LORD has
2: 1 Hannah **p** and said: "My heart
2:20 one she **p** for and gave to the LORD.
8: 6 so he **p** to the LORD.
14:41 Saul **p** to the LORD, the God of
2Sa 15:31 So David **p**, "O LORD, turn
1Ki 8:59 which I have **p** before the LORD, be
18:36 stepped forward and **p**: "O LORD,
19: 4 under it and **p** that he might die.
2Ki 4:33 the two of them and **p** to the LORD.
6:17 Elisha **p**, "O LORD, open his eyes so
6:18 Elisha **p** to the LORD, "Strike these
19:15 Hezekiah **p** to the LORD: "O LORD, God
20: 2 face to the wall and **p** to the LORD,
2Ch 30:18 But Hezekiah **p** for them, saying,
32:24 He **p** to the LORD, who answered him
33:13 he **p** to him, the LORD was moved by
Ezr 9: 6 and **p**: "O my God, I am too ashamed
Ne 1: 4 and **p** before the God of heaven.
2: 4 Then I **p** to the God of heaven,
4: 9 we **p** to our God and posted a guard
6: 9 ⌊But I **p**,⌋ "Now strengthen my hands
Job 42:10 After Job had **p** for his friends, the
Isa 37:15 Hezekiah **p** to the LORD:
37:21 Because you have **p** to me concerning
38: 2 face to the wall and **p** to the LORD,
Jer 32:16 son of Neriah, I **p** to the LORD:
Da 6:10 day he got down on his knees and **p**,
9: 4 I **p** to the LORD my God and confessed:
Jnh 2: 1 From inside the fish Jonah **p** to the
4: 2 He **p** to the LORD, "O LORD, is this
Mt 26:39 with his face to the ground and **p**,
26:42 He went away a second time and **p**,
26:44 away once more and **p** the third time,
Mk 1:35 off to a solitary place, where he **p**.
14:35 he fell to the ground and **p** that if
14:39 he went away and **p** the same thing.
Lk 5:16 withdrew to lonely places and **p**.
18:11 The Pharisee stood up and **p** about
22:32 I have **p** for you, Simon, that your
22:41 throw beyond them, knelt down and **p**,
22:44 in anguish, he **p** more earnestly,
Jn 17: 1 he looked towards heaven and **p**:
Ac 1:24 they **p**, "Lord, you know everyone's
4:31 After they **p**, the place where they
6: 6 who **p** and laid their hands on them.
7:59 Stephen **p**, "Lord Jesus, receive my
8:15 they arrived, they **p** for them that
9:40 then he got down on his knees and **p**.
10: 2 in need and **p** to God regularly.
13: 3 after they had fasted and **p**, they
20:36 knelt down with all of them and **p**.
27:29 from the stern and **p** for daylight.
Jas 5:17 He **p** earnestly that it would not
5:18 Again he **p**, and the heavens gave

Prayer (Pray)

Ge 25:21 The LORD answered his **p**, and his
Ex 9:29 out my hands in **p** to the LORD.
2Sa 7:27 found courage to offer you this **p**.
2Sa 21:14 God answered **p** on behalf of the land.
24:25 Then the LORD answered **p** on behalf
1Ki 8:28 servant's **p** and his plea for mercy,
8:28 Hear the cry and the **p** that your
8:29 will hear the **p** your servant prays
8:38 a **p** or plea is made by any of your
8:45 hear from heaven their **p** and their
8:49 hear their **p** and their plea, and
9: 3 "I have heard the **p** and plea you
2Ki 19:20 says: I have heard your **p** concerning
20: 5 says: I have heard your **p** and seen
2Ch 6:19 servant's **p** and his plea for mercy,
6:19 Hear the cry and the **p** that your
6:20 May you hear the **p** your servant
6:29 a **p** or plea is made by any of your
6:35 hear from heaven their **p** and their
6:39 hear their **p** and their pleas, and
7:12 "I have heard your **p** and have chosen
30:27 for their **p** reached heaven, his
32:20 cried out in **p** to heaven about this.
33:18 including his **p** to his God and the
33:19 His **p** and how God was moved by his
Ezr 8:23 about this, and he answered our **p**.
Ne 1: 6 your eyes open to hear the **p** your
1:11 let your ear be attentive to the **p**
1:11 to the **p** of your servants who
11:17 who led in thanksgiving and **p**;
Job 16:17 free of violence and my **p** is pure.
42: 8 and I will accept his **p** and not deal
42: 9 and the LORD accepted Job's **p**.
Ps 4: 1 be merciful to me and hear my **p**.
6: 9 for mercy; the LORD accepts my **p**.
17: T A **p** of David.
17: 1 Give ear to my **p**—it does not rise
17: 6 give ear to me and hear my **p**.
39:12 "Hear my **p**, O LORD, listen to my cry
42: 8 with me—a **p** to the God of my life.
54: 2 Hear my **p**, O God; listen to the
55: 1 Listen to my **p**, O God, do not ignore
61: 1 Hear my cry, O God; listen to my **p**.
65: 2 O you who hear **p**, to you all men
66:19 listened and heard my voice in **p**.
66:20 who has not rejected my **p** or
84: 8 Hear my **p**, O LORD God Almighty;
86: T A **p** of David.
86: 6 Hear my **p**, O LORD; listen to my cry
88: 2 May my **p** come before you; turn your
88:13 the morning my **p** comes before you.
90: T A **p** of Moses the man of God.
102: T A **p** of an afflicted man. When he is
102: 1 Hear my **p**, O LORD; let my cry for
102:17 He will respond to the **p** of the
109: 4 they accuse me, but I am a man of **p**.
141: 2 May my **p** be set before you like
141: 5 Yet my **p** is ever against the deeds
142: T When he was in the cave. A **p**.
143: 1 O LORD, hear my **p**, listen to my cry
Pr 15: 8 the **p** of the upright pleases him.
15:29 but he hears the **p** of the righteous.
Isa 1:15 you spread out your hands in **p**, I
26:16 them, they could barely whisper a **p**.
38: 5 says: I have heard your **p** and seen
56: 7 and give them joy in my house of **p**.
56: 7 a house of **p** for all nations."
Lam 3: 8 or cry for help, he shuts out my **p**.
3:44 cloud so that no **p** can get through.
Da 9: 3 pleaded with him in **p** and petition,
9:21 while I was still in **p**, Gabriel, the
Jnh 2: 7 and my **p** rose to you, to your holy
Hab 3: 1 A **p** of Habakkuk the prophet.
Mt 21:13 house will be called a house of **p**,'
21:22 receive whatever you ask for in **p**."
Mk 9:29 "This kind can come out only by **p**.
11:17 a house of **p** for all nations'?
11:24 whatever you ask for in **p**, believe
Lk 1:13 Zechariah; your **p** has been heard.
19:46 'My house will be a house of **p**';
22:45 he rose from **p** and went back to the
Jn 17:15 My **p** is not that you take them out
17:20 "My **p** is not for them alone. I pray
Ac 1:14 all joined together constantly in **p**,
2:42 to the breaking of bread and to **p**.
3: 1 of **p**—at three in the afternoon.
4:24 their voices together in **p** to God.
6: 4 will give our attention to **p** and the
10:31 'Cornelius, God has heard your **p** and
Ac 14:23 with **p** and fasting, committed them
16:13 we expected to find a place of **p**.
16:16 we were going to the place of **p**,
28: 8 Paul went in to see him and, after **p**,
Ro 10: 1 Brothers, my heart's desire and **p** to
12:12 in affliction, faithful in **p**.
1Co 7: 5 that you may devote yourselves to **p**.
2Co 13: 9 and our **p** is for your perfection.
Php 1: 9 this is my **p**: that your love may
4: 6 but in everything, by **p** and petition,
Col 4: 2 Devote yourselves to **p**, being
4:12 He is always wrestling in **p** for you,
1Ti 2: 8 lift up holy hands in **p**, without
4: 5 by the word of God and **p**.
Jas 5:15 the **p** offered in faith will make the
5:16 The **p** of a righteous man is powerful
1Pe 3:12 his ears are attentive to their **p**,

Prayers (Pray)

1Ki 8:54 Solomon had finished all these **p** and
1Ch 5:20 He answered their **p**, because they
2Ch 6:40 to the **p** offered in this place.
7:15 to the **p** offered in this place.
Ps 35:13 When my **p** returned to me unanswered,
72:20 This concludes the **p** of David son of
80: 4 against the **p** of your people?
109: 7 guilty, and may his **p** condemn him.
Pr 28: 9 the law, even his **p** are detestable.
Isa 1:15 you offer many **p**, I will not listen.
Da 9:17 "Now, our God, hear the **p** and
Mk 12:40 and for a show make lengthy **p**.
Lk 20:47 and for a show make lengthy **p**.
Ac 10: 4 "Your **p** and gifts to the poor have
Ro 1:10 in my **p** at all times; and I pray
2Co 1:11 you help us by your **p**. Then many
1:11 us in answer to the **p** of many.
9:14 in their **p** for you their hearts will
Eph 1:16 for you, remembering you in my **p**.
6:18 with all kinds of **p** and requests.
Php 1: 4 In all my **p** for all of you, I always
1:19 for I know that through your **p** and
1Th 1: 2 all of you, mentioning you in our **p**.
1Ti 2: 1 that requests, **p**, intercession and
2Ti 1: 3 I constantly remember you in my **p**.
Phm : 4 my God as I remember you in my **p**,
:22 restored to you in answer to your **p**.
Heb 5: 7 he offered up **p** and petitions with
1Pe 3: 7 so that nothing will hinder your **p**.
Rev 5: 8 which are the **p** of the saints.
8: 3 with the **p** of all the saints, on the
8: 4 together with the **p** of the saints,

Praying (Pray)

Ge 24:15 Before he had finished **p**, Rebekah
24:45 "Before I finished **p** in my heart,
1Sa 1:12 she kept on **p** to the LORD, Eli
1:13 Hannah was **p** in her heart, and her
1:16 I have been **p** here out of my great
1:26 stood here beside you **p** to the LORD.
1Ki 8:28 the prayer that your servant is **p**
8:33 **p** and making supplication to you in
2Ch 6:19 the prayer that your servant is **p**
6:24 **p** and making supplication before you
7: 1 Solomon finished **p**, fire came down
Ezr 10: 1 While Ezra was **p** and confessing,
Ne 1: 6 your servant is **p** before you day
Job 21:15 What would we gain by **p** to him?'
Da 6:11 Daniel **p** and asking God for help.
9:20 While I was speaking and **p**,
Mk 11:25 you stand **p**, if you hold anything
Lk 1:10 worshippers were **p** outside.
2:37 night and day, fasting and **p**.
3:21 And as he was **p**, heaven was opened
6:12 pray, and spent the night **p** to God.
9:18 Once when Jesus was **p** in private and
9:29 he was **p**, the appearance of his face
11: 1 One day Jesus was **p** in a certain
Jn 17: 9 I am not **p** for the world, but for
18: 1 he had finished **p**, Jesus left with
Ac 9:11 from Tarsus named Saul, for he is **p**.
10:30 "Four days ago I was in my house **p**
11: 5 "I was in the city of Joppa **p**, and
12: 5 was earnestly **p** to God for him.
12:12 many people had gathered and were **p**.
16:25 About midnight Paul and Silas were **p**

Ac 22:17 and was **p** at the temple, I fell
Ro 15:30 in my struggle by **p** to God for me.
Eph 6:18 always keep on **p** for all the saints.
Col 1: 9 we have not stopped **p** for you and

Prays (Pray)

1Ki 8:29 your servant **p** towards this place.
8:42 he comes and **p** towards this temple,
2Ch 6:20 your servant **p** towards this place.
6:32 he comes and **p** towards this temple,
Job 33:26 He **p** to God and finds favour with
Isa 44:17 He **p** to it and says, "Save me;
Da 6: 7 enforce the decree that anyone who **p**
6:12 **p** to any god or man except to you,
6:13 He still **p** three times a day."
1Co 11: 4 Every man who **p** or prophesies with
11: 5 every woman who **p** or prophesies with
14:14 spirit **p**, but my mind is unfruitful.

Preach (Preached, Preacher, Preaches, Preaching)

Isa 61: 1 me to **p** good news to the poor.
Eze 20:46 **p** against the south and prophesy
21: 2 and **p** against the sanctuary.
Jnh 1: 2 city of Nineveh and **p** against it,
Mt 4:17 From that time on Jesus began to **p**,
10: 7 you go, **p** this message: 'The kingdom
11: 1 teach and **p** in the towns of Galilee.
23: 3 they do not practise what they **p**.
Mk 1:38 that I can **p** there also.
3:14 and that he might send them out to **p**
16:15 and **p** the good news to all creation.
Lk 4:18 me to **p** good news to the poor.
4:43 he said, "I must **p** the good news of
9: 2 he sent them out to **p** the kingdom of
Ac 9:20 At once he began to **p** in the
10:42 He commanded us to **p** to the people
14: 7 where they continued to **p** the good
16:10 called us to **p** the gospel to them.
20:20 not hesitated to **p** anything that
Ro 1:15 why I am so eager to **p** the gospel
2:21 You who **p** against stealing, do you
10:15 how can they **p** unless they are sent?
15:20 been my ambition to **p** the gospel
1Co 1:17 but to **p** the gospel—not with words
1:23 we **p** Christ crucified: a
9:14 those who **p** the gospel should
9:16 Yet when I **p** the gospel, I cannot
9:16 boast, for I am compelled to **p**.
9:16 Woe to me if I do not **p** the gospel!
9:17 If I **p** voluntarily, I have a reward;
15:11 this is what we **p**, and this is what
2Co 2:12 I went to Troas to **p** the gospel
4: 5 For we do not **p** ourselves, but Jesus
10:16 that we can **p** the gospel in the
Gal 1: 8 should **p** a gospel other than the
1:16 I might **p** him among the Gentiles,
2: 2 gospel that I **p** among the Gentiles.
Eph 3: 8 to **p** to the Gentiles the
Php 1:15 is true that some **p** Christ out of
1:17 The former **p** Christ out of selfish
2Ti 4: 2 **P** the Word; be prepared in season

Preached (Preach)

Dt 13: 5 because he **p** rebellion against the
Jer 28:16 have **p** rebellion against the LORD.
29:32 he has **p** rebellion against me.
Mt 11: 5 and the good news is **p** to the poor.
24:14 this gospel of the kingdom will be **p**
26:13 wherever this gospel is **p** throughout
Mk 2: 2 the door, and he **p** the word to them.
6:12 They went out and **p** that people
13:10 the gospel must first be **p** to all
14: 9 wherever the gospel is **p** throughout
16:20 the disciples went out and **p**
Lk 3:18 people and **p** the good news to them.
7:22 and the good news is **p** to the poor.
16:16 of the kingdom of God is being **p**,
24:47 be **p** in his name to all nations,
Ac 8: 4 Those who had been scattered **p** the
8:12 when they believed Philip as he **p**
9:27 **p** fearlessly in the name of Jesus.
10:37 after the baptism that John **p**—
13:24 John **p** repentance and baptism to
14:21 They **p** the good news in that city
Ac 14:25 they had **p** the word in Perga, they
15:21 For Moses has been **p** in every city
15:35 taught and **p** the word of the Lord.
15:36 where we **p** the word of the Lord
26:20 I **p** that they should repent and
28:31 Boldly and without hindrance he **p**
1Co 1:21 the foolishness of what was **p** to
9:27 so that after I have **p** to others,
15: 1 remind you of the gospel I **p** to you,
15: 2 hold firmly to the word I **p** to you.
15:12 if it is **p** that Christ has been
2Co 1:19 Jesus Christ, who was **p** among you by
11: 4 a Jesus other than the Jesus we **p**,
Gal 1: 8 other than the one we **p** to you,
1:11 the gospel I **p** is not something
4:13 that I first **p** the gospel to you.
Eph 2:17 He came and **p** peace to you who were
Php 1:18 false motives or true, Christ is **p**.
1Th 2: 9 while we **p** the gospel of God to you.
1Ti 3:16 was seen by angels, was **p** among the
Heb 4: 2 For we also have had the gospel **p** to
4: 6 the gospel **p** to them did not go in,
1Pe 1:12 those who have **p** the gospel to you
1:25 this is the word that was **p** to you.
3:19 through whom also he went and **p** to
4: 6 **p** even to those who are now dead,

Preacher (Preach)

2Pe 2: 5 **p** of righteousness, and seven others;

Preaches (Preach)

Ac 19:13 Jesus, whom Paul **p**, I command you
2Co 11: 4 someone comes to you and **p** a Jesus

Preaching (Preach)

Ezr 6:14 prosper under the **p** of Haggai the
Am 7:16 stop **p** against the house of Isaac.'
Mt 3: 1 came, **p** in the Desert of Judea
4:23 **p** the good news of the kingdom, and
9:35 **p** the good news of the kingdom and
12:41 for they repented at the **p** of Jonah,
Mk 1: 4 **p** a baptism of repentance for the
1:39 **p** in their synagogues and driving
Lk 3: 3 **p** a baptism of repentance for the
4:44 he kept on **p** in the synagogues of
9: 6 **p** the gospel and healing people
11:32 for they repented at the **p** of Jonah,
20: 1 the temple courts and **p** the gospel,
Ac 8:25 **p** the gospel in many Samaritan
8:40 **p** the gospel in all the towns until
16: 6 **p** the word in the province of Asia.
17:13 Paul was **p** the word of God at Berea,
17:18 because Paul was **p** the good news
18: 5 devoted himself exclusively to **p**,
20:25 I have gone about **p** the kingdom
Ro 1: 9 heart in **p** the gospel of his Son,
10:14 they hear without someone **p** to them?
1Co 2: 4 My message and my **p** were not with
9:18 that in **p** the gospel I may offer it
9:18 not make use of my rights in **p** it.
15:14 not been raised, our **p** is useless
2Co 11: 7 by **p** the gospel of God to you free
Gal 1: 9 I say again: If anybody is **p** to you
1:23 **p** the faith he once tried to destroy.
2: 7 of **p** the gospel to the Gentiles,
5:11 if I am still **p** circumcision, why
1Ti 4:13 of Scripture, to **p** and to teaching.
5:17 those whose work is **p** and teaching.
Tit 1: 3 through the **p** entrusted to me by

Precede (Preceded, Preceding)

1Th 4:15 not **p** those who have fallen asleep.

Preceded (Precede)

2Ki 17: 2 like the kings of Israel who **p** him.
21:11 evil than the Amorites who **p** him
Jer 28: 8 the prophets who **p** you and me have
34: 5 the former kings who **p** you, so they

Preceding (Precede)

Ne 5:15 the earlier governors—those **p** me

Precepts

Dt 33:10 He teaches your **p** to Jacob and your
Ps 19: 8 The **p** of the LORD are right, giving
103:18 covenant and remember to obey his **p**.
105:45 that they might keep his **p** and
111: 7 and just; all his **p** are trustworthy.
111:10 his **p** have good understanding.
119: 4 You have laid down **p** that are to be
119:15 I meditate on your **p** and consider
119:27 understand the teaching of your **p**;
119:40 How I long for your **p**! Preserve my
119:45 for I have sought out your **p**.
119:56 has been my practice: I obey your **p**.
119:63 fear you, to all who follow your **p**.
119:69 I keep your **p** with all my heart.
119:78 but I will meditate on your **p**.
119:87 but I have not forsaken your **p**.
119:93 I will never forget your **p**, for by
119:94 I am yours; I have sought out your **p**.
119:100 than the elders, for I obey your **p**.
119:104 I gain understanding from your **p**;
119:110 but I have not strayed from your **p**.
119:128 I consider all your **p** right, I hate
119:134 of men, that I may obey your **p**.
119:141 despised, I do not forget your **p**.
119:159 See how I love your **p**; preserve my
119:168 I obey your **p** and your statutes, for
119:173 help me, for I have chosen your **p**.

Precincts

Eze 42:14 Once the priests enter the holy **p**,

Precious

Ge 30:20 "God has presented me with a **p** gift.
Ex 28:17 mount four rows of **p** stones on it.
39:10 they mounted four rows of **p** stones
Dt 33:13 with the **p** dew from heaven above
1Sa 26:21 Because you considered my life **p**
2Sa 12:30 and it was set with **p** stones—and it
1Ki 10: 2 quantities of gold, and **p** stones
10:10 quantities of spices, and **p** stones.
10:11 cargoes of almug-wood and **p** stones.
1Ch 20: 2 and it was set with **p** stones—and it
29: 8 Any who had **p** stones gave them to
2Ch 3: 6 He adorned the temple with **p** stones.
9: 1 quantities of gold, and **p** stones
9: 9 quantities of spices, and **p** stones.
9:10 brought algum-wood and **p** stones.
32:27 and gold and for his **p** stones,
Ezr 8:27 polished bronze, as **p** as gold.
Job 28:16 of Ophir, with **p** onyx or sapphires.
29:24 the light of my face was **p** to them.
Ps 19:10 They are more **p** than gold, than much
22:20 my **p** life from the power of the
35:17 ravages, my **p** life from these lions.
72:14 for **p** is their blood in his sight.
116:15 **P** in the sight of the LORD is the
119:72 The law from your mouth is more **p** to
133: 2 is like **p** oil poured on the head,
139:17 How **p** to me are your thoughts, O God!
Pr 3:15 She is more **p** than rubies;
8:11 for wisdom is more **p** than rubies,
Isa 28:16 a tested stone, a **p** cornerstone for
43: 4 Since you are **p** and honoured in my
54:12 and all your walls of **p** stones.
Lam 4: 2 How the **p** sons of Zion, once worth
Eze 22:25 take treasures and **p** things and make
27:22 of spices and **p** stones, and gold.
28:13 the garden of God; every **p** stone
Da 11:38 with **p** stones and costly gifts.
1Pe 1:19 with the **p** blood of Christ, a lamb
2: 4 men but chosen by God and **p** to him—
2: 6 a chosen and **p** cornerstone, and the
2: 7 to you who believe, this stone is **p**.
2Pe 1: 1 have received a faith as **p** as ours:
1: 4 us his very great and **p** promises,
Rev 17: 4 with gold, **p** stones and pearls.
18:12 cargoes of gold, silver, **p** stones
18:16 with gold, **p** stones and pearls!
21:11 was like that of a very **p** jewel,
21:19 with every kind of **p** stone.

Predecessor (Predecessors)

1Ch 17:13 him, as I took it away from your **p**.

Predecessors (Predecessor)
Dt 19:14 boundary stone set up by your **p** in
Ezr 4:15 be made in the archives of your **p**.

Predestined (Destine)
Ro 8:29 For those God foreknew he also **p** to
8:30 those he **p**, he also called; those he
Eph 1: 5 he **p** us to be adopted as his sons
1:11 having been **p** according to the plan

Predicted (Prediction)
1Sa 28:17 The LORD has done what he **p** through
Ac 7:52 **p** the coming of the Righteous One.
11:28 **p** that a severe famine would spread
16:16 a spirit by which she **p** the future.
1Pe 1:11 when he **p** the sufferings of Christ

Predicting (Prediction)
1Ki 22:13 prophets are **p** success for the king.
2Ch 18:12 prophets are **p** success for the king.

Prediction (Predicted, Predicting, Predictions)
Jer 28: 9 the LORD only if his **p** comes true."

Predictions (Prediction)
Isa 44:26 and fulfils the **p** of his messengers,
47:13 those stargazers who make **p** month by

Pre-eminent
Est 10: 3 **p** among the Jews, and held in high

Prefects
Da 3: 2 He then summoned the satraps, **p**,
3: 3 the satraps, **p**, governors, advisers,
3:27 the satraps, **p**, governors and royal
6: 7 The royal administrators, **p**, satraps,

Prefer (Preference)
1Ki 21: 2 if you **p**, I will pay you whatever it
21: 6 'sell me your vineyard; or if you **p**,
Job 7:15 that I **p** strangling and death,
36:21 which you seem to **p** to affliction.
Jer 8: 3 evil nation will **p** death to life,
Eze 16:32 You **p** strangers to your own husband
1Co 4:21 What do you **p**? Shall I come to you
2Co 5: 8 and would **p** to be away from the

Preference (Prefer)
Dt 21:16 loves in **p** to his actual firstborn,

Pregnancy (Pregnant)
Hos 9:11 no birth, no **p**, no conception.

Pregnant (Pregnancy)
Ge 4: 1 she became **p** and gave birth to Cain.
4:17 became **p** and gave birth to Enoch.
16: 4 When she knew she was **p**, she began
16: 5 she knows she is **p**, she despises me.
19:36 both of Lot's daughters became **p** by
21: 2 Sarah became **p** and bore a son to
25:21 and his wife Rebekah became **p**.
29:32 Leah became **p** and gave birth to a
30: 5 she became **p** and bore him a son.
30:17 became **p** and bore Jacob a fifth son.
30:23 She became **p** and gave birth to a son
38: 3 she became **p** and gave birth to a son,
38:18 with her, and she became **p** by him.
38:24 and as a result she is now **p**.
38:25 "I am **p** by the man who owns these,"
Ex 2: 2 she became **p** and gave birth to a son.
21:22 men who are fighting hit a **p** woman
Lev 12: 2 'A woman who becomes **p** and gives
1Sa 4:19 was **p** and near the time of delivery.
2Sa 11: 5 sent word to David, saying, "I am **p**.
2Ki 4:17 the woman became **p**, and the next
8:12 ground, and rip open their **p** women."
15:16 and ripped open all the **p** women.
1Ch 7:23 became **p** and gave birth to a son.
Ps 7:14 He who is **p** with evil and conceives
Hos 13:16 ground, their **p** women ripped open."
Am 1:13 Because he ripped open the **p** women
Mt 24:19 for **p** women and nursing mothers!
Mk 13:17 for **p** women and nursing mothers!
Lk 1:24 this his wife Elizabeth became **p**
21:23 for **p** women and nursing mothers!
1Th 5: 3 as labour pains on a **p** woman, and
Rev 12: 2 She was **p** and cried out in pain as

Prematurely
Ex 21:22 she gives birth **p** but there is no

Preparation (Prepare)
Nu 11:18 'Consecrate yourselves in **p** for
Jos 7:13 'Consecrate yourselves in **p** for
1Sa 23:22 Go and make further **p**. Find out
Mt 27:62 The next day, the one after **P** Day,
Mk 15:42 was **P** Day (that is, the day before
Lk 23:54 was **P** Day, and the Sabbath was about
Jn 19:14 was the day of **P** of Passover Week,
19:31 Now it was the day of **P**, and the
19:42 it was the Jewish day of **P** and since

Preparations (Prepare)
1Ch 22: 5 Therefore I will make **p** for it."
22: 5 made extensive **p** before his death.
2Ch 35:14 After this, they made **p** for
35:14 So the Levites made **p** for themselves
35:15 fellow Levites made the **p** for them.
Mt 26:17 make **p** for you to eat the Passover?"
Mk 14:12 make **p** for you to eat the Passover?"
14:15 Make **p** for us there."
Lk 10:40 Martha was distracted by all the **p**
22: 8 make **p** for us to eat the Passover."
22:12 room, all furnished. Make **p** there."

Prepare (Preparation, Preparations, Prepared, Prepares, Preparing)
Ge 18: 7 to a servant, who hurried to **p** it.
27: 4 **P** me the kind of tasty food I like
27: 7 'Bring me some game and **p** me some
27: 9 so that I can **p** some tasty food for
43:16 slaughter an animal and **p** dinner;
Ex 12:16 except to **p** food for everyone to eat
12:39 have time to **p** food for themselves.
16: 5 they are to **p** what they bring in,
19:15 he said to the people, "**P** yourselves
Lev 6:21 **P** it with oil on a griddle; bring it
6:22 him as anointed priest shall **p** it.
Nu 15: 5 **p** a quarter of a hin of wine as a
15: 6 "'With a ram **p** a grain offering of
15: 8 "'When you **p** a young bull as a
15:12 for each one, for as many as you **p**.
23: 1 **p** seven bulls and seven rams for me."
23:29 **p** seven bulls and seven rams for me."
28: 4 **P** one lamb in the morning and the
28: 8 **P** the second lamb at twilight, along
28: 8 offering that you **p** in the morning.
28:20 With each bull **p** a grain offering of
28:23 **P** these in addition to the regular
28:24 In this way **p** the food for the
28:31 **P** these together with their drink
29: 2 **p** a burnt offering of one young
29: 3 With the bull **p** a grain offering of
29: 9 With the bull **p** a grain offering of
29:14 With each of the thirteen bulls **p** a
29:17 "'On the second day **p** twelve young
29:18 **p** their grain offerings and drink
29:20 "'On the third day **p** eleven bulls,
29:21 **p** their grain offerings and drink
29:23 "'On the fourth day **p** ten bulls,
29:24 **p** their grain offerings and drink
29:26 "'On the fifth day **p** nine bulls,
29:27 **p** their grain offerings and drink
29:29 "'On the sixth day **p** eight bulls,
29:30 **p** their grain offerings and drink
29:32 "'On the seventh day **p** seven bulls,
29:33 **p** their grain offerings and drink
29:37 the ram and the lambs, **p** their grain
29:39 **p** these for the LORD at your
Jdg 13:15 until we **p** a young goat for you."
13:16 But if you **p** a burnt offering, offer
2Sa 12: 4 to **p** a meal for the traveller who
13: 5 Let her **p** the food in my sight so
13: 7 Amnon and **p** some food for him."
1Ki 18:23 I will **p** the other bull and put it
18:25 "Choose one of the bulls and **p** it
20:12 he ordered his men: "**P** to attack.
2Ki 20: 7 Isaiah said, "**P** a poultice of figs."
1Ch 22: 2 stonecutters to **p** dressed stone for
2Ch 31:11 Hezekiah gave orders to **p** storerooms
35: 4 **P** yourselves by families in your
35: 6 consecrate yourselves and **p** the
Est 5: 8 to the banquet I will **p** for them.
Job 33: 5 **p** yourself and confront me.
Ps 23: 5 You **p** a table before me in the
Isa 8: 9 **P** for battle, and be shattered!
8: 9 **P** for battle, and be shattered!
14:21 **P** a place to slaughter his sons for
25: 6 the LORD Almighty will **p** a feast of
38:21 Isaiah had said, "**P** a poultice of
40: 3 "In the desert **p** the way for the
57:14 "Build up, build up, **p** the road!
62:10 the gates! **P** the way for the people.
Jer 6: 4 "**P** for battle against her!
46: 3 "**P** your shields, both large and
51:12 station the watchmen, **p** an ambush!
51:27 **P** the nations for battle against her;
51:28 **P** the nations for battle against her
Eze 7:23 "**P** chains, because the land is full
Da 11:10 His sons will **p** for war and assemble
Joel 3: 9 this among the nations: **P** for war!
Am 4:12 you, **p** to meet your God, O Israel."
Mic 3: 5 not, they **p** to wage war against him.
Na 1:14 **p** your grave, for you are vile."
Mal 3: 1 who will **p** the way before me.
Mt 3: 3 '**P** the way for the Lord, make
11:10 who will **p** your way before you.'
26:12 body, she did it to **p** me for burial.
Mk 1: 2 ahead of you, who will **p** your way"—
1: 3 '**P** the way for the Lord, make
14: 8 body beforehand to **p** for my burial.
Lk 1:76 the Lord to **p** the way for him,
3: 4 '**P** the way for the Lord, make
7:27 who will **p** your way before you.'
17: 8 '**P** my supper, get yourself ready
22: 9 "Where do you want us to **p** for it?"
Jn 14: 2 am going there to **p** a place for you.
14: 3 if I go and **p** a place for you, I
Eph 4:12 to **p** God's people for works of
Phm :22 one thing more: **P** a guest room for
1Pe 1:13 Therefore, **p** your minds for action;
Rev 16:12 and its water was dried up to **p** the

Prepared (Prepare)
Ge 18: 8 and the calf that had been **p**, and
19: 3 He **p** a meal for them, baking bread
24:31 I have **p** the house and a place for
27:14 and she **p** some tasty food, just the
27:31 He too **p** some tasty food and brought
43:25 They **p** their gifts for Joseph's
Ex 23:20 to bring you to the place I have **p**.
Lev 2: 5 If your grain offering is **p** on a
10:12 eat it **p** without yeast beside the
Nu 15:11 goat, is to be **p** in this manner.
23: 4 "I have **p** seven altars, and on each
28:24 it is to be **p** in addition to the
Jos 24: 9 the king of Moab, **p** to fight against
Jdg 6: 2 the Israelites **p** shelters for
6:19 Gideon went in, **p** a young goat, and
19: 5 they got up early and he **p** to leave,
Ru 1: 6 **p** to return home from there.
2Sa 3:20 David **p** a feast for him and his men.
12: 4 **p** it for the one who had come to him.
13:10 And Tamar took the bread she had **p**
1Ki 5:18 the men of Gebal cut and **p** the timber
6:19 He **p** the inner sanctuary within the
18:26 took the bull given them and **p** it.
20:12 So they **p** to attack the city.
2Ki 6:23 he **p** a great feast for them, and
1Ch 12:33 experienced soldiers **p** for battle
12:36 experienced soldiers **p** for battle—
15: 1 he **p** a place for the ark of God and
15: 3 LORD to the place he had **p** for it.
15:12 Israel, to the place I have **p** for it.
2Ch 1: 4 to the place he had **p** for it,
29:19 We have **p** and consecrated all the
Ezr 1: 5 heart God had moved—**p** to go up
Ne 5:18 and some poultry were **p** for me,
8:10 some to those who have nothing **p**.
Est 5: 4 to a banquet I have **p** for him."

Est 5: 5 went to the banquet Esther had **p**.
6:14 away to the banquet Esther had **p**.
7:10 the gallows he had **p** for Mordecai.
Job 13:18 Now that I have **p** my case, I know I
Ps 7:13 He has **p** his deadly weapons;
78:50 He **p** a path for his anger; he did
Pr 9: 2 She has **p** her meat and mixed her
19:29 Penalties are **p** for mockers, and
SS 3: 8 **p** for the terrors of the night.
Isa 30:33 Topheth has long been **p**; it has been
Eze 28:13 day you were created they were **p**.
38: 7 "'Get ready; be **p**, you and all the
Zep 1: 7 The Lord has **p** a sacrifice; he has
Mt 20:23 whom they have been **p** by my Father."
22: 2 who **p** a wedding banquet for his son.
22: 4 invited that I have **p** my dinner:
25:34 the kingdom **p** for you since the
25:41 fire **p** for the devil and his angels.
26:19 directed them and **p** the Passover.
Mk 10:40 to those for whom they have been **p**."
14:16 told them. So they **p** the Passover.
Lk 1:17 make ready a people **p** for the Lord."
2:31 which you have **p** in the sight of all
12:20 get what you have **p** for yourself?'
22:13 told them. So they **p** the Passover.
23:56 they went home and **p** spices and
24: 1 they had **p** and went to the tomb.
Jn 19:19 Pilate had a notice **p** and fastened
Ac 10:10 was being **p**, he fell into a trance.
Ro 9:22 of his wrath—**p** for destruction?
9:23 whom he **p** in advance for glory—
1Co 2: 9 God has **p** for those who love him"—
Eph 2:10 which God **p** in advance for us to do.
2Ti 2:21 Master and **p** to do any good work.
4: 2 Preach the Word; be **p** in season and
Heb 10: 5 not desire, but a body you **p** for me;
11:16 God, for he has **p** a city for them.
1Pe 3:15 Always be **p** to give an answer to
Rev 8: 6 the seven trumpets **p** to sound them.
9: 7 The locusts looked like horses **p** for
12: 6 desert to a place **p** for her by God,
12:14 the place **p** for her in the desert,
21: 2 **p** as a bride beautifully dressed for

Prepares (Prepare)

Ps 50:23 and he **p** the way so that I may show
85:13 him and **p** the way for his steps.
Isa 44:16 in the fire; over it he **p** his meal,

Preparing (Prepare)

1Ch 9:32 in charge of **p** for every Sabbath
Jer 18:11 Look! I am **p** a disaster for you and
Eze 39:17 to the sacrifice I am **p** for you,
39:19 At the sacrifice I am **p** for you, you
Am 7: 1 He was **p** swarms of locusts after the
Mt 4:21 their father Zebedee, **p** their nets.
Mk 1:19 John in a boat, **p** their nets.
Lk 14:16 certain man was **p** a great banquet
Ac 25: 3 for they were **p** an ambush to kill

Prescribed

Lev 5:10 as a burnt offering in the **p** way
9:16 and offered it in the **p** way.
Nu 15:24 along with its **p** grain offering and
1Sa 2:29 offering that I **p** for my dwelling?
1Ch 15:13 about how to do it in the **p** way."
23:31 number and in the way **p** for them.
24:19 according to the regulations **p** for
2Ch 4:20 front of the inner sanctuary as **p**;
29:25 harps and lyres in the way **p** by
30:16 **p** in the Law of Moses the man of God.
35:13 Passover animals over the fire as **p**,
35:15 were in the places **p** by David, Asaph,
Ezr 3: 4 of burnt offerings **p** for each day.
3:10 Lord, as **p** by David king of Israel.
7:23 Whatever the God of heaven has **p**,
Ne 12:24 other, as **p** by David the man of God.
12:36 musical instruments ⌊**p** by⌋ David
13: 5 new wine and oil **p** for the Levites,
Est 2:12 beauty treatments **p** for the women,
9:27 the way **p** and at the time appointed.
Job 36:23 Who has **p** his ways for him, or said
Eze 45:14 The **p** portion of oil, measured by
Heb 8: 4 who offer the gifts **p** by the law.

Presence (*Bread of the presence, Presence of the Lord, Presence of the Lord, Present*[1])

Ge 4:14 and I will be hidden from your **p**;
4:16 Cain went out from the Lord's **p** and
23:11 I give it to you in the **p** of my
23:18 in the **p** of all the Hittites
27:30 had scarcely left his father's **p**,
31:32 In the **p** of our relatives, see for
31:35 that I cannot stand up in your **p**;
40:20 baker in the **p** of his officials:
41:46 Joseph went out from Pharoah's **p** and
45: 1 "Make everyone leave my **p**!" So there
45: 3 they were terrified at his **p**.
47:10 Pharaoh and went out from his **p**.
Ex 7:20 He raised his staff in the **p** of
9: 8 it into the air in the **p** of Pharaoh.
10:11 Aaron were driven out of Pharaoh's **p**.
18:12 Moses' father-in-law in the **p** of God.
29:11 Slaughter it in the Lord's **p** at the
33:14 The Lord replied, "My **P** will go with
33:15 Moses said to him, "If your **P** does
33:19 my name, the Lord, in your **p**.
34:34 whenever he entered the Lord's **p** to
35:20 community withdrew from Moses' **p**,
Lev 19:32 "'Rise in the **p** of the aged, show
22: 3 person must be cut off from my **p**.
Nu 4: 7 "Over the table of the **P** they are to
6: 9 "'If someone dies suddenly in his **p**,
6:11 by being in the **p** of the dead body.
17: 9 the Lord's **p** to all the Israelites.
19: 3 the camp and slaughtered in his **p**.
20: 9 took the staff from the Lord's **p**,
27:19 and commission him in their **p**.
Dt 4:37 by his **P** and his great strength,
25: 2 have him flogged in his **p** with the
25: 9 go up to him in the **p** of the elders,
31: 7 said to him in the **p** of all Israel,
32:51 in the **p** of the Israelites at the
Jos 8:32 There, in the **p** of the Israelites,
10:12 Joshua said to the Lord in the **p** of
Ru 4: 4 buy it in the **p** of these seated
4: 4 in the **p** of the elders of my people.
1Sa 2:28 and to wear an ephod in my **p**.
16:13 him in the **p** of his brothers,
19:24 and also prophesied in Samuel's **p**.
21:13 he feigned insanity in their **p**;
2Sa 3:13 Do not come into my **p** unless you
22:13 Out of the brightness of his **p** bolts
24: 4 so they left the **p** of the king to
1Ki 1:28 the king's **p** and stood before him.
8: 1 King Solomon summoned into his **p** at
8:28 is praying in your **p** this day.
2Ki 3:14 respect for the **p** of Jehoshaphat
5:27 Then Gehazi went from Elisha's **p**
13:23 them or banish them from his **p**.
17:18 Israel and removed them from his **p**.
17:20 until he thrust them from his **p**.
17:23 the Lord removed them from his **p**,
22:10 read from it in the **p** of the king.
22:19 tore your robes and wept in my **p**,
23:27 "I will remove Judah also from my **p**
24: 3 in order to remove them from his **p**
24:20 the end he thrust them from his **p**.
1Ch 12: 1 he was banished from the **p** of Saul
24: 6 recorded their names in the **p** of the
24:31 in the **p** of King David and of Zadok,
29:10 David praised the Lord in the **p** of
2Ch 6:19 your servant is praying in your **p**.
20: 9 we will stand in your **p** before this
26:19 in their **p** before the incense altar
28:14 plunder in the **p** of the officials
34:18 read from it in the **p** of the king.
34:24 read in the **p** of the king of Judah.
34:27 tore your robes and wept in my **p**,
Ezr 4:18 been read and translated in my **p**.
9:15 not one of us can stand in your **p**."
Ne 1:11 him favour in the **p** of this man.
2: 1 I had not been sad in his **p** before;
4: 2 in the **p** of his associates and the
8: 3 the Water Gate in the **p** of the men,
Est 1:16 Memucan replied in the **p** of the king
1:19 again to enter the **p** of King Xerxes.
2:23 of the annals in the **p** of the king.
3: 7 in the **p** of Haman to select a day
Est 4: 8 into the king's **p** to beg for mercy
5: 9 rose nor showed fear in his **p**,
8: 1 And Mordecai came into the **p** of the
8:15 Mordecai left the king's **p** wearing
Job 30:11 they throw off restraint in my **p**.
Ps 5: 5 The arrogant cannot stand in your **p**;
9:19 let the nations be judged in your **p**.
16:11 you will fill me with joy in your **p**,
18:12 Out of the brightness of his **p**
21: 6 him glad with the joy of your **p**.
23: 5 before me in the **p** of my enemies.
31:20 In the shelter of your **p** you hide
39: 1 as long as the wicked are in my **p**."
41:12 me and set me in your **p** for ever.
51:11 Do not cast me from your **p** or take
52: 9 praise you in the **p** of your saints.
61: 7 May he be enthroned in God's **p** for
89:15 walk in the light of your **p**, O Lord.
90: 8 secret sins in the light of your **p**.
101: 7 speaks falsely will stand in my **p**.
102:28 your servants will live in your **p**;
114: 7 Lord, at the **p** of the God of Jacob,
116:14 the Lord in the **p** of all his people.
116:18 the Lord in the **p** of all his people,
139: 7 Where can I flee from your **p**?
Pr 8:30 day, rejoicing always in his **p**,
14:19 Evil men will bow down in the **p** of
18:16 ushers him into the **p** of the great.
25: 5 remove the wicked from the king's **p**,
25: 6 Do not exalt yourself in the king's **p**
Ecc 8: 3 be in a hurry to leave the king's **p**.
Isa 3: 8 the Lord, defying his glorious **p**.
26:17 pain, so were we in your **p**, O Lord.
63: 9 and the angel of his **p** saved them.
Jer 5:22 "Should you not tremble in my **p**?
7:15 I will thrust you from my **p**, just as
15: 1 send them away from my **p**! Let them
23:39 cast you out of my **p** along with the
28: 1 in the **p** of the priests and all the
32:12 in the **p** of my cousin Hanamel and
32:13 "In their **p** I gave Baruch these
52: 3 the end he thrust them from his **p**.
Eze 28: 9 "I am a god," in the **p** of those who
38:20 of the earth will tremble at my **p**.
44:12 they served them in the **p** of their
Da 4: 8 Finally, Daniel came into my **p** and I
7:13 of Days and was led into his **p**.
Hos 6: 2 us, that we may live in his **p**.
Na 1: 5 The earth trembles at his **p**,
Mal 3:16 was written in his **p** concerning
Mk 7:24 yet he could not keep his **p** secret.
Lk 1:19 I stand in the **p** of God, and I have
8:47 In the **p** of all the people, she told
14:10 in the **p** of all your fellow guests.
15:10 there is rejoicing in the **p** of the
23:14 I have examined him in your **p** and
24:43 he took it and ate it in their **p**.
Jn 8:38 what I have seen in the Father's **p**,
12:37 these miraculous signs in their **p**,
17: 5 now, Father, glorify me in your **p**
20:30 signs in the **p** of his disciples,
Ac 2:28 will fill me with joy in your **p**.'
10:33 Now we are all here in the **p** of God
24:21 I shouted as I stood in their **p**:
2Co 4:14 and present us with you in his **p**.
Php 2:12 always obeyed—not only in my **p**,
1Th 2:19 glory in the **p** of our Lord Jesus
3: 9 in the **p** of our God because of you?
3:13 holy in the **p** of our God and Father
1Ti 6:12 in the **p** of many witnesses.
2Ti 2: 2 say in the **p** of many witnesses
4: 1 In the **p** of God and of Christ Jesus,
Heb 2:12 in the **p** of the congregation I will
9:24 now to appear for us in God's **p**.
1Jn 3:19 we set our hearts at rest in his **p**
Jude :24 present you before his glorious **p**
Rev 14:10 in the **p** of the holy angels and of
20:11 Earth and sky fled from his **p**, and

Presence of the Lord

Ge 27: 7 my blessing in the **p** before I die.'
Ex 28:30 heart whenever he enters the **p**.
Lev 9:24 Fire came out from the **p** and
10: 2 fire came out from the **p** and
Dt 12: 7 There, in the **p** your God, you and

Dt 12:18 Instead, you are to eat them in the **p**
14:23 flocks in the **p** your God at the
14:26 there in the **p** your God and rejoice.
15:20 your family are to eat them in the **p**
18: 7 Levites who serve there in the **p**.
19:17 stand in the **p** before the priests
27: 7 and rejoicing in the **p** your God.
29:10 in the **p** your God—your leaders
29:15 here with us today in the **p** our God
Jos 18: 6 cast lots for you in the **p** our God.
18: 8 for you here at Shiloh in the **p**."
18:10 lots for them in Shiloh in the **p**,
19:51 assigned by lot at Shiloh in the **p**
1Sa 2:21 the boy Samuel grew up in the **p**.
6:20 "Who can stand in the **p**, this holy
11:15 and confirmed Saul as king in the **p**.
12: 3 Testify against me in the **p** and his
26:20 fall to the ground far from the **p**.
1Ki 19:11 stand on the mountain in the **p**, for
2Ki 23: 3 renewed the covenant in the **p**—to
1Ch 29:22 with great joy in the **p** that day.
2Ch 34:31 renewed the covenant in the **p**—to
Job 1:12 Then Satan went out from the **p**.
2: 7 Satan went out from the **p** and
Eze 44: 3 inside the gateway to eat in the **p**.
46: 3 worhsip in the **p** at the entrance to

Presence of the Lord

Ps 114: 7 Tremble, O earth, at the **p**, at the
Lam 2:19 out your heart like water in the **p**.
Zec 6: 5 in the **p** of the whole world.
2Th 1: 9 shut out from the **p** and from the
2Pe 2:11 against such beings in the **p**.

Present[1] (Ever-present, Presence)

Ex 22:14 is not **p**, he must make restitution.
2Sa 14:20 did this to change the **p** situation.
1Ch 9:18 Gate on the east, up to the **p** time.
2Ch 29:29 the king and everyone **p** with him
30:21 Israelites who were **p** in Jerusalem
34:33 all who were **p** in Israel serve the
35:17 The Israelites who were **p** celebrated
Ezr 5:16 From that day to the **p** it has been
8:25 his officials and all Israel **p** there
Est 1: 3 the nobles of the provinces were **p**.
Ps 14: 5 for God is **p** in the company of the
Jer 44:15 along with all the women who were **p**—
Hag 2: 9 'The glory of this **p** house will be
Mk 8: 9 About four thousand men were **p**.
10:30 times as much in this **p** age (homes,
14: 4 Some of those **p** were saying
Lk 5:17 Lord was **p** for him to heal the sick.
12:56 know how to interpret this **p** time?
13: 1 Now there were some **p** at that time
22: 6 over to them when no crowd was **p**.
Ac 1:13 Those **p** were Peter, John, James and
5:38 Therefore, in the **p** case I advise
21:18 James, and all the elders were **p**.
25:24 "King Agrippa, and all who are **p**
Ro 3:26 his justice at the **p** time,
8:18 I consider that our **p** sufferings are
8:22 childbirth right up to the **p** time.
8:38 neither the **p** nor the future, nor
11: 5 at the **p** time there is a remnant
13:11 do this, understanding the **p** time.
1Co 3:22 the **p** or the future—all are yours,
5: 3 Even though I am not physically **p**, I
5: 3 who did this, just as if I were **p**.
5: 4 the power of our Lord Jesus is **p**,
7:26 Because of the **p** crisis, I think
7:31 world in its **p** form is passing away.
2Co 8:14 At the **p** time your plenty will
10:11 be in our actions when we are **p**.
Gal 1: 4 to rescue us from the **p** evil age,
4:25 to the **p** city of Jerusalem,
Eph 1:21 not only in the **p** age but also in
Col 2: 5 I am **p** with you in spirit and
1Ti 4: 8 the **p** life and the life to come.
6:17 those who are rich in this **p** world
Tit 2:12 and godly lives in this **p** age,
Heb 2: 8 Yet at **p** we do not see everything
9: 9 is an illustration for the **p** time,
2Pe 3: 7 By the same word the **p** heavens and

Present[2] (Presentable, Presented, Presenting, Presents)

Ex 10:25 offerings to **p** to the LORD our God.
29: 3 Put them in a basket and **p** them in
34: 2 **P** yourself to me there on top of the
Lev 1: 3 He must **p** it at the entrance to the
2: 8 to the LORD; **p** it to the priest,
3: 1 he is to **p** before the LORD an
3: 7 If he offers a lamb, he is to **p** it
3:12 goat, he is to **p** it before the LORD.
4: 4 He is to **p** the bull at the entrance
4:14 and **p** it before the Tent of Meeting.
6:21 bring it well-mixed and **p** the grain
7:11 offering a person may **p** to the LORD:
7:13 he is to **p** an offering with cakes
9: 2 defect, and **p** them before the LORD.
13:19 he must **p** himself to the priest.
14:11 shall **p** both the one to be cleansed
16: 7 take the two goats and **p** them
17: 4 to **p** it as an offering to the LORD
18:23 A woman must not **p** herself to an
21: 6 Because they **p** the offerings made to
21:21 to **p** the offerings made to the LORD
22:15 the Israelites **p** to the LORD
22:19 you must **p** a male without defect
22:23 You may, however, **p** as a freewill
23: 8 For seven days **p** an offering made to
23:16 and then **p** an offering of new grain
23:18 **P** with this bread seven male lambs,
23:25 but **p** an offering made to the LORD
23:27 and **p** an offering made to the LORD
23:36 For seven days **p** offerings made to
23:36 **p** an offering made to the LORD by
27: 8 he is to **p** the person to the priest,
Nu 3: 6 "Bring the tribe of Levi and **p** them
6:14 There he is to **p** his offerings to
6:16 "'The priest is to **p** them before
6:17 He is to **p** the basket of unleavened
8:11 Aaron is to **p** the Levites before the
8:13 and then **p** them as a wave offering
9:13 he did not **p** the LORD's offering at
15: 3 you **p** to the LORD offerings made by
15: 4 shall **p** to the LORD a grain
15:19 **p** a portion as an offering to the
15:20 **P** a cake from the first of your
15:20 **p** it as an offering from the
16:17 in all—and **p** it before the LORD.
16:17 Aaron are to **p** your censers also."
18:19 the Israelites **p** to the LORD I give
18:24 **p** as an offering to the LORD.
18:26 you must **p** a tenth of that tithe as
18:28 way you also will **p** an offering
18:29 You must **p** as the LORD's portion the
18:30 "Say to the Levites: 'When you **p** the
28: 2 'see that you **p** to me at the
28: 3 fire that you are to **p** to the LORD:
28:11 **p** to the LORD a burnt offering of
28:19 **P** to the LORD an offering made by
28:26 when you **p** to the LORD an offering
28:27 **P** a burnt offering of two young
29: 8 **P** as an aroma pleasing to the LORD a
29:13 **P** an offering made by fire as an
29:36 **P** an offering made by fire as an
Dt 12:27 **P** your burnt offerings on the altar
31:14 Call Joshua and **p** yourselves at the
Jos 7:14 "'In the morning, **p** yourselves
1Sa 1:22 I will take him and **p** him before the
10:19 So now **p** yourselves before the LORD
1Ki 18: 1 "Go and **p** yourself to Ahab, and I
18: 2 Elijah went to **p** himself to Ahab.
18:15 will surely **p** myself to Ahab today."
1Ch 16:40 to **p** burnt offerings to the LORD on
2Ch 13:11 and evening they **p** burnt offerings
23:18 to **p** the burnt offerings of the LORD
29: 7 incense or **p** any burnt offerings
Ezr 6: 3 rebuilt as a place to **p** sacrifices,
Job 1: 6 the angels came to **p** themselves
2: 1 the angels came to **p** themselves
2: 1 with them to **p** himself before him.
23: 7 an upright man could **p** his case
Ps 56:12 I will **p** my thank-offerings to you.
72:10 of Sheba and Seba will **p** him gifts.
Pr 4: 9 **p** you with a crown of splendour."
18:17 The first to **p** his case seems right,
Isa 40:20 A man too poor to **p** such an offering
41:21 "**P** your case," says the LORD.
45:21 Declare what is to be, **p** it—let
Jer 33:18 grain offerings and to **p** sacrifices."
42: 9 sent me to **p** your petition, says:
Eze 43:27 the priests are to **p** your burnt
45: 1 you are to **p** to the LORD a portion
48: 8 you are to **p** as a special gift.
Lk 2:22 to Jerusalem to **p** him to the
Ac 23:30 to **p** to you their case against him.
24:17 for the poor and to **p** offerings.
2Co 4:14 and **p** us with you in his presence.
11: 2 might **p** you as a pure virgin to him.
Eph 5:27 to **p** her to himself as a radiant
Php 4: 6 **p** your requests to God.
Col 1:22 death to **p** you holy in his sight,
1:25 to **p** to you the word of God in its
1:28 we may **p** everyone perfect in Christ.
2Ti 2:15 Do your best to **p** yourself to God as
Jude :24 to **p** you before his glorious

Present[3] (Presents)

Ge 33:11 Please accept the **p** that was brought
1Sa 30:26 "Here is a **p** for you from the
Jer 40: 5 provisions and a **p** and let him go.

Presentable (Present[2])

1Co 12:24 while our **p** parts need no special

Presented (Present[2])

Ge 30:20 Leah said, "God has **p** me with a
43:15 to Egypt and **p** themselves to Joseph.
43:26 Joseph came home, they **p** to him the
47: 2 brothers and **p** them before Pharaoh.
47: 7 Jacob in and **p** him before Pharaoh.
Ex 29:27 was waved and the thigh that was **p**.
32: 6 and **p** fellowship offerings.
35:22 They all **p** their gold as a wave
Lev 7:34 the thigh that is **p** and have given
7:35 were **p** to serve the LORD as priests.
8:14 He then **p** the bull for the sin
8:18 He then **p** the ram for the burnt
8:22 He then **p** the other ram, the ram for
10:14 was waved and the thigh that was **p**.
10:15 The thigh that was **p** and the breast
16:10 shall be **p** alive before the LORD to
27:11 animal must be **p** to the priest,
Nu 6:20 was waved and the thigh that was **p**.
7: 3 These they **p** before the tabernacle.
7:10 and **p** them before the altar.
8:15 and **p** them as a wave offering,
8:21 Then Aaron **p** them as a wave offering
16:38 for they were **p** before the LORD and
18: 8 in charge of the offerings **p** to me;
28:15 be **p** to the LORD as a sin offering.
31:52 **p** as a gift to the LORD weighed
Dt 31:14 **p** themselves at the Tent of Meeting.
Jos 24: 1 and they **p** themselves before God.
Jdg 3:17 He **p** the tribute to Eglon king of
3:18 After Ehud had **p** the tribute, he
20:26 **p** burnt offerings and fellowship
21: 4 **p** burnt offerings and fellowship
1Sa 18:27 and **p** the full number to the king
2Ki 11:12 he **p** him with a copy of the covenant
16:12 approached it and **p** offerings on it.
1Ch 6:49 were the ones who **p** offerings on
16: 1 and they **p** burnt offerings and
23:31 whenever burnt offerings were **p** to
29:21 LORD and **p** burnt offerings to him:
2Ch 23:11 they **p** him with a copy of the
24:14 burnt offerings were **p** continually
28:21 and **p** them to the king of Assyria,
29:24 **p** their blood on the altar for a sin
Ezr 3: 5 After that, they **p** the regular burnt
10:19 for their guilt they each **p** a ram
Est 8: 2 from Haman, and **p** it to Mordecai.
Eze 20:28 **p** their fragrant incense and poured
Da 1:18 official **p** them to Nebuchadnezzar.
2:46 an offering and incense be **p** to him.
Mt 2:11 **p** him with gifts of gold and of
Mk 6:28 He **p** it to the girl, and she gave it
Ac 6: 6 They **p** these men to the apostles,
9:41 the widows and **p** her to them alive.
24: 2 Tertullus **p** his case before Felix:
25: 2 him and **p** the charges against Paul.
Ro 3:25 God **p** him as a sacrifice of

Presenting (Present[2])
Ex 30:20 by **p** an offering made to the LORD
35:24 Those **p** an offering of silver or
Nu 9: 7 but why should we be kept from **p** the
18:32 By **p** the best part of it you will
Eze 46:14 The **p** of this grain offering to the
Ac 17:19 this new teaching is that you are **p**?

Presents[1] (Present[2])
Lev 6: 5 on the day he **p** his guilt offering.
22:18 **p** a gift for a burnt offering to the
Nu 15:14 among you **p** an offering made by
Isa 66: 3 is like one who **p** pig's blood,

Presents[2] (Present[3])
Est 9:19 a day for giving **p** to each other.
9:22 and giving **p** of food to one another

Preserve (Preserved, Preserves)
Ge 19:32 **p** our family line through our father.
19:34 **p** our family line through our father.
45: 7 God sent me ahead of you to **p** for
Job 33:18 to **p** his soul from the pit, his life
Ps 36: 6 O LORD, you **p** both man and beast.
41: 2 will protect him and **p** his life;
79:11 your arm **p** those condemned to die.
119:25 **p** my life according to your word.
119:37 **p** my life according to your word.
119:40 **P** my life in your righteousness.
119:88 **P** my life according to your love,
119:107 **p** my life, O LORD, according to
119:149 **p** my life, O LORD, according to
119:154 **p** my life according to your promise
119:156 **p** my life according to your laws.
119:159 **p** my life, O LORD, according to
138: 7 you **p** my life; you stretch out your
143:11 name's sake, O LORD, **p** my life;
Pr 3:21 My son, **p** sound judgment and
5: 2 and your lips may **p** knowledge.
Eze 7:13 not one of them will **p** his life.
13:18 lives of my people but **p** your own?
Mal 2: 7 of a priest ought to **p** knowledge,
Lk 17:33 whoever loses his life will **p** it.

Preserved (Preserve)
2Sa 22:44 have **p** me as the head of nations.
Ps 66: 9 he has **p** our lives and kept our feet
119:93 for by them you have **p** my life.
Mt 9:17 into new wineskins, and both are **p**."

Preserves (Preserve)
Ps 31:23 The LORD **p** the faithful, but the
119:50 is this: Your promise **p** my life.
Ecc 7:12 wisdom **p** the life of its possessor.

Presides
Ps 82: 1 God **p** in the great assembly;

Press (Pressed, Presses, Pressing, Pressure)
Jdg 14:17 her, because she continued to **p** him.
2Sa 11:25 **P** the attack against the city and
Job 23: 6 he would not **p** charges against me.
Ps 56: 1 all day long they **p** their attack.
Pr 6: 3 **p** your plea with your neighbour!
Hos 6: 3 let us **p** on to acknowledge him.
Mic 6:15 you will **p** olives but not use the
Ac 19:38 They can **p** charges.
25: 5 and **p** charges against the man there,
Php 3:12 but I **p** on to take hold of that for
3:14 I **p** on towards the goal to win the
Rev 14:20 and blood flowed out of the **p**,

Pressed (Press)
Ex 27:20 clear oil of **p** olives for the light
29:40 of a hin of oil from **p** olives,
Lev 24: 2 clear oil of **p** olives for the light
Nu 22:25 she **p** close to the wall, crushing
28: 5 of a hin of oil from **p** olives.
Jdg 1:28 they **p** the Canannites into forced
1:35 they too were **p** into forced labour.
9:45 All that day Abimelech **p** his attack
1Sa 13: 6 and that their army was hard **p**,
25:18 two hundred cakes of **p** figs, and
30:12 part of a cake of **p** figs and two
31: 2 The Philistines **p** hard after Saul
1Ki 5:11 thousand baths, of **p** olive oil.
1Ch 10: 2 The Philistines **p** hard after Saul
Mk 5:24 crowd followed and **p** around him.
Lk 6:38 A good measure, **p** down, shaken
2Co 4: 8 We are hard **p** on every side, but not
8:13 be relieved while you are hard **p**,

Presses (Press)
Isa 16:10 no-one treads out wine at the **p**,
Jer 48:33 stopped the flow of wine from the **p**;

Pressing (Press)
Ex 5:13 The slave drivers kept **p** them,
Jdg 20:45 They kept **p** after the Benjamites as
Lk 8:45 are crowding and **p** against you."

Pressure (Press)
Ge 19: 9 They kept bringing **p** on Lot and
2Co 1: 8 We were under great **p**, far beyond
11:28 **p** of my concern for all the churches.

Presume (Presumes, Presumption, Presumptuously)
Jas 3: 1 Not many of you should **p** to be

Presumes (Presume)
Dt 18:20 a prophet who **p** to speak in my name

Presumption (Presume)
Nu 14:44 Nevertheless, in their **p** they went

Presumptuously (Presume)
Dt 18:22 That prophet has spoken **p**. Do not be

Pretence (Pretend)
1Ki 14: 6 Why this **p**? I have been sent to you
Jer 3:10 but only in **p**," declares the LORD.

Pretend (Pretence, Pretended, Pretending, Pretends, Pretension)
2Sa 13: 5 "Go to bed and **p** to be ill," Jonadab
14: 2 He said to her, "**P** you are in
1Ki 14: 5 she will **p** to be someone else."
Pr 12: 9 **p** to be somebody and have no food.

Pretended (Pretend)
Ge 42: 7 he recognised them, but he **p** to be a
2Sa 13: 6 Amnon lay down and **p** to be ill.
Ps 34: T he **p** to be insane before Abimelech
Lk 20:20 they sent spies, who **p** to be honest.

Pretending (Pretend)
Ac 27:30 **p** they were going to lower some

Pretends (Pretend)
Pr 13: 7 One man **p** to be rich, yet has
13: 7 **p** to be poor, yet has great wealth.

Pretension (Pretend)
2Co 10: 5 We demolish arguments and every **p**

Pretext
Ac 23:15 on the **p** of wanting more accurate
23:20 on the **p** of wanting more accurate

Prevail (Prevailed, Prevails, Prevalent)
2Ch 14:11 do not let man **p** against you."
Isa 54:17 no weapon forged against you will **p**,
Jer 5:22 waves may roll, but they cannot **p**;
20:10 then we will **p** over him and take our
20:11 persecutors will stumble and not **p**.
Ro 3: 4 you speak and **p** when you judge."

Prevailed (Prevail)
Jdg 19: 4 the girl's father, **p** upon him to
Jer 20: 7 you overpowered me and **p**.
Lam 1:16 destitute because the enemy has **p**."
Lk 23:23 he be crucified, and their shouts **p**.

Prevails (Prevail)
1Sa 2: 9 "It is not by strength that one **p**;
Pr 19:21 but it is the LORD's purpose that **p**.
Hab 1: 4 is paralysed, and justice never **p**.

Prevalent (Prevail)
Jas 1:21 filth and the evil that is so **p**,

Prevent (Prevented)
2Sa 14:11 to **p** the avenger of blood from
1Ki 15:17 fortified Ramah to **p** anyone from
2Ch 16: 1 fortified Ramah to **p** anyone from
Mal 3:11 I will **p** pests from devouring your
Jn 18:36 fight to **p** my arrest by the Jews.
Ac 27:42 to **p** any of them from swimming away
Rev 7: 1 to **p** any wind from blowing on the

Prevented (Prevent)
Ro 1:13 (but have been **p** from doing so
Heb 7:23 **p** them from continuing in office;

Previous (Previously)
Nu 6:12 The **p** days do not count, because he
Jdg 3: 2 had not had **p** battle experience):
Gal 1:13 For you have heard of my **p** way of

Previously (Previous)
1Sa 14:21 Those Hebrews who had **p** been with
1Ch 6:65 they allotted the **p** named towns.
Ac 21:29 (They had **p** seen Trophimus the
Ro 9:29 is just as Isaiah said **p**: "Unless
Gal 3:17 the covenant **p** established by God
1Th 2: 2 We had **p** suffered and been insulted

Prey (Preys)
Ge 15:11 birds of **p** came down on the
49: 9 you return from the **p**, my son.
49:27 in the morning he devours the **p**,
Nu 23:24 does not rest till he devours his **p**
Job 4:11 The lion perishes for lack of **p**, and
9:26 eagles swooping down on their **p**.
24:21 They **p** on the barren and childless
28: 7 No bird of **p** knows that hidden path,
38:39 "Do you hunt the **p** for the lioness
Ps 17:12 They are like a lion hungry for **p**,
22:13 Roaring lions tearing their **p** open
104:21 The lions roar for their **p** and seek
Isa 5:29 they growl as they seize their **p** and
10: 2 making widows their **p** and robbing
18: 6 birds of **p** and to the wild animals;
31: 4 a great lion over his **p**—and though
46:11 From the east I summon a bird of **p**;
59:15 and whoever shuns evil becomes a **p**.
Jer 12: 9 like a speckled bird of **p**
12: 9 that other birds of **p** surround and
Eze 13:21 will no longer fall **p** to your power.
19: 3 He learned to tear the **p** and he
19: 6 He learned to tear the **p** and he
22:25 like a roaring lion tearing its **p**;
22:27 her are like wolves tearing their **p**;
Am 3: 4 in the thicket when he has no **p**?
Na 2:12 and strangled the **p** for his mate,
2:12 the kill and his dens with the **p**.
2:13 I will leave you no **p** on the earth.

Preys (Prey)
Pr 6:26 adulteress **p** upon your very life.

Price (Bride-price, Priced, Priceless)
Ge 23: 9 sell it to me for the full **p** as a
23:13 I will pay the **p** of the field.
23:16 weighed out for him the **p** he had
34:12 Make the **p** for the bride and the
Lev 25:16 you are to increase the **p**, and when
25:16 you are to decrease the **p**, because
25:50 The **p** for his release is to be based
25:51 larger share of the **p** paid for him.
Nu 18:16 **p** set at five shekels of silver,
Dt 2:28 to drink for their **p** in silver.
1Sa 13:21 The **p** was two thirds of a shekel for

1Sa 18:25 'The king wants no other **p** for the
2Sa 3:14 **p** of a hundred Philistine foreskins."
1Ch 21:22 Sell it to me at the full **p**."
21:24 "No, I insist on paying the full **p**.
Job 28:15 nor can its **p** be weighed in silver.
28:18 the **p** of wisdom is beyond rubies.
Pr 27:26 and the goats with the **p** of a field.
Isa 45:13 but not for a **p** or reward, says the
Lam 5: 4 our wood can be had only at a **p**.
Da 11:39 and will distribute the land at a **p**.
Am 8: 5 boosting the **p** and cheating with
Mic 3:11 her priests teach for a **p**, and her
Zec 11:13 handsome **p** at which they priced me!
Mt 26: 9 could have been sold at a high **p**
27: 9 **p** set on him by the people of Israel,
Ac 5: 8 "Tell me, is this the **p** you and
5: 8 "Yes," she said, "that is the **p**.
22:28 to pay a big **p** for my citizenship.
1Co 6:20 you were bought at a **p**. Therefore
7:23 You were bought at a **p**; do not

Priced (Price)

Zec 11:13 handsome price at which they **p** me!

Priceless (Price)

Ps 36: 7 How **p** is your unfailing love!

Pride (Proud)

Lev 26:19 I will break down your stubborn **p**
2Ki 19:22 and lifted your eyes in **p**?
2Ch 26:16 his **p** led to his downfall.
32:26 Hezekiah repented of the **p** of his
Job 20: 6 Though his **p** reaches to the heavens
33:17 from wrongdoing and keep him from **p**,
Ps 10: 4 In his **p** the wicked does not seek
31:18 for with **p** and contempt they speak
47: 4 us, the **p** of Jacob, whom he loved.
56: 2 many are attacking me in their **p**.
59:12 lips, let them be caught in their **p**.
62:10 or take **p** in stolen goods;
73: 6 Therefore **p** is their necklace;
Pr 8:13 I hate **p** and arrogance, evil
11: 2 **p** comes, then comes disgrace, but
13:10 **P** only breeds quarrels, but wisdom
16:18 **P** goes before destruction, a haughty
17: 6 parents are the **p** of their children.
21:24 he behaves with overweening **p**.
29:23 A man's **p** brings him low, but a man
Ecc 7: 8 and patience is better than **p**.
Isa 2:11 and the **p** of men brought low;
2:17 low and the **p** of men humbled;
4: 2 the land will be the **p** and glory of
9: 9 say with **p** and arrogance of heart,
10:12 for the wilful **p** of his heart
13:11 will humble the **p** of the ruthless.
13:19 the glory of the Babylonians' **p**,
16: 6 We have heard of Moab's **p**—her
16: 6 her overweening **p** and conceit,
16: 6 her **p** and her insolence—
23: 9 to bring low the **p** of all glory and
25:11 God will bring down their **p** despite
28: 1 the **p** of Ephraim's drunkards,
28: 1 the **p** of those laid low by wine!
28: 3 the **p** of Ephraim's drunkards,
37:23 and lifted your eyes in **p**?
43:14 in the ships in which they took **p**.
60:15 **p** and the joy of all generations.
Jer 13: 9 same way I will ruin the **p** of Judah
13: 9 Judah and the great **p** of Jerusalem.
13:17 weep in secret because of your **p**;
48:29 "We have heard of Moab's **p**—her
48:29 her overweening **p** and conceit,
48:29 her **p** and arrogance and the
49:16 you inspire and the **p** of your heart
Eze 7:24 put an end to the **p** of the mighty,
16:56 sister Sodom in the day of your **p**,
24:21 stronghold in which you take **p**,
28: 2 'In the **p** of your heart you say, "I
32:12 They will shatter the **p** of Egypt,
Da 4:37 who walk in **p** he is able to humble.
5:20 became arrogant and hardened with **p**,
11:12 will be filled with **p** and will
Am 6: 8 "I abhor the **p** of Jacob and detest
8: 7 The LORD has sworn by the **P** of Jacob:
Ob : 3 The **p** of your heart has deceived you,
Zep 2:10 they will get in return for their **p**,
3:11 city those who rejoice in their **p**.
Zec 9: 6 cut off the **p** of the Philistines.
10:11 Assyria's **p** will be brought down and
1Co 4: 6 **p** in one man over against another.
2Co 5:12 you an opportunity to take **p** in us,
5:12 those who take **p** in what is seen
7: 4 in you; I take great **p** in you.
8:24 and the reason for our **p** in you,
Gal 6: 4 Then he can take **p** in himself,
Jas 1: 9 to take **p** in his high position.
1:10 the one who is rich should take **p** in

Priest (*High priest*, Priest's, Priesthood, Priestly, Priests, Priests')

Ge 14:18 He was **p** of God Most High,
41:45 Potiphera, **p** of On, to be his wife.
41:50 daughter of Potiphera, **p** of On.
46:20 daughter of Potiphera, **p** of On.
Ex 2:16 Now a **p** of Midian had seven
3: 1 the **p** of Midian, and he led the
18: 1 Now Jethro, the **p** of Midian and
28: 3 so that he may serve me as **p**.
29:30 The son who succeeds him as **p** and
30:33 a **p** must be cut off from his people.
31:10 the sacred garments for Aaron the **p**
35:19 the sacred garments for Aaron the **p**
38:21 of Ithamar son of Aaron, the **p**.
39:41 the sacred garments for Aaron the **p**
40:13 him so that he may serve me as **p**.
Lev 1: 7 The sons of Aaron the **p** are to put
1: 9 **p** is to burn all of it on the altar.
1:12 and the **p** shall arrange them,
1:13 and the **p** is to bring all of it and
1:15 The **p** shall bring it to the altar,
1:17 and then the **p** shall burn it on the
2: 2 The **p** shall take a handful of the
2: 8 present it to the **p**, who shall take
2:16 The **p** shall burn the memorial
3:11 The **p** shall burn them on the altar
3:16 The **p** shall burn them on the altar
4: 3 "'If the anointed **p** sins, bringing
4: 5 the anointed **p** shall take some of
4: 7 The **p** shall then put some of the
4:10 Then the **p** shall burn them on the
4:16 the anointed **p** is to take some of
4:20 In this way the **p** will make
4:25 the **p** shall take some of the blood
4:26 In this way the **p** will make
4:30 the **p** is to take some of the blood
4:31 and the **p** shall burn it on the altar
4:31 In this way the **p** will make
4:34 the **p** shall take some of the blood
4:35 and the **p** shall burn it on the altar
4:35 In this way the **p** will make
5: 6 the **p** shall make atonement for him
5: 8 He is to bring them to the **p**, who
5:10 The **p** shall then offer the other as
5:12 He is to bring it to the **p**, who
5:13 In this way the **p** will make
5:13 the offering will belong to the **p**,
5:16 to that and give it all to the **p**,
5:18 He is to bring to the **p** as a guilt
5:18 In this way the **p** will make
6: 6 a penalty he must bring to the **p**,
6: 7 In this way the **p** will make
6:10 The **p** shall then put on his linen
6:12 Every morning the **p** is to add
6:15 The **p** is to take a handful of fine
6:22 him as anointed **p** shall prepare it.
6:23 Every grain offering of a **p** shall be
6:26 The **p** who offers it shall eat it;
7: 5 The **p** shall burn them on the altar
7: 7 the **p** who makes atonement with them.
7: 8 The **p** who offers a burnt offering
7: 9 belongs to the **p** who offers it,
7:14 it belongs to the **p** who sprinkles
7:31 The **p** shall burn the fat on the
7:32 to the **p** as a contribution.
7:34 have given them to Aaron the **p** and
12: 6 she is to bring to the **p** at the
12: 8 In this way the **p** will make
13: 2 he must be brought to Aaron the **p**
13: 2 or to one of his sons who is a **p**.
13: 3 The **p** is to examine the sore on his
Lev 13: 3 When the **p** examines him, he shall
13: 4 the **p** is to put the infected person
13: 5 On the seventh day the **p** is to
13: 6 On the seventh day the **p** is to
13: 6 the **p** shall pronounce him clean;
13: 7 to the **p** to be pronounced clean,
13: 7 he must appear before the **p** again.
13: 8 The **p** is to examine him, and if the
13: 9 he must be brought to the **p**.
13:10 The **p** is to examine him, and if
13:11 the **p** shall pronounce him unclean.
13:12 so far as the **p** can see, it covers
13:13 the **p** is to examine him, and if the
13:15 the **p** sees the raw flesh, he shall
13:16 and turn white, he must go to the **p**.
13:17 The **p** is to examine him, and if the
13:17 the **p** shall pronounce the infected
13:19 he must present himself to the **p**.
13:20 The **p** is to examine it, and if it
13:20 the **p** shall pronounce him unclean.
13:21 if, when the **p** examines it, there is
13:21 then the **p** is to put him in
13:22 the **p** shall pronounce him unclean;
13:23 and the **p** shall pronounce him clean.
13:25 the **p** is to examine the spot, and if
13:25 The **p** shall pronounce him unclean;
13:26 if the **p** examines it and there is no
13:26 then the **p** is to put him in
13:27 On the seventh day the **p** is to
13:27 the **p** shall pronounce him unclean;
13:28 and the **p** shall pronounce him clean;
13:30 the **p** is to examine the sore, and if
13:30 the **p** shall pronounce that person
13:31 if, when the **p** examines this kind of
13:31 then the **p** is to put the infected
13:32 On the seventh day the **p** is to
13:33 and the **p** is to keep him in
13:34 On the seventh day the **p** is to
13:34 the **p** shall pronounce him clean.
13:36 the **p** is to examine him, and if the
13:36 the **p** does not need to look for
13:37 and the **p** shall pronounce him clean.
13:39 the **p** is to examine them, and if the
13:43 The **p** is to examine him, and if the
13:44 The **p** shall pronounce him unclean
13:49 mildew and must be shown to the **p**.
13:50 The **p** is to examine the mildew and
13:53 "But if, when the **p** examines it, the
13:55 the **p** is to examine it, and if the
13:56 If, when the **p** examines it, the
14: 2 when he is brought to the **p**:
14: 3 The **p** is to go outside the camp and
14: 4 the **p** shall order that two live
14: 5 the **p** shall order that one of the
14:11 The **p** who pronounces him clean shall
14:12 "Then the **p** is to take one of the
14:13 belongs to the **p**; it is most holy.
14:14 The **p** is to take some of the blood
14:15 The **p** shall then take some of the
14:17 The **p** is to put some of the oil
14:18 the **p** shall put on the head of the
14:19 "Then the **p** is to sacrifice the sin
14:19 **p** shall slaughter the burnt
14:23 for his cleansing to the **p** at the
14:24 The **p** is to take the lamb for the
14:26 The **p** is to pour some of the oil
14:29 the **p** shall put on the head of the
14:31 In this way the **p** will make
14:35 of the house must go and tell the **p**,
14:36 The **p** is to order the house to be
14:36 **p** is to go in and inspect the house.
14:38 the **p** shall go out of the doorway of
14:39 On the seventh day the **p** shall
14:44 the **p** is to go and examine it and,
14:48 "But if the **p** comes to examine it
15:14 of Meeting and give them to the **p**.
15:15 The **p** is to sacrifice them, the one
15:29 bring them to the **p** at the entrance
15:30 The **p** is to sacrifice one for a sin
16:32 The **p** who is anointed and ordained
17: 5 They must bring them to the **p**, that
17: 6 The **p** is to sprinkle the blood
19:22 the **p** is to make atonement for him
21: 1 'A **p** must not make himself
21:21 No descendant of Aaron the **p** who has
22:10 guest of a **p** or his hired worker

Lev 22:11 if a **p** buys a slave with money, or
22:12 marries anyone other than a **p**,
22:14 he must make restitution to the **p**
23:10 bring to the **p** a sheaf of the first
23:11 the **p** is to wave it on the day after
23:20 The **p** is to wave the two lambs
23:20 offering to the LORD for the **p**.
27: 8 is to present the person to the **p**,
27:11 animal must be presented to the **p**,
27:12 Whatever value the **p** then sets,
27:14 the **p** will judge its quality as good
27:14 Whatever value the **p** then sets,
27:18 the **p** will determine the value
27:23 the **p** will determine its value up to
Nu 3: 6 them to Aaron the **p** to assist him.
3:32 was Eleazar son of Aaron, the **p**.
4:16 "Eleazar son of Aaron, the **p**, is to
4:28 of Ithamar son of Aaron, the **p**.
4:33 of Ithamar son of Aaron, the **p**."
5: 8 the LORD and must be given to the **p**,
5: 9 bring to a **p** will belong to him.
5:10 gives to the **p** will belong to the **p**.
5:15 he is to take his wife to the **p**.
5:16 "'The **p** shall bring her and make
5:18 After the **p** has made the woman stand
5:19 the **p** shall put the woman under oath
5:21 here the **p** is to put the woman under
5:23 "'The **p** is to write these curses on
5:25 The **p** is to take from her hands the
5:26 The **p** is then to take a handful of
5:30 The **p** is to make her stand before
6:10 or two young pigeons to the **p** at
6:11 The **p** is to offer one as a sin
6:16 "'The **p** is to present them before
6:19 the **p** is to place in his hands a
6:20 The **p** shall then wave them before
6:20 they are holy and belong to the **p**,
7: 8 of Ithamar son of Aaron, the **p**.
15:25 The **p** is to make atonement for the
15:28 The **p** is to make atonement before
16:37 "Tell Eleazar son of Aaron, the **p**,
16:39 Eleazar the **p** collected the bronze
18:28 the LORD's portion to Aaron the **p**.
19: 3 Give it to Eleazar the **p**; it is to
19: 4 Eleazar the **p** is to take some of its
19: 6 The **p** is to take some cedar wood,
19: 7 After that, the **p** must wash his
25: 7 the son of Aaron, the **p**, saw this,
25:11 the son of Aaron, the **p**, has turned
26: 1 and Eleazar son of Aaron, the **p**,
26: 3 the **p** spoke with them and said,
26:63 Eleazar the **p** when they counted the
26:64 Aaron the **p** when they counted the
27: 2 Eleazar the **p**, the leaders and the
27:19 Make him stand before Eleazar the **p**
27:21 He is to stand before Eleazar the **p**,
27:22 Eleazar the **p** and the whole assembly.
31: 6 Phinehas son of Eleazar, the **p**, who
31:12 plunder to Moses and Eleazar the **p**
31:13 Moses, Eleazar the **p** and all the
31:21 Eleazar the **p** said to the soldiers
31:26 "You and Eleazar the **p** and the
31:29 to Eleazar the **p** as the LORD's part.
31:31 Moses and Eleazar the **p** did as the
31:41 to Eleazar the **p** as the LORD's part,
31:51 Moses and Eleazar the **p** accepted
31:54 Moses and Eleazar the **p** accepted the
32: 2 they came to Moses and Eleazar the **p**
32:28 orders about them to Eleazar the **p**
33:38 At the LORD's command Aaron the **p**
34:17 Eleazar the **p** and Joshua son of Nun.
Dt 10: 6 Eleazar his son succeeded him as **p**.
17:12 for the **p** who stands ministering
20: 2 the **p** shall come forward and address
26: 3 say to the **p** in office at the time,
26: 4 The **p** shall take the basket from
Jos 14: 1 which Eleazar the **p**, Joshua son of
17: 4 They went to Eleazar the **p**, Joshua
19:51 the territories that Eleazar the **p**,
21: 1 Levites approached Eleazar the **p**,
21: 4 descendants of Aaron the **p** were
21:13 to the descendants of Aaron the **p**
22:13 Phinehas son of Eleazar, the **p**,
22:30 Phinehas the **p** and the leaders of
22:31 Phinehas son of Eleazar, the **p**, said
22:32 Phinehas son of Eleazar, the **p**, and
Jdg 17: 5 installed one of his sons as his **p**.
17:10 "Live with me and be my father and **p**,
17:12 became his **p** and lived in his house.
17:13 since this Levite has become my **p**."
18: 4 "He has hired me and I am his **p**.
18: 6 The **p** answered them, "Go in peace.
18:17 the cast idol while the **p** and the
18:18 the **p** said to them, "What are you
18:19 with us, and be our father and **p**.
18:19 clan in Israel as **p** rather than just
18:20 the **p** was glad. He took the ephod,
18:24 I made, and my **p**, and went away.
18:27 and his **p**, and went on to Laish,
1Sa 1: 9 Now Eli the **p** was sitting on a chair
2:11 before the LORD under Eli the **p**.
2:13 the servant of the **p** would come with
2:14 and the **p** would take for himself
2:15 the servant of the **p** would come and
2:15 "Give the **p** some meat to roast;
2:28 all the tribes of Israel to be my **p**,
2:35 raise up for myself a faithful **p**,
14: 3 son of Eli, the LORD's **p** in Shiloh.
14:19 While Saul was talking to the **p**, the
14:19 So Saul said to the **p**, "Withdraw
14:36 But the **p** said, "Let us enquire of
21: 1 David went to Nob, to Ahimelech the **p**
21: 2 David answered Ahimelech the **p**, "The
21: 4 the **p** answered David, "I don't have
21: 6 the **p** gave him the consecrated bread,
21: 9 The **p** replied, "The sword of Goliath
22:11 the king sent for the **p** Ahimelech
23: 9 to Abiathar the **p**, "Bring the ephod.
30: 7 David said to Abiathar the **p**, the
2Sa 15:27 The king also said to Zadok the **p**,
20:26 Ira the Jairite was David's **p**.
1Ki 1: 7 and with Abiathar the **p**, and they
1: 8 Zadok the **p**, Benaiah son of Jehoiada,
1:19 Abiathar the **p** and Joab the
1:25 of the army and Abiathar the **p**.
1:26 me your servant, and Zadok the **p**,
1:32 King David said, "Call in Zadok the **p**
1:34 There shall Zadok the **p** and Nathan
1:38 Zadok the **p**, Nathan the prophet,
1:39 Zadok the **p** took the horn of oil
1:42 son of Abiathar the **p** arrived.
1:44 king has sent with him Zadok the **p**,
1:45 Zadok the **p** and Nathan the prophet
2:22 for Abiathar the **p** and Joab son of
2:26 To Abiathar the **p** the king said, "Go
2:35 replaced Abiathar with Zadok the **p**.
4: 2 Azariah son of Zadok—the **p**;
4: 5 **p** and personal adviser to the king;
13:33 to become a **p** he consecrated for
2Ki 11: 9 did just as Jehoiada the **p** ordered.
11: 9 duty—and came to Jehoiada the **p**.
11:15 Jehoiada the **p** ordered the
11:15 For the **p** had said, "She must not
11:18 killed Mattan the **p** of Baal in
11:18 Then Jehoiada the **p** posted guards at
12: 2 years Jehoiada the **p** instructed him.
12: 5 Let every **p** receive the money from
12: 7 King Joash summoned Jehoiada the **p**
12: 9 Jehoiada the **p** took a chest and
16:10 Uriah the **p** a sketch of the altar,
16:11 Uriah the **p** built an altar in
16:15 gave these orders to Uriah the **p**:
16:16 Uriah the **p** did just as King Ahaz
22:10 "Hilkiah the **p** has given me a book.
22:12 He gave these orders to Hilkiah the **p**
22:14 Hilkiah the **p**, Ahikam, Acbor,
23:24 that Hilkiah the **p** had discovered
25:18 as prisoners Seraiah the chief **p**,
25:18 Zephaniah the **p** next in rank and the
1Ch 6:10 served as **p** in the temple Solomon
16:39 David left Zadok the **p** and his
24: 6 and of the officials: Zadok the **p**,
27: 5 was Benaiah son of Jehoiada the **p**.
29:22 LORD to be ruler and Zadok to be **p**.
2Ch 13: 9 may become a **p** of what are not gods.
15: 3 without a **p** to teach and without
19:11 "Amariah the chief **p** will be over
22:11 Jehoram and wife of the **p** Jehoiada,
23: 8 did just as Jehoiada the **p** ordered.
23: 8 for Jehoiada the **p** had not released
23:14 Jehoiada the **p** sent out the
23:14 For the **p** had said, "Do not put her
2Ch 23:17 killed Mattan the **p** of Baal in
24: 2 LORD all the years of Jehoiada the **p**.
24: 6 Jehoiada the chief **p** and said to him,
24:11 the officer of the chief **p** would
24:20 Zechariah son of Jehoiada the **p**.
24:25 the son of Jehoiada the **p**, and they
26:17 Azariah the **p** with eighty other
26:20 Azariah the chief **p** and all the
31:10 Azariah the chief **p**, from the family
34:14 Hilkiah the **p** found the Book of the
34:18 "Hilkiah the **p** has given me a book.
Ezr 2:63 was a **p** ministering with the Urim
7: 5 the son of Aaron the chief **p**—
7:11 had given to Ezra the **p** and teacher,
7:12 To Ezra the **p**, a teacher of the Law
7:21 with diligence whatever Ezra the **p**,
8:33 of Meremoth son of Uriah, the **p**.
10:10 Ezra the **p** stood up and said to them,
10:16 Ezra the **p** selected men who were
Ne 7:65 be a **p** ministering with the Urim
8: 2 Ezra the **p** brought the Law before
8: 9 Nehemiah the governor, Ezra the **p**
10:38 A **p** descended from Aaron is to
12:26 and of Ezra the **p** and scribe.
13: 4 Before this, Eliashib the **p** had been
13:13 I put Shelemiah the **p**, Zadok the
Ps 110: 4 "You are a **p** for ever, in the order
Isa 8: 2 I will call in Uriah the **p** and
24: 2 will be the same for **p** as for people,
61:10 bridegroom adorns his head like a **p**,
Jer 14:18 Both prophet and **p** have gone to a
18:18 the law by the **p** will not be lost,
20: 1 the **p** Pashhur son of Immer, the
21: 1 and the **p** Zephaniah son of Maaseiah.
23:11 "Both prophet and **p** are godless;
23:33 or a prophet or a **p**, ask you, 'What
23:34 If a prophet or a **p** or anyone else
29:25 to Zephaniah son of Maaseiah the **p**,
29:26 'The LORD has appointed you **p** in
29:29 Zephaniah the **p**, however, read the
37: 3 the **p** Zephaniah son of Maaseiah
52:24 as prisoners Seraiah the chief **p**,
52:24 Zephaniah the **p** next in rank and the
Lam 2: 6 he has spurned both king and **p**.
2:20 Should **p** and prophet be killed in
Eze 1: 3 of the LORD came to Ezekiel the **p**,
7:26 of the law by the **p** will be lost,
44:21 No **p** is to drink wine when he enters
44:25 "'A **p** must not defile himself by
45:19 The **p** is to take some of the blood
Hos 4: 4 those who bring charges against a **p**.
Am 7:10 Amaziah the **p** of Bethel sent a
Zec 6:13 And he will be a **p** on his throne.
Mal 2: 7 "For the lips of a **p** ought to
Mt 8: 4 But go, show yourself to the **p** and
Mk 1:44 But go, show yourself to the **p** and
Lk 1: 5 Judea there was a **p** named Zechariah,
1: 8 and he was serving as **p** before God,
5:14 but go, show yourself to the **p** and
10:31 A **p** happened to be going down the
Ac 14:13 The **p** of Zeus, whose temple was just
19:14 Seven sons of Sceva, a Jewish chief **p**
Heb 5: 6 "You are a **p** for ever, in the order
7: 1 of Salem and **p** of God Most High.
7: 3 Son of God he remains a **p** for ever.
7:11 still need for another **p** to come
7:15 another **p** like Melchizedek appears,
7:16 one who has become a **p** not on the
7:17 "You are a **p** for ever, in the order
7:21 he became a **p** with an oath when God
7:21 his mind: 'You are a **p** for ever.
8: 4 he would not be a **p**, for there are
10:11 Day after day every **p** stands and
10:12 when this **p** had offered for all time
10:21 since we have a great **p** over thezaz

Priest's (Priest)

Lev 6:29 Any male in a **p** family may eat it;
7: 6 Any male in a **p** family may eat it,
21: 9 "'If a **p** daughter defiles herself
22:10 "'No-one outside a **p** family may eat
22:12 If a **p** daughter marries anyone other
22:13 if a **p** daughter becomes a widow or
Jn 18:10 struck the high **p** servant, cutting
18:15 Jesus into the high **p** courtyard,

Jn 18:26 One of the high **p** servants, a
Ac 4: 6 the other men of the high **p** family.

Priesthood (Priest)

Ex 29: 9 The **p** is theirs by a lasting
40:15 Their anointing will be to a **p** that
Nu 16:10 now you are trying to get the **p** too.
18: 1 for offences against the **p**.
18: 7 I am giving you the service of the **p**
25:13 will have a covenant of a lasting **p**,
1Ki 2:27 Solomon removed Abiathar from the **p**
Ezr 2:62 were excluded from the **p** as unclean.
Ne 7:64 were excluded from the **p** as unclean.
13:29 the covenant of the **p** and of the
Lk 1: 9 according to the custom of the **p**, to
3: 2 during the high **p** of Annas and
Heb 7:11 attained through the Levitical **p**
7:12 For when there is a change of the **p**,
7:24 for ever, he has a permanent **p**.
1Pe 2: 5 a spiritual house to be a holy **p**,
2: 9 you are a chosen people, a royal **p**,

Priestly (Priest)

Lev 21:10 ordained to wear the **p** garments,
Jos 18: 7 because the **p** service of the LORD is
1Sa 2:36 "Appoint me to some **p** office so that
Ezr 2:69 minas of silver and 100 **p** garments.
Ne 12:12 were the heads of the **p** families:
13:29 because they defiled the **p** office
Lk 1: 5 who belonged to the **p** division of
Ro 15:16 with the **p** duty of proclaiming the

Priests (*Chief priests*, Priest, *Priests and Levites, Priests and the Levites*)

Ge 47:22 he did not buy the land of the **p**,
47:26 the **p** that did not become Pharaoh's.
Ex 19: 6 you will be for me a kingdom of **p**
19:22 Even the **p**, who approach the LORD,
19:24 But the **p** and the people must not
28: 1 so that they may serve me as **p**.
28: 4 so that they may serve me as **p**.
28:41 them so they may serve me as **p**.
29: 1 so that they may serve me as **p**: Take
29:44 Aaron and his sons to serve me as **p**.
30:30 them so they may serve me as **p**.
31:10 for his sons when they serve as **p**,
35:19 for his sons when they serve as **p**."
39:41 for his sons when serving as **p**.
40:15 so that they may serve me as **p**.
Lev 1: 5 and then Aaron's sons the **p** shall
1: 8 Aaron's sons the **p** shall arrange the
1:11 and Aaron's sons the **p** shall
2: 2 take it to Aaron's sons the **p**.
3: 2 Then Aaron's sons the **p** shall
7:35 presented to serve the LORD as **p**.
16:33 and for the **p** and all the people of
21: 1 "Speak to the **p**, the sons of Aaron,
21: 5 "'**P** must not shave their heads or
21: 7 because **p** are holy to their God.
22: 9 "'The **p** are to keep my requirements
22:15 The **p** must not desecrate the sacred
27:21 will become the property of the **p**.
Nu 3: 3 of Aaron's sons, the anointed **p**,
3: 3 who were ordained to serve as **p**.
3: 4 Ithamar served as **p** during the
3:10 Aaron and his sons to serve as **p**;
10: 8 "The sons of Aaron, the **p**, are to
18: 7 only you and your sons may serve as **p**
Dt 17: 9 Go to the **p**, who are Levites, and to
17:18 from that of the **p**, who are Levites.
18: 1 The **p**, who are Levites—indeed the
18: 3 This is the share due to the **p** from
19:17 presence of the LORD before the **p**
21: 5 The **p**, the sons of Levi, shall step
24: 8 **p**, who are Levites, instruct you.
27: 9 Moses and the **p**, who are Levites,
31: 9 down this law and gave it to the **p**,
Jos 3: 3 and the **p**, who are Levites, carrying
3: 6 Joshua said to the **p**, "Take up the
3: 8 Tell the **p** who carry the ark of the
3:13 soon as the **p** who carry the ark of
3:14 the **p** carrying the ark of the
3:15 Yet as soon as the **p** who carried the
3:17 The **p** who carried the ark of the
4: 3 Jordan from right where the **p** stood
Jos 4: 9 where the **p** who carried the ark of
4:10 Now the **p** who carried the ark
4:11 and the **p** came to the other side
4:16 "Command the **p** carrying the ark of
4:17 Joshua commanded the **p**, "Come up out
4:18 the **p** came up out of the river
6: 4 Make seven **p** carry trumpets of rams'
6: 4 with the **p** blowing the trumpets.
6: 6 Joshua son of Nun called the **p** and
6: 6 **p** carry trumpets in front of it."
6: 8 the seven **p** carrying the seven
6: 9 of the **p** who blew the trumpets,
6:12 the **p** took up the ark of the LORD.
6:13 The seven **p** carrying the seven
6:16 when the **p** sounded the trumpet
8:33 carried it—the **p**, who were Levites.
21:19 All the towns for the **p**, the
Jdg 18:30 and his sons were **p** for the tribe of
1Sa 1: 3 two sons of Eli, were **p** of the LORD.
2:13 Now it was the practice of the **p**
5: 5 neither the **p** of Dagon nor any
6: 2 the Philistines called for the **p** and
22:11 who were the **p** at Nob, and they all
22:17 "Turn and kill the **p** of the LORD,
22:17 a hand to strike the **p** of the LORD.
22:18 "You turn and strike down the **p**.
22:19 the town of the **p**, with its men and
22:21 Saul had killed the **p** of the LORD.
2Sa 8:17 Ahimelech son of Abiathar were **p**;
15:35 Won't the **p** Zadok and Abiathar be
17:15 Hushai told Zadok and Abiathar, the **p**
19:11 to Zadok and Abiathar, the **p**: "Ask
20:25 Zadok and Abiathar were **p**;
1Ki 4: 4 Zadok and Abiathar—**p**;
8: 3 had arrived, the **p** took up the ark,
8: 6 The **p** then brought the ark of the
8:10 the **p** withdrew from the Holy Place,
8:11 the **p** could not perform their
12:31 **p** from all sorts of people,
12:32 installed **p** at the high places he
13: 2 On you he will sacrifice the **p** of
13:33 but once more appointed **p** for the
2Ki 10:11 his close friends and his **p**,
10:19 all his ministers and all his **p**.
12: 4 Joash said to the **p**, "Collect all
12: 6 **p** still had not repaired the temple.
12: 7 and the other **p** and asked them,
12: 8 The **p** agreed that they would not
12: 9 The **p** who guarded the entrance put
12:16 of the LORD; it belonged to the **p**.
17:27 "Make one of the **p** you took captive
17:28 one of the **p** who had been exiled
17:32 **p** in the shrines at the high places.
19: 2 the secretary and the leading **p**,
23: 2 the **p** and the prophets—all the
23: 4 the **p** next in rank and the
23: 5 He did away with the pagan **p**
23: 8 Josiah brought all the **p** from the
23: 8 where the **p** had burned incense.
23: 9 Although the **p** of the high places
23: 9 bread with their fellow **p**.
23:20 Josiah slaughtered all the **p** of
1Ch 9: 2 **p**, Levites and temple servants.
9:10 Of the **p**: Jedaiah; Jehoiarib; Jakin;
9:13 The **p**, who were heads of families,
9:30 some of the **p** took care of mixing
15:11 summoned Zadok and Abiathar the **p**,
15:24 Benaiah and Eliezer the **p** were to
16: 6 Benaiah and Jahaziel the **p** were to
16:39 his fellow **p** before the tabernacle
18:16 Ahimelech son of Abiathar were **p**;
24: 2 Eleazar and Ithamar served as the **p**.
24: 6 the heads of families of the **p** and
24:31 of the **p** and of the Levites.
2Ch 4: 6 was to be used by the **p** for washing.
4: 9 He made the courtyard of the **p**, and
5: 5 **p**, who were Levites, carried them up;
5: 7 The **p** then brought the ark of the
5:11 The **p** then withdrew from the Holy
5:11 All the **p** who were there had
5:12 They were accompanied by 120 **p**
5:14 the **p** could not perform their
6:41 May your **p**, O LORD God, be clothed
7: 2 The **p** could not enter the temple of
7: 6 The **p** took their positions, as did
7: 6 Opposite the Levites, the **p** blew
2Ch 8:14 he appointed the divisions of the **p**
8:14 to assist the **p** according to each
8:15 to the **p** or to the Levites in any
11:14 had rejected them as **p** of the LORD.
11:15 he appointed his own **p** for the high
13: 9 didn't you drive out the **p** of the
13: 9 and make **p** of your own as the
13:10 The **p** who serve the LORD are sons of
13:12 His **p** with their trumpets will sound
13:14 The **p** blew their trumpets
17: 8 —and the **p** Elishama and Jehoram.
19: 8 **p** and heads of Israelite families to
23:18 of the LORD in the hands of the **p**,
26:17 **p** of the LORD followed him in.
26:18 That is for the **p**, the descendants
26:19 While he was raging at the **p** in
26:20 and all the other **p** looked at him,
29:16 The **p** went into the sanctuary of the
29:21 The king commanded the **p**, the
29:22 and the **p** took the blood and
29:24 The **p** then slaughtered the goats and
29:26 and the **p** with their trumpets.
29:34 The **p**, however, were too few to skin
29:34 until other **p** had been consecrated,
29:34 themselves than the **p** had been.
30: 3 enough **p** had consecrated themselves
30:16 The **p** sprinkled the blood handed to
30:21 while the Levites and **p** sang to the
30:24 number of **p** consecrated themselves.
31: 2 to their duties as **p** or Levites—
31:15 faithfully in the towns of the **p**,
31:15 distributing to their fellow **p**
31:17 they distributed to the **p** enrolled
31:19 for the **p**, the descendants of Aaron,
34: 5 He burned the bones of the **p** on
35: 2 He appointed the **p** to their duties
35: 8 gave the **p** two thousand six hundred
35:10 and the **p** stood in their places
35:11 and the **p** sprinkled the blood handed
35:14 for themselves and for the **p**,
35:14 because the **p**, the descendants of
35:14 themselves and for the Aaronic **p**.
35:18 with the **p**, the Levites and all
36:14 Furthermore, all the leaders of the **p**
Ezr 2:36 The **p**: the descendants of Jedaiah
2:61 from among the **p**: The descendants of
2:70 The **p**, the Levites, the singers, the
3: 2 his fellow **p** and Zerubbabel son of
3:10 the **p** in their vestments and with
6: 9 as requested by the **p** in Jerusalem
6:16 the people of Israel—the **p**, the
6:18 they installed the **p** in their
6:20 brothers the **p** and for themselves.
7: 7 Some of the Israelites, including **p**,
7:16 **p** for the temple of their God in
7:24 tribute or duty on any of the **p**,
8:15 checked among the people and the **p**,
8:24 I set apart twelve of the leading **p**,
9: 7 we and our kings and our **p** have been
10:18 Among the descendants of the **p**, the
Ne 2:16 or the **p** or nobles or officials
3: 1 his fellow **p** went to work and
3:22 the **p** from the surrounding region.
3:28 Above the Horse Gate, the **p** made
5:12 Then I summoned the **p** and made the
7:39 The **p**: the descendants of Jedaiah
7:63 from among the **p**: the descendants of
7:70 50 bowls and 530 garments for **p**.
7:72 of silver and 67 garments for **p**.
7:73 The **p**, the Levites, the gatekeepers,
9:32 upon our **p** and prophets, upon our
9:34 Our kings, our leaders, our **p** and
9:38 **p** are affixing their seals to it."
10: 8 These were the **p**.
10:28 "The rest of the people—**p**, Levites,
10:34 "We—the **p**, the Levites and the
10:36 our God, to the **p** ministering there.
10:37 to the **p**, the first of our ground
10:39 kept and where the ministering **p**,
11: 3 **p**, Levites, temple servants and
11:10 From the **p**: Jedaiah; the son of
12: 7 These were the leaders of the **p** and
12:22 as well as those of the **p**, were
12:35 well as some **p** with trumpets, and
12:41 well as the **p**—Eliakim, Maaseiah,
13: 5 well as the contributions for the **p**.

Job 12:19 He leads **p** away stripped and
Ps 78:64 their **p** were put to the sword, and
99: 6 Moses and Aaron were among his **p**,
132: 9 May your **p** be clothed with
132:16 I will clothe her **p** with salvation,
Isa 28: 7 **P** and prophets stagger from beer and
37: 2 and the leading **p**, all wearing
61: 6 you will be called **p** of the LORD,
Jer 1: 1 one of the **p** at Anathoth in the
1:18 its **p** and the people of the land.
2: 8 The **p** did not ask, 'Where is the
2:26 their **p** and their prophets.
4: 9 the **p** will be horrified, and the
5:31 the **p** rule by their own authority,
6:13 prophets and **p** alike, all practise
8: 1 the bones of the **p** and prophets, and
8:10 prophets and **p** alike, all practise
13:13 the **p**, the prophets and all those
19: 1 elders of the people and of the **p**
26: 7 The **p**, the prophets and all the
26: 8 the **p**, the prophets and all the
26:11 the **p** and the prophets said to the
26:16 said to the **p** and the prophets,
27:16 I said to the **p** and all these people,
28: 1 of the **p** and all the people:
28: 5 before the **p** and all the people
29: 1 among the exiles and to the **p**,
29:25 the priest, and to all the other **p**.
31:14 I will satisfy the **p** with abundance,
32:32 officials, their **p** and prophets,
33:18 nor will the **p**, who are Levites,
33:21 who are **p** ministering before me—
34:19 the **p** and all the people of the
48: 7 together with his **p** and officials.
49: 3 together with his **p** and officials.
Lam 1: 4 gateways are desolate, her **p** groan,
1:19 My **p** and my elders perished in the
4:13 and the iniquities of her **p**,
4:16 The **p** are shown no honour, the
Eze 22:26 Her **p** do violence to my law and
40:45 the **p** who have charge of the temple,
40:46 the room facing north is for the **p**
42:13 where the **p** who approach the LORD
42:14 Once the **p** enter the holy precincts,
43:19 bull as a sin offering to the **p**,
43:24 and the **p** are to sprinkle salt on
43:27 from the eighth day on, the **p** are to
44:13 near to serve me as **p** or come near
44:15 "'But the **p**, who are Levites and
44:22 of Israelite descent or widows of **p**.
44:24 the **p** are to serve as judges and
44:28 be the only inheritance the **p** have.
44:30 special gifts will belong to the **p**.
44:31 The **p** must not eat anything, bird or
45: 4 portion of the land for the **p**,
46: 2 The **p** are to sacrifice his burnt
46:19 which belonged to the **p**, and showed
46:20 "This is the place where the **p** will
48:10 be the sacred portion for the **p**.
48:11 This will be for the consecrated **p**,
48:13 "Alongside the territory of the **p**,
Hos 4: 6 I also reject you as my **p**;
4: 7 The more the **p** increased, the more
4: 9 will be: Like people, like **p**. I will
5: 1 "Hear this, you **p**! Pay attention,
6: 9 so do bands of **p**; they murder on the
10: 5 and so will its idolatrous **p**, those
Joel 1: 9 The **p** are in mourning, those who
1:13 Put on sackcloth, O **p**, and mourn;
2:17 Let the **p**, who minister before the
Mic 3:11 her **p** teach for a price,
Zep 1: 4 of the pagan and the idolatrous **p**—
3: 4 Her **p** profane the sanctuary and do
Hag 2:11 says: 'Ask the **p** what the law says:
2:12 The **p** answered, "No."
2:13 the **p** replied, "it becomes defiled.
Zec 7: 3 by asking the **p** of the house of the
7: 5 the people of the land and the **p**,
Mal 1: 6 "It is you, O **p**, who show contempt
2: 1 now this admonition is for you, O **p**.
Mt 12: 4 for them to do, but only for the **p**.
12: 5 **p** in the temple desecrate the day
Mk 2:26 which is lawful only for **p** to eat.
Lk 6: 4 what is lawful only for **p** to eat.
17:14 said, "Go, show yourselves to the **p**.
Ac 4: 1 The **p** and the captain of the temple
Ac 6: 7 a large number of **p** became obedient
Heb 7: 5 **p** to collect a tenth from the people
7:14 tribe Moses said nothing about **p**.
7:20 Others became **p** without any oath,
7:23 Now there have been many of those **p**,
7:27 Unlike the other high **p**, he does not
7:28 For the law appoints as high **p** men
9: 6 the **p** entered regularly into the
Rev 1: 6 and **p** to serve his God and Father
5:10 be a kingdom and **p** to serve our God,
20: 6 but they will be **p** of God and of

Priests and Levites

1Ki 8: 4 The **p** carried them up,
1Ch 13: 2 and also to the **p** who are with them
15:14 the **p** consecrated themselves in
23: 2 leaders of Israel, as well as the **p**.
28:13 for the divisions of the **p**, and for
28:21 The divisions of the **p** are ready for
2Ch 11:13 The **p** from all their districts
23: 4 A third of you **p** who are going on
23: 6 of the LORD except the **p** on duty;
24: 5 He called together the **p** and said to
30:25 along with the **p** and all who had
31: 2 Hezekiah assigned the **p** to divisions
31: 4 to give the portion due to the **p** so
31: 9 Hezekiah asked the **p** about the heaps;
35: 8 voluntarily to the people and the **p**.
Ezr 1: 5 and the **p**—everyone whose heart God
3:12 many of the older **p** and family heads,
6:20 The **p** had purified themselves and
7:13 including **p**, who wish to go to
8:30 the **p** received the silver and gold
10: 5 Ezra rose up and put the leading **p**
Ne 11:20 with the **p**, were in all the towns of
12: 1 These were the **p** who returned with
12:30 the **p** had purified themselves
12:44 was pleased with the ministering **p**.
Isa 66:21 them also to be **p**," says the LORD.
Jn 1:19 sent **p** to ask him who he was.

Priests and the Levites

2Ch 29: 4 He brought in the **p**, assembled them
30:15 The **p** were ashamed and consecrated
30:27 The **p** stood to bless the people, and
34:30 the people of Jerusalem, the **p**—all
Ezr 3: 8 (the **p** and all who had returned
8:29 **p** and the family heads of Israel."
9: 1 including the **p**, have not kept
Ne 8:13 along with the **p**, gathered round
12:44 required by the Law for the **p**,
13:30 I purified the **p** of everything

Priests' (Priest)

Eze 41:10 the ⌊**p**⌋ rooms was twenty cubits
42:13 temple courtyard are the **p** rooms,

Prime

1Sa 2:33 will die in the **p** of life.
Job 29: 4 Oh, for the days when I was in my **p**,
Isa 38:10 I said, "In the **p** of my life must I

Prince (*Prince of this world*, Prince's, Princely, Princes, Princess)

Ge 23: 6 You are a mighty **p** among us.
49:26 brow of the **p** among his brothers.
Dt 33:16 brow of the **p** among his brothers.
Jdg 8:18 "each one with the bearing of a **p**.
2Sa 3:38 "Do you not realise that a **p** and a
2Ch 11:22 be the chief **p** among his brothers,
Ezr 1: 8 out to Sheshbazzar the **p** of Judah.
Job 31:37 like a **p** I would approach him.
Pr 14:28 but without subjects a **p** is ruined.
Isa 9: 6 God, Everlasting Father, **P** of Peace.
Eze 7:27 the **p** will be clothed with despair,
12:10 oracle concerns the **p** in Jerusalem
12:12 "The **p** among them will put his
21:25 "'O profane and wicked **p** of Israel,
30:13 No longer will there be a **p** in Egypt,
34:24 servant David will be **p** among them.
37:25 my servant will be their **p** for ever.
38: 2 the chief **p** of Meshech and Tubal;
38: 3 O Gog, chief **p** of Meshech and Tubal.
39: 1 O Gog, chief **p** of Meshech and Tubal.
Eze 44: 3 The **p** himself is the only one who
45: 7 "'The **p** will have the land
45:16 gift for the use of the **p** in Israel.
45:17 will be the duty of the **p** to provide
45:22 On that day the **p** is to provide a
46: 2 The **p** is to enter from the outside
46: 4 The burnt offering the **p** brings to
46: 8 the **p** enters, he is to go in through
46:10 The **p** is to be among them, going in
46:12 the **p** provides a freewill offering
46:16 If the **p** makes a gift from his
46:17 then it will revert to the **p**.
46:18 The **p** must not take any of the
48:21 city property will belong to the **p**.
48:21 portions will belong to the **p**,
48:22 of the area that belongs to the **p**.
48:22 The area belonging to the **p** will lie
Da 8:11 set itself up to be as great as the **P**
8:25 his stand against the **P** of princes.
10:13 the **p** of the Persian kingdom
10:20 to fight against the **p** of Persia,
10:20 I go, the **p** of Greece will come;
10:21 against them except Michael, your **p**.
11:22 **p** of the covenant will be destroyed.
12: 1 Michael, the great **p** who protects
Hos 3: 4 for many days without king or **p**,
Mt 9:34 "It is by the **p** if demons that he
12:24 only by Beelzebub, the **p** of demons,
Mk 3:22 By the **p** of demons he is driving out
Lk 11:15 "By Beelzebub, the **p** of demons, he
Ac 5:31 him to his own right hand as **P** and

Prince of this world

Jn 12:31 now the **p** will be driven out.
14:30 much longer, for the **p** is coming.
16:11 because the **p** now stands condemned.

Prince's (Prince)

SS 7: 1 O **p** daughter! Your graceful legs are

Princely (Prince)

Ps 49:14 grave, far from their **p** mansions.

Princes (Prince)

Nu 21:18 about the well that the **p** dug, that
22: 8 So the Moabite **p** stayed with him.
22:13 Balaam got up and said to Balak's **p**,
22:14 the Moabite **p** returned to Balak and
22:15 Balak sent other **p**, more numerous
22:21 donkey and went with the **p** of Moab.
22:35 So Balaam went with the **p** of Balak.
22:40 Balaam and the **p** who were with him.
23: 6 offering, with all the **p** of Moab.
23:17 his offering, with the **p** of Moab.
Jos 13:21 Hur and Reba—**p** allied with Sihon
Jdg 5: 2 "When the **p** in Israel take the lead,
5: 9 My heart is with Israel's **p**, with
5:15 The **p** of Issachar were with Deborah;
1Sa 2: 8 he seats them with **p** and has them
2Sa 13:32 think that they killed all the **p**;
2Ki 10: 6 Now the royal **p**, seventy of them,
10: 7 these men took the **p** and slaughtered
10: 8 They have brought the heads of the **p**.
11: 2 him away from among the royal **p**,
2Ch 21: 4 along with some of the **p** of Israel.
22: 8 he found the **p** of Judah and the sons
22:11 him away from among the royal **p**
28:21 from the royal palace and from the **p**
Est 1: 3 the **p**, and the nobles of the
6: 9 to one of the king's most noble **p**.
Job 34:19 who shows no partiality to **p** and
Ps 45:16 make them **p** throughout the land.
68:27 there the great throng of Judah's **p**,
68:27 the **p** of Zebulun and of Naphtali.
83:11 all their **p** like Zebah and Zalmunna,
105:22 to instruct his **p** as he pleased and
113: 8 he seats them with **p**, with the **p** of
118: 9 in the LORD than to trust in **p**.
146: 3 Do not put your trust in **p**, in
148:11 you **p** and all rulers on earth,
Pr 8:16 by me **p** govern, and all nobles who
19:10 worse for a slave to rule over **p**!
Ecc 10: 7 while **p** go on foot like slaves.
10:16 and whose **p** feast in the morning.

Ecc 10:17 whose **p** eat at a proper time—for
Isa 23: 8 whose merchants are **p**, whose traders
34:12 kingdom, all her **p** will vanish away.
40:23 He brings **p** to naught and reduces
49: 7 **p** will see and bow down,
Lam 1: 6 Her **p** are like deer that find no
2: 2 her kingdom and its **p** down to the
2: 9 Her king and her **p** are exiled among
4: 7 Their **p** were brighter than snow and
5:12 **P** have been hung up by their hands;
Eze 19: 1 "Take up a lament concerning the **p**
21:12 it is against all the **p** of Israel.
22: 6 "'see how each of the **p** of Israel
22:25 There is a conspiracy of her **p**
26:16 all the **p** of the coast will step
27:21 "'Arabia and all the **p** of Kedar
32:29 is there, her kings and all her **p**;
32:30 "All the **p** of the north and all the
39:18 drink the blood of the **p** of the
45: 8 And my **p** will no longer oppress my
45: 9 O **p** of Israel! Give up your violence
Da 8:25 his stand against the Prince of **p**.
9: 6 our **p** and our fathers, and to all
9: 8 O LORD, we and our kings, our **p** and
10:13 Then Michael, one of the chief **p**,
Hos 7: 3 wickedness, the **p** with their lies.
7: 5 the **p** become inflamed with wine,
8: 4 they choose **p** without my approval.
13:10 you said, 'Give me a king and **p**'?
Zep 1: 8 LORD's sacrifice I will punish the **p**
Rev 6:15 the kings of the earth, the **p**, the

Princess (Prince)
Ps 45:13 All glorious is the **p** within her

Principal
1Ch 9:26 the four **p** gatekeepers, who were

Principle (Principles)
Ro 3:27 On what **p**? On that of observing the

Principles (Principle)
Gal 4: 3 under the basic **p** of the world.
4: 9 back to those weak and miserable **p**?
Col 2: 8 the basic **p** of this world rather
2:20 Christ to the basic **p** of this world,

Priscilla
Also called Prisca. Wife of Aquila. Disciples from Rome (Ac 18:2); co-workers with Paul (Ro 16:3; 1Co 16:19; 2Ti 4:19), accompanied him to Ephesus (Ac 18:18–19); instructed Apollos (Ac 18:26).

Ac 18: 2 come from Italy with his wife **P**,
18:18 Syria, accompanied by **P** and Aquila.
18:19 where Paul left **P** and Aquila.
18:26 When **P** and Aquila heard him, they
Ro 16: 3 Greet **P** and Aquila, my
1Co 16:19 Aquila and **P** greet you warmly in the
2Ti 4:19 Greet **P** and Aquila and the household

Prison (Prisoner, Prisoners, Prisons)
Ge 39:20 master took him and put him in **p**,
39:20 while Joseph was there in the **p**,
39:21 favour in the eyes of the **p** warder.
39:22 charge of all those held in the **p**,
40: 3 same **p** where Joseph was confined.
40: 5 who were being held in **p**—had a
40:14 to Pharaoh and get me out of this **p**.
42:16 the rest of you will be kept in **p**,
42:19 one of your brothers stay here in **p**,
Jdg 16:21 they set him to grinding in the **p**.
16:25 So they called Samson out of the **p**,
1Ki 22:27 Put this fellow in **p** and give him
2Ki 17: 4 seized him and put him in **p**.
25:27 he released Jehoiachin from **p** on the
25:29 Jehoiachin put aside his **p** clothes
2Ch 16:10 was so enraged that he put him in **p**.
18:26 Put this fellow in **p** and give him
Job 11:10 you in **p** and convenes a court,
Ps 66:11 You brought us into **p** and laid
142: 7 Set me free from my **p**, that I may
Ecc 4:14 The youth may have come from **p** to
Isa 24:22 they will be shut up in **p** and be
42: 7 to free captives from **p** and to
Jer 37: 4 for he had not yet been put in **p**.
37:15 which they had made into a **p**.
37:18 people, that you have put me in **p**?
52:11 him in **p** till the day of his death.
52:31 freed him from **p** on the twenty-fifth
52:33 Jehoiachin put aside his **p** clothes
Eze 19: 9 They put him in **p**, so his roar was
Mt 4:12 heard that John had been put in **p**,
5:25 and you may be thrown into **p**.
11: 2 John heard in **p** what Christ was
14: 3 put him in **p** because of Herodias,
14:10 had John beheaded in the **p**.
18:30 into **p** until he could pay the debt.
25:36 I was in **p** and you came to visit me.'
25:39 did we see you sick or in **p** and go
25:43 in **p** and you did not look after me.'
25:44 sick or in **p**, and did not help you?'
Mk 1:14 After John was put in **p**, Jesus went
6:17 and he had him bound and put in **p**.
6:27 The man went, beheaded John in the **p**,
15: 7 A man called Barabbas was in **p** with
Lk 3:20 to them all: He locked John up in **p**.
12:58 and the officer throw you into **p**.
22:33 to go with you to **p** and to death."
23:19 Barabbas had been thrown into **p** for
23:25 into **p** for insurrection and murder,
Jn 3:24 (This was before John was put in **p**.)
Ac 8: 3 off men and women and put them in **p**.
12: 4 After arresting him, he put him in **p**,
12: 5 Peter was kept in **p**, but the church
12: 9 Peter followed him out of the **p**, but
12:17 the Lord had brought him out of **p**.
16:23 they were thrown into **p**, and the
16:26 foundations of the **p** were shaken.
16:26 At once all the **p** doors flew open,
16:27 and when he saw the **p** doors open, he
16:37 Roman citizens, and threw us into **p**.
16:39 and escorted them from the **p**,
16:40 Paul and Silas came out of the **p**,
20:23 that **p** and hardships are facing me.
22: 4 and women and throwing them into **p**,
24:27 to the Jews, he left Paul in **p**.
26:10 I put many of the saints in **p**, and
Ro 16: 7 who have been in **p** with me.
2Co 11:23 harder, been in **p** more frequently,
Heb 10:34 You sympathised with those in **p** and
11:36 others were chained and put in **p**.
13: 3 Remember those in **p** as if you were
1Pe 3:19 and preached to the spirits in **p**
Rev 2:10 the devil will put some of you in **p**
20: 7 Satan will be released from his **p**

Prisoner (Prison)
Ex 12:29 to the firstborn of the **p**, who was
Jdg 15:10 "We have come to take Samson **p**,"
2Ki 24:12 of Babylon, he took Jehoiachin **p**.
2Ch 33:11 who took Manasseh **p**, put a hook in
Isa 22: 3 All you who were caught were taken **p**
Mt 27:15 to release a **p** chosen by the crowd.
27:16 At that time they had a notorious **p**,
Mk 15: 6 a **p** whom the people requested.
Jn 18:39 one **p** at the time of the Passover.
Ac 23:18 The centurion said, "Paul, the **p**,
25:14 a man here whom Felix left as a **p**.
25:27 unreasonable to send on a **p** without
Ro 7:23 making me a **p** of the law of sin at
Gal 3:22 that the whole world is a **p** of sin,
Eph 3: 1 I, Paul, the **p** of Christ Jesus
4: 1 a **p** for the Lord, then, I urge you
2Ti 1: 8 our Lord, or ashamed of me his **p**.
Phm : 1 Paul, a **p** of Christ Jesus, and
: 9 and now also a **p** of Christ Jesus—

Prisoners (Prison)
Ge 39:20 where the king's **p** were confined.
2Ki 25:18 took as **p** Seraiah the chief priest
2Ch 28: 5 took many of his people as **p** and
28:11 countrymen that you have taken as **p**,
28:13 "You must not bring those **p** here,"
28:14 the soldiers gave up the **p** and
28:15 The men designated by name took the **p**
28:17 attacked Judah and carried away **p**,
Ps 68: 6 he leads forth the **p** with singing;
79:11 May the groans of the **p** come before
102:20 to hear the groans of the **p** and
107:10 gloom, **p** suffering in iron chains,
146: 7 The LORD sets **p** free,
Isa 24:22 They will be herded together like **p**
51:14 The cowering **p** will soon be set free;
61: 1 and release from darkness for the **p**,
Jer 52:24 took as **p** Seraiah the chief priest,
Lam 3:34 To crush underfoot all **p** in the land,
Hab 1: 9 desert wind and gather **p** like sand.
Zec 9:11 free your **p** from the waterless pit.
9:12 Return to your fortress, O **p** of hope;
Lk 4:18 me to proclaim freedom for the **p**
21:24 be taken as **p** to all the nations.
Ac 9: 2 he might take them **p** to Jerusalem.
9:21 them as **p** to the chief priests?"
16:25 the other **p** were listening to them.
16:27 he thought the **p** had escaped.
22: 5 as **p** to Jerusalem to be punished.
27: 1 Paul and some other **p** were handed
27:42 The soldiers planned to kill the **p**
Gal 3:23 we were held **p** by the law, locked up

Prisons (Prison)
Isa 42:22 trapped in pits or hidden away in **p**.
Lk 21:12 deliver you to synagogues and **p**,

Private (Privately)
Ge 43:30 went into his **p** room and wept there.
Dt 25:11 out and seizes him by his **p** parts,
Mt 17:19 the disciples came to Jesus in **p** and
Lk 9:18 Once when Jesus was praying in **p** and

Privately (Private)
1Sa 18:22 "Speak to David **p** and say, 'Look,
2Sa 3:27 as though to speak with him **p**.
Jer 37:17 where he asked him **p**, "Is there any
40:15 Johanan son of Kareah said **p** to
Mt 14:13 by boat **p** to a solitary place.
24: 3 the disciples came to him **p**.
Mk 9:28 his disciples asked him **p**, "Why
13: 3 James, John and Andrew asked him **p**,
Lk 10:23 he turned to his disciples and said **p**
Gal 2: 2 But I did this **p** to those who seemed

Privilege
2Co 8: 4 for the **p** of sharing in this

Prize (Prizes)
1Co 9:24 but only one gets the **p**?
9:24 Run in such a way as to get the **p**.
9:27 will not be disqualified for the **p**.
Php 3:14 win the **p** for which God has called
Col 2:18 of angels disqualify you for the **p**.

Prizes (Prize)
Pr 12:27 the diligent man **p** his possessions.

Probe
Dt 13:14 you must enquire, **p** and investigate
Job 10: 6 out my faults and **p** after my sin—
11: 7 Can you **p** the limits of the Almighty?
Ps 17: 3 Though you **p** my heart and examine me
Jer 20:12 righteous and **p** the heart and mind,

Problems
Dt 1:12 how can I bear your **p** and your
Da 5:12 riddles and solve difficult **p**.
5:16 and to solve difficult **p**.

Procedure (Proceed)
Ecc 8: 5 will know the proper time and **p**.
8: 6 For there is a proper time and **p** for

Proceed (Procedure, Proceeded, Proceedings, Procession)
Ne 12:31 One was to **p** on top of the wall to

Proceeded (Proceed)
Ge 9:20 Noah, a man of the soil, **p** to plant
42:20 may not die." This they **p** to do.
44:12 the steward **p** to search, beginning
2Ki 8: 2 The woman **p** to do as the man of God

2Ki 11: 1 **p** to destroy the whole royal family.
2Ch 22:10 she **p** to destroy the whole royal
Ne 12:38 The second choir **p** in the opposite
Ac 12: 3 the Jews, he **p** to seize Peter also.

Proceedings (Proceed)
Ac 24:22 with the Way, adjourned the **p**.

Procession (Proceed)
1Sa 10: 5 you will meet a **p** of prophets coming
10:10 at Gibeah, a **p** of prophets met him;
Ne 12:36 Ezra the scribe led the **p**.
Ps 42: 4 leading the **p** to the house of God,
68:24 Your **p** has come into view, O God,
68:24 the **p** of my God and King into the
118:27 **p** up to the horns of the altar.
SS 6:10 the sun, majestic as the stars in **p**?
Isa 60:11 their kings led in triumphal **p**.
1Co 4: 9 on display at the end of the **p**,
2Co 2:14 who always leads us in triumphal **p**

Proclaim (Proclaimed, Proclaiming, Proclaims, Proclamation)
Ex 33:19 and I will **p** my name, the LORD, in
Lev 23: 2 you are to **p** as sacred assemblies.
23: 4 are to **p** at their appointed times:
23:21 day you are to **p** a sacred assembly
23:37 which you are to **p** as sacred
25:10 and **p** liberty throughout the land
Dt 11:29 you are to **p** on Mount Gerizim the
30:12 **p** it to us so that we may obey it?"
30:13 **p** it to us so that we may obey it?"
32: 3 I will **p** the name of the LORD.
1Sa 31: 9 to **p** the news in the temple of
2Sa 1:20 **p** it not in the streets of Ashkelon
1Ki 21: 9 "**P** a day of fasting and seat Naboth
1Ch 10: 9 to **p** the news among their idols
16:23 **p** his salvation day after day.
Ne 8:15 that they should **p** this word and
Ps 2: 7 I will **p** the decree of the LORD:
9:11 **p** among the nations what he has done.
19: 1 the skies **p** the work of his hands.
22:31 They will **p** his righteousness to a
30: 9 Will it **p** your faithfulness?
40: 9 I **p** righteousness in the great
50: 6 the heavens **p** his righteousness, for
64: 9 they will **p** the works of God
68:34 **P** the power of God, whose majesty is
71:16 I will come and **p** your mighty acts,
71:16 **p** your righteousness, yours alone.
92: 2 to **p** your love in the morning and
96: 2 **p** his salvation day after day.
97: 6 The heavens **p** his righteousness, and
106: 2 Who can **p** the mighty acts of the
118:17 and will **p** what the LORD has done
145: 6 and I will **p** your great deeds.
Isa 12: 4 and **p** that his name is exalted.
40: 2 tenderly to Jerusalem, and **p** to her
42:12 and **p** his praise in the islands.
43:21 myself that they may **p** my praise.
44: 7 Who then is like me? Let him **p** it.
44: 8 Did I not **p** this and foretell it
48:20 this with shouts of joy and **p** it.
52: 7 who **p** peace, who bring good tidings,
52: 7 who **p** salvation, who say to Zion,
61: 1 to **p** freedom for the captives and
61: 2 to **p** the year of the LORD's favour
66:19 will **p** my glory among the nations.
Jer 2: 2 "Go and **p** in the hearing of
3:12 Go, **p** this message towards the north:
4: 5 in Judah and **p** in Jerusalem and say
4:16 to the nations, **p** it to Jerusalem:
5:20 house of Jacob and **p** it in Judah:
7: 2 house and there **p** this message:
11: 6 "**P** all these words in the towns of
19: 2 There **p** the words I tell you,
22: 1 of Judah and **p** this message there:
31:10 **p** it in distant coastlands:
34: 8 to **p** freedom for the slaves.
34:17 So I now **p** 'freedom' for you,
46:14 this in Egypt, and **p** it in Migdol;
46:14 **p** it also in Memphis and Tahpanhes:
50: 2 "Announce and **p** among the nations,
50: 2 lift up a banner and **p** it;
Hos 5: 9 of Israel I **p** what is certain.
Joel 3: 9 **P** this among the nations: Prepare
Am 3: 9 **P** to the fortresses of Ashdod and to
Jnh 3: 2 and **p** to it the message I give you."
Mic 3: 5 if one feeds them, they **p** 'peace';
Zec 1:14 "**P** this word: This is what the LORD
1:17 "**P** further: This is what the LORD
9:10 He will **p** peace to the nations.
Mt 10:27 in your ear, **p** from the roofs.
12:18 he will **p** justice to the nations.
Lk 4:18 He has sent me to **p** freedom for the
4:19 to **p** the year of the Lord's favour."
9:60 you go and **p** the kingdom of God."
Ac 17:23 unknown I am going to **p** to you.
20:27 For I have not hesitated to **p** to you
26:23 would **p** light to his own people and
1Co 11:26 **p** the Lord's death until he comes.
Col 1:28 We **p** him, admonishing and teaching
4: 3 so that we may **p** the mystery of
4: 4 Pray that I may **p** it clearly, as I
1Jn 1: 1 we **p** concerning the Word of life.
1: 2 and we **p** to you the eternal life,
1: 3 We **p** to you what we have seen and
Rev 14: 6 and he had the eternal gospel to **p**

Proclaimed (Proclaim)
Ex 9:16 my name might be **p** in all the earth.
34: 5 with him and **p** his name, the LORD.
Dt 1: 3 Moses **p** to the Israelites all that
5:22 These are the commandments the LORD **p**
9:10 the commandments the LORD **p** to you
10: 4 the Ten Commandments he had **p** to you
15: 2 for cancelling debts has been **p**.
1Ki 16:16 they **p** Omri, the commander of the
21:12 They **p** a fast and seated Naboth in a
2Ki 10:20 in honour of Baal." So they **p** it.
11:12 copy of the covenant and **p** him king.
23:16 word of the LORD **p** by the man of
24: 2 word of the LORD **p** by his servants
2Ch 20: 3 LORD, and he **p** a fast for all Judah.
23:11 copy of the covenant and **p** him king.
Ezr 8:21 by the Ahava Canal, I **p** a fast,
Est 1:20 the king's edict is **p** throughout all
2: 8 the king's order and edict had been **p**
2:18 He **p** a holiday throughout the
Ps 68:11 was the company of those who **p** it:
Isa 43: 9 this and **p** to us the former things?
43:12 I have revealed and saved and **p**—
Jer 23:22 they would have **p** my words to my
34:15 of you **p** freedom to his countrymen.
34:17 **p** freedom for your fellow countrymen.
36: 9 **p** for all the people in Jerusalem
Da 3: 4 the herald loudly **p**, "This is what
5:29 and he was **p** the third highest ruler
Jnh 3: 4 He **p**: "Forty more days and Nineveh
Zec 1: 4 to whom the earlier prophets **p**: This
7: 7 Are these not the words the LORD **p**
Lk 12: 3 rooms will be **p** from the roofs.
16:16 "The Law and the Prophets were **p**
Ac 8: 5 in Samaria and **p** the Christ there.
8:25 they had testified and **p** the word of
13: 5 at Salamis, they **p** the word of God
13:38 the forgiveness of sins is **p** to you.
Ro 9:17 name might be **p** in all the earth."
15:19 I have fully **p** the gospel of Christ.
1Co 2: 1 I **p** to you the testimony about God.
Col 1:23 **p** to every creature under heaven,
2Ti 4:17 the message might be fully **p** and
Heb 9:19 Moses had **p** every commandment of the

Proclaiming (Proclaim)
Ex 34: 6 he passed in front of Moses, **p**, "The
1Sa 11: 7 throughout Israel, **p**, "This is what
Est 1:22 **p** in each people's tongue that every
6: 9 **p** before him, 'This is what is done
6:11 **p** before him, "This is what is done
Ps 26: 7 **p** aloud your praise and telling of
92:15 **p**, "The LORD is upright; he is my
Isa 60: 6 and **p** the praise of the LORD.
Jer 4:15 **p** disaster from the hills of
20: 8 cry out **p** violence and destruction.
Mk 1:14 Galilee, **p** the good news of God.
Lk 8: 1 **p** the good news of the kingdom of
Ac 4: 2 **p** in Jesus the resurrection of the
5:42 they never stopped teaching and **p**
17: 3 "This Jesus I am **p** to you is the
Ro 10: 8 that is, the word of faith we are **p**:
15:16 duty of **p** the gospel of God,
2Th 2: 4 God's temple, **p** himself to be God.
Rev 5: 2 I saw a mighty angel **p** in a loud

Proclaims (Proclaim)
Dt 18:22 If what a prophet **p** in the name of
Na 1:15 who brings good news, who **p** peace!

Proclamation (Proclaim)
2Ch 24: 9 A **p** was then issued in Judah and
30: 5 They decided to send a **p** throughout
36:22 to make a **p** throughout his realm
Ezr 1: 1 to make a **p** throughout his realm
10: 7 A **p** was then issued throughout Judah
Ne 6: 7 make this **p** about you in Jerusalem:
Isa 62:11 The LORD has made **p** to the ends of
Jnh 3: 7 he issued a **p** in Nineveh: "By the
Ro 16:25 my gospel and the **p** of Jesus Christ,

Proconsul (Proconsuls)
Ac 13: 7 who was an attendant of the **p**,
13: 7 The **p**, an intelligent man, sent for
13: 8 tried to turn the **p** from the faith.
13:12 the **p** saw what had happened, he
18:12 While Gallio was **p** of Achaia, the

Proconsuls (Proconsul)
Ac 19:38 the courts are open and there are **p**.

Procorus
Ac 6: 5 **P**, Nicanor, Timon, Parmenas, and

Prodded
Jdg 16:16 With such nagging she **p** him day

Produce (Produced, Produces, Producing, Product, Products)
Ge 1:11 God said, "Let the land **p** vegetation:
1:24 "Let the land **p** living creatures
3:18 will **p** thorns and thistles for you,
38: 8 to **p** offspring for your brother."
47:26 a fifth of the **p** belongs to Pharaoh.
Ex 5:18 must **p** your full quota of bricks."
8:18 when the magicians tried to **p** gnats
Dt 8:18 gives you the ability to **p** wealth,
11:17 rain and the ground will yield no **p**,
14:22 of all that your fields **p** each year.
14:28 of that year's **p** and store it in
16:13 the **p** of your threshing-floor
26: 2 all that you **p** from the soil of the
26:12 of all your **p** in the third year,
28:33 eat what your land and labour **p**,
Jos 5:11 they ate some of the **p** of the land:
5:12 year they ate of the **p** of Canaan.
1Ch 27:27 in charge of the **p** of the vineyards
Job 40:20 The hills bring him their **p**, and all
Ps 78:46 grasshopper, their **p** to the locust.
105:35 land, ate up the **p** of their soil.
Pr 13:23 A poor man's field may **p** abundant
Isa 5:10 A ten-acre vineyard will **p** only a
Jer 2: 7 land to eat its fruit and rich **p**.
29: 5 plant gardens and eat what they **p**.
29:28 plant gardens and eat what they **p**.
Eze 17: 8 water so that it would **p** branches,
17:23 it will **p** branches and bear fruit
36: 8 will **p** branches and fruit for my
48:18 Its **p** will supply food for the
Hos 8: 7 has no head; it will **p** no flour.
Hab 3:17 crop fails and the fields **p** no food,
Zec 8:12 the ground will **p** its crops, and the
Mt 3: 8 **P** fruit in keeping with repentance.
3:10 and every tree that does not **p** good
21:43 to a people who will **p** its fruit.
Mk 4:20 the word, accept it, and **p** a crop
Lk 3: 8 **P** fruit in keeping with repentance.
3: 9 and every tree that does not **p** good
8:15 it, and by persevering **p** a crop.
2Ti 2:23 because you know they **p** quarrels.
Jas 3:12 can a salt spring **p** fresh water.

Produced (Produce)
Ge 1:12 The land **p** vegetation: plants
41:47 of abundance the land **p** plentifully.
41:48 Joseph collected all the food **p** in
Nu 17: 8 had budded, blossomed and **p** almonds.
Dt 8:17 my hands have **p** this wealth for me."
2Ch 31: 5 and honey and all that the fields **p**.
Eze 17: 6 **p** branches and put out leafy boughs.
Mt 13: 8 where it **p** a crop—a hundred, sixty
Mk 4: 8 It came up, grew and **p** a crop,
Lk 12:16 of a certain rich man **p** a good crop.
Ac 6:13 They **p** false witnesses, who
Ro 7: 8 **p** in me every kind of covetous
7:13 it **p** death in me through what was
2Co 7:11 See what this godly sorrow has **p** in
1Th 1: 3 God and Father your work **p** by faith,
Jas 5:18 rain, and the earth **p** its crops.

Produces (Produce)
Lev 25: 7 Whatever the land **p** may be eaten.
Dt 29:18 among you that **p** such bitter poison.
Ne 9:36 and the other good things it **p**.
Job 37:10 The breath of God **p** ice, and the
Pr 30:33 For as churning the milk **p** butter,
30:33 and as twisting the nose **p** blood,
30:33 so stirring up anger **p** strife."
Hag 1:11 the oil and whatever the ground **p**,
Mt 13:23 He **p** a crop, yielding a hundred,
Mk 4:28 All by itself the soil **p** corn—first
Jn 12:24 But if it dies, it **p** many seeds.
Ro 5: 3 know that suffering **p** perseverance;
2Co 1: 6 which **p** in you patient endurance of
Heb 6: 7 that **p** a crop useful to those for
6: 8 land that **p** thorns and thistles is
12:11 Later on, however, it **p** a harvest of

Producing (Produce)
Ge 38: 9 from **p** offspring for his brother.

Product (Produce)
Nu 18:30 be reckoned to you as the **p** of the

Products (Produce)
Ge 43:11 Put some of the best **p** of the land
Isa 45:14 "The **p** of Egypt and the merchandise
Jer 20: 5 the wealth of this city—all its **p**,
Eze 27:16 with you because of your many **p**;
27:18 because of your many **p** and great

Profane (Profaned)
Lev 18:21 you must not **p** the name of your God.
19:12 name and so **p** the name of your God.
21: 6 must not **p** the name of their God.
22: 2 that they will not **p** my holy name.
22:32 Do not **p** my holy name. I must be
Eze 20:39 no longer **p** my holy name with your
21:25 "'O **p** and wicked prince of Israel,
22:26 to my law and **p** my holy things;
Am 2: 7 the same girl and so **p** my holy name.
Zep 3: 4 Her priests **p** the sanctuary and do
Mal 1:12 "But you **p** it by saying of the
2:10 Why do we **p** the covenant of our

Profaned (Profane)
Lev 20: 3 my sanctuary and **p** my holy name.
Jer 34:16 have turned round and **p** my name;
Eze 13:19 You have **p** me among my people for a
20: 9 from being **p** in the eyes of the
20:14 from being **p** in the eyes of the
20:22 from being **p** in the eyes of the
22:26 Sabbaths, so that I am **p** among them.
36:20 the nations they **p** my holy name,
36:21 which the house of Israel **p** among
36:22 which you have **p** among the nations
36:23 which has been **p** among the nations,
36:23 the name you have **p** among them.
39: 7 no longer let my holy name be **p**,

Profess (Professed)
1Ti 2:10 for women who **p** to worship God.
Heb 4:14 us hold firmly to the faith we **p**.
10:23 hold unswervingly to the hope we **p**,

Professed (Profess)
1Ti 6:21 which some have **p** and in so doing

Profit (Profitable, Profits)
Lev 25:37 at interest or sell him food at a **p**.
Job 20:18 not enjoy the **p** from his trading.
35: 3 Yet you ask him, 'What **p** is it to me,
Pr 14:23 All hard work brings a **p**, but mere
21: 5 The plans of the diligent lead to **p**
Ecc 6:11 meaning, and how does that **p** anyone?
10:11 there is no **p** for the charmer.
Isa 23:18 Yet her **p** and her earnings will be
44:10 an idol, which can **p** him nothing?
2Co 2:17 do not peddle the word of God for **p**.
Php 3: 7 whatever was to my **p** I now consider
Jude :11 they have rushed for **p** into Balaam's

Profitable (Profit)
Pr 3:14 for she is more **p** than silver and
31:18 She sees that her trading is **p**, and
Tit 3: 8 are excellent and **p** for everyone.

Profits (Profit)
Job 34: 9 For he says, 'It **p** a man nothing
Ecc 5: 9 the king himself **p** from the fields.
Isa 23:18 Her **p** will go to those who live

Profligate
Dt 21:20 He is a **p** and a drunkard."

Profound
Job 9: 4 His wisdom is **p**, his power is vast.
Ps 92: 5 works, O LORD, how **p** your thoughts!
Ecc 7:24 and most **p**—who can discover it?
Ac 24: 3 acknowledge this with **p** gratitude.
Eph 5:32 This is a **p** mystery—but I am

Progress (Progressed)
Ezr 5: 8 rapid **p** under their direction.
Php 1:25 you for your **p** and joy in the faith,
1Ti 4:15 so that everyone may see your **p**.

Progressed (Progress)
2Ch 24:13 and the repairs **p** under them.

Project (Projected, Projecting, Projection, Projections, Projects)
1Ki 5:16 who supervised the **p** and directed
Ne 6: 3 on a great **p** and cannot go down.
Eze 43:15 four horns **p** upward from the hearth.

Projected (Project)
1Ki 6: 3 and **p** ten cubits from the front of

Projecting (Project)
1Ki 7:34 on each corner, **p** from the stand.
Ne 3:25 the tower **p** from the upper palace
3:26 towards the east and the **p** tower.
3:27 great **p** tower to the wall of Ophel.
Eze 40: 7 and the **p** walls between the alcoves
40:10 and the faces of the **p** walls on each
40:14 along the faces of the **p** walls all
40:16 The alcoves and the **p** walls inside
40:16 The faces of the **p** walls were
40:21 on each side—its **p** walls and its
40:26 faces of the **p** walls on each side.
40:29 Its alcoves, its **p** walls and its
40:33 Its alcoves, its **p** walls and its
40:36 did its alcoves, its **p** walls and its
40:48 its **p** walls were three cubits wide
41: 2 and the **p** walls on each side of it
41: 3 and the **p** walls on each side of it

Projection (Project)
Ex 26:19 for each frame, one under each **p**.
36:24 for each frame, one under each **p**.

Projections (Project)
Ex 26:17 with two **p** set parallel to each
36:22 with two **p** set parallel to each

Projects (Project)
1Ki 9:23 officials in charge of Solomon's **p**
Ecc 2: 4 I undertook great **p**: I built houses

Prolong (Prolonged)
Dt 5:33 prosper and **p** your days in the land
Ps 85: 5 **p** your anger through all generations?
Pr 3: 2 for they will **p** your life many years
Isa 53:10 see his offspring and **p** his days,
Lam 4:22 will end; he will not **p** your exile.

Prolonged (Prolong)
Dt 28:59 harsh and **p** disasters, and severe
Isa 13:22 at hand, and her days will not be **p**.

Prominent
1Ki 21: 9 Naboth in a **p** place among the people.
21:12 Naboth in a **p** place among the people.
Est 9: 4 Mordecai was **p** in the palace;
Isa 9:15 the elders and **p** men are the head,
Da 8: 5 suddenly a goat with a **p** horn
8: 8 and in its place four **p** horns grew
Mk 15:43 Joseph of Arimathea, a **p** member of
Lk 14: 1 to eat in the house of a **p** Pharisee,
Ac 17: 4 Greeks and not a few **p** women.
17:12 of **p** Greek women and many Greek men.

Promiscuity (Promiscuous)
Eze 16:25 with increasing **p** to anyone who
16:26 me to anger with your increasing **p**.
16:29 you increased your **p** to include
16:36 in your **p** with your lovers,
23:29 be exposed. Your lewdness and **p**

Promiscuous (Promiscuity)
Dt 22:21 **p** while still in her father's house.
Eze 23:19 Yet she became more and more **p** as

Promise (Promised, Promises)
Ge 47:29 under my thigh and **p** that you will
Nu 23:19 not act? Does he **p** and not fulfil?
30: 6 utter a rash **p** by which she binds
30: 8 rash **p** by which she binds herself,
Jos 9:21 So the leaders' **p** to them was kept.
23:14 Every **p** has been fulfilled; not one
23:15 just as every good **p** of the LORD
2Sa 7:25 LORD God, keep for ever the **p** you
1Ki 2: 4 that the LORD may keep his **p** to me:
6:12 the **p** I gave to David your father.
8:20 "The LORD has kept the **p** he made:
8:24 You have kept your **p** to your servant
1Ch 17:23 "And now, LORD, let the **p** you have
2Ch 1: 9 Now, LORD God, let your **p** to my
6:10 "The LORD has kept the **p** he made.
6:15 You have kept your **p** to your servant
Ne 5:13 every man who does not keep this **p**.
9: 8 You have kept your **p** because you
10:30 "We **p** not to give our daughters in
Ps 77: 8 Has his **p** failed for all time?
105:42 For he remembered his holy **p** given
106:24 they did not believe his **p**.
119:38 Fulfil your **p** to your servant, so
119:41 your salvation according to your **p**;
119:50 is this: Your **p** preserves my life.
119:58 gracious to me according to your **p**.
119:76 according to your **p** to your servant.
119:82 My eyes fail, looking for your **p**;
119:116 Sustain me according to your **p**, and
119:123 looking for your righteous **p**.
119:154 my life according to your **p**.
119:162 I rejoice in your **p** like one who
119:170 deliver me according to your **p**.
Jer 29:10 **p** to bring you back to this place.
33:14 'when I will fulfil the gracious **p** I
34: 4 "'Yet hear the **p** of the LORD,
34: 5 I myself make this **p**, declares the
Ac 2:39 The **p** is for you and your children
7:17 for God to fulfil his **p** to Abraham,
26: 7 This is the **p** our twelve tribes are
Ro 4:13 **p** that he would be heir of the world,
4:14 has no value and the **p** is worthless,
4:16 Therefore, the **p** comes by faith, so
4:20 unbelief regarding the **p** of God,
9: 8 but it is the children of the **p** who

Ro 9: 9 For this was how the **p** was stated:
Gal 3:14 might receive the **p** of the Spirit.
3:17 by God and thus do away with the **p**.
3:18 then it no longer depends on a **p**;
3:18 gave it to Abraham through a **p**.
3:19 Seed to whom the **p** referred had come.
3:29 seed, and heirs according to the **p**.
4:23 woman was born as the result of a **p**.
4:28 like Isaac, are children of **p**.
Eph 2:12 to the covenants of the **p**, without
3: 6 together in the **p** in Christ Jesus.
6: 2 is the first commandment with a **p**—
1Ti 4: 8 holding **p** for both the present life
2Ti 1: 1 **p** of life that is in Christ Jesus,
Heb 4: 1 Therefore, since the **p** of entering
6:13 God made his **p** to Abraham, since
11: 9 were heirs with him of the same **p**.
11:11 him faithful who had made the **p**.
2Pe 2:19 They **p** them freedom, while they
3: 9 The Lord is not slow in keeping his **p**
3:13 in keeping with his **p** we are looking

Promised (Promise)

Ge 18:19 for Abraham what he has **p** him."
21: 1 LORD did for Sarah what he had **p**.
21: 2 age, at the very time God had **p** him.
24: 7 who spoke to me and **p** me on oath,
28:15 I have done what I have **p** you."
50:24 to the land he **p** on oath to Abraham,
Ex 3:17 I have **p** to bring you up out of your
12:25 LORD will give you as he **p**,
13:11 as he **p** on oath to you and your
32:13 descendants all this land I **p** them,
33: 1 and go up to the land I **p** on oath to
Lev 19:20 slave girl **p** to another man but who
Nu 10:29 LORD has **p** good things to Israel."
11:12 you **p** on oath to their forefathers?
14:16 into the land he **p** them on oath;
14:23 I **p** on oath to their forefathers.
14:40 will go up to the place the LORD **p**."
32:11 see the land I **p** on oath to Abraham,
32:24 flocks, but do what you have **p**."
Dt 1:11 times and bless you as he has **p**!
6: 3 LORD, the God of your fathers, **p** you.
6:18 LORD **p** on oath to your forefathers,
6:23 he **p** on oath to our forefathers.
8: 1 LORD **p** on oath to your forefathers.
9: 3 them quickly, as the LORD has **p** you.
9:28 them into the land he had **p** them,
11:25 The LORD your God, as he **p** you, will
12:20 enlarged your territory as he **p** you,
13:17 as he **p** on oath to your forefathers,
15: 6 your God will bless you as he has **p**,
18: 2 is their inheritance, as he **p** them.
19: 8 as he **p** on oath to your forefathers,
19: 8 gives you the whole land he **p** them,
26:15 as you **p** on oath to our forefathers,
26:18 his treasured possession as he **p**,
26:19 holy to the LORD your God, as he **p**.
27: 3 LORD, the God of your fathers, **p** you.
28: 9 as he **p** you on oath, if you keep the
29:13 that he may be your God as he **p** you
31:20 the land I **p** on oath to their
31:21 into the land I **p** them on oath."
31:23 into the land I **p** them on oath,
34: 4 "This is the land I **p** on oath to
Jos 1: 3 you set your foot, as I **p** Moses.
5: 6 solemnly **p** their fathers to give us,
13:14 are their inheritance, as he **p** them.
13:33 is their inheritance, as he **p** them.
14:10 "Now then, just as the LORD **p**, he
14:12 country that the LORD **p** me that day.
22: 4 given your brothers rest as he **p**,
23: 5 land, as the LORD your God **p** you.
23:10 God fights for you, just as he **p**.
Jdg 1:20 Moses had **p**, Hebron was given to
6:36 Israel by my hand as you have **p**—
11:36 Do to me just as you **p**, now that the
1Sa 2:30 'I **p** that your house and your
25:30 good thing he **p** concerning him
2Sa 3: 9 David what the LORD **p** him on oath
3:18 Now do it! For the LORD **p** David, 'By
7:25 servant and his house. Do as you **p**,
7:28 **p** these good things to your servant.
19:23 And the king **p** him on oath.
1Ki 2:24 has founded a dynasty for me as he **p**
5:12 Solomon wisdom, just as he had **p** him.
8:15 fulfilled what he **p** with his own
8:20 just as the LORD **p**, and I have built
8:24 with your mouth you have **p** and with
8:26 let your word that you **p** your
8:56 to his people Israel just as he **p**.
9: 5 as I **p** David your father when I said,
2Ki 8:19 He had **p** to maintain a lamp for
10:10 he **p** through his servant Elijah."
20: 9 that the LORD will do what he has **p**:
1Ch 11: 3 as the LORD had **p** through Samuel.
11:10 the whole land, as the LORD had **p**—
17:23 established for ever. Do as you **p**,
17:26 You have **p** these good things to
27:23 because the LORD had **p** to make
2Ch 2:15 and the olive oil and wine he **p**,
6: 4 **p** with his mouth to my father David.
6:10 just as the LORD **p**, and I have built
6:15 with your mouth you have **p** and with
6:17 let your word that you **p** your
6:42 great love **p** to David your servant."
21: 7 He had **p** to maintain a lamp for him
23: 3 as the LORD **p** concerning the
Ne 5:12 take an oath to do what they had **p**.
5:13 And the people did as they had **p**.
Est 4: 7 money Haman had **p** to pay into the
Ps 66:14 vows my lips **p** and my mouth spoke
119:57 I have **p** to obey your words.
Isa 38: 7 that the LORD will do what he has **p**:
55: 3 you, my faithful love **p** to David.
Jer 32:42 all the prosperity I have **p** them.
44:25 actions what you **p** when you said,
44:25 then, do what you **p**! Keep your vows!
Mt 14: 7 that he **p** with an oath to give her
Mk 6:23 he **p** her with an oath, "Whatever you
14:11 hear this and **p** to give him money.
Lk 2:29 "Sovereign Lord, as you have **p**, you
24:49 to send you what my Father has **p**;
Ac 1: 4 but wait for the gift my Father **p**,
2:30 knew that God had **p** him on oath that
2:33 from the Father the **p** Holy Spirit
3:21 **p** long ago through his holy prophets.
7: 5 But God **p** him that he and his
13:23 Israel the Saviour Jesus, as he **p**.
13:32 good news: What God **p** our fathers
13:34 holy and sure blessings **p** to David.'
18:21 as he left, he **p**, "I will come back
26: 6 what God has **p** our fathers that I
Ro 1: 2 the gospel he **p** beforehand through
4:21 God had power to do what he had **p**.
2Co 9: 5 for the generous gift you had **p**.
11: 2 I **p** you to one husband, to Christ,
Gal 3:22 so that what was **p**, being given
Eph 1:13 him with a seal, the **p** Holy Spirit,
Tit 1: 2 lie, **p** before the beginning of time,
Heb 6:12 patience inherit what has been **p**.
6:15 Abraham received what was **p**.
6:17 clear to the heirs of what was **p**,
9:15 receive the **p** eternal inheritance
10:23 profess, for he who **p** is faithful.
10:36 God, you will receive what he has **p**.
11: 9 he made his home in the **p** land
11:13 They did not receive the things **p**;
11:33 justice, and gained what was **p**;
11:39 of them received what had been **p**.
12:26 but now he has **p**, "Once more I will
Jas 1:12 God has **p** to those who love him.
2: 5 the kingdom he **p** those who love him?
2Pe 3: 4 "Where is this 'coming' he **p**?
1Jn 2:25 this is what he **p** us—even eternal

Promises (Promise)

Jos 21:45 Not one of all the LORD's good **p** to
23:14 not one of all the good **p** the LORD
1Ki 8:25 the **p** you made to him when you said,
8:56 **p** he gave through his servant Moses.
1Ch 17:19 and made known all these great **p**.
25: 5 given to him through the **p** of God
2Ch 6:16 the **p** you made to him when you said,
Ps 85: 8 he **p** peace to his people, his saints
106:12 they believed his **p** and sang his
119:140 Your **p** have been thoroughly tested,
119:148 that I may meditate on your **p**.
145:13 The LORD is faithful to all his **p**
Hos 10: 4 They make many **p**, take false oaths
Ro 9: 4 law, the temple worship and the **p**.
15: 8 the **p** made to the patriarchs
2Co 1:20 For no matter how many **p** God has
7: 1 Since we have these **p**, dear friends,
Gal 3:16 The **p** were spoken to Abraham and to
3:21 therefore, opposed to the **p** of God?
Heb 7: 6 and blessed him who had the **p**.
8: 6 one, and it is founded on better **p**.
11:17 He who had received the **p** was about
2Pe 1: 4 us his very great and precious **p**,

Promote (Promoted, Promotes)

Ne 2:10 to **p** the welfare of the Israelites.
Pr 12:20 evil, but joy for those who **p** peace.
16:21 and pleasant words **p** instruction.
16:23 mouth, and his lips **p** instruction.
Da 5:19 those he wanted to **p**, he promoted;
Hab 1: 7 themselves and **p** their own honour.
1Ti 1: 4 These **p** controversies rather than

Promoted (Promote)

2Ch 28:19 for he had **p** wickedness in Judah and
Da 3:30 the king **p** Shadrach, Meshach and
5:19 those he wanted to promote, he **p**;

Promotes (Promote)

Pr 17: 9 He who covers over an offence **p** love,
Gal 2:17 does that mean that Christ **p** sin?

Prompt (Prompted, Prompts)

Job 20: 2 "My troubled thoughts **p** me to answer

Prompted (Prompt)

Mt 14: 8 **P** by her mother, she said, "Give me
Jn 13: 2 and the devil had already **p** Judas
1Th 1: 3 your labour **p** by love, and your
2Th 1:11 yours and every act **p** by your faith.

Prompts (Prompt)

Ex 25: 2 each man whose heart **p** him to give.
Job 15: 5 Your sin **p** your mouth; you adopt the

Prone

Ex 32:22 know how **p** these people are to evil.

Pronounce (Pronounced, Pronounces, Pronouncing)

Ge 48:20 "In your name will Israel **p** this
Lev 13: 3 he shall **p** him ceremonially unclean.
13: 6 the priest shall **p** him clean;
13: 8 he shall **p** him unclean; it is an
13:11 and the priest shall **p** him unclean.
13:13 body, he shall **p** that person clean.
13:15 raw flesh, he shall **p** him unclean.
13:17 the priest shall **p** the infected
13:20 the priest shall **p** him unclean.
13:22 the priest shall **p** him unclean;
13:23 and the priest shall **p** him clean.
13:25 The priest shall **p** him unclean;
13:27 the priest shall **p** him unclean;
13:28 and the priest shall **p** him clean;
13:30 the priest shall **p** that person
13:34 deep, the priest shall **p** him clean.
13:37 and the priest shall **p** him clean.
13:44 The priest shall **p** him unclean
14: 7 infectious disease and **p** him clean.
14:48 he shall **p** the house clean, because
Dt 10: 8 and to **p** blessings in his name,
21: 5 to **p** blessings in the name of the
23: 4 Aram Naharaim to **p** a curse on you.
27:13 stand on Mount Ebal to **p** curses:
Jdg 12: 6 because he could not **p** the word
1Ch 23:13 to **p** blessings in his name for ever.
Job 9:20 blameless, it would **p** me guilty.
Ps 109:17 He loved to **p** a curse—may it come
Jer 1:16 I will **p** my judgments on my people
4:12 Now I **p** my judgments against them."

Pronounced (Pronounce)

Lev 13: 7 himself to the priest to be **p** clean,
13:35 in the skin after he is **p** clean,
14:36 in the house will be **p** unclean.

Dt 33: 1 the man of God **p** on the Israelites
Jos 6:26 At that time Joshua **p** this solemn
1Ki 20:40 "You have **p** it yourself."
2Ki 23:17 **p** against the altar of Bethel the
25: 6 Riblah, where sentence was **p** on him.
1Ch 16:12 miracles, and the judgments he **p**,
Ps 76: 8 From heaven you **p** judgment, and the
105: 5 miracles, and the judgments he **p**,
Jer 19:15 it every disaster I **p** against them,
26:13 the disaster he has **p** against you.
26:19 the disaster he **p** against them?
35:17 every disaster I **p** against them.
36: 7 for the anger and wrath **p** against
36:31 every disaster I **p** against them,
39: 5 Hamath, where he **p** sentence on him.
52: 9 Hamath, where he **p** sentence on him.
Da 7:22 Ancient of Days came and **p** judgment

Pronounces (Pronounce)
Lev 14:11 The priest who **p** him clean shall

Pronouncing (Pronounce)
Lev 13:59 for **p** them clean or unclean.

Proof (Prove)
Dt 22:14 I did not find **p** of her virginity,"
22:15 mother shall bring **p** that she was a
22:17 But here is the **p** of my daughter's
22:20 the charge is true and no **p** of the
Ac 17:31 He has given **p** of this to all men by
2Co 8:24 Therefore show these men the **p** of
13: 3 since you are demanding **p** that

Proofs (Prove)
Ac 1: 3 many convincing **p** that he was alive.

Proper (Properly)
Lev 5:15 without defect and of the **p** value
5:18 without defect and of the **p** value.
6: 6 without defect and of the **p** value.
Jdg 6:26 build a **p** kind of altar to the LORD
2Sa 15: 3 "Look, your claims are valid and **p**,
1Ki 4:28 They also brought to the **p** place
1Ch 23:31 the LORD regularly in the **p** number
Ezr 4:14 **p** for us to see the king dishonoured,
Ps 104:27 give them their food at the **p** time.
145:15 give them their food at the **p** time.
Ecc 5:18 I realised that it is good and **p** for
6: 3 and does not receive **p** burial,
8: 5 will know the **p** time and procedure.
8: 6 For there is a **p** time and procedure
10:17 whose princes eat at a **p** time—for
Jer 30:18 palace will stand in its **p** place.
Mt 3:15 it is **p** for us to do this to fulfil
24:45 give them their food at the **p** time?
Lk 1:20 will come true at their **p** time."
12:42 their food allowance at the **p** time?
Ac 13:28 Though they found no **p** ground for a
1Co 11:13 Is it **p** for a woman to pray to God
2Co 10:13 will not boast beyond **p** limits, but
Gal 6: 9 for at the **p** time we will reap a
2Th 2: 6 he may be revealed at the **p** time.
1Ti 2: 6 testimony given in its **p** time.
3: 4 children obey him with **p** respect.
5: 3 Give **p** recognition to those widows
1Pe 2:17 Show **p** respect to everyone: Love the

Properly (Proper)
1Ti 1: 8 the law is good if one uses it **p**.

Property
Ge 23: 4 Sell me some **p** for a burial site
23:18 to Abraham as his **p** in the presence
34:10 trade in it, and acquire **p** in it."
34:23 Won't their livestock, their **p** and
47:11 them **p** in the best part of the land,
47:27 They acquired **p** there and were
Ex 21:21 or two, since the slave is his **p**.
22: 8 laid his hands on the other man's **p**.
22: 9 a garment, or any other lost **p** about
22:11 lay hands on the other person's **p**.
Lev 6: 3 or if he finds lost **p** and lies about
6: 4 to him, or the lost **p** he found,
25:10 family **p** and each to his own clan.
Lev 25:13 everyone is to return to his own **p**.
25:25 poor and sells some of his **p**,
25:27 he can then go back to his own **p**.
25:28 and he can then go back to his **p**.
25:33 the **p** of the Levites is redeemable
25:33 are their **p** among the Israelites.
25:41 and to the **p** of his forefathers.
25:45 and they will become your **p**.
25:46 to your children as inherited **p** and
27:21 it will become the **p** of the priests.
Nu 27: 4 us **p** among our father's relatives."
27: 7 You must certainly give them **p** as an
32:32 but the **p** we inherit will be on this
35:28 priest may he return to his own **p**.
36: 4 and their **p** will be taken from the
Dt 21:16 he wills his **p** to his sons, he must
Ru 4: 5 the name of the dead with his **p**."
4: 7 and transfer of **p** to become final,
4: 9 **p** of Elimelech, Kilion and Mahlon.
4:10 the name of the dead with his **p**,
1Sa 25: 2 A certain man in Maon, who had **p**
25:21 all my watching over this fellow's **p**
1Ki 21:19 not murdered a man and seized his **p**?'
1Ch 9: 2 first to resettle on their own **p**
27:31 in charge of King David's **p**.
28: 1 the officials in charge of all the **p**
2Ch 11:14 abandoned their pasture-lands and **p**,
31: 1 their own towns and to their own **p**.
Ezr 7:26 confiscation of **p**, or imprisonment.
10: 8 three days would forfeit all his **p**,
Ne 11: 3 on his own **p** in the various towns,
11:20 of Judah, each on his ancestral **p**.
Est 8:11 to plunder the **p** of their enemies.
Job 5:24 take stock of your **p** and find
Jer 37:12 of the **p** among the people there.
Eze 45: 6 "'You are to give the city as its **p**
45: 7 district and the **p** of the city.
46:16 it is to be their **p** by inheritance.
46:18 people, driving them off their **p**.
46:18 their inheritance out of his own **p**,
46:18 people will be separated from his **p**.
48:20 along with the **p** of the city.
48:21 city **p** will belong to the prince.
48:22 the **p** of the Levites and the **p** of
Mt 25:14 and entrusted his **p** to them.
Lk 15:12 So he divided his **p** between them.
15:30 squandered your **p** with prostitutes
16:12 trustworthy with someone else's **p**,
16:12 who will give you **p** of your own?
Ac 5: 1 Sapphira, also sold a piece of **p**.
Heb 10:34 accepted the confiscation of your **p**,

Prophecies (Prophecy)
2Ch 24:27 The account of his sons, the many **p**
1Co 13: 8 But where there are **p**, they will
1Th 5:20 do not treat **p** with contempt.
1Ti 1:18 with the **p** once made about you,

Prophecy (Prophecies)
2Ki 9:25 when the LORD made this **p** about him:
2Ch 9:29 in the **p** of Ahijah the Shilonite and
15: 8 these words and the **p** of Azariah
Eze 14: 9 the prophet is enticed to utter a **p**,
Da 9:24 to seal up vision and **p** and to
Mt 13:14 In them is fulfilled the **p** of Isaiah:
1Co 12:10 miraculous powers, to another **p**,
13: 2 If I have the gift of **p** and can
14: 1 gifts, especially the gift of **p**.
14: 6 or **p** or word of instruction?
14:22 **p**, however, is for believers, not
2Th 2: 2 unsettled or alarmed by some **p**,
2Pe 1:20 understand that no **p** of Scripture
1:21 For **p** never had its origin in the
Rev 1: 3 one who reads the words of this **p**,
19:10 of Jesus is the spirit of **p**."
22: 7 the words of the **p** in this book."
22:10 "Do not seal up the words of the **p**
22:18 the words of the **p** of this book:
22:19 words away from this book of **p**,

Prophesied (Prophesy)
Nu 11:25 Spirit rested on them, they **p**, but
11:26 on them, and they **p** in the camp.
1Sa 19:20 upon Saul's men and they also **p**.
19:21 he sent more men, and they **p** too.
1Sa 19:21 men a third time, and they also **p**.
19:24 He stripped off his robes and also **p**
1Ch 25: 2 who **p** under the king's supervision.
25: 3 who **p**, using the harp in thanking
2Ch 20:37 Eliezer son of Dodavahu of Mareshah **p**
Ezr 5: 1 a descendant of Iddo, **p** to the Jews
Ne 6:12 but that he had **p** against me because
Jer 2: 8 **p** by Baal, following worthless idols.
20: 6 friends to whom you have **p** lies.
23:13 They **p** by Baal and led my people
23:21 not speak to them, yet they have **p**.
25:13 **p** by Jeremiah against all the
26:11 because he has **p** against this city.
26:18 "Micah of Moresheth **p** in the days of
26:20 man who **p** in the name of the LORD;
26:20 he **p** the same things against this
28: 6 LORD fulfil the words you have **p**
28: 8 who preceded you and me have **p** war,
29:31 Because Shemaiah has **p** to you,
37:19 Where are your prophets who **p** to you,
Eze 13:16 those prophets of Israel who **p** to
37: 7 I **p** as I was commanded. And as I was
37:10 I **p** as he commanded me, and breath
38:17 At that time they **p** for years that I
Mt 11:13 Prophets and the Law **p** until John.
15: 7 Isaiah was right when he **p** about you:
Mk 7: 6 "Isaiah was right when he **p** about
Lk 1:67 filled with the Holy Spirit and **p**:
Jn 11:51 that year he **p** that Jesus would die
Ac 19: 6 and they spoke in tongues and **p**.
21: 9 He had four unmarried daughters who **p**
Jude :14 Enoch, the seventh from Adam, **p**

Prophesies (Prophesy)
1Ki 22: 8 because he never **p** anything good
22:18 he never **p** anything good about me,
2Ch 18: 7 because he never **p** anything good
18:17 he never **p** anything good about me,
Jer 28: 9 the prophet who **p** peace will be
Eze 12:27 and he **p** about the distant future.'
Zec 13: 3 if anyone still **p**, his father and
13: 3 he **p**, his own parents will stab him.
1Co 11: 4 Every man who prays or **p** with his
11: 5 every woman who prays or **p** with her
14: 3 everyone who **p** speaks to men for
14: 4 but he who **p** edifies the church.
14: 5 He who **p** is greater than one who

Prophesy (Prophesied, Prophesies, Prophesying)
1Sa 10: 6 and you will **p** with them; and you
Isa 30:10 Tell us pleasant things, **p** illusions.
Jer 5:31 The prophets **p** lies, the priests
11:21 'Do not **p** in the name of the LORD or
19:14 where the LORD had sent him to **p**,
23:25 prophets say who **p** lies in my name.
23:26 **p** the delusions of their own minds?
23:32 against those who **p** false dreams,"
25:30 "Now **p** all these words against them
26: 9 Why do you **p** in the LORD's name that
26:12 "The LORD sent me to **p** against this
27:10 They **p** lies to you that will only
27:15 you and the prophets who **p** to you.
32: 3 "Why do you **p** as you do? You say,
Eze 4: 7 and with bared arm **p** against her.
6: 2 mountains of Israel; **p** against them
11: 4 Therefore **p** against them; **p**, son of
13: 2 "Son of man, **p** against the prophets
13: 2 Say to those who **p** out of their
13:17 who **p** out of their own imagination.
13:17 **P** against them
20:46 preach against the south and **p**
21: 2 **P** against the land of Israel
21: 9 "Son of man, **p** and say, 'This is
21:14 "So then, son of man, **p** and strike
21:28 "And you, son of man, **p** and say,
25: 2 the Ammonites and **p** against them.
28:21 face against Sidon; **p** against her
29: 2 **p** against him and against all Egypt.
30: 2 "Son of man, **p** and say: 'This is
34: 2 "Son of man, **p** against the shepherds
34: 2 **p** and say to them: 'This is what
35: 2 against Mount Seir; **p** against it
36: 1 "Son of man, **p** to the mountains of
36: 3 Therefore **p** and say, 'This is what

Eze 36: 6 Therefore **p** concerning the land of
37: 4 he said to me, "**P** to these bones and
37: 9 he said to me, "**P** to the breath;
37: 9 **p**, son of man, and say to it,
37:12 Therefore **p** and say to them: 'This
38: 2 of Meshech and Tubal; **p** against him
38:14 "Therefore, son of man, **p** and say to
39: 1 "Son of man, **p** against Gog and say:
Joel 2:28 Your sons and daughters will **p**, your
Am 2:12 and commanded the prophets not to **p**.
3: 8 LORD has spoken—who can but **p**?
7:13 Don't **p** any more at Bethel, because
7:15 to me, 'Go, **p** to my people Israel.'
7:16 You say, "'Do not **p** against Israel,
Mic 2: 6 "Do not **p**," their prophets say. "Do
2: 6 "Do not **p** about these things;
2:11 'I will **p** for you plenty of wine and
Mt 7:22 'Lord, Lord, did we not **p** in your
26:68 said, "**P** to us, Christ. Who hit you?"
Mk 14:65 with their fists, and said, "**P**!"
Lk 22:64 him and demanded, "**P**! Who hit you?"
Ac 2:17 Your sons and daughters will **p**, your
2:18 in those days, and they will **p**.
1Co 13: 9 For we know in part and we **p** in part,
14: 5 but I would rather have you **p**.
14:31 For you can all **p** in turn so that
14:39 Therefore, my brothers, be eager to **p**
Rev 10:11 I was told, "You must **p** again about
11: 3 and they will **p** for 1,260 days,

Prophesying (Prophesy)

Nu 11:27 "Eldad and Medad are **p** in the camp.
1Sa 10: 5 before them, and they will be **p**.
10:10 in power, and he joined in their **p**.
10:11 him saw him **p** with the prophets,
10:13 After Saul stopped **p**, he went to the
18:10 He was **p** in his house, while David
19:20 when they saw a group of prophets **p**,
19:23 he walked along **p** until he came to
1Ki 18:29 and they continued their frantic **p**
22:10 with all the prophets **p** before them.
22:12 All the other prophets were **p** the
1Ch 25: 1 and Jeduthun for the ministry of **p**,
2Ch 18: 9 with all the prophets **p** before them.
18:11 All the other prophets were **p** the
Jer 14:14 "The prophets are **p** lies in my name.
14:14 They are **p** to you false visions,
14:15 prophets who are **p** in my name:
14:16 the people they are **p** to will be
20: 1 LORD, heard Jeremiah **p** these things,
23:16 to what the prophets are **p** to you;
27:14 Babylon,' for they are **p** lies to you.
27:15 'They are **p** lies in my name.
27:16 They are **p** lies to you.
29: 9 They are **p** lies to you in my name.
29:21 who are **p** lies to you in my name:
Eze 11:13 Now as I was **p**, Pelatiah son of
13: 2 prophets of Israel who are now **p**.
37: 7 And as I was **p**, there was a noise, a
Am 7:12 bread there and do your **p** there.
Ro 12: 6 If a man's gift is **p**, let him use it
1Co 14:24 comes in while everybody is **p**,
Rev 11: 6 not rain during the time they are **p**;

Prophet (*False prophet*, Prophet's, Prophetess, Prophetic, Prophets)

Ge 20: 7 for he is a **p**, and he will pray for
Ex 7: 1 your brother Aaron will be your **p**.
Nu 12: 6 "When a **p** of the LORD is among you,
Dt 13: 1 If a **p**, or one who foretells by
13: 3 to the words of that **p** or dreamer.
13: 5 That **p** or dreamer must be put to
18:15 a **p** like me from among your own
18:18 I will raise up for them a **p** like
18:19 words that the **p** speaks in my name,
18:20 a **p** who presumes to speak in my name
18:20 or a **p** who speaks in the name of
18:22 If what a **p** proclaims in the name of
18:22 That **p** has spoken presumptuously.
34:10 Since then, no **p** has risen in Israel
Jdg 6: 8 he sent them a **p**, who said, "This is
1Sa 3:20 was attested as a **p** of the LORD.
9: 9 **p** of today used to be called a seer.)
22: 5 the **p** Gad said to David, "Do not
2Sa 7: 2 he said to Nathan the **p**, "Here I am,
2Sa 12:25 Nathan the **p** to name him Jedidiah.
24:11 had come to Gad the **p**, David's seer:
1Ki 1: 8 Nathan the **p**, Shimei and Rei and
1:10 he did not invite Nathan the **p** or
1:22 with the king, Nathan the **p** arrived.
1:23 the king, "Nathan the **p** is here."
1:32 Nathan the **p** and Benaiah son of
1:34 Nathan the **p** anoint him king
1:38 Zadok the priest, Nathan the **p**,
1:44 Nathan the **p**, Benaiah son of
1:45 Zadok the priest and Nathan the **p**
11:29 and Ahijah the **p** of Shiloh met him
13:11 Now there was a certain old **p** living
13:15 the **p** said to him, "Come home with
13:18 The old **p** answered, "I too am a **p**,
13:20 the old **p** who had brought him back.
13:23 the **p** who had brought him back
13:25 in the city where the old **p** lived.
13:26 the **p** who had brought him back from
13:27 The **p** said to his sons, "Saddle the
13:29 the **p** picked up the body of the man
14: 2 Ahijah the **p** is there—the one who
14:18 through his servant the **p** Ahijah.
16: 7 the **p** Jehu son of Hanani to Baasha
16:12 against Baasha through the **p** Jehu—
18:36 the **p** Elijah stepped forward and
19:16 Abel Meholah to succeed you as **p**.
20:13 Meanwhile a **p** came to Ahab king of
20:14 The **p** replied, "This is what the
20:14 The **p** answered, "You will."
20:22 Afterwards, the **p** came to the king
20:36 the **p** said, "Because you have not
20:37 The **p** found another man and said,
20:38 the **p** went and stood by the road
20:39 the king passed by, the **p** called out
20:41 the **p** quickly removed the headband
22: 7 "Is there not a **p** of the LORD here
2Ki 3:11 "Is there no **p** of of the LORD here,
5: 3 "If only my master would see the **p**
5: 8 know that there is a **p** in Israel."
5:13 "My father, if the **p** had told you to
5:16 The **p** answered, "As surely as the
6:12 "but Elisha, the **p** who is in Israel,
6:16 "Don't be afraid," the **p** answered.
9: 1 The **p** Elisha summoned a man from the
9: 4 the young man, the **p**, went to Ramoth
9: 6 Then the **p** poured the oil on Jehu's
14:25 of Amittai, the **p** from Gath Hepher.
19: 2 to the **p** Isaiah son of Amoz.
20: 1 The **p** Isaiah son of Amoz went to him
20:11 the **p** Isaiah called upon the LORD,
20:14 Isaiah the **p** went to King Hezekiah
20:15 The **p** asked, "What did they see in
23:18 of the **p** who had come from Samaria.
1Ch 17: 1 he said to Nathan the **p**, "Here I am,
29:29 the records of Nathan the **p** and the
2Ch 9:29 in the records of Nathan the **p**,
12: 5 the **p** Shemaiah came to Rehoboam and
12:15 in the records of Shemaiah the **p**
13:22 in the annotations of the **p** Iddo.
15: 8 of Azariah son of Oded the **p**,
18: 6 "Is there not a **p** of the LORD here
21:12 received a letter from Elijah the **p**,
25:15 and he sent a **p** to him, who said,
25:16 So the **p** stopped but said, "I know
26:22 by the **p** Isaiah son of Amoz.
28: 9 a **p** of the LORD named Oded was there,
29:25 Gad the king's seer and Nathan the **p**
32:20 King Hezekiah and the **p** Isaiah son
32:32 the vision of the **p** Isaiah son of
35:18 since the days of the **p** Samuel;
36:12 before Jeremiah the **p**, who spoke
Ezr 5: 1 Now Haggai the **p** and Zechariah the **p**
6:14 of Haggai the **p** and Zechariah,
Ps 51: T **p** Nathan came to him after David
Isa 3: 2 hero and warrior, the judge and **p**
37: 2 to the **p** Isaiah son of Amoz.
38: 1 The **p** Isaiah son of Amoz went to him
39: 3 Isaiah the **p** went to King Hezekiah
39: 4 The **p** asked, "What did they see in
Jer 1: 5 you as a **p** to the nations."
14:18 Both **p** and priest have gone to a
20: 2 he had Jeremiah the **p** beaten and put
23:11 "Both **p** and priest are godless;
23:28 Let the **p** who has a dream tell his
23:33 "When these people, or a **p** or a
Jer 23:34 If a **p** or a priest or anyone else
23:37 This is what you keep saying to a **p**:
25: 2 Jeremiah the **p** said to all the
28: 1 the **p** Hananiah son of Azzur, who was
28: 5 the **p** Jeremiah replied to the **p**
28: 9 the **p** who prophesies peace will be
28:10 the **p** Hananiah took the yoke off the
28:10 neck of the **p** Jeremiah and broke it,
28:11 the **p** Jeremiah went on his way.
28:12 Shortly after the **p** Hananiah had
28:12 yoke off the neck of the **p** Jeremiah,
28:15 the **p** Jeremiah said to Hananiah the **p**
28:17 that same year, Hananiah the **p** died.
29: 1 letter that the **p** Jeremiah sent
29:26 any madman who acts like a **p** into
29:27 Anathoth, who poses as a **p** among you?
29:29 read the letter to Jeremiah the **p**.
32: 2 and Jeremiah the **p** was confined in
34: 6 Jeremiah the **p** told all this to
36: 8 Jeremiah the **p** told him to do;
36:26 Baruch the scribe and Jeremiah the **p**.
37: 2 had spoken through Jeremiah the **p**.
37: 3 to Jeremiah the **p** with this message:
37: 6 of the LORD came to Jeremiah the **p**:
38: 9 they have done to Jeremiah the **p**.
38:10 lift Jeremiah the **p** out of the
38:14 King Zedekiah sent for Jeremiah the **p**
42: 2 Jeremiah the **p** and said to him,
42: 4 heard you," replied Jeremiah the **p**.
43: 6 Jeremiah the **p** and Baruch son of
45: 1 This is what Jeremiah the **p** told
46: 1 came to Jeremiah the **p** concerning
46:13 spoke to Jeremiah the **p** about the
47: 1 came to Jeremiah the **p** concerning
49:34 to Jeremiah the **p** concerning Elam,
50: 1 Jeremiah the **p** concerning Babylon
Lam 2:20 Should priest and **p** be killed in the
Eze 2: 5 know that a **p** has been among them.
7:26 will try to get a vision from the **p**;
14: 4 his face and then goes to a **p**,
14: 7 then goes to a **p** to enquire of me,
14: 9 "'And if the **p** is enticed to utter
14: 9 I the LORD have enticed that **p**, and
14:10 the **p** will be as guilty as the one
33:33 know that a **p** has been among them."
Da 9: 2 of the LORD given to Jeremiah the **p**,
Hos 9: 7 the **p** is considered a fool, the
9: 8 The **p**, along with my God, is the
12:13 The LORD used a **p** to bring Israel up
12:13 from Egypt, by a **p** he cared for him.
Am 7:14 "I was neither a **p** nor a prophet's
Mic 2:11 would be just the **p** for this people!
Hab 1: 1 that Habakkuk the **p** received.
3: 1 A prayer of Habakkuk the **p**.
Hag 1: 1 through the **p** Haggai to Zerubbabel
1: 3 the LORD came through the **p** Haggai:
1:12 God and the message of the **p** Haggai,
2: 1 the LORD came through the **p** Haggai:
2:10 of the LORD came to the **p** Haggai:
Zec 1: 1 of the LORD came to the **p** Zechariah
1: 7 of the LORD came to the **p** Zechariah
13: 4 "On that day every **p** will be ashamed
13: 5 He will say, 'I am not a **p**. I am a
Mal 4: 5 "See, I will send you the **p** Elijah
Mt 1:22 the Lord had said through the **p**:
2: 5 this is what the **p** has written:
2:15 the Lord had said through the **p**:
2:17 what was said through the **p** Jeremiah
3: 3 was spoken of through the **p** Isaiah:
4:14 what was said through the **p** Isaiah:
8:17 was spoken through the **p** Isaiah:
10:41 Anyone who receives a **p** because he
10:41 a **p** will receive a prophet's reward,
11: 9 what did you go out to see? A **p**?
11: 9 Yes, I tell you, and more than a **p**.
12:17 was spoken through the **p** Isaiah:
12:39 it except the sign of the **p** Jonah.
13:35 what was spoken through the **p**:
13:57 own house is a **p** without honour."
14: 5 because they considered him a **p**.
21: 4 what was spoken through the **p**:
21:11 the **p** from Nazareth in Galilee."
21:26 they all hold that John was a **p**."
21:46 the people held that he was a **p**.
24:15 spoken of through the **p** Daniel—let
27: 9 what was spoken by Jeremiah the **p**

Mk 1: 2 is written in Isaiah the **p**: “I will
6: 4 own house is a **p** without honour.”
6:15 “He is a **p**, like one of the prophets
11:32 held that John really was a **p**.)
Lk 1:76 be called a **p** of the Most High;
3: 4 book of the words of Isaiah the **p**:
4:17 The scroll of the **p** Isaiah was
4:24 “no **p** is accepted in his home town.
4:27 leprosy in the time of Elisha the **p**,
7:16 “A great **p** has appeared among us,”
7:26 what did you go out to see? A **p**?
7:26 Yes, I tell you, and more than a **p**.
7:39 “If this man were a **p**, he would know
13:33 no **p** can die outside Jerusalem!
20: 6 are persuaded that John was a **p**.”
24:19 “He was a **p**, powerful in word and
Jn 1:21 “Are you the **P**?” He answered, “No.”
1:23 in the words of Isaiah the **p**,
1:25 the Christ, nor Elijah, nor the **P**?”
4:19 said, “I can see that you are a **p**.
4:44 **p** has no honour in his own country.)
6:14 **P** who is to come into the world.”
7:40 said, “Surely this man is the **P**.”
7:52 a **p** does not come out of Galilee.”
9:17 The man replied, “He is a **p**.”
12:38 the word of Isaiah the **p**: “Lord,
Ac 2:16 No, this is what was spoken by the **p**
2:30 he was a **p** and knew that God had
3:22 send you a **p** like me from among
7:37 a **p** like me from your own people.’
7:48 houses made by men. As the **p** says:
7:52 Was there ever a **p** your fathers did
8:28 reading the book of Isaiah the **p**.
8:30 heard the man reading Isaiah the **p**.
8:34 please, who is the **p** talking about,
13:20 until the time of Samuel the **p**.
21:10 **p** named Agabus came down from Judea.
28:25 when he said through Isaiah the **p**:
1Co 14:37 If anybody thinks he is a **p** or

Prophet's (Prophet)

Am 7:14 “I was neither a prophet nor a **p** son,
Zec 13: 4 He will not put on a **p** garment of
Mt 10:41 a prophet will receive a **p** reward,
2Pe 1:20 about by the **p** own interpretation.
2:16 voice and restrained the **p** madness.

Prophetess (Prophet)

Ex 15:20 Miriam the **p**, Aaron's sister, took a
Jdg 4: 4 Deborah, a **p**, the wife of Lappidoth,
2Ki 22:14 Asaiah went to speak to the **p** Huldah,
2Ch 34:22 him went to speak to the **p** Huldah,
Ne 6:14 remember also the **p** Noadiah and the
Isa 8: 3 I went to the **p**, and she conceived
Lk 2:36 There was also a **p**, Anna, the
Rev 2:20 Jezebel, who calls herself a **p**.

Prophetic (Prophet)

Zec 13: 4 will be ashamed of his **p** vision.
Ro 16:26 made known through the **p** writings by
1Ti 4:14 was given you through a **p** message

Prophets (*False prophets*, Prophet)

Nu 11:29 that all the LORD's people were **p**
1Sa 10: 5 you will meet a procession of **p**
10:10 a procession of **p** met him;
10:11 him saw him prophesying with the **p**,
10:11 Is Saul also among the **p**?”
10:12 “Is Saul also among the **p**?”
19:20 But when they saw a group of **p**
19:24 “Is Saul also among the **p**?”
28: 6 answer him by dreams or Urim or **p**.
28:15 He no longer answers me, either by **p**
1Ki 18: 4 Jezebel was killing off the LORD's **p**,
18: 4 Obadiah had taken a hundred **p** and
18:13 was killing the **p** of the LORD?
18:13 of the LORD's **p** in two caves,
18:19 four hundred and fifty **p** of Baal
18:19 and the four hundred **p** of Asherah,
18:20 and assembled the **p** on Mount Carmel.
18:22 “I am the only one of the LORD's **p**
18:22 Baal has four hundred and fifty **p**.
18:25 Elijah said to the **p** of Baal,
18:40 Elijah commanded them, “Seize the **p**
1Ki 19: 1 had killed all the **p** with the sword.
19:10 put your **p** to death with the sword.
19:14 put your **p** to death with the sword.
20:35 sons of the **p** said to his companion,
20:41 recognised him as one of the **p**.
22: 6 the **p**—about four hundred men—
22:10 all the **p** prophesying before them.
22:12 All the other **p** were prophesying the
22:13 “Look, as one man the other **p** are
22:22 the mouths of all his **p**,’ he said.
22:23 the mouths of all these **p** of yours.
2Ki 2: 3 The company of the **p** at Bethel came
2: 5 The company of the **p** at Jericho went
2: 7 Fifty men of the company of the **p**
2:15 The company of the **p** from Jericho,
3:13 the **p** of your father and the **p** of
4: 1 of the **p** cried out to Elisha,
4:38 While the company of the **p** was
5:22 young men from the company of the **p**
6: 1 The company of the **p** said to Elisha,
9: 1 company of the **p** and said to him,
9: 7 the blood of my servants the **p**
10:19 Now summon all the **p** of Baal, all
17:13 Judah through all his **p** and seers:
17:13 to you through my servants the **p**.”
17:23 through all his servants the **p**.
21:10 LORD said through his servants the **p**:
23: 2 the priests and the **p**—all the
24: 2 proclaimed by his servants the **p**.
1Ch 16:22 my anointed ones; do my **p** no harm.”
2Ch 18: 5 together the **p**—four hundred men—
18: 9 all the **p** prophesying before them.
18:11 All the other **p** were prophesying the
18:12 “Look, as one man the other **p** are
18:21 the mouths of all his **p**,’ he said.
18:22 in the mouths of these **p** of yours.
20:20 have faith in his **p** and you will be
24:19 Although the LORD sent **p** to the
29:25 commanded by the LORD through his **p**.
36:16 scoffed at his **p** until the wrath of
Ezr 5: 2 And the **p** of God were with them,
9:11 you gave through your servants the **p**
Ne 6: 7 have even appointed **p** to make this
6:14 the rest of the **p** who have been
9:26 They killed your **p**, who had
9:30 you admonished them through your **p**.
9:32 upon our priests and **p**, upon our
Ps 74: 9 no **p** are left, and none of us knows
105:15 my anointed ones; do my **p** no harm.”
Isa 9:15 the **p** who teach lies are the tail.
28: 7 Priests and **p** stagger from beer and
29:10 He has sealed your eyes (the **p**);
30:10 and to the **p**, “Give us no more
Jer 2: 8 The **p** prophesied by Baal, following
2:26 their priests and their **p**.
2:30 Your sword has devoured your **p**
4: 9 and the **p** will be appalled.”
5:13 The **p** are but wind and the word is
5:31 The **p** prophesy lies, the priests
6:13 **p** and priests alike, all practise
7:25 again I sent you my servants the **p**.
8: 1 the bones of the priests and **p**, and
8:10 **p** and priests alike, all practise
13:13 **p** and all those living in Jerusalem.
14:13 LORD, the **p** keep telling them,
14:14 “The **p** are prophesying lies in my
14:15 **p** who are prophesying in my name:
14:15 **p** will perish by sword and famine.
18:18 the wise, nor the word from the **p**.
23: 9 Concerning the **p**: My heart is broken
23:10 The **p** follow an evil course and use
23:13 “Among the **p** of Samaria I saw this
23:14 among the **p** of Jerusalem I have seen
23:15 LORD Almighty says concerning the **p**:
23:15 because from the **p** of Jerusalem
23:16 “Do not listen to what the **p** are
23:21 I did not send these **p**, yet they
23:25 “I have heard what the **p** say who
23:26 in the hearts of these lying **p**,
23:30 “I am against the **p** who steal from
23:31 “I am against the **p** who wag their
25: 4 sent all his servants the **p** to you
26: 5 to the words of my servants the **p**,
26: 7 The priests, the **p** and all the
26: 8 the priests, the **p** and all the
26:11 the priests and the **p** said to the
Jer 26:16 said to the priests and the **p**,
27: 9 do not listen to your **p**, your
27:14 Do not listen to the words of the **p**
27:15 you and the **p** who prophesy to you.
27:16 Do not listen to the **p** who say,
27:18 If they are **p** and have the word of
28: 8 From early times the **p** who preceded
29: 1 the **p** and all the other people
29: 8 **p** and diviners among you deceive you.
29:15 has raised up **p** for us in Babylon,”
29:19 and again by my servants the **p**.
32:32 their priests and **p**, the men of
35:15 I sent all my servants the **p** to you.
37:19 Where are your **p** who prophesied to
44: 4 and again I sent my servants the **p**,
Lam 2: 9 and her **p** no longer find visions
2:14 The visions of your **p** were false and
4:13 happened because of the sins of her **p**
Eze 13: 2 “Son of man, prophesy against the **p**
13: 3 Woe to the foolish **p** who follow
13: 4 Your **p**, O Israel, are like jackals
13: 9 My hand will be against the **p** who
13:16 those **p** of Israel who prophesied to
22:28 Her **p** whitewash these deeds for them
38:17 days by my servants the **p** of Israel?
Da 9: 6 not listened to your servants the **p**,
9:10 gave us through his servants the **p**.
Hos 4: 5 and the **p** stumble with you.
6: 5 I cut you in pieces with my **p**,
12:10 I spoke to the **p**, gave them many
Am 2:11 I also raised up **p** from among your
2:12 and commanded the **p** not to prophesy.
3: 7 his plan to his servants the **p**.
Mic 2: 6 “Do not prophesy,” their **p** say.
3: 5 “As for the **p** who lead my people
3: 6 The sun will set for the **p**,
3:11 and her **p** tell fortunes for money.
Zep 3: 4 Her **p** are arrogant; they are
Zec 1: 4 to whom the earlier **p** proclaimed:
1: 5 And the **p**, do they live for ever?
1: 6 which I commanded my servants the **p**,
7: 3 of the LORD Almighty and the **p**,
7: 7 the earlier **p** when Jerusalem
7:12 by his Spirit through the earlier **p**.
8: 9 spoken by the **p** who were there when
13: 2 “I will remove both the **p** and the
Mt 2:23 what was said through the **p**:
5:12 persecuted the **p** who were before
5:17 come to abolish the Law or the **P**;
7:12 for this sums up the Law and the **P**.
11:13 For all the **P** and the Law prophesied
13:17 many **p** and righteous men longed to
16:14 others, Jeremiah or one of the **p**.”
22:40 All the Law and the **P** hang on these
23:29 You build tombs for the **p** and
23:30 in shedding the blood of the **p**.’
23:31 of those who murdered the **p**.
23:34 Therefore I am sending you **p** and
23:37 Jerusalem, you who kill the **p** and
26:56 that the writings of the **p** might be
Mk 6:15 like one of the **p** of long ago.”
8:28 and still others, one of the **p**.”
Lk 1:70 (as he said through his holy **p** of
6:23 is how their fathers treated the **p**.
9: 8 one of the **p** of long ago had come
9:19 one of the **p** of long ago has come
10:24 For I tell you that many **p** and kings
11:47 because you build tombs for the **p**,
11:48 they killed the **p**, and you build
11:49 ‘I will send them **p** and apostles,
11:50 blood of all the **p** that has been
13:28 Isaac and Jacob and all the **p** in the
13:34 Jerusalem, you who kill the **p** and
16:16 “The Law and the **P** were proclaimed
16:29 ‘They have Moses and the **P**;
16:31 do not listen to Moses and the **P**,
18:31 everything that is written by the **p**
24:25 believe all that the **p** have spoken!
24:27 beginning with Moses and all the **P**,
24:44 Law of Moses, the **P** and the Psalms.”
Jn 1:45 and about whom the **p** also wrote—
6:45 is written in the **P**: ‘They will all
8:52 Abraham died and so did the **p**,
8:53 He died, and so did the **p**.
Ac 3:18 he had foretold through all the **p**,
3:21 long ago through his holy **p**.

Ac 3:24 "Indeed, all the **p** from Samuel on,
3:25 you are heirs of the **p** and of the
7:42 is written in the book of the **p**:
10:43 All the **p** testify about him that
11:27 During this time some **p** came down
13: 1 In the church at Antioch there were **p**
13:15 the reading from the Law and the **P**,
13:27 the **p** that are read every Sabbath.
13:40 Take care that what the **p** have said
15:15 The words of the **p** are in agreement
15:32 who themselves were **p**, said much to
24:14 Law and that is written in the **P**,
26:22 the **p** and Moses said would happen—
26:27 King Agrippa, do you believe the **p**?
28:23 the Law of Moses and from the **P**.
Ro 1: 2 his **p** in the Holy Scriptures
3:21 to which the Law and the **P** testify.
11: 3 "Lord, they have killed your **p** and
1Co 12:28 second **p**, third teachers, then
12:29 Are all apostles? Are all **p**? Are all
14:29 Two or three **p** should speak, and the
14:32 The spirits of **p** are subject to the
14:32 subject to the control of **p**.
Eph 2:20 foundation of the apostles and **p**,
3: 5 Spirit to God's holy apostles and **p**.
4:11 some to be **p**, some to be evangelists,
1Th 2:15 who killed the Lord Jesus and the **p**
Tit 1:12 Even one of their own **p** has said,
Heb 1: 1 through the **p** at many times and in
11:32 Jephthah, David, Samuel and the **p**,
Jas 5:10 **p** who spoke in the name of the Lord.
1Pe 1:10 Concerning this salvation, the **p**,
2Pe 1:19 we have the word of the **p** made more
3: 2 spoken in the past by the holy **p**
Rev 10: 7 he announced to his servants the **p**."
11:10 because these two **p** had tormented
11:18 for rewarding your servants the **p**
16: 6 shed the blood of your saints and **p**,
18:20 saints and apostles and **p**! God has
18:24 In her was found the blood of **p** and
22: 6 the God of the spirits of the **p**,
22: 9 with your brothers the **p** and of all

Proportion
Nu 35: 8 given in **p** to the inheritance of
Dt 16:10 freewill offering in **p** to the
16:17 must bring a gift in **p** in the way
Ro 12: 6 let him use it in **p** to his faith.

Proposal (Propose)
Ge 34:18 Their **p** seemed good to Hamor and his
Ac 6: 5 This **p** pleased the whole group.

Propose (Proposal, Proposed)
Dt 1:14 "What you **p** to do is good."
Isa 8:10 **p** your plan, but it will not stand,

Proposed (Propose)
Ezr 10:16 the exiles did as was **p**. Ezra the
Est 1:21 so the king did as Memucan **p**.
2: 2 the king's personal attendants **p**,
Ac 1:23 they **p** two men: Joseph called

Propped
1Ki 22:35 and the king was **p** up in his chariot
2Ch 18:34 and the king of Israel **p** himself up

Propriety
1Ti 2: 9 with decency and **p**, not with braided
2:15 in faith, love and holiness with **p**.

Prospect (Prospects)
Pr 10:28 The **p** of the righteous is joy, but

Prospects (Prospect)
Job 6:11 What **p**, that I should be patient?

Prosper (Prospered, Prosperity, Prosperous, Prospers)
Ge 32: 9 relatives, and I will make you **p**,'
32:12 'I will surely make you **p** and will
Dt 5:33 so that you may live and **p** and
6:24 so that we might always **p** and be
28:63 make you **p** and increase in number,
29: 9 that you may **p** in everything you do.
1Ki 2: 3 **p** in all you do and wherever you go,
2Ch 24:20 the LORD's commands? You will not **p**.
Ezr 6:14 **p** under the preaching of Haggai the
Ps 49:18 and men praise you when you **p**—
51:18 In your good pleasure make Zion **p**;
Pr 11:10 the righteous **p**, the city rejoices;
11:25 A generous man will **p**; he who
17:20 A man of perverse heart does not **p**;
28:13 He who conceals his sins does not **p**,
28:25 he who trusts in the LORD will **p**.
Isa 53:10 will of the LORD will **p** in his hand.
Jer 10:21 they do not **p** and all their flock
12: 1 Why does the way of the wicked **p**?
22:30 a man who will not **p** in his lifetime,
22:30 for none of his offspring will **p**,
29: 7 if it prospers, you too will **p**."
29:11 "plans to **p** you and not to harm you,
Eze 26: 2 that she lies in ruins I will **p**,'
36:11 will make you **p** more than before.
Da 4: 1 in all the world: May you **p** greatly!
6:25 "May you **p** greatly!
8:25 He will cause deceit to **p**, and he
Mal 3:15 Certainly the evildoers **p**, and even
Ac 13:17 people **p** during their stay in Egypt,

Prospered (Prosper)
Ge 39: 2 The LORD was with Joseph and he **p**,
1Ch 29:23 He **p** and all Israel obeyed him.
2Ch 14: 7 So they built and **p**.
31:21 worked wholeheartedly. And so he **p**.
Da 6:28 Daniel **p** during the reign of Darius
8:12 It **p** in everything it did, and
Hos 10: 1 as his land **p**, he adorned his

Prosperity (Prosper)
Dt 28:11 The LORD will grant you abundant **p**
28:47 and gladly in the time of **p**,
30:15 life and **p**, death and destruction.
Job 20:21 to devour; his **p** will not endure.
21:13 They spend their years in **p** and go
21:16 their **p** is not in their own hands,
22:21 in this way **p** will come to you.
36:11 spend the rest of their days in **p**
Ps 25:13 He will spend his days in **p**, and his
72: 3 The mountains will bring **p** to the
72: 7 **p** will abound till the moon is no
73: 3 when I saw the **p** of the wicked.
106: 5 that I may enjoy the **p** of your
122: 9 LORD our God, I will seek your **p**.
128: 2 blessings and **p** will be yours.
128: 5 may you see the **p** of Jerusalem,
Pr 3: 2 life many years and bring you **p**.
8:18 and honour, enduring wealth and **p**.
13:21 **p** is the reward of the righteous.
21:21 and love finds life, **p** and honour.
Ecc 6: 3 if he cannot enjoy his **p** and does
6: 6 twice over but fails to enjoy his **p**.
Isa 45: 7 I bring **p** and create disaster;
Jer 17: 6 he will not see **p** when it comes.
29: 7 Also, seek the peace and **p** of the
32:42 them all the **p** I have promised them.
33: 9 **p** and peace I provide for it.'
39:16 this city through disaster, not **p**.
Lam 3:17 I have forgotten what **p** is.
Da 4:27 be that then your **p** will continue."
Zec 1:17 'My towns will again overflow with **p**,

Prosperous (Prosper)
Ge 30:43 the man grew exceedingly **p** and came
Dt 30: 5 more **p** and numerous than your
30: 9 **p** in all the work of your hands
30: 9 again delight in you and make you **p**,
Jos 1: 8 Then you will be **p** and successful.
Jdg 18: 7 land lacked nothing, they were **p**.
Job 8: 7 humble, so **p** will your future be.
42:10 the LORD made him **p** again and gave
Ps 10: 5 His ways are always **p**; he is haughty
Da 4: 4 home in my palace, contented and **p**.
Zec 7: 7 towns were at rest and **p**,

Prospers (Prosper)
Lev 25:26 redeem it for him but he himself **p**
25:49 Or if he **p**, he may redeem himself.
Ps 1: 3 Whatever he does **p**.
Pr 16:20 Whoever gives heed to instruction **p**,
19: 8 he who cherishes understanding **p**.
Jer 29: 7 if it **p**, you too will prosper."

Prostitute (Prostitute's, Prostituted, Prostitutes, Prostituting, Prostitution, Shrine-prostitute)
Ge 34:31 have treated our sister like a **p**?"
38:15 Judah saw her, he thought she was a **p**
Ex 34:15 for when they **p** themselves to their
34:16 **p** themselves to their gods,
Lev 17: 7 idols to whom they **p** themselves.
19:29 your daughter by making her a **p**,
20: 6 to **p** himself by following them,
21: 9 defiles herself by becoming a **p**,
Nu 15:39 obey them and not **p** yourselves
Dt 23:18 of a female **p** or of a male **p** into
31:16 these people will soon **p** themselves
Jos 2: 1 of a **p** named Rahab and stayed there.
6:17 Only Rahab the **p** and all who are
6:25 Joshua spared Rahab the **p**, with her
Jdg 11: 1 was Gilead; his mother was a **p**.
16: 1 went to Gaza, where he saw a **p**.
2Ch 21:11 people of Jerusalem to **p** themselves
21:13 people of Jerusalem to **p** themselves,
Pr 6:26 for the **p** reduces you to a loaf of
7:10 like a **p** and with crafty intent.
23:27 for a **p** is a deep pit and a wayward
Isa 23:15 to Tyre as in the song of the **p**:
23:16 walk through the city, O **p** forgotten;
23:17 She will return to her hire as a **p**
Jer 2:20 spreading tree you lay down as a **p**.
3: 1 But you have lived as a **p** with many
3: 3 you have the brazen look of a **p**;
Eze 16:15 and used your fame to become a **p**.
16:30 things, acting like a brazen **p**!
16:31 you were unlike a **p**, because you
16:33 Every **p** receives a fee, but you give
16:35 "'Therefore, you **p**, hear the word
23: 7 She gave herself as a **p** to all the
23:19 youth, when she was a **p** in Egypt.
23:43 her as a **p**, for that is all she is.'
23:44 As men sleep with a **p**, so they slept
Hos 3: 3 be a **p** or be intimate with any man,
9: 1 of a **p** at every threshing-floor.
Am 7:17 'Your wife will become a **p** in the
1Co 6:15 and unite them with a **p**? Never!
6:16 with a **p** is one with her in body?
Heb 11:31 By faith the **p** Rahab, because she
Jas 2:25 was not even Rahab the **p** considered
Rev 17: 1 punishment of the great **p**, who sits
17:15 waters you saw, where the **p** sits,
17:16 ten horns you saw will hate the **p**.
19: 2 He has condemned the great **p** who

Prostitute's (Prostitute)
Jos 6:22 "Go into the **p** house and bring her

Prostituted (Prostitute)
Jdg 2:17 but **p** themselves to other gods
8:27 All Israel **p** themselves by
8:33 again **p** themselves to the Baals.
1Ch 5:25 **p** themselves to the gods of the
Ps 106:39 by their deeds they **p** themselves.

Prostitutes (Prostitute, Shrine-prostitutes)
1Ki 3:16 Now two **p** came to the king and stood
22:38 in Samaria (where the **p** bathed),
Job 36:14 They die in their youth, among male **p**
Pr 29: 3 companion of **p** squanders his wealth.
Isa 57: 3 you offspring of adulterers and **p**!
Jer 5: 7 and thronged to the houses of **p**.
Eze 23: 3 They became **p** in Egypt, engaging in
Joel 3: 3 for my people and traded boys for **p**;
Mic 1: 7 her gifts from the wages of **p**,
1: 7 wages of **p** they will again be used."
Mt 21:31 the tax collectors and the **p** are
21:32 the tax collectors and the **p** did.
Lk 15:30 your property with **p** comes home,

1Co 6: 9 nor male **p** nor homosexual offenders
Rev 17: 5 THE MOTHER OF **P** AND OF THE

Prostituting (Prostitute)
Lev 20: 5 him in **p** themselves to Molech.

Prostitution (Prostitute)
Ge 38:24 Tamar is guilty of **p**, and as a
Lev 19:29 the land will turn to **p** and be
21: 7 women defiled by **p** or divorced from
21:14 or a woman defiled by **p**, but only a
Jer 3: 2 the land with your **p** and wickedness.
13:27 your shameless **p**! I have seen your
Eze 16:16 places, where you carried on your **p**.
16:17 idols and engaged in **p** with them.
16:20 Was your **p** not enough?
16:22 your **p** you did not remember the days
16:26 You engaged in **p** with the Egyptians,
16:28 You engaged in **p** with the Assyrians
16:34 in your **p** you are the opposite of
16:41 I will put a stop to your **p**, and you
23: 3 engaging in **p** from their youth.
23: 5 "Oholah engaged in **p** while she was
23: 8 She did not give up the **p** she began
23:11 yet in her lust and **p** she was more
23:14 "But she carried her **p** still further.
23:18 she carried on her **p** openly and
23:27 lewdness and **p** you began in Egypt.
23:29 the shame of your **p** will be exposed.
23:35 of your lewdness and **p**."
43: 7 by their **p** and the lifeless idols
43: 9 Now let them put away from me their **p**
Hos 4:10 will engage in **p** but not increase,
4:11 to **p**, to old wine and new, which
4:12 A spirit of **p** leads them astray;
4:13 Therefore your daughters turn to **p**
4:14 your daughters when they turn to **p**,
4:18 they continue their **p**; their rulers
5: 3 now turned to **p**; Israel is corrupt.
5: 4 A spirit of **p** is in their heart;
6:10 is given to **p** and Israel is defiled.
Na 3: 4 who enslaved nations by her **p** and

Prostrate (Prostrated)
Nu 24: 4 falls **p**, and whose eyes are opened:
24:16 falls **p**, and whose eyes are opened:
Dt 9:18 once again I fell **p** before the LORD
9:25 I lay **p** before the LORD those forty
2Sa 19:18 Jordan, he fell **p** before the
1Ki 18:39 all the people saw this, they fell **p**
1Ch 29:20 fell **p** before the LORD and the king.
Isa 15: 3 they all wail, **p** with weeping.
51:23 'Fall **p** that we may walk over you.
Da 2:46 King Nebuchadnezzar fell **p** before
8:17 I was terrified and fell **p**.

Prostrated (Prostrate)
1Sa 24: 8 David bowed down and **p** himself with
28:14 and he bowed down and **p** himself with

Protect (Protected, Protection, Protective, Protects)
Nu 35:25 The assembly must **p** the one accused
Dt 23:14 moves about in your camp to **p** you
2Sa 18:12 **P** the young man Absalom for my sake.'
Ezr 8:22 to **p** us from enemies on the road,
Est 8:11 right to assemble and **p** themselves;
9:16 also assembled to **p** themselves
Ps 12: 5 **p** them from those who malign them."
12: 7 and **p** us from such people for ever.
20: 1 the name of the God of Jacob **p** you.
25:21 May integrity and uprightness **p** me,
32: 7 you will **p** me from trouble
40:11 love and your truth always **p** me.
41: 2 The LORD will **p** him and preserve his
59: 1 **p** me from those who rise up against
61: 7 your love and faithfulness to **p** him.
64: 1 **p** my life from the threat of the
69:29 may your salvation, O God, **p** me.
91:14 **p** him, for he acknowledges my name.
140: 1 **p** me from men of violence,
140: 4 **p** me from men of violence who plan
Pr 2:11 Discretion will **p** you, and
4: 6 Do not forsake wisdom, and she will **p**
Pr 14: 3 but the lips of the wise **p** them.
Jer 49:11 your orphans; I will **p** their lives.
Da 11: 1 took my stand to support and **p** him.)
Jn 17:11 Holy Father, **p** them by the power of
17:15 that you **p** them from the evil one.
2Th 3: 3 and **p** you from the evil one.

Protected (Protect)
Jos 24:17 He **p** us on our entire journey and
1Sa 30:23 He has **p** us and handed over to us
Ezr 8:31 and he **p** us from enemies and bandits
Job 5:21 You will be **p** from the lash of the
Ps 37:28 They will be **p** for ever, but the
Mk 6:20 Herod feared John and **p** him, knowing
Jn 17:12 While I was with them, I **p** them and
2Pe 2: 5 but **p** Noah, a preacher of

Protection (Protect)
Ge 19: 8 have come under the **p** of my roof."
Nu 14: 9 Their **p** is gone, but the LORD is
32:17 **p** from the inhabitants of the land.
Jos 20: 3 find **p** from the avenger of blood.
Ezr 9: 9 a wall of **p** in Judah and Jerusalem.
Ps 5:11 Spread your **p** over them, that those
Isa 30: 2 who look for help to Pharoah's **p**,
30: 3 Pharaoh's **p** will be to your shame,
Mic 1:11 mourning; its **p** is taken from you.

Protective (Protect)
Na 2: 5 the **p** shield is put in place.

Protects (Protect)
Ps 34:20 he **p** all his bones, not one of them
116: 6 The LORD **p** the simple-hearted;
Pr 2: 8 and **p** the way of his faithful ones.
Da 12: 1 who **p** your people, will arise.
1Co 13: 7 always **p**, always trusts, always

Protest (Protested)
Ecc 5: 6 And do not **p** to the temple messenger,
Ac 13:51 **p** against them and went to Iconium.
18: 6 he shook out his clothes in **p** and

Protested (Protest)
Jn 8:41 not illegitimate children," they **p**.
19:21 The chief priests of the Jews **p** to

Proud (Pride, Proudly)
Dt 8:14 your heart will become **p** and you
2Ch 25:19 Edom, and now you are arrogant and **p**.
32:25 Hezekiah's heart was **p** and he did
Job 28: 8 **P** beasts do not set foot on it, and
38:11 here is where your **p** waves halt'?
39:20 striking terror with his **p** snorting?
40:11 at every **p** man and bring him low,
40:12 look at every **p** man and humble him,
41:34 he is king over all that are **p**."
Ps 31:23 but the **p** he pays back in full.
36:11 May the foot of the **p** not come
40: 4 who does not look to the **p**, to those
94: 2 pay back to the **p** what they deserve.
101: 5 has haughty eyes and a **p** heart,
123: 4 endured much ridicule from the **p**,
131: 1 My heart is not **p**, O LORD, my eyes
138: 6 lowly, but the **p** he knows from afar.
140: 5 **P** men have hidden a snare for me;
140: 8 succeed, or they will become **p**.
Pr 3:34 He mocks **p** mockers but gives grace
15:25 LORD tears down the **p** man's house
16: 5 The LORD detests all the **p** of heart.
16:19 than to share plunder with the **p**.
18:12 his downfall a man's heart is **p**,
21: 4 Haughty eyes and a **p** heart, the lamp
21:24 The **p** and arrogant man—"Mocker" is
Isa 2:12 in store for all the **p** and lofty,
Eze 7:20 They were **p** of their beautiful
28: 5 your wealth your heart has grown **p**.
28:17 Your heart became **p** on account of
30: 6 fall and her **p** strength will fail.
30:18 her **p** strength will come to an end.
31:10 and because it was **p** of its height,
33:28 and her **p** strength will come to an
Hos 13: 6 they became **p**; then they forgot me.
Zec 10: 3 make them like a **p** horse in battle.
Lk 1:51 who are **p** in their inmost thoughts.
Ro 12:16 Do not be **p**, but be willing to
1Co 5: 2 you are **p**! Shouldn't you rather have
13: 4 it does not boast, it is not **p**.
2Ti 3: 2 lovers of money, boastful, **p**,
Jas 4: 6 "God opposes the **p** but gives grace
1Pe 5: 5 "God opposes the **p** but gives grace
Rev 13: 5 was given a mouth to utter **p** words

Proudly (Proud)
1Sa 2: 3 "Do not keep talking so **p** or let
Eze 31:14 waters are ever to tower **p** on high,
Mic 2: 3 You will no longer walk **p**,

Prove (Proof, Proofs, Proved, Proves, Proving)
Ge 44:16 we say? How can we **p** our innocence?
Job 6:25 But what do your arguments **p**?
24:25 "If this is not so, who can **p** me
Pr 29:25 Fear of man will **p** to be a snare,
30: 6 he will rebuke you and **p** you a liar.
Isa 43: 9 witnesses to **p** they were right,
Jer 17:11 in the end he will **p** to be a fool.
Mic 1:14 **p** deceptive to the kings of Israel.
Hab 2: 3 of the end and will not **p** false.
Jn 2:18 to **p** your authority to do all this?"
8:46 Can any of you **p** me guilty of sin?
Ac 24:13 they cannot **p** to you the charges
25: 7 against him, which they could not **p**.
26:20 **p** their repentance by their deeds.
1Co 4: 2 been given a trust must **p** faithful.
2Co 9: 3 in this matter should not **p** hollow,
Gal 2:18 I **p** that I am a law-breaker.
Heb 9:16 **p** the death of the one who made it,

Proved (Prove)
Dt 13:14 And if it is true and it has been **p**
17: 4 If it is true and it has been **p** that
1Ki 16:22 Omri's followers **p** stronger than
Job 6:21 Now you too have **p** to be of no help;
32:12 But not one of you has **p** Job wrong;
Ps 51: 4 so that you are **p** right when you
105:19 the word of the LORD **p** him true.
Ecc 2: 1 But that also **p** to be meaningless.
Mt 11:19 wisdom is **p** right by her actions."
Lk 7:35 wisdom is **p** right by all her
Ro 3: 4 "So that you may be **p** right when you
2Co 7:11 At every point you have **p** yourselves
7:14 to Titus has **p** to be true as well.
8:22 who has often **p** to us in many ways
9:13 by which you have **p** yourselves,
Php 2:22 you know that Timothy has **p** himself,
Col 4:11 God, and they have **p** a comfort to me.
1Pe 1: 7 **p** genuine and may result in praise,

Proverb (Proverbs)
Ps 49: 4 I will turn my ear to a **p**; with the
Pr 26: 7 limp is a **p** in the mouth of a fool.
26: 9 hand is a **p** in the mouth of a fool.
Eze 12:22 "Son of man, what is this **p** you have
12:23 I am going to put an end to this **p**,
16:44 this **p** about you: "Like mother,
18: 2 this **p** about the land of Israel:
18: 3 no longer quote this **p** in Israel.
Lk 4:23 "Surely you will quote this **p** to me:

Proverbs (Proverb)
1Ki 4:32 He spoke three thousand **p** and his
Job 13:12 Your maxims are **p** of ashes;
Pr 1: 1 The **p** of Solomon son of David, king
1: 6 for understanding **p** and parables,
10: 1 The **p** of Solomon: A wise son brings
25: 1 These are more **p** of Solomon, copied
Ecc 12: 9 out and set in order many **p**.
Eze 16:44 "Everyone who quotes **p** will quote
2Pe 2:22 Of them the **p** are true: "A dog

Proves (Prove)
Dt 19:18 and if the witness **p** to be a liar,

Provide (Provided, Provides, Providing, Provision, Provisions)

Ge 22: 8 Abraham answered, "God himself will **p**
22:14 called that place The LORD Will **P**.
45:11 I will **p** for you there, because five
49:16 "Dan will **p** justice for his people
49:20 he will **p** delicacies fit for a king
50:21 I will **p** for you and your children.
Ex 21:11 If he does not **p** her with these
27:16 **p** a curtain twenty cubits long,
Lev 25:24 **p** for the redemption of the land.
Dt 6:11 kinds of good things you did not **p**,
11:15 I will **p** grass in the fields for
Jdg 21: 7 "How can we **p** wives for those who
21:16 we **p** wives for the men who are left?
2Sa 7:10 I will **p** a place for my people
19:33 in Jerusalem, and I will **p** for you."
1Ki 4: 7 **p** supplies for one month in the year.
5:17 to **p** a foundation of dressed stone
1Ch 17: 9 I will **p** a place for my people
22:14 "I have taken great pains to **p** for
2Ch 2: 9 to **p** me with plenty of timber,
Ezr 1: 4 are to **p** him with silver and gold,
7:20 you may **p** from the royal treasury.
7:21 to **p** with diligence whatever Ezra
Ne 2: 7 so that they will **p** me safe-conduct
Ps 65: 9 water to **p** the people with corn,
Pr 27:26 the lambs will **p** you with clothing,
Isa 4: 1 our own food and **p** our own clothes;
43:20 because I **p** water in the desert and
50:11 **p** yourselves with flaming torches,
58: 7 to **p** the poor wanderer with shelter—
61: 3 **p** for those who grieve in Zion—to
Jer 33: 9 prosperity and peace I **p** for it.'
Eze 34:29 I will **p** for them a land renowned
43:25 "For seven days you are to **p** a male
43:25 you are also to **p** a young bull and a
45:17 prince to **p** the burnt offerings,
45:17 He will **p** the sin offerings, grain
45:22 that day the prince is to **p** a bull
45:23 of the Feast he is to **p** seven bulls
45:24 He is to **p** as a grain offering an
46: 7 He is to **p** as a grain offering one
46:13 you are to **p** a year-old lamb
46:13 morning by morning you shall **p** it.
46:14 You are also to **p** with it morning by
Lk 12:33 **P** purses for yourselves that will
Ac 7:46 favour and asked that he might **p** a
11:29 decided to **p** help for the brothers
23:24 **P** mounts for Paul so that he may be
27: 3 so they might **p** for his needs.
1Co 10:13 he will also **p** a way out so that you
Col 4: 1 Masters, **p** your slaves with what is
1Ti 5: 8 If anyone does not **p** for his
Tit 3:14 in order that they may **p** for daily

Provided (Provide)

Ge 22:14 mountain of the LORD it will be **p**."
43:24 feet and **p** fodder for their donkeys.
47:12 Joseph also **p** his father and his
Ru 3: 1 you, where you will be well **p** for?
1Sa 21: 4 **p** the men have kept themselves from
2Sa 9:10 your master's grandson may be **p** for.
15: 1 Absalom **p** himself with a chariot
19:32 He had **p** for the king during his
20: 3 He **p** for them, but did not lie with
1Ki 8:21 I have **p** a place there for the ark,
11:18 house and land and **p** him with food.
2Ki 13: 5 The LORD **p** a deliverer for Israel,
1Ch 22: 3 He **p** a large amount of iron to make
22: 4 He also **p** more cedar logs than could
23: 5 I have **p** for that purpose."
29: 2 I have **p** for the temple of my God
29: 3 I have **p** for this holy temple:
29:16 we have **p** for building you a temple
29:19 structure for which I have **p**."
2Ch 2: 7 craftsmen, whom my father David **p**.
3: 1 the Jebusite, the place **p** by David.
26:14 Uzziah **p** shields, spears, helmets,
28:15 They **p** them with clothes and sandals,
30:24 Hezekiah king of Judah **p** a thousand
30:24 and the officials **p** them with a
35: 7 Josiah **p** for all the lay people who
35: 9 the leaders of the Levites, **p** five
Ne 13: 5 he had **p** him with a large room
Est 2: 9 Immediately he **p** her with her beauty
Ps 68:10 bounty, O God, you **p** for the poor.
111: 9 He **p** redemption for his people;
Eze 16:19 Also the food I **p** for you—the fine
46:15 the oil shall be **p** morning by
Jnh 1:17 the LORD **p** a great fish to swallow
4: 6 the LORD God **p** a vine and made it
4: 7 at dawn the next day God **p** a worm,
4: 8 rose, God **p** a scorching east wind,
Ro 11:22 **p** that you continue in his kindness.
Gal 4:18 is fine to be zealous, **p** the purpose
Heb 1: 3 After he had **p** purification for sins,

Providence

Job 10:12 in your **p** watched over my spirit.

Provides (Provide)

Job 24: 5 wasteland **p** food for their children.
36:31 the nations and **p** food in abundance.
38:41 Who **p** food for the raven when its
Ps 111: 5 He **p** food for those who fear him;
147: 9 He **p** food for the cattle and for the
Pr 31:15 she **p** food for her family and
Eze 18: 7 hungry and **p** clothing for the naked.
18:16 hungry and **p** clothing for the naked.
46:12 the prince **p** a freewill offering to
Ac 14:17 he **p** you with plenty of food and
1Ti 6:17 who richly **p** us with everything for
1Pe 4:11 do it with the strength God **p**,

Providing (Provide)

Ru 1: 6 of his people by **p** food for them,
1Ki 5: 8 want in **p** the cedar and pine logs.
5: 9 by **p** food for my royal household."
Ne 13: 7 Eliashib had done in **p** Tobiah
Da 4:21 **p** food for all, giving shelter to

Province (Provinces, Provincial)

Ezr 2: 1 Now these are the people of the **p**
6: 2 of Ecbatana in the **p** of Media,
6: 6 of that **p**, stay away from there.
7:16 may obtain from the **p** of Babylon,
Ne 1: 3 **p** are in great trouble and disgrace.
7: 6 These are the people of the **p** who
Est 1:22 to each **p** in its own script and to
2: 3 commissioners in every **p** of his
3:12 wrote out in the script of each **p**
3:14 was to be issued as law in every **p**
4: 3 In every **p** to which the edict and
8: 9 written in the script of each **p**
8:11 or **p** that might attack them
8:13 was to be issued as law in every **p**
8:17 In every **p** and in every city,
9:28 and in every **p** and in every city.
Da 2:48 He made him ruler over the entire **p**
2:49 over the **p** of Babylon, while Daniel
3: 1 plain of Dura in the **p** of Babylon.
3:12 of the **p** of Babylon—Shadrach,
3:30 and Abednego in the **p** of Babylon.
8: 2 citadel of Susa in the **p** of Elam;
Ac 16: 6 preaching the word in the **p** of Asia.
19:10 **p** of Asia heard the word of the Lord.
19:22 in the **p** of Asia a little longer.
19:26 in practically the whole **p** of Asia.
19:27 who is worshipped throughout the **p**
19:31 Even some of the officials of the **p**,
20: 4 and Trophimus from the **p** of Asia.
20:16 spending time in the **p** of Asia,
20:18 first day I came into the **p** of Asia.
21:27 some Jews from the **p** of Asia saw
23:34 letter and asked what **p** he was from.
24:19 are some Jews from the **p** of Asia,
25: 1 Three days after arriving in the **p**,
27: 2 along the coast of the **p** of Asia,
Ro 16: 5 convert to Christ in the **p** of Asia.
1Co 16:19 The churches in the **p** of Asia send
2Co 1: 8 we suffered in the **p** of Asia.
2Ti 1:15 know that everyone in the **p** of Asia
Rev 1: 4 the seven churches in the **p** of Asia:

Provinces (Province)

Ezr 4:15 troublesome to kings and **p**, a place
Est 1: 1 **p** stretching from India to Cush:
1: 3 the nobles of the **p** were present.
Est 1:16 peoples of all the **p** of King Xerxes.
2:18 a holiday throughout the **p**
3: 8 in all the **p** of your kingdom whose
3:12 the governors of the various **p** and
3:13 king's **p** with the order to destroy,
4:11 the people of the royal **p** know that
8: 5 the Jews in all the king's **p**.
8: 9 127 **p** stretching from India to Cush.
8:12 in all the **p** of King Xerxes was the
9: 2 in all the **p** of King Xerxes to
9: 3 all the nobles of the **p**, the satraps,
9: 4 reputation spread throughout the **p**,
9:12 done in the rest of the king's **p**?
9:16 in the king's **p** also assembled to
9:20 the **p** of King Xerxes, near and far,
9:30 the 127 **p** of the kingdom of Xerxes—
Ecc 2: 8 and the treasure of kings and **p**.
Lam 1: 1 among the **p** has now become a slave.
Da 11:24 the richest **p** feel secure, he will
Ac 6: 9 well as the **p** of Cilicia and Asia.

Provincial (Province)

1Ki 20:14 of the **p** commanders will do it.
20:15 of the **p** commanders, 232 men.
20:17 young officers of the **p** commanders
20:19 young officers of the **p** commanders
Ne 11: 3 These are the **p** leaders who settled
Da 3: 2 and all the other **p** officials to
3: 3 and all the other **p** officials

Proving (Prove)

Ac 9:22 by **p** that Jesus is the Christ.
17: 3 explaining and **p** that the Christ had
18:28 **p** from the Scriptures that Jesus was

Provision (Provide)

Ne 13:31 I also made **p** for contributions of
Ps 144:13 will be filled with every kind of **p**.
Eze 45:25 he is to make the same **p** for sin
Ro 5:17 receive God's abundant **p** of grace

Provisions (Provide)

Ge 42:25 to give them **p** for their journey.
45:21 also gave them **p** for their journey.
45:23 bread and other **p** for his journey.
Jos 9:11 'Take **p** for your journey; go and
9:14 The men of Israel sampled their **p**
Jdg 7: 8 the **p** and trumpets of the others.
20:10 ten thousand, to get **p** for the army.
1Sa 22:10 he also gave him **p** and the sword of
2Sa 19:42 Have we eaten any of the king's **p**?
1Ki 4: 7 who supplied **p** for the king and the
4:22 Solomon's daily **p** were thirty cors
4:27 supplied **p** for King Solomon and all
20:27 and given **p**, they marched out to
1Ch 12:39 families had supplied **p** for them.
2Ch 11:23 He gave them abundant **p** and took
Ps 132:15 I will bless her with abundant **p**;
Pr 6: 8 yet it stores its **p** in summer and
Jer 40: 5 commander gave him **p** and a present
Da 11:26 Those who eat from the king's **p** will

Provocation (Provoke)

Pr 27: 3 **p** by a fool is heavier than both.

Provoke (Provocation, Provoked, Provokes, Provoking)

Dt 2: 5 Do not **p** them to war, for I will not
2: 9 the Moabites or **p** them to war,
2:19 do not harass them or **p** them to war,
31:29 **p** him to anger by what your hands
1Ki 16: 2 and to **p** me to anger by their sins.
16:33 pole and did more to **p** the LORD,
2Ki 23:26 Manasseh had done to **p** him to anger.
Job 12: 6 and those who **p** God are secure—
Isa 65: 3 a people who continually **p** me to my
Jer 7:18 to other gods to **p** me to anger.
25: 6 do not **p** me to anger with what your
32:30 **p** me with what their hands have made,
44: 8 Why **p** me to anger with what your
Eze 8:17 and continually **p** me to anger?

Provoked (Provoke)
Dt 9: 7 never forget how you **p** the LORD your
Jdg 2:12 They **p** the LORD to anger
1Sa 1: 7 her rival **p** her till she wept and
1Ki 14: 9 you have **p** me to anger and thrust
14:15 because they **p** the LORD to anger by
15:30 and because he **p** the LORD, the God
16:13 so that they **p** the LORD, the God of
16:26 so that they **p** the LORD, the God of
21:22 because you have **p** me to anger and
22:53 and worshipped Baal and **p** the LORD,
2Ki 17:11 things that **p** the LORD to anger.
21:15 have **p** me to anger from the day
22:17 to other gods and **p** me to anger
23:19 Samaria that had **p** the LORD to anger.
2Ch 28:25 to other gods and **p** the LORD,
34:25 to other gods and **p** me to anger by
Ps 106:29 they **p** the LORD to anger by their
Ecc 7: 9 Do not be quickly **p** in your spirit,
Jer 8:19 "Why have they **p** me to anger with
11:17 **p** me to anger by burning incense to
25: 7 "and you have **p** me with what your
32:29 the people **p** me to anger by burning
32:32 of Israel and Judah have **p** me by
44: 3 They **p** me to anger by burning
Eze 16:26 and **p** me to anger with your
20:28 made offerings that **p** me to anger,
Hos 12:14 Ephraim has bitterly **p** him to anger;

Provokes (Provoke)
Eze 8: 3 the idol that **p** to jealousy stood.

Provoking (Provoke)
Dt 4:25 LORD your God and **p** him to anger,
9:18 LORD's sight and so **p** him to anger.
1Sa 1: 6 kept **p** her in order to irritate her.
1Ki 16: 7 **p** him to anger by the things he did,
2Ki 17:17 eyes of the LORD, **p** him to anger.
21: 6 eyes of the LORD, **p** him to anger.
2Ch 33: 6 eyes of the LORD, **p** him to anger.
Jer 7:19 am I the one they are **p**? declares
Gal 5:26 Let us not become conceited, **p** and

Prowl (Prowled, Prowling, Prowls)
Ps 55:10 Day and night they **p** about on its
59: 6 like dogs, and **p** about the city.
59:14 like dogs, and **p** about the city.
104:20 and all the beasts of the forest **p**.

Prowled (Prowl)
Eze 19: 6 He **p** among the lions, for he was now

Prowling (Prowl)
Lam 5:18 desolate, with jackals **p** over it.

Prowls (Prowl)
Job 28: 8 set foot on it, and no lion **p** there.
1Pe 5: 8 Your enemy the devil **p** around like a

Prudence (Prudent)
Pr 1: 4 for giving **p** to the simple,
8: 5 You who are simple, gain **p**; you who
8:12 "I, wisdom, dwell together with **p**;
15: 5 whoever heeds correction shows **p**.
19:25 and the simple will learn **p**;

Prudent (Prudence)
Pr 1: 3 acquiring a disciplined and **p** life,
12:16 but a **p** man overlooks an insult.
12:23 A **p** man keeps his knowledge to
13:16 Every **p** man acts out of knowledge,
14: 8 The wisdom of the **p** is to give
14:15 a **p** man gives thought to his steps.
14:18 the **p** are crowned with knowledge.
19:14 but a **p** wife is from the LORD.
22: 3 A **p** man sees danger and takes refuge,
27:12 The **p** see danger and take refuge,
Jer 49: 7 Has counsel perished from the **p**?
Am 5:13 Therefore the **p** man keeps quiet in

Prune (Pruned, Prunes, Pruning)
Lev 25: 3 and for six years **p** your vineyards
25: 4 sow your fields or **p** your vineyards.

Pruned (Prune)
Isa 5: 6 wasteland, neither **p** nor cultivated

Prunes (Prune)
Jn 15: 2 does bear fruit he **p** so that it

Pruning (Prune)
Isa 2: 4 and their spears into **p** hooks.
18: 5 cut off the shoots with **p** knives,
Joel 3:10 swords and your **p** hooks into spears.
Mic 4: 3 and their spears into **p** hooks.

Psalm (Psalms)
1Ch 16: 7 this **p** of thanks to the LORD:
Ps 3: T A **p** of David. When he fled from his
4: T stringed instruments. A **p** of David.
5: T of music. For flutes. A **p** of David.
6: T According to sheminith. A **p** of David.
8: T According to gittith. A **p** of David.
9: T The Death of the Son." A **p** of David.
12: T According to sheminith. A **p** of David.
13: T the director of music. A **p** of David.
15: T A **p** of David.
19: T the director of music. A **p** of David.
20: T the director of music. A **p** of David.
21: T the director of music. A **p** of David.
22: T Doe of the Morning." A **p** of David.
23: T A **p** of David.
24: T Of David. A **p**.
29: T A **p** of David.
30: T A **p**. A song. For the dedication of
31: T the director of music. A **p** of David.
38: T A **p** of David. A petition.
39: T music. For Jeduthun. A **p** of David.
40: T director of music. Of David. A **p**.
41: T the director of music. A **p** of David.
47: T music. Of the Sons of Korah. A **p**.
47: 7 sing to him a **p** of praise.
48: T A song. A **p** of the Sons of Korah.
49: T music. Of the Sons of Korah. A **p**.
50: T A **p** of Asaph.
51: T the director of music. A **p** of David.
62: T music. For Jeduthun. A **p** of David.
63: T A **p** of David. When he was in the
64: T the director of music. A **p** of David.
65: T the director of music. A **p** of David.
66: T the director of music. A song. A **p**.
67: T stringed instruments. A **p**. A song.
68: T of music. Of David. A **p**. A song.
73: T A **p** of Asaph.
75: T "Do Not Destroy." A **p** of Asaph.
76: T stringed instruments. A **p** of Asaph.
77: T music. For Jeduthun. Of Asaph. A **p**.
79: T A **p** of Asaph.
80: T of the Covenant." Of Asaph. A **p**.
82: T A **p** of Asaph.
83: T A song. A **p** of Asaph.
84: T Of the Sons of Korah. A **p**.
85: T music. Of the Sons of Korah. A **p**.
87: T Of the Sons of Korah. A **p**. a song.
88: T A song. A **p** of the Sons of Korah.
92: T A **p**. A song. For the Sabbath day.
98: T A **p**.
100: T A **p**. For giving thanks.
101: T Of David. A **p**.
108: T A song. A **p** of David.
109: T director of music. Of David. A **p**.
110: T Of David. A **p**.
139: T director of music. Of David. A **p**.
140: T director of music. A **p** of David.
141: T A **p** of David.
143: T A **p** of David.
145: T A **p** of praise. Of David.
Ac 13:33 As it is written in the second **P**:

Psalms (Psalm)
Lk 20:42 himself declares in the Book of **P**:
24:44 of Moses, the Prophets and the **P**."
Ac 1:20 "it is written in the Book of **P**,
Eph 5:19 Speak to one another with **p**, hymns
Col 3:16 and as you sing **p**, hymns and

Ptolemais
Ac 21: 7 voyage from Tyre and landed at **P**,

Puah (Puite)
Ge 46:13 The sons of Issachar: Tola, **P**,
Ex 1:15 whose names were Shiphrah and **P**,
Nu 26:23 through **P**, the Puite clan;
Jdg 10: 1 Tola son of **P**, the son of Dodo, rose
1Ch 7: 1 The sons of Issachar: Tola, **P**,

Public (Publicly)
Lev 5: 1 when he hears a **p** charge to testify
Dt 13:16 into the middle of the **p** square
2Sa 21:12 from the **p** square at Beth Shan,
Job 29: 7 and took my seat in the **p** square,
Pr 1:20 raises her voice in the **p** squares;
5:16 streams of water in the **p** squares?
Isa 15: 3 and in the **p** squares they all wail,
Jer 9:21 the young men from the **p** squares.
48:38 roofs in Moab and in the **p** squares
Eze 16:24 a lofty shrine in every **p** square.
16:31 lofty shrines in every **p** square,
Am 5:16 cries of anguish in every **p** square.
Mt 1:19 want to expose her to **p** disgrace,
Lk 20:26 him in what he had said there in **p**.
Jn 7: 4 who wants to become a **p** figure
Ac 5:18 apostles and put them in the **p** jail.
12: 4 out for **p** trial after the Passover.
12:21 delivered a **p** address to the people.
18:28 refuted the Jews in **p** debate,
Ro 16:23 is the city's director of **p** works,
Col 2:15 he made a **p** spectacle of them,
1Ti 4:13 devote yourself to the **p** reading of
Heb 6: 6 and subjecting him to **p** disgrace.

Publicly (Public)
Lk 1:80 until he appeared **p** to Israel.
Jn 7:10 he went also, not **p**, but in secret.
7:13 no-one would say anything **p** about
7:26 Here he is, speaking **p**, and they are
11:54 longer moved about **p** among the Jews.
Ac 16:37 "They beat us **p** without a trial,
19: 9 to believe and **p** maligned the Way.
19:19 scrolls together and burned them **p**.
20:20 have taught you **p** and from house to
1Ti 5:20 Those who sin are to be rebuked **p**,
Heb 10:33 Sometimes you were **p** exposed to

Publish (Published)
Da 6:12 "Did you not **p** a decree that during

Published (Publish)
Est 4: 8 which had been **p** in Susa, to show to
Da 6:10 learned that the decree had been **p**,

Publius
Ac 28: 7 **P**, the chief official of the island.

Pudens
2Ti 4:21 Eubulus greets you, and so do **P**,

Puffed (Puffs)
Hab 2: 4 "See, he is **p** up; his desires are

Puffs (Puffed)
1Co 8: 1 Knowledge **p** up, but love builds up.
Col 2:18 mind **p** him up with idle notions.

Puite (Puah)
Nu 26:23 through Puah, the **P** clan;

Pul
2Ki 15:19 **P** king of Assyria invaded the land,
1Ch 5:26 of **P** king of Assyria (that is,

Pull (Pulled, Pulling, Pulls)
Jdg 3:22 Ehud did not **p** the sword out, and
Ru 2:16 Rather, **p** out some stalks for her
1Ki 13: 4 up, so that he could not **p** it back.
Job 41: 1 "Can you **p** in the leviathan with a
Jer 13:26 I will **p** up your skirts over your
22:24 right hand, I would still **p** you off.
Eze 17: 9 many people to **p** it up by the roots.
26: 4 walls of Tyre and **p** down her towers;
29: 4 I will **p** you out from among your

Hos 7:12 **p** them down like birds of the air.
Am 3:11 he will **p** down your strongholds and
Mt 9:16 for the patch will **p** away from the
13:28 you want us to go and **p** them up?'
Mk 2:21 the new piece will **p** away from
Lk 14: 5 will you not immediately **p** him out?"

Pulled (Pull)
Ge 19:10 reached out and **p** Lot back into
37:28 his brothers **p** Joseph up out of the
Jdg 8:17 He also **p** down the tower of Peniel
16:14 sleep and **p** up the pin and the loom,
1Ki 19:13 Elijah heard it, he **p** his cloak over
2Ki 23:12 He **p** down the altars the kings of
Ezr 6:11 a beam is to be **p** from his house and
9: 3 **p** hair from my head and beard
Ne 13:25 of the men and **p** out their hair.
Job 4:21 Are not the cords of their tent **p** up,
Isa 33:20 its stakes will never be **p** up,
38:12 has been **p** down and taken from me.
50: 6 my cheeks to those who **p** out my
Jer 38:13 they **p** him up with the ropes and
Eze 19: 9 With hooks they **p** him into a cage
Mt 13:40 "As the weeds are **p** up and burned in
13:48 was full, the fishermen **p** it up on
15:13 planted will be **p** up by the roots.
Lk 5:11 they **p** their boats up on shore, left
Ac 11:10 then it was **p** up to heaven again.

Pulling (Pull)
Mt 13:29 'because while you are **p** the weeds,
2Co 10: 8 you up rather than **p** you down,

Pulls (Pull)
Job 20:25 He **p** it out of his back, the
Pr 21:22 **p** down the stronghold in which they
Hab 1:15 The wicked foe **p** all of them up with

Punish (Punished, Punishes, Punishing, Punishment, Punishments)
Ge 15:14 I will **p** the nation they serve as
Ex 32:34 comes for me to **p**, I will **p** them
Lev 26:18 **p** you for your sins seven times over.
26:28 **p** you for your sins seven times over.
Dt 22:18 shall take the man and **p** him.
1Sa 15: 2 'I will **p** the Amalekites for what
2Sa 7:14 When he does wrong, I will **p** him
Job 37:13 He brings the clouds to **p** men, or to
Ps 59: 5 rouse yourself to **p** all the nations;
89:32 I will **p** their sin with the rod,
94:10 Does he who disciplines nations not **p**
119:84 When will you **p** my persecutors?
120: 4 He will **p** you with a warrior's sharp
Pr 17:26 is not good to **p** an innocent man, or
23:13 **p** him with the rod, he will not die.
23:14 **P** him with the rod and save his soul
Isa 10:12 "I will **p** the king of Assyria for
13:11 I will **p** the world for its evil, the
24:21 In that day the LORD will **p** the
26:21 to **p** the people of the earth for
27: 1 the LORD will **p** with his sword,
64:12 keep silent and **p** us beyond measure?
Jer 2:19 Your wickedness will **p** you;
5: 9 Should I not **p** them for this?"
5:29 Should I not **p** them for this?"
6:15 down when I **p** them," says the LORD.
9: 9 Should I not **p** them for this?"
9:25 "when I will **p** all who are
11:22 LORD Almighty says: 'I will **p** them.
14:10 and **p** them for their sins."
21:14 I will **p** you as your deeds deserve,
23:34 I will **p** that man and his household.
25:12 I will **p** the king of Babylon and his
27: 8 I will **p** that nation with the sword,
29:32 I will surely **p** Shemaiah the
30:20 I will **p** all who oppress them.
36:31 I will **p** him and his children and
44:13 I will **p** those who live in Egypt
44:29 you that I will **p** you in this place,'
49: 8 on Esau at the time I **p** him.
50:18 "I will **p** the king of Babylon and
51:44 I will **p** Bel in Babylon and make him
51:47 when I will **p** the idols of Babylon;
51:52 "when I will **p** her idols, and
Lam 4:22 he will **p** your sin and expose your
Eze 7:11 Violence has grown into a rod to **p**
23:24 **p** you according to their standards.
25:17 on them and **p** them in my wrath.
Hos 1: 4 because I will soon **p** the house of
2:13 I will **p** her for the days she burned
4: 9 I will **p** both of them for their ways
4:14 "I will not **p** your daughters when
8:13 their wickedness and **p** their sins:
9: 9 and **p** them for their sins.
10:10 I please, I will **p** them; nations
12: 2 he will **p** Jacob according to his
Am 3: 2 I will **p** you for all your sins."
3:14 "On the day I **p** Israel for her sins,
Hab 1:12 O Rock, you have ordained them to **p**.
Zep 1: 8 sacrifice I will **p** the princes
1: 9 On that day I will **p** all who avoid
1:12 and **p** those who are complacent,
Zec 10: 3 and I will **p** the leaders; for the
Lk 23:16 Therefore, I will **p** him and then
Ac 4:21 They could not decide how to **p** them,
7: 7 I will **p** the nation they serve as
2Co 10: 6 we will be ready to **p** every act of
1Th 4: 6 The Lord will **p** men for all such
2Th 1: 8 He will **p** those who do not know God
1Pe 2:14 who are sent by him to **p** those who

Punished (Punish)
Ge 19:15 be swept away when the city is **p**."
42:21 are being **p** because of our brother.
Ex 21:20 as a direct result, he must be **p**,
21:21 he is not to be **p** if the slave gets
Lev 18:25 Even the land was defiled; so I **p** it
1Sa 28:10 lives, you will not be **p** for this."
1Ch 21: 7 in the sight of God; so he **p** Israel.
Ezr 7:26 the king must surely be **p** by death,
9:13 and yet, our God, you have **p** us less
Ps 73:14 I have been **p** every morning.
99: 8 God, though you **p** their misdeeds.
Pr 21:11 a mocker is **p**, the simple gain
Isa 24:22 in prison and be **p** after many days.
26:14 You **p** them and brought them to ruin;
57:17 I **p** him, and hid my face in anger,
Jer 2:30 "In vain I **p** your people; they did
6: 6 This city must be **p**; it is filled
8:12 down when they are **p**, says the LORD.
23:12 year they are **p**," declares the LORD.
30:14 would and **p** you as would the cruel,
44:13 famine and plague, as I **p** Jerusalem.
46:21 them, the time for them to be **p**.
50:18 his land as I **p** the king of Assyria.
50:27 has come, the time for them to be **p**.
50:31 has come, the time for you to be **p**.
Lam 3:39 man complain when **p** for his sins?
Mk 12:40 Such men will be **p** most severely."
Lk 20:47 Such men will be **p** most severely."
23:22 have him **p** and then release him."
23:41 We are **p** justly, for we are getting
Ac 22: 5 as prisoners to Jerusalem to be **p**.
26:11 synagogue to another to have them **p**,
2Th 1: 9 They will be **p** with everlasting
Heb 10:29 a man deserves to be **p** who has

Punishes (Punish)
Ex 34: 7 he **p** the children and their children
Nu 14:18 he **p** the children for the sin of the
Job 34:26 He **p** them for their wickedness where
35:15 further, that his anger never **p** and
Heb 12: 6 he **p** everyone he accepts as a son."

Punishing (Punish)
Ex 20: 5 am a jealous God, **p** the children for
Dt 5: 9 am a jealous God, **p** the children for
Jdg 8:16 **p** them with desert thorns and briers.
Isa 30:32 LORD lays on them with his **p** rod

Punishment (Punish)
Ge 4:13 Cain said to the LORD, "My **p** is more
Lev 19:20 her freedom, there must be due **p**.
1Sa 14:47 he turned, he inflicted **p** on them.
2Ki 7: 9 until daylight, **p** will overtake us.
Job 19:29 for wrath will bring **p** by the sword,
21:19 is said, 'God stores up a man's **p**
Ps 81:15 and their **p** would last for ever.
91: 8 eyes and see the **p** of the wicked.
149: 7 on the nations and **p** on the peoples,
Pr 10:16 income of the wicked brings them **p**.
16:22 it, but folly brings **p** to fools.
Isa 53: 5 **p** that brought us peace was upon him,
Jer 4:18 This is your **p**. How bitter it is!
11:15 Can consecrated meat avert your **p**?
11:23 of Anathoth in the year of their **p**.
23: 2 **p** on you for the evil you have done,"
32:18 bring the **p** for the fathers' sins
46:25 "I am about to bring **p** on Amon god
48:44 bring upon Moab the year of her **p**,"
Lam 4: 6 The **p** of my people is greater than
4:22 O Daughter of Zion, your **p** will end;
5: 7 are no more, and we bear their **p**.
Eze 5: 8 **p** on you in the sight of the nations.
5:10 I will inflict **p** on you and will
5:15 when I inflict **p** on you in anger
11: 9 to foreigners and inflict **p** on you.
16:38 I will sentence you to the **p** of
16:41 **p** on you in the sight of many women.
21:25 time of **p** has reached its climax,
21:29 time of **p** has reached its climax.
23:10 women, and **p** was inflicted on her.
23:24 I will turn you over to them for **p**,
23:45 the **p** of women who commit adultery
25:11 I will inflict **p** on Moab. Then they
28:22 when I inflict **p** on her and show
28:26 when I inflict **p** on all their
30:14 to Zoan and inflict **p** on Thebes.
30:19 I will inflict **p** on Egypt, and they
32:27 The **p** for their sins rested on their
35: 5 the time their **p** reached its climax,
39:21 and all the nations will see the **p** I
Hos 9: 7 The days of **p** are coming, the days
Zep 3:15 The LORD has taken away your **p**, he
Zec 14:19 the **p** of Egypt and the **p** of all the
Mt 25:46 "Then they will go away to eternal **p**,
Lk 12:48 **p** will be beaten with few blows.
21:22 For this is the time of **p** in
Ro 13: 4 wrath to bring **p** on the wrongdoer.
13: 5 because of possible **p** but also
2Co 2: 6 The **p** inflicted on him by the
Heb 2: 2 disobedience received its just **p**,
2Pe 2: 9 judgment, while continuing their **p**.
1Jn 4:18 fear, because fear has to do with **p**.
Jude : 7 who suffer the **p** of eternal fire.
Rev 17: 1 "Come, I will show you the **p** of the

Punishments (Punish)
Zep 3: 7 cut off, nor all my **p** come upon her.

Punon
Nu 33:42 They left Zalmonah and camped at **P**.
33:43 They left **P** and camped at Oboth.

Pur
Est 3: 7 they cast the **p** (that is, the lot)
9:24 them and had cast the **p** (that is,
9:26 called Purim, from the word **p**.)

Purah
Jdg 7:10 down to the camp with your servant **P**
7:11 So he and **P** his servant went down

Purchase (Purchased)
2Ki 22: 6 Also make them **p** timber and dressed
2Ch 34:11 and builders to **p** dressed stone,
Pr 20:14 off he goes and boasts about his **p**.
Jer 32:11 I took the deed of **p**—the sealed
32:14 unsealed copies of the deed of **p**,
32:16 "After I had given the deed of **p** to

Purchased (Purchase)
1Ki 10:28 royal merchants **p** them from Kue.
2Ki 12:12 They **p** timber and dressed stone for
2Ch 1:16 royal merchants **p** them from Kue.
Ps 74: 2 Remember the people you **p** of old,
Rev 5: 9 and with your blood you **p** men for
14: 4 They were **p** from among men and

Pure (Purest, Purification, Purified, Purifier, Purifies, Purify, Purifying, Purity)

Ex 25:11 Overlay it with **p** gold, both inside
25:17 "Make an atonement cover of **p** gold
25:24 Overlay it with **p** gold and make a
25:29 make its plates and dishes of **p** gold,
25:31 "Make a lampstand of **p** gold and
25:36 lampstand, hammered out of **p** gold.
25:38 and trays are to be of **p** gold.
25:39 A talent of **p** gold is to be used for
28:14 two braided chains of **p** gold, like a
28:22 chains of **p** gold, like a rope.
28:36 "Make a plate of **p** gold and engrave
30: 3 the sides and the horns with **p** gold,
30:34 **p** frankincense, all in equal amounts,
30:35 It is to be salted and **p** and sacred.
31: 8 the **p** gold lampstand and all its
37: 2 He overlaid it with **p** gold, both
37: 6 made the atonement cover of **p** gold
37:11 they overlaid it with **p** gold and
37:16 they made from **p** gold the articles
37:17 They made the lampstand of **p** gold
37:22 lampstand, hammered out of **p** gold.
37:23 wick trimmers and trays, of **p** gold.
37:24 from one talent of **p** gold.
37:26 the sides and the horns with **p** gold,
37:29 oil and the **p**, fragrant incense
39:15 chains of **p** gold, like a rope.
39:25 they made bells of **p** gold and
39:30 the sacred diadem, out of **p** gold and
39:37 the **p** gold lampstand with its row of
Lev 24: 4 The lamps on the **p** gold lampstand
24: 6 the table of **p** gold before the LORD.
24: 7 Along each row put some **p** incense as
2Sa 22:27 to the **p** you show yourself **p**, but to
1Ki 6:20 He overlaid the inside with **p** gold,
6:21 inside of the temple with **p** gold,
7:49 the lampstands of **p** gold (five on
7:50 the **p** gold dishes, wick trimmers,
10:21 the Forest of Lebanon were **p** gold.
2Ki 25:15 that were made of **p** gold or silver.
1Ch 28:17 the weight of **p** gold for the forks,
2Ch 3: 4 He overlaid the inside with **p** gold.
4:20 the lampstands of **p** gold with their
4:22 the **p** gold wick trimmers, sprinkling
9:17 with ivory and overlaid with **p** gold.
9:20 the Forest of Lebanon were **p** gold.
Job 4:17 Can a man be more **p** than his Maker?
8: 6 if you are **p** and upright, even now
11: 4 flawless and I am **p** in your sight.'
14: 4 Who can bring what is **p** from the
15:14 "What is man, that he could be **p**, or
15:15 the heavens are not **p** in his eyes,
16:17 free of violence and my prayer is **p**.
25: 4 How can one born of woman be **p**?
25: 5 and the stars are not **p** in his eyes,
28:19 it cannot be bought with **p** gold.
31:24 to **p** gold, 'You are my security,'
33: 9 'I am **p** and without sin; I am clean
Ps 18:26 to the **p** you show yourself **p**, but to
19: 9 The fear of the LORD is **p**, enduring
19:10 than gold, than much **p** gold;
21: 3 a crown of **p** gold on his head.
24: 4 He who has clean hands and a **p** heart,
51:10 Create in me a **p** heart, O God, and
73: 1 Israel, to those who are **p** in heart.
73:13 Surely in vain have I kept my heart **p**
119: 9 How can a young man keep his way **p**?
119:127 more than gold, more than **p** gold,
Pr 15:26 those of the **p** are pleasing to him.
20: 9 Who can say, "I have kept my heart **p**;
20:11 whether his conduct is **p** and right.
22:11 He who loves a **p** heart and whose
30:12 those who are **p** in their own eyes
SS 5:15 of marble set on bases of **p** gold.
Isa 13:12 I will make man scarcer than **p** gold,
52:11 Come out from it and be **p**, you who
Jer 52:19 that were made of **p** gold or silver.
Da 2:32 of the statue was made of **p** gold,
Hab 1:13 Your eyes are too **p** to look on evil;
Mal 1:11 every place incense and **p** offerings
Mt 5: 8 Blessed are the **p** in heart, for they
Mk 14: 3 expensive perfume, made of **p** nard.
Jn 12: 3 Mary took about a pint of **p** nard, an
2Co 11: 2 present you as a **p** virgin to him.
11: 3 sincere and **p** devotion to Christ.
Php 1:10 may be **p** and blameless until the day
2:15 that you may become blameless and **p**,
4: 8 whatever is right, whatever is **p**,
1Ti 1: 5 which comes from a **p** heart and a
5:22 sins of others. Keep yourself **p**.
2Ti 2:22 call on the Lord out of a **p** heart.
Tit 1:15 To the **p**, all things are **p**, but to
1:15 and do not believe, nothing is **p**.
2: 5 to be self-controlled and **p**, to be
Heb 7:26 blameless, **p**, set apart from sinners,
10:22 our bodies washed with **p** water.
13: 4 and the marriage bed kept **p**, for God
Jas 1: 2 Consider it **p** joy, my brothers,
1:27 accepts as **p** and faultless is this:
3:17 from heaven is first of all **p**;
1Pe 2: 2 crave **p** spiritual milk, so that by
1Jn 3: 3 purifies himself, just as he is **p**.
Rev 14: 4 women, for they kept themselves **p**.
21:18 the city of **p** gold, as **p** as glass.
21:21 of **p** gold, like transparent glass.

Purest (Pure)

SS 5:11 His head is **p** gold; his hair is wavy

Purge (Purged)

Dt 13: 5 You must **p** the evil from among you.
17: 7 You must **p** the evil from among you.
17:12 You must **p** the evil from Israel.
19:13 You must **p** from Israel the guilt of
19:19 You must **p** the evil from among you.
21: 9 you will **p** from yourselves the guilt
21:21 You must **p** the evil from among you.
22:21 You must **p** the evil from among you.
22:22 You must **p** the evil from Israel.
22:24 You must **p** the evil from among you.
24: 7 You must **p** the evil from among you.
Jdg 20:13 to death and **p** the evil from Israel.
2Ch 34: 3 he began to **p** Judah and Jerusalem
Pr 20:30 and beatings **p** the inmost being.
Isa 1:25 I will thoroughly **p** away your dross
Eze 20:38 I will **p** you of those who revolt and

Purged (Purge)

2Ch 34: 5 and so he **p** Judah and Jerusalem.
Jer 6:29 in vain; the wicked are not **p** out.

Purification (Pure)

Lev 12: 4 until the days of her **p** are over.
12: 6 "'When the days of her **p** for a son
Nu 19: 9 of cleansing; it is for **p** from sin.
19:17 ashes from the burned **p** offering
1Ch 23:28 the **p** of all sacred things and the
Ne 12:45 of their God and the service of **p**,
Lk 2:22 the time of their **p** according to the
Ac 21:24 Take these men, join in their **p**
21:26 date when the days of **p** would end
Heb 1: 3 After he had provided **p** for sins, he

Purified (Pure)

Lev 12: 4 days to be **p** from her bleeding.
12: 5 days to be **p** from her bleeding.
Nu 8:15 "After you have **p** the Levites and
8:21 The Levites **p** themselves and washed
31:23 But it must also be **p** with the water
2Sa 11: 4 (She had **p** herself from her
2Ch 29:18 "We have **p** the entire temple of the
30:18 and Zebulun had not **p** themselves,
Ezr 6:20 and Levites had **p** themselves
Ne 12:30 and Levites had **p** themselves
12:30 **p** the people, the gates and the wall.
13:30 I **p** the priests and the Levites of
Job 1: 5 Job would send and have them **p**.
Ps 12: 6 in a furnace of clay, **p** seven times.
Eze 43:22 to be **p** as it was **p** with the bull.
Da 11:35 so that they may be refined, **p** and
12:10 Many will be **p**, made spotless and
Ac 15: 9 for he **p** their hearts by faith.
21:26 Paul took the men and **p** himself
Heb 9:23 to be **p** with these sacrifices,
1Pe 1:22 Now that you have **p** yourselves by

Purifier (Pure)

Mal 3: 3 He will sit as a refiner and **p** of

Purifies (Pure)

1Jn 1: 7 Jesus, his Son, **p** us from all sin.
3: 3 who has this hope in him **p** himself,

Purify (Pure)

Ge 35: 2 **p** yourselves and change your clothes.
Ex 29:36 **P** the altar by making atonement for
Lev 8:15 horns of the altar to **p** the altar.
14:49 To **p** the house he is to take two
14:52 He shall **p** the house with the bird's
Nu 8: 7 To **p** them, do this: Sprinkle the
8: 7 their clothes, and so **p** themselves.
8:21 made atonement for them to **p** them.
19:12 He must **p** himself with the water on
19:12 But if he does not **p** himself on the
19:13 fails to **p** himself defiles the
19:19 on the seventh day he is to **p** him.
19:20 who is unclean does not **p** himself.
31:19 must **p** yourselves and your captives.
31:20 **P** every garment as well as
2Ch 29:15 they went in to **p** the temple of the
29:16 the sanctuary of the LORD to **p** it.
34: 8 to **p** the land and the temple, he
Ne 13: 9 I gave orders to **p** the rooms, and
13:22 the Levites to **p** themselves and go
Isa 66:17 who consecrate and **p** themselves
Eze 43:20 and so **p** the altar and make
45:18 without defect and **p** the sanctuary.
Zep 3: 9 "Then will I **p** the lips of the
Mal 3: 3 he will **p** the Levites and refine
2Co 7: 1 dear friends, let us **p** ourselves
Tit 2:14 to **p** for himself a people that are
Jas 4: 8 **p** your hearts, you double-minded.
1Jn 1: 9 and **p** us from all unrighteousness.

Purifying (Pure)

Eze 43:23 you have finished **p** it, you are to

Purim

Est 9:26 (Therefore these days were called **P**,
9:28 And these days of **P** should never
9:29 this second letter concerning **P**.
9:31 to establish these days of **P** at
9:32 confirmed these regulations about **P**,

Purity (Pure)

Hos 8: 5 How long will they be incapable of **p**?
2Co 6: 6 in **p**, understanding, patience and
1Ti 4:12 in life, in love, in faith and in **p**.
5: 2 women as sisters, with absolute **p**.
1Pe 3: 2 they see the **p** and reverence of your

Purple

Ex 25: 4 blue, **p** and scarlet yarn and fine
26: 1 and blue, **p** and scarlet yarn, with
26:31 "Make a curtain of blue, **p** and
26:36 **p** and scarlet yarn and finely
27:16 of blue, **p** and scarlet yarn and
28: 5 Make them use gold, and blue, **p** and
28: 6 and of blue, **p** and scarlet yarn, and
28: 8 and with blue, **p** and scarlet yarn,
28:15 and of blue, **p** and scarlet yarn, and
28:33 Make pomegranates of blue, **p** and
35: 6 blue, **p** and scarlet yarn and fine
35:23 Everyone who had blue, **p** or scarlet
35:25 **p** or scarlet yarn or fine linen.
35:35 embroiderers in blue, **p** and scarlet
36: 8 and blue, **p** and scarlet yarn, with
36:35 They made the curtain of blue, **p** and
36:37 of blue, **p** and scarlet yarn and
38:18 of blue, **p** and scarlet yarn and
38:23 in blue, **p** and scarlet yarn and
39: 1 From the blue, **p** and scarlet yarn
39: 2 and of blue, **p** and scarlet yarn, and
39: 3 into the blue, **p** and scarlet yarn
39: 5 and with blue, **p** and scarlet yarn,
39: 8 and of blue, **p** and scarlet yarn, and
39:24 made pomegranates of blue, **p** and
39:29 **p** and scarlet yarn—the work of an
Nu 4:13 altar and spread a **p** cloth over it.
Jdg 8:26 the pendants and the **p** garments worn

2Ch 2: 7 bronze and iron, and in **p**, crimson
2:14 stone and wood, and with **p** and blue
3:14 He made the curtain of blue, **p** and
Est 1: 6 **p** material to silver rings on marble
8:15 of gold and a **p** robe of fine linen.
Pr 31:22 she is clothed in fine linen and **p**.
SS 3:10 Its seat was upholstered with **p**, its
Jer 10: 9 is then dressed in blue and **p**—
Lam 4: 5 nurtured in **p** now lie on ash heaps.
Eze 27: 7 and **p** from the coasts of Elishah.
27:16 **p** fabric, embroidered work, fine
Da 5: 7 what it means will be clothed in **p**
5:16 you will be clothed in **p** and have a
5:29 Daniel was clothed in **p**, a gold
Mk 15:17 They put a **p** robe on him, then
15:20 they took off the **p** robe and put his
Lk 16:19 was a rich man who was dressed in **p**
Jn 19: 2 They clothed him in a **p** robe
19: 5 the crown of thorns and the **p** robe,
Ac 16:14 a dealer in **p** cloth from the city of
Rev 17: 4 The woman was dressed in **p** and
18:12 linen, **p**, silk and scarlet cloth;
18:16 dressed in fine linen, **p** and scarlet,

Purpose (Purposed, Purposes)

Ex 9:16 I have raised you up for this very **p**,
Lev 7:24 may be used for any other **p**, but
1Ch 23: 5 I have provided for that **p**."
Job 36: 5 he is mighty, and firm in his **p**.
Ps 57: 2 to God, who fulfils ⌊his **p**⌋ for me.
138: 8 The LORD will fulfil his **p** for me;
Pr 19:21 it is the LORD's **p** that prevails.
Isa 10: 7 his **p** is to destroy, to put an end
46:10 I say: My **p** will stand, and I will
46:11 far-off land, a man to fulfil my **p**.
48:14 carry out his **p** against Babylon;
49: 4 I said, "I have laboured to no **p**;
55:11 achieve the **p** for which I sent it.
Jer 15:11 I will deliver you for a good **p**;
51:11 because his **p** is to destroy Babylon.
51:12 The LORD will carry out his **p**,
Lk 7:30 law rejected God's **p** for themselves,
Ac 2:23 by God's set **p** and foreknowledge;
5:38 **p** or activity is of human origin,
13:36 "For when David had served God's **p**
Ro 8:28 have been called according to his **p**.
9:11 God's **p** in election might stand:
9:17 "I raised you up for this very **p**,
1Co 3: 8 and the man who waters have one **p**,
2Co 5: 5 God who has made us for this very **p**
Gal 3:19 What, then, was the **p** of the law?
4:18 be zealous, provided the **p** is good,
Eph 1:11 conformity with the **p** of his will,
2:15 His **p** was to create in himself one
3:11 according to his eternal **p** which he
6:22 sending him to you for this very **p**,
Php 2: 2 love, being one in spirit and **p**.
2:13 and to act according to his good **p**.
Col 2: 2 My **p** is that they may be encouraged
4: 8 for the express **p** that you may know
2Th 1:11 he may fulfil every good **p** of yours
1Ti 2: 7 for this **p** I was appointed a herald
2Ti 1: 9 but because of his own **p** and grace.
3:10 **p**, faith, patience, love, endurance,
Heb 6:17 nature of his **p** very clear to the
Rev 17:13 They have one **p** and will give their
17:17 to accomplish his **p** by agreeing to

Purposed (Purpose)

Isa 14:24 and as I have **p**, so it will stand.
14:27 For the LORD Almighty has **p**, and who
Jer 49:20 what he has **p** against those who live
50:45 what he has **p** against the land of
Eph 1: 9 good pleasure, which he **p** in Christ,

Purposes (Purpose)

Ps 33:10 he thwarts the **p** of the peoples.
33:11 the **p** of his heart through all
Pr 20: 5 The **p** of a man's heart are deep
Jer 23:20 accomplishes the **p** of his heart.
30:24 accomplishes the **p** of his heart.
32:19 great are your **p** and mighty are your
51:29 for the LORD's **p** against Babylon
Ro 9:21 for noble **p** and some for common use?
2Ti 2:20 for noble **p** and some for ignoble.
2:21 will be an instrument for noble **p**,

Purse (Purses)

Pr 1:14 us, and we will share a common **p**"—
7:20 He took his **p** filled with money and
Hag 1: 6 put them in a **p** with holes in it."
Lk 10: 4 Do not take a **p** or bag or sandals;
22:35 "When I sent you without **p**, bag or
22:36 "But now if you have a **p**, take it,

Purses (Purse)

Pr 16:30 he who **p** his lips is bent on evil.
Isa 3:22 and the capes and cloaks, the **p**
Lk 12:33 Provide **p** for yourselves that will

Pursue (Pursued, Pursuer, Pursuers, Pursues, Pursuing, Pursuit)

Ex 14: 4 Pharaoh's heart, and he will **p** them.
15: 9 "The enemy boasted, 'I will **p**, I
Lev 26: 7 You will **p** your enemies, and they
26:33 will draw out my sword and **p** you.
Dt 19: 6 the avenger of blood might **p** him in
28:45 They will **p** you and overtake you
Jos 8: 6 They will **p** us until we have lured
8:16 men of Ai were called to **p** them,
10:19 **P** your enemies, attack them from
1Sa 30: 8 "Shall I **p** this raiding party?
30: 8 "**P** them," he answered. "You will
2Sa 20: 6 Take your master's men and **p** him, or
20: 7 Jerusalem to **p** Sheba son of Bicri.
20:13 with Joab to **p** Sheba son of Bicri.
24:13 from your enemies while they **p** you?
Job 19:22 Why do you **p** me as God does?
Ps 7: 1 and deliver me from all who **p** me,
7: 5 let my enemy **p** and overtake me;
31:15 my enemies and from those who **p** me.
34:14 and do good; seek peace and **p** it.
35: 3 and javelin against those who **p** me.
38:20 slander me when I **p** what is good.
56: 1 O God, for men hotly **p** me; all day
56: 2 My slanderers **p** me all day long;
57: 3 rebuking those who hotly **p** me;
71:11 **p** him and seize him, for no-one
83:15 **p** them with your tempest and terrify
142: 6 rescue me from those who **p** me,
Pr 15: 9 he loves those who **p** righteousness.
Isa 51: 1 you who **p** righteousness and who
Jer 2:24 that **p** her need not tire themselves;
9:16 and I will **p** them with the sword
29:18 I will **p** them with the sword, famine
48: 2 be silenced; the sword will **p** you.
49:37 "I will **p** them with the sword until
50:21 **P**, kill and completely destroy them,"
Lam 1: 3 All who **p** her have overtaken her in
3:66 **P** them in anger and destroy them
5: 5 Those who **p** us are at our heels;
Eze 5: 2 For I will **p** them with drawn sword.
5:12 to the winds and **p** with drawn sword.
12:14 I will **p** them with drawn sword.
35: 6 over to bloodshed and it will **p** you.
35: 6 bloodshed, bloodshed will **p** you.
Hos 8: 3 what is good; an enemy will **p** him.
Na 1: 8 he will **p** his foes into darkness.
Mt 23:34 synagogues and **p** from town to town.
Ro 9:30 who did not **p** righteousness, have
1Ti 6:11 and **p** righteousness, godliness,
2Ti 2:22 and **p** righteousness, faith, love
1Pe 3:11 he must seek peace and **p** it.

Pursued (Pursue)

Ge 31:23 he **p** Jacob for seven days and
35: 5 around them so that no-one **p** them.
Ex 14: 8 so that he **p** the Israelites, who
14: 9 and troops—**p** the Israelites
14:23 The Egyptians **p** them, and all
Jos 8:16 and they **p** Joshua and were lured
10:10 Israel **p** them along the road going
11: 8 They defeated them and **p** them all
24: 6 and the Egyptians **p** them with
Jdg 4:16 Barak **p** the chariots and army as far
7:23 out, and they **p** the Midianites.
7:25 They **p** the Midianites and brought
8:12 fled, but he **p** them and captured
1Sa 7:11 out of Mizpah and **p** the Philistines,
17:52 **p** the Philistines to the entrance of
2Sa 2:19 right nor to the left as he **p** him.
2:24 Joab and Abishai **p** Abner, and as the
2:28 to a halt; they no longer **p** Israel,
20:10 Abishai **p** Sheba son of Bicri.
22:38 "I **p** my enemies and crushed them;
2Ki 25: 5 the Babylonian army **p** the king and
2Ch 13:19 Abijah **p** Jeroboam and took from him
14:13 Asa and his army **p** them as far as
Ps 18:37 I **p** my enemies and overtook them;
Jer 39: 5 the Babylonian army **p** them and
52: 8 the Babylonian army **p** King Zedekiah
Lam 3:43 yourself with anger and **p** us;
Am 1:11 Because he **p** his brother with a
Ro 9:31 Israel, who **p** a law of righteousness,
9:32 Why not? Because they **p** it not by
Rev 12:13 he **p** the woman who had given birth

Pursuer (Pursue)

Lam 1: 6 they have fled before the **p**.

Pursuers (Pursue)

Jos 2: 7 and as soon as the **p** had gone out,
2:16 so that the **p** will not find you.
2:22 until the **p** had searched all along
8:20 had turned back against their **p**.
Ne 9:11 but you hurled their **p** into the
Isa 30:16 Therefore your **p** will be swift!
Lam 4:19 Our **p** were swifter than eagles in

Pursues (Pursue)

Jos 20: 5 If the avenger of blood **p** him, they
Ps 143: 3 The enemy **p** me, he crushes me to the
Pr 11:19 but he who **p** evil goes to his death.
13:21 Misfortune **p** the sinner, but
18: 1 An unfriendly man **p** selfish ends;
19: 7 Though he **p** them with pleading,
21:21 He who **p** righteousness and love
28: 1 The wicked man flees though no-one **p**,
Isa 41: 3 He **p** them and moves on unscathed, by
Jer 8: 6 Each **p** his own course like a horse
Hos 12: 1 he **p** the east wind all day

Pursuing (Pursue)

Ge 14:15 **p** them as far as Hobah, north of
Lev 26:17 will flee even when no-one is **p** you.
26:36 fall, even though no-one is **p** them.
26:37 sword, even though no-one is **p** them.
Dt 11: 4 of the Red Sea as they were **p** you,
Jdg 8: 5 and I am still **p** Zebah and Zalmunna,
1Sa 14:46 Saul stopped **p** the Philistines, and
24: 1 returned from **p** the Philistines,
24:14 Whom are you **p**? A dead dog? A flea?
25:29 Even though someone is **p** you to take
26:18 "Why is my lord **p** his servant?
2Sa 2:26 your men to stop **p** their brothers?"
2:30 Joab returned from **p** Abner and
18:16 the troops stopped **p** Israel, for
1Ki 22:33 king of Israel and stopped **p** him.
2Ch 18:32 king of Israel, they stopped **p** him.
Ps 35: 6 with the angel of the LORD **p** them.
Isa 65: 2 not good, **p** their own imaginations—
Jer 2:33 How skilled you are at **p** love!
Hos 5:11 in judgment, intent on **p** idols.
1Ti 3: 8 much wine, and not **p** dishonest gain.
Tit 1: 7 not violent, not **p** dishonest gain.

Pursuit (Pursue)

Ge 14:14 and went in **p** as far as Dan.
Jos 2: 7 the men set out in **p** of the spies on
8:17 city open and went in **p** of Israel.
Jdg 4:22 Barak came by in **p** of Sisera, and
8: 4 yet keeping up the **p**, came to the
1Sa 14:22 they joined the battle in hot **p**.
23:25 the Desert of Maon in **p** of David.
23:28 Saul broke off his **p** of David and
30:10 four hundred men continued the **p**.
2Sa 2:23 Asahel refused to give up the **p**;
2:27 continued the **p** of their brothers
17: 1 and set out tonight in **p** of David.
1Ki 20:20 fled, with the Israelites in **p**.

Push (Pushed, Pushes, Pushing)
Dt 15:17 take an awl and **p** it through his ear
Jos 23: 5 He will **p** them out before you, and
2Ki 4:27 Gehazi came over to **p** her away, but
Ps 44: 5 Through you we **p** back our enemies;
Jer 46:15 for the LORD will **p** them down.

Pushed (Push)
Jdg 16:30 Then he **p** with all his might,
Ps 118:13 I was **p** back and about to fall, but
Isa 16: 2 Like fluttering birds **p** from the
Zec 5: 8 "This is wickedness," and he **p** her
5: 8 **p** the lead cover down over its mouth.
Ac 7:27 the other **p** Moses aside and said,
19:33 The Jews **p** Alexander to the front,

Pushes (Push)
Nu 35:20 with malice aforethought **p** another
35:22 someone suddenly **p** another or
2Co 11:20 or **p** himself forward or slaps you

Pushing (Push)
Joel 2:20 **p** it into a parched and barren land,
Mk 3:10 were **p** forward to touch him.

Put to the sword
Dt 13:15; 20:13; Jos 8:24; 10:30, 32; 11:11, 14; 13:22; Jdg 21:10; 1Sa 22:19; 2Ki 11:15; 2Ch 23:14; Ps 78:64

Puteoli
Ac 28:13 on the following day we reached **P**.

Puthites
1Ch 2:53 **P**, Shumathites and Mishraites.

Putiel
Ex 6:25 married one of the daughters of **P**,

Puzzled
Mk 6:20 Herod heard John, he was greatly **p**;
Ac 5:24 the chief priests were **p**, wondering

Pyrrhus
Ac 20: 4 by Sopater son of **P** from Berea,

Quail
Ex 16:13 That evening **q** came and covered the
Nu 11:31 LORD and drove **q** in from the sea.
11:32 the people went out and gathered **q**.
Ps 105:40 They asked, and he brought them **q**

Quake (Earthquake, Earthquakes, Quaked, Quaking)
Job 26:11 The pillars of the heavens **q**, aghast
Ps 46: 3 the mountains **q** with their surging.
75: 3 the earth and all its people **q**, it
Isa 64: 2 cause the nations to **q** before you!
Eze 27:28 The shorelands will **q** when your
Na 1: 5 The mountains **q** before him and the
Rev 16:18 on earth, so tremendous was the **q**.

Quaked (Quake)
Jdg 5: 5 The mountains **q** before the LORD, the
2Sa 22: 8 "The earth trembled and **q**, the
Ps 18: 7 The earth trembled and **q**, and the
77:18 the world; the earth trembled and **q**.

Quaking (Quake)
1Sa 13: 7 troops with him were **q** with fear.
Ps 60: 2 mend its fractures, for it is **q**.
Jer 4:24 at the mountains, and they were **q**;

Qualified
Da 1: 4 and **q** to serve in the king's palace.
Col 1:12 the Father, who has **q** you to share
2Ti 2: 2 who will also be **q** to teach others.

Qualities (Quality)
Da 6: 3 the satraps by his exceptional **q**
Ro 1:20 God's invisible **q**—his eternal power
2Pe 1: 8 For if you possess these **q** in

Quality (Qualities)
Lev 27:12 who will judge its **q** as good or bad.
27:14 will judge its **q** as good or bad.
1Ki 5:17 large blocks of **q** stone to provide a
7:10 laid with large stones of good **q**,
1Co 3:13 will test the **q** of each man's work.

Qualm
Jude :12 with you without the slightest **q**

Quantities (Quantity)
Ge 41:49 Joseph stored up huge **q** of grain,
1Ki 10: 2 large **q** of gold, and precious stones
10:10 **q** of spices, and precious stones.
1Ch 22:14 of silver, **q** of bronze and iron too
29: 2 and marble—all of these in large **q**.
2Ch 9: 1 large **q** of gold, and precious stones
9: 9 **q** of spices, and precious stones.
25:13 and carried off great **q** of plunder.
Zec 14:14 **q** of gold and silver and clothing.

Quantity (Quantities)
Lev 19:35 when measuring length, weight or **q**.
Jos 22: 8 and iron, and a great **q** of clothing
2Sa 8: 8 King David took a great **q** of bronze.
12:30 a great **q** of plunder from the
1Ch 18: 8 David took a great **q** of bronze,
20: 2 a great **q** of plunder from the
23:29 and all measurements of **q** and size.

Quarrel (Quarrelled, Quarrelling, Quarrels, Quarrelsome)
Ge 45:24 said to them, "Don't **q** on the way!"
Ex 17: 2 Moses replied, "Why do you **q** with
21:18 "If men **q** and one hits the other
Jdg 11:25 **q** with Israel or fight with them?
2Ki 5: 7 he is trying to pick a **q** with me!"
2Ch 35:21 "What **q** is there between you and me,
Pr 15:18 but a patient man calms a **q**.
17:14 Starting a **q** is like breaching a dam
17:19 He who loves a **q** loves sin; he who
20: 3 but every fool is quick to **q**.
26:17 who meddles in a **q** not his own.
26:20 without gossip a **q** dies down.
Mt 12:19 He will not **q** or cry out; no-one
2Ti 2:24 the Lord's servant must not **q**;
Jas 4: 2 You **q** and fight. You do not have,

Quarrelled (Quarrel)
Ge 26:20 the herdsmen of Gerar **q** with Isaac's
26:21 they dug another well, but they **q**
26:22 another well, and no-one **q** over it.
Ex 17: 2 they **q** with Moses and said, "Give us
17: 7 Meribah because the Israelites **q** and
Nu 20: 3 They **q** with Moses and said, "If only
20:13 where the Israelites **q** with the LORD

Quarrelling (Quarrel)
Ge 13: 7 **q** arose between Abram's herdsmen and
13: 8 "Let's not have any **q** between you
Isa 58: 4 Your fasting ends in **q** and strife,
Ac 12:20 He had been **q** with the people of
1Co 3: 3 For since there is jealousy and **q**
2Co 12:20 I fear that there may be **q**, jealousy,
2Ti 2:14 Warn them before God against **q** about

Quarrels (Quarrel)
Pr 13:10 Pride only breeds **q**, but wisdom is
22:10 **q** and insults are ended.
Isa 45: 9 "Woe to him who **q** with his Maker, to
1Co 1:11 me that there are **q** among you.
1Ti 6: 4 **q** about words that result in envy,
2Ti 2:23 because you know they produce **q**.
Tit 3: 9 and arguments and **q** about the law,
Jas 4: 1 What causes fights and **q** among you?

Quarrelsome (Quarrel)
Pr 19:13 **q** wife is like a constant dripping.
21: 9 than share a house with a **q** wife.
21:19 than with a **q** and ill-tempered wife.
25:24 than share a house with a **q** wife.
26:21 so is a **q** man for kindling strife.
27:15 A **q** wife is like a constant dripping
1Ti 3: 3 gentle, not **q**, not a lover of money.

Quarries (Quarry)
Jos 7: 5 as far as the stone **q** and struck
Ecc 10: 9 Whoever **q** stones may be injured by

Quarry (Quarries)
1Ki 5:17 removed from the **q** large blocks of
6: 7 only blocks dressed at the **q** were
Isa 51: 1 to the **q** from which you were hewn;

Quart (Quarts)
Rev 6: 6 "A **q** of wheat for a day's wages,

Quarters
2Sa 19:11 Israel has reached the king at his **q**?
2Ki 23: 7 He also tore down the **q** of the male
Ne 3:30 made repairs opposite his living **q**.
Isa 11:12 Judah from the four **q** of the earth.
Jer 49:36 from the four **q** of the heavens;

Quarts (Quart)
Rev 6: 6 three **q** of barley for a day's wages

Quartus
Ro 16:23 brother **Q** send you their greetings.

Queen (Queen's, Queens)
1Ki 10: 1 the **q** of Sheba heard about the fame
10: 4 the **q** of Sheba saw all the wisdom of
10:10 the **q** of Sheba gave to King Solomon.
10:13 King Solomon gave the **q** of Sheba all
11:19 own wife, **Q** Tahpenes, in marriage.
15:13 Maacah from her position as **q** mother,
2Ki 10:13 of the king and of the **q** mother."
2Ch 9: 1 the **q** of Sheba heard of Solomon's
9: 3 the **q** of Sheba saw the wisdom of
9: 9 the **q** of Sheba gave to King Solomon.
9:12 King Solomon gave the **q** of Sheba all
15:16 Maacah from her position as **q** mother
Ne 2: 6 king, with the **q** sitting beside him
Est 1: 9 **Q** Vashti also gave a banquet for the
1:11 to bring before him **Q** Vashti,
1:12 command, **Q** Vashti refused to come.
1:15 must be done to **Q** Vashti?" he asked.
1:16 "**Q** Vashti has done wrong, not only
1:17 King Xerxes commanded **Q** Vashti to be
2: 4 who pleases the king be **q** instead
2:17 and made her **q** instead of Vashti.
2:22 about the plot and told **Q** Esther,
5: 2 he saw **Q** Esther standing in the
5: 3 king asked, "What is it, **Q** Esther
5:12 "I'm the only person **Q** Esther
7: 1 Haman went to dine with **Q** Esther,
7: 2 "**Q** Esther, what is your petition?
7: 3 **Q** Esther answered, "If I have found
7: 5 King Xerxes asked **Q** Esther, "Who is
7: 6 was terrified before the king and **q**.
7: 7 behind to beg **Q** Esther for his life.
7: 8 "Will he even molest the **q** while she
8: 1 same day King Xerxes gave **Q** Esther
8: 7 King Xerxes replied to **Q** Esther and
9:12 The king said to **Q** Esther, "The Jews
9:29 **Q** Esther, daughter of Abihail, along
9:31 as Mordecai the Jew and **Q** Esther had
Isa 47: 5 will you be called **q** of kingdoms.
47: 7 continue for ever—the eternal **q**!'
Jer 7:18 cakes of bread for the **Q** of Heaven.
13:18 Say to the king and to the **q** mother,
29: 2 King Jehoiachin and the **q** mother,
44:17 will burn incense to the **Q** of Heaven
44:18 burning incense to the **Q** of Heaven
44:19 we burned incense to the **Q** of Heaven
44:25 drink offerings to the **Q** of Heaven.
Lam 1: 1 She who was **q** among the provinces
Eze 16:13 very beautiful and rose to be a **q**.
Da 5:10 The **q**, hearing the voices of the
Mt 12:42 The **Q** of the South will rise at the
Lk 11:31 The **Q** of the South will rise at the
Ac 8:27 of Candace, **q** of the Ethiopians.
Rev 18: 7 In her heart she boasts, 'I sit as **q**

Queen's (Queen)
Est 1:17 For the **q** conduct will become known
1:18 who have heard about the **q** conduct

Queens (Queen)
SS 6: 8 Sixty **q** there may be, and eighty
6: 9 the **q** and concubines praised her.
Isa 49:23 and their **q** your nursing mothers.
Jer 44: 9 by the kings and **q** of Judah and the

Quench (Quenched)
Ps 104:11 the wild donkeys **q** their thirst.
SS 8: 7 Many waters cannot **q** love; rivers
Isa 1:31 with no-one to **q** the fire."
Jer 4: 4 done—burn with no-one to **q** it.
21:12 done—burn with no-one to **q** it.
Am 5: 6 and Bethel will have no-one to **q** it.

Quenched (Quench)
2Ki 22:17 this place and will not be **q**.'
2Ch 34:25 on this place and will not be **q**.'
Isa 34:10 will not be **q** night and day; its
66:24 nor will their fire be **q**, and they
Jer 7:20 and it will burn and not be **q**.
46:10 till it has **q** its thirst with blood.
Eze 20:47 The blazing flame will not be **q**,
20:48 have kindled it; it will not be **q**.
Mk 9:48 not die, and the fire is not **q**.'
Heb 11:34 **q** the fury of the flames, and

Question (Questioned, Questioning, Questions)
Jdg 11:12 to the Ammonite king with the **q**:
Est 5: 8 Then I will answer the king's **q**."
Job 38: 3 I will **q** you, and you shall answer
40: 7 I will **q** you, and you shall answer
42: 4 **q** you, and you shall answer me.'
Ps 35:11 **q** me on things I know nothing about.
Isa 45:11 do you **q** me about my children, or
Jer 38:27 did come to Jeremiah and **q** him,
Mt 21:24 replied, "I will also ask you one **q**.
22:23 resurrection, came to him with a **q**.
22:35 in the law, tested him with this **q**:
Mk 8:11 The Pharisees came and began to **q**
11:29 replied, "I will ask you one **q**.
12:18 resurrection, came to him with a **q**.
Lk 20: 3 replied, "I will also ask you a **q**.
20:27 came to Jesus with a **q**.
22:23 They began to **q** among themselves
Jn 8: 6 They were using this **q** as a trap,
18:21 Why **q** me? Ask those who heard me.
Ac 4: 7 before them and began to **q** them:
15: 2 apostles and elders about this **q**.
15: 6 and elders met to consider this **q**.
22:29 Those who were about to **q** him
1Ti 3:16 Beyond all **q**, the mystery of

Questioned (Question)
Ge 43: 7 They replied, "The man **q** us closely
Jdg 8:14 a young man of Succoth and **q** him,
Ezr 5: 9 We **q** the elders and asked them, "Who
Ne 1: 2 and I **q** them about the Jewish
Job 21:29 Have you never **q** those who travel?
Da 1:20 about which the king **q** them,
Lk 20:21 the spies **q** him: "Teacher, we know
Jn 1:25 **q** him, "Why then do you baptise if
18:19 Meanwhile, the high priest **q** Jesus
Ac 5:27 Sanhedrin to be **q** by the high priest.
22:24 He directed that he be flogged and **q**

Questioning (Question)
Jn 8: 7 they kept on **q** him, he straightened

Questions (Question)
Ge 43: 7 brother?' We simply answered his **q**.
1Ki 10: 1 she came to test him with hard **q**.
10: 3 Solomon answered all her **q**; nothing
2Ch 9: 1 Jerusalem to test him with hard **q**.
9: 2 Solomon answered all her **q**; nothing
Pr 18:17 another comes forward and **q** him.
Ecc 7:10 For it is not wise to ask such **q**.
Mt 22:46 no-one dared to ask him any more **q**.
Mk 12:34 on no-one dared ask him any more **q**.
Lk 2:46 listening to them and asking them **q**.
11:53 fiercely and to besiege him with **q**,
20:40 no-one dared to ask him any more **q**.
23: 9 He plied him with many **q**, but Jesus
Jn 16:30 even need to have anyone ask you **q**.
Ac 18:15 since it involves **q** about words and
23:29 had to do with **q** about their law,
1Co 10:25 without raising **q** of conscience,
10:27 you without raising **q** of conscience.

Quick (Quickly, Quick-tempered)
Ge 18: 6 "**Q**," he said, "get three seahs of
25:30 He said to Jacob, "**Q**, let me have
Ex 32: 8 They have been **q** to turn away from
Jdg 9:48 "**Q**! Do what you have seen me do!"
1Ki 20:33 sign and were **q** to pick up his word.
Pr 6:18 feet that are **q** to rush into evil,
20: 3 but every fool is **q** to quarrel.
Ecc 5: 2 Do not be **q** with your mouth, do not
Da 1: 4 well informed, **q** to understand, and
Jnh 4: 2 why I was so **q** to flee to Tarshish
Mal 3: 5 I will be **q** to testify against
Lk 15:22 '**Q**! Bring the best robe and put it
Ac 12: 7 "**Q**, get up!" he said, and the chains
22:18 saw the Lord speaking. '**Q**!' he said
Jas 1:19 Everyone should be **q** to listen,

Quickly (Quick)
Ge 19:22 flee there **q**, because I cannot do
24:18 and **q** lowered the jar to her hands
24:20 she **q** emptied her jar into the
24:46 "She **q** lowered her jar from her
27:20 "How did you find it so **q**, my son?"
41:14 for Joseph, and he was **q** brought
44:11 Each of them **q** lowered his sack to
45:13 And bring my father down here **q**."
Ex 10:16 Pharaoh **q** summoned Moses and Aaron
Dt 4:26 you will **q** perish from the land
7: 4 against you and will **q** destroy you.
9: 3 them out and annihilate them **q**,
9:12 They have turned away **q** from what I
9:16 You had turned aside **q** from the way
Jos 2: 5 Go after them **q**. You may catch up
8:19 the men in the ambush rose **q** from
8:19 captured it and **q** set it on fire.
10: 6 Come up to us **q** and save us! Help us
23:16 and you will **q** perish from the good
Jdg 2:17 Unlike their fathers, they **q** turned
1Sa 17:48 David ran **q** towards the battle line
20:38 shouted, "Hurry! Go **q**! Don't stop!
23:27 "Come **q**! The Philistines are raiding
25:23 Abigail saw David, she **q** got off her
25:34 if you had not come **q** to meet me,
25:42 Abigail **q** got on a donkey and,
2Sa 5:24 move **q**, because that will mean the
15:14 or he will move **q** to overtake us and
17:18 So the two of them left **q** and went
1Ki 20:41 the prophet **q** removed the headband
2Ki 4:22 go to the man of God **q** and return."
2Ch 29:36 people, because it was done so **q**.
35:13 and served them **q** to all the people.
Job 8:12 they wither more **q** than grass.
Ps 22:19 O my Strength, come **q** to help me.
31: 2 your ear to me, come **q** to my rescue
38:22 Come **q** to help me, O Lord my Saviour
40:13 Be pleased, O LORD, to save me;
69:17 answer me **q**, for I am in trouble.
70: 1 Hasten, O God, to save me; O LORD,
70: 5 poor and needy; come **q** to me, O God
71:12 come **q**, O my God, to help me.
79: 8 may your mercy come **q** to meet us,
81:14 how **q** would I subdue their enemies
90:10 for they **q** pass, and we fly away.
102: 2 ear to me; when I call, answer me **q**.
118:12 died out as **q** as burning thorns;
141: 1 O LORD, I call to you; come **q** to me.
143: 7 Answer me **q**, O LORD; my spirit fails
Pr 20:21 An inheritance **q** gained at the
Ecc 4:12 of three strands is not **q** broken.
7: 9 Do not be **q** provoked in your spirit
8:11 for a crime is not **q** carried out,
Isa 58: 8 and your healing will **q** appear; then
Jer 9:18 Let them come **q** and wail over us
48:16 at hand; her calamity will come **q**.
49:30 "Flee **q** away! Stay in deep caves,
Joel 3:11 Come **q**, all you nations from every
Zep 1:14 LORD is near— near and coming **q**.
Mt 5:25 "Settle matters **q** with your
13: 5 sprang up **q**, because the soil was
13:21 of the word, he **q** falls away.
21:20 "How did the fig-tree wither so **q**?"
28: 7 go **q** and tell his disciples: 'He has
Mk 1:28 News about him spread **q** over the
4: 5 sprang up **q**, because the soil was
4:17 of the word, they **q** fall away.
Lk 14:21 'Go out **q** into the streets and
16: 6 'Take you bill, sit down **q**, and
18: 8 see that they get justice, and **q**.
Jn 11:29 Mary heard this, she got up **q** and
11:31 noticed how **q** she got up and went
13:27 "What you are about to do, do **q**,"
Gal 1: 6 you are so **q** deserting the one who
2Ti 4: 9 Do your best to come to me **q**,

Quick-tempered (Quick, Temper)
Pr 14:17 A **q** man does foolish things, and a
14:29 but a **q** man displays folly.
Tit 1: 7 not **q**, not given to drunkenness,

Quiet (Quietened, Quietly, Quietness)
Ge 25:27 Jacob was a **q** man, staying among
34: 5 kept **q** about it until they came home
Jdg 3:19 The king said, "**Q**!" And all his
18:19 They answered him, "Be **q**! Don't say
2Sa 13:20 **q** now, my sister; he is your brother
2Ki 11:20 And the city was **q**, because Athaliah
1Ch 4:40 land was spacious, peaceful and **q**.
22: 9 Israel peace and **q** during his reign.
2Ch 23:21 And the city was **q**, because Athaliah
Ne 5: 8 to be sold back to us!" They kept **q**,
Est 7: 4 I would have kept **q**, because no such
Job 6:24 "Teach me, and I will be **q**; show me
Ps 23: 2 he leads me beside **q** waters,
76: 8 and the land feared and was **q**—
83: 1 O God, do not keep silent; be not **q**,
Pr 17: 1 Better a dry crust with peace and **q**
Ecc 9:17 The **q** words of the wise are more to
Isa 18: 4 "I will remain **q** and will look on
42:14 I have been **q** and held myself back.
62: 1 Jerusalem's sake I will not remain **q**
Am 5:13 Therefore the prudent man keeps **q** in
Zep 3:17 he will **q** you with his love, he will
Mt 20:31 rebuked them and told them to be **q**,
Mk 1:25 "Be **q**!" said Jesus sternly. "Come
4:39 "**Q**! Be still!" Then the wind died
6:31 to a **q** place and get some rest."
9:34 they kept **q** because on the way they
10:48 rebuked him and told him to be **q**
Lk 4:35 "Be **q**!" Jesus said sternly. "Come
18:39 rebuked him and told him to be **q**,
19:40 if they keep **q**, the stones will cry
Ac 12:17 with his hand for them to be **q**
19:36 to be **q** and not do anything rash.
22: 2 them in Aramaic, they became very **q**.
1Co 14:28 the speaker should keep **q** in the
1Th 4:11 it your ambition to lead a **q** life,
1Ti 2: 2 we may live peaceful and **q** lives
1Pe 3: 4 beauty of a gentle and **q** spirit,

Quietened (Quiet)
Ps 131: 2 I have stilled and **q** my soul; like a
Ac 19:35 The city clerk **q** the crowd and said:

Quietly (Quiet)
Jdg 4:21 **q** to him while he lay fast asleep,
Ru 3: 7 Ruth approached **q**, uncovered his
Ps 35:20 those who live **q** in the land.
Lam 3:26 is good to wait **q** for the salvation
Eze 24:17 Groan **q**; do not mourn for the dead.
Mt 1:19 he had in mind to divorce her **q**.
Ac 16:37 now do they want to get rid of us **q**?

Quietness (Quiet)
Job 3:26 I have no peace, no **q**; I have no
Isa 30:15 in **q** and trust is your strength,
32:17 will be **q** and confidence for ever.
1Ti 2:11 A woman should learn in **q** and full

Quirinius
Lk 2: 2 while **Q** was governor of Syria.)

Quiver (Quivers)
Ge 27: 3 get your weapons—your **q** and bow—
Job 39:23 The **q** rattles against his side,
Ps 127: 5 Blessed is the man whose **q** is full
Isa 22: 6 Elam takes up the **q**, with her
49: 2 arrow and concealed me in his **q**.
Lam 3:13 my heart with arrows from his **q**.

Quivered
Hab 3:16 my lips **q** at the sound; decay crept

Quivers (Quiver)
Jer 5:16 Their **q** are like an open grave;

Quota (Quotas)
Ex 5: 8 as before; don't reduce the **q**.
5:14 Why didn't you meet your **q** of bricks
5:18 must produce your full **q** of bricks."

Quotas (Quota)
1Ki 4:28 the proper place their **q** of barley

Quote (Quotes, Quoting)
Eze 12:23 they will no longer **q** it in Israel.
16:44 who quotes proverbs will **q** this
18: 3 no longer **q** this proverb in Israel.
Lk 4:23 "Surely you will **q** this proverb to

Quotes (Quote)
Eze 16:44 "'Everyone who **q** proverbs will

Quoting (Quote)
Eze 18: 2 "What do you people mean by **q** this

Raamah
Ge 10: 7 Seba, Havilah, Sabtah, **R** and Sabteca.
10: 7 The sons of **R**: Sheba and Dedan.
1Ch 1: 9 Seba, Havilah, Sabta, **R** and Sabteca.
1: 9 The sons of **R**: Sheba and Dedan.
Eze 27:22 "'The merchants of Sheba and **R**

Raamiah
Ne 7: 7 Jeshua, Nehemiah, Azariah, **R**,

Rabbah
1. Chief city of the Ammonites on eastern border of the territory of Gad (Dt 3:11; Jos 13:24–25; 2Sa 12:26; 17:27; Jer 49:2; Eze 21:20). Uriah the Hittite was slain here under orders from David (2Sa 11:1, 15). Eventually conquered by David (2Sa 12:27–31; 1Ch 20:1). Its eventual destruction was prophesied (Jer 49:2–3; Eze 21:20; 25:5; Am 1:14). **2.** City in the Judean hill country, mentioned with Kiriath Jearim (Jos 15:60). Exact location unknown.

Dt 3:11 It is still in **R** of the Ammonites.)
Jos 13:25 country as far as Aroer, near **R**;
15:60 and **R**—two towns and their villages.
2Sa 11: 1 the Ammonites and besieged **R**.
12:26 Meanwhile Joab fought against **R** of
12:27 **R** and taken its water supply.
12:29 to **R**, and attacked and captured it.
17:27 Shobi son of Nahash from **R** of the
1Ch 20: 1 and went to **R** and besieged it,
20: 1 Joab attacked **R** and left it in ruins.
Jer 49: 2 cry against **R** of the Ammonites;
49: 3 O inhabitants of **R**! Put on sackcloth
Eze 21:20 to come against **R** of the Ammonites
25: 5 I will turn **R** into a pasture for
Am 1:14 I will set fire to the walls of **R**

Rabbi (Rabboni)
Mt 23: 7 and to have men call them '**R**'.
23: 8 "But you are not to be called '**R**',
26:25 **R**?" Jesus answered, "Yes, it is you.
26:49 "Greetings, **R**!" and kissed him.
Mk 9: 5 Peter said to Jesus, "**R**, it is good
10:51 The blind man said, "**R**, I want to
11:21 "**R**, look! The fig-tree you cursed
14:45 Judas said, "**R**!" and kissed him.
Jn 1:38 "What do you want?" They said, "**R**"
1:49 Nathanael declared, "**R**, you are the
3: 2 "**R**, we know you are a teacher who
3:26 They came to John and said to him, "**R**
4:31 his disciples urged him, "**R**, eat
6:25 "**R**, when did you get here?
9: 2 His disciples asked him, "**R**, who
11: 8 "But **R**," they said, "a short while

Rabbit
Lev 11: 6 The **r**, though it chews the cud, does
Dt 14: 7 eat the camel, the **r** or the coney.

Rabbith
Jos 19:20 **R**, Kishion, Ebez,

Rabble
Nu 11: 4 The **r** with them began to crave other
Eze 23:42 desert along with men from the **r**,

Rabboni (Rabbi)
Jn 20:16 Aramaic, "**R**!" (which means Teacher).

Raca
Mt 5:22 '**R**,' is answerable to the Sanhedrin.

Racal
1Sa 30:29 and **R**; to those in the towns of the

Race[1] (Raced)
Ecc 9:11 The **r** is not to the swift or the
Ac 20:24 if only I may finish the **r** and
1Co 9:24 Do you not know that in a **r** all the
Gal 2: 2 was running or had run my **r** in vain.
5: 7 You were running a good **r**. Who cut
2Ti 4: 7 the **r**, I have kept the faith.
Heb 12: 1 the **r** marked out for us.

Race[2]
Ezr 9: 2 holy **r** with the peoples around them.
Ro 9: 3 of my brothers, those of my own **r**,

Raced (Race[1])
Est 8:14 riding the royal horses, **r** out,
Jer 12: 5 "If you have **r** with men on foot and

Rachel (Rachel's)
Daughter of Laban (Ge 29:9–13); became Jacob's wife (Ge 29:28); mother of Joseph and Benjamin (Ge 30:22–24; 35:16–18,24); died in childbirth; buried by Jacob (Ge 35:16–20; 48:7).

Ge 29: 6 his daughter **R** with the sheep."
29: 9 **R** came with her father's sheep, for
29:10 Jacob saw **R** daughter of Laban, his
29:11 Jacob kissed **R** and began to weep
29:12 He had told **R** that he was a relative
29:16 and the name of the younger was **R**.
29:17 Leah had weak eyes, but **R** was lovely
29:18 Jacob was in love with **R** and said,
29:18 return for your younger daughter **R**."
29:20 Jacob served seven years to get **R**,
29:25 have done to me? I served you for **R**,
29:28 him his daughter **R** to be his wife.
29:29 his daughter **R** as her maidservant.
29:30 Jacob lay with **R** also, and he loved **R**
29:31 opened her womb, but **R** was barren.
30: 1 **R** saw that she was not bearing Jacob
30: 6 **R** said, "God has vindicated me; he
30: 8 **R** said, "I have had a great struggle
30:14 **R** said to Leah, "Please give me some
30:15 "Very well," **R** said, "he can sleep
30:22 God remembered **R**; he listened to her
30:25 After **R** gave birth to Joseph, Jacob
31: 4 Jacob sent word to **R** and Leah to
31:14 **R** and Leah replied, "Do we still
31:19 **R** stole her father's household gods
31:32 not know that **R** had stolen the gods.
31:34 Now **R** had taken the household gods
31:35 **R** said to her father, "Don't be
33: 1 Leah, **R** and the two maidservants.
33: 2 next, and **R** and Joseph in the rear.
Ge 33: 7 and **R**, and they too bowed down.
35:16 **R** began to give birth and had great
35:19 **R** died and was buried on the way to
35:24 The sons of **R**: Joseph and Benjamin.
46:19 The sons of Jacob's wife **R**: Joseph
46:22 These were the sons of **R** who were
46:25 to his daughter **R**—seven in all.
48: 7 to my sorrow **R** died in the land of
Ru 4:11 into your home like **R** and Leah,
Jer 31:15 and great weeping, **R** weeping
Mt 2:18 and great mourning, **R** weeping

Rachel's (Rachel)
Ge 30: 7 **R** servant Bilhah conceived again and
31:33 of Leah's tent, he entered **R** tent.
35:20 this day that pillar marks **R** tomb.
35:25 The sons of **R** maidservant Bilhah:
1Sa 10: 2 you will meet two men near **R** tomb,

Racked
Isa 21: 3 At this my body is **r** with pain,
Lam 4: 9 who die of famine; **r** with hunger,

Raddai
1Ch 2:14 the fourth Nethanel, the fifth **R**,

Radiance (Radiant)
Job 31:26 if I have regarded the sun in its **r**
Eze 1:28 rainy day, so was the **r** around him.
10: 4 of the **r** of the glory of the LORD.
2Co 3:13 at it while the **r** was fading away.
Heb 1: 3 The Son is the **r** of God's glory and

Radiant (Radiance)
Ex 34:29 his face was **r** because he had
34:30 his face was **r**, and they were afraid
34:35 they saw that his face was **r**. Then
Ps 19: 8 commands of the LORD are **r**, giving
34: 5 Those who look to him are **r**; their
SS 5:10 My lover is **r** and ruddy, outstanding
Isa 60: 5 you will look and be **r**, your heart
Eze 43: 2 and the land was **r** with his glory.
Eph 5:27 as a **r** church, without stain or

Rafters
Ecc 10:18 If a man is lazy, the **r** sag; if his
SS 1:17 house are cedars; our **r** are firs.

Rafts
1Ki 5: 9 **r** by sea to the place you specify.
2Ch 2:16 them in **r** by sea down to Joppa.

Rage (Enraged, Outrageous, Raged, Rages, Raging)
Dt 19: 6 of blood might pursue him in a **r**,
2Ki 5:12 So he turned and went off in a **r**.
19:27 and go and how you **r** against me.
19:28 you **r** against me and your insolence
2Ch 25:10 Judah and left for home in a great **r**.
28: 9 them in a **r** that reaches to heaven.
Est 5: 9 was filled with **r** against Mordecai.
7: 7 The king got up in a **r**, left his
Job 15:13 that you vent your **r** against God and
Ps 7: 6 rise up against the **r** of my enemies.
Pr 19:12 A king's **r** is like the roar of a
Isa 17:12 the raging of many nations—they **r**
37:28 and go and how you **r** against me.
37:29 you **r** against me and because your
41:11 "All who **r** against you will surely
Jer 51:55 Waves of enemies will **r** like great
Da 3:13 Furious with **r**, Nebuchadnezzar
8: 6 canal and charged at him in great **r**.
11:11 of the South will march out in a **r**
11:44 **r** to destroy and annihilate many.
Hab 3: 8 Did you **r** against the sea when you
Ac 4:25 Why do the nations **r** and the
Gal 5:20 discord, jealousy, fits of **r**,
Eph 4:31 Get rid of all bitterness, **r** and
Col 3: 8 **r**, malice, slander and filthy

Raged (Rage)
1Ki 22:35 All day long the battle **r**, and the
2Ch 18:34 All day long the battle **r**, and the

Isa 45:24 All who have **r** against him will
Jer 44: 6 it **r** against the towns of Judah and
Am 1:11 because his anger **r** continually and

Rages (Rage)

Job 40:23 the river **r**, he is not alarmed; he
Ps 50: 3 him, and around him a tempest **r**.
Pr 19: 3 yet his heart **r** against the LORD.
29: 9 **r** and scoffs, and there is no peace.

Raging (Rage)

2Ch 26:19 While he was **r** at the priests in
Ps 124: 5 the **r** waters would have swept us
Isa 17:12 Oh, the **r** of many nations—they
17:12 they rage like the **r** sea! Oh,
30:30 with **r** anger and consuming fire,
Jnh 1:15 overboard, and the **r** sea grew calm.
Lk 8:24 the **r** waters; the storm subsided,
Ac 27:20 many days and the storm continued **r**,
Heb 10:27 of **r** fire that will consume the

Rags

Pr 23:21 and drowsiness clothes them in **r**.
Isa 64: 6 righteous acts are like filthy **r**;
Jer 38:11 He took some old **r** and worn-out
38:12 "Put these old **r** and worn-out
1Co 4:11 we are in **r**, we are brutally treated,

Rahab

1. Prostitute in Jericho; sheltered Israelite spies and helped them escape (Jos 2; Jas 2:25); spared when city fell (Jos 6:22–25; Heb 11:31). Mother of Boaz (Mt 1:5). **2.** Female chaos monster (Job 26:12; Ps 89:10; Isa 51:9); figurative name for Egypt (Ps 87:4; Isa 30:7).

Jos 2: 1 prostitute named **R** and stayed there.
2: 3 of Jericho sent this message to **R**:
6:17 Only **R** the prostitute and all who
6:23 spying went in and brought out **R**,
6:25 Joshua spared **R** the prostitute, with
Job 9:13 cohorts of **R** cowered at his feet.
26:12 by his wisdom he cut **R** to pieces.
Ps 87: 4 "I will record **R** and Babylon among
89:10 You crushed **R** like one of the slain;
Isa 30: 7 I call her **R** the Do-Nothing.
51: 9 Was it not you who cut **R** to pieces,
Mt 1: 5 whose mother was **R**, Boaz the father
Heb 11:31 By faith the prostitute **R**, because
Jas 2:25 In the same way, was not even **R** the

Raham

1Ch 2:44 Shema was the father of **R**, and **R** the

Raid (Raided, Raiders, Raiding)

2Sa 3:22 Joab returned from a **r** and brought
Pr 24:15 house, do not **r** his dwelling-place;

Raided (Raid)

1Sa 27: 8 Now David and his men went up and **r**
30: 1 Now the Amalekites had **r** the Negev
30:14 We **r** the Negev of the Kerethites and
1Ch 14: 9 Now the Philistines had come and **r**
14:13 Once more the Philistines **r** the
2Ch 25:13 **r** Judean towns from Samaria to
28:18 while the Philistines had **r** towns in

Raiders (Raid)

Ge 49:19 "Gad will be attacked by a band of **r**,
Jdg 2:14 them over to **r** who plundered them.
2:16 them out of the hands of these **r**.
2Ki 13:20 Now Moabite **r** used to enter the
13:21 suddenly they saw a band of **r**; so
24: 2 Moabite and Ammonite **r** against him.
2Ch 22: 1 king in his place, since the **r**, who

Raiding (Raid)

1Sa 13:17 **R** parties went out from the
14:15 and **r** parties—and the ground shook.
23:27 The Philistines are **r** the land."
27:10 Achish asked, "Where did you go **r**
30: 8 "Shall I pursue this **r** party? Will I
30:15 you lead me down to this **r** party?
2Sa 4: 2 two men who were leaders of **r** bands.
2Ki 6:23 Aram stopped **r** Israel's territory.
1Ch 12:18 made them leaders of his **r** bands.
12:21 They helped David against **r** bands,
Job 1:17 Chaldeans formed three **r** parties

Rail

Ps 102: 8 **r** against me use my name as a curse.

Rain (Rainbow, Rained, Raining, Rains, Rainy)

Ge 2: 5 for the LORD God had not sent **r** on
7: 4 Seven days from now I will send **r** on
7:12 **r** fell on the earth for forty days
8: 2 **r** had stopped falling from the sky.
Ex 9:33 **r** no longer poured down on the land.
9:34 Pharaoh saw that the **r** and hail and
16: 4 said to Moses, "I will **r** down bread
Lev 26: 4 I will send you **r** in its season, and
Dt 11:11 valleys that drinks **r** from heaven.
11:14 I will send **r** on your land in its
11:17 the heavens so that it will not **r**
28:12 to send **r** on your land in season and
28:24 The LORD will turn the **r** of your
32: 2 Let my teaching fall like **r** and my
32: 2 like abundant **r** on tender plants.
1Sa 12:17 upon the LORD to send thunder and **r**.
12:18 day the LORD sent thunder and **r**.
2Sa 1:21 may you have neither dew nor **r**, nor
21:10 till the **r** poured down from the
22:12 him—the dark **r** clouds of the sky.
23: 4 like the brightness after **r** that
1Ki 8:35 there is no **r** because your people
8:36 and send **r** on the land you gave your
17: 1 there will be neither dew nor **r** in
17: 7 there had been no **r** in the land.
17:14 day the LORD gives **r** on the land.
18: 1 Ahab, and I will send **r** on the land."
18:41 there is the sound of a heavy **r**."
18:44 and go down before the **r** stops you.
18:45 the wind rose, a heavy **r** came on and
2Ki 3:17 You will see neither wind nor **r**,
2Ch 6:26 there is no **r** because your people
6:27 and send **r** on the land that you gave
7:13 the heavens so that there is no **r**,
Ezr 10: 9 the occasion and because of the **r**.
Job 5:10 He bestows **r** on the earth; he sends
20:23 him and **r** down his blows upon him.
28:26 he made a decree for the **r** and a
29:23 drank in my words as the spring **r**.
36:27 which distil as **r** to the streams;
37: 6 **r** shower, 'Be a mighty downpour.'
38:25 a channel for the torrents of **r**,
38:28 Does the **r** have a father? Who
Ps 11: 6 On the wicked he will **r** fiery coals
18:11 him—the dark **r** clouds of the sky.
68: 8 the heavens poured down **r**, before
72: 6 He will be like **r** falling on a mown
105:32 He turned their **r** into hail, with
135: 7 he sends lightning with the **r** and
147: 8 **r** and makes grass grow on the hills.
Pr 16:15 favour is like a **r** cloud in spring.
25:14 Like clouds and wind without **r** is a
25:23 a north wind brings **r**, so a sly
26: 1 Like snow in summer or **r** in harvest,
28: 3 a driving **r** that leaves no crops.
Ecc 11: 3 water, they pour **r** upon the earth.
12: 2 and the clouds return after the **r**;
Isa 4: 6 hiding-place from the storm and **r**.
5: 6 command the clouds not to **r** on it."
28: 2 like a driving **r** and a flooding
30:23 He will also send you **r** for the seed
44:14 a pine, and the **r** made it grow.
45: 8 heavens above, **r** down righteousness
55:10 the **r** and the snow come down from
Jer 10:13 He sends lightning with the **r** and
14: 4 because there is no **r** in the land;
14:22 idols of the nations bring **r**?
51:16 He sends lightning with the **r** and
Eze 13:11 **R** will come in torrents, and I will
13:13 **r** will fall with destructive fury.
22:24 **r** or showers in the day of wrath.'
38:22 I will pour down torrents of **r**,
Am 4: 7 "I also withheld **r** from you when the
4: 7 I sent **r** on one town, but withheld
4: 7 One field had **r**; another had none
Zec 10: 1 Ask the LORD for **r** in the springtime;
10: 1 He gives showers of **r** to men, and
14:17 LORD Almighty, they will have no **r**.
14:18 and take part, they will have no **r**.
Mt 5:45 and sends **r** on the righteous and the
7:25 The **r** came down, the streams rose,
7:27 The **r** came down, the streams rose,
Lk 12:54 say, 'It's going to **r**,' and it does.
Ac 14:17 giving you **r** from heaven and crops
Heb 6: 7 Land that drinks in the **r** often
Jas 5:17 earnestly that it would not **r**,
5:17 and it did not **r** on the land for
5:18 **r**, and the earth produced its crops.
Jude :12 They are clouds without **r**, blown
Rev 11: 6 the sky so that it will not **r**

Rainbow (Rain)

Ge 9:13 I have set my **r** in the clouds, and
9:14 and the **r** appears in the clouds,
9:16 Whenever the **r** appears in the clouds,
Eze 1:28 Like the appearance of a **r** in the
Rev 4: 3 A **r**, resembling an emerald,
10: 1 He was robed in a cloud, with a **r**

Rained (Rain)

Ge 19:24 the LORD **r** down burning sulphur on
Ex 9:23 LORD **r** hail on the land of Egypt;
Ps 78:24 he **r** down manna for the people to
78:27 He **r** meat down on them like dust,
Lk 17:29 fire and sulphur **r** down from heaven

Raining (Rain)

Ac 28: 2 us all because it was **r** and cold.

Rains (Rain)

Dt 11:14 both autumn and spring **r**, so that
Job 24: 8 They are drenched by mountain **r** and
Ps 84: 6 autumn **r** also cover it with pools.
SS 2:11 See! The winter is past; the **r** are
Jer 3: 3 and no spring **r** have fallen.
5:24 who gives autumn and spring **r** in
Hos 6: 3 will come to us like the winter **r**,
6: 3 the spring **r** that water the earth."
Joel 2:23 you the autumn **r** in righteousness.
2:23 both autumn and spring **r**, as before.
Jas 5: 7 he is for the autumn and spring **r**.

Rainy (Rain)

Ezr 10:13 **r** season; so we cannot stand outside.
Pr 27:15 like a constant dripping on a **r** day;
Eze 1:28 a rainbow in the clouds on a **r** day,

Raise (Raised, Raises, Raising, Upraised)

Ge 4:20 who live in tents and **r** livestock.
Ex 14:16 **R** your staff and stretch out your
24:11 God did not **r** his hand against these
Dt 18:15 The LORD your God will **r** up for you
18:18 I will **r** up for them a prophet like
Jos 6:10 "Do not give a war cry, do not **r**
Jdg 8:28 and did not **r** its head again.
1Sa 2:35 I will **r** up for myself a faithful
18:17 "I will not **r** a hand against him.
22:17 not willing to **r** a hand to strike
2Sa 7:12 I will **r** up your offspring to
1Ki 14:14 "The LORD will **r** up for himself a
20:25 You must also **r** an army like the one
2Ki 4:28 I tell you, 'Don't **r** my hopes'?"
1Ch 17:11 I will **r** up your offspring to
Job 38:34 "Can you **r** your voice to the clouds
Ps 41:10 O LORD, have mercy on me; **r** me up,
Pr 8: 1 Does not understanding **r** her voice?
8: 4 "To you, O men, I call out; I **r** my
Isa 8: 9 **R** the war cry, you nations, and be
10:15 Does the axe **r** itself above him who
10:26 he will **r** his staff over the waters,
11:12 He will **r** a banner for the nations
13: 2 **R** a banner on a bare hilltop, shout
14:13 I will **r** my throne above the stars
24:14 They **r** their voices, they shout for
42: 2 He will not shout or cry out, or **r**
42:11 Let the desert and its towns **r** their
42:13 with a shout he will **r** the battle
45:13 will **r** up Cyrus in my righteousness

Isa 58: 1 do not hold back. **R** your voice
58:12 will **r** up the age-old foundations;
62:10 **R** a banner for the nations.
Jer 4: 6 **R** the signal to go to Zion! Flee for
6: 1 Sound the trumpet in Tekoa! **R** the
23: 5 "when I will **r** up to David a
30: 9 king, whom I will **r** up for them.
Eze 26: 8 walls and **r** his shields against you.
27:30 They will **r** their voice and cry
Da 11:11 who will **r** a large army, but it will
Hos 5: 8 **R** the battle cry in Beth Aven; lead
Mic 5: 5 we will **r** against him seven
Zec 1:21 so that no-one could **r** his head,
2: 9 I will surely **r** my hand against them
11:16 For I am going to **r** up a shepherd
Mt 3: 9 God can **r** up children for Abraham.
10: 8 Heal the sick, **r** the dead, cleanse
Lk 3: 8 God can **r** up children for Abraham.
Jn 2:19 I will **r** it again in three days."
2:20 are going to **r** it in three days?"
6:39 me, but **r** them up at the last day.
6:40 I will **r** him up at the last day."
6:44 and I will **r** him up at the last day.
6:54 and I will **r** him up at the last day.
Ac 3:22 'The Lord your God will **r** up for you
1Co 6:14 the dead, and he will **r** us also.
15:15 But he did not **r** him if in fact the
2Co 4:14 the dead will also **r** us with Jesus
Heb 11:19 Abraham reasoned that God could **r**
Jas 3:18 Peacemakers who sow in peace **r** a
5:15 person well; the Lord will **r** him up.

Raised (Raise, *Raised from the dead*)

Ge 14:22 "I have **r** my hand to the LORD, God
Ex 7:20 He **r** his staff in the presence of
9:16 I have **r** you up for this very
Nu 14: 1 **r** their voices and wept aloud.
20:11 Moses **r** his arm and struck the rock
Jos 5: 7 he **r** up their sons in their place,
8:29 And they **r** a large pile of rocks
Jdg 2:16 the LORD **r** up judges, who saved them
2:18 Whenever the LORD **r** up a judge for
3: 9 when they cried out to the LORD, he **r**
1Sa 4: 5 all Israel **r** such a great shout that
14:27 He **r** his hand to his mouth, and his
2Sa 12: 3 He **r** it, and it grew up with him and
23: 8 was chief of the Three; he **r** his
23:18 He **r** his spear against three hundred
1Ki 11:14 the LORD **r** up against Solomon an
11:23 God **r** up against Solomon another
14: 7 'I **r** you up from among the people
2Ki 3: 4 Now Mesha king of Moab **r** sheep, and
19:22 Against whom have you **r** your voice
1Ch 11:11 was chief of the officers; he **r** his
11:20 He **r** his spear against three hundred
2Ch 5:13 they **r** their voices in praise to the
13:15 the men of Judah **r** the battle cry.
Ne 5: 1 Now the men and their wives **r** a
Est 10: 2 Mordecai to which the king had **r** him,
Job 31:21 if I have **r** my hand against the
Ps 60: 4 who fear you, you have **r** a banner
80:15 the son you have **r** up for yourself.
80:17 of man you have **r** up for yourself.
148:14 He has **r** up for his people a horn,
Isa 2: 2 it will be **r** above the hills,
5:25 hand is **r** and he strikes them down.
18: 3 when a banner is **r** on the mountains,
23:13 they **r** up their siege towers,
37:23 Against whom have you **r** your voice
40: 4 Every valley shall be **r** up, every
49:11 roads, and my highways will be **r** up.
52:13 **r** and lifted up and highly exalted.
Jer 12: 6 they have **r** a loud cry against you.
29:15 You may say, "The LORD has **r** up
Lam 2: 7 they have **r** a shout in the house of
Eze 2: 2 the Spirit came into me and **r** me to
3:24 the Spirit came into me and **r** me to
41: 8 I saw that the temple had a **r** base
Da 4:34 I, Nebuchadnezzar, **r** my eyes towards
7: 5 It was **r** up on one of its sides, and
8:18 he touched me and **r** me to my feet.
Am 2:11 I also **r** up prophets from among your
Mic 4: 1 it will be **r** above the hills,
Zec 5: 7 the cover of lead was **r**, and there
14:10 But Jerusalem will be **r** up and
Mt 11: 5 the deaf hear, the dead are **r**, and
16:21 and on the third day be **r** to life.
17:23 the third day he will be **r** to life.
20:19 the third day he will be **r** to life!"
27:52 people who had died were **r** to life.
Lk 1:69 He has **r** up a horn of salvation for
7:22 the deaf hear, the dead are **r**, and
9:22 and on the third day be **r** to life."
24: 7 and on the third day be **r** again.
Jn 12:17 **r** him from the dead continued to
Ac 2:14 Peter stood up with the Eleven, **r**
2:24 God **r** him from the dead, freeing him
2:32 God has **r** this Jesus to life, and we
3:15 life, but God **r** him from the dead.
3:26 God **r** up his servant, he sent him
4:24 they heard this, they **r** their voices
5:30 The God of our fathers **r** Jesus from
10:40 God **r** him from the dead on the third
13:30 God **r** him from the dead,
13:34 The fact that God **r** him from the
22:22 Then they **r** their voices and shouted,
Ro 4:24 who **r** Jesus our Lord from the dead.
4:25 was **r** to life for our justification.
8:11 if the Spirit of him who **r** Jesus
8:11 he who **r** Christ from the dead will
8:34 who died—more than that, who was **r**
9:17 "I **r** you up for this very purpose,
10: 9 heart that God **r** him from the dead,
1Co 6:14 By his power God **r** the Lord from the
15: 4 that he was buried, that he was **r** on
15:13 then not even Christ has been **r**.
15:14 if Christ has not been **r**, our
15:15 God that he **r** Christ from the dead.
15:15 him if in fact the dead are not **r**.
15:16 For if the dead are not **r**, then
15:16 then Christ has not been **r** either.
15:17 if Christ has not been **r**, your faith
15:29 dead? If the dead are not **r** at all,
15:32 I gained? If the dead are not **r**,
15:35 someone may ask, "How are the dead **r**?
15:42 is perishable, it is **r** imperishable;
15:43 is sown in dishonour, it is **r** in
15:43 sown in weakness, it is **r** in power;
15:44 is sown a natural body, it is **r** a
15:52 the dead will be **r** imperishable, and
2Co 4:14 we know that the one who **r** the Lord
5:15 who died for them and was **r** again.
Gal 1: 1 Father, who **r** him from the dead—
Eph 1:20 which he exerted in Christ when he **r**
2: 6 God **r** us up with Christ and seated
Col 2:12 **r** with him through your faith in the
2:12 of God, who **r** him from the dead.
3: 1 Since, then, you have been **r** with
Heb 11:35 received back their dead, **r** to llife
1Pe 1:21 Through him you believe in God, who **r**
Rev 10: 5 the land **r** his right hand to heaven.

Raised from the dead

Mt 17: 9 until the Son of Man has been **r**."
27:64 tell the people that he has been **r**.
Mk 6:14 "John the Baptist has been **r**, and
6:16 the man I beheaded, has been **r**!"
Lk 9: 7 were saying that John had been **r**,
Jn 2:22 After he was **r**, his disciples
12: 1 Lazarus lived, whom Jesus had **r**.
12: 9 also to see Lazarus, whom he had **r**.
21:14 to his disciples after he was **r**.
Ac 4:10 whom you crucified but whom God **r**,
13:37 the one whom God **r** did not see decay.
Ro 6: 4 just as Christ was **r** through the
6: 9 For we know that since Christ was **r**,
7: 4 to him who was **r**, in order that we
1Co 15:12 is preached that Christ has been **r**,
15:20 Christ has indeed been **r**, the
1Th 1:10 whom he **r**—Jesus, who rescues us
2Ti 2: 8 Remember Jesus Christ, **r**, descended

Raises (Raise)

1Sa 2: 6 brings down to the grave and **r** up.
2: 8 He **r** the poor from the dust and
Ps 113: 7 He **r** the poor from the dust and
Pr 1:20 **r** her voice in the public squares;
Isa 19:16 the LORD Almighty **r** against them.
Jn 5:21 For just as the Father **r** the dead
Ac 26: 8 it incredible that God **r** the dead?
2Co 1: 9 but on God, who **r** the dead.

Raisin (Raisins)

1Ch 12:40 fig cakes, **r** cakes, wine, oil,
Hos 3: 1 gods and love the sacred **r** cakes."

Raising (Raise)

Jdg 21: 2 **r** their voices and weeping bitterly.
1Ki 15: 4 by **r** up a son to succeed him
Ps 55:12 I could endure it; if a foe were **r**
Jer 4:16 **r** a war cry against the cities of
Am 7:10 "Amos is **r** a conspiracy against you
Hab 1: 6 I am **r** up the Babylonians, that
Ac 10:29 when I was sent for, I came without **r**
13:33 us, their children, by **r** up Jesus.
17:31 to all men by **r** him from the dead."
1Co 10:25 without **r** questions of conscience,
10:27 without **r** questions of conscience.

Raisins (Raisin)

Nu 6: 3 grape juice or eat grapes or **r**.
1Sa 25:18 a hundred cakes of **r** and two hundred
30:12 of pressed figs and two cakes of **r**.
2Sa 6:19 a cake of dates and a cake of **r** to
16: 1 a hundred cakes of **r**, a hundred
1Ch 16: 3 **r** to each Israelite man and woman.
SS 2: 5 Strengthen me with **r**, refresh me

Rakem

1Ch 7:15 and his sons were Ulam and **R**.

Rakkath

Jos 19:35 Ziddim, Zer, Hammath, **R**, Kinnereth,

Rakkon

Jos 19:46 Me Jarkon and **R**, with the area

Rallied (Rally)

Ge 48: 2 **r** his strength and sat up on the bed.
Ex 32:26 And all the Levites **r** to him.
2Sa 2:25 the men of Benjamin **r** behind Abner.
Ac 5:36 and about four hundred men **r** to him.

Rally (Rallied)

Isa 11:10 peoples; the nations will **r** to him,

Ram (Ram's, Rams, Rams')

Ge 15: 9 "Bring me a heifer, a goat and a **r**,
22:13 he saw a **r** caught by its horns.
22:13 He went over and took the **r** and
Ex 25: 5 **r** skins dyed red and hides of sea
26:14 Make for the tent a covering of **r**
29:17 Cut the **r** into pieces and wash the
29:18 burn the entire **r** on the altar. It
29:19 "Take the other **r**, and Aaron and his
29:22 "Take from this **r** the fat, the fat
29:22 (This is the **r** for the ordination.)
29:26 After you take the breast of the **r**
29:27 **r** that belong to Aaron and his sons:
29:31 "Take the **r** for the ordination and
29:32 sons are to eat the meat of the **r**
29:34 any of the meat of the ordination **r**
35: 7 **r** skins dyed red and hides of sea
35:23 or goat hair, **r** skins dyed red or
36:19 tent a covering of **r** skins dyed red,
39:34 the covering of **r** skins dyed red,
Lev 5:15 LORD as a penalty a **r** from the flock,
5:16 him with the **r** as a guilt offering,
5:18 a guilt offering a **r** from the flock,
6: 6 his guilt offering, a **r** from the
8:18 He then presented the **r** for the
8:19 Moses slaughtered the **r** and
8:20 He cut the **r** into pieces and burned
8:21 **r** on the altar as a burnt offering,
8:22 He then presented the other **r**, the **r**
8:23 Moses slaughtered the **r** and took
8:29 Moses' share of the ordination **r**
9: 2 and a **r** for your burnt offering,
9: 4 an ox and a **r** for a fellowship
9:18 He slaughtered the ox and the **r** as
9:19 the fat portions of the ox and the **r**
16: 3 and a **r** for a burnt offering.

Lev 16: 5 and a **r** for a burnt offering.
19:21 The man, however, must bring a **r** to
19:22 With the **r** of the guilt offering the
Nu 5: 8 along with the **r** with which
6:14 a **r** without defect for a fellowship
6:17 is to sacrifice the **r** as a
6:19 hands a boiled shoulder of the **r**,
7:15 one young bull, one **r** and one male
7:21 one young bull, one **r** and one male
7:27 one young bull, one **r** and one male
7:33 one young bull, one **r** and one male
7:39 one young bull, one **r** and one male
7:45 one young bull, one **r** and one male
7:51 one young bull, one **r** and one male
7:57 one young bull, one **r** and one male
7:63 one young bull, one **r** and one male
7:69 one young bull, one **r** and one male
7:75 one young bull, one **r** and one male
7:81 one young bull, one **r** and one male
15: 6 "'With a **r** prepare a grain offering
15:11 Each bull or **r**, each lamb or young
23: 2 a bull and a **r** on each altar.
23: 4 I have offered a bull and a **r**."
23:14 a bull and a **r** on each altar.
23:30 a bull and a **r** on each altar.
28:11 one **r** and seven male lambs a year
28:12 flour mixed with oil; with the **r**,
28:14 of half a hin of wine; with the **r**,
28:19 one **r** and seven male lambs a year
28:20 with oil; with the **r**, two-tenths;
28:27 one **r** and seven male lambs a year
28:28 with oil; with the **r**, two-tenths;
29: 2 one **r** and seven male lambs a year
29: 3 with oil; with the **r**, two-tenths;
29: 8 one **r** and seven male lambs a year
29: 9 with oil; with the **r**, two-tenths;
29:36 a burnt offering of one bull, one **r**
29:37 With the bull, the **r** and the lambs,
Ru 4:19 Hezron the father of **R**, **R** the father
1Ch 2: 9 Hezron were: Jerahmeel, **R** and Caleb.
2:10 **R** was the father of Amminadab, and
2:25 of Hezron: **R** his firstborn,
2:27 The sons of **R** the firstborn of
Ezr 10:19 **r** from the flock as a guilt offering.
Job 32: 2 of the family of **R**, became very
Eze 43:23 a young bull and a **r** from the flock,
43:25 a young bull and a **r** from the flock,
45:24 each bull and an ephah for each **r**,
46: 4 lambs and a **r**, all without defect.
46: 5 The grain offering given with the **r**
46: 6 lambs and a **r**, all without defect.
46: 7 one ephah with the **r**, and with the
46:11 an ephah with a **r**, and with the
Da 8: 3 and there before me was a **r** with two
8: 4 I watched the **r** as he charged
8: 6 He came towards the two-horned **r** I
8: 7 I saw him attack the **r** furiously,
8: 7 the **r** and shattering his two horns.
8: 7 The **r** was powerless to stand against
8: 7 could rescue the **r** from his power
8:20 The two-horned **r** that you saw
Mt 1: 3 of Hezron, Hezron the father of **R**,
1: 4 **R** the father of Amminadab, Amminadab
Lk 3:33 the son of Amminadab, the son of **R**,

Ram's (Ram)

Ex 19:13 Only when the **r** horn sounds a long
Ps 81: 3 Sound the **r** horn at the New Moon,
98: 6 trumpets and the blast of the **r** horn

Ramah

1. Town in territory of Benjamin (Jos 18:25), near Gibeah (Jdg 19:13–14). Deborah held court between here and Bethel (Jdg 4:5). On border between the divided kingdoms, so was heavily fortified (1Ki 15:17; 2Ch 16:1), but Judah weakened its defences (1Ki 15:22; 2Ch 16:6). On Nebuchadnezzar's invasion route (Isa 10:29; Hos 5:8); he detained Jewish captives here (Jer 31:15; 40:1). **2.** Town in territory of Ephraim, exact location unknown. Known also as Ramathaim (1Sa 1:1). Home and burial place of Samuel (1Sa 7:17; 25:1), where the people demanded a king (1Sa 8:4–6). David fled here from Saul (1Sa 19:18). **3.** Town on border of territory of Asher (Jos 19:29). Exact location unknown. **4.** Fortified town in territory of Naphtali (Jos 19:36). **5.** Town in territory of Simeon in the Negev (Jos 19:8). Exact location unknown.

Jos 18:25 Gibeon, **R**, Beeroth,
19: 8 as Baalath Beer (**R** in the Negev).
19:29 boundary then turned back towards **R**
19:36 Adamah, **R**, Hazor,
Jdg 4: 5 under the Palm of Deborah between **R**
19:13 let's try to reach Gibeah or **R** and
1Sa 1:19 then went back to their home at **R**.
2:11 Elkanah went home to **R**, but the boy
7:17 he always went back to **R**, where his
8: 4 together and came to Samuel at **R**.
15:34 Samuel left for **R**, but Saul went up
16:13 Samuel then went to **R**.
19:18 he went to Samuel at **R** and told him
19:19 "David is in Naioth at **R**"
19:22 Finally, he himself left for **R** and
19:22 "Over in Naioth at **R**," they said.
19:23 Saul went to Naioth at **R**. But the
20: 1 David fled from Naioth at **R** and went
25: 1 they buried him at his home in **R**.
28: 3 and buried him in his own town of **R**.
1Ki 15:17 fortified **R** to prevent anyone from
15:21 building **R** and withdrew to Tirzah.
15:22 they carried away from **R** the stones
2Ch 16: 1 fortified **R** to prevent anyone from
16: 5 building **R** and abandoned his work.
16: 6 and they carried away from **R** the
Ezr 2:26 of **R** and Geba 621
Ne 7:30 of **R** and Geba 621
11:33 in Hazor, **R** and Gittaim,
Isa 10:29 **R** trembles; Gibeah of Saul flees.
Jer 31:15 "A voice is heard in **R**, mourning and
40: 1 guard had released him at **R**.
Hos 5: 8 trumpet in Gibeah, the horn in **R**.
Mt 2:18 "A voice is heard in **R**, weeping and

Ramath Lehi

Jdg 15:17 and the place was called **R**.

Ramath Mizpah

Jos 13:26 from Heshbon to **R** and Betonim, and

Ramathaim See Ramah

1Sa 1: 1 There was a certain man from **R**, a

Ramathite

1Ch 27:27 Shimei the **R** was in charge of the

Rameses

Ge 47:11 district of **R**, as Pharaoh directed.
Ex 1:11 and **R** as store cities for Pharaoh.
12:37 The Israelites journeyed from **R** to
Nu 33: 3 The Israelites set out from **R** on the
33: 5 The Israelites left **R** and camped at

Ramiah

Ezr 10:25 From the descendants of Parosh: **R**,

Ramoth

Dt 4:43 for the Reubenites; **R** in Gilead, for
Jos 20: 8 **R** in Gilead in the tribe of Gad, and
21:38 from the tribe of Gad, **R** in Gilead
2Ki 8:29 at **R** in his battle with Hazael king
1Ch 6:73 **R** and Anem, together with their
6:80 from the tribe of Gad they received **R**
2Ch 22: 6 at **R** in his battle with Hazael king

Ramoth Gilead

Fortified city in territory of Gad, about 25 miles east of River Jordan. Designated as a town of refuge (Dt 4:43; Jos 20:8), and assigned to the Levites (Jos 21:38; 1Ch 6:80). Its people received Amalekite plunder from David (1Sa 30:27), and it was one of Solomon's 12 districts (1Ki 4:13). Ahab tried to retake the city from the Arameans, rejecting Micaiah's advice and was killed by a random arrow (1Ki 22:1–38; 2Ch 18:2–34; 22:5–6). Ahab's son Joram also fought the Arameans here and was injured (2Ki 8:28–29). Jehu was anointed king here (2Ki 9:1–6).

1Ki 4:13 Ben-Geber—in **R** (the settlements of
22: 3 "Don't you know that **R** belongs to us
22: 4 you go with me to fight against **R**?"
22: 6 "Shall I go to war against **R**, or
22:12 "Attack **R** and be victorious," they
22:15 war against **R**, or shall I refrain?"
22:20 king **R** and going to his death there?'
22:29 king of Judah went up to **R**.
2Ki 8:28 against Hazael king of Aram at **R**.
9: 1 flask of oil with you and go to **R**.
9: 4 the young man, the prophet, went to **R**
9:14 **R** against Hazael king of Aram,
2Ch 18: 2 with him and urged him to attack **R**.
18: 3 "Will you go with me against **R**?"
18: 5 "Shall we go to war against **R**, or
18:11 "Attack **R** and be victorious," they
18:14 war against **R**, or shall I refrain?"
18:19 king **R** and going to his death there?'
18:28 king of Judah went up to **R**.
22: 5 against Hazael king of Aram at **R**.

Ramoth Negev

1Sa 30:27 who were in Bethel, **R** and Jattir;

Ramp (Ramps)

2Sa 20:15 They built a siege **r** up to the city,
2Ki 19:32 or build a siege **r** against it.
Job 19:12 they build a siege **r** against me and
Isa 37:33 or build a siege **r** against it.
Eze 4: 2 build a **r** up to it, set up camps
21:22 build a **r** and to erect siege works.
26: 8 build a **r** up to your walls and raise

Rampart (Ramparts)

Ps 91: 4 will be your shield and **r**.

Ramparts (Rampart)

Ps 48:13 consider well her **r**, view her
Isa 26: 1 God makes salvation its walls and **r**.
Lam 2: 8 He made **r** and walls lament; together
Hab 2: 1 watch and station myself on the **r**;

Ramps (Ramp)

Job 30:12 they build their siege **r** against me.
Jer 6: 6 and build siege **r** against Jerusalem.
32:24 "See how the siege **r** are built up to
33: 4 against the siege **r** and the
Eze 17:17 when **r** are built and siege works
Da 11:15 seige **r** and will capture a fortified
Hab 1:10 build earthen **r** and capture them.

Rams (Ram)

Ge 31:38 nor have I eaten **r** from your flocks.
32:14 two hundred ewes and twenty **r**,
Ex 29: 1 young bull and two **r** without defect.
29: 3 with the bull and the two **r**.
29:15 "Take one of the **r**, and Aaron and
Lev 8: 2 the two **r** and the basket containing
23:18 defect, one young bull and two **r**.
Nu 7:17 two oxen, five **r**, five male goats
7:23 two oxen, five **r**, five male goats
7:29 two oxen, five **r**, five male goats
7:35 two oxen, five **r**, five male goats
7:41 two oxen, five **r**, five male goats
7:47 two oxen, five **r**, five male goats
7:53 two oxen, five **r**, five male goats
7:59 two oxen, five **r**, five male goats
7:65 two oxen, five **r**, five male goats
7:71 two oxen, five **r**, five male goats
7:77 two oxen, five **r**, five male goats
7:83 two oxen, five **r**, five male goats
7:87 twelve **r** and twelve male lambs a
7:88 sixty **r**, sixty male goats and sixty
23: 1 seven bulls and seven **r** for me."
23:29 seven bulls and seven **r** for me."
29:13 two **r** and fourteen male lambs a year
29:14 with each of the two **r**, two-tenths;
29:17 two **r** and fourteen male lambs a year
29:18 With the bulls, **r** and lambs, prepare
29:20 two **r** and fourteen male lambs a year
29:21 With the bulls, **r** and lambs, prepare
29:23 two **r** and fourteen male lambs a year
29:24 With the bulls, **r** and lambs, prepare
29:26 two **r** and fourteen male lambs a year
29:27 With the bulls, **r** and lambs, prepare
29:29 two **r** and fourteen male lambs a year

Nu 29:30 With the bulls, **r** and lambs, prepare
29:32 two **r** and fourteen male lambs a year
29:33 With the bulls, **r** and lambs, prepare
Dt 32:14 with choice **r** of Bashan and the
1Sa 15:22 to heed is better than the fat of **r**.
2Ki 3: 4 the wool of a hundred thousand **r**.
1Ch 15:26 bulls and seven **r** were sacrificed.
29:21 a thousand **r** and a thousand male
2Ch 13: 9 seven **r** may become a priest of what
17:11 seven thousand seven hundred **r** and
29:21 They brought seven bulls, seven **r**,
29:22 next they slaughtered the **r** and
29:32 a hundred **r** and two hundred male
Ezr 6: 9 Whatever is needed—young bulls, **r**,
6:17 two hundred **r**, four hundred male
7:17 **r** and male lambs, together with
8:35 ninety-six **r**, seventy-seven male
Job 42: 8 now take seven bulls and seven **r** and
Ps 66:15 an offering of **r**; I will offer
114: 4 the mountains skipped like **r**, the
114: 6 like **r**, you hills, like lambs?
Isa 1:11 of **r** and the fat of fattened animals;
34: 6 goats, fat from the kidneys of **r**.
60: 7 the **r** of Nebaioth will serve you;
Jer 51:40 to the slaughter, like **r** and goats.
Eze 27:21 with you in lambs, **r** and goats.
34:17 another, and between **r** and goats.
39:18 earth as if they were **r** and lambs,
45:23 seven **r** without defect as a burnt
Mic 6: 7 LORD be pleased with thousands of **r**,

Rams' (Ram)

Jos 6: 4 of **r** horns in front of the ark.
1Ch 15:28 with the sounding of **r** horns and

Ran (Run)

Ge 18: 7 he **r** to the herd and selected a
24:20 **r** back to the well to draw more
24:28 The girl **r** and told her mother's
29:12 So she **r** and told her father.
33: 4 Esau **r** to meet Jacob and embraced
39:12 in her hand and **r** out of the house.
39:15 beside me and **r** out of the house."
39:18 beside me and **r** out of the house."
Ex 4: 3 it became a snake, and he **r** from it.
Nu 11:27 A young man **r** and told Moses, "Eldad
16:47 Aaron did as Moses said, and **r** into
Jos 4:18 place and **r** in flood as before.
7:22 Joshua sent messengers, and they **r**
15: 3 Then it **r** past Hezron up to Addar
15: 8 **r** up the Valley of Ben Hinnom along
15:10 **r** along the northern slope of Mount
17: 7 The boundary **r** southward from there
18:17 and **r** down to the Stone of Bohan son
19:11 Going west it **r** to Maralah, touched
19:34 The boundary **r** west through Aznoth
Jdg 7:21 **r**, crying out as they fled.
9:54 servant **r** him through, and he died.
1Sa 3: 5 he **r** to Eli and said, "Here I am;
4:12 That same day a Benjamite **r** from the
10:23 They **r** and brought him out, and as
17:22 **r** to the battle lines and greeted
17:24 they all **r** from him in great fear.
17:48 David **r** quickly towards the battle
17:51 David **r** and stood over him. He took
17:51 hero was dead, they turned and **r**.
20:36 boy **r**, he shot an arrow beyond him.
2Sa 18:21 bowed down before Joab and **r** off.
18:23 So Joab said, "Run!" Then Ahimaaz **r**
1Ki 2:39 two of Shimei's slaves **r** off to
18:35 The water **r** down around the altar
18:46 he **r** ahead of Ahab all the way to
19: 3 Elijah was afraid and **r** for his life.
19:20 Elisha then left his oxen and **r**
22:35 The blood from his wound **r** onto the
2Ki 7: 7 as it was and **r** for their lives.
9:10 Then he opened the door and **r**.
Jnh 1: 3 Jonah **r** away from the LORD and
Mt 8:33 Those tending the pigs **r** off, went
27:48 Immediately one of them **r** and got a
28: 8 joy, and **r** to tell his disciples.
Mk 5: 6 he saw Jesus from a distance, he **r**
5:14 Those tending the pigs **r** off and
6:33 **r** on foot from all the towns and got
6:55 They **r** throughout that whole region
Mk 9:15 with wonder and **r** to greet him.
10:17 Jesus started on his way, a man **r** up
15:36 One man **r**, filled a sponge with wine
Lk 8:34 they **r** off and reported this in the
15:20 compassion for him; he **r** to his son,
19: 4 he **r** ahead and climbed a
24:12 Peter, however, got up and **r** to the
Ac 8:30 Philip **r** up to the chariot and heard
12:14 she was so overjoyed she **r** back
19:16 that they **r** out of the house naked
21:32 soldiers and **r** down to the crowd.
27:41 the ship struck a sand-bar and **r**

Random

1Ki 22:34 someone drew his bow at **r** and hit
2Ch 18:33 someone drew his bow at **r** and hit
Pr 26:10 Like an archer who wounds at **r** is he

Rang

Mt 25: 6 "At midnight the cry **r** out: 'Here's
1Th 1: 8 The Lord's message **r** out from you

Range (Ranges)

Nu 27:12 "Go up this mountain in the Abarim **R**
Dt 32:49 "Go up into the Abarim **R** to Mount
2Ch 16: 9 For the eyes of the LORD **r**
Isa 32:20 your cattle and donkeys **r** free.
Zec 4:10 LORD, which **r** throughout the earth.)"

Ranges (Range)

Job 39: 8 He **r** the hills for his pasture and

Rank (Ranking, Ranks)

1Sa 18: 5 Saul gave him a high **r** in the army.
2Ki 23: 4 the priests next in **r** and the
25:18 next in **r** and the three doorkeepers.
1Ch 15:18 with them their brothers next in **r**:
2Ch 31:12 his brother Shimei was next in **r**.
Est 10: 3 Mordecai the Jew was second in **r** to
Isa 3: 3 the captain of fifty and man of **r**,
5:13 their men of **r** will die of hunger
Jer 52:24 next in **r** and the three doorkeepers.
Eze 23:23 of high **r**, all mounted on horses.

Ranking (Rank)

Ac 25:23 room with the high **r** officers

Ranks (Rank)

1Sa 17: 8 Goliath stood and shouted to the **r**
17:10 "This day I defy the **r** of Israel!
2Ki 11: 8 Anyone who approaches your **r** must be
11:15 "Bring her out between the **r** and put
1Ch 12:38 who volunteered to serve in the **r**.
2Ch 23:14 "Bring her out between the **r** and put
Job 40:19 He **r** first among the works of God,
Pr 30:27 yet they advance together in **r**;
Isa 14:31 there is not a straggler in its **r**.
Jer 46:21 The mercenaries in her **r** are like
50:37 in her **r**! They will become women.
Joel 2: 8 through defences without breaking **r**.
Gal 2: 4 infiltrated our **r** to spy on the

Ransacked

Ob : 6 how Esau will be **r**, his hidden
Zec 14: 2 the houses **r**, and the women raped.

Ransom (Ransomed, Ransoms)

Ex 30:12 each one must pay the LORD a **r** for
Nu 35:31 "'Do not accept a **r** for the life of
35:32 "'Do not accept a **r** for anyone who
Job 5:20 In famine he will **r** you from death,
6:22 pay a **r** for me from your wealth,
6:23 **r** me from the clutches of the
33:24 the pit; I have found a **r** for him'—
Ps 49: 7 another or give to God a **r** for him—
49: 8 the **r** for a life is costly, no
Pr 13: 8 A man's riches may **r** his life, but a
21:18 The wicked become a **r** for the
Isa 43: 3 your **r**, Cush and Seba in your stead.
47:11 that you cannot ward off with a **r**;
50: 2 Was my arm too short to **r** you? Do I
Jer 31:11 For the LORD will **r** Jacob and redeem
Hos 13:14 "I will **r** them from the power of the
Mt 20:28 to give his life as a **r** for many."
Mk 10:45 to give his life as a **r** for many."
1Ti 2: 6 who gave himself as a **r** for all men—
Heb 9:15 now that he has died as a **r** to set

Ransomed (Ransom)

Lev 19:20 has not been **r** or given her freedom,
27:29 may be **r**; he must be put to death.
Isa 35:10 the **r** of the LORD will return. They
51:11 The **r** of the LORD will return. They

Ransoms (Ransom)

Ps 55:18 He **r** me unharmed from the battle

Raped (Rapes)

Ge 34: 2 saw her, he took her and **r** her.
Jdg 19:25 and they **r** her and abused her
20: 5 They **r** my concubine, and she died.
2Sa 13:14 he was stronger than she, he **r** her.
13:32 day that Amnon **r** his sister Tamar.
Zec 14: 2 houses ransacked, and the women **r**.

Rapes (Raped)

Dt 22:25 pledged to be married and **r** her,
22:28 and **r** her and they are discovered,

Rapha

2Sa 21:16 one of the descendants of **R**, whose
21:18 Saph, one of the descendants of **R**.
21:20 He also was descended from **R**.
21:22 These four were descendants of **R** in
1Ch 8: 2 Nohah the fourth and **R** the fifth.
20: 6 He also was descended from **R**.
20: 8 These were descendants of **R** in Gath,

Raphah

1Ch 8:37 the father of Binea; **R** was his son,

Raphu

Nu 13: 9 tribe of Benjamin, Palti son of **R**;

Rapid

Ezr 5: 8 **r** progress under their direction.

Rare

1Sa 3: 1 was **r**; there were not many visions.
Pr 20:15 that speak knowledge are a **r** jewel.
24: 4 with **r** and beautiful treasures.
Isa 13:12 gold, more **r** than the gold of Ophir.

Rash (Rashly)

Lev 13: 2 "When anyone has a swelling or a **r**
13: 6 pronounce him clean; it is only a **r**.
13: 7 if the **r** does spread in his skin
13: 8 and if the **r** has spread in the skin,
13:39 it is a harmless **r** that has broken
14:56 for a swelling, a **r** or a bright spot,
Nu 30: 6 **r** promise by which she binds herself
30: 8 **r** promise by which she binds herself,
Ps 106:33 and **r** words came from Moses' lips.
Isa 32: 4 The mind of the **r** will know and
Ac 19:36 to be quiet and not do anything **r**.
2Ti 3: 4 treacherous, **r**, conceited, lovers of

Rashly (Rash)

Pr 13: 3 he who speaks **r** will come to ruin.
20:25 for a man to dedicate something **r**

Rat (Rats)

Lev 11:29 the **r**, any kind of great lizard,

Rate

Lev 25:50 based on the **r** paid to a hired man

Ratified

Jos 9:15 of the assembly **r** it by oath.

Rationed

Eze 4:16 The people will eat **r** food in
4:16 and drink **r** water in despair,

Rats (Rat)
1Sa 6: 4 "Five gold tumours and five gold **r**,
6: 5 **r** that are destroying the country,
6:11 **r** and the models of the tumours.
6:18 the number of the gold **r** was
Isa 66:17 **r** and other abominable things—they

Rattles (Rattling)
Job 39:23 The quiver **r** against his side, along

Rattling (Rattles)
Job 41:29 he laughs at the **r** of the lance.
Eze 37: 7 there was a noise, a **r** sound, and

Ravage (Ravaged, Ravages, Ravaging)
Ge 41:30 and the famine will **r** the land.
Jdg 6: 5 they invaded the land to **r** it.
Ps 80:13 Boars from the forest **r** it and the
Jer 5: 6 a wolf from the desert will **r** them,
5:10 "Go through her vineyards and **r** them,
Eze 26: 8 He will **r** your settlements on the

Ravaged (Ravage)
Isa 6:11 and the fields ruined and **r**,
Eze 26: 6 the mainland will be **r** by the sword.
36: 3 Because they **r** and hounded you from

Ravages (Ravage)
Ps 35:17 Rescue my life from their **r**, my
Jer 14:18 the city, I see the **r** of famine.

Ravaging (Ravage)
1Ch 21:12 of the LORD **r** every part of Israel.

Raven (Ravens)
Ge 8: 7 sent out a **r**, and it kept flying
Lev 11:15 any kind of **r**,
Dt 14:14 any kind of **r**,
Job 38:41 Who provides food for the **r** when its
SS 5:11 his hair is wavy and black as a **r**.
Isa 34:11 great owl and the **r** will nest there.

Ravening (Ravenous)
Jer 2:30 your prophets like a **r** lion.

Ravenous (Ravening)
Ge 49:27 "Benjamin is a **r** wolf; in the
Ps 57: 4 I lie among **r** beasts—men whose

Ravens (Raven)
1Ki 17: 4 ordered the **r** to feed you there."
17: 6 The **r** brought him bread and meat in
Ps 147: 9 and for the young **r** when they call.
Pr 30:17 will be pecked out by the **r** of the
Lk 12:24 Consider the **r**: They do not sow or

Ravine (Ravines)
Jos 16: 8 to the Kanah **R** and ended at the sea.
17: 9 continued south to the Kanah **R**.
17: 9 side of the **r** and ended at the sea.
19:11 and extended to the **r** near Jokneam.
1Sa 15: 5 Amalek and set an ambush in the **r**.
25:20 riding her donkey into a mountain **r**,
30: 9 Besor **R**, where some stayed behind,
30:10 were too exhausted to cross the **r**.
30:21 who were left behind at the Besor **R**.
1Ki 17: 3 in the Kerith **R**, east of the Jordan.
17: 5 He went to the Kerith **R**, east of the
Isa 15: 7 away over the **R** of the Poplars.
Zec 1: 8 among the myrtle trees in a **r**.

Ravines (Ravine)
Nu 21:14 Waheb in Suphah and the **r**, the
21:15 the slopes of the **r** that lead to the
2Sa 23:30 Hiddai from the **r** of Gaash,
1Ch 11:32 Hurai from the **r** of Gaash, Abiel the
Job 22:24 gold of Ophir to the rocks in the **r**,
Ps 104:10 springs pour water into the **r**;
Isa 7:19 **r** and in the crevices in the rocks,
57: 5 **r** and under the overhanging crags.
57: 6 of the **r** are your portion; they,
Eze 6: 3 to the **r** and valleys: I am about to
31:12 lay broken in all the **r** of the land.
32: 6 **r** will be filled with your flesh.
34:13 in the **r** and in all the settlements
35: 8 in your valleys and in all your **r**.
36: 4 to the **r** and valleys, to the
36: 6 to the **r** and valleys: 'This is what
Joel 3:18 the **r** of Judah will run with water.

Raving
Jn 10:20 "He is demon-possessed and **r** mad.

Ravish (Ravished)
Dt 28:30 but another will take her and **r** her.

Ravished (Ravish)
Isa 13:16 will be looted and their wives **r**.
Jer 3: 2 any place where you have not been **r**?
Lam 5:11 Women have been **r** in Zion, and

Raw
Ex 12: 9 Do not eat the meat **r** or cooked in
Lev 13:10 if there is **r** flesh in the swelling,
13:14 whenever **r** flesh appears on him, he
13:15 the priest sees the **r** flesh, he
13:15 The **r** flesh is unclean; he has an
13:16 Should the **r** flesh change and turn
13:24 appears in the **r** flesh of the burn,
1Sa 2:15 boiled meat from you, but only **r**."
Eze 29:18 bare and every shoulder made **r**.

Ray (Rays)
Am 5:20 without a **r** of brightness?

Rays (Ray)
Job 3: 9 and not see the first **r** of dawn,
41:18 his eyes are like the **r** of dawn.
Hab 3: 4 like the sunrise; **r** flashed from

Razor
Nu 6: 5 no **r** may be used on his head.
Jdg 13: 5 No **r** may be used on his head,
16:17 he told her everything. "No **r** has
1Sa 1:11 No **r** will ever be used on his head
Ps 52: 2 like a sharpened **r**, you who
Isa 7:20 In that day the Lord will use a **r**
Eze 5: 1 **r** to shave your head and your beard.

Read (Reader, Reading, Reads)
Ex 24: 7 the Covenant and **r** it to the people.
Dt 17:19 is to be with him, and he is to **r** it
31:11 you shall **r** this law before them in
Jos 8:34 Afterwards, Joshua **r** all the words
8:35 **r** to the whole assembly of Israel,
2Ki 5: 6 he took to the king of Israel **r**:
5: 7 soon as the king of Israel **r** the
19:14 letter from the messengers and **r** it.
22: 8 He gave it to Shaphan, who **r** it.
22:10 And Shaphan **r** from it in the
22:16 in the book the king of Judah has **r**.
23: 2 He **r** in their hearing all the words
2Ch 30: 6 which **r**: "People of Israel, return
34:18 And Shaphan **r** from it in the
34:24 **r** in the presence of the king of
34:30 He **r** in their hearing all the words
Ezr 4:18 The letter you sent us has been **r**
4:23 of King Artaxerxes was **r** to Rehum
5: 7 The report they sent him **r** as
Ne 8: 3 He **r** it aloud from daybreak till
8: 8 They **r** from the Book of the Law of
8: 8 could understand what was being **r**.
8:18 **r** from the Book of the Law of God.
9: 3 They stood where they were and **r**
13: 1 On that day the Book of Moses was **r**
Est 6: 1 to be brought in and **r** to him.
Isa 29:11 **r**, and say to him, "**R** this, please,"
29:12 cannot **r**, and say, "**R** this, please,"
29:12 will answer, "I don't know how to **r**.
34:16 Look in the scroll of the LORD and **r**:
37:14 letter from the messengers and **r** it.
Jer 29:29 Zephaniah the priest, however, **r** the
36: 6 **r** to the people from the scroll the
36: 6 **R** them to all the people of Judah
Jer 36: 8 at the LORD's temple he **r** the words
36:10 Baruch **r** to all the people at the
36:13 **r** to the people from the scroll,
36:14 you have **r** to the people and come.
36:15 "Sit down, please, and **r** it to us.
36:15 So Baruch **r** it to them.
36:21 **r** it to the king and all the
36:23 Whenever Jehudi had **r** three or four
51:61 that you **r** all these words aloud.
Da 5: 8 but they could not **r** the writing or
5:15 brought before me to **r** this writing
5:16 If you can **r** this writing and tell
5:17 Nevertheless, I will **r** the writing
Mt 12: 3 He answered, "Haven't you **r** what
12: 5 Or haven't you **r** in the Law that on
19: 4 "Haven't you **r**," he replied, "that
21:16 "have you never **r**, "'From the lips
21:42 Jesus said to them, "Have you never **r**
22:31 you not **r** what God said to you,
Mk 2:25 He answered, "Have you never **r** what
12:10 Haven't you **r** this scripture: "'The
12:26 you not **r** in the book of Moses,
15:26 him **r**: THE KING OF THE JEWS.
Lk 4:16 And he stood up to **r**.
6: 3 "Have you never **r** what David did
10:26 "How do you **r** it?"
23:38 **r**: THIS IS THE KING OF THE JEWS.
Jn 19:19 It **r**: JESUS OF NAZARETH, THE KING
19:20 Many of the Jews **r** this sign, for
Ac 13:27 prophets that are **r** every Sabbath.
15:21 **r** in the synagogues on every Sabbath.
15:31 The people **r** it and were glad for
23:34 The governor **r** the letter and asked
2Co 1:13 anything you cannot **r** or understand.
3: 2 hearts, known and **r** by everybody.
3:14 remains when the old covenant is **r**.
3:15 Even to this day when Moses is **r**, a
Col 4:16 After this letter has been **r** to you,
4:16 see that it is also **r** in the church
4:16 in turn **r** the letter from Laodicea.
1Th 5:27 this letter **r** to all the brothers.

Reader (Read)
Mt 24:15 Daniel—let the **r** understand—
Mk 13:14 let the **r** understand—then let those

Readiness (Ready)
2Co 7:11 concern, what **r** to see justice done.
Eph 6:15 with your feet fitted with the **r**

Reading (Read)
Jer 51:63 you finish **r** this scroll, tie a
Ac 8:28 **r** the book of Isaiah the prophet.
8:30 heard the man **r** Isaiah the prophet.
8:30 "Do you understand what you are **r**?"
8:32 The eunuch was **r** this passage of
13:15 After the **r** from the Law and the
Eph 3: 4 In **r** this, then, you will be able to
1Ti 4:13 devote yourself to the public **r** of

Reads (Read)
Da 5: 7 "Whoever **r** this writing and tells me
Rev 1: 3 Blessed is the one who **r** the words

Ready (Readiness)
Ge 24:61 Rebekah and her maids got **r** and
46:29 Joseph had his chariot made **r** and
46:30 Israel said to Joseph, "Now I am **r**
Ex 14: 6 he had his chariot made **r** and took
17: 4 They are almost **r** to stone me."
19:11 be **r** by the third day, because on
34: 2 Be **r** in the morning, and then come
Nu 4:15 and when the camp is **r** to move, the
8:11 may be **r** to do the work of the LORD.
32:17 we are **r** to arm ourselves and go
Jos 1: 2 you and all these people, get **r** to
1:11 the people, 'Get your supplies **r**.
22:26 "That is why we said, 'Let us get **r**
1Sa 6: 7 "Now then, get a new cart **r**, with
9:26 **r**, and I will send you on your way.
9:26 When Saul got **r**, he and Samuel went
25:41 "Here is your maidservant, **r** to
2Sa 15:15 "Your servants are **r** to do whatever
15:26 not pleased with you,' then I am **r**;

1Ki 1: 5 So he got chariots and horses **r**,
2Ki 22: 4 make him get **r** the money that has
1Ch 5:18 44,760 men **r** for military service
7: 4 they had 36,000 men **r** for battle,
7:11 fighting men **r** to go out to war.
7:40 The number of men **r** for battle, as
12: 8 They were brave warriors, **r** for
12:17 I am **r** to have you unite with me.
12:25 men of Simeon, warriors **r** for battle
12:35 men of Dan, **r** for battle—28,600;
28:21 Levites are **r** for all the work on
2Ch 25: 5 thousand men **r** for military service,
26:11 Uzziah had a well-trained army, **r** to
26:19 **r** to burn incense, became angry.
29:26 the Levites stood **r** with David's
Est 3:14 that they would be **r** for that day.
8:13 **r** on that day to avenge themselves
Job 3: 8 those who are **r** to rouse Leviathan.
18:12 disaster is **r** for him when he falls.
32:19 wine, like new wineskins **r** to burst.
Ps 7:13 he makes **r** his flaming arrows.
59: 4 I have done no wrong, yet they are **r**
119:173 May your hand be **r** to help me, for I
Pr 21:31 The horse is made **r** for the day of
22:18 and have all of them **r** on your lips.
24:27 get your fields **r**; after that,
Isa 30:33 it has been made **r** for the king.
Jer 1:17 "Get yourself **r**! Stand up and say to
9: 3 "They make **r** their tongue like a bow,
46:14 'Take your positions and get **r**, for
Lam 2: 4 strung his bow; his right hand is **r**.
Eze 7:14 the trumpet and get everything **r**,
21:11 made **r** for the hand of the slayer.
38: 7 "'Get **r**; be prepared, you and all
Da 3:15 if you are **r** to fall down and
Hos 2: 9 and my new wine when it is **r**.
Na 2: 3 are made **r**; the spears of pine are
Zec 5:11 When it is **r**, the basket will be set
Mt 22: 4 slaughtered, and everything is **r**.
22: 8 'The wedding banquet is **r**, but those
24:44 you also must be **r**, because the Son
25:10 The virgins who were **r** went in with
Mk 3: 9 to have a small boat **r** for him,
14:15 a large upper room, furnished and **r**.
Lk 1:17 **r** a people prepared for the Lord."
1:39 At that time Mary got **r** and hurried
9:52 village to get things **r** for him;
12:35 "Be dressed **r** for service and keep
12:38 servants whose master finds them **r**,
12:40 You also must be **r**, because the Son
12:47 does not get **r** or does not do what
14:17 'Come, for everything is now **r**.'
17: 8 'Prepare my supper, get yourself **r**
22:33 he replied, "Lord, I am **r** to go with
Jn 8:37 Yet you are **r** to kill me, because
Ac 16:10 we got **r** at once to leave for
21:13 heart? I am **r** not only to be bound,
21:15 After this, we got **r** and went up to
23:15 **r** to kill him before he gets here."
23:21 They are **r** now, waiting for your
23:23 "Get **r** a detachment of two hundred
28:10 ways and when we were **r** to sail,
1Co 3: 2 food, for you were not yet **r** for it.
3: 2 Indeed, you are still not **r**.
14: 8 call, who will get **r** for battle?
2Co 9: 2 year you in Achaia were **r** to give;
9: 3 may be **r**, as I said you would be.
9: 5 Then it will be **r** as a generous gift,
10: 6 we will be **r** to punish every act of
12:14 Now I am **r** to visit you for the
Tit 3: 1 to be **r** to do whatever is good,
1Pe 1: 5 **r** to be revealed in the last time.
4: 5 **r** to judge the living and the dead.
Rev 9:15 the four angels who had been kept **r**
19: 7 and his bride has made herself **r**.

Reaffirm (Affirm)

1Sa 11:14 to Gilgal and there **r** the kingship."
20:17 Jonathan made David **r** his oath out
2Co 2: 8 urge you, therefore, to **r** your love

Reaiah

1Ch 4: 2 **R** son of Shobal was the father of
5: 5 Micah his son, **R** his son, Baal his
Ezr 2:47 Giddel, Gahar, **R**,
Ne 7:50 **R**, Rezin, Nekoda,

Real (Realities, Reality, Really)

Jn 6:55 For my flesh is **r** food and my blood
6:55 is **r** food and my blood is **r** drink.
1Jn 2:27 things and as that anointing is **r**,

Realise (Realised, Realising)

Ge 42:23 They did not **r** that Joseph could
Ex 10: 7 you not yet **r** that Egypt is ruined?"
Nu 22:34 I did not **r** you were standing in the
Jdg 13:16 **r** that it was the angel of the LORD.)
15:11 "Don't you **r** that the Philistines
20:34 did not **r** how near disaster was.
1Sa 12:17 And you will **r** what an evil thing
2Sa 2:26 Don't you **r** that this will end in
3:38 "Do you not **r** that a prince and a
Ecc 2:14 but I came to **r** that the same fate
Jer 2:19 Consider then and **r** how evil and
11:19 **r** that they had plotted against me,
Da 2: 8 because you **r** that this is what I
Hos 7: 2 they do not **r** that I remember all
7: 9 his strength, but he does not **r** it.
11: 3 did not **r** it was I who healed them.
14: 9 Who is wise? He will **r** these things.
Jn 2: 9 He did not **r** where it had come from,
11:50 You do not **r** that it is better for
12:16 did they **r** that these things had
13: 7 Jesus replied, "You do not **r** now
14:20 On that day you will **r** that I am in
19:10 "Don't you **r** I have power either to
20:14 but she did not **r** that it was Jesus.
21: 4 did not **r** that it was Jesus.
Ac 7:25 would **r** that God was using him to
10:34 Peter began to speak: "I now **r** how
23: 5 Paul replied, "Brothers, I did not **r**
1Co 11: 3 Now I want you to **r** that the head of
2Co 10:11 Such people should **r** that what we
13: 5 Do you not **r** that Christ Jesus is in
Rev 3:17 But you do not **r** that you are

Realised (Realise)

Ge 3: 7 and they **r** that they were naked; so
28: 8 Esau then **r** how displeasing the
Ex 5:19 The Israelite foremen **r** they were in
Jdg 6:22 Gideon **r** that it was the angel of
13:21 **r** that it was the angel of the LORD.
20:41 **r** that disaster had come upon them.
Ru 1:18 Naomi **r** that Ruth was determined to
1Sa 3: 8 **r** that the LORD was calling the boy.
18:28 Saul **r** that the LORD was with David
2Sa 10: 6 the Ammonites **r** that they had become
12:19 and he **r** that the child was dead.
20:12 When he **r** that everyone who came up
1Ki 3:15 Solomon awoke—and he **r** it had been
1Ch 19: 6 the Ammonites **r** that they had become
Ne 6:12 I **r** that God had not sent him, but
6:16 because they **r** that this work had
Ecc 5:18 I **r** that it is good and proper for a
SS 6:12 Before I **r** it, my desire set me
Eze 10:20 and I **r** that they were cherubim.
Mt 2:16 Herod **r** that he had been outwitted
Mk 5:30 At once Jesus **r** that power had gone
Lk 1:22 They **r** he had seen a vision in the
Jn 4:53 the father **r** that this was the exact
6:22 **r** that only one boat had been there,
6:24 Once the crowd **r** that neither Jesus
Ac 4:13 John and **r** that they were unschooled,
16:19 the owners of the slave girl **r** that
19:34 when they **r** he was a Jew, they all
22:29 when he **r** that he had put Paul,

Realising (Realise)

Ge 38:16 Not **r** that she was his
Est 7: 7 But Haman, **r** that the king had
Ro 2: 4 tolerance and patience, not **r** that

Realities (Real)

Heb 10: 1 are coming—not the **r** themselves.

Reality (Real)

Col 2:17 the **r**, however, is found in Christ.

Really (Real)

Ge 3: 1 He said to the woman, "Did God **r** say,
18:13 I **r** have a child, now that I am old?'
18:24 Will you **r** sweep it away and not
20:12 Besides, she **r** is my sister, the
26: 9 "She is **r** your wife! Why did you say,
27:21 you **r** are my son Esau or not."
27:24 "Are you **r** my son Esau?" he asked.
45:12 it is **r** I who am speaking to you.
Lev 25:16 **r** selling you is the number of crops.
Nu 22:37 me? Am I **r** not able to reward you?"
Jdg 6:17 sign that it is **r** you talking to me.
6:31 by morning! If Baal **r** is a god,
9:15 'If you **r** want to anoint me king
11: 9 them to me—will I **r** be your head?"
14:16 "You hate me! You don't **r** love me.
15: 3 Philistines; I will **r** harm them."
1Ki 8:27 "But will God **r** dwell on earth? The
18: 7 "Is it **r** you, my lord Elijah?
2Ch 6:18 "But will God **r** dwell on earth with
Ecc 8:17 he knows, he cannot **r** comprehend it.
Jer 7: 5 If you **r** change your ways and your
9:26 For all these nations are **r**
Zec 7: 5 was it **r** for me that you fasted?
Mk 11:32 held that John **r** was a prophet.)
Jn 4:42 man **r** is the Saviour of the world."
7:26 **r** concluded that he is the Christ?
8:31 my teaching, you are **r** my disciples.
13:38 Jesus answered, "Will you **r** lay down
14: 7 If you **r** knew me, you would know my
Ac 9:26 believing that he **r** was a disciple.
12: 9 the angel was doing was **r** happening;
Ro 7: 7 **r** was if the law had not said,
1Co 4: 8 How I wish that you **r** had become
5: 7 batch without yeast—as you **r** are.
14:25 exclaiming, "God is **r** among you!
Gal 1: 7 which is **r** no gospel at all.
3: 4 nothing—if it **r** was for nothing?
Php 1:12 has **r** served to advance the gospel.
1Th 3: 8 For now we **r** live, since you are
1Ti 5: 3 to those widows who are **r** in need.
5: 5 The widow who is **r** in need and left
5:16 help those widows who are **r** in need.
Jas 2: 8 If you **r** keep the royal law found in
1Jn 2:19 us, but they did not **r** belong to us.

Realm (Realms)

Dt 32:22 that burns to the **r** of death below.
Jos 13:21 **r** of Sihon king of the Amorites,
13:27 Zaphon with the rest of the **r** of
13:30 the entire **r** of Og king of Bashan
2Ch 36:22 his **r** and to put it in writing:
Ezr 1: 1 his **r** and to put it in writing:
7:23 the **r** of the king and of his sons?
Est 1:20 throughout all his vast **r**, all the
2: 3 in every province of his **r** to bring
Da 11: 9 will invade the **r** of the king of
Hab 2: 9 "Woe to him who builds his **r** by

Realms (Realm)

Eph 1: 3 blessed us in the heavenly **r** with
1:20 at his right hand in the heavenly **r**,
2: 6 in the heavenly **r** in Christ Jesus,
3:10 and authorities in the heavenly **r**,
6:12 forces of evil in the heavenly **r**.

Reap (Reaped, Reaper, Reapers, Reaping, Reaps)

Lev 19: 9 "'When you **r** the harvest of your
19: 9 do not **r** to the very edges of your
23:10 to give you and you **r** its harvest,
23:22 "'When you **r** the harvest of your
23:22 do not **r** to the very edges of your
25: 5 Do not **r** what grows of itself or
25:11 do not sow and do not **r** what grows
1Sa 8:12 plough his ground and **r** his harvest,
2Ki 19:29 But in the third year sow and **r**,
Job 4: 8 evil and those who sow trouble **r** it.
Ps 126: 5 Those who sow in tears will **r** with
Ecc 11: 4 looks at the clouds will not **r**.
Isa 37:30 But in the third year sow and **r**,
Jer 12:13 They will sow wheat but **r** thorns;
Hos 8: 7 "They sow the wind and **r** the
10:12 Sow for yourselves righteousness, **r**
Mt 6:26 not sow or **r** or store away in barns,

Lk 12:24 the ravens: They do not sow or **r**,
19:21 put in and **r** what you did not sow.'
Jn 4:38 I sent you to **r** what you have not
Ro 6:21 What benefit did you **r** at that time
6:22 the benefit you **r** leads to holiness,
1Co 9:11 if we **r** a material harvest from you?
2Co 9: 6 sparingly will also **r** sparingly,
9: 6 generously will also **r** generously.
Gal 6: 8 from that nature will **r** destruction;
6: 8 from the Spirit will **r** eternal life.
6: 9 **r** a harvest if we do not give up.
Rev 14:15 "Take your sickle and **r**, because the
14:15 because the time to **r** has come, for

Reaped (Reap)

Ge 26:12 and the same year **r** a hundredfold,
Hos 10:13 you have **r** evil, you have eaten the
Jn 4:38 **r** the benefits of their labour."

Reaper (Reap)

Ps 129: 7 with it the **r** cannot fill his hands,
Isa 17: 5 will be as when a **r** gathers the
Jer 9:22 the **r**, with no-one to gather them.
50:16 the **r** with his sickle at harvest.
Am 9:13 "when the **r** will be overtaken by the
Jn 4:36 Even now the **r** draws his wages, even
4:36 and the **r** may be glad together.

Reapers (Reap)

2Ki 4:18 to his father, who was with the **r**.

Reaping (Reap)

Ge 45: 6 there will not be ploughing and **r**.
Lk 19:22 put in, and **r** what I did not sow?

Reappears (Appear)

Lev 13:57 if it **r** in the clothing, or in the
14:43 "If the mildew **r** in the house after

Reaps (Reap)

Pr 11:18 sows righteousness **r** a sure reward.
22: 8 He who sows wickedness **r** trouble,
Jn 4:37 'One sows and another **r**' is true.
Gal 6: 7 A man **r** what he sows.

Reason (Reasonable, Reasoned, Reasoning, Reasons)

Ge 2:24 For this **r** a man will leave his
20:10 "What was your **r** for doing this?
41:32 The **r** the dream was given to Pharaoh
1Sa 19: 5 like David by killing him for no **r**?"
Job 2: 3 him to ruin him without any **r**."
9:17 and multiply my wounds for no **r**.
12:24 the leaders of the earth of their **r**;
22: 6 from your brothers for no **r**;
Ps 35:19 without **r** maliciously wink the eye.
38:19 who hate me without **r** are numerous.
69: 4 Those who hate me without **r**
Pr 3:30 Do not accuse a man for no **r**—when
Isa 1:18 "Come now, let us **r** together," says
Mt 12:10 Looking for a **r** to accuse Jesus,
19: 3 his wife for any and every **r**?"
19: 5 said, 'For this **r** a man will leave
Mk 3: 2 Some of them were looking for a **r** to
10: 7 'For this **r** a man will leave his
Lk 6: 7 looking for a **r** to accuse Jesus,
Jn 1:31 the **r** I came baptising with water
5:18 For this **r** the Jews tried all the
8:47 The **r** you do not hear is that you do
10:17 The **r** my Father loves me is that I
12:27 for this very **r** I came to this hour.
12:39 For this **r** they could not believe,
15:25 Law: 'They hated me without **r**.'
18:37 In fact, for this **r** I was born, and
Ac 19:40 since there is no **r** for it."
28:20 For this **r** I have asked to see you
Ro 14: 9 For this very **r**, Christ died and
1Co 4:17 For this **r** I am sending to you
11:10 For this **r**, and because of the
12:15 that **r** cease to be part of the body.
12:16 that **r** cease to be part of the body.
14:13 For this **r** anyone who speaks in a
2Co 2: 9 The **r** I wrote to you was to see if
8:24 love and the **r** for our pride in you,
Gal 6:12 The only **r** they do this is to avoid
Eph 1:15 For this **r**, ever since I heard about
3: 1 For this **r** I, Paul, the prisoner of
3:14 For this **r** I kneel before the Father,
5:31 "For this **r** a man will leave his
Col 1: 9 For this **r**, since the day we heard
1Th 3: 5 For this **r**, when I could stand it no
2Th 2:11 For this **r** God sends them a powerful
1Ti 1:16 for that very **r** I was shown mercy so
2Ti 1: 6 For this **r** I remind you to fan into
Tit 1: 5 The **r** I left you in Crete was that
Phm :15 Perhaps the **r** he was separated from
Heb 2:17 For this **r** he had to be made like
9:15 For this **r** Christ is the mediator of
10: 1 For this **r** it can never, by the same
Jas 4: 5 you think Scripture says without **r**
1Pe 3:15 the **r** for the hope that you have.
4: 6 For this is the **r** the gospel was
2Pe 1: 5 For this very **r**, make every effort
1Jn 3: 1 The **r** the world does not know us
3: 8 The **r** the Son of God appeared was to

Reasonable (Reason)

Ac 18:14 would be **r** for me to listen to you.
26:25 "What I am saying is true and **r**.

Reasoned (Reason)

Ac 17: 2 he **r** with them from the Scriptures,
17:17 he **r** in the synagogue with the Jews
18: 4 Every Sabbath he **r** in the synagogue,
18:19 the synagogue and **r** with the Jews.
1Co 13:11 like a child, I **r** like a child.
Heb 11:19 Abraham **r** that God could raise the

Reasoning (Reason)

Job 32:11 I listened to your **r**; while you were

Reasons (Reason)

1Co 15:32 in Ephesus for merely human **r**,
Php 3: 4 though I myself have **r** for such
3: 4 If anyone else thinks he has **r** to

Reassign (Assign)

Isa 49: 8 and to **r** its desolate inheritances,

Reassure (Assure, Reassured)

2Ki 25:24 Gedaliah took an oath to **r** them and
Jer 40: 9 an oath to **r** them and their men.

Reassured (Reassure)

Ge 50:21 he **r** them and spoke kindly to them.

Reba

Nu 31: 8 Hur and **R**—the five kings of Midian.
Jos 13:21 Evi, Rekem, Zur, Hur and **R**—princes

Rebekah (Rebekah's)

Sister of Laban (Ge 25:20); left Haran with Abraham's servant to marry Isaac (Ge 24). Mother of Esau and Jacob (Ge 25:21–26). In Gerar, pretended to be Isaac's sister (Ge 26:1–11). Helped Jacob deceive Jacob and steal blessing (Ge 27).

Ge 22:23 Bethuel became the father of **R**.
24:15 Before he had finished praying, **R**
24:29 Now **R** had a brother named Laban, and
24:30 and had heard **R** tell what the man
24:45 **R** came out, with her jar on her
24:51 Here is **R**; take her and go, and let
24:53 of clothing and gave them to **R**;
24:58 they called **R** and asked her, "Will
24:59 they sent their sister **R** on her way,
24:60 they blessed **R** and said to her, "Our
24:61 **R** and her maids got ready and
24:61 So the servant took **R** and left.
24:64 **R** also looked up and saw Isaac. She
24:67 his mother Sarah, and he married **R**.
25:20 he married **R** daughter of Bethuel
25:21 and his wife **R** became pregnant.
25:26 years old when **R** gave birth to them.
25:28 game, loved Esau, but **R** loved Jacob.
26: 7 of **R**, because she is beautiful."
Ge 26: 8 and saw Isaac caressing his wife **R**.
26:35 a source of grief to Isaac and **R**.
27: 5 Now **R** was listening as Isaac spoke
27: 6 **R** said to her son Jacob, "Look, I
27:11 Jacob said to **R** his mother, "But my
27:15 **R** took the best clothes of Esau her
27:42 **R** was told what her older son Esau
27:46 **R** said to Isaac, "I'm disgusted with
28: 5 the brother of **R**, who was the mother
29:12 of her father and a son of **R**.
49:31 there Isaac and his wife **R** were

Rebekah's (Rebekah)

Ge 35: 8 Now Deborah, **R** nurse, died and was
Ro 9:10 Not only that, but **R** children had

Rebel (Rebelled, Rebelling, Rebellion, Rebellious, Rebels)

Ex 23:21 Do not **r** against him; he will not
Nu 14: 9 Only do not **r** against the LORD. And
Dt 31:27 much more will you **r** after I die!
Jos 22:18 'If you **r** against the LORD today,
22:19 But do not **r** against the LORD or
22:29 "Far be it from us to **r** against the
1Sa 12:14 and do not **r** against his commands,
12:15 and if you **r** against his commands,
2Ki 18:20 depending, that you **r** against me?
Job 24:13 "There are those who **r** against the
Isa 1:20 if you resist and **r**, you will be
36: 5 depending, that you **r** against me?
48: 8 are; you were called a **r** from birth.
Eze 2: 8 Do not **r** like that rebellious house;
20:38 those who revolt and **r** against me.
Da 11:14 will **r** in fulfilment of the vision,
Mt 10:21 children will **r** against their
Mk 13:12 Children will **r** against their

Rebelled (Rebel)

Ge 14: 4 but in the thirteenth year they **r**.
Nu 20:24 because both of you **r** against my
26: 9 officials who **r** against Moses
26: 9 when they **r** against the LORD.
27:14 for when the community **r** at the
Dt 1:26 you were unwilling to go up; you **r**
1:43 You **r** against the LORD's command and
9:23 But you **r** against the command of
1Sa 22:13 so that he has **r** against me and lies
1Ki 11:26 Also, Jeroboam son of Nebat **r**
11:27 Here is the account of how he **r**
2Ki 1: 1 After Ahab's death, Moab **r** against
3: 5 after Ahab died, the king of Moab **r**
3: 7 "The king of Moab has **r** against me.
8:20 In the time of Jehoram, Edom **r**
18: 7 He **r** against the king of Assyria and
24: 1 mind and **r** against Nebuchadnezzar.
24:20 **r** against the king of Babylon.
2Ch 13: 6 son of David, **r** against his master.
21: 8 In the time of Jehoram, Edom **r**
36:13 He also **r** against King
Ne 9:26 "But they were disobedient and **r**
Ps 5:10 sins, for they have **r** against you.
78:40 How often they **r** against him in the
78:56 they put God to the test and **r**
105:28 had they not **r** against his words?
106: 7 and they **r** by the sea, the Red Sea.
106:33 for they **r** against the Spirit of God,
107:11 for they had **r** against the words of
Isa 1: 2 them up, but they have **r** against me.
43:27 sinned; your spokesmen **r** against me.
63:10 Yet they **r** and grieved his Holy
66:24 bodies of those who **r** against me;
Jer 2: 8 know me; the leaders **r** against me.
2:29 **r** against me," declares the LORD.
3:13 have **r** against the LORD your God,
4:17 **r** against me,'" declares the LORD.
52: 3 **r** against the king of Babylon.
Lam 1:18 "The LORD is righteous, yet I **r**
3:42 "We have sinned and **r** and you have
Eze 2: 3 to a rebellious nation that has **r**
5: 6 Yet in her wickedness she has **r**
17:15 the king **r** against him by sending
20: 8 "'But they **r** against me and would
20:13 "'Yet the people of Israel **r**
20:21 "'But the children **r** against me:
Da 9: 5 We have been wicked and have **r**; we

Da 9: 9 even though we have **r** against him;
Hos 7:13 because they have **r** against me! I
8: 1 my covenant and **r** against my law.
13:16 they have **r** against their God.
Heb 3:16 Who were they who heard and **r**? Were

Rebelling (Rebel)
Ne 2:19 "Are you **r** against the king?"
Ps 78:17 they continued to sin against him, **r**
Ro 13: 2 **r** against what God has instituted,

Rebellion (Rebel)
Ex 23:21 he will not forgive your **r**, since
34: 7 and forgiving wickedness, **r** and sin.
Lev 16:16 uncleanness and **r** of the Israelites,
16:21 **r** of the Israelites—all their sins—
Nu 14:18 in love and forgiving sin and **r**.
Dt 13: 5 because he preached **r** against the
Jos 22:16 an altar in **r** against him now?
22:22 in **r** or disobedience to the LORD,
24:19 not forgive your **r** and your sins.
1Sa 15:23 For **r** is like the sin of divination,
24:11 I am not guilty of wrongdoing or **r**.
1Ki 12:19 Israel has been in **r** against the
16:20 and the **r** he carried out, are they
2Ki 8:22 To this day Edom has been in **r**
2Ch 10:19 Israel has been in **r** against the
21:10 To this day Edom has been in **r**
Ezr 4:15 a place of **r** from ancient times.
4:19 has been a place of **r** and sedition.
Ne 9:17 in their **r** appointed a leader in
Job 34:37 To his sin he adds **r**; scornfully he
Ps 106:43 bent on **r** and they wasted away in
Pr 17:11 An evil man is bent only on **r**;
Isa 1: 5 Why do you persist in **r**? Your whole
24:20 **r** that it falls—never to rise again.
58: 1 Declare to my people their **r** and to
59:13 **r** and treachery against the LORD,
Jer 5: 6 for their **r** is great and their
28:16 have preached **r** against the LORD.
29:32 he has preached **r** against me.
33: 8 all their sins of **r** against me.
Eze 21:24 to mind your guilt by your open **r**,
Da 8:12 Because of **r**, the host ⌊of the saints⌋
8:13 the **r** that causes desolation, and
Mt 26:55 "Am I leading a **r**, that you have
Mk 14:48 "Am I leading a **r**," said Jesus,
Lk 22:52 "Am I leading a **r**, that you have
23:14 who was inciting the people to **r**.
Jn 18:40 Now Barabbas had taken part in a **r**.
2Th 2: 3 until the **r** occurs and the man of
Heb 3: 8 your hearts as you did in the **r**,
3:15 your hearts as you did in the **r**."
Jude :11 have been destroyed in Korah's **r**.

Rebellious (Rebel, *Rebellious house*,)
Nu 17:10 to be kept as a sign to the **r**.
Dt 9: 7 you have been **r** against the LORD.
9:24 You have been **r** against the LORD
21:18 If a man has a stubborn and **r** son
21:20 "This son of ours is stubborn and **r**.
31:27 For I know how **r** and stiff-necked
31:27 If you have been **r** against the LORD
1Sa 20:30 "You son of a perverse and **r** woman!
Ezr 4:12 rebuilding that **r** and wicked city.
4:15 find that this city is a **r** city,
Ps 25: 7 the sins of my youth and my **r** ways;
66: 7 let not the **r** rise up against him.
68: 6 the **r** live in a sun-scorched land.
68:18 even from the **r**—that you, O LORD
78: 8 a stubborn and **r** generation,
107:17 became fools through their **r** ways
Pr 24:21 my son, and do not join with the **r**,
28: 2 a country is **r**, it has many rulers,
Isa 30: 9 These are **r** people, deceitful
50: 5 not been **r**; I have not drawn back.
Jer 5:23 these people have stubborn and **r**
Lam 1:20 disturbed, for I have been most **r**.
Eze 2: 3 to a **r** nation that has rebelled
2: 7 or fail to listen, for they are **r**.
12: 2 "Son of man, you are living among a **r**
12: 2 not hear, for they are a **r** people.
Hos 9:15 love them; all their leaders are **r**.
14: 9 in them, but the **r** stumble in them.
Zep 3: 1 Woe to the city of oppressors, **r** and
Tit 1:10 For there are many **r** people, mere

Rebellious house
Eze 2: 5 for they are a **r**—they will know
2: 6 by them, though they are a **r**.
2: 8 Do not rebel like that **r**; open your
3: 9 by them, though they are a **r**."
3:26 to rebuke them, though they are a **r**.
3:27 let him refuse; for they are a **r**.
12: 3 understand, though they are a **r**.
12: 9 "Son of man, did not that **r** of
12:25 For in your days, you **r**, I will
17:12 "Say to this **r**, 'Do you not know
24: 3 Tell this **r** a parable and say to
44: 6 Say to the **r** of Israel, 'This is

Rebels (Rebel)
Nu 20:10 "Listen, you **r**, must we bring you
Jos 1:18 Whoever **r** against your word and does
1Ki 11:24 became the leader of a band of **r**
11:24 of Zobah; the **r** went to Damascus,
Isa 1:23 Your rulers are **r**, companions of
1:28 **r** and sinners will both be broken,
46: 8 it in mind, take it to heart, you **r**.
57: 4 brood of **r**, the offspring of liars?
Jer 6:28 They are all hardened **r**, going about
Da 8:23 when **r** have become completely wicked,
Hos 5: 2 The **r** are deep in slaughter. I will
Ro 13: 2 Consequently, he who **r** against the
1Ti 1: 9 righteous but for lawbreakers and **r**,

Rebirth (Bear[1])
Tit 3: 5 of **r** and renewal by the Holy Spirit,

Rebuild (Build, Rebuilding, Rebuilt)
Jos 6:26 man who undertakes to **r** this city,
Ezr 5: 2 to **r** the house of God in Jerusalem.
5: 3 "Who authorised you to **r** this temple
5: 9 "Who authorised you to **r** this temple
5:13 a decree to **r** this house of God.
5:15 And **r** the house of God on its site.'
5:17 to **r** this house of God in Jerusalem.
6: 7 **r** this house of God on its site.
9: 9 He has granted us new life to **r** the
Ne 2: 5 are buried so that I can **r** it."
2:17 Come, let us **r** the wall of Jerusalem,
4:10 rubble that we cannot **r** the wall."
Ps 69:35 for God will save Zion and **r** the
102:16 For the LORD will **r** Zion and appear
Isa 9:10 but we will **r** with dressed stone;
45:13 He will **r** my city and set my exiles
58:12 Your people will **r** the ancient ruins
60:10 "Foreigners will **r** your walls, and
61: 4 They will **r** the ancient ruins and
Jer 33: 7 and will **r** them as they were before.
Da 9:25 **r** Jerusalem until the Anointed One,
Am 9:14 **r** the ruined cities and live in them.
Mal 1: 4 been crushed, we will **r** the ruins.
Mt 26:61 of God and **r** it in three days.
Ac 15:16 "'After this I will return and **r**
15:16 I will **r**, and I will restore it,
Gal 2:18 If I **r** what I destroyed, I prove

Rebuilding (Rebuild)
Ezr 2:68 **r** of the house of God on its site.
4:12 **r** that rebellious and wicked city.
5:11 and we are **r** the temple that was
Ne 2:18 They replied, "Let us start **r**." So
2:20 We his servants will start **r**, but as
4: 1 Sanballat heard that we were **r** the

Rebuilt (Rebuild)
Nu 21:27 be **r**; let Sihon's city be restored.
32:37 the Reubenites **r** Heshbon, Elealeh
32:38 They gave names to the cities they **r**.
Dt 13:16 a ruin for ever, never to be **r**.
Jdg 18:28 Danites **r** the city and settled there.
21:23 and **r** the towns and settled in them.
1Ki 9:17 Solomon **r** Gezer.) He built up Lower
16:34 In Ahab's time, Hiel of Bethel **r**
2Ki 14:22 He was the one who **r** Elath and
15:35 Jotham **r** the Upper Gate of the
21: 3 He **r** the high places his father
2Ch 8: 2 Solomon **r** the villages that Hiram
8: 5 He **r** Upper Beth Horon and Lower Beth
24:13 They **r** the temple of God according
26: 2 He was the one who **r** Elath and
26: 6 He then **r** towns near Ashdod and
27: 3 Jotham **r** the Upper Gate of the
33: 3 He **r** the high places his father
33:14 Afterwards he **r** the outer wall of
Ezr 4:21 city will not be **r** until I so order.
6: 3 **r** as a place to present sacrifices,
Ne 3: 1 went to work and **r** the Sheep Gate.
3: 3 The Fish Gate was **r** by the sons of
3:13 They **r** it and put its doors and
3:14 He **r** it and put its doors and bolts
3:15 He **r** it, roofing it over and putting
4: 6 we **r** the wall till all of it reached
6: 1 the rest of our enemies that I had **r**
7: 1 After the wall had been **r** and I had
7: 4 and the houses had not yet been **r**.
Job 12:14 What he tears down cannot be **r**; the
Isa 25: 2 a city no more; it will never be **r**.
44:28 "Let it be **r**," and of the temple,
Jer 30:18 the city will be **r** on her ruins,
31: 4 and you will be **r**, O Virgin Israel.
31:38 "when this city will be **r** for me
Eze 26:14 You will never be **r**, for I the LORD
36:10 will be inhabited and the ruins **r**.
36:33 your towns, and the ruins will be **r**.
36:36 I the LORD have **r** what was destroyed
Da 9:25 It will be **r** with streets and a
Zec 1:16 mercy, and there my house will be **r**.

Rebuke (Rebuked, Rebukes, Rebuking)
Lev 19:17 **R** your neighbour frankly so that you
Dt 28:20 confusion and **r** in everything you
Ru 2:16 her to pick up, and don't **r** her."
1Sa 2:25 did not listen to their father's **r**,
2Sa 22:16 laid bare at the **r** of the LORD,
2Ki 19: 3 day of distress and **r** and disgrace,
19: 4 and that he will **r** him for the words
Job 11: 3 Will no-one **r** you when you mock?
13:10 He would surely **r** you if you
20: 3 I hear a **r** that dishonours me, and
26:11 the heavens quake, aghast at his **r**.
Ps 6: 1 O LORD, do not **r** me in your anger or
18:15 of the earth laid bare at your **r**,
38: 1 O LORD, do not **r** me in your anger or
39:11 You **r** and discipline men for their
50: 8 I do not **r** you for your sacrifices
50:21 **r** you and accuse you to your face.
68:30 **R** the beast among the reeds, the
76: 6 At your **r**, O God of Jacob, both
80:16 fire; at your **r** your people perish.
104: 7 at your **r** the waters fled, at the
119:21 You **r** the arrogant, who are cursed
141: 5 let him **r** me—it is oil on my head.
Pr 1:23 If you had responded to my **r**, I
1:25 my advice and would not accept my **r**,
1:30 accept my advice and spurned my **r**,
3:11 discipline and do not resent his **r**,
9: 8 Do not **r** a mocker or he will hate
9: 8 **r** a wise man and he will love you.
13: 1 but a mocker does not listen to **r**.
15:31 He who listens to a life-giving **r**
17:10 A **r** impresses a man of discernment
19:25 learn prudence; **r** a discerning man,
25:12 a wise man's **r** to a listening ear.
27: 5 Better is open **r** than hidden love.
30: 6 Do not add to his words, or he will **r**
Ecc 7: 5 is better to heed a wise man's **r**
Isa 37: 3 day of distress and **r** and disgrace,
37: 4 and that he will **r** him for the words
50: 2 you? By a mere **r** I dry up the sea,
51:20 of the LORD and the **r** of your God.
54: 9 with you, never to **r** you again.
66:15 fury, and his **r** with flames of fire.
Jer 2:19 you; your backsliding will **r** you.
Eze 3:26 will be silent and unable to **r** them,
5:15 and in wrath and with stinging **r**.
Hos 2: 2 "**R** your mother, **r** her, for she is
Zec 3: 2 LORD said to Satan, "The LORD **r** you
3: 2 who has chosen Jerusalem, **r** you! Is
Mal 2: 3 "Because of you I will **r** your
Mt 16:22 Peter took him aside and began to **r**

Mk 8:32 took him aside and began to **r** him.
Lk 17: 3 "If your brother sins, **r** him, and if
19:39 "Teacher, **r** your disciples!
1Ti 5: 1 Do not **r** an older man harshly, but
2Ti 4: 2 **r** and encourage—with great patience
Tit 1:13 is true. Therefore, **r** them sharply,
2:15 Encourage and **r** with all authority.
Jude : 9 but said, "The Lord **r** you!"
Rev 3:19 Those whom I love I **r** and discipline.

Rebuked (Rebuke)

Ge 31:42 my hands, and last night he **r** you."
37:10 his father **r** him and said, "What is
1Sa 24: 7 With these words David **r** his men and
1Ch 16:21 them; for their sake he **r** kings:
Ne 13:11 I **r** the officials and asked them,
13:17 I **r** the nobles of Judah and said to
13:25 I **r** them and called curses down on
Ps 9: 5 You have **r** the nations and destroyed
105:14 them; for their sake he **r** kings:
106: 9 He **r** the Red Sea, and it dried up;
Mt 8:26 up and **r** the winds and the waves,
17:18 Jesus **r** the demon, and it came out
19:13 disciples **r** those who brought them.
20:31 The crowd **r** them and told them to be
Mk 4:39 He got up, **r** the wind and said to
8:33 looked at his disciples, he **r** Peter.
9:25 to the scene, he **r** the evil spirit.
10:13 them, but the disciples **r** them.
10:48 Many **r** him and told him to be quiet,
14: 5 And they **r** her harshly.
16:14 he **r** them for their lack of faith
Lk 3:19 when John **r** Herod the tetrarch
4:39 he bent over her and **r** the fever,
4:41 he **r** them and would not allow them
8:24 **r** the wind and the raging waters;
9:42 But Jesus **r** the evil spirit, healed
9:55 Jesus turned and **r** them,
18:15 the disciples saw this, they **r** them.
18:39 Those who led the way **r** him and told
23:40 the other criminal **r** him. "Don't you
1Ti 5:20 Those who sin are to be **r** publicly,
2Pe 2:16 he was **r** for his wrongdoing by a

Rebukes (Rebuke)

Job 22: 4 "Is it for your piety that he **r** you
Ps 2: 5 he **r** them in his anger and terrifies
Pr 9: 7 whoever **r** a wicked man incurs abuse.
28:23 He who **r** a man will in the end gain
29: 1 many **r** will suddenly be destroyed
Isa 17:13 when he **r** them they flee far away,
Na 1: 4 He **r** the sea and dries it up; he
Heb 12: 5 and do not lose heart when he **r** you,

Rebuking (Rebuke)

Ps 57: 3 saves me, **r** those who hotly pursue
2Ti 3:16 **r**, correcting and training in

Recab (Recabite, Recabites)

2Sa 4: 2 One was named Baanah and the other **R**;
4: 5 Now **R** and Baanah, the sons of Rimmon
4: 6 Then **R** and his brother Baanah
4: 9 David answered **R** and his brother
2Ki 10:15 **R**, who was on his way to meet him.
10:23 Jehu and Jehonadab son of **R** went
1Ch 2:55 the father of the house of **R**.
Ne 3:14 was repaired by Malkijah son of **R**,
Jer 35: 6 son of **R** gave us this command:
35: 8 Jonadab son of **R** commanded us.
35:14 'Jonadab son of **R** ordered his sons
35:16 The descendants of Jonadab son of **R**
35:19 'Jonadab son of **R** shall never fail

Recabite (Recab)

Jer 35: 2 "Go to the **R** family and invite them
35: 5 of the **R** family and said to them,

Recabites (Recab)

Jer 35: 3 his sons—the whole family of the **R**.
35:18 Jeremiah said to the family of the **R**,

Recah

1Ch 4:12 These were the men of **R**.

Recall (Recalled, Recalling)

2Pe 3: 2 I want you to **r** the words spoken in

Recalled (Recall)

Isa 63:11 his people **r** the days of old, the
Eze 23:19 as she **r** the days of her youth,
Jn 2:22 his disciples **r** what he had said.

Recalling (Recall)

Job 11:16 **r** it only as waters gone by.
2Ti 1: 4 **R** your tears, I long to see you, so

Recapture (Capture, Recaptured)

Eze 14: 5 I will do this to **r** the hearts of

Recaptured (Recapture)

2Ki 13:25 Jehoash son of Jehoahaz **r** from

Recede (Receded)

Ge 8: 5 The waters continued to **r** until the

Receded (Recede)

Ge 8: 1 over the earth, and the waters **r**.
8: 3 The water **r** steadily from the earth.
8: 8 **r** from the surface of the ground.
8:11 that the water had **r** from the earth.
Rev 6:14 The sky **r** like a scroll, rolling up,

Receive (Received, Receives, Receiving, Reception)

Ge 4:11 which opened its mouth to **r** your
32:20 I see him, perhaps he will **r** me."
Ex 25: 2 You are to **r** the offering for me
25: 3 These are the offerings you are to **r**
30:16 **R** the atonement money from the
Nu 18:23 They will **r** no inheritance among the
18:26 'When you **r** from the Israelites the
18:28 tithes you **r** from the Israelites.
26:54 each is to **r** its inheritance
32:19 We will not **r** any inheritance with
Dt 9: 9 I went up on the mountain to **r** the
19:14 the inheritance you **r** in the land
33: 3 down, and from you **r** instruction,
2Ki 12: 5 Let every priest **r** the money from
Ne 10:38 the Levites when they **r** the tithes,
Job 3:12 Why were there knees to **r** me and
35: 7 or what does he **r** from your hand?
Ps 24: 5 He will **r** blessing from the LORD and
27:10 forsake me, the LORD will **r** me.
110: 3 you will **r** the dew of your youth.
Pr 11:31 If the righteous **r** their due on
28:10 blameless will **r** a good inheritance.
Ecc 6: 3 and does not **r** proper burial,
8:10 go from the holy place and **r** praise
Isa 50:11 This is what you shall **r** from my
61: 7 my people will **r** a double portion,
Eze 16:61 be ashamed when you **r** your sisters,
Da 2: 6 you will **r** from me gifts and rewards
7:18 of the Most High will **r** the kingdom
11:34 they fall, they will **r** a little help,
12:13 to **r** your allotted inheritance."
Hos 14: 2 "Forgive all our sins and **r** us
Mt 10:41 a prophet will **r** a prophet's reward,
10:41 will **r** a righteous man's reward.
11: 5 The blind **r** sight, the lame walk,
19:29 sake will **r** a hundred times as much
20:10 first, they expected to **r** more.
21:22 If you believe, you will **r** whatever
Mk 4:16 the word and at once **r** it with joy.
10:15 anyone who will not **r** the kingdom of
10:30 will fail to **r** a hundred times as
Lk 7:22 seen and heard: The blind **r** sight,
8:13 Those on the rock are the ones who **r**
18:17 anyone who will not **r** the kingdom of
18:30 will fail to **r** many times as much in
18:42 Jesus said to him, "**R** your sight;
Jn 1:11 his own, but his own did not **r** him.
3:27 To this John replied, "A man can **r**
7:39 who believed in him were later to **r**.
16:24 **r**, and your joy will be complete.
20:22 them and said, "**R** the Holy Spirit.
Ac 1: 8 you will **r** power when the Holy
2:38 will **r** the gift of the Holy Spirit.
Ac 7:59 prayed, "Lord Jesus, **r** my spirit.
8:15 that they might **r** the Holy Spirit,
8:19 lay my hands may **r** the Holy Spirit."
19: 2 asked them, "Did you **r** the Holy
19: 3 what baptism did you **r**?" "John's
19:25 **r** a good income from this business.
20:35 It is more blessed to give than to **r**.
22:13 'Brother Saul, **r** your sight!' And at
26:18 so that they may **r** forgiveness of
Ro 5:17 how much more will those who **r** God's
8:15 For you did not **r** a spirit that
11:31 that they too may now **r** mercy as a
16: 2 I ask you to **r** her in the Lord in a
1Co 3:14 survives, he will **r** his reward.
4: 5 each will **r** his praise from God.
4: 7 you did not **r**? And if you did **r** it,
9:14 **r** their living from the gospel.
2Co 5:10 that each one may **r** what is due to
6: 1 you not to **r** God's grace in vain.
6:17 no unclean thing, and I will **r** you."
11: 4 or if you **r** a different spirit from
11:16 But if you do, then **r** me just as you
Gal 1:12 I did not **r** it from any man, nor was
3: 2 **r** the Spirit by observing the law,
3:14 might **r** the promise of the Spirit.
4: 5 we might **r** the full rights of sons.
Php 2:19 be cheered when I **r** news about you.
Col 3:24 since you know that you will **r** an
1Th 5: 9 to suffer wrath but to **r** salvation
1Ti 1:16 believe on him and **r** eternal life.
2Ti 2: 5 he does not **r** the victor's crown
2: 6 the first to **r** a share of the crops.
Heb 4:16 so that we may **r** mercy and find
9:15 that those who are called may **r** the
10:36 God, you will **r** what he has promised.
11: 8 he would later **r** as his inheritance,
11:13 They did not **r** the things promised;
11:19 he did **r** Isaac back from death.
Jas 1: 7 That man should not think he will **r**
1:12 he will **r** the crown of life that God
4: 3 you ask, you do not **r**, because you
1Pe 2:20 how is it to your credit if you **r** a
5: 4 you will **r** the crown of glory that
2Pe 1:11 you will **r** a rich welcome into the
1Jn 3:22 **r** from him anything we ask, because
Rev 4:11 our Lord and God, to **r** glory and
5:12 who was slain, to **r** power and wealth
13:16 to **r** a mark on his right hand or on
17:12 who for one hour will **r** authority
18: 4 you will not **r** any of her plagues;

Received (Receive)

Ge 33:10 now that you have **r** me favourably.
43:23 in your sacks; I **r** your silver.
47:22 because they **r** a regular allotment
Ex 18: 2 his father-in-law Jethro **r** her
36: 3 They **r** from Moses all the offerings
Nu 23:20 I have **r** a command to bless; he has
26:62 they **r** no inheritance among them.
32:18 Israelite has **r** his inheritance.
34:14 Manasseh have **r** their inheritance.
34:15 These two and a half tribes have **r**
Dt 18: 8 has **r** money from the sale of family
Jos 13: 8 the Gadites had **r** the inheritance
14: 1 the areas the Israelites **r** as an
14: 4 The Levites **r** no share of the land
16: 4 of Joseph, **r** their inheritance.
17: 1 who had **r** Gilead and Bashan because
17: 6 **r** an inheritance among the sons.
18: 2 who had not yet **r** their inheritance.
18: 7 **r** their inheritance on the east side
19: 9 So the Simeonites **r** their
21: 7 clan by clan, **r** twelve towns from
21:23 Also from the tribe of Dan they **r**
21:25 they **r** Taanach and Gath Rimmon,
1Ki 5: 8 Hiram sent word to Solomon: "I have **r**
10:14 The weight of the gold that Solomon **r**
2Ki 12: 4 the money **r** from personal vows and
19: 9 Now Sennacherib **r** a report that
19:14 Hezekiah **r** the letter from the
20:13 Hezekiah **r** the messengers and showed
1Ch 6:71 The Gershonites **r** the following:
6:71 **r** Golan in Bashan and also Ashtaroth,
6:72 from the tribe of Issachar they **r**
6:74 from the tribe of Asher they **r**

1Ch 6:76 from the tribe of Naphtali they **r**
6:77 of the Levites) **r** the following:
6:77 the tribe of Zebulun they **r** Jokneam,
6:78 they **r** Bezer in the desert, Jahzah,
6:80 from the tribe of Gad they **r** Ramoth
11: 6 up first, and so he **r** the command.
12:18 So David **r** them and made them
2Ch 9:13 The weight of the gold that Solomon **r**
21:12 Jehoram **r** a letter from Elijah the
Ezr 5: 5 Darius and his written reply be **r**.
8:30 the priests and Levites **r** the silver
Est 6: 3 Mordecai **r** for this?" the king asked.
Job 15:18 hiding nothing **r** from their
Ps 68:18 in your train; you **r** gifts from men,
Isa 37: 9 Now Sennacherib **r** a report that
37:14 Hezekiah **r** the letter from the
39: 2 Hezekiah **r** the envoys gladly and
40: 2 that she has **r** from the LORD's hand
47:13 All the counsel you have **r** has only
Hab 1: 1 oracle that Habakkuk the prophet **r**.
Mt 6: 2 they have **r** their reward in full.
6: 5 they have **r** their reward in full.
6:16 they have **r** their reward in full.
10: 8 Freely you have **r**, freely give.
13:20 The one who **r** the seed that fell on
13:22 The one who **r** the seed that fell
13:23 the one who **r** the seed that fell on
15: 5 **r** from me is a gift devoted to God,'
20: 9 hour came and each **r** a denarius.
20:10 each one of them also **r** a denarius.
20:11 they **r** it, they began to grumble
20:34 they **r** their sight and followed him.
25:16 The man who had **r** the five talents
25:18 the man who had **r** the one talent
25:20 The man who had **r** the five talents
25:24 "Then the man who had **r** the one
25:27 I would have **r** it back with interest.
Mk 7:11 otherwise have **r** from me is Corban'
10:52 Immediately he **r** his sight and
11:24 you have **r** it, and it will be yours.
Lk 6:24 for you have already **r** your comfort.
16:25 lifetime you **r** your good things,
16:25 while Lazarus **r** bad things, but now
18:43 Immediately he **r** his sight and
Jn 1:12 Yet to all who **r** him, to those who
1:16 all **r** one blessing after another.
9:15 asked him how he had **r** his sight.
9:18 had **r** his sight until they sent for
10:18 This command I **r** from my Father."
19:30 he had **r** the drink, Jesus said, "It
Ac 2:33 he has **r** from the Father the
5: 3 of the money you **r** for the land?
7:38 he **r** living words to pass on to us.
7:45 Having **r** the tabernacle, our fathers
7:53 you who have **r** the law that was put
8:17 on them, and they **r** the Holy Spirit.
10:47 **r** the Holy Spirit just as we have."
11: 1 Gentiles also had **r** the word of God.
17:11 for they **r** the message with great
21:17 Jerusalem, the brothers **r** us warmly.
21:40 Having **r** the commander's permission,
28:21 They replied, "We have not **r** any
Ro 1: 5 we **r** grace and apostleship to call
1:27 and **r** in themselves the due penalty
4:11 he **r** the sign of circumcision, a
4:13 his offspring **r** the promise that he
5:11 whom we have now **r** reconciliation.
8:15 but you **r** the Spirit of sonship.
11:30 have now **r** mercy as a result of
15:28 sure that they have **r** this fruit,
1Co 2:12 We have not **r** the spirit of the
6:19 **r** from God? You are not your own;
11:23 For I **r** from the Lord what I also
15: 1 which you **r** and on which you have
15: 3 For what I **r** I passed on to you as
2Co 1: 4 we ourselves have **r** from God.
11: 4 different spirit from the one you **r**,
11:24 Five times I **r** from the Jews the
Gal 1:12 **r** it by revelation from Jesus Christ.
Eph 4: 1 worthy of the calling you have **r**.
Php 4: 9 Whatever you have learned or **r** or
4:18 I have **r** full payment and even more;
4:18 now that I have **r** from Epaphroditus
Col 2: 6 then, just as you **r** Christ Jesus as
4:10 (You have **r** instructions about him;
4:17 the work you have **r** in the Lord."
1Th 2:13 when you **r** the word of God, which
2Th 3: 6 to the teaching you **r** from us.
1Ti 4: 3 which God created to be **r** with
4: 4 if it is **r** with thanksgiving,
Heb 2: 2 disobedience **r** its just punishment,
6:15 after waiting patiently, Abraham **r**
8: 6 the ministry Jesus has **r** is as
10:26 have **r** the knowledge of the truth,
10:32 days after you had **r** the light,
11:17 He who had **r** the promises was about
11:35 Women **r** back their dead, raised to
11:39 of them **r** what had been promised.
1Pe 2:10 **r** mercy, but now you have **r** mercy.
4:10 gift he has **r** to serve others,
2Pe 1: 1 have **r** a faith as precious as ours:
1:17 For he **r** honour and glory from God
1Jn 2:27 for you, the anointing you **r** from
Rev 2:27 I have **r** authority from my Father.
3: 3 Remember, therefore, what you have **r**
17:12 kings who have not yet **r** a kingdom,
19:20 who had **r** the mark of the beast
20: 4 had not **r** his mark on their

Receives (Receive)

2Sa 15: 4 and I would see that he **r** justice."
Job 27:13 a ruthless man **r** from the Almighty:
Pr 8:35 finds me finds life and **r** favour
18:22 is good and **r** favour from the LORD.
27:21 man is tested by the praise he **r**.
28:27 his eyes to them **r** many curses.
Eze 16:33 Every prostitute **r** a fee, but you
Mt 7: 8 For everyone who asks **r**; he who
10:40 "He who **r** you **r** me, and he who **r** me **r**
10:41 Anyone who **r** a prophet because he is
10:41 and anyone who **r** a righteous man
13:20 the word and at once **r** it with joy.
Lk 11:10 For everyone who asks **r**; he who
Ac 10:43 believes in him **r** forgiveness of sins
Gal 6: 6 Anyone who **r** instruction in the word
Heb 6: 7 it is farmed **r** the blessing of God.
Rev 2:17 on it, known only to him who **r** it.
14: 9 his image and **r** his mark on the
14:11 anyone who **r** the mark of his name."

Receiving (Receive)

2Sa 16:12 good for the cursing I am **r** today."
Ac 16:24 Upon **r** such orders, he put them in
Ro 9: 4 the covenants, the **r** of the law, the
2Co 7:15 **r** him with fear and trembling.
11: 8 I robbed other churches by **r** support
Php 4:15 of giving and **r**, except you only;
Heb 12:28 Therefore, since we are **r** a kingdom
1Pe 1: 9 for you are **r** the goal of your faith,
3Jn : 7 went out, **r** no help from the pagans.

Reception (Receive)

1Th 1: 9 report what kind of **r** you gave us.

Recesses

Job 28: 3 **r** for ore in the blackest darkness.
38:16 sea or walked in the **r** of the deep?

Recite (Recited, Reciting)

Dt 27:14 The Levites shall **r** to all the
Jdg 5:11 They **r** the righteous acts of the
Ps 45: 1 theme as I **r** my verses for the king;
50:16 "What right have you to **r** my laws or

Recited (Recite)

Dt 31:30 Moses **r** the words of this song from

Reciting (Recite)

Dt 32:45 Moses finished **r** all these words to

Reckless

Nu 22:32 your path is a **r** one before me.
Jdg 9: 4 used it to hire **r** adventurers,
Pr 12:18 **R** words pierce like a sword, but the
14:16 evil, but a fool is hotheaded and **r**.
Jer 23:32 my people astray with their **r** lies,

Reckoned (Reckoning)

Ge 21:12 Isaac that your offspring will be **r**.
48: 5 I came to you here will be **r** as mine;
48: 6 **r** under the names of their brothers.
Nu 18:27 Your offering will be **r** to you as
18:30 it will be **r** to you as the product
Ro 9: 7 Isaac that your offspring will be **r**."
Heb 11:18 Isaac that your offspring will be **r**."

Reckoning (Reckoned)

Isa 10: 3 What will you do on the day of **r**,
Hos 5: 9 will be laid waste on the day of **r**.
9: 7 coming, the days of **r** are at hand.

Reclaim (Claim, Reclaimed)

Isa 11:11 a second time to **r** the remnant that

Reclaimed (Reclaim)

Est 8: 2 which he had **r** from Haman, and

Recline (Reclined, Reclining)

Lk 12:37 will have them **r** at the table and

Reclined (Recline)

Lk 7:36 Pharisee's house and **r** at the table.
11:37 so he went in and **r** at the table.
22:14 and his apostles **r** at the table.

Reclining (Recline)

Est 7: 8 on the couch where Esther was **r**.
Mt 26: 7 his head as he was **r** at the table.
26:20 evening came, Jesus was **r** at the
Mk 14: 3 While he was in Bethany, **r** at the
14:18 While they were **r** at the table
Jn 12: 2 among those **r** at the table with him.
13:23 whom Jesus loved, was **r** next to him.

Recognise (Recognised, Recognises, Recognising, Recognition)

Ge 27:23 He did not **r** him, for his hands were
38:25 And she added, "See if you **r** whose
42: 8 his brothers, they did not **r** him.
Dt 33: 9 He did not **r** his brothers or
1Sa 24:11 Now understand and **r** that I am not
Job 2:12 they could hardly **r** him; they began
Mt 7:16 By their fruit you will **r** them. Do
7:20 Thus, by their fruit you will **r** them.
17:12 and they did not **r** him, but have
Lk 19:44 **r** the time of God's coming to you."
Jn 1:10 him, the world did not **r** him.
10: 5 they do not **r** a stranger's voice."
Ac 13:27 and their rulers did not **r** Jesus,
27:39 daylight came, they did not **r** the
1Jn 4: 2 This is how you can **r** the Spirit of
4: 6 This is how we **r** the Spirit of truth

Recognised (Recognise)

Ge 37:33 He **r** it and said, "It is my son's
38:26 Judah **r** them and said, "She is more
42: 7 Joseph saw his brothers, he **r** them,
42: 8 Although Joseph **r** his brothers, they
Jdg 18: 3 near Micah's house, they **r** the voice
Ru 3:14 but got up before anyone could be **r**;
1Sa 3:20 all Israel from Dan to Beersheba **r**
26:17 Saul **r** David's voice and said, "Is
1Ki 14: 2 won't be **r** as the wife of Jeroboam.
18: 7 Obadiah **r** him, bowed down to the
20:41 Israel **r** him as one of the prophets.
Jer 28: 9 **r** as one truly sent by the LORD
Lam 4: 8 soot; they are not **r** in the streets.
Mt 12:33 bad, for a tree is **r** by its fruit.
14:35 the men of that place **r** Jesus, they
Mk 6:33 many who saw them leaving **r** them and
6:54 got out of the boat, people **r** Jesus.
Lk 6:44 Each tree is **r** by its own fruit.
24:31 their eyes were opened and they **r**
24:35 **r** by them when he broke the bread.
Ac 3:10 they **r** him as the same man who used
12:14 she **r** Peter's voice, she was so
Ro 7:13 in order that sin might be **r** as sin,
Gal 2: 9 when they **r** the grace given to me.

Recognises (Recognise)

Job 11:11 Surely he **r** deceitful men; and when

Recognising (Recognise)

Lk 24:16 they were kept from **r** him.
1Co 11:29 drinks without **r** the body of the

Recognition (Recognise)

Est 6: 3 "What honour and **r** has Mordecai
1Co 16:18 Such men deserve **r**.
1Ti 5: 3 Give proper **r** to those widows who

Recoil (Recoils)

Ps 54: 5 Let evil **r** on those who slander me;

Recoils (Recoil)

Ps 7:16 The trouble he causes **r** on himself;

Recommendation (Recommended)

2Co 3: 1 letters of **r** to you or from you?

Recommended (Recommendation)

Est 6:10 Do not neglect anything you have **r**."

Recompense

Isa 40:10 with him, and his **r** accompanies him.
62:11 with him, and his **r** accompanies him.

Reconcile (Reconciled, Reconciliation, Reconciling)

Ac 7:26 He tried to **r** them by saying, 'Men,
Eph 2:16 in this one body to **r** both of them
Col 1:20 through him to **r** to himself all

Reconciled (Reconcile)

Mt 5:24 First go and be **r** to your brother;
Lk 12:58 try hard to be **r** to him on the way,
Ro 5:10 we were **r** to him through the death
5:10 how much more, having been **r**, shall
1Co 7:11 or else be **r** to her husband.
2Co 5:18 All this is from God, who **r** us to
5:20 you on Christ's behalf: Be **r** to God.
Col 1:22 now he has **r** you by Christ's

Reconciliation (Reconcile)

Ro 5:11 through whom we have now received **r**.
11:15 For if their rejection is the **r** of
2Co 5:18 Christ and gave us the ministry of **r**:
5:19 committed to us the message of **r**.

Reconciling (Reconcile)

2Co 5:19 that God was **r** the world to himself

Reconsecrated (Consecrate)

Da 8:14 then the sanctuary will be **r**."

Reconsider (Consider)

Job 6:29 Relent, do not be unjust; **r**, for my
Jer 18:10 then I will **r** the good I had

Record (Recorded, Recorder, Records)

1Ch 4:33 And they kept a genealogical **r**.
5: 1 **r** in accordance with his birthright,
7: 7 **r** listed 22,034 fighting men.
7: 9 Their genealogical **r** listed the
2Ch 24:27 and the **r** of the restoration of the
Ne 7: 5 I found the genealogical **r** of those
Est 6: 1 the **r** of his reign, to be brought in
Ps 56: 8 **R** my lament; list my tears on your
56: 8 scroll—are they not in your **r**?
87: 4 "I will **r** Rahab and Babylon among
130: 3 If you, O LORD, kept a **r** of sins,
Jer 22:30 This is what the LORD says: "**R** this
Eze 24: 2 "Son of man, **r** this date, this very
Hos 13:12 stored up, his sins are kept on **r**.
Mt 1: 1 A **r** of the genealogy of Jesus Christ
1Co 13: 5 angered, it keeps no **r** of wrongs.

Recorded (Record)

Ex 38:21 **r** at Moses' command by the Levites
Nu 33: 2 At the LORD's command Moses **r** the
Dt 28:61 not **r** in this Book of the Law,
Jos 24:26 Joshua **r** these things in the Book of
1Ki 8: 5 that they could not be **r** or counted.
1Ch 24: 6 a Levite, **r** their names in the
2Ch 5: 6 that they could not be **r** or counted.
20:34 **r** in the book of the kings of Israel.
26:22 **r** by the prophet Isaiah son of Amoz.
31:19 **r** in the genealogies of the Levites.
Ezr 8:34 entire weight was **r** at that time.
Ne 12:22 **r** in the reign of Darius the Persian.
12:23 were **r** in the book of the annals.
Est 2:23 All this was **r** in the book of the
6: 2 was found **r** there that Mordecai had
9:20 Mordecai **r** these events, and he sent
Job 19:23 "Oh, that my words were **r**, that they
Isa 4: 3 are **r** among the living in Jerusalem.
Jer 51:60 that had been **r** concerning Babylon.
Jn 20:30 which are not **r** in this book.
Rev 20:12 they had done as **r** in the books.

Recorder (Record)

2Sa 8:16 Jehoshaphat son of Ahilud was **r**;
20:24 Jehoshaphat son of Ahilud was **r**;
1Ki 4: 3 Jehoshaphat son of Ahilud—**r**;
2Ki 18:18 son of Asaph the **r** went out to them.
18:37 son of Asaph the **r** went to Hezekiah,
1Ch 18:15 Jehoshaphat son of Ahilud was **r**;
2Ch 34: 8 with Joah son of Joahaz, the **r**, to
Isa 36: 3 son of Asaph the **r** went out to him.
36:22 and Joah son of Asaph the **r** went to

Records (Record)

Ge 41:49 **r** because it was beyond measure.
Ex 6:16 their **r**: Gershon, Kohath and Merari.
6:19 clans of Levi according to their **r**.
Nu 1:20 the **r** of their clans and families.
1:22 the **r** of their clans and families.
1:24 the **r** of their clans and families.
1:26 the **r** of their clans and families.
1:28 the **r** of their clans and families.
1:30 the **r** of their clans and families.
1:32 the **r** of their clans and families.
1:34 the **r** of their clans and families.
1:36 the **r** of their clans and families.
1:38 the **r** of their clans and families.
1:40 the **r** of their clans and families.
1:42 the **r** of their clans and families.
Ru 4:10 among his family or from the town **r**.
1Ch 4:22 (These **r** are from ancient times.)
5: 7 according to their genealogical **r**:
5:17 were entered in the genealogical **r**
26:31 genealogical **r** of their families.
26:31 reign a search was made in the **r**,
29:29 they are written in the **r** of Samuel
29:29 **r** of Nathan the prophet and the **r**
2Ch 9:29 are they not written in the **r** of
12:15 are they not written in the **r** of
31:16 names were in the genealogical **r**
31:17 families in the genealogical **r**
31:18 listed in these genealogical **r**.
33:19 are written in the **r** of the seers.
Ezr 2:62 These searched for their family **r**,
4:15 In these **r** you will find that this
Ne 7:64 These searched for their family **r**,
Est 9:32 and it was written down in the **r**.
Eze 13: 9 in the **r** of the house of Israel,

Recount (Recounted)

Ps 40: 5 planned for us no-one can **r** to you;
79:13 to generation we will **r** your praise.
119:13 With my lips I **r** all the laws that

Recounted (Recount)

Ps 119:26 I **r** my ways and you answered me;

Recover (Recovered, Recovery)

2Ki 1: 2 see if I will **r** from this injury."
8: 8 him, 'Will I **r** from this illness?'
8: 9 ask, 'Will I **r** from this illness?'
8:10 'You will certainly **r**'; but the LORD
8:14 told me that you would certainly **r**."
8:29 King Joram returned to Jezreel to **r**
9:15 to **r** from the wounds the Arameans
20: 1 are going to die; you will not **r**."
2Ch 14:13 Cushites fell that they could not **r**;
22: 6 he returned to Jezreel to **r** from the
Isa 38: 1 are going to die; you will not **r**."
38:21 it to the boil, and he will **r**."
Eze 7:13 The seller will not **r** the land he

Recovered (Recover)

Ge 14:16 He **r** all the goods and brought back
38:12 When Judah had **r** from his grief, he
1Sa 30:18 David **r** everything the Amalekites
30:22 share with them the plunder we **r**.
2Sa 14:14 which cannot be **r**, so we must die.
2Ki 13:25 and so he **r** the Israelite towns.
14:28 including how he **r** for Israel both
16: 6 At that time, Rezin king of Aram **r**
20: 7 applied it to the boil, and he **r**.
Jer 41:16 survivors from Mizpah whom he had **r**
Eze 38: 8 invade a land that has **r** from war,
Rev 18:14 have vanished, never to be **r**.'

Recovery (Recover)

Isa 38: 9 of Judah after his illness and **r**:
39: 1 he had heard of his illness and **r**.
Lk 4:18 and **r** of sight for the blind,
Ro 11:11 fall beyond **r**? Not at all! Rather,

Rectangular

1Ki 7: 5 All the doorways had **r** frames; they
Eze 41:21 sanctuary had a **r** door-frame,

Red (Red Sea, Reddish)

Ge 25:25 The first to come out was **r**, and his
25:30 let me have some of that **r** stew!
Ex 25: 5 ram skins dyed **r** and hides of
26:14 tent a covering of ram skins dyed **r**,
35: 7 ram skins dyed **r** and hides of
35:23 ram skins dyed **r** or hides of
36:19 tent a covering of ram skins dyed **r**,
39:34 the covering of ram skins dyed **r**,
Lev 11:14 the **r** kite, any kind of black kite,
Nu 19: 2 **r** heifer without defect or blemish
Dt 14:13 the **r** kite, the black kite, any kind
2Ki 3:22 way, the water looked **r**—like blood.
Job 16:16 My face is **r** with weeping, deep
Pr 23:31 Do not gaze at wine when it is **r**,
Isa 1:18 snow; though they are **r** as crimson,
63: 2 Why are your garments **r**, like those
Jer 22:14 it with cedar and decorates it in **r**.
Eze 23:14 figures of Chaldeans portrayed in **r**,
Na 2: 3 The shields of his soldiers are **r**;
Zec 1: 8 me was a man riding a **r** horse!
1: 8 him were **r**, brown and white horses.
6: 2 The first chariot had **r** horses, the
Mt 16: 2 be fair weather, for the sky is **r**,'
16: 3 for the sky is **r** and overcast.
Rev 6: 4 another horse came out, a fiery **r**
6:12 hair, the whole moon turned blood **r**,
9:17 **r**, dark blue, and yellow as sulphur.
12: 3 an enormous **r** dragon with seven

Red Sea

Sometimes called "Sea of Reeds" as this is an alternative translation of the Hebrew expression. Stretch of water separating Arabia from Egypt and Ethiopia. Locusts sent upon Egypt were carried away to here (Ex 10:19). When Moses led the Israelites out of Egypt, its waters parted for them to cross over (Ex 14:16; Jos 2:10; 4:23) and then returned to drown the pursuing Egyptians (Ex 15:4; Dt 11:4; 24:6–7). The southern border of the promised land (Ex 23:31) and an important trade route for Israel (1Ki 9:26).

Ex 10:19 and carried them into the **R**.
13:18 the desert road towards the **R**.
15: 4 officers are drowned in the **R**.
15:22 Moses led Israel from the **R** and
23:31 **R** to the Sea of the Philistines,
Nu 14:25 along the route to the **R**."
21: 4 route to the **R**, to go round Edom.
33:10 They left Elim and camped by the **R**
33:11 They left the **R** and camped in the
Dt 1:40 along the route to the **R**."

Dt 2: 1 along the route of the **R**, as the
11: 4 with the waters of the **R** Sea as they
Jos 2:10 the LORD dried up the water of the **R**
4:23 just what he had done to the **R**
24: 6 and horsemen as far as the **R**.
Jdg 11:16 to the **R** and on to Kadesh.
1Ki 9:26 in Edom, on the shore of the **R**.
Ne 9: 9 you heard their cry at the **R**.
Ps 106: 7 they rebelled by the sea, the **R**.
106: 9 He rebuked the **R**, and it dried up;
106:22 of Ham and awesome deeds by the **R**.
136:13 to him who divided the **R** asunder
136:15 Pharaoh and his army into the **R**
Jer 49:21 their cry will resound to the **R**.
Ac 7:36 at the **R** and for forty years in
Heb 11:29 through the **R** as on dry land;

Reddish (Red)
Lev 13:49 is greenish or **r**, it is a spreading
14:37 it has greenish or **r** depressions

Reddish-white (Red, White)
Lev 13:19 a white swelling or **r** spot appears,
13:24 a **r** or white spot appears in the raw
13:42 if he has a **r** sore on his bald head
13:43 **r** like an infectious skin disease,

Redeem (Kinsman-redeemer, Kinsman-redeemers, Redeemable, Redeemed, Redeemer, Redeems, Redemption)
Ex 6: 6 will **r** you with an outstretched arm
13:13 **R** with a lamb every firstborn donkey,
13:13 if you do not **r** it, break its neck.
13:13 **R** every firstborn among your sons.
13:15 and **r** each of my firstborn sons.'
21:30 he may **r** his life by paying whatever
34:20 **R** the firstborn donkey with a lamb,
34:20 if you do not **r** it, break its neck.
34:20 **R** all your firstborn sons. "No-one
Lev 25:25 and **r** what his countryman has sold.
25:26 If, however, a man has no-one to **r**
25:26 acquires sufficient means to **r** it,
25:29 During that time he may **r** it.
25:32 to **r** their houses in the Levitical
25:48 One of his relatives may **r** him:
25:49 in his clan may **r** him.
25:49 Or if he prospers, he may **r** himself.
27:13 If the owner wishes to **r** the animal,
27:19 dedicates the field wishes to **r** it,
27:20 If, however, he does not **r** the field,
27:27 If he does not **r** it, it is to be
Nu 3:46 To **r** the 273 firstborn Israelites
18:15 But you must **r** every firstborn son
18:16 are a month old, you must **r** them
18:17 "But you must not **r** the firstborn of
Ru 3:13 if he wants to **r**, good; let him **r**.
4: 4 If you will **r** it, do so. But if you
4: 4 "I will **r** it," he said.
4: 6 "Then I cannot **r** it because I might
4: 6 You **r** it yourself. I cannot do it."
2Sa 7:23 out to **r** as a people for himself,
1Ch 17:21 went out to **r** a people for himself,
Ps 25:22 **R** Israel, O God, from all their
26:11 I lead a blameless life; **r** me and be
31: 5 I commit my spirit; **r** me, O LORD,
44:26 Rise up and help us; **r** us because of
49: 7 No man can **r** the life of another or
49:15 God will **r** my life from the grave;
69:18 Come near and rescue me; **r** me
119:134 **R** me from the oppression of men,
119:154 Defend my cause and **r** me; preserve
130: 8 He himself will **r** Israel from all
Jer 15:21 **r** you from the grasp of the cruel."
31:11 For the LORD will ransom Jacob and **r**
32: 8 Since it is your right to **r** it and
Hos 7:13 I long to **r** them but they speak lies
13:14 the grave; I will **r** them from death.
Mic 4:10 There the LORD will **r** you out of the
Zec 10: 8 Surely I will **r** them; they will be
Lk 24:21 the one who was going to **r** Israel.
Gal 4: 5 to **r** those under law, that we might
Tit 2:14 who gave himself for us to **r** us from

Redeemable (Redeem)
Lev 25:33 the property of the Levites is **r**

Redeemed (Redeem)
Ex 15:13 you will lead the people you have **r**.
21: 8 for himself, he must let her be **r**.
Lev 25:30 If it is not **r** before a full year
25:31 They can be **r**, and they are to be
25:54 "'Even if he is not **r** in any of
27:20 to someone else, it can never be **r**.
27:28 or family land—may be sold or **r**;
27:33 become holy and cannot be **r**.
Nu 3:49 the number **r** by the Levites.
Dt 7: 8 and **r** you from the land of slavery,
9:26 your own inheritance that you **r** by
13: 5 who brought you out of Egypt and **r**
15:15 Egypt and the LORD your God **r** you.
21: 8 whom you have **r**, O LORD, and do not
24:18 the LORD your God **r** you from there.
2Sa 7:23 your people, whom you **r** from Egypt?
1Ch 17:21 your people, whom you **r** from Egypt?
Ne 1:10 whom you **r** by your great strength
Job 33:28 He **r** my soul from going down to the
Ps 71:23 praise to you—I, whom you have **r**.
74: 2 you **r**—Mount Zion, where you dwelt.
77:15 With your mighty arm you **r** your
78:42 day he **r** them from the oppressor,
106:10 the hand of the enemy he **r** them.
107: 2 Let the **r** of the LORD say this—
107: 2 those he **r** from the hand of the foe,
Isa 1:27 Zion will be **r** with justice, her
29:22 who **r** Abraham, says to the house of
35: 9 But only the **r** will walk there,
43: 1 "Fear not, for I have **r** you; I have
44:22 Return to me, for I have **r** you."
44:23 for the LORD has **r** Jacob, he
48:20 "The LORD has **r** his servant Jacob.
51:10 sea so that the **r** might cross over?
52: 3 and without money you will be **r**."
52: 9 his people, he has **r** Jerusalem.
62:12 the **R** of the LORD; and you will be
63: 9 In his love and mercy he **r** them; he
Lam 3:58 O Lord, you took up my case; you **r**
Mic 6: 4 out of Egypt and **r** you from the
Lk 1:68 he has come and has **r** his people.
Gal 3:13 Christ **r** us from the curse of the
3:14 He **r** us in order that the blessing
1Pe 1:18 were **r** from the empty way of life
Rev 14: 3 who had been **r** from the earth.

Redeemer (Redeem)
Job 19:25 I know that my **R** lives, and that in
Ps 19:14 O LORD, my Rock and my **R**.
78:35 Rock, that God Most High was their **R**.
Isa 41:14 LORD, your **R**, the Holy One of Israel.
43:14 This is what the LORD says—your **R**,
44: 6 the LORD says—Israel's King and **R**,
44:24 "This is what the LORD says—your **R**,
47: 4 Our **R**—the LORD Almighty is his name
48:17 This is what the LORD says—your **R**,
49: 7 This is what the LORD says—the **R**
49:26 your **R**, the Mighty One of Jacob."
54: 5 the Holy One of Israel is your **R**;
54: 8 on you," says the LORD your **R**.
59:20 "The **R** will come to Zion, to those
60:16 your **R**, the Mighty One of Jacob.
63:16 our **R** from of old is your name.
Jer 50:34 Yet their **R** is strong; the LORD

Redeems (Redeem)
Lev 27:15 If the man who dedicates his house **r**
27:31 If a man **r** any of his tithe, he must
Ps 34:22 The LORD **r** his servants; no-one will
103: 4 who **r** your life from the pit and

Redemption (Redeem)
Lev 25:24 must provide for the **r** of the land.
25:29 of **r** a full year after its sale.
25:48 he retains the right of **r** after he
25:51 he must pay for his **r** a larger share
25:52 that and pay for his **r** accordingly.
Nu 3:48 Give the money for the **r** of the
3:49 Moses collected the **r** money from
3:51 Moses gave the **r** money to Aaron and
18:16 you must redeem them at the **r** price
Ru 4: 7 for the **r** and transfer of property
Ps 111: 9 He provided **r** for his people; he
130: 7 love and with him is full **r**.
Isa 63: 4 and the year of my **r** has come.
Lk 2:38 forward to the **r** of Jerusalem.
21:28 because your **r** is drawing near."
Ro 3:24 the **r** that came by Christ Jesus.
8:23 as sons, the **r** of our bodies.
1Co 1:30 our righteousness, holiness and **r**.
Eph 1: 7 In him we have **r** through his blood,
1:14 **r** of those who are God's possession
4:30 you were sealed for the day of **r**.
Col 1:14 in whom we have **r**, the forgiveness
Heb 9:12 blood, having obtained eternal **r**.

Reduce (Reduced, Reduces)
Ex 5: 8 bricks as before; don't **r** the quota.
5:19 "You are not to **r** the number of
2Ki 10:32 began to **r** the size of Israel,
Job 11: 3 Will your idle talk **r** men to silence?
24:25 me false and **r** my words to nothing?"
Isa 41:15 them, and **r** the hills to chaff.
Jer 10:24 anger, lest you **r** me to nothing.

Reduced (Reduce)
Ge 47:21 Joseph **r** the people to servitude,
Ex 5:11 but your work will not be **r** at all.
Lev 27:18 Jubilee, and its set value will be **r**.
Job 30:19 me into the mud, and I am **r** to dust
Ps 79: 1 they have **r** Jerusalem to rubble.
89:40 and **r** his strongholds to ruins.
102: 5 of my loud groaning I am **r** to skin
Isa 25: 5 heat is **r** by the shadow of a cloud,
Eze 16:27 against you and **r** your territory;
28:18 and it consumed you, and I **r** you to
Am 5: 5 and Bethel will be **r** to nothing."

Reduces (Reduce)
Pr 6:26 for the prostitute **r** you to a loaf
Isa 40:23 and **r** the rulers of this world to

Reed (Reeds)
1Ki 14:15 be like a **r** swaying in the water.
2Ki 18:21 that splintered **r** of a staff, which
Isa 9:14 palm branch and **r** in a single day;
19:15 do—head or tail, palm branch or **r**.
36: 6 that splintered **r** of a staff, which
42: 3 A bruised **r** he will not break, and a
58: 5 only for bowing one's head like a **r**
Eze 29: 6 staff of **r** for the house of Israel.
Mt 11: 7 to see? A **r** swayed by the wind?
12:20 A bruised **r** he will not break, and a
Lk 7:24 to see? A **r** swayed by the wind?
Rev 11: 1 I was given a **r** like a measuring rod

Reeds (Reed)
Ge 41: 2 fat, and they grazed among the **r**.
41:18 sleek, and they grazed among the **r**.
Ex 2: 3 the **r** along the bank of the Nile.
2: 5 saw the basket among the **r** and sent
Job 8:11 marsh? Can **r** thrive without water?
40:21 hidden among the **r** in the marsh.
41:20 from a boiling pot over a fire of **r**.
Ps 68:30 Rebuke the beast among the **r**, the
Isa 19: 6 The **r** and rushes will wither,
35: 7 grass and **r** and papyrus will grow.

Reeked
Ex 8:14 into heaps, and the land **r** of them.

Reel (Reeled, Reeling, Reels)
Isa 28: 7 these also stagger from wine and **r**
28: 7 with wine; they **r** from beer,

Reelaiah
Ezr 2: 2 Jeshua, Nehemiah, Seraiah, **R**,

Reeled (Reel)
Ps 107:27 They **r** and staggered like drunken

Reeling (Reel)
Zec 12: 2 sends all the surrounding peoples **r**.

Reels (Reel)
Isa 24:20 The earth **r** like a drunkard, it

Re-entered (Enter)
Ne 2:15 back and **r** through the Valley Gate.

Re-established (Establish)
2Ch 29:35 of the temple of the LORD was **r**.

Refer (Referred, Referring)
1Jn 5:16 I **r** to those whose sin does not lead

Referred (Refer)
Gal 3:19 Seed to whom the promise **r** had come.

Referring (Refer)
Ex 4:26 of blood", **r** to circumcision.
Jn 13:18 "I am not **r** to all of you; I know

Refine (Refined, Refiner, Refiner's, Refining)
Jer 9: 7 "See, I will **r** and test them, for
Zec 13: 9 I will **r** them like silver and test
Mal 3: 3 and **r** them like gold and silver.

Refined (Refine)
1Ch 28:18 the weight of the **r** gold for the
29: 4 seven thousand talents of **r** silver,
Job 28: 1 silver and a place where gold is **r**.
Ps 12: 6 like silver **r** in a furnace of clay,
66:10 For you, O God, tested us; you **r** us
Isa 48:10 See, I have **r** you, though not as
Da 11:35 so that they may be **r**, purified and
12:10 made spotless and **r**, but the wicked
1Pe 1: 7 which perishes even though **r** by fire
Rev 3:18 I counsel you to buy from me gold **r**

Refiner (Refine)
Mal 3: 3 He will sit as a **r** and purifier of

Refiner's (Refine)
Mal 3: 2 like a **r** fire or a launderer's soap.

Refining (Refine)
Jer 6:29 but the **r** goes on in vain; the

Reflect (Reflected, Reflection, Reflects)
Isa 47: 7 things or **r** on what might happen.
2Co 3:18 we, who with unveiled faces all **r**
2Ti 2: 7 **R** on what I am saying, for the Lord

Reflected (Reflect)
Ecc 9: 1 I **r** on all this and concluded that

Reflection (Reflect)
1Co 13:12 Now we see but a poor **r** as in a

Reflects (Reflect)
Pr 27:19 water **r** a face, so a man's heart **r**
Ecc 5:20 He seldom **r** on the days of his life,

Reform (Reforms)
Jer 7: 3 the God of Israel, says: **R** your ways
18:11 and **r** your ways and your actions.'
26:13 Now **r** your ways and your actions and
35:15 your wicked ways and **r** your actions;

Reforms (Reform)
Ac 24: 2 has brought about **r** in this nation.

Refrain (Refrained)
Dt 23:22 if you **r** from making a vow, you will
1Sa 18: 8 Saul was very angry; this **r** galled
1Ki 22: 6 Ramoth Gilead, or shall I **r**?"
22:15 Ramoth Gilead, or shall I **r**?"
2Ch 18: 5 Ramoth Gilead, or shall I **r**?"
18:14 Ramoth Gilead, or shall I **r**?"
Job 16: 6 and if I **r**, it does not go away.
Ps 37: 8 **R** from anger and turn from wrath; do
Ecc 3: 5 a time to embrace and a time to **r**,
2Co 12: 6 But I **r**, so no-one will think more

Refrained (Refrain)
2Sa 12: 4 but the rich man **r** from taking one
Job 29: 9 the chief men **r** from speaking and

Refresh (Refreshed, Refreshes, Refreshing)
Jdg 19: 5 "**R** yourself with something to eat;
19: 8 the girl's father said, "**R** yourself.
2Sa 16: 2 and the wine is to **r** those who
SS 2: 5 Strengthen me with raisins, **r** me
Jer 31:25 I will **r** the weary and satisfy the
Phm :20 in the Lord; **r** my heart in Christ.
2Pe 1:13 I think it is right to **r** your memory

Refreshed (Refresh)
Ge 18: 5 so you can be **r** and then go on your
Ex 23:12 and the alien as well, may be **r**.
2Sa 16:14 And there he **r** himself.
Ps 68: 9 O God; you **r** your weary inheritance.
Pr 11:25 refreshes others will himself be **r**.
Ro 15:32 with joy and together with you be **r**.
1Co 16:18 For they **r** my spirit and yours also.
2Co 7:13 his spirit has been **r** by all of you.
2Ti 1:16 because he often **r** me and was not
Phm : 7 have **r** the hearts of the saints.

Refreshes (Refresh)
Pr 11:25 he who **r** others will himself be
25:13 him; he **r** the spirit of his masters.

Refreshing (Refresh)
Ac 3:19 times of **r** may come from the Lord,

Refuge (*Cities of refuge*, Refugees)
Nu 35:12 They will be places of **r** from the
35:15 These six towns will be a place of **r**
35:25 to the city of **r** to which he fled.
35:26 the city of **r** to which he has
35:28 **r** until the death of the high priest;
35:32 anyone who has fled to a city of **r**
Dt 23:15 If a slave has taken **r** with you, do
32:37 their gods, the rock they took **r** in,
33:27 The eternal God is your **r**, and
Jos 21:13 **r** for one accused of murder), Libnah,
21:21 of **r** for one accused of murder)
21:27 Golan in Bashan (a city of **r** for one
21:32 Kedesh in Galilee (a city of **r** for
21:38 Ramoth in Gilead (a city of **r** for
Jdg 9:15 come and take **r** in my shade; but if
Ru 2:12 wings you have come to take **r**."
2Sa 22: 3 my God is my rock, in whom I take **r**,
22: 3 He is my stronghold, my **r** and my
22:31 a shield for all who take **r** in him.
1Ch 6:57 were given Hebron (a city of **r**),
6:67 Shechem (a city of **r**), and Gezer,
Ps 2:12 Blessed are all who take **r** in him.
5:11 let all who take **r** in you be glad;
7: 1 O LORD my God, I take **r** in you; save
9: 9 The LORD is a **r** for the oppressed, a
11: 1 In the LORD I take **r**. How then can
14: 6 the poor, but the LORD is their **r**.
16: 1 me safe, O God, for in you I take **r**.
17: 7 who take **r** in you from their foes.
18: 2 my God is my rock, in whom I take **r**.
18:30 a shield for all who take **r** in him.
25:20 put to shame, for I take **r** in you.
31: 1 In you, O LORD, I have taken **r**; let
31: 2 be my rock of **r**, a strong fortress
31: 4 is set for me, for you are my **r**.
31:19 of men on those who take **r** in you.
34: 8 is the man who takes **r** in him.
34:22 be condemned who takes **r** in him.
36: 7 find **r** in the shadow of your wings.
37:40 them, because they take **r** in him.
46: 1 God is our **r** and strength, an
57: 1 on me, for in you my soul takes **r**.
57: 1 I will take **r** in the shadow of your
59:16 fortress, my **r** in times of trouble.
61: 3 For you have been my **r**, a strong
61: 4 take **r** in the shelter of your wings.
62: 7 on God; he is my mighty rock, my **r**.
Ps 62: 8 hearts to him, for God is our **r**.
64:10 in the LORD and take **r** in him;
71: 1 In you, O LORD, I have taken **r**; let
71: 3 Be my rock of **r**, to which I can
71: 7 to many, but you are my strong **r**.
73:28 my **r**; I will tell of all your deeds.
91: 2 I will say of the LORD, "He is my **r**
91: 4 and under his wings you will find **r**;
91: 9 even the LORD, who is my **r**—
94:22 my God the rock in whom I take **r**.
104:18 the crags are a **r** for the conies.
118: 8 is better to take **r** in the LORD than
118: 9 is better to take **r** in the LORD than
119:114 You are my **r** and my shield; I have
141: 8 in you I take **r**—do not give me
142: 4 have no **r**; no-one cares for my life.
142: 5 "You are my **r**, my portion in the
144: 2 my shield, in whom I take **r**, who
Pr 10:29 The way of the LORD is a **r** for the
14:26 and for his children it will be a **r**.
14:32 in death the righteous have a **r**.
22: 3 A prudent man sees danger and takes **r**
27:12 The prudent see danger and take **r**,
30: 5 a shield to those who take **r** in him.
Isa 4: 6 and a **r** and hiding-place from the
14:32 his afflicted people will find **r**."
25: 4 You have been a **r** for the poor, a **r**
27: 5 Or else let them come to me for **r**;
28:15 made a lie our **r** and falsehood
28:17 hail will sweep away your **r**,
30: 2 protection, to Egypt's shade for **r**.
32: 2 the wind and a **r** from the storm,
33:16 **r** will be the mountain fortress.
57:13 But the man who makes me his **r** will
Jer 16:19 my strength and my fortress, my **r** in
17:17 you are my **r** in the day of disaster.
21:13 against us? Who can enter our **r**?"
Joel 3:16 But the LORD will be a **r** for his
Na 1: 7 The LORD is good, a **r** in times of
3:11 hiding and seek **r** from the enemy.

Refugees (Refuge)
Isa 16: 3 the fugitives, do not betray the **r**.
Jer 50:28 Listen to the fugitives and **r** from

Refund
Lev 25:27 **r** the balance to the man to whom he

Refusal (Refuse[1])
Mk 16:14 their stubborn **r** to believe those

Refuse[1] (Refusal, Refused, Refuses, Refusing)
Ge 23: 6 None of us will **r** you his tomb for
24:41 even if they **r** to give her to you
Ex 8: 2 If you **r** to let them go, I will
9: 2 If you **r** to let them go and continue
10: 3 'How long will you **r** to humble
10: 4 If you **r** to let them go, I will
11: 9 "Pharaoh will **r** to listen to you—so
16:28 "How long will you **r** to keep my
Lev 26:21 towards me and **r** to listen to me,
Nu 14:11 long will they **r** to believe in me,
Dt 20:12 If they **r** to make peace and they
1Ki 2:16 Do not **r** me." "You may make it," she
2:17 he will not **r** you—to give me
2:20 "Do not **r** me." The king replied,
2:20 it, my mother; I will not **r** you."
20: 7 and my gold, I did not **r** him."
2Ki 2:17 until he was too ashamed to **r**.
Job 6: 7 I **r** to touch it; such food makes me
34:33 when you **r** to repent? You must
Ps 26: 5 and **r** to sit with the wicked.
141: 5 My head will not **r** it. Yet my prayer
Pr 6:35 **r** the bribe, however great it is.
21: 7 for they **r** to do what is right.
21:25 of him, because his hands **r** to work.
30: 7 O LORD; do not **r** me before I die:
Jer 3: 3 you **r** to blush with shame.
8: 5 cling to deceit; they **r** to return.
9: 6 deceit they **r** to acknowledge me,"
13:10 These wicked people, who **r** to listen
25:28 if they **r** to take the cup from your
38:21 if you **r** to surrender, this is what

Eze 3:27 and whoever will **r** let him **r**; for
Hos 11: 5 over them because they **r** to repent?
Mk 6:26 guests, he did not want to **r** her.
Jn 5:40 yet you **r** to come to me to have life.
19:10 "Do you **r** to speak to me?" Pilate
Ac 25:11 deserving death, I do not **r** to die.
1Co 16:11 No-one, then, should **r** to accept him.
Heb 12:25 See to it that you do not **r** him who
Rev 11: 9 on their bodies and **r** them burial.

Refuse[2]

2Ki 9:37 Jezebel's body will be like **r** on the
Ps 83:10 and became like **r** on the ground.
Isa 5:25 bodies are like **r** in the streets.
Jer 8: 2 will be like **r** lying on the ground.
9:22 will lie like **r** on the open field,
16: 4 will be like **r** lying on the ground.
25:33 will be like **r** lying on the ground.
Lam 3:45 You have made us scum and **r** among
1Co 4:13 of the earth, the **r** of the world.

Refused (Refuse[1])

Ge 37:35 him, but he **r** to be comforted.
39: 8 he **r**. "With me in charge," he told
39:10 he **r** to go to bed with her or even
48:19 his father **r** and said, "I know, my
Ex 4:23 But you **r** to let him go; so I will
13:15 Pharaoh stubbornly **r** to let us go,
Nu 20:21 Since Edom **r** to let them go through
22:13 LORD has **r** to let me go with you."
22:14 and said, "Balaam **r** to come with us.
Dt 2:30 Sihon king of Heshbon **r** to let us
Jdg 2:19 They **r** to give up their evil
11:17 also to the king of Moab, and he **r**.
1Sa 8:19 the people **r** to listen to Samuel.
28:23 He **r** and said, "I will not eat." But
2Sa 2:23 Asahel **r** to give up the pursuit; so
12:17 but he **r**, and he would not eat any
13: 9 him the bread, but he **r** to eat.
13:14 he **r** to listen to her, and since he
13:16 But he **r** to listen to her.
13:25 **r** to go, but gave him his blessing.
14:29 the king, but Joab **r** to come to him.
14:29 a second time, but he **r** to come.
23:16 But he **r** to drink it; instead, he
1Ki 12:16 all Israel saw that the king **r** to
20:35 me with your weapon," but the man **r**.
21: 4 lay on his bed sulking and **r** to eat.
21:15 Jezreelite that he **r** to sell you.
22:49 with your men," but Jehoshaphat **r**.
2Ki 5:16 even though Naaman urged him, he **r**.
15:16 because they **r** to open their gates.
1Ch 11:18 But he **r** to drink it; instead, he
2Ch 10:16 all Israel saw that the king **r** to
Ne 9:17 They **r** to listen and failed to
9:29 became stiff-necked and **r** to listen.
Est 1:12 command, Queen Vashti **r** to come.
3: 4 spoke to him but he **r** to comply.
Ps 77: 2 hands and my soul **r** to be comforted.
78:10 covenant and **r** to live by his law.
Ecc 2:10 desired; I **r** my heart no pleasure.
Jer 5: 3 crushed them but they **r** correction.
5: 3 harder than stone and **r** to repent.
11:10 who **r** to listen to my words.
Zec 7:11 "But they **r** to pay attention;
Mt 18:30 "But he **r**. Instead, he went off and
22: 3 them to come, but they **r** to come.
27:34 after tasting it, he **r** to drink it.
Lk 15:28 "The older brother became angry and **r**
18: 4 "For some time he **r**. But finally he
Ac 7:39 "But our fathers **r** to obey him.
14: 2 the Jews who **r** to believe stirred up
19: 9 some of them became obstinate; they **r**
2Th 2:10 **r** to love the truth and so be saved.
Heb 11:24 when he had grown up, **r** to be known
11:35 Others were tortured and **r** to be
12:25 If they did not escape when they **r**
Rev 13:15 **r** to worship the image to be killed.
16: 9 they **r** to repent and glorify him.
16:11 **r** to repent of what they had done.

Refuses (Refuse[1])

Ex 7:14 he **r** to let the people go.
22:17 If her father absolutely **r** to give
Dt 25: 7 "My husband's brother **r** to carry on
Pr 11:15 **r** to strike hands in pledge is safe.
Mt 18:17 If he **r** to listen to them, tell it
18:17 tell it to the church; and if he **r**
3Jn :10 he **r** to welcome the brothers.

Refusing (Refuse[1])

Jer 31:15 her children and **r** to be comforted,
50:33 hold them fast, **r** to let them go.
Da 9:11 law and turned away, **r** to obey you.
Mt 2:18 her children and **r** to be comforted,

Refute (Refuted)

Job 32: 3 to **r** Job, and yet had condemned him.
32:13 wisdom; let God **r** him, not man.'
Isa 54:17 **r** every tongue that accuses you.
Tit 1: 9 doctrine and **r** those who oppose it.

Refuted (Refute)

Ac 18:28 For he vigorously **r** the Jews in

Regain (Gain, Regained)

1Sa 29: 4 How better could he **r** his master's
1Ki 12:21 to **r** the kingdom for Rehoboam son of
2Ch 11: 1 and to **r** the kingdom for Rehoboam.
13:20 Jeroboam did not **r** power during the
Job 9:18 He would not let me **r** my breath but

Regained (Regain)

Ac 9:19 taking some food, he **r** his strength

Regard (Regarded, Regards)

Ge 31:15 Does he not **r** us as foreigners? Not
Lev 5:15 **r** to any of the LORD's holy things,
5:16 to do in **r** to the holy things,
11:35 and you are to **r** them as unclean.
19:23 tree, **r** its fruit as forbidden.
21: 8 **R** them as holy, because they offer
Nu 18:10 eat it. You must **r** it as holy.
Dt 33: 9 and mother, 'I have no **r** for them.
Jos 7: 1 in **r** to the devoted things;
1Sa 2:12 men; they had no **r** for the LORD.
Ezr 7:14 with **r** to the Law of your God,
Est 9:31 their descendants in **r** to their
Job 21:29 you paid no **r** to their accounts—
34:27 and had no **r** for any of his ways.
37:24 have **r** for all the wise in heart?"
Ps 28: 5 Since they show no **r** for the works
41: 1 Blessed is he who has **r** for the weak;
54: 3 my life—men without **r** for God.
74:20 Have **r** for your covenant, because
86:14 my life—men without **r** for you.
119:117 always have **r** for your decrees.
Isa 5:12 but they have no **r** for the deeds of
8:13 is the one you are to **r** as holy,
17: 8 and they will have no **r** for the
22:11 or have **r** for the One who planned it
26:10 and **r** not the majesty of the LORD.
Jer 24: 5 'Like these good figs, I **r** as good
33:24 and no longer **r** them as a nation.
Eze 44: 8 your duty in **r** to my holy things,
Da 11:37 He will show no **r** for the gods of
11:37 nor will he **r** any god, but will
Am 5:22 I will have no **r** for them.
Jn 16: 8 the world of guilt in **r** to sin
16: 9 in **r** to sin, because men do not
16:10 in **r** to righteousness, because I am
16:11 in **r** to judgment, because the prince
1Co 4: 1 then, men ought to **r** us as servants
14:20 In **r** to evil be infants, but in your
2Co 5:16 from now on we **r** no-one from a
Eph 4:22 You were taught, with **r** to your
Php 3: 5 Hebrews; in **r** to the law, a Pharisee;
Col 1:24 in **r** to Christ's afflictions,
2:16 or with **r** to a religious festival, a
1Th 5:13 Hold them in the highest **r** in love
2Th 3:15 Yet do not **r** him as an enemy, but
Heb 7:14 and in **r** to that tribe Moses said
11:20 Jacob and Esau in **r** to their future.
1Pe 4: 6 according to men in **r** to the body,
4: 6 according to God in **r** to the spirit.
5:12 With the help of Silas, whom I **r** as

Regarded (Regard)

Ex 11: 3 and Moses himself was highly **r** in
Dt 24:13 and it will be **r** as a righteous act
2Sa 16:23 Absalom **r** all of Ahithophel's advice.
2Ki 5: 1 sight of his master and highly **r**,
2Ch 32:23 he was highly **r** by all the nations.
Job 18: 3 Why are we **r** as cattle and
31:26 if I have **r** the sun in its radiance
Isa 40:15 they are **r** as dust on the scales; he
40:17 they are **r** by him as worthless and
Da 4:35 All the peoples of the earth are **r**
Hos 8:12 but they **r** them as something alien.
Mk 10:42 "You know that those who are **r** as
Ac 5:13 they were highly **r** by the people.
Ro 2:26 **r** as though they were circumcised?
9: 8 who are **r** as Abraham's offspring.
2Co 5:16 Though we once **r** Christ in this way,
6: 8 report; genuine, yet **r** as impostors;
6: 9 known, yet **r** as unknown; dying, and
Heb 11:26 He **r** disgrace for the sake of Christ

Regards (Regard)

Est 5: 8 If the king **r** me with favour and if
8: 5 "and if he **r** me with favour and
Ro 14: 6 He who **r** one day as special, does so
14:14 But if anyone **r** something as unclean,

Regem

1Ch 2:47 The sons of Jahdai: **R**, Jotham,

Regem-Melech

Zec 7: 2 of Bethel had sent Sharezer and **R**,

Regiment

Ac 10: 1 in what was known as the Italian **R**.
27: 1 who belonged to the Imperial **R**.

Region (Regions)

Ge 10:30 The **r** where they lived stretched
20: 1 from there into the **r** of the Negev
22: 2 you love, and go to the **r** of Moriah.
35:22 While Israel was living in that **r**,
36:20 the **r**: Lotan, Shobal, Zibeon, Anah,
45:10 You shall live in the **r** of Goshen
46:28 When they arrived in the **r** of Goshen,
46:34 to settle in the **r** of Goshen,
47:13 however, in the whole **r** because the
47:27 settled in Egypt in the **r** of Goshen.
Dt 2:18 you are to pass by the **r** of Moab
3: 4 **r** of Argob, Og's kingdom in Bashan.
3:13 (The whole **r** of Argob in Bashan used
3:14 took the whole **r** of Argob as far as
34: 3 the Negev and the whole **r** from the
Jos 7: 2 told them, "Go up and spy out the **r**.
10:40 Joshua subdued the whole **r**,
10:41 the whole **r** of Goshen to Gibeon.
11: 3 below Hermon in the **r** of Mizpah.
11:16 all the Negev, the whole **r** of Goshen,
13: 4 far as Aphek, the **r** of the Amorites,
16: 3 as far as the **r** of Lower Beth Horon
17:12 were determined to live in that **r**.
19:29 out at the sea in the **r** of Aczib,
Jdg 20: 6 to each **r** of Israel's inheritance,
2Sa 20:14 through the entire **r** of the Berites,
24: 6 They went to Gilead and the **r** of
2Ki 4:38 and there was a famine in that **r**.
10:33 the land of Gilead (the **r** of Gad,
1Ch 5:10 the entire **r** east of Gilead.
Ne 3:22 the priests from the surrounding **r**.
12:28 from the **r** around Jerusalem—from
Ps 78:12 the land of Egypt, in the **r** of Zoan.
78:43 Egypt, his wonders in the **r** of Zoan.
Isa 49:12 the west, some from the **r** of Aswan."
Eze 47: 8 flows towards the eastern **r** and
Mt 3: 5 Judea and the whole **r** of the Jordan.
4:25 **r** across the Jordan followed him.
8:28 other side in the **r** of the Gadarenes
8:34 pleaded with him to leave their **r**.
9:26 of this spread through all that **r**.
9:31 the news about him all over that **r**.
15:21 withdrew to the **r** of Tyre and Sidon.
16:13 Jesus came to the **r** of Caesarea
19: 1 he left Galilee and went into the **r**
Mk 1: 4 John came, baptising in the desert **r**

Mk 1:28 quickly over the whole **r** of Galilee.
5: 1 They went across the lake to the **r**
5:17 plead with Jesus to leave their **r**.
6:55 They ran throughout that whole **r** and
7:31 and into the **r** of the Decapolis.
8:10 and went to the **r** of Dalmanutha.
10: 1 **r** of Judea and across the Jordan.
Lk 4:26 in Zarephath in the **r** of Sidon.
8:26 sailed to the **r** of the Gerasenes
8:37 all the people of the **r** of the
Jn 11:54 Instead he withdrew to a **r** near the
Ac 13:49 the Lord spread through the whole **r**.
13:50 and expelled them from their **r**.
16: 6 the **r** of Phrygia and Galatia,
18:23 the **r** of Galatia and Phrygia,

Regions (Region)

Ge 36:40 clans and **r**: Timna, Alvah, Jetheth,
Jos 13: 2 **r** of the Philistines and Geshurites:
13: 6 **r** from Lebanon to Misrephoth Maim,
Eze 19: 8 him, those from **r** round about.
Joel 3: 4 O Tyre and Sidon and all you **r** of
Mk 3: 8 Jerusalem, Idumea, and the **r** across
Ro 15:23 place for me to work in these **r**,
2Co 10:16 the gospel in the **r** beyond you.
11:10 nobody in the **r** of Achaia will stop
Eph 4: 9 descended to the lower, earthly **r**?

Register (Registered, Registration)

Ps 87: 6 The LORD will write in the **r** of the
Lk 2: 3 everyone went to his own town to **r**.
2: 5 He went there to **r** with Mary, who

Registered (Register)

1Ch 9:22 They were **r** by genealogy in their
23:24 as they were **r** under their names
Ezr 8: 1 those **r** with them who came up with
8: 3 and with him were **r** 150 men;
8:20 All were **r** by name.

Registration (Register)

Ne 7: 5 the common people for **r** by families.

Regret

2Ch 21:20 He passed away, to no-one's **r**, and
2Co 7: 8 sorrow by my letter, I do not **r** it.
7: 8 Though I did **r** it—I see that my
7:10 leads to salvation and leaves no **r**,

Regrouped (Group)

2Sa 10:15 had been routed by Israel, they **r**.

Regular (Regularly)

Ge 47:22 because they received a **r** allotment
Ex 29:28 This is always to be the **r** share
Lev 6:18 It is his **r** share of the offerings
6:20 of fine flour as a **r** grain offering,
6:22 It is the LORD's **r** share and is to
7:34 their **r** share from the Israelites.
7:36 **r** share for the generations to come.
10:15 This will be the **r** share for you and
14:32 the **r** offerings for his cleansing.
15:19 "'When a woman has her **r** flow of
16:24 place and put on his **r** garments.
23: 7 a sacred assembly and do no **r** work.
23: 8 a sacred assembly and do no **r** work.
23:21 a sacred assembly and do no **r** work.
23:25 Do no **r** work, but present an
23:35 is a sacred assembly; do no **r** work.
23:36 the closing assembly; do no **r** work.
24: 9 their **r** share of the offerings made
Nu 4:16 the fragrant incense, the **r** grain
8:25 their **r** service and work no longer.
18: 8 sons as your portion and **r** share.
18:11 sons and daughters as your **r** share.
18:19 sons and daughters as your **r** share.
28: 3 as a **r** burnt offering each day.
28: 6 This is the **r** burnt offering
28:10 in addition to the **r** burnt offering
28:15 Besides the **r** burnt offering with
28:18 a sacred assembly and do no **r** work.
28:23 in addition to the **r** morning
28:24 in addition to the **r** burnt offering
28:25 a sacred assembly and do no **r** work.
Nu 28:26 a sacred assembly and do no **r** work.
28:31 in addition to the **r** burnt offering
29: 1 a sacred assembly and do no **r** work.
29:11 the **r** burnt offering with its grain
29:12 a sacred assembly and do no **r** work.
29:16 in addition to the **r** burnt offering
29:19 in addition to the **r** burnt offering
29:22 in addition to the **r** burnt offering
29:25 in addition to the **r** burnt offering
29:28 in addition to the **r** burnt offering
29:31 in addition to the **r** burnt offering
29:34 in addition to the **r** burnt offering
29:35 hold an assembly and do no **r** work.
29:38 in addition to the **r** burnt offering
2Ki 25:30 a **r** allowance as long as he lived.
2Ch 30: 3 able to celebrate it at the **r** time
30:16 they took up their **r** positions as
Ezr 3: 5 presented the **r** burnt offerings
Ne 10:33 for the **r** grain offerings and burnt
Job 1: 5 This was Job's **r** custom.
Jer 5:24 us of the **r** weeks of harvest.'
52:34 a **r** allowance as long as he lived,
Eze 41:17 on the walls at **r** intervals all
46:15 by morning for a **r** burnt offering.

Regularly (Regular)

Ex 29:38 **r** each day: two lambs a year old.
29:42 burnt offering is to be made **r**
30: 8 incense will burn **r** before the LORD
Lev 24: 8 is to be set out before the LORD **r**,
2Ki 25:29 his life ate **r** at the king's table.
1Ch 16: 6 blow the trumpets **r** before the ark
16:37 of the LORD to minister there **r**,
16:40 on the altar of burnt offering **r**,
23:31 They were to serve before the LORD **r**
2Ch 2: 4 setting out the consecrated bread **r**,
24:11 They did this **r** and collected a
Jer 52:33 his life ate **r** at the king's table.
Eze 39:14 "'Men will be **r** employed to cleanse
Ac 10: 2 those in need and prayed to God **r**.
Heb 9: 6 the priests entered **r** into the outer

Regulated (Regulation)

Ne 11:23 which **r** their daily activity.

Regulation (Regulated, Regulations)

Ne 8:18 with the **r**, there was an assembly.
Heb 7:16 a priest not on the basis of a **r**
7:18 The former **r** is set aside because it

Regulations (Regulation)

Ex 12:43 "These are the **r** for the Passover:
Lev 6: 9 'These are the **r** for the burnt
6:14 "'These are the **r** for the grain
6:25 'These are the **r** for the sin
7: 1 "'These are the **r** for the guilt
7:11 are the **r** for the fellowship
7:37 These, then, are the **r** for the burnt
11:46 the **r** concerning animals, birds
12: 7 "'These are the **r** for the woman who
13:59 **r** concerning contamination by
14: 2 "These are the **r** for the diseased
14:32 These are the **r** for anyone who has
14:54 These are the **r** for any infectious
14:57 These are the **r** for infectious skin
15:32 These are the **r** for a man with a
26:46 the laws and the **r** that the LORD
Nu 9: 3 with all its rules and **r**."
9:12 Passover, they must follow all the **r**.
9:14 in accordance with its rules and **r**.
9:14 You must have the same **r** for the
15:16 The same laws and **r** will apply both
30:16 These are the **r** the LORD gave Moses
35:24 of blood according to these **r**.
36:13 These are the commands and **r** the
Dt 12:28 Be careful to obey all these **r** I am
1Sa 10:25 Samuel explained to the people the **r**
1Ki 6:12 carry out my **r** and keep all my
8:58 decrees and **r** he gave our fathers.
2Ki 23: 3 **r** and decrees with all his heart and
1Ch 6:32 to the **r** laid down for them.
24:19 according to the **r** prescribed for
2Ch 34:31 **r** and decrees with all his heart and
Ne 9:13 You gave them **r** and laws that are
Ne 10:29 **r** and decrees of the LORD our Lord.
Est 9:32 Esther's decree confirmed these **r**
Eze 43:11 whole design and all its **r** and laws.
43:11 to its design and follow all its **r**.
43:18 These will be the **r** for sacrificing
44: 5 **r** regarding the temple of the LORD.
Lk 1: 6 commandments and **r** blamelessly.
Eph 2:15 the law with its commandments and **r**.
Col 2:14 with its **r**, that was against us and
2:23 Such **r** indeed have an appearance of
Heb 9: 1 Now the first covenant had **r** for
9:10 external **r** applying until the time

Rehabiah

1Ch 23:17 The descendants of Eliezer: **R** was
23:17 the sons of **R** were very numerous.
24:21 for **R**, from his sons: Isshiah was
26:25 His relatives through Eliezer: **R** his

Rehob

Nu 13:21 Zin as far as **R**, towards Lebo Hamath.
Jos 19:28 went to Abdon, **R**, Hammon and Kanah,
19:30 Ummah, Aphek and **R**. There were
21:31 Helkath and **R**, together with their
Jdg 1:31 or Aczib or Helbah or Aphek or **R**,
2Sa 8: 3 David fought Hadadezer son of **R**,
8:12 Hadadezer son of **R**, king of Zobah.
10: 8 while the Arameans of Zobah and **R**
1Ch 6:75 Hukok and **R**, together with their
Ne 10:11 Mica, **R**, Hashabiah,

Rehoboam (Rehoboam's)

Son of Solomon; succeeded him as king (1Ki 11:43; 2Ch 9:31). Refusal to ease burden on people led to breaking away of northern tribes under Jeroboam (1Ki 12; 2Ch 10). In his evil reign temple plundered by Egyptians (1Ki 14:21–28; 2Ch 12:9–16).

1Ki 11:43 And **R** his son succeeded him as king.
12: 1 **R** went to Shechem, for all the
12: 3 of Israel went to **R** and said to him:
12: 5 **R** answered, "Go away for three days
12: 6 King **R** consulted the elders who had
12: 8 **R** rejected the advice the elders
12:12 and all the people returned to **R**,
12:17 of Judah, **R** still ruled over them.
12:18 King **R** sent out Adoniram, who was in
12:18 King **R**, however, managed to get into
12:21 **R** arrived in Jerusalem, he mustered
12:21 the kingdom for **R** son of Solomon.
12:23 "Say to **R** son of Solomon king of
12:27 to their lord, **R** king of Judah.
12:27 will kill me and return to King **R**."
14:21 **R** son of Solomon was king in Judah.
14:25 In the fifth year of King **R**, Shishak
14:27 King **R** made bronze shields to
14:30 There was continual warfare between **R**
14:31 **R** rested with his fathers and was
15: 6 There was war between **R** and Jeroboam
1Ch 3:10 Solomon's son was **R**, Abijah his son,
2Ch 9:31 And **R** his son succeeded him as king.
10: 1 **R** went to Shechem, for all the
10: 3 Israel went to **R** and said to him:
10: 5 **R** answered, "Come back to me in
10: 6 King **R** consulted the elders who had
10: 8 **R** rejected the advice the elders
10:12 and all the people returned to **R**,
10:17 of Judah, **R** still ruled over them.
10:18 King **R** sent out Adoniram, who was in
10:18 King **R**, however, managed to get into
11: 1 **R** arrived in Jerusalem, he mustered
11: 1 and to regain the kingdom for **R**.
11: 3 "Say to **R** son of Solomon king of
11: 5 **R** lived in Jerusalem and built up
11:17 **R** son of Solomon for three years,
11:18 **R** married Mahalath, who was the
11:21 **R** loved Maacah daughter of Absalom
11:22 **R** appointed Abijah son of Maacah to
12: 2 in the fifth year of King **R**.
12: 5 the prophet Shemaiah came to **R** and
12:10 King **R** made bronze shields to
12:12 **R** humbled himself, the LORD's anger
12:13 King **R** established himself firmly in
12:15 warfare between **R** and Jeroboam.
12:16 **R** rested with his fathers and was

2Ch 13: 7 opposed **R** son of Solomon when he was
Mt 1: 7 Solomon the father of **R**, **R** the

Rehoboam's (Rehoboam)

1Ki 14:29 for the other events of **R** reign, and
2Ch 12: 1 After **R** position as king was
12:15 for the events of **R** reign, from

Rehoboth

Ge 26:22 He named it **R**, saying, "Now the LORD
36:37 Samlah died, Shaul from **R** on the
1Ch 1:48 Samlah died, Shaul from **R** on the

Rehoboth Ir

Ge 10:11 where he built Nineveh, **R**,

Rehum

Ezr 2: 2 Bilshan, Mispar, Bigvai, **R** and
4: 8 **R** the commanding officer and
4: 9 **R** the commanding officer and
4:17 The king sent this reply: To **R** the
4:23 of King Artaxerxes was read to **R**
Ne 3:17 by the Levites under **R** son of Bani.
10:25 **R**, Hashabnah, Maaseiah,
12: 3 Shecaniah, **R**, Meremoth,

Rei

1Ki 1: 8 Nathan the prophet, Shimei and **R** and

Reign (Reigned, Reigning, Reigns)

Ge 37: 8 "Do you intend to **r** over us? Will
Ex 15:18 The LORD will **r** for ever and ever."
Dt 17:20 Then he and his descendants will **r** a
32:25 in their homes terror will **r**.
1Sa 8: 9 king who will **r** over them will do."
8:11 "This is what the king who will **r**
11:12 'Shall Saul **r** over us?' Bring these
2Sa 21: 1 During the **r** of David, there was a
1Ki 1:35 sit on my throne and **r** in my place.
6: 1 in the fourth year of Solomon's **r**
11:41 for the other events of Solomon's **r**—
14:19 The other events of Jeroboam's **r**,
14:29 for the other events of Rehoboam's **r**,
15: 1 In the eighteenth year of the **r** of
15: 7 for the other events of Abijah's **r**,
15:23 for all the other events of Asa's **r**,
15:29 soon as he began to **r**, he killed
15:31 for the other events of Nadab's **r**,
16: 5 for the other events of Baasha's **r**,
16:11 soon as he began to **r** and was seated
16:14 for the other events of Elah's **r**,
16:20 for the other events of Zimri's **r**,
16:27 for the other events of Omri's **r**,
22:39 for the other events of Ahab's **r**,
22:45 the other events of Jehoshaphat's **r**,
22:46 even after the **r** of his father Asa.
2Ki 1:18 all the other events of Ahaziah's **r**,
8:16 began his **r** as king of Judah.
8:23 for the other events of Jehoram's **r**,
8:25 of Jehoram king of Judah began to **r**.
10:34 for the other events of Jehu's **r**,
11:21 seven years old when he began his **r**.
12:19 the other events of the **r** of Joash
13: 8 other events of the **r** of Jehoahaz
13:12 other events of the **r** of Jehoash
13:22 Israel throughout the **r** of Jehoahaz.
14: 1 of Joash king of Judah began to **r**.
14:15 other events of the **r** of Jehoash
14:18 for the other events of Amaziah's **r**,
14:28 for the other events of Jeroboam's **r**,
15: 1 of Amaziah king of Judah began to **r**.
15: 6 for the other events of Azariah's **r**,
15:11 The other events of Zechariah's **r**
15:15 The other events of Shallum's **r**, and
15:18 During his entire **r** he did not turn
15:21 for the other events of Menahem's **r**,
15:26 The other events of Pekahiah's **r**,
15:31 for the other events of Pekah's **r**,
15:32 of Uzziah king of Judah began to **r**.
15:36 for the other events of Jotham's **r**,
16: 1 of Jotham king of Judah began to **r**.
16:19 the other events of the **r** of Ahaz
18: 1 of Ahaz king of Judah began to **r**.
18:13 year of King Hezekiah's **r**,
2Ki 20:20 for the other events of Hezekiah's **r**,
21:17 for the other events of Manasseh's **r**,
21:25 for the other events of Amon's **r**,
22: 3 In the eighteenth year of his **r**,
23:28 for the other events of Josiah's **r**,
23:33 so that he might not **r** in Jerusalem,
24: 1 During Jehoiakim's **r**, Nebuchadnezzar
24: 5 for the other events of Jehoiakim's **r**
24:12 In the eighth year of the **r** of the
25: 1 in the ninth year of Zedekiah's **r**,
1Ch 4:31 their towns until the **r** of David.
5:10 During Saul's **r** they waged war
7: 2 During the **r** of David, the
13: 3 enquire of it during the **r** of Saul."
22: 9 Israel peace and quiet during his **r**.
26:31 In the fortieth year of David's **r** a
29:29 for the events of King David's **r**,
29:30 together with the details of his **r**
2Ch 3: 2 month in the fourth year of his **r**.
9:29 for the other events of Solomon's **r**,
12:15 for the events of Rehoboam's **r**, from
13: 1 In the eighteenth year of the **r** of
13:22 The other events of Abijah's **r**, what
15:10 of the fifteenth year of Asa's **r**.
15:19 the thirty-fifth year of Asa's **r**.
16: 1 In the thirty-sixth year of Asa's **r**
16:11 The events of Asa's **r**, from
16:12 In the thirty-ninth year of his **r**
16:13 in the forty-first year of his **r** Asa
17: 7 In the third year of his **r** he sent
20:34 The other events of Jehoshaphat's **r**,
22: 1 of Jehoram king of Judah began to **r**.
23: 3 "The king's son shall **r**, as the LORD
25:26 for the other events of Amaziah's **r**,
26:22 The other events of Uzziah's **r**, from
27: 7 The other events in Jotham's **r**,
28:26 The other events of his **r** and all
29: 3 month of the first year of his **r**,
32:32 The other events of Hezekiah's **r** and
33:18 The other events of Manasseh's **r**,
34: 3 In the eighth year of his **r**, while
34: 8 In the eighteenth year of Josiah's **r**,
35:19 the eighteenth year of Josiah's **r**.
35:26 The other events of Josiah's **r** and
36: 8 The other events of Jehoiakim's **r**,
Ezr 4: 5 entire **r** of Cyrus king of Persia
4: 5 to the **r** of Darius king of Persia.
4: 6 At the beginning of the **r** of Xerxes,
4:24 of the **r** of Darius king of Persia.
6:15 sixth year of the **r** of King Darius.
7: 1 during the **r** of Artaxerxes king of
8: 1 during the **r** of King Artaxerxes:
Ne 12:22 in the **r** of Darius the Persian.
Est 1: 3 in the third year of his **r** he gave a
2:16 Tebeth, in the seventh year of his **r**.
6: 1 the chronicles, the record of his **r**
Ps 68:16 the mountain where God chooses to **r**,
Pr 8:15 By me kings **r** and rulers make laws
Isa 9: 7 He will **r** on David's throne and over
24:23 **r** on Mount Zion and in Jerusalem,
32: 1 See, a king will **r** in righteousness
36: 1 year of King Hezekiah's **r**,
Jer 1: 2 thirteenth year of the **r** of Josiah
1: 3 through the **r** of Jehoiakim son of
3: 6 During the **r** of King Josiah, the
23: 5 a King who will **r** wisely and do what
26: 1 Early in the **r** of Jehoiakim son of
27: 1 Early in the **r** of Zedekiah son of
28: 1 the fourth year, early in the **r** of
33:21 a descendant to **r** on his throne.
35: 1 during the **r** of Jehoiakim son of
36: 2 to you in the **r** of Josiah till now.
49:34 in the **r** of Zedekiah king of Judah:
51:59 Judah in the fourth year of his **r**.
52: 4 in the ninth year of Zedekiah's **r**,
Lam 5:19 You, O LORD, **r** for ever; your throne
Da 1: 1 third year of the **r** of Jehoiakim
2: 1 In the second year of his **r**,
5:26 of your **r** and brought it to an end.
6:28 Daniel prospered during the **r** of
6:28 and the **r** of Cyrus the Persian.
8: 1 third year of King Belshazzar's **r**,
8:23 "In the latter part of their **r**, when
9: 2 in the first year of his **r**, I,
Hos 1: 1 kings of Judah, and during the **r** of
Am 6: 3 day and bring near a **r** of terror.
Zep 1: 1 the son of Hezekiah, during the **r** of
Lk 1:33 he will **r** over the house of Jacob
3: 1 In the fifteenth year of the **r** of
Ac 11:28 happened during the **r** of Claudius.)
Ro 5:17 **r** in life through the one man,
5:21 so also grace might **r** through
6:12 Therefore do not let sin **r** in your
1Co 15:25 For he must **r** until he has put all
2Ti 2:12 if we endure, we will also **r** with
Rev 5:10 God, and they will **r** on the earth."
11:15 and he will **r** for ever and ever."
11:17 great power and have begun to **r**.
20: 6 **r** with him for a thousand years.
22: 5 And they will **r** for ever and ever.

Reigned (Reign)

Ge 36:31 These were the kings who **r** in Edom
36:31 in Edom before any Israelite king **r**:
Nu 21:34 of the Amorites, who **r** in Heshbon."
Dt 1: 4 who **r** in Heshbon, and at Edrei had
1: 4 king of Bashan, who **r** in Ashtaroth.
3: 2 of the Amorites, who **r** in Heshbon."
4:46 who **r** in Heshbon and was defeated by
Jos 9:10 king of Bashan, who **r** in Ashtaroth.
12: 2 Sihon king of the Amorites, who **r** in
12: 4 who **r** in Ashtaroth and Edrei.
13:12 who had **r** in Ashtaroth and Edrei and
Jdg 4: 2 a king of Canaan, who **r** in Hazor.
1Sa 13: 1 he **r** over Israel for ⌊forty-⌋ two
2Sa 2:10 over Israel, and he **r** two years.
5: 4 king, and he **r** for forty years.
5: 5 In Hebron he **r** over Judah for seven
5: 5 and in Jerusalem he **r** over all
8:15 David **r** over all Israel, doing what
16: 8 of Saul, in whose place you have **r**.
1Ki 2:11 He had **r** for forty years over Israel
11:42 Solomon **r** in Jerusalem over all
14:20 He **r** for twenty-two years and then
14:21 and he **r** for seventeen years in
15: 2 he **r** in Jerusalem for three years.
15:10 he **r** in Jerusalem for forty-one
15:25 and he **r** over Israel for two years.
15:33 and he **r** for twenty-four years.
16: 8 and he **r** in Tirzah for two years.
16:15 Zimri **r** in Tirzah for seven days.
16:23 and he **r** for twelve years, six of
16:29 and he **r** in Samaria over Israel for
22:42 **r** in Jerusalem for twenty-five years.
22:51 and he **r** over Israel for two years.
2Ki 3: 1 of Judah, and he **r** for twelve years.
8:17 he **r** in Jerusalem for eight years.
8:26 and he **r** in Jerusalem for one year.
10:36 The time that Jehu **r** over Israel in
12: 1 he **r** in Jerusalem for forty years.
13: 1 and he **r** for seventeen years.
13:10 Samaria, and he **r** for sixteen years.
14: 2 **r** in Jerusalem for twenty-nine years.
14:23 and he **r** for forty-one years.
15: 2 **r** in Jerusalem for fifty-two years.
15: 8 in Samaria, and he **r** for six months.
15:13 and he **r** in Samaria for one month.
15:17 and he **r** in Samaria for ten years.
15:23 in Samaria, and he **r** for two years.
15:27 Samaria, and he **r** for twenty years.
15:33 he **r** in Jerusalem for sixteen years.
16: 2 he **r** in Jerusalem for sixteen years.
17: 1 in Samaria, and he **r** for nine years.
18: 2 **r** in Jerusalem for twenty-nine years.
21: 1 **r** in Jerusalem for fifty-five years.
21:19 and he **r** in Jerusalem for two years.
22: 1 **r** in Jerusalem for thirty-one years.
23:31 he **r** in Jerusalem for three months.
23:36 he **r** in Jerusalem for eleven years.
24: 8 he **r** in Jerusalem for three months.
24:18 he **r** in Jerusalem for eleven years.
1Ch 1:43 These were the kings who **r** in Edom
1:43 Israelite king **r**: Bela son of Beor,
3: 4 he **r** for seven years and six months.
3: 4 David **r** in Jerusalem for
18:14 David **r** over all Israel, doing what
2Ch 1:13 And he **r** over Israel.
9:30 Solomon **r** in Jerusalem over all
12:13 and he **r** for seventeen years in
13: 2 he **r** in Jerusalem for three years.
20:31 Jehoshaphat **r** over Judah. He was

2Ch 20:31 **r** in Jerusalem for twenty-five years.
21: 5 he **r** in Jerusalem for eight years.
21:20 he **r** in Jerusalem for eight years.
22: 2 and he **r** in Jerusalem for one year.
24: 1 he **r** in Jerusalem for forty years.
25: 1 **r** in Jerusalem for twenty-nine years.
26: 3 **r** in Jerusalem for fifty-two years.
27: 1 he **r** in Jerusalem for sixteen years.
27: 8 he **r** in Jerusalem for sixteen years.
28: 1 he **r** in Jerusalem for sixteen years.
29: 1 **r** in Jerusalem for twenty-nine years.
33: 1 **r** in Jerusalem for fifty-five years.
33:21 and he **r** in Jerusalem for two years.
34: 1 **r** in Jerusalem for thirty-one years.
36: 2 he **r** in Jerusalem for three months.
36: 5 he **r** in Jerusalem for eleven years.
36: 9 and he **r** in Jerusalem for three
36:11 he **r** in Jerusalem for eleven years.
Est 1: 2 At that time King Xerxes **r** from his
Jer 37: 1 he **r** in place of Jehoiachin son of
52: 1 he **r** in Jerusalem for eleven years.
Ro 5:14 Nevertheless, death **r** from the time
5:17 death **r** through that one man, how
5:21 that, just as sin **r** in death, so
Rev 20: 4 **r** with Christ for a thousand years.

Reigning (Reign)

Mt 2:22 when he heard that Archelaus was **r**

Reigns (Reign)

1Sa 12:14 and if both you and the king who **r**
1Ki 15:16 king of Israel throughout their **r**.
15:32 king of Israel throughout their **r**.
1Ch 5:17 the **r** of Jotham king of Judah
16:31 say among the nations, "The LORD **r**!
Ps 9: 7 The LORD **r** for ever; he has
47: 8 God **r** over the nations; God is
93: 1 The LORD **r**, he is robed in majesty;
96:10 Say among the nations, "The LORD **r**."
97: 1 The LORD **r**, let the earth be glad;
99: 1 The LORD **r**, let the nations tremble;
146:10 The LORD **r** for ever, your God,
Isa 1: 1 of Amoz saw during the **r** of Uzziah,
52: 7 who say to Zion, "Your God **r**!"
Hos 1: 1 son of Beeri during the **r** of Uzziah,
Mic 1: 1 of Moresheth during the **r** of Jotham,
Lk 22:53 this is your hour—when darkness **r**."
Rev 19: 6 For our Lord God Almighty **r**.

Reimburse

Lk 10:35 'and when I return, I will **r** you for

Rein

Job 10: 1 I will give free **r** to my complaint
Jas 1:26 not keep a tight **r** on his tongue,

Reinforce (Reinforced, Reinforcements)

Jer 51:12 the walls of Babylon! **R** the guard,

Reinforced (Reinforce)

2Ch 24:13 to its original design and **r** it.
32: 5 **r** the supporting terraces of the

Reinforcements (Reinforce)

Isa 43:17 the army and **r** together, and they

Reject (Rejected, Rejecting, Rejection, Rejects)

Lev 26:15 if you **r** my decrees and abhor my
26:44 I will not **r** them or abhor them so
1Sa 12:22 name the LORD will not **r** his people,
1Ki 9: 7 will **r** this temple I have
2Ki 23:27 and I will **r** Jerusalem, the city I
1Ch 28: 9 forsake him, he will **r** you for ever.
2Ch 6:42 O LORD God, do not **r** your anointed
7:20 which I have given them, and will **r**
Job 8:20 "Surely God does not **r** a blameless
Ps 27: 9 **r** me or forsake me, O God my Saviour.
36: 4 course and does not **r** what is wrong.
44:23 Rouse yourself! Do not **r** us for ever.
77: 7 "Will the Lord **r** for ever? Will he
88:14 Why, O LORD, do you **r** me and hide
Ps 94:14 For the LORD will not **r** his people;
119:118 You **r** all who stray from your
132:10 servant, do not **r** your anointed one.
Isa 7:15 to **r** the wrong and choose the right.
7:16 before the boy knows enough to **r** the
31: 7 of you will **r** the idols of silver
Jer 31:37 will I **r** all the descendants of
33:26 I will **r** the descendants of Jacob
Hos 4: 6 I also **r** you as my priests; because
9:17 My God will **r** them because they have
Lk 6:22 insult you and **r** your name as evil,
Ac 13:46 Since you **r** it and do not consider
Ro 2: 8 and who **r** the truth and follow evil,
11: 1 I ask then: Did God **r** his people? By
11: 2 God did not **r** his people, whom he
1Th 4: 8 instruction does not **r** man but God,
Tit 1:14 commands of those who **r** the truth.
Jude : 8 **r** authority and slander celestial

Rejected (Reject)

Lev 26:43 **r** my laws and abhorred my decrees.
Nu 11:20 it—because you have **r** the LORD,
14:31 in to enjoy the land you have **r**.
Dt 32:15 made him and **r** the Rock his Saviour.
32:19 The LORD saw this and **r** them because
1Sa 8: 7 **r**, but they have **r** me as their king.
10:19 you have now **r** your God, who saves
15:23 Because you have **r** the word of the
15:23 of the LORD, he has **r** you as king."
15:26 You have **r** the word of the LORD, and
15:26 LORD has **r** you as king over Israel!"
16: 1 since I have **r** him as king over
16: 7 or his height, for I have **r** him.
1Ki 12: 8 Rehoboam **r** the advice the elders
19:10 The Israelites have **r** your covenant,
19:14 The Israelites have **r** your covenant,
2Ki 17:15 They **r** his decrees and the covenant
17:20 Therefore the LORD **r** all the people
2Ch 10: 8 Rehoboam **r** the advice the elders
11:14 had **r** them as priests of the LORD.
Ps 43: 2 Why have you **r** me? Why must I go
44: 9 now you have **r** and humbled us; you
60: 1 You have **r** us, O God, and burst
60:10 you, O God, you who have **r** us
66:20 Praise be to God, who has not **r** my
74: 1 Why have you **r** us for ever, O God?
78:59 very angry; he **r** Israel completely.
78:67 he **r** the tents of Joseph, he did not
89:38 you have **r**, you have spurned, you
108:11 you, O God, you who have **r** us
118:22 The stone the builders **r** has become
Pr 1:24 since you **r** me when I called and
Isa 5:24 for they have **r** the law of the LORD
8: 6 "Because this people has **r** the
14:19 out of your tomb like a **r** branch;
30:12 "Because you have **r** this message,
41: 9 I have chosen you and have not **r** you.
49:21 and barren; I was exiled and **r**.
53: 3 He was despised and **r** by men, a man
54: 6 young, only to be **r**," says your God.
Jer 2:37 for the LORD has **r** those you trust;
6:19 to my words and have **r** my law.
6:30 They are called **r** silver, because
6:30 because the LORD has **r** them."
7:29 for the LORD has **r** and abandoned
8: 9 Since they have **r** the word of the
14:19 Have you **r** Judah completely? Do you
15: 6 You have **r** me," declares the LORD.
33:24 'The LORD has **r** the two kingdoms he
Lam 1:15 "The Lord has **r** all the warriors in
2: 7 The Lord has **r** his altar and
5:22 unless you have utterly **r** us and are
Eze 5: 6 She has **r** my laws and has not
20:13 not follow my decrees but **r** my laws
20:16 they **r** my laws and did not follow my
20:24 they had not obeyed my laws but had **r**
Hos 4: 6 "Because you have **r** knowledge, I
8: 3 Israel has **r** what is good; an enemy
Am 2: 4 Because they have **r** the law of the
Zec 10: 6 will be as though I had not **r** them.
Mt 21:42 'The stone the builders **r** has become
Mk 8:31 many things and be **r** by the elders,
9:12 Son of Man must suffer much and be **r**?
12:10 builders **r** has become the capstone;
Lk 7:30 law **r** God's purpose for themselves,
Lk 9:22 many things and be **r** by the elders,
17:25 things and be **r** by this generation.
20:17 The stone the builders **r** has become
Ac 4:11 He is "'the stone you builders **r**,
7:35 Moses whom they had **r** with the words,
7:39 Instead, they **r** him and in their
1Ti 1:19 Some have **r** these and so have
4: 4 and nothing is to be **r** if it is
2Ti 3: 8 as the faith is concerned, are **r**.
Heb 10:28 Anyone who **r** the law of Moses died
12:17 to inherit this blessing, he was **r**.
1Pe 2: 4 to him, the living Stone—**r** by men
2: 7 The stone the builders **r** has become

Rejecting (Reject)

Dt 31:20 them, **r** me and breaking my covenant.
1Ki 12:13 **R** the advice given him by the elders,
2Ch 10:13 answered them harshly. **R** the advice

Rejection (Reject)

Ro 11:15 For if their **r** is the reconciliation

Rejects (Reject)

Isa 33:15 who **r** gain from extortion and keeps
Lk 10:16 he who **r** you **r** me; but he who **r** me **r**
Jn 3:36 but whoever **r** the Son will not see
12:48 There is a judge for the one who **r**
1Th 4: 8 Therefore, he who **r** this instruction

Rejoice (Joy, Rejoiced, Rejoices, Rejoicing)

Lev 23:40 and poplars, and **r** before the LORD
Dt 12: 7 your families shall eat and shall **r**
12:12 there **r** before the LORD your God,
12:18 you are to **r** before the LORD your
14:26 presence of the LORD your God and **r**.
16:11 **r** before the LORD your God at the
26:11 the aliens among you shall **r** in all
32:43 **R**, O nations, with his people, for
33:18 About Zebulun he said: "**R**, Zebulun,
2Sa 1:20 daughters of the uncircumcised **r**.
1Ch 16:10 hearts of those who seek the LORD **r**.
16:31 Let the heavens **r**, let the earth be
2Ch 6:41 may your saints **r** in your goodness.
20:27 them cause to **r** over their enemies.
Job 3:22 who are filled with gladness and **r**
22:19 "The righteous see their ruin and **r**;
Ps 2:11 Serve the LORD with fear and **r** with
5:11 who love your name may **r** in you.
9: 2 I will be glad and **r** in you; I will
9:14 Zion and there **r** in your salvation.
13: 4 and my foes will **r** when I fall.
14: 7 let Jacob **r** and Israel be glad!
31: 7 I will be glad and **r** in your love,
32:11 **R** in the LORD and be glad, you
33:21 In him our hearts **r**, for we trust in
34: 2 LORD; let the afflicted hear and **r**.
35: 9 my soul will **r** in the LORD and
39:13 Look away from me, that I may **r**
40:16 may all who seek you **r** and be glad
51: 8 let the bones you have crushed **r**.
53: 6 let Jacob **r** and Israel be glad!
63:11 the king will **r** in God; all who
64:10 Let the righteous **r** in the LORD and
66: 6 on foot—come, let us **r** in him.
68: 3 may the righteous be glad and **r**
68: 4 name is the LORD—and **r** before him.
70: 4 may all who seek you **r** and be glad
85: 6 that your people may **r** in you?
89:16 They **r** in your name all day long;
89:42 you have made all his enemies **r**.
96:11 Let the heavens **r**, let the earth be
97: 1 be glad; let the distant shores **r**.
97:12 **R** in the LORD, you who are righteous,
104:31 ever; may the LORD **r** in his works—
104:34 pleasing to him, as I **r** in the LORD.
105: 3 hearts of those who seek the LORD **r**.
107:42 The upright see and **r**, but all the
109:28 to shame, but your servant will **r**.
118:24 made; let us **r** and be glad in it.
119:14 I **r** in following your statutes as
119:74 May those who fear you **r** when they
119:162 I **r** in your promise like one who
149: 2 Let Israel **r** in their Maker; let the

Ps 149: 5 Let the saints **r** in this honour and
Pr 2:14 who delight in doing wrong and **r** in
5:18 may you **r** in the wife of your youth.
23:16 my inmost being will **r** when your
23:25 glad; may she who gave you birth **r**!
24:17 stumbles, do not let your heart **r**,
29: 2 the righteous thrive, the people **r**;
SS 1: 4 We **r** and delight in you; we will
Isa 9: 3 they **r** before you as people **r** at the
9: 3 as men **r** when dividing the plunder.
13: 3 wrath—those who **r** in my triumph.
14:29 Do not **r**, all you Philistines, that
25: 9 us **r** and be glad in his salvation."
29:19 Once more the humble will **r** in the
29:19 will **r** in the Holy One of Israel.
30:29 your hearts will **r** as when people go
35: 1 the wilderness will **r** and blossom.
35: 2 will burst into bloom; it will **r**
41:16 But you will **r** in the LORD and glory
42:11 the settlements where Kedar lives **r**.
49:13 Shout for joy, O heavens; **r**, O earth;
61: 7 and instead of disgrace they will **r**
62: 5 bride, so will your God **r** over you.
65:13 my servants will **r**, but you will
65:18 be glad and **r** for ever in what I
65:19 I will **r** over Jerusalem and take
66:10 "**R** with Jerusalem and be glad for
66:10 all you who love her; **r** greatly with
66:14 you see this, your heart will **r** and
Jer 11:15 in your wickedness, then you **r**."
31:12 they will **r** in the bounty of the
32:41 I will **r** in doing them good and will
50:11 "Because you **r** and are glad, you who
Lam 1:21 they **r** at what you have done.
4:21 **R** and be glad, O Daughter of Edom,
Eze 7:12 Let not the buyer **r** nor the seller
21:10 'Shall we **r** in the sceptre of my son
Hos 9: 1 Do not **r**, O Israel; do not be
Joel 2:21 Be not afraid, O land; be glad and **r**.
2:23 Be glad, O people of Zion, **r** in the
Am 6:13 who **r** in the conquest of Lo Debar
Ob :12 nor **r** over the people of Judah in
Hab 3:18 yet I will **r** in the LORD, I will be
Zep 3:11 city those who **r** in their pride.
3:14 O Israel! Be glad and **r** with all
3:17 he will **r** over you with singing."
Zec 4:10 Men will **r** when they see the
9: 9 **R** greatly, O Daughter of Zion! Shout,
10: 7 their hearts will **r** in the LORD.
Mt 5:12 **R** and be glad, because great is your
Lk 1:14 many will **r** because of his birth,
6:23 "**R** in that day and leap for joy,
10:20 However, do not **r** that the spirits
10:20 but **r** that your names are written in
15: 6 '**R** with me; I have found my lost
15: 9 **R** with me; I have found my lost coin.
Jn 16:22 I will see you again and you will **r**,
Ro 5: 2 **r** in the hope of the glory of God.
5: 3 Not only so, but we also **r** in our
5:11 Not only is this so, but we also **r**
12:15 **R** with those who **r**; mourn with those
15:10 Again, it says, "**R**, O Gentiles, with
2Co 2: 3 by those who ought to make me **r**.
Php 1:18 And because of this I **r**. Yes, and I
1:18 Yes, and I will continue to **r**,
2:17 I am glad and **r** with all of you.
2:18 you too should be glad and **r** with me.
3: 1 Finally, my brothers, **r** in the Lord!
4: 4 **R** in the Lord always. I will say it
4: 4 I will say it again: **R**!
4:10 I **r** greatly in the Lord that at last
Col 1:24 Now I **r** in what was suffered for you,
1Pe 1: 6 In this you greatly **r**, though now
4:13 **r** that you participate in the
Rev 12:12 Therefore **r**, you heavens and you who
18:20 **R** over her, O heaven! **R**, saints and
19: 7 Let us **r** and be glad and give him

Rejoiced (Rejoice)

1Sa 6:13 saw the ark, they **r** at the sight.
2Ki 11:20 all the people of the land **r**. And
1Ch 29: 9 The people **r** at the willing response
29: 9 David the king also **r** greatly.
2Ch 15:15 All Judah **r** about the oath because
23:21 all the people of the land **r**. And
29:36 Hezekiah and all the people **r** at
30:25 The entire assembly of Judah **r**,
Ne 12:43 The women and children also **r**. The
Job 31:25 if I have **r** over my great wealth,
31:29 "If I have **r** at my enemy's
Ps 122: 1 I **r** with those who said to me, "Let
SS 3:11 of his wedding, the day his heart **r**.
Eze 35:15 you **r** when the inheritance of the
Hos 10: 5 those who had **r** over its splendour,
Jn 8:56 Your father Abraham **r** at the thought

Rejoices (Rejoice)

1Sa 2: 1 Hannah prayed and said: "My heart **r**
Ps 13: 5 my heart **r** in your salvation.
16: 9 my heart is glad and my tongue **r**;
21: 1 O LORD, the king **r** in your strength.
48:11 Mount Zion **r**, the villages of Judah
97: 8 Zion hears and **r** and the villages of
119:14 statutes as one **r** in great riches.
Pr 11:10 the righteous prosper, the city **r**;
Isa 8: 6 **r** over Rezin and the son of Remaliah,
61:10 in the LORD; my soul **r** in my God.
62: 5 as a bridegroom **r** over his bride,
Eze 35:14 While the whole earth **r**, I will
Hab 1:15 drag-net; and so he **r** and is glad.
Lk 1:47 my spirit **r** in God my Saviour,
Jn 16:20 weep and mourn while the world **r**.
Ac 2:26 my tongue **r**; my body also will
1Co 12:26 is honoured, every part **r** with it.
13: 6 Love does not delight in evil but **r**

Rejoicing (Rejoice)

Nu 10:10 Also at your times of **r**—your
Dt 27: 7 eating them and **r** in the presence of
2Sa 6:12 to the City of David with **r**.
1Ki 1:40 playing flutes and **r** greatly, so
2Ki 11:14 land were **r** and blowing trumpets.
1Ch 15:25 from the house of Obed-Edom, with **r**.
2Ch 23:13 land were **r** and blowing trumpets,
23:18 **r** and singing, as David had ordered.
30:21 Bread for seven days with great **r**,
Ne 12:43 **r** because God had given them great
12:43 The sound of **r** in Jerusalem could be
Job 39:21 He paws fiercely, **r** in his strength,
Ps 19: 5 like a champion **r** to run his course.
30: 5 a night, but **r** comes in the morning.
105:43 He brought out his people with **r**,
Pr 8:30 after day, **r** always in his presence,
8:31 **r** in his whole world and delighting
Jer 30:19 of thanksgiving and the sound of **r**.
Eze 25: 6 **r** with all the malice of your heart
Lk 15: 7 **r** in heaven over one sinner who
15:10 I tell you, there is **r** in the
Ac 5:41 The apostles left the Sanhedrin, **r**
8:39 him again, but went on his way **r**.
2Co 6:10 sorrowful, yet always **r**; poor, yet

Rejoined (Join)

Jdg 14: 9 When he **r** his parents, he gave them

Rekem

Nu 31: 8 Among their victims were Evi, **R**, Zur,
Jos 13:21 Evi, **R**, Zur, Hur and Reba—princes
18:27 **R**, Irpeel, Taralah,
1Ch 2:43 The sons of Hebron: Korah, Tappuah, **R**
2:44 **R** was the father of Shammai.

Related (Relation, Relations, Relationship, Relationships, Relative, Relatives)

Lev 21: 4 for people **r** to him by marriage,
Nu 3:26 everything **r** to their use.
3:31 and everything **r** to their use.
3:36 and everything **r** to their use,
4:32 and everything **r** to their use.
2Sa 19:42 because the king is closely **r** to us.
2Ki 8:27 was **r** by marriage to Ahab's family.
2Ch 4:16 meat forks and all **r** articles.
Est 8: 1 Esther had told how he was **r** to her.
Ac 19:25 along with the workmen in **r** trades,
Heb 5: 1 represent them in matters **r** to God,

Relation (Related)

1Ki 10: 1 and his **r** to the name of the LORD,

Relations (Related)

Ex 19:15 Abstain from sexual **r**."
22:19 "Anyone who has sexual **r** with an
Lev 18: 6 any close relative to have sexual **r**.
18: 7 by having sexual **r** with your mother.
18: 7 your mother; do not have **r** with her.
18: 8 "'Do not have sexual **r** with your
18: 9 "'Do not have sexual **r** with your
18:10 "'Do not have sexual **r** with your
18:11 "'Do not have sexual **r** with the
18:12 "'Do not have sexual **r** with your
18:13 "'Do not have sexual **r** with your
18:14 to have sexual **r**; she is your aunt.
18:15 "'Do not have sexual **r** with your
18:15 son's wife; do not have **r** with her.
18:16 "'Do not have sexual **r** with your
18:17 "'Do not have sexual **r** with both a
18:17 Do not have sexual **r** with either her
18:18 **r** with her while your wife is living.
18:19 sexual **r** during the uncleanness of
18:20 "'Do not have sexual **r** with your
18:23 "'Do not have sexual **r** with an
18:23 **r** with it; that is a perversion.
20:15 "'If a man has sexual **r** with an
20:16 an animal to have sexual **r** with it,
20:17 have sexual **r**, it is a disgrace.
20:18 period and has sexual **r** with her,
20:19 "'Do not have sexual **r** with the
Dt 27:21 "Cursed is the man who has sexual **r**
Jdg 4:17 because there were friendly **r**
1Ki 1: 4 the king had no intimate **r** with her.
5:12 There were peaceful **r** between Hiram
Ro 1:26 natural **r** for unnatural ones.
1:27 also abandoned natural **r** with women
2Co 1:12 and especially in our **r** with you, in

Relationship (Related)

Jdg 18: 7 and had no **r** with anyone else.
18:28 Sidon and had no **r** with anyone else.
Ro 2:17 law and brag about your **r** to God;

Relationships (Related)

Nu 30:16 **r** between a man and his wife,

Relative (Blood-relative, Related)

Ge 14:14 Abram heard that his **r** had been
14:16 back his **r** Lot and his possessions,
29:12 He had told Rachel that he was a **r**
29:15 "Just because you are a **r** of mine,
Lev 18: 6 "'No-one is to approach any close **r**
18:12 she is your father's close **r**.
18:13 she is your mother's close **r**.
20:19 for that would dishonour a close **r**;
21: 2 except for a close **r**, such as his
25:25 his nearest **r** is to come and redeem
Nu 5: 8 if that person has no close **r** to
27:11 to the nearest **r** in his clan,
Ru 2: 1 Now Naomi had a **r** on her husband's
2:20 She added, "That man is our close **r**;
1Ki 16:11 a single male, whether **r** or friend.
Jer 23:35 keeps on saying to his friend or **r**:
32: 7 because as nearest **r** it is your
Am 6:10 if a **r** who is to burn the bodies
Lk 1:36 Even Elizabeth your **r** is going to
Jn 18:26 a **r** of the man whose ear Peter had
Ro 16:11 Greet Herodion, my **r**. Greet those in

Relatives (Blood-relatives, Related)

Ge 24: 4 will go to my country and my own **r**
24:27 to the house of my master's **r**."
27:37 have made all his **r** his servants,
31: 3 to your **r**, and I will be with you."
31:23 Taking his **r** with him, he pursued
31:25 Laban and his **r** camped there too.
31:32 In the presence of our **r**, see for
31:37 it here in front of your **r** and mine,
31:46 He said to his **r**, "Gather some
31:54 country and invited his **r** to a meal.
32: 9 Go back to your country and your **r**,
Lev 10: 6 But your **r**, all the house of Israel,
18:17 daughter; they are her close **r**.
25:48 One of his **r** may redeem him:
Nu 27: 4 us property among our father's **r**."
27: 7 inheritance among their father's **r**

Jdg 14: 3 your **r** or among all our people?
2Ki 10:13 he met some **r** of Ahaziah king of
10:13 "Who are you?" They said, "We are **r**
1Ch 5: 7 Their **r** by clans, listed according
5:13 Their **r**, by families, were: Michael,
7: 5 The **r** who were fighting men
7:22 days, and his **r** came to comfort him.
8:32 too lived near their **r** in Jerusalem.
9:38 too lived near their **r** in Jerusalem.
12:32 all their **r** under their command;
15: 5 Kohath, Uriel the leader and 120 **r**;
15: 6 Merari, Asaiah the leader and 220 **r**;
15: 7 Gershon, Joel the leader and 130 **r**;
15: 8 Shemaiah the leader and 200 **r**;
15: 9 Hebron, Eliel the leader and 80 **r**;
15:10 Amminadab the leader and 112 **r**.
25: 7 Along with their **r**—all of them
25: 9 fell to Joseph, his sons and **r**, 12
25: 9 Gedaliah, he and his **r** and sons, 12
25:10 the third to Zaccur, his sons and **r**,
25:11 the fourth to Izri, his sons and **r**,
25:12 to Nethaniah, his sons and **r**, 12
25:13 the sixth to Bukkiah, his sons and **r**,
25:14 to Jesarelah, his sons and **r**, 12
25:15 to Jeshaiah, his sons and **r**, 12
25:16 to Mattaniah, his sons and **r**, 12
25:17 the tenth to Shimei, his sons and **r**,
25:18 to Azarel, his sons and **r**, 12
25:19 to Hashabiah, his sons and **r**, 12
25:20 to Shubael, his sons and **r**, 12
25:21 to Mattithiah, his sons and **r**, 12
25:22 to Jerimoth, his sons and **r**, 12
25:23 to Hananiah, his sons and **r**, 12
25:24 to Joshbekashah, his sons and **r**, 12
25:25 to Hanani, his sons and **r**, 12
25:26 to Mallothi, his sons and **r**, 12
25:27 to Eliathah, his sons and **r**, 12
25:28 to Hothir, his sons and **r**, 12
25:29 to Giddalti, his sons and **r**, 12
25:30 to Mahazioth, his sons and **r**, 12
25:31 to Romamti-Ezer, his sons and **r**,
26: 7 Rephael, Obed and Elzabad; his **r**
26: 8 they and their sons and their **r** were
26: 9 Meshelemiah had sons and **r**, who were
26:11 sons and **r** of Hosah were 13 in all.
26:12 of the LORD, just as their **r** had.
26:25 His **r** through Eliezer: Rehabiah his
26:26 Shelomith and his **r** were in charge
26:28 in the care of Shelomith and his **r**.
26:30 Hashabiah and his **r**—seventeen
26:32 had two thousand seven hundred **r**,
2Ch 5:12 Jeduthun and their sons and **r**—stood
22: 8 Judah and the sons of Ahaziah's **r**,
Pr 19: 7 A poor man is shunned by all his **r**—
Jer 49:10 His children, **r** and neighbours will
Mk 6: 4 "Only in his home town, among his **r**
Lk 1:58 Her neighbours and **r** heard that the
1:61 among your **r** who has that name."
2:44 for him among their **r** and friends.
14:12 your brothers or **r**, or your rich
21:16 brothers, **r** and friends, and they
Ac 10:24 together his **r** and close friends.
Ro 16: 7 Greet Andronicus and Junias, my **r**
16:21 Lucius, Jason and Sosipater, my **r**.
1Ti 5: 8 If anyone does not provide for his **r**,

Release (Released, Releases)

Lev 14: 7 **r** the live bird in the open fields.
14:53 he is to **r** the live bird in the open
16:22 the man shall **r** it in the desert.
25:50 The price for his **r** is to be based
Nu 30: 5 the LORD will **r** her because her
30: 8 herself, and the LORD will **r** her.
30:12 them, and the LORD will **r** her.
Dt 15:13 you **r** him, do not send him away
Ps 25:15 he will **r** my feet from the snare.
102:20 and **r** those condemned to death."
Ecc 8: 8 will not **r** those who practise it.
Isa 42: 7 to **r** from the dungeon those who sit
61: 1 **r** from darkness for the prisoners,
Mt 27:15 to **r** a prisoner chosen by the crowd.
27:17 "Which one do you want me to **r** to
27:21 "Which of the two do you want me to **r**
Mk 15: 6 custom at the Feast to **r** a prisoner
15: 9 "Do you want me to **r** to you the king
15:11 to have Pilate **r** Barabbas instead.
Lk 4:18 for the blind, to **r** the oppressed,
23:16 I will punish him and then **r** him."
23:18 with this man! **R** Barabbas to us!"
23:20 Wanting to **r** Jesus, Pilate appealed
23:22 have him punished and then **r** him."
Jn 18:39 is your custom for me to **r** to you
18:39 me to **r** 'the king of the Jews'?"
Ac 4:23 On their **r**, Peter and John went back
16:35 jailer with the order: "**R** those men.
28:18 They examined me and wanted to **r** me,
Rev 9:14 "**R** the four angels who are bound at

Released (Release)

Ge 24: 8 will be **r** from this oath of mine.
24:41 you will be **r** from my oath even if
24:41 to you—you will be **r** from my oath.'
Lev 25:41 he and his children are to be **r**, and
25:54 are to be **r** in the Year of Jubilee,
27:21 the field is **r** in the Jubilee, it
Jos 2:20 **r** from the oath you made us swear."
2Ki 25:27 he **r** Jehoiachin from prison on the
2Ch 23: 8 had not **r** any of the divisions.
Job 12:14 the man he imprisons cannot be **r**.
Ps 105:20 The king sent and **r** him, the ruler
Jer 20: 3 The next day, when Pashhur **r** him
40: 1 imperial guard had **r** him at Ramah.
52:31 he **r** Jehoiachin king of Judah and
Mal 4: 2 leap like calves **r** from the stall.
Mt 27:26 he **r** Barabbas to them. But he had
Mk 15:15 crowd, Pilate **r** Barabbas to them.
Lk 23:25 He **r** the man who had been thrown
Ac 3:14 asked that a murderer be **r** to you.
16:36 ordered that you and Silas be **r**.
22:30 he **r** him and ordered the chief
Ro 7: 2 she is **r** from the law of marriage.
7: 3 But if her husband dies, she is **r**
7: 6 we have been **r** from the law so that
Heb 11:35 were tortured and refused to be **r**,
13:23 that our brother Timothy has been **r**.
Rev 9:15 were **r** to kill a third of mankind.
20: 7 Satan will be **r** from his prison

Releases (Release)

Lev 16:26 "The man who **r** the goat as a

Relent (Relented, Relents)

Ex 32:12 **r** and do not bring disaster on your
Job 6:29 **R**, do not be unjust; reconsider, for
Ps 7:12 If he does not **r**, he will sharpen
90:13 **R**, O LORD! How long will it be? Have
Isa 57: 6 light of these things, should I **r**?
Jer 4:28 I have spoken and will not **r**,
18: 8 then I will **r** and not inflict on it
26: 3 Then I will **r** and not bring on them
26:13 Then the LORD will **r** and not bring
26:19 his favour? And did not the LORD **r**,
Eze 24:14 I will not have pity, nor will I **r**.
Jnh 3: 9 Who knows? God may yet **r** and with

Relented (Relent)

Ex 32:14 the LORD **r** and did not bring on his
Ps 106:45 and out of his great love he **r**.
Am 7: 3 the LORD **r**. "This will not happen,"
7: 6 the LORD **r**. "This will not happen

Relentless

Isa 14: 6 subdued nations with **r** aggression.

Relents (Relent)

Joel 2:13 and he **r** from sending calamity.
Jnh 4: 2 a God who **r** from sending calamity.

Reliable (Rely)

1Sa 29: 6 you have been **r**, and I would be
Pr 22:21 teaching you true and **r** words, so
Isa 8: 2 Jeberekiah as **r** witnesses for me."
Jer 2:21 a choice vine of sound and **r** stock.
Jn 8:26 But he who sent me is **r**, and what I
2Ti 2: 2 entrust to **r** men who will also be

Reliance (Rely)

Pr 25:19 a lame foot is **r** on the unfaithful

Relied (Rely)

Jdg 20:36 because they **r** on the ambush they
2Ch 13:18 because they **r** on the LORD,
16: 7 "Because you **r** on the king of Aram
16: 8 Yet when you **r** on the LORD,
Ps 71: 6 From my birth I have **r** on you; you
Isa 20: 6 'See what has happened to those we **r**
30:12 **r** on oppression and depended on

Relief (Relieve)

Ex 8:15 when Pharaoh saw that there was **r**,
1Sa 8:18 you will cry out for **r** from the king
16:23 Then **r** would come to Saul; he would
Ezr 9: 8 eyes and a little **r** in our bondage.
Est 4:14 **r** and deliverance for the Jews will
9:16 and get **r** from their enemies.
9:22 the time when the Jews got **r** from
Job 16: 5 from my lips would bring you **r**.
32:20 I must speak and find **r**; I must open
35: 9 for **r** from the arm of the powerful.
Ps 4: 1 Give me **r** from my distress; be
94:13 you grant him **r** from days of trouble,
143: 1 and righteousness come to my **r**.
Isa 1:24 "Ah, I will get **r** from my foes and
14: 3 On the day the LORD gives you **r** from
Lam 2:18 yourself no **r**, your eyes no rest.
3:49 will flow unceasingly, without **r**,
3:56 close your ears to my cry for **r**."
Mic 1:12 waiting for **r**, because disaster has
2Th 1: 7 give **r** to you who are troubled, and

Relies (Rely)

Job 8:14 what he **r** on is a spider's web.

Relieve (Relief, Relieved, Relieving)

Dt 23:12 camp where you can go to **r** yourself.
23:13 and when you **r** yourself, dig a hole
1Sa 24: 3 and Saul went in to **r** himself.

Relieved (Relieve)

Job 16: 6 "Yet if I speak, my pain is not **r**;
2Co 8:13 be **r** while you are hard pressed,

Relieving (Relieve)

Jdg 3:24 They said, "He must be **r** himself in

Religion (Religious)

Ac 25:19 dispute with him about their own **r**
26: 5 of our **r**, I lived as a Pharisee.
1Ti 5: 4 put their **r** into practice by caring
Jas 1:26 himself and his **r** is worthless.
1:27 **R** that God our Father accepts as

Religious (Religion)

Am 5:21 "I hate, I despise your **r** feasts;
8:10 I will turn your **r** feasts into
Ac 17:22 that in every way you are very **r**.
Col 2:16 or with regard to a **r** festival, a
Heb 10:11 stands and performs his **r** duties;
Jas 1:26 If anyone considers himself **r** and

Relish

Hos 4: 8 of my people and **r** their wickedness.

Rely (Reliable, Reliance, Relied, Relies)

2Ch 14:11 out God, for we **r** on you, and in
Job 39:11 Will you **r** on him for his great
Isa 10:20 will no longer **r** on him who struck
10:20 down but will truly **r** on the LORD,
31: 1 who **r** on horses, who trust in the
48: 2 **r** on the God of Israel—the LORD
50:10 name of the LORD and **r** on his God.
59: 4 They **r** on empty arguments and speak
Jer 46:25 and on those who **r** on Pharaoh.
Eze 33:26 You **r** on your sword, you do
Ro 2:17 if you **r** on the law and brag about
2Co 1: 9 might not **r** on ourselves but on God,
Gal 3:10 All who **r** on observing the law are
1Jn 4:16 we know and **r** on the love God has

Remain (Remainder, Remained, Remaining, Remains)

Ge 15: 2 can you give me since I **r** childless
24:55 "Let the girl **r** with us ten days or
36: 7 too great for them to **r** together;
44:33 "Now then, please let your servant **r**
Ex 8: 9 for those that **r** in the Nile."
8:11 they will **r** only in the Nile."
25:15 The poles are to **r** in the rings of
34:25 the Passover Feast **r** until morning.
Lev 6: 9 The burnt offering is to **r** on the
11:37 are to be planted, they **r** clean.
22:27 to **r** with its mother for seven days.
25:28 what he sold will **r** in the
25:51 If many years **r**, he must pay for his
25:52 If only a few years **r** until the Year
26:21 "'If you **r** hostile towards me and
27:14 the priest then sets, so it will **r**.
27:18 **r** until the next Year of Jubilee,
Nu 4: 7 is continually there is to **r** on it.
9:22 the Israelites would **r** in camp and
32:26 will **r** here in the cities of Gilead.
33:55 those you allow to **r** will become
Dt 13:16 It is to **r** a ruin for ever, never to
16: 4 of the first day **r** until morning.
31:26 it will **r** as a witness against you.
Jos 18: 5 Judah is to **r** in its territory on
23: 4 all the land of the nations that **r**
23: 7 with these nations that **r** among you;
23:12 of these nations that **r** among you
Jdg 2:23 LORD had allowed those nations to **r**;
Ru 1:13 Would you **r** unmarried for them? No,
1Sa 16:22 "Allow David to **r** in my service, for
2Sa 14:14 person may not **r** estranged from him.
16:18 I will be, and I will **r** with him.
1Ki 2:45 **r** secure before the LORD for ever."
1Ch 21:17 do not let this plague **r** on your
2Ch 32:10 that you **r** in Jerusalem under siege?
33: 4 Name will **r** in Jerusalem for ever."
Est 4:14 For if you **r** silent at this time,
Job 29:20 My glory will **r** fresh in me, the bow
37: 8 The animals take cover; they **r** in
Ps 28: 1 For if you **r** silent, I shall be like
30: 5 lifetime; weeping may **r** for a night,
49:11 Their tombs will **r** their houses for
102:26 They will perish, but you **r**; they
102:27 you **r** the same, and your years will
109: 1 God, whom I praise, do not **r** silent
109:15 May their sins always **r** before the
125: 3 The sceptre of the wicked will not **r**
Pr 2:21 and the blameless will **r** in it;
10:30 the wicked will not **r** in the land.
Isa 4: 3 Those who are left in Zion, who **r** in
7:22 All who **r** in the land will eat curds
10: 4 Nothing will **r** but to cringe among
15: 9 and upon those who **r** in the land.
17: 6 Yet some gleanings will **r**, as when
18: 4 "I will **r** quiet and will look on
22:18 there your splendid chariots will **r**—
46: 3 O house of Jacob, all you who **r** of
62: 1 for Jerusalem's sake I will not **r**
Jer 24: 8 **r** in this land or live in Egypt.
27:11 I will let that nation **r** in its own
27:22 ill **r** until the day I come for them,'
29:16 all the people who **r** in this city,
32: 5 where he will **r** until I deal with
51:30 they **r** in their strongholds.
Eze 36:36 the nations around you that **r** will
39:14 bury those that **r** on the ground.
44: 2 said to me, "This gate is to **r** shut.
44: 2 It is to **r** shut because the LORD,
Da 2:43 be a mixture and will not **r** united,
4:15 bound with iron and bronze, **r** in the
4:23 while its roots **r** in the ground.
11:12 yet he will not **r** triumphant.
Hos 9: 3 They will not **r** in the LORD's land;
Zec 5: 4 It will **r** in his house and destroy
12: 6 Jerusalem will **r** intact in her place.
14:10 be raised up and **r** in its place,
Jn 1:32 from heaven as a dove and **r** on him.
1:33 see the Spirit come down and **r** is
12:34 Law that the Christ will **r** for ever,
15: 4 **R** in me, and I will **r** in you. No
15: 4 by itself; it must **r** in the vine.
15: 4 you bear fruit unless you **r** in me.
Jn 15: 6 If anyone does not **r** in me, he is
15: 7 If you **r** in me and my words **r** in you,
15: 9 have I loved you. Now **r** in my love.
15:10 If you obey my commands, you will **r**
15:10 Father's commands and **r** in his love.
17:11 I will **r** in the world no longer, but
21:22 Jesus answered, "If I want him to **r**
21:23 "If I want him to **r** alive until I
Ac 3:21 He must **r** in heaven until the time
11:23 encouraged them all to **r** true to the
14:22 them to **r** true to the faith.
Ro 13: 8 Let no debt **r** outstanding, except
1Co 7:11 if she does, she must **r** unmarried or
7:20 Each one should **r** in the situation
7:24 **r** in the situation God called him to.
7:26 it is good for you to **r** as you are.
13:13 now these three **r**: faith, hope and
14:34 women should **r** silent in the
Gal 2: 5 of the gospel might **r** with you.
Php 1:24 is more necessary for you that I **r**
1:25 I know that I will **r**, and I will
2Ti 2:13 if we are faithless, he will **r**
Heb 1:11 They will perish, but you **r**; they
1:12 But you **r** the same, and your years
8: 9 because they did not **r** faithful to
12:27 that what cannot be shaken may **r**.
1Jn 2:24 will **r** in the Son and in the Father.
2:27 as it has taught you, **r** in him.
Rev 2:13 Yet you **r** true to my name. You did
14:12 and **r** faithful to Jesus.
17:10 come, he must **r** for a little while.

Remainder (Remain)

Est 9:16 Meanwhile, the **r** of the Jews who

Remained (Remain)

Ge 18:22 Abraham **r** standing before the LORD.
32: 4 Laban and have **r** there till now.
49:24 his bow **r** steady, his strong arms
Ex 8:31 and his people; not a fly **r**.
10:15 Nothing green **r** on tree or plant in
17:12 that his hands **r** steady till sunset.
20:21 The people **r** at a distance, while
Lev 10: 3 will be honoured.'" Aaron **r** silent.
Nu 9:18 over the tabernacle, they **r** in camp.
9:19 the cloud **r** over the tabernacle a
11:26 Eldad and Medad, had **r** in the camp.
36:12 **r** in their father's clan and tribe.
Jos 4:10 Now the priests who carried the ark **r**
5: 8 they **r** where they were in camp until
8:17 Not a man **r** in Ai or Bethel who did
Jdg 1:30 who **r** among them; but they did
5:17 Asher **r** on the coast and stayed in
7: 3 men left, while ten thousand **r**.
13: 2 who was sterile and **r** childless.
19: 4 prevailed upon him to stay; so he **r**
1Sa 5: 4 on the threshold; only his body **r**.
7: 2 twenty years in all, that the ark **r**
13: 7 Saul **r** at Gilgal, and all the troops
18:29 **r** his enemy for the rest of his days.
23:18 went home, but David **r** at Horesh.
2Sa 6:11 The ark of the LORD **r** in the house
11: 1 But David **r** in Jerusalem.
11:12 **r** in Jerusalem that day and the next.
1Ki 12:20 Judah **r** loyal to the house of David.
22:46 the male shrine-prostitutes who **r**
2Ki 2:22 the water has **r** wholesome to this
10:11 Jehu killed everyone in Jezreel who **r**
11: 3 He **r** hidden with his nurse at the
13: 6 Asherah pole **r** standing in Samaria.
18:36 the people **r** silent and said nothing
25:11 exile the people who **r** in the city,
1Ch 12:29 **r** loyal to Saul's house until then;
13:14 The ark of God **r** with the family of
20: 1 it, but David **r** in Jerusalem.
2Ch 22:12 He **r** hidden with them at the temple
Isa 36:21 the people **r** silent and said nothing
Jer 35:11 So we have **r** in Jerusalem."
37:16 a dungeon, where he **r** a long time.
37:21 **r** in the courtyard of the guard.
38:13 **r** in the courtyard of the guard.
38:28 Jeremiah **r** in the courtyard of the
39: 9 Babylon the people who **r** in the city,
39:14 So he **r** among his own people.
52:15 people and those who **r** in the city,
Eze 17: 6 him, but its roots **r** under it.
Da 1:21 Daniel **r** there until the first year
2:49 Daniel himself **r** at the royal court.
Hos 10: 9 O Israel, and there you have **r**.
Mt 11:23 Sodom, it would have **r** to this day.
26:63 Jesus **r** silent. The high priest said
Mk 3: 4 life or to kill?" But they **r** silent.
14:61 Jesus **r** silent and gave no answer.
Lk 1:22 signs to them but **r** unable to speak.
1:24 and for five months **r** in seclusion.
14: 4 they **r** silent. So taking hold of the
Ac 7:45 It **r** in the land until the time of
15:35 Paul and Barnabas **r** in Antioch,
1Jn 2:19 they would have **r** with us; but their

Remaining (Remain)

Ex 28:10 stone and the **r** six on the other.
Lev 10:12 Moses said to Aaron and his **r** sons,
10:16 Ithamar, Aaron's **r** sons, and asked,
14:17 the oil **r** in his palm on the lobe
Nu 31:32 The plunder **r** from the spoils that
Jos 7: 6 of the LORD, **r** there till evening.
1Ki 9:21 that is, their descendants **r** in the
1Ch 4:43 They killed the **r** Amalekites who had
2Ch 8: 8 that is, their descendants **r** in the
Ne 11: 1 the holy city, while the **r** nine were
Isa 10:19 the **r** trees of his forests will be
Jer 27:18 **r** in the house of the LORD
Eze 25:16 and destroy those **r** along the coast.
48:15 "The **r** area, 5,000 cubits wide and
Jn 19:23 of them, with the undergarment **r**.

Remains (Remain)

Ex 22:13 he shall bring in the **r** as evidence
Lev 11:36 or a cistern for collecting water **r**
13:46 long as he has the infection he **r**
27:17 the value that has been set **r**.
Nu 15:31 be cut off; his guilt **r** on him.
16:37 censers out of the smouldering **r**
19:13 unclean; his uncleanness **r** on him.
Dt 24:20 Leave what **r** for the alien, the
24:21 Leave what **r** for the alien, the
Jos 7:26 pile of rocks, which **r** to this day.
8:29 rocks over it, which **r** to this day.
13: 2 "This is the land that **r**: all the
2Sa 7: 2 while the ark of God **r** in a tent."
1Ki 20:10 if enough dust **r** in Samaria to give
2Ki 6:31 Shaphat **r** on his shoulders today!"
Ne 9:10 for yourself, which **r** to this day.
Job 19: 4 astray, my error **r** my concern alone.
34:29 if he **r** silent, who can condemn him?
Ps 146: 6 the LORD, who **r** faithful for ever.
Pr 29: 1 A man who **r** stiff-necked after many
Ecc 1: 4 go, but the earth **r** for ever.
Isa 6:13 though a tenth **r** in the land, it
29: 8 but he awakens, and his hunger **r**; as
Eze 32: 5 and fill the valleys with your **r**.
48:18 What **r** of the area, bordering on the
48:21 "What **r** on both sides of the area
Mic 7: 2 the land; not one upright man **r**.
Hag 1: 4 houses, while this house **r** a ruin?"
1: 9 "Because of my house, which **r** a ruin,
2: 5 And my Spirit **r** among you. Do not
Jn 3:36 see life, for God's wrath **r** on him."
6:56 my blood **r** in me, and I in him.
9:41 you claim you can see, your guilt **r**.
12:24 and dies, it **r** only a single seed.
15: 5 If a man **r** in me and I in him, he
1Co 11:21 One **r** hungry, another gets drunk.
2Co 3:14 **r** when the old covenant is read.
Heb 4: 6 still **r** that some will enter that
4: 9 There **r**, then, a Sabbath-rest for
7: 3 Son of God he **r** a priest for ever.
1Jn 2:24 heard from the beginning **r** in you.
2:27 you received from him **r** in you,
3: 9 because God's seed **r** in him; he
3:14 Anyone who does not love **r** in death.
Rev 3: 2 Wake up! Strengthen what **r** and is

Remaliah (Remaliah's)

2Ki 15:25 son of **R**, conspired against him.
15:27 Pekah son of **R** became king of Israel
15:30 conspired against Pekah son of **R**.
15:32 In the second year of Pekah son of **R**
15:37 and Pekah son of **R** against Judah.)

2Ki 16: 1 seventeenth year of Pekah son of **R**,
16: 5 Rezin king of Aram and Pekah son of **R**
2Ch 28: 6 In one day Pekah son of **R** killed a
Isa 7: 1 Pekah son of **R** king of Israel
7: 4 Rezin and Aram and of the son of **R**.
8: 6 over Rezin and the son of **R**,

Remaliah's (Remaliah)

Isa 7: 5 Aram, Ephraim and **R** son have plotted
7: 9 the head of Samaria is only **R** son.

Remarkable

Lk 5:26 said, "We have seen **r** things today.
Jn 9:30 The man answered, "Now that is **r**!

Remarked (Remarking)

Ac 17:18 babbler trying to say?" Others **r**,

Remarking (Remarked)

Lk 21: 5 Some of his disciples were **r** about

Remedies (Remedy)

Jer 46:11 But you multiply **r** in vain; there is

Remedy (Remedies)

2Ch 36:16 his people and there was no **r**.
Pr 6:15 suddenly be destroyed—without **r**.
29: 1 suddenly be destroyed—without **r**.
Isa 3: 7 day he will cry out, "I have no **r**.
Jer 30:13 **r** for your sore, no healing for you.
Mic 2:10 defiled, it is ruined, beyond all **r**.

Remember (Remembered, Remembering, Remembers, Remembrance)

Ge 9:15 I will **r** my covenant between me and
9:16 I will see it and **r** the everlasting
31:50 **r** that God is a witness between you
40:14 when all goes well with you, **r** me
40:23 did not **r** Joseph; he forgot him.
Ex 20: 8 "**R** the Sabbath day by keeping it
32:13 **R** your servants Abraham, Isaac and
33:13 **R** that this nation is your people."
Lev 26:42 I will **r** my covenant with Jacob and
26:42 with Abraham, and I will **r** the land.
26:45 for their sake I will **r** the covenant
Nu 11: 5 We **r** the fish we ate in Egypt at no
15:39 will **r** all the commands of the LORD,
15:40 you will **r** to obey all my commands
Dt 4:10 **R** the day you stood before the LORD
5:15 **R** that you were slaves in Egypt and
7:18 do not be afraid of them; **r** well
8: 2 **R** how the LORD your God led you all
8:18 **r** the LORD your God, for it is he
9: 7 **R** this and never forget how you
9:27 **R** your servants Abraham, Isaac and
11: 2 **R** today that your children were not
15:15 **R** that you were slaves in Egypt and
16: 3 **r** the time of your departure from
16:12 **R** that you were slaves in Egypt, and
24: 9 **R** what the LORD your God did to
24:18 **R** that you were slaves in Egypt and
24:22 **R** that you were slaves in Egypt.
25:17 **R** what the Amalekites did to you
32: 7 **R** the days of old; consider the
Jos 1:13 "**R** the command that Moses the
23: 4 **R** how I have allotted as an
Jdg 8:34 did not **r** the LORD their God, who
9: 2 man?' **R**, I am your flesh and blood."
16:28 the LORD, "O Sovereign LORD, **r** me.
1Sa 1:11 your servant's misery and **r** me,
20:23 the matter you and I discussed—**r**,
25:31 my master success, **r** your servant."
2Sa 19:19 Do not **r** how your servant did wrong
1Ki 2: 8 "And **r**, you have with you Shimei son
2Ki 9:25 **R** how you and I were riding together
20: 3 "**R**, O LORD, how I have walked before
1Ch 16:12 **R** the wonders he has done, his
2Ch 6:42 **R** the great love promised to David
24:22 King Joash did not **r** the kindness
Ne 1: 8 "**R** the instruction you gave your
4:14 **R** the Lord, who is great and awesome,
5:19 **R** me with favour, O my God, for all
Ne 6:14 **R** Tobiah and Sanballat, O my God,
6:14 because of what they have done; **r**
9:17 failed to **r** the miracles you
13:14 **R** me for this, O my God, and do not
13:22 **R** me for this also, O my God, and
13:29 **R** them, O my God, because they
13:31 **R** me with favour, O my God.
Job 7: 7 **R**, O God, that my life is but a
10: 9 **R** that you moulded me like clay.
14:13 would set me a time and then **r** me!
36:24 **R** to extol his work, which men have
41: 8 If you lay a hand on him, you will **r**
Ps 20: 3 May he **r** all your sacrifices and
22:27 All the ends of the earth will **r** and
25: 6 **R**, O LORD, your great mercy and love,
25: 7 **R** not the sins of my youth and my
25: 7 according to your love **r** me, for
42: 4 These things I **r** as I pour out my
42: 6 **r** you from the land of the Jordan,
63: 6 On my bed I **r** you; I think of you
74: 2 **R** the people you purchased of old,
74:18 **R** how the enemy has mocked you,
74:22 **r** how fools mock you all day long.
77:11 I will **r** the deeds of the LORD; yes,
77:11 I will **r** your miracles of long ago.
78:42 They did not **r** his power—the day
88: 5 whom you **r** no more, who are cut off
89:47 **R** how fleeting is my life. For what
89:50 **R**, Lord, how your servant has been
103:18 covenant and **r** to obey his precepts.
105: 5 **R** the wonders he has done, his
106: 4 **R** me, O LORD, when you show favour
106: 7 they did not **r** your many kindnesses,
119:49 **R** your word to your servant, for you
119:52 I **r** your ancient laws, O LORD, and I
119:55 In the night I **r** your name, O LORD,
132: 1 O LORD, **r** David and all the
137: 6 roof of my mouth if I do not **r** you,
137: 7 **R**, O LORD, what the Edomites did on
143: 5 I **r** the days of long ago; I meditate
Pr 31: 7 poverty and **r** their misery no more.
Ecc 11: 8 But let him **r** the days of darkness,
12: 1 **R** your Creator in the days of your
12: 6 **R** him—before the silver cord is
Isa 38: 3 "**R**, O LORD, how I have walked before
44:21 "**R** these things, O Jacob, for you
46: 8 "**R** this, fix it in mind, take it to
46: 9 **R** the former things, those of long
54: 4 **r** no more the reproach of your
64: 5 gladly do right, who **r** your ways.
64: 9 O LORD; do not **r** our sins for ever.
Jer 2: 2 'I **r** the devotion of your youth, how
14:10 he will now **r** their wickedness and
14:21 **R** your covenant with us and do not
15:15 You understand, O LORD; **r** me and
17: 2 Even their children **r** their altars
18:20 **R** that I stood before you and spoke
31:20 speak against him, I still **r** him.
31:34 and will **r** their sins no more."
44:21 "Did not the LORD **r** and think about
51:50 leave and do not linger! **R** the LORD
Lam 3:19 I **r** my affliction and my wandering,
3:20 I well **r** them, and my soul is
5: 1 **R**, O LORD, what has happened to us;
Eze 6: 9 those who escape will **r** me—how I
16:22 did not **r** the days of your youth,
16:43 "'Because you did not **r** the days of
16:60 Yet I will **r** the covenant I made
16:61 you will **r** your ways and be ashamed
16:63 you will **r** and be ashamed and never
20:43 There you will **r** your conduct and
23:27 with longing or **r** Egypt any more.
36:31 you will **r** your evil ways and wicked
Da 6:15 "**R**, O king, that according to the
Hos 7: 2 they do not realise that I **r** all
8:13 Now he will **r** their wickedness and
9: 9 God will **r** their wickedness and
Mic 6: 5 My people, **r** what Balak king of Moab
6: 5 **R** your journey from Shittim to
Hab 3: 2 make them known; in wrath **r** mercy.
Zec 10: 9 yet in distant lands they will **r** me.
Mal 4: 4 "**R** the law of my servant Moses, the
Mt 5:23 there **r** that your brother has
16: 9 Don't you **r** the five loaves for the
27:63 "Sir," they said, "we **r** that while
Mk 8:18 but fail to hear? And don't you **r**?
Lk 1:72 to show mercy to our fathers and to **r**
16:25 "But Abraham replied, 'Son, **r** that
17:32 **R** Lot's wife!
23:42 he said, "Jesus, **r** me when you come
24: 6 He is not here; he has risen! **R** how
Jn 15:20 **R** the words I spoke to you: 'No
16: 4 comes you will **r** that I warned you.
Ac 20:31 be on your guard! **R** that for three
Ro 1: 9 is my witness how constantly I **r**
1Co 1:16 I don't **r** if I baptised anyone else.)
2Co 9: 6 **R** this: Whoever sows sparingly will
Gal 2:10 we should continue to **r** the poor,
Eph 2:11 Therefore, **r** that formerly you who
2:12 **r** that at that time you were
Php 1: 3 I thank my God every time I **r** you.
Col 4:18 **R** my chains. Grace be with you.
1Th 1: 3 We continually **r** before our God and
2: 9 Surely you **r**, brothers, our toil and
2Th 2: 5 Don't you **r** that when I was with you
2Ti 1: 3 I constantly **r** you in my prayers.
2: 8 **R** Jesus Christ, raised from the dead,
Phm : 4 I always thank my God as I **r** you in
Heb 8:12 and will **r** their sins no more."
10:17 and lawless acts I will **r** no more."
10:32 **R** those earlier days after you had
13: 3 **R** those in prison as if you were
13: 7 **R** your leaders, who spoke the word
Jas 5:20 **r** this: Whoever turns a sinner from
2Pe 1:15 always be able to **r** these things.
Jude :17 dear friends, **r** what the apostles
Rev 2: 5 **R** the height from which you have
3: 3 **R**, therefore, what you have received

Remembered (Remember)

Ge 8: 1 God **r** Noah and all the wild animals
19:29 he **r** Abraham, and he brought Lot out
30:22 God **r** Rachel; he listened to her and
41:31 abundance in the land will not be **r**,
42: 9 he **r** his dreams about them and said
Ex 2:24 God heard their groaning and he **r**
3:15 be **r** from generation to generation.
6: 5 enslaving, and I have **r** my covenant.
17:14 **r** and make sure that Joshua hears it,
Nu 10: 9 Then you will be **r** by the LORD your
1Sa 1:19 Hannah his wife, and the LORD **r** her.
Est 2: 1 he **r** Vashti and what she had done
9:28 These days should be **r** and observed
Job 24:20 longer **r** but are broken like a tree.
Ps 77: 3 I **r** you, O God, and I groaned; I
77: 6 I **r** my songs in the night. My heart
78:35 They **r** that God was their Rock, that
78:39 He **r** that they were but flesh, a
83: 4 the name of Israel be **r** no more."
98: 3 He has **r** his love and his
105:42 For he **r** his holy promise given to
106:45 for their sake he **r** his covenant and
109:14 May the iniquity of his fathers be **r**
111: 4 He has caused his wonders to be **r**;
112: 6 a righteous man will be **r** for ever.
136:23 to the One who **r** us in our low
137: 1 we sat and wept when we **r** Zion.
Ecc 1:11 will not be **r** by those who follow.
2:16 like the fool, will not be long **r**;
9:15 But nobody **r** that poor man.
Isa 17:10 have not **r** the Rock, your fortress.
23:16 many a song, so that you will be **r**."
57:11 and have neither **r** me nor pondered
65:17 be **r**, nor will they come to mind.
Jer 3:16 or be **r**; it will not be missed,
11:19 living, that his name be **r** no more."
Lam 2: 1 he has not **r** his footstool in the
Eze 3:20 things he did will not be **r**,
18:22 has committed will be **r** against him.
18:24 things he has done will be **r**.
21:32 you will be **r** no more; for I the
25:10 will not be **r** among the nations;
33:13 things he has done will be **r**;
33:16 has committed will be **r** against him.
Jnh 2: 7 "When my life was ebbing away, I **r**
Zec 13: 2 land, and they will be **r** no more,"
Mt 26:75 Peter **r** the word Jesus had spoken:
Mk 11:21 Peter **r** and said to Jesus, "Rabbi,
14:72 Then Peter **r** the word Jesus had
Lk 22:61 Then Peter **r** the word the Lord had
24: 8 Then they **r** his words.

Jn 2:17 His disciples **r** that it is written:
Ac 10:31 prayer and **r** your gifts to the poor.
11:16 I **r** what the Lord had said: 'John
Rev 16:19 God **r** Babylon the Great and gave her
18: 5 to heaven, and God has **r** her crimes.

Remembering (Remember)
Lk 1:54 He has helped his servant Israel, **r**
Ac 20:35 **r** the words the Lord Jesus himself
1Co 11: 2 I praise you for **r** me in everything
Eph 1:16 thanks for you, **r** you in my prayers.

Remembers (Remember)
1Ch 16:15 He **r** his covenant for ever, the word
Ps 6: 5 No-one **r** you when he is dead. Who
9:12 For he who avenges blood **r**; he does
103:14 for he knows how we are formed, he **r**
103:16 is gone, and its place **r** it no more.
105: 8 He **r** his covenant for ever, the word
111: 5 him; he **r** his covenant for ever.
115:12 The LORD **r** us and will bless us: He
Isa 43:25 own sake, and **r** your sins no more.
Lam 1: 7 wandering Jerusalem **r** all the
2Co 7:15 he **r** that you were all obedient,

Remembrance (Remember)
Ecc 1:11 There is no **r** of men of old, and
Mal 3:16 A scroll of **r** was written in his
Lk 22:19 given for you; do this in **r** of me."
1Co 11:24 is for you; do this in **r** of me."
11:25 whenever you drink it, in **r** of me."

Remeth
Jos 19:21 **R**, En Gannim, En Haddah and Beth

Remind (Reminded, Reminder, Reminders, Reminding)
Nu 16:40 This was to **r** the Israelites that
1Ki 17:18 to **r** me of my sin and kill my son?"
Eze 21:23 but he will **r** them of their guilt
Jn 14:26 will **r** you of everything I have said
Ro 15:15 as if to **r** you of them again,
1Co 4:17 He will **r** you of my way of life in
15: 1 Now, brothers, I want to **r** you of
2Ti 1: 6 For this reason I **r** you to fan into
Tit 3: 1 **R** the people to be subject to rulers
2Pe 1:12 I will always **r** you of these things,
Jude : 5 I want to **r** you that the Lord

Reminded (Remind)
Ge 41: 9 "Today I am **r** of my shortcomings.
2Ti 1: 5 I have been **r** of your sincere faith,

Reminder (Remind)
Ex 13: 9 a **r** on your forehead that the law of
Nu 5:15 a **r** offering to draw attention to
5:18 place in her hands the **r** offering,
Eze 29:16 a **r** of their sin in turning to her
Heb 10: 3 those sacrifices are an annual **r** of

Reminders (Remind)
2Pe 3: 1 I have written both of them as **r** to

Reminding (Remind)
2Ti 2:14 Keep **r** them of these things. Warn

Remnant
Ge 45: 7 to preserve for you a **r** on earth
Dt 3:11 was left of the **r** of the Rephaites.
2Ki 19: 4 pray for the **r** that still survives."
19:30 Once more a **r** of the house of Judah
19:31 For out of Jerusalem will come a **r**,
21:14 I will forsake the **r** of my
2Ch 34: 9 Ephraim and the entire **r** of Israel
34:21 for the **r** in Israel and Judah about
36:20 the **r** who escaped from the sword,
Ezr 9: 8 has been gracious in leaving us a **r**
9:13 and have given us a **r** like this.
9:14 us, leaving us no **r** or survivor?
9:15 We are left this day as a **r**.
Ne 1: 2 Jewish **r** that survived the exile,
Isa 10:20 In that day the **r** of Israel, the
10:21 A **r** will return, a **r** of Jacob will
10:22 by the sea, only a **r** will return.
11:11 to reclaim the **r** that is left of
11:16 There will be a highway for the **r** of
17: 3 the **r** of Aram will be like the glory
28: 5 wreath for the **r** of his people.
37: 4 pray for the **r** that still survives."
37:31 Once more a **r** of the house of Judah
37:32 For out of Jerusalem will come a **r**,
Jer 6: 9 "Let them glean the **r** of Israel as
11:23 Not even a **r** will be left to them,
23: 3 "I myself will gather the **r** of my
31: 7 save your people, the **r** of Israel.'
40:11 of Babylon had left a **r** in Judah
40:15 and the **r** of Judah to perish?"
42: 2 the LORD your God for this entire **r**.
42:15 hear the word of the LORD, O **r** of
42:19 "O **r** of Judah, the LORD has told you,
43: 5 led away all the **r** of Judah who had
44: 7 and so leave yourselves without a **r**?
44:12 I will take away the **r** of Judah who
44:14 None of the **r** of Judah who have gone
44:28 Then the whole **r** of Judah who came
47: 4 the **r** from the coasts of Caphtor.
47: 5 O **r** on the plain, how long will you
50:20 for I will forgive the **r** I spare.
50:26 destroy her and leave her no **r**.
Eze 9: 8 you going to destroy the entire **r**
11:13 completely destroy the **r** of Israel?"
Am 5:15 will have mercy on the **r** of Joseph.
9:12 that they may possess the **r** of Edom
Mic 2:12 bring together the **r** of Israel.
4: 7 I will make the lame a **r**, those
5: 7 The **r** of Jacob will be in the midst
5: 8 The **r** of Jacob will be among the
7:18 of the **r** of his inheritance?
Zep 1: 4 off from this place every **r** of Baal,
2: 7 will belong to the **r** of the house of
2: 9 The **r** of my people will plunder them;
3:13 The **r** of Israel will do no wrong;
Hag 1:12 the high priest, and the whole **r** of
1:14 spirit of the whole **r** of the people.
2: 2 priest, and to the **r** of the people.
Zec 8: 6 "It may seem marvellous to the **r** of
8:11 now I will not deal with the **r** of
8:12 inheritance to the **r** of this people.
Ac 15:17 that the **r** of men may seek the Lord,
Ro 9:27 the sea, only the **r** will be saved.
11: 5 too, at the present time there is a **r**

Remorse
Mt 27: 3 he was seized with **r** and returned

Remote (Remotest)
Jdg 19: 1 Now a Levite who lived in a **r** area
19:18 from Bethlehem in Judah to a **r** area
Mt 14:15 "This is a **r** place, and it's already
15:33 this **r** place to feed such a crowd?"
Mk 6:35 "This is a **r** place," they said, "and
8: 4 "But where in this **r** place can
Lk 9:12 because we are in a **r** place here."

Remotest (Remote)
2Ki 19:23 **r** parts, the finest of its forests.
Ne 9:22 to them even the **r** frontiers.
Isa 37:24 **r** heights, the finest of its forests.

Removal (Remove)
Isa 27: 9 full fruitage of the **r** of his sin:
1Pe 3:21 not the **r** of dirt from the body but

Remove (Removal, Removed, Removes, Removing)
Ge 30:32 **r** from them every speckled or
Ex 12:15 On the first day **r** the yeast from
27: 3 of bronze—its pots to **r** the ashes,
33:23 I will **r** my hand and you will see my
Lev 1:16 He is to **r** the crop with its
3: 4 which he will **r** with the kidneys.
3:10 which he will **r** with the kidneys.
3:15 which he will **r** with the kidneys.
4: 8 He shall **r** all the fat from the bull
4: 9 which he will **r** with the kidneys—
4:19 He shall **r** all the fat from it and
4:31 He shall **r** all the fat, just as the
Lev 4:35 He shall **r** all the fat, just as the
6:10 and shall **r** the ashes of the burnt
26: 6 I will **r** savage beasts from the land,
Nu 4:13 "They are to **r** the ashes from the
20:26 **R** Aaron's garments and put them on
Jos 7:13 against your enemies until you **r** it.
1Ki 15:14 Although he did not **r** the high
20:24 Do this: **R** all the kings from their
2Ki 23: 4 the doorkeepers to **r** from the temple
23:27 the LORD said, "I will **r** Judah also
24: 3 in order to **r** them from his presence
2Ch 15:17 Although he did not **r** the high
29: 5 **R** all defilement from the sanctuary.
32:12 Did not Hezekiah himself **r** this
Job 9:34 someone to **r** God's rod from me, that
22:23 you **r** wickedness far from your
Ps 39:10 **R** your scourge from me; I am
119:22 **R** from me scorn and contempt, for I
Pr 25: 4 **R** the dross from the silver, and out
25: 5 **r** the wicked from the king's
27:22 you will not **r** his folly from him.
Isa 1:25 dross and **r** all your impurities.
25: 8 he will **r** the disgrace of his people
57:14 prepare the road! **R** the obstacles
62:10 build up the highway! **R** the stones
Jer 27:10 serve to **r** you far from your lands;
28:16 to **r** you from the face of the earth.
32:31 that I must **r** it from my sight.
Eze 11:18 "They will return to it and **r** all
11:19 I will **r** from them their heart of
21:26 Take off the turban, **r** the crown.
34:10 I will **r** them from tending the flock
36:26 I will **r** from you your heart of
Hos 2: 2 Let her **r** the adulterous look from
2:17 I will **r** the names of the Baals from
Zep 3:11 because I will **r** from this city
3:18 appointed feasts I will **r** from you;
Zec 3: 9 'and I will **r** the sin of this land
13: 2 "I will **r** both the prophets and the
Mt 7: 5 **r** the speck from your brother's eye.
Lk 6:42 **r** the speck from your brother's eye.
Rev 2: 5 and **r** your lampstand from its place.

Removed (Remove)
Ge 8:13 Noah then **r** the covering from the
30:35 That same day he **r** all the male
48:12 Joseph **r** them from Israel's knees
Ex 25:15 of this ark; they are not to be **r**.
34:34 he **r** the veil until he came out.
Lev 4:10 just as the fat is **r** from the ox
4:31 just as the fat is **r** from the
4:35 just as the fat is **r** from the lamb
7: 4 which is to be **r** with the kidneys.
Nu 20:28 Moses **r** Aaron's garments and put
Dt 26:13 say to the LORD your God: "I have **r**
26:14 nor have I **r** any of it while I was
Ru 4: 8 And he **r** his sandal.
1Sa 21: 6 had been **r** from before the LORD
2Sa 7:15 from Saul, whom I **r** from before you.
20:13 After Amasa had been **r** from the road,
1Ki 2:27 Solomon **r** Abiathar from the
5:17 At the king's command they **r** from
20:41 the prophet quickly **r** the headband
22:43 The high places, however, were not **r**,
2Ki 12: 3 The high places, however, were not **r**;
14: 4 The high places, however, were not **r**;
15: 4 The high places, however, were not **r**;
15:35 The high places, however, were not **r**;
16:17 **r** the basins from the movable stands.
16:17 He **r** the Sea from the bronze bulls
16:18 **r** the royal entrance outside the
17:18 Israel and **r** them from his presence.
17:23 until the LORD **r** them from his
18: 4 He **r** the high places, smashed the
18:22 high places and altars Hezekiah **r**,
23:11 He **r** from the entrance to the temple
23:12 He **r** them from there, smashed them
23:16 he had the bones **r** from them and
23:19 Josiah **r** and defiled all the shrines
23:27 also from my presence as I **r** Israel,
24:13 Nebuchadnezzar **r** all the treasures
2Ch 14: 3 He **r** the foreign altars and the high
14: 5 He **r** the high places and incense
15: 8 He **r** the detestable idols from the
17: 6 he **r** the high places and the Asherah

2Ch 20:33 The high places, however, were not **r**,
29:19 all the articles that King Ahaz **r**
30:14 They **r** the altars in Jerusalem and
33:15 He got rid of the foreign gods and **r**
34:33 Josiah **r** all the detestable idols
Ezr 5:14 He even **r** from the temple of Babylon
Job 19: 9 He has stripped me of my honour and **r**
34:20 the mighty are **r** without human hand.
Ps 30:11 you **r** my sackcloth and clothed me
81: 6 He says, "I **r** the burden from their
103:12 has he **r** our transgressions from us.
Pr 27:25 the hay is **r** and new growth appears
Isa 10:13 I **r** the boundaries of nations, I
14:25 his burden **r** from their shoulders."
36: 7 high places and altars Hezekiah **r**,
54:10 be shaken and the hills be **r**,
54:10 nor my covenant of peace be **r**,"
54:14 be far **r**; it will not come near you.
Jer 8: 1 will be **r** from their graves.
28: 3 **r** from here and took to Babylon.
Eze 24:12 has not been **r**, not even by fire.
Jn 20: 1 stone had been **r** from the entrance.
2Co 3:14 It has not been **r**, because only in
Rev 6:14 and island was **r** from its place.

Removes (Remove)

1Sa 17:26 and **r** this disgrace from Israel?

Removing (Remove)

Ac 13:22 After **r** Saul, he made David their
Heb 12:27 The words "once more" indicate the **r**

Rend

Isa 64: 1 Oh, that you would **r** the heavens and
Joel 2:13 **R** your heart and not your garments.

Render (Rendering)

Isa 16: 3 "Give us counsel, **r** a decision. Make
Zec 8:16 and **r** true and sound judgment in

Rendering (Render)

Isa 28: 7 they stumble when **r** decisions.

Renegades

Jdg 12: 4 are **r** from Ephraim and Manasseh."

Renew (Renewal, Renewed, Renewing)

Ru 4:15 He will **r** your life and sustain you
Ps 51:10 and **r** a steadfast spirit within me.
104:30 and you **r** the face of the earth.
Isa 40:31 those who hope in the LORD will **r**
41: 1 Let the nations **r** their strength!
61: 4 they will **r** the ruined cities that
Lam 5:21 we may return; **r** our days as of old
Hab 3: 2 **R** them in our day, in our time make

Renewal (Renew)

Job 14:14 I will wait for my **r** to come.
Isa 57:10 You found **r** of your strength, and
Mt 19:28 "I tell you the truth, at the **r** of
Tit 3: 5 of rebirth and **r** by the Holy Spirit,

Renewed (Renew)

2Ki 23: 3 by the pillar and **r** the covenant
2Ch 34:31 The king stood by his pillar and **r**
Job 33:25 his flesh is **r** like a child's; it is
Ps 103: 5 your youth is **r** like the eagle's.
2Co 4:16 inwardly we are being **r** day by day.
Php 4:10 last you have **r** your concern for me.
Col 3:10 which is being **r** in knowledge in the

Renewing (Renew)

Ro 12: 2 transformed by the **r** of your mind.

Renounce (Renounced, Renounces)

Eze 14: 6 and **r** all your detestable practices!
Da 4:27 accept my advice: **R** your sins
Rev 2:13 You did not **r** your faith in me, even

Renounced (Renounce)

Ps 89:39 You have **r** the covenant with your
Mt 19:12 and others have **r** marriage because
2Co 4: 2 Rather, we have **r** secret and

Renounces (Renounce)

Pr 28:13 confesses and **r** them finds mercy.

Renown (Renowned)

Ge 6: 4 were the heroes of old, men of **r**.
Ps 102:12 **r** endures through all generations.
135:13 endures for ever, your **r**, O LORD,
Isa 26: 8 and **r** are the desire of our hearts.
55:13 This will be for the LORD's **r**, for
63:12 to gain for himself everlasting **r**,
Jer 13:11 for my **r** and praise and honour.
32:20 gained the **r** that is still yours.
33: 9 this city will bring me **r**, joy,
49:25 Why has the city of **r** not been
Eze 26:17 'How you are destroyed, O city of **r**,
Hos 12: 5 Almighty, the LORD is his name of **r**!

Renowned (Renown)

Isa 23: 8 whose traders are **r** in the earth?
23: 9 humble all who are **r** on the earth.
Eze 34:29 I will provide for them a land **r** for

Rent (Rented)

Mt 21:41 "and he will **r** the vineyard to other

Rented (Rent)

Mt 21:33 Then he **r** the vineyard to some
Mk 12: 1 Then he **r** the vineyard to some
Lk 20: 9 "A man planted a vineyard, **r** it to
Ac 28:30 Paul stayed there in his own **r** house

Repaid (Repay)

Ge 44: 4 'Why have you **r** good with evil?
Jdg 9:56 Thus God **r** the wickedness that
2Sa 16: 8 The LORD has **r** you for all the blood
Pr 14:14 The faithless will be fully **r** for
Jer 18:20 Should good be **r** with evil? Yet they
Lk 6:34 expecting to be **r** in full.
14:12 you back and so you will be **r**.
14:14 you will be **r** at the resurrection of
Col 3:25 Anyone who does wrong will be **r** for

Repair (Repaired, Repairer, Repairing, Repairs)

2Ki 12: 5 and let it be used to **r** whatever
12: 8 would not **r** the temple themselves.
12:12 for the **r** of the temple of the LORD,
12:14 who used it to **r** the temple.
22: 5 who **r** the temple of the LORD—
22: 6 and dressed stone to **r** the temple.
1Ch 26:27 for the **r** of the temple of the LORD.
2Ch 24: 5 Israel, to **r** the temple of your God.
24:12 in iron and bronze to **r** the temple.
34: 8 to **r** the temple of the LORD his God.
Ezr 9: 9 house of our God and **r** its ruins,
Eze 13: 5 to the breaks in the wall to **r** it
Am 9:11 I will **r** its broken places, restore
Na 3:14 tread the mortar, **r** the brickwork!

Repaired (Repair)

1Ki 18:30 They came to him, and he **r** the
2Ki 12: 6 priests still had not **r** the temple.
2Ch 15: 8 He **r** the altar of the LORD that was
29: 3 the temple of the LORD and **r** them.
34:10 who **r** and restored the temple.
Ne 3: 4 son of Hakkoz, **r** the next section.
3: 5 The next section was **r** by the men of
3: 6 The Jeshanah Gate was **r** by Joiada
3: 8 one of the goldsmiths, **r** the next
3: 9 of Jerusalem, **r** the next section.
3:11 Hasshub son of Pahath-Moab **r** another
3:12 **r** the next section with the help of
3:13 The Valley Gate was **r** by Hanun and
3:13 They also **r** five hundred yards of
3:14 The Dung Gate was **r** by Malkijah son
3:15 The Fountain Gate was **r** by Shallun
3:15 He also **r** the wall of the Pool of
3:19 ruler of Mizpah, **r** another section,
Ne 3:20 Baruch son of Zabbai zealously **r**
3:21 the son of Hakkoz, **r** another section,
3:24 Next to him, Binnui son of Henadad **r**
3:27 Next to them, the men of Tekoa **r**
3:30 son of Zalaph, **r** another section.
Jer 19:11 jar is smashed and cannot be **r**.

Repairer (Repair)

Isa 58:12 will be called **R** of Broken Walls,

Repairing (Repair)

2Ki 12: 7 "Why aren't you **r** the damage done to
12: 7 but hand it over for **r** the temple."
2Ch 32: 5 he worked hard **r** all the broken
Ezr 4:12 the walls and **r** the foundations.

Repairs (Repair)

2Ch 24:13 and the **r** progressed under them.
Ne 3: 4 the son of Meshezabel, made **r**, and
3: 4 him Zadok son of Baana also made **r**.
3: 7 Next to them, **r** were made by men
3: 8 perfume-makers, made **r** next to that.
3:10 Jedaiah son of Harumaph made **r**
3:10 of Hashabneiah made **r** next to him.
3:16 made **r** up to a point opposite the
3:17 Next to him, the **r** were made by the
3:17 carried out **r** for his district.
3:18 Next to him, the **r** were made by
3:22 The **r** next to him were made by the
3:23 Benjamin and Hasshub made **r** in front
3:23 of Ananiah, made **r** beside his house.
3:26 made **r** up to a point opposite the
3:28 **r**, each in front of his own house.
3:29 of Immer made **r** opposite his house.
3:29 the guard at the East Gate, made **r**.
3:30 made **r** opposite his living quarters.
3:31 one of the goldsmiths, made **r** as far
3:32 the goldsmiths and merchants made **r**.
4: 7 the men of Ashdod heard that the **r**

Repay (Pay, Repaid, Repaying, Repayment, Repays)

Lev 25:28 he does not acquire the means to **r**
Dt 7:10 those who hate him he will **r** to
7:10 **r** to their face those who hate him.
32: 6 Is this the way you **r** the LORD,
32:35 is mine to avenge; I will **r**. In due
32:41 adversaries and **r** those who hate me.
Ru 2:12 May the LORD **r** you for what you have
2Sa 3:39 May the LORD **r** the evildoer
16:12 **r** me with good for the cursing I am
1Ki 2:32 The LORD will **r** him for the blood he
2:44 LORD will **r** you for your wrongdoing.
Job 21:19 Let him **r** the man himself, so that
Ps 28: 4 **R** them for their deeds and for their
28: 4 **r** them for what their hands have
35:12 They **r** me evil for good and leave my
37:21 The wicked borrow and do not **r**, but
38:20 Those who **r** my good with evil
41:10 me; raise me up, that I may **r** them.
94:23 He will **r** them for their sins and
103:10 or **r** us according to our iniquities.
109: 5 They **r** me evil for good, and hatred
116:12 How can I **r** the LORD for all his
Pr 24:12 Will he not **r** each person according
Isa 59:18 so will he **r** wrath to his enemies
59:18 he will **r** the islands their due.
Jer 16:18 I will **r** them double for their
25:14 I will **r** them according to their
50:29 **R** her for her deeds; do to her as
51:24 "Before your eyes I will **r** Babylon
51:56 of retribution; he will **r** in full.
Eze 7: 3 **r** you for all your detestable
7: 4 I will surely **r** you for your conduct
7: 8 **r** you for all your detestable
7: 9 I will **r** you in accordance with your
Hos 4: 9 ways and **r** them for their deeds.
12: 2 and **r** him according to his deeds.
12:14 and will **r** him for his contempt.
Joel 2:25 **r** you for the years the locusts
Mt 18:25 that he had be sold to **r** the debt.
Lk 14:14 Although they cannot **r** you, you will
Ro 11:35 to God, that God should **r** him?"
12:17 Do not **r** anyone evil for evil. Be

Ro 12:19 to avenge; I will **r**," says the Lord.
2Ti 4:14 Lord will **r** him for what he has done.
Heb 10:30 "It is mine to avenge; I will **r**,"
1Pe 3: 9 Do not **r** evil with evil or insult
Rev 2:23 and I will **r** each of you according

Repaying (Repay)
2Ch 6:23 Judge between your servants, **r** the
20:11 See how they are **r** us by coming to
Isa 66: 6 LORD **r** his enemies all they deserve.
Joel 3: 4 Are you **r** me for something I have
1Ti 5: 4 so **r** their parents and grandparents,

Repayment (Repay)
Lk 6:34 to those from whom you expect **r**,

Repays (Repay)
Job 21:31 Who **r** him for what he has done?
34:11 He **r** a man for what he has done; he
Ps 137: 8 **r** you for what you have done to us—

Repealed
Est 1:19 which cannot be **r**, that Vashti is
Da 6: 8 and Persians, which cannot be **r**."
6:12 and Persians, which cannot be **r**."

Repeat (Repeated, Repeats)
2Co 11:16 I **r**: Let no-one take me for a fool.
13: 2 I now **r** it while absent: On my

Repeated (Repeat)
Ge 44: 6 he caught up with them, he **r** these
Jdg 9: 3 the brothers **r** all this to the
11:11 And he **r** all his words before the
1Sa 8:21 said, he **r** it before the LORD.
11: 5 Why are they weeping?" Then they **r**
17:27 They **r** to him what they had been
18:23 They **r** these words to David. But
Heb 10: 1 by the same sacrifices **r** endlessly

Repeats (Repeat)
Pr 17: 9 **r** the matter separates close friends.
26:11 to its vomit, so a fool **r** his folly.

Repent (Penitent, *Repent and believe*, Repentance, Repented, Repents)
1Ki 8:47 and **r** and plead with you in the land
2Ch 6:37 and **r** and plead with you in the land
Job 34:33 when you refuse to **r**? You must
36:10 commands them to **r** of their evil.
42: 6 Therefore I despise myself and **r** in
Isa 59:20 **r** of their sins," declares the LORD.
Jer 5: 3 harder than stone and refused to **r**.
15:19 "If you **r**, I will restore you that
Eze 14: 6 **R**! Turn from your idols and renounce
18:30 **R**! Turn away from all your offences;
18:32 the Sovereign LORD. **R** and live!
Hos 11: 5 over them because they refuse to **r**?
Mt 3: 2 saying, "**R**, for the kingdom of
4:17 **R**, for the kingdom of heaven is near.
11:20 performed, because they did not **r**.
Mk 6:12 and preached that people should **r**.
Lk 13: 3 I tell you, no! But unless you **r**,
13: 5 I tell you, no! But unless you **r**,
15: 7 persons who do not need to **r**.
16:30 the dead goes to them, they will **r**.'
17: 4 you and says, 'I **r**,' forgive him."
Ac 2:38 Peter replied, "**R** and be baptised,
3:19 **R**, then, and turn to God, so that
8:22 **R** of this wickedness and pray to the
17:30 commands all people everywhere to **r**.
26:20 I preached that they should **r** and
Rev 2: 5 **R** and do the things you did at first.
2: 5 If you do not **r**, I will come to you
2:16 **R** therefore! Otherwise, I will soon
2:21 I have given her time to **r** of her
2:22 unless they **r** of her ways.
3: 3 received and heard; obey it, and **r**.
3:19 So be earnest, and **r**.
9:20 not **r** of the work of their hands;
9:21 Nor did they **r** of their murders,
Rev 16: 9 they refused to **r** and glorify him.
16:11 refused to **r** of what they had done.

Repent and believe
Mt 21:32 you saw this, you did not **r** him.
Mk 1:15 "The kingdom of God is near. **R** the

Repentance (*Baptism of repentance*, Repent)
Isa 30:15 "In **r** and rest is your salvation, in
Mt 3: 8 Produce fruit in keeping with **r**.
3:11 "I baptise you with water for **r**. But
Lk 3: 8 Produce fruit in keeping with **r**. And
5:32 the righteous, but sinners to **r**."
24:47 **r** and forgiveness of sins will be
Ac 5:31 **r** and forgiveness of sins to Israel.
11:18 even the Gentiles **r** unto life."
13:24 John preached **r** and baptism to all
20:21 turn to God in **r** and have faith in
26:20 God and prove their **r** by their deeds.
Ro 2: 4 God's kindness leads you towards **r**?
2Co 7: 9 because your sorrow led you to **r**.
7:10 Godly sorrow brings **r** that leads to
2Ti 2:25 hope that God will grant them **r**
Heb 6: 1 of **r** from acts that lead to death,
6: 6 to be brought back to **r**, because to
2Pe 3: 9 perish, but everyone to come to **r**.

Repented (Repent)
2Ch 32:26 Hezekiah **r** of the pride of his heart,
Jer 31:19 After I strayed, I **r**; after I came
34:15 Recently you **r** and did what is right
Zec 1: 6 "Then they **r** and said, 'The LORD
Mt 11:21 **r** long ago in sackcloth and ashes.
12:41 they **r** at the preaching of Jonah,
Lk 10:13 they would have **r** long ago, sitting
11:32 they **r** at the preaching of Jonah,
2Co 12:21 and have not **r** of the impurity,

Repents (Repent)
Jer 8: 6 No-one **r** of his wickedness, saying,
18: 8 if that nation I warned **r** of its
Lk 15: 7 in heaven over one sinner who **r**
15:10 of God over one sinner who **r**."
17: 3 him, and if he **r**, forgive him.

Rephael
1Ch 26: 7 The sons of Shemaiah: Othni, **R**, Obed

Rephah
1Ch 7:25 **R** was his son, Resheph his son,

Rephaiah
1Ch 3:21 and the sons of **R**, of Arnan, of
4:42 led by Pelatiah, Neariah, **R** and
7: 2 The sons of Tola: Uzzi, **R**, Jeriel,
9:43 the father of Binea; **R** was his son,
Ne 3: 9 **R** son of Hur, ruler of a

Rephaim
Jos 15: 8 the northern end of the Valley of **R**.
18:16 Ben Hinnom, north of the Valley of **R**.
2Sa 5:18 and spread out in the Valley of **R**;
5:22 and spread out in the Valley of **R**;
23:13 was encamped in the Valley of **R**.
1Ch 11:15 was encamped in the Valley of **R**.
14: 9 had come and raided the Valley of **R**;
Isa 17: 5 ears of corn in the Valley of **R**.

Rephaites
Ge 14: 5 defeated the **R** in Ashteroth Karnaim,
15:20 Hittites, Perizzites, **R**,
Dt 2:11 they too were considered **R**, but the
2:20 too was considered a land of the **R**,
3:11 was left of the remnant of the **R**.
3:13 used to be known as a land of the **R**.
Jos 12: 4 one of the last of the **R**, who
13:12 as one of the last of the **R**.
17:15 the land of the Perizzites and **R**."
1Ch 20: 4 one of the descendants of the **R**, and

Rephan
Ac 7:43 your god **R**, the idols you made to

Rephidim
Ex 17: 1 They camped at **R**, but there was no
17: 8 and attacked the Israelites at **R**.
19: 2 After they set out from **R**, they
Nu 33:14 They left Alush and camped at **R**,
33:15 They left **R** and camped in the Desert

Replace (Replaced)
Lev 14:42 to take other stones to **r** these
1Ki 14:27 made bronze shields to **r** them
20:24 and **r** them with other officers.
2Ki 17:24 of Samaria to **r** the Israelites.
2Ch 12:10 made bronze shields to **r** them
Isa 9:10 but we will **r** them with cedars."

Replaced (Replace)
1Sa 21: 6 **r** by hot bread on the day it was
1Ki 2:35 **r** Abiathar with Zadok the priest.
Da 8:22 The four horns that **r** the one that

Replanted (Plant)
Eze 36:36 and have **r** what was desolate.

Replica
Jos 22:28 we will answer: Look at the **r** of the

Repointing
1Sa 13:21 forks and axes and for **r** goads.

Report (Reported, Reporting, Reports)
Ge 37: 2 their father a bad **r** about them.
Nu 13:32 **r** about the land they had explored.
14:15 heard this **r** about you will say,
14:36 him by spreading a bad **r** about it—
14:37 **r** about the land were struck down
Dt 1:22 bring back a **r** about the route we
Jos 14: 7 a **r** according to my convictions,
22:33 They were glad to hear the **r** and
1Sa 2:24 No, my sons; it is not a good **r** that
2Sa 1: 5 the young man who brought him the **r**,
1:13 him the **r**, "Where are you from?"
13:30 the **r** came to David: "Absalom has
13:33 **r** that all the king's sons are dead.
1Ki 10: 6 She said to the king, "The **r** I heard
10: 7 you have far exceeded the **r** I heard.
2Ki 6:13 The **r** came back: "He is in Dothan."
7: 9 and **r** this to the royal palace."
19: 7 him that when he hears a certain **r**,
19: 9 Now Sennacherib received a **r** that
1Ch 21: 2 Then **r** back to me so that I may know
2Ch 9: 5 She said to the king, "The **r** I heard
9: 6 you have far exceeded the **r** I heard.
Ezr 5: 5 and they were not stopped until a **r**
5: 7 The **r** they sent him read as follows:
Ne 6: 7 **r** will get back to the king; so come,
Est 2:23 the **r** was investigated and found to
Job 38:35 Do they **r** to you, 'Here we are'?
Ecc 10:20 bird on the wing may **r** what you say.
Isa 21: 6 lookout and have him **r** what he sees.
23: 5 be in anguish at the **r** from Tyre.
37: 7 so that when he hears a certain **r**,
37: 9 Now Sennacherib received a **r** that
Jer 10:22 Listen! The **r** is coming—a great
20:10 "Terror on every side! **R** him! Let's **r**
36:16 must **r** all these words to the king."
37: 5 Jerusalem heard the **r** about them,
Mt 2: 8 As soon as you find him, **r** to me, so
11: 4 Jesus replied, "Go back and **r** to
28:14 If this **r** gets to the governor, we
Lk 7:22 "Go back and **r** to John what you have
Jn 11:57 **r** it so that they might arrest him.
Ac 5:24 On hearing this **r**, the captain of
2Co 6: 8 and dishonour, bad **r** and good **r**;
Gal 1:23 They only heard the **r**: "The man who
1Th 1: 9 for they themselves **r** what kind of
2Th 2: 2 **r** or letter supposed to have come

Reported (Report)
Ge 14:13 One who had escaped came and **r** this
Ex 6: 9 Moses **r** this to the Israelites, but
16:22 community came and **r** this to Moses.
Nu 13:26 There they **r** to them and to the

Nu 14:39 Moses **r** this to all the Israelites,
Dt 1:25 they brought it down to us and **r**,
Jos 22:32 in Gilead and **r** to the Israelites.
Jdg 9:25 by, and this was **r** to Abimelech.
9:42 fields, and this was **r** to Abimelech.
1Sa 11: 4 Saul and **r** these terms to the people,
11: 9 When the messengers went and **r**
17:31 What David said was overheard and **r**
25:12 When they arrived, they **r** every word.
2Sa 7:17 Nathan **r** to David all the words of
18:25 called out to the king and **r** it.
24: 9 Joab **r** the number of the fighting
1Ki 2:30 Benaiah **r** to the king, "This is how
13:25 and they went and **r** it in the city
18:44 The seventh time the servant **r**, "A
20:17 **r**, "Men are advancing from Samaria.
2Ki 7:11 and it was **r** within the palace.
7:15 returned and **r** to the king.
9:18 The lookout **r**, "The messenger has
9:20 The lookout **r**, "He has reached them,
17:26 was **r** to the king of Assyria: "The
22: 9 went to the king and **r** to him:
1Ch 17:15 Nathan **r** to David all the words of
21: 5 Joab **r** the number of the fighting
2Ch 29:18 they went in to King Hezekiah and **r**:
34:16 the book to the king and **r** to him:
Ne 6: 6 in which was written: "It is **r** among
Est 2:22 who in turn **r** it to the king, giving
4: 9 Hathach went back and **r** to Esther
4:12 Esther's words were **r** to Mordecai,
9:11 Susa was **r** to the king that same day.
Jer 36:20 courtyard and **r** everything to him.
Zec 1:11 they **r** to the angel of the LORD, who
Mt 8:33 went into the town and **r** all this,
28:11 **r** to the chief priests everything
Mk 5:14 Those tending the pigs ran off and **r**
6:30 **r** to him all they had done and
16:13 These returned and **r** it to the rest;
Lk 8:34 **r** this in the town and countryside,
9:10 the apostles returned, they **r** to
14:21 "The servant came back and **r** this to
Ac 4:23 **r** all that the chief priests and
5:22 there. So they went back and **r**,
14:27 **r** all that God had done through them
15: 4 to whom they **r** everything God had
16:38 The officers **r** this to the
21:19 Paul greeted them and **r** in detail
22:26 he went to the commander and **r** it.
23:22 anyone that you have **r** this to me."
28:21 **r** or said anything bad about you.
Ro 1: 8 faith is being **r** all over the world.
3: 8 are being slanderously **r** as saying
1Co 5: 1 is actually **r** that there is sexual

Reporting (Report)
Ne 6:19 Moreover, they kept **r** to me his good

Reports (Report)
Ex 23: 1 "Do not spread false **r**. Do not help
Dt 2:25 They will hear **r** of you and will
Jos 9: 9 **r** of him: all that he did in Egypt,
Ne 6: 6 **r** you are about to become their
Jer 6:24 We have heard **r** about them, and our
50:43 The king of Babylon has heard **r**
Da 11:44 **r** from the east and the north will
Mt 14: 1 tetrarch heard the **r** about Jesus,
Ac 9:13 "I have heard many **r** about this man
21:24 is no truth in these **r** about you,

Repose (Reposes)
Dt 28:65 those nations you will find no **r**,
Isa 28:12 place of **r**"—but they would not
34:14 the night creatures will also **r**

Reposes (Repose)
Pr 14:33 Wisdom **r** in the heart of the

Represent (Representation, Representative, Representatives, Represented, Representing, Represents)
Lev 24: 7 a memorial portion to **r** the bread
Jer 40:10 I myself will stay in Mizpah to **r**
Da 8:22 **r** four kingdoms that will emerge
Gal 3:20 A mediator, however, does not **r** just
Gal 4:24 for the women **r** two covenants.
Heb 5: 1 to **r** them in matters related to God,

Representation (Represent)
Heb 1: 3 glory and the exact **r** of his being,

Representative (Represent)
Ex 18:19 You must be the people's **r** before
2Sa 15: 3 is no **r** of the king to hear you."

Representatives (Represent)
2Co 8:23 they are **r** of the churches and an

Represented (Represent)
Nu 17: 8 which **r** the house of Levi, had not
Jdg 18: 2 These men **r** all their clans. They

Representing (Represent)
Ex 24: 4 **r** the twelve tribes of Israel.
Nu 1:44 of Israel, each one **r** his family.

Represents (Represent)
Da 8:20 The two-horned ram that you saw **r**

Reprimanded
Jer 29:27 why have you not **r** Jeremiah from

Reproach (Reproached)
Jos 5: 9 rolled away the **r** of Egypt from you.
Ne 5: 9 avoid the **r** of our Gentile enemies?
Job 27: 6 will not **r** me as long as I live.
Ps 44:13 You have made us a **r** to our
44:16 at the taunts of those who **r** and
79: 4 We are objects of **r** to our
79:12 **r** they have hurled at you, O Lord.
Isa 51: 7 Do not fear the **r** of men or be
54: 4 no more the **r** of your widowhood.
Jer 15:15 of how I suffer **r** for your sake.
20: 8 me insult and **r** all day long.
24: 9 a **r** and a byword, an object of
29:18 of scorn and **r**, among all the
42:18 of condemnation and **r**; you will
44: 8 **r** among all the nations on earth.
44:12 and horror, of condemnation and **r**.
49:13 of **r** and of cursing; and all its
Eze 5:14 "I will make you a ruin and a **r**
5:15 You will be a **r** and a taunt, a
Zep 3:18 they are a burden and a **r** to you.
1Ti 3: 2 Now the overseer must be above **r**,

Reproached (Reproach)
Job 19: 3 Ten times now you have **r** me;

Reproves
Am 5:10 you hate the one who **r** in court and

Reptiles
1Ki 4:33 about animals and birds, **r** and fish.
Ac 10:12 **r** of the earth and birds of the air.
11: 6 beasts, **r**, and birds of the air.
Ro 1:23 man and birds and animals and **r**.
Jas 3: 7 All kinds of animals, birds, **r** and

Repulse (Repulsive)
2Ki 18:24 How can you **r** one officer of the
Isa 36: 9 How then can you **r** one officer of

Repulsive (Repulse)
1Ki 15:13 she had made a **r** Asherah pole.
1Ch 21: 6 the king's command was **r** to him.
2Ch 15:16 she had made a **r** Asherah pole.
Job 33:20 that his very being finds food **r** and
Ps 88: 8 friends and have made me **r** to them.
Jer 23:13 of Samaria I saw this **r** thing:

Reputation (Reputed)
Est 9: 4 **r** spread throughout the provinces,
Pr 25:10 and you will never lose your bad **r**.
1Ti 3: 7 He must also have a good **r** with
Rev 3: 1 **r** of being alive, but you are dead.

Reputed (Reputation)
Gal 2: 9 James, Peter and John, those **r** to be

Request (Requested, Requesting, Requests)
Ge 19:21 "Very well, I will grant this **r** too;
Jdg 6:39 Let me make just one more **r**. Allow
8: 8 Peniel and made the same **r** of them,
8:24 he said, "I do have one **r**, that each
11:37 grant me this one **r**," she said.
1Sa 25:35 your words and granted your **r**."
2Sa 12:20 **r** they served him food, and he ate.
14:22 king has granted his servant's **r**."
1Ki 2:16 Now I have one **r** to make of you. Do
2:20 "I have one small **r** to make of you,"
2:22 "Why do you **r** Abishag the Shunammite
2:22 **r** the kingdom for him—after all,
2:23 not pay with his life for this **r**!
1Ch 4:10 from pain." And God granted his **r**.
Est 5: 3 Queen Esther? What is your **r**? Even
5: 6 And what is your **r**? Even up to half
5: 7 Esther replied, "My petition and my **r**
5: 8 grant my petition and fulfil my **r**,
7: 2 What is your **r**? Even up to half the
7: 3 And spare my people—this is my **r**.
9:12 is your **r**? It will also be granted."
Job 6: 8 "Oh, that I might have my **r**, that
Ps 21: 2 have not withheld the **r** of his lips.
Da 2:49 Moreover, at Daniel's **r** the king
9:20 making my **r** to the LORD my God for
Mt 14: 9 he ordered that her **r** be granted
15:28 have great faith! Your **r** is granted.
Mk 6:25 hurried in to the king with the **r**:
Jn 12:21 from Bethsaida in Galilee, with a **r**.
Ac 23:21 for your consent to their **r**."
24: 4 I would **r** that you be kind enough to

Requested (Request)
Ex 12:31 Go, worship the LORD as you have **r**.
Ezr 6: 9 and wheat, salt, wine and oil, as **r**
Jer 42: 4 to the LORD your God as you have **r**;
Mk 15: 6 a prisoner whom the people **r**.
Ac 25: 3 They urgently **r** Festus, as a favour

Requesting (Request)
Ac 16:39 prison, **r** them to leave the city.

Requests (Request)
Ne 2: 8 was upon me, the king granted my **r**.
Ps 5: 3 **r** before you and wait in expectation.
20: 5 May the LORD grant all your **r**.
Da 9:18 We do not make **r** of you because we
Eph 6:18 with all kinds of prayers and **r**.
Php 4: 6 thanksgiving, present your **r** to God.
1Ti 2: 1 I urge, then, first of all, that **r**,

Require (Required, Requirement, Requirements, Requires, Requiring)
Ex 5: 8 **r** them to make the same number of
Dt 15: 2 He shall not **r** payment from his
15: 3 You may **r** payment from a foreigner,
2Ki 12:15 They did not **r** an accounting from
Ps 40: 6 and sin offerings you did not **r**.
Eze 18:16 He does not oppress anyone or **r** a
20:40 There I will **r** your offerings and
Mic 6: 8 And what does the LORD **r** of you? To

Required (Require)
Ge 50: 3 that was the time **r** for embalming.
Ex 5:13 "Complete the work **r** of you for each
5:19 of bricks **r** of you for each day."
22:11 this, and no restitution is **r**.
22:13 not be **r** to pay for the torn animal.
Lev 23:37 and drink offerings **r** for each day.
27:16 to the amount of seed **r** for it
Nu 7: 7 to the Gershonites, as their work **r**,
7: 8 to the Merarites, as their work **r**.
Jos 16:10 but are **r** to do forced labour.
1Ki 8:31 is **r** to take an oath and he comes
2Ch 6:22 is **r** to take an oath and he comes
24: 6 "Why haven't you **r** the Levites to
24: 9 God had **r** of Israel in the desert.
24:12 work **r** for the temple of the LORD.
Ezr 3: 4 the **r** number of burnt offerings

Ne 12:44 **r** by the Law for the priests
Jnh 3: 3 city—a visit **r** three days.
Lk 2:27 him what the custom of the Law **r**,
2:39 Joseph and Mary had done everything **r**
3:13 than you are **r** to," he told them.
Ac 15: 5 and **r** to obey the law of Moses."
Ro 2:14 do by nature things **r** by the law,
1Co 4: 2 Now it is **r** that those who have been
Gal 5: 3 that he is **r** to obey the whole law.
Heb 10: 8 (although the law **r** them to be made).

Requirement (Require)

Nu 19: 2 "This is a **r** of the law that the
27:11 This is to be a legal **r** for the
31:21 "This is the **r** of the law that the
2Ch 8:13 according to the daily **r** for
8:14 priests according to each day's **r**.

Requirements (Require)

Ge 26: 5 Abraham obeyed me and kept my **r**, my
Lev 18:30 Keep my **r** and do not follow any of
22: 9 "'The priests are to keep my **r** so
Nu 35:29 "'These are to be legal **r** for you
Dt 11: 1 Love the LORD your God and keep his **r**
1Ki 2: 3 his laws and **r**, as written in the
2Ki 23:24 This he did to fulfil the **r** of the
1Ch 16:37 according to each day's **r**.
29:19 **r** and decrees and to do everything
2Ch 13:11 We are observing the **r** of the LORD
Jer 5: 4 way of the LORD, the **r** of their God.
5: 5 way of the LORD, the **r** of their God.
8: 7 do not know the **r** of the LORD.
Zec 3: 7 will walk in my ways and keep my **r**,
Mal 3:14 did we gain by carrying out his **r**
Ac 15:28 anything beyond the following **r**:
Ro 2:15 since they show that the **r** of the
2:26 not circumcised keep the law's **r**,
8: 4 in order that the righteous **r** of the

Requires (Require)

Lev 8:35 seven days and do what the LORD **r**,
Nu 7: 5 the Levites as each man's work **r**."
1Ki 2: 3 observe what the LORD your God **r**:
2Ki 17:26 know what the god of that country **r**.
17:26 the people do not know what he **r**."
17:27 people what the god of the land **r**."
Jn 6:28 must we do to do the works God **r**?"
Heb 7: 5 Now the law **r** the descendants of
9:22 In fact, the law **r** that nearly

Requiring (Require)

Lev 22:16 so bring upon them guilt **r** payment.

Rescue (Rescued, Rescues, Rescuing)

Ge 37:21 Reuben heard this, he tried to **r** him
37:22 Reuben said this to **r** him from them
Ex 2:17 to their **r** and watered their flock.
3: 8 I have come down to **r** them from the
Dt 22:27 screamed, there was no-one to **r** her.
25:11 to **r** her husband from his assailant,
28:29 and robbed, with no-one to **r** you.
28:31 enemies, and no-one will **r** them.
Jdg 9:17 to **r** you from the hand of Midian
10:15 think best, but please **r** us now."
18:28 There was no-one to **r** them because
1Sa 7: 8 that he may **r** us from the hand of
11: 3 to **r** us, we will surrender to you."
12:21 **r** you, because they are useless.
30: 8 overtake them and succeed in the **r**."
2Sa 3:18 'By my servant David I will **r** my
10:11 then you are to come to my **r**; but if
10:11 for you, then I will come to **r** you.
21:17 son of Zeruiah came to David's **r**;
1Ch 19:12 then you are to **r** me; but if the
19:12 strong for you, then I will **r** you.
2Ch 32:17 did not **r** their people from my hand,
32:17 will not **r** his people from my hand."
Job 5:19 From six calamities he will **r** you;
10: 7 that no-one can **r** me from your hand?
Ps 7: 2 me to pieces with no-one to **r** me.
17:13 **r** me from the wicked by your sword.
22: 8 in the LORD; let the LORD **r** him.
22:21 **R** me from the mouth of the lions;
25:20 Guard my life and **r** me; let me not
Ps 31: 2 come quickly to my **r**; be my rock of
35:10 "Who is like you, O LORD? You **r** the
35:17 how long will you look on? **R** my life
43: 1 **r** me from deceitful and wicked men.
50:22 tear you to pieces, with none to **r**:
69:14 **R** me from the mire, do not let me
69:18 Come near and **r** me; redeem me
71: 2 **R** me and deliver me in your
71:11 seize him, for no-one will **r** him."
72:14 He will **r** them from oppression and
82: 4 **R** the weak and needy; deliver them
91:14 "I will **r** him; I will protect him,
140: 1 **R** me, O LORD, from evil men; protect
142: 6 for I am in desperate need; **r** me
143: 9 **R** me from my enemies, O LORD, for I
144: 7 me and **r** me from the mighty waters,
144:11 Deliver me and **r** me from the hands
Pr 19:19 **r** him, you will have to do it again.
24:11 **R** those being led away to death;
Isa 5:29 and carry it off with no-one to **r**.
19:20 and defender, and he will **r** them.
31: 5 will 'pass over' it and will **r** it."
42:22 with no-one to **r** them; they have
46: 2 together; unable to **r** the burden,
46: 4 I will sustain you and I will **r** you.
50: 2 Do I lack the strength to **r** you? By
Jer 1: 8 and will **r** you," declares the LORD.
1:19 and will **r** you," declares the LORD.
15:20 **r** and save you," declares the LORD.
21:12 **r** from the hand of his oppressor the
22: 3 **R** from the hand of his oppressor the
39:17 I will **r** you on that day, declares
Eze 34:10 I will **r** my flock from their mouths,
34:12 I will **r** them from all the places
34:27 **r** them from the hands of those who
Da 3:15 will be able to **r** you from my hand?"
3:17 he will **r** us from your hand, O king.
6:14 he was determined to **r** Daniel and
6:16 whom you serve continually, **r** you!"
6:20 been able to **r** you from the lions?"
8: 4 and none could **r** from his power.
8: 7 none could **r** the ram from his power.
Hos 5:14 them off, with no-one to **r** them.
Mic 5: 8 as it goes, and no-one can **r**.
Zep 3:19 I will **r** the lame and gather those
Zec 11: 6 I will not **r** them from their hands."
Mt 27:43 He trusts in God. Let God **r** him now
Lk 1:74 to **r** us from the hand of our enemies,
Ac 7:25 him to **r** them, but they did not.
26:17 I will **r** you from your own people
Ro 7:24 wretched man I am! Who will **r** me
Gal 1: 4 gave himself for our sins to **r** us
2Ti 4:18 The Lord will **r** me from every evil
2Pe 2: 9 the Lord knows how to **r** godly men

Rescued (Rescue)

Ex 2:19 They answered, "An Egyptian **r** us
5:23 you have not **r** your people at all."
18:10 "Praise be to the LORD, who **r** you
18:10 and who **r** the people from the hand
Nu 10: 9 your God and **r** from your enemies.
Jos 22:31 Now you have **r** the Israelites from
Jdg 8:34 who had **r** them from the hands of all
1Sa 11:13 for this day the LORD has **r** Israel."
14:23 the LORD **r** Israel that day, and the
14:45 So the men **r** Jonathan, and he was
17:35 I went after it, struck it and **r** the
2Sa 19: 9 he is the one who **r** us from the hand
22:18 He **r** me from my powerful enemy, from
22:20 he **r** me because he delighted in me.
22:49 my foes; from violent men you **r** me.
2Ki 18:34 Have they **r** Samaria from my hand?
Ne 9:27 who **r** them from the hand of their
Job 29:12 I **r** the poor who cried for help, and
Ps 18:17 He **r** me from my powerful enemy, from
18:19 he **r** me because he delighted in me.
18:48 my foes; from violent men you **r** me.
81: 7 In your distress you called and I **r**
107:20 them; he **r** them from the grave.
Pr 11: 8 The righteous man is **r** from trouble,
Isa 36:19 Have they **r** Samaria from my hand?
49:24 or captives **r** from the fierce?
Da 3:28 who has sent his angel and **r** his
6:27 He has **r** Daniel from the power of
Mic 4:10 go to Babylon; there you will be **r**.
Ac 7:10 **r** him from all his troubles. He gave
12:11 **r** me from Herod's clutches and from
23:27 but I came with my troops and **r** him,
Ro 15:31 Pray that I may be **r** from the
Col 1:13 For he has **r** us from the dominion of
2Ti 3:11 Yet the Lord **r** me from all of them.
2Pe 2: 7 if he **r** Lot, a righteous man, who

Rescues (Rescue)

1Sa 14:39 surely as the LORD who **r** Israel
Pr 12: 6 the speech of the upright **r** them.
Jer 20:13 Give praise to the LORD! He **r** the
Da 6:27 He **r** and he saves; he performs signs
1Th 1:10 who **r** us from the coming wrath.

Rescuing (Rescue)

Ex 18: 9 had done for Israel in **r** them from

Resembled (Resembling)

Rev 9: 7 gold, and their faces **r** human faces.
9:17 The heads of the horses **r** the heads
13: 2 The beast I saw **r** a leopard, but had

Resembling (Resembled)

Rev 4: 3 **r** an emerald, encircled the throne.

Resen

Ge 10:12 **R**, which is between Nineveh and

Resent (Resentful, Resentment, Resents)

Pr 3:11 discipline and do not **r** his rebuke,

Resentful (Resent)

2Ti 2:24 to everyone, able to teach, not **r**.

Resentment (Resent)

Jdg 8: 3 this, their **r** against him subsided.
Job 5: 2 **R** kills a fool, and envy slays the
36:13 "The godless in heart harbour **r**;

Resents (Resent)

Pr 15:12 A mocker **r** correction; he will not

Reserve (Reserved)

Ge 41:36 This food should be held in **r** for
Dt 32:34 "Have I not kept this in **r** and
1Ki 19:18 Yet I **r** seven thousand in Israel
Job 38:23 which I **r** for times of trouble, for

Reserved (Reserve)

Ge 27:36 "Haven't you **r** any blessing for me?
Isa 26:11 **r** for your enemies consume them.
Ro 11: 4 "I have **r** for myself seven thousand
2Pe 2:17 Blackest darkness is **r** for them.
3: 7 heavens and earth are **r** for fire,
Jude :13 darkness has been **r** for ever.

Reservoir (Reservoirs)

Isa 22:11 You built a **r** between the two walls

Reservoirs (Reservoir)

Ex 7:19 the **r**'—and they will turn to blood.
Ecc 2: 6 I made **r** to water groves of

Resettle (Settle, Resettled)

1Ch 9: 2 Now the first to **r** on their own
Eze 36:33 I will **r** your towns, and the ruins

Resettled (Resettle)

2Ki 17:26 "The people you deported and **r** in
Eze 38:12 turn my hand against the **r** ruins

Resheph

1Ch 7:25 Rephah was his son, **R** his son, Telah

Reside (Residence, Resident, Residents, Resides)

Job 38:19 of light? And where does darkness **r**?

Residence (Reside)
2Sa 5: 9 David then took up **r** in the fortress
1Ch 11: 7 David then took up **r** in the fortress,
Ne 2: 8 wall and for the **r** I will occupy?"
Est 2:16 in the royal **r** in the tenth month,
Da 4:30 Babylon I have built as the royal **r**,

Resident (Reside)
Ex 12:45 a temporary **r** and a hired worker may
Lev 25: 6 and temporary **r** who live among you,
25:35 you would an alien or a temporary **r**,
25:40 worker or a temporary **r** among you;
25:47 "'If an alien or a temporary **r**

Residents (Reside)
Lev 25:45 of the temporary **r** living among you
Ne 3:13 by Hanun and the **r** of Zanoah.
7: 3 Also appoint **r** of Jerusalem as
Ac 2: 9 Parthians, Medes and Elamites; **r** of

Resides (Reside)
Job 18:15 Fire **r** in his tent; burning sulphur
41:22 Strength **r** in his neck; dismay goes
Ecc 7: 9 for anger **r** in the lap of fools.

Resin
Ge 2:12 aromatic **r** and onyx are also there.)
Ex 30:34 "Take fragrant spices—gum **r**, onycha
Nu 11: 7 coriander seed and looked like **r**.

Resist (Resisted, Resists)
Jdg 2:14 whom they were no longer able to **r**.
2Ki 10: 4 kings could not **r** him, how can we?"
2Ch 13: 7 and not strong enough to **r** them.
13: 8 "And now you plan to **r** the kingdom
Pr 28: 4 but those who keep the law **r** them.
Isa 1:20 if you **r** and rebel, you will be
Da 11:15 of the South will be powerless to **r**;
11:32 know their God will firmly **r** him.
Mt 5:39 I tell you, Do not **r** an evil person.
Lk 21:15 will be able to **r** or contradict.
Ac 7:51 You always **r** the Holy Spirit!
Jas 4: 7 **R** the devil, and he will flee from
1Pe 5: 9 **R** him, standing firm in the faith,

Resisted (Resist)
Job 9: 4 Who has **r** him and come out unscathed?
Da 10:13 prince of the Persian kingdom **r** me
Heb 12: 4 you have not yet **r** to the point of

Resists (Resist)
Ro 9:19 still blame us? For who **r** his will?"

Resolved
2Ch 20: 3 Alarmed, Jehoshaphat **r** to enquire of
Ps 17: 3 I have **r** that my mouth will not sin.
Da 1: 8 Daniel **r** not to defile himself with
1Co 2: 2 For I **r** to know nothing while I was

Resort (Resorted)
Nu 24: 1 he did not **r** to sorcery as at other

Resorted (Resort)
Jos 9: 4 they **r** to a ruse: They went as a

Resound (Resounded, Resounding, Resounds)
1Ch 16:32 Let the sea **r**, and all that is in it;
Ps 96:11 the sea **r**, and all that is in it;
98: 7 Let the sea **r**, and everything in it,
118:15 Shouts of joy and victory **r** in the
Jer 6: 7 Violence and destruction **r** in her;
25:31 The tumult will **r** to the ends of the
49:21 their cry will **r** to the Red Sea.
50:46 its cry will **r** among the nations.
51:55 the roar of their voices will **r**.

Resounded (Resound)
2Sa 22:14 the voice of the Most High **r**.
Ps 18:13 the voice of the Most High **r**.
77:17 the skies **r** with thunder; your

Resounding (Resound)
Ps 150: 5 cymbals, praise him with **r** cymbals.
1Co 13: 1 only a **r** gong or a clanging cymbal.

Resounds (Resound)
1Ki 1:45 up cheering, and the city **r** with it.
Job 37: 4 his voice **r**, he holds nothing back.

Resources
1Ch 29: 2 With all my **r** I have provided for

Respect (Respectable, Respected, Respects)
Ge 41:40 Only with **r** to the throne will I be
Lev 19: 3 "'Each of you must **r** his mother and
19:32 show **r** for the elderly and revere
22: 2 his sons to treat with **r** the sacred
Dt 28:50 a fierce-looking nation without **r**
2Ki 1:13 "please have **r** for my life and the
1:14 But now have **r** for my life!"
3:14 if I did not have **r** for the presence
Est 1:20 all the women will **r** their husbands,
Pr 11:16 A kind-hearted woman gains **r**, but
Isa 5:12 LORD, no **r** for the work of his hands.
Lam 5:12 their hands; elders are shown no **r**.
Mal 1: 6 **r** due to me?" says the LORD Almighty.
Mt 21:37 'They will **r** my son,' he said.
Mk 12: 6 all, saying, 'They will **r** my son.'
Lk 20:13 I love; perhaps they will **r** him.'
Ro 13: 7 **r**, then **r**; if honour, then honour.
Eph 5:33 and the wife must **r** her husband.
6: 5 obey your earthly masters with **r** and
1Th 4:12 that your daily life may win the **r**
5:12 Now we ask you, brothers, to **r** those
1Ti 3: 4 his children obey him with proper **r**.
3: 8 likewise, are to be men worthy of **r**,
3:11 wives are to be women worthy of **r**,
6: 1 their masters worthy of full **r**,
6: 2 **r** for them because they are brothers.
Tit 2: 2 worthy of **r**, self-controlled, and
1Pe 2:17 Show proper **r** to everyone: Love the
2:18 to your masters with all **r**,
3: 7 and treat them with **r** as the weaker
3:15 But do this with gentleness and **r**,

Respectable (Respect)
1Ti 3: 2 **r**, hospitable, able to teach,

Respected (Respect)
Dt 1:13 Choose some wise, understanding and **r**
1:15 wise and **r** men, and appointed them
1Sa 9: 6 is highly **r**, and everything he says
22:14 and highly **r** in your household?
Pr 31:23 Her husband is **r** at the city gate,
Isa 32: 5 noble nor the scoundrel be highly **r**.
33: 8 witnesses are despised, no-one is **r**.
Ac 10:22 who is **r** by all the Jewish people.
22:12 **r** by all the Jews living there.
Heb 12: 9 disciplined us and we **r** them for it.

Respects (Respect)
Pr 13:13 but he who **r** a command is rewarded.
Ac 25:13 Caesarea to pay their **r** to Festus.

Respite
Job 20:20 "Surely he will have no **r** from his

Resplendent
Ps 76: 4 You are **r** with light, more majestic
132:18 the crown on his head shall be **r**."

Respond (Responded, Responding, Response, Responsive)
1Sa 4:20 she did not **r** or pay any attention.
2Ch 32:25 did not **r** to the kindness shown him;
Est 1:18 about the queen's conduct will **r** to
Ps 102:17 He will **r** to the prayer of the
Pr 29:19 he understands, he will not **r**.
Isa 14:10 They will all **r**, they will say to
19:22 will **r** to their pleas and heal them.
Jer 2:30 they did not **r** to correction.
17:23 would not listen or **r** to discipline.
32:33 would not listen or **r** to discipline.
Hos 2:21 "In that day I will **r**," declares the
2:21 **r** to the skies, and they will **r**
2:22 and oil, and they will **r** to Jezreel.
Ac 16:14 her heart to **r** to Paul's message.
Rev 16: 7 I heard the altar **r**: "Yes, Lord God

Responded (Respond)
Ex 19: 8 The people all **r** together, "We will
24: 3 they **r** with one voice, "Everything
24: 7 They **r**, "We will do everything the
Jdg 7:14 His friend **r**, "This can be nothing
20:28 The LORD **r**, "Go, for tomorrow I
2Sa 19:43 men of Judah **r** even more harshly
Ezr 10:12 The whole assembly **r** with a loud
Ne 8: 6 their hands and **r**, "Amen! Amen!"
Job 9:16 Even if I summoned him and he **r**, I
Pr 1:23 If you had **r** to my rebuke, I would
Jer 7:28 the LORD its God or **r** to correction.
Lk 20:39 Some of the teachers of the law **r**,

Responding (Respond)
Ne 12:24 one section **r** to the other, as

Response (Respond)
1Ki 18:26 But there was no **r**; no-one answered.
18:29 But there was no **r**, no-one answered,
2Ki 4:31 face, but there was no sound or **r**.
1Ch 29: 9 The people rejoiced at the willing **r**
Job 19: 7 'I've been wronged!' I get no **r**;
Da 10:12 heard, and I have come in **r** to them.
Ro 8:31 What, then, shall we say in **r** to
Gal 2: 2 I went in **r** to a revelation and set

Responsibilities (Responsible)
Nu 8:26 are to assign the **r** of the Levites."
1Ch 23:32 the Levites carried out their **r** for
2Ch 31:16 to their **r** and their divisions.
31:17 to their **r** and their divisions.

Responsibility (Responsible)
Nu 4:27 as their **r** all they are to carry.
18: 1 **r** for offences against the sanctuary,
18: 1 your sons alone are to bear the **r**
18:23 bear the **r** for offences against it.
1Ch 9:26 were entrusted with the **r** for the
9:31 the **r** for baking the offering bread.
15:22 his **r** because he was skilful at it.
Ne 10:32 "We assume the **r** for carrying out
10:35 "We also assume **r** for bringing to
Mt 27: 4 they replied. "That's your **r**."
27:24 he said. "It is your **r**!"
Ac 6: 3 We will turn this **r** over to
18: 6 your own heads! I am clear of my **r**.

Responsible (Responsibilities, Responsibility)
Ge 16: 5 Sarai said to Abram, "You are **r** for
39:22 made **r** for all that was done there.
43: 9 can hold me personally **r** for him.
Ex 21:19 not be held **r** if the other gets up
21:28 of the bull will not be held **r**.
Lev 5: 1 or learned about, he will be held **r**.
5:17 it, he is guilty and will be held **r**.
7:18 who eats any of it will be held **r**.
17:16 bathe himself, he will be held **r**.
19: 8 Whoever eats it will be held **r**
20:17 his sister and will be held **r**.
20:19 both of you would be held **r**.
20:20 be held **r**; they will die childless.
24:15 curses his God, he will be held **r**;
Nu 1:53 The Levites are to be **r** for the care
3:25 **r** for the care of the tabernacle
3:28 **r** for the care of the sanctuary.
3:31 They were **r** for the care of the ark,
3:32 **r** for the care of the sanctuary.
3:38 They were **r** for the care of the
7: 9 holy things, for which they were **r**.
14:37 these men **r** for spreading the bad
18: 3 They are to be **r** to you and are to
18: 4 They are to join you and be **r** for
18: 5 "You are to be **r** for the care of the
30:15 them, then he is **r** for her guilt."
31:30 Give them to the Levites, who are **r**
31:47 who were **r** for the care of the

Jos 2:19 on his own head; we will not be **r**.
1Sa 22:22 I am **r** for the death of your
23:20 **r** for handing him over to the king."
1Ch 9:13 able men, **r** for ministering in the
9:19 **r** for guarding the thresholds of
9:19 as their fathers had been **r** for
9:33 were **r** for the work day and night.
16:42 Heman and Jeduthun were **r** for the
26:30 seventeen hundred able men—were **r**
Ne 11:22 who were the singers **r** for the
13:10 that all the Levites and singers **r**
13:13 They were made **r** for distributing
Jnh 1: 7 find out who is **r** for this calamity.
1: 8 they asked him, "Tell us, who is **r**
Lk 11:50 this generation will be held **r** for
11:51 will be held **r** for it all.
1Co 7:24 Brothers, each man, as **r** to God,

Responsive (Respond)

2Ki 22:19 your heart was **r** and you humbled
2Ch 34:27 your heart was **r** and you humbled

Rest[1] (Rested, Resting, Resting-place, Rests, Sabbath-rest)

Ge 8: 4 to **r** on the mountains of Ararat.
18: 4 your feet and **r** under this tree.
47:30 I **r** with my fathers, carry me out of
49:26 Let all these **r** on the head of
Ex 16:23 of **r**, a holy Sabbath to the LORD.
23:12 your donkey may **r** and the slave born
31:15 is a Sabbath of **r**, holy to the LORD.
33:14 go with you, and I will give you **r**."
34:21 but on the seventh day you shall **r**;
34:21 season and harvest you must **r**.
35: 2 day, a Sabbath of **r** to the LORD.
Lev 16:31 is a sabbath of **r**, and you must deny
23: 3 of **r**, a day of sacred assembly.
23:24 month you are to have a day of **r**,
23:32 is a sabbath of **r** for you, and you
23:39 days; the first day is a day of **r**,
23:39 the eighth day also is a day of **r**.
25: 4 sabbath of **r**, a sabbath to the LORD.
25: 5 The land is to have a year of **r**.
26:34 land will **r** and enjoy its sabbaths.
26:35 the land will have the **r** it did not
Nu 10:12 came to **r** in the Desert of Paran.
10:33 days to find them a place to **r**.
10:36 Whenever it came to **r**, he said,
23:24 does not **r** till he devours his prey
Dt 3:20 until the LORD gives **r** to your
5:14 and maidservant may **r**, as you do.
12:10 and he will give you **r** from all your
25:19 the LORD your God gives you **r** from
31:16 "You are going to **r** with your
33:12 "Let the beloved of the LORD **r**
33:16 Let all these **r** on the head of
Jos 1:13 'The LORD your God is giving you **r**
1:15 until the LORD gives them **r**, as he
11:23 Then the land had **r** from war.
14:15 Then the land had **r** from war.
21:44 The LORD gave them **r** on every side,
22: 4 your brothers **r** as he promised,
23: 1 **r** from all their enemies around them,
Ru 1: 9 **r** in the home of another husband.
2: 7 for a short **r** in the shelter."
3:18 **r** until the matter is settled today."
2Sa 4: 5 while he was taking his noonday **r**.
7: 1 **r** from all his enemies around him,
7:11 I will also give you **r** from all your
7:12 your days are over and you **r** with
14: 9 "My lord the king, let the blame **r**
14:17 word of my lord the king bring me **r**,
1Ki 1:21 king is laid to **r** with his fathers,
2:33 May the guilt of their blood **r** on
5: 4 now the LORD my God has given me **r**
8:56 who has given **r** to his people Israel
1Ch 6:31 LORD after the ark came to **r** there.
22: 9 who will be a man of peace and **r**,
22: 9 **r** from all his enemies on every side.
22:18 And has he not granted you **r** on
23:25 the God of Israel, has granted **r** to
28: 2 a place of **r** for the ark of the
2Ch 14: 6 years, for the LORD gave him **r**.
14: 7 and he has given us **r** on every side.
15:15 the LORD gave them **r** on every side.
20:30 God had given him **r** on every side.
Ne 9:28 "But as soon as they were at **r**, they
Job 3:13 in peace; I would be asleep and at **r**
3:17 and there the weary are at **r**.
3:26 I have no **r**, but only turmoil."
11:18 about you and take your **r** in safety.
16:18 may my cry never be laid to **r**!
24:23 He may let them **r** in a feeling of
30:17 my bones; my gnawing pains never **r**.
Ps 16: 9 my body also will **r** secure,
33:22 May your unfailing love **r** upon us,
55: 6 dove! I would fly away and be at **r**
62: 1 My soul finds **r** in God alone; my
62: 5 Find **r**, O my soul, in God alone; my
80:17 Let your hand **r** on the man at your
90:17 May the favour of the Lord our God **r**
91: 1 **r** in the shadow of the Almighty.
95:11 anger, "They shall never enter my **r**.
116: 7 Be at **r** once more, O my soul, for
Pr 6:10 a little folding of the hands to **r**—
21:16 to **r** in the company of the dead.
24:33 a little folding of the hands to **r**—
26: 2 undeserved curse does not come to **r**.
Ecc 2:23 even at night his mind does not **r**.
6: 5 it has more **r** than does that man—
10: 4 calmness can lay great errors to **r**.
SS 1: 7 where you **r** your sheep at midday.
Isa 11: 2 The Spirit of the LORD will **r** on him
11:10 and his place of **r** will be glorious.
13:20 no shepherd will **r** his flocks there.
14: 7 All the lands are at **r** and at peace;
23:12 even there you will find no **r**."
25:10 The hand of the LORD will **r** on this
28:12 let the weary **r**"; and, "This is the
30:15 "In repentance and **r** is your
32:18 homes, in undisturbed places of **r**.
34:14 and find for themselves places of **r**.
57: 2 they find **r** as they lie in death.
57:20 the tossing sea, which cannot **r**,
62: 6 on the LORD, give yourselves no **r**,
62: 7 give him no **r** till he establishes
63:14 given **r** by the Spirit of the LORD.
Jer 6:16 and you will find **r** for your souls.
31: 2 I will come to give **r** to Israel."
33:12 for shepherds to **r** their flocks.
45: 3 out with groaning and find no **r**.
47: 6 'how long till you **r**? Return to your
47: 7 how can it **r** when the LORD has
48:11 "Moab has been at **r** from youth, like
50:34 that he may bring **r** to their land,
Lam 2:18 yourself no relief, your eyes no **r**.
5: 5 heels; we are weary and find no **r**.
Eze 44:30 a blessing may **r** on your household.
Da 12:13 You will **r**, and then at the end of
Na 3:18 slumber; your nobles lie down to **r**.
Hab 2: 5 him; he is arrogant and never at **r**.
Zec 1:11 the whole world at **r** and in peace."
6: 8 Spirit **r** in the land of the north."
7: 7 towns were at **r** and prosperous,
9: 1 will **r** upon Damascus—for the eyes
Mt 10:13 let your peace **r** on it; if it is not,
11:28 and burdened, and I will give you **r**.
11:29 and you will find **r** for your souls.
12:43 seeking **r** and does not find it.
Mk 6:31 to a quiet place and get some **r**."
Lk 10: 6 your peace will **r** on him; if not, it
11:24 seeking **r** and does not find it.
Ac 2: 3 and came to **r** on each of them.
1Co 2: 5 that your faith might not **r** on men's
2Co 7: 5 this body of ours had no **r**, but we
12: 9 so that Christ's power may **r** on me.
Heb 3:11 anger, 'They shall never enter my **r**.
3:18 his **r** if not to those who disobeyed?
4: 1 since the promise of entering his **r**
4: 3 Now we who have believed enter that **r**
4: 3 anger, 'They shall never enter my **r**.
4: 5 says, "They shall never enter my **r**.
4: 6 remains that some will enter that **r**,
4: 8 For if Joshua had given them **r**, God
4:10 for anyone who enters God's **r** also
4:11 make every effort to enter that **r**,
1Jn 3:19 set our hearts at **r** in his presence
Rev 14:11 There is no **r** day or night for those
14:13 "Yes," says the Spirit, "they will **r**

Rest[2]

Ge 14:10 them and the **r** fled to the hills.
30:36 to tend the **r** of Laban's flocks.
30:40 but made the **r** face the streaked and
42:16 the **r** of you will be kept in prison,
42:19 while the **r** of you go and take grain
44: 9 **r** of us will become my lord's slaves.
44:10 **r** of you will be free from blame."
44:17 The **r** of you, go back to your father
Ex 4: 7 restored, like the **r** of his flesh.
29:12 **r** of it at the base of the altar.
Lev 2: 3 The **r** of the grain offering belongs
2:10 The **r** of the grain offering belongs
4: 7 The **r** of the bull's blood he shall
4:12 that is, all the **r** of the bull—he
4:18 The **r** of the blood he shall pour out
4:25 pour out the **r** of the blood at the
4:30 pour out the **r** of the blood at the
4:34 pour out the **r** of the blood at the
5: 9 the **r** of the blood must be drained
5:13 The **r** of the offering will belong to
6:16 Aaron and his sons shall eat the **r**
8:15 He poured out the **r** of the blood at
8:32 burn up the **r** of the meat and the
9: 9 the **r** of the blood he poured out at
14: 9 his eyebrows and the **r** of his hair.
14:18 The **r** of the oil in his palm the
14:29 The **r** of the oil in his palm the
Nu 16: 9 the **r** of the Israelite community
18:31 You and your households may eat the **r**
31:27 battle and the **r** of the community.
Dt 3:13 The **r** of Gilead and also all of
19:20 The **r** of the people will hear of
Jos 7:25 had stoned the **r**, they burned them.
13:27 Succoth and Zaphon with the **r** of the
14: 3 Levites an inheritance among the **r**,
17: 2 this allotment was for the **r** of the
17: 6 **r** of the descendants of Manasseh.
21: 5 The **r** of Kohath's descendants were
21:20 The **r** of the Kohathite clans of the
21:26 to the **r** of the Kohathite clans.
21:34 The Merarite clans (the **r** of the
21:40 the **r** of the Levites, were twelve.
Jdg 7: 6 **r** got down on their knees to drink.
7: 8 Gideon sent the **r** of the Israelites
1Sa 13: 2 The **r** of the men he sent back to
15:15 God, but we totally destroyed the **r**."
18:29 his enemy for the **r** of his days.
18:30 than the **r** of Saul's officers,
2Sa 10:10 He put the **r** of the men under the
12:28 Now muster the **r** of the troops and
13:27 Amnon and the **r** of the king's sons.
1Ki 12:23 Benjamin, and to the **r** of the people,
20:15 **r** of the Israelites, 7,000 in all.
20:30 The **r** of them escaped to the city of
22:46 He rid the land of the **r** of the male
2Ki 13: 7 king of Aram had destroyed the **r**
25:11 along with the **r** of the populace and
25:29 for the **r** of his life ate regularly
1Ch 6:61 The **r** of Kohath's descendants were
6:70 to the **r** of the Kohathite clans.
6:77 The Merarites (the **r** of the Levites)
11: 8 Joab restored the **r** of the city.
12:38 All the **r** of the Israelites were
13: 2 wide to the **r** of our brothers
16:41 Jeduthun and the **r** of those chosen
19:11 He put the **r** of the men under the
24:20 for the **r** of the descendants of Levi:
2Ch 24:14 they had finished, they brought the **r**
Ezr 2:70 and the **r** of the Israelites settled
3: 8 Jeshua son of Jozadak and the **r** of
4: 3 Zerubbabel, Jeshua and the **r** of the
4: 7 Mithredath, Tabeel and the **r** of his
4: 9 together with the **r** of their
4:17 Shimshai the secretary and the **r** of
6:16 the Levites and the **r** of the exiles—
7:18 with the **r** of the silver and gold,
Ne 4:14 the officials and the **r** of the
4:19 the officials and the **r** of the
6: 1 Tobiah, Geshem the Arab and the **r** of
6:14 the **r** of the prophets who have been
7:72 The total given by the **r** of the
7:73 people and the **r** of the Israelites,
10:28 "The **r** of the people—priests,
11: 1 and the **r** of the people cast lots to

Ne 11:20 The **r** of the Israelites, with the
Est 9:12 What have they done in the **r** of the
Job 36:11 they will spend the **r** of their days
Isa 38:10 and be robbed of the **r** of my years?"
44:17 From the **r** he makes a god, his idol;
Jer 39: 9 to him, and the **r** of the people.
41:10 Ishmael made captives of all the **r**
52:15 along with the **r** of the craftsmen
52:16 Nebuzaradan left behind the **r** of the
52:33 for the **r** of his life ate regularly
Eze 34:18 Must you also trample the **r** of your
34:18 you also muddy the **r** with your feet?
36: 3 possession of the **r** of the nations
36: 4 by the **r** of the nations around you—
36: 5 spoken against the **r** of the nations,
48:23 "As for the **r** of the tribes:
Da 2:18 the **r** of the wise men of Babylon.
Mic 5: 3 the **r** of his brothers return to join
Zec 12:14 all the **r** of the clans and their
14: 2 but the **r** of the people will not be
Mt 22: 6 The **r** seized his servants,
27:49 The **r** said, "Now leave him alone.
Mk 16:13 returned and reported it to the **r**;
Lk 12:26 thing, why do you worry about the **r**?
Jn 11:16 Thomas (called Didymus) said to the **r**
Ac 5: 2 **r** and put it at the apostles' feet.
16:17 This girl followed Paul and the **r** of
21:18 The next day Paul and the **r** of us
27:44 The **r** were to get there on planks or
28: 9 this had happened, the **r** of the sick
1Co 7:12 To the **r** I say this (I, not the Lord)
Eph 2: 3 Like the **r**, we were by nature
Php 4: 3 along with Clement and the **r** of my
1Th 4:13 like the **r** of men, who have no hope.
1Pe 4: 2 a result, he does not live the **r** of
Rev 2:24 Now I say to the **r** of you in
9:20 The **r** of mankind that were not
12:17 went off to make war against the **r**
19:21 The **r** of them were killed with the
20: 5 (The **r** of the dead did not come to

Rested (Rest[1])

Ge 2: 2 seventh day he **r** from all his work.
2: 3 because on it he **r** from all the work
Ex 16:30 the people **r** on the seventh day.
20:11 them, but he **r** on the seventh day.
31:17 day he abstained from work and **r**.
Nu 11:25 When the Spirit **r** on them, they
11:26 Yet the Spirit also **r** on them, and
1Ki 2:10 David **r** with his fathers and was
7: 3 **r** on the columns—forty-five beams,
7:25 The Sea **r** on top of them, and their
11:21 Hadad heard that David **r** with his
11:43 he **r** with his fathers and was buried
14:20 years and then **r** with his fathers.
14:31 Rehoboam **r** with his fathers and was
15: 8 Abijah **r** with his fathers and was
15:24 Asa **r** with his fathers and was
16: 6 Baasha **r** with his fathers and was
16:28 Omri **r** with his fathers and was
22:40 Ahab **r** with his fathers. And Ahaziah
22:50 Jehoshaphat **r** with his fathers and
2Ki 8:24 Jehoram **r** with his fathers and was
10:35 Jehu **r** with his fathers and was
13: 9 Jehoahaz **r** with his fathers and was
13:13 Jehoash **r** with his fathers, and
14:16 Jehoash **r** with his fathers and was
14:22 after Amaziah **r** with his fathers.
14:29 Jeroboam **r** with his fathers, the
15: 7 Azariah **r** with his fathers and was
15:22 Menahem **r** with his fathers. And
15:38 Jotham **r** with his fathers and was
16:20 Ahaz **r** with his fathers and was
20:21 Hezekiah **r** with his fathers. And
21:18 Manasseh **r** with his fathers and was
24: 6 Jehoiakim **r** with his fathers. And
2Ch 4: 4 The Sea **r** on top of them, and their
9:31 he **r** with his fathers and was buried
12:16 Rehoboam **r** with his fathers and was
14: 1 Abijah **r** with his fathers and was
16:13 Asa died and **r** with his fathers.
21: 1 Jehoshaphat **r** with his fathers and
26: 2 after Amaziah **r** with his fathers.
26:23 Uzziah **r** with his fathers and was
27: 9 Jotham **r** with his fathers and was
28:27 Ahaz **r** with his fathers and was
32:33 Hezekiah **r** with his fathers and was
33:20 Manasseh **r** with his fathers and was
36:21 all the time of its desolation it **r**,
Ezr 8:32 we arrived in Jerusalem, where we **r**
Est 9:17 and on the fourteenth they **r** and
9:18 and then on the fifteenth they **r** and
Eze 32:27 for their sins **r** on their bones,
Am 5:19 **r** his hand on the wall only to have
Lk 23:56 But they **r** on the Sabbath in
Heb 4: 4 day God **r** from all his work."

Resting (Rest[1])

Ge 28:12 he saw a stairway **r** on the earth,
49:15 he sees how good is his **r** place and
Dt 12: 9 have not yet reached the **r** place
28:65 **r** place for the sole of your foot.
1Ki 7:30 and each had a basin **r** on four
2Ki 2:15 spirit of Elijah is **r** on Elisha.
9:16 because Joram was **r** there and
2Ch 6:41 O LORD God, and come to your **r** place,
Ps 132: 8 O LORD, and come to your **r** place
132:14 "This is my **r** place for ever and
SS 1:13 My lover is to me a sachet of myrrh **r**
Isa 22:16 chiselling your **r** place in the rock?
65:10 and the Valley of Achor a **r** place
66: 1 for me? Where will my **r** place be?
Jer 50: 6 hill and forgot their own **r** place.
Lam 1: 3 the nations; she finds no **r** place.
Eze 25: 5 and Ammon into a **r** place for sheep.
Mic 2:10 For this is not your **r** place
Mt 26:45 "Are you still sleeping and **r**? Look,
Mk 14:41 and **r**? Enough! The hour has come.
Ac 7:49 Or where will my **r** place be?
Tit 1: 2 a faith and knowledge **r** on the hope

Resting-place (Rest[1])

Isa 28:12 to whom he said, "This is the **r**, let

Restitution

Ex 22: 3 "A thief must certainly make **r**, but
22: 5 he must make **r** from the best of his
22: 6 who started the fire must make **r**.
22:11 accept this, and no **r** is required.
22:12 he must make **r** to the owner.
22:14 is not present, he must make **r**.
Lev 5:16 He must make **r** for what he has
6: 5 He must make **r** in full, add a fifth
22:14 he must make **r** to the priest for the
24:18 animal must make **r**—life for life.
24:21 Whoever kills an animal must make **r**,
Nu 5: 7 He must make full **r** for his wrong,
5: 8 to whom **r** can be made for the wrong,
5: 8 the **r** belongs to the LORD and must

Restless

Ge 4:12 will be a **r** wanderer on the earth."
4:14 I will be a **r** wanderer on the earth,
27:40 But when you grow **r**, you will throw
Jer 49:23 troubled like the **r** sea.
Jas 3: 8 can tame the tongue. It is a **r** evil

Restoration (Restore)

2Ch 24:27 and the record of the **r** of the

Restore (Restoration, Restored, Restorer, Restores, Restoring)

Ge 40:13 head and **r** you to your position,
Dt 30: 3 the LORD your God will **r** your
2Sa 8: 3 king of Zobah, when he went to **r** his
9: 7 I will **r** to you all the land that
2Ch 24: 4 Some time later Joash decided to **r**
24:12 carpenters to **r** the LORD's temple,
Ezr 5: 3 this temple and **r** this structure?"
5: 9 this temple and **r** this structure?"
Ne 4: 2 Will they **r** their wall? Will they
Job 8: 6 and **r** you to your rightful place.
Ps 41: 3 and **r** him from his bed of illness.
51:12 **R** to me the joy of your salvation
60: 1 us; you have been angry—now **r** us!
69: 4 am forced to **r** what I did not steal.
71:20 many and bitter, you will **r** my life
80: 3 **R** us, O God; make your face shine
80: 7 **R** us, O God Almighty; make your face
80:19 **R** us, O LORD God Almighty; make your
85: 4 **R** us again, O God our Saviour, and
126: 4 **R** our fortunes, O LORD, like streams
Isa 1:26 I will **r** your judges as in days of
44:26 and of their ruins, 'I will **r** them,'
49: 6 my servant to **r** the tribes of Jacob
49: 8 to **r** the land and to reassign its
57:18 will guide him and **r** comfort to him,
61: 4 and **r** the places long devastated;
Jer 15:19 "If you repent, I will **r** you that
16:15 For I will **r** them to the land I
27:22 'Then I will bring them back and **r**
30: 3 Judah back from captivity and **r** them
30:17 I will **r** you to health and heal your
30:18 'I will **r** the fortunes of Jacob's
31:18 **R** me, and I will return, because you
32:44 **r** their fortunes, declares the LORD."
33:11 For I will **r** the fortunes of the
33:26 For I will **r** their fortunes and have
42:12 on you and **r** you to your land.'
48:47 "Yet I will **r** the fortunes of Moab
49: 6 "Yet afterwards, I will **r** the
49:39 "Yet I will **r** the fortunes of Elam
Lam 1:16 comfort me, no-one to **r** my spirit.
5:21 **R** us to yourself, O LORD, that we
Eze 16:53 I will **r** the fortunes of Sodom and
Da 9:25 From the issuing of the decree to **r**
Hos 6: 2 us; on the third day he will **r** us,
6:11 I would **r** the fortunes of my people,
Joel 3: 1 when I **r** the fortunes of Judah and
Am 9:11 "In that day I will **r** David's fallen
9:11 repair its broken places, **r** its
Na 2: 2 The LORD will **r** the splendour of
Zep 2: 7 for them; he will **r** their fortunes.
3:20 when I **r** your fortunes before your
Zec 9:12 that I will **r** twice as much to you.
10: 6 I will **r** them because I have
Mt 17:11 Elijah comes and will **r** all things.
Ac 1: 6 going to **r** the kingdom to Israel?"
3:21 time comes for God to **r** everything,
9:12 his hands on him to **r** his sight."
15:16 I will rebuild, and I will **r** it,
Gal 6: 1 are spiritual should **r** him gently.
1Pe 5:10 will himself **r** you and make you

Restored (Restore)

Ge 40:21 He **r** the chief cupbearer to his
41:13 them to us: I was **r** to my position,
Ex 4: 7 was **r**, like the rest of his flesh.
Nu 21:27 be rebuilt; let Sihon's city be **r**.
1Sa 7:14 captured from Israel were **r** to her,
1Ki 13: 6 pray for me that my hand may be **r**.
13: 6 was **r** and became as it was before.
2Ki 5:10 will be **r** and you will be cleansed."
5:14 and his flesh was **r** and became clean
8: 1 woman whose son he had **r** to life,
8: 5 how Elisha had **r** the dead to life,
8: 5 is her son whom Elisha **r** to life."
14:22 **r** it to Judah after Amaziah rested
14:25 He was the one who **r** the boundaries
1Ch 11: 8 while Joab **r** the rest of the city.
2Ch 26: 2 **r** it to Judah after Amaziah rested
33:16 he **r** the altar of the LORD and
34:10 who repaired and **r** the temple.
Ezr 4:13 city is built and its walls are **r**,
4:16 city is built and its walls are **r**,
Ne 3: 8 **r** Jerusalem as far as the Broad Wall.
Job 22:23 you will be **r**: If you remove
33:25 it is **r** as in the days of his youth.
33:26 is **r** by God to his righteous state.
Ps 85: 1 O LORD; you **r** the fortunes of Jacob.
Isa 38:16 You **r** me to health and let me live.
Eze 21:27 It will not be **r** until he comes to
Da 4:26 your kingdom will be **r** to you when
4:34 towards heaven, and my sanity was **r**.
4:36 At the same time that my sanity was **r**
4:36 and I was **r** to my throne and became
Mic 4: 8 the former dominion will be **r** to you;
Mt 9:30 their sight was **r**. Jesus warned them
12:13 **r**, just as sound as the other.
Mk 3: 5 out, and his hand was completely **r**.
8:25 **r**, and he saw everything clearly.
Lk 6:10 so, and his hand was completely **r**.
Phm :22 **r** to you in answer to your prayers.
Heb 13:19 pray so that I may be **r** to you soon.

Restorer (Restore)
Isa 58:12 Walls, **R** of Streets with Dwellings.

Restores (Restore)
Ps 14: 7 LORD **r** the fortunes of his people,
23: 3 he **r** my soul. He guides me in paths
53: 6 God **r** the fortunes of his people,
Mk 9:12 does come first, and **r** all things.

Restoring (Restore)
2Ki 12:12 the other expenses of **r** the temple.
Ezr 4:12 They are **r** the walls and repairing

Restrain (Restrained, Restraining, Restraint)
1Sa 3:13 and he failed to **r** them.
Job 9:13 God does not **r** his anger; even the
Jer 2:24 craving—in her heat who can **r** her?
14:10 to wander; they do not **r** their feet.
31:16 This is what the LORD says: "**R** your

Restrained (Restrain)
Ex 36: 6 people were **r** from bringing more,
Est 5:10 Nevertheless, Haman **r** himself and
Ps 76:10 the survivors of your wrath are **r**.
78:38 Time after time he **r** his anger and
Eze 31:15 and its abundant waters were **r**.
2Pe 2:16 voice and **r** the prophet's madness.

Restraining (Restrain)
Pr 27:16 **r** her is like **r** the wind or grasping
Col 2:23 any value in **r** sensual indulgence.

Restraint (Restrain)
Job 30:11 me, they throw off **r** in my presence.
Ps 119:51 The arrogant mock me without **r**, but
Pr 17:27 A man of knowledge uses words with **r**,
23: 4 get rich; have the wisdom to show **r**.
29:18 the people cast off **r**; but blessed
Eze 35:13 me without **r**, and I heard it.

Restrict (Restricted, Restriction)
1Co 7:35 not to **r** you, but that you may live

Restricted (Restrict)
Jer 36: 5 Jeremiah told Baruch, "I am **r**; I

Restriction (Restrict)
Job 36:16 to a spacious place free from **r**,

Rests (Rest[1])
Dt 33:12 LORD loves **r** between his shoulders."
2Ch 28:11 the LORD's fierce anger **r** on you."
28:13 and his fierce anger **r** on Israel."
36:21 The land enjoyed its sabbath **r**; all
Pr 19:23 one **r** content, untouched by trouble.
21:31 battle, but victory **r** with the LORD.
Lk 2:14 peace to men on whom his favour **r**."
Heb 4:10 God's rest also **r** from his own work,
1Pe 4:14 Spirit of glory and of God **r** on you.

Result
Ge 38:24 and as a **r** she is now pregnant.
Ex 21:20 as a direct **r**, he must be punished,
Lev 7:16 "'If, however, his offering is the **r**
Nu 25:18 the plague came as a **r** of Peor."
Ezr 9:13 "What has happened to us is a **r** of
Mic 7:13 as the **r** of their deeds.
Mk 1:45 As a **r**, Jesus could no longer enter
Lk 21:13 This will **r** in your being witnesses
Ac 5:15 As a **r**, people brought the sick
25:26 King Agrippa, so that as a **r** of this
Ro 3: 8 "Let us do evil that good may **r**"?
5:16 the gift of God is not like the **r** of
5:18 Consequently, just as the **r** of one
5:18 so also the **r** of one act of
6:21 ashamed of? Those things **r** in death!
6:22 holiness, and the **r** is eternal life.
11:30 mercy as a **r** of their disobedience,
11:31 mercy as a **r** of God's mercy to you.
1Co 9: 1 not the **r** of my work in the Lord?
11:34 together it may not **r** in judgment.
2Co 3: 3 the **r** of our ministry, written not
9:11 will **r** in thanksgiving to God.
Gal 4:23 was born as the **r** of a promise.
Php 1:13 a **r**, it has become clear throughout
2Th 1: 5 and as a **r** you will be counted
1Ti 6: 4 quarrels about words that **r** in envy,
1Pe 1: 7 proved genuine and may **r** in praise,
4: 2 a **r**, he does not live the rest of

Resurrection (*Resurrection from the dead, Resurrection of the dead*)
Mt 22:23 no **r**, came to him with a question.
22:28 Now then, at the **r**, whose wife will
22:30 At the **r** people will neither marry
27:53 and after Jesus' **r** they went into
Mk 12:18 the Sadducees, who say there is no **r**,
12:23 At the **r** whose wife will she be,
Lk 14:14 repaid at the **r** of the righteous."
20:27 no **r**, came to Jesus with a question.
20:33 Now then, at the **r** whose wife will
20:36 since they are children of the **r**.
Jn 11:24 again in the **r** at the last day."
11:25 Jesus said to her, "I am the **r** and
Ac 1:22 become a witness with us of his **r**."
2:31 he spoke of the **r** of the Christ,
4:33 testify to the **r** of the Lord Jesus,
17:18 the good news about Jesus and the **r**.
23: 8 (The Sadducees say that there is no **r**
24:15 that there will be a **r** of both the
Ro 6: 5 also be united with him in his **r**.
1Co 15:29 Now if there is no **r**, what will
Php 3:10 the power of his **r** and the
2Ti 2:18 They say that the **r** has already
Heb 11:35 so that they might gain a better **r**.
1Pe 1: 3 the **r** of Jesus Christ from the dead,
3:21 saves you by the **r** of Jesus Christ,
Rev 20: 5 were ended.) This is the first **r**.
20: 6 those who have part in the first **r**.

Resurrection from the dead
Lk 20:35 in the **r** will neither marry nor be
Ro 1: 4 God, by his **r**: Jesus Christ our Lord.
Php 3:11 so, somehow, to attain to the **r**.

Resurrection of the dead
Mt 22:31 about the **r**—have you not read what
Ac 4: 2 and proclaiming in Jesus the **r**.
17:32 they heard about the **r**, some of them
23: 6 trial because of my hope in the **r**."
24:21 'It is concerning the **r** that I am on
1Co 15:12 some of you say that there is no **r**?
15:13 If there is no **r**, then not even
15:21 man, the **r** comes also through a man.
15:42 will it be with the **r**. The body that
Heb 6: 2 hands, the **r**, and eternal judgment.

Retain (Retains)
2Ch 22: 9 powerful enough to **r** the kingdom.
Da 11: 6 but she will not **r** her power, and he
Lk 8:15 who hear the word, **r** it, and by
Ro 1:28 worth while to **r** the knowledge of
1Co 7:17 each one should **r** the place in life

Retains (Retain)
Lev 25:29 he **r** the right of redemption a full
25:48 he **r** the right of redemption after

Retake
Jdg 11:26 didn't you **r** them during that time?
1Ki 22: 3 to **r** it from the king of Aram?"

Retaliate
1Pe 2:23 he did not **r**; when he suffered, he

Retinue
1Ki 10:13 with her **r** to her own country.
2Ch 9:12 with her **r** to her own country.

Retire
Nu 8:25 at the age of fifty, they must **r**

Retorted
Jn 7:47 deceived you also?" the Pharisees **r**.

Retreat (Retreated, Retreating, Retreats)
Jdg 20:32 "Let's **r** and draw them away from the
Job 41:25 they **r** before his thrashing.
Ps 44:10 You made us **r** before the enemy, and
74:21 Do not let the oppressed **r** in
Da 11: 9 South but will **r** to his own country.

Retreated (Retreat)
2Sa 23: 9 battle. Then the men of Israel **r**,

Retreating (Retreat)
Jer 46: 5 are **r**, their warriors are defeated.

Retreats (Retreat)
Pr 30:30 a lion, mighty among beasts, who **r**

Retribution
Ps 69:22 a snare; may it become **r** and a trap.
Isa 34: 8 a year of **r**, to uphold Zion's cause.
35: 4 divine **r** he will come to save you."
59:18 to his enemies and **r** to his foes;
Jer 51:56 a God of **r**; he will repay in full.
Ro 11: 9 a stumbling-block and a **r** for them.

Retrieved
Isa 49:25 and plunder **r** from the fierce; I

Return (*Return to the LORD*, Returned, Returning, Returns)
Ge 3:19 your food until you **r** to the ground,
3:19 you are and to dust you will **r**."
8:12 but this time it did not **r** to him.
18:10 the LORD said, "I will surely **r** to
18:14 I will **r** to you at the appointed
20: 7 Now **r** the man's wife, for he is a
20: 7 But if you do not **r** her, you may be
28:21 that I **r** safely to my father's house,
29: 3 Then they would **r** the stone to its
29:18 in **r** for your younger daughter
29:27 in **r** for another seven years of work
30:15 in **r** for your son's mandrakes."
31:30 longed to **r** to your father's house.
43:12 for you must **r** the silver that was
44:33 and let the boy **r** with his brothers.
45:17 animals and **r** to the land of Canaan,
49: 9 Judah; you **r** from the prey, my son.
50: 5 and bury my father; then I will **r**.
Ex 4:21 The LORD said to Moses, "When you **r**
13:17 change their minds and **r** to Egypt."
22:26 as a pledge, **r** it to him by sunset,
33:11 Then Moses would **r** to the camp, but
Lev 6: 4 he must **r** what he has stolen or
14:39 On the seventh day the priest shall **r**
25:10 each one of you is to **r** to his
25:13 is to **r** to his own property.
Nu 10:36 it came to rest, he said, "**R**, O LORD
18:21 their inheritance in **r** for the work
32:18 We will not **r** to our homes until
32:22 you may **r** and be free from your
35:28 priest may he **r** to his own property.
Dt 5:30 "Go, tell them to **r** to their tents.
16: 7 Then in the morning **r** to your tents.
17:16 **r** to Egypt to get more of them,
23:11 and at sunset he may **r** to the camp.
24:13 **R** his cloak to him by sunset so that
Jos 2:16 they **r**, and then go on your way."
18: 4 Then they will **r** to me.
18: 8 Then **r** to me, and I will cast lots
22: 4 **r** to your homes in the land that
22: 8 saying, "**R** to your homes with your
22: 9 at Shiloh in Canaan to **r** to Gilead,
Jdg 6:18 LORD said, "I will wait until you **r**.
8: 9 "When I **r** in triumph, I will tear
11:31 of my house to meet me when I **r**
19: 3 went to her to persuade her to **r**.
20: 8 not one of us will **r** to his house.
Ru 1: 6 prepared to **r** home from there.
1:11 Naomi said, "**R** home, my daughters.
1:12 **R** home, my daughters; I am too old
1Sa 6: 3 They answered, "If you **r** the ark of
18: 2 not let him **r** to his father's house.
29: 4 may **r** to the place you assigned him.
2Sa 1:22 sword of Saul did not **r** unsatisfied.

2Sa 12:23 go to him, but he will not **r** to me."
15:34 if you **r** to the city and say to
17: 3 man you seek will mean the **r** of all;
19:14 They sent word to the king, "**R**, you
19:37 Let your servant **r**, that I may die
1Ki 11:21 so that I may **r** to my own country."
12:27 kill me and **r** to King Rehoboam."
13: 9 water or **r** by the way you came.
13:10 he took another road and did not **r**
13:17 there or **r** by the way you came.
17:21 God, let this boy's life **r** to him!"
20:34 "I will **r** the cities my father took
22:27 bread and water until I **r** safely.
22:28 Micaiah declared, "If you ever **r**
2Ki 4:22 go to the man of God quickly and **r**."
19: 7 he will **r** to his own country, and
19:28 make you **r** by the way you came.'
19:33 By the way that he came he will **r**;
2Ch 18:26 bread and water until I **r** safely.
18:27 Micaiah declared, "If you ever **r**
30: 6 Isaac and Israel, that he may **r** to
30: 9 his face from you if you **r** to him."
Ne 1: 9 if you **r** to me and obey my commands,
7: 5 those who had been the first to **r**.
9:17 in order to **r** to their slavery.
9:29 "You warned them to **r** to your law,
Est 2:14 in the morning **r** to another part of
2:14 She would not **r** to the king unless
Job 7: 9 goes down to the grave does not **r**.
10:21 before I go to the place of no **r**, to
15:31 for he will get nothing in **r**.
16:22 before I go on the journey of no **r**.
22:23 If you **r** to the Almighty, you will
34:15 and man would **r** to the dust.
39: 4 the wilds; they leave and do not **r**.
Ps 9:17 The wicked **r** to the grave, all the
59: 6 They **r** at evening, snarling like
59:14 They **r** at evening, snarling like
78:39 a passing breeze that does not **r**.
80:14 **R** to us, O God Almighty! Look down
85: 8 but let them not **r** to folly.
90: 3 saying, "**R** to dust, O sons of men."
104:22 they **r** and lie down in their dens.
104:29 breath, they die and **r** to the dust.
109: 4 In **r** for my friendship they accuse
126: 6 carrying seed to sow, will **r** with
146: 4 their spirit departs, they **r** to the
Pr 2:19 None who go to her **r** or attain the
Ecc 1: 7 come from, there they **r** again.
3:20 come from dust, and to dust all **r**.
4: 9 they have a good **r** for their work:
12: 2 and the clouds **r** after the rain;
Isa 10:21 A remnant will **r**, a remnant of Jacob
10:21 of Jacob will **r** to the Mighty God.
10:22 by the sea, only a remnant will **r**.
13:14 each will **r** to his own people, each
23:17 She will **r** to her hire as a
31: 6 **R** to him you have so greatly
35:10 the ransomed of the LORD will **r**.
37: 7 he will **r** to his own country, and
37:29 will make you **r** by the way you came.
37:34 By the way that he came he will **r**;
44:22 **R** to me, for I have redeemed you."
51:11 The ransomed of the LORD will **r**.
55:10 and do not **r** to it without watering
55:11 my mouth: It will not **r** to me empty,
63:17 **R** for the sake of your servants,
Jer 3: 1 should he **r** to her again? Would not
3: 1 you now **r** to me?" declares the LORD.
3: 7 she would **r** to me but she did not,
3:10 did not **r** to me with all her heart,
3:12 '**R**, faithless Israel,' declares the
3:14 "**R**, faithless people," declares the
3:22 "**R**, faithless people; I will cure
4: 1 "If you will **r**, O Israel, **r** to me,"
8: 4 When a man turns away, does he not **r**?
8: 5 cling to deceit; they refuse to **r**.
14: 3 They **r** with their jars unfilled;
22:10 never **r** nor see his native land
22:11 from this place: "He will never **r**.
22:27 back to the land you long to **r** to."
24: 7 will **r** to me with all their heart.
31: 8 in labour; a great throng will **r**.
31:16 will **r** from the land of the enemy.
31:17 children will **r** to their own land.
31:18 **r**, because you are the LORD my God.
Jer 31:21 **R**, O Virgin Israel, **r** to your towns.
37: 8 the Babylonians will **r** and attack
44:14 survive to **r** to the land of Judah,
44:14 to which they long to **r** and live;
44:14 none will **r** except a few fugitives."
44:28 Those who escape the sword and **r** to
47: 6 'how long till you rest? **R** to your
50: 9 warriors who do not **r** empty-handed.
50:16 let everyone **r** to his own people,
Lam 5:21 we may **r**; renew our days as of
Eze 11:18 "They will **r** to it and remove all
16:55 will **r** to what they were before; and
16:55 will **r** to what you were before.
18:12 He commits robbery. He does not **r**
21: 5 its scabbard; it will not **r** again.'
21:30 **R** the sword to its scabbard. In the
26:20 and you will not **r** or take your
29:14 captivity and **r** them to Upper Egypt,
46: 9 No-one is to **r** through the gate by
Da 10:20 Soon I will **r** to fight against the
11:28 The king of the North will **r** to his
11:28 it and then **r** to his own country.
11:30 He will **r** and show favour to those
Hos 3: 5 Afterwards the Israelites will **r** and
5: 4 "Their deeds do not permit them to **r**
8:13 their sins: They will **r** to Egypt.
9: 3 Ephraim will **r** to Egypt and eat
11: 5 "Will they not **r** to Egypt and will
12: 6 you must **r** to your God; maintain
14: 1 **R**, O Israel, to the LORD your God.
Joel 2:12 "Even now," declares the LORD, "**r** to
3: 4 I will swiftly and speedily **r** on
3: 7 and I will **r** on your own heads what
Ob :15 deeds will **r** upon your own head.
Mic 5: 3 brothers **r** to join the Israelites.
Zep 2:10 This is what they will get in **r** for
Zec 1: 3 '**R** to me,' declares the LORD
1: 3 I will **r** to you,' says the LORD
1:16 'I will **r** to Jerusalem with mercy,
8: 3 This is what the LORD says: "I will **r**
9:12 **R** to your fortress, O prisoners of
10: 9 will survive, and they will **r**.
Mal 3: 7 **R** to me, and I will **r** to you," says
3: 7 "But you ask, 'How are we to **r**?'
Mt 10:13 it is not, let your peace **r** to you.
12:44 says, 'I will **r** to the house I left.'
Lk 8:39 "**R** home and tell how much God has
10: 6 on him; if not, it will **r** to you.
10:35 'and when I **r**, I will reimburse you
11:24 'I will **r** to the house I left.'
12:36 master to **r** from a wedding banquet,
17:18 Was no-one found to **r** and give
19:12 appointed king and then to **r**.
Jn 21:22 I want him to remain alive until I **r**,
21:23 until I **r**, what is that to you?"
Ac 13:13 John left them to **r** to Jerusalem.
15:16 "'After this I will **r** and rebuild
15:33 to **r** to those who had sent them.
Ro 9: 9 I will **r**, and Sarah will have a son."
1Co 16:11 way in peace so that he may **r** to me.
2Co 1:23 you that I did not **r** to Corinth.
13: 2 On my **r** I will not spare those who
1Th 3: 9 you in **r** for all the joy we have
Heb 11:15 would have had opportunity to **r**.

Return to the LORD

Dt 4:30 you will **r** your God and obey him.
30: 2 you and your children **r** your God and
2Ch 30: 6 "People of Israel, **r**, the God of
30: 9 If you **r**, then your brothers and
Lam 3:40 ways and test them, and let us **r**.
Hos 6: 1 "Come, let us **r**. He has torn us to
7:10 not **r** his God or search for him.
14: 2 Take words with you and **r**. Say to
Joel 2:13 **R** your God, for he is gracious and

Returned (Return)

Ge 8: 9 earth; so it **r** to Noah in the ark.
8:11 the dove **r** to him in the evening,
14:17 After Abram **r** from defeating
18:33 Abraham, he left, and Abraham **r** home.
19:27 **r** to the place where he had stood
20:14 and he **r** Sarah his wife to him.
21:32 **r** to the land of the Philistines.
22:19 Abraham **r** to his servants, and they
Ge 31:55 Then he left and **r** home.
32: 6 the messengers **r** to Jacob, they said,
35: 9 After Jacob **r** from Paddan Aram, God
37:29 Reuben **r** to the cistern and saw that
42:28 "My silver has been **r**," he said to
43:10 we could have gone and **r** twice."
44:13 their donkeys and **r** to the city.
50:14 After burying his father, Joseph **r**
Ex 2:18 the girls **r** to Reuel their father,
2:18 "Why have you **r** so early today?
5:22 Moses **r** to the LORD and said, "O
18:27 and Jethro **r** to his own country.
Lev 25:28 It will be **r** in the Jubilee, and he
25:30 It is not to be **r** in the Jubilee.
25:31 and they are to be **r** in the Jubilee.
25:33 hold—and is to be **r** in the Jubilee,
Nu 11:30 Moses and the elders of Israel **r** to
13:25 At the end of forty days they **r** from
14:36 who **r** and made the whole community
16:50 Aaron **r** to Moses at the entrance to
22:14 the Moabite princes **r** to Balak and
24:25 Balaam got up and **r** home and Balak
31:14 of hundreds—who **r** from the battle.
Dt 28:31 taken from you and will not be **r**.
Jos 2:22 the road and **r** without finding them.
4:18 of the Jordan **r** to their place
6:11 **r** to camp and spent the night there.
6:14 the city once and **r** to the camp.
7: 3 they **r** to Joshua, they said, "Not
8:24 all the Israelites **r** to Ai and
10:15 Joshua **r** with all Israel to the camp
10:21 The whole army then **r** safely to
10:43 Joshua **r** with all Israel to the camp
18: 9 **r** to Joshua in the camp at Shiloh.
22:32 the priest, and the leaders **r** to
Jdg 2:19 when the judge died, the people **r** to
7:15 He **r** to the camp of Israel and
8:13 Gideon son of Joash then **r** from the
11:34 Jephthah **r** to his home in Mizpah,
11:39 After the two months, she **r** to her
14: 2 he **r**, he said to his father and
15:19 When Samson drank, his strength **r**
16:18 **r** with the silver in their hands.
17: 3 he **r** the eleven hundred shekels of
17: 4 he **r** the silver to his mother, and
18: 8 they **r** to Zorah and Eshtaol, their
21:14 the Benjamites **r** at that time and
21:23 Then they **r** to their inheritance and
Ru 1:22 Naomi **r** from Moab accompanied by
1Sa 4: 3 the soldiers **r** to camp, the elders
6:16 and then **r** that same day to Ekron.
6:21 have **r** the ark of the LORD.
17:53 the Israelites **r** from chasing the
17:57 soon as David **r** from killing the
20:38 up the arrow and **r** to his master.
24: 1 After Saul **r** from pursuing the
24:22 Then Saul **r** home, but David and his
26:25 went on his way, and Saul **r** home.
27: 9 and clothes. Then he **r** to Achish.
2Sa 1: 1 After the death of Saul, David **r**
2:30 Joab **r** from pursuing Abner and
3:22 Just then David's men and Joab **r**
3:27 Now when Abner **r** to Hebron, Joab
6:20 David **r** home to bless his household,
8:13 David became famous after he **r** from
10:14 So Joab **r** from fighting the
12:31 and his entire army **r** to Jerusalem.
17:20 no-one, so they **r** to Jerusalem.
19:15 the king **r** and went as far as the
19:24 king left until the day he **r** safely.
19:39 and Barzillai **r** to his home.
20: 3 David **r** to his palace in Jerusalem,
23:10 The troops **r** to Eleazar, but only to
1Ki 2:41 from Jerusalem to Gath and had **r**,
3:15 He **r** to Jerusalem, stood before the
10:13 Then she left and **r** with her retinue
10:22 Once every three years it **r** carrying
12: 2 from King Solomon), he **r** from Egypt.
12:12 and all the people **r** to Rehoboam,
12:20 Israelites heard that Jeroboam had **r**,
13:19 the man of God **r** with him and ate
14:28 they **r** them to the guardroom.
17:22 boy's life **r** to him, and he lived.
2Ki 1: 5 the messengers **r** to the king, he
2:18 they **r** to Elisha, who was staying in
2:25 Carmel and from there **r** to Samaria.

2Ki 3:27 withdrew and **r** to their own land.
4:38 Elisha **r** to Gilgal and there was a
4:39 When he **r**, he cut them up into the
6:23 away, and they **r** to their master.
7: 8 They **r** and entered another tent and
7:15 **r** and reported to the king.
8:14 Hazael left Elisha and **r** to his
8:29 King Joram **r** to Jezreel to recover
9:15 King Joram had **r** to Jezreel to
14:14 also took hostages and **r** to Samaria.
16:11 and finished it before King Ahaz **r**.
19:36 He **r** to Nineveh and stayed there.
1Ch 16:43 David **r** home to bless his family.
20: 3 and his entire army **r** to Jerusalem.
2Ch 9:12 Then she left and **r** with her retinue
9:21 Once every three years it **r**,
10: 2 from King Solomon), he **r** from Egypt.
10:12 and all the people **r** to Rehoboam,
12:11 they **r** them to the guardroom.
14:15 Then they **r** to Jerusalem.
19: 1 Jehoshaphat king of Judah **r** safely
20:27 Jerusalem **r** joyfully to Jerusalem,
22: 6 he **r** to Jezreel to recover from the
25:14 Amaziah **r** from slaughtering the
25:24 and the hostages, and **r** to Samaria.
28: 9 meet the army when it **r** to Samaria.
28:15 the City of Palms, and **r** to Samaria.
31: 1 the Israelites **r** to their own towns
Ezr 2: 1 (they **r** to Jerusalem and Judah,
3: 8 the Levites and all who had **r** from
6: 5 are to be **r** to their places in the
6:21 the Israelites who had **r** from the
8:35 the exiles who had **r** from captivity
Ne 4:15 **r** to the wall, each to his own work.
7: 6 (they **r** to Jerusalem and Judah,
8:17 The whole company that had **r** from
12: 1 Levites who **r** with Zerubbabel son of
13: 6 king of Babylon I had **r** to the king.
Est 6:12 Afterwards Mordecai **r** to the king's
7: 8 Just as the king **r** from the palace
Ps 35:13 When my prayers **r** to me unanswered,
60: T and when Joab **r** and struck down
Isa 9:13 the people have not **r** to him who
37:37 He **r** to Nineveh and stayed there.
Jer 11:10 They have **r** to the sins of their
19:14 Jeremiah then **r** from Topheth, where
Da 2:17 Daniel **r** to his house and explained
4:36 **r** to me for the glory of my kingdom.
6:18 the king **r** to his palace and spent
Am 4: 6 not **r** to me," declares the LORD.
4: 8 not **r** to me," declares the LORD.
4: 9 not **r** to me," declares the LORD.
4:10 not **r** to me," declares the LORD.
4:11 not **r** to me," declares the LORD.
Zec 4: 1 the angel who talked with me **r** and
Mt 2:12 **r** to their country by another route.
4:12 been put in prison, he **r** to Galilee.
25:19 **r** and settled accounts with them.
25:27 so that when I **r** I would have
26:40 he **r** to his disciples and found them
26:45 he **r** to the disciples and said to
27: 3 he was seized with remorse and **r** the
Mk 14:37 he **r** to his disciples and found them
16:13 These **r** and reported it to the rest;
Lk 1:23 of service was completed, he **r** home.
1:56 about three months and then **r** home.
2:20 The shepherds **r**, glorifying and
2:39 they **r** to Galilee to their own town
4: 1 Jesus, full of the Holy Spirit, **r**
4:14 Jesus **r** to Galilee in the power of
7:10 the men who had been sent **r** to the
8:40 Now when Jesus **r**, a crowd welcomed
8:55 Her spirit **r**, and at once she stood
9:10 the apostles **r**, they reported to
10:17 The seventy-two **r** with joy and said,
19:15 "He was made king, however, and **r**
24:33 They got up and **r** at once to
24:52 they worshipped him and **r** to
Jn 4:27 Just then his disciples **r** and were
13:12 on his clothes and **r** to his place.
20:17 for I have not yet **r** to the Father.
Ac 1:12 they **r** to Jerusalem from the hill
8:25 Peter and John **r** to Jerusalem,
12:25 they **r** from Jerusalem, taking with
14:21 **r** to Lystra, Iconium and Antioch,
21: 6 aboard the ship, and they **r** home.
Ac 22:17 "When I **r** to Jerusalem and was
23:32 him, while they **r** to the barracks.
Ro 14: 9 Christ died and **r** to life so that he
Gal 1:17 into Arabia and later **r** to Damascus.
1Pe 2:25 but now you have **r** to the Shepherd

Returning (Return)

Ge 48: 7 I was **r** from Paddan, to my sorrow
1Sa 7: 3 "If you are **r** to the LORD with all
11: 5 Just then Saul was **r** from the fields,
18: 6 the men were **r** home after David had
2Sa 20:22 from the city, each **r** to his home.
Ecc 1: 6 round it goes, ever **r** on its course.
Mic 2: 8 a care, like men **r** from battle.
Mk 14:41 **R** the third time, he said to them,
Lk 2:43 while his parents were **r** home, the
Jn 13: 3 had come from God and was **r** to God;
20:17 'I am **r** to my Father and your Father,
Heb 7: 1 He met Abraham **r** from the defeat of

Returns (Return)

Lev 22:13 yet has no children, and she **r** to
Pr 3:14 and yields better **r** than gold.
26:11 a dog **r** to its vomit, so a fool
Ecc 12: 7 the dust **r** to the ground it came
12: 7 and the spirit **r** to God who gave it.
Isa 52: 8 When the LORD **r** to Zion, they will
Eze 18: 7 He does not oppress anyone, but **r**
33:15 **r** what he has stolen, follows the
Mt 24:46 master finds him doing so when he **r**.
Lk 12:43 the master finds doing so when he **r**.
2Pe 2:22 "A dog **r** to its vomit," and, "A sow

Reu

Ge 11:18 30 years, he became the father of **R**.
11:19 after he became the father of **R**,
11:20 **R** had lived 32 years, he became the
11:21 **R** lived 207 years and had other sons
1Ch 1:25 Eber, Peleg, **R**,
Lk 3:35 the son of Serug, the son of **R**, the

Reuben (Reubenite, Reubenites)

1. Jacob's firstborn, by Leah (Ge 29:32; 35:23; 46:8). Wanted to save Joseph (Ge 37:19–30). Lost position because slept with Bilhah (Ge 35:22; 49:4). Blessed by Jacob (Ge 49:3–4). **2.** Tribe descended from Reuben. Blessed by Moses (Dt 33:6). Included in census (Nu 1:20–21; 26:5–11). Apportioned land east of Jordan (Nu 32; 34:14–15; Jos 18:7; 22); crossed into Canaan to fight alongside other tribes (Nu 32:16–31). Place restored in land (Eze 48:6). **3.** Territory east of Dead Sea, and south of territory of Gad. Allotted to the descendants of Jacob's eldest son, who liked it for its good grazing (Nu 32:1). Its towns and borders were clearly listed (Jos 13:15–23).

Ge 29:32 She named him **R**, for she said, "It
30:14 During wheat harvest, **R** went out
35:22 **R** went in and slept with his
35:23 The sons of Leah: **R** the firstborn of
37:21 **R** heard this, he tried to rescue him
37:22 **R** said this to rescue him from them
37:29 **R** returned to the cistern and saw
42:22 **R** replied, "Didn't I tell you not to
42:37 **R** said to his father, "You may put
46: 8 to Egypt: **R** the firstborn of Jacob.
46: 9 The sons of **R**: Hanoch, Pallu, Hezron
48: 5 mine, just as **R** and Simeon are mine.
49: 3 "**R**, you are my firstborn, my might,
Ex 1: 2 **R**, Simeon, Levi and Judah;
6:14 The sons of **R** the firstborn son of
6:14 These were the clans of **R**.
Nu 1: 5 you: from **R**, Elizur son of Shedeur;
1:20 From the descendants of **R** the
1:21 The number from the tribe of **R** was
2:10 the camp of **R** under their standard.
2:10 of **R** is Elizur son of Shedeur.
2:16 All the men assigned to the camp of **R**
7:30 people of **R**, brought his offering.
10:18 The divisions of the camp of **R** went
13: 4 tribe of **R**, Shammua son of Zaccur;
26: 5 The descendants of **R**, the firstborn
26: 7 These were the clans of **R**; those
34:14 the families of the tribe of **R**, the
Dt 27:13 Mount Ebal to pronounce curses: **R**,
Dt 33: 6 "Let **R** live and not die, nor his men
Jos 4:12 The men of **R**, Gad and the half-tribe
13:15 to the tribe of **R**, clan by clan:
15: 6 to the Stone of Bohan son of **R**.
18: 7 And Gad, **R** and the half-tribe of
18:17 down to the Stone of Bohan son of **R**.
20: 8 on the plateau in the tribe of **R**,
21: 7 the tribes of **R**, Gad and Zebulun.
21:36 from the tribe of **R**, Bezer, Jahaz,
22:13 to the land of Gilead—to **R**, Gad and
22:15 they went to Gilead—to **R**, Gad and
22:21 **R**, Gad and the half-tribe of
22:30 of the Israelites—heard what **R**,
22:31 the priest, said to **R**, Gad and
Jdg 5:15 In the districts of **R** there was
5:16 In the districts of **R** there was
2Ki 10:33 **R** and Manasseh), from Aroer by the
1Ch 2: 1 These were the sons of Israel: **R**,
5: 1 The sons of **R** the firstborn of
5: 3 the sons of **R** the firstborn of
6:63 the tribes of **R**, Gad and Zebulun.
6:78 from the tribe of **R** across the
12:37 from east of the Jordan, men of **R**,
Eze 48: 6 "**R** will have one portion; it will
48: 7 territory of **R** from east to west.
48:31 north side will be the gate of **R**,
Rev 7: 5 from the tribe of **R** 12,000, from the

Reubenite (Reuben)

Dt 11: 6 sons of Eliab the **R**, when the earth
1Ch 11:42 Adina son of Shiza the **R**, who was

Reubenites (Reuben)

Nu 16: 1 the son of Levi, and certain **R**—
32: 1 The **R** and Gadites, who had very
32: 6 Moses said to the Gadites and **R**,
32:25 The Gadites and **R** said to Moses, "We
32:29 "If the Gadites and **R**, every man
32:31 The Gadites and **R** answered, "Your
32:33 Moses gave to the Gadites, the **R** and
32:37 the **R** rebuilt Heshbon, Elealeh and
Dt 3:12 I gave the **R** and the Gadites the
3:16 to the **R** and the Gadites I gave the
4:43 for the **R**; Ramoth in Gilead, for the
29: 8 gave it as an inheritance to the **R**,
Jos 1:12 to the **R**, the Gadites and the
12: 6 the LORD gave their land to the **R**,
13: 8 The other half of Manasseh, the **R**
13:23 The boundary of the **R** was the bank
13:23 inheritance of the **R**, clan by clan.
22: 1 Joshua summoned the **R**, the Gadites
22: 9 So the **R**, the Gadites and the
22:10 the **R**, the Gadites and the
22:25 us and you—you **R** and Gadites!
22:32 Canaan from their meeting with the **R**
22:33 where the **R** and the Gadites lived.
22:34 the **R** and the Gadites gave the altar
1Ch 5: 6 Beerah was a leader of the **R**.
5:18 The **R**, the Gadites and the
5:26 who took the **R**, the Gadites and the
11:42 of the **R**, and the thirty with him,
26:32 David put them in charge of the **R**,
27:16 over the **R**: Eliezer son of Zicri;

Reuel

Ge 36: 4 Eliphaz to Esau, Basemath bore **R**,
36:10 **R**, the son of Esau's wife Basemath.
36:13 The sons of **R**: Nahath, Zerah,
36:17 The sons of Esau's son **R**: Chiefs
36:17 the chiefs descended from **R** in Edom;
Ex 2:18 the girls returned to **R** their father,
Nu 10:29 Now Moses said to Hobab son of **R** the
1Ch 1:35 The sons of Esau: Eliphaz, **R**, Jeush,
1:37 The sons of **R**: Nahath, Zerah,
9: 8 the son of **R**, the son of Ibnijah.

Reumah

Ge 22:24 His concubine, whose name was **R**,

Reunited (Unite)

Hos 1:11 and the people of Israel will be **r**,

Reveal (Revealed, Revealer, Revealing, Reveals, Revelation, Revelations)

Nu 12: 6 I **r** myself to him in visions, I
1Sa 2:27 'Did I not clearly **r** myself to your
Da 2:11 No-one can **r** it to the king except
2:47 you were able to **r** this mystery."
Mt 11:27 to whom the Son chooses to **r** him.
Lk 10:22 to whom the Son chooses to **r** him."
Gal 1:16 to **r** his Son in me so that I might

Revealed (Reveal)

Ge 35: 7 because it was there that God **r**
41:25 **r** to Pharaoh what he is about to do.
Dt 29:29 but the things **r** belong to us and to
1Sa 3: 7 the LORD had not yet been **r** to him.
3:21 **r** himself to Samuel through his word.
9:15 came, the LORD had **r** this to Samuel:
2Sa 7:27 God of Israel, you have **r** this to
2Ki 8:10 **r** to me that he will in fact die."
1Ch 17:25 "You, my God, have **r** to your servant
Est 2:10 Esther had not **r** her nationality and
Ps 98: 2 **r** his righteousness to the nations.
147:19 He has **r** his word to Jacob, his laws
Isa 22:14 The LORD Almighty has **r** this in my
40: 5 the glory of the LORD will be **r**, and
43:12 I have **r** and saved and proclaimed—
53: 1 whom has the arm of the LORD been **r**?
56: 1 and my righteousness will soon be **r**.
65: 1 "I **r** myself to those who did not ask
Jer 11:18 the LORD **r** their plot to me, I knew
38:21 this is what the LORD has **r** to me:
Eze 20: 5 Jacob and **r** myself to them in Egypt.
20: 9 in whose sight I had **r** myself to the
Da 2:19 During the night the mystery was **r**
2:30 for me, this mystery has been **r** to
Hos 7: 1 exposed and the crimes of Samaria **r**.
Mt 11:25 and **r** them to little children.
16:17 for this was not **r** to you by man,
Lk 2:26 had been **r** to him by the Holy Spirit
2:35 thoughts of many hearts will be **r**.
10:21 and **r** them to little children.
17:30 this on the day the Son of Man is **r**.
Jn 1:31 was that he might be **r** to Israel."
2:11 He thus **r** his glory, and his
12:38 has the arm of the Lord been **r**?"
17: 6 "I have **r** you to those whom you gave
Ro 1:17 a righteousness from God is **r**,
1:18 The wrath of God is being **r** from
2: 5 his righteous judgment will be **r**.
8:18 with the glory that will be **r** in us.
8:19 for the sons of God to be **r**.
10:20 I **r** myself to those who did not ask
16:26 now **r** and made known through the
1Co 1: 7 for our Lord Jesus Christ to be **r**.
2:10 God has **r** it to us by his Spirit.
3:13 It will be **r** with fire, and the fire
2Co 4:10 of Jesus may also be **r** in our body.
4:11 life may be **r** in our mortal body.
Gal 3:23 locked up until faith should be **r**.
Eph 3: 5 been **r** by the Spirit to God's holy
2Th 1: 7 the Lord Jesus is **r** from heaven in
2: 3 and the man of lawlessness is **r**,
2: 6 that he may be **r** at the proper time.
2: 8 the lawless one will be **r**, whom the
2Ti 1:10 has now been **r** through the appearing
1Pe 1: 5 is ready to be **r** in the last time.
1: 7 and honour when Jesus Christ is **r**.
1:12 was **r** to them that they were not
1:13 be given you when Jesus Christ is **r**.
1:20 **r** in these last times for your sake.
4:13 be overjoyed when his glory is **r**.
5: 1 will share in the glory to be **r**:
Rev 15: 4 your righteous acts have been **r**."

Revealer (Reveal)

Da 2:29 and the **r** of mysteries showed you
2:47 Lord of kings and a **r** of mysteries,

Revealing (Reveal)

Eze 21:24 **r** your sins in all that you
Am 3: 7 does nothing without **r** his plan

Reveals (Reveal)

Nu 23: 3 Whatever he **r** to me I will tell you."
Job 12:22 He **r** the deep things of darkness and
Da 2:22 He **r** deep and hidden things; he
2:28 there is a God in heaven who **r**
Am 4:13 creates the wind, and **r** his thoughts

Revelation (Reveal)

2Sa 7:17 David all the words of this entire **r**.
1Ch 17:15 David all the words of this entire **r**.
Pr 29:18 Where there is no **r**, the people cast
Da 10: 1 a **r** was given to Daniel (who was
Hab 2: 2 the LORD replied: "Write down the **r**
2: 3 For the **r** awaits an appointed time;
Lk 2:32 a light for **r** to the Gentiles and
Ro 16:25 according to the **r** of the mystery
1Co 14: 6 unless I bring you some **r** or
14:26 a **r**, a tongue or an interpretation.
14:30 if a **r** comes to someone who is
Gal 1:12 I received it by **r** from Jesus Christ.
2: 2 I went in response to a **r** and set
Eph 1:17 **r**, so that you may know him better.
3: 3 the mystery made know to me by **r**,
Rev 1: 1 The **r** of Jesus Christ, which God

Revelations (Reveal)

2Co 12: 1 on to visions and **r** from the Lord.
12: 7 of these surpassingly great **r**,

Revelled (Revelry)

Ne 9:25 they **r** in your great goodness.

Revellers (Revelry)

Isa 5:14 with all their brawlers and **r**.
24: 8 the noise of the **r** has stopped, the
Jer 15:17 I never sat in the company of **r**,

Revelling (Revelry)

1Sa 30:16 eating, drinking and **r** because of
Isa 23:12 He said, "No more of your **r**,
2Pe 2:13 blots and blemishes, **r** in their

Revelry (Revelled, Revellers, Revelling)

Ex 32: 6 drink and got up to indulge in **r**.
Isa 22: 2 O city of tumult and **r**? Your slain
22:13 But see, there is joy and **r**,
23: 7 Is this your city of **r**, the old, old
32:13 of merriment and for this city of **r**.
1Co 10: 7 and got up to indulge in pagan **r**."

Revenge (Vengeance)

Lev 19:18 "'Do not seek **r** or bear a grudge
Jdg 15: 7 won't stop until I get my **r** on you."
16:28 **r** on the Philistines for my two eyes.
1Sa 18:25 foreskins, to take **r** on his enemies.
Ps 44:16 of the enemy, who is bent on **r**.
Pr 6:34 will show no mercy when he takes **r**.
Jer 20:10 over him and take our **r** on him."
Eze 24: 8 To stir up wrath and take **r** I put
25:12 'Because Edom took **r** on the house of
25:15 took **r** with malice in their hearts,
Ro 12:19 Do not take **r**, my friends, but leave

Revenue (Revenues)

Isa 23: 3 of the Nile was the **r** of Tyre,
33:18 Where is the one who took the **r**?
Ro 13: 7 pay taxes; if **r**, then **r**; if respect,

Revenues (Revenue)

1Ki 10:15 not including the **r** from merchants
2Ch 9:14 not including the **r** brought in by
Ezr 4:13 paid, and the royal **r** will suffer.
6: 8 from the **r** of Trans-Euphrates, so

Revere (Revered, Reverence, Reverent, Revering)

Lev 19:32 for the elderly and **r** your God.
Dt 4:10 they may learn to **r** me as long as
13: 4 you must follow, and him you must **r**.
14:23 learn to **r** the LORD your God always.
17:19 he may learn to **r** the LORD his God
28:58 and do not **r** this glorious and
Job 37:24 Therefore, men **r** him, for does he
Ps 22:23 **R** him, all you descendants of Israel!
33: 8 all the people of the world **r** him.
102:15 of the earth will **r** your glory.
Ecc 3:14 God does it so that men will **r** him.
Isa 25: 3 of ruthless nations will **r** you.
59:19 of the sun, they will **r** his glory.
63:17 our hearts so we do not **r** you?
Jer 10: 7 Who should not **r** you, O King of the
Hos 10: 3 king because we did not **r** the LORD.
Mal 4: 2 for you who **r** my name, the sun of

Revered (Revere)

Jos 4:14 they **r** him all the days of his life,
4:14 his life, just as they had **r** Moses.
2Ki 4: 1 and you know that he **r** the LORD.
Mal 2: 5 he **r** me and stood in awe of my name.

Reverence (Revere)

Lev 19:30 "'Observe my Sabbaths and have **r**
26: 2 "'Observe my Sabbaths and have **r**
Jos 5:14 fell face down to the ground in **r**,
Ne 5:15 **r** for God I did not act like that.
Ps 5: 7 will come into your house; in **r** will
Jer 44:10 not humbled themselves or shown **r**,
Da 6:26 must fear and **r** the God of Daniel.
Mal 2: 5 this called for **r** and he revered me
Ac 10:25 met him and fell at his feet in **r**.
2Co 7: 1 holiness out of **r** for God.
Eph 5:21 Submit to one another out of **r** for
Col 3:22 of heart and **r** for the Lord.
Heb 12:28 God acceptably with **r** and awe,
1Pe 3: 2 they see the purity and **r** of your
Rev 11:18 saints and those who **r** your name,

Reverent (Revere)

Ecc 8:12 men, who are **r** before God.
Tit 2: 3 teach the older women to be **r** in the
Heb 5: 7 heard because of his **r** submission.
1Pe 1:17 lives as strangers here in **r** fear.

Revering (Revere)

Dt 8: 6 God, walking in his ways and **r** him.
Ne 1:11 servants who delight in **r** your name.

Reverse (Reversed)

Isa 43:13 When I act, who can **r** it?"

Reversed (Reverse)

Eze 7:13 the whole crowd will not be **r**.

Revert

Lev 27:24 Year of Jubilee the field will **r** to
1Ki 12:26 likely to **r** to the house of David.
Eze 46:17 then it will **r** to the prince.

Review

Isa 43:26 **R** the past for me, let us argue the

Revile (Reviled, Reviles)

Ps 10:13 Why does the wicked man **r** God? Why
44:16 of those who reproach and **r** me,
55: 3 upon me and **r** me in their anger.
74:10 Will the foe **r** your name for ever?
Ecc 10:20 Do not **r** the king even in your

Reviled (Revile)

Ps 74:18 how foolish people have **r** your name.

Reviles (Revile)

Ps 10: 3 blesses the greedy and **r** the LORD.

Revive (Revived, Reviving)

Ps 80:18 we will not turn away from you; **r** us,
85: 6 Will you not **r** us again, that your
Isa 57:15 to **r** the spirit of the lowly and to **r**
Hos 6: 2 After two days he will **r** us; on the

Revived (Revive)
Ge 45:27 the spirit of their father Jacob **r**.
Jdg 15:19 his strength returned and he **r**.
1Sa 30:12 He ate and was **r**, for he had not

Reviving (Revive)
Ps 19: 7 The law of the LORD is perfect, **r**

Revoke (Revoked, Revoking)
Ps 132:11 a sure oath that he will not **r**: "One

Revoked (Revoke)
Est 8: 8 and sealed with his ring can be **r**."
Isa 45:23 integrity a word that will not be **r**:
Zec 11:11 was **r** on that day, and so the

Revoking (Revoke)
Zec 11:10 **r** the covenant I had made with all

Revolt (Revolted)
Ezr 4:19 a long history of **r** against kings
Ne 6: 6 you and the Jews are plotting to **r**,
Isa 59:13 fomenting oppression and **r**, uttering
Eze 2: 3 in **r** against me to this very day.
20:38 I will purge you of those who **r** and
Ac 5:37 and led a band of people in **r**.
21:38 you the Egyptian who started a **r**

Revolted (Revolt)
Jdg 9:18 (but today you have **r** against my
2Ki 8:22 Libnah **r** at the same time.
2Ch 21:10 Libnah **r** at the same time, because
Isa 31: 6 Return to him you have so greatly **r**

Revolutions
Lk 21: 9 you hear of wars and **r**, do not be

Reward (Rewarded, Rewarding, Rewards)
Ge 15: 1 I am your shield, your very great **r**."
Nu 22:17 I will **r** you handsomely and do
22:37 me? Am I really not able to **r** you?"
24:11 I said I would **r** you handsomely,
1Sa 24:19 May the LORD **r** you well for the way
2Sa 4:10 was the **r** I gave him for his news!
18:22 any news that will bring you a **r**."
19:36 should the king **r** me in this way?
Job 17: 5 If a man denounces his friends for **r**,
34:33 Should God then **r** you on your terms,
Ps 17:14 this world whose **r** is in this life.
19:11 in keeping them there is great **r**.
62:12 Surely you will **r** each person
127: 3 the LORD, children a **r** from him.
Pr 9:12 If you are wise, your wisdom will **r**
11:18 sows righteousness reaps a sure **r**.
13:21 is the **r** of the righteous.
19:17 he will **r** him for what he has done.
25:22 his head, and the LORD will **r** you.
31:31 Give her the **r** she has earned, and
Ecc 2:10 this was the **r** for all my labour.
9: 5 nothing; they have no further **r**,
Isa 40:10 See, his **r** is with him, and his
45:13 not for a price or **r**, says the LORD
49: 4 hand, and my **r** is with my God."
61: 8 In my faithfulness I will **r** them and
62:11 'See, your Saviour comes! See, his **r**
Jer 17:10 to **r** a man according to his conduct,
32:19 you **r** everyone according to his
Eze 29:18 Yet he and his army got no **r** from
29:20 I have given him Egypt as a **r** for
Mt 5:12 because great is your **r** in heaven,
5:46 what **r** will you get? Are not even
6: 1 no **r** from your Father in heaven.
6: 2 they have received their **r** in full.
6: 4 what is done in secret, will **r** you.
6: 5 they have received their **r** in full.
6: 6 what is done in secret, will **r** you.
6:16 they have received their **r** in full.
6:18 what is done in secret, will **r** you.
10:41 prophet will receive a prophet's **r**,
10:41 will receive a righteous man's **r**.
10:42 he will certainly not lose his **r**."
16:27 and then he will **r** each person
Mk 9:41 will certainly not lose his **r**.
Lk 6:23 because great is your **r** in heaven.
6:35 Then your **r** will be great, and you
Ac 1:18 (With the **r** he got for his
1Co 3:14 survives, he will receive his **r**.
9:17 If I preach voluntarily, I have a **r**;
9:18 What then is my **r**? Just this: that
Eph 6: 8 you know that the Lord will **r**
Col 3:24 an inheritance from the Lord as a **r**.
Heb 11:26 he was looking ahead to his **r**.
Rev 22:12 I am coming soon! My **r** is with me

Rewarded (Reward)
Ge 30:18 Leah said, "God has **r** me for giving
Nu 24:11 the LORD has kept you from being **r**."
Ru 2:12 May you be richly **r** by the LORD, the
2Sa 22:21 cleanness of my hands he has **r** me.
22:25 The LORD has **r** me according to my
2Ch 15: 7 give up, for your work will be **r**."
Ps 18:20 cleanness of my hands he has **r** me.
18:24 The LORD has **r** me according to my
58:11 "Surely the righteous still are **r**;
Pr 13:13 but he who respects a command is **r**.
14:14 ways, and the good man **r** for his.
Jer 31:16 work will be **r**," declares the LORD.
1Co 3: 8 be **r** according to his own labour.
Heb 10:35 confidence; it will be richly **r**.
2Jn : 8 for, but that you may be **r** fully.

Rewarding (Reward)
Rev 11:18 and for **r** your servants the prophets

Rewards (Reward)
1Sa 26:23 The LORD **r** every man for his
Pr 12:14 as the work of his hands **r** him.
Da 2: 6 me gifts and **r** and great honour.
5:17 and give your **r** to someone else.
Heb 11: 6 he **r** those who earnestly seek him.

Rezeph
2Ki 19:12 Haran, **R** and the people of Eden who
Isa 37:12 Haran, **R** and the people of Eden who

Rezin (Rezin's)
2Ki 15:37 LORD began to send **R** king of Aram
16: 5 **R** king of Aram and Pekah son of
16: 6 At that time, **R** king of Aram
16: 9 to Kir and put **R** to death.
Ezr 2:48 **R**, Nekoda, Gazzam,
Ne 7:50 Reaiah, **R**, Nekoda,
Isa 7: 1 was king of Judah, King **R** of Aram
7: 4 of the fierce anger of **R** and Aram
7: 8 and the head of Damascus is only **R**.
8: 6 over **R** and the son of Remaliah,

Rezin's (Rezin)
Isa 9:11 the LORD has strengthened **R** foes

Rezon
1Ki 11:23 **R** son of Eliada, who had fled from
11:25 **R** was Israel's adversary as long as
11:25 So **R** ruled in Aram and was hostile

Rhegium
Ac 28:13 there we set sail and arrived at **R**.

Rhesa
Lk 3:27 the son of Joanan, the son of **R**, the

Rhoda
Ac 12:13 named **R** came to answer the door.

Rhodes
Eze 27:15 "'The men of **R** traded with you, and
Ac 21: 1 went to **R** and from there to Patara.

Rib (Ribs)
Ge 2:22 the LORD God made a woman from the **r**

Ribai
2Sa 23:29 son of **R** from Gibeah in Benjamin,
1Ch 11:31 Ithai son of **R** from Gibeah in

Ribbon
SS 4: 3 Your lips are like a scarlet **r**; your

Riblah
1. Town on River Orontes, between Hamath and Damascus. Pharaoh Neco put Jehoahaz in chains here to prevent him from ruling in Jerusalem (2Ki 23:33). During his siege of Jerusalem, Nebuchadnezzar established his base here (2Ki 25:6, 20–21; Jer 39:5–6; 52:9–10, 26–27). **2.** Landmark given by Moses for the eastern boundary of Israel, between Shepham and the Sea of Kinnereth (Nu 34:11).

Nu 34:11 Shepham to **R** on the east side of Ain
2Ki 23:33 Pharaoh Neco put him in chains at **R**
25: 6 taken to the king of Babylon at **R**,
25:20 them to the king of Babylon at **R**.
25:21 There at **R**, in the land of Hamath,
Jer 39: 5 Babylon at **R** in the land of Hamath,
39: 6 There at **R** the king of Babylon
52: 9 Babylon at **R** in the land of Hamath,
52:10 There at **R** the king of Babylon
52:26 them to the king of Babylon at **R**.
52:27 There at **R**, in the land of Hamath,

Ribs (Rib)
Ge 2:21 took one of the man's **r** and closed
Da 7: 5 **r** in its mouth between its teeth.

Rich (Richer, Riches, Richest, Richness)
Ge 14:23 be able to say, 'I made Abram **r**.'
26:13 The man became **r**, and his wealth
49:20 "Asher's food will be **r**; he will
Ex 30:15 The **r** are not to give more than a
Lev 25:47 resident among you becomes **r**
Ru 3:10 the younger men, whether **r** or poor.
2Sa 12: 1 town, one **r** and the other poor.
12: 2 The **r** man had a very large number of
12: 4 "Now a traveller came to the **r** man,
12: 4 but the **r** man refrained from taking
1Ch 4:40 They found **r**, good pasture, and the
Job 15:29 He will no longer be **r** and his
21:24 his body well nourished, his bones **r**
34:19 does not favour the **r** over the poor,
Ps 21: 3 You welcomed him with **r** blessings
22:29 All the **r** of the earth will feast
49: 2 both low and high, **r** and poor alike:
49:16 Do not be overawed when a man grows **r**
76: 4 majestic than mountains **r** with game.
145: 8 slow to anger and **r** in love.
Pr 10:15 The wealth of the **r** is their
13: 7 One man pretends to be **r**, yet has
14:20 but the **r** have many friends.
18:11 The wealth of the **r** is their
18:23 mercy, but a **r** man answers harshly.
21:17 loves wine and oil will never be **r**.
22: 2 **R** and poor have this in common: The
22: 7 The **r** rule over the poor, and the
22:16 to the **r**—both come to poverty.
23: 4 Do not wear yourself out to get **r**;
24:25 and **r** blessing will come upon them.
28: 6 a **r** man whose ways are perverse.
28:11 A **r** man may be wise in his own eyes,
28:20 to get **r** will not go unpunished.
28:22 A stingy man is eager to get **r** and
Ecc 5:12 of a **r** man permits him no sleep.
10: 6 while the **r** occupy the low ones.
10:20 or curse the **r** in your bedroom,
Isa 5:17 will feed among the ruins of the **r**.
25: 6 a feast of **r** food for all peoples,
30:23 the land will be **r** and plentiful.
33: 6 a **r** store of salvation and wisdom
53: 9 and with the **r** in his death, though
Jer 2: 7 land to eat its fruit and **r** produce.
5:27 they have become **r** and powerful
9:23 or the **r** man boast of his riches,
49:19 thickets to a **r** pasture-land,
50:44 thickets to a **r** pasture-land,
51:13 You who live by many waters and are **r**
Eze 34:14 **r** pasture on the mountains of Israel.
38:12 **r** in livestock and goods, living at
Hos 12: 8 Ephraim boasts, "I am very **r**; I have
Mic 2: 8 You strip off the **r** robe from those
6:12 Her **r** men are violent; her people

Zec 3: 4 and I will put **r** garments on you."
11: 3 their **r** pastures are destroyed!
11: 5 'Praise the LORD, I am **r**!' Their own
Mt 19:23 **r** man to enter the kingdom of heaven.
19:24 **r** man to enter the kingdom of God."
27:57 evening approached, there came a **r**
Mk 10:23 the **r** to enter the kingdom of God!"
10:25 **r** man to enter the kingdom of God."
12:41 Many **r** people threw in large amounts.
Lk 1:53 but has sent the **r** away empty.
6:24 "But woe to you who are **r**, for you
12:16 certain **r** man produced a good crop.
12:21 himself but is not **r** towards God."
14:12 or your **r** neighbours; if you do,
16: 1 "There was a **r** man whose manager was
16:19 "There was a **r** man who was dressed
16:21 longing to eat what fell from the **r**
16:22 The **r** man also died and was buried.
18:24 the **r** to enter the kingdom of God!
18:25 **r** man to enter the kingdom of God."
21: 1 Jesus saw the **r** putting their gifts
1Co 4: 8 Already you have become **r**! You have
2Co 6:10 yet making many **r**; having nothing,
8: 2 poverty welled up in **r** generosity.
8: 9 that though he was **r**, yet for your
8: 9 through his poverty might become **r**.
9:11 You will be made **r** in every way so
Eph 2: 4 love for us, God, who is **r** in mercy,
1Ti 6: 9 People who want to get **r** fall into
6:17 Command those who are **r** in this
6:18 Command them to do good, to be **r** in
Jas 1:10 the one who is **r** should take pride
1:11 In the same way, the **r** man will fade
2: 5 eyes of the world to be **r** in faith
2: 6 Is it not the **r** who are exploiting
5: 1 Now listen, you **r** people, weep and
2Pe 1:11 you will receive a **r** welcome into
Rev 2: 9 and your poverty—yet you are **r**!
3:17 You say, 'I am **r**; I have acquired
3:18 so that you can become **r**; and white
6:15 the princes, the generals, the **r**,
13:16 small and great, **r** and poor, free
18: 3 grew **r** from her excessive luxuries."
18:19 the sea became **r** through her wealth!

Richer (Rich)

Da 11: 2 will be far **r** than all the others.

Riches (Rich)

1Ki 3:13 what you have not asked for—both **r**
10:23 King Solomon was greater in **r** and
2Ch 1:11 not asked for wealth, **r** or honour,
1:12 And I will also give you wealth, **r**
9:22 King Solomon was greater in **r** and
32:27 Hezekiah had very great **r** and honour,
32:29 for God had given him very great **r**.
Job 20:15 He will spit out the **r** he swallowed;
36:18 that no-one entices you by **r**;
Ps 49: 6 wealth and boast of their great **r**?
49:12 man, despite his **r**, does not endure;
49:20 man who has **r** without understanding
62:10 goods; though your **r** increase,
112: 3 Wealth and **r** are in his house, and
119:14 statutes as one rejoices in great **r**.
Pr 3:16 in her left hand are **r** and honour.
8:18 With me are **r** and honour, enduring
11:28 Whoever trusts in his **r** will fall,
13: 8 A man's **r** may ransom his life, but a
22: 1 name is more desirable than great **r**;
23: 5 Cast but a glance at **r**, and they are
27:24 for **r** do not endure for ever, and a
30: 8 give me neither poverty nor **r**,
Isa 10: 3 help? Where will you leave your **r**?
30: 6 the envoys carry their **r** on donkeys'
45: 3 **r** stored in secret places, so that
60: 5 you the **r** of the nations will come.
61: 6 and in their **r** you will boast.
Jer 9:23 or the rich man boast of his **r**,
17:11 the man who gains **r** by unjust means.
48: 7 Since you trust in your deeds and **r**,
49: 4 you trust in your **r** and say, 'Who
Da 11:43 and silver and all the **r** of Egypt,
Joel 2:22 fig-tree and the vine yield their **r**.
Lk 8:14 choked by life's worries, **r** and
16:11 who will trust you with true **r**?
Ro 2: 4 Or do you show contempt for the **r** of
9:23 What if he did this to make the **r** of
11:12 if their transgression means **r** for
11:12 and their loss means **r** for the
11:12 greater **r** will their fulness bring!
11:33 Oh, the depth of the **r** of the wisdom
Eph 1: 7 accordance with the **r** of God's
1:18 the **r** of his glorious inheritance in
2: 7 the incomparable **r** of his grace,
3: 8 the unsearchable **r** of Christ,
3:16 I pray that out of his glorious **r** he
Php 4:19 to his glorious **r** in Christ Jesus.
Col 1:27 the glorious **r** of this mystery,
2: 2 so that they may have the full **r** of
Rev 18:14 All your **r** and splendour have

Richest (Rich)

Ps 63: 5 be satisfied as with the **r** of foods;
Isa 55: 2 soul will delight in the **r** of fare.
Da 11:24 the **r** provinces feel secure, he will

Richness (Rich)

Ge 27:28 of earth's **r**—an abundance of grain
27:39 away from the earth's **r**, away from

Rid

Ge 21:10 she said to Abraham, "Get **r** of that
35: 2 "Get **r** of the foreign gods you have
Ex 8: 9 your houses may be **r** of the frogs,
Lev 13:58 been washed and is **r** of the mildew,
Nu 17: 5 and I will **r** myself of this constant
Jdg 9:29 command! Then I would get **r** of him.
10:16 they got **r** of the foreign gods among
1Sa 1:14 getting drunk? Get **r** of your wine."
7: 3 then **r** yourselves of the foreign
2Sa 4:11 your hand and **r** the earth of you!"
13:13 Where could I get **r** of my disgrace?
14: 7 we will get **r** of the heir as well.
1Ki 15:12 got **r** of all the idols his fathers
22:46 He **r** the land of the rest of the
2Ki 3: 2 He got **r** of the sacred stone of Baal
23:24 Josiah got **r** of the mediums
2Ch 19: 3 some good in you, for you have **r** the
33:15 He got **r** of the foreign gods and
Eze 18:31 **R** yourselves of all the offences you
20: 7 I said to them, "Each of you, get **r**
20: 8 they did not get **r** of the vile
34:25 **r** the land of wild beasts so that
Zec 11: 8 In one month I got **r** of the three
Lk 22: 2 for some way to get **r** of Jesus,
Ac 16:37 And now do they want to get **r** of us
22:22 "**R** the earth of him! He's not fit to
1Co 5: 7 Get **r** of the old yeast that you may
Gal 4:30 what does the Scripture say? "Get **r**
Eph 4:31 Get **r** of all bitterness, rage and
Col 3: 8 now you must **r** yourselves of all
Jas 1:21 Therefore, get **r** of all moral filth
1Pe 2: 1 **r** yourselves of all malice and

Ridden (Ride)

Nu 22:30 which you have always **r**, to this day?
Est 6: 8 has worn and a horse the king has **r**,
Mk 11: 2 tied there, which no-one has ever **r**.
Lk 19:30 tied there, which no-one has ever **r**.

Riddle (Riddles)

Jdg 14:12 "Let me tell you a **r**," Samson said
14:13 "Tell us your **r**," they said. "Let's
14:15 into explaining the **r** for us,
14:16 You've given my people a **r**, but you
14:17 turn explained the **r** to her people.
14:18 you would not have solved my **r**."
14:19 to those who had explained the **r**.
Ps 49: 4 with the harp I will expound my **r**:

Riddles (Riddle)

Nu 12: 8 face to face, clearly and not in **r**;
Pr 1: 6 the sayings and **r** of the wise.
Da 5:12 explain **r** and solve difficult

Ride (Ridden, Rider, Riders, Rides, Riding, Rode)

Ge 41:43 He had him **r** in a chariot as his
Dt 32:13 He made him **r** on the heights of the
Jdg 5:10 "You who **r** on white donkeys, sitting
2Sa 16: 2 for the king's household to **r** on,
19:26 my donkey saddled and will **r** on it,
2Ki 10:16 Then he made him **r** in his chariot.
Ps 45: 4 In your majesty **r** forth victoriously
66:12 You let men **r** over our heads; we
Isa 30:16 'We will **r** off on swift horses.'
33:21 No galley with oars will **r** them, no
58:14 and I will cause you to **r** on the
Jer 6:23 sea as they **r** on their horses;
50:42 sea as they **r** on their horses;

Rider (Ride)

Ge 49:17 so that its **r** tumbles backwards.
Ex 15: 1 its **r** he has hurled into the sea.
15:21 its **r** he has hurled into the sea."
Job 39:18 to run, she laughs at horse and **r**.
Jer 51:21 with you I shatter horse and **r**, with
Zec 12: 4 with panic and its **r** with madness,"
Rev 6: 2 was a white horse! Its **r** held a bow,
6: 4 Its **r** was given power to take peace
6: 5 Its **r** was holding a pair of scales
6: 8 a pale horse! Its **r** was named Death,
19:11 whose **r** is called Faithful and True.
19:19 the **r** on the horse and his army.
19:21 of the mouth of the **r** on the horse,

Riders (Ride)

2Sa 1: 6 the chariots and **r** almost upon him.
2Ki 18:23 horses—if you can put **r** on them!
Isa 21: 7 **r** on donkeys or **r** on camels, let him
36: 8 horses—if you can put **r** on them!
Eze 39:20 will eat your fill of horses and **r**,
Hag 2:22 horses and their **r** will fall,
Rev 9:17 The horses and **r** I saw in my vision
19:18 of horses and their **r**, and the flesh

Rides (Ride)

Dt 33:26 who **r** on the heavens to help you and
Ps 68: 4 extol him who **r** on the clouds—his
68:33 to him who **r** the ancient skies above,
104: 3 and **r** on the wings of the wind.
Isa 19: 1 the LORD **r** on a swift cloud and is
Rev 17: 7 of the woman and of the beast she **r**,

Ridge (Ridges)

Ge 48:22 I give the **r** of land I took from the

Ridges (Ridge)

Ps 65:10 drench its furrows and level its **r**;

Ridicule (Ridiculed)

Dt 28:37 an object of scorn and **r** to all the
1Ki 9: 7 an object of **r** among all peoples.
2Ki 19: 4 the king of Assyria, has sent to **r**
2Ch 7:20 an object of **r** among all peoples.
Job 19:18 scorn me; when I appear, they **r** me.
Ps 123: 4 We have endured much **r** from the
Isa 37: 4 the king of Assyria, has sent to **r**
Jer 24: 9 an object of **r** and cursing, wherever
48:26 vomit; let her be an object of **r**.
48:27 Was not Israel the object of your **r**?
48:39 Moab has become an object of **r**,
Mic 2: 4 In that day men will **r** you; they
Hab 2: 6 him with **r** and scorn, saying,
Lk 14:29 it, everyone who sees it will **r** him,

Ridiculed (Ridicule)

Jdg 9:38 men you **r**? Go out and fight them!"
2Ch 30:10 but the people scorned and **r** them.
Ne 2:19 about it, they mocked and **r** us.
4: 1 greatly incensed. He **r** the Jews,
Jer 20: 7 **r** all day long; everyone mocks me.
Eze 36: 4 **r** by the rest of the nations around
Hos 7:16 they will be **r** in the land of Egypt.
Lk 23:11 Herod and his soldiers **r** and mocked

Riding (Ride)

Lev 15: 9 "'Everything the man sits on when **r**
Nu 22:22 Balaam was **r** on his donkey, and his
1Sa 25:20 she came **r** her donkey into a
2Sa 18: 9 He was **r** his mule, and as the mule
18: 9 the mule he was **r** kept on going.
2Ki 9:25 Remember how you and I were **r**
Ne 2:12 with me except the one I was **r** on.
Est 8:14 The couriers, **r** the royal horses,
Jer 17:25 They and their officials will come **r**
22: 4 **r** in chariots and on horses,
Eze 38:15 all of them **r** on horses, a great
Zec 1: 8 before me was a man **r** a red horse!
9: 9 gentle and **r** on a donkey, on a colt,
Mt 21: 5 gentle and **r** on a donkey, on a colt,
Rev 19:14 **r** on white horses and dressed in

Rifts

Jer 2: 6 through a land of deserts and **r**, a

Rigging

Pr 23:34 high seas, lying on top of the **r**.
Isa 33:23 Your **r** hangs loose: The mast is not

Right (Aright, *Right hand*, *Right in the eyes of the Lord*, Rightful, Right-handed, Rights)

Ge 4: 7 If you do what is **r**, will you not be
4: 7 But if you do not do what is **r**,
13: 9 I'll go to the **r**; if you go to the **r**,
18:19 LORD by doing what is **r** and just,
18:25 the Judge of all the earth do **r**?"
24:48 who had led me on the **r** road to get
43:23 "It's all **r**," he said. "Don't be
48:13 Ephraim on his **r** towards Israel's
Ex 8:26 Moses said, "That would not be **r**.
9:27 "The LORD is in the **r**, and I and my
14:22 water on their **r** and on their left.
14:29 water on their **r** and on their left.
15:26 God and do what is **r** in his eyes,
21: 8 He has no **r** to sell her to
29:20 of the **r** ears of Aaron and his sons,
29:20 on the thumbs of their **r** hands, and
29:20 and on the big toes of their **r** feet.
29:22 the fat on them, and the **r** thigh.
Lev 7:32 You are to give the **r** thigh of your
7:33 shall have the **r** thigh as his share.
8:23 put it on the lobe of Aaron's **r** ear,
8:23 and on the big toe of his **r** foot.
8:24 blood on the lobes of their **r** ears,
8:24 on the thumbs of their **r** hands and
8:24 and on the big toes of their **r** feet.
8:25 and their fat and the **r** thigh.
8:26 the fat portions and on the **r** thigh.
9:21 waved the breasts and the **r** thigh
14:14 the **r** ear of the one to be cleansed,
14:14 and on the big toe of his **r** foot.
14:16 dip his **r** forefinger into the oil in
14:17 the **r** ear of the one to be cleansed,
14:17 and on the big toe of his **r** foot,
14:25 the **r** ear of the one to be cleansed,
14:25 and on the big toe of his **r** foot.
14:27 with his **r** forefinger sprinkle some
14:28 the **r** ear of the one to be cleansed,
14:28 and on the big toe of his **r** foot.
25:29 he retains the **r** of redemption a
25:32 "'The Levites always have the **r** to
25:48 he retains the **r** of redemption after
Nu 11:15 put me to death **r** now—if I have
18:18 offering and the **r** thigh are yours.
20:17 not turn to the **r** or to the left
22:26 either to the **r** or to the left.
22:29 in my hand, I would kill you **r** now."
25: 6 woman **r** before the eyes of Moses
27: 7 daughters are saying is **r**.
36: 5 of Joseph is saying is **r**.
Dt 2:27 turn aside to the **r** or to the left.
5:32 turn aside to the **r** or to the left.
6:18 Do what is **r** and good in the LORD's
11: 6 when the earth opened its mouth **r** in
13:18 and doing what is **r** in his eyes.
17:11 tell you, to the **r** or to the left.
17:20 the law to the **r** or to the left.
21:17 **r** of the firstborn belongs to him.
Dt 28:14 to the **r** or to the left, following
Jos 1: 7 from it to the **r** or to the left,
4: 3 from **r** where the priests stood
9:25 whatever seems good and **r** to you."
23: 6 aside to the **r** or to the left.
Jdg 3:16 to his **r** thigh under his clothing.
3:21 drew the sword from his **r** thigh and
4:18 to him, "Come, my lord, come **r** in.
7:20 holding in their **r** hands the
11:23 what **r** have you to take it over?
12: 6 they said, "All **r**, say 'Shibboleth'."
14: 3 She's the **r** one for me."
15: 3 "This time I have a **r** to get even
Ru 4: 4 For no-one has the **r** to do it except
1Sa 6:12 not turn to the **r** or to the left.
11: 2 out the **r** eye of every one of you
12: 3 any of these, I will make it **r**."
12:23 you the way that is good and **r**.
14:13 with his armour-bearer **r** behind him.
14:41 God of Israel, "Give me the **r** answer.
2Sa 2:14 "All **r**, let them do it," Joab said.
2:19 Abner, turning neither to the **r** nor
2:21 "Turn aside to the **r** or to the left;
8:15 was just and **r** for all his people.
14:19 no-one can turn to the **r** or to the
16: 6 guard were on David's **r** and left.
18:11 strike him to the ground **r** there?
19:28 So what **r** do I have to make any more
21: 4 "We have no **r** to demand silver or
21: 4 **r** to put anyone in Israel to death.
23: 5 "Is not my house **r** with God? Has he
1Ki 3: 9 to distinguish between **r** and wrong.
7:49 (five on the **r** and five on the left,
8:36 Teach them the **r** way to live, and
11:33 nor done what is **r** in my eyes, nor
11:38 walk in my ways and do what is **r** in
14: 8 doing only what was **r** in my eyes.
22:19 round him on his **r** and on his left.
2Ki 2: 8 The water divided to the **r** and to
2:14 it divided to the **r** and to the left,
4:23 "It's all **r**," she said.
4:26 ask her, 'Are you all **r**? Is your
4:26 husband all **r**? Is your child all **r**?'
5:21 "Is everything all **r**?" he asked.
5:22 "Everything is all **r**," Gehazi
7: 9 to each other, "We're not doing **r**.
9:11 "Is everything all **r**? Why did this
10:30 accomplishing what is **r** in my eyes
12: 9 on the **r** side as one enters the
17: 9 the LORD their God that were not **r**.
22: 2 aside to the **r** or to the left.
1Ch 13: 4 it seemed **r** to all the people.
18:14 was just and **r** for all his people.
2Ch 6:27 Teach them the **r** way to live, and
18:18 standing on his **r** and on his left.
26:18 "It is not **r** for you, Uzziah, to
30: 4 The plan seemed **r** both to the king
31:20 doing what was good and **r** and
34: 2 aside to the **r** or to the left.
Ezr 10:12 "You are **r**! We must do as you say.
Ne 2:20 or any claim or historic **r** to it."
4:11 we will be **r** there among them and
5: 9 "What you are doing is not **r**.
8: 4 Beside him on his **r** stood Mattithiah,
9:13 and laws that are just and **r**,
12:31 to the **r**, towards the Dung Gate.
Est 8: 5 and thinks it the **r** thing to do,
8:11 **r** to assemble and protect themselves;
Job 8: 3 Does the Almighty pervert what is **r**?
27: 5 I will never admit you are in the **r**;
30:12 On my **r** the tribe attacks; they lay
32: 9 the aged who understand what is **r**.
33:12 not **r**, for God is greater than man.
33:23 to tell a man what is **r** for him,
33:27 sinned, and perverted what was **r**,
34: 4 us discern for ourselves what is **r**;
34: 6 Although I am **r**, I am considered a
42: 7 me what is **r**, as my servant Job has.
42: 8 what is **r**, as my servant Job has."
Ps 4: 5 Offer **r** sacrifices and trust in the
9: 4 For you have upheld my **r** and my
17: 2 you; may your eyes see what is **r**.
19: 8 The precepts of the LORD are **r**,
25: 9 He guides the humble in what is **r**
26:10 whose **r** hands are full of bribes.
33: 4 For the word of the LORD is **r** and
Ps 50:16 to the wicked, God says: "What **r**
51: 4 so that you are proved **r** when you
99: 4 you have done what is just and **r**.
106: 3 who constantly do what is **r**.
119:128 I consider all your precepts **r**, I
119:137 you, O LORD, and your laws are **r**.
119:144 Your statutes are for ever **r**; give
142: 4 Look to my **r** and see; no-one is
144: 8 lies, whose **r** hands are deceitful.
144:11 lies, whose **r** hands are deceitful.
Pr 1: 3 doing what is **r** and just and fair;
2: 9 you will understand what is **r** and
4:27 Do not swerve to the **r** or the left;
8: 6 I open my lips to speak what is **r**.
8: 9 To the discerning all of them are **r**;
12:15 The way of a fool seems **r** to him,
14:12 There is a way that seems **r** to a man,
16:25 There is a way that seems **r** to a man,
18:17 The first to present his case seems **r**
20:11 whether his conduct is pure and **r**.
21: 2 All a man's ways seem **r** to him, but
21: 3 To do what is **r** and just is more
21: 7 for they refuse to do what is **r**.
23:16 when your lips speak what is **r**.
23:19 and keep your heart on the **r** path.
Ecc 7:20 who does what is **r** and never sins.
10: 2 heart of the wise inclines to the **r**,
12:10 searched to find just the **r** words,
SS 1: 4 How **r** they are to adore you!
2: 6 my head, and his **r** arm embraces me.
8: 3 my head and his **r** arm embraces me.
Isa 1: 7 stripped by foreigners **r** before you,
1:17 learn to do **r**! Seek justice,
7:15 reject the wrong and choose the **r**.
7:16 reject the wrong and choose the **r**,
9:20 On the **r** they will devour, but still
28:26 him and teaches him the **r** way.
30:10 what is **r**! Tell us pleasant things,
30:21 Whether you turn to the **r** or to the
33:15 righteously and speaks what is **r**,
40:14 and who taught him the **r** way? Who
41:26 'He was **r**'? No-one told of this,
43: 9 witnesses to prove they were **r**,
45:19 the truth; I declare what is **r**.
51: 7 "Hear me, you who know what is **r**,
54: 3 For you will spread out to the **r** and
56: 1 "Maintain justice and do what is **r**,
58: 2 were a nation that does what is **r**
64: 5 gladly do **r**, who remember your ways.
Jer 8: 6 but they do not say what is **r**.
22: 3 LORD says: Do what is just and **r**.
22:15 drink? He did what was **r** and just,
23: 5 do what is just and **r** in the land.
26:14 me whatever you think is good and **r**.
32: 7 it is your **r** and duty to buy it.'
32: 8 Since it is your **r** to redeem it and
33:15 do what is just and **r** in the land.
34:15 and did what is **r** in my sight:
Eze 1:10 and on the **r** side each had the face
4: 6 lie down again, this time on your **r**
18: 5 man who does what is just and **r**.
18:19 the son has done what is just and **r**
18:21 decrees and does what is just and **r**,
18:27 just and **r**, he will save his life.
21:16 O sword, slash to the **r**, then to the
33:14 sin and does what is just and **r**—
33:16 is just and **r**; he will surely live.
33:19 and **r**, he will live by doing so.
45: 9 and do what is just and **r**.
Da 4:27 your sins by doing what is **r**,
4:37 does is **r** and all his ways are just.
Hos 14: 9 The ways of the LORD are **r**; the
Am 3:10 "They do not know how to do **r**,"
Jnh 4: 4 the LORD replied, "Have you any **r** to
4: 9 God said to Jonah, "Do you have a **r**
Mic 3: 9 justice and distort all that is **r**;
7: 9 pleads my case and establishes my **r**.
Zec 3: 1 at his **r** side to accuse him.
4: 3 one on the **r** of the bowl and the
4:11 **r** and the left of the lampstand?"
11:17 sword strike his arm and his **r** eye!
11:17 his **r** eye totally blinded!"
12: 6 They will consume **r** and left all the
Mt 5:29 If your **r** eye causes you to sin,
5:39 the **r** cheek, turn to him the other
11:19 wisdom is proved **r** by her actions."

Mt 15: 7 You hypocrites! Isaiah was **r** when he
15:26 He replied, "It is not **r** to take the
20: 4 and I will pay you whatever is **r**.'
20:15 Don't I have the **r** to do what I want
20:21 two sons of mine may sit at your **r**
20:23 my **r** or left is not for me to grant.
21: 3 them, and he will send them **r** away."
22:17 it **r** to pay taxes to Caesar or not?"
22:26 brother, **r** on down to the seventh.
24:33 know that it is near, **r** at the door.
25:33 He will put the sheep on his **r** and
25:34 the King will say to those on his **r**,
26:58 Peter followed him at a distance, **r**
27:38 one on his **r** and one on his left.
Mk 5:15 in his **r** mind; and they were afraid.
6:25 "I want you to give me **r** now the
7: 6 He replied, "Isaiah was **r** when he
7:27 "for it is not **r** to take the
10:37 "Let one of us sit at your **r** and the
10:40 to sit at my **r** or left is not for me
12:14 it **r** to pay taxes to Caesar or not?
12:32 "You are **r** in saying that God is one
13:29 know that it is near, **r** at the door.
14:54 Peter followed him at a distance, **r**
15:27 one on his **r** and one on his left.
16: 5 the **r** side, and they were alarmed.
Lk 1:11 the **r** side of the altar of incense.
4:30 he walked **r** through the crowd and
5:19 of the crowd, **r** in front of Jesus.
7:29 acknowledged that God's way was **r**,
7:35 wisdom is proved **r** by all her
8:35 in his **r** mind; and they were afraid.
12:57 you judge for yourselves what is **r**?
20:21 that you speak and teach what is **r**,
20:22 Is it **r** for us to pay taxes to
21: 9 but the end will not come **r** away."
22:50 high priest, cutting off his **r** ear.
22:70 replied, "You are **r** in saying I am.
23:33 on his **r**, the other on his left.
Jn 1:12 the **r** to become children of God—
4:17 **r** when you say you have no husband.
7: 6 Jesus told them, "The **r** time for
7: 6 not yet come; for you any time is **r**.
7: 8 for me the **r** time has not yet come."
7:24 appearances, and make a **r** judgment."
8:16 if I do judge, my decisions are **r**,
8:48 The Jews answered him, "Aren't we **r**
18:10 servant, cutting off his **r** ear.
18:31 "But we have no **r** to execute anyone,
18:37 Jesus answered, "You are **r** in saying
21: 6 He said, "Throw your net on the **r**
Ac 4:19 whether it is **r** in God's sight to
6: 2 "It would not be **r** for us to neglect
8:21 your heart is not **r** before God.
10:35 who fear him and do what is **r**.
11:11 "**R** then three men who had been sent
13:10 an enemy of everything that is **r**!
13:10 perverting the **r** ways of the Lord?
25:11 has the **r** to hand me over to them.
Ro 3: 4 "So that you may be proved **r** when
5: 6 You see, at just the **r** time, when we
7:21 to do good, evil is **r** there with me.
8:22 childbirth **r** up to the present time.
9:21 Does not the potter have the **r** to
12:17 what is **r** in the eyes of everybody.
13: 3 hold no terror for those who do **r**,
13: 3 what is **r** and he will commend you.
1Co 7:35 but that you may live in a **r** way in
7:37 man also does the **r** thing.
7:38 he who marries the virgin does **r**,
9: 4 Don't we have the **r** to food and
9: 5 Don't we have the **r** to take a
9:12 If others have this **r** of support
9:12 the more? But we did not use this **r**.
2Co 5:13 we are in our **r** mind, it is for you.
8:21 we are taking pains to do what is **r**,
13: 7 you will do what is **r** even though
Eph 6: 1 parents in the Lord, for this is **r**.
Php 1: 7 is **r** for me to feel this way about
4: 8 whatever is noble, whatever is **r**,
Col 4: 1 provide your slaves with what is **r**
2Th 1: 5 evidence that God's judgment is **r**,
3: 9 not because we do not have the **r** to
3:13 never tire of doing what is **r**.
Heb 13:10 at the tabernacle have no **r** to eat.
Jas 2: 8 as yourself," you are doing **r**.
1Pe 2:14 wrong and to commend those who do **r**.
3: 6 is **r** and do not give way to fear.
3:14 for what is **r**, you are blessed.
2Pe 1:13 I think it is **r** to refresh your
1Jn 2:29 does what is **r** has been born of him.
3: 7 He who does what is **r** is righteous,
3:10 Anyone who does not do what is **r** is
Rev 2: 7 I will give the **r** to eat from the
3:21 I will give the **r** to sit with me on
10: 2 He planted his **r** foot on the sea and
22:11 let him who does **r** continue to do **r**;
22:14 that they may have the **r** to the tree

Right hand

Ge 48:13 Israel's **r**, and brought them close
48:14 Israel reached out his **r** and put it
48:17 Joseph saw his father placing his **r**
48:18 firstborn; put your **r** on his head."
Ex 15: 6 "Your **r**, O LORD, was majestic in
15: 6 Your **r**, O LORD, shattered the enemy.
15:12 You stretched out your **r** and the
Lev 8:23 on the thumb of his **r** and on the big
14:14 on the thumb of his **r** and on the big
14:17 on the thumb of his **r** and on the big
14:25 on the thumb of his **r** and on the big
14:28 on the thumb of his **r** and on the big
Jdg 5:26 peg, her **r** for the workman's hammer.
16:29 Bracing himself against them, his **r**
2Sa 20: 9 by the beard with his **r** to kiss him.
1Ki 2:19 mother, and she sat down at his **r**.
1Ch 6:39 who served at his **r**: Asaph son of
Job 40:14 to you that your own **r** can save you.
Ps 16: 8 is at my **r**, I shall not be shaken.
16:11 with eternal pleasures at your **r**.
17: 7 you who save by your **r** those who
18:35 and your **r** sustains me; you stoop
20: 6 with the saving power of his **r**.
21: 8 your **r** will seize your foes.
44: 3 bring them victory; it was your **r**,
45: 4 let your **r** display awesome deeds.
45: 9 at your **r** is the royal bride in gold
48:10 your **r** is filled with righteousness.
60: 5 Save us and help us with your **r**,
63: 8 clings to you; your **r** upholds me.
73:23 with you; you hold me by my **r**.
74:11 your **r**? Take it from the folds of
77:10 years of the **r** of the Most High."
78:54 to the hill country his **r** had taken.
80:15 the root your **r** has planted, the son
80:17 your hand rest on the man at your **r**,
89:13 your hand is strong, your **r** exalted.
89:25 over the sea, his **r** over the rivers.
89:42 You have exalted the **r** of his foes;
91: 7 ten thousand at your **r**, but it will
98: 1 his **r** and his holy arm have worked
108: 6 Save us and help us with your **r**,
109: 6 him; let an accuser stand at his **r**.
109:31 For he stands at the **r** of the needy
110: 1 "Sit at my **r** until I make your
110: 5 The Lord is at your **r**; he will crush
118:15 "The LORD's **r** has done mighty
118:16 The LORD's **r** is lifted high; the
118:16 LORD's **r** has done mighty things!"
121: 5 the LORD is your shade at your **r**;
137: 5 Jerusalem, may my **r** forget its skill.
138: 7 of my foes, with your **r** you save me.
139:10 guide me, your **r** will hold me fast.
Pr 3:16 Long life is in her **r**; in her left
Isa 41:10 will uphold you with my righteous **r**.
41:13 your God, who takes hold of your **r**
44:20 "Is not this thing in my **r** a lie?
45: 1 to Cyrus, whose **r** I take hold of to
48:13 and my **r** spread out the heavens;
62: 8 The LORD has sworn by his **r** and by
63:12 arm of power to be at Moses' **r**,
Jer 22:24 on my **r**, I would still pull you off.
Lam 2: 3 He has withdrawn his **r** at the
2: 4 has strung his bow; his **r** is ready.
Eze 21:22 Into his **r** will come the lot for
39: 3 make your arrows drop from your **r**.
Da 12: 7 lifted his **r** and his left hand
Jnh 4:11 cannot tell their **r** from their left,
Hab 2:16 the LORD's **r** is coming round to you,
Mt 5:30 if your **r** causes you to sin, cut it
6: 3 left hand know what your **r** is doing,
Mt 22:44 "Sit at my **r** until I put your
26:64 sitting at the **r** of the Mighty One
27:29 They put a staff in his **r** and knelt
Mk 12:36 "Sit at my **r** until I put your
14:62 sitting at the **r** of the Mighty One
16:19 heaven and he sat at the **r** of God.
Lk 6: 6 was there whose **r** was shrivelled.
20:42 Lord said to my Lord: "Sit at my **r**
22:69 seated at the **r** of the mighty God."
Ac 2:25 he is at my **r**, I will not be shaken.
2:33 Exalted to the **r** of God, he has
2:34 Lord said to my Lord: "Sit at my **r**
3: 7 Taking him by the **r**, he helped him
5:31 God exalted him to his own **r** as
7:55 and Jesus standing at the **r** of God.
7:56 Son of Man standing at the **r** of God."
Ro 8:34 who was raised to life—is at the **r**
2Co 6: 7 in the **r** and in the left;
Gal 2: 9 me and Barnabas the **r** of fellowship
Eph 1:20 him at his **r** in the heavenly realms,
Col 3: 1 Christ is seated at the **r** of God.
Heb 1: 3 at the **r** of the Majesty in heaven.
1:13 "Sit at my **r** until I make your
8: 1 who sat down at the **r** of the throne
10:12 sins, he sat down at the **r** of God.
12: 2 down at the **r** of the throne of God.
1Pe 3:22 and is at God's **r**—with angels,
Rev 1:16 In his **r** he held seven stars, and
1:17 Then he placed his **r** on me and said:
1:20 seven stars that you saw in my **r**
2: 1 who holds the seven stars in his **r**
5: 1 I saw in the **r** of him who sat on the
5: 7 the **r** of him who sat on the throne.
10: 5 on the land raised his **r** to heaven.
13:16 a mark on his **r** or on his forehead,

Right in the eyes of the LORD

Dt 12:25 because you will be doing what is **r**.
12:28 doing what is good and **r** your God.
21: 9 since you have done what is **r**.
1Ki 15: 5 For David had done what was **r** and
15:11 Asa did what was **r**, as his father
22:43 stray from them; he did what was **r**.
2Ki 12: 2 Joash did what was **r** all the years
14: 3 He did what was **r**, but not as his
15: 3 He did what was **r**, just as his
15:34 He did what was **r**, just as his
16: 2 he did not do what was **r** his God.
18: 3 He did what was **r**, just as his
22: 2 He did what was **r** and walked in all
2Ch 14: 2 Asa did what was good and **r** his God.
20:32 stray from them; he did what was **r**.
24: 2 Joash did what was **r** all the years
25: 2 He did what was **r**, but not
26: 4 He did what was **r**, just as his
27: 2 He did what was **r**, just as his
28: 1 father, he did not do what was **r**.
29: 2 He did what was **r**, just as his
34: 2 He did what was **r** and walked in the

Righteous (Over-righteous, *Righteous man, Righteous one*, Righteously, Righteousness)

Ge 7: 1 have found you **r** in this generation.
18:23 sweep away the **r** with the wicked?
18:24 What if there are fifty **r** people in
18:24 sake of the fifty **r** people in it?
18:25 kill the **r** with the wicked,
18:25 treating the **r** and the wicked alike.
18:26 The LORD said, "If I find fifty **r**
18:28 what if the number of the **r** is five
38:26 "She is more **r** than I, since I
Ex 23: 8 see and twists the words of the **r**.
Nu 23:10 Let me die the death of the **r**, and
Dt 4: 8 so great as to have such **r** decrees
16:19 wise and twists the words of the **r**.
24:13 and it will be regarded as a **r** act
33:21 he carried out the LORD's **r** will,
Jdg 5:11 They recite the **r** acts of the LORD,
5:11 **r** acts of his warriors in Israel.
1Sa 12: 7 **r** acts performed by the LORD for you
24:17 "You are more **r** than I," he said.
1Ki 3: 6 to you and **r** and upright in heart.
Ezr 9:15 O LORD, God of Israel, you are **r**! We
Ne 9: 8 kept your promise because you are **r**.

Job 4:17 'Can a mortal be more **r** than God?
9: 2 But how can a mortal be **r** before God?
12: 4 though **r** and blameless!
15:14 born of woman, that he could be **r**?
17: 9 the **r** will hold to their ways,
22: 3 it give the Almighty if you were **r**?
22:19 "The **r** see their ruin and rejoice;
25: 4 How then can a man be **r** before God?
27:17 what he lays up the **r** will wear, and
32: 1 because he was **r** in his own eyes.
33:26 is restored by God to his **r** state.
35: 7 If you are **r**, what do you give to
36: 7 He does not take his eyes off the **r**;
Ps 1: 5 sinners in the assembly of the **r**.
1: 6 LORD watches over the way of the **r**,
4: 1 when I call to you, O my **r** God.
5:12 For surely, O LORD, you bless the **r**;
7: 9 O **r** God, who searches minds and
7: 9 of the wicked and make the **r** secure.
7:11 God is a **r** judge, a God who
11: 3 being destroyed, what can the **r** do?"
11: 5 The LORD examines the **r**, but the
11: 7 For the LORD is **r**, he loves justice;
14: 5 is present in the company of the **r**.
15: 2 is blameless and who does what is **r**,
17: 1 Hear, O LORD, my **r** plea; listen to
19: 9 the LORD are sure and altogether **r**.
31:18 they speak arrogantly against the **r**.
32:11 you **r**; sing, all you who are upright
33: 1 Sing joyfully to the LORD, you **r**; it
34:15 The eyes of the LORD are on the **r**
34:17 The **r** cry out, and the LORD hears
34:21 the foes of the **r** will be condemned.
37:12 The wicked plot against the **r** and
37:16 Better the little that the **r** have
37:17 broken, but the LORD upholds the **r**.
37:21 repay, but the **r** give generously;
37:25 yet I have never seen the **r** forsaken
37:29 the **r** will inherit the land and
37:32 The wicked lie in wait for the **r**,
37:39 The salvation of the **r** comes from
51:19 there will be **r** sacrifices, whole
52: 6 The **r** will see and fear; they will
55:22 you; he will never let the **r** fall.
58:10 The **r** will be glad when they are
58:11 men will say, "Surely the **r** still
64:10 Let the **r** rejoice in the LORD and
68: 3 may the **r** be glad and rejoice before
69:28 life and not be listed with the **r**.
71:24 My tongue will tell of your **r** acts
72: 7 In his days the **r** will flourish;
75:10 horns of the **r** shall be lifted up.
88:12 **r** deeds in the land of oblivion?
92:12 The **r** will flourish like a palm tree,
94:21 They band together against the **r** and
97:11 Light is shed upon the **r** and joy on
97:12 Rejoice in the LORD, you who are **r**,
116: 5 The LORD is gracious and **r**; our God
118:15 resound in the tents of the **r**:
118:20 LORD through which the **r** may enter.
119: 7 heart as I learn your **r** laws.
119:62 to give you thanks for your **r** laws.
119:75 I know, O LORD, that your laws are **r**,
119:106 it, that I will follow your **r** laws.
119:121 I have done what is **r** and just; do
119:123 looking for your **r** promise.
119:137 **R** are you, O LORD, and your laws are
119:138 The statutes you have laid down are **r**
119:160 all your **r** laws are eternal.
119:164 a day I praise you for your **r** laws.
119:172 word, for all your commands are **r**.
125: 3 over the land allotted to the **r**,
125: 3 **r** might use their hands to do evil.
129: 4 the LORD is **r**; he has cut me free
140:13 Surely the **r** will praise your name
142: 7 Then the **r** will gather about me
143: 2 for no-one living is **r** before you.
145:17 The LORD is **r** in all his ways and
146: 8 bowed down, the LORD loves the **r**.
Pr 2:20 men and keep to the paths of the **r**.
3:33 but he blesses the home of the **r**.
4:18 The path of the **r** is like the first
10: 3 The LORD does not let the **r** go
10: 6 Blessings crown the head of the **r**,
10: 7 The memory of the **r** will be a
10:11 The mouth of the **r** is a fountain of
Pr 10:16 The wages of the **r** bring them life,
10:20 The tongue of the **r** is choice silver,
10:21 The lips of the **r** nourish many, but
10:24 what the **r** desire will be granted.
10:25 gone, but the **r** stand firm for ever.
10:28 The prospect of the **r** is joy, but
10:29 of the LORD is a refuge for the **r**,
10:30 The **r** will never be uprooted, but
10:31 The mouth of the **r** brings forth
10:32 The lips of the **r** know what is
11: 9 but through knowledge the **r** escape.
11:10 the **r** prosper, the city rejoices;
11:21 but those who are **r** will go free.
11:23 The desire of the **r** ends only in
11:28 the **r** will thrive like a green leaf.
11:30 The fruit of the **r** is a tree of life,
11:31 If the **r** receive their due on earth,
12: 3 but the **r** cannot be uprooted.
12: 5 The plans of the **r** are just, but the
12: 7 but the house of the **r** stands firm.
12:12 but the root of the **r** flourishes.
12:21 No harm befalls the **r**, but the
13: 5 The **r** hate what is false, but the
13: 9 The light of the **r** shines brightly,
13:21 prosperity is the reward of the **r**.
13:22 wealth is stored up for the **r**.
13:25 The **r** eat to their hearts' content,
14:19 the wicked at the gates of the **r**.
14:32 even in death the **r** have a refuge.
15: 6 The house of the **r** contains great
15:28 The heart of the **r** weighs its
15:29 but he hears the prayer of the **r**.
16:31 it is attained by a **r** life.
18:10 tower; the **r** run to it and are safe.
21:15 brings joy to the **r** but terror to
21:18 The wicked become a ransom for the **r**,
21:26 but the **r** give without sparing.
24:15 an outlaw against a **r** man's house,
28: 1 but the **r** are as bold as a lion.
28:12 the **r** triumph, there is great
28:28 the wicked perish, the **r** thrive.
29: 2 the **r** thrive, the people rejoice;
29: 7 The **r** care about justice for the
29:16 but the **r** will see their downfall.
29:27 The **r** detest the dishonest; the
Ecc 3:17 judgment both the **r** and the wicked,
8:14 **r** men who get what the wicked
8:14 men who get what the **r** deserve.
9: 1 concluded that the **r** and the wise
9: 2 All share a common destiny—the **r**
Isa 3:10 Tell the **r** it will be well with them,
10:22 been decreed, overwhelming and **r**.
26: 2 Open the gates that the **r** nation may
26: 7 The path of the **r** is level;
26: 7 you make the way of the **r** smooth.
41:10 uphold you with my **r** right hand.
45:21 a **r** God and a Saviour; there is none
45:25 will be found **r** and will exult.
53:11 my **r** servant will justify many,
57: 1 The **r** perish, and no-one ponders it
57: 1 the **r** are taken away to be spared
60:21 will all your people be **r** and they
64: 6 and all our **r** acts are like filthy
Jer 3:11 is more **r** than unfaithful Judah.
4: 2 if in a truthful, just and **r** way you
12: 1 You are always **r**, O LORD, when I
20:12 you who examine the **r** and probe the
23: 5 will raise up to David a **r** Branch,
31:23 O **r** dwelling, O sacred mountain.'
33:15 a **r** Branch sprout from David's line;
Lam 1:18 "The LORD is **r**, yet I rebelled
4:13 shed within her the blood of the **r**.
Eze 3:20 The **r** things he did will not be
13:22 you disheartened the **r** with your
16:51 **r** by all these things you have done.
16:52 theirs, they appear more **r** than you.
16:52 you have made your sisters appear **r**.
18: 9 That man is **r**; he will surely live,
18:22 **r** things he has done, he will live.
18:24 None of the **r** things he has done
21: 3 from you both the **r** and the wicked.
21: 4 I am going to cut off the **r** and the
23:45 **r** men will sentence them to the
33:13 none of the **r** things he has done
Da 9: 7 "Lord, you are **r**, but this day we
9:14 our God is **r** in everything he does;
Da 9:16 in keeping with all your **r** acts,
9:18 because we are **r**, but because of
Hos 14: 9 LORD are right; the **r** walk in them,
Am 2: 6 They sell the **r** for silver, and the
5:12 You oppress the **r** and take bribes
Mic 6: 5 may know the **r** acts of the LORD."
Hab 1: 4 the **r**, so that justice is perverted.
1:13 up those more **r** than themselves?
2: 4 but the **r** will live by his faith—
Zep 3: 5 The LORD within her is **r**; he does no
Zec 8: 8 and **r** to them as their God."
9: 9 your king comes to you, **r** and having
Mal 3:18 between the **r** and the wicked,
Mt 5:45 rain on the **r** and the unrighteous.
9:13 come to call the **r**, but sinners."
10:41 will receive a **r** man's reward.
13:17 many prophets and **r** men longed to
13:43 the **r** will shine like the sun in the
13:49 and separate the wicked from the **r**
23:28 outside you appear to people as **r**
23:29 and decorate the graves of the **r**.
23:35 upon you will come all the **r** blood
23:35 from the blood of **r** Abel to the
25:37 "Then the **r** will answer him, 'Lord,
25:46 but the **r** to eternal life."
Mk 2:17 come to call the **r**, but sinners."
6:20 knowing him to be a **r** and holy man.
Lk 1:17 disobedient to the wisdom of the **r**
2:25 called Simeon, who was **r** and devout.
5:32 I have not come to call the **r**, but
14:14 at the resurrection of the **r**."
15: 7 **r** persons who do not need to repent.
Jn 17:25 "**R** Father, though the world does not
Ac 10:22 He is a **r** and God-fearing man, who
24:15 of both the **r** and the wicked.
Ro 1:17 written: "The **r** will live by faith.
1:32 Although they know God's **r** decree
2: 5 his **r** judgment will be revealed.
2:13 the law who are **r** in God's sight,
2:13 obey the law who will be declared **r**.
3:10 is written: "There is no-one **r**, not
3:20 Therefore no-one will be declared **r**
5:19 the one man the many will be made **r**.
7:12 the commandment is holy, **r** and good.
8: 4 in order that the **r** requirements of
Gal 3:11 because, "The **r** will live by faith.
1Th 2:10 and so is God, of how holy, **r** and
1Ti 1: 9 **r** but for lawbreakers and rebels,
2Ti 4: 8 which the Lord, the **r** Judge, will
Tit 3: 5 he saved us, not because of **r** things
Heb 12:23 the spirits of **r** men made perfect,
Jas 1:20 about the **r** life that God desires.
2:21 Abraham considered **r** for what he
2:25 Rahab the prostitute considered **r**
1Pe 3:12 For the eyes of the Lord are on the **r**
3:18 the **r** for the unrighteous, to bring
4:18 And, "If it is hard for the **r** to be
2Pe 2: 8 was tormented in his **r** soul by the
1Jn 2:29 If you know that he is **r**, you know
3: 7 what is right is **r**, just as he is **r**.
3:12 were evil and his brother's were **r**.
Rev 15: 4 for your **r** acts have been revealed."
19: 8 for the **r** acts of the saints.)

Righteous man

Ge 6: 9 Noah was a **r**, blameless among the
Ps 34:19 A **r** may have many troubles, but the
37:30 The mouth of the **r** utters wisdom,
112: 4 gracious and compassionate and **r**.
112: 6 a **r** will be remembered for ever.
141: 5 Let a **r** strike me—it is a kindness;
Pr 9: 9 a **r** and he will add to his learning.
11: 8 The **r** is rescued from trouble, and
11:19 The truly **r** attains life, but he who
12:10 A **r** cares for the needs of his
12:13 talk, but a **r** escapes trouble.
12:26 A **r** is cautious in friendship, but
20: 7 The **r** leads a blameless life;
23:24 The father of a **r** has great joy; he
24:16 for though a **r** falls seven times, he
25:26 is a **r** who gives way to the wicked.
Ecc 7:15 a **r** perishing in his righteousness,
7:20 There is not a **r** on earth who does
Eze 3:20 "Again, when a **r** turns from his
3:21 if you do warn the **r** not to sin and

Eze 18: 5 "Suppose there is a **r** who does what
18:20 The righteousness of the **r** will be
18:24 "But if a **r** turns from his
18:26 If a **r** turns from his righteousness
33:12 'The righteousness of the **r** will not
33:12 The **r**, if he sins, will not be
33:13 If I tell the **r** that he will surely
33:18 If a **r** turns from his righteousness
Mt 1:19 Joseph her husband was a **r** and did
10:41 and anyone who receives a **r** because
10:41 because he is a **r** will receive
Lk 23:47 God and said, "Surely this was a **r**.
Ro 5: 7 Very rarely will anyone die for a **r**,
Heb 11: 4 By faith he was commended as a **r**,
Jas 5:16 of a **r** is powerful and effective.
2Pe 2: 7 if he rescued Lot, a **r**, who was
2: 8 (for that **r**, living among them day

Righteous one

Pr 21:12 The **R** takes note of the house of
29: 6 sin, but a **r** can sing and be glad.
Isa 24:16 we hear singing: "Glory to the **R**.
Heb 10:38 my **r** will live by faith. And if he

Righteously (Righteous)

Ps 9: 4 have sat on your throne, judging **r**.
Isa 33:15 He who walks **r** and speaks what is
Jer 11:20 But, O LORD Almighty, you who judge **r**

Righteousness (Righteous, *Righteousness and justice,*)

Ge 15: 6 LORD, and he credited it to him as **r**.
Dt 6:25 commanded us, that will be our **r**."
9: 4 of this land because of my **r**.
9: 5 is not because of your **r** or your
9: 6 that it is not because of your **r**
33:19 and there offer sacrifices of **r**;
1Sa 26:23 The LORD rewards every man for his **r**
2Sa 22:21 has dealt with me according to my **r**;
22:25 has rewarded me according to my **r**,
23: 3 'When one rules over men in **r**, when
1Ki 10: 9 king, to maintain justice and **r**."
2Ch 9: 8 them, to maintain justice and **r**."
Job 27: 6 I will maintain my **r** and never let
29:14 I put on **r** as my clothing; justice
35: 8 and your **r** only the sons of men.
37:23 and great **r**, he does not oppress.
Ps 5: 8 Lead me, O LORD, in your **r** because
7: 8 Judge me, O LORD, according to my **r**,
7:17 thanks to the LORD because of his **r**
9: 8 He will judge the world in **r**; he
17:15 I—in **r** I shall see your face; when
18:20 has dealt with me according to my **r**;
18:24 has rewarded me according to my **r**,
22:31 They will proclaim his **r** to a people
23: 3 in paths of **r** for his name's sake.
31: 1 put to shame; deliver me in your **r**.
35:24 Vindicate me in your **r**, O LORD my
35:28 My tongue will speak of your **r** and
36: 6 Your **r** is like the mighty mountains,
36:10 you, your **r** to the upright in heart.
37: 6 He will make your **r** shine like the
40: 9 I proclaim **r** in the great assembly;
40:10 I do not hide your **r** in my heart; I
45: 4 humility and **r**; let your right hand
45: 7 You love **r** and hate wickedness;
48:10 your right hand is filled with **r**.
50: 6 the heavens proclaim his **r**, for God
51:14 and my tongue will sing of your **r**.
65: 5 You answer us with awesome deeds of **r**
71: 2 Rescue me and deliver me in your **r**;
71:15 My mouth will tell of your **r**, of
71:16 I will proclaim your **r**, yours alone.
71:19 Your **r** reaches to the skies, O God,
72: 1 O God, the royal son with your **r**.
72: 2 He will judge your people in **r**, your
72: 3 people, the hills the fruit of **r**.
85:10 **r** and peace kiss each other.
85:11 earth, and **r** looks down from heaven.
85:13 **R** goes before him and prepares the
89:16 all day long; they exult in your **r**.
94:15 Judgment will again be founded on **r**,
96:13 He will judge the world in **r** and
97: 6 The heavens proclaim his **r**, and all
98: 2 and revealed his **r** to the nations.
Ps 98: 9 in **r** and the peoples with equity.
103:17 **r** with their children's children—
106:31 This was credited to him as **r** for
111: 3 deeds, and his **r** endures for ever.
112: 3 house, and his **r** endures for ever.
112: 9 his **r** endures for ever; his horn
118:19 Open for me the gates of **r**; I will
119:40 Preserve my life in your **r**.
119:142 Your **r** is everlasting and your law
132: 9 May your priests be clothed with **r**;
143: 1 and **r** come to my relief.
143:11 in your **r**, bring me out of trouble.
145: 7 and joyfully sing of your **r**.
Pr 8:20 I walk in the way of **r**, along the
10: 2 no value, but **r** delivers from death.
11: 4 of wrath, but **r** delivers from death.
11: 5 The **r** of the blameless makes a
11: 6 The **r** of the upright delivers them,
11:18 he who sows **r** reaps a sure reward.
12:28 In the way of **r** there is life; along
13: 6 **R** guards the man of integrity, but
14:34 **R** exalts a nation, but sin is a
15: 9 but he loves those who pursue **r**.
16: 8 Better a little with **r** than much
16:12 a throne is established through **r**.
21:21 He who pursues **r** and love finds life,
25: 5 will be established through **r**.
Ecc 7:15 a righteous man perishing in his **r**,
Isa 1:21 **r** used to dwell in her—but now
1:26 the City of **R**, the Faithful City."
1:27 justice, her penitent ones with **r**.
5: 7 for **r**, but heard cries of distress.
5:16 God will show himself holy by his **r**.
9: 7 **r** from that time on and for ever.
11: 4 with **r** he will judge the needy, with
11: 5 **R** will be his belt and faithfulness
16: 5 justice and speeds the cause of **r**.
26: 9 the people of the world learn **r**.
26:10 they do not learn **r**; even in a land
28:17 measuring line and **r** the plumb-line;
32: 1 See, a king will reign in **r** and
32:16 and **r** live in the fertile field.
32:17 The fruit of **r** will be peace; the
32:17 the effect of **r** will be quietness
33: 5 will fill Zion with justice and **r**.
41: 2 calling him in **r** to his service? He
42: 6 "I, the LORD, have called you in **r**;
42:21 the LORD for the sake of his **r**
45: 8 "You heavens above, rain down **r**; let
45: 8 let salvation spring up, let **r** grow
45:13 I will raise up Cyrus in my **r**: I
45:24 In the LORD alone are **r** and strength.
46:12 you who are far from **r**.
46:13 I am bringing my **r** near, it is not
48: 1 of Israel—but not in truth or **r**—
48:18 your **r** like the waves of the sea.
51: 1 "Listen to me, you who pursue **r** and
51: 5 My **r** draws near speedily, my
51: 6 last for ever, my **r** will never fail.
51: 8 But my **r** will last for ever, my
54:14 In **r** you will be established:
56: 1 hand and my **r** will soon be revealed.
57:12 I will expose your **r** and your works,
58: 8 then your **r** will go before you,
59: 9 justice is far from us, and **r** does
59:14 justice is driven back, and **r** stands
59:16 him, and his own **r** sustained him.
59:17 He put on **r** as his breastplate, and
60:17 your governor and **r** your ruler.
61: 3 They will be called oaks of **r**, a
61:10 and arrayed me in a robe of **r**,
61:11 so the Sovereign LORD will make **r**
62: 1 till her **r** shines out like the dawn,
62: 2 The nations will see your **r**, and all
63: 1 I, speaking in **r**, mighty to save."
Jer 9:24 **r** on earth, for in these I delight,"
23: 6 he will be called: The LORD Our **R**.
33:16 it will be called: The LORD Our **R**.'
Eze 3:20 man turns from his **r** and does evil,
14:14 by their **r**, declares the Sovereign
14:20 save only themselves by their **r**.
18:20 The **r** of the righteous man will be
18:24 if a righteous man turns from his **r**
18:26 If a righteous man turns from his **r**
33:12 'The **r** of the righteous man will not
33:12 to live because of his former **r**.'
Eze 33:13 but then he trusts in his **r** and does
33:18 If a righteous man turns from his **r**
Da 9:24 to bring in everlasting **r**, to seal
12: 3 **r**, like the stars for ever and ever.
Hos 10:12 Sow for yourselves **r**, reap the fruit
10:12 until he comes and showers **r** on you.
Joel 2:23 has given you the autumn rains in **r**.
Am 5: 7 bitterness and cast **r** to the
5:24 let justice roll on like a river, **r**
6:12 and the fruit of **r** into bitterness—
Mic 7: 9 into the light; I will see his **r**.
Zep 2: 3 Seek **r**, seek humility; perhaps you
Mal 3: 3 men who will bring offerings in **r**,
4: 2 the sun of **r** will rise with healing
Mt 3:15 for us to do this to fulfil all **r**.
5: 6 hunger and thirst for **r**, for they
5:10 who are persecuted because of **r**,
5:20 For I tell you that unless your **r**
6: 1 "Be careful not to do your 'acts of **r**
6:33 seek first his kingdom and his **r**,
21:32 to you to show you the way of **r**,
Lk 1:75 in holiness and **r** before him all our
18: 9 confident of their own **r** and looked
Jn 16: 8 in regard to sin and **r** and judgment:
16:10 in regard to **r**, because I am going
Ac 24:25 Paul discoursed on **r**, self-control
Ro 1:17 For in the gospel a **r** from God is
1:17 a **r** that is by faith from first to
3: 5 brings out God's **r** more clearly,
3:21 now a **r** from God, apart from law,
3:22 This **r** from God comes through faith
4: 3 and it was credited to him as **r**."
4: 5 wicked, his faith is credited as **r**.
4: 6 whom God credits **r** apart from works:
4: 9 faith was credited to him as **r**.
4:11 a seal of the **r** that he had by faith
4:11 that **r** might be credited to them.
4:13 through the **r** that comes by faith.
4:22 is why "it was credited to him as **r**.
4:24 to whom God will credit **r**—for us
5:17 **r** reign in life through the one man,
5:18 so also the result of one act of **r**
5:21 so also grace might reign through **r**
6:13 body to him as instruments of **r**.
6:16 or to obedience, which leads to **r**?
6:18 sin and have become slaves to **r**.
6:19 in slavery to **r** leading to holiness.
6:20 you were free from the control of **r**.
8:10 your spirit is alive because of **r**.
9:30 who did not pursue **r**, have obtained
9:30 obtained it, a **r** that is by faith;
9:31 Israel, who pursued a law of **r**, has
10: 3 Since they did not know the **r** that
10: 3 own, they did not submit to God's **r**.
10: 4 may be **r** for everyone who believes.
10: 5 Moses describes in this way the **r**
10: 6 the **r** that is by faith says: "Do not
14:17 **r**, peace and joy in the Holy Spirit,
1Co 1:30 is, our **r**, holiness and redemption.
2Co 3: 9 is the ministry that brings **r**!
5:21 in him we might become the **r** of God.
6: 7 **r** in the right hand and in the left;
6:14 For what do **r** and wickedness have in
9: 9 the poor; his **r** endures for ever."
9:10 will enlarge the harvest of your **r**.
11:15 masquerade as servants of **r**.
Gal 2:21 for if **r** could be gained through the
3: 6 and it was credited to him as **r**."
3:21 then **r** would certainly have come by
5: 5 the Spirit the **r** for which we hope.
Eph 4:24 be like God in true **r** and holiness.
5: 9 in all goodness, **r** and truth)
6:14 with the breastplate of **r** in place,
Php 1:11 filled with the fruit of **r** that
3: 6 as for legalistic **r**, faultless.
3: 9 be found in him, not having a **r** of
3: 9 Christ—the **r** that comes from God
1Ti 6:11 flee from all this, and pursue **r**,
2Ti 2:22 and pursue **r**, faith, love and peace,
3:16 correcting and training in **r**,
4: 8 is in store for me the crown of **r**,
Heb 1: 8 **r** will be the sceptre of your
1: 9 You have loved **r** and hated
5:13 with the teaching about **r**.
7: 2 First, his name means "king of **r**";
11: 7 heir of the **r** that comes by faith.

Heb 12:11 however, it produces a harvest of r
Jas 2:23 credited to him as r," and he was
3:18 sow in peace raise a harvest of r.
1Pe 2:24 we might die to sins and live for r;
2Pe 1: 1 To those who through the r of our
2: 5 a preacher of r, and seven others;
2:21 them not to have known the way of r,
3:13 and a new earth, the home of r.

Righteousness and justice
Ps 33: 5 The LORD loves r; the earth is full
89:14 R are the foundation of your throne;
97: 2 r are the foundation of his throne.
103: 6 The LORD works r for all the
Hos 2:19 you in r, in love and compassion.

Rightful (Right)
Job 8: 6 and restore you to your r place.

Right-handed (Hand, Right)
1Ch 12: 2 or to sling stones r or left-handed;

Rights (Right)
Ex 21: 9 must grant her the r of a daughter.
21:10 of her food, clothing and marital r.
Dt 21:16 he must not give the r of the
1Ch 5: 1 his r as firstborn were given to the
5: 2 the r of the firstborn belonged to
Job 36: 6 but gives the afflicted their r.
Ps 82: 3 the r of the poor and oppressed.
Pr 31: 5 all the oppressed of their r.
31: 8 for the r of all who are destitute.
31: 9 defend the r of the poor and needy."
Ecc 5: 8 and justice and r denied, do not be
Isa 10: 2 to deprive the poor of their r and
Jer 5:28 do not defend the r of the poor.
Lam 3:35 to deny a man his r before the Most
1Co 9:15 I have not used any of these r. And
9:18 make use of my r in preaching it.
Gal 4: 5 we might receive the full r of sons.
Heb 12:16 his inheritance r as the oldest son.

Rigid
Mk 9:18 gnashes his teeth and becomes r.

Rim (Rims)
Ex 25:25 make around it a r a handbreadth
25:25 and put a gold moulding on the r.
25:27 The rings are to be close to the r
37:12 They also made around it a r a
37:12 and put a gold moulding on the r.
37:14 The rings were put close to the r to
Dt 2:36 From Aroer on the r of the Arnon
4:48 from Aroer on the r of the Arnon
Jos 12: 2 He ruled from Aroer on the r of the
13: 9 extended from Aroer on the r of the
13:16 The territory from Aroer on the r of
1Ki 7:23 from r to r and five cubits high.
7:24 Below the r, gourds encircled
7:26 and its r was like the r of a cup,
2Ch 4: 2 from r to r and five cubits high.
4: 3 Below the r, figures of bulls
4: 5 and its r was like the r of a cup,
Eze 43:13 a r of one span around the edge.
43:17 with a r of half a cubit and a
43:20 the upper ledge and all round the r,

Rimmon
1. Town in the Negev region of southern Judah (Jos 15:32; Zec 14:10), later reassigned to the tribe of Simeon (Jos 19:7; 1Ch 4:32). **2.** Town marking the eastern border of the territory of Zebulun (Jos 19:13). **3.** A rock in the territory of Benjamin, where 600 of the tribe found refuge from the other Israelite tribes, after they had sinned at Gibeah (Jdg 20:45, 47). They were eventually offered peace (Jdg 21:13).

Jos 15:32 Lebaoth, Shilhim, Ain and R—a total
19: 7 Ain, R, Ether and Ashan—four towns
19:13 out at R and turned towards Neah.
Jdg 20:45 towards the desert to the rock of R,
20:47 R, where they stayed for four months.
21:13 to the Benjamites at the rock of R.
2Sa 4: 2 they were sons of R the Beerothite
4: 5 Now Recab and Baanah, the sons of R
4: 9 the sons of R the Beerothite, "As
2Ki 5:18 enters the temple of R to bow down
5:18 I bow down in the temple of R,
1Ch 4:32 Ain, R, Token and Ashan—five towns—
Zec 14:10 The whole land, from Geba to R,

Rimmon Perez
Nu 33:19 They left Rithmah and camped at R.
33:20 They left R and camped at Libnah.

Rimmono
1Ch 6:77 Kartah, R and Tabor, together with

Rims (Rim)
1Ki 7:33 r, spokes and hubs were all of cast
Eze 1:18 Their r were high and awesome, and
1:18 four r were full of eyes all around.

Ring (Ear-ring, Ear-rings, Ringed, Rings)
Ge 24:22 the man took out a gold nose r
24:30 soon as he had seen the nose r, and
24:47 "Then I put the r in her nose and
41:42 Pharaoh took his signet r from his
Ex 26:24 a single r; both shall be like that.
27: 4 and make a bronze r at each of the
36:29 a single r; both were made alike.
Jdg 8:25 threw a r from his plunder onto it.
Est 3:10 the king took his signet r from his
3:12 himself and sealed with his own r.
8: 2 The king took off his signet r,
8: 8 seal it with the king's signet r
8: 8 sealed with his r can be revoked."
8:10 dispatches with the king's signet r,
Job 16:16 weeping, deep shadows r my eyes;
42:11 him a piece of silver and a gold r.
Pr 11:22 Like a gold r in a pig's snout is a
Jer 22:24 were a signet r on my right hand, I
Eze 16:12 I put a r on your nose, ear-rings on
Da 6:17 r and with the rings of his nobles,
Hag 2:23 my signet r, for I have chosen you,'
Lk 15:22 Put a r on his finger and sandals on
Jas 2: 2 wearing a gold r and fine clothes,

Ringed (Ring)
Job 41:14 r about with his fearsome teeth?

Ringleader (Lead[1])
Ac 24: 5 He is a r of the Nazarene sect

Rings (Ear-rings, Ring)
Ge 35: 4 they had and the r in their ears,
Ex 25:12 Cast four gold r for it and fasten
25:12 r on one side and two r on the other.
25:14 Insert the poles into the r on the
25:15 The poles are to remain in the r of
25:26 Make four gold r for the table and
25:27 The r are to be close to the rim to
26:29 make gold r to hold the crossbars.
27: 7 poles are to be inserted into the r
28:23 Make two gold r for it and fasten
28:24 Fasten the two gold chains to the r
28:26 Make two gold r and attach them to
28:27 Make two more gold r and attach them
28:28 The r of the breastpiece are to be
28:28 the r of the ephod with blue cord,
30: 4 Make two gold r for the altar below
35:22 ear-rings, r and ornaments.
36:34 made gold r to hold the crossbars.
37: 3 He cast four gold r for it and
37: 3 r on one side and two r on the other.
37: 5 he inserted the poles into the r on
37:13 They cast four gold r for the table
37:14 The r were put close to the rim to
37:27 They made two gold r below the
38: 5 They cast bronze r to hold the poles
38: 7 They inserted the poles into the r
39:16 filigree settings and two gold r,
39:16 and fastened the r to two of the
39:17 r at the corners of the breastpiece,
39:19 They made two gold r and attached
39:20 they made two more gold r and
Ex 39:21 They tied the r of the breastpiece
39:21 the r of the ephod with blue cord,
Nu 31:50 bracelets, signet r, ear-rings and
Jdg 8:26 The weight of the gold r he asked
Est 1: 6 to silver r on marble pillars.
Isa 3:21 the signet r and nose r,
Da 6:17 ring and with the r of his nobles,
Hos 2:13 decked herself with r and jewellery,

Rinnah
1Ch 4:20 The sons of Shimon: Amnon, R,

Rinsed (Rinsing)
Lev 6:28 is to be scoured and r with water.
15:12 article is to be r with water.
2Ch 4: 6 used for the burnt offerings were r,

Rinsing (Rinsed)
Lev 15:11 touches without r his hands with

Riot (Rioters, Rioting, Riots)
Mt 26: 5 there may be a r among the people."
Mk 14: 2 they said, "or the people may r.
Ac 17: 5 a mob and started a r in the city.

Rioters (Riot)
Ac 21:32 When the r saw the commander and his

Rioting (Riot)
Ac 19:40 with r because of today's events.

Riots (Riot)
Ac 24: 5 r among the Jews all over the world.
2Co 6: 5 in beatings, imprisonments and r; in

Rip (Ripped)
2Ki 8:12 and r open their pregnant women."
Ps 7: 2 r me to pieces with no-one to rescue
Hos 13: 8 I will attack them and r them open.

Ripe (Ripen, Ripened, Ripening, Ripens)
Nu 13:20 the season for the first r grapes.)
2Ki 4:42 bread baked from the first r corn,
Isa 28: 4 will be like a fig r before harvest—
Joel 3:13 the sickle, for the harvest is r.
Am 8: 1 LORD showed me: a basket of r fruit.
8: 2 "A basket of r fruit," I answered.
8: 2 "The time is r for my people Israel;
Na 3:12 first r fruit; when they are shaken,
Zec 8: 4 "Once again men and women of r old
Mk 4:29 soon as the grain is r, he puts the
Jn 4:35 the fields! They are r for harvest.
Rev 14:15 for the harvest of the earth is r."
14:18 vine, because its grapes are r."

Ripen (Ripe)
Ex 9:32 destroyed, because they r later.)
Jer 24: 2 like those that r early; the other

Ripened (Ripe)
Ge 40:10 and its clusters r into grapes.
Isa 16: 9 The shouts of joy over your r fruit
Jer 48:32 fallen on your r fruit and grapes.

Ripening (Ripe)
Isa 18: 5 and the flower becomes a r grape,

Ripens (Ripe)
Hos 2: 9 I will take away my grain when it r

Riphath
Ge 10: 3 The sons of Gomer: Ashkenaz, R and
1Ch 1: 6 The sons of Gomer: Ashkenaz, R and

Ripped (Rip)
2Ki 15:16 and r open all the pregnant women.
Hos 13:16 their pregnant women r open."
Am 1:13 Because he r open the pregnant women

Rise (Arise, Arisen, Arises, Arose, Risen, Rises, Rising, Rose)

Lev 19:32 "'**R** in the presence of the aged,
Nu 10:35 "**R** up, O LORD! May your enemies be
23:24 The people **r** like a lioness; they
24:17 a sceptre will **r** out of Israel.
Dt 28: 7 enemies who **r** up against you will
28:43 The alien who lives among you will **r**
32:38 Let them **r** up to help you! Let them
33:11 Smite the loins of those who **r** up
33:11 his foes till they **r** no more."
Jos 8: 7 you are to **r** up from ambush and take
Jdg 20:40 when the column of smoke began to **r**
1Sa 16:12 Then the LORD said, "**R** and anoint
2Sa 18:32 all who **r** up to harm you be like
22:39 not **r**; they fell beneath my feet.
Ezr 10: 4 **R** up; this matter is in your hands.
Job 14:12 man lies down and does not **r**; till
20:27 the earth will **r** up against him.
24:12 The groans of the dying **r** from the
25: 3 Upon whom does his light not **r**?
Ps 3: 1 my foes! How many **r** up against me!
7: 6 Arise, O LORD, in your anger; **r** up
17: 1 it does not **r** from deceitful lips.
17:13 **R** up, O LORD, confront them, bring
18:38 not **r**; they fell beneath my feet.
20: 8 fall, but we **r** up and stand firm.
27:12 for false witnesses **r** up against me,
32: 6 waters **r**, they will not reach him.
35:23 Awake, and **r** to my defence! Contend
36:12 fallen—thrown down, not able to **r**!
44:26 **R** up and help us; redeem us because
59: 1 me from those who **r** up against me.
66: 7 not the rebellious **r** up against him.
74:22 **R** up, O God, and defend your cause;
82: 8 **R** up, O God, judge the earth, for
88:10 are dead **r** up and praise you?
94: 2 **R** up, O Judge of the earth; pay back
94:16 Who will **r** up for me against the
119:62 At midnight I **r** to give you thanks
119:147 I **r** before dawn and cry for help; I
127: 2 In vain you **r** early and stay up late,
135: 7 He makes clouds **r** from the ends of
139: 2 You know when I sit and when I **r**;
139: 9 If I **r** on the wings of the dawn, if
139:21 abhor those who **r** up against you?
140:10 fire, into miry pits, never to **r**.
Pr 28:12 **r** to power, men go into hiding.
28:28 the wicked **r** to power, people go
Ecc 12: 4 when men **r** up at the sound of birds,
Isa 3: 5 The young will **r** up against the old,
5:11 Woe to those who **r** early in the
14: 9 it makes them **r** from their thrones—
14:21 they are not to **r** to inherit the
14:22 "I will **r** up against them," declares
24:20 that it falls—never to **r** again.
26:14 those departed spirits do not **r**.
26:19 dead will live; their bodies will **r**.
28:21 The LORD will **r** up as he did at
31: 2 He will **r** up against the house of
32: 9 You women who are so complacent, **r**
33: 3 when you **r** up, the nations scatter.
34:10 and day; its smoke will **r** for ever.
43:17 and they lay there, never to **r** again,
49: 7 "Kings will see you and **r** up,
51:17 Awake, awake! **R** up, O Jerusalem, you
52: 2 Shake off your dust; **r** up, sit
58:10 then your light will **r** in the
Jer 10:13 clouds **r** from the ends of the earth.
25:27 get drunk and vomit, and fall to **r**
46: 8 She says, 'I will **r** and cover the
49:14 to attack it! **R** up for battle!"
51:16 clouds **r** from the ends of the earth.
51:42 The sea will **r** over Babylon; its
51:64 say, 'So will Babylon sink to **r** no
Eze 1:20 and the wheels would **r** along with
10:16 their wings to **r** from the ground,
17:14 unable to **r** again, surviving only by
Da 2:39 "After you, another kingdom will **r**,
7:17 kingdoms that will **r** from the earth.
11:14 "In those times many will **r** against
11:23 a few people he will **r** to power.
11:31 "His armed forces will **r** up to
12:13 at the end of the days you will **r**
Hos 10:14 the roar of battle will **r** against
Joel 2:20 stench will go up; its smell will **r**.
Am 5: 2 "Fallen is Virgin Israel, never to **r**
7: 9 **r** against the house of Jeroboam."
8: 8 The whole land will **r** like the Nile;
8:14 they will fall, never to **r** again."
Ob : 1 "**R**, and let us go against her for
Mic 4:13 "**R** and thresh, O Daughter of Zion,
7: 8 Though I have fallen, I will **r**.
Mal 4: 2 will **r** with healing in its wings.
Mt 5:45 He causes his sun to **r** on the evil
12:42 The Queen of the South will **r** at the
24: 7 Nation will **r** against nation, and
26:46 **R**, let us go! Here comes my betrayer!
27:63 'After three days I will **r** again.'
Mk 8:31 killed and after three days **r** again.
9:31 and after three days he will **r**."
10:34 Three days later he will **r**."
12:25 the dead **r**, they will neither marry
13: 8 Nation will **r** against nation, and
14:42 **R**! Let us go! Here comes my betrayer!
Lk 11:31 The Queen of the South will **r** at the
17:19 he said to him, "**R** and go; your
18:33 On the third day he will **r** again."
20:37 even Moses showed that the dead **r**,
21:10 he said to them: "Nation will **r**
24:38 and why do doubts **r** in your minds?
24:46 **r** from the dead on the third day,
Jn 5:29 who have done good will **r** to live,
5:29 done evil will **r** to be condemned.
11:23 to her, "Your brother will **r** again.
11:24 Martha answered, "I know he will **r**
20: 9 that Jesus had to **r** from the dead.)
Ac 17: 3 had to suffer and **r** from the dead.
26:23 as the first to **r** from the dead,
Eph 5:14 "Wake up, O sleeper, **r** from the dead,
1Th 4:16 and the dead in Christ will **r** first.

Risen (Rise)

Ge 19:23 Zoar, the sun had **r** over the land.
Dt 34:10 Since then, no prophet has **r** in
2Sa 14: 7 Now the whole clan has **r** up against
Eze 47: 5 because the water had **r** and was deep
Mic 2: 8 Lately my people have **r** up like an
Mt 11:11 has not **r** anyone greater than John
14: 2 "This is John the Baptist; he has **r**
26:32 after I have **r**, I will go ahead of
28: 6 He is not here; he has **r**, just as he
28: 7 'He has **r** from the dead and is going
Mk 9: 9 the Son of Man had **r** from the dead.
14:28 after I have **r**, I will go ahead of
16: 6 He has **r**! He is not here. See the
16:14 who had seen him after he had **r**.
Lk 24: 6 He is not here; he has **r**! Remember
24:34 saying, "It is true! The Lord has **r**

Rises (Rise)

Jos 11:17 from Mount Halak, which **r** towards
12: 7 which **r** towards Seir (their lands
Jdg 5:31 the sun when it **r** in its strength.
Job 16: 8 **r** up and testifies against me.
24:14 daylight is gone, the murderer **r** up
41:25 he **r** up, the mighty are terrified;
Ps 19: 6 **r** at one end of the heavens and
74:23 your enemies, which **r** continually.
104:22 The sun **r**, and they steal away; they
Pr 24:16 he **r** again, but the wicked are
Ecc 1: 5 The sun **r** and the sun sets, and
1: 5 and hurries back to where it **r**.
3:21 Who knows if the spirit of man **r**
10: 4 If a ruler's anger **r** against you, do
Isa 2:19 when he **r** to shake the earth.
2:21 when he **r** to shake the earth.
3:13 in court; he **r** to judge the people.
30:18 to you; he **r** to show you compassion.
60: 1 the glory of the LORD **r** upon you.
60: 2 but the LORD **r** upon you and his
Jer 46: 7 "Who is this that **r** like the Nile,
46: 8 Egypt **r** like the Nile, like rivers
48:34 "The sound of their cry **r** from
51: 9 skies, it **r** as high as the clouds.'
Hos 6: 3 As surely as the sun **r**, he will
7: 4 the kneading of the dough till it **r**.
Am 9: 5 the whole land **r** like the Nile,
Mic 7: 6 a daughter **r** up against her mother,
Lk 16:31 even if someone **r** from the dead.
Eph 2:21 **r** to become a holy temple in the
Jas 1:11 For the sun **r** with scorching heat
2Pe 1:19 the morning star **r** in your hearts.
Rev 14:11 the smoke of their torment **r** for

Rising (Rise)

Ge 19:28 and he saw dense smoke **r** from the
Jos 8:20 smoke of the city **r** against the sky,
1Ki 18:44 as a man's hand is **r** from the sea.
Ps 50: 1 summons the earth from the **r** of the
113: 3 From the **r** of the sun to the place
Isa 13:10 The **r** sun will be darkened and the
30:28 a rushing torrent, **r** up to the neck.
41:25 from the **r** sun who calls on my name.
45: 6 that from the **r** of the sun to the
59:19 and from the **r** of the sun, they will
Jer 25:32 is **r** from the ends of the earth."
47: 2 "See how the waters are **r** in the
Eze 8:11 a fragrant cloud of incense was **r**.
Mal 1:11 the **r** to the setting of the sun.
Mk 9:10 what "**r** from the dead" meant.
12:26 Now about the dead **r**—have you not
Lk 1:78 **r** sun will come to us from heaven
2:34 the falling and **r** of many in Israel,
12:54 "When you see a cloud **r** in the west,
ev 14:20 out of the press, **r** as high as the

Risk (Risked, Risking)

2Sa 17:17 not **r** being seen entering the city.
23:17 who went at the **r** of their lives?"
1Ch 11:19 who went at the **r** of their lives?"
Lam 5: 9 We get our bread at the **r** of our

Risked (Risk)

Jdg 5:18 The people of Zebulun **r** their very
9:17 **r** his life to rescue you from the
1Ch 11:19 they **r** their lives to bring it back,
Ac 15:26 men who have **r** their lives for the
Ro 16: 4 They **r** their lives for me. Not only

Risking (Risk)

Php 2:30 **r** his life to make up for the help

Rissah

Nu 33:21 They left Libnah and camped at **R**.
33:22 They left **R** and camped at Kehelathah.

Rites

Ac 21:24 join in their purification **r** and pay

Rithmah

Nu 33:18 They left Hazeroth and camped at **R**.
33:19 They left **R** and camped at Rimmon

Rival (Rivalry)

Lev 18:18 take your wife's sister as a **r** wife
1Sa 1: 6 the LORD had closed her womb, her **r**
1: 7 her **r** provoked her till she wept and
Eze 31: 8 in the garden of God could not **r** it,

Rivalry (Rival)

Php 1:15 preach Christ out of envy and **r**,

River (Riverbank, Rivers)

Ge 2:10 A **r** watering the garden flowed from
2:13 The name of the second **r** is the
2:14 The name of the third **r** is the
2:14 And the fourth **r** is the Euphrates.
15:18 from the **r** of Egypt to the great **r**,
31:21 and crossing the **R**, he headed for
36:37 on the **r** succeeded him as king.
41: 2 out of the **r** there came up seven
41:18 out of the **r** there came up seven
Ex 2: 5 were walking along the **r** bank.
4: 9 **r** will become blood on the ground."
7:18 and the **r** will stink; the Egyptians
7:21 The fish in the Nile died, and the **r**
7:24 could not drink the water of the **r**.
23:31 and from the desert to the **R**.
Nu 22: 5 near the **R**, in his native land.
24: 6 like gardens beside a **r**, like aloes
Dt 1: 7 far as the great **r**, the Euphrates.
3:16 the border) and out to the Jabbok **R**,

Dt 11:24 the Euphrates **R** to the western sea.
Jos 1: 2 get ready to cross the Jordan **R** into
1: 4 and from the great **r**, the Euphrates—
2:23 forded the **r** and came to Joshua son
3: 8 waters, go and stand in the **r**.
4:18 the priests came up out of the **r**
12: 2 of the gorge—to the Jabbok **R**,
13: 3 from the Shihor **R** on the east of
24: 2 the **R** and worshipped other gods.
24: 3 Abraham from the land beyond the **R**
24:14 beyond the **R** and in Egypt, and serve
24:15 forefathers served beyond the **R**,
Jdg 4: 7 to the Kishon **R** and give him
4:13 Harosheth Haggoyim to the Kishon **R**.
5:21 The **r** Kishon swept them away, the
5:21 away, the age-old **r**, the **r** Kishon.
2Sa 8: 3 his control along the Euphrates **R**.
10:16 beyond the **R**; they went to Helam,
17:21 "Set out and cross the **r** at once;
1Ki 4:21 **R** to the land of the Philistines,
4:24 over all the kingdoms west of the **R**,
14:15 and scatter them beyond the **R**,
2Ki 17: 6 in Gozan on the Habor **R** and in
18:11 Habor **R**, and in towns of the Medes.
23:29 **R** to help the king of Assyria.
24: 7 Wadi of Egypt to the Euphrates **R**.
1Ch 1:48 on the **r** succeeded him as king.
5: 9 that extends to the Euphrates **R**,
5:26 Habor, Hara and the **r** of Gozan,
13: 5 from the Shihor **R** in Egypt to Lebo
18: 3 his control along the Euphrates **R**.
19:16 Arameans brought from beyond the **R**,
2Ch 9:26 **R** to the land of the Philistines,
Job 14:11 water disappears from the sea or a **r**
40:23 the **r** rages, he is not alarmed; he
Ps 36: 8 them drink from your **r** of delights.
46: 4 There is a **r** whose streams make glad
72: 8 from the **R** to the ends of the earth.
80:11 the Sea, its shoots as far as the **R**.
83: 9 to Sisera and Jabin at the **r** Kishon,
105:41 like a **r** it flowed in the desert.
Isa 7:20 use a razor hired from beyond the **R**
8: 7 the mighty floodwaters of the **R**
11:15 sweep his hand over the Euphrates **R**.
19: 5 The waters of the **r** will dry up, and
19: 5 the **r** bed will be parched and dry.
19: 7 the Nile, at the mouth of the **r**.
48:18 your peace would have been like a **r**,
66:12 "I will extend peace to her like a **r**,
Jer 2:18 Assyria to drink water from the **R**?
46: 2 at Carchemish on the Euphrates **R**
46: 6 **R** Euphrates they stumble and fall.
46:10 of the north by the **R** Euphrates.
51:32 the **r** crossings seized, the marshes
Lam 2:18 let your tears flow like a **r** day and
Eze 1: 1 was among the exiles by the Kebar **R**,
1: 3 **R** in the land of the Babylonians.
3:15 lived at Tel Abib near the Kebar **R**.
3:23 the Kebar **R**, and I fell face down.
10:15 creatures I had seen by the Kebar **R**.
10:20 the God of Israel by the Kebar **R**,
10:22 as those I had seen by the Kebar **R**.
43: 3 the Kebar **R**, and I fell face down.
47: 5 but now it was a **r** that I could not
47: 5 in—a **r** that no-one could cross.
47: 6 he led me back to the bank of the **r**.
47: 7 of trees on each side of the **r**.
47: 9 will live wherever the **r** flows.
47: 9 the **r** flows everything will live.
47:12 will grow on both banks of the **r**.
Da 7:10 A **r** of fire was flowing, coming out
10: 4 the bank of the great **r**, the Tigris,
12: 5 the **r** and one on the opposite bank.
12: 6 who was above the waters of the **r**,
12: 7 who was above the waters of the **r**,
Am 5:24 let justice roll on like a **r**,
8: 8 and then sink like the **r** of Egypt.
9: 5 then sinks like the **r** of Egypt—
Na 2: 6 The **r** gates are thrown open and the
3: 8 with water around her? The **r** was her
Zec 9:10 from the **R** to the ends of the earth.
Mt 3: 6 baptised by him in the Jordan **R**.
Mk 1: 5 baptised by him in the Jordan **R**.
Ac 16:13 went outside the city gate to the **r**,
Rev 9:14 are bound at the great **r** Euphrates."
12:15 the serpent spewed water like a **r**,
Rev 12:16 swallowing the **r** that the dragon had
16:12 his bowl on the great **r** Euphrates,
22: 1 the angel showed me the **r** of the
22: 2 On each side of the **r** stood the tree

Riverbank (Bank, River)

Ge 41: 3 Nile and stood beside those on the **r**.

Rivers (River)

2Ki 5:12 Are not Abana and Pharpar, the **r** of
Job 20:17 He will not enjoy the streams, the **r**
28:11 He searches the sources of the **r** and
Ps 74:15 you dried up the ever-flowing **r**.
78:16 and made water flow down like **r**.
78:44 He turned their **r** to blood; they
89:25 the sea, his right hand over the **r**.
98: 8 Let the **r** clap their hands, let the
107:33 He turned **r** into a desert, flowing
137: 1 By the **r** of Babylon we sat and wept
SS 8: 7 Many waters cannot quench love; **r**
Isa 18: 1 whirring wings along the **r** of Cush,
18: 2 speech, whose land is divided by **r**.
18: 7 whose land is divided by **r**—the
33:21 It will be like a place of broad **r**
41:18 I will make **r** flow on barren heights,
42:15 **r** into islands and dry up the pools.
43: 2 the **r**, they will not sweep over you.
50: 2 I turn **r** into a desert; their fish
Jer 46: 7 the Nile, like **r** of surging waters?
46: 8 Egypt rises like the Nile, like **r** of
Mic 6: 7 with ten thousand **r** of oil? Shall I
Na 1: 4 it up; he makes all the **r** run dry.
Hab 3: 8 Were you angry with the **r**, O LORD?
3: 9 Selah You split the earth with **r**;
Zep 3:10 From beyond the **r** of Cush my
2Co 11:26 I have been in danger from **r**, in
Rev 8:10 the **r** and on the springs of water—
16: 4 bowl on the **r** and springs of water,

Rizia

1Ch 7:39 The sons of Ulla: Arah, Hanniel and **R**

Rizpah

2Sa 3: 7 Now Saul had had a concubine named **R**
21: 8 the two sons of Aiah's daughter **R**,
21:10 **R** daughter of Aiah took sackcloth
21:11 David was told what Aiah's daughter **R**

Road (Crossroads, Roads, Roadside)

Ge 16: 7 spring that is beside the **r** to Shur.
24:48 who had led me on the right **r** to get
38:14 Enaim, which is on the **r** to Timnah.
38:21 who was beside the **r** at Enaim?"
48: 7 So I buried her there beside the **r**
Ex 13:17 God did not lead them on the **r**
13:18 by the desert **r** towards the Red Sea.
Nu 20:19 "We will go along the main **r**, and if
21: 1 was coming along the **r** to Atharim,
21:33 they turned and went up along the **r**
22:22 LORD stood in the **r** to oppose him.
22:23 in the **r** with a drawn sword in
22:23 she turned off the **r** into a field.
22:23 beat her to get her back on the **r**.
22:31 in the **r** with his sword drawn.
22:34 were standing in the **r** to oppose me.
Dt 1: 2 Kadesh Barnea by the Mount Seir **r**.)
2: 8 We turned from the Arabah **r**, which
2: 8 along the desert **r** of Moab.
2:27 We will stay on the main **r**; we will
3: 1 went up along the **r** towards Bashan,
6: 7 home and when you walk along the **r**,
11:19 home and when you walk along the **r**,
11:30 west of the **r**, towards the setting
22: 4 fallen on the **r**, do not ignore it.
22: 6 across a bird's nest beside the **r**,
27:18 who leads the blind astray on the **r**.
Jos 2: 7 in pursuit of the spies on the **r**
2:22 **r** and returned without finding them.
10:10 Israel pursued them along the **r**
10:11 they fled before Israel on the **r**
Jdg 5:10 you who walk along the **r**, consider
21:19 and east of the **r** that goes from
Ru 1: 7 set out on the **r** that would take
1Sa 4:13 on his chair by the side of the **r**,
1Sa 6:12 keeping on the **r** and lowing all the
17:52 the Shaaraim **r** to Gath and Ekron.
26: 3 Saul made his camp beside the **r** on
2Sa 13:34 many people on the **r** west of him,
15: 2 of the **r** leading to the city gate.
16:13 his men continued along the **r** while
20:12 in his blood in the middle of the **r**,
20:12 he dragged him from the **r** into a
20:13 Amasa had been removed from the **r**,
1Ki 13:10 he took another **r** and did not return
13:12 showed him which **r** the man of God
13:24 a lion met him on the **r** and killed
13:24 his body was thrown down on the **r**,
13:28 found the body thrown down on the **r**,
20:38 the prophet went and stood by the **r**
2Ki 2:23 As he was walking along the **r**, some
6:19 Elisha told them, "This is not the **r**
7:15 and they found the whole **r** strewn
9:27 he fled up the **r** to Beth Haggan.
12:20 Beth Millo, on the **r** down to Silla.
18:17 on the **r** to the Washerman's Field.
1Ch 26:16 upper **r** fell to Shuppim and Hosah.
26:18 the **r** and two at the court itself.
Ezr 8:22 to protect us from enemies on the **r**,
Job 30:13 They break up my **r**; they succeed in
Pr 26:13 "There is a lion in the **r**, a fierce
Ecc 10: 3 Even as he walks along the **r**, the
Isa 7: 3 on the **r** to the Washerman's Field.
15: 5 weeping as they go; on the **r** to
36: 2 on the **r** to the Washerman's Field,
51:10 who made a **r** in the depths of the
57:14 "Build up, build up, prepare the **r**!
Jer 31:21 "Set up **r** signs; put up guideposts.
31:21 Take note of the highway, the **r** that
48: 5 on the **r** down to Horonaim anguished
48:19 Stand by the **r** and watch, you who
Eze 21:19 the **r** branches off to the city.
21:20 Mark out one **r** for the sword to come
21:21 will stop at the fork in the **r**,
47:15 Hethlon **r** past Lebo Hamath to Zedad,
48: 1 it will follow the Hethlon **r** to Lebo
Hos 6: 9 they murder on the **r** to Shechem,
Na 2: 1 Guard the fortress, watch the **r**,
Mt 7:13 is the **r** that leads to destruction,
7:14 small is the gate and narrow the **r**
21: 8 crowd spread their cloaks on the **r**,
21: 8 the trees and spread them on the **r**.
21:19 Seeing a fig-tree by the **r**, he went
Mk 9:33 were you arguing about on the **r**?"
10:52 and followed Jesus along the **r**.
11: 8 people spread their cloaks on the **r**,
Lk 9:57 they were walking along the **r**, a man
10: 4 and do not greet anyone on the **r**.
10:31 to be going down the same **r**,
19:36 people spread their cloaks on the **r**.
19:37 he came near the place where the **r**
24:32 **r** and opened the Scriptures to us?"
Ac 8:26 "Go south to the **r**—the desert **r**—
8:36 they travelled along the **r**, they
9:17 who appeared to you on the **r** as you
19: 1 Paul took the **r** through the interior
26:13 About noon, O King, as I was on the **r**

Roads (Road)

Lev 26:22 number that your **r** will be deserted.
Dt 19: 3 Build **r** to them and divide into
Jdg 5: 6 in the days of Jael, the **r** were
20:31 on the **r**—the one leading to Bethel
20:32 them away from the city to the **r**."
20:45 down five thousand men along the **r**.
Isa 33: 8 no travellers are on the **r**.
49: 9 "They will feed beside the **r** and
49:11 I will turn all my mountains into **r**,
59: 8 They have turned them into crooked **r**;
Jer 6:25 out to the fields or walk on the **r**,
18:15 in bypaths and on **r** not built up.
Lam 1: 4 The **r** to Zion mourn, for no-one
Eze 21:19 "Son of man, mark out two **r** for the
21:21 at the junction of the two **r**, to
Lk 3: 5 The crooked **r** shall become straight,
14:23 'Go out to the **r** and country lanes

Roadside (Road)

Ge 38:16 he went over to her by the **r** and
49:17 Dan will be a serpent by the **r**, a

Jer 3: 2 By the **r** you sat waiting for lovers,
Mt 20:30 Two blind men were sitting by the **r**,
Mk 10:46 was sitting by the **r** begging.
Lk 18:35 man was sitting by the **r** begging.

Roam (Roamed, Roaming)
Jdg 11:37 "Give me two months to **r** the hills
Isa 8:21 Distressed and hungry, they will **r**
Jer 2:31 my people say, 'We are free to **r**;
50: 6 caused them to **r** on the mountains.

Roamed (Roam)
1Sa 30:31 where David and his men had **r**.
Job 30: 3 Haggard from want and hunger, they **r**

Roaming (Roam)
Job 1: 7 "From **r** through the earth and going
2: 2 "From **r** through the earth and going
Pr 26:13 road, a fierce lion **r** the streets!"

Roar (Roared, Roaring, Roars)
Job 4:10 The lions may **r** and growl, yet the
37: 2 Listen! Listen to the **r** of his voice,
37: 4 After that comes the sound of his **r**;
Ps 42: 7 Deep calls to deep in the **r** of your
46: 3 though its waters **r** and foam and the
104:21 The lions **r** for their prey and seek
Pr 19:12 A king's rage is like the **r** of a
20: 2 A king's wrath is like the **r** of a
Isa 5:29 Their **r** is like that of the lion,
5:29 they **r** like young lions; they growl
5:30 In that day they will **r** over it like
17:12 **r** like the roaring of great waters!
17:13 Although the peoples **r** like the **r** of
51:15 its waves **r**—the LORD Almighty is
Jer 5:22 may **r**, but they cannot cross it.
10:13 the waters in the heavens **r**; he
11:16 But with the **r** of a mighty storm he
25:30 'The LORD will **r** from on high; he
25:30 and **r** mightily against his land.
31:35 its waves **r**—the LORD Almighty is
51:16 the waters in the heavens **r**; he
51:38 Her people all **r** like young lions,
51:55 the **r** of their voices will resound.
Eze 1:24 like the **r** of rushing waters, like
19: 9 They put him in prison, so his **r** was
43: 2 His voice was like the **r** of rushing
Hos 10:14 the **r** of battle will rise against
11:10 They will follow the LORD; he will **r**
Joel 3:16 The LORD will **r** from Zion and
Am 3: 4 Does a lion **r** in the thicket when he
Zec 9:15 They will drink and **r** as with wine;
11: 3 Listen to the **r** of the lions;
2Pe 3:10 The heavens will disappear with a **r**;
Rev 10: 3 he gave a loud shout like the **r** of a
14: 2 heaven like the **r** of rushing waters
19: 1 like the **r** of a great multitude in
19: 6 like the **r** of rushing waters and

Roared (Roar)
Ps 74: 4 Your foes **r** in the place where you
Jer 2:15 Lions have **r**; they have growled at
Am 3: 8 The lion has **r**—who will not fear?
Hab 3:10 deep **r** and lifted its waves on high.

Roaring (Roar)
Jdg 14: 5 a young lion came **r** towards him.
Ps 22:13 **R** lions tearing their prey open
65: 7 who stilled the **r** of the seas, the **r**
Pr 28:15 Like a **r** lion or a charging bear is
Isa 5:30 roar over it like the **r** of the sea.
17:12 roar like the **r** of great waters!
Jer 6:23 They sound like the **r** sea as they
50:42 They sound like the **r** sea as they
51:42 The sea will rise over Babylon; its **r**
Eze 19: 7 were in it were terrified by his **r**.
22:25 her like a **r** lion tearing its prey;
Zep 3: 3 Her officials are **r** lions, her
Lk 21:25 at the **r** and tossing of the sea.
1Pe 5: 8 **r** lion looking for someone to devour.

Roars (Roar)
Jer 12: 8 She **r** at me; therefore I hate her.
Hos 11:10 When he **r**, his children will come
Am 1: 2 He said: "The LORD **r** from Zion and

Roast (Roasted, Roasts)
Ex 12: 9 but **r** it over the fire—head, legs
Dt 16: 7 **R** it and eat it at the place the
1Sa 2:15 "Give the priest some meat to **r**; he
Pr 12:27 The lazy man does not **r** his game,

Roasted (Roast)
Ex 12: 8 are to eat the meat **r** over the fire,
Lev 2:14 heads of new grain **r** in the fire.
23:14 You must not eat any bread, or **r** or
Jos 5:11 land: unleavened bread and **r** grain.
Ru 2:14 he offered her some **r** grain.
1Sa 17:17 "Take this ephah of **r** grain and
25:18 dressed sheep, five seahs of **r** grain
2Sa 17:28 and **r** grain, beans and lentils,
2Ch 35:13 They **r** the Passover animals over the
Isa 44:19 over its coals, I **r** meat and I ate.

Roasts (Roast)
Isa 44:16 he **r** his meat and eats his fill.

Rob (Robbed, Robber, Robbers, Robbery, Robbing, Robs)
Lev 19:13 "'Do not defraud your neighbour or **r**
26:22 and they will **r** you of your children,
Jdg 9:25 ambush and **r** everyone who passed by,
14:15 Did you invite us here to **r** us?"
Ps 35:10 and needy from those who **r** them."
Hos 7: 1 houses, bandits **r** in the streets;
Mal 3: 8 "Will a man **r** God? Yet you **r** me.
3: 8 "But you ask, 'How do we **r** you?' "In
Mt 12:29 strong man? Then he can **r** his house.
Mk 3:27 strong man. Then he can **r** his house.
Ro 2:22 who abhor idols, do you **r** temples?

Robbed (Rob)
Dt 28:29 and **r**, with no-one to rescue you.
2Sa 17: 8 fierce as a wild bear **r** of her cubs.
Ps 7: 4 me or without cause have **r** my foe—
Pr 4:16 they are **r** of slumber till they make
17:12 Better to meet a bear **r** of her cubs
Isa 38:10 and be **r** of the rest of my years?"
Jer 21:12 oppressor the one who has been **r**,
22: 3 oppressor the one who has been **r**.
Eze 18:18 because he practised extortion, **r**
Hos 13: 8 Like a bear **r** of her cubs, I will
Mk 9:17 a spirit that has **r** him of speech.
Ac 19:27 will be **r** of her divine majesty."
19:37 **r** temples nor blasphemed our goddess.
2Co 11: 8 I **r** other churches by receiving
1Ti 6: 5 who have been **r** of the truth and who

Robber (Rob)
Jn 10: 1 some other way, is a thief and a **r**.

Robbers (Rob)
Jer 7:11 become a den of **r** to you? But I have
Eze 7:22 **r** will enter it and desecrate it.
Ob : 5 "If thieves came to you, if **r** in the
Mt 21:13 but you are making it a 'den of **r**'.
27:38 Two **r** were crucified with him, one
27:44 In the same way the **r** who were
Mk 11:17 But you have made it 'a den of **r**'.
15:27 They crucified two **r** with him, one
Lk 10:30 when he fell into the hands of **r**.
10:36 man who fell into the hands of **r**?"
18:11 you that I am not like other men—**r**,
19:46 but you have made it 'a den of **r**'.
Jn 10: 8 came before me were thieves and **r**,

Robbery (Rob)
Isa 61: 8 love justice; I hate **r** and iniquity.
Eze 18: 7 He does not commit **r**, but gives his
18:12 He commits **r**. He does not return
18:16 He does not commit **r**, but gives his
22:29 practise extortion and commit **r**;

Robbing (Rob)
Isa 10: 2 their prey and **r** the fatherless.
Mal 3: 9 nation of you—because you are **r** me.

Robe (Robed, Robes)
Ge 37: 3 made a richly ornamented **r** for him.
37:23 they stripped him of his **r**—the
37:23 richly ornamented **r** he was wearing—
37:31 they got Joseph's **r**, slaughtered a
37:31 goat and dipped the **r** in the blood.
37:32 They took the ornamented **r** back to
37:32 to see whether it is your son's **r**."
37:33 "It is my son's **r**! Some ferocious
Ex 28: 4 an ephod, a **r**, a woven tunic, a
28:31 "Make the **r** of the ephod entirely of
28:33 the **r**, with gold bells between them.
28:34 alternate around the hem of the **r**.
29: 5 the **r** of the ephod, the ephod itself
39:22 They made the **r** of the ephod
39:23 the **r** like the opening of a collar,
39:24 linen around the hem of the **r**.
39:26 of the **r** to be worn for ministering,
Lev 8: 7 with the **r** and put the ephod on him.
Jos 7:21 I saw in the plunder a beautiful **r**
7:24 the silver, the **r**, the gold wedge,
1Sa 2:19 year his mother made him a little **r**
15:27 of the hem of his **r**, and it tore.
18: 4 Jonathan took off the **r** he was
24: 4 and cut off a corner of Saul's **r**.
24: 5 having cut off a corner of his **r**.
24:11 look at this piece of your **r** in my
24:11 of your **r** but did not kill you.
28:14 "An old man wearing a **r** is coming up,
2Sa 13:18 was wearing a richly ornamented **r**,
13:19 the ornamented **r** she was wearing.
15:32 his **r** torn and dust on his head.
1Ch 15:27 Now David was clothed in a **r** of fine
Ne 5:13 I also shook out the folds of my **r**
Est 6: 8 have them bring a royal **r** the king
6: 9 let the **r** and horse be entrusted to
6: 9 Let them **r** the man the king delights
6:10 "Get the **r** and the horse and do just
6:11 Haman got the **r** and the horse. He
8:15 gold and a purple **r** of fine linen.
Job 1:20 At this, Job got up and tore his **r**
29:14 justice was my **r** and my turban.
SS 5: 3 I have taken off my **r**—must I put
Isa 6: 1 train of his **r** filled the temple.
22:21 I will clothe him with your **r** and
61:10 arrayed me in a **r** of righteousness,
Mic 2: 8 You strip off the rich **r** from those
Zec 8:23 one Jew by the hem of his **r** and say,
Mt 27:28 They stripped him and put a scarlet **r**
27:31 took off the **r** and put his own
Mk 15:17 They put a purple **r** on him, then
15:20 took off the purple **r** and put his
16: 5 a white **r** sitting on the right side,
Lk 15:22 Bring the best **r** and put it on him.
23:11 in an elegant **r**, they sent him back
Jn 19: 2 They clothed him in a purple **r**
19: 5 crown of thorns and the purple **r**,
Heb 1:12 You will roll them up like a **r**; like
Rev 1:13 "like a son of man", dressed in a **r**
6:11 each of them was given a white **r**,
19:13 He is dressed in a **r** dipped in blood,
19:16 On his **r** and on his thigh he has

Robed (Robe)
Est 6:11 He **r** Mordecai, and led him on
Ps 93: 1 The LORD reigns, he is **r** in majesty;
93: 1 he is **r** in majesty; the LORD is **r** in
Isa 63: 1 **r** in splendour, striding forward in
Rev 10: 1 He was **r** in a cloud, with a rainbow

Robes (Robe)
Ge 41:42 He dressed him in **r** of fine linen
49:11 wine, his **r** in the blood of grapes.
1Sa 19:24 He stripped off his **r** and also
1Ki 10: 5 the attending servants in their **r**,
10:25 **r**, weapons and spices, and horses
22:10 Dressed in their royal **r**, the king
22:30 disguise, but you wear your royal **r**.
2Ki 5: 7 he tore his **r** and said, "Am I God?
5: 8 the king of Israel had torn his **r**,
5: 8 "Why have you torn your **r**? Make the

2Ki 6:30 the woman's words, he tore his **r**.
10:22 **r** for all the ministers of Baal.
10:22 So he brought out **r** for them.
11:14 Then Athaliah tore her **r** and called
22:11 the Book of the Law, he tore his **r**.
22:19 and because you tore your **r** and wept
2Ch 9: 4 the attending servants in their **r**,
9: 4 the cupbearers in their **r** and the
9:24 and **r**, weapons and spices, and
18: 9 Dressed in their royal **r**, the king
18:29 disguise, but you wear your royal **r**.
23:13 Then Athaliah tore her **r** and shouted,
34:19 the words of the Law, he tore his **r**.
34:27 tore your **r** and wept in my presence,
Est 5: 1 third day Esther put on her royal **r**
Job 2:12 tore their **r** and sprinkled dust on
Ps 45: 8 All your **r** are fragrant with myrrh
133: 2 down upon the collar of his **r**.
Isa 3:22 the fine **r** and the capes and cloaks,
Eze 26:16 lay aside their **r** and take off their
Da 3:21 these men, wearing their **r**, trousers,
3:27 singed; their **r** were not scorched,
Jnh 3: 6 took off his royal **r**, covered
Mk 12:38 like to walk around in flowing **r**
Lk 20:46 like to walk around in flowing **r**
Ac 9:39 crying and showing him the **r** and
12:21 wearing his royal **r**, sat on his
Rev 7: 9 They were wearing white **r** and were
7:13 "These in white **r**—who are they, and
7:14 they have washed their **r** and made
22:14 "Blessed are those who wash their **r**,

Robs (Rob)

Pr 19:26 He who **r** his father and drives out
28:24 He who **r** his father or mother and

Rock (*God is my rock*, *Lord is my rock*, Rocks, Rocky)

Ge 49:24 of the Shepherd, the **R** of Israel,
Ex 17: 6 there before you by the **r** at Horeb.
17: 6 Strike the **r**, and water will come
33:21 near me where you may stand on a **r**.
33:22 I will put you in a cleft in the **r**
Nu 20: 8 Speak to that **r** before their eyes
20: 8 You will bring water out of the **r**
20:10 of the **r** and Moses said to them,
20:10 we bring you water out of this **r**?"
20:11 Moses raised his arm and struck the **r**
24:21 is secure, your nest is set in a **r**;
Dt 8:15 He brought you water out of hard **r**.
32: 4 He is the **R**, his works are perfect,
32:13 nourished him with honey from the **r**,
32:15 him and rejected the **R** his Saviour.
32:18 You deserted the **R**, who fathered you;
32:30 unless their **R** had sold them, unless
32:31 For their **r** is not like our **R**, as
32:37 gods, the **r** they took refuge in,
Jdg 6:20 on this **r**, and pour out the broth.
6:21 Fire flared from the **r**, consuming
7:25 They killed Oreb at the **r** of Oreb,
13:19 sacrificed it on a **r** to the Lord.
15: 8 stayed in a cave in the **r** of Etam.
15:11 in the **r** of Etam and said to Samson,
15:13 new ropes and led him up from the **r**.
20:45 the desert to the **r** of Rimmon,
20:47 into the desert to the **r** of Rimmon,
21:13 the Benjamites at the **r** of Rimmon.
1Sa 2: 2 you; there is no **R** like our God.
6:14 there it stopped beside a large **r**.
6:15 and placed them on the large **r**.
6:18 The large **r**, on which they set the
23:25 went down to the **r** and stayed in
2Sa 20: 8 While they were at the great **r** in
21:10 spread it out for herself on a **r**.
22:32 And who is the **R** except our God?
22:47 "The Lord lives! Praise be to my **R**!
22:47 to my **R**! Exalted be God, the **R**,
23: 3 The God of Israel spoke, the **R** of
1Ch 11:15 to the **r** at the cave of Adullam,
Ne 9:15 you brought them water from the **r**;
Job 14:18 and as a **r** is moved from its place,
19:24 on lead, or engraved in **r** for ever!
28: 9 Man's hand assaults the flinty **r** and
28:10 He tunnels through the **r**; his eyes
29: 6 the **r** poured out for me streams of
Job 41:24 His chest is hard as **r**, hard as a
Ps 18:31 And who is the **R** except our God?
18:46 The Lord lives! Praise be to my **R**!
19:14 O Lord, my **R** and my Redeemer.
27: 5 tabernacle and set me high upon a **r**.
28: 1 To you I call, O Lord my **R**; do not
31: 2 come quickly to my rescue; be my **r**
31: 3 Since you are my **r** and my fortress,
40: 2 he set my feet on a **r** and gave me
42: 9 I say to God my **R**, "Why have you
61: 2 me to the **r** that is higher than I.
62: 2 He alone is my **r** and my salvation;
62: 6 He alone is my **r** and my salvation;
62: 7 God; he is my mighty **r**, my refuge.
71: 3 Be my **r** of refuge, to which I can
71: 3 for you are my **r** and my fortress.
78:20 he struck the **r**, water gushed out,
78:35 They remembered that God was their **R**,
81:16 from the **r** I would satisfy you."
89:26 Father, my God, the **R** my Saviour.'
92:15 **R**, and there is no wickedness in him.
94:22 my God the **r** in whom I take refuge.
95: 1 aloud to the **R** of our salvation.
105:41 He opened the **r**, and water gushed
114: 8 who turned the **r** into a pool, the
114: 8 the hard **r** into springs of water.
144: 1 Praise be to the Lord my **R**, who
Pr 30:19 the way of a snake on a **r**, the way
SS 2:14 My dove in the clefts of the **r**, in
Isa 8:14 and a **r** that makes them fall.
10:26 struck down Midian at the **r** of Oreb;
17:10 not remembered the **R**, your fortress.
22:16 your resting place in the **r**?
26: 4 Lord, the Lord, is the **R** eternal.
30:29 of the Lord, to the **R** of Israel.
32: 2 of a great **r** in a thirsty land.
44: 8 is no other **R**; I know not one."
48:21 made water flow for them from the **r**;
48:21 he split the **r** and water gushed out.
51: 1 Look to the **r** from which you were
Jer 23:29 a hammer that breaks a **r** in pieces?
51:26 No **r** will be taken from you for a
Eze 24: 7 She poured it on the bare **r**; she
24: 8 I put her blood on the bare **r**, so
26: 4 her rubble and make her a bare **r**.
26:14 I will make you a bare **r**, and you
Da 2:34 While you were watching, a **r** was cut
2:35 But the **r** that struck the statue
2:45 of the **r** cut out of a mountain,
2:45 but not by human hands—a **r** that
Hab 1:12 **R**, you have ordained them to punish.
Zec 12: 3 an immovable **r** for all the nations.
Mt 7:24 man who built his house on the **r**.
7:25 it had its foundation on the **r**.
16:18 and on this **r** I will build my church,
27:60 tomb that he had cut out of the **r**.
Mk 15:46 placed it in a tomb cut out of **r**.
Lk 6:48 deep and laid the foundation on **r**.
8: 6 Some fell on **r**, and when it came up,
8:13 Those on the **r** are the ones who
23:53 placed it in a tomb cut in the **r**,
Ro 9:33 and a **r** that makes them fall,
1Co 10: 4 spiritual **r** that accompanied them,
10: 4 them, and that **r** was Christ.
1Pe 2: 8 to stumble a **r** that makes them fall.

Rocks (Rock)

Dt 8: 9 a land where the **r** are iron and you
Jos 7:26 of **r**, which remains to this day.
8:29 **r** over it, which remains to this day.
10:18 he said, "Roll large **r** up to the
10:27 **r**, which are there to this day.
1Sa 13: 6 the **r**, and in pits and cisterns.
2Sa 18:17 piled up a large heap of **r** over him.
1Ki 19:11 and shattered the **r** before the Lord,
Job 8:17 entwines its roots around a pile of **r**
18: 4 the **r** be moved from their place?
22:24 of Ophir to the **r** in the ravines,
24: 8 and hug the **r** for lack of shelter.
28: 6 sapphires come from its **r**, and its
30: 6 the **r** and in holes in the ground.
Ps 78:15 He split the **r** in the desert and
137: 9 and dashes them against the **r**.
Isa 2:10 Go into the **r**, hide in the ground
2:19 Men will flee to caves in the **r** and
Isa 2:21 They will flee to caverns in the **r**
7:19 and in the crevices in the **r**,
Jer 4:29 thickets; some climb up among the **r**.
13: 4 it there in a crevice in the **r**."
16:16 hill and from the crevices of the **r**.
48:28 among the **r**, you who live in Moab.
49:16 you who live in the clefts of the **r**,
Ob : 3 you who live in the clefts of the **r**
Na 1: 6 the **r** are shattered before him.
Mt 27:51 The earth shook and the **r** split.
Ac 27:29 we would be dashed against the **r**,
Rev 6:15 and among the **r** of the mountains.
6:16 called to the mountains and the **r**,

Rocky (Rock)

Nu 23: 9 From the **r** peaks I see them, from
Job 39:28 night; a **r** crag is his stronghold.
Ps 78:16 he brought streams out of a **r** crag
Jer 18:14 ever vanish from its **r** slopes?
21:13 above this valley on the **r** plateau,
Am 6:12 Do horses run on the **r** crags? Does
Mt 13: 5 Some fell on **r** places, where it did
13:20 the seed that fell on **r** places is
Mk 4: 5 Some fell on **r** places, where it did
4:16 Others, like seed sown on **r** places,

Rod (Rods)

Ex 21:20 his male or female slave with a **r**
Lev 27:32 under the shepherd's **r**—will be
1Sa 17: 7 His spear shaft was like a weaver's **r**
2Sa 7:14 I will punish him with the **r** of men,
21:19 with a shaft like a weaver's **r**.
1Ch 11:23 spear like a weaver's **r** in his hand,
20: 5 with a shaft like a weaver's **r**.
Job 9:34 someone to remove God's **r** from me,
21: 9 fear; the **r** of God is not upon them.
Ps 23: 4 **r** and your staff, they comfort me.
89:32 I will punish their sin with the **r**,
Pr 10:13 but a **r** is for the back of him who
13:24 He who spares the **r** hates his son,
14: 3 A fool's talk brings a **r** to his back,
22: 8 the **r** of his fury will be destroyed.
22:15 but the **r** of discipline will drive
23:13 him with the **r**, he will not die.
23:14 Punish him with the **r** and save his
26: 3 and a **r** for the backs of fools!
29:15 The **r** of correction imparts wisdom,
Isa 9: 4 shoulders, the **r** of their oppressor.
10: 5 "Woe to the Assyrian, the **r** of my
10:15 As if a **r** were to wield him who
10:24 who beat you with a **r** and lift up a
11: 4 He will strike the earth with the **r**
14: 5 The Lord has broken the **r** of the
14:29 all you Philistines, that the **r** that
28:27 with a **r**, and cummin with a stick.
30:32 lays on them with his punishing **r**
Lam 3: 1 affliction by the **r** of his wrath.
Eze 7:10 the **r** has budded, arrogance has
7:11 Violence has grown into a **r** to
20:37 note of you as you pass under my **r**,
40: 3 cord and a measuring **r** in his hand.
40: 5 The length of the measuring **r** in the
40: 5 measuring **r** thick and one **r** high.
40: 6 of the gate; it was one **r** deep.
40: 7 The alcoves for the guards were one **r**
40: 7 were one **r** long and one **r** wide,
41: 8 length of the **r**, six long cubits.
42:16 the east side with the measuring **r**;
42:17 hundred cubits by the measuring **r**.
42:18 hundred cubits by the measuring **r**.
42:19 hundred cubits by the measuring **r**.
Mic 5: 1 Israel's ruler on the cheek with a **r**.
6: 9 the **r** and the One who appointed it.
Rev 11: 1 I was given a reed like a measuring **r**
21:15 **r** of gold to measure the city,
21:16 He measured the city with the **r** and

Rodanim

Ge 10: 4 Tarshish, the Kittim and the **R**.
1Ch 1: 7 Tarshish, the Kittim and the **R**.

Rode (Ride)

Jdg 10: 4 He had thirty sons, who **r** thirty
12:14 grandsons, who **r** on seventy donkeys.

1Sa 30:17 men who **r** off on camels and fled.
1Ki 13:14 **r** after the man of God. He found him
18:45 came on and Ahab **r** off to Jezreel.
2Ki 9:16 he got into his chariot and **r** to
9:18 The horseman **r** off to meet Jehu and
9:21 and Ahaziah king of Judah **r** out,
Est 8:10 who **r** fast horses especially bred
Hab 3: 8 the sea when you **r** with your horses
Rev 6: 2 and he was given a crown, and he **r**

Rodents
Isa 2:20 day men will throw away to the **r**

Rods (Rod)
Job 40:18 of bronze, his limbs like **r** of iron.
SS 5:14 His arms are **r** of gold set with
2Co 11:25 Three times I was beaten with **r**,

Roe (Roebucks)
Dt 14: 5 the deer, the gazelle, the **r** deer,

Roebucks (Roe)
1Ki 4:23 deer, gazelles, **r** and choice fowl.

Rogelim
2Sa 17:27 and Barzillai the Gileadite from **R**
19:31 down from **R** to cross the Jordan

Rohgah
1Ch 7:34 The sons of Shomer: Ahi, **R**, Hubbah

Roll (Rolled, Rolling, Rolls)
Ge 29: 3 the shepherds would **r** the stone away
Jos 10:18 he said, "**R** large rocks up to the
1Sa 14:33 "**R** a large stone over here at once."
Pr 26:27 a stone, it will **r** back on him.
Isa 22:18 He will **r** you up tightly like a ball
Jer 5:22 The waves may **r**, but they cannot
6:26 O my people, put on sackcloth and **r**
25:34 wail, you shepherds; **r** in the dust
51:25 **r** you off the cliffs, and make you a
Eze 27:30 dust on their heads and **r** in ashes.
Am 5:24 let justice **r** on like a river,
Mic 1:10 In Beth Ophrah **r** in the dust.
Mk 16: 3 they asked each other, "Who will **r**
Heb 1:12 You will **r** them up like a robe; like

Rolled (Roll)
Ge 29: 8 **r** away from the mouth of the well.
29:10 he went over and **r** the stone away
Jos 5: 9 "Today I have **r** away the reproach of
2Ki 2: 8 Elijah took his cloak, **r** it up and
Isa 9: 5 every garment **r** in blood will be
28:27 nor is a cartwheel **r** over cummin;
34: 4 and the sky **r** up like a scroll;
38:12 Like a weaver I have **r** up my life,
Mt 27:60 He **r** a big stone in front of the
28: 2 **r** back the stone and sat on it.
Mk 9:20 and **r** around, foaming at the mouth.
15:46 Then he **r** a stone against the
16: 4 was very large, had been **r** away.
Lk 4:20 he **r** up the scroll, gave it back to
24: 2 They found the stone **r** away from the

Rolling (Roll)
Job 30:14 amid the ruins they come **r** in.
Rev 6:14 The sky receded like a scroll, **r** up,

Rolls (Roll)
Pr 26:27 **r** a stone, it will roll back on him.
Isa 9:18 it **r** upward in a column of smoke.

Romamti-Ezer
1Ch 25: 4 Hanani, Eliathah, Giddalti and **R**;
25:31 the twenty-fourth to **R**, his sons and

Roman (Rome)
Lk 2: 1 be taken of the entire **R** world.
Jn 18:28 to the palace of the **R** governor.
Ac 11:28 spread over the entire **R** world.
16:12 a **R** colony and the leading city of
16:37 **R** citizens, and threw us into prison.
Ac 16:38 were **R** citizens, they were alarmed.
21:31 news reached the commander of the **R**
22:25 "Is it legal for you to flog a **R**
22:26 "This man is a **R** citizen."
22:27 **R** citizen?" "Yes, I am," he answered.
22:29 put Paul, a **R** citizen, in chains.
23:27 I had learned that he is a **R** citizen.
25:16 it is not the **R** custom to hand over

Romans (Rome)
Jn 11:48 and then the **R** will come and take
Ac 16:21 for us **R** to accept or practise."
28:17 Jerusalem and handed over to the **R**.

Rome (Roman, Romans)
Capital city of Roman Empire, about 15 miles from Mediterranean coast of Italy. Its inhabitants were at Pentecost (Ac 2:10). Aquila and Priscilla were ordered out of here by Claudius (Ac 18:2). Paul possessed Roman citizenship (Ac 16:37; 22:28) and resolved to preach here (Ac 19:21; 23:11; Ro 1:15; 15:24). After appealing to Caesar for justice (Ac 25:11) he was brought here as a prisoner (Ac 25:24–25; 28:16). The fall of Rome is anticipated in Revelation (Rev 17–18).

Ac 2:10 Libya near Cyrene; visitors from **R**
18: 2 had ordered all the Jews to leave **R**.
19:21 he said, "I must visit **R** also.
23:11 so you must also testify in **R**."
25:25 Emperor I decided to send him to **R**.
28:14 And so we came to **R**.
28:16 we got to **R**, Paul was allowed to
Ro 1: 7 To all in **R** who are loved by God and
1:15 the gospel also to you who are at **R**.
2Ti 1:17 On the contrary, when he was in **R**,

Roof (Roofed, Roofing, Roofs)
Ge 6:16 Make a **r** for it and finish the ark
19: 8 come under the protection of my **r**."
Dt 22: 8 make a parapet around your **r** so that
22: 8 house if someone falls from the **r**.
Jos 2: 6 (But she had taken them up to the **r**
2: 6 of flax she had laid out on the **r**.)
2: 8 for the night, she went up on the **r**
Jdg 9:51 in and climbed up on the tower **r**.
16:27 and on the **r** were about three
1Sa 9:25 with Saul on the **r** of his house.
9:26 and Samuel called to Saul on the **r**,
2Sa 11: 2 around on the **r** of the palace.
11: 2 From the **r** he saw a woman bathing.
16:22 pitched a tent for Absalom on the **r**,
18:24 to the **r** of the gateway by the wall.
1Ki 7: 6 were pillars and an overhanging **r**.
2Ki 4:10 Let's make a small room on the **r** and
19:26 like grass sprouting on the **r**,
23:12 the **r** near the upper room of Ahaz,
Job 29:10 stuck to the **r** of their mouths.
Ps 22:15 and my tongue sticks to the **r** of my
102: 7 become like a bird alone on a **r**.
129: 6 May they be like grass on the **r**,
137: 6 May my tongue cling to the **r** of my
Pr 21: 9 Better to live on a corner of the **r**
25:24 Better to live on a corner of the **r**
Isa 37:27 like grass sprouting on the **r**,
Lam 4: 4 tongue sticks to the **r** of its mouth;
Eze 3:26 tongue stick to the **r** of your mouth
Da 4:29 **r** of the royal palace of Babylon,
Mt 8: 8 deserve to have you come under my **r**.
24:17 Let no-one on the **r** of his house go
Mk 2: 4 they made an opening in the **r** above
13:15 Let no-one on the **r** of his house go
Lk 5:19 they went up on the **r** and lowered
7: 6 deserve to have you come under my **r**.
17:31 On that day no-one who is on the **r**
Ac 10: 9 Peter went up on the **r** to pray.

Roofed (Roof)
1Ki 7: 3 was **r** with cedar above the beams

Roofing (Roof)
1Ki 6: 9 **r** it with beams and cedar planks.
Ne 3:15 He rebuilt it, **r** it over and putting

Roofs (Roof)
Ne 8:16 themselves booths on their own **r**,
Isa 15: 3 on the **r** and in the public squares
22: 1 that you have all gone up on the **r**,
Jer 19:13 on the **r** to all the starry hosts
32:29 by burning incense on the **r** to Baal
48:38 On all the **r** in Moab and in the
Zep 1: 5 those who bow down on the **r** to
Mt 10:27 in your ear, proclaim from the **r**.
Lk 12: 3 rooms will be proclaimed from the **r**.

Room (Bedroom, Bedrooms, Rooms, Storeroom, Storerooms)
Ge 24:23 is there **r** in your father's house
24:25 as **r** for you to spend the night."
26:22 has given us **r** and we will flourish
34:21 the land has plenty of **r** for them.
43:30 into his private **r** and wept there.
Lev 26:10 move it out to make **r** for the new.
Nu 22:26 place where there was no **r** to turn,
Jdg 3:20 **r** of his summer palace and said,
3:23 upper **r** behind him and locked them.
3:24 the doors of the upper **r** locked.
3:24 in the inner **r** of the house."
3:25 did not open the doors of the **r**,
15: 1 He said, "I'm going to my wife's **r**."
16: 9 With men hidden in the **r**, she called
16:12 Then, with men hidden in the **r**, she
2Sa 18:33 He went up to the **r** over the gateway
1Ki 1:15 went to see the aged king in his **r**,
6:17 The main hall in front of this **r** was
6:27 the innermost **r** of the temple,
6:27 each other in the middle of the **r**.
7:50 for the doors of the innermost **r**,
17:19 carried him to the upper **r** where he
17:23 him down from the **r** into the house.
20:30 to the city and hid in an inner **r**.
22:25 day you go to hide in an inner **r**."
2Ki 1: 2 **r** in Samaria and injured himself.
4:10 Let's make a small **r** on the roof and
4:11 went up to his **r** and lay down there.
4:35 walked back and forth in the **r** and
9: 2 and take him into an inner **r**.
23:11 They were in the court near the **r** of
23:12 the roof near the upper **r** of Ahaz,
2Ch 18:24 day you go to hide in an inner **r**."
Ezr 10: 6 the **r** of Jehohanan son of Eliashib.
Ne 2:14 **r** for my mount to get through;
3:31 as far as the **r** above the corner;
3:32 between the **r** above the corner and
13: 5 he had provided him with a large **r**
13: 7 **r** in the courts of the house of God.
13: 8 household goods out of the **r**.
Ps 10: 4 his thoughts there is no **r** for God.
SS 3: 4 the **r** of the one who conceived me.
Jer 7:32 in Topheth until there is no more **r**.
19:11 in Topheth until there is no more **r**.
35: 4 into the **r** of the sons of Hanan son
35: 4 It was next to the **r** of the
36:10 From the **r** of Gemariah son of
36:12 he went down to the secretary's **r** in
36:20 After they put the scroll in the **r**
36:21 and Jehudi brought it from the **r** of
38:11 **r** under the treasury in the palace.
Eze 40:38 A **r** with a doorway was by the
40:45 He said to me, "The **r** facing south
40:46 the **r** facing north is for the
41: 5 and each side **r** round the temple was
Da 6:10 he went home to his upstairs **r** where
Joel 2:16 his **r** and the bride her chamber.
Zec 10:10 there will not be **r** enough for them.
Mal 3:10 you will not have **r** enough for it.
Mt 6: 6 when you pray, go into your **r**, close
Mk 2: 2 many gathered that there was no **r**
14:14 Teacher asks: Where is my guest **r**,
14:15 He will show you a large upper **r**,
Lk 2: 7 there was no **r** for them in the inn.
14:22 been done, but there is still **r**.'
22:11 Teacher asks: Where is the guest **r**,
22:12 He will show you a large upper **r**,
Jn 8:37 because you have no **r** for my word.
21:25 would not have **r** for the books that
Ac 1:13 to the **r** where they were staying.
9:37 washed and placed in an upstairs **r**.
9:39 he was taken upstairs to the **r**.

Ac 9:40 Peter sent them all out of the **r**;
20: 8 upstairs **r** where we were meeting.
25:23 entered the audience **r** with the high
26:31 They left the **r**, and while talking
Ro 12:19 my friends, but leave **r** for God's
2Co 7: 2 Make **r** for us in your hearts. We
Phm :22 one thing more: Prepare a guest **r**
Heb 9: 2 In its first **r** were the lampstand,
9: 3 Behind the second curtain was a **r**
9: 6 outer **r** to carry on their ministry.
9: 7 the high priest entered the inner **r**,

Rooms (Room)
Ge 6:14 make **r** in it and coat it with pitch
1Ki 6: 5 in which there were side **r**.
6:10 he built the side **r** all along the
6:29 in both the inner and outer **r**, he
6:30 and outer **r** of the temple with gold.
1Ch 9:26 **r** and treasuries in the house of God.
9:33 stayed in the **r** of the temple and
23:28 the side **r**, the purification of all
28:11 inner **r** and the place of atonement.
28:12 the LORD and all the surrounding **r**,
Ne 13: 9 I gave orders to purify the **r**, and
Pr 24: 4 through knowledge its **r** are filled
Isa 26:20 Go, my people, enter your **r** and shut
Jer 22:13 his upper **r** by injustice, making his
22:14 great palace with spacious upper **r**.
35: 2 the side **r** of the house of the LORD
Eze 40:17 There I saw some **r** and a pavement
40:17 were thirty **r** along the pavement.
40:44 within the inner court, were two **r**,
41: 6 The side **r** were on three levels, one
41: 6 to serve as supports for the side **r**,
41: 7 The side **r** all round the temple were
41: 7 the **r** widened as one went upward.
41: 8 the foundation of the side **r**.
41: 9 The outer wall of the side **r** was
41: 9 between the side **r** of the temple
41:10 the ⌊priests'⌋ **r** was twenty cubits
41:11 There were entrances to the side **r**
41:26 **r** of the temple also had overhangs.
42: 1 brought me to the **r** opposite the
42: 4 In front of the **r** was an inner
42: 5 Now the upper **r** were narrower, for
42: 5 them than from the **r** on the lower
42: 6 The **r** on the third floor had no
42: 7 to the **r** and the outer court;
42: 7 in front of the **r** for fifty cubits.
42: 8 While the row of **r** on the side next
42: 9 The lower **r** had an entrance on the
42:10 and opposite the outer wall, were **r**
42:11 These were like the **r** on the north;
42:12 were the doorways of the **r** on the
42:12 eastward, by which one enters the **r**.
42:13 he said to me, "The north and south **r**
42:13 temple courtyard are the priests' **r**,
44:19 in and leave them in the sacred **r**,
46:19 gate to the sacred **r** facing north,
Mt 24:26 in the inner **r**,' do not believe it.
Lk 12: 3 in the inner **r** will be proclaimed
Jn 14: 2 In my Father's house are many **r**; if

Roost
Zep 2:14 screech owl will **r** on her columns.

Root (Rooted, Roots)
Dt 29:18 make sure there is no **r** among you
2Ki 19:30 take **r** below and bear fruit above.
Job 5: 3 I myself have seen a fool taking **r**,
19:28 the **r** of the trouble lies in him,'
30: 4 food was the **r** of the broom tree.
Ps 80: 9 and it took **r** and filled the land.
80:15 the **r** your right hand has planted,
Pr 12:12 the **r** of the righteous flourishes.
Isa 11:10 In that day the **R** of Jesse will
14:29 from the **r** of that snake will spring
14:30 But your **r** I will destroy by famine;
27: 6 In days to come Jacob will take **r**,
37:31 take **r** below and bear fruit above.
40:24 no sooner do they take **r** in the
53: 2 and like a **r** out of dry ground.
Jer 12: 2 taken **r**; they grow and bear fruit.
Hos 9:16 Ephraim is blighted, their **r** is
Mal 4: 1 **r** or a branch will be left to them.
Mt 3:10 The axe is already at the **r** of the
13: 6 they withered because they had no **r**.
13:21 since he has no **r**, he lasts only a
13:29 you may **r** up the wheat with them.
Mk 4: 6 they withered because they had no **r**.
4:17 since they have no **r**, they last only
Lk 3: 9 The axe is already at the **r** of the
8:13 they hear it, but they have no **r**.
Ro 11:16 the **r** is holy, so are the branches.
11:17 the nourishing sap from the olive **r**,
11:18 the **r**, but the **r** supports you.
15:12 again, Isaiah says, "The **R** of Jesse
1Ti 6:10 For the love of money is a **r** of all
Heb 12:15 that no bitter **r** grows up to cause
Rev 5: 5 Judah, the **R** of David, has triumphed.
22:16 I am the **R** and the Offspring of

Rooted (Root)
Eph 3:17 being **r** and established in love,
Col 2: 7 **r** and built up in him, strengthened

Roots (Root)
Jdg 5:14 Some came from Ephraim, whose **r** were
Job 8:17 entwines its **r** around a pile of
14: 8 Its **r** may grow old in the ground and
18:16 His **r** dry up below and his branches
28: 9 lays bare the **r** of the mountains.
29:19 My **r** will reach to the water, and
Isa 5:24 so their **r** will decay and their
11: 1 from his **r** a Branch will bear fruit.
Jer 17: 8 that sends out its **r** by the stream.
Eze 17: 6 him, but its **r** remained under it.
17: 7 The vine now sent out its **r** towards
17: 9 many people to pull it up by the **r**.
31: 7 its **r** went down to abundant waters.
Da 4:15 let the stump and its **r**, bound with
4:23 while its **r** remain in the ground.
4:26 the stump of the tree with its **r**
Hos 14: 5 of Lebanon he will send down his **r**;
Am 2: 9 his fruit above and his **r** below.
Jnh 2: 6 To the **r** of the mountains I sank
Mt 15:13 planted will be pulled up by the **r**.
Mk 11:20 the fig-tree withered from the **r**.

Rope (Ropes)
Ex 28:14 like a **r**, and attach the chains to
28:22 chains of pure gold, like a **r**.
39:15 chains of pure gold, like a **r**.
Jos 2:15 she let them down by a **r** through the
Job 41: 1 or tie down his tongue with a **r**?
Isa 3:24 instead of a sash, a **r**; instead of

Ropes (Rope)
Ex 35:18 and for the courtyard, and their **r**;
39:40 the **r** and tent pegs for the
Nu 3:26 and the **r**—and everything related to
3:37 with their bases, tent pegs and **r**.
4:26 the curtain for the entrance, the **r**
4:32 tent pegs, **r**, all their equipment
Jdg 15:13 new **r** and led him up from the rock.
15:14 The **r** on his arms became like
16:11 new **r** that have never been used,
16:12 Delilah took new **r** and tied him with
16:12 But he snapped the **r** off his arms
2Sa 17:13 then all Israel will bring **r** to that
1Ki 20:31 our waists and **r** round our heads.
20:32 waists and **r** round their heads,
Job 39: 5 donkey go free? Who untied his **r**?
Ps 119:61 Though the wicked bind me with **r**, I
Isa 5:18 and wickedness as with cart **r**,
33:20 pulled up, nor any of its **r** broken.
Jer 10:20 My tent is destroyed; all its **r** are
38: 6 They lowered Jeremiah by **r** into the
38:11 with **r** to Jeremiah in the cistern.
38:12 under your arms to pad the **r**.
38:13 they pulled him up with the **r** and
Eze 3:25 you, son of man, they will tie with **r**
4: 8 I will tie you up with **r** so that you
Ac 27:17 they passed **r** under the ship itself
27:32 the soldiers cut the **r** that held the
27:40 untied the **r** that held the rudders.

Rose[1] (Rise)
Ge 7:18 The waters **r** and increased greatly
7:19 They **r** greatly on the earth, and all
7:20 The waters **r** and covered the
23: 3 Abraham **r** from beside his dead wife
23: 7 Abraham **r** and bowed down before the
32:31 The sun **r** above him as he passed
37: 7 my sheaf **r** and stood upright,
Ex 32: 6 the next day the people **r** early and
33: 8 all the people **r** and stood at the
Nu 16: 2 **r** up against Moses. With them were
Jos 8:19 the men in the ambush **r** quickly from
Jdg 3:20 As the king **r** from his seat,
6:38 that is what happened. Gideon **r**
9:43 of the city, he **r** to attack them.
10: 1 the son of Dodo, **r** to save Israel.
19: 8 when he **r** to go, the girl's father
20: 8 All the people **r** as one man, saying,
1Sa 5: 3 the people of Ashdod **r** early the
5: 4 the following morning when they **r**,
9:26 They **r** about daybreak and Samuel
2Sa 18:31 from all who **r** up against you."
22: 9 Smoke **r** from his nostrils; consuming
1Ki 1:49 At this, all Adonijah's guests **r** in
8:54 he **r** from before the altar of the
18:45 the wind **r**, a heavy rain came on and
2Ki 3:24 **r** up and fought them until they fled.
8:21 but he **r** up and broke through by
1Ch 21: 1 Satan **r** up against Israel and
28: 2 King David **r** to his feet and said:
2Ch 20:23 The men of Ammon and Moab **r** up
21: 9 he **r** up and broke through by night.
Ezr 9: 5 Then, at the evening sacrifice, I **r**
10: 5 Ezra **r** up and put the leading
Est 5: 9 **r** nor showed fear in his presence,
Job 29: 8 and the old men **r** to their feet;
Ps 18: 8 Smoke **r** from his nostrils; consuming
76: 9 you, O God, **r** up to judge, to save
78:21 and his wrath **r** against Israel,
78:31 God's anger **r** against them; he put
Eze 1:19 **r** from the ground, the wheels also **r**.
1:21 the creatures **r** from the ground,
1:21 the wheels **r** along with them,
10: 4 the glory of the LORD **r** from above
10:15 the cherubim **r** upwards. These were
10:17 still; and when the cherubim **r**,
10:17 they **r** with them, because the spirit
10:19 their wings and **r** from the ground,
16:13 very beautiful and **r** to be a queen.
Jnh 2: 7 my prayer **r** to you, to your holy
3: 6 he **r** from his throne, took off his
4: 8 the sun **r**, God provided a scorching
Mt 7:25 The rain came down, the streams **r**,
7:27 The rain came down, the streams **r**,
Mk 16: 9 Jesus **r** early on the first day of
Lk 22:45 he **r** from prayer and went back to
23: 1 the whole assembly **r** and led him off
Ac 10:41 with him after he **r** from the dead.
26:30 The king **r**, and with him the
1Th 4:14 We believe that Jesus died and **r**
Rev 9: 2 he opened the Abyss, smoke **r** from it

Rose[2]
SS 2: 1 I am a **r** of Sharon, a lily of the

Rosh
Ge 46:21 Ehi, **R**, Muppim, Huppim and Ard.

Rot (Rots, Rotted, Rotten)
Pr 10: 7 but the name of the wicked will **r**.
Isa 40:20 selects wood that will not **r**.
50: 2 their fish **r** for lack of water and
Hos 5:12 I am like a moth to Ephraim, like **r**
Zec 14:12 Their flesh will **r** while they are
14:12 their eyes will **r** in their sockets,
14:12 tongues will **r** in their mouths.

Rots (Rot)
Pr 14:30 to the body, but envy **r** the bones.

Rotted (Rot)
Jas 5: 2 Your wealth has **r**, and moths have

Rotten (Rot)
Job 13:28 "So man wastes away like something **r**,
41:27 like straw and bronze like **r** wood.

Rough (Rougher, Roughs)
Isa 40: 4 the **r** ground shall become level,
42:16 them and make the **r** places smooth.
Lk 3: 5 become straight, the **r** ways smooth.
Jn 6:18 was blowing and the waters grew **r**.

Rougher (Rough)
Jnh 1:11 The sea was getting **r** and **r**. So they

Roughs (Rough)
Isa 44:13 he **r** it out with chisels and marks

Rounded
1Ki 10:19 six steps, and its back had a **r** top.
SS 7: 2 Your navel is a **r** goblet that never
Ac 17: 5 the Jews were jealous; so they **r** up

Rounds
SS 3: 3 me as they made their **r** in the city.
5: 7 me as they made their **r** in the city.

Rouse (Arouse, Aroused, Arouses, Roused, Rouses)
Ge 49: 9 like a lioness—who dares to **r** him?
Nu 23:24 they **r** themselves like a lion that
24: 9 like a lioness—who dares to **r** them?
Job 3: 8 those who are ready to **r** Leviathan.
8: 6 even now he will **r** himself on your
41:10 No-one is fierce enough to **r** him.
Ps 44:23 Lord! Why do you sleep? **R** yourself!
59: 5 the God of Israel, **r** yourself to
Isa 28:21 he will **r** himself as in the Valley
Joel 3: 7 "See, I am going to **r** them out of
3: 9 Prepare for war! **R** the warriors! Let
Zec 9:13 I will **r** your sons, O Zion, against

Roused (Rouse)
Job 14:12 not awake or be **r** from their sleep.
SS 8: 5 lover? Under the apple tree I **r** you;
Eze 7: 6 come! It has **r** itself against you.
Joel 3:12 "Let the nations be **r**; let them
Zec 2:13 **r** himself from his holy dwelling."

Rouses (Rouse)
Isa 14: 9 it **r** the spirits of the departed to

Rout (Routed, Routing, Routs)
Jdg 1: 5 to **r** the Canaanites and Perizzites.
Ps 92:11 have heard the **r** of my wicked foes.
144: 6 shoot your arrows and **r** them.

Route (Routes)
Nu 14:25 desert along the **r** to the Red Sea."
21: 4 **r** to the Red Sea, to go round Edom.
Dt 1:22 bring back a report about the **r** we
1:40 desert along the **r** to the Red Sea."
2: 1 desert along the **r** to the Red Sea,
Jdg 8:11 Gideon went up by the **r** of the
2Ki 3: 8 "By what **r** shall we attack?" he
Mt 2:12 to their country by another **r**.

Routed (Rout)
Ge 14:15 men to attack them and he **r** them,
Jos 7: 4 but they were **r** by the men of Ai,
7: 8 Israel has been **r** by its enemies?
Jdg 4:15 Barak's advance, the LORD **r** Sisera
1Sa 7:10 they were **r** before the Israelites.
2Sa 10:15 been **r** by Israel, they regrouped.
22:15 bolts of lightning and **r** them.
2Ki 14:12 Judah was **r** by Israel, and every man
1Ch 19:16 saw that they had been **r** by Israel,
2Ch 13:15 God **r** Jeroboam and all Israel before
25:22 Judah was **r** by Israel, and every man
Ps 18:14 great bolts of lightning and **r** them.
Heb 11:34 in battle and **r** foreign armies.

Routes (Route)
Job 6:18 Caravans turn aside from their **r**;

Routing (Rout)
Jdg 8:12 captured them, **r** their entire army.

Routs (Rout)
Jos 23:10 One of you **r** a thousand, because the

Roving
Ecc 6: 9 Better what the eye sees than the **r**

Row[1] (Rows)
Ex 28:17 In the first **r** there shall be a ruby,
28:18 in the second **r** a turquoise, a
28:19 in the third **r** a jacinth, an agate
28:20 in the fourth **r** a chrysolite, an
39:10 In the first **r** there was a ruby, a
39:11 in the second **r** a turquoise, a
39:12 in the third **r** a jacinth, an agate
39:13 in the fourth **r** a chrysolite, an
39:37 the pure gold lampstand with its **r**
Lev 24: 6 Set them in two rows, six in each **r**,
24: 7 Along each **r** put some pure incense
1Ki 7: 3 beams, fifteen to a **r**.
Eze 42: 8 While the **r** of rooms on the side
42: 8 the **r** on the side nearest the

Row[2] (Rowed)
Jnh 1:13 Instead, the men did their best to **r**

Rowed (Row[2])
Jn 6:19 they had **r** three or three and a half

Rows (Row[1])
Ex 28:17 mount four **r** of precious stones on
39:10 they mounted four **r** of precious
Lev 24: 6 Set them in two **r**, six in each row,
1Ki 7: 2 with four **r** of cedar columns
7:18 He made pomegranates in two **r**
7:20 pomegranates in **r** all around.
7:24 in two **r** in one piece with the Sea.
7:42 **r** of pomegranates for each network,
2Ch 4: 3 in two **r** in one piece with the Sea.
4:13 **r** of pomegranates for each network,
Job 41:15 His back has **r** of shields tightly

Royal (Royalty)
Jos 10: 2 like one of the **r** cities; it was
11:12 Joshua took all these **r** cities and
13:31 Edrei (the **r** cities of Og in Bashan).
1Sa 27: 5 live in the **r** city with you?"
2Sa 8:18 and David's sons were **r** advisers.
12:26 Ammonites and captured the **r** citadel.
14:26 hundred shekels by the **r** standard.
1Ki 1: 9 men of Judah who were **r** officials,
1:46 has taken his seat on the **r** throne.
1:47 Also, the **r** officials have come to
4: 7 for the king and the **r** household.
5: 9 providing food for my **r** household."
9: 1 temple of the LORD and the **r** palace,
9: 5 I will establish your **r** throne over
9:10 of the LORD and the **r** palace—
10:12 of the LORD and for the **r** palace,
10:13 had given her out of his **r** bounty.
10:28 **r** merchants purchased them from Kue.
11: 3 had seven hundred wives of **r** birth
11:14 Edomite, from the **r** line of Edom.
11:20 Tahpenes brought up in the **r** palace.
14:26 and the treasures of the **r** palace.
14:27 at the entrance to the **r** palace.
16:18 into the citadel of the **r** palace
22:10 Dressed in their **r** robes, the king
22:30 disguise, but you wear your **r** robes.
2Ki 7: 9 and report this to the **r** palace."
10: 6 Now the **r** princes, seventy of them,
11: 1 to destroy the whole **r** family.
11: 2 him away from among the **r** princes,
11: 5 third of you guarding the **r** palace,
11:19 then took his place on the **r** throne,
12:10 the **r** secretary and the high priest
12:18 of the LORD and of the **r** palace,
14:14 in the treasuries of the **r** palace.
15:25 citadel of the **r** palace at Samaria.
16: 8 in the treasuries of the **r** palace
16:18 removed the **r** entrance outside the
2Ki 18:15 in the treasuries of the **r** palace.
24:13 of the LORD and from the **r** palace,
25: 9 the **r** palace and all the houses of
25:19 fighting men and five **r** advisers.
25:25 son of Elishama, who was of **r** blood
1Ch 27:25 was in charge of the **r** storehouses.
27:34 Joab was the commander of the **r** army.
29:25 bestowed on him **r** splendour such as
2Ch 1:16 **r** merchants purchased them from Kue.
2: 1 the LORD and a **r** palace for himself.
7:11 temple of the LORD and the **r** palace,
7:18 I will establish your **r** throne, as I
9:11 of the LORD and for the **r** palace,
12: 9 and the treasures of the **r** palace.
12:10 at the entrance to the **r** palace.
18: 9 Dressed in their **r** robes, the king
18:29 disguise, but you wear your **r** robes.
22:10 **r** family of the house of Judah.
22:11 him away from among the **r** princes
23: 5 a third of you at the **r** palace and a
23:20 and seated the king on the **r** throne,
24:11 the **r** secretary and the officer of
26:11 of Hananiah, one of the **r** officials.
28:21 from the **r** palace and from the
Ezr 4:13 and the **r** revenues will suffer.
4:22 to the detriment of the **r** interests?
5:17 a search be made in the **r** archives
6: 4 are to be paid by the **r** treasury.
6: 8 be fully paid out of the **r** treasury,
7:20 you may provide from the **r** treasury.
8:36 the king's orders to the **r** satraps
Est 1: 2 his **r** throne in the citadel of Susa,
1: 7 and the **r** wine was abundant, in
1: 9 in the **r** palace of King Xerxes.
1:11 wearing her **r** crown, in order to
1:19 let him issue a **r** decree and let it
1:19 let the king give her **r** position to
2:16 to King Xerxes in the **r** residence
2:17 So he set a **r** crown on her head and
2:18 distributed gifts with **r** liberality.
3: 2 All the **r** officials at the king's
3: 3 the **r** officials at the king's gate
3: 9 of silver into the **r** treasury for
3:12 the **r** secretaries were summoned.
4: 7 promised to pay into the **r** treasury
4:11 the people of the **r** provinces know
4:14 **r** position for such a time as this?"
5: 1 third day Esther put on her **r** robes
5: 1 The king was sitting on his **r** throne
6: 8 have them bring a **r** robe the king
6: 8 with a **r** crest placed on its head.
8: 9 At once the **r** secretaries were
8:14 The couriers, riding the **r** horses,
8:15 **r** garments of blue and white,
Ps 45: 9 is the **r** bride in gold of Ophir.
72: 1 the **r** son with your righteousness.
SS 6:12 among the **r** chariots of my people.
7: 5 Your hair is like **r** tapestry; the
Isa 17: 3 and **r** power from Damascus; the
60:16 nations and be nursed at **r** breasts.
62: 3 a **r** diadem in the hand of your God.
Jer 21:11 "Moreover, say to the **r** house of
26:10 they went up from the **r** palace to
32: 2 the guard in the **r** palace of Judah.
33: 4 the **r** palaces of Judah that have
36:12 secretary's room in the **r** palace,
38: 7 an official in the **r** palace,
39: 8 set fire to the **r** palace and the
41: 1 son of Elishama, who was of **r** blood
43:10 will spread his **r** canopy above them.
52:13 the **r** palace and all the houses of
52:25 fighting men, and seven **r** advisers.
Eze 17:13 he took a member of the **r** family and
Da 1: 3 from the **r** family and the nobility—
1: 8 himself with the **r** food and wine,
1:13 of the young men who eat the **r** food,
1:15 of the young men who ate the **r** food.
2:49 himself remained at the **r** court.
3:27 and **r** advisers crowded around them.
4:29 the roof of the **r** palace of Babylon,
4:30 I have built as the **r** residence,
4:31 **r** authority has been taken from you.
5: 5 near the lampstand in the **r** palace.
5:20 **r** throne and stripped of his glory.
6: 7 The **r** administrators, prefects,
6:12 and spoke to him about his **r** decree:

Da 11: 6 together with her **r** escort and her
11:20 to maintain the **r** splendour.
11:45 He will pitch his **r** tents between
Hos 5: 1 you Israelites! Listen, O **r** house!
Jnh 3: 6 took off his **r** robes, covered
Hag 2:22 I will overturn **r** thrones and
Zec 14:10 of Hananel to the **r** winepresses.
Jn 4:46 And there was a certain **r** official
4:49 The **r** official said, "Sir, come down
Ac 12:21 wearing his **r** robes, sat on his
Jas 2: 8 If you really keep the **r** law found
1Pe 2: 9 a chosen people, a **r** priesthood,

Royalty (Royal)
Da 11:21 has not been given the honour of **r**.

Rub (Rubbed)
Lk 6: 1 **r** them in their hands and eat the

Rubbed (Rub)
2Sa 1:21 of Saul—no longer **r** with oil.
Eze 16: 4 **r** with salt or wrapped in cloths.
29:18 **r** bare and every shoulder made raw.

Rubbish
Php 3: 8 them **r**, that I may gain Christ

Rubble
2Ki 23:12 threw the **r** into the Kidron Valley.
Ezr 6:11 his house is to be made a pile of **r**.
Ne 4: 2 heaps of **r**—burned as they are?"
4:10 **r** that we cannot rebuild the wall."
Job 15:28 no-one lives, houses crumbling to **r**.
Ps 79: 1 they have reduced Jerusalem to **r**.
Isa 25: 2 You have made the city a heap of **r**,
Jer 26:18 Jerusalem will become a heap of **r**,
Eze 26: 4 away her **r** and make her a bare rock.
26:12 stones, timber and **r** into the sea.
Da 2: 5 your houses turned into piles of **r**.
3:29 houses be turned into piles of **r**,
Mic 1: 6 **r**, a place for planting vineyards.
3:12 Jerusalem will become a heap of **r**,
Zep 1: 3 The wicked will have only heaps of **r**
2:14 **r** will be in the doorways, the beams

Rubies (Ruby)
Job 28:18 the price of wisdom is beyond **r**.
Pr 3:15 She is more precious than **r**; nothing
8:11 for wisdom is more precious than **r**,
20:15 Gold there is, and **r** in abundance,
31:10 find? She is worth far more than **r**.
Isa 54:12 I will make your battlements of **r**,
Lam 4: 7 their bodies more ruddy than **r**,
Eze 27:16 coral and **r** for your merchandise.

Ruby (Rubies)
Ex 28:17 shall be a **r**, a topaz and a beryl;
39:10 there was a **r**, a topaz and a beryl;
Eze 28:13 every precious stone adorned you: **r**,

Rudder (Rudders)
Jas 3: 4 steered by a very small **r** wherever

Rudders (Rudder)
Ac 27:40 untied the ropes that held the **r**.

Ruddy
1Sa 16:12 He was **r**, with a fine appearance and
17:42 **r** and handsome, and he despised him.
SS 5:10 My lover is radiant and **r**,
Lam 4: 7 their bodies more **r** than rubies,

Rude
1Co 13: 5 is not **r**, it is not self-seeking, it

Rue
Lk 11:42 **r** and all other kinds of garden

Rufus
Mk 15:21 the father of Alexander and **R**, was
Ro 16:13 Greet **R**, chosen in the Lord, and his

Rugged
Ps 68:15 **r** are the mountains of Bashan.
68:16 Why gaze in envy, O **r** mountains, at
SS 2:17 or like a young stag on the **r** hills.
Isa 40: 4 become level, the **r** places a plain.

Rugs
Isa 21: 5 they spread the **r**, they eat, they
Eze 27:24 multicoloured **r** with cords twisted

Ruin (Ruined, Ruining, Ruins)
Nu 11:15 do not let me face my own **r**."
24:20 but he will come to **r** at last."
24:24 Eber, but they too will come to **r**."
Dt 11: 4 the LORD brought lasting **r** on them.
13:16 a **r** for ever, never to be rebuilt.
28:20 come to sudden **r** because of the evil
28:63 please him to **r** and destroy you.
2Sa 15:14 bring **r** upon us and put the city to
16: 8 **r** because you are a man of blood!"
2Ki 3:19 and **r** every good field with stones."
2Ch 34:11 of Judah had allowed to fall into **r**.
Est 6:13 him—you will surely come to **r**!"
9:24 lot) for their **r** and destruction.
Job 2: 3 him to **r** him without any reason."
22:19 "The righteous see their **r** and
31: 3 Is it not **r** for the wicked, disaster
Ps 9: 6 Endless **r** has overtaken the enemy,
35: 4 plot my **r** be turned back in dismay.
35: 8 may **r** overtake them by surprise—
35: 8 they fall into the pit, to their **r**.
38:12 of my **r**; all day long they plot
40:14 my **r** be turned back in disgrace.
52: 5 bring you down to everlasting **r**:
64: 8 against them and bring them to **r**;
70: 2 my **r** be turned back in disgrace.
73:18 ground; you cast them down to **r**.
Pr 3:25 of the **r** that overtakes the wicked,
5:14 I have come to the brink of utter **r**
10: 8 but a chattering fool comes to **r**.
10:10 and a chattering fool comes to **r**.
10:14 but the mouth of a fool invites **r**.
10:15 but poverty is the **r** of the poor.
10:29 it is the **r** of those who do evil.
13: 3 he who speaks rashly will come to **r**.
18:24 of many companions may come to **r**,
19:13 A foolish son is his father's **r**, and
21:12 wicked and brings the wicked to **r**.
26:28 and a flattering mouth works **r**.
31: 3 your vigour on those who **r** kings.
SS 2:15 little foxes that **r** the vineyards,
Isa 7: 5 son have plotted your **r**, saying,
23:13 bare and turned it into a **r**.
24: 1 he will **r** its face and scatter its
25: 2 of rubble, the fortified town a **r**,
26:14 punished them and brought them to **r**
51:19 comfort you?—**r** and destruction,
59: 7 **r** and destruction mark their ways.
60:18 nor **r** or destruction within your
Jer 12:10 Many shepherds will **r** my vineyard
13: 9 'In the same way I will **r** the pride
19: 7 "'In this place I will **r** the plans
22: 5 that this palace will become a **r**.
25: 9 and scorn, and an everlasting **r**.
25:18 to make them a **r** and an object of
27:17 Why should this city become a **r**?
38: 4 good of these people but their **r**."
48:18 you and **r** your fortified cities.
49:13 "that Bozrah will become a **r** and an
Lam 3:47 and pitfalls, **r** and destruction."
Eze 5:14 "I will make you a **r** and a reproach
21:27 A **r**! A **r**! I will make it a **r**! It
23:33 the cup of **r** and desolation, the cup
29:10 I will make the land of Egypt a **r**
Hos 2:12 I will **r** her vines and her fig-trees,
4:14 understanding will come to **r**!
Am 5: 9 and brings the fortified city to **r**),
6: 6 do not grieve over the **r** of Joseph.
Mic 6:13 you, to **r** you because of your sins.
6:16 Therefore I will give you over to **r**
Hab 2: 9 high, to escape the clutches of **r**!
2:10 You have plotted the **r** of many
Zep 1:15 a day of trouble and **r**, a day of
2:15 What a **r** she has become, a lair for
Hag 1: 4 while this house remains a **r**?"
Hag 1: 9 which remains a **r**, while each of you
Ro 3:16 **r** and misery mark their ways,
1Ti 6: 9 plunge men into **r** and destruction.
Rev 17:16 They will bring her to **r** and leave
18:17 great wealth has been brought to **r**!'
18:19 one hour she has been brought to **r**!

Ruined (Ruin)
Ge 41:36 country may not be **r** by the famine."
Ex 8:24 Egypt the land was **r** by the flies.
10: 7 not yet realise that Egypt is **r**?"
Dt 28:51 of your flocks until you are **r**.
Jdg 6: 4 They camped on the land and **r** the
Job 15:28 he will inhabit **r** towns and houses
Ps 109:10 they be driven from their **r** homes.
Pr 14:28 but without subjects a prince is **r**.
Isa 3:14 "It is you who have **r** my vineyard;
6: 5 "Woe to me!" I cried. "I am **r**! For I
6:11 "Until the cities lie **r** and without
6:11 and the fields **r** and ravaged,
15: 1 concerning Moab: Ar in Moab is **r**,
15: 1 Kir in Moab is **r**, destroyed in a
24:10 The **r** city lies desolate; the
49:19 "Though you were **r** and made desolate
60:12 will perish; it will be utterly **r**.
61: 4 they will renew the **r** cities that
Jer 4:13 than eagles. Woe to us! We are **r**!
4:27 "The whole land will be **r**, though I
9:12 Why has the land been **r** and laid
9:19 'How **r** we are! How great is our
13: 7 now it was **r** and completely useless.
48: 1 "Woe to Nebo, for it will be **r**.
48: 8 The valley will be **r** and the plateau
Eze 6: 6 your idols smashed and **r**, your
29:12 for forty years among **r** cities.
30: 7 cities will lie among **r** cities.
36:38 So will the **r** cities be filled with
Joel 1: 7 has laid waste my vines and **r** my
1:10 The fields are **r**, the ground is
Am 7: 9 the sanctuaries of Israel will be **r**;
9:14 the **r** cities and live in them.
Mic 2: 4 'We are utterly **r**; my people's
2:10 defiled, it is **r**, beyond all remedy.
Na 2: 2 them waste and have **r** their vines.
Zep 1:11 all who trade with silver will be **r**.
Zec 11: 2 the stately trees are **r**! Wail,
11: 3 the lush thicket of the Jordan is **r**!
Mt 9:17 run out and the wineskins will be **r**.
12:25 divided against itself will be **r**,
Mk 2:22 wine and the wineskins will be **r**.
Lk 5:37 run out and the wineskins will be **r**.
11:17 divided against itself will be **r**,

Ruining (Ruin)
Tit 1:11 because they are **r** whole households

Ruins (Ruin)
Lev 26:31 I will turn your cities into **r** and
26:33 and your cities will lie in **r**.
Jos 8:28 of **r**, a desolate place to this day.
1Ki 18:30 altar of the LORD, which was in **r**.
1Ch 20: 1 attacked Rabbah and left it in **r**.
2Ch 34: 6 Naphtali, and in the **r** around them,
Ezr 9: 9 house of our God and repair its **r**,
Ne 2: 3 my fathers are buried lies in **r**,
2:17 we are in: Jerusalem lies in **r**,
Job 3:14 themselves places now lying in **r**,
30:14 amid the **r** they come rolling in.
Ps 74: 3 steps towards these everlasting **r**,
89:40 and reduced his strongholds to **r**.
102: 6 desert owl, like an owl among the **r**.
Pr 19: 3 A man's own folly **r** his life, yet
24:31 weeds, and the stone wall was in **r**.
Ecc 4: 5 fool folds his hands and **r** himself.
Isa 3: 6 take charge of this heap of **r**!"
5:17 will feed among the **r** of the rich.
17: 1 a city but will become a heap of **r**.
24:12 The city is left in **r**, its gate is
44:26 of their **r**, 'I will restore them,'
51: 3 look with compassion on all her **r**;
52: 9 you **r** of Jerusalem, for the LORD has
58:12 people will rebuild the ancient **r**
61: 4 They will rebuild the ancient **r** and
64:11 and all that we treasured lies in **r**.
Jer 4: 7 will lie in **r** without inhabitant.

Jer 4:20 disaster; the whole land lies in **r**.
4:26 its towns lay in **r** before the LORD,
9:11 "I will make Jerusalem a heap of **r**,
9:19 land because our houses are in **r**.
30:18 the city will be rebuilt on her **r**,
44: 2 Today they lie deserted and in **r**
44: 6 them the desolate **r** they are today.
46:19 and lie in **r** without inhabitant.
49: 2 it will become a mound of **r**,
49:13 its towns will be in **r** for ever."
51:37 Babylon will be a heap of **r**, a haunt
Eze 13: 4 O Israel, are like jackals among **r**.
26: 2 that she lies in **r** I will prosper,'
26:20 as in ancient **r**, with those who go
33:24 the people living in those **r** in the
33:27 those who are left in the **r** will
35: 4 I will turn your towns into **r** and
36: 4 to the desolate **r** and the deserted
36:10 will be inhabited and the **r** rebuilt.
36:33 towns, and the **r** will be rebuilt.
36:35 the cities that were lying in **r**,
38:12 turn my hand against the resettled **r**
Joel 1:17 The storehouses are in **r**, the
Am 9:11 restore its **r**, and build it as it
Na 3: 7 'Nineveh is in **r**—who will mourn for
Zep 2: 4 be abandoned and Ashkelon left in **r**.
Mal 1: 4 been crushed, we will rebuild the **r**.
Ac 15:16 Its **r** I will rebuild, and I will
2Ti 2:14 value, and only **r** those who listen.

Rule (Ruled, Ruler, Ruler's, Rulers, Rules, Ruling)

Ge 1:26 in our likeness, and let them **r** over
1:28 **R** over the fish of the sea and the
3:16 husband, and he will **r** over you."
37: 8 over us? Will you actually **r** us?"
Lev 25:43 Do not **r** over them ruthlessly, but
25:46 but you must not **r** over your fellow
25:53 does not **r** over him ruthlessly.
26:17 those who hate you will **r** over you,
Dt 15: 6 You will **r** over many nations but
15: 6 nations but none will **r** over you.
19: 4 This is the **r** concerning the man who
Jdg 8:22 said to Gideon, "**R** over us—you,
8:23 Gideon told them, "I will not **r** over
8:23 you, nor will my son **r** over you.
8:23 The LORD will **r** over you."
9: 2 Jerub-Baal's sons **r** over you, or
13:12 the **r** for the boy's life and work?"
1Sa 12:12 'No, we want a king to **r** over us'—
14:47 After Saul had assumed **r** over Israel,
2Sa 3:21 **r** over all that your heart desires.
19:10 Absalom, whom we anointed to **r** over
1Ki 2:12 and his **r** was firmly established.
5: 7 son to **r** over this great nation."
8:16 chosen David to **r** my people Israel.'
11:37 I will take you, and you will **r** over
2Ch 6: 6 chosen David to **r** my people Israel.'
7:18 to have a man to **r** over Israel.'
9: 8 as king to **r** for the LORD your God.
20: 6 You **r** over all the kingdoms of the
Ne 9:37 They **r** over our bodies and our
Ps 2: 9 You will **r** them with an iron sceptre;
7: 7 round you. **R** over them from on high;
19:13 wilful sins; may they not **r** over me.
49:14 The upright will **r** over them in the
67: 4 for you **r** the peoples justly and
72: 8 He will **r** from sea to sea and from
89: 9 You **r** over the surging sea; when its
110: 2 will **r** in the midst of your enemies.
119:133 to your word; let no sin **r** over me.
Pr 8:16 and all nobles who **r** on earth.
12:24 Diligent hands will **r**, but laziness
17: 2 A wise servant will **r** over a
19:10 worse for a slave to **r** over princes!
22: 7 The rich **r** over the poor, and the
29: 2 when the wicked **r**, the people groan.
Isa 3:12 Youths oppress my people, women **r**
14: 2 captors and **r** over their oppressors.
19: 4 and a fierce king will **r** over them,"
28:10 do and do, **r** on **r**, **r** on **r**; a little
28:13 do and do, **r** on **r**, **r** on **r**; a little
28:14 who **r** this people in Jerusalem.
32: 1 and rulers will **r** with justice.
52: 5 who **r** them mock," declares the LORD.
Jer 5:31 the priests **r** by their own authority,
22:30 of David or **r** any more in Judah."
33:26 **r** over the descendants of Abraham,
51:28 and all the countries they **r**.
Lam 5: 8 Slaves **r** over us, and there is none
Eze 20:33 I will **r** over you with a mighty hand
29:15 will never again **r** over the nations.
Da 2:39 bronze, will **r** over the whole earth.
6: 1 satraps to **r** throughout the kingdom,
7: 6 and it was given authority to **r**.
11: 3 a mighty king will appear, who will **r**
11: 5 **r** his own kingdom with great power.
Hos 11: 5 will not Assyria **r** over them because
Mic 4: 7 The LORD will **r** over them in Mount
5: 6 They will **r** the land of Assyria with
Zec 6:13 and will sit and **r** on his throne.
9:10 His **r** will extend from sea to sea
Ro 13: 9 summed up in this one **r**: "Love
15:12 one who will arise to **r** over the
1Co 7:17 **r** I lay down in all the churches.
Gal 6:16 this **r**, even to the Israel of God.
Eph 1:21 far above all **r** and authority, power
Col 3:15 Let the peace of Christ **r** in your
2Th 3:10 we gave you this **r**: "If a man will
Rev 2:27 'He will **r** them with an iron sceptre;
12: 5 a male child, who will **r** all the
17:17 give the beast their power to **r**,
19:15 "He will **r** them with an iron sceptre.

Ruled (Rule)

Jos 12: 2 He **r** from Aroer on the rim of the
12: 3 He also **r** over the eastern Arabah
12: 5 He **r** over Mount Hermon, Salecah, all
13:10 who **r** in Heshbon, out to the border
13:21 of the Amorites, who **r** at Heshbon.
Jdg 11:19 who **r** in Heshbon, and said to him,
Ru 1: 1 In the days when the judges **r**, there
1Ki 4: 1 King Solomon **r** over all Israel.
4:21 Solomon **r** over all the kingdoms from
4:24 For he **r** over all the kingdoms west
9:19 throughout all the territory he **r**.
11:25 So Rezon **r** in Aram and was hostile
12:17 Judah, Rehoboam still **r** over them.
14:19 his wars and how he **r**, are written
22:47 then no king in Edom; a deputy **r**.
2Ki 11: 3 six years while Athaliah **r** the land.
1Ch 4:22 who **r** in Moab and Jashubi Lehem.
29:27 He **r** over Israel for forty years—
2Ch 8: 6 all the territory that he **r**.
9:26 He **r** over all the kings from the
10:17 Judah, Rehoboam still **r** over them.
22:12 six years while Athaliah **r** the land.
Ne 9:28 enemies so that they **r** over them.
Est 1: 1 the Xerxes who **r** over 127 provinces
Ps 106:41 nations, and their foes **r** over them.
Ecc 1:16 who has **r** over Jerusalem before me;
Isa 26:13 other lords besides you have **r** over
63:19 old; but you have not **r** over them,
Jer 34: 1 peoples in the empire he **r** were
Eze 34: 4 You have **r** them harshly and brutally.
Ac 13:21 of Benjamin, who **r** for forty years.

Ruler (Rule)

Ge 34: 2 the **r** of that area, saw her, he took
45: 8 entire household and **r** of all Egypt.
45:26 In fact, he is **r** of all Egypt.
Ex 2:14 The man said, "Who made you **r** and
22:28 "Do not blaspheme God or curse the **r**
Nu 24:19 A **r** will come out of Jacob and
2Sa 5: 2 Israel, and you shall become their **r**.
6:21 me **r** over the LORD's people Israel
7: 8 flock to be **r** over my people Israel.
1Ki 1:35 him **r** over Israel and Judah."
11:34 I have made him **r** all the days of
22:26 send him back to Amon the **r** of the
1Ch 5: 2 his brothers and a **r** came from him,
11: 2 Israel, and you will become their **r**.
17: 7 to be **r** over my people Israel.
29:12 you; you are the **r** of all things.
29:22 LORD to be **r** and Zadok to be priest.
2Ch 18:25 send him back to Amon the **r** of the
34: 8 and Maaseiah the **r** of the city,
Ne 3: 9 Rephaiah son of Hur, **r** of a
3:12 Shallum son of Hallohesh, **r** of a
3:14 **r** of the district of Beth Hakkerem.
Ne 3:15 **r** of the district of Mizpah.
3:16 Beyond him, Nehemiah son of Azbuk, **r**
3:17 Beside him, Hashabiah, **r** of half the
3:18 **r** of the other half-district of
3:19 Ezer son of Jeshua, **r** of Mizpah,
Est 1:22 should be **r** over his own household.
Ps 8: 6 You made him **r** over the works of
82: 7 you will fall like every other **r**."
105:20 released him, the **r** of peoples set
105:21 household, **r** over all he possessed,
Pr 6: 7 has no commander, no overseer or **r**,
17: 7 how much worse lying lips to a **r**!
19: 6 Many curry favour with a **r**, and
23: 1 you sit to dine with a **r**, note well
25:15 Through patience a **r** can be
28: 3 A **r** who oppresses the poor is like a
28:16 A tyrannical **r** lacks judgment, but
29:12 If a **r** listens to lies, all his
29:26 Many seek an audience with a **r**, but
Ecc 9:17 than the shouts of a **r** of fools.
10: 5 sort of error that arises from a **r**:
Isa 16: 1 Send lambs as tribute to the **r** of
60:17 governor and righteousness your **r**.
Jer 30:21 their **r** will arise from among them.
51:46 in the land and of **r** against **r**.
Eze 28: 2 "Son of man, say to the **r** of Tyre,
31:11 I handed it over to the **r** of the
Da 2:38 he has made you **r** over them all.
2:48 He made him **r** over the entire
5: 7 the third highest **r** in the kingdom."
5:16 the third highest **r** in the kingdom."
5:29 the third highest **r** in the kingdom.
9: 1 made **r** over the Babylonian kingdom—
9:25 until the Anointed One, the **r**, comes
9:26 The people of the **r** who will come
Am 2: 3 I will destroy her **r** and kill all
Mic 5: 1 Israel's **r** on the cheek with a rod.
5: 2 me one who will be **r** over Israel,
7: 3 in doing evil; the **r** demands gifts,
Hab 1:14 like sea creatures that have no **r**.
Zec 10: 4 the battle-bow, from him every **r**.
Mt 2: 6 for out of you will come a **r** who
9:18 While he was saying this, a **r** came
Mk 5:35 house of Jairus, the synagogue **r**.
5:36 Jesus told the synagogue **r**, "Don't
5:38 came to the home of the synagogue **r**,
Lk 8:41 a man named Jairus, a **r** of the
8:49 house of Jairus, the synagogue **r**.
13:14 the synagogue **r** said to the people,
18:18 A certain **r** asked him, "Good teacher,
Ac 7:10 him **r** over Egypt and all his palace.
7:18 about Joseph, became **r** of Egypt.
7:27 'Who made you **r** and judge over us?
7:35 'Who made you **r** and judge?' He was
7:35 **r** and deliverer by God himself,
18: 8 Crispus, the synagogue **r**, and his
18:17 turned on Sosthenes the synagogue **r**
23: 5 evil about the **r** of your people.'"
Eph 2: 2 of the **r** of the kingdom of the air,
1Ti 6:15 the blessed and only **R**, the King of
Rev 1: 5 and the **r** of the kings of the earth.
3:14 witness, the **r** of God's creation.

Ruler's (Rule)

Ge 49:10 nor the **r** staff from between his
Ecc 10: 4 If a **r** anger rises against you, do
Eze 19:11 were strong, fit for a **r** sceptre.
19:14 is left on it fit for a **r** sceptre.
Mt 9:23 Jesus entered the **r** house and saw

Rulers (Rule)

Ge 17:20 He will be the father of twelve **r**,
25:16 **r** according to their settlements
Jos 13: 3 of the five Philistine **r** in Gaza,
Jdg 3: 3 the five **r** of the Philistines, all
5: 3 "Hear this, you kings! Listen, you **r**!
15:11 the Philistines are **r** over us? What
16: 5 The **r** of the Philistines went to her
16: 8 the **r** of the Philistines brought her
16:18 she sent word to the **r** of the
16:18 the **r** of the Philistines returned
16:23 Now the **r** of the Philistines
16:27 the **r** of the Philistines were there,
16:30 on the **r** and all the people in it.
1Sa 5: 8 they called together all the **r** of

1Sa 5:11 they called together all the **r** of
6: 4 to the number of the Philistine **r**,
6: 4 has struck both you and your **r**.
6:12 The **r** of the Philistines followed
6:16 The five **r** of the Philistines saw
6:18 towns belonging to the five **r**—
7: 7 the **r** of the Philistines came up to
29: 2 the Philistine **r** marched with their
29: 6 you, but the **r** don't approve of you.
29: 7 to displease the Philistine **r**."
2Sa 7: 7 did I ever say to any of their **r**
1Ch 12:19 consultation, their **r** sent him away.
2Ch 23:20 the nobles, the **r** of the people and
32:31 when envoys were sent by the **r** of
Job 3:15 with **r** who had gold, who filled
Ps 2: 2 the **r** gather together against the
2:10 wise; be warned, you **r** of the earth.
58: 1 Do you **r** indeed speak justly? Do you
76:12 He breaks the spirit of **r**; he is
105:30 up into the bedrooms of their **r**.
110: 6 crushing the **r** of the whole earth.
119:23 Though **r** sit together and slander me,
119:161 **R** persecute me without cause, but my
141: 6 their **r** will be thrown down from the
148:11 you princes and all **r** on earth,
Pr 8:15 By me kings reign and **r** make laws
28: 2 is rebellious, it has many **r**, but a
31: 4 drink wine, not for **r** to crave beer,
Ecc 7:19 more powerful than ten **r** in a city.
Isa 1:10 Hear the word of the LORD, you **r** of
1:23 Your **r** are rebels, companions of
14: 5 of the wicked, the sceptre of the **r**,
16: 8 The **r** of the nations have trampled
32: 1 and **r** will rule with justice.
40:23 the **r** of this world to nothing.
41:25 He treads on **r** as if they were
49: 7 to the servant of **r**: "Kings will see
Da 7:27 all **r** will worship and obey him.'
9:12 against our **r** by bringing upon us
11:39 He will make them **r** over many people
Hos 4:18 their **r** dearly love shameful ways.
7: 7 hot as an oven; they devour their **r**.
13:10 Where are your **r** in all your towns,
Mic 3: 1 Jacob, you **r** of the house of Israel.
3: 9 you **r** of the house of Israel, who
Hab 1:10 They deride kings and scoff at **r**.
Zep 3: 3 her **r** are evening wolves, who leave
Mt 2: 6 are by no means least among the **r** of
20:25 "You know that the **r** of the Gentiles
Mk 5:22 one of the synagogue **r**, named Jairus,
10:42 **r** of the Gentiles lord it over them,
Lk 1:52 He has brought down **r** from their
12:11 **r** and authorities, do not worry
23:13 chief priests, the **r** and the people,
23:35 The people stood watching, and the **r**
24:20 The chief priests and our **r** handed
Jn 7:48 "Has any of the **r** or of the
Ac 4: 5 The next day the **r**, elders and
4: 8 "**R** and elders of the people!
4:26 the **r** gather together against the
13:15 the synagogue **r** sent word to them,
13:27 The people of Jerusalem and their **r**
Ro 13: 3 For **r** hold no terror for those who
1Co 2: 6 of this age or of the **r** of this age,
2: 8 None of the **r** of this age understood
Eph 3:10 God should be made known to the **r**
6:12 but against the **r**, against the
Col 1:16 whether thrones or powers or **r** or
Tit 3: 1 Remind the people to be subject to **r**

Rules (Rule)

Nu 9: 3 with all its **r** and regulations."
9:14 with its **r** and regulations.
15:15 The community is to have the same **r**
2Sa 23: 3 said to me: 'When one **r** over men in
23: 3 when he **r** in the fear of God,
1Ki 21:18 king of Israel, who **r** in Samaria.
2Ch 30:19 to the **r** of the sanctuary."
Ps 22:28 the LORD and he **r** over the nations.
59:13 of the earth that God **r** over Jacob.
66: 7 He **r** for ever by his power, his eyes
103:19 heaven, and his kingdom **r** over all.
Isa 29:13 is made up only of **r** taught by men.
40:10 with power, and his arm **r** for him.
Da 4:26 when you acknowledge that Heaven **r**.
Mt 15: 9 teachings are but **r** taught by men.'"
Mk 7: 7 teachings are but **r** taught by men.'
Lk 22:26 one who **r** like the one who serves.
Col 2:20 to it, do you submit to its **r**:
2Ti 2: 5 he competes according to the **r**.
Rev 17:18 that **r** over the kings of the earth."

Ruling (Rule)

Jdg 14: 4 that time they were **r** over Israel.)
1Ki 3:27 the king gave his **r**: "Give the
15:18 king of Aram, who was **r** in Damascus.
2Ch 16: 2 king of Aram, who was **r** in Damascus.
Ezr 4:20 Jerusalem has had powerful kings **r**
Job 34:30 to keep a godless man from **r**, from
Pr 28:15 wicked man **r** over a helpless people.
Jn 3: 1 a member of the Jewish **r** council.

Rumah

2Ki 23:36 daughter of Pedaiah; she was from **R**.

Rumble (Rumbling, Rumblings)

Jer 47: 3 chariots and the **r** of their wheels.

Rumbling (Rumble)

Job 37: 2 to the **r** that comes from his mouth.
Eze 3:12 and I heard behind me a loud **r** sound
3:13 wheels beside them, a loud **r** sound.

Rumblings (Rumble)

Rev 4: 5 lightning, **r** and peals of thunder.
8: 5 **r**, flashes of lightning and an
11:19 **r**, peals of thunder, an earthquake
16:18 there came flashes of lightning, **r**,

Rumour (Rumours)

Job 28:22 Destruction and Death say, 'Only a **r**
Jer 51:46 in the land; one **r** comes this year,
Eze 7:26 calamity will come, and **r** upon **r**.
Jn 21:23 of this, the **r** spread among the

Rumours (Rumour)

Jer 51:46 Do not lose heart or be afraid when **r**
51:46 another the next, **r** of violence in
Mt 24: 6 You will hear of wars and **r** of wars,
Mk 13: 7 you hear of wars and **r** of wars, do

Run (Outran, Overran, Overrun, Ran, Runner, Runners, Running, Runs)

Ge 19:20 here is a town near enough to **r** to
31:27 Why did you **r** off secretly and
39:13 her hand and had **r** out of the house,
Ex 23:27 your enemies turn their backs and **r**.
Lev 26:36 They will **r** as though fleeing from
Nu 34: 7 your northern boundary, **r** a line
34:10 your eastern boundary, **r** a line
Jos 7:12 they turn their backs and **r** because
Ru 3:10 You have not **r** after the younger men,
1Sa 8:11 will **r** in front of his chariots.
14:22 that the Philistines were on the **r**,
19:11 "If you don't **r** for your life
20:36 he said to the boy, "**R** and find the
21:13 and letting saliva **r** down his beard.
31: 4 "Draw your sword and **r** me through,
31: 4 come and **r** me through and abuse me.
2Sa 15: 1 with fifty men to **r** ahead of him.
18:19 "Let me **r** and take the news to the
18:22 please let me **r** behind the Cushite.
18:23 He said, "Come what may, I want to **r**.
18:23 So Joab said, "**R**!" Then Ahimaaz ran
1Ki 1: 5 with fifty men to **r** ahead of him.
17:14 the jug of oil will not **r** dry until
17:16 up and the jug of oil did not **r** dry,
2Ki 4:26 **R** to meet her and ask her, 'Are you
4:29 take my staff in your hand and **r**.
5:20 I will **r** after him and get something
9: 3 open the door and **r**; don't delay!"
1Ch 10: 4 "Draw your sword and **r** me through,
Ne 6:11 I said, "Should a man like me **r** away?
Job 1: 5 period of feasting had **r** its course
39:18 spreads her feathers to **r**, she
Ps 16: 4 increase who **r** after other gods.
19: 5 champion rejoicing to **r** his course.
119:32 I **r** in the path of your commands,
Pr 4:12 when you **r**, you will not stumble.
18:10 the righteous **r** to it and are safe.
Isa 5:11 the morning to **r** after their drinks,
7:25 are turned loose and where sheep **r**.
8: 7 its channels, **r** over all its
10: 3 To whom will you **r** for help? Where
40:31 they will **r** and not grow weary,
Jer 2:23 'I am not defiled; I have not **r**
2:25 Do not **r** until your feet are bare
17:16 I have not **r** away from being your
23:21 yet they have **r** with their message;
48: 6 Flee! **R** for your lives; become like
51: 6 "Flee from Babylon! **R** for your lives!
51:45 **R** for your lives! **R** from the fierce
Eze 47:15 "On the north side it will **r** from
47:18 "On the east side the boundary will **r**
47:19 "On the south side it will **r** from
48:28 "The southern boundary of Gad will **r**
Joel 2: 9 They rush upon the city; they **r**
3:18 ravines of Judah will **r** with water.
Am 6:12 Do horses **r** on the rocky crags? Does
Na 1: 4 up; he makes all the rivers **r** dry.
Hab 2: 2 so that a herald may **r** with it.
Zec 2: 4 said to him: "**R**, tell that young man,
Mt 6:32 For the pagans **r** after all these
9:17 will burst, the wine will **r** out and
Lk 5:37 burst the skins, the wine will **r** out
Jn 10: 5 they will **r** away from him because
Ac 27:17 Fearing that they would **r** aground on
27:26 Nevertheless, we must **r** aground on
27:39 to **r** the ship aground if they could.
1Co 9:24 that in a race all the runners **r**,
9:24 **R** in such a way as to get the prize
9:26 Therefore I do not **r** like a man
Gal 2: 2 running or had **r** my race in vain.
Php 2:16 I did not **r** or labour for nothing.
Heb 12: 1 and let us **r** with perseverance the

Runner (Run)

Job 9:25 "My days are swifter than a **r**; they

Runners (Run)

1Co 9:24 know that in a race all the **r** run,

Running (Run)

Ge 16: 8 "I'm **r** away from my mistress Sarai,"
31:20 by not telling him he was **r** away.
Ex 32:25 Moses saw that the people were **r**
Lev 21:20 or **r** sores or damaged testicles.
22:22 with warts or festering or **r** sores.
Jos 8: 6 **r** away from us as they did before.
2Sa 3:29 who has a **r** sore or leprosy or who
18:24 he looked out, he saw a man **r** alone.
18:26 the watchman saw another man **r**, and
18:26 "Look, another man **r** alone!" The
2Ki 5:21 When Naaman saw him **r** towards him,
2Ch 23:12 the people **r** and cheering the king,
Ps 133: 2 **r** down on the beard, **r** down on
Pr 5:15 water from your own cistern, **r** water
Jer 2:23 a swift she-camel **r** here and there,
Eze 45: 7 **r** lengthwise from the western to the
48:18 portion and **r** the length of it,
48:21 Both these areas **r** the length of the
Jnh 1:10 knew he was **r** away from the LORD,
Mk 9:25 Jesus saw that a crowd was **r** to the
Lk 6:38 **r** over, will be poured into your lap.
17:23 he is!' Do not go **r** off after them.
Jn 20: 2 she came **r** to Simon Peter and the
20: 4 Both were **r**, but the other disciple
Ac 3:11 came **r** to them in the place called
21:30 people came **r** from all directions.
1Co 9:26 I do not run like a man **r** aimlessly
Gal 2: 2 I was **r** or had run my race in vain.
5: 7 You were **r** a good race. Who cut in

Runs (Run)

Ge 2:14 it **r** along the east side of Asshur.
2Sa 18:27 one **r** like Ahimaaz son of Zadok.
Ps 147:15 to the earth; his word **r** swiftly.
Eze 16:34 no-one **r** after you for your favours.
Lk 12:30 For the pagan world **r** after all such
Jn 10:12 he abandons the sheep and **r** away.
10:13 The man **r** away because he is a hired
2Jn : 9 Anyone who **r** ahead and does not

Rural
Est 9:19 That is why **r** Jew's—those living in

Ruse
Jos 9: 4 they resorted to a **r**: They went as a

Rush (Rushed, Rushes, Rushing)
Jdg 21:21 then **r** from the vineyards and each
Pr 1:16 for their feet **r** into sin, they are
6:18 feet that are quick to **r** into evil,
Isa 59: 7 Their feet **r** into sin; they are
Jer 49: 3 **r** here and there inside the walls,
Joel 2: 9 They **r** upon the city; they run along

Rushed (Rush)
Jos 8:19 from their position and **r** forward.
Jdg 9:44 the companies with him **r** forward to
9:44 Then two companies **r** upon those in
1Sa 7:11 The men of Israel **r** out of Mizpah
2Sa 19:17 **r** to the Jordan, where the king was.
Est 6:12 But Haman **r** home, with his head
Mt 8:32 and the whole herd **r** down the steep
Mk 5:13 about two thousand in number, **r** down
Lk 8:33 and the herd **r** down the steep bank
Ac 7:57 of their voices, they all **r** at him,
14:14 and **r** out into the crowd, shouting:
16:29 The jailer called for lights, **r** in
17: 5 They **r** to Jason's house in search of
19:29 and **r** as one man into the theatre.
Jude :11 they have **r** for profit into Balaam's

Rushes[1] (Rush)
Dt 32:35 is near and their doom **r** upon them."
Job 16:14 upon me; he **r** at me like a warrior.

Rushes[2]
Isa 19: 6 The reeds and **r** will wither,

Rushing (Rush)
Jdg 5:15 Barak, **r** after him into the valley.
Job 20:28 will carry off his house, **r** waters
Isa 30:28 His breath is like a **r** torrent,
Eze 1:24 like the roar of **r** waters, like the
43: 2 His voice was like the roar of **r**
Mic 1: 4 the fire, like water **r** down a slope.
Na 2: 4 **r** back and forth through the squares.
Rev 1:15 was like the sound of **r** waters.
9: 9 horses and chariots **r** into battle.
14: 2 heaven like the roar of **r** waters
19: 6 like the roar of **r** waters and like

Rust
Mt 6:19 where moth and **r** destroy, and where
6:20 where moth and **r** do not destroy, and

Ruth
Moabitess at time of Judges; widow of Naomi's son, Mahlon (Ru 1:4–5; 4:10). Refused to leave Naomi; accompanied her to Bethlehem (Ru 1:11–22). Gleaned in field of Boaz and treated kindly (Ru 2). Claimed protection from Boaz as kinsman-redeemer (Ru 3). Married Boaz; gave birth to Obed, grandfather of David (Ru 4).

Ru 1: 4 one named Orpah and the other **R**.
1:14 good-bye, but **R** clung to her.
1:16 **R** replied, "Don't urge me to leave
1:18 Naomi realised that **R** was determined
1:22 Moab accompanied by **R** the Moabitess,
2: 2 **R** the Moabitess said to Naomi, "Let
2: 8 Boaz said to **R**, "My daughter, listen
2:17 **R** gleaned in the field until evening.
2:18 **R** also brought out and gave her what
2:19 **R** told her mother-in-law about the
2:21 **R** the Moabitess said, "He even said
2:22 Naomi said to **R** her daughter-in-law,
2:23 **R** stayed close to the servant girls
3: 5 do whatever you say," **R** answered.
3: 7 **R** approached quietly, uncovered his
3: 9 "I am your servant **R**," she said.
3:16 **R** came to her mother-in-law, Naomi
4: 5 from Naomi and from **R** the Moabitess,
4:10 I have also acquired **R** the Moabitess,
4:13 Boaz took **R** and she became his wife.
Mt 1: 5 was **R**, Obed the father of Jesse,

Ruthless (Ruthlessly)
Job 6:23 me from the clutches of the **r**'?
15:20 the **r** through all the years stored
27:13 a **r** man receives from the Almighty:
Ps 35:11 **R** witnesses come forward; they
37:35 I have seen a wicked and **r** man
54: 3 Strangers are attacking me; **r** men
86:14 O God; a band of **r** men seeks my life
Pr 11:16 respect, but **r** men gain only wealth.
Isa 13:11 and will humble the pride of the **r**.
25: 3 cities of **r** nations will revere you.
25: 4 For the breath of the **r** is like a
25: 5 so the song of the **r** is stilled.
29: 5 dust, the **r** hordes like blown chaff.
29:20 The **r** will vanish, the mockers will
Eze 28: 7 the most **r** of nations; they will
30:11 He and his army—the most **r** of
31:12 the most **r** of foreign nations cut it
32:12 men—the most **r** of all nations.
Hab 1: 6 that **r** and impetuous people, who
Ro 1:31 senseless, faithless, heartless, **r**.

Ruthlessly (Ruthless)
Ex 1:13 and worked them **r**.
1:14 labour the Egyptians used them **r**.
Lev 25:43 Do not rule over them **r**, but fear
25:46 rule over your fellow Israelites **r**.
25:53 his owner does not rule over him **r**.
Job 30:21 You turn on me **r**; with the might of

Sabachthani
Mt 27:46 "Eloi, Eloi, lama **s**?"—which means,
Mk 15:34 "Eloi, Eloi, lama **s**?"—which means,

Sabbath (Sabbaths)
Ex 16:23 a day of rest, a holy **S** to the LORD.
16:25 "because today is a **S** to the LORD.
16:26 but on the seventh day, the **S**,
16:29 that the LORD has given you the **S**;
20: 8 "Remember the **S** day by keeping it
20:10 the seventh day is a **S** to the LORD
20:11 blessed the **S** day and made it holy.
31:14 "'Observe the **S**, because it is holy
31:15 but the seventh day is a **S** of rest,
31:15 on the **S** day must be put to death.
31:16 The Israelites are to observe the **S**,
35: 2 holy day, a **S** of rest to the LORD.
35: 3 any of your dwellings on the **S** day."
Lev 16:31 is a **s** of rest, and you must deny
23: 3 but the seventh day is a **S** of rest,
23: 3 you live, it is a **S** to the LORD.
23:11 to wave it on the day after the **S**.
23:15 "'From the day after the **S**, the day
23:16 up to the day after the seventh **S**,
23:32 is a **s** of rest for you, and you must
23:32 evening you are to observe your **s**."
24: 8 **S** after **S**, on behalf of the
25: 2 itself must observe a **s** to the LORD.
25: 4 have a **s** of rest, a **s** to the LORD.
25: 6 Whatever the land yields during the **s**
26:34 the land will enjoy its **s** years all
Nu 15:32 found gathering wood on the **S** day.
28: 9 "'On the **S** day, make an offering of
28:10 is the burnt offering for every **S**,
Dt 5:12 "Observe the **S** day by keeping it
5:14 the seventh day is a **S** to the LORD
5:15 commanded you to observe the **S** day.
2Ki 4:23 "It's not the New Moon or the **S**."
11: 5 that are going on duty on the **S**
11: 7 that normally go off **S** duty are all
11: 9 who were going on duty on the **S**
16:18 He took away the **S** canopy that had
1Ch 9:32 preparing for every **S** the bread set
2Ch 23: 4 on duty on the **S** are to keep watch
23: 8 who were going on duty on the **S**
36:21 The land enjoyed its **s** rests;
Ne 9:14 You made known to them your holy **S**
10:31 or grain to sell on the **S**,
10:31 we will not buy from them on the **S**
13:15 Judah treading winepresses on the **S**
13:15 all this into Jerusalem on the **S**.
Ne 13:16 on the **S** to the people of Judah.
13:17 are doing—desecrating the **S** day?
13:18 Israel by desecrating the **S**."
13:19 the gates of Jerusalem before the **S**,
13:19 and not opened until the **S** was over.
13:19 could be brought in on the **S** day.
13:21 on they no longer came on the **S**.
13:22 in order to keep the **S** day holy.
Ps 92: T A psalm. A song. For the **S** day.
Isa 56: 2 who keeps the **S** without desecrating
56: 6 all who keep the **S** without
58:13 keep your feet from breaking the **S**
58:13 if you call the **S** a delight and the
66:23 another and from one **S** to another,
Jer 17:21 not to carry a load on the **S** day
17:22 your houses or do any work on the **S**,
17:22 but keep the **S** day holy, as I
17:24 the gates of this city on the **S**,
17:24 but keep the **S** day holy by not doing
17:27 if you do not obey me to keep the **S**
17:27 the gates of Jerusalem on the **S** day,
Eze 46: 1 but on the **S** day and on the day of
46: 4 brings to the LORD on the **S** day is
46:12 offerings as he does on the **S** day.
Hos 2:11 **S** days—all her appointed feasts.
Am 8: 5 and the **S** be ended that we may
Mt 12: 1 through the cornfields on the **S**.
12: 2 doing what is unlawful on the **S**."
12: 5 on the **S** the priests in the temple
12: 8 For the Son of Man is Lord of the **S**."
12:10 "Is it lawful to heal on the **S**?"
12:11 and it falls into a pit on the **S**,
12:12 it is lawful to do good on the **S**."
24:20 take place in winter or on the **S**.
28: 1 After the **S**, at dawn on the first
Mk 1:21 and when the **S** came, Jesus went into
2:23 One **S** Jesus was going through the
2:24 doing what is unlawful on the **S**?"
2:27 he said to them, "The **S** was made for
2:27 was made for man, not man for the **S**.
2:28 the Son of Man is Lord even of the **S**.
3: 2 see if he would heal him on the **S**.
3: 4 "Which is lawful on the **S**: to do
6: 2 the **S** came, he began to teach in the
15:42 Day (that is, the day before the **S**).
16: 1 the **S** was over, Mary Magdalene, Mary
Lk 4:16 and on the **S** day he went into the
4:31 on the **S** began to teach the people.
6: 1 One **S** Jesus was going through the
6: 2 doing what is unlawful on the **S**?"
6: 5 "The Son of Man is Lord of the **S**.
6: 6 On another **S** he went into the
6: 7 to see if he would heal on the **S**.
6: 9 "I ask you, which is lawful on the **S**:
13:10 On a **S** Jesus was teaching in one of
13:14 because Jesus had healed on the **S**,
13:14 healed on those days, not on the **S**."
13:15 Doesn't each of you on the **S** untie
13:16 on the **S** day from what bound her?"
14: 1 One **S**, when Jesus went to eat in the
14: 3 it lawful to heal on the **S** or not?"
14: 5 that falls into a well on the **S** day,
23:54 and the **S** was about to begin.
23:56 they rested on the **S** in obedience
Jn 5: 9 on which this took place was a **S**,
5:10 "It is the **S**; the law forbids you to
5:16 on the **S**, the Jews persecuted him.
5:18 not only was he breaking the **S**,
7:22 you circumcise a child on the **S**.
7:23 a child can be circumcised on the **S**
7:23 for healing the whole man on the **S**?
9:14 and opened the man's eyes was a **S**.
9:16 God, for he does not keep the **S**.
19:31 the next day was to be a special **S**.
19:31 left on the crosses during the **S**,
Ac 1:12 Olives, a **S** day's walk from the city.
13:14 On the **S** they entered the synagogue
13:27 the prophets that are read every **S**.
13:42 about these things on the next **S**.
13:44 On the next **S** almost the whole city
15:21 read in the synagogues on every **S**."
16:13 On the **S** we went outside the city
17: 2 and on three **S** days he reasoned with
18: 4 Every **S** he reasoned in the synagogue,
Col 2:16 a New Moon celebration or a **S** day.

Sabbath-rest (Rest[1])
Heb 4: 9 There remains, then, a **S** for the

Sabbaths (Sabbath)
Ex 31:13 Israelites, 'You must observe my **S**.
Lev 19: 3 father, and you must observe my **S**.
19:30 "'Observe my **S** and have reverence
23:38 addition to those for the LORD's **S**
25: 8 "'Count off seven **s** of years—seven
25: 8 so that the seven **s** of years amount
26: 2 "'Observe my **S** and have reverence
26:34 the land will rest and enjoy its **s**.
26:35 have during the **s** you lived in it.
26:43 will enjoy its **s** while it lies
1Ch 23:31 were presented to the LORD on **S**
2Ch 2: 4 evening and on **S** and New Moons and
8:13 offerings commanded by Moses for **S**,
31: 3 for the burnt offerings on the **S**,
Ne 10:33 for the offerings on the **S**,
Isa 1:13 New Moons, **S** and convocations—
56: 4 "To the eunuchs who keep my **S**, who
Lam 2: 6 her appointed feasts and her **S**;
Eze 20:12 Also I gave them my **S** as a sign
20:13 they utterly desecrated my **S**.
20:16 my decrees and desecrated my **S**.
20:20 Keep my **S** holy, that they may be a
20:21 by them—and they desecrated my **S**.
20:24 my decrees and desecrated my **S**,
22: 8 my holy things and desecrated my **S**.
22:26 their eyes to the keeping of my **S**,
23:38 my sanctuary and desecrated my **S**.
44:24 and they are to keep my **S** holy.
45:17 the New Moons and the **S**—at all the
46: 3 On the **S** and New Moons the people of

Sabeans
Job 1:15 the **S** attacked and carried them off.
Isa 45:14 and those tall **S**—they will come
Eze 23:42 **S** were brought from the desert along
Joel 3: 8 them to the **S**, a nation far away.

Sabta
1Ch 1: 9 The sons of Cush: Seba, Havilah, **S**,

Sabtah
Ge 10: 7 The sons of Cush: Seba, Havilah, **S**,

Sabteca
Ge 10: 7 Seba, Havilah, Sabtah, Raamah and **S**.
1Ch 1: 9 Seba, Havilah, Sabta, Raamah and **S**.

Sacar
1Ch 11:35 Ahiam son of **S** the Hararite, Eliphal
26: 4 **S** the fourth, Nethanel the fifth,

Sachet
SS 1:13 My lover is to me a **s** of myrrh

Sack (Sacks)
Ge 42:25 put each man's silver back in his **s**,
42:27 opened his **s** to get feed for his
42:27 his silver in the mouth of his **s**.
42:28 "Here it is in my **s**." Their hearts
42:35 there in each man's **s** was his pouch
43:21 exact weight—in the mouth of his **s**.
44: 1 man's silver in the mouth of his **s**.
44: 2 the mouth of the youngest one's **s**,
44:11 Each of them quickly lowered his **s**
44:12 the cup was found in Benjamin's **s**.

Sackcloth (*Sackcloth and ashes*)
Ge 37:34 Jacob tore his clothes, put on **s** and
Lev 11:32 is made of wood, cloth, hide or **s**.
2Sa 3:31 "Tear your clothes and put on **s** and
21:10 Rizpah daughter of Aiah took **s** and
1Ki 20:31 of Israel with **s** round our waists
20:32 Wearing **s** round their waists and
21:27 his clothes, put on **s** and fasted.
21:27 He lay in **s** and went around meekly.
2Ki 6:30 underneath, he had **s** on his body.
19: 1 he tore his clothes and put on **s** and
19: 2 wearing **s**, to the prophet Isaiah
1Ch 21:16 clothed in **s**, fell face down.
Ne 9: 1 fasting and wearing **s** and having
Est 4: 2 no-one clothed in **s** was allowed to
4: 4 instead of his **s**, but he would not
Job 16:15 "I have sewed **s** over my skin and
Ps 30:11 you removed my **s** and clothed me
35:13 Yet when they were ill, I put on **s**
69:11 I put on **s**, people make sport of me.
Isa 3:24 instead of fine clothing, **s**;
15: 3 In the streets they wear **s**; on the
20: 2 He said to him, "Take off the **s** from
22:12 to tear out your hair and put on **s**.
32:11 clothes, put **s** round your waists.
37: 1 he tore his clothes and put on **s** and
37: 2 wearing **s**, to the prophet Isaiah
50: 3 darkness and make **s** its covering."
Jer 4: 8 put on **s**, lament and wail, for the
6:26 O my people, put on **s** and roll in
48:37 and every waist is covered with **s**.
49: 3 Put on **s** and mourn; rush here and
Lam 2:10 dust on their heads and put on **s**.
Eze 7:18 They will put on **s** and be clothed
27:31 because of you and will put on **s**.
Joel 1: 8 Mourn like a virgin in **s** grieving
1:13 Put on **s**, O priests, and mourn; wail,
1:13 Come, spend the night in **s**, you who
Am 8:10 I will make all of you wear **s** and
Jnh 3: 5 the greatest to the least, put on **s**.
3: 6 covered himself with **s** and sat down
3: 8 let man and beast be covered with **s**.
Rev 6:12 The sun turned black like **s** made of
11: 3 for 1,260 days, clothed in **s**."

Sackcloth and ashes
Est 4: 1 he tore his clothes, put on **s**, and
4: 3 weeping and wailing. Many lay in **s**.
Isa 58: 5 and for lying on **s**? Is that what
Da 9: 3 and petition, in fasting, and in **s**.
Mt 11:21 would have repented long ago in **s**.
Lk 10:13 repented long ago, sitting in **s**.

Sacked
2Ki 15:16 He **s** Tiphsah and ripped open all the

Sacks (Sack)
Ge 42:35 they were emptying their **s**, there in
43:12 put back into the mouths of your **s**.
43:18 put back into our **s** the first time.
43:21 for the night we opened our **s**
43:22 know who put our silver in our **s**."
43:23 has given you treasure in your **s**;
44: 1 "Fill the men's **s** with as much food
44: 8 we found inside the mouths of our **s**.
Jos 9: 4 with worn-out **s** and old wineskins,
1Sa 9: 7 the man? The food in our **s** is gone.

Sacred
Ex 12:16 On the first day hold a **s** assembly,
23:24 and break their **s** stones to pieces.
28: 2 Make **s** garments for your brother
28: 4 They are to make these **s** garments
28:38 **s** gifts the Israelites consecrate,
29: 6 attach the **s** diadem to the turban.
29:29 "Aaron's **s** garments will belong to
29:31 and cook the meat in a **s** place.
29:33 may eat them, because they are **s**.
29:34 must not be eaten, because it is **s**.
30:25 Make these into a **s** anointing oil, a
30:25 It will be the **s** anointing oil.
30:31 'This is to be my **s** anointing oil
30:32 is **s**, and you are to consider it **s**.
30:35 It is to be salted and pure and **s**.
31:10 both the **s** garments from Aaron the
34:13 smash their **s** stones and cut down
35:19 the **s** garments for Aaron the priest
35:21 its service, and for the **s** garments.
37:29 They also made the **s** anointing oil
39: 1 They also made **s** garments for Aaron,
39:30 They made the plate, the **s** diadem,
39:41 both the **s** garments for Aaron the
40:13 dress Aaron in the **s** garments,
Lev 8: 9 the **s** diadem, on the front of it, as
12: 4 She must not touch anything **s** or go
16: 4 He is to put on the **s** linen tunic,
16: 4 These are **s** garments; so he must
Lev 16:32 He is to put on the **s** linen
22: 2 treat with respect the **s** offerings
22: 3 yet comes near the **s** offerings that
22: 4 he may not eat the **s** offerings
22: 6 must not eat any of the **s** offerings
22: 7 he may eat the **s** offerings, for
22:10 family may eat the **s** offering,
22:12 not eat any of the **s** contributions.
22:14 "'If anyone eats a **s** offering by
22:15 must not desecrate the **s** offerings
22:16 them to eat the **s** offerings and so
23: 2 you are to proclaim as **s** assemblies.
23: 3 Sabbath of rest, a day of **s** assembly.
23: 4 the **s** assemblies you are to proclaim
23: 7 On the first day hold a **s** assembly
23: 8 the seventh day hold a **s** assembly
23:20 They are a **s** offering to the LORD
23:21 you are to proclaim a **s** assembly
23:24 a **s** assembly commemorated with
23:27 Hold a **s** assembly and deny
23:35 The first day is a **s** assembly; do no
23:36 on the eighth day hold a **s** assembly
23:37 which you are to proclaim as **s**
26: 1 image or a **s** stone for yourselves,
Nu 5: 9 All the **s** contributions the
5:10 Each man's **s** gifts are his own, but
28:18 On the first day hold a **s** assembly
28:25 On the seventh day hold a **s** assembly
28:26 a **s** assembly and do no regular work.
29: 1 a **s** assembly and do no regular work.
29: 7 seventh month hold a **s** assembly.
29:12 a **s** assembly and do no regular work.
Dt 7: 5 smash their **s** stones, cut down their
12: 3 smash their **s** stones and burn their
16:22 do not erect a **s** stone, for these
26:13 removed from my house the **s** portion
26:14 have not eaten any of the **s** portion
Jos 6:19 iron are **s** to the LORD and must go
1Ki 1:39 the horn of oil from the **s** tent
8: 4 and all the **s** furnishings in it.
14:23 **s** stones and Asherah poles on every
2Ki 3: 2 He got rid of the **s** stone of Baal
10:26 They brought the **s** stone out of the
10:27 They demolished the **s** stone of Baal
12: 4 is brought as **s** offerings to the
12:18 took all the **s** objects dedicated
17:10 They set up **s** stones and Asherah
18: 4 smashed the **s** stones and cut down
23:14 Josiah smashed the **s** stones and cut
1Ch 16:42 of the other instruments for **s** song.
22:19 the **s** articles belonging to God into
23:28 the purification of all **s** things and
2Ch 5: 5 and all the **s** furnishings in it.
14: 3 smashed the **s** stones and cut down
24: 7 even its **s** objects for the Baals.
31: 1 smashed the **s** stones and cut down
35: 3 "Put the **s** ark in the temple that
Ezr 2:63 not to eat any of the most **s** food
3: 5 the appointed **s** feasts of the LORD,
8:30 gold and **s** articles that had been
8:33 gold and the **s** articles into the
Ne 7:65 not to eat any of the most **s** food
8: 9 "This day is **s** to the LORD your God.
8:10 This day is **s** to our Lord. Do not
8:11 "Be still, for this is a **s** day.
Ps 89:20 with my **s** oil I have anointed him.
Isa 1:29 be ashamed because of the **s** oaks
14:13 utmost heights of the **s** mountain.
64:10 Your **s** cities have become a desert;
65: 5 near me, for I am too **s** for you!'
Jer 31:23 O righteous dwelling, O **s** mountain.'
43:13 Egypt he will demolish the **s** pillars
Lam 4: 1 The **s** gems are scattered at the
Eze 44:19 in and leave them in the **s** rooms,
45: 1 portion of the land as a **s** district,
45: 3 In the **s** district, measure off a
45: 4 will be the **s** portion of the land
45: 6 adjoining the **s** portion; it will
45: 7 the area formed by the **s** district
46:19 gate to the **s** rooms facing north,
48:10 This will be the **s** portion for the
48:12 them from the **s** portion of the land,
48:18 bordering on the **s** portion and
48:20 you will set aside the **s** portion,
48:21 of the area formed by the **s** portion
48:21 the **s** portion to the eastern border,

Eze 48:21 and the **s** portion with the temple
Hos 3: 1 gods and love the **s** raisin cakes."
3: 4 without sacrifice or **s** stones,
10: 1 prospered, he adorned his **s** stones.
10: 2 altars and destroy their **s** stones.
Joel 1:14 a holy fast; call a **s** assembly.
2:15 a holy fast, call a **s** assembly.
Mic 5:13 and your **s** stones from among you;
Zec 14:20 the **s** bowls in front of the altar.
Mt 7: 6 "Do not give dogs what is **s**; do not
23:17 or the temple that makes the gold **s**?
23:19 or the altar that makes the gift **s**?
Ro 14: 5 One man considers one day more **s**
1Co 3:17 for God's temple is **s**, and you are
2Pe 1:18 we were with him on the **s** mountain.
2:21 **s** command that was passed on to them.

Sacrifice (Sacrificed, Sacrifices, Sacrificing)

Ge 22: 2 **S** him there as a burnt offering on
31:54 He offered a **s** there in the hill
Ex 5: 8 out, 'Let us go and **s** to our God.'
5:17 'Let us go and **s** to the LORD.'
8:25 "Go, **s** to your God here in the land.
12:27 tell them, 'It is the Passover **s** to
13:15 This is why I **s** to the LORD the
20:24 altar of earth for me and **s** on it
23:18 "Do not offer the blood of a **s** to me
29:36 **S** a bull each day as a sin offering
29:41 **S** the other lamb at twilight with
34:15 to their gods and **s** to them,
34:25 "Do not offer the blood of a **s** to me
34:25 and do not let any of the **s** from the
Lev 3: 3 bring a **s** made to the LORD by fire:
3: 9 **s** made to the LORD by fire: its fat,
7:16 the **s** shall be eaten on the day he
7:17 Any meat of the **s** left over till the
7:29 part of it as his **s** to the LORD.
9: 4 offering to **s** before the LORD,
9: 7 "Come to the altar and **s** your sin
9: 7 **s** the offering that is for the
14:19 "Then the priest is to **s** the sin
14:30 he shall **s** the doves or the young
15:15 The priest is to **s** them, the one for
15:30 The priest is to **s** one for a sin
16: 9 LORD and **s** it for a sin offering.
16:24 Then he shall come out and **s** the
17: 5 and **s** them as fellowship offerings.
17: 8 who offers a burnt offering or **s**
17: 9 Tent of Meeting to **s** it to the LORD
19: 5 "'When you **s** a fellowship offering
19: 5 **s** it in such a way that it will be
19: 6 shall be eaten on the day you **s** it
22:29 "When you **s** a thank-offering to the
22:29 **s** it in such a way that it will be
23:12 you must **s** as a burnt offering to
23:19 **s** one male goat for a sin offering
Nu 6:17 is to **s** the ram as a fellowship
6:18 the **s** of the fellowship offering.
7:88 total number of animals for the **s**
15: 5 for the burnt offering or the **s**,
15: 8 young bull as a burnt offering or **s**,
Dt 12:13 Be careful not to **s** your burnt
15:21 must not **s** it to the LORD your God.
16: 2 **S** as the Passover to the LORD your
16: 4 Do not let any of the meat you **s** on
16: 5 You must not **s** the Passover in any
16: 6 There you must **s** the Passover in the
17: 1 Do not **s** to the LORD your God an ox
18: 3 the people who **s** a bull or a sheep:
27: 7 **S** fellowship offerings there, eating
Jos 22:23 or to **s** fellowship offerings on it,
Jdg 11:31 I will **s** it as a burnt offering."
16:23 offer a great **s** to Dagon their god
1Sa 1: 3 **s** to the LORD Almighty at Shiloh,
1: 4 the day came for Elkanah to **s**,
1:21 **s** to the LORD and to fulfil his vow,
2:13 that whenever anyone offered a **s**
2:19 her husband to offer the annual **s**.
2:29 Why do you scorn my **s** and offering
3:14 be atoned for by **s** or offering.
9:12 people have a **s** at the high place.
9:13 because he must bless the **s**;
10: 8 I will surely come down to you to **s**
15:15 cattle to **s** to the LORD your God,
1Sa 15:21 in order to **s** them to the LORD your
15:22 To obey is better than **s**, and to
16: 2 say, 'I have come to **s** to the LORD.'
16: 3 Invite Jesse to the **s**, and I will
16: 5 I have come to **s** to the LORD.
16: 5 and come to the **s** with me.
16: 5 his sons and invited them to the **s**.
20: 6 because an annual **s** is being made
20:29 because our family is observing a **s**
2Sa 24:24 I will not **s** to the LORD my God
1Ki 8:63 Solomon offered a **s** of fellowship
13: 2 On you he will **s** the priests of the
18:29 until the time for the evening **s**.
18:36 At the time of **s**, the prophet Elijah
18:38 the LORD fell and burned up the **s**,
2Ki 3:20 about the time for offering the **s**,
3:27 offered him as a **s** on the city wall.
10:19 am going to hold a great **s** for Baal.
17:35 to them, serve them or **s** to them.
23:10 so no-one could use it to **s** his son
1Ch 21:24 or **s** a burnt offering that costs me
2Ch 7: 5 King Solomon offered a **s** of
28:23 **s** to them so that they will help me.
29:27 Hezekiah gave the order to **s** the
29:28 All this continued until the **s** of
33:17 The people, however, continued to **s**
Ezr 3: 2 Israel to **s** burnt offerings on it,
7:17 and **s** them on the altar of the
9: 4 there appalled until the evening **s**.
9: 5 Then, at the evening **s**, I rose from
Job 1: 5 Early in the morning he would **s** a
42: 8 **s** a burnt offering for yourselves.
Ps 27: 6 at his tabernacle will I **s** with
40: 6 **S** and offering you did not desire,
50: 5 who made a covenant with me by **s**."
50:14 **S** thank-offerings to God, fulfil
51:16 You do not delight in **s**, or I would
54: 6 I will **s** a freewill offering to you;
66:15 I will **s** fat animals to you and an
107:22 Let them **s** thank-offerings and tell
116:17 I will **s** a thank-offering to you and
141: 2 of my hands be like the evening **s**.
Pr 15: 8 The LORD detests the **s** of the wicked,
21: 3 more acceptable to the LORD than **s**.
21:27 The **s** of the wicked is detestable—
Ecc 5: 1 rather than to offer the **s** of fools,
Isa 34: 6 For the LORD has a **s** in Bozrah and a
57: 5 you **s** your children in the ravines
Jer 32:35 **s** their sons and daughters to Molech,
46:10 the LORD Almighty, will offer **s** in
Eze 20:26 the **s** of every firstborn—that I
20:31 —the **s** of your sons in the fire—
39:17 to the **s** I am preparing for you,
39:17 great **s** on the mountains of Israel.
39:19 At the **s** I am preparing for you, you
43:24 **s** them as a burnt offering to the
46: 2 The priests are to **s** his burnt
Da 8:11 it took away the daily **s** from him,
8:12 and the daily **s** were given over to
8:13 vision concerning the daily **s**,
9:21 about the time of the evening **s**.
9:27 will put an end to **s** and offering.
11:31 and will abolish the daily **s**.
12:11 "From the time that the daily **s** is
Hos 3: 4 without **s** or sacred stones, without
4:13 They **s** on the mountaintops and burn
4:14 **s** with shrine-prostitutes—a people
6: 6 For I desire mercy, not **s**, and
12:11 Do they **s** bulls in Gilgal?
13: 2 "They offer human **s** and kiss the
Jnh 1:16 **s** to the LORD and made vows to him.
2: 9 song of thanksgiving, will **s** to you.
Zep 1: 7 The LORD has prepared a **s**; he has
1: 8 On the day of the LORD's **s** I will
Zec 14:21 and all who come to **s** will take some
Mal 1: 8 you bring blind animals for **s**, is
1: 8 When you **s** crippled or diseased
Mt 9:13 this means: 'I desire mercy, not **s**.
12: 7 'I desire mercy, not **s**,' you would
Mk 14:12 customary to **s** the Passover lamb,
Lk 2:24 to offer a **s** in keeping with what is
Ro 3:25 presented him as a **s** of atonement
1Co 10:19 Do I mean then that a **s** offered to
10:28 "This has been offered in **s**," then
Eph 5: 2 as a fragrant offering and **s** to God.
Php 2:17 **s** and service coming from your faith,
Php 4:18 an acceptable **s**, pleasing to God.
Heb 9:26 away with sin by the **s** of himself.
10: 5 "**S** and offering you did not desire,
10:10 through the **s** of the body of Jesus
10:12 offered for all time one **s** for sins,
10:14 by one **s** he has made perfect for
10:18 there is no longer any **s** for sin.
10:26 of the truth, no **s** for sins is left,
11: 4 By faith Abel offered God a better **s**
11:17 God tested him, offered Isaac as a **s**.
11:17 was about to **s** his one and only son,
13:15 let us continually offer to God a **s**
1Jn 2: 2 He is the atoning **s** for our sins,
4:10 Son as an atoning **s** for our sins.

Sacrificed (Sacrifice)

Ge 8:20 birds, he **s** burnt offerings on it.
22:13 and took the ram and **s** it as a
Ex 24: 5 burnt offerings and **s** young bulls
32: 6 **s** burnt offerings and presented
32: 8 have bowed down to it and **s** to it
Lev 4:10 the ox **s** as a fellowship offering.
9:22 And having **s** the sin offering, the
10:19 "Today they **s** their sin offering
18:21 of your children to be **s** to Molech,
Nu 7:17 to be **s** as a fellowship offering.
7:23 to be **s** as a fellowship offering.
7:29 to be **s** as a fellowship offering.
7:35 to be **s** as a fellowship offering.
7:41 to be **s** as a fellowship offering.
7:47 to be **s** as a fellowship offering.
7:53 to be **s** as a fellowship offering.
7:59 to be **s** as a fellowship offering.
7:65 to be **s** as a fellowship offering.
7:71 to be **s** as a fellowship offering.
7:77 to be **s** as a fellowship offering.
7:83 to be **s** as a fellowship offering.
22:40 Balak **s** cattle and sheep, and gave
Dt 32:17 They **s** to demons, which are not God
Jos 8:31 and **s** fellowship offerings.
Jdg 6:28 bull **s** on the newly-built altar!
13:19 and **s** it on a rock to the LORD.
1Sa 6:14 **s** the cows as a burnt offering to
11:15 There they **s** fellowship offerings
2Sa 6:13 he **s** a bull and a fattened calf.
6:17 and David **s** burnt offerings and
24:25 **s** burnt offerings and fellowship
1Ki 1: 9 Adonijah then **s** sheep, cattle and
1:19 He has **s** great numbers of cattle,
1:25 and **s** great numbers of cattle
3:15 **s** burnt offerings and fellowship
9:25 year Solomon **s** burnt offerings and
2Ki 16: 3 and even **s** his son in the fire,
17:17 They **s** their sons and daughters in
21: 6 He **s** his own son in the fire,
1Ch 15:26 seven bulls and seven rams were **s**.
21:26 **s** burnt offerings and fellowship
2Ch 8:12 **s** burnt offerings to the LORD,
15:11 At that time they **s** to the LORD
28: 3 Hinnom and **s** his sons in the fire,
33: 6 He **s** his sons in the fire in the
33:16 **s** fellowship offerings and
34: 4 graves of those who had **s** to them.
Ezr 3: 3 **s** burnt offerings on it to the LORD,
8:35 **s** burnt offerings to the God of
Ps 106:37 They **s** their sons and their
106:38 whom they **s** to the idols of Canaan,
Eze 16:20 me and **s** them as food to the idols.
16:21 slaughtered my children and **s** them
23:37 they even **s** their children, whom
23:39 the very day they **s** their children
Hos 11: 2 They **s** to the Baals and they burned
Lk 22: 7 which the Passover lamb had to be **s**.
Ac 15:29 to abstain from food **s** to idols,
21:25 should abstain from food **s** to idols,
1Co 5: 7 our Passover lamb, has been **s**.
8: 1 Now about food **s** to idols: We know
8: 4 then, about eating food **s** to idols:
8: 7 of it as having been **s** to an idol,
8:10 to eat what has been **s** to idols?
Heb 7:27 He **s** for their sins once for all
9:28 Christ was **s** once to take away the
Rev 2:14 to sin by eating food **s** to idols
2:20 and the eating of food **s** to idols.

Sacrifices (Sacrifice)
Ge 46: 1 s to the God of his father Isaac.
Ex 3:18 to offer s to the LORD our God.'
5: 3 to offer s to the LORD our God,
8: 8 people go to offer s to the LORD."
8:26 The s we offer the LORD our God
8:26 And if we offer s that are
8:27 to offer s to the LORD our God,
8:28 'I will let you go to offer s to the
8:29 people go to offer s to the LORD."
10:25 "You must allow us to have s and
18:12 a burnt offering and other s to God,
22:20 "Whoever s to any god other than the
34:15 invite you and you will eat their s.
Lev 17: 3 Any Israelite who s an ox, a lamb or
17: 5 the s they are now making in the
17: 7 no longer offer any of their s to
23:37 s and drink offerings required for
Nu 15: 3 LORD—whether burnt offerings or s,
25: 2 who invited them to the s to their
Dt 12: 6 bring your burnt offerings and s,
12:11 you: your burnt offerings and s,
12:27 The blood of your s must be poured
12:31 in the fire as s to their gods.
18:10 be found among you who s his son or
32:38 the gods who ate the fat of their s
33:19 and there offer s of righteousness;
Jos 22:26 not for burnt offerings or s.'
22:27 s and fellowship offerings.
22:28 not for burnt offerings and s, but
22:29 grain offerings and s, other than
Jdg 2: 5 There they offered s to the LORD.
1Sa 6:15 offerings and made s to the LORD.
15:22 delight in burnt offerings and s
2Sa 15:12 While Absalom was offering s, he
15:24 and Abiathar offered s until all the
1Ki 3: 3 except that he offered s and burned
3: 4 The king went to Gibeon to offer s,
8:62 with him offered s before the LORD.
11: 8 incense and offered s to their gods.
12:27 If these people go up to offer s at
12:32 Judah, and offered s on the altar.
12:33 he offered s on the altar he had
22:43 to offer s and burn incense there.
2Ki 5:17 and s to any other god but the LORD.
10:24 they went in to make s and burnt
12: 3 to offer s and burn incense there.
14: 4 to offer s and burn incense there.
15: 4 to offer s and burn incense there.
15:35 to offer s and burn incense there.
16: 4 He offered s and burned incense at
16:15 blood of the burnt offerings and s.
17:31 as s to Adrammelech and Anammelech,
17:36 shall bow down and to him offer s.
1Ch 21:28 the Jebusite, he offered s there.
23:13 to offer s before the LORD, to
29:21 The next day they made s to the LORD
29:21 other s in abundance for all Israel.
2Ch 2: 6 as a place to burn s before him?
7: 1 the burnt offering and the s,
7: 4 the king and all the people offered s
7:12 place for myself as a temple for s.
11:16 to Jerusalem to offer s to the LORD,
25:14 down to them and burned s to them.
28: 3 burned s in the Valley of Ben Hinnom
28: 4 He offered s and burned incense at
28:23 He offered s to the gods of Damascus,
28:25 high places to burn s to other gods
29:31 Come and bring s and thank-offerings
29:31 So the assembly brought s and
29:33 The animals consecrated as s
32:12 before one altar and burn s on it'?
33:22 s to all the idols Manasseh had made.
Ezr 3: 3 LORD, both the morning and evening s.
3: 5 the New Moon s and the s for all the
6: 3 rebuilt as a place to present s,
6:10 that they may offer s pleasing to
Ne 4: 2 Will they offer s? Will they finish
12:43 on that day they offered great s,
Ps 4: 5 Offer right s and trust in the LORD.
20: 3 May he remember all your s and
50: 8 I do not rebuke you for your s or
50:23 He who s thank-offerings honours me,
51:17 The s of God are a broken spirit;
51:19 there will be righteous s, whole
106:28 and ate s offered to lifeless gods;
Ecc 9: 2 who offer s and those who do not.
Isa 1:11 "The multitude of your s—what are
19:21 They will worship with s and grain
43:23 nor honoured me with your s.
43:24 or lavished on me the fat of your s.
56: 7 Their burnt offerings and s will be
57: 7 there you went up to offer your s.
65: 3 offering s in gardens and burning
65: 7 "Because they burned s on the
66: 3 whoever s a bull is like one who
Jer 6:20 your s do not please me."
7:21 other s and eat the meat yourselves!
7:22 about burnt offerings and s,
17:26 bringing burnt offerings and s,
19: 4 they have burned s in it to gods
33:18 grain offerings and to present s.
Eze 20:28 there they offered their s, made
20:40 gifts, along with all your holy s.
40:41 —on which the s were slaughtered.
40:42 the burnt offerings and the other s.
44:11 s for the people and stand before
44:15 me to offer s of fat and blood,
46:24 will cook the s of the people."
Hos 4:19 and their s will bring them shame.
8:13 They offer s given to me and they
9: 4 LORD, nor will their s please him.
9: 4 Such s will be to them like the
Am 4: 4 Bring your s every morning, your
5:25 "Did you bring me s and offerings
Hab 1:16 Therefore he s to his net and burns
Mal 1:13 animals and offer them as s,
1:14 s a blemished animal to the Lord.
2: 3 the offal from your festival s,
Mk 1:44 offer the s that Moses commanded for
12:33 than all burnt offerings and s."
Lk 5:14 offer the s that Moses commanded for
13: 1 blood Pilate had mixed with their s.
Ac 7:41 They brought s to it and held a
7:42 'Did you bring me s and offerings
14:13 the crowd wanted to offer s to them.
Ro 12: 1 to offer your bodies as living s,
1Co 10:18 eat the s participate in the altar?
10:20 No, but the s of pagans are offered
Heb 5: 1 God, to offer gifts and s for sins.
5: 3 This is why he has to offer s for
7:27 does not need to offer s day after
8: 3 appointed to offer both gifts and s,
9: 9 indicating that the gifts and s
9:23 things to be purified with these s,
9:23 themselves with better s than these.
10: 1 by the same s repeated endlessly
10: 3 those s are an annual reminder of
10: 8 First he said, "S and offerings,
10:11 he offers the same s, which can
13:16 for with such s God is pleased.
1Pe 2: 5 offering spiritual s acceptable to

Sacrificing (Sacrifice)
1Sa 2:15 come and say to the man who was s,
7:10 While Samuel was s the burnt
2Sa 6:18 After he had finished s the burnt
1Ki 3: 2 The people, however, were still s at
8: 5 s so many sheep and cattle that they
12:32 he did in Bethel, s to the calves
1Ch 16: 2 After David had finished s the burnt
2Ch 5: 6 s so many sheep and cattle that they
35:14 the descendants of Aaron, were s the
Ezr 4: 2 we seek your God and have been s to
Eze 43:18 regulations for s burnt offerings
Ac 14:18 keeping the crowd from s to them.

Sad (Saddened, Sadness)
Ge 40: 7 "Why are your faces so s today?
Ne 2: 1 not been s in his presence before;
2: 2 "Why does your face look so s when
2: 3 Why should my face not look s when
Ecc 7: 3 a s face is good for the heart.
Mt 19:22 he went away s, because he had
26:22 They were very s and began to say to
Mk 10:22 He went away s, because he had
Lk 18:23 he heard this, he became very s,

Saddened (Sad)
Mk 14:19 They were s, and one by one they

Saddle (Saddlebags, Saddled)
Ge 31:34 put them inside her camel's s and
Jdg 5:10 sitting on your s blankets, and you
1Ki 13:13 to his sons, "S the donkey for me."
13:27 to his sons, "S the donkey for me,"
Eze 27:20 "'Dedan traded in s blankets with

Saddlebags (Saddle)
Ge 49:14 donkey lying down between two s.

Saddled (Saddle)
Ge 22: 3 Abraham got up and s his donkey.
Nu 22:21 in the morning, s his donkey and
Jdg 19:10 his two s donkeys and his concubine.
2Sa 16: 1 He had a string of donkeys s and
17:23 he s his donkey and set out for his
19:26 'I will have my donkey s and will
1Ki 2:40 At this, he s his donkey and went to
13:13 s the donkey for him, he mounted
13:23 him back s his donkey for him.
2Ki 4:24 She s the donkey and said to her

Sadducees
Mt 3: 7 many of the Pharisees and S coming
16: 1 The Pharisees and S came to Jesus
16: 6 the yeast of the Pharisees and S."
16:11 the yeast of the Pharisees and S."
16:12 the teaching of the Pharisees and S.
22:23 That same day the S, who say there
22:34 Hearing that Jesus had silenced the S
Mk 12:18 the S, who say there is no
Lk 20:27 Some of the S, who say there is no
Ac 4: 1 the S came up to Peter and John
5:17 were members of the party of the S,
23: 6 knowing that some of them were S and
23: 7 out between the Pharisees and the S,
23: 8 (The S say that there is no

Sadness (Sad)
Ne 2: 2 This can be nothing but s of heart.

Safe (Safe-conduct, Safeguard, Safekeeping, Safely, Safety)
Dt 29:19 "I will be s, even though I persist
1Sa 20: 7 'Very well,' then your servant is s.
20:21 you are s; there is no danger.
22:23 You will be s with me."
2Sa 18:29 "Is the young man Absalom s?"
18:32 "Is the young man Absalom s?"
2Ch 15: 5 In those days it was not s to travel
Ezr 8:21 a s journey for us and our children,
Job 21: 9 Their homes are s and free from fear;
Ps 12: 7 O LORD, you will keep us s and
16: 1 Keep me s, O God, for in you I take
27: 5 he will keep me s in his dwelling;
31:20 keep them s from accusing tongues.
37: 3 in the land and enjoy s pasture.
Pr 11:15 to strike hands in pledge is s.
18:10 the righteous run to it and are s.
20:28 Love and faithfulness keep a king s;
28:18 He whose walk is blameless is kept s,
28:26 he who walks in wisdom is kept s.
29:25 trusts in the LORD is kept s.
Jer 7:10 "We are s"—s to do all these
12: 5 If you stumble in s country, how will
12:12 land to the other; no-one will be s.
Lk 11:21 own house, his possessions are s.
15:27 he has him back s and sound.'
Jn 17:12 I protected them and kept them s
1Jn 5:18 who was born of God keeps him s,

Safe-conduct (Safe, Conduct)
Ne 2: 7 they will provide me s until I

Safeguard (Safe, Guard)
Php 3: 1 to you again, and it is a s for you.

Safekeeping (Safe, Keep)
Ex 22: 7 his neighbour silver or goods for s
22:10 other animal to his neighbour for s

Safely (Safe)
Ge 19:16 and led them s out of the city,
28:21 that I return s to my father's house,
33:18 he arrived s at the city of Shechem
Lev 25:18 and you will live s in the land.
Jos 10:21 The whole army then returned s to
1Sa 20:13 let you know and send you away s.
2Sa 19:24 left until the day he returned s.
19:30 lord the king has arrived home s."
1Ki 22:27 bread and water until I return s.
22:28 "If you ever return s, the LORD has
2Ch 18:26 bread and water until I return s.
18:27 "If you ever return s, the LORD has
19: 1 Jehoshaphat king of Judah returned s
Ps 78:53 He guided them s, so they were
Zec 8:10 No-one could go about his business s
Ac 23:24 may be taken s to Governor Felix."
28: 1 Once s on shore, we found out that
2Ti 4:18 bring me s to his heavenly kingdom.

Safety (Safe)
Ge 43: 9 I myself will guarantee his s; you
44:32 Your servant guaranteed the boy's s
Lev 25:19 eat your fill and live there in s.
26: 5 you want and live in s in your land.
Dt 12:10 you so that you will live in s.
33:28 Israel will live in s alone; Jacob's
Jdg 18: 7 that the people were living in s,
1Ki 4:25 from Dan to Beersheba, lived in s,
Job 5: 4 His children are far from s, crushed
5:11 and those who mourn are lifted to s.
11:18 about you and take your rest in s.
30:15 wind, my s vanishes like a cloud.
Ps 4: 8 alone, O LORD, make me dwell in s.
141:10 own nets, while I pass by in s.
Pr 1:33 whoever listens to me will live in s
3:23 you will go on your way in s, and
Isa 14:30 and the needy will lie down in s.
Jer 4: 6 Flee for s without delay! For I am
6: 1 "Flee for s, people of Benjamin!
23: 6 be saved and Israel will live in s.
32:37 this place and let them live in s.
33:16 saved and Jerusalem will live in s.
Eze 28:26 They will live there in s and will
28:26 they will live in s when I inflict
34:25 and sleep in the forests in s.
34:28 They will live in s, and no-one
38: 8 and now all of them live in s.
38:14 my people Israel are living in s,
39: 6 who live in s in the coastlands,
39:26 when they lived in s in their land
Hos 2:18 land, so that all may lie down in s.
Zep 2:15 the carefree city that lived in s.
Ac 27:44 this way everyone reached land in s.
1Th 5: 3 people are saying, "Peace and s

Saffron
SS 4:14 nard and s, calamus and cinnamon,

Sag
Ecc 10:18 If a man is lazy, the rafters s;

Sail (Foresail, Sailed, Sailing, Sailors)
1Ki 22:48 but they never set s—they were
22:49 "Let my men s with your men," but
2Ch 20:37 and were not able to set s to trade.
Isa 33:21 them, no mighty ship will s them.
33:23 held secure, the s is not spread.
Eze 27: 7 linen from Egypt was your s and
Ac 18:21 Then he set s from Ephesus.
20: 3 just as he was about to s for Syria,
20:15 The next day we set s from there and
20:16 Paul had decided to s past Ephesus
21: 2 Phoenicia, went on board and set s.
27: 1 decided that we would s for Italy,
27: 2 to s for ports along the coast of
27:12 decided that we should s on,
27:21 taken my advice not to s from Crete;
27:24 the lives of all who s with you.'
28:10 ways and when we were ready to s,
28:13 From there we set s and arrived at

Sailed (Sail)
1Ki 9:28 They s to Ophir and brought back 420
2Ch 8:18 with Solomon's men, s to Ophir
Jnh 1: 3 s for Tarshish to flee from the LORD.
Lk 8:23 they s, he fell asleep. A squall
8:26 They s to the region of the
Ac 13: 4 Seleucia and s from there to Cyprus.
13:13 Paul and his companions s to Perga
14:26 From Attalia they s back to Antioch,
15:39 Barnabas took Mark and s for Cyprus,
16:11 to sea and s straight for Samothrace,
18:18 left the brothers and s for Syria,
18:18 Before he s, he had his hair cut off
20: 6 we s from Philippi after the Feast
20:13 ahead to the ship and s for Assos,
21: 1 out to sea and s straight to Cos.
21: 3 the south of it, we s on to Syria.
27: 5 we had s across the open sea off the
27: 7 we s to the lee of Crete, opposite
27:13 and s along the shore of Crete.

Sailing (Sail)
Ac 27: 6 an Alexandrian ship s for Italy
27: 9 and s had already become dangerous

Sailors (Sail)
1Ki 9:27 Hiram sent his men—s who knew the
Eze 27: 9 All the ships of the sea and their s
Jnh 1: 5 All the s were afraid and each cried
1: 7 the s said to each other, "Come, let
Ac 27:27 s sensed they were approaching land.
27:30 the s let the lifeboat down into the
Rev 18:17 and all who travel by ship, the s,

Saints
1Sa 2: 9 He will guard the feet of his s, but
2Ch 6:41 may your s rejoice in your goodness.
Ps 16: 3 for the s who are in the land, they
30: 4 Sing to the LORD, you s of his;
31:23 Love the LORD, all his s! The LORD
34: 9 Fear the LORD, you his s, for those
52: 9 you in the presence of your s.
79: 2 the flesh of your s to the beasts
85: 8 promises peace to his people, his s
116:15 of the LORD is the death of his s.
132: 9 may your s sing for joy."
132:16 and her s shall ever sing for joy.
145:10 you, O LORD; your s will extol you.
148:14 the praise of all his s, of Israel,
149: 1 his praise in the assembly of the s.
149: 5 Let the s rejoice in this honour and
149: 9 This is the glory of all his s.
Da 7:18 the s of the Most High will receive
7:21 against the s and defeating them,
7:22 in favour of the s of the Most High,
7:25 oppress his s and try to change the
7:25 The s will be handed over to him for
7:27 will be handed over to the s,
8:12 the host ⌊of the s⌋ and the daily
Ac 9:13 he has done to your s in Jerusalem.
9:32 he went to visit the s in Lydda.
26:10 I put many of the s in prison,
Ro 1: 7 are loved by God and called to be s:
8:27 the s in accordance with God's will.
15:25 in the service of the s there.
15:26 the poor among the s in Jerusalem.
15:31 may be acceptable to the s there,
16: 2 the Lord in a way worthy of the s
16:15 and Olympas and all the s with them.
1Co 6: 1 judgment instead of before the s?
6: 2 Do you not know that the s will
14:33 As in all the congregations of the s,
16:15 themselves to the service of the s.
2Co 1: 1 with all the s throughout Achaia:
8: 4 of sharing in this service to the s.
9: 1 to you about this service to the s.
13:13 All the s send their greetings.
Eph 1: 1 To the s in Ephesus, the faithful in
1:15 Jesus and your love for all the s,
1:18 his glorious inheritance in the s,
3:18 together with all the s, to grasp
6:18 keep on praying for all the s.
Php 1: 1 To all the s in Christ Jesus at
4:21 Greet all the s in Christ Jesus.
4:22 All the s send you greetings,
Col 1: 4 of the love you have for all the s
1:12 of the s in the kingdom of light.
1:26 but is now disclosed to the s.
1Ti 5:10 washing the feet of the s, helping
Phm : 5 Jesus and your love for all the s.
: 7 have refreshed the hearts of the s.
Jude : 3 was once for all entrusted to the s.
Rev 5: 8 which are the prayers of the s.
8: 3 with the prayers of all the s, on
8: 4 together with the prayers of the s,
11:18 and your s and those who reverence
13: 7 against the s and to conquer them.
13:10 faithfulness on the part of the s.
14:12 the s who obey God's commandments
16: 6 the blood of your s and prophets,
17: 6 was drunk with the blood of the s,
18:20 O heaven! Rejoice, s and apostles
18:24 the blood of prophets and of the s,
19: 8 for the righteous acts of the s.)

Sake (Sakes)
Ge 12:13 I will be treated well for your s
12:16 He treated Abram well for her s, and
18:24 not spare the place for the s of the
18:26 spare the whole place for their s."
18:29 the s of forty, I will not do it."
18:31 "For the s of twenty, I will not
18:32 "For the s of ten, I will not
26:24 for the s of my servant Abraham."
Ex 18: 8 the Egyptians for Israel's s and
Lev 26:45 for their s I will remember the
Nu 11:29 "Are you jealous for my s? I wish
Jos 23: 3 to all these nations for your s;
1Sa 12:22 For the s of his great name the LORD
2Sa 5:12 for the s of his people Israel.
7:21 For the s of your word and according
9: 1 can show kindness for Jonathan's s?"
9: 7 for the s of your father Jonathan.
18: 5 with the young man Absalom for my s.
18:12 the young man Absalom for my s.'
1Ki 11:12 Nevertheless, for the s of David
11:13 tribe for the s of David my servant
11:13 and for the s of Jerusalem, which I
11:32 for the s of my servant David and
11:34 life for the s of David my servant,
15: 4 Nevertheless, for David's s the LORD
2Ki 8:19 for the s of his servant David,
19:34 for my s and for the s of David my
20: 6 I will defend this city for my s
20: 6 and for the s of my servant David.
1Ch 14: 2 for the s of his people Israel.
16:21 for their s he rebuked kings:
17:19 For the s of your servant and
Ne 10:28 peoples for the s of the Law of God,
Job 18: 4 earth to be abandoned for your s?
Ps 23: 3 of righteousness for his name's s.
25:11 For the s of your name, O LORD,
31: 3 for the s of your name lead and
44:22 Yet for your s we face death all day
69: 7 For I endure scorn for your s, and
79: 9 forgive our sins for your name's s.
105:14 for their s he rebuked kings:
106: 8 Yet he saved them for his name's s,
106:45 for their s he remembered his
109:21 deal well with me for your name's s;
122: 8 For the s of my brothers and friends,
122: 9 For the s of the house of the LORD
132:10 For the s of David your servant, do
143:11 For your name's s, O LORD, preserve
Isa 37:35 for my s and for the s of David my
42:21 pleased the LORD for the s of his
43:14 "For your s I will send to Babylon
43:25 your transgressions, for my own s,
45: 4 For the s of Jacob my servant, of
48: 9 For my own name's s I delay my wrath;
48: 9 for the s of my praise I hold it
48:11 For my own s, for my own s, I do
62: 1 For Zion's s I will not keep silent,
62: 1 for Jerusalem's s I will not remain
63:17 Return for the s of your servants,
Jer 14: 7 do something for the s of your name.
14:21 For the s of your name do not
15:15 of how I suffer reproach for your s.
Eze 20: 9 for the s of my name I did what
20:14 for the s of my name I did what

Eze 20:22 and for the s of my name I did what
20:44 I deal with you for my name's s
36:22 LORD says: It is not for your s,
36:22 but for the s of my holy name, which
36:32 I am not doing this for your s,
Da 9:17 For your s, O Lord, look with favour
9:19 For your s, O my God, do not delay,
Mt 10:39 his life for my s will find it.
15: 3 of God for the s of your tradition?
15: 6 of God for the s of your tradition.
19:29 for my s will receive a hundred
24:22 but for the s of the elect those
Mk 13:20 But for the s of the elect, whom he
Lk 18:29 for the s of the kingdom of God
Jn 11:15 for your s I am glad I was not there,
Ro 1: 5 Through him and for his name's s, we
8:36 "For your s we face death all day
9: 3 Christ for the s of my brothers,
14:20 the work of God for the s of food.
1Co 9:23 I do all this for the s of the
10:28 both for the s of the man who told
10:28 who told you and for conscience' s—
2Co 2:10 in the sight of Christ for your s,
4: 5 as your servants for Jesus' s.
4:11 given over to death for Jesus' s,
5:13 it is for the s of God; if we are in
12:10 That is why, for Christ's s, I
Eph 3: 1 Jesus for the s of you Gentiles—
Php 3: 7 consider loss for the s of Christ.
3: 8 for whose s I have lost all things.
Col 1:24 for the s of his body, which is the
1Th 1: 5 how we lived among you for your s.
2Ti 2:10 everything for the s of the elect,
Tit 1:11 that for the s of dishonest gain.
Heb 11:26 disgrace for the s of Christ as of
1Pe 1:20 in these last times for your s.
2:13 Submit yourselves for the Lord's s
3Jn : 7 was for the s of the Name that they

Sakes (Sake)
2Co 8: 9 yet for your s he became poor, so

Sakia
1Ch 8:10 Jeuz, **S** and Mirmah. These were his

Salamis
Ac 13: 5 they arrived at **S**, they proclaimed

Sale (Sell)
Lev 25:29 redemption a full year after its s.
Dt 18: 8 from the s of family possessions.
28:68 for s to your enemies as male
Ps 44:12 gaining nothing from their s.

Salecah
Dt 3:10 and all Bashan as far as **S** and Edrei,
Jos 12: 5 He ruled over Mount Hermon, **S**, all
13:11 Hermon and all Bashan as far as **S**—
1Ch 5:11 next to them in Bashan, as far as **S**:

Salem
Ge 14:18 Melchizedek king of **S** brought out
Ps 76: 2 His tent is in **S**, his dwelling-place
Heb 7: 1 This Melchizedek was king of **S** and
7: 2 "king of **S**" means "king of peace".

Sales (Sell)
Ac 4:34 them, brought the money from the s

Salim
Jn 3:23 also was baptising at Aenon near **S**,

Saliva
1Sa 21:13 and letting s run down his beard.
Jn 9: 6 made some mud with the s, and put

Sallai
Ne 11: 8 his followers, Gabbai and **S**—928 men

Sallu (Sallu's)
1Ch 9: 7 the Benjamites: **S** son of Meshullam,
Ne 11: 7 From the descendants of Benjamin: **S**
12: 7 **S**, Amok, Hilkiah and Jedaiah. These

Sallu's (Sallu)
Ne 12:20 of **S**, Kallai; of Amok's, Eber;

Salma
1Ch 2:51 **S** the father of Bethlehem, and
2:54 The descendants of **S**: Bethlehem, the

Salmon
Ru 4:20 of Nahshon, Nahshon the father of **S**,
4:21 **S** the father of Boaz, Boaz the
1Ch 2:11 Nahshon was the father of **S**,
2:11 **S** the father of Boaz,
Mt 1: 4 of Nahshon, Nahshon the father of **S**,
1: 5 **S** the father of Boaz, whose mother
Lk 3:32 the son of **S**, the son of Nahshon,

Salmone
Ac 27: 7 to the lee of Crete, opposite **S**.

Salome
Mk 15:40 the younger and of Joses, and **S**.
16: 1 Mary the mother of James, and **S**

Salt (Salted, Saltiness, Salty)
Ge 14: 3 in the Valley of Siddim (the **S** Sea).
19:26 back, and she became a pillar of s.
Lev 2:13 all your grain offerings with s.
2:13 Do not leave the s of the covenant
2:13 add s to all your offerings.
Nu 18:19 It is an everlasting covenant of s
34: 3 start from the end of the **S** Sea,
34:12 the Jordan and end at the **S** Sea.
Dt 3:17 the Sea of the Arabah (the **S** Sea),
29:23 a burning waste of s and sulphur—
Jos 3:16 the Sea of the Arabah (the **S** Sea)
12: 3 the Sea of the Arabah (the **S** Sea),
15: 2 at the southern end of the **S** Sea,
15: 5 The eastern boundary is the **S** Sea as
15:62 Nibshan, the City of **S** and En Gedi
18:19 at the northern bay of the **S** Sea,
Jdg 9:45 the city and scattered s over it.
2Sa 8:13 Edomites in the Valley of **S**.
2Ki 2:20 bowl," he said, "and put s in it."
2:21 the spring and threw the s into it,
14: 7 Edomites in the Valley of **S** and
1Ch 18:12 Edomites in the Valley of **S**.
2Ch 13: 5 for ever by a covenant of s?
25:11 and led his army to the Valley of **S**,
Ezr 6: 9 and wheat, s, wine and oil, as
7:22 of olive oil, and s without limit.
Job 6: 6 Is tasteless food eaten without s,
30: 4 In the brush they gathered s herbs,
39: 6 home, the s flats as his habitat.
Ps 60: T Edomites in the Valley of **S**.
107:34 fruitful land into a s waste,
Jer 17: 6 in a s land where no-one lives.
48: 9 Put s on Moab, for she will be laid
Eze 16: 4 rubbed with s or wrapped in cloths.
43:24 and the priests are to sprinkle s on
47: 9 there and makes the s water fresh;
47:11 they will be left for s.
Zep 2: 9 a place of weeds and s pits,
Mt 5:13 "You are the s of the earth.
5:13 But if the s loses its saltiness,
Mk 9:50 "**S** is good, but if it loses its
9:50 "s is good, but if it loses its
Lk 14:34 "**S** is good, but if it loses its
Col 4: 6 seasoned with s, so that you may
Jas 3:11 Can both fresh water and s water
3:12 can a s spring produce fresh water.

Salt Sea See **Dead Sea**

Salted (Salt)
Ex 30:35 It is to be s and pure and sacred.
Mk 9:49 Everyone will be s with fire.

Saltiness (Salt)
Mt 5:13 But if the salt loses its s, how can
Mk 9:50 "Salt is good, but if it loses its s,
Lk 14:34 "Salt is good, but if it loses its s,

Salty (Salt)
Mt 5:13 how can it be made s again? It is no
Mk 9:50 how can you make it s again?
Lk 14:34 how can it be made s again?

Salu
Nu 25:14 **S**, the leader of a Simeonite family.

Salvation (Save)
Ex 15: 2 and my song; he has become my s.
2Sa 22: 3 my shield and the horn of my s.
23: 5 Will he not bring to fruition my s
1Ch 16:23 proclaim his s day after day.
2Ch 6:41 O LORD God, be clothed with s, may
Ps 9:14 of Zion and there rejoice in your s.
13: 5 my heart rejoices in your s.
14: 7 Oh, that s for Israel would come out
18: 2 and the horn of my s, my stronghold.
27: 1 The LORD is my light and my s—whom
28: 8 fortress of s for his anointed one.
35: 3 Say to my soul, "I am your s."
35: 9 in the LORD and delight in his s.
37:39 The s of the righteous comes from
40:10 I speak of your faithfulness and s.
40:16 those who love your s always say,
50:23 that I may show him the s of God."
51:12 Restore to me the joy of your s and
53: 6 Oh, that s for Israel would come out
62: 1 in God alone; my s comes from him.
62: 2 He alone is my rock and my s; he is
62: 6 He alone is my rock and my s; he is
62: 7 My s and my honour depend on God;
67: 2 on earth, your s among all nations.
69:13 O God, answer me with your sure s.
69:27 do not let them share in your s.
69:29 may your s, O God, protect me.
70: 4 those who love your s always say,
71:15 of your s all day long, though I
74:12 of old; you bring s upon the earth.
85: 7 love, O LORD, and grant us your s.
85: 9 Surely his s is near those who fear
91:16 I satisfy him and show him my s."
95: 1 us shout aloud to the Rock of our s.
96: 2 proclaim his s day after day.
98: 1 his holy arm have worked s for him.
98: 2 The LORD has made his s known and
98: 3 earth have seen the s of our God.
116:13 I will lift up the cup of s and call
118:14 and my song; he has become my s.
118:21 answered me; you have become my s.
119:41 your s according to your promise;
119:81 soul faints with longing for your s,
119:123 My eyes fail, looking for your s,
119:155 **S** is far from the wicked, for they
119:166 I wait for your s, O LORD, and I
119:174 I long for your s, O LORD, and your
132:16 I will clothe her priests with s,
149: 4 he crowns the humble with s.
Isa 12: 2 Surely God is my s; I will trust and
12: 2 and my song; he has become my s."
12: 3 will draw water from the wells of s.
25: 9 us rejoice and be glad in his s."
26: 1 God makes s its walls and ramparts.
26:18 We have not brought s to the earth;
30:15 "In repentance and rest is your s,
33: 2 morning, our s in time of distress.
33: 6 a rich store of s and wisdom and
45: 8 earth open wide, let s spring up,
45:17 by the LORD with an everlasting s;
46:13 and my s will not be delayed.
46:13 I will grant s to Zion, my splendour
49: 6 my s to the ends of the earth."
49: 8 and in the day of s I will help you;
51: 5 my s is on the way, and my arm will
51: 6 But my s will last for ever, my
51: 8 ever, my s through all generations."
52: 7 who proclaim s, who say to Zion,
52:10 the earth will see the s of our God.
56: 1 for my s is close at hand and my
59:16 so his own arm worked s for him,

Isa 59:17 and the helmet of **s** on his head;
60:18 your walls **S** and your gates Praise.
61:10 has clothed me with garments of **s**
62: 1 dawn, her **s** like a blazing torch.
63: 5 so my own arm worked **s** for me,
Jer 3:23 the LORD our God is the **s** of Israel.
Lam 3:26 wait quietly for the **s** of the LORD.
Jnh 2: 9 **S** comes from the LORD."
Zec 9: 9 righteous and having **s**, gentle and
Lk 1:69 He has raised up a horn of **s** for us
1:71 **s** from our enemies and from the hand
1:77 to give his people the knowledge of **s**
2:30 For my eyes have seen your **s**,
3: 6 all mankind will see God's **s**.'
19: 9 Jesus said to him, "Today **s** has come
Jn 4:22 we do know, for **s** is from the Jews.
Ac 4:12 **S** is found in no-one else, for there
13:26 this message of **s** has been sent.
13:47 bring **s** to the ends of the earth.'"
28:28 **s** has been sent to the Gentiles,
Ro 1:16 for the **s** of everyone who believes:
11:11 **s** has come to the Gentiles to make
13:11 because our **s** is nearer now than
2Co 1: 6 it is for your comfort and **s**; if we
6: 2 and in the day of **s** I helped you.
6: 2 God's favour, now is the day of **s**.
7:10 leads to **s** and leaves no regret,
Eph 1:13 word of truth, the gospel of your **s**.
6:17 Take the helmet of **s** and the sword
Php 2:12 out your **s** with fear and trembling,
1Th 5: 8 and the hope of **s** as a helmet.
5: 9 **s** through our Lord Jesus Christ.
2Ti 2:10 that they too may obtain the **s** that
3:15 for **s** through faith in Christ Jesus.
Tit 2:11 For the grace of God that brings **s**
Heb 1:14 to serve those who will inherit **s**?
2: 3 escape if we ignore such a great **s**?
2: 3 This **s**, which was first announced
2:10 their **s** perfect through suffering.
5: 9 of eternal **s** for all who obey
6: 9 your case—things that accompany **s**.
9:28 **s** to those who are waiting for him.
1Pe 1: 5 until the coming of the **s** that is
1: 9 of your faith, the **s** of your souls.
1:10 Concerning this **s**, the prophets, who
2: 2 by it you may grow up in your **s**,
2Pe 3:15 that our Lord's patience means **s**,
Jude :3 write to you about the **s** we share,
Rev 7:10 "**S** belongs to our God, who sits on
12:10 "Now have come the **s** and the power
19: 1 "Hallelujah! **S** and glory and power

Salve

Rev 3:18 and **s** to put on your eyes,

Samaria (Samaritan, Samaritans)

1. City built by King Omri on hill of Samaria, which he bought from Shemer (1Ki 16:24). It replaced Tirzah as capital of northern kingdom (1Ki 16:23, 28–29), and remained the royal residence until the Assyrian conquest (2Ki 17:5–6). Site of ornate palace built by Ahab (1Ki 22:39; Am 3:15), and also his temple to Baal (1Ki 16:32–33). Prophets condemned its pride and idolatry (Isa 9:9; Jer 23:13; Eze 16:46–55; Am 6:1; Mic 1:1). The prophets Elisha (2Ki 5:3) and Oded (2Ch 28:9) lived here. Site of assassinations of Ahab's sons (2Ki 10:1–17), Shallum (2Ki 15:14) and Pekahiah (2Ki 15:25). Twice under Syrian siege (1Ki 20:1; 2Ki 6:24), but did not fall until the Assyrian conquest. Became inhabited by refugees from other conquered countries (2Ki 17:24); led to intermarriage with remaining Jews, and the birth of a despised people (Jn 4:9). Philip preached here (Ac 8:5) and Peter and John were sent to support the new church (Ac 8:14; 9:31).
2. The name of the city extended to include the surrounding region, which became a province under Roman occupation (Lk 17:11; Ac 1:8; 8:1; 9:31; 15:3).

1Ki 13:32 high places in the towns of **S** will
16:24 He bought the hill of **S** from Shemer
16:24 calling it **S**, after Shemer, the name
16:28 his fathers and was buried in **S**.
16:29 and he reigned in **S** over Israel for
16:32 temple of Baal that he built in **S**.
18: 2 Now the famine was severe in **S**,
20: 1 up and besieged **S** and attacked it.
20:10 if enough dust remains in **S** to give
20:17 reported, "Men are advancing from **S**.
20:34 in Damascus, as my father did in **S**.
20:43 of Israel went to his palace in **S**.
21: 1 to the palace of Ahab king of **S**.
21:18 Ahab king of Israel, who rules in **S**.
22:10 by the entrance of the gate of **S**,
22:37 the king died and was brought to **S**,
22:38 in **S** (where the prostitutes bathed),
22:51 became king of Israel in **S** in the
2Ki 1: 2 upper room in **S** and injured himself.
1: 3 of the king of **S** and ask them,
2:25 Carmel and from there returned to **S**.
3: 1 became king of Israel in **S** in the
3: 6 King Joram set out from **S** and
5: 3 would see the prophet who is in **S**!
6:19 And he led them to **S**.
6:20 and there they were, inside **S**.
6:24 and marched up and laid siege to **S**.
7: 1 for a shekel at the gate of **S**."
7:18 for a shekel at the gate of **S**."
10: 1 Now there were in **S** seventy sons of
10: 1 wrote letters and sent them to **S**:
10:12 Jehu then set out and went towards **S**
10:17 Jehu came to **S**, he killed all who
10:35 his fathers and was buried in **S**.
10:36 Israel in **S** was twenty-eight years.
13: 1 of Jehu became king of Israel in **S**,
13: 6 Asherah pole remained standing in **S**.
13: 9 his fathers and was buried in **S**.
13:10 became king of Israel in **S**, and he
13:13 in **S** with the kings of Israel.
14:14 took hostages and returned to **S**.
14:16 in **S** with the kings of Israel.
14:23 king of Israel became king in **S**,
15: 8 became king of Israel in **S**, and he
15:13 and he reigned in **S** for one month.
15:14 of Gadi went from Tirzah up to **S**.
15:14 attacked Shallum son of Jabesh in **S**,
15:17 and he reigned in **S** for ten years.
15:23 became king of Israel in **S**, and he
15:25 citadel of the royal palace at **S**.
15:27 became king of Israel in **S**, and he
17: 1 became king in Israel in **S**, and he
17: 5 marched against **S** and laid siege to
17: 6 the king of Assyria captured **S** and
17:24 settled them in the towns of **S** to
17:24 took over **S** and lived in its towns.
17:26 resettled in the towns of **S** do not
17:27 from **S** go back to live there
17:28 from **S** came to live in Bethel
17:29 shrines the people of **S** had made at
18: 9 against **S** and laid siege to it.
18:10 So **S** was captured in Hezekiah's
18:34 Have they rescued **S** from my hand?
21:13 the measuring line used against **S**
23:18 of the prophet who had come from **S**.
23:19 had built in the towns of **S** that
2Ch 18: 2 he went down to visit Ahab in **S**.
18: 9 by the entrance to the gate of **S**,
22: 9 him while he was hiding in **S**.
25:13 Judean towns from **S** to Beth Horon.
25:24 and the hostages, and returned to **S**.
28: 8 which they carried back to **S**.
28: 9 meet the army when it returned to **S**.
28:15 City of Palms, and returned to **S**.
Ezr 4:10 **S** and elsewhere in Trans-Euphrates.
4:17 **S** and elsewhere in Trans-Euphrates:
Ne 4: 2 of his associates and the army of **S**,
Isa 7: 9 The head of Ephraim is **S**, and the
7: 9 head of **S** is only Remaliah's son.
8: 4 the plunder of **S** will be carried off
9: 9 the inhabitants of **S**—who say with
10: 9 like Arpad, and **S** like Damascus?
10:10 excelled those of Jerusalem and **S**—
10:11 as I dealt with **S** and her idols?'
36:19 Have they rescued **S** from my hand?
Jer 23:13 "Among the prophets of **S** I saw this
31: 5 plant vineyards on the hills of **S**;
41: 5 Shiloh and **S**, bringing grain
Eze 16:46 Your older sister was **S**, who lived
16:51 **S** did not commit half the sins you
16:53 and of **S** and her daughters,
16:55 and **S** with her daughters, will
23: 4 Oholah is **S**, and Oholibah is
23:33 the cup of your sister **S**.
Hos 7: 1 and the crimes of **S** revealed.
8: 5 Throw out your calf-idol, O **S**!
8: 6 be broken in pieces, that calf of **S**.
10: 5 The people who live in **S** fear for
10: 7 **S** and its king will float away like
13:16 The people of **S** must bear their
Am 3: 9 yourselves on the mountains of **S**;
3:12 those who sit in **S** on the edge of
4: 1 you cows of Bashan on Mount **S**, you
6: 1 to you who feel secure on Mount **S**,
8:14 They who swear by the shame of **S**, or
Ob :19 occupy the fields of Ephraim and **S**,
Mic 1: 1 he saw concerning **S** and Jerusalem.
1: 5 Is it not **S**? What is Judah's high
1: 6 "Therefore I will make **S** a heap of
Lk 17:11 the border between **S** and Galilee.
Jn 4: 4 Now he had to go through **S**.
4: 5 he came to a town in **S** called Sychar,
Ac 1: 8 and in all Judea and **S**, and to the
8: 1 scattered throughout Judea and **S**.
8: 5 Philip went down to a city in **S** and
8: 9 city and amazed all the people of **S**.
8:14 that **S** had accepted the word of God,
9:31 and **S** enjoyed a time of peace.
15: 3 travelled through Phoenicia and **S**,

Samaritan (Samaria)

Lk 9:52 who went into a **S** village to get
10:33 a **S**, as he travelled, came where the
17:16 and thanked him—and he was a **S**.)
Jn 4: 7 a **S** woman came to draw water, Jesus
4: 9 The **S** woman said to him, "You are a
4: 9 "You are a Jew and I am a **S** woman.
8:48 you are a **S** and demon-possessed?"
Ac 8:25 the gospel in many **S** villages.

Samaritans (Samaria)

Mt 10: 5 Gentiles or enter any town of the **S**.
Jn 4: 9 (For Jews do not associate with **S**.)
4:22 You **S** worship what you do not know;
4:39 Many of the **S** from that town
4:40 when the **S** came to him, they urged

Samgar

Jer 39: 3 Middle Gate: Nergal-Sharezer of **S**,

Samlah

Ge 36:36 Hadad died, **S** from Masrekah
36:37 **S** died, Shaul from Rehoboth on the
1Ch 1:47 Hadad died, **S** from Masrekah
1:48 **S** died, Shaul from Rehoboth on the

Samos

Ac 20:15 day after that we crossed over to **S**,

Samothrace

Ac 16:11 to sea and sailed straight for **S**,

Sample (Sampled)

Pr 23:30 who go to **s** bowls of mixed wine.

Sampled (Sample)

Jos 9:14 The men of Israel **s** their provisions

Samson (Samson's)

Judge. Birth promised (Jdg 13:2–3); set apart as Nazirite (Jdg 13:4–7); great strength linked with uncut hair (Jdg 16:17,22). Married Philistine (Jdg 14); killed lion, 30 Philistines (Jdg 14:6,19). Took vengeance on Philistines when wife given away (Jdg 15); killed 1,000 with jaw-bone (Jdg 15:15–16). Carried off gates of Gaza (Jdg 16:1–3). Betrayed by Delilah and captured (Jdg 16:4–21); died when brought temple of Dagon down on Philistines (Jdg 16:23–30).

Jdg 13:24 gave birth to a boy and named him **S**.
14: 1 **S** went down to Timnah and saw there
14: 3 But **S** said to his father, "Get her
14: 5 **S** went down to Timnah together with
14:10 And **S** made a feast there, as was
14:12 "Let me tell you a riddle," **S** said
14:18 **S** said to them, "If you had not

Jdg 15: 1 **S** took a young goat and went to
15: 3 **S** said to them, "This time I have a
15: 6 told, "**S**, the Timnite's son-in-law
15: 7 **S** said to them, "Since you've acted
15:10 "We have come to take **S** prisoner,"
15:11 in the rock of Etam and said to **S**,
15:12 **S** said, "Swear to me that you won't
15:16 **S** said, "With a donkey's jaw-bone I
15:19 When **S** drank, his strength returned
15:20 **S** led Israel for twenty years in the
16: 1 One day **S** went to Gaza, where he saw
16: 2 of Gaza were told, "**S** is here!"
16: 3 **S** lay there only until the middle of
16: 6 Delilah said to **S**, "Tell me the
16: 7 **S** answered her, "If anyone ties me
16: 9 "**S**, the Philistines are upon you!"
16:10 Delilah said to **S**, "You have made a
16:12 "**S**, the Philistines are upon you!"
16:13 Delilah then said to **S**, "Until now,
16:14 Again she called to him, "**S**, the
16:20 she called, "**S**, the Philistines are
16:23 has delivered **S**, our enemy, into our
16:25 "Bring out **S** to entertain us.
16:25 So they called **S** out of the prison,
16:26 **S** said to the servant who held his
16:27 men and women watching **S** perform.
16:28 **S** prayed to the LORD, "O Sovereign
16:29 **S** reached towards the two central
16:30 **S** said, "Let me die with the
Heb 11:32 Barak, **S**, Jephthah, David, Samuel

Samson's (Samson)

Jdg 14:15 the fourth day, they said to **S** wife,
14:16 **S** wife threw herself on him, sobbing,
14:20 **S** wife was given to the friend who

Samuel (Samuel's)

Judge and prophet (Ac 3:24; 13:20). Born to Hannah, who vowed to dedicate him to God (1Sa 1:9–20). Taken to temple to be raised by Eli (1Sa 1:21–28; 2:11,18–21). Called by God (1Sa 3). Led Israel to victory over Philistines (1Sa 7). Asked by people for a king (1Sa 8); anointed Saul (1Sa 9–10). Farewell speech (1Sa 12). Rebuked Saul (1Sa 13:8–14; 15); and announced his rejection by God (1Sa 13:13–14; 15:22–26). Anointed David (1Sa 16:1–13); protected David (1Sa 19:18–24). Death (1Sa 25:1). Spirit called up by Saul (1Sa 28:11–19).

1Sa 1:20 She named him **S**, saying, "Because I
2:18 **S** was ministering before the LORD—a
2:21 Meanwhile, the boy **S** grew up in the
2:26 the boy **S** continued to grow in
3: 1 The boy **S** ministered before the LORD
3: 3 and **S** was lying down in the temple
3: 4 the LORD called **S**. **S** answered, "Here
3: 6 Again the LORD called, "**S**!"
3: 6 And **S** got up and went to Eli and
3: 7 Now **S** did not yet know the LORD: The
3: 8 The LORD called **S** a third time, and
3: 8 and **S** got up and went to Eli and
3: 9 Eli told **S**, "Go and lie down, and if
3: 9 So **S** went and lay down in his place.
3:10 "**S**! **S**!" Then **S** said, "Speak, for
3:11 the LORD said to **S**: "See, I am about
3:15 **S** lay down until morning and then
3:16 Eli called him and said, "**S**, my son."
3:16 **S** answered, "Here I am."
3:18 **S** told him everything, hiding
3:19 The LORD was with **S** as he grew up,
3:20 recognised that **S** was attested as a
3:21 himself to **S** through his word.
7: 3 **S** said to the whole house of Israel,
7: 5 **S** said, "Assemble all Israel at
7: 6 And **S** was leader of Israel at Mizpah.
7: 8 They said to **S**, "Do not stop crying
7: 9 **S** took a suckling lamb and offered
7:10 While **S** was sacrificing the burnt
7:12 **S** took a stone and set it up between
7:15 **S** continued as judge over Israel all
8: 1 **S** grew old, he appointed his sons as
8: 4 together and came to **S** at Ramah.
8: 6 this displeased **S**; so he prayed to
8:10 **S** told all the words of the LORD to
8:19 the people refused to listen to **S**.
1Sa 8:21 **S** heard all that the people said, he
8:22 Then **S** said to the men of Israel,
9:14 there was **S**, coming towards them on
9:15 the LORD had revealed this to **S**:
9:17 **S** caught sight of Saul, the LORD
9:18 Saul approached **S** in the gateway and
9:19 "I am the seer," **S** replied. "Go up
9:22 **S** brought Saul and his servant into
9:23 **S** said to the cook, "Bring the piece
9:24 **S** said, "Here is what has been kept
9:24 And Saul dined with **S** that day.
9:25 **S** talked with Saul on the roof of
9:26 and **S** called to Saul on the roof
9:26 he and **S** went outside together.
9:27 **S** said to Saul, "Tell the servant to
10: 1 **S** took a flask of oil and poured it
10: 9 Saul turned to leave **S**, God changed
10:14 were not to be found, we went to **S**."
10:15 "Tell me what **S** said to you."
10:16 what **S** had said about the kingship.
10:17 **S** summoned the people of Israel to
10:20 **S** brought all the tribes of Israel
10:24 **S** said to all the people, "Do you
10:25 **S** explained to the people the
10:25 Then **S** dismissed the people, each to
11: 7 who does not follow Saul and **S**.
11:12 The people then said to **S**, "Who was
11:14 **S** said to the people, "Come, let us
12: 1 **S** said to all Israel, "I have
12: 5 **S** said to them, "The LORD is witness
12: 6 **S** said to the people, "It is the
12:11 Barak, Jephthah and **S**, and he
12:18 **S** called upon the LORD, and that
12:18 stood in awe of the LORD and of **S**.
12:19 The people all said to **S**, "Pray to
12:20 "Do not be afraid," **S** replied. "You
13: 8 the time set by **S**; but **S** did not
13:10 **S** arrived, and Saul went out to
13:11 "What have you done?" asked **S**.
13:13 "You acted foolishly," **S** said.
13:15 **S** left Gilgal and went up to Gibeah
15: 1 **S** said to Saul, "I am the one the
15:10 the word of the LORD came to **S**:
15:11 **S** was troubled, and he cried out to
15:12 Early in the morning **S** got up and
15:13 **S** reached him, Saul said, "The LORD
15:14 **S** said, "What then is this bleating
15:16 "Stop!" **S** said to Saul. "Let me tell
15:17 **S** said, "Although you were once
15:22 **S** replied: "Does the LORD delight in
15:24 Saul said to **S**, "I have sinned.
15:26 **S** said to him, "I will not go back
15:27 **S** turned to leave, Saul caught hold
15:28 **S** said to him, "The LORD has torn
15:31 **S** went back with Saul, and Saul
15:32 **S** said, "Bring me Agag king of the
15:33 **S** said, "As your sword has made
15:33 And **S** put Agag to death before the
15:34 **S** left for Ramah, but Saul went up
15:35 Until the day **S** died, he did not go
15:35 Saul again, though **S** mourned for him.
16: 1 The LORD said to **S**, "How long will
16: 2 **S** said, "How can I go? Saul will
16: 4 **S** did what the LORD said. When he
16: 5 **S** replied, "Yes, in peace; I have
16: 6 they arrived, **S** saw Eliab and
16: 7 the LORD said to **S**, "Do not consider
16: 8 and made him pass in front of **S**.
16: 8 But **S** said, "The LORD has not chosen
16: 9 but **S** said, "Nor has the LORD chosen
16:10 seven of his sons pass before **S**,
16:10 but **S** said to him, "The LORD has not
16:11 **S** said, "Send for him; we will not
16:13 **S** took the horn of oil and anointed
16:13 **S** then went to Ramah.
19:18 he went to **S** at Ramah and told him
19:18 **S** went to Naioth and stayed there.
19:20 with **S** standing there as their
19:22 And he asked, "Where are **S** and David?
25: 1 Now **S** died, and all Israel assembled
28: 3 Now **S** was dead, and all Israel had
28:11 up for you?" "Bring up **S**," he said.
28:12 the woman saw **S**, she cried out at
28:14 Then Saul knew it was **S**, and he
28:15 **S** said to Saul, "Why have you
28:16 **S** said, "Why do you consult me, now
1Ch 6:27 son, Elkanah his son and **S** his son.
6:28 The sons of **S**: Joel the firstborn
6:33 the son of Joel, the son of **S**,
7: 2 Ibsam and **S**—heads of their families.
9:22 of trust by David and **S** the seer.
11: 3 as the LORD had promised through **S**.
26:28 everything dedicated by **S** the seer
29:29 in the records of **S** the seer,
2Ch 35:18 since the days of the prophet **S**;
Ps 99: 6 **S** was among those who called on his
Jer 15: 1 "Even if Moses and **S** were to stand
Ac 3:24 "Indeed, all the prophets from **S** on,
13:20 until the time of **S** the prophet.
Heb 11:32 Jephthah, David, **S** and the prophets,

Samuel's (Samuel)

1Sa 4: 1 **S** word came to all Israel. Now the
7:13 Throughout **S** lifetime, the hand of
19:24 and also prophesied in **S** presence.
28:20 filled with fear because of **S** words.

Sanballat

Horonite; governor of Samaria; leading opponent of Nehemiah in his task to rebuild walls of Jerusalem (Ne 2:10,19; 4:1–9; 6).

Ne 2:10 **S** the Horonite and Tobiah the
2:19 when **S** the Horonite, Tobiah the
4: 1 **S** heard that we were rebuilding the
4: 7 when **S**, Tobiah, the Arabs, the
6: 1 word came to **S**, Tobiah, Geshem the
6: 2 **S** and Geshem sent me this message:
6: 5 Then, the fifth time, **S** sent his
6:12 because Tobiah and **S** had hired him.
6:14 Remember Tobiah and **S**, O my God,
13:28 was son-in-law to **S** the Horonite.

Sanctified (Sanctify)

Jn 17:19 that they too may be truly s.
Ac 20:32 among all those who are s.
26:18 those who are s by faith in me.'
Ro 15:16 to God, s by the Holy Spirit.
1Co 1: 2 to those s in Christ Jesus and
6:11 But you were washed, you were s, you
7:14 husband has been s through his wife,
7:14 s through her believing husband.
1Th 4: 3 is God's will that you should be s:
Heb 10:29 blood of the covenant that s him,

Sanctify (Sanctified, Sanctifying)

Jn 17:17 **S** them by the truth; your word is
17:19 For them I s myself, that they too
1Th 5:23 peace, s you through and through.
Heb 9:13 s them so that they are outwardly

Sanctifying (Sanctify)

2Th 2:13 through the s work of the Spirit
1Pe 1: 2 through the s work of the Spirit,

Sanctuaries (Sanctuary)

Lev 26:31 into ruins and lay waste your s,
Eze 7:24 and their s will be desecrated.
28:18 trade you have desecrated your s.
Am 7: 9 and the s of Israel will be ruined;

Sanctuary (Sanctuaries)

Ex 15:17 s, O Lord, your hands established.
25: 8 "Then have them make a s for me, and
30:13 s shekel, which weighs twenty gerahs.
30:24 —all according to the s shekel—
35:19 worn for ministering in the s—
36: 1 all the work of constructing the s
36: 3 out the work of constructing the s.
36: 4 the work on the s left their
36: 6 else as an offering for the s.
38:24 used for all the work on the s was
38:24 shekels, according to the s shekel.
38:25 shekels, according to the s shekel—
38:26 according to the s shekel, from
38:27 used to cast the bases for the s
39: 1 garments for ministering in the s.
39:41 worn for ministering in the s,
Lev 4: 6 in front of the curtain of the s.
5:15 silver, according to the s shekel.

Lev 10: 4 camp, away from the front of the s.”
10:17 eat the sin offering in the s area?
10:18 goat in the s area, as I commanded.”
12: 4 or go to the s until the days of
16: 3 “This is how Aaron is to enter the s
19:30 Sabbaths and have reverence for my s
20: 3 he has defiled my s and profaned my
21:12 nor leave the s of his God or
21:23 the altar, and so desecrate my s.
26: 2 Sabbaths and have reverence for my s
27: 3 silver, according to the s shekel;
27:25 to be set according to the s shekel,
Nu 3:10 who approaches the s must be put to
3:28 responsible for the care of the s.
3:31 the altars, the articles of the s
3:32 responsible for the care of the s.
3:38 responsible for the care of the s
3:38 who approached the s was to be put
3:47 s shekel, which weighs twenty gerahs.
3:50 according to the s shekel.
4:12 used for ministering in the s,
4:19 his sons are to go into the s and
7:13 both according to the s shekel, each
7:19 both according to the s shekel, each
7:25 both according to the s shekel, each
7:31 both according to the s shekel, each
7:37 both according to the s shekel, each
7:43 both according to the s shekel, each
7:49 both according to the s shekel, each
7:55 both according to the s shekel, each
7:61 both according to the s shekel, each
7:67 both according to the s shekel, each
7:73 both according to the s shekel, each
7:79 both according to the s shekel, each
7:85 shekels, according to the s shekel.
7:86 each, according to the s shekel.
8:19 Israelites when they go near the s.”
18: 1 for offences against the s,
18: 3 furnishings of the s or the altar,
18: 5 for the care of the s and the altar,
18: 7 near the s must be put to death.”
18:16 s shekel, which weighs twenty gerahs.
19:20 he has defiled the s of the LORD.
28: 7 drink offering to the LORD at the s.
31: 6 articles from the s and the
Jos 22:27 at his s with our burnt offerings,
1Ki 6: 5 inner s he built a structure around
6:16 an inner s, the Most Holy Place.
6:19 He prepared the inner s within the
6:20 The inner s was twenty cubits long,
6:21 across the front of the inner s,
6:22 altar that belonged to the inner s.
6:23 In the inner s he made a pair of
6:31 For the entrance of the inner s he
7:49 the left, in front of the inner s);
8: 6 place in the inner s of the temple,
8: 8 Holy Place in front of the inner s,
1Ch 9:29 and all the other articles of the s,
22:19 Begin to build the s of the LORD God,
24: 5 for there were officials of the s
28:10 chosen you to build a temple as a s.
2Ch 4:20 front of the inner s as prescribed;
5: 7 place in the inner s of the temple,
5: 9 seen from in front of the inner s,
20: 8 in it a s for your Name, saying,
26:18 Leave the s, for you have been
29: 5 Remove all defilement from the s.
29: 7 at the s to the God of Israel.
29:16 The priests went into the s of the
29:21 kingdom, for the s and for Judah.
30: 8 Come to the s, which he has
30:19 according to the rules of the s.”
36:17 young men with the sword in the s,
Ezr 9: 8 and giving us a firm place in his s,
Ne 10:39 the articles for the s are kept
Ps 15: 1 LORD, who may dwell in your s? Who
20: 2 May he send you help from the s and
60: 6 God has spoken from his s: “In
63: 2 I have seen you in the s and beheld
68:17 ⌊has come⌋ from Sinai into his s.
68:24 of my God and King into the s.
68:35 You are awesome, O God, in your s;
73:17 till I entered the s of God; then I
74: 3 the enemy has brought on the s.
74: 7 They burned your s to the ground;
78:69 He built his s like the heights,
Ps 96: 6 strength and glory are in his s.
102:19 “The LORD looked down from his s on
108: 7 God has spoken from his s: “In
114: 2 Judah became God’s s, Israel his
134: 2 Lift up your hands in the s and
150: 1 Praise the LORD. Praise God in his s
Isa 8:14 he will be a s; but for both houses
60:13 to adorn the place of my s; and I
62: 9 drink it in the courts of my s.”
63:18 enemies have trampled down your s.
Jer 17:12 beginning, is the place of our s.
Lam 1:10 she saw pagan nations enter her s—
2: 7 his altar and abandoned his s.
2:20 be killed in the s of the Lord?
Eze 5:11 because you have defiled my s with
8: 6 that will drive me far from my s?
9: 6 Begin at my s.” So they began with
11:16 I have been a s for them in the
21: 2 Jerusalem and preach against the s.
23:38 they defiled my s and desecrated my
23:39 they entered my s and desecrated it.
24:21 I am about to desecrate my s—the
25: 3 “Aha!” over my s when it was
37:26 I will put my s among them for ever.
37:28 when my s is among them for ever.
41: 1 the man brought me to the outer s
41: 2 He also measured the outer s; it was
41: 3 he went into the inner s and
41: 4 measured the length of the inner s
41: 4 across the end of the outer s.
41:15 The outer s, the inner s and the
41:17 of the entrance to the inner s
41:17 all round the inner and outer s
41:20 carved on the wall of the outer s.
41:21 The outer s had a rectangular
41:23 Both the outer s and the Most Holy
41:25 on the doors of the outer s were
42: 8 the s was a hundred cubits long.
43:21 of the temple area outside the s.
44: 1 me back to the outer gate of the s,
44: 5 temple and all the exits of the s.
44: 7 in heart and flesh into my s,
44: 8 you put others in charge of my s.
44: 9 in heart and flesh is to enter my s,
44:11 They may serve in my s, having
44:15 carried out the duties of my s when
44:16 They alone are to enter my s;
44:27 court of the s to minister in the s,
45: 2 cubits square is to be for the s,
45: 3 will be the s, the Most Holy Place.
45: 4 who minister in the s and who draw
45: 4 as well as a holy place for the s.
45:18 without defect and purify the s.
47:12 the water from the s flows to them.
48: 8 the s will be in the centre of it.
48:10 of it will be the s of the LORD.
48:21 s will be in the centre of them.
Da 8:11 the place of his s was brought low.
8:13 and the surrender of the s and of
8:14 then the s will be reconsecrated.”
9:17 look with favour on your desolate s.
9:26 will destroy the city and the s.
Am 7:13 this is the king’s s and the temple
Zep 3: 4 Her priests profane the s and do
Mal 2:11 has desecrated the s the LORD loves,
Lk 11:51 killed between the altar and the s.
Heb 6:19 the inner s behind the curtain,
8: 2 who serves in the s, the true
8: 5 They serve at a s that is a copy and
9: 1 for worship and also an earthly s.
9:24 For Christ did not enter a man-made s

Sand (Sandy)

Ge 22:17 sky and as the s on the seashore.
32:12 descendants like the s of the sea,
41:49 like the s of the sea; it was so
Ex 2:12 the Egyptian and hid him in the s.
Dt 33:19 on the treasures hidden in the s.”
Jos 11: 4 numerous as the s on the seashore.
Jdg 7:12 counted than the s on the seashore.
1Sa 13: 5 numerous as the s on the seashore.
2Sa 17:11 as numerous as the s on the seashore
1Ki 4:20 as numerous as the s on the seashore;
4:29 as the s on the seashore.
Job 6: 3 surely outweigh the s of the seas
Job 29:18 days as numerous as the grains of s.
39:14 ground and lets them warm in the s,
Ps 78:27 flying birds like s on the seashore.
139:18 would outnumber the grains of s.
Pr 27: 3 Stone is heavy and s a burden, but
Isa 10:22 O Israel, be like the s by the sea,
35: 7 The burning s will become a pool,
48:19 would have been like the s,
Jer 5:22 I made the s a boundary for the sea,
15: 8 more numerous than the s of the sea.
33:22 as the s on the seashore.’”
Hos 1:10 will be like the s on the seashore,
Hab 1: 9 wind and gather prisoners like s.
Mt 7:26 man who built his house on s.
Ro 9:27 Israelites be like the s by the sea,
Heb 11:12 countless as the s on the seashore.
Rev 20: 8 they are like the s on the seashore.

Sandal (Sandalled, Sandals)

Ge 14:23 even a thread or the thong of a s,
Ru 4: 7 one party took off his s and gave
4: 8 And he removed his s.
Ps 60: 8 upon Edom I toss my s;
108: 9 upon Edom I toss my s;
Isa 5:27 the waist, not a s thong is broken.

Sandalled (Sandal)

SS 7: 1 How beautiful your s feet,

Sandals (Sandal)

Ex 3: 5 “Take off your s, for the place
12:11 your s on your feet and your staff
Dt 25: 9 take off one of his s, spit in his
29: 5 out, nor did the s on your feet.
Jos 5:15 “Take off your s, for the place
9: 5 The men put worn and patched s on
9:13 And our clothes and s are worn out
1Ki 2: 5 his waist and the s on his feet.
2Ch 28:15 s, food and drink, and healing balm.
Isa 11:15 so that men can cross over in s.
20: 2 your body and the s from your feet.
Eze 16:10 dress and put leather s on you.
24:17 fastened and your s on your feet;
24:23 your heads and your s on your feet.
Am 2: 6 and the needy for a pair of s.
8: 6 and the needy for a pair of s,
Mt 3:11 I, whose s I am not fit to carry.
10:10 or extra tunic, or s or a staff;
Mk 1: 7 the thongs of whose s I am not
6: 9 Wear s but not an extra tunic.
Lk 3:16 of whose s I am not worthy to untie.
10: 4 Do not take a purse or bag or s;
15:22 on his finger and s on his feet.
22:35 I sent you without purse, bag or s,
Jn 1:27 whose s I am not worthy to untie.”
Ac 7:33 ‘Take off your s; the place where
12: 8 “Put on your clothes and s.”
13:25 whose s I am not worthy to untie.’

Sand-bar (Sand-bars)

Ac 27:41 the ship struck a s and ran aground.

Sand-bars (Sand-bar)

Ac 27:17 run aground on the s of Syrtis,

Sandy (Sand)

Ac 27:39 but they saw a bay with a s beach,

Sang (Sing)

Ex 15: 1 Moses and the Israelites s this song
15:21 Miriam s to them: “Sing to the LORD,
Nu 21:17 Israel s this song: “Spring up,
Jdg 5: 1 Barak son of Abinoam s this song:
1Sa 18: 7 they danced, they s: “Saul has slain
29: 5 Isn’t this the David they s about in
2Sa 3:33 The king s this lament for Abner:
22: 1 David s to the LORD the words of
2Ch 5:13 voices in praise to the LORD and s:
29:28 singers s and the trumpeters played.
29:30 So they s praises with gladness and
30:21 while the Levites and priests s to
Ezr 3:11 With praise and thanksgiving they s
Ne 12:42 s under the direction of Jezrahiah.
Job 38: 7 while the morning stars s together

Ps 7: T of David, which he **s** to the LORD
18: T He **s** to the LORD words of this song
106:12 his promises and **s** his praise.
Mt 11:17 **s** a dirge, and you did not mourn.'
Lk 7:32 we **s** a dirge, and you did not cry.'
Rev 5: 9 they **s** a new song: "You are worthy
5:12 In a loud voice they **s**: "Worthy is
14: 3 they **s** a new song before the throne
15: 3 **s** the song of Moses the servant of

Sanhedrin
Mt 5:22 'Raca,' is answerable to the **S**.
26:59 The chief priests and the whole **S**
Mk 14:55 The chief priests and the whole **S**
15: 1 and the whole **S**, reached a decision.
Jn 11:47 Pharisees called a meeting of the **S**.
Ac 4:15 ordered them to withdraw from the **S**
5:21 they called together the **S**—the full
5:27 they made them appear before the **S**
5:34 stood up in the **S** and ordered that
5:41 The apostles left the **S**, rejoicing
6:12 Stephen and brought him before the **S**.
6:15 All who were sitting in the **S** looked
22:30 priests and all the **S** to assemble.
23: 1 Paul looked straight at the **S** and
23: 6 called out in the **S**, "My brothers, I
23:15 Now then, you and the **S** petition the
23:20 to bring Paul before the **S** tomorrow
23:28 him, so I brought him to their **S**.
24:20 in me when I stood before the **S**—

Sanity
Da 4:34 heaven, and my **s** was restored.
4:36 same time that my **s** was restored.

Sank (Sink)
Ge 42:28 Their hearts **s** and they turned to
Ex 15: 5 they **s** to the depths like a stone.
15:10 **s** like lead in the mighty waters.
Nu 21:18 that the nobles of the people **s**—
Jos 2:11 we heard of it, our hearts **s** and
5: 1 their hearts **s** and they no longer
Jdg 3:22 Even the handle **s** in after the blade,
5:27 At her feet he **s**, he fell;
5:27 At her feet he **s**, he fell;
5:27 where he **s**, there he fell—dead.
1Sa 17:49 The stone **s** into his forehead, and
SS 5: 6 My heart **s** at his departure.
Jer 38: 6 and Jeremiah **s** down into the mud.
Jnh 2: 6 To the roots of the mountains I **s**

Sansannah
Jos 15:31 Ziklag, Madmannah, **S**,

Sap (Sapped)
Hos 7: 9 Foreigners **s** his strength, but he
Ro 11:17 nourishing **s** from the olive root,

Saph
2Sa 21:18 **S**, one of the descendants of Rapha.

Sapped (Sap)
Ps 32: 4 my strength was **s** as in the heat of
Lam 1:14 neck and the Lord has **s** my strength.

Sapphira
Ac 5: 1 together with his wife **S**, also sold

Sapphire (Sapphires)
Ex 24:10 made of **s**, clear as the sky itself.
28:18 in the second row a turquoise, a **s**
39:11 in the second row a turquoise, a **s**
Eze 1:26 was what looked like a throne of **s**,
10: 1 I saw the likeness of a throne of **s**
28:13 and jasper, **s**, turquoise and beryl.
Rev 21:19 the second **s**, the third chalcedony,

Sapphires (Sapphire)
Job 28: 6 **s** come from its rocks, and its dust
28:16 of Ophir, with precious onyx or **s**.
SS 5:14 polished ivory decorated with **s**.
Isa 54:11 turquoise, your foundations with **s**.
Lam 4: 7 rubies, their appearance like **s**.

Sarah (Sarah's, Sarai)
Wife of Abraham; formerly Sarai; barren (Ge 11:29–30). Taken by Pharaoh when pretending to be Abraham's sister (Ge 12:10–20). Gave Hagar to Abraham (Ge 16:1–3). Name changed; promised a son (Ge 17:15–21; 18:9–10; Ro 9:9; Heb 11:11); laughed in disbelief (Ge 18:10–15). Taken by Abimelech when pretending to be Abraham's sister; returned (Ge 20:1–18). Gave birth to Isaac (Ge 21:1–7); sent away Hagar and Ishmael (Ge 21:8–14). Death and burial (Ge 23).

Ge 17:15 call her Sarai; her name will be **S**.
17:17 **S** bear a child at the age of ninety?
17:19 your wife **S** will bear you a son,
17:21 whom **S** will bear to you by this time
18: 6 Abraham hurried into the tent to **S**.
18: 9 "Where is your wife **S**?" they asked
18:10 and **S** your wife will have a son.
18:10 Now **S** was listening at the entrance
18:11 Abraham and **S** were already old and
18:11 **S** was past the age of childbearing.
18:12 **S** laughed to herself as she thought,
18:13 Abraham, "Why did **S** laugh and say,
18:14 next year and **S** will have a son."
18:15 **S** was afraid, so she lied and said,
20: 2 there Abraham said of his wife **S**,
20: 2 of Gerar sent for **S** and took her.
20:14 and he returned **S** his wife to him.
20:16 To **S** he said, "I am giving your
20:18 because of Abraham's wife **S**.
21: 1 Now the LORD was gracious to **S** as he
21: 1 LORD did for **S** what he had promised.
21: 2 **S** became pregnant and bore a son to
21: 3 name Isaac to the son **S** bore him.
21: 6 **S** said, "God has brought me laughter,
21: 7 Abraham that **S** would nurse children?
21: 9 **S** saw that the son whom Hagar the
21:12 Listen to whatever **S** tells you,
23: 1 **S** lived to be a hundred and
23: 2 to mourn for **S** and to weep over her.
23:19 Afterwards Abraham buried his wife **S**
24:36 My master's wife **S** has borne him a
24:67 her into the tent of his mother **S**,
25:10 Abraham was buried with his wife **S**.
49:31 There Abraham and his wife **S** were
Isa 51: 2 and to **S**, who gave you birth.
Ro 9: 9 will return, and **S** will have a son."
Heb 11:11 age—and **S** herself was barren—
1Pe 3: 6 like **S**, who obeyed Abraham and

Sarah's (Sarah)
Ge 25:12 whom **S** maidservant, Hagar the
Ro 4:19 old—and that **S** womb was also dead.

Sarai (Sarah)
Ge 11:29 The name of Abram's wife was **S**, and
11:30 Now **S** was barren; she had no
11:31 and his daughter-in-law **S**, the wife
12: 5 He took his wife **S**, his nephew Lot,
12:11 he said to his wife **S**, "I know what
12:17 household because of Abram's wife **S**.
16: 1 Now **S**, Abram's wife, had borne him
16: 2 Abram agreed to what **S** said.
16: 3 **S** his wife took her Egyptian
16: 5 **S** said to Abram, "You are
16: 6 Then **S** ill-treated Hagar; so she
16: 8 he said, "Hagar, servant of **S**, where
16: 8 from my mistress **S**," she answered.
17:15 to Abraham, "As for **S** your wife,
17:15 you are no longer to call her **S**;

Saraph
1Ch 4:22 the men of Cozeba, and Joash and **S**,

Sardis
Capital city of Lydia in Asia Minor, situated on River Pactolus east of Smyrna. One of the 7 letters of Revelation was addressed to the church here (Rev 1:11), which was encouraged to turn from complacency (Rev 3:1–6).

Rev 1:11 **S**, Philadelphia and Laodicea."
3: 1 "To the angel of the church in **S**
3: 4 Yet you have a few people in **S** who

Sardonyx
Rev 21:20 the fifth **s**, the sixth carnelian,

Sargon
Isa 20: 1 sent by **S** king of Assyria, came to

Sarid
Jos 19:10 their inheritance went as far as **S**.
19:12 turned east from **S** towards the

Sash (Sashes)
Ex 28: 4 a woven tunic, a turban and a **s**.
28:39 The **s** is to be the work of an
39:29 The **s** was of finely twisted linen
Lev 8: 7 He put the tunic on Aaron, tied the **s**
16: 4 he is to tie the linen **s** around him
Isa 3:24 instead of a **s**, a rope;
11: 5 faithfulness the **s** round his waist.
22:21 fasten your **s** around him and hand
Rev 1:13 and with a golden **s** round his chest.

Sashes (Sash)
Ex 28:40 Make tunics, **s** and headbands for
29: 9 Then tie **s** on Aaron and his sons.
Lev 8:13 tunics on them, tied **s** around them
Pr 31:24 and supplies the merchants with **s**.
Isa 3:20 ankle chains and **s**, the perfume
Rev 15: 6 wore golden **s** round their chests.

Sat (Sit)
Ge 21:16 she went off and **s** down nearby,
21:16 And as she **s** there nearby, she
37:25 they **s** down to eat their meal, they
38:14 and then **s** down at the entrance to
48: 2 his strength and **s** up on the bed.
Ex 2:15 Midian, where he **s** down by a well.
12:29 of Pharaoh, who **s** on the throne,
16: 3 There we **s** round pots of meat and
17:12 and put it under him and he **s** on it.
32: 6 Afterwards they **s** down to eat and
Lev 15: 6 the man with a discharge **s** on must
Jdg 6:11 angel of the LORD came and **s** down
19: 6 the two of them **s** down to eat and
19:15 They went and **s** in the city square,
20:26 they **s** weeping before the LORD.
21: 2 where they **s** before God until
Ru 2:14 When she **s** down with the harvesters,
4: 1 up to the town gate and **s** there.
4: 1 So he went over and **s** down.
1Sa 20:24 came, the king **s** down to eat.
20:25 He **s** in his customary place by the
20:25 and Abner **s** next to Saul, but
28:23 from the ground and **s** on the couch.
2Sa 2:13 One group **s** down on one side of the
7:18 King David went in and **s** before the
1Ki 2:12 Solomon **s** on the throne of his
2:19 to her and **s** down on his throne.
2:19 and she **s** down at his right hand.
19: 4 He came to a broom tree, **s** down
21:13 two scoundrels came and **s** opposite
2Ki 4:20 the boy **s** on her lap until noon, and
1Ch 17:16 King David went in and **s** before the
29:23 Solomon **s** on the throne of the LORD
Ezr 9: 3 head and beard and **s** down appalled.
9: 4 And I **s** there appalled until the
10:16 **s** down to investigate the cases,
Ne 1: 4 I heard these things, I **s** down and
Est 3:15 The king and Haman **s** down to drink,
Job 2: 8 with it as he **s** among the ashes.
2:13 they **s** on the ground with him for
29:25 way for them and **s** as their chief;
Ps 9: 4 my cause; you have **s** on your throne,
107:10 Some **s** in darkness and the deepest
137: 1 By the rivers of Babylon we **s** and
Jer 3: 2 roadside you **s** waiting for lovers,
3: 2 **s** like a nomad in the desert.
15:17 I never **s** in the company of
15:17 I **s** alone because your hand was
Eze 3:15 I **s** among them for seven days—
14: 1 to me and **s** down in front of me.
20: 1 LORD, and they **s** down in front of me.
23:41 You **s** on an elegant couch, with a
Jnh 3: 6 sackcloth and **s** down in the dust.
4: 5 Jonah went out and **s** down at a place

Jnh 4: 5 shelter, **s** in its shade and waited
Zec 5: 7 and there in the basket **s** a woman!
Mt 5: 1 up on a mountainside and **s** down.
13: 1 out of the house and **s** by the lake.
13: 2 that he got into a boat and **s** in it,
13:48 Then they **s** down and collected the
15:29 up on a mountainside and **s** down.
21: 7 cloaks on them, and Jesus **s** on them.
26:55 I **s** in the temple courts teaching,
26:58 He entered and **s** down with the
28: 2 rolled back the stone and **s** on it.
Mk 4: 1 a boat and **s** in it out on the lake,
6:40 they **s** down in groups of hundreds
11: 7 their cloaks over it, he **s** on it.
12:41 Jesus **s** down opposite the place
14:54 There he **s** with the guards and
16:19 and he **s** at the right hand of God.
Lk 4:20 it back to the attendant and **s** down.
5: 3 Then he **s** down and taught the people
7:15 The dead man **s** up and began to talk,
9:15 The disciples did so, and everybody **s**
10:39 Mary, who **s** at the Lord's feet
22:55 courtyard and had **s** down together,
22:55 together, Peter **s** down with them.
Jn 4: 6 the journey, **s** down by the well.
6: 3 and **s** down with his disciples.
6:10 the men **s** down, about five thousand
8: 2 him, and he **s** down to teach them.
12:14 found a young donkey and **s** upon it,
19:13 he brought Jesus out and **s** down on
Ac 9:40 her eyes, and seeing Peter she **s** up.
12:21 his royal robes, **s** on his throne
13:14 entered the synagogue and **s** down.
14: 8 In Lystra there **s** a man crippled in
16:13 We **s** down and began to speak to the
1Co 10: 7 "The people **s** down to eat and drink
Heb 1: 3 he **s** down at the right hand of the
8: 1 who **s** down at the right hand of the
10:12 he **s** down at the right hand of God.
12: 2 and **s** down at the right hand of the
Rev 3:21 **s** down with my Father on his throne.
4: 3 the one who **s** there had the
5: 1 hand of him who **s** on the throne
5: 7 hand of him who **s** on the throne.

Satan (Satan's)

1Ch 21: 1 **S** rose up against Israel and incited
Job 1: 6 the LORD, and **S** also came with them.
1: 7 The LORD said to **S**, "Where have you
1: 7 **S** answered the LORD, "From roaming
1: 8 the LORD said to **S**, "Have you
1: 9 fear God for nothing?" **S** replied.
1:12 The LORD said to **S**, "Very well, then,
1:12 Then **S** went out from the presence
2: 1 and **S** also came with them to present
2: 2 the LORD said to **S**, "Where have you
2: 2 **S** answered the LORD, "From roaming
2: 3 the LORD said to **S**, "Have you
2: 4 "Skin for skin!" **S** replied. "A man
2: 6 The LORD said to **S**, "Very well, then,
2: 7 **S** went out from the presence of the
Zec 3: 1 and **S** standing at his right side to
3: 2 The LORD said to **S**, "The LORD rebuke
3: 2 "The LORD rebuke you, **S**! The LORD,
Mt 4:10 Jesus said to him, "Away from me, **S**!
12:26 If **S** drives out **S**, he is divided
16:23 "Get behind me, **S**! You are a
Mk 1:13 for forty days, being tempted by **S**.
3:23 "How can **S** drive out **S**?
3:26 if **S** opposes himself and is divided,
4:15 As soon as they hear it, **S** comes and
8:33 "Get behind me, **S**!" he said. "You do
Lk 10:18 He replied, "I saw **S** fall like
11:18 If **S** is divided against himself, how
13:16 a daughter of Abraham, whom **S** has
22: 3 **S** entered Judas, called Iscariot,
22:31 "Simon, Simon, **S** has asked to sift
Jn 13:27 took the bread, **S** entered into him.
Ac 5: 3 "Ananias, how is it that **S** has so
26:18 and from the power of **S** to God, so
Ro 16:20 The God of peace will soon crush **S**
1Co 5: 5 hand this man over to **S**, so that the
7: 5 so that **S** will not tempt you
2Co 2:11 in order that **S** might not outwit us.
11:14 no wonder, for **S** himself masquerades
2Co 12: 7 a messenger of **S**, to torment me.
1Th 2:18 again and again—but **S** stopped us.
2Th 2: 9 the work of **S** displayed in all
1Ti 1:20 to **S** to be taught not to blaspheme.
5:15 already turned away to follow **S**.
Rev 2: 9 are not, but are a synagogue of **S**.
2:13 you live—where **S** has his throne.
2:13 death in your city—where **S** lives.
3: 9 those who are of the synagogue of **S**,
12: 9 **S**, who leads the whole world astray.
20: 2 who is the devil, or **S**, and bound
20: 7 **S** will be released from his prison

Satan's (Satan)

Rev 2:24 have not learned **S** so-called deep

Sated

Lam 3:15 bitter herbs and **s** me with gall.

Satisfaction (Satisfy)

Est 5:13 all this gives me no **s** as long as I
Ecc 2:24 and drink and find **s** in his work.
3:13 and find **s** in all his toil—this is
5:18 and to find **s** in his toilsome labour

Satisfied (Satisfy)

Ex 18:23 all these people will go home **s**."
Lev 10:20 Moses heard this, he was **s**.
26:26 You will eat, but you will not be **s**.
Dt 6:11 plant—then when you eat and are **s**,
8:10 you have eaten and are **s**, praise the
8:12 Otherwise, when you eat and are **s**,
11:15 cattle, and you will eat and be **s**.
14:29 towns may come and eat and be **s**,
26:12 they may eat in your towns and be **s**.
Ps 17:15 be **s** with seeing your likeness.
22:26 The poor will eat and be **s**; they who
59:15 about for food and howl if not **s**.
63: 5 My soul will be **s** as with the
104:13 earth is **s** by the fruit of his work.
104:28 hand, they are **s** with good things.
105:40 and **s** them with the bread of heaven.
Pr 13: 4 desires of the diligent are fully **s**.
18:20 the harvest from his lips he is **s**.
27:20 Death and Destruction are never **s**,
30:15 are three things that are never **s**,
30:16 land, which is never **s** with water,
Ecc 5:10 wealth is never **s** with his income.
6: 7 mouth, yet his appetite is never **s**.
Isa 9:20 left they will eat, but not be **s**.
53:11 will see the light of life and be **s**;
66:11 For you will nurse and be **s** at her
Jer 46:10 The sword will devour till it is **s**,
50:19 his appetite will be **s** on the hills
Eze 16:28 after that, you still were not **s**.
16:29 but even with this you were not **s**.
27:33 you **s** many nations; with your great
Hos 13: 6 I fed them, they were **s**; when they
13: 6 they were **s**, they became proud;
Mic 6:14 You will eat but not be **s**; your
Hab 2: 5 the grave and like death is never **s**,
Mt 14:20 They all ate and were **s**, and the
15:37 They all ate and were **s**. Afterwards
Mk 6:42 They all ate and were **s**,
8: 8 The people ate and were **s**.
Lk 6:21 who hunger now, for you will be **s**.
9:17 They all ate and were **s**, and the
3Jn :10 Not **s** with that, he refuses to

Satisfies (Satisfy)

Ps 103: 5 who **s** your desires with good things
107: 9 for he **s** the thirsty and fills the
147:14 and **s** you with the finest of wheat.

Satisfy (Satisfaction, Satisfied, Satisfies)

Job 38:27 to **s** a desolate wasteland and make
38:39 and **s** the hunger of the lions
Ps 81:16 honey from the rock I would **s** you."
90:14 **S** us in the morning with your
91:16 With long life will I **s** him and show
132:15 her poor will I **s** with food.
145:16 You open your hand and **s** the desires
Pr 5:19 may her breasts **s** you always,
Pr 6:30 to **s** his hunger when he is starving.
Isa 55: 2 and your labour on what does not **s**?
58:10 and **s** the needs of the oppressed,
58:11 he will **s** your needs in a
Jer 31:14 I will **s** the priests with abundance,
31:25 refresh the weary and **s** the faint."
Eze 7:19 They will not **s** their hunger or fill
Joel 2:19 new wine and oil, enough to **s** you
Mt 28:14 **s** him and keep you out of trouble."
Mk 15:15 Wanting to **s** the crowd, Pilate

Satraps

Ezr 8:36 the king's orders to the royal **s**
Est 3:12 all Haman's orders to the king's **s**,
8: 9 and to the **s**, governors and nobles
9: 3 the **s**, the governors and the king's
Da 3: 2 He then summoned the **s**, prefects,
3: 3 the **s**, prefects, governors, advisers,
3:27 the **s**, prefects, governors and royal
6: 1 pleased Darius to appoint 120 **s** to
6: 2 The **s** were made accountable to them
6: 3 among the administrators and the **s**
6: 4 At this, the administrators and the **s**
6: 6 the administrators and the **s** went as
6: 7 The royal administrators, prefects, **s**

Saul (Paul, Saul's)

Benjamite; Israel's first king. Chosen by God (1Sa 9:15–16); anointed by Samuel (1Sa 10:1); acknowledged publicly (1Sa 10:17–25). Defeated Ammonites (1Sa 11). Rebuked by Samuel, when offered sacrifices (1Sa 13) and for disobedience (1Sa 15); rejected as king (1Sa 13:13–14; 15:23,26–28; 28:17). Defeated Philistines (1Sa 14). Troubled by evil spirit; soothed by David's playing (1Sa 16:14–23). Sent David to fight Goliath (1Sa 17). Gave David his daughter Michal as wife (1Sa 18:20–21). Became jealous; tried to kill David (1Sa 18:1–11; 19:1–10). Anger at Jonathan (1Sa 20:26–34). Pursued David; killed priests at Nob (1Sa 22); life spared by David (1Sa 24; 26). Consulted medium at Endor; rebuked by Samuel's spirit (1Sa 28). Defeated by Philistines on Mt Gilboa; wounded, took own life (1Sa 31; 1Ch 10). Mourned by David (2Sa 1:19–27). Children (1Sa 14:49–51; 1Ch 8).

1Sa 9: 2 He had a son named **S**, an impressive
9: 3 and Kish said to his son **S**, "Take
9: 5 **S** said to the servant who was with
9: 7 **S** said to his servant, "If we go,
9:10 "Good," **S** said to his servant. "Come,
9:15 Now the day before **S** came, the LORD
9:17 Samuel caught sight of **S**, the LORD
9:18 **S** approached Samuel in the gateway
9:21 **S** answered, "But am I not a
9:22 Samuel brought **S** and his servant
9:24 was on it and set it in front of **S**.
9:24 And **S** dined with Samuel that day.
9:25 with **S** on the roof of his house.
9:26 and Samuel called to **S** on the roof,
9:26 When **S** got ready, he and Samuel
9:27 Samuel said to **S**, "Tell the servant
10: 9 **S** turned to leave Samuel, God
10:11 Is **S** also among the prophets?"
10:12 "Is **S** also among the prophets?"
10:13 After **S** stopped prophesying, he went
10:16 **S** replied, "He assured us that the
10:21 Finally **S** son of Kish was chosen.
10:26 **S** also went to his home in Gibeah,
10:27 him no gifts. But **S** kept silent.
11: 4 the messengers came to Gibeah of **S**
11: 5 Just then **S** was returning from the
11: 6 **S** heard their words, the Spirit of
11: 7 who does not follow **S** and Samuel.
11: 8 **S** mustered them at Bezek, the men of
11:11 The next day **S** separated his men
11:12 'Shall **S** reign over us?' Bring these
11:13 **S** said, "No-one shall be put to
11:15 confirmed **S** as king in the presence
11:15 and **S** and all the Israelites held a
13: 1 **S** was thirty years old when he
13: 2 **S** chose three thousand men from
13: 3 Then **S** had the trumpet blown
13: 4 "**S** has attacked the Philistine
13: 4 were summoned to join **S** at Gilgal.

1Sa 13: 7 **S** remained at Gilgal, and all the
13: 9 And **S** offered up the burnt offering.
13:10 and **S** went out to greet him.
13:11 **S** replied, "When I saw that the men
13:15 **S** counted the men who were with him.
13:16 **S** and his son Jonathan and the men
13:22 not a soldier with **S** and Jonathan
13:22 **S** and his son Jonathan had them.
14: 1 One day Jonathan son of **S** said to
14: 2 **S** was staying on the outskirts of
14:17 **S** said to the men who were with him,
14:18 **S** said to Ahijah, "Bring the ark of
14:19 While **S** was talking to the priest,
14:19 So **S** said to the priest, "Withdraw
14:20 **S** and all his men assembled and went
14:21 who were with **S** and Jonathan.
14:24 because **S** had bound the people under
14:33 someone said to **S**, "Look, the men
14:35 **S** built an altar to the LORD; it was
14:36 **S** said, "Let us go down after the
14:37 **S** asked God, "Shall I go down after
14:38 **S** therefore said, "Come here, all
14:40 **S** then said to all the Israelites,
14:41 **S** prayed to the LORD, the God of
14:41 And Jonathan and **S** were taken by
14:42 **S** said, "Cast the lot between me and
14:43 **S** said to Jonathan, "Tell me what
14:44 **S** said, "May God deal with me, be it
14:45 the men said to **S**, "Should Jonathan
14:46 **S** stopped pursuing the Philistines,
14:47 After **S** had assumed rule over Israel,
14:52 All the days of **S** there was bitter
14:52 and whenever **S** saw a mighty or brave
15: 1 Samuel said to **S**, "I am the one the
15: 4 **S** summoned the men and mustered them
15: 5 **S** went to the city of Amalek and set
15: 7 **S** attacked the Amalekites all the
15: 9 **S** and the army spared Agag and the
15:11 grieved that I have made **S** king.
15:12 Samuel got up and went to meet **S**,
15:12 he was told, "**S** has gone to Carmel.
15:13 Samuel reached him, **S** said, "The
15:15 **S** answered, "The soldiers brought
15:16 "Stop!" Samuel said to **S**. "Let me
15:16 "Tell me," **S** replied.
15:20 "But I did obey the LORD," **S** said.
15:24 **S** said to Samuel, "I have sinned.
15:27 **S** caught hold of the hem of his
15:30 **S** replied, "I have sinned.
15:31 Samuel went back with **S**,
15:31 and **S** worshipped the LORD.
15:34 **S** went up to his home in Gibeah of **S**.
15:35 he did not go to see **S** again, though
15:35 that he had made **S** king over Israel.
16: 1 "How long will you mourn for **S**,
16: 2 "How can I go? **S** will hear about it.
16:14 of the LORD had departed from **S**,
16:17 **S** said to his attendants, "Find
16:19 **S** sent messengers to Jesse and said,
16:20 sent them with his son David to **S**.
16:21 David came to **S** and entered his
16:21 **S** liked him very much, and David
16:22 **S** sent word to Jesse, saying, "Allow
16:23 the spirit from God came upon **S**,
16:23 Then relief would come to **S**;
17: 2 **S** and the Israelites assembled and
17: 8 and are you not the servants of **S**?
17:11 **S** and all the Israelites were
17:13 sons had followed **S** to the war:
17:14 The three oldest followed **S**,
17:15 David went back and forth from **S** to
17:19 They are with **S** and all the men of
17:31 reported to **S**, and **S** sent for him.
17:32 David said to **S**, "Let no-one lose
17:33 **S** replied, "You are not able to go
17:34 David said to **S**, "Your servant has
17:37 **S** said to David, "Go, and the LORD
17:38 **S** dressed David in his own tunic.
17:39 "I cannot go in these," he said to **S**,
17:55 **S** watched David going out to meet
17:57 took him and brought him before **S**,
17:58 are you, young man?" **S** asked him.
18: 1 David had finished talking with **S**,
18: 2 From that day **S** kept David with him
18: 5 Whatever **S** sent him to do, David did
18: 5 **S** gave him a high rank in the army.

1Sa 18: 6 to meet King **S** with singing and
18: 7 sang: "**S** has slain his thousands,
18: 8 **S** was very angry; this refrain
18: 9 from that time on **S** kept a jealous
18:10 from God came forcefully upon **S**.
18:10 **S** had a spear in his hand
18:12 **S** was afraid of David, because the
18:12 LORD was with David but had left **S**.
18:15 **S** saw how successful he was, he was
18:17 **S** said to David, "Here is my older
18:17 For **S** said to himself, "I will not
18:18 David said to **S**, "Who am I, and what
18:20 told **S** about it, he was pleased.
18:21 So **S** said to David, "Now you have a
18:22 **S** ordered his attendants: "Speak to
18:25 **S** replied, "Say to David, 'The king
18:27 Then **S** gave him his daughter Michal
18:28 **S** realised that the LORD was with
18:29 **S** became still more afraid of him,
19: 1 **S** told his son Jonathan and all the
19: 2 warned him, "My father **S** is looking
19: 4 Jonathan spoke well of David to **S**
19: 6 **S** listened to Jonathan and took this
19: 7 He brought him to **S**, and
19: 7 and David was with **S** as before.
19: 9 came upon **S** as he was sitting in
19:10 **S** tried to pin him to the wall with
19:10 as **S** drove the spear into the wall.
19:11 **S** sent men to David's house to watch
19:14 **S** sent the men to capture David,
19:15 **S** sent the men back to see David and
19:17 **S** said to Michal, "Why did you
19:18 told him all that **S** had done to him.
19:19 Word came to **S**: "David is in Naioth
19:21 **S** was told about it, and he sent
19:21 **S** sent men a third time, and they
19:23 **S** went to Naioth at Ramah. But the
19:24 "Is **S** also among the prophets?"
20:25 Abner sat next to **S**, but David's
20:26 **S** said nothing that day, for he
20:27 Then **S** said to his son Jonathan,
20:33 **S** hurled his spear at him to kill
21:10 That day David fled from **S** and went
21:11 '**S** has slain his thousands, and
22: 6 Now **S** heard that David and his men
22: 6 And **S**, spear in hand, was seated
22: 7 **S** said to them, "Listen, men of
22:12 **S** said, "Listen now, son of Ahitub."
22:13 **S** said to him, "Why have you
22:21 He told David that **S** had killed the
22:22 I knew he would be sure to tell **S**.
23: 7 **S** was told that David had gone to
23: 8 **S** called up all his forces for
23: 9 David learned that **S** was plotting
23:10 **S** plans to come to Keilah and
23:11 Will **S** come down, as your servant
23:12 surrender me and my men to **S**?"
23:13 When **S** was told that David had
23:14 Day after day **S** searched for him,
23:15 **S** had come out to take his life.
23:17 "My father **S** will not lay a hand on
23:17 Even my father **S** knows this."
23:19 The Ziphites went up to **S** at Gibeah
23:21 **S** replied, "The LORD bless you for
23:24 set out and went to Ziph ahead of **S**.
23:25 **S** and his men began the search, and
23:25 When **S** heard this, he went into the
23:26 **S** was going along one side of the
23:26 side, hurrying to get away from **S**.
23:26 As **S** and his forces were closing in
23:27 a messenger came to **S**, saying, "Come
23:28 **S** broke off his pursuit of David and
24: 1 After **S** returned from pursuing the
24: 2 **S** took three thousand chosen men
24: 3 and **S** went in to relieve himself.
24: 7 and did not allow them to attack **S**.
24: 7 And **S** left the cave and went his way.
24: 8 called out to **S**, "My lord the king!"
24: 8 When **S** looked behind him, David
24: 9 He said to **S**, "Why do you listen
24:16 David finished saying this, **S** asked,
24:22 David gave his oath to **S**.
24:22 Then **S** returned home, but David
25:44 **S** had given his daughter Michal,
26: 1 The Ziphites went to **S** at Gibeah and
26: 2 **S** went down to the Desert of Ziph,

1Sa 26: 3 **S** made his camp beside the road on
26: 3 saw that **S** had followed him there,
26: 4 that **S** had definitely arrived.
26: 5 to the place where **S** had camped.
26: 5 He saw where **S** and Abner son of Ner,
26: 5 **S** was lying inside the camp, with
26: 6 down into the camp with me to **S**?"
26: 7 and there was **S**, lying asleep inside
26:17 **S** recognised David's voice and said,
26:21 **S** said, "I have sinned. Come back,
26:25 **S** said to David, "May you be blessed,
26:25 on his way, and **S** returned home.
27: 1 shall be destroyed by the hand of **S**.
27: 1 Then **S** will give up searching for me
27: 4 **S** was told that David had fled to
28: 3 **S** had expelled the mediums and
28: 4 while **S** gathered all the Israelites
28: 5 **S** saw the Philistine army, he was
28: 7 **S** then said to his attendants, "Find
28: 8 **S** disguised himself, putting on
28: 9 "Surely you know what **S** has done.
28:10 **S** swore to her by the LORD, "As
28:12 the top of her voice and said to **S**,
28:12 Why have you deceived me? You are **S**!"
28:14 Then **S** knew it was Samuel, and he
28:15 Samuel said to **S**, "Why have you
28:15 "I am in great distress," **S** said.
28:20 Immediately **S** fell full length on
28:21 the woman came to **S** and saw that he
28:25 she set it before **S** and his men, and
29: 3 an officer of **S** king of Israel?
29: 3 and from the day he left **S** until now,
29: 5 '**S** has slain his thousands, and
31: 2 The Philistines pressed hard after **S**
31: 3 The fighting grew fierce around **S**,
31: 4 **S** said to his armour-bearer, "Draw
31: 4 **S** took his own sword and fell on it.
31: 5 armour-bearer saw that **S** was dead
31: 6 **S** and his three sons and his
31: 7 and that **S** and his sons had died,
31: 8 they found **S** and his three sons
31:11 what the Philistines had done to **S**,
31:12 They took down the bodies of **S** and
2Sa 1: 1 After the death of **S**, David returned
1: 4 And **S** and his son Jonathan are dead."
1: 5 **S** and his son Jonathan are dead?"
1: 6 "and there was **S**, leaning on his
1:12 evening for **S** and his son Jonathan,
1:17 concerning **S** and his son Jonathan,
1:21 the shield of **S**—no longer rubbed
1:22 the sword of **S** did not return
1:23 "**S** and Jonathan—in life they were
1:24 "O daughters of Israel, weep for **S**,
2: 4 of Jabesh Gilead who had buried **S**,
2: 5 this kindness to **S** your master by
2: 7 brave, for **S** your master is dead,
2: 8 taken Ish-Bosheth son of **S** and
2:10 Ish-Bosheth son of **S** was forty years
2:12 the men of Ish-Bosheth son of **S**,
2:15 and Ish-Bosheth son of **S**, and
3: 1 The war between the house of **S** and
3: 1 house of **S** grew weaker and weaker.
3: 6 the war between the house of **S**
3: 6 his own position in the house of **S**.
3: 7 Now **S** had had a concubine named
3: 8 loyal to the house of your father **S**
3:10 the kingdom from the house of **S**
3:13 bring Michal daughter of **S** when you
3:14 messengers to Ish-Bosheth son of **S**,
4: 1 Ish-Bosheth son of **S** heard that
4: 4 (Jonathan son of **S** had a son who was
4: 4 **S** and Jonathan came from Jezreel.
4: 8 is the head of Ish-Bosheth son of **S**,
4: 8 king against **S** and his offspring."
4:10 a man told me, '**S** is dead,' and
5: 2 In the past, while **S** was king over
6:16 daughter of **S** watched from a window.
6:20 Michal daughter of **S** came out to
6:23 Michal daughter of **S** had no children
7:15 **S**, whom I removed from before you.
9: 1 anyone still left of the house of **S**
9: 3 **S** to whom I can show God's kindness?"
9: 6 the son of **S**, came to David, he
9: 7 that belonged to your grandfather **S**,
9: 9 that belonged to **S** and his family.
12: 7 I delivered you from the hand of **S**.

2Sa 16: 8 you shed in the household of **S**,
21: 1 "It is on account of **S** and his
21: 2 but **S** in his zeal for Israel and
21: 4 silver or gold from **S** or his family,
21: 6 Gibeah of **S**—the LORD's chosen one.
21: 7 the son of **S**, because of the oath
21: 7 between David and Jonathan son of **S**.
21: 8 whom she had borne to **S**, together
21:12 he went and took the bones of **S** and
21:12 after they struck **S** down on Gilboa.)
21:13 David brought the bones of **S** and his
21:14 They buried the bones of **S** and his
22: 1 his enemies and from the hand of **S**.
1Ch 8:33 Kish the father of **S**, and **S** the
9:39 Kish the father of **S**, and **S** the
10: 2 The Philistines pressed hard after **S**
10: 3 The fighting grew fierce around **S**,
10: 4 **S** said to his armour-bearer, "Draw
10: 4 **S** took his own sword and fell on it.
10: 5 armour-bearer saw that **S** was dead,
10: 6 **S** and his three sons died, and all
10: 7 and that **S** and his sons had died,
10: 8 they found **S** and his sons fallen on
10:11 the Philistines had done to **S**,
10:12 took the bodies of **S** and his sons
10:13 **S** died because he was unfaithful to
11: 2 In the past, even while **S** was king,
12: 1 was banished from the presence of **S**
12: 2 they were kinsmen of **S** from the
12:19 the Philistines to fight against **S**.
12:19 if he deserts to his master **S**.")
13: 3 of it during the reign of **S**."
15:29 daughter of **S** watched from a window.
26:28 Samuel the seer and by **S** son of Kish,
Ps 18: T his enemies and from the hand of **S**.
52: T When Doeg the Edomite had gone to **S**
54: T When the Ziphites had gone to **S** and
57: T he had fled from **S** into the cave.
59: T When **S** had sent men to watch David's
Isa 10:29 Ramah trembles; Gibeah of **S** flees.
Ac 7:58 at the feet of a young man named **S**.
8: 1 **S** was there, giving approval to his
8: 3 **S** began to destroy the church.
9: 1 Meanwhile, **S** was still breathing out
9: 4 "**S**, **S**, why do you persecute me?"
9: 5 "Who are you, Lord?" **S** asked. "I am
9: 7 The men travelling with **S** stood
9: 8 **S** got up from the ground, but when
9:11 ask for a man from Tarsus named **S**,
9:17 Placing his hands on **S**, he said,
9:17 "Brother **S**, the Lord—Jesus, who
9:19 **S** spent several days with the
9:22 Yet **S** grew more and more powerful
9:24 **S** learned of their plan. Day and
9:27 He told them how **S** on his journey
9:28 **S** stayed with them and moved about
11:25 Barnabas went to Tarsus to look for **S**
11:26 Barnabas and **S** met with the church
11:30 to the elders by Barnabas and **S**.
12:25 Barnabas and **S** had finished their
13: 1 up with Herod the tetrarch) and **S**.
13: 2 "Set apart for me Barnabas and **S** for
13: 7 sent for Barnabas and **S** because he
13: 9 **S**, who was also called Paul, filled
13:21 and he gave them **S** son of Kish, of
13:22 After removing **S**, he made David
22: 7 me, '**S**! **S**! Why do you persecute me?"
22:13 'Brother **S**, receive your sight!'
26:14 '**S**, **S**, why do you persecute me?

Saul's (Paul, Saul)

1Sa 9: 3 donkeys belonging to **S** father Kish
10: 1 poured it on **S** head and kissed him,
10: 9 God changed **S** heart, and all these
10:14 Now **S** uncle asked him and his
10:15 **S** uncle said, "Tell me what Samuel
13: 8 Gilgal, and **S** men began to scatter.
14:16 **S** lookouts at Gibeah in Benjamin saw
14:49 **S** sons were Jonathan, Ishvi and
14:50 The name of the commander of **S** army
14:50 son of Ner, and Ner was **S** uncle.
14:51 **S** father Kish and Abner's father Ner
16:15 **S** attendants said to him, "See, an
17:12 Jesse had eight sons, and in **S** time
18: 5 the people, and **S** officers as well.
1Sa 18:19 time came for Merab, **S** daughter, to
18:20 Now **S** daughter Michal was in love
18:24 **S** servants told him what David had
18:25 **S** plan was to have David fall by
18:30 success than the rest of **S** officers,
19:20 the Spirit of God came upon **S** men
20:30 **S** anger flared up at Jonathan and he
21: 7 Now one of **S** servants was there that
21: 7 Doeg the Edomite, **S** head shepherd.
22: 9 who was standing with **S** officials,
23:16 **S** son Jonathan went to David at
24: 4 and cut off a corner of **S** robe.
26:12 jug near **S** head, and they left.
2Sa 1: 2 a man arrived from **S** camp, with
2: 8 the commander of **S** army, had taken
4: 2 Now **S** son had two men who were
9: 2 there was a servant of **S** household
9: 9 the king summoned Ziba, **S** servant,
16: 5 as **S** family came out from there.
19:17 Ziba, the steward of **S** household,
19:24 Mephibosheth, **S** grandson, also went
21: 8 the five sons of **S** daughter Merab,
21:11 Rizpah, **S** concubine, had done,
21:14 in the tomb of **S** father Kish,
1Ch 5:10 During **S** reign they waged war
12:23 Hebron to turn **S** kingdom over to him,
12:29 men of Benjamin, **S** kinsmen—3,000,
12:29 loyal to **S** house until then;
Ac 9:18 scales fell from **S** eyes, and he

Savage

Lev 26: 6 I will remove **s** beasts from the land,
Ac 20:29 after I leave, **s** wolves will come

Save (Salvation, Saved, Saves, Saving, Saviour)

Ge 32:11 **S** me, I pray, from the hand of my
45: 5 because it was to **s** lives that God
45: 7 **s** your lives by a great deliverance.
Ex 16:23 **S** whatever is left and keep it until
Nu 31:18 **s** for yourselves every girl who has
Dt 4:42 one of these cities and **s** his life.
19: 4 flees there to **s** his life—one who
19: 5 one of these cities and **s** his life.
Jos 2:13 and that you will **s** us from death."
10: 6 Come up to us quickly and **s** us! Help
Jdg 6:14 and **s** Israel out of Midian's hand.
6:15 "how can I **s** Israel? My clan is the
6:31 Are you trying to **s** him? Whoever
6:36 "If you will **s** Israel by my hand as
6:37 you will **s** Israel by my hand, as
7: 7 men that lapped I will **s** you
10: 1 the son of Dodo, rose to **s** Israel.
10:12 did I not **s** you from their hands?
10:13 gods, so I will no longer **s** you.
10:14 them **s** you when you are in trouble!"
12: 2 you didn't **s** me out of their hands.
1Sa 4: 3 **s** us from the hand of our enemies."
10:27 "How can this fellow **s** us?"
23: 2 the Philistines and **s** Keilah."
2Sa 22: 3 saviour—from violent men you **s** me.
22:28 You **s** the humble, but your eyes are
22:42 but there was no-one to **s** them—to
1Ki 1:12 let me advise you how you can **s** your
2Ki 16: 7 Come up and **s** me out of the hand of
18:35 has been able to **s** his land from me?
19:34 I will defend this city and **s** it,
1Ch 16:35 Cry out, "**S** us, O God our Saviour;
2Ch 20: 9 and you will hear us and **s** us.'
25:15 **s** their own people from your hand?"
32:11 'The LORD our God will **s** us from the
32:14 been able to **s** his people from me?
Ne 6:11 go into the temple to **s** his life?
Job 20:20 he cannot **s** himself by his treasure.
22:29 up!' then he will **s** the downcast.
40:14 that your own right hand can **s** you.
Ps 6: 4 **s** me because of your unfailing love
7: 1 **s** and deliver me from all who
17: 7 you who **s** by your right hand those
17:14 O LORD, by your hand **s** me from such
18:27 You **s** the humble but bring low those
18:41 but there was no-one to **s** them—to
20: 9 O LORD, **s** the king! Answer us when
22:21 **s** me from the horns of the wild oxen.
28: 9 **S** your people and bless your
Ps 31: 2 refuge, a strong fortress to **s** me.
31:16 **s** me in your unfailing love.
33:17 all its great strength it cannot **s**.
39: 8 **S** me from all my transgressions;
40:13 Be pleased, O LORD, to **s** me; O LORD,
51:14 **S** me from bloodguilt, O God, the God
54: 1 **S** me, O God, by your name; vindicate
59: 2 Deliver me from evildoers and **s** me
60: 5 **S** us and help us with your right
69: 1 **S** me, O God, for the waters have
69:35 for God will **s** Zion and rebuild the
70: 1 Hasten, O God, to **s** me; O LORD, come
71: 2 turn your ear to me and **s** me.
71: 3 always go; give the command to **s** me,
72: 4 and **s** the children of the needy;
72:13 needy and **s** the needy from death.
76: 9 to **s** all the afflicted of the land.
80: 2 Awaken your might; come and **s** us.
86: 2 **s** your servant who trusts in you.
86:16 and **s** the son of your maidservant.
89:48 or **s** himself from the power of the
91: 3 Surely he will **s** you from the
106: 4 come to my aid when you **s** them,
106:47 **S** us, O LORD our God, and gather us
108: 6 **S** us and help us with your right
109:26 **s** me in accordance with your love.
109:31 to **s** his life from those who condemn
116: 4 "O LORD, **s** me!"
118:25 O LORD, **s** us; O LORD, grant us
119:94 **S** me, for I am yours; I have sought
119:146 I call out to you; **s** me and I will
120: 2 **S** me, O LORD, from lying lips and
138: 7 foes, with your right hand you **s** me.
146: 3 in mortal men, who cannot **s**.
Pr 2:12 Wisdom will **s** you from the ways of
2:16 will **s** you also from the adulteress,
23:14 the rod and **s** his soul from death.
Isa 33:22 is our king; it is he who will **s** us.
35: 4 retribution he will come to **s** you."
36:20 has been able to **s** his land from me?
37:35 "I will defend this city and **s** it,
38:20 The LORD will **s** me, and we will sing
44:17 and says, "**S** me; you are my god."
44:20 he cannot **s** himself, or say,
45:20 who pray to gods that cannot **s**.
46: 7 it cannot **s** him from his troubles.
47:13 **s** you from what is coming upon you.
47:14 They cannot even **s** themselves from
47:15 there is not one that can **s** you.
49:25 you, and your children I will **s**.
57:13 let your collection of idols **s** you!
59: 1 of the LORD is not too short to **s**,
63: 1 in righteousness, mighty to **s**."
Jer 2:27 trouble, they say, 'Come and **s** us!'
2:28 Let them come if they can **s** you when
14: 9 like a warrior powerless to **s**? You
15:20 I am with you to rescue and **s** you,"
15:21 "I will **s** you from the hands of the
17:14 **s** me and I shall be saved, for you
30:10 'I will surely **s** you out of a
30:11 I am with you and will **s** you,'
31: 7 **s** your people, the remnant of Israel.
39:18 I will **s** you; you will not fall by
42:11 **s** you and deliver you from his hands.
46:27 I will surely **s** you out of a distant
Lam 4:17 for a nation that could not **s** us.
Eze 3:18 evil ways in order to **s** his life,
7:19 gold will not be able to **s** them in
13:21 and **s** my people from your hands,
13:22 evil ways and so **s** their lives,
13:23 I will **s** my people from your hands.
14:14 they could **s** only themselves by
14:16 not **s** their own sons or daughters.
14:18 not **s** their own sons or daughters.
14:20 could **s** neither son nor daughter.
14:20 They would **s** only themselves by
18:27 just and right, he will **s** his life.
33:12 man will not **s** him when he disobeys,
34:22 I will **s** my flock, and they will no
36:29 I will **s** you from all your
37:23 for I will **s** them from all their
Da 3:17 the God we serve is able to **s** us
3:29 for no other god can **s** in this way."
6:14 every effort until sundown to **s** him.
Hos 1: 7 and I will **s** them—not by bow,
13:10 Where is your king, that he may **s**

Hos 14: 3 Assyria cannot s us; we will not
Am 2:14 and the warrior will not s his life.
2:15 the horseman will not s his life.
Mic 2: 3 from which you cannot s yourselves.
6:14 You will store up but s nothing,
6:14 what you s I will give to the sword.
Hab 1: 2 "Violence!" but you do not s?
3:13 your people, to s your anointed one.
Zep 1:18 will be able to s them on the day
3:17 God is with you, he is mighty to s.
Zec 8: 7 "I will s my people from the
8:13 I s you, and you will be a blessing.
9:16 The LORD their God will s them on
10: 6 of Judah and s the house of Joseph.
12: 7 "The LORD will s the dwellings of
Mt 1:21 will s his people from their sins."
8:25 "Lord, s us! We're going to drown!
14:30 to sink, cried out, "Lord, s me!"
16:25 For whoever wants to s his life will
27:40 s yourself! Come down from the cross,
27:42 "but he can't s himself! He's the
27:49 Let's see if Elijah comes to s him."
Mk 3: 4 to do evil, to s life or to kill?"
8:35 For whoever wants to s his life will
8:35 for me and for the gospel will s it.
15:30 down from the cross and s yourself!"
15:31 they said, "but he can't s himself!
Lk 6: 9 evil, to s life or to destroy it?"
9:24 For whoever wants to s his life will
9:24 loses his life for me will s it.
19:10 to seek and to s what was lost."
23:35 "He saved others; let him s himself
23:37 the king of the Jews, s yourself."
23:39 you the Christ? S yourself and us!"
Jn 3:17 but to s the world through him.
12: 7 she should s this perfume for the
12:27 'Father, s me from this hour'?
12:47 to judge the world, but to s it.
Ac 2:40 "S yourselves from this corrupt
Ro 11:14 people to envy and s some of them.
1Co 1:21 was preached to s those who believe.
7:16 whether you will s your husband?
7:16 whether you will s your wife?
9:22 all possible means I might s some.
2Co 12:14 children should not have to s up for
1Ti 1:15 s sinners—of whom I am the worst.
4:16 s both yourself and your hearers.
Heb 5: 7 the one who could s him from death,
7:25 Therefore he is able to s completely
11: 7 fear built an ark to s his family.
Jas 1:21 planted in you, which can s you.
2:14 has no deeds? Can such faith s him?
4:12 one who is able to s and destroy.
5:20 of his way will s him from death
Jude :23 others from the fire and s them;

Saved (Save)

Ge 47:25 "You have s our lives," they said.
Ex 14:30 That day the LORD s Israel from the
16:24 they s it until morning, as Moses
18: 4 he s me from the sword of Pharaoh."
18: 8 the way and how the LORD had s them.
Dt 33:29 a people s by the LORD? He is your
Jos 9:26 Joshua s them from the Israelites,
Jdg 2:16 LORD raised up judges, who s them
2:18 he was with the judge and s them out
3: 9 Caleb's younger brother, who s them.
3:31 with an ox-goad. He too s Israel.
7: 2 me that her own strength has s her,
8:22 s us out of the hand of Midian."
1Sa 23: 5 and s the people of Keilah.
2Sa 19: 5 who have just s your life and the
22: 4 praise, and I am s from my enemies.
2Ki 14:27 he s them by the hand of Jeroboam
2Ch 32:22 the LORD s Hezekiah and the people
Job 26: 2 you have s the arm that is feeble!
Ps 18: 3 praise, and I am s from my enemies.
22: 5 They cried to you and were s; in you
33:16 No king is s by the size of his army;
34: 6 he s him out of all his troubles.
80: 3 shine upon us, that we may be s.
80: 7 shine upon us, that we may be s.
80:19 shine upon us, that we may be s.
106: 8 Yet he s them for his name's sake,
106:10 He s them from the hand of the foe;
106:21 They forgot the God who s them, who
107:13 and he s them from their distress.
107:19 and he s them from their distress.
116: 6 when I was in great need, he s me.
Ecc 9:15 and he s the city by his wisdom.
Isa 25: 9 we trusted in him, and he s us.
43:12 I have revealed and s and proclaimed
45:17 Israel will be s by the LORD with an
45:22 "Turn to me and be s, all you ends
63: 9 the angel of his presence s them.
64: 5 How then can we be s?
Jer 4:14 the evil from your heart and be s.
8:20 summer has ended, and we are not s."
17:14 save me and I shall be s, for you
23: 6 In his days Judah will be s and
30: 7 Jacob, but he will be s out of it.
33:16 In those days Judah will be s and
Eze 3:19 but you will have s yourself.
3:21 and you will have s yourself."
14:16 They alone would be s, but the land
14:18 They alone would be s.
33: 5 warning, he would have s himself.
33: 9 his sin, but you will be s yourself.
Joel 2:32 on the name of the LORD will be s;
Am 3:12 so will the Israelites be s, those
Mt 10:22 stands firm to the end will be s.
19:25 and asked, "Who then can be s?"
24:13 stands firm to the end will be s.
27:42 "He s others," they said, "but he
Mk 10:26 to each other, "Who then can be s?"
13:13 stands firm to the end will be s.
15:31 "He s others," they said, "but he
16:16 believes and is baptised will be s,
Lk 7:50 "Your faith has s you; go in peace.
8:12 that they may not believe and be s.
13:23 only a few people going to be s?"
18:26 this asked, "Who then can be s?"
23:35 They said, "He s others; let him
Jn 2:10 but you have s the best till now."
5:34 but I mention it that you may be s.
10: 9 whoever enters through me will be s.
Ac 2:21 on the name of the Lord will be s.'
2:47 number daily those who were being s.
4:12 given to men by which we must be s."
11:14 and all your household will be s.'
15: 1 taught by Moses, you cannot be s."
15:11 that we are s, just as they are."
16:17 are telling you the way to be s."
16:30 "Sirs, what must I do to be s?"
16:31 will be s—you and your household."
27:20 finally gave up all hope of being s.
27:31 with the ship, you cannot be s."
Ro 5: 9 be s from God's wrath through him!
5:10 shall we be s through his life!
8:24 For in this hope we were s. But hope
9:27 the sea, only the remnant will be s.
10: 1 Israelites is that they may be s.
10: 9 him from the dead, you will be s.
10:10 mouth that you confess and are s.
10:13 on the name of the Lord will be s."
11:26 all Israel will be s, as it is
1Co 1:18 are being s it is the power of God.
3:15 he himself will be s, but only as
5: 5 his spirit s on the day of the Lord.
10:33 good of many, so that they may be s.
15: 2 By this gospel you are s, if you
2Co 2:15 among those who are being s and
Eph 2: 5 —it is by grace you have been s.
2: 8 For it is by grace you have been s,
Php 1:28 that you will be s—and that by God.
1Th 2:16 the Gentiles so that they may be s.
2Th 2:10 to love the truth and so be s.
2:13 God chose you to be s through the
1Ti 2: 4 who wants all men to be s and to
2:15 women will be s through childbearing
2Ti 1: 9 who has s us and called us to a holy
Tit 3: 5 he s us, not because of righteous
3: 5 He s us through the washing of
Heb 10:39 but of those who believe and are s.
1Pe 3:20 eight in all, were s through water,
4:18 is hard for the righteous to be s,

Saves (Save)

1Sa 10:19 now rejected your God, who s you
17:47 by sword or spear that the LORD s;
Job 5:15 He s the needy from the sword in
5:15 he s them from the clutches of the
Ps 7:10 High, who s the upright in heart.
18:48 who s me from my enemies. You
20: 6 know that the LORD s his anointed;
34:18 s those who are crushed in spirit.
37:40 them from the wicked and s them,
51:14 O God, the God who s me, and my
55:16 I call to God, and the LORD s me.
57: 3 He sends from heaven and s me,
68:20 Our God is a God who s; from the
88: 1 O LORD, the God who s me, day and
145:19 he hears their cry and s them.
Pr 14:25 A truthful witness s lives, but a
Da 6:27 He rescues and he s; he performs
Am 3:12 "As a shepherd s from the lion's
1Pe 3:21 baptism that now s you also—
3:21 It s you by the resurrection of

Saving (Save)

Ge 50:20 now being done, the s of many lives.
1Sa 14: 6 nothing can hinder the LORD from s,
Ps 20: 6 with the s power of his right hand.
22: 1 Why are you so far from s me,
1Co 16: 2 s it up, so that when I come no

Saviour (Save)

Dt 32:15 him and rejected the Rock his S.
2Sa 22: 3 my stronghold, my refuge and my s—
22:47 Exalted be God, the Rock, my S!
1Ch 16:35 Cry out, "Save us, O God our S;
Ps 18:46 be to my Rock! Exalted be God my S!
24: 5 LORD and vindication from God his S.
25: 5 for you are God my S, and my hope is
27: 9 reject me or forsake me, O God my S.
38:22 Come quickly to help me, O Lord my S
42: 5 for I will yet praise him, my S
42:11 yet praise him, my S and my God.
43: 5 yet praise him, my S and my God.
65: 5 O God our S, the hope of all the
68:19 Praise be to the Lord, to God our S,
79: 9 Help us, O God our S, for the glory
85: 4 Restore us again, O God our S, and
89:26 my Father, my God, the Rock my S.'
Isa 17:10 You have forgotten God your S;
19:20 he will send them a s and defender,
43: 3 the Holy One of Israel, your S;
43:11 and apart from me there is no s.
45:15 himself, O God and S of Israel.
45:21 from me, a righteous God and a S;
49:26 the LORD, am your S, your Redeemer,
60:16 the LORD, am your S, your Redeemer,
62:11 'See, your S comes! See, his reward
63: 8 to me"; and so he became their S.
Jer 14: 8 O Hope of Israel, its S in times of
Hos 13: 4 no God but me, no S except me.
Mic 7: 7 I wait for God my S; my God will
Hab 3:18 LORD, I will be joyful in God my S.
Lk 1:47 my spirit rejoices in God my S,
2:11 Today in the town of David a S has
Jn 4:42 man really is the S of the world."
Ac 5:31 as Prince and S that he might give
13:23 Israel the S Jesus, as he promised.
Eph 5:23 his body, of which he is the S.
Php 3:20 we eagerly await a S from there,
1Ti 1: 1 of God our S and of Christ Jesus
2: 3 This is good, and pleases God our S,
4:10 who is the S of all men, and
2Ti 1:10 through the appearing of our S,
Tit 1: 3 to me by the command of God our S,
1: 4 the Father and Christ Jesus our S.
2:10 teaching about God our S attractive.
2:13 our great God and S, Jesus Christ,
3: 4 and love of God our S appeared,
3: 6 through Jesus Christ our S,
2Pe 1: 1 of our God and S Jesus Christ have
1:11 of our Lord and S Jesus Christ.
2:20 knowing our Lord and S Jesus Christ
3: 2 Lord and S through your apostles.
3:18 of our Lord and S Jesus Christ.
1Jn 4:14 his Son to be the S of the world.
Jude :25 to the only God our S be glory,

Sawdust
Mt 7: 3 "Why do you look at the speck of s
Lk 6:41 "Why do you look at the speck of s

Sawn (Saws)
Heb 11:37 They were stoned; they were s in two;

Saws (Sawn)
2Sa 12:31 consigning them to labour with s and
1Ch 20: 3 with s and with iron picks and axes.

Scabbard
1Sa 17:51 sword and drew it from the s.
Jer 47: 6 Return to your s; cease and be
Eze 21: 3 I will draw my sword from its s and
21: 5 have drawn my sword from its s;
21:30 Return the sword to its s. In the

Scabs
Job 7: 5 My body is clothed with worms and s,

Scale (Scales)
1Sa 17: 5 wore a coat of s armour of bronze
2Sa 22:30 a troop; with my God I can s a wall.
Ps 18:29 a troop; with my God I can s a wall.
Joel 2: 7 they s walls like soldiers.

Scales (Scale)
Lev 11: 9 may eat any that have fins and s.
11:10 that do not have fins and s—
11:12 that does not have fins and s is
19:36 Use honest s and honest weights, an
Dt 14: 9 you may eat any that has fins and s.
14:10 not have fins and s you may not eat;
Job 6: 2 all my misery be placed on the s!
31: 6 let God weigh me in honest s and he
Pr 11: 1 The LORD abhors dishonest s, but
16:11 Honest s and balances are from the
20:23 and dishonest s do not please him.
Isa 40:12 on the s and the hills in a balance?
40:15 they are regarded as dust on the s;
46: 6 bags and weigh out silver on the s;
Jer 32:10 and weighed out the silver on the s.
Eze 5: 1 a set of s and divide up the hair.
29: 4 of your streams stick to your s.
29: 4 all the fish sticking to your s.
45:10 You are to use accurate s, an
Da 5:27 weighed on the s and found wanting.
Hos 12: 7 The merchant uses dishonest s;
Am 8: 5 price and cheating with dishonest s,
Mic 6:11 Shall I acquit a man with dishonest s
Ac 9:18 Immediately, something like s fell
Rev 6: 5 was holding a pair of s in his hand.

Scalp (Scalps)
Lev 13:41 his hair from the front of his s

Scalps (Scalp)
Isa 3:17 the LORD will make their s bald."

Scapegoat (Goat)
Lev 16: 8 the LORD and the other for the s.
16:10 the goat chosen by lot as the s
16:10 sending it into the desert as a s.
16:26 The man who releases the goat as a s

Scar
Lev 13:23 it is only a s from the boil, and
13:28 it is only a s from the burn.

Scarce (Scarcer, Scarcity)
Dt 8: 9 a land where bread will not be s and
Eze 4:17 for food and water will be s.

Scarcer (Scarce)
Isa 13:12 I will make man s than pure gold,

Scarcity (Scarce)
Pr 6:11 a bandit and s like an armed man.
24:34 a bandit and s like an armed man.

Scarecrow
Jer 10: 5 Like a s in a melon patch, their

Scarlet
Ge 38:28 so the midwife took a s thread and
38:30 his brother, who had the s thread on
Ex 25: 4 blue, purple and s yarn and fine
26: 1 purple and s yarn, with cherubim
26:31 "Make a curtain of blue, purple and s
26:36 purple and s yarn and finely twisted
27:16 of blue, purple and s yarn and
28: 5 purple and s yarn, and fine linen.
28: 6 and of blue, purple and s yarn, and
28: 8 and with blue, purple and s yarn,
28:15 and of blue, purple and s yarn,
28:33 purple and s yarn around the hem of
35: 6 blue, purple and s yarn and fine
35:23 Everyone who had blue, purple or s
35:25 purple or s yarn or fine linen.
35:35 embroiderers in blue, purple and s
36: 8 purple and s yarn, with cherubim
36:35 purple and s yarn and finely twisted
36:37 purple and s yarn and finely twisted
38:18 purple and s yarn and finely twisted
38:23 purple and s yarn and fine linen.)
39: 1 From the blue, purple and s yarn
39: 2 and of blue, purple and s yarn,
39: 3 purple and s yarn and fine linen—
39: 5 and with blue, purple and s yarn,
39: 8 and of blue, purple and s yarn,
39:24 purple and s yarn and finely twisted
39:29 purple and s yarn—the work of an
Lev 14: 4 s yarn and hyssop be brought for the
14: 6 wood, the s yarn and the hyssop,
14:49 some cedar wood, s yarn and hyssop.
14:51 the hyssop, the s yarn and the live
14:52 wood, the hyssop and the s yarn.
Nu 4: 8 these they are to spread a s cloth,
19: 6 hyssop and s wool and throw them
Jos 2:18 you have tied this s cord in the
2:21 she tied the s cord in the window.
2Sa 1:24 weep for Saul, who clothed you in s
Pr 31:21 for all of them are clothed in s.
SS 4: 3 Your lips are like a s ribbon;
Isa 1:18 "Though your sins are like s, they
Jer 4:30 Why dress yourself in s and put on
Na 2: 3 are red; the warriors are clad in s.
Mt 27:28 They stripped him and put a s robe
Heb 9:19 together with water, s wool and
Rev 17: 3 I saw a woman sitting on a s beast
17: 4 The woman was dressed in purple and s
18:12 purple, silk and s cloth; every sort
18:16 dressed in fine linen, purple and s,

Scatter (Scattered, Scattering, Scatters)
Ge 49: 7 I will s them in Jacob and disperse
Lev 26:33 I will s you among the nations and
Nu 16:37 and s the coals some distance away,
Dt 4:27 The LORD will s you among the
28:64 the LORD will s you among all
32:26 I said I would s them and blot out
1Sa 13: 8 Gilgal, and Saul's men began to s.
1Ki 14:15 and s them beyond the River,
Ne 1: 8 I will s you among the nations,
Ps 68:30 S the nations who delight in war.
106:27 and s them throughout the lands.
144: 6 lightning and s ⌞the enemies⌟;
Ecc 3: 5 a time to s stones and a time to
Isa 24: 1 its face and s its inhabitants—
28:25 does he not sow caraway and s cummin
33: 3 when you rise up, the nations s.
Jer 9:16 I will s them among nations that
13:24 "I will s you like chaff driven by
18:17 I will s them before their enemies;
30:11 all the nations among which I s you,
46:28 all the nations among which I s you,
49:32 I will s to the winds those who are
49:36 I will s them to the four winds,
Eze 5: 2 And s a third to the wind. For I
5:10 s all your survivors to the winds.
5:12 and a third I will s to the winds
6: 5 s your bones around your altars.
10: 2 cherubim and s them over the city.
12:14 I will s to the winds all those
12:15 and s them through the countries.
20:23 and s them through the countries,
22:15 and s you through the countries;
29:12 and s them through the countries.
30:23 and s them through the countries.
30:26 and s them through the countries.
Da 4:14 off its leaves and s its fruit.
Hab 3:14 his warriors stormed out to s us,
Zec 1:21 the land of Judah to s its people."
10: 9 Though I s them among the peoples,

Scattered (Scatter)
Ge 9:19 people who were s over the earth.
10:18 Later the Canaanite clans s
11: 4 s over the face of the whole earth."
11: 8 the LORD s them from there over all
11: 9 From there the LORD s them over the
Ex 5:12 the people s all over Egypt to
32:20 s it on the water and made the
Nu 10:35 May your enemies be s; may your
Dt 30: 3 from all the nations where he s you.
Jdg 9:45 the city and s salt over it.
1Sa 11:11 Those who survived were s, so that
30:16 and there they were, s over the
2Sa 17:19 of the well and s grain over it.
22:15 He shot arrows and s the enemies,
1Ki 22:17 "I saw all Israel s on the hills
2Ki 23: 6 and s the dust over the graves
25: 5 were separated from him and s,
2Ch 18:16 "I saw all Israel s on the hills
34: 4 These he broke to pieces and s over
Est 3: 8 s among the peoples in all the
Job 4:11 and the cubs of the lioness are s.
18:15 sulphur is s over his dwelling.
38:24 the east winds are s over the earth?
Ps 18:14 He shot his arrows and s the enemies,
44:11 and have s us among the nations.
53: 5 God s the bones of those who
68: 1 May God arise, may his enemies be s;
68:14 the Almighty s the kings in the land,
89:10 your strong arm you s your enemies.
92: 9 all evildoers will be s.
112: 9 He has s abroad his gifts to the
141: 7 been s at the mouth of the grave."
Isa 11:12 he will assemble the s people of
Jer 3:13 you have s your favours to foreign
10:21 prosper and all their flock is s.
23: 2 "Because you have s my flock and
31:10 'He who s Israel will gather them
40:12 the countries where they had been s.
40:15 gathered around you to be s and the
43: 5 the nations where they had been s.
50:17 "Israel is a s flock that lions have
52: 8 were separated from him and s,
Lam 4: 1 are s at the head of every street.
4:16 The LORD himself has s them; he no
Eze 6: 8 are s among the lands and nations.
11:16 and s them among the countries,
11:17 the countries where you have been s,
17:21 survivors will be s to the winds.
20:34 you have been s—with a mighty hand
20:41 the countries where you have been s,
28:25 the nations where they have been s,
29:13 from the nations where they were s.
34: 5 they were s because there was no
34: 5 and when they were s they became
34: 6 They were s over the whole earth,
34:12 a shepherd looks after his s flock
34:12 s on a day of clouds and darkness.
36:19 and they were s through the
Da 9: 7 countries where you have s us
Joel 3: 2 for they s my people among the
Na 3:18 Your people are s on the mountains
Zep 3:10 my worshippers, my s people, will
3:19 and gather those who have been s.
Zec 1:19 that s Judah, Israel and Jerusalem."
1:21 "These are the horns that s Judah so
2: 6 "for I have s you to the four winds
7:14 'I s them with a whirlwind among all
13: 7 and the sheep will be s, and I will
Mt 25:24 gathering where you have not s seed.
25:26 and gather where I have not s seed?
26:31 the sheep of the flock will be s.'
Mk 14:27 shepherd, and the sheep will be s.'
Lk 1:51 he has s those who are proud in

Jn 2:15 he s the coins of the money-changers
7:35 our people live s among the Greeks,
11:52 but also for the s children of God,
16:32 you will be s, each to his own home.
Ac 5:37 and all his followers were s.
8: 1 were s throughout Judea and Samaria.
8: 4 Those who had been s preached the
11:19 Now those who had been s by the
1Co 10: 5 their bodies were s over the desert.
2Co 9: 9 "He has s abroad his gifts to the
Jas 1: 1 twelve tribes s among the nations:
1Pe 1: 1 strangers in the world, s throughout

Scattering (Scatter)
1Sa 13:11 "When I saw that the men were s, and
Jer 23: 1 and s the sheep of my pasture!"
Mt 13: 4 he was s the seed, some fell along
Mk 4: 4 he was s the seed, some fell along
Lk 8: 5 As he was s the seed, some fell

Scatters (Scatter)
Job 36:30 See how he s his lightning about him,
37:11 he s his lightning through them.
Ps 147:16 and s the frost like ashes.
Mt 12:30 he who does not gather with me s.
Mk 4:26 A man s seed on the ground.
Lk 11:23 he who does not gather with me, s.
Jn 10:12 the wolf attacks the flock and s it.

Scene
Mk 9:25 a crowd was running to the s, he

Scent
Job 14: 9 yet at the s of water it will bud
39:25 He catches the s of battle from

Sceptre (Sceptres)
Ge 49:10 The s will not depart from Judah,
Nu 24:17 a s will rise out of Israel.
Est 4:11 king to extend the gold s to him
5: 2 her the gold s that was in his hand.
5: 2 and touched the tip of the s.
8: 4 the king extended the gold s to
Ps 2: 9 You will rule them with an iron s;
45: 6 and ever; a s of justice will be
45: 6 will be the s of your kingdom.
60: 7 Ephraim is my helmet, Judah my s.
108: 8 Ephraim is my helmet, Judah my s.
110: 2 The LORD will extend your mighty s
125: 3 The s of the wicked will not remain
Isa 14: 5 of the wicked, the s of the rulers,
30:31 with his s he will strike them down.
Jer 48:17 say, 'How broken is the mighty s,
Eze 19:11 were strong, fit for a ruler's s.
19:14 is left on it fit for a ruler's s.
21:10 'Shall we rejoice in the s of my son
21:13 And what if the s of Judah, which
Am 1: 5 one who holds the s in Beth Eden.
1: 8 the one who holds the s in Ashkelon.
Zec 10:11 down and Egypt's s will pass away.
Heb 1: 8 will be the s of your kingdom.
Rev 2:27 'He will rule them with an iron s;
12: 5 rule all the nations with an iron s.
19:15 "He will rule them with an iron s."

Sceptres (Sceptre)
Nu 21:18 sank—the nobles with s and staffs.

Sceva
Ac 19:14 Seven sons of S, a Jewish chief

Scheme (Schemer, Schemes, Scheming)
Est 9:25 that the evil s Haman had devised
Ecc 7:25 to search out wisdom and the s of
7:27 to discover the s of things—
Eze 38:10 mind and you will devise an evil s.

Schemer (Scheme)
Pr 24: 8 who plots evil will be known as a s.

Schemes (Scheme)
Ex 21:14 if a man s and kills another man
Job 5:13 the s of the wily are swept away.
10: 3 you smile on the s of the wicked?
18: 7 weakened; his own s throw him down.
21:27 the s by which you would wrong me.
Ps 10: 2 who are caught in the s he devises.
21:11 wicked s, they cannot succeed;
26:10 in whose hands are wicked s, whose
37: 7 when they carry out their wicked s.
119:150 Those who devise wicked s are near,
Pr 1:31 be filled with the fruit of their s.
6:18 a heart that devises wicked s, feet
24: 9 The s of folly are sin, and men
Ecc 7:29 men have gone in search of many s."
8:11 are filled with s to do wrong.
Isa 32: 7 he makes up evil s to destroy the
Jer 6:19 the fruit of their s, because they
11:15 she works out her evil s with many?
2Co 2:11 For we are not unaware of his s.
Eph 6:11 your stand against the devil's s.

Scheming (Scheme)
Ne 6: 2 But they were s to harm me;
Eph 4:14 of men in their deceitful s.

Scholar
1Co 1:20 Where is the wise man? Where is the s

Scoff (Scoffed, Scoffers, Scoffing, Scoffs)
1Ki 9: 8 will be appalled and will s and say,
Ps 59: 8 you s at all those nations.
73: 8 They s, and speak with malice; in
Jer 19: 8 will s because of all its wounds.
49:17 will s because of all its wounds.
50:13 and s because of all her wounds.
Lam 2:15 they s and shake their heads at the
2:16 s and gnash their teeth and say,
Hab 1:10 They deride kings and s at rulers.
Zep 2:15 pass by her s and shake their fists.

Scoffed (Scoff)
2Ch 36:16 despised his words and s at his

Scoffers (Scoff)
Isa 28:14 s who rule this people in Jerusalem.
Ac 13:41 "'Look, you s, wonder and perish,
2Pe 3: 3 that in the last days s will come,
Jude :18 "In the last times there will be s

Scoffing (Scoff)
2Pe 3: 3 s and following their own evil

Scoffs (Scoff)
Ps 2: 4 heaven laughs; the Lord s at them.
Pr 29: 9 rages and s, and there is no peace.

Scoop (Scooped, Scooping, Scoops)
Pr 6:27 Can a man s fire into his lap

Scooped (Scoop)
Jdg 14: 9 which he s out with his hands and

Scooping (Scoop)
Isa 30:14 hearth or s water out of a cistern."

Scoops (Scoop)
Ps 7:15 He who digs a hole and s it out

Scorch (Scorched, Scorching, Sun-scorched)
Rev 16: 8 given power to s people with fire.

Scorched (Scorch)
Ge 41: 6 and s by the east wind.
41:23 and thin and s by the east wind.
41:27 ears of corn s by the east wind:
2Ki 19:26 on the roof, s before it grows up.
Pr 6:28 hot coals without his feet being s?
Isa 9:19 LORD Almighty the land will be s
37:27 on the roof, s before it grows up.
Eze 20:47 from south to north will be s by it.
Da 3:27 their robes were not s, and there
Mt 13: 6 the plants were s, and they withered
Mk 4: 6 the plants were s, and they withered

Scorching (Scorch)
Dt 28:22 with fever and inflammation, with s
Ps 11: 6 a s wind will be their lot.
Pr 16:27 and his speech is like a s fire.
Isa 11:15 with a s wind he will sweep his hand
Jer 4:11 "A s wind from the barren heights in
Jnh 4: 8 God provided a s east wind, and
Jas 1:11 For the sun rises with s heat and
Rev 7:16 not beat upon them, nor any s heat.

Scorn (Scorned, Scornfully, Scorning, Scorns)
Dt 28:37 an object of s and ridicule to all
1Sa 2:29 Why do you s my sacrifice and
2Ch 29: 8 an object of dread and horror and s,
Job 16:10 they strike my cheek in s and unite
19:18 Even the little boys s me; when I
34: 7 What man is like Job, who drinks s
Ps 39: 8 do not make me the s of fools.
44:13 s and derision of those around us.
64: 8 them will shake their heads in s.
69: 7 For I endure s for your sake, and
69:10 I weep and fast, I must endure s;
69:20 S has broken my heart and has left
71:13 me be covered with s and disgrace.
79: 4 s and derision to those around us.
89:41 has become the s of his neighbours.
109:25 I am an object of s to my accusers;
119:22 Remove from me s and contempt, for I
Pr 23: 9 for he will s the wisdom of your
Isa 43:28 Jacob to destruction and Israel to s.
Jer 18:16 an object of lasting s; all who pass
19: 8 city and make it an object of s;
25: 9 them an object of horror and s,
25:18 object of horror and s and cursing,
29:18 of s and reproach, among all the
48:27 head in s whenever you speak of her?
51:37 an object of horror and s,
Eze 22: 4 you an object of s to the nations
23:32 it will bring s and derision, for
34:29 land or bear the s of the nations.
36: 6 have suffered the s of the nations.
36: 7 around you will also suffer s.
36:15 and no longer will you suffer the s
Da 9:16 object of s to all those around us.
Joel 2:17 your inheritance an object of s,
2:19 you an object of s to the nations.
Mic 6:16 you will bear the s of the nations."
Hab 2: 6 him with ridicule and s, saying,
Gal 4:14 did not treat me with contempt or s.

Scorned (Scorn)
2Ch 30:10 but the people s and ridiculed them.
Est 3: 6 s the idea of killing only Mordecai.
Ps 22: 6 s by men and despised by the people
69:19 You know how I am s, disgraced and
SS 8: 7 for love, it would be utterly s.
Eze 16:31 a prostitute, because you s payment.
16:57 you are now s by the daughters of

Scornfully (Scorn)
Job 34:37 s he claps his hands among us

Scorning (Scorn)
Heb 12: 2 s its shame, and sat down at the

Scorns (Scorn)
Pr 13:13 He who s instruction will pay for it,
30:17 that s obedience to a mother,

Scorpion (Scorpions)
Nu 34: 4 cross south of S Pass, continue on
Jos 15: 3 crossed south of S Pass, continued
Jdg 1:36 was from S Pass to Sela and beyond.
Lk 11:12 asks for an egg, will give him a s?
Rev 9: 5 sting of a s when it strikes a man.

Scorpions (Scorpion)
Dt 8:15 with its venomous snakes and s.
1Ki 12:11 I will scourge you with s.'"
12:14 I will scourge you with s."
2Ch 10:11 I will scourge you with s.'"
10:14 I will scourge you with s."
Eze 2: 6 all around you and you live among s.
Lk 10:19 to trample of snakes and s
Rev 9: 3 power like that of s of the earth.
9:10 They had tails and stings like s,

Scoundrel (Scoundrel's, Scoundrels)
2Sa 16: 7 get out, you man of blood, you s!
Pr 6:12 A s and villain, who goes about with
16:27 A s plots evil, and his speech is
Isa 32: 5 noble nor the s be highly respected.

Scoundrel's (Scoundrel)
Isa 32: 7 The s methods are wicked, he makes

Scoundrels (Scoundrel)
1Ki 21:10 seat two s opposite him and have
21:13 two s came and sat opposite him and
2Ch 13: 7 Some worthless s gathered around him

Scoured
Lev 6:28 is to be s and rinsed with water.

Scourge (Scourged)
1Ki 12:11 I will s you with scorpions.'"
12:14 I will s you with scorpions."
2Ch 10:11 I will s you with scorpions.'"
10:14 I will s you with scorpions."
Job 9:23 a s brings sudden death, he mocks
Ps 39:10 Remove your s from me; I am overcome
Isa 28:15 When an overwhelming s sweeps by, it
28:18 When the overwhelming s sweeps by,

Scourged (Scourge)
1Ki 12:11 My father s you with whips; I will
12:14 My father s you with whips; I will
2Ch 10:11 My father s you with whips; I will
10:14 My father s you with whips; I will

Scouts
1Sa 26: 4 he sent out s and learned that Saul
1Ki 20:17 Now Ben-Hadad had dispatched s, who

Scrape (Scraped)
Eze 26: 4 I will s away her rubble and make

Scraped (Scrape)
Lev 14:41 all the inside walls of the house s
14:41 the material that is s off dumped
14:43 out and the house s and plastered,
Job 2: 8 s himself with it as he sat among

Scraps
Jdg 1: 7 off have picked up s under my table.
Eze 13:19 handfuls of barley and s of bread.

Scrawny
Ge 41:19 came up—s and very ugly and lean.
49:14 "Issachar is a s donkey lying down

Scream (Screamed, Screams)
Ge 39:15 he heard me s for help, he left his
Dt 22:24 in a town and did not s for help,

Screamed (Scream)
Ge 39:14 in here to sleep with me, but I s.
39:18 as soon as I s for help, he left his
Dt 22:27 the betrothed girl s, there was

Screams (Scream)
Lk 9:39 A spirit seizes him and he suddenly s

Screech
Lev 11:16 the horned owl, the s owl, the gull,
Dt 14:15 the horned owl, the s owl, the gull,
Isa 34:11 The desert owl and s owl will
Zep 2:14 The desert owl and the s owl will

Scribe (Scribe's, Scribes)
1Ch 24: 6 The s Shemaiah son of Nethanel, a
27:32 a man of insight and a s.
Ne 8: 1 They told Ezra the s to bring out
8: 4 Ezra the s stood on a high wooden
8: 9 Ezra the priest and s, and the
8:13 gathered round Ezra the s to give
12:26 and of Ezra the priest and s.
12:36 Ezra the s led the procession.
13:13 Zadok the s, and a Levite named
Jer 36:26 arrest Baruch the s and Jeremiah
36:32 it to the s Baruch son of Neriah,

Scribe's (Scribe)
Jer 36:23 the king cut them off with a s knife

Scribes (Scribe)
1Ch 2:55 the clans of s who lived at Jabez:
2Ch 34:13 were secretaries, s and doorkeepers.
Jer 8: 8 pen of the s has handled it falsely?

Script
Ezr 4: 7 The letter was written in Aramaic s
Est 1:22 to each province in its own s and to
3:12 They wrote out in the s of each
8: 9 written in the s of each province
8: 9 Jews in their own s and language.

Scripture (Scriptures)
Mk 12:10 Haven't you read this s: "'The
Lk 4:21 s is fulfilled in your hearing."
Jn 2:22 Then they believed the **S** and the
7:38 believes in me, as the **S** has said,
7:42 Does not the **S** say that the Christ
10:35 came—and the **S** cannot be broken—
13:18 But this is to fulfil the s: 'He who
17:12 so that **S** would be fulfilled.
19:24 This happened that the s might be
19:28 and so that the **S** would be fulfilled,
19:36 so that the s would be fulfilled:
19:37 and, as another s says, "They will
20: 9 They still did not understand from **S**
Ac 1:16 said, "Brothers, the **S** had to be
8:32 was reading this passage of **S**:
8:35 began with that very passage of **S**
Ro 4: 3 What does the **S** say? "Abraham
9:17 For the **S** says to Pharaoh: "I raised
10:11 the **S** says, "Anyone who trusts in
11: 2 Don't you know what the **S** says in
Gal 3: 8 The **S** foresaw that God would justify
3:16 The **S** does not say "and to seeds",
3:22 the **S** declares that the whole world
4:30 what does the **S** say? "Get rid of the
1Ti 4:13 to the public reading of **S**, to
5:18 For the **S** says, "Do not muzzle the
2Ti 3:16 All **S** is God-breathed and is useful
Jas 2: 8 keep the royal law found in **S**,
2:23 the s was fulfilled that says,
4: 5 Or do you think **S** says without
4: 6 us more grace. That is why **S** says:
1Pe 2: 6 For in **S** it says: "See, I lay a
2Pe 1:20 no prophecy of **S** came about by the

Scriptures (Scripture)
Da 9: 2 I, Daniel, understood from the **S**,
Mt 21:42 "Have you never read in the **S**:
22:29 not know the **S** or the power of God.
26:54 how then would the **S** be fulfilled
Mk 12:24 not know the **S** or the power of God?
14:49 But the **S** must be fulfilled."
Lk 24:27 in all the **S** concerning himself.
24:32 on the road and opened the **S** to us?"
24:45 so they could understand the **S**.
Jn 5:39 You diligently study the **S** because
5:39 are the **S** that testify about me,
Ac 17: 2 he reasoned with them from the **S**,
17:11 examined the **S** every day to see if
18:24 with a thorough knowledge of the **S**.
18:28 proving from the **S** that Jesus was
Ro 1: 2 through his prophets in the Holy **S**
15: 4 of the **S** we might have hope.
1Co 15: 3 for our sins according to the **S**,
15: 4 on the third day according to the **S**,
2Ti 3:15 infancy you have known the holy **S**,
2Pe 3:16 as they do the other **S**, to their

Scroll (Scrolls)
Ex 17:14 "Write this on a s as something to
Nu 5:23 is to write these curses on a s
Dt 17:18 he is to write for himself on a s a
Jos 18: 9 They wrote its description on a s,
1Sa 10:25 He wrote them down on a s and
Ezr 6: 2 A s was found in the citadel of
Job 19:23 that they were written on a s,
Ps 40: 7 it is written about me in the s.
56: 8 list my tears on your s—are they not
Isa 8: 1 The LORD said to me, "Take a large s
29:11 is nothing but words sealed in a s.
29:11 And if you give the s to someone who
29:12 Or if you give the s to someone who
29:18 deaf will hear the words of the s,
30: 8 inscribe it on a s, that for the
34: 4 and the sky rolled up like a s;
34:16 Look in the s of the LORD and read:
Jer 36: 2 "Take a s and write on it all the
36: 4 to him, Baruch wrote them on the s.
36: 6 read to the people from the s the
36: 8 the words of the LORD from the s.
36:10 the words of Jeremiah from the s.
36:11 the words of the LORD from the s,
36:13 Baruch read to the people from the s,
36:14 "Bring the s from which you have
36:14 went to them with the s in his hand.
36:18 and I wrote them in ink on the s."
36:20 After they put the s in the room of
36:21 The king sent Jehudi to get the s,
36:23 read three or four columns of the s,
36:23 the entire s was burned in the fire.
36:25 urged the king not to burn the s,
36:27 After the king burned the s
36:28 "Take another s and write on it all
36:28 the words that were on the first s,
36:29 says: You burned that s and said,
36:32 Jeremiah took another s and gave it
36:32 the words of the s that Jehoiakim
45: 1 after Baruch had written on a s the
51:60 Jeremiah had written on a s about
51:63 you finish reading this s, tie a
Eze 2: 9 stretched out to me. In it was a s,
3: 1 eat what is before you, eat this s;
3: 2 mouth, and he gave me the s to eat.
3: 3 "Son of man, eat this s I am giving
Da 12: 4 seal the words of the s until the
Zec 5: 1 there before me was a flying s!
5: 2 "I see a flying s, thirty feet long
Mal 3:16 A s of remembrance was written in
Lk 4:17 The s of the prophet Isaiah was
4:20 he rolled up the s, gave it back to
Heb 9:19 sprinkled the s and all the people.
10: 7 it is written about me in the s—
Rev 1:11 which said: "Write on a s what you
5: 1 a s with writing on both sides
5: 2 to break the seals and open the s?"
5: 3 open the s or even look inside it.
5: 4 worthy to open the s or look inside.
5: 5 to open the s and its seven seals."
5: 7 He came and took the s from the
5: 9 "You are worthy to take the s and to
6:14 The sky receded like a s, rolling up,
10: 2 He was holding a little s, which lay
10: 8 "Go, take the s that lies open in
10: 9 asked him to give me the little s.
10:10 I took the little s from the angel's

Scrolls (Scroll)
Ac 19:19 brought their s together and burned
19:19 they calculated the value of the s,
2Ti 4:13 and my s, especially the parchments.

Sculptured
2Ch 3:10 Place he made a pair of s cherubim

Scum
Lam 3:45 You have made us s and refuse among
1Co 4:13 we have become the s of the earth,

Scythian
Col 3:11 barbarian, **S**, slave or free, but

Sea (Dead Sea, Great Sea, Red Sea, Seafarers, Seamen, Seas, Seashore, Seaweed)
Ge 1:21 the great creatures of the **s**
1:26 rule over the fish of the **s** and the
1:28 Rule over the fish of the **s** and the
9: 2 and upon all the fish of the **s**;
14: 3 the Valley of Siddim (the Salt **S**).
32:12 like the sand of the **s**, which
41:49 of grain, like the sand of the **s**;
Ex 14: 2 Hahiroth, between Migdol and the **s**.
14: 2 They are to camp by the **s**, directly
14: 9 camped by the **s** near Pi Hahiroth,
14:16 stretch out your hand over the **s** to
14:16 can go through the **s** on dry ground.
14:21 stretched out his hand over the **s**,
14:21 all that night the LORD drove the **s**
14:22 the Israelites went through the **s** on
14:23 horsemen followed them into the **s**.
14:26 "Stretch out your hand over the **s** so
14:27 stretched out his hand over the **s**,
14:27 the **s** went back to its place.
14:27 and the LORD swept them into the **s**.
14:28 followed the Israelites into the **s**.
14:29 the Israelites went through the **s** on
15: 1 its rider he has hurled into the **s**.
15: 4 his army he has hurled into the **s**.
15: 8 congealed in the heart of the **s**.
15:10 breath, and the **s** covered them.
15:19 and horsemen went into the **s**,
15:19 the waters of the **s** back over them,
15:19 walked through the **s** on dry ground.
15:21 its rider he has hurled into the **s**."
20:11 the **s**, and all that is in them, but
25: 5 skins dyed red and hides of **s** cows;
26:14 that a covering of hides of **s** cows.
35: 7 skins dyed red and hides of **s** cows;
35:23 red or hides of **s** cows brought them.
36:19 that a covering of hides of **s** cows.
39:34 the covering of hides of **s** cows
Nu 4: 6 to cover this with hides of **s** cows,
4: 8 cover that with hides of **s** cows and
4:10 in a covering of hides of **s** cows
4:11 cover that with hides of **s** cows and
4:12 cover that with hides of **s** cows and
4:14 a covering of hides of **s** cows and
4:25 outer covering of hides of **s** cows,
11:22 fish in the **s** were caught for them?"
11:31 LORD and drove quail in from the **s**.
13:29 near the **s** and along the Jordan."
33: 8 through the **s** into the desert,
34: 3 start from the end of the Salt **S**,
34: 5 the Wadi of Egypt and end at the **S**.
34:11 slopes east of the **S** of Kinnereth.
34:12 the Jordan and end at the Salt **S**.
Dt 3:17 the **S** of the Arabah (the Salt **S**),
4:49 as far as the **S** of the Arabah, below
11:24 Euphrates River to the western **s**.
30:13 Nor is it beyond the **s**, so that you
30:13 "Who will cross the **s** to get it and
34: 2 of Judah as far as the western **s**,
Jos 3:16 the **S** of the Arabah (the Salt **S**)
12: 3 from the **S** of Kinnereth to the
12: 3 to the **S** of the Arabah (the Salt **S**),
13:27 to the end of the **S** of Kinnereth).
15: 2 at the southern end of the Salt **S**,
15: 4 the Wadi of Egypt, ending at the **s**.
15: 5 The eastern boundary is the Salt **S**
15: 5 of the **s** at the mouth of the Jordan,
15:11 The boundary ended at the **s**.
16: 3 and on to Gezer, ending at the **s**.
16: 6 continued to the **s**. From Micmethath
16: 8 the Kanah Ravine and ended at the **s**.
17: 9 of the ravine and ended at the **s**.
17:10 territory of Manasseh reached the **s**
18:19 at the northern bay of the Salt **S**,
19:29 out at the **s** in the region of Aczib,
24: 6 you came to the **s**, and the Egyptians
24: 7 the **s** over them and covered them.
2Sa 22:16 The valleys of the **s** were exposed
1Ki 5: 9 them down from Lebanon to the **s**,
5: 9 rafts by **s** to the place you specify.
1Ki 7:23 He made the **S** of cast metal,
7:24 in two rows in one piece with the **S**.
7:25 The **S** stood on twelve bulls, three
7:25 The **S** rested on top of them, and
7:39 He placed the **S** on the south side,
7:44 the **S** and the twelve bulls under it;
9:27 sailors who knew the **s**—to serve in
10:22 at **s** along with the ships of Hiram.
18:43 "Go and look towards the **s**," he told
18:44 a man's hand is rising from the **s**.
2Ki 14:25 Lebo Hamath to the **S** of the Arabah,
16:17 He removed the **S** from the bronze
25:13 the movable stands and the bronze **S**
25:16 the **S** and the movable stands, which
1Ch 16:32 Let the **s** resound, and all that is
18: 8 Solomon used to make the bronze **S**,
2Ch 2:16 them in rafts by **s** down to Joppa.
4: 2 He made the **S** of cast metal,
4: 3 in two rows in one piece with the **S**.
4: 4 The **S** stood on twelve bulls, three
4: 4 The **S** rested on top of them, and
4: 6 but the **S** was to be used by the
4:10 He placed the **S** on the south side,
4:15 the **S** and the twelve bulls under it;
8:18 own officers, men who knew the **s**.
20: 2 Edom, from the other side of the **S**.
Ezr 3: 7 logs by **s** from Lebanon to Joppa,
Ne 9:11 You divided the **s** before them, so
Job 7:12 Am I the **s**, or the monster of the
9: 8 and treads on the waves of the **s**.
11: 9 than the earth and wider than the **s**.
12: 8 or let the fish of the **s** inform you.
14:11 water disappears from the **s** or a
26:12 By his power he churned up the **s**;
28:14 the **s** says, 'It is not with me.'
36:30 him, bathing the depths of the **s**.
38: 8 "Who shut up the **s** behind doors when
38:16 journeyed to the springs of the **s**
41:31 and stirs up the **s** like a pot of
Ps 8: 8 and the fish of the **s**, all that swim
18:15 The valleys of the **s** were exposed
33: 7 He gathers the waters of the **s** into
46: 2 fall into the heart of the **s**,
66: 6 He turned the **s** into dry land, they
68:22 bring them from the depths of the **s**,
72: 8 He will rule from **s** to **s** and from
74:13 was you who split open the **s** by your
77:19 Your path led through the **s**, your
78:13 He divided the **s** and led them
78:53 but the **s** engulfed their enemies.
80:11 sent out its boughs to the **S**, its
89: 9 You rule over the surging **s**;
89:25 I will set his hand over the **s**, his
93: 4 mightier than the breakers of the **s**
95: 5 The **s** is his, for he made it, and
96:11 let the **s** resound, and all that is
98: 7 Let the **s** resound, and everything in
104:25 There is the **s**, vast and spacious,
107:23 Others went out on the **s** in ships;
107:29 the waves of the **s** were hushed.
114: 3 The **s** looked and fled, the Jordan
114: 5 Why was it, O **s**, that you fled,
139: 9 I settle on the far side of the **s**,
146: 6 the Maker of heaven and earth, the **s**
148: 7 **s** creatures and all ocean depths,
Pr 8:29 he gave the **s** its boundary so that
Ecc 1: 7 All streams flow into the **s**,
1: 7 yet the **s** is never full.
Isa 5:30 over it like the roaring of the **s**.
9: 1 the way of the **s**, along the Jordan—
10:22 be like the sand by the **s**, only a
11: 9 the LORD as the waters cover the **s**.
11:11 Hamath and from the islands of the **s**.
11:15 dry up the gulf of the Egyptian **s**;
16: 8 spread out and went as far as the **s**.
17:12 they rage like the raging **s**!
18: 2 which sends envoys by **s** in papyrus
21: 1 concerning the Desert by the **S**:
23: 4 and you, O fortress of the **s**,
23: 4 for the **s** has spoken: "I have
23:11 stretched out his hand over the **s**
24:15 of Israel, in the islands of the **s**.
27: 1 he will slay the monster of the **s**.
42:10 you who go down to the **s**, and all
43:16 he who made a way through the **s**,
48:18 like the waves of the **s**.
Isa 50: 2 By a mere rebuke I dry up the **s**,
51:10 Was it not you who dried up the **s**,
51:10 made a road in the depths of the **s**
51:15 who churns up the **s** so that its
57:20 the wicked are like the tossing **s**,
63:11 he who brought them through the **s**,
Jer 5:22 I made the sand a boundary for the **s**
6:23 They sound like the roaring **s** as
15: 8 numerous than the sand of the **s**.
25:22 of the coastlands across the **s**;
27:19 the **S**, the movable stands and the
31:35 who stirs up the **s** so that its waves
46:18 the mountains, like Carmel by the **s**.
48:32 Your branches spread as far as the **s**
48:32 reached as far as the **s** of Jazer.
49:23 troubled like the restless **s**.
50:42 They sound like the roaring **s** as
51:36 I will dry up her **s** and make her
51:42 The **s** will rise over Babylon;
52:17 the movable stands and the bronze **S**
52:20 the **S** and the twelve bronze bulls
Lam 2:13 Your wound is as deep as the **s**.
Eze 26: 3 like the **s** casting up its waves.
26: 5 Out in the **s** she will become a place
26:12 timber and rubble into the **s**.
26:17 of renown, peopled by men of the **s**!
26:18 the islands in the **s** are terrified
27: 3 situated at the gateway to the **s**,
27: 9 All the ships of the **s** and their
27:25 heavy cargo in the heart of the **s**.
27:26 you to pieces in the heart of the **s**.
27:27 the **s** on the day of your shipwreck.
27:32 like Tyre, surrounded by the **s**?"
27:34 Now you are shattered by the **s** in
38:20 The fish of the **s**, the birds of the
39:11 those who travel east towards the **S**.
47: 8 the Arabah, where it enters the **S**.
47: 8 When it empties into the **S**, the
47:17 The boundary will extend from the **s**
47:18 the eastern **s** and as far as Tamar.
Da 7: 2 of heaven churning up the great **s**.
7: 3 the others, came up out of the **s**.
Hos 4: 3 air and the fish of the **s** are dying.
Joel 2:20 columns going into the eastern **s**
2:20 in the rear into the western **s**.
Am 5: 8 who calls for the waters of the **s**
8:12 Men will stagger from **s** to **s** and
9: 3 hide from me at the bottom of the **s**,
9: 6 who calls for the waters of the **s**
Jnh 1: 4 the LORD sent a great wind on the **s**,
1: 5 And they threw the cargo into the **s**
1: 9 who made the **s** and the land."
1:11 The **s** was getting rougher and
1:11 you to make the **s** calm down for us?"
1:12 "Pick me up and throw me into the **s**,"
1:13 the **s** grew even wilder than before.
1:15 and the raging **s** grew calm.
Mic 7:12 **s** to **s** and from mountain to mountain.
7:19 iniquities into the depths of the **s**.
Na 1: 4 He rebukes the **s** and dries it up;
Hab 1:14 You have made men like fish in the **s**,
1:14 like **s** creatures that have no ruler.
2:14 the LORD, as the waters cover the **s**.
3: 8 Did you rage against the **s** when you
3:15 You trampled the **s** with your horses,
Zep 1: 3 of the air and the fish of the **s**.
2: 5 Woe to you who live by the **s**,
2: 6 The land by the **s**, where the
Hag 2: 6 the earth, the **s** and the dry land.
Zec 9: 4 and destroy her power on the **s**,
9:10 His rule will extend from **s** to **s** and
10:11 will pass through the **s** of trouble;
10:11 the surging **s** will be subdued and
14: 8 Jerusalem, half to the eastern **s**
14: 8 and half to the western **s**, in
Mt 4:15 the way to the **s**, along the Jordan,
4:18 walking beside the **S** of Galilee,
15:29 and went along the **S** of of Galilee.
18: 6 be drowned in the depths of the **s**.
21:21 'Go, throw yourself into the **s**,'
23:15 land and **s** to win a single convert,
Mk 1:16 Jesus walked beside the **S** of Galilee,
7:31 down to the **S** of Galilee and into
9:42 for him to be thrown into the **s**
11:23 'Go, throw yourself into the **s**,' and
Lk 17: 2 for him to be thrown into the **s**

Lk 17: 6 'Be uprooted and planted in the s,'
21:25 at the roaring and tossing of the s.
Jn 6: 1 the far shore of the S of Galilee
6: 1 Galilee (that is, the S of Tiberias),
21: 1 his disciples, by the S of Tiberias.
Ac 4:24 and the s, and everything in them.
10: 6 tanner, whose house is by the s."
10:32 the tanner, who lives by the s.'
14:15 earth and s and everything in them.
16:11 From Troas we put out to s and
21: 1 out to s and sailed straight to Cos.
27: 2 of Asia, and we put out to s.
27: 4 From there we put out to s again and
27: 5 we had sailed across the open s off
27:17 they lowered the s anchor and let
27:27 being driven across the Adriatic S,
27:30 let the lifeboat down into the s,
27:38 by throwing the grain into the s.
27:40 they left them in the s and at the
28: 4 for though he escaped from the s,
28:11 After three months we put out to s
Ro 9:27 be like the sand by the s,
1Co 10: 1 that they all passed through the s.
10: 2 Moses in the cloud and in the s.
2Co 11:25 a night and a day in the open s,
11:26 in danger at s; and in danger from
Jas 1: 6 who doubts is like a wave of the s,
3: 7 reptiles and creatures of the s are
Jude :13 They are wild waves of the s,
Rev 4: 6 like a s of glass, clear as crystal.
5:13 and under the earth and on the s,
7: 1 the land or on the s or on any tree.
7: 2 power to harm the land and the s:
7: 3 "Do not harm the land or the s or
8: 8 all ablaze, was thrown into the s.
8: 8 A third of the s turned into blood,
8: 9 the living creatures in the s died,
10: 2 He planted his right foot on the s
10: 5 angel I had seen standing on the s
10: 6 and the s and all that is in it, and
10: 8 standing on the s and on the land."
12:12 But woe to the earth and the s,
13: 1 dragon stood on the shore of the s.
13: 1 I saw a beast coming out of the s.
14: 7 the s and the springs of water."
15: 2 I saw what looked like a s of glass
15: 2 standing beside the s, those who had
16: 3 angel poured out his bowl on the s,
16: 3 every living thing in the s died.
18:17 "Every s captain, and all who travel
18:17 who earn their living from the s,
18:19 where all who had ships on the s
18:21 millstone and threw it into the s,
20:13 The s gave up the dead that were in
21: 1 away, and there was no longer any s.

Seafarers (Sea)
Isa 23: 2 of Sidon, whom the s have enriched.

Seah (Seahs)
2Ki 7: 1 a s of flour will sell for a shekel
7:16 So a s of flour sold for a shekel,
7:18 a s of flour will sell for a shekel

Seahs (Seah)
Ge 18: 6 "Quick," he said, "get three s of
1Sa 25:18 sheep, five s of roasted grain,
1Ki 18:32 large enough to hold two s of seed.
2Ki 7: 1 two s of barley for a shekel at the
7:16 and two s of barley sold for a
7:18 two s of barley for a shekel at the

Seal (Sealed, Sealing, Seals)
Ge 38:18 "Your s and its cord, and the staff
38:25 recognise whose s and cord and
Ex 28:11 the way a gem cutter engraves a s.
28:21 each engraved like a s with the name
28:36 and engrave on it as on a s:
39: 6 engraved them like a s with the
39:14 each engraved like a s with the name
39:30 on it, like an inscription on a s:
1Ki 21: 8 placed his s on them, and sent them
Est 8: 8 and s it with the king's signet ring
Job 38:14 takes shape like clay under a s;
Ps 40: 9 not s my lips, as you know, O LORD.
SS 8: 6 Place me like a s over your heart,
8: 6 like a s on your arm; for love is as
Isa 8:16 Bind up the testimony and s up the
Da 8:26 but s up the vision, for it concerns
9:24 to s up vision and prophecy and to
12: 4 Daniel, close up and s the words
Mt 27:66 by putting a s on the stone and
Jn 6:27 Father has placed his s of approval."
Ro 4:11 a s of the righteousness that he had
1Co 9: 2 the s of my apostleship in the Lord.
2Co 1:22 set his s of ownership on us, and
Eph 1:13 with a s, the promised Holy Spirit,
Rev 6: 3 the Lamb opened the second s, I
6: 5 the Lamb opened the third s, I heard
6: 7 the Lamb opened the fourth s, I
6: 9 he opened the fifth s, I saw under
6:12 I watched as he opened the sixth s.
7: 2 having the s of the living God.
7: 3 until we put a s on the foreheads
8: 1 he opened the seventh s, there was
9: 4 the s of God on their foreheads.
10: 4 "S up what the seven thunders have
22:10 he told me, "Do not s up the words

Sealed (Seal)
Dt 32:34 in reserve and s it in my vaults?
Ne 10: 1 Those who s it were: Nehemiah the
Est 3:12 himself and s with his own ring.
8: 8 and s with his ring can be revoked."
8:10 s the dispatches with the king's
Job 14:17 My offences will be s up in a bag;
41:15 rows of shields tightly s together;
SS 4:12 are a spring enclosed, a s fountain.
Isa 29:10 He has s your eyes (the prophets);
29:11 is nothing but words s in a scroll.
29:11 he will answer, "I can't; it is s.
Jer 32:10 I signed and s the deed, had it
32:11 the s copy containing the terms and
32:14 both the s and unsealed copies of
32:44 and deeds will be signed, s and
Da 6:17 and the king s it with his own
12: 9 up and s until the time of the end.
Eph 4:30 were s for the day of redemption.
2Ti 2:19 s with this inscription: "The Lord
Rev 5: 1 both sides and s with seven seals.
7: 4 the number of those who were s:
7: 5 From the tribe of Judah 12,000 were s
20: 3 and locked and s it over him, to

Sealing (Seal)
Dt 29:12 you this day and s with an oath,

Seals (Seal)
Ne 9:38 priests are affixing their s to it."
Job 9: 7 he s off the light of the stars.
Rev 5: 1 both sides and sealed with seven s.
5: 2 to break the s and open the scroll?"
5: 5 to open the scroll and its seven s."
5: 9 take the scroll and to open its s,
6: 1 Lamb opened the first of the seven s.

Seam (Seams)
Ex 28:27 close to the s just above the
39:20 close to the s just above the

Seamen (Sea)
Eze 27: 8 men, O Tyre, were aboard as your s.
27:27 your mariners, s and shipwrights,
27:28 will quake when your s cry out.
27:29 all the s will stand on the shore.

Seamless
Jn 19:23 This garment was s, woven in one

Seams (Seam)
Eze 27: 9 as shipwrights to caulk your s.

Search (Searched, Searches, Searching)
Ge 44:12 the steward proceeded to s,
Dt 1:33 to s out places for you to camp and
Jdg 17: 8 left that town in s of some other
1Sa 16:16 s for someone who can play the harp.
23:25 Saul and his men began the s, and
26: 2 men of Israel, to s there for David.
2Sa 5:17 they went up in full force to s for
1Ki 2:40 Achish at Gath in s of his slaves.
20: 6 send my officials to s your palace
1Ch 4:39 in s of pasture for their flocks.
14: 8 they went up in full force to s for
26:31 reign a s was made in the records,
2Ch 22: 9 He then went in s of Ahaziah, and
Ezr 4:15 that a s may be made in the archives
4:19 I issued an order and a s was made,
5:17 let a s be made in the royal
Est 2: 2 "Let a s be made for beautiful young
Job 3:21 who s for it more than for hidden
7:21 s for me, but I shall be no more."
10: 6 that you must s out my faults and
Ps 4: 4 beds, s your hearts and be silent.
139:23 S me, O God, and know my heart;
Pr 2: 4 and s for it as for hidden treasure,
25: 2 s out a matter is the glory of kings.
Ecc 3: 6 a time to s and a time to give up,
7:25 to investigate and to s out wisdom
7:29 men have gone in s of many schemes."
8:17 Despite all his efforts to s it out,
SS 3: 2 I will s for the one my heart loves.
Isa 41:12 Though you s for your enemies, you
41:17 "The poor and needy s for water, but
Jer 5: 1 and consider, s through her squares.
17:10 "I the LORD s the heart and examine
50:20 "s will be made for Israel's guilt,
Lam 1:11 All her people groan as they s for
Eze 34: 8 my shepherds did not s for my flock
34:11 s for my sheep and look after them.
34:16 I will s for the lost and bring back
39:14 months they will begin their s.
Hos 7:10 to the LORD his God or s for him.
Zep 1:12 At that time I will s Jerusalem with
Mt 2: 8 and make a careful s for the child.
2:13 to s for the child to kill him."
10:11 s for some worthy person there and
Lk 15: 8 and s carefully until she finds it?
Jn 6:24 and went to Capernaum in s of Jesus.
Ac 12:19 After Herod had a thorough s made
17: 5 rushed to Jason's house in s of Paul

Searched (Search)
Ge 31:34 Laban s through everything in the
31:35 So he s but could not find the
31:37 Now that you have s through all my
Jos 2:22 until the pursuers had s all along
1Sa 23:14 Day after day Saul s for him, but
27: 4 to Gath, he no longer s for him.
2Sa 17:20 The men s but found no-one, so they
1Ki 1: 3 they s throughout Israel for a
2Ki 2:17 fifty men, who s for three days
Ezr 2:62 These s for their family records,
6: 1 and they s in the archives stored in
Ne 7:64 These s for their family records,
Ps 139: 1 O LORD, you have s me and you know
Ecc 12: 9 s out and set in order many proverbs.
12:10 The Teacher s to find just the right
Jer 31:37 foundations of the earth below be s
Eze 20: 6 into a land I had s out for them,
34: 4 back the strays or s for the lost.
34: 6 and no-one s or looked for them.
2Ti 1:17 he s hard for me until he found me.
1Pe 1:10 s intently and with the greatest

Searches (Search)
1Ch 28: 9 for the LORD s every heart and
Job 28: 3 he s the farthest recesses for ore
28:11 He s the sources of the rivers and
39: 8 pasture and s for any green thing.
Ps 7: 9 O righteous God, who s minds and
Pr 11:27 but evil comes to him who s for it.
20:27 The lamp of the LORD s the spirit of
20:27 of a man; it s out his inmost being.
Ro 8:27 he who s our hearts knows the mind
1Co 2:10 The Spirit s all things, even the
Rev 2:23 that I am he who s hearts and minds,

Searching (Search)
Jdg 5:15 of Reuben there was much s of heart.
5:16 of Reuben there was much s of heart.

1Sa 27: 1 Then Saul will give up s for me
Job 32:11 while you were s for words,
Ecc 7:28 while I was still s but not finding
Am 8:12 s for the word of the LORD, but they
Lk 2:48 I have been anxiously s for you."
2:49 "Why were you s for me?" he asked.

Seared (Searing)
1Ti 4: 2 have been s as with a hot iron.
Rev 16: 9 They were s by the intense heat and

Searing (Seared)
Ps 38: 7 My back is filled with s pain;

Seas (Sea)
Ge 1:10 the gathered waters he called "s".
1:22 number and fill the water in the s,
Lev 11: 9 the water of the s and the streams,
11:10 all creatures in the s or streams
Dt 33:19 feast on the abundance of the s,
Ne 9: 6 it, the s and all that is in them.
Job 6: 3 surely outweigh the sand of the s
Ps 8: 8 all that swim the paths of the s.
24: 2 for he founded it upon the s and
65: 5 of the earth and of the farthest s,
65: 7 who stilled the roaring of the s,
69:34 the s and all that move in them,
78:15 them water as abundant as the s;
93: 3 The s have lifted up, O LORD,
93: 3 the s have lifted up their voice;
93: 3 the s have lifted up their pounding
135: 6 in the s and all their depths.
Pr 23:34 like one sleeping on the high s,
30:19 the way of a ship on the high s, and
Isa 60: 5 the wealth on the s will be brought
Eze 26:17 You were a power on the s, you and
27: 4 Your domain was on the high s;
27:26 oarsmen take you out to the high s.
27:33 your merchandise went out on the s,
28: 2 of a god in the heart of the s.
28: 8 violent death in the heart of the s.
32: 2 you are like a monster in the s
Da 11:45 between the s at the beautiful holy
Jnh 2: 3 into the very heart of the s, and

Seashore (Sea, Shore)
Ge 22:17 in the sky and as the sand on the s.
49:13 "Zebulun will live by the s and
Jos 11: 4 as numerous as the sand on the s.
Jdg 7:12 be counted than the sand on the s.
1Sa 13: 5 as numerous as the sand on the s.
2Sa 17:11 sand on the s—be gathered to you,
1Ki 4:20 as numerous as the sand on the s;
4:29 as measureless as the sand on the s.
Ps 78:27 flying birds like sand on the s.
Jer 33:22 as measureless as the sand on the s.
Hos 1:10 will be like the sand on the s,
Heb 11:12 as countless as the sand on the s.
Rev 20: 8 they are like the sand on the s.

Season (Seasoned, Seasons)
Ge 31:10 "In the breeding s I once had a
Ex 34:21 during the ploughing s and harvest
Lev 2:13 S all your grain offerings with salt.
26: 4 I will send you rain in its s, and
Nu 13:20 the s for the first ripe grapes.)
Dt 11:14 send rain on your land in its s,
28:12 to send rain on your land in s and
Ezr 10:13 it is the rainy s; so we cannot
Job 5:26 vigour, like sheaves gathered in s.
6:17 that cease to flow in the dry s, and
Ps 1: 3 which yields its fruit in s and
Pr 20: 4 A sluggard does not plough in s;
Ecc 3: 1 a s for every activity under heaven:
SS 2:12 the s of singing has come,
Jer 5:24 gives autumn and spring rains in s,
Eze 34:26 I will send down showers in s;
Mk 11:13 because it was not the s for figs.
2Ti 4: 2 be prepared in s and out of s;
Tit 1: 3 at his appointed s he brought his

Seasoned (Season)
Col 4: 6 s with salt, so that you may know

Seasons (Season)
Ge 1:14 signs to mark s and days and years,
Job 38:32 forth the constellations in their s
Ps 104:19 The moon marks off the s, and the
Jer 8: 7 in the sky knows her appointed s,
Da 2:21 He changes times and s; he sets up
Ac 14:17 from heaven and crops in their s;
Gal 4:10 days and months and s and years!

Seat (Seated, Seating, Seats)
Ex 18:13 The next day Moses took his s to
Jdg 3:20 As the king rose from his s,
1Sa 20:18 because your s will be empty.
2Sa 19: 8 the king got up and took his s in
1Ki 1:46 Moreover, Solomon has taken his s on
10:19 On both sides of the s were armrests,
21: 9 and s Naboth in a prominent place
21:10 s two scoundrels opposite him and
2Ki 25:28 gave him a s of honour higher than
2Ch 9:18 On both sides of the s were armrests,
Est 3: 1 him and giving him a s of honour
Job 29: 7 and took my s in the public square,
Ps 1: 1 sinners or sit in the s of mockers.
Pr 9:14 s at the highest point of the city,
31:23 his s among the elders of the land.
SS 3:10 Its s was upholstered with purple,
Isa 22:23 he will be a s of honour for the
Jer 52:32 gave him a s of honour higher than
Da 7: 9 and the Ancient of Days took his s.
Mt 23: 2 and the Pharisees sit in Moses' s.
27:19 Pilate was sitting on the judge's s,
Lk 14: 9 say to you, 'Give this man your s.
Jn 19:13 sat down on the judge's s at a place
Ro 14:10 all stand before God's judgment s.
2Co 5:10 before the judgment s of Christ,
Jas 2: 3 "Here's a good s for you," but say

Seated (Seat, *Seated on the throne*)
Ge 43:33 The men had been s before him in the
Ru 4: 4 it in the presence of these s here
1Sa 9:22 his servant into the hall and s them
22: 6 And Saul, spear in hand, was s under
1Ki 21:12 They proclaimed a fast and s Naboth
2Ch 23:20 and s the king on the royal throne,
Ps 47: 8 God is s on his holy throne.
Isa 6: 1 I saw the Lord s on a throne, high
Da 7:10 The court was s, and the books were
Zec 3: 8 and your associates s before you,
Mk 3:34 he looked at those s in a circle
Lk 22:56 A servant girl saw him s there in
22:69 Son of Man will be s at the right
Jn 6:11 who were s as much as they wanted.
12:15 is coming, s on a donkey's colt."
20:12 saw two angels in white, s where
Ac 20: 9 S in a window was a young man named
Eph 1:20 s him at his right hand in the
2: 6 us up with Christ and s us with him
Col 3: 1 Christ is s at the right hand of God.
Rev 4: 4 s on them were twenty-four elders.
11:16 who were s on their thrones before
14:14 and s on the cloud was one "like a
14:16 he who was s on the cloud swung his
20: 4 I saw thrones on which were s those
20:11 throne and him who was s on it.

Seated on the throne
1Ki 16:11 soon as he began to reign and was s,
Rev 19: 4 down and worshipped God, who was s.
21: 5 He who was s said, "I am making

Seating (Seat)
1Ki 10: 5 his table, the s of his officials,
2Ch 9: 4 his table, the s of his officials,

Seats (Seat)
1Sa 2: 8 he s them with princes and has them
Ps 113: 8 he s them with princes, with the
Jer 39: 3 came and took s in the Middle Gate:
Mt 23: 6 most important s in the synagogues;
Mk 12:39 have the most important s in the
Lk 11:43 most important s in the synagogues
20:46 have the most important s in the

Seaweed (Sea, Weed)
Jnh 2: 5 s was wrapped around my head.

Seba
Ge 10: 7 The sons of Cush: S, Havilah, Sabtah,
1Ch 1: 9 The sons of Cush: S, Havilah, Sabta,
Ps 72:10 Sheba and S will present him gifts.
Isa 43: 3 ransom, Cush and S in your stead.

Sebam
Nu 32: 3 Heshbon, Elealeh, S, Nebo and Beon—

Secacah
Jos 15:61 In the desert: Beth Arabah, Middin, S

Seclusion
Lk 1:24 and for five months remained in s.

Second-in-command (Command)
Ge 41:43 He had him ride in a chariot as his s

Secret (Secretly, Secrets)
Ex 7:11 did the same things by their s arts:
7:22 did the same things by their s arts,
8: 7 did the same things by their s arts;
8:18 by their s arts, they could not.
Dt 27:15 hands—and sets it up in s.
29:29 The s things belong to the LORD our
Jdg 3:19 "I have a s message for you, O king.
16: 5 you the s of his great strength
16: 6 "Tell me the s of your great
16: 9 s of his strength was not discovered.
16:15 me the s of your great strength."
2Sa 12:12 You did it in s, but I will do this
15:10 Absalom sent s messengers throughout
Est 2:20 Esther had kept s her family
Ps 10: 8 watching in s for his victims.
90: 8 s sins in the light of your presence.
101: 5 Whoever slanders his neighbour in s,
139:15 you when I was made in the s place.
Pr 9:17 food eaten in s is delicious!"
11:13 but a trustworthy man keeps a s.
17:23 A wicked man accepts a bribe in s to
21:14 A gift given in s soothes anger, and
Isa 45: 3 riches stored in s places, so that
45:19 I have not spoken in s, from
48:16 I have not spoken in s; at the time
65: 4 spend their nights keeping s vigil;
Jer 13:17 I will weep in s because of your
23:24 Can anyone hide in s places so that
Eze 28: 3 Is no s hidden from you?
Mt 6: 4 that your giving may be in s.
6: 4 what is done in s, will reward you.
6: 6 what is done in s, will reward you.
6:18 what is done in s, will reward you.
Mk 4:11 He told them, "The s of the kingdom
7:24 he could not keep his presence s.
Jn 7: 4 to become a public figure acts in s.
7:10 went also, not publicly, but in s.
18:20 come together. I said nothing in s.
1Co 2: 7 No, we speak of God's s wisdom, a
4: 1 entrusted with the s things of God.
2Co 4: 2 have renounced s and shameful ways;
Eph 5:12 what the disobedient do in s.
Php 4:12 I have learned the s of being
2Th 2: 7 For the s power of lawlessness is

Secretaries (Secretary)
1Ki 4: 3 and Ahijah, sons of Shisha—s;
2Ch 34:13 were s, scribes and doorkeepers.
Est 3:12 month the royal s were summoned.
8: 9 At once the royal s were

Secretary (Secretaries, Secretary's)
2Sa 8:17 Abiathar were priests; Seraiah was s
20:25 Sheva was s; Zadok and Abiathar were
2Ki 12:10 the royal s and the high priest came
18:18 Shebna the s, and Joah son of Asaph
18:37 Shebna the s and Joah son of Asaph
19: 2 Shebna the s and the leading priests
22: 3 King Josiah sent the s, Shaphan son
22: 8 high priest said to Shaphan the s,
22: 9 Shaphan the s went to the king and

2Ki 22:10 Shaphan the s informed the king,
22:12 Shaphan the s and Asaiah the king's
25:19 He also took the s who was chief
1Ch 18:16 Abiathar were priests; Shavsha was s
2Ch 24:11 the royal s and the officer of the
26:11 numbers as mustered by Jeiel the s
34:15 Hilkiah said to Shaphan the s, "I
34:18 Shaphan the s informed the king,
34:20 Shaphan the s and Asaiah the king's
Ezr 4: 8 Shimshai the s wrote a letter
4: 9 officer and Shimshai the s,
4:17 Shimshai the s and the rest of their
4:23 Shimshai the s and their associates,
Isa 36: 3 Shebna the s, and Joah son of Asaph
36:22 Shebna the s, and Joah son of Asaph
37: 2 Shebna the s, and the leading
Jer 36:10 of Gemariah son of Shaphan the s,
36:12 were sitting: Elishama the s,
36:20 in the room of Elishama the s,
36:21 it from the room of Elishama the s
37:15 in the house of Jonathan the s,
37:20 to the house of Jonathan the s,
52:25 He also took the s who was chief

Secretary's (Secretary)

Jer 36:12 he went down to the s room in the

Secretly (Secret)

Ge 31:27 Why did you run off s and deceive me
Dt 13: 6 or your closest friend s entices you
27:24 the man who kills his neighbour s.
28:57 For she intends to eat them s during
Jos 2: 1 Joshua son of Nun s sent two spies
2Sa 21:12 (They had taken them s from the
2Ki 17: 9 The Israelites s did things against
Job 4:12 "A word was s brought to me, my ears
13:10 you if you s showed partiality.
31:27 that my heart was s enticed and my
Jer 38:16 King Zedekiah swore this oath s to
Mt 2: 7 Herod called the Magi s and found
Jn 19:38 but s because he feared the Jews.
Ac 6:11 they s persuaded some men to say,
2Pe 2: 1 They will s introduce destructive
Jude : 4 ago have s slipped in among you.

Secrets (Secret)

Job 11: 6 disclose to you the s of wisdom, for
Ps 44:21 since he knows the s of the heart?
Mt 13:11 knowledge of the s of the kingdom
Lk 8:10 knowledge of the s of the kingdom
Ro 2:16 judge men's s through Jesus Christ,
1Co 14:25 the s of his heart will be laid bare.
Rev 2:24 learned Satan's so-called deep s

Sect

Lk 5:30 their s complained to his disciples,
Ac 24: 5 He is a ringleader of the Nazarene s
24:14 of the Way, which they call a s.
26: 5 that according to the strictest s of
28:22 are talking against this s."

Section (Sections)

2Ki 14:13 s about six hundred feet long.
2Ch 25:23 s about six hundred feet long.
Ne 3: 2 of Jericho built the adjoining s,
3: 4 son of Hakkoz, repaired the next s.
3: 5 The next s was repaired by the men
3: 8 goldsmiths, repaired the next s;
3: 9 of Jerusalem, repaired the next s.
3:11 repaired another s and the Tower of
3:12 repaired the next s with the help
3:19 ruler of Mizpah, repaired another s,
3:20 Zabbai zealously repaired another s,
3:21 repaired another s, from the
3:24 son of Henadad repaired another s,
3:27 the men of Tekoa repaired another s,
3:30 son of Zalaph, repaired another s.
12:24 one s responding to the other, as
Eze 42: 3 Both in the s twenty cubits from the
42: 3 in the s opposite the pavement of
45: 2 Of this, a s 500 cubits square is to
45: 3 measure off a s 25,000 cubits long

Sections (Section)

1Ki 22:34 Israel between the s of his armour.
2Ch 18:33 Israel between the s of his armour.
32: 5 all the broken s of the wall

Secu

1Sa 19:22 and went to the great cistern at S.

Secundus

Ac 20: 4 Aristarchus and S from Thessalonica,

Secure (Secured, Securely, Secures, Security)

Nu 24:21 "Your dwelling-place is s, your
Dt 33:12 "Let the beloved of the LORD rest s
33:28 s in a land of grain and new wine,
Jdg 18: 7 the Sidonians, unsuspecting and s.
1Ki 2:45 remain s before the LORD for ever."
Job 5:24 You will know that your tent is s;
11:18 You will be s, because there is hope
12: 6 and those who provoke God are s—
21:23 vigour, completely s and at ease,
40:23 he is s, though the Jordan should
Ps 7: 9 the wicked and make the righteous s.
16: 5 and my cup; you have made my lot s.
16: 9 rejoices; my body also will rest s,
30: 6 I felt s, I said, "I shall never be
48: 8 our God: God makes her s for ever.
112: 8 His heart is s, he will have no fear
122: 6 "May those who love you be s.
Pr 14:26 fears the LORD has a s fortress,
20:28 through love his throne is made s.
27:24 crown is not s for all generations.
29:14 his throne will always be s.
Isa 32: 9 who feel s, hear what I have to say!
32:10 a year you who feel s will tremble;
32:11 you daughters who feel s! Strip off
32:18 in s homes, in undisturbed places of
33:23 The mast is not held s, the sail is
Jer 22:21 I warned you when you felt s, but
Eze 34:27 the people will be s in their land.
Da 8:25 When they feel s, he will destroy
11:21 the kingdom when its people feel s,
11:24 the richest provinces feel s, he
Am 6: 1 you who feel s on Mount Samaria,
Zec 1:15 angry with the nations that feel s.
14:11 be destroyed. Jerusalem will be s.
Mt 27:64 to be made s until the third day.
27:65 make the tomb as s as you know how."
27:66 they went and made the tomb s by
Ac 27:16 hardly able to make the lifeboat s.
Heb 6:19 an anchor for the soul, firm and s.
2Pe 3:17 men and fall from your s position.

Secured (Secure)

2Sa 23: 5 arranged and s in every part?
Ac 12:20 Having s the support of Blastus, a

Securely (Secure)

Jdg 16:11 He said, "If anyone ties me s with
1Sa 12:11 on every side, so that you lived s.
25:29 life of my master will be bound s
1Ki 2:24 established me s on the throne of
Pr 8:28 fixed s the fountains of the deep,
10: 9 The man of integrity walks s, but he
Mic 5: 4 And they will live s, for then his
Ac 5:23 "We found the jail s locked, with

Secures (Secure)

Ps 140:12 I know that the LORD s justice for

Security (Secure)

Dt 24: 6 even the upper one—as s for a debt,
24: 6 be taking a man's livelihood as s.
2Ki 20:19 not be peace and s in my lifetime?"
Job 17: 3 Who else will put up s for me?
18:14 He is torn from the s of his tent
22: 6 You demanded s from your brothers
24:23 let them rest in a feeling of s,
31:24 said to pure gold, 'You are my s,'
Ps 122: 7 walls and s within your citadels."
Pr 6: 1 My son, if you have put up s for
11:15 He who puts up s for another will
Pr 17:18 and puts up s for his neighbour.
20:16 Take the garment of one who puts up s
22:26 in pledge or puts up s for debts;
27:13 Take the garment of one who puts up s
Isa 39: 8 will be peace and s in my lifetime."
47: 8 lounging in your s and saying to
Jer 30:10 Jacob will again have peace and s,
33: 6 let them enjoy abundant peace and s.
46:27 Jacob will again have peace and s,

Sedition

Ezr 4:19 has been a place of rebellion and s.

Seduce (Seduced, Seduces, Seductive)

2Pe 2:14 stop sinning; they s the unstable;

Seduced (Seduce)

Pr 7:21 she s him with her smooth talk.

Seduces (Seduce)

Ex 22:16 "If a man s a virgin who is not

Seductive (Seduce)

Pr 2:16 the wayward wife with her s words,
7: 5 the wayward wife with her s words.

See visions

Joel 2:28; Zec 10:2; Ac 2:17

Seed (Seed-bearing, Seeds, Seedtime)

Ge 1:11 land that bear fruit with s in it,
1:12 plants bearing s according to their
1:12 s in it according to their kinds.
1:29 tree that has fruit with s in it.
47:19 Give us s so that we may live and
47:23 here is s for you so you can plant
47:24 you may keep as s for the fields
Ex 16:31 It was white like coriander s and
Lev 11:38 if water has been put on the s and
19:19 your field with two kinds of s.
26:16 You will plant s in vain, because
27:16 to the amount of s required for it
27:16 of silver to a homer of barley s.
Nu 11: 7 The manna was like coriander s and
24: 7 their s will have abundant water.
Dt 11:10 where you planted your s and
22: 9 Do not plant two kinds of s in your
28:38 You will sow much s in the field but
1Ki 18:32 large enough to hold two seahs of s.
2Ki 6:25 of a cab of s pods for five shekels.
Ps 126: 6 He who goes out weeping, carrying s
Ecc 11: 6 Sow your s in the morning, and at
Isa 5:10 homer of s only an ephah of grain."
6:13 so the holy s will be the stump in
30:23 He will also send you rain for the s
32:20 sowing your s by every stream, and
55:10 so that it yields s for the sower
Jer 35: 7 sow s or plant vineyards; you must
Eze 17: 5 "'He took some of the s of your
Hag 2:19 Is there yet any s left in the barn?
Zec 8:12 "The s will grow well, the vine will
Mt 13: 3 "A farmer went out to sow his s.
13: 4 he was scattering the s, some fell
13: 7 Other s fell among thorns, which
13: 8 Still other s fell on good soil,
13:19 This is the s sown along the path.
13:20 The one who received the s that fell
13:22 The one who received the s that fell
13:23 the one who received the s that fell
13:24 a man who sowed good s in his field.
13:27 'Sir, didn't you sow good s in your
13:31 of heaven is like a mustard s,
13:37 sowed the good s is the Son of Man.
13:38 good s stands for the sons of the
17:20 have faith as small as a mustard s,
25:24 where you have not scattered s.
25:26 gather where I have not scattered s?
Mk 4: 3 A farmer went out to sow his s.
4: 4 he was scattering the s, some fell
4: 7 Other s fell among thorns, which
4: 8 Still other s fell on good soil.

Mk 4:15 Some people are like s along the
4:16 Others, like s sown on rocky places,
4:18 Still others, like s sown among
4:20 Others, like s sown on good soil,
4:26 A man scatters s on the ground.
4:27 gets up, the s sprouts and grows,
4:31 is like a mustard s, which is the
4:31 smallest s you plant in the ground.
Lk 8: 5 "A farmer went out to sow his s.
8: 5 As he was scattering the s, some
8: 7 Other s fell among thorns, which
8: 8 Still other s fell on good soil.
8:11 parable: The s is the word of God.
8:14 The s that fell among thorns stands
8:15 the s on good soil stands for those
13:19 is like a mustard s, which a man
17: 6 have faith as small as a mustard s,
Jn 12:24 dies, it remains only a single s.
1Co 3: 6 I planted the s, Apollos watered it,
9:11 If we have sown spiritual s among
15:37 but just a s, perhaps of wheat or of
15:38 kind of s he gives its own body.
2Co 9:10 Now he who supplies s to the sower
9:10 increase your store of s and will
Gal 3:16 were spoken to Abraham and to his s.
3:16 but "and to your s", meaning many
3:19 until the S to whom the promise
3:29 then you are Abraham's s, and heirs
1Pe 1:23 not of perishable s, but of
1Jn 3: 9 because God's s remains in him;

Seed-bearing (Seed)

Ge 1:11 vegetation: s plants and trees on
1:29 God said, "I give you every s plant

Seeds (Seed)

Lev 11:37 If a carcass falls on any s that are
Nu 6: 4 grapevine, not even the s or skins.
Isa 61:11 up and a garden causes s to grow,
Joel 1:17 The s are shrivelled beneath the
Mt 13:32 it is the smallest of all your s,
Jn 12:24 But if it dies, it produces many s.
Gal 3:16 The Scripture does not say "and to s"

Seedtime (Seed)

Ge 8:22 the earth endures, s and harvest,

Seek (Seeking, Seeks, Self-seeking, Sought)

Ex 18:15 people come to me to s God's will.
Lev 19:18 "'Do not s revenge or bear a grudge
19:31 turn to mediums or s out spiritists
Dt 4:29 if from there you s the LORD your
12: 5 you are to s the place the LORD your
23: 6 Do not s a treaty of friendship with
2Sa 17: 3 The death of the man you s will mean
1Ki 22: 5 "First s the counsel of the LORD.
1Ch 16:10 of those who s the LORD rejoice.
16:11 his strength; s his face always.
28: 9 If you s him, he will be found by
2Ch 7:14 pray and s my face and turn from
14: 4 He commanded Judah to s the LORD,
15: 2 If you s him, he will be found by
15:12 into a covenant to s the LORD,
15:13 All who would not s the LORD, the
16:12 he did not s help from the LORD.
18: 4 "First s the counsel of the LORD.
20: 4 together to s help from the LORD;
20: 4 from every town in Judah to s him.
34: 3 to s the God of his father David.
Ezr 4: 2 like you, we s your God and have
6:21 to s the LORD, the God of Israel.
9:12 Do not s a treaty of friendship with
Ps 4: 2 love delusions and s false gods?
9:10 have never forsaken those who s you.
10: 4 pride the wicked does not s him;
14: 2 any who understand, any who s God.
22:26 they who s the LORD will praise him—
24: 6 is the generation of those who s him;
24: 6 who s your face, O God of Jacob.
27: 4 this is what I s: that I may dwell
27: 4 the LORD and to s him in his temple.
27: 8 My heart says of you, "S his face!"
27: 8 Your face, LORD, I will s.
Ps 34:10 who s the LORD lack no good thing.
34:14 and do good; s peace and pursue it.
35: 4 May those who s my life be disgraced
38:12 Those who s my life set their traps,
40:14 May all who s to take my life be put
40:16 may all who s you rejoice and be
45:12 men of wealth will s your favour.
53: 2 any who understand, any who s God.
54: 3 ruthless men s my life—men without
63: 1 you are my God, earnestly I s you;
63: 9 They who s my life will be destroyed;
69: 4 cause, those who s to destroy me.
69: 6 may those who s you not be put to
69:32 you who s God, may your hearts live!
70: 2 May those who s my life be put to
70: 4 may all who s you rejoice and be
78:34 God slew them, they would s him;
83:16 that men will s your name, O LORD.
104:21 prey and s their food from God.
105: 3 of those who s the LORD rejoice.
105: 4 his strength; s his face always.
119: 2 and s him with all their heart.
119:10 I s you with all my heart; do not
119:155 for they do not s out your decrees.
119:176 S your servant, for I have not
122: 9 our God, I will s your prosperity.
Pr 8:17 love me, and those who s me find me.
18:15 the ears of the wise s it out.
25:27 it honourable to s one's own honour.
28: 5 who s the LORD understand it fully.
29:10 integrity and s to kill the upright.
29:26 Many s an audience with a ruler, but
Isa 1:17 S justice, encourage the oppressed.
31: 1 of Israel, or s help from the LORD.
45:19 Jacob's descendants, 'S me in vain.
51: 1 righteousness and who s the LORD:
55: 6 S the LORD while he may be found;
58: 2 For day after day they s me out;
65: 1 was found by those who did not s me.
65:10 for herds, for my people who s me.
Jer 4:30 despise you; they s your life.
19: 7 at the hands of those who s their
19: 9 by the enemies who s their lives.'
21: 7 to their enemies who s their lives.
22:25 you over to those who s your life,
26:19 fear the LORD and s his favour?
29: 7 Also, s the peace and prosperity of
29:13 You will s me and find me when
29:13 you s me with all your heart.
34:20 to their enemies who s their lives.
34:21 to their enemies who s their lives,
44:30 over to his enemies who s his life,
45: 5 Should you then s great things for
45: 5 things for yourself? S them not.
46:26 them over to those who s their lives,
49:37 before those who s their lives;
50: 4 go in tears to s the LORD their God.
Eze 7:25 terror comes, they will s peace, but
21:21 to s an omen: He will cast lots with
Hos 3: 5 s the LORD their God and David their
5: 6 flocks and herds to s the LORD,
5:15 And they will s my face; in their
5:15 misery they will earnestly s me."
10:12 for it is time to s the LORD,
Am 5: 4 "S me and live;
5: 5 do not s Bethel, do not go to Gilgal,
5: 6 S the LORD and live, or he will
5:14 S good, not evil, that you may live.
Na 3:11 hiding and s refuge from the enemy.
Zep 1: 6 s the LORD nor enquire of him.
2: 3 S the LORD, all you humble of the
2: 3 S righteousness, s humility; perhaps
Zec 8:21 the LORD and s the LORD Almighty.
8:22 to Jerusalem to s the LORD Almighty
11:16 or s the young, or heal the injured,
Mal 2: 7 his mouth men should s instruction
Mt 6:33 s first his kingdom and his
7: 7 given to you; s and you will find;
Lk 11: 9 given to you; s and you will find;
12:31 s his kingdom, and these things will
19:10 For the Son of Man came to s and to
Jn 5:30 for I s not to please myself but
Ac 15:17 the remnant of men may s the LORD,
17:27 God did this so that men would s him
Ro 2: 7 persistence in doing good s glory,
10:20 "I was found by those who did not s
1Co 7:27 Are you married? Do not s a divorce.
10:24 Nobody should s his own good, but
Gal 2:17 "If, while we s to be justified in
Heb 11: 6 rewards those who earnestly s him.
1Pe 3:11 he must s peace and pursue it.
Rev 9: 6 During those days men will s death,

Seeking (Seek)

Jdg 14: 4 who was s an occasion to confront
18: 1 tribe of the Danites was s a place
1Sa 22:23 who is s your life is s mine also.
1Ki 12:28 After s advice, the king made two
2Ki 16:15 the bronze altar for s guidance."
1Ch 22:19 your heart and soul to s the LORD
2Ch 11:16 who set their hearts on s the LORD,
12:14 had not set his heart on s the LORD.
19: 3 and have set your heart on s God."
30:19 who sets his heart on s God—the
Est 9: 2 to attack those s their destruction.
Ps 37:32 the righteous, s their very lives;
Pr 20:18 Make plans by s advice; if you wage
Jer 11:21 who are s your life and saying,
38: 4 This man is not s the good of these
38:16 over to those who are s your life."
44:30 the enemy who was s his life.
Mal 2:15 Because he was s godly offspring.
3: 1 Then suddenly the Lord you are s
Mt 12:43 places s rest and does not find it.
Lk 11:24 places s rest and does not find it.
Jn 8:50 I am not s glory for myself;
Ac 13:11 s someone to lead him by the hand.
1Co 10:33 For I am not s my own good but the

Seeks (Seek)

Job 39:29 From there he s out his food; his
Ps 86:14 a band of ruthless men s my life—
Pr 11:27 He who s good finds goodwill, but
14: 6 The mocker s wisdom and finds none,
15:14 The discerning heart s knowledge,
Isa 16: 5 David— one who in judging s justice
56:11 their own way, each s his own gain.
Jer 5: 1 who deals honestly and s the truth,
Lam 3:25 is in him, to the one who s him;
Mt 7: 8 he who s finds; and to him who
Lk 11:10 he who s finds; and to him who
Jn 4:23 kind of worshippers the Father s.
8:50 one who s it, and he is the judge.
Ro 3:11 who understands, no-one who s God.

Seer (Seer's, Seers)

1Sa 9: 9 "Come, let us go to the s," because
9: 9 of today used to be called a s.)
9:11 they asked them, "Is the s here?"
9:19 "I am the s," Samuel replied. "Go up
2Sa 15:27 "Aren't you a s? Go back to the city
24:11 come to Gad the prophet, David's s:
1Ch 9:22 of trust by David and Samuel the s.
21: 9 The LORD said to Gad, David's s,
25: 5 were sons of Heman the king's s.
26:28 everything dedicated by Samuel the s
29:29 in the records of Samuel the s,
29:29 and the records of Gad the s,
2Ch 9:29 visions of Iddo the s concerning
12:15 and of Iddo the s that deal with
16: 7 At that time Hanani the s came to
16:10 Asa was angry with the s because of
19: 2 Jehu the s, the son of Hanani, went
29:25 the king's s and Nathan the prophet;
29:30 words of David and of Asaph the s.
35:15 Heman and Jeduthun the king's s.
Am 7:12 Amaziah said to Amos, "Get out, you s

Seer's (Seer)

1Sa 9:18 tell me where the s house is?"

Seers (Seer)

2Ki 17:13 through all his prophets and s:
2Ch 33:18 the words the s spoke to him in the
33:19 are written in the records of the s.
Isa 29:10 he has covered your heads (the s).
30:10 They say to the s, "See no more
Mic 3: 7 The s will be ashamed and the

Segub
1Ki 16:34 at the cost of his youngest son **S**,
1Ch 2:21 years old), and she bore him **S**.
2:22 **S** was the father of Jair, who

Seir See Edom
Ge 14: 6 the Horites in the hill country of **S**,
32: 3 the land of **S**, the country of Edom.
33:14 until I come to my lord in **S**."
33:16 Esau started on his way back to **S**.
36: 8 settled in the hill country of **S**.
36: 9 Edomites in the hill country of **S**.
36:20 These were the sons of **S** the Horite,
36:21 of **S** in Edom were Horite chiefs.
36:30 their divisions, in the land of **S**.
Nu 24:18 **S**, his enemy, will be conquered,
Dt 1: 2 Kadesh Barnea by the Mount **S** road.)
1:44 down from **S** all the way to Hormah.
2: 1 way around the hill country of **S**.
2: 4 descendants of Esau, who live in **S**.
2: 5 the hill country of **S** as his own.
2: 8 descendants of Esau, who live in **S**.
2:12 Horites used to live in **S**, but the
2:22 who lived in **S**, when he destroyed
2:29 who live in **S**, and the Moabites, who
33: 2 and dawned over them from **S**;
Jos 11:17 which rises towards **S**, to Baal Gad
12: 7 which rises towards **S** (their lands
15:10 westward from Baalah to Mount **S**,
24: 4 I assigned the hill country of **S** to
Jdg 5: 4 "O LORD, when you went out from **S**,
1Ch 1:38 The sons of **S**: Lotan, Shobal, Zibeon,
4:42 Ishi, invaded the hill country of **S**.
2Ch 20:10 Moab and Mount **S**, whose territory
20:22 and Mount **S** who were invading Judah,
20:23 against the men from Mount **S** to
20:23 slaughtering the men from **S**,
25:11 he killed ten thousand men of **S**.
25:14 back the gods of the people of **S**.
Isa 21:11 Dumah: Someone calls to me from **S**,
Eze 25: 8 'Because Moab and **S** said, "Look, the
35: 2 set your face against Mount **S**;
35: 3 I am against you, Mount **S**, and I
35: 7 I will make Mount **S** a desolate waste
35:15 You will be desolate, O Mount **S**, you

Seirah
Jdg 3:26 by the idols and escaped to **S**.

Seize (Seized, Seizes, Seizing, Seizures)
Ge 43:18 **s** us as slaves and take our donkeys."
Jdg 7:24 **s** the waters of the Jordan ahead of
21:21 each of you **s** a wife from the girls
1Ki 13: 4 "**S** him!" But the hand he stretched
18:40 "**S** the prophets of Baal. Don't let
20: 6 They will **s** everything you value and
1Ch 7:21 they went down to **s** their livestock.
Job 3: 6 That night—may thick darkness **s** it;
Ps 21: 8 your right hand will **s** your foes.
71:11 pursue him and **s** him, for no-one
109:11 May a creditor **s** all he has; may
Isa 3: 6 A man will **s** one of his brothers at
5:29 they growl as they **s** their prey and
10: 6 to **s** loot and snatch plunder, and to
13: 8 Terror will **s** them, pain and anguish
21: 3 pangs **s** me, like those of a woman in
Jer 12:14 neighbours who **s** the inheritance
Eze 38:13 and goods and to **s** much plunder?"'
Da 11: 8 He will also **s** their gods, their
11:21 and he will **s** it through intrigue.
Am 9: 3 I will hunt them down and **s** them.
Ob :13 nor **s** their wealth in the day of
Mic 2: 2 They covet fields and **s** them, and
Hab 1: 6 to **s** dwelling-places not their own.
Zec 14:13 Each man will **s** the hand of another,
Jn 7:30 At this they tried to **s** him, but
7:44 Some wanted to **s** him, but no-one
10:39 Again they tried to **s** him, but he
Ac 12: 3 Jews, he proceeded to **s** Peter also.

Seized (Seize)
Ge 14:11 The four kings **s** all the goods of
21:25 that Abimelech's servants had **s**.
34:28 They **s** their flocks and herds and
Ex 15:15 the leaders of Moab will be **s** with
Jdg 12: 6 they **s** him and killed him at the
16:21 the Philistines **s** him, gouged out
1Sa 17:35 When it turned on me, I **s** it by its
2Sa 4:10 **s** him and put him to death in Ziklag.
10: 4 Hanun **s** David's men, shaved off half
1Ki 18:40 They **s** them, and Elijah had them
21:19 murdered a man and **s** his property?'
2Ki 11:16 they **s** her as she reached the place
17: 4 **s** him and put him in prison.
1Ch 5:21 They **s** the livestock of the Hagrites
19: 4 Hanun **s** David's men, shaved them,
2Ch 23:15 they **s** her as she reached the
Est 8:17 because fear of the Jews had **s** them.
9: 3 because fear of Mordecai had **s** them.
Job 4:14 fear and trembling **s** me and made all
16:12 he **s** me by the neck and crushed me.
18:20 men of the east are **s** with horror.
20:19 he has **s** houses he did not build.
24: 9 infant of the poor is **s** for a debt.
Ps 48: 6 Trembling **s** them there, pain like
56: T the Philistines had **s** him in Gath.
Isa 10:10 my hand **s** the kingdoms of the idols,
Jer 26: 8 and all the people **s** him and said,
49:24 anguish and pain have **s** her,
51:32 the river crossings **s**, the marshes
51:41 the boast of the whole earth **s**!
Mt 21:35 "The tenants **s** his servants;
22: 6 The rest **s** his servants, ill-treated
26:50 forward, **s** Jesus and arrested him.
27: 3 he was **s** with remorse and returned
Mk 12: 3 they **s** him, beat him and sent him
14:46 The men **s** Jesus and arrested him.
14:51 following Jesus. When they **s** him,
Lk 8:29 Many times it had **s** him, and though
23:26 they led him away, they **s** Simon from
Jn 8:20 Yet no-one **s** him, because his time
Ac 4: 3 They **s** Peter and John, and because
5: 5 great fear **s** all who heard what had
5:11 Great fear **s** the whole church and
6:12 They **s** Stephen and brought him
16:19 they **s** Paul and Silas and dragged
19:17 they were all **s** with fear, and the
19:29 The people **s** Gaius and Aristarchus,
21:27 up the whole crowd and **s** him,
23:27 This man was **s** by the Jews and they
24: 6 desecrate the temple; so we **s** him.
26:21 That is why the Jews **s** me in the
1Co 10:13 No temptation has **s** you except what
Rev 20: 2 He **s** the dragon, that ancient

Seizes (Seize)
Dt 25:11 out and **s** him by his private parts,
Job 18: 9 A trap **s** him by the heel; a snare
21: 6 I am terrified; trembling **s** my body.
Ps 137: 9 he who **s** your infants and dashes
Pr 26:17 Like one who **s** a dog by the ears is
Mic 4: 9 **s** you like that of a woman in labour?
Mk 9:18 Whenever it **s** him, it throws him to
Lk 9:39 A spirit **s** him and he suddenly

Seizing (Seize)
Lk 22:54 **s** him, they led him away and took
Ac 21:30 **S** Paul, they dragged him from the
Ro 7: 8 sin, **s** the opportunity afforded by
7:11 For sin, **s** the opportunity afforded

Seizures (Seize)
Mt 4:24 the demon-possessed, those having **s**,
17:15 "He has **s** and is suffering greatly.

Sela
Jdg 1:36 from Scorpion Pass to **S** and beyond.
2Ki 14: 7 captured **S** in battle, calling it
Isa 16: 1 from **S**, across the desert, to the
42:11 Let the people of **S** sing for joy;

Sela Hammahlekoth
1Sa 23:28 That is why they call this place **S**.

Selah
Ps 3: 2 "God will not deliver him." **S**
3: 4 he answers me from his holy hill. **S**
3: 8 your blessing be on your people. **S**
4: 2 delusions and seek false gods? **S**
4: 4 search your hearts and be silent. **S**
7: 5 and make me sleep in the dust. **S**
9:16 work of their hands. Higgaion. **S**
9:20 nations know they are but men. **S**
20: 3 and accept your burnt offerings. **S**
21: 2 withheld the request of his lips. **S**
24: 6 seek your face, O God of Jacob. **S**
24:10 he is the King of glory. **S**
32: 4 as in the heat of summer. **S**
32: 5 you forgave the guilt of my sin. **S**
32: 7 me with songs of deliverance. **S**
39: 5 Each man's life is but a breath. **S**
39:11 each man is but a breath. **S**
44: 8 will praise your name for ever. **S**
46: 3 quake with their surging. **S**
46: 7 the God of Jacob is our fortress. **S**
46:11 the God of Jacob is our fortress. **S**
47: 4 pride of Jacob, whom he loved. **S**
48: 8 God makes her secure for ever. **S**
49:13 who approve their sayings. **S**
49:15 will surely take me to himself. **S**
50: 6 for God himself is judge. **S**
52: 3 rather than speaking the truth. **S**
52: 5 from the land of the living. **S**
54: 3 life—men without regard for God. **S**
55: 7 far away and stay in the desert; **S**
55:19 will hear them and afflict them—**S**
57: 3 those who hotly pursue me; **S**
57: 6 have fallen into it themselves. **S**
59: 5 show no mercy to wicked traitors. **S**
59:13 earth that God rules over Jacob. **S**
60: 4 to be unfurled against the bow. **S**
61: 4 in the shelter of your wings. **S**
62: 4 but in their hearts they curse. **S**
62: 8 for God is our refuge. **S**
66: 4 they sing praise to your name." **S**
66: 7 rebellious rise up against him. **S**
66:15 I will offer bulls and goats. **S**
67: 1 make his face shine upon us, **S**
67: 4 guide the nations of the earth. **S**
68: 7 marched through the wasteland, **S**
68:19 who daily bears our burdens. **S**
68:32 sing praise to the Lord, **S**
75: 3 I who hold its pillars firm. **S**
76: 3 the swords, the weapons of war. **S**
76: 9 all the afflicted of the land. **S**
77: 3 and my spirit grew faint. **S**
77: 9 in anger withheld his compassion?" **S**
77:15 descendants of Jacob and Joseph. **S**
81: 7 you at the waters of Meribah. **S**
82: 2 show partiality to the wicked? **S**
83: 8 to the descendants of Lot. **S**
84: 4 they are ever praising you. **S**
84: 8 listen to me, O God of Jacob. **S**
85: 2 and covered all theirs sins. **S**
87: 3 are said of you, O city of God: **S**
87: 6 "This one was born in Zion." **S**
88: 7 me with all your waves. **S**
88:10 are dead rise uup and praise you?
89: 4 firm through all generations.'" **S**
89:37 the faithful witness in the sky." **S**
89:45 him with a mantle of shame. **S**
89:48 from the power of the grave? **S**
140: 3 poison of vipers is on their lips. **S**
140: 5 set traps for me along my path. **S**
140: 8 or they will become proud. **S**
143: 6 for you like a parched land. **S**
Hab 3: 3 the Holy One from Mount Paran. **S**
3: 9 you called for many arrows. **S**
3:13 stripped him from head to foot. **S**

Select (Selected, Selects)
Ex 12:21 "Go at once and **s** the animals for
18:21 **s** capable men from all the
Nu 31:30 From the Israelites' half, **s** one out
35:11 **s** some towns to be your cities of
Est 3: 7 of Haman to **s** a day and month.
Isa 66:21 I will **s** some of them also to be

Selected (Select)
Ge 18: 7 he ran to the herd and **s** a choice,
32:13 he **s** a gift for his brother Esau:
Ex 21: 8 master who has **s** her for himself,

Nu 18: 6 I myself have s your fellow Levites
31:47 Moses s one out of every fifty
Dt 1:23 so I s twelve of you, one man from
2Sa 10: 9 so he s some of the best troops in
2Ki 7:14 they s two chariots with their
1Ch 19:10 so he s some of the best troops in
Ezr 10:16 Ezra the priest s men who were
Est 2: 9 seven maids s from the king's
Heb 5: 1 Every high priest is s from among

Selects (Select)
Ex 21: 9 If he s her for his son, he must
Pr 31:13 She s wool and flax and works with
Isa 40:20 offering s wood that will not rot.

Seled
1Ch 2:30 The sons of Nadab: **S** and Appaim.
2:30 **S** died without children.

Seleucia
Ac 13: 4 went down to **S** and sailed from

Self (Selfish)
Ex 32:13 to whom you swore by your own s: 'I
Lk 9:25 and yet lose or forfeit his very s?
Ro 6: 6 For we know that our old s was
Eph 4:22 to put off your old s, which is
4:24 to put on the new s, created to be
Col 3: 9 off your old s with its practices
3:10 have put on the new s, which is
Phm :19 mention that you owe me your very s.
1Pe 3: 4 it should be that of your inner s,

Self-abasement
Ezr 9: 5 I rose from my s, with my tunic and

Self-condemned (Condemn)
Tit 3:11 a man is warped and sinful; he is s.

Self-confidence (Confidence)
Ne 6:16 were afraid and lost their s,

Self-confident (Confidence)
2Co 11:17 In this s boasting I am not talking

Self-control (Control)
Pr 25:28 broken down is a man who lacks s.
Ac 24:25 Paul discoursed on righteousness, s
1Co 7: 5 tempt you because of your lack of s.
Gal 5:23 gentleness and s. Against such
2Ti 3: 3 without s, brutal, not lovers of
2Pe 1: 6 to knowledge, s; and to s,

Self-controlled (Control)
1Th 5: 6 asleep, but let us be alert and s.
5: 8 let us be s, putting on faith and
1Ti 3: 2 temperate, s, respectable,
Tit 1: 8 is s, upright, holy and disciplined.
2: 2 worthy of respect, s, and sound in
2: 5 to be s and pure, to be busy at home,
2: 6 encourage the young men to be s.
2:12 and to live s, upright and godly
1Pe 1:13 prepare your minds for action; be s;
4: 7 be clear minded and s so that you
5: 8 Be s and alert. Your enemy the devil

Self-discipline (Discipline)
2Ti 1: 7 a spirit of power, of love and of s.

Self-imposed (Impose)
Col 2:23 with their s worship, their false

Self-indulgence (Indulge)
Mt 23:25 inside they are full of greed and s.
Jas 5: 5 have lived on earth in luxury and s.

Selfish (Self)
Ps 119:36 statutes and not towards s gain.
Pr 18: 1 An unfriendly man pursues s ends;
Gal 5:20 s ambition, dissensions, factions
Php 1:17 preach Christ out of s ambition
2: 3 Do nothing out of s ambition or vain
Jas 3:14 harbour bitter envy and s ambition
3:16 where you have envy and s ambition

Self-seeking (Seek)
Ro 2: 8 for those who are s and who reject
1Co 13: 5 is not rude, it is not s, it is not

Sell (Sale, Sales, Seller, Sellers, Selling, Sells, Sold)
Ge 23: 4 **S** me some property for a burial site
23: 9 that he will s me the cave of
23: 9 Ask him to s it to me for the full
25:31 Jacob replied, "First s me your
37:27 Come, let's s him to the Ishmaelites
47:16 "I will s you food in exchange for
47:22 is why they did not s their land.
Ex 21: 8 He has no right to s her to
21:35 they are to s the live one and
Lev 25:14 "'If you s land to one of your
25:15 And he is to s to you on the basis
25:37 interest or s him food at a profit.
Dt 2:28 **S** us food to eat and water to drink
14:21 it, or you may s it to a foreigner.
21:14 You must not s her or treat her as a
1Ki 21: 6 '**S** me your vineyard; or if you
21:15 Jezreelite that he refused to s you.
2Ki 4: 7 "Go, s the oil and pay your debts.
7: 1 a seah of flour will s for a shekel
7:18 a seah of flour will s for a shekel
1Ch 21:22 **S** it to me at the full price."
Ne 10:31 or grain to s on the Sabbath,
Pr 11:26 crowns him who is willing to s.
23:23 Buy the truth and do not s it;
Isa 50: 1 to which of my creditors did I s you?
Eze 30:12 the Nile and s the land to evil men;
48:14 They must not s or exchange any of
Joel 3: 8 I will s your sons and daughters to
3: 8 and they will s them to the Sabeans,
Am 2: 6 They s the righteous for silver, and
8: 5 New Moon be over that we may s grain,
Zec 11: 5 Those who s them say, 'Praise the
Mt 19:21 be perfect, go, s your possessions
25: 9 s oil and buy some for yourselves.'
Mk 10:21 "Go, s everything you have and give
Lk 12:33 **S** your possessions and give to the
18:22 **S** everything you have and give to
22:36 a sword, s your cloak and buy one.
Rev 13:17 that no-one could buy or s unless he

Seller (Sell)
Isa 24: 2 as for maid, for s as for buyer,
Eze 7:12 Let not the buyer rejoice nor the s
7:13 The s will not recover the land he

Sellers (Sell)
Ne 13:20 the merchants and s of all kinds of

Selling (Sell)
Ge 25:33 to him, s his birthright to Jacob.
45: 5 angry with yourselves for s me here,
Lev 25:16 really s you is the number of crops.
Ru 4: 3 from Moab, is s the piece of land
Ne 5: 8 Now you are s your brothers, only
13:15 them against s food on that day.
13:16 all kinds of merchandise and s them
Am 8: 6 s even the sweepings with the wheat.
Mt 21:12 out all who were buying and s there.
21:12 and the benches of those s doves.
Mk 11:15 those who were buying and s there.
11:15 and the benches of those s doves,
Lk 17:28 buying and s, planting and building.
19:45 began driving out those who were s.
Jn 2:14 he found men s cattle, sheep and
Ac 2:45 **S** their possessions and goods, they

Sells (Sell)
Ex 21: 7 "If a man s his daughter as a
21:16 either s him or still has him when
22: 1 a sheep and slaughters it or s it,
Lev 25:25 poor and s some of his property,
25:29 "'If a man s a house in a walled
25:39 poor among you and s himself to you,
25:47 s himself to the alien living among
Dt 15:12 a man or woman, s himself to you
24: 7 treats him as a slave or s him, the
Pr 31:24 She makes linen garments and s them,

Semakiah
1Ch 26: 7 Elihu and **S** were also able men.

Semein
Lk 3:26 the son of Mattathias, the son of **S**,

Semen
Ge 38: 9 he spilled his s on the ground to
Lev 15:16 "'When a man has an emission of s,
15:17 Any clothing or leather that has s
15:18 woman and there is an emission of s,
15:32 made unclean by an emission of s,
22: 4 by anyone who has an emission of s,

Senaah
Ezr 2:35 of **S** 3,630
Ne 7:38 of **S** 3,930

Send (Sending, Sends, Sent)
Ge 7: 4 Seven days from now I will s rain on
24: 7 he will s his angel before you so
24:40 will s his angel with you and make
24:54 said, "**S** me on my way to my master.
24:56 **S** me on my way so I may go to my
27:45 I'll s word for you to come back
30:25 "**S** me on my way so that I can go
31:27 so that I could s you away with joy
37:13 Come, I am going to s you to them."
38:17 "I'll s you a young goat from my
38:17 a pledge until you s it?" she asked.
38:23 After all, I did s her this young
42: 4 Jacob did not s Benjamin, Joseph's
42:16 **S** one of your number to get your
43: 4 If you will s our brother along with
43: 5 if you will not s him, we will not
43: 8 "**S** the boy along with me and we
Ex 4:13 "O Lord, please s someone else to
8:21 I will s swarms of flies on you and
9:14 or this time I will s the full force
9:18 at this time tomorrow I will s the
23:27 "I will s my terror ahead of you and
23:28 I will s the hornet ahead of you to
33: 2 I will s an angel before you and
33:12 let me know whom you will s with me.
33:15 with us, do not s us up from here.
Lev 16:21 He shall s the goat away into the
25:21 I will s you such a blessing in the
26: 4 I will s you rain in its season, and
26:22 I will s wild animals against you,
26:25 I will s a plague among you, and you
Nu 5: 2 "Command the Israelites to s away
5: 3 **S** away male and female alike;
5: 3 s them outside the camp so that
13: 2 "**S** some men to explore the land of
13: 2 tribe s one of its leaders."
22:37 "Did I not s you an urgent summons?
31: 4 **S** into battle a thousand men from
35:25 s him back to the city of refuge to
Dt 1:22 "Let us s men ahead to spy out the
7:20 the Lord your God will s the hornet
11:14 I will s rain on your land in its
15:13 you release him, do not s him away
19:12 the elders of his town shall s for
28: 8 The Lord will s a blessing on your
28:12 to s rain on your land in season
28:20 The Lord will s on you curses,
28:59 the Lord will s fearful plagues on
28:68 The Lord will s you back in ships to
32:24 I will s wasting famine against them,
32:24 I will s against them the fangs of
Jos 1:16 and wherever you s us we will go.
7: 3 **S** two or three thousand men to take
18: 4 I will s them out to make a survey
Jdg 20:38 they should s up a great cloud
1Sa 5:11 "**S** the ark of the god of Israel away;
6: 2 we should s it back to its place."
6: 3 do not s it away empty, but by all
6: 3 all means s a guilt offering to him.
6: 4 "What guilt offering should we s to
6: 6 did they not s the Israelites out so
6: 8 a guilt offering. **S** it on its way,

1Sa 9:16 time tomorrow I will s you a man
9:26 ready, and I will s you on your way.
11: 3 days so that we can s messengers
12:17 upon the LORD to s thunder and rain.
16:11 Samuel said, "S for him; we will
16:19 "S me your son David, who is with
19:17 s my enemy away so that he escaped?"
20:12 I not s you word and let you know?
20:13 let you know and s you away safely.
20:21 I will s a boy and say, 'Go, find
20:31 Now s and bring him to me, for he
29: 4 "S the man back, that he may return
2Sa 11: 6 to Joab: "S me Uriah the Hittite."
11:12 day, and tomorrow I will s you back.
13: 9 "S everyone out of here," Amnon said.
14:29 Joab in order to s him to the king,
14:32 'Come here so that I can s you to
15:36 S them to me with anything you hear."
17:16 Now s a message immediately and tell
18:29 to s the king's servant and me,
19:31 and to s him on his way from there.
1Ki 8:36 and s rain on the land you gave your
8:44 wherever you s them, and when they
18: 1 Ahab, and I will s rain on the land."
20: 6 s my officials to search your palace
22:26 "Take Micaiah and s him back to Amon
2Ki 2:16 Elisha replied, "do not s them."
2:17 So he said, "S them." And they sent
4:22 "Please s me one of the servants and
5: 5 "I will s a letter to the king of
5: 7 Why does this fellow s someone to me
6:13 that I can s men and capture him.
7:13 s them to find out what happened."
9:17 "S him to meet them and ask,
15:37 days the LORD began to s Rezin
1Ch 13: 2 let us s word far and wide to the
2Ch 2: 3 "S me cedar logs as you did for my
2: 7 "S me, therefore, a man skilled to
2: 8 "S me also cedar, pine and algum
2:15 "Now let my lord s his servants the
6:27 and s rain on the land that you gave
6:34 wherever you s them, and when they
7:13 land or s a plague among my people,
18:25 "Take Micaiah and s him back to Amon
28:11 Now listen to me! S back your fellow
30: 5 They decided to s a proclamation
Ezr 5:17 s us his decision in this matter.
10: 3 our God to s away all these women
Ne 2: 5 let him s me to the city in Judah
2: 6 It pleased the king to s me;
8:10 and s some to those who have nothing
8:12 to s portions of food and to
Job 1: 5 Job would s and have them purified.
14:20 his countenance and s him away.
21:11 They s forth their children as a
38:35 Do you s the lightning bolts on
Ps 20: 2 May he s you help from the sanctuary
43: 3 S forth your light and your truth,
104:30 you s your Spirit, they are created,
144: 6 S forth lightning and scatter the
Pr 10:26 so is a sluggard to those who s him.
24:22 those two will s sudden destruction
25:13 messenger to those who s him;
SS 7:13 The mandrakes s out their fragrance,
Isa 6: 8 "Whom shall I s? And who will go for
6: 8 And I said, "Here am I. S me!"
10: 6 I s him against a godless nation, I
10:16 will s a wasting disease upon his
16: 1 S lambs as tribute to the ruler of
19:20 he will s them a saviour and
30:23 He will also s you rain for the seed
34: 3 their dead bodies will s up a stench
42:19 and deaf like the messenger I s?
42:22 with no-one to say, "S them back.
43:14 "For your sake I will s to Babylon
48:20 S it out to the ends of the earth;
66:19 and I will s some of those who
Jer 1: 7 You must go to everyone I s you to
2:10 s to Kedar and observe closely;
8:17 "See, I will s venomous snakes among
9:17 s for the most skilful of them.
14: 3 The nobles s their servants for
14:15 in my name: I did not s them,
14:22 skies themselves s down showers?
15: 1 S them away from my presence!
15: 3 "I will s four kinds of destroyers
Jer 16:16 "But now I will s for many fishermen,
16:16 After that I will s for many hunters,
22: 7 I will s destroyers against you,
23:21 I did not s these prophets, yet they
23:32 yet I did not s or appoint them.
24:10 I will s the sword, famine and
25:15 nations to whom I s you drink it.
25:16 of the sword I will s among them."
25:27 of the sword I will s among you.'
27: 3 s word to the kings of Edom, Moab,
29:17 "I will s the sword, famine and
29:31 "S this message to all the exiles:
29:31 even though I did not s him, and has
37:20 Do not s me back to the house of
38:26 not to s me back to Jonathan's
43:10 says: I will s for my servant
48:12 "when I will s men who pour from
51: 2 I will s foreigners to Babylon to
51:27 s up horses like a swarm of locusts.
51:53 I will s destroyers against her,"
Eze 5:17 I will s famine and wild beasts
13:11 and I will s hailstones hurtling
14:13 s famine upon it and kill its men
14:15 "Or if I s wild beasts through that
14:19 "Or if I s a plague into that land
14:21 it be when I s against Jerusalem
28:23 I will s a plague upon her and make
34:26 I will s down showers in season;
39: 2 s you against the mountains of
39: 6 I will s fire on Magog and on those
Da 11:20 "His successor will s out a tax
Hos 8:14 But I will s fire upon their cities
14: 5 of Lebanon he will s down his roots;
Joel 3: 6 s them far from their homeland.
Am 1: 4 I will s fire upon the house of
1: 7 I will s fire upon the walls of Gaza
1:10 I will s fire upon the walls of Tyre
1:12 I will s fire upon Teman that will
2: 2 I will s fire upon Moab that will
2: 5 I will s fire upon Judah that will
5:27 Therefore I will s you into exile
8:11 "when I will s a famine through the
Zec 5: 4 Almighty declares, 'I will s it out,
Mal 2: 2 "I will s a curse upon you, and I
3: 1 "See, I will s my messenger, who
4: 5 "See, I will s you the prophet
Mt 8:31 us out, s us into the herd of pigs."
9:38 s out workers into his harvest field.
11:10 'I will s my messenger ahead of you,
13:41 The Son of Man will s out his angels,
14:15 S the crowds away, so that they can
15:23 "S her away, for she keeps crying
15:32 I do not want to s them away hungry,
19: 7 of divorce and s her away?"
21: 3 and he will s them right away."
24:31 he will s his angels with a loud
Mk 1: 2 "I will s my messenger ahead of you,
3:14 that he might s them out to
5:10 again not to s them out of the area.
5:12 The demons begged Jesus, "S us among
6:36 S the people away so that they can
8: 3 If I s them home hungry, they will
10: 4 of divorce and s her away."
11: 3 it and will s it back here shortly.
12: 6 "He had one left to s, a son, whom
13:27 he will s his angels and gather his
Lk 7:27 'I will s my messenger ahead of you,
9:12 "S the crowd away so they can go to
10: 2 s out workers into his harvest field.
11:49 'I will s them prophets and apostles,
14:32 he will s a delegation while the
16:24 have pity on me and s Lazarus to dip
16:27 s Lazarus to my father's house,
20:13 'What shall I do? I will s my son,
24:49 I am going to s you what my Father
Jn 3:17 For God did not s his Son into the
13:20 whoever accepts anyone I s accepts
14:26 whom the Father will s in my name,
15:26 whom I will s to you from the Father,
16: 7 but if I go, I will s him to you.
Ac 3:20 that he may s the Christ, who has
7:34 come, I will s you back to Egypt.'
7:37 'God will s you a prophet like me
7:43 s you into exile' beyond Babylon.
10: 5 Now s men to Joppa to bring back a
10:32 S to Joppa for Simon who is called
Ac 11:13 'S to Joppa for Simon who is called
15:22 s them to Antioch with Paul and
15:25 s them to you with our dear friends
22:21 will s you far away to the Gentiles.
24:25 it convenient, I will s for you."
25:21 held until I could s him to Caesar."
25:25 Emperor I decided to s him to Rome.
25:27 is unreasonable to s on a prisoner
Ro 16:16 the churches of Christ s greetings.
16:23 Quartus s you their greetings.
1Co 1:17 For Christ did not s me to baptise,
16: 3 s them with your gift to Jerusalem.
16:11 S him on his way in peace so that he
16:19 province of Asia s you greetings.
16:20 the brothers here s you greetings.
2Co 1:16 to have you s me on my way to Judea.
13:13 All the saints s their greetings.
Php 2:19 hope in the Lord Jesus to s Timothy
2:23 I hope, therefore, to s him as soon
2:25 I think it is necessary to s back to
2:28 I am all the more eager to s him,
4:21 who are with me s greetings.
4:22 All the saints s you greetings,
Col 4:14 the doctor, and Demas s greetings.
Tit 3:12 soon as I s Artemas or Tychicus to
Heb 13:24 from Italy s you their greetings.
2Jn :13 chosen sister s their greetings.
3Jn : 6 You will do well to s them on their
:14 The friends here s their greetings.
Rev 1:11 see and s it to the seven churches:

Sending (Send)

Ge 32: 5 Now I am s this message to my lord,
32:20 these gifts I am s on ahead; later,
Ex 3:10 I am s you to Pharaoh to bring
23:20 "See, I am s an angel ahead of you
Lev 16:10 s it into the desert as a scapegoat.
Jdg 6:14 of Midian's hand. Am I not s you?"
1Sa 6: 8 gold objects you are s back to him
16: 1 I am s you to Jesse of Bethlehem.
2Sa 10: 3 by s men to you to express sympathy?
13:16 "No!" she said to him. "S me away
1Ki 15:19 See, I am s you a gift of silver and
2Ki 1: 6 you are s men to consult Baal-Zebub,
5: 6 "With this letter I am s my servant
6:32 s someone to cut off my head?
1Ch 19: 3 by s men to you to express sympathy?
2Ch 2:13 "I am s you Huram-Abi, a man of
16: 3 See, I am s you silver and gold.
Ezr 4:14 s this message to inform the king,
Ne 6:17 Judah were s many letters to Tobiah,
Pr 26: 6 s of a message by the hand of a fool.
Jer 42: 6 to whom we are s you, so that it
Eze 2: 3 He said: "Son of man, I am s you to
2: 4 The people to whom I am s you are
17:15 against him by s his envoys to
Joel 2:13 and he relents from s calamity.
2:19 "I am s you grain, new wine and oil
Jnh 4: 2 a God who relents from s calamity.
Mt 10:16 I am s you out like sheep among
23:34 Therefore I am s you prophets and
Lk 10: 3 Go! I am s you out like lambs among
Jn 20:21 the Father has sent me, I am s you."
Ac 11:30 This they did, s their gift to the
15:27 Therefore we are s Judas and Silas
26:17 the Gentiles. I am s you to them
Ro 8: 3 God did by s his own Son in the
1Co 4:17 For this reason I am s to you
2Co 8:18 we are s along with him the brother
8:22 In addition, we are s with them our
9: 3 I am s the brothers in order that
Eph 6:22 I am s him to you for this very
Col 4: 8 I am s him to you for the express
Phm :12 I am s him—who is my very heart
Rev 1: 1 by s his angel to his servant John,
11:10 celebrate by s each other gifts,

Sends (Send)

Dt 24: 1 it to her and s her from his house,
24: 3 s her from his house, or if he dies,
28:48 the enemies the LORD s against you.
1Sa 2: 7 The LORD s poverty and wealth;
Job 5:10 he s water upon the countryside.
12:24 he s them wandering through a
37: 3 and s it to the ends of the earth.

Ps 57: 3 He s from heaven and saves me,
57: 3 God s his love and his faithfulness.
135: 7 he s lightning with the rain and
147:15 He s his command to the earth;
147:18 He s his word and melts them;
Isa 18: 2 which s envoys by sea in papyrus
Jer 10:13 He s lightning with the rain and
17: 8 that s out its roots by the stream.
42: 5 the LORD your God s you to tell us.
51:16 He s lightning with the rain and
Hos 12: 1 Assyria and s olive oil to Egypt.
Joel 2:23 He s you abundant showers, both
Zec 12: 2 a cup that s all the surrounding
Mt 5:45 and s rain on the righteous and the
Ro 16:21 Timothy, my fellow-worker, s his
16:23 here enjoy, s you his greetings.
Col 4:10 Aristarchus s you his greetings,
4:11 is called Justus, also s greetings.
4:12 of Christ Jesus, s greetings.
2Th 2:11 For this reason God s them a
Tit 3:15 Everyone with me s you greetings.
Phm :23 in Christ Jesus, s you greetings.
1Pe 5:13 chosen together with you, s you her

Seneh

1Sa 14: 4 was called Bozez, and the other **S**.

Senir

Dt 3: 9 Sidonians; the Amorites call it **S**.)
1Ch 5:23 Hermon, that is, to **S** (Mount Hermon).
SS 4: 8 from the top of **S**, the summit of
Eze 27: 5 your timbers of pine trees from **S**;

Sennacherib (Sennacherib's)

King of Assyria. Attacked Judah and laid siege to Jerusalem (2Ki 18:13–19:13; Isa 36:1–37:13; 2Ch 32). Pride brought God's judgment (Isa 10:12–19). Fall prophesied by Isaiah, following Hezekiah's prayer (2Ki 19:14–34; Isa 37:14–35); defeat and death (2Ki 19:35–37; Isa 37:36–38).

2Ki 18:13 **S** king of Assyria attacked all the
19: 9 Now **S** received a report that
19:16 listen to the words **S** has sent to
19:20 prayer concerning **S** king of Assyria.
19:36 **S** king of Assyria broke camp and
2Ch 32: 1 **S** king of Assyria came and invaded
32: 2 Hezekiah saw that **S** had come and
32: 9 Later, when **S** king of Assyria and
32:10 "This is what **S** king of Assyria says:
32:22 from the hand of **S** king of Assyria
Isa 36: 1 **S** king of Assyria attacked all the
37: 9 Now **S** received a report that
37:17 listen to all the words **S** has sent
37:21 to me concerning **S** king of Assyria,
37:37 **S** king of Assyria broke camp and

Sennacherib's (Sennacherib)

2Ch 32:16 **S** officers spoke further against the

Sense (Sensed, Senses)

Dt 32:28 They are a nation without s, there
Job 39:17 or give her a share of good s.
Ecc 10: 3 the fool lacks s and shows everyone
1Co 12:17 where would the s of hearing be?
12:17 ear, where would the s of smell be?

Sensed (Sense)

Ac 27:27 the sailors s they were approaching

Senseless

Ps 49:10 the foolish and the s alike perish
73:22 I was s and ignorant; I was a brute
92: 6 The s man does not know, fools do
94: 8 Take heed, you s ones among the
Isa 19:11 of Pharaoh give s advice.
Jer 4:22 They are s children; they have no
5:21 Hear this, you foolish and s people,
10: 8 They are all s and foolish; they are
10:14 Everyone is s and without knowledge;
10:21 The shepherds are s and do not
51:17 "Every man is s and without
Hos 7:11 easily deceived and s—now calling
Ro 1:31 they are s, faithless, heartless,

Senses (Sense)

Lk 15:17 "When he came to his s, he said,
1Co 15:34 Come back to your s as you ought,
2Ti 2:26 that they will come to their s and

Sensible

Job 18: 2 Be s, and then we can talk.
1Co 10:15 I speak to s people; judge for

Sensitive (Sensitivity)

Dt 28:54 Even the most gentle and s man among
28:56 The most gentle and s woman among
28:56 s woman among you—so s and gentle

Sensitivity (Sensitive)

Eph 4:19 Having lost all s, they have given

Sensual (Sensuality)

Col 2:23 value in restraining s indulgence.
1Ti 5:11 For when their s desires overcome

Sensuality (Sensual)

Eph 4:19 given themselves over to s so as to

Sent (Send)

Ge 2: 5 for the LORD God had not s rain on
8: 1 and he s a wind over the earth, and
8: 7 s out a raven, and it kept flying
8: 8 he s out a dove to see if the water
8:10 and again s out the dove from the
8:12 more days and s the dove out again,
12:20 and they s him on his way, with his
19:13 that he has s us to destroy it."
20: 2 of Gerar s for Sarah and took her.
21:14 and then s her off with the boy.
24:59 they s their sister Rebekah on her
25: 6 s them away from his son Isaac to
26:27 were hostile to me and s me away?"
26:29 you well and s you away in peace.
26:31 Then Isaac s them on their way, and
27:42 she s for her younger son Jacob and
28: 5 Isaac s Jacob on his way, and he
28: 6 had s him to Paddan Aram to take a
31: 4 Jacob s word to Rachel and Leah to
31:42 surely have s me away empty-handed.
32: 3 Jacob s messengers ahead of him to
32:18 They are a gift s to my lord Esau,
32:23 After he had s them across the
32:23 he s over all his possessions.
37:14 Then he s him off from the Valley
38:20 Meanwhile Judah s the young goat by
38:25 being brought out, she s a message
41: 8 so he s for all the magicians and
41:14 Pharaoh s for Joseph, and he was
44: 3 morning dawned, the men were s on
45: 5 lives that God s me ahead of you.
45: 7 God s me ahead of you to preserve
45: 8 "So then, it was not you who s me
45:23 this is what he s to his father: ten
45:24 he s his brothers away, and as they
45:27 Joseph had s to carry him back,
46: 5 that Pharaoh had s to transport him.
46:28 Now Jacob s Judah ahead of him to
50:16 they s word to Joseph, saying, "Your
Ex 2: 5 and s her slave girl to get it.
3:12 to you that it is I who have s you:
3:13 'The God of your fathers has s me to
3:14 I AM has s me to you.'"
3:15 the God of Jacob—has s me to you.
4:28 the LORD had s him to say,
5:22 this people? Is this why you s me?
7:16 the God of the Hebrews, has s me to
9: 7 Pharaoh s men to investigate and
9:23 the LORD s thunder and hail, and
18: 2 After Moses had s away his wife
18: 6 Jethro had s word to him, "I, your
18:27 Moses s his father-in-law on his way,
24: 5 he s young Israelite men, and they
36: 6 Moses gave an order and they s this
Lev 26:41 so that I s them into the land of
Nu 5: 4 they s them outside the camp.
13: 3 at the LORD's command Moses s them
13:16 the men Moses s to explore the land.
13:17 Moses s them to explore Canaan, he
Nu 13:27 into the land to which you s us,
14:36 the men Moses had s to explore the
16:28 LORD has s me to do all these things
16:29 to men, then the LORD has not s me.
20:14 Moses s messengers from Kadesh to
20:16 he heard our cry and s an angel and
21: 6 the LORD s venomous snakes among
21:21 Israel s messengers to say to Sihon
21:32 After Moses had s spies to Jazer,
22: 5 s messengers to summon Balaam son of
22:10 king of Moab, s me this message:
22:15 Balak s other princes, more numerous
24:12 I not tell the messengers you s me,
31: 6 Moses s them into battle, a thousand
32: 8 when I s them from Kadesh Barnea to
Dt 2:26 I s messengers to Sihon king of
6:22 the LORD s miraculous signs and
9:23 the LORD s you out from Kadesh
24: 5 he must not be s to war or have any
34:11 wonders the LORD s him to do in
Jos 2: 1 Joshua son of Nun secretly s two
2: 3 the king of Jericho s this message
2:21 So she s them away and they
6:17 because she hid the spies we s.
6:25 Joshua had s as spies to Jericho
7: 2 Now Joshua s men from Jericho to Ai,
7:22 Joshua s messengers, and they ran to
8: 3 fighting men and s them out at
8: 9 Joshua s them off, and they went to
10: 6 The Gibeonites then s word to Joshua
11: 1 he s word to Jobab king of Madon, to
14: 7 Moses the servant of the LORD s me
14:11 today as the day Moses s me out;
22: 6 Joshua blessed them and s them away,
22: 7 Joshua s them home, he blessed them,
22:13 the Israelites s Phinehas son of
22:14 With him they s ten of the chief men,
24: 5 "'Then I s Moses and Aaron, and I
24: 9 he s for Balaam son of Beor to put a
24:12 I s the hornet ahead of you, which
24:28 Joshua s the people away, each to
Jdg 1:23 they s men to spy out Bethel
3:15 The Israelites s him with tribute to
3:18 he s on their way the men who had
4: 6 She s for Barak son of Abinoam from
6: 8 he s them a prophet, who said, "This
6:35 He s messengers throughout Manasseh,
7: 8 Gideon s the rest of the Israelites
7:24 Gideon s messengers throughout the
9:23 God s an evil spirit between
9:31 Under cover he s messengers to
11:12 Jephthah s messengers to the
11:14 Jephthah s back messengers to the
11:17 Israel s messengers to the king of
11:17 They s also to the king of Moab, and
11:19 "Then Israel s messengers to Sihon
11:28 to the message Jephthah s him.
13: 8 let the man of God you s to us come
16:18 she s word to the rulers of the
18: 2 the Danites s five warriors from
19:25 his concubine and s her outside
19:29 s them into all the areas of Israel.
20: 6 cut her into pieces and s one piece
20:12 tribes of Israel s men throughout
21:10 the assembly s twelve thousand
21:13 the whole assembly s an offer of
1Sa 4: 4 the people s men to Shiloh, and they
4:13 happened, the whole town s up a cry.
5:10 they s the ark of God to Ekron.
6:17 Philistines s as a guilt offering
6:21 they s messengers to the people of
11: 7 and s the pieces by messengers
12: 8 and the LORD s Moses and Aaron, who
12:11 the LORD s Jerub-Baal, Barak,
12:18 day the LORD s thunder and rain.
13: 2 of the men he s back to their homes.
14:15 It was a panic s by God.
15: 1 "I am the one the LORD s to anoint
15:18 he s you on a mission, saying, 'Go
16:12 he s and had him brought in. He was
16:19 Saul s messengers to Jesse and said,
16:20 s them with his son David to Saul.
16:22 Saul s word to Jesse, saying, "Allow
17:31 to Saul, and Saul s for him.
18: 5 Whatever Saul s him to do, David did
18:13 he s David away from him and gave

1Sa 19:11 Saul s men to David's house to watch
19:14 Saul s the men to capture David,
19:15 Saul s the men back to see David and
19:20 he s men to capture him. But when
19:21 told about it, and he s more men,
19:21 Saul s men a third time, and they
20:22 go, because the LORD has s you away.
22:11 the king s for the priest Ahimelech
25: 5 he s ten young men and said to them,
25:14 "David s messengers from the desert
25:25 I did not see the men my master s.
25:32 who has s you today to meet me.
25:39 Then David s word to Abigail,
25:40 "David has s us to you to take you
26: 4 he s out scouts and learned that
30:26 he s some of the plunder to the
30:27 He s it to those who were in Bethel,
31: 9 and they s messengers throughout the
2Sa 2: 5 he s messengers to the men of Jabesh
3:12 Abner s messengers on his behalf to
3:14 David s messengers to Ish-Bosheth
3:21 s Abner away, and he went in peace.
3:22 s him away, and he had gone in peace.
3:23 that the king had s him away and
3:26 and s messengers after Abner,
5:11 Now Hiram king of Tyre s messengers
8:10 he s his son Joram to King David to
10: 2 So David s a delegation to express
10: 3 Hasn't David s them to you to
10: 4 at the buttocks, and s them away.
10: 5 he s messengers to meet the men,
10: 7 On hearing this, David s Joab out
11: 1 David s Joab out with the king's men
11: 3 David s someone to find out about
11: 4 David s messengers to get her.
11: 5 The woman conceived and s word to
11: 6 David s this word to Joab: "Send me
11: 6 And Joab s him to David.
11: 8 gift from the king was s after him.
11:14 letter to Joab and s it with Uriah.
11:18 Joab s David a full account of the
11:22 everything Joab had s him to say.
12: 1 The LORD s Nathan to David. When he
12:25 him, he s word through Nathan the
12:27 Joab then s messengers to David,
13: 7 David s word to Tamar at the palace:
13:27 Absalom urged him, so he s with him
14: 2 Joab s someone to Tekoa and had a
14:29 Absalom s for Joab in order to send
14:29 So he s a second time, but he
14:32 "Look, I s word to you and said,
15:10 Absalom s secret messengers
15:12 he also s for Ahithophel the
18: 2 David s the troops out—a third
19:11 King David s this message to Zadok
19:14 They s word to the king, "Return,
24:13 I should answer the one who s me."
24:15 the LORD s a plague on Israel from
1Ki 1:44 The king has s with him Zadok the
1:53 King Solomon s men, and they brought
2:36 the king s for Shimei and said to
4:34 s by all the kings of the world, who
5: 1 he s his envoys to Solomon, because
5: 2 Solomon s back this message to Hiram:
5: 8 Hiram s word to Solomon: "I have
5: 8 received the message you s me and
5:14 He s them off to Lebanon in shifts
7:13 King Solomon s to Tyre and brought
8:66 On the following day he s the people
9:14 Hiram had s to the king 120 talents
9:27 Hiram s his men—sailors who knew
12: 3 they s for Jeroboam, and he and the
12:18 King Rehoboam s out Adoniram, who
12:20 they s and called him to the
14: 6 I have been s to you with bad news.
15:18 s them to Ben-Hadad son of Tabrimmon,
15:20 with King Asa and s the commanders
18:10 has not s someone to look for you.
18:20 Ahab s word throughout all Israel
19: 2 Jezebel s a messenger to Elijah to
20: 2 He s messengers into the city to
20: 5 'I s to demand your silver and gold,
20: 7 he s for my wives and my children,
20:10 Ben-Hadad s another message to Ahab:
21: 8 and s them to the elders and nobles
21:14 they s word to Jezebel: "Naboth has

2Ki 1: 2 So he s messengers, saying to them,
1: 6 'Go back to the king who s you and
1: 9 he s to Elijah a captain with his
1:11 At this the king s to Elijah another
1:13 the king s a third captain with his
1:16 s messengers to consult Baal-Zebub,
2: 2 the LORD has s me to Bethel.
2: 4 the LORD has s me to Jericho.
2: 6 the LORD has s me to the Jordan.
2:17 And they s fifty men, who searched
3: 7 also s this message to Jehoshaphat
5: 8 he s him this message: "Why have you
5:10 Elisha s a messenger to say to him,
5:22 "My master s me to say, 'Two young
5:24 He s the men away and they left.
6: 9 The man of God s word to the king of
6:14 he s horses and chariots and a
6:23 he s them away, and they returned to
6:32 The king s a messenger ahead, but
7:14 king s them after the Aramean army.
8: 9 king of Aram has s me to ask,
9:19 the king s out a second horseman.
10: 1 So Jehu wrote letters and s them to
10: 5 the elders and the guardians s this
10: 7 and s them to Jehu in Jezreel.
10:21 he s word throughout Israel, and all
11: 4 In the seventh year Jehoiada s for
12:18 and he s them to Hazael king of Aram,
14: 8 Amaziah s messengers to Jehoash son
14: 9 "A thistle in Lebanon s a message to
14:19 but they s men after him to Lachish
16: 7 Ahaz s messengers to say to
16: 8 s it as a gift to the king of
16:10 altar in Damascus and s to Uriah
16:11 that King Ahaz had s from Damascus
17: 4 for he had s envoys to So king of
17:25 so he s lions among them and they
17:26 He has s lions among them, which are
18:14 Hezekiah king of Judah s this
18:17 The king of Assyria s his supreme
18:27 my master s me to say these things,
19: 2 He s Eliakim the palace
19: 4 king of Assyria, has s to ridicule
19: 9 So he again s messengers to
19:16 words Sennacherib has s to insult
19:20 Isaiah son of Amoz s a message to
20:12 s Hezekiah letters and a gift,
22: 3 King Josiah s the secretary, Shaphan
22:15 says: Tell the man who s you to me,
22:18 Tell the king of Judah, who s you to
24: 2 The LORD s Babylonian, Aramean,
24: 2 He s them to destroy Judah, in
1Ch 6:15 was deported when the LORD s Judah
10: 9 and s messengers throughout the land
12:19 their rulers s him away.
14: 1 Now Hiram king of Tyre s messengers
18:10 he s his son Hadoram to King David
19: 2 So David s a delegation to express
19: 4 at the buttocks, and s them away.
19: 5 he s messengers to meet them, for
19: 6 Hanun and the Ammonites s a thousand
19: 8 On hearing this, David s Joab out
19:16 they s messengers and had Arameans
21:12 I should answer the one who s me."
21:14 the LORD s a plague on Israel, and
21:15 God s an angel to destroy Jerusalem.
2Ch 2: 3 Solomon s this message to Hiram king
2: 3 you s him cedar to build a palace
7:10 he s the people to their homes,
8:18 Hiram s him ships commanded by his
10: 3 they s for Jeroboam, and he and all
10:18 King Rehoboam s out Adoniram, who
13:13 Now Jeroboam had s troops round to
16: 2 and s it to Ben-Hadad king of Aram,
16: 4 Ben-Hadad agreed with King Asa and s
17: 7 of his reign he s his officials
23:14 Jehoiada the priest s out the
24:19 Although the LORD s prophets to the
24:23 They s all the plunder to their king
25:10 to him from Ephraim and s them home.
25:13 the troops that Amaziah had s back
25:15 and he s a prophet to him, who said,
25:17 he s this challenge to Jehoash son
25:18 "A thistle in Lebanon s a message to
25:27 but they s men after him to Lachish
28:16 At that time King Ahaz s to the king

2Ch 30: 1 Hezekiah s word to all Israel and
32: 9 he s his officers to Jerusalem with
32:21 the LORD s an angel, who annihilated
32:31 when envoys were s by the rulers of
34: 8 he s Shaphan son of Azaliah and
34:22 Hilkiah and those the king had s
34:23 says: Tell the man who s you to me,
34:26 Tell the king of Judah, who s you to
35:21 Neco s messengers to him saying,
36:10 King Nebuchadnezzar s for him and
36:15 the God of their fathers, s word to
Ezr 4:11 (This is a copy of the letter they s
4:17 The king s this reply: To Rehum the
4:18 The letter you s us has been read
5: 6 Trans-Euphrates, s to King Darius.
5: 7 The report they s him read as
6:13 of the decree King Darius had s,
7:14 You are s by the king and his seven
8:17 I s them to Iddo, the leader in
Ne 2: 9 s army officers and cavalry with me.
6: 2 Sanballat and Geshem s me this
6: 3 I s messengers to them with this
6: 4 Four times they s me the same
6: 5 Sanballat s his assistant to me
6: 8 I s him this reply: "Nothing like
6:12 I realised that God had not s him,
6:19 Tobiah s letters to intimidate me.
9:10 You s miraculous signs and wonders
Est 1:22 He s dispatches to all parts of the
3:13 Dispatches were s by couriers to all
4: 4 She s clothes for him to put on
4:13 he s back this answer: "Do not think
4:15 Esther s this reply to Mordecai:
8:10 and s them by mounted couriers, who
9:20 and he s letters to all the Jews
9:30 Mordecai s letters to all the Jews
Job 22: 9 you s widows away empty-handed and
Ps 59: T Saul had s men to watch David's
78:25 he s them all the food they could
78:45 He s swarms of flies that devoured
78:61 He s the ark of his might into
80:11 s out its boughs to the Sea, its
105:17 he s a man before them—Joseph,
105:20 The king s and released him, the
105:26 He s Moses his servant, and Aaron,
105:28 He s darkness and made the land dark
106:15 but s a wasting disease upon them.
107:20 He s forth his word and healed them;
135: 9 He s his signs and wonders into your
Pr 9: 3 She has s out her maids, and she
17:11 official will be s against him.
22:21 give sound answers to him who s you?
Isa 6:12 until the LORD has s everyone far
9: 8 The Lord has s a message against
20: 1 s by Sargon king of Assyria, came to
36: 2 the king of Assyria s his field
36:12 my master s me to say these things,
37: 2 He s Eliakim the palace
37: 4 king of Assyria, has s to ridicule
37: 9 he s messengers to Hezekiah with
37:17 words Sennacherib has s to
37:21 Isaiah son of Amoz s a message to
39: 1 s Hezekiah letters and a gift,
48:16 LORD has s me, with his Spirit.
50: 1 of divorce with which I s her away?
50: 1 your mother was s away.
55:11 the purpose for which I s it.
57: 9 You s your ambassadors far away; you
61: 1 He has s me to bind up the
63:12 who s his glorious arm of power to
Jer 3: 8 s her away because of all her
7:25 I s you my servants the prophets.
14:14 I have not s them or appointed them
19:14 where the LORD had s him to prophesy,
21: 1 s to him Pashhur son of Malkijah
24: 5 whom I s away from this place to the
25: 4 though the LORD has s all his
25:17 nations to whom he s me drink it:
26: 5 whom I have s to you again and again
26:12 "The LORD s me to prophesy against
26:15 for in truth the LORD has s me to
26:22 King Jehoiakim, however, s Elnathan
27:15 'I have not s them,' declares the
28: 9 one truly s by the LORD only if his
28:15 The LORD has not s you, yet you
29: 1 Jeremiah s from Jerusalem to the

Jer 29: 3 s to King Nebuchadnezzar in Babylon.
29: 9 I have not s them," declares the
29:19 "words that I s to them again and
29:20 s away from Jerusalem to Babylon.
29:25 You s letters in your own name to
29:28 He has s this message to us in
35:15 Again and again I s all my servants
36:14 all the officials s Jehudi son of
36:21 The king s Jehudi to get the scroll,
37: 3 King Zedekiah, however, s Jehucal
37: 7 king of Judah, who s you to enquire
37:17 King Zedekiah s for him and had him
38:14 King Zedekiah s for Jeremiah the
39:14 s and had Jeremiah taken out of the
40:14 king of the Ammonites has s Ishmael
42: 9 to whom you s me to present your
42:20 s me to the LORD your God and said,
42:21 your God in all he s me to tell you.
43: 1 the LORD had s him to tell them—
43: 2 LORD our God has not s you to say,
44: 4 Again and again I s my servants the
49:14 An envoy was s to the nations to say,
Lam 1:13 "From on high he s fire, s it down
Eze 3: 5 You are not being s to a people of
3: 6 Surely if I had s you to them, they
11:16 Although I s them far away among the
13: 6 when the LORD has not s them;
17: 7 The vine now s out its roots towards
23:16 and s messengers to them in Chaldea.
23:40 "They even s messengers for men who
31: 4 s their channels to all the trees of
39:28 for though I s them into exile among
Da 2:13 and men were s to look for Daniel
3:28 Meshach and Abednego, who has s his
5:24 Therefore he s the hand that wrote
6:22 My God s his angel, and he shut the
10:11 up, for I have now been s to you.
Hos 5:13 and s to the great king for help.
Joel 2:25 my great army that I s among you.
Am 4: 7 I s rain on one town, but withheld
4:10 "I s plagues among you as I did to
7:10 Amaziah the priest of Bethel s a
Ob : 1 An envoy was s to the nations to say,
Jnh 1: 4 the LORD s a great wind on the sea,
Mic 6: 4 I s Moses to lead you, also Aaron
Hag 1:12 the LORD their God had s him.
Zec 1:10 has s to go throughout the earth."
2: 8 honoured me and has s me against
2: 9 that the LORD Almighty has s me.
2:11 the LORD Almighty has s me to you.
4: 9 the LORD Almighty has s me to you.
6:15 the LORD Almighty has s me to you.
7: 2 The people of Bethel had s Sharezer
7:12 LORD Almighty had s by his Spirit
Mal 2: 4 you will know that I have s you this
Mt 2: 8 He s them to Bethlehem and said, "Go
10: 5 These twelve Jesus s out with the
10:40 me receives the one who s me.
11: 2 Christ was doing, he s his
14:35 they s word to all the surrounding
15:24 He answered, "I was s only to the
15:39 After Jesus had s the crowd away, he
20: 2 day and s them into his vineyard.
21: 1 of Olives, Jesus s two disciples,
21:34 he s his servants to the tenants
21:36 he s other servants to them, more
21:37 Last of all, he s his son to them.
22: 3 He s his servants to those who had
22: 4 "Then he s some more servants and
22: 7 The king was enraged. He s his army
22:16 They s their disciples to him along
23:37 prophets and stone those s to you,
26:47 s from the chief priests and the
27:19 his wife s him this message: "Don't
Mk 1:12 At once the Spirit s him out into
1:43 Jesus s him away at once with a
3:31 they s someone in to call him.
6: 7 Calling the Twelve to him, he s them
6:27 he immediately s an executioner with
8: 9 And having s them away,
8:26 Jesus s him home, saying, "Don't go
9:37 welcome me but the one who s me."
11: 1 Olives, Jesus s two of his disciples,
12: 2 At harvest time he s a servant to
12: 3 they seized him, beat him and s him
12: 4 he s another servant to them;
Mk 12: 5 He s still another, and that one
12: 5 He s many others; some of them they
12: 6 He s him last of all, saying, 'They
12:13 Later they s some of the Pharisees
14:13 he s two of his disciples, telling
14:43 s from the chief priests, the
Lk 1:19 and I have been s to speak to you
1:26 In the sixth month, God s the angel
1:53 but has s the rich away empty.
4:18 He has s me to proclaim freedom for
4:26 Yet Elijah was not s to any of them,
4:43 also, because that is why I was s."
7: 3 heard of Jesus and s some elders of
7: 6 centurion s friends to say to him:
7:10 the men who had been s returned to
7:19 he s them to the Lord to ask, "Are
7:20 "John the Baptist s us to you to ask,
8:38 him, but Jesus s him away, saying,
9: 2 he s them out to preach the kingdom
9:48 me welcomes the one who s me.
9:52 he s messengers on ahead, who went
10: 1 s them two by two ahead of him to
10:16 rejects me rejects him who s me."
13:34 prophets and stone those s to you,
14: 4 man, he healed him and s him away.
14:17 At the time of the banquet he s his
15:15 s him to his fields to feed pigs.
19:14 hated him and s a delegation after
19:15 Then he s for the servants to whom
19:29 he s two of his disciples, saying to
19:32 Those who were s ahead went and
20:10 At harvest time he s a servant to
20:10 him and s him away empty-handed.
20:11 He s another servant, but that one
20:11 shamefully and s away empty-handed.
20:12 He s still a third, and they wounded
20:20 they s spies, who pretended to be
22: 8 Jesus s Peter and John, saying, "Go
22:35 Jesus asked them, "When I s you
23: 7 he s him to Herod, who was also in
23:11 robe, they s him back to Pilate.
23:15 Neither has Herod, for he s him back
Jn 1: 6 There came a man who was s from God;
1:19 the Jews of Jerusalem s priests
1:22 to take back to those who s us.
1:24 Now some Pharisees who had been s
1:33 except that the one who s me to
3:28 the Christ but am s ahead of him.'
3:34 For the one whom God has s speaks
4:34 him who s me and to finish his work.
4:38 I s you to reap what you have not
5:23 not honour the Father, who s him.
5:24 believes him who s me has eternal
5:30 to please myself but him who s me.
5:33 "You have s to John and he has
5:36 testifies that the Father has s me.
5:37 the Father who s me has himself
5:38 for you do not believe the one he s.
6:29 to believe in the one he has s."
6:38 but to do the will of him who s me.
6:39 this is the will of him who s me,
6:44 the Father who s me draws him,
6:57 Just as the living Father s me and I
7:16 It comes from him who s me.
7:18 the one who s him is a man of truth;
7:28 on my own, but he who s me is true.
7:29 because I am from him and he s me."
7:32 s temple guards to arrest him.
7:33 and then I go to the one who s me.
8:16 I stand with the Father, who s me.
8:18 witness is the Father, who s me."
8:26 But he who s me is reliable, and
8:29 The one who s me is with me; he has
8:42 not come on my own; but he s me.
9: 4 we must do the work of him who s me.
9: 7 Pool of Siloam" (this word means S).
9:18 until they s for the man's parents.
10:36 his very own and s into the world?
11: 3 the sisters s word to Jesus, "Lord,
11:42 they may believe that you s me."
12:44 in me only, but in the one who s me.
12:45 at me, he sees the one who s me
12:49 but the Father who s me commanded me
13:16 greater than the one who s him.
13:20 me accepts the one who s me."
14:24 they belong to the Father who s me.
Jn 15:21 they do not know the One who s me.
16: 5 "Now I am going to him who s me, yet
17: 3 and Jesus Christ, whom you have s.
17: 8 and they believed that you s me.
17:18 you s me into the world, I have s
17:21 may believe that you have s me.
17:23 to let the world know that you s me
17:25 and they know that you have s me.
18:24 Annas s him, still bound, to
20:21 Father has s me, I am sending you."
Ac 3:26 God raised up his servant, he s him
5:21 s to the jail for the apostles.
7: 4 God s him to this land where you
7:12 s our fathers on their first visit.
7:14 After this, Joseph s for his father
7:35 He was s to be their ruler and
8:14 God, they s Peter and John to them.
9:17 s me so that you may see again
9:30 to Caesarea and s him off to Tarsus.
9:38 they s two men to him and urged him,
9:40 Peter s them all out of the room;
10: 8 had happened and s them to Joppa.
10:17 the men s by Cornelius found out
10:20 to go with them, for I have s them."
10:29 when I was s for, I came without
10:29 May I ask why you s for me?"
10:33 I s for you immediately, and it was
10:36 You know the message God s to the
11:11 then three men who had been s to me
11:22 and they s Barnabas to Antioch.
12:11 a doubt that the Lord s his angel
13: 3 their hands on them and s them off.
13: 4 The two of them, s on their way by
13: 7 an intelligent man, s for Barnabas
13:15 the synagogue rulers s word to them,
13:26 message of salvation has been s.
15: 3 The church s them on their way, and
15:23 With them they s the following
15:30 The men were s off and went down to
15:33 they were s off by the brothers with
15:33 to return to those who had s them.
16:35 the magistrates s their officers to
17:10 the brothers s Paul and Silas away
17:14 The brothers immediately s Paul to
19:22 He s two of his helpers, Timothy and
19:31 friends of Paul, s him a message
20: 1 the uproar had ended, Paul s for the
20:17 From Miletus, Paul s to Ephesus for
23:18 "Paul, the prisoner, s for me and
23:30 the man, I s him to you at once.
24:24 He s for Paul and listened to him as
24:26 so he s for him frequently and
28:28 has been s to the Gentiles,
Ro 10:15 can they preach unless they are s?
2Co 2:17 with sincerity, like men s from God.
12:17 you through any of the men I s you?
12:18 you and I s our brother with him.
Gal 1: 1 Paul, an apostle—s not from men nor
4: 4 God s his Son, born of a woman,
4: 6 God s the Spirit of his Son into
Php 2:25 whom you s to take care of my needs.
4:16 you s me aid again and again when I
4:18 from Epaphroditus the gifts you s.
1Th 3: 2 We s Timothy, who is our brother and
3: 5 I s to find out about your faith.
2Ti 4:12 I s Tychicus to Ephesus.
Heb 1:14 ministering spirits s to serve
Jas 2:25 s them off in a different direction?
1Pe 1:12 by the Holy Spirit s from heaven.
2:14 or to governors, who are s by him to
2Pe 2: 4 but s them to hell, putting them
1Jn 4: 9 He s his one and only Son into the
4:10 but that he loved us and s his Son
4:14 testify that the Father has s his
Rev 5: 6 of God s out into all the earth.
22: 6 s his angel to show his servants the
22:16 "I, Jesus, have s my angel to give

Sentence (Sentenced)

1Ki 20:40 "That is your s," the king of
2Ki 25: 6 where s was pronounced on him.
Ps 149: 9 to carry out the s written against
Ecc 8:11 the s for a crime is not quickly
Jer 39: 5 Hamath, where he pronounced s on him.
52: 9 Hamath, where he pronounced s on him.

Eze 16:38 I will **s** you to the punishment of
23:45 righteous men will **s** them to the
Lk 23:40 "since you are under the same **s**
Ac 13:28 no proper ground for a death **s**,
Ro 9:28 For the Lord will carry out his **s** on
2Co 1: 9 our hearts we felt the **s** of death.

Sentenced (Sentence)
Jer 26:11 "This man should be **s** to death
26:16 "This man should not be **s** to death!
Lk 24:20 handed him over to be **s** to death,

Sentries
Ac 12: 6 and **s** stood guard at the entrance.

Seorim
1Ch 24: 8 the third to Harim, the fourth to **S**,

Separate (Separated, Separates, Separation)
Ge 1: 6 the waters to **s** water from water."
1:14 the sky to **s** the day from the night,
1:18 night, and to **s** light from darkness.
30:40 Thus he made **s** flocks for himself
Ex 26:33 The curtain will **s** the Holy Place
Lev 15:31 "'You must keep the Israelites **s**
Nu 16:21 "**S** yourselves from this assembly so
Jdg 7: 5 "**S** those who lap the water with
2Sa 14: 6 and no-one was there to **s** them.
1Ki 5: 9 There I will **s** them and you can take
2Ki 15: 5 he died, and he lived in a **s** house.
2Ch 26:21 He lived in a **s** house—leprous, and
Ezr 9: 1 have not kept themselves **s** from the
10:11 **S** yourselves from the peoples around
Eze 42:20 wide, to **s** the holy from the common.
Mt 13:49 **s** the wicked from the righteous
19: 6 has joined together, let man not **s**."
25:32 and he will **s** the people one from
Mk 10: 9 has joined together, let man not **s**."
Jn 20: 7 up by itself, **s** from the linen.
Ro 8:35 Who shall **s** us from the love of
8:39 will be able to **s** us from the love
1Co 7:10 A wife must not **s** from her husband.
2Co 6:17 from them and be **s**, says the Lord.
Gal 2:12 he began to draw back and **s** himself
Eph 2:12 that time you were **s** from Christ,

Separated (Separate)
Ge 1: 4 he **s** the light from the darkness.
1: 7 God made the expanse and **s** the water
2:10 there it was **s** into four headwaters.
25:23 peoples from within you will be **s**;
Nu 16: 9 the God of Israel has **s** you from
1Sa 11:11 The next day Saul **s** his men into
2Ki 2:11 fire appeared and **s** the two of them,
25: 5 were **s** from him and scattered,
1Ch 24: 3 David **s** them into divisions for
Ezr 6:21 all who had **s** themselves from the
Ne 4:19 **s** from each other along the wall.
9: 2 Israelite descent had **s** themselves
10:28 and all who **s** themselves from the
Isa 59: 2 your iniquities have **s** you from your
Jer 52: 8 were **s** from him and scattered,
Eze 46:18 people will be **s** from his property.
Ac 2: 3 tongues of fire that **s** and came to
Eph 4:18 **s** from the life of God because of
Phm :15 Perhaps the reason he was **s** from you

Separates (Separate)
Ru 1:17 if anything but death **s** you and me."
Pr 16:28 and a gossip **s** close friends.
17: 9 repeats the matter **s** close friends.
Eze 14: 7 living in Israel **s** himself from me
Mt 25:32 shepherd **s** the sheep from the goats.

Separation (Separate)
Nu 6: 2 vow of **s** to the LORD as a Nazirite,
6: 5 vow of **s** no razor may be used on
6: 5 period of his **s** to the LORD is over;
6: 6 Throughout the period of his **s** to
6: 7 of his **s** to God is on his head.
6: 8 Throughout the period of his **s** he is
6:12 to the LORD for the period of his **s**
6:12 he became defiled during his **s**.
6:13 when the period of his **s** is over.
6:21 the LORD in accordance with his **s**,

Sephar
Ge 10:30 **S**, in the eastern hill country.

Sepharad
Ob :20 exiles from Jerusalem who are in **S**

Sepharvaim (Sepharvites)
2Ki 17:24 Cuthah, Avva, Hamath and **S** and
17:31 and Anammelech, the gods of **S**.
18:34 Where are the gods of **S**, Hena and
19:13 the city of **S**, or of Hena or Ivvah?"
Isa 36:19 Where are the gods of **S**? Have they
37:13 the city of **S**, or of Hena or Ivvah?"

Sepharvites (Sepharvaim)
2Ki 17:31 and the **S** burned their children in

Serah
Ge 46:17 Their sister was **S**. The sons of
Nu 26:46 (Asher had a daughter named **S**.)
1Ch 7:30 Their sister was **S**.

Seraiah (Seraiah's)
2Sa 8:17 were priests; **S** was secretary;
2Ki 25:18 as prisoners **S** the chief priest,
25:23 **S** son of Tanhumeth the Netophathite
1Ch 4:13 The sons of Kenaz: Othniel and **S**.
4:14 **S** was the father of Joab,
4:35 the son of **S**, the son of Asiel,
6:14 Azariah the father of **S**, and **S** the
Ezr 2: 2 Jeshua, Nehemiah, **S**, Reelaiah,
7: 1 Ezra son of **S**, the son of Azariah,
Ne 10: 2 **S**, Azariah, Jeremiah,
11:11 **S** son of Hilkiah, the son of
12: 1 and with Jeshua: **S**, Jeremiah, Ezra,
Jer 36:26 a son of the king, **S** son of Azriel
40: 8 **S** son of Tanhumeth, the sons of
51:59 the staff officer **S** son of Neriah,
51:61 He said to **S**, "When you get to
52:24 as prisoners **S** the chief priest,

Seraiah's (Seraiah)
Ne 12:12 the priestly families: of **S** family,

Seraphs
Isa 6: 2 Above him were **s**, each with six
6: 6 one of the **s** flew to me with a live

Sered (Seredite)
Ge 46:14 The sons of Zebulun: **S**, Elon and
Nu 26:26 by their clans were: through **S**,

Seredite (Sered)
Nu 26:26 through Sered, the **S** clan;

Sergius (Paulus)
Ac 13: 7 of the proconsul, **S** Paulus.

Serious (Seriousness)
Ge 12:17 the LORD inflicted **s** diseases on
Ex 21:22 but there is no **s** injury,
21:23 if there is **s** injury, you are to
Dt 15:21 is lame or blind, or has any **s** flaw,
Jer 6:14 my people as though it were not **s**.
8:11 my people as though it were not **s**.
Ac 18:14 about some misdemeanour or **s** crime,
25: 7 bringing many **s** charges against him,

Seriousness (Serious)
Tit 2: 7 In your teaching show integrity, **s**

Serpent (Serpent's, Serpents)
Ge 3: 1 Now the **s** was more crafty than any
3: 2 The woman said to the **s**, "We may eat
3: 4 will not surely die," the **s** said
3:13 said, "The **s** deceived me, and I ate.
3:14 the LORD God said to the **s**, "Because
49:17 Dan will be a **s** by the roadside, a
Job 26:13 his hand pierced the gliding **s**.
Ps 91:13 trample the great lion and the **s**.
Isa 14:29 fruit will be a darting, venomous **s**.
27: 1 Leviathan the gliding **s**,
27: 1 Leviathan the coiling **s**; he will
Jer 46:22 Egypt will hiss like a fleeing **s** as
51:34 Like a **s** he has swallowed us and
Am 9: 3 I will command the **s** to bite them.
Rev 12: 9 ancient **s** called the devil,
12:15 from his mouth the **s** spewed water
20: 2 He seized the dragon, that ancient **s**,

Serpent's (Serpent)
Ps 140: 3 their tongues as sharp as a **s**;
Isa 65:25 the ox, but dust will be the **s** food.
2Co 11: 3 Eve was deceived by the **s** cunning,
Rev 12:14 and half a time, out of the **s** reach.

Serpents (Serpent)
Dt 32:33 Their wine is the venom of **s**, the
Job 20:14 become the venom of **s** within him.
20:16 He will suck the poison of **s**;

Serug
Ge 11:20 32 years, he became the father of **S**.
11:21 after he became the father of **S**, Reu
11:22 **S** had lived 30 years, he became the
11:23 **S** lived 200 years and had other sons
1Ch 1:26 **S**, Nahor, Terah
Lk 3:35 the son of **S**, the son of Reu, the

Servant (Fellow-servant, Fellow-servants, Maidservant, Maidservants, Manservant, Menservants, *Moses the servant of the LORD, My servant Moses, Servant David, Servant of God, Servant of the LORD, Servant of the Lord*, Servant's, Servants, Servants')
Ge 15: 3 **s** in my household will be my heir."
16: 5 I put my **s** in your arms, and now
16: 6 "Your **s** is in your hands," Abram
16: 8 he said, "Hagar, **s** of Sarai, where
18: 3 my lord, do not pass your **s** by.
18: 5 that you have come to your **s**.
18: 7 to a **s**, who hurried to prepare it.
19:19 Your **s** has found favour in your eyes,
24: 2 He said to the chief **s** in his
24: 5 The **s** asked him, "What if the woman
24: 9 the **s** put his hand under the thigh
24:10 the **s** took ten of his master's
24:14 you have chosen for your **s** Isaac.
24:17 The **s** hurried to meet her and said,
24:34 he said, "I am Abraham's **s**.
24:52 Abraham's **s** heard what they said, he
24:53 the **s** brought out gold and silver
24:59 nurse and Abraham's **s** and his men.
24:61 So the **s** took Rebekah and left.
24:65 asked the **s**, "Who is that man in the
24:65 "He is my master," the **s** answered.
24:66 the **s** told Isaac all he had done.
26:24 for the sake of my **s** Abraham."
29:24 Laban gave his **s** girl Zilpah to his
29:29 Laban gave his **s** girl Bilhah to his
30: 4 she gave him her **s** Bilhah as a wife.
30: 7 Rachel's **s** Bilhah conceived again
30:10 Leah's **s** Zilpah bore Jacob a son.
30:12 Leah's **s** Zilpah bore Jacob a second
32: 4 'Your **s** Jacob says, I have been
32:10 faithfulness you have shown your **s**.
32:18 say, 'They belong to your **s** Jacob.
32:20 be sure to say, 'Your **s** Jacob is
33: 5 God has graciously given your **s**."
33:14 let my lord go on ahead of his **s**,
41:12 us, a **s** of the captain of the guard.
43:28 They replied, "Your **s** our father is
44:18 let your **s** speak a word to my lord.
44:18 Do not be angry with your **s**, though
44:24 we went back to your **s** my father, we
44:27 "Your **s** my father said to us, 'You
44:30 your **s** my father and if my father,
44:32 Your **s** guaranteed the boy's safety
44:33 "Now then, please let your **s** remain
Ex 4:10 nor since you have spoken to your **s**.

Ex 14:31 trust in him and in Moses his s.
21: 2 "If you buy a Hebrew s, he is to
21: 5 "But if the s declares, 'I love my
21: 6 Then he will be his s for life.
21: 7 "If a man sells his daughter as a s,
21:26 he must let the s go free to
21:27 he must let the s go free to
Nu 11:11 you brought this trouble on your s?
14:24 my s Caleb has a different spirit
Dt 3:24 you have begun to show to your s
15:16 if your s says to you, "I do not
15:17 and he will become your s for life.
15:18 it a hardship to set your s free,
Jos 1: 2 "Moses my s is dead. Now then, you
5:14 does my Lord have for his s?"
9:24 commanded his s Moses to give you
11:15 the LORD commanded his s Moses, so
12: 6 Moses, the s of the LORD, and the
Jdg 7:10 down to the camp with your s Purah
7:11 So he and Purah his s went down to
9:54 his s ran him through, and he died.
15:18 given your s this great victory.
16:26 Samson said to the s who held his
19: 3 He had with him his s and two
19: 9 man, with his concubine and his s
19:11 the s said to his master, "Come,
Ru 2: 8 Stay here with my s girls.
2:13 have spoken kindly to your s—though
2:13 standing of one of your s girls."
2:23 Ruth stayed close to the s girls of
3: 2 Is not Boaz, with whose s girls you
3: 9 "I am your s Ruth," she said.
1Sa 1:11 and not forget your s but give her
1:16 Do not take your s for a wicked
1:18 She said, "May your s find favour in
2:13 the s of the priest would come with
2:15 the s of the priest would come and
2:16 you want," the s would then answer,
3: 9 Speak, LORD, for your s is listening.
3:10 "Speak, for your s is listening.
9: 5 Saul said to the s who was with him,
9: 6 the s replied, "Look, in this town
9: 7 Saul said to his s, "If we go, what
9: 8 The s answered him again. "Look," he
9:10 "Good," Saul said to his s. "Come,
9:22 Samuel brought Saul and his s into
9:27 "Tell the s to go on ahead of
9:27 and the s did so—"but you stay
10:14 Now Saul's uncle asked him and his s,
17:32 your s will go and fight him."
17:34 "Your s has been keeping his
17:36 Your s has killed both the lion and
17:58 son of your s Jesse of Bethlehem."
20: 7 'Very well,' then your s is safe.
20: 8 for you, show kindness to your s,
22: 8 incited my s to lie in wait for me,
22:15 accuse your s or any of his
22:15 for your s knows nothing at all
23:10 your s has heard definitely that
23:11 come down, as your s has heard?
23:11 O LORD, God of Israel, tell your s.
25:24 Please let your s speak to you;
25:24 to you; hear what your s has to say.
25:25 But as for me, your s, I did not see
25:27 let this gift, which your s has
25:31 my master success, remember your s."
25:39 He has kept his s from doing wrong
26:18 "Why is my lord pursuing his s?
27: 5 why should your s live in the royal
27:12 that he will be my s for ever."
28: 2 see for yourself what your s can do.
28:22 Now please listen to your s and let
29: 8 "What have you found against your s
2Sa 7:19 the future of the house of your s.
7:20 you know your s, O Sovereign LORD.
7:21 thing and made it known to your s.
7:25 concerning your s and his house.
7:27 you have revealed this to your s,
7:27 So your s has found courage to
7:28 these good things to your s.
7:29 to bless the house of your s,
7:29 the house of your s will be blessed
9: 2 Now there was a s of Saul's
9: 2 "Your s," he replied.
9: 6 "Your s," he replied.
9: 8 "What is your s, that you should
2Sa 9: 9 the king summoned Ziba, Saul's s,
9:11 "Your s will do whatever my lord
9:11 lord the king commands his s to do.
11:21 your s Uriah the Hittite is dead.
11:24 your s Uriah the Hittite is dead."
13:17 He called his personal s and said,
13:18 his s put her out and bolted the
13:24 said, "Your s has had shearers come.
13:35 has happened just as your s said."
14: 6 I your s had two sons. They got into
14: 7 clan has risen up against your s;
14:12 "Let your s speak a word to my lord
14:15 Your s thought, 'I will speak to the
14:15 perhaps he will do what his s asks.
14:16 agree to deliver his s from the
14:17 "And now your s says, 'May the word
14:19 Yes, it was your s Joab who
14:19 words into the mouth of your s.
14:20 Your s Joab did this to change the
14:22 Joab said, "Today your s knows that
15: 2 "Your s is from one of the tribes of
15: 8 While your s was living at Geshur in
15:21 or death, there will your s be."
15:34 'I will be your s, O king; I was
15:34 I was your father's s in the past,
15:34 the past, but now I will be your s,'
17:17 A s girl was to go and inform them,
18:29 Joab was about to send the king's s
18:29 and me, your s, but I don't know
19:19 Do not remember how your s did wrong
19:20 For I your s know that I have sinned,
19:26 "My lord the king, since I your s am
19:26 But Ziba my s betrayed me.
19:27 he has slandered your s to my lord
19:28 but you gave your s a place among
19:35 Can your s taste what he eats and
19:35 Why should your s be an added burden
19:36 Your s will cross over the Jordan
19:37 Let your s return, that I may die in
19:37 But here is your s Kimham. Let him
20:17 "Listen to what your s has to say."
24:10 take away the guilt of your s.
24:21 has my lord the king come to his s?"
1Ki 1:13 did you not swear to me your s:
1:17 you yourself swore to me your s by
1:19 he has not invited Solomon your s.
1:26 me your s, and Zadok the priest, and
1:26 your s Solomon he did not invite.
1:51 put his s to death with the sword.
2:38 Your s will do as my lord the king
3: 6 have shown great kindness to your s,
3: 7 you have made your s king in place
3: 8 Your s is here among the people you
3: 9 give your s a discerning heart to
3:20 my side while I your s was asleep.
8:28 the prayer that your s is praying
8:29 your s prays towards this place.
8:30 Hear the supplication of your s and
8:53 you declared through your s Moses
8:56 he gave through his s Moses.
8:59 he may uphold the cause of his s
11:13 for the sake of David my s and for
11:34 his life for the sake of David my s,
11:36 so that David my s may always have
11:38 David my s did, I will be with you.
12: 7 "If today you will be a s to these
14:18 through his s the prophet Ahijah.
15:29 through his s Ahijah the Shilonite
18: 9 handing over s over to Ahab to be
18:12 Yet I your s have worshipped the
18:36 that I am your s and have done all
18:43 towards the sea," he told his s.
18:44 The seventh time the s reported,
19: 3 in Judah, he left his s there,
20: 9 'Your s will do all you demanded the
20:32 "Your s Ben-Hadad says: 'Please let
20:39 "Your s went into the thick of the
20:40 While your s was busy here and there,
2Ki 4: 1 "Your s my husband is dead, and you
4: 2 "Your s has nothing there at all,"
4:12 He said to his s Gehazi, "Call the
4:16 "Don't mislead your s, O man of God!"
4:19 His father told a s, "Carry him to
4:20 After the s had lifted him up and
4:24 the donkey and said to her s,
4:25 the man of God said to his s Gehazi,
2Ki 4:38 he said to his s, "Put on the large
4:43 before a hundred men?" his s asked.
5: 6 I am sending my s Naaman to you so
5:15 accept now a gift from your s."
5:17 "please let me, your s, be given as
5:17 for your s will never again make
5:18 may the LORD forgive your s for this
5:18 the LORD forgive your s for this."
5:20 Gehazi, the s of Elisha the man of
5:25 "Your s didn't go anywhere," Gehazi
6:15 the s of the man of God got up and
6:15 what shall we do?" the s asked.
8: 4 to Gehazi, the s of the man of God,
8:13 "How could your s, a mere dog,
9:36 through his s Elijah the Tishbite:
10:10 he promised through his s Elijah."
14:25 spoken through his s Jonah son of
16: 7 of Assyria, "I am your s and vassal.
19:34 and for the sake of David my s."
1Ch 2:34 He had an Egyptian s named Jarha.
2:35 in marriage to his s Jarha,
16:13 O descendants of Israel his s,
17:17 the future of the house of your s.
17:18 say to you for honouring your s?
17:18 For you know your s,
17:19 For the sake of your s and
17:23 you have made concerning your s
17:25 You, my God, have revealed to your s
17:25 So your s has found courage to pray
17:26 these good things to your s.
17:27 to bless the house of your s,
21: 8 you, take away the guilt of your s.
2Ch 1: 3 the LORD's s had made in the desert.
6:19 the prayer that your s is praying
6:20 your s prays towards this place.
6:21 Hear the supplications of your s and
6:42 love promised to David your s."
32:16 LORD God and against his s Hezekiah.
Ne 1: 6 your s is praying before you day
1: 7 and laws you gave your s Moses.
1: 8 instruction you gave your s Moses,
1:11 to the prayer of this your s and
1:11 Give your s success today by
2: 5 if your s has found favour in his
9:14 and laws through your s Moses.
Job 1: 8 "Have you considered my s Job?
2: 3 "Have you considered my s Job?
19:16 I summon my s, but he does not
42: 7 me what is right, as my s Job has.
42: 8 seven rams and go to my s Job and
42: 8 My s Job will pray for you, and I
42: 8 me what is right, as my s Job has."
Ps 19:11 By them is your s warned; in keeping
19:13 Keep your s also from wilful sins;
27: 9 do not turn your s away in anger;
31:16 Let your face shine on your s;
35:27 in the well-being of his s."
69:17 Do not hide your face from your s;
78:70 He chose David his s and took him
86: 2 save your s who trusts in you.
86: 4 Bring joy to your s, for to you,
86:16 grant your strength to your s and
89: 3 one, I have sworn to David my s,
89:20 I have found David my s; with my
89:39 renounced the covenant with your s
89:50 Remember, Lord, how your s has been
105: 6 O descendants of Abraham his s,
105:26 He sent Moses his s, and Aaron, whom
105:42 holy promise given to his s Abraham.
109:28 to shame, but your s will rejoice.
116:16 O LORD, truly I am your s;
116:16 I am your s, the son of your
119:17 Do good to your s, and I will live;
119:23 s will meditate on your decrees.
119:38 Fulfil your promise to your s, so
119:49 Remember your word to your s, for
119:65 Do good to your s according to your
119:76 according to your promise to your s.
119:84 How long must your s wait? When will
119:124 Deal with your s according to your
119:125 I am your s; give me discernment
119:135 Make your face shine upon your s and
119:140 tested, and your s loves them.
119:176 Seek your s, for I have not
132:10 For the sake of David your s, do not
136:22 an inheritance to his s Israel;

Ps 143: 2 Do not bring your s into judgment,
143:12 all my foes, for I am your s.
Pr 11:29 and the fool will be s to the wise.
12: 9 yet have a s than pretend to be
14:35 A king delights in a wise s, but a
14:35 but a shameful s incurs his wrath.
17: 2 A wise s will rule over a
22: 7 and the borrower is s to the lender.
27:27 family and to nourish your s girls.
29:19 A s cannot be corrected by mere
29:21 If a man pampers his s from youth,
30:10 "Do not slander a s to his master,
30:22 a s who becomes king, a fool who is
31:15 family and portions for her s girls.
Ecc 7:21 or you may hear your s cursing you—
10:16 Woe to you, O land whose king was a s
Isa 16:14 "Within three years, as a s bound by
20: 3 the LORD said, "Just as my s Isaiah
21:16 "Within one year, as a s bound by
22:20 "In that day I will summon my s,
24: 2 for master as for s, for mistress as
37:35 and for the sake of David my s!"
41: 8 "But you, O Israel, my s, Jacob,
41: 9 I said, 'You are my s'; I have
42: 1 "Here is my s, whom I uphold, my
42:19 Who is blind but my s, and deaf like
43:10 "and my s whom I have chosen, so
44: 1 "But now listen, O Jacob, my s,
44: 2 my s, Jeshurun, whom I have chosen.
44:21 O Jacob, for you are my s, O Israel.
44:21 I have made you, you are my s;
45: 4 For the sake of Jacob my s, of
48:20 "The LORD has redeemed his s Jacob.
49: 3 He said to me, "You are my s, Israel,
49: 5 be his s to bring Jacob back to him
49: 6 small a thing for you to be my s
49: 7 to the s of rulers: "Kings will see
50:10 and obeys the word of his s?
52:13 See, my s will act wisely; he will
53:11 my righteous s will justify many,
Jer 2:14 Is Israel a s, a slave by birth?
25: 9 my s Nebuchadnezzar king of Babylon,
27: 6 my s Nebuchadnezzar king of Babylon;
30:10 "'So do not fear, O Jacob my s;
33:21 my covenant with David my s—and my
33:22 make the descendants of David my s
33:26 descendants of Jacob and David my s
43:10 I will send for my s Nebuchadnezzar
46:27 "Do not fear, O Jacob my s; do not
46:28 Do not fear, O Jacob my s, for I am
Eze 28:25 land, which I gave to my s Jacob.
37:25 in the land I gave to my s Jacob,
37:25 my s will be their prince for ever.
46:17 the s may keep it until the year of
Da 6:20 "Daniel, s of the living God, has
9:17 the prayers and petitions of your s.
10:17 How can I, your s, talk with you, my
Hag 2:23 'I will take you, my s Zerubbabel
Zec 3: 8 I am going to bring my s, the Branch.
Mal 1: 6 his father, and a s his master.
Mt 8: 6 "Lord," he said, "my s lies at home
8: 8 the word, and my s will be healed.
8: 9 I say to my s, 'Do this,' and he does
8:13 his s was healed at that very hour.
10:24 teacher, nor a s above his master.
10:25 teacher, and the s like his master.
12:18 "Here is my s whom I have chosen,
18:26 "The s fell on his knees before him.
18:28 "But when that s went out, he found
18:32 "Then the master called the s in.
18:32 'You wicked s,' he said, 'I
20:26 great among you must be your s,
23:11 The greatest among you will be your s
24:45 "Who then is the faithful and wise s,
24:46 will be good for that s whose master
24:48 suppose that s is wicked and says to
24:50 The master of that s will come on a
25:21 'Well done, good and faithful s!
25:23 'Well done, good and faithful s!
25:26 'You wicked, lazy s! So you knew
25:30 throw that worthless s outside, into
26:51 drew it out and struck the s of the
26:69 courtyard, and a s girl came to him.
Mk 9:35 be the very last, and the s of all."
10:43 great among you must be your s,
12: 2 At harvest time he sent a s to the
Mk 12: 4 he sent another s to them;
14:47 and struck the s of the high priest,
14:66 s girls of the high priest came by.
14:69 the s girl saw him there, she said
Lk 1:38 "I am the Lord's s," Mary answered.
1:48 of the humble state of his s.
1:54 He has helped his s Israel,
2:29 you now dismiss your s in peace.
7: 2 There a centurion's s, whom his
7: 3 asking him to come and heal his s.
7: 7 the word, and my s will be healed.
7: 8 I say to my s, 'Do this', and he does
7:10 to the house and found the s well.
12:43 will be good for that s whom the
12:45 suppose the s says to himself, 'My
12:46 The master of that s will come on a
12:47 "That s who knows his master's will
14:17 he sent his s to tell those who had
14:21 "The s came back and reported this
14:21 became angry and ordered his s,
14:22 "'Sir,' the s said, 'what you
14:23 "Then the master told his s, 'Go out
16:13 "No s can serve two masters. Either
17: 7 "Suppose one of you had a s
17: 7 Would he say to the s when he comes
17: 9 Would he thank the s because he did
19:17 "'Well done, my good s!' his master
19:20 "Then another s came and said, 'Sir,
19:22 you wicked s! You knew, did you,
20:10 At harvest time he sent a s to the
20:11 He sent another s, but that one also
22:50 one of them struck the s of the high
22:56 A s girl saw him seated there in the
Jn 12:26 and where I am, my s also will be.
13:16 no s is greater than his master,
15:15 because a s does not know his
15:20 'No s is greater than his master.
18:10 struck the high priest's s, cutting
Ac 3:13 fathers, has glorified his s Jesus.
3:26 God raised up his s, he sent him
4:25 mouth of your s, our father David:
4:27 holy s Jesus, whom you anointed.
4:30 the name of your holy s Jesus."
12:13 and a s girl named Rhoda came to
12:20 a trusted personal s of the king,
26:16 to you to appoint you as a s
Ro 1: 1 Paul, a s of Christ Jesus, called to
13: 4 For he is God's s to do you good.
13: 4 He is God's s, an agent of wrath to
14: 4 Who are you to judge someone else's s
15: 8 Christ has become a s of the Jews
16: 1 a s of the church in Cenchrea.
Gal 1:10 men, I would not be a s of Christ.
Eph 3: 7 I became a s of this gospel by the
6:21 the dear brother and faithful s in
Php 2: 7 taking the very nature of a s,
Col 1:23 of which I, Paul, have become a s.
1:25 I have become its s by the
4:12 one of you and a s of Christ Jesus,
2Ti 2:24 the Lord's s must not quarrel;
Heb 3: 5 Moses was faithful as a s in all God'
2Pe 1: 1 Simon Peter, a s and apostle of
Jude : 1 Jude, a s of Jesus Christ and a
Rev 1: 1 by sending his angel to his s John,

Servant David

1Sa 19: 4 "Let not the king do wrong to his s;
2Sa 3:18 'By my s I will rescue my people
7: 5 "Go and tell my s, 'This is what the
7: 8 "Now then, tell my s, 'This is what
7:26 the house of your s will be
1Ki 8:24 You have kept your promise to your s
8:25 keep for your s my father the
8:26 promised your s my father come true.
8:66 for his s and his people Israel.
11:32 for the sake of my s and the city of
14: 8 but you have not been like my s, who
2Ki 8:19 Nevertheless, for the sake of his s,
20: 6 my sake and for the sake of my s.
1Ch 17: 4 "Go and tell my s, 'This is what the
17: 7 "Now then, tell my s, 'This is what
17:24 the house of your s will be
2Ch 6:15 You have kept your promise to your s
6:16 keep for your s my father the
6:17 that you promised your s come true.
Ps 144:10 his s from the deadly sword.
Eze 34:23 one shepherd, my s, and he will
34:24 and my s will be prince among them.
37:24 "'My s will be king over them, and
Lk 1:69 for us in the house of his s

Servant of God

1Ch 6:49 all that Moses the s had commanded.
2Ch 24: 9 tax that Moses the s had required
Ne 10:29 Law of God given through Moses the s
Da 9:11 written in the Law of Moses, the s,
Tit 1: 1 Paul, a s and an apostle of Jesus
Jas 1: 1 James, a s and of the Lord Jesus
Rev 15: 3 sang the song of Moses the s and the

Servant of the LORD (Moses the servant of the LORD)

Jos 12: 6 Moses, the s, and the Israelites
13: 8 he, the s, had assigned it to them.
24:29 Joshua son of Nun, the s, died at
Jdg 2: 8 Joshua son of Nun, the s, died at
Ps 18: T Of David the s. He sang to the LORD
36: T director of music. Of David the s.
Isa 42:19 committed to me, blind like the s?

Servant's (Servant)

Ge 19: 2 "please turn aside to your s house.
1Sa 1:11 look upon your s misery and
25:28 Please forgive your s offence, for
26:19 lord the king listen to his s words.
2Sa 14:22 the king has granted his s request."
1Ki 8:28 Yet give attention to your s prayer
8:52 your eyes be open to your s plea
2Ki 6:17 Then the LORD opened the s eyes,
2Ch 6:19 Yet give attention to your s prayer
Ps 119:122 Ensure your s well-being; let not
Mt 18:27 The s master took pity on him,
Jn 18:10 (The s name was Malchus.)

Servants (Servant)

Ge 21:25 water that Abimelech's s had seized.
22: 3 He took with him two of his s and
22: 5 He said to his s, "Stay here with
22:19 Abraham returned to his s, and they
26:14 He had so many flocks and herds and s
26:15 wells that his father's s had dug
26:19 Isaac's s dug in the valley and
26:25 tent, and there his s dug a well.
26:32 That day Isaac's s came and told him
27:37 have made all his relatives his s,
32:16 He put them in the care of his s,
32:16 and said to his s, "Go ahead of me,
39:11 none of the household s was inside.
39:14 she called her household s. "Look,"
41:10 Pharaoh was once angry with his s,
42:10 "Your s have come to buy food.
42:11 Your s are honest men, not spies."
42:13 "Your s were twelve brothers, the
44: 7 your s to do anything like that!
44: 9 If any of your s is found to have it,
44:19 My lord asked his s, 'Do you have a
44:21 "Then you said to your s, 'Bring him
44:23 you told your s, 'Unless your
44:31 Your s will bring the grey head of
46:34 'Your s have tended livestock from
47: 3 "Your s are shepherds," they
47: 4 please let your s settle in Goshen."
50:17 of the s of the God of your father.
Ex 5:15 Why have you treated your s this way?
5:16 Your s are given no straw, yet we
5:16 Your s are being beaten, but the
32:13 Remember your s Abraham, Isaac and
Lev 25:42 the Israelites are my s, whom I
25:55 for the Israelites belong to me as s.
25:55 They are my s, whom I brought out of
Nu 22:22 donkey, and his two s were with him.
31:49 "Your s have counted the soldiers
32: 4 and your s have livestock.
32: 5 given to your s as our possession.
32:25 your s will do as our lord commands.
32:27 your s, every man armed for battle,
32:31 s will do what the LORD has said.
Dt 9:27 Remember your s Abraham, Isaac and
32:36 have compassion on his s when he

Dt 32:43 he will avenge the blood of his s;
Jos 9: 8 "We are your s," they said to Joshua.
9: 9 They answered: "Your s have come
9:11 We are your s; make a treaty with us.
9:24 "Your s were clearly told how the
10: 6 at Gilgal: "Do not abandon your s.
Jdg 3:24 After he had gone, the s came and
6:27 Gideon took ten of his s and did as
19:19 and wine for ourselves your s—me,
1Sa 9: 3 "Take one of the s with you and go
12:19 for your s so that we will not die,
16:16 Let our lord command his s here to
16:18 One of the s answered, "I have seen
17: 8 and are you not the s of Saul?
18:24 Saul's s told him what David had
21: 7 Now one of Saul's s was there that
21:11 the s of Achish said to him, "Isn't
21:14 Achish said to his s, "Look at the
22:14 "Who of all your s is as loyal as
25: 8 Ask your own s and they will tell
25: 8 Please give your s and your son
25:10 Nabal answered David's s, "Who is
25:10 Many s are breaking away from their
25:14 One of the s told Nabal's wife
25:19 she told her s, "Go on ahead;
25:40 His s went to Carmel and said to
25:41 and wash the feet of my master's s."
29:10 along with your master's s who have
2Sa 6:20 the slave girls of his s as any
9:10 You and your sons and your s are to
9:10 Ziba had fifteen sons and twenty s.)
9:12 household were s of Mephibosheth.
11: 9 with all his master's s and did not
11:13 on his mat among his master's s;
11:24 the archers shot arrows at your s
12:18 David's s were afraid to tell him
12:19 David noticed that his s were
12:21 His s asked him, "Why are you acting
13:31 s stood by with their clothes torn.
13:36 and all his s wept very bitterly.
14:30 he said to his s, "Look, Joab's
14:30 So Absalom's s set the field on fire.
14:31 have your s set my field on fire?"
15:15 "Your s are ready to do whatever our
19:17 and his fifteen sons and twenty s.
1Ki 1: 2 his s said to him, "Let us look for
1:27 without letting his s know who
1:33 "Take your lord's s with you and
8:23 covenant of love with your s who
8:32 Judge between your s, condemning the
8:36 sin of your s, your people Israel.
10: 5 the attending s in their robes, his
12: 7 answer, they will always be your s."
2Ki 1:13 lives of these fifty men, your s!
2:16 "Look," they said, "we your s have
4:22 "Please send me one of the s and a
5:13 Naaman's s went to him and said, "My
5:23 He gave them to two of his s, and
5:24 he took the things from the s and
6: 3 Won't you please come with your s?"
9: 7 and I will avenge the blood of my s
9: 7 of all the LORD's s shed by Jezebel.
9:28 His s took him by chariot to
10: 5 "We are your s and we will do
10:23 see that no s of the LORD are here
17:13 to you through my s the prophets."
17:23 through all his s the prophets.
18:26 "Please speak to your s in Aramaic,
21:10 The LORD said through his s the
23:30 Josiah's s brought his body in a
24: 2 proclaimed by his s the prophets.
1Ch 9: 2 priests, Levites and temple s.
2Ch 2:10 I will give your s, the woodsmen who
2:15 "Now let my lord send his s the
6:14 covenant of love with your s who
6:23 Judge between your s, repaying the
6:27 sin of your s, your people Israel.
9: 4 the attending s in their robes, the
10: 7 answer, they will always be your s."
36:20 and they became s to him and his
Ezr 2:43 The temple s: the descendants of
2:55 The descendants of the s of Solomon:
2:58 The temple s and the descendants of
2:58 descendants of the s of Solomon 392
2:70 the gatekeepers and the temple s
4:11 your s, the men of Trans-Euphrates:
Ezr 5:11 "We are the s of the God of heaven
7: 7 singers, gatekeepers and temple s,
7:24 singers, gatekeepers, temple s or
8:17 the temple s in Casiphia, so that
8:20 They also brought 220 of the temple s
9:11 you gave through your s the prophets
Ne 1: 6 for your s, the people of Israel.
1:10 "They are your s and your people,
1:11 s who delight in revering your name.
2:20 We his s will start rebuilding, but
3:26 the temple s living on the hill of
3:31 of the temple s and the merchants,
7:46 The temple s: the descendants of
7:57 The descendants of the s of Solomon:
7:60 The temple s and the descendants of
7:60 descendants of the s of Solomon 392
7:73 the singers and the temple s, along
10:28 gatekeepers, singers, temple s and
11: 3 priests, Levites, temple s and
11: 3 s lived in the towns of Judah,
11:21 The temple s lived on the hill of
Job 1: 3 and had a large number of s.
1:15 They put the s to the sword, and I
1:16 and burned up the sheep and the s,
1:17 They put the s to the sword, and I
4:18 If God places no trust in his s, if
Ps 34:22 The LORD redeems his s; no-one will
69:36 the children of his s will inherit
79: 2 the dead bodies of your s as food
79:10 the outpoured blood of your s.
90:13 Have compassion on your s.
90:16 May your deeds be shown to your s,
102:14 For her stones are dear to your s;
102:28 The children of your s will live in
103:21 hosts, you his s who do his will.
104: 4 messengers, flames of fire his s.
105:25 people, to conspire against his s.
113: 1 Praise, O s of the LORD, praise the
134: 1 Praise the LORD, all you s of the
135: 1 praise him, you s of the LORD,
135: 9 Egypt, against Pharaoh and all his s.
135:14 people and have compassion on his s.
Isa 36:11 "Please speak to your s in Aramaic,
44:26 who carries out the words of his s
54:17 This is the heritage of the s of the
63:17 Return for the sake of your s,
65: 8 so will I do on behalf of my s;
65: 9 them, and there will my s live.
65:13 "My s will eat, but you will go
65:13 my s will drink, but you will go
65:13 my s will rejoice, but you will be
65:14 My s will sing out of the joy of
65:15 to his s he will give another name.
66:14 LORD will be made known to his s,
Jer 7:25 again I sent you my s the prophets.
14: 3 The nobles send their s for water;
25: 4 though the LORD has sent all his s
26: 5 to the words of my s the prophets,
29:19 and again by my s the prophets.
35:15 again I sent all my s the prophets
44: 4 again I sent my s the prophets, who
Eze 38:17 days by my s the prophets of Israel?
46:17 his inheritance to one of his s,
Da 1:12 "Please test your s for ten days:
1:13 treat your s in accordance with
2: 4 Tell your s the dream, and we will
2: 7 "Let the king tell his s the dream,
3:26 s of the Most High God, come out!
3:28 sent his angel and rescued his s!
9: 6 We have not listened to your s the
9:10 gave us through his s the prophets.
Joel 2:29 Even on my s, both men and women, I
Am 3: 7 his plan to his s the prophets.
Zec 1: 6 which I commanded my s the prophets,
Mt 13:27 "The owner's s came to him and said,
13:28 "The s asked him, 'Do you want us to
18:23 to settle accounts with his s.
18:31 the other s saw what had happened,
21:34 he sent his s to the tenants to
21:35 "The tenants seized his s; they beat
21:36 he sent other s to them, more than
22: 3 He sent his s to those who had been
22: 4 "Then he sent some more s and said,
22: 6 The rest seized his s, ill-treated
22: 8 "Then he said to his s, 'The wedding
22:10 the s went out into the streets and
Mt 24:45 charge of the s in his household
25:14 who called his s and entrusted his
25:19 time the master of those s returned
Mk 13:34 his house and puts his s in charge,
Lk 1: 2 eye-witnesses and s of the word.
12:37 will be good for those s whose
12:38 will be good for those s whose
12:42 puts in charge of his s to give
15:22 "But the father said to his s,
15:26 he called one of the s and asked him
17:10 'We are unworthy s; we have only
19:13 he called ten of his s and gave them
19:15 Then he sent for the s to whom he
Jn 2: 5 His mother said to the s, "Do
2: 7 Jesus said to the s, "Fill the jars
2: 9 the s who had drawn the water knew.
4:51 his s met him with the news that
15:15 I no longer call you s, because a
18:18 was cold, and the s and officials
18:26 One of the high priest's s, a
18:36 If it were, my s would fight to
Ac 2:18 Even on my s, both men and women, I
4:29 enable your s to speak your word
10: 7 Cornelius called two of his s and a
16:17 "These men are s of the Most High
Ro 13: 6 for the authorities are God's s, who
1Co 3: 5 Only s, through whom you came to
4: 1 ought to regard us as s of Christ
2Co 4: 5 ourselves as your s for Jesus' sake.
6: 4 Rather, as s of God we commend
11:15 is not surprising, then, if his s
11:15 masquerade as s of righteousness.
11:23 Are they s of Christ? (I am out of
Php 1: 1 Paul and Timothy, s of Christ Jesus,
Heb 1: 7 angels winds, his s flames of fire."
1Pe 2:16 cover-up for evil; live as s of God.
Rev 1: 1 his s what must soon take place.
2:20 By her teaching she misleads my s
7: 3 the foreheads of the s of our God."
10: 7 he announced to his s the prophets."
11:18 for rewarding your s the prophets
19: 2 avenged on her the blood of his s."
19: 5 "Praise our God, all you his s, you
22: 3 the city, and his s will serve him.
22: 6 sent his angel to show his s the

Servants' (Servant)

Ge 44:16 God has uncovered your s guilt.
47: 4 and your s flocks have no pasture.

Serve (Served, Serves, Service, Services, Serving, Servitude)

Ge 1:14 and let them s as signs to mark
15:14 I will punish the nation they s as
25:23 and the older will s the younger."
27:29 May nations s you and peoples bow
27:40 sword and you will s your brother.
31:44 let it s as a witness between us."
43:31 himself, said, "S the food."
Ex 14:12 us alone; let us s the Egyptians'?
14:12 better for us to s the Egyptians
18:13 Moses took his seat to s as judge
18:22 Have them s as judges for the people
21: 2 he is to s you for six years.
28: 1 so that they may s me as priests.
28: 3 so that he may s me as priest.
28: 4 so that they may s me as priests.
28:41 them so they may s me as priests.
29: 1 so that they may s me as priests:
29:44 and his sons to s me as priests.
30:30 them so they may s me as priests.
31:10 for his sons when they s as priests,
35:19 his sons when they s as priests."
40:13 him so that he may s me as priest.
40:15 so that they may s me as priests.
Lev 7:35 presented to s the LORD as priests.
Nu 1: 3 more who are able to s in the army.
1:20 who were able to s in the army were
1:22 able to s in the army were counted
1:24 who were able to s in the army were
1:26 who were able to s in the army were
1:28 who were able to s in the army were
1:30 who were able to s in the army were
1:32 who were able to s in the army were
1:34 who were able to s in the army were

Nu 1:36 who were able to s in the army were
1:38 who were able to s in the army were
1:40 who were able to s in the army were
1:42 who were able to s in the army were
1:45 who were able to s in Israel's army
3: 3 who were ordained to s as priests.
3:10 Appoint Aaron and his sons to s as
4: 3 s in the work in the Tent of Meeting.
4:23 s in the work at the Tent of Meeting.
4:30 s in the work at the Tent of Meeting.
4:35 s in the work in the Tent of Meeting,
4:39 s in the work at the Tent of Meeting,
4:43 s in the work at the Tent of Meeting,
18: 7 only you and your sons may s as
26: 2 able to s in the army of Israel."
Dt 6:13 Fear the LORD your God, s him only
7: 4 from following me to s other gods,
7:16 with pity and do not s their gods,
10:12 to love him, to s the LORD your God
10:20 Fear the LORD your God and s him.
11:13 to s him with all your heart and
12:30 "How do these nations s their gods?
13: 4 s him and hold fast to him.
18: 7 s there in the presence of the LORD.
28:47 you did not s the LORD your God
28:48 you will s the enemies the LORD
Jos 4: 6 to s as a sign among you. In the
9:23 You will never cease to s as
22: 5 to hold fast to him and to s him
23: 7 must not s them or bow down to them.
23:16 and go and s other gods and bow down
24:14 "Now fear the LORD and s him with
24:14 River and in Egypt, and s the LORD.
24:15 yourselves this day whom you will s,
24:15 my household, we will s the LORD."
24:16 to forsake the LORD to s other gods!
24:18 s the LORD, because he is our God."
24:19 "You are not able to s the LORD.
24:20 forsake the LORD and s foreign gods
24:21 to Joshua, "No! We will s the LORD.
24:22 that you have chosen to s the LORD.
24:24 "We will s the LORD our God and
Jdg 9:28 S the men of Hamor, Shechem's
9:28 Why should we s Abimelech?
18:19 Isn't it better that you s a tribe
1Sa 7: 3 to the LORD and s him only,
8:11 them s with his chariots and horses,
12:10 of our enemies, and we will s you.'
12:14 If you fear the LORD and s and obey
12:20 but s the LORD with all your heart.
12:24 be sure to fear the LORD and s him
17: 9 will become our subjects and s us."
18:17 only s me bravely and fight the
25:41 ready to s you and wash the feet of
26:19 and have said, 'Go, s other gods.'
29: 6 to have you s with me in the army.
2Sa 16:19 Furthermore, whom should I s?
16:19 whom should I s? Should I not s the
1Ki 9: 6 to s other gods and worship them,
9:27 s in the fleet with Solomon's men.
12: 4 he put on us, and we will s you."
12: 7 s them and give them a favourable
16:31 and began to s Baal and worship him.
17: 1 the God of Israel, lives, whom I s,
18:15 the LORD Almighty lives, whom I s,
2Ki 3:14 the LORD Almighty lives, whom I s,
4:41 "S it to the people to eat."
5:16 as the LORD lives, whom I s,
10:18 Baal a little; Jehu will s him much.
17:35 them, s them or sacrifice to them.
18: 7 king of Assyria and did not s him.
23: 9 did not s at the altar of the LORD
25:24 "Settle down in the land and s the
1Ch 12:38 who volunteered to s in the ranks.
23:31 They were to s before the LORD
28: 9 and s him with wholehearted devotion
2Ch 7:19 to s other gods and worship them,
10: 4 he put on us, and we will s you."
13:10 The priests who s the LORD are sons
19: 9 "You must s faithfully and
19:11 will s as officials before you.
29:11 you to stand before him and s him,
30: 8 S the LORD your God, so that his
33:16 to s the LORD, the God of Israel.
34:33 in Israel s the LORD their God.
35: 3 Now s the LORD your God and his
Ne 4:22 so that they can s us as guards by
9:35 they did not s you or turn from
Est 1: 8 to s each man what he wished.
Job 21:15 the Almighty, that we should s him?
36:11 If they obey and s him, they will
39: 9 "Will the wild ox consent to s you?
Ps 2:11 S the LORD with fear and rejoice
22:30 Posterity will s him; future
72:11 to him and all nations will s him.
119:91 to this day, for all things s you.
Pr 22:29 in his work? He will s before kings;
22:29 he will not s before obscure men.
Isa 56: 6 themselves to the LORD to s him,
60: 7 the rams of Nebaioth will s you;
60:10 walls, and their kings will s you.
60:12 that will not s you will perish;
Jer 2:20 'I will not s you!' Indeed, on every
5:19 s foreigners in a land not your own.'
11:10 have followed other gods to s them.
13:10 other gods to s and worship them,
15:19 I will restore you that you may s me;
16:13 and there you will s other gods day
25: 6 other gods to s and worship them;
25:11 and these nations will s the king of
27: 7 All nations will s him and his son
27: 8 any nation or kingdom will not s
27: 9 will not s the king of Babylon.'
27:10 s to remove you far from your lands;
27:11 of the king of Babylon and s him,
27:12 of Babylon; s him and his people,
27:13 that will not s the king of Babylon?
27:14 'You will not s the king of Babylon,
27:17 S the king of Babylon, and you will
28:14 s Nebuchadnezzar king of Babylon,
28:14 of Babylon, and they will s him.
30: 9 Instead, they will s the LORD their
35:15 do not follow other gods to s them.
35:19 never fail to have a man to s me.
40: 9 "Do not be afraid to s the
40: 9 "Settle down in the land and s the
Eze 20:32 of the world, who s wood and stone.
20:39 LORD says: Go and s your idols,
20:40 entire house of Israel will s me,
27:25 "'The ships of Tarshish s as
41: 6 to s as supports for the side rooms,
44:11 They may s in my sanctuary, having
44:11 stand before the people and s them.
44:13 They are not to come near to s me as
44:24 the priests are to s as judges and
45: 5 who s in the temple, as their
47:12 Their fruit will s for food and
Da 1: 4 qualified to s in the king's palace.
3:12 They neither s your gods nor worship
3:14 that you do not s my gods or worship
3:17 the God we s is able to save us from
3:18 O king, that we will not s your gods
3:28 rather than s or worship any god
6:16 whom you s continually, rescue you!"
6:20 has your God, whom you s continually,
Zep 3: 9 LORD and s him shoulder to shoulder.
Zec 4:14 to s the Lord of all the earth."
Mal 3:14 have said, 'It is futile to s God.
3:18 who s God and those who do not.
Mt 4:10 the Lord your God, and s him only.'"
6:24 "No-one can s two masters. Either he
6:24 You cannot s both God and Money.
20:28 but to s, and to give his life as a
Mk 10:45 but to s, and to give his life as a
Lk 1:74 to enable us to s him without
4: 8 the Lord your God and s him only.'"
12:37 he will dress himself to s, will
16:13 "No servant can s two masters.
16:13 You cannot s both God and Money."
Ac 7: 7 I will punish the nation they s as
26: 7 they earnestly s God day and night.
27:23 I am and whom I s stood beside
Ro 1: 9 God, whom I s with my whole heart in
7: 6 we s in the new way of the Spirit,
9:12 told, "The older will s the younger.
12: 7 If it is serving, let him s; if it
1Co 9:13 and those who s at the altar share
2Co 11: 8 support from them so as to s you.
13: 4 we will live with him to s you.
Gal 5:13 rather, s one another in love.
Eph 6: 7 S wholeheartedly, as if you were
1Th 1: 9 idols to s the living and true God,
1Ti 3:10 against them, let them s as deacons.
6: 2 Instead, they are to s them even
2Ti 1: 3 I thank God, whom I s, as my
Heb 1:14 s those who will inherit salvation?
8: 5 They s at a sanctuary that is a copy
9:14 so that we may s the living God!
1Pe 4:10 gift he has received to s others,
5: 2 greedy for money, but eager to s;
Jude : 7 They s as an example of those who
Rev 1: 6 priests to s his God and Father—to
5:10 a kingdom and priests to s our God,
7:15 s him day and night in his temple;
22: 3 city, and his servants will s him.

Served (Serve)

Ge 29:20 Jacob s seven years to get Rachel,
29:25 have done to me? I s you for Rachel,
30:26 have s you, and I will be on my way.
43:32 They s him by himself, the brothers
43:34 portions were s to them from
Ex 18:26 They s as judges for the people at
38: 8 mirrors of the women who s at the
Nu 3: 4 so only Eleazar and Ithamar s as
4:37 clans who s in the Tent of Meeting.
4:41 clans who s at the Tent of Meeting.
26:10 And they s as a warning sign.
Jos 24:15 whether the gods your forefathers s
24:31 Israel s the LORD throughout the
Jdg 2: 7 The people s the LORD throughout the
2:11 eyes of the LORD and s the Baals.
2:13 they forsook him and s Baal and the
3: 6 to their sons, and s their gods.
3: 7 God and s the Baals and the Asherahs.
10: 6 They s the Baals and the Ashtoreths,
10: 6 the LORD and no longer s him,
10:13 you have forsaken me and s other
10:16 gods among them and s the LORD.
1Sa 2:22 slept with the women who s at the
7: 4 and Ashtoreths, and s the LORD only.
8: 2 was Abijah, and they s at Beersheba.
12:10 and s the Baals and the Ashtoreths.
2Sa 12:20 request they s him food, and he ate.
13: 9 she took the pan and s him the bread
16:19 s your father, so I will serve you."
1Ki 11:17 officials who had s his father.
12: 6 elders who had s his father Solomon
22:53 He s and worshipped Baal and
2Ki 5: 2 Israel, and she s Naaman's wife.
10:18 "Ahab s Baal a little; Jehu will
17:33 but they also s their own gods in
1Ch 6:10 (it was he who s as priest in the
6:33 Here are the men who s, together
6:39 Asaph, who s at his right hand:
23:24 who s in the temple of the LORD.
24: 2 Eleazar and Ithamar s as the priests.
27: 1 and their officers, who s the king
2Ch 10: 6 elders who had s his father Solomon
17:19 These were the men who s the king,
35:13 s them quickly to all the people.
Ne 12:26 They s in the days of Joiakim son of
Est 1: 7 Wine was s in goblets of gold, each
1:10 seven eunuchs who s him—Mehuman,
Jer 5:19 have forsaken me and s foreign gods
8: 2 which they have loved and s and
16:11 gods and s and worshipped them.
22: 9 have worshipped and s other gods.
34:14 After he has s you for six years,
52:12 who s the king of Babylon, came to
Eze 27: 7 was your sail and s as your banner;
27:10 "'Men of Persia, Lydia and Put s as
44:12 they s them in the presence of their
Hos 12:12 Israel s to get a wife, and to pay
Mt 20:28 the Son of Man did not come to be s,
Mk 10:45 the Son of Man did not come to be s,
Jn 12: 2 Martha s, while Lazarus was among
13: 2 The evening meal was being s, and
Ac 1:16 who s as guide for those who
13:36 "For when David had s God's purpose
17:25 he is not s by human hands, as if he
20:19 I s the Lord with great humility and
Ro 1:25 and worshipped and s created things
Php 1:12 has really s to advance the gospel.
2:22 s with me in the work of the gospel.
1Ti 3:13 Those who have s well gain an
Heb 7:13 that tribe has ever s at the altar.

Serves (Serve)

Dt 15:12 sells himself to you and **s** you six
Mal 3:17 a man spares his son who **s** him.
Lk 22:26 one who rules like the one who **s**.
22:27 is at the table or the one who **s**?
22:27 But I am among you as one who **s**.
Jn 12:26 Whoever **s** me must follow me;
12:26 Father will honour the one who **s** me.
Ro 14:18 anyone who **s** Christ in this way is
1Co 9: 7 Who **s** as a soldier at his own
Heb 8: 2 who **s** in the sanctuary, the true
1Pe 4:11 If anyone **s**, he should do it with

Service (Serve)

Ge 41:46 the **s** of Pharaoh king of Egypt.
50: 2 his **s** to embalm his father Israel.
Ex 27:19 used in the **s** of the tabernacle,
30:16 it for the **s** of the Tent of Meeting.
35:21 its **s**, and for the sacred garments.
Nu 4:24 "This is the **s** of the Gershonite
4:26 and all the equipment used in its **s**.
4:27 All their **s**, whether carrying or
4:28 This is the **s** of the Gershonite
4:31 This is their duty as they perform **s**
4:33 This is the **s** of the Merarite clans
8:25 their regular **s** and work no longer.
18: 7 I am giving you the **s** of the
Dt 15:18 because his **s** to you these six years
Jos 18: 7 **s** of the LORD is their inheritance.
1Sa 14:52 brave man, he took him into his **s**.
16:21 David came to Saul and entered his **s**.
16:22 "Allow David to remain in my **s**, for
1Ki 8:11 priests could not perform their **s**
2Ki 25:14 articles used in the temple **s**.
1Ch 5:18 had 44,760 men ready for military **s**
9:28 the articles used in the temple **s**;
23:26 any of the articles used in its **s**."
23:28 in the **s** of the temple of the LORD:
23:32 for the **s** of the temple of the LORD.
25: 1 of the men who performed this **s**:
26:30 of the LORD and for the king's **s**.
28: 1 the divisions in the **s** of the king,
28:13 the articles to be used in its **s**.
28:14 to be used in various kinds of **s**,
28:14 to be used in various kinds of **s**:
28:20 work for the **s** of the temple of the
2Ch 5:14 priests could not perform their **s**
17:16 for the **s** of the LORD, with 200,000.
24:14 the **s** and for the burnt offerings,
25: 5 thousand men ready for military **s**,
29:35 So the **s** of the temple of the LORD
30:22 understanding of the **s** of the LORD.
31:21 undertook in the **s** of God's temple
35: 2 them in the **s** of the LORD's temple.
35:10 The **s** was arranged and the priests
35:16 at that time the entire **s** of the
Ezr 6:18 for the **s** of God at Jerusalem,
Ne 10:32 for the **s** of the house of our God:
11:22 for the **s** of the house of God.
12:45 They performed the **s** of their God
12:45 their God and the **s** of purification,
13:10 and singers responsible for the **s**
Job 7: 1 "Does not man have hard **s** on earth?
14:14 All the days of my hard **s** I will
Isa 40: 2 that her hard **s** has been completed,
41: 2 him in righteousness to his **s**?
Jer 52:18 articles used in the temple **s**.
Eze 44:16 minister before me and perform my **s**.
Da 1: 5 they were to enter the king's **s**.
1:19 so they entered the king's **s**.
Lk 1:23 his time of **s** was completed, he
9:62 is fit for **s** in the kingdom of God."
12:35 "Be dressed ready for **s** and keep
Jn 16: 2 think he is offering a **s** to God.
Ro 15:17 in Christ Jesus in my **s** to God.
15:25 in the **s** of the saints there.
15:31 that my **s** in Jerusalem may be
1Co 12: 5 There are different kinds of **s**, but
16:15 themselves to the **s** of the saints.
2Co 8: 4 of sharing in this **s** to the saints.
8:18 churches for his **s** to the gospel.
9: 1 to you about this **s** to the saints.
9:12 This **s** that you perform is not only
9:13 of the **s** by which you have proved
Eph 4:12 prepare God's people for works of **s**,
Php 2:17 and **s** coming from your faith,
1Ti 1:12 me faithful, appointing me to his **s**.
6: 2 benefit from their **s** are believers,
Heb 2:17 faithful high priest in **s** to God,
Rev 2:19 your love and faith, your **s** and

Services (Serve)

Ex 14: 5 Israelites go and have lost their **s**!"
Ne 12: 9 stood opposite them in the **s**.
13:14 for the house of my God and its **s**.

Serving (Serve)

Ex 39:41 for his sons when **s** as priests.
Nu 4:47 **s** and carrying the Tent of
18:21 do while **s** at the Tent of Meeting.
Dt 28:14 following other gods and **s** them.
Jos 20: 6 high priest who is **s** at that time.
24:15 if **s** the LORD seems undesirable to
Jdg 2:19 gods and **s** and worshipping them.
10:10 forsaking our God and **s** the Baals."
1Sa 8: 8 forsaking me and **s** other gods, so
1Ki 9: 9 worshipping and **s** them—that is why
12: 8 grown up with him and were **s** him.
2Ki 17:41 the LORD, they were **s** their idols.
1Ch 28:13 and for all the work of **s** in the
2Ch 7:22 worshipping and **s** them—that is why
10: 8 grown up with him and were **s** him.
12: 8 **s** me and **s** the kings of other lands."
Eze 44:11 the gates of the temple and **s** in it;
48:11 who were faithful in **s** me and did
Lk 1: 8 and he was **s** as priest before God,
Ro 12: 7 If it is **s**, let him serve; if it is
12:11 your spiritual fervour, **s** the Lord.
16:18 For such people are not **s** our Lord
Eph 6: 7 as if you were **s** the Lord, not men,
Col 3:24 It is the Lord Christ you are **s**.
2Ti 2: 4 No-one **s** as a soldier gets involved
1Pe 1:12 they were not **s** themselves but you,
5: 2 **s** as overseers—not because you must,

Servitude (Serve)

Ge 47:21 Joseph reduced the people to **s**, from

Set my face

Lev 17:10; 20:3, 5, 6; 26:17; Isa 50:7; Eze 14:8; 15:7

Set your face

Eze 6:2; 13:17; 20:46; 21:2; 25:2; 28:21; 29:2; 35:2; 38:2

Seth

Ge 4:25 gave birth to a son and named him **S**,
4:26 **S** also had a son, and he named him
5: 3 his own image; and he named him **S**.
5: 4 After **S** was born, Adam lived 800
5: 6 **S** had lived 105 years, he became the
5: 7 **S** lived 807 years and had other sons
5: 8 Altogether, **S** lived 912 years, and
1Ch 1: 1 Adam, **S**, Enosh,
Lk 3:38 the son of Enosh, the son of **S**, the

Sethur

Nu 13:13 tribe of Asher, **S** son of Michael;

Settle (Resettle, Settled, Settlement, Settlements, Settles)

Ge 34:10 You can **s** among us; the land is open
34:16 We'll **s** among you and become one
34:23 to them, and they will **s** among us."
35: 1 "Go up to Bethel and **s** there, and
46:34 Then you will be allowed to **s** in
47: 4 let your servants **s** in Goshen."
47: 6 **s** your father and your brothers in
Nu 33:53 Take possession of the land and **s** in
Dt 8:12 you build fine houses and **s** down,
12:10 you will cross the Jordan and **s** in
Jdg 18: 1 of their own where they might **s**,
2Ki 25:24 "**S** down in the land and serve the
2Ch 19: 8 law of the LORD and to **s** disputes.
Job 3: 5 may a cloud **s** over it; may blackness
Ps 69:35 people will **s** there and possess it;
107: 4 no way to a city where they could **s**.
107: 7 way to a city where they could **s**.
Ps 107:36 founded a city where they could **s**.
139: 9 if I **s** on the far side of the sea,
Isa 2: 4 will **s** disputes for many peoples.
7:19 They will all come and **s** in the
14: 1 and will **s** them in their own land.
23: 7 taken her to **s** in far-off lands?
54: 3 and **s** in their desolate cities.
Jer 29: 5 "Build houses and **s** down;
29:28 Therefore build houses and **s** down;
40: 9 "**S** down in the land and serve the
42:15 to Egypt and you do go to **s** there,
42:17 to **s** there will die by the sword,
42:22 place where you want to go to **s**."
43: 2 You must not go to Egypt to **s** there.
44:12 to go to Egypt to **s** there.
Eze 32: 4 all the birds of the air **s** on you
32:14 I will let her waters **s** and make her
36:11 I will **s** people on you as in the
37:14 and I will **s** you in your own land.
Hos 11:11 I will **s** them in their homes,"
Mic 4: 3 will **s** disputes for strong nations
Na 3:17 that **s** in the walls on a cold day
Mt 5:25 "**S** matters quickly with your
18:23 to **s** accounts with his servants.
Ac 18:15 own law—**s** the matter yourselves.
2Th 3:12 **s** down and earn the bread they eat.

Settled (Settle)

Ge 11: 2 found a plain in Shinar and **s** there.
11:31 they came to Haran, they **s** there.
19:30 left Zoar and **s** in the mountains,
25:18 His descendants **s** in the area from
26:17 in the Valley of Gerar and **s** there.
36: 8 Esau (that is, Edom) **s** in the hill
47:11 Joseph **s** his father and his brothers
47:27 Now the Israelites **s** in Egypt in the
Ex 10: 6 day they **s** in this land till now.
10:14 they invaded all Egypt and **s** down in
16:35 they came to a land that was **s**;
22:11 the issue between them will be **s** by
24:16 the glory of the LORD **s** on Mount
40:35 because the cloud had **s** upon it,
Nu 9:17 cloud **s**, the Israelites encamped.
11: 9 the dew **s** on the camp at night, the
21:31 Israel **s** in the land of the Amorites.
22: 5 of the land and have **s** next to me.
31:10 Towns where the Midianites had **s**,
32:40 of Manasseh, and they **s** there.
Dt 2:12 before them and **s** in their place,
2:21 drove them out and **s** in their place.
2:23 them and **s** in their place.)
12:29 driven them out and **s** in their land,
17:14 taken possession of it and **s** in it,
19: 1 out and **s** in their towns and houses,
26: 1 taken possession of it and **s** in it,
Jos 19:47 They **s** in Leshem and named it Dan
19:50 And he built up the town and **s** there.
21:43 took possession of it and **s** there.
Jdg 7:12 **s** in the valley, thick as locusts.
11: 3 brothers and **s** in the land of Tob,
18:28 Danites rebuilt the city and **s** there.
21:23 and rebuilt the towns and **s** in them.
Ru 3:18 rest until the matter is **s** today."
1Sa 12: 8 of Egypt and **s** them in this place.
27: 3 David and his men **s** in Gath with
2Sa 2: 3 and they **s** in Hebron and its towns.
7: 1 After the king was **s** in his palace
20:18 your answer at Abel,' and that **s** it.
1Ki 11:24 where they **s** and took control.
2Ki 17: 6 He **s** them in Halah, in Gozan on the
17:24 and **s** them in the towns of Samaria
17:29 in the several towns where they **s**,
18:11 to Assyria and **s** them in Halah,
1Ch 4:41 Then they **s** in their place, because
5: 8 They **s** in the area from Aroer to
5:23 they **s** in the land from Bashan to
17: 1 After David was **s** in his palace, he
2Ch 8: 2 given him, and **s** Israelites in them.
15: 9 Manasseh and Simeon who had **s** among
Ezr 2:70 servants **s** in their own towns,
2:70 of the Israelites **s** in their towns.
3: 1 the Israelites had **s** in their towns,
4:10 **s** in the city of Samaria and
Ne 7:73 Israelites, **s** in their own towns.
7:73 the Israelites had **s** in their towns,

Ne 11: 1 Now the leaders of the people s in
11: 3 leaders who s in Jerusalem
11:36 the Levites of Judah s in Benjamin.
Ps 68:10 Your people s in it, and from your
78:55 he s the tribes of Israel in their
Pr 8:25 before the mountains were s in place,
Isa 29: 1 Ariel, the city where David s!
Eze 31:13 All the birds of the air s on the
47:22 s among you and who have children.
Zec 7: 7 and the western foothills were s?'
Mt 25:19 returned and s accounts with them.
Ac 7: 4 of the Chaldeans and s in Haran.
7:29 s as a foreigner and had two sons.
19:39 it must be s in a legal assembly.
1Co 7:37 the man who has s the matter in his

Settlement (Settle)
Isa 27:10 an abandoned s, forsaken like the
Mt 18:24 he began the s, a man who owed him

Settlements (Settle)
Ge 25:16 according to their s and camps.
36:43 their s in the land they occupied.
Nu 21:25 Heshbon and all its surrounding s.
21:32 captured its surrounding s
32:41 captured their s and called them
32:42 Kenath and its surrounding s and
Jos 13:30 s of Jair in Bashan, sixty towns,
15:45 Ekron, with its surrounding s and
15:47 Ashdod, its surrounding s and
15:47 its s and villages, as far as the
17:11 together with their surrounding s
17:16 Beth Shan and its s and those in
Jdg 1:27 or Megiddo and their surrounding s,
11:26 the surrounding s and all the towns
1Ki 4:13 in Ramoth Gilead (the s of Jair son
1Ch 2:23 with its surrounding s—sixty towns.
4:33 These were their s. And they kept a
6:54 These were the locations of their s
7:28 Their lands and s included Bethel
Ne 11:25 Kiriath Arba and its surrounding s,
11:25 in Dibon and its s, in Jekabzeel
11:27 Hazar Shual, in Beersheba and its s,
11:28 in Ziklag, in Meconah and its s,
11:30 its fields, and in Azekah and its s.
11:31 in Michmash, Aija, Bethel and its s,
Isa 42:11 let the s where Kedar lives rejoice.
Eze 26: 6 her s on the mainland will be
26: 8 He will ravage your s on the
34:13 and in all the s in the land.

Settles (Settle)
2Sa 17:12 fall on him as dew s on the ground.
Ps 113: 9 He s the barren woman in her home as
Pr 18:18 Casting the lot s disputes and keeps
Eze 47:23 In whatever tribe the alien s, there

Seven (*Seven days*, Seven-day, Sevenfold, Sevens, Seventh)
Ge 4:15 will suffer vengeance s times over.
4:24 If Cain is avenged s times, then
7: 2 Take with you s of every kind of
7: 3 also s of every kind of bird, male
8:10 He waited s more days and again sent
8:12 He waited s more days and sent the
21:28 Abraham set apart s ewe lambs from
21:29 "What is the meaning of these s ewe
21:30 He replied, "Accept these s lambs
29:18 "I'll work for you s years in return
29:20 Jacob served s years to get Rachel,
29:27 return for another s years of work."
29:30 he worked for Laban another s years.
33: 3 bowed down to the ground s times
41: 2 of the river there came up s cows,
41: 3 After them, s other cows, ugly and
41: 4 gaunt ate up the s sleek, fat cows.
41: 5 had a second dream: S ears of corn,
41: 6 After them, s other ears of corn
41: 7 up the s healthy, full ears.
41:18 out of the river there came up s
41:19 After them, s other cows came
41:20 ugly cows ate up the s fat cows
41:22 "In my dreams I also saw s ears of
41:23 After them, s other ears sprouted
Ge 41:24 corn swallowed up the s good ears.
41:26 The s good cows are s years, and the
41:26. the s good ears of corn are s years
41:27 The s lean, ugly cows that came up
41:27 that came up afterwards are s years,
41:27 and so are the s worthless ears of
41:27 wind: They are s years of famine.
41:29 S years of great abundance are
41:30 s years of famine will follow them.
41:34 during the s years of abundance.
41:36 to be used during the s years of
41:47 During the s years of abundance the
41:48 those s years of abundance in Egypt
41:53 The s years of abundance in Egypt
41:54 the s years of famine began, just as
46:25 to his daughter Rachel—s in all.
Ex 2:16 a priest of Midian had s daughters,
25:37 "Then make its s lamps and set them
37:23 They made its s lamps, as well as
Lev 4: 6 some of it s times before the LORD,
4:17 LORD s times in front of the curtain.
8:11 of the oil on the altar s times,
14: 7 S times he shall sprinkle the one to
14:16 some of it before the LORD s times.
14:27 his palm s times before the LORD.
14:51 and sprinkle the house s times.
16:14 s times before the atonement cover.
16:19 his finger s times to cleanse it
23:15 offering, count off s full weeks.
23:18 Present with this bread s male lambs,
25: 8 "'Count off s sabbaths of years—
25: 8 s times s years—so that the
25: 8 the s Sabbaths of years amount to
26:18 you for your sins s times over.
26:21 s times over, as your sins deserve.
26:24 you for your sins s times over.
26:28 you for your sins s times over.
Nu 8: 2 'When you set up the s lamps, they
13:22 built s years before Zoan in Egypt.)
19: 4 sprinkle it s times towards the
23: 1 Balaam said, "Build me s altars here,
23: 1 prepare s bulls and s rams for me."
23: 4 "I have prepared s altars, and on
23:14 and there he built s altars and
23:29 Balaam said, "Build me s altars here,
23:29 prepare s bulls and s rams for me."
28:11 one ram and s male lambs a year old,
28:19 one ram and s male lambs a year old,
28:21 with each of the s lambs, one-tenth.
28:27 one ram and s male lambs a year old
28:29 with each of the s lambs, one-tenth.
29: 2 one ram and s male lambs a year old,
29: 4 with each of the s lambs, one-tenth.
29: 8 one ram and s male lambs a year old,
29:10 with each of the s lambs, one-tenth.
29:32 the seventh day prepare s bulls,
29:36 one ram and s male lambs a year old,
Dt 7: 1 Hivites and Jebusites, s nations
15: 1 At the end of every s years you must
16: 9 Count off s weeks from the time you
28: 7 direction but flee from you in s.
28:25 direction but flee from them in s,
31:10 "At the end of every s years, in the
Jos 6: 4 Make s priests carry trumpets of
6: 4 march around the city s times,
6: 6 make s priests carry trumpets in
6: 8 s priests carrying the s trumpets
6:13 s priests carrying the s trumpets
6:15 the city s times in the same manner,
6:15 day they circled the city s times.
18: 2 there were still s Israelite tribes
18: 5 to divide the land into s parts.
18: 6 of the s parts of the land, bring
18: 9 town by town, in s parts, and
Jdg 6: 1 and for s years he gave them into
6:25 father's herd, the one s years old.
12: 9 Ibzan led Israel for s years.
16: 7 "If anyone ties me with s fresh
16: 8 brought her s fresh thongs that had
16:13 "If you weave the s braids of
16:13 Delilah took the s braids of his
16:19 shave off the s braids of his hair,
20:15 in addition to s hundred chosen men
20:16 there were s hundred chosen men
Ru 4:15 who is better to you than s sons,
1Sa 2: 5 was barren has borne s children,
1Sa 6: 1 Philistine territory for s months,
16:10 Jesse made s of his sons pass before
2Sa 2:11 of Judah was s years and six months.
5: 5 reigned over Judah for s years and
8: 4 s thousand charioteers and twenty
10:18 and David killed s hundred of their
21: 6 let s of his male descendants be
21: 9 All s of them fell together;
1Ki 2:11 over Israel—s years in Hebron
6: 6 six cubits and the third floor s.
6:38 He had spent s years building it.
7:17 of the pillars, s for each capital.
11: 3 He had s hundred wives of royal
18:43 S times Elijah said, "Go back."
19:18 Yet I reserve s thousand in
2Ki 3:26 he took with him s hundred swordsmen
4:35 sneezed s times and opened his eyes.
5:10 "Go, wash yourself s times in the
5:14 himself in the Jordan s times,
8: 1 in the land that will last s years."
8: 2 land of the Philistines for s years.
8: 3 At the end of the s years she came
11:21 Joash was s years old when he began
24:16 force of s thousand fighting men,
1Ch 3: 4 reigned for s years and six months.
3:24 Johanan, Delaiah and Anani—s in all.
5:13 Jorai, Jacan, Zia and Eber—s in all.
11:23 was s and a half feet tall.
15:26 s bulls and s rams were sacrificed.
18: 4 s thousand charioteers and twenty
19:18 and David killed s thousand of their
26:32 Jeriah had two thousand s hundred
29: 4 s thousand talents of refined silver,
29:27 Israel for forty years—s in Hebron
2Ch 13: 9 with a young bull and s rams may
15:11 the LORD s hundred head of cattle
15:11 s thousand sheep and goats from the
17:11 s thousand s hundred rams and
17:11 s thousand s hundred goats.
24: 1 Joash was s years old when he became
29:21 They brought s bulls, s rams,
29:21 s male lambs and s male goats as a
30:23 celebrate the festival s more days;
30:24 s thousand sheep and goats for the
Ezr 7:14 sent by the king and his s advisers
Est 1:10 he commanded the s eunuchs who
1:14 the s nobles of Persia and Media
2: 9 He assigned to her s maids selected
Job 1: 2 He had s sons and three daughters,
1: 3 he owned s thousand sheep, three
2:13 with him for s days and s nights.
5:19 in s no harm will befall you.
42: 8 now take s bulls and s rams and go
42:13 he also had s sons and three
Ps 12: 6 a furnace of clay, purified s times.
79:12 s times the reproach they have
119:164 S times a day I praise you for your
Pr 6:16 hates, s that are detestable to him:
9: 1 she has hewn out its s pillars.
24:16 a righteous man falls s times, he
26:16 than s men who answer discreetly.
26:25 for s abominations fill his heart.
Ecc 11: 2 Give portions to s, yes to eight,
Isa 4: 1 In that day s women will take hold
11:15 He will break it up into s streams
30:26 and the sunlight will be s times
30:26 like the light of s full days, when
Jer 15: 9 The mother of s will grow faint and
52:25 fighting men, and s royal advisers.
Eze 39: 9 s years they will use them for fuel.
39:12 "'For s months the house of Israel
39:14 At the end of the s months they will
40:22 S steps led up to it, with its
40:26 S steps led up to it, with its
41: 3 each side of it were s cubits wide.
45:23 the Feast he is to provide s bulls
45:23 s rams without defect as a burnt
Da 3:19 be heated s times hotter than
4:16 till s times pass by for him.
4:23 until s times pass by for him.'
4:25 S times will pass by for you until
4:32 S times will pass by for you until
9:25 s 'sevens', and sixty-two 'sevens'.
9:27 a covenant with many for one 's'.
9:27 In the middle of the 's' he will put
Mic 5: 5 will raise against him s shepherds,

Zec 3: 9 There are s eyes on that one stone,
4: 2 bowl at the top and s lights on it,
4: 2 it, with s channels to the lights.
4:10 "(These s are the eyes of the LORD,
Mt 12:45 goes and takes with it s other
15:34 "S," they replied, "and a few small
15:36 he took the s loaves and the fish,
15:37 disciples picked up s basketfuls
16:10 the s loaves for the four thousand
18:21 he sins against me? Up to s times?"
18:22 Jesus answered, "I tell you, not s
22:25 Now there were s brothers among us.
22:28 whose wife will she be of the s,
Mk 8: 5 "S," they replied.
8: 6 When he had taken the s loaves and
8: 8 disciples picked up s basketfuls
8:20 "And when I broke the s loaves for
8:20 did you pick up?" They answered, "S.
12:20 Now there were s brothers. The first
12:22 In fact, none of the s left any
12:23 since the s were married to her?"
16: 9 out of whom he had driven s demons.
Lk 2:36 husband s years after her marriage,
8: 2 from whom s demons had come out;
11:26 goes and takes s other spirits more
17: 4 If he sins against you s times in a
17: 4 and s times comes back to you and
20:29 Now there were s brothers. The first
20:31 way the s died, leaving no children.
20:33 since the s were married to her?"
24:13 Emmaus, about s miles from Jerusalem.
Ac 6: 3 Brothers, choose s men from among
13:19 he overthrew s nations in Canaan and
19:14 S sons of Sceva, a Jewish chief
21: 8 Philip the evangelist, one of the S.
Ro 11: 4 have reserved for myself s thousand
2Pe 2: 5 of righteousness, and s others;
Rev 1: 4 John, To the s churches in the
1: 4 the s spirits before his throne,
1:11 it to the s churches: to Ephesus,
1:12 I turned I saw s golden lampstands,
1:16 In his right hand he held s stars,
1:20 The mystery of the s stars that you
1:20 of the s golden lampstands is this:
1:20 The s stars are the angels of the s
1:20 the s lampstands are the s churches.
2: 1 holds the s stars in his right hand
2: 1 walks among the s golden lampstands:
3: 1 s spirits of God and the s stars.
4: 5 Before the throne, s lamps were
4: 5 These are the s spirits of God.
5: 1 both sides and sealed with s seals.
5: 5 to open the scroll and its s seals."
5: 6 He had s horns and s eyes, which are
5: 6 the s spirits of God sent out into
6: 1 Lamb opened the first of the s seals.
8: 2 I saw the s angels who stand before
8: 2 and to them were given s trumpets.
8: 6 the s angels who had the s trumpets
10: 3 the voices of the s thunders spoke.
10: 4 the s thunders spoke, I was about to
10: 4 "Seal up what the s thunders have
11:13 S thousand people were killed in the
12: 3 an enormous red dragon with s heads
12: 3 ten horns and s crowns on his heads.
13: 1 He had ten horns and s heads, with
15: 1 s angels with the s last plagues—
15: 6 the s angels with the s plagues.
15: 7 gave to the s angels s golden bowls
15: 8 the s plagues of the s angels were
16: 1 the temple saying to the s angels,
16: 1 s bowls of God's wrath on the earth."
17: 1 the s angels who had the s bowls
17: 3 names and had s heads and ten horns.
17: 7 which has the s heads and ten horns.
17: 9 The s heads are s hills on which the
17:10 They are also s kings. Five have
17:11 He belongs to the s and is going to
21: 9 the s angels who had the s bowls
21: 9 s last plagues came and said to me,

Seven days

Ge 7: 4 S from now I will send rain on the
7:10 after the s the floodwaters came on
31:23 he pursued Jacob for s and caught up
Ex 7:25 S passed after the LORD struck the
12:15 For s you are to eat bread made
12:19 For s no yeast is to be found in
13: 6 For s eat bread made without yeast
13: 7 Eat unleavened bread during those s;
22:30 them stay with their mothers for s,
23:15 for s eat bread made without yeast,
29:30 in the Holy Place is to wear them s.
29:35 you, taking s to ordain them.
29:37 For s make atonement for the altar
34:18 For s eat bread made without yeast,
Lev 8:33 to the Tent of Meeting for s,
8:33 for your ordination will last s.
8:35 for s and do what the LORD requires,
12: 2 will be ceremonially unclean for s,
13: 4 infected person in isolation for s.
13: 5 to keep him in isolation another s.
13:21 is to put him in isolation for s.
13:26 is to put him in isolation for s.
13:31 infected person in isolation for s.
13:33 to keep him in isolation another s.
13:50 isolate the affected article for s.
13:54 he is to isolate it for another s.
14: 8 he must stay outside his tent for s.
14:38 of the house and close it up for s.
15:13 he is to count off s for his
15:19 of her monthly period will last s,
15:24 he will be unclean for s; any bed he
15:28 she must count off s, and after that
22:27 is to remain with its mother for s.
23: 6 for s you must eat bread made
23: 8 For s present an offering made to
23:34 begins, and it lasts for s.
23:36 For s present offerings made to the
23:39 the festival to the LORD for s;
23:40 before the LORD your God for s.
23:41 to the LORD for s each year.
23:42 Live in booths for s: All
Nu 12:14 she not have been in disgrace for s?
12:14 Confine her outside the camp for s;
12:15 was confined outside the camp for s,
19:11 of anyone will be unclean for s.
19:14 who is in it will be unclean for s,
19:16 or a grave, will be unclean for s.
28:17 for s eat bread made without yeast.
28:24 fire every day for s as an aroma
29:12 a festival to the LORD for s.
31:19 killed must stay outside the camp s.
Dt 16: 3 but for s eat unleavened bread, the
16: 4 possession in all your land for s.
16:13 Feast of Tabernacles for s after
16:15 For s celebrate the Feast to the
Jdg 14:12 answer within the s of the feast,
14:17 She cried the whole s of the feast.
1Sa 10: 8 but you must wait s until I come to
11: 3 "Give us s so that we can send
13: 8 He waited for s, the time set by
31:13 tree at Jabesh, and they fasted s.
1Ki 8:65 s and s more, fourteen days in all.
16:15 Judah, Zimri reigned in Tirzah for s
20:29 For s they camped opposite each
2Ki 3: 9 After a roundabout march of s, the
1Ch 10:12 tree in Jabesh, and they fasted s.
2Ch 7: 8 the festival at that time for s,
7: 9 for s and the festival for s more.
30:21 Bread for s with great rejoicing,
30:22 For the s they ate their assigned
30:23 another s they celebrated joyfully.
35:17 the Feast of Unleavened Bread for s.
Ezr 6:22 For s they celebrated with joy the
Ne 8:18 They celebrated the feast for s, and
Est 1: 5 the king gave a banquet, lasting s,
Job 2:13 sat on the ground with him for s
Eze 3:15 I sat among them for s—overwhelmed.
3:16 At the end of s the word of the LORD
43:25 "For s you are to provide a male
43:26 For s they are to make atonement for
44:26 After he is cleansed, he must wait s.
45:21 a feast lasting s, during which you
45:23 Every day during the s of the Feast
45:25 "'During the s of the Feast, which
Ac 20: 6 others at Troas, where we stayed s.
21: 4 there, we stayed with them s.
21:27 the s were nearly over, some Jews
Heb 11:30 had marched around them for s.

Seven-day (Day)

Ge 50:10 s period of mourning for his father.
1Ch 9:25 share their duties for s periods.

Sevenfold (Seven)

Pr 6:31 Yet if he is caught, he must pay s,

Sevens (Seven)

Da 9:24 "Seventy 's' are decreed for your
9:25 be seven 's', and sixty-two 's'.
9:26 After the sixty-two 's', the

Seventh (Seven, *Seventh day*)

Ge 8: 4 seventeenth day of the s month
Ex 12:15 the s must be cut off from Israel.
21: 2 But in the s year, he shall go free,
23:11 during the s year let the land lie
Lev 16:29 On the tenth day of the s month you
23:16 up to the day after the s Sabbath,
23:24 'On the first day of the s month you
23:27 "The tenth day of this s month is
23:34 'On the fifteenth day of the s month
23:39 the fifteenth day of the s month,
23:41 celebrate it in the s month.
25: 4 in the s year the land is to have a
25: 9 on the tenth day of the s month;
25:20 "What will we eat in the s year if
Nu 19:12 himself on the third and s days,
19:19 person on the third and s days,
29: 1 "'On the first day of the s month
29: 7 "'On the tenth day of this s month
29:12 On the fifteenth day of the s month
31:19 On the third and s days you must
Dt 15: 9 "The s year, the year for cancelling
15:12 the s year you must let him go free.
Jos 6:16 The s time around, when the priests
19:40 The s lot came out for the tribe of
1Ki 8: 2 the month of Ethanim, the s month.
18:44 The s time the servant reported,
2Ki 11: 4 In the s year Jehoiada sent for the
12: 1 In the s year of Jehu, Joash became
18: 9 which was the s year of Hoshea son
25:25 In the s month, however, Ishmael son
1Ch 2:15 the sixth Ozem and the s David.
12:11 Attai the sixth, Eliel the s,
24:10 the s to Hakkoz, the eighth to
25:14 the s to Jesarelah, his sons and
26: 3 the sixth and Eliehoenai the s.
26: 5 Ammiel the sixth, Issachar the s and
27:10 The s, for the s month, was Helez
2Ch 5: 3 time of the festival in the s month.
7:10 twenty-third day of the s month
23: 1 In the s year Jehoiada showed his
31: 7 month and finished in the s month.
Ezr 3: 1 the s month came and the Israelites
3: 6 On the first day of the s month they
7: 7 in the s year of King Artaxerxes.
7: 8 month of the s year of the king.
Ne 7:73 When the s month came and the
8: 2 on the first day of the s month,
8:14 during the feast of the s month
10:31 Every s year we will forgo working
Est 2:16 Tebeth, in the s year of his reign.
Jer 28:17 In the s month of that same year,
34:14 'Every s year each of you must free
41: 1 In the s month Ishmael son of
52:28 exile: in the s year, 3,023 Jews;
Eze 20: 1 In the s year, in the fifth month on
45:25 which begins in the s month on the
Hag 2: 1 twenty-first day of the s month
Zec 7: 5 mourned in the fifth and s months
8:19 "The fasts of the fourth, fifth, s
Mt 22:26 brother, right on down to the s.
Jn 4:52 left him yesterday at the s hour."
Jude :14 Enoch, the s from Adam, prophesied
Rev 8: 1 he opened the s seal, there was
10: 7 in the days when the s angel is
11:15 The s angel sounded his trumpet, and
16:17 The s angel poured out his bowl into
21:20 sixth carnelian, the s chrysolite,

Seventh day

Ge 2: 2 By the s God had finished the work
2: 2 the s he rested from all his work.

Ge 2: 3 God blessed the s and made it holy,
Ex 12:16 assembly, and another one on the s.
13: 6 the s hold a festival to the LORD.
16:26 but on the s, the Sabbath, there
16:27 went out on the s to gather it, but
16:29 is to stay where he is on the s;
16:30 the people rested on the s.
20:10 the s is a Sabbath to the LORD your
20:11 is in them, but he rested on the s.
23:12 but on the s do not work, so that
24:16 and on the s the LORD called to
31:15 but the s is a Sabbath of rest,
31:17 s he abstained from work and rested.
34:21 but on the s you shall rest;
35: 2 but the s shall be your holy day,
Lev 13: 5 On the s the priest is to examine
13: 6 On the s the priest is to examine
13:27 On the s the priest is to examine
13:32 On the s the priest is to examine
13:34 On the s the priest is to examine
13:51 On the s he is to examine it, and if
14: 9 On the s he must shave off all his
14:39 On the s the priest shall return to
23: 3 but the s is a Sabbath of rest, a
23: 8 And on the s hold a sacred assembly
Nu 6: 9 on the day of his cleansing—the s.
7:48 On the s Elishama son of Ammihud,
19:12 on the third day and on the s;
19:19 on the s he is to purify him.
28:25 On the s hold a sacred assembly and
29:32 "'On the s prepare seven bulls, two
31:24 On the s wash your clothes and you
Dt 5:14 the s is a Sabbath to the LORD your
16: 8 on the s hold an assembly to the
Jos 6: 4 On the s, march around the city
6:15 On the s, they got up at daybreak
Jdg 14:17 So on the s he finally told her,
14:18 Before sunset on the s the men of
2Sa 12:18 On the s the child died.
1Ki 20:29 and on the s the battle was joined.
2Ki 25: 8 On the s of the fifth month, in the
Est 1:10 On the s, when King Xerxes was in
Eze 30:20 in the first month on the s, the
45:20 You are to do the same on the s of
Heb 4: 4 spoken about the s in these words:
4: 4 the s God rested from all his work."

Severe (Severely)

Ge 12:10 a while because the famine was s.
41:31 famine that follows it will be so s.
41:56 the famine was s throughout Egypt.
41:57 the famine was s in all the world.
43: 1 Now the famine was still s in the
47: 4 because the famine is s in Canaan
47:13 region because the famine was s;
47:20 the famine was too s for them.
Nu 11:33 and he struck them with a s plague.
Dt 28:59 and s and lingering illnesses.
1Ki 18: 2 Now the famine was s in Samaria,
2Ki 25: 3 become so s that there was no food
2Ch 16:12 Though his disease was s, even in
Jer 52: 6 become so s that there was no food
Mt 4:24 those suffering s pain, the
Lk 4:25 was a s famine throughout the land.
15:14 there was a s famine in that whole
Ac 11:28 predicted that a s famine would
2Co 8: 2 Out of the most s trial, their
1Th 1: 6 in spite of s suffering, you
Rev 11:13 very hour there was a s earthquake
16:18 peals of thunder and a s earthquake.

Severed (Severing)

Ecc 12: 6 him—before the silver cord is s,

Severely (Severe)

Ru 1:17 be it ever so s, if anything but
1Sa 3:17 be it ever so s, if you hide from me
14:44 be it ever so s, if you do not die,
20:13 be it ever so s, if I do not let you
25:22 be it ever so s, if by morning I
2Sa 3: 9 be it ever so s, if I do not do for
3:35 be it ever so s, if I taste bread or
19:13 be it ever so s, if from now on you
1Ki 2:23 be it ever so s, if Adonijah does
19: 2 be it ever so s, if by this time
1Ki 20:10 be it ever so s, if enough dust
2Ki 6:31 be it ever so s, if the head of
13: 4 for he saw how s the king of Aram
2Ch 24:25 withdrew, they left Joash s wounded.
Ps 118:18 The LORD has chastened me s, but he
Mk 12:40 Such men will be punished most s."
Lk 20:47 Such men will be punished most s."
Ac 16:23 After they had been s flogged, they
20:19 s tested by the plots of the Jews.
2Co 2: 5 to some extent—not to put it too s.
11:23 been flogged more s, and been
Heb 10:29 How much more s do you think a man

Severing (Severed)

Lev 1:17 not s it completely, and then the
5: 8 from its neck, not s it completely,

Sew (Sewed, Sews)

Eze 13:18 Woe to the women who s magic charms

Sewed (Sew)

Ge 3: 7 so they s fig leaves together and
Job 16:15 "I have s sackcloth over my skin and

Sews (Sew)

Mt 9:16 "No-one s a patch of unshrunk cloth
Mk 2:21 "No-one s a patch of unshrunk cloth
Lk 5:36 new garment and s it on an old one.

Sex (Sexual, Sexually)

Ge 19: 5 us so that we can have s with them."
Jdg 19:22 house so we can have s with him."

Sexual (Sex)

Ex 19:15 Abstain from s relations."
22:19 "Anyone who has s relations with an
Lev 18: 6 close relative to have s relations.
18: 7 having s relations with your mother.
18: 8 "'Do not have s relations with your
18: 9 "'Do not have s relations with your
18:10 "'Do not have s relations with your
18:11 "'Do not have s relations with the
18:12 "'Do not have s relations with your
18:13 "'Do not have s relations with your
18:14 have s relations; she is your aunt.
18:15 "'Do not have s relations with your
18:16 "'Do not have s relations with your
18:17 "'Do not have s relations with both
18:17 Do not have s relations with either
18:18 have s relations with her while your
18:19 approach a woman to have s relations
18:20 "'Do not have s relations with your
18:23 "'Do not have s relations with an
18:23 animal to have s relations with it;
20:15 "'If a man has s relations with an
20:16 animal to have s relations with it,
20:17 have s relations, it is a disgrace.
20:18 period and has s relations with her,
20:19 "'Do not have s relations with the
Nu 25: 1 in s immorality with Moabite women,
Dt 27:21 the man who has s relations with
Mt 15:19 murder, adultery, s immorality,
Mk 7:21 come evil thoughts, s immorality,
Ac 15:20 from s immorality, from the meat of
15:29 animals and from s immorality.
21:25 animals and from s immorality."
Ro 1:24 to s impurity for the degrading of
13:13 not in s immorality and debauchery,
1Co 5: 1 there is s immorality among you,
6:13 body is not meant for s immorality,
6:18 Flee from s immorality. All other
10: 8 We should not commit s immorality,
2Co 12:21 s sin and debauchery in which they
Gal 5:19 nature are obvious: s immorality,
Eph 5: 3 not be even a hint of s immorality,
Col 3: 5 your earthly nature: s immorality,
1Th 4: 3 that you should avoid s immorality;
Jude : 7 up to s immorality and perversion.
Rev 2:14 and by committing s immorality.
2:20 my servants into s immorality
9:21 their s immorality or their thefts.

Sexually (Sex)

1Co 5: 9 to associate with s immoral people—
5:11 brother but is s immoral or greedy,
6: 9 Neither the s immoral nor idolaters
6:18 sins s sins against his own body.
Heb 12:16 See that no-one is s immoral, or is
13: 4 the adulterer and all the s immoral.
Rev 21: 8 vile, the murderers, the s immoral,
22:15 the s immoral, the murderers, the

Shaalabbin

Jos 19:42 S, Aijalon, Ithlah,

Shaalbim

Jdg 1:35 Aijalon and S, but when the power of
1Ki 4: 9 Ben-Deker—in Makaz, S, Beth Shemesh

Shaalbonite

2Sa 23:32 Eliahba the S, the sons of Jashen,
1Ch 11:33 the Baharumite, Eliahba the S,

Shaalim

1Sa 9: 4 They went on into the district of S,

Shaaph

1Ch 2:47 Jotham, Geshan, Pelet, Ephah and S.
2:49 She also gave birth to S the father

Shaaraim

Jos 15:36 S, Adithaim and Gederah (or
1Sa 17:52 along the S road to Gath and Ekron.
1Ch 4:31 Hazar Susim, Beth Biri and S.

Shaashgaz

Est 2:14 part of the harem to the care of S,

Shabbethai

Ezr 10:15 and S the Levite, opposed this.
Ne 8: 7 Bani, Sherebiah, Jamin, Akkub, S,
11:16 S and Jozabad, two of the heads of

Shabby

Jas 2: 2 poor man in s clothes also comes in.

Shackles

Jdg 16:21 Binding him with bronze s, they set
2Ki 25: 7 bound him with bronze s and took
2Ch 33:11 bound him with bronze s and took
36: 6 bound him with bronze s to take him
Job 12:18 He takes off the s put on by kings
13:27 You fasten my feet in s; you keep
33:11 He fastens my feet in s; he keeps
Ps 105:18 They bruised his feet with s, his
149: 8 their nobles with s of iron,
Jer 39: 7 bound him with bronze s to take him
52:11 bound him with bronze s and took him
Na 1:13 your neck and tear your s away."

Shade

Jdg 9:15 come and take refuge in my s; but if
Ne 8:15 and from myrtles, palms and s trees,
Ps 80:10 The mountains were covered with its s
121: 5 LORD is your s at your right hand;
SS 2: 3 I delight to sit in his s, and his
Isa 4: 6 will be a shelter and s from the
25: 4 the storm and a s from the heat.
30: 2 protection, to Egypt's s for refuge.
30: 3 Egypt's s will bring you disgrace.
Jer 4:30 Why s your eyes with paint?
Eze 17:23 shelter in the s of its branches.
31: 6 the great nations lived in its s.
31:12 out from under its s and left it.
31:17 Those who lived in its s, its allies
Hos 4:13 terebinth, where the s is pleasant.
14: 7 Men will dwell again in his s.
Jnh 4: 5 sat in its s and waited to see what
4: 6 made it grow up over Jonah to give s
Mk 4:32 of the air can perch in its s."

Shadow (*Shadow of death*, Shadows)

2Ki 20: 9 Shall the s go forward ten steps,
20:10 "It is a simple matter for the s to
20:11 and the LORD made the s go back the
1Ch 29:15 on earth are like a s, without hope.
Job 3: 5 May darkness and deep s claim it
8: 9 and our days on earth are but a s.
10:21 to the land of gloom and deep s,
10:22 of deep s and disorder, where even
14: 2 a fleeting s, he does not endure.
17: 7 my whole frame is but a s.
34:22 There is no dark place, no deep s,
40:22 The lotuses conceal him in their s;
Ps 17: 8 hide me in the s of your wings
36: 7 find refuge in the s of your wings.
57: 1 I will take refuge in the s of your
63: 7 I sing in the s of your wings.
91: 1 will rest in the s of the Almighty.
102:11 My days are like the evening s;
109:23 I fade away like an evening s;
144: 4 his days are like a fleeting s.
Ecc 6:12 days he passes through like a s?
8:13 days will not lengthen like a s.
Isa 16: 3 Make your s like night—at high
25: 5 heat is reduced by the s of a cloud,
32: 2 s of a great rock in a thirsty land.
34:15 and care for her young under the s
38: 8 I will make the s cast by the sun go
49: 2 in the s of his hand he hid me;
51:16 covered you with the s of my hand—
Jer 48:45 "In the s of Heshbon the fugitives
Lam 4:20 We thought that under his s we would
Ac 5:15 that at least Peter's s might fall
Col 2:17 These are a s of the things that
Heb 8: 5 a copy and s of what is in heaven.
10: 1 The law is only a s of the good

Shadow of death

Job 38:17 Have you seen the gates of the s?
Ps 23: 4 I walk through the valley of the s,
Isa 9: 2 land of the s a light has dawned.
Mt 4:16 land of the s a light has dawned."
Lk 1:79 living in darkness and in the s,

Shadows (Shadow)

Jdg 9:36 the s of the mountains for men."
Ne 13:19 evening s fell on the gates of
Job 7: 2 a slave longing for the evening s,
12:22 and brings deep s into the light.
16:16 with weeping, deep s ring my eyes;
Ps 11: 2 from the s at the upright in heart.
SS 2:17 Until the day breaks and the s flee,
4: 6 Until the day breaks and the s flee,
Isa 59: 9 brightness, but we walk in deep s.
Jer 6: 4 and the s of evening grow long.
Jas 1:17 who does not change like shifting s.

Shadrach

Formerly Hananiah; member of Jewish nobility taken to Babylon with Daniel, Meshach and Abednego (Da 1:3–7). Refused unclean food (Da 1:8–16); appointed as administrator (Da 2:49). Refused to worship golden image; kept safe in fiery furnace (Da 3).

Da 1: 7 to Hananiah, S; to Mishael, Meshach
2:49 request the king appointed S,
3:12 of Babylon—S, Meshach and Abednego
3:13 summoned S, Meshach and Abednego.
3:14 "Is it true, S, Meshach and Abednego,
3:16 S, Meshach and Abednego replied to
3:19 Nebuchadnezzar was furious with S,
3:20 soldiers in his army to tie up S,
3:22 who took up S, Meshach and Abednego,
3:26 "S, Meshach and Abednego, servants
3:26 So S, Meshach and Abednego came
3:28 "Praise be to the God of S, Meshach
3:29 say anything against the God of S,
3:30 the king promoted S, Meshach and

Shaft

Ex 25:31 gold and hammer it out, base and s;
37:17 and hammered it out, base and s;
1Sa 17: 7 His spear s was like a weaver's rod,
2Sa 5: 8 have to use the water s to reach
2Sa 21:19 spear with a s like a weaver's rod.
23: 7 a tool of iron or the s of a spear;
1Ch 20: 5 spear with a s like a weaver's rod.
Job 28: 4 from where people dwell he cuts a s,
Rev 9: 1 given the key to the s of the Abyss.

Shagee

1Ch 11:34 Jonathan son of S the Hararite,

Shaggy

Da 8:21 The s goat is the king of Greece,

Shaharaim

1Ch 8: 8 Sons were born to S in Moab after he

Shahazumah

Jos 19:22 The boundary touched Tabor, S and

Shake (Shaken, Shakes, Shaking, Shook)

Jdg 16:20 go out as before and s myself free.
Ne 5:13 "In this way may God s out of his
Job 4:14 seized me and made all my bones s.
16: 4 against you and s my head at you.
38:13 edges and s the wicked out of it?
Ps 10: 6 says to himself, "Nothing will s me
44:14 the peoples s their heads at us.
64: 8 them will s their heads in scorn.
99: 1 the cherubim, let the earth s.
109:25 they see me, they s their heads.
Isa 2:19 when he rises to s the earth.
2:21 when he rises to s the earth.
5:25 The mountains s, and the dead bodies
10:32 they will s their fist at the mount
13:13 and the earth will s from its place
24:18 the foundations of the earth s.
52: 2 S off your dust; rise up, sit
Jer 18:16 be appalled and will s their heads.
48:27 that you s your head in scorn
Lam 2:15 they scoff and s their heads at the
Am 9: 1 pillars so that the thresholds s.
9: 9 and I will s the house of Israel
Zep 2:15 pass by her scoff and s their fists.
Hag 2: 6 more s the heavens and the earth,
2: 7 I will s all nations, and the
2:21 I will s the heavens and the earth.
Mt 10:14 s the dust off your feet when you
Mk 6:11 s the dust off your feet when you
Lk 6:48 not s it, because it was well built.
9: 5 s the dust off your feet when you
Heb 12:26 "Once more I will s not only the

Shaken (Shake)

1Sa 28:21 Saul and saw that he was greatly s,
2Sa 18:33 The king was s. He went up to the
Ne 5:13 So may such a man be s out and
Job 34:20 the people are s and they pass away;
Ps 15: 5 does these things will never be s.
16: 8 at my right hand, I shall not be s.
21: 7 of the Most High he will not be s.
30: 6 secure, I said, "I shall never be s.
60: 2 You have s the land and torn it open;
62: 2 is my fortress, I shall never be s.
62: 6 he is my fortress, I shall not be s.
82: 5 the foundations of the earth are s.
109:23 I am s off like a locust.
112: 6 Surely he will never be s;
125: 1 cannot be s but endures for ever.
Isa 7: 2 of Ahaz and his people were s,
7: 2 of the forest are s by the wind.
24:19 asunder, the earth is thoroughly s.
54:10 Though the mountains be s and the
54:10 love for you will not be s nor
Am 9: 9 nations as grain is s in a sieve,
Na 3:12 when they are s, the figs fall into
Mt 24:29 and the heavenly bodies will be s.'
Mk 13:25 and the heavenly bodies will be s.'
Lk 6:38 down, s together and running over,
21:26 for the heavenly bodies will be s.
Ac 2:25 at my right hand, I will not be s.
4:31 place where they were meeting was s.
16:26 foundations of the prison were s.
Heb 12:27 removing of what can be s—that is,
12:27 that what cannot be s may remain.
Heb 12:28 a kingdom that cannot be s,
Rev 6:13 a fig-tree when s by a strong wind.

Shakes (Shake)

Job 9: 6 He s the earth from its place and
15:25 he s his fist at God and vaunts
Ps 29: 8 The voice of the LORD s the desert;
29: 8 the LORD s the Desert of Kadesh.
Isa 30:28 He s the nations in the sieve of
Joel 2:10 Before them the earth s, the sky

Shaking (Shake)

Ps 22: 7 they hurl insults, s their heads:
Mt 27:39 insults at him, s their heads
Mk 15:29 s their heads and saying, "So! You

Shalisha

1Sa 9: 4 through the area around S, but they

Shalleketh

1Ch 26:16 the West Gate and the S Gate on the

Shallow

Mt 13: 5 up quickly, because the soil was s.
Mk 4: 5 up quickly, because the soil was s.

Shallum (Shallum's)

2Ki 15:10 S son of Jabesh conspired against
15:13 S son of Jabesh became king in the
15:14 He attacked S son of Jabesh in
22:14 who was the wife of S son of Tikvah,
1Ch 2:40 of Sismai, Sismai the father of S,
2:41 S the father of Jekamiah, and
3:15 Zedekiah the third, S the fourth.
4:25 S was Shaul's son, Mibsam his son
6:12 of Zadok, Zadok the father of S,
6:13 S the father of Hilkiah, Hilkiah the
9:17 The gatekeepers: S, Akkub, Talmon,
9:17 and their brothers, S their chief
9:19 S son of Kore, the son of Ebiasaph,
9:31 the firstborn son of S the Korahite,
2Ch 28:12 Jehizkiah son of S, and Amasa son of
34:22 who was the wife of S son of Tokhath,
Ezr 2:42 of the temple: the descendants of S,
7: 2 the son of S, the son of Zadok, the
10:24 the gatekeepers: S, Telem and Uri.
10:42 S, Amariah and Joseph.
Ne 3:12 S son of Hallohesh, ruler of a
7:45 The gatekeepers: the descendants of S
Jer 22:11 the LORD says about S son of Josiah,
32: 7 Hanamel son of S your uncle is going
35: 4 Maaseiah son of S the door-keeper.

Shallum's (Shallum)

2Ki 15:15 The other events of S reign, and the

Shallun

Ne 3:15 The Fountain Gate was repaired by S

Shalmai

Ezr 2:46 Hagab, S, Hanan,
Ne 7:48 Lebana, Hagaba, S,

Shalman

Hos 10:14 as S devastated Beth Arbel on the

Shalmaneser (Shalmaneser's)

2Ki 17: 3 S king of Assyria came up to attack
17: 4 S seized him and put him in prison.
18: 9 S king of Assyria marched against

Shalmaneser's (Shalmaneser)

2Ki 17: 3 who had been S vassal and had paid

Shama

1Ch 11:44 Uzzia the Ashterathite, S and Jeiel

Shame (Ashamed, Shamed, Shameful, Shamefully, Shaming)

Ge 2:25 were both naked, and they felt no s.
Dt 32: 5 to their s they are no longer his

1Sa 20:30 with the son of Jesse to your own s
20:30 to the s of the mother who bore you?
2Ki 19:26 of power, are dismayed and put to s.
Job 8:22 Your enemies will be clothed in s,
10:15 for I am full of s and drowned in
11:15 you will lift up your face without s
Ps 4: 2 will you turn my glory into s?
25: 2 Do not let me be put to s, nor let
25: 3 is in you will ever be put to s,
25: 3 but they will be put to s who are
25:20 let me not be put to s, for I take
31: 1 let me never be put to s;
31:17 Let me not be put to s, O LORD, for
31:17 but let the wicked be put to s
34: 5 faces are never covered with s.
35: 4 my life be disgraced and put to s;
35:26 distress be put to s and confusion;
35:26 me be clothed with s and disgrace.
40:14 my life be put to s and confusion;
40:15 Aha!" be appalled at their own s.
44: 7 you put our adversaries to s.
44:15 long, and my face is covered with s
53: 5 them to s, for God despised them.
69: 6 not be put to s because of me,
69: 7 for your sake, and s covers my face.
70: 2 my life be put to s and confusion;
70: 3 Aha!" turn back because of their s.
71: 1 let me never be put to s.
71:13 May my accusers perish in s;
71:24 me have been put to s and confusion.
78:66 he put them to everlasting s.
83:16 Cover their faces with s so that men
86:17 enemies may see it and be put to s,
89:45 have covered him with a mantle of s.
97: 7 All who worship images are put to s,
109:28 they will be put to s, but your
109:29 and wrapped in s as in a cloak.
119: 6 I would not be put to s when I
119:31 do not let me be put to s.
119:46 kings and will not be put to s,
119:78 May the arrogant be put to s for
119:80 decrees, that I may not be put to s.
127: 5 They will not be put to s when they
129: 5 who hate Zion be turned back in s.
132:18 I will clothe his enemies with s,
Pr 3:35 honour, but fools he holds up to s.
6:33 and his s will never be wiped away;
13: 5 but the wicked bring s and disgrace.
13:18 discipline comes to poverty and s,
18: 3 contempt, and with s comes disgrace.
18:13 that is his folly and his s.
19:26 is a son who brings s and disgrace.
25: 8 end if your neighbour puts you to s?
25:10 or he who hears it may s you and you
Isa 20: 4 with buttocks bared—to Egypt's s.
20: 5 Egypt will be afraid and put to s.
26:11 for your people and be put to s;
30: 3 protection will be to your s,
30: 5 everyone will be put to s because of
30: 5 advantage, but only s and disgrace."
37:27 of power, are dismayed and put to s.
42:17 will be turned back in utter s.
44: 9 they are ignorant, to their own s.
44:11 He and his kind will be put to s;
45:16 will be put to s and disgraced;
45:17 never be put to s or disgraced,
45:24 will come to him and be put to s.
47: 3 be exposed and your s uncovered.
50: 7 and I know I will not be put to s.
54: 4 be afraid; you will not suffer s.
54: 4 You will forget the s of your youth
61: 7 Instead of their s my people will
65:13 rejoice, but you will be put to s.
66: 5 Yet they will be put to s.
Jer 3: 3 you refuse to blush with s.
3:25 Let us lie down in our s, and let
6:15 they have no s at all; they do not
7:19 harming themselves, to their own s?
8: 9 The wise will be put to s; they will
8:12 they have no s at all; they do not
9:19 How great is our s! We must leave
12:13 So bear the s of your harvest
13:26 your face that your s may be seen—
17:13 who forsake you will be put to s.
17:18 Let my persecutors be put to s, but
17:18 but keep me from s; let them be
Jer 20:18 and sorrow and to end my days in s?
23:40 s that will not be forgotten."
46:12 The nations will hear of your s;
46:24 Daughter of Egypt will be put to s,
48:39 How Moab turns her back in s!
50: 2 Bel will be put to s, Marduk filled
50: 2 Her images will be put to s and her
51:51 insulted and s covers our faces,
Eze 7:18 Their faces will be covered with s
23:29 and the s of your prostitution will
32:24 s with those who go down to the pit.
32:25 they bear their s with those who go
32:30 s with those who go down to the pit.
39:26 They will forget their s and all the
44:13 the s of their detestable practices.
Da 9: 7 but this day we are covered with s
9: 8 are covered with s because we have
12: 2 to s and everlasting contempt.
Hos 4:19 their sacrifices will bring them s.
Am 8:14 They who swear by the s of Samaria,
Ob :10 you will be covered with s;
Mic 1:11 Pass on in nakedness and s, you who
7:10 see it and will be covered with s,
Na 3: 5 nakedness and the kingdoms your s.
Hab 2:16 You will be filled with s instead of
Zep 3: 5 fail, yet the unrighteous know no s.
3:11 On that day you will not be put to s
3:19 every land where they were put to s.
Ro 9:33 in him will never be put to s."
10:11 in him will never be put to s."
1Co 1:27 things of the world to s the wise;
1:27 things of the world to s the strong.
4:14 I am not writing this to s you, but
6: 5 I say this to s you. Is it possible
15:34 of God—I say this to your s.
2Co 11:21 To my s I admit that we were too
Php 3:19 and their glory is in their s.
Heb 12: 2 scorning its s, and sat down at the
1Pe 2: 6 in him will never be put to s."
Jude :13 of the sea, foaming up their s;

Shamed (Shame)
Ps 69:19 how I am scorned, disgraced and s;
Jer 10:14 every goldsmith is s by his idols.
51:17 every goldsmith is s by his idols.
Joel 2:26 never again will my people be s.
2:27 never again will my people be s.

Shameful (Shame)
1Sa 20:34 his father's s treatment of David.
Job 31:11 For that would have been s, a sin to
Pr 14:35 but a s servant incurs his wrath.
Jer 3:24 From our youth s gods have consumed
11:13 to burn incense to that s god Baal
Hos 4:18 their rulers dearly love s ways.
6: 9 to Shechem, committing s crimes.
9:10 themselves to that s idol
Zep 2: 1 gather together, O s nation,
Ro 1:26 God gave them over to s lusts.
2Co 4: 2 we have renounced secret and s ways;
Eph 5:12 For it is s even to mention what the
2Pe 2: 2 Many will follow their s ways and
Rev 3:18 you can cover your s nakedness;
21:27 nor will anyone who does what is s

Shamefully (Shame)
Eze 22:11 s defiles his daughter-in-law,
Mk 12: 4 man on the head and treated him s.
Lk 20:11 they beat and treated s and sent
Rev 16:15 may not go naked and be s exposed."

Shameless
Jer 13:27 neighings, your s prostitution!

Shamgar
Jdg 3:31 After Ehud came S son of Anath, who
5: 6 "In the days of S son of Anath, in

Shamhuth
1Ch 27: 8 was the commander S the Izrahite.

Shaming (Shame)
Hab 2:10 s your own house and forfeiting your

Shamir
Jos 15:48 In the hill country: S, Jattir,
Jdg 10: 1 He lived in S, in the hill country
10: 2 then he died, and was buried in S.
1Ch 24:24 from the sons of Micah: S.

Shamma
1Ch 7:37 Bezer, Hod, S, Shilshah, Ithran and

Shammah
Ge 36:13 The sons of Reuel: Nahath, Zerah, S
36:17 Chiefs Nahath, Zerah, S and Mizzah.
1Sa 16: 9 Jesse then made S pass by, but
17:13 second, Abinadab; and the third, S.
2Sa 23:11 Next to him was S son of Agee the
23:12 S took his stand in the middle of
23:25 S the Harodite, Elika the Harodite,
23:33 son of S the Hararite, Ahiam son of
1Ch 1:37 The sons of Reuel: Nahath, Zerah, S

Shammai (Shammai's)
1Ch 2:28 The sons of Onam: S and Jada.
2:28 The sons of S: Nadab and Abishur.
2:44 Rekem was the father of S.
2:45 The son of S was Maon, and Maon was
4:17 S and Ishbah the father of Eshtemoa.

Shammai's (Shammai)
1Ch 2:32 The sons of Jada, S brother: Jether

Shammoth
1Ch 11:27 S the Harorite, Helez the Pelonite,

Shammua
Nu 13: 4 tribe of Reuben, S son of Zaccur;
2Sa 5:14 there: S, Shobab, Nathan, Solomon,
1Ch 3: 5 S, Shobab, Nathan and Solomon.
14: 4 there: S, Shobab, Nathan, Solomon,
Ne 11:17 his associates; and Abda son of S,
12:18 of Bilgah's, S; of Shemaiah's,

Shamsherai
1Ch 8:26 S, Sheheriah, Athaliah,

Shape (Shaped, Shapes, Shaping)
Ex 32: 4 an idol cast in the s of a calf,
32: 8 an idol cast in the s of a calf.
Dt 4:16 an image of any s, whether formed
9:16 an idol cast in the s of a calf.
1Ki 6:25 were identical in size and s.
7:19 the s of lilies, four cubits high.
7:22 The capitals on top were in the s of
7:23 circular in s, measuring ten cubits
7:37 and were identical in size and s.
2Ki 17:16 two idols cast in the s of calves,
2Ch 4: 2 circular in s, measuring ten cubits
Job 38:14 The earth takes s like clay under a

Shaped (Shape)
Ex 25:33 Three cups s like almond flowers
25:34 s like almond flowers with buds
37:19 Three cups s like almond flowers
37:20 four cups s like almond flowers
Job 10: 8 "Your hands s me and made me.

Shapes (Shape)
Isa 44:10 Who s a god and casts an idol, which
44:12 he s an idol with hammers,
44:13 He s it in the form of man, of man
Jer 10: 3 a craftsman s it with his chisel.

Shapham
1Ch 5:12 Joel was the chief, S the second,

Shaphan
2Ki 22: 3 King Josiah sent the secretary, S
22: 8 Hilkiah the high priest said to S
22: 8 He gave it to S, who read it.
22: 9 S the secretary went to the king and
22:10 S the secretary informed the king,
22:10 And S read from it in the presence
22:12 Ahikam son of S, Acbor son of

2Ki 22:12 **S** the secretary and Asaiah the
22:14 Hilkiah the priest, Ahikam, Acbor, **S**
25:22 the son of **S**, to be over the people
2Ch 34: 8 he sent **S** son of Azaliah and
34:15 Hilkiah said to **S** the secretary,
34:15 He gave it to **S**.
34:16 **S** took the book to the king and
34:18 **S** the secretary informed the king,
34:18 And **S** read from it in the presence
34:20 Ahikam son of **S**, Abdon son of Micah,
34:20 Abdon son of Micah, **S** the secretary
Jer 26:24 Ahikam son of **S** supported Jeremiah,
29: 3 letter to Elasah son of **S** and to
36:10 From the room of Gemariah son of **S**
36:11 Micaiah son of Gemariah, the son of **S**
36:12 Gemariah son of **S**, Zedekiah son of
39:14 Ahikam, the son of **S**, to take him
40: 5 the son of **S**, whom the king of
40: 9 Gedaliah son of Ahikam, the son of **S**,
40:11 the son of **S**, as governor over them,
41: 2 the son of **S**, with the sword,
43: 6 the son of **S**, and Jeremiah the
Eze 8:11 son of **S** was standing among them.

Shaphat
Nu 13: 5 the tribe of Simeon, **S** son of Hori;
1Ki 19:16 and anoint Elisha son of **S** from Abel
19:19 there and found Elisha son of **S**.
2Ki 3:11 "Elisha son of **S** is here. He used
6:31 the head of Elisha son of **S** remains
1Ch 3:22 Bariah, Neariah and **S**—six in all.
5:12 second, then Janai and **S**, in Bashan.
27:29 **S** son of Adlai was in charge of the

Shaphir
Mic 1:11 and shame, you who live in **S**.

Shaping (Shape)
Jer 18: 4 the pot he was s from the clay was
18: 4 pot, s it as seemed best to him.

Sharai
Ezr 10:40 Macnadebai, Shashai, **S**,

Sharar
2Sa 23:33 Ahiam son of **S** the Hararite,

Share (Shared, Sharers, Shares, Sharing)
Ge 14:24 the s that belongs to the men who
14:24 Let them have their s."
21:10 will never s in the inheritance
31:14 "Do we still have any s in the
Ex 12: 4 they must s one with their nearest
18:22 because they will s it with you.
29:26 offering, and it will be your s.
29:28 This is always to be the regular s
Lev 6:17 I have given it as their s of the
6:18 It is his regular s of the offerings
6:22 It is the LORD's regular s and is
7:33 shall have the right thigh as his s.
7:34 their regular s from the Israelites.
7:36 their regular s for the generations
8:29 —Moses' s of the ordination ram—
10:13 it is your s and your sons' s of
10:14 children as your s of the Israelites'
10:15 This will be the regular s for you
19:17 so that you will not s in his guilt.
24: 9 their regular s of the offerings
25:51 larger s of the price paid for him.
Nu 10:32 we will s with you whatever good
18: 8 sons as your portion and regular s.
18:11 and daughters as your regular s.
18:19 and daughters as your regular s.
18:20 nor will you have any s among them;
18:20 I am your s and your inheritance
31:29 Take this tribute from their half s
31:36 The half s of those who fought in
Dt 10: 9 That is why the Levites have no s or
18: 3 This is the s due to the priests
18: 8 He is to s equally in their benefits
21:17 giving him a double s of all he has.
Jos 14: 4 The Levites received no s of the
17: 5 Manasseh's s consisted of ten tracts
Jos 19: 9 was taken from the s of Judah,
22:19 stands, and s the land with us.
22:25 You have no s in the LORD.
22:27 ours, 'You have no s in the LORD.'
Jdg 8:24 ear-ring from your s of the plunder.
1Sa 26:19 They have now driven me from my s in
30:22 s with them the plunder we recovered.
30:24 The s of the man who stayed with the
30:24 to the battle. All shall s alike."
2Sa 20: 1 "We have no s in David, no part in
1Ki 12:16 "What s do we have in David, what
1Ch 9:25 s their duties for seven-day periods.
2Ch 10:16 "What s do we have in David, what
Ne 2:20 but as for you, you have no s in
Job 39:17 or give her a s of good sense.
Ps 68:23 tongues of your dogs have their s."
69:27 do not let them s in your salvation.
106: 5 that I may s in the joy of your
Pr 1:14 us, and we will s a common purse"–
14:10 and no-one else can s its joy.
16:19 than to s plunder with the proud.
17: 2 and will s the inheritance as one of
21: 9 s a house with a quarrelsome wife.
25:24 s a house with a quarrelsome wife.
Ecc 9: 2 All s a common destiny—the
Isa 58: 7 Is it not to s your food with the
Jer 37:12 to get his s of the property among
Eze 18:19 'Why does the son not s the guilt
18:20 The son will not s the guilt of the
18:20 the father s the guilt of the son.
Am 7: 1 the king's s had been harvested
Mt 21:41 his s of the crop at harvest time."
25:21 Come and s your master's happiness!'
25:23 Come and s your master's happiness!'
Lk 3:11 "The man with two tunics should s
15:12 'Father, give me my s of the estate.
Ac 8:21 You have no part or s in this
Ro 8:17 if indeed we s in his sufferings in
8:17 that we may also s in his glory.
11:17 now s in the nourishing sap from the
12:13 **S** with God's people who are in need.
15:27 s with them their material blessings.
1Co 9:13 s in what is offered on the altar?
9:23 that I may s in its blessings.
2Co 1: 7 just as you s in our sufferings,
1: 7 so also you s in our comfort.
2: 3 of you, that you would all s my joy.
Gal 4:30 will never s in the inheritance
6: 6 must s all good things with his
Eph 4:28 something to s with those in need.
Php 1: 7 all of you s in God's grace with me.
4:14 Yet it was good of you to s in my
Col 1:12 who has qualified you to s in the
1Th 2: 8 we were delighted to s with you not
2Th 2:14 that you might s in the glory of our
1Ti 5:22 and do not s in the sins of others.
6:18 and to be generous and willing to s.
2Ti 2: 6 first to receive a s of the crops.
Heb 3: 1 who s in the heavenly calling,
3:14 We have come to s in Christ if we
12:10 good, that we may s in his holiness.
13:16 to do good and to s with others,
1Pe 5: 1 will s in the glory to be revealed:
Jude : 3 to you about the salvation we s,
Rev 18: 4 so that you will not s in her sins,
22:19 God will take away from him his s in

Shared (Share)
2Sa 12: 3 It s his food, drank from his cup
1Ki 2:26 and s all my father's hardships."
Ps 41: 9 whom I trusted, he who s my bread,
Pr 5:17 alone, never to be s with strangers.
Lk 1:58 her great mercy, and they s her joy.
Ac 1:17 our number and s in this ministry."
4:32 own, but they s everything they had.
Ro 15:27 For if the Gentiles have s in the
Php 4:15 not one church s with me in the
Heb 2:14 he too s in their humanity so that
6: 4 gift, who have s in the Holy Spirit,
Rev 18: 9 s her luxury see the smoke of her

Sharers (Share)
Eph 3: 6 and s together in the promise in

Shares (Share)
2Sa 19:43 "We have ten s in the king;
Pr 22: 9 for he s his food with the poor.
Jn 13:18 'He who s my bread has lifted up his
19:23 dividing them into four s, one for
2Jn :11 Anyone who welcomes him s in his

Sharezer
2Ki 19:37 his sons Adrammelech and **S** cut him
Isa 37:38 his sons Adrammelech and **S** cut him
Zec 7: 2 The people of Bethel had sent **S** and

Sharing (Share)
Job 31:17 not s it with the fatherless—
1Co 9:10 so in the hope of s in the harvest.
2Co 8: 4 of s in this service to the saints.
9:13 s with them and with everyone else.
Php 3:10 fellowship of s in his sufferings,
Phm : 6 you may be active in s your faith,

Sharon (Sharonite)
1. Large plain on Mediterranean coast of Palestine, stretching from the foot of Mount Carmel to Joppa. Rich in pasture (1Ch 27:29; Isa 65:10) and known for its fruitfulness and beauty (SS 2:1; Isa 33:9; 35:2). Peter enjoyed a fruitful ministry here (Ac 9:35).
2. District to the east of River Jordan; occupied by tribe of Gad; boasted good pasture land (1Ch 5:16).

1Ch 5:16 all the pasture-lands of **S** as far
27:29 in charge of the herds grazing in **S**.
SS 2: 1 I am a rose of **S**, a lily of the
Isa 33: 9 **S** is like the Arabah, and Bashan and
35: 2 the splendour of Carmel and **S**; they
65:10 **S** will become a pasture for flocks,
Ac 9:35 All those who lived in Lydda and **S**

Sharonite (Sharon)
1Ch 27:29 Shitrai the **S** was in charge of the

Sharp (Sharpen, Sharpened, Sharpening, Sharpens, Sharper)
Ps 45: 5 Let your s arrows pierce the hearts
57: 4 arrows, whose tongues are s swords.
120: 4 punish you with a warrior's s arrows,
140: 3 their tongues as s as a serpent's
Pr 5: 4 s as a double-edged sword.
25:18 Like a club or a sword or a s arrow
Isa 5:28 Their arrows are s, all their bows
41:15 new and s, with many teeth.
Eze 5: 1 "Now, son of man, take a s sword and
28:24 who are painful briers and s thorns.
Ac 15: 2 Paul and Barnabas into s dispute
15:39 They had such a s disagreement that
Rev 1:16 mouth came a s double-edged sword.
2:12 who has the s, double-edged sword.
14:14 his head and a s sickle in his hand.
14:17 heaven, and he too had a s sickle.
14:18 voice to him who had the s sickle,
14:18 "Take your s sickle and gather the
19:15 Out of his mouth comes a s sword

Sharpen (Sharp)
Dt 32:41 I s my flashing sword and my hand
Ps 7:12 not relent, he will s his sword;
64: 3 They s their tongues like swords and
Jer 51:11 "**S** the arrows, take up the shields!

Sharpened (Sharp)
1Sa 13:20 mattocks, axes and sickles s.
Ps 52: 2 it is like a s razor, you who
Isa 49: 2 He made my mouth like a s sword, in
Eze 21: 9 'A sword, a sword, s and polished
21:10 s for the slaughter, polished to
21:11 with the hand; it is s and polished,

Sharpening (Sharp)
1Sa 13:21 for s ploughshares and mattocks,
13:21 and a third of a shekel for s forks

Sharpens (Sharp)
Pr 27:17 iron s iron, so one man s another.

Sharper (Sharp)
Heb 4:12 S than any double-edged sword, it

Sharuhen
Jos 19: 6 Beth Lebaoth and S—thirteen towns

Shashai
Ezr 10:40 Macnadebai, S, Sharai,

Shashak
1Ch 8:14 Ahio, S, Jeremoth,
8:25 and Penuel were the sons of S.

Shatter (Shattered, Shattering, Shatters)
Isa 30:31 The voice of the LORD will s Assyria;
Jer 49:37 I will s Elam before their foes,
51:20 with you I s nations, with you I
51:21 with you I s horse and rider, with
51:21 with you I s chariot and driver,
51:22 with you I s man and woman, with you
51:22 with you I s old man and youth,
51:22 with you I s young man and maiden,
51:23 with you I s shepherd and flock,
51:23 with you I s farmer and oxen, with
51:23 you I s governors and officials.
Eze 32:12 They will s the pride of Egypt, and
Hag 2:22 and s the power of the foreign

Shattered (Shatter)
Ex 15: 6 Your right hand, O LORD, s the enemy.
Jdg 5:26 head, she s and pierced his temple.
10: 8 who that year s and crushed them.
1Sa 2:10 those who oppose the LORD will be s.
1Ki 19:11 and s the rocks before the LORD,
Job 16:12 All was well with me, but he s me;
17:11 My days have passed, my plans are s,
Ps 48: 7 ships of Tarshish s by an east wind.
105:33 and s the trees of their country.
Ecc 12: 6 the pitcher is s at the spring,
Isa 7: 8 Ephraim will be too s to be a people.
8: 9 the war cry, you nations, and be s!
8: 9 be s! Prepare for battle, and be s!
9: 4 you have s the yoke that burdens
21: 9 of its gods lie s on the ground!'
30:14 s so mercilessly that among its
Jer 25:34 fall and be s like fine pottery.
48: 1 stronghold will be disgraced and s.
48:20 Moab is disgraced, for she is s.
48:39 "How s she is! How they wail!
50:23 How broken and s is the hammer of
Eze 27:34 Now you are s by the sea in the
Na 1: 6 the rocks are s before him.

Shattering (Shatter)
Da 8: 7 the ram and s his two horns.

Shatters (Shatter)
Job 34:24 Without enquiry he s the mighty and
Ps 46: 9 he breaks the bow and s the spear,

Shaul (Shaul's, Shaulite)
Ge 36:37 Samlah died, S from Rehoboth on the
36:38 S died, Baal-Hanan son of Acbor
46:10 and S the son of a Canaanite woman.
Ex 6:15 and S the son of a Canaanite woman.
Nu 26:13 through S, the Shaulite clan.
1Ch 1:48 Samlah died, S from Rehoboth on the
1:49 S died, Baal-Hanan son of Acbor
4:24 Nemuel, Jamin, Jarib, Zerah and S;
6:24 son, Uzziah his son and S his son.

Shaul's (Shaul)
1Ch 4:25 Shallum was S son, Mibsam his son

Shaulite (Shaul)
Nu 26:13 through Shaul, the S clan.

Shave (Shaved)
Lev 14: 8 s off all his hair and bathe with
14: 9 On the seventh day he must s off all
14: 9 he must s his head, his beard, his
Lev 21: 5 "'Priests must not s their heads or
21: 5 or s off the edges of their beards
Nu 6: 9 he must s his head on the day of his
6:18 s off the hair that he dedicated.
8: 7 then make them s their whole bodies
Dt 14: 1 Do not cut yourselves or s the front
21:12 make her s her head, trim her
Jdg 16:19 she called a man to s off the seven
Isa 7:20 king of Assyria—to s your head
Jer 16: 6 cut himself or s his head for them.
47: 5 Gaza will s her head in mourning;
Eze 5: 1 razor to s your head and your beard.
27:31 They will s their heads because of
44:20 "'They must not s their heads or
Am 8:10 you wear sackcloth and s your heads.
Mic 1:16 S your heads in mourning for the

Shaved (Shave)
Ge 41:14 When he had s and changed his
Lev 13:33 he must be s except for the diseased
Nu 6:19 "'After the Nazirite has s off the
Jdg 16:17 If my head were s, my strength would
16:22 to grow again after it had been s.
2Sa 10: 4 Hanun seized David's men, s off half
1Ch 19: 4 Hanun seized David's men, s them,
Job 1:20 up and tore his robe and s his head.
Isa 15: 2 head is s and every beard cut off.
Jer 2:16 have s the crown of your head.
41: 5 eighty men who had s off their
48:37 Every head is s and every beard cut
Eze 7:18 shame and their heads will be s.
Ac 21:24 so that they can have their heads s.
1Co 11: 5 is just as though her head were s.
11: 6 or s off, she should cover her head.

Shaveh
Ge 14:17 to meet him in the Valley of S

Shaveh Kiriathaim
Ge 14: 5 the Zuzites in Ham, the Emites in S

Shavsha
1Ch 18:16 were priests; S was secretary;

Shawl (Shawls)
Ru 3:15 "Bring me the s you are wearing

Shawls (Shawl)
Isa 3:23 the linen garments and tiaras and s.

Sheaf (Sheaves)
Ge 37: 7 my s rose and stood upright,
Lev 23:10 a s of the first grain you harvest.
23:11 He is to wave the s before the LORD
23:12 On the day you wave the s, you must
23:15 the day you brought the s of the
Dt 24:19 you overlook a s, do not go back to

Sheal
Ezr 10:29 Adaiah, Jashub, S and Jeremoth.

Shealtiel
1Ch 3:17 Jehoiachin the captive: S his son,
Ezr 3: 2 Zerubbabel son of S and his
3: 8 Zerubbabel son of S, Jeshua son of
5: 2 Zerubbabel son of S and Jeshua son
Ne 12: 1 returned with Zerubbabel son of S
Hag 1: 1 Haggai to Zerubbabel son of S,
1:12 Zerubbabel son of S, Joshua son of
1:14 the spirit of Zerubbabel son of S,
2: 2 "Speak to Zerubbabel son of S,
2:23 you, my servant Zerubbabel son of S,
Mt 1:12 Jeconiah was the father of S,
1:12 S the father of Zerubbabel,
Lk 3:27 the son of S, the son of Neri,

Shear (Sheared, Shearer, Shearers, Shearing, Sheep-shearers, Sheep-shearing, Shorn)
Ge 31:19 Laban had gone to s his sheep,
38:13 his way to Timnah to s his sheep,"
Dt 15:19 not s the firstborn of your sheep.

Sheared (Shear)
Isa 22:25 it will be s off and will fall,

Shearer (Shear)
Ac 8:32 and as a lamb before the s is silent,

Shearers (Shear)
1Sa 25:11 meat I have slaughtered for my s,
2Sa 13:24 said, "Your servant has had s come.
Isa 53: 7 as a sheep before her s is silent,

Sheariah
1Ch 8:38 Ishmael, S, Obadiah and Hanan.
9:44 Ishmael, S, Obadiah and Hanan.

Shearing (Shear)
Ge 38:12 to the men who were s his sheep, and
Dt 18: 4 first wool from the s of your sheep,
1Sa 25: 2 sheep, which he was s in Carmel.
25: 4 he heard that Nabal was s sheep.

Shear-Jashub
Isa 7: 3 "Go out, you and your son S, to meet

Sheath (Sheathed)
2Sa 20: 8 was a belt with a dagger in its s.
20: 8 forward, it dropped out of its s.
1Ch 21:27 he put his sword back into its s.

Sheathed (Sheath)
Ps 68:13 the wings of my dove are s with

Sheaves (Sheaf)
Ge 37: 7 We were binding s of corn out in the
37: 7 while your s gathered round mine and
Ru 2: 7 among the s behind the harvesters.
2:15 among the s, don't embarrass her.
Job 5:26 vigour, like s gathered in season.
24:10 carry the s, but still go hungry.
Ps 126: 6 songs of joy, carrying s with him.
Mic 4:12 them like s to the threshing-floor.
Zec 12: 6 like a flaming torch among s.

Sheba
1. City in territory of Judah, assigned to tribe of Simeon (Jos 19:2). **2.** Kingdom of the Sabeans, location uncertain but probably in south-west Arabia. Its queen travelled to Jerusalem to test Solomon's reputed wisdom (1Ki 10:1–13; 2Ch 9:1–12; Mt 12:42; Lk 11:31). Renowned for the quality of its goods (Job 6:19; Ps 72:10, 15; Isa 60:6; Jer 6:20; Eze 27:22–23).

Ge 10: 7 The sons of Raamah: S and Dedan.
10:28 Obal, Abimael, S,
25: 3 Jokshan was the father of S and
Jos 19: 2 included: Beersheba (or S), Moladah
2Sa 20: 1 Now a troublemaker named S son of
20: 2 David to follow S son of Bicri.
20: 6 "Now S son of Bicri will do us more
20: 7 Jerusalem to pursue S son of Bicri.
20:10 Abishai pursued S son of Bicri.
20:13 with Joab to pursue S son of Bicri.
20:14 S passed through all the tribes of
20:15 and besieged S in Abel Beth Maacah.
20:21 A man named S son of Bicri, from
20:22 cut off the head of S son of Bicri
1Ki 10: 1 the queen of S heard about the fame
10: 4 the queen of S saw all the wisdom of
10:10 the queen of S gave to King Solomon.
10:13 King Solomon gave the queen of S all
1Ch 1: 9 The sons of Raamah: S and Dedan.
1:22 Obal, Abimael, S,
1:32 The sons of Jokshan: S and Dedan.
5:13 were: Michael, Meshullam, S, Jorai,
2Ch 9: 1 the queen of S heard of Solomon's
9: 3 the queen of S saw the wisdom of
9: 9 the queen of S gave to King Solomon.
9:12 King Solomon gave the queen of S all
Job 6:19 merchants of S look in hope.
Ps 72:10 S and Seba will present him gifts.
72:15 May gold from S be given to him.
Isa 60: 6 And all from S will come, bearing
Jer 6:20 What do I care about incense from S

Eze 27:22 "'The merchants of **S** and Raamah
27:23 **S**, Asshur and Kilmad traded with you.
38:13 **S** and Dedan and the merchants of

Shebaniah

1Ch 15:24 **S**, Joshaphat, Nethanel, Amasai,
Ne 9: 4 Bani, Kadmiel, **S**, Bunni, Sherebiah,
9: 5 Hashabneiah, Sherebiah, Hodiah, **S**
10: 4 Hattush, **S**, Malluch,
10:10 their associates: **S**, Hodiah, Kelita,
10:12 Zaccur, Sherebiah, **S**,

Shebat

Zec 1: 7 the month of **S**, in the second year

Sheber

1Ch 2:48 was the mother of **S** and Tirhanah.

Shebna

2Ki 18:18 **S** the secretary, and Joah son of
18:26 Eliakim son of Hilkiah, and **S** and
18:37 **S** the secretary and Joah son of
19: 2 **S** the secretary and the leading
Isa 22:15 **S**, who is in charge of the palace:
36: 3 **S** the secretary, and Joah son of
36:11 Eliakim, **S** and Joah said to the
36:22 **S** the secretary, and Joah son of
37: 2 **S** the secretary, and the leading

She-camel (Camel)

Jer 2:23 a swift **s** running here and there,

Shecaniah (Shecaniah's)

1Ch 3:21 of Arnan, of Obadiah and of **S**.
3:22 The descendants of **S**: Shemaiah and
24:11 the ninth to Jeshua, the tenth to **S**,
2Ch 31:15 Jeshua, Shemaiah, Amariah and **S**
Ezr 8: 3 of the descendants of **S**;
8: 5 of Zattu, **S** son of Jahaziel, and
10: 2 **S** son of Jehiel, one of the
Ne 3:29 Next to him, Shemaiah son of **S**, the
6:18 he was son-in-law to **S** son of Arah
12: 3 **S**, Rehum, Meremoth,

Shecaniah's (Shecaniah)

Ne 12:14 Malluch's, Jonathan; of **S**, Joseph;

Shechem (Shechem's, Shechemite)

1. Son of Hamor, a ruling Hivite (Ge 34:2). Raped Jacob's daughter, Dinah, and asked to marry her (Ge 34:2–12). Shechemites treacherously killed by Simeon and Levi in revenge (Ge 34:13–31). **2.** Town in hill country of Ephraim, between Mounts Ebal and Gerizim. Where the LORD promised Abram the land (Ge 12:6–7). Abram erected an altar, so it became an important sanctuary (Ge 12:7). Jacob built an altar here to mark his return from Paddan Aram (Ge 33:18–20), and later buried foreign gods under its great oak tree (Ge 35:4). Jacob gave it to Joseph for his burial site (Jos 24:32; Ac 7:16). Allotted to tribe of Ephraim; became a city of refuge (Jos 20:7; 1Ch 6:67). Here Joshua drew up the covenant and laws (Jos 24). Home of Abimelech (Jdg 8:31; 9:1) who was crowned here after executing the sons of Jerub-Baal (Jdg 9:1–6). Jotham chastised its people for this (Jdg 9:7–20), and so they revolted against Abimelech (Jdg 9:22–57). Rehoboam was crowned here (1Ki 12:1; 2Ch 10:1). Jeroboam made it the capital of the northern kingdom (1Ki 12:25). After the exile, inhabited by Samaritans, and became Sychar, where Jesus met a woman at Jacob's well (Jn 4:5–40).

Ge 12: 6 of the great tree of Moreh at **S**.
33:18 he arrived safely at the city of **S**
33:19 the father of **S**, the plot of ground
34: 2 **S** son of Hamor the Hivite, the ruler
34: 4 **S** said to his father Hamor, "Get me
34: 7 because **S** had done a disgraceful
34: 8 "My son **S** has his heart set on your
34:11 **S** said to Dinah's father and
34:13 spoke to **S** and his father Hamor.
34:18 seemed good to Hamor and his son **S**.
34:20 Hamor and his son **S** went to the gate
34:24 agreed with Hamor and his son **S**,
34:26 They put Hamor and his son **S** to the
35: 4 Jacob buried them under the oak at **S**.
37:12 graze their father's flocks near **S**,
37:13 are grazing the flocks near **S**.
37:14 When Joseph arrived at **S**,
Nu 26:31 through **S**, the Shechemite clan;
Jos 17: 2 Helek, Asriel, **S**, Hepher and Shemida.
17: 7 from Asher to Micmethath east of **S**.
20: 7 **S** in the hill country of Ephraim,
21:21 they were given **S** (a city of refuge
24: 1 all the tribes of Israel at **S**.
24:25 and there at **S** he drew up for them
24:32 were buried at **S** in the tract of
24:32 the sons of Hamor, the father of **S**.
Jdg 8:31 His concubine, who lived in **S**, also
9: 1 went to his mother's brothers in **S**
9: 2 "Ask all the citizens of **S**, 'Which
9: 3 all this to the citizens of **S**,
9: 6 all the citizens of **S** and Beth Millo
9: 6 pillar in **S** to crown Abimelech king.
9: 7 "Listen to me, citizens of **S**, so
9:18 king over the citizens of **S** because
9:20 citizens of **S** and Beth Millo, and
9:20 citizens of **S** and Beth Millo, and
9:23 Abimelech and the citizens of **S**,
9:24 Abimelech and on the citizens of **S**,
9:25 citizens of **S** set men on the
9:26 Ebed moved with his brothers into **S**,
9:28 "Who is Abimelech, and who is **S**,
9:31 his brothers have come to **S** and are
9:34 positions near **S** in four companies.
9:39 Gaal led out the citizens of **S** and
9:41 Gaal and his brothers out of **S**.
9:42 The next day the people of **S** went
9:46 the citizens in the tower of **S** went
9:49 So all the people in the tower of **S**,
9:57 God also made the men of **S** pay for
21:19 road that goes from Bethel to **S**,
1Ki 12: 1 Rehoboam went to **S**, for all the
12:25 Jeroboam fortified **S** in the hill
1Ch 6:67 **S** (a city of refuge), and Gezer,
7:19 The sons of Shemida were: Ahian, **S**,
7:28 and **S** and its villages all the way
2Ch 10: 1 Rehoboam went to **S**, for all the
Ps 60: 6 "In triumph I will parcel out **S** and
108: 7 "In triumph I will parcel out **S** and
Jer 41: 5 and cut themselves came from **S**,
Hos 6: 9 they murder on the road to **S**,
Ac 7:16 Their bodies were brought back to **S**
7:16 at **S** for a certain sum of money.

Shechem's (Shechem)

Ge 34: 6 **S** father Hamor went out to talk with
34:26 took Dinah from **S** house and left.
Jdg 9:28 Serve the man of Hamor, **S** father!

Shechemite (Shechem)

Nu 26:31 through Shechem, the **S** clan;

Shed (Shedding, Sheds)

Ge 9: 6 by man shall his blood be **s**; for in
37:22 "Don't **s** any blood. Throw him into
Lev 17: 4 he has **s** blood and must be cut off
Nu 35:33 the land on which blood has been **s**,
35:33 by the blood of the one who **s** it.
Dt 19:10 blood will not be **s** in your land,
21: 7 "Our hands did not **s** this blood, nor
2Sa 16: 8 you **s** in the household of Saul,
1Ki 2:31 of the innocent blood that Joab **s**.
2:32 will repay him for the blood he **s**,
2Ki 9: 7 the LORD's servants **s** by Jezebel.
21:16 Moreover, Manasseh also **s** so much
1Ch 22: 8 'You have **s** much blood and have
22: 8 because you have **s** much blood on the
28: 3 you are a warrior and have **s** blood.'
Ps 97:11 Light is **s** upon the righteous and
106:38 They **s** innocent blood, the blood of
Pr 1:16 into sin, they are swift to **s** blood.
6:17 tongue, hands that **s** innocent blood,
Isa 26:21 The earth will disclose the blood **s**
59: 7 they are swift to **s** innocent blood.
Jer 7: 6 not **s** innocent blood in this place,
22: 3 not **s** innocent blood in this place.
Lam 4:13 who **s** within her the blood of the
Eze 16:38 who commit adultery and who **s** blood;
21:32 your blood will be **s** in your land,
22: 4 because of the blood you have **s**
22: 6 in you uses his power to **s** blood.
22:12 In you men accept bribes to **s** blood;
22:13 the blood you have **s** in your midst.
22:27 they **s** blood and kill people to make
23:45 who commit adultery and **s** blood,
24: 7 "'For the blood she **s** is in her
24:16 not lament or weep or **s** any tears.
33:25 and look to your idols and **s** blood,
36:18 they had **s** blood in the land
Joel 3:19 in whose land they **s** innocent blood.
Mic 7: 2 All men lie in wait to **s** blood;
Hab 2: 8 For you have **s** man's blood; you have
2:17 For you have **s** man's blood; you have
Mt 23:35 blood that has been **s** on earth,
Lk 11:50 **s** since the beginning of the world,
Ac 22:20 blood of your martyr Stephen was **s**,
Ro 3:15 "Their feet are swift to **s** blood;
Col 1:20 through his blood, **s** on the cross.
Rev 16: 6 for they have **s** the blood of your

Shedding (Shed)

Dt 19:13 Israel the guilt of **s** innocent blood,
21: 9 the guilt of **s** innocent blood,
Jdg 9:24 the **s** of their blood, might be
1Ki 2: 5 He killed them, **s** their blood in
2Ki 24: 4 including the **s** of innocent blood.
Job 15:33 like an olive tree **s** its blossoms.
Jer 22:17 on **s** innocent blood and on
Eze 22: 3 doom by **s** blood in her midst
22: 9 are slanderous men bent on **s** blood;
Mt 23:30 in **s** the blood of the prophets.'
Heb 9:22 without the **s** of blood there is no
12: 4 to the point of **s** your blood.

Shedeur

Nu 1: 5 you: from Reuben, Elizur son of **S**;
2:10 people of Reuben is Elizur son of **S**.
7:30 On the fourth day Elizur son of **S**,
7:35 was the offering of Elizur son of **S**.
10:18 Elizur son of **S** was in command.

Sheds (Shed)

Ge 9: 6 "Whoever **s** the blood of man, by man
Eze 18:10 he has a violent son, who **s** blood

Sheep (Sheep's, Sheep-shearers, Sheep-shearing, Sheepskins)

Ge 12:16 and Abram acquired **s** and cattle,
20:14 Abimelech brought **s** and cattle and
21:27 Abraham brought **s** and cattle and
24:35 He has given him **s** and cattle,
29: 2 with three flocks of **s** lying near it
29: 3 the well's mouth and water the **s**.
29: 6 his daughter Rachel with the **s**."
29: 7 Water the **s** and take them back to
29: 8 Then we will water the **s**."
29: 9 Rachel came with her father's **s**,
29:10 his mother's brother, and Laban's **s**,
29:10 the well and watered his uncle's **s**.
30:32 them every speckled or spotted **s**,
31:19 Laban had gone to shear his **s**,
31:38 Your **s** and goats have not miscarried,
32: 5 I have cattle and donkeys, **s** and
38:12 to the men who were shearing his **s**,
38:13 his way to Timnah to shear his **s**,"
47:17 their **s** and goats, their cattle and
Ex 9: 3 and on your cattle and **s** and goats.
12: 5 take them from the **s** or the goats.
20:24 your **s** and goats and your cattle.
22: 1 "If a man steals an ox or a **s** and
22: 1 for the ox and four **s** for the **s**.
22: 4 whether ox or donkey or **s**—he must
22: 9 a donkey, a **s**, a garment, or any
22:10 "If a man gives a donkey, an ox, a **s**
22:30 same with your cattle and your **s**.
Lev 1:10 from either the **s** or the goats, he
7:23 of the fat of cattle, **s** or goats.
22:19 **s** or goats in order that it may be
22:23 or a **s** that is deformed or stunted,
22:28 Do not slaughter a cow or a **s** and
27:26 an ox or a **s**, it is the LORD's.
Nu 18:17 an ox, a **s** or a goat; they are holy.
22:40 Balak sacrificed cattle and **s**, and
27:17 not be like **s** without a shepherd."

Nu 31:28 cattle, donkeys, s or goats.
31:30 donkeys, s, goats or other animals.
31:32 the soldiers took was 675,000 s,
31:36 fought in the battle was: 337,500 s,
31:43 the community's half—was 337,500 s,
Dt 14: 4 may eat: the ox, the s, the goat,
14: 5 the antelope and the mountain s.
14:26 s, wine or other fermented drink, or
15:19 not shear the firstborn of your s.
17: 1 s that has any defect or flaw in it,
18: 3 people who sacrifice a bull or a s:
18: 4 wool from the shearing of your s,
22: 1 If you see your brother's ox or s
28:31 Your s will be given to your enemies,
Jos 6:21 and old, cattle, s and donkeys.
7:24 his cattle, donkeys and s, his tent
Jdg 6: 4 neither s nor cattle nor donkeys.
1Sa 14:32 taking s, cattle and calves, they
14:34 of you bring me your cattle and s,
15: 3 cattle and s, camels and donkeys.
15: 9 and the best of the s and cattle,
15:14 "What then is this bleating of s in
15:15 they spared the best of the s and
15:21 The soldiers took s and cattle from
16:11 answered, "but he is tending the s.
16:19 your son David, who is with the s."
17:15 to tend his father's s at Bethlehem.
17:28 you leave those few s in the desert?
17:34 has been keeping his father's s.
17:34 and carried off a s from the flock,
17:35 it and rescued the s from its mouth.
22:19 and its cattle, donkeys and s.
24: 3 He came to the s pens along the way;
25: 2 s, which he was shearing in Carmel.
25: 4 he heard that Nabal was shearing s.
25:16 we were herding our s near them.
25:18 two skins of wine, five dressed s,
27: 9 but took s and cattle, donkeys and
2Sa 12: 2 a very large number of s and cattle,
12: 4 one of his own s or cattle to prepare
17:29 honey and curds, s, and cheese from
24:17 These are but s. What have they done?
1Ki 1: 9 Adonijah then sacrificed s, cattle
1:19 fattened calves, and s, and has
1:25 of cattle, fattened calves, and s.
4:23 cattle and a hundred s and goats,
8: 5 sacrificing so many s and cattle
8:63 and twenty thousand s and goats.
22:17 the hills like s without a shepherd,
2Ki 3: 4 Now Mesha king of Moab raised s, and
1Ch 5:21 two hundred and fifty thousand s
12:40 wine, oil, cattle and s, for there was
21:17 These are but s. What have they done?
2Ch 5: 6 sacrificing so many s and cattle
7: 5 and twenty thousand s and goats.
14:15 droves of s and goats and camels.
15:11 seven thousand s and goats from the
18: 2 Ahab slaughtered many s and cattle
18:16 the hills like s without a shepherd,
29:33 and three thousand s and goats.
30:24 s and goats for the assembly,
30:24 bulls and ten thousand s and goats.
35: 7 there a total of thirty thousand s
Ne 3: 1 went to work and rebuilt the S Gate.
3:32 the S Gate the goldsmiths and
5:18 Each day one ox, six choice s and
12:39 the Hundred, as far as the S Gate.
Job 1: 3 he owned seven thousand s, three
1:16 burned up the s and the servants,
30: 1 disdained to put with my s dogs.
31:20 him with the fleece from my s,
42:12 He had fourteen thousand s, six
Ps 44:11 You gave us up to be devoured like s
44:22 considered as s to be slaughtered.
49:14 Like s they are destined for the
74: 1 against the s of your pasture?
78:52 led them like s through the desert.
78:70 and took him from the s pens;
78:71 from tending the s he brought him to
79:13 your people, the s of your pasture,
100: 3 his people, the s of his pasture.
119:176 I have strayed like a lost s.
144:13 Our s will increase by thousands, by
SS 1: 7 and where you rest your s at midday.
1: 8 follow the tracks of the s and graze
4: 2 Your teeth are like a flock of s
SS 6: 6 Your teeth are like a flock of s
Isa 5:17 s will graze as in their own pasture;
7:25 are turned loose and where s run.
13:14 Like a hunted gazelle, like s
22:13 of cattle and killing of s,
43:23 You have not brought me s for burnt
53: 6 We all, like s, have gone astray,
53: 7 and as a s before her shearers is
Jer 12: 3 Drag them off like s to be butchered!
13:20 to you, the s of which you boasted?
23: 1 scattering the s of my pasture!"
50: 6 "My people have been lost s;
Eze 25: 5 Ammon into a resting place for s.
34: 6 My s wandered over all the mountains
34:11 search for my s and look after them.
34:12 them, so will I look after my s.
34:15 I myself will tend my s and make
34:17 judge between one s and another,
34:20 between the fat s and the lean s.
34:21 butting all the weak s with your
34:22 judge between one s and another.
34:31 You my s, the s of my pasture, are
36:37 make their people as numerous as s,
45:15 Also one s is to be taken from every
Hos 12:12 and to pay for her he tended s.
Joel 1:18 even the flocks of s are suffering.
Mic 2:12 I will bring them together like s in
5: 8 like a young lion among flocks of s,
Hab 3:17 though there are no s in the pen and
Zep 2: 6 be a place for shepherds and s pens.
Zec 10: 2 Therefore the people wander like s
11:16 will eat the meat of the choice s,
13: 7 "Strike the shepherd, and the s will
Mt 9:36 helpless, like s without a shepherd.
10: 6 Go rather to the lost s of Israel.
10:16 I am sending you out like s among
12:11 "If any of you has a s and it falls
12:12 more valuable is a man than a s!
15:24 sent only to the lost s of Israel."
18:12 If a man owns a hundred s, and one
18:13 he is happier about that one s than
25:32 separates the s from the goats.
25:33 He will put the s on his right and
26:31 s of the flock will be scattered.'
Mk 6:34 they were like s without a shepherd.
14:27 and the s will be scattered.'
Lk 15: 4 "Suppose one of you has a hundred s
15: 4 after the lost s until he finds it?
15: 6 with me; I have found my lost s.'
17: 7 ploughing or looking after the s.
Jn 2:14 men selling cattle, s and doves, and
2:15 the temple area, both s and cattle;
5: 2 is in Jerusalem near the S Gate
10: 1 the man who does not enter the s pen
10: 2 the gate is the shepherd of his s.
10: 3 him, and the s listen to his voice.
10: 3 He calls his own s by name and
10: 4 and his s follow him because they
10: 7 the truth, I am the gate for the s.
10: 8 but the s did not listen to them.
10:11 lays down his life for the s.
10:12 is not the shepherd who owns the s.
10:12 he abandons the s and runs away.
10:13 hand and cares nothing for the s.
10:14 I know my s and my s know me—
10:15 I lay down my life for the s.
10:16 other s that are not of this s pen.
10:26 believe because you are not my s.
10:27 My s listen to my voice; I know them,
21:16 Jesus said, "Take care of my s."
21:17 Jesus said, "Feed my s.
Ac 8:32 "He was led like a s to the
Ro 8:36 considered as s to be slaughtered."
Heb 13:20 Jesus, that great Shepherd of the s,
1Pe 2:25 For you were like s going astray,
Rev 18:13 cattle and s; horses and carriages;

Sheep's (Sheep)
Mt 7:15 They come to you in s clothing, but

Sheep-shearers (Shear)
2Sa 13:23 when Absalom's s were at Baal Hazor

Sheep-shearing (Shear)
1Sa 25: 7 "'Now I hear that it is s time.

Sheepskins (Sheep, Skins)
Heb 11:37 They went about in s and goatskins,

Sheer
Isa 28:19 of this message will bring s terror.

Sheerah
1Ch 7:24 His daughter was S, who built Lower

Sheet (Sheets)
Isa 25: 7 the s that covers all nations;
Ac 10:11 something like a large s being let
10:16 the s was taken back to heaven.
11: 5 I saw something like a large s being

Sheets (Sheet)
Ex 39: 3 They hammered out thin s of gold and
Nu 16:38 Hammer the censers into s to overlay

Shehariah
1Ch 8:26 Shamsherai, S, Athaliah,

Shekel (Shekels)
Ex 30:13 already counted is to give a half s,
30:13 according to the sanctuary s, which
30:13 half s is an offering to the LORD.
30:15 are not to give more than a half s
30:24 all according to the sanctuary s
38:24 according to the sanctuary s.
38:25 according to the sanctuary s—
38:26 that is, half a s, according to the
38:26 according to the sanctuary s, from
Lev 5:15 according to the sanctuary s.
27: 3 according to the sanctuary s;
27:25 sanctuary s, twenty gerahs to the s.
Nu 3:47 according to the sanctuary s, which
3:50 according to the sanctuary s.
7:13 both according to the sanctuary s,
7:19 both according to the sanctuary s,
7:25 both according to the sanctuary s,
7:31 both according to the sanctuary s,
7:37 both according to the sanctuary s,
7:43 both according to the sanctuary s,
7:49 both according to the sanctuary s,
7:55 both according to the sanctuary s,
7:61 both according to the sanctuary s,
7:67 both according to the sanctuary s,
7:73 both according to the sanctuary s,
7:79 both according to the sanctuary s,
7:85 according to the sanctuary s.
7:86 each, according to the sanctuary s.
18:16 according to the sanctuary s, which
1Sa 9: 8 "I have a quarter of a s of silver.
13:21 The price was two thirds of a s for
13:21 and a third of a s for sharpening
2Ki 7: 1 a seah of flour will sell for a s
7: 1 two seahs of barley for a s at the
7:16 So a seah of flour sold for a s, and
7:16 sold for a s, as the LORD had said.
7:18 a seah of flour will sell for a s
7:18 two seahs of barley for a s at the
Ne 10:32 give a third of a s each year for
Eze 45:12 The s is to consist of twenty gerahs.

Shekels (Shekel)
Ge 20:16 your brother a thousand s of silver.
23:15 is worth four hundred s of silver,
23:16 Hittites: four hundred s of silver,
24:22 two gold bracelets weighing ten s.
37:28 sold him for twenty s of silver to
45:22 three hundred s of silver and five
Ex 21:32 owner must pay thirty s of silver
30:23 fine spices: 500 s of liquid myrrh,
30:23 half as much (that is, 250 s) of
30:23 cinnamon, 250 s of fragrant cane,
30:24 500 s of cassia—all according to
38:24 29 talents and 730 s, according to
38:25 census was 100 talents and 1,775 s,
38:28 They used the 1,775 s to make the
38:29 was 70 talents and 2,400 s.
Lev 27: 3 and sixty at fifty s of silver,
27: 4 a female, set her value at thirty s.
27: 5 twenty s and of a female at ten s.

Lev 27: 6 set the value of a male at five **s** of
27: 6 of a female at three **s** of silver.
27: 7 fifteen **s** and of a female at ten **s**.
27:16 fifty **s** of silver to a homer of
Nu 3:47 collect five **s** for each one,
3:50 collected silver weighing 1,365 **s**,
7:13 weighing a hundred and thirty **s**,
7:13 sprinkling bowl weighing seventy **s**,
7:14 one gold dish weighing ten **s**, filled
7:19 weighing a hundred and thirty **s**,
7:19 sprinkling bowl weighing seventy **s**,
7:20 one gold dish weighing ten **s**, filled
7:25 weighing a hundred and thirty **s**,
7:25 sprinkling bowl weighing seventy **s**,
7:26 one gold dish weighing ten **s**, filled
7:31 weighing a hundred and thirty **s**,
7:31 sprinkling bowl weighing seventy **s**,
7:32 one gold dish weighing ten **s**, filled
7:37 weighing a hundred and thirty **s**,
7:37 sprinkling bowl weighing seventy **s**,
7:38 one gold dish weighing ten **s**, filled
7:43 weighing a hundred and thirty **s**,
7:43 sprinkling bowl weighing seventy **s**,
7:44 one gold dish weighing ten **s**, filled
7:49 weighing a hundred and thirty **s**,
7:49 sprinkling bowl weighing seventy **s**,
7:50 one gold dish weighing ten **s**, filled
7:55 weighing a hundred and thirty **s**,
7:55 sprinkling bowl weighing seventy **s**,
7:56 one gold dish weighing ten **s**, filled
7:61 weighing a hundred and thirty **s**,
7:61 sprinkling bowl weighing seventy **s**,
7:62 one gold dish weighing ten **s**, filled
7:67 weighing a hundred and thirty **s**,
7:67 sprinkling bowl weighing seventy **s**,
7:68 one gold dish weighing ten **s**, filled
7:73 weighing a hundred and thirty **s**,
7:73 sprinkling bowl weighing seventy **s**,
7:74 one gold dish weighing ten **s**, filled
7:79 weighing a hundred and thirty **s**,
7:79 sprinkling bowl weighing seventy **s**,
7:80 one gold dish weighing ten **s**, filled
7:85 weighed a hundred and thirty **s**,
7:85 and each sprinkling bowl seventy **s**.
7:85 two thousand four hundred **s**,
7:86 with incense weighed ten **s** each,
7:86 weighed a hundred and twenty **s**.
18:16 price set at five **s** of silver,
31:52 a gift to the LORD weighed 16,750 **s**.
Dt 22:19 They shall fine him a hundred **s** of
22:29 the girl's father fifty **s** of silver.
Jos 7:21 Babylonia, two hundred **s** of silver
7:21 a wedge of gold weighing fifty **s**,
Jdg 8:26 for came to seventeen hundred **s**,
9: 4 They gave him seventy **s** of silver
16: 5 you eleven hundred **s** of silver."
17: 2 "The eleven hundred **s** of silver that
17: 3 he returned the eleven hundred **s** of
17: 4 and she took two hundred **s** of silver
17:10 and I'll give you ten **s** of silver a
1Sa 17: 5 of bronze weighing five thousand **s**;
17: 7 iron point weighed six hundred **s**.
2Sa 14:26 two hundred **s** by the royal standard.
18:11 ten **s** of silver and a warrior's belt
18:12 "Even if a thousand **s** were weighed
21:16 spearhead weighed three hundred **s**
24:24 and paid fifty **s** of silver for them.
1Ki 10:29 Egypt for six hundred **s** of silver,
2Ki 5: 5 six thousand **s** of gold and ten sets
6:25 head sold for eighty **s** of silver,
6:25 of a cab of seed pods for five **s**.
15:20 had to contribute fifty **s** of silver
1Ch 21:25 David paid Araunah six hundred **s** of
2Ch 1:17 Egypt for six hundred **s** of silver,
3: 9 The gold nails weighed fifty **s**.
Ne 5:15 took forty **s** of silver from them in
SS 8:11 its fruit a thousand **s** of silver.
8:12 thousand **s** are for you, O Solomon,
Isa 7:23 vines worth a thousand silver **s**,
Jer 32: 9 out for him seventeen **s** of silver.
Eze 4:10 Weigh out twenty **s** of food to eat
45:12 Twenty **s** plus twenty-five **s** plus
45:12 plus fifteen **s** equal one mina.
Hos 3: 2 I bought her for fifteen **s** of silver

Shelah (Shelanite)

Ge 10:24 Arphaxad was the father of **S**,
10:24 and **S** the father of Eber.
11:12 35 years, he became the father of **S**.
11:13 after he became the father of **S**,
11:14 **S** had lived 30 years, he became the
11:15 **S** lived 403 years and had other
38: 5 still another son and named him **S**.
38:11 house until my son **S** grows up.
38:14 For she saw that, though **S** had now
38:26 I wouldn't give her to my son **S**.
46:12 The sons of Judah: Er, Onan, **S**,
Nu 26:20 Judah by their clans were: through **S**,
1Ch 1:18 Arphaxad was the father of **S**,
1:18 and **S** the father of Eber.
1:24 Shem, Arphaxad, **S**,
2: 3 The sons of Judah: Er, Onan and **S**.
4:21 The sons of **S** son of Judah: Er the
Ne 11: 5 son of Zechariah, a descendant of **S**.
Lk 3:35 Peleg, the son of Eber, the son of **S**,

Shelanite (Shelah)

Nu 26:20 through Shelah, the **S** clan;

Shelemiah

1Ch 26:14 The lot for the East Gate fell to **S**.
Ezr 10:39 **S**, Nathan, Adaiah,
10:41 Azarel, **S**, Shemariah,
Ne 3:30 Next to him, Hananiah son of **S**, and
13:13 I put **S** the priest, Zadok the scribe,
Jer 36:14 the son of **S**, the son of Cushi, to
36:26 son of Azriel and **S** son of Abdeel
37: 3 however, sent Jehucal son of **S** with
37:13 whose name was Irijah son of **S**, the
38: 1 Jehucal son of **S**, and Pashhur son of

Sheleph

Ge 10:26 Joktan was the father of Almodad, **S**,
1Ch 1:20 Joktan was the father of Almodad, **S**,

Shelesh

1Ch 7:35 Helem: Zophah, Imna, **S** and Amal.

Shelomi

Nu 34:27 Ahihud son of **S**, the leader from the

Shelomith

Lev 24:11 **S**, the daughter of Dibri the Danite.)
1Ch 3:19 **S** was their sister.
23:18 The sons of Izhar: **S** was the first.
26:25 son, Zicri his son and **S** his son.
26:26 **S** and his relatives were in charge
26:28 in the care of **S** and his relatives.
2Ch 11:20 bore him Abijah, Attai, Ziza and **S**.
Ezr 8:10 of Bani, **S** son of Josiphiah,

Shelomoth

1Ch 23: 9 The sons of Shimei: **S**, Haziel and
24:22 From the Izharites: **S**;
24:22 from the sons of **S**: Jahath.

Shelter (Sheltered, Shelters)

Ex 9:19 have in the field to a place of **s**,
Dt 32:38 up to help you! Let them give you **s**!
Ru 2: 7 except for a short rest in the **s**."
1Ch 28:18 **s** the ark of the covenant of the
Job 24: 8 and hug the rocks for lack of **s**.
Ps 27: 5 he will hide me in the **s** of his
31:20 In the **s** of your presence you hide
55: 8 I would hurry to my place of **s**, far
61: 4 take refuge in the **s** of your wings.
91: 1 dwells in the **s** of the Most High
Ecc 7:12 Wisdom is a **s** as money is a **s**, but
Isa 1: 8 The Daughter of Zion is left like a **s**
4: 6 will be a **s** and shade from the heat
16: 4 be their **s** from the destroyer.
25: 4 a **s** from the storm and a shade from
32: 2 Each man will be like a **s** from the
58: 7 provide the poor wanderer with **s**—
Jer 4:20 are destroyed, my **s** in a moment.
10:20 to pitch my tent or to set up my **s**.
Eze 17:23 find **s** in the shade of its branches.
Da 4:12 it the beasts of the field found **s**,
Da 4:21 giving **s** to the beasts of the field
Jnh 4: 5 There he made himself a **s**, sat in

Sheltered (Shelter)

Zep 2: 3 be **s** on the day of the LORD'S anger.

Shelters (Shelter)

Ge 33:17 and made **s** for his livestock.
Jdg 6: 2 the Israelites prepared **s** for
Jer 49:29 their **s** will be carried off with all
Mt 17: 4 If you wish, I will put up three **s**
Mk 9: 5 Let us put up three **s**—one for you,
Lk 9:33 Let us put up three **s**—one for you,

Shelumiel

Nu 1: 6 from Simeon, **S** son of Zurishaddai;
2:12 of Simeon is **S** son of Zurishaddai.
7:36 the fifth day **S** son of Zurishaddai,
7:41 offering of **S** son of Zurishaddai.
10:19 **S** son of Zurishaddai was over the

Shem

Son of Noah (Ge 5:32; 6:10; 1Ch 1:4). Saved in ark (Ge 7:13; 9:18–19). Blessed by Noah (Ge 9:26); descendants (Ge 10:21–31); ancestor of Abraham (Ge 11:10–32).

Ge 5:32 the father of **S**, Ham and Japheth.
6:10 Noah had three sons: **S**, Ham and
7:13 Noah and his sons, **S**, Ham and
9:18 of the ark were **S**, Ham and Japheth.
9:23 **S** and Japheth took a garment and
9:26 "Blessed be the LORD, the God of **S**!
9:26 May Canaan be the slave of **S**.
9:27 may Japheth live in the tents of **S**,
10: 1 This is the account of **S**, Ham and
10:21 Sons were also born to **S**, whose
10:21 **S** was the ancestor of all the sons
10:22 The sons of **S**: Elam, Asshur,
10:31 These are the sons of **S** by their
11:10 This is the account of **S**. Two years
11:10 when **S** was 100 years old, he became
11:11 **S** lived 500 years and had other sons
1Ch 1: 4 The sons of Noah: **S**, Ham and Japheth.
1:17 The sons of **S**: Elam, Asshur,
1:24 **S**, Arphaxad, Shelah,
Lk 3:36 the son of Arphaxad, the son of **S**,

Shema

Jos 15:26 Amam, **S**, Moladah,
1Ch 2:43 Hebron: Korah, Tappuah, Rekem and **S**.
2:44 **S** was the father of Raham, and Raham
5: 8 Bela son of Azaz, the son of **S**, the
8:13 Beriah and **S**, who were heads of
Ne 8: 4 **S**, Anaiah, Uriah, Hilkiah and

Shemaah

1Ch 12: 3 Joash the sons of **S** the Gibeathite;

Shemaiah (Shemaiah's)

1Ki 12:22 this word of God came to **S** the man
1Ch 3:22 The descendants of Shecaniah: **S** and
4:37 the son of Shimri, the son of **S**.
5: 4 The descendants of Joel: **S** his son,
9:14 Of the Levites: **S** son of Hasshub,
9:16 Obadiah son of **S**, the son of Galal,
15: 8 from the descendants of Elizaphan, **S**
15:11 **S**, Eliel and Amminadab the Levites.
24: 6 The scribe **S** son of Nethanel, a
26: 4 also had sons: **S** the firstborn,
26: 6 His son **S** also had sons, who were
26: 7 The sons of **S**: Othni, Rephael, Obed
2Ch 11: 2 this word of the LORD came to **S** the
12: 5 the prophet **S** came to Rehoboam and
12: 7 this word of the LORD came to **S**:
12:15 in the records of **S** the prophet
17: 8 With them were certain Levites—**S**,
29:14 of Jeduthun, **S** and Uzziel.
31:15 Eden, Miniamin, Jeshua, **S**, Amariah
35: 9 Also Conaniah along with **S** and
Ezr 8:13 Jeuel and **S**, and with them 60 men;
8:16 I summoned Eliezer, Ariel, **S**,
10:21 Elijah, **S**, Jehiel and Uzziah.
10:31 Ishijah, Malkijah, **S**, Shimeon,

Ne 3:29 Next to him, **S** son of Shecaniah, the
6:10 to the house of **S** son of Delaiah,
10: 8 Maaziah, Bilgai and **S**. These were
11:15 From the Levites: **S** son of Hasshub,
12: 6 **S**, Joiarib, Jedaiah,
12:34 Judah, Benjamin, **S**, Jeremiah,
12:35 the son of **S**, the son of Mattaniah,
12:36 his associates—**S**, Azarel, Milalai,
12:42 also Maaseiah, **S**, Eleazar, Uzzi,
Jer 26:20 (Now Uriah son of **S** from Kiriath
29:24 Tell **S** the Nehelamite,
29:31 'This is what the LORD says about **S**
29:31 Because **S** has prophesied to you,
29:32 **S** the Nehelamite and his descendants.
36:12 Delaiah son of **S**, Elnathan son of

Shemaiah's (Shemaiah)
Ne 12:18 of **S**, Jehonathan;

Shemariah
1Ch 12: 5 Eluzai, Jerimoth, Bealiah, **S** and
2Ch 11:19 She bore him sons: Jeush, **S** and
Ezr 10:32 Benjamin, Malluch and **S**.
10:41 Azarel, Shelemiah, **S**,

Shemeber
Ge 14: 2 king of Admah, **S** king of Zeboiim,

Shemed
1Ch 8:12 The sons of Elpaal: Eber, Misham, **S**

Shemer
1Ki 16:24 He bought the hill of Samaria from **S**
16:24 calling it Samaria, after **S**, the
1Ch 6:46 Amzi, the son of Bani, the son of **S**,

Shemida (Shemidaite)
Nu 26:32 through **S**, the Shemidaite clan;
Jos 17: 2 Helek, Asriel, Shechem, Hepher and **S**.
1Ch 7:19 The sons of **S** were: Ahian, Shechem,

Shemidaite (Shemida)
Nu 26:32 through Shemida, the **S** clan;

Sheminith
1Ch 15:21 harps, directing according to **s**.
Ps 6: T According to **s**. A psalm of David.
12: T According to **s**. A psalm of David.

Shemiramoth
1Ch 15:18 Jaaziel, **S**, Jehiel, Unni, Eliab,
15:20 Zechariah, Aziel, **S**, Jehiel, Unni,
16: 5 Zechariah second, then Jeiel, **S**,
2Ch 17: 8 Nethaniah, Zebadiah, Asahel, **S**,

Shemuel
Nu 34:20 **S** son of Ammihud, from the tribe of

Shen
1Sa 7:12 and set it up between Mizpah and **S**.

Shenazzar
1Ch 3:18 Malkiram, Pedaiah, **S**, Jekamiah,

Shepham
Nu 34:10 run a line from Hazar Enan to **S**.
34:11 The boundary will go down from **S** to

Shephatiah
2Sa 3: 4 the fifth, **S** the son of Abital;
1Ch 3: 3 the fifth, **S** the son of Abital;
9: 8 of Micri; and Meshullam son of **S**,
12: 5 Shemariah and **S** the Haruphite;
27:16 the Simeonites: **S** son of Maacah;
2Ch 21: 2 Zechariah, Azariahu, Michael and **S**.
Ezr 2: 4 of **S** 372
2:57 **S**, Hattil, Pokereth-Hazzebaim and
8: 8 of the descendants of **S**, Zebadiah
Ne 7: 9 of **S** 372
7:59 **S**, Hattil, Pokereth-Hazzebaim and
11: 4 the son of Amariah, the son of **S**,
Jer 38: 1 **S** son of Mattan, Gedaliah son of

Shepher
Nu 33:23 Kehelathah and camped at Mount **S**.
33:24 They left Mount **S** and camped at

Shepherd (*Good shepherd*, Shepherd's, Shepherded, Shepherdess, Shepherds)
Ge 48:15 been my **s** all my life to this day,
49:24 of the **S**, the Rock of Israel,
Nu 27:17 will not be like sheep without a **s**."
1Sa 17:20 David left the flock with a **s**,
21: 7 was Doeg the Edomite, Saul's head **s**.
2Sa 5: 2 'You shall **s** my people Israel, and
7: 7 I commanded to **s** my people Israel,
1Ki 22:17 on the hills like sheep without a **s**,
1Ch 11: 2 'You will **s** my people Israel, and
17: 6 whom I commanded to **s** my people,
2Ch 18:16 on the hills like sheep without a **s**,
Ps 23: 1 The LORD is my **s**, I shall not be in
28: 9 be their **s** and carry them for ever.
78:71 him to be the **s** of his people Jacob,
80: 1 Hear us, O **S** of Israel, you who lead
Ecc 12:11 embedded nails—given by one **S**.
Isa 13:14 like sheep without a **s**, each will
13:20 no **s** will rest his flocks there.
40:11 He tends his flock like a **s**:
44:28 who says of Cyrus, 'He is my **s** and
61: 5 Aliens will **s** your flocks;
63:11 with the **s** of his flock? Where is he
Jer 17:16 I have not run away from being your **s**
31:10 will watch over his flock like a **s**.'
43:12 As a **s** wraps his garment round him,
49:19 And what **s** can stand against me?"
50:44 And what **s** can stand against me?"
51:23 with you I shatter **s** and flock, with
Eze 34: 5 scattered because there was no **s**,
34: 8 because my flock lacks a **s** and so
34:12 a **s** looks after his scattered flock
34:16 I will **s** the flock with justice.
34:23 I will place over them one **s**, my
34:23 he will tend them and be their **s**.
37:24 them, and they will all have one **s**.
Am 3:12 "As a **s** saves from the lion's mouth
7:14 but I was a **s**, and I also took care
Mic 5: 4 He will stand and **s** his flock in the
7:14 **S** your people with your staff, the
Zec 10: 2 sheep oppressed for lack of a **s**.
11: 9 said, "I will not be your **s**. Let the
11:15 again the equipment of a foolish **s**.
11:16 For I am going to raise up a **s** over
11:17 "Woe to the worthless **s**, who deserts
13: 7 "Awake, O sword, against my **s**,
13: 7 "Strike the **s**, and the sheep will be
Mt 2: 6 will be the **s** of my people Israel.'"
9:36 helpless, like sheep without a **s**.
25:32 **s** separates the sheep from the goats.
26:31 'I will strike the **s**, and the sheep
Mk 6:34 they were like sheep without a **s**.
14:27 "I will strike the **s**, and the
Jn 10: 2 by the gate is the **s** of his sheep.
10:12 The hired hand is not the **s** who owns
10:16 there shall be one flock and one **s**.
Heb 13:20 Jesus, that great **S** of the sheep,
1Pe 2:25 to the **S** and Overseer of your souls.
5: 4 the Chief **S** appears, you will
Rev 7:17 of the throne will be their **s**;

Shepherd's (Shepherd)
Lev 27:32 that passes under the **s** rod—will
1Sa 17:40 put them in the pouch of his **s** bag
Isa 38:12 Like a **s** tent my house has been

Shepherded (Shepherd)
Ps 78:72 David **s** them with integrity of heart;

Shepherdess (Shepherd)
Ge 29: 9 her father's sheep, for she was a **s**.

Shepherds (Shepherd)
Ge 29: 3 the **s** would roll the stone away from
29: 4 Jacob asked the **s**, "My brothers,
46:32 The men are **s**; they tend livestock,
46:34 **s** are detestable to the Egyptians."
47: 3 "Your servants are **s**," they replied
Ex 2:17 Some **s** came along and drove them
2:19 "An Egyptian rescued us from the **s**.
Nu 14:33 Your children will be **s** here for
1Sa 25: 7 When your **s** were with us, we did not
2Ki 10:12 At Beth Eked of the **S**,
SS 1: 8 young goats by the tents of the **s**.
Isa 31: 4 and though a whole band of **s** is
56:11 They are **s** who lack understanding;
Jer 3:15 I will give you **s** after my own heart,
6: 3 **S** with their flocks will come
10:21 The **s** are senseless and do not
12:10 Many **s** will ruin my vineyard and
22:22 The wind will drive all your **s** away,
23: 1 "Woe to the **s** who are destroying and
23: 2 the God of Israel, says to the **s** who
23: 4 I will place **s** over them who will
25:34 Weep and wail, you **s**; roll in the
25:35 The **s** will have nowhere to flee, the
25:36 Hear the cry of the **s**, the wailing
33:12 pastures for **s** to rest their flocks.
50: 6 their **s** have led them astray and
Eze 34: 2 "Son of man, prophesy against the **s**
34: 2 Woe to the **s** of Israel who only take
34: 2 Should not **s** take care of the flock?
34: 7 "'Therefore, you **s**, hear the word
34: 8 and because my **s** did not search for
34: 9 therefore, O **s**, hear the word of the
34:10 I am against the **s** and will hold
34:10 the **s** can no longer feed themselves.
Am 1: 1 of Amos, one of the **s** of Tekoa
1: 2 the pastures of the **s** dry up,
Mic 5: 5 seven **s**, even eight leaders of men.
Na 3:18 O king of Assyria, your **s** slumber;
Zep 2: 6 be a place for **s** and sheep pens.
Zec 10: 3 "My anger burns against the **s**, and I
11: 3 Listen to the wail of the **s**: their
11: 5 Their own **s** do not spare them.
11: 8 In one month I got rid of the three **s**
Lk 2: 8 there were **s** living out in the
2:15 the **s** said to one another, "Let's go
2:18 amazed at what the **s** said to them.
2:20 The **s** returned, glorifying and
Ac 20:28 Be **s** of the church of God, which he
1Pe 5: 2 Be **s** of God's flock that is under
Jude :12 qualm—**s** who feed only themselves.

Shepho
Ge 36:23 Alvan, Manahath, Ebal, **S** and Onam.
1Ch 1:40 Alvan, Manahath, Ebal, **S** and Onam.

Shephuphan
1Ch 8: 5 Gera, **S** and Huram.

Sherebiah (Sherebiah's)
Ezr 8:18 they brought us **S**, a capable man,
8:24 together with **S**, Hashabiah and ten
Ne 8: 7 The Levites—Jeshua, Bani, **S**, Jamin,
9: 4 Bani, Kadmiel, Shebaniah, Bunni, **S**,
9: 5 Kadmiel, Bani, Hashabneiah, **S**,
10:12 Zaccur, **S**, Shebaniah,
12: 8 Binnui, Kadmiel, **S**, Judah, and also
12:24 **S**, Jeshua son of Kadmiel, and their

Sherebiah's (Sherebiah)
Ezr 8:18 and **S** sons and brothers, 18 men;

Sheresh
1Ch 7:16 His brother was named **S**, and his

She's
Jdg 14: 3 **S** the right one for me."

Sheshach
Jer 25:26 the king of **S** will drink it too.
51:41 "How **S** will be captured, the boast

Sheshai
Nu 13:22 where Ahiman, **S** and Talmai, the
Jos 15:14 drove out the three Anakites—**S**,
Jdg 1:10 and defeated **S**, Ahiman and Talmai.

Sheshan
1Ch 2:31 Ishi, who was the father of **S**.
2:31 **S** was the father of Ahlai.
2:34 **S** had no sons—only daughters.
2:35 **S** gave his daughter in marriage to

Sheshbazzar
Ezr 1: 8 them out to **S** the prince of Judah.
1:11 **S** brought all these along when the
5:14 **S**, whom he had appointed governor,
5:16 this **S** came and laid the foundations

Sheth
Nu 24:17 the skulls of all the sons of **S**.

Shethar
Est 1:14 were closest to the king—Carshena, **S**

Shethar-Bozenai
Ezr 5: 3 and **S** and their associates went to
5: 6 and **S** and their associates, the
6: 6 and **S** and you, their fellow
6:13 and **S** and their associates carried

Sheva
2Sa 20:25 **S** was secretary; Zadok and Abiathar
1Ch 2:49 **S** the father of Macbenah and Gibea.

Shibah
Ge 26:33 He called it **S**, and to this day the

Shibboleth
Jdg 12: 6 they said, "All right, say '**S**'."

Shield (Shield-bearer, Shielded, Shielding, Shields)
Ge 15: 1 I am your **s**, your very great reward."
Ex 40: 3 it and **s** the ark with the curtain.
Dt 13: 8 Do not spare him or **s** him.
33:29 He is your **s** and helper and your
Jdg 5: 8 and not a **s** or spear was seen among
2Sa 1:21 For there the **s** of the mighty was
1:21 **s** of Saul—no longer rubbed with oil.
22: 3 my **s** and the horn of my salvation.
22:31 a **s** for all who take refuge in him.
22:36 You give me your **s** of victory;
1Ki 10:16 bekas of gold went into each **s**.
10:17 with three minas of gold in each **s**.
2Ki 19:32 He will not come before it with **s**
1Ch 5:18 men who could handle **s** and sword,
12: 8 and able to handle the **s** and spear.
12:24 men of Judah, carrying **s** and spear—
2Ch 9:15 of hammered gold went into each **s**.
9:16 hundred bekas of gold in each **s**.
25: 5 able to handle the spear and **s**.
Job 15:26 against him with a thick, strong **s**.
Ps 3: 3 you are a **s** around me, O LORD;
5:12 them with your favour as with a **s**.
7:10 My **s** is God Most High, who saves the
18: 2 He is my **s** and the horn of my
18:30 a **s** for all who take refuge in him.
18:35 You give me your **s** of victory, and
28: 7 The LORD is my strength and my **s**;
33:20 the LORD; he is our help and our **s**.
35: 2 Take up **s** and buckler; arise and
59:11 do not kill them, O Lord our **s**, or
84: 9 Look upon our **s**, O God; look with
84:11 For the LORD God is a sun and **s**;
89:18 Indeed, our **s** belongs to the LORD,
91: 4 will be your **s** and rampart.
115: 9 the LORD—he is their help and **s**.
115:10 the LORD—he is their help and **s**.
115:11 the LORD—he is their help and **s**.
119:114 You are my refuge and my **s**; I have
144: 2 my **s**, in whom I take refuge, who
Pr 2: 7 **s** to those whose walk is blameless,
30: 5 a **s** to those who take refuge in him.
Isa 22: 6 and horses; Kir uncovers the **s**.
31: 5 the LORD Almighty will **s** Jerusalem;
31: 5 he will **s** it and deliver it,
37:33 He will not come before it with **s**
Na 2: 5 the protective **s** is put in place.
Zec 9:15 the LORD Almighty will **s** them. They
Zec 12: 8 On that day the LORD will **s** those
Eph 6:16 take up the **s** of faith, with which

Shield-bearer (Shield)
1Sa 17: 7 His **s** went ahead of him.
17:41 the Philistine, with his **s** in front

Shielded (Shield)
Ex 40:21 and **s** the ark of the Testimony,
Dt 32:10 He **s** him and cared for him;
1Pe 1: 5 who through faith are **s** by God's

Shielding (Shield)
Ex 39:34 hides of sea cows and the **s** curtain;
40:21 hung the **s** curtain and shielded the
Nu 4: 5 take down the **s** curtain and cover

Shields (Shield)
Ex 35:12 cover and the curtain that **s** it;
Dt 33:12 for he **s** him all day long, and the
2Sa 8: 7 David took the gold **s** that belonged
1Ki 10:16 King Solomon made two hundred large **s**
10:17 He also made three hundred small **s**
14:26 all the gold **s** Solomon had made.
14:27 King Rehoboam made bronze **s** to
14:28 the guards bore the **s**, and
2Ki 11:10 **s** that had belonged to King David
1Ch 12:34 37,000 men carrying **s** and spears;
18: 7 David took the gold **s** carried by the
2Ch 9:15 King Solomon made two hundred large **s**
9:16 He also made three hundred small **s**
11:12 He put **s** and spears in all the
12: 9 the gold **s** that Solomon had made.
12:10 King Rehoboam made bronze **s** to
12:11 bearing the **s**, and afterwards they
14: 8 equipped with large **s** and with
14: 8 armed with small **s** and with bows.
17:17 200,000 men armed with bows and **s**;
23: 9 the large and small **s** that had
26:14 Uzziah provided **s**, spears, helmets,
32: 5 made large numbers of weapons and **s**.
32:27 **s** and all kinds of valuables.
Ne 4:16 with spears, **s**, bows and armour.
Job 41:15 His back has rows of **s** tightly
Ps 46: 9 the spear, he burns the **s** with fire.
76: 3 **s** and the swords, the weapons of war.
140: 7 who **s** my head in the day of battle—
SS 4: 4 on it hang a thousand **s**,
4: 4 all of them **s** of warriors.
Isa 21: 5 Get up, you officers, oil the **s**!
Jer 46: 3 "Prepare your **s**, both large and
46: 9 men of Cush and Put who carry **s**,
51:11 "Sharpen the arrows, take up the **s**!
Eze 23:24 large and small **s** and with helmets.
26: 8 walls and raise his **s** against you.
27:10 They hung their **s** and helmets on
27:11 They hung their **s** around your walls;
38: 4 great horde with large and small **s**,
38: 5 with them, all with **s** and helmets,
39: 9 burn them up—the small and large **s**,
Na 2: 3 The **s** of his soldiers are red;

Shifting
Jas 1:17 who does not change like **s** shadows.

Shiftless
Pr 19:15 sleep, and the **s** man goes hungry.

Shifts
1Ki 5:14 He sent them off to Lebanon in **s** of

Shiggaion
Ps 7: T A **s** of David, which he sang to the

Shigionoth
Hab 3: 1 of Habbakkuk the prophet. On **s**.

Shihor
Jos 13: 3 from the **S** River on the east of
1Ch 13: 5 from the **S** River in Egypt to Lebo
Isa 23: 3 waters came the grain of the **S**;
Jer 2:18 to Egypt to drink water from the **S**?

Shihor Libnath
Jos 19:26 the boundary touched Carmel and **S**.

Shikkeron
Jos 15:11 turned towards **S**, passed along to

Shilhi
1Ki 22:42 name was Azubah daughter of **S**.
2Ch 20:31 name was Azubah daughter of **S**.

Shilhim
Jos 15:32 Lebaoth, **S**, Ain and Rimmon—a total

Shillem (Shillemite)
Ge 46:24 Naphtali: Jahziel, Guni, Jezer and **S**.
Nu 26:49 through **S**, the Shillemite clan.
1Ch 7:13 Jahziel, Guni, Jezer and **S**—the

Shillemite (Shillem)
Nu 26:49 through Shillem, the **S** clan.

Shiloah
Isa 8: 6 the gently flowing waters of **S**

Shiloh
City in hill country of Ephraim, north of Bethel, and east of the road that connects Bethel to Shechem (Jdg 21:19). The Tent of Meeting was first set up here; it became an important sanctuary (Jos 18:1, 8–10; 19:51; 21:2; 22:9, 12; Jdg 18:31; 21:12, 19, 21). Samuel grew up here under Eli's care (1Sa 1:24–28; 3:19–21). The ark of the covenant was kept here until it was captured by the Philistines (1Sa 4:1–22), and it never returned (2Sa 6:2–17). Base for Ahijah the prophet (1Ki 14:2, 4), who pronounced the downfall of Jeroboam (1Ki 14:7–16). Laid in ruins during the time of Jeremiah's ministry (Jer 7:12–14; 26:6, 9).

Jos 18: 1 of the Israelites gathered at **S**
18: 8 at **S** in the presence of the LORD."
18: 9 returned to Joshua in the camp at **S**.
18:10 Joshua then cast lots for them in **S**
19:51 assigned by lot at **S** in the presence
21: 2 at **S** in Canaan and said to them,
22: 9 left the Israelites at **S** in Canaan
22:12 gathered at **S** to go to war against
Jdg 18:31 the time the house of God was in **S**.
21:12 them to the camp at **S** in Canaan.
21:19 annual festival of the LORD in **S**,
21:21 When the girls of **S** come out to
21:21 seize a wife from the girls of **S**
1Sa 1: 3 sacrifice to the LORD Almighty at **S**,
1: 9 and drinking in **S**, Hannah stood up.
1:24 him to the house of the LORD at **S**.
2:14 all the Israelites who came to **S**.
3:21 The LORD continued to appear at **S**,
4: 3 ark of the LORD's covenant from **S**,
4: 4 the people sent men to **S**, and they
4:12 from the battle line and went to **S**,
14: 3 son of Eli, the LORD's priest in **S**.
1Ki 2:27 spoken at **S** about the house of Eli.
11:29 and Ahijah the prophet of **S** met him
14: 2 Then go to **S**. Ahijah the prophet is
14: 4 and went to Ahijah's house in **S**.
Ps 78:60 He abandoned the tabernacle of **S**,
Jer 7:12 "'Go now to the place in **S** where I
7:14 Therefore, what I did to **S** I will
26: 6 I will make this house like **S** and
26: 9 name that this house will be like **S**
41: 5 from Shechem, **S** and Samaria,

Shilonite (Shilonites)
1Ki 12:15 son of Nebat through Ahijah the **S**.
15:29 through his servant Ahijah the **S**—
2Ch 9:29 in the prophecy of Ahijah the **S** and
10:15 son of Nebat through Ahijah the **S**.

Shilonites (Shilonite)
1Ch 9: 5 Of the **S**: Asaiah the firstborn and

Shilshah
1Ch 7:37 Bezer, Hod, Shamma, **S**, Ithran and

Shimea

1Ch 2:13 son was Abinadab, the third **S**,
6:30 **S** his son, Haggiah his son and
6:39 Asaph son of Berekiah, the son of **S**,
20: 7 he taunted Israel, Jonathan son of **S**,

Shimeah

2Sa 13: 3 Jonadab son of **S**, David's brother.
13:32 Jonadab son of **S**, David's brother,
21:21 he taunted Israel, Jonathan son of **S**,
1Ch 8:32 Mikloth, who was the father of **S**.

Shimeam

1Ch 9:38 Mikloth was the father of **S**.

Shimeath (Shimeathites)

2Ki 12:21 Jozabad son of **S** and Jehozabad son
2Ch 24:26 son of **S** an Ammonite woman, and

Shimeathites (Shimeath)

1Ch 2:55 the Tirathites, **S** and Sucathites.

Shimei (Shimei's, Shimeites)

Ex 6:17 Gershon, by clans, were Libni and **S**.
Nu 3:18 the Gershonite clans: Libni and **S**.
2Sa 16: 5 His name was **S** son of Gera, and he
16: 7 he cursed, **S** said, "Get out, get out
16:13 while **S** was going along the hillside
19:16 **S** son of Gera, the Benjamite from
19:18 When **S** son of Gera crossed the
19:21 "Shouldn't **S** be put to death for
19:23 the king said to **S**, "You shall not
1Ki 1: 8 Nathan the prophet, **S** and Rei and
2: 8 "And remember, you have with you **S**
2:36 the king sent for **S** and said to him,
2:38 **S** answered the king, "What you say
2:38 And **S** stayed in Jerusalem for a
2:39 **S** was told, "Your slaves are in Gath.
2:40 So **S** went away and brought the
2:41 Solomon was told that **S** had gone
2:42 the king summoned **S** and said to him,
2:44 The king also said to **S**, "You know
2:46 and struck **S** down and killed him.
4:18 **S** son of Ela—in Benjamin;
1Ch 3:19 The sons of Pedaiah: Zerubbabel and **S**
4:26 son, Zaccur his son and **S** his son.
4:27 **S** had sixteen sons and six daughters,
5: 4 his son, Gog his son, **S** his son,
6:17 of the sons of Gershon: Libni and **S**.
6:29 his son, **S** his son, Uzzah his son,
6:42 the son of Zimmah, the son of **S**,
8:21 and Shimrath were the sons of **S**.
23: 7 to the Gershonites: Ladan and **S**.
23: 9 The sons of **S**: Shelomoth, Haziel and
23:10 the sons of **S**: Jahath, Ziza, Jeush
23:10 were the sons of **S**—four in all.
25: 3 Zeri, Jeshaiah, **S**, Hashabiah and
25:17 the tenth to **S**, his sons and
27:27 **S** the Ramathite was in charge of the
2Ch 29:14 descendants of Heman, Jehiel and **S**;
31:12 and his brother **S** was next in rank.
31:13 under Conaniah and **S** his brother,
Ezr 10:23 Among the Levites: Jozabad, **S**,
10:33 Eliphelet, Jeremai, Manasseh and **S**.
10:38 From the descendants of Binnui: **S**,
Est 2: 5 Jair, the son of **S**, the son of Kish,
Zec 12:13 the clan of **S** and their wives,

Shimei's (Shimei)

1Ki 2:39 three years later, two of **S** slaves

Shimeites (Shimei)

Nu 3:21 the clans of the Libnites and **S**;

Shimeon

Ezr 10:31 Ishijah, Malkijah, Shemaiah, **S**,

Shimmering

Isa 18: 4 like **s** heat in the sunshine, like a

Shimon

1Ch 4:20 The sons of **S**: Amnon, Rinnah,

Shimrath

1Ch 8:21 Adaiah, Beraiah and **S** were the sons

Shimri

1Ch 4:37 the son of **S**, the son of Shemaiah.
11:45 Jediael son of **S**, his brother Joha
26:10 the Merarite had sons: **S** the first
2Ch 29:13 from the descendants of Elizaphan, **S**

Shimrith

2Ch 24:26 Jehozabad, son of **S** a Moabite woman.

Shimron (Shimronite)

Ge 46:13 Issachar: Tola, Puah, Jashub and **S**.
Nu 26:24 through **S**, the Shimronite clan.
Jos 11: 1 Madon, to the kings of **S** and Acshaph,
19:15 Included were Kattath, Nahalal, **S**,
1Ch 7: 1 Puah, Jashub and **S**—four in all.

Shimron Meron

Jos 12:20 the king of **S** one

Shimronite (Shimron)

Nu 26:24 through Shimron, the **S** clan.

Shimshai

Ezr 4: 8 and **S** the secretary wrote a letter
4: 9 officer and **S** the secretary,
4:17 **S** the secretary and the rest of
4:23 **S** the secretary and their associates,

Shinab

Ge 14: 2 king of Gomorrah, **S** king of Admah,

Shinar

Ge 10:10 Erech, Akkad and Calneh, in **S**.
11: 2 a plain in **S** and settled there.
14: 1 At this time Amraphel king of **S**,
14: 9 Amraphel king of **S** and Arioch king

Shine (Shines, Shining, Shone)

Nu 6:25 the LORD make his face **s** upon you
Ne 9:19 to **s** on the way they were to take.
Job 3: 4 about it; may no light **s** upon it.
9: 7 speaks to the sun and it does not **s**;
22:28 done, and light will **s** on your ways.
33:30 that the light of life may **s** on him.
Ps 4: 6 the light of your face **s** upon us,
31:16 Let your face **s** on your servant;
37: 6 He will make your righteousness **s**
67: 1 and make his face **s** upon us,
80: 1 between the cherubim, **s** forth
80: 3 make your face **s** upon us, that we
80: 7 make your face **s** upon us, that we
80:19 make your face **s** upon us, that we
94: 1 avenges, O God who avenges, **s** forth.
104:15 oil to make his face **s**, and bread
118:27 and he has made his light **s** upon us.
119:135 Make your face **s** upon your servant
139:12 the night will **s** like the day,
Isa 30:26 The moon will **s** like the sun, and
60: 1 "Arise, **s**, for your light has come,
60:19 the brightness of the moon **s** on you,
Jer 31:35 he who appoints the sun to **s** by day,
31:35 who decrees the moon and stars to **s**
Da 12: 3 Those who are wise will **s** like the
Joel 2:10 darkened, and the stars no longer **s**.
3:15 darkened, and the stars no longer **s**.
Mt 5:16 In the same way, let your light **s**
13:43 the righteous will **s** like the sun in
Lk 1:79 to **s** on those living in darkness and
2Co 4: 6 "Let light **s** out of darkness,"
4: 6 made his light **s** in our hearts to
Eph 5:14 the dead, and Christ will **s** on you."
Php 2:15 you **s** like stars in the universe
Rev 18:23 The light of a lamp will never **s** in
21:23 need the sun or the moon to **s** on it,

Shines (Shine)

Ps 50: 2 perfect in beauty, God **s** forth.
Pr 13: 9 light of the righteous **s** brightly,
Isa 62: 1 till her righteousness **s** out like
Lk 11:36 when the light of a lamp **s** on you."
Jn 1: 5 The light **s** in the darkness, but the

Shining (Shine)

2Ki 3:22 morning, the sun was **s** on the water.
Ps 68:13 silver, its feathers with **s** gold."
148: 3 moon, praise him, all you **s** stars.
Pr 4:18 **s** ever brighter till the full light
Eze 28: 7 wisdom and pierce your **s** splendour.
32: 8 All the **s** lights in the heavens I
Lk 23:45 for the sun stopped **s**. And the
Ac 10:30 a man in **s** clothes stood before
2Pe 1:19 as to a light **s** in a dark place,
1Jn 2: 8 and the true light is already **s**.
Rev 1:16 the sun **s** in all its brilliance.
15: 6 They were dressed in clean, **s** linen

Shion

Jos 19:19 Hapharaim, **S**, Anaharath,

Ship (Ship's, Ships, Shipwreck, Shipwrecked, Shipwrights)

Pr 30:19 the way of a **s** on the high seas, and
Isa 2:16 for every trading **s** and every
33:21 them, no mighty **s** will sail them.
Jnh 1: 3 he found a **s** bound for that port.
1: 4 that the **s** threatened to break up.
1: 5 cargo into the sea to lighten the **s**.
Ac 20:13 We went on ahead to the **s** and sailed
20:38 Then they accompanied him to the **s**.
21: 2 We found a **s** crossing over to
21: 3 where our **s** was to unload its cargo.
21: 6 we went aboard the **s**, and they
27: 2 We boarded a **s** from Adramyttium
27: 6 an Alexandrian **s** sailing for Italy
27:10 and bring great loss to **s** and cargo,
27:11 the pilot and of the owner of the **s**.
27:15 The **s** was caught by the storm and
27:17 passed ropes under the **s** itself to
27:17 and let the **s** be driven along.
27:22 only the **s** will be destroyed.
27:30 In an attempt to escape from the **s**,
27:31 with the **s**, you cannot be saved."
27:38 lightened the **s** by throwing the
27:39 to run the **s** aground if they could.
27:41 the **s** struck a sand-bar and ran
27:44 on planks or on pieces of the **s**.
28:11 a **s** that had wintered in the island.
28:11 It was an Alexandrian **s** with the
Rev 18:17 and all who travel by **s**, the sailors,

Ship's (Ship)

Ac 27:19 they threw the **s** tackle overboard

Shiphi

1Ch 4:37 Ziza son of **S**, the son of Allon, the

Shiphmite

1Ch 27:27 Zabdi the **S** was in charge of the

Shiphrah

Ex 1:15 whose names were **S** and Puah,

Shiphtan

Nu 34:24 Kemuel son of **S**, the leader from the

Ships (Ship)

Ge 49:13 seashore and become a haven for **s**;
Nu 24:24 **S** will come from the shores of
Dt 28:68 The LORD will send you back in **s** to
Jdg 5:17 And Dan, why did he linger by the **s**?
1Ki 9:26 Solomon also built **s** at Ezion Geber
10:11 (Hiram's **s** brought gold from Ophir;
10:22 The king had a fleet of trading **s** at
10:22 at sea along with the **s** of Hiram.
22:48 trading **s** to go to Ophir for gold,
2Ch 8:18 Hiram sent him **s** commanded by his
9:21 The king had a fleet of trading **s**
20:36 to construct a fleet of trading **s**.
20:37 The **s** were wrecked and were not
Ps 48: 7 destroyed them like **s** of Tarshish
104:26 There the **s** go to and fro, and the
107:23 Others went out on the sea in **s**;

Pr 31:14 She is like the merchant s, bringing
Isa 23: 1 Wail, O s of Tarshish!
23:14 Wail, you s of Tarshish;
43:14 in the s in which they took pride.
60: 9 in the lead are the s of Tarshish,
Eze 27: 9 All the s of the sea and their
27:25 "The s of Tarshish serve as
27:29 the oars will abandon their s;
30: 9 out from me in s to frighten Cush
Da 11:30 S of the western coastlands will
11:40 and cavalry and a great fleet of s.
Jas 3: 4 Or take s as an example. Although
Rev 8: 9 and a third of the s were destroyed.
18:19 city, where all who had s on the sea

Shipwreck (Ship, Wrecked)
Eze 27:27 of the sea on the day of your s.

Shipwrecked (Ship, Wrecked)
2Co 11:25 three times I was s, I spent a night
1Ti 1:19 these and so have s their faith.

Shipwrights (Ship)
Eze 27: 9 on board as s to caulk your seams.
27:27 your mariners, seamen and s, your

Shisha
1Ki 4: 3 Elihoreph and Ahijah, sons of S—

Shishak
1Ki 11:40 but Jeroboam fled to Egypt, to S the
14:25 S king of Egypt attacked Jerusalem.
2Ch 12: 2 S king of Egypt attacked Jerusalem
12: 5 in Jerusalem for fear of S,
12: 5 therefore I now abandon you to S.
12: 7 poured out on Jerusalem through S.
12: 9 S king of Egypt attacked Jerusalem,

Shitrai
1Ch 27:29 S the Sharonite was in charge of the

Shittim
An abbreviation of Abel Shittim. Israel's last encampment east of River Jordan, before entering promised land (Nu 33:49–50). Here the Israelites sinned (Nu 25:1–3) and were punished with a plague (Nu 25:4–9). Joshua sent out spies from here (Jos 2:1) before all the people left to cross the River Jordan (Jos 3:1; Mic 6:5).
Nu 25: 1 While Israel was staying in S, the
Jos 2: 1 Nun secretly sent two spies from S.
3: 1 out from S and went to the Jordan,
Mic 6: 5 Remember your journey from S to

Shiza
1Ch 11:42 Adina son of S the Reubenite, who

Shoa
Eze 23:23 the men of Pekod and S and Koa, and

Shobab
2Sa 5:14 there: Shammua, S, Nathan, Solomon,
1Ch 2:18 were her sons: Jesher, S and Ardon.
3: 5 Shammua, S, Nathan and Solomon.
14: 4 there: Shammua, S, Nathan, Solomon,

Shobach
2Sa 10:16 with S the commander of Hadadezer's
10:18 He also struck down S the commander

Shobai
Ezr 2:42 Ater, Talmon, Akkub, Hatita and S 139
Ne 7:45 Ater, Talmon, Akkub, Hatita and S 138

Shobal
Ge 36:20 the region: Lotan, S, Zibeon, Anah,
36:23 The sons of S: Alvan, Manahath, Ebal,
36:29 chiefs: Lotan, S, Zibeon, Anah,
1Ch 1:38 The sons of Seir: Lotan, S, Zibeon,
1:40 The sons of S: Alvan, Manahath, Ebal,
2:50 S the father of Kiriath Jearim,
2:52 The descendants of S the father of
4: 1 Perez, Hezron, Carmi, Hur and S.
4: 2 Reaiah son of S was the father of

Shobek
Ne 10:24 Hallohesh, Pilha, S,

Shobi
2Sa 17:27 S son of Nahash from Rabbah of the

Shocked (Shocking)
Eze 16:27 who were s by your lewd conduct.

Shocking (Shocked)
Jer 5:30 "A horrible and s thing has happened

Shocks
Ex 22: 6 it burns s of grain or standing corn
Jdg 15: 5 He burned up the s and standing corn

Shoham
1Ch 24:27 Jaaziah: Beno, S, Zaccur and Ibri.

Shomer
2Ki 12:21 of Shimeath and Jehozabad son of S.
1Ch 7:32 Heber was the father of Japhlet, S
7:34 The sons of S: Ahi, Rohgah, Hubbah

Shone (Shine)
Dt 33: 2 he s forth from Mount Paran.
Job 29: 3 his lamp s upon my head and by his
Mt 17: 2 His face s like the sun, and his
Lk 2: 9 and the glory of the Lord s around
Ac 12: 7 appeared and a light s in the cell.
Rev 21:11 s with the glory of God, and its

Shook (Shake)
Jdg 5: 4 the earth s, the heavens poured, the
1Sa 4: 5 a great shout that the ground s.
14:15 raiding parties—and the ground s.
2Sa 22: 8 the foundations of the heavens s;
1Ki 1:40 so that the ground s with the sound.
Ne 5:13 I also s out the folds of my robe
Ps 18: 7 the foundations of the mountains s;
68: 8 the earth s, the heavens poured down
Isa 6: 4 thresholds s and the temple was
14:16 "Is this the man who s the earth and
Hab 3: 6 He stood, and s the earth; he looked
Mt 27:51 The earth s and the rocks split.
28: 4 they s and became like dead men.
Mk 1:26 The evil spirit s the man violently
Ac 13:51 they s the dust from their feet in
18: 6 he s out his clothes in protest and
28: 5 Paul s the snake off into the fire
Heb 12:26 At that time his voice s the earth,

Shoot (Shooting, Shoots, Shot)
1Sa 20:20 I will s three arrows to the side of
20:36 boy, "Run and find the arrows I s.
2Sa 11:20 they would s arrows from the wall?
2Ki 13:17 "S!" Elisha said, and he shot.
19:32 enter this city or s an arrow here.
1Ch 12: 2 were able to s arrows or to sling
2Ch 26:15 to s arrows and hurl large stones.
Job 41:19 his mouth; sparks of fire s out.
Ps 11: 2 to s from the shadows at the
64: 4 They s from ambush at the innocent
64: 4 s at him suddenly, without fear.
64: 7 God will s them with arrows;
144: 6 s your arrows and rout them.
Isa 11: 1 A s will come up from the stump of
37:33 enter this city or s an arrow here.
53: 2 He grew up before him like a tender s
60:21 They are the s I have planted, the
Jer 9: 3 their tongue like a bow, to s lies;
50:14 S at her! Spare no arrows, for she
Eze 5:16 I s at you with my deadly and
5:16 of famine, I will s to destroy you.
17: 4 he broke off its topmost s and
17:22 I myself will take a s from the very
Ro 11:17 and you, though a wild olive s, have

Shooting (Shoot)
1Sa 20:20 it, as though I were s at a target.
Pr 26:18 Like a madman s firebrands or deadly

Shoots (Shoot)
2Ki 19:26 like tender green s, like grass
Job 8:16 spreading its s over the garden;
14: 7 again, and its new s will not fail.
14: 9 bud and put forth s like a plant.
15:30 a flame will wither his s, and the
Ps 80:11 the Sea, its s as far as the River
128: 3 be like olive s round your table.
Isa 16: 8 Their s spread out and went as far
18: 5 he will cut off the s with pruning
37:27 like tender green s, like grass
Eze 17:22 a tender sprig from its topmost s
Hos 14: 6 his young s will grow. His splendour

Shophach
1Ch 19:16 with S the commander of Hadadezer's
19:18 S the commander of their army.

Shore (Ashore, Seashore, Shorelands, Shores)
Ex 14:30 the Egyptians lying dead on the s.
1Ki 9:26 in Edom, on the s of the Red Sea.
Eze 27:29 all the seamen will stand on the s.
47:10 Fishermen will stand along the s;
Zep 2:11 The nations on every s will worship
Mt 13: 2 while all the people stood on the s.
13:48 the fishermen pulled it up on the s.
Mk 4: 1 along the s at the water's edge.
Lk 5: 3 him to put out a little from s.
5:11 they pulled their boats up on s,
Jn 6: 1 Jesus crossed to the far s of the
6:21 the s where they were heading.
6:22 the opposite s of the lake realised
21: 4 Jesus stood on the s, but the
21: 8 far from s, about a hundred yards.
Ac 27:13 and sailed along the s of Crete.
28: 1 Once safely on s, we found out that
Rev 13: 1 the dragon stood on the s of the sea.

Shorelands (Land, Shore)
Eze 27:28 The s will quake when your seamen

Shores (Shore)
Nu 24:24 Ships will come from the s of Kittim;
Est 10: 1 the empire, to its distant s.
Ps 72:10 kings of Tarshish and of distant s
97: 1 be glad; let the distant s rejoice.

Shorn (Shear)
SS 4: 2 just s, coming up from the washing.

Short (Shortened, Short-sighted)
Nu 11:23 "Is the LORD's arm too s? You will
Ru 2: 7 except for a s rest in the shelter."
1Sa 2:31 The time is coming when I will cut s
21:15 Am I so s of madmen that you have to
2Sa 16: 1 David had gone a s distance beyond
19:36 with the king for a s distance,
Job 17: 1 days are cut s, the grave awaits me.
Ps 89:45 You have cut s the days of his youth;
102:23 broke my strength; he cut s my days.
Pr 10:27 the years of the wicked are cut s.
Isa 28:20 The bed is too s to stretch out on,
29:17 In a very s time, will not Lebanon
50: 2 Was my arm too s to ransom you? Do I
59: 1 of the LORD is not too s to save,
Mic 6:10 and the s ephah, which is accursed?
Mt 13:21 has no root, he lasts only a s time.
24:22 If those days had not been cut s,
Mk 4:17 no root, they last only a s time.
13:20 If the Lord had not cut s those days,
Lk 19: 3 but being a s man he could not,
Jn 7:33 "I am with you for only a s time,
11: 8 "a s while ago the Jews tried to
Ac 26:28 "Do you think that in such a s time
26:29 Paul replied, "S time or long—I
27:28 A s time later they took soundings
Ro 3:23 for all have sinned and fall s of
1Co 7:29 brothers, is that the time is s.

1Th 2:17 from you for a **s** time (in person,
Heb 4: 1 you be found to have fallen **s** of it.
11:25 the pleasures of sin for a **s** time.
13:22 I have written you only a **s** letter.
Rev 12:12 he knows that his time is **s**."
20: 3 he must be set free for a **s** time.

Shortcomings

Ge 41: 9 "Today I am reminded of my **s**.

Shortened (Short)

Mt 24:22 of the elect those days will be **s**.
Mk 13:20 whom he has chosen, he has **s** them.

Short-sighted (Short)

2Pe 1: 9 if anyone does not have them, he is **s**

Shot (Shoot)

Ge 49:23 they **s** at him with hostility.
Ex 19:13 He shall surely be stoned or **s** with
1Sa 20:36 boy ran, he **s** an arrow beyond him.
2Sa 11:24 the archers **s** arrows at your
22:15 He **s** arrows and scattered the
2Ki 9:24 Jehu drew his bow and **s** Joram
13:17 "Shoot!" Elisha said, and he **s**.
2Ch 35:23 Archers **s** King Josiah, and he told
Ps 18:14 He **s** his arrows and scattered the

Shoulder (Shoulders)

Ge 24:15 came out with her jar on her **s**.
24:45 came out, with her jar on her **s**.
24:46 lowered her jar from her **s** and said,
49:15 he will bend his **s** to the burden and
Ex 28: 7 is to have two **s** pieces attached to
28:12 fasten them on the **s** pieces of the
28:25 attaching them to the **s** pieces of
28:27 to the bottom of the **s** pieces on
39: 4 They made **s** pieces for the ephod,
39: 7 they fastened them on the **s** pieces
39:18 attaching them to the **s** pieces of
39:20 to the bottom of the **s** pieces on
Nu 6:19 in his hands a boiled **s** of the ram,
Dt 18: 3 **s**, the jowls and the inner parts.
Jos 4: 5 you is to take up a stone on his **s**,
Job 31:22 let my arm fall from the **s**, let it
31:36 Surely I would wear it on my **s**, I
Isa 22:22 I will place on his **s** the key to the
Eze 12: 6 Put them on your **s** as they are
12:12 things on his **s** at dusk and leave,
24: 4 choice pieces—the leg and the **s**.
29:18 rubbed bare and every **s** made raw.
34:21 you shove with flank and **s**, butting
Zep 3: 9 of the LORD and serve him **s** to **s**.

Shoulders (Shoulder)

Ge 9:23 garment and laid it across their **s**;
21:14 He set them on her **s** and then sent
Ex 12:34 and carried it on their **s** in
28:12 bear the names on his **s** as a
Nu 7: 9 to carry on their **s** the holy things,
Dt 33:12 the LORD loves rests between his **s**."
Jdg 9:48 branches, which he lifted to his **s**.
16: 3 He lifted them to his **s** and carried
2Ki 6:31 of Shaphat remains on his **s** today!"
9:24 bow and shot Joram between the **s**.
1Ch 15:15 of God with the poles on their **s**,
2Ch 35: 3 not to be carried about on your **s**.
Ne 3: 5 would not put their **s** to the work
Ps 81: 6 "I removed the burden from their **s**;
Isa 9: 4 the bar across their **s**, the rod of
9: 6 and the government will be on his **s**.
10:27 burden will be lifted from your **s**,
14:25 his burden removed from their **s**."
46: 7 They lift it to their **s** and carry it;
49:22 and carry your daughters on their **s**.
Eze 12: 7 them on my **s** while they watched.
29: 7 and you tore open their **s**;
Mt 23: 4 heavy loads and put them on men's **s**,
Lk 15: 5 it, he joyfully puts it on his **s**

Shout (Shouted, Shouting, Shouts)

Nu 23:21 the **s** of the King is among them.
Jos 6: 5 make all the people give a loud **s**;
6:10 the day I tell you to **s**. Then **s**!"
Jos 6:16 "**S**! For the LORD has given you the
6:20 when the people gave a loud **s**, the
Jdg 7:18 and **s**, 'For the LORD and for Gideon.
1Sa 4: 5 a great **s** that the ground shook.
17:52 Judah surged forward with a **s** and
1Ki 1:34 and **s**, 'Long live King Solomon!'
18:27 "**S** louder!" he said. "Surely he is a
Ezr 3:11 And all the people gave a great **s**
Job 3: 7 may no **s** of joy be heard in it.
3:18 no longer hear the slave driver's **s**.
39: 7 he does not hear a driver's **s**.
39:25 **s** of commanders and the battle cry.
Ps 20: 5 We will **s** for joy when you are
33: 3 play skilfully, and **s** for joy.
35:27 vindication **s** for joy and gladness;
47: 1 **s** to God with cries of joy.
60: 8 over Philistia I **s** in triumph."
65:13 with corn; they **s** for joy and sing.
66: 1 **S** with joy to God, all the earth!
71:23 My lips will **s** for joy when I sing
81: 1 **s** aloud to the God of Jacob!
95: 1 **s** aloud to the Rock of our salvation.
98: 4 **S** for joy to the LORD, all the earth,
98: 6 **s** for joy before the LORD, the King.
100: 1 **S** for joy to the LORD, all the earth.
108: 9 over Philistia I **s** in triumph."
Isa 12: 6 **S** aloud and sing for joy, people of
13: 2 a banner on a bare hilltop, **s** to them
24:14 raise their voices, they **s** for joy;
26:19 in the dust, wake up and **s** for joy.
35: 2 will rejoice greatly and **s** for joy.
35: 6 deer, and the mute tongue **s** for joy.
40: 9 lift up your voice with a **s**, lift it
42: 2 He will not **s** or cry out, or raise
42:11 let them **s** from the mountaintops.
42:13 with a **s** he will raise the battle
44:23 done this; **s** aloud, O earth beneath.
49:13 **S** for joy, O heavens; rejoice,
52: 8 together they **s** for joy.
54: 1 **s** for joy, you who were never in
58: 1 "**S** it aloud, do not hold back.
Jer 25:30 He will **s** like those who tread the
25:30 **s** against all who live on the earth.
31: 7 **s** for the foremost of the nations.
31:12 They will come and **s** for joy on the
49:29 **s** to them, 'Terror on every side!'
50:15 **S** against her on every side!
51:14 and they will **s** in triumph over you.
51:39 so that they **s** with laughter—then
51:48 in them will **s** for joy over Babylon,
Lam 2: 7 they have raised a **s** in the house of
Eze 8:18 Although they **s** in my ears, I will
Zep 3:14 of Zion; **s** aloud, O Israel!
Zec 2:10 "**S** and be glad, O Daughter of Zion.
9: 9 **S**, Daughter of Jerusalem!
Mk 10:47 he began to **s**, "Jesus, Son of David,
Rev 10: 3 he gave a loud **s** like the roar of a

Shouted (Shout)

Ge 41:43 and men **s** before him, "Make way!"
Lev 9:24 they **s** for joy and fell face down.
Jos 6:20 the trumpets sounded, the people **s**,
Jdg 7:20 they **s**, "A sword for the LORD and
9: 7 top of Mount Gerizim and **s** to them,
16:25 **s**, "Bring out Samson to entertain us.
18:23 they **s** after them, the Danites
19:22 Pounding on the door, they **s** to the
1Sa 10:24 Then the people **s**, "Long live the
14:12 The men of the outpost **s** to Jonathan
17: 8 Goliath stood and **s** to the ranks of
17:23 his lines and **s** his usual defiance,
20:38 he **s**, "Hurry! Go quickly! Don't stop!
2Sa 20: 1 He sounded the trumpet and **s**, "We
1Ki 1:39 the trumpet and all the people **s**,
18:26 "O Baal, answer us!" they **s**.
18:28 they **s** louder and slashed themselves
2Ki 7:11 The gatekeepers **s** the news, and it
9:13 Then they blew the trumpet and **s**,
11:12 people clapped their hands and **s**,
2Ch 23:11 They anointed him and **s**, "Long live
23:13 Then Athaliah tore her robes and **s**,
Ezr 3:12 laid, while many others **s** for joy.
Job 30: 5 **s** at as if they were thieves.
38: 7 and all the angels **s** for joy?
Isa 21: 8 the lookout **s**, "Day after day, my
Da 3:26 of the blazing furnace and **s**,
Mt 8:29 want with us, Son of God?" they **s**.
20:30 they **s**, "Lord, Son of David, have
20:31 but they **s** all the louder, "Lord,
21: 9 **s**, "Hosanna to the Son of David!"
27:23 But they **s** all the louder, "Crucify
Mk 5: 7 He **s** at the top of his voice, "What
10:48 but he **s** all the more, "Son of David,
11: 9 and those who followed **s**, "Hosanna!"
15:13 "Crucify him!" they **s**.
15:14 But they **s** all the louder, "Crucify
Lk 18:39 but he **s** all the more, "Son of David,
Jn 18:40 They **s** back, "No, not him! Give us
19: 6 saw him, they **s**, "Crucify! Crucify!"
19:15 they **s**, "Take him away! Take him
Ac 12:22 They **s**, "This is the voice of a god,
14:11 they **s** in the Lycaonian language,
16:28 Paul **s**, "Don't harm yourself! We are
19:33 of the crowd **s** instructions to him.
19:34 they all **s** in unison for about two
21:34 Some in the crowd **s** one thing and
22:22 Then they raised their voices and **s**,
24:21 unless it was this one thing I **s** as
26:24 are out of your mind, Paul!" he **s**.
Rev 10: 3 When he **s**, the voices of the seven
18: 2 With a mighty voice he **s**: "Fallen!
19: 3 again they **s**: "Hallelujah! The smoke

Shouting (Shout)

Ex 32:17 heard the noise of the people **s**,
Nu 16:34 **s**, "The earth is going to swallow us
Jdg 15:14 the Philistines came towards him **s**.
1Sa 4: 6 "What's all this **s** in the Hebrew
17:20 its battle positions, **s** the war cry.
2Ki 9:27 Jehu chased him, **s**, "Kill him too!"
2Ch 15:14 with **s** and with trumpets and horns.
Isa 16:10 for I have put an end to the **s**.
Zep 1:14 bitter, the **s** of the warrior there.
Mt 21:15 the children **s** in the temple area,
Lk 4:41 people, **s**, "You are the Son of God!"
8:28 **s** at the top of his voice, "What do
23:21 they kept **s**, "Crucify him! Crucify
Jn 12:13 went out to meet him, **s**, "Hosanna!"
19:12 but the Jews kept **s**, "If you let
Ac 14:14 and rushed out into the crowd, **s**:
16:17 **s**, "These men are servants of the
17: 6 **s**: "These men who have caused
19:28 they were furious and began **s**:
19:32 Some were **s** one thing, some another.
21:28 **s**, "Men of Israel, help us! This is
21:36 The crowd that followed kept **s**,
22:23 they were **s** and throwing off their
22:24 the people were **s** at him like this.
25:24 **s** that he ought not to live any
Rev 19: 1 of a great multitude in heaven **s**:
19: 6 **s**: "Hallelujah! For our Lord God

Shouts (Shout)

2Sa 6:15 with **s** and the sound of trumpets.
1Ch 15:28 with **s**, with the sounding of
Ezr 3:13 the sound of the **s** of joy from the
Job 8:21 and your lips with **s** of joy.
33:26 he sees God's face and **s** for joy;
Ps 27: 6 will I sacrifice with **s** of joy;
42: 4 with **s** of joy and thanksgiving among
47: 5 God has ascended amid **s** of joy, the
105:43 his chosen ones with **s** of joy;
118:15 **S** of joy and victory resound in the
Pr 11:10 wicked perish, there are **s** of joy.
Ecc 9:17 than the **s** of a ruler of fools.
Isa 16: 9 The **s** of joy over your ripened
16:10 no-one sings or **s** in the vineyards;
31: 4 he is not frightened by their **s** or
48:20 this with **s** of joy and proclaim it.
Jer 48:33 no-one treads them with **s** of joy.
48:33 there are **s**, they are not **s** of joy.
Zec 4: 7 **s** of 'God bless it! God bless it!'
Lk 23:23 with loud **s** they insistently
23:23 be crucified, and their **s** prevailed.

Shove

Eze 34:21 you **s** with flank and shoulder,

Shovel (Shovels)
Isa 30:24 mash, spread out with fork and **s**.

Shovels (Shovel)
Ex 27: 3 and its **s**, sprinkling bowls, meat
38: 3 **s**, sprinkling bowls, meat forks and
Nu 4:14 meat forks, **s** and sprinkling bowls.
1Ki 7:40 He also made the basins and **s** and
7:45 the pots, **s** and sprinkling bowls.
2Ki 25:14 They also took away the pots, **s**,
2Ch 4:11 He also made the pots and **s** and
4:16 the pots, **s**, meat forks and all
Jer 52:18 They also took away the pots, **s**,

Show (Showed, Showing, Shown, Shows)
Ge 12: 1 and go to the land I will **s** you.
20:13 'This is how you can **s** your love to
21:23 **S** to me and the country where you
24:12 and **s** kindness to my master Abraham
24:49 Now if you will **s** kindness and
40:14 remember me and **s** me kindness;
47:29 will **s** me kindness and faithfulness.
Ex 9:16 that I might **s** you my power and that
18:20 and **s** them the way to live and the
23: 3 do not **s** favouritism to a poor man
25: 9 like the pattern I will **s** you.
33:18 Moses said, "Now **s** me your glory."
Lev 10: 3 approach me I will **s** myself holy;
19:15 do not **s** partiality to the poor or
19:32 **s** respect for the elderly and
Nu 16: 5 "In the morning the LORD will **s** who
Dt 1:17 Do not **s** partiality in judging;
1:33 and to **s** you the way you should go.
3:24 you have begun to **s** to your servant
4: 6 for this will **s** your wisdom and
7: 2 with them, and **s** them no mercy.
13: 8 **S** him no pity. Do not spare him or
13:17 fierce anger; he will **s** you mercy,
15: 9 so that you do not **s** ill will
16:19 not pervert justice or **s** partiality.
19:13 **S** him no pity. You must purge from
19:21 **S** no pity: life for life, eye for
25:12 cut off her hand. **S** her no pity.
Jos 2:12 you will **s** kindness to my family,
Jdg 1:24 "**S** us how to get into the city and
4:22 "Come," she said, "I will **s** you the
8:35 They also failed to **s** kindness to
13:21 angel of the LORD did not **s** himself
Ru 1: 8 May the LORD **s** kindness to you, as
1Sa 16: 3 and I will **s** you what to do.
20: 8 for you, **s** kindness to your servant,
20:14 **s** me unfailing kindness like that of
2Sa 2: 6 May the LORD now **s** you kindness and
2: 6 and I too will **s** you the same favour
9: 1 can **s** kindness for Jonathan's sake?"
9: 3 Saul to whom I can **s** God's kindness?"
9: 7 "for I will surely **s** you kindness
10: 2 "I will **s** kindness to Hanun son of
12:14 of the LORD **s** utter contempt,
16:17 "Is this the love you **s** your friend?
22:26 "To the faithful you **s** yourself
22:26 blameless you **s** yourself blameless,
22:27 to the pure you **s** yourself pure, but
22:27 the crooked you **s** yourself shrewd.
1Ki 2: 2 "So be strong, **s** yourself a man,
2: 7 "But **s** kindness to the sons of
8:50 their conquerors to **s** them mercy;
2Ki 20:13 that Hezekiah did not **s** them.
20:15 my treasures that I did not **s** them."
1Ch 19: 2 "I will **s** kindness to Hanun son of
Ezr 2:59 but they could not **s** that their
Ne 7:61 but they could not **s** that their
13:22 and **s** mercy to me according to your
Est 4: 8 to **s** to Esther and explain it to her,
Job 6:24 **s** me where I have been wrong.
13: 8 Will you **s** him partiality? Will you
13:23 **S** me my offence and my sin.
24:21 and to the widow **s** no kindness.
32:21 I will **s** partiality to no-one, nor
36: 2 I will **s** you that there is more to
37:13 to water his earth and **s** his love.
Ps 4: 6 Many are asking, "Who can **s** us any
17: 7 **S** the wonder of your great love, you
18:25 To the faithful you **s** yourself
18:25 blameless you **s** yourself blameless,
18:26 to the pure you **s** yourself pure, but
18:26 the crooked you **s** yourself shrewd.
25: 4 **S** me your ways, O LORD, teach me
28: 5 Since they **s** no regard for the works
39: 4 "**S** me, O LORD, my life's end and the
50:23 I may **s** him the salvation of God."
59: 5 **s** no mercy to wicked traitors.
68:28 **s** us your strength, O God, as you
77: 7 Will he never **s** his favour again?
82: 2 **s** partiality to the wicked?
85: 7 **S** us your unfailing love, O LORD,
88:10 Do you **s** your wonders to the dead?
91:16 satisfy him and **s** him my salvation."
102:13 for it is time to **s** favour to her;
106: 4 when you **s** favour to your people,
143: 8 **S** me the way I should go, for to you
Pr 6:34 **s** no mercy when he takes revenge.
23: 4 have the wisdom to **s** restraint.
24:23 **s** partiality in judging is not good:
28:21 To **s** partiality is not good—yet a
SS 2:14 **s** me your face, let me hear your
Isa 5:16 **s** himself holy by his righteousness.
13:10 will not **s** their light.
19:12 Let them **s** you and make known what
30:18 he rises to **s** you compassion.
39: 2 that Hezekiah did not **s** them.
39: 4 my treasures that I did not **s** them."
60:10 in favour I will **s** you compassion.
Jer 6:23 they are cruel and **s** no mercy.
15: 6 I can no longer **s** compassion.
16: 5 do not go to mourn or **s** sympathy,
16:13 night, for I will **s** you no favour.'
18:17 I will **s** them my back and not my
21: 7 he will **s** them no mercy or pity or
32:18 You **s** love to thousands but bring
42:12 I will **s** you compassion so that he
Lam 3:32 brings grief, he will **s** compassion,
Eze 20:41 and I will **s** myself holy among you
28:22 on her and **s** myself holy within her.
28:25 I will **s** myself holy among them in
36:23 I will **s** the holiness of my great
36:23 when I **s** myself holy through you
38:16 when I **s** myself holy through you
38:23 I will **s** my greatness and my
39:27 I will **s** myself holy through them in
40: 4 to everything I am going to **s** you,
44:23 the common and **s** them how to
Da 1: 9 to **s** favour and sympathy to Daniel,
11:30 He will return and **s** favour to those
11:37 He will **s** no regard for the gods of
Hos 1: 6 for I will no longer **s** love to the
1: 7 Yet I will **s** love to the house of
2: 4 I will not **s** my love to her children,
2:23 I will **s** my love to the one I called
3: 1 "Go, **s** your love to your wife again
Joel 2:30 I will **s** wonders in the heavens and
Mic 7:15 of Egypt, I will **s** them my wonders."
7:18 for ever but delight to **s** mercy.
7:20 to Jacob, and **s** mercy to Abraham,
Na 3: 5 I will **s** the nations your nakedness
Zec 1: 9 "I will **s** you what they are."
7: 9 **s** mercy and compassion to one
Mal 1: 6 who **s** contempt for my name.
Mt 6:16 faces to **s** men they are fasting.
8: 4 But go, **s** yourself to the priest and
16: 1 him to **s** them a sign from heaven.
18:15 go and **s** him his fault, just between
21:32 For John came to you to **s** you the
22:19 **S** me the coin used for paying the
Mk 1:44 But go, **s** yourself to the priest and
12:40 and for a **s** make lengthy prayers.
14:15 He will **s** you a large upper room,
Lk 1:72 to **s** mercy to our fathers and to
5:14 but go, **s** yourself to the priest
6:47 I will **s** you what he is like who
12: 5 I will **s** you whom you should fear:
17:14 "Go, **s** yourselves to the priests."
18: 1 **s** them that they should always pray
20:21 and that you do not **s** partiality but
20:24 "**S** me a denarius. Whose portrait and
20:47 and for a **s** make lengthy prayers.
22:12 He will **s** you a large upper room,
Jn 2:18 "What miraculous sign can you **s** us
5:20 **s** him even greater things than these.
7: 4 things, **s** yourself to the world."
12:33 He said this to **s** the kind of death
14: 8 Philip said, "Lord, **s** us the Father
14: 9 How can you say, '**S** us the Father'?
14:21 will love him and **s** myself to him."
14:22 why do you intend to **s** yourself
Ac 1:24 **S** us which of these two you have
2:19 I will **s** wonders in the heaven above
7: 3 'and go to the land I will **s** you.'
9:16 I will **s** him how much he must suffer
10:34 is that God does not **s** favouritism
26:16 seen of me and what I will **s** you.
Ro 2: 4 Or do you **s** contempt for the riches
2:11 For God does not **s** favouritism.
2:15 since they **s** that the requirements
9:22 What if God, choosing to **s** his wrath
1Co 11:19 **s** which of you have God's approval.
12:31 I will **s** you the most excellent way.
2Co 3: 3 You **s** that you are a letter from
4: 7 to **s** that this all-surpassing power
8:19 and to **s** our eagerness to help.
8:24 Therefore **s** these men the proof of
11:30 of the things that **s** my weakness.
Eph 2: 7 he might **s** the incomparable riches
Php 4:10 but you had no opportunity to **s** it.
1Ti 6: 2 are not to **s** less respect for them
2Ti 1:16 May the Lord **s** mercy to the
Tit 2: 7 In your teaching **s** integrity,
2:10 but to **s** that they can be fully
3: 2 to **s** true humility towards all men.
Heb 6:11 We want each of you to **s** this same
11:14 People who say such things **s** that
Jas 2: 1 Jesus Christ, don't **s** favouritism.
2: 3 If you **s** special attention to the
2: 9 if you **s** favouritism, you sin and
2:18 **S** me your faith without deeds, and
2:18 I will **s** you my faith by what I do.
3:13 Let him **s** it by his good life,
1Pe 2:17 **S** proper respect to everyone: Love
3Jn : 8 We ought therefore to **s** hospitality
Jude :23 to others **s** mercy, mixed with fear
Rev 1: 1 which God gave him to **s** his servants
4: 1 "Come up here, and I will **s** you what
17: 1 "Come, I will **s** you the punishment
21: 9 "Come, I will **s** you the bride, the
22: 6 sent his angel to **s** his servants the

Showed (Show)
Ge 39:21 he **s** him kindness and granted him
Ex 15:25 and the LORD **s** him a piece of wood.
Nu 13:26 and **s** them the fruit of the land.
20:13 where he **s** himself holy among them.
Dt 4:36 On earth he **s** you his great fire,
34: 1 There the LORD **s** him the whole land—
Jdg 1:25 he **s** them, and they put the city to
Ru 3:10 than that which you **s** earlier:
1Sa 14:11 both of them **s** themselves to the
15: 6 for you **s** kindness to all the
2Sa 10: 2 just as his father **s** kindness to me.
1Ki 3: 3 Solomon **s** his love for the LORD by
13:12 And his sons **s** him which road the
2Ki 6: 6 When he **s** him the place, Elisha cut
11: 4 Then he **s** them the king's son.
13:23 had compassion and **s** concern for
20:13 **s** them all that was in his
1Ch 19: 2 because his father **s** kindness to me.
2Ch 23: 1 Jehoiada **s** his strength. He made a
30:22 who **s** good understanding of the
Est 5: 9 rose nor **s** fear in his presence,
Job 10:12 You gave me life and **s** me kindness,
13:10 you if you secretly **s** partiality.
Ps 31:21 for he **s** his wonderful love to me
85: 1 You **s** favour to your land, O LORD;
Isa 39: 2 **s** them what was in his
40:14 or **s** him the path of understanding?
47: 6 your hand, and you **s** them no mercy.
Jer 11:18 time he **s** me what they were doing.
24: 1 the LORD **s** me two baskets of figs
36:24 who heard all these words **s** no fear,
Eze 35:11 jealousy you **s** in your hatred of
39:26 all the unfaithfulness they **s**
46:19 and **s** me a place at the western end.
Da 2:29 **s** you what is going to happen.
Am 7: 1 This is what the Sovereign LORD **s** me:
7: 4 This is what the Sovereign LORD **s** me:
7: 7 This is what he **s** me: the Lord was

Am 8: 1 This is what the Sovereign LORD s me:
Mic 6: 8 He has s you, O man, what is good.
Zec 1:20 the LORD s me four craftsmen.
3: 1 he s me Joshua the high priest
8:14 s no pity when your fathers angered
Mt 4: 8 s him all the kingdoms of the world
Lk 4: 5 s him in an instant all the kingdoms
20:37 even Moses s that the dead rise, for
24:40 he s them his hands and feet.
Jn 13: 1 s them the full extent of his love.
20:20 he s them his hands and side.
Ac 1: 3 After his suffering, he s himself to
15: 8 God, who knows the heart, s that he
15:14 how God at first s his concern by
18:17 But Gallio s no concern whatever.
20:35 In everything I did, I s you that by
28: 2 The islanders s us unusual kindness.
1Jn 2:19 s that none of them belonged to us.
4: 9 This is how God s his love among us:
Rev 21:10 and s me the Holy City, Jerusalem,
22: 1 the angel s me the river of the

Shower (Showering, Showers)
Job 37: 6 the rain s, 'Be a mighty downpour.'
Isa 45: 8 let the clouds s it down.

Showering (Shower)
2Sa 16:13 stones at him and s him with dirt.

Showers (Shower)
Dt 32: 2 like s on new grass, like abundant
Job 29:23 They waited for me as for s and
36:28 and abundant s fall on mankind.
Ps 65:10 you soften it with s and bless its
68: 9 You gave abundant s, O God; you
72: 6 field, like s watering the earth.
Jer 3: 3 Therefore the s have been withheld,
14:22 the skies themselves send down s?
Eze 22:24 no rain or s in the day of wrath.'
34:26 I will send down s in season;
34:26 there will be s of blessing.
Hos 10:12 he comes and s righteousness on you.
Joel 2:23 He sends you abundant s, both autumn
Mic 5: 7 like s on the grass, which do not
Zec 10: 1 He gives s of rain to men, and

Showing (Show)
Ex 20: 6 s love to a thousand generations of
Dt 5:10 s love to a thousand generations of
Jdg 16: 5 "See if you can lure him into s you
Ru 2:20 "He has not stopped s his kindness
2Sa 2: 5 "The LORD bless you for s this
Eze 9: 5 kill, without s pity or compassion.
Da 1: 4 handsome, s aptitude for every kind
Jn 15: 8 s yourselves to be my disciples.
Ac 9:39 crying and s him the robes and other
Ro 12: 8 s mercy, let him do it cheerfully.
1Ti 5:10 bringing up children, s hospitality
Heb 9: 8 The Holy Spirit was s by this that
Rev 22: 8 the angel who had been s them to me.

Shown (Show)
Ge 19:19 and you have s great kindness to me
21:23 the same kindness I have s to you."
24:14 you have s kindness to my master."
32:10 you have s your servant.
41:28 s Pharaoh what he is about to do.
Ex 25:40 the pattern s you on the mountain.
26:30 to the plan s you on the mountain.
27: 8 just as you were s on the mountain.
Lev 13: 7 after he has s himself to the priest
13:49 mildew and must be s to the priest.
Nu 8: 4 the pattern the LORD had s Moses.
Dt 4:35 You were s these things so that you
5:24 "The LORD our God has s us his glory
34:12 For no-one has ever s the mighty
Jos 2:12 because I have s kindness to you.
Jdg 13:23 nor s us all these things or now
Ru 1: 8 you have s to your dead and to me.
1Ki 3: 6 "You have s great kindness to your
2Ki 8:13 "The LORD has s me that you will
2Ch 1: 8 Solomon answered God, "You have s
24:22 had s him but killed his son,
30: 9 your children will be s compassion
32:25 not respond to the kindness s him;
Ezr 9: 9 He has s us kindness in the sight of
Job 38:12 morning, or s the dawn its place,
38:17 Have the gates of death been s to
Ps 48: 3 he has s himself to be her fortress
60: 3 You have s your people desperate
78:11 had done, the wonders he had s them.
90:16 May your deeds be s to your servants,
111: 6 He has s his people the power of his
Isa 21: 2 A dire vision has been s to me: The
26:10 Though grace is s to the wicked,
66:14 but his fury will be s to his foes.
Jer 44:10 humbled themselves or s reverence,
44:25 You and your wives have s by your
Lam 4:16 The priests are s no honour, the
5:12 elders are s no respect.
Eze 11:25 exiles everything the LORD had s me.
Da 2:28 He has s King Nebuchadnezzar what
2:45 "The great God has s the king what
Mal 1: 6 have we s contempt for your name?'
2: 9 s partiality in matters of the law."
Mt 5: 7 merciful, for they will be s mercy.
Lk 1:25 "In these days he has s his favour
1:58 that the Lord had s her great mercy,
Jn 10:32 "I have s you many great miracles
Ac 4: 9 an act of kindness s to a cripple
10:28 But God has s me that I should not
14:17 He has s kindness by giving you rain
1Co 3:13 his work will be s for what it is,
1Ti 1:13 I was s mercy because I acted in
1:16 for that very reason I was s mercy
Heb 6:10 the love you have s him as you have
8: 5 the pattern s you on the mountain."
Jas 2:13 judgment without mercy will be s to

Shows (Show)
Dt 10:17 who s no partiality and accepts no
17:12 The man who s contempt for the judge
2Sa 22:51 s unfailing kindness to his anointed,
1Ki 1:52 Solomon replied, "If he s himself to
Job 34:19 who s no partiality to princes and
Ps 18:50 s unfailing kindness to his anointed,
123: 2 LORD our God, till he s us his mercy.
Pr 10:17 He who heeds discipline s the way to
11:22 beautiful woman who s no discretion.
12:16 A fool s his annoyance at once, but
14:31 He who oppresses the poor s contempt
15: 5 whoever heeds correction s prudence.
17: 5 He who mocks the poor s contempt for
Ecc 10: 3 and s everyone how stupid he is.
Isa 27:11 and their Creator s them no favour.
Jn 5:20 loves the Son and s him all he does

Shrewd (Shrewdly)
2Sa 13: 3 Jonadab was a very s man.
22:27 to the crooked you show yourself s.
Ps 18:26 to the crooked you show yourself s.
Mt 10:16 s as snakes and as innocent as doves.
Lk 16: 8 are more s in dealing with their

Shrewdly (Shrewd)
Ex 1:10 Come, we must deal s with them or
Lk 16: 8 manager because he had acted s.

Shriek (Shrieked, Shrieks)
Mk 1:26 and came out of him with a s.

Shrieked (Shriek)
Mk 9:26 The spirit s, convulsed him

Shrieks (Shriek)
Ac 8: 7 With s, evil spirits came out of

Shrine (Shrines)
Jdg 17: 5 Now this man Micah had a s, and he
2Ki 10:25 the inner s of the temple of Baal.
Isa 16:12 when she goes to her s to pray, it
44:13 his glory, that it may dwell in a s.
Eze 8:12 each at the s of his own idol?
16:24 a lofty s in every public square.
Am 5:26 You have lifted up the s of your
Ac 7:43 You have lifted up the s of Molech

Shrine-prostitute (Shrine, Prostitute)
Ge 38:21 "Where is the s who was beside the
38:21 hasn't been any s here," they said.
38:22 said, 'There hasn't been any s here.
Dt 23:17 man or woman is to become a s.

Shrine-prostitutes (Shrine, Prostitutes)
1Ki 14:24 There were even male s in the land;
15:12 He expelled the male s from the land
22:46 the male s who remained there even
2Ki 23: 7 down the quarters of the male s,
Hos 4:14 sacrifice with s—a people without

Shrines (Shrine)
1Ki 12:31 Jeroboam built s on high places and
13:32 against all the s on the high places
2Ki 17:29 and set them up in the s the people
17:32 priests in the s at the high places.
23: 8 He broke down the s at the gates—at
23:19 defiled all the s at the high places
Job 36:14 among male prostitutes of the s.
Eze 16:25 you built your lofty s and degraded
16:31 your lofty s in every public square,
16:39 mounds and destroy your lofty s.
18: 6 He does not eat at the mountain s or
18:11 "He eats at the mountain s.
18:15 "He does not eat at the mountain s
22: 9 those who eat at the mountain s and
Ac 19:24 who made silver s of Artemis,

Shrink (Shrinks)
Heb 10:39 we are not of those who s back and
Rev 12:11 lives so much as to s from death.

Shrinks (Shrink)
Heb 10:38 And if he s back, I will not be

Shrivel (Shrivelled)
Isa 64: 6 we all s up like a leaf,
Eze 19:12 The east wind made it s, it was

Shrivelled (Shrivel)
1Ki 13: 4 stretched out towards the man s up,
Isa 34: 4 vine, like s figs from the fig-tree.
Lam 4: 8 Their skin has s on their bones;
Joel 1:17 The seeds are s beneath the clods.
Mt 12:10 a man with a s hand was there.
Mk 3: 1 and a man with a s hand was there.
3: 3 said to the man with the s hand,
Lk 6: 6 was there whose right hand was s.
6: 8 and said to the man with the s hand,

Shroud (Shrouded)
Job 40:13 s their faces in the grave.
Isa 25: 7 the s that enfolds all peoples,

Shrouded (Shroud)
Job 19: 8 he has s my paths in darkness.
Ecc 6: 4 and in darkness its name is s.

Shrub
Ge 2: 5 no s of the field had yet appeared

Shua
Ge 38: 2 daughter of a Canaanite man named **S**.
38:12 wife, the daughter of **S**, died.
1Ch 2: 3 Canaanite woman, the daughter of **S**.
7:32 and Hotham and of their sister **S**.

Shuah
Ge 25: 2 Jokshan, Medan, Midian, Ishbak and **S**.
1Ch 1:32 Jokshan, Medan, Midian, Ishbak and **S**.

Shual
1Sa 13:17 towards Ophrah in the vicinity of **S**,
1Ch 7:36 Suah, Harnepher, **S**, Beri, Imrah,

Shubael
1Ch 23:16 of Gershom: **S** was the first.
24:20 from the sons of Amram: **S**;

1Ch 24:20 from the sons of **S**: Jehdeiah.
25: 4 Mattaniah, Uzziel, **S** and Jerimoth;
25:20 the thirteenth to **S**, his sons and
26:24 **S**, a descendant of Gershom son of

Shudder
Isa 19:16 They will **s** with fear at the
32:11 **s**, you daughters who feel secure!
Jer 2:12 O heavens, and **s** with great horror,"
Eze 12:18 **s** in fear as you drink your water.
27:35 their kings **s** with horror and their
32:10 and their kings will **s** with horror
Jas 2:19 Even the demons believe that—and **s**.

Shuhah's
1Ch 4:11 Kelub, **S** brother, was the father of

Shuham (Shuhamite)
Nu 26:42 through **S**, the Shuhamite clan.

Shuhamite (Shuham)
Nu 26:42 clans: through Shuham, the **S** clan.
26:43 All of them were **S** clans; and those

Shuhite
Job 2:11 Eliphaz the Temanite, Bildad the **S**
8: 1 Bildad the **S** replied:
18: 1 Bildad the **S** replied:
25: 1 Bildad the **S** replied:
42: 9 Eliphaz the Temanite, Bildad the **S**

Shulammite
SS 6:13 Come back, come back, O **S**; come back,
6:13 Why would you gaze on the **S** as on

Shumathites
1Ch 2:53 Ithrites, Puthites, **S** and Mishraites.

Shun (Shunned, Shuns)
Job 28:28 and to **s** evil is understanding.
Pr 3: 7 own eyes; fear the LORD and **s** evil.

Shunammite
1Ki 1: 3 found Abishag, a **S**, and brought her
1:15 Abishag the **S** was attending him.
2:17 give me Abishag the **S** as my wife."
2:21 "Let Abishag the **S** be given in
2:22 "Why do you request Abishag the **S**
2Ki 4:12 to his servant Gehazi, "Call the **S**.
4:25 "Look! There's the **S**!
4:36 Gehazi and said, "Call the **S**."

Shunem
Town in territory of Issachar (Jos 19:18), where the Philistines camped before meeting Saul in battle (1Sa 28:4). Home of Abishag, who cared for the aged David (1Ki 1:3). Elisha occasionally lodged here with a wealthy couple, and foretold the birth of their long-desired son (2Ki 4:8–17). He later restored the boy to life (2Ki 4:32–37).

Jos 19:18 included: Jezreel, Kesulloth, **S**,
1Sa 28: 4 and came and set up camp at **S**,
2Ki 4: 8 One day Elisha went to **S**. And a

Shuni (Shunite)
Ge 46:16 The sons of Gad: Zephon, Haggi, **S**,
Nu 26:15 through **S**, the Shunite clan;

Shunite (Shuni)
Nu 26:15 through Shuni, the **S** clan;

Shunned (Shun)
Job 1: 1 he feared God and **s** evil.
Pr 14:20 The poor are **s** even by their
19: 7 A poor man is **s** by all his relatives

Shuns (Shun)
Job 1: 8 a man who fears God and **s** evil."
2: 3 a man who fears God and **s** evil.
Pr 14:16 A wise man fears the LORD and **s** evil,
Isa 59:15 and whoever **s** evil becomes a prey.

Shupham (Shuphamite)
Nu 26:39 through **S**, the Shuphamite clan;

Shuphamite (Shupham)
Nu 26:39 through Shupham, the **S** clan;

Shuppim
1Ch 26:16 the upper road fell to **S** and Hosah.

Shuppites
1Ch 7:12 The **S** and Huppites were the
7:15 wife from among the Huppites and **S**.

Shur
Desert region between Egypt and the Negev. Hagar was on her way here when the angel found her (Ge 16:7). Abraham stayed near here (Ge 20:1). Ishmael's descendants settled here (Ge 25:18). Moses led the Israelites through this parched land (Ex 15:22). Saul pursued the Amalekites this far (1Sa 15:7); David attacked its inhabitants (1Sa 27:8).

Ge 16: 7 spring that is beside the road to **S**.
20: 1 Negev and lived between Kadesh and **S**.
25:18 in the area from Havilah to **S**,
Ex 15:22 and they went into the Desert of **S**.
1Sa 15: 7 Havilah to **S**, to the east of Egypt.
27: 8 the land extending to **S** and Egypt.)

Shut (Shuts)
Ge 7:16 Then the LORD **s** him in.
19: 6 meet them and **s** the door behind him
19:10 back into the house and **s** the door.
Dt 11:17 and he will **s** the heavens so that it
Jos 2: 7 had gone out, the gate was **s**.
6: 1 Now Jericho was tightly **s** up because
Jdg 3:23 he **s** the door of the upper room
1Sa 12: 3 a bribe to make me **s** my eyes?
1Ki 8:35 "When the heavens are **s** up and there
2Ki 4: 4 go inside and **s** the door behind you
4: 5 and afterwards **s** the door behind
4:21 God, then **s** the door and went out.
4:33 He went in, **s** the door on the two of
6:32 **s** the door and hold it **s** against him.
2Ch 6:26 "When the heavens are **s** up and there
7:13 "When I **s** up the heavens so that
28:24 He **s** the doors of the LORD's temple
29: 7 They also **s** the doors of the portico
Ne 6:10 Mehetabel, who was **s** in at his home.
7: 3 make them **s** the doors and bar them.
13:19 I ordered the doors to be **s** and not
Job 3:10 for it did not **s** the doors of the
24:16 but by day they **s** themselves in;
38: 8 "Who **s** up the sea behind doors when
Ps 107:42 but all the wicked **s** their mouths.
Isa 22:22 what he opens no-one can **s**,
24:22 they will be **s** up in prison and be
26:20 rooms and **s** the doors behind you;
45: 1 him so that gates will not be **s**:
52:15 will **s** their mouths because of him.
60:11 they will never be **s**, day or night,
Jer 13:19 The cities in the Negev will be **s** up,
20: 9 a fire, a fire **s** up in my bones.
Eze 3:24 "Go, **s** yourself inside your house.
22:26 and they **s** their eyes to the keeping
44: 1 the one facing east, and it was **s**.
44: 2 to me, "This gate is to remain **s**.
44: 2 It is to remain **s** because the LORD,
46: 1 is to be **s** on the six working days,
46: 2 gate will not be **s** until evening.
46:12 he has gone out, the gate will be **s**.
Da 6:22 and he **s** the mouths of the lions.
Mal 1:10 one of you would **s** the temple doors,
Mt 23:13 You **s** the kingdom of heaven in
25:10 And the door was **s**.
Lk 4:25 was **s** for three and a half years
Ac 21:30 and immediately the gates were **s**.
2Th 1: 9 **s** out from the presence of the Lord
Heb 11:33 promised; who **s** the mouths of lions,
Rev 3: 7 What he opens no-one can **s**,
3: 8 you an open door that no-one can **s**.
11: 6 These men have power to **s** up the sky
21:25 On no day will its gates ever be **s**,

Shuthelah (Shuthelahite)
Nu 26:35 through **S**, the Shuthelahite clan;
26:36 These were the descendants of **S**:
1Ch 7:20 The descendants of Ephraim: **S**, Bered
7:21 Zabad his son and **S** his son.

Shuthelahite (Shuthelah)
Nu 26:35 through Shuthelah, the **S** clan;

Shuts (Shut)
Job 5:16 hope, and injustice **s** its mouth.
Pr 21:13 If a man **s** his ears to the cry of
Isa 22:22 shut, and what he **s** no-one can open.
33:15 **s** his eyes against contemplating
Lam 3: 8 or cry for help, he **s** out my prayer.
Rev 3: 7 shut, and what he **s** no-one can open.

Shuttle
Job 7: 6 days are swifter than a weaver's **s**,

Shy
Job 39:22 he does not **s** away from the sword.

Sia
Ne 7:47 Keros, **S**, Padon,

Siaha
Ezr 2:44 Keros, **S**, Padon,

Sibbecai
2Sa 21:18 At that time **S** the Hushathite killed
1Ch 11:29 **S** the Hushathite, Ilai the Ahohite,
20: 4 At that time **S** the Hushathite killed
27:11 was **S** the Hushathite, a Zerahite.

Sibboleth
Jdg 12: 6 If he said, "**S**", because he could

Sibmah
Town east of Jordan, near Heshbon. Probably also known as Sebam. One of the towns requested by the Reubenites and Gadites (Nu 32:1–3). Eventually allotted to the tribe of Reuben, who rebuilt it (Nu 32:37–38; Jos 13:19). Renowned for its vines (Isa 16:8–9; Jer 48:32).

Nu 32:38 (these names were changed) and **S**.
Jos 13:19 Kiriathaim, **S**, Zereth Shahar on the
Isa 16: 8 Heshbon wither, the vines of **S** also.
16: 9 as Jazer weeps, for the vines of **S**.
Jer 48:32 you, as Jazer weeps, O vines of **S**.

Sibraim
Eze 47:16 Berothah and **S** (which lies on the

Sick (Sick-bed, Sickness, Sicknesses)
Pr 13:12 Hope deferred makes the heart **s**, but
Isa 10:18 as when a **s** man wastes away.
19:10 the wage earners will be **s** at heart.
Eze 34: 4 healed the **s** or bound up the
Mt 8:16 with a word and healed all the **s**.
9:12 who need a doctor, but the **s**.
10: 8 Heal the **s**, raise the dead, cleanse
12:15 him, and he healed all their **s**,
14:14 on them and healed their **s**.
14:35 People brought all their **s** to him
14:36 begged him to let the **s** just touch
25:36 I was **s** and you looked after me, I
25:39 did we see you **s** or in prison and go
25:43 I was **s** and in prison and you did
25:44 needing clothes or **s** or in prison,
Mk 1:32 Jesus all the **s** and demon-possessed.
2:17 who need a doctor, but the **s**.
6: 5 on a few **s** people and heal them.
6:13 anointed many **s** people with oil and
6:55 carried the **s** on mats to wherever
6:56 placed the **s** in the market-places.
16:18 will place their hands on **s** people,
Lk 5:17 was present for him to heal the **s**.
5:31 who need a doctor, but the **s**.
7: 2 highly, was **s** and about to die.
9: 2 kingdom of God and to heal the **s**.
10: 9 Heal the **s** who are there and tell

Jn 4:46 whose son lay s at Capernaum.
6: 2 signs he had performed on the s.
11: 1 Now a man named Lazarus was s.
11: 2 whose brother Lazarus now lay s, was
11: 3 "Lord, the one you love is s."
11: 6 Yet when he heard that Lazarus was s,
Ac 5:15 brought the s into the streets
5:16 bringing their s and those tormented
9:37 About that time she became s and
19:12 had touched him were taken to the s,
28: 8 His father was s in bed, suffering
28: 9 the rest of the s on the island
1Co 11:30 why many among you are weak and s,
2Ti 4:20 and I left Trophimus s in Miletus.
Jas 5:14 Is any one of you s? He should call
5:15 faith will make the s person well;

Sick-bed (Bed, Sick)
Ps 41: 3 The LORD will sustain him on his s

Sickle (Sickles)
Dt 16: 9 to put the s to the standing corn.
23:25 not put a s to his standing corn.
Jer 50:16 the reaper with his s at harvest.
Joel 3:13 Swing the s, for the harvest is ripe.
Mk 4:29 he puts the s to it, because the
Rev 14:14 his head and a sharp s in his hand.
14:15 "Take your s and reap, because the
14:16 cloud swung his s over the earth,
14:17 in heaven, and he too had a sharp s.
14:18 voice to him who had the sharp s,
14:18 "Take your sharp s and gather the
14:19 The angel swung his s on the earth,

Sickles (Sickle)
1Sa 13:20 mattocks, axes and s sharpened.

Sickness (Sick)
Ex 23:25 I will take away s from among you,
Dt 28:61 also bring on you every kind of s
Pr 18:14 A man's spirit sustains him in s,
Jer 6: 7 her s and wounds are ever before me.
10:19 "This is my s, and I must endure it.
Hos 5:13 "When Ephraim saw his s, and Judah
Mt 4:23 disease and s among the people.
9:35 and healing every disease and s.
10: 1 and to heal every disease and s.
Lk 4:40 Jesus all who had various kinds of s,
Jn 11: 4 "This s will not end in death.

Sicknesses (Sick)
Lk 5:15 him and to be healed of their s.
7:21 had diseases, s and evil spirits,

Siddim
Ge 14: 3 in the Valley of **S** (the Salt Sea).
14: 8 battle lines in the Valley of **S**
14:10 Now the Valley of **S** was full of tar

Side (Sided, Sides, Siding)
Ge 2:14 it runs along the east s of Asshur.
3:24 he placed on the east s of the
6:16 Put a door in the s of the ark and
31:52 this heap to your s to harm you
31:52 heap and pillar to my s to harm me.
Ex 3: 1 and he led the flock to the far s of
14:20 to the one s and light to the other;
17:12 —one on one s, one on the other—
25:12 with two rings on one s and two
25:32 three on one s and three on the
26:18 Make twenty frames for the south s
26:20 For the other s, the north s of the
26:26 frames on one s of the tabernacle,
26:27 five for those on the other s, and
26:35 on the north s of the tabernacle
26:35 opposite it on the south s.
27: 9 The south s shall be a hundred
27:11 The north s shall also be a hundred
27:14 are to be on one s of the entrance,
27:15 on the other s, with three posts
32:27 'Each man strap a sword to his s.
36:23 for the south s of the tabernacle
36:25 For the other s, the north s of the
36:31 frames on one s of the tabernacle,
Ex 36:32 five for those on the other s, and
37: 3 with two rings on one s and two
37:18 three on one s and three on the
38: 9 The south s was a hundred cubits
38:11 The north s was also a hundred
38:14 long were on one s of the entrance,
38:15 the other s of the entrance to the
40:22 on the north s of the tabernacle
40:24 on the south s of the tabernacle
Lev 1:11 He is to slaughter it at the north s
1:15 drained out on the s of the altar.
1:16 throw it to the east s of the altar
5: 9 offering against the s of the altar;
13:55 has affected one s or the other.
Nu 3:29 on the south s of the tabernacle.
3:35 on the north s of the tabernacle.
32:19 them on the other s of the Jordan,
32:19 to us on the east s of the Jordan."
32:32 will be on this s of the Jordan."
34: 3 "'Your southern s will include some
34:11 to Riblah on the east s of Ain
34:12 with its boundaries on every s.
34:15 the east s of the Jordan of Jericho,
35: 5 three thousand feet on the east s,
35: 5 three thousand on the south s, three
35:14 Give three on this s of the Jordan
36:11 their cousins on their father's s.
Jos 4:11 the priests came to the other s
7: 7 stay on the other s of the Jordan!
12: 1 all the eastern s of the Arabah:
12: 7 on the west s of the Jordan,
13:27 Heshbon (the east s of the Jordan,
17: 9 the northern s of the ravine and
18: 7 on the east s of the Jordan.
18:12 On the north s their boundary began
18:14 turned south along the western s
18:14 This was the western s.
18:15 The southern s began at the
18:20 the boundary on the eastern s.
20: 8 On the east s of the Jordan of
21:44 The LORD gave them rest on every s,
22: 4 you on the other s of the Jordan.
22: 7 land on the west s of the Jordan
22:11 near the Jordan on the Israelite s,
Jdg 8:34 of all their enemies on every s.
10: 8 the east s of the Jordan in Gilead,
11:18 passed along the eastern s of the
11:18 camped on the other s of the Arnon.
Ru 2: 1 had a relative on her husband's s,
1Sa 4:13 on his chair by the s of the road,
4:18 off his chair by the s of the gate.
12:11 hands of your enemies on every s,
14: 1 Philistine outpost on the other s.
14: 4 On each s of the pass that Jonathan
14:47 their enemies on every s: Moab,
20:20 I will shoot three arrows to the s
20:21 'Look, the arrows are on this s of
20:41 David got up from the south s of the
22:17 the king ordered the guards at his s:
23:26 Saul was going along one s of the
23:26 and his men were on the other s,
26:13 David crossed over to the other s
2Sa 2:13 One group sat down on one s of the
2:13 pool and one group on the other s.
2:16 his dagger into his opponent's s,
3: 8 "Am I a dog's head—on Judah's s?
13:34 him, coming down the s of the hill.
13:34 of Horonaim, on the s of the hill."
15: 2 stand by the s of the road leading
1Ki 3:20 took my son from my s while I your
5: 4 my God has given me rest on every s,
6: 5 in which there were s rooms.
6: 8 was on the south s of the temple;
6:10 he built the s rooms all along the
7:28 had s panels attached to uprights.
7:30 cast with wreaths on each s.
7:39 stands on the south s of the temple
7:39 He placed the Sea on the south s, at
2Ki 4: 4 as each is filled, put it to one s."
6:11 is on the s of the king of Israel?"
9:32 "Who is on my s? Who?" Two or three
10: 6 "If you are on my s and will obey me,
11:11 from the south s to the north s of
12: 9 on the right s as one enters the
16:14 it on the north s of the new altar.
16:17 King Ahaz took away the s panels and
1Ch 18:17 chief officials at the king's s.
22: 9 from all his enemies on every s.
22:18 he not granted you rest on every s?
23:28 the s rooms, the purification of all
2Ch 4: 6 five on the south s and five on the
4: 7 five on the south s and five on the
4: 8 five on the south s and five on the
4:10 He placed the Sea on the south s, at
5:12 on the east s of the altar,
14: 7 and he has given us rest on every s.
15:15 the LORD gave them rest on every s.
20: 2 Edom, from the other s of the Sea.
20:30 God had given him rest on every s.
23:10 from the south s to the north s of
29: 4 them in the square on the east s
32:22 He took care of them on every s.
32:30 to the west s of the City of David.
Ne 4: 3 Tobiah the Ammonite, who was at his s
4:18 his sword at his s as he worked.
Job 15:10 and the aged are on our s,
18:11 Terrors startle him on every s and
19:10 He tears me down on every s till I
21:26 **S** by s they lie in the dust, and
33:23 "Yet if there is an angel on his s
39:23 The quiver rattles against his s,
Ps 3: 6 drawn up against me on every s.
31:13 there is terror on every s;
45: 3 Gird your sword upon your s,
91: 7 A thousand may fall at your s, ten
97: 3 and consumes his foes on every s.
118:11 They surrounded me on every s, but
124: 1 If the LORD had not been on our s—
124: 2 if the LORD had not been on our s
139: 9 if I settle on the far s of the sea,
Pr 8:30 I was the craftsman at his s. I was
Ecc 4: 1 power was on the s of their
SS 3: 8 each with his sword at his s,
Jer 6:25 and there is terror on every s.
20:10 "Terror on every s! Report him!
35: 2 them to come to one of the s rooms
46: 5 and there is terror on every s,"
49:29 shout to them, 'Terror on every s!'
49:32 disaster on them from every s,"
50:15 Shout against her on every s!
51: 2 they will oppose her on every s in
Lam 2:22 against me terrors on every s.
Eze 1:10 and on the right s each had the face
1:11 of another creature on either s,
4: 4 "Then lie on your left s and put the
4: 4 number of days you lie on your s.
4: 6 this time on your right s, and bear
4: 8 cannot turn from one s to the other
4: 9 the 390 days you lie on your s.
9: 2 who had a writing kit at his s.
9: 3 who had the writing kit at his s
9:11 kit at his s brought back word,
10: 3 standing on the south s of the
10:16 the wheels did not leave their s.
21:14 closing in on them from every s.
23:22 them against you from every s—
23:24 against you on every s with large
27:11 manned your walls on every s;
28:23 the sword against her on every s.
36: 3 hounded you from every s so that you
40: 2 on whose south s were some buildings
40:10 gate were three alcoves on each s;
40:10 on each s had the same measurements.
40:19 the east s as well as on the north.
40:21 Its alcoves—three on each s—its
40:24 he led me to the south s and I saw a
40:26 of the projecting walls on each s.
40:27 to the outer gate on the south s;
40:32 me to the inner court on the east s,
40:34 decorated the jambs on either s,
40:37 decorated the jambs on either s,
40:39 gateway were two tables on each s,
40:40 s of the steps were two tables.
40:41 there were four tables on one s of
40:44 were two rooms, one at the s of the
40:44 another at the s of the south gate
40:48 were five cubits wide on either s.
40:48 were three cubits wide on either s.
40:49 were pillars on each s of the jambs.
41: 1 the jambs was six cubits on each s.
41: 2 each s of it were five cubits wide.
41: 3 each s of it were seven cubits wide.

Eze 41: 5 and each **s** room round the temple was
41: 6 The **s** rooms were on three levels,
41: 6 serve as supports for the **s** rooms,
41: 7 The **s** rooms all round the temple
41: 8 the foundation of the **s** rooms.
41: 9 The outer wall of the **s** rooms was
41: 9 between the **s** rooms of the temple
41:11 There were entrances to the **s** rooms
41:12 the west **s** was seventy cubits wide.
41:15 including its galleries on each **s**;
41:19 man towards the palm tree on one **s**
41:26 On the **s** walls of the portico were
41:26 with palm trees carved on each **s**.
41:26 The **s** rooms of the temple also had
42: 1 the outer wall on the north **s**.
42: 8 While the row of rooms on the **s** next
42: 8 the row on the **s** nearest the
42: 9 rooms had an entrance on the east **s**
42:10 On the south **s** along the length of
42:16 He measured the east **s** with the
42:17 He measured the north **s**; it was five
42:18 He measured the south **s**; it was five
42:19 he turned to the west **s** and measured;
45: 7 land bordering each **s** of the area
45: 7 west **s** and eastward from the east **s**,
46:19 the entrance at the **s** of the gate
47: 1 **s** of the temple, south of the altar.
47: 2 water was flowing from the south **s**.
47: 7 of trees on each **s** of the river.
47:15 "On the north **s** it will run from the
47:18 "On the east **s** the boundary will run
47:19 "On the south **s** it will run from
47:20 "On the west **s**, the Great Sea will
48: 1 from the east **s** to the west **s**.
48:10 25,000 cubits long on the north **s**,
48:10 10,000 cubits wide on the west **s**,
48:10 10,000 cubits wide on the east **s** and
48:10 25,000 cubits long on the south **s**.
48:16 the north **s** 4,500 cubits
48:16 the south **s** 4,500 cubits,
48:16 the east **s** 4,500 cubits, and the
48:16 and the west **s** 4,500 cubits.
48:18 will be 10,000 cubits on the east **s**
48:18 and 10,000 cubits on the west **s**.
48:20 a square, 25,000 cubits on each **s**.
48:23 from the east **s** to the west **s**.
48:30 north **s**, which is 4,500 cubits long,
48:31 The three gates on the north **s** will
48:32 "On the east **s**, which is 4,500
48:33 "On the south **s**, which measures
48:34 "On the west **s**, which is 4,500
Joel 3:11 all you nations from every **s**,
3:12 to judge all the nations on every **s**.
Zec 3: 1 at his right **s** to accuse him.
5: 3 according to what it says on one **s**,
Mt 8:18 to cross to the other **s** of the lake.
8:28 he arrived at the other **s** in the
14:22 go on ahead of him to the other **s**,
19: 1 Judea to the other **s** of the Jordan.
Mk 4:35 "Let us go over to the other **s**.
5:21 by boat to the other **s** of the lake,
8:13 the boat and crossed to the other **s**.
16: 5 sitting on the right **s**, and they
Lk 1:11 the right **s** of the altar of incense.
8:22 go over to the other **s** of the lake.
10:31 man, he passed by on the other **s**.
10:32 saw him, passed by on the other **s**.
16:22 angels carried him to Abraham's **s**.
16:23 far away, with Lazarus by his **s**.
19:43 you and hem you in on every **s**.
Jn 1:18 who is at the Father's **s**, has made
1:28 Bethany on the other **s** of the Jordan,
3:26 you on the other **s** of the Jordan—
6:25 they found him on the other **s** of the
18: 1 On the other **s** there was an olive
18:37 on the **s** of truth listens to me."
19:18 on each **s** and Jesus in the middle.
19:34 pierced Jesus' **s** with a spear,
20:20 he showed them his hands and **s**.
20:25 put my hand into his **s**, I will not
20:27 out your hand and put it into my **s**.
21: 6 net on the right **s** of the boat and
Ac 12: 7 He struck Peter on the **s** and woke
2Co 4: 8 We are hard pressed on every **s**, but
Php 4: 3 at my **s** in the cause of the gospel,
2Ti 4:17 the Lord stood at my **s** and gave me
Heb 10:33 at other times you stood **s** by **s** with
Rev 22: 2 On each **s** of the river stood the

Sided (Side)

1Sa 20:30 Don't I know that you have **s** with
22:17 because they too have **s** with David.
2Ch 11:13 throughout Israel **s** with him.
Ac 14: 4 some **s** with the Jews, others with

Sides (Side)

Ex 12: 7 put it on the **s** and tops of the
12:22 top and on both **s** of the door-frame.
12:23 **s** of the door-frame and will pass
25:14 on the **s** of the chest to carry it.
25:32 Six branches are to extend from the **s**
26:13 will be a cubit longer on both **s**;
26:13 what is left will hang over the **s** of
27: 7 be on two **s** of the altar when it is
29:16 it against the altar on all **s**.
29:20 blood against the altar on all **s**.
30: 3 Overlay the top and all the **s** and
30: 4 two on opposite **s**—to hold the poles
32:15 inscribed on both **s**, front and back.
37: 5 on the **s** of the ark to carry it.
37:18 Six branches extended from the **s** of
37:26 They overlaid the top and all the **s**
37:27 two on opposite **s**—to hold the poles
38: 7 the **s** of the altar for carrying it.
Lev 1: 5 against the altar on all **s** at the
1:11 blood against the altar on all **s**.
3: 2 blood against the altar on all **s**.
3: 8 blood against the altar on all **s**.
3:13 blood against the altar on all **s**.
7: 2 against the altar on all **s**.
8:19 blood against the altar on all **s**.
8:24 blood against the altar on all **s**.
9:12 it against the altar on all **s**.
9:18 it against the altar on all **s**.
19:27 "'Do not cut the hair at the **s** of
Nu 22:24 two vineyards, with walls on both **s**.
33:55 in your eyes and thorns in your **s**.
Jos 8:22 middle, with Israelites on both **s**.
8:33 were standing on both **s** of the ark
18:20 of the clans of Benjamin on all **s**.
Jdg 2: 3 they will be ⌊thorns⌋ in your **s**
1Ki 4:24 to Gaza, and had peace on all **s**.
5: 3 against my father David from all **s**,
10:19 On both **s** of the seat were armrests,
1Ch 9:24 The gatekeepers were on the four **s**:
2Ch 9:18 On both **s** of the seat were armrests,
Job 11: 6 wisdom, for true wisdom has two **s**.
Jer 52:23 ninety-six pomegranates on the **s**;
Eze 1: 8 Under their wings on their four **s**
2:10 On both **s** of it were written words
40:18 abutted the **s** of the gateways and
41:22 its base and its **s** were of wood.
42:20 he measured the area on all four **s**.
48:21 "What remains on both **s** of the area
Da 7: 5 It was raised up on one of its **s**,
Rev 5: 1 with writing on both **s** and sealed

Siding (Side)

Ex 23: 2 pervert justice by **s** with the crowd,

Sidon (Sidonians)

Ancient city on Mediterranean coast of Lebanon, about 20 miles north of Tyre, founded by the son of Canaan (Ge 10:15; 1Ch 1:13). Israel pursued the defeated Canaanites to here (Jos 11:8); it formed the northernmost border of Asher's territory (Jos 19:28). Asher failed to drive out its Canaanite inhabitants (Jdg 1:31) and Israel was punished for serving their gods (Jdg 10:6, 12). The city's importance grew so the King of Tyre was known as "king of the Sidonians" (1Ki 16:31), and its name was used for that whole area (1Ki 17:9). Despite its power, wealth and security (Ezr 3:7; Isa 23:2), the prophets emphasised its fragility (Isa 23:12; Jer 27:3, 6; 47:4; Eze 28:21–26; Joel 3:4–8; Zec 9:1–4). Jesus spoke of it more favourably than some of the towns of Galilee (Mt 11:21–22; Lk 4:26; 10:13–14). Here he praised a Canaanite woman's faith and healed her daughter (Mt 15:21–28; Mk 7:24–31). Its people went to Galilee to hear Jesus preach (Mk 3:8; Lk 6:17); they sought peace with King Herod (Ac 12:20); and Paul found kind hospitality here (Ac 27:3).

Ge 10:15 Canaan was the father of **S** his
10:19 the borders of Canaan reached from **S**
49:13 his border will extend towards **S**.
Jos 11: 8 them all the way to Greater **S**,
19:28 and Kanah, as far as Greater **S**.
Jdg 1:31 those living in Acco or **S** or Ahlab
10: 6 and the gods of Aram, the gods of **S**,
18:28 they lived a long way from **S** and
2Sa 24: 6 on to Dan Jaan and around towards **S**.
1Ki 17: 9 "Go at once to Zarephath of **S** and
1Ch 1:13 Canaan was the father of **S** his
Ezr 3: 7 and oil to the people of **S** and Tyre,
Isa 23: 2 and you merchants of **S**, whom the
23: 4 Be ashamed, O **S**, and you, O fortress
23:12 O Virgin Daughter of **S**, now crushed!
Jer 25:22 all the kings of Tyre and **S**;
27: 3 Moab, Ammon, Tyre and **S** through the
47: 4 survivors who could help Tyre and **S**.
Eze 27: 8 Men of **S** and Arvad were your oarsmen;
28:21 "Son of man, set your face against **S**;
28:22 "'I am against you, O **S**, and I will
Joel 3: 4 O Tyre and **S** and all you regions of
Zec 9: 2 and upon Tyre and **S**, though they
Mt 11:21 had been performed in Tyre and **S**,
11:22 more bearable for Tyre and **S** on the
15:21 to the region of Tyre and **S**.
Mk 3: 8 the Jordan and around Tyre and **S**.
7:31 vicinity of Tyre and went through **S**,
Lk 4:26 in Zarephath in the region of **S**.
6:17 and from the coast of Tyre and **S**,
10:13 had been performed in Tyre and **S**,
10:14 will be more bearable for Tyre and **S**
Ac 12:20 with the people of Tyre and **S**;
27: 3 The next day we landed at **S**;

Sidonians (Sidon)

Dt 3: 9 (Hermon is called Sirion by the **S**;
Jos 13: 4 from Arah of the **S** as far as Aphek,
13: 6 that is, all the **S**, I myself will
Jdg 3: 3 all the Canaanites, the **S**, and the
10:12 the **S**, the Amalekites and the
18: 7 like the **S**, unsuspecting and secure.
18: 7 they lived a long way from the **S** and
1Ki 5: 6 skilled in felling timber as the **S**."
11: 1 Ammonites, Edomites, **S** and Hittites.
11: 5 Ashtoreth the goddess of the **S**,
11:33 Ashtoreth the goddess of the **S**,
16:31 daughter of Ethbaal king of the **S**,
2Ki 23:13 Ashtoreth the vile goddess of the **S**,
1Ch 22: 4 for the **S** and Tyrians had brought
Eze 32:30 the north and all the **S** are there;

Siege (Besiege, Besieged, Besieges, Besieging, Siegeworks)

Dt 20:12 you in battle, lay **s** to that city.
20:19 you lay **s** to a city for a long time,
20:20 use them to build **s** works until the
28:52 They will lay **s** to all the cities
28:53 will inflict on you during the **s**,
28:55 you during the **s** of all your cities.
28:57 to eat them secretly during the **s**
2Sa 11:16 while Joab had the city under **s**, he
20:15 They built a **s** ramp up to the city,
1Ki 16:17 from Gibbethon and laid **s** to Tirzah.
2Ki 6:24 marched up and laid **s** to Samaria.
6:25 the **s** lasted so long that a donkey's
17: 5 and laid **s** to it for three years.
18: 9 against Samaria and laid **s** to it.
19:32 shield or build a **s** ramp against it.
24:10 on Jerusalem and laid **s** to it,
25: 1 and built **s** works all around it.
25: 2 The city was kept under **s** until the
2Ch 32: 1 He laid **s** to the fortified cities,
32: 9 his forces were laying **s** to Lachish,
32:10 you remain in Jerusalem under **s**?
Job 19:12 they build a **s** ramp against me and
30:12 they build their **s** ramps against me.
Isa 1: 8 of melons, like a city under **s**.
21: 2 Elam, attack! Media, lay **s**! I will
23:13 they raised up their **s** towers,
29: 3 and set up my **s** works against you.
37:33 shield or build a **s** ramp against it.

Jer 6: 6 and build s ramps against Jerusalem.
10:17 the land, you who live under s.
19: 9 stress of the s imposed on them by
32:24 "See how the s ramps are built up to
33: 4 against the s ramps and the
39: 1 his whole army and laid s to it.
52: 4 and built s works all around it.
52: 5 The city was kept under s until the
Eze 4: 2 lay s to it: Erect s works against
4: 3 It will be under s, and you shall
4: 7 Turn your face towards the s of
4: 8 have finished the days of your s.
5: 2 the days of your s come to an end,
17:17 and s works erected to destroy many
21:22 build a ramp and to erect s works.
24: 2 laid s to Jerusalem this very day.
26: 8 he will set up s works against you,
Da 11:15 build up s ramps and will capture a
Mic 5: 1 troops, for a s is laid against us.
Na 3:14 Draw water for the s, strengthen

Siegeworks (Siege)
Ecc 9:14 it and built huge s against it.

Sieve
Isa 30:28 nations in the s of destruction;
Am 9: 9 nations as grain is shaken in a s,

Sift
Jdg 7: 4 and I will s them out for you there.
Lk 22:31 Satan has asked to s you as wheat.

Sigh (Sighed, Sighing)
Mk 7:34 a deep s said to him, "Ephphatha!"

Sighed (Sigh)
Mk 8:12 He s deeply and said, "Why does this

Sighing (Sigh)
Job 3:24 For s comes to me instead of food;
Ps 5: 1 to my words, O LORD, consider my s.
38: 9 O Lord: my s is not hidden from you.
Isa 35:10 and sorrow and s will flee away.
51:11 and sorrow and s will flee away.

Sight (Sights)
Ge 6:11 Now the earth was corrupt in God's s
33:18 and camped within s of the city.
38: 7 was wicked in the LORD's s;
38:10 was wicked in the LORD's s;
43:30 Deeply moved at the s of his brother,
Ex 3: 3 and see this strange s—why the
4:11 Who give him s or makes him blind?
10:28 "Get out of my s! Make sure you do
17: 6 in the s of the elders of Israel.
19:11 Sinai in the s of all the people.
40:38 in the s of all the house of Israel
Lev 10: 3 in the s of all the people I will be
26:16 destroy your s and drain away your
26:45 in the s of the nations to be their
Nu 20:12 as holy in the s of the Israelites,
20:27 Hor in the s of the whole community.
32:13 who had done evil in his s was gone.
Dt 6:18 is right and good in the LORD's s,
9:18 doing what was evil in the LORD's s
24:13 act in the s of the LORD your God.
31:29 will do evil in the s of the LORD
34:12 Moses did in the s of all Israel.
Jos 4:14 Joshua in the s of all Israel;
1Sa 2:17 men was very great in the LORD's s,
6:13 saw the ark, they rejoiced at the s.
9:17 Samuel caught s of Saul, the LORD
2Sa 6:20 disrobing in the s of the slave
7:19 if this were not enough in your s,
7:29 it may continue for ever in your s;
10:12 LORD will do what is good in his s."
13: 5 Let her prepare the food in my s so
13: 6 make some special bread in my s,
13: 8 the bread in his s and baked it.
16:22 concubines in the s of all Israel.
22:25 according to my cleanness in his s.
1Ki 14: 4 his s was gone because of his age.
2Ki 5: 1 He was a great man in the s of his
1Ch 2: 3 was wicked in the LORD's s;
1Ch 17:17 if this were not enough in your s,
17:27 it may continue for ever in your s;
19:13 LORD will do what is good in his s."
21: 7 was also evil in the s of God;
22: 5 in the s of all the nations.
22: 8 much blood on the earth in my s.
28: 8 "So now I charge you in the s of all
29:15 We are aliens and strangers in your s
29:25 Solomon in the s of all Israel
Ezr 9: 9 He has shown us kindness in the s of
Ne 2: 5 servant has found favour in his s,
4: 5 or blot out their sins from your s,
9:28 again did what was evil in your s.
Job 11: 4 flawless and I am pure in your s.'
18: 3 and considered stupid in your s?
41: 9 the mere s of him is overpowering.
Ps 18:24 the cleanness of my hands in his s.
19:14 be pleasing in your s, O LORD, my
31:19 which you bestow in the s of men on
31:22 "I am cut off from your s!" Yet you
51: 4 and done what is evil in your s,
72:14 precious is their blood in his s.
78:12 He did miracles in the s of their
90: 4 For a thousand years in your s are
116:15 Precious in the s of the LORD is the
146: 8 the LORD gives s to the blind, the
Pr 3: 4 a good name in the s of God and man.
3:21 do not let them out of your s;
4:21 Do not let them out of your s, keep
29:13 The LORD gives s to the eyes of both.
Isa 1:16 Take your evil deeds out of my s!
5:21 own eyes and clever in their own s.
31: 9 at s of the battle standard their
43: 4 are precious and honoured in my s,
52:10 arm in the s of all the nations,
59:12 For our offences are many in your s,
65:12 You did evil in my s and chose what
66: 4 They did evil in my s and chose what
Jer 4: 1 out of my s and no longer go astray,
18:10 if it does evil in my s and does not
18:23 or blot out their sins from your s.
31:36 if these decrees vanish from my s,"
32:30 but evil in my s from their youth;
32:31 that I must remove it from my s.
34:15 and did what is right in my s:
Eze 4:12 bake it in the s of the people,
4:17 They will be appalled at the s of
5: 8 on you in the s of the nations.
5:14 you, in the s of all who pass by.
16:41 on you in the s of many women.
20: 9 in whose s I had revealed myself to
20:14 in whose s I had brought them out.
20:22 in whose s I had brought them out.
20:41 among you in the s of the nations.
28:18 in the s of all who were watching.
28:25 among them in the s of the nations.
36:17 woman's monthly uncleanness in my s.
36:34 in the s of all who pass through it.
38:23 known in the s of many nations.
39:27 them in the s of many nations.
Da 6:22 I was found innocent in his s.
Joel 2: 6 At the s of them, nations are in
Jnh 2: 4 'I have been banished from your s;
Hag 2:14 nation in my s,' declares the LORD.
Mt 9:30 their s was restored. Jesus warned
11: 5 The blind receive s, the lame walk,
20:33 "Lord," they answered, "we want our s
20:34 received their s and followed him.
Mk 8:25 were opened, his s was restored,
10:52 Immediately he received his s and
Lk 1: 6 them were upright in the s of God,
1:15 for he will be great in the s of the
2:31 which you have prepared in the s of
4:18 and recovery of s for the blind,
7:21 and gave s to many who were blind.
7:22 The blind receive s, the lame walk
16:15 among men is detestable in God's s.
18:42 Jesus said to him, "Receive your s;
18:43 Immediately he received his s and
23:48 witness this s saw what took place,
24:31 and he disappeared from their s.
Jn 9:15 asked him how he had received his s.
9:18 had received his s until they sent
Ac 1: 9 and a cloud hid him from their s.
4:19 right in God's s to obey you rather
7:31 he saw this, he was amazed at the s.
Ac 9:12 his hands on him to restore his s."
22:13 'Brother Saul, receive your s!'
28:15 At the s of these men Paul thanked
Ro 2:13 law who are righteous in God's s,
3:20 righteous in his s by observing the
4:17 He is our father in the s of God,
1Co 3:19 world is foolishness in God's s.
2Co 2:10 in the s of Christ for your sake,
4: 2 man's conscience in the s of God.
5: 7 We live by faith, not by s.
12:19 in the s of God as those in Christ;
Eph 1: 4 to be holy and blameless in his s.
Col 1:22 death to present you holy in his s,
1Ti 5:21 I charge you, in the s of God and
6:13 In the s of God, who gives life to
Heb 4:13 all creation is hidden from God's s.
12:21 The s was so terrifying that Moses
1Pe 3: 4 which is of great worth in God's s.
Rev 3: 2 deeds complete in the s of my God.

Sightless
Isa 29: 9 blind yourselves and be s; be drunk,

Sights (Sight)
Dt 28:34 The s you see will drive you mad.
28:67 and the s that your eyes will see.
Pr 23:33 Your eyes will see strange s and

Sign (Signed, Signs)
Ge 9:12 "This is the s of the covenant
9:13 and it will be the s of the covenant
9:17 "This is the s of the covenant
17:11 s of the covenant between me and you.
49: 3 my might, the first s of my strength,
Ex 3:12 And this will be the s to you that
4: 8 the first miraculous s, they may
8:23 This miraculous s will occur
12:13 The blood will be a s for you on the
13: 9 be for you like a s on your hand
13:16 will be like a s on your hand and a
31:13 This will be a s between me and you
31:17 will be a s between me and the
Nu 16:38 Let them be a s to the Israelites."
17:10 to be kept as a s to the rebellious.
26:10 And they served as a warning s.
Dt 13: 1 to you a miraculous s or wonder,
13: 2 if the s or wonder of which he has
21:17 That son is the first s of his
28:46 They will be a s and a wonder to you
Jos 2:12 kindness to you. Give me a sure s
4: 6 to serve as a s among you. In the
Jdg 6:17 give me a s that it is really you
1Sa 2:34 Hophni and Phinehas, will be a s to
14:10 because that will be our s that the
1Ki 13: 3 That same day the man of God gave a s
13: 3 "This is the s the LORD has declared:
13: 5 according to the s given by the man
20:33 The men took this as a good s and
2Ki 19:29 "This will be the s for you,
20: 8 "What will be the s that the LORD
20: 9 "This is the LORD's s to you that
2Ch 32:24 him and gave him a miraculous s.
32:31 s that had occurred in the land,
Job 31:35 I s now my defence—let the
Ps 86:17 Give me a s of your goodness, that
Isa 7:11 "Ask the LORD your God for a s,
7:14 the Lord himself will give you a s:
19:20 will be a s and witness to the LORD
20: 3 s and portent against Egypt and Cush,
37:30 "This will be the s for you,
38: 7 "'This is the LORD's s to you that
38:22 "What will be the s that I will go
55:13 for an everlasting s, which will
66:19 "I will set a s among them, and I
Jer 44:29 "'This will be the s to you that I
Eze 4: 3 will be a s to the house of Israel.
12: 6 you a s to the house of Israel."
12:11 Say to them, 'I am a s to you.'
20:12 Also I gave them my Sabbaths as a s
20:20 that they may be a s between us.
24:24 Ezekiel will be a s to you; you will
24:27 So you will be a s to them, and they
Mt 12:38 to see a miraculous s from you."
12:39 generation asks for a miraculous s!
12:39 except the s of the prophet Jonah.

Mt 16: 1 him to show them a s from heaven.
16: 4 generation looks for a miraculous s,
16: 4 be given it except the s of Jonah.
24: 3 and what will be the s of your
24:30 "At that time the s of the Son of
Mk 8:11 they asked him for a s from heaven.
8:12 generation ask for a miraculous s?
8:12 truth, no s will be given to it."
13: 4 And what will be the s that they are
Lk 2:12 This will be a s to you: You will
2:34 be a s that will be spoken against,
11:16 Others tested him by asking for a s
11:29 It asks for a miraculous s, but none
11:29 be given it except the s of Jonah.
11:30 For as Jonah was a s to the
21: 7 s that they are about to take place?
Jn 2:18 "What miraculous s can you show us
4:54 This was the second miraculous s
6:14 the people saw the miraculous s
6:30 "What miraculous s then will you
10:41 John never performed a miraculous s,
12:18 he had given this miraculous s,
19:20 Many of the Jews read this s, for
19:20 and the s was written in Aramaic,
Ro 4:11 he received the s of circumcision, a
1Co 11:10 have a s of authority on her head.
14:22 Tongues, then, are a s, not for
Php 1:28 This is a s to them that they will
Rev 12: 1 A great and wondrous s appeared in
12: 3 another s appeared in heaven: an
15: 1 another great and marvellous s:

Signal (Signalled, Signalling, Signals)
Nu 10: 6 blast will be the s for setting out.
10: 7 trumpets, but not with the same s.
Jer 4: 6 Raise the s to go to Zion! Flee for
6: 1 Raise the s over Beth Hakkerem!
Zec 10: 8 I will s for them and gather them in
Mt 26:48 Now the betrayer had arranged a s
Mk 14:44 Now the betrayer had arranged a s

Signalled (Signal)
Lk 5: 7 they s to their partners in the

Signalling (Signal)
Nu 31: 6 sanctuary and the trumpets for s.

Signals (Signal)
Pr 6:13 winks with his eye, s with his feet

Signed (Sign)
Jer 32:10 I s and sealed the deed, had it
32:12 of the witnesses who had s the deed
32:44 and deeds will be s, sealed and

Signet
Ge 41:42 Pharaoh took his s ring from his
Nu 31:50 bracelets, s rings, ear-rings and
Est 3:10 the king took his s ring from his
8: 2 The king took off his s ring, which
8: 8 and seal it with the king's s ring
8:10 dispatches with the king's s ring,
Isa 3:21 the s rings and nose rings,
Jer 22:24 were a s ring on my right hand, I
Da 6:17 king sealed it with his own s ring
Hag 2:23 'and I will make you like my s ring,

Signpost
Eze 21:19 Make a s where the road branches off

Signs (*Miraculous signs*, *Miraculous signs and wonders*, Sign, *Signs and wonders*)
Ge 1:14 s to mark seasons and days and years,
Ex 4: 9 if they do not believe these two s
4:30 performed the s before the people,
10: 2 and how I performed my s among them,
Dt 11: 3 the s he performed and the things he
Jos 24:17 those great s before our eyes.
1Sa 10: 7 Once these s are fulfilled, do
10: 9 all these s were fulfilled that day.
Ps 74: 4 they set up their standards as s.
Isa 8:18 We are s and symbols in Israel from
44:25 who foils the s of false prophets
Jer 10: 2 or be terrified by s in the sky,
31:21 "Set up road s; put up guideposts.
Da 4: 3 How great are his s, how mighty his
Mt 16: 3 cannot interpret the s of the times.
24:24 perform great s and miracles to
Mk 13:22 perform s and miracles to deceive
16:17 these s will accompany those who
16:20 word by the s that accompanied it.
Lk 1:22 for he kept making s to them but
1:62 they made s to his father, to find
21:11 events and great s from heaven.
21:25 "There will be s in the sun, moon
Ac 2:19 above and s on the earth below,
2:22 wonders and s, which God did among
8:13 by the great s and miracles he saw.
Ro 15:19 by the power of s and miracles,
2Co 12:12 that mark an apostle—s, wonders
Heb 2: 4 God also testified to it by s,
Rev 13:14 of the s he was given power to do on
19:20 With these s he had deluded those

Signs and wonders (*Miraculous signs and wonders*)
Ps 135: 9 He sent his s into your midst,
Jer 32:21 people Israel out of Egypt with s,
Da 6:27 he performs s in the heavens and on
2Th 2: 9 kinds of counterfeit miracles, s,

Sihon (Sihon's)
Nu 21:21 Israel sent messengers to say to S
21:23 S would not let Israel pass through
21:26 Heshbon was the city of S king of
21:28 Heshbon, a blaze from the city of S.
21:29 captives to S king of the Amorites.
21:34 Do to him what you did to S king of
32:33 kingdom of S king of the Amorites
Dt 1: 4 This was after he had defeated S
2:24 See, I have given into your hand S
2:26 to S king of Heshbon offering peace
2:30 S king of Heshbon refused to let us
2:31 S and his country over to you.
2:32 S and all his army came out to meet
3: 2 Do to him what you did to S king of
3: 6 we had done with S king of Heshbon
4:46 the land of S king of the Amorites,
29: 7 S king of Heshbon and Og King of
31: 4 do to them what he did to S and Og,
Jos 2:10 and what you did to S and Og, the
9:10 of the Jordan—S king of Heshbon,
12: 2 S king of the Amorites, who reigned
12: 5 to the border of S king of Heshbon.
13:10 all the towns of S king of the
13:21 realm of S king of the Amorites,
13:21 with S—who lived in that country.
13:27 of the realm of S king of Heshbon
Jdg 11:19 "Then Israel sent messengers to S
11:20 S, however, did not trust Israel to
11:21 gave S and all his men into
1Ki 4:19 country of S king of the Amorites
Ne 9:22 They took over the country of S king
Ps 135:11 S king of the Amorites, Og king of
136:19 S king of the Amorites
Jer 48:45 a blaze from the midst of S;

Sihon's (Sihon)
Nu 21:27 be rebuilt; let S city be restored.

Silas
Prophet and a leader in Jerusalem church; sent to Antioch from Council of Jerusalem (Ac 15:22–32). Accompanied Paul on second missionary journey (Ac 15:40–18:22; 2Co 1:19). Assisted Peter with first letter (1Pe 5:12); and Paul (1Th 1:1; 2Th 1:1).

Ac 15:22 Judas (called Barsabbas) and S,
15:27 Therefore we are sending Judas and S
15:32 Judas and S, who themselves were
15:40 Paul chose S and left, commended by
16:19 they seized Paul and S and dragged
16:22 in the attack against Paul and S,
16:25 About midnight Paul and S were
16:29 fell trembling before Paul and S.
16:36 ordered that you and S be released.
16:38 heard that Paul and S were Roman
16:40 After Paul and S came out of the
17: 4 persuaded and joined Paul and S,
17: 5 in search of Paul and S in order to
17:10 sent Paul and S away to Berea.
17:14 but S and Timothy stayed at Berea.
17:15 then left with instructions for S
18: 5 S and Timothy came from Macedonia,
2Co 1:19 among you by me and S and Timothy,
1Th 1: 1 Paul, S and Timothy, To the church
2Th 1: 1 Paul, S and Timothy, To the church
1Pe 5:12 With the help of S, whom I regard as

Silence (Silenced, Silences, Silent)
Job 11: 3 Will your idle talk reduce men to s?
29:21 waiting in s for my counsel.
Ps 8: 2 to s the foe and the avenger.
94:17 soon have dwelt in the s of death.
101: 5 in secret, him will I put to s;
101: 8 Every morning I will put to s all
115:17 the LORD, those who go down to s;
143:12 In your unfailing love, s my enemies;
Isa 25: 5 You s the uproar of foreigners;
47: 5 "Sit in s, go into darkness,
Jer 51:55 he will s her noisy din.
Lam 2:10 of Zion sit on the ground in s;
3:28 Let him sit alone in s, for the LORD
Am 8: 3 many bodies—flung everywhere! S!"
Ac 19:33 He motioned for s in order to make a
1Pe 2:15 s the ignorant talk of foolish men.
Rev 8: 1 s in heaven for about half an hour.

Silenced (Silence)
Nu 13:30 Caleb s the people before Moses and
1Sa 2: 9 the wicked will be s in darkness.
Job 23:17 Yet I am not s by the darkness, by
Ps 31:18 Let their lying lips be s, for with
63:11 while the mouths of liars will be s.
Jer 47: 5 in mourning; Ashkelon will be s.
48: 2 You too, O Madmen, will be s;
49:26 her soldiers will be s in that day,"
50:30 all her soldiers will be s in that
Eze 27:32 "Who was ever s like Tyre,
Mt 22:34 Hearing that Jesus had s the
Ro 3:19 so that every mouth may be s and the
Tit 1:11 They must be s, because they are

Silences (Silence)
Job 12:20 He s the lips of trusted advisers

Silent (Silence)
Lev 10: 3 " Aaron remained s.
Dt 27: 9 "Be s, O Israel, and listen!
1Sa 10:27 But Saul kept s.
2Ki 18:36 the people remained s and said
Est 4:14 For if you remain s at this time,
Job 7:11 "Therefore I will not keep s; I will
13: 5 If only you would be altogether s!
13:13 "Keep s and let me speak; then let
13:19 If so, I will be s and die.
31:34 I kept s and would not go outside—
32:16 Must I wait, now that they are s,
33:31 be s, and I will speak.
33:33 be s, and I will teach you wisdom."
34:29 if he remains s, who can condemn him?
Ps 4: 4 beds, search your hearts and be s.
22: 2 not answer, by night, and am not s.
28: 1 For if you remain s, I shall be like
30:12 heart may sing to you and not be s.
31:17 put to shame and lie s in the grave.
32: 3 I kept s, my bones wasted away
35:22 O LORD, you have seen this; be not s.
39: 2 I was s and still, not even saying
39: 9 I was s; I would not open my mouth,
50: 3 Our God comes and will not be s;
50:21 things you have done and I kept s;
83: 1 O God, do not keep s; be not quiet,
109: 1 O God, whom I praise, do not remain s
Pr 17:28 fool is thought wise if he keeps s,
Ecc 3: 7 a time to be s and a time to speak,
Isa 23: 2 Be s, you people of the island and
24: 8 has stopped, the joyful harp is s.
36:21 the people remained s and said
41: 1 "Be s before me, you islands!

Isa 42:14 "For a long time I have kept **s**, I
53: 7 a sheep before her shearers is **s**,
57:11 because I have long been **s** that you
62: 1 For Zion's sake I will not keep **s**,
62: 6 they will never be **s** day or night.
64:12 keep **s** and punish us beyond measure?
65: 6 I will not keep **s** but will pay back
Jer 4:19 pounds within me, I cannot keep **s**.
Eze 3:26 will be **s** and unable to rebuke them,
24:27 with him and will no longer be **s**.
33:22 was opened and I was no longer **s**.
Hab 1:13 Why are you **s** while the wicked
2:20 let all the earth be **s** before him."
Zep 1: 7 Be **s** before the Sovereign Lord, for
Mt 26:63 Jesus remained **s**. The high priest
Mk 3: 4 or to kill?" But they remained **s**.
14:61 Jesus remained **s** and gave no answer.
Lk 1:20 now you will be **s** and not able to
14: 4 they remained **s**. So taking hold of
20:26 by his answer, they became **s**.
Ac 8:32 as a lamb before the shearer is **s**,
15:12 The whole assembly became **s** as they
18: 9 keep on speaking, do not be **s**.
21:40 When they were all **s**, he said to
1Co 14:34 women should remain **s** in the
1Ti 2:12 authority over a man; she must be **s**.

Silk

Rev 18:12 linen, purple, **s** and scarlet cloth;

Silla

2Ki 12:20 Beth Millo, on the road down to **S**.

Siloam

Ne 3:15 repaired the wall of the Pool of **S**,
Lk 13: 4 when the tower in **S** fell on them
Jn 9: 7 "wash in the Pool of **S**" (this word
9:11 He told me to go to **S** and wash. So I

Silver (*Silver and gold*)

Ge 20:16 brother a thousand shekels of **s**.
23:15 is worth four hundred shekels of **s**,
23:16 Hittites: four hundred shekels of **s**,
24:53 the servant brought out gold and **s**
33:19 For a hundred pieces of **s**, he bought
37:28 sold him for twenty shekels of **s** to
42:25 to put each man's **s** back in his sack,
42:27 saw his **s** in the mouth of his sack.
42:28 "My **s** has been returned," he said to
42:35 each man's sack was his pouch of **s**!
43:12 Take double the amount of **s** with you,
43:12 for you must return the **s** that was
43:15 gifts and double the amount of **s**,
43:18 because of the **s** that was put back
43:21 each of us found his **s**—the exact
43:22 We have also brought additional **s**
43:22 know who put our **s** in our sacks."
43:23 in your sacks; I received your **s**.
44: 1 put each man's **s** in the mouth of
44: 2 put my cup, the **s** one, in the mouth
44: 2 along with the **s** for his grain.
44: 8 the **s** we found inside the mouths of
44: 8 why should we steal **s** or gold from
45:22 three hundred shekels of **s** and five
Ex 20:23 gods of **s** or gods of gold.
21:32 pay thirty shekels of **s** to the
22: 7 "If a man gives his neighbour **s** or
25: 3 from them: gold, **s** and bronze;
26:19 make forty **s** bases to go under them—
26:21 forty **s** bases—two under each frame.
26:25 sixteen **s** bases—two under each
26:32 gold and standing on four **s** bases.
27:10 with **s** hooks and bands on the posts.
27:11 with **s** hooks and bands on the posts.
27:17 **s** bands and hooks, and bronze bases.
31: 4 for work in gold, **s** and bronze,
35: 5 an offering of gold, **s** and bronze;
35:24 Those presenting an offering of **s** or
35:32 for work in gold, **s** and bronze,
36:24 made forty **s** bases to go under them—
36:26 forty **s** bases—two under each frame.
36:30 eight frames and sixteen **s** bases
36:36 them and cast their four **s** bases.
38:10 with **s** hooks and bands on the posts.
Ex 38:11 with **s** hooks and bands on the posts.
38:12 with **s** hooks and bands on the posts.
38:17 hooks and bands on the posts were **s**,
38:17 and their tops were overlaid with **s**;
38:17 posts of the courtyard had **s** bands.
38:19 Their hooks and bands were **s**, and
38:19 and their tops were overlaid with **s**.
38:25 The **s** obtained from those of the
38:27 The 100 talents of **s** were used to
Lev 5:15 of the proper value in **s**, according
27: 3 at fifty shekels of **s**, according to
27: 6 of a male at five shekels of **s**
27: 6 of a female at three shekels of **s**.
27:16 fifty shekels of **s** to a homer of
Nu 3:50 Israelites he collected **s** weighing
7:13 His offering was one **s** plate
7:13 and one **s** sprinkling bowl weighing
7:19 offering he brought was one **s** plate
7:19 and one **s** sprinkling bowl weighing
7:25 His offering was one **s** plate
7:25 and one **s** sprinkling bowl weighing
7:31 His offering was one **s** plate
7:31 and one **s** sprinkling bowl weighing
7:37 His offering was one **s** plate
7:37 and one **s** sprinkling bowl weighing
7:43 His offering was one **s** plate
7:43 and one **s** sprinkling bowl weighing
7:49 His offering was one **s** plate
7:49 and one **s** sprinkling bowl weighing
7:55 His offering was one **s** plate
7:55 and one **s** sprinkling bowl weighing
7:61 His offering was one **s** plate
7:61 and one **s** sprinkling bowl weighing
7:67 His offering was one **s** plate
7:67 and one **s** sprinkling bowl weighing
7:73 His offering was one **s** plate
7:73 and one **s** sprinkling bowl weighing
7:79 His offering was one **s** plate
7:79 and one **s** sprinkling bowl weighing
7:84 it was anointed: twelve **s** plates,
7:84 twelve **s** sprinkling bowls and twelve
7:85 Each **s** plate weighed a hundred and
7:85 Altogether, the **s** dishes weighed
10: 2 "Make two trumpets of hammered **s**,
18:16 price set at five shekels of **s**,
31:22 Gold, **s**, bronze, iron, tin,
Dt 2: 6 You are to pay them in **s** for the
2:28 water to drink for their price in **s**.
14:25 exchange your tithe for **s**, and take
14:25 and take the **s** with you and go to
14:26 Use the **s** to buy whatever you like:
22:19 fine him a hundred shekels of **s** and
22:29 girl's father fifty shekels of **s**.
Jos 7:21 two hundred shekels of **s** and a wedge
7:21 my tent, with the **s** underneath."
7:22 in his tent, with the **s** underneath.
7:24 took Achan son of Zerah, the **s**, the
22: 8 with **s**, gold, bronze and iron, and a
24:32 bought for a hundred pieces of **s**
Jdg 5:19 they carried off no **s**, no plunder.
9: 4 They gave him seventy shekels of **s**
16: 5 you eleven hundred shekels of **s**."
16:18 returned with the **s** in their hands.
17: 2 "The eleven hundred shekels of **s**
17: 2 I have that **s** with me; I took it.
17: 3 eleven hundred shekels of **s** to his
17: 3 "I solemnly consecrate my **s** to the
17: 4 he returned the **s** to his mother, and
17: 4 took two hundred shekels of **s** and
17:10 give you ten shekels of **s** a year,
1Sa 2:36 a piece of **s** and a crust of bread
9: 8 "I have a quarter of a shekel of **s**.
2Sa 18:11 ten shekels of **s** and a warrior's
21: 4 "We have no right to demand **s** or
24:24 paid fifty shekels of **s** for them.
1Ki 10:21 Nothing was made of **s**, because **s** was
10:22 **s** and ivory, and apes and baboons.
10:27 The king made **s** as common in
10:29 Egypt for six hundred shekels of **s**,
16:24 for two talents of **s** and built a
20: 7 and my children, my **s** and my gold,
20:39 or you must pay a talent of **s**.'
2Ki 5: 5 taking with him ten talents of **s**,
5:22 Please give them a talent of **s** and
5:23 up the two talents of **s** in two bags,
6:25 head sold for eighty shekels of **s**,
2Ki 7: 8 and carried away **s**, gold and clothes,
12:13 was not spent for making **s** basins,
12:13 or **s** for the temple of the Lord;
14:14 He took all the gold and **s** and all
15:19 gave him a thousand talents of **s** to
15:20 contribute fifty shekels of **s** to be
18:14 three hundred talents of **s** and
18:15 Hezekiah gave him all the **s** that was
20:13 in his storehouses—the **s**, the gold,
23:33 levy of a hundred talents of **s** and
25:15 that were made of pure gold or **s**.
1Ch 18:10 articles of gold and **s** and bronze.
19: 6 a thousand talents of **s** to hire
22:14 a million talents of **s**, quantities
22:16 in gold and **s**, bronze and iron—
28:14 weight of **s** for all the **s** articles
28:15 weight of **s** for each **s** lampstand
28:16 the weight of **s** for the **s** tables;
28:17 the weight of **s** for each **s** dish;
29: 2 **s** for the **s**, bronze for the bronze,
29: 3 gold and **s** for the temple of my God,
29: 4 seven thousand talents of refined **s**,
29: 5 for the gold work and the **s** work,
29: 7 ten thousand talents of **s**, eighteen
2Ch 1:17 Egypt for six hundred shekels of **s**,
2: 7 a man skilled to work in gold and **s**,
2:14 He is trained to work in gold and **s**,
9:14 land brought gold and **s** to Solomon.
9:20 Nothing was made of **s**, because **s** was
9:21 **s** and ivory, and apes and baboons.
9:27 The king made **s** as common in
17:11 Jehoshaphat gifts and **s** as tribute,
24:14 and other objects of gold and **s**.
25: 6 Israel for a hundred talents of **s**.
25:24 He took all the gold and **s** and all
27: 5 paid him a hundred talents of **s**,
36: 3 levy of a hundred talents of **s** and
Ezr 1: 9 dishes 30 **s** dishes 1,000 **s** pans 29
1:10 gold bowls 30 matching **s** bowls 410
1:11 5,400 articles of gold and of **s**.
2:69 5,000 minas of **s** and 100 priestly
5:14 and **s** articles of the house of God,
6: 5 Also, the gold and **s** articles of the
7:22 up to a hundred talents of **s**, a
8:26 out to them 650 talents of **s**,
8:26 **s** articles weighing 100 talents, 100
Ne 5:15 took forty shekels of **s** from them in
7:71 of gold and 2,200 minas of **s**.
7:72 2,000 minas of **s** and 67 garments
Est 1: 6 to **s** rings on marble pillars.
1: 6 There were couches of gold and **s** on
3: 9 I will put ten thousand talents of **s**
Job 3:15 who filled their houses with **s**.
22:25 your gold, the choicest **s** for you.
27:16 Though he heaps up **s** like dust and
27:17 and the innocent will divide his **s**.
28: 1 "There is a mine for **s** and a place
28:15 nor can its price be weighed in **s**.
42:11 him a piece of **s** and a gold ring.
Ps 12: 6 like **s** refined in a furnace of clay,
66:10 tested us; you refined us like **s**.
68:13 of ⌊my⌋ dove are sheathed with **s**,
68:30 Humbled, may it bring bars of **s**.
Pr 2: 4 if you look for it as for **s** and
3:14 for she is more profitable than **s**
8:10 Choose my instruction instead of **s**,
8:19 what I yield surpasses choice **s**.
10:20 tongue of the righteous is choice **s**,
16:16 choose understanding rather than **s**!
17: 3 The crucible for **s** and the furnace
22: 1 esteemed is better than **s** or gold.
25: 4 Remove the dross from the **s**, and out
25:11 apples of gold in settings of **s**.
27:21 The crucible for **s** and the furnace
Ecc 12: 6 Remember him—before the **s** cord is
SS 1:11 ear-rings of gold, studded with **s**.
3:10 Its posts he made of **s**, its base of
8: 9 we will build towers of **s** on her.
8:11 its fruit a thousand shekels of **s**.
Isa 1:22 Your **s** has become dross, your choice
2:20 their idols of **s** and idols of gold,
7:23 vines worth a thousand **s** shekels,
13:17 who do not care for **s** and have no
30:22 defile your idols overlaid with **s**
39: 2 his storehouses—the **s**, the gold,
40:19 gold and fashions **s** chains for it.

Isa 46: 6 bags and weigh out **s** on the scales;
48:10 I have refined you, though not as **s**;
60:17 you gold, and **s** in place of iron.
Jer 6:30 They are called rejected **s**, because
10: 9 Hammered **s** is brought from Tarshish
32: 9 out for him seventeen shekels of **s**.
32:10 and weighed out the **s** on the scales.
32:25 'Buy the field with **s** and have the
32:44 Fields will be bought for **s**, and
52:19 that were made of pure gold or **s**.
Eze 7:19 They will throw their **s** into the
16:13 you were adorned with gold and **s**;
16:17 the jewellery made of my gold and **s**,
22:18 They are but the dross of **s**.
22:20 men gather **s**, copper, iron, lead and
22:22 **s** is melted in a furnace, so you
27:12 they exchanged **s**, iron, tin and
28: 4 gold and **s** in your treasuries.
Da 2:32 its chest and arms of **s**, its belly
2:35 iron, the clay, the bronze, the **s**
2:45 clay, the **s** and the gold to pieces.
5: 2 **s** goblets that Nebuchadnezzar his
5: 4 praised the gods of gold and **s**, of
11:38 he will honour with gold and **s**,
11:43 the treasures of gold and **s** and all
Hos 3: 2 bought her for fifteen shekels of **s**
9: 6 Their treasures of **s** will be taken
13: 2 idols for themselves from their **s**,
Joel 3: 5 For you took my **s** and my gold and
Am 2: 6 They sell the righteous for **s**, and
8: 6 buying the poor with **s** and the needy
Na 2: 9 Plunder the **s**! Plunder the gold!
Hab 2:19 It is covered with gold and **s**;
Zep 1:11 all who trade with **s** will be ruined.
1:18 Neither their **s** nor their gold will
Hag 2: 8 'The **s** is mine and the gold is mine,'
Zec 9: 3 she has heaped up **s** like dust,
11:12 So they paid me thirty pieces of **s**.
11:13 So I took the thirty pieces of **s** and
13: 9 I will refine them like **s** and test
14:14 great quantities of gold and **s** and
Mal 3: 3 sit as a refiner and purifier of **s**;
3: 3 and refine them like gold and **s**.
Mt 10: 9 Do not take along any gold or **s** or
26:15 counted out for him thirty **s** coins.
27: 3 returned the thirty **s** coins to the
27: 9 "They took the thirty **s** coins, the
Lk 10:35 The next day he took out two **s** coins
15: 8 "Or suppose a woman has ten **s** coins
Ac 3: 6 Peter said, "**S** or gold I do not have,
17:29 divine being is like gold or **s** or
19:24 who made **s** shrines of Artemis,
20:33 I have not coveted anyone's **s** or
1Co 3:12 **s**, costly stones, wood, hay or straw,
2Ti 2:20 are articles not only of gold and **s**,
Jas 5: 3 Your gold and **s** are corroded.
1Pe 1:18 perishable things such as **s** or gold
Rev 9:20 and idols of gold, **s**, bronze, stone
18:12 cargoes of gold, **s**, precious stones

Silver and gold

Ge 13: 2 very wealthy in livestock and in **s**.
24:35 He has given him sheep and cattle, **s**,
Ex 3:22 for articles of **s** and for clothing,
11: 2 their neighbours for articles of **s**."
12:35 for articles of **s** and for clothing.
Nu 22:18 gave me his palace filled with **s**,
24:13 gave me his palace filled with **s**,
Dt 7:25 Do not covet the **s** on them, and do
8:13 grow large and your **s** increase and
17:17 not accumulate large amounts of **s**.
29:17 and idols of wood and stone, of **s**.
Jos 6:19 All the **s** and the articles of bronze
6:24 but they put the **s** and the articles
2Sa 8:10 with him articles of **s** and bronze.
8:11 as he had done with the **s** from all
1Ki 7:51 —the **s** and the furnishings—and he
10:25 articles of **s**, robes, weapons and
15:15 into the temple of the LORD the **s**
15:18 Asa then took all the **s** that was
15:19 See, I am sending you a gift of **s**.
20: 3 'Your **s** are mine, and the best of
20: 5 **s**, your wives and your children.
2Ki 16: 8 Ahaz took the **s** found in the temple
23:35 Jehoiakim paid Pharaoh Neco the **s** he
2Ki 23:35 he taxed the land and exacted the **s**
1Ch 18:11 as he had done with the **s** he had
2Ch 1:15 The king made **s** as common in
5: 1 —the **s** and all the furnishings—
9:24 articles of **s**, and robes, weapons
15:18 into the temple of God the **s**
16: 2 Asa then took the **s** out of the
16: 3 See, I am sending you **s**. Now break
21: 3 gifts of **s** and articles of value,
32:27 and he made treasuries for his **s** and
Ezr 1: 4 be living are to provide him with **s**,
1: 6 assisted them with articles of **s**,
7:15 you are to take with you the **s** that
7:16 together with all the **s** you may
7:18 seems best with the rest of the **s**,
8:25 the offering of **s** and the articles
8:28 The **s** are a freewill offering to the
8:30 Levites received the **s** and sacred
8:33 we weighed out the **s** and the sacred
Ps 105:37 He brought out Israel, laden with **s**,
115: 4 their idols are **s**, made by the hands
119:72 to me than thousands of pieces of **s**.
135:15 The idols of the nations are **s**, made
Ecc 2: 8 I amassed **s** for myself, and the
Isa 2: 7 Their land is full of **s**; there is no
31: 7 reject the idols of **s** your sinful
60: 9 your sons from afar, with their **s**,
Jer 10: 4 They adorn it with **s**; they fasten it
Eze 7:19 Their **s** will not be able to save
38:13 to carry off **s**, to take away
Da 5:23 You praised the gods of **s**, of bronze,
11: 8 their valuable articles of **s** and
Hos 2: 8 who lavished on her the **s**—which
8: 4 With their **s** they make idols for
Zec 6:10 "Take **s** from the exiles Heldai,
6:11 Take the **s** and make a crown, and set

Silversmith

Jdg 17: 4 of silver and gave them to a **s**,
Pr 25: 4 and out comes material for the **s**;
Ac 19:24 A **s** named Demetrius, who made silver

Simeon (Simeonite, Simeonites)

1. Son of Jacob by Leah (Ge 29:33; 35:23; 1Ch 2:1). With Levi killed Shechemites to avenge rape of sister Dinah (Ge 34). Left in Egypt as hostage (Ge 42:24–43:23). Blessed by Jacob (Ge 49:5–7). **2.** Tribe descended from Simeon. Included in census (Nu 1:22–23; 26:12–14). Given territory in restored land (Eze 48:24). **3.** Territory at southernmost end of Palestine, in the Negev Desert. Allotted to the descendants of Jacob's second son, taken from Judah's territory which was more than was needed (Jos 19:1–9). **4.** Righteous and devout man in Jerusalem; recognised the child Jesus as the Messiah when he was brought into the temple (Lk 2:25–35).

Ge 29:33 So she named him **S**.
34:25 two of Jacob's sons, **S** and Levi,
34:30 Jacob said to **S** and Levi, "You have
35:23 **S**, Levi, Judah, Issachar and Zebulun.
42:24 He had **S** taken from them and bound
42:36 Joseph is no more and **S** is no more,
43:23 Then he brought **S** out to them.
46:10 The sons of **S**: Jemuel, Jamin, Ohad,
48: 5 mine, just as Reuben and **S** are mine.
49: 5 "**S** and Levi are brothers—their
Ex 1: 2 Reuben, **S**, Levi and Judah;
6:15 The sons of **S** were Jemuel, Jamin,
6:15 These were the clans of **S**.
Nu 1: 6 from **S**, Shelumiel son of Zurishaddai
1:22 From the descendants of **S**: All the
1:23 The number from the tribe of **S** was
2:12 The tribe of **S** will camp next to
2:12 The leader of the people of **S** is
7:36 the leader of the people of **S**,
10:19 over the division of the tribe of **S**,
13: 5 from the tribe of **S**, Shaphat son of
26:12 The descendants of **S** by their clans
26:14 These were the clans of **S**;
34:20 son of Ammihud, from the tribe of **S**;
Dt 27:12 **S**, Levi, Judah, Issachar, Joseph
Jos 19: 1 for the tribe of **S**, clan by clan.
21: 4 the tribes of Judah, **S** and Benjamin.
21: 9 From the tribes of Judah and **S** they
1Ch 2: 1 **S**, Levi, Judah, Issachar, Zebulun,
4:24 The descendants of **S**: Nemuel, Jamin,
6:65 From the tribes of Judah, **S** and
12:25 men of **S**, warriors ready for battle—
2Ch 15: 9 Manasseh and **S** who had settled among
34: 6 Ephraim and **S**, as far as Naphtali,
Eze 48:24 "**S** will have one portion; it will
48:25 territory of **S** from east to west.
48:33 will be three gates: the gate of **S**,
Lk 2:25 **S**, who was righteous and devout.
2:28 **S** took him in his arms and praised
2:34 **S** blessed them and said to Mary, his
3:30 the son of **S**, the son of Judah, the
Ac 13: 1 **S** called Niger, Lucius of Cyrene,
Rev 7: 7 from the tribe of **S** 12,000, from the

Simeonite (Simeon)

Nu 25:14 of Salu, the leader of a **S** family.

Simeonites (Simeon)

Jos 19: 8 of the tribe of the **S**, clan by clan.
19: 9 The inheritance of the **S** was taken
19: 9 So the **S** received their inheritance
Jdg 1: 3 the men of Judah said to the **S** their
1: 3 So the **S** went with them.
1:17 the men of Judah went with the **S**
1Ch 4:42 five hundred of these **S**, led by
27:16 the **S**: Shephatiah son of Maacah;

Simon (Peter, Simon's)

1. Apostle; called "the Zealot" (Mt 10:4; Mk 3:18; Lk 6:15; Ac 1:13). **2.** Brother of Jesus (Mt 13:55; Mk 6:3). **3.** Leper from Bethany, in whose house Jesus was anointed with oil (Mt 26:6; Mk 14:3). **4.** Pharisee, in whose house Jesus' feet were washed with tears (Lk 7:40). **5.** Man from Cyrene, forced to carry Jesus' cross (Mk 15:21). **6.** Sorcerer, who amazed Samaritans with his magic (Ac 8:9–11). Believed Philip and was baptised (Ac 8:12–13); rebuked by Peter for trying to buy spiritual power (Ac 8:18–24). **7.** Tanner, with whom Peter lodged (Ac 9:43).

Mt 4:18 he saw two brothers, **S** called Peter
10: 2 **S** (who is called Peter) and his
10: 4 **S** the Zealot and Judas Iscariot, who
13:55 brothers James, Joseph, **S** and Judas?
16:16 **S** Peter answered, "You are the
16:17 "Blessed are you, **S** son of Jonah,
17:25 "What do you think, **S**?" he asked.
26: 6 home of a man known as **S** the Leper,
27:32 they met a man from Cyrene, named **S**,
Mk 1:16 he saw **S** and his brother Andrew
1:29 John to the home of **S** and Andrew.
1:36 **S** and his companions went to look
3:16 **S** (to whom he gave the name Peter);
3:18 Alphaeus, Thaddaeus, **S** the Zealot
6: 3 of James, Joseph, Judas and **S**?
14: 3 home of a man known as **S** the Leper,
14:37 "**S**," he said to Peter, "are you
15:21 A certain man from Cyrene, **S**, the
Lk 4:38 synagogue and went to the home of **S**.
5: 3 the one belonging to **S**, and asked
5: 4 he said to **S**, "Put out into deep
5: 5 **S** answered, "Master, we've worked
5: 8 **S** Peter saw this, he fell at Jesus'
5:10 Then Jesus said to **S**, "Don't be
6:14 **S** (whom he named Peter), his brother
6:15 **S** who was called the Zealot,
7:40 "**S**, I have something to tell you."
7:43 **S** replied, "I suppose the one who
7:44 towards the woman and said to **S**,
22:31 "**S**, **S**, Satan has asked to sift you
22:32 I have prayed for you, **S**, that your
23:26 they seized **S** from Cyrene, who was
24:34 has risen and has appeared to **S**."
Jn 1:40 Andrew, **S** Peter's brother, was one
1:41 to find his brother **S** and tell him,
1:42 and said, "You are **S** son of John.
6: 8 Andrew, **S** Peter's brother, spoke up
6:68 **S** Peter answered him, "Lord, to whom
6:71 meant Judas, the son of **S** Iscariot
13: 2 Judas Iscariot, son of **S**, to betray Jesus
13: 6 He came to **S** Peter, who said to him,
13: 9 "Then, Lord," **S** Peter replied, "not
13:24 **S** Peter motioned to this disciple

Jn 13:26 gave it to Judas Iscariot, son of **S**.
13:36 **S** Peter asked him, "Lord, where are
18:10 **S** Peter, who had a sword, drew it
18:15 **S** Peter and another disciple were
18:25 **S** Peter stood warming himself, he
20: 2 she came running to **S** Peter and the
20: 6 **S** Peter, who was behind him, arrived
21: 2 **S** Peter, Thomas (called Didymus),
21: 3 out to fish," **S** Peter told them,
21: 7 As soon as **S** Peter heard him say,
21:11 **S** Peter climbed aboard and dragged
21:15 Jesus said to **S** Peter, "**S** son of
21:16 "**S** son of John, do you truly love me?
21:17 "**S** son of John, do you love me?"
Ac 1:13 **S** the Zealot, and Judas son of James.
8: 9 Now for some time a man named **S** had
8:13 **S** himself believed and was baptised.
8:18 **S** saw that the Spirit was given at
8:24 **S** answered, "Pray to the Lord for me
9:43 for some time with a tanner named **S**.
10: 5 a man named **S** who is called Peter.
10: 6 He is staying with **S** the tanner,
10:18 asking if **S** who was known as Peter
10:19 "**S**, three men are looking for you.
10:32 Send to Joppa for **S** who is called
10:32 **S** the tanner, who lives by the sea.'
11:13 to Joppa for **S** who is called Peter.
15:14 **S** has described to us how God at
2Pe 1: 1 **S** Peter, a servant and apostle of

Simon's (Peter, Simon)

Mk 1:30 **S** mother-in-law was in bed with a
Lk 4:38 Now **S** mother-in-law was suffering
5:10 the sons of Zebedee, **S** partners.
Ac 10:17 found out where **S** house was and

Simple (Simple-hearted)

Ex 18:22 **s** cases they can decide themselves.
18:26 the **s** ones they decided themselves.
2Ki 20:10 "It is a **s** matter for the shadow to
Job 5: 2 kills a fool, and envy slays the **s**.
Ps 19: 7 are trustworthy, making wise the **s**.
119:130 it gives understanding to the **s**.
Pr 1: 4 for giving prudence to the **s**,
1:22 will you **s** ones love your **s** ways?
1:32 For the waywardness of the **s** will
7: 7 I saw among the **s**, I noticed among
8: 5 You who are **s**, gain prudence;
9: 4 "Let all who are **s** come in here!"
9: 6 Leave your **s** ways and you will live;
9:16 "Let all who are **s** come in here!"
14:15 A **s** man believes anything, but a
14:18 The **s** inherit folly, but the prudent
19:25 Flog a mocker, and the **s** will learn
21:11 a mocker is punished, the **s** gain
22: 3 the **s** keep going and suffer for it.
27:12 the **s** keep going and suffer for it.

Simple-hearted (Simple, Heart)

Ps 116: 6 The LORD protects the **s**; when I was

Sin, Desert of

Wilderness area "between Elim and Sinai" (Ex 16:1), near the Red Sea and Dophkah (Nu 33:11-12), exact location unknown. Here the Israelites grumbled to Moses, but were fed with quails and manna (Ex 16).

Ex 16: 1 Elim and came to the Desert of **S**
17: 1 set out from the Desert of **S**,
Nu 33:11 Sea and camped in the Desert of **S**.
33:12 They left the Desert of **S** and camped

Sin (*Sin offering, Sin offerings*, Sin's, Sinful, Sinfulness, Sinned, Sinner, Sinner's, Sinners, Sinning, Sins)

Ge 4: 7 **s** is crouching at your door;
15:16 for the **s** of the Amorites has not
18:20 is so great and their **s** so grievous
31:36 "What **s** have I committed that you
39: 9 a wicked thing and **s** against God?"
42:22 "Didn't I tell you not to **s** against
Ex 10:17 Now forgive my **s** once more and pray
20: 5 punishing the children for the **s** of
23:33 or they will cause you to **s** against
Ex 32:21 you led them into such great **s**?"
32:30 "You have committed a great **s**.
32:30 I can make atonement for your **s**."
32:31 "Oh, what a great **s** these people
32:32 now, please forgive their **s**—but if
32:34 I will punish them for their **s**."
34: 7 wickedness, rebellion and **s**.
34: 7 their children for the **s** of the
34: 9 forgive our wickedness and our **s**,
Lev 4: 3 offering for the **s** he has committed.
4:14 they become aware of the **s** they
4:23 made aware of the **s** he committed,
4:26 make atonement for the man's **s**, and
4:28 made aware of the **s** he committed,
4:28 his offering for the **s** he committed
4:35 for him for the **s** he has committed,
5: 6 and, as a penalty for the **s** he has
5: 6 make atonement for him for his **s**.
5: 7 to the LORD as a penalty for his **s**
5:10 for him for the **s** he has committed,
5:11 to bring as an offering for his **s**
6: 3 any such **s** that people may do—
18:25 so I punished it for its **s**,
19:22 the LORD for the **s** he has committed,
19:22 and his **s** will be forgiven.
26:41 humbled and they pay for their **s**,
Nu 5: 7 must confess the **s** he has committed.
5:31 will bear the consequences of her **s**.
9:13 will bear the consequences of his **s**.
12:11 **s** we have so foolishly committed.
14:18 love and forgiving **s** and rebellion.
14:18 children for the **s** of the fathers
14:19 forgive the **s** of these people, just
18: 9 grain or **s** or guilt offerings
18:22 bear the consequences of their **s**
19: 9 it is for purification from **s**.
27: 3 died for his own **s** and left no sons.
32:23 sure that your **s** will find you out.
Dt 5: 9 punishing the children for the **s** of
9:18 because of all the **s** you had
9:27 their wickedness and their **s**.
15: 9 and you will be found guilty of **s**.
20:18 will **s** against the LORD your God.
22:26 has committed no **s** deserving death.
23:21 of you and you will be guilty of **s**.
24: 4 Do not bring **s** upon the land the
24:15 you, and you will be guilty of **s**.
24:16 each is to die for his own **s**.
Jos 22:17 Was not the **s** of Peor enough for us?
22:17 not cleansed ourselves from that **s**,
22:20 not the only one who died for his **s**.
1Sa 2:17 This **s** of the young men was very
3:13 ever because of the **s** he knew about;
12:23 far be it from me that I should **s**
14:34 Do not **s** against the LORD by eating
14:38 out what **s** has been committed today.
15:23 For rebellion is like the **s** of
15:25 Now I beg you, forgive my **s** and come
2Sa 12:13 "The LORD has taken away your **s**.
22:24 him and have kept myself from **s**.
1Ki 8:34 forgive the **s** of your people Israel
8:35 turn from their **s** because you have
8:36 and forgive the **s** of your servants,
8:46 "When they **s** against you—for there
8:46 there is no-one who does not **s**—and
12:30 this thing became a **s**; the people
13:34 This was the **s** of the house of
15:26 the ways of his father and in his **s**,
15:34 the ways of Jeroboam and in his **s**,
16: 2 caused my people Israel to **s** and to
16:19 in the **s** he had committed and had
16:26 Jeroboam son of Nebat and in his **s**,
17:18 remind me of my **s** and kill my son?"
21:22 anger and have caused Israel to **s**.'
22:52 of Nebat, who caused Israel to **s**.
2Ki 17:21 and caused them to commit a great **s**.
21:11 has led Judah into **s** with his idols.
21:16 **s** that he had caused Judah to commit,
21:17 did, including the **s** he committed,
23:15 who had caused Israel to **s**—even
2Ch 6:25 hear from heaven and forgive the **s**
6:26 turn from their **s** because you have
6:27 and forgive the **s** of your servants,
6:36 "When they **s** against you—for there
6:36 for there is no-one who does not **s**
7:14 will forgive their **s** and will heal
2Ch 19:10 warn them not to **s** against the LORD;
19:10 Do this, and you will not **s**.
28:13 Do you intend to add to our **s** and
Ne 6:13 I would commit a **s** by doing this,
13:26 he was led into **s** by foreign women.
Job 1:22 In all this, Job did not **s** by
2:10 this, Job did not **s** in what he said.
8: 4 them over to the penalty of their **s**.
10: 6 out my faults and probe after my **s**—
11: 6 has even forgotten some of your **s**.
11:14 if you put away the **s** that is in
13:23 Show me my offence and my **s**.
14:16 my steps but not keep track of my **s**.
14:17 in a bag; you will cover over my **s**.
15: 5 Your **s** prompts your mouth; you adopt
31:11 been shameful, a **s** to be judged.
31:30 I have not allowed my mouth to **s** by
31:33 if I have concealed my **s** as men do,
33: 9 'I am pure and without **s**; I am clean
34:37 To his **s** he adds rebellion;
35: 6 If you **s**, how does that affect him?
Ps 4: 4 In your anger do not **s**; when you are
17: 3 resolved that my mouth will not **s**.
18:23 him and have kept myself from **s**.
32: 2 Blessed is the man whose **s** the LORD
32: 5 I acknowledged my **s** to you and did
32: 5 and you forgave the guilt of my **s**.
36: 2 too much to detect or hate his **s**.
38: 3 have no soundness because of my **s**.
38:18 my iniquity; I am troubled by my **s**.
39: 1 my ways and keep my tongue from **s**;
39:11 and discipline men for their **s**;
51: 2 iniquity and cleanse me from my **s**.
51: 3 and my **s** is always before me.
59: 3 for no offence or **s** of mine, O LORD.
66:18 If I had cherished **s** in my heart,
78:17 they continued to **s** against him,
89:32 I will punish their **s** with the rod,
106:43 and they wasted away in their **s**.
109:14 **s** of his mother never be blotted out.
119:11 that I might not **s** against you.
119:133 to your word; let no **s** rule over me.
Pr 1:16 for their feet rush into **s**, they are
5:22 the cords of his **s** hold him fast.
10:19 words are many, **s** is not absent, but
14: 9 Fools mock at making amends for **s**,
14:34 but **s** is a disgrace to any people.
16: 6 Through love and faithfulness **s** is
17:19 He who loves a quarrel loves **s**;
20: 9 I am clean and without **s**"?
21: 4 the lamp of the wicked, are **s**!
24: 9 The schemes of folly are **s**, and men
29: 6 An evil man is snared by his own **s**,
29:16 the wicked thrive, so does **s**, but
Ecc 5: 6 Do not let your mouth lead you into **s**
Isa 3: 9 they parade their **s** like Sodom;
5:18 Woe to those who draw **s** along with
6: 7 taken away and your **s** atoned for."
22:14 "Till your dying day this **s** will not
27: 9 fruitage of the removal of his **s**:
30: 1 not by my Spirit, heaping **s** upon **s**;
30:13 this **s** will become for you like a
40: 2 that her **s** has been paid for, that
53:12 For he bore the **s** of many, and made
59: 7 Their feet rush into **s**; they are
64: 5 But when we continued to **s** against
Jer 9: 3 They go from one **s** to another;
9: 7 I do because of the **s** of my people?
16:10 What **s** have we committed against
16:17 is their **s** concealed from my eyes.
16:18 for their wickedness and their **s**,
17: 1 "Judah's **s** is engraved with an iron
17: 3 because of **s** throughout your
31:30 everyone will die for his own **s**;
32:35 thing and so make Judah **s**.
33: 8 I will cleanse them from all the **s**
36: 3 their wickedness and their **s**."
Lam 2:14 they did not expose your **s** to ward
4:22 he will punish your **s** and expose
Eze 3:18 that wicked man will die for his **s**,
3:19 he will die for his **s**; but you will
3:20 warn him, he will die for his **s**.
3:21 man not to **s** and he does not **s**,
4: 4 put the **s** of the house of Israel
4: 4 You are to bear their **s** for the
4: 5 of days as the years of their **s**.

Eze 4: 5 bear the s of the house of Israel.
4: 6 bear the s of the house of Judah.
4:17 will waste away because of their s.
7:19 for it has made them stumble into s.
9: 9 "The s of the house of Israel and
16:49 "'Now this was the s of your sister
18:17 He withholds his hand from s and
18:17 He will not die for his father's s;
18:18 his father will die for his own s,
18:24 commits s and does the same
18:26 his righteousness and commits s,
18:26 the s he has committed he will die.
18:30 then s will not be your downfall.
29:16 a reminder of their s in turning to
33: 6 will be taken away because of his s,
33: 8 that wicked man will die for his s,
33: 9 he will die for his s, but you will
33:14 turns away from his s and does what
39:23 Israel went into exile for their s,
44:10 bear the consequences of their s.
44:12 the house of Israel fall into s,
44:12 bear the consequences of their s,
Da 9:20 confessing my s and the s of my
9:24 to put an end to s, to atone for
Hos 5: 5 even Ephraim, stumble in their s;
10: 8 destroyed—it is the s of Israel.
10:10 them in bonds for their double s.
12: 8 not find in me any iniquity or s."
13: 2 Now they s more and more; they make
Am 4: 4 "Go to Bethel and s;
4: 4 go to Gilgal and s yet more.
Mic 1:13 You were the beginning of s to the
3: 8 his transgression, to Israel his s.
6: 7 of my body for the s of my soul?
7:18 Who is a God like you, who pardons s
Zec 3: 4 "See, I have taken away your s, and
3: 9 the s of this land in a single day.
13: 1 to cleanse them from s and impurity.
Mal 2: 6 uprightness, and turned many from s.
Mt 5:29 If your right eye causes you to s,
5:30 if your right hand causes you to s,
6:14 For if you forgive men when they s
12:31 I tell you, every s and blasphemy
13:41 that causes s and all who do evil.
18: 6 little ones who believe in me to s,
18: 7 the things that cause people to s!
18: 8 hand or your foot causes you to s,
18: 9 if your eye causes you to s, gouge
23:32 Fill up, then, the measure of the s
Mk 3:29 he is guilty of an eternal s."
9:42 little ones who believe in me to s,
9:43 If your hand causes you to s, cut it
9:45 if your foot causes you to s, cut it
9:47 if your eye causes you to s, pluck
Lk 17: 1 "Things that cause people to s are
17: 2 cause one of these little ones to s.
Jn 1:29 who takes away the s of the world!
8: 7 "If any one of you is without s, let
8:11 "Go now and leave your life of s."
8:21 for me, and you will die in your s.
8:34 everyone who sins is a slave to s.
8:46 Can any of you prove me guilty of s?
9:34 "You were steeped in s at birth;
9:41 you would not be guilty of s;
15:22 them, they would not be guilty of s.
15:22 they have no excuse for their s.
15:24 did, they would not be guilty of s.
16: 8 to s and righteousness and judgment:
16: 9 in regard to s, because men do not
19:11 to you is guilty of a greater s."
Ac 7:60 do not hold this s against them.
8:23 of bitterness and captive to s."
Ro 2:12 All who s apart from the law will
2:12 and all who s under the law will be
3: 9 and Gentiles alike are all under s.
3:20 the law we become conscious of s.
4: 8 Blessed is the man whose s the Lord
5:12 Therefore, just as s entered the
5:12 and death through s, and in this way
5:13 law was given, s was in the world.
5:13 But s is not taken into account when
5:14 even over those who did not s by
5:16 like the result of the one man's s:
5:16 The judgment followed one s and
5:20 But where s increased, grace
5:21 that, just as s reigned in death, so
Ro 6: 2 We died to s; how can we live in it
6: 6 body of s might be done away with,
6: 6 we should no longer be slaves to s—
6: 7 who has died has been freed from s.
6:10 he died, he died to s once for all;
6:11 count yourselves dead to s but alive
6:12 Therefore do not let s reign in your
6:13 offer the parts of your body to s,
6:14 For s shall not be your master,
6:15 What then? Shall we s because we are
6:16 obey—whether you are slaves to s,
6:17 though you used to be slaves to s,
6:18 You have been set free from s and
6:20 you were slaves to s, you were free
6:22 you have been set free from s
6:23 For the wages of s is death, but the
7: 7 Is the law s? Certainly not!
7: 7 what s was except through the law.
7: 8 s, seizing the opportunity afforded
7: 8 For apart from law, s is dead.
7: 9 came, s sprang to life and I died.
7:11 For s, seizing the opportunity
7:13 that s might be recognised as s,
7:13 s might become utterly sinful.
7:14 unspiritual, sold as a slave to s.
7:17 who do it, but it is s living in me.
7:20 it is s living in me that does it.
7:23 law of s at work within my members.
7:25 nature a slave to the law of s.
8: 2 me free from the law of s and death.
8: 3 And so he condemned s in sinful man,
8:10 your body is dead because of s, yet
14:23 that does not come from faith is s.
1Co 8:12 you s against your brothers in this
8:12 conscience, you s against Christ.
8:13 causes my brother to fall into s,
15:56 The sting of death is s, and the
15:56 and the power of s is the law.
2Co 5:21 God made him who had no s to be s
11: 7 Was it a s for me to lower myself in
11:29 Who is led into s, and I do not
12:21 sexual s and debauchery in which
Gal 2:17 that mean that Christ promotes s?
3:22 the whole world is a prisoner of s,
6: 1 Brothers, if someone is caught in a s
Eph 4:26 "In your anger do not s": Do not let
1Ti 5:20 Those who s are to be rebuked
Heb 4:15 just as we are—yet was without s.
9:26 to do away with s by the sacrifice
9:28 not to bear s, but to bring
10:18 is no longer any sacrifice for s.
11:25 the pleasures of s for a short time.
12: 1 and the s that so easily entangles,
12: 4 In your struggle against s, you have
Jas 1:15 has conceived, it gives birth to s;
1:15 and s, when it is full-grown, gives
2: 9 if you show favouritism, you s and
1Pe 2:22 "He committed no s, and no deceit
4: 1 suffered in his body is done with s.
1Jn 1: 7 his Son, purifies us from all s.
1: 8 If we claim to be without s, we
2: 1 this to you so that you will not s.
2: 1 But if anybody does s, we have one
3: 4 in fact, s is lawlessness.
3: 5 And in him is no s.
3: 6 No-one who continues to s has
3: 9 is born of God will continue to s,
5:16 If anyone sees his brother commit a s
5:16 I refer to those whose s does not
5:16 There is a s that leads to death.
5:17 All wrongdoing is s, and there
5:17 is s that does not lead to death.
5:18 born of God does not continue to s;
Rev 2:14 s by eating food sacrificed to idols

Sin offering

Ex 29:14 It is a s.
29:36 Sacrifice a bull each day as a s to
30:10 s for the generations to come.
Lev 4: 3 as a s for the sin he has committed.
4: 8 all the fat from the bull of the s
4:14 must bring a young bull as a s
4:20 as he did with the bull for the s.
4:21 This is the s for the community.
4:24 It is a s.
Lev 4:25 the blood of the s with his finger
4:29 lay his hand on the head of the s
4:32 "'If he brings a lamb as his s, he
4:33 slaughter it for a s at the place
4:34 the blood of the s with his finger
5: 6 lamb or goat from the flock as a s;
5: 7 one for a s and the other for a
5: 8 shall first offer the one for the s.
5: 9 the s against the side of the altar;
5: 9 It is a s.
5:11 of an ephah of fine flour for a s.
5:11 or incense on it, because it is a s.
5:12 It is a s.
6:17 Like the s and the guilt offering,
6:25 'These are the regulations for the s:
6:25 The s is to be slaughtered before
6:30 any s whose blood is brought into
7: 7 "'The same law applies to both the s
7:37 the grain offering, the s, the guilt
8: 2 the bull for the s, the two rams and
8:14 He then presented the bull for the s,
9: 2 "Take a bull calf for your s and a
9: 3 'Take a male goat for a s, a calf
9: 7 sacrifice your s and your burnt
9: 8 the calf as a s for himself.
9:10 covering of the liver from the s,
9:15 He took the goat for the people's s
9:15 offered it for a s as he did with
9:22 And having sacrificed the s, the
10:16 enquired about the goat of the s
10:17 "Why didn't you eat the s in the
10:19 "Today they sacrificed their s and
10:19 pleased if I had eaten the s today?"
12: 6 a young pigeon or a dove for a s.
12: 8 offering and the other for a s.
14:13 the holy place where the s and the
14:13 Like the s, the guilt offering
14:19 the priest is to sacrifice the s
14:22 one for a s and the other for a
14:31 one as a s and the other as a burnt
15:15 the one for a s and the other for a
15:30 one for a s and the other for a
16: 3 with a young bull for a s and a ram
16: 5 two male goats for a s and a ram
16: 6 offer the bull for his own s to make
16: 9 the LORD and sacrifice it for a s.
16:11 bring the bull for his own s to
16:11 to slaughter the bull for his own s.
16:15 the goat for the s for the people
16:25 He shall also burn the fat of the s
23:19 sacrifice one male goat for a s and
Nu 6:11 The priest is to offer one as a s
6:14 ewe lamb without defect for a s,
6:16 make the s and the burnt offering.
7:16 one male goat for a s;
7:22 one male goat for a s;
7:28 one male goat for a s;
7:34 one male goat for a s;
7:40 one male goat for a s;
7:46 one male goat for a s;
7:52 one male goat for a s;
7:58 one male goat for a s;
7:64 one male goat for a s;
7:70 one male goat for a s;
7:76 one male goat for a s;
7:82 one male goat for a s;
7:87 male goats were used for the s.
8: 8 to take a second young bull for a s.
8:12 use the one for a s to the LORD and
15:24 offering, and a male goat for a s.
15:25 an offering made by fire and a s.
15:27 a year-old female goat for a s.
28:15 to be presented to the LORD as a s.
28:22 Include one male goat as a s to make
29: 5 Include one male goat as a s to make
29:11 Include one male goat as a s, in
29:11 in addition to the s for atonement
29:16 Include one male goat as a s, in
29:19 Include one male goat as a s, in
29:22 Include one male goat as a s, in
29:25 Include one male goat as a s, in
29:28 Include one male goat as a s, in
29:31 Include one male goat as a s, in
29:34 Include one male goat as a s, in
29:38 Include one male goat as a s, in
2Ch 29:21 male goats as a s for the kingdom,

2Ch 29:23 The goats for the s were brought
29:24 for a s to atone for all Israel,
29:24 offering and the s for all Israel.
Ezr 6:17 as a s for all Israel, twelve male
8:35 and, as a s, twelve male goats.
Eze 43:19 You are to give a young bull as a s
43:21 You are to take the bull for the s
43:22 a male goat without defect for a s,
43:25 provide a male goat daily for a s;
44:27 he is to offer a s for himself,
45:19 to take some of the blood of the s
45:22 provide a bull as a s for himself
45:23 the LORD, and a male goat for a s.
46:20 cook the guilt offering and the s
Ro 8: 3 likeness of sinful man to be a s.
Heb 13:11 into the Most Holy Place as a s,

Sin offerings

Lev 16:27 The bull and the goat for the s,
2Ki 12:16 from the guilt offerings and s was
Ne 10:33 for s to make atonement for Israel;
Ps 40: 6 offerings and s you did not require.
Eze 40:39 on which the burnt offerings, s and
42:13 the s and the guilt offerings—for
44:29 the s and the guilt offerings;
45:17 He will provide the s, grain
45:25 is to make the same provision for s,
Hos 8:11 Ephraim built many altars for s,
Heb 10: 6 with burnt offerings and s you were
10: 8 burnt offerings and s you did not

Sin's (Sin)

Heb 3:13 may be hardened by s deceitfulness.

Sinai (Mount Sinai)

1. Mountain situated in Sinai Peninsula, also known as Horeb, exact location unknown. Here God spoke to Moses from the burning bush (Ex 3:1–4; Ac 7:30), and later provided water for the Israelites (Ex 17:6). God appeared here again after the exodus (Ex 19; Nu 3:1), revealing to Moses the law (Ex 31:18; 34:29; Lev 7:38; 25:1; 26:46; 27:34; Nu 28:6; Ne 9:13; Ac 7:38). Used figuratively by Paul when writing about slavery to the law (Gal 4:24–25). **2.** Wilderness area around the mountain (Ex 19:1), where the Israelites camped while God met with Moses (Ex 19:2; Lev 7:38). Here the Tent of Meeting was set up (Nu 1:1) in which Moses was instructed to take a census of the people (Nu 1:2, 19; 3:14; 26:64). Two of Aaron's sons were struck down for making an unauthorised offering (Nu 3:4). The people celebrated Passover (Nu 9:1, 5) before moving on (Nu 10:12). They returned to this place later (Nu 33:15–16).

Ex 16: 1 which is between Elim and **S**, on the
19: 1 day—they came to the Desert of **S**.
19: 2 they entered the Desert of **S**, and
Lev 7:38 to the LORD, in the Desert of **S**.
Nu 1: 1 Tent of Meeting in the Desert of **S**
1:19 he counted them in the Desert of **S**:
3: 4 fire before him in the Desert of **S**.
3:14 said to Moses in the Desert of **S**,
9: 1 spoke to Moses in the Desert of **S**
9: 5 they did so in the Desert of **S** at
10:12 set out from the Desert of **S**
26:64 the Israelites in the Desert of **S**.
33:15 and camped in the Desert of **S**.
33:16 They left the Desert of **S** and camped
Dt 33: 2 "The LORD came from **S** and dawned
Jdg 5: 5 before the LORD, the One of **S**,
Ps 68: 8 before God, the One of **S**,
68:17 the Lord ⌊has come⌋ from **S** into his

Sincere (Sincerity)

Da 11:34 many who are not s will join them.
Ac 2:46 ate together with glad and s hearts,
Ro 12: 9 Love must be s. Hate what is evil;
2Co 6: 6 in the Holy Spirit and in s love;
11: 3 your s and pure devotion to Christ.
1Ti 1: 5 and a good conscience and a s faith.
3: 8 are to be men worthy of respect, s,
2Ti 1: 5 I have been reminded of your s faith,
Heb 10:22 draw near to God with a s heart
Jas 3:17 and good fruit, impartial and s.
1Pe 1:22 you have s love for your brothers,

Sincerity (Sincere)

1Co 5: 8 yeast, the bread of s and truth.
2Co 1:12 holiness and s that are from God.
2:17 Christ we speak before God with s,
8: 8 but I want to test the s of your
Eph 6: 5 and with s of heart, just as you
Col 3:22 but with s of heart and reverence

Sinews

Job 10:11 knit me together with bones and s?
40:17 the s of his thighs are close-knit.
Isa 48: 4 the s of your neck were iron,
Col 2:19 held together by its ligaments and s

Sinful (Sin, *Sinful nature*)

Dt 9:21 Also I took that s thing of yours,
Ps 36: 4 he commits himself to a s course and
38: 5 are loathsome because of my s folly.
51: 5 Surely I was s at birth, s from the
Pr 12:13 An evil man is trapped by his s talk
Isa 1: 4 Ah, s nation, a people loaded with
31: 7 and gold your s hands have made.
57:17 I was enraged by his s greed;
Eze 37:23 them from all their s backsliding,
Hos 9:15 Because of their s deeds, I will
Am 9: 8 Sovereign LORD are on the s kingdom.
Mk 8:38 in this adulterous and s generation,
Lk 5: 8 Go away from me, Lord; I am a s man!
7:37 a woman who had lived a s life in
24: 7 delivered into the hands of s men,
Ro 1:24 over in the s desires of the hearts
7: 5 the s passions aroused by the law
7:13 sin might become utterly s.
8: 3 own Son in the likeness of s man
8: 3 And so he condemned sin in s man,
8: 6 The mind of s man is death, but the
8: 7 the s mind is hostile to God.
1Ti 1: 9 the ungodly and s, the unholy and
Tit 3:11 that such a man is warped and s;
Heb 3:12 of you has a s, unbelieving heart
12: 3 endured such opposition from s men,
1Pe 2:11 to abstain from s desires, which war
2Pe 2:18 lustful desires of s human nature,
1Jn 2:16 in the world—the cravings of s man,
3: 8 He who does what is s is of the

Sinful nature

Ro 7: 5 For when we were controlled by the s
7:18 good lives in me, that is, in my s.
7:25 in the s a slave to the law of sin.
8: 3 do in that it was weakened by the s,
8: 4 who do not live according to the s
8: 5 Those who live according to the s
8: 8 Those controlled by the s cannot
8: 9 are controlled not by the s but by
8:12 but it is not to the s, to live
8:13 For if you live according to the s,
13:14 how to gratify the desires of the s.
1Co 5: 5 so that the s may be destroyed and
Gal 5:13 use your freedom to indulge the s;
5:16 not gratify the desires of the s.
5:17 For the s desires what is contrary
5:17 Spirit what is contrary to the s.
5:19 The acts of the s are obvious:
5:24 the s with its passions and desires.
6: 8 The one who sows to please his s,
Eph 2: 3 gratifying the cravings of our s and
Col 2:11 in the putting off of the s, not
2:13 in the uncircumcision of your s,
2Pe 2:10 follow the corrupt desire of the s

Sinfulness (Sin)

Ps 36: 1 concerning the s of the wicked:

Sing (Sang, *Sing praise, Sing praises, Sing to the LORD*, Singer, Singers, Singing, Sings, Song, Songs, Sung)

Nu 21:17 "Spring up, O well! **S** about it,
Dt 31:19 the Israelites and make them s it,
Jdg 5: 3 I will s; I will make music to the
1Sa 21:11 one they s about in their dances:
1Ch 15:16 as singers to s joyful songs,
16: 9 **S** to him, s praise to him; tell of
16:33 the trees of the forest will s, they
1Ch 16:33 they will s for joy before the LORD,
2Ch 20:22 they began to s and praise, the LORD
Job 21:12 They s to the music of tambourine
29:13 I made the widow's heart s.
Ps 5:11 be glad; let them ever s for joy.
21:13 we will s and praise your might.
27: 6 I will s and make music to the LORD.
30:12 that my heart may s to you and not
32:11 s, all you who are upright in heart!
33: 1 **S** joyfully to the LORD, you
33: 3 **S** to him a new song; play skilfully,
47: 7 s to him a psalm of praise.
51:14 tongue will s of your righteousness.
57: 7 I will s and make music.
57: 9 I will s of you among the peoples.
59:16 I will s of your strength, in the
59:16 in the morning I will s of your love
63: 7 I s in the shadow of your wings,
65:13 with corn; they shout for joy and s.
66: 2 **S** the glory of his name; make his
67: 4 the nations be glad and s for joy,
68: 4 **S** to God, s praise to his name,
68:32 **S** to God, O kingdoms of the earth,
81: 1 **S** for joy to God our strength;
87: 7 they make music they will s, "All my
89: 1 I will s of the LORD's great love
89:12 and Hermon s for joy at your name.
90:14 s for joy and be glad all our days.
92: 4 s for joy at the work of your hands.
95: 1 Come, let us s for joy to the LORD;
96:12 trees of the forest will s for joy;
96:13 they will s before the LORD, for he
98: 8 the mountains s together for joy;
98: 9 let them s before the LORD, for he
101: 1 to you, O LORD, I will s praise.
104:12 they s among the branches.
105: 2 **S** to him, s praise to him; tell of
108: 1 s and make music with all my soul.
108: 3 I will s of you among the peoples.
119:172 May my tongue s of your word, for
132: 9 may your saints s for joy."
132:16 and her saints shall ever s for joy.
137: 3 "**S** us one of the songs of Zion!
137: 4 How can we s the songs of the LORD
138: 1 the "gods" I will s your praise.
138: 5 May they s of the ways of the LORD,
144: 9 I will s a new song to you, O God;
145: 7 joyfully s of your righteousness.
149: 5 honour and s for joy on their beds.
Pr 29: 6 a righteous one can s and be glad.
Isa 5: 1 I will s for the one I love a song
12: 6 Shout aloud and s for joy, people of
23:16 s many a song, so that you will be
27: 2 "**S** about a fruitful vineyard:
30:29 you will s as on the night you
38:18 death cannot s your praise;
38:20 we will s with stringed instruments
42:11 Let the people of Sela s for joy;
44:23 **S** for joy, O heavens, for the LORD
54: 1 "**S**, O barren woman, you who never
65:14 My servants will s out of the joy of
Jer 31: 7 "**S** with joy for Jacob;
Hos 2:15 There she will s as in the days of
Zep 3:14 **S**, O Daughter of Zion; shout aloud,
Ro 15: 9 I will s hymns to your name."
1Co 14:15 my mind; I will s with my spirit,
14:15 but I will also s with my mind.
Eph 5:19 **S** and make music in your heart to
Col 3:16 and as you s psalms, hymns and
Heb 2:12 congregation I will s your praises."
Jas 5:13 Let him s songs of praise.

Sing praise

1Ch 16: 9 Sing to him, s to him; tell of all
Ps 7:17 s to the name of the LORD Most High.
9: 2 I will s to your name, O Most High.
59:17 O my Strength, I s to you; you, O
61: 8 will I ever s to your name and
66: 4 they s to you, they s to your name.
68: 4 Sing to God, s to his name, extol
68:32 of the earth, s to the Lord,
71:22 I will s to you with the lyre,
71:23 My lips will shout for joy when I s
75: 9 I will s to the God of Jacob.
101: 1 to you, O LORD, I will s.

Ps 104:33 I will s to my God as long as I live.
105: 2 Sing to him, s to him; tell of all
135: 3 s to his name, for that is pleasant.
146: 2 I will s to my God as long as I live.

Sing praises
2Sa 22:50 the nations; I will s to your name.
2Ch 31: 2 to give thanks and to s at the gates
Ps 9:11 S to the LORD, enthroned in Zion;
18:49 O LORD; I will s to your name.
47: 6 S to God, s; s to our King, s.
147: 1 How good it is to s to our God,
Ro 15:11 and s to him, all you peoples."

Sing to the LORD
Ex 15: 1 "I will s, for he is highly exalted.
15:21 "S, for he is highly exalted.
Jdg 5: 3 I will s, I will sing;
1Ch 16:23 S, all the earth; proclaim his
2Ch 20:21 Jehoshaphat appointed men to s and
Ps 13: 6 I will s, for he has been good to me.
30: 4 S, you saints of his; praise his
96: 1 S a new song; s, all the earth.
96: 2 S, praise his name; proclaim his
98: 1 S a new song, for he has done
104:33 I will s all my life; I will sing
147: 7 S with thanksgiving; make music to
149: 1 S a new song, his praise in the
Isa 12: 5 S, for he has done glorious things;
42:10 S a new song, his praise from the
Jer 20:13 S! Give praise to the LORD!

Singed
Da 3:27 nor was a hair of their heads s;

Singer (Sing)
2Sa 23: 1 God of Jacob, Israel's s of songs:

Singers (Sing)
Jdg 5:11 the voice of the s at the watering
2Sa 19:35 hear the voices of men and women s?
1Ch 15:16 brothers as s to sing joyful songs,
15:27 and as were the s, and Kenaniah, who
2Ch 5:13 The trumpeters and s joined in
23:13 and s with musical instruments were
29:28 s sang and the trumpeters played.
35:25 s commemorate Josiah in the laments.
Ezr 2:41 The s: the descendants of Asaph 128
2:65 they also had 200 men and women s.
2:70 The priests, the Levites, the s, the
7: 7 including priests, Levites, s,
7:24 Levites, s, gatekeepers, temple
10:24 From the s: Eliashib.
Ne 7: 1 s and the Levites were appointed.
7:44 The s: the descendants of Asaph 148
7:67 they also had 245 men and women s.
7:73 the Levites, the gatekeepers, the s
10:28 Levites, gatekeepers, s, temple
10:39 the gatekeepers and the s stay.
11:22 who were the s responsible for the
11:23 The s were under the king's orders,
12:28 The s also were brought together
12:29 for the s had built villages for
12:45 as did also the s and gatekeepers,
12:46 there had been directors for the s
12:47 portions for the s and gatekeepers.
13: 5 for the Levites, s and gatekeepers,
13:10 and that all the Levites and s
Ps 68:25 In front are the s, after them the
Ecc 2: 8 I acquired men and women s, and a

Singing (Sing)
Ge 31:27 s to the music of tambourines and
Ex 32:18 it is the sound of s that I hear."
1Sa 18: 6 meet King Saul with s and dancing,
1Ch 15:22 head Levite was in charge of the s;
15:27 in charge of the s of the choirs.
2Ch 23:18 with rejoicing and s, as David had
29:27 s to the LORD began also,
Ps 63: 5 s lips my mouth will praise you.
68: 6 he leads forth the prisoners with s;
98: 5 with the harp and the sound of s,
SS 2:12 the season of s has come,
Isa 14: 7 and at peace; they break into s.
Isa 24:16 From the ends of the earth we hear s:
35:10 They will enter Zion with s;
51: 3 thanksgiving and the sound of s.
51:11 They will enter Zion with s;
Am 8:10 and all your s into weeping.
Zep 3:17 he will rejoice over you with s."
Ac 16:25 were praying and s hymns to God,
Rev 5:13 and all that is in them, s: "To him

Single (Singled, Singleness)
Ge 41: 5 and good, were growing on a s stalk.
41:22 full and good, growing on a s stalk.
Ex 23:29 not drive them out in a s year,
26:24 the top, and fitted into a s ring;
36:29 the top and fitted into a s ring;
Nu 13:23 bearing a s cluster of grapes.
Dt 29:21 The LORD will s him out from all the
Jdg 9:18 his seventy sons on a s stone,
1Ki 16:11 s male, whether relative or friend.
Est 3:13 and little children—on a s day,
Isa 9:14 palm branch and reed in a s day;
10:17 in a s day it will burn and consume
47: 9 in a moment, on a s day:
Eze 37:19 making them a s stick of wood, and
Zec 3: 9 the sin of this land in a s day.
Mt 6:27 by worrying can add a s hour to his
23:15 land and sea to win a s convert,
27:14 no reply, not even to a s charge
Lk 12:25 by worrying can add a s hour to his
Jn 12:24 and dies, it remains only a s seed.
Ac 27:34 will lose a s hair from his head."
Gal 5:14 law is summed up in a s command:
Heb 12:16 for a s meal sold his inheritance
Rev 21:21 pearls, each gate made of a s pearl.

Singled (Single)
1Ki 8:53 For you s them out from all the

Singleness (Single)
Jer 32:39 I will give them s of heart and

Sings (Sing)
Pr 25:20 is one who s songs to a heavy heart.
Isa 16:10 no-one s or shouts in the vineyards;
Eze 33:32 s love songs with a beautiful voice

Sinites
Ge 10:17 Hivites, Arkites, S,
1Ch 1:15 Hivites, Arkites, S,

Sink (Sank, Sinking, Sinks, Sunk)
Dt 28:43 but you will s lower and lower.
Jos 14: 8 me made the hearts of the people s.
Ps 69: 2 I s in the miry depths, where there
69:14 do not let me s; deliver me from
Jer 51:64 'so will Babylon s to rise no more
Eze 27:27 and everyone else on board will s
Am 8: 8 and then s like the river of Egypt.
Mt 14:30 he was afraid and, beginning to s,
Lk 5: 7 boats so full that they began to s.

Sinking (Sink)
Ac 20: 9 who was s into a deep sleep as Paul

Sinks (Sink)
Isa 5:24 as dry grass s down in the flames,
Am 9: 5 then s like the river of Egypt—

Sinned (Sin)
Ex 9:27 "This time I have s," he said to
9:34 thunder had stopped, he s again:
10:16 "I have s against the LORD your God
32:33 "Whoever has s against me I will
Lev 5: 5 he must confess in what way he has s
Nu 6:11 he s by being in the presence of
14:40 "We have s," they said. "We will go
16:38 the censers of the men who s at the
21: 7 "We s when we spoke against the LORD
22:34 to the angel of the LORD, "I have s.
Dt 1:41 "We have s against the LORD.
9:16 I saw that you had s against the
Jos 7:11 Israel has s; they have violated my
7:20 I have s against the LORD,
Jdg 10:10 "We have s against you, forsaking
10:15 said to the LORD, "We have s. Do with
1Sa 7: 6 "We have s against the LORD."
12:10 'We have s; we have forsaken the
15:24 Saul said to Samuel, "I have s.
15:30 Saul replied, "I have s. But please
26:21 Saul said, "I have s. Come back,
2Sa 12:13 "I have s against the LORD."
19:20 For I your servant know that I have s
24:10 I have s greatly in what I have done.
24:17 am the one who has s and done wrong.
1Ki 8:33 because they have s against you,
8:35 your people have s against you,
8:47 'We have s, we have done wrong, we
8:50 forgive your people, who have s
16:25 s more than all those before him.
2Ki 17: 7 had s against the LORD their God,
1Ch 21: 8 David said to God, "I have s greatly
21:17 am the one who has s and done wrong.
2Ch 6:24 because they have s against you
6:26 your people have s against you,
6:37 'We have s, we have done wrong and
6:39 your people, who have s against you.
Ezr 10:13 we have s greatly in this thing.
Ne 9:29 They s against your ordinances, by
13:26 these that Solomon king of Israel s?
Job 1: 5 s and cursed God in their hearts.
7:20 If I have s, what have I done to you,
8: 4 your children s against him, he gave
10:14 If I s, you would be watching me and
24:19 snatches away those who have s.
33:27 he comes to men and says, 'I have s,
36: 9 done—that they have s arrogantly.
Ps 41: 4 heal me, for I have s against you."
51: 4 Against you, you only, have I s and
106: 6 We have s, even as our fathers did;
Isa 42:24 the LORD, against whom we have s?
43:27 Your first father s; your spokesmen
Jer 2:35 you because you say, 'I have not s.'
3:25 We have s against the LORD our God,
8:14 because we have s against him.
14: 7 is great; we have s against you.
14:20 we have indeed s against you.
40: 3 you people s against the LORD
44:23 incense and have s against the LORD
50: 7 for they s against the LORD, their
50:14 for she has s against the LORD.
Lam 1: 8 Jerusalem has s greatly and so has
3:42 "We have s and rebelled and you have
5: 7 Our fathers s and are no more, and
5:16 Woe to us, for we have s!
Eze 28:16 filled with violence, and you s.
Da 9: 5 we have s and done wrong. We have
9: 8 because we have s against you.
9:11 us, because we have s against you.
9:15 day, we have s, we have done wrong.
Hos 4: 7 the more they s against me;
10: 9 "Since the days of Gibeah, you have s
Mic 7: 9 I have s against him, I will bear
Zep 1:17 they have s against the LORD.
Mt 27: 4 "I have s," he said, "for I have
Lk 15:18 s against heaven and against you.
15:21 s against heaven and against you.
Jn 9: 2 "Rabbi, who s, this man or his
9: 3 "Neither this man nor his parents s,
Ro 3:23 for all have s and fall short of the
5:12 came to all men, because all s—
1Co 7:28 if you do marry, you have not s;
7:28 if a virgin marries, she has not s.
2Co 12:21 over many who have s earlier
13: 2 will not spare those who s earlier
Heb 3:17 was it not those who s, whose
Jas 5:15 If he has s, he will be forgiven.
2Pe 2: 4 God did not spare angels when they s
1Jn 1:10 If we claim we have not s, we make

Sinner (Sin)
Pr 11:31 how much more the ungodly and the s
13: 6 but wickedness overthrows the s.
13:21 Misfortune pursues the s, but
Ecc 2:26 but to the s he gives the task of
7:26 her, but the s she will ensnare.
9: 2 with the good man, so with the s;
9:18 war, but one s destroys much good.
Lk 7:39 of woman she is—that she is a s."

Lk 15: 7 over one s who repents than over
15:10 of God over one s who repents."
18:13 said, 'God, have mercy on me, a s.'
19: 7 has gone to be the guest of a 's'."
Jn 9:16 "How can a s do such miraculous
9:24 "We know this man is a s."
9:25 He replied, "Whether he is a s or
Ro 3: 7 why am I still condemned as a s?"
1Co 14:24 he is a s and will be judged by all,
1Ti 2:14 who was deceived and became a s.
Jas 5:20 Whoever turns a s from the error of
1Pe 4:18 become of the ungodly and the s?"

Sinner's (Sin)

Pr 13:22 but a s wealth is stored up for the

Sinners (Sin)

Nu 32:14 "And here you are, a brood of s,
Ps 1: 1 or stand in the way of s or sit in
1: 5 s in the assembly of the righteous.
25: 8 he instructs s in his ways.
26: 9 not take away my soul along with s
37:38 all s will be destroyed; the future
51:13 ways, and s will turn back to you.
104:35 may s vanish from the earth and the
Pr 1:10 My son, if s entice you, do not give
23:17 Do not let your heart envy s, but
Isa 1:28 rebels and s will both be broken,
13: 9 and destroy the s within it.
33:14 The s in Zion are terrified;
Am 9:10 All the s among my people will die
Mt 9:10 "s" came and ate with him and his
9:11 eat with tax collectors and 's'?"
9:13 come to call the righteous, but s."
11:19 a friend of tax collectors and "s".
26:45 Man is betrayed into the hands of s.
Mk 2:15 "s" were eating with him and his
2:16 with the "s" and tax collectors,
2:16 he eat with tax collectors and 's'?"
2:17 come to call the righteous, but s."
14:41 is betrayed into the hands of s.
Lk 5:30 drink with tax collectors and 's'?"
5:32 the righteous, but s to repentance."
6:32 Even 's' love those who love them.
6:33 is that to you? Even 's' do that.
6:34 's' lend to 's', expecting to be
7:34 a friend of tax collectors and "s".
13: 2 worse s than all the other
15: 1 Now the tax collectors and "s" were
15: 2 man welcomes s, and eats with them."
Jn 9:31 We know that God does not listen to s
Ro 5: 8 we were still s, Christ died for us.
5:19 of the one man the many were made s,
Gal 2:15 Jews by birth and not 'Gentile s'
2:17 evident that we ourselves are s,
1Ti 1:15 to save s—of whom I am the worst.
1:16 in me, the worst of s, Christ Jesus
Heb 7:26 set apart from s, exalted above the
Jas 4: 8 Wash your hands, you s, and purify
Jude :15 ungodly s have spoken against him."

Sinning (Sin)

Ge 13:13 and were s greatly against the LORD.
20: 6 I have kept you from s against me.
Ex 20:20 be with you to keep you from s."
Nu 15:28 one who erred by s unintentionally,
32:23 you will be s against the LORD;
1Sa 14:33 "Look, the men are s against the
Job 35: 3 to me, and what do I gain by not s?'
Ps 78:32 In spite of all this, they kept on s;
Jer 9: 5 they weary themselves with s.
Hos 8:11 these have become altars for s.
Jn 5:14 Stop s or something worse may happen
Ro 6: 1 go on s, so that grace may increase?
1Co 7:36 He is not s. They should get married.
11:27 be guilty of s against the body
15:34 senses as you ought, and stop s;
Heb 10:26 If we deliberately keep on s after
2Pe 2:14 of adultery, they never stop s;
1Jn 3: 6 No-one who lives in him keeps on s.
3: 8 devil has been s from the beginning.
3: 9 he cannot go on s, because he has

Sins (*Forgiveness of sins*, Sin)

Ge 50:17 you to forgive your brothers the s
50:17 Now please forgive the s of the
Lev 4: 2 'When anyone s unintentionally and
4: 3 "'If the anointed priest s,
4:13 "'If the whole Israelite community s
4:22 "'When a leader s unintentionally
4:27 "'If a member of the community s
5: 1 "'If a person s because he does not
5:13 for any of these s he has committed,
5:15 s unintentionally in regard to any
5:17 "If a person s and does what is
6: 2 "If anyone s and is unfaithful to
6: 4 he thus s and becomes guilty, he
16:16 whatever their s have been.
16:21 —all their s—and put them on the
16:22 all their s to a solitary place;
16:30 you will be clean from all your s.
16:34 for all the s of the Israelites.
26:18 you for your s seven times over.
26:21 seven times over, as your s deserve.
26:24 you for your s seven times over.
26:28 you for your s seven times over.
26:39 their enemies because of their s;
26:39 because of their fathers' s they
26:40 "'But if they will confess their s
26:40 the s of their fathers—their
26:43 They will pay for their s because
Nu 14:34 land—you will suffer for your s
15:27 "'But if just one person s
15:29 to everyone who s unintentionally,
15:30 "'But anyone who s defiantly,
16:22 assembly when only one man s?"
16:26 swept away because of all their s."
Jos 24:19 forgive your rebellion and your s.
1Sa 2:25 If a man s against another man, God
2:25 but if a man s against the LORD,
12:19 added to all our other s the evil
1Ki 14:16 of the s Jeroboam has committed
14:22 By the s they committed they stirred
15: 3 He committed all the s his father
15:30 of the s Jeroboam had committed and
16: 2 to provoke me to anger by their s.
16:13 of all the s Baasha and his son Elah
16:19 of the s he had committed, doing
16:31 the s of Jeroboam son of Nebat,
2Ki 3: 3 Nevertheless he clung to the s of
10:29 he did not turn away from the s of
10:31 He did not turn away from the s of
13: 2 the s of Jeroboam son of Nebat,
13: 6 they did not turn away from the s of
13:11 of the s of Jeroboam son of Nebat,
14: 6 each is to die for his own s."
14:24 of the s of Jeroboam son of Nebat,
15: 9 He did not turn away from the s of
15:18 from the s of Jeroboam son of Nebat,
15:24 He did not turn away from the s of
15:28 He did not turn away from the s of
17:22 The Israelites persisted in all the s
21:11 has committed these detestable s.
24: 3 s of Manasseh and all he had done,
2Ch 25: 4 each is to die for his own s."
28:10 of s against the LORD your God?
33:19 as all his s and unfaithfulness,
Ezr 9: 6 my God, because our s are higher
9: 7 Because of our s, we and our kings
9:13 us less than our s have deserved
Ne 1: 6 I confess the s we Israelites,
4: 5 or blot out their s from your sight,
9: 2 confessed their s and the wickedness
9:37 Because of our s, its abundant
Job 7:21 pardon my offences and forgive my s?
13:23 How many wrongs and s have I
13:26 make me inherit the s of my youth.
22: 5 Are not your s endless?
31:28 these also would be s to be judged,
35: 6 s are many, what does that do to him?
Ps 5:10 Banish them for their many s, for
19:13 Keep your servant also from wilful s;
25: 7 Remember not the s of my youth and
25:18 my distress and take away all my s.
32: 1 are forgiven, whose s are covered.
40:12 my s have overtaken me, and I
51: 9 Hide your face from my s and blot
59:12 For the s of their mouths, for the
Ps 65: 3 we were overwhelmed by s, you
68:21 of those who go on in their s.
79: 8 Do not hold against us the s of the
79: 9 forgive our s for your name's sake.
85: 2 your people and covered all their s.
90: 8 s in the light of your presence.
94:23 He will repay them for their s and
103: 3 who forgives all your s and heals
103:10 does not treat us as our s deserve
109:15 May their s always remain before the
130: 3 If you, O LORD, kept a record of s,
130: 8 will redeem Israel from all their s.
Pr 14:21 He who despises his neighbour s, but
28:13 He who conceals his s does not
29:22 a hot-tempered one commits many s.
Ecc 7:20 who does what is right and never s.
Isa 1:18 "Though your s are like scarlet,
13:11 its evil, the wicked for their s.
14:21 sons for the s of their forefathers;
26:21 the people of the earth for their s.
33:24 and the s of those who dwell there
38:17 have put all my s behind your back.
40: 2 LORD's hand double for all her s.
43:24 you have burdened me with your s
43:25 sake, and remembers your s no more.
44:22 cloud, your s like the morning mist.
50: 1 Because of your s you were sold;
58: 1 and to the house of Jacob their s.
59: 2 s have hidden his face from you,
59:12 sight, and our s testify against us.
59:20 in Jacob who repent of their s,"
64: 6 like the wind our s sweep us away.
64: 7 made us waste away because of our s.
64: 9 do not remember our s for ever.
65: 7 your s and the s of your fathers,"
Jer 2:13 "My people have committed two s:
5:25 your s have deprived you of good.
11:10 They have returned to the s of their
13:22 it is because of your many s that
14: 7 Although our s testify against us,
14:10 and punish them for their s."
15:13 all your s throughout your country.
18:23 or blot out their s from your sight.
30:14 is so great and your s so many.
30:15 of your great guilt and many s
31:34 and will remember their s no more."
32:18 punishment for the fathers' s into
33: 8 all their s of rebellion against me.
50:20 and for the s of Judah, but none
51: 6 Do not be destroyed because of her s.
Lam 1: 5 her grief because of her many s.
1:14 "My s have been bound into a yoke;
1:22 dealt with me because of all my s.
3:39 complain when punished for his s?
4:13 happened because of the s of her
Eze 7:13 Because of their s, not one of them
7:16 the valleys, each because of his s.
14:11 any more with all their s.
14:13 "Son of man, if a country s against
16:51 Samaria did not commit half the s
16:52 Because your s were more vile than
18: 4 soul who s is the one who will die.
18:14 sees all the s his father commits,
18:20 The soul who s is the one who will
18:21 from all the s he has committed
18:24 the s he has committed, he will die.
21:24 revealing your s in all that you do—
23:49 consequences of your s of idolatry.
24:23 waste away because of your s and
28:18 By your many s and dishonest trade
32:27 for their s rested on their bones,
33:10 "Our offences and s weigh us down,
33:12 The righteous man, if he s, will not
33:16 None of the s he has committed will
36:31 for your s and detestable practices.
36:33 day I cleanse you from all your s,
43:10 that they may be ashamed of their s.
45:20 for anyone who s unintentionally or
Da 4:27 Renounce your s by doing what is
9:13 by turning from our s and giving
9:16 Our s and the iniquities of our
Hos 4: 8 They feed on the s of my people and
7: 1 the s of Ephraim are exposed.
7: 2 Their s engulf them; they are always
8:13 wickedness and punish their s:
9: 7 Because your s are so many and your

Hos 9: 9 and punish them for their s.
13:12 stored up, his s are kept on record.
14: 1 Your s have been your downfall!
14: 2 Say to him: "Forgive all our s and
Am 1: 3 "For three s of Damascus, even for
1: 6 "For three s of Gaza, even for four,
1: 9 "For three s of Tyre, even for four,
1:11 "For three s of Edom, even for four,
1:13 "For three s of Ammon, even for four,
2: 1 "For three s of Moab, even for four,
2: 4 "For three s of Judah, even for four,
2: 6 "For three s of Israel, even for
3: 2 I will punish you for all your s."
3:14 On the day I punish Israel for her s
5:12 your offences and how great your s.
Mic 1: 5 of the s of the house of Israel.
6:13 you, to ruin you because of your s.
7:19 you will tread our s underfoot and
Mt 1:21 will save his people from their s."
3: 6 Confessing their s, they were
6:15 if you do not forgive men their s,
6:15 your Father will not forgive your s.
9: 2 heart, son; your s are forgiven."
9: 5 to say, 'Your s are forgiven,' or
9: 6 has authority on earth to forgive s.
18:15 "If your brother s against you, go
18:21 my brother when he s against me?
Mk 1: 5 Confessing their s, they were
2: 5 "Son, your s are forgiven."
2: 7 Who can forgive s but God alone?"
2: 9 'Your s are forgiven,' or to say,
2:10 authority on earth to forgive s
3:28 all the s and blasphemies of men
11:25 in heaven may forgive you your s."
Lk 1:77 through the forgiveness of their s,
5:20 said, "Friend, your s are forgiven.
5:21 Who can forgive s but God alone?"
5:23 to say, 'Your s are forgiven,' or
5:24 has authority on earth to forgive s.
7:47 her many s have been forgiven—
7:48 said to her, "Your s are forgiven."
7:49 "Who is this who even forgives s?
11: 4 Forgive us our s, for we also
11: 4 forgive everyone who s against us.
17: 3 "If your brother s, rebuke him,
17: 4 If he s against you seven times in a
Jn 8:24 you that you would die in your s;
8:24 be, you will indeed die in your s."
8:34 everyone who s is a slave to sin.
20:23 If you forgive anyone his s, they
Ac 2:38 Christ for the forgiveness of your s.
3:19 and turn to God, so that your s may
22:16 and wash your s away, calling on
Ro 3:25 had left the s committed beforehand
4: 7 are forgiven, whose s are covered.
4:25 delivered over to death for our s
11:27 with them when I take away their s."
1Co 6:18 All other s a man commits are
6:18 s sexually s against his own body.
15: 3 Christ died for our s according to
15:17 is futile; you are still in your s.
2Co 5:19 not counting men's s against them.
Gal 1: 4 who gave himself for our s to rescue
Eph 2: 1 dead in your transgressions and s,
Col 2:13 you were dead in your s and in the
2:13 He forgave us all our s,
1Th 2:16 always heap up their s to the limit.
4: 6 Lord will punish men for all such s,
1Ti 5:22 and do not share in the s of others.
5:24 The s of some men are obvious,
5:24 the s of others trail behind them.
2Ti 3: 6 who are loaded down with s and are
Heb 1: 3 he had provided purification for s,
2:17 atonement for the s of the people.
5: 1 to offer gifts and sacrifices for s.
5: 3 to offer sacrifices for his own s,
5: 3 as well as for the s of the people.
7:27 first for his own s, and then
7:27 and then for the s of the people.
7:27 He sacrificed for their s once for
8:12 and will remember their s no more."
9: 7 for the s the people had committed
9:15 s committed under the first covenant.
9:28 to take away the s of many people;
10: 2 longer have felt guilty for their s.
10: 3 are an annual reminder of s,
Heb 10: 4 of bulls and goats to take away s.
10:11 which can never take away s.
10:12 for all time one sacrifice for s,
10:17 he adds: "Their s and lawless acts I
10:26 truth, no sacrifice for s is left,
Jas 4:17 he ought to do and doesn't do it, s.
5:16 Therefore confess your s to each
5:20 and cover over a multitude of s.
1Pe 2:24 He himself bore our s in his body on
2:24 so that we might die to s and live
3:18 For Christ died for s once for all,
4: 8 love covers over a multitude of s.
2Pe 1: 9 has been cleansed from his past s.
1Jn 1: 9 If we confess our s, he is faithful
1: 9 just and will forgive us our s and
2: 2 He is the atoning sacrifice for our s
2: 2 also for the s of the whole world.
2:12 because your s have been forgiven
3: 4 Everyone who s breaks the law;
3: 5 so that he might take away our s.
4:10 as an atoning sacrifice for our s.
Rev 1: 5 freed us from our s by his blood,
18: 4 so that you will not share in her s,
18: 5 for her s are piled up to heaven,

Siphmoth

1Sa 30:28 to those in Aroer, S, Eshtemoa

Sippai

1Ch 20: 4 Sibbecai the Hushathite killed S,

Sirah

2Sa 3:26 brought him back from the well of S.

Sirion

Dt 3: 9 (Hermon is called S by the Sidonians;
Ps 29: 6 S like a young wild ox.

Sisera (Sisera's)

Jdg 4: 2 S, who lived in Harosheth Haggoyim.
4: 7 I will lure S, the commander of
4: 9 LORD will hand S over to a woman.
4:12 they told S that Barak son of
4:13 S gathered together his nine hundred
4:14 LORD has given S into your hands.
4:15 At Barak's advance, the LORD routed S
4:15 and S abandoned his chariot and fled
4:16 All the troops of S fell by the
4:17 S, however, fled on foot to the tent
4:18 Jael went out to meet S and said to
4:22 Barak came by in pursuit of S, and
4:22 and there lay S with the tent peg
5:20 their courses they fought against S.
5:26 She struck S, she crushed his head,
5:30 colourful garments as plunder for S,
1Sa 12: 9 so he sold them into the hands of S,
Ezr 2:53 Barkos, S, Temah,
Ne 7:55 Barkos, S, Temah,
Ps 83: 9 to S and Jabin at the river Kishon,

Sisera's (Sisera)

Jdg 5:28 "Through the window peered S mother;

Sismai

1Ch 2:40 Eleasah the father of S,
2:40 S the father of Shallum,

Sister (Sister's, Sister-in-law, Sisters)

Ge 4:22 Tubal-Cain's s was Naamah.
12:13 Say you are my s, so that I will be
12:19 Why did you say, 'She is my s,' so
20: 2 of his wife Sarah, "She is my s."
20: 5 Did he not say to me, 'She is my s,'
20:12 Besides, she really is my s, the
24:59 they sent their s Rebekah on her way,
24:60 "Our s, may you increase to
25:20 Aram and s of Laban the Aramean.
26: 7 "She is my s," because he was afraid
26: 9 'she is my s'?" Isaac answered him,
28: 9 the s of Nebaioth and daughter of
30: 1 she became jealous of her s.
30: 8 struggle with my s, and I have won.
Ge 34:13 their s Dinah had been defiled,
34:14 s to a man who is not circumcised.
34:17 we'll take our s and go."
34:27 city where their s had been defiled.
34:31 treated our s like a prostitute?"
36: 3 of Ishmael and s of Nebaioth.
36:22 Timna was Lotan's s.
46:17 Their s was Serah. The sons of
Ex 2: 4 His s stood at a distance to see
2: 7 his s asked Pharaoh's daughter,
6:20 Amram married his father's s
6:23 of Amminadab and s of Nahshon,
15:20 Miriam the prophetess, Aaron's s,
Lev 18: 9 have sexual relations with your s,
18:11 born to your father; she is your s.
18:12 relations with your father's s;
18:13 relations with your mother's s,
18:18 "'Do not take your wife's s as a
20:17 "'If a man marries his s, the
20:17 He has dishonoured his s and will
20:19 sexual relations with the s of
21: 3 or an unmarried s who is dependent
Nu 6: 7 or mother or brother or s dies,
25:18 affair of Peor and their s Cozbi,
26:59 Aaron, Moses and their s Miriam.
Dt 27:22 is the man who sleeps with his s,
Jdg 15: 2 Isn't her younger s more attractive
2Sa 13: 1 beautiful s of Absalom son of David.
13: 2 illness on account of his s Tamar,
13: 4 with Tamar, my brother Absalom's s."
13: 5 'I would like my s Tamar to come and
13: 6 "I would like my s Tamar to come and
13:11 said, "Come to bed with me, my s."
13:20 quiet now, my s; he is your brother.
13:22 he had disgraced his s Tamar.
13:32 day that Amnon raped his s Tamar.
17:25 and s of Zeruiah the mother of Joab.
1Ki 11:19 he gave him a s of his own wife,
11:20 The s of Tahpenes bore him a son
2Ki 11: 2 of King Jehoram and s of Ahaziah,
1Ch 1:39 Timna was Lotan's s.
3: 9 And Tamar was their s.
3:19 Shelomith was their s.
4: 3 Their s was named Hazzelelponi.
4:19 of Hodiah's wife, the s of Naham:
7:18 His s Hammoleketh gave birth to
7:30 Their s was Serah.
7:32 and Hotham and of their s Shua.
2Ch 22:11 was Ahaziah's s, she hid the child
Job 17:14 to the worm, 'My mother' or 'My s',
Pr 7: 4 Say to wisdom, "You are my s," and
SS 4: 9 You have stolen my heart, my s, my
4:10 How delightful is your love, my s,
4:12 You are a garden locked up, my s, my
5: 1 I have come into my garden, my s, my
5: 2 "Open to me, my s, my darling, my
8: 8 We have a young s, and her breasts
8: 8 our s for the day she is spoken for?
Jer 3: 7 and her unfaithful s Judah saw it.
3: 8 her unfaithful s Judah had no fear;
3:10 her unfaithful s Judah did not
22:18 'Alas, my brother! Alas, my s!
Eze 16:45 you are a true s of your sisters,
16:46 Your older s was Samaria, who lived
16:46 and your younger s, who lived to
16:48 your s Sodom and her daughters
16:49 "'Now this was the sin of your s
16:56 You would not even mention your s
22:11 his s, his own father's daughter.
23: 4 Oholah, and her s was Oholibah.
23:11 "Her s Oholibah saw this, yet in her
23:11 she was more depraved than her s.
23:18 as I had turned away from her s.
23:31 You have gone the way of your s;
23:33 the cup of your s Samaria.
23:42 arms of the women and her s and
44:25 brother or unmarried s, then he may
Mt 12:50 is my brother and s and mother."
Mk 3:35 is my brother and s and mother."
Lk 10:39 She had a s called Mary, who sat at
10:40 "Lord, don't you care that my s has
Jn 11: 1 village of Mary and her s Martha.
11: 5 Jesus loved Martha and her s and
11:28 back and called her s Mary aside.
11:39 "But, Lord," said Martha, the s of

Jn 19:25 his mother's s, Mary the wife of
Ac 23:16 when the son of Paul's s heard of
Ro 16: 1 I commend to you our s Phoebe, a
16:15 Julia, Nereus and his s, and Olympas
Phm : 2 to Apphia our s, to Archippus our
Jas 2:15 Suppose a brother or s is without
2Jn :13 The children of your chosen s send

Sister's (Sister)
Ge 24:30 and the bracelets on his s arms, and
29:13 Jacob, his s son, he hurried to meet
1Ch 7:15 His s name was Maacah.
Eze 23:32 "You will drink your s cup, a cup

Sister-in-law (Sister)
Ru 1:15 "Look," said Naomi, "your s is going

Sisters (Sister)
Jos 2:13 my brothers and s, and all who
1Ch 2:16 Their s were Zeruiah and Abigail.
Job 1: 4 three s to eat and drink with them.
42:11 All his brothers and s and everyone
Eze 16:45 and you are a true sister of your s,
16:51 and have made your s seem righteous
16:52 some justification for your s.
16:52 have made your s appear righteous.
16:55 your s, Sodom with her daughters and
16:61 be ashamed when you receive your s,
Hos 2: 1 and of your s, 'My loved one'.
Mt 13:56 Aren't all his s with us? Where then
19:29 left houses or brothers or s or
Mk 6: 3 Aren't his s here with us?"
10:29 has left home or brothers or s or
10:30 brothers, s, mothers, children and
Lk 14:26 his brothers and s—yes, even his
Jn 11: 3 the s sent word to Jesus, "Lord, the
1Ti 5: 2 women as s, with absolute purity.

Sistrums
2Sa 6: 5 lyres, tambourines, s and cymbals.

Sit (Sat, Sits, Sitting)
Ge 27:19 Please s up and eat some of my game
27:31 "My father, s up and eat some of my
Ex 18:14 Why do you alone s as judge,
Nu 32: 6 go to war while you s here?
Dt 6: 7 Talk about them when you s at home
11:19 talking about them when you s at
Ru 4: 1 over here, my friend, and s down.
4: 2 and said, "**S** here," and they did so.
1Sa 16:11 will not s down until he arrives."
1Ki 1:13 and he will s on my throne"?
1:17 me, and he will s on my throne.'
1:20 to learn from you who will s on the
1:24 and that he will s on your throne?
1:27 who should s on the throne of my
1:30 he will s on my throne in my place."
1:35 s on my throne and reign in my place.
3: 6 to s on his throne this very day.
8:20 and now I s on the throne of Israel,
8:25 s before me on the throne of Israel,
2Ki 10:30 your descendants will s on the
15:12 "Your descendants will s on the
1Ch 28: 5 my son Solomon to s on the throne
2Ch 6:10 and now I s on the throne of Israel,
6:16 s before me on the throne of Israel,
Ps 1: 1 sinners or s in the seat of mockers.
26: 4 I do not s with deceitful men, nor
26: 5 and refuse to s with the wicked.
69:12 Those who s at the gate mock me, and
80: 1 s enthroned between the cherubim,
102:12 you, O LORD, s enthroned for ever;
110: 1 to my Lord: "**S** at my right hand.
119:23 Though rulers s together and slander
132:12 s on your throne for ever and ever."
132:14 here I will s enthroned, for I have
139: 2 You know when I s and when I rise;
Pr 23: 1 you s to dine with a ruler, note
SS 2: 3 I delight to s in his shade, and his
Isa 3:26 destitute, she will s on the ground.
14:13 s enthroned on the mount of assembly,
16: 5 in faithfulness a man will s on it—
42: 7 the dungeon those who s in darkness.
47: 1 "Go down, s in the dust, Virgin
Isa 47: 1 s on the ground without a throne,
47: 5 "**S** in silence, go into darkness,
47:14 here is no fire to s by.
52: 2 rise up, s enthroned, O Jerusalem.
65: 4 who s among the graves and spend
Jer 13:13 the kings who s on David's throne
16: 8 and s down to eat and drink.
17:25 kings who s on David's throne will
22: 2 O king of Judah, you who s on
22: 4 then kings who s on David's throne
22:30 none will s on the throne of David
33:17 a man to s on the throne of the
36:15 They said to him, "**S** down, please,
36:30 He will have no-one to s on the
48:18 glory and s on the parched ground,
Lam 2:10 of Zion s on the ground in silence;
3:28 Let him s alone in silence, for the
Eze 26:16 Clothed with terror, they will s on
28: 2 I s on the throne of a god in the
33:31 and s before you to listen to your
44: 3 who may s inside the gateway to eat
Da 7:26 "'But the court will s, and his
11:27 will s at the same table and lie to
Joel 3:12 for there I will s to judge all the
Am 3:12 those who s in Samaria on the edge
Mic 4: 4 Every man will s under his own vine
7: 8 Though I s in darkness, the LORD
Zec 3:10 to s under his vine and fig-tree,'
6:13 and will s and rule on his throne.
8: 4 will s in the streets of Jerusalem,
Mal 3: 3 He will s as a refiner and purifier
Mt 14:19 he directed the people to s down on
15:35 He told the crowd to s down on the
19:28 me will also s on twelve thrones,
20:21 sons of mine may s at your right
20:23 but to s at my right or left is not
22:44 "**S** at my right hand until I put
23: 2 and the Pharisees s in Moses' seat.
25:31 s on his throne in heavenly glory.
26:36 "**S** here while I go over there and
Mk 6:39 s down in groups on the green grass.
8: 6 He told the crowd to s down on the
10:37 "Let one of us s at your right
10:40 to s at my right or left is not for
12:36 "**S** at my right hand until I put
14:32 his disciples, "**S** here while I pray.
Lk 9:14 s down in groups of about fifty each.
14:28 Will he not first s down and
14:31 Will he not first s down and
16: 6 'Take your bill, s down quickly, and
17: 7 'Come along now and s down to eat'?
20:42 to my Lord: "**S** at my right hand
22:30 in my kingdom and s on thrones,
Jn 6:10 Jesus said, "Make the people s down."
9: 8 the same man who used to s and beg?"
Ac 2:34 to my Lord: "**S** at my right hand
3:10 who used to s begging at the temple
8:31 Philip to come up and s with him.
23: 3 You s there to judge me according
1Co 9: 3 This is my defence to those who s in
Heb 1:13 "**S** at my right hand until I make
Jas 2: 3 "You stand there" or "**S** on the floor
Rev 3:21 I will give the right to s with me
18: 7 'I s as queen; I am not a widow,

Site (Sites)
Ge 12: 6 as far as the s of the great tree
23: 4 for a burial s here so that I can
23: 9 full price as a burial s among you."
23:20 by the Hittites as a burial s.
Nu 21:15 ravines that lead to the s of Ar
1Ki 6: 7 temple s while it was being built.
1Ch 17: 5 I have moved from one tent s to
21:22 to him, "Let me have the s of your
21:25 hundred shekels of gold for the s.
Ezr 2:68 of the house of God on its s.
5:15 rebuild the house of God on its s.'
6: 7 rebuild this house of God on its s.
Zec 14:10 from the Benjamin Gate to the s of

Sites (Site)
2Ki 23:14 and covered the s with human bones.
2Ch 33:19 and the s where he built high places

Sithri
Ex 6:22 Uzziel were Mishael, Elzaphan and **S**.

Sitnah
Ge 26:21 that one also; so he named it **S**.

Sits (Sit)
Ex 11: 5 who s on the throne, to the
Lev 15: 4 anything he s on will be unclean.
15: 6 Whoever s on anything that the man
15: 9 "'Everything the man s on when
15:20 anything she s on will be unclean.
15:22 Whoever touches anything she s on
15:26 and anything she s on will be
Est 6:10 the Jew, who s at the king's gate.
Ps 29:10 The LORD s enthroned over the flood;
99: 1 he s enthroned between the cherubim
113: 5 God, the One who s enthroned on high,
Pr 9:14 She s at the door of her house, on a
20: 8 a king s on his throne to judge, he
Isa 28: 6 of justice to him who s in judgment,
40:22 He s enthroned above the circle of
Jer 29:16 the king who s on David's throne
Mt 19:28 when the Son of Man s on his
23:22 throne and by the one who s on it.
Rev 4: 9 honour and thanks to him who s on
4:10 down before him who s on the throne,
5:13 "To him who s on the throne and to
6:16 the face of him who s on the throne
7:10 to our God, who s on the throne,
7:15 and he who s on the throne will
17: 1 prostitute, who s on many waters.
17: 9 seven hills on which the woman s.
17:15 where the prostitute s, are peoples,

Sitting (Sit)
Ge 18: 1 while he was s at the entrance to
19: 1 Lot was s in the gateway of the city.
23:10 Ephron the Hittite was s among his
31:34 camel's saddle and was s on them.
Lev 15:23 is the bed or anything she was s on,
Dt 22: 6 and the mother is s on the young or
Jdg 3:20 while he was s alone in the upper
5:10 donkeys, s on your saddle blankets,
1Sa 1: 9 Now Eli the priest was s on a chair
4:13 there was Eli s on his chair by
19: 9 as he was s in his house with his
2Sa 18:24 While David was s between the inner
19: 8 "The king is s in the gateway," they
1Ki 13:14 He found him s under an oak tree and
13:20 While they were s at the table, the
22:10 Jehoshaphat king of Judah were s on
22:19 I saw the LORD s on his throne with
2Ki 1: 9 who was s on the top of a hill, and
6:32 Now Elisha was s in his house, and
6:32 and the elders were s with him.
9: 5 found the army officers s together.
18:27 and not to the men s on the wall—
2Ch 18: 9 Jehoshaphat king of Judah were s on
18:18 I saw the LORD s on his throne with
Ezr 10: 9 all the people were s in the square
Ne 2: 6 the king, with the queen s beside
Est 2:19 Mordecai was s at the king's gate.
2:21 During the time Mordecai was s at
5: 1 The king was s on his royal throne
5:13 Jew Mordecai s at the king's gate."
Isa 36:12 and not to the men s on the wall—
Jer 8:14 "Why are we s here? Gather together!
32:12 Jews s in the courtyard of the guard.
36:12 where all the officials were s:
36:22 king was s in the winter apartment,
38: 7 the king was s in the Benjamin Gate,
Lam 3:63 Look at them! **S** or standing, they
Eze 8: 1 while I was s in my house and the
8: 1 elders of Judah were s before me,
8:14 women s there, mourning for Tammuz.
Mt 9: 9 s at the tax collector's booth.
11:16 They are like children s in the
20:30 Two blind men were s by the roadside,
24: 3 Jesus was s on the Mount of Olives,
26:64 the Son of Man s at the right hand
26:69 Now Peter was s out in the courtyard,
27:19 While Pilate was s on the judge's
27:36 s down, they kept watch over him
27:61 Mary were s there opposite the tomb.

Mk 2: 6 teachers of the law were s there,
2:14 s at the tax collector's booth.
3:32 A crowd was s around him, and they
5:15 s there, dressed and in his right
9:35 S down, Jesus called the Twelve and
10:46 was s by the roadside begging.
13: 3 Jesus was s on the Mount of Olives
14:62 the Son of Man s at the right hand
16: 5 in a white robe s on the right side,
Lk 2:46 s among the teachers, listening to
5:17 Judea and Jerusalem, were s there.
5:27 the name of Levi s at his tax booth.
7:32 They are like children s in the
8:35 s at Jesus' feet, dressed and in
10:13 long ago, s in sackcloth and ashes.
18:35 man was s by the roadside begging.
Jn 2:14 others s at tables exchanging money.
Ac 2: 2 the whole house where they were s.
6:15 All who were s in the Sanhedrin
8:28 on his way home was s in his chariot
26:30 and Bernice and those s with them.
1Co 14:30 comes to someone who is s down,
Jas 4:11 keeping it, but s in judgment on it.
Rev 4: 2 in heaven with someone s on it.
14:15 voice to him who was s on the cloud,
17: 3 There I saw a woman s on a scarlet

Situated (Situation)

2Ki 2:19 "Look, our lord, this town is well s,
Eze 27: 3 Say to Tyre, s at the gateway to the
Na 3: 8 Are you better than Thebes, s on the

Situation (Situated, Situations)

Ge 31:40 This was my s: The heat consumed me
1Sa 13: 6 saw that their s was critical
2Sa 14:20 did this to change the present s.
Da 2: 9 things, hoping the s will change.
6:17 Daniel's s might not be changed.
Mt 19:10 "If this is the s between a husband
1Co 7:20 Each one should remain in the s
7:24 remain in the s God called him to.
Php 4:12 of being content in any and every s,

Situations (Situation)

2Ti 4: 5 you, keep your head in all s, endure

Sivan

Est 8: 9 of the third month, the month of S.

Six days

Ex 16:26; 20:9, 11; 23:12; 24:16; 31:15, 17; 34:21; 35:2; Lev 23:3; Dt 5:13; 16:8; Jos 6:3, 14; Mt 17:1; Mk 9:2; Lk 13:14; Jn 12:1

Siyon

Dt 4:48 Gorge to Mount S (that is, Hermon),

Size

Ex 26: 2 All the curtains are to be the same s
26: 8 be the same s—thirty cubits long
36: 9 All the curtains were the same s—
36:15 All eleven curtains were the same s—
Nu 13:32 people we saw there are of great s.
1Ki 6:25 were identical in s and shape.
7: 9 blocks of high-grade stone cut to s
7:11 stones, cut to s, and cedar beams.
7:37 and were identical in s and shape.
2Ki 10:32 LORD began to reduce the s of Israel.
1Ch 23:29 all measurements of quantity and s.
Ps 33:16 No king is saved by the s of his
Eze 45:11 and the bath are to be the same s,
46:22 in the four corners was the same s.
Rev 18:21 boulder the s of a large millstone

Sketch

2Ki 16:10 Uriah the priest a s of the altar,

Skies (Sky)

Dt 28:24 from the s until you are destroyed.
Job 26: 7 He spreads out the northern s over
26:13 By his breath the s became fair;
37:18 join him in spreading out the s,
37:21 bright as it is in the s after the
Ps 19: 1 s proclaim the work of his hands.
36: 5 heavens, your faithfulness to the s.
57:10 your faithfulness reaches to the s.
68:33 to him who rides the ancient s above,
68:34 Israel, whose power is in the s.
71:19 Your righteousness reaches to the s,
77:17 the s resounded with thunder;
78:23 Yet he gave a command to the s above
89: 6 For who in the s above can compare
108: 4 your faithfulness reaches to the s.
148: 4 heavens and you waters above the s.
Jer 14:22 s themselves send down showers?
51: 9 for her judgment reaches to the s,
Hos 2:21 "I will respond to the s, and they
Mt 11:23 will you be lifted up to the s?
Lk 10:15 will you be lifted up to the s?

Skilful (Skill)

Ge 25:27 grew up, and Esau became a s hunter,
1Ch 15:22 because he was s at it.
2Ch 26:15 by s men for use on the towers
Ps 45: 1 my tongue is the pen of a s writer.
58: 5 however s the enchanter may be.
78:72 of heart; with s hands he led them.
Jer 9:17 send for the most s of them.
Zec 9: 2 and Sidon, though they are very s.

Skilfully (Skill)

Ex 28: 8 Its s woven waistband is to be like
29: 5 on him by its s woven waistband.
39: 5 Its s woven waistband was like
Lev 8: 7 to him by its s woven waistband;
Ps 33: 3 play s, and shout for joy.

Skill (Skilful, Skilfully, Skilled, Skills)

Ex 31: 3 with s, ability and knowledge in all
31: 6 Also I have given s to all the
35:26 and had the s spun the goat hair.
35:31 with s, ability and knowledge in all
35:35 He has filled them with s to do all
36: 1 person to whom the LORD has given s
2Ch 2:13 you Huram-Abi, a man of great s,
Ps 137: 5 may my right hand forget ⌊its s⌋.
Ecc 2:19 my effort and s under the sun.
2:21 work with wisdom, knowledge and s,
10:10 is needed but s will bring success.
Eze 28: 5 By your great s in trading you have
Ac 17:29 image made by man's design and s.

Skilled (Skill)

Ex 26: 1 worked into them by a s craftsman.
26:31 worked into it by a s craftsman.
28: 3 Tell all the s men to whom I have
28: 6 linen—the work of a s craftsman.
28:15 —the work of a s craftsman.
35:10 "All who are s among you are to come
35:25 Every s woman spun with her hands
36: 1 Bezalel, Oholiab and every s person
36: 2 Oholiab and every s person to whom
36: 4 all the s craftsmen who were doing
36: 8 All the s men among the workmen made
36: 8 worked into them by a s craftsman.
36:35 worked into it by a s craftsman.
39: 3 linen—the work of a s craftsman.
39: 8 —the work of a s craftsman.
1Ki 5: 6 You know that we have no-one so s in
7:14 Huram was highly s and experienced
1Ch 22:15 well as men s in every kind of
25: 7 s in music for the LORD—they
28:21 and every willing man s in any craft
2Ch 2: 7 "Send me, therefore, a man s to work
2: 7 and Jerusalem with my s craftsmen,
2: 8 men are s in cutting timber there.
34:12 s in playing musical instruments—
Job 32:22 for if I were s in flattery, my
Pr 22:29 Do you see a man s in his work?
Isa 3: 3 s craftsman and clever enchanter.
40:20 He looks for a s craftsman to set up
Jer 2:33 How s you are at pursuing love!
4:22 They are s in doing evil; they know
10: 9 and purple—all made by s workers.
50: 9 Their arrows will be like s warriors
Eze 21:31 to brutal men, men s in destruction.
Eze 27: 8 your s men, O Tyre, were aboard as
Mic 7: 3 Both hands are s in doing evil;

Skills (Skill)

Dt 33:11 Bless all his s, O LORD, and be

Skim

Job 9:26 They s past like boats of papyrus,

Skimping

Am 8: 5 s the measure, boosting the price

Skin (Skinned, Skins, Smooth-skinned)

Ge 3:21 The LORD God made garments of s for
21:14 a s of water and gave them to Hagar.
21:15 the water in the s was gone, she put
21:19 So she went and filled the s with
27:11 man, and I'm a man with smooth s.
Lev 1: 6 He is to s the burnt offering and
13: 2 or a rash or a bright spot on his s
13: 2 may become an infectious s disease,
13: 3 is to examine the sore on his s,
13: 3 sore appears to be more than s deep,
13: 3 deep, it is an infectious s disease.
13: 4 If the spot on his s is white but
13: 4 not appear to be more than s deep
13: 5 and has not spread in the s,
13: 6 faded and has not spread in the s,
13: 7 if the rash does spread in his s
13: 8 and if the rash has spread in the s,
13: 9 anyone has an infectious s disease,
13:10 s that has turned the hair white
13:11 is a chronic s disease and the
13:12 breaks out all over his s and,
13:12 it covers all the s of the infected
13:18 "When someone has a boil on his s
13:20 it appears to be more than s deep
13:20 It is an infectious s disease that
13:21 not more than s deep and has faded,
13:22 If it is spreading in the s, the
13:24 "When someone has a burn on his s
13:25 appears to be more than s deep,
13:25 it is an infectious s disease.
13:26 not more than s deep and has faded,
13:27 and if it is spreading in the s, the
13:27 it is an infectious s disease.
13:28 not spread in the s but has faded,
13:30 it appears to be more than s deep
13:31 not seem to be more than s deep
13:32 not appear to be more than s deep,
13:34 and if it has not spread in the s
13:34 appears to be no more than s deep,
13:35 if the itch does spread in the s
13:36 and if the itch has spread in the s,
13:38 or woman has white spots on the s,
13:39 rash that has broken out on the s;
13:43 like an infectious s disease,
14: 3 healed of his infectious s disease,
14:32 who has an infectious s disease
14:54 infectious s disease, for an itch,
14:57 infectious s diseases and mildew.
22: 4 s disease or a bodily discharge,
Nu 5: 2 s disease or a discharge of any kind,
Jdg 4:19 She opened a s of milk, gave him a
1Sa 1:24 an ephah of flour and a s of wine,
10: 3 of bread, and another a s of wine.
16:20 a s of wine and a young goat and
2Sa 16: 1 cakes of figs and a s of wine.
2Ch 29:34 however, were too few to s all the
Job 2: 4 "S for s!" Satan replied.
7: 5 scabs, my s is broken and festering.
10:11 clothe me with s and flesh and knit
16:15 "I have sewed sackcloth over my s
18:13 eats away parts of his s;
19:20 I am nothing but s and bones; I have
19:20 escaped by only the s of my teeth.
19:26 after my s has been destroyed, yet
30:30 My s grows black and peels; my body
Ps 102: 5 I am reduced to s and bones.
Jer 13:23 Can the Ethiopian change his s or
Lam 3: 4 He has made my s and my flesh grow
4: 8 Their s has shrivelled on their
5:10 Our s is hot as an oven, feverish

Eze 37: 6 come upon you and cover you with s;
37: 8 appeared on them and s covered them,
Mic 3: 2 who tear the s from my people and
3: 3 strip off their s and break their

Skink
Lev 11:30 lizard, the s and the chameleon.

Skinned (Skin)
2Ch 35:11 while the Levites s the animals.

Skins (Sheepskins, Skin)
Ex 25: 5 ram s dyed red and hides of sea cows;
26:14 Make for the tent a covering of ram s
35: 7 ram s dyed red and hides of sea cows;
35:23 or goat hair, ram s dyed red or
36:19 tent a covering of ram s dyed red,
39:34 the covering of ram s dyed red, the
Nu 6: 4 grapevine, not even the seeds or s.
1Sa 25:18 two s of wine, five dressed sheep,
Mt 9:17 If they do, the s will burst, the
Mk 2:22 the wine will burst the s, and both
Lk 5:37 the new wine will burst the s, the

Skip (Skipped)
Ps 29: 6 He makes Lebanon s like a calf,

Skipped (Skip)
Ps 114: 4 the mountains s like rams, the hills
114: 6 you mountains, that you s like rams,

Skirted (Skirts)
Jdg 11:18 s the lands of Edom and Moab, passed

Skirts (Skirted)
Isa 47: 2 Lift up your s, bare your legs, and
Jer 13:22 sins that your s have been torn off
13:26 I will pull up your s over your face
Lam 1: 9 Her filthiness clung to her s;
Na 3: 5 "I will lift your s over your face.

Skull (Skulls)
Jdg 9:53 on his head and cracked his s.
2Ki 9:35 her s, her feet and her hands.
Mt 27:33 (which means The Place of the S).
Mk 15:22 (which means The Place of the S).
Lk 23:33 they came to the place called the S,
Jn 19:17 he went out to the place of the S

Skulls (Skull)
Nu 24:17 Moab, the s of all the sons of Sheth.
Jer 48:45 Moab, the s of the noisy boasters.

Sky (Skies)
Ge 1: 8 God called the expanse "s".
1: 9 God said, "Let the water under the s
1:14 s to separate the day from the night,
1:15 of the s to give light on the earth.
1:17 God set them in the expanse of the s
1:20 earth across the expanse of the s."
8: 2 rain had stopped falling from the s.
22:17 as numerous as the stars in the s
26: 4 as numerous as the stars in the s
Ex 9:22 "Stretch out your hand towards the s
9:23 out his staff towards the s,
10:21 "Stretch out your hand towards the s
10:22 out his hand towards the s,
24:10 of sapphire, clear as the s itself.
32:13 as numerous as the stars in the s
Lev 26:19 make the s above you like iron and
Dt 1:10 are as many as the stars in the s.
1:28 are large, with walls up to the s.
4:19 you look up to the s and see the sun,
9: 1 cities that have walls up to the s.
10:22 as numerous as the stars in the s.
17: 3 or the moon or the stars of the s,
28:23 The s over your head will be bronze,
28:62 as numerous as the stars in the s
Jos 8:20 of the city rising against the s,
10:11 hailstones down on them from the s,
10:13 sun stopped in the middle of the s
Jdg 20:40 the whole city going up into the s.
2Sa 22:12 him—the dark rain clouds of the s.
1Ki 18:45 Meanwhile, the s grew black with
1Ch 27:23 as numerous as the stars in the s.
Ne 9:23 as numerous as the stars in the s,
Job 1:16 "The fire of God fell from the s and
Ps 18:11 him—the dark rain clouds of the s.
89:37 moon, the faithful witness in the s.
147: 8 He covers the s with clouds;
Pr 23: 5 and fly off to the s like an eagle.
30:19 the way of an eagle in the s, the
Isa 34: 4 and the s rolled up like a scroll;
50: 3 I clothe the s with darkness and
Jer 4:25 every bird in the s had flown away.
8: 7 Even the stork in the s knows her
10: 2 or be terrified by signs in the s,
33:22 as countless as the stars of the s
51:53 Even if Babylon reaches the s and
Lam 4:19 were swifter than eagles in the s;
Da 4:11 strong and its top touched the s;
4:20 with its top touching the s,
4:22 has grown until it reaches the s,
Joel 2:10 the earth shakes, the s trembles,
3:16 the earth and the s will tremble.
Na 3:16 are more than the stars of the s,
Mt 16: 2 be fair weather, for the s is red,'
16: 3 for the s is red and overcast.
16: 3 interpret the appearance of the s,
24:29 the stars will fall from the s,
24:30 the Son of Man will appear in the s,
24:30 coming on the clouds of the s, with
Mk 13:25 the stars will fall from the s, and
Lk 4:25 when the s was shut for three and a
12:56 appearance of the earth and the s.
17:24 lights up the s from one end to the
Ac 1:10 up into the s as he was going,
1:11 you stand here looking into the s?
Heb 11:12 as numerous as the stars in the s
Rev 6:13 the stars in the s fell to earth, as
6:14 The s receded like a scroll, rolling
8:10 fell from the s on a third of the
9: 1 had fallen from the s to the earth.
9: 2 The sun and s were darkened by the
11: 6 These men have power to shut up the s
12: 4 stars out of the s and flung them
16:21 From the s huge hailstones of about
20:11 Earth and s fled from his presence,

Slack
Pr 18: 9 One who is s in his work is brother

Slain (Slay)
Dt 21: 1 If a man is found s, lying in a
32:42 the blood of the s and the captives,
Jos 11: 6 hand all of them over to Israel, s.
13:22 In addition to those s in battle,
Jdg 16:24 our land and multiplied our s."
1Sa 18: 7 "Saul has s his thousands, and
21:11 'saul has s his thousands, and David
29: 5 'saul has s his thousands, and David
31: 1 and many fell s on Mount Gilboa.
2Sa 1:19 "Your glory, O Israel, lies s on
1:22 From the blood of the s, from the
1:25 Jonathan lies s on your heights.
2Ki 11:20 been s with the sword at the palace.
1Ch 5:22 many others fell s, because the
10: 1 and many fell s on Mount Gilboa.
2Ch 23:21 Athaliah had been s with the sword.
Est 9:11 The number of those s in the citadel
Job 39:30 and where the s are, there is he."
Ps 88: 5 like the s who lie in the grave,
89:10 You crushed Rahab like one of the s;
Pr 7:26 her s are a mighty throng.
Isa 10: 4 the captives or fall among the s.
14:19 you are covered with the s,
22: 2 Your s were not killed by the sword,
26:21 she will conceal her s no longer.
34: 3 Their s will be thrown out, their
66:16 many will be those s by the LORD.
Jer 9: 1 and night for the s of my people.
14:18 I see those s by the sword; if I go
18:21 young men s by the sword in battle.
25:33 At that time those s by the LORD
51: 4 They will fall down s in Babylon,
51:47 s will all lie fallen within her.
51:49 must fall because of Israel's s,
51:49 just as the s in all the earth have
Lam 2: 4 Like a foe he has s all who were
2:21 You have s them in the day of your
3:43 pursued us; you have s without pity.
Eze 6: 7 Your people will fall s among you,
6:13 when their people lie s among their
9: 7 and fill the courts with the s.
21:29 necks of the wicked who are to be s,
28:23 The s will fall within her, with the
30: 4 When the s fall in Egypt, her wealth
30:11 Egypt and fill the land with the s.
32:22 by the graves of all her s,
32:23 living are s, fallen by the sword.
32:24 All of them are s, fallen by the
32:25 A bed is made for her among the s,
32:25 they are laid among the s.
32:30 they went down with the s in disgrace
35: 8 I will fill your mountains with the s
37: 9 breathe into these s, that they may
Da 5:30 king of the Babylonians, was s,
7:11 I kept looking until the beast was s
Zep 2:12 "You too, O Cushites, will be s by
Rev 5: 6 looking as if it had been s,
5: 9 because you were s, and with your
5:12 "Worthy is the Lamb, who was s, to
6: 9 been s because of the word of God
13: 8 belonging to the Lamb that was s

Slander (Slandered, Slanderer, Slanderers, Slandering, Slanderous, Slanderously, Slanders)
Lev 19:16 "'Do not go about spreading s among
Ps 15: 3 has no s on his tongue, who does his
31:13 For I hear the s of many; there is
38:20 Those who repay my good with evil s
41: 6 falsely, while his heart gathers s;
50:20 brother and s your own mother's son.
54: 5 Let evil recoil on those who s me;
59:10 let me gloat over those who s me.
119:23 Though rulers sit together and s me,
Pr 10:18 and whoever spreads s is a fool.
30:10 "Do not s a servant to his master,
Jer 6:28 hardened rebels, going about to s.
Eze 36: 3 of people's malicious talk and s,
Mt 15:19 theft, false testimony, s.
Mk 7:22 envy, s, arrogance and folly.
2Co 12:20 s, gossip, arrogance and disorder.
Eph 4:31 brawling and s, along with every
Col 3: 8 s and filthy language from your lips.
1Ti 5:14 give the enemy no opportunity for s.
Tit 3: 2 to s no-one, to be peaceable and
Jas 4:11 Brothers, do not s one another.
1Pe 2: 1 envy, and s of every kind.
3:16 in Christ may be ashamed of their s.
2Pe 2:10 not afraid to s celestial beings;
Jude : 8 authority and s celestial beings.
Rev 2: 9 I know the s of those who say they
13: 6 and to s his name and his

Slandered (Slander)
Dt 22:17 Now he has s her and said, 'I did
2Sa 19:27 he has s your servant to my lord the
Ps 35:15 They s me without ceasing.
1Co 4:13 we are s, we answer kindly. Up to
1Ti 6: 1 name and our teaching may not be s.

Slanderer (Slander)
Jer 9: 4 is a deceiver, and every friend a s.
1Co 5:11 or a s, a drunkard or a swindler.

Slanderers (Slander)
Ps 56: 2 My s pursue me all day long;
140:11 Let s not be established in the land;
Ro 1:30 s, God-haters, insolent, arrogant
1Co 6:10 nor drunkards nor s nor swindlers
Tit 2: 3 not to be s or addicted to much wine,

Slandering (Slander)
Jas 2: 7 Are they not the ones who are s the

Slanderous (Slander)
Eze 22: 9 In you are s men bent on shedding
2Ti 3: 3 without love, unforgiving, s,
2Pe 2:11 do not bring s accusations against
Jude : 9 did not dare to bring a s accusation

Slanderously (Slander)
Ro 3: 8 we are being s reported as saying

Slanders (Slander)
Dt 22:14 s her and gives her a bad name,
Ps 101: 5 Whoever s his neighbour in secret,

Slapped (Slaps)
1Ki 22:24 went up and s Micaiah in the face.
2Ch 18:23 went up and s Micaiah in the face.
Mt 26:67 him with their fists. Others s him

Slaps (Slapped)
2Co 11:20 forward or s you in the face.

Slash (Slashed)
Eze 21:16 O sword, s to the right, then to the

Slashed (Slash)
1Ki 18:28 they shouted louder and s themselves
Jer 48:37 every hand is s and every waist is

Slaughter (Slaughtered, Slaughtering, Slaughters)
Ge 43:16 s an animal and prepare dinner;
Ex 12: 6 of Israel must s them at twilight.
12:21 families and s the Passover lamb.
29:11 S it in the LORD's presence at the
29:16 S it and take the blood and sprinkle
29:20 S it, take some of its blood and put
Lev 1: 5 He is to s the young bull before the
1:11 He is to s it at the north side of
3: 2 s it at the entrance to the Tent of
3: 8 s it in front of the Tent of Meeting.
3:13 s it in front of the Tent of Meeting.
4: 4 its head and s it before the LORD.
4:24 s it at the place where the burnt
4:29 s it at the place of the burnt
4:33 s it for a sin offering at the place
14:13 He is to s the lamb in the holy
14:19 priest shall s the burnt offering
14:25 He shall s the lamb for the guilt
16:11 s the bull for his own sin offering.
16:15 "He shall then s the goat for the
22:28 Do not s a cow or a sheep and its
Dt 12:15 Nevertheless, you may s your animals
12:21 you may s animals from the herds and
1Sa 4:10 The s was very great; Israel lost
14:30 Would not the s of the Philistines
14:34 sheep, and s them here and eat them.
2Sa 17: 9 'There has been a s among the troops
2Ch 35: 6 S the Passover lambs, consecrate
Est 7: 4 destruction and s and annihilation.
Pr 7:22 like an ox going to the s,
24:11 back those staggering towards s.
Isa 14:21 Prepare a place to s his sons for
30:25 In the day of great s, when the
34: 2 them, he will give them over to s.
34: 6 in Bozrah and a great s in Edom.
53: 7 he was led like a lamb to the s,
65:12 you will all bend down for the s;
Jer 7:32 but the Valley of S, for they will
11:19 like a gentle lamb led to the s;
12: 3 Set them apart for the day of s!
19: 6 of Ben Hinnom, but the Valley of S.
48:15 young men will go down in the s,"
50:27 let them go down to the s!
51:40 lambs to the s, like rams and goats.
Eze 9: 6 S old men, young men and maidens,
21:10 sharpened for the s, polished to
21:14 It is a sword for s—a sword for
21:14 a sword for great s, closing in on
21:15 the sword for s at all their gates.
21:15 like lightning, it is grasped for s.
21:22 to give the command to s, to sound
21:28 'A sword, a sword, drawn for the s,
26:15 groan and the s takes place in you?
34: 3 the wool and s the choice animals,
44:11 they may s the burnt offerings and
Da 11:12 pride and will s many thousands,
Hos 5: 2 The rebels are deep in s. I will
Ob : 9 mountains will be cut down in the s.
Zec 11: 4 "Pasture the flock marked for s.
11: 5 Their buyers s them and go
Zec 11: 7 I pastured the flock marked for s,
Ac 8:32 "He was led like a sheep to the s,
Jas 5: 5 fattened yourselves in the day of s.

Slaughtered (Slaughter)
Ge 37:31 they got Joseph's robe, s a goat and
Lev 4:15 the bull shall be s before the LORD.
4:24 burnt offering is s before the LORD.
4:33 place where the burnt offering is s.
6:25 The sin offering is to be s before
6:25 where the burnt offering is s;
7: 2 The guilt offering is to be s in the
7: 2 place where the burnt offering is s,
8:15 Moses s the bull and took some of
8:19 Moses s the ram and sprinkled the
8:23 Moses s the ram and took some of its
9: 8 Aaron came to the altar and s the
9:12 he s the burnt offering. His sons
9:15 s it and offered it for a sin
9:18 He s the ox and the ram as the
14:13 and the burnt offering are s.
Nu 11:22 if flocks and herds were s for them?
14:16 so he s them in the desert.'
19: 3 the camp and s in his presence.
Dt 28:31 Your ox will be s before your eyes,
Jdg 15: 8 them viciously and s many of them.
1Sa 1:25 they had s the bull, they brought
11:11 s them until the heat of the day.
14:34 his ox that night and s it there.
25:11 and the meat I have s for my
28:24 at the house, which she s at once.
1Ki 18:40 to the Kishon Valley and s there.
19:21 He took his yoke of oxen and s them.
2Ki 3:23 must have fought and s each other.
3:24 invaded the land and s the Moabites.
10: 7 princes and s all seventy of them.
10:14 So they took them alive and s them
23:20 Josiah s all the priests of those
2Ch 18: 2 Ahab s many sheep and cattle for him
28: 9 But you have s them in a rage that
29:22 they s the bulls, and the priests
29:22 next they s the rams and sprinkled
29:22 then they s the lambs and sprinkled
29:24 The priests then s the goats and
30:15 They s the Passover lamb on the
35: 1 and the Passover lamb was s on the
35:11 The Passover lambs were s, and the
Ezr 6:20 The Levites s the Passover lamb for
Ps 44:22 we are considered as sheep to be s.
Jer 25:34 For your time to be s has come;
39: 6 There at Riblah the king of Babylon s
41: 7 s them and threw them into a cistern.
52:10 the king of Babylon s the sons of
Lam 2:21 you have s them without pity.
Eze 16:21 You s my children and sacrificed
40:39 and guilt offerings were s.
40:41 all—on which the sacrifices were s.
Mt 22: 4 and fattened cattle have been s,
Ro 8:36 we are considered as sheep to be s."

Slaughtering (Slaughter)
1Sa 7:11 s them along the way to a point
2Ch 20:23 After they finished s the men from
25:14 Amaziah returned from s the Edomites,
Isa 22:13 s of cattle and killing of sheep,
Eze 40:42 utensils for s the burnt offerings

Slaughters (Slaughter)
Ex 22: 1 ox or a sheep and s it or sells it,

Slave (Slavery, Slaves, Slaving)
Ge 9:26 May Canaan be the s of Shem.
9:27 of Shem, and may Canaan be his s."
20:17 his wife and his s girls so they
21:10 "Get rid of that s woman and her son,
21:10 for that s woman's son will never
39:17 "That Hebrew s you brought us came
39:19 "This is how your s treated me,"
44:10 found to have it will become my s;
44:17 to have the cup will become my s.
44:33 as my lord's s in place of the boy,
Ex 1:11 they put s masters over them to
2: 5 reeds and sent her s girl to get it.
3: 7 out because of their s drivers,
Ex 5: 6 gave this order to the s drivers
5:10 the s drivers and the foremen went
5:13 The s drivers kept pressing them,
5:14 s drivers were beaten and were asked,
11: 5 to the firstborn son of the s girl,
12:44 Any s you have bought may eat of it
21:20 "If a man beats his male or female s
21:20 and the s dies as a direct result,
21:21 not to be punished if the s gets up
21:21 or two, since the s is his property.
21:32 If the bull gores a male or female s,
21:32 to the master of the s, and the
23:12 and the s born in your household,
Lev 19:20 a s girl promised to another man
22:11 if a priest buys a s with money, or
22:11 or if a s is born in his household,
22:11 household, that s may eat his food.
25:39 to you, do not make him work as a s.
Dt 21:14 not sell her or treat her as a s,
23:15 If a s has taken refuge with you, do
24: 7 and treats him as a s or sells him,
32:36 gone and no-one is left, s or free.
Jdg 9:18 the son of his s girl, king over the
1Sa 30:13 an Egyptian, the s of an Amalekite.
2Sa 6:20 disrobing in the sight of the s
6:22 But by these s girls you spoke of, I
1Ki 9:21 conscripted for his s labour force,
14:10 last male in Israel—s or free.
21:21 last male in Israel—s or free.
2Ki 9: 8 last male in Israel—s or free.
14:26 whether s or free, was suffering;
2Ch 8: 8 conscripted for his s labour force,
Job 3:18 no longer hear the s driver's shout.
3:19 and the s is freed from his master.
7: 2 Like a s longing for the evening
41: 4 you to take him as your s for life?
Ps 105:17 before them—Joseph, sold as a s.
Pr 12:24 rule, but laziness ends in s labour.
19:10 worse for a s to rule over princes!
Jer 2:14 Is Israel a servant, a s by birth?
Lam 1: 1 the provinces has now become a s.
Na 2: 7 Its s girls moan like doves and beat
Mt 20:27 wants to be first must be your s—
Mk 10:44 wants to be first must be s of all.
Jn 8:34 everyone who sins is a s to sin.
8:35 Now a s has no permanent place in
Ac 7: 9 they sold him as a s into Egypt.
16:16 we were met by a s girl who had a
16:19 the owners of the s girl realised
Ro 7:14 I am unspiritual, sold as a s to sin.
7:25 I myself in my mind am a s to God's
7:25 sinful nature a s to the law of sin.
8:15 that makes you a s again to fear,
1Co 7:21 Were you a s when you were called?
7:22 For he who was a s when he was
7:22 when he was called is Christ's s.
9:19 I make myself a s to everyone, to
9:27 No, I beat my body and make it my s
12:13 whether Jews or Greeks, s or free—
Gal 3:28 neither Jew nor Greek, s nor free,
4: 1 he is no different from a s,
4: 7 you are no longer a s, but a son;
4:22 one by the s woman and the other by
4:23 His son by the s woman was born in
4:30 "Get rid of the s woman and her son,
4:30 for the s woman's son will never
4:31 we are not children of the s woman,
Eph 6: 8 he does, whether he is s or free.
Col 3:11 barbarian, Scythian, s or free, but
1Ti 1:10 for s traders and liars and
Phm :16 no longer as a s, but better than a s
2Pe 2:19 is a s to whatever has mastered him.
Rev 6:15 the rich, the mighty, and every s
13:16 rich and poor, free and s, to
19:18 free and s, small and great."

Slavery (Slave)
Ex 2:23 The Israelites groaned in their s
2:23 because of their s went up to God.
13: 3 out of the land of s, because the
13:14 out of Egypt, out of the land of s.
20: 2 out of Egypt, out of the land of s.
Dt 5: 6 out of Egypt, out of the land of s.
6:12 out of Egypt, out of the land of s.
7: 8 and redeemed you from the land of s,

Dt 8:14 out of Egypt, out of the land of s.
13: 5 and redeemed you from the land of s;
13:10 out of Egypt, out of the land of s.
Jos 24:17 from that land of s, and performed
Jdg 6: 8 out of Egypt, out of the land of s.
Ne 5: 5 subject our sons and daughters to s.
9:17 in order to return to their s.
Jer 34:13 out of Egypt, out of the land of s.
Mic 6: 4 and redeemed you from the land of s.
Ro 6:19 parts of your body in s to impurity
6:19 offer them in s to righteousness
Gal 4: 3 when we were children, we were in s
4:25 she is in s with her children.
5: 1 be burdened again by a yoke of s.
1Ti 6: 1 All who are under the yoke of s
Heb 2:15 held in s by their fear of death.

Slaves (Slave)

Ge 9:25 The lowest of s will he be to his
15:14 punish the nation they serve as s,
20:14 female s and gave them to Abraham,
43:18 seize us as s and take our donkeys."
44: 9 rest of us will become my lord's s."
44:16 We are now my lord's s—we ourselves
50:18 "We are your s," they said.
Ex 6: 6 I will free you from being s to them,
9:20 their s and their livestock inside.
9:21 their s and livestock in the field.
Lev 25:42 Egypt, they must not be sold as s.
25:44 "'Your male and female s are to
25:44 around you; from them you may buy s.
25:46 and can make them s for life,
26:13 no longer be s to the Egyptians;
Dt 5:15 Remember that you were s in Egypt
6:21 "We were s of Pharaoh in Egypt,
15:15 Remember that you were s in Egypt
16:12 Remember that you were s in Egypt,
24:18 Remember that you were s in Egypt
24:22 Remember that you were s in Egypt.
28:68 your enemies as male and female s,
1Sa 8:17 you yourselves will become his s.
1Ki 2:39 two of Shimei's s ran off to Achish
2:39 Shimei was told, "Your s are in Gath.
2:40 Achish at Gath in search of his s.
2:40 and brought the s back from Gath.
9:22 Solomon did not make s of any of the
2Ki 4: 1 to take my two boys as his s."
2Ch 8: 9 Solomon did not make s of the
28:10 women of Judah and Jerusalem your s.
Ezr 9: 9 Though we are s, our God has not
Ne 9:36 we are s today, s in the land you
Est 7: 4 been sold as male and female s,
Ps 123: 2 the eyes of s look to the hand of
Ecc 2: 7 I bought male and female s and had
2: 7 other s who were born in my house.
10: 7 I have seen s on horseback, while
10: 7 while princes go on foot like s.
Jer 34: 8 to proclaim freedom for the s.
34: 9 Everyone was to free his Hebrew s,
34:10 free their male and female s and no
34:11 took back the s they had freed and
34:16 female s you had set free to go
34:16 forced them to become your s again.
Lam 5: 8 S rule over us, and there is none to
Eze 27:13 they exchanged s and articles of
Zec 2: 9 so that their s will plunder them.
Jn 8:33 and have never been s of anyone.
Ac 7: 7 punish the nation they serve as s,'
Ro 6: 6 we should no longer be s to sin—
6:16 to someone to obey him as s,
6:16 you are s to the one whom you
6:16 you obey—whether you are s to sin,
6:17 though you used to be s to sin, you
6:18 and have become s to righteousness.
6:20 you were s to sin, you were free
6:22 from sin and have become s to God,
1Co 7:23 at a price; do not become s of men.
Gal 2: 4 in Christ Jesus and to make us s.
4: 8 you were s to those who by nature
4:24 and bears children who are to be s:
Eph 6: 5 S, obey your earthly masters with
6: 6 but like s of Christ, doing the will
6: 9 masters, treat your s in the same
Col 3:22 S, obey your earthly masters in
4: 1 Masters, provide your s with what is
Tit 2: 9 Teach s to be subject to their
1Pe 2:18 S, submit yourselves to your masters
2Pe 2:19 while they themselves are s of

Slaving (Slave)

Lk 15:29 'Look! All these years I've been s

Slay (Slain, Slayer, Slays, Slew)

Ge 22:10 and took the knife to s his son.
Job 13:15 Though he s me, yet will I hope in
Ps 34:21 Evil will s the wicked; the foes of
37:14 to s those whose ways are upright.
94: 6 They s the widow and the alien;
139:19 If only you would s the wicked,
Isa 11: 4 of his lips he will s the wicked.
14:30 by famine; it will s your survivors.
27: 1 he will s the monster of the sea.
Jer 33: 5 men I will s in my anger and wrath.
Eze 6: 4 s your people in front of your idols.
28: 9 in the hands of those who s you.
Hos 2: 3 parched land, and s her with thirst.
9:16 I will s their cherished offspring."
Am 9: 4 I will command the sword to s them.
Rev 6: 4 earth and to make men s each other.

Slayer (Slay)

Eze 21:11 made ready for the hand of the s.
Hos 9:13 bring out their children to the s."

Slays (Slay)

Job 5: 2 a fool, and envy s the simple.

Sledge (Sledges, Threshing-sledge, Threshing-sledges)

Isa 28:27 Caraway is not threshed with a s,

Sledges (Sledge)

Am 1: 3 Gilead with s having iron teeth,

Sleek

Ge 41: 2 came up seven cows, s and fat, and
41: 4 gaunt ate up the seven s, fat cows.
41:18 came up seven cows, fat and s, and
Dt 32:15 with food, he became heavy and s.
Jer 5:28 have grown fat and s. Their evil
Eze 34:16 the s and the strong I will destroy.

Sleep (Asleep, Sleeper, Sleeping, Sleeps, Sleepy, Slept)

Ge 2:21 the man to fall into a deep s;
15:12 Abram fell into a deep s, and a
16: 2 Go, s with my maidservant; perhaps I
28:11 it under his head and lay down to s.
28:16 Jacob awoke from his s, he thought,
30: 3 S with her so that she can bear
30:15 said, "he can s with you tonight in
30:16 "You must s with me," she said.
31:40 at night, and s fled from my eyes.
38:16 said, "Come now, let me s with you.
38:16 will you give me to s with you?"
38:26 And he did not s with her again.
39:14 here to s with me, but I screamed.
Ex 22:27 What else will he s in? When he
Dt 24:12 do not go to s with his pledge in
24:13 by sunset so that he may s in it.
Jdg 16:14 He awoke from his s and pulled up
16:19 Having put him to s on her lap, she
16:20 He awoke from his s and thought,
1Sa 26:12 the LORD had put them into a deep s.
2Sa 3: 7 you s with my father's concubine?"
11:13 Uriah went out to s on his mat
Est 6: 1 That night the king could not s;
Job 4:13 the night, when deep s falls on men,
14:12 not awake or be roused from their s.
31:10 grain, and may other men s with her.
33:15 when deep s falls on men as they
Ps 3: 5 I lie down and s; I wake again,
4: 8 I will lie down and s in peace, for
7: 5 ground and make me s in the dust.
13: 3 to my eyes, or I will s in death;
44:23 Awake, O Lord! Why do you s?
68:13 Even while you s among the campfires,
76: 5 lie plundered, they s their last s;
78:65 the Lord awoke as from s, as a man
90: 5 You sweep men away in the s of death;
121: 4 Israel will neither slumber nor s.
127: 2 for he grants s to those he loves.
132: 4 I will allow no s to my eyes, no
Pr 3:24 you lie down, your s will be sweet.
4:16 For they cannot s till they do evil;
6: 4 Allow no s to your eyes, no slumber
6: 9 When will you get up from your s?
6:10 A little s, a little slumber, a
6:22 when you s, they will watch over
19:15 Laziness brings on deep s, and the
20:13 Do not love s or you will grow poor;
24:33 A little s, a little slumber, a
Ecc 5:12 The s of a labourer is sweet,
5:12 of a rich man permits him no s.
8:16 eyes not seeing s day or night—
Isa 29:10 LORD has brought over you a deep s:
56:10 around and dream, they love to s.
Jer 31:26 My s had been pleasant to me.
51:39 then s for ever and not awake,"
51:57 they will s for ever and not awake,"
Eze 23:44 As men s with a prostitute, so they
34:25 and s in the forests in safety.
Da 2: 1 was troubled and he could not s.
6:18 And he could not s.
8:18 I was in a deep s, with my face to
10: 9 I fell into a deep s, my face to
12: 2 Multitudes who s in the dust of the
Jnh 1: 5 he lay down and fell into a deep s.
1: 6 "How can you s? Get up and call on
Zec 4: 1 me, as a man is wakened from his s.
Jn 11:13 thought he meant natural s.
Ac 20: 9 a deep s as Paul talked on and on.
1Co 15:51 We will not all s, but we will all
2Co 11:27 and have often gone without s;
1Th 5: 7 For those who s, s at night, and

Sleeper (Sleep)

Eph 5:14 "Wake up, O s, rise from the dead,

Sleeping (Sleep)

Ge 2:21 and while he was s, he took one of
Nu 5:13 by s with another man, and this is
5:20 you have defiled yourself by s with
Dt 22:22 If a man is found s with another
Jdg 16:13 So while he was s, Delilah took the
19: 4 eating and drinking, and s there.
1Sa 26:12 They were all s, because the LORD
1Ki 18:27 Maybe he is s and must be awakened."
Pr 23:34 You will be like one s on the high
Mt 8:24 But Jesus was s.
13:25 while everyone was s, his enemy came
26:40 to his disciples and found them s.
26:43 he came back, he again found them s,
26:45 "Are you still s and resting?
Mk 4:38 was in the stern, s on a cushion.
13:36 suddenly, do not let him find you s.
14:37 to his disciples and found them s.
14:40 he came back, he again found them s,
14:41 "Are you still s and resting? Enough!
Lk 22:46 "Why are you s?" he asked them.
Ac 12: 6 Peter was s between two soldiers,
2Pe 2: 3 their destruction has not been s.

Sleepless

2Co 6: 5 in hard work, s nights and hunger;

Sleeps (Sleep)

Ex 22:16 to be married and s with her,
Lev 14:47 Anyone who s or eats in the house
19:20 "'If a man s with a woman who is a
20:11 "'If a man s with his father's wife,
20:12 a man s with his daughter-in-law,
20:20 "'If a man s with his aunt, he has
Dt 22:23 to be married and he s with her,
27:20 "Cursed is the man who s with his
27:22 "Cursed is the man who s with his
27:23 "Cursed is the man who s with his
Pr 6:29 is he who s with another man's wife;
10: 5 but he who s during harvest is a
Isa 5:27 or stumbles, not one slumbers or s;
Mk 4:27 Night and day, whether he s or gets
Jn 11:12 "Lord, if he s, he will get better.

Sleepy (Sleep)
Lk 9:32 Peter and his companions were very s,

Sleet
Ps 78:47 hail and their sycamore-figs with s.

Slept (Sleep)
Ge 16: 4 He s with Hagar, and she conceived.
19: 8 who have never s with a man.
26:10 might well have s with your wife,
30: 4 Jacob s with her,
30:16 So he s with her that night.
35:22 Reuben went in and s with his
38:18 he gave them to her and s with her,
Nu 5:19 "If no other man has s with you and
31:17 every woman who has s with a man,
31:18 girl who has never s with a man.
31:35 32,000 women who had never s with a
Dt 22:22 both the man who s with her and the
Jdg 21:12 women who had never s with a man,
1Sa 2:22 how they s with the women who served
2Sa 11: 4 She came to him, and he s with her.
11: 9 Uriah s at the entrance to the
12: 3 from his cup and even s in his arms.
SS 5: 2 I s but my heart was awake. Listen!
Eze 23: 8 when during her youth men s with her,
23:44 they s with her. As men sleep with a
23:44 so they s with those lewd women,

Slew (Slay)
Ps 78:34 Whenever God s them, they would seek

Slightest
Jude :12 eating with you without the s qualm—

Slime (Slimy)
Job 9:31 you would plunge me into a s pit so

Slimy (Slime)
Ps 40: 2 He lifted me out of the s pit, out

Sling (Slings, Slung)
Jdg 20:16 s a stone at a hair and not miss.
1Sa 17:40 with his s in his hand, approached
17:50 the Philistine with a s and a stone;
25:29 hurl away as from the pocket of a s.
1Ch 12: 2 s stones right-handed or left-handed;
Pr 26: 8 Like tying a stone in a s is the

Slings (Sling)
2Ki 3:25 but men armed with s surrounded it

Slingstones (Stone)
2Ch 26:14 bows and s for the entire army.
Job 41:28 s are like chaff to him.
Zec 9:15 will destroy and overcome with s.

Slip (Slipped, Slippery, Slipping, Slips)
Dt 4: 9 or let them s from your heart as
32:35 In due time their foot will s;
1Sa 27: 1 and I will s out of his hand."
2Ki 9:15 don't let anyone s out of the city
Ps 37:31 is in his heart; his feet do not s.
121: 3 He will not let your foot s—he who
Jer 20:10 my friends are waiting for me to s,

Slipped (Slip)
2Sa 4: 6 Recab and his brother Baanah s away.
Ps 17: 5 to your paths; my feet have not s.
73: 2 But as for me, my feet had almost s;
Jn 5:13 s away into the crowd that was there.
2Co 11:33 in the wall and s through his hands.
Jude : 4 ago have secretly s in among you.

Slippery (Slip)
Ps 35: 6 may their path be dark and s, with
73:18 Surely you place them on s ground;
Jer 23:12 "Therefore their path will become s;

Slipping (Slip)
Job 12: 5 the fate of those whose feet are s.
Ps 66: 9 our lives and kept our feet from s.
94:18 I said, "My foot is s," your love,
Jn 8:59 s away from the temple grounds.

Slips (Slip)
Ps 38:16 themselves over me when my foot s."

Slope (Slopes)
Jos 15: 8 southern s of the Jebusite city
15:10 the northern s of Mount Jearim
15:11 went to the northern s of Ekron,
18:12 passed the northern s of Jericho and
18:13 From there it crossed to the south s
18:16 the southern s of the Jebusite city
18:18 to the northern s of Beth Arabah
18:19 to the northern s of Beth Hoglah
Mic 1: 4 fire, like water rushing down a s.

Slopes (Slope)
Nu 21:15 the s of the ravines that lead to
34:11 the s east of the Sea of Kinnereth.
Dt 3:17 Salt Sea), below the s of Pisgah.
4:49 the Arabah, below the s of Pisgah.
33: 2 from the south, from his mountain s.
Jos 7: 5 and struck them down on the s.
10:40 foothills and the mountain s,
12: 3 southward below the s of Pisgah.
12: 8 the Arabah, the mountain s, the
13:20 the s of Pisgah, and Beth Jeshimoth
Isa 11:14 They will swoop down on the s of
Jer 18:14 Lebanon ever vanish from its rocky s?

Slow (*Slow to anger*, Slowness)
Ex 4:10 I am s of speech and tongue."
Dt 7:10 he will not be s to repay to their
23:21 do not be s to pay it, for the LORD
2Ki 4:24 s down for me unless I tell you."
Lk 24:25 and how s of heart to believe all
Ac 27: 7 We made s headway for many days and
Heb 5:11 explain because you are s to learn.
Jas 1:19 s to speak and s to become angry,
2Pe 3: 9 The Lord is not s in keeping his

Slow to anger
Ex 34: 6 s, abounding in love and
Nu 14:18 'The LORD is s, abounding in love
Ne 9:17 s and abounding in love.
Ps 86:15 s, abounding in love and
103: 8 and gracious, s, abounding in love.
145: 8 compassionate, s and rich in love.
Joel 2:13 s and abounding in love, and he
Jnh 4: 2 s and abounding in love, a God who
Na 1: 3 The LORD is s and great in power;

Slowness (Slow)
2Pe 3: 9 his promise, as some understand s.

Slug
Ps 58: 8 Like a s melting away as it moves

Sluggard (Sluggard's)
Pr 6: 6 Go to the ant, you s; consider its
6: 9 How long will you lie there, you s?
10:26 so is a s to those who send him.
13: 4 The s craves and gets nothing, but
15:19 The way of the s is blocked with
19:24 The s buries his hand in the dish;
20: 4 A s does not plough in season; so at
22:13 The s says, "There is a lion outside!
24:30 I went past the field of the s, past
26:13 The s says, "There is a lion in the
26:14 hinges, so a s turns on his bed.
26:15 The s buries his hand in the dish;
26:16 The s is wiser in his own eyes than

Sluggard's (Sluggard)
Pr 21:25 The s craving will be the death of

Slumber (Slumbers)
Job 33:15 on men as they s in their beds,
Ps 121: 3 he who watches over you will not s;
121: 4 Israel will neither s nor sleep.
132: 4 to my eyes, no s to my eyelids,
Pr 4:16 they are robbed of s till they make
6: 4 to your eyes, no s to your eyelids.
6:10 A little sleep, a little s, a little
24:33 A little sleep, a little s, a little
Na 3:18 O king of Assyria, your shepherds s;
Ro 13:11 come for you to wake up from your s,

Slumbers (Slumber)
Isa 5:27 or stumbles, not one s or sleeps;

Slumped
2Ki 9:24 heart and he s down in his chariot.

Slung (Sling)
1Sa 17: 6 a bronze javelin was s on his back.
17:49 he s it and struck the Philistine on

Slur
Ps 15: 3 and casts no s on his fellow-man,

Sly
Pr 25:23 so a s tongue brings angry looks.
Mt 26: 4 Jesus in some s way and kill him.
Mk 14: 1 s way to arrest Jesus and kill him.

Small (Smallest)
Ge 19:20 near enough to run to, and it is s.
19:20 Let me flee to it—it is very s,
Ex 12: 4 If any household is too s for a
Nu 22:18 I could not do anything great or s
Dt 1:17 hear both s and great alike.
25:14 in your house—one large, one s.
Jos 17:15 country of Ephraim is too s for you,
1Sa 15:17 "Although you were once s in your
18:23 "Do you think it is a s matter to
20: 2 great or s, without confiding in me.
20:35 He had a s boy with him,
1Ki 2:20 "I have one s request to make of you,
8:64 too s to hold the burnt offerings,
10:17 He also made three hundred s shields
17:13 But first make a s cake of bread for
18:44 "A cloud as s as a man's hand is
20:27 them like two s flocks of goats,
22:31 "Do not fight with anyone, s or
2Ki 4:10 Let's make a s room on the roof and
6: 1 we meet with you is too s for us.
2Ch 9:16 He also made three hundred s shields
14: 8 armed with s shields and with bows.
15:13 whether s or great, man or woman.
18:30 "Do not fight with anyone, s or
23: 9 the large and s shields that had
36:18 both large and s, and the treasures
Job 3:19 The s and the great are there, and
Ps 104:25 living things both large and s.
115:13 fear the LORD—s and great alike.
148:10 s creatures and flying birds,
Pr 24:10 of trouble, how s is your strength!
30:24 "Four things on earth are s, yet
Ecc 9:14 There was once a s city with only a
Isa 49: 6 "It is too s a thing for you to
49:19 now you will be too s for your
49:20 'This place is too s for us; give us
Jer 46: 3 your shields, both large and s,
49:15 "Now I will make you s among the
Eze 23:24 and s shields and with helmets.
38: 4 horde with large and s shields,
39: 9 them up—the s and large shields,
Da 8: 9 which started s but grew in power to
Am 6:11 pieces and the s house into bits.
7: 2 How can Jacob survive? He is so s!"
7: 5 How can Jacob survive? He is so s!"
Ob : 2 "See, I will make you s among the
Mic 5: 2 though you are s among the clans of
Zec 4:10 "Who despises the day of s things?
Mt 7:14 s is the gate and narrow the road
15:34 they replied, "and a few s fish."
17:20 have faith as s as a mustard seed,
Mk 3: 9 to have a s boat ready for him,
8: 7 They had a few s fish as well;
12:42 and put in two very s copper coins,
Lk 17: 6 have faith as s as a mustard seed,
19:17 trustworthy in a very s matter,

Lk 21: 2 put in two very s copper coins.
Jn 6: 9 five s barley loaves and two s fish,
Ac 12:18 there was no s commotion among the
26:22 and testify to s and great alike.
27:16 we passed to the lee of a s island
Jas 3: 4 they are steered by a very s rudder
3: 5 Likewise the tongue is a s part of
3: 5 forest is set on fire by a s spark.
Rev 11:18 your name, both s and great—and
13:16 He also forced everyone, s and great,
19: 5 you who fear him, both s and great!"
19:18 free and slave, s and great."
20:12 I saw the dead, great and s,

Smallest (Small)
1Sa 9:21 from the s tribe of Israel, and is
Isa 60:22 a thousand, the s a mighty nation.
Mt 5:18 not the s letter, not the least
13:32 Though it is the s of all your seeds,
Mk 4:31 the s seed you plant in the ground.

Smash (Smashed, Smashes)
Ex 34:13 s their sacred stones and cut down
Dt 7: 5 s their sacred stones, cut down
12: 3 s their sacred stones and burn
Jer 13:14 I will s them one against the other,
19:11 I will s this nation and this city
48:12 will empty her jars and s her jugs.
Am 6:11 and he will s the great house into

Smashed (Smash)
Jdg 7:20 blew the trumpets and s the jars.
2Ki 11:18 They s the altars and idols to
18: 4 s the sacred stones and cut down
23:12 them from there, s them to pieces
23:14 Josiah s the sacred stones and cut
2Ch 14: 3 s the sacred stones and cut down the
23:17 They s the altars and idols and
31: 1 s the sacred stones and cut down the
34: 4 and s the Asherah poles, the idols
Ps 74: 6 They s all the carved panelling with
Jer 19:11 jar is s and cannot be repaired.
Eze 6: 4 and your incense altars will be s;
6: 6 your idols s and ruined, your
Da 2:34 feet of iron and clay and s them.

Smashes (Smash)
Da 2:40 for iron breaks and s everything—

Smear (Smeared)
Job 13: 4 You, however, s me with lies;

Smeared (Smear)
Ps 119:69 Though the arrogant have s me with

Smell (Smelled)
Ge 27:27 Isaac caught the s of his clothes,
27:27 the s of my son is like the s of a
Ex 16:20 was full of maggots and began to s.
Dt 4:28 cannot see or hear or eat or s.
Ps 115: 6 hear, noses, but they cannot s;
Ecc 10: 1 dead flies give perfume a bad s, so
Da 3:27 and there was no s of fire on them.
Joel 2:20 stench will go up; its s will rise.
1Co 12:17 ear, where would the sense of s be?
2Co 2:16 To the one we are the s of death;

Smelled (Smell)
Ge 8:21 The LORD s the pleasing aroma and
Ex 7:21 and the river s so bad that the

Smelted
Job 28: 2 the earth, and copper is s from ore.

Smile (Smiled)
Job 9:27 I will change my expression, and s,'
10: 3 you s on the schemes of the wicked?

Smiled (Smile)
Job 29:24 I s at them, they scarcely believed

Smite (Smitten)
Dt 33:11 S the loins of those who rise up

Smitten (Smite)
Isa 53: 4 by God, s by him, and afflicted.

Smoke (Smoking)
Ge 19:28 and he saw dense s rising from the
19:28 the land, like s from a furnace.
Ex 19:18 Mount Sinai was covered with s,
19:18 The s billowed up from it
19:18 like s from a furnace, the whole
20:18 and saw the mountain in s, they
Lev 16:13 and the s of the incense will
Jos 8:20 s of the city rising against the sky,
8:21 that s was going up from the city,
Jdg 20:38 up a great cloud of s from the city,
20:40 when the column of s began to rise
20:40 the Benjamites turned and saw the s
2Sa 22: 9 S rose from his nostrils;
Job 41:20 S pours from his nostrils as from a
Ps 18: 8 S rose from his nostrils;
37:20 they will vanish—vanish like s.
68: 2 s is blown away by the wind, may you
102: 3 For my days vanish like s;
104:32 touches the mountains, and they s.
119:83 Though I am like a wineskin in the s,
144: 5 touch the mountains, so that they s.
Pr 10:26 to the teeth and s to the eyes,
SS 3: 6 from the desert like a column of s,
Isa 4: 5 assemble there a cloud of s by day
6: 4 and the temple was filled with s.
9:18 it rolls upward in a column of s.
14:31 A cloud of s comes from the north,
30:27 burning anger and dense clouds of s
34:10 its s will rise for ever.
51: 6 the heavens will vanish like s,
65: 5 Such people are s in my nostrils,
Hos 13: 3 like s escaping through a window.
Joel 2:30 blood and fire and billows of s.
Na 2:13 "I will burn up your chariots in s,
Ac 2:19 blood and fire and billows of s.
Rev 8: 4 The s of the incense, together with
9: 2 he opened the Abyss, s rose from it
9: 2 like the s from a gigantic furnace.
9: 2 darkened by the s from the Abyss.
9: 3 out of the s locusts came down upon
9:17 mouths came fire, s and sulphur.
9:18 s and sulphur that came out of their
14:11 the s of their torment rises for
15: 8 the temple was filled with s from
18: 9 her luxury see the s of her burning,
18:18 they see the s of her burning, they
19: 3 s from her goes up for ever and ever.

Smoking (Smoke)
Ge 15:17 a s brazier with a blazing torch

Smooth (Smooth-skinned)
Ge 27:11 man, and I'm a man with s skin.
27:16 hands and the s part of his neck
1Sa 17:40 chose five s stones from the stream,
Ps 55:21 His speech is s as butter, yet war
Pr 6:24 the s tongue of the wayward wife.
7:21 she seduced him with her s talk.
Isa 26: 7 you make the way of the righteous s.
42:16 them and make the rough places s.
57: 6 The idols among the s stones of the
Lk 3: 5 become straight, the rough ways s.
Ro 16:18 By s talk and flattery they deceive

Smooth-skinned (Skin, Smooth)
Isa 18: 2 to a people tall and s, to a people
18: 7 Almighty from a people tall and s,

Smoulder (Smouldering, Smoulders)
Ps 74: 1 Why does your anger s against the
80: 4 how long will your anger s against

Smouldering (Smoulder)
Nu 16:37 the censers out of the s remains
Isa 7: 4 of these two s stubs of firewood
Isa 42: 3 and a s wick he will not snuff out.
Mt 12:20 and a s wick he will not snuff out,

Smoulders (Smoulder)
Hos 7: 6 Their passion s all night;

Smyrna
Wealthy city in western Asia Minor, about 40 miles north of Ephesus. One of the 7 cities John addressed in which they are described as "in poverty" due to their afflictions and are encouraged to persevere (Rev 2:8–11).

Rev 1:11 S, Pergamum, Thyatira, Sardis,
2: 8 "To the angel of the church in S

Snake (Snakes)
Ex 4: 3 it became a s, and he ran from it.
4: 4 took hold of the s and it turned
7: 9 Pharaoh,' and it will become a s."
7:10 his officials, and it became a s.
7:12 down his staff and it became a s.
7:15 the staff that was changed into a s.
Nu 21: 8 "Make a s and put it up on a pole;
21: 9 Moses made a bronze s and put it up
21: 9 Then when anyone was bitten by a s
21: 9 looked at the bronze s, he lived.
2Ki 18: 4 He broke into pieces the bronze s
Ps 58: 4 Their venom is like the venom of a s,
Pr 23:32 In the end it bites like a s and
30:19 the way of a s on a rock, the way of
Ecc 10: 8 through a wall may be bitten by a s.
10:11 If a s bites before it is charmed,
Isa 14:29 of that s will spring up a viper,
Am 5:19 the wall only to have a s bite him.
Mic 7:17 They will lick dust like a s, like
Mt 7:10 asks for a fish, will give him a s?
Lk 11:11 a fish, will give him a s instead?
Jn 3:14 Just as Moses lifted up the s in the
Ac 28: 4 the islanders saw the s hanging from
28: 5 Paul shook the s off into the fire

Snakes (Snake)
Nu 21: 6 the LORD sent venomous s among them;
21: 7 Pray that the LORD will take the s
Dt 8:15 with its venomous s and scorpions.
Isa 30: 6 of adders and darting s, the envoys
Jer 8:17 "See, I will send venomous s among
Mt 10:16 Therefore be as shrewd as s and as
23:33 "You s! You brood of vipers!
Mk 16:18 they will pick up s with their hands;
Lk 10:19 given you authority to trample on s
1Co 10: 9 of them did—and were killed by s.
Rev 9:19 for their tails were like s,

Snapped (Snaps)
Jdg 16: 9 But he s the thongs as easily as a
16:12 But he s the ropes off his arms as
Jer 10:20 is destroyed; all its ropes are s.

Snaps (Snapped)
Jdg 16: 9 s when it comes close to a flame.

Snare (Snared, Snares)
Ex 10: 7 "How long will this man be a s to us?
23:33 gods will certainly be a s to you."
34:12 or they will be a s among you.
Dt 7:16 gods, for that will be a s to you.
Jdg 2: 3 their gods will be a s to you."
8:27 became a s to Gideon and his family.
1Sa 18:21 "so that she may be a s to him and
Job 18: 9 by the heel; a s holds him fast.
Ps 25:15 he will release my feet from the s.
69:22 table set before them become a s;
91: 3 will save you from the fowler's s
106:36 idols, which became a s to them.
119:110 The wicked have set a s for me, but
124: 7 like a bird out of the fowler's s;
124: 7 the s has been broken, and we have
140: 5 Proud men have hidden a s for me;
142: 3 I walk men have hidden a s for me.
Pr 6: 5 a bird from the s of the fowler.
7:23 like a bird darting into a s, little
18: 7 and his lips are a s to his soul.

Pr 21: 6 is a fleeting vapour and a deadly s.
29:25 Fear of man will prove to be a s,
Ecc 7:26 than death the woman who is a s,
9:12 or birds are taken in a s, so men
Isa 8:14 Jerusalem he will be a trap and a s.
24:17 Terror and pit and s await you,
24:18 of the pit will be caught in a s.
Jer 5:26 lie in wait like men who s birds
48:43 Terror and pit and s await you,
48:44 of the pit will be caught in a s;
Eze 12:13 and he will be caught in my s;
17:20 him, and he will be caught in my s.
Hos 5: 1 You have been a s at Mizpah,
Am 3: 5 the ground where no s has been set?
Ro 11: 9 "May their table become a s and a

Snared (Snare)
Pr 3:26 will keep your foot from being s.
29: 6 An evil man is s by his own sin, but
Isa 8:15 they will be s and captured."
28:13 be injured and s and captured.

Snares (Snare)
Jos 23:13 Instead, they will become s and
2Sa 22: 6 the s of death confronted me.
Job 22:10 That is why s are all around you,
30:12 they lay s for my feet,
34:30 from laying s for the people.
Ps 18: 5 the s of death confronted me.
64: 5 they talk about hiding their s;
141: 9 Keep me from the s they have laid
Pr 13:14 turning a man from the s of death.
14:27 turning a man from the s of death.
22: 5 of the wicked lie thorns and s,
Jer 18:22 me and have hidden s for my feet.
Hos 9: 8 yet s await him on all his paths,

Snarling
Ps 59: 6 They return at evening, s like dogs,
59:14 They return at evening, s like dogs,

Snatch (Snatched, Snatches)
Job 24:19 heat and drought s away the melted
30:22 You s me up and drive me before the
Ps 52: 5 He will s you up and tear you from
119:43 Do not s the word of truth from my
Isa 3:18 In that day the Lord will s away
10: 6 to seize loot and s plunder, and to
Jn 10:28 no-one can s them out of my hand.
10:29 can s them out of my Father's hand.
Jude :23 s others from the fire and save them;

Snatched (Snatch)
Jdg 6: 9 I s you from the power of Egypt and
2Sa 23:21 He s the spear from the Egyptian's
1Ch 11:23 He s the spear from the Egyptian's
Job 24: 9 The fatherless child is s from the
29:17 and s the victims from their teeth.
Pr 22:27 very bed will be s from under you.
Joel 1: 5 for it has been s from your lips.
Am 4:11 You were like a burning stick s from
Zec 3: 2 a burning stick s from the fire?"
Rev 12: 5 was s up to God and to his throne.

Snatches (Snatch)
Job 9:12 If he s away, who can stop him?
24:19 grave s away those who have sinned.
27:20 a tempest s him away in the night.
Mt 13:19 s away what was sown in his heart.

Sneer (Sneered, Sneering, Sneers)
Isa 57: 4 At whom do you s and stick out your

Sneered (Sneer)
Lk 23:35 and the rulers even s at him.
Ac 17:32 some of them s, but others said, "We

Sneering (Sneer)
Lk 16:14 heard all this and were s at Jesus.

Sneers (Sneer)
Ps 10: 5 he s at all his enemies.

Sneezed
2Ki 4:35 s seven times and opened his eyes.

Sniff (Sniffing)
Mal 1:13 and you s at it contemptuously,"

Sniffing (Sniff)
Jer 2:24 s the wind in her craving—

Snorting (Snorts)
Job 39:20 striking terror with his proud s?
41:18 His s throws out flashes of light;
Jer 8:16 The s of the enemy's horses is heard

Snorts (Snorting)
Job 39:25 At the blast of the trumpet he s,

Snout
Pr 11:22 Like a gold ring in a pig's s is a

Snow (Snows, Snowy)
Ex 4: 6 took it out, it was leprous, like s.
Nu 12:10 there stood Miriam—leprous, like s.
2Ki 5:27 and he was leprous, as white as s.
Job 6:16 ice and swollen with melting s,
24:19 drought snatch away the melted s,
37: 6 He says to the s, 'Fall on the earth,
38:22 entered the storehouses of the s
Ps 51: 7 me, and I shall be whiter than s.
68:14 it was like s fallen on Zalmon.
147:16 He spreads the s like wool and
148: 8 lightning and hail, s and clouds,
Pr 25:13 Like the coolness of s at harvest
26: 1 Like s in summer or rain in harvest,
Isa 1:18 they shall be as white as s;
55:10 the rain and the s come down from
Jer 18:14 Does the s of Lebanon ever vanish
Lam 4: 7 Their princes were brighter than s
Da 7: 9 His clothing was as white as s;
Mt 28: 3 and his clothes were white as s.
Rev 1:14 white like wool, as white as s,

Snows (Snow)
Pr 31:21 When it s, she has no fear for her

Snowy (Snow)
2Sa 23:20 went down into a pit on a s day
1Ch 11:22 went down into a pit on a s day

Snuff (Snuffed)
Isa 42: 3 smouldering wick he will not s out.
Eze 32: 7 I s you out, I will cover the
Mt 12:20 smouldering wick he will not s out,

Snuffed (Snuff)
Job 18: 5 "The lamp of the wicked is s out;
21:17 is the lamp of the wicked s out?
Pr 13: 9 but the lamp of the wicked is s out.
20:20 will be s out in pitch darkness.
24:20 lamp of the wicked will be s out.
Isa 43:17 extinguished, s out like a wick:

So
2Ki 17: 4 had sent envoys to **S** king of Egypt,

Soaked
2Ki 8:15 a thick cloth, s it in water and
Isa 34: 3 will be s with their blood.
34: 7 and the dust will be s with fat.
Jn 19:29 so they s a sponge in it, put the

Soap
Job 9:30 Even if I washed myself with s and
Jer 2:22 with soda and use an abundance of s,
Mal 3: 2 a refiner's fire or a launderer's s.

Soar (Soared)
Job 39:27 Does the eagle s at your command and
Isa 40:31 They will s on wings like eagles;
Jer 49:22 Look! An eagle will s and swoop down,
Ob : 4 Though you s like the eagle and make

Soared (Soar)
2Sa 22:11 he s on the wings of the wind.
Ps 18:10 he s on the wings of the wind.

Sob (Sobbing)
Ge 21:16 sat there nearby, she began to s.

Sobbing (Sob)
Jdg 14:16 Samson's wife threw herself on him, s

Sober
1Sa 25:37 in the morning, when Nabal was s,
Ro 12: 3 think of yourself with s judgment,

So-called (Call)
1Co 8: 5 For even if there are s gods,
Rev 2:24 not learned Satan's s deep secrets

Socket (Sockets)
Ge 32:25 he touched the s of Jacob's hip so
32:32 tendon attached to the s of the hip,
32:32 because the s of Jacob's hip was

Sockets (Socket)
1Ki 6:34 having two leaves that turned in s.
7:50 and the gold s for the doors of the
Zec 14:12 their eyes will rot in their s, and

Soco
1Ch 4:18 Heber the father of **S**, and Jekuthiel
2Ch 11: 7 Beth Zur, **S**, Adullam,
28:18 Aijalon and Gederoth, as well as **S**,

Socoh
Jos 15:35 Jarmuth, Adullam, **S**, Azekah,
15:48 the hill country: Shamir, Jattir, **S**,
1Sa 17: 1 for war and assembled at **S** in Judah.
17: 1 Ephes Dammim, between **S** and Azekah.
1Ki 4:10 (**S** and all the land of Hepher were

Soda
Job 9:30 soap and my hands with washing s,
Pr 25:20 or like vinegar poured on s, is one
Jer 2:22 Although you wash yourself with s

Sodi
Nu 13:10 tribe of Zebulun, Gaddiel son of **S**;

Sodom (*Sodom and Gomorrah*)
City in Valley of Siddim (Ge 14:2–3), at south end of the Dead Sea, exact location unknown. Often paired with Gomorrah as a place of wickedness. Lot and his family chose to settle near here (Ge 13:12). When its king and army were defeated by a Mesopotamian alliance (Ge 14:8–11), Lot was captured (Ge 14:12) and then rescued by Abram (Ge 14:14–16). God threatened to destroy it (Ge 18:20–21) but Abraham pleaded on its behalf (Ge 18:23–33). It was destroyed because of its depravity but Lot and his daughters survived (Ge 19:1–29). Frequently used as an example of man's depravity and God's judgment (Dt 29:23; Isa 1:9–10; Jer 23:14; La 4:6; Eze 16:46–56; Am 4:11; Zep 2:9; Mt 10:15; Lk 10:12; Ro 9:29; 2Pe 2:6; Jude 7; Rev 11:8). See *Gomorrah*.

Ge 10:19 and then towards **S**, Gomorrah, Admah
13:12 plain and pitched his tents near **S**.
13:13 Now the men of **S** were wicked and
14: 2 went to war against Bera king of **S**,
14: 8 the king of **S**, the king of Gomorrah,
14:12 since he was living in **S**.
14:17 the king of **S** came out to meet him
14:21 The king of **S** said to Abram, "Give
14:22 Abram said to the king of **S**, "I have
18:16 they looked down towards **S**, and
18:22 men turned away and went towards **S**,
18:26 righteous people in the city of **S**,
19: 1 The two angels arrived at **S** in the
19: 4 from every part of the city of **S**
Dt 32:32 Their vine comes from the vine of **S**
Isa 1: 9 we would have become like **S**,
1:10 word of the LORD, you rulers of **S**;
3: 9 they parade their sin like **S**;

Jer 23:14 They are all like **S** to me; the
Lam 4: 6 my people is greater than that of **S**,
Eze 16:46 of you with her daughters, was **S**.
16:48 your sister **S** and her daughters
16:49 this was the sin of your sister **S**:
16:53 I will restore the fortunes of **S** and
16:55 your sisters, **S** with her daughters
16:56 sister **S** in the day of your pride,
Zep 2: 9 "surely Moab will become like **S**, the
Mt 11:23 in you had been performed in **S**,
11:24 it will be more bearable for **S** on
Lk 10:12 that day for **S** than for that town.
17:29 the day Lot left **S**, fire and sulphur
Ro 9:29 we would have become like **S**,
Rev 11: 8 which is figuratively called **S** and

Sodom and Gomorrah

Ge 13:10 was before the LORD destroyed **S**.)
14:10 and when the kings of **S** fled, some
14:11 the goods of **S** and all their food;
18:20 "The outcry against **S** is so great
19:24 rained down burning sulphur on **S**
19:28 He looked down towards **S**, towards
Dt 29:23 It will be like the destruction of **S**,
Isa 13:19 will be overthrown by God like **S**.
Jer 49:18 **S** were overthrown, along with their
50:40 God overthrew **S** along with their
Am 4:11 some of you as I overthrew **S**.
Mt 10:15 it will be more bearable for **S** on
2Pe 2: 6 if he condemned the cities of **S** by
Jude : 7 **S** and the surrounding towns gave

Soften

Ps 65:10 you **s** it with showers and bless its

Soil (Soiled)

Ge 4: 2 kept flocks, and Cain worked the **s**.
4: 3 the fruits of the **s** as an offering
9:20 Noah, a man of the **s**, proceeded to
Ex 23:19 firstfruits of your **s** to the house
34:26 firstfruits of your **s** to the house
Lev 26:20 because your **s** will not yield its
27:30 whether grain from the **s** or fruit
Nu 13:20 How is the **s**? Is it fertile or poor?
Dt 26: 2 from the **s** of the land that the
26:10 now I bring the firstfruits of the **s**
1Ki 18:38 the wood, the stones and the **s**, and
2Ch 26:10 fertile lands, for he loved the **s**.
Job 5: 6 hardship does not spring from the **s**,
8:19 and from the **s** other plants grow.
14: 8 ground and its stump die in the **s**,
14:19 and torrents wash away the **s**,
21:33 The **s** in the valley is sweet to him;
Ps 37:35 like a green tree in its native **s**,
105:35 land, ate up the produce of their **s**.
SS 5: 3 my feet—must I **s** them again?
Isa 28:24 on breaking up and harrowing the **s**?
30:24 The oxen and donkeys that work the **s**
61:11 For as the **s** makes the young plant
Eze 17: 5 your land and put it in fertile **s**.
17: 8 had been planted in good **s** by
Mt 13: 5 where it did not have much **s**.
13: 5 quickly, because the **s** was shallow.
13: 8 Still other seed fell on good **s**,
13:23 the seed that fell on good **s** is the
Mk 4: 5 where it did not have much **s**.
4: 5 quickly, because the **s** was shallow.
4: 8 Still other seed fell on good **s**.
4:20 Others, like seed sown on good **s**,
4:28 All by itself the **s** produces
Lk 8: 8 Still other seed fell on good **s**.
8:15 the seed on good **s** stands for those
13: 7 Why should it use up the **s**?'
14:35 is fit neither for the **s** nor for the

Soiled (Soil)

Rev 3: 4 Sardis who have not **s** their clothes.

Sold (Sell)

Ge 31:15 Not only has he **s** us, but he has
37:28 **s** him for twenty shekels of silver
37:36 Meanwhile, the Midianites **s** Joseph
41:56 opened the storehouses and **s** grain
42: 6 one who **s** grain to all its people.
45: 4 Joseph, the one you **s** into Egypt!
47:20 The Egyptians, one and all, **s** their
Ex 22: 3 he must be **s** to pay for his theft.
Lev 25:23 The land must not be **s** permanently,
25:25 redeem what his countryman has **s**.
25:27 value for the years since he **s** it
25:27 balance to the man to whom he **s** it;
25:28 what he **s** will remain in the
25:33 a house **s** in any town they hold—and
25:34 to their towns must not be **s**;
25:42 Egypt, they must not be **s** as slaves.
25:48 redemption after he has **s** himself.
25:50 **s** himself up to the Year of Jubilee.
27:20 or if he has **s** it to someone else,
27:27 it, it is to be **s** at its set value.
27:28 family land—may be **s** or redeemed;
Dt 32:30 unless their Rock had **s** them, unless
Jdg 2:14 He **s** them to their enemies all
3: 8 so that he **s** them into the hands of
4: 2 the LORD **s** them into the hands of
10: 7 He **s** them into the hands of the
1Sa 12: 9 he **s** them into the hands of Sisera,
1Ki 21:20 "because you have **s** yourself to do
21:25 who **s** himself to do evil in the eyes
2Ki 6:25 donkey's head **s** for eighty shekels
7:16 So a seah of flour **s** for a shekel,
7:16 two seahs of barley **s** for a shekel,
17:17 sorcery and **s** themselves to do evil
Ne 5: 8 brothers who were **s** to the Gentiles.
5: 8 only for them to be **s** back to us!"
Est 7: 4 For I and my people have been **s** for
7: 4 If we had merely been **s** as male and
Ps 44:12 You **s** your people for a pittance,
105:17 before them—Joseph, **s** as a slave.
Isa 50: 1 Because of your sins you were **s**;
52: 3 "You were **s** for nothing, and without
Jer 34:14 Hebrew who has **s** himself to you.
Eze 7:13 not recover the land he has **s** as
Hos 8: 9 Ephraim has **s** herself to lovers.
8:10 Although they have **s** themselves
Joel 3: 3 they **s** girls for wine that they
3: 6 You **s** the people of Judah and
3: 7 of the places to which you **s** them,
Am 1: 6 communities and **s** them to Edom,
1: 9 Because she **s** whole communities of
Mt 10:29 Are not two sparrows **s** for a penny?
13:44 **s** all he had and bought that field.
13:46 **s** everything he had and bought it.
18:25 that he had be **s** to repay the debt.
26: 9 "This perfume could have been **s** at a
Mk 14: 5 could have been **s** for more than a
Lk 12: 6 Are not five sparrows **s** for two
Jn 2:16 To those who **s** doves he said, "Get
12: 5 "Why wasn't this perfume **s** and the
Ac 4:34 who owned lands or houses **s** them,
4:37 **s** a field he owned and brought the
5: 1 Sapphira, also **s** a piece of property.
5: 4 it belong to you before it was **s**?
5: 4 And after it was **s**, wasn't the
7: 9 they **s** him as a slave into Egypt.
Ro 7:14 am unspiritual, **s** as a slave to sin.
1Co 10:25 Eat anything **s** in the meat market
Heb 12:16 Esau, who for a single meal **s** his
Rev 18:15 The merchants who **s** these things and

Soldier (Fellow-soldier, Soldiers)

Nu 31:53 Each **s** had taken plunder for himself.
1Sa 13:22 day of the battle not a **s** with Saul
2Sa 17:10 even the bravest **s**, whose heart is
2Ki 5: 1 was a valiant **s**, but he had leprosy.
2Ch 17:17 From Benjamin: Eliada, a valiant **s**,
Am 2:15 the fleet-footed **s** will not get away,
Ac 10: 7 **s** who was one of his attendants.
28:16 by himself, with a **s** to guard him.
1Co 9: 7 Who serves as a **s** at his own expense?
2Ti 2: 3 Endure hardship with us like a good **s**
2: 4 No-one serving as a **s** gets involved

Soldiers (Soldier)

Nu 31:21 Eleazar the priest said to the **s** who
31:27 Divide the spoils between the **s** who
31:28 From the **s** who fought in the battle,
31:32 that the **s** took was 675,000 sheep,
31:49 "Your servants have counted the **s**
Jos 8:13 They had the **s** take up their
17: 1 because the Makirites were great **s**.
Jdg 9:35 **s** came out from their hiding-place.
20: 2 four hundred thousand **s** armed with
20:16 Among all these **s** there were seven
1Sa 4: 3 the **s** returned to camp, the elders
4:10 Israel lost thirty thousand foot **s**.
13: 5 and **s** as numerous as the sand on
14:28 one of the **s** told him, "Your father
15: 4 two hundred thousand foot **s** and
15:15 Saul answered, "The **s** brought them
15:21 The **s** took sheep and cattle from the
26: 7 Abner and the **s** were lying round him.
2Sa 3:23 Joab and all the **s** with him arrived,
8: 4 and twenty thousand foot **s**.
10: 6 foot **s** from Beth Rehob and Zobah,
10:18 and forty thousand of their foot **s**.
11: 7 how the **s** were and how the war was
1Ki 20:29 on the Aramean foot **s** in one day.
2Ki 13: 7 chariots and ten thousand foot **s**,
25: 5 All his **s** were separated from him
1Ch 12:33 experienced **s** prepared for battle
12:36 experienced **s** prepared for battle
18: 4 and twenty thousand foot **s**.
19:18 and forty thousand of their foot **s**.
2Ch 28: 6 a hundred and twenty thousand **s** in
28:14 the **s** gave up the prisoners and
Ezr 8:22 I was ashamed to ask the king for **s**
Jer 38: 4 He is discouraging the **s** who are
39: 4 Zedekiah king of Judah and all the **s**
41: 3 as the Babylonian **s** who were there.
41:16 the **s**, women, children and court
49:26 her **s** will be silenced in that day,"
50:30 her **s** will be silenced in that day,"
51:32 set on fire, and the **s** terrified."
52: 8 All his **s** were separated from him
Eze 27:10 and Put served as **s** in your army.
27:27 your merchants and all your **s**, and
39:20 mighty men and **s** of every kind,'
Da 3:20 commanded some of the strongest **s** in
3:22 killed the **s** who took up Shadrach,
Joel 2: 7 warriors; they scale walls like **s**.
Na 2: 3 The shields of his **s** are red;
Mt 8: 9 under authority, with **s** under me.
27:27 the governor's **s** took Jesus into the
27:27 the whole company of **s** round him.
28:12 gave the **s** a large sum of money,
28:15 the **s** took the money and did as they
Mk 15:16 The **s** led Jesus away into the palace
15:16 together the whole company of **s**.
Lk 3:14 some **s** asked him, "And what should
7: 8 under authority, with **s** under me.
23:11 Herod and his **s** ridiculed and mocked
23:36 The **s** also came up and mocked him.
Jn 18: 3 guiding a detachment of **s** and some
18:12 the detachment of **s** with its
19: 2 The **s** twisted together a crown of
19:16 So the **s** took charge of Jesus.
19:23 the **s** crucified Jesus, they took his
19:24 So this is what the **s** did.
19:32 The **s** therefore came and broke the
19:34 one of the **s** pierced Jesus' side
Ac 12: 4 by four squads of four **s** each.
12: 6 Peter was sleeping between two **s**,
12:18 no small commotion among the **s** as
21:32 He at once took some officers and **s**
21:32 saw the commander and his **s**, they
21:35 great he had to be carried by the **s**.
21:37 the **s** were about to take Paul into
23:23 ready a detachment of two hundred **s**,
23:31 the **s**, carrying out their orders,
27:31 Paul said to the centurion and the **s**,
27:32 the **s** cut the ropes that held the
27:42 The **s** planned to kill the prisoners

Sole (Soles)

Dt 28:56 the ground with the **s** of her foot
28:65 place for the **s** of your foot.
2Sa 14:25 top of his head to the **s** of his foot
Isa 1: 6 From the **s** of your foot to the top

Solemn

Ge 50:11 holding a **s** ceremony of mourning.
Jos 6:26 time Joshua pronounced this **s** oath:
Jdg 21: 5 For they had taken a **s** oath that

Eze 16: 8 I gave you my **s** oath and entered
Ac 23:14 "We have taken a **s** oath not to eat

Soles (Sole)

Dt 28:35 spreading from the **s** of your feet to
2Ki 19:24 With the **s** of my feet I have dried
Job 2: 7 **s** of his feet to the top of his head.
13:27 putting marks on the **s** of my feet.
Isa 37:25 With the **s** of my feet I have dried
Eze 43: 7 and the place for the **s** of my feet.
Mal 4: 3 be ashes under the **s** of your feet

Solid

Nu 4: 6 spread a cloth of **s** blue over that
2Ch 4:21 lamps and tongs (they were **s** gold);
Zec 4: 2 "I see a **s** gold lampstand with a
1Co 3: 2 I gave you milk, not **s** food, for you
2Ti 2:19 Nevertheless, God's **s** foundation
Heb 5:12 You need milk, not **s** food!
5:14 **s** food is for the mature, who by

Solitary

Lev 16:22 itself all their sins to a **s** place;
Mt 14:13 by boat privately to a **s** place.
Mk 1:35 off to a **s** place, where he prayed.
6:32 themselves in a boat to a **s** place.
Lk 4:42 Jesus went out to a **s** place.
8:29 driven by the demon into **s** places.

Solomon (Solomon's)

Third king of Israel; son of David and Bathsheba (2Sa 12:24). Appointed by David; anointed by Nathan and Zadok (1Ki 1; 1Ch 29:21–25). Given charge by David (1Ki 2:1–9); had Adonijah, Joab and Shimei killed (1Ki 2:13–46). Asked God for wisdom (1Ki 3:5–15; 2Ch 1:7–12); gave wise judgment (1Ki 3:16–28); noted for his wisdom (1Ki 4:29–34; 10:23–24). Wrote proverbs (1Ki 4:32; Pr 1:1; 10:1–22:16; 25–29); psalms (Ps 72:1; 127:1); Song of Songs (SS 1:1). Built temple (1Ki 5–7; 2Ch 2–4); brought ark; prayer of dedication (1Ki 8–9; 2Ch 5–7). Established trading fleet (1Ki 9:26–28; 2Ch 8:17). Visited by Queen of Sheba (1Ki 10:1–13; 2Ch 9:1–12; Mt 12:42; Lk 11:31). Acquired great wealth (1Ki 10:14–29; 2Ch 1:14–17; 9:13–28). Foreign wives turned his heart from God (1Ki 11:1–10), causing him to break covenant with God and so to lose part of kingdom (1Ki 11:11–13, 29–39). Death (1Ki 11:41–43; 2Ch 9:29–31).

2Sa 5:14 there: Shammua, Shobab, Nathan, **S**,
12:24 to a son, and they named him **S**.
1Ki 1:10 the special guard or his brother **S**.
1:12 own life and the life of your son **S**.
1:13 "Surely **S** your son shall be king
1:17 '**S** your son shall become king after
1:19 he has not invited **S** your servant.
1:21 son **S** will be treated as criminals."
1:26 your servant **S** he did not invite.
1:30 **S** your son shall be king after me,
1:33 set **S** my son on my own mule and take
1:34 and shout, 'Long live King **S**!'
1:37 so may he be with **S** to make his
1:38 down and put **S** on Kind David's mule
1:39 from the sacred tent and anointed **S**.
1:39 "Long live King **S**!"
1:43 "Our lord King David has made **S** king.
1:46 Moreover, **S** has taken his seat on
1:50 Adonijah, in fear of **S**, went and
1:51 **S** was told, "Adonijah is afraid of
1:51 "Adonijah is afraid of King **S** and is
1:51 He says, 'Let King **S** swear to me
1:52 **S** replied, "If he shows himself to
1:53 King **S** sent men, and they brought
1:53 bowed down to King **S**, and **S** said,
2: 1 die, he gave a charge to **S** his son.
2:12 **S** sat on the throne of his father
2:17 "Please ask King **S**—he will not
2:19 Bathsheba went to King **S** to speak to
2:22 King **S** answered his mother, "Why do
2:23 King **S** swore by the LORD: "May God
2:25 King **S** gave orders to Benaiah son of
2:27 **S** removed Abiathar from the
1Ki 2:29 King **S** was told that Joab had fled
2:29 Then **S** ordered Benaiah son of
2:41 **S** was told that Shimei had gone from
2:45 King **S** will be blessed, and David's
3: 1 **S** made an alliance with Pharaoh king
3: 3 **S** showed his love for the LORD by
3: 4 and **S** offered a thousand burnt
3: 5 At Gibeon the LORD appeared to **S**
3: 6 **S** answered, "You have shown great
3:10 The Lord was pleased that **S** had
3:15 **S** awoke—and he realised it had been
4: 1 King **S** ruled over all Israel.
4: 7 **S** also had twelve district governors
4:11 married to Taphath daughter of **S**);
4:15 had married Basemath daughter of **S**);
4:21 **S** ruled over all the kingdoms from
4:26 **S** had four thousand stalls for
4:27 supplied provisions for King **S** and
4:29 God gave **S** wisdom and very great
5: 1 Hiram king of Tyre heard that **S** had
5: 1 he sent his envoys to **S**, because he
5: 2 **S** sent back this message to Hiram:
5: 8 Hiram sent word to **S**: "I have
5:10 In this way Hiram kept **S** supplied
5:11 **S** gave Hiram twenty thousand cors of
5:11 **S** continued to do this for Hiram
5:12 The LORD gave **S** wisdom, just as he
5:12 relations between Hiram and **S**,
5:13 King **S** conscripted labourers from
5:15 **S** had seventy thousand carriers and
5:18 The craftsmen of **S** and Hiram and the
6: 2 The temple that King **S** built for the
6:11 The word of the LORD came to **S**:
6:14 **S** built the temple and completed it.
6:21 **S** covered the inside of the temple
7: 1 took **S** thirteen years, however, to
7: 8 **S** also made a palace like this hall
7:13 King **S** sent to Tyre and brought
7:14 He came to King **S** and did all the
7:40 work he had undertaken for King **S**
7:45 objects that Huram made for King **S**
7:47 **S** left all these things unweighed,
7:48 **S** also made all the furnishings that
7:51 all the work King **S** had done for the
8: 1 King **S** summoned into his presence at
8: 2 came together to King **S** at the time
8: 5 King **S** and the entire assembly of
8:12 **S** said, "The LORD has said that he
8:22 **S** stood before the altar of the LORD
8:54 **S** had finished all these prayers and
8:63 **S** offered a sacrifice of fellowship
8:65 **S** observed the festival at that time,
9: 1 **S** had finished building the temple
9:10 during which **S** built these two
9:11 King **S** gave twenty towns in Galilee
9:12 see the towns that **S** had given him,
9:15 forced labour King **S** conscripted to
9:17 **S** rebuilt Gezer.) He built up Lower
9:21 these **S** conscripted for his slave
9:22 **S** did not make slaves of any of the
9:24 to the palace **S** had built for her,
9:25 Three times a year **S** sacrificed
9:26 King **S** also built ships at
9:28 which they delivered to King **S**.
10: 1 of Sheba heard about the fame of **S**
10: 2 she came to **S** and talked with him
10: 3 **S** answered all her questions;
10: 4 saw all the wisdom of **S** and the
10:10 the queen of Sheba gave to King **S**.
10:13 King **S** gave the queen of Sheba all
10:14 weight of the gold that **S** received
10:16 King **S** made two hundred large
10:23 King **S** was greater in riches and
10:24 world sought audience with **S** to
10:26 **S** accumulated chariots and horses;
11: 1 King **S**, however, loved many foreign
11: 2 **S** held fast to them in love.
11: 4 **S** grew old, his wives turned his
11: 6 **S** did evil in the eyes of the LORD;
11: 7 **S** built a high place for Chemosh
11: 9 The LORD became angry with **S** because
11:10 Although he had forbidden **S** to
11:10 **S** did not keep the LORD's command.
11:11 the LORD said to **S**, "Since this is
11:14 raised up against **S** an adversary,
11:23 God raised up against **S** another
1Ki 11:25 adversary as long as **S** lived,
11:27 **S** had built the supporting terraces
11:28 and when **S** saw how well the young
11:40 **S** tried to kill Jeroboam, but
11:41 in the book of the annals of **S**?
11:42 **S** reigned in Jerusalem over all
12: 2 where he had fled from King **S**),
12: 6 his father **S** during his lifetime.
12:21 the kingdom for Rehoboam son of **S**.
12:23 "Say to Rehoboam son of **S** king of
14:21 Rehoboam son of **S** was king in Judah.
14:26 all the gold shields **S** had made.
2Ki 21: 7 had said to David and to his son **S**,
23:13 the ones **S** king of Israel had built
24:13 gold articles that **S** king of Israel
25:16 which **S** had made for the temple of
1Ch 3: 5 Shammua, Shobab, Nathan and **S**.
6:10 in the temple **S** built in Jerusalem),
6:32 until **S** built the temple of the
14: 4 there: Shammua, Shobab, Nathan, **S**,
18: 8 which **S** used to make the bronze Sea,
22: 5 David said, "My son **S** is young and
22: 6 he called for his son **S** and charged
22: 7 David said to **S**: "My son, I had it
22: 9 His name will be **S**, and I will grant
22:17 leaders of Israel to help his son **S**.
23: 1 he made his son **S** king over Israel.
28: 5 he has chosen my son **S** to sit on the
28: 6 '**S** your son is the one who will
28: 9 "And you, my son **S**, acknowledge the
28:11 David gave his son **S** the plans for
28:20 David also said to **S** his son, "Be
29: 1 "My son **S**, the one whom God has
29:19 give my son **S** the wholehearted
29:22 they acknowledged **S** son of David
29:23 **S** sat on the throne of the LORD as
29:24 pledged their submission to King **S**.
29:25 The LORD highly exalted **S** in the
29:28 His son **S** succeeded him as king.
2Ch 1: 1 **S** son of David established himself
1: 2 **S** spoke to all Israel—to the
1: 3 **S** and the whole assembly went to the
1: 5 so **S** and the assembly enquired of
1: 6 **S** went up to the bronze altar before
1: 7 That night God appeared to **S** and
1: 8 **S** answered God, "You have shown
1:11 God said to **S**, "Since this is your
1:13 **S** went to Jerusalem from the high
1:14 **S** accumulated chariots and horses;
2: 1 **S** gave orders to build a temple for
2: 3 **S** sent this message to Hiram king of
2:11 king of Tyre replied by letter to **S**:
2:17 **S** took a census of all the aliens
3: 1 **S** began to build the temple of the
3: 3 The foundation **S** laid for building
4:11 for King **S** in the temple of God:
4:16 that Huram-Abi made for King **S** for
4:18 All these things that **S** made
4:19 **S** also made all the furnishings that
5: 1 all the work **S** had done for the
5: 2 **S** summoned to Jerusalem the elders
5: 6 King **S** and the entire assembly of
6: 1 **S** said, "The LORD has said that he
6:12 **S** stood before the altar of the LORD
7: 1 **S** finished praying, fire came down
7: 5 King **S** offered a sacrifice of
7: 7 **S** consecrated the middle part of the
7: 8 **S** observed the festival at that time
7:10 the LORD had done for David and **S**
7:11 **S** had finished the temple of the
8: 1 during which **S** built the temple of
8: 2 **S** rebuilt the villages that Hiram
8: 3 **S** then went to Hamath Zobah and
8: 8 these **S** conscripted for his slave
8: 9 **S** did not make slaves of the
8:11 **S** brought Pharaoh's daughter up from
8:12 **S** sacrificed burnt offerings to the
8:17 **S** went to Ezion Geber and Elath on
8:18 which they delivered to King **S**.
9: 1 she came to **S** and talked with him
9: 2 **S** answered all her questions;
9: 3 queen of Sheba saw the wisdom of **S**,
9: 9 the queen of Sheba gave to King **S**.
9:10 (The men of Hiram and the men of **S**
9:12 King **S** gave the queen of Sheba all
9:13 weight of the gold that **S** received

2Ch 9:14 land brought gold and silver to **S**.
9:15 King **S** made two hundred large
9:22 King **S** was greater in riches and
9:23 sought audience with **S** to hear the
9:25 **S** had four thousand stalls for
9:30 **S** reigned in Jerusalem over all
10: 2 where he had fled from King **S**),
10: 6 his father **S** during his lifetime.
11: 3 "Say to Rehoboam son of **S** king of
11:17 Rehoboam son of **S** for three years,
11:17 of David and **S** during this time.
12: 9 the gold shields that **S** had made.
13: 6 an official of **S** son of David,
13: 7 opposed Rehoboam son of **S** when he
30:26 for since the days of **S** son of David
33: 7 had said to David and to his son **S**,
35: 3 **S** son of David king of Israel built.
35: 4 king of Israel and by his son **S**.
Ezr 2:55 The descendants of the servants of **S**:
2:58 descendants of the servants of **S** 392
Ne 7:57 The descendants of the servants of **S**:
7:60 descendants of the servants of **S** 392
12:45 the commands of David and his son **S**.
13:26 these that **S** king of Israel sinned?
Ps 72: T Of **S**.
127: T A song of ascents. Of **S**.
Pr 1: 1 The proverbs of **S** son of David, king
10: 1 The proverbs of **S**: A wise son brings
25: 1 These are more proverbs of **S**, copied
SS 1: 5 Kedar, like the tent curtains of **S**.
3: 9 King **S** made for himself the carriage;
3:11 and look at King **S** wearing the crown,
8:11 **S** had a vineyard in Baal Hamon;
8:12 thousand shekels are for you, O **S**,
Jer 52:20 which King **S** had made for the temple
Mt 1: 6 David was the father of **S**, whose
1: 7 **S** the father of Rehoboam, Rehoboam
6:29 not even **S** in all his splendour
12:42 and now one greater than **S** is here.
Lk 11:31 and now one greater than **S** is here.
12:27 not even **S** in all his splendour
Ac 7:47 was **S** who built the house for him.

Solomon's (Solomon)

1Ki 1:11 Nathan asked Bathsheba, **S** mother,
1:47 'May your God make **S** name more
2:13 Haggith, went to Bathsheba, **S** mother.
2:46 now firmly established in **S** hands.
4:21 and were **S** subjects all his life.
4:22 **S** daily provisions were thirty cors
4:25 During **S** lifetime Judah and Israel,
4:30 **S** wisdom was greater than the wisdom
4:34 nations came to listen to **S** wisdom,
5: 7 Hiram heard **S** message, he was
6: 1 in the fourth year of **S** reign over
9:16 gift to his daughter, **S** wife.
9:23 officials in charge of **S** projects
9:27 serve in the fleet with **S** men.
10:21 All King **S** goblets were gold, and
10:21 of little value in **S** days.
10:28 **S** horses were imported from Egypt
11:26 He was one of **S** officials, an
11:31 to tear the kingdom out of **S** hand
11:33 and laws as David, **S** father, did.
11:34 the whole kingdom out of **S** hand;
11:40 and stayed there until **S** death.
11:41 for the other events of **S** reign—all
1Ch 3:10 **S** son was Rehoboam, Abijah his son,
2Ch 1:16 **S** horses were imported from Egypt
8:10 were also King **S** chief officials
8:16 All **S** work was carried out, from the
8:18 These, with **S** men, sailed to Ophir
9: 1 the queen of Sheba heard of **S** fame,
9:20 All King **S** goblets were gold, and
9:20 considered of little value in **S** day.
9:28 **S** horses were imported from Egypt
9:29 for the other events of **S** reign,
Ne 11: 3 descendants of **S** servants lived in
SS 1: 1 **S** Song of Songs.
3: 7 Look! It is **S** carriage, escorted by
Mt 12:42 of the earth to listen to **S** wisdom,
Lk 11:31 of the earth to listen to **S** wisdom,
Jn 10:23 temple area walking in **S** Colonnade.
Ac 3:11 in the place called **S** Colonnade.
5:12 to meet together in **S** Colonnade.

Solve (Solved)

Da 5:12 riddles and **s** difficult problems.
5:16 and to **s** difficult problems.

Solved (Solve)

Jdg 14:18 you would not have **s** my riddle."

Sombre

Mt 6:16 "When you fast, do not look **s** as the

Son (Grandson, Grandsons, *My son, Only son, Son of David, Son of God, Son of man*, Son's, Son-in-law, Sons, Sons', Sonship, Sons-in-law)

Ge 4:17 and he named it after his **s** Enoch.
4:22 Zillah also had a **s**, Tubal-Cain, who
4:25 and she gave birth to a **s** and named
4:26 Seth also had a **s**, and he named him
5: 3 Adam had lived 130 years, he had a **s**
5:28 had lived 182 years, he had a **s**.
9:24 what his youngest **s** had done to him,
11:31 Terah took his **s** Abram, his grandson
11:31 his grandson Lot **s** of Haran, and his
11:31 Sarai, the wife of his **s** Abram,
15: 4 but a **s** coming from your own body
16:11 with child and you will have a **s**.
16:15 Hagar bore Abram a **s**, and Abram gave
16:15 name Ishmael to the **s** she had borne.
17:16 and will surely give you a **s** by her.
17:17 "Will a **s** be born to a man a hundred
17:19 your wife Sarah will bear you a **s**,
17:23 On that very day Abraham took his **s**
17:25 his **s** Ishmael was thirteen;
17:26 Abraham and his **s** Ishmael were both
18:10 and Sarah your wife will have a **s**.
18:14 next year and Sarah will have a **s**."
19:37 The older daughter had a **s**, and she
19:38 The younger daughter also had a **s**,
21: 2 Sarah became pregnant and bore a **s**
21: 3 the name Isaac to the **s** Sarah bore
21: 4 his **s** Isaac was eight days old,
21: 5 when his **s** Isaac was born to him.
21: 7 I have borne him a **s** in his old age."
21: 9 Sarah saw that the **s** whom Hagar the
21:10 rid of that slave woman and her **s**,
21:10 for that slave woman's **s** will never
21:11 greatly because it concerned his **s**.
21:13 I will make the **s** of the maidservant
22: 2 God said, "Take your **s**, your only **s**,
22: 3 two of his servants and his **s** Isaac.
22: 6 and placed it on his **s** Isaac,
22: 9 He bound his **s** Isaac and laid him on
22:10 and took the knife to slay his **s**.
22:12 not withheld from me your **s**,
22:13 a burnt offering instead of his **s**.
22:16 and have not withheld your **s**,
23: 8 with Ephron **s** of Zohar on my
24: 5 take your **s** back to the country you
24:15 the daughter of Bethuel **s** of Milcah,
24:24 the **s** that Milcah bore to Nahor."
24:36 has borne him a **s** in her old age,
24:44 LORD has chosen for my master's **s**.'
24:47 The daughter of Bethuel **s** of Nahor,
24:48 of my master's brother for his **s**.
24:51 the wife of your master's **s**, as the
25: 6 sent them away from his **s** Isaac to
25: 9 of Ephron **s** of Zohar the Hittite,
25:11 God blessed his **s** Isaac, who then
25:12 This is the account of Abraham's **s**
25:19 This is the account of Abraham's **s**
27: 1 he called for Esau his older **s** and
27: 5 as Isaac spoke to his **s** Esau.
27: 6 Rebekah said to her **s** Jacob, "Look,
27:15 best clothes of Esau her older **s**,
27:15 and put them on her younger **s** Jacob.
27:17 she handed to her **s** Jacob the tasty
27:20 Isaac asked his **s**, "How did you find
27:32 "I am your **s**," he answered, "your
27:42 told what her older **s** Esau had said
27:42 she sent for her younger **s** Jacob and
28: 5 to Laban **s** of Bethuel the Aramean,
28: 9 daughter of Ishmael **s** of Abraham,
29:12 of her father and a **s** of Rebekah.
29:13 news about Jacob, his sister's **s**,
Ge 29:32 pregnant and gave birth to a **s**.
29:33 and when she gave birth to a **s** she
29:34 and when she gave birth to a **s** she
29:35 and when she gave birth to a **s** she
30: 5 she became pregnant and bore him a **s**.
30: 6 to my plea and given me a **s**.
30: 7 again and bore Jacob a second **s**.
30:10 Leah's servant Zilpah bore Jacob a **s**.
30:12 Zilpah bore Jacob a second **s**.
30:17 pregnant and bore Jacob a fifth **s**.
30:19 again and bore Jacob a sixth **s**.
30:23 and gave birth to a **s** and said,
30:24 "May the LORD add to me another **s**.
34: 2 Shechem **s** of Hamor the Hivite, the
34:18 good to Hamor and his **s** Shechem.
34:20 Hamor and his **s** Shechem went to the
34:24 agreed with Hamor and his **s** Shechem,
34:26 They put Hamor and his **s** Shechem to
35:17 be afraid, for you have another **s**."
35:18 was dying—she named her **s** Ben-Oni.
36:10 Eliphaz, the **s** of Esau's wife Adah,
36:10 Reuel, the **s** of Esau's wife Basemath.
36:12 Esau's **s** Eliphaz also had a
36:17 The sons of Esau's **s** Reuel: Chiefs
36:32 Bela **s** of Beor became king of Edom.
36:33 Bela died, Jobab **s** of Zerah from
36:35 Husham died, Hadad **s** of Bedad, who
36:38 Baal-Hanan **s** of Acbor succeeded
36:39 Baal-Hanan **s** of Acbor died, Hadad
37:34 and mourned for his **s** many days.
38: 3 gave birth to a **s**, who was named Er.
38: 4 birth to a **s** and named him Onan.
38: 5 She gave birth to still another **s**
41:52 The second **s** he named Ephraim and
43:29 Benjamin, his own mother's **s**, he
44:20 young **s** born to him in his old age.
45: 9 'This is what your **s** Joseph says:
46:10 Shaul the **s** of a Canaanite woman.
46:23 The **s** of Dan: Hushim.
47:29 he called for his **s** Joseph and said
48: 2 "Your **s** Joseph has come to you,"
50:23 children of Makir **s** of Manasseh
Ex 2: 2 pregnant and gave birth to a **s**.
2:10 daughter and he became her **s**.
2:22 Zipporah gave birth to a **s**, and
4:22 LORD says: Israel is my firstborn **s**,
4:23 so I will kill your firstborn **s**.
6:14 Reuben the firstborn **s** of Israel
6:15 Shaul the **s** of a Canaanite woman.
6:25 Eleazar **s** of Aaron married one of
11: 5 Every firstborn **s** in Egypt will die,
11: 5 from the firstborn **s** of Pharaoh, who
11: 5 to the firstborn **s** of the slave girl,
13: 8 On that day tell your **s**, 'I do this
13:14 "In days to come when your **s** asks
18: 3 One **s** was named Gershom, for Moses
20:10 neither you, nor your **s** or daughter,
21: 9 If he selects her for his **s**, he must
21:31 if the bull gores a **s** or a daughter.
29:30 The **s** who succeeds him as priest and
31: 2 "See I have chosen Bezalel **s** of Uri,
31: 2 the **s** of Hur, of the tribe of Judah,
31: 6 appointed Oholiab **s** of Ahisamach,
33:11 Joshua **s** of Nun did not leave the
35:30 LORD has chosen Bezalel **s** of Uri,
35:30 the **s** of Hur, of the tribe of Judah,
35:34 him and Oholiab **s** of Ahisamach,
38:21 of Ithamar **s** of Aaron, the priest.
38:22 (Bezalel **s** of Uri, the **s** of Hur, of
38:23 with him was Oholiab **s** of Ahisamach,
Lev 6:22 The **s** who is to succeed him as
7:33 The **s** of Aaron who offers the blood
12: 2 gives birth to a **s** will be
12: 6 for a **s** or daughter are over,
21: 2 his **s** or daughter, his brother,
24:10 Now the **s** of an Israelite mother and
24:11 The **s** of the Israelite woman
Nu 1: 5 from Reuben, Elizur **s** of Shedeur;
1: 6 Shelumiel **s** of Zurishaddai;
1: 7 from Judah, Nahshon **s** of Amminadab;
1: 8 from Issachar, Nethanel **s** of Zuar;
1: 9 from Zebulun, Eliab **s** of Helon;
1:10 from Ephraim, Elishama **s** of Ammihud;
1:10 Manasseh, Gamaliel **s** of Pedahzur;
1:11 from Benjamin, Abidan **s** of Gideoni;
1:12 from Dan, Ahiezer **s** of Ammishaddai;

Nu 1:13 from Asher, Pagiel **s** of Ocran;
1:14 from Gad, Eliasaph **s** of Deuel;
1:15 from Naphtali, Ahira **s** of Enan."
1:20 of Reuben the firstborn **s** of Israel:
2: 3 of Judah is Nahshon **s** of Amminadab.
2: 5 of Issachar is Nethanel **s** of Zuar.
2: 7 of Zebulun is Eliab **s** of Helon.
2:10 of Reuben is Elizur **s** of Shedeur.
2:12 Simeon is Shelumiel **s** of Zurishaddai.
2:14 of Gad is Eliasaph **s** of Deuel.
2:18 of Ephraim is Elishama **s** of Ammihud.
2:20 Manasseh is Gamaliel **s** of Pedahzur.
2:22 of Benjamin is Abidan **s** of Gideoni.
2:25 of Dan is Ahiezer **s** of Ammishaddai.
2:27 of Asher is Pagiel **s** of Ocran.
2:29 of Naphtali is Ahira **s** of Enan.
3:24 Gershonites was Eliasaph **s** of Lael.
3:30 clans was Elizaphan **s** of Uzziel.
3:32 was Eleazar **s** of Aaron, the priest.
3:35 clans was Zuriel **s** of Abihail;
4:16 "Eleazar **s** of Aaron, the priest, is
4:28 of Ithamar **s** of Aaron, the priest.
4:33 of Ithamar **s** of Aaron, the priest."
7: 8 of Ithamar **s** of Aaron, the priest.
7:12 Nahshon **s** of Amminadab of the tribe
7:17 offering of Nahshon **s** of Amminadab.
7:18 On the second day Nethanel **s** of Zuar,
7:23 the offering of Nethanel **s** of Zuar.
7:24 On the third day, Eliab **s** of Helon,
7:29 the offering of Eliab **s** of Helon.
7:30 the fourth day Elizur **s** of Shedeur,
7:35 the offering of Elizur **s** of Shedeur.
7:36 fifth day Shelumiel **s** of Zurishaddai,
7:41 of Shelumiel **s** of Zurishaddai.
7:42 On the sixth day Eliasaph **s** of Deuel,
7:47 the offering of Eliasaph **s** of Deuel.
7:48 seventh day Elishama **s** of Ammihud,
7:53 offering of Elishama **s** of Ammihud.
7:54 eighth day Gamaliel **s** of Pedahzur,
7:59 offering of Gamaliel **s** of Pedahzur.
7:60 On the ninth day Abidan **s** of Gideoni,
7:65 the offering of Abidan **s** of Gideoni.
7:66 tenth day Ahiezer **s** of Ammishaddai,
7:71 of Ahiezer **s** of Ammishaddai.
7:72 the eleventh day Pagiel **s** of Ocran,
7:77 the offering of Pagiel **s** of Ocran.
7:78 On the twelfth day Ahira **s** of Enan,
7:83 was the offering of Ahira **s** of Enan.
10:14 Nahshon **s** of Amminadab was in
10:15 Nethanel **s** of Zuar was over the
10:16 Eliab **s** of Helon was over the
10:18 Elizur **s** of Shedeur was in command.
10:19 Shelumiel **s** of Zurishaddai was over
10:20 Eliasaph **s** of Deuel was over the
10:22 Elishama **s** of Ammihud was in command.
10:23 Gamaliel **s** of Pedahzur was over the
10:24 Abidan **s** of Gideoni was over the
10:25 Ahiezer **s** of Ammishaddai was in
10:26 Pagiel **s** of Ocran was over the
10:27 Ahira **s** of Enan was over the
10:29 Now Moses said to Hobab **s** of Reuel
11:28 Joshua **s** of Nun, who had been Moses'
13: 4 of Reuben, Shammua **s** of Zaccur;
13: 5 tribe of Simeon, Shaphat **s** of Hori;
13: 6 of Judah, Caleb **s** of Jephunneh;
13: 7 of Issachar, Igal **s** of Joseph;
13: 8 tribe of Ephraim, Hoshea **s** of Nun;
13: 9 tribe of Benjamin, Palti **s** of Raphu;
13:10 tribe of Zebulun, Gaddiel **s** of Sodi;
13:11 (a tribe of Joseph), Gaddi **s** of Susi;
13:12 tribe of Dan, Ammiel **s** of Gemalli;
13:13 tribe of Asher, Sethur **s** of Michael;
13:14 tribe of Naphtali, Nahbi **s** of Vophsi;
13:15 tribe of Gad, Geuel **s** of Maki.
13:16 Hoshea **s** of Nun the name Joshua.)
14: 6 Joshua **s** of Nun and Caleb **s** of
14:30 except Caleb **s** of Jephunneh
14:30 and Joshua **s** of Nun.
14:38 only Joshua **s** of Nun and Caleb **s** of
16: 1 Korah **s** of Izhar, the **s** of Kohath,
16: 1 the **s** of Levi, and certain
16: 1 and On **s** of Peleth—became insolent
16:37 "Tell Eleazar **s** of Aaron, the priest,
18:15 you must redeem every firstborn **s**
20:25 Call Aaron and his **s** Eleazar and
20:26 and put them on his **s** Eleazar,
Nu 20:28 and put them on his **s** Eleazar.
22: 2 Now Balak **s** of Zippor saw all that
22: 4 So Balak **s** of Zippor, who was king
22: 5 to summon Balaam **s** of Beor, who was
22:10 "Balak **s** of Zippor, king of Moab,
22:16 "This is what Balak **s** of Zippor says:
23:18 and listen; hear me, **s** of Zippor.
24: 3 "The oracle of Balaam **s** of Beor, the
24:15 "The oracle of Balaam **s** of Beor, the
25: 7 Phinehas **s** of Eleazar, the **s** of
25:11 "Phinehas **s** of Eleazar, the **s** of
25:14 Midianite woman was Zimri **s** of Salu,
26: 1 and Eleazar **s** of Aaron, the priest,
26: 5 the firstborn **s** of Israel, were:
26: 8 The **s** of Pallu was Eliab,
26:33 (Zelophehad **s** of Hepher had no sons;
26:65 **s** of Jephunneh and Joshua **s** of Nun.
27: 1 The daughters of Zelophehad **s** of
27: 1 the **s** of Gilead, the **s** of Makir, the
27: 1 the **s** of Makir, the **s** of Manasseh,
27: 4 from his clan because he had no **s**?
27: 8 'If a man dies and leaves no **s**, give
27:18 "Take Joshua **s** of Nun, a man in whom
31: 6 along with Phinehas **s** of Eleazar,
31: 8 Balaam **s** of Beor with the sword.
32:12 not one except Caleb **s** of Jephunneh
32:12 the Kenizzite and Joshua **s** of Nun,
32:28 Joshua **s** of Nun and to the family
32:33 the half-tribe of Manasseh **s** of
32:39 The descendants of Makir **s** of
34:17 the priest and Joshua **s** of Nun.
34:19 Caleb **s** of Jephunneh, from the
34:20 Shemuel **s** of Ammihud, from the tribe
34:21 Elidad **s** of Kislon, from the tribe
34:22 Bukki **s** of Jogli, the leader from
34:23 Hanniel **s** of Ephod, the leader from
34:23 the tribe of Manasseh **s** of Joseph;
34:24 Kemuel **s** of Shiphtan, the leader
34:24 the tribe of Ephraim **s** of Joseph;
34:25 Elizaphan **s** of Parnach, the leader
34:26 Paltiel **s** of Azzan, the leader from
34:27 Ahihud **s** of Shelomi, the leader from
34:28 Pedahel **s** of Ammihud, the leader
36: 1 of the clan of Gilead **s** of Makir,
36: 1 the **s** of Manasseh, who were from the
36:12 descendants of Manasseh **s** of Joseph,
Dt 1:31 as a father carries his **s**, all the
1:36 except Caleb **s** of Jephunneh. He will
1:38 your assistant, Joshua **s** of Nun,
5:14 neither you, nor your **s** or daughter,
6:20 In the future, when your **s** asks you,
8: 5 that as a man disciplines his **s**,
10: 6 his **s** succeeded him as priest.
13: 6 If your very own brother, or your **s**
18:10 his **s** or daughter in the fire,
21:15 the **s** of the wife he does not love,
21:16 to the **s** of the wife he loves in
21:16 the **s** of the wife he does not love.
21:17 He must acknowledge the **s** of his
21:17 That **s** is the first sign of his
21:18 rebellious **s** who does not obey his
21:20 "This **s** of ours is stubborn and
23: 4 and they hired Balaam **s** of Beor from
25: 5 and one of them dies without a **s**,
25: 6 The first **s** she bears shall carry on
28:56 she loves and her own **s** or daughter
31:23 this command to Joshua **s** of Nun:
32:44 Moses came with Joshua **s** of Nun and
34: 9 Now Joshua **s** of Nun was filled with
Jos 1: 1 Joshua **s** of Nun, Moses' assistant:
2: 1 Joshua **s** of Nun secretly sent two
2:23 came to Joshua **s** of Nun and told him
6: 6 Joshua **s** of Nun called the priests
6:26 "At the cost of his firstborn **s** will
7: 1 Achan **s** of Carmi, the **s** of Zimri,
7: 1 the **s** of Zerah, of the tribe of
7:18 and Achan **s** of Carmi, the **s** of Zimri,
7:18 the **s** of Zerah, of the tribe of
7:24 took Achan **s** of Zerah, the silver,
13:22 Balaam **s** of Beor, who practised
13:31 descendants of Makir **s** of Manasseh
14: 1 Eleazar the priest, Joshua **s** of Nun
14: 6 and Caleb **s** of Jephunneh the
14:13 Joshua blessed Caleb **s** of Jephunneh
14:14 Hebron has belonged to Caleb **s** of
15: 6 to the Stone of Bohan **s** of Reuben.
Jos 15:13 Joshua gave to Caleb **s** of Jephunneh
15:17 Othniel **s** of Kenaz, Caleb's brother,
17: 2 Manasseh **s** of Joseph by their clans.
17: 3 Now Zelophehad **s** of Hepher, the **s** of
17: 3 the **s** of Gilead, the **s** of Makir, the
17: 4 Joshua **s** of Nun, and the leaders and
18:17 to the Stone of Bohan **s** of Reuben.
19:49 gave Joshua **s** of Nun an inheritance
19:51 Joshua **s** of Nun and the heads of the
21: 1 Joshua **s** of Nun, and the heads of
21:12 given to Caleb **s** of Jephunneh as
22:13 the Israelites sent Phinehas **s** of
22:20 Achan **s** of Zerah acted unfaithfully
22:31 Phinehas **s** of Eleazar, the priest,
22:32 Phinehas **s** of Eleazar, the priest,
24: 9 Balak **s** of Zippor, the king of Moab,
24: 9 he sent for Balaam **s** of Beor to put
24:29 After these things, Joshua **s** of Nun,
24:33 Eleazar **s** of Aaron died and was
24:33 which had been allotted to his **s**
Jdg 1:13 Othniel **s** of Kenaz, Caleb's younger
2: 8 Joshua **s** of Nun, the servant of the
3: 9 Othniel **s** of Kenaz, Caleb's younger
3:11 until Othniel **s** of Kenaz died.
3:15 man, the **s** of Gera the Benjamite.
3:31 After Ehud came Shamgar **s** of Anath,
4: 6 She sent for Barak **s** of Abinoam from
4:12 they told Sisera that Barak **s** of
5: 1 On that day Deborah and Barak **s** of
5: 6 "In the days of Shamgar **s** of Anath,
5:12 your captives, O **s** of Abinoam.'
6:11 where his **s** Gideon was threshing
6:29 told, "Gideon **s** of Joash did it.
6:30 "Bring out your **s**. He must die,
7:14 of Gideon **s** of Joash, the Israelite.
8:13 Gideon **s** of Joash then returned from
8:20 Turning to Jether, his oldest **s**, he
8:22 "Rule over us—you, your **s** and your
8:29 Jerub-Baal **s** of Joash went back home
8:31 him a **s**, whom he named Abimelech.
8:32 Gideon **s** of Joash died at a good old
9: 1 Abimelech **s** of Jerub-Baal went to
9: 5 the youngest **s** of Jerub-Baal,
9:18 and made Abimelech, the **s** of his
9:26 Now Gaal **s** of Ebed moved with his
9:28 Gaal **s** of Ebed said, "Who is
9:28 Isn't he Jerub-Baal's **s**, and
9:30 heard what Gaal **s** of Ebed said, he
9:31 "Gaal **s** of Ebed and his brothers
9:35 Now Gaal **s** of Ebed had gone out and
9:57 Jotham **s** of Jerub-Baal came on them.
10: 1 Tola **s** of Puah, the **s** of Dodo, rose
11: 2 you are the **s** of another woman."
11:25 Are you better than Balak **s** of
11:34 her he had neither **s** nor daughter.
12:13 After him, Abdon **s** of Hillel, from
12:15 Abdon **s** of Hillel died, and was
13: 3 are going to conceive and have a **s**.
13: 5 will conceive and give birth to a **s**.
13: 7 will conceive and give birth to a **s**.
18:30 and Jonathan **s** of Gershom, the **s** of
20:28 with Phinehas **s** of Eleazar, the **s** of
Ru 4:13 conceive, and she gave birth to a **s**.
4:17 living there said, "Naomi has a **s**.
1Sa 1: 1 whose name was Elkanah **s** of Jeroham,
1: 1 the **s** of Elihu, the **s** of Tohu, the **s**
1:11 but give her a **s**, then I will give
1:20 conceived and gave birth to a **s**.
1:23 her **s** until she had weaned him.
4:20 you have given birth to a **s**.
7: 1 his **s** to guard the ark of the LORD.
9: 1 whose name was Kish **s** of Abiel, the **s**
9: 1 the **s** of Zeror, the **s** of Becorath,
9: 2 He had a **s** named Saul, an impressive
9: 3 and Kish said to his **s** Saul, "Take
10:11 that has happened to the **s** of Kish?
10:21 Finally Saul **s** of Kish was chosen.
13:16 Saul and his **s** Jonathan and the men
13:22 Saul and his **s** Jonathan had them.
14: 1 One day Jonathan **s** of Saul said to
14: 3 He was a **s** of Ichabod's brother
14: 3 brother Ahitub **s** of Phinehas,
14: 3 the **s** of Eli, the LORD's priest in
14:50 Abner **s** of Ner, and Ner was Saul's
16:18 "I have seen a **s** of Jesse of

1Sa 16:19 "Send me your s David, who is with
16:20 sent them with his s David to Saul.
17:12 Now David was the s of an Ephrathite
17:17 Now Jesse said to his s David, "Take
17:55 "Abner, whose s is that young man?"
17:56 The king said, "Find out whose s
17:58 "Whose s are you, young man?" Saul
17:58 "I am the s of your servant Jesse
19: 1 Saul told his s Jonathan and all the
20:27 Then Saul said to his s Jonathan,
20:27 "Why hasn't the s of Jesse come to
20:30 "You s of a perverse and rebellious
20:30 the s of Jesse to your own shame
20:31 long as the s of Jesse lives on this
22: 7 Will the s of Jesse give all of you
22: 8 a covenant with the s of Jesse.
22: 9 "I saw the s of Jesse come to
22: 9 to Ahimelech s of Ahitub at Nob.
22:11 the priest Ahimelech s of Ahitub
22:12 Saul said, "Listen now, s of Ahitub."
22:13 you and the s of Jesse, giving him
22:20 Abiathar, s of Ahimelech s of Ahitub,
23: 6 (Now Abiathar s of Ahimelech had
23:16 Saul's s Jonathan went to David at
25: 8 Please give your servants and your s
25:10 "Who is this David? Who is this s of
25:44 to Paltiel s of Laish, who was from
26: 5 He saw where Saul and Abner s of Ner,
26: 6 Hittite and Abishai s of Zeruiah,
26:14 to the army and to Abner s of Ner,
27: 2 to Achish s of Maoch king of Gath.
30: 7 Abiathar the priest, the s of
2Sa 1: 4 Saul and his s Jonathan are dead."
1: 5 Saul and his s Jonathan are dead?"
1:12 evening for Saul and his s Jonathan,
1:13 "I am the s of an alien, an
1:17 concerning Saul and his s Jonathan,
2: 8 Meanwhile, Abner s of Ner, the
2: 8 had taken Ish-Bosheth s of Saul and
2:10 Ish-Bosheth s of Saul was forty
2:12 Abner s of Ner, together with the
2:12 the men of Ish-Bosheth s of Saul,
2:13 Joab s of Zeruiah and David's men
2:15 and Ish-Bosheth s of Saul, and
3: 2 Amnon the s of Ahinoam of Jezreel;
3: 3 his second, Kileab the s of Abigail
3: 3 Absalom the s of Maacah daughter of
3: 4 fourth, Adonijah the s of Haggith;
3: 4 fifth, Shephatiah the s of Abital;
3: 5 the sixth, Ithream the s of David's
3:14 messengers to Ish-Bosheth s of Saul,
3:15 from her husband Paltiel s of Laish.
3:23 he was told that Abner s of Ner had
3:25 You know Abner s of Ner; he came to
3:28 the blood of Abner s of Ner.
3:37 in the murder of Abner s of Ner.
4: 1 Ish-Bosheth s of Saul heard that
4: 2 Now Saul's s had two men who were
4: 4 (Jonathan s of Saul had a s who was
4: 8 the head of Ish-Bosheth s of Saul,
8: 3 David fought Hadadezer s of Rehob,
8:10 he sent his s Joram to King David to
8:12 Hadadezer s of Rehob, king of Zobah.
8:16 Joab s of Zeruiah was over the army;
8:16 Jehoshaphat s of Ahilud was recorder;
8:17 Zadok s of Ahitub and Ahimelech s of
8:18 Benaiah s of Jehoiada was over the
9: 3 "There is still a s of Jonathan;
9: 4 of Makir s of Ammiel in Lo Debar."
9: 5 from the house of Makir s of Ammiel.
9: 6 Mephibosheth s of Jonathan, the s of
9:12 Mephibosheth had a young s named
10: 1 his s Hanun succeeded him as king.
10: 2 "I will show kindness to Hanun s of
11:21 killed Abimelech s of Jerub-Besheth
11:27 became his wife and bore him a s.
12:14 the s born to you will die."
12:24 She gave birth to a s, and they
13: 3 s of Shimeah, David's brother.
13: 4 "Why do you, the king's s, look so
13:25 "No, my s," the king replied.
13:32 Jonadab s of Shimeah, David's
13:37 Absalom fled and went to Talmai s of
13:37 David mourned for his s every day.
14: 1 Joab s of Zeruiah knew that the
14:13 has not brought back his banished s?
2Sa 14:16 s from the inheritance God gave us.'
15:27 s Ahimaaz and Jonathan s of Abiathar.
15:36 Their two sons, Ahimaaz s of Zadok
15:36 and Jonathan s of Abiathar, are
16: 5 His name was Shimei s of Gera, and
16: 8 the kingdom over to your s Absalom.
16: 9 Abishai s of Zeruiah said to the
16:19 Should I not serve the s? Just as I
17:25 Amasa was the s of a man named
17:27 David came to Mahanaim, Shobi s of
17:27 and Makir s of Ammiel from Lo Debar,
18: 2 Joab's brother Abishai s of Zeruiah,
18:12 lift my hand against the king's s.
18:18 s to carry on the memory of my name.
18:19 Now Ahimaaz s of Zadok said, "Let me
18:20 because the king's s is dead."
18:22 Ahimaaz s of Zadok again said to
18:27 one runs like Ahimaaz s of Zadok.
19: 2 "The king is grieving for his s.
19:16 Shimei s of Gera, the Benjamite from
19:18 When Shimei s of Gera crossed the
19:21 Abishai s of Zeruiah said,
20: 1 Now a troublemaker named Sheba s of
20: 1 in David, no part in Jesse's s!
20: 2 David to follow Sheba s of Bicri.
20: 6 "Now Sheba s of Bicri will do us
20: 7 Jerusalem to pursue Sheba s of Bicri.
20:10 Abishai pursued Sheba s of Bicri.
20:13 Joab to pursue Sheba s of Bicri.
20:21 A man named Sheba s of Bicri, from
20:22 off the head of Sheba s of Bicri
20:23 Benaiah s of Jehoiada was over the
20:24 Jehoshaphat s of Ahilud was recorder;
21: 7 The king spared Mephibosheth s of
21: 7 the s of Saul, because of the oath
21: 7 David and Jonathan s of Saul.
21: 8 s of Barzillai the Meholathite.
21:12 took the bones of Saul and his s
21:13 Saul and his s Jonathan from there,
21:14 his s Jonathan in the tomb of Saul's
21:17 Abishai s of Zeruiah came to David's
21:19 Elhanan s of Jaare-Oregim the
21:21 Jonathan s of Shimeah, David's
23: 1 "The oracle of David s of Jesse, the
23: 9 Next to him was Eleazar s of Dodai
23:11 Next to him was Shammah s of Agee
23:18 Abishai the brother of Joab s of
23:20 Benaiah s of Jehoiada was a valiant
23:22 exploits of Benaiah s of Jehoiada;
23:24 Elhanan s of Dodo from Bethlehem,
23:26 Helez the Paltite, Ira s of Ikkesh
23:29 Heled s of Baanah the Netophathite,
23:29 s of Ribai from Gibeah in Benjamin,
23:33 s of Shammah the Hararite,
23:33 Ahiam s of Sharar the Hararite,
23:34 Eliphelet s of Ahasbai the
23:34 Eliam s of Ahithophel the Gilonite,
23:36 Igal s of Nathan from Zobah, the s
23:37 armour-bearer of Joab s of Zeruiah,
1Ki 1: 7 Adonijah conferred with Joab s of
1: 8 the priest, Benaiah s of Jehoiada,
1:11 the s of Haggith, has become king
1:12 life and the life of your s Solomon.
1:13 "Surely Solomon your s shall be king
1:17 'solomon your s shall become king
1:26 the priest, and Benaiah s of Jehoiada
1:30 Solomon your s shall be king after
1:32 prophet and Benaiah s of Jehoiada.
1:36 Benaiah s of Jehoiada answered the
1:38 the prophet, Benaiah s of Jehoiada,
1:42 Jonathan s of Abiathar the priest
1:44 the prophet, Benaiah s of Jehoiada,
2: 1 he gave a charge to Solomon his s.
2: 5 what Joab s of Zeruiah did to me
2: 5 Abner s of Ner and Amasa s of Jether.
2: 8 you have with you Shimei s of Gera,
2:13 Now Adonijah, the s of Haggith, went
2:22 the priest and Joab s of Zeruiah!"
2:25 orders to Benaiah s of Jehoiada,
2:29 Then Solomon ordered Benaiah s of
2:32 Both of them—Abner s of Ner,
2:32 and Amasa s of Jether, commander of
2:34 Benaiah s of Jehoiada went up and
2:35 The king put Benaiah s of Jehoiada
2:39 ran off to Achish s of Maacah,
2:46 the order to Benaiah s of Jehoiada,
1Ki 3: 6 given him a s to sit on his throne
3:19 "During the night this woman's s
3:20 and put her dead s by my breast.
3:21 that it wasn't the s I had borne."
3:23 'My s is alive and your s is dead,'
3:23 Your s is dead and mine is alive.'"
3:26 The woman whose s was alive was
3:26 for her s and said to the king,
4: 2 Azariah s of Zadok—the priest;
4: 3 Jehoshaphat s of Ahilud—recorder;
4: 4 Benaiah s of Jehoiada—
4: 5 Azariah s of Nathan—in charge of
4: 5 Zabud s of Nathan—a priest and
4: 6 Adoniram s of Abda—in charge of
4:12 Baana s of Ahilud—in Taanach and
4:13 Jair s of Manasseh in Gilead were
4:14 Ahinadab s of Iddo—in Mahanaim;
4:16 Baana s of Hushai—in Asher and in
4:17 Jehoshaphat s of Paruah—in Issachar;
4:18 Shimei s of Ela—in Benjamin;
4:19 Geber s of Uri—in Gilead (the
5: 5 'Your s whom I will put on the
5: 7 s to rule over this great nation."
8:19 but your s, who is your own flesh
11:12 tear it out of the hand of your s.
11:20 The sister of Tahpenes bore him a s
11:23 Rezon s of Eliada, who had fled from
11:26 Also, Jeroboam s of Nebat rebelled
11:36 I will give one tribe to his s so
11:43 Rehoboam his s succeeded him as king.
12: 2 Jeroboam s of Nebat heard this (he
12:15 had spoken to Jeroboam s of Nebat
12:16 in David, what part in Jesse's s?
12:21 kingdom for Rehoboam s of Solomon.
12:23 "Say to Rehoboam s of Solomon king
13: 2 'A s named Josiah will be born to
14: 1 At that time Abijah s of Jeroboam
14: 5 is coming to ask you about her s,
14:20 Nadab his s succeeded him as king.
14:21 Rehoboam s of Solomon was king in
14:31 Abijah his s succeeded him as king.
15: 1 of the reign of Jeroboam s of Nebat,
15: 4 by raising up a s to succeed him
15: 8 And Asa his s succeeded him as king.
15:18 them to Ben-Hadad s of Tabrimmon,
15:18 the s of Hezion, the king of Aram,
15:24 his s succeeded him as king.
15:25 Nadab s of Jeroboam became king of
15:27 Baasha s of Ahijah of the house of
15:33 Baasha s of Ahijah became king of
16: 1 the LORD came to Jehu s of Hanani
16: 3 like that of Jeroboam s of Nebat.
16: 6 And Elah his s succeeded him as king.
16: 7 the prophet Jehu s of Hanani to
16: 8 Elah s of Baasha became king of
16:13 of all the sins Baasha and his s
16:21 Tibni s of Ginath for king,
16:22 than those of Tibni s of Ginath.
16:26 Jeroboam s of Nebat and in his sin,
16:28 And Ahab his s succeeded him as king.
16:29 Ahab s of Omri became king of Israel,
16:30 Ahab s of Omri did more evil in the
16:31 the sins of Jeroboam s of Nebat,
16:34 the cost of his firstborn s Abiram,
16:34 at the cost of his youngest s Segub,
16:34 the LORD spoken by Joshua s of Nun.
17:13 something for yourself and your s.
17:17 Some time later the s of the woman
17:19 "Give me your s," Elijah replied.
17:20 by causing her s to die?"
17:23 "Look, your s is alive!"
19:16 Also, anoint Jehu s of Nimshi king
19:16 and anoint Elisha s of Shaphat from
19:19 there and found Elisha s of Shaphat.
21:22 like that of Jeroboam s of Nebat
21:22 Nebat and that of Baasha s of Ahijah,
21:29 on his house in the days of his s."
22: 8 He is Micaiah s of Imlah."
22: 9 "Bring Micaiah s of Imlah at once."
22:11 Now Zedekiah s of Kenaanah had made
22:24 Zedekiah s of Kenaanah went up and
22:26 the city and to Joash the king's s
22:40 Ahaziah his s succeeded him as king.
22:41 Jehoshaphat s of Asa became king of
22:49 At that time Ahaziah s of Ahab said
22:50 And Jehoram his s succeeded him.

1Ki 22:51 Ahaziah s of Ahab became king of
22:52 in the ways of Jeroboam s of Nebat,
2Ki 1:17 Because Ahaziah had no s, Joram
1:17 s of Jehoshaphat king of Judah.
3: 1 Joram s of Ahab became king of
3: 3 to the sins of Jeroboam s of Nebat,
3:11 "Elisha s of Shaphat is here.
3:27 he took his firstborn s, who was to
4: 6 to her s, "Bring me another one."
4:14 has no s and her husband is old."
4:16 "you will hold a s in your arms.
4:17 she gave birth to a s, just as
4:28 "Did I ask you for a s, my lord?"
4:36 When she came, he said, "Take your s.
4:37 Then she took her s and went out.
6:28 'Give up your s so that we may eat
6:29 'Give up your s so that we may eat
6:31 if the head of Elisha s of Shaphat
8: 1 whose s he had restored to life,
8: 5 the woman whose s Elisha had brought
8: 5 her s whom Elisha restored to life."
8: 9 "Your s Ben-Hadad king of Aram has
8:16 In the fifth year of Joram s of Ahab
8:16 Jehoram s of Jehoshaphat began his
8:24 Ahaziah his s succeeded him as king.
8:25 In the twelfth year of Joram s of
8:25 Ahaziah s of Jehoram king of Judah
8:28 Ahaziah went with Joram s of Ahab to
8:29 Then Ahaziah s of Jehoram king of
8:29 to Jezreel to see Joram s of Ahab,
9: 2 s of Jehoshaphat, the s of Nimshi.
9: 9 the house of Jeroboam s of Nebat
9: 9 the house of Baasha s of Ahijah.
9:14 Jehu s of Jehoshaphat, the s of
9:20 is like that of Jehu s of Nimshi
9:29 (In the eleventh year of Joram s of
10:15 he came upon Jehonadab s of Recab,
10:23 Jehu and Jehonadab s of Recab went
10:29 the sins of Jeroboam s of Nebat,
10:35 Jehoahaz his s succeeded him as king.
11: 1 of Ahaziah saw that her s was dead,
11: 2 took Joash s of Ahaziah and stole
11: 4 Then he showed them the king's s.
11:12 Jehoiada brought out the king's s
12:21 him were Jozabad s of Shimeath
12:21 Shimeath and Jehozabad s of Shomer.
12:21 Amaziah his s succeeded him as king.
13: 1 Joash s of Ahaziah king of Judah,
13: 1 Jehoahaz s of Jehu became king of
13: 2 the sins of Jeroboam s of Nebat,
13: 3 king of Aram and Ben-Hadad his s.
13: 9 Jehoash his s succeeded him as king.
13:10 Jehoash s of Jehoahaz became king of
13:11 of the sins of Jeroboam s of Nebat,
13:24 his s succeeded him as king.
13:25 Jehoash s of Jehoahaz recaptured
13:25 from Ben-Hadad s of Hazael the
14: 1 In the second year of Jehoash s of
14: 1 Amaziah s of Joash king of Judah
14: 8 messengers to Jehoash s of Jehoahaz
14: 8 the s of Jehu, king of Israel, with
14:13 the s of Joash, the s of Ahaziah, at
14:16 Jeroboam his s succeeded him as king.
14:17 Amaziah s of Joash king of Judah
14:17 Jehoash s of Jehoahaz king of Israel.
14:23 Amaziah s of Joash king of Judah,
14:23 Jeroboam s of Jehoash king of Israel
14:24 of the sins of Jeroboam s of Nebat,
14:25 his servant Jonah s of Amittai,
14:27 the hand of Jeroboam s of Jehoash.
14:29 his s succeeded him as king.
15: 1 Azariah s of Amaziah king of Judah
15: 5 Jotham the king's s had charge of
15: 7 Jotham his s succeeded him as king.
15: 8 Zechariah s of Jeroboam became king
15: 9 the sins of Jeroboam s of Nebat,
15:10 Shallum s of Jabesh conspired
15:13 Shallum s of Jabesh became king in
15:14 Menahem s of Gadi went from Tirzah
15:14 He attacked Shallum s of Jabesh in
15:17 Menahem s of Gadi became king of
15:18 the sins of Jeroboam s of Nebat,
15:22 Pekahiah his s succeeded him as king.
15:23 Pekahiah s of Menahem became king of
15:24 the sins of Jeroboam s of Nebat,
15:25 chief officers, Pekah s of Remaliah
2Ki 15:27 Pekah s of Remaliah became king of
15:28 the sins of Jeroboam s of Nebat,
15:30 Hoshea s of Elah conspired against
15:30 against Pekah s of Remaliah.
15:30 year of Jotham s of Uzziah.
15:32 In the second year of Pekah s of
15:32 Jotham s of Uzziah king of Judah
15:37 Pekah s of Remaliah against Judah.)
15:38 And Ahaz his s succeeded him as king.
16: 1 the seventeenth year of Pekah s of
16: 1 Ahaz s of Jotham king of Judah began
16: 3 even sacrificed his s in the fire,
16: 5 Rezin king of Aram and Pekah s of
16:20 Hezekiah his s succeeded him as king.
17: 1 Hoshea s of Elah became king of
17:21 made Jeroboam s of Nebat their king.
18: 1 In the third year of Hoshea s of
18: 1 Hezekiah s of Ahaz king of Judah
18: 9 of Hoshea s of Elah king of Israel,
18:18 and Eliakim s of Hilkiah the palace
18:18 and Joah s of Asaph the recorder
18:26 Eliakim s of Hilkiah, and Shebna and
18:37 Eliakim s of Hilkiah the palace
18:37 and Joah s of Asaph the recorder
19: 2 to the prophet Isaiah s of Amoz.
19:20 Isaiah s of Amoz sent a message to
19:37 his s succeeded him as king.
20: 1 The prophet Isaiah s of Amoz went to
20:12 At that time Merodach-Baladan s of
20:21 Manasseh his s succeeded him as king.
21: 6 He sacrificed his own s in the fire,
21: 7 said to David and to his s Solomon,
21:18 And Amon his s succeeded him as king.
21:24 made Josiah his s king in his place.
21:26 Josiah his s succeeded him as king.
22: 3 Shaphan s of Azaliah, the s of
22:12 Ahikam s of Shaphan, Acbor s of
22:14 the wife of Shallum s of Tikvah,
22:14 s of Harhas, keeper of the wardrobe.
23:10 s or daughter in the fire to Molech.
23:15 the high place made by Jeroboam s of
23:30 the land took Jehoahaz s of Josiah
23:34 Pharaoh Neco made Eliakim s of
24: 6 his s succeeded him as king.
25:22 appointed Gedaliah s of Ahikam,
25:22 the s of Shaphan, to be over the
25:23 at Mizpah—Ishmael s of Nethaniah,
25:23 Johanan s of Kareah, Seraiah s of
25:23 s of the Maacathite, and their men.
25:25 Ishmael s of Nethaniah, the s of
1Ch 1:41 The s of Anah: Dishon. The sons of
1:43 king reigned: Bela s of Beor,
1:44 Bela died, Jobab s of Zerah from
1:46 Husham died, Hadad s of Bedad, who
1:49 Shaul died, Baal-Hanan s of Acbor
2: 7 The s of Carmi: Achar, who brought
2: 8 The s of Ethan: Azariah.
2:13 the second s was Abinadab,
2:18 Caleb s of Hezron had children by
2:31 The s of Appaim: Ishi, who was the
2:42 and his s Mareshah, who was the
2:45 The s of Shammai was Maon, and Maon
3: 1 Amnon the s of Ahinoam of Jezreel;
3: 1 Daniel the s of Abigail of Carmel;
3: 2 the third, Absalom the s of Maacah
3: 2 fourth, Adonijah the s of Haggith;
3: 3 fifth, Shephatiah the s of Abital;
3:10 Solomon's s was Rehoboam, Abijah his
3:10 his s, Asa his s, Jehoshaphat his s,
3:11 Jehoram his s, Ahaziah his s,
3:11 Joash his s,
3:12 Amaziah his s, Azariah his s,
3:12 Jotham his s,
3:13 Ahaz his s, Hezekiah his s,
3:13 Manasseh his s,
3:14 Amon his s, Josiah his s.
3:15 Jehoiakim the second s, Zedekiah the
3:16 Jehoiachin his s, and Zedekiah.
3:17 the captive: Shealtiel his s,
4: 2 Reaiah s of Shobal was the father of
4: 8 of the clans of Aharhel s of Harum.
4:15 The sons of Caleb s of Jephunneh:
4:15 The s of Elah: Kenaz.
4:21 The sons of Shelah s of Judah: Er
4:25 Shallum was Shaul's s, Mibsam his
4:25 Mibsam his s and Mishma his s.
1Ch 4:26 of Mishma: Hammuel his s,
4:26 Zaccur his s and Shimei his s.
4:34 Meshobab, Jamlech, Joshah s of
4:35 Joel, Jehu s of Joshibiah, the s of
4:35 the s of Seraiah, the s of Asiel,
4:37 Ziza s of Shiphi, the s of Allon,
4:37 the s of Allon, the s of Jedaiah,
4:37 the s of Shimri, the s of Shemaiah.
5: 1 to the sons of Joseph s of Israel;
5: 4 his s, Gog his s, Shimei his s,
5: 5 Micah his s, Reaiah his s, Baal his s
5: 6 Beerah his s, whom Tiglath-Pileser
5: 8 Bela s of Azaz, the s of Shema, the s
5:14 were the sons of Abihail s of Huri,
5:14 the s of Jaroah, the s of Gilead,
5:14 the s of Michael, the s of Jeshishai,
5:14 the s of Jahdo, the s of Buz.
5:15 Ahi s of Abdiel, the s of Guni, was
6:20 Of Gershon: Libni his s, Jehath his
6:20 Jehath his s, Zimmah his s,
6:21 Joah his s, Iddo his s, Zerah his
6:21 Zerah his s and Jeatherai his s.
6:22 Amminadab his s, Korah his s,
6:22 Assir his s,
6:23 Elkanah his s, Ebiasaph his s,
6:23 Assir his s,
6:24 Tahath his s, Uriel his s,
6:24 Uzziah his s and Shaul his s.
6:26 Elkanah his s, Zophai his s,
6:26 Nahath his s,
6:27 Eliab his s, Jeroham his s,
6:27 Elkanah his s and Samuel his s.
6:28 firstborn and Abijah the second s.
6:29 Mahli, Libni his s,
6:29 Shimei his s, Uzzah his s,
6:30 Shimea his s, Haggiah his s and
6:30 and Asaiah his s.
6:33 the s of Joel, the s of Samuel,
6:34 the s of Elkanah, the s of Jeroham,
6:34 the s of Eliel, the s of Toah,
6:35 the s of Zuph, the s of Elkanah,
6:35 the s of Mahath, the s of Amasai,
6:36 the s of Elkanah, the s of Joel,
6:36 the s of Azariah, the s of Zephaniah
6:37 the s of Tahath, the s of Assir,
6:37 the s of Ebiasaph, the s of Korah,
6:38 the s of Izhar, the s of Kohath,
6:38 the s of Levi, the s of Israel;
6:39 Asaph s of Berekiah, the s of Shimea,
6:40 the s of Michael, the s of Baaseiah,
6:40 s of Baaseiah, the s of Malkijah,
6:41 the s of Ethni, the s of Zerah, the s
6:42 the s of Ethan, the s of Zimmah, the
6:42 the s of Zimmah, the s of Shimei,
6:43 the s of Jahath, the s of Gershon,
6:43 the s of Gershon, the s of Levi;
6:44 at his left hand: Ethan s of Kishi,
6:44 the s of Abdi, the s of Malluch,
6:45 the s of Hashabiah, the s of Amaziah,
6:45 the s of Amaziah, the s of Hilkiah,
6:46 the s of Amzi, the s of Bani, the s
6:47 the s of Mahli, the s of Mushi, the s
6:47 the s of Merari, the s of Levi.
6:50 of Aaron: Eleazar his s,
6:50 Phinehas his s, Abishua his s,
6:51 Bukki his s, Uzzi his s,
6:51 Zerahiah his s,
6:52 Meraioth his s, Amariah his s,
6:52 Ahitub his s,
6:53 Zadok his s and Ahimaaz his s.
6:56 were given to Caleb s of Jephunneh.
7: 3 The s of Uzzi: Izrahiah.
7:10 The s of Jediael: Bilhan.
7:16 birth to a s and named him Peresh.
7:17 The s of Ulam: Bedan.
7:17 Gilead s of Makir, the s of
7:20 Bered his s, Tahath his s,
7:20 Eleadah his s, Tahath his s,
7:21 Zabad his s and Shuthelah his s.
7:23 pregnant and gave birth to a s.
7:25 Rephah was his s, Resheph his s,
7:25 Telah his s, Tahan his s,
7:26 Ladan his s, Ammihud his s,
7:26 Elishama his s,
7:27 Nun his s and Joshua his s.
7:29 descendants of Joseph s of Israel

1Ch 8: 1 Ashbel the second **s**, Aharah the
8:30 his firstborn **s** was Abdon, followed
8:34 The **s** of Jonathan: Merib-Baal, who
8:37 his **s**, Eleasah his **s** and Azel his **s**.
8:39 Jeush the second **s** and Eliphelet
9: 4 Uthai **s** of Ammihud, the **s** of Omri,
9: 4 the **s** of Imri, the **s** of Bani,
9: 7 Of the Benjamites: Sallu **s** of
9: 7 **s** of Hodaviah, the **s** of Hassenuah;
9: 8 Ibneiah **s** of Jeroham;
9: 8 Elah **s** of Uzzi, the **s** of Micri;
9: 8 and Meshullam **s** of Shephatiah,
9: 8 the **s** of Reuel, the **s** of Ibnijah.
9:11 Azariah **s** of Hilkiah, the **s** of
9:11 the **s** of Meshullam, the **s** of Zadok,
9:11 the **s** of Meraioth, the **s** of Ahitub,
9:12 Adaiah **s** of Jeroham, the **s** of
9:12 the **s** of Pashhur, the **s** of Malkijah;
9:12 and Maasai **s** of Adiel,
9:12 **s** of Jahzerah, the **s** of Meshullam,
9:12 **s** of Meshillemith, the **s** of Immer.
9:14 Of the Levites: Shemaiah **s** of Hasshub
9:14 the **s** of Azrikam, the **s** of Hashabiah,
9:15 Galal and Mattaniah **s** of Mica,
9:15 the **s** of Zicri, the **s** of Asaph;
9:16 Obadiah **s** of Shemaiah, the **s** of
9:16 the **s** of Galal, the **s** of Jeduthun;
9:16 and Berekiah **s** of Asa,
9:16 the **s** of Elkanah, who lived in the
9:19 Shallum **s** of Kore, the **s** of Ebiasaph,
9:19 the **s** of Korah, and his fellow
9:20 Phinehas **s** of Eleazar was in charge
9:21 Zechariah **s** of Meshelemiah was the
9:31 the firstborn **s** of Shallum the
9:36 his firstborn **s** was Abdon, followed
9:40 The **s** of Jonathan: Merib-Baal, who
9:43 his **s**, Eleasah his **s** and Azel his **s**.
10:14 kingdom over to David **s** of Jesse.
11: 6 Joab **s** of Zeruiah went up first,
11:12 Next to him was Eleazar **s** of Dodai
11:22 Benaiah **s** of Jehoiada was a valiant
11:24 exploits of Benaiah **s** of Jehoiada;
11:26 Elhanan **s** of Dodo from Bethlehem,
11:28 Ira **s** of Ikkesh from Tekoa, Abiezer
11:30 Heled **s** of Baanah the Netophathite,
11:31 Ithai **s** of Ribai from Gibeah in
11:34 Jonathan **s** of Shagee the Hararite,
11:35 Ahiam **s** of Sacar the Hararite,
11:35 Sacar the Hararite, Eliphal **s** of Ur,
11:37 the Carmelite, Naarai **s** of Ezbai,
11:38 brother of Nathan, Mibhar **s** of Hagri
11:39 armour-bearer of Joab **s** of Zeruiah,
11:41 Uriah the Hittite, Zabad **s** of Ahlai,
11:42 Adina **s** of Shiza the Reubenite, who
11:43 Hanan **s** of Maacah, Joshaphat the
11:45 Jediael **s** of Shimri, his brother
12: 1 from the presence of Saul **s** of Kish
12:18 We are with you, O **s** of Jesse!
15:17 Levites appointed Heman **s** of Joel;
15:17 his brothers, Asaph **s** of Berekiah;
15:17 the Merarites, Ethan **s** of Kushaiah;
16:38 Obed-Edom **s** of Jeduthun, and also
18:10 he sent his **s** Hadoram to King David
18:12 Abishai **s** of Zeruiah struck down
18:15 Joab **s** of Zeruiah was over the army;
18:15 Jehoshaphat **s** of Ahilud was recorder;
18:16 Zadok **s** of Ahitub and Ahimelech **s** of
18:17 Benaiah **s** of Jehoiada was over the
19: 1 and his **s** succeeded him as king.
19: 2 "I will show kindness to Hanun **s** of
20: 5 Elhanan **s** of Jair killed Lahmi the
20: 7 Jonathan **s** of Shimea, David's
22: 6 he called for his **s** Solomon and
22: 9 you will have a **s** who will be a man
22:17 of Israel to help his **s** Solomon.
23: 1 made his **s** Solomon king over Israel.
24: 6 The scribe Shemaiah **s** of Nethanel, a
24: 6 Ahimelech **s** of Abiathar and the
24:24 The **s** of Uzziel: Micah; from the
24:26 The **s** of Jaaziah: Beno.
24:29 From Kish: the **s** of Kish: Jerahmeel.
26: 1 Meshelemiah **s** of Kore, one of the
26: 6 His **s** Shemaiah also had sons, who
26:14 Then lots were cast for his **s**
26:24 a descendant of Gershom **s** of Moses,
26:25 through Eliezer: Rehabiah his **s**,

1Ch 26:25 Jeshaiah his **s**, Joram his **s**, Zicri
26:25 Zicri his **s** and Shelomith his **s**.
26:28 the seer and by Saul **s** of Kish,
26:28 Abner **s** of Ner and Joab **s** of Zeruiah,
27: 2 month, was Jashobeam **s** of Zabdiel.
27: 5 Benaiah **s** of Jehoiada the priest.
27: 6 His **s** Ammizabad was in charge of his
27: 7 his **s** Zebadiah was his successor.
27: 9 was Ira the **s** of Ikkesh the Tekoite.
27:16 the Reubenites: Eliezer **s** of Zicri;
27:16 Simeonites: Shephatiah **s** of Maacah;
27:17 over Levi: Hashabiah **s** of Kemuel;
27:18 over Issachar: Omri **s** of Michael;
27:19 over Zebulun: Ishmaiah **s** of Obadiah;
27:19 over Naphtali: Jerimoth **s** of Azriel;
27:20 Ephraimites: Hoshea **s** of Azaziah;
27:20 of Manasseh: Joel **s** of Pedaiah;
27:21 in Gilead: Iddo **s** of Zechariah;
27:21 over Benjamin: Jaasiel **s** of Abner;
27:22 over Dan: Azarel **s** of Jeroham.
27:24 Joab **s** of Zeruiah began to count the
27:25 Azmaveth **s** of Adiel was in charge of
27:25 Jonathan **s** of Uzziah was in charge
27:26 Ezri **s** of Kelub was in charge of the
27:29 Shaphat **s** of Adlai was in charge of
27:32 Jehiel **s** of Hacmoni took care of the
27:34 succeeded by Jehoiada **s** of Benaiah
28: 6 He said to me, 'Solomon your **s** is
28:11 David gave his **s** Solomon the plans
28:20 David also said to Solomon his **s**,
29:26 David **s** of Jesse was king over all
29:28 His **s** Solomon succeeded him as king.
2Ch 1: 5 bronze altar that Bezalel **s** of Uri
1: 5 the **s** of Hur, had made was in Gibeon
2:12 He has given King David a wise **s**,
6: 9 but your **s**, who is your own flesh
9:29 seer concerning Jeroboam **s** of Nebat?
9:31 Rehoboam his **s** succeeded him as king.
10: 2 Jeroboam **s** of Nebat heard this (he
10:15 had spoken to Jeroboam **s** of Nebat
10:16 in David, what part in Jesse's **s**?
11: 3 "Say to Rehoboam **s** of Solomon king
11:17 **s** of Solomon for three years,
11:18 who was the daughter of David's **s**
11:18 the daughter of Jesse's **s** Eliab.
11:22 Rehoboam appointed Abijah **s** of
12:16 Abijah his **s** succeeded him as king.
13: 6 Yet Jeroboam **s** of Nebat, an official
13: 7 opposed Rehoboam **s** of Solomon when
14: 1 Asa his **s** succeeded him as king, and
15: 1 of God came upon Azariah **s** of Oded.
15: 8 of Azariah **s** of Oded the prophet,
17: 1 Jehoshaphat his **s** succeeded him as
17:16 next, Amasiah **s** of Zicri, who
18: 7 He is Micaiah **s** of Imlah."
18: 8 "Bring Micaiah **s** of Imlah at once.
18:10 Now Zedekiah **s** of Kenaanah had made
18:23 Zedekiah **s** of Kenaanah went up and
18:25 the city and to Joash the king's **s**,
19: 2 Jehu the seer, the **s** of Hanani, went
19:11 and Zebadiah **s** of Ishmael, the
20:14 came upon Jahaziel **s** of Zechariah,
20:14 the **s** of Benaiah, the **s** of Jeiel,
20:14 the **s** of Jeiel, the **s** of Mattaniah,
20:34 in the annals of Jehu **s** of Hanani,
20:37 Eliezer **s** of Dodavahu of Mareshah
21: 1 Jehoram his **s** succeeded him as king.
21: 3 because he was his firstborn **s**.
21:17 Not a **s** was left to him except
22: 1 Jehoram's youngest **s**, king in his
22: 1 Ahaziah, Jehoram's youngest **s**,
22: 5 went with Joram **s** of Ahab king of
22: 6 Then Ahaziah **s** of Jehoram king of
22: 6 to see Joram **s** of Ahab because he
22: 7 with Joram to meet Jehu **s** of Nimshi,
22: 9 "He was a **s** of Jehoshaphat, who
22:10 of Ahaziah saw that her **s** was dead,
22:11 took Joash **s** of Ahaziah and stole
23: 1 of a hundred: Azariah **s** of Jeroham,
23: 1 Ishmael **s** of Jehohanan, Azariah **s** of
23: 1 **s** of Obed, Maaseiah **s** of Adaiah,
23: 1 and Elishaphat **s** of Zicri.
23: 3 "The king's **s** shall reign, as the
23:11 brought out the king's **s** and put
24:20 Zechariah **s** of Jehoiada the priest.
24:22 had shown him but killed his **s**,

2Ch 24:25 the **s** of Jehoiada the priest,
24:26 **s** of Shimeath an Ammonite woman, and
24:26 **s** of Shimrith a Moabite woman.
24:27 Amaziah his **s** succeeded him as king.
25:17 challenge to Jehoash **s** of Jehoahaz,
25:17 the **s** of Jehu, king of Israel: "Come,
25:23 the **s** of Joash, the **s** of Ahaziah, at
25:25 Amaziah **s** of Joash king of Judah
25:25 Jehoash **s** of Jehoahaz king of Israel.
26:21 Jotham his **s** had charge of the
26:22 by the prophet Isaiah **s** of Amoz.
26:23 Jotham his **s** succeeded him as king.
27: 9 And Ahaz his **s** succeeded him as king.
28: 6 In one day Pekah **s** of Remaliah
28: 7 killed Maaseiah the king's **s**,
28:12 in Ephraim—Azariah **s** of Jehohanan,
28:12 Berekiah **s** of Meshillemoth,
28:12 Jehizkiah **s** of Shallum, and
28:12 and Amasa **s** of Hadlai—confronted
28:27 Hezekiah his **s** succeeded him as king.
29:12 Mahath **s** of Amasai and Joel **s** of
29:12 Kish **s** of Abdi and Azariah **s** of
29:12 Joah **s** of Zimmah and Eden **s** of Joah;
31:14 Kore **s** of Imnah the Levite, keeper
32:20 the prophet Isaiah **s** of Amoz cried
32:32 the prophet Isaiah **s** of Amoz in the
32:33 Manasseh his **s** succeeded him as king.
33: 7 said to David and to his **s** Solomon,
33:20 And Amon his **s** succeeded him as king.
33:25 made Josiah his **s** king in his place.
34: 8 he sent Shaphan **s** of Azaliah and
34: 8 with Joah **s** of Joahaz, the recorder,
34:20 Ahikam **s** of Shaphan, Abdon **s** of
34:22 wife of Shallum **s** of Tokhath,
34:22 **s** of Hasrah, keeper of the wardrobe.
35: 4 king of Israel and by his **s** Solomon.
36: 1 the land took Jehoahaz **s** of Josiah
36: 8 his **s** succeeded him as king.
Ezr 3: 2 Jeshua **s** of Jozadak and his fellow
3: 2 and Zerubbabel **s** of Shealtiel
3: 8 Zerubbabel **s** of Shealtiel, Jeshua **s**
5: 2 Zerubbabel **s** of Shealtiel and Jeshua
5: 2 Jeshua **s** of Jozadak set to work to
7: 1 Ezra **s** of Seraiah, the **s** of Azariah,
7: 1 the **s** of Azariah, the **s** of Hilkiah,
7: 2 the **s** of Shallum, the **s** of Zadok,
7: 2 the **s** of Zadok, the **s** of Ahitub,
7: 3 the **s** of Amariah, the **s** of Azariah,
7: 3 the **s** of Azariah, the **s** of Meraioth,
7: 4 the **s** of Zerahiah, the **s** of Uzzi,
7: 4 the **s** of Uzzi, the **s** of Bukki,
7: 5 the **s** of Abishua, the **s** of Phinehas,
7: 5 the **s** of Eleazar, the **s** of Aaron
8: 4 Eliehoenai **s** of Zerahiah, and with
8: 5 Shecaniah **s** of Jahaziel, and with
8: 6 of Adin, Ebed **s** of Jonathan,
8: 7 Jeshaiah **s** of Athaliah, and with
8: 8 Zebadiah **s** of Michael, and with
8: 9 of Joab, Obadiah **s** of Jehiel, and
8:10 Shelomith **s** of Josiphiah, and with
8:11 Zechariah **s** of Bebai, and with
8:12 Johanan **s** of Hakkatan, and with
8:18 Mahli **s** of Levi, the **s** of Israel,
8:33 of Meremoth **s** of Uriah, the priest.
8:33 Eleazar **s** of Phinehas was with him,
8:33 **s** of Jeshua and Noadiah **s** of Binnui.
10: 2 Shecaniah **s** of Jehiel, one of the
10: 6 the room of Jehohanan **s** of Eliashib.
10:15 Only Jonathan **s** of Asahel and
10:15 and Jahzeiah **s** of Tikvah, supported
10:18 descendants of Jeshua **s** of Jozadak,
Ne 1: 1 The words of Nehemiah **s** of Hacaliah:
3: 2 Zaccur **s** of Imri built next to them.
3: 4 Meremoth **s** of Uriah, the **s** of Hakkoz,
3: 4 Next to him Meshullam **s** of Berekiah,
3: 4 the **s** of Meshezabel, made repairs,
3: 4 Zadok **s** of Baana also made repairs.
3: 6 was repaired by Joiada **s** of Paseah
3: 6 Paseah and Meshullam **s** of Besodeiah.
3: 8 Uzziel **s** of Harhaiah, one of the
3: 9 Rephaiah **s** of Hur, ruler of a
3:10 Jedaiah **s** of Harumaph made repairs
3:10 and Hattush **s** of Hashabneiah made
3:11 Malkijah **s** of Harim and Hasshub **s** of
3:12 Shallum **s** of Hallohesh, ruler of a
3:14 was repaired by Malkijah **s** of Recab,

Ne 3:15 repaired by Shallun s of Col-Hozeh,
3:16 Beyond him, Nehemiah s of Azbuk,
3:17 the Levites under Rehum s of Bani.
3:18 under Binnui s of Henadad,
3:19 Next to him, Ezer s of Jeshua, ruler
3:20 Next to him, Baruch s of Zabbai
3:21 Meremoth s of Uriah, the s of Hakkoz,
3:23 Azariah s of Maaseiah, the s of
3:24 Next to him, Binnui s of Henadad
3:25 Palal s of Uzai worked opposite the
3:25 Next to him, Pedaiah s of Parosh
3:29 Next to them, Zadok s of Immer made
3:29 Next to him, Shemaiah s of Shecaniah,
3:30 Next to him, Hananiah s of Shelemiah,
3:30 and Hanun, the sixth s of Zalaph,
3:30 Meshullam s of Berekiah made
6:10 the house of Shemaiah s of Delaiah,
6:10 the s of Mehetabel, who was shut in
6:18 son-in-law to Shecaniah s of Arah,
6:18 and his s Jehohanan had married the
6:18 daughter of Meshullam s of Berekiah.
8:17 From the days of Joshua s of Nun
10: 1 the governor, the s of Hacaliah.
10: 9 The Levites: Jeshua s of Azaniah,
11: 4 of Judah: Athaiah s of Uzziah,
11: 4 the s of Zechariah, the s of Amariah,
11: 4 the s of Shephatiah, the s of
11: 5 Maaseiah s of Baruch, the s of
11: 5 the s of Col-Hozeh, the s of Hazaiah,
11: 5 the s of Adaiah, the s of Joiarib,
11: 5 the s of Zechariah, a descendant of
11: 7 of Benjamin: Sallu s of Meshullam,
11: 7 the s of Joed, the s of Pedaiah, the
11: 7 the s of Kolaiah, the s of Maaseiah
11: 7 the s of Ithiel, the s of Jeshaiah,
11: 9 Joel s of Zicri was their chief
11: 9 and Judah s of Hassenuah was over
11:10 priests: Jedaiah; the s of Joiarib;
11:11 Seraiah s of Hilkiah, the s of
11:11 the s of Meshullam, the s of Zadok,
11:11 the s of Meraioth, the s of Ahitub,
11:12 Adaiah s of Jeroham,
11:12 the s of Pelaliah, the s of Amzi,
11:12 the s of Amzi, the s of Zechariah,
11:12 the s of Pashhur, the s of Malkijah,
11:13 Amashsai s of Azarel,
11:13 the s of Ahzai, the s of
11:13 s of Meshillemoth, the s of Immer,
11:14 officer was Zabdiel s of Haggedolim.
11:15 the Levites: Shemaiah s of Hasshub,
11:15 the s of Azrikam, the s of Hashabiah,
11:15 the s of Hashabiah, the s of Bunni;
11:17 Mattaniah s of Mica, the s of Zabdi,
11:17 the s of Asaph, the director who
11:17 and Abda s of Shammua,
11:17 the s of Galal, the s of Jeduthun.
11:22 in Jerusalem was Uzzi s of Bani,
11:22 the s of Hashabiah, the s of
11:22 the s of Mattaniah, the s of Mica.
11:24 Pethahiah s of Meshezabel, one of
11:24 descendants of Zerah s of Judah,
12: 1 Zerubbabel s of Shealtiel and with
12:23 the time of Johanan s of Eliashib
12:24 Sherebiah, Jeshua s of Kadmiel, and
12:26 in the days of Joiakim s of Jeshua,
12:26 the s of Jozadak, and in the days of
12:35 and also Zechariah s of Jonathan,
12:35 the s of Shemaiah, the s of
12:35 the s of Mattaniah, the s of Micaiah,
12:35 the s of Zaccur, the s of Asaph,
12:45 commands of David and his s Solomon.
13:13 and made Hanan s of Zaccur,
13:13 the s of Mattaniah, their assistant,
13:28 One of the sons of Joiada s of
Est 2: 5 named Mordecai s of Jair, the s of
2: 5 the s of Shimei, the s of Kish,
3: 1 King Xerxes honoured Haman s of
3:10 gave it to Haman s of Hammedatha,
8: 5 that Haman s of Hammedatha,
9:10 ten sons of Haman s of Hammedatha,
9:24 For Haman s of Hammedatha, the
Job 32: 2 Elihu s of Barakel the Buzite, of
32: 6 Elihu s of Barakel the Buzite said:
Ps 2:12 Kiss the **S**, lest he be angry and you
3: T When he fled from his s Absalom.
9: T ⌊the tune of⌋ "The Death of the **S**".
Ps 50:20 and slander your own mother's s.
72: 1 the royal s with your righteousness.
72:20 the prayers of David s of Jesse.
80:15 s you have raised up for yourself.
86:16 and save the s of your maidservant.
116:16 servant, the s of your maidservant;
Pr 3:12 as a father the s he delights in.
10: 1 A wise s brings joy to his father,
10: 1 but a foolish s grief to his mother.
10: 5 gathers crops in summer is a wise s,
10: 5 during harvest is a disgraceful s.
13: 1 A wise s heeds his father's
13:24 He who spares the rod hates his s,
15:20 A wise s brings joy to his father,
17: 2 will rule over a disgraceful s,
17:21 To have a fool for a s brings grief;
17:25 A foolish s brings grief to his
19:13 A foolish s is his father's ruin,
19:18 Discipline your s, for in that there
19:26 a s who brings shame and disgrace.
23:24 he who has a wise s delights in him.
28: 7 who keeps the law is a discerning s,
29:17 Discipline your s, and he will give
30: 1 The sayings of Agur s of Jakeh—an
30: 4 is his name, and the name of his s?
31: 2 O s of my womb, O s of my vows,
Ecc 4: 8 alone; he had neither s nor brother.
5:14 a s there is nothing left for him.
Isa 1: 1 Jerusalem that Isaiah s of Amoz saw
2: 1 This is what Isaiah s of Amoz saw
7: 1 Ahaz s of Jotham, the s of Uzziah,
7: 1 Pekah s of Remaliah king of Israel
7: 3 "Go out, you and your s Shear-Jashub,
7: 4 and Aram and of the s of Remaliah.
7: 5 Aram, Ephraim and Remaliah's s have
7: 6 make the s of Tabeel king over it."
7: 9 of Samaria is only Remaliah's s.
7:14 will give birth to a s, and will
8: 2 Zechariah s of Jeberekiah as
8: 3 she conceived and gave birth to a s.
8: 6 over Rezin and the s of Remaliah,
9: 6 child is born, to us a s is given,
13: 1 Babylon that Isaiah s of Amoz saw:
14:12 O morning star, s of the dawn!
20: 2 LORD spoke through Isaiah s of Amoz.
22:20 my servant, Eliakim s of Hilkiah.
36: 3 Eliakim s of Hilkiah the palace
36: 3 Shebna the secretary, and Joah s of
36:22 Eliakim s of Hilkiah the palace
36:22 Shebna the secretary, and Joah s of
37: 2 to the prophet Isaiah s of Amoz.
37:21 Isaiah s of Amoz sent a message to
37:38 his s succeeded him as king.
38: 1 The prophet Isaiah s of Amoz went to
39: 1 Merodach-Baladan s of Baladan king
66: 7 come upon her, she delivers a s.
Jer 1: 1 The words of Jeremiah s of Hilkiah,
1: 2 of Josiah s of Amon king of Judah,
1: 3 the reign of Jehoiakim s of Josiah
1: 3 Zedekiah s of Josiah king of Judah,
6:26 bitter wailing as for an only s,
15: 4 Manasseh s of Hezekiah king of
20: 1 the priest Pashhur s of Immer, the
20:15 "A child is born to you—a s!
21: 1 sent to him Pashhur s of Malkijah
21: 1 the priest Zephaniah s of Maaseiah.
22:11 LORD says about Shallum s of Josiah,
22:18 Jehoiakim s of Josiah king of Judah:
22:24 "even if you, Jehoiachin s of
24: 1 After Jehoiachin s of Jehoiakim king
25: 1 Jehoiakim s of Josiah king of Judah,
25: 3 thirteenth year of Josiah s of Amon
26: 1 Early in the reign of Jehoiakim s of
26:20 (Now Uriah s of Shemaiah from
26:22 however, sent Elnathan s of Acbor to
26:24 Furthermore, Ahikam s of Shaphan
27: 1 Early in the reign of Zedekiah s of
27: 7 All nations will serve him and his s
27:20 carried Jehoiachin s of Jehoiakim
28: 1 the prophet Hananiah s of Azzur, who
28: 4 s of Jehoiakim king of Judah
29: 3 the letter to Elasah s of Shaphan
29: 3 Shaphan and to Gemariah s of Hilkiah,
29:21 says about Ahab s of Kolaiah and
29:21 Kolaiah and Zedekiah s of Maaseiah,
29:25 to Zephaniah s of Maaseiah the
Jer 31: 9 and Ephraim is my firstborn s.
31:20 Is not Ephraim my dear s, the child
32: 7 Hanamel s of Shallum your uncle is
32:12 I gave this deed to Baruch s of
32:12 the s of Mahseiah, in the presence
32:16 of purchase to Baruch s of Neriah,
35: 1 Jehoiakim s of Josiah king of Judah:
35: 3 I went to get Jaazaniah s of
35: 3 the s of Habazziniah, and his
35: 4 Hanan s of Igdaliah the man of God.
35: 4 s of Shallum the door-keeper.
35: 6 because our forefather Jonadab s of
35: 8 Jonadab s of Recab commanded us.
35:14 'Jonadab s of Recab ordered his sons
35:16 The descendants of Jonadab s of
35:19 'Jonadab s of Recab shall never fail
36: 1 In the fourth year of Jehoiakim s of
36: 4 Jeremiah called Baruch s of Neriah,
36: 8 Baruch s of Neriah did everything
36: 9 Jehoiakim s of Josiah king of Judah,
36:10 From the room of Gemariah s of
36:11 Micaiah s of Gemariah, the s of
36:12 Delaiah s of Shemaiah, Elnathan s of
36:12 Gemariah s of Shaphan, Zedekiah s of
36:14 all the officials sent Jehudi s of
36:14 the s of Shelemiah, the s of Cushi,
36:14 So Baruch s of Neriah went to them
36:26 a s of the king, Seraiah s of Azriel
36:26 and Shelemiah s of Abdeel to arrest
36:32 it to the scribe Baruch s of Neriah,
37: 1 Zedekiah s of Josiah was made king
37: 1 place of Jehoiachin s of Jehoiakim.
37: 3 however, sent Jehucal s of Shelemiah
37: 3 the priest Zephaniah s of Maaseiah
37:13 whose name was Irijah s of Shelemiah,
37:13 the s of Hananiah, arrested him and
38: 1 Shephatiah s of Mattan, Gedaliah s
38: 1 Gedaliah s of Pashhur, Jehucal s of
38: 1 and Pashhur s of Malkijah heard
38: 6 the king's s, which was in the
39:14 him over to Gedaliah s of Ahikam
39:14 the s of Shaphan, to take him back
40: 5 "Go back to Gedaliah s of Ahikam,
40: 5 the s of Shaphan, whom the king of
40: 6 Jeremiah went to Gedaliah s of
40: 7 had appointed Gedaliah s of Ahikam
40: 8 at Mizpah—Ishmael s of Nethaniah,
40: 8 Seraiah s of Tanhumeth, the sons of
40: 8 Jaazaniah the s of the Maacathite
40: 9 Gedaliah s of Ahikam, the s of
40:11 had appointed Gedaliah s of Ahikam,
40:11 s of Shaphan, as governor over them,
40:13 Johanan s of Kareah and all the army
40:14 s of Nethaniah to take your life?"
40:14 s of Ahikam did not believe them.
40:15 Johanan s of Kareah said privately
40:15 "Let me go and kill Ishmael s of
40:16 Gedaliah s of Ahikam said to Johanan
40:16 Ahikam said to Johanan s of Kareah,
41: 1 In the seventh month Ishmael s of
41: 1 the s of Elishama, who was of royal
41: 1 to Gedaliah s of Ahikam at Mizpah.
41: 2 Ishmael s of Nethaniah and the ten
41: 2 struck down Gedaliah s of Ahikam,
41: 2 the s of Shaphan, with the sword,
41: 6 Ishmael s of Nethaniah went out from
41: 6 said, "Come to Gedaliah s of Ahikam.
41: 7 Ishmael s of Nethaniah and the men
41: 9 Ishmael s of Nethaniah filled it
41:10 had appointed Gedaliah s of Ahikam.
41:10 Ishmael s of Nethaniah took them
41:11 Johanan s of Kareah and all the army
41:11 Ishmael s of Nethaniah had committed,
41:12 to fight Ishmael s of Nethaniah.
41:13 with him saw Johanan s of Kareah
41:14 went over to Johanan s of Kareah.
41:15 Ishmael s of Nethaniah and eight of
41:16 Johanan s of Kareah and all the army
41:16 from Ishmael s of Nethaniah after
41:16 assassinated Gedaliah s of Ahikam:
41:18 because Ishmael s of Nethaniah had
41:18 had killed Gedaliah s of Ahikam,
42: 1 including Johanan s of Kareah and
42: 1 Kareah and Jezaniah s of Hoshaiah,
42: 8 he called together Johanan s of
43: 2 Azariah s of Hoshaiah and Johanan s

Jer 43: 3 Baruch s of Neriah is inciting you
43: 4 Johanan s of Kareah and all the army
43: 5 Instead, Johanan s of Kareah and all
43: 6 had left with Gedaliah s of Ahikam,
43: 6 the s of Shaphan, and Jeremiah the
43: 6 the prophet and Baruch s of Neriah.
45: 1 the prophet told Baruch s of Neriah
45: 1 Jehoiakim s of Josiah king of Judah,
46: 2 Jehoiakim s of Josiah king of Judah:
51:59 staff officer Seraiah s of Neriah,
51:59 the s of Mahseiah, when he went to
Eze 1: 3 Ezekiel the priest, the s of Buzi,
8:11 s of Shaphan was standing among them.
11: 1 saw among them Jaazaniah s of Azzur
11: 1 Pelatiah s of Benaiah, leaders of
11:13 Pelatiah s of Benaiah died.
14:20 could save neither s nor daughter.
18: 4 the father as well as the s—both
18:10 "Suppose he has a violent s, who
18:14 "But suppose this s has a s who sees
18:19 "Yet you ask, 'Why does the s not
18:19 Since the s has done what is just
18:20 The s will not share the guilt of
18:20 the father share the guilt of the s.
44:25 s or daughter, brother or unmarried
Da 3:25 fourth looks like a s of the gods."
5:22 "But you his s, O Belshazzar, have
9: 1 first year of Darius s of Xerxes
Hos 1: 1 LORD that came to Hosea s of Beeri
1: 1 Jeroboam s of Joash king of Israel:
1: 3 and she conceived and bore him a s.
1: 8 Lo-Ruhamah, Gomer had another s.
Joel 1: 1 LORD that came to Joel s of Pethuel.
Am 1: 1 s of Jehoash was king of Israel.
2: 7 Father and s use the same girl and
7:14 neither a prophet nor a prophet's s,
8:10 time like mourning for an only s
Jnh 1: 1 LORD came to Jonah s of Amittai:
Mic 6: 5 and what Balaam s of Beor answered.
7: 6 For a s dishonours his father, a
Zep 1: 1 that came to Zephaniah s of Cushi,
1: 1 the s of Gedaliah, the s of Amariah,
1: 1 the s of Amariah, the s of Hezekiah,
Hag 1: 1 Haggai to Zerubbabel s of Shealtiel,
1: 1 s of Jehozadak, the high priest:
1:12 Zerubbabel s of Shealtiel, Joshua s
1:14 spirit of Zerubbabel s of Shealtiel,
1:14 spirit of Joshua s of Jehozadak,
2: 2 "Speak to Zerubbabel s of Shealtiel,
2: 2 governor of Judah, to Joshua s of
2: 4 'Be strong, O Joshua s of Jehozadak,
2:23 servant Zerubbabel s of Shealtiel,'
Zec 1: 1 s of Berekiah, the s of Iddo:
1: 7 s of Berekiah, the s of Iddo.
6:10 house of Josiah s of Zephaniah.
6:11 high priest, Joshua s of Jehozadak.
6:14 Tobijah, Jedaiah and Hen s of
12:10 as one grieves for a firstborn s.
Mal 1: 6 "A s honours his father, and a
3:17 a man spares his s who serves him.
Mt 1: 1 the s of David, the s of Abraham:
1:21 She will give birth to a s, and you
1:23 child and will give birth to a s,
1:25 her until she gave birth to a s.
4:21 s of Zebedee and his brother John.
7: 9 "Which of you, if his s asks for
9: 2 "Take heart, s; your sins are
10: 2 s of Zebedee, and his brother John;
10: 3 James s of Alphaeus, and Thaddaeus;
10:37 anyone who loves his s or daughter
11:27 No-one knows the S except the Father,
11:27 no-one knows the Father except the S
11:27 to whom the S chooses to reveal him.
13:55 "Isn't this the carpenter's s?
16:16 Christ, the S of the living God."
16:17 "Blessed are you, Simon s of Jonah,
21:28 'S, go and work today in the
21:30 "Then the father went to the other s
21:37 Last of all, he sent his s to them.
21:38 "But when the tenants saw the s,
22: 2 a wedding banquet for his s.
22:42 about the Christ? Whose s is he?"
22:45 him 'Lord', how can he be his s?"
23:15 as much a s of hell as you are.
23:35 blood of Zechariah s of Barakiah,
24:36 nor the S, but only the Father.

Mt 28:19 and of the S and of the Holy Spirit,
Mk 1:19 he saw James s of Zebedee and his
2: 5 "S, your sins are forgiven."
2:14 he saw Levi s of Alphaeus sitting
3:17 James s of Zebedee and his brother
3:18 Matthew, Thomas, James s of Alphaeus,
5: 7 Jesus, S of the Most High God?
6: 3 Mary's s and the brother of James,
10:46 (that is, the S of Timaeus),
12: 6 "He had one left to send, a s, whom
12:37 How then can he be his s?" The large
13:32 nor the S, but only the Father.
14:61 Christ, the S of the Blessed One?"
Lk 1:13 wife Elizabeth will bear you a s,
1:31 be with child and give birth to a s,
1:32 be called the S of the Most High.
1:57 her baby, she gave birth to a s.
2: 7 she gave birth to her firstborn, a s.
2:48 "S, why have you treated us like
3: 2 John s of Zechariah in the desert.
3:23 He was the s, so it was thought, of
3:23 thought, of Joseph, the s of Heli,
3:24 the s of Matthat, the s of Levi, the
3:24 the s of Levi, the s of Melki, the s
3:25 the s of Mattathias, the s of Amos,
3:25 the s of Nahum, the s of Esli,
3:25 the s of Naggai
3:26 the s of Maath, the s of Mattathias,
3:26 the s of Mattathias, the s of Semein,
3:26 the s of Josech, the s of Joda,
3:27 the s of Joanan, the s of Rhesa, the
3:27 the s of Rhesa, the s of Zerubbabel,
3:27 the s of Shealtiel, the s of Neri,
3:28 the s of Melki, the s of Addi, the s
3:28 Cosam, the s of Elmadam, the s of Er,
3:29 the s of Joshua, the s of Eliezer,
3:29 the s of Eliezer, the s of Jorim,
3:29 the s of Matthat, the s of Levi,
3:30 the s of Simeon, the s of Judah, the
3:30 the s of Judah, the s of Joseph, the
3:30 the s of Jonam, the s of Eliakim,
3:31 the s of Melea, the s of Menna, the s
3:31 the s of Nathan, the s of David,
3:32 the s of Jesse, the s of Obed, the s
3:32 the s of Salmon, the s of Nahshon,
3:33 the s of Amminadab, the s of Ram,
3:33 the s of Ram, the s of Hezron,
3:33 the s of Perez, the s of Judah,
3:34 the s of Jacob, the s of Isaac, the s
3:34 the s of Terah, the s of Nahor,
3:35 the s of Serug, the s of Reu, the s
3:35 the s of Eber, the s of Shelah,
3:36 the s of Cainan, the s of Arphaxad,
3:36 the s of Arphaxad, the s of Shem,
3:36 Shem, the s of Noah, the s of Lamech,
3:37 the s of Methuselah, the s of Enoch,
3:37 the s of Jared, the s of Mahalalel,
3:37 the s of Kenan,
3:38 the s of Enosh, the s of Seth, the s
3:38 Seth, the s of Adam, the s of God.
4:22 "Isn't this Joseph's s?" they asked.
6:15 Matthew, Thomas, James s of Alphaeus,
6:16 Judas s of James, and Judas Iscariot,
8:28 Jesus, S of the Most High God?
9:41 put up with you? Bring your s here."
10:22 No-one knows who the S is except the
10:22 who the Father is except the S and
10:22 whom the S chooses to reveal him."
11:11 fathers, if your s asks for a fish,
12:53 father against s and s against
14: 5 he asked them, "If one of you has a s
15:13 "Not long after that, the younger s
15:19 longer worthy to be called your s;
15:20 he ran to his s, threw his arms
15:21 "The s said to him, 'Father, I have
15:21 longer worthy to be called your s.'
15:24 For this s of mine was dead and is
15:25 "Meanwhile, the older s was in the
15:30 this s of yours who has squandered
16:25 "But Abraham replied, 'S, remember
19: 9 this man, too, is a s of Abraham.
20:44 How then can he be his s?"
Jn 1:42 and said, "You are Simon s of John.
1:45 of Nazareth, the s of Joseph."
3:17 For God did not send his S into the
3:35 The Father loves the S and has

Jn 3:36 Whoever believes in the S has
3:36 but whoever rejects the S will not
4: 5 Jacob had given to his s Joseph.
4:46 whose s lay sick at Capernaum.
4:47 heal his s, who was close to death.
4:50 "You may go. Your s will live."
4:52 to the time when his s got better,
4:53 said to him, "Your s will live."
5:19 "I tell you the truth, the S can do
5:19 the Father does the S also does.
5:20 For the Father loves the S and shows
5:21 even so the S gives life to whom he
5:22 has entrusted all judgment to the S,
5:23 that all may honour the S just as
5:23 He who does not honour the S does
5:26 the S to have life in himself.
6:40 is that everyone who looks to the S
6:42 "Is this not Jesus, the s of Joseph,
6:71 (He meant Judas, the s of Simon
8:35 but a s belongs to it for ever.
8:36 if the S sets you free, you will be
9:19 "Is this your s?" they asked.
9:20 "We know he is our s," the parents
10:36 because I said, 'I am God's S'?
11: 4 God's S may be glorified through it."
13: 2 Judas Iscariot, s of Simon, to
13:26 it to Judas Iscariot, s of Simon.
13:32 God will glorify the S in himself,
14:13 the S may bring glory to the Father.
17: 1 your S, that your S may glorify you.
19:26 "Dear woman, here is your s,
21:15 "Simon s of John, do you truly love
21:16 Again Jesus said, "Simon s of John,
21:17 "Simon s of John, do you love me?"
Ac 1:13 James s of Alphaeus and Simon the
1:13 the Zealot, and Judas s of James.
4:36 (which means S of Encouragement),
7:21 him and brought him up as her own s.
13:21 and he gave them Saul s of Kish, of
13:22 'I have found David s of Jesse a man
20: 4 accompanied by Sopater s of Pyrrhus
23: 6 I am a Pharisee, the s of a Pharisee.
23:16 when the s of Paul's sister heard of
Ro 1: 3 regarding his S, who as to his human
1: 9 in preaching the gospel of his S,
5:10 to him through the death of his S,
8: 3 God did by sending his own S in the
8:29 conformed to the likeness of his S,
8:32 He who did not spare his own S, but
9: 9 return, and Sarah will have a s."
1Co 1: 9 with his S Jesus Christ our Lord,
15:28 then the S himself will be made
Gal 1:16 to reveal his S in me so that I
4: 4 God sent his S, born of a woman,
4: 6 God sent the Spirit of his S into
4: 7 you are no longer a slave, but a s;
4: 7 and since you are a s, God has made
4:23 His s by the slave woman was born in
4:23 but his s by the free woman was born
4:29 At that time the s born in the
4:29 s born by the power of the Spirit.
4:30 Get rid of the slave woman and her s,
4:30 for the slave woman's s will never
4:30 with the free woman's s."
Php 2:22 because as a s with his father he
Col 1:13 into the kingdom of the S he loves,
1Th 1:10 to wait for his S from heaven, whom
1Ti 1: 2 To Timothy my true s in the faith:
2Ti 1: 2 To Timothy, my dear s: Grace, mercy
Tit 1: 4 To Titus, my true s in our common
Heb 1: 2 days he has spoken to us by his S,
1: 3 The S is the radiance of God's glory
1: 8 about the S he says, "Your throne,
3: 6 Christ is faithful as a s over God's
5: 8 Although he was a s, he learned
7:28 appointed the S, who has been made
11:24 as the s of Pharaoh's daughter.
12: 6 everyone he accepts as a s."
12: 7 s is not disciplined by his father?
12:16 inheritance rights as the oldest s.
Jas 2:21 he offered his s Isaac on the altar?
2Pe 2:15 follow the way of Balaam s of Beor,
1Jn 1: 3 Father and with his S, Jesus Christ.
1: 7 and the blood of Jesus, his S,
2:22 denies the Father and the S.
2:23 No-one who denies the S has the

1Jn 2:23 whoever acknowledges the **S** has the
2:24 remain in the **S** and in the Father.
3:23 to believe in the name of his **S**,
4:10 but that he loved us and sent his **S**
4:14 **S** to be the Saviour of the world.
5: 9 God, which he has given about his **S**.
5:10 testimony God has given about his **S**.
5:11 life, and this life is in his **S**.
5:12 He who has the **S** has life; he who
5:20 is true—even in his **S** Jesus Christ.
2Jn : 3 from Jesus Christ, the Father's **S**,
: 9 has both the Father and the **S**.
Rev 12: 5 She gave birth to a **s**, a male child,

Son of David

2Sa 13: 1 In the course of time, Amnon **s** fell
13: 1 the beautiful sister of Absalom **s**.
1Ch 29:22 Then they acknowledged Solomon **s** as
2Ch 1: 1 Solomon **s** established himself firmly
13: 6 an official of Solomon **s**, rebelled
30:26 for since the days of Solomon **s** king
35: 3 that Solomon **s** king of Israel built.
Pr 1: 1 The proverbs of Solomon **s**, king of
Ecc 1: 1 The words of the Teacher, **s**, king of
Mt 1: 1 Christ the **s**, the son of Abraham:
1:20 "Joseph **s**, do not be afraid to take
9:27 "Have mercy on us, **S**!"
12:23 "Could this be the **S**?"
15:22 "Lord, **S**, have mercy on me!
20:30 "Lord, **S**, have mercy on us!"
20:31 "Lord, **S**, have mercy on us!"
21: 9 "Hosanna to the **S**!"
21:15 "Hosanna to the **S**," they were
22:42 "The **s**," they replied.
Mk 10:47 "Jesus, **S**, have mercy on me!"
10:48 "**S**, have mercy on me!"
12:35 law say that the Christ is the **s**?
Lk 3:31 Mattatha, the son of Nathan, the **s**,
18:38 He called out, "Jesus, **S**, have mercy
18:39 "**S**, have mercy on me!"
20:41 that they say the Christ is the **S**?

Son of God

Mt 4: 3 "If you are the **S**, tell these
4: 6 "If you are the **S**," he said, "throw
8:29 "What do you want with us, **S**?" they
14:33 him, saying, "Truly you are the **S**.
26:63 us if you are the Christ, the **S**."
27:40 from the cross, if you are the **S**!"
27:43 wants him, for he said, 'I am the **S**.
27:54 "Surely he was the **S**!"
Mk 1: 1 gospel about Jesus Christ, the **S**.
3:11 him and cried out, "You are the **S**.
15:39 "Surely this man was the **S**!"
Lk 1:35 one to be born will be called the **S**.
3:38 son of Seth, the son of Adam, the **s**.
4: 3 "If you are the **S**, tell this stone
4: 9 "If you are the **S**," he said, "throw
4:41 people, shouting, "You are the **S**!"
22:70 They all asked, "Are you then the **S**?"
Jn 1:34 and I testify that this is the **S**."
1:49 "Rabbi, you are the **S**; you are the
5:25 hear the voice of the **S** and those
11:27 **S**, who was to come into the world."
19: 7 because he claimed to be the **S**."
20:31 that Jesus is the Christ, the **S**,
Ac 9:20 the synagogues that Jesus is the **S**.
Ro 1: 4 was declared with power to be the **S**,
2Co 1:19 For the **S**, Jesus Christ, who was
Gal 2:20 I live by faith in the **S**, who loved
Eph 4:13 in the knowledge of the **S** and
Heb 4:14 Jesus the **S**, let us hold firmly to
6: 6 are crucifying the **S** all over again
7: 3 like the **S** he remains a priest for
10:29 who has trampled the **S** under foot,
1Jn 3: 8 The reason the **S** appeared was to
4:15 acknowledges that Jesus is the **S**,
5: 5 he who believes that Jesus is the **S**.
5:10 Anyone who believes in the **S** has
5:12 not have the **S** does not have life.
5:13 who believe in the name of the **S**
5:20 We know also that the **S** has come and
Rev 2:18 write: These are the words of the **S**,

Son of man

Nu 23:19 a **s**, that he should change his mind.
Job 25: 6 a maggot—a **s**, who is only a worm!"
Ps 8: 4 of him, the **s** that you care for him?
80:17 **s** you have raised up for yourself.
144: 3 him, the **s** that you think of him?
Eze 2: 1 He said to me, "**S**, stand up on your
2: 3 He said: "**S**, I am sending you to the
2: 6 you, **s**, do not be afraid of them or
2: 8 you, **s**, listen to what I say to you.
3: 1 he said to me, "**S**, eat what is
3: 3 he said to me, "**S**, eat this scroll I
3: 4 He then said to me: "**S**, go now to
3:10 he said to me, "**S**, listen carefully
3:17 "**S**, I have made you a watchman for
3:25 you, **s**, they will tie with ropes;
4: 1 "Now, **s**, take a clay tablet, put it
4:16 He then said to me: "**S**, I will cut
5: 1 "Now, **s**, take a sharp sword and use
6: 2 "**S**, set your face against the
7: 2 "**S**, this is what the Sovereign LORD
8: 5 "**S**, look towards the north."
8: 6 "**S**, do you see what they are doing
8: 8 He said to me, "**S**, now dig into the
8:12 He said to me, "**S**, have you seen
8:15 He said to me, "Do you see this, **s**?
8:17 He said to me, "Have you seen this, **s**
11: 2 The LORD said to me, "**S**, these are
11: 4 prophesy against them; prophesy, **s**."
11:15 "**S**, your brothers—your brothers who
12: 2 "**S**, you are living among a
12: 3 "Therefore, **s**, pack your belongings
12: 9 "**S**, did not that rebellious house of
12:18 "**S**, tremble as you eat your food,
12:22 "**S**, what is this proverb you have in
12:27 "**S**, the house of Israel is saying,
13: 2 "**S**, prophesy against the prophets of
13:17 "Now, **s**, set your face against the
14: 3 "**S**, these men have set up idols in
14:13 "**S**, if a country sins against me by
15: 2 "**S**, how is the wood of a vine better
16: 2 "**S**, confront Jerusalem with her
17: 2 "**S**, set forth an allegory and tell
20: 3 "**S**, speak to the elders of Israel
20: 4 Will you judge them, **s**?
20:27 "Therefore, **s**, speak to the people
20:46 "**S**, set your face towards the south;
21: 2 "**S**, set your face against Jerusalem
21: 6 "Therefore groan, **s**! Groan before
21: 9 "**S**, prophesy and say, 'This is what
21:12 Cry out and wail, **s**, for it is
21:14 "So then, **s**, prophesy and strike
21:19 "**S**, mark out two roads for the sword
21:28 "And you, **s**, prophesy and say, 'This
22: 2 "**S**, will you judge her? Will you
22:18 "**S**, the house of Israel has become
22:24 "**S**, say to the land, 'You are a land
23: 2 "**S**, there were two women, daughters
23:36 The LORD said to me: "**S**, will you
24: 2 "**S**, record this date, this very date,
24:16 "**S**, with one blow I am about to take
24:25 "And you, **s**, on the day I take away
25: 2 "**S**, set your face against the
26: 2 "**S**, because Tyre has said of
27: 2 "**S**, take up a lament concerning Tyre.
28: 2 "**S**, say to the ruler of Tyre, 'This
28:12 "**S**, take up a lament concerning the
28:21 "**S**, set your face against Sidon;
29: 2 "**S**, set your face against Pharaoh
29:18 "**S**, Nebuchadnezzar king of Babylon
30: 2 "**S**, prophesy and say: 'This is what
30:21 "**S**, I have broken the arm of Pharaoh
31: 2 "**S**, say to Pharaoh king of Egypt and
32: 2 "**S**, take up a lament concerning
32:18 "**S**, wail for the hordes of Egypt and
33: 2 "**S**, speak to your countrymen and say
33: 7 "**S**, I have made you a watchman for
33:10 "**S**, say to the house of Israel,
33:12 "Therefore, **s**, say to your
33:24 "**S**, the people living in those ruins
33:30 "As for you, **s**, your countrymen are
34: 2 "**S**, prophesy against the shepherds
35: 2 "**S**, set your face against Mount Seir;
36: 1 "**S**, prophesy to the mountains of
36:17 "**S**, when the people of Israel were
Eze 37: 3 He asked me, "**S**, can these bones
37: 9 "Prophesy to the breath; prophesy, **s**,
37:11 "**S**, these bones are the whole house
37:16 "**S**, take a stick of wood and write
38: 2 "**S**, set your face against Gog, of
38:14 "Therefore, **s**, prophesy and say to
39: 1 "**S**, prophesy against Gog and say:
39:17 "**S**, this is what the Sovereign LORD
40: 4 The man said to me, "**S**, look with
43: 7 He said: "**S**, this is the place of my
43:10 "**S**, describe the temple to the
43:18 he said to me, "**S**, this is what the
44: 5 LORD said to me, "**S**, look carefully,
47: 6 He asked me, "**S**, do you see this?"
Da 7:13 there before me was one like a **s**,
8:17 "**S**," he said to me, "understand that
Mt 8:20 the **S** has nowhere to lay his head."
9: 6 so that you may know that the **S** has
10:23 cities of Israel before the **S** comes.
11:19 The **S** came eating and drinking, and
12: 8 For the **S** is Lord of the Sabbath."
12:32 word against the **S** will be forgiven,
12:40 so the **S** will be three days and
13:37 who sowed the good seed is the **S**.
13:41 The **S** will send out his angels, and
16:13 "Who do people say the **S** is?"
16:27 For the **S** is going to come in his
16:28 see the **S** coming in his kingdom."
17: 9 **S** has been raised from the dead."
17:12 **S** is going to suffer at their hands."
17:22 "The **S** is going to be betrayed into
19:28 when the **S** sits on his glorious
20:18 and the **S** will be betrayed to the
20:28 just as the **S** did not come to be
24:27 so will be the coming of the **S**.
24:30 "At that time the sign of the **S** will
24:30 They will see the **S** coming on the
24:37 it will be at the coming of the **S**.
24:39 it will be at the coming of the **S**.
24:44 because the **S** will come at an hour
25:31 "When the **S** comes in his glory, and
26: 2 the **S** will be handed over to be
26:24 The **S** will go just as it is written
26:24 woe to that man who betrays the **S**!
26:45 the hour is near, and the **S** is
26:64 In the future you will see the **S**
Mk 2:10 that you may know that the **S** has
2:28 the **S** is Lord even of the Sabbath."
8:31 that the **S** must suffer many things
8:38 the **S** will be ashamed of him when he
9: 9 until the **S** had risen from the dead.
9:12 **S** must suffer much and be rejected?
9:31 He said to them, "The **S** is going to
10:33 "and the **S** will be betrayed to the
10:45 For even the **S** did not come to be
13:26 "At that time men will see the **S**
14:21 The **S** will go just as it is written
14:21 woe to that man who betrays the **S**!
14:41 Look, the **S** is betrayed into the
14:62 "And you will see the **S** sitting at
Lk 5:24 that you may know that the **S** has
6: 5 Jesus said to them, "The **S** is Lord
6:22 your name as evil, because of the **S**.
7:34 The **S** came eating and drinking, and
9:22 "The **S** must suffer many things
9:26 the **S** will be ashamed of him when he
9:44 The **S** is going to be betrayed into
9:58 the **S** has nowhere to lay his head."
11:30 will the **S** be to this generation.
12: 8 the **S** will also acknowledge him
12:10 word against the **S** will be forgiven,
12:40 because the **S** will come at an hour
17:22 one of the days of the **S**, but you
17:24 For the **S** in his day will be like
17:26 will it be in the days of the **S**.
17:30 this on the day the **S** is revealed.
18: 8 However, when the **S** comes, will he
18:31 about the **S** will be fulfilled.
19:10 For the **S** came to seek and to save
21:27 At that time they will see the **S**
21:36 may be able to stand before the **S**."
22:22 The **S** will go as it has been decreed,
22:48 you betraying the **S** with a kiss?"
22:69 from now on, the **S** will be seated at
24: 7 'The **S** must be delivered into the
Jn 1:51 ascending and descending on the **S**."

Jn 3:13 the one who came from heaven—the **S**.
3:14 desert, so the **S** must be lifted up,
5:27 to judge because he is the **S**.
6:27 life, which the **S** will give you.
6:53 unless you eat the flesh of the **S**
6:62 What if you see the **S** ascend to
8:28 "When you have lifted up the **S**, then
9:35 "Do you believe in the **S**?"
12:23 has come for the **S** to be glorified.
12:34 'The **S** must be lifted up'? Who is
12:34 be lifted up'? Who is this '**S**'?"
13:31 "Now is the **S** glorified and God is
Ac 7:56 **S** standing at the right hand of God."
Heb 2: 6 of him, the **s** that you care for him?
Rev 1:13 "like a **s**", dressed in a robe
14:14 "like a **s**" with a crown of gold on

Son's (Son)

Ge 30:14 give me some of your **s** mandrakes."
30:15 Will you take my **s** mandrakes too?"
30:15 in return for your **s** mandrakes."
30:16 hired you with my **s** mandrakes."
37:32 to see whether it is your **s** robe."
37:33 "It is my **s** robe! Some ferocious
Ex 4:25 cut off her **s** foreskin and touched
Lev 18:10 relations with your **s** daughter or
18:15 She is your **s** wife; do not have
18:17 with either her **s** daughter or her
2Sa 14:11 **s** head will fall to the ground."
1Ki 11:35 take the kingdom from his **s** hands

Song (*New song*, Sing)

Ex 15: 1 Moses and the Israelites sang this **s**
15: 2 The LORD is my strength and my **s**;
Nu 21:17 Israel sang this **s**: "Spring up, O
Dt 31:19 "Now write down for yourselves this **s**
31:21 this **s** will testify against them,
31:22 Moses wrote down this **s** that day and
31:30 Moses recited the words of this **s**
32:44 this **s** in the hearing of the people.
Jdg 5: 1 Barak son of Abinoam sang this **s**:
5:12 Wake up, wake up, break out in **s**!
2Sa 22: 1 the words of this **s** when the LORD
1Ch 16:42 the other instruments for sacred **s**.
Job 30: 9 "And now their sons mock me in **s**;
36:24 work, which men have praised in **s**.
Ps 18: T sang to the LORD the words of this **s**
28: 7 and I will give thanks to him in **s**.
30: T A psalm. A **s**. For the dedication of
42: 8 at night his **s** is with me—a prayer
45: T Sons of Korah A maskil. A wedding **s**.
46: T According to alamoth. A **s**.
65: T of music. A psalm of David. A **s**.
66: T director of music. A **s**. A psalm.
67: T stringed instruments. A psalm. A **s**.
68: T of music. Of David. A psalm. A **s**.
69:12 me, and I am the **s** of the drunkards.
69:30 I will praise God's name in **s** and
75: T A psalm of Asaph. A **s**.
76: T instruments. A psalm of Asaph. A **s**.
83: T A **s**. A psalm of Asaph.
87: T Of the Sons of Korah. A psalm. A **s**.
88: T A **s**. A psalm of the Sons of Korah.
92: T A psalm. A **s**. For the Sabbath Day.
95: 2 and extol him with music and **s**.
98: 4 burst into jubilant **s** with music;
108: T A **s**. A psalm of David.
118:14 The LORD is my strength and my **s**;
119:54 Your decrees are the theme of my **s**
120: T A **s** of ascents.
121: T A **s** of ascents.
122: T A **s** of ascents. Of David.
123: T A **s** of ascents.
124: T A **s** of ascents. Of David.
125: T A **s** of ascents.
126: T A **s** of ascents.
127: T A **s** of ascents. Of Solomon.
128: T A **s** of ascents.
129: T A **s** of ascents.
130: T A **s** of ascents.
131: T A **s** of ascents. Of David.
132: T A **s** of ascents.
133: T A **s** of ascents. Of David.
134: T A **s** of ascents.
Ecc 7: 5 than to listen to the **s** of fools.
SS 1: 1 Solomon's **S** of Songs.
Isa 5: 1 I will sing for the one I love a **s**
12: 2 the LORD, is my strength and my **s**;
23:15 Tyre as in the **s** of the prostitute:
23:16 play the harp well, sing many a **s**,
24: 9 No longer do they drink wine with a **s**
25: 5 so the **s** of the ruthless is stilled.
26: 1 In that day this **s** will be sung in
44:23 Burst into **s**, you mountains, you
49:13 O earth; burst into **s**, O mountains!
54: 1 burst into **s**, shout for joy,
55:12 hills will burst into **s** before you,
Lam 3:14 they mock me in **s** all day long.
Jnh 2: 9 I, with a **s** of thanksgiving, will
Mic 2: 4 will taunt you with this mournful **s**:
Rev 14: 3 No-one could learn the **s** except the
15: 3 sang the **s** of Moses the servant of
15: 3 of God and the **s** of the Lamb:

Songs (Sing)

1Sa 18: 6 with joyful **s** and with tambourines
2Sa 6: 5 with **s** and with harps, lyres,
23: 1 God of Jacob, Israel's singer of **s**:
1Ki 4:32 his **s** numbered a thousand and five.
1Ch 13: 8 with **s** and with harps, lyres,
15:16 as singers to sing joyful **s**,
Ne 12: 8 in charge of the **s** of thanksgiving.
12:27 dedication with **s** of thanksgiving
12:46 **s** of praise and thanksgiving to God.
Job 35:10 my Maker, who gives **s** in the night,
Ps 32: 7 surround me with **s** of deliverance.
65: 8 fades you call forth **s** of joy.
77: 6 I remembered my **s** in the night.
78:63 and their maidens had no wedding **s**;
100: 2 come before him with joyful **s**.
107:22 and tell of his works with **s** of joy.
126: 2 laughter, our tongues with **s** of joy.
126: 5 in tears will reap with **s** of joy.
126: 6 will return with **s** of joy, carrying
137: 3 for there our captors asked us for **s**,
137: 3 our tormentors demanded **s** of joy;
137: 3 "Sing us one of the **s** of Zion!"
137: 4 How can we sing the **s** of the LORD
Pr 25:20 is one who sings **s** to a heavy heart.
Ecc 12: 4 birds, but all their **s** grow faint;
SS 1: 1 Solomon's Song of **S**.
Isa 52: 9 Burst into **s** of joy together, you
Jer 30:19 them will come **s** of thanksgiving
Lam 3:63 standing, they mock me in their **s**.
Eze 26:13 I will put an end to your noisy **s**,
33:32 sings love **s** with a beautiful voice
Am 5:23 Away with the noise of your **s**!
8: 3 **s** in the temple will turn to wailing.
Eph 5:19 with psalms, hymns and spiritual **s**.
Col 3:16 hymns and spiritual **s** with gratitude
Jas 5:13 Let him sing **s** of praise.

Son-in-law (Son)

Jdg 15: 6 "Samson, the Timnite's **s**, because
19: 5 but the girl's father said to his **s**,
1Sa 18:18 that I should become the king's **s**?"
18:21 second opportunity to become my **s**."
18:22 all like you; now become his **s**.
18:23 small matter to become the king's **s**?
18:26 was pleased to become the king's **s**.
18:27 that he might become the king's **s**.
22:14 the king's **s**, captain of your
Ne 6:18 since he was **s** to Shecaniah son of
13:28 was **s** to Sanballat the Horonite.

Sons (Son, *Sons of God*)

Ge 5: 4 years and had other **s** and daughters.
5: 7 years and had other **s** and daughters.
5:10 years and had other **s** and daughters.
5:13 years and had other **s** and daughters.
5:16 years and had other **s** and daughters.
5:19 years and had other **s** and daughters.
5:22 years and had other **s** and daughters.
5:26 years and had other **s** and daughters.
5:30 years and had other **s** and daughters.
6:10 Noah had three **s**: Shem, Ham and
6:18 **s** and your wife and your sons' wives
7: 7 Noah and his **s** and his wife and his
7:13 On that very day Noah and his **s**,
7:13 of his three **s**, entered the ark.
Ge 8:16 wife and your **s** and their wives.
8:18 Noah came out, together with his **s**
9: 1 God blessed Noah and his **s**, saying
9: 8 God said to Noah and to his **s** with
9:18 The **s** of Noah who came out of the
9:19 These were the three **s** of Noah, and
10: 1 Ham and Japheth, Noah's **s**, who
10: 1 themselves had **s** after the flood.
10: 2 The **s** of Japheth: Gomer, Magog,
10: 3 The **s** of Gomer: Ashkenaz, Riphath
10: 4 The **s** of Javan: Elishah, Tarshish,
10: 6 The **s** of Ham: Cush, Mizraim, Put and
10: 7 The **s** of Cush: Seba, Havilah, Sabtah,
10: 7 The **s** of Raamah: Sheba and Dedan.
10:20 These are the **s** of Ham by their
10:21 **S** were also born to Shem, whose
10:21 the ancestor of all the **s** of Eber.
10:22 The **s** of Shem: Elam, Asshur,
10:23 The **s** of Aram: Uz, Hul, Gether and
10:25 Two **s** were born to Eber: One was
10:29 All these were **s** of Joktan.
10:31 These are the **s** of Shem by their
10:32 These are the clans of Noah's **s**,
11:11 years and had other **s** and daughters.
11:13 years and had other **s** and daughters.
11:15 years and had other **s** and daughters.
11:17 years and had other **s** and daughters.
11:19 years and had other **s** and daughters.
11:21 years and had other **s** and daughters.
11:23 years and had other **s** and daughters.
11:25 years and had other **s** and daughters.
19:12 **s** or daughters, or anyone else in
22:20 has borne **s** to your brother Nahor:
22:23 eight **s** to Abraham's brother Nahor.
22:24 also had **s**: Tebah, Gaham, Tahash
25: 4 The **s** of Midian were Ephah, Epher,
25: 6 he gave gifts to the **s** of his
25: 9 His **s** Isaac and Ishmael buried him
25:13 These are the names of the **s** of
25:16 These were the **s** of Ishmael, and
27:29 **s** of your mother bow down to you.
29:34 because I have borne him three **s**.
30:20 because I have borne him six **s**.
30:35 he placed them in the care of his **s**.
31: 1 Jacob heard that Laban's **s** were
32:22 two maidservants and his eleven **s**
33:19 he bought from the **s** of Hamor, the
34: 5 his **s** were in the fields with his
34: 7 Now Jacob's **s** had come in from the
34:13 Jacob's **s** replied deceitfully as
34:25 two of Jacob's **s**, Simeon and Levi,
34:27 The **s** of Jacob came upon the dead
35:22 Jacob had twelve **s**:
35:23 The **s** of Leah: Reuben the firstborn
35:24 The **s** of Rachel: Joseph and Benjamin.
35:25 The **s** of Rachel's maidservant Bilhah:
35:26 The **s** of Leah's maidservant Zilpah:
35:26 These were the **s** of Jacob, who were
35:29 And his **s** Esau and Jacob buried him.
36: 5 These were the **s** of Esau, who were
36: 6 Esau took his wives and **s** and
36:10 These are the names of Esau's **s**:
36:11 The **s** of Eliphaz: Teman, Omar, Zepho,
36:13 The **s** of Reuel: Nahath, Zerah,
36:14 The **s** of Esau's wife Oholibamah
36:15 The **s** of Eliphaz the firstborn of
36:17 The **s** of Esau's son Reuel: Chiefs
36:18 The **s** of Esau's wife Oholibamah:
36:19 These were the **s** of Esau (that is,
36:20 These were the **s** of Seir the Horite,
36:21 These **s** of Seir in Edom were Horite
36:22 The **s** of Lotan: Hori and Homam.
36:23 The **s** of Shobal: Alvan, Manahath,
36:24 The **s** of Zibeon: Aiah and Anah.
36:26 The **s** of Dishon: Hemdan, Eshban,
36:27 The **s** of Ezer: Bilhan, Zaavan and
36:28 The **s** of Dishan: Uz and Aran.
37: 2 the **s** of Bilhah and the **s** of Zilpah,
37: 3 Joseph more than any of his other **s**,
37:35 All his **s** and daughters came to
41:50 two **s** were born to Joseph by Asenath
42: 1 he said to his **s**, "Why do you just
42: 5 Israel's **s** were among those who went
42:11 We are all the **s** of one man.
42:13 the **s** of one man, who lives in the
42:32 We were twelve brothers, **s** of one

Ge 42:37 "You may put both of my **s** to death
44:20 only one of his mother's **s** left,
44:27 know that my wife bore me two **s**.
45:21 the **s** of Israel did this.
46: 5 and Israel's **s** took their father
46: 7 He took with him to Egypt his **s** and
46: 8 These are the names of the **s** of
46: 9 The **s** of Reuben: Hanoch, Pallu,
46:10 The **s** of Simeon: Jemuel, Jamin, Ohad,
46:11 The **s** of Levi: Gershon, Kohath and
46:12 The **s** of Judah: Er, Onan, Shelah,
46:12 The **s** of Perez: Hezron and Hamul.
46:13 The **s** of Issachar: Tola, Puah,
46:14 The **s** of Zebulun: Sered, Elon and
46:15 These were the **s** Leah bore to Jacob
46:15 These **s** and daughters of his were
46:16 The **s** of Gad: Zephon, Haggi, Shuni,
46:17 The **s** of Asher: Imnah, Ishvah, Ishvi
46:17 The **s** of Beriah: Heber and Malkiel.
46:19 The **s** of Jacob's wife Rachel: Joseph
46:21 The **s** of Benjamin: Bela, Beker,
46:22 These were the **s** of Rachel who were
46:24 The **s** of Naphtali: Jahziel, Guni,
46:25 These were the **s** born to Jacob by
46:27 With the two **s** who had been born to
48: 1 he took his two **s** Manasseh and
48: 5 "Now then, your two **s** born to you in
48: 8 Israel saw the **s** of Joseph, he asked,
48: 9 "They are the **s** God has given me
48:10 So Joseph brought his **s** close to him,
49: 1 Jacob called for his **s** and said:
49: 2 "Assemble and listen, **s** of Jacob;
49: 8 father's **s** will bow down to you.
49:33 giving instructions to his **s**,
50:12 Jacob's **s** did as he had commanded
50:25 Joseph made the **s** of Israel swear an
Ex 1: 1 These are the names of the **s** of
3:22 will put on your **s** and daughters.
4:20 Moses took his wife and **s**, put them
6:14 The **s** of Reuben the firstborn son of
6:15 The **s** of Simeon were Jemuel, Jamin,
6:16 These were the names of the **s** of
6:17 The **s** of Gershon, by clans, were
6:18 The **s** of Kohath were Amram, Izhar,
6:19 The **s** of Merari were Mahli and Mushi.
6:21 The **s** of Izhar were Korah, Nepheg
6:22 The **s** of Uzziel were Mishael,
6:24 The **s** of Korah were Assir, Elkanah
10: 9 with our **s** and daughters, and with
13:13 Redeem every firstborn among your **s**.
13:15 and redeem each of my firstborn **s**.'
13:19 made the **s** of Israel swear an oath.
18: 3 her two **s**. One son was named Gershom,
18: 5 together with Moses' **s** and wife,
18: 6 you with your wife and her two **s**."
21: 4 and she bears him **s** or daughters,
22:29 give me the firstborn of your **s**.
27:21 Aaron and his **s** are to keep the
28: 1 with his **s** Nadab and Abihu, Eleazar
28: 4 for your brother Aaron and his **s**,
28: 9 on them the names of the **s** of Israel
28:11 Engrave the names of the **s** of Israel
28:12 memorial stones for the **s** of Israel.
28:21 of the names of the **s** of Israel,
28:29 he will bear the names of the **s** of
28:40 sashes and headbands for Aaron's **s**,
28:41 on your brother Aaron and his **s**,
28:43 Aaron and his **s** must wear them
29: 4 bring Aaron and his **s** to the
29: 8 Bring his **s** and dress them in
29: 9 Then tie sashes on Aaron and his **s**.
29: 9 you shall ordain Aaron and his **s**.
29:10 **s** shall lay their hands on its head.
29:15 **s** shall lay their hands on its head.
29:19 **s** shall lay their hands on its head.
29:20 the right ears of Aaron and his **s**,
29:21 and on his **s** and their garments.
29:21 Then he and his **s** and their garments
29:24 in the hands of Aaron and his **s** and
29:27 ram that belong to Aaron and his **s**:
29:28 the Israelites for Aaron and his **s**.
29:32 Aaron and his **s** are to eat the meat
29:35 "Do for Aaron and his **s** everything I
29:44 and his **s** to serve me as priests.
30:19 Aaron and his **s** are to wash their
30:30 "Anoint Aaron and his **s** and

Ex 31:10 his **s** when they serve as priests,
32: 2 your **s** and your daughters are
32:29 for you were against your own **s** and
34:16 their daughters as wives for your **s**
34:16 will lead your **s** to do the same.
34:20 Redeem all your firstborn **s**.
35:19 his **s** when they serve as priests."
39: 6 with the names of the **s** of Israel.
39: 7 memorial stones for the **s** of Israel,
39:14 of the names of the **s** of Israel.
39:27 For Aaron and his **s**, they made
39:41 for his **s** when serving as priests.
40:12 "Bring Aaron and his **s** to the
40:14 Bring his **s** and dress them in tunics.
40:31 Moses and Aaron and his **s** used it to
Lev 1: 5 and then Aaron's **s** the priests shall
1: 7 The **s** of Aaron the priest are to put
1: 8 Aaron's **s** the priests shall arrange
1:11 and Aaron's **s** the priests shall
2: 2 take it to Aaron's **s** the priests.
2: 3 offering belongs to Aaron and his **s**;
2:10 offering belongs to Aaron and his **s**;
3: 2 Then Aaron's **s** the priests shall
3: 5 Aaron's **s** are to burn it on the
3: 8 Then Aaron's **s** shall sprinkle its
3:13 Then Aaron's **s** shall sprinkle its
6: 9 "Give Aaron and his **s** this command:
6:14 **s** are to bring it before the LORD,
6:16 Aaron and his **s** shall eat the rest
6:20 offering Aaron and his **s** are to bring
6:25 "Say to Aaron and his **s**: 'These are
7:10 equally to all the **s** of Aaron.
7:31 breast belongs to Aaron and his **s**.
7:34 his **s** as their regular share from
7:35 his **s** on the day they were presented
8: 2 "Bring Aaron and his **s**, their
8: 6 Moses brought Aaron and his **s**
8:13 he brought Aaron's **s** forward, put
8:14 his **s** laid their hands on its head.
8:18 his **s** laid their hands on its head.
8:22 his **s** laid their hands on its head.
8:24 Moses also brought Aaron's **s** forward
8:27 in the hands of Aaron and his **s** and
8:30 and on his **s** and their garments.
8:30 and his **s** and their garments.
8:31 Moses then said to Aaron and his **s**,
8:31 'Aaron and his **s** are to eat it.'
8:36 Aaron and his **s** did everything the
9: 1 and his **s** and the elders of Israel.
9: 9 His **s** brought the blood to him, and
9:12 His **s** handed him the blood, and he
9:18 His **s** handed him the blood, and he
10: 1 Aaron's **s** Nadab and Abihu took their
10: 4 **s** of Aaron's uncle Uzziel, and said
10: 6 Moses said to Aaron and his **s**
10: 9 "You and your **s** are not to drink
10:12 said to Aaron and his remaining **s**,
10:14 you and your **s** and your daughters
10:16 Aaron's remaining **s**, and asked,
13: 2 or to one of his **s** who is a priest.
16: 1 death of the two **s** of Aaron who died
17: 2 "Speak to Aaron and his **s** and to all
21: 1 "Speak to the priests, the **s** of
21:24 Moses told this to Aaron and his **s**
22: 2 "Tell Aaron and his **s** to treat with
22:18 "Speak to Aaron and his **s** and to all
24: 9 belongs to Aaron and his **s**, who are
26:29 You will eat the flesh of your **s** and
Nu 1:10 from the **s** of Joseph: from Ephraim,
1:32 From the **s** of Joseph: From the
3: 2 The names of the **s** of Aaron were
3: 3 Those were the names of Aaron's **s**,
3: 4 They had no **s**; so only Eleazar and
3: 9 Give the Levites to Aaron and his **s**;
3:10 Appoint Aaron and his **s** to serve as
3:17 These were the names of the **s** of
3:38 Moses and Aaron and his **s** were to
3:48 Israelites to Aaron and his **s**."
3:51 redemption money to Aaron and his **s**,
4: 5 Aaron and his **s** are to go in and
4:15 "After Aaron and his **s** have finished
4:19 Aaron and his **s** are to go into
4:27 the direction of Aaron and his **s**.
6:23 "Tell Aaron and his **s**, 'This is how
8:13 stand in front of Aaron and his **s**
8:18 of all the firstborn **s** in Israel.

Nu 8:19 his **s** to do the work at the Tent of
8:22 the supervision of Aaron and his **s**.
10: 8 "The **s** of Aaron, the priests, are to
16: 1 —Dathan and Abiram, **s** of Eliab,
16:12 Dathan and Abiram, the **s** of Eliab.
18: 1 "You, your **s** and your father's
18: 1 and you and your **s** alone are to bear
18: 2 when you and your **s** minister before
18: 7 only you and your **s** may serve as
18: 8 I give to you and your **s** as your
18: 9 that part belongs to you and your **s**.
18:11 I give this to you and your **s** and
18:19 your **s** and daughters as your regular
21:29 He has given up his **s** as fugitives
21:35 together with his **s** and his whole
24:17 the skulls of all the **s** of Sheth.
26: 9 the **s** of Eliab were Nemuel, Dathan
26:19 Er and Onan were **s** of Judah, but
26:33 (Zelophehad son of Hepher had no **s**;
27: 3 died for his own sin and left no **s**.
Dt 2:33 with his **s** and his whole army.
7: 3 not give your daughters to their **s**
7: 3 or take their daughters for your **s**,
7: 4 for they will turn your **s** away from
11: 6 to Dathan and Abiram, **s** of Eliab
12:12 you, your **s** and daughters, your
12:18 —you, your **s** and daughters, your
12:31 They even burn their **s** and daughters
16:11 —you, your **s** and daughters, your
16:14 Be joyful at your Feast—you, your **s**
21: 5 The priests, the **s** of Levi, shall
21:15 and both bear him **s** but the
21:16 he wills his property to his **s**, he
28:32 Your **s** and daughters will be given
28:41 You will have **s** and daughters but
28:53 the flesh of the **s** and daughters the
31: 9 the **s** of Levi, who carried the ark
32: 8 to the number of the **s** of Israel.
32:19 was angered by his **s** and daughters.
33:24 "Most blessed of **s** is Asher; let him
Jos 5: 7 he raised up their **s** in their place,
7:24 the robe, the gold wedge, his **s** and
13:31 of the **s** of Makir, clan by clan.
14: 4 for the **s** of Joseph had become two
17: 3 the son of Manasseh, had no **s** but
17: 6 received an inheritance among the **s**.
24: 4 Jacob and his **s** went down to Egypt.
24:32 **s** of Hamor, the father of Shechem.
Jdg 1:20 drove from it the three **s** of Anak.
3: 6 to their **s**, and served their gods.
8:19 my brothers, the **s** of my own mother.
8:30 He had seventy **s** of his own, for he
9: 2 all seventy of Jerub-Baal's **s** rule
9: 5 brothers, the **s** of Jerub-Baal.
9:18 murdered his seventy **s** on a single
9:24 against Jerub-Baal's seventy **s**,
10: 4 He had thirty **s**, who rode thirty
11: 2 Gilead's wife also bore him **s**, and
12: 9 He had thirty **s** and thirty daughters.
12: 9 and for his **s** he brought in thirty
12:14 He had forty **s** and thirty grandsons,
17: 5 one of his **s** as his priest.
17:11 man was to him like one of his **s**.
18:30 and his **s** were priests for the
Ru 1: 1 together with his wife and two **s**,
1: 2 of his two **s** were Mahlon and Kilion.
1: 3 and she was left with her two **s**.
1: 5 without her two **s** and her husband.
1:11 Am I going to have any more **s**,
1:12 tonight and then gave birth to **s**—
4:15 than seven **s**, has given him birth."
1Sa 1: 3 **s** of Eli, were priests of the LORD.
1: 4 and to all her **s** and daughters.
1: 8 Don't I mean more to you than ten **s**?"
2: 5 she who has had many **s** pines away.
2:12 Eli's **s** were wicked men; they had no
2:21 birth to three **s** and two daughters.
2:22 heard about everything his **s** were
2:24 No, my **s**; it is not a good report
2:25 His **s**, however, did not listen to
2:29 Why do you honour your **s** more than
2:34 "'And what happens to your two **s**,
3:13 his **s** made themselves contemptible,
4: 4 And Eli's two **s**, Hophni and Phinehas,
4:11 two **s**, Hophni and Phinehas, died.
4:17 Also your two **s**, Hophni and Phinehas,

1Sa 8: 1 Samuel grew old, he appointed his **s**
8: 3 his **s** did not walk in his ways.
8: 5 "You are old, and your **s** do not walk
8:11 He will take your **s** and make them
12: 2 grey, and my **s** are here with you.
14:49 Saul's **s** were Jonathan, Ishvi and
14:51 Abner's father Ner were **s** of Abiel.
16: 1 chosen one of his **s** to be king."
16: 5 he consecrated Jesse and his **s** and
16:10 Jesse made seven of his **s** pass
16:11 "Are these all the **s** you have?"
17:12 Jesse had eight **s**, and in Saul's
17:13 Jesse's three oldest **s** had followed
28:19 you and your **s** will be with me.
30: 3 and **s** and daughters taken captive.
30: 6 because of his **s** and daughters.
31: 2 pressed hard after Saul and his **s**,
31: 2 **s** Jonathan, Abinadab and Malki-Shua.
31: 6 Saul and his three **s** and his
31: 7 and that Saul and his **s** had died,
31: 8 his three **s** fallen on Mount Gilboa.
31:12 his **s** from the wall of Beth Shan and
2Sa 2:18 The three **s** of Zeruiah were there:
3: 2 **S** were born to David in Hebron: His
3:39 **s** of Zeruiah are too strong for me.
4: 2 they were **s** of Rimmon the Beerothite
4: 5 Now Recab and Baanah, the **s** of
4: 9 the **s** of Rimmon the Beerothite, "As
5:13 **s** and daughters were born to him.
6: 3 Uzzah and Ahio, **s** of Abinadab, were
8:18 and David's **s** were royal advisers.
9:10 You and your **s** and your servants are
9:10 had fifteen **s** and twenty servants.)
9:11 table like one of the king's **s**.
13:23 all the king's **s** to come there.
13:27 Amnon and the rest of the king's **s**.
13:29 Then all the king's **s** got up,
13:30 has struck down all the king's **s**;
13:33 that all the king's **s** are dead.
13:35 "See, the king's **s** are here; it has
13:36 the king's **s** came in, wailing
14: 6 I your servant had two **s**. They got
14:27 Three **s** and a daughter were born to
15:27 Abiathar take your two **s** with you.
15:36 Their two **s**, Ahimaaz son of Zadok
16:10 have in common, you **s** of Zeruiah?
19: 5 the lives of your **s** and daughters
19:17 his fifteen **s** and twenty servants.
19:22 have in common, you **s** of Zeruiah?
21: 8 the two **s** of Aiah's daughter Rizpah,
21: 8 together with the five **s** of Saul's
23:32 Eliahba the Shaalbonite, the **s** of
1Ki 1: 9 the king's **s**, and all the men of
1:19 and has invited all the king's **s**,
1:25 He has invited all the king's **s**, the
2: 7 "But show kindness to the **s** of
4: 3 Elihoreph and Ahijah, **s** of Shisha—
4:31 Calcol and Darda, the **s** of Mahol.
8:25 if only your **s** are careful in all
9: 6 "But if you or your **s** turn away from
13:11 whose **s** came and told him all that
13:12 And his **s** showed him which road the
13:13 he said to his **s**, "Saddle the donkey
13:27 The prophet said to his **s**, "Saddle
13:31 After burying him, he said to his **s**,
20:35 By the word of the LORD one of the **s**
2Ki 4: 4 shut the door behind you and your **s**.
4: 5 shut the door behind her and her **s**.
4: 7 your **s** can live on what is left."
9:26 of Naboth and the blood of his **s**,
10: 1 Now there were in Samaria seventy **s**
10: 2 since your master's **s** are with you
10: 3 and most worthy of your master's **s**
10: 6 take the heads of your master's **s**
14: 6 Yet he did not put the **s** of the
17:17 sacrificed their **s** and daughters in
19:37 his **s** Adrammelech and Sharezer cut
25: 7 They killed the **s** of Zedekiah before
1Ch 1: 4 The **s** of Noah: Shem, Ham and Japheth.
1: 5 The **s** of Japheth: Gomer, Magog,
1: 6 The **s** of Gomer: Ashkenaz, Riphath
1: 7 The **s** of Javan: Elishah, Tarshish,
1: 8 The **s** of Ham: Cush, Mizraim, Put and
1: 9 The **s** of Cush: Seba, Havilah, Sabta,
1: 9 The **s** of Raamah: Sheba and Dedan.
1:17 The **s** of Shem: Elam, Asshur,
1Ch 1:17 The **s** of Aram: Uz, Hul, Gether and
1:19 Two **s** were born to Eber: One was
1:23 All these were **s** of Joktan.
1:28 The **s** of Abraham: Isaac and Ishmael.
1:31 These were the **s** of Ishmael.
1:32 The **s** born to Keturah, Abraham's
1:32 The **s** of Jokshan: Sheba and Dedan.
1:33 The **s** of Midian: Ephah, Epher,
1:34 The **s** of Isaac: Esau and Israel.
1:35 The **s** of Esau: Eliphaz, Reuel, Jeush,
1:36 The **s** of Eliphaz: Teman, Omar, Zepho,
1:37 The **s** of Reuel: Nahath, Zerah,
1:38 The **s** of Seir: Lotan, Shobal, Zibeon,
1:39 The **s** of Lotan: Hori and Homam.
1:40 The **s** of Shobal: Alvan, Manahath,
1:40 The **s** of Zibeon: Aiah and Anah.
1:41 The **s** of Dishon: Hemdan, Eshban,
1:42 The **s** of Ezer: Bilhan, Zaavan and
1:42 The **s** of Dishan: Uz and Aran.
2: 1 These were the **s** of Israel: Reuben,
2: 3 The **s** of Judah: Er, Onan and Shelah.
2: 4 Judah had five **s** in all.
2: 5 The **s** of Perez: Hezron and Hamul.
2: 6 The **s** of Zerah: Zimri, Ethan, Heman,
2: 9 The **s** born to Hezron were: Jerahmeel,
2:16 **s** were Abishai, Joab and Asahel.
2:18 her **s**: Jesher, Shobab and Ardon.
2:25 The **s** of Jerahmeel the firstborn of
2:27 The **s** of Ram the firstborn of
2:28 The **s** of Onam: Shammai and Jada.
2:28 The **s** of Shammai: Nadab and Abishur.
2:30 The **s** of Nadab: Seled and Appaim.
2:32 The **s** of Jada, Shammai's brother:
2:33 The **s** of Jonathan: Peleth and Zaza.
2:34 Sheshan had no **s**—only daughters.
2:42 The **s** of Caleb the brother of
2:43 The **s** of Hebron: Korah, Tappuah,
2:47 The **s** of Jahdai: Regem, Jotham,
2:50 The **s** of Hur the firstborn of
3: 1 These were the **s** of David born to
3: 9 All these were the **s** of David,
3: 9 besides his **s** by his concubines.
3:15 The **s** of Josiah: Johanan the
3:19 The **s** of Pedaiah: Zerubbabel and
3:19 The **s** of Zerubbabel: Meshullam and
3:21 and the **s** of Rephaiah, of Arnan, of
3:22 Shemaiah and his **s**: Hattush,
3:23 The **s** of Neariah: Elioenai, Hizkiah
3:24 The **s** of Elioenai: Hodaviah,
4: 3 These were the **s** of Etam: Jezreel,
4: 7 The **s** of Helah: Zereth, Zohar,
4:13 The **s** of Kenaz: Othniel and Seraiah.
4:13 **s** of Othniel: Hathath and Meonothai.
4:15 The **s** of Caleb son of Jephunneh: Iru,
4:16 The **s** of Jehallelel: Ziph, Ziphah,
4:17 The **s** of Ezrah: Jether, Mered, Epher
4:19 The **s** of Hodiah's wife, the sister
4:20 The **s** of Shimon: Amnon, Rinnah,
4:21 The **s** of Shelah son of Judah: Er the
4:27 Shimei had sixteen **s** and six
4:42 Rephaiah and Uzziel, the **s** of Ishi,
5: 1 The **s** of Reuben the firstborn of
5: 1 to the **s** of Joseph son of Israel;
5: 3 the **s** of Reuben the firstborn of
5:14 These were the **s** of Abihail son of
6: 1 The **s** of Levi: Gershon, Kohath and
6: 2 The **s** of Kohath: Amram, Izhar,
6: 3 The **s** of Aaron: Nadab, Abihu,
6:16 The **s** of Levi: Gershon, Kohath and
6:17 These are the names of the **s** of
6:18 The **s** of Kohath: Amram, Izhar,
6:19 The **s** of Merari: Mahli and Mushi.
6:28 The **s** of Samuel: Joel the firstborn
6:33 who served, together with their **s**:
7: 1 The **s** of Issachar: Tola, Puah,
7: 2 The **s** of Tola: Uzzi, Rephaiah,
7: 3 The **s** of Izrahiah: Michael, Obadiah
7: 6 Three **s** of Benjamin: Bela, Beker and
7: 7 The **s** of Bela: Ezbon, Uzzi, Uzziel,
7: 8 The **s** of Beker: Zemirah, Joash,
7: 8 All these were the **s** of Beker.
7:10 The **s** of Bilhan: Jeush, Benjamin,
7:11 All these **s** of Jediael were heads of
7:13 The **s** of Naphtali: Jahziel, Guni,
7:15 and his **s** were Ulam and Rakem.
7:17 These were the **s** of Gilead son of
1Ch 7:19 The **s** of Shemida were: Ahian,
7:30 The **s** of Asher: Imnah, Ishvah, Ishvi
7:31 The **s** of Beriah: Heber and Malkiel,
7:33 The **s** of Japhlet: Pasach, Bimhal and
7:33 These were Japhlet's **s**.
7:34 The **s** of Shomer: Ahi, Rohgah, Hubbah
7:35 The **s** of his brother Helem: Zophah,
7:36 The **s** of Zophah: Suah, Harnepher,
7:38 The **s** of Jether: Jephunneh, Pispah
7:39 The **s** of Ulla: Arah, Hanniel and
8: 3 The **s** of Bela were: Addar, Gera,
8: 8 **S** were born to Shaharaim in Moab
8:10 These were his **s**, heads of families.
8:12 The **s** of Elpaal: Eber, Misham,
8:16 Michael, Ishpah and Joha were the **s**
8:18 Ishmerai, Izliah and Jobab were the **s**
8:21 and Shimrath were the **s** of Shimei.
8:25 Iphdeiah and Penuel were the **s** of
8:27 and Zicri were the **s** of Jeroham.
8:35 The **s** of Micah: Pithon, Melech,
8:38 Azel had six **s**, and these were their
8:38 All these were the **s** of Azel.
8:39 The **s** of his brother Eshek: Ulam his
8:40 The **s** of Ulam were brave warriors
8:40 They had many **s** and grandsons—150
9: 5 Asaiah the firstborn and his **s**.
9:41 The **s** of Micah: Pithon, Melech,
9:44 Azel had six **s**, and these were their
9:44 These were the **s** of Azel.
10: 2 pressed hard after Saul and his **s**,
10: 2 killed his **s** Jonathan, Abinadab and
10: 6 Saul and his three **s** died, and all
10: 7 and that Saul and his **s** had died,
10: 8 and his **s** fallen on Mount Gilboa.
10:12 took the bodies of Saul and his **s**
11:34 the **s** of Hashem the Gizonite,
11:44 Jeiel the **s** of Hotham the Aroerite,
11:46 the **s** of Elnaam, Ithmah the Moabite,
12: 3 chief and Joash the **s** of Shemaah
12: 3 Jeziel and Pelet the **s** of Azmaveth;
12: 7 Joelah and Zebadiah the **s** of Jeroham
14: 3 the father of more **s** and daughters.
16:13 O **s** of Jacob, his chosen ones.
16:42 The **s** of Jeduthun were stationed at
17:11 one of your own **s**, and I will
18:17 and David's **s** were chief officials
21:20 **s** who were with him hid themselves.
23: 6 corresponding to the **s** of Levi:
23: 8 The **s** of Ladan: Jehiel the first,
23: 9 The **s** of Shimei: Shelomoth, Haziel
23:10 the **s** of Shimei: Jahath, Ziza, Jeush
23:10 were the **s** of Shimei—four in all.
23:11 Jeush and Beriah did not have many **s**;
23:12 The **s** of Kohath: Amram, Izhar,
23:13 The **s** of Amram: Aaron and Moses.
23:14 The **s** of Moses the man of God were
23:15 The **s** of Moses: Gershom and Eliezer.
23:17 Eliezer had no other **s**, but the **s** of
23:18 The **s** of Izhar: Shelomith was the
23:19 The **s** of Hebron: Jeriah the first,
23:20 The **s** of Uzziel: Micah the first and
23:21 The **s** of Merari: Mahli and Mushi.
23:21 The **s** of Mahli: Eleazar and Kish.
23:22 Eleazar died without having **s**: he
23:22 the **s** of Kish, married them.
23:23 The **s** of Mushi: Mahli, Eder and
24: 1 the divisions of the **s** of Aaron:
24: 1 The **s** of Aaron were Nadab, Abihu,
24: 2 their father did, and they had no **s**
24:20 from the **s** of Amram: Shubael;
24:20 from the **s** of Shubael: Jehdeiah.
24:21 for Rehabiah, from his **s**: Isshiah
24:22 from the **s** of Shelomoth: Jahath.
24:23 The **s** of Hebron: Jeriah the first,
24:24 from the **s** of Micah: Shamir.
24:25 from the **s** of Isshiah: Zechariah.
24:26 The **s** of Merari: Mahli and Mushi.
24:27 The **s** of Merari: from Jaaziah: Beno,
24:28 From Mahli: Eleazar, who had no **s**.
24:30 the **s** of Mushi: Mahli, Eder and
25: 1 set apart some of the **s** of Asaph,
25: 2 From the **s** of Asaph: Zaccur, Joseph,
25: 2 The **s** of Asaph were under the
25: 3 for Jeduthun, from his **s**: Gedaliah,
25: 4 for Heman, from his **s**: Bukkiah,
25: 5 All these were **s** of Heman the king's

1Ch 25: 5 Heman fourteen s and three daughters.
25: 9 fell to Joseph, his s and relatives,
25: 9 Gedaliah, he and his relatives and s,
25:10 to Zaccur, his s and relatives,
25:11 fourth to Izri, his s and relatives
25:12 to Nethaniah, his s and relatives,
25:13 to Bukkiah, his s and relatives,
25:14 to Jesarelah, his s and relatives,
25:15 to Jeshaiah, his s and relatives,
25:16 to Mattaniah, his s and relatives,
25:17 to Shimei, his s and relatives,
25:18 to Azarel, his s and relatives,
25:19 to Hashabiah, his s and relatives,
25:20 to Shubael, his s and relatives,
25:21 to Mattithiah, his s and relatives,
25:22 to Jerimoth, his s and relatives,
25:23 to Hananiah, his s and relatives,
25:24 to Joshbekashah, his s and relatives
25:25 to Hanani, his s and relatives,
25:26 to Mallothi, his s and relatives,
25:27 to Eliathah, his s and relatives,
25:28 to Hothir, his s and relatives,
25:29 to Giddalti, his s and relatives,
25:30 to Mahazioth, his s and relatives,
25:31 Romamti-Ezer, his s and relatives.
26: 1 son of Kore, one of the s of Asaph.
26: 2 Meshelemiah had s: Zechariah the
26: 4 Obed-Edom also had s: Shemaiah the
26: 6 His son Shemaiah also had s, who
26: 7 The s of Shemaiah: Othni, Rephael,
26: 8 they and their s and their relatives
26: 9 Meshelemiah had s and relatives, who
26:10 Hosah the Merarite had s: Shimri the
26:11 The s and relatives of Hosah were 13
26:15 for the storehouse fell to his s.
26:22 the s of Jehieli, Zetham and his
26:29 Kenaniah and his s were assigned
27:32 Hacmoni took care of the king's s.
28: 1 belonging to the king and his s,
28: 4 and from my father's s he was
28: 5 Of all my s—and the LORD has given
29:24 as well as all of King David's s,
2Ch 5:12 Heman, Jeduthun and their s and
6:16 if only your s are careful in all
11:14 because Jeroboam and his s had
11:19 She bore him s: Jeush, Shemariah and
11:21 twenty-eight s and sixty daughters.
11:23 dispersing some of his s throughout
13: 9 the s of Aaron, and the Levites, and
13:10 The priests who serve the LORD are s
13:21 twenty-two s and sixteen daughters.
21: 2 Jehoram's brothers, the s of
21: 2 s of Jehoshaphat king of Israel.
21:14 your s, your wives and everything
21:17 together with his s and wives.
22: 1 camp, had killed all the older s.
22: 8 and the s of Ahaziah's relatives,
23:11 Jehoiada and his s brought out the
24: 3 for him, and he had s and daughters.
24: 7 Now the s of that wicked woman
24:27 The account of his s, the many
25: 4 Yet he did not put their s to death,
28: 3 and sacrificed his s in the fire,
28: 8 thousand wives, s and daughters.
29: 9 why our s and daughters and our
29:11 My s, do not be negligent now, for
31:18 the wives, and the s and daughters
32:21 his s cut him down with the sword.
33: 6 He sacrificed his s in the fire in
36:20 servants to him and his s until the
Ezr 3: 9 Jeshua and his s and brothers and
3: 9 brothers and Kadmiel and his s
3: 9 the s of Henadad and their s and
3:10 and the Levites (the s of Asaph)
6:10 well-being of the king and his s.
7:23 the realm of the king and of his s?
8:18 Sherebiah's s and brothers, 18 men;
9: 2 as wives for themselves and their s,
9:12 daughters in marriage to their s
9:12 or take their daughters for your s.
Ne 3: 3 The Fish Gate was rebuilt by the s
4:14 and fight for your brothers, your s
5: 2 "We and our s and daughters are
5: 5 though our s are as good as theirs,
5: 5 our s and daughters to slavery.
9:23 You made their s as numerous as the
Ne 9:24 Their s went in and took possession
10: 9 Binnui of the s of Henadad, Kadmiel,
10:28 all their s and daughters who are
10:30 or take their daughters for our s.
10:36 of our s and of our cattle,
13:25 daughters in marriage to their s,
13:25 for your s or for yourselves.
13:28 One of the s of Joiada son of
Est 5:11 his many s, and all the ways the
9:10 the ten s of Haman son of Hammedatha,
9:12 s of Haman in the citadel of Susa.
9:13 Haman's ten s be hanged on gallows."
9:14 and they hanged the ten s of Haman.
9:25 s should be hanged on the gallows.
Job 1: 2 He had seven s and three daughters,
1: 4 His s used to take turns holding
1:13 One day when Job's s and daughters
1:18 "Your s and daughters were feasting
14:21 If his s are honoured, he does not
21:19 up a man's punishment for his s.
30: 9 "And now their s mock me in song;
35: 8 righteousness only the s of men.
42:13 he also had seven s and three
Ps 11: 4 He observes the s of men; his eyes
14: 2 down from heaven on the s of men to
17:14 their s have plenty, and they store
42: T A maskil of the S of Korah.
44: T Of the S of Korah. A maskil.
45: T Of the S of Korah. A maskil.
45:16 Your s will take the place of your
46: T Of the S of Korah. According to
47: T Of the S of Korah. A psalm.
48: T A song. A psalm of the S of Korah.
49: T Of the S of Korah. A psalm.
53: 2 God looks down from heaven on the s
69: 8 an alien to my own mother's s;
82: 6 you are all s of the Most High.
84: T Of the S of Korah. A psalm.
85: T Of the S of Korah. A psalm.
87: T Of the S of Korah. A psalm. A song.
88: T A song. A psalm of the S of Korah.
89:30 "If his s forsake my law and do not
90: 3 "Return to dust, O s of men."
105: 6 O s of Jacob, his chosen ones.
106:37 They sacrificed their s and their
106:38 the blood of their s and daughters,
127: 3 S are a heritage from the LORD,
127: 4 a warrior are s born in one's youth.
128: 3 your s will be like olive shoots
132:12 if your s keep my covenant and the
132:12 then their s shall sit on your
144:12 our s in their youth will be like
Pr 4: 1 Listen, my s, to a father's
5: 7 Now then, my s, listen to me;
7:24 Now then, my s, listen to me;
8:32 "Now then, my s, listen to me;
SS 1: 6 My mother's s were angry with me and
Isa 14:21 Prepare a place to slaughter his s
23: 4 reared s nor brought up daughters."
37:38 his s Adrammelech and Sharezer cut
43: 6 Bring my s from afar and my
49:17 Your s hasten back, and those who
49:18 all your s gather and come to you.
49:22 they will bring your s in their arms
51:12 the s of men, who are but grass,
51:18 Of all the s she bore there was none
51:18 of all the s she brought up there
51:20 Your s have fainted; they lie at the
54:13 All your s will be taught by the
56: 5 a name better than s and daughters;
57: 3 "But you—come here, you s of a
60: 4 your s come from afar, and your
60: 9 bringing your s from afar, with
60:14 The s of your oppressors will come
62: 5 a maiden, so will your s marry you;
63: 8 s who will not be false to me";
Jer 3:19 'How gladly would I treat you like s
3:24 and herds, their s and daughters.
5:17 devour your s and daughters;
6:21 Fathers and s alike will stumble
7:31 Valley of Ben Hinnom to burn their s
10:20 My s are gone from me and are no
11:22 their s and daughters by famine.
13:14 and s alike, declares the LORD.
14:16 wives, their s or their daughters.
16: 2 "You must not marry and have s or
Jer 16: 3 is what the LORD says about the s
19: 5 s in the fire as offerings to Baal
19: 9 the flesh of their s and daughters,
29: 6 Marry and have s and daughters;
29: 6 find wives for your s and give your
29: 6 they too may have s and daughters.
32:35 their s and daughters to Molech,
33:26 will not choose one of his s to rule
35: 3 his brothers and all his s—the
35: 4 into the room of the s of Hanan son
35: 8 s and daughters have ever drunk
35:14 'Jonadab son of Recab ordered his s
39: 6 the s of Zedekiah before his eyes
40: 8 Johanan and Jonathan the s of Kareah,
40: 8 the s of Ephai the Netophathite,
48:46 your s are taken into exile and your
49: 1 "Has Israel no s? Has she no heirs?
52:10 the s of Zedekiah before his eyes;
Lam 4: 2 How the precious s of Zion, once
Eze 14:16 not save their own s or daughters.
14:18 not save their own s or daughters.
14:22 be some survivors—s and daughters
16:20 "'And you took your s and daughters
20:31 the sacrifice of your s in the fire—
23: 4 They were mine and gave birth to s
23:10 took away her s and daughters and
23:25 They will take away your s and
23:47 they will kill their s and daughters
24:21 The s and daughters you left behind
24:25 and their s and daughters as well—
40:46 These are the s of Zadok, who are
46:16 his inheritance to one of his s,
46:17 belongs to his s only; it is theirs.
46:18 He is to give his s their
Da 11:10 His s will prepare for war and
Hos 1:10 be called 's of the living God'.
Joel 2:28 Your s and daughters will prophesy,
3: 8 I will sell your s and daughters to
Am 2:11 up prophets from among your s
7:17 and your s and daughters will fall
Zep 1: 8 the king's s and all those clad in
Zec 9:13 I will rouse your s, O Zion, against
9:13 O Zion, against your s, O Greece,
Mt 5:45 that you may be s of your Father in
13:38 stands for the s of the kingdom.
13:38 The weeds are the s of the evil one,
17:25 from their own s or from others?"
17:26 "Then the s are exempt," Jesus said
20:20 the mother of Zebedee's s came to
20:20 came to Jesus with her s and,
20:21 "Grant that one of these two s of
21:28 There was a man who had two s.
26:37 He took Peter and the two s of
27:56 Joses, and the mother of Zebedee's s.
Mk 3:17 Boanerges, which means S of Thunder);
10:35 James and John, the s of Zebedee,
Lk 5:10 James and John, the s of Zebedee,
6:35 and you will be s of the Most High,
15:11 "There was a man who had two s.
Jn 4:12 his s and his flocks and herds?"
12:36 so that you may become s of light.
21: 2 the s of Zebedee, and two other
Ac 2:17 Your s and daughters will prophesy,
7:16 had bought from the s of Hamor
7:29 as a foreigner and had two s.
19:14 Seven s of Sceva, a Jewish chief
Ro 8:23 wait eagerly for our adoption as s,
9: 4 Theirs is the adoption as s;
9:26 be called 's of the living God'."
2Co 6:18 and you will be my s and daughters,
Gal 4: 5 might receive the full rights of s.
4: 6 you are s, God sent the Spirit of
4:22 is written that Abraham had two s,
Eph 1: 5 as his s through Jesus Christ,
1Th 5: 5 You are all s of the light and s of
Heb 2:10 In bringing many s to glory, it was
11:21 blessed each of Joseph's s, and
12: 5 that addresses you as s:
12: 7 God is treating you as s.
12: 8 children and not true s.

Sons of God

Ge 6: 2 the s saw that the daughters of men
6: 4 the s went to the daughters of men
Mt 5: 9 for they will be called s.

Ro 8:14 are led by the Spirit of God are s.
8:19 for the s to be revealed.
Gal 3:26 You are all s through faith in

Sons' (Son)
Ge 6:18 your wife and your s wives with you.
7: 7 sons and his wife and his s wives
8:18 sons and his wife and his s wives.
46:26 not counting his s wives—numbered
Lev 10:13 it is your share and your s share

Sonship (Son)
Ro 8:15 but you received the Spirit of s.

Sons-in-law (Son)
Ge 19:12 else here—s, sons or daughters,
19:14 Lot went out and spoke to his s, who
19:14 But his s thought he was joking.

Soot
Ex 9: 8 "Take handfuls of s from a furnace
9:10 they took s from a furnace and stood
Lam 4: 8 now they are blacker than s;

Soothed (Soothes, Soothing)
Isa 1: 6 cleansed or bandaged or s with oil.

Soothes (Soothed)
Pr 21:14 A gift given in secret s anger, and

Soothing (Soothed)
Ps 55:21 his words are more s than oil,

Soothsayer (Soothsayers')
Isa 3: 2 judge and prophet, the s and elder,

Soothsayers' (Soothsayer)
Jdg 9:37 from the direction of the s tree."

Sopater
Ac 20: 4 He was accompanied by **S** son of

Sophereth
Ne 7:57 the descendants of Sotai, **S**, Perida,

Sorcerer (Sorcery)
Ac 13: 6 s and false prophet named Bar-Jesus,
13: 8 Elymas the s (for that is what his

Sorcerers (Sorcery)
Ex 7:11 then summoned the wise men and s,
Jer 27: 9 your mediums or your s who tell you,
Da 2: 2 enchanters, s and astrologers to
Mal 3: 5 I will be quick to testify against s,

Sorceress (Sorcery)
Ex 22:18 "Do not allow a s to live.
Isa 57: 3 "But you—come here, you sons of a s,

Sorceries (Sorcery)
Isa 47: 9 many s and all your potent spells.
47:12 magic spells and with your many s,
Na 3: 4 alluring, the mistress of s, who

Sorcery (Sorcerer, Sorcerers, Sorceress, Sorceries)
Lev 19:26 "'Do not practise divination or s.
Nu 23:23 There is no s against Jacob, no
24: 1 he did not resort to s as at other
Dt 18:10 who practises divination or s,
18:14 those who practise s or divination.
2Ki 17:17 They practised divination and s and
21: 6 practised s and divination, and
2Ch 33: 6 practised s, divination and
Ac 8: 9 Simon had practised s in the city
19:19 A number who had practised s brought

Sore (Sores)
Lev 13: 3 The priest is to examine the s on
13: 3 and if the hair in the s has turned
13: 3 s appears to be more than skin deep,
Lev 13: 5 if he sees that the s is unchanged
13: 6 and if the s has faded and has not
13:29 "If a man or woman has a s on the
13:30 the priest is to examine the s, and
13:31 the priest examines this kind of s,
13:32 day the priest is to examine the s,
13:42 if he has a reddish-white s on his
13:43 and if the swollen s on his head or
13:44 because of the s on his head.
2Sa 3:29 who has a running s or leprosy or
Jer 30:13 no remedy for your s, no healing

Sorek
Jdg 16: 4 Valley of **S** whose name was Delilah.

Sores (Sore)
Lev 13:17 and if the s have turned white, the
21:20 or running s or damaged testicles.
22:22 warts or festering or running s.
Dt 28:27 festering s and the itch, from which
Job 2: 7 afflicted Job with painful s from
Isa 1: 6 only wounds and bruises and open s,
3:17 Therefore the Lord will bring s on
Hos 5:13 saw his sickness, and Judah his s,
5:13 cure you, not able to heal your s.
Lk 16:20 beggar named Lazarus, covered with s
16:21 Even the dogs came and licked his s.
Rev 16: 2 and ugly and painful s broke out on
16:11 because of their pains and their s,

Sorrow (Sorrowful, Sorrows)
Ge 42:38 grey head down to the grave in s."
44:31 our father down to the grave in s.
48: 7 to my s Rachel died in the land of
Est 9:22 and as the month when their s was
Ps 6: 7 My eyes grow weak with s; they fail
13: 2 and every day have s in my heart?
31: 9 my eyes grow weak with s, my soul
90:10 yet their span is but trouble and s,
107:39 by oppression, calamity and s;
116: 3 I was overcome by trouble and s.
119:28 My soul is weary with s; strengthen
Pr 23:29 Who has woe? Who has s? Who has
Ecc 1:18 For with much wisdom comes much s;
7: 3 **S** is better than laughter, because a
Isa 35:10 and s and sighing will flee away.
51:11 and s and sighing will flee away.
60:20 light, and your days of s will end.
Jer 8:18 O my Comforter in s, my heart is
20:18 to see trouble and s and to end my
31:12 garden, and they will s no more.
31:13 them comfort and joy instead of s.
45: 3 The LORD has added s to my pain;
Eze 23:33 be filled with drunkenness and s,
Mt 26:38 with s to the point of death.
Mk 14:34 "My soul is overwhelmed with s to
Lk 22:45 found them asleep, exhausted from s.
Ro 9: 2 I have great s and unceasing anguish
2Co 2: 7 not be overwhelmed by excessive s.
7: 7 your deep s, your ardent concern for
7: 8 Even if I caused you s by my letter,
7: 9 your s led you to repentance.
7:10 Godly s brings repentance that leads
7:10 regret, but worldly s brings death.
7:11 See what this godly s has produced
Php 2:27 also on me, to spare me s upon s.

Sorrowful (Sorrow)
Mt 26:37 and he began to be s and troubled.
2Co 6:10 s, yet always rejoicing; poor, yet
7: 9 For you became s as God intended and

Sorrows (Sorrow)
Ps 16: 4 The s of those will increase who run
Isa 53: 3 a man of s, and familiar with
53: 4 our infirmities and carried our s,
Zep 3:18 "The s for the appointed feasts I

Sorry
Ex 2: 6 He was crying, and she felt s for
2Co 7: 9 not because you were made s, but

Sort (Sorts)
2Ki 9:11 man and the s of things he says,"
Ecc 10: 5 s of error that arises from a ruler:
2Th 2:10 in every s of evil that deceives
Rev 18:12 every s of citron wood, and

Sorts (Sort)
1Ki 12:31 priests from all s of people,
13:33 high places from all s of people.
2Ki 17:32 but they also appointed all s of
Pr 1:13 we will get all s of valuable things
1Co 14:10 there are all s of languages in the

Sosipater
Ro 16:21 Lucius, Jason and **S**, my relatives.

Sosthenes
Ac 18:17 they all turned on **S** the synagogue
1Co 1: 1 the will of God, and our brother **S**,

Sotai
Ezr 2:55 the descendants of **S**, Hassophereth,
Ne 7:57 descendants of **S**, Sophereth, Perida,

Sought (Seek)
Ex 32:11 Moses s the favour of the LORD his
1Sa 7: 2 Israel mourned and s after the LORD.
13:12 and I have not s the LORD's favour.
13:14 the LORD has s out a man after his
2Sa 21: 1 so David s the face of the LORD.
1Ki 10:24 The whole world s audience with
2Ki 13: 4 Jehoahaz s the LORD's favour, and
2Ch 9:23 the kings of the earth s audience
14: 7 because we have s the LORD our God;
14: 7 we s him and he has given us rest on
15: 4 and s him, and he was found by them.
15:15 They s God eagerly, and he was found
17: 4 s the God of his father and followed
22: 9 who s the LORD with all his heart.
25:20 because they s the gods of Edom.
26: 5 He s God during the days of
26: 5 he s the LORD, God gave him success.
31:21 s his God and worked wholeheartedly.
33:12 In his distress he s the favour of
Ne 12:27 the Levites were s out from where
Ps 34: 4 I s the LORD, and he answered me;
77: 2 I was in distress, I s the Lord;
119:45 for I have s out your precepts.
119:58 I have s your face with all my heart;
119:94 I have s out your precepts.
Isa 9:13 nor have they s the LORD Almighty.
62:12 and you will be called **S** After, the
Jer 26:21 the king s to put him to death.
Eze 25:15 hostility s to destroy Judah,
26:21 You will be s, but you will never
Da 4:36 My advisers and nobles s me out, and
9:13 yet we have not s the favour of the
Ac 12:20 together and s an audience with him.
Ro 10: 3 God and s to establish their own,
11: 7 What Israel s so earnestly it did
Heb 8: 7 place would have been s for another.
12:17 though he s the blessing with tears.

Soul (Souls)
Dt 4:29 all your heart and with all your s.
6: 5 your s and with all your strength.
10:12 all your heart and with all your s,
11:13 all your heart and with all your s—
13: 3 all your heart and with all your s.
26:16 all your heart and with all your s.
30: 2 with all your s according to
30: 6 heart and with all your s, and live.
30:10 all your heart and with all your s.
Jos 22: 5 with all your heart and all your s."
23:14 You know with all your heart and s
Jdg 5:21 March on, my s; be strong!
1Sa 1:10 In bitterness of s Hannah wept much
1:15 I was pouring out my s to the LORD.
14: 7 Go ahead; I am with you heart and s."
1Ki 2: 4 me with all their heart and s,
8:48 with all their heart and s in the
2Ki 23: 3 with all his heart and all his s,
23:25 all his s and with all his strength,
1Ch 22:19 Now devote your heart and s to

2Ch 6:38 with all their heart and s in the
15:12 fathers, with all their heart and s.
34:31 with all his heart and all his s,
Job 3:20 misery, and life to the bitter of s,
7:11 complain in the bitterness of my s.
10: 1 speak out in the bitterness of my s.
21:25 Another man dies in bitterness of s,
27: 2 has made me taste bitterness of s,
30:25 Has not my s grieved for the poor?
33:18 to preserve his s from the pit, his
33:20 and his s loathes the choicest meal.
33:22 His s draws near to the pit, and his
33:28 He redeemed my s from going down to
33:30 to turn back his s from the pit,
Ps 6: 3 My s is in anguish. How long, O LORD,
11: 5 those who love violence his s hates.
19: 7 the LORD is perfect, reviving the s.
23: 3 he restores my s. He guides me in
24: 4 who does not lift up his s to an
25: 1 To you, O LORD, I lift up my s;
26: 9 Do not take away my s along with
31: 7 and knew the anguish of my s.
31: 9 sorrow, my s and my body with grief.
34: 2 My s will boast in the LORD; let the
35: 3 Say to my s, "I am your salvation."
35: 9 my s will rejoice in the LORD and
35:12 for good and leave my s forlorn.
42: 1 water, so my s pants for you, O God.
42: 2 My s thirsts for God, for the living
42: 4 I remember as I pour out my s:
42: 5 Why are you downcast, O my s?
42: 6 My s is downcast within me;
42:11 Why are you downcast, O my s?
43: 5 Why are you downcast, O my s?
57: 1 on me, for in you my s takes refuge.
57: 8 Awake, my s! Awake, harp and lyre!
62: 1 My s finds rest in God alone;
62: 5 Find rest, O my s, in God alone;
63: 1 my s thirsts for you, my body longs
63: 5 My s will be satisfied as with the
63: 8 My s clings to you; your right hand
77: 2 and my s refused to be comforted.
84: 2 My s yearns, even faints, for the
86: 4 for to you, O Lord, I lift up my s.
88: 3 For my s is full of trouble and my
94:19 consolation brought joy to my s.
103: 1 Praise the LORD, O my s;
103: 2 Praise the LORD, O my s, and forget
103:22 Praise the LORD, O my s.
104: 1 Praise the LORD, O my s.
104:35 Praise the LORD, O my s.
108: 1 sing and make music with all my s.
116: 7 Be at rest once more, O my s, for
116: 8 For you, O LORD, have delivered my s
119:20 My s is consumed with longing for
119:28 My s is weary with sorrow;
119:81 My s faints with longing for your
130: 5 I wait for the LORD, my s waits, and
130: 6 My s waits for the Lord more than
131: 2 I have stilled and quietened my s;
131: 2 a weaned child is my s within me.
143: 6 my s thirsts for you like a parched
143: 8 go, for to you I lift up my s.
146: 1 Praise the LORD, O my s.
Pr 1:11 blood, let's waylay some harmless s;
2:10 will be pleasant to your s.
13:19 A longing fulfilled is sweet to the s
16:24 sweet to the s and healing to the
18: 7 and his lips are a snare to his s.
19: 8 He who gets wisdom loves his own s;
22: 5 guards his s stays far from them.
23:14 the rod and save his s from death.
24:14 that wisdom is sweet to your s;
25:25 Like cold water to a weary s is good
29:17 he will bring delight to your s.
Isa 1:14 your appointed feasts my s hates.
26: 9 My s yearns for you in the night;
38:15 because of this anguish of my s.
53:11 After the suffering of his s, he
55: 2 and your s will delight in the
55: 3 hear me, that your s may live.
61:10 my s rejoices in my God.
Jer 32:41 this land with all my heart and s.
Lam 3:20 and my s is downcast within me.
3:51 What I see brings grief to my s
Eze 18: 4 For every living s belongs to me,
Eze 18: 4 s who sins is the one who will die.
18:20 The s who sins is the one who will
27:31 of s and with bitter mourning.
Mic 6: 7 of my body for the sin of my s?
Mt 10:28 kill the body but cannot kill the s.
10:28 can destroy both s and body in hell.
16:26 whole world, yet forfeits his s?
16:26 a man give in exchange for his s?
22:37 all your s and with all your mind.'
26:38 "My s is overwhelmed with sorrow to
Mk 8:36 the whole world, yet forfeit his s?
8:37 a man give in exchange for his s?
12:30 with all your s and with all your
14:34 "My s is overwhelmed with sorrow to
Lk 1:46 Mary said: "My s glorifies the Lord
2:35 a sword will pierce your own s too."
10:27 with all your s and with all your
1Th 5:23 May your whole spirit, s and body be
Heb 4:12 it penetrates even to dividing s and
6:19 anchor for the s, firm and secure.
1Pe 2:11 desires, which war against your s.
2Pe 2: 8 was tormented in his righteous s by
3Jn : 2 as your s is getting along well.

Souls (Soul)

Job 24:12 s of the wounded cry out for help.
Pr 11:30 of life, and he who wins s is wise.
Isa 66: 3 s delight in their abominations;
Jer 6:16 and you will find rest for your s.
Mt 11:29 and you will find rest for your s.
1Pe 1: 9 your faith, the salvation of your s.
2:25 the Shepherd and Overseer of your s.
Rev 6: 9 I saw under the altar the s of those
18:13 carriages; and bodies and s of men.
20: 4 And I saw the s of those who had

Sound[1] (Fine-sounding, Sounded, Sounding, Sounds)

Ge 3: 8 the man and his wife heard the s of
Ex 19:19 the s of the trumpet grew louder and
28:35 The s of the bells will be heard
32:17 "There is the s of war in the camp.
32:18 "It is not the s of victory,
32:18 it is not the s of defeat; it is the
32:18 it is the s of singing that I hear."
Lev 25: 9 s the trumpet throughout your land.
26:36 the s of a wind-blown leaf will put
Nu 10: 9 you, s a blast on the trumpets.
10:10 you are to s the trumpets over your
29: 1 is a day for you to s the trumpets.
Dt 4:12 You heard the s of words but saw no
Jos 6: 5 you hear them s a long blast on the
6:20 and at the s of the trumpet, when
Jdg 11:34 dancing to the s of tambourines!
2Sa 5:24 soon as you hear the s of marching
6:15 with shouts and the s of trumpets.
15:10 "As soon as you hear the s of the
1Ki 1:40 so that the ground shook with the s.
1:41 On hearing the s of the trumpet,
14: 6 when Ahijah heard the s of her
18:41 for there is the s of a heavy rain."
2Ki 4:31 but there was no s or response.
6:32 Is not the s of his master's
7: 6 Arameans to hear the s of chariots
7:10 not a man was there—not a s of
1Ch 14:15 soon as you hear the s of marching
15:19 Ethan were to s the bronze cymbals;
16: 5 harps, Asaph was to s the cymbals,
2Ch 13:12 will s the battle cry against you.
13:15 At the s of their battle cry, God
Ezr 3:13 No-one could distinguish the s of
3:13 shouts of joy from the s of weeping,
3:13 And the s was heard far away.
Ne 4:20 Wherever you hear the s of the
12:43 The s of rejoicing in Jerusalem
Job 21:12 make merry to the s of the flute.
30:31 and my flute to the s of wailing.
37: 4 After that comes the s of his roar;
Ps 66: 8 let the s of his praise be heard;
81: 3 S the ram's horn at the New Moon,
98: 5 with the harp and the s of singing,
104: 7 at the s of your thunder they took
115: 7 they utter a s with their throats.
Ecc 12: 4 closed and the s of grinding fades;
12: 4 when men rise up at the s of birds,
Isa 6: 4 At the s of their voices the
24:18 Whoever flees at the s of terror
27:13 in that day a great trumpet will s.
51: 3 thanksgiving and the s of singing.
65:19 the s of weeping and of crying will
66: 6 It is the s of the LORD repaying his
Jer 4: 5 'S the trumpet throughout the land!'
4:19 For I have heard the s of the
4:21 and hear the s of the trumpet?
4:29 At the s of horsemen and archers
6: 1 S the trumpet in Tekoa!
6:17 'Listen to the s of the trumpet!'
6:23 They s like the roaring sea as they
9:19 The s of wailing is heard from Zion:
25:10 the s of millstones and the light of
30:19 thanksgiving and the s of rejoicing.
47: 3 at the s of the hoofs of galloping
48:34 "The s of their cry rises from
49: 2 "when I will s the battle cry
49:21 At the s of their fall the earth
50:42 They s like the roaring sea as they
50:46 At the s of Babylon's capture the
51:54 "The s of a cry comes from Babylon,
51:54 the s of great destruction from the
Eze 1:24 I heard the s of their wings, like
3:12 I heard behind me a loud rumbling s—
3:13 the s of the wings of the living
3:13 and the s of the wheels beside them,
3:13 beside them, a loud rumbling s.
10: 5 The s of the wings of the cherubim
21:22 to s the battle cry, to set
26:15 tremble at the s of your fall,
31:16 I made the nations tremble at the s
33: 5 Since he heard the s of the trumpet
37: 7 there was a noise, a rattling s, and
Da 3: 5 soon as you hear the s of the horn,
3: 7 as soon as they heard the s of the
3:10 that everyone who hears the s of the
3:15 Now when you hear the s of the horn,
10: 6 his voice like the s of a multitude.
Hos 5: 8 "S the trumpet in Gibeah, the horn
Joel 2: 1 s the alarm on my holy hill.
Hab 3:16 my lips quivered at the s;
Zec 9:14 Sovereign LORD will s the trumpet;
Lk 1:44 soon as the s of your greeting
Jn 3: 8 You hear its s, but you cannot tell
Ac 2: 2 Suddenly a s like the blowing of a
2: 6 they heard this s, a crowd came
9: 7 heard the s but did not see anyone.
1Co 14: 8 Again, if the trumpet does not s a
15:52 For the trumpet will s, the dead
Rev 1:15 was like the s of rushing waters.
8: 6 seven trumpets prepared to s them.
9: 9 and the s of their wings was like
10: 7 angel is about to s his trumpet,
14: 2 I heard a s from heaven like the
14: 2 The s I heard was like that of
18:22 The s of a millstone will never be

Sound[2] (Soundness)

Pr 3:21 My son, preserve s judgment and
4: 2 I give you s learning, so do not
8:14 Counsel and s judgment are mine;
18: 1 he defies all s judgment.
22:21 give s answers to him who sent you?
Jer 2:21 choice vine of s and reliable stock.
Zec 8:16 true and s judgment in your courts;
Mt 12:13 restored, just as s as the other.
Lk 15:27 because he has him back safe and s.'
Ac 20: 9 When he was s asleep, he fell to the
1Ti 1:10 else is contrary to the s doctrine
6: 3 does not agree to the s instruction
2Ti 1:13 keep as the pattern of s teaching,
4: 3 men will not put up with s doctrine.
Tit 1: 9 can encourage others by s doctrine
1:13 so that they will be s in the
2: 1 what is in accord with s doctrine.
2: 2 s in faith, in love and in endurance.

Sound[3] (Soundings)

1Sa 20:12 I will surely s out my father by

Sounded (Sound[1])

Lev 25: 9 have the trumpet s everywhere on the
Nu 10: 3 both are s, the whole community is

Nu 10: 4 If only one is s, the leaders—the
10: 5 a trumpet blast is s, the tribes
Jos 6:16 when the priests s the trumpet blast,
6:20 the trumpets s, the people shouted,
Jdg 7:22 the three hundred trumpets s, the
2Sa 18:16 Joab s the trumpet, and the troops
20: 1 He s the trumpet and shouted, "We
20:22 So he s the trumpet, and his men
1Ki 1:39 Then they s the trumpet and all the
Ne 4:18 who s the trumpet stayed with me.
Rev 6: 6 I heard what s like a voice among
8: 7 The first angel s his trumpet, and
8: 8 The second angel s his trumpet, and
8:10 The third angel s his trumpet, and a
8:12 The fourth angel s his trumpet, and
8:13 to be s by the other three angels!"
9: 1 The fifth angel s his trumpet, and I
9:13 The sixth angel s his trumpet, and I
11:15 The seventh angel s his trumpet, and
19: 1 After this I heard what s like the
19: 6 I heard what s like a great

Sounding (Sound[1])

Nu 10: 6 At the s of a second blast, the
Jos 6: 9 All this time the trumpets were s.
6:13 the LORD, while the trumpets kept s.
1Ch 15:28 with the s of rams' horns and
16:42 were responsible for the s of the
2Ch 5:12 by 120 priests s trumpets.
Ps 47: 5 the LORD amid the s of trumpets.
150: 3 Praise him with the s of the trumpet,

Soundings (Sound[3])

Ac 27:28 They took s and found that the water
27:28 A short time later they took s again

Soundness (Sound[2])

Ps 38: 3 bones have no s because of my sin.
Isa 1: 6 there is no s—only wounds and
Tit 2: 8 s of speech that cannot be condemned,

Sounds (Sound[1])

Ex 19:13 Only when the ram's horn s a long
Job 15:21 Terrifying s fill his ears; when all
39:24 stand still when the trumpet s.
Isa 18: 3 when a trumpet s, you will hear it.
Jer 7:34 I will bring an end to the s of joy
16: 9 I will bring an end to the s of joy
25:10 I will banish from them the s of joy
33:11 the s of joy and gladness, the
Am 3: 6 a trumpet s in a city, do not the
1Co 14: 7 case of lifeless things that make s,

Sour

Job 20:14 yet his food will turn s in his
Jer 31:29 'The fathers have eaten s grapes,
31:30 whoever eats s grapes—his own teeth
Eze 18: 2 'The fathers eat s grapes, and the
Rev 10: 9 It will turn your stomach s, but in
10:10 I had eaten it, my stomach turned s.

Source (Sources)

Ge 26:35 They were a s of grief to Isaac and
Lev 20:18 he has exposed the s of her flow,
Ps 80: 6 You have made us a s of contention
Isa 28: 6 a s of strength to those who turn
Eze 29:16 Egypt will no longer be a s of
Heb 5: 9 became the s of eternal salvation

Sources (Source)

Job 28:11 He searches the s of the rivers and
Jer 18:14 from distant s ever cease to flow?

South (South-east, Southern, Southernmost, Southland, Southward, South-west)

Ge 13:14 and look north and s, east and west.
28:14 the east, to the north and to the s.
Ex 26:18 Make twenty frames for the s side of
26:35 lampstand opposite it on the s side.
27: 9 The s side shall be a hundred cubits
36:23 made twenty frames for the s side
38: 9 The s side was a hundred cubits
Ex 40:24 on the s side of the tabernacle
Nu 2:10 On the s will be the divisions of
3:29 on the s side of the tabernacle.
10: 6 the camps on the s are to set out.
34: 4 cross s of Scorpion Pass, continue
34: 4 on to Zin and go s of Kadesh Barnea.
35: 5 three thousand on the s side, three
Dt 3:27 look west and north and s and east.
33: 2 the s, from his mountain slopes.
Jos 11: 2 in the Arabah s of Kinnereth, in the
13: 4 from the s, all the land of the
15: 1 the Desert of Zin in the extreme s.
15: 3 crossed s of Scorpion Pass,
15: 3 went over to the s of Kadesh Barnea.
15: 7 the Pass of Adummim s of the gorge.
17: 9 the boundary continued s to the
17:10 On the s the land belonged to
18: 5 to remain in its territory on the s
18:13 From there it crossed to the s slope
18:13 on the hill s of Lower Beth Horon.
18:14 the hill facing Beth Horon on the s
18:14 turned s along the western side
18:19 at the mouth of the Jordan in the s.
19:34 It touched Zebulun on the s, Asher
Jdg 21:19 Shechem, and to the s of Lebonah."
1Sa 14: 5 the other to the s towards Geba.
20:41 David got up from the s side of the
23:19 the hill of Hakilah, s of Jeshimon?
23:24 Maon, in the Arabah s of Jeshimon.
2Sa 24: 5 they camped near Aroer, s of the
1Ki 6: 8 was on the s side of the temple;
7:21 The pillar to the s he named Jakin
7:25 facing s and three facing east.
7:39 He placed five of the stands on the s
7:39 He placed the Sea on the s side, at
2Ki 11:11 from the s side to the north side of
23:13 on the s of the Hill of Corruption
1Ch 9:24 four sides: east, west, north and s.
26:15 The lot for the S Gate fell to
26:17 four a day on the s and two at a
2Ch 3:17 one to the s and one to the north.
3:17 The one to the s he named Jakin and
4: 4 facing s and three facing east.
4: 6 on the s side and five on the north.
4: 7 on the s side and five on the north.
4: 8 on the s side and five on the north.
4:10 He placed the Sea on the s side, at
23:10 from the s side to the north side of
Job 9: 9 and the constellations of the s.
23: 9 when he turns to the s, I catch no
37:17 land lies hushed under the s wind,
39:26 and spread his wings towards the s?
Ps 78:26 led forth the s wind by his power.
89:12 You created the north and the s;
107: 3 east and west, from north and s.
Ecc 1: 6 The wind blows to the s and turns to
11: 3 Whether a tree falls to the s or to
SS 4:16 Awake, north wind, and come, s wind!
Isa 43: 6 to the s, 'Do not hold them back.'
Eze 10: 3 were standing on the s side of the
16:46 who lived to the s of you with her
20:46 set your face towards the s;
20:46 preach against the s and prophesy
20:47 s to north will be scorched by it.
21: 4 against everyone from s to north.
40: 2 on whose s side were some buildings
40:24 he led me to the s side and I saw a
40:24 and I saw a gate facing s.
40:27 court also had a gate facing s,
40:27 to the outer gate on the s side;
40:28 the inner court through the s gate,
40:28 and he measured the s gate; it had
40:44 side of the north gate and facing s,
40:44 side of the s gate and facing north.
40:45 He said to me, "The room facing s is
41:11 on the north and another on the s;
42:10 On the s side along the length of
42:12 the doorways of the rooms on the s.
42:13 "The north and s rooms facing the
42:18 He measured the s side; it was five
46: 9 worship is to go out by the s gate;
46: 9 and whoever enters by the s gate is
47: 1 s side of the temple, s of the altar.
47: 2 water was flowing from the s side.
47:19 "On the s side it will run from
47:19 This will be the s boundary.
Eze 48:10 25,000 cubits long on the s side.
48:16 the s side 4,500 cubits, the east
48:17 250 cubits on the s, 250 cubits on
48:28 will run s from Tamar to the waters
48:33 "On the s side, which measures
Da 8: 4 the west and the north and the s.
8: 9 small but grew in power to the s
11: 5 "The king of the S will become
11: 6 The daughter of the king of the S
11: 9 realm of the king of the S but will
11:11 "Then the king of the S will march
11:12 the king of the S will be filled
11:14 will rise against the king of the S.
11:15 The forces of the S will be
11:17 an alliance with the king of the S.
11:25 courage against the king of the S.
11:25 The king of the S will wage war with
11:29 time he will invade the S again,
11:40 king of the S will engage him in
Zec 6: 6 the dappled horses towards the s."
9:14 will march in the storms of the s,
14: 4 moving north and half moving s.
14:10 from Geba to Rimmon, s of Jerusalem,
Mt 12:42 The Queen of the S will rise at the
Lk 11:31 The Queen of the S will rise at the
12:55 the s wind blows, you say, 'It's
13:29 from east and west and north and s,
Ac 8:26 "Go s to the road—the desert
21: 3 passing to the s of it, we sailed on to
27:13 a gentle s wind began to blow, they
28:13 The next day the s wind came up, and
Rev 21:13 three on the s and three on the west

South-east (East, South)

1Ki 7:39 side, at the s corner of the temple.
2Ch 4:10 on the south side, at the s corner.

Southern (South)

Nu 34: 3 "'Your s side will include some of
34: 3 On the east, your s boundary will
Jos 15: 2 Their s boundary started from the
15: 2 bay at the s end of the Salt Sea,
15: 4 This is their s boundary.
15: 8 along the s slope of the Jebusite
18:15 The s side began at the outskirts of
18:16 the s slope of the Jebusite city
18:19 This was the s boundary.
Eze 20:47 Say to the s forest: 'Hear the word
48:28 "The s boundary of Gad will run

Southernmost (South)

Jos 15:21 The s towns of the tribe of Judah in

Southland (South)

Isa 21: 1 whirlwinds sweeping through the s,
Eze 20:46 against the forest of the s.

Southward (South)

Dt 33:23 he will inherit s to the lake."
Jos 12: 3 then s below the slopes of Pisgah.
17: 7 The boundary ran s from there to

South-west (South, West)

Ac 27:12 Crete, facing both s and north-west.

Sovereign (*Sovereign Lord*, *Sovereign Lord*, Sovereignty)

Da 4:17 is s over the kingdoms of men
4:25 is s over the kingdoms of men
4:32 is s over the kingdoms of men
5:21 God is s over the kingdoms of men
Da 7:14 given authority, glory and s power;
Jude : 4 Jesus Christ our only S and Lord.

Sovereign Lord

Ge 15: 2 Abram said, "O S, what can you give
15: 8 Abram said, "O S, how can I know
Ex 23:17 the men are to appear before the S.
34:23 before the S, the God of Israel.
Dt 3:24 "O S, you have begun to show to your
9:26 I prayed to the LORD and said, "O S,
Jos 7: 7 Joshua said, "Ah, S, why did you
Jdg 6:22 "Ah, S! I have seen the angel of the

Jdg 16:28 "O **S**, remember me. O God, please
2Sa 7:18 "Who am I, O **S**, and what is my
7:19 O **S**, you have also spoken about the
7:19 usual way of dealing with man, O **S**?
7:20 For you know your servant, O **S**.
7:22 "How great you are, O **S**! There is
7:28 O **S**, you are God! Your words are
7:29 for you, O **S**, have spoken, and with
1Ki 2:26 ark of the **S** before my father David
8:53 when you, O **S**, brought our fathers
Ps 68:20 from the **S** comes escape from death.
71: 5 For you have been my hope, O **S**, my
71:16 and proclaim your mighty acts, O **S**;
73:28 I have made the **S** my refuge; I will
109:21 you, O **S**, deal well with me for your
140: 7 O **S**, my strong deliverer, who
141: 8 my eyes are fixed on you, O **S**;
Isa 7: 7 Yet this is what the **S** says: "'It
25: 8 The **S** will wipe away the tears from
28:16 this is what the **S** says: "See, I lay
30:15 This is what the **S**, the Holy One of
40:10 See, the **S** comes with power, and his
48:16 the **S** has sent me, with his Spirit.
49:22 This is what the **S** says: "See, I
50: 4 The **S** has given me an instructed
50: 5 The **S** has opened my ears, and I have
50: 7 the **S** helps me, I will not be
50: 9 is the **S** who helps me. Who is he who
51:22 This is what your **S** says, your God,
52: 4 For this is what the **S** says: "At
56: 8 The **S** declares—he who gathers the
61: 1 The Spirit of the **S** is on me,
61:11 so the **S** will make righteousness and
65:13 Therefore this is what the **S** says:
65:15 the **S** will put you to death,
Jer 1: 6 "Ah, **S**," I said, "I do not know how
2:22 is still before me," declares the **S**.
4:10 I said, "Ah, **S**, how completely you
7:20 "'Therefore this is what the **S** says:
14:13 I said, "Ah, **S**, the prophets keep
32:17 "Ah, **S**, you have made the heavens
32:25 you, O **S**, say to me, 'Buy the field
44:26 or swear, "As surely as the **S** lives.
50:25 for the **S** Almighty has work to do in
Eze 2: 4 to them, 'This is what the **S** says.'
3:11 to them, 'This is what the **S** says,'
3:27 to them, 'This is what the **S** says.
4:14 I said, "Not so, **S**! I have never
5: 5 "This is what the **S** says: This is
5: 7 "Therefore this is what the **S** says:
5: 8 "Therefore this is what the **S** says:
5:11 surely as I live, declares the **S**,
6: 3 of Israel, hear the word of the **S**.
6: 3 This is what the **S** says to the
6:11 "'This is what the **S** says: Strike
7: 2 "Son of man, this is what the **S** says
7: 5 "This is what the **S** says: Disaster!
8: 1 hand of the **S** came upon me there.
9: 8 "Ah, **S**! Are you going to destroy the
11: 7 "Therefore this is what the **S** says:
11: 8 bring against you, declares the **S**.
11:13 "Ah, **S**! Will you completely destroy
11:16 say: 'This is what the **S** says:
11:17 say: 'This is what the **S** says:
11:21 they have done, declares the **S**."
12:10 to them, 'This is what the **S** says:
12:19 'This is what the **S** says about those
12:23 'This is what the **S** says: I am
12:25 whatever I say, declares the **S**.'"
12:28 'This is what the **S** says: None of my
12:28 be fulfilled, declares the **S**.'"
13: 3 This is what the **S** says: Woe to the
13: 8 "'Therefore this is what the **S** says:
13: 8 I am against you, declares the **S**.
13: 9 Then you will know that I am the **S**.
13:13 "'Therefore this is what the **S** says:
13:16 was no peace, declares the **S**.'"
13:18 'This is what the **S** says: Woe to the
13:20 "'Therefore this is what the **S** says:
14: 4 'This is what the **S** says: When any
14: 6 'This is what the **S** says: Repent!
14:11 be their God, declares the **S**.'"
14:14 their righteousness, declares the **S**.
14:16 surely as I live, declares the **S**,
14:18 surely as I live, declares the **S**,
14:20 surely as I live, declares the **S**,
Eze 14:21 "For this is what the **S** says: How
14:23 it without cause, declares the **S**."
15: 6 "Therefore this is what the **S** says:
15: 8 been unfaithful, declares the **S**."
16: 3 say, 'This is what the **S** says to
16: 8 covenant with you, declares the **S**,
16:14 your beauty perfect, declares the **S**.
16:19 is what happened, declares the **S**.
16:23 "'Woe! Woe to you, declares the **S**.
16:30 weak-willed you are, declares the **S**
16:36 This is what the **S** says: Because you
16:43 what you have done, declares the **S**.
16:48 surely as I live, declares the **S**,
16:59 "'This is what the **S** says: I will
16:63 your humiliation, declares the **S**.'"
17: 3 'This is what the **S** says: A great
17: 9 'This is what the **S** says: Will it
17:16 'As surely as I live, declares the **S**,
17:19 "'Therefore this is what the **S** says:
17:22 "'This is what the **S** says: I myself
18: 3 "As surely as I live, declares the **S**,
18: 9 will surely live, declares the **S**.
18:23 death of the wicked? declares the **S**.
18:30 to his ways, declares the **S**.
18:32 the death of anyone, declares the **S**.
20: 3 'This is what the **S** says: Have you
20: 3 you enquire of me, declares the **S**.'
20: 5 'This is what the **S** says: On the
20:27 'This is what the **S** says: In this
20:30 'This is what the **S** says: Will you
20:31 As surely as I live, declares the **S**,
20:33 surely as I live, declares the **S**, I
20:36 so I will judge you, declares the **S**.
20:39 this is what the **S** says: Go and
20:40 mountain of Israel, declares the **S**,
20:44 house of Israel, declares the **S**.'"
20:47 This is what the **S** says: I am about
20:49 I said, "Ah, **S**! They are saying of
21: 7 surely take place, declares the **S**."
21:13 does not continue? declares the **S**.'
21:24 "Therefore this is what the **S** says:
21:26 this is what the **S** says: Take off
21:28 'This is what the **S** says about the
22: 3 'This is what the **S** says: O city
22:12 have forgotten me, declares the **S**.
22:19 Therefore this is what the **S** says:
22:28 They say, 'This is what the **S** says'—
22:31 all they have done, declares the **S**."
23:22 Oholibah, this is what the **S** says:
23:28 "For this is what the **S** says: I am
23:32 "This is what the **S** says: "You will
23:34 I have spoken, declares the **S**.
23:35 "Therefore this is what the **S** says:
23:46 "This is what the **S** says: Bring a
23:49 Then you will know that I am the **S**."
24: 3 'This is what the **S** says: "'Put on
24: 6 "'For this is what the **S** says:
24: 9 "'Therefore this is what the **S** says:
24:14 and your actions, declares the **S**.'"
24:21 'This is what the **S** says: I am about
24:24 you will know that I am the **S**.'
25: 3 Say to them, 'Hear the word of the **S**.
25: 3 This is what the **S** says: Because you
25: 6 For this is what the **S** says: Because
25: 8 "This is what the **S** says: 'Because
25:12 "This is what the **S** says: 'Because
25:13 therefore this is what the **S** says:
25:14 know my vengeance, declares the **S**.'
25:15 "This is what the **S** says: 'Because
25:16 therefore this is what the **S** says:
26: 3 therefore this is what the **S** says:
26: 5 for I have spoken, declares the **S**.
26: 7 "For this is what the **S** says:
26:14 LORD have spoken, declares the **S**.
26:15 "This is what the **S** says to Tyre:
26:19 "This is what the **S** says: When I
26:21 again be found, declares the **S**."
27: 3 'This is what the **S** says:
28: 2 'This is what the **S** says:
28: 6 "'Therefore this is what the **S** says:
28:10 I have spoken, declares the **S**.'"
28:12 'This is what the **S** says:
28:22 say: 'This is what the **S** says:
28:24 Then they will know that I am the **S**.
28:25 "'This is what the **S** says: When I
29: 3 'This is what the **S** says:
Eze 29: 8 "'Therefore this is what the **S** says:
29:13 "'Yet this is what the **S** says:
29:16 Then they will know that I am the **S**.
29:19 Therefore this is what the **S** says:
29:20 army did it for me, declares the **S**.
30: 2 'This is what the **S** says:
30: 6 sword within her, declares the **S**.
30:10 "'This is what the **S** says:
30:13 "'This is what the **S** says:
30:22 Therefore this is what the **S** says:
31:10 "'Therefore this is what the **S** says:
31:15 "'This is what the **S** says: On the
31:18 all his hordes, declares the **S**.'"
32: 3 "'This is what the **S** says:
32: 8 over your land, declares the **S**.
32:11 "'For this is what the **S** says:
32:14 flow like oil, declares the **S**.
32:16 they will chant it, declares the **S**."
32:31 killed by the sword, declares the **S**.
32:32 by the sword, declares the **S**."
33:11 'As surely as I live, declares the **S**,
33:25 'This is what the **S** says: Since you
33:27 'This is what the **S** says: As surely
34: 2 'This is what the **S** says: Woe to the
34: 8 surely as I live, declares the **S**,
34:10 This is what the **S** says: I am
34:11 "'For this is what the **S** says:
34:15 make them lie down, declares the **S**.
34:17 my flock, this is what the **S** says:
34:20 "'Therefore this is what the **S** says
34:30 are my people, declares the **S**.
34:31 I am your God, declares the **S**.'"
35: 3 say: 'This is what the **S** says: I am
35: 6 as surely as I live, declares the **S**,
35:11 as surely as I live, declares the **S**,
35:14 This is what the **S** says: While the
36: 2 This is what the **S** says: The enemy
36: 3 'This is what the **S** says: Because
36: 4 hear the word of the **S**: This is what
36: 4 **S** says to the mountains and hills,
36: 5 this is what the **S** says: In my
36: 6 'This is what the **S** says: I speak in
36: 7 Therefore this is what the **S** says:
36:13 "'This is what the **S** says: Because
36:14 nation childless, declares the **S**.
36:15 nation to fall, declares the **S**.'"
36:22 'This is what the **S** says: It is not
36:23 that I am the LORD, declares the **S**,
36:32 this for your sake, declares the **S**.
36:33 "'This is what the **S** says: On the
36:37 "This is what the **S** says: Once again
37: 3 I said, "O **S**, you alone know."
37: 5 This is what the **S** says to these
37: 9 'This is what the **S** says: Come from
37:12 'This is what the **S** says: O my
37:19 'This is what the **S** says: I am
37:21 'This is what the **S** says: I will
38: 3 say: 'This is what the **S** says: I am
38:10 "'This is what the **S** says: On that
38:14 'This is what the **S** says: In that
38:17 "'This is what the **S** says: Are you
38:18 will be aroused, declares the **S**.
38:21 on all my mountains, declares the **S**.
39: 1 'This is what the **S** says: I am
39: 5 for I have spoken, declares the **S**.
39: 8 surely take place, declares the **S**.
39:10 who looted them, declares the **S**.
39:13 day for them, declares the **S**.
39:17 "Son of man, this is what the **S** says:
39:20 of every kind,' declares the **S**.
39:25 "Therefore this is what the **S** says:
39:29 house of Israel, declares the **S**."
43:18 "Son of man, this is what the **S** says:
43:19 minister before me, declares the **S**.
43:27 I will accept you, declares the **S**."
44: 6 'This is what the **S** says: Enough of
44: 9 This is what the **S** says:
44:12 of their sin, declares the **S**.
44:15 of fat and blood, declares the **S**.
44:27 for himself, declares the **S**.
45: 9 "'This is what the **S** says: You have
45: 9 my people, declares the **S**.
45:15 for the people, declares the **S**.
45:18 "'This is what the **S** says: In the
46: 1 "'This is what the **S** says: The gate
46:16 "'This is what the **S** says: If the

Eze 47:13 This is what the **S** says: "These are
47:23 his inheritance," declares the **S**.
48:29 be their portions," declares the **S**.
Am 1: 8 Philistines is dead," says the **S**.
3: 7 Surely the **S** does nothing without
3: 8 **S** has spoken—who can but prophesy?
3:11 Therefore this is what the **S** says:
4: 2 The **S** has sworn by his holiness:
4: 5 you love to do," declares the **S**.
5: 3 This is what the **S** says: "The city
6: 8 The **S** has sworn by himself—the LORD
7: 1 This is what the **S** showed me: He was
7: 2 "**S**, forgive! How can Jacob survive?
7: 4 This is what the **S** showed me:
7: 4 The **S** was calling for judgment by
7: 5 I cried out, "**S**, I beg you, stop!
7: 6 will not happen either," the **S** said.
8: 1 This is what the **S** showed me:
8: 3 "In that day," declares the **S**,
8: 9 "In that day," declares the **S**,
8:11 "The days are coming," declares the **S**
9: 8 "Surely the eyes of the **S** are on the
Ob : 1 This is what the **S** says about Edom—
Mic 1: 2 that the **S** may witness against you,
Hab 3:19 The **S** is my strength; he makes my
Zep 1: 7 Be silent before the **S**, for the day
Zec 9:14 The **S** will sound the trumpet;

Sovereign Lord
Lk 2:29 "**S**, as you have promised, you now
Ac 4:24 "**S**," they said, "you made the heaven
2Pe 2: 1 even denying the **s** who bought them
Rev 6:10 "How long, **S**, holy and true, until

Sovereignty (Sovereign)
Da 5:18 gave your father Nebuchadnezzar **s**
7:27 the **s**, power and greatness of the

Sow[1] (Sowed, Sower, Sowing, Sown, Sows)
Ex 23:10 "For six years you are to **s** your
23:16 of the crops you **s** in your field.
Lev 25: 3 For six years **s** your fields, and for
25: 4 Do not **s** your fields or prune your
25:11 do not **s** and do not reap what grows
Dt 28:38 You will **s** much seed in the field
2Ki 19:29 But in the third year **s** and reap,
Job 4: 8 and those who **s** trouble reap it.
Ps 126: 5 Those who **s** in tears will reap with
126: 6 carrying seed to **s**, will return with
Ecc 11: 6 **S** your seed in the morning, and at
Isa 28:25 does he not **s** caraway and scatter
30:23 for the seed you **s** in the ground,
37:30 But in the third year **s** and reap,
Jer 4: 3 ground and do not **s** among thorns.
12:13 They will **s** wheat but reap thorns;
35: 7 must never build houses, **s** seed or
Hos 8: 7 "They **s** the wind and reap the
10:12 **S** for yourselves righteousness, reap
Mt 6:26 **s** or reap or store away in barns,
13: 3 "A farmer went out to **s** his seed.
13:27 'sir, didn't you **s** good seed in your
Mk 4: 3 A farmer went out to **s** his seed.
Lk 8: 5 "A farmer went out to **s** his seed.
12:24 Consider the ravens: They do not **s**
19:21 put in and reap what you did not **s**.'
19:22 in, and reaping what I did not **s**?
1Co 15:36 What you **s** does not come to life
15:37 you **s**, you do not plant the body
Jas 3:18 Peacemakers who **s** in peace raise a

Sow[2]
2Pe 2:22 "A **s** that is washed goes back to her

Sowed (Sow[1])
Ps 107:37 They **s** fields and planted vineyards
Mt 13:24 a man who **s** good seed in his field.
13:25 his enemy came and **s** weeds among the
13:37 "The one who **s** the good seed is the

Sower (Sow[1])
Isa 55:10 so that it yields seed for the **s**
Jer 50:16 Cut off from Babylon the **s**, and the
Mt 13:18 to what the parable of the **s** means:
Jn 4:36 so that the **s** and the reaper may be
2Co 9:10 Now he who supplies seed to the **s**

Sowing (Sow[1])
Isa 32:20 **s** your seed by every stream,

Sown (Sow[1])
Job 31: 8 may others eat what I have **s**, and
Isa 19: 7 Every **s** field along the Nile will
40:24 no sooner are they **s**, no sooner do
Jer 2: 2 the desert, through a land not **s**.
Eze 36: 9 you will be ploughed and **s**,
Mt 13: 8 sixty or thirty times what was **s**.
13:19 away what was **s** in his heart.
13:19 This is the seed **s** along the path.
13:23 sixty or thirty times what was **s**."
25:24 harvesting where you have not **s** and
25:26 that I harvest where I have not **s**
Mk 4:15 along the path, where the word is **s**.
4:15 away the word that was **s** in them.
4:16 Others, like seed **s** on rocky places,
4:18 Still others, like seed **s** among
4:20 Others, like seed **s** on good soil,
4:20 or even a hundred times what was **s**."
Lk 8: 8 a hundred times more than was **s**.
1Co 9:11 If we have **s** spiritual seed among
15:42 The body that is **s** is perishable, it
15:43 is **s** in dishonour, it is raised in
15:43 **s** in weakness, it is raised in power;
15:44 is **s** a natural body, it is raised a

Sows (Sow[1])
Pr 11:18 **s** righteousness reaps a sure reward.
22: 8 He who **s** wickedness reaps trouble,
Mt 13:39 the enemy who **s** them is the devil.
Mk 4:14 The farmer **s** the word.
Jn 4:37 'One **s** and another reaps' is true.
2Co 9: 6 Whoever **s** sparingly will also reap
9: 6 and whoever **s** generously will also
Gal 6: 7 A man reaps what he **s**.
6: 8 The one who **s** to please his sinful
6: 8 the one who **s** to please the Spirit,

Space (Spacious)
Ge 32:16 and keep some **s** between the herds."
Ex 25:37 they light the **s** in front of it.
1Sa 26:13 there was a wide **s** between them.
1Ki 7:36 in every available **s**, with wreaths
Job 26: 7 out the northern skies over empty **s**;
Isa 5: 8 join field to field till no **s** is
49:20 for us; give us more **s** to live in.'
Eze 41:17 In the **s** above the outside of the
42: 5 for the galleries took more **s** from
42: 6 so they were smaller in floor **s** than

Spacious (Space)
Ex 3: 8 of that land into a good and **s** land,
Jdg 18:10 a **s** land that God has put into your
2Sa 22:20 He brought me out into a **s** place;
1Ch 4:40 the land was **s**, peaceful and quiet.
Ne 7: 4 Now the city was large and **s**, but
9:35 **s** and fertile land you gave them,
Job 36:16 to a **s** place free from restriction,
Ps 18:19 He brought me out into a **s** place;
31: 8 but have set my feet in a **s** place.
104:25 There is the sea, vast and **s**,
Jer 22:14 a great palace with **s** upper rooms.

Spain
Ro 15:24 I plan to do so when I go to **S**.
15:28 go to **S** and visit you on the way.

Span
Ex 23:26 I will give you a full life **s**.
28:16 be square—a **s** long and a **s** wide
39: 9 was square—a **s** long and a **s** wide
Ps 39: 5 the **s** of my years is as nothing
90:10 their **s** is but trouble and sorrow,
Isa 23:15 years, the **s** of a king's life.
Eze 43:13 with a rim of one **s** around the edge.

Spare (Spared, Spares, Sparing, Sparingly)
Ge 18:24 not **s** the place for the sake of the
18:26 **s** the whole place for their sake."
Dt 13: 8 Show him no pity. Do not **s** him or
Jos 2:13 that you will **s** the lives of my
22:22 to the LORD, do not **s** us this day.
Jdg 6: 4 did not **s** a living thing for Israel,
1Sa 15: 3 Do not **s** them; put to death men and
2Sa 21: 2 Israelites had sworn to ⌊**s**⌋ them,
1Ki 16:11 He did not **s** a single male, whether
20:31 Perhaps he will **s** your life."
2Ki 7: 4 If they **s** us, we live; if they kill
2Ch 31:10 had enough to eat and plenty to **s**,
Est 4:11 gold sceptre to him and **s** his life.
7: 3 And **s** my people—this is my request.
Job 2: 6 but you must **s** his life."
33:24 '**S** him from going down to the pit;
Ps 78:50 he did not **s** them from death but
Pr 20:13 awake and you will have food to **s**.
Isa 9:19 the fire; no-one will **s** his brother.
47: 3 take vengeance; I will **s** no-one."
Jer 50:14 Shoot at her! **S** no arrows, for she
50:20 for I will forgive the remnant I **s**.
51: 3 Do not **s** her young men; completely
Eze 5:11 not look on you with pity or **s** you.
6: 8 "'But I will **s** some, for some of
7: 4 not look on you with pity or **s** you;
7: 9 not look on you with pity or **s** you;
8:18 not look on them with pity or **s** them.
9:10 not look on them with pity or **s** them,
12:16 I will **s** a few of them from the
Da 5:19 those he wanted to **s**, he spared;
Joel 2:17 Let them say, "**S** your people, O LORD.
Am 7: 8 I will **s** them no longer.
8: 2 I will **s** them no longer.
Zec 11: 5 Their own shepherds do not **s** them.
Mal 3:17 I will **s** them, just as in compassion
Lk 15:17 father's hired men have food to **s**,
Ac 20:29 among you and will not **s** the flock.
27:43 the centurion wanted to **s** Paul's
Ro 8:32 He who did not **s** his own Son, but
11:21 For if God did not **s** the natural
11:21 branches, he will not **s** you either.
1Co 7:28 this life, and I want to **s** you this.
2Co 1:23 it was in order to **s** you that I did
13: 2 On my return I will not **s** those who
Php 2:27 on me, to **s** me sorrow upon sorrow.
2Pe 2: 4 For if God did not **s** angels when
2: 5 if he did not **s** the ancient world

Spared (Spare)
Ge 12:13 my life will be **s** because of you."
19:20 isn't it? Then my life will be **s**."
32:30 to face, and yet my life was **s**."
Ex 12:27 **s** our homes when he struck down the
Nu 22:33 you by now, but I would have **s** her."
Jos 6:17 with her in her house shall be **s**,
6:25 Joshua **s** Rahab the prostitute, with
Jdg 1:25 but **s** the man and his whole family.
8:19 if you had **s** their lives, I would not
21:14 of Jabesh Gilead who had been **s**.
1Sa 2:33 **s** only to blind your eyes with tears
15: 9 Saul and the army **s** Agag and the
15:15 they **s** the best of the sheep and
24:10 urged me to kill you, but I **s** you;
2Sa 21: 7 The king **s** Mephibosheth son of
2Ki 23:18 So they **s** his bones and those of
2Ch 36:17 and **s** neither young man nor young
Job 21:30 that the evil man is **s** from the day
Ps 30: 3 **s** me from going down into the pit.
Isa 57: 1 are taken away to be **s** from evil.
Jer 38:17 your life will be **s** and this city
38:20 with you, and your life will be **s**.
Eze 6:12 and is **s** will die of famine.
13:19 have **s** those who should not live.
Da 5:19 those he wanted to spare, he **s**;
Ac 27:21 **s** yourselves this damage and loss.

Spares (Spare)
Pr 13:24 He who **s** the rod hates his son, but
Mal 3:17 a man **s** his son who serves him.

Sparing (Spare)
Ge 19:19 great kindness to me in s my life.
Jos 11:11 not s anything that breathed,
11:14 them, not s anyone that breathed.
Pr 21:26 but the righteous give without s.

Sparingly (Spare)
2Co 9: 6 Whoever sows s will also reap s,

Spark (Sparks)
Isa 1:31 become tinder and his work a s;
Jas 3: 5 forest is set on fire by a small s.

Sparkle (Sparkled, Sparkles, Sparkling)
Zec 9:16 s in his land like jewels in a crown.

Sparkled (Sparkle)
Eze 1:16 the wheels: They s like chrysolite,
10: 9 the wheels s like chrysolite.

Sparkles (Sparkle)
Pr 23:31 when it s in the cup, when it goes

Sparkling (Sparkle)
Isa 54:12 your gates of s jewels, and all your
Eze 1:22 an expanse, s like ice, and awesome.

Sparks (Spark)
Job 5: 7 trouble as surely as s fly upward.
41:19 his mouth; s of fire shoot out.

Sparrow (Sparrows)
Ps 84: 3 Even the s has found a home, and the
Pr 26: 2 Like a fluttering s or a darting

Sparrows (Sparrow)
Mt 10:29 Are not two s sold for a penny?
10:31 you are worth more than many s.
Lk 12: 6 Are not five s sold for two pennies?
12: 7 you are worth more than many s.

Spat (Spit)
Nu 12:14 "If her father had s in her face,
Mt 26:67 they s in his face and struck him
27:30 They s on him, and took the staff
Mk 7:33 he s and touched the man's tongue.
8:23 When he had s on the man's eyes and
15:19 the head with a staff and s on him.
Jn 9: 6 Having said this, he s on the ground,

Spattered
Lev 6:27 and if any of the blood is s on a
2Ki 9:33 and some of her blood s the wall and
Isa 63: 3 their blood s my garments, and I

Speaker (Spokesman, Spokesmen)
Ac 14:12 Hermes because he was the chief s.
1Co 14:11 I am a foreigner to the s, and he
14:28 the s should keep quiet in the
14:30 down, the first s should stop.
2Co 11: 6 I may not be a trained s, but I do

Spear (Spearhead, Spearmen, Spears)
Nu 25: 7 the assembly, took a s in his hand
25: 8 He drove the s through both of them—
Jdg 5: 8 and not a shield or s was seen among
1Sa 13:22 had a sword or s in his hand;
17: 7 His s shaft was like a weaver's rod,
17:45 me with sword and s and javelin,
17:47 by sword or s that the LORD saves;
18:10 Saul had a s in his hand
19: 9 in his house with his s in his hand.
19:10 to pin him to the wall with his s,
19:10 as Saul drove the s into the wall.
20:33 Saul hurled his s at him to kill him.
21: 8 "Don't you have a s or sword here?
22: 6 And Saul, s in hand, was seated
26: 7 s stuck in the ground near his head.
26: 8 the ground with one thrust of my s;
26:11 Now get the s and water jug that are
1Sa 26:12 David took the s and water jug near
26:16 Where are the king's s and water jug
26:22 "Here is the king's s," David
2Sa 1: 6 there was Saul leaning on his s,
2:23 butt of his s into Asahel's stomach,
2:23 and the s came out through his back.
21:19 s with a shaft like a weaver's rod.
23: 7 a tool of iron or the shaft of a s;
23: 8 his s against eight hundred men,
23:18 He raised his s against three
23:21 Although the Egyptian had a s in his
23:21 snatched the s from the Egyptian's
23:21 hand and killed him with his own s.
1Ch 11:11 his s against three hundred men,
11:20 He raised his s against three
11:23 Although the Egyptian had a s like a
11:23 snatched the s from the Egyptian's
11:23 hand and killed him with his own s.
12: 8 and able to handle the shield and s.
12:24 men of Judah, carrying shield and s—
20: 5 s with a shaft like a weaver's rod.
2Ch 25: 5 able to handle the s and shield.
Job 39:23 along with the flashing s and lance.
41:26 the s or the dart or the javelin.
Ps 35: 3 Brandish s and javelin against those
46: 9 breaks the bow and shatters the s,
Jer 6:23 They are armed with bow and s;
Hab 3:11 at the lightning of your flashing s.
3:14 With his own s you pierced his head
Jn 19:34 pierced Jesus' side with a s,

Spearhead (Spear)
2Sa 21:16 whose bronze s weighed three hundred

Spearmen (Spear)
Ac 23:23 s to go to Caesarea at nine tonight.

Spears (Spear)
1Sa 13:19 the Hebrews will make swords or s!"
1Ki 18:28 themselves with swords and s,
2Ki 11:10 he gave the commanders the s and
1Ch 12:34 37,000 men carrying shields and s;
2Ch 11:12 He put shields and s in all the
14: 8 with large shields and with s,
23: 9 the s and the large and small
26:14 Uzziah provided shields, s, helmets,
Ne 4:13 with their swords, s and bows.
4:16 with s, shields, bows and armour.
4:21 work with half the men holding s,
Job 41: 7 harpoons or his head with fishing s?
Ps 57: 4 men whose teeth are s and arrows,
Isa 2: 4 and their s into pruning hooks.
Jer 46: 4 Polish your s, put on your armour!
50:42 They are armed with bows and s;
Eze 39: 9 and arrows, the war clubs and s.
Joel 3:10 and your pruning hooks into s.
Mic 4: 3 and their s into pruning hooks.
Na 2: 3 the s of pine are brandished.
3: 3 flashing swords and glittering s!

Special
Ge 47: 6 of any among them with s ability,
Lev 22:21 a s vow or as a freewill offering,
27: 2 'If anyone makes a s vow to dedicate
Nu 6: 2 a man or woman wants to make a s vow
15: 3 for s vows or freewill offerings or
15: 8 for a s vow or a fellowship offering
Dt 12: 6 your tithes and s gifts, what you
12:11 your tithes and s gifts, and all the
12:17 your freewill offerings or s gifts.
Jos 15:19 She replied, "Do me a s favour.
Jdg 1:15 She replied, "Do me a s favour.
2Sa 13: 6 and make some s bread in my sight,
16: 6 all the troops and the s guard
1Ki 1: 8 s guard did not join Adonijah.
1:10 the s guard or his brother Solomon.
Est 1:14 Media who had s access to the king
2: 9 her beauty treatments and s food.
Jer 13:21 you cultivated as your s allies?
Eze 44:30 s gifts will belong to the priests.
45:13 "'This is the s gift you are to
45:16 participate in this s gift for the
48: 8 you are to present as a s gift.
48: 9 "The s portion you are to offer to
Eze 48:12 will be a s gift to them from the
48:20 As a s gift you will set aside the
Jn 19:31 the next day was to be a s Sabbath.
Ro 14: 6 He who regards one day as s, does so
1Co 12:23 honourable we treat with s honour.
12:23 are treated with s modesty,
12:24 parts need no s treatment.
Gal 4:10 You are observing s days and months
2Th 3:14 in this letter, take s note of him.
Jas 2: 3 If you show s attention to the man

Specific (Specify)
Nu 4:32 man the s things he is to carry.

Specifications (Specify)
1Ki 6:38 all its details according to its s.
2Ch 4: 7 according to the s for them

Specified (Specify)
Lev 27: 8 vow is too poor to pay the s amount,
Nu 29: 6 offerings and drink offerings as s.
29:18 offerings according to the number s.
29:21 offerings according to the number s.
29:24 offerings according to the number s.
29:27 offerings according to the number s.
29:30 offerings according to the number s.
29:33 offerings according to the number s.
29:37 offerings according to the number s.

Specify (Specific, Specifications, Specified, Specifying)
1Ki 5: 9 in rafts by sea to the place you s.

Specifying (Specify)
Ac 25:27 without s the charges against him."

Speck (Speckled)
Mt 7: 3 "Why do you look at the s of sawdust
7: 4 'Let me take the s out of your eye,'
7: 5 the s from your brother's eye.
Lk 6:41 "Why do you look at the s of sawdust
6:42 'Brother, let me take the s out of
6:42 the s from your brother's eye.

Speckled (Speck)
Ge 30:32 from them every s or spotted sheep,
30:32 lamb and every spotted or s goat.
30:33 possession that is not s or spotted,
30:35 and all the s or spotted female
30:39 that were streaked or s or spotted.
31: 8 'The s ones will be your wages,'
31: 8 the flocks gave birth to s young;
31:10 flock were streaked, s or spotted.
31:12 flock are streaked, s or spotted,
Jer 12: 9 like a s bird of prey that other

Spectacle
Eze 28:17 I made a s of you before kings.
Na 3: 6 you with contempt and make you a s.
1Co 4: 9 We have been made a s to the whole
Col 2:15 he made a public s of them,

Sped (Speed)
Eze 1:14 The creatures s back and forth like

Speech (Speeches)
Ge 11: 1 had one language and a common s.
Ex 4:10 I am slow of s and tongue."
Ps 19: 2 Day after day they pour forth s;
19: 3 There is no s or language where
55: 9 O Lord, confound their s, for I see
55:21 His s is smooth as butter, yet war
Pr 1:21 of the city she makes her s:
5: 3 and her s is smoother than oil;
8:13 evil behaviour and perverse s.
12: 6 the s of the upright rescues them.
16:27 and his s is like a scorching fire.
22:11 pure heart and whose s is gracious
26:25 Though his s is charming, do not
Ecc 5: 3 so the s of a fool when there are
Isa 18: 2 an aggressive nation of strange s,
18: 7 an aggressive nation of strange s,
29: 4 your s will mumble out of the dust.

Isa 29: 4 out of the dust your **s** will whisper.
33:19 those people of an obscure **s**, with
Jer 5:15 know, whose **s** you do not understand.
Eze 3: 5 of obscure **s** and difficult language,
3: 6 not to many peoples of obscure **s** and
Mk 9:17 a spirit that has robbed him of **s**.
Jn 10: 6 Jesus used this figure of **s**, but
16:29 clearly and without figures of **s**.
Ac 5:40 His **s** persuaded them. They called
7:22 and was powerful in **s** and action.
2Co 6: 7 in truthful **s** and in the power of
8: 7 in **s**, in knowledge, in complete
1Ti 4:12 an example for the believers in **s**,
Tit 2: 8 soundness of **s** that cannot be
1Pe 3:10 evil and his lips from deceitful **s**.
2Pe 2:16 a beast without **s**—who spoke with a

Speeches (Speech)
Job 15: 3 words, with **s** that have no value?
16: 3 Will your long-winded **s** never end?
16: 4 I could make fine **s** against you and
18: 2 "When will you end these **s**?

Speechless
Da 10:15 face towards the ground and was **s**.
Mt 22:12 The man was **s**.
Ac 9: 7 travelling with Saul stood there **s**;

Speed (Sped, Speeds)
Ro 9:28 on earth with **s** and finality."
2Pe 3:12 to the day of God and **s** its coming.

Speeds (Speed)
Isa 16: 5 and **s** the cause of righteousness.

Spell (Spells)
Rev 18:23 By your magic **s** all the nations

Spells (Spell)
Dt 18:11 or casts **s**, or who is a medium or
Isa 47: 9 sorceries and all your potent **s**.
47:12 "Keep on, then, with your magic **s**
Mic 5:12 and you will no longer cast **s**.

Spelt
Ex 9:32 The wheat and **s**, however, were not
Isa 28:25 in its plot, and **s** in its field?
Eze 4: 9 beans and lentils, millet and **s**;

Spend (Spending, Spent)
Ge 19: 2 wash your feet and **s** the night
19: 2 "we will **s** the night in the square.
24:23 house for us to **s** the night?"
24:25 as room for you to **s** the night."
Nu 22: 8 "**S** the night here," Balaam said to
Jdg 16: 1 He went in to **s** the night with her.
19: 9 **S** the night here; the day is nearly
19:11 of the Jebusites and **s** the night."
19:13 **s** the night in one of those places."
19:15 There they stopped to **s** the night.
19:20 don't **s** the night in the square."
20: 4 Gibeah in Benjamin to **s** the night.
2Sa 17: 8 not **s** the night with the troops.
17:16 'Do not **s** the night at the fords in
1Ch 9:27 They would **s** the night stationed
Ne 13:21 "Why do you **s** the night by the wall
Job 21:13 They **s** their years in prosperity and
24: 7 Lacking clothes, they **s** the night
31:32 no stranger had to **s** the night in
36:11 they will **s** the rest of their days
Ps 25:13 He will **s** his days in prosperity,
Pr 31: 3 do not **s** your strength on women,
SS 7:11 let us **s** the night in the villages.
Isa 55: 2 Why **s** money on what is not bread,
58:10 if you **s** yourselves on behalf of the
65: 4 who sit among the graves and **s** their
Eze 6:12 So will I **s** my wrath upon them.
7: 8 on you and **s** my anger against you;
13:15 I will **s** my wrath against the wall
20: 8 **s** my anger against them in Egypt.
20:21 **s** my anger against them in the
Joel 1:13 Come, **s** the night in sackcloth, you
Mk 6:37 Are we to go and **s** that much on
Lk 21:37 he went out to **s** the night on the
Ac 18:20 they asked him to **s** more time with
28:14 invited us to **s** a week with them.
1Co 16: 6 or even **s** the winter, so that you
16: 7 I hope to **s** some time with you,
2Co 12:15 I will very gladly **s** for you
Jas 4: 3 **s** what you get on your pleasures.
4:13 **s** a year there, carry on business

Spending (Spend)
Ac 15:33 After **s** some time there, they were
18:23 After **s** some time in Antioch, Paul
20:16 **s** time in the province of Asia,
25: 6 After **s** eight or ten days with them,
25:14 Since they were **s** many days there,

Spent (Spend)
Ge 24:54 ate and drank and **s** the night there.
31:54 had eaten, they **s** the night there.
32:13 He **s** the night there, and from what
32:21 he himself **s** the night in the camp.
Lev 26:20 Your strength will be **s** in vain,
Dt 1:46 many days—all the time you **s** there.
Jos 6:11 to camp and **s** the night there.
8: 9 Joshua **s** that night with the people.
Jdg 18: 2 of Micah, where they **s** the night.
2Sa 12:16 **s** the nights lying on the ground.
14: 2 **s** many days grieving for the dead.
1Ki 5:14 so that they **s** one month in Lebanon
6:38 He had **s** seven years building it.
19: 9 went into a cave and **s** the night.
2Ki 12:13 was not **s** for making silver basins,
1Ch 12:39 The men **s** three days there with
Ne 9: 3 and **s** another quarter in confession
13:20 goods **s** the night outside Jerusalem.
Pr 5:11 when your flesh and body are **s**.
Isa 49: 4 I have **s** my strength in vain and for
Eze 5:13 And when I have **s** my wrath upon them,
Da 6:18 and **s** the night without eating
Mt 21:17 to Bethany, where he **s** the night.
Mk 5:26 many doctors and had **s** all she had,
Lk 6:12 and **s** the night praying to God.
15:14 After he had **s** everything, there was
Jn 1:39 staying, and **s** that day with him.
3:22 **s** some time with them, and baptised.
Ac 9:19 Saul **s** several days with the
14: 3 Paul and Barnabas **s** considerable
17:21 who lived there **s** their time doing
2Co 11:25 **s** a night and a day in the open sea,
1Pe 4: 3 For you have **s** enough time in the

Spew (Spewed)
Ps 59: 7 See what they **s** from their mouths—
59: 7 they **s** out swords from their lips,
Jer 51:44 him **s** out what he has swallowed.

Spewed (Spew)
Jer 51:34 delicacies, and then has **s** us out.
Rev 12:15 from his mouth the serpent **s** water
12:16 the dragon had **s** out of his mouth.

Spice (Spiced, Spice-laden, Spices)
SS 4:10 of your perfume than any **s**!
5: 1 I have gathered my myrrh with my **s**.
5:13 His cheeks are like beds of **s**
Rev 18:13 cargoes of cinnamon and **s**, of

Spiced (Spice)
SS 8: 2 I would give you **s** wine to drink,

Spice-laden (Load, Spice)
SS 8:14 a young stag on the **s** mountains.

Spices (Spice)
Ge 37:25 Their camels were loaded with **s**,
43:11 some **s** and myrrh, some pistachio
Ex 25: 6 **s** for the anointing oil and for the
30:23 "Take the following fine **s**: 500
30:34 "Take fragrant **s**—gum resin, onycha
35: 8 **s** for the anointing oil and for the
35:28 They also brought **s** and olive oil
1Ki 10: 2 caravan—with camels carrying **s**,
10:10 large quantities of **s**, and precious
1Ki 10:10 Never again were so many **s** brought
10:25 weapons and **s**, and horses and mules.
2Ki 20:13 the gold, the **s** and the fine
1Ch 9:29 wine, and the oil, incense and **s**.
9:30 priests took care of mixing the **s**.
2Ch 9: 1 caravan—with camels carrying **s**,
9: 9 large quantities of **s**, and precious
9: 9 There had never been such **s** as those
9:24 weapons and **s**, and horses and mules.
16:14 with **s** and various blended perfumes,
32:27 precious stones, **s**, shields and all
Ps 75: 8 full of foaming wine mixed with **s**;
SS 3: 6 made from all the **s** of the merchant?
4:14 and aloes and all the finest **s**.
6: 2 to his garden, to the beds of **s**,
Isa 39: 2 the gold, the **s**, the fine oil, his
Eze 24:10 Cook the meat well, mixing in the **s**;
27:22 of **s** and precious stones, and gold.
Mt 23:23 You give a tenth of your **s**—mint,
Mk 16: 1 and Salome bought **s** so that they
Lk 23:56 they went home and prepared **s** and
24: 1 the women took the **s** they had
Jn 19:40 it, with the **s**, in strips of linen.

Spider's
Job 8:14 what he relies on is a **s** web.
Isa 59: 5 the eggs of vipers and spin a **s** web.

Spied (Spy)
Jos 6:22 Joshua said to the two men who had **s**
7: 2 So the men went up and **s** out Ai.
Jdg 18:14 the five men who had **s** out the land
18:17 The five men who had **s** out the land

Spies (Spy)
Ge 42: 9 "You are **s**! You have come to see
42:11 Your servants are honest men, not **s**."
42:14 "It is just as I told you: You are **s**
42:16 surely as Pharaoh lives, you are **s**!"
42:31 'We are honest men; we are not **s**.
42:34 that you are not **s** but honest men.
Nu 21:32 After Moses had sent **s** to Jazer, the
Jos 2: 1 Joshua son of Nun secretly sent two **s**
2: 7 the men set out in pursuit of the **s**
2: 8 Before the **s** lay down for the night,
6:17 because she hid the **s** we sent.
6:25 men Joshua had sent as **s** to Jericho
Jdg 1:24 the **s** saw a man coming out of the
Lk 20:20 sent **s**, who pretended to be honest.
20:21 the **s** questioned him: "Teacher, we
Heb 11:31 because she welcomed the **s**, was not
Jas 2:25 did when she gave lodging to the **s**

Spilled (Spills)
Ge 38: 9 he **s** his semen on the ground to keep
2Sa 14:14 Like water **s** on the ground, which
20:10 his intestines **s** out on the ground.
Ac 1:18 open and all his intestines **s** out.

Spills (Spilled)
Job 16:13 kidneys and **s** my gall on the ground.

Spin (Spun)
Isa 59: 5 eggs of vipers and **s** a spider's web
Mt 6:28 They do not labour or **s**.
Lk 12:27 They do not labour or **s**. Yet I tell

Spindle
Pr 31:19 and grasps the **s** with her fingers.

Spirit (*Evil spirit, Holy Spirit, My spirit, Spirit of God, Spirit of the Lord, Spirit of the Lord*, Spirit's, Spiritist, Spiritists, Spirits, Spiritual, Spiritually)
Ge 45:27 the **s** of their father Jacob revived.
Nu 11:17 and I will take of the **S** that is on
11:17 is on you and put the **S** on them.
11:25 and he took of the **S** that was on him
11:25 and put the **S** on the seventy elders.
11:25 When the **S** rested on them, they
11:26 Yet the **S** also rested on them, and
11:29 the Lord would put his **S** on them!"
14:24 my servant Caleb has a different **s**

Nu 27:18 a man in whom is the **s**, and lay
Dt 2:30 For the LORD your God had made his **s**
34: 9 filled with the **s** of wisdom because
1Sa 16:23 Whenever the **s** from God came upon
18: 1 Jonathan became one in **s** with David,
28: 8 "Consult a **s** for me," he said, "and
28:13 a **s** coming up out of the ground."
30: 6 each one was bitter in **s** because of
2Sa 13:39 the **s** of the king longed to go to
1Ki 22:21 Finally, a **s** came forward, stood
22:22 "'I will go out and be a lying **s** in
22:23 "So now the LORD has put a lying **s**
22:24 "Which way did the **s** from the LORD
2Ki 2: 9 inherit a double portion of your **s**,
2:15 The **s** of Elijah is resting on Elisha.
19: 7 I am going to put such a **s** in him
1Ch 5:26 God of Israel stirred up the **s** of Pul
12:18 the **S** came upon Amasai, chief of the
28:12 all that the **S** had put in his mind
2Ch 18:20 Finally, a **s** came forward, stood
18:21 "'I will go and be a lying **s** in the
18:22 "So now the LORD has put a lying **s**
18:23 "Which way did the **s** from the LORD
Ne 9:20 You gave your good **S** to instruct
9:30 By your **S** you admonished them
Job 4:15 A **s** glided past my face, and the
6: 4 my **s** drinks in their poison;
26: 4 And whose **s** spoke from your mouth?
31:39 or broken the **s** of its tenants,
32: 8 is the **s** in a man, the breath of the
32:18 and the **s** within me compels me;
34:14 and he withdrew his **s** and breath,
Ps 32: 2 him and in whose **s** is no deceit.
34:18 saves those who are crushed in **s**.
51:10 and renew a steadfast **s** within me.
51:12 grant me a willing **s**, to sustain me.
51:17 The sacrifices of God are a broken **s**;
76:12 He breaks the **s** of rulers;
104:30 you send your **S**, they are created,
139: 7 Where can I go from your **S**?
143:10 your good **S** lead me on level ground.
146: 4 their **s** departs, they return to the
Pr 15: 4 a deceitful tongue crushes the **s**.
15:13 but heartache crushes the **s**.
16:18 a haughty **s** before a fall.
16:19 Better to be lowly in **s** and among
17:22 but a crushed **s** dries up the bones.
18:14 A man's **s** sustains him in sickness,
18:14 but a crushed **s** who can bear?
20:27 The lamp of the LORD searches the **s**
25:13 he refreshes the **s** of his masters.
29:23 but a man of lowly **s** gains honour.
Ecc 3:21 Who knows if the **s** of man rises
3:21 if the **s** of the animal goes down
7: 9 Do not be quickly provoked in your **s**,
12: 7 the **s** returns to God who gave it.
Isa 4: 4 by a **s** of judgment and a **s** of fire.
11: 2 **S** of wisdom and of understanding,
11: 2 the **S** of counsel and of power,
11: 2 the **S** of knowledge and of the fear
19:14 The LORD has poured into them a **s** of
28: 6 He will be a **s** of justice to him who
29:24 Those who are wayward in **s** will gain
31: 3 their horses are flesh and not **s**.
32:15 till the **S** is poured upon us from on
34:16 and his **S** will gather them together.
37: 7 Listen! I am going to put a **s** in him
48:16 LORD has sent me, with his **S**.
54: 6 a wife deserted and distressed in **s**
57:15 him who is contrite and lowly in **s**,
57:15 to revive the **s** of the lowly and to
57:16 for then the **s** of man would grow
61: 1 The **S** of the Sovereign LORD is on me,
61: 3 of praise instead of a **s** of despair.
65:14 heart and wail in brokenness of **s**.
66: 2 he who is humble and contrite in **s**,
Jer 51: 1 "See, I will stir up the **s** of a
Eze 1:12 Wherever the **s** would go, they would
1:20 Wherever the **s** would go, they would
1:20 the **s** of the living creatures was
1:21 the **s** of the living creatures was
2: 2 he spoke, the **S** came into me and
3:12 the **S** lifted me up, and I heard
3:14 The **S** then lifted me up and took me
3:24 the **S** came into me and raised me to
8: 3 The **S** lifted me up between earth and

Eze 10:17 the **s** of the living creatures was
11: 1 the **S** lifted me up and brought me to
11:19 heart and put a new **s** in them;
11:24 The **S** lifted me up and brought me to
13: 3 their own **s** and have seen nothing!
18:31 and get a new heart and a new **s**.
21: 7 every **s** will become faint and every
36:26 a new heart and put a new **s** in you;
43: 5 the **S** lifted me up and brought me
Da 4: 8 the **s** of the holy gods is in him.)
4: 9 I know that the **s** of the holy gods
4:18 the **s** of the holy gods is in you."
5:11 has the **s** of the holy gods in him.
5:14 I have heard that the **s** of the gods
7:15 "I, Daniel, was troubled in **s**, and
Hos 4:12 A **s** of prostitution leads them
5: 4 A **s** of prostitution is in their
Hag 1:14 LORD stirred up the **s** of Zerubbabel
1:14 the **s** of Joshua son of Jehozadak.
1:14 **s** of the whole remnant of the people.
Zec 7:12 his **S** through the earlier prophets.
12: 1 the **s** of man within him, declares:
12:10 a **s** of grace and supplication.
13: 2 and the **s** of impurity from the land.
Mal 2:15 So guard yourself in your **s**, and do
2:15 In flesh and **s** they are his.
2:16 So guard yourself in your **s**, and do
Mt 4: 1 Jesus was led by the **S** into the
5: 3 "Blessed are the poor in **s**, for
10:20 but the **S** of your Father speaking
12:18 I will put my **S** on him, and he will
12:31 against the **S** will not be forgiven.
22:43 speaking by the **S**, calls him 'Lord'?
26:41 **s** is willing, but the body is weak."
27:50 in a loud voice, he gave up his **s**.
Mk 1:10 the **S** descending on him like a dove.
1:12 At once the **S** sent him out into the
2: 8 Immediately Jesus knew in his **s** that
9:17 a **s** that has robbed him of speech.
9:18 out the **s**, but they could not."
9:20 When the **s** saw Jesus, it
9:25 "You deaf and mute **s**," he said, "I
9:26 The **s** shrieked, convulsed him
14:38 **s** is willing, but the body is weak."
Lk 1:17 in the **s** and power of Elijah, to
1:80 the child grew and became strong in **s**
2:27 Moved by the **S**, he went into the
4: 1 and was led by the **S** in the desert,
4:14 to Galilee in the power of the **S**,
8:55 Her **s** returned, and at once she
9:39 A **s** seizes him and he suddenly
13:11 crippled by a **s** for eighteen years.
Jn 1:32 "I saw the **S** come down from heaven
1:33 'The man on whom you see the **S** come
3: 5 he is born of water and the **S**.
3: 6 flesh, but the **S** gives birth to **s**.
3: 8 it is with everyone born of the **S**."
3:34 for God gives the **S** without limit.
4:23 worship the Father in **s** and truth,
4:24 God is **s**, and his worshippers must
4:24 must worship in **s** and in truth."
6:63 The **S** gives life; the flesh counts
6:63 to you are **s** and they are life.
7:39 By this he meant the **S**, whom those
7:39 Up to that time the **S** had not been
11:33 was deeply moved in **s** and troubled.
13:21 Jesus was troubled in **s** and
14:17 the **S** of truth. The world cannot
15:26 the **S** of truth who goes out from the
16:13 when he, the **S** of truth, comes, he
16:15 That is why I said the **S** will take
19:30 he bowed his head and gave up his **s**.
Ac 2: 4 other tongues as the **S** enabled them.
6: 3 to be full of the **S** and wisdom.
6:10 wisdom or the **S** by whom he spoke.
8:18 Simon saw that the **S** was given at
8:29 The **S** told Philip, "Go to that
10:19 the **S** said to him, "Simon, three men
11:12 The **S** told me to have no hesitation
11:28 stood up and through the **S** predicted
16: 7 **S** of Jesus would not allow them to.
16:16 **s** by which she predicted the future.
16:18 he turned round and said to the **s**,
16:18 At that moment the **s** left her.
20:22 "And now, compelled by the **S**, I am
21: 4 Through the **S** they urged Paul not to

Ac 23: 9 a **s** or an angel has spoken to him?"
Ro 1: 4 who through the **S** of holiness was
2:29 by the **S**, not by the written code.
7: 6 we serve in the new way of the **S**,
8: 2 through Christ Jesus the law of the **S**
8: 4 nature but according to the **S**.
8: 5 who live in accordance with the **S**
8: 5 minds set on what the **S** desires.
8: 6 by the **S** is life and peace;
8: 9 by the sinful nature but by the **S**,
8: 9 anyone does not have the **S** of Christ
8:10 **s** is alive because of righteousness.
8:11 if the **S** of him who raised Jesus
8:11 through his **S**, who lives in you.
8:13 but if by the **S** you put to death
8:15 For you did not receive a **s** that
8:15 but you received the **S** of sonship.
8:16 The **S** himself testifies with our **s**
8:23 who have the firstfruits of the **S**,
8:26 In the same way, the **S** helps us in
8:26 but the **S** himself intercedes for us
8:27 our hearts knows the mind of the **S**,
8:27 because the **S** intercedes for the
11: 8 "God gave them a **s** of stupor,
15: 5 encouragement give you a **s** of unity
15:19 through the power of the **S**.
15:30 Christ and by the love of the **S**,
1Co 2:10 God has revealed it to us by his **S**.
2:10 The **S** searches all things, even the
2:11 a man except the man's **s** within him?
2:12 We have not received the **s** of the
2:12 the world but the **S** who is from God,
2:13 wisdom but in words taught by the **S**,
2:14 The man without the **S** does not
3:16 and that God's **S** lives in you?
4:21 or in love and with a gentle **s**?
5: 3 present, I am with you in **s**.
5: 4 Lord Jesus and I am with you in **s**,
5: 5 his **s** saved on the day of the Lord.
6:11 Jesus Christ and by the **S** of our God.
6:17 with the Lord is one with him in **s**.
7:34 to the Lord in both body and **s**.
12: 4 kinds of gifts, but the same **S**.
12: 7 the **S** is given for the common good.
12: 8 To one there is given through the **S**
12: 8 of knowledge by means of the same **S**,
12: 9 to another faith by the same **S**, to
12: 9 gifts of healing by that one **S**,
12:11 are the work of one and the same **S**,
12:13 For we were all baptised by one **S**
12:13 were all given the one **S** to drink.
14: 2 he utters mysteries with his **s**.
14:16 If you are praising God with your **s**,
15:45 the last Adam, a life-giving **s**.
2Co 1:22 and put his **S** in our hearts as a
3: 3 written not with ink but with the **S**
3: 6 not of the letter but of the **S**;
3: 6 letter kills, but the **S** gives life.
3: 8 will not the ministry of the **S** be
3:17 Now the Lord is the **S**, and where the
3:18 comes from the Lord, who is the **S**.
4:13 With that same **s** of faith we also
5: 5 and has given us the **S** as a deposit,
7: 1 that contaminates body and **s**,
7:13 **s** has been refreshed by all of you.
11: 4 or if you receive a different **s** from
12:18 same **s** and follow the same course?
Gal 3: 2 receive the **S** by observing the law,
3: 3 After beginning with the **S**, are you
3: 5 Does God give you his **S** and work
3:14 might receive the promise of the **S**.
4: 6 God sent the **S** of his Son into our
4: 6 **S** who calls out, "Abba, Father."
4:29 the son born by the power of the **S**.
5: 5 through the **S** the righteousness for
5:16 I say, live by the **S**, and you will
5:17 desires what is contrary to the **S**,
5:17 and the **S** what is contrary to the
5:18 if you are led by the **S**, you are not
5:22 the fruit of the **S** is love, joy,
5:25 Since we live by the **S**, let us keep
5:25 let us keep in step with the **S**.
6: 8 the one who sows to please the **S**,
6: 8 from the **S** will reap eternal life.
6:18 Christ be with your **s**, brothers.
Eph 1:17 may give you the **S** of wisdom and

Eph 2: 2 the s who is now at work in those
2:18 have access to the Father by one **S**.
2:22 in which God lives by his **S**.
3: 5 by the **S** to God's holy apostles
3:16 through his **S** in your inner being,
4: 3 of the **S** through the bond of peace.
4: 4 There is one body and one **S**—just as
5:18 Instead, be filled with the **S**.
6:17 the sword of the **S**, which is the
6:18 pray in the **S** on all occasions with
Php 1:19 help given by the **S** of Jesus Christ,
1:27 know that you stand firm in one **s**,
2: 1 if any fellowship with the **S**,
2: 2 love, being one in **s** and purpose.
4:23 Lord Jesus Christ be with your **s**.
Col 1: 8 also told us of your love in the **S**.
2: 5 I am present with you in **s** and
1Th 5:23 May your whole **s**, soul and body be
2Th 2:13 the sanctifying work of the **S** and
1Ti 3:16 was vindicated by the **S**, was seen by
4: 1 The **S** clearly says that in later
2Ti 1: 7 God did not give us a **s** of timidity
1: 7 but a **s** of power, of love and of
4:22 The Lord be with your **s**. Grace be
Phm :25 Lord Jesus Christ be with your **s**.
Heb 4:12 even to dividing soul and **s**,
9:14 who through the eternal **S** offered
10:29 and who has insulted the **S** of grace?
Jas 2:26 the body without the **s** is dead, so
4: 5 the **s** he caused to live in us
1Pe 1: 2 the sanctifying work of the **S**,
1:11 circumstances to which the **S** of
3: 4 beauty of a gentle and quiet **s**,
3:18 in the body but made alive by the **S**,
4: 6 according to God in regard to the **s**.
4:14 **S** of glory and of God rests on you.
1Jn 3:24 We know it by the **S** he gave us.
4: 1 Dear friends, do not believe every **s**,
4: 2 Every **s** that acknowledges that Jesus
4: 3 every **s** that does not acknowledge
4: 3 This is the **s** of the antichrist,
4: 6 **S** of truth and the **s** of falsehood.
4:13 because he has given us of his **S**.
5: 6 And it is the **S** who testifies,
5: 6 because the **S** is the truth.
5: 8 the **S**, the water and the blood;
Jude :19 instincts and do not have the **S**.
Rev 1:10 On the Lord's Day I was in the **S**,
2: 7 what the **S** says to the churches.
2:11 what the **S** says to the churches.
2:17 what the **S** says to the churches.
2:29 what the **S** says to the churches.
3: 6 what the **S** says to the churches.
3:13 what the **S** says to the churches.
3:22 what the **S** says to the churches."
4: 2 At once I was in the **S**, and there
14:13 "Yes," says the **S**, "they will rest
17: 3 the angel carried me away in the **S**
19:10 of Jesus is the **s** of prophecy."
21:10 he carried me away in the **S** to a
22:17 The **S** and the bride say, "Come!"

Spirit of God

Ge 1: 2 the **S** was hovering over the waters.
41:38 this man, one in whom is the **s**?"
Ex 31: 3 I have filled him with the **S**, with
35:31 he has filled him with the **S**, with
Nu 24: 2 tribe by tribe, the **S** came upon
1Sa 10:10 the **S** came upon him in power,
11: 6 Saul heard their words, the **S** came
19:20 the **S** came upon Saul's men and they
19:23 But the **S** came even upon him, and he
2Ch 15: 1 The **S** came upon Azariah son of Oded.
24:20 the **S** came upon Zechariah son of
Job 33: 4 The **S** has made me; the breath of the
Ps 106:33 for they rebelled against the **S**, and
Eze 11:24 in the vision given by the **S**.
Mt 3:16 and he saw the **S** descending like a
12:28 if I drive out demons by the **S**, then
Ro 8: 9 the Spirit, if the **S** lives in you.
8:14 those who are led by the **S** are sons
1Co 2:11 the thoughts of God except the **S**.
2:14 the things that come from the **S**,
7:40 I think that I too have the **S**.
12: 3 by the **S** says, "Jesus be cursed,"
Eph 4:30 do not grieve the Holy **S**, with whom
Php 3: 3 we who worship by the **S**, who glory
1Jn 4: 2 This is how you can recognise the **S**:

Spirit of the LORD

Jdg 3:10 The **S** came upon him, so that he
6:34 the **S** came upon Gideon, and he blew
11:29 the **S** came upon Jephthah. He crossed
13:25 the **S** began to stir him while he was
14: 6 The **S** came upon him in power so that
14:19 the **S** came upon him in power.
15:14 The **S** came upon him in power.
1Sa 10: 6 The **S** will come upon you in power,
16:13 on the **S** came upon David in power.
16:14 Now the **S** had departed from Saul,
2Sa 23: 2 "The **S** spoke through me; his word
1Ki 18:12 I don't know where the **S** may carry
2Ki 2:16 Perhaps the **S** has picked him up and
2Ch 20:14 the **S** came upon Jahaziel son of
Isa 11: 2 The **S** will rest on him—the Spirit
63:14 they were given rest by the **S**.
Eze 11: 5 the **S** came upon me, and he told me
37: 1 and he brought me out by the **S** and
Mic 2: 7 "Is the **S** angry? Does he do such
3: 8 I am filled with power, with the **S**,

Spirit of the Lord

Lk 4:18 "The **S** is on me, because he has
Ac 5: 9 "How could you agree to test the **S**?
8:39 the **S** suddenly took Philip away,
2Co 3:17 where the **S** is, there is freedom.

Spirit's (Spirit)

1Co 2: 4 with a demonstration of the **S** power,
1Th 5:19 Do not put out the **S** fire;

Spiritist (Spirit)

Lev 20:27 or **s** among you must be put to death.
Dt 18:11 or **s** or who consults the dead.

Spiritists (Spirit)

Lev 19:31 or seek out **s**, for you will be
20: 6 to mediums and **s** to prostitute
1Sa 28: 3 the mediums and **s** from the land.
28: 9 He has cut off the mediums and **s**
2Ki 21: 6 and consulted mediums and **s**.
23:24 Josiah got rid of the mediums and **s**,
2Ch 33: 6 and consulted mediums and **s**.
Isa 8:19 men tell you to consult mediums and **s**
19: 3 of the dead, the mediums and the **s**.

Spirits (*Evil spirits*, Spirit)

Nu 16:22 "O God, God of the **s** of all mankind,
27:16 "May the LORD, the God of the **s** of
Jdg 16:25 While they were in high **s**, they
Ru 3: 7 and drinking and was in good **s**,
1Sa 25:36 He was in high **s** and very drunk.
2Sa 13:28 "Listen! When Amnon is in high **s**
Est 1:10 when King Xerxes was in high **s** from
5: 9 out that day happy and in high **s**.
Ps 78: 8 whose **s** were not faithful to him.
Pr 2:18 and her paths to the **s** of the dead.
Isa 14: 9 it rouses the **s** of the departed to
19: 3 the idols and the **s** of the dead,
26:14 those departed **s** do not rise.
Zec 6: 5 "These are the four **s** of heaven,
Mt 8:16 and he drove out the **s** with a word
12:45 goes and takes with it seven other **s**
Lk 10:20 However, do not rejoice that the **s**
11:26 goes and takes seven other **s** more
Ac 23: 8 that there are neither angels nor **s**,
1Co 12:10 to another distinguishing between **s**,
14:32 The **s** of prophets are subject to the
1Ti 4: 1 deceiving **s** and things taught by
Heb 1:14 Are not all angels ministering **s**
12: 9 to the Father of our **s** and live!
12:23 the **s** of righteous men made perfect,
1Pe 3:19 went and preached to the **s** in
1Jn 4: 1 but test the **s** to see whether they
Rev 1: 4 from the seven **s** before his throne,
3: 1 seven **s** of God and the seven stars.
4: 5 These are the seven **s** of God.
5: 6 seven **s** of God sent out into all the
16:14 They are **s** of demons performing
22: 6 The Lord, the God of the **s** of the

Spiritual (Spirit, *Spiritual gifts*)

Ro 1:11 you some **s** gift to make you strong—
7:14 We know that the law is **s**; but I am
12: 1 God—this is your **s** act of worship.
12:11 your **s** fervour, serving the Lord.
15:27 shared in the Jews' **s** blessings,
1Co 1: 7 Therefore you do not lack any **s** gift
2:13 expressing **s** truths in **s** words.
2:15 The **s** man makes judgments about all
3: 1 I could not address you as **s** but as
9:11 If we have sown **s** seed among you, is
10: 3 They all ate the same **s** food
10: 4 drank the same **s** drink; for they
10: 4 the **s** rock that accompanied them,
15:44 natural body, it is raised a **s** body.
15:44 body, there is also a **s** body.
15:46 The **s** did not come first, but the
15:46 the natural, and after that the **s**.
Gal 6: 1 who are **s** should restore him gently.
Eph 1: 3 with every **s** blessing in Christ.
5:19 with psalms, hymns and **s** songs.
6:12 against the **s** forces of evil in the
Col 1: 9 all **s** wisdom and understanding.
3:16 you sing psalms, hymns and **s** songs
1Pe 2: 2 newborn babies, crave pure **s** milk,
2: 5 are being built into a **s** house to be
2: 5 offering **s** sacrifices acceptable to

Spiritual gifts

1Co 12: 1 Now about **s**, brothers, I do not want
14: 1 eagerly desire **s**, especially the
14:12 Since you are eager to have **s**, try

Spiritually (Spirit)

1Co 2:14 them, because they are **s** discerned.
14:37 thinks he is a prophet or **s** gifted,

Spit (Spat, Spits, Spitting)

Dt 25: 9 his sandals, **s** in his face and say,
Job 17: 6 a man in whose face people **s**.
20:15 He will **s** out the riches he
30:10 do not hesitate to **s** in my face.
Mk 10:34 who will mock him and **s** on him, flog
14:65 some began to **s** at him;
Lk 18:32 **s** on him, flog him and kill him.
Rev 3:16 am about to **s** you out of my mouth.

Spits (Spit)

Lev 15: 8 "'If the man with the discharge **s**

Spitting (Spit)

Isa 50: 6 not hide my face from mocking and **s**.

Splendid (Splendour)

Isa 22:18 there your **s** chariots will remain
Eze 17: 8 bear fruit and become a **s** vine.'
17:23 and bear fruit and become a **s** cedar.

Splendour (Splendid)

1Ch 16:27 **S** and majesty are before him;
16:29 the LORD in the **s** of his holiness.
22: 5 **s** in the sight of all the nations.
29:11 the glory and the majesty and the **s**,
29:25 bestowed on him royal **s** such as no
2Ch 20:21 to praise him for the **s** of his
Est 1: 4 and the **s** and glory of his majesty.
Job 13:11 Would not his **s** terrify you?
31:23 of his **s** I could not do such things.
31:26 radiance or the moon moving in **s**,
37:22 Out of the north he comes in golden **s**
40:10 adorn yourself with glory and **s**, and
Ps 21: 5 have bestowed on him **s** and majesty.
29: 2 the LORD in the **s** of his holiness.
45: 3 clothe yourself with **s** and majesty.
49:16 when the **s** of his house increases;
49:17 his **s** will not descend with him.
71: 8 declaring your **s** all day long.
78:61 his **s** into the hands of the enemy.
89:44 You have put an end to his **s** and
90:16 servants, your **s** to their children.

Ps 96: 6 **S** and majesty are before him;
96: 9 Worship the LORD in the **s** of his
104: 1 you are clothed with **s** and majesty.
145: 5 They will speak of the glorious **s** of
145:12 and the glorious **s** of your kingdom.
148:13 **s** is above the earth and the heavens.
Pr 4: 9 and present you with a crown of **s**."
16:31 Grey hair is a crown of **s**; it is
20:29 grey hair the **s** of the old.
Isa 2:10 the LORD and the **s** of his majesty!
2:19 the LORD and the **s** of his majesty,
2:21 the LORD and the **s** of his majesty,
10:18 The **s** of his forests and fertile
16:14 Moab's **s** and all her many people
35: 2 the **s** of Carmel and Sharon;
35: 2 glory of the LORD, the **s** of our God.
46:13 salvation to Zion, my **s** to Israel.
49: 3 Israel, in whom I will display my **s**."
52: 1 Put on your garments of **s**,
55: 5 for he has endowed you with **s**."
60: 9 for he has endowed you with **s**.
60:21 my hands, for the display of my **s**.
61: 3 the LORD for the display of his **s**.
62: 3 You will be a crown of **s** in the
63: 1 robed in **s**, striding forward in the
Jer 22:18 'Alas, my master! Alas, his **s**!'
Lam 1: 6 All the **s** has departed from the
2: 1 **s** of Israel from heaven to earth;
3:18 I say, "My **s** is gone and all that I
Eze 16:14 because the **s** I had given you made
27:10 on your walls, bringing you **s**.
28: 7 wisdom and pierce your shining **s**.
28:17 your wisdom because of your **s**.
31:18 compared with you in **s** and majesty?
Da 4:36 my honour and **s** were returned to me
5:18 and greatness and glory and **s**.
11:20 collector to maintain the royal **s**.
Hos 10: 5 those who had rejoiced over its **s**,
14: 6 His **s** will be like an olive tree,
Na 2: 2 The LORD will restore the **s** of Jacob
2: 2 the **s** of Jacob like the **s** of Israel,
Hab 3: 4 His **s** was like the sunrise;
Mt 4: 8 kingdoms of the world and their **s**.
6:29 Solomon in all his **s** was dressed
Lk 4: 6 give you all their authority and **s**,
9:31 appeared in glorious **s**, talking with
12:27 Solomon in all his **s** was dressed
1Co 15:40 **s** of the heavenly bodies is one kind,
15:40 **s** of the earthly bodies is another.
15:41 The sun has one kind of **s**, the moon
15:41 and star differs from star in **s**.
2Th 2: 8 and destroy by the **s** of his coming.
Rev 18: 1 the earth was illuminated by his **s**.
18:14 All your riches and **s** have vanished,
21:24 earth will bring their **s** into it.

Splint
Eze 30:21 or put in a **s** so as to become

Splintered
2Ki 18:21 on Egypt, that **s** reed of a staff,
Isa 36: 6 on Egypt, that **s** reed of a staff,
Eze 29: 7 you **s** and you tore open their

Split (Splits)
Lev 11: 3 eat any animal that has a **s** hoof
11: 4 or only have a **s** hoof, but you must
11: 4 chew the cud, does not have a **s** hoof;
11: 5 chews the cud, does not have a **s** hoof;
11: 6 chews the cud, does not have a **s** hoof;
11: 7 the pig, though it has a **s** hoof
11:26 "'Every animal that has a **s** hoof
Nu 16:31 this, the ground under them **s** apart
Dt 14: 6 eat any animal that has a **s** hoof
14: 7 chew the cud or that have a **s** hoof
14: 7 they do not have a **s** hoof; they are
14: 8 although it has a **s** hoof, it does
1Ki 13: 3 The altar will be **s** apart and the
13: 5 Also, the altar was **s** apart and its
16:21 the people of Israel were **s** into two
Ps 74:13 was you who **s** open the sea by your
78:15 He **s** the rocks in the desert and
Isa 24:19 the earth is **s** asunder, the earth is
48:21 he **s** the rock and water gushed out.
Mic 1: 4 beneath him and the valleys **s** apart,
Hab 3: 9 You **s** the earth with rivers;
Zec 14: 4 and the Mount of Olives will be **s** in
Mt 27:51 The earth shook and the rocks **s**.
Rev 16:19 The great city **s** into three parts,

Splits (Split)
Ecc 10: 9 whoever **s** logs may be endangered by

Spoil (Despoil, Spoils)
Ps 119:162 promise like one who finds great **s**.
Jer 30:16 who make **s** of you I will despoil.
1Pe 1: 4 that can never perish **s** or fade—

Spoils (Spoil)
Ex 15: 9 I will divide the **s**; I will gorge
Nu 31:11 They took all the plunder and **s**,
31:12 brought the captives, **s** and plunder
31:27 Divide the **s** between the soldiers
31:32 The plunder remaining from the **s**
Jdg 5:30 not finding and dividing the **s**:
Isa 33:23 Then an abundance of **s** will be
53:12 and he will divide the **s** with the
Lk 11:22 man trusted and divides up the **s**.
Jn 6:27 Do not work for food that **s**, but for

Spokesman (Speaker, Man)
Jer 15:19 worthless, words, you will be my **s**.

Spokesmen (Speaker, Man)
Isa 43:27 your **s** rebelled against me.

Sponge
Mt 27:48 one of them ran and got a **s**.
Mk 15:36 One man ran, filled a **s** with wine
Jn 19:29 so they soaked a **s** in it, put the **s**

Spontaneous
Phm :14 you do will be **s** and not forced.

Sport
Ge 39:14 been brought to us to make **s** of us!
39:17 us came to me to make **s** of me.
Ps 69:11 on sackcloth, people make **s** of me.

Spot (Spots, Spotted)
Lev 13: 2 a rash or a bright **s** on his skin
13: 4 If the **s** on his skin is white but
13:19 a white swelling or reddish-white **s**
13:23 if the **s** is unchanged and has not
13:24 a reddish-white or white **s** appears
13:25 the priest is to examine the **s**, and
13:26 there is no white hair in the **s** and
13:28 If, however, the **s** is unchanged and
14:56 for a swelling, a rash or a bright **s**,
Jos 4: 9 at the **s** where the priests who
2Sa 2:23 He fell there and died on the **s**.
2Ki 5:11 wave his hand over the **s** and cure me
Job 8:18 is torn from its **s**, that place
Isa 28: 8 and there is not a **s** without filth.
46: 7 From that **s** it cannot move.
Lk 19: 5 Jesus reached the **s**, he looked up
1Ti 6:14 to keep this command without **s** or

Spotless
Da 11:35 purified and made **s** until the time
12:10 Many will be purified, made **s** and
2Pe 3:14 **s**, blameless and at peace with him.

Spots (Spot)
Lev 13:38 "When a man or woman has white **s** on
13:39 and if the **s** are dull white, it is a
Jer 13:23 his skin or the leopard its **s**?

Spotted (Spot)
Ge 30:32 from them every speckled or **s** sheep,
30:32 lamb and every **s** or speckled goat.
30:33 that is not speckled or **s**, or any
30:35 male goats that were streaked or **s**,
30:35 all the speckled or **s** female goats
30:39 that were streaked or speckled or **s**.
31:10 flock were streaked, speckled or **s**.
31:12 flock are streaked, speckled or **s**,

Sprang (Spring[1])
Jnh 4:10 It **s** up overnight and died overnight.
Mt 13: 5 It **s** up quickly, because the soil
Mk 4: 5 It **s** up quickly, because the soil
Ro 7: 9 came, sin **s** to life and I died.

Spread (Outspread, Spreading, Spreads, Widespread)
Ge 10: 5 (From these the maritime peoples **s**
10:32 **s** out over the earth after the flood.
28:14 and you will **s** out to the west and
41:56 the famine had **s** over the whole
Ex 1:12 the more they multiplied and **s**;
9:29 **s** out my hands in prayer to the LORD.
9:33 He **s** out his hands towards the LORD;
10:21 so that darkness will **s** over Egypt
23: 1 "Do not **s** false reports. Do not help
25:20 are to have their wings **s** upwards,
29: 2 with oil, and wafers **s** with oil.
37: 9 The cherubim had their wings **s**
40:19 he **s** the tent over the tabernacle
Lev 2: 4 made without yeast and **s** with oil.
7:12 wafers made without yeast and **s** with
13: 5 unchanged and has not **s** in the skin,
13: 6 has faded and has not **s** in the skin,
13: 7 if the rash does **s** in his skin after
13: 8 and if the rash has **s** in the skin,
13:23 the spot is unchanged and has not **s**,
13:28 the spot is unchanged and has not **s**
13:32 and if the itch has not **s** and there
13:34 and if it has not **s** in the skin and
13:35 if the itch does **s** in the skin after
13:36 and if the itch has **s** in the skin,
13:51 if the mildew has **s** in the clothing
13:53 the mildew has not **s** in the clothing,
13:55 though it has not **s**, it is unclean.
14:39 If the mildew has **s** on the walls,
14:44 if the mildew has **s** in the house, it
14:48 **s** after the house has been plastered,
Nu 4: 6 **s** a cloth of solid blue over that
4: 7 Presence they are to **s** a blue cloth
4: 8 Over these they are to **s** a scarlet
4:11 "Over the gold altar they are to **s** a
4:13 altar and **s** a purple cloth over it.
4:14 Over it they are to **s** a covering of
6:15 with oil, and wafers **s** with oil.
11:32 they **s** them out all around the camp.
13:32 they **s** among the Israelites a bad
24: 6 "Like valleys they **s** out, like
Jos 6:27 and his fame **s** throughout the land.
7:23 and **s** them out before the LORD.
Jdg 8:25 So they **s** out a garment, and each
20:37 **s** out and put the whole city to the
Ru 3: 9 "**S** the corner of your garment over
1Sa 4: 2 and as the battle **s**, Israel was
2Sa 5:18 the Philistines had come and **s** out
5:22 and **s** out in the Valley of Rephaim;
17:19 His wife took a covering and **s** it
18: 8 The battle **s** out over the whole
21:10 and **s** it out for herself on a rock.
1Ki 4:31 **s** to all the surrounding nations.
6:27 the temple, with their wings **s** out.
8: 7 The cherubim **s** their wings over the
8:22 **s** out his hands towards heaven
8:54 with his hands **s** out towards heaven.
22:36 the sun was setting, a cry **s** through
2Ki 8:15 soaked it in water and **s** it over the
9:13 **s** them under him on the bare steps.
19:14 LORD and **s** it out before the LORD.
1Ch 14:17 David's fame **s** throughout every land,
28:18 the cherubim of gold that **s** their
2Ch 5: 8 The cherubim **s** their wings over the
6:12 of Israel and **s** out his hands.
6:13 and **s** out his hands towards heaven.
26: 8 and his fame **s** as far as the border
26:15 His fame **s** far and wide, for he was
Ezr 9: 5 my hands **s** out to the LORD my God
Ne 4:19 "The work is extensive and **s** out,
8:15 **s** it throughout their towns and in
Est 9: 4 his reputation **s** throughout the
Job 1:10 and herds are **s** throughout the land.
15:29 his possessions **s** over the land.
17:13 if I **s** out my bed in darkness,
39:26 and **s** his wings towards the south?
Ps 5:11 **S** your protection over them, that

Ps 44:20 or s out our hands to a foreign god,
57: 6 They s a net for my feet—I was
78:19 "Can God s a table in the desert?
88: 9 I s out my hands to you.
105:39 He s out a cloud as a covering, and
136: 6 who s out the earth upon the waters,
140: 5 they have s out the cords of their
143: 6 I s out my hands to you; my soul
Pr 1:17 How useless to s a net in full view
15: 7 The lips of the wise s knowledge;
SS 1:12 table, my perfume s its fragrance.
2:13 blossoming vines s their fragrance.
4:16 that its fragrance may s abroad.
Isa 1:15 you s out your hands in prayer, I
14:11 maggots are s out beneath you and
16: 8 Jazer and s towards the desert.
16: 8 s out and went as far as the sea.
21: 5 They set the tables, they s the rugs,
25:11 They will s out their hands in it,
30:24 mash, s out with fork and shovel.
33:23 not held secure, the sail is not s.
37:14 LORD and s it out before the LORD.
42: 5 who s out the earth and all that
44:24 who s out the earth by myself,
48:13 and my right hand s out the heavens;
54: 3 For you will s out to the right and
65:11 who s a table for Fortune and fill
Jer 23:15 has s throughout the land."
43:10 will s his royal canopy above them.
48:32 Your branches s as far as the sea;
Lam 1:13 He s a net for my feet and turned me
Eze 1:11 Their wings were s out upwards;
1:22 S out above the heads of the living
5: 4 A fire will s from there to the
10:16 and when the cherubim s their wings
10:19 the cherubim s their wings and rose
11:22 with the wheels beside them, s their
12:13 I will s my net for him, and he will
16: 8 I s the corner of my garment over
16:14 your fame s among the nations on
17:20 I will s my net for him, and he will
19: 8 They s their net for him, and he was
19:14 Fire s from one of its main branches
23:41 with a table s before it on which
26: 5 become a place to s fishing nets,
26:14 become a place to s fishing nets.
30:13 I will s fear throughout the land.
32: 5 I will s your flesh on the mountains
32:23 All who had s terror in the land of
32:24 All who had s terror in the land of
32:25 Because their terror had s in the
32:26 because they s terror in the land
32:32 Although I had him s terror in the
Hos 5: 1 at Mizpah, a net s out on Tabor.
Mal 2: 3 I will s on your faces the offal
Mt 4:24 News about him s all over Syria, and
9:26 News of this s through all that
9:31 they went out and s the news about
21: 8 A very large crowd s their cloaks on
21: 8 the trees and s them on the road.
Mk 1:28 News about him s quickly over the
11: 8 Many people s their cloaks on the
11: 8 while others s branches they had cut
Lk 2:17 they had seen him, they s the word
4:14 him s through the whole countryside.
4:37 the news about him s throughout the
5:15 Yet the news about him s all the
7:17 This news about Jesus s throughout
19:36 he went along, people s their cloaks
Jn 12:17 the dead continued to s the word.
21:23 of this, the rumour s among the
Ac 6: 7 the word of God s. The number of
11:28 would s over the entire Roman world.
12:24 of God continued to increase and s.
13:49 The word of the Lord s through the
19:20 In this way the word of the Lord s
2Th 3: 1 Lord may s rapidly and be honoured,
2Ti 2:17 Their teaching will s like gangrene.
Rev 7:15 throne will s his tent over them.

Spreading (Spread)

Lev 13:22 If it is s in the skin, the priest
13:27 and if it is s in the skin, the
13:49 or reddish, it is a s mildew
13:57 or in the leather article, it is s,
14:34 a s mildew in a house in that land,
19:16 "'Do not go about s slander among
Nu 14:36 him by s a bad report about it—
14:37 these men responsible for s the bad
Dt 12: 2 on the hills and under every s tree
28:35 s from the soles of your feet to the
Jdg 15: 9 camped in Judah, s out near Lehi.
1Sa 2:24 I hear s among the LORD's people.
1Ki 8:38 s out his hands towards this temple—
14:23 high hill and under every s tree.
2Ki 16: 4 the hilltops and under every s tree.
17:10 high hill and under every s tree.
2Ch 6:29 s out his hands towards this temple—
28: 4 the hilltops and under every s tree.
Job 8:16 s its shoots over the garden;
26: 9 the full moon, s his clouds over it.
37:18 can you join him in s out the skies,
Pr 29: 5 neighbour is s a net for his feet.
Isa 18: 5 down and take away the s branches.
57: 5 the oaks and under every s tree;
Jer 2:20 and under every s tree you lay down
3: 6 under every s tree and has committed
3:13 foreign gods under every s tree,
17: 2 the s trees and on the high hills.
25:32 "Look! Disaster is s from nation to
48:40 down, s its wings over Moab.
49:22 swoop down, s its wings over Bozrah.
Eze 6:13 under every s tree and every leafy
17: 6 sprouted and became a low, s vine.
31: 5 long, s because of abundant waters.
31: 7 in beauty, with its s boughs,
47:10 there will be places for s nets.
Hos 10: 1 Israel was a s vine; he brought
Joel 2: 2 Like dawn s across the mountains a
Mk 1:45 began to talk freely, s the news.
Ac 4:17 to stop this thing from s any
1Th 3: 2 in s the gospel of Christ,

Spreads (Spread)

Ex 22: 6 "If a fire breaks out and s into
Dt 32:11 that s its wings to catch them and
Job 26: 7 He s out the northern skies over
36:29 Who can understand how he s out the
39:18 Yet when she s her feathers to run,
Ps 41: 6 then he goes out and s it abroad.
147:16 He s the snow like wool and scatters
Pr 10:18 and whoever s slander is a fool.
Isa 25:11 a swimmer s out his hands to swim.
32: 6 He practises ungodliness and s error
40:22 s them out like a tent to live in.
2Co 2:14 through us s everywhere the

Sprig

Eze 17:22 I will break off a tender s from its

Spring[1] (Sprang, Springing, Springs, Sprung)

Nu 21:17 Israel sang this song: "S up, O well!
Job 5: 6 For hardship does not s from the
Ps 92: 7 that though the wicked s up like
Ecc 4: 4 s from man's envy of his neighbour.
Isa 14:29 of that snake will s up a viper,
42: 9 before they s into being I announce
44: 4 They will s up like grass in a
45: 8 let salvation s up, let
61:11 and praise s up before all nations.
Hos 10: 4 therefore lawsuits s up like
Am 3: 5 Does a trap s up from the earth when
Ro 15:12 "The Root of Jesse will s up, one
Col 1: 5 the faith and love that s from the
1Th 2: 3 we make does not s from error or

Spring[2] (Springs, Springtime, Wellspring)

Ge 16: 7 found Hagar near a s in the desert;
16: 7 s that is beside the road to Shur.
24:13 See, I am standing beside this s,
24:16 She went down to the s, filled her
24:29 he hurried out to the man at the s.
24:30 standing by the camels near the s.
24:42 "When I came to the s today, I said,
24:43 See, I am standing beside this s;
24:45 She went down to the s and drew
49:22 a fruitful vine near a s, whose
Lev 11:36 A s, however, or a cistern for
Dt 11:14 both autumn and s rains, so that you
33:28 Jacob's s is secure in a land of
Jos 15: 9 the s of the waters of Nephtoah,
18:15 at the s of the waters of Nephtoah.
Jdg 7: 1 his men camped at the s of Harod.
15:19 So the s was called En Hakkore, and
1Sa 29: 1 Israel camped by the s in Jezreel.
2Sa 11: 1 In the s, at the time when kings go
1Ki 20:22 because next s the king of Aram will
20:26 The next s Ben-Hadad mustered the
2Ki 2:21 he went out to the s and threw the
13:20 used to enter the country every s.
1Ch 20: 1 In the s, at the time when kings go
2Ch 32:30 the upper outlet of the Gihon s
33:14 west of the Gihon s in the valley,
36:10 In the s, King Nebuchadnezzar sent
Job 29:23 and drank in my words as the s rain.
Pr 16:15 favour is like a rain cloud in s.
25:26 Like a muddied s or a polluted well
Ecc 12: 6 the pitcher is shattered at the s,
SS 4:12 are a s enclosed, a sealed fountain.
Isa 58:11 like a s whose waters never fail.
Jer 2:13 the s of living water, and have dug
3: 3 and no s rains have fallen.
5:24 who gives autumn and s rains in
9: 1 Oh, that my head were a s of water
15:18 brook, like a s that fails?
17:13 the LORD, the s of living water.
Hos 6: 3 the s rains that water the earth."
13:15 his s will fail and his well dry up.
Joel 2:23 both autumn and s rains, as before.
Jn 4:14 will become in him a s of water
Jas 3:11 and salt water flow from the same s?
3:12 can a salt s produce fresh water.
5: 7 he is for the autumn and s rains.
Rev 21: 6 from the s of the water of life.

Springing (Spring[1])

Dt 33:22 is a lion's cub, s out of Bashan."

Springs (Spring[1])

2Ki 19:29 the second year what s from that.
Job 14: 2 He s up like a flower and withers
Ps 85:11 Faithfulness s forth from the earth,
90: 6 though in the morning it s up new,
Pr 27: 9 friend s from his earnest counsel.
Isa 37:30 the second year what s from that.
43:19 Now it s up; do you not perceive it

Springs (Spring[2])

Ge 7:11 the s of the great deep burst forth,
8: 2 Now the s of the deep and the
36:24 discovered the hot s in the desert
Ex 15:27 where there were twelve s and
Nu 33: 9 where there were twelve s and
Dt 8: 7 s flowing in the valleys and hills;
Jos 15:19 the Negev, give me also s of water.
15:19 Caleb gave her the upper and lower s.
Jdg 1:15 the Negev, give me also s of water.
1:15 Caleb gave her the upper and lower s.
1Ki 18: 5 the land to all the s and valleys.
2Ki 3:19 stop up all the s, and ruin every
3:25 They stopped up all the s and cut
2Ch 32: 3 water from the s outside the city,
32: 4 and they blocked all the s and the
Job 38:16 "Have you journeyed to the s of the
Ps 74:15 was you who opened up s and streams;
84: 6 they make it a place of s;
104:10 He makes s pour water into the
107:33 flowing s into thirsty ground,
107:35 the parched ground into flowing s;
114: 8 pool, the hard rock into s of water.
Pr 5:16 Should your s overflow in the
8:24 were no s abounding with water;
Isa 35: 7 pool, the thirsty ground bubbling s.
41:18 heights, and s within the valleys.
41:18 and the parched ground into s.
49:10 and lead them beside s of water.
Jer 51:36 dry up her sea and make her s dry.
Eze 31: 4 deep s made it grow tall;
31:15 I covered the deep s with mourning
2Pe 2:17 These men are s without water and
Rev 7:17 will lead them to s of living water.
8:10 the rivers and on the s of water—

Rev 14: 7 earth, the sea and the **s** of water."
16: 4 bowl on the rivers and **s** of water,

Springtime (Spring²)
Zec 10: 1 Ask the LORD for rain in the **s**;

Sprinkle (Sprinkled, Sprinkles, Sprinkling)
Ex 29:16 and take the blood and **s** it against the
29:20 Then **s** blood against the altar on
29:21 some of the anointing oil and **s** it
Lev 1: 5 **s** it against the altar on all sides
1:11 Aaron's sons the priests shall **s** its
3: 2 the priests shall **s** the blood against
3: 8 Then Aaron's sons shall **s** its blood
3:13 Then Aaron's sons shall **s** its blood
4: 6 **s** some of it seven times before the
4:17 **s** it before the LORD seven times in
5: 9 is to **s** some of the blood of the sin
14: 7 Seven times he shall **s** the one to be
14:16 and with his finger **s** some of it
14:27 with his right forefinger **s** some of
14:51 water, and **s** the house seven times.
16:14 with his finger **s** it on the front of
16:14 then he shall **s** some of it with his
16:15 He shall **s** it on the atonement cover
16:19 He shall **s** some of the blood on it
17: 6 The priest is to **s** the blood against
Nu 8: 7 **S** the water of cleansing on them;
18:17 **S** their blood on the altar and burn
19: 4 **s** it seven times towards the front
19:18 dip it in the water and **s** the tent
19:18 He must also **s** anyone who has
19:19 The man who is clean is to **s** the
2Ki 16:15 **S** on the altar all the blood of the
Isa 52:15 will he **s** many nations, and kings
Eze 27:30 they will **s** dust on their heads and
36:25 I will **s** clean water on you, and you
43:24 and the priests are to **s** salt on

Sprinkled (Sprinkle)
Ex 24: 6 the other half he **s** on the altar.
24: 8 Moses then took the blood, **s** it on
Lev 7: 2 be **s** against the altar on all sides.
8:11 He **s** some of the oil on the altar
8:19 slaughtered the ram and **s** the blood
8:24 Then he **s** blood against the altar on
8:30 **s** them on Aaron and his garments and
9:12 **s** it against the altar on all sides.
9:18 **s** it against the altar on all sides.
Nu 19:13 of cleansing has not been **s** on him,
19:20 of cleansing has not been **s** on him,
Jos 7: 6 the same, and **s** dust on their heads.
2Ki 16:13 and **s** the blood of his fellowship
2Ch 29:22 the blood and **s** it on the altar;
29:22 rams and **s** their blood on the altar;
29:22 and **s** their blood on the altar.
30:16 The priests **s** the blood handed to
35:11 and the priests **s** the blood handed
Job 2:12 robes and **s** dust on their heads.
Lam 2:10 they have **s** dust on their heads and
Hos 7: 9 His hair is **s** with grey, but he
Heb 9:13 and the ashes of a heifer **s** on those
9:19 and **s** the scroll and all the people.
9:21 In the same way, he **s** with the blood
10:22 having our hearts **s** to cleanse us
12:24 and to the **s** blood that speaks a

Sprinkles (Sprinkle)
Lev 7:14 it belongs to the priest who **s** the
Nu 19:21 "The man who **s** the water of

Sprinkling (Sprinkle)
Ex 27: 3 **s** bowls, meat forks and firepans.
38: 3 **s** bowls, meat forks and firepans.
Nu 4:14 meat forks, shovels and **s** bowls.
7:13 and one silver **s** bowl weighing
7:19 and one silver **s** bowl weighing
7:25 and one silver **s** bowl weighing
7:31 and one silver **s** bowl weighing
7:37 and one silver **s** bowl weighing
7:43 and one silver **s** bowl weighing
7:49 and one silver **s** bowl weighing
7:55 and one silver **s** bowl weighing
Nu 7:61 and one silver **s** bowl weighing
7:67 and one silver **s** bowl weighing
7:73 and one silver **s** bowl weighing
7:79 and one silver **s** bowl weighing
7:84 **s** bowls and twelve gold dishes.
7:85 and each **s** bowl seventy shekels.
1Ki 7:40 the basins and shovels and **s** bowls.
7:45 the pots, shovels and **s** bowls.
7:50 wick trimmers, **s** bowls, dishes and
2Ki 12:13 wick trimmers, **s** bowls, trumpets or
25:15 took away the censers and **s** bowls—
1Ch 28:17 the forks, **s** bowls and pitchers;
2Ch 4: 8 He also made a hundred gold **s** bowls.
4:11 the pots and shovels and **s** bowls.
4:22 the pure gold wick trimmers, **s** bowls,
Jer 52:18 shovels, wick trimmers, **s** bowls,
52:19 censers, **s** bowls, pots, lampstands,
Eze 43:18 **s** blood upon the altar when it is
Zec 9:15 used for **s** the corners of the altar.
Heb 11:28 the Passover and the **s** of blood,
1Pe 1: 2 to Jesus Christ and **s** by his blood:

Sprout (Sprouted, Sprouting, Sprouts)
Nu 17: 5 to the man I choose will **s**,
Job 5: 6 nor does trouble **s** from the ground.
14: 7 it will **s** again, and its new shoots
38:27 wasteland and make it **s** with grass?
Pr 23: 5 for they will surely **s** wings and fly
Jer 33:15 Branch **s** from David's line;
Lk 21:30 they **s** leaves, you can see for

Sprouted (Sprout)
Ge 41: 6 seven other ears of corn **s**—thin and
41:23 After them, seven other ears **s**—
Nu 17: 8 had not only **s** but had budded,
Eze 17: 6 **s** and became a low, spreading vine.
Mt 13:26 the wheat **s** and formed ears, then

Sprouting (Sprout)
Dt 29:23 nothing planted, nothing **s**, no
2Ki 19:26 like grass **s** on the roof, scorched
Isa 37:27 like grass **s** on the roof, scorched

Sprouts (Sprout)
Mk 4:27 the seed **s** and grows, though he does

Sprung (Spring¹)
Ge 2: 5 no plant of the field had yet **s** up,

Spun (Spin)
Ex 35:25 Every skilled woman **s** with her hands
35:25 and brought what she had **s**—blue,
35:26 and had the skill **s** the goat hair.

Spur (Spurred, Spurs)
Heb 10:24 how we may **s** one another on towards

Spurn (Spurned, Spurns)
Job 10: 3 to **s** the work of your hands, while

Spurned (Spurn)
Ps 89:38 you have rejected, you have **s**, you
Pr 1:30 accept my advice and **s** my rebuke,
5:12 How my heart **s** correction!
Isa 1: 4 they have **s** the Holy One of Israel
5:24 **s** the word of the Holy One of Israel.
Lam 2: 6 anger he has **s** both king and priest.

Spurns (Spurn)
Pr 15: 5 A fool **s** his father's discipline,

Spurred (Spur)
Est 3:15 **S** on by the king's command, the
8:14 out, **s** on by the king's command.
Isa 9:11 them and has **s** their enemies on.

Spurs (Spur)
Isa 41: 7 **s** on him who strikes the anvil.

Spy (Spied, Spies, Spying)
Dt 1:22 "Let us send men ahead to **s** out the
Jos 2: 2 here tonight to **s** out the land."
2: 3 have come to **s** out the whole land."
7: 2 "Go up and **s** out the region."
Jdg 1:23 they sent men to **s** out Bethel
18: 2 to **s** out the land and explore it.
2Sa 10: 3 city and **s** it out and overthrow it?"
1Ch 19: 3 **s** out the country and overthrow it?"
Gal 2: 4 to **s** on the freedom we have in

Spying (Spy)
Ge 42:30 us as though we were **s** on the land.
Jos 6:23 the young men who had done the **s**

Squads
Ac 12: 4 by four **s** of four soldiers each.

Squall
Mk 4:37 A furious **s** came up, and the waves
Lk 8:23 A **s** came down on the lake, so that

Squandered (Squanders)
Lk 15:13 there **s** his wealth in wild living.
15:30 of yours who has **s** your property

Squanders (Squandered)
Pr 29: 3 of prostitutes **s** his wealth.

Square (Squares)
Ge 19: 2 "we will spend the night in the **s**.
Ex 27: 1 it is to be **s**, five cubits long
28:16 is to be **s**—a span long and a span
30: 2 is to be **s**, a cubit long and a cubit
37:25 It was **s**, a cubit long and a cubit
38: 1 it was **s**, five cubits long
39: 9 was **s**—a span long and a span wide
Dt 13:16 into the middle of the public **s**
Jdg 19:15 They went and sat in the city **s**, but
19:17 and saw the traveller in the city **s**,
19:20 Only don't spend the night in the **s**."
2Sa 21:12 from the public **s** at Beth Shan,
1Ki 7:31 of the stands were **s**, not round.
2Ch 29: 4 them in the **s** on the east side
32: 6 assembled them before him in the **s**
Ezr 10: 9 in the **s** before the house of God,
Ne 8: 1 man in the **s** before the Water Gate.
8: 3 faced the **s** before the Water Gate
8:16 in the **s** by the Water Gate and the
Est 4: 6 in the open **s** of the city in front
Job 29: 7 and took my seat in the public **s**,
Eze 16:24 a lofty shrine in every public **s**.
16:31 lofty shrines in every public **s**,
40:12 and the alcoves were six cubits **s**.
40:47 he measured the court: It was **s**—a
41:22 three cubits high and two cubits **s**;
43:16 The altar hearth is **s**, twelve cubits
43:17 The upper ledge also is **s**, fourteen
45: 2 Of this, a section 500 cubits **s** is
48:20 The entire portion will be a **s**,
Am 5:16 cries of anguish in every public **s**.
Rev 21:16 The city was laid out like a **s**, as

Squares (Square)
Pr 1:20 raises her voice in the public **s**;
5:16 streams of water in the public **s**?
7:12 now in the street, now in the **s**, at
SS 3: 2 through its streets and **s**;
Isa 15: 3 and in the public **s** they all wail,
Jer 5: 1 and consider, search through her **s**.
9:21 and the young men from the public **s**.
48:38 roofs in Moab and in the public **s**
Na 2: 4 back and forth through the **s**.

Squeezed
Ge 40:11 and I took the grapes, **s** them into
Jdg 6:38 he **s** the fleece and wrung out the

Stab (Stabbed)
Zec 13: 3 his own parents will **s** him.

Stabbed (Stab)
2Sa 3:27 s him in the stomach, and he died.
4: 6 and they s him in the stomach.
4: 7 After they s and killed him, they
20:10 Without being s again, Amasa died.

Stability
Pr 29: 4 By justice a king gives a country s,

Stachys
Ro 16: 9 in Christ, and my dear friend S.

Stadia
Rev 14:20 for a distance of 1,600 s.
21:16 found it to be 12,000 s in length,

Staff (*Aaron's staff*, Flagstaff, Staffs)
Ge 32:10 I had only my s when I crossed this
38:18 its cord, and the s in your hand,"
38:25 seal and cord and s these are."
47:31 as he leaned on the top of his s.
49:10 nor the ruler's s from between his
Ex 4: 2 "A s," he replied.
4: 4 it turned back into a s in his hand.
4:17 take this s in your hand so that you
4:20 And he took the s of God in his hand.
7: 9 'Take your s and throw it down
7:10 Aaron threw his s down in front of
7:12 Each one threw down his s and it
7:15 the s that was changed into a snake.
7:17 With the s that is in my hand I will
7:19 'Take your s and stretch out your
7:20 He raised his s in the presence of
8: 5 'stretch out your hand with your s
8:16 'stretch out your s and strike the
8:17 stretched out his hand with the s
9:23 Moses stretched out his s towards
10:13 Moses stretched out his s over Egypt,
12:11 your feet and your s in your hand.
14:16 Raise your s and stretch out your
17: 5 s with which you struck the Nile,
17: 9 hill with the s of God in my hands."
21:19 walks around outside with his s;
Nu 17: 2 Write the name of each man on his s.
17: 3 On the s of Levi write Aaron's name,
17: 3 for there must be one s for the head
17: 5 The s belonging to the man I choose
17: 9 them, and each man took his own s.
20: 8 "Take the s, and you and your
20: 9 Moses took the s from the LORD's
20:11 struck the rock twice with his s.
22:27 was angry and beat her with his s.
Jdg 5:14 those who bear a commander's s.
6:21 With the tip of the s that was in
1Sa 14:27 so he reached out the end of the s
14:43 a little honey with the end of my s.
17:40 he took his s in his hand, chose
2Ki 4:29 take my s in your hand and run.
4:29 Lay my s on the boy's face."
4:31 and laid the s on the boy's face,
18:21 that splintered reed of a s, which
2Ch 32: 3 military s about blocking off the
Ps 23: 4 rod and your s, they comfort me.
Isa 10:26 he will raise his s over the waters,
36: 6 that splintered reed of a s, which
Jer 48:17 sceptre, how broken the glorious s!'
51:59 the s officer Seraiah son of Neriah,
Eze 12:14 —his s and all his troops—
29: 6 a s of reed for the house of Israel.
Mic 7:14 Shepherd your people with your s,
Zec 11:10 I took my s called Favour and broke
11:14 I broke my second s called Union,
Mt 10:10 or extra tunic, or sandals or a s;
27:29 They put a s in his right hand and
27:30 They spat on him, and took the s and
Mk 6: 8 the journey except a s—no bread,
15:19 the head with a s and spat on him.
Lk 9: 3 "Take nothing for the journey—no s,
Heb 11:21 as he leaned on the top of his s.

Staffs (Staff)
Ex 7:12 Aaron's staff swallowed up their s.
Nu 17: 2 and get twelve s from them,
17: 6 and their leaders gave him twelve s,
17: 7 Moses placed the s before the LORD
17: 9 Moses brought out all the s from the
21:18 the nobles with sceptres and s.
Zec 11: 7 Then I took two s and called one

Stag
SS 2: 9 is like a gazelle or a young s.
2:17 like a young s on the rugged hills.
8:14 s on the spice-laden mountains.

Stages
Nu 33: 1 Here are the s in the journey of the
33: 2 recorded the s in their journey.
33: 2 This is their journey by s:
Eze 41: 7 the temple was built in ascending s,

Stagger (Staggered, Staggering, Staggers)
Job 12:25 he makes them s like drunkards.
Ps 60: 3 have given us wine that makes us s.
Isa 19:14 make Egypt s in all that she does,
28: 7 these also s from wine and reel from
28: 7 Priests and prophets s from beer and
28: 7 they s when seeing visions, they
29: 9 not from wine, s, but not from beer.
51:17 dregs the goblet that makes men s.
51:22 your hand the cup that made you s;
Jer 25:16 they will s and go mad because of
Lam 5:13 boys s under loads of wood.
Am 8:12 Men will s from sea to sea and

Staggered (Stagger)
Ps 107:27 They reeled and s like drunken men;
Isa 21: 3 I am s by what I hear,
Am 4: 8 People s from town to town for water

Staggering (Stagger)
1Sa 25:31 the s burden of needless bloodshed
Pr 24:11 hold back those s towards slaughter.

Staggers (Stagger)
Isa 3: 8 Jerusalem s, Judah is falling;
19:14 as a drunkard s around in his vomit.

Stain (Stained)
Jer 2:22 s of your guilt is still before me,"
Eph 5:27 without s or wrinkle or any other

Stained (Stain)
1Ki 2: 5 and with that blood s the belt round
Isa 59: 3 For your hands are s with blood,
63: 1 Bozrah, with his garments s crimson
63: 3 garments, and I s all my clothing.
Hos 6: 8 men, s with footprints of blood.
Jude :23 the clothing s by corrupted flesh.

Stairs (Downstairs, Stairway, Upstairs)
Ne 9: 4 Standing on the s were the Levites
Eze 40:49 It was reached by a flight of s, and

Stairway (Stairs)
Ge 28:12 He had a dream in which he saw a s
1Ki 6: 8 a s led up to the middle level and
2Ki 20:11 it had gone down on the s of Ahaz.
Isa 38: 8 it has gone down on the s of Ahaz.
Eze 41: 7 A s went up from the lowest floor to

Stake (Stakes)
Job 6:29 for my integrity is at s.

Stakes (Stake)
Isa 33:20 its s will never be pulled up,
54: 2 your cords, strengthen your s.

Stalk (Stalked, Stalks)
Ge 41: 5 good, were growing on a single s.
41:22 and good, growing on a single s.
Job 10:16 If I hold my head high, you s me
Hos 8: 7 The s has no head; it will produce
Mk 4:28 the soil produces corn—first the s,
Jn 19:29 put the sponge on a s of the hyssop

Stalked (Stalk)
Lam 4:18 Men s us at every step, so we could
Eze 32:27 s through the land of the living.

Stalks (Stalk)
Jos 2: 6 hidden them under the s of flax she
Ru 2:16 Rather, pull out some s for her from
Ps 91: 6 nor the pestilence that s in the

Stall (Stalls)
Ps 50: 9 I have no need of a bull from your s
Mal 4: 2 like calves released from the s.
Lk 13:15 donkey from the s and lead it out

Stall-fed (Feed)
1Ki 4:23 ten head of s cattle, twenty of

Stallions
Jer 5: 8 They are well-fed, lusty s, each
8:16 at the neighing of their s the
50:11 threshing corn and neigh like s,

Stalls (Stall)
1Ki 4:26 Solomon had four thousand s for
2Ch 9:25 Solomon had four thousand s for
32:28 and he made s for various kinds of
Hab 3:17 in the pen and no cattle in the s,

Stammering
Isa 32: 4 s tongue will be fluent and clear.

Stamp (Stamped)
Eze 6:11 and s your feet and cry out "Alas!"

Stamped (Stamp)
Eze 25: 6 clapped your hands and s your feet,

Stand (*Stand firm*, Standing, Stands, Stood)
Ge 31:35 my lord, that I cannot s up in your
Ex 9:11 The magicians could not s before
17: 6 I will s there before you by the
17: 9 Tomorrow I will s on top of the hill
18:14 while all these people s round you
18:23 you will be able to s the strain,
30:18 with its bronze s, for washing.
30:28 utensils, and the basin with its s.
31: 9 its utensils, the basin with its s—
33:21 near me where you may s on a rock.
35:16 the bronze basin with its s;
38: 8 its bronze s from the mirrors of the
39:39 its utensils; the basin with its s;
40:11 Anoint the basin and its s and
Lev 8:11 the basin with its s, to consecrate
26:37 be able to s before your enemies.
Nu 5:16 her and make her s before the LORD.
5:18 made the woman s before the LORD,
5:30 The priest is to make her s before
8:13 Make the Levites s in front of Aaron
11:16 that they may s there with you.
11:24 and made them s round the Tent.
16: 9 to s before the community and
27:19 Make him s before Eleazar the priest
27:21 He is to s before Eleazar the priest,
27:22 He took Joshua and made him s before
30: 4 by which she bound herself will s.
30: 5 by which she bound herself will s;
30: 7 by which she bound herself will s.
30:11 by which she bound herself will s.
30:12 that came from her lips will s.
Dt 7:24 No-one will be able to s up against
9: 2 "Who can s up against the Anakites?
10: 8 to s before the LORD to minister and
11:25 No man will be able to s against you.
18: 5 all your tribes to s and minister
19:16 If a malicious witness takes the s
19:17 must s in the presence of the LORD
27:12 tribes shall s on Mount Gerizim
27:13 these tribes shall s on Mount Ebal
Jos 1: 5 No-one will be able to s up against

Jos 3: 8 waters, go and s in the river.
3:13 will be cut off and s up in a heap."
7:10 The LORD said to Joshua, "S up!
7:12 That is why the Israelites cannot s
7:13 You cannot s against your enemies
10:12 "O sun, s still over Gibeon, O moon,
20: 4 he is to s in the entrance of the
Jdg 4:20 "S in the doorway of the tent," he
1Sa 6:20 "Who can s in the presence of the
12: 3 Here I s. Testify against me in the
12: 7 Now then, s here, because I am going
12:16 "Now then, s still and see this
14:40 "You s over there; I and Jonathan my
14:40 Jonathan my son will s over here.
17:16 morning and evening and took his s.
19: 3 I will go out and s with my father
2Sa 1: 9 "Then he said to me, 'S over me and
2:25 and took their s on top of a hill.
15: 2 He would get up early and s by the
18:30 The king said, "S aside and wait
22:34 he enables me to s on the heights.
23:12 Shammah took his s in the middle of
1Ki 7:30 Each s had four bronze wheels with
7:31 On the inside of the s there was an
7:32 the wheels were attached to the s.
7:34 Each s had four handles, one on each
7:34 each corner, projecting from the s.
7:35 At the top of the s there was a
7:35 were attached to the top of the s.
10: 8 s before you and hear your wisdom!
19:11 "Go out and s on the mountain
2Ki 5:11 s and call on the name of the LORD
1Ch 11:14 they took their s in the middle of
23:30 They were also to s every morning to
2Ch 9: 7 s before you and hear your wisdom!
20: 9 we will s in your presence before
29:11 LORD has chosen you to s before him
35: 5 "S in the holy place with a group of
Ezr 9:15 one of us can s in your presence."
10:13 so we cannot s outside.
Ne 9: 5 "S up and praise the LORD your God,
Est 6:13 origin, you cannot s against him
9: 2 No-one could s against them, because
Job 19:25 in the end he will s upon the earth.
21:16 so I s aloof from the counsel of the
22:18 so I s aloof from the counsel of the
30:20 I s up, but you merely look at me.
30:28 I s up in the assembly and cry for
32:16 now that they s there with no reply?
38:14 s out like those of a garment.
39:24 s still when the trumpet sounds.
40:12 him, crush the wicked where they s.
41:10 Who then is able to s against me?
Ps 1: 1 or s in the way of sinners or sit
1: 5 Therefore the wicked will not s in
2: 2 The kings of the earth take their s
5: 5 The arrogant cannot s in your
10: 1 Why, O LORD, do you s far off?
18:33 he enables me to s on the heights.
24: 3 Who may s in his holy place?
26:12 My feet s on level ground;
40: 2 rock and gave me a firm place to s.
76: 7 Who can s before you when you are
94:16 take a s for me against evildoers?
101: 7 falsely will s in my presence.
109: 6 let an accuser s at his right hand.
119:120 I s in awe of your laws.
122: 5 There the thrones for judgment s,
127: 1 city, the watchmen s guard in vain.
130: 3 record of sins, O Lord, who could s?
Pr 8: 2 the paths meet, she takes her s;
27: 4 but who can s before jealousy?
Ecc 5: 7 Therefore s in awe of God.
8: 3 Do not s up for a bad cause, for he
Isa 7: 9 your faith, you will not s at all.
8:10 it will not s, for God is with us.
11:10 In that day the Root of Jesse will s
14:24 as I have purposed, so it will s.
21: 8 "Day after day, my lord, I s on the
28:18 agreement with the grave will not s.
29:23 will s in awe of the God of Israel.
44:11 all come together and take their s;
46:10 I say: My purpose will s, and I will
48:13 summon them, they all s up together.
60:11 Your gates will always s open, they
Jer 1:17 "Get yourself ready! S up and say to
1:18 a bronze wall to s against the whole
6:16 "S at the crossroads and look;
7: 2 "S at the gate of the LORD's house
7:10 come and s before me in this house,
14: 6 Wild donkeys s on the barren heights
15: 1 Moses and Samuel were to s before
17:19 "Go and s at the gate of the people,
17:19 s also at all the other gates of
26: 2 S in the courtyard of the LORD's
30:18 palace will s in its proper place.
33:18 ever fail to have a man to s before
44:28 whose word will s—mine or theirs.
44:29 of harm against you will surely s.'
46:15 They cannot s, for the LORD will
46:21 they will not s their ground, for
48:19 S by the road and watch, you who
48:45 of Heshbon the fugitives s helpless,
49:19 And what shepherd can s against me?"
50:44 And what shepherd can s against me?"
51:29 LORD's purposes against Babylon s
Eze 2: 1 He said to me, "Son of man, s up on
22:30 s before me in the gap on behalf of
27:29 all the seamen will s on the shore.
44:11 s before the people and serve them.
44:15 they are to s before me to offer
46: 2 the gateway and s by the gatepost.
47:10 Fishermen will s along the shore;
Da 8: 4 No animal could s against him, and
8: 7 The ram was powerless to s against
8:25 his s against the Prince of princes.
10:11 and s up, for I have now been sent
11: 1 my s to support and protect him.)
11:15 will not have the strength to s.
11:16 will be able to s against him.
11:25 but he will not be able to s because
Am 2:15 The archer will not s his ground,
5:21 I cannot s your assemblies.
Mic 5: 4 He will s and shepherd his flock in
6: 1 "S up, plead your case before the
Hab 2: 1 I will s at my watch and station
3: 2 I s in awe of your deeds, O LORD.
Zep 3: 8 "for the day I will s up to testify.
Zec 14: 4 On that day his feet will s on the
Mal 3: 2 Who can s when he appears? For he
Mt 4: 5 s on the highest point of the temple.
5:15 Instead they put it on its s, and it
12:25 divided against itself will not s.
12:26 How then can his kingdom s?
12:41 The men of Nineveh will s up at the
18: 2 child and had him s among them.
Mk 3: 3 hand, "S up in front of everyone."
3:24 itself, that kingdom cannot s.
3:25 against itself, that house cannot s.
3:26 he cannot s; his end has come.
4:21 Instead, don't you put it on its s?
9:36 child and had him s among them.
11:25 you s praying, if you hold anything
13: 9 On account of me you will s before
Lk 1:19 I s in the presence of God, and I
4: 9 s on the highest point of the temple.
6: 8 "Get up and s in front of everyone."
8:16 Instead, he puts it on a s, so that
9:47 child and made him s beside him.
11:18 himself, how can his kingdom s?
11:32 The men of Nineveh will s up at the
11:33 Instead he puts it on its s, so that
13:25 you will s outside knocking and
21:28 s up and lift up your heads,
21:36 be able to s before the Son of Man."
Jn 8: 3 They made her s before the group
8:16 I s with the Father, who sent me.
Ac 1:11 "why do you s here looking into the
4:26 The kings of the earth take their s
5:20 "Go, s in the temple courts," he
6:10 they could not s up against his
10:26 "S up," he said, "I am only a man
14:10 called out, "S up on your feet!"
22:30 Paul and had him s before them.
23: 6 I s on trial because of my hope in
25: 9 s trial before me there on these
25:20 and s trial there on these charges.
26: 2 fortunate to s before you today as
26:16 'Now get up and s on your feet.
26:22 and so I s here and testify to small
27:24 You must s trial before Caesar;
Ro 5: 2 into this grace in which we now s.
9:11 God's purpose in election might s:
11:20 of unbelief, and you s by faith.
14: 4 And he will s, for the Lord is able
14: 4 for the Lord is able to make him s.
14:10 all s before God's judgment seat.
1Co 10:13 out so that you can s up under it.
15: 1 and on which you have taken your s.
2Co 2: 9 was to see if you would s the test
Eph 6:11 your s against the devil's schemes.
6:13 you may be able to s your ground,
6:13 you have done everything, to s.
1Th 3: 1 when we could s it no longer, we
3: 5 For this reason, when I could s it
Jas 2: 3 "You s there" or "Sit on the floor
1Pe 5:12 true grace of God. S fast in it.
Rev 3:20 Here I am! I s at the door and knock.
6:17 wrath has come, and who can s?"
8: 2 I saw the seven angels who s before
11: 4 that s before the Lord of the earth.
18:10 they will s far off and cry:
18:15 s far off, terrified at her torment.
18:17 living from the sea, will s far off.

Stand firm

Ex 14:13 S and you will see the deliverance
2Ch 20:17 Take up your positions; s and see
Job 11:15 you will s and without fear.
Ps 20: 8 and fall, but we rise up and s.
30: 7 you made my mountain s; but when you
33:11 the plans of the LORD s for ever,
78:13 he made the water s like a wall.
93: 5 Your statutes s; holiness adorns
Pr 10:25 gone, but the righteous s for ever.
Isa 7: 9 If you do not s in your faith, you
Eze 13: 5 so that it will s in the battle on
1Co 15:58 Therefore, my dear brothers, s.
16:13 Be on your guard; s in the faith;
2Co 1:21 makes both us and you s in Christ.
1:24 joy, because it is by faith you s.
Gal 5: 1 S, then, and do not let yourselves
Eph 6:14 S then, with the belt of truth
Php 1:27 I will know that you s in one spirit,
4: 1 should s in the Lord, dear friends!
Col 4:12 that you may s in all the will of
2Th 2:15 then, brothers, s and hold to the
Jas 5: 8 You too, be patient and s, because

Standard (Standards)

Nu 1:52 man in his own camp under his own s.
2: 2 each man under his s with the
2: 3 Judah are to encamp under their s.
2:10 of the camp of Reuben under their s.
2:17 each in his own place under his s.
2:18 the camp of Ephraim under their s.
2:25 of the camp of Dan, under their s.
10:14 of Judah went first, under their s.
10:18 of Reuben went next, under their s.
10:22 of Ephraim went next, under their s.
10:25 camp of Dan set out, under their s.
2Sa 14:26 two hundred shekels by the royal s.
2Ch 3: 3 wide (using the cubit of the old s).
Isa 31: 9 at the sight of the battle s their
Jer 4:21 How long must I see the battle s and
Eze 45:11 is to be the s measure for both.

Standards (Standard)

Lev 19:35 "'Do not use dishonest s when
Nu 2:31 will set out last, under their s.
2:34 the way they encamped under their s,
Ps 74: 4 they set up their s as signs.
Eze 5: 7 to the s of the nations around you.
7:27 by their own s I will judge them.
11:12 to the s of the nations around you."
23:24 punish you according to their s.
Jn 8:15 You judge by human s; I pass
1Co 1:26 Not many of you were wise by human s;
3:18 he is wise by the s of this age,
2Co 10: 2 that we live by the s of this world.

Standing (Stand)

Ge 18: 2 Abraham looked up and saw three men s
18:22 Abraham remained s before the LORD.
24:13 See, I am s beside this spring, and
24:30 him s by the camels near the spring.

Ge 24:31 "Why are you s out here? I have
24:43 See, I am s beside this spring; if a
41: 1 had a dream: He was s by the Nile,
41:17 I was s on the bank of the Nile,
Ex 3: 5 where you are s is holy ground."
22: 6 grain or s corn or the whole field,
26:32 gold and s on four silver bases.
33:10 cloud s at the entrance to the tent,
Nu 16:27 out and were s with their wives,
22:23 the angel of the LORD s in the road
22:31 s in the road with his sword drawn.
22:34 I did not realise you were s in the
23: 6 and found him s beside his offering
23:17 and found him s beside his offering
32:14 a brood of sinners, s in the place
Dt 16: 9 to put the sickle to the s corn.
23:25 must not put a sickle to his s corn.
29:10 All of you are s today in the
29:12 You are s here in order to enter
29:15 who are s here with us today in the
Jos 4:10 remained s in the middle of the
5:13 he looked up and saw a man s in
5:15 the place where you are s is holy.
8:33 officials and judges, were s on both
20: 9 to s trial before the assembly.
Jdg 9:35 was s at the entrance to the city
15: 5 in the s corn of the Philistines.
15: 5 He burned up the shocks and s corn,
Ru 2: 1 a man of s, whose name was Boaz.
2:13 the s of one of your servant girls."
4:11 May you have s in Ephrathah and be
1Sa 9: 1 There was a Benjamite, a man of s,
17:26 David asked the men s near him,
19:20 with Samuel s there as their leader,
22: 6 with all his officials s round him.
22: 9 Doeg the Edomite, who was s with
2Sa 13:34 Now the man s watch looked up and
1Ki 8:14 assembly of Israel was s there,
10:19 with a lion s beside each of them.
11:28 Now Jeroboam was a man of s, and
13: 1 s by the altar to make an offering.
13:24 the donkey and the lion s beside it.
13:25 with the lion s beside the body, and
13:28 the donkey and the lion s beside it.
22:19 of heaven s round him on his right
2Ki 9:17 the lookout s on the tower in
11:14 there was the king, s by the pillar
13: 6 Asherah pole remained s in Samaria.
1Ch 21:15 The angel of the LORD was then s at
21:16 the LORD s between heaven and earth,
2Ch 6: 3 assembly of Israel was s there,
7: 6 and all the Israelites were s.
9:18 with a lion s beside each of them.
18:18 s on his right and on his left.
23:13 there was the king, s by his pillar
Ne 8: 5 him because he was s above them;
8: 7 Law while the people were s there.
9: 4 S on the stairs were the Levites
Est 5: 2 he saw Queen Esther s in the court,
6: 5 answered, "Haman is s in the court."
Ps 122: 2 Our feet are s in your gates,
Isa 17: 5 as when a reaper gathers the s corn
27: 9 or incense altars will be left s.
Jer 28: 5 who were s in the house of the LORD.
36:21 and all the officials s beside him.
Lam 3:63 Look at them! Sitting or s, they
Eze 3:23 the glory of the LORD was s there,
8:11 son of Shaphan was s among them.
10: 3 Now the cherubim were s on the south
40: 3 he was s in the gateway with a linen
43: 6 While the man was s beside me, I
Da 7:16 I approached one of those s there
8: 3 s beside the canal, and the horns
8: 6 ram I had seen s beside the canal
8:17 he came near the place where I was s,
10: 4 as I was s on the bank of the great
10:16 I said to the one s before me, "I am
Am 7: 7 the Lord was s by a wall that had
9: 1 I saw the Lord s by the altar, and
Zec 1: 8 s among the myrtle trees in a ravine.
1:10 the man s among the myrtle trees
1:11 who was s among the myrtle trees,
3: 1 Joshua the high priest s before the
3: 1 s at his right side to accuse him.
3: 4 The angel said to those who were s
3: 7 give you a place among these s here.
Zec 6: 5 going out from s in the presence of
14:12 they are still s on their feet,
Mt 6: 5 for they love to pray s in the
12:47 s outside, wanting to speak to you."
16:28 some who are s here will not taste
20: 3 s in the market-place doing nothing.
20: 6 out and found still others s around.
20: 6 s here all day long doing nothing?'
24:15 "So when you see s in the holy place
26:73 those s there went up to Peter and
27:47 some of those s there heard this,
Mk 3:31 S outside, they sent someone in to
9: 1 some who are s here will not taste
11: 5 some people s there asked, "What are
13:14 s where it does not belong—let the
14:47 one of those s near drew his sword
14:69 she said again to those s around,
14:70 After a little while, those s near
15:35 some of those s near heard this,
Lk 1:11 s at the right side of the altar of
5: 1 One day as Jesus was s by the Lake
8:20 are s outside, wanting to see you."
9:27 some who are s here will not taste
9:32 glory and the two men s with him.
19:24 "Then he said to those s by, 'Take
21:19 By s firm you will gain life.
23:10 s there, vehemently accusing him.
Jn 8: 9 left, with the woman still s there.
11:42 the benefit of the people s here,
18: 5 the traitor was s there with them.)
18:18 was s with them, warming himself.
19:26 disciple whom he loved s near by
20:14 turned round and saw Jesus s there
Ac 4:14 had been healed s there with them,
5:23 with the guards s at the doors;
5:25 The men you put in jail are s in the
7:33 where you are s is holy ground.
7:55 Jesus s at the right hand of God.
7:56 Son of Man s at the right hand of
13:16 S up, Paul motioned with his hand
13:50 God-fearing women of high s and the
16: 9 man of Macedonia s and begging him,
22:25 Paul said to the centurion s there,
23: 2 Ananias ordered those s near Paul
23: 4 Those who were s near Paul said,
25:10 "I am now s before Caesar's court
1Co 10:12 So, if you think you are s firm, be
1Th 3: 8 since you are s firm in the Lord.
1Ti 3:13 served well gain an excellent s
Heb 9: 8 as the first tabernacle was still s.
Jas 5: 9 The Judge is s at the door!
1Pe 5: 9 Resist him, s firm in the faith,
Rev 4: 1 me was a door s open in heaven.
5: 6 s in the centre of the throne,
7: 1 After this I saw four angels s at
7: 9 and language, s before the throne
7:11 All the angels were s round the
10: 5 the angel I had seen s on the sea
10: 8 is s on the sea and on the land."
14: 1 me was the Lamb, s on Mount Zion,
15: 2 s beside the sea, those who had been
19:11 I saw heaven s open and there before
19:17 I saw an angel s in the sun, who
20:12 and small, s before the throne,

Stands (Stand)

Nu 35:12 he s trial before the assembly.
Dt 17:12 the priest who s ministering there
Jos 22:19 where the LORD's tabernacle s, and
22:29 God that s before his tabernacle."
Jdg 6:24 it s in Ophrah of the Abiezrites.
1Sa 16: 6 anointed s here before the LORD."
1Ki 7:27 He also made ten movable s of bronze;
7:28 This is how the s were made: They
7:31 The panels of the s were square,
7:37 This is the way he made the ten s.
7:38 basin to go on each of the ten s.
7:39 He placed five of the s on the south
7:43 the ten s with their ten basins;
2Ki 16:17 the basins from the movable s.
25:13 the movable s and the bronze Sea
25:16 the Sea and the movable s, which
2Ch 4:14 the s with their basins;
Est 7: 9 feet high s by Haman's house.
Job 9:35 but as it now s with me, I cannot.
Job 23:13 "But he s alone, and who can oppose
Ps 89: 2 I will declare that your love s firm
109:31 For he s at the right hand of the
119:89 it s firm in the heavens.
Pr 12: 7 the house of the righteous s firm.
SS 2: 9 Look! There he s behind our wall,
Isa 27:10 The fortified city s desolate, an
32: 8 plans, and by noble deeds he s.
40: 8 but the word of our God s for ever."
46: 7 it up in its place, and there it s.
59:14 and righteousness s at a distance;
65: 6 "See, it s written before me; I will
Jer 27:19 the Sea, the movable s and the other
52:17 the movable s and the bronze Sea
52:20 the movable s, which King Solomon
Da 6:12 "The decree s—in accordance with
Mt 10:22 who s firm to the end will be saved.
13:38 seed s for the sons of the kingdom.
24:13 he who s firm to the end will be
Mk 13:13 who s firm to the end will be saved.
Lk 8:14 fell among thorns s for those who
8:15 the seed on good soil s for those
Jn 1:26 among you s one you do not know.
3:18 does not believe s condemned
16:11 of this world now s condemned.
Ac 4:10 that this man s before you healed.
Ro 14: 4 To his own master he s or falls.
Gal 4:25 Now Hagar s for Mount Sinai in
2Ti 2:19 God's solid foundation s firm,
Heb 4: 1 of entering his rest still s,
10:11 Day after day every priest s and
1Pe 1:25 the word of the Lord s for ever."
Rev 19: 8 (Fine linen s for the righteous

Standstill

Ezr 4:24 came to a s until the second year

Star (Stargazers, Starry, Stars)

Nu 24:17 A s will come out of Jacob;
Isa 14:12 O morning s, son of the dawn!
Am 5:26 of your idols, the s of your god—
Mt 2: 2 We saw his s in the east and have
2: 7 the exact time the s had appeared.
2: 9 and the s they had seen in the east
2:10 they saw the s, they were overjoyed.
Ac 7:43 Molech and the s of your god Rephan,
1Co 15:41 and s differs from s in splendour.
2Pe 1:19 the morning s rises in your hearts.
Rev 2:28 I will also give him the morning s.
8:10 and a great s, blazing like a torch,
8:11 the name of the s is Wormwood.
9: 1 and I saw a s that had fallen from
9: 1 The s was given the key to the shaft
22:16 of David, and the bright Morning S."

Stare (Stared, Stares)

Ps 22:17 people s and gloat over me.
SS 1: 6 Do not s at me because I am dark,
Isa 14:16 Those who see you s at you, they
Ac 3:12 Why do you s at us as if by our own

Stared (Stare)

2Ki 8:11 He s at him with a fixed gaze until
Jn 13:22 His disciples s at one another, at a
Ac 10: 4 Cornelius s at him in fear.

Stares (Stare)

Ps 55: 3 the enemy, at the s of the wicked;

Stargazers (Star)

Isa 47:13 those s who make predictions month

Starry (Star)

2Ki 17:16 They bowed down to all the s hosts,
21: 3 all the s hosts and worshipped them.
21: 5 he built altars to all the s hosts.
23: 4 Baal and Asherah and all the s hosts.
23: 5 and to all the s hosts.
2Ch 33: 3 all the s hosts and worshipped them.
33: 5 he built altars to all the s hosts.
Ne 9: 6 and all their s host, the earth and
Ps 33: 6 s host by the breath of his mouth.
Isa 34: 4 all the s host will fall like
40:26 brings out the s host one by one,

Isa 45:12 I marshalled their s hosts.
Jer 19:13 on the roofs to all the s hosts
Da 8:10 and it threw some of the s host down
Zep 1: 5 on the roofs to worship the s host,

Stars (Star)

Ge 1:16 He also made the s.
15: 5 up at the heavens and count the s
22:17 as numerous as the s in the sky
26: 4 as numerous as the s in the sky
37: 9 eleven s were bowing down to me."
Ex 32:13 as numerous as the s in the sky
Dt 1:10 you are as many as the s in the sky.
4:19 the moon and the s—all the heavenly
10:22 you as numerous as the s in the sky.
17: 3 sun or the moon or the s of the sky,
28:62 You who were as numerous as the s in
Jdg 5:20 From the heavens the s fought, from
1Ch 27:23 as numerous as the s in the sky.
Ne 4:21 light of dawn till the s came out.
9:23 as numerous as the s in the sky,
Job 3: 9 May its morning s become dark;
9: 7 he seals off the light of the s.
22:12 And see how lofty are the highest s!
25: 5 and the s are not pure in his eyes,
38: 7 while the morning s sang together
Ps 8: 3 the moon and the s, which you have
136: 9 the moon and s to govern the night;
147: 4 He determines the number of the s
148: 3 moon, praise him, all you shining s.
Ecc 12: 2 and the moon and the s grow dark,
SS 6:10 majestic as the s in procession?
Isa 13:10 The s of heaven and their
14:13 I will raise my throne above the s
34: 4 All the s of the heavens will be
Jer 8: 2 moon and all the s of the heavens,
31:35 who decrees the moon and s to shine
33:22 me as countless as the s of the sky
Eze 32: 7 the heavens and darken their s;
Da 12: 3 like the s for ever and ever.
Joel 2:10 darkened, and the s no longer shine.
3:15 darkened, and the s no longer shine.
Ob : 4 s, from there I will bring you down,"
Na 3:16 they are more than the s of the sky,
Mt 24:29 the s will fall from the sky,
Mk 13:25 the s will fall from the sky, and
Lk 21:25 be signs in the sun, moon and s.
Ac 27:20 neither sun nor s appeared for many
1Co 15:41 the moon another and the s another;
Php 2:15 you shine like s in the
Heb 11:12 as numerous as the s in the sky
Jude :13 wandering s, for whom blackest
Rev 1:16 In his right hand he held seven s,
1:20 The mystery of the seven s that you
1:20 The seven s are the angels of the
2: 1 holds the seven s in his right hand
3: 1 spirits of God and the seven s.
6:13 the s in the sky fell to earth, as
8:12 and a third of the s, so that a
12: 1 and a crown of twelve s on her head.
12: 4 His tail swept a third of the s out

Start (Started, Starting)

Nu 34: 3 will s from the end of the Salt Sea,
1Sa 9: 5 donkeys and s worrying about us."
1Ki 20:14 "And who will s the battle?" he
Ne 2:18 They replied, "Let us s rebuilding."
2:20 We his servants will s rebuilding,

Started (Start)

Ge 33:16 that day Esau s on his way back to
Ex 4:20 on a donkey and s back to Egypt.
22: 6 s the fire must make restitution.
Nu 11: 4 and again the Israelites s wailing
16:46 from the LORD; the plague has s."
16:47 The plague had already s among the
Jos 2:23 the two men s back. They went down
15: 2 Their southern boundary s from the
15: 5 The northern boundary s from the bay
18: 8 the men s on their way to map out
Est 6:13 before whom your downfall has s, is
Jer 37:12 Jeremiah s to leave the city to go
Da 8: 9 which s small but grew in power to
Jnh 3: 4 On the first day, Jonah s into the
Mk 10:17 Jesus s on his way, a man ran up to
Lk 9:46 An argument s among the disciples as
23: 5 He s in Galilee and has come all the
Jn 8: 6 But Jesus bent down and s to write
20: 3 Peter and the other disciple s for
Ac 8:27 he s out, and on his way he met an
10:23 The next day Peter s out with them,
17: 5 a mob and s a riot in the city.
21:38 "Aren't you the Egyptian who s a

Starting (Start)

2Ki 15:16 At that time Menahem, s out from
Pr 17:14 S a quarrel is like breaching a dam;
Eze 21:19 take, both s from the same country.
Mt 27:24 but that instead an uproar was s, he

Startle (Startled)

Job 18:11 Terrors s him on every side and dog

Startled (Startle)

Ru 3: 8 of the night something s the man,
Lk 1:12 Zechariah saw him, he was s and was
24:37 They were s and frightened, thinking

Starvation (Starve)

Jer 15: 2 to the sword; those for s, to s;

Starve (Starvation, Starving)

Ex 16: 3 to s this entire assembly to death."
Jer 38: 9 where he will s to death when there

Starving (Starve)

Ge 42:19 grain back for your s households.
42:33 food for your s households and go.
2Ki 7:12 They know we are s; so they have
Pr 6:30 to satisfy his hunger when he is s.
Lk 15:17 to spare, and here I am s to death!

State (Stated, Statement, Statements)

Jos 20: 4 s his case before the elders of that
Job 23: 4 I would s my case before him and
33:26 restored by God to his righteous s.
Isa 14:18 All the kings of the nations lie in s
43:26 s the case for your innocence.
Lk 1:48 of the humble s of his servant.
Ac 24:20 Or these who are here should s what

Stated (State)

Ac 13:34 to decay, is s in these words:
13:35 So it is s elsewhere:
Ro 9: 9 For this was how the promise was s:

Stately

Pr 30:29 "There are three things that are s
30:29 four that move with s bearing:
Isa 2:16 trading ship and every s vessel.
Zec 11: 2 the s trees are ruined!

Statement (State)

Ac 20:38 What grieved them most was his s
28:25 after Paul had made this final s:

Statements (State)

Mk 14:56 him, but their s did not agree.

Station (Stationed)

2Ki 11: 8 S yourselves round the king, each
2Ch 23: 7 The Levites are to s themselves
Jer 51:12 s the watchmen, prepare an ambush!
Hab 2: 1 and s myself on the ramparts;

Stationed (Station)

Jdg 20:22 they had s themselves the first day.
2Ki 3:21 was called up and s on the border.
11:11 s themselves round the king—near
1Ch 9:18 being s at the King's Gate on the
9:27 They would spend the night s round
16:42 sons of Jeduthun were s at the gate.
2Ch 17: 2 He s troops in all the fortified
17:19 besides those he s in the fortified
23:10 He s all the men, each with his
23:19 He also s doorkeepers at the gates
29:25 He s the Levites in the temple of
33:14 He s military commanders in all the
Ne 4:13 Therefore I s some of the people
13:11 together and s them at their posts.
13:19 I s some of my own men at the gates
Eze 21:15 I have s the sword for slaughter at

Statue

Da 2:31 there before you stood a large s
2:31 dazzling s, awesome in appearance.
2:32 The head of the s was made of pure
2:34 It struck the s on its feet of iron
2:35 But the rock that struck the s

Stature

1Sa 2:26 the boy Samuel continued to grow in s
SS 7: 7 Your s is like that of the palm, and
Lk 2:52 Jesus grew in wisdom and s, and in

Statute (Statutes)

1Sa 30:25 David made this a s and ordinance
Ps 81: 5 He established it as a s for Joseph
122: 4 according to the s given to Israel.

Statutes (Statute)

1Ki 3: 3 to the s of his father David,
3:14 if you walk in my ways and obey my s
11:33 nor kept my s and laws as David,
11:34 and who observed my commands and s.
11:38 eyes by keeping my s and commands,
Ps 19: 7 The s of the LORD are trustworthy,
78: 5 He decreed s for Jacob and
78:56 they did not keep his s.
89:30 my law and do not follow my s,
93: 5 Your s stand firm; holiness adorns
99: 7 his s and the decrees he gave them.
119: 2 Blessed are they who keep his s and
119:14 I rejoice in following your s as one
119:22 and contempt, for I keep your s.
119:24 Your s are my delight; they are my
119:31 I hold fast to your s, O LORD;
119:36 Turn my heart towards your s and not
119:46 I will speak of your s before kings
119:59 and have turned my steps to your s.
119:79 to me, those who understand your s.
119:88 and I will obey the s of your mouth.
119:95 me, but I will ponder your s.
119:99 teachers, for I meditate on your s.
119:111 Your s are my heritage for ever;
119:119 therefore I love your s.
119:125 that I may understand your s.
119:129 Your s are wonderful; therefore I
119:138 The s you have laid down are
119:144 Your s are for ever right; give me
119:146 save me and I will keep your s.
119:152 Long ago I learned from your s that
119:157 but I have not turned from your s.
119:167 I obey your s, for I love them
119:168 I obey your precepts and your s, for
132:12 my covenant and the s I teach them,
Isa 24: 5 violated the s and broken the
Eze 20:18 "Do not follow the s of your fathers
20:25 I also gave them over to s that were
Mic 6:16 You have observed the s of Omri and

Stay (Stayed, Staying, Stays)

Ge 13: 6 they were not able to s together.
19:30 for he was afraid to s in Zoar.
22: 5 "S here with the donkey while I and
26: 3 S in this land for a while, and I
27:44 S with him for a while until your
29:19 some other man. S here with me."
30:27 found favour in your eyes, please s.
38: 1 s with a man of Adullam named Hirah.
42:19 let one of your brothers s here in
Ex 2:21 Moses agreed to s with the man, who
9:28 you don't have to s any longer."
16:29 Everyone is to s where he is on the
22:30 Let them s with their mothers for
24:12 to me on the mountain and s here,
33: 9 come down and s at the entrance,
Lev 8:35 You must s at the entrance to the
14: 8 s outside his tent for seven days.
Nu 22:19 Now s here tonight as the others did,

Nu 23: 3 "**S** here beside your offering while
23:15 "**S** here beside your offering while
31:19 must **s** outside the camp seven days.
35:25 He must **s** there until the death of
35:28 The accused must **s** in his city of
Dt 2:27 We will **s** on the main road; we will
3:19 may **s** in the towns I have given you,
5:31 you **s** here with me so that I may
23:10 to go outside the camp and **s** there.
24: 5 For one year he is to be free to **s**
24:11 **S** outside and let the man to whom
Jos 1:14 your livestock may **s** in the land
4: 3 at the place where you **s** tonight."
7: 7 **s** on the other side of the Jordan!
20: 6 He is to **s** in that city until he has
Jdg 5:16 Why did you **s** among the campfires to
13:15 "We would like you to **s** until we
17: 8 in search of some other place to **s**.
17: 9 "and I'm looking for a place to **s**.
19: 4 prevailed upon him to **s**; so he
19: 6 Please **s** tonight and enjoy yourself."
19: 9 **S** and enjoy yourself. Early tomorrow
19:10 But, unwilling to **s** another night,
Ru 1:16 I will go, and where you **s** I will **s**.
2: 8 **S** here with my servant girls.
2:21 '**S** with my workers until they finish
3:13 **S** here for the night, and in the
1Sa 1:23 "**S** here until you have weaned him;
5: 7 of Israel must not **s** here with us,
9:27 but you **s** here awhile, so that I
14: 9 **s** where we are and not go up to them.
19: 2 go into hiding and **s** there.
22: 3 mother come and **s** with you until I
22: 5 David, "Do not **s** in the stronghold.
22:23 **S** with me; don't be afraid; the man
2Sa 10: 5 The king said, "**S** at Jericho till
11:12 David said to him, "**S** here one more
15:19 Go back and **s** with King Absalom.
19:32 the king during his **s** in Mahanaim,
19:33 "Cross over with me and **s** with me in
1Ki 17: 9 to Zarephath of Sidon and **s** there.
2Ki 2: 2 Elijah said to Elisha, "**S** here;
2: 4 Elijah said to him, "**S** here, Elisha;
2: 6 Elijah said to him, "**S** here;
4: 8 who urged him to **s** for a meal.
4:10 **s** there whenever he comes to us."
7: 3 "Why **s** here until we die?
7: 4 And if we **s** here, we will die.
8: 1 "Go away with your family and **s** for
11: 8 **S** close to the king wherever he goes.
14:10 Glory in your victory, but **s** at home!
19:27 "But I know where you **s** and when
1Ch 19: 5 "**S** at Jericho till your beards have
2Ch 23: 7 **S** close to the king wherever he goes.
25:19 But **s** at home! Why ask for trouble
Ezr 6: 6 of that province, **s** away from there.
Ne 4:22 every man and his helper **s** inside
5: 2 eat and **s** alive, we must get grain."
10:39 the gatekeepers and the singers **s**.
11: 1 nine were to **s** in their own towns.
Job 24:13 not know its ways or **s** in its paths.
39: 9 Will he **s** by your manger at night?
Ps 38:11 my neighbours **s** far away.
55: 7 I would flee far away and **s** in the
92:14 age, they will **s** fresh and green,
119:148 My eyes **s** open through the watches
127: 2 In vain you rise early and **s** up late,
Pr 7:11 defiant, her feet never **s** at home;
14: 7 **S** away from a foolish man, for you
20:13 **s** awake and you will have food to
Isa 5:11 who **s** up late at night till they are
16: 4 Let the Moabite fugitives **s** with you;
21: 8 every night I **s** at my post.
37:28 "But I know where you **s** and when you
Jer 25: 5 and you can **s** in the land the LORD
40:10 I myself will **s** in Mizpah to
42:10 'If you **s** in this land, I will build
42:13 'We will not **s** in this land,'
43: 4 command to **s** in the land of Judah.
49:30 "Flee quickly away! **S** in deep caves,
Lam 4:15 say, "They can **s** here no longer.
Mic 7:18 You do not **s** angry for ever but
Mt 2:13 **S** there until I tell you, for Herod
10:11 and **s** at his house until you leave.
17:17 "how long shall I **s** with you?
26:38 **S** here and keep watch with me."
Mk 6:10 **s** there until you leave that town.
9:19 "how long shall I **s** with you?
14:34 "**S** here and keep watch."
Lk 9: 4 **s** there until you leave that town.
9:41 "how long shall I **s** with you and put
10: 7 **S** in that house, eating and drinking
19: 5 I must **s** at your house today."
24:29 they urged him strongly, "**S** with us,
24:29 So he went in to **s** with them.
24:49 but **s** in the city until you have
Jn 4:40 **s** with them, and he stayed two days.
12:46 believes in me should **s** in darkness.
Ac 8:29 "Go to that chariot and **s** near it.
10:48 Peter to **s** with them for a few days.
13:17 prosper during their **s** in Egypt,
16:15 she said, "come and **s** at my house.
21:16 home of Mnason, where we were to **s**.
27:31 **s** with the ship, you cannot be saved.
1Co 7: 8 for them to **s** unmarried, as I am.
16: 6 Perhaps I will **s** with you awhile, or
16: 8 I will **s** on at Ephesus until
1Ti 1: 3 **s** there in Ephesus so that you may

Stayed (Stay)

Ge 13: 6 support them while they **s** together,
20: 1 For a while he **s** in Gerar,
21:34 Abraham **s** in the land of the
22:19 And Abraham **s** in Beersheba.
26: 6 Isaac **s** in Gerar.
29:14 had **s** with him for a whole month,
35:27 where Abraham and Isaac had **s**.
37: 1 in the land where his father had **s**,
49:24 his strong arms **s** supple, because of
50:22 Joseph **s** in Egypt, along with all
Ex 20:18 They **s** at a distance
24:18 And he **s** on the mountain forty days
Nu 9:18 As long as the cloud **s** over the
9:21 Sometimes the cloud **s** only from
9:22 Whether the cloud **s** over the
11:35 travelled to Hazeroth and **s** there.
20: 1 Desert of Zin, and they **s** at Kadesh.
22: 8 So the Moabite princes **s** with him.
Dt 1: 6 have **s** long enough at this mountain.
1:46 you **s** in Kadesh many days—all the
3:29 we **s** in the valley near Beth Peor.
9: 9 I **s** on the mountain forty days and
10:10 Now I had **s** on the mountain forty
Jos 2: 1 prostitute named Rahab and **s** there.
2:22 they went into the hills and **s** there
Jdg 5:17 Gilead **s** beyond the Jordan. And Dan,
5:17 on the coast and **s** in his coves.
9:41 Abimelech **s** in Arumah, and Zebul
11:17 So Israel **s** at Kadesh.
15: 8 and **s** in a cave in the rock of Etam.
19: 7 him, so he **s** there that night.
20:47 Rimmon, where they **s** for four months.
Ru 2:23 Ruth **s** close to the servant girls of
1Sa 1:23 So the woman **s** at home and nursed
19:18 Samuel went to Naioth and **s** there.
22: 4 and they **s** with him as long as David
23:14 David **s** in the desert strongholds
23:25 rock and **s** in the Desert of Maon.
25:13 two hundred **s** with the supplies.
26: 3 Jeshimon, but David **s** in the desert.
30: 9 Besor Ravine, where some **s** behind,
30:24 The share of the man who **s** with the
2Sa 1: 1 Amalekites and **s** in Ziklag two days.
13:38 Geshur, he **s** there for three years.
15:29 God back to Jerusalem and **s** there.
20: 2 But the men of Judah **s** by their king
1Ki 2:38 **s** in Jerusalem for a long time.
11:16 Joab and all the Israelites **s** there
11:40 and **s** there until Solomon's death.
17: 5 east of the Jordan, and **s** there.
2Ki 8: 2 **s** in the land of the Philistines
10:21 of Baal came; not one **s** away.
15:20 and **s** in the land no longer.
19:36 He returned to Nineveh and **s** there.
1Ch 4:23 **s** there and worked for the king.
9:33 **s** in the rooms of the temple and
Ne 4:18 who sounded the trumpet **s** with me.
Est 7: 7 **s** behind to beg Queen Esther for his
Ecc 2: 9 In all this my wisdom **s** with me.
Isa 37:37 He returned to Nineveh and **s** there.
Jer 40: 6 **s** with him among the people who were
Mt 2:15 where he **s** until the death of Herod.
Mk 1:45 but **s** outside in lonely places.
Lk 1:21 why he **s** so long in the temple.
1:56 Mary **s** with Elizabeth for about
2:43 the boy Jesus **s** behind in Jerusalem,
24:53 they **s** continually at the temple,
Jn 2:12 There they **s** for a few days.
4:40 stay with them, and he **s** two days.
6:22 The next day the crowd that had **s** on
7: 9 Having said this, he **s** in Galilee.
10:40 in the early days. Here he **s**
11: 6 he **s** where he was two more days.
11:20 out to meet him, but Mary **s** at home.
11:54 where he **s** with his disciples.
Ac 9:28 Saul **s** with them and moved about
9:43 Peter **s** in Joppa for some time with
12:19 to Caesarea and **s** there a while.
14:28 they **s** there a long time with the
16:12 And we **s** there several days.
17:14 but Silas and Timothy **s** at Berea.
18: 3 he **s** and worked with them.
18:11 Paul **s** for a year and a half,
18:18 Paul **s** on in Corinth for some time.
19:22 while he **s** in the province of Asia
20: 3 where he **s** three months. Because the
20: 6 at Troas, where we **s** seven days.
21: 4 there, we **s** with them seven days.
21: 7 brothers and **s** with them for a day.
21: 8 we reached Caesarea and **s** at the
28:12 We put in at Syracuse and **s** there
28:30 For two whole years Paul **s** there in
Gal 1:18 Peter and **s** with him fifteen days.
2Ti 4:20 Erastus **s** in Corinth, and I left

Staying (Stay)

Ge 25:27 was a quiet man, **s** among the tents.
32: 4 I have been **s** with Laban and have
36: 7 the land where they were **s** could not
Nu 25: 1 While Israel was **s** in Shittim, the
Jdg 19:26 to the house where her master was **s**,
1Sa 13:16 them were **s** in Gibeah of Benjamin,
14: 2 Saul was **s** on the outskirts of
2Sa 11:11 and Israel and Judah are **s** in tents
16: 3 "He is **s** in Jerusalem, because he
17:17 Jonathan and Ahimaaz were **s** at
1Ki 17:19 to the upper room where he was **s**,
17:20 upon this widow I am **s** with,
2Ki 2:18 to Elisha, who was **s** in Jericho,
Ne 2:11 and after **s** there three days
Mt 24:48 'My master is **s** away a long time,'
Jn 1:38 "where are you **s**?"
1:39 So they went and saw where he was **s**,
7: 1 purposely **s** away from Judea because
Ac 1:13 to the room where they were **s**.
2: 5 Now there were **s** in Jerusalem
10: 6 He is **s** with Simon the tanner, whose
10:18 who was known as Peter was **s** there.
11:11 stopped at the house where I was **s**.
28:23 numbers to the place where he was **s**.

Stays (Stay)

Nu 14:14 that your cloud **s** over them.
Job 39:28 He dwells on a cliff and **s** there at
Pr 22: 5 who guards his soul **s** far from them.
Jer 14: 8 like a traveller who **s** only a night?
21: 9 Whoever **s** in this city will die by
38: 2 'Whoever **s** in this city will die by
1Co 7:40 she is happier if she **s** as she
Rev 16:15 Blessed is he who **s** awake and keeps

Steadfast (Steadfastly)

Ps 51:10 God, and renew a **s** spirit within me.
57: 7 My heart is **s**, O God, my heart is **s**;
108: 1 My heart is **s**, O God; I will sing
111: 8 They are **s** for ever and ever, done
112: 7 heart is **s**, trusting in the LORD.
119: 5 Oh, that my ways were **s** in obeying
Isa 26: 3 mind is **s**, because he trusts in you.
1Pe 5:10 you and make you strong, firm and **s**.

Steadfastly (Steadfast)

2Ch 27: 6 he walked **s** before the LORD his God.

Steady
Ge 49:24 his bow remained s, his strong arms
Ex 17:12 his hands remained s till sunset.
1Ch 13: 9 s the ark, because the oxen stumbled.
Isa 35: 3 s the knees that give way;

Steal (Stealing, Steals, Stole, Stolen)
Ge 31:30 But why did you s my gods?"
44: 8 So why would we s silver or gold
Ex 20:15 "You shall not s.
Lev 19:11 "'Do not s.
Dt 5:19 "You shall not s.
2Sa 19: 3 as men s in who are ashamed when
19:41 s the king away and bring him and
Ps 69: 4 forced to restore what I did not s.
104:22 The sun rises, and they s away;
Pr 30: 9 Or I may become poor and s,
Jer 7: 9 "'Will you s and murder, commit
23:30 "I am against the prophets who s
49: 9 not s only as much as they wanted?
Ob : 5 not s only as much as they wanted?
Mt 6:19 and where thieves break in and s.
6:20 where thieves do not break in and s.
19:18 do not commit adultery, do not s,
27:64 his disciples may come and s the
Mk 10:19 do not commit adultery, do not s, do
Lk 18:20 do not murder, do not s, do not give
Jn 10:10 The thief comes only to s and kill
Ro 2:21 preach against stealing, do you s?
13: 9 "Do not murder," "Do not s," "Do not
Eph 4:28 has been stealing must s no longer
Tit 2:10 not to s from them, but to show that

Stealing (Steal)
Hos 4: 2 lying and murder, s and adultery;
Ro 2:21 who preach against s, do you steal?
Eph 4:28 has been s must steal no longer

Steals (Steal)
Ex 22: 1 "If a man s an ox or a sheep and
Job 24:14 the night he s forth like a thief.
Pr 6:30 Men do not despise a thief if he s

Steeds
Jdg 5:22 galloping go his mighty s.
Jer 46: 4 Harness the horses, mount the s!
47: 3 sound of the hoofs of galloping s,

Steep
Isa 7:19 settle in the s ravines and in the
Mt 8:32 whole herd rushed down the s bank
Mk 5:13 rushed down the s bank into the lake
Lk 8:33 herd rushed down the s bank into

Steeped
Jn 9:34 "You were s in sin at birth;

Steered
Jas 3: 4 they are s by a very small rudder

Stench
Ge 34:30 making me a s to the Canaanites
Ex 5:21 You have made us a s to Pharaoh and
Isa 3:24 of fragrance there will be a s;
34: 3 their dead bodies will send up a s;
Joel 2:20 And its s will go up; its smell will
Am 4:10 I filled your nostrils with the s of

Step (Footsteps, Overstep, Stepped, Stepping, Steps)
Dt 21: 5 the sons of Levi, shall s forward,
1Sa 5: 5 temple at Ashdod s on the threshold.
20: 3 is only a s between me and death."
1Ki 10:20 steps, one at either end of each s.
2Ch 9:19 steps, one at either end of each s.
Job 18: 7 The vigour of his s is weakened;
18:11 on every side and dog his every s.
31: 4 see my ways and count my every s?
31:37 give him an account of my every s;
34:21 ways of men; he sees their every s.
Ps 89:51 mocked every s of your anointed one.
Lam 4:18 Men stalked us at every s, so we
Eze 26:16 princes of the coast will s down
Gal 5:25 let us keep in s with the Spirit.

Stephanas
1Co 1:16 I also baptised the household of **S**;
16:15 You know that the household of **S**
16:17 I was glad when **S**, Fortunatus and

Stephen
Deacon (Ac 6:5–6). Performed miracles; aroused opposition; arrested (Ac 6:8–15). Defence to Sanhedrin (Ac 7:1–53); killed by stoning (Ac 7:54–8:1; 22:20).

Ac 6: 5 They chose **S**, a man full of faith
6: 8 Now **S**, a man full of God's grace and
6: 9 These men began to argue with **S**,
6:11 "We have heard **S** speak words of
6:12 They seized **S** and brought him before
6:15 the Sanhedrin looked intently at **S**,
7:55 **S**, full of the Holy Spirit, looked
7:59 **S** prayed, "Lord Jesus, receive my
8: 2 Godly men buried **S** and mourned
11:19 **S** travelled as far as Phoenicia,
22:20 the blood of your martyr **S** was shed,

Stepped (Step)
Lev 9:22 the fellowship offering, he s down.
Nu 12: 5 When both of them s forward,
Jdg 8:21 So Gideon s forward and killed
19:27 and s out to continue on his way,
1Sa 17:23 s out from his lines and shouted his
2Sa 18:30 So he s aside and stood there.
20: 8 As he s forward, it dropped out of
1Ki 14:17 As soon as she s over the threshold
18:36 the prophet Elijah s forward and
Job 29: 8 the young men saw me and s aside and
Jer 26:17 the elders of the land s forward
Mt 9: 1 Jesus s into a boat, crossed over
26:50 Then the men s forward, seized
Lk 8:27 Jesus s ashore, he was met by a

Stepping (Step)
Pr 7:22 like a deer s into a noose
Zep 1: 9 all who avoid s on the threshold,

Steps (Step)
Ex 20:26 do not go up to my altar on s, lest
2Sa 6:13 the ark of the LORD had taken six s,
1Ki 10:19 The throne had six s, and its back
10:20 Twelve lions stood on the six s, one
2Ki 9:13 spread them under him on the bare s.
20: 9 ten s, or shall it go back ten s?"
20:10 to go forward ten s," said Hezekiah.
20:10 "Rather, have it go back ten s."
20:11 made the shadow go back the ten s
2Ch 9:11 make s for the temple of the LORD
9:18 The throne had six s, and a
9:19 Twelve lions stood on the six s, one
Ne 3:15 s going down from the City of David.
12:37 up the s of the City of David on
Job 14:16 Surely then you will count my s but
23:11 My feet have closely followed his s;
31: 7 if my s have turned from the path,
Ps 17: 5 My s have held to your paths;
37:23 in a man's way, he makes his s firm;
56: 6 watch my s, eager to take my life.
74: 3 Turn your s towards these
85:13 him and prepares the way for his s.
119:59 have turned my s to your statutes.
Pr 4:12 walk, your s will not be hampered;
5: 5 her s lead straight to the grave.
14:15 prudent man gives thought to his s.
16: 9 but the LORD determines his s.
20:24 A man's s are directed by the LORD.
Ecc 5: 1 Guard your s when you go to the
Isa 3:16 tripping along with mincing s, with
38: 8 go back the ten s it has gone down
38: 8 back the ten s it had gone down.
Jer 10:23 it is not for man to direct his s.
Eze 40: 6 He climbed its s and measured the
40:22 Seven s led up to it, with its
40:26 Seven s led up to it, with its
40:31 its jambs, and eight s led up to it.
40:34 side, and eight s led up to it.
40:37 side, and eight s led up to it.
Eze 40:40 near the s at the entrance to the
40:40 other side of the s were two tables.
43:17 The s of the altar face east."
Hab 3: 5 pestilence followed his s.
Ac 21:35 Paul reached the s, the violence of
21:40 on the s and motioned to the crowd.
1Pe 2:21 that you should follow in his s.

Sterile
Jdg 13: 2 who was s and remained childless.
13: 3 "You are s and childless, but you

Stern (Stern-faced, Sternly, Sternness)
Pr 15:10 **S** discipline awaits him who leaves
Mk 4:38 Jesus was in the s, sleeping on a
Ac 27:29 dropped four anchors from the s
27:41 and the s was broken to pieces by

Stern-faced (Face, Stern)
Da 8:23 a s king, a master of intrigue, will

Sternly (Stern)
Mt 9:30 Jesus warned them s, "See that
Mk 1:25 "Be quiet!" said Jesus s. "Come out
Lk 4:35 "Be quiet!" Jesus said s. "Come out

Sternness (Stern)
Ro 11:22 therefore the kindness and s of God:
11:22 s to those who fell, but kindness

Stew
Ge 25:29 Once when Jacob was cooking some s,
25:30 let me have some of that red s!
25:34 Esau some bread and some lentil s.
2Ki 4:38 pot and cook some s for these men."
4:39 he cut them up into the pot of s,
4:40 The s was poured out for the men,
Hag 2:12 that fold touches some bread or s,

Steward (Stewards)
Ge 43:16 he said to the s of his house, "Take
43:19 they went up to Joseph's s and spoke
43:24 The s took the men into Joseph's
44: 1 instructions to the s of his house:
44: 4 the city when Joseph said to his s,
44:12 the s proceeded to search, beginning
2Sa 16: 1 was Ziba, the s of Mephibosheth
19:17 along with Ziba, the s of Saul's
Isa 22:15 "Go, say to this s, to Shebna, who

Stewards (Steward)
Est 1: 8 s to serve each man what he wished.

Stick[1] (Sticks[1])
2Ki 6: 6 Elisha cut a s and threw it there,
Isa 28:27 out with a rod, and cummin with a s.
Lam 4: 8 it has become as dry as a s.
Eze 21:10 The sword despises every such s.
37:16 "Son of man, take a s of wood and
37:16 Then take another s of wood, and
37:16 'Ephraim's s, belonging to Joseph
37:17 Join them together into one s so
37:19 I am going to take the s of Joseph
37:19 and join it to Judah's s, making
37:19 making them a single s of wood, and
Hos 4:12 and are answered by a s of wood.
Am 4:11 You were like a burning s snatched
Zec 3: 2 a burning s snatched from the fire?"
Mt 27:48 put it on a s, and offered it to
Mk 15:36 put it on a s, and offered it to

Stick[2] (Sticking, Sticks[2], Stuck)
Job 33:21 his bones, once hidden, now s out.
38:38 and the clods of earth s together?
Isa 57: 4 At whom do you sneer and s out your
Eze 3:26 I will make your tongue s to the
29: 4 of your streams s to your scales.

Sticking (Stick[2])
Eze 29: 4 with all the fish s to your scales.

Sticks[1] (Stick[1])
1Sa 17:43 I a dog, that you come at me with s?"
1Ki 17:10 gate, a widow was there gathering s.
17:12 I am gathering a few s to take home
Eze 37:20 Hold before their eyes the s you

Sticks[2] (Stick[2])
Ps 22:15 and my tongue s to the roof of my
Pr 18:24 friend who s closer than a brother.
Lam 4: 4 of thirst the infant's tongue s to
Lk 10:11 of your town that s to our feet

Stiff-necked (Neck)
Ex 32: 9 to Moses, "and they are a s people.
33: 3 because you are a s people and I
33: 5 the Israelites, 'You are a s people.
34: 9 Although this is a s people, forgive
Dt 9: 6 to possess, for you are a s people.
9:13 and they are a s people indeed!
10:16 and do not be s any longer.
31:27 know how rebellious and s you are.
2Ki 17:14 and were as s as their fathers,
2Ch 30: 8 Do not be s, as your fathers were;
36:13 He became s and hardened his heart
Ne 9:16 became arrogant and s, and did not
9:17 They became s and in their rebellion
9:29 you, became s and refused to listen.
Pr 29: 1 A man who remains s after many
Jer 7:26 They were s and did more evil than
17:23 they were s and would not listen or
19:15 s and would not listen to my words.
Ac 7:51 "You s people, with uncircumcised

Stifling
Am 1:11 s all compassion, because his anger

Still (Stilled)
Ex 14:14 for you; you need only to be s."
15:16 arm they will be as s as a stone
Jos 10:12 "O sun, stand s over Gibeon, O moon,
10:13 the sun stood s, and the moon
1Sa 12:16 "Now then, stand s and see this
Ne 8:11 "Be s, for this is a sacred day.
Job 39:24 stand s when the trumpet sounds.
Ps 17:14 You s the hunger of those you
37: 7 Be s before the LORD and wait
39: 2 I was silent and s, not even saying
46:10 "Be s, and know that I am God;
76: 6 Jacob, both horse and chariot lie s.
83: 1 be not quiet, O God, be not s.
89: 9 when its waves mount up, you s them.
Jer 47: 6 to your scabbard; cease and be s.'
Eze 1:21 when the creatures stood s,
1:21 they also stood s; and when the
1:24 stood s, they lowered their wings.
10:17 the cherubim stood s, they also
10:17 they also stood s; and when the
Hab 3:11 Sun and moon stood s in the heavens
Zec 2:13 Be s before the LORD, all mankind,
Mk 4:39 "Quiet! Be s!" Then the wind died
Lk 7:14 and those carrying it stood s.
24:17 They stood s, their faces downcast.

Stillborn (Bear[1])
Nu 12:12 Do not let her be like a s infant
Job 3:16 hidden in the ground like a s child,
Ps 58: 8 a s child, may they not see the sun.
Ecc 6: 3 a s child is better off than he.

Stilled (Still)
Ps 65: 7 who s the roaring of the seas, the
107:29 He s the storm to a whisper;
131: 2 I have s and quietened my soul;
Isa 16: 9 and over your harvests have been s.
24: 8 The gaiety of the tambourines is s,
25: 5 so the song of the ruthless is s.
1Co 13: 8 there are tongues, they will be s;

Stimulate
2Pe 3: 1 to s you to wholesome thinking.

Sting (Stinging, Stings)
1Co 15:55 Where, O death, is your s?"
15:56 The s of death is sin, and the power
Rev 9: 5 like that of the s of a scorpion

Stinging (Sting)
Eze 5:15 and in wrath and with s rebuke.

Stings (Sting)
Rev 9:10 They had tails and s like scorpions,

Stingy
Pr 23: 6 Do not eat the food of a s man, do
28:22 A s man is eager to get rich and is

Stink
Ex 7:18 will die, and the river will s;
16:24 it did not s or get maggots in it.
Isa 19: 6 The canals will s; the streams of

Stipulations
Dt 4:45 These are the s, decrees and laws
6:17 the s and decrees he has given you.
6:20 "What is the meaning of the s,
Jer 44:23 his law or his decrees or his s,

Stir (Astir, Stirred, Stirring, Stirs)
Jdg 13:25 the Spirit of the LORD began to s
Ne 4: 8 and s up trouble against it.
Ps 78:38 and did not s up his full wrath.
140: 2 their hearts and s up war every day.
Pr 29: 8 Mockers s up a city, but wise men
Isa 13:17 See, I will s up against them the
19: 2 "I will s up Egyptian against
42:13 like a warrior he will s up his zeal;
Jer 50: 9 For I will s up and bring against
51: 1 "See, I will s up the spirit of a
Eze 23:22 I will s up your lovers against you,
24: 8 To s up wrath and take revenge I put
Da 11: 2 he will s up everyone against the
11:25 "With a large army he will s up his
Hos 7: 4 whose fire the baker need not s
Am 6:14 "I will s up a nation against you,
Php 1:17 supposing that they can s up trouble

Stirred (Stir)
Ru 1:19 the whole town was s because of them,
1Ki 14:22 they s up his jealous anger more
1Ch 5:26 the God of Israel s up the spirit of
Ps 45: 1 My heart is s by a noble theme as I
107:25 For he spoke and s up a tempest that
Ecc 12: 5 along and desire no longer is s.
Isa 41: 2 "Who has s up one from the east,
41:25 "I have s up one from the north, and
Jer 6:22 s up from the ends of the earth.
50:41 s up from the ends of the earth.
51:11 The LORD has s up the kings of the
Eze 32:13 no longer to be s by the foot of man
Am 8: 8 it will be s up and then sink like
Hag 1:14 the LORD s up the spirit of
Mt 21:10 the whole city was s and asked, "Who
Mk 15:11 the chief priests s up the crowd to
Jn 5: 7 into the pool when the water is s.
Ac 6:12 they s up the people and the elders
13:50 They s up persecution against Paul
14: 2 the Jews who refused to believe s up
21:27 s up the whole crowd and seized him,
2Co 9: 2 has s most of them to action.

Stirring (Stir)
Jdg 9:31 and are s up the city against you.
Ne 13:18 Now you are s up more wrath against
Pr 30:33 so s up anger produces strife."
Ac 17:13 agitating the crowds and s them up.
24: 5 s up riots among the Jews all over
24:12 or s up a crowd in the synagogues or

Stirs (Stir)
Dt 32:11 like an eagle that s up its nest and
Job 41:31 s up the sea like a pot of ointment.
Ps 147:18 he s up his breezes, and the waters
Pr 6:14 heart—he always s up dissension.
6:19 who s up dissension among brothers.
10:12 Hatred s up dissension, but love
15: 1 wrath, but a harsh word s up anger.
15:18 A hot-tempered man s up dissension,
16:28 A perverse man s up dissension, and
28:25 A greedy man s up dissension, but he
29:22 An angry man s up dissension, and a
Jer 31:35 who s up the sea so that its waves
Lk 23: 5 "He s up the people all over Judea

Stock (Stocks)
Job 5:24 you will take s of your property and
Jer 2:21 choice vine of sound and reliable s.

Stocks (Stock)
Jer 20: 2 put in the s at the Upper Gate of
20: 3 Pashhur released him from the s,
29:26 a prophet into the s and neck-irons.
Ac 16:24 and fastened their feet in the s.

Stoic
Ac 17:18 Epicurean and S philosophers began

Stole (Steal)
Ge 31:19 Rachel s her father's household gods.
2Sa 15: 6 s the hearts of the men of Israel.
19: 3 The men s into the city that day as
2Ki 11: 2 took Joash son of Ahaziah and s him
2Ch 22:11 took Joash son of Ahaziah and s him
Mt 28:13 s him away while we were asleep.'

Stolen (Steal)
Ge 30:33 will be considered s."
31:32 not know that Rachel had s the gods.
31:39 for whatever was s by day or night.
Ex 22: 4 "If the s animal is found alive in
22: 7 are s from the neighbour's house,
22:12 if the animal was s from the
Lev 6: 2 left in his care or s, or if he
6: 4 he must return what he has s or
Jos 7:11 they have s, they have lied,
Job 24: 2 they pasture flocks they have s.
Ps 62:10 extortion or take pride in s goods;
Pr 9:17 "S water is sweet; food eaten in
SS 4: 9 You have s my heart, my sister, my
4: 9 you have s my heart with one glance
Eze 33:15 returns what he has s, follows the
Hab 2: 6 'Woe to him who piles up s goods and

Stomach (Stomachs)
2Sa 2:23 butt of his spear into Asahel's s,
3:27 stabbed him in the s, and he died.
4: 6 and they stabbed him in the s.
Job 20:14 yet his food will turn sour in his s;
20:15 God will make his s vomit them up.
Pr 13:25 but the s of the wicked goes hungry.
18:20 of his mouth a man's s is filled;
Jer 30: 6 on his s like a woman in labour,
51:34 filled his s with our delicacies,
Eze 3: 3 giving you and fill your s with it.
Mic 6:14 your s will still be empty.
Mt 15:17 into the s and then out of the body?
Mk 7:19 go into his heart but into his s,
Lk 15:16 He longed to fill his s with the
1Co 6:13 "Food for the s and the s for food"—
Php 3:19 their god is their s, and their
1Ti 5:23 your s and your frequent illnesses.
Rev 10: 9 It will turn your s sour, but in
10:10 I had eaten it, my s turned sour.

Stomachs (Stomach)
Eze 7:19 hunger or fill their s with it,
Am 4: 6 "I gave you empty s in every city

Stone (Capstone, Cornerstone, Cornerstones, Millstone, Millstones, Slingstones, Stone's, Stonecutters, Stoned, Stonemasons, Stones, Stoning, Stumbling-stone, Tombstone)
Ge 11: 3 They used brick instead of s, and
28:18 the s he had placed under his head
28:22 this s that I have set up as a
29: 2 The s over the mouth of the well was
29: 3 the shepherds would roll the s away

Ge 29: 3 Then they would return the s to its
29: 8 the s has been rolled away from the
29:10 he went over and rolled the s away
31:45 Jacob took a s and set it up as a
35:14 Jacob set up a s pillar at the place
Ex 7:19 in the wooden buckets and s jars."
8:26 in their eyes, will they not s us?
15: 5 they sank to the depths like a s.
15:16 they will be as still as a s—
17: 4 They are almost ready to s me."
17:12 they took a s and put it under him
21:18 one hits the other with a s or with
24: 4 set up twelve s pillars representing
24:12 I will give you the tablets of s,
28:10 six names on one s and the
31:18 of s inscribed by the finger of God.
34: 1 "Chisel out two s tablets like the
34: 4 Moses chiselled out two s tablets
34: 4 the two s tablets in his hands.
Lev 20: 2 of the community are to s him.
20:27 You are to s them; their blood will
24:14 and the entire assembly is to s him.
24:16 The entire assembly must s him.
26: 1 image or a sacred s for yourselves,
26: 1 do not place a carved s in your
Nu 15:35 must s him outside the camp."
35:17 Or if anyone has a s in his hand
35:23 or, without seeing him, drops a s on
Dt 4:13 then wrote them on two s tablets.
4:28 worship man-made gods of wood and s,
5:22 two s tablets and gave them to me.
9: 9 to receive the tablets of s,
9:10 The LORD gave me two s tablets
9:11 the LORD gave me the two s tablets,
10: 1 "Chisel out two s tablets like the
10: 3 two s tablets like the first ones,
13:10 S him to death, because he tried to
16:22 do not erect a sacred s, for these
17: 5 gate and s that person to death.
19:14 your neighbour's boundary s set up
21:21 all the men of his town shall s him
22:21 of her town shall s her to death.
22:24 of that town and s them to death—
27:17 moves his neighbour's boundary s.
28:36 other gods, gods of wood and s.
28:64 other gods—gods of wood and s,
29:17 of wood and s, of silver and gold.
Jos 4: 5 Each of you is to take up a s on his
7: 5 city gate as far as the s quarries
15: 6 to the S of Bohan son of Reuben.
18:17 to the S of Bohan son of Reuben.
24:26 Then he took a large s and set it up
24:27 "This s will be a witness against us.
Jdg 9: 5 one s murdered his seventy brothers,
9:18 his seventy sons on a single s,
20:16 sling a s at a hair and not miss.
1Sa 7:12 Samuel took a s and set it up
14:33 "Roll a large s over here at once."
17:49 into his bag and taking out a s,
17:49 The s sank into his forehead, and he
17:50 the Philistine with a sling and a s;
20:19 began, and wait by the s Ezel.
20:41 up from the south side ⌊of the s⌋
25:37 failed him and he became like a s.
1Ki 1: 9 at the S of Zoheleth near En Rogel.
5:17 large blocks of quality s to provide
5:17 of dressed s for the temple.
5:18 s for the building of the temple.
6:18 was cedar; no s was to be seen.
6:36 of three courses of dressed s
7: 9 were made of blocks of high-grade s
7:12 wall of three courses of dressed s
8: 9 the two s tablets that Moses had
21:10 take him out and s him to death."
2Ki 3: 2 s of Baal that his father had made.
3:25 and each man threw a s on every good
10:26 They brought the sacred s out of the
10:27 They demolished the sacred s of Baal
12:12 They purchased timber and dressed s
16:17 supported it and set it on a s base.
19:18 were not gods but only wood and s,
19:25 fortified cities into piles of s.
22: 6 and dressed s to repair the temple.
1Ch 22: 2 s for building the house of God.
22:14 great to be weighed, and wood and s.
29: 2 and all kinds of fine s and marble—
2Ch 2:14 bronze and iron, s and wood, and
34:11 and builders to purchase dressed s,
Ne 9:11 depths, like a s into mighty waters.
Job 6:12 Do I have the strength of s?
38:30 the waters become hard as s, when
Ps 91:12 not strike your foot against a s.
118:22 The s the builders rejected has
Pr 22:28 Do not move an ancient boundary s
23:10 Do not move an ancient boundary s or
24:31 weeds, and the s wall was in ruins.
26: 8 Like tying a s in a sling is the
26:27 rolls a s, it will roll back on him.
27: 3 S is heavy and sand a burden, but
Isa 8:14 be a s that causes men to stumble
9:10 but we will rebuild with dressed s;
28:16 "See, I lay a s in Zion, a tested s,
37:19 were not gods but only wood and s,
37:26 fortified cities into piles of s.
Jer 2:27 and to s, 'You gave me birth.'
3: 9 committed adultery with s and wood.
5: 3 harder than s and refused to repent.
51:26 nor any s for a foundation, for you
51:63 tie a s to it and throw it into the
Lam 3: 9 He has barred my way with blocks of s
Eze 3: 9 the hardest s, harder than flint.
11:19 remove from them their heart of s
16:40 who will s you and hack you to
20:32 of the world, who serve wood and s.
23:47 The mob will s them and cut them
28:13 every precious s adorned you: ruby,
36:26 remove from you your heart of s
40:42 dressed s for the burnt offerings,
46:23 of the four courts was a ledge of s,
Da 5: 4 silver, of bronze, iron, wood and s.
5:23 of bronze, iron, wood and s, which
6:17 A s was brought and placed over the
Am 5:11 though you have built s mansions,
Hab 2:19 Or to lifeless s, 'Wake up!'
Hag 2:15 before one s was laid on another
Zec 3: 9 See, the s I have set in front of
3: 9 There are seven eyes on that one s,
Mt 4: 6 not strike your foot against a s.'"
7: 9 asks for bread, will give him a s?
21:42 'The s the builders rejected has
21:44 He who falls on this s will be
23:37 prophets and s those sent to you,
24: 2 not one s here will be left on
27:60 He rolled a big s in front of the
27:66 seal on the s and posting the guard.
28: 2 rolled back the s and sat on it.
Mk 12:10 'The s the builders rejected has
13: 2 "Not one s here will be left on
15:46 s against the entrance of the tomb.
16: 3 "Who will roll the s away from the
16: 4 they saw that the s, which was very
Lk 4: 3 God, tell this s to become bread."
4:11 not strike your foot against a s.'"
13:34 prophets and s those sent to you,
19:44 They will not leave one s on another,
20: 6 'From men', all the people will s us,
20:17 'The s the builders rejected has
20:18 Everyone who falls on that s will be
21: 6 the time will come when not one s
24: 2 They found the s rolled away from
Jn 2: 6 Nearby stood six s water jars, the
8: 5 Moses commanded us to s such women.
8: 7 be the first to throw a s at her."
8:59 they picked up stones to s him,
10:31 the Jews picked up stones to s him,
10:32 For which of these do you s me?"
11: 8 while ago the Jews tried to s you,
11:38 with a s laid across the entrance.
11:39 "Take away the s," he said.
11:41 they took away the s. Then Jesus
19:13 at a place known as the S Pavement
20: 1 s had been removed from the entrance.
Ac 4:11 "'the s you builders rejected,
5:26 feared that the people would s them.
7:58 out of the city and began to s him.
14: 5 to ill-treat them and s them.
17:29 being is like gold or silver or s
Ro 9:33 "See, I lay in Zion a s that causes
2Co 3: 3 not on tablets of s but on tablets
3: 7 which was engraved in letters on s,
Heb 9: 4 and the s tablets of the covenant.
1Pe 2: 4 you come to him, the living S—
1Pe 2: 6 "See, I lay a s in Zion, a chosen
2: 7 Now to you who believe, this s is
2: 7 "The s the builders rejected has
2: 8 "A s that causes men to stumble
Rev 2:17 I will also give him a white s with
9:20 silver, bronze, s and wood—idols
21:19 with every kind of precious s.

Stone's (Stone)

Lk 22:41 He withdrew about a s throw beyond

Stonecutters (Stone)

1Ki 5:15 and eighty thousand s in the hills,
2Ki 12:12 the masons and s. They purchased
1Ch 22: 2 and from among them he appointed s
22:15 You have many workmen: s, masons and
2Ch 2: 2 eighty thousand as s in the hills
2:18 and 80,000 to be s in the hills,

Stoned (Stone)

Ex 19:13 He shall surely be s or shot with
21:28 the bull must be s to death, and its
21:29 the bull must be s and the owner
21:32 the slave, and the bull must be s.
Lev 24:23 outside the camp and s him.
Nu 15:36 outside the camp and s him to death,
Jos 7:25 Then all Israel s him, and after
7:25 had s the rest, they burned them.
1Ki 12:18 but all Israel s him to death.
21:13 outside the city and s him to death.
21:14 "Naboth has been s and is dead.
21:15 that Naboth had been s to death,
2Ch 10:18 but the Israelites s him to death.
24:21 and by order of the king they s him
Mt 21:35 one, killed another, and s a third.
Ac 14:19 They s Paul and dragged him outside
2Co 11:25 once I was s, three times I was
Heb 11:37 They were s; they were sawn in two;
12:20 touches the mountain, it must be s."

Stonemasons (Stone)

2Sa 5:11 cedar logs and carpenters and s,
1Ch 14: 1 with cedar logs, s and carpenters

Stones (Stone)

Ge 28:11 Taking one of the s there, he put it
31:46 to his relatives, "Gather some s."
31:46 So they took s and piled them in a
Ex 20:25 If you make an altar of s for me, do
20:25 do not build it with dressed s, for
23:24 and break their sacred s to pieces.
25: 7 onyx s and other gems to be mounted
28: 9 "Take two onyx s and engrave on them
28:11 the sons of Israel on the two s
28:11 Then mount the s in gold filigree
28:12 memorial s for the sons of Israel.
28:17 mount four rows of precious s on it.
28:21 There are to be twelve s, one for
31: 5 to cut and set s, to work in wood,
34:13 smash their sacred s and cut down
35: 9 onyx s and other gems to be mounted
35:27 The leaders brought onyx s and other
35:33 to cut and set s, to work in wood
39: 6 They mounted the onyx s in gold
39: 7 memorial s for the sons of Israel,
39:10 they mounted four rows of precious s
39:14 There were twelve s, one for each of
Lev 14:40 that the contaminated s be torn out
14:42 they are to take other s to replace
14:43 after the s have been torn out
14:45 must be torn down—its s, timbers
Dt 7: 5 smash their sacred s, cut down their
12: 3 smash their sacred s and burn their
27: 2 large s and coat them with plaster.
27: 4 set up these s on Mount Ebal, as I
27: 5 to the LORD your God, an altar of s.
27: 6 LORD your God with s from the field
27: 8 law on these s you have set up."
Jos 4: 3 tell them to take up twelve s from
4: 6 ask you, 'What do these s mean?'
4: 7 These s are to be a memorial to the
4: 8 They took twelve s from the middle
4: 9 Joshua set up the twelve s that had
4:20 Joshua set up at Gilgal the twelve s

Jos 4:21 fathers, 'What do these s mean?'
8:31 Law of Moses—an altar of uncut s,
8:32 Joshua copied on s the law of Moses,
1Sa 17:40 chose five smooth s from the stream,
2Sa 12:30 and it was set with precious s
16: 6 and all the king's officials with s,
16:13 throwing s at him and showering him
1Ki 7:10 laid with large s of good quality,
7:11 Above were high-grade s, cut to size,
10: 2 quantities of gold and precious s
10:10 quantities of spices, and precious s.
10:11 of almug-wood and precious s.
10:27 silver as common in Jerusalem as s,
14:23 sacred s and Asherah poles on every
15:22 they carried away from Ramah the s
18:31 Elijah took twelve s, one for each
18:32 With the s he built an altar in the
18:38 the wood, the s and the soil, and
2Ki 3:19 and ruin every good field with s."
3:25 was left with its s in place,
17:10 set up sacred s and Asherah poles
18: 4 smashed the sacred s and cut down
23:14 Josiah smashed the sacred s and cut
1Ch 12: 2 sling s right-handed or left-handed;
20: 2 and it was set with precious s—
29: 2 turquoise, s of various colours, and
29: 8 Any who had precious s gave them to
2Ch 1:15 gold as common in Jerusalem as s,
3: 6 He adorned the temple with precious s
9: 1 quantities of gold and precious s
9: 9 quantities of spices, and precious s.
9:10 brought algum-wood and precious s.
9:27 silver as common in Jerusalem as s,
14: 3 smashed the sacred s and cut down
16: 6 s and timber Baasha had been using.
26:15 to shoot arrows and hurl large s.
31: 1 smashed the sacred s and cut down
32:27 and gold and for his precious s,
Ezr 5: 8 people are building it with large s
6: 4 with three courses of large s and
Ne 4: 2 Can they bring the s back to life
4: 3 would break down their wall of s!"
Est 1: 6 mother-of-pearl and other costly s.
Job 5:23 a covenant with the s of the field,
8:17 and looks for a place among the s.
14:19 water wears away s and torrents wash
24: 2 Men move boundary s; they pasture
Ps 102:14 For her s are dear to your servants;
Ecc 3: 5 a time to scatter s and a time to
10: 9 Whoever quarries s may be injured by
Isa 5: 2 He dug it up and cleared it of s and
14:19 who descend to the s of the pit.
27: 9 When he makes all the altar s to be
27: 9 be like chalk s crushed to pieces,
54:11 I will build you with s of turquoise,
54:12 and all your walls of precious s.
57: 6 The idols among the smooth s of the
60:17 you bronze, and iron in place of s.
62:10 build up the highway! Remove the s.
Jer 43: 9 take some large s with you and bury
43:10 over these s I have buried here;
Lam 3:53 my life in a pit and threw s at me;
Eze 26:12 s, timber and rubble into the sea.
27:22 of spices and precious s, and gold.
28:14 you walked among the fiery s.
28:16 cherub, from among the fiery s.
Da 11:38 with precious s and costly gifts.
Hos 3: 4 or sacred s, without ephod or idol.
5:10 are like those who move boundary s.
10: 1 prospered, he adorned his sacred s.
10: 2 altars and destroy their sacred s.
12:11 like piles of s on a ploughed field.
Mic 1: 6 I will pour her s into the valley
5:13 and your sacred s from among you;
Hab 2:11 The s of the wall will cry out, and
Zec 5: 4 it, both its timbers and its s.
Mt 3: 9 I tell you that out of these s God
4: 3 God, tell these s to become bread."
Mk 5: 5 cry out and cut himself with s.
13: 1 What massive s! What magnificent
Lk 3: 8 For I tell you that out of these s
19:40 keep quiet, the s will cry out."
21: 5 adorned with beautiful s and with
Jn 8:59 At this, they picked up s to stone
10:31 Again the Jews picked up s to stone
1Co 3:12 costly s, wood, hay or straw,
1Pe 2: 5 you also, like living s, are being
Rev 17: 4 with gold, precious s and pearls.
18:12 cargoes of gold, silver, precious s
18:16 with gold, precious s and pearls!

Stoning (Stone)

Nu 14:10 the whole assembly talked about s
1Sa 30: 6 the men were talking of s him;
Jn 10:33 "We are not s you for any of these,"
Ac 7:59 While they were s him, Stephen

Stood (Stand)

Ge 18: 8 ate, he s near them under a tree.
19:27 where he had s before the LORD.
28:13 There above it s the LORD, and he
37: 7 my sheaf rose and s upright,
41: 3 and s beside those on the riverbank.
Ex 2: 4 His sister s at a distance to see
9:10 a furnace and s before Pharaoh.
14:19 from in front and s behind them,
15: 8 The surging waters s firm like a
18:13 and they s round him from morning
19:17 they s at the foot of the mountain.
32:26 he s at the entrance to the camp and
33: 8 all the people rose and s at the
33:10 they all s and worshipped, each at
34: 5 in the cloud and s there with him
Lev 9: 5 came near and s before the LORD.
Nu 12: 5 he s at the entrance to the Tent and
12:10 there s Miriam—leprous, like snow.
16:18 and s with Moses and Aaron at the
16:48 He s between the living and the dead,
22:22 LORD s in the road to oppose him.
22:24 the angel of the LORD s in a narrow
22:26 s in a narrow place where there was
27: 2 Tent of Meeting and s before Moses,
Dt 4:10 Remember the day you s before the
4:11 You came near and s at the foot of
5: 5 (At that time I s between the LORD
31:15 s over the entrance to the Tent.
Jos 3:17 s firm on dry ground in the middle
4: 3 from right where the priests s
4: 9 the ark of the covenant had s.
8:33 Half of the people s in front of
10:13 the sun s still, and the moon
20: 6 he has s trial before the assembly
Jdg 16:25 When they s him among the pillars,
16:29 pillars on which the temple s.
18:16 s at the entrance to the gate.
18:17 men s at the entrance to the gate.
1Sa 1: 9 and drinking in Shiloh, Hannah s up.
1:26 my lord, I am the woman who s here
3:10 The LORD came and s there, calling
10:23 and as he s among the people he was
12:18 s in awe of the LORD and of Samuel.
14: 5 One cliff s to the north towards
17: 8 Goliath s and shouted to the ranks
17:51 David ran and s over him. He took
26:13 s on top of the hill some distance
2Sa 1:10 "So I s over him and killed him,
2:15 they s up and were counted off—
12:17 The elders of his household s beside
13:31 The king s up, tore his clothes and
13:31 s by with their clothes torn.
18: 4 So the king s beside the gate while
18:30 So he stepped aside and s there.
20:11 One of Joab's men s beside Amasa and
20:15 s against the outer fortifications.
23:10 he s his ground and struck down the
1Ki 1:28 king's presence and s before him.
2: 7 They s by me when I fled from your
2:19 the king s up to meet her, bowed
3:15 s before the ark of the Lord's
3:16 came to the king and s before him.
7:25 The Sea s on twelve bulls, three
8:22 Solomon s before the altar of the
8:55 He s and blessed the whole assembly
10:20 Twelve lions s on the six steps, one
19:13 out and s at the mouth of the cave.
20:38 the prophet went and s by the road
22:21 came forward, s before the LORD and
2Ki 2: 7 prophets went and s at a distance,
2:13 and s on the bank of the Jordan.
4:12 he called her, and she s before him.
4:15 her, and she s in the doorway.
2Ki 5:15 He s before him and said, "Now I
5:25 he went in and s before his master
8: 9 He went in and s before him, and
10: 9 He s before all the people and said
13:21 came to life and s up on his feet.
16:14 The bronze altar that s before the
18:28 the commander s and called out in
23: 3 The king s by the pillar and renewed
2Ch 3:13 They s on their feet, facing the
4: 4 The Sea s on twelve bulls, three
5:12 s on the east side of the altar,
6:12 Solomon s before the altar of the
6:13 He s on the platform and then knelt
9:19 Twelve lions s on the six steps, one
13: 4 Abijah s on Mount Zemaraim, in the
18:20 came forward, s before the LORD and
20: 5 Jehoshaphat s up in the assembly of
20:13 ones, s there before the LORD.
20:14 of Asaph, as he s in the assembly.
20:19 Korahites s up and praised the LORD,
20:20 As they set out, Jehoshaphat s and
24:20 He s before the people and said,
29:26 the Levites s ready with David's
30:27 The priests and the Levites s to
34:31 The king s by his pillar and renewed
35:10 the priests s in their places with
Ezr 10:10 Ezra the priest s up and said to
Ne 4:14 After I looked things over, I s up
8: 4 Ezra the scribe s on a high wooden
8: 4 Beside him on his right s Mattithiah,
8: 5 he opened it, the people all s up.
9: 2 They s in their places and confessed
9: 3 They s where they were and read from
12: 9 s opposite them in the services.
12:24 and their associates, who s opposite
Est 5: 1 s in the inner court of the palace,
8: 4 and she arose and s before him.
Job 4:15 and the hair on my body s on end.
4:16 A form s before my eyes, and I heard
Ps 33: 9 he commanded, and it s firm.
104: 6 the waters s above the mountains.
106:23 s in the breach before him to keep
106:30 Phinehas s up and intervened, and
Isa 36:13 the commander s and called out in
Jer 18:20 Remember that I s before you and
19:14 and s in the court of the LORD's
23:18 which of them has s in the council
23:22 if they had s in my council, they
Eze 1:21 when the creatures s still,
1:21 they also s still; and when the
1:24 s still, they lowered their wings.
1:25 heads as they s with lowered wings.
8: 3 idol that provokes to jealousy s.
8:11 In front of them s seventy elders of
9: 2 in and s beside the bronze altar.
10: 6 man went in and s beside a wheel.
10:17 the cherubim s still, they also s
37:10 and s up on their feet—a vast army.
Da 2: 2 they came in and s before the king,
2:31 and there before you s a large
3: 3 had set up, and they s before it.
4:10 s a tree in the middle of the land.
7: 4 so that it s on two feet like a man,
7:10 times ten thousand s before him.
8:15 me s one who looked like a man.
10:11 said this to me, I s up trembling.
12: 5 and there before me s two others,
Ob :11 On the day you s aloof while
Hab 3: 6 He s, and shook the earth; he looked,
3:11 Sun and moon s still in the heavens
Zec 3: 3 clothes as he s before the angel.
3: 5 while the angel of the LORD s by.
Mal 2: 5 revered me and s in awe of my name.
Mt 12:46 s outside, wanting to speak to him.
13: 2 while all the people s on the shore.
26:62 the high priest s up and said to
27:11 Meanwhile Jesus s before the
Mk 5:42 Immediately the girl s up and walked
9:27 lifted him to his feet, and he s up.
14:57 some s up and gave this false
14:60 the high priest s up before them and
15:39 the centurion, who s there in front
Lk 4:16 And he s up to read.
5:25 Immediately he s up in front of them,
6: 8 So he got up and s there.
6:17 He went down with them and s on a

Lk 7:14 and those carrying it s still.
7:38 she s behind him at his feet weeping,
8:55 returned, and at once she s up.
10:25 in the law s up to test Jesus.
17:12 They s at a distance
18:11 The Pharisee s up and prayed about
18:13 "But the tax collector s at a
19: 8 Zacchaeus s up and said to the Lord,
22:28 You are those who have s by me in my
23:35 The people s watching, and the
23:49 s at a distance, watching these
24: 4 like lightning s beside them.
24:17 They s still, their faces downcast.
24:36 Jesus himself s among them and said
Jn 2: 6 Nearby s six stone water jars, the
7:37 Jesus s and said in a loud voice,
11:56 and as they s in the temple area
18:18 and the servants and officials s
18:25 Simon Peter s warming himself, he
19:25 Near the cross of Jesus s his mother,
20:11 Mary s outside the tomb crying.
20:19 Jesus came and s among them and said,
20:26 Jesus came and s among them and said,
21: 4 Early in the morning, Jesus s on the
Ac 1:10 men dressed in white s beside them.
1:15 In those days Peter s up among the
2:14 Peter s up with the Eleven, raised
5:34 s up in the Sanhedrin and ordered
9: 7 The men travelling with Saul s there
9:39 All the widows s around him, crying
10:30 a man in shining clothes s before
11:28 One of them, named Agabus, s up and
12: 6 sentries s guard at the entrance.
15: 5 of the Pharisees s up and said,
17:22 Paul then s up in the meeting of the
21:40 Paul s on the steps and motioned to
22:13 He s beside me and said, 'Brother
22:20 I s there giving my approval and
23: 9 Pharisees s up and argued vigorously.
23:11 The following night the Lord s near
24:20 me when I s before the Sanhedrin—
24:21 I shouted as I s in their presence:
25: 7 down from Jerusalem s around him,
27:21 Paul s up before them and said: "Men,
27:23 I am and whom I serve s beside
2Co 13: 7 will see that we have s the test
Col 2:14 against us and that s opposed to us
2Ti 4:17 the Lord s at my side and gave me
Heb 10:32 when you s your ground in a great
10:33 at other times you s side by side
Jas 1:12 because when he has s the test, he
Rev 8: 3 censer, came and s at the altar.
11:11 and they s on their feet, and terror
12: 4 The dragon s in front of the woman
13: 1 the dragon s on the shore of the sea.
22: 2 On each side of the river s the tree

Stool (Footstool)
Ex 1:16 and observe them on the delivery s,

Stoop (Stooped, Stoops)
2Sa 22:36 you s down to make me great.
Ps 18:35 you s down to make me great.
Ecc 12: 3 and the strong men s, when the
Isa 46: 2 They s and bow down together;
Mk 1: 7 I am not worthy to s down and untie.

Stooped (Stoop)
Jn 8: 8 Again he s down and wrote on the

Stoops (Stoop)
Ps 113: 6 who s down to look on the heavens
Isa 46: 1 Bel bows down, Nebo s low;

Stop (Stopped, Stopping, Stops)
Ge 19:17 and don't s anywhere in the plain!
Ex 9:29 The thunder will s and there will be
Nu 11:28 "Moses, my lord, s them!"
Jos 10:19 don't s! Pursue your enemies, attack
22:25 cause ours to s fearing the LORD.
Jdg 15: 7 I won't s until I get my revenge
19:11 "Come, let's s at this city of the
1Sa 7: 8 "Do not s crying out to the LORD
9: 5 or my father will s thinking about
1Sa 15:16 "S!" Samuel said to Saul. "Let me
20:38 "Hurry! Go quickly! Don't s!"
2Sa 2:21 But Asahel would not s chasing him.
2:22 Abner warned Asahel, "S chasing me!
2:26 men to s pursuing their brothers?"
2Ki 3:19 good tree, s up all the springs,
2Ch 25:16 S! Why be struck down?"
35:21 so s opposing God, who is with me,
Ezr 4:21 Now issue an order to these men to s
4:23 and compelled them by force to s.
6: 8 so that the work will not s.
Ne 5:10 But let the exacting of usury s!
6: 3 Why should the work s while I leave
Job 9:12 If he snatches away, who can s him?
13:21 and s frightening me with your
37:14 s and consider God's wonders.
Pr 19:27 S listening to instruction, my son,
Isa 1:13 S bringing meaningless offerings!
1:16 out of my sight! S doing wrong,
2:22 S trusting in man, who has but a
28:22 Now s your mocking, or your chains
30:11 get off this path, and s confronting
33: 1 When you s destroying, you will be
33: 1 s betraying, you will be betrayed.
Jer 15: 5 Who will s to ask how you are?
32:40 I will never s doing good to them,
44: 5 or s burning incense to other gods.
Eze 16:41 I will put a s to your prostitution,
21:21 For the king of Babylon will s at
23:27 I will put a s to the lewdness and
45: 9 S dispossessing my people, declares
Hos 2:11 I will s all her celebrations: her
Am 7: 5 "Sovereign LORD, I beg you, s!
7:16 and s preaching against the house of
Na 2: 8 "S! S!" they cry, but no-one turns
Mk 9:38 and we told him to s, because he
9:39 "Do not s him," Jesus said. "No-one
Lk 6:29 do not s him from taking your tunic.
8:52 "S wailing," Jesus said. "She is not
9:49 and we tried to s him, because he
9:50 "Do not s him," Jesus said, "for
Jn 5:14 S sinning or something worse may
6:43 "S grumbling among yourselves,"
7:24 S judging by mere appearances, and
20:27 S doubting and believe."
Ac 4:17 to s this thing from spreading any
5:39 you will not be able to s these men;
8:38 he gave orders to s the chariot.
13:10 Will you never s perverting the
Ro 14:13 Therefore let us s passing judgment
1Co 14:20 Brothers, s thinking like children.
14:30 down, the first speaker should s.
15:34 senses as you ought, and s sinning;
2Co 11:10 Achaia will s this boasting of mine.
1Ti 5:23 S drinking only water, and use a
2Pe 2:14 of adultery, they never s sinning;
Rev 4: 8 Day and night they never s saying:
9:20 they did not s worshipping demons,

Stopped (Stop)
Ge 8: 2 the rain had s falling from the sky.
11: 8 earth, and they s building the city.
26:15 the Philistines s up, filling them
26:18 which the Philistines had s up after
28:11 he s for the night because the sun
29:35 Then she s having children.
30: 9 Leah saw that she had s having
41:49 it was so much that he s keeping
42:27 At the place where they s for the
43:21 at the place where we s for the
Ex 9:33 the thunder and hail s, and the
9:34 the rain and hail and thunder had s,
Nu 16:48 and the dead, and the plague s.
16:50 of Meeting, for the plague had s.
25: 8 plague against the Israelites was s;
Jos 3:16 the water from upstream s flowing.
5:12 The manna s the day after they ate
10:13 the sun stood still, and the moon s,
10:13 The sun s in the middle of the sky
Jdg 19:15 There they s to spend the night.
Ru 1:18 to go with her, she s urging her.
2:20 "He has not s showing his kindness
1Sa 6:14 and there it s beside a large rock.
10: 2 And now your father has s thinking
10:13 After Saul s prophesying, he went to
1Sa 14:46 Saul s pursuing the Philistines, and
2Sa 2:23 And every man s when he came to the
18:16 and the troops s pursuing Israel,
20:12 everyone who came up to Amasa s,
24:21 the plague on the people may be s."
24:25 and the plague on Israel was s.
1Ki 15:21 Baasha heard this, he s building
17:17 and worse, and finally s breathing.
22:33 king of Israel and s pursuing him.
2Ki 2: 7 and Elisha had s at the Jordan.
3:25 They s up all the springs and cut
4: 6 Then the oil s flowing.
4: 8 he came by, he s there to eat.
5: 9 and s at the door of Elisha's house.
6:23 Aram s raiding Israel's territory.
13:18 He struck it three times and s.
18:17 They came up to Jerusalem and s at
1Ch 21:22 the plague on the people may be s.
2Ch 16: 5 Baasha heard this, he s building
18:32 king of Israel, they s pursuing him.
25:16 So the prophet s but said, "I know
Ezr 5: 5 and they were not s until a report
Ne 12:39 At the Gate of the Guard they s.
Job 4:16 s, but I could not tell what it was.
32: 1 these three men s answering Job,
Ps 58: 4 that of a cobra that has s its ears,
Isa 24: 8 the noise of the revellers has s,
36: 2 When the commander s at the aqueduct
Jer 44:18 ever since we s burning incense to
48:33 I have s the flow of wine from the
51:30 Babylon's warriors have s fighting;
Lam 5:14 the young men have s their music.
Eze 10:18 the temple and s above the cherubim.
10:19 They s at the entrance to the east
11:23 and s above the mountain east of it.
Zec 7:11 their backs and s up their ears.
Mt 2: 9 s over the place where the child was.
20:32 Jesus s and called them. "What do
Mk 5:29 Immediately her bleeding s and she
10:49 Jesus s and said, "Call him."
Lk 7:45 I entered, has not s kissing my feet.
8:44 and immediately her bleeding s.
18:40 Jesus s and ordered the man to be
23:45 for the sun s shining. And the
Ac 5:42 they never s teaching and
10:17 Simon's house was and s at the gate.
11:11 s at the house where I was staying.
20:31 I never s warning each of you night
21:32 his soldiers, they s beating Paul.
Eph 1:16 I have not s giving thanks for you,
Col 1: 9 we have not s praying for you and
1Th 2:18 again and again—but Satan s us.
Heb 10: 2 would they not have s being offered

Stopping (Stop)
Ex 5: 5 and you are s them from working."
Jer 41:17 they went on, s at Geruth Kimham

Stops (Stop)
1Ki 18:44 and go down before the rain s you.
Job 18: 5 the flame of his fire s burning.
30:27 The churning inside me never s;
37: 7 he s every man from his labour.
Isa 33:15 who s his ears against plots of
44:19 No-one s to think, no-one has the
Ac 6:13 "This fellow never s speaking
3Jn :10 He also s those who want to do so

Storage (Store)
Jer 40:10 and put them in your s jars, and
Eze 4: 9 put them in a s jar and use them to

Store (Storage, Stored, Storehouse, Storehouses, Storeroom, Storerooms, Stores, Storing)
Ge 6:21 s it away as food for you and for
41:35 s up the grain under the authority
Ex 1:11 and Rameses as s cities for Pharaoh.
Dt 14:28 produce and s it in your towns,
1Ki 9:19 well as all his s cities and the
2Ch 8: 4 the s cities he had built in Hamath.
8: 6 well as Baalath and all his s cities,
16: 4 and all the s cities of Naphtali.
17:12 he built forts and s cities in

2Ch 32:28 He also made buildings to s the
Ne 13: 5 used to s the grain offerings
Job 23:14 many such plans he still has in s.
Ps 17:14 they s up wealth for their children.
Pr 2: 1 and s up my commands within you,
2: 7 He holds victory in s for the
7: 1 My son, keep my words and s up my
10:14 Wise men s up knowledge, but the
30:25 they s up their food in the summer;
Isa 2:12 The LORD Almighty has a day in s for
10:28 they s supplies at Michmash.
33: 6 a rich s of salvation and wisdom and
Mic 6:14 You will s up but save nothing,
Mt 6:19 "Do not s up for yourselves
6:20 s up for yourselves treasures in
6:26 not sow or reap or s away in barns,
Lk 12:17 I have no place to s my crops.'
12:18 I will s all my grain and my goods.
2Co 9:10 increase your s of seed and will
2Ti 4: 8 Now there is in s for me the crown

Stored (Store)

Ge 41:48 in Egypt and s it in the cities.
41:49 Joseph s up huge quantities of grain,
2Ki 20:17 and all that your fathers have s up
Ezr 6: 1 s in the treasury at Babylon.
Job 15:20 through all the years s up for him.
Ps 31:19 which you have s up for those who
Pr 13:22 wealth is s up for the righteous.
SS 7:13 that I have s up for you, my lover.
Isa 15: 7 the wealth they have acquired and s
22: 9 you s up water in the Lower Pool.
23:18 they will not be s up or hoarded.
39: 6 and all that your fathers have s up
45: 3 riches s in secret places, so that
Hos 13:12 The guilt of Ephraim is s up, his
Mt 12:35 things out of the good s up in him,
12:35 things out of the evil s up in him.
Lk 6:45 out of the good s up in his heart,
6:45 out of the evil s up in his heart.
Col 1: 5 hope that is s up for you in heaven

Storehouse (House, Store)

Dt 28:12 the heavens, the s of his bounty,
1Ch 26:15 the lot for the s fell to his sons.
26:17 south and two at a time at the s.
Hos 13:15 His s will be plundered of all its
Mal 3:10 Bring the whole tithe into the s,

Storehouses (House, Store)

Ge 41:56 Joseph opened the s and sold grain
2Ki 20:13 all that was in his s—the silver,
1Ch 27:25 Adiel was in charge of the royal s.
27:25 of the s in the outlying districts,
Job 38:22 "Have you entered the s of the snow
38:22 the snow or seen the s of the hail,
Ps 33: 7 into jars; he puts the deep into s.
135: 7 and brings out the wind from his s.
Isa 39: 2 them what was in his s—the silver,
Jer 10:13 and brings out the wind from his s.
51:16 and brings out the wind from his s.
Joel 1:17 The s are in ruins, the granaries

Storeroom (Room, Store)

Mt 13:52 brings out of his s new treasures
Lk 12:24 they have no s or barn; yet God

Storerooms (Room, Store)

1Ch 28:11 its buildings, its s, its upper
2Ch 31:11 Hezekiah gave orders to prepare s in
Ne 10:37 "Moreover, we will bring to the s of
10:38 our God, to the s of the treasury.
10:39 new wine and oil to the s where the
12:25 who guarded the s at the gates.
12:44 to be in charge of the s for the
12:44 to bring into the s the portions
13: 4 of the s of the house of our God.
13:12 grain, new wine and oil into the s.
13:13 Pedaiah in charge of the s and made

Stores (Store)

Job 21:19 'God s up a man's punishment for
Pr 6: 8 yet it s its provisions in summer

Pr 21:20 In the house of the wise are s of
Lk 12:21 anyone who s up things for himself

Storey

Ac 20: 9 fell to the ground from the third s

Stories (Story)

2Pe 1:16 We did not follow cleverly invented s
2: 3 you with s they have made up.

Storing (Store)

Ecc 2:26 s up wealth to hand it over to the
Ro 2: 5 you are s up wrath against yourself

Stork

Lev 11:19 the s, any kind of heron, the hoopoe
Dt 14:18 the s, any kind of heron, the hoopoe
Job 39:13 the pinions and feathers of the s.
Ps 104:17 s has its home in the pine trees.
Jer 8: 7 Even the s in the sky knows her
Zec 5: 9 They had wings like those of a s,

Storm (Stormed, Storms, Stormy, Thunderstorm, Windstorm)

Ex 9:24 It was the worst s in all the land
Job 9:17 He would crush me with a s and
30:22 you toss me about in the s.
36:33 His thunder announces the coming s;
38: 1 the LORD answered Job out of the s.
40: 6 the LORD spoke to Job out of the s:
Ps 55: 8 far from the tempest and s."
83:15 and terrify them with your s.
107:29 He stilled the s to a whisper;
Pr 1:27 calamity overtakes you like a s,
10:25 the s has swept by, the wicked are
Isa 4: 6 hiding-place from the s and rain.
25: 4 a shelter from the s and a shade
25: 4 is like a s driving against a
32: 2 the wind and a refuge from the s,
Jer 11:16 But with the roar of a mighty s he
23:19 See, the s of the LORD will burst
25:32 a mighty s is rising from the ends
30:23 See, the s of the LORD will burst
Eze 30:16 Thebes will be taken by s;
38: 9 you will go up, advancing like a s;
Da 11:40 and the king of the North will s out
Jnh 1: 4 and such a violent s arose that the
1:12 this great s has come upon you."
Na 1: 3 way is in the whirlwind and the s,
2: 4 The chariots s through the streets,
Zec 10: 1 is the LORD who makes the s clouds.
Mt 8:24 Without warning, a furious s came up
Lk 8:24 the s subsided, and all was calm.
Ac 27:15 The ship was caught by the s and
27:18 battering from the s that the
27:20 days and the s continued raging,
Heb 12:18 with fire; to darkness, gloom and s;
2Pe 2:17 water and mists driven by a s.

Stormed (Storm)

Jdg 9:52 Abimelech went to the tower and s it.
Hab 3:14 his warriors s out to scatter us,

Storms (Storm)

Isa 54:11 "O afflicted city, lashed by s and
Zec 9:14 he will march in the s of the south,

Stormy (Storm)

Ps 148: 8 clouds, s winds that do his bidding,
Am 1:14 amid violent winds on a s day.
Mt 16: 3 'Today it will be s, for the sky is

Story (Stories)

Ge 39:17 she told him this s: "That Hebrew
39:19 his master heard the s his wife told
Mt 28:15 this s has been widely circulated

Stout-hearted (Heart)

Ps 138: 3 answered me; you made me bold and s.

Straggler

Isa 14:31 and there is not a s in its ranks.

Straight (Straighten, Straightened)

Jos 6: 5 people will go up, every man s in."
6:20 so every man charged s in, and they
1Sa 6:12 cows went s up towards Beth Shemesh
2Sa 5:23 "Do not go s up, but circle round
1Ch 14:14 "Do not go s up, but circle round
Job 10:19 s from the womb to the grave!
Ps 5: 8 enemies—make s your way before me.
27:11 a s path because of my oppressors.
107: 7 He led them by a s way to a city
Pr 2:13 who leave the s paths to walk in
3: 6 him, and he will make your paths s.
4:11 wisdom and lead you along s paths.
4:25 Let your eyes look s ahead, fix your
5: 5 her steps lead s to the grave.
9:15 who pass by, who go s on their way.
11: 5 blameless makes a s way for them,
15:21 of understanding keeps a s course.
SS 7: 9 May the wine go s to my lover,
Isa 40: 3 make s in the wilderness a highway
45:13 I will make all his ways s.
Jer 31:39 from there s to the hill of Gareb
Eze 1: 7 Their legs were s; their feet were
1: 9 Each one went s ahead; they did not
1:12 Each one went s ahead. Wherever the
10:22 Each one went s ahead.
Joel 2: 8 each other; each marches s ahead.
Am 4: 3 You will each go s out through
Mt 3: 3 for the Lord, make s paths for him.
Mk 1: 3 for the Lord, make s paths for him.
Lk 3: 4 for the Lord, make s paths for him.
3: 5 The crooked roads shall become s,
22:61 The Lord turned and looked s at
Jn 1:23 'Make s the way for the Lord.'"
Ac 3: 4 Peter looked s at him, as did John.
9:11 to the house of Judas on S Street
13: 9 Spirit, looked s at Elymas and said,
16:11 to sea and sailed s for Samothrace,
21: 1 put out to sea and sailed s to Cos.
23: 1 Paul looked s at the Sanhedrin and
2Pe 2:15 They have left the s way and

Straighten (Straight)

Ecc 7:13 Who can s what he has made crooked?
Lk 13:11 bent over and could not s up at all.
Tit 1: 5 s out what was left unfinished

Straightened (Straight)

Ecc 1:15 What is twisted cannot be s; what is
Lk 13:13 she s up and praised God.
Jn 8: 7 he s up and said to them, "If any
8:10 Jesus s up and asked her, "Woman,

Strain (Straining)

Ex 18:23 you will be able to stand the s, and
Mt 23:24 You s out a gnat but swallow a

Straining (Strain)

Zec 6: 7 were s to go throughout the earth.
Mk 6:48 He saw the disciples s at the oars,
Php 3:13 behind and s towards what is ahead,

Strands

Ex 39: 3 cut s to be worked into the blue,
Ecc 4:12 of three s is not quickly broken.
Eze 5: 3 take a few s of hair and tuck them

Strange (Stranger, Stranger's, Strangers)

Ex 3: 3 "I will go over and see this s sight
Pr 23:33 Your eyes will see s sights and your
Isa 18: 2 an aggressive nation of s speech,
18: 7 an aggressive nation of s speech,
28:11 with foreign lips and s tongues God
28:21 to do his work, his s work,
33:19 their s, incomprehensible tongue.
Ac 17:20 You are bringing some s ideas to our
1Co 14:21 "Through men of s tongues and
Heb 13: 9 away by all kinds of s teachings.
1Pe 4: 4 They think it s that you do not
4:12 something s were happening to you.

Stranger (Strange)
Ge 23: 4 "I am an alien and a s among you.
42: 7 but he pretended to be a s and
Job 19:15 and my maidservants count me a s;
29:16 I took up the case of the s.
31:32 no s had to spend the night in the
Ps 39:12 alien, a s, as all my fathers were.
69: 8 I am a s to my brothers, an alien to
119:19 I am a s on earth; do not hide your
Pr 20:16 of one who puts up security for a s;
27:13 of one who puts up security for a s;
Ecc 6: 2 them, and a s enjoys them instead.
Jer 14: 8 why are you like a s in the land,
Mt 25:35 I was a s and you invited me in,
25:38 did we see you a s and invite you in,
25:43 I was a s and you did not invite me
25:44 hungry or thirsty or a s or needing
Jn 10: 5 they will never follow a s; in fact,
Heb 11: 9 land like a s in a foreign country;

Stranger's (Strange)
Jn 10: 5 they do not recognise a s voice."

Strangers (Strange)
Ge 15:13 be s in a country not their own,
1Ch 16:19 in number, few indeed, and s in it,
29:15 We are aliens and s in your sight,
Ps 54: 3 S are attacking me; ruthless men
105:12 in number, few indeed, and s in it,
109:11 s plunder the fruits of his labour.
Pr 5:10 lest s feast on your wealth and your
5:17 alone, never to be shared with s.
Isa 1: 7 laid waste as when overthrown by s.
Eze 16:32 You prefer s to your own husband!
Ob :11 while s carried off his wealth
Zec 7:14 all the nations, where they were s.
Ac 7: 6 'Your descendants will be s in a
Heb 11:13 they were aliens and s on earth.
13: 2 Do not forget to entertain s, for by
1Pe 1: 1 To God's elect, s in the world,
1:17 lives as s here in reverent fear.
2:11 I urge you, as aliens and s in the
3Jn : 5 even though they are s to you.

Strangled (Strangling)
Na 2:12 cubs and s the prey for his mate,
Ac 15:20 meat of s animals and from blood.
15:29 from the meat of s animals and from
21:25 from the meat of s animals and from

Strangling (Strangled)
Job 7:15 that I prefer s and death, rather

Strap (Strapped, Straps)
Ex 32:27 'Each man s a sword to his side.

Strapped (Strap)
Jdg 3:16 which he s to his right thigh under
2Sa 20: 8 and s over it at his waist was a

Straps (Strap)
Jer 27: 2 "Make a yoke out of s and crossbars

Strategy
2Ki 18:20 You say you have s and military
Isa 8:10 Devise your s, but it will be
36: 5 You say you have s and military

Straw
Ge 24:25 "We have plenty of s and fodder,
24:32 S and fodder were brought for the
Ex 5: 7 the people with s for making bricks;
5: 7 let them go and gather their own s.
5:10 'I will not give you any more s.
5:11 Go and get your own s wherever you
5:12 Egypt to gather stubble to use for s.
5:13 each day, just as when you had s."
5:16 Your servants are given no s, yet we
5:18 You will not be given any s, yet you
Jdg 19:19 We have both s and fodder for our
1Ki 4:28 s for the chariot horses and the
Job 21:18 How often are they like s before the
41:27 Iron he treats like s and bronze
Job 41:29 A club seems to him but a piece of s;
Isa 5:24 as tongues of fire lick up s and as
11: 7 and the lion will eat s like the ox.
25:10 as s is trampled down in the manure.
33:11 conceive chaff, you give birth to s;
65:25 and the lion will eat s like the ox,
Jer 23:28 For what has s to do with grain?"
1Co 3:12 costly stones, wood, hay or s,

Stray (Astray, Strayed, Straying, Strays)
Ex 22: 5 lets them s and they graze in
1Ki 22:43 father Asa and did not s from them;
2Ch 20:32 father Asa and did not s from them;
Ps 119:10 do not let me s from your commands.
119:21 cursed and who s from your commands.
119:118 You reject all who s from your
Pr 7:25 to her ways or s into her paths.
19:27 will s from the words of knowledge.
Eze 14:11 the people of Israel will no longer s

Strayed (Stray)
Ps 44:18 our feet had not s from your path.
119:110 but I have not s from your precepts.
119:176 I have s like a lost sheep.
Jer 2: 5 that they s so far from me?
31:19 After I s, I repented; after I came
Hos 7:13 Woe to them, because they have s

Straying (Stray)
Dt 22: 1 see your brother's ox or sheep s,

Strays (Stray)
Pr 21:16 A man who s from the path of
27: 8 Like a bird that s from its nest is
27: 8 nest is a man who s from his home.
Eze 34: 4 You have not brought back the s or
34:16 for the lost and bring back the s.

Streaked
Ge 30:35 male goats that were s or spotted,
30:39 that were s or speckled or spotted.
30:40 but made the rest face the s and
31: 8 'The s ones will be your wages,'
31: 8 then all the flocks bore s young.
31:10 flock were s, speckled or spotted.
31:12 goats mating with the flock are s,

Stream (Downstream, Streaming, Streams, Upstream)
Ge 32:23 After he had sent them across the s,
Dt 9:21 a s that flowed down the mountain.
21: 4 and where there is a flowing s.
1Sa 17:40 chose five smooth stones from the s,
2Ch 32: 4 the s that flowed through the land.
Job 30: 6 They were forced to live in the dry s
40:22 the poplars by the s surround him.
41:19 Firebrands s from his mouth;
Isa 2: 2 hills, and all nations will s to it.
30:33 s of burning sulphur, sets it ablaze.
32:20 sowing your seed by every s, and
66:12 wealth of nations like a flooding s;
Jer 17: 8 that sends out its roots by the s.
51:44 The nations will no longer s to him.
Am 5:24 like a never-failing s!
Mic 4: 1 the hills, and peoples will s to it.

Streaming (Stream)
SS 4:15 flowing water s down from Lebanon.

Streams (Stream)
Ge 2: 6 s came up from the earth and watered
Ex 7:19 of Egypt—over the s and canals,
8: 5 over the s and canals and ponds,
Lev 11: 9 in the water of the seas and the s,
11:10 all creatures in the seas or s that
Dt 8: 7 land with s and pools of water,
10: 7 Jotbathah, a land with s of water.
2Ki 19:24 I have dried up all the s of Egypt."
Job 6:15 undependable as intermittent s,
6:15 as the s that overflow
20:17 He will not enjoy the s, the rivers
29: 6 poured out for me s of olive oil.
Job 36:27 which distil as rain to the s;
Ps 1: 3 He is like a tree planted by s of
42: 1 the deer pants for s of water, so my
46: 4 There is a river whose s make glad
65: 9 The s of God are filled with water
74:15 was you who opened up springs and s;
78:16 he brought s out of a rocky crag and
78:20 gushed out, and s flowed abundantly.
78:44 they could not drink from their s.
119:136 S of tears flow from my eyes, for
126: 4 O LORD, like s in the Negev.
Pr 5:16 s of water in the public squares?
Ecc 1: 7 All s flow into the sea, yet the sea
1: 7 To the place the s come from, there
SS 5:12 eyes are like doves by the water s,
Isa 7:18 flies from the distant s of Egypt
11:15 He will break it up into seven s so
19: 6 the s of Egypt will dwindle and dry
30:25 s of water will flow on every high
32: 2 like s of water in the desert and
33:21 like a place of broad rivers and s.
34: 9 Edom's s will be turned into pitch,
35: 6 the wilderness and s in the desert.
37:25 I have dried up all the s of Egypt.'
43:19 the desert and s in the wasteland.
43:20 the desert and s in the wasteland,
44: 3 and s on the dry ground; I will pour
44: 4 like poplar trees by flowing s.
44:27 'Be dry, and I will dry up your s,'
47: 2 your legs, and wade through the s.
Jer 9:18 tears and water s from our eyelids.
31: 9 I will lead them beside s of water
Lam 3:48 S of tears flow from my eyes because
Eze 29: 3 great monster lying among your s.
29: 4 fish of your s stick to your scales.
29: 4 will pull you out from among your s,
29: 5 you and all the fish of your s.
29:10 I am against you and against your s,
30:12 I will dry up the s of the Nile and
31: 4 their s flowed all around its base
31:15 I held back its s, and its abundant
32: 2 the seas thrashing about in your s,
32: 2 with your feet and muddying the s.
32:14 settle and make her s flow like oil,
Joel 1:20 the s of water have dried up and
Hab 3: 8 Was your wrath against the s?
Mt 7:25 The rain came down, the s rose, and
7:27 The rain came down, the s rose, and
Jn 7:38 s of living water will flow from

Street (Streets)
Dt 32:25 In the s the sword will make them
Jos 2:19 goes outside your house into the s,
2Ch 28:24 at every s corner in Jerusalem.
Job 31:32 had to spend the night in the s,
Ps 31:11 who see me on the s flee from me.
Pr 1:20 Wisdom calls aloud in the s, she
7: 8 He was going down the s near her
7:12 now in the s, now in the squares, at
Ecc 12: 4 the doors to the s are closed and
Isa 51:20 they lie at the head of every s,
51:23 ground, like a s to be walked over."
Jer 6:11 Pour it out on the children in the s
37:21 given bread from the s of the bakers
Lam 2:19 from hunger at the head of every s.
4: 1 scattered at the head of every s.
Eze 16:25 At the head of every s you built
16:31 your mounds at the head of every s
Na 3:10 to pieces at the head of every s.
Mt 6: 5 on the s corners to be seen by men.
22: 9 Go to the s corners and invite to
Mk 11: 4 outside in the s, tied at a doorway.
Ac 9:11 to the house of Judas on Straight S
12:10 had walked the length of one s,
Rev 11: 8 Their bodies will lie in the s of
21:21 The great s of the city was of pure
22: 2 down the middle of the great s of

Streets (Street)
2Sa 1:20 proclaim it not in the s of Ashkelon,
22:43 and trampled them like mud in the s.
Est 6: 9 him on the horse through the city s,
6:11 him on horseback through the city s,
Ps 18:42 I poured them out like mud in the s.

Ps 55:11 threats and lies never leave its s.
144:14 no cry of distress in our s.
Pr 1:21 at the head of the noisy s she cries
5:16 Should your springs overflow in the s
22:13 "I will be murdered in the s!"
26:13 road, a fierce lion roaming the s!"
Ecc 12: 5 of heights and of dangers in the s;
12: 5 home and mourners go about the s.
SS 3: 2 the city, through its s and squares;
Isa 5:25 bodies are like refuse in the s.
10: 6 trample them down like mud in the s.
15: 3 In the s they wear sackcloth; on the
24:11 In the s they cry out for wine;
33: 7 their brave men cry aloud in the s;
42: 2 out, or raise his voice in the s.
58:12 Walls, Restorer of **S** with Dwellings.
59:14 truth has stumbled in the s,
Jer 5: 1 "Go up and down the s of Jerusalem,
7:17 of Judah and in the s of Jerusalem?
7:34 of Judah and the s of Jerusalem,
9:21 has cut off the children from the s
11: 6 of Judah and in the s of Jerusalem:
11:13 are as many as the s of Jerusalem.'
14:16 thrown out into the s of Jerusalem
33:10 of Judah and the s of Jerusalem
44: 6 the s of Jerusalem and made them the
44: 9 of Judah and the s of Jerusalem?
44:17 of Judah and in the s of Jerusalem.
44:21 the s of Jerusalem by you and your
49:26 her young men will fall in the s;
50:30 her young men will fall in the s;
51: 4 Babylon, fatally wounded in her s.
Lam 2:11 infants faint in the s of the city.
2:12 wounded men in the s of the city,
2:21 lie together in the dust of the s;
4: 5 delicacies are destitute in the s.
4: 8 they are not recognised in the s.
4:14 Now they grope through the s like
4:18 step, so we could not walk in our s.
Eze 7:19 will throw their silver into the s,
11: 6 city and filled its s with the dead.
26:11 his horses will trample all your s;
28:23 her and make blood flow in her s.
Da 9:25 It will be rebuilt with s and a
Hos 7: 1 into houses, bandits rob in the s;
Am 5:16 "There will be wailing in all the s
Mic 7:10 underfoot like mire in the s.
Na 2: 4 The chariots storm through the s,
Zep 3: 6 I have left their s deserted, with
Zec 8: 4 age will sit in the s of Jerusalem,
8: 5 The city s will be filled with boys
9: 3 and gold like the dirt of the s.
10: 5 men trampling the muddy s in battle.
Mt 6: 2 in the synagogues and on the s,
12:19 no-one will hear his voice in the s.
22:10 the servants went out into the s and
Lk 10:10 not welcomed, go into its s and say,
13:26 with you, and you taught in our s.'
14:21 'Go out quickly into the s and
Ac 5:15 people brought the sick into the s

Strength (Strong)

Ge 31: 6 for your father with all my s,
48: 2 rallied his s and sat up on the bed.
49: 3 my might, the first sign of my s,
Ex 15: 2 The LORD is my s and my song; he has
15:13 In your s you will guide them to
Lev 26:20 Your s will be spent in vain,
Nu 14:17 "Now may the Lord's s be displayed,
23:22 they have the s of a wild ox.
24: 8 they have the s of a wild ox.
Dt 4:37 by his Presence and his great s,
6: 5 all your soul and with all your s.
8:17 "My power and the s of my hands have
11: 8 so that you may have the s to go in
21:17 is the first sign of his father's s.
32:36 their s is gone and no-one is left,
33:25 and your s will equal your days.
34: 7 eyes were not weak nor his s gone.
Jdg 5:31 like the sun when it rises in its s.
6:14 "Go in the s you have and save
7: 2 me that her own s has saved her,
8:21 'As is the man, so is his s.'"
15:19 When Samson drank, his s returned
16: 5 you the secret of his great s
Jdg 16: 6 "Tell me the secret of your great s
16: 9 secret of his s was not discovered.
16:15 told me the secret of your great s."
16:17 If my head were shaved, my s would
16:19 And his s left him.
1Sa 2: 4 those who stumbled are armed with s.
2: 9 "It is not by s that one prevails;
2:10 "He will give s to his king and
2:31 your s and the s of your father's
23:16 and helped him to find s in God.
28:20 His s was gone, for he had eaten
28:22 and have the s to go on your way."
30: 4 until they had no s left to weep.
30: 6 David found s in the LORD his God.
2Sa 15:12 And so the conspiracy gained s, and
22:33 is God who arms me with s and makes
22:40 You armed me with s for battle; you
2Ki 18:20 you have strategy and military s—
19: 3 and there is no s to deliver them.
23:25 all his soul and with all his s,
1Ch 16:11 Look to the LORD and his s; seek his
16:27 s and joy in his dwelling-place.
16:28 ascribe to the LORD glory and s,
26: 8 men with the s to do the work
29:12 In your hands are s and power to
29:12 power to exalt and give s to all.
2Ch 13:21 Abijah grew in s. He married
23: 1 seventh year Jehoiada showed his s.
25:11 Amaziah then marshalled his s and
Ne 1:10 your great s and your mighty hand.
4:10 "The s of the labourers is giving
8:10 for the joy of the LORD is your s."
Job 6:11 "What s do I have, that I should
6:12 Do I have the s of stone?
9:19 If it is a matter of s, he is mighty!
12:16 To him belong s and victory; both
22: 9 and broke the s of the fatherless.
30: 2 Of what use was the s of their hands
39:11 Will you rely on him for his great s?
39:19 "Do you give the horse his s or
39:21 He paws fiercely, rejoicing in his s,
40:16 What s he has in his loins, what
41:12 limbs, his s and his graceful form.
41:22 **S** resides in his neck; dismay goes
Ps 10:10 they fall under his s.
18: 1 I love you, O LORD, my s.
18:32 is God who arms me with s and makes
18:39 You armed me with s for battle;
21: 1 O LORD, the king rejoices in your s.
21:13 Be exalted, O LORD, in your s;
22:15 My s is dried up like a potsherd,
22:19 O my **S**, come quickly to help me.
28: 7 The LORD is my s and my shield;
28: 8 The LORD is the s of his people, a
29: 1 ascribe to the LORD glory and s.
29:11 The LORD gives s to his people;
31:10 my s fails because of my affliction,
32: 4 my s was sapped as in the heat of
33:16 no warrior escapes by his great s.
33:17 all its great s it cannot save.
38:10 My heart pounds, my s fails me;
46: 1 God is our refuge and s, an
59: 9 O my **S**, I watch for you;
59:16 I will sing of your s, in the
59:17 O my **S**, I sing praise to you;
65: 6 power, having armed yourself with s,
68:28 show us your s, O God, as you have
68:35 gives power and s to his people.
71: 9 do not forsake me when my s is gone.
73:26 but God is the s of my heart and my
79:11 by the s of your arm preserve those
81: 1 Sing for joy to God our s;
83: 8 to lend s to the descendants of Lot.
84: 5 Blessed are those whose s is in you,
84: 7 They go from s to s, till each
86:16 grant your s to your servant and
88: 4 I am like a man without s.
89:17 For you are their glory and s, and
89:19 "I have bestowed s on a warrior;
90:10 or eighty, if we have the s;
93: 1 in majesty and is armed with s.
96: 6 s and glory are in his sanctuary.
96: 7 ascribe to the LORD glory and s.
102:23 course of my life he broke my s;
105: 4 Look to the LORD and his s;
118:14 The LORD is my s and my song;
Ps 147:10 His pleasure is not in the s of the
Pr 5: 9 lest you give your best s to others
14: 4 s of an ox comes an abundant harvest.
20:29 The glory of young men is their s,
24: 5 and a man of knowledge increases s;
24:10 of trouble, how small is your s!
30:25 Ants are creatures of little s, yet
31: 3 do not spend your s on women, your
31:25 She is clothed with s and dignity;
Ecc 9:16 I said, "Wisdom is better than s."
10:10 more s is needed but skill will
10:17 for s and not for drunkenness.
Isa 10:13 "'By the s of my hand I have done
12: 2 The LORD, the LORD, is my s and my
28: 6 a source of s to those who turn back
30:15 in quietness and trust is your s,
31: 1 in the great s of their horsemen,
33: 2 Be our s every morning, our
36: 5 you have strategy and military s—
37: 3 and there is no s to deliver them.
40:26 of his great power and mighty s,
40:29 He gives s to the weary and
40:31 hope in the LORD will renew their s.
41: 1 Let the nations renew their s!
44:12 He gets hungry and loses his s;
45:24 LORD alone are righteousness and s.
49: 4 spent my s in vain and for nothing.
49: 5 the LORD and my God has been my s—
50: 2 Do I lack the s to rescue you?
51: 9 Awake, awake! Clothe yourself with s,
52: 1 O Zion, clothe yourself with s.
57:10 You found renewal of your s, and so
63: 1 forward in the greatness of his s?
Jer 9:23 the strong man boast of his s or
16:19 O LORD, my s and my fortress, my
17: 5 who depends on flesh for his s and
51:30 Their s is exhausted; they have
Lam 1:14 neck and the Lord has sapped my s.
Eze 30: 6 will fall and her proud s will fail.
30:18 her proud s will come to an end.
33:28 and her proud s will come to an end,
Da 2:41 have some of the s of iron in it,
10: 8 I had no s left, my face turned
10:17 s is gone and I can hardly breathe."
10:18 like a man touched me and gave me s.
10:19 my lord, since you have given me s."
11:15 troops will not have the s to stand.
11:25 a large army he will stir up his s
Hos 7: 9 Foreigners sap his s, but he does
10:13 you have depended on your own s
Am 2:14 the strong will not muster their s,
6:13 we not take Karnaim by our own s?"
Mic 5: 4 his flock in the s of the LORD,
Na 2: 1 yourselves, marshal all your s!
3: 9 Cush and Egypt were her boundless s;
Hab 1:11 men, whose own s is their god."
3:19 The Sovereign LORD is my s;
Mk 12:30 all your mind and with all your s.'
12:33 understanding and with all your s,
Lk 10:27 your s and with all your mind';
Ac 9:19 taking some food, he regained his s.
1Co 1:25 of God is stronger than man's s.
Eph 1:19 is like the working of his mighty s,
Php 4:13 through him who gives me s.
1Ti 1:12 Jesus our Lord, who has given me s,
2Ti 4:17 Lord stood at my side and gave me s,
Heb 11:34 whose weakness was turned to s;
1Pe 4:11 do it with the s God provides, so
Rev 3: 8 I know that you have little s, yet
5:12 s and honour and glory and praise!"
7:12 power and s be to our God for ever
14:10 full s into the cup of his wrath.

Strengthen (Strong)

Dt 3:28 and encourage and s him, for he will
Jdg 16:28 O God, please s me just once more,
1Ki 20:22 "**S** your position and see what must
2Ki 15:19 and s his own hold on the kingdom.
2Ch 16: 9 to s those whose hearts are fully
Ne 6: 9 ⌞But I prayed,⌟ "Now s my hands."
Job 8:20 man or s the hands of evildoers.
Ps 89:21 surely my arm will s him.
119:28 s me according to your word.
SS 2: 5 **S** me with raisins, refresh me with
Isa 22:10 and tore down houses to s the wall.

Isa 35: 3 **S** the feeble hands, steady the knees
41:10 I will s you and help you; I will
45: 5 I will s you, though you have not
54: 2 lengthen your cords, s your stakes.
58:11 land and will s your frame.
Jer 23:14 They s the hands of evildoers, so
Eze 30:24 I will s the arms of the king of
30:25 I will s the arms of the king of
34:16 I will bind up the injured and s the
Na 3:14 for the siege, s your defences!
Zec 10: 6 "I will s the house of Judah and
10:12 I will s them in the LORD and in his
Lk 22:32 have turned back, s your brothers."
Ac 15:32 to encourage and s the brothers.
Eph 3:16 he may s you with power through his
1Th 3: 2 s and encourage you in your faith,
3:13 May he s your hearts so that you
2Th 2:17 encourage your hearts and s you in
3: 3 and he will s and protect you from
Heb 12:12 Therefore, s your feeble arms and
Rev 3: 2 Wake up! **S** what remains and is about

Strengthened (Strong)
2Sa 16:21 of everyone with you will be s."
1Ki 19: 8 **S** by that food, he travelled for
2Ch 11:11 He s their defences and put
11:17 They s the kingdom of Judah and
17: 1 king and s himself against Israel.
Job 4: 3 many, how you have s feeble hands.
4: 4 you have s faltering knees.
Isa 9:11 the LORD has s Rezin's foes against
Eze 34: 4 You have not s the weak or healed
Da 10:19 When he spoke to me, I was s and
Hos 7:15 I trained them and s them, but they
Lk 22:43 heaven appeared to him and s him.
Ac 9:31 It was s; and encouraged by the Holy
16: 5 the churches were s in the faith and
Ro 4:20 s in his faith and gave glory to God,
Col 1:11 being s with all power according to
2: 7 s in the faith as you were taught,
Heb 13: 9 It is good for our hearts to be s by

Strengthening (Strong)
2Sa 3: 6 Abner had been s his own position in
Ac 14:22 s the disciples and encouraging them
15:41 Syria and Cilicia, s the churches.
18:23 and Phrygia, s all the disciples.
1Co 14: 3 their s, encouragement and comfort.
14:26 be done for the s of the church.
2Co 12:19 we do, dear friends, is for your s.

Strengthens (Strong)
Ps 147:13 for he s the bars of your gates and

Stress
Jer 19: 9 during the s of the siege imposed
Tit 3: 8 And I want you to s these things, so

Stretch (Outstretched, Stretched, Stretches, Stretching)
Ex 3:20 I will s out my hand and strike the
7: 5 when I s out my hand against Egypt
7:19 'Take your staff and s out your hand
8: 5 '**S** out your hand with your staff
8:16 '**S** out your staff and strike the
9:22 "**S** out your hand towards the sky so
10:12 "**S** out your hand over Egypt so that
10:21 "**S** out your hand towards the sky so
14:16 Raise your staff and s out your hand
14:26 "**S** out your hand over the sea so
2Ki 21:13 I will s out over Jerusalem the
Job 1:11 s out your hand and strike
2: 5 s out your hand and strike his flesh
11:13 to him and s out your hands to him,
Ps 138: 7 you s out your hand against the
Isa 28:20 The bed is too short to s out on,
34:11 God will s out over Edom the
54: 2 s your tent curtains wide,
Jer 6:12 when I s out my hand against those
31:39 The measuring line will s from there
51:25 "I will s out my hand against you,
Eze 6:14 I will s out my hand against them
14: 9 and I will s out my hand against him
14:13 I s out my hand against it to cut
25: 7 therefore I will s out my hand
25:13 I will s out my hand against Edom
25:16 I am about to s out my hand against
35: 3 Mount Seir, and I will s out my hand
Zep 1: 4 "I will s out my hand against Judah
2:13 He will s out his hand against the
Mt 12:13 said to the man, "**S** out your hand."
Mk 3: 5 said to the man, "**S** out your hand."
Lk 6:10 said to the man, "**S** out your hand."
Jn 21:18 are old you will s out your hands,
Ac 4:30 **S** out your hand to heal and perform

Stretched (Stretch)
Ge 10:30 The region where they lived s from
Ex 8: 6 Aaron s out his hand over the waters
8:17 and when Aaron s out his hand with
9:15 For by now I could have s out my
9:23 Moses s out his staff towards the
10:13 Moses s out his staff over Egypt,
10:22 Moses s out his hand towards the sky,
14:21 Moses s out his hand over the sea,
14:27 Moses s out his hand over the sea,
15:12 You s out your right hand and the
2Sa 24:16 the angel s out his hand to destroy
1Ki 13: 4 he s out his hand from the altar and
13: 4 But the hand he s out towards the
17:21 he s himself out on the boy three
2Ki 4:34 As he s himself out upon him, the
4:35 bed and s out upon him once more.
Job 38: 5 Who s a measuring line across it?
Ps 77: 2 at night I s out untiring hands
Pr 1:24 gave heed when I s out my hand,
Isa 14:26 is the hand s out over all nations.
14:27 His hand is s out, and who can turn
23:11 The LORD has s out his hand over the
42: 5 created the heavens and s them out,
44:24 who alone s out the heavens, who
45:12 My own hands s out the heavens;
51:13 who s out the heavens and laid the
Jer 10:12 s out the heavens by his
51:15 s out the heavens by his
Lam 2: 8 He s out a measuring line and did
Eze 1:23 Under the expanse their wings were s
2: 9 I looked, and I saw a hand s out to
8: 3 He s out what looked like a hand and
16:27 I s out my hand against you and
17: 7 s out its branches to him for water.
Zec 1:16 And the measuring line will be s out
Mt 12:13 So he s it out and it was
Mk 3: 5 He s it out, and his hand was
Ac 22:25 they s him out to flog him, Paul

Stretches (Stretch)
Job 9: 8 He alone s out the heavens and
Ps 104: 2 he s out the heavens like a
Isa 31: 3 When the LORD s out his hand, he who
33:17 beauty and view a land that s afar.
40:22 He s out the heavens like a canopy,
Lam 1:17 Zion s out her hands, but there is
Zec 12: 1 The LORD, who s out the heavens, who

Stretching (Stretch)
Est 1: 1 provinces s from India to Cush:
8: 9 127 provinces s from India to Cush.
Jer 4:31 s out her hands and saying, "Alas!

Strewn
1Sa 17:52 Their dead were s along the Shaaraim
2Ki 7:15 and they found the whole road s with

Stricken
Isa 53: 4 yet we considered him s by God,
53: 8 transgression of my people he was s.
Zec 14:13 On that day men will be s by the

Strict (Strictest, Strictly)
1Sa 14:28 bound the army under a s oath,
Mk 3:12 he gave them s orders not to tell
5:43 He gave s orders not to let anyone
Ac 5:28 "We gave you s orders not to teach
1Co 9:25 in the games goes into s training.

Strictest (Strict)
Ac 26: 5 that according to the s sect of our

Strictly (Strict)
Lk 9:21 Jesus s warned them not to tell this
Jas 3: 1 we who teach will be judged more s.

Stride (Striding, Strode)
Pr 30:29 things that are stately in their s,

Striding (Stride)
Isa 63: 1 robed in splendour, s forward in the

Strife (Strive)
Ps 55: 9 I see violence and s in the city.
Pr 17: 1 a house full of feasting, with s.
18: 6 A fool's lips bring him s, and his
20: 3 is to a man's honour to avoid s, but
22:10 Drive out the mocker, and out goes s;
23:29 Who has sorrow? Who has s? Who has
26:21 is a quarrelsome man for kindling s.
30:33 so stirring up anger produces s."
Isa 58: 4 fasting ends in quarrelling and s,
Hab 1: 3 there is s, and conflict abounds.
Ro 1:29 They are full of envy, murder, s,
1Ti 6: 4 s, malicious talk, evil suspicions

Strike (Strikes, Striking, Stroke, Struck)
Ge 3:15 your head, and you will s his heel."
Ex 3:20 I will stretch out my hand and s the
5: 3 s us with plagues or with the sword."
7:17 hand I will s the water of the Nile,
8:16 'stretch out your staff and s the
12:12 s down every firstborn—both men and
12:13 will touch you when I s Egypt.
12:23 the LORD goes through the land to s
12:23 to enter your houses and s you down.
17: 6 **S** the rock, and water will come out
Nu 8:19 no plague will s the Israelites when
14:12 I will s them down with a plague and
Dt 28:22 The LORD will s you with wasting
33:11 s his foes till they rise no more."
Jdg 6:16 s down all the Midianites together."
1Sa 17:46 s you down and cut off your head.
22:17 a hand to s the priests of the LORD.
22:18 "You turn and s down the priests."
26: 8 of my spear; I won't s him twice."
26:10 "the LORD himself will s him;
2Sa 1:15 "Go, s him down!" So he struck him
2:22 "Stop chasing me! Why should I s you
5:24 of you to s the Philistine army."
13:28 you, '**S** Amnon down,' then kill him.
17: 2 I would s him with terror, and then
17: 2 I would s down only the king
18:11 Why didn't you s him to the ground
1Ki 2:29 "Go, s him down!"
2:31 **S** him down and bury him, and so
14:15 the LORD will s Israel, so that it
20:35 "**S** me with your weapon," but the man
20:37 another man and said, "**S** me, please.
2Ki 6:18 LORD, "**S** these people with blindness.
13:18 Elisha told him, "**S** the ground."
1Ch 14:15 of you to s the Philistine army."
2Ch 21:14 now the LORD is about to s your
Job 1:11 stretch out your hand and s
2: 5 stretch out your hand and s his
16:10 they s my cheek in scorn and unite
36:32 and commands it to s its mark.
Ps 3: 7 **S** all my enemies on the jaw;
9:20 **S** them with terror, O LORD;
81: 2 Begin the music, s the tambourine,
89:23 him and s down his adversaries.
91:12 not s your foot against a stone.
141: 5 Let a righteous man s me—it is a
Pr 11:15 to s hands in pledge is safe.
Isa 11: 4 He will s the earth with the rod of
13:18 Their bows will s down the young men;
19:22 The LORD will s Egypt with a plague;
19:22 he will s them and heal them.
30:31 his sceptre he will s them down.
Jer 21: 6 I will s down those who live in this
Lam 3:30 his cheek to one who would s him,
Eze 5: 2 Take a third and s it with the sword
6:11 **S** your hands together and stamp your
21:14 prophesy and s your hands together.
21:14 Let the sword s twice, even three

Eze 21:17 I too will s my hands together, and
22:13 "'I will surely s my hands together
32:15 when I s down all who live there,
39: 3 I will s your bow from your left
Am 9: 1 "S the tops of the pillars so that
Mic 5: 1 They will s Israel's ruler on the
Zec 11:17 May the sword s his arm and his
12: 4 On that day I will s every horse
13: 7 "S the shepherd, and the sheep will
14:12 the LORD will s all the nations
14:15 A similar plague will s the horses
Mal 4: 6 come and s the land with a curse."
Mt 4: 6 not s your foot against a stone.'"
26:31 'I will s the shepherd, and the
Mk 14:27 'I will s the shepherd, and the
Lk 4:11 not s your foot against a stone.'"
22:49 "Lord, should we s with our swords?
Jn 18:23 I spoke the truth, why did you s me?"
Ac 23: 2 near Paul to s him on the mouth.
23: 3 Paul said to him, "God will s you,
Rev 2:23 I will s her children dead. Then all
11: 6 to s the earth with every kind of
19:15 with which to s down the nations.

Strikes (Strike)

Ex 21:12 "Anyone who s a man and kills him
Nu 35:16 "'If a man s someone with an iron
35:17 and he s someone so that he dies, he
Job 4: 5 it s you, and you are dismayed.
Ps 29: 7 The voice of the LORD s with flashes
Pr 17:18 A man lacking in judgment s hands in
22:26 Do not be a man who s hands in
27:10 brother's house when disaster s you
Isa 5:25 hand is raised and he s them down.
41: 7 hammer spurs on him who s the anvil.
Jer 11:12 help them at all when disaster s.
Eze 7: 9 it is I the LORD who s the blow.
17:10 completely when the east wind s it
Mt 5:39 If someone s you on the right cheek,
Lk 6:29 If someone s you on one cheek, turn
Rev 9: 5 sting of a scorpion when it s a man.

Striking (Strike)

1Sa 14:20 s each other with their swords.
2Sa 8:13 after he returned from s down
24:17 David saw the angel who was s down
Job 39:20 s terror with his proud snorting?
Isa 58: 4 in s each other with wicked fists.
Da 8: 7 s the ram and shattering his two

String (Stringed, Strings, Strung, Ten-stringed)

Jdg 16: 9 as easily as a piece of s snaps
2Sa 16: 1 He had a s of donkeys saddled and
Ps 7:12 he will bend and s his bow.
Jer 51: 3 Let not the archer s his bow, nor

Stringed (String)

Ps 4: T With s instruments. A psalm of David
6: T With s instruments. According to
54: T With s instruments. A maskil of
55: T With s instruments. A maskil of
61: T With s instruments. Of David.
67: T With s instruments. A psalm. A song
76: T With s instruments. A psalm of Asaph
Isa 38:20 and we will sing with s instruments
Hab 3:19 On my s instruments.

Strings (String)

Ps 11: 2 they set their arrows against the s
45: 8 the music of the s makes you glad.
150: 4 praise him with the s and flute,
SS 1:10 your neck with s of jewels.

Strip (Stripped, Strips)

1Sa 31: 8 when the Philistines came to s the
2Sa 2:21 young men and s him of his weapons.
23:10 to Eleazar, but only to s the dead.
1Ch 10: 8 when the Philistines came to s the
Job 41:13 Who can s off his outer coat? Who
Isa 27:10 they s its branches bare.
32:11 S off your clothes, put sackcloth
45: 1 him and to s kings of their armour,
Jer 5:10 S off her branches, for these people
49:10 I will s Esau bare; I will uncover
Eze 16:37 and will s you in front of them,
16:39 They will s you of your clothes and
23:26 They will also s you of your clothes
32:15 I make Egypt desolate and s the land
Da 4:14 s off its leaves and scatter its
Hos 2: 3 Otherwise I will s her naked and
Mic 2: 8 You s off the rich robe from those
3: 3 s off their skin and break their
Na 3:16 they s the land and then fly away.

Stripes

Ge 30:37 plane trees and made white s on them

Stripped (Strip)

Ge 37:23 they s him of his robe—the richly
Ex 9:25 in the fields and s every tree.
33: 6 the Israelites s off their ornaments
Jdg 14:19 s them of their belongings and gave
1Sa 19:24 He s off his robes and also
31: 9 They cut off his head and s off his
2Ki 18:16 Hezekiah king of Judah s off the
1Ch 10: 9 They s him and took his head and his
Job 12:17 He leads counsellors away s and
12:19 He leads priests away s and
15:33 He will be like a vine s of its
19: 9 He has s me of my honour and removed
22: 6 you s men of their clothing,
Isa 1: 7 s by foreigners right before you,
20: 2 did so, going around s and barefoot.
20: 3 gone s and barefoot for three years,
20: 4 will lead away s and barefoot the
22: 8 the defences of Judah are s away.
23:13 they s its fortresses bare and
Lam 4:21 you will be drunk and s naked.
Eze 12:19 their land will be s of everything
17: 9 Will it not be uprooted and s of its
19:12 it was s of its fruit;
23:10 They s her naked, took away her sons
Da 5:20 his royal throne and s of his glory.
7:12 (The other beasts had been s of
Joel 1: 7 It has s off their bark and thrown
Am 7: 2 they had s the land clean, I cried
Na 2:10 She is pillaged, plundered, s!
Hab 3:13 you s him from head to foot.
Mt 27:28 They s him and put a scarlet robe on
Lk 10:30 They s him of his clothes, beat him
Ac 16:22 ordered them to be s and beaten.

Strips (Strip)

Ps 29: 9 the oaks and s the forests bare.
Lk 24:12 Bending over, he saw the s of linen
Jn 11:44 his hands and feet wrapped with s of
19:40 it, with the spices, in s of linen.
20: 5 and looked in at the s of linen
20: 6 He saw the s of linen lying there,

Strive (Strife, Strives, Striving)

Ac 24:16 I s always to keep my conscience
1Ti 4:10 (and for this we labour and s), that

Strives (Strive)

Isa 64: 7 your name or s to lay hold of you;
Jer 15:10 a man with whom the whole land s and

Striving (Strive)

Ecc 2:22 anxious s with which he labours

Strode (Stride)

Hab 3:12 In wrath you s through the earth and

Stroke (Strike)

Job 5:20 in battle from the s of the sword.
Isa 30:32 Every s the LORD lays on them with
Mt 5:18 not the least s of a pen, will by
Lk 16:17 s of a pen to drop out of the Law.

Strong (Strength, Strengthen, Strengthened, Strengthening, Strengthens, *Strong and courageous*, Stronger, Strongest)

Ge 30:42 to Laban and the s ones to Jacob.
49:24 steady, his s arms stayed supple,
Ex 10:19 the wind to a very s west wind,
14:21 the sea back with a s east wind
Nu 13:18 there are s or weak, few or many.
24:18 conquered, but Israel will grow s.
Dt 2:10 live there—a people s and numerous,
2:21 They were a people s and numerous,
2:36 not one town was too s for us.
3:24 your greatness and your s hand.
9: 2 The people are s and tall—Anakites!
Jos 1: 7 Be s and very courageous. Be careful
14:11 I am still as s today as the day
17:18 they are s, you can drive them out."
23: 6 "Be very s; be careful to obey all
Jdg 1:28 Israel became s, they pressed the
3:29 Moabites, all vigorous and s;
5:21 March on, my soul; be s!
9:51 the city, however, was a s tower
14:14 out of the s, something sweet.
18:26 seeing that they were too s for him,
1Sa 4: 9 Be s, Philistines! Be men, or you
2Sa 2: 7 Now then, be s and brave, for Saul
3:39 sons of Zeruiah are too s for me.
10:11 "If the Arameans are too s for me,
10:11 if the Ammonites are too s for you,
10:12 Be s and let us fight bravely for
13:28 you this order? Be s and brave."
22:18 from my foes, who were too s for me.
1Ki 2: 2 "So be s, show yourself a man,
15: 4 him and by making Jerusalem s.
20:23 That is why they were too s for us.
2Ki 6:14 horses and chariots and a s force
24:16 fighting men, s and fit for war,
1Ch 11:10 gave his kingship s support to
19:12 "If the Arameans are too s for me,
19:12 if the Ammonites are too s for you,
19:13 Be s and let us fight bravely for
28:10 Be s and do the work."
2Ch 11:12 the cities, and made them very s.
12: 1 was established and he had become s,
13: 7 and not s enough to resist them.
15: 7 as for you, be s and do not give up,
Ezr 9:12 that you may be s and eat the good
Job 15:26 against him with a thick, s shield.
39: 4 Their young thrive and grow s in the
Ps 18:17 from my foes, who were too s for me.
22:12 s bulls of Bashan encircle me.
24: 8 The LORD s and mighty, the LORD
27:14 be s and take heart and wait for
31: 2 of refuge, a s fortress to save me.
31:24 Be s and take heart, all you who
35:10 the poor from those too s for them,
52: 7 and grew s by destroying others!"
61: 3 refuge, a s tower against the foe.
62:11 I heard: that you, O God, are s,
71: 7 to many, but you are my s refuge.
73: 4 their bodies are healthy and s.
89:10 s arm you scattered your enemies.
89:13 hand is s, your right hand exalted.
140: 7 O Sovereign LORD, my s deliverer,
142: 6 me, for they are too s for me.
Pr 18:10 The name of the LORD is a s tower;
18:18 and keeps s opponents apart.
23:11 for their Defender is s; he will
31:17 her arms are s for her tasks.
Ecc 9:11 to the swift or the battle to the s,
12: 3 and the s men stoop, when the
SS 8: 6 for love is as s as death,
Isa 8:11 The LORD spoke to me with his s hand
17: 9 In that day their s cities, which
25: 3 Therefore s peoples will honour you;
26: 1 We have a s city; God makes
28: 2 Lord has one who is powerful and s.
35: 4 "Be s, do not fear; your God will
41: 6 and says to his brother, "Be s!"
53:12 will divide the spoils with the s,
59:10 among the s, we are like the dead.
Jer 4:12 a wind too s for that comes from me.
9:23 or the s man boast of his strength
30: 6 Then why do I see every s man with
46: 6 swift cannot flee nor the s escape.
50:34 Yet their Redeemer is s; the LORD
Eze 3:14 with the s hand of the LORD upon me.
17: 9 It will not take a s arm or many
19: 3 of her cubs, and he became a s lion.
19: 5 of her cubs and made him a s lion.
19: 6 the lions, for he was now a s lion.

Eze 19:11 Its branches were s, fit for a
19:12 its s branches withered and fire
19:14 No s branch is left on it fit for a
22:14 be s in the day I deal with you?
26:11 s pillars will fall to the ground.
30:21 to become s enough to hold a sword.
34:16 the sleek and the s I will destroy.
Da 2:40 will be a fourth kingdom, s as iron
2:42 will be partly s and partly brittle.
4:11 The tree grew large and s and its
4:20 which grew large and s, with its top
4:22 You have become great and s;
8:24 He will become very s, but not by
10:19 "Peace! Be s now; be s."
11: 5 "The king of the South will become s,
Joel 3:10 Let the weakling say, "I am s!"
Am 2: 9 as the cedars and s as the oaks.
2:14 the s will not muster their
5: 3 marches out a thousand s for Israel
5: 3 hundred s will have only ten left."
8:13 lovely young women and s young men
Mic 4: 3 disputes for s nations far and wide.
4: 7 those driven away a s nation.
Hag 2: 4 now be s, O Zerubbabel,' declares
2: 4 'Be s, O Joshua son of Jehozadak,
2: 4 Be s, all you people of the land,'
Zec 8: 9 let your hands be s so that the
8:13 be afraid, but let your hands be s."
12: 5 'The people of Jerusalem are s,
Mt 12:29 can anyone enter a s man's house
12:29 unless he first ties up the s man?
Mk 1:43 him away at once with a s warning:
3:27 no-one can enter a s man's house
3:27 unless he first ties up the s man.
5: 4 No-one was s enough to subdue him.
Lk 1:80 the child grew and became s in
2:40 the child grew and became s; he was
11:21 "When a s man, fully armed, guards
16: 3 I'm not s enough to dig, and I'm
Jn 6:18 A s wind was blowing and the waters
Ac 3: 7 the man's feet and ankles became s.
3:16 whom you see and know was made s.
Ro 1:11 some spiritual gift to make you s—
15: 1 We who are s ought to bear with the
1Co 1: 8 He will keep you s to the end, so
1:27 things of the world to shame the s.
4:10 We are weak, but you are s!
16:13 the faith; be men of courage; be s.
2Co 12:10 For when I am weak, then I am s.
13: 9 whenever we are weak but you are s;
Eph 6:10 Finally, be s in the Lord and in his
1Th 2: 2 his gospel in spite of s opposition.
2Ti 2: 1 You then, my son, be s in the grace
Jas 3: 4 so large and are driven by s winds,
1Pe 5:10 and make you s, firm and steadfast.
1Jn 2:14 young men, because you are s, and
Rev 6:13 a fig-tree when shaken by a s wind.
12: 8 he was not s enough, and they lost

Strong and courageous

Dt 31: 6 Be s. Do not be afraid or terrified
31: 7 "Be s, for you must go with this
31:23 "Be s, for you will bring the
Jos 1: 6 "Be s, because you will lead these
1: 9 Have I not commanded you? Be s.
1:18 will be put to death. Only be s!"
10:25 Be s. This is what the LORD will do
1Ch 22:13 Be s. Do not be afraid or
28:20 his son, "Be s, and do the work.
2Ch 32: 7 "Be s. Do not be afraid or

Stronger (Strong)

Ge 25:23 one people will be s than the other,
30:41 Whenever the s females were in heat,
Nu 13:31 they are s than we are."
14:12 a nation greater and s than they."
Dt 1:28 They say, 'The people are s and
4:38 nations greater and s than you and
7: 1 nations larger and s than you—
7:17 "These nations are s than we are.
9: 1 nations greater and s than you,
9:14 s and more numerous than they."
11:23 nations larger and s than you.
Jos 17:13 However, when the Israelites grew s,
Jdg 4:24 the hand of the Israelites grew s
Jdg 4:24 grew s and s against Jabin,
14:18 What is s than a lion?"
2Sa 1:23 than eagles, they were s than lions.
3: 1 David grew s and s, while the house
13:14 he was s than she, he raped her.
1Ki 16:22 Omri's followers proved s than those
20:23 surely we will be s than they.
20:25 Then surely we will be s than they."
Job 17: 9 those with clean hands will grow s.
Ecc 6:10 contend with one who is s than he.
Jer 31:11 from the hand of those s than they.
Da 11: 5 will become even s than he and will
Lk 11:22 someone s attacks and overpowers
1Co 1:25 of God is s than man's strength.
10:22 Lord's jealousy? Are we s than he?
2Pe 2:11 yet even angels, although they are s

Strongest (Strong)

2Sa 11:16 where he knew the s defenders were.
1Ch 5: 2 though Judah was the s of his
Da 3:20 commanded some of the s soldiers in

Stronghold (Strongholds)

Jdg 9:46 the s of the temple of El-Berith.
9:49 They piled them against the s and
1Sa 22: 4 him as long as David was in the s.
22: 5 to David, "Do not stay in the s.
24:22 David and his men went up to the s.
2Sa 5:17 about it and went down to the s.
22: 3 He is my s, my refuge and my saviour
23:14 At that time David was in the s, and
1Ch 11:16 At that time David was in the s, and
12: 8 to David at his s in the desert.
12:16 Judah also came to David in his s.
Job 39:28 a rocky crag is his s.
Ps 9: 9 oppressed, a s in times of trouble.
18: 2 and the horn of my salvation, my s.
27: 1 The LORD is the s of my life—of
37:39 he is their s in time of trouble.
43: 2 You are God my s. Why have you
52: 7 who did not make God his s but
144: 2 my s and my deliverer, my shield, in
Pr 21:22 pulls down the s in which they trust.
Isa 25: 2 the foreigners' s a city no more;
31: 9 Their s will fall because of terror;
Jer 48: 1 s will be disgraced and shattered.
51:53 the sky and fortifies her lofty s,
Eze 24:21 s in which you take pride,
24:25 on the day I take away their s,
30:15 wrath on Pelusium, the s of Egypt,
Joel 3:16 a s for the people of Israel.
Am 5: 9 he flashes destruction on the s and
Mic 4: 8 O s of the Daughter of Zion,
Zec 9: 3 Tyre has built herself a s; she has

Strongholds (Stronghold)

Jdg 6: 2 in mountain clefts, caves and s.
1Sa 23:14 David stayed in the desert s and in
23:19 hiding among us in the s at Horesh,
23:29 there and lived in the s of En Gedi.
2Sa 22:46 they come trembling from their s.
Ps 18:45 they come trembling from their s.
89:40 walls and reduced his s to ruins.
Isa 13:22 Hyenas will howl in her s, jackals
34:13 nettles and brambles her s.
Jer 48:41 will be captured and the s taken.
51:30 they remain in their s.
Lam 2: 2 down the s of the Daughter of Judah.
2: 5 all her palaces and destroyed her s.
Eze 19: 7 He broke down their s and devastated
33:27 in s and caves will die of a plague.
Am 3:11 he will pull down your s and
Mic 5:11 your land and tear down all your s.
Zep 3: 6 their s are demolished.
2Co 10: 4 have divine power to demolish s.

Struck (Strike)

Ge 19:11 they s the men who were at the door
Ex 7:20 and s the water of the Nile,
7:25 Seven days passed after the LORD s
8:17 staff and s the dust of the ground,
9:15 s you and your people with a plague
9:25 Throughout Egypt hail s everything
12:27 homes when he s down the Egyptians.
Ex 12:29 At midnight the LORD s down all the
17: 5 with which you s the Nile, and go.
21:19 the one who s the blow will not be
22: 2 in and is s so that he dies,
32:35 the LORD s the people with a plague
Nu 3:13 When I s down all the firstborn in
8:17 When I s down all the firstborn in
11:33 and he s them with a severe plague.
14:37 report about the land were s down
20:11 Moses raised his arm and s the rock
21:35 they s him down, together with his
24:10 He s his hands together and said to
31:16 that a plague s the LORD's people.
33: 4 whom the LORD had s down among them;
Dt 2:33 him over to us and we s him down,
3: 3 We s them down, leaving no survivors.
Jos 7: 5 and s them down on the slopes.
10:26 Joshua s and killed the kings and
11:17 s them down, putting them to death.
Jdg 1: 4 s down ten thousand men at Bezek.
3:29 At that time they s down about ten
3:31 who s down six hundred Philistines
5:26 She s Sisera, she crushed his head,
7:13 It s the tent with such force that
9:44 those in the fields and s them down.
12: 4 The Gileadites s them down because
14:19 s down thirty of their men,
15:15 it and s down a thousand men.
20:35 on that day the Israelites s down
20:45 Gidom and s down two thousand more.
1Sa 4: 8 are the gods who s the Eyptians
6: 4 has s both you and your rulers.
6: 9 that it was not his hand that s us
6:19 God s down some of the men of Beth
14:15 panic s the whole army—those in the
14:31 after the Israelites had s down the
17:35 I went after it, s it and rescued
17:35 it by its hair, s it and killed it.
17:49 s the Philistine on the forehead.
17:50 s down the Philistine and killed him.
19: 8 He s them with such force that they
22:18 Doeg the Edomite turned and s them
25:38 the LORD s Nabal and he died.
2Sa 1:15 So he s him down, and he died.
5:25 and he s down the Philistines all
6: 7 therefore God s him down and he died
8: 5 s down twenty-two thousand of them.
10:18 He also s down Shobach the commander
11:15 so that he will be s down and die."
12: 9 You s down Uriah the Hittite with
12:15 the LORD s the child that Uriah's
13:30 "Absalom has s down all the king's
14: 6 One s the other and killed him.
14: 7 'Hand over the one who s his brother
18:15 Absalom, s him and killed him.
21:12 after they s Saul down on Gilboa.)
21:17 s the Philistine down and killed him.
23:10 he stood his ground and s down the
23:12 He defended it and s the Philistines
23:20 He s down two of Moab's best men.
23:21 he s down a huge Egyptian.
1Ki 2:25 and he s down Adonijah and he died.
2:34 went up and s down Joab and killed
2:46 and s Shimei down and killed him.
11:15 had s down all the men in Edom.
15:27 and he s him down at Gibbethon, a
16:10 Zimri came in, s him down and killed
20:20 each one s down his opponent.
20:37 So the man s him and wounded him.
2Ki 2: 8 it up and s the water with it.
2:14 from him and s the water with it.
2:14 When he s the water, it divided to
6:18 So he s them with blindness, as
13:18 He s it three times and stopped.
13:19 "You should have s the ground five
1Ch 11:14 defended it and s the Philistines
11:22 He s down two of Moab's best men.
11:23 he s down an Egyptian who was seven
13:10 and he s him down because he had put
14:16 and they s down the Philistine army,
18: 5 s down twenty-two thousand of them.
18:12 Abishai son of Zeruiah s down
2Ch 13:20 And the LORD s him down and he died.
14:12 The LORD s down the Cushites before
25:16 to the king? Stop! Why be s down?"
Est 9: 5 The Jews s down all their enemies

Job 1:19 and s the four corners of the house.
19:21 pity, for the hand of God has s me.
Ps 60: T Joab returned and s down twelve
64: 7 suddenly they will be s down.
78:20 he s the rock, water gushed out, and
78:51 He s down all the firstborn of Egypt,
105:33 he s down their vines and fig-trees
105:36 he s down all the firstborn in their
135: 8 He s down the firstborn of Egypt,
135:10 He s down many nations and killed
136:10 to him who s down the firstborn of
136:17 who s down great kings,
Pr 6: 1 have s hands in pledge for another,
Isa 9:13 have not returned to him who s them,
10:20 longer rely on him who s them down
10:26 as when he s down Midian at the rock
14: 6 which in anger s down peoples with
14:29 that the rod that s you is broken;
27: 7 s her as he s down those who s her?
60:10 Though in anger I s you, in favour I
Jer 5: 3 You s them, but they felt no pain;
26:23 who had him s down with a sword and
30:14 I have s you as an enemy would and
41: 2 and s down Gedaliah son of Ahikam,
Da 2:34 It s the statue on its feet of iron
2:35 But the rock that s the statue
Am 4: 9 "Many times I s your gardens and
4: 9 I s them with blight and mildew.
Hag 2:17 I s all the work of your hands with
Zec 13: 8 "two-thirds will be s down and
Mt 26:51 drew it out and s the servant of the
26:67 they spat in his face and s him with
27:30 s him on the head again and again.
Mk 12: 4 they s this man on the head and
14:47 s the servant of the high priest,
14:65 s him with their fists, and said,
15:19 Again and again they s him on the
Lk 6:48 When the flood came, the torrent s
6:49 The moment the torrent s that house,
22:50 one of them s the servant of the
Jn 18:10 who had a sword, drew it and s the
18:22 officials near by s him in the face.
19: 3 And they s him in the face.
Ac 7:11 "Then a famine s all Egypt and
12: 7 He s Peter on the side and woke him
12:23 an angel of the Lord s him down, and
23: 3 the law by commanding that I be s!"
27:41 ship s a sand-bar and ran aground.
2Co 4: 9 s down, but not destroyed.
Rev 8:12 and a third of the sun was s, a
11:11 and terror s those who saw them.

Structure (Structures)
1Ki 6: 5 he built a s around the building,
1Ch 29: 1 because this palatial s is not for
29:19 s for which I have provided."
Ezr 5: 3 this temple and restore this s?"
5: 9 this temple and restore this s?"
Eze 1:16 This was the appearance and s of the
41: 7 The s surrounding the temple was

Structures (Structure)
1Ki 7: 9 All these s, from the outside to the

Struggle (Struggled, Struggles, Struggling)
Ge 30: 8 Rachel said, "I have had a great s
Jdg 12: 2 in a great s with the Ammonites,
Job 9:29 guilty, why should I s in vain?
41: 8 you will remember the s and never
Ro 15:30 me in my s by praying to God for me.
Eph 6:12 For our s is not against flesh and
Php 1:30 through the same s you saw I had,
Heb 12: 4 In your s against sin, you have not

Struggled (Struggle)
Ge 32:28 because you have s with God and
Hos 12: 3 as a man he s with God.
12: 4 He s with the angel and overcame him;

Struggles (Struggle)
Ps 73: 4 They have no s; their bodies are

Struggling (Struggle)
Col 1:29 To this end I labour, s with all his
2: 1 I want you to know how much I am s

Strum
Am 6: 5 You s away on your harps like David

Strung (String)
Isa 5:28 are sharp, all their bows are s;
Lam 2: 4 Like an enemy he has s his bow;

Strut (Strutting)
Ps 12: 8 The wicked freely s about when what

Strutting (Strut)
Pr 30:31 a s cock, a he-goat, and a king with

Stubble
Ex 5:12 Egypt to gather s to use for straw.
15: 7 it consumed them like s.
Isa 47:14 Surely they are like s; the fire
Joel 2: 5 like a crackling fire consuming s,
Ob :18 the house of Esau will be s,
Na 1:10 they will be consumed like dry s.
Mal 4: 1 and every evildoer will be s,

Stubborn (Stubborn-hearted, Stubbornly, Stubbornness)
Lev 26:19 I will break down your s pride and
Dt 2:30 LORD your God had made his spirit s
21:18 If a man has a s and rebellious son
21:20 This son of ours is s and rebellious.
Jdg 2:19 up their evil practices and s ways.
Ps 78: 8 a s and rebellious generation,
81:12 I gave them over to their s hearts
Isa 48: 4 For I knew how s you were;
Jer 5:23 these people have s and rebellious
7:24 s inclinations of their evil hearts.
Eze 2: 4 I am sending you are obstinate and s.
Hos 4:16 Israelites are s, like a s heifer.
Mk 3: 5 deeply distressed at their s hearts,
16:14 their s refusal to believe those who

Stubborn-hearted (Heart, Stubborn)
Isa 46:12 Listen to me, you s, you who are far

Stubbornly (Stubborn)
Ex 13:15 Pharaoh s refused to let us go, the
Ne 9:29 S they turned their backs on you,
Zec 7:11 s they turned their backs and

Stubbornness (Stubborn)
Dt 9:27 Overlook the s of this people, their
Jer 3:17 follow the s of their evil hearts.
9:14 Instead, they have followed the s of
11: 8 followed the s of their evil hearts.
13:10 who follow the s of their hearts and
16:12 following the s of his evil heart
18:12 will follow the s of his evil heart.
23:17 who follow the s of their hearts
Ro 2: 5 of your s and your unrepentant heart,

Stubs
Isa 7: 4 these two smouldering s of firewood

Stuck (Stick[2])
1Sa 26: 7 spear s in the ground near his head.
Job 29:10 s to the roof of their mouths.
Ac 27:41 The bow s fast and would not move,

Studded
SS 1:11 ear-rings of gold, s with silver.

Student
1Ch 25: 8 teacher as well as s, cast lots for
Mt 10:24 "A s is not above his teacher, nor a
10:25 is enough for the s to be like his
Lk 6:40 A s is not above his teacher, but

Studied (Study)
Jn 7:15 get such learning without having s?"

Study (Studied)
Ezr 7:10 For Ezra had devoted himself to the s
Ecc 1:13 I devoted myself to s and to explore
12:12 no end, and much s wearies the body.
Jn 5:39 You diligently s the Scriptures

Stumble (Stumbled, Stumbles, Stumbling, Stumbling-block, Stumbling-blocks, Stumbling-stone)
Lev 26:37 They will s over one another as
Ps 9: 3 they s and perish before you.
27: 2 attack me, they will s and fall.
37:24 though he s, he will not fall, for
119:165 law, and nothing can make them s.
Pr 3:23 in safety, and your foot will not s;
4:12 when you run, you will not s.
4:19 they do not know what makes them s.
Isa 8:14 a stone that causes men to s and a
8:15 Many of them will s; they will fall
28: 7 they s when rendering decisions.
31: 3 he who helps will s, he who is
40:30 and weary, and young men s and fall;
59:10 At midday we s as if it were
63:13 in open country, they did not s;
Jer 6:21 Fathers and sons alike will s over
12: 5 If you s in safe country,
13:16 your feet s on the darkening hills.
18:15 which made them s in their ways and
20:11 persecutors will s and not prevail.
31: 9 a level path where they will not s,
46: 6 the River Euphrates they s and fall.
46:12 One warrior will s over another;
46:16 They will s repeatedly; they will
50:32 The arrogant one will s and fall and
Eze 7:19 it, for it has made them s into sin.
Da 11:19 will s and fall, to be seen no more.
11:35 Some of the wise will s, so that
Hos 4: 5 You s day and night, and the
4: 5 night, and the prophets s with you.
5: 5 even Ephraim, s in their sin;
14: 9 them, but the rebellious s in them.
Na 2: 5 troops, yet they s on their way.
Mal 2: 8 your teaching have caused many to s;
Jn 11: 9 A man who walks by day will not s,
Ro 9:33 a stone that causes men to s and a
11:11 Again I ask: Did they s so as to
14:20 that causes someone else to s.
1Co 10:32 Do not cause anyone to s, whether
Jas 3: 2 We all s in many ways. If anyone is
1Pe 2: 8 "A stone that causes men to s
2: 8 They s because they disobey the
1Jn 2:10 is nothing in him to make him s.

Stumbled (Stumble)
1Sa 2: 4 those who s are armed with strength.
2Sa 6: 6 the ark of God, because the oxen s.
1Ch 13: 9 steady the ark, because the oxen s.
Job 4: 4 Your words have supported those who s
Ps 35:15 But when I s, they gathered in glee;
107:12 s, and there was no-one to help.
Isa 59:14 truth has s in the streets,
Ro 9:32 They s over the "stumbling-stone".

Stumbles (Stumble)
Pr 24:17 he s, do not let your heart rejoice,
Isa 5:27 Not one of them grows tired or s,
Hos 5: 5 Judah also s with them.
Jn 11:10 is when he walks by night that he s,
Jas 2:10 yet s at just one point is guilty of

Stumbling (Stumble)
Ps 56:13 me from death and my feet from s,
116: 8 my eyes from tears, my feet from s,
Na 3: 3 number, people s over the corpses—

Stumbling-block (Stumble)
Lev 19:14 or put a s in front of the blind,
Eze 3:20 I put a s before him, he will die.
14: 4 puts a wicked s before his face and
14: 7 puts a wicked s before his face and
Mt 16:23 You are a s to me; you do not have
Ro 11: 9 a s and a retribution for them.
14:13 s or obstacle in your brother's way.
1Co 1:23 we preach Christ crucified: a s to

1Co 8: 9 does not become a s to the weak.
2Co 6: 3 We put no s in anyone's path, so

Stumbling-blocks (Stumble)
Eze 14: 3 and put wicked s before their faces.

Stumbling-stone (Stone, Stumble)
Ro 9:32 They stumbled over the "s".

Stump (Stumps)
Job 14: 8 ground and its s die in the soil,
Isa 6:13 seed will be the s in the land."
11: 1 A shoot will come up from the s of
Da 4:15 let the s and its roots, bound with
4:23 but leave the s, bound with iron and
4:26 The command to leave the s of the

Stumps (Stump)
Isa 6:13 leave s when they are cut down,

Stunned
Ge 45:26 Jacob was s; he did not believe them.
Isa 29: 9 Be s and amazed, blind yourselves

Stunted
Lev 22:23 ox or a sheep that is deformed or s,

Stupid (Stupidity)
Job 18: 3 and considered s in your sight?
Pr 12: 1 but he who hates correction is s.
Ecc 10: 3 and shows everyone how s he is.
2Ti 2:23 to do with foolish and s arguments,

Stupidity (Stupid)
Ecc 7:25 to understand the s of wickedness

Stupor
Ps 78:65 as a man wakes from the s of wine.
Ro 11: 8 "God gave them a spirit of s, eyes

Sturdiest (Sturdy)
Ps 78:31 he put to death the s among them,

Sturdy (Sturdiest)
Isa 10:16 wasting disease upon his s warriors;

Suah
1Ch 7:36 The sons of Zophah: S, Harnepher,

Sub-division (Divide, Sub-divisions)
2Ch 35: 5 for each s of the families of your

Sub-divisions (Divide, Sub-division)
2Ch 35:12 give them to the s of the families

Subdue (Subdued, Subdues, Subduing)
Ge 1:28 in number; fill the earth and s it.
Nu 24:24 they will s Asshur and Eber,
Dt 9: 3 He will destroy them; he will s them
Jdg 16: 5 so that we may tie him up and s him.
16:19 of his hair, and so began to s him.
1Ch 17:10 I will also s all your enemies.
Ps 81:14 how quickly would I s their enemies
Isa 45: 1 hold of to s nations before him
Da 7:24 earlier ones; he will s three kings.
Mk 5: 4 No-one was strong enough to s him.

Subdued (Subdue)
Nu 32: 4 the land the LORD s before the
32:22 the land is s before the LORD, you
32:29 then when the land is s before you,
Jos 10:40 Joshua s the whole region, including
10:41 Joshua s them from Kadesh Barnea to
Jdg 4:23 On that day God s Jabin, the
8:28 Thus Midian was s before the
11:33 Thus Israel s Ammon.
16: 6 and how you can be tied up and s."
1Sa 7:13 the Philistines were s and did not
2Sa 8: 1 defeated the Philistines and s them,
8:11 gold from all the nations he had s:
1Ch 18: 1 defeated the Philistines and s them,
2Ch 13:18 The men of Israel were s on that
Ne 9:24 You s before them the Canaanites,
Ps 47: 3 He s nations under us, peoples under
Isa 10:13 like a mighty one I s their kings.
14: 6 s nations with relentless aggression.
Zec 10:11 the surging sea will be s and all

Subdues (Subdue)
Ps 18:47 avenges me, who s nations under me,
144: 2 take refuge, who s peoples under me.
Isa 41: 2 over to him and s kings before him.

Subduing (Subdue)
Job 41: 9 Any hope of s him is false; the mere

Subject (Subjected, Subjecting, Subjects)
Ge 14: 4 For twelve years they had been s to
Dt 20:11 all the people in it shall be s to
Jdg 1:30 they did s them to forced labour.
3: 8 Israelites were s for eight years.
3:14 The Israelites were s to Eglon king
3:30 That day Moab was made s to Israel,
9:28 Shechem, that we should be s to him?
9:38 that we should be s to him?'
1Sa 4: 9 or you will be s to the Hebrews, as
11: 1 with us, and we will be s to you."
2Sa 8: 2 s to David and brought tribute.
8: 6 became s to him and brought tribute.
8:14 all the Edomites became s to David.
10:19 the Israelites and became s to them.
22:44 People I did not know are s to me,
1Ch 18: 2 became s to him and brought tribute.
18: 6 became s to him and brought tribute.
18:13 all the Edomites became s to David.
19:19 with David and became s to him.
22:18 is s to the LORD and to his people.
2Ch 12: 8 They will, however, become s to him,
Ne 5: 5 s our sons and daughters to slavery.
Ps 18:43 people I did not know are s to me.
89:22 No enemy will s him to tribute;
Isa 11:14 and the Ammonites will be s to them.
Jer 27: 6 make even the wild animals s to him.
Mt 5:21 who murders will be s to judgment.'
5:22 his brother will be s to judgment.
9:20 Just then a woman who had been s to
Mk 5:25 a woman was there who had been s to
Lk 8:43 a woman was there who had been s to
Ac 17:32 We want to hear you again on this s."
1Co 2:15 is not s to any man's judgment:
14:32 The spirits of prophets are s to the
15:28 then the Son himself will be made s
Gal 4: 2 He is s to guardians and trustees
Tit 2: 5 and to be s to their husbands,
2: 9 Teach slaves to be s to their
3: 1 Remind the people to be s to rulers
Heb 2: 8 left nothing that is not s to him.
2: 8 we do not see everything s to him.
5: 2 since he himself is s to weakness.

Subjected (Subject)
Jos 17:13 they s the Canaanites to forced
Ezr 9: 7 been s to the sword and captivity,
Ps 106:42 them and s them to their power.
107:12 he s them to bitter labour;
Ro 8:20 the creation was s to frustrations,
8:20 will of the one who s it, in
Heb 2: 5 that he has s the world to come,

Subjecting (Subject)
Heb 6: 6 again and s him to public disgrace.

Subjects (Subject)
1Sa 17: 9 and kill me, we will become your s;
17: 9 you will become our s and serve us."
1Ki 4:21 and were Solomon's s all his life.
1Ch 21: 3 are they not all my lord's s?
Pr 14:28 but without s a prince is ruined.
Mt 8:12 the s of the kingdom will be thrown
Lk 19:14 "But his s hated him and sent a

Subjugate (Subjugated)
Jer 27: 7 nations and great kings will s him.

Subjugated (Subjugate)
1Ch 20: 4 and the Philistines were s.

Submission (Submit)
1Ch 29:24 pledged their s to King Solomon.
Da 11:43 with the Libyans and Nubians in s.
1Co 14:34 but must be in s, as the Law says.
1Ti 2:11 learn in quietness and full s.
Heb 5: 7 was heard because of his reverent s.
1Pe 3:22 authorities and powers in s to him.

Submissive (Submit)
Jas 3:17 considerate, s, full of mercy and
1Pe 3: 1 Wives, in the same way be s to your
3: 5 They were s to their own husbands,
5: 5 Young men, in the same way be s to

Submit (Submission, Submissive, Submits, Submitted)
Ge 16: 9 back to your mistress and s to her."
41:40 my people are to s to your orders.
49:15 the burden and s to forced labour.
2Ch 30: 8 as your fathers were; s to the LORD.
Job 22:21 "S to God and be at peace with him;
Ps 68:31 Cush will s herself to God.
81:11 Israel would not s to me.
Lk 10:17 the demons s to us in your name."
10:20 do not rejoice that the spirits s to
Ro 8: 7 It does not s to God's law, nor can
10: 3 did not s to God's righteousness.
13: 1 Everyone must s himself to the
13: 5 necessary to s to the authorities,
1Co 16:16 to s to such as these and to
Eph 5:21 S to one another out of reverence
5:22 Wives, s to your husbands as to the
5:24 s to their husbands in everything.
Col 2:20 to it, do you s to its rules:
3:18 Wives, s to your husbands, as is
Heb 12: 9 How much more should we s to the
13:17 Obey your leaders and s to their
Jas 4: 7 S yourselves, then, to God.
1Pe 2:13 S yourselves for the Lord's sake to
2:18 Slaves, s yourselves to your masters

Submits (Submit)
Eph 5:24 Now as the church s to Christ, so

Submitted (Submit)
Lam 5: 6 We s to Egypt and Assyria to get

Subordinates
1Ki 11:11 you and give it to one of your s.

Subside (Subsided, Subsides)
Eze 5:13 my wrath against them will s, and I
16:42 my wrath against you will s and my
21:17 hands together, and my wrath will s.

Subsided (Subside)
Jdg 8: 3 their resentment against him s.
Est 2: 1 when the anger of King Xerxes had s,
7:10 Then the king's fury s.
Eze 24:13 until my wrath against you has s.
Lk 8:24 the storm s, and all was calm.

Subsides (Subside)
Ge 27:44 a while until your brother's fury s.

Substance
Da 7: 1 He wrote down the s of his dream.

Substitute (Substitution)
Lev 27:10 He must not exchange it or s a good
27:10 he should s one animal for another,
27:10 both it and the s become holy.
27:33 the animal and its s become holy

Substitution (Substitute)
Lev 27:33 the good from the bad or make any s.
27:33 If he does make a s, both the animal

Subtract
Dt 4: 2 I command you and do not s from it,

Subverting
Lk 23: 2 have found this man s our nation.

Sucathites
1Ch 2:55 the Tirathites, Shimeathites and S.

Succeed (Succeeded, Succeeds, Success, Successful, Successive, Successor, Successors)
Lev 6:22 The son who is to s him as anointed
16:32 ordained to s his father as high
Nu 14:41 the LORD's command? This will not s!
1Sa 30: 8 overtake them and s in the rescue."
2Sa 7:12 I will raise up your offspring to s
1Ki 5: 1 anointed king to s his father David,
15: 4 by raising up a son to s him and by
19:16 Abel Meholah to s you as prophet.
22:22 "'You will s in enticing him,' said
2Ki 3:27 who was to s him as king, and
1Ch 17:11 I will raise up your offspring to s
2Ch 13:12 your fathers, for you will not s."
18:21 "'You will s in enticing him,' said
Job 30:13 they s in destroying me—without
Ps 20: 4 heart and make all your plans s.
21:11 wicked schemes, they cannot s;
37: 7 not fret when men s in their ways,
140: 8 do not let their plans s, or they
Pr 15:22 but with many advisers they s.
16: 3 you do, and your plans will s.
21:30 no plan that can s against the LORD.
Ecc 11: 6 for you do not know which will s,
Isa 47:12 Perhaps you will s, perhaps you
48:15 him, and he will s in his mission.
Jer 32: 5 the Babylonians, you will not s.
Eze 17:15 Will he s? Will he who does such
Da 8:24 and will s in whatever he does.
11:17 his plans will not s or help him.

Succeeded (Succeed)
Ge 36:33 of Zerah from Bozrah s him as king.
36:34 land of the Temanites s him as king.
36:35 the country of Moab, s him as king.
36:36 Samlah from Masrekah s him as king.
36:37 Rehoboth on the river s him as king.
36:38 Baal-Hanan son of Acbor s him as king
36:39 of Acbor died, Hadad s him as king.
Dt 10: 6 and Eleazar his son s him as priest.
2Sa 10: 1 and his son Hanun s him as king.
1Ki 8:20 I have s David my father and now I
11:43 And Rehoboam his son s him as king.
14:20 And Nadab his son s him as king.
14:31 And Abijah his son s him as king.
15: 8 And Asa his son s him as king.
15:24 Jehoshaphat his son s him as king.
15:28 Asa king of Judah and s him as king.
16: 6 And Elah his son s him as king.
16:10 Then he s him as king.
16:28 And Ahab his son s him as king.
22:40 And Ahaziah his son s him as king.
22:50 And Jehoram his son s him.
2Ki 1:17 had no son, Joram s him as king
8:15 Then Hazael s him as king.
8:24 And Ahaziah his son s him as king.
10:35 And Jehoahaz his son s him as king.
12:21 And Amaziah his son s him as king.
13: 9 And Jehoash his son s him as king.
13:13 and Jeroboam s him on the throne.
13:24 and Ben-Hadad his son s him as king.
14:16 And Jeroboam his son s him as king.
14:29 And Zechariah his son s him as king.
15: 7 And Jotham his son s him as king.
15:10 assassinated him and s him as king.
15:14 assassinated him and s him as king.
15:22 And Pekahiah his son s him as king.
15:25 killed Pekahiah and s him as king.
15:30 and then s him as king in the
15:38 And Ahaz his son s him as king.
2Ki 16:20 And Hezekiah his son s him as king.
19:37 And Esarhaddon his son s him as king.
20:21 And Manasseh his son s him as king.
21:18 And Amon his son s him as king.
21:26 And Josiah his son s him as king.
24: 6 And Jehoiachin his son s him as king.
1Ch 1:44 of Zerah from Bozrah s him as king.
1:45 land of the Temanites s him as king.
1:46 the country of Moab, s him as king.
1:47 Samlah from Masrekah s him as king.
1:48 Rehoboth on the river s him as king.
1:49 Baal-Hanan son of Acbor s him as king
1:50 Baal-Hanan died, Hadad s him as king.
19: 1 died, and his son s him as king.
27:34 Ahithophel was s by Jehoiada son of
29:28 His son Solomon s him as king.
2Ch 6:10 I have s David my father and now I
7:11 and had s in carrying out all he had
9:31 And Rehoboam his son s him as king.
12:16 And Abijah his son s him as king.
14: 1 Asa his son s him as king, and in
17: 1 Jehoshaphat his son s him as king
21: 1 And Jehoram his son s him as king.
24:27 And Amaziah his son s him as king.
26:23 And Jotham his son s him as king.
27: 9 And Ahaz his son s him as king.
28:27 And Hezekiah his son s him as king.
32:30 He s in everything he undertook.
32:33 And Manasseh his son s him as king.
33:20 And Amon his son s him as king.
36: 8 And Jehoiachin his son s him as king.
Isa 37:38 And Esarhaddon his son s him as king.
Jer 22:11 who s his father as king of Judah
Da 11:21 "He will be s by a contemptible
Ac 24:27 Felix was s by Porcius Festus, but

Succeeds (Succeed)
Ex 29:30 The son who s him as priest and
Pr 17: 8 wherever he turns, he s.

Success (Succeed)
Ge 24:12 give me s today, and show kindness
24:40 with you and make your journey a s,
24:42 please grant s to the journey on
24:56 LORD has granted s to my journey.
27:20 LORD your God gave me s," he replied.
39: 3 LORD gave him s in everything he did,
39:23 and gave him s in whatever he did.
1Sa 18:14 In everything he did he had great s,
18:30 David met with more s than the rest
25:31 the LORD has brought my master s,
1Ki 22:13 are predicting s for the king.
1Ch 12:18 S, s to you, and s to those who
22:11 and may you have s and build the
22:13 you will have s if you are careful
2Ch 18:12 are predicting s for the king.
26: 5 he sought the LORD, God gave him s.
Ne 1:11 Give your servant s today by
2:20 "The God of heaven will give us s.
Job 5:12 so that their hands achieve no s.
6:13 now that s has been driven from me?
Ps 118:25 O LORD, save us; O LORD, grant us s.
Ecc 10:10 is needed but skill will bring s.
Da 11:14 of the vision, but without s.

Successful (Succeed)
Ge 24:21 not the LORD had made his journey s.
Jos 1: 7 that you may be s wherever you go.
1: 8 Then you will be prosperous and s.
Jdg 18: 5 whether our journey will be s."
1Sa 18:15 Saul saw how s he was, he was afraid
2Ki 18: 7 he was s in whatever he undertook.
2Ch 20:20 in his prophets and you will be s."
Da 11:36 He will be s until the time of wrath

Successive (Succeed)
2Sa 21: 1 there was a famine for three s years;
Eze 41: 7 temple were wider at each s level.

Successor (Succeed)
1Ki 1:48 eyes to see a s on my throne today.
1Ch 27: 7 of Joab; his son Zebadiah was his s.
Ecc 2:12 What more can the king's s do
4:15 followed the youth, the king's s.
Ecc 4:16 later were not pleased with the s.
Da 11:20 "His s will send out a tax collector

Successors (Succeed)
1Ch 3:16 The s of Jehoiakim: Jehoiachin his

Succoth
1. Town east of the Jordan in territory of Gad (Jos 13:27), where Jacob stayed after reconciliation with Esau (Ge 33:16–17). Gideon punished its inhabitants for not helping his troops when they pursued the Midianites (Jdg 8:5–16). Solomon had foundries in this valley (1Ki 7:46; 2Ch 4:17). The Psalmist mentions it to emphasise God's sovereignty (Ps 60:6; 108:7). Exact location unknown. **2.** Region where the Israelites first encamped having left Egypt (Ex 12:37; 13:20; Nu 33:5–6). Located in the north-east of the Egyptian delta, close to Rameses.

Ge 33:17 Jacob, however, went to S, where he
33:17 That is why the place is called S.
Ex 12:37 journeyed from Rameses to S.
13:20 After leaving S they camped at Etham
Nu 33: 5 left Rameses and camped at S.
33: 6 They left S and camped at Etham, on
Jos 13:27 Beth Haram, Beth Nimrah, S and
Jdg 8: 5 He said to the men of S, "Give my
8: 6 the officials of S said, "Do you
8: 8 they answered as the men of S had.
8:14 He caught a young man of S and
8:14 the seventy-seven officials of S,
8:15 Gideon came and said to the men of S,
8:16 taught the men of S a lesson by
1Ki 7:46 the Jordan between S and Zarethan.
2Ch 4:17 the Jordan between S and Zarethan.
Ps 60: 6 and measure off the Valley of S.
108: 7 and measure off the Valley of S.

Succoth Benoth
2Ki 17:30 The men from Babylon made S, the men

Suck (Suckling)
Job 20:16 He will s the poison of serpents;

Suckling (Suck)
1Sa 7: 9 Samuel took a s lamb and offered it

Sudden (Suddenly)
Lev 26:16 you: I will bring upon you s terror,
Dt 28:20 come to s ruin because of the evil
Jdg 20:37 in ambush made a s dash into Gibeah,
Job 9:23 a scourge brings s death, he mocks
22:10 you, why s peril terrifies you,
Ps 6:10 they will turn back in s disgrace.
Pr 3:25 Have no fear of s disaster or of the
24:22 those two will send s destruction
Isa 17:14 In the evening, s terror! Before the
Zep 1:18 s end of all who live in the earth."
Jn 19:34 a s flow of blood and water.

Suddenly (Sudden)
Ge 37: 7 s my sheaf rose and stood upright,
Nu 6: 9 "'If someone dies s in his presence,
16:42 s the cloud covered it and the glory
35:22 hostility someone s pushes another
Jos 11: 7 his whole army came against them s
Jdg 14: 5 s a young lion came roaring towards
2Ki 2:11 s a chariot of fire and horses of
13:21 s they saw a band of raiders;
Job 1:19 s a mighty wind swept in from the
5: 3 root, but s his house was cursed.
Ps 64: 4 they shoot at him s, without fear.
64: 7 s they will be struck down.
73:19 How s are they destroyed, completely
Pr 6:15 will s be destroyed—without remedy.
28:18 whose ways are perverse will s fall.
29: 1 will s be destroyed—without remedy.
Isa 29: 5 S, in an instant,
30:13 that collapses s, in an instant.
47:11 cannot foresee will s come upon you.
48: 3 s I acted, and they came to pass.
Jer 6:26 s the destroyer will come upon us.
15: 8 s I will bring down on them anguish
18:22 you s bring invaders against them,

Jer 51: 8 Babylon will s fall and be broken.
Da 5: 5 S the fingers of a human hand
8: 5 s a goat with a prominent horn
Hab 2: 7 Will not your debtors s arise?
Mal 3: 1 Then s the Lord you are seeking will
Mt 28: 9 S Jesus met them. "Greetings," he
Mk 9: 8 S, when they looked round, they no
13:36 If he comes s, do not let him find
Lk 2:13 S a great company of the heavenly
9:39 A spirit seizes him and he s screams;
24: 4 s two men in clothes that gleamed
Ac 1:10 when s two men dressed in white
2: 2 S a sound like the blowing of a
8:39 the Spirit of the Lord s took Philip
9: 3 s a light from heaven flashed
10:30 S a man in shining clothes stood
12: 7 S an angel of the Lord appeared and
12:10 of one street, s the angel left him.
16:26 S there was such a violent
22: 6 s a bright light from heaven flashed
28: 6 him to swell up or s fall dead,
1Th 5: 3 destruction will come on them s, as

Sue
Mt 5:40 if someone wants to s you and take

Suffer (Long-suffering, Suffered, Suffering, Sufferings, Suffers)
Ge 4:15 will s vengeance seven times over.
Nu 14:34 the land—you will s for your sins
Dt 26: 6 ill-treated us and made us s,
Ezr 4:13 paid, and the royal revenues will s.
Job 24:11 tread the winepresses, yet s thirst.
36:15 those who s he delivers in their
Ps 42:10 My bones s mortal agony as my foes
Pr 9:12 you are a mocker, you alone will s."
11:15 security for another will surely s,
22: 3 the simple keep going and s for it.
27:12 the simple keep going and s for it.
Isa 47: 8 a widow or s the loss of children.'
53:10 to crush him and cause him to s,
54: 4 not be afraid; you will not s shame
Jer 14:13 will not see the sword or s famine.
15:15 of how I s reproach for your sake.
Eze 23:49 You will s the penalty for your
36: 7 around you will also s scorn.
36:15 and no longer will you s the scorn
36:30 that you will no longer s disgrace
Da 6: 2 so that the king might not s loss.
Mt 16:21 s many things at the hands of the
17:12 Man is going to s at their hands."
Mk 8:31 the Son of Man must s many things
9:12 the Son of Man must s much and be
Lk 9:22 "The Son of Man must s many things
17:25 first he must s many things and be
22:15 this Passover with you before I s.
24:26 Did not the Christ have to s these
24:46 The Christ will s and rise from the
Ac 3:18 saying that his Christ would s.
9:16 I will show him how much he must s
17: 3 had to s and rise from the dead.
26:23 that the Christ would s and, as the
1Co 3:15 If it is burned up, he will s loss;
2Co 1: 6 of the same sufferings we s.
Php 1:29 on him, but also to s for him,
1Th 5: 9 God did not appoint us to s wrath
Heb 9:26 Christ would have had to s many
1Pe 1: 6 to s grief in all kinds of trials.
2:20 s for doing good and you endure it,
3:14 even if you should s for what is
3:17 is better, if it is God's will, to s
4:15 If you s, it should not be as a
4:16 However, if you s as a Christian, do
4:19 those who s according to God's will
Jude : 7 s the punishment of eternal fire.
Rev 2:10 afraid of what you are about to s.
2:10 you will s persecution for ten days.
2:22 adultery with her s intensely,

Suffered (Suffer)
1Sa 4:17 and the army has s heavy losses.
Ps 88:15 s your terrors and am in despair.
107:17 s affliction because of their
119:107 I have s much; preserve my life,
Isa 38:17 Surely it was for my benefit that I s
Jer 14:17 s a grievous wound, a crushing blow.
44:17 and were well off and s no harm.
Lam 3:47 We have s terror and pitfalls, ruin
Eze 36: 6 you have s the scorn of the nations.
Mt 27:19 for I have s a great deal today in a
Mk 5:26 She had s a great deal under the
Lk 13: 2 Galileans because they s this way?
Ac 28: 5 into the fire and s no ill effects.
2Co 1: 8 we s in the province of Asia.
Gal 3: 4 Have you s so much for nothing—if
Col 1:24 Now I rejoice in what was s for you,
1Th 2: 2 We had previously s and been
2:14 You s from your own countrymen the
2:14 those churches s from the Jews,
Heb 2: 9 glory and honour because he s death,
2:18 he himself s when he was tempted, he
5: 8 he learned obedience from what he s
13:12 Jesus also s outside the city gate
1Pe 2:21 because Christ s for you, leaving
2:23 when he s, he made no threats.
4: 1 Therefore, since Christ s in his
4: 1 has s in his body is done with sin.
5:10 after you have s a little while,
Rev 9: 5 And the agony they s was like that

Suffering (Suffer)
Ge 16: 5 responsible for the wrong I am s.
41:52 me fruitful in the land of my s."
Ex 3: 7 and I am concerned about their s.
Nu 5:24 will enter her and cause bitter s.
5:27 will go into her and cause bitter s;
14:33 s for your unfaithfulness, until the
Dt 28:53 of the s that your enemy will
28:55 of the s that your enemy will
2Ki 13:14 Now Elisha was s from the illness
14:26 whether slave or free, was s;
Ne 9: 9 "You saw the s of our forefathers in
Job 2:13 they saw how great his s was.
30:16 my life ebbs away; days of s grip me.
30:27 never stops; days of s confront me.
36:15 who suffer he delivers in their s;
Ps 22:24 the s of the afflicted one;
55: 3 for they bring down s upon me and
107:10 gloom, prisoners s in iron chains,
119:50 My comfort in my s is this: Your
119:153 Look upon my s and deliver me, for I
Isa 14: 3 s and turmoil and cruel bondage,
53: 3 man of sorrows, and familiar with s.
53:11 After the s of his soul, he will see
Lam 1:12 Is any s like my s that was
1:18 all you peoples; look upon my s.
Joel 1:18 even the flocks of sheep are s.
Mt 4:24 diseases, those s severe pain, the
8: 6 home paralysed and in terrible s."
15:22 s terribly from demon-possession."
17:15 "He has seizures and is s greatly.
Mk 5:29 body that she was freed from her s.
5:34 in peace and be freed from your s."
Lk 4:38 Now Simon's mother-in-law was s from
14: 2 front of him was a man s from dropsy
Ac 1: 3 After his s, he showed himself to
5:41 worthy of s disgrace for the Name.
7:11 bringing great s, and our fathers
28: 8 His father was sick in bed, s from
Ro 5: 3 know that s produces perseverance;
1Th 1: 6 in spite of severe s, you welcomed
2Th 1: 5 kingdom of God, for which you are s.
2Ti 1: 8 But join with me in s for the gospel,
1:12 That is why I am s as I am. Yet I am
2: 9 for which I am s even to the point
Heb 2:10 their salvation perfect through s.
10:32 in a great contest in the face of s.
13: 3 as if you yourselves were s.
Jas 5:10 of patience in the face of s,
1Pe 2:19 the pain of unjust s because he is
4:12 at the painful trial you are s,
Rev 1: 9 your brother and companion in the s
2:22 I will cast her on a bed of s, and I

Sufferings (Suffer)
Job 9:28 I still dread all my s, for I know
Ro 5: 3 but we also rejoice in our s,
8:17 if indeed we share in his s in order
8:18 I consider that our present s are
2Co 1: 5 For just as the s of Christ flow
1: 6 endurance of the same s we suffer.
1: 7 as you share in our s, so also you
Eph 3:13 my s for you, which are your glory.
Php 3:10 the fellowship of sharing in his s,
2Ti 3:11 persecutions, s—what kinds of
1Pe 1:11 when he predicted the s of Christ
4:13 you participate in the s of Christ,
5: 1 a witness of Christ's s and one who
5: 9 are undergoing the same kind of s.

Suffers (Suffer)
Job 15:20 All his days the wicked man s
Pr 13:20 but a companion of fools s harm.
1Co 12:26 If one part s, every part s with it;

Sufficient
Lev 25:26 and acquires s means to redeem it,
Isa 40:16 Lebanon is not s for altar fires,
2Co 2: 6 on him by the majority is s for him.
12: 9 "My grace is s for you, for my
Php 1:20 but will have s courage so that now

Suggest (Suggested, Suggestion)
Ru 4: 4 s that you buy it in the presence of

Suggested (Suggest)
1Ki 22:20 "One s this, and another that.
2Ch 18:19 "One s this, and another that.
Ezr 10: 5 under oath to do what had been s.
Est 2:15 who was in charge of the harem, s.
6:10 as you have s for Mordecai the Jew,

Suggestion (Suggest)
Est 5:14 This s delighted Haman, and he had

Suit
2Ti 4: 3 Instead, to s their own desires,

Suitable
Ge 2:18 I will make a helper s for him."
2:20 But for Adam no s helper was found.
Nu 32: 1 and Gilead were s for livestock.
32: 4 of Israel—are s for livestock,

Sukkites
2Ch 12: 3 S and Cushites that came with him

Sulking
1Ki 21: 4 lay on his bed s and refused to eat.

Sullen
1Ki 20:43 S and angry, the king of Israel went
21: 4 Ahab went home, s and angry because
21: 5 Why are you so s? Why won't you eat?"

Sulphur
Ge 19:24 the LORD rained down burning s on
Dt 29:23 of salt and s—nothing planted,
Job 18:15 burning s is scattered over his
Ps 11: 6 will rain fiery coals and burning s;
Isa 30:33 stream of burning s, sets it ablaze.
34: 9 into pitch, her dust into burning s;
Eze 38:22 hailstones and burning s on him and
Lk 17:29 fire and s rained down from heaven
Rev 9:17 red, dark blue, and yellow as s.
9:17 their mouths came fire, smoke and s.
9:18 and s that came out of their mouths.
14:10 He will be tormented with burning s
19:20 into the fiery lake of burning s.
20:10 thrown into the lake of burning s,
21: 8 be in the fiery lake of burning s.

Sum (Summed, Sums)
Ps 139:17 How vast is the s of them!
Mt 28:12 the soldiers a large s of money,
Ac 7:16 at Shechem for a certain s of money.
1Co 16: 2 should set aside a s of money

Summed (Sum)
Ro 13: 9 are s up in this one rule: "Love
Gal 5:14 The entire law is s up in a single

Summer
Ge 8:22 cold and heat, s and winter, day and
Jdg 3:20 upper room of his s palace and said,
Ps 32: 4 was sapped as in the heat of s.
74:17 you made both s and winter.
Pr 6: 8 yet it stores its provisions in s
10: 5 He who gathers crops in s is a wise
26: 1 Like snow in s or rain in harvest,
30:25 they store up their food in the s;
Isa 18: 6 the birds will feed on them all s,
Jer 8:20 "The harvest is past, the s has
40:10 harvest the wine, s fruit and oil,
40:12 an abundance of wine and s fruit.
Da 2:35 chaff on a threshing-floor in the s.
Am 3:15 winter house along with the s house;
Mic 7: 1 I am like one who gathers s fruit at
Zec 14: 8 the western sea, in s and in winter.
Mt 24:32 come out, you know that s is near.
Mk 13:28 come out, you know that s is near.
Lk 21:30 yourselves and know that s is near.

Summit
2Sa 15:32 David arrived at the s, where people
16: 1 gone a short distance beyond the s,
SS 4: 8 the top of Senir, the s of Hermon,
Jer 22: 6 like the s of Lebanon, I will surely

Summon (Summoned, Summoning, Summons)
Nu 22: 5 sent messengers to s Balaam son of
22:20 "Since these men have come to s you,
Dt 25: 8 the elders of his town shall s him
33:19 They will s peoples to the mountain
2Sa 17: 5 "S also Hushai the Arkite, so that
20: 4 the king said to Amasa, "S the men
20: 5 when Amasa went to s Judah, he took
1Ki 18:19 Now s the people from all over
22:13 messenger who had gone to s Micaiah
2Ki 10:19 Now s all the prophets of Baal, all
2Ch 18:12 messenger who had gone to s Micaiah
Job 9:19 a matter of justice, who will s him?
13:22 s me and I will answer, or let me
19:16 I s my servant, but he does not
Ps 68:28 S your power, O God; show us your
Isa 22:20 "In that day I will s my servant,
45: 4 of Israel my chosen, I s you by name
46:11 From the east I s a bird of prey;
48:13 I s them, they all stand up together.
55: 5 Surely you will s nations you know
Jer 1:15 I am about to s all the peoples of
25: 9 I will s all the peoples of the
50:29 "S archers against Babylon, all
51:27 s against her these kingdoms: Ararat,
Lam 2:22 "As you s to a feast day, so you
Eze 38:21 I will s a sword against Gog on all
Joel 1:14 S the elders and all who live in the

Summoned (Summon)
Ge 12:18 Pharaoh s Abram. "What have you done
20: 8 Abimelech s all his officials,
26: 9 Abimelech s Isaac and said, "She is
Ex 1:18 the king of Egypt s the midwives and
7:11 Pharaoh then s the wise men and
8: 8 Pharaoh s Moses and Aaron and said,
8:25 Pharaoh s Moses and Aaron and said,
9:27 Pharaoh s Moses and Aaron.
10:16 Pharaoh quickly s Moses and Aaron
10:24 Pharaoh s Moses and said, "Go,
12:21 Moses s all the elders of Israel and
12:31 During the night Pharaoh s Moses and
19: 7 Moses went back and s the elders of
36: 2 Moses s Bezalel and Oholiab and
Lev 9: 1 On the eighth day Moses s Aaron and
10: 4 Moses s Mishael and Elzaphan, sons
Nu 12: 5 to the Tent and s Aaron and Miriam.
16:12 Moses s Dathan and Abiram, the sons
24:10 "I s you to curse my enemies, but
Dt 5: 1 Moses s all Israel and said: Hear,
29: 2 Moses s all the Israelites and said
31: 7 Moses s Joshua and said to him in
Jos 9:22 Joshua s the Gibeonites and said,
10:24 he s all the men of Israel and said
22: 1 Joshua s the Reubenites, the Gadites
23: 2 s all Israel—their elders, leaders,
24: 1 He s the elders, leaders, judges and
Jdg 4:10 where he s Zebulun and Naphtali.
1Sa 10:17 Samuel s the people of Israel to the
13: 4 were s to join Saul at Gilgal.
15: 4 Saul s the men and mustered them at
2Sa 9: 9 the king s Ziba, Saul's servant, and
14:33 Then the king s Absalom, and he came
21: 2 The king s the Gibeonites and spoke
1Ki 2:42 the king s Shimei and said to him,
8: 1 King Solomon s into his presence at
18: 3 Ahab had s Obadiah, who was in
20: 7 The king of Israel s all the elders
20:15 Ahab s the young officers of the
2Ki 4:36 Elisha s Gehazi and said, "Call the
6:11 He s his officers and demanded of
9: 1 The prophet Elisha s a man from the
12: 7 Therefore King Joash s Jehoiada the
1Ch 15:11 David s Zadok and Abiathar the
28: 1 David s all the officials of Israel
2Ch 5: 2 Solomon s to Jerusalem the elders of
24: 6 Therefore the king s Jehoiada the
Ezr 8:16 I s Eliezer, Ariel, Shemaiah,
Ne 5:12 Then I s the priests and made the
Est 2:14 pleased with her and s her by name.
3:12 month the royal secretaries were s.
4: 5 Esther s Hathach, one of the king's
4:11 being s the king has but one law:
8: 9 At once the royal secretaries were s
Job 9:16 Even if I s him and he responded, I
Isa 13: 3 I have s my warriors to carry out my
43: 1 I have s you by name; you are mine.
Lam 1:15 he has s an army against me to crush
2:22 s against me terrors on every side.
Da 2: 2 the king s the magicians, enchanters,
3: 2 He then s the satraps, prefects,
3:13 Nebuchadnezzar s Shadrach, Meshach
Am 5:16 The farmers will be s to weep and the
Jn 9:24 A second time they s the man who had
18:33 s Jesus and asked him, "Are you the

Summoning (Summon)
Jdg 6:34 s the Abiezrites to follow him.
Mk 15:44 S the centurion, he asked him if

Summons (Summon)
Nu 22:37 "Did I not send you an urgent s?
Ps 50: 1 God, the LORD, speaks and s the
50: 4 He s the heavens above, and the
Isa 45: 3 God of Israel, who s you by name.
Na 2: 5 He s his picked troops, yet they

Sums (Sum)
Mt 7:12 this s up the Law and the Prophets.

Sun (Sundown, Sunrise, Sunset, Sunshine, *Under the sun*)
Ge 15:12 the s was setting, Abram fell into a
15:17 the s had set and darkness had
19:23 the s had risen over the land.
28:11 for the night because the s had set.
29: 7 "Look," he said, "the s is still
32:31 The s rose above him as he passed
37: 9 and this time the s and moon and
Ex 16:21 when the s grew hot, it melted away.
Lev 22: 7 the s goes down, he will be clean,
Dt 4:19 you look up to the sky and see the s,
11:30 towards the setting s, near the
16: 6 when the s goes down, on the
17: 3 bowing down to them or to the s or
33:14 with the best the s brings forth and
Jos 10:12 "O s, stand still over Gibeon,
10:13 the s stood still, and the moon
10:13 The s stopped in the middle of the
Jdg 5:31 may they who love you be like the s
19:14 and the s set as they neared Gibeah
1Sa 11: 9 'By the time the s is hot tomorrow,
2Sa 2:24 and as the s was setting, they came
3:35 or anything else before the s sets!"
1Ki 22:36 the s was setting, a cry spread
2Ki 3:22 the s was shining on the water.
23: 5 incense to Baal, to the s and moon,
23:11 of Judah had dedicated to the s.
23:11 the chariots dedicated to the s.
Ne 7: 3 not to be opened until the s is hot.
Job 9: 7 He speaks to the s and it does not
30:28 about blackened, but not by the s;
Job 31:26 if I have regarded the s in its
37:21 Now no-one can look at the s, bright
Ps 19: 4 he has pitched a tent for the s,
37: 6 of your cause like the noonday s.
50: 1 of the s to the place where it sets.
58: 8 child, may they not see the s.
72: 5 He will endure as long as the s, as
72:17 may it continue as long as the s.
74:16 you established the s and moon.
84:11 For the LORD God is a s and shield;
89:36 throne endure before me like the s;
104:19 and the s knows when to go down.
104:22 The s rises, and they steal away;
113: 3 From the rising of the s to the
121: 6 the s will not harm you by day, nor
136: 8 the s to govern the day,
148: 3 Praise him, s and moon, praise him,
Ecc 1: 5 The s rises and the s sets, and
6: 5 Though it never saw the s or knew
7:11 and benefits those who see the s.
11: 7 it pleases the eyes to see the s.
12: 2 before the s and the light and the
SS 1: 6 because I am darkened by the s.
6:10 fair as the moon, bright as the s,
Isa 13:10 The rising s will be darkened and
24:23 moon will be abashed, the s ashamed
30:26 The moon will shine like the s, and
38: 8 I will make the shadow cast by the s
41:25 the rising s who calls on my name.
45: 6 that from the rising of the s to the
49:10 desert heat or the s beat upon them.
59:19 and from the rising of the s, they
60:19 The s will no more be your light by
60:20 Your s will never set again, and
Jer 8: 2 They will be exposed to the s and
15: 9 Her s will set while it is still day;
31:35 he who appoints the s to shine by
43:13 There in the temple of the s in
Eze 8:16 bowing down to the s in the east.
32: 7 I will cover the s with a cloud,
Hos 6: 3 As surely as the s rises, he will
Joel 2:10 the sky trembles, the s and moon are
2:31 The s will be turned to darkness and
3:15 The s and moon will be darkened, and
Am 8: 9 "I will make the s go down at noon
Jnh 4: 8 the s rose, God provided a scorching
4: 8 and the s blazed on Jonah's head so
Mic 3: 6 The s will set for the prophets, and
Na 3:17 when the s appears they fly away,
Hab 3:11 S and moon stood still in the
Mal 1:11 the rising to the setting of the s.
4: 2 the s of righteousness will rise
Mt 5:45 He causes his s to rise on the evil
13: 6 when the s came up, the plants were
13:43 the righteous will shine like the s
17: 2 His face shone like the s, and his
24:29 'the s will be darkened, and the
Mk 4: 6 when the s came up, the plants were
13:24 'the s will be darkened, and the
Lk 1:78 rising s will come to us from
4:40 the s was setting, the people
21:25 "There will be signs in the s, moon
23:45 for the s stopped shining. And the
Ac 2:20 The s will be turned to darkness and
13:11 be unable to see the light of the s.
26:13 brighter than the s, blazing around
27:20 neither s nor stars appeared for
1Co 15:41 The s has one kind of splendour, the
Eph 4:26 s go down while you are still angry,
Jas 1:11 For the s rises with scorching heat
Rev 1:16 the s shining in all its brilliance.
6:12 The s turned black like sackcloth
7:16 The s will not beat upon them, nor
8:12 and a third of the s was struck, a
9: 2 The s and sky were darkened by the
10: 1 his face was like the s, and his
12: 1 heaven: a woman clothed with the s,
16: 8 angel poured out his bowl on the s,
16: 8 and the s was given power to scorch
19:17 I saw an angel standing in the s,
21:23 The city does not need the s or the
22: 5 of a lamp or the light of the s,

Sundown (Sun)
Da 6:14 every effort until s to save him.

Sung (Sing)
Isa 26: 1 In that day this song will be s in
Mt 26:30 they had s a hymn, they went out to
Mk 14:26 they had s a hymn, they went out to

Sunk (Sink)
Jer 38:22 Your feet are s in the mud; your
Lam 2: 9 Her gates have s into the ground;
Hos 9: 9 They have s deep into corruption, as

Sunlight (Light[1])
Isa 30:26 and the s will be seven times
38: 8 So the s went back the ten steps

Sunrise (Sun)
Ex 22: 3 if it happens after s, he is guilty
27:13 On the east end, towards the s, the
38:13 The east end, towards the s, was
Nu 2: 3 On the east, towards the s, the
3:38 towards the s, in front of the Tent
21:11 that faces Moab towards the s.
34:15 Jordan of Jericho, towards the s."
Jos 1:15 east of the Jordan towards the s."
19:12 turned east from Sarid towards the s
Jdg 9:33 In the morning at s, advance against
2Sa 23: 4 he is like the light of morning at s
Hab 3: 4 His splendour was like the s;
Mk 16: 2 just after s, they were on their way

Sun-scorched (Scorch)
Ps 68: 6 but the rebellious live in a s land.
Isa 58:11 will satisfy your needs in a s land

Sunset (Sun)
Ex 17:12 his hands remained steady till s.
22:26 as a pledge, return it to him by s,
Dt 23:11 and at s he may return to the camp.
24:13 Return his cloak to him by s so that
24:15 Pay him his wages each day before s,
Jos 8:29 At s, Joshua ordered them to take
10:27 At s Joshua gave the order and they
Jdg 14:18 Before s on the seventh day the men
2Ch 18:34 Then at s he died.
Mk 1:32 That evening after s the people

Sunshine (Sun)
Job 8:16 like a well-watered plant in the s,
Isa 18: 4 like shimmering heat in the s, like

Super-apostles (Apostle)
2Co 11: 5 in the least inferior to those "s".
12:11 in the least inferior to the "s",

Superior
Da 8:25 and he will consider himself s.
Ro 2:18 approve of what is s because you are
1Co 2: 1 not come with eloquence or s wisdom
Heb 1: 4 he became as much s to the angels as
1: 4 he has inherited is s to theirs.
8: 6 is as s to theirs as the covenant
8: 6 he is mediator is s to the old one,

Superstitions
Isa 2: 6 They are full of s from the East;

Supervise (Supervised, Supervising, Supervision, Supervisor, Supervisors)
2Ki 12:11 to s the work on the temple.
22: 5 to s the work on the temple.
1Ch 23: 4 twenty-four thousand are to s the
2Ch 34:10 to s the work on the LORD's temple.
Ezr 3: 8 older to s the building of the house

Supervised (Supervise)
1Ki 5:16 hundred foremen who s the project
2Ch 34:13 and s all the workers from job to

Supervising (Supervise)
1Ki 9:23 s the men who did the work.
2Ch 8:10 and fifty officials s the men.
Ezr 3: 9 s those working on the house of God.

Supervision (Supervise)
Nu 8:22 under the s of Aaron and his sons.
1Ch 25: 2 of Asaph were under the s of Asaph,
25: 2 who prophesied under the king's s.
25: 3 six in all, under the s of their
25: 6 All these men were under the s of
25: 6 Heman were under the s of the king.
Gal 3:25 no longer under the s of the law.

Supervisor (Supervise)
Ne 11:11 of Ahitub, s in the house of God,

Supervisors (Supervise)
2Ki 22: 9 to the workers and s at the temple."
2Ch 31:13 Ismakiah, Mahath and Benaiah were s
34:17 entrusted it to the s and workers."
Ne 3: 5 shoulders to the work under their s.

Suph
Dt 1: 1 in the Arabah—opposite S, between

Suphah
Nu 21:14 Waheb in S and the ravines, the

Supper
Lk 17: 8 'Prepare my s, get yourself ready
22:20 In the same way, after the s he took
Jn 21:20 against Jesus at the s and had said,
1Co 11:20 it is not the Lord's S you eat,
11:25 In the same way, after s he took the
Rev 19: 9 invited to the wedding s of the Lamb!
19:17 together for the great s of God,

Supple
Ge 49:24 his strong arms stayed s, because of

Supplication (Supplications)
1Ki 8:30 Hear the s of your servant and of
8:33 and making s to you in this temple,
2Ch 6:24 making s before you in this temple,
Ps 119:170 May my s come before you; deliver me
Zec 12:10 Jerusalem a spirit of grace and s.

Supplications (Supplication)
1Ki 8:54 all these prayers and s to the LORD,
2Ch 6:21 Hear the s of your servant and of

Supplied (Supply)
Nu 31: 5 were s from the clans of Israel.
1Ki 4: 7 who s provisions for the king and
4:27 each in his month, s provisions for
5:10 In this way Hiram kept Solomon s
9:11 because Hiram had s him with all the
18: 4 and had s them with food and water.)
18:13 and s them with food and water.
1Ch 12:39 families had s provisions for them.
Isa 33:16 His bread will be s, and water will
Jer 5: 7 I s all their needs, yet they
Ac 20:34 hands of mine have s my own needs
1Co 16:17 have s what was lacking from you.
2Co 11: 9 came from Macedonia s what I needed.
Php 4:18 I am amply s, now that I have

Supplies (Supply)
Jos 1:11 tell the people, 'Get your s ready.
1Sa 17:22 his things with the keeper of s,
25:13 while two hundred stayed with the s.
30:24 the man who stayed with the s is to
1Ki 4: 7 provide s for one month in the year.
1Ch 12:40 There were plentiful s of flour, fig
27:28 was in charge of the s of olive oil.
2Ch 11:11 with s of food, olive oil and wine.
17:13 had large s in the towns of Judah.
Ne 13:13 the s to their brothers.
Ps 105:16 and destroyed all their s of food;
147: 8 he s the earth with rain and makes
Pr 31:24 and s the merchants with sashes.
Isa 3: 1 all s of food and all s of water,
10:28 they store s at Michmash.
Ac 28:10 furnished us with the s we needed.
2Co 9:10 Now he who s seed to the sower and

Supply (Supplied, Supplies, Supplying)
Ex 5: 7 "You are no longer to s the people
Lev 26:26 I cut off your s of bread, ten women
Nu 4: 9 its jars for the oil used to s it.
Dt 15:14 S him liberally from your flock,
Jos 9: 5 of their food s was dry and mouldy.
Jdg 19:20 "Let me s whatever you need.
2Sa 12:27 Rabbah and taken its water s.
1Ki 17: 9 in that place to s you with food."
2Ki 3: 4 and he had to s the king of Israel
Ezr 7:20 God that you may have occasion to s,
Ne 5:18 an abundant s of wine of all kinds.
Ps 78:20 Can he s meat for his people?"
Isa 3: 1 and Judah both s and support:
Eze 4:16 cut off the s of food in Jerusalem.
5:16 upon you and cut off your s of food.
14:13 against it to cut off its food s
48:18 s food for the workers of the city.
Na 2: 9 The s is endless, the wealth from
Ac 12:20 the king's country for their food s.
2Co 8:14 your plenty will s what they need,
8:14 their plenty will s what you need.
9:10 bread for food will also s and
1Th 3:10 and s what is lacking in your faith.

Supplying (Supply)
2Co 9:12 not only s the needs of God's people

Support (Supported, Supporting, Supports)
Ge 13: 6 the land could not s them while they
36: 7 could not s them both because of
Lev 25:35 is unable to s himself among you,
Jdg 16:26 feel the pillars that s the temple,
2Sa 18: 3 for you to give us s from the city."
22:19 my disaster, but the LORD was my s.
1Ki 1: 7 priest, and they gave him their s.
2Ki 15:19 talents of silver to gain his s
1Ch 11:10 gave his kingship strong s to extend
2Ch 26:13 to s the king against his enemies.
Ezr 10: 4 We will s you, so take courage and
Ps 18:18 my disaster, but the LORD was my s.
20: 2 sanctuary and grant you s from Zion.
Pr 28:17 till death; let no-one s him.
Isa 3: 1 and Judah both supply and s:
63: 5 I was appalled that no-one gave s;
Jer 37: 7 which has marched out to s you, will
Da 11: 1 took my stand to s and protect him.)
Lk 8: 3 to s them out of their own means.
Ac 12:20 Having secured the s of Blastus, a
Ro 11:18 consider this: You do not s the root,
1Co 9:12 If others have this right of s from
2Co 11: 8 s from them so as to serve you.
2Ti 4:16 no-one came to my s, but everyone

Supported (Support)
1Ki 16:21 half s Tibni son of Ginath for king,
16:21 for king, and the other half s Omri.
2Ki 16:17 from the bronze bulls that s it and
2Ch 11:17 s Rehoboam son of Solomon for three
Ezr 10:15 s by Meshullam and Shabbethai the
Job 4: 4 Your words have s those who stumbled;
Ps 89:43 sword and have not s him in battle.
94:18 your love, O LORD, s me.
Jer 26:24 Ahikam son of Shaphan s Jeremiah,
Da 11: 6 her father and the one who s her.
Col 2:19 from whom the whole body, s and held

Supporting (Support)
2Sa 5: 9 it, from the s terraces inward.
1Ki 7: 2 cedar columns s trimmed cedar beams.
9:15 his own palace, the s terraces, the
9:24 her, he constructed the s terraces.
11:27 Solomon had built the s terraces and
1Ch 11: 8 from the s terraces to the
2Ch 32: 5 the s terraces of the City of David.
Eph 4:16 held together by every s ligament,

Supports (Support)
1Ki 7:30 each had a basin resting on four s,
7:35 The s and panels were attached to
7:36 surfaces of the s and on the panels,
10:12 make s for the temple of the LORD

Eze 41: 6 to serve as s for the side rooms,
41: 6 so that the s were not inserted into
Da 10:21 (No-one s me against them except
Ro 11:18 the root, but the root s you.

Suppose (Supposed, Supposing)
Ex 3:13 "S I go to the Israelites and say
Nu 36: 3 Now s they marry men from other
Jdg 11: 9 "S you take me back to fight the
Job 34:31 "S a man says to God, 'I am guilty
Eze 18: 5 "S there is a righteous man who does
18:10 "S he has a violent son, who sheds
18:14 "But s this son has a son who sees
Mt 10:34 "Do not s that I have come to bring
24:48 s that servant is wicked and says to
Lk 7:43 Simon replied, "I s the one who had
11: 5 "S one of you has a friend, and he
12:45 s the servant says to himself, 'My
14:28 "S one of you wants to build a tower.
14:31 "Or s a king is about to go to war
15: 4 "S one of you has a hundred sheep
15: 8 "Or s a woman has ten silver coins
17: 7 "S one of you had a servant
Jn 21:25 I s that even the whole world would
Ac 2:15 These men are not drunk, as you s.
Jas 2: 2 S a man comes into your meeting
2:15 S a brother or sister is without

Supposed (Suppose)
1Sa 20: 5 and I am s to dine with the king;
2Th 2: 2 report or letter s to have come from

Supposing (Suppose)
Jn 11:31 they followed her, s she was going
Php 1:17 not sincerely, s that they can stir

Suppress
Ro 1:18 who s the truth by their wickedness,

Supremacy (Supreme)
Col 1:18 in everything he might have the s.

Supreme (Supremacy)
2Ki 18:17 of Assyria sent his s commander,
Pr 4: 7 Wisdom is s; therefore get wisdom.
Ecc 8: 4 Since a king's word is s, who can
Isa 20: 1 In the year that the s commander,
1Pe 2:13 to the king, as the s authority,

Sur
2Ki 11: 6 a third at the S Gate, and a third

Sure
Ge 20: 7 you may be s that you and all yours
24: 6 "Make s that you do not take my son
32:20 be s to say, 'Your servant Jacob is
Ex 8:29 Only be s that Pharaoh does not act
10:28 Make s you do not appear before me
17:14 and make s that Joshua hears it,
23: 4 off, be s to take it back to him.
23: 5 it there; be s you help him with it.
Nu 26:55 Be s that the land is distributed by
28:31 Be s the animals are without defect.
32:23 s that your sin will find you out.
Dt 5: 1 Learn them and be s to follow them.
6:17 Be s to keep the commands of the
11:32 be s that you obey all the decrees
12:23 be s you do not eat the blood,
14:22 Be s to set aside a tenth of all
17:15 be s to appoint over you the king
21:23 Be s to bury him that same day,
22: 1 it but be s to take it back to him.
22: 7 but be s to let the mother go,
23:23 your lips utter you must be s to do,
28:66 night and day, never s of your life.
29:18 Make s there is no man or woman,
29:18 make s there is no root among you
31:29 you are s to become utterly corrupt
Jos 2:12 Give me a s sign
13: 6 Be s to allocate this land to Israel
23:13 you may be s that the LORD your God
Jdg 15: 2 "I was so s you thoroughly hated her,
1Sa 12:24 be s to fear the LORD and serve him
1Sa 20: 7 s that he is determined to harm me.
22:22 I knew he would be s to tell Saul.
1Ki 2:37 you can be s you will die;
2:42 you can be s you will die'?
Ezr 7:17 With this money be s to buy bulls,
Ps 19: 9 LORD are s and altogether righteous.
69:13 God, answer me with your s salvation.
132:11 a s oath that he will not revoke:
Pr 11:14 but many advisers make victory s.
11:18 sows righteousness reaps a s reward.
11:21 Be s of this: The wicked will not go
16: 5 Be s of this: They will not go
27:23 Be s you know the condition of your
Isa 28:16 cornerstone for a s foundation;
33: 6 He will be the s foundation for your
Jer 42:19 Be s of this: I warn you today
42:22 now, be s of this: You will die by
Eze 30: 9 Egypt's doom, for it is s to come.
Mt 17:11 "To be s, Elijah comes and will
Mk 9:12 "To be s, Elijah does come first,
Lk 1:18 "How can I be s of this? I am an old
10:11 Yet be s of this: The kingdom of God
Ac 13:34 and s blessings promised to David.'
Ro 15:28 s that they have received this fruit,
2Co 13: 4 For to be s, he was crucified in
Eph 5: 5 For of this you can be s: No immoral,
1Th 5:15 Make s that nobody pays back wrong
Tit 3:11 You may be s that such a man is
Heb 6:11 end, in order to make your hope s.
11: 1 Now faith is being s of what we hope
13:18 Pray for us. We are s that we have a
2Pe 1:10 to make your calling and election s.

Surf
Ac 27:41 to pieces by the pounding of the s.

Surface (Surfaces)
Ge 1: 2 darkness was over the s of the deep,
2: 6 watered the whole s of the ground—
7:18 ark floated on the s of the water.
8: 8 receded from the s of the ground.
8: 9 water over all the s of the earth;
8:13 that the s of the ground was dry.
Lev 14:37 to be deeper than the s of the wall,
Job 24:18 "Yet they are foam on the s of the
38:30 when the s of the deep is frozen?
Isa 28:25 he has levelled the s, does he not
Hos 10: 7 like a twig on the s of the waters.
2Co 10: 7 You are looking only on the s of

Surfaces (Surface)
1Ki 7:36 lions and palm trees on the s of the

Surge (Surged, Surging)
Job 40:23 Jordan should s against his mouth.
Isa 54: 8 In a s of anger I hid my face from

Surged (Surge)
1Sa 17:52 men of Israel and Judah s forward

Surging (Surge)
Ex 15: 8 The s waters stood firm like a wall;
Ps 46: 3 the mountains quake with their s.
89: 9 You rule over the s sea; when its
Isa 17:13 roar like the roar of s waters,
Jer 46: 7 the Nile, like rivers of s waters?
46: 8 the Nile, like rivers of s waters.
Zec 10:11 the s sea will be subdued and all

Surly
1Sa 25: 3 was s and mean in his dealings.

Surmounted
Eze 40:16 were s by narrow parapet openings

Surpass (All-surpassing, Surpassed, Surpasses, Surpassing)
Pr 31:29 noble things, but you s them all."

Surpassed (Surpass)
Jn 1:15 has s me because he was before me.
1:30 has s me because he was before me.'

Surpasses (Surpass)
Pr 8:19 what I yield s choice silver.
Mt 5:20 s that of the Pharisees and the
Eph 3:19 to know this love that s knowledge

Surpassing (Surpass)
Ps 150: 2 praise him for his s greatness.
2Co 3:10 now in comparison with the s glory.
9:14 of the s grace God has given you.
Php 3: 8 s greatness of knowing Christ Jesus

Surprise (Surprised, Surprising)
Jos 10: 9 from Gilgal, Joshua took them by s.
Ps 35: 8 may ruin overtake them by s—may
55:15 Let death take my enemies by s;
Jer 14: 9 Why are you like a man taken by s,
Ac 3:12 "Men of Israel, why does this s you?
1Th 5: 4 this day should s you like a thief.

Surprised (Surprise)
Ecc 5: 8 do not be s at such things; for one
Mk 15:44 Pilate was s to hear that he was
Lk 11:38 first wash before the meal, was s.
Jn 3: 7 You should not be s at my saying,
4:27 s to find him talking with a woman.
1Pe 4:12 Dear friends, do not be s at the
1Jn 3:13 Do not be s, my brothers, if the

Surprising (Surprise)
2Co 11:15 is not s, then, if his servants

Surrender (Surrendered, Surrenders)
Jos 20: 5 they must not s the one accused,
Jdg 20:13 Now s those wicked men of Gibeah so
1Sa 11: 3 to rescue us, we will s to you."
11:10 "Tomorrow we will s to you, and you
23:11 Will the citizens of Keilah s me to
23:12 "Will the citizens of Keilah s me
2Ki 7: 4 to the camp of the Arameans and s.
Ps 41: 2 not s him to the desire of his foes.
Isa 54:15 whoever attacks you will s to you.
Jer 38:17 'If you s to the officers of the
38:18 if you will not s to the officers of
38:21 if you refuse to s, this is what the
Da 8:13 and the s of the sanctuary and of
1Co 13: 3 poor and s my body to the flames,

Surrendered (Surrender)
2Ki 24:12 and his officials all s to him.
Lk 23:25 for, and s Jesus to their will.

Surrenders (Surrender)
Jer 21: 9 But whoever goes out and s to the
50:15 She s, her towers fall, her walls

Surround (Surrounded, Surrounding, Surrounds)
Jos 7: 9 they will s us and wipe out our name
Job 16:13 his archers s me. Without pity, he
17: 2 Surely mockers s me; my eyes must
40:22 the poplars by the stream s him.
Ps 5:12 you s them with your favour as with
17: 9 me, from my mortal enemies who s me.
17:11 have tracked me down, they now s me,
22:12 Many bulls s me; strong bulls of
27: 6 exalted above the enemies who s me;
32: 7 and s me with songs of deliverance.
40:12 For troubles without number s me;
49: 5 come, when wicked deceivers s me—
88:17 All day long they s me like a flood;
89: 7 is more awesome than all who s him.
97: 2 Clouds and thick darkness s him;
109: 3 With words of hatred they s me;
125: 2 the mountains s Jerusalem, so the
140: 9 Let the heads of those who s me be
Jer 4:17 They s her like men guarding a field,
12: 9 other birds of prey s and attack?
31:22 on earth—a woman will s a man."

Surrounded (Surround)
Ge 19: 4 young and old—s the house.
Jdg 16: 2 So they s the place and lay in wait
19:22 wicked men of the city s the house.

Jdg 20: 5 came after me and s the house,
20:43 They s the Benjamites, chased them
2Sa 18:15 Joab's armour-bearers s Absalom,
1Ki 7:12 The great courtyard was s by a wall
2Ki 3:25 slings s it and attacked it as well.
6:14 They went by night and s the city.
6:15 horses and chariots had s the city.
8:21 The Edomites s him and his chariot
1Ch 29:30 and the circumstances that s him and
2Ch 21: 9 The Edomites s him and his chariot
Ps 22:16 Dogs have s me; a band of evil men
118:10 All the nations s me, but in the
118:11 They s me on every side, but in the
Ecc 9:14 s it and built huge siegeworks
Lam 3: 5 He has besieged me and s me with
Eze 1: 4 lightning and s by brilliant light.
1:27 and brilliant light s him.
27:32 silenced like Tyre, s by the sea?"
32:22 is s by the graves of all her slain,
Hos 11:12 Ephraim has s me with lies, the
Jnh 2: 5 waters threatened me, the deep s me
Lk 21:20 "When you see Jerusalem being s by
Jn 5: 2 is s by five covered colonnades.
Heb 12: 1 Therefore, since we are s by such a
Rev 20: 9 and s the camp of God's people,

Surrounding (Surround)

Ge 41:48 the food grown in the fields s it.
Ex 38:20 and of the s courtyard were bronze.
38:31 the bases for the s courtyard and
38:31 and those for the s courtyard.
Nu 3:26 s the tabernacle and altar,
3:37 well as the posts of the s courtyard
4:26 the curtains of the courtyard s the
4:32 well as the posts of the s courtyard
21:25 Heshbon and all its s settlements.
21:32 captured its s settlements and
32:42 Kenath and its s settlements and
Jos 15:45 Ekron, with its s settlements and
15:47 Ashdod, its s settlements and
17:11 together with their s settlements
21:11 Hebron), with its s pasture-land, in
21:42 these towns had pasture-lands s it;
Jdg 1:27 or Megiddo and their s settlements,
11:26 Aroer, the s settlements and all the
1Ki 4:31 fame spread to all the s nations.
2Ki 25: 4 the Babylonians were s the city.
1Ch 2:23 with its s settlements—sixty towns.
4:32 Their s villages were Etam, Ain,
6:55 in Judah with its s pasture-lands.
7:28 included Bethel and its s villages,
8:12 Ono and Lod with its s villages),
11: 8 supporting terraces to the s wall,
18: 1 and he took Gath and its s villages
28:12 of the LORD and all the s rooms,
2Ch 13:19 and Ephron, with their s villages.
17:10 the kingdoms of the lands s Judah,
28:18 and Gimzo, with their s villages.
Ne 3:22 by the priests from the s region.
5:17 who came to us from the s nations.
6:16 all the s nations were afraid and
11:25 Kiriath Arba and its s settlements,
Jer 1:15 will come against all her s walls
25: 9 and against all the s nations.
34: 1 Jerusalem and all its s towns,
49: 2 its s villages will be set on fire.
52: 7 the Babylonians were s the city.
52:23 above the s network was a hundred.
Eze 34:26 bless them and the places s my hill
40: 5 I saw a wall completely s the temple
41: 7 The structure s the temple was built
43:12 All the s area on top of the
Zec 7: 7 s towns were at rest and prosperous,
12: 2 sends all the s peoples reeling.
12: 6 right and left all the s peoples,
14:14 The wealth of all the s nations will
Mt 14:35 they sent word to all the s country.
Mk 6:36 they can go to the s countryside
Lk 4:37 him spread throughout the s area.
7:17 throughout Judea and the s country.
9:12 so they can go to the s villages
Ac 14: 6 and Derbe and to the s country,
Jude : 7 Sodom and Gomorrah and the s towns
Rev 4: 4 S the throne were twenty-four other

Surrounds (Surround)

Ps 32:10 love s the man who trusts in him.
89: 8 and your faithfulness s you.
125: 2 so the LORD s his people both now

Survey (Surveyed)

Jos 18: 4 I will send them out to make a s of
18: 8 "Go and make a s of the land and

Surveyed (Survey)

Ecc 2:11 Yet when I s all that my hands had

Survive (Survived, Survives, Surviving, Survivor, Survivors)

Dt 4:27 and only a few of you will s among
Jos 11:22 in Gaza, Gath and Ashdod did any s.
2Sa 1:10 after he had fallen he could not s.
Job 27:15 The plague will bury those who s him,
Isa 66:19 and I will send some of those who s
Jer 21: 7 in this city who s the plague,
31: 2 "The people who s the sword will
42:17 not one of them will s or escape the
44:14 or s to return to the land of Judah,
Eze 7:16 All who s and escape will be in the
Am 7: 2 How can Jacob s? He is so small!"
7: 5 How can Jacob s? He is so small!"
Zec 10: 9 They and their children will s,
Mt 24:22 not been cut short, no-one would s,
Mk 13:20 short those days, no-one would s.
Ac 27:34 You need it to s. Not one of you

Survived (Survive)

Ex 14:28 Not one of them s.
Nu 14:38 of Nun and Caleb son of Jephunneh s.
Dt 5:26 out of fire, as we have, and s?
Jos 13:12 Edrei and had s as one of the last
1Sa 11:11 Those who s were scattered, so that
Ne 1: 2 the Jewish remnant that s the exile,
1: 3 "Those who s the exile and are back
Ps 106:11 not one of them s.
Lam 2:22 LORD's anger no-one escaped or s;

Survives (Survive)

2Ki 19: 4 pray for the remnant that still s."
Isa 37: 4 pray for the remnant that still s."
Eze 6:12 s and is spared will die of famine.
1Co 3:14 If what he has built s, he will

Surviving (Survive)

Dt 28:54 the wife he loves or his s children,
Jer 29: 1 to the s elders among the exiles
Eze 17:14 again, s only by keeping his treaty.

Survivor (Survive)

Jdg 12: 5 and whenever a s of Ephraim said,
2Ki 10:11 and his priests, leaving him no s.
10:14 He left no s.
Ezr 9:14 us, leaving us no remnant or s?
Job 18:19 people, no s where once he lived.

Survivors (Survive)

Nu 21:35 his whole army, leaving them no s.
24:19 Jacob and destroy the s of the city."
Dt 2:34 We left no s.
3: 3 We struck them down, leaving no s.
7:20 s who hide from you have perished.
Jos 8:22 them neither s nor fugitives.
10:28 He left no s. And he did to the king
10:30 He left no s there. And he did to
10:33 and his army—until no s were left.
10:37 They left no s. Just as at Eglon,
10:39 They left no s. They did to Debir
10:40 He left no s. He totally destroyed
11: 8 on the east, until no s were left.
23:12 ally yourselves with the s of these
Jdg 21:17 The Benjamite s must have heirs,"
2Sa 21: 2 Israel but were s of the Amorites;
2Ki 19:31 and out of Mount Zion a band of s.
Ezr 1: 4 the people of any place where s may
Ps 76:10 the s of your wrath are restrained.
Isa 1: 9 LORD Almighty had left us some s,
4: 2 pride and glory of the s in Israel.
10:20 the s of the house of Jacob, will no
14:22 from Babylon her name and s,
14:30 by famine; it will slay your s.
16:14 her s will be very few and feeble."
21:17 The s of the bowmen, the warriors of
37:32 and out of Mount Zion a band of s.
Jer 8: 3 Wherever I banish them, all the s of
15: 9 I will put the s to the sword before
24: 8 his officials and the s from
41:16 led away all the s from Mizpah whom.
47: 4 all s who could help Tyre and Sidon.
Eze 5:10 scatter all your s to the winds.
14:22 Yet there will be some s—sons and
17:21 s will be scattered to the winds.
Joel 2:32 among the s whom the LORD calls.
Ob :14 their s in the day of their trouble.
:18 There will be no s from the house of
Zep 2: 9 the s of my nation will inherit
Zec 14:16 the s from all the nations that have
Rev 11:13 and the s were terrified and gave

Susa

Capital city of Elam, situated about 150 miles north of the Persian Gulf. Favoured by the kings of Persia as a winter residence, and therefore is the backdrop to the book of Esther. Some of its deported officials wrote to Artaxerxes warning of the rebuilding of Jerusalem (Ezr 4:9–10). Here Nehemiah served as Artaxerxes' cup-bearer (Ne 1:1) and Daniel received his vision about Belshazzar (Da 8:2).

Ezr 4: 9 Erech and Babylon, the Elamites of S,
Ne 1: 1 while I was in the citadel of S,
Est 1: 2 royal throne in the citadel of S,
1: 5 who were in the citadel of S.
2: 3 into the harem at the citadel of S.
2: 5 Now there was in the citadel of S a
2: 8 were brought to the citadel of S
3:15 was issued in the citadel of S.
3:15 but the city of S was bewildered.
4: 8 which had been published in S, to
4:16 Jews who are in S, and fast for me.
8:14 was also issued in the citadel of S.
8:15 city of S held a joyous celebration.
9: 6 In the citadel of S, the Jews killed
9:11 those slain in the citadel of S was
9:12 sons of Haman in the citadel of S.
9:13 "give the Jews in S permission to
9:14 An edict was issued in S, and they
9:15 The Jews in S came together on the
9:15 put to death in S three hundred
9:18 The Jews in S, however, had
Da 8: 2 of S in the province of Elam;

Susanna

Lk 8: 3 household; S; and many others.

Susi

Nu 13:11 (a tribe of Joseph), Gaddi son of S;

Suspects (Suspicions)

Nu 5:14 he s his wife and she is impure—or
5:14 s her even though she is not impure—
5:30 over a man because he s his wife.

Suspends

Job 26: 7 he s the earth over nothing.

Suspense

Dt 28:66 You will live in constant s, filled
Jn 10:24 "How long will you keep us in s?
Ac 27:33 "you have been in constant s and

Suspicions (Suspects)

1Ti 6: 4 envy, strife, malicious talk, evil s

Sustain (Sustained, Sustaining, Sustains)

Ru 4:15 He will renew your life and s you in
Job 36:19 all your mighty efforts s you so you
Ps 41: 3 The LORD will s him on his sick-bed
51:12 grant me a willing spirit, to s me.
55:22 cares on the LORD and he will s you;
89:21 My hand will s him; surely my arm
119:116 S me according to your promise, and

Ps 119:175 praise you, and may your laws s me.
Isa 46: 4 I am he, I am he who will s you.
46: 4 I will s you and I will rescue you.

Sustained (Sustain)
Ge 27:37 I have s him with grain and new wine.
Ne 9:21 For forty years you s them in the
Isa 59:16 and his own righteousness s him.
63: 5 for me, and my own wrath s me.

Sustaining (Sustain)
Heb 1: 3 s all things by his powerful word.

Sustains (Sustain)
Ps 3: 5 I wake again, because the LORD s me.
18:35 and your right hand s me;
54: 4 the Lord is the one who s me.
104:15 shine, and bread that s his heart.
146: 9 and s the fatherless and the widow,
147: 6 The LORD s the humble but casts the
Pr 18:14 A man's spirit s him in sickness,
Isa 50: 4 to know the word that s the weary.

Swallow[1] (Swallowed, Swallowing, Swallows)
Nu 14: 9 the land, because we will s them up.
16:34 "The earth is going to s us too!
2Sa 20:19 to s up the LORD's inheritance?"
20:20 Far be it from me to s up or destroy!
Ps 21: 9 In his wrath the LORD will s them up,
69:15 or the depths s me up or the pit
Pr 1:12 let's s them alive, like the grave,
Isa 25: 8 he will s up death for ever.
Hos 8: 7 grain, foreigners would s it up.
Jnh 1:17 the LORD provided a great fish to s
Hab 1:13 while the wicked s up those more
Mt 23:24 You strain out a gnat but s a camel.

Swallow[2]
Ps 84: 3 and the s a nest for herself, where
Pr 26: 2 a fluttering sparrow or a darting s,

Swallowed (Swallow[1])
Ge 41: 7 The thin ears of corn s up the seven
41:24 The thin ears of corn s up the seven
Ex 7:12 But Aaron's staff s up their staffs.
15:12 right hand and the earth s them.
Nu 16:32 earth opened its mouth and s them,
26:10 earth opened its mouth and s them
Dt 11: 6 and s them up with their households,
2Sa 17:16 the people with him will be s up.
Job 20:15 He will spit out the riches he s;
37:20 Would any man ask to be s up?
Ps 35:25 or say, "We have s him up."
106:17 The earth opened up and s Dathan;
124: 3 us, they would have s us alive;
Jer 51:34 Like a serpent he has s us and
51:44 and make him spew out what he has s.
Lam 2: 2 Without pity the Lord has s up all
2: 5 like an enemy; he has s up Israel.
2: 5 He has s up all her palaces and
2:16 teeth and say, "We have s her up.
Hos 8: 8 Israel is s up; now she is among the
1Co 15:54 "Death has been s up in victory."
2Co 5: 4 what is mortal may be s up by life.

Swallowing (Swallow[1])
Rev 12:16 s the river that the dragon had

Swallows (Swallow[1])
Nu 16:30 earth opens its mouth and s them,
Isa 28: 4 and takes it in his hand, he s it.

Swamped (Swampland, Swamps)
Mk 4:37 the boat, so that it was nearly s.
Lk 8:23 so that the boat was being s, and

Swampland (Land, Swamped)
Isa 14:23 into a place for owls and into s;

Swamps (Swamped)
Eze 47:11 the s and marshes will not become

Swarm (Swarmed, Swarming, Swarms)
Ge 7:21 creatures that s over the earth,
Ex 10:12 that locusts will s over the land
Dt 1:44 they chased you like a s of bees and
14:19 All flying insects that s are
Jdg 14: 8 In it was a s of bees and some honey,
Isa 33: 4 a s of locusts men pounce on it.
Jer 12:12 in the desert destroyers will s,
51:14 as with a s of locusts, and they
51:27 send up horses like a s of locusts.
Joel 1: 4 What the locust s has left the great
2:25 the other locusts and the locust s—

Swarmed (Swarm)
Ps 118:12 They s around me like bees, but they

Swarming (Swarm)
Lev 11:10 —whether among all the s things or

Swarms (Swarm)
Ex 8:21 I will send s of flies on you and
8:22 no s of flies will be there, so
8:24 Dense s of flies poured into
Dt 28:42 S of locusts will take over all your
Jdg 6: 5 and their tents like s of locusts.
Ps 78:45 He sent s of flies that devoured
105:31 He spoke, and there came s of flies,
Eze 47: 9 S of living creatures will live
Am 7: 1 He was preparing s of locusts after
Na 3:17 your officials like s of locusts

Sway (Swayed, Swaying, Sways)
Jdg 9: 9 honoured, to hold s over the trees?'
9:11 sweet, to hold s over the trees?'
9:13 and men, to hold s over the trees?'
Ps 72:16 on the tops of the hills may it s.

Swayed (Sway)
Mt 11: 7 desert to see? A reed s by the wind?
22:16 You aren't s by men, because you pay
Mk 12:14 You aren't s by men, because you pay
Lk 7:24 desert to see? A reed s by the wind?
2Ti 3: 6 are s by all kinds of evil desires,

Swaying (Sway)
1Ki 14:15 will be like a reed s in the water.
Jer 4:24 were quaking; all the hills were s.

Sways (Sway)
Job 28: 4 far from men he dangles and s.
40:17 His tail s like a cedar; the sinews
Isa 24:20 it s like a hut in the wind;

Swear (Swearing, Swears, Swore, Sworn)
Ge 21:23 Now s to me here before God that you
21:24 Abraham said, "I s it."
22:16 "I s by myself, declares the LORD,
24: 3 I want you to s by the LORD, the God
24:37 my master made me s an oath, and
25:33 Jacob said, "S to me first." So he
47:31 "S to me," he said. Then Joseph
50: 5 'My father made me s an oath and
50: 6 father, as he made you s to do."
50:25 made the sons of Israel s an oath
Ex 13:19 made the sons of Israel s an oath.
Lev 5: 4 in any matter one might carelessly s
19:12 "'Do not s falsely by my name and
Jos 2:12 Now then, please s to me by the LORD
2:17 made us s will not be binding on
2:20 from the oath you made us s."
23: 7 names of their gods or s by them.
Jdg 15:12 "S to me that you won't kill me
1Sa 24:21 Now s to me by the LORD that you
30:15 "S to me before God that you will
2Sa 19: 7 I s by the LORD that if you don't go
1Ki 1:13 did you not s to me your servant:
1:51 He says, 'Let King Solomon s to me
2:42 "Did I not make you s by the LORD
18:10 made them s they could not find you.
22:16 "How many times must I make you s to
2Ch 18:15 "How many times must I make you s to

Ps 24: 4 to an idol or s by what is false.
63:11 who s by God's name will praise him,
Isa 19:18 s allegiance to the LORD Almighty.
45:23 will bow; by me every tongue will s.
65:16 the land will s by the God of truth.
Jer 4: 2 you s, 'As surely as the LORD lives,'
12:16 ways of my people and s by my name,
12:16 once taught my people to s by Baal
22: 5 I s by myself that this palace will
44:26 'I s by my great name,' says the
44:26 ever again invoke my name or s,
49:13 I s by myself," declares the LORD,
Eze 36: 7 I s with uplifted hand that the
Da 12: 7 and I heard him s by him who lives
Hos 4:15 And do not s, 'As surely as the
Am 8:14 They who s by the shame of Samaria,
Zep 1: 5 those who bow down and s by the LORD
1: 5 the LORD and who also s by Molech,
Zec 8:17 and do not love to s falsely.
Mt 5:34 I tell you, Do not s at all: either
5:36 do not s by your head, for you
Mk 5: 7 S to God that you won't torture me!"
Heb 3:18 to whom did God s that they would
6:13 no-one greater for him to s by, he
6:16 Men s by someone greater than
Jas 5:12 Above all, my brothers, do not s

Swearing (Swear)
Jer 5: 2 still they are s falsely."

Swears (Swear)
Lev 6: 3 or if he s falsely, or if he commits
1Ki 8:31 he comes and s the oath before your
2Ch 6:22 he comes and s the oath before your
Zec 5: 3 who s falsely will be banished.
5: 4 of him who s falsely by my name.
Mt 23:16 'If anyone s by the temple, it means
23:16 but if anyone s by the gold of the
23:18 'If anyone s by the altar, it means
23:18 but if anyone s by the gift on it,
23:20 he who s by the altar s by it
23:21 he who s by the temple s by it and
23:22 he who s by heaven s by God's throne

Sweat
Ge 3:19 By the s of your brow you will eat
Lk 22:44 and his s was like drops of blood

Sweep (Sweeping, Sweepings, Sweeps, Swept)
Ge 18:23 s away the righteous with the wicked?
18:24 Will you really s it away and not
Ps 90: 5 You s men away in the sleep of death;
Isa 8: 8 s on into Judah, swirling over it,
11:15 s his hand over the Euphrates River.
14:23 s her with the broom of destruction,"
28:17 hail will s away your refuge,
28:19 day and by night, it will s through.
43: 2 rivers, they will not s over you.
64: 6 like the wind our sins s us away.
Eze 5:17 Plague and bloodshed will s through
Da 11:10 which will s on like an irresistible
11:40 and s through them like a flood.
Hos 4:19 A whirlwind will s them away, and
Am 5: 6 or he will s through the house of
Hab 1: 6 who s across the whole earth to
1:11 they s past like the wind and go on—
Zep 1: 2 "I will s away everything from the
1: 3 "I will s away both men and animals;
1: 3 I will s away the birds of the air
Lk 15: 8 light a lamp, s the house and
Rev 12:15 and s her away with the torrent.

Sweeping (Sweep)
Isa 21: 1 whirlwinds s through the southland,

Sweepings (Sweep)
Am 8: 6 selling even the s with the wheat.

Sweeps (Sweep)
Job 27:21 it s him out of his place.
Pr 1:27 when disaster s over you like a
13:23 food, but injustice s it away.

Isa 28:15 When an overwhelming scourge s by,
28:18 When the overwhelming scourge s by,
40:24 a whirlwind s them away like chaff.
Zep 2: 2 and that day s on like chaff,

Sweet (Sweeter, Sweetness)
Ex 15:25 the water, and the water became s.
Jdg 9:11 I give up my fruit, so good and s,
14:14 out of the strong, something s.
Ne 8:10 and enjoy choice food and s drinks,
Job 20:12 "Though evil is s in his mouth and
21:33 The soil in the valley is s to him;
Ps 55:14 whom I once enjoyed s fellowship
119:103 How s are your words to my taste,
Pr 3:24 you lie down, your sleep will be s.
9:17 "Stolen water is s; food eaten in
13:19 A longing fulfilled is s to the soul,
16:24 s to the soul and healing to the
20:17 Food gained by fraud tastes s to a
24:13 from the comb is s to your taste.
24:14 Know also that wisdom is s to your
27: 7 hungry even what is bitter tastes s.
Ecc 5:12 The sleep of a labourer is s,
11: 7 Light is s, and it pleases the eyes
SS 2: 3 and his fruit is s to my taste.
2:14 voice is s, and your face is lovely.
Isa 5:20 put bitter for s and s for bitter.
Jer 6:20 or s calamus from a distant land?
Eze 3: 3 it tasted as s as honey in my mouth.
Rev 10: 9 mouth it will be as s as honey."
10:10 It tasted as s as honey in my mouth,

Sweeter (Sweet)
Jdg 14:18 "What is s than honey? What is
Ps 19:10 they are s than honey, than honey
119:103 my taste, s than honey to my mouth!

Sweetness (Sweet)
SS 4:11 Your lips drop s as the honeycomb,
5:16 His mouth is s itself; he is

Swell (Swelling, Swells, Swollen)
Nu 5:21 to waste away and your abdomen to s.
5:27 her abdomen will s and her thigh
Dt 8: 4 did not s during these forty years.
Isa 60: 5 your heart will throb and s with joy;
Ac 28: 6 The people expected him to s up or

Swelling (Swell)
Lev 13: 2 "When anyone has a s or a rash or a
13:10 and if there is a white s in the
13:10 and if there is raw flesh in the s,
13:19 a white s or reddish-white spot
13:28 it is a s from the burn, and the
14:56 for a s, a rash or a bright spot,

Swells (Swell)
Nu 5:22 your abdomen s and your thigh

Swelter
Job 37:17 You who s in your clothes when the

Swept (Sweep)
Ge 19:15 s away when the city is punished."
19:17 mountains or you will be s away!"
Ex 14:27 and the LORD s them into the sea.
Nu 16:26 s away because of all their sins."
Jdg 5:21 The river Kishon s them away, the
1Sa 12:25 you and your king will be s away."
1Ch 21:12 three months of being s away before
Job 1:17 s down on your camels and carried
1:19 suddenly a mighty wind s in from the
5:13 the schemes of the wily are s away.
21:18 wind, like chaff s away by a gale?
37:21 after the wind has s them clean.
Ps 42: 7 waves and breakers have s over me.
58: 9 or dry—the wicked will be s away.
73:19 completely s away by terrors!
88:16 Your wrath has s over me;
124: 4 the torrent would have s over us,
124: 5 the raging waters would have s us
136:15 s Pharaoh and his army into the Red
Pr 10:25 the storm has s by, the wicked are
Isa 44:22 I have s away your offences like a
Da 2:35 The wind s them away without leaving
11:22 an overwhelming army will be s away
11:26 his army will be s away, and many
Jnh 2: 3 your waves and breakers s over me.
Mic 7: 2 The godly have been s from the land;
Hab 3:10 Torrents of water s by; the deep
Mt 8:24 so that the waves s over the boat.
12:44 s clean and put in order.
Lk 11:25 arrives, it finds the house s clean
Ac 27:14 s down from the island.
Rev 12: 4 His tail s a third of the stars out

Swerve (Swerving)
Pr 4: 5 not forget my words or s from them.
4:27 Do not s to the right or the left;

Swerving (Swerve)
Joel 2: 7 in line, not s from their course.

Swift (Swifter)
1Ch 12: 8 as s as gazelles in the mountains.
Pr 1:16 into sin, they are s to shed blood.
Ecc 9:11 The race is not to the s or the
Isa 18: 2 Go, s messengers, to a people tall
19: 1 See, the LORD rides on a s cloud
30:16 'We will ride off on s horses.'
30:16 Therefore your pursuers will be s!
38:14 I cried like a s or thrush, I moaned
59: 7 they are s to shed innocent blood.
Jer 2:23 s she-camel running here and there,
8: 7 and the dove, the s and the thrush
46: 6 "The s cannot flee nor the strong
Da 9:21 came to me in s flight about the
Am 2:14 The s will not escape, the strong
Ro 3:15 "Their feet are s to shed blood;
2Pe 2: 1 s destruction on themselves.

Swifter (Swift)
2Sa 1:23 They were s than eagles, they were
Job 7: 6 "My days are s than a weaver's
9:25 "My days are s than a runner;
Jer 4:13 his horses are s than eagles.
Lam 4:19 Our pursuers were s than eagles in
Hab 1: 8 Their horses are s than leopards,

Swim (Swimmer, Swimming)
Ps 8: 8 all that s the paths of the seas.
Isa 25:11 swimmer spreads out his hands to s.
Eze 47: 5 was deep enough to s in—a river
Ac 27:43 He ordered those who could s to jump

Swimmer (Swim)
Isa 25:11 a s spreads out his hands to swim.

Swimming (Swim)
Ac 27:42 of them from s away and escaping.

Swindler (Swindlers)
1Co 5:11 or a slanderer, a drunkard or a s.

Swindlers (Swindler)
1Co 5:10 or the greedy and s, or idolaters.
6:10 nor slanderers nor s will inherit

Swing (Swings, Swung)
Ex 28:28 will not s out from the ephod.
39:21 would not s out from the ephod
Joel 3:13 S the sickle, for the harvest is

Swings (Swing)
Dt 19: 5 and as he s his axe to fell a tree,
Isa 10:15 axe raise itself above him who s it,

Swirl (Swirled, Swirling)
Job 37:12 At his direction they s around over

Swirled (Swirl)
2Sa 22: 5 "The waves of death s about me;
Jnh 2: 3 and the currents s about me;

Swirling (Swirl)
Isa 8: 8 sweep on into Judah, s over it,
Jer 23:19 s down on the heads of the wicked.
30:23 s down on the heads of the wicked.
Hos 13: 3 like chaff s from a threshing-floor,

Swollen (Swell)
Lev 13:43 and if the s sore on his head or
Ne 9:21 out nor did their feet become s.
Job 6:16 darkened by thawing ice and s with

Swoop (Swooping)
Isa 11:14 They will s down on the slopes of
Jer 49:22 Look! An eagle will soar and s down,

Swooping (Swoop)
Dt 28:49 like an eagle s down, a nation whose
Job 9:26 like eagles s down on their prey.
Jer 48:40 "Look! An eagle is s down, spreading
Hab 1: 8 They fly like a vulture s to devour;

Sword (*Put to the sword*, Swords, Swordsmen)
Ge 3:24 a flaming s flashing back and forth
27:40 You will live by the s and you will
34:26 his son Shechem to the s and took
48:22 the Amorites with my s and my bow."
Ex 5: 3 us with plagues or with the s."
5:21 put a s in their hand to kill us."
15: 9 my s and my hand will destroy them.'
17:13 the Amalekite army with the s.
18: 4 he saved me from the s of Pharaoh."
22:24 and I will kill you with the s;
32:27 'Each man strap a s to his side.
Lev 26: 6 s will not pass through your country.
26: 7 they will fall by the s before you.
26: 8 will fall by the s before you.
26:25 I will bring the s upon you to
26:33 will draw out my s and pursue you.
26:36 run as though fleeing from the s,
26:37 as though fleeing from the s,
Nu 14: 3 land only to let us fall by the s?
14:43 you and you will fall by the s."
19:16 who has been killed with a s or
20:18 out and attack you with the s."
21:24 Israel, however, put him to the s
22:23 the road with a drawn s in his hand,
22:29 If I had a s in my hand, I would
22:31 in the road with his s drawn.
31: 8 Balaam son of Beor with the s.
Dt 32:25 In the street the s will make them
32:41 I sharpen my flashing s and my hand
32:42 while my s devours flesh: the blood
33:29 and helper and your glorious s.
Jos 5:13 of him with a drawn s in his hand.
6:21 destroyed with the s every living
10:28 its king to the s and totally
10:35 put it to the s and totally
10:37 took the city and put it to the s,
10:39 its villages, and put them to the s.
11:10 Hazor and put its king to the s.
11:12 their kings and put them to the s.
19:47 it, put it to the s and occupied it.
24:12 not do it with your own s and bow.
Jdg 1: 8 city to the s and set it on fire.
1:25 and they put the city to the s but
3:16 Now Ehud had made a double-edged s
3:21 drew the s from his right thigh and
3:22 Ehud did not pull the s out, and
4:15 all his chariots and army by the s,
4:16 the troops of Sisera fell by the s;
7:14 than the s of Gideon son of Joash,
7:20 "A s for the LORD and for Gideon!"
8:20 But Jether did not draw his s,
9:54 "Draw your s and kill me, so that
18:27 They attacked them with the s and
20:37 out and put the whole city to the s.
20:48 and put all the towns to the s,
1Sa 13:22 had a s or spear in his hand;
15: 8 he totally destroyed with the s.
15:33 "As your s has made women childless
17:39 David fastened on his s over the
17:45 "You come against me with a s and
17:47 by s or spear that the LORD saves;

1Sa 17:50 without a s in his hand he struck
17:51 He took hold of the Philistine's s
17:51 him, he cut off his head with the s.
18: 4 even his s, his bow and his belt.
21: 8 "Don't you have a spear or s here?
21: 8 brought my s or any other weapon,
21: 9 "The s of Goliath the Philistine,
21: 9 there is no s here but that one.
22:10 the s of Goliath the Philistine."
22:13 giving him bread and a s and
31: 4 "Draw your s and run me through, or
31: 4 Saul took his own s and fell on it.
31: 5 too fell on his s and died with him.
2Sa 1:12 because they had fallen by the s.
1:22 s of Saul did not return unsatisfied.
2:26 "Must the s devour for ever?
3:29 falls by the s or who lacks food."
11:25 s devours one as well as another.
12: 9 down Uriah the Hittite with the s
12: 9 him with the s of the Ammonites.
12:10 Now, therefore, the s shall never
15:14 upon us and put the city to the s."
18: 8 more lives that day than the s.
21:16 who was armed with a new ⌊s⌋, said
23:10 hand grew tired and froze to the s.
24: 9 men who could handle a s, and in
1Ki 1:51 put his servant to death with the s.
2: 8 will not put you to death by the s.'
2:32 two men and killed them with the s.
3:24 the king said, "Bring me a s."
3:24 So they brought a s for the king.
19: 1 killed all the prophets with the s.
19:10 your prophets to death with the s.
19:14 your prophets to death with the s.
19:17 any who escape the s of Hazael,
19:17 death any who escape the s of Jehu.
2Ki 6:22 captured with your own s or bow?
8:12 kill their young men with the s,
10:25 So they cut them down with the s.
11:20 been slain with the s at the palace.
19: 7 I will have him cut down with the s.
19:37 Sharezer cut him down with the s,
1Ch 5:18 men who could handle shield and s,
10: 4 "Draw your s and run me through, or
10: 4 Saul took his own s and fell on it.
10: 5 dead, he too fell on his s and died.
21: 5 thousand men who could handle a s,
21:12 or three days of the s of the
21:16 with a drawn s in his hand extended
21:27 he put his s back into its sheath.
21:30 of the s of the angel of the LORD.
2Ch 20: 9 whether the s of judgment, or plague
21: 4 he put all his brothers to the s
23:21 Athaliah had been slain with the s.
29: 9 our fathers have fallen by the s
32:21 of his sons cut him down with the s.
36:17 men with the s in the sanctuary,
36:20 the remnant who escaped from the s,
Ezr 9: 7 subjected to the s and captivity,
Ne 4:18 each of the builders wore his s at
Est 9: 5 down all their enemies with the s,
Job 1:15 They put the servants to the s, and
1:17 They put the servants to the s, and
5:15 He saves the needy from the s in
5:20 in battle from the stroke of the s.
15:22 he is marked for the s.
19:29 you should fear the s yourselves;
19:29 will bring punishment by the s,
27:14 his children, their fate is the s;
33:18 his life from perishing by the s.
36:12 they will perish by the s and die
39:22 he does not shy away from the s.
40:19 Maker can approach him with his s.
41:26 The s that reaches him has no effect,
Ps 7:12 not relent, he will sharpen his s;
17:13 rescue me from the wicked by your s.
22:20 Deliver my life from the s, my
37:14 The wicked draw the s and bend the
44: 3 was not by their s that they won the
44: 6 my s does not bring me victory;
45: 3 Gird your s upon your side, O mighty
63:10 They will be given over to the s and
78:62 He gave his people over to the s;
89:43 have turned back the edge of his s
144:10 his servant David from the deadly s.
149: 6 and a double-edged s in their hands,
Pr 5: 4 as gall, sharp as a double-edged s.
12:18 Reckless words pierce like a s, but
25:18 Like a club or a s or a sharp arrow
SS 3: 8 all of them wearing the s, all
3: 8 each with his s at his side,
Isa 1:20 you will be devoured by the s.
2: 4 Nation will not take up s against
3:25 Your men will fall by the s, your
13:15 who are caught will fall by the s.
14:19 with those pierced by the s, those
21:15 flee from the s, from the drawn s,
22: 2 Your slain were not killed by the s
27: 1 the LORD will punish with his s, his
27: 1 his fierce, great and powerful s,
31: 8 "Assyria will fall by a s that is
31: 8 s, not of mortals, will devour them.
31: 8 They will flee before the s and
34: 5 My s has drunk its fill in the
34: 6 The s of the LORD is bathed in blood,
37: 7 I will have him cut down with the s.
37:38 Sharezer cut him down with the s,
41: 2 He turns them to dust with his s,
49: 2 He made my mouth like a sharpened s,
51:19 ruin and destruction, famine and s
65:12 I will destine you for the s, and
66:16 For with fire and with his s the
Jer 2:30 Your s has devoured your prophets
4:10 when the s is at our throats."
5:12 we will never see s or famine.
5:17 With the s they will destroy the
6:25 for the enemy has a s, and there is
9:16 I will pursue them with the s until
11:22 Their young men will die by the s,
12:12 for the s of the LORD will devour
14:12 them with the s, famine and plague."
14:13 will not see the s or suffer famine.
14:15 'No s or famine will touch this land.
14:15 will perish by s and famine.
14:16 because of the famine and s.
14:18 I see those slain by the s; if I go
15: 2 those for the s, to the s;
15: 3 "the s to kill and the dogs to drag
15: 9 I will put the survivors to the s
16: 4 They will perish by s and famine,
18:21 them over to the power of the s.
18:21 young men slain by the s in battle.
19: 7 I will make them fall by the s
20: 4 them fall by the s of their enemies.
20: 4 to Babylon or put them to the s.
21: 7 survive the plague, s and famine,
21: 7 He will put them to the s; he will
21: 9 will die by the s, famine or plague.
24:10 I will send the s, famine and plague
25:16 of the s I will send among them."
25:27 of the s I will send among you.'
25:29 for I am calling down a s upon all
25:31 and put the wicked to the s,'"
25:38 because of the s of the oppressor
26:23 who had him struck down with a s and
27: 8 I will punish that nation with the s,
27:13 you and your people die by the s,
29:17 "I will send the s, famine and
29:18 I will pursue them with the s,
31: 2 "The people who survive the s will
32:24 Because of the s, famine and plague,
32:36 'By the s, famine and plague it will
33: 4 against the siege ramps and the s
34: 4 You will not die by the s;
34:17 to fall by the s, plague and famine.
38: 2 in this city will die by the s,
39:18 you will not fall by the s but will
41: 2 the son of Shaphan, with the s,
42:16 the s you fear will overtake you
42:17 to settle there will die by the s,
42:22 sure of this: You will die by the s,
43:11 the s to those destined for the s.
44:12 fall by the s or die from famine.
44:12 they will die by s or famine.
44:13 those who live in Egypt with the s,
44:18 been perishing by s and famine."
44:27 the Jews in Egypt will perish by s
44:28 Those who escape the s and return to
46:10 The s will devour till it is
46:14 for the s devours those around you.'
46:16 away from the s of the oppressor.'
47: 6 "'Ah, s of the LORD,' you cry, 'how
Jer 48: 2 be silenced; the s will pursue you.
48:10 him who keeps his s from bloodshed!
49:37 "I will pursue them with the s
50:16 Because of the s of the oppressor
50:35 "A s against the Babylonians!"
50:36 A s against her false prophets!
50:36 A s against her warriors! They will
50:37 A s against her horses and chariots
50:37 A s against her treasures! They will
51:50 You who have escaped the s, leave
Lam 1:20 Outside, the s bereaves; inside,
2:21 and maidens have fallen by the s.
4: 9 Those killed by the s are better off
5: 9 because of the s in the desert.
Eze 5: 1 "Now, son of man, take a sharp s and
5: 2 it with the s all around the city.
5: 2 For I will pursue them with drawn s.
5:12 a third will fall by the s outside
5:12 the winds and pursue with drawn s.
5:17 and I will bring the s against you.
6: 3 I am about to bring a s against you,
6: 8 for some of you will escape the s
6:11 fall by the s, famine and plague.
6:12 he that is near will fall by the s,
7:15 "Outside is the s, inside are plague
7:15 in the country will die by the s,
11: 8 You fear the s, and the s is what I
11:10 You will fall by the s, and I will
12:14 I will pursue them with drawn s.
12:16 I will spare a few of them from the s
14:17 "Or if I bring a s against that
14:17 'Let the s pass throughout the land,'
14:21 my four dreadful judgments—s and
17:21 fleeing troops will fall by the s,
21: 3 I will draw my s from its scabbard
21: 4 my s will be unsheathed against
21: 5 have drawn my s from its scabbard;
21: 9 "'A s, a s, sharpened and polished
21:10 The s despises every such stick.
21:11 "'The s is appointed to be polished,
21:12 They are thrown to the s along with
21:13 which the s despises, does not
21:14 Let the s strike twice, even three
21:14 It is a s for slaughter—a s for
21:15 I have stationed the s for
21:16 O s, slash to the right, then to the
21:19 mark out two roads for the s of the
21:20 Mark out one road for the s to come
21:28 'A s, a s, drawn for the slaughter,
21:30 Return the s to its scabbard.
23:10 daughters and killed her with the s.
23:25 you who are left will fall by the s.
24:21 you left behind will fall by the s.
25:13 to Dedan they will fall by the s.
26: 6 mainland will be ravaged by the s.
26: 8 on the mainland with the s;
26:11 he will kill your people with the s,
28:23 the s against her on every side.
29: 8 I will bring a s against you and
30: 4 A s will come against Egypt, and
30: 5 will fall by the s along with Egypt.
30: 6 they will fall by the s within her,
30:17 and Bubastis will fall by the s,
30:21 to become strong enough to hold a s.
30:22 and make the s fall from his hand.
30:24 of Babylon and put my s in his hand,
30:25 when I put my s into the hand of the
31:17 it, joining those killed by the s.
31:18 with those killed by the s.
32:10 when I brandish my s before them.
32:11 'The s of the king of Babylon will
32:20 fall among those killed by the s.
32:20 The s is drawn; let her be dragged
32:21 with those killed by the s.'
32:22 slain, all who have fallen by the s.
32:23 living are slain, fallen by the s.
32:24 of them are slain, fallen by the s.
32:25 are uncircumcised, killed by the s.
32:26 killed by the s because they spread
32:28 with those killed by the s.
32:29 are laid with those killed by the s.
32:30 with those killed by the s and bear
32:31 hordes that were killed by the s,
32:32 with those skilled by the s,
33: 2 'When I bring the s against a land,
33: 3 he sees the s coming against the

Eze 33: 4 and the s comes and takes his life,
33: 6 if the watchman sees the s coming
33: 6 the s comes and takes the life of
33:26 You rely on your s, you do
33:27 in the ruins will fall by the s,
35: 5 Israelites over to the s at the
35: 8 those killed by the s will fall on
38:21 I will summon a s against Gog on all
38:21 man's s will be against his brother.
39:23 enemies, and they all fell by the s.
Da 11:33 will fall by the s or be burned or
Hos 1: 7 not by bow, s or battle, or by
2:18 Bow and s and battle I will abolish
7:16 Their leaders will fall by the s
13:16 They will fall by the s; their
Am 1:11 he pursued his brother with a s,
4:10 I killed your young men with the s,
7: 9 with my s I will rise against the
7:11 'Jeroboam will die by the s, and
7:17 and daughters will fall by the s.
9: 1 who are left I will kill with the s.
9: 4 I will command the s to slay them.
9:10 among my people will die by the s,
Mic 4: 3 Nation will not take up s against
5: 6 the land of Assyria with the s,
5: 6 the land of Nimrod with drawn s.
6:14 what you save I will give to the s.
Na 2:13 the s will devour your young lions.
3:15 the s will cut you down and, like
Zep 2:12 O Cushites, will be slain by my s."
Hag 2:22 fall, each by the s of his brother.
Zec 9:13 and make you like a warrior's s.
11:17 May the s strike his arm and his
13: 7 "Awake, O s, against my shepherd,
Mt 10:34 not come to bring peace, but a s.
26:51 Jesus' companions reached for his s,
26:52 "Put your s back in its place,"
26:52 who draw the s will die by the s.
Mk 14:47 one of those standing near drew his s
Lk 2:35 a s will pierce your own soul too."
21:24 They will fall by the s and will be
22:36 if you don't have a s, sell your
Jn 18:10 Simon Peter, who had a s, drew it
18:11 "Put your s away! Shall I not drink
Ac 12: 2 of John, put to death with the s.
16:27 he drew his s and was about to kill
Ro 8:35 famine or nakedness or danger or s?
13: 4 he does not bear the s for nothing.
Eph 6:17 salvation and the s of the Spirit,
Heb 4:12 Sharper than any double-edged s, it
11:34 and escaped the edge of the s;
11:37 they were put to death by the s.
Rev 1:16 mouth came a sharp double-edged s.
2:12 who has the sharp, double-edged s.
2:16 against them with the s of my mouth.
6: 4 To him was given a large s.
6: 8 a fourth of the earth to kill by s,
13:10 If anyone is to be killed with the s,
13:10 with the s he will be killed.
13:14 was wounded by the s and yet lived.
19:15 Out of his mouth comes a sharp s
19:21 killed with the s that came out of

Swords (Sword)

Ge 34:25 took their s and attacked the
49: 5 their s are weapons of violence.
Jos 10:11 killed by the s of the Israelites.
Jdg 7:22 to turn on each other with their s.
20: 2 thousand soldiers armed with s.
20:25 Israelites, all of them armed with s.
20:35 25,100 Benjamites, all armed with s.
1Sa 13:19 the Hebrews will make s or spears!"
14:20 striking each other with their s.
25:13 David said to his men, "Put on your s
25:13 So they put on their s, and David
1Ki 18:28 themselves with s and spears,
1Ch 21:12 with their s overtaking you, or
Ne 4:13 with their s, spears and bows.
Ps 37:15 their s will pierce their own hearts,
55:21 than oil, yet they are drawn s.
57: 4 arrows, whose tongues are sharp s.
59: 7 they spew out s from their lips,
64: 3 They sharpen their tongues like s
76: 3 the shields and the s, the weapons
Pr 30:14 those whose teeth are s and whose
Isa 2: 4 will beat their s into ploughshares
Eze 16:40 and hack you to pieces with their s.
23:47 them and cut them down with their s;
28: 7 they will draw their s against your
30:11 They will draw their s against Egypt
32:12 to fall by the s of mighty men
32:27 whose s were placed under their
38: 4 all of them brandishing their s.
Hos 11: 6 S will flash in their cities, will
Joel 3:10 Beat your ploughshares into s and
Mic 4: 3 will beat their s into ploughshares
Na 3: 3 Charging cavalry, flashing s and
Mt 26:47 large crowd armed with s and clubs,
26:55 that you have come out with s and
Mk 14:43 With him was a crowd armed with s
14:48 out with s and clubs to capture me?
Lk 22:38 "See, Lord, here are two s."
22:49 "Lord, should we strike with our s?
22:52 that you have come with s and clubs?

Swordsmen (Sword)

Jdg 8:10 and twenty thousand s had fallen.
20:15 Twenty-six thousand s from their
20:17 four hundred thousand s, all of
20:46 Benjamite s fell, all of them valiant
2Ki 3:26 he took with him seven hundred s to

Swore (Swear)

Ge 21:31 because the two men s an oath there.
24: 9 s an oath to him concerning this
25:33 So he s an oath to him, selling his
26: 3 the oath I s to your father Abraham.
26:31 the next morning the men s an oath
47:31 Then Joseph s to him, and Israel
Ex 6: 8 will bring you to the land I s with
13: 5 s to your forefathers to give you,
32:13 Isaac and Israel, to whom you s by
Lev 6: 5 or whatever it was he s falsely
Nu 14:30 the land I s with uplifted hand to
32:10 aroused that day and he s this oath:
Dt 1: 8 LORD s he would give to your fathers
1:34 said, he was angry and solemnly s:
1:35 land I s to give your forefathers,
4:21 and he solemnly s that I would not
6:10 into the land he s to your fathers,
7: 8 the oath he s to your forefathers
7:12 you, as he s to your forefathers.
7:13 s to your forefathers to give you.
8:18 which he s to your forefathers, as
9: 5 to accomplish what he s to your
10:11 I s to their fathers to give them."
11: 9 the LORD s to your forefathers to
11:21 the LORD s to give your forefathers,
26: 3 s to our forefathers to give us."
28:11 s to your forefathers to give you.
29:13 you and as he s to your fathers,
30:20 land he s to give to your fathers,
31: 7 s to their forefathers to give them,
Jos 1: 6 s to their forefathers to give them.
9:20 for breaking the oath we s to them."
14: 9 on that day Moses s to me, 'The land
Jdg 2: 1 I s to give to your forefathers.
1Sa 3:14 Therefore, I s to the house of Eli,
28:10 Saul s to her by the LORD, "As
2Sa 21:17 Then David's men s to him, saying,
1Ki 1:17 "My lord, you yourself s to me your
1:30 today what I s to you by the LORD,
2: 8 I s to him by the LORD: 'I will not
2:23 King Solomon s by the LORD: "May God
1Ch 16:16 Abraham, the oath he s to Isaac.
Ps 89:49 in your faithfulness you s to David?
105: 9 Abraham, the oath he s to Isaac.
106:26 he s to them with uplifted hand that
132: 2 He s an oath to the LORD and made a
132:11 The LORD s an oath to David, a sure
Isa 54: 9 when I s that the waters of Noah
Jer 11: 5 I will fulfil the oath I s to your
38:16 King Zedekiah s this oath secretly
Eze 20: 5 I s with uplifted hand to the
20: 6 On that day I s to them that I would
20:15 Also with uplifted hand I s to them
20:23 Also with uplifted hand I s to them
47:14 Because I s with uplifted hand to
Mt 26:74 s to them, "I don't know the man!"
Mk 14:71 and he s to them, "I don't know this
Lk 1:73 the oath he s to our father Abraham:
Heb 6:13 him to swear by, he s by himself,
Rev 10: 6 he s by him who lives for ever and

Sworn (Swear)

Ge 26:28 'There ought to be a s agreement
Nu 30:13 or any s pledge to deny herself.
Dt 2:14 the camp, as the LORD had s to them.
Jos 5: 6 For the LORD had s to them that they
9:18 had s an oath to them by the LORD,
21:43 he had s to give their forefathers,
21:44 as he had s to their forefathers.
Jdg 2:15 them, just as he had s to them.
1Sa 20:42 for we have s friendship with each
2Sa 21: 2 the Israelites had s to spare them,
2Ch 15:15 they had s it wholeheartedly.
Ne 9:15 s with uplifted hand to give them.
Ps 89: 3 one, I have s to David my servant,
89:35 Once for all, I have s by my
110: 4 The LORD has s and will not change
Isa 14:24 The LORD Almighty has s, "Surely, as
45:23 By myself I have s, my mouth has
54: 9 So now I have s not to be angry with
62: 8 The LORD has s by his right hand and
Jer 5: 7 me and s by gods that are not gods.
32:22 You gave them this land you had s to
51:14 The LORD Almighty has s by himself:
Eze 20:28 into the land I had s to give them
20:42 the land I had s with uplifted hand
21:23 those who have s allegiance to him,
44:12 therefore I have s with uplifted
Da 9:11 curses and s judgments written in
Am 4: 2 The Sovereign LORD has s by his
6: 8 The Sovereign LORD has s by himself—
8: 7 The LORD has s by the Pride of Jacob:
Heb 7:21 "The Lord has s and will not change

Swung (Swing)

Eze 26: 2 and its doors have s open to me;
Rev 14:16 he who was seated on the cloud s his
14:19 The angel s his sickle on the earth,

Sycamore-fig (Fig)

1Ki 10:27 as s trees in the foothills.
1Ch 27:28 s trees in the western foothills.
2Ch 1:15 as s trees in the foothills.
9:27 as s trees in the foothills.
Am 7:14 and I also took care of s trees.
Lk 19: 4 he ran ahead and climbed a s tree to

Sycamore-figs (Fig)

Ps 78:47 with hail and their s with sleet.

Sychar

City in Samaria near Jacob's well where Jesus spoke with a Samaritan woman (Jn 4:5-43). Probably built on the site of the ancient town of Shechem (Ge 33:18).

Jn 4: 5 he came to a town in Samaria called S

Symbol (Symbolic, Symbolises, Symbols)

Ex 13:16 a s on your forehead that the LORD
Nu 6: 7 because the s of his separation to

Symbolic (Symbol)

Zec 3: 8 who are men s of things to come:

Symbolises (Symbol)

1Pe 3:21 this water s baptism that now saves

Symbols (Symbol)

Dt 6: 8 Tie them as s on your hands and bind
11:18 tie them as s on your hands and bind
Isa 8:18 We are signs and s in Israel from
57: 8 doorposts you have put your pagan s.

Sympathetic (Sympathy)

1Pe 3: 8 be s, love as brothers, be

Sympathise (Sympathy)

Job 2:11 go and s with him and comfort him.
Heb 4:15 is unable to s with our weaknesses,

Sympathised (Sympathy)
Heb 10:34 You **s** with those in prison and

Sympathy (Sympathetic, Sympathise, Sympathised)
2Sa 10: 2 **s** to Hanun concerning his father.
10: 3 by sending men to you to express **s**?
1Ch 19: 2 **s** to Hanun concerning his father.
19: 2 the Ammonites to express **s** to him,
19: 3 by sending men to you to express **s**?
Ps 69:20 I looked for **s**, but there was none,
Jer 16: 5 do not go to mourn or show **s**,
Da 1: 9 to show favour and **s** to Daniel,

Synagogue (Synagogues)
Mt 12: 9 that place, he went into their **s**,
13:54 teaching the people in their **s**,
Mk 1:21 went into the **s** and began to teach.
1:23 Just then a man in their **s** who was
1:29 soon as they left the **s**, they went
3: 1 Another time he went into the **s**, and
5:22 one of the **s** rulers, named Jairus,
5:35 the house of Jairus, the **s** ruler.
5:36 Jesus told the **s** ruler, "Don't be
5:38 they came to the home of the **s** ruler,
6: 2 he began to teach in the **s**, and many
Lk 4:16 went into the **s**, as was his custom.
4:20 in the **s** were fastened on him,
4:28 All the people in the **s** were furious
4:33 In the **s** there was a man possessed
4:38 Jesus left the **s** and went to the
6: 6 On another Sabbath he went into the **s**
7: 5 our nation and has built our **s**."
8:41 a man named Jairus, a ruler of the **s**,
8:49 the house of Jairus, the **s** ruler.
13:14 the **s** ruler said to the people,
Jn 6:59 He said this while teaching in the **s**
9:22 Christ would be put out of the **s**.
12:42 fear they would be put out of the **s**;
16: 2 They will put you out of the **s**;
Ac 6: 9 members of the **S** of the Freedmen
13:14 they entered the **s** and sat down.
13:15 the **s** rulers sent word to them,
13:42 Paul and Barnabas were leaving the **s**,
14: 1 went as usual into the Jewish **s**.
17: 1 where there was a Jewish **s**.
17: 2 his custom was, Paul went into the **s**,
17:10 there, they went to the Jewish **s**.
17:17 he reasoned in the **s** with the Jews
18: 4 Every Sabbath he reasoned in the **s**,
18: 7 Paul left the **s** and went next door
18: 8 Crispus, the **s** ruler, and his entire
18:17 turned on Sosthenes the **s** ruler
18:19 He himself went into the **s** and
18:26 He began to speak boldly in the **s**.
19: 8 Paul entered the **s** and spoke boldly
22:19 from one **s** to another to imprison
26:11 Many a time I went from one **s** to
Rev 2: 9 and are not, but are a **s** of Satan.
3: 9 I will make those who are of the **s**

Synagogues (Synagogue)
Mt 4:23 teaching in their **s**, preaching the
6: 2 as the hypocrites do in the **s** and on
6: 5 they love to pray standing in the **s**
9:35 teaching in their **s**, preaching the
10:17 councils and flog you in their **s**.
23: 6 the most important seats in the **s**;
23:34 flog in your **s** and pursue from town
Mk 1:39 preaching in their **s** and driving
12:39 the most important seats in the **s**
13: 9 local councils and flogged in the **s**.
Lk 4:15 He taught in their **s**, and everyone
4:44 he kept on preaching in the **s** of
11:43 the most important seats in the **s**
12:11 "When you are brought before **s**,
13:10 Jesus was teaching in one of the **s**,
20:46 the most important seats in the **s**
21:12 They will deliver you to **s** and
Jn 18:20 "I always taught in **s** or at the
Ac 9: 2 asked him for letters to the **s** in
9:20 At once he began to preach in the **s**
13: 5 the word of God in the Jewish **s**.
15:21 is read in the **s** on every Sabbath."
24:12 or stirring up a crowd in the **s**

Syntyche
Php 4: 2 I plead with **S** to agree with each

Syracuse
Ac 28:12 We put in at **S** and stayed there

Syria See Aram (Syrian)
Mt 4:24 News about him spread all over **S**,
Lk 2: 2 while Quirinius was governor of **S**.)
Ac 15:23 Antioch, **S** and Cilicia: Greetings.
15:41 He went through **S** and Cilicia,
18:18 left the brothers and sailed for **S**,
20: 3 just as he was about to sail for **S**,
21: 3 the south of it, we sailed on to **S**.
Gal 1:21 Later I went to **S** and Cilicia.

Syrian (Syria)
Mk 7:26 was a Greek, born in **S** Phoenicia.
Lk 4:27 was cleansed—only Naaman the **S**."

Syrtis
Ac 27:17 run aground on the sand-bars of **S**,

Taanach
Royal city of the Canaanites, situated in the hills south of Valley of Jezreel, about 5 miles south—east of Megiddo. After its defeat by Joshua (Jos 12:21), it was allotted to the tribe of Manasseh (Jos 17:11; 1Ch 7:29) and assigned to the Levites (Jos 21:25). Its Canaanite inhabitants were never driven out, so it retained some independence (Jdg 1:27). Canaanite kings fought against Deborah and Barak here (Jdg 5:19). Part of one of Solomon's 12 districts (1Ki 4:12).

Jos 12:21 the king of **T** one the king of
17:11 Endor, **T** and Megiddo, together with
21:25 they received **T** and Gath Rimmon,
Jdg 1:27 or **T** or Dor or Ibleam or Megiddo
5:19 at **T** by the waters of Megiddo,
1Ki 4:12 Baana son of Ahilud—in **T** and
1Ch 7:29 **T**, Megiddo and Dor, together with

Taanath Shiloh
Jos 16: 6 the north it curved eastward to **T**,

Tabaliah
1Ch 26:11 Hilkiah the second, **T** the third and

Tabbaoth
Ezr 2:43 the descendants of Ziha, Hasupha, **T**,
Ne 7:46 the descendants of Ziha, Hasupha, **T**,

Tabbath
Jdg 7:22 the border of Abel Meholah near **T**.

Tabeel
Ezr 4: 7 Bishlam, Mithredath, **T** and the rest
Isa 7: 6 and make the son of **T** king over it."

Taberah
Nu 11: 3 that place was called **T**, because
Dt 9:22 You also made the LORD angry at **T**,

Tabernacle (*Feast of Tabernacles*)
Ex 25: 9 Make this **t** and all its furnishings
26: 1 "Make the **t** with ten curtains of
26: 6 together so that the **t** is a unit.
26: 7 tent over the **t**—eleven altogether.
26:12 to hang down at the rear of the **t**.
26:13 sides of the **t** so as to cover it.
26:15 frames of acacia wood for the **t**.
26:17 all the frames of the **t** in this way.
26:18 frames for the south side of the **t**
26:20 side of the **t**, make twenty frames
26:22 end, that is, the west end of the **t**,
26:26 for the frames on one side of the **t**,
26:27 the west, at the far end of the **t**.
26:30 "Set up the **t** according to the plan
26:35 curtain on the north side of the **t**
27: 9 "Make a courtyard for the **t**. The
27:19 used in the service of the **t**,
35:11 the **t** with its tent and its covering,
35:15 doorway at the entrance to the **t**;
Ex 35:18 the tent pegs for the **t** and for the
36: 8 the workmen made the **t** with ten
36:13 together so that the **t** was a unit.
36:14 tent over the **t**—eleven altogether.
36:20 frames of acacia wood for the **t**.
36:22 all the frames of the **t** in this way.
36:23 frames for the south side of the **t**
36:25 of the **t**, they made twenty frames
36:27 end, that is, the west end of the **t**,
36:28 the corners of the **t** at the far end.
36:31 for the frames on one side of the **t**,
36:32 the west, at the far end of the **t**.
38:20 All the tent pegs of the **t** and of
38:21 of the materials used for the **t**,
38:21 the **t** of the Testimony, which were
38:31 all the tent pegs for the **t** and
39:32 all the work on the **t**, the Tent of
39:33 they brought the **t** to Moses: the
39:40 for the **t**, the Tent of Meeting;
40: 2 "Set up the **t**, the Tent of Meeting,
40: 5 curtain at the entrance to the **t**.
40: 6 to the **t**, the Tent of Meeting;
40: 9 anoint the **t** and everything in it;
40:17 the **t** was set up on the first day of
40:18 Moses set up the **t**, he put the bases
40:19 he spread the tent over the **t** and
40:21 he brought the ark into the **t** and
40:22 side of the **t** outside the curtain
40:24 the table on the south side of the **t**
40:28 curtain at the entrance to the **t**.
40:29 offering near the entrance to the **t**,
40:33 set up the courtyard around the **t**
40:34 the glory of the LORD filled the **t**.
40:35 the glory of the LORD filled the **t**.
40:36 above the **t**, they would set out;
40:38 the cloud of the LORD was over the **t**
Lev 8:10 anointed the **t** and everything in it,
17: 4 LORD in front of the **t** of the LORD
Nu 1:50 in charge of the **t** of the Testimony
1:50 They are to carry the **t** and all its
1:51 Whenever the **t** is to move, the
1:51 and whenever the **t** is to be set up,
1:53 to set up their tents round the **t**
1:53 the care of the **t** of the Testimony."
3: 7 Meeting by doing the work of the **t**.
3: 8 by doing the work of the **t**.
3:23 to camp on the west, behind the **t**.
3:25 for the care of the **t** and tent,
3:26 surrounding the **t** and altar,
3:29 to camp on the south side of the **t**.
3:35 to camp on the north side of the **t**.
3:36 to take care of the frames of the **t**,
3:38 were to camp to the east of the **t**,
4:16 the entire **t** and everything in it,
4:25 are to carry the curtains of the **t**,
4:26 surrounding the **t** and altar,
4:31 **t**, its crossbars, posts and bases,
5:17 from the **t** floor into the water.
7: 1 Moses finished setting up the **t**, he
7: 3 These they presented before the **t**.
9:15 On the day the **t**, the Tent of the
9:15 cloud above the **t** looked like fire.
9:18 over the **t**, they remained in camp.
9:19 the cloud remained over the **t** a long
9:20 Sometimes the cloud was over the **t**
9:22 Whether the cloud stayed over the **t**
10:11 from above the **t** of the Testimony.
10:17 the **t** was taken down, and the
10:21 The **t** was to be set up before they
16: 9 to do the work at the LORD's **t**
17:13 Anyone who even comes near the **t** of
19:13 purify himself defiles the LORD's **t**.
31:30 for the care of the LORD's **t**."
31:47 for the care of the LORD's **t**.
Jos 22:19 **t** stands, and share the land with us.
22:29 our God that stands before his **t**."
1Ch 6:32 ministered with music before the **t**,
6:48 duties of the **t**, the house of God.
16:39 his fellow priests before the **t** of
21:29 The **t** of the LORD, which Moses had
23:26 no longer need to carry the **t** or
2Ch 1: 5 Gibeon in front of the **t** of the LORD;
Ps 27: 5 his **t** and set me high upon a rock.
27: 6 at his **t** will I sacrifice with
78:60 He abandoned the **t** of Shiloh, the
Ac 7:44 "Our forefathers had the **t** of the

Ac 7:45 Having received the t, our fathers
Heb 8: 2 t set up by the Lord, not by man.
8: 5 when he was about to build the t:
9: 2 A t was set up. In its first room
9: 8 as the first t was still standing.
9:11 more perfect t that is not man—made,
9:21 sprinkled with the blood both the t
13:10 at the t have no right to eat.
Rev 15: 5 the t of the Testimony, was opened.

Tabitha See Dorcas

Ac 9:36 In Joppa there was a disciple named T
9:40 the dead woman, he said, "T, get up.

Table (Tables)

Ge 43:34 were served to them from Joseph's t,
Ex 25:23 "Make a t of acacia wood—two cubits
25:26 Make four gold rings for the t and
25:27 the poles used in carrying the t.
25:28 with gold and carry the t with them.
25:30 this t to be before me at all times.
26:35 Place the t outside the curtain on
30:27 the t and all its articles, the
31: 8 the t and its articles, the pure
35:13 the t with its poles and all its
37:10 They made the t of acacia wood—two
37:13 They cast four gold rings for the t
37:14 the poles used in carrying the t.
37:15 The poles for carrying the t were
37:16 the articles for the t—its plates
39:36 the t with all its articles and the
40: 4 Bring in the t and set out what
40:22 Moses placed the t in the Tent of
40:24 opposite the t on the south side
Lev 24: 6 the t of pure gold before the LORD.
Nu 3:31 the t, the lampstand, the altars,
4: 7 "Over the t of the Presence they are
Jdg 1: 7 have picked up scraps under my t.
1Sa 20:29 he has not come to the king's t."
20:34 Jonathan got up from the t in fierce
2Sa 9: 7 and you will always eat at my t."
9:10 master, will always eat at my t.
9:11 Mephibosheth ate at David's t like
9:13 ate at the king's t, and he was
19:28 place among those who eat at your t.
1Ki 2: 7 be among those who eat at your t.
4:27 and all who came to the king's t.
7:48 the golden altar; the golden t on
10: 5 the food on his t, the seating of
13:20 While they were sitting at the t,
18:19 of Asherah, who eat at Jezebel's t."
2Ki 4:10 and a t, a chair and a lamp for him.
25:29 life ate regularly at the king's t.
1Ch 9:32 Sabbath the bread set out on the t.
23:29 of the bread set out on the t,
28:16 the weight of gold for each t for
2Ch 9: 4 the food on his t, the seating of
13:11 bread on the ceremonially clean t
29:18 and the t for setting out the
Ne 5:17 Jews and officials ate at my t,
10:33 for the bread set out on the t; for
Job 36:16 of your t laden with choice food.
Ps 23: 5 You prepare a t before me in the
69:22 May the t set before them become a
78:19 "Can God spread a t in the
128: 3 be like olive shoots round your t.
Pr 9: 2 her wine; she has also set her t.
SS 1:12 While the king was at his t, my
Isa 65:11 who spread a t for Fortune and fill
Jer 52:33 life ate regularly at the king's t.
Eze 23:41 You sat on an elegant couch, with a t
39:20 At my t you will eat your fill of
41:22 is the t that is before the LORD."
44:16 they alone are to come near my t to
Da 1: 5 of food and wine from the king's t.
11:27 will sit at the same t and lie to
Mal 1: 7 that the LORD's t is contemptible.
1:12 it by saying of the Lord's t,
Mt 15:27 that fall from their masters' t."
26: 7 head as he was reclining at the t.
26:20 reclining at the t with the Twelve.
Mk 7:28 the t eat the children's crumbs."
14: 3 reclining at the t in the home of a
14:18 While they were reclining at the t
Lk 7:36 house and reclined at the t.
Lk 11:37 so he went in and reclined at the t.
12:37 will have them recline at the t and
14: 7 at the t, he told them this parable:
14:15 one of those at the t with him heard
16:21 eat what fell from the rich man's t.
22:14 and his apostles reclined at the t.
22:21 to betray me is with mine on the t.
22:27 the one who is at the t or the one
22:27 Is it not the one who is at the t?
22:30 that you may eat and drink at my t
24:30 he was at the t with them, he took
Jn 12: 2 those reclining at the t with him.
Ro 11: 9 David says: "May their t become a
1Co 10:21 the Lord's t and the t of demons.
Heb 9: 2 the t and the consecrated bread;

Tables (Table)

1Ch 28:16 weight of silver for the silver t;
2Ch 4: 8 He made ten t and placed them in the
4:19 the golden altar; the t on which was
Est 9: 1 but now the t were turned and the
Isa 21: 5 They set the t, they spread the rugs,
28: 8 All the t are covered with vomit and
Eze 40:39 the gateway were two t on each side,
40:40 to the north gateway were two t,
40:40 other side of the steps were two t.
40:41 there were four t on one side of the
40:41 four on the other—eight t in all—
40:42 There were also four t of dressed
40:43 The t were for the flesh of the
Mt 21:12 He overturned the t of the
Mk 11:15 He overturned the t of the
Jn 2:14 sitting at t exchanging money.
2:15 and overturned their t.
Ac 6: 2 word of God in order to wait on t.

Tablet (Tablets)

Pr 3: 3 write them on the t of your heart.
7: 3 write them on the t of your heart.
Isa 30: 8 Go now, write it on a t for them,
Eze 4: 1 "Now, son of man, take a clay t, put
Lk 1:63 He asked for a writing t, and to

Tablets (Tablet)

Ex 24:12 and I will give you the t of stone,
31:18 he gave him the two t of the
31:18 the t of stone inscribed by the
32:15 two t of the Testimony in his hands.
32:16 The t were the work of God; the
32:16 writing of God, engraved on the t.
32:19 his anger burned and he threw the t
34: 1 "Chisel out two stone t like the
34: 1 on the first t, which you broke.
34: 4 Moses chiselled out two stone t like
34: 4 the two stone t in his hands.
34:28 And he wrote on the t the words of
34:29 two t of the Testimony in his hands,
Dt 4:13 and then wrote them on two stone t.
5:22 on two stone t and gave them to me.
9: 9 mountain to receive the t of stone,
9: 9 the t of the covenant that the LORD
9:10 The LORD gave me two stone t
9:11 two stone t, the t of the covenant.
9:15 t of the covenant were in my hands.
9:17 I took the two t and threw them out
10: 1 "Chisel out two stone t like the
10: 2 I will write on the t the words that
10: 2 on the first t, which you broke.
10: 3 out two stone t like the first ones,
10: 3 mountain with the two t in my hands.
10: 4 The LORD wrote on these t what he
10: 5 and put the t in the ark I had made,
1Ki 8: 9 in the ark except the two stone t
2Ch 5:10 nothing in the ark except the two t
Jer 17: 1 on the t of their hearts and on the
Hab 2: 2 t so that a herald may run with it.
2Co 3: 3 t of stone but on t of human hearts.
Heb 9: 4 and the stone t of the covenant.

Tabor

1. Isolated mountain on the border between Issachar, Zebulun and Naphtali (Jos 19:22), about 6 miles east of Nazareth. Here Barak gathered his troops to attack the Canaanite army of Sisera (Jdg 4:6, 12, 14), and Gideon's brothers were killed by the Midianite kings (Jdg 8:18–19). Its greatness was equated with Mount Carmel (Jer 46:18) and Mount Hermon (Ps 89:13), but it became a sanctuary for idolatry (Hos 5:1). **2.** Levite city in the territory of Zebulun (1Ch 6:77). **3.** Site of a great tree where Samuel told Saul he would receive a sign of God's favour (1Sa 10:3).

Jos 19:22 The boundary touched T, Shahazumah
Jdg 4: 6 Zebulun and lead the way to Mount T.
4:12 of Abinoam had gone up to Mount T,
4:14 Barak went down Mount T, followed
8:18 "What kind of men did you kill at T?"
1Sa 10: 3 until you reach the great tree of T.
1Ch 6:77 Rimmono and T, together with their
Ps 89:12 T and Hermon sing for joy at your
Jer 46:18 "one will come who is like T among
Hos 5: 1 at Mizpah, a net spread out on T.

Tabrimmon

1Ki 15:18 and sent them to Ben-Hadad son of T,

Tackle

Ac 27:19 they threw the ship's t overboard

Tact

Da 2:14 spoke to him with wisdom and t.

Tadmor

1Ki 9:18 Baalath, and T in the desert, within
2Ch 8: 4 He also built up T in the desert and

Tahan (Tahanite)

Nu 26:35 clan; through T, the Tahanite clan.
1Ch 7:25 his son, Telah his son, T his son,

Tahanite (Tahan)

Nu 26:35 clan; through Tahan, the T clan.

Tahash

Ge 22:24 sons: Tebah, Gaham, T and Maacah.

Tahath

Nu 33:26 They left Makheloth and camped at T.
33:27 They left T and camped at Terah.
1Ch 6:24 T his son, Uriel his son, Uzziah his
6:37 the son of T, the son of Assir, the
7:20 Bered his son, T his son, Eleadah
7:20 his son, Eleadah his son, T his son,

Tahkemonite

2Sa 23: 8 a T, was chief of the Three; he

Tahpanhes

City on the eastern side of the Nile Delta, often associated with Memphis (Jer 2:16; 44:1; 46:14). The Judeans fled here after the murder of Gedaliah (Jer 43:7) and Jeremiah was instructed by God to warn the people against putting their faith in Egypt, for it too would fall (Jer 43:7–13; Eze 30:18–19).

Jer 2:16 Also, the men of Memphis and T have
43: 7 to the LORD and went as far as T.
43: 8 In T the word of the LORD came to
43: 9 entrance to Pharaoh's palace in T.
44: 1 T and Memphis—and in Upper Egypt:
46:14 proclaim it also in Memphis and T:
Eze 30:18 Dark will be the day at T when I

Tahpenes

1Ki 11:19 his own wife, Queen T, in marriage.
11:20 The sister of T bore him a son named
11:20 T brought up in the royal palace.

Tahrea
1Ch 9:41 The sons of Micah: Pithon, Melech, T

Tahtim Hodshi
2Sa 24: 6 went to Gilead and the region of T,

Tail (Tails)
Ex 4: 4 out your hand and take it by the t.
29:22 the fat t, the fat around the inner
Lev 3: 9 the entire fat t cut off close to
7: 3 the fat t and the fat that covers
8:25 He took the fat, the fat t, all the
9:19 of the ox and the ram—the fat t,
Dt 28:13 will make you the head, not the t.
28:44 be the head, but you will be the t.
Jdg 15: 4 foxes and tied them t to t in pairs.
Job 40:17 His t sways like a cedar; the sinews
Isa 9:14 cut off from Israel both head and t,
9:15 prophets who teach lies are the t.
19:15 do—head or t, palm branch or reed.
Rev 12: 4 His t swept a third of the stars out

Tails (Tail)
Jdg 15: 4 fastened a torch to every pair of t,
Rev 9:10 They had t and stings like scorpions,
9:10 and in their t they had power to
9:19 in their t; for their t were like

Talent (Talents)
Ex 25:39 A t of pure gold is to be used for
37:24 accessories from one t of pure gold.
38:27 100 talents, one t for each base.
2Sa 12:30 king—its weight was a t of gold,
1Ki 20:39 or you must pay a t of silver.'
2Ki 5:22 Please give them a t of silver and
23:33 talents of silver and a t of gold.
1Ch 20: 2 weight was found to be a t of gold,
2Ch 36: 3 talents of silver and a t of gold.
Mt 25:15 t, each according to his ability.
25:18 the man who had received the one t
25:24 man who had received the one t came.
25:25 out and hid your t in the ground.
25:28 "'Take the t from him and give it

Talents (Talent)
Ex 38:24 sanctuary was 29 t and 730 shekels,
38:25 counted in the census was 100 t
38:27 The 100 t of silver were used to
38:27 the 100 t, one talent for each base.
38:29 was 70 t and 2,400 shekels.
1Ki 9:14 Now Hiram had sent to the king 120 t
9:28 Ophir and brought back 420 t of gold,
10:10 she gave the king 120 t of gold,
10:14 Solomon received yearly was 666 t,
16:24 from Shemer for two t of silver
2Ki 5: 5 taking with him ten t of silver, six
5:23 "By all means, take two t," said
5:23 and then tied up the two t of silver
15:19 and Menahem gave him a thousand t of
18:14 t of silver and thirty t of gold.
23:33 t of silver and a talent of gold.
1Ch 19: 6 the Ammonites sent a thousand t of
22:14 LORD a hundred thousand t of gold,
22:14 a million t of silver, quantities of
29: 4 three thousand t of gold (gold of
29: 4 seven thousand t of refined silver,
29: 7 t and ten thousand darics of gold,
29: 7 ten thousand t of silver, eighteen
29: 7 eighteen thousand t of bronze and a
29: 7 and a hundred thousand t of iron.
2Ch 3: 8 with six hundred t of fine gold.
8:18 four hundred and fifty t of gold,
9: 9 she gave the king 120 t of gold,
9:13 Solomon received yearly was 666 t,
25: 6 Israel for a hundred t of silver.
25: 9 "But what about the hundred t I paid
27: 5 paid him a hundred t of silver,
36: 3 t of silver and a talent of gold.
Ezr 7:22 up to a hundred t of silver, a
8:26 I weighed out to them 650 t of
8:26 weighing 100 t, 100 t of gold,
Est 3: 9 and I will put ten thousand t of
Mt 18:24 ten thousand t was brought to him.
25:15 To one he gave five t of money, to
25:15 to another two t, and to another one
25:16 The man who had received the five t
25:17 also, the one with the two t gained
25:20 The man who had received the five t
25:20 said, 'you entrusted me with five t.
25:22 "The man with the two t also came.
25:22 two t; see, I have gained two more.'
25:28 it to the one who has the ten t.

Tales
1Ti 4: 7 myths and old wives' t; rather,

Talitha
Mk 5:41 "T koum!" (which means, "Little

Tall (Taller, Tallest)
Dt 2:10 numerous, and as t as the Anakites.
2:21 numerous, and as t as the Anakites.
9: 2 The people are strong and t—
1Sa 17: 4 He was over nine feet t.
1Ch 11:23 who was seven and a half feet t.
Job 8:11 Can papyrus grow t where there is no
Isa 2:13 for all the cedars of Lebanon, t and
10:33 the t ones will be brought low.
18: 2 Go, swift messengers, to a people t
18: 7 from a people t and smooth-skinned,
45:14 and those t Sabeans—they will come
Eze 17:24 t tree and make the low tree grow t.
31: 4 deep springs made it grow t; their
Am 2: 9 though he was t as the cedars and

Taller (Tall)
Dt 1:28 'The people are stronger and t than
1Sa 9: 2 head t than any of the others.
10:23 was a head t than any of the others.

Tallest (Tall)
2Ki 19:23 I have cut down its t cedars, the
Isa 37:24 I have cut down its t cedars, the

Talmai
Nu 13:22 T, the descendants of Anak, lived.
Jos 15:14 Ahiman and T—descendants of Anak.
Jdg 1:10 and defeated Sheshai, Ahiman and T.
2Sa 3: 3 Maacah daughter of T king of Geshur;
13:37 Absalom fled and went to T son of
1Ch 3: 2 of T king of Geshur; the fourth,

Talmon
1Ch 9:17 The gatekeepers: Shallum, Akkub, T,
Ezr 2:42 Ater, T, Akkub, Hatita and Shobai 139
Ne 7:45 Ater, T, Akkub, Hatita and Shobai 138
11:19 The gatekeepers: Akkub, T and their
12:25 Bakbukiah, Obadiah, Meshullam, T and

Tamar
1. Married in turn to Judah's sons Er and Onan (Ge 38:6–10). Pretended to be prostitute and became pregnant by Judah when he withheld third son (Ge 38:11–30). Mother of Perez and Zerah (Ge 38:27–30; Ru 4:12). **2.** Daughter of David. Raped by Amnon; avenged by brother Absalom (2Sa 13). **3.** Town at south end of the Dead Sea. Precise location unknown but near the border of Judah and Edom. It would form part of the southern boundary of the restored land (Eze 47:19). Also known as Tadmor (1Ki 9:18; 2Ch 8:4), which Solomon rebuilt.

Ge 38: 6 his firstborn, and her name was T.
38:11 then said to his daughter-in-law T,
38:11 T went to live in her father's house.
38:13 T was told, "Your father-in-law is
38:24 "Your daughter-in-law T is guilty of
Ru 4:12 of Perez, whom T bore to Judah."
2Sa 13: 1 son of David fell in love with T,
13: 2 illness on account of his sister T,
13: 4 T, my brother Absalom's sister."
13: 5 'I would like my sister T to come
13: 6 "I would like my sister T to come
13: 7 David sent word to T at the palace:
13: 8 T went to the house of her brother
13:10 Amnon said to T, "Bring the food
13:10 And T took the bread she had
13:19 T put ashes on her head and tore the
2Sa 13:20 T lived in her brother Absalom's
13:22 he had disgraced his sister T.
13:32 day that Amnon raped his sister T.
14:27 T, and she became a beautiful woman.
1Ch 2: 4 T, Judah's daughter-in-law, bore him
3: 9 concubines. And T was their sister.
Eze 47:18 to the eastern sea and as far as T.
47:19 "On the south side it will run from T
48:28 T to the waters of Meribah Kadesh,
Mt 1: 3 whose mother was T, Perez the father

Tamarisk
Ge 21:33 Abraham planted a t tree in
1Sa 22: 6 was seated under the t tree on the
31:13 them under a t tree at Jabesh,

Tambourine (Tambourines)
Ex 15:20 Aaron's sister, took a t in her hand,
Job 21:12 They sing to the music of t and harp;
Ps 81: 2 Begin the music, strike the t, play
149: 3 make music to him with t and harp.
150: 4 praise him with t and dancing,

Tambourines (Tambourine)
Ge 31:27 singing to the music of t and harps?
Ex 15:20 followed her, with t and dancing.
Jdg 11:34 sound of t! She was an only child.
1Sa 10: 5 t, flutes and harps being played
18: 6 joyful songs and with t and lutes.
2Sa 6: 5 lyres, t, sistrums and cymbals.
1Ch 13: 8 lyres, t, cymbals and trumpets.
Ps 68:25 with them are the maidens playing t.
Isa 5:12 t and flutes and wine, but they have
24: 8 The gaiety of the t is stilled, the
30:32 will be to the music of t and harps,
Jer 31: 4 Again you will take up your t and go

Tame (Tamed)
Jas 3: 8 no man can t the tongue. It is a

Tamed (Tame)
Jas 3: 7 are being t and have been t by man,

Tammuz
Eze 8:14 women sitting there, mourning for T.

Tanhumeth
2Ki 25:23 Seraiah son of T the Netophathite,
Jer 40: 8 Seraiah son of T, the sons of Ephai

Tanner
Ac 9:43 for some time with a t named Simon.
10: 6 He is staying with Simon the t,
10:32 Simon the t, who lives by the sea.'

Tapestry
SS 7: 5 Your hair is like royal t; the king

Taphath
1Ki 4:11 married to T daughter of Solomon);

Tappuah
Jos 12:17 the king of T one the king of Hepher
15:34 Zanoah, En Gannim, T, Enam,
16: 8 From T the border went west to the
17: 8 (Manasseh had the land of T, but T
1Ch 2:43 The sons of Hebron: Korah, T, Rekem

Tar
Ge 14:10 Valley of Siddim was full of t pits,
Ex 2: 3 him and coated it with t and pitch.

Taralah
Jos 18:27 Rekem, Irpeel, T,

Tarea
1Ch 8:35 The sons of Micah: Pithon, Melech, T

Target
1Sa 20:20 as though I were shooting at a t.
Job 7:20 Why have you made me your t? Have

Job 16:12 crushed me. He has made me his **t**;
Lam 3:12 He drew his bow and made me the **t**

Tarshish

City or territory at western end of Mediterranean Sea, possibly in southern Spain, renowned for its shipping (Ps 48:7; Isa 23:1, 14; 60:9; Eze 27:25) and valuable merchandise (Ps 72:10; Jer 10:9; Eze 38:13). Jonah tried to flee here from God's call to Nineveh (Jnh 1:3; 4:2).

Ge 10: 4 The sons of Javan: Elishah, **T**, the
1Ch 1: 7 The sons of Javan: Elishah, **T**, the
7:10 Kenaanah, Zethan, **T** and Ahishahar.
Est 1:14 Shethar, Admatha, **T**, Meres, Marsena
Ps 48: 7 You destroyed them like ships of **T**
72:10 The kings of **T** and of distant shores
Isa 23: 1 O ships of **T**! For Tyre is destroyed
23: 6 Cross over to **T**; wail, you people of
23:10 **T**, for you no longer have a harbour.
23:14 Wail, you ships of **T**; your fortress
60: 9 me; in the lead are the ships of **T**,
66:19 who survive to the nations—to **T**,
Jer 10: 9 Hammered silver is brought from **T**
Eze 27:12 "'**T** did business with you because
27:25 "'The ships of **T** serve as carriers
38:13 Dedan and the merchants of **T** and all
Jnh 1: 3 away from the LORD and headed for **T**.
1: 3 sailed for **T** to flee from the LORD.
4: 2 Why I was so quick to flee to **T**.

Tarsus

Principal city of Cilicia in Asia Minor. Birthplace of Paul (Ac 9:11; 21:39; 22:3), he was sent here to escape a Jewish death threat (Ac 9:30). Barnabas fetched him and took him to Antioch (Ac 11:25).

Ac 9:11 ask for a man from **T** named Saul,
9:30 to Caesarea and sent him off to **T**.
11:25 Barnabas went to **T** to look for Saul,
21:39 Paul answered, "I am a Jew, from **T**
22: 3 "I am a Jew, born in **T** of Cilicia,

Tartak

2Ki 17:31 the Avvites made Nibhaz and **T**, and

Task (Tasks)

Ge 31:36 Jacob was angry and took Laban to **t**.
Lev 16:21 care of a man appointed for the **t**.
1Ch 29: 1 The **t** is great, because this
2Ch 29:34 them until the **t** was finished
Ne 13:30 them duties, each to his own **t**.
Ecc 2:26 but to the sinner he gives the **t** of
Isa 28:21 and perform his **t**, his alien **t**.
Mk 13:34 each with his assigned **t**, and tells
Ac 20:24 complete the **t** the Lord Jesus has
20:24 the **t** of testifying to the gospel of
Ro 15:28 after I have completed this **t** and
1Co 3: 5 the Lord has assigned to each his **t**.
2Co 2:16 And who is equal to such a **t**?
Gal 2: 7 entrusted with the **t** of preaching
1Ti 3: 1 an overseer, he desires a noble **t**.

Tasks (Task)

2Ch 31:16 the daily duties of their various **t**,
Pr 31:17 her arms are strong for her **t**.

Tassel (Tassels)

Nu 15:38 with a blue cord on each **t**.

Tassels (Tassel)

Nu 15:38 **t** on the corners of your garments,
15:39 You will have these **t** to look at and
Dt 22:12 Make **t** on the four corners of the
Mt 23: 5 and the **t** on their garments long;

Taste (Tasted, Tastes, Tasting, Tasty)

Ge 25:28 Isaac, who had a **t** for wild game,
2Sa 3:35 be it ever so severely, if I **t** bread
19:35 Can your servant **t** what he eats and
Job 27: 2 has made me **t** bitterness of soul,
Ps 34: 8 **T** and see that the LORD is good;
119:103 How sweet are your words to my **t**,
Pr 24:13 from the comb is sweet to your **t**.
SS 2: 3 and his fruit is sweet to my **t**.
4:16 his garden and **t** its choice fruits.
Jnh 3: 7 herd or flock, **t** anything; do not
Mt 16:28 standing here will not **t** death
Mk 9: 1 standing here will not **t** death
Lk 9:27 standing here will not **t** death
14:24 invited will get a **t** of my banquet.
Jn 8:52 your word, he will never **t** death.
Col 2:21 "Do not handle! Do not **t**! Do not
Heb 2: 9 God he might **t** death for everyone.

Tasted (Taste)

Ex 16:31 and **t** like wafers made with honey.
Nu 11: 8 **t** like something made with olive oil.
1Sa 14:24 So none of the troops **t** food.
14:29 when I **t** a little of this honey.
14:43 So Jonathan told him, "I merely **t** a
Eze 3: 3 it **t** as sweet as honey in my mouth.
Jn 2: 9 the master of the banquet **t** the
Heb 6: 4 who have **t** the heavenly gift, who
6: 5 who have **t** the goodness of the word
1Pe 2: 3 now that you have **t** that the Lord is
Rev 10:10 It **t** as sweet as honey in my mouth,

Tasteless

Job 6: 6 Is **t** food eaten without salt, or is

Tastes (Taste)

Job 12:11 ear test words as the tongue **t** food?
34: 3 tests words as the tongue **t** food.
Pr 20:17 Food gained by fraud **t** sweet to a
27: 7 hungry even what is bitter **t** sweet.
Jer 48:11 So she **t** as she did, and her aroma

Tasting (Taste)

Mt 27:34 after **t** it, he refused to drink it.

Tasty (Taste)

Ge 27: 4 Prepare me the kind of **t** food I like
27: 7 and prepare me some **t** food to eat,
27: 9 so that I can prepare some **t** food
27:14 and she prepared some **t** food, just
27:17 handed to her son Jacob the **t** food
27:31 He too prepared some **t** food and

Tattenai

Ezr 5: 3 At that time **T**, governor of
5: 6 This is a copy of the letter that **T**,
6: 6 Now then, **T**, governor of
6:13 **T**, governor of Trans-Euphrates, and

Tattoo

Lev 19:28 dead or put **t** marks on yourselves.

Taught (Teach)

Dt 4: 5 See, I have **t** you decrees and laws
31:22 that day and **t** it to the Israelites.
Jdg 8:16 He took the elders of the town and **t**
2Sa 1:18 ordered that the men of Judah be **t**
1Ki 4:33 He also **t** about animals and birds,
2Ki 17:28 and **t** them how to worship the LORD.
2Ch 17: 9 They **t** throughout Judah, taking with
17: 9 the towns of Judah and **t** the people.
Ps 71:17 Since my youth, O God, you have **t** me,
119:102 laws, for you yourself have **t** me.
Pr 4: 4 he **t** me and said, "Lay hold of my
31: 1 Lemuel—an oracle his mother **t** him:
SS 8: 2 mother's house—she who has **t** me.
Isa 29:13 is made up only of rules **t** by men.
40:14 and who **t** him the right way? Who was
40:14 Who was it that **t** him knowledge or
50: 4 my ear to listen like one being **t**.
54:13 All your sons will be **t** by the LORD,
Jer 9: 5 They have **t** their tongues to lie;
9:14 the Baals, as their fathers **t** them."
10: 8 are **t** by worthless wooden idols.
12:16 even as they once **t** my people to
32:33 though I **t** them again and again,
Hos 11: 3 was I who **t** Ephraim to walk, taking
Mt 7:29 he **t** as one who had authority, and
15: 9 teachings are but rules **t** by men.'"
Mk 1:22 because he **t** them as one who had
4: 2 He **t** them many things by parables,
6:30 to him all they had done and **t**.
7: 7 teachings are but rules **t** by men.'
10: 1 and as was his custom, he **t** them.
11:17 he **t** them, he said, "Is it not
12:38 he **t**, Jesus said, "Watch out for the
Lk 1: 4 of the things you have been **t**.
4:15 He **t** in their synagogues, and
5: 3 down and **t** the people from the boat.
11: 1 pray, just as John **t** his disciples."
13:26 with you, and you **t** in our streets.'
Jn 6:45 Prophets: 'They will all be **t** by God.
8:28 speak just what the father has **t** me
18:20 "I always **t** in synagogues or at the
Ac 11:26 and **t** great numbers of people.
15: 1 **t** by Moses, you cannot be saved."
15:35 **t** and preached the word of the Lord.
18:25 and **t** about Jesus accurately,
20:20 to you but have **t** you publicly
28:31 and **t** about the Lord Jesus Christ.
1Co 2:13 what we speak, not in words **t** us by
2:13 wisdom but in words **t** by the Spirit,
Gal 1:12 nor was I **t** it; rather, I received
Eph 4:21 Surely you heard of him and were **t**
4:22 You were **t**, with regard to your
Col 2: 7 in the faith as you were **t**, and
1Th 4: 9 been **t** by God to love each other.
1Ti 1:20 to Satan to be **t** not to blaspheme.
4: 1 spirits and things **t** by demons.
Tit 1: 9 message as it has been **t**, so that
1Jn 2:27 as it has **t** you, remain in him.
Rev 2:14 who **t** Balak to entice the Israelites

Taunt (Taunted, Taunts)

Dt 32:27 I dreaded the **t** of the enemy, lest
1Ki 18:27 At noon Elijah began to **t** them.
Ps 42:10 suffer mortal agony as my foes **t** me,
102: 8 All day long my enemies **t** me; those
Isa 14: 4 you will take up this **t** against the
Eze 5:15 You will be a reproach and a **t**, a
Mic 2: 4 will **t** you with this mournful song:
Hab 2: 6 "Will not all of them **t** him with

Taunted (Taunt)

Jdg 8:15 about whom you **t** me by saying, 'Do
2Sa 21:21 he **t** Israel, Jonathan son of Shimeah,
23: 9 he was with David when they **t** the
1Ch 20: 7 he **t** Israel, Jonathan son of Shimea,

Taunts (Taunt)

Ps 44:16 at the **t** of those who reproach and
89:50 my heart the **t** of all the nations,
89:51 the **t** with which your enemies have
119:42 I will answer the one who **t** me, for
Eze 36:15 No longer will I make you hear the **t**
Zep 2: 8 of Moab and the **t** of the Ammonites,

Tax (Taxed, Taxes)

2Ch 24: 6 Jerusalem the **t** imposed by Moses the
24: 9 bring to the LORD the **t** that Moses
Ne 5: 4 **t** on our fields and vineyards.
Da 11:20 "His successor will send out a **t**
Mt 5:46 even the **t** collectors doing that?
9: 9 sitting at the **t** collector's booth.
9:10 many **t** collectors and "sinners"
9:11 with **t** collectors and 'sinners'?"
10: 3 Thomas and Matthew the **t** collector;
11:19 of **t** collectors and "sinners".
17:24 the collectors of the two-drachma **t**
17:24 your teacher pay the temple **t**?"
17:27 give it to them for my **t** and yours."
18:17 you would a pagan or a **t** collector.
21:31 **t** collectors and prostitutes are
21:32 **t** collectors and the prostitutes did.
22:19 me the coin used for paying the **t**.
Mk 2:14 sitting at the **t** collector's booth.
2:15 many **t** collectors and "sinners"
2:16 "sinners" and **t** collectors, they
2:16 with **t** collectors and 'sinners'?"
Lk 3:12 **T** collectors also came to be
5:27 Jesus went out and saw a **t** collector
5:27 name of Levi sitting at his **t** booth.
5:29 and a large crowd of **t** collectors
5:30 with **t** collectors and 'sinners'?"

Lk 7:29 All the people, even the **t**
7:34 of **t** collectors and "sinners".
15: 1 Now the **t** collectors and "sinners"
18:10 Pharisee and the other a **t** collector.
18:11 even like this **t** collector.
18:13 "But the **t** collector stood at a
19: 2 a chief **t** collector and was wealthy.

Taxed (Tax)

2Ki 23:35 In order to do so, he **t** the land and

Taxes (Tax)

1Sa 17:25 father's family from **t** in Israel."
Ezr 4:13 no more **t**, tribute or duty will be
4:20 and **t**, tribute and duty were paid to
7:24 you have no authority to impose **t**,
Mt 17:25 **t**—from their own sons or from
22:17 it right to pay **t** to Caesar or not?"
Mk 12:14 it right to pay **t** to Caesar or not?
Lk 20:22 Is it right for us to pay **t** to
23: 2 He opposes payment of **t** to Caesar
Ro 13: 6 This is also why you pay **t**, for the
13: 7 If you owe **t**, pay **t**; if revenue,

Teach (Taught, Teacher, Teachers, Teaches, Teaching, Teachings)

Ex 4:12 speak and will **t** you what to say."
4:15 you speak and will **t** you what to do.
18:20 **T** them the decrees and laws, and
33:13 If you are pleased with me, **t** me
35:34 of Dan, the ability to **t** others.
Lev 10:11 you must **t** the Israelites all the
Dt 4: 1 and laws I am about to **t** you.
4: 9 **T** them to your children and to their
4:10 and may **t** them to their children."
4:14 at that time to **t** you the decrees
5:31 decrees and laws that you are to **t**
6: 1 directed me to **t** you to observe
8: 3 to **t** you that man does not live on
11:19 **T** them to your children, talking
17:11 Act according to the law they **t** you
20:18 Otherwise, they will **t** you to follow
31:19 **t** it to the Israelites and make them
Jdg 3: 2 (he did this only to **t** warfare to
13: 8 to **t** us how to bring up the boy who
1Sa 12:23 **t** you the way that is good and right.
14:12 up to us and we'll **t** you a lesson.
1Ki 8:36 **T** them the right way to live, and
2Ki 17:27 **t** the people what the god of the
2Ch 6:27 **T** them the right way to live, and
15: 3 a priest to **t** and without the law.
17: 7 Micaiah to **t** in the towns of Judah.
Ezr 7:25 are to **t** any who do not know them.
Job 6:24 "**T** me, and I will be quiet; show me
12: 7 "But ask the animals, and they will **t**
12: 8 or speak to the earth, and it will **t**
21:22 "Can anyone **t** knowledge to God,
27:11 "I will **t** you about the power of God;
32: 7 advanced years should **t** wisdom.'
33:33 be silent, and I will **t** you wisdom."
34:32 **T** me what I cannot see; if I have
Ps 25: 4 Show me your ways, O LORD, **t** me your
25: 5 guide me in your truth and **t** me, for
27:11 **T** me your way, O LORD; lead me in a
32: 8 I will instruct you and **t** you in the
34:11 I will **t** you the fear of the LORD.
51: 6 you **t** me wisdom in the inmost place.
51:13 I will **t** transgressors your ways,
78: 5 our forefathers to **t** their children,
86:11 **T** me your way, O LORD, and I will
90:12 **T** us to number our days aright, that
94:12 O LORD, the man you **t** from your law;
105:22 he pleased and **t** his elders wisdom.
119:12 Praise be to you, O LORD; **t** me your
119:26 you answered me; **t** me your decrees.
119:33 **T** me, O LORD, to follow your decrees;
119:64 love, O LORD; **t** me your decrees.
119:66 **T** me knowledge and good judgment,
119:68 you do is good; **t** me your decrees.
119:108 of my mouth, and **t** me your laws.
119:124 to your love and **t** me your decrees.
119:135 your servant and **t** me your decrees.
119:171 praise, for you **t** me your decrees.
132:12 covenant and the statutes I **t** them,
143:10 **T** me to do your will, for you are my
Pr 9: 9 **t** a righteous man and he will add to
22:17 wise; apply your heart to what I **t**,
22:19 the LORD, I **t** you today, even you.
Isa 2: 3 He will **t** us his ways, so that we
9:15 prophets who **t** lies are the tail.
28: 9 "Who is it he is trying to **t**? To
Jer 9:20 **T** your daughters how to wail; **t** one
16:21 "Therefore I will **t** them—this time
16:21 I will **t** them my power and might.
31:34 No longer will a man **t** his neighbour,
Eze 22:26 they **t** that there is no difference
44:23 They are to **t** my people the
Da 1: 4 He was to **t** them the language and
Mic 3:11 her priests **t** for a price, and her
4: 2 He will **t** us his ways, so that we
Mt 5: 2 he began to **t** them, saying:
11: 1 **t** and preach in the towns of Galilee.
22:16 you **t** the way of God in accordance
Mk 1:21 into the synagogue and began to **t**.
2:13 came to him, and he began to **t** them.
4: 1 Again Jesus began to **t** by the lake.
6: 2 the Sabbath came, he began to **t** in
8:31 He then began to **t** them that the Son
12:14 you **t** the way of God in accordance
Lk 4:31 the Sabbath began to **t** the people.
11: 1 "Lord, **t** us to pray, just as John
12:12 for the Holy Spirit will **t** you at
20:21 you speak and **t** what is right,
20:21 but **t** the way of God in accordance
Jn 7:14 to the temple courts and begin to **t**.
7:35 among the Greeks, and **t** the Greeks?
8: 2 him, and he sat down to **t** them.
14:26 will **t** you all things and will
Ac 1: 1 all that Jesus began to do and to **t**
4:18 or **t** at all in the name of Jesus.
5:21 told, and began to **t** the people.
5:28 "We gave you strict orders not to **t**
21:21 They have been informed that you **t**
Ro 2:21 you, then, who **t** others, do you not **t**
12: 7 serve; if it is teaching, let him **t**;
15: 4 in the past was written to **t** us,
1Co 4:17 what I **t** everywhere in every church.
11:14 Does not the very nature of things **t**
Col 3:16 Christ dwell in you richly as you **t**
1Ti 1: 3 not to **t** false doctrines any
2:12 I do not permit a woman to **t** or to
3: 2 respectable, hospitable, able to **t**,
4:11 Command and **t** these things.
6: 2 you are to **t** and urge on them.
2Ti 2: 2 will also be qualified to **t** others.
2:24 everyone, able to **t**, not resentful.
Tit 1:11 teaching things they ought not to **t**
2: 1 You must **t** what is in accord with
2: 2 **T** the older men to be temperate,
2: 3 Likewise, **t** the older women to be
2: 3 to much wine, but to **t** what is good.
2: 9 **T** slaves to be subject to their
2:15 then, are the things you should **t**.
Heb 5:12 you need someone to **t** you the
8:11 No longer will a man **t** his neighbour,
Jas 3: 1 who **t** will be judged more strictly.
1Jn 2:27 and you do not need anyone to **t** you.

Teacher (Teach)

1Ch 25: 8 Young and old alike, **t** as well as
Ezr 7: 6 He was a **t** well versed in the Law of
7:11 had given to Ezra the priest and **t**,
7:12 To Ezra the priest, a **t** of the Law
7:21 a **t** of the Law of the God of heaven,
Job 36:22 in his power. Who is a **t** like him?
Ecc 1: 1 The words of the **T**, son of David,
1: 2 Meaningless!" says the **T**.
1:12 I, the **T**, was king over Israel in
7:27 "Look," says the **T**, "this is what I
12: 8 Meaningless!" says the **T**.
12: 9 Not only was the **T** wise, but also he
12:10 The **T** searched to find just the
Mt 8:19 a **t** of the law came to him and said,
8:19 **T**, I will follow you wherever you go.
9:11 "Why does your **t** eat with tax
10:24 "A student is not above his **t**, nor a
10:25 for the student to be like his **t**,
12:38 "**T**, we want to see miraculous
13:52 He said to them, "Therefore every **t**
17:24 "Doesn't your **t** pay the temple tax?
Mt 19:16 "**T**, what good thing must I do to get
22:16 "**T**," they said, "we know you are a
22:24 "**T**," they said, "Moses told us that
22:36 "**T**, which is the greatest
23:10 Nor are you to be called '**t**', for
23:10 for you have one **T**, the Christ.
26:18 **T** says: My appointed time is near.
Mk 4:38 "**T**, don't you care if we drown?
5:35 "Why bother the **t** any more?"
9:17 A man in the crowd answered, "**T**, I
9:38 "**T**," said John, "we saw a man
10:17 "Good **t**," he asked, "what must I do
10:20 "**T**," he declared, "all these I have
10:35 "**T**," they said, "we want you to do
12:14 They came to him and said, "**T**, we
12:19 "**T**," they said, "Moses wrote for us
12:32 "Well said, **t**," the man replied.
13: 1 "Look, **T**! What massive stones! What
14:14 'The **T** asks: Where is my guest room,
Lk 3:12 "**T**," they asked, "what should we do?"
6:40 A student is not above his **t**, but
6:40 is fully trained will be like his **t**.
7:40 to tell you." "Tell me, **t**," he said.
8:49 "Don't bother the **t** any more."
9:38 A man in the crowd called out, "**T**, I
10:25 "**T**," he asked, "what must I do to
11:45 "**T**, when you say these things, you
12:13 Someone in the crowd said to him, "**T**,
18:18 A certain ruler asked him, "Good **t**,
19:39 "**T**, rebuke your disciples!
20:21 the spies questioned him: "**T**, we
20:28 "**T**," they said, "Moses wrote for us
20:39 responded, "Well said, **t**!"
21: 7 "**T**," they asked, "when will these
22:11 say to the owner of the house, 'The **T**
Jn 1:38 "Rabbi" (which means **T**), "where are
3: 2 you are a **t** who has come from God.
3:10 "You are Israel's **t**," said Jesus,
8: 4 said to Jesus, "**T**, this woman was
11:28 "The **T** is here," she said, "and is
13:13 "You call me '**T**' and 'Lord', and
13:14 Now that I, your Lord and **T**, have
20:16 Aramaic, "Rabboni!" (which means **T**).
Ac 5:34 a Pharisee named Gamaliel, a **t** of
Ro 2:20 an instructor of the foolish, a **t** of
1Ti 2: 7 **t** of the true faith to the Gentiles.
2Ti 1:11 a herald and an apostle and a **t**.

Teachers (Teach, *Teachers of the law*)

Ps 119:99 I have more insight than all my **t**,
Pr 5:13 I would not obey my **t** or listen to
Isa 30:20 your **t** will be hidden no more; with
Mt 23:34 you prophets and wise men and **t**.
Lk 2:46 sitting among the **t**, listening to
Ac 13: 1 there were prophets and **t**: Barnabas,
23: 9 and some of the **t** of the law who
1Co 12:28 second prophets, third **t**, then
12:29 Are all **t**? Do all work miracles?
Eph 4:11 and some to be pastors and **t**,
2Ti 4: 3 a great number of **t** to say what
Heb 5:12 by this time you ought to be **t**,
Jas 3: 1 many of you should presume to be **t**,
2Pe 2: 1 as there will be false **t** among you.
2: 3 In their greed these **t** will exploit

Teachers of the law

Mt 2: 4 the people's chief priests and **t**,
5:20 that of the Pharisees and the **t**,
7:29 had authority, and not as their **t**.
9: 3 At this, some of the **t** said to
12:38 some of the Pharisees and **t** said to
15: 1 some Pharisees and **t** came to Jesus
16:21 chief priests and **t**, and that he
17:10 **t** say that Elijah must come first?"
20:18 to the chief priests and the **t**.
21:15 when the chief priests and the **t** saw
23: 2 "The **t** and the Pharisees sit in
23:13 "Woe to you, **t** and Pharisees, you
23:15 "Woe to you, **t** and Pharisees, you
23:23 "Woe to you, **t** and Pharisees, you
23:25 "Woe to you, **t** and Pharisees, you
23:27 "Woe to you, **t** and Pharisees, you
23:29 "Woe to you, **t** and Pharisees, you
26:57 the **t** and the elders had assembled.

Mt 27:41 the **t** and the elders mocked him.
Mk 1:22 one who had authority, not as the **t**.
2: 6 Now some **t** were sitting there,
2:16 the **t** who were Pharisees saw him
3:22 the **t** who came down from Jerusalem
7: 1 The Pharisees and some of the **t** who
7: 5 the Pharisees and **t** asked Jesus,
8:31 chief priests and **t**, and that he
9:11 they asked him, "Why do the **t** say
9:14 them and the **t** arguing with them.
10:33 betrayed to the chief priests and **t**.
11:18 The chief priests and the **t** heard
11:27 the **t** and the elders came to him.
12:28 One of the **t** came and heard them
12:35 "How is it that the **t** say that the
12:38 Jesus said, "Watch out for the **t**.
14: 1 and the chief priests and the **t** were
14:43 priests, the **t**, and the elders.
14:53 priests, elders and **t** came together.
15: 1 with the elders, the **t** and the whole
15:31 the **t** mocked him among themselves.
Lk 5:17 Pharisees and **t**, who had come from
5:21 The Pharisees and the **t** began
5:30 the Pharisees and the **t** who belonged
6: 7 The Pharisees and the **t** were looking
9:22 chief priests and **t**, and he must be
11:53 the Pharisees and the **t** began to
15: 2 the Pharisees and the **t** muttered,
19:47 But the chief priests, the **t** and the
20: 1 the chief priests and the **t**,
20:19 The **t** and the chief priests looked
20:39 Some of the **t** responded, "Well said,
20:46 "Beware of the **t**. They like to walk
22: 2 the chief priests and the **t** were
22:66 both the chief priests and **t**, met
23:10 The chief priests and the **t** were
Jn 8: 3 The **t** and the Pharisees brought in a
Ac 4: 5 The next day the rulers, elders and **t**
6:12 the people and the elders and the **t**.
23: 9 and some of the **t** who were Pharisees
1Ti 1: 7 They want to be **t**, but they do not

Teaches (Teach)

Dt 33:10 He **t** your precepts to Jacob and your
Job 35:11 who **t** more to us than to the beasts
Ps 25: 9 in what is right and **t** them his way.
94:10 Does he who **t** man lack knowledge?
Pr 15:33 The fear of the LORD **t** a man wisdom,
Isa 28:26 His God instructs him and **t** him the
48:17 "I am the LORD your God, who **t** you
Hab 2:18 Or an image that **t** lies? For he who
Mt 5:19 **t** others to do the same will be
5:19 but whoever practises and **t** these
Ac 21:28 help us! This is the man who **t** all
1Ti 6: 3 If anyone **t** false doctrines and does
Tit 2:12 **t** us to say "No" to ungodliness and
1Jn 2:27 But as his anointing **t** you about all

Teaching (Teach)

Dt 32: 2 Let my **t** fall like rain and my words
Ezr 7:10 to **t** its decrees and laws in Israel.
Ps 60: T For **t**. When he fought Aram Naharaim
78: 1 O my people, hear my **t**; listen to
119:27 Let me understand the **t** of your
Pr 1: 8 and do not forsake your mother's **t**.
3: 1 My son, do not forget my **t**, but keep
4: 2 learning, so do not forsake my **t**.
6:20 and do not forsake your mother's **t**.
6:23 For these commands are a lamp, this **t**
13:14 The **t** of the wise is a fountain of
22:21 **t** you true and reliable words, so
Jer 18:18 for the **t** of the law by the priest
Eze 7:26 the **t** of the law by the priest will
Mal 2: 8 your **t** have caused many to stumble;
Mt 4:23 Jesus went throughout Galilee, **t** in
7:28 the crowds were amazed at his **t**,
9:35 **t** in their synagogues, preaching the
13:54 Coming to his home town, he began **t**
16:12 **t** of the Pharisees and Sadducees.
21:23 and, while he was **t**, the chief
22:33 this, they were astonished at his **t**.
26:55 courts **t**, and you did not arrest me.
28:20 **t** them to obey everything I have
Mk 1:22 The people were amazed at his **t**,
1:27 "What is this? A new **t**—and with
Mk 4: 2 by parables, and in his **t** said:
6: 6 round **t** from village to village.
6:34 So he began **t** them many things.
9:31 he was **t** his disciples. He said to
11:18 the whole crowd was amazed at his **t**.
12:35 While Jesus was **t** in the temple
14:49 Every day I was with you, **t** in the
Lk 4:32 They were amazed at his **t**, because
4:36 "What is this **t**? With authority and
5:17 One day as he was **t**, Pharisees and
6: 6 went into the synagogue and was **t**,
13:10 On a Sabbath Jesus was **t** in one of
13:22 **t** as he made his way to Jerusalem.
19:47 Every day he was **t** at the temple.
20: 1 One day as he was **t** the people in
21:37 Each day Jesus was **t** at the temple,
23: 5 the people all over Judea by his **t**.
Jn 6:59 He said this while **t** in the
6:60 disciples said, "This is a hard **t**.
7:16 Jesus answered, "My **t** is not my own.
7:17 he will find out whether my **t** comes
7:28 Jesus, still **t** in the temple courts,
8:20 He spoke these words while **t** in the
8:31 my **t**, you are really my disciples.
14:23 anyone loves me, he will obey my **t**.
14:24 does not love me will not obey my **t**.
15:20 my **t**, they will obey yours also.
18:19 Jesus about his disciples and his **t**.
Ac 2:42 apostles' **t** and to the fellowship,
4: 2 the apostles were **t** the people
5:25 in the temple courts **t** the people."
5:28 have filled Jerusalem with your **t**
5:42 they never stopped **t** and proclaiming
13:12 was amazed at the **t** about the Lord.
15: 1 to Antioch and were **t** the brothers:
17:19 new **t** is that you are presenting?
18:11 Paul stayed for a year and a half, **t**
Ro 6:17 of **t** to which you were entrusted.
12: 7 serve; if it is **t**, let him teach;
16:17 contrary to the **t** you have learned.
Eph 4:14 there by every wind of **t** and by the
Col 1:28 We proclaim him, admonishing and **t**
2Th 3: 6 to the **t** you received from us.
1Ti 4: 6 the good **t** that you have followed.
4:13 of Scripture, to preaching and to **t**.
5:17 those whose work is preaching and **t**.
6: 1 name and our **t** may not be slandered.
6: 3 Lord Jesus Christ and to godly **t**,
2Ti 1:13 keep as the pattern of sound **t**, with
2:17 Their **t** will spread like gangrene.
3:10 You, however, know all about my **t**,
3:16 is God-breathed and is useful for **t**,
Tit 1:11 by **t** things they ought not to teach
2: 7 is good. In your **t** show integrity,
2:10 **t** about God our Saviour attractive.
Heb 5:13 with the **t** about righteousness.
2Jn : 9 the **t** of Christ does not have God;
: 9 **t** has both the Father and the Son.
:10 to you and does not bring this **t**,
Rev 2:14 there who hold to the **t** of Balaam,
2:15 hold to the **t** of the Nicolaitans.
2:20 By her **t** she misleads my servants
2:24 to you who do not hold to her **t** and

Teachings (Teach)

Pr 7: 2 guard my **t** as the apple of your eye.
Mt 15: 9 They worship me in vain; their **t** are
Mk 7: 7 They worship me in vain; their **t** are
1Co 11: 2 holding on to the **t**, just as I passed
Col 2:22 are based on human commands and **t**.
2Th 2:15 stand firm and hold to the **t** we
1Ti 4: 2 Such **t** come through hypocritical
Heb 6: 1 **t** about Christ and go on to maturity,
13: 9 away by all kinds of strange **t**.

Team (Teams)

Isa 21: 9 man in a chariot with a **t** of horses.
Mic 1:13 harness the **t** to the chariot.

Teams (Team)

Isa 21: 7 he sees chariots with **t** of horses,

Tear[1] (Tears)

Rev 7:17 wipe away every **t** from their eyes."
21: 4 He will wipe every **t** from their eyes.

Tear[2] (Tearing, Tears, Tore, Torn)

Ex 28:32 this opening, so that it will not **t**.
39:23 opening, so that it would not **t**.
Lev 1:17 He shall **t** it open by the wings, not
10: 6 and do not **t** your clothes, or you
13:56 he is to **t** the contaminated part out
21:10 become unkempt or **t** his clothes.
Jdg 6:25 **T** down your father's altar to Baal
8: 7 I will **t** your flesh with desert
8: 9 triumph, I will **t** down this tower."
2Sa 3:31 "**T** your clothes and put on sackcloth
1Ki 11:11 I will most certainly **t** the kingdom
11:12 **t** it out of the hand of your son.
11:13 Yet I will not **t** the whole kingdom
11:31 'See, I am going to **t** the kingdom
Job 18: 4 You who **t** yourself to pieces in your
Ps 7: 2 or they will **t** me like a lion and
28: 5 he will **t** them down and never build
50:22 **t** you to pieces, with none to rescue:
52: 5 He will snatch you up and **t** you from
58: 6 O God; **t** out, O LORD, the fangs of
137: 7 "**T** it down," they cried, "**t** it down
Ecc 3: 3 time to **t** down and a time to build,
3: 7 a time to **t** and a time to mend, a
Isa 7: 6 "Let us invade Judah; let us **t** it
22:12 **t** out your hair and put on sackcloth.
Jer 1:10 and kingdoms to uproot and **t** down,
5: 6 to **t** to pieces any who venture out,
24: 6 I will build them up and not **t** them
30: 8 necks and will **t** off their bonds;
31:28 over them to uproot and **t** down,
36:24 fear, nor did they **t** their clothes.
42:10 I will build you up and not **t** you
Lam 2: 8 The LORD determined to **t** down the
Eze 13:14 I will **t** down the wall you have
13:20 and I will **t** them from your arms;
13:21 I will **t** off your veils and save my
16:39 and they will **t** down your mounds and
19: 3 to **t** the prey and he devoured men.
19: 6 to **t** the prey and he devoured men.
23:34 it to pieces and **t** your breasts.
Hos 5:14 I will **t** them to pieces and go away;
13: 8 a wild animal will **t** them apart.
Am 3:15 I will **t** down the winter house along
Mic 3: 2 who **t** the skin from my people and
5:11 and **t** down all your strongholds.
Na 1:13 your neck and **t** your shackles away."
Mt 7: 6 and then turn and **t** you to pieces.
9:16 the garment, making the **t** worse.
Mk 2:21 from the old, making the **t** worse.
Lk 12:18 I will **t** down my barns and build
Jn 19:24 "Let's not **t** it," they said to one

Tearing (Tear[2])

Dt 33:20 there like a lion, **t** at arm or head.
Ps 22:13 Roaring lions **t** their prey open
Eze 22:25 lion **t** its prey; they devour people,
22:27 her are like wolves **t** their prey;
Zec 11:16 the choice sheep, **t** off their hoofs.
2Co 13:10 building you up, not for **t** you down.

Tears[1] (Tear[1])

1Sa 2:33 with **t** and to grieve your heart,
2Ki 20: 5 and seen your **t**; I will heal you.
Job 16:20 friend as my eyes pour out **t** to God;
31:38 and all its furrows are wet with **t**,
Ps 6: 6 weeping and drench my couch with **t**.
42: 3 My **t** have been my food day and night,
56: 8 Record my lament; list my **t** on your
80: 5 You have fed them with the bread of **t**
80: 5 made them drink **t** by the bowlful.
102: 9 my food and mingle my drink with **t**
116: 8 eyes from **t**, my feet from stumbling,
119:136 Streams of **t** flow from my eyes, for
126: 5 Those who sow in **t** will reap with
Ecc 4: 1 I saw the **t** of the oppressed—and
Isa 16: 9 O Elealeh, I drench you with **t**! The
25: 8 will wipe away the **t** from all faces;
38: 5 heard your prayer and seen your **t**;
Jer 9: 1 water and my eyes a fountain of **t**!
9:18 our eyes overflow with **t** and water
13:17 overflowing with **t**, because the
14:17 'Let my eyes overflow with **t** night
31:16 your eyes from **t**, for your work
50: 4 go in **t** to seek the LORD their God.

Lam 1: 2 Bitterly she weeps at night, **t** are
1:16 I weep and my eyes overflow with **t**.
2:18 let your **t** flow like a river day and
3:48 Streams of **t** flow from my eyes
Eze 24:16 do not lament or weep or shed any **t**.
Mal 2:13 You flood the LORD's altar with **t**.
Lk 7:38 began to wet his feet with her **t**.
7:44 her **t** and wiped them with her hair.
Ac 20:19 Lord with great humility and with **t**,
20:31 each of you night and day with **t**.
2Co 2: 4 anguish of heart and with many **t**,
Php 3:18 and now say again even with **t**,
2Ti 1: 4 Recalling your **t**, I long to see you,
Heb 5: 7 petitions with loud cries and **t** to
12:17 he sought the blessing with **t**.

Tears[2] (Tear[2])
Job 12:14 What he **t** down cannot be rebuilt;
16: 9 God assails me and **t** me in his anger
19:10 He **t** me down on every side till I am
Pr 14: 1 hands the foolish one **t** hers down.
15:25 The LORD **t** down the proud man's
29: 4 who is greedy for bribes **t** it down.
Lk 5:36 this parable: "No-one **t** a patch

Tebah
Ge 22:24 sons: **T**, Gaham, Tahash and Maacah.
2Sa 8: 8 From **T** and Berothai, towns that
1Ch 18: 8 From **T** and Cun, towns that belonged

Tebeth
Est 2:16 the month of **T**, in the seventh year

Teem (Teemed, Teeming, Teems)
Ge 1:20 God said, "Let the water **t** with
Ex 8: 3 The Nile will **t** with frogs. They

Teemed (Teem)
Ps 105:30 Their land **t** with frogs, which went

Teeming (Teem)
Ps 104:25 vast and spacious, **t** with creatures

Teems (Teem)
Ge 1:21 moving thing with which the water **t**,

Teeth (Tooth, *Weeping and gnashing of teeth*)
Ge 49:12 than wine, his **t** whiter than milk.
Nu 11:33 the meat was still between their **t**
Job 4:10 the **t** of the great lions are broken.
16: 9 his anger and gnashes his **t** at me;
19:20 escaped by only the skin of my **t**.
29:17 snatched the victims from their **t**.
41:14 ringed about with his fearsome **t**?
Ps 3: 7 the jaw; break the **t** of the wicked.
35:16 mocked; they gnashed their **t** at me.
37:12 righteous and gnash their **t** at them;
57: 4 men whose **t** are spears and arrows,
58: 6 Break the **t** in their mouths, O God;
112:10 he will gnash his **t** and waste away;
124: 6 has not let us be torn by their **t**.
Pr 10:26 vinegar to the **t** and smoke to the
30:14 those whose **t** are swords and whose
SS 4: 2 Your **t** are like a flock of sheep
6: 6 Your **t** are like a flock of sheep
7: 9 flowing gently over lips and **t**.
Isa 41:15 new and sharp, with many **t**.
Jer 31:29 the children's **t** are set on edge.'
31:30 his own **t** will be set on edge.
Lam 2:16 scoff and gnash their **t** and say,
3:16 He has broken my **t** with gravel; he
Eze 18: 2 the children's **t** are set on edge'?
Da 7: 5 ribs in its mouth between its **t**.
7: 7 It had large iron **t**; it crushed and
7:19 with its iron **t** and bronze claws
Joel 1: 6 **t** of a lion, the fangs of a lioness.
Am 1: 3 Gilead with sledges having iron **t**,
Zec 9: 7 forbidden food from between their **t**.
Mk 9:18 He foams at the mouth, gnashes his **t**
Lk 13:28 weeping there, and gnashing of **t**,
Ac 7:54 furious and gnashed their **t** at him.
Rev 9: 8 and their **t** were like lions' **t**.

Tehinnah
1Ch 4:12 Paseah and **T** the father of Ir Nahash.

Tekel
Da 5:25 written: MENE, MENE, **T**, PARSIN
5:27 **T**: You have been weighed on the

Tekoa (Tekoite)
Town in hill country of Judah, about 6 miles south of Bethlehem, and 10 miles south of Jerusalem. Home of the wise woman used by Joab to bring reconciliation between David and Absalom (2Sa 14:2–21). Also home of David's bodyguard Ira (2Sa 23:26). Rehoboam fortified it (2Ch 11:6) because it was a strategic warning point overlooking Jerusalem (Jer 6:1). Birthplace of Amos, where he received his call from God (Am 1:1).

2Sa 14: 2 Joab sent someone to **T** and had a
14: 4 the woman from **T** went to the king,
14: 9 the woman from **T** said to him, "My
23:26 Paltite, Ira son of Ikkesh from **T**,
1Ch 2:24 bore him Ashhur the father of **T**.
4: 5 Ashhur the father of **T** had two wives,
11:28 Ira son of Ikkesh from **T**, Abiezer
2Ch 11: 6 Bethlehem, Etam, **T**,
20:20 they left for the Desert of **T**.
Ne 3: 5 was repaired by the men of **T**,
3:27 Next to them, the men of **T** repaired
Jer 6: 1 Sound the trumpet in **T**! Raise the
Am 1: 1 one of the shepherds of **T**—what he

Tekoite (Tekoa)
1Ch 27: 9 was Ira the son of Ikkesh the **T**.

Tel Abib
Eze 3:15 I came to the exiles who lived at **T**

Tel Assar
2Ki 19:12 the people of Eden who were in **T**?
Isa 37:12 the people of Eden who were in **T**?

Tel Harsha
Ezr 2:59 **T**, Kerub, Addon and Immer, but they
Ne 7:61 **T**, Kerub, Addon and Immer, but they

Tel Melah
Ezr 2:59 came up from the towns of **T**,
Ne 7:61 came up from the towns of **T**,

Telah
1Ch 7:25 his son, **T** his son, Tahan his son,

Telaim
1Sa 15: 4 mustered them at **T**—two hundred

Telem
Jos 15:24 Ziph, **T**, Bealoth,
Ezr 10:24 the gatekeepers: Shallum, **T** and Uri.

Tema
Ge 25:15 Hadad, **T**, Jetur, Naphish and Kedemah.
1Ch 1:30 Mishma, Dumah, Massa, Hadad, **T**,
Job 6:19 The caravans of **T** look for water,
Isa 21:14 in **T**, bring food for the fugitives.
Jer 25:23 Dedan, **T**, Buz and all who are in

Temah
Ezr 2:53 Barkos, Sisera, **T**,
Ne 7:55 Barkos, Sisera, **T**,

Teman (Temanite, Temanites)
Town and region in the south of Edom, probably named after one of Esau's grandsons (Ge 36:11; 1Ch 1:36). Its inhabitants were famous for their wisdom (Jer 49:7; Ob 8), one being Job's advisor (Job 2:11). Its destruction was foretold along with all of Edom (Eze 25:13).

Ge 36:11 The sons of Eliphaz: **T**, Omar, Zepho,
36:15 Esau: Chiefs **T**, Omar, Zepho, Kenaz,
36:42 Kenaz, **T**, Mibzar,
1Ch 1:36 The sons of Eliphaz: **T**, Omar, Zepho,
1:53 Kenaz, **T**, Mibzar,
Jer 49: 7 "Is there no longer wisdom in **T**? Has
49:20 against those who live in **T**:
Eze 25:13 I will lay it waste, and from **T** to
Am 1:12 I will send fire upon **T** that will
Ob : 9 Your warriors, O **T**, will be
Hab 3: 3 God came from **T**, the Holy One from

Temanite (Teman)
Job 2:11 Job's three friends, Eliphaz the **T**,
4: 1 Then Eliphaz the **T** replied:
15: 1 Then Eliphaz the **T** replied:
22: 1 Then Eliphaz the **T** replied:
42: 7 he said to Eliphaz the **T**, "I am
42: 9 Eliphaz the **T**, Bildad the Shuhite

Temanites (Teman)
Ge 36:34 land of the **T** succeeded him as king.
1Ch 1:45 land of the **T** succeeded him as king.

Temeni
1Ch 4: 6 Naarah bore him Ahuzzam, Hepher, **T**

Temper (Even-tempered, Hot-tempered, Ill-tempered, Quick-tempered)
1Sa 20: 7 But if he loses his **t**, you can be
Pr 16:32 his **t** than one who takes a city.

Temperate
1Ti 3: 2 the husband of but one wife, **t**,
3:11 but **t** and trustworthy in everything.
Tit 2: 2 Teach the older men to be **t**, worthy

Tempest
Job 27:20 a **t** snatches him away in the night.
37: 9 The **t** comes out from its chamber,
Ps 50: 3 him, and around him a **t** rages.
55: 8 shelter, far from the **t** and storm."
83:15 pursue them with your **t** and terrify
107:25 For he spoke and stirred up a **t** that
Isa 29: 6 **t** and flames of a devouring fire.

Temple (*Curtain of the temple, Temple of the LORD*, Temples)
Jdg 4:21 his **t** into the ground, and he died.
4:22 the tent peg through his **t**—dead.
5:26 she shattered and pierced his **t**.
9: 4 of silver from the **t** of Baal-Berith,
9:27 a festival in the **t** of their god.
9:46 stronghold of the **t** of El-Berith.
16:26 that support the **t**, so that I may
16:27 Now the **t** was crowded with men and
16:29 pillars on which the **t** stood.
16:30 and down came the **t** on the rulers
1Sa 1: 9 by the doorpost of the LORD's **t**.
5: 2 they carried the ark into Dagon's **t**
5: 5 who enter Dagon's **t** at Ashdod step
31: 9 the news in the **t** of their idols
31:10 They put his armour in the **t** of the
2Sa 22: 7 From his **t** he heard my voice; my cry
1Ki 3: 2 because a **t** had not yet been built
5: 3 he could not build a **t** for the Name
5: 5 I intend, therefore, to build a **t**
5: 5 place will build the **t** for my Name.'
5:17 of dressed stone for the **t**.
5:18 and stone for the building of the **t**.
6: 2 The **t** that King Solomon built for
6: 3 the **t** extended the width of the **t**,
6: 3 ten cubits from the front of the **t**.
6: 4 narrow clerestory windows in the **t**.
6: 6 ledges around the outside of the **t**
6: 6 would be inserted into the **t** walls.
6: 7 In building the **t**, only blocks
6: 7 the **t** site while it was being built.
6: 8 was on the south side of the **t**;
6: 9 he built the **t** and completed it,
6:10 the side rooms all along the **t**.
6:10 attached to the **t** by beams of cedar.
6:12 "As for this **t** you are building, if
6:14 Solomon built the **t** and completed it.
6:15 the floor of the **t** to the ceiling,
6:15 floor of the **t** with planks of pine.

1Ki 6:16 twenty cubits at the rear of the **t**
6:16 within the **t** an inner sanctuary,
6:18 The inside of the **t** was cedar,
6:19 the inner sanctuary within the **t** to
6:21 Solomon covered the inside of the **t**
6:27 the **t**, with their wings spread out.
6:29 On the walls all round the **t**, in
6:30 and outer rooms of the **t** with gold.
6:38 the eighth month, the **t** was finished
7:21 the pillars at the portico of the **t**.
7:39 side of the **t** and five on the north.
7:39 at the south-east corner of the **t**.
7:48 that were in the LORD's **t**:
7:50 the doors of the main hall of the **t**.
7:51 in the treasuries of the LORD's **t**.
8: 6 in the inner sanctuary of the **t**,
8:11 the glory of the LORD filled his **t**.
8:13 I have indeed built a magnificent **t**
8:16 a **t** built for my Name to be there,
8:17 build a **t** for the Name of the LORD,
8:18 your heart to build a **t** for my Name,
8:19 you are not the one to build the **t**,
8:19 who will build the **t** for my Name.'
8:20 and I have built the **t** for the Name
8:27 How much less this **t** I have built!
8:29 May your eyes be open towards this **t**
8:31 oath before your altar in this **t**,
8:33 supplication to you in this **t**,
8:38 out his hands towards this **t**—
8:42 he comes and prays towards this **t**,
8:44 the **t** I have built for your Name,
8:48 the **t** I have built for your Name;
9: 3 me; I have consecrated this **t**,
9: 7 **t** I have consecrated for my Name.
9: 8 though this **t** is now imposing, all
9: 8 a thing to this land and to this **t**?'
9:15 conscripted to build the LORD's **t**,
9:25 and so fulfilled the **t** obligations.
14:28 the king went to the LORD's **t**,
15:18 the LORD's **t** and of his own palace.
16:32 He set up an altar for Baal in the **t**
2Ki 5:18 When my master enters the **t** of
5:18 I bow down in the **t** of Rimmon,
10:21 They crowded into the **t** of Baal
10:23 of Recab went into the **t** of Baal.
10:25 the inner shrine of the **t** of Baal.
10:26 out of the **t** of Baal and burned it.
10:27 of Baal and tore down the **t** of Baal,
11: 6 who take turns guarding the **t**—
11: 7 are all to guard the **t** for the king.
11:11 the king—near the altar and the **t**,
11:11 side to the north side of the **t**.
11:18 to the **t** of Baal and tore it down.
12: 4 money brought voluntarily to the **t**.
12: 5 whatever damage is found in the **t**."
12: 6 still had not repaired the **t**.
12: 7 repairing the damage done to the **t**?
12: 7 hand it over for repairing the **t**."
12: 8 would not repair the **t** themselves.
12:11 to supervise the work on the **t**.
12:12 other expenses of restoring the **t**.
12:13 The money brought into the **t** was not
12:14 who used it to repair the **t**.
16:14 the **t**—from between the new altar
16:18 canopy that had been built at the **t**
19:37 while he was worshipping in the **t** of
21: 7 he had made and put it in the **t**,
21: 7 "In this **t** and in Jerusalem, which I
22: 5 to supervise the work on the **t**.
22: 6 and dressed stone to repair the **t**.
22: 9 workers and supervisors at the **t**."
23:27 the city I chose, and this **t**, about
25:14 articles used in the **t** service.
1Ch 6:10 the **t** Solomon built in Jerusalem),
9: 2 priests, Levites and **t** servants.
9:28 the articles used in the **t** service;
9:33 stayed in the rooms of the **t** and
10:10 They put his armour in the **t** of
10:10 hung up his head in the **t** of Dagon.
22:19 articles belonging to God into the **t**
26:29 assigned duties away from the **t**,
28:10 you to build a **t** as a sanctuary.
28:11 the plans for the portico of the **t**,
28:12 for the treasuries of the **t** of God
28:21 for all the work on the **t** of God,
29: 2 **t** of my God—gold for the gold work,
1Ch 29: 3 in my devotion to the **t** of my God
29: 3 gold and silver for the **t** of my God,
29: 3 I have provided for this holy **t**:
29: 7 They gave towards the work on the **t**
29:16 for building you a **t** for your Holy
2Ch 2: 1 Solomon gave orders to build a **t** for
2: 4 Now I am about to build a **t** for the
2: 5 "The **t** I am going to build will be
2: 6 who is able to build a **t** for him,
2: 6 Who then am I to build a **t** for him,
2: 9 because the **t** I build must be large
2:12 who will build a **t** for the LORD and
3: 3 the **t** of God was sixty cubits long
3: 4 The portico at the front of the **t**
3: 6 He adorned the **t** with precious
3: 7 walls and doors of the **t** with gold,
3: 8 width of the **t**—twenty cubits long
3:11 cubits long and touched the **t** wall,
3:12 long and touched the other **t** wall,
3:15 In the front of the **t** he made two
3:17 the pillars in the front of the **t**,
4: 7 for them and placed them in the **t**,
4: 8 ten tables and placed them in the **t**,
4:11 for King Solomon in the **t** of God:
4:19 furnishings that were in God's **t**:
4:22 and the gold doors of the **t**:
5: 1 them in the treasuries of God's **t**.
5: 7 in the inner sanctuary of the **t**,
5:14 of the LORD filled the **t** of God.
6: 2 I have built a magnificent **t** for you,
6: 5 a **t** built for my Name to be there,
6: 7 build a **t** for the Name of the LORD,
6: 8 your heart to build a **t** for my Name,
6: 9 you are not the one to build the **t**,
6: 9 who will build the **t** for my Name.'
6:10 and I have built the **t** for the Name
6:18 much less this **t** that I have built!
6:20 May your eyes be open towards this **t**
6:22 oath before your altar in this **t**,
6:24 supplication before you in this **t**,
6:29 out his hands towards this **t**—
6:32 he comes and prays towards this **t**,
6:34 the **t** I have built for your Name,
6:38 **t** that I have built for your Name;
7: 1 the glory of the LORD filled the **t**.
7: 3 the glory of the LORD above the **t**,
7: 5 the people dedicated the **t** of God.
7:12 for myself as a **t** for sacrifices.
7:16 I have chosen and consecrated this **t**
7:20 and will reject this **t** which I have
7:21 though this **t** is now so imposing,
7:21 a thing to this land and to this **t**?'
12:11 the king went to the LORD's **t**,
15: 8 of the portico of the LORD's **t**.
15:18 He brought into the **t** of God the
16: 2 of the treasuries of the LORD's **t**
20: 9 before this **t** that bears your Name
22:12 He remained hidden with them at the **t**
23: 3 with the king at the **t** of God.
23: 7 Anyone who enters the **t** must be put
23: 9 David and that were in the **t** of God.
23:10 the king—near the altar and the **t**,
23:10 side to the north side of the **t**.
23:17 All the people went to the **t** of Baal
23:18 David had made assignments in the **t**,
23:19 at the gates of the LORD's **t** so
24: 5 Israel, to repair the **t** of your God.
24: 7 had broken into the **t** of God
24:12 carpenters to restore the LORD's **t**,
24:12 in iron and bronze to repair the **t**.
24:13 They rebuilt the **t** of God according
24:14 were made articles for the LORD's **t**:
24:16 done in Israel for God and his **t**.
24:21 in the courtyard of the LORD's **t**.
24:27 record of the restoration of the **t**
25:24 all the articles found in the **t** of
26:19 in the LORD's **t**, leprosy broke out
28:24 the **t** of God and took them away.
28:24 He shut the doors of the LORD's **t**
29:16 to the courtyard of the LORD's **t**
31:13 official in charge of the **t** of God.
31:21 undertook in the service of God's **t**
32:21 And when he went into the **t** of his
33: 7 he had made and put it in God's **t**,
33: 7 "In this **t** and in Jerusalem, which I
33:15 on the **t** hill and in Jerusalem;
2Ch 34: 8 to purify the land and the **t**, he
34: 9 had been brought into the **t** of God,
34:10 supervise the work on the LORD's **t**.
34:10 who repaired and restored the **t**.
35: 2 them in the service of the LORD's **t**.
35: 3 "Put the sacred ark in the **t** that
35: 8 the administrators of God's **t**, gave
35:20 when Josiah had set the **t** in order,
36: 7 LORD and put them in his **t** there.
36:18 all the articles from the **t** of God,
36:18 and the treasures of the LORD's **t**
36:19 They set fire to God's **t** and broke
36:23 a **t** for him at Jerusalem in Judah.
Ezr 1: 2 a **t** for him at Jerusalem in Judah.
1: 4 for the **t** of God in Jerusalem.
1: 7 and had placed in the **t** of his god.
2:42 The gatekeepers of the **t**: the
2:43 The **t** servants: the descendants of
2:58 The **t** servants and the descendants
2:70 the gatekeepers and the **t** servants
3: 6 the LORD's **t** had not yet been laid.
3:12 who had seen the former **t**, wept
3:12 the foundation of this **t** being laid,
4: 1 a **t** for the LORD, the God of Israel,
4: 3 with us in building a **t** to our God.
5: 3 this **t** and restore this structure?"
5: 8 of Judah, to the **t** of the great God.
5: 9 this **t** and restore this structure?"
5:11 and we are rebuilding the **t** that was
5:12 destroyed this **t** and deported the
5:14 He even removed from the **t** of
5:14 had taken from the **t** in Jerusalem
5:14 and brought to the **t** in Babylon.
5:15 deposit them in the **t** in Jerusalem.
6: 3 the **t** of God in Jerusalem:
6: 3 Let the **t** be rebuilt as a place to
6: 5 took from the **t** in Jerusalem
6: 5 their places in the **t** in Jerusalem;
6: 7 with the work on this **t** of God.
6:12 or to destroy this **t** in Jerusalem.
6:14 They finished building the **t**
6:15 The **t** was completed on the third day
7: 7 singers, gatekeepers and **t** servants
7:16 for the **t** of their God in Jerusalem.
7:17 of the **t** of your God in Jerusalem.
7:19 for worship in the **t** of your God.
7:20 anything else needed for the **t** of
7:23 for the **t** of the God of heaven.
7:24 singers, gatekeepers, **t** servants
8:17 the **t** servants in Casiphia, so that
8:20 also brought 220 of the **t** servants
Ne 2: 8 the gates of the citadel by the **t**
3:26 the **t** servants living on the hill of
3:31 of the **t** servants and the merchants,
6:10 inside the **t**, and let us close the **t**
6:11 go into the **t** to save his life?
7:46 The **t** servants: the descendants of
7:60 The **t** servants and the descendants
7:73 the singers and the **t** servants,
10:28 gatekeepers, singers, **t** servants
11: 3 priests, Levites, **t** servants and
11:12 who carried on work for the **t**—822
11:21 The **t** servants lived on the hill of
13: 5 and incense and **t** articles,
Ps 5: 7 will I bow down towards your holy **t**.
11: 4 The LORD is in his holy **t**; the LORD
18: 6 From his **t** he heard my voice; my cry
27: 4 the LORD and to seek him in his **t**.
29: 9 And in his **t** all cry, "Glory!"
30: T A song. For the dedication of the **t**
48: 9 Within your **t**, O God, we meditate on
65: 4 of your house, of your holy **t**.
66:13 I will come to your **t** with burnt
68:29 of your **t** at Jerusalem kings will
79: 1 they have defiled your holy **t**,
138: 2 I will bow down towards your holy **t**
Ecc 5: 6 do not protest to the ⌊**t**⌋ messenger
Isa 2: 2 mountain of the LORD's **t** will be
6: 1 the train of his robe filled the **t**.
6: 4 and the **t** was filled with smoke.
15: 2 Dibon goes up to its **t**, to its high
37:38 while he was worshipping in the **t** of
43:28 disgrace the dignitaries of your **t**,
44:28 the **t**, "Let its foundations be laid.
56: 5 to them I will give within my **t** and
60: 7 and I will adorn my glorious **t**.

Isa 64:11 Our holy and glorious **t**, where our
66: 6 hear that noise from the **t**! It is
Jer 7:14 the **t** you trust in, the place I gave
11:15 "What is my beloved doing in my **t** as
19:14 LORD's **t** and said to all the people,
20: 2 Gate of Benjamin at the LORD's **t**.
23:11 in my **t** I find their wickedness,"
26:18 the **t** hill a mound overgrown with
36: 5 I cannot go to the LORD's **t**.
36: 8 at the LORD's **t** he read the words of
36:10 entrance of the New Gate of the **t**,
36:10 to all the people at the LORD's **t**
43:13 There in the **t** of the sun in Egypt
50:28 vengeance, vengeance for his **t**.
51:11 take vengeance, vengeance for his **t**.
52:18 articles used in the **t** service.
Eze 8:16 and there at the entrance to the **t**,
9: 3 and moved to the threshold of the **t**.
9: 6 elders who were in front of the **t**.
9: 7 he said to them, "Defile the **t** and
10: 3 side of the **t** when the man went in,
10: 4 and moved to the threshold of the **t**.
10: 4 The cloud filled the **t**, and the
10:18 **t** and stopped above the cherubim.
40: 5 completely surrounding the **t** area.
40: 7 facing the **t** was one rod deep.
40: 9 portico of the gateway faced the **t**.
40:45 priests who have charge of the **t**,
40:47 And the altar was in front of the **t**.
40:48 He brought me to the portico of the **t**
41: 5 he measured the wall of the **t**; it
41: 5 round the **t** was four cubits wide.
41: 6 ledges all round the wall of the **t**
41: 6 not inserted into the wall of the **t**.
41: 7 The side rooms all round the **t** were
41: 7 The structure surrounding the **t** was
41: 8 I saw that the **t** had a raised base
41: 9 area between the side rooms of the **t**
41:10 twenty cubits wide all round the **t**.
41:12 The building facing the **t** courtyard
41:13 he measured the **t**; it was a hundred
41:13 and the **t** courtyard and the building
41:14 The width of the **t** courtyard on the
41:14 of the **t**, was a hundred cubits.
41:15 the courtyard at the rear of the **t**,
41:19 were carved all round the whole **t**.
41:26 rooms of the **t** also had overhangs.
42: 1 the rooms opposite the **t** courtyard
42:10 adjoining the **t** courtyard and
42:13 rooms facing the **t** courtyard are
42:15 what was inside the **t** area,
43: 4 The glory of the LORD entered the **t**
43: 5 the glory of the LORD filled the **t**.
43: 6 speaking to me from inside the **t**.
43:10 "Son of man, describe the **t** to the
43:11 design of the **t**—its arrangement,
43:12 "This is the law of the **t**: All the
43:12 Such is the law of the **t**.
43:21 of the **t** area outside the sanctuary.
44: 4 north gate to the front of the **t**.
44: 5 **t** and all the exits of the sanctuary.
44: 7 desecrating my **t** while you offered
44:11 having charge of the gates of the **t**
44:14 in charge of the duties of the **t**
44:17 of the inner court or inside the **t**.
45: 5 who serve in the **t**, as their
45:19 put it on the doorposts of the **t**,
45:20 you are to make atonement for the **t**.
46:24 who minister at the **t** will cook
47: 1 me back to the entrance of the **t**,
47: 1 from under the threshold of the **t**
47: 1 the east (for the **t** faced east).
47: 1 side of the **t**, south of the altar.
48:21 portion with the **t** sanctuary
Da 1: 2 of the articles from the **t** of God.
1: 2 These he carried off to the **t** of his
5: 2 had taken from the **t** in Jerusalem,
5: 3 from the **t** of God in Jerusalem,
5:23 You had the goblets from his **t**
9:27 And on a wing of the **t** he will set
11:31 rise up to desecrate the **t** fortress
Joel 2:17 between the **t** porch and the altar.
Am 7:13 sanctuary and the **t** of the kingdom."
8: 3 songs in the **t** will turn to wailing.
Jnh 2: 4 look again towards your holy **t**.'
2: 7 prayer rose to you, to your holy **t**.
Mic 1: 2 you, the Lord from his holy **t**.
1: 7 all her **t** gifts will be burned with
3:12 the **t** hill a mound overgrown with
4: 1 mountain of the LORD's **t** will be
Na 1:14 that are in the **t** of your gods.
Hab 2:20 the LORD is in his holy **t**; let all
Zep 1: 9 who fill the **t** of their gods with
Hag 2:15 was laid on another in the LORD's **t**.
2:18 foundation of the LORD's **t** was laid.
Zec 4: 9 laid the foundation of this **t**; his
8: 9 strong so that the **t** may be built.
Mal 1:10 "Oh, that one of you would shut the **t**
3: 1 will come to his **t**; the messenger
Mt 4: 5 stand on the highest point of the **t**.
12: 5 priests in the **t** desecrate the day
12: 6 that one greater than the **t** is here.
17:24 "Doesn't your teacher pay the **t** tax?
21:12 Jesus entered the **t** area and drove
21:14 to him at the **t**, and he healed them.
21:15 the children shouting in the **t** area,
21:23 Jesus entered the **t** courts, and,
23:16 'If anyone swears by the **t**, it means
23:16 of the **t**, he is bound by his oath.'
23:17 or the **t** that makes the gold sacred?
23:21 he who swears by the **t** swears by it
23:35 between the **t** and the altar.
24: 1 Jesus left the **t** and was walking
26:55 day I sat in the **t** courts teaching,
26:61 'I am able to destroy the **t** of God
27: 5 Judas threw the money into the **t** and
27:40 "You who are going to destroy the **t**
Mk 11:11 entered Jerusalem and went to the **t**.
11:15 Jesus entered the **t** area and began
11:16 merchandise through the **t** courts.
11:27 Jesus was walking in the **t** courts,
12:35 While Jesus was teaching in the **t**
12:41 their money into the **t** treasury.
13: 1 he was leaving the **t**, one of his
13: 3 the Mount of Olives opposite the **t**,
14:49 teaching in the **t** courts, and you
14:58 'I will destroy this man-made **t** and
15:29 the **t** and build it in three days,
Lk 1:21 why he stayed so long in the **t**.
1:22 he had seen a vision in the **t**,
2:27 Spirit, he went into the **t** courts.
2:37 She never left the **t** but worshipped
2:46 days they found him in the **t** courts,
4: 9 stand on the highest point of the **t**.
18:10 "Two men went up to the **t** to pray,
19:45 he entered the **t** area and began
19:47 Every day he was teaching at the **t**.
20: 1 **t** courts and preaching the gospel,
21: 1 their gifts into the **t** treasury.
21: 5 **t** was adorned with beautiful stones
21:37 Each day Jesus was teaching at the **t**,
21:38 in the morning to hear him at the **t**.
22: 4 the officers of the **t** guard and
22:52 the officers of the **t** guard, and the
22:53 Every day I was with you in the **t**
24:53 they stayed continually at the **t**,
Jn 2:14 In the **t** courts he found men selling
2:15 and drove all from the **t** area, both
2:19 Jesus answered them, "Destroy this **t**,
2:20 forty-six years to build this **t**,
2:21 the **t** he had spoken of was his body.
5:14 Later Jesus found him at the **t** and
7:14 to the **t** courts and begin to teach.
7:28 Jesus, still teaching in the **t**
7:32 sent **t** guards to arrest him.
7:45 Finally the **t** guards went back to
8: 2 At dawn he appeared again in the **t**
8:20 while teaching in the **t** area near
8:59 slipping away from the **t** grounds.
10:23 Jesus was in the **t** area walking in
11:56 and as they stood in the **t** area they
18:20 **t**, where all the Jews come together.
Ac 2:46 to meet together in the **t** courts.
3: 1 John were going up to the **t** at the
3: 2 to the **t** gate called Beautiful,
3: 2 from those going into the **t** courts.
3: 8 Then he went with them into the **t**
3:10 at the **t** gate called Beautiful,
4: 1 The priests and the captain of the **t**
5:20 "Go, stand in the **t** courts," he said,
5:21 At daybreak they entered the **t**
5:24 the captain of the **t** guard and the
Ac 5:25 the **t** courts teaching the people."
5:42 Day after day, in the **t** courts and
14:13 The priest of Zeus, whose **t** was just
19:27 that the **t** of the great goddess
19:35 of the **t** of the great Artemis
21:26 Then he went to the **t** to give notice
21:27 province of Asia saw Paul at the **t**.
21:28 **t** area and defiled this holy place."
21:29 had brought him into the **t** area.)
21:30 they dragged him from the **t**, and
22:17 at the **t**, I fell into a trance
24: 6 even tried to desecrate the **t**; so we
24:12 me arguing with anyone at the **t**,
24:18 found me in the **t** courts doing this.
25: 8 or against the **t** or against Caesar."
26:21 the **t** courts and tried to kill me.
Ro 9: 4 law, the **t** worship and the promises.
1Co 3:16 you yourselves are God's **t** and that
3:17 If anyone destroys God's **t**, God will
3:17 **t** is sacred, and you are that **t**.
6:19 Do you not know that your body is a **t**
8:10 knowledge eating in an idol's **t**,
9:13 in the **t** get their food from the **t**,
2Co 6:16 What agreement is there between the **t**
6:16 For we are the **t** of the living God.
Eph 2:21 to become a holy **t** in the Lord.
2Th 2: 4 he sets himself up in God's **t**,
Rev 3:12 make a pillar in the **t** of my God.
7:15 serve him day and night in his **t**;
11: 1 "Go and measure the **t** of God and the
11:19 God's **t** in heaven was opened, and
11:19 within his **t** was seen the ark of
14:15 another angel came out of the **t** and
14:17 Another angel came out of the **t** in
15: 5 this I looked and in heaven the **t**,
15: 6 Out of the **t** came the seven angels
15: 8 the **t** was filled with smoke from the
15: 8 and no-one could enter the **t** until
16: 1 I heard a loud voice from the **t**
16:17 and out of the **t** came a loud voice
21:22 I did not see a **t** in the city,
21:22 God Almighty and the Lamb are its **t**.

Temple of the LORD/Lord

1Sa 3: 3 in the **t**, where the ark of God was.
1Ki 3: 1 building his palace and the **t**, and
6: 1 month, he began to build the **t**.
6:37 The foundation of the **t** was laid in
7:12 courtyard of the **t** with its portico.
7:40 for King Solomon in the **t**:
7:45 for the **t** were of burnished bronze.
7:51 had done for the **t** was finished,
8:10 Holy Place, the cloud filled the **t**.
8:63 all the Israelites dedicated the **t**.
8:64 of the courtyard in front of the **t**,
9: 1 Solomon had finished building the **t**
9:10 two buildings—the **t** and the royal
10: 5 made at the **t**, she was overwhelmed.
10:12 for the **t** and for the royal palace,
12:27 sacrifices at the **t** in Jerusalem,
14:26 He carried off the treasures of the **t**
15:15 He brought into the **t** the silver and
2Ki 11: 3 hidden with his nurse at the **t**
11: 4 had them brought to him at the **t**.
11: 4 and put them under oath at the **t**.
11:10 King David and that were in the **t**.
11:13 she went to the people at the **t**.
11:15 must not be put to death in the **t**."
11:18 the priest posted guards at the **t**.
11:19 from the **t** and went into the palace,
12: 4 **t**—the money collected in the census,
12: 9 the right side as one enters the **t**.
12: 9 the money that was brought to the **t**.
12:10 into the **t** and put it into bags.
12:11 the **t**—the carpenters and builders,
12:12 stone for the repair of the **t**,
12:13 of gold or silver for the **t**;
12:16 the **t**; it belonged to the priests.
12:18 of the **t** and of the royal palace,
14:14 all the articles found in the **t** and
15:35 rebuilt the Upper Gate of the **t**.
16: 8 gold found in the **t** and in the
16:14 the **t**—and put it on the north side
16:18 the royal entrance outside the **t**,
18:15 the silver that was found in the **t**

2Ki 18:16 the doors and doorposts of the **t**,
19: 1 on sackcloth and went into the **t**.
19:14 **t** and spread it out before the LORD.
20: 5 from now you will go up to the **t**.
20: 8 to the **t** on the third day from now?"
21: 4 He built altars in the **t**, of which
21: 5 In both courts of the **t**, he built
22: 3 the son of Meshullam, to the **t**.
22: 4 that has been brought into the **t**,
22: 5 pay the workers who repair the **t**—
22: 8 found the Book of the Law in the **t**.
22: 9 out the money that was in the **t**
23: 2 He went up to the **t** with the men of
23: 2 which had been found in the **t**.
23: 4 the doorkeepers to remove from the **t**
23: 6 He took the Asherah pole from the **t**
23: 7 which were in the **t** and where women
23:11 He removed from the entrance to the **t**
23:12 built in the two courts of the **t**.
23:24 the priest had discovered in the **t**.
24:13 the **t** and from the royal palace,
24:13 king of Israel had made for the **t**.
25: 9 He set fire to the **t**, the royal
25:13 the bronze Sea that were at the **t**
25:16 which Solomon had made for the **t**,
1Ch 6:32 Solomon built the **t** in Jerusalem.
22:14 provide for the **t** a hundred thousand
23: 4 are to supervise the work of the **t**
23:24 old or more who served in the **t**.
23:28 in the service of the **t**: to be in
23:32 of Aaron, for the service of the **t**.
24:19 ministering when they entered the **t**,
25: 6 fathers for the music of the **t**,
26:12 the **t**, just as their relatives had.
26:22 charge of the treasuries of the **t**.
26:27 dedicated for the repair of the **t**.
28:12 the **t** and all the surrounding rooms,
28:13 all the work of serving in the **t**,
28:20 the service of the **t** is finished.
29: 8 gave them to the treasury of the **t**
2Ch 3: 1 Solomon began to build the **t** in
4:16 for the **t** were of polished bronze.
5: 1 had done for the **t** was finished,
5:13 Then the **t** was filled with a cloud,
7: 2 The priests could not enter the **t**
7: 7 of the courtyard in front of the **t**,
7:11 Solomon had finished the **t** and the
7:11 do in the **t** and in his own palace,
8: 1 built the **t** and his own palace,
8:16 the **t** was laid until its completion.
8:16 So the **t** was finished.
9: 4 made at the **t**, she was overwhelmed.
9:11 for the **t** and for the royal palace,
12: 9 carried off the treasures of the **t**
20: 5 at the **t** in the front of the new
20:28 **t** with harps and lutes and trumpets.
23: 5 to be in the courtyards of the **t**.
23: 6 No-one is to enter the **t** except the
23:12 the king, she went to them at the **t**.
23:14 "Do not put her to death at the **t**.
23:18 the **t** in the hands of the priests,
23:20 brought the king down from the **t**.
24: 4 Joash decided to restore the **t**.
24: 8 outside, at the gate of the **t**.
24:12 out the work required for the **t**.
24:14 were presented continually in the **t**.
24:18 They abandoned the **t**, the God of
26:16 and entered the **t** to burn incense on
26:21 —leprous, and excluded from the **t**.
27: 2 unlike him he did not enter the **t**.
27: 3 rebuilt the Upper Gate of the **t**
28:21 took some of the things from the **t**
29: 3 doors of the **t** and repaired them.
29: 5 the **t**, the God of your fathers.
29:15 they went in to purify the **t**, as the
29:16 unclean that they found in the **t**.
29:17 days they consecrated the **t** itself,
29:18 "We have purified the entire **t**, the
29:20 together and went up to the **t**.
29:25 He stationed the Levites in the **t**
29:31 and thank-offerings to the **t**.
29:35 service of the **t** was re-established.
30: 1 inviting them to come to the **t** in
30:15 brought burnt offerings to the **t**.
31:10 bring their contributions to the **t**,
31:11 in the **t**, and this was done.
2Ch 31:16 all who would enter the **t** to perform
33: 4 He built altars in the **t**, of which
33: 5 In both courts of the **t**, he built
33:15 and removed the image from the **t**,
34: 8 recorder, to repair the **t** his God.
34:14 that had been taken into the **t**,
34:15 found the Book of the Law in the **t**.
34:17 out the money that was in the **t**
34:30 He went up to the **t** with the men of
34:30 which had been found in the **t**.
36: 7 took to Babylon articles from the **t**
36:10 with articles of value from the **t**,
36:14 of the nations and defiling the **t**,
Ezr 1: 3 Jerusalem in Judah and build the **t**,
1: 7 out the articles belonging to the **t**,
3:10 laid the foundation of the **t**,
Isa 37: 1 on sackcloth and went into the **t**.
37:14 **t** and spread it out before the LORD.
38:20 all the days of our lives in the **t**.
38:22 sign that I will go up to the **t**?"
66:20 the **t** in ceremonially clean vessels.
Jer 7: 4 "This is the **t**, the **t**, the **t**!
20: 1 the chief officer in the **t**, heard
24: 1 of figs placed in front of the **t**.
38:14 to the third entrance to the **t**.
52:13 He set fire to the **t**, the royal
52:17 the bronze Sea that were at the **t**
52:20 King Solomon had made for the **t**,
Eze 8:16 With their backs towards the **t** and
44: 4 filling the **t**, and I fell face down.
44: 5 all the regulations regarding the **t**.
Hos 9: 4 it will not come into the **t**.
Zec 6:12 out from his place and build the **t**.
6:13 is he who will build the **t**, and he
6:14 of Zephaniah as a memorial in the **t**.
6:15 will come and help to build the **t**,
Lk 1: 9 to go into the **t** and burn incense.

Temples (Temple)

SS 4: 3 Your **t** behind your veil are like the
6: 7 Your **t** behind your veil are like the
Jer 43:12 He will set fire to the **t** of the
43:12 their **t** and take their gods captive.
43:13 down the **t** of the gods of Egypt.
Joel 3: 5 off my finest treasures to your **t**.
Ac 17:24 does not live in **t** built by hands.
19:37 robbed **t** nor blasphemed our goddess.
Ro 2:22 You who abhor idols, do you rob **t**?

Temporary

Ex 12:45 a **t** resident and a hired worker may
Lev 25: 6 and **t** resident who live among you,
25:35 you would an alien or a **t** resident,
25:40 worker or a **t** resident among you;
25:45 also buy some of the **t** residents
25:47 "'If an alien or a **t** resident among
2Co 4:18 is **t**, but what is unseen is eternal.

Tempt (Temptation, Tempted, Tempter, Tempting)

1Co 7: 5 that Satan will not **t** you because
Jas 1:13 by evil, nor does he **t** anyone;

Temptation (Tempt)

Mt 6:13 lead us not into **t**, but deliver us
26:41 so that you will not fall into **t**.
Mk 14:38 so that you will not fall into **t**.
Lk 11: 4 And lead us not into **t**.'
22:40 "Pray that you will not fall into **t**."
22:46 so that you will not fall into **t**."
1Co 10:13 No **t** has seized you except what is
1Ti 6: 9 who want to get rich fall into **t**

Tempted (Tempt)

Mt 4: 1 the desert to be **t** by the devil.
Mk 1:13 for forty days, being **t** by Satan.
Lk 4: 2 where for forty days he was **t** by the
1Co 10:13 you be **t** beyond what you can bear.
10:13 But when you are **t**, he will also
Gal 6: 1 yourself, or you also may be **t**.
1Th 3: 5 way the tempter might have **t** you
Heb 2:18 he himself suffered when he was **t**,
2:18 able to help those who are being **t**.
4:15 but we have one who has been **t** in
Jas 1:13 When **t**, no-one should say, "God is
1:13 God cannot be **t** by evil, nor does
1:14 each one is **t** when, by his own evil

Tempter (Tempt)

Mt 4: 3 The **t** came to him and said, "If you
1Th 3: 5 I was afraid that in some way the **t**

Tempting (Tempt)

Lk 4:13 the devil had finished all this **t**,
Jas 1:13 no-one should say, "God is **t** me."

Ten (Tens, Ten-stringed, Tenth, Tithe, Tithes)

Ge 16: 3 had been living in Canaan **t** years,
18:32 What if only **t** can be found there?"
18:32 sake of **t**, I will not destroy it."
24:10 the servant took **t** of his master's
24:22 gold bracelets weighing **t** shekels.
24:55 us **t** days or so; then you may go."
31: 7 me by changing my wages **t** times.
31:41 and you changed my wages **t** times.
32:15 forty cows and **t** bulls, and twenty
32:15 female donkeys and **t** male donkeys.
42: 3 **t** of Joseph's brothers went down to
45:23 he sent to his father: **t** donkeys
45:23 and **t** female donkeys loaded with
50:22 He lived a hundred and **t** years
50:26 died at the age of a hundred and **t**.
Ex 26: 1 "Make the tabernacle with **t** curtains
26:16 Each frame is to be **t** cubits long
27:12 curtains, with **t** posts and **t** bases.
34:28 of the covenant—the **T** Commandments.
36: 8 **t** curtains of finely twisted linen
36:21 Each frame was **t** cubits long and a
38:12 with **t** posts and **t** bases, with
Lev 26: 8 will chase **t** thousand, and your
26:26 **t** women will be able to bake your
27: 5 and of a female at **t** shekels.
27: 7 and of a female at **t** shekels.
Nu 7:14 one gold dish weighing **t** shekels,
7:20 one gold dish weighing **t** shekels,
7:26 one gold dish weighing **t** shekels,
7:32 one gold dish weighing **t** shekels,
7:38 one gold dish weighing **t** shekels,
7:44 one gold dish weighing **t** shekels,
7:50 one gold dish weighing **t** shekels,
7:56 one gold dish weighing **t** shekels,
7:62 one gold dish weighing **t** shekels,
7:68 one gold dish weighing **t** shekels,
7:74 one gold dish weighing **t** shekels,
7:80 one gold dish weighing **t** shekels,
7:86 with incense weighed **t** shekels each,
11:19 two days, or five, **t** or twenty days,
11:32 No-one gathered less than **t** homers.
14:22 disobeyed me and tested me **t** times—
29:23 "'On the fourth day prepare **t** bulls,
Dt 4:13 the **T** Commandments, which he
10: 4 written before, the **T** Commandments
32:30 or two put **t** thousand to flight,
33:17 Such are the **t** thousands of Ephraim;
Jos 15:57 Kain, Gibeah and Timnah—**t** towns and
17: 5 share consisted of **t** tracts of
21: 5 allotted **t** towns from the clans of
21:26 All these **t** towns and their
22:14 With him they sent **t** of the chief
24:29 died at the age of a hundred and **t**.
Jdg 1: 4 struck down **t** thousand men at Bezek.
2: 8 died at the age of a hundred and **t**.
3:29 struck down about **t** thousand
4: 6 'Go, take with you **t** thousand men of
4:10 **T** thousand men followed him, and
4:14 Tabor, followed by **t** thousand men.
6:27 Gideon took **t** of his servants and
7: 3 men left, while **t** thousand remained.
12:11 Zebulunite led Israel for **t** years.
17:10 and I'll give you **t** shekels of
20:10 We'll take **t** men out of every
20:10 and a thousand from **t** thousand, to
20:34 **t** thousand of Israel's finest men
Ru 1: 4 they had lived there about **t** years,
4: 2 Boaz took **t** of the elders of the
1Sa 1: 8 I mean more to you than **t** sons?"
15: 4 and **t** thousand men from Judah.
17:17 these **t** loaves of bread for your

1Sa 17:18 Take along these t cheeses to the
25: 5 he sent t young men and said to them,
25:38 About t days later, the LORD struck
2Sa 15:16 but he left t concubines to take
18: 3 but you are worth t thousand of us.
18:11 have had to give you t shekels of
18:15 t of Joab's armour-bearers
19:43 "We have t shares in the king; and
20: 3 he took the t concubines he had left
1Ki 4:23 t head of stall-fed cattle, twenty
5:14 in shifts of t thousand a month,
6: 3 and projected t cubits from the
6:23 of olive wood, each t cubits high.
6:24 t cubits from wing tip to wing tip.
6:25 The second cherub also measured t
6:26 height of each cherub was t cubits
7:10 measuring t cubits and some eight.
7:23 measuring t cubits from rim to rim
7:24 gourds encircled it—t to a cubit.
7:27 He also made t movable stands of
7:37 This is the way he made the t stands.
7:38 He then made t bronze basins, each
7:38 basin to go on each of the t stands.
7:43 the t stands with their t basins;
11:31 he said to Jeroboam, "Take t pieces
11:31 Solomon's hand and give you t tribes.
11:35 son's hands and give you t tribes.
14: 3 Take t loaves of bread with you,
2Ki 5: 5 left, taking with him t talents
5: 5 of gold and t sets of clothing.
13: 7 t chariots and t thousand foot
14: 7 who defeated t thousand Edomites
15:17 he reigned in Samaria for t years.
20: 9 Shall the shadow go forward t steps,
20: 9 steps, or shall it go back t steps?"
20:10 go forward t steps," said Hezekiah.
20:10 "Rather, have it go back t steps."
20:11 made the shadow go back the t steps
24:14 and artisans—a total of t thousand.
25:25 came with t men and assassinated
1Ch 6:61 allotted t towns from the clans of
29: 7 and t thousand darics of gold,
29: 7 t thousand talents of silver,
2Ch 4: 1 cubits wide and t cubits high.
4: 2 measuring t cubits from rim to rim
4: 3 of bulls encircled it—t to a cubit.
4: 6 He then made t basins for washing
4: 7 He made t gold lampstands according
4: 8 He made t tables and placed them in
14: 1 country was at peace for t years.
25:11 he killed t thousand men of Seir.
25:12 also captured t thousand men alive,
27: 5 t thousand cors of wheat and t
30:24 and t thousand sheep and goats.
36: 9 for three months and t days.
Ezr 8:24 Hashabiah and t of their brothers,
Ne 4:12 them came and told us t times over,
5:18 and every t days an abundant supply
11: 1 out of every t to live in Jerusalem,
Est 3: 9 and I will put t thousand talents of
9:10 the t sons of Haman son of
9:12 men and the t sons of Haman in
9:13 Haman's t sons be hanged on gallows."
9:14 and they hanged the t sons of Haman.
Job 19: 3 T times now you have reproached me;
Ps 91: 7 fall at your side, t thousand at
Ecc 7:19 powerful than t rulers in a city.
SS 5:10 ruddy, outstanding among t thousand.
Isa 38: 8 cast by the sun go back the t steps
38: 8 back the t steps it had gone down.
Jer 41: 1 came with t men to Gedaliah son of
41: 2 son of Nethaniah and the t men
41: 8 t of them said to Ishmael, "Don't
42: 7 T days later the word of the LORD
Eze 40:11 it was t cubits and its length was
41: 2 The entrance was t cubits wide, and
42: 4 an inner passageway t cubits wide
45:14 consists of t baths or one homer,
45:14 t baths are equivalent to a homer).
Da 1:12 test your servants for t days:
1:14 to this and tested them for t days.
1:15 At the end of the t days they looked
1:20 he found them t times better than
7: 7 former beasts, and it had t horns.
7:10 t thousand times t thousand stood
7:20 wanted to know about the t horns
Da 7:24 The t horns are t kings who will
Am 5: 3 strong will have only t left."
6: 9 If t men are left in one house, they
Mic 6: 7 with t thousand rivers of oil? Shall
Hag 2:16 twenty measures, there were only t.
Zec 8:23 "In those days t men from all
Mt 18:24 a man who owed him t thousand
20:24 the t heard about this, they were
25: 1 like t virgins who took their lamps
25:28 it to the one who has the t talents.
Mk 10:41 the t heard about this, they became
Lk 14:31 whether he is able with t thousand
15: 8 "Or suppose a woman has t silver
17:12 he was going into a village, t men
17:17 asked, "Were not all t cleansed?
19:13 he called t of his servants and gave
19:13 his servants and gave them t minas.
19:16 'Sir, your mina has earned t more.'
19:17 matter, take charge of t cities.'
19:24 give it to the one who has t minas.'
19:25 "'Sir,' they said, 'he already has t
Ac 25: 6 After spending eight or t days with
1Co 4:15 Even though you have t thousand
14:19 than t thousand words in a tongue.
Rev 2:10 will suffer persecution for t days.
5:11 and t thousand times t thousand.
12: 3 t horns and seven crowns on his
13: 1 He had t horns and seven heads, with
13: 1 with t crowns on his horns, and on
17: 3 and had seven heads and t horns.
17: 7 has the seven heads and t horns.
17:12 "The t horns you saw are t kings who
17:16 The beast and the t horns you saw

Tenants

Lev 25:23 and you are but aliens and my t.
Job 31:39 or broken the spirit of its t,
SS 8:11 Hamon; he let out his vineyard to t.
Mt 21:34 to the t to collect his fruit.
21:35 "The t seized his servants; they
21:36 the t treated them in the same way.
21:38 "But when the t saw the son, they
21:40 comes, what will he do to those t?"
21:41 will rent the vineyard to other t,
Mk 12: 2 sent a servant to the t to collect
12: 7 "But the t said to one another,
12: 9 kill those t and give the vineyard
Lk 20:10 sent a servant to the t so they
20:10 But the t beat him and sent him away
20:14 "But when the t saw him, they talked
20:16 He will come and kill those t and

Tend (Tended, Tending, Tends)

Ge 30:36 to t the rest of Laban's flocks.
46:32 are shepherds; they t livestock
Lev 24: 3 Aaron is to t the lamps before the
1Sa 17:15 t his father's sheep at Bethlehem.
SS 8:12 are for those who t its fruit.
Jer 23: 2 says to the shepherds who t my
23: 4 shepherds over them who will t them,
Eze 34:14 I will t them in a good pasture, and
34:15 I myself will t my sheep and make
34:23 my servant David, and he will t them;
34:23 will t them and be their shepherd.
Jnh 4:10 you did not t it or make it grow.

Tended (Tend)

Ge 46:34 'Your servants have t livestock from
Lev 24: 4 the LORD must be t continually.
Hos 12:12 wife, and to pay for her he t sheep.

Tender (Tenderly, Tenderness)

Ge 18: 7 t calf and gave it to a servant, who
33:13 lord knows that the children are t
Dt 32: 2 like abundant rain on t plants.
2Ki 19:26 like t green shoots, like grass
Pr 4: 3 t, and an only child of my mother,
Isa 37:27 like t green shoots, like grass
47: 1 will you be called t or delicate.
53: 2 He grew up before him like a t shoot,
Eze 17:22 I will break off a t sprig from its
Mt 24:32 twigs get t and its leaves come out,
Mk 13:28 twigs get t and its leaves come out,
Lk 1:78 of the t mercy of our God, by which

Tenderly (Tender)

Ge 34: 3 loved the girl and spoke t to her.
Isa 40: 2 Speak t to Jerusalem, and proclaim
Hos 2:14 into the desert and speak t to her.

Tenderness (Tender)

Isa 63:15 Your t and compassion are withheld
Php 2: 1 the Spirit, if any t and compassion,

Tending (Tend)

Ge 30:31 t your flocks and watching over them:
37: 2 a young man of seventeen, was t the
Ex 3: 1 Now Moses was t the flock of Jethro
1Sa 16:11 answered, "but he is t the sheep.
Ps 78:71 from t the sheep he brought him to
Jer 6: 3 round her, each t his own portion."
Eze 34:10 I will remove them from t the flock
Am 7:15 the LORD took me from t the flock
Mt 8:33 Those t the pigs ran off, went into
Mk 5:14 Those t the pigs ran off and
Lk 8:34 those t the pigs saw what had

Tendon (Tendons)

Ge 32:32 t attached to the socket of the hip,
32:32 Jacob's hip was touched near the t.

Tendons (Tendon)

Eze 37: 6 I will attach t to you and make
37: 8 I looked, and t and flesh appeared

Tends (Tend)

Ex 30: 7 every morning when he t the lamps.
Pr 27:18 He who t a fig-tree will eat its
Isa 40:11 He t his flock like a shepherd: He
1Co 9: 7 Who t a flock and does not drink of

Tens (Ten)

Ex 18:21 thousands, hundreds, fifties and t.
18:25 thousands, hundreds, fifties and t.
Dt 1:15 and of t and as tribal officials.
1Sa 18: 7 and David his t of thousands."
18: 8 "They have credited David with t of
21:11 and David his t of thousands'?"
29: 5 and David his t of thousands'?"
Ps 3: 6 I will not fear the t of thousands
68:17 The chariots of God are t of
144:13 by t of thousands in our fields;

Ten-stringed (String, Ten)

Ps 33: 2 make music to him on the t lyre.
92: 3 to the music of the t lyre and the
144: 9 the t lyre I will make music to you,

Tent (*Tent of meeting*, Tent-dwelling, Tentmaker, Tents)

Ge 9:21 and lay uncovered inside his t.
12: 8 east of Bethel and pitched his t,
13: 3 and Ai where his t had been
18: 1 to his t in the heat of the day.
18: 2 the entrance of his t to meet them
18: 6 Abraham hurried into the t to Sarah.
18: 9 "There, in the t," he said.
18:10 to the t, which was behind him.
24:67 Isaac brought her into the t of his
26:25 There he pitched his t, and there
31:25 Jacob had pitched his t in the hill
31:33 Laban went into Jacob's t and into
31:33 into Leah's t and into the t of the
31:33 of Leah's t, he entered Rachel's t.
31:34 in the t but found nothing.
33:19 of ground where he pitched his t.
35:21 pitched his t beyond Migdal Eder.
Ex 16:16 for each person you have in your t.
18: 7 each other and then went into the t.
26: 7 "Make curtains of goat hair for the t
26: 9 double at the front of the t.
26:11 to fasten the t together as a unit.
26:12 for the additional length of the t
26:13 The t curtains will be a cubit
26:14 Make for the t a covering of ram
26:36 "For the entrance to the t make a
27:19 including all the t pegs for it and
31: 7 all the other furnishings of the t—

Ex 33: 7 Now Moses used to take a **t** and pitch
33: 8 whenever Moses went out to the **t**,
33: 8 Moses until he entered the **t**.
33: 9 Moses went into the **t**, the pillar of
33:10 standing at the entrance to the **t**,
33:10 each at the entrance to his **t**.
33:11 son of Nun did not leave the **t**.
35:11 the tabernacle with its **t** and its
35:18 the **t** pegs for the tabernacle and
36:14 hair for the **t** over the tabernacle
36:18 to fasten the **t** together as a unit.
36:19 they made for the **t** a covering of
36:37 For the entrance to the **t** they made
38:20 All the **t** pegs of the tabernacle and
38:31 for its entrance and all the **t** pegs
39:33 Moses: the **t** and all its furnishings,
39:38 curtain for the entrance to the **t**;
39:40 the ropes and **t** pegs for the
40:19 he spread the **t** over the tabernacle
40:19 the **t**, as the LORD commanded him.
Lev 14: 8 stay outside his **t** for seven days.
Nu 3:25 the care of the tabernacle and **t**,
3:37 with their bases, **t** pegs and ropes.
4:32 **t** pegs, ropes, all their equipment
9:15 tabernacle, the **T** of the Testimony
9:17 the cloud lifted from above the **T**,
11:10 each at the entrance to his **t**.
11:24 and made them stand round the **T**.
11:26 elders, but did not go out to the **T**.
12: 5 the **T** and summoned Aaron and Miriam.
12:10 the cloud lifted from above the **T**,
17: 7 the LORD in the **T** of the Testimony.
17: 8 Moses entered the **T** of the Testimony
18: 2 before the **T** of the Testimony.
18: 3 to perform all the duties of the **T**,
18: 4 all the work at the **T**—and no-one
19:14 applies when a person dies in a **t**:
19:14 Anyone who enters the **t** and anyone
19:18 sprinkle the **t** and all the
25: 8 followed the Israelite into the **t**.
Dt 31:15 the LORD appeared at the **T** in a
31:15 stood over the entrance to the **T**.
Jos 7:21 my **t**, with the silver underneath."
7:22 and they ran to the **t**, and there it
7:22 his **t**, with the silver underneath.
7:23 They took the things from the **t**,
7:24 donkeys and sheep, his **t** and all
Jdg 4:11 and pitched his **t** by the great tree
4:17 however, fled on foot to the **t** of
4:18 he entered her **t**, and she put a
4:20 "Stand in the doorway of the **t**," he
4:21 Heber's wife, picked up a **t** peg
4:22 the **t** peg through his temple—dead.
5:26 Her hand reached for the **t** peg, her
7:13 It struck the **t** with such force that
7:13 the **t** overturned and collapsed."
1Sa 4:10 and every man fled to his **t**.
17:54 Philistine's weapons in his own **t**.
2Sa 6:17 the **t** that David had pitched for it,
7: 2 the ark of God remains in a **t**."
7: 6 to place with a **t** as my dwelling.
16:22 they pitched a **t** for Absalom on the
20: 1 son! Every man to his **t**, O Israel!"
1Ki 1:39 the sacred **t** and anointed Solomon.
2:28 he fled to the **t** of the LORD and
2:29 Joab had fled to the **t** of the LORD
2:30 Benaiah entered the **t** of the LORD
2Ki 7: 8 They returned and entered another **t**
1Ch 9:19 guarding the thresholds of the **T**
9:23 of the LORD—the house called the **T**.
15: 1 ark of God and pitched a **t** for it.
16: 1 the **t** that David had pitched for it,
17: 1 covenant of the LORD is under a **t**."
17: 5 I have moved from one **t** site to
2Ch 1: 4 had pitched a **t** for it in Jerusalem.
24: 6 Israel for the **T** of the Testimony?"
Job 4:21 Are not the cords of their **t** pulled
5:24 You will know that your **t** is secure;
11:14 allow no evil to dwell in your **t**,
18: 6 The light in his **t** becomes dark; the
18:14 He is torn from the security of his **t**
18:15 Fire resides in his **t**; burning
19:12 against me and encamp around my **t**.
20:26 and devour what is left in his **t**.
22:23 remove wickedness far from your **t**
Ps 19: 4 he has pitched a **t** for the sun,
Ps 52: 5 you up and tear you from your **t**;
61: 4 I long to dwell in your **t** for ever
76: 2 His **t** is in Salem, his
78:60 the **t** he had set up among men.
91:10 no disaster will come near your **t**.
104: 2 stretches out the heavens like a **t**
Pr 14:11 the **t** of the upright will flourish.
SS 1: 5 like the **t** curtains of Solomon.
Isa 13:20 no Arab will pitch his **t** there,
33:20 a peaceful abode, a **t** that will not
38:12 Like a shepherd's **t** my house has
40:22 them out like a **t** to live in.
54: 2 "Enlarge the place of your **t**,
54: 2 stretch your **t** curtains wide, do not
Jer 10:20 My **t** is destroyed; all its ropes are
10:20 pitch my **t** or to set up my shelter.
Lam 2: 4 on the **t** of the Daughter of Zion.
Am 9:11 day I will restore David's fallen **t**.
Zec 10: 4 from him the **t** peg, from him the
Ac 15:16 return and rebuild David's fallen **t**.
2Co 5: 1 Now we know that if the earthly **t** we
5: 4 For while we are in this **t**, we groan
2Pe 1:13 as I live in the **t** of this body,
Rev 7:15 throne will spread his **t** over them.

Tent of meeting

Ex 27:21 In the **T**, outside the curtain that
28:43 wear them whenever they enter the **T**
29: 4 to the **T** and wash them with water.
29:10 "Bring the bull to the front of the **T**
29:11 presence at the entrance to the **T**.
29:30 comes to the **T** to minister in the
29:32 At the entrance to the **T**, Aaron and
29:42 entrance to the **T** before the LORD.
29:44 "So I will consecrate the **T** and the
30:16 and use it for the service of the **T**.
30:18 **T** and the altar, and put water in it.
30:20 Whenever they enter the **T**, they
30:26 use it to anoint the **T**, the ark of
30:36 the **T**, where I will meet with you.
31: 7 the **T**, the ark of the Testimony with
33: 7 distance away, calling it the "**t**".
33: 7 would go to the **t** outside the camp.
35:21 to the LORD for the work on the **T**,
38: 8 who served at the entrance to the **T**.
38:30 the bases for the entrance to the **T**,
39:32 all the work on the tabernacle, the **T**
39:40 for the tabernacle, the **T**;
40: 2 "Set up the tabernacle, the **T**, on
40: 6 entrance to the tabernacle, the **T**;
40: 7 place the basin between the **T** and
40:12 to the **T** and wash them with water.
40:22 Moses placed the table in the **T** on
40:24 He placed the lampstand in the **T**
40:26 Moses placed the gold altar in the **T**
40:29 the **T**, and offered on it burnt
40:30 He placed the basin between the **T**
40:32 the **T** or approached the altar,
40:34 the cloud covered the **T**, and the
40:35 Moses could not enter the **T** because
Lev 1: 1 Moses and spoke to him from the **T**.
1: 3 present it at the entrance to the **T**
1: 5 all sides at the entrance to the **T**.
3: 2 it at the entrance to the **T**.
3: 8 and slaughter it in front of the **T**.
3:13 and slaughter it in front of the **T**.
4: 4 entrance to the **T** before the LORD.
4: 5 blood and carry it into the **T**.
4: 7 that is before the LORD in the **T**.
4: 7 offering at the entrance to the **T**.
4:14 and present it before the **T**.
4:16 some of the bull's blood into the **T**.
4:18 that is before the LORD in the **T**.
4:18 offering at the entrance to the **T**.
6:16 to eat it in the courtyard of the **T**.
6:26 place, in the courtyard of the **T**.
6:30 into the **T** to make atonement
8: 3 assembly at the entrance to the **T**."
8: 4 gathered at the entrance to the **T**.
8:31 the meat at the entrance to the **T**
8:33 Do not leave the entrance to the **T**
8:35 stay at the entrance to the **T** day
9: 5 commanded to the front of the **T**,
9:23 Moses and Aaron then went into the **T**.
10: 7 Do not leave the entrance to the **T**
Lev 10: 9 you go into the **T**, or you will die.
12: 6 the priest at the entrance to the **T**
14:11 the LORD at the entrance to the **T**.
14:23 entrance to the **T**, before the LORD.
15:14 the **T** and give them to the priest.
15:29 the priest at the entrance to the **T**.
16: 7 the LORD at the entrance to the **T**.
16:16 He is to do the same for the **T**,
16:17 No-one is to be in the **T** from the
16:20 the **T** and the altar, he shall bring
16:23 "Then Aaron is to go into the **T** and
16:33 for the **T** and the altar, and for the
17: 4 the entrance to the **T** to present it
17: 5 at the entrance to the **T** and
17: 6 the LORD at the entrance to the **T**
17: 9 the **T** to sacrifice it to the LORD
19:21 **T** for a guilt offering to the LORD.
24: 3 curtain of the Testimony in the **T**,
Nu 1: 1 The LORD spoke to Moses in the **T** in
2: 2 round the **T** some distance from it,
2:17 the **T** and the camp of the Levites
3: 7 for the whole community at the **T** by
3: 8 of all the furnishings of the **T**,
3:25 At the **T** the Gershonites were
3:25 curtain at the entrance to the **T**,
3:38 the sunrise, in front of the **T**.
4: 3 come to serve in the work in the **T**.
4: 4 **T**: the care of the most holy things.
4:15 those things that are in the **T**.
4:23 come to serve in the work at the **T**.
4:25 the **T**, its covering and the outer
4:25 curtains for the entrance to the **T**,
4:28 of the Gershonite clans at the **T**.
4:30 come to serve in the work at the **T**.
4:31 as they perform service at the **T**:
4:33 Merarite clans as they work at the **T**
4:35 came to serve in the work in the **T**,
4:37 Kohathite clans who served in the **T**.
4:39 came to serve in the work at the **T**,
4:41 Gershonite clans who served at the **T**.
4:43 came to serve in the work at the **T**,
4:47 work of serving and carrying the **T**
6:10 the priest at the entrance to the **T**.
6:13 be brought to the entrance to the **T**.
6:18 "'Then at the entrance to the **T**,
7: 5 may be used in the work at the **T**.
7:89 Moses entered the **T** to speak with
8: 9 the Levites to the front of the **T**
8:15 to come to do their work at the **T**.
8:19 his sons to do the work at the **T** on
8:22 **T** under the supervision of Aaron
8:24 to take part in the work at the **T**,
8:26 in performing their duties at the **T**,
10: 3 before you at the entrance to the **T**.
11:16 Make them come to the **T**, that they
12: 4 out to the **T**, all three of you.
14:10 at the **T** to all the Israelites.
16:18 and Aaron at the entrance to the **T**.
16:19 to them at the entrance to the **T**,
16:42 and Aaron and turned towards the **T**,
16:43 Aaron went to the front of the **T**,
16:50 the **T**, for the plague had stopped.
17: 4 Place them in the **T** in front of the
18: 4 be responsible for the care of the **T**
18: 6 to the LORD to do the work at the **T**.
18:21 work they do while serving at the **T**.
18:22 Israelites must not go near the **T**,
18:23 who are to do the work at the **T**
18:31 your wages for your work at the **T**.
19: 4 times towards the front of the **T**.
20: 6 to the **T** and fell face down,
25: 6 weeping at the entrance to the **T**.
27: 2 the entrance to the **T** and stood
31:54 brought it into the **T** as a memorial
Dt 31:14 the **T**, where I will commission him.
31:14 and presented themselves at the **T**.
Jos 18: 1 at Shiloh and set up the **T** there.
19:51 the LORD at the entrance to the **T**.
1Sa 2:22 who served at the entrance to the **T**.
1Ki 8: 4 the **T** and all the sacred furnishings
1Ch 6:32 the **T**, until Solomon built the
9:21 gatekeeper at the entrance to the **T**.
23:32 their responsibilities for the **T**,
2Ch 1: 3 for God's **T** was there, which Moses
1: 6 altar before the LORD in the **T**

2Ch 1:13 place at Gibeon, from before the T.
5: 5 they brought up the ark and the T

Tent-dwelling (Dwell, Tent)

Jdg 5:24 the Kenite, most blessed of t women.

Tenth (Ten)

Ge 8: 5 to recede until the t month,
8: 5 and on the first day of the t month
14:20 Abram gave him a t of everything.
28:22 you give me I will give you a t."
Ex 12: 3 on the t day of this month each man
16:36 (An omer is one t of an ephah.)
29:40 With the first lamb offer a t of an
Lev 5:11 for his sin a t of an ephah of fine
6:20 a t of an ephah of fine flour as a
14:21 together with a t of an ephah of
16:29 On the t day of the seventh month
23:27 "The t day of this seventh month is
25: 9 on the t day of the seventh month;
27:32 flock—every t animal that passes
Nu 5:15 take an offering of a t of an ephah
7:66 On the t day Ahiezer son of
15: 4 a grain offering of a t of an ephah
18:26 you must present a t of that tithe
28: 5 together with a grain offering of a t
28:13 a grain offering of a t of an ephah
29: 7 "'On the t day of this seventh
Dt 14:22 Be sure to set aside a t of all that
23: 2 LORD, even down to the t generation.
23: 3 LORD, even down to the t generation.
26:12 you have finished setting aside a t
Jos 4:19 On the t day of the first month the
1Sa 8:15 He will take a t of your grain and
8:17 He will take a t of your flocks, and
2Ki 25: 1 on the t day of the t month,
1Ch 12:13 Jeremiah the t and Macbannai the
24:11 the ninth to Jeshua, the t to
25:17 the t to Shimei, his sons and
27:13 The t, for the t month, was Maharai
Ezr 10:16 On the first day of the t month they
Ne 10:38 and the Levites are to bring a t of
Est 2:16 the royal residence in the t month,
Isa 6:13 though a t remains in the land, it
Jer 32: 1 t year of Zedekiah king of Judah,
39: 1 in the t month, Nebuchadnezzar king
52: 4 on the t day of the t month,
52:12 On the t day of the fifth month, in
Eze 20: 1 in the fifth month on the t day,
24: 1 In the ninth year, in the t month on
24: 1 in the t month on the t day, the
29: 1 In the t year, in the t month on the
33:21 in the t month on the fifth day, a
40: 1 on the t of the month, in the
45:11 the bath containing a t of a homer
45:11 homer and the ephah a t of a homer;
45:14 measured by the bath, is a t of a
Zec 8:19 fifth, seventh and t months will
Mt 23:23 you hypocrites! You give a t of your
Lk 11:42 because you give God a t of your
18:12 I fast twice a week and give a t of
Jn 1:39 with him. It was about the t hour.
Heb 7: 2 Abraham gave him a t of everything.
7: 4 Abraham gave him a t of the plunder!
7: 5 a t from the people—that is,
7: 6 yet he collected a t from Abraham
7: 8 In the one case, the t is collected
7: 9 the t, paid the t through Abraham,
Rev 11:13 and a t of the city collapsed.
21:20 the ninth topaz, the t chrysoprase,

Tentmaker (Tent)

Ac 18: 3 he was a t as they were, he stayed

Tents (Tent)

Ge 4:20 who live in t and raise livestock.
9:27 may Japheth live in the t of Shem,
13: 5 also had flocks and herds and t.
13:12 plain and pitched his t near Sodom.
13:18 Abram moved his t and went to live
25:27 a quiet man, staying among the t.
Ex 33: 8 stood at the entrances to their t,
Nu 1:52 The Israelites are to set up their t
1:53 however, are to set up their t round
16:24 the t of Korah, Dathan and Abiram.
16:26 "Move back from the t of these
16:27 they moved away from the t of Korah,
16:27 ones at the entrances to their t.
24: 5 "How beautiful are your t, O Jacob,
Dt 1:27 You grumbled in your t and said,
5:30 "Go, tell them to return to their t.
11: 6 their t and every living thing that
16: 7 Then in the morning return to your t.
33:18 out, and you, Issachar, in your t.
Jdg 6: 5 and their t like swarms of locusts.
7: 8 their t but kept the three hundred,
2Sa 11:11 Israel and Judah are staying in t,
1Ki 12:16 what part in Jesse's son? To your t,
20:12 the kings were drinking in their t,
20:16 him were in their t getting drunk.
2Ki 7: 7 t and their horses and donkeys.
7: 8 the camp and entered one of the t.
7:10 and the t left just as they were."
2Ch 10:16 what part in Jesse's son? To your t,
Job 8:22 t of the wicked will be no more."
12: 6 The t of marauders are undisturbed,
15:34 the t of those who love bribes.
21:28 the t where wicked men lived?'
Ps 69:25 there be no-one to dwell in their t.
78:28 their camp, all around their t.
78:51 of manhood in the t of Ham.
78:67 he rejected the t of Joseph, he did
83: 6 the t of Edom and the Ishmaelites,
84:10 than dwell in the t of the wicked.
106:25 They grumbled in their t and did not
118:15 resound in the t of the righteous:
120: 5 that I live among the t of Kedar!
SS 1: 5 dark like the t of Kedar, like the
1: 8 goats by the t of the shepherds.
Jer 4:20 In an instant my t are destroyed, my
6: 3 they will pitch their t round her,
30:18 restore the fortunes of Jacob's t
35: 7 things, but must always live in t.
35:10 We have lived in t and have fully
37:10 wounded men were left in their t,
49:29 Their t and their flocks will be
Eze 25: 4 camps and pitch their t among you;
Da 11:45 He will pitch his royal t between
Hos 9: 6 and thorns will overrun their t.
12: 9 I will make you live in t again,
Hab 3: 7 I saw the t of Cushan in distress,
Mal 2:12 may the LORD cut him off from the t
Heb 11: 9 in a foreign country; he lived in t,

Terah

Ge 11:24 29 years, he became the father of T.
11:25 after he became the father of T,
11:26 After T had lived 70 years, he
11:27 This is the account of T. T became
11:28 While his father T was still alive,
11:31 T took his son Abram, his grandson
11:32 T lived 205 years, and he died in
Nu 33:27 They left Tahath and camped at T.
33:28 They left T and camped at Mithcah.
Jos 24: 2 including T the father of Abraham
1Ch 1:26 Serug, Nahor, T
Lk 3:34 the son of T, the son of Nahor,

Terebinth

Isa 6:13 But as the t and oak leave stumps
Hos 4:13 and t, where the shade is pleasant.

Teresh

Est 2:21 Bigthana and T, two of the king's
6: 2 Mordecai had exposed Bigthana and T,

Terraces

2Sa 5: 9 it, from the supporting t inward.
1Ki 9:15 his own palace, the supporting t,
9:24 he constructed the supporting t.
11:27 Solomon had built the supporting t
1Ch 11: 8 from the supporting t to the
2Ch 32: 5 supporting t of the City of David.
Job 24:11 They crush olives among the t; they
Jer 31:40 and all the t out to the Kidron

Terrible (Terror)

Ex 9: 3 the LORD will bring a t plague
Nu 20: 5 t place? It has no grain or figs,
Dt 6:22 wonders—great and t—upon Egypt and
Ne 13:27 too are doing all this t wickedness
Jer 4: 6 from the north, even t destruction."
6: 1 of the north, even t destruction.
21: 6 they will die of a t plague.
26:19 to bring a t disaster on ourselves!"
Mt 8: 6 home paralysed and in t suffering."
2Ti 3: 1 mark this: There will be t times in
Rev 16:21 hail, because the plague was so t.

Terrified (Terror)

Ge 45: 3 because they were t at his presence.
Ex 14:10 were t and cried out to the LORD.
15:15 The chiefs of Edom will be t, the
Nu 22: 3 Moab was t because there were so
Dt 1:29 I said to you, "Do not be t; do not
7:21 Do not be t by them, for the LORD
20: 3 t or give way to panic before them.
31: 6 Do not be afraid or t because of
Jos 1: 9 Do not be t; do not be discouraged,
Jdg 20:41 and the men of Benjamin were t,
1Sa 17:11 the Israelites were dismayed and t.
31: 4 But the armour-bearer was t and
2Ki 10: 4 they were t and said, "If two kings
1Ch 10: 4 But his armour-bearer was t and
Est 7: 6 was t before the king and queen.
Job 21: 6 I think about this, I am t;
23:15 That is why I am t before him; when
23:16 heart faint; the Almighty has t me.
41:25 he rises up, the mighty are t; they
Ps 90: 7 We are consumed by your anger and t
104:29 you hide your face, they are t; when
Isa 19:17 whom Judah is mentioned will be t,
33:14 The sinners in Zion are t; trembling
51: 7 of men or be t by their insults.
Jer 1:17 Do not be t by them, or I will
10: 2 nations or be t by signs in the sky,
10: 2 though the nations are t by them.
17:18 them be t, but keep me from terror.
23: 4 or t, nor will any be missing,"
46: 5 What do I see? They are t, they are
51:32 set on fire, and the soldiers t."
Eze 2: 6 of what they say or t by them,
3: 9 Do not be afraid of them or t by
19: 7 were in it were t by his roaring.
26:18 in the sea are t at your collapse.'
Da 4: 5 that passed through my mind t me.
4:19 for a time, and his thoughts t him.
5: 9 King Belshazzar became even more t
8:17 I was t and fell prostrate.
Ob : 9 Your warriors, O Teman, will be t,
Jnh 1:10 This t them and they asked, "What
Mt 14:26 walking on the lake, they were t.
17: 6 fell face down to the ground, t.
27:54 they were t, and exclaimed, "Surely
Mk 4:41 They were t and asked each other,
6:50 they all saw him and were t.
Lk 2: 9 shone around them, and they were t.
Jn 6:19 on the water; and they were t.
Rev 11:13 and the survivors were t and gave
18:10 T at her torment, they will stand
18:15 stand far off, t at her torment.

Terrifies (Terror)

Job 22:10 around you, why sudden peril t you,
Ps 2: 5 he rebukes them in his anger and t

Terrify (Terror)

2Ch 32:18 to t them and make them afraid in
Job 7:14 with dreams and t me with visions,
13:11 Would not his splendour t you? Would
33:16 he may speak in their ears and t
Ps 10:18 who is of the earth, may t no more.
83:15 pursue them with your tempest and t
Jer 1:17 them, or I will t you before them.
Hab 2:17 destruction of animals will t you.
Zec 1:21 the craftsmen have come to t them

Terrifying (Terror)

Job 15:21 T sounds fill his ears; when all
Da 7: 7 a fourth beast—t and frightening

Da 7:19 from all the others and most t,
Heb 12:21 The sight was so t that Moses said,

Territories (Territory)

Ge 10: 5 spread out into their t by their
10:20 languages, in their t and nations.
10:31 languages, in their t and nations.
Jos 19:51 These are the t that Eleazar the
1Ch 13: 2 brothers throughout the t of Israel,

Territory (Territories)

Ge 9:27 May God extend the t of Japheth; may
14: 7 and they conquered the whole t of
48: 6 in the t they inherit they will be
Ex 34:24 before you and enlarge your t,
Nu 20:16 Kadesh, a town on the edge of your t.
20:17 we have passed through your t."
20:21 to let them go through their t,
21:13 the desert extending into Amorite t.
21:22 we have passed through your t."
21:23 not let Israel pass through his t.
22:36 Arnon border, at the edge of his t.
32:33 its cities and the t around them.
Dt 1: 5 East of the Jordan in the t of Moab,
2: 4 'You are about to pass through the t
3: 8 Amorites the t east of the Jordan,
3:12 t north of Aroer by the Arnon Gorge,
3:16 the Gadites I gave the t extending
11:24 Your t will extend from the desert
11:30 in the t of those Canaanites living
12:20 the LORD your God has enlarged your t
19: 8 If the LORD your God enlarges your t,
34: 2 all of Naphtali, the t of Ephraim
Jos 1: 4 Your t will extend from the desert
11:22 No Anakites were left in Israelite t;
12: 1 t they took over east of the Jordan,
12: 4 the t of Og king of Bashan, one of
13: 3 Egypt to the t of Ekron on the north,
13: 3 the t of the five Philistine rulers
13:11 also included Gilead, the t of the
13:16 The t from Aroer on the rim of the
13:25 The t of Jazer, all the towns of
13:26 and from Mahanaim to the t of Debir;
13:27 the t up to the end of the Sea of
13:30 The t extending from Mahanaim and
15: 1 extended down to the t of Edom, to
16: 2 to the t of the Arkites in Ataroth,
16: 3 descended westward to the t of the
16: 5 This was the t of Ephraim, clan by
17: 7 The t of Manasseh extended from
17:10 The t of Manasseh reached the sea
18: 5 Judah is to remain in its t on the
18: 5 of Joseph in its t on the north.
18:11 Their allotted t lay between the
19: 1 lay within the t of Judah.
19: 9 inheritance within the t of Judah.
19:12 sunrise to the t of Kisloth Tabor
19:18 Their t included: Jezreel, Kesulloth,
19:25 Their t included: Helkath, Hali,
19:41 The t of their inheritance included:
19:47 taking possession of their t,
21:41 The towns of the Levites in the t
Jdg 1: 3 "Come up with us into the t allotted
1:18 and Ekron—each city with its t.
11:18 They did not enter the t of Moab,
11:20 trust Israel to pass through his t.
1Sa 6: 1 in Philistine t for seven months,
6: 9 If it goes up to its own t, towards
7:13 did not invade Israelite t again.
7:14 delivered the neighbouring t from
9: 4 Then he passed through the t of
27: 7 David lived in Philistine t for a
27:11 as long as he lived in Philistine t.
30:14 the t belonging to Judah and the
1Ki 9:19 and throughout all the t he ruled.
15:17 entering the t of Asa king of Judah.
2Ki 6:23 Aram stopped raiding Israel's t.
10:32 the Israelites throughout their t
18: 8 as far as Gaza and its t.
24: 7 king of Babylon had taken all his t,
1Ch 4:10 would bless me and enlarge my t!
6:54 settlements allotted as their t
6:66 given as their t towns from the
2Ch 8: 6 throughout all the t that he ruled.
16: 1 entering the t of Asa king of Judah.
2Ch 20:10 Moab and Mount Seir, whose t you
34:33 the t belonging to the Israelites,
Jer 1: 1 at Anathoth in the t of Benjamin.
17:26 from the t of Benjamin and the
32: 8 at Anathoth in the t of Benjamin.
32:44 sealed and witnessed in the t of
33:13 in the t of Benjamin, in the
37:12 to leave the city to go to the t of
Eze 16:27 hand against you and reduced your t;
48: 2 the t of Dan from east to west.
48: 3 the t of Asher from east to west.
48: 4 the t of Naphtali from east to west.
48: 5 the t of Manasseh from east to west.
48: 6 the t of Ephraim from east to west.
48: 7 the t of Reuben from east to west.
48: 8 "Bordering the t of Judah from east
48:12 bordering the t of the Levites.
48:13 "Alongside the t of the priests, the
48:24 the t of Benjamin from east to west.
48:25 the t of Simeon from east to west.
48:26 the t of Issachar from east to west.
48:27 the t of Zebulun from east to west.
2Co 10:16 already done in another man's t.

Terror (Terrible, Terrified, Terrifies, Terrify, Terrifying, Terrorists, Terrors)

Ge 35: 5 they set out, and the t of God fell
Ex 15:16 t and dread will fall upon them. By
23:27 "I will send my t ahead of you and
Lev 26:16 you: I will bring upon you sudden t,
Dt 2:25 very day I will begin to put the t
11:25 as he promised you, will put the t
26: 8 with great t and with miraculous
28:67 of the t that will fill your hearts
32:25 in their homes t will reign.
1Sa 11: 7 Then the t of the LORD fell on the
28: 5 he was afraid; t filled his heart.
2Sa 17: 2 I would strike him with t, and then
2Ch 14:14 t of the LORD had fallen upon them.
Job 9:34 his t would frighten me no more.
15:24 Distress and anguish fill him with t;
39:20 striking t with his proud snorting?
Ps 9:20 Strike them with t, O LORD; let the
31:13 there is t on every side; they
48: 5 and were astounded; they fled in t.
78:33 in futility and their years in t.
91: 5 You will not fear the t of night,
Pr 21:15 to the righteous but t to evildoers.
Isa 13: 8 T will seize them, pain and anguish
17:14 In the evening, sudden t! Before the
19:17 the land of Judah will bring t to
21: 1 from the desert, from a land of t.
22: 5 and t in the Valley of Vision,
24:17 T and pit and snare await you,
24:18 Whoever flees at the sound of t will
28:19 of this message will bring sheer t.
31: 9 stronghold will fall because of t;
33:18 you will ponder the former t:
44:11 be brought down to t and infamy.
47:12 succeed, perhaps you will cause t.
51:13 that you live in constant t every
54:14 T will be far removed; it will not
Jer 6:25 sword, and there is t on every side.
8:15 of healing but there was only t.
14:19 time of healing but there is only t.
15: 8 bring down on them anguish and t.
17:17 Do not be a t to me; you are my
17:18 be terrified, but keep me from t.
20: 4 'I will make you a t to yourself and
20:10 I hear many whispering, "T on every
30: 5 of fear are heard—t, not peace.
32:21 outstretched arm and with great t.
46: 5 t on every side," declares the LORD.
48:43 T and pit and snare await you,
48:44 "Whoever flees from the t will fall
49: 5 I will bring t on you from all those
49:16 The t you inspire and the pride of
49:29 shout to them, 'T on every side!'
50: 2 put to shame, Marduk filled with t.
50: 2 shame and her idols filled with t.'
50:36 They will be filled with t.
50:38 idols that will go mad with t.
Lam 3:47 We have suffered t and pitfalls,
Eze 7:18 on sackcloth and be clothed with t.
7:25 t comes, they will seek peace, but
Eze 23:46 and give them over to t and plunder.
26:16 Clothed with t, they will sit on the
26:17 put your t on all who lived there.
32:23 All who had spread t in the land of
32:24 All who had spread t in the land of
32:25 Because their t had spread in the
32:26 their t in the land of the living.
32:27 though the t of these warriors had
32:30 despite the t caused by their power.
32:32 Although I had him spread t in the
Da 10: 7 but such t overwhelmed them that
Am 6: 3 day and bring near a reign of t.
Lk 21:26 Men will faint from t, apprehensive
Ro 13: 3 For rulers hold no t for those who
Rev 11:11 and t struck those who saw them.

Terrorists (Terror)

Ac 21:38 led four thousand t out into the

Terrors (Terror)

Job 6: 4 God's t are marshalled against me.
13:21 and stop frightening me with your t.
18:11 T startle him on every side and dog
18:14 and marched off to the king of t.
20:25 T will come over him;
24:17 make friends with the t of darkness.
27:20 T overtake him like a flood; a
30:15 T overwhelm me; my dignity is driven
Ps 55: 4 within me; the t of death assail me.
73:19 completely swept away by t!
88:15 suffered your t and am in despair.
88:16 over me; your t have destroyed me.
SS 3: 8 prepared for the t of the night.
Lam 2:22 summoned against me t on every side.

Tertius

Ro 16:22 I, T, who wrote down this letter,

Tertullus

Ac 24: 1 of the elders and a lawyer named T,
24: 2 Paul was called in, T presented his

Test (Tested, Tester, Testing, Testings, Tests)

Ex 16: 4 In this way I will t them and see
17: 2 Why do you put the LORD to the t?"
20:20 God has come to t you, so that the
Dt 6:16 Do not t the LORD your God as you
8: 2 to humble you and to t you in order
8:16 to humble and to t you so that in
Jdg 2:22 I will use them to t Israel and see
3: 1 the nations the LORD left to t all
3: 4 They were left to t the Israelites
6:39 Allow me one more t with the fleece.
1Ki 10: 1 came to t him with hard questions.
1Ch 29:17 I know, my God, that you t the heart
2Ch 9: 1 to t him with hard questions.
32:31 God left him to t him and to know
Job 7:18 morning and t him every moment?
12:11 Does not the ear t words as the
Ps 17: 3 though you t me, you will find
26: 2 T me, O LORD, and try me, examine my
78:18 They wilfully put God to the t by
78:41 Again and again they put God to the t
78:56 they put God to the t and rebelled
106:14 the wasteland they put God to the t.
139:23 t me and know my anxious thoughts.
Ecc 2: 1 "Come now, I will t you with
Isa 7:12 I will not put the LORD to the t."
Jer 6:27 you may observe and t their ways.
9: 7 "See, I will refine and t them, for
11:20 you who judge righteously and t the
12: 3 see me and t my thoughts about you.
Lam 3:40 Let us examine our ways and t them,
Da 1:12 "Please t your servants for ten days:
Zec 13: 9 like silver and t them like gold.
Mal 3:10 T me in this," says the LORD
Mt 4: 7 put the Lord your God to the t.'"
19: 3 Some Pharisees came to him to t him.
Mk 8:11 To t him, they asked him for a sign
Lk 4:12 put the Lord your God to the t.'"
10:25 in the law stood up to t Jesus.
Jn 6: 6 He asked this only to t him, for he
Ac 5: 9 "How could you agree to t the Spirit

Ac 15:10 Now then, why do you try to t God by
Ro 12: 2 Then you will be able to t and
1Co 3:13 t the quality of each man's work.
10: 9 We should not t the Lord, as some of
2Co 2: 9 stand the t and be obedient in
8: 8 but I want to t the sincerity of
13: 5 you are in the faith; t yourselves.
13: 5 of course, you fail the t?
13: 6 that we have not failed the t.
13: 7 will see that we have stood the t
Gal 6: 4 Each one should t his own actions.
1Th 5:21 T everything. Hold on to the good.
Jas 1:12 because when he has stood the t, he
1Jn 4: 1 do not believe every spirit, but t
Rev 2:10 put some of you in prison to t you,
3:10 to t those who live on the earth.

Tested (Test)
Ge 22: 1 Some time later God t Abraham. He
42:15 this is how you will be t: As surely
42:16 so that your words may be t to see
Ex 15:25 a law for them, and there he t them.
17: 7 and because they t the LORD saying,
Nu 14:22 disobeyed me and t me ten times—
Dt 33: 8 You t him at Massah; you contended
Job 23:10 t me, I shall come forth as gold.
28:27 it; he confirmed it and t it.
34:36 Oh, that Job might be t to the
Ps 66:10 For you, O God, t us; you refined us
81: 7 I t you at the waters of Meribah.
95: 9 where your fathers t and tried me,
119:140 Your promises have been thoroughly t,
Pr 27:21 man is t by the praise he receives.
Ecc 7:23 All this I t by wisdom and I said,
Isa 28:16 I lay a stone in Zion, a t stone
48:10 t you in the furnace of affliction.
Da 1:14 he agreed to this and t them for ten
Mt 16: 1 Sadducees came to Jesus and t him by
22:35 an expert in the law, t him with
Mk 10: 2 Some Pharisees came and t him by
Lk 11:16 Others t him by asking for a sign
Ac 20:19 severely t by the plots of the Jews.
Ro 16:10 Greet Apelles, t and approved in
1Ti 3:10 They must first be t; and then if
Heb 3: 9 where your fathers t and tried me
11:17 By faith Abraham, when God t him,
Rev 2: 2 that you have t those who claim to

Tester (Test)
Jer 6:27 "I have made you a t of metals and

Testicles
Lev 21:20 or running sores or damaged t.
22:24 t are bruised, crushed, torn or cut.

Testified (Testify)
2Sa 1:16 Your own mouth t against you when
2Ch 24:19 and though they t against them, they
Mk 14:56 Many t falsely against him, but
Jn 3:26 Jordan—the one you t about—well,
5:33 "You have sent to John and he has t
5:37 the Father who sent me has himself t
13:21 Jesus was troubled in spirit and t,
Ac 6:13 They produced false witnesses, who t,
8:25 they had t and proclaimed the word
13:22 He t concerning him: 'I have found
23:11 "Take courage! As you have t about
1Co 15:15 for we have t about God that he
Heb 2: 4 God also t to it by signs, wonders
2: 6 there is a place where someone has t:

Testifies (Testify)
Job 16: 8 gauntness rises up and t against me.
Isa 3: 9 The look on their faces t against
Hos 5: 5 Israel's arrogance t against them;
7:10 Israel's arrogance t against him,
Jn 1:15 John t concerning him. He cries out,
3:32 He t to what he has seen and heard,
5:32 There is another who t in my favour,
5:36 t that the Father has sent me.
8:18 I am one who t for myself; my other
19:35 he t so that you also may believe.
21:24 This is the disciple who t to these
Ro 8:16 The Spirit himself t with our spirit
2Co 1:12 Our conscience t that we have
Heb 10:15 The Holy Spirit also t to us about
1Jn 5: 6 it is the Spirit who t, because the
Rev 1: 2 who t to everything he saw—that is,
22:20 He who t to these things says, "Yes,

Testify (Testified, Testifies, Testifying, Testimony)
Ge 30:33 my honesty will t for me in the
Lev 5: 1 t regarding something he has seen
Dt 8:19 I t against you today that you will
31:21 this song will t against them,
31:28 heaven and earth to t against them.
1Sa 12: 3 Here I stand. T against me in the
1Ki 21:10 have them t that he has cursed both
Job 15: 6 mine; your own lips t against you.
Ps 50: 7 t against you: I am God, your God.
Pr 24:28 Do not t against your neighbour
29:24 he is put under oath and dare not t.
Isa 59:12 sight, and our sins t against us.
Jer 14: 7 Although our sins t against us,
Am 3:13 "Hear this and t against the house
Zep 3: 8 "for the day I will stand up to t.
Mal 3: 5 I will be quick to t against
Mt 23:31 you t against yourselves that you
Lk 11:48 you t that you approve of what your
Jn 1: 7 He came as a witness to t concerning
1:34 I have seen and I t that this is the
3:11 we speak of what we know, and we t
3:28 You yourselves can t that I said, 'I
5:31 "If I t about myself, my testimony
5:39 are the Scriptures that t about me,
7: 7 I t that what it does is evil.
8:14 Jesus answered, "Even if I t on my
15:26 from the Father, he will t about me.
15:27 you also must t, for you have been
18:23 replied, "t as to what is wrong.
18:37 into the world, to t to the truth.
Ac 4:33 power the apostles continued to t
10:42 to t that he is the one whom God
10:43 All the prophets t about him that
22: 5 priest and all the Council can t.
23:11 so you must also t in Rome."
26: 5 known me for a long time and can t,
26:22 here and t to small and great alike.
Ro 3:21 to which the Law and the Prophets t.
10: 2 For I can t about them that they are
2Co 8: 3 For I t that they gave as much as
Gal 4:15 to all your joy? I can t that,
Php 1: 8 God can t how I long for all of you
2Ti 1: 8 do not be ashamed to t about our
Jas 5: 3 Their corrosion will t against you
1Jn 1: 2 we have seen it and t to it,
4:14 we have seen and t that the Father
5: 7 For there are three that t:

Testifying (Testify)
Ac 18: 5 t to the Jews that Jesus was the
20:24 of t to the gospel of God's grace.
1Ti 6:13 and of Christ Jesus, who while t
Heb 3: 5 t to what would be said in the
1Pe 5:12 t that this is the true grace of God.

Testimony (*Ark of the testimony*, *False testimony*, Testify)
Ex 16:34 put the manna in front of the T,
23: 2 When you give t in a lawsuit, do not
25:16 put in the ark the T, which I will
25:21 ark the T, which I will give you.
27:21 curtain that is in front of the T,
30: 6 the T—where I will meet with you.
30:36 of the T in the Tent of Meeting,
31:18 gave him the two tablets of the T,
32:15 two tablets of the T in his hands.
34:29 two tablets of the T in his hands,
38:21 the T, which were recorded at Moses'
40:20 He took the T and placed it in the
Lev 16:13 the T, so that he will not die.
24: 3 Outside the curtain of the T in the
Nu 1:50 of the T—over all its furnishings
1:53 tents round the tabernacle of the T
1:53 care of the tabernacle of the T."
9:15 T, was set up, the cloud covered it.
10:11 from above the tabernacle of the T.
17: 4 of the T, where I meet with you.
17: 7 the LORD in the Tent of the T.
17: 8 of the T and saw that Aaron's staff,
17:10 Aaron's staff in front of the T,
18: 2 minister before the Tent of the T.
35:30 murderer only on the t of witnesses.
35:30 death on the t of only one witness.
Dt 17: 6 On the t of two or three witnesses a
17: 6 death on the t of only one witness.
19:15 by the t of two or three witnesses.
2Ch 24: 6 of Israel for the Tent of the T?"
Pr 12:17 A truthful witness gives honest t,
Isa 8:16 Bind up the t and seal up the law
8:20 To the law and to the t! If they do
Mt 8: 4 Moses commanded, as a t to them."
18:16 by the t of two or three witnesses.'
24:14 whole world as a t to all nations,
26:62 What is this t that these men are
27:13 t they are bringing against you?"
Mk 1:44 for your cleansing, as a t to them."
6:11 you leave, as a t against them."
14:59 Yet even then their t did not agree.
14:60 What is this t that these men are
Lk 5:14 for your cleansing, as a t to them."
9: 5 their town, as a t against them."
22:71 they said, "Why do we need any more t
Jn 1:19 Now this was John's t when the Jews
1:32 John gave this t: "I saw the Spirit
2:25 He did not need man's t about man,
3:11 you people do not accept our t.
3:32 and heard, but no-one accepts his t.
4:39 woman's t, "He told me everything
5:31 "If I testify about myself, my t is
5:32 I know that his t about me is valid.
5:34 Not that I accept human t; but I
5:36 "I have t weightier than that of
8:13 own witness; your t is not valid."
8:14 my t is valid, for I know where I
8:17 that the t of two men is valid.
19:35 The man who saw it has given t, and
19:35 it has given t, and his t is true.
21:24 We know that his t is true.
Ac 7:44 of the T with them in the desert.
14:17 Yet he has not left himself without t
22:18 will not accept your t about me.'
1Co 1: 6 our t about Christ was confirmed in
2: 1 I proclaimed to you the t about God.
2Co 13: 1 by the t of two or three witnesses."
2Th 1:10 because you believed our t to you.
1Ti 2: 6 men—the t given in its proper time.
Tit 1:13 This t is true. Therefore, rebuke
Heb 10:28 on the t of two or three witnesses.
1Jn 5: 9 We accept man's t, but God's t is
5: 9 greater because it is the t of God,
5:10 Son of God has this t in his heart.
5:10 the t God has given about his Son.
5:11 this is the t: God has given us
3Jn :12 and you know that our t is true.
Rev 1: 2 of God and the t of Jesus Christ.
1: 9 the word of God and the t of Jesus.
6: 9 God and the t they had maintained.
11: 7 Now when they have finished their t,
12:11 the Lamb and by the word of their t;
12:17 and hold to the t of Jesus.
15: 5 the tabernacle of the T, was opened.
17: 6 blood of those who bore t to Jesus.
19:10 brothers who hold to the t of Jesus.
19:10 Worship God! For the t of Jesus is
20: 4 because of their t for Jesus
22:16 to give you this t for the churches.

Testing (Test)
Dt 13: 3 The LORD your God is t you to find
Eze 21:13 "'T will surely come. And what if
Lk 8:13 but in the time of t they fall away.
Heb 3: 8 during the time of t in the desert,
Jas 1: 3 you know that the t of your faith

Testings (Test)
Dt 4:34 by t, by miraculous signs and

Tests (Test)
Job 34: 3 For the ear t words as the tongue
Pr 17: 3 for gold, but the LORD t the heart.
Ecc 3:18 I also thought, "As for men, God t
1Th 2: 4 men but God, who t our hearts.

Tether (Tethered)

Ge 49:11 He will **t** his donkey to a vine, his

Tethered (Tether)

2Ki 7:10 anyone—only **t** horses and donkeys,

Tetrarch

Mt 14: 1 At that time Herod the **t** heard the
Lk 3: 1 Herod **t** of Galilee, his brother
3: 1 his brother Philip **t** of Iturea and
3: 1 and Lysanias **t** of Abilene—
3:19 when John rebuked Herod the **t**
9: 7 Now Herod the **t** heard about all that
Ac 13: 1 up with Herod the **t**) and Saul.

Text

Est 3:14 A copy of the **t** of the edict was to
4: 8 He also gave him a copy of the **t** of
8:13 A copy of the **t** of the edict was to
Jer 29: 1 This is the **t** of the letter that the

Thaddaeus See **Judas 2.**

Mt 10: 3 James son of Alphaeus, and **T**;
Mk 3:18 son of Alphaeus, **T**, Simon the

Thank (Thanked, Thankful, Thankfulness, Thanking, Thank-offering, Thank-offerings, Thanks, Thanksgiving)

Dt 24:13 Then he will **t** you, and it will be
1Ch 23:30 morning to **t** and praise the LORD.
Da 2:23 I **t** and praise you, O God of my
Lk 17: 9 Would he **t** the servant because he
18:11 'God, I **t** you that I am not like
Jn 11:41 I **t** you that you have heard me.
Ro 1: 8 First, I **t** my God through Jesus
1Co 1: 4 I always **t** God for you because of
10:30 because of something I **t** God for?
14:18 I **t** God that I speak in tongues more
2Co 8:16 I **t** God, who put into the heart of
Php 1: 3 I **t** my God every time I remember you.
Col 1: 3 We always **t** God, the Father of our
1Th 1: 2 We always **t** God for all of you,
2:13 we also **t** God continually because,
3: 9 How can we **t** God enough for you in
2Th 1: 3 We ought always to **t** God for you,
2:13 we ought always to **t** God for you,
1Ti 1:12 I **t** Christ Jesus our Lord, who has
2Ti 1: 3 I **t** God, whom I serve, as my
Phm : 4 I always **t** my God as I remember you

Thanked (Thank)

Lk 17:16 He threw himself at Jesus' feet and **t**
Ac 28:15 men Paul **t** God and was encouraged.

Thankful (Thank)

1Co 1:14 I am **t** that I did not baptise any of
Col 3:15 you were called to peace. And be **t**.
4: 2 to prayer, being watchful and **t**.
Heb 12:28 let us be **t**, and so worship God

Thankfulness (Thank)

Lev 7:12 he offers it as an expression of **t**,
1Co 10:30 If I take part in the meal with **t**,
Col 2: 7 were taught, and overflowing with **t**.

Thanking (Thank)

1Ch 25: 3 the harp in **t** and praising the LORD.

Thank-offering (Thank, Thank-offerings)

Lev 7:12 then along with this **t** he is to
22:29 "When you sacrifice a **t** to the LORD,
Ps 116:17 I will sacrifice a **t** to you and call
Am 4: 5 Burn leavened bread as a **t** and brag

Thank-offerings (Thank, Thank-offering)

2Ch 29:31 Come and bring sacrifices and **t** to
29:31 assembly brought sacrifices and **t**,
33:16 fellowship offerings and **t** on it,
Ps 50:14 Sacrifice **t** to God, fulfil your vows
50:23 He who sacrifices **t** honours me, and
56:12 O God; I will present my **t** to you.
107:22 Let them sacrifice **t** and tell of his
Jer 17:26 and **t** to the house of the LORD.
33:11 and the voices of those who bring **t**

Thanks (*Give thanks*, Thank)

1Ch 16: 7 this psalm of **t** to the LORD:
29:13 Now, our God, we give you **t**, and
2Ch 5:13 to give praise and **t** to the LORD.
7: 3 and they worshipped and gave **t** to
7: 6 and which were used when he gave **t**,
Ne 12:40 The two choirs that gave **t** then took
Ps 30:12 O LORD my God, I will give you **t**
35:18 I will give you **t** in the great
100: T A psalm. For giving **t**.
118:21 I will give you **t**, for you answered
119:62 At midnight I rise to give you **t** for
Da 6:10 giving **t** to his God, just as he had
Mt 14:19 he gave **t** and broke the loaves.
15:36 and when he had given **t**, he broke
26:26 Jesus took bread, gave **t** and broke
26:27 he took the cup, gave **t** and offered
Mk 6:41 he gave **t** and broke the loaves.
8: 6 taken the seven loaves and given **t**,
8: 7 he gave **t** for them also and told the
14:22 Jesus took bread, gave **t** and broke
14:23 he took the cup, gave **t** and offered
Lk 2:38 she gave **t** to God and spoke about
9:16 to heaven, he gave **t** and broke them.
22:17 After taking the cup, he gave **t** and
22:19 he took bread, gave **t** and broke it,
24:30 he took bread, gave **t**, broke it and
Jn 6:11 Jesus then took the loaves, gave **t**,
6:23 bread after the Lord had given **t**.
Ac 27:35 gave **t** to God in front of them all.
Ro 1:21 him as God nor gave **t** to him,
6:17 **t** be to God that, though you used to
7:25 **T** be to God—through Jesus Christ
14: 6 eats to the Lord, for he gives **t** to
14: 6 so to the Lord and gives **t** to God.
1Co 11:24 he had given **t**, he broke it and said,
14:17 You may be giving **t** well enough, but
15:57 **t** be to God! He gives us the victory
2Co 2:14 **t** be to God, who always leads us in
9:12 in many expressions of **t** to God.
9:15 **T** be to God for his indescribable
Eph 1:16 I have not stopped giving **t** for you,
5:20 always giving **t** to God the Father
Col 1:12 giving **t** to the Father, who has
3:17 **t** to God the Father through him.
Rev 4: 9 honour and **t** to him who sits on the
7:12 Praise and glory and wisdom and **t**

Thanksgiving (Thank)

Lev 7:13 his fellowship offering of **t**
7:15 his fellowship offering of **t** must
Ezr 3:11 With praise and **t** they sang to the
Ne 11:17 the director who led in **t** and prayer;
12: 8 was in charge of the songs of **t**.
12:24 opposite them to give praise and **t**,
12:27 of **t** and with the music of cymbals,
12:46 the songs of praise and **t** to God.
Ps 42: 4 joy and **t** among the festive throng.
69:30 name in song and glorify him with **t**.
95: 2 Let us come before him with **t** and
100: 4 Enter his gates with **t** and his
147: 7 Sing to the LORD with **t**; make music
Isa 51: 3 in her, **t** and the sound of singing.
Jer 30:19 From them will come songs of **t** and
Jnh 2: 9 I, with a song of **t**, will sacrifice
1Co 10:16 Is not the cup of **t** for which we
14:16 "Amen" to your **t**, since he does not
2Co 4:15 **t** to overflow to the glory of God.
9:11 generosity will result in **t** to God.
Eph 5: 4 are out of place, but rather **t**.
Php 4: 6 with **t**, present your requests to
1Ti 2: 1 and **t** be made for everyone—
4: 3 with **t** by those who believe
4: 4 rejected if it is received with **t**,

Thawing

Job 6:16 darkened by **t** ice and swollen with

Theatre

Ac 19:29 and rushed as one man into the **t**.
19:31 him not to venture into the **t**.

Thebes

City in Upper Egypt, on eastern bank of the Nile, also known as No or No-Amon. Its destruction was foretold (Jer 46:25; Eze 30:14–16), to emphasise that no city, however great, could escape God's judgment (Na 3:8).

Jer 46:25 bring punishment on Amon god of **T**,
Eze 30:14 to Zoan and inflict punishment on **T**.
30:15 Egypt, and cut off the hordes of **T**.
30:16 **T** will be taken by storm; Memphis
Na 3: 8 Are you better than **T**, situated on

Thebez

Jdg 9:50 Next Abimelech went to **T** and
2Sa 11:21 so that he died in **T**? Why did you

Theft (Thief)

Ex 22: 3 he must be sold to pay for his **t**.
Mt 15:19 **t**, false testimony, slander.
Mk 7:21 immorality, **t**, murder, adultery,

Thefts (Thief)

Rev 9:21 their sexual immorality or their **t**.

Theme

Ps 22:25 From you comes the **t** of my praise in
45: 1 My heart is stirred by a noble **t** as
119:54 Your decrees are the **t** of my song

Theophilus

Lk 1: 3 account for you, most excellent **T**,
Ac 1: 1 In my former book, **T**, I wrote about

Thessalonians (Thessalonica)

Ac 17:11 of more noble character than the **T**,
1Th 1: 1 To the church of the **T** in God the
2Th 1: 1 To the church of the **T** in God our

Thessalonica (Thessalonians)

Chief seaport of province of Macedonia. Paul established a church here (Ac 17:1–4; 1Th 1:9–10). A deep affection grew between Paul and the church (1Th 2:1–12). Home of two of his co-workers, Aristarchus and Secundus (Ac 20:4; 27:2), Demas moved here after deserting Paul (2Ti 4:10).

Ac 17: 1 they came to **T**, where there was a
17:13 the Jews in **T** learned that Paul was
20: 4 Aristarchus and Secundus from **T**,
27: 2 a Macedonian from **T**, was with us.
Php 4:16 for even when I was in **T**, you sent
2Ti 4:10 has deserted me and has gone to **T**.

Theudas

Ac 5:36 Some time ago **T** appeared, claiming

Thicket (Thickets)

Ge 22:13 Abraham looked up and there in a **t**
Job 38:40 in their dens or lie in wait in a **t**?
Ps 74: 5 axes to cut through a **t** of trees.
Hos 2:12 make them a **t**, and wild animals
Am 3: 4 Does a lion roar in the **t** when he
Zec 11: 3 the lush **t** of the Jordan is ruined!

Thickets (Thicket)

1Sa 13: 6 they hid in caves and **t**, among the
Isa 9:18 it sets the forest **t** ablaze, so that
10:34 He will cut down the forest **t** with
17: 9 abandoned to **t** and undergrowth.
21:13 who camp in the **t** of Arabia,
Jer 4:29 Some go into the **t**; some climb up
12: 5 you manage in the **t** by the Jordan?
26:18 hill a mound overgrown with **t**.'
49:19 Jordan's **t** to a rich pasture-land,
50:44 Like a lion coming up from Jordan's **t**
Mic 3:12 hill a mound overgrown with **t**.

Thief (Theft, Thefts, Thieves)
Ex 22: 2 "If a **t** is caught breaking in and is
22: 3 "A **t** must certainly make restitution,
22: 7 the **t**, if he is caught, must pay
22: 8 if the **t** is not found, the owner of
Job 24:14 the night he steals forth like a **t**.
Ps 50:18 you see a **t**, you join with him; you
Pr 6:30 Men do not despise a **t** if he steals
29:24 The accomplice of a **t** is his own
Jer 2:26 "As a **t** is disgraced when he is
Zec 5: 3 every **t** will be banished, and
5: 4 it will enter the house of the **t** and
Mt 24:43 what time of night the **t** was coming,
Lk 12:33 where no **t** comes near and no moth
12:39 known at what hour the **t** was coming,
Jn 10: 1 some other way, is a **t** and a robber.
10:10 The **t** comes only to steal and kill
12: 6 was a **t**; as keeper of the money bag,
1Th 5: 2 Lord will come like a **t** in the night.
5: 4 day should surprise you like a **t**.
1Pe 4:15 it should not be as a murderer or **t**
2Pe 3:10 day of the Lord will come like a **t**.
Rev 3: 3 I will come like a **t**, and you will
16:15 "Behold, I come like a **t**! Blessed is

Thieves (Thief)
Job 30: 5 shouted at as if they were **t**.
Isa 1:23 companions of **t**; they all love
Jer 48:27 ridicule? Was she caught among **t**,
49: 9 If **t** came during the night, would
Hos 7: 1 They practise deceit, **t** break into
Joel 2: 9 **t** they enter through the windows.
Ob : 5 "If **t** came to you, if robbers in the
Mt 6:19 and where **t** break in and steal.
6:20 where **t** do not break in and steal.
Jn 10: 8 All who ever came before me were **t**
1Co 6:10 nor **t** nor the greedy nor drunkards

Thigh (Thighs)
Ge 24: 2 he had, "Put your hand under my **t**.
24: 9 the servant put his hand under the **t**
47:29 put your hand under my **t** and promise
Ex 28:42 reaching from the waist to the **t**.
29:22 the fat on them, and the right **t**.
29:27 waved and the **t** that was presented.
Lev 7:32 You are to give the right **t** of your
7:33 shall have the right **t** as his share.
7:34 the **t** that is presented and have
8:25 and their fat and the right **t**.
8:26 the fat portions and on the right **t**.
9:21 **t** before the LORD as a wave offering,
10:14 waved and the **t** that was presented.
10:15 The **t** that was presented and the
Nu 5:21 denounce you when he causes your **t**
5:22 swells and your **t** wastes away.
5:27 will swell and her **t** waste away,
6:20 waved and the **t** that was presented.
18:18 offering and the right **t** are yours.
Jdg 3:16 to his right **t** under his clothing.
3:21 drew the sword from his right **t** and
Rev 19:16 On his robe and on his **t** he has this

Thighs (Thigh)
Job 40:17 the sinews of his **t** are close-knit.
Da 2:32 silver, its belly and **t** of bronze,

Thin
Ge 41: 6 —**t** and scorched by the east wind.
41: 7 The **t** ears of corn swallowed up the
41:23 and **t** and scorched by the east wind.
41:24 The **t** ears of corn swallowed up the
Ex 16:14 the dew was gone, **t** flakes like
39: 3 They hammered out **t** sheets of gold
Lev 13:30 and the hair in it is yellow and **t**,
Ps 109:24 fasting; my body is **t** and gaunt.

Think (Thinking, Thinks, Thought, Thoughts)
Ge 16: 6 "Do with her whatever you **t** best."
Ex 14: 3 Pharaoh will **t**, 'The Israelites are
Jdg 9:17 to **t** that my father fought for you,
10:15 Do with us whatever you think **t** best,
19:30 **T** about it! Consider it! Tell us
1Sa 18:23 But David said, "Do you **t** it is a
1Sa 25:17 Now **t** it over and see what you can
2Sa 10: 3 "Do you **t** David is honouring your
13:32 "My lord should not **t** that they
24:13 **t** it over and decide how I should
1Ki 20:28 'Because the Arameans **t** the LORD is
2Ki 10: 5 king; you do whatever you **t** best."
1Ch 19: 3 "Do you **t** David is honouring your
Est 4:13 he sent back this answer: "Do not **t**
Job 4: 3 **T** how you have instructed many, how
7: 4 I lie down I **t**, 'How long before I
7:13 I **t** my bed will comfort me and my
21: 6 I **t** about this, I am terrified;
23:15 when I **t** of all this, I fear him.
35: 2 "Do you **t** this is just? You say, 'I
41:32 one would **t** the deep had white hair.
Ps 35:25 Do not let them **t**, "Aha, just what
40:17 and needy; may the Lord **t** of me.
63: 6 On my bed I remember you; I **t** of you
144: 3 the son of man that you **t** of him?
Isa 29:15 who do their work in darkness and **t**,
44:19 No-one stops to **t**, no-one has the
Jer 15:15 **t** of how I suffer reproach for your
23:27 They **t** the dreams they tell one
26:14 me whatever you **t** is good and right.
44:21 "Did not the LORD remember and **t**
51:50 a distant land, and **t** on Jerusalem."
Eze 28: 2 you **t** you are as wise as a god.
28: 6 **t** you are wise, as wise as a god,
Zep 1:12 who **t**, 'The LORD will do nothing,
Zec 7:10 hearts do not **t** evil of each other.'
11:12 I told them, "If you **t** it best, give
Mt 3: 9 do not **t** you can say to yourselves,
5:17 "Do not **t** that I have come to
6: 7 for they **t** they will be heard
17:25 "What do you **t**, Simon?" he asked.
18:12 "What do you **t**? If a man owns a
21:28 "What do you **t**? There was a man who
22:42 "What do you **t** about the Christ?
26:53 Do you **t** I cannot call on my Father,
26:66 What do you **t**?" "He is worthy of
Mk 14:64 What do you **t**?" They all condemned
Lk 10:36 "Which of these three do you **t** was a
12:51 Do you **t** I came to bring peace on
13: 2 Jesus answered, "Do you **t** that these
13: 4 do you **t** they were more guilty than
Jn 5:39 study the Scriptures because you **t**
5:45 "But do not **t** I will accuse you
8:53 Who do you **t** you are?"
11:56 "What do you **t**? Isn't he coming to
16: 2 **t** he is offering a service to God.
Ac 5: 4 What made you **t** of doing such a
11:17 was I to **t** that I could oppose God?"
13:25 Who do you **t** I am? I am not that one.
15:38 Paul did not **t** it wise to take him,
17:29 we should not **t** that the divine
25:27 For I **t** it is unreasonable to send
26:28 Agrippa said to Paul, "Do you **t** that
Ro 1:28 Furthermore, since they did not **t** it
2: 3 **t** you will escape God's judgment?
12: 3 Do not **t** of yourself more highly
12: 3 but rather **t** of yourself with sober
13:14 and do not **t** about how to gratify
1Co 1:26 Brothers, **t** of what you were when
7:26 of the present crisis, I **t** that it
7:40 **t** that I too have the Spirit of God.
8: 7 when they eat such food they **t** of
10:12 So, if you **t** you are standing firm,
12:23 the parts that we **t** are less
2Co 10: 2 people who **t** that we live by the
11: 5 I do not **t** I am in the least
12: 6 But I refrain, so no-one will **t** more
Php 2:25 I **t** it is necessary to send back to
3:15 if on some point you **t** differently
4: 8 praiseworthy—**t** about such things.
1Ti 6: 5 who **t** that godliness is a means to
Heb 7: 4 Just **t** how great he was: Even the
10:29 How much more severely do you **t** a
Jas 1: 7 That man should not **t** he will
4: 5 Or do you **t** Scripture says without
1Pe 4: 4 They **t** it strange that you do not
2Pe 1:13 I **t** it is right to refresh your

Thinking (Think)
Ex 2:14 Are you **t** of killing me as you
Dt 1:41 **t** it easy to go up into the hill
1Sa 9: 5 or my father will stop **t** about the
10: 2 And now your father has stopped **t**
15:32 Agag came to him confidently, **t**,
2Ki 7:12 **t**, 'They will surely come out, and
2Ch 32: 1 **t** to conquer them for himself.
Ne 6: 9 **t**, "Their hands will get too weak
Job 1: 5 **t**, "Perhaps my children have sinned
21:27 "I know full well what you are **t**,
Pr 23: 7 man who is always **t** about the cost.
Jer 37: 9 **t**, 'The Babylonians will surely
Da 7: 8 "While I was **t** about the horns,
8: 5 I was **t** about this, suddenly a goat
Mk 2: 6 were sitting there, **t** to themselves,
2: 8 what they were **t** in their hearts,
2: 8 "Why are you **t** these things?
Lk 2:44 **T** he was in their company, they
5:21 of the law began **t** to themselves,
5:22 Jesus knew what they were **t** and
5:22 you **t** these things in your hearts?
6: 8 Jesus knew what they were **t** and said
24:37 They were startled and frightened, **t**
Jn 20:15 looking for?" **T** he was the gardener,
Ac 10:19 While Peter was still **t** about the
14:19 him outside the city, **t** he was dead.
Ro 1:21 but their **t** became futile and their
1Co 14:20 Brothers, stop **t** like children. In
14:20 be infants, but in your **t** be adults.
2Co 12:19 Have you been **t** all along that we
Eph 4:17 do, in the futility of their **t**.
Heb 11:15 If they had been **t** of the country
2Pe 3: 1 to stimulate you to wholesome **t**.

Thinks (Think)
Dt 29:19 blessing on himself and therefore **t**,
2Sa 16: 3 because he **t**, 'Today the house of
Est 8: 5 and **t** it the right thing to do,
Job 24:15 for dusk; he **t**, 'No eye will see me,'
Lk 8:18 he **t** he has will be taken from him."
1Co 3:18 If any one of you **t** he is wise by
7:36 If anyone **t** he is acting improperly
8: 2 The man who **t** he knows something
14:37 If anybody **t** he is a prophet or
Gal 6: 3 If anyone **t** he is something when he
Php 3: 4 If anyone else **t** he has reasons to

Third day
Ge 1:13; 22:4; 31:22; 40:20; 42:18; Ex 19:11, 15, 16; Lev 7:17, 18; 19:6, 7; Nu 7:24; 19:12; 29:20; Jos 9:17; Jdg 20:30; 1Sa 30:1; 2Sa 1:2; 1Ki 3:18; 2Ki 20:5, 8; Ezr 6:15; Est 5:1; Hos 6:2; Mt 16:21; 17:23; 20:19; 27:64; Lk 9:22; 13:32; 18:33; 24:7, 21, 46; Jn 2:1; Ac 10:40; 27:19; 1Co 15:4

Thirst (Thirsts, Thirsty)
Ex 17: 3 children and livestock die of **t**?"
Dt 28:48 therefore in hunger and **t**, in
Jdg 15:18 Must I now die of **t** and fall into
2Ch 32:11 you, to let you die of hunger and **t**.
Ne 9:15 in their **t** you brought them water
9:20 and you gave them water for their **t**.
Job 24:11 tread the winepresses, yet suffer **t**.
Ps 69:21 food and gave me vinegar for my **t**.
104:11 the wild donkeys quench their **t**.
Isa 5:13 their masses will be parched with **t**.
29: 8 faint, with his **t** unquenched.
41:17 their tongues are parched with **t**.
48:21 They did not **t** when he led them
49:10 They will neither hunger nor **t**, nor
50: 2 rot for lack of water and die of **t**.
Jer 46:10 it has quenched its **t** with blood.
Lam 4: 4 of **t** the infant's tongue sticks to
Hos 2: 3 a parched land, and slay her with **t**.
Am 8:11 a famine of food or a **t** for water,
8:13 young men will faint because of **t**.
Mt 5: 6 Blessed are those who hunger and **t**
Jn 4:14 the water I give him will never **t**.
2Co 11:27 I have known hunger and **t** and have
Rev 7:16 hunger; never again will they **t**.

Thirsts (Thirst)
Ps 42: 2 My soul **t** for God, for the living
63: 1 earnestly I seek you; my soul **t** for
143: 6 soul **t** for you like a parched land.

Thirsty (Thirst)

Ex 17: 3 the people were **t** for water there,
Dt 8:15 that **t** and waterless land, with its
Jdg 4:19 "I'm **t**," he said. "Please give me
15:18 he was very **t**, he cried out to the
Ru 2: 9 And whenever you are **t**, go and get a
2Sa 17:29 and tired and **t** in the desert."
Job 5: 5 and the **t** pant after his wealth.
Ps 107: 5 They were hungry and **t**, and their
107: 9 for he satisfies the **t** and fills the
107:33 flowing springs into **t** ground,
Pr 25:21 if he is **t**, give him water to drink.
Isa 21:14 bring water for the **t**; you who live
29: 8 his hunger remains; as when a **t** man
32: 2 shadow of a great rock in a **t** land.
32: 6 and from the **t** he withholds water.
35: 7 pool, the **t** ground bubbling springs.
44: 3 For I will pour water on the **t** land,
55: 1 "Come, all you who are **t**, come to
65:13 but you will go **t**; my servants will
Eze 19:13 in the desert, in a dry and **t** land.
Mt 25:35 I was **t** and you gave me something to
25:37 **t** and give you something to drink?
25:42 **t** and you gave me nothing to drink,
25:44 when did we see you hungry or **t** or a
Jn 4:13 drinks this water will be **t** again,
4:15 me this water so that I won't get **t**
6:35 who believes in me will never be **t**.
7:37 is **t**, let him come to me and drink.
19:28 be fulfilled, Jesus said, "I am **t**."
Ro 12:20 is **t**, give him something to drink.
1Co 4:11 To this very hour we go hungry and **t**,
Rev 21: 6 To him who is **t** I will give to drink
22:17 "Come!" Whoever is **t**, let him come;

Thistle (Thistles)

2Ki 14: 9 "A **t** in Lebanon sent a message to a
14: 9 along and trampled the **t** underfoot.
2Ch 25:18 "A **t** in Lebanon sent a message to a
25:18 along and trampled the **t** underfoot.

Thistles (Thistle)

Ge 3:18 will produce thorns and **t** for you,
Hos 10: 8 Thorns and **t** will grow up and cover
Mt 7:16 from thornbushes, or figs from **t**?
Heb 6: 8 land that produces thorns and **t** is

Thomas

Apostle (Mt 10:3; Mk 3:18; Lk 6:15; Ac 1:13); called Didymus, the Twin (Jn 11:16). Asked where Jesus was going (Jn 14:5). Doubted resurrection (Jn 20:24–25); saw Jesus alive; confessed him as Lord and God (Jn 20:26–29). Present at miraculous catch of fish after resurrection (Jn 21:2–14).

Mt 10: 3 Philip and Bartholomew; **T** and
Mk 3:18 Philip, Bartholomew, Matthew, **T**,
Lk 6:15 Matthew, **T**, James son of Alphaeus,
Jn 11:16 **T** (called Didymus) said to the rest
14: 5 **T** said to him, "Lord, we don't know
20:24 Now **T** (called Didymus), one of the
20:26 house again, and **T** was with them.
20:27 he said to **T**, "Put your finger here;
20:28 **T** said to him, "My Lord and my God!"
21: 2 Simon Peter, **T** (called Didymus),
Ac 1:13 James and Andrew; Philip and **T**,

Thong (Thongs)

Ge 14:23 not even a thread or the **t** of a
Isa 5:27 the waist, not a sandal **t** is broken.

Thongs (Thong)

Jdg 16: 7 fresh **t** that have not been dried,
16: 8 fresh **t** that had not been dried,
16: 9 snapped the **t** as easily as a piece
Mk 1: 7 the **t** of whose sandals I am not
Lk 3:16 the **t** of whose sandals I am not
Jn 1:27 the **t** of whose sandals I am not

Thorn (Thornbush, Thornbushes, Thorn-bushes, Thorns)

Mic 7: 4 most upright worse than a **t** hedge.
2Co 12: 7 there was given me a **t** in my flesh,

Thornbush (Thorn)

Jdg 9:14 "Finally all the trees said to the **t**,
9:15 "The **t** said to the trees, 'If you
9:15 let fire come out of the **t** and
Pr 26: 9 Like a **t** in a drunkard's hand is a
Isa 55:13 Instead of the **t** will grow the pine

Thornbushes (Thorn)

Ex 22: 6 spreads into **t** so that it burns
Isa 7:19 the **t** and at all the water holes.
33:12 like cut **t** they will be set ablaze."
Hos 2: 6 I will block her path with **t**;
Mt 7:16 Do people pick grapes from **t**, or

Thorn-bushes (Thorn)

Lk 6:44 figs from **t**, or grapes from briers.

Thorns (Thorn)

Ge 3:18 will produce **t** and thistles for you,
Nu 33:55 in your eyes and **t** in your sides.
Jos 23:13 whips on your backs and **t** in your
Jdg 2: 3 they will be ⌊**t**⌋ in your sides and
8: 7 flesh with desert **t** and briers."
8:16 them with desert **t** and briers.
2Sa 23: 6 men are all to be cast aside like **t**,
23: 7 Whoever touches **t** uses a tool of
Job 5: 5 taking it even from among **t**, and the
Ps 58: 9 pots can feel the heat of the **t**
118:12 died out as quickly as burning **t**;
Pr 15:19 of the sluggard is blocked with **t**,
22: 5 In the paths of the wicked lie **t** and
24:31 **t** had come up everywhere, the ground
Ecc 7: 6 Like the crackling of **t** under the
SS 2: 2 Like a lily among **t** is my darling
Isa 5: 6 and briers and **t** will grow there.
7:23 there will be only briers and **t**.
7:24 will be covered with briers and **t**.
7:25 there for fear of the briers and **t**;
9:18 a fire; it consumes briers and **t**,
10:17 and consume his **t** and his briers.
27: 4 If only there were briers and **t**
32:13 a land overgrown with **t** and briers—
34:13 **T** will overrun her citadels, nettles
Jer 4: 3 ground and do not sow among **t**.
12:13 They will sow wheat but reap **t**; they
Eze 2: 6 though briers and **t** are all around
28:24 who are painful briers and sharp **t**.
Hos 9: 6 and **t** will overrun their tents.
10: 8 **T** and thistles will grow up and
Na 1:10 They will be entangled among **t** and
Mt 13: 7 Other seed fell among **t**, which grew
13:22 the **t** is the man who hears the word,
27:29 twisted together a crown of **t** and
Mk 4: 7 Other seed fell among **t**, which grew
4:18 Still others, like seed sown among **t**,
15:17 a crown of **t** and set it on him.
Lk 8: 7 Other seed fell among **t**, which grew
8:14 The seed that fell among **t** stands
Jn 19: 2 a crown of **t** and put it on his head.
19: 5 Jesus came out wearing the crown of **t**
Heb 6: 8 land that produces **t** and thistles is

Thought (Think)

Ge 18:12 Sarah laughed to herself as she **t**,
19:14 But his sons-in-law **t** he was joking.
21:16 she **t**, "I cannot watch the boy die.
26: 7 He **t**, "The men of this place might
26: 9 "Because I **t** I might lose my life on
27:42 himself with the **t** of killing you.
28:16 Jacob awoke from his sleep, he **t**,
31:31 "I was afraid, because I **t** you would
32: 8 He **t**, "If Esau comes and attacks one
32:20 For he **t**, "I will pacify him with
38:11 For he **t**, "He may die too, just
38:15 Judah saw her, he **t** she was a
43:18 They **t**, "We were brought here
Ex 2:14 Then Moses was afraid and **t**,
3: 3 Moses **t**, "I will go over and see
Dt 15: 9 this wicked **t**: "The seventh year,
Jdg 16:20 He awoke from his sleep and **t**,
Ru 1:12 Even if I **t** there was still hope for
4: 4 I **t** I should bring the matter to
1Sa 1:13 not heard. Eli **t** she was drunk
13:12 I **t**, 'Now the Philistines will come
1Sa 16: 6 they arrived, Samuel saw Eliab and **t**,
18: 8 he **t**, "but me with only thousands.
18:21 "I will give her to him," he **t**, "so
20:26 Saul said nothing that day, for he **t**,
27: 1 David **t** to himself, "One of these
27:11 for he **t**, "They might inform on us
2Sa 4:10 a man told me, 'Saul is dead,' and **t**
5: 6 They **t**, "David cannot get in here."
10: 2 David **t**, "I will show kindness to
12:18 for they **t**, "While the child was
12:22 I **t**, 'Who knows? The LORD may be
14:15 Your servant **t**, 'I will speak to the
18:18 for he **t**, "I have no son to carry on
1Ki 12:26 Jeroboam **t** to himself, "The kingdom
18:27 deep in **t**, or busy, or travelling.
22:32 they **t**, "Surely this is the king of
2Ki 5:11 Naaman went away angry and said, "I **t**
20:19 For he **t**, "Will there not be peace
1Ch 19: 2 David **t**, "I will show kindness to
2Ch 18:31 they **t**, "This is the king of Israel.
28:23 who had defeated him; for he **t**,
Est 6: 6 Now Haman **t** to himself, "Who is
Job 29:18 "I **t**, 'I shall die in my own house,
32: 7 I **t**, 'Age should speak; advanced
Ps 50:21 you **t** I was altogether like you.
77: 5 I **t** about the former days, the years
77:10 I **t**, "To this I will appeal: the
106: 7 they gave no **t** to your miracles;
109:16 For he never **t** of doing a kindness,
Pr 5: 6 She gives no **t** to the way of life;
14: 8 prudent is to give **t** to their ways,
14:15 a prudent man gives **t** to his steps.
17:28 Even a fool is **t** wise if he keeps
21:29 an upright man gives **t** to his ways.
Ecc 1:16 I **t** to myself, "Look, I have grown
2: 1 I **t** in my heart, "Come now, I will
2:15 I **t** in my heart, "The fate of the
3:17 I **t** in my heart, "God will bring to
3:18 I also **t**, "As for men, God tests
Isa 29:16 as if the potter were **t** to be like
39: 8 For he **t**, "There will be peace and
65:20 he who dies at a hundred will be **t** a
Jer 3: 7 I **t** that after she had done all this
3:19 I **t** you would call me 'Father' and
5: 4 I **t**, "These are only the poor; they
Lam 3:54 and I **t** I was about to be cut off.
4:20 We **t** that under his shadow we would
Hag 1: 5 says: "Give careful **t** to your ways.
1: 7 says: "Give careful **t** to your ways.
2:15 "Now give careful **t** to this from
2:18 give careful **t** to the day when the
2:18 temple was laid. Give careful **t**:
Mk 5:28 she **t**, "If I just touch his clothes,
6:49 on the lake, they **t** he was a ghost.
Lk 3:23 the son, so it was **t**, of Joseph,
12:17 He **t** to himself, 'What shall I do? I
19:11 the people **t** that the kingdom of God
Jn 8:56 Your father Abraham rejoiced at the **t**
11:13 disciples **t** he meant natural sleep.
13:29 some **t** Jesus was telling him to buy
Ac 7:25 Moses **t** that his own people would
8:20 because you **t** you could buy the gift
8:22 for having such a **t** in your heart.
12: 9 he **t** he was seeing a vision.
16:27 he **t** the prisoners had escaped.
27:13 they **t** they had obtained what they
1Co 1:10 be perfectly united in mind and **t**.
13:11 I talked like a child, I **t** like a
2Co 9: 5 I **t** it necessary to urge the
10: 5 **t** to make it obedient to Christ.
1Th 2:17 not in **t**), out of our intense
3: 1 we **t** it best to be left by ourselves
Heb 12:10 for a little while as they **t** best;

Thoughts (Think)

Ge 6: 5 and that every inclination of the **t**
1Ch 28: 9 every motive behind the **t**.
Job 20: 2 "My troubled **t** prompt me to answer
Ps 10: 4 all his **t** there is no room for God.
13: 2 How long must I wrestle with my **t**
55: 2 hear me and answer me. My **t** trouble
92: 5 works, O LORD, how profound your **t**!
94:11 The LORD knows the **t** of man; he
139: 2 I rise; you perceive my **t** from afar.
139:17 How precious to me are your **t**, O God!

Ps 139:23 test me and know my anxious **t**.
Pr 1:23 to you and made my **t** known to you.
15:26 The LORD detests the **t** of the wicked,
Ecc 2:12 I turned my **t** to consider wisdom,
10:20 Do not revile the king even in your **t**
Isa 33:18 In your **t** you will ponder the former
55: 7 his way and the evil man his **t**.
55: 8 "For my **t** are not your **t**, neither
55: 9 than your ways and my **t** than your **t**.
59: 7 Their **t** are evil **t**; ruin and
Jer 4:14 How long will you harbour wicked **t**?
12: 3 you see me and test my **t** about you.
Eze 38:10 On that day **t** will come into your
Da 4:19 for a time, and his **t** terrified him.
7:28 Daniel, was deeply troubled by my **t**,
Am 4:13 creates the wind, and reveals his **t**
Mic 4:12 they do not know the **t** of the LORD;
Mt 9: 4 Knowing their **t**, Jesus said, "Why do
9: 4 you entertain evil **t** in your hearts?
12:25 Jesus knew their **t** and said to them,
15:19 For out of the heart come evil **t**,
Mk 7:21 out of men's hearts, come evil **t**,
Lk 1:51 who are proud in their inmost **t**.
2:35 that the **t** of many hearts will be
9:47 Jesus, knowing their **t**, took a
11:17 Jesus knew their **t** and said to them:
Ro 2:15 and their **t** now accusing, now even
1Co 2:11 For who among men knows the **t** of a
2:11 **t** of God except the Spirit of God.
3:20 again, "The Lord knows that the **t** of
Eph 2: 3 and following its desires and **t**.
Heb 3: 1 fix your **t** on Jesus, the apostle and
4:12 the **t** and attitudes of the heart.
Jas 2: 4 and become judges with evil **t**?

Thousand (Thousands)

Ge 20:16 your brother a **t** shekels of silver.
Ex 12:37 There were about six hundred **t** men
20: 6 showing love to a **t** generations of
32:28 about three **t** of the people died.
Lev 26: 8 a hundred of you will chase ten **t**,
Nu 7:85 the silver dishes weighed two **t** four
11:21 "Here I am among six hundred **t** men
31: 4 Send into battle a **t** men from each
31: 5 twelve **t** men armed for battle, a **t**
31: 6 Moses sent them into battle, a **t**
35: 5 measure three **t** feet on the east
35: 5 three **t** on the south side, three
35: 5 three **t** on the west and three **t** on
Dt 1:11 increase you a **t** times and bless you
5:10 showing love to a **t** generations of
7: 9 keeping his covenant of love to a **t**
32:30 How could one man chase a **t**, or two
32:30 or two put ten **t** to flight, unless
Jos 3: 4 keep a distance of about a **t** yards
4:13 About forty **t** armed for battle
7: 3 Send two or three **t** men to take it
7: 4 about three **t** men went up; but they
8: 3 He chose thirty **t** of his best
8:12 Joshua had taken about five **t** men
8:25 Twelve **t** men and women fell that day
23:10 One of you routs a **t**, because the
Jdg 1: 4 they struck down ten **t** men at Bezek.
3:29 struck down about ten **t** Moabites,
4: 6 'Go, take with you ten **t** men of
4:10 Ten **t** men followed him, and Deborah
4:14 Mount Tabor, followed by ten **t** men.
5: 8 was seen among forty **t** in Israel.
7: 3 **t** men left, while ten **t** remained.
8:10 with a force of about fifteen **t** men,
8:10 and twenty **t** swordsmen had fallen.
9:49 about a **t** men and women, also died.
12: 6 Forty-two **t** Ephraimites were killed
15:11 three **t** men from Judah went down to
15:15 grabbed it and struck down a **t** men.
15:16 jaw-bone I have killed a **t** men."
16:27 on the roof were about three **t** men
20: 2 four hundred **t** soldiers armed with
20:10 and a hundred from a **t**, and a **t** from
20:10 from ten **t**, to get provisions for
20:15 mobilised twenty-six **t** swordsmen
20:17 mustered four hundred **t** swordsmen,
20:21 cut down twenty-two **t** Israelites on
20:25 they cut down another eighteen **t**
20:34 ten **t** of Israel's finest men made a
Jdg 20:44 Eighteen **t** Benjamites fell, all of
20:45 cut down five **t** men along the roads.
20:45 as Gidom and struck down two **t** more.
20:46 On that day twenty-five **t** Benjamite
21:10 the assembly sent twelve **t** fighting
1Sa 4: 2 four **t** of them on the battlefield.
4:10 Israel lost thirty **t** foot soldiers.
11: 8 **t** and the men of Judah thirty **t**.
13: 2 Saul chose three **t** men from Israel;
13: 2 two **t** were with him at Michmash and
13: 2 and a **t** were with Jonathan at Gibeah
13: 5 three **t** chariots, six **t** charioteers
15: 4 Telaim—two hundred **t** foot soldiers
15: 4 soldiers and ten **t** men from Judah.
17: 5 of bronze weighing five **t** shekels;
18:13 and gave him command over a **t** men,
24: 2 Saul took three **t** chosen men from
25: 2 He had a **t** goats and three **t** sheep,
26: 2 with his three **t** chosen men of
2Sa 6: 1 Israel chosen men, thirty **t** in all.
8: 4 David captured a **t** of his chariots,
8: 4 seven **t** charioteers and twenty **t**
8: 5 struck down twenty-two **t** of them.
8:13 eighteen **t** Edomites in the Valley
10: 6 they hired twenty **t** Aramean foot
10: 6 as the king of Maacah with a **t** men,
10: 6 men, and also twelve **t** men from Tob.
10:18 and forty **t** of their foot soldiers.
17: 1 "I would choose twelve **t** men and set
18: 3 care; but you are worth ten **t** of us.
18: 7 that day were great—twenty **t** men.
18:12 man replied, "Even if a **t** shekels
19:17 With him were a **t** Benjamites, along
24: 9 eight hundred **t** able-bodied men who
24: 9 sword, and in Judah five hundred **t**.
24:15 and seventy **t** of the people from Dan
1Ki 3: 4 a **t** burnt offerings on that altar.
4:26 Solomon had four **t** stalls for
4:26 chariot horses, and twelve **t** horses.
4:32 He spoke three **t** proverbs and his
4:32 and his songs numbered a **t** and five.
5:11 Solomon gave Hiram twenty **t** cors of
5:11 twenty **t** baths of pressed olive oil
5:13 from all Israel—thirty **t** men.
5:14 Lebanon in shifts of ten **t** a month,
5:15 Solomon had seventy **t** carriers and
5:15 eighty **t** stonecutters in the hills,
7:26 It held two **t** baths.
8:63 twenty-two **t** cattle and a hundred
8:63 and twenty **t** sheep and goats.
10:26 chariots and twelve **t** horses,
12:21 eighty **t** fighting men—to make war
19:18 Yet I reserve seven **t** in Israel—all
20:29 inflicted a hundred **t** casualties on
20:30 collapsed on twenty-seven **t** of them.
2Ki 3: 4 of Israel with a hundred **t** lambs
3: 4 with the wool of a hundred **t** rams.
5: 5 six **t** shekels of gold and ten sets
13: 7 ten chariots and ten **t** foot soldiers,
14: 7 He was the one who defeated ten **t**
15:19 and Menahem gave him a **t** talents of
18:23 I will give you two **t** horses—if you
19:35 **t** men in the Assyrian camp.
24:14 and artisans—a total of ten **t**.
24:16 force of seven **t** fighting men,
24:16 war, and a **t** craftsmen and artisans.
1Ch 5:21 of the Hagrites—fifty **t** camels,
5:21 and fifty **t** sheep and two **t** donkeys.
5:21 took one hundred **t** people captive,
12:14 a hundred, and the greatest for a **t**.
12:20 leaders of units of a **t** in Manasseh.
15:25 the commanders of units of a **t** went
16:15 he commanded, for a **t** generations,
18: 4 David captured a **t** of his chariots,
18: 4 seven **t** charioteers and twenty **t**
18: 5 struck down twenty-two **t** of them.
18:12 eighteen **t** Edomites in the Valley
19: 6 the Ammonites sent a **t** talents of
19: 7 They hired thirty-two **t** chariots and
19:18 and David killed seven **t** of their
19:18 and forty **t** of their foot soldiers.
21: 5 **t** men who could handle a sword,
21: 5 four hundred and seventy **t** in Judah.
21:14 seventy **t** men of Israel fell dead.
22:14 LORD a hundred **t** talents of gold,
23: 3 number of men was thirty-eight **t**.
1Ch 23: 4 David said, "Of these, twenty-four **t**
23: 4 six **t** are to be officials and
23: 5 Four **t** are to be gatekeepers and
23: 5 four **t** are to praise the LORD with
26:32 Jeriah had two **t** seven hundred
29: 4 three **t** talents of gold (gold of
29: 4 seven **t** talents of refined silver,
29: 7 **t** talents and ten **t** darics of gold,
29: 7 ten **t** talents of silver, eighteen **t**
29: 7 and a hundred **t** talents of iron.
29:21 burnt offerings to him: a **t** bulls,
29:21 a **t** rams and a **t** male lambs,
2Ch 1: 6 offered a **t** burnt offerings on it.
1:14 chariots and twelve **t** horses,
2: 2 He conscripted seventy **t** men as
2: 2 eighty **t** as stonecutters in the
2:10 twenty **t** cors of ground wheat,
2:10 twenty **t** cors of barley, twenty **t**
2:10 and twenty **t** baths of olive oil."
4: 5 It held three **t** baths.
7: 5 of twenty-two **t** head of cattle
7: 5 and twenty **t** sheep and goats.
9:25 Solomon had four **t** stalls for horses
9:25 and twelve **t** horses, which he kept
11: 1 Benjamin—a hundred and eighty **t**
12: 3 sixty **t** horsemen and the innumerable
13: 3 of four hundred **t** able fighting men,
13: 3 with eight hundred **t** able troops.
13:17 **t** casualties among Israel's able men
14: 8 Asa had an army of three hundred **t**
14: 8 and two hundred and eighty **t** from
15:11 seven **t** sheep and goats from the
17:11 seven **t** seven hundred rams and seven
17:11 and seven **t** seven hundred goats.
25: 5 **t** men ready for military service,
25: 6 He also hired a hundred **t** fighting
25:11 where he killed ten **t** men of Seir.
25:12 army of Judah also captured ten **t**
25:13 They killed three **t** people and
27: 5 ten **t** cors of wheat and ten **t** cors
28: 6 twenty **t** soldiers in Judah—because
28: 8 hundred **t** wives, sons and daughters.
29:33 bulls and three **t** sheep and goats.
30:24 king of Judah provided a **t** bulls
30:24 **t** sheep and goats for the assembly,
30:24 a **t** bulls and ten **t** sheep and goats.
35: 7 there a total of thirty **t** sheep
35: 7 and also three **t** cattle—all from
35: 8 gave the priests two **t** six hundred
35: 9 provided five **t** Passover offerings
Est 3: 9 and I will put ten **t** talents of
9:16 They killed seventy-five **t** of them
Job 1: 3 he owned seven **t** sheep, three **t**
9: 3 not answer him one time out of a **t**.
33:23 one out of a **t**, to tell a man what
42:12 had fourteen **t** sheep, six **t** camels
42:12 a **t** yoke of oxen and a **t** donkeys.
Ps 50:10 mine, and the cattle on a **t** hills.
60: T struck down twelve **t** Edomites in
84:10 in your courts than a **t** elsewhere;
90: 4 For a **t** years in your sight are like
91: 7 A **t** may fall at your side, ten **t** at
105: 8 he commanded, for a **t** generations,
Ecc 6: 6 even if he lives a **t** years twice
7:28 I found one upright man among a **t**,
SS 4: 4 elegance; on it hang a **t** shields,
5:10 and ruddy, outstanding among ten **t**.
8:11 for its fruit a **t** shekels of silver.
8:12 to give; the **t** shekels are for you,
Isa 7:23 a **t** vines worth a **t** silver shekels,
30:17 A **t** will flee at the threat of one;
36: 8 I will give you two **t** horses—if you
37:36 **t** men in the Assyrian camp.
60:22 The least of you will become a **t**,
Eze 47: 3 he measured off a **t** cubits and then
47: 4 He measured off another **t** cubits and
47: 4 He measured off another **t** and led me
47: 5 He measured off another **t**, but now
Da 5: 1 great banquet for a **t** of his nobles
7:10 ten **t** times ten **t** stood before him.
Am 5: 3 city that marches out a **t** strong
Jnh 4:11 twenty **t** people who cannot tell
Mic 6: 7 with ten **t** rivers of oil? Shall I
Mt 14:21 those who ate was about five **t** men,
15:38 four **t**, besides women and children.
16: 9 the five loaves for the five **t**,

Mt 16:10 Or the seven loaves for the four t,
18:24 ten t talents was brought to him.
Mk 5:13 The herd, about two t in number,
6:44 of the men who had eaten was five t.
8: 9 About four t men were present. And
8:19 the five loaves for the five t,
8:20 the seven loaves for the four t,
Lk 9:14 (About five t men were there.) But
14:31 whether he is able with ten t men
14:31 coming against him with twenty t?
16: 7 'A t bushels of wheat,' he replied.
Jn 6:10 men sat down, about five t of them.
Ac 2:41 and about three t were added to
4: 4 number of men grew to about five t.
19:19 the total came to fifty t drachmas.
21:38 led four t terrorists out into the
Ro 11: 4 "I have reserved for myself seven t
1Co 4:15 Even though you have ten t guardians
10: 8 one day twenty-three t of them died.
14:19 others than ten t words in a tongue.
2Pe 3: 8 the Lord a day is like a t years,
3: 8 years, and a t years are like a day.
Rev 5:11 thousands, and ten t times ten t.
11:13 Seven t people were killed in the
20: 2 Satan, and bound him for a t years.
20: 3 more until the t years were ended.
20: 4 reigned with Christ for a t years.
20: 5 life until the t years were ended.
20: 6 will reign with him for a t years.
20: 7 the t years are over, Satan will be

Thousands (Thousand)

Ge 24:60 may you increase to t upon t; may
Ex 18:21 over t, hundreds, fifties and tens.
18:25 over t, hundreds, fifties and tens.
34: 7 maintaining love to t, and forgiving
Nu 10:36 LORD, to the countless t of Israel."
31:14 of the army—the commanders of t
31:48 of the army—the commanders of t
31:52 All the gold from the commanders of t
31:54 the gold from the commanders of t
Dt 1:15 over you—as commanders of t,
33:17 Such are the ten t of Ephraim; such
33:17 Ephraim; such are the t of Manasseh."
1Sa 8:12 of t and commanders of fifties,
18: 7 his t, and David his tens of t."
18: 8 t," he thought, "but me with only t.
21:11 his t, and David his tens of t'?"
22: 7 of t and commanders of hundreds?
29: 2 with their units of hundreds and t,
29: 5 his t, and David his tens of t'?"
2Sa 18: 1 of t and commanders of hundreds.
18: 4 out in units of hundreds and of t.
1Ch 13: 1 of t and commanders of hundreds.
26:26 of t and commanders of hundreds,
27: 1 commanders of t and commanders of
28: 1 the commanders of t and commanders
29: 6 the commanders of t and commanders
2Ch 1: 2 of t and commanders of hundreds,
25: 5 their families to commanders of t
Ps 3: 6 I will not fear the tens of t drawn
68:17 of God are tens of t and t of t;
119:72 than t of pieces of silver and gold.
144:13 by t, by tens of t in our fields;
Jer 32:18 You show love to t but bring the
Da 7:10 T upon t attended him; ten thousand
11:12 slaughter many t, yet he will not
Mic 6: 7 Will the LORD be pleased with t of
Lk 12: 1 Meanwhile, when a crowd of many t
Ac 21:20 "You see, brother, how many t of
Heb 12:22 You have come to t upon t of angels
Jude :14 with t upon t of his holy ones
Rev 5:11 numbering t upon t, and ten thousand

Thrashing

Job 41:25 they retreat before his t.
Eze 32: 2 in the seas t about in your streams,

Thread (Threads)

Ge 14:23 not even a t or the thong of a
38:28 t and tied it on his wrist and said,
38:30 his brother, who had the scarlet t

Threads (Thread)

Jdg 16:12 off his arms as if they were t.

Threat (Threaten, Threatened, Threats)

Ezr 4:22 Why let this t grow, to the
Ne 4: 9 guard day and night to meet this t.
Ps 64: 1 my life from the t of the enemy.
Pr 13: 8 his life, but a poor man hears no t.
Isa 30:17 A thousand will flee at the t of one;
30:17 t of five you will all flee away,

Threaten (Threat)

Ps 73: 8 their arrogance they t oppression.
Eze 6:10 I did not t in vain to bring this
Eph 6: 9 Do not t them, since you know that

Threatened (Threat)

Ex 32:14 on his people the disaster he had t.
Jos 23:15 bring on you all the evil he has t,
Jer 27:13 plague with which the LORD has t any
Jnh 1: 4 arose that the ship t to break up.
2: 5 The engulfing waters t me, the deep
3:10 upon them the destruction he had t.

Threats (Threat)

Ps 10: 7 is full of curses and lies and t;
55:11 t and lies never leave its streets.
Jer 44:29 'so that you will know that my t of
Zep 2: 8 and made t against their land.
Ac 4:21 After further t they let them go.
4:29 Now, Lord, consider their t and
9: 1 t against the Lord's disciples.
1Pe 2:23 when he suffered, he made no t.

Three (*Three days*, Three-day)

Ge 6:10 Noah had t sons: Shem, Ham and
7:13 of his t sons, entered the ark.
9:19 These were the t sons of Noah, and
15: 9 a goat and a ram, each t years old,
18: 2 Abraham looked up and saw t men
18: 6 "Quick," he said, "get t seahs of
29: 2 with t flocks of sheep lying near it
29:34 me, because I have borne him t sons.
38:24 About t months later Judah was told,
40:10 on the vine were t branches. As soon
40:12 Joseph said to him. "The t branches
40:16 On my head were t baskets of bread.
40:18 Jospeh said. "The t baskets are
45:22 but to Benjamin he gave t hundred
Ex 2: 2 child, she hid him for t months.
21:11 not provide her with these t things,
23:14 "T times a year you are to celebrate
23:17 "T times a year all the men are to
25:32 on one side and t on the other.
25:32 on one side and t on the other.
25:33 T cups shaped like almond flowers
25:33 t on the next branch, and the same
27: 1 an altar of acacia wood, t cubits
27:14 entrance, with t posts and t bases,
27:15 side, with t posts and t bases.
32:28 about t thousand of the people died.
34:23 T times a year all your men are to
34:24 go up t times each year to appear
37:18 on one side and t on the other.
37:18 on one side and t on the other.
37:19 T cups shaped like almond flowers
37:19 t on the next branch and the same
38: 1 t cubits high; it was square, five
38:14 entrance, with t posts and t bases,
38:15 courtyard, with t posts and t bases.
Lev 19:23 For t years you are to consider it
25:21 land will yield enough for t years.
27: 6 of a female at t shekels of silver.
Nu 11:31 to about t feet above the ground,
12: 4 the Tent of Meeting, all t of you.
12: 4 So the t of them came out.
22:28 to make you beat me these t times?"
22:32 beaten your donkey these t times?
22:33 turned away from me these t times.
24:10 you have blessed them these t times.
35: 5 Outside the town, measure t thousand
35: 5 side, t thousand on the south side,
35: 5 t thousand on the west and t
Nu 35:14 Give t on this side of the Jordan
35:14 and t in Canaan as cities of refuge.
Dt 4:41 Moses set aside t cities east of the
14:28 At the end of every t years, bring
16:16 T times a year all your men must
17: 6 On the testimony of two or t
19: 2 set aside for yourselves t cities
19: 3 Build roads to them and divide into t
19: 7 set aside for yourselves t cities.
19: 9 you are to set aside t more cities.
19:15 the testimony of two or t witnesses.
Jos 7: 3 Send two or t thousand men to take
7: 4 about t thousand men went up; but
15:14 Caleb drove out the t Anakites
18: 4 Appoint t men from each tribe. I
21:32 with their pasture-lands—t towns.
Jdg 1:20 drove from it the t sons of Anak.
7: 6 T hundred men lapped with their
7: 7 The LORD said to Gideon, "With the t
7: 8 their tents but kept the t hundred,
7:16 Dividing the t hundred men into t
7:20 The t companies blew the trumpets
7:22 the t hundred trumpets sounded, the
8: 4 Gideon and his t hundred men,
9:22 had governed Israel for t years,
9:43 he took his men, divided them into t
11:26 For t hundred years Israel occupied
15: 4 he went out and caught t hundred
15:11 t thousand men from Judah went down
16:27 on the roof were about t thousand
1Sa 2:21 birth to t sons and two daughters.
10: 3 T men going up to God at Bethel will
10: 3 One will be carrying t young goats,
10: 3 another t loaves of bread, and
11: 8 the men of Israel numbered t hundred
11:11 separated his men into t divisions;
13: 2 Saul chose t thousand men from
13: 5 with t thousand chariots, six
13:17 Philistine camp in t detachments.
17:13 Jesse's t oldest sons had followed
17:14 David was the youngest. The t oldest
20:20 I will shoot t arrows to the side of
20:41 bowed down before Jonathan t times
24: 2 Saul took t thousand chosen men from
25: 2 and t thousand sheep, which he was
26: 2 with his t thousand chosen men of
30:12 any water for t days and t nights.
31: 6 Saul and his t sons and his
31: 8 his t sons fallen on Mount Gilboa.
2Sa 2:18 The t sons of Zeruiah were there:
6:11 Obed-Edom the Gittite for t months,
13:38 Geshur, he stayed there for t years.
14:27 T sons and a daughter were born to
18:14 So he took t javelins in his hand
21: 1 there was a famine for t successive
21:16 whose bronze spearhead weighed t
23: 8 a Tahkemonite, was chief of the T;
23: 9 As one of the t mighty men, he was
23:13 During harvest time, t of the thirty
23:16 the t mighty men broke through the
23:17 the exploits of the t mighty men.
23:18 son of Zeruiah was chief of the T.
23:18 raised his spear against t hundred
23:18 and so he became as famous as the T.
23:19 the T? He became their commander,
23:22 was as famous as the t mighty men.
23:23 but he was not included among the T.
24:12 LORD says: I am giving you t options.
24:13 "Shall there come upon you t years
24:13 Or t months of fleeing from your
1Ki 2:39 t years later, two of Shimei's
4:32 He spoke t thousand proverbs and his
6:36 inner courtyard of t courses of
7: 4 in sets of t, facing each other.
7: 5 in sets of t, facing each other.
7:12 wall of t courses of dressed stone
7:25 on twelve bulls, t facing north,
7:25 t facing west, t facing south and t
7:27 cubits long, four wide and t high.
9:25 T times a year Solomon sacrificed
10:17 He also made t hundred small shields
10:17 with t minas of gold in each shield.
10:22 Once every t years it returned
11: 3 birth and t hundred concubines,
15: 2 he reigned in Jerusalem for t years.
17:21 stretched himself out on the boy t

1Ki 22: 1 For **t** years there was no war between
2Ki 3:10 "Has the LORD called us **t** kings
3:13 was the LORD who called us **t** kings
9:32 Two or **t** eunuchs looked down at him.
11: 5 You who are in the **t** companies that
13:18 He struck it **t** times and stopped.
13:19 you will defeat it only **t** times."
13:25 **T** times Jehoash defeated him, and so
17: 5 and laid siege to it for **t** years.
18:10 At the end of **t** years the Assyrians
18:14 Judah **t** hundred talents of silver
23:31 reigned in Jerusalem for **t** months.
24: 1 became his vassal for **t** years.
24: 8 reigned in Jerusalem for **t** months.
25:18 next in rank and the **t** doorkeepers.
1Ch 2: 3 These **t** were born to him by a
2:16 **t** sons were Abishai, Joab and Asahel.
3:23 Hizkiah and Azrikam—**t** in all.
7: 6 **T** sons of Benjamin: Bela, Beker and
10: 6 Saul and his **t** sons died, and all
11:11 his spear against **t** hundred men,
11:12 Ahohite, one of the **t** mighty men.
11:15 **T** of the thirty chiefs came down to
11:18 the **T** broke through the Philistine
11:19 the exploits of the **t** mighty men.
11:20 brother of Joab was chief of the **T**.
11:20 raised his spear against **t** hundred
11:20 and so he became as famous as the **T**.
11:21 He was doubly honoured above the **T**
11:24 was as famous as the **t** mighty men.
11:25 but he was not included among the **T**.
13:14 Obed-Edom in his house for **t** months,
21:10 LORD says: I am giving you **t** options.
21:12 **t** years of famine, **t** months of being
23: 8 first, Zetham and Joel—**t** in all.
23: 9 Haziel and Haran—**t** in all.
23:23 Mahli, Eder and Jerimoth—**t** in all.
25: 5 Heman fourteen sons and **t** daughters.
29: 4 **t** thousand talents of gold (gold of
2Ch 4: 4 on twelve bulls, **t** facing north,
4: 4 **t** facing west, **t** facing south and **t**
4: 5 It held **t** thousand baths.
6:13 five cubits wide and **t** cubits high,
8:13 New Moons and the **t** annual feasts
9:16 He also made **t** hundred small shields
9:16 with **t** hundred bekas of gold in each
9:21 Once every **t** years it returned,
11:17 Rehoboam son of Solomon for **t** years,
13: 2 he reigned in Jerusalem for **t** years.
14: 8 Asa had an army of **t** hundred
14: 9 a vast army and **t** hundred chariots,
25: 5 found that there were **t** hundred
25:13 They killed **t** thousand people and
29:33 and **t** thousand sheep and goats.
31:16 distributed to the males **t** years old
35: 7 and also **t** thousand cattle—all from
35: 8 offerings and **t** hundred cattle.
36: 2 reigned in Jerusalem for **t** months.
36: 9 Jerusalem for **t** months and ten days.
Ezr 6: 4 with **t** courses of large stones and
Est 9:15 put to death in Susa **t** hundred
Job 1: 2 He had seven sons and **t** daughters,
1: 3 he owned seven thousand sheep, **t**
1: 4 **t** sisters to eat and drink with them.
1:17 "The Chaldeans formed **t** raiding
2:11 Job's **t** friends, Eliphaz the
32: 1 these **t** men stopped answering Job,
32: 3 He was also angry with the **t** friends,
32: 5 when he saw that the **t** men had
33:29 to a man—twice, even **t** times—
42:13 had seven sons and **t** daughters
Pr 30:15 **t** things that are never satisfied,
30:18 "There are **t** things that are too
30:21 "Under **t** things the earth trembles,
30:29 "There are **t** things that are stately
Ecc 4:12 of **t** strands is not quickly broken.
Isa 16:14 now the LORD says: "Within **t** years,
17: 6 leaving two or **t** olives on the
20: 3 stripped and barefoot for **t** years,
Jer 36:23 Whenever Jehudi had read **t** or four
52:24 next in rank and the **t** doorkeepers.
Eze 14:14 even if these **t** men—Noah, Daniel
14:16 even if these **t** men were in it, they
14:18 even if these **t** men were in it, they
21:14 Let the sword strike twice, even **t**
40:10 Inside the east gate were **t** alcoves
Eze 40:10 the **t** had the same measurements,
40:21 Its alcoves—**t** on each side—its
40:48 were **t** cubits wide on either side.
41: 6 The side rooms were on **t** levels, one
41:16 galleries round the **t** of them—
41:22 There was a wooden altar **t** cubits
42: 3 faced gallery at the **t** levels.
48:31 The **t** gates on the north side will
48:32 will be **t** gates: the gate of Joseph
48:33 will be **t** gates: the gate of Simeon,
48:34 will be **t** gates: the gate of Gad,
Da 1: 5 They were to be trained for **t** years,
3:23 these **t** men, firmly tied, fell into
3:24 "Weren't there **t** men that we tied up
6: 2 with **t** administrators over them, one
6:10 **T** times a day he got down on his
6:13 He still prays **t** times a day."
7: 5 and it had **t** ribs in its mouth
7: 8 **t** of the first horns were uprooted
7:20 before which **t** of them fell—the
7:24 ones; he will subdue **t** kings.
10: 2 I, Daniel, mourned for **t** weeks.
10: 3 at all until the **t** weeks were over.
11: 2 the truth: **T** more kings will appear
Am 1: 3 LORD says: "For **t** sins of Damascus
1: 6 the LORD says: "For **t** sins of Gaza
1: 9 the LORD says: "For **t** sins of Tyre
1:11 the LORD says: "For **t** sins of Edom
1:13 LORD says: "For **t** sins of Ammon
2: 1 the LORD says: "For **t** sins of Moab
2: 4 LORD says: "For **t** sins of Judah
2: 6 LORD says: "For **t** sins of Israel
4: 4 morning, your tithes every **t** years.
4: 7 the harvest was still **t** months away.
Jnh 1:17 inside the fish **t** days and **t** nights.
Zec 11: 8 I got rid of the **t** shepherds.
Mt 12:40 **t** nights in the belly of a huge fish
12:40 **t** nights in the heart of the earth.
17: 4 you wish, I will put up **t** shelters
18:16 testimony of two or **t** witnesses.'
18:20 For where two or **t** come together in
26:34 crows, you will disown me **t** times."
26:75 crows, you will disown me **t** times.
Mk 9: 5 Let us put up **t** shelters—one for
14:30 yourself will disown me **t** times."
14:72 twice you will disown me **t** times.
Lk 1:56 **t** months and then returned home.
4:25 when the sky was shut for **t** and a
9:33 Let us put up **t** shelters—one for
10:36 "Which of these **t** do you think was a
11: 5 'Friend, lend me **t** loaves of bread,
12:52 **t** against two and two against **t**.
13: 7 'For **t** years now I've been coming to
22:34 will deny **t** times that you know me."
22:61 today, you will disown me **t** times."
Jn 6:19 they had rowed **t** or **t** and a half
13:38 crows, you will disown me **t** times!
Ac 2:41 and about **t** thousand were added to
3: 1 of prayer—at **t** in the afternoon.
5: 7 About **t** hours later his wife came in,
7:20 For **t** months he was cared for in his
10: 3 One day at about **t** in the afternoon
10:16 This happened **t** times, and
10:19 "Simon, **t** men are looking for you.
10:30 at this hour, at **t** in the afternoon.
11:10 This happened **t** times, and then it
11:11 "Right then **t** men who had been sent
17: 2 and on **t** Sabbath days he reasoned
19: 8 and spoke boldly there for **t** months,
20: 3 where he stayed **t** months. Because
20:31 Remember that for **t** years I never
28:11 After **t** months we put out to sea in
1Co 13:13 now these **t** remain: faith, hope and
14:27 two—or at the most **t**—should speak,
14:29 Two or **t** prophets should speak, and
2Co 11:25 **T** times I was beaten with rods, once
11:25 stoned, **t** times I was shipwrecked
12: 8 **T** times I pleaded with the Lord to
13: 1 testimony of two or **t** witnesses."
Gal 1:18 after **t** years, I went up to
1Ti 5:19 it is brought by two or **t** witnesses.
Heb 10:28 the testimony of two or **t** witnesses.
11:23 By faith Moses' parents hid him for **t**
Jas 5:17 on the land for **t** and a half years.
1Jn 5: 7 For there are **t** that testify:
5: 8 blood; and the **t** are in agreement.
Rev 6: 6 and **t** quarts of barley for a day's
8:13 be sounded by the other **t** angels!"
9:18 was killed by the **t** plagues of fire,
11: 9 For **t** and a half days men from every
11:11 after the **t** and a half days a breath
16:13 I saw **t** evil spirits that looked
16:19 The great city split into **t** parts,
21:13 There were **t** gates on the east, **t** on
21:13 **t** on the south and **t** on the west.

Three days

Ge 34:25 **T** later, while all of them were
40:12 "The three branches are **t**.
40:13 Within **t** Pharaoh will lift up your
40:18 "The three baskets are **t**.
40:19 Within **t** Pharaoh will lift off your
42:17 he put them all in custody for **t**.
Ex 10:22 darkness covered all Egypt for **t**.
10:23 else or leave his place for **t**.
15:22 For **t** they travelled in the desert
Nu 10:33 of the LORD and travelled for **t**.
10:33 **t** to find them a place to rest.
33: 8 and when they had travelled for **t** in
Jos 1:11 **T** from now you will cross the Jordan
2:16 Hide yourselves there **t** until they
2:22 into the hills and stayed there **t**,
3: 2 After **t** the officers went throughout
9:16 **T** after they made the treaty with
Jdg 14:14 For **t** they could not give the answer.
19: 4 to stay; so he remained with him **t**,
1Sa 9:20 for the donkeys you lost **t** ago, do
30:12 any water for **t** and three nights.
30:13 me when I became ill **t** ago.
2Sa 20: 4 me within **t**, and be here yourself."
24:13 **t** of plague in your land? Now then,
1Ki 12: 5 Rehoboam answered, "Go away for **t**
12:12 **T** later Jeroboam and all the people
12:12 had said, "Come back to me in **t**.
2Ki 2:17 searched for **t** but did not find him.
1Ch 12:39 The men spent **t** there with David,
21:12 or **t** of the sword of the LORD—days
2Ch 10: 5 answered, "Come back to me in **t**.
10:12 **T** later Jeroboam and all the people
10:12 had said, "Come back to me in **t**.
20:25 that it took **t** to collect it.
Ezr 8:15 Ahava, and we camped there **t**.
8:32 in Jerusalem, where we rested **t**.
10: 8 Anyone who failed to appear within **t**
10: 9 Within the **t**, all the men of Judah
Ne 2:11 Jerusalem, and after staying there **t**
Est 4:16 Do not eat or drink for **t**, night or
Jnh 1:17 inside the fish **t** and three nights.
3: 3 important city—a visit required **t**.
Mt 12:40 For as Jonah was **t** and three nights
12:40 so the Son of Man will be **t** and
15:32 with me **t** and have nothing to eat.
26:61 temple of God and rebuild it in **t**.
27:40 the temple and build it in **t**,
27:63 said, 'After **t** I will rise again.'
Mk 8: 2 with me **t** and have nothing to eat.
8:31 be killed and after **t** rise again.
9:31 kill him, and after **t** he will rise."
10:34 and kill him. **T** later he will rise."
14:58 temple and in **t** will build another,
15:29 the temple and build it in **t**,
Lk 2:46 After **t** they found him in the temple
Jn 2:19 and I will raise it again in **t**."
2:20 and you are going to raise it in **t**?"
Ac 9: 9 For **t** he was blind, and did not eat
25: 1 **T** after arriving in the province,
28: 7 and for **t** entertained us hospitably.
28:12 in Syracuse and stayed there **t**.
28:17 **T** later he called together the

Three Taverns

Ac 28:15 Forum of Appius and the **T** to meet us.

Three-day (Day, Three)

Ge 30:36 he put a **t** journey between himself
Ex 3:18 Let us take a **t** journey into the
5: 3 Now let us take a **t** journey into the
8:27 We must take a **t** journey into the

Thresh (Threshed, Thresher, Threshes, Threshing, Threshing-cart, Threshing-floor, Threshing-floors, Threshing-sledge, Threshing-sledges)

Isa 27:12 In that day the LORD will **t** from the
41:15 You will **t** the mountains and crush
Hos 10:11 is a trained heifer that loves to **t**;
Mic 4:13 "Rise and **t**, O Daughter of Zion, for

Threshed (Thresh)

Ru 2:17 Then she **t** the barley she had
Isa 28:27 Caraway is not **t** with a sledge, nor
Am 1: 3 Because she **t** Gilead with sledges
Hab 3:12 and in anger you **t** the nations.

Thresher (Thresh)

1Co 9:10 ploughs and the **t** threshes,

Threshes (Thresh)

1Co 9:10 ploughs and the thresher **t**,

Threshing (Thresh)

Lev 26: 5 Your **t** will continue until grape
Jdg 6:11 where his son Gideon was **t** wheat in
2Ki 13: 7 made them like the dust at **t** time.
1Ch 21:20 While Araunah was **t** wheat, he turned
Pr 20:26 he drives the **t** wheel over them.
Isa 28:28 so one does not go on **t** it for ever.
Jer 50:11 **t** corn and neigh like stallions,

Threshing-cart (Thresh, Cart)

Isa 28:28 Though he drives the wheels of his **t**

Threshing-floor (Thresh, Floor)

Ge 50:10 they reached the **t** of Atad, near the
50:11 saw the mourning at the **t** of Atad,
Nu 15:20 it as an offering from the **t**.
18:27 the **t** or juice from the winepress.
18:30 product of the **t** or the winepress.
Dt 15:14 flock, your **t** and your winepress.
16:13 of your **t** and your winepress.
Jdg 6:37 I will place a wool fleece on the **t**.
Ru 3: 2 will be winnowing barley on the **t**.
3: 3 Then go down to the **t**, but don't let
3: 6 she went down to the **t** and did
3:14 known that a woman came to the **t**."
2Sa 6: 6 they came to the **t** of Nacon, Uzzah
24:16 at the **t** of Araunah the Jebusite.
24:18 on the **t** of Araunah the Jebusite."
24:21 "To buy your **t**," David answered, "so
24:24 So David bought the **t** and the oxen
1Ki 22:10 sitting on their thrones at the **t**
2Ki 6:27 From the **t**? From the winepress?"
1Ch 13: 9 they came to the **t** of Kidon, Uzzah
21:15 at the **t** of Araunah the Jebusite.
21:18 on the **t** of Araunah the Jebusite.
21:21 he left the **t** and bowed down before
21:22 "Let me have the site of your **t** so
21:28 on the **t** of Araunah the Jebusite,
2Ch 3: 1 It was on the **t** of Araunah the
18: 9 sitting on their thrones at the **t**
Job 39:12 your grain and gather it to your **t**?
Isa 21:10 O my people, crushed on the **t**, I
Jer 51:33 "The Daughter of Babylon is like a **t**
Da 2:35 like chaff on a **t** in the summer.
Hos 9: 1 wages of a prostitute at every **t**.
13: 3 like chaff swirling from a **t**, like
Mic 4:12 gathers them like sheaves to the **t**.
Mt 3:12 and he will clear his **t**, gathering
Lk 3:17 fork is in his hand to clear his **t**

Threshing-floors (Thresh, Floor)

1Sa 23: 1 Keilah and are looting the **t**,"
Hos 9: 2 **T** and winepresses will not feed the
Joel 2:24 The **t** will be filled with grain; the

Threshing-sledge (Thresh, Sledge)

Job 41:30 leaving a trail in the mud like a **t**.
Isa 41:15 "See, I will make you into a **t**, new

Threshing-sledges (Thresh, Sledge)

2Sa 24:22 are **t** and ox yokes for the wood.
1Ch 21:23 the **t** for the wood, and the wheat

Threshold (Thresholds)

Jdg 19:27 the house, with her hands on the **t**.
1Sa 5: 4 on the **t**; only his body remained.
5: 5 temple at Ashdod step on the **t**.
1Ki 14:17 the **t** of the house, the boy died.
Eze 9: 3 and moved to the **t** of the temple.
10: 4 and moved to the **t** of the temple.
10:18 from over the **t** of the temple
40: 6 **t** of the gate; it was one rod deep.
40: 7 And the **t** of the gate next to the
41:16 the **t** was covered with wood.
43: 8 they placed their **t** next to my **t** and
46: 2 He is to worship at the **t** of the
47: 1 water coming out from under the **t**
Zep 1: 9 all who avoid stepping on the **t**,

Thresholds (Threshold)

1Ch 9:19 for guarding the **t** of the Tent
9:22 gatekeepers at the **t** numbered 212.
Isa 6: 4 **t** shook and the temple was filled
Eze 41:16 well as the **t** and the narrow windows
Am 9: 1 of the pillars so that the **t** shake.

Threw (Throw)

Ge 33: 4 he **t** his arms around his neck and
37:24 they took him and **t** him into the
44:14 and they **t** themselves to the ground
45:14 he **t** his arms around his brother
46:29 he **t** his arms around his father and
50: 1 Joseph **t** himself upon his father and
50:18 His brothers then came and **t**
Ex 4: 3 Moses **t** it on the ground and it
7:10 Aaron **t** his staff down in front of
7:12 Each one **t** down his staff and it
14:24 army and **t** it into confusion.
15: 7 you **t** down those who opposed you.
15:25 He **t** it into the water, and the
32:19 his anger burned and he **t** the
32:24 Then they gave me the gold, and I **t**
Dt 9:17 I took the two tablets and **t** them
9:21 **t** the dust into a stream that flowed
Jos 10:10 The LORD **t** them into confusion
10:27 **t** them into the cave where they had
Jdg 8:25 **t** a ring from his plunder onto it.
14:16 Samson's wife **t** herself on him,
15:17 he finished speaking, he **t** away the
1Sa 7:10 **t** them into such a panic that they
2Sa 18:17 They took Absalom, **t** him into a big
20:12 a field and **t** a garment over him.
20:22 Sheba son of Bicri and **t** it to Joab.
1Ki 19:19 to him and **t** his cloak around him.
2Ki 2:21 he went out to the spring and **t** the
3:25 and each man **t** a stone on every good
6: 6 **t** it there, and made the iron float.
9:33 So they **t** her down, and some of her
10:25 The guards and officers **t** the bodies
13:21 **t** the man's body into Elisha's tomb.
23:12 **t** the rubble into the Kidron Valley.
2Ch 25:12 **t** them down so that all were dashed
30:14 and **t** them into the Kidron Valley.
33:15 and he **t** them out of the city.
Ne 13: 8 I was greatly displeased and **t** all
Jer 36:23 knife and **t** them into the brazier,
41: 7 them and **t** them into a cistern.
41: 9 Now the cistern where he **t** all the
Lam 3:53 my life in a pit and **t** stones at me;
Eze 28:17 So I **t** you to the earth; I made a
Da 3:24 we tied up and **t** into the fire?"
6:16 Daniel and **t** him into the lions' den.
8:10 and it **t** some of the starry host
Jnh 1: 5 And they **t** the cargo into the sea to
1:15 they took Jonah and **t** him overboard,
Zec 11:13 **t** them into the house of the LORD to
Mt 13:48 fish in baskets, but **t** the bad away.
21:39 they took him and **t** him out of the
27: 5 Judas **t** the money into the temple
Mk 9:20 **t** the boy into a convulsion. He fell
11: 7 they brought the colt to Jesus and **t**
12: 8 they took him and killed him, and **t**
12:41 Many rich people **t** in large amounts.
Lk 4:35 "Come out of him!" Then the demon **t**
9:42 **t** him to the ground in a convulsion.
15:20 **t** his arms around him and kissed him.
17:16 He **t** himself at Jesus' feet and
19:35 They brought it to Jesus, **t** their
Lk 20:12 and they wounded him and **t** him out.
20:15 they **t** him out of the vineyard and
Jn 9:34 you lecture us!" And they **t** him out.
Ac 16:37 Roman citizens, and **t** us into prison.
20:10 Paul went down, **t** himself on the
27:19 On the third day, they **t** the ship's
Rev 14:19 gathered its grapes and **t** them into
18:21 millstone and **t** it into the sea,
20: 3 He **t** him into the Abyss, and locked

Thrive (Thrives, Thriving)

Dt 31:20 and when they eat their fill and **t**,
Job 8:11 no marsh? Can reeds **t** without water?
39: 4 Their young **t** and grow strong in the
Ps 72:16 it **t** like the grass of the field.
Pr 11:28 righteous will **t** like a green leaf.
28:28 the wicked perish, the righteous **t**.
29: 2 the righteous **t**, the people rejoice;
29:16 the wicked **t**, so does sin, but the
Eze 17: 9 Will it **t**? Will it not be uprooted
17:10 Even if it is transplanted, will it **t**
Zec 9:17 Grain will make the young men **t**,

Thrives (Thrive)

Hos 13:15 even though he **t** among his brothers.

Thriving (Thrive)

Jer 11:16 The LORD called you a **t** olive tree

Throat (Throats)

Ps 5: 9 Their **t** is an open grave; with their
69: 3 calling for help; my **t** is parched.
Pr 23: 2 put a knife to your **t** if you are
Jer 2:25 feet are bare and your **t** is dry.

Throats (Throat)

Ps 115: 7 can they utter a sound with their **t**.
Jer 4:10 peace,' when the sword is at our **t**."
Ro 3:13 "Their **t** are open graves; their

Throb

Isa 60: 5 your heart will **t** and swell with joy

Throes

2Sa 1: 9 **t** of death, but I'm still alive.'

Throne (*Seated on the throne*, Thrones)

Ge 41:40 Only with respect to the **t** will I
Ex 11: 5 who sits on the **t**, to the firstborn
12:29 who sat on the **t**, to the firstborn
17:16 were lifted up to the **t** of the LORD.
Dt 17:18 he takes the **t** of his kingdom, he is
1Sa 2: 8 and has them inherit a **t** of honour.
2Sa 3:10 establish David's **t** over Israel and
7:13 the **t** of his kingdom for ever.
7:16 **t** shall be established for ever.
14: 9 king and his **t** be without guilt."
1Ki 1:13 and he will sit on my **t**"? Why then
1:17 after me, and he will sit on my **t**.'
1:20 the **t** of my lord the king after him.
1:24 you, and that he will sit on your **t**?
1:27 **t** of my lord the king after him?"
1:30 he will sit on my **t** in my place."
1:35 sit on my **t** and reign in my place.
1:37 Solomon to make his **t** even greater
1:37 than the **t** of my lord King David!"
1:46 has taken his seat on the royal **t**.
1:47 yours and his **t** greater than yours!'
1:48 to see a successor on my **t** today.
2: 4 to have a man on the **t** of Israel.'
2:12 Solomon sat on the **t** of his father
2:19 down to her and sat down on his **t**.
2:19 He had a **t** brought for the king's
2:24 on the **t** of my father David
2:33 his house and his **t**, may there be
2:45 and David's **t** will remain secure
3: 6 a son to sit on his **t** this very day.
5: 5 'Your son whom I will put on the **t**
7: 7 He built the **t** hall, the Hall of
8:20 and now I sit on the **t** of Israel,
8:25 to sit before me on the **t** of Israel,
9: 5 I will establish your royal **t** over

1Ki 9: 5 to have a man on the **t** of Israel.'
10: 9 and placed you on the **t** of Israel.
10:18 the king made a great **t** inlaid with
10:19 The **t** had six steps, and its back
22:19 I saw the LORD sitting on his **t** with
2Ki 10: 3 sons and set him on his father's **t**.
10:30 **t** of Israel to the fourth generation.
11:19 then took his place on the royal **t**,
13:13 and Jeroboam succeeded him on the **t**.
15:12 **t** of Israel to the fourth generation.
1Ch 17:12 and I will establish his **t** for ever.
17:14 his **t** will be established for ever.
22:10 And I will establish the **t** of his
28: 5 my son Solomon to sit on the **t**
29:23 Solomon sat on the **t** of the LORD as
2Ch 6:10 and now I sit on the **t** of Israel,
6:16 to sit before me on the **t** of Israel,
7:18 I will establish your royal **t**, as I
9: 8 placed you on his **t** as king to rule
9:17 the king made a great **t** inlaid with
9:18 The **t** had six steps, and a footstool
18:18 I saw the LORD sitting on his **t** with
23:20 and seated the king on the royal **t**,
Est 1: 2 his royal **t** in the citadel of Susa,
5: 1 **t** in the hall, facing the entrance.
Ps 9: 4 sat on your **t**, judging righteously.
9: 7 has established his **t** for judgment.
11: 4 the LORD is on his heavenly **t**.
45: 6 Your **t**, O God, will last for ever
47: 8 God is seated on his holy **t**.
89: 4 your **t** firm through all generations.
89:14 are the foundation of your **t**;
89:29 his **t** as long as the heavens endure.
89:36 his **t** endure before me like the sun;
89:44 and cast his **t** to the ground.
93: 2 Your **t** was established long ago; you
94:20 Can a corrupt **t** be allied with you—
97: 2 justice are the foundation of his **t**.
103:19 The LORD has established his **t** in
123: 1 to you, to you whose **t** is in heaven.
132:11 descendants I will place on your **t**—
132:12 sit on your **t** for ever and ever."
Pr 16:12 Kings detest wrongdoing, for a **t** is
20: 8 a king sits on his **t** to judge, he
20:28 through love his **t** is made secure.
25: 5 and his **t** will be established
29:14 his **t** will always be secure.
Isa 6: 1 I saw the Lord seated on a **t**, high
9: 7 He will reign on David's **t** and over
14:13 I will raise my **t** above the stars of
16: 5 In love a **t** will be established; in
47: 1 sit on the ground without a **t**,
63:15 your lofty **t**, holy and glorious.
66: 1 Heaven is my **t**, and the earth is my
Jer 3:17 call Jerusalem The **T** of the LORD,
13:13 the kings who sit on David's **t**,
14:21 do not dishonour your glorious **t**.
17:12 A glorious **t**, exalted from the
17:25 kings who sit on David's **t** will come
22: 2 you who sit on David's **t**—you, your
22: 4 then kings who sit on David's **t** will
22:30 **t** of David or rule any more in Judah.
29:16 the king who sits on David's **t**
33:17 sit on the **t** of the house of Israel,
33:21 have a descendant to reign on his **t**.
36:30 He will have no-one to sit on the **t**
43:10 and I will set his **t** over these
49:38 I will set my **t** in Elam and destroy
Lam 5:19 your **t** endures from generation to
Eze 1:26 what looked like a **t** of sapphire,
1:26 **t** was a figure like that of a man.
10: 1 and I saw the likeness of a **t** of
17:16 of the king who put him on the **t**,
28: 2 **t** of a god in the heart of the seas.
43: 7 this is the place of my **t** and the
Da 4:36 and I was restored to my **t** and
5:20 royal **t** and stripped of his glory.
7: 9 His **t** was flaming with fire, and its
Jnh 3: 6 he rose from his **t**, took off his
Zec 6:13 and will sit and rule on his **t**.
6:13 And he will be a priest on his **t**.
Mt 5:34 either by heaven, for it is God's **t**;
19:28 Son of Man sits on his glorious **t**,
23:22 swears by God's **t** and by the one
25:31 will sit on his **t** in heavenly glory.
Lk 1:32 give him the **t** of his father David,
Ac 2:30 one of his descendants on his **t**.
7:49 "'Heaven is my **t**, and the earth is
12:21 sat on his **t** and delivered a public
Heb 1: 8 about the Son he says, "Your **t**,
4:16 Let us then approach the **t** of grace
8: 1 of the **t** of the Majesty in heaven,
12: 2 at the right hand of the **t** of God.
Rev 1: 4 from the seven spirits before his **t**,
2:13 you live—where Satan has his **t**.
3:21 the right to sit with me on my **t**,
3:21 sat down with my Father on his **t**.
4: 2 and there before me was a **t** in
4: 3 an emerald, encircled the **t**.
4: 4 Surrounding the **t** were twenty-four
4: 5 From the **t** came flashes of lightning
4: 5 Before the **t**, seven lamps were
4: 6 Also before the **t** there was what
4: 6 In the centre, around the **t**, were
4: 9 and thanks to him who sits on the **t**
4:10 down before him who sits on the **t**,
4:10 their crowns before the **t** and say:
5: 1 right hand of him who sat on the **t**
5: 6 standing in the centre of the **t**,
5: 7 right hand of him who sat on the **t**.
5:11 They encircled the **t** and the living
5:13 "To him who sits on the **t** and to the
6:16 **t** and from the wrath of the Lamb!
7: 9 the **t** and in front of the Lamb.
7:10 who sits on the **t**, and to the Lamb."
7:11 angels were standing round the **t**
7:11 before the **t** and worshipped God,
7:15 they are before the **t** of God and
7:15 **t** will spread his tent over them.
7:17 For the Lamb at the centre of the **t**
8: 3 on the golden altar before the **t**.
12: 5 was snatched up to God and to his **t**.
13: 2 power and his **t** and great authority.
14: 3 they sang a new song before the **t**
16:10 out his bowl on the **t** of the beast,
16:17 temple came a loud voice from the **t**,
19: 5 a voice came from the **t**, saying:
20:11 I saw a great white **t** and him who
20:12 before the **t**, and books were opened.
21: 3 I heard a loud voice from the **t**
22: 1 from the **t** of God and of the
22: 3 The **t** of God and of the Lamb will be

Thrones (Throne)

1Ki 22:10 were sitting on their **t** at the
2Ch 18: 9 were sitting on their **t** at the
Ps 122: 5 There the **t** for judgment stand, the **t**
Isa 14: 9 it makes them rise from their **t**—
Jer 1:15 set up their **t** in the entrance of
13:18 "Come down from your **t**, for your
Eze 26:16 coast will step down from their **t**
Da 7: 9 As I looked, "**t** were set in place,
Hag 2:22 I will overturn royal **t** and shatter
Mt 19:28 me will also sit on twelve **t**,
Lk 1:52 brought down rulers from their **t**
22:30 my table in my kingdom and sit on **t**,
Col 1:16 visible and invisible, whether **t** or
Rev 4: 4 the throne were twenty-four other **t**,
11:16 who were seated on their **t** before
20: 4 I saw **t** on which were seated those

Throng (Thronged, Throngs)

Job 21:33 and a countless **t** goes before him.
Ps 42: 4 thanksgiving among the festive **t**.
55:14 with the **t** at the house of God.
68:27 leading them, there the great **t** of
109:30 in the great **t** I will praise him.
Pr 7:26 down; her slain are a mighty **t**.
Jer 31: 8 in labour; a great **t** will return.
Eze 23:24 chariots and wagons and with a **t** of
32: 3 'With a great **t** of people I will
Mic 2:12 the place will **t** with people.

Thronged (Throng)

Jer 5: 7 and **t** to the houses of prostitutes.

Throngs (Throng)

Ps 35:18 among **t** of people I will praise you.

Throw (Threw, Throwing, Thrown, Throws)

Ge 27:40 will **t** his yoke from off your neck."
37:20 "Come now, let's kill him and **t** him
37:22 "Don't shed any blood. **T** him into
Ex 1:22 "Every boy that is born you must **t**
4: 3 The LORD said, "**T** it on the ground."
7: 9 'Take your staff and **t** it down
22:31 by wild beasts; **t** it to the dogs.
23:27 **t** into confusion every nation you
Lev 1:16 **t** it to the east side of the altar,
Nu 19: 6 and **t** them onto the burning heifer.
Jos 8:29 **t** it down at the entrance of the
24:14 **T** away the gods your forefathers
24:23 "Now then," said Joshua, "**t** away the
2Sa 11:21 Didn't a woman **t** an upper millstone
2Ki 9:25 "Pick him up and **t** him on the field
9:26 Now then, pick him up and **t** him on
9:33 "**T** her down!" Jehu said. So they
Job 18: 7 his own schemes **t** him down.
30:11 they **t** off restraint in my presence.
Ps 2: 3 they say, "and **t** off their fetters.
17:11 eyes alert, to **t** me to the ground.
50:18 you **t** in your lot with adulterers.
62: 3 you **t** him down—this leaning wall,
Pr 1:14 **t** in your lot with us, and we will
Ecc 3: 6 a time to keep and a time to **t** away,
Isa 2:20 In that day men will **t** away to the
19: 8 **t** nets on the water will pine away.
22:18 ball and **t** you into a large country.
28: 2 will **t** it forcefully to the ground.
30:22 you will **t** them away like a
Jer 7:29 Cut off your hair and **t** it away;
16:13 I will **t** you out of this land into a
22: 7 beams and **t** them into the fire.
51:63 to it and **t** it into the Euphrates.
Eze 5: 4 Again, take a few of these and **t**
7:19 They will **t** their silver into the
26:12 your fine houses and **t** your stones,
32: 4 I will **t** you on the land and hurl
Da 3:20 and **t** them into the blazing furnace.
Hos 7:12 they go, I will **t** my net over them;
8: 5 **T** out your calf-idol, O Samaria! My
Jnh 1:12 "Pick me up and **t** me into the sea,"
Zec 1:21 **t** down these horns of the nations
11:13 the LORD said to me, "**T** it to the
Mal 3:10 "and see if I will not **t** open the
Mt 4: 6 of God," he said, "**t** yourself down.
5:29 to sin, gouge it out and **t** it away.
5:30 to sin, cut it off and **t** it away.
7: 6 do not **t** your pearls to pigs.
13:42 They will **t** them into the fiery
13:50 **t** them into the fiery furnace, where
17:27 go to the lake and **t** out your line.
18: 8 to sin, cut it off and **t** it away.
18: 9 to sin, gouge it out and **t** it away.
21:21 'Go, **t** yourself into the sea,' and
22:13 'Tie him hand and foot, and **t** him
25:30 **t** that worthless servant outside,
Mk 11:23 'Go, **t** yourself into the sea,' and
Lk 4: 9 he said, "**t** yourself down from here.
4:29 in order to **t** him down the cliff.
12: 5 body, has power to **t** you into hell.
12:58 and the officer **t** you into prison.
22:41 He withdrew about a stone's **t** beyond
Jn 8: 7 be the first to **t** a stone at her."
21: 6 He said, "**T** your net on the right
Ac 7:19 forcing them to **t** out their newborn
27:18 they began to **t** the cargo overboard.
Heb 10:35 do not **t** away your confidence; it
12: 1 let us **t** off everything that hinders
Rev 18:19 They will **t** dust on their heads, and

Throwing (Throw)

Dt 7:23 **t** them into great confusion until
1Sa 5: 9 that city, **t** it into a great panic.
2Sa 16:13 cursing as he went and **t** stones at
Ezr 10: 1 weeping and **t** himself down before
Mk 10:50 **T** his cloak aside, he jumped to his
Ac 16:20 and are **t** our city into an
22: 4 and women and **t** them into prison,
22:23 they were shouting and **t** off their
27:38 ship by **t** the grain into the sea.
Gal 1: 7 Evidently some people are **t** you into
5:10 The one who is **t** you into confusion

Thrown (Throw)

Lev 4:12 where the ashes are t, and burn it
14:40 t into an unclean place outside the
2Sa 20:21 will be t to you from the wall."
1Ki 13:24 and his body was t down on the road,
13:25 passed by saw the body t down there,
13:28 he went out and found the body t
2Ki 7:15 had t away in their headlong flight.
19:18 They have t their gods into the fire
Ne 4: 5 for they have t insults in the face
Job 16:11 t me into the clutches of the wicked.
Ps 36:12 how the evildoers lie fallen—t down
102:10 you have taken me up and t me aside.
140:10 them; may they be t into the fire,
141: 6 their rulers will be t down from the
Isa 34: 3 Their slain will be t out, their
37:19 They have t their gods into the fire
Jer 14:16 t out into the streets of Jerusalem
22:19 t outside the gates of Jerusalem."
26:23 his body t into the burial place of
31:40 where dead bodies and ashes are t,
36:30 his body will be t out and exposed
38: 9 They have t him into a cistern,
51:34 he has t us into confusion, he has
Eze 11: 7 The bodies you have t there are the
15: 4 after it is t on the fire as fuel
16: 5 Rather, you were t out into the open
19:12 was uprooted in fury and t to the
21:12 They are t to the sword along with
Da 3: 6 be t into a blazing furnace."
3:11 will be t into a blazing furnace.
3:15 t immediately into a blazing furnace.
3:17 If we are t into the blazing furnace,
3:21 and t into the blazing furnace.
6: 7 shall be t into the lions' den.
6:12 would be t into the lions' den?
6:24 brought in and t into the lions' den
7:11 and t into the blazing fire.
8:12 and truth was t to the ground.
Joel 1: 7 It has stripped off their bark and t
Na 2: 6 The river gates are t open and the
Mt 3:10 be cut down and t into the fire.
5:13 to be t out and trampled by men.
5:25 and you may be t into prison.
5:29 your whole body to be t into hell.
6:30 and tomorrow is t into the fire,
7:19 is cut down and t into the fire.
8:12 the subjects of the kingdom will be t
18: 8 two feet and be t into eternal fire.
18: 9 eyes and be t into the fire of hell.
18:30 he went off and had the man t into
24: 2 another; every one will be t down."
Mk 9:22 "It has often t him into fire or
9:42 it would be better for him to be t
9:45 to have two feet and be t into hell.
9:47 to have two eyes and be t into hell,
13: 2 another; every one will be t down."
Lk 3: 9 be cut down and t into the fire."
12:28 and tomorrow is t into the fire, how
13:28 of God, but you yourselves t out.
14:35 for the manure heap; it is t out.
17: 2 would be better for him to be t into
21: 6 every one of them will be t down."
23:19 Barabbas had been t into prison for
23:25 He released the man who had been t
Jn 9:35 Jesus heard that they had t him out,
15: 6 he is like a branch that is t away
15: 6 up, t into the fire and burned.
Ac 16:23 they were t into prison, and the
17: 8 city officials were t into turmoil.
Rev 8: 8 all ablaze, was t into the sea.
18:21 be t down, never to be found again.
19:20 The two of them were t alive into
20:10 the devil, who deceived them, was t
20:10 and the false prophet had been t.
20:14 death and Hades were t into the lake
20:15 he was t into the lake of fire.

Throws (Throw)

Nu 35:20 pushes another or t something at
35:22 t something at him unintentionally
Job 30:19 He t me into the mud, and I am
41:18 His snorting t out flashes of light;
Mk 9:18 Whenever it seizes him, it t him to
Lk 9:39 it t him into convulsions so that he

Thrush

Isa 38:14 I cried like a swift or t, I moaned
Jer 8: 7 and the dove, the swift and the t

Thrust (Thrusting)

Dt 29:28 land and t them into another land,
1Sa 26: 8 the ground with one t of my spear;
2Sa 2:16 t his dagger into his opponent's
2:23 so Abner t the butt of his spear
1Ki 14: 9 to anger and t me behind your back.
2Ki 17:20 until he t them from his presence.
24:20 the end he t them from his presence.
Job 18: 8 His feet t him into a net and he
24: 4 They t the needy from the path and
SS 5: 4 My lover t his hand through the
Isa 8:22 they will be t into utter darkness.
13:15 Whoever is captured will be t
Jer 7:15 I will t you from my presence, just
52: 3 the end he t them from his presence.
Eze 23:35 me and t me behind your back,

Thrusting (Thrust)

Dt 6:19 t out all your enemies before you,

Thumb (Thumbs)

Lev 8:23 on the t of his right hand and on
14:14 on the t of his right hand and on
14:17 on the t of his right hand and on
14:25 on the t of his right hand and on
14:28 on the t of his right hand and on

Thumbs (Thumb)

Ex 29:20 on the t of their right hands, and
Lev 8:24 on the t of their right hands and on
Jdg 1: 6 him, and cut off his t and big toes.
1: 7 "Seventy kings with their t and big

Thummim (*Urim and thummim*)

Ex 28:30 Also put the Urim and the T in the
Dt 33: 8 About Levi he said: "Your T and Urim

Thunder (Thundercloud, Thundered, Thundering, Thunders, Thunderstorm)

Ex 9:23 the LORD sent t and hail, and
9:28 for we have had enough t and hail.
9:29 The t will stop and there will be no
9:33 the LORD; the t and hail stopped,
9:34 the rain and hail and t had stopped,
19:16 third day there was t and lightning,
20:18 the people saw the t and lightning
1Sa 2:10 He will t against them from heaven;
7:10 with loud t against the Philistines
12:17 upon the LORD to send t and rain.
12:18 same day the LORD sent t and rain.
Job 26:14 can understand the t of his power?"
36:33 His t announces the coming storm;
40: 9 God's, and can your voice t like his?
Ps 77:17 the skies resounded with t; your
77:18 Your t was heard in the whirlwind,
93: 4 Mightier than the t of the great
104: 7 sound of your t they took to flight;
Isa 29: 6 the LORD Almighty will come with t
33: 3 At the t of your voice, the peoples
Jer 25:30 he will t from his holy dwelling and
Joel 3:16 The LORD will roar from Zion and t
Mk 3:17 Boanerges, which means Sons of T);
Rev 4: 5 lightning, rumblings and peals of t.
6: 1 creatures say in a voice like t,
8: 5 earth; and there came peals of t,
11:19 rumblings, peals of t, an earthquake
14: 2 waters and like a loud peal of t.
16:18 peals of t and a severe earthquake.
19: 6 waters and like loud peals of t,

Thundercloud (Cloud, Thunder)

Ps 81: 7 I answered you out of a t; I tested

Thundered (Thunder)

Jdg 5:22 t the horses' hoofs—galloping,
1Sa 7:10 But that day the LORD t with loud
2Sa 22:14 The LORD t from heaven; the voice of
Ps 18:13 The LORD t from heaven; the voice of
Jn 12:29 there and heard it said it had t;

Thundering (Thunder)

Rev 9: 9 wings was like the t of many horses

Thunders (Thunder)

Job 36:29 clouds, how he t from his pavilion?
37: 4 roar; he t with his majestic voice.
37: 5 God's voice t in marvellous ways; he
Ps 29: 3 t, the LORD t over the mighty waters.
68:33 above, who t with mighty voice.
Jer 10:13 he t, the waters in the heavens roar;
51:16 he t, the waters in the heavens roar;
Joel 2:11 The LORD t at the head of his army;
Am 1: 2 "The LORD roars from Zion and t from
Rev 10: 3 the voices of the seven t spoke.
10: 4 the seven t spoke, I was about to
10: 4 "Seal up what the seven t have said

Thunderstorm (Storm, Thunder)

Job 28:26 for the rain and a path for the t,
38:25 of rain, and a path for the t,
Isa 30:30 fire, with cloudburst, t and hail.

Thwart (Thwarted, Thwarts)

Isa 14:27 and who can t him? His hand is

Thwarted (Thwart)

Job 42: 2 things; no plan of yours can be t.
Isa 8:10 but it will be t; propose your plan,

Thwarts (Thwart)

Job 5:12 He t the plans of the crafty, so
Ps 33:10 he t the purposes of the peoples.
Pr 10: 3 but he t the craving of the wicked.

Thyatira

Town in province of Lydia in western Asia Minor. Home of Lydia, a dealer in purple cloth (Ac 16:14). Though not large, this town was known for its thriving manufacturing industry and the pagan customs of some of its trade guilds. One of the 7 letters of Revelation was addressed to its church warning against the immoral teaching of Jezebel (Rev 2:18–29).

Ac 16:14 of T, who was a worshipper of God.
Rev 1:11 T, Sardis, Philadelphia and Laodicea.
2:18 "To the angel of the church in T
2:24 Now I say to the rest of you in T,

Tiaras

Isa 3:23 and the linen garments and t

Tiberias

City on the western shore of the Sea of Galilee, which is sometimes referred to as the Sea of Tiberias (Jn 6:1; 21:1). Some of its inhabitants travelled to hear Jesus (Jn 6:23–25) but there is no record of Jesus visiting here.

Jn 6: 1 of Galilee (that is, the Sea of T),
6:23 some boats from T landed near the
21: 1 to his disciples, by the Sea of T.

Tiberius

Lk 3: 1 year of the reign of T Caesar

Tibni

1Ki 16:21 supported T son of Ginath for king,
16:22 than those of T son of Ginath.
16:22 So T died and Omri became king.

Tidal

Ge 14: 1 of Elam and T king of Goiim
14: 9 king of Elam, T king of Goiim

Tidings

Isa 40: 9 You who bring good t to Zion, go up
40: 9 You who bring good t to Jerusalem,
41:27 to Jerusalem a messenger of good t.
52: 7 who bring good t, who proclaim

Tidy
Ac 9:34 Get up and **t** up your mat."

Tie (Tied, Ties, Tying)
Ex 29: 9 put headbands on them. Then **t** sashes
Lev 16: 4 he is to **t** the linen sash around him
Dt 6: 8 **T** them as symbols on your hands and
11:18 **t** them as symbols on your hands and
Jdg 15:12 said to him, "We've come to **t** you
15:13 "We will only **t** you up and hand you
16: 5 that we may **t** him up and subdue him.
Job 41: 1 or **t** down his tongue with a rope?
Jer 51:63 you finish reading this scroll, **t** a
Eze 3:25 you, son of man, they will **t** with
4: 8 I will **t** you up with ropes so that
Da 3:20 in his army to **t** up Shadrach,
Mt 13:30 First collect the weeds and **t** them
22:13 '**T** him hand and foot, and throw him
23: 4 They **t** up heavy loads and put them

Tied (Tie)
Ge 38:28 and **t** it on his wrist and said,
Ex 28:28 **t** to the rings of the ephod with
39:21 They **t** the rings of the breastpiece
Lev 8: 7 He put the tunic on Aaron, **t** the
8: 7 He also **t** the ephod to him by its
8:13 put tunics on them, **t** sashes around
Jos 2:18 when we enter the land, you have **t**
2:21 **t** the scarlet cord in the window.
Jdg 15: 4 and **t** them tail to tail in pairs.
16: 6 how you can be **t** up and subdued."
16: 8 been dried, and she **t** him with them.
16:10 Come now, tell me how you can be **t**."
16:12 Delilah took new ropes and **t** him
16:13 Tell me how you can be **t**." He
2Ki 5:23 and then **t** up the two talents of
Ps 109:19 like a belt **t** for ever round him.
Da 3:23 these three men, firmly **t**, fell into
3:24 "Weren't there three men that we **t**
Mt 21: 2 **t** there, with her colt by her.
Mk 9:42 a large millstone **t** around his neck.
11: 2 you will find a colt **t** there, which
11: 4 in the street, **t** at a doorway.
Lk 17: 2 with a millstone **t** round his neck
19:30 you will find a colt **t** there, which
Ac 21:11 he took Paul's belt, **t** his own hands

Ties (Tie)
Jdg 16: 7 Samson answered her, "If anyone **t** me
16:11 He said, "If anyone **t** me securely
Job 12:18 and **t** a loincloth round their waist.
Hos 11: 4 with **t** of love; I lifted the yoke
Mt 12:29 unless he first **t** up the strong man?
Mk 3:27 unless he first **t** up the strong man.

Tight (Tighten, Tightened, Tight-fisted)
Jas 1:26 not keep a **t** rein on his tongue,

Tighten (Tight)
Jdg 16:13 and **t** it with the pin, I'll become

Tightened (Tight)
Jdg 16:14 **t** it with the pin. Again she called

Tight-fisted (Fist, Tight)
Dt 15: 7 or **t** towards your poor brother.

Tiglath-Pileser
2Ki 15:29 **T** king of Assyria came and took Ijon,
16: 7 Ahaz sent messengers to say to **T**
16:10 King Ahaz went to Damascus to meet **T**
1Ch 5: 6 Beerah his son, whom **T** king of
5:26 **T** king of Assyria), who took the
2Ch 28:20 **T** king of Assyria came to him, but

Tigris, River
Major river in south-west Asia (about 1,150 miles), which with the River Euphrates gives Mesopotamia its name. One of the four rivers of Paradise (Ge 2:14). Daniel was standing on its banks when he received his vision (Da 10:4–7).

Ge 2:14 The name of the third river is the **T**;
Da 10: 4 the bank of the great river, the **T**,

Tikvah
2Ki 22:14 was the wife of Shallum son of **T**,
Ezr 10:15 son of Asahel and Jahzeiah son of **T**,

Tiles
Lk 5:19 the **t** into the middle of the crowd,

Till
Job 39:10 Will he **t** the valleys behind you?
Isa 23:10 **T** your land as along the Nile,
Jer 27:11 own land to **t** it and to live there,

Tilon
1Ch 4:20 Amnon, Rinnah, Ben-Hanan and **T**.

Tilting
Jer 1:13 **t** away from the north," I answered.

Timaeus
Mk 10:46 Bartimaeus (that is, the Son of **T**),

Timber (Timbers)
1Ki 5: 6 in felling **t** as the Sidonians."
5:18 prepared the **t** and stone for the
15:22 and **t** Baasha had been using there.
2Ki 12:12 They purchased **t** and dressed stone
22: 6 Also make them purchase **t** and
2Ch 2: 8 men are skilled in cutting **t** there.
2: 9 to provide me with plenty of **t**,
2:10 the woodsmen who cut the **t**, twenty
16: 6 stones and **t** Baasha had been using.
34:11 and **t** for joists and beams for the
Ne 2: 8 so he will give me **t** to make beams
Eze 26:12 stones, **t** and rubble into the sea.
Hag 1: 8 bring down **t** and build the house,

Timbers (Timber)
Lev 14:45 must be torn down—its stones, **t** and
Ezr 5: 8 and placing the **t** in the walls.
6: 4 of large stones and one of **t**.
Eze 27: 5 They made all your **t** of pine trees
Zec 5: 4 it, both its **t** and its stones.

Time (*Time is coming*, Times)
Ge 4: 3 In the course of **t** Cain brought some
4:26 At that **t** men began to call on the
6: 5 his heart was only evil all the **t**.
6: 9 of his **t**, and he walked with God.
8:12 but this **t** it did not return to him.
10:25 because in his **t** the earth was
12: 6 **t** the Canaanites were in the land.
13: 7 also living in the land at that **t**.
14: 1 At this **t** Amraphel king of Shinar,
17:21 bear to you by this **t** next year."
18:10 to you about this **t** next year,
18:14 to you at the appointed **t** next year
19:23 By the **t** Lot reached Zoar, the sun
21: 2 at the very **t** God had promised him.
21:22 At that **t** Abimelech and Phicol the
21:34 of the Philistines for a long **t**.
22: 1 Some **t** later God tested Abraham. He
22:15 to Abraham from heaven a second **t**
22:20 Some **t** later Abraham was told,
24:11 **t** the women go out to draw water.
25:24 the **t** came for her to give birth,
26: 1 the earlier famine of Abraham's **t**
26: 8 Isaac had been there a long **t**,
26:15 dug in the **t** of his father Abraham,
26:18 dug in the **t** of his father Abraham,
29: 7 not **t** for the flocks to be gathered.
29:21 My **t** is completed, and I want to lie
29:35 "This **t** I will praise the LORD.
30:20 This **t** my husband will treat me with
30:21 Some **t** later she gave birth to a
34:19 lost no **t** in doing what they said,
37: 9 "I had another dream, and this **t** the
38: 1 At that **t**, Judah left his brothers
38:12 After a long **t** Judah's wife, the
38:27 the **t** came for her to give birth,
39: 5 From the **t** he put him in charge of
Ge 40: 1 Some **t** later, the cupbearer and the
40: 4 they had been in custody for some **t**,
43:18 put back into our sacks the first **t**.
43:20 down here the first **t** to buy food.
46:29 his father and wept for a long **t**.
47:29 the **t** drew near for Israel to die,
48: 1 Some **t** later Joseph was told, "Your
50: 3 was the **t** required for embalming.
Ex 4:26 At that **t** she said "bridegroom of
8: 9 the **t** for me to pray for you
8:32 this **t** also Pharaoh hardened his
9: 5 The LORD set a **t** and said, "Tomorrow
9:14 or this **t** I will send the full force
9:18 Therefore, at this **t** tomorrow I will
9:27 "This **t** I have sinned," he said to
12:39 **t** to prepare food for themselves.
12:40 Now the length of **t** the Israelite
13:10 at the appointed **t** year after year.
21:19 injured man for the loss of his **t**
23:15 Do this at the appointed **t** in the
30:12 for his life at the **t** he is counted.
32:34 However, when the **t** comes for me to
34:18 Do this at the appointed **t** in the
Lev 14: 2 the **t** of his ceremonial cleansing,
15:25 of blood for many days at a **t**
16:17 the **t** Aaron goes in to make
19:10 go over your vineyard a second **t**
25:29 During that **t** he may redeem it.
25:50 He and his buyer are to count the **t**
26:34 all the **t** that it lies desolate
26:35 All the **t** that it lies desolate, the
Nu 3: 1 Moses at the **t** the LORD talked with
9: 2 the Passover at the appointed **t**.
9: 3 Celebrate it at the appointed **t**, at
9: 7 Israelites at the appointed **t**?"
9:13 LORD's offering at the appointed **t**.
9:19 over the tabernacle a long **t**,
10:13 They set out, this first **t**, at the
14:15 these people to death all at one **t**,
14:19 the **t** they left Egypt until now."
22: 4 who was king of Moab at that **t**,
28: 2 present to me at the appointed **t**
30:15 however, he nullifies them some **t**
Dt 1: 9 At that **t** I said to you, "You are
1:16 I charged your judges at that **t**:
1:18 at that **t** I told you everything you
1:46 days—all the **t** you spent there.
2: 1 For a long **t** we made our way around
2:14 Thirty-eight years passed from the **t**
2:34 At that **t** we took all his towns and
3: 4 At that **t** we took all his cities.
3: 8 at that **t** we took from these two
3:12 land that we took over at that **t**,
3:18 I commanded you at that **t**: "The LORD
3:21 At that **t** I commanded Joshua: "You
3:23 At that **t** I pleaded with the LORD:
4:14 the LORD directed me at that **t** to
4:25 have lived in the land a long **t**—if
4:32 long before your **t**, from the day God
4:40 LORD your God gives you for all **t**.
5: 5 (At that **t** I stood between the LORD
9:20 at that **t** I prayed for Aaron too.
10: 1 At that **t** the LORD said to me,
10: 8 At that **t** the LORD set apart the
10:10 as I did the first **t**, and the LORD
10:10 LORD listened to me at this **t** also.
15: 2 because the LORD's **t** for cancelling
16: 3 the **t** of your departure from Egypt.
16: 9 Count off seven weeks from the **t** you
17: 9 judge who is in office at that **t**.
17:20 a long **t** over his kingdom in Israel.
19:17 judges who are in office at the **t**.
20:19 you lay siege to a city for a long **t**,
24:20 not go over the branches a second **t**.
26: 3 say to the priest in office at the **t**,
28:47 and gladly in the **t** of prosperity,
32:35 In due **t** their foot will slip; their
34: 8 **t** of weeping and mourning was over.
Jos 2: 5 At dusk, when it was **t** to close the
5: 2 At that **t** the LORD said to Joshua,
6: 9 this **t** the trumpets were sounding.
6:16 The seventh **t** around, when the
6:26 At that **t** Joshua pronounced this
11: 6 because by this **t** tomorrow I will
11:10 At that **t** Joshua turned back and
11:18 all these kings for a long **t**.

Jos 11:21 At that **t** Joshua went and destroyed
14:10 since the **t** he said this to Moses,
20: 6 priest who is serving at that **t**.
22: 3 For a long **t** now—to this very
23: 1 After a long **t** had passed and the
24: 7 lived in the desert for a long **t**.
Jdg 3:29 At that **t** they struck down about ten
4: 4 was leading Israel at that **t**.
6:39 This **t** make the fleece dry and the
10: 1 After the **t** of Abimelech a man of
11: 4 Some **t** later, when the Ammonites
11:26 you retake them during that **t**?
12: 6 Ephraimites were killed at that **t**.
14: 4 **t** they were ruling over Israel.)
14: 8 Some **t** later, when he went back to
15: 1 Later on, at the **t** of wheat harvest,
15: 3 Samson said to them, "This **t** I have
16: 4 Some **t** later, he fell in love with a
16:15 This is the third **t** you have made a
18:30 the **t** of the captivity of the land.
18:31 **t** the house of God was in Shiloh.
20:25 This **t**, when the Benjamites came out
21:14 the Benjamites returned at that **t**
21:24 At that **t** the Israelites left that
1Sa 1:20 in the course of **t** Hannah conceived
3: 8 The LORD called Samuel a third **t**,
3:12 At that **t** I will carry out against
4:19 pregnant and near the **t** of delivery.
7: 2 was a long **t**, twenty years in all,
9:13 you should find him about this **t**."
9:16 "About this **t** tomorrow I will send
9:24 **t** I said, 'I have invited guests.
11: 9 'By the **t** the sun is hot tomorrow,
13: 8 He waited for seven days, the **t** set
13:11 that you did not come at the set **t**,
13:13 your kingdom over Israel for all **t**.
14:18 that **t** it was with the Israelites.)
14:35 it was the first **t** he had done this.
17:12 and in Saul's **t** he was old and well
18: 9 from that **t** on Saul kept a jealous
18:19 when the **t** came for Merab, Saul's
18:26 So before the allotted **t** elapsed,
19:21 a third **t**, and they also prophesied.
20:12 by this **t** the day after tomorrow!
22:15 Was that day the first **t** I enquired
25: 7 I hear that it is sheep-shearing **t**.
25: 7 and the whole **t** they were at Carmel
25: 8 men, since we come at a festive **t**.
25:15 and the whole **t** we were out in the
25:16 all the **t** we were herding our sheep
25:18 Abigail lost no **t**. She took two
26:10 his **t** will come and he will die,
2Sa 2: 1 In the course of **t**, David enquired
2:11 The length of **t** David was king in
3: 1 the house of David lasted a long **t**.
3:17 "For some **t** you have wanted to make
7:11 have done ever since the **t** I
8: 1 In the course of **t**, David defeated
10: 1 In the course of **t**, the king of the
11: 1 In the spring, at the **t** when kings
11:27 After the **t** of mourning was over,
13: 1 In the course of **t**, Amnon son of
14:26 he used to cut his hair from **t** to **t**
14:29 a second **t**, but he refused to come.
15: 1 In the course of **t**, Absalom provided
17: 7 has given is not good this **t**.
18:20 "You may take the news another **t**,
20: 5 than the **t** the king had set for him.
21:18 In the course of **t**, there was
21:18 At that **t** Sibbecai the Hushathite
23:13 During harvest **t**, three of the
23:14 At that **t** David was in the
24:15 until the end of the **t** designated,
1Ki 2: 1 the **t** drew near for David to die, he
2:38 stayed in Jerusalem for a long **t**.
2:42 will die'? At that **t** you said to me,
8: 2 Solomon at the **t** of the festival
8:40 that they will fear you all the **t**
8:61 obey his commands, as at this **t**."
8:65 observed the festival at that **t**,
9: 2 the LORD appeared to him a second **t**,
11:29 About that **t** Jeroboam was going out
14: 1 At that **t** Abijah son of Jeroboam
16: 9 Elah was in Tirzah at the **t**, getting
16:34 In Ahab's **t**, Hiel of Bethel rebuilt
17: 7 Some **t** later the brook dried up
1Ki 17:17 Some **t** later the son of the woman
18: 1 After a long **t**, in the third year,
18:29 the **t** for the evening sacrifice.
18:34 "Do it a third **t**," he ordered, and
18:34 and they did it the third **t**.
18:36 At the **t** of sacrifice, the prophet
18:44 The seventh **t** the servant reported,
19: 2 if by this **t** tomorrow I do not make
19: 7 a second **t** and touched him and said,
20: 6 about this **t** tomorrow I am going to
20: 9 do all you demanded the first **t**,
21: 1 Some **t** later there was an incident
22:49 At that **t** Ahaziah son of Ahab said
2Ki 3: 6 at that **t** King Joram set out from
3:20 The next morning, about the **t** for
4:16 "About this **t** next year," Elisha
4:17 and the next year about that same **t**
5:26 you? Is this the **t** to take money,
6:10 **T** and again Elisha warned the king,
6:24 Some **t** later, Ben-Hadad king of Aram
7: 1 LORD says: About this **t** tomorrow,
7:18 "About this **t** tomorrow, a seah of
8:20 In the **t** of Jehoram, Edom rebelled
8:22 Libnah revolted at the same **t**.
10: 6 to me in Jezreel by this **t** tomorrow.
10:36 The **t** that Jehu reigned over Israel
12:17 About this **t** Hazael king of Aram
13: 3 and for a long **t** he kept them under
13: 7 them like the dust at threshing **t**.
15:16 At that **t** Menahem, starting out from
15:29 In the **t** of Pekah king of Israel,
16: 6 At that **t**, Rezin king of Aram
18: 4 for up to that **t** the Israelites had
18:16 At this **t** Hezekiah king of Judah
20:12 At that **t** Merodach-Baladan son of
20:17 The **t** will surely come when
24:10 At that **t** the officers of
1Ch 1:19 because in his **t** the earth was
9:18 on the east, up to the present **t**.
9:25 villages had to come from **t** to **t**
11:16 At that **t** David was in the
15:13 did not bring it up the first **t** that
17:10 have done ever since the **t** I
18: 1 In the course of **t**, David defeated
19: 1 In the course of **t**, Nahash king of
20: 1 In the spring, at the **t** when kings
20: 4 In the course of **t**, war broke out
20: 4 At that **t** Sibbecai the Hushathite
21:28 At that **t**, when David saw that the
21:29 that **t** on the high place at Gibeon.
26:17 and two at a **t** at the storehouse.
28: 7 laws, as is being done at this **t**.'
29:22 son of David as king a second **t**,
2Ch 5: 3 the king at the **t** of the festival
6:31 walk in your ways all the **t** they
7: 8 festival at that **t** for seven days,
11:17 of David and Solomon during this **t**.
13:20 regain power during the **t** of Abijah.
15: 3 For a long **t** Israel was without the
15:11 At that **t** they sacrificed to the
16: 7 At that **t** Hanani the seer came to
16:10 At the same **t** Asa brutally oppressed
21: 8 In the **t** of Jehoram, Edom rebelled
21:10 Libnah revolted at the same **t**,
21:19 In the course of **t**, at the end of
24: 4 Some **t** later Joash decided to
25:27 From the **t** that Amaziah turned away
28:16 At that **t** King Ahaz sent to the king
28:22 In his **t** of trouble King Ahaz became
30: 3 to celebrate it at the regular **t**
35:16 at that **t** the entire service of the
35:17 celebrated the Passover at that **t**
35:21 is not you I am attacking at this **t**,
36:21 the **t** of its desolation it rested,
Ezr 4: 2 the **t** of Esarhaddon king of Assyria,
5: 3 At that **t** Tattenai, governor of
8:34 weight was recorded at that **t**.
9:12 of friendship with them at any **t**,
10:14 a foreign woman come at a set **t**,
Ne 2: 6 the king to send me; so I set a **t**.
4:22 At that **t** I also said to the people,
6: 1 though up to that **t** I had not set
6: 4 each **t** I gave them the same answer.
6: 5 Then, the fifth **t**, Sanballat sent
9:28 you delivered them **t** after **t**.
12:23 up to the **t** of Johanan son of
Ne 12:44 At that **t** men were appointed to be
13: 6 Some **t** later I asked his
13:21 From that **t** on they no longer came
Est 1: 1 This is what happened during the **t**
1: 2 At that **t** King Xerxes reigned from
2:19 virgins were assembled a second **t**
2:21 During the **t** Mordecai was sitting at
4:14 For if you remain silent at this **t**,
4:14 position for such a **t** as this?"
8:16 For the Jews it was a **t** of happiness
9:22 the **t** when the Jews got relief from
9:27 prescribed and at the **t** appointed.
Job 9: 3 answer him one **t** out of a thousand.
14: 6 has put in his **t** like a hired man.
14:13 set me a **t** and then remember me!
15:32 Before his **t** he will be paid in full,
22:16 They were carried off before their **t**,
39: 2 Do you know the **t** they give birth?
Ps 21: 9 At the **t** of your appearing you will
37:39 is their stronghold in **t** of trouble.
51: 5 from the **t** my mother conceived me.
69:13 I pray to you, O LORD, in the **t** of
75: 2 You say, "I choose the appointed **t**;
77: 8 Has his promise failed for all **t**?
78:38 **T** after **t** he restrained his anger
102:13 for it is **t** to show favour to her;
102:13 to her; the appointed **t** has come.
104:27 them their food at the proper **t**.
119:126 is **t** for you to act, O LORD; your
145:15 them their food at the proper **t**.
Pr 20: 4 at harvest **t** he looks but finds
25:13 the coolness of snow at harvest **t**
Ecc 1:10 long ago; it was here before our **t**.
3: 1 There is a **t** for everything, and a
3: 2 a **t** to be born and a **t** to die,
3: 2 a **t** to plant and a **t** to uproot,
3: 3 a **t** to kill and a **t** to heal,
3: 3 a **t** to tear down and a **t** to build,
3: 4 a **t** to weep and a **t** to laugh,
3: 4 a **t** to mourn and a **t** to dance,
3: 5 a **t** to scatter stones and a **t** to
3: 5 a **t** to embrace and a **t** to refrain,
3: 6 a **t** to search and a **t** to give up,
3: 6 a **t** to keep and a **t** to throw away,
3: 7 a **t** to tear and a **t** to mend,
3: 7 a **t** to be silent and a **t** to speak,
3: 8 a **t** to love and a **t** to hate,
3: 8 a **t** for war and a **t** for peace.
3:11 made everything beautiful in its **t**.
3:17 a **t** for every activity, a **t** for
7:17 be a fool—why die before your **t**?
8: 5 know the proper **t** and procedure.
8: 6 For there is a proper **t** and
8: 8 As no-one is discharged in **t** of war,
8: 9 There is a **t** when a man lords it
8:12 crimes and still lives a long **t**,
9:11 but **t** and chance happen to them all.
10:17 whose princes eat at a proper **t**—
Isa 7:17 on the house of your father a **t**
9: 7 from that **t** on and for ever.
11:11 reach out his hand a second **t** to
13:22 Her **t** is at hand, and her days will
18: 7 At that **t** gifts will be brought to
20: 2 at that **t** the LORD spoke through
23:15 At that **t** Tyre will be forgotten for
29:17 In a very short **t**, will not Lebanon
33: 2 our salvation in **t** of distress.
39: 1 At that **t** Merodach-Baladan son of
39: 6 The **t** will surely come when
42:14 "For a long **t** I have kept silent, I
42:23 or pay close attention in **t** to come?
48:16 at the **t** it happens, I am there.
49: 8 is what the LORD says: "In the **t**
59:21 **t** on and for ever," says the LORD.
60:22 in its **t** I will do this swiftly."
Jer 2:24 at mating **t** they will find her.
3:17 At that **t** they will call Jerusalem
4:11 At that **t** this people and Jerusalem
7:25 From the **t** your forefathers left
8: 1 "'At that **t**, declares the LORD, the
8: 7 observe the **t** of their migration.
8:15 for a **t** of healing but there was
10:18 "At this **t** I will hurl out those who
11: 7 From the **t** I brought your
11:14 to me in the **t** of their distress.
11:18 **t** he showed me what they were doing.

Jer 13: 3 of the LORD came to me a second **t**:
14:19 for a **t** of healing but there is only
16:19 my refuge in **t** of distress, to you
16:21 "Therefore I will teach them—this **t**
18: 7 If at any **t** I announce that a nation
18: 9 if at another **t** I announce that a
18:23 with them in the **t** of your anger.
25:33 At that **t** those slain by the LORD
25:34 For your **t** to be slaughtered has
27: 7 until the **t** for his land comes;
29:28 us in Babylon: It will be a long **t**.
30: 7 It will be a **t** of trouble for Jacob,
31: 1 "At that **t**," declares the LORD, "I
31:33 after that **t**," declares the LORD.
32:14 jar so that they will last a long **t**.
33: 1 of the LORD came to him a second **t**:
33:15 "'In those days and at that **t** I
33:20 no longer come at their appointed **t**,
35: 7 **t** in the land where you are nomads.'
36: 2 all the other nations from the **t** I
36: 9 a **t** of fasting before the LORD was
37:16 dungeon, where he remained a long **t**.
39:10 **t** he gave them vineyards and fields.
39:16 At that **t** they will be fulfilled
44:17 At that **t** we had plenty of food and
46:21 them, the **t** for them to be punished.
49: 8 on Esau at the **t** I punish him.
50: 4 "In those days, at that **t**," declares
50:20 In those days, at that **t**," declares
50:27 come, the **t** for them to be punished.
50:31 come, the **t** for you to be punished.
51: 6 It is **t** for the LORD's vengeance; he
51:13 come, the **t** for you to be cut off.
51:33 at the **t** it is trampled; the **t** to
51:47 For the **t** will surely come when I
Eze 4: 6 lie down again, this **t** on your right
7: 7 The **t** has come, the day is near;
7:12 The **t** has come, the day has arrived.
11: 3 They say, 'Will it not soon be **t** to
21:25 whose day has come, whose **t** of
21:29 whose day has come, whose **t** of
23:38 At that same **t** they defiled my
24:14 "'I the LORD have spoken. The **t** has
24:27 At that **t** your mouth will be opened;
30: 3 clouds, a **t** of doom for the nations.
35: 5 sword at the **t** of their calamity,
35: 5 the **t** their punishment reached its
38:17 At that **t** they prophesied for years
38:19 fiery wrath I declare that at that **t**
48:35 the name of the city from that **t** on
Da 1:18 At the end of the **t** set by the king
2: 8 that you are trying to gain **t**,
2:16 went in to the king and asked for **t**,
2:35 were broken to pieces at the same **t**
2:44 "In the **t** of those kings, the God of
3: 8 At this **t** some astrologers came
4:19 was greatly perplexed for a **t**, and
4:34 At the end of that **t**, I,
4:36 At the same **t** that my sanity was
5:11 In the **t** of your father he was found
7:12 allowed to live for a period of **t**.)
7:22 and the **t** came when they possessed
7:25 to him for a **t**, times and half a **t**.
8:17 vision concerns the **t** of the end."
8:19 will happen later in the **t** of wrath,
8:19 concerns the appointed **t** of the end.
9:21 the **t** of the evening sacrifice.
10: 2 At that **t** I, Daniel, mourned for
10:14 vision concerns a **t** yet to come."
11:24 of fortresses—but only for a **t**.
11:27 will still come at the appointed **t**.
11:29 "At the appointed **t** he will invade
11:29 but this **t** the outcome will be
11:33 though for a **t** they will fall by the
11:35 spotless until the **t** of the end,
11:35 will still come at the appointed **t**.
11:36 He will be successful until the **t** of
11:40 "At the **t** of the end the king of the
12: 1 "At that **t** Michael, the great prince
12: 1 There will be a **t** of distress such
12: 1 But at that **t** your people—everyone
12: 4 the scroll until the **t** of the end.
12: 7 will be for a **t**, times and half a **t**.
12: 9 and sealed until the **t** of the end.
12:11 "From the **t** that the daily sacrifice
Hos 10:12 for it is **t** to seek the LORD,
Hos 13:13 without wisdom; when the **t** arrives,
Joel 3: 1 "In those days and at that **t**, when I
Am 4: 2 "The **t** will surely come when you
8: 2 Then the LORD said to me, "The **t** is
8:10 I will make that **t** like mourning for
Jnh 3: 1 the LORD came to Jonah a second **t**:
Mic 2: 3 for it will be a **t** of calamity.
3: 4 At that **t** he will hide his face from
5: 3 Israel will be abandoned until the **t**
7: 4 Now is the **t** of their confusion.
Na 1: 9 trouble will not come a second **t**.
Hab 2: 3 revelation awaits an appointed **t**;
3: 2 Renew them in our day, in our **t** make
Zep 1:12 At that **t** I will search Jerusalem
2: 2 before the appointed **t** arrives and
3:19 At that **t** I will deal with all who
3:20 At that **t** I will gather you; at that
3:20 at that **t** I will bring you home.
Hag 1: 2 'The **t** has not yet come for the LORD'
1: 4 "Is it a **t** for you yourselves to be
2:20 the LORD came to Haggai a second **t**
Zec 8: 6 remnant of this people at that **t**,
8:10 Before that **t** there were no wages
Mal 3: 7 Ever since the **t** of your forefathers
Mt 1:11 at the **t** of the exile to Babylon.
2: 1 during the **t** of King Herod, Magi
2: 7 the exact **t** the star had appeared.
2:16 the **t** he had learned from the Magi.
4:17 From that **t** on Jesus began to preach,
7: 4 **t** there is a plank in your own eye?
8:29 torture us before the appointed **t**?"
9:15 The **t** will come when the bridegroom
10:19 **t** you will be given what to say,
11:25 At that **t** Jesus said, "I praise you,
12: 1 At that **t** Jesus went through the
13:21 no root, he lasts only a short **t**.
13:30 At that **t** I will tell the harvesters
14: 1 At that **t** Herod the tetrarch heard
16:21 From that **t** on Jesus began to
18: 1 At that **t** the disciples came to
21:34 the harvest **t** approached, he sent
21:36 more than the first **t**, and the
21:41 his share of the crop at harvest **t**."
24:10 At that **t** many will turn away from
24:23 At that **t** if anyone says to you,
24:25 See, I have told you ahead of **t**.
24:30 "At that **t** the sign of the Son of
24:43 **t** of night the thief was coming,
24:45 them their food at the proper **t**?
24:48 master is staying away a long **t**,'
25: 1 "At that **t** the kingdom of heaven
25: 5 The bridegroom was a long **t** in
25:19 "After a long **t** the master of those
26:18 Teacher says: My appointed **t** is near.
26:42 He went away a second **t** and prayed,
26:44 the third **t**, saying the same thing.
26:55 At that **t** Jesus said to the crowd,
27:16 At that **t** they had a notorious
Mk 1: 9 At that **t** Jesus came from Nazareth
1:15 "The **t** has come," he said. "The
2:20 the **t** will come when the bridegroom
3: 1 Another **t** he went into the synagogue,
4:17 no root, they last only a short **t**.
6:21 Finally the opportune **t** came. On his
6:35 By this **t** it was late in the day, so
12: 2 At harvest **t** he sent a servant to
13:11 say whatever is given you at the **t**,
13:21 At that **t** if anyone says to you,
13:23 have told you everything ahead of **t**.
13:26 "At that **t** men will see the Son of
13:33 do not know when that **t** will come.
14: 7 you can help them any **t** you want.
14:41 Returning the third **t**, he said to
14:72 the cock crowed the second **t**.
Lk 1: 5 In the **t** of Herod king of Judea
1:10 the **t** for the burning of incense
1:20 will come true at their proper **t**."
1:23 his **t** of service was completed, he
1:39 At that **t** Mary got ready and hurried
1:57 was **t** for Elizabeth to have her baby,
2: 6 While they were there, the **t** came
2:21 On the eighth day, when it was **t** to
2:22 When the **t** of their purification
4:13 he left him until an opportune **t**.
4:25 many widows in Israel in Elijah's **t**,
4:27 in the **t** of Elisha the prophet,
Lk 5:35 the **t** will come when the bridegroom
7:21 At that very **t** Jesus cured many who
7:45 but this woman, from the **t** I entered,
8:13 in the **t** of testing they fall away.
8:27 For a long **t** this man had not worn
9:36 no-one at that **t** what they had seen.
9:51 the **t** approached for him to be taken
10:21 At that **t** Jesus, full of joy through
12:12 you at that **t** what you should say."
12:42 food allowance at the proper **t**?
12:45 'My master is taking a long **t** in
12:56 how to interpret this present **t**?
13: 1 there were some present at that **t**
13:31 At that **t** some Pharisees came to
14:17 At the **t** of the banquet he sent his
16:16 Since that **t**, the good news of the
16:22 "The **t** came when the beggar died and
18: 4 "For some **t** he refused. But finally
19:44 the **t** of God's coming to you."
20: 9 farmers and went away for a long **t**.
20:10 At harvest **t** he sent a servant to
21: 6 "As for what you see here, the **t**
21: 8 'I am he,' and 'The **t** is near.
21:22 For this is the **t** of punishment in
21:27 At that **t** they will see the Son of
23: 7 who was also in Jerusalem at that **t**.
23: 8 **t** he had been wanting to see him.
23:22 For the third **t** he spoke to them:
23:29 For the **t** will come when you will
Jn 2: 4 "My **t** has not yet come."
2:13 was almost **t** for the Jewish Passover,
3: 4 a second **t** into his mother's womb
3:22 some **t** with them, and baptised.
4:52 he enquired as to the **t** when his son
4:53 **t** at which Jesus had said to him,
5: 1 Some **t** later, Jesus went up to
5: 6 been in this condition for a long **t**,
5:35 chose for a **t** to enjoy his light.
6: 1 Some **t** after this, Jesus crossed to
6:66 From this **t** many of his disciples
7: 6 The right **t** for me has not yet come;
7: 6 yet come; for you any **t** is right.
7: 8 me the right **t** has not yet come."
7:30 him, because his **t** had not yet come.
7:33 "I am with you for only a short **t**,
7:39 Up to that **t** the Spirit had not been
8: 9 heard began to go away one at a **t**,
8:20 him, because his **t** had not yet come.
9:24 A second **t** they summoned the man who
11:39 "by this **t** there is a bad odour, for
11:55 was almost **t** for the Jewish Passover,
12:31 Now is the **t** for judgment on this
12:42 Yet at the same **t** many even among
13: 1 Jesus knew that the **t** had come for
14: 9 I have been among you such a long **t**?
16: 4 so that when the **t** comes you will
16:21 has pain because her **t** has come;
16:22 with you: Now is your **t** of grief,
17: 1 and prayed: "Father, the **t** has come.
18:39 prisoner at the **t** of the Passover.
19:27 From that **t** on, this disciple took
21:14 This was now the third **t** Jesus
21:17 The third **t** he said to him, "Simon
21:17 him the third **t**, "Do you love me?"
Ac 1: 6 "Lord, are you at this **t** going to
1:21 the whole **t** the Lord Jesus went in
1:22 **t** when Jesus was taken up from us.
3: 1 up to the temple at the **t** of prayer
3:21 He must remain in heaven until the **t**
4:34 For from **t** to **t** those who owned
5:36 Some **t** ago Theudas appeared,
7: 5 at that **t** Abraham had no child.
7:17 "As the **t** drew near for God to
7:20 "At that **t** Moses was born, and he
7:41 That was the **t** they made an idol in
7:45 in the land until the **t** of David,
8: 9 Now for some **t** a man named Simon had
8:11 them for a long **t** with his magic.
9:31 and Samaria enjoyed a **t** of peace.
9:37 About that **t** she became sick and
9:43 Peter stayed in Joppa for some **t**
10:15 The voice spoke to him a second **t**,
11: 9 voice spoke from heaven a second **t**,
11:27 During this **t** some prophets came
12: 1 was about this **t** that King Herod
13:11 and for a **t** you will be unable to

Ac 13:20 until the **t** of Samuel the prophet.
14: 3 Barnabas spent considerable **t** there,
14:28 they stayed there a long **t** with the
15: 7 "Brothers, you know that some **t** ago
15:33 After spending some **t** there, they
15:36 Some **t** later Paul said to Barnabas,
17:21 their **t** doing nothing but talking
18:18 Paul stayed on in Corinth for some **t**
18:20 they asked him to spend more **t** with
18:23 After spending some **t** in Antioch,
19:23 About that **t** there arose a great
20:16 spending **t** in the province of Asia,
20:18 "You know how I lived the whole **t** I
21: 5 when our **t** was up, we left and
21:38 out into the desert some **t** ago?"
24:26 At the same **t** he was hoping that
26: 5 They have known me for a long **t** and
26:11 Many a **t** I went from one synagogue
26:28 "Do you think that in such a short **t**
26:29 Paul replied, "Short **t** or long—I
27: 9 Much **t** had been lost, and sailing
27:21 After the men had gone a long **t**
27:28 A short **t** later they took soundings
27:40 at the same **t** untied the ropes that
28: 6 but after waiting a long **t** and
Ro 3:26 his justice at the present **t**,
5: 6 You see, at just the right **t**, when
5:14 the **t** of Adam to the **t** of Moses,
6:21 What benefit did you reap at that **t**
8:22 right up to the present **t**.
9: 9 "At the appointed **t** I will return,
11: 5 too, at the present **t** there is a
11:30 Just as you who were at one **t**
13: 6 who give their full **t** to governing.
13:11 do this, understanding the present **t**
1Co 2: 7 for our glory before **t** began.
4: 5 judge nothing before the appointed **t**
4: 5 At that **t** each will receive his
7: 5 by mutual consent and for a **t**,
7:29 brothers, is that the **t** is short.
14:27 at a **t**, and someone must interpret.
15: 6 of the brothers at the same **t**,
16: 7 **t** with you, if the Lord permits.
2Co 6: 2 For he says, "In the **t** of my favour
6: 2 I tell you, now is the **t** of God's
8:14 At the present **t** your plenty will
12:14 ready to visit you for the third **t**,
13: 2 when I was with you the second **t**.
Gal 2: 1 to Jerusalem, this **t** with Barnabas.
4: 2 until the **t** set by his father.
4: 4 when the **t** had fully come, God sent
4:29 At that **t** the son born in the
6: 9 for at the proper **t** we will reap a
Eph 2: 3 us also lived among them at one **t**,
2:12 remember that at that **t** you were
Php 1: 3 I thank my God every **t** I remember
1Th 2:17 from you for a short **t** (in person,
2Th 2: 6 he may be revealed at the proper **t**.
1Ti 2: 6 testimony given in its proper **t**.
6:15 will bring about in his own **t**—God,
2Ti 1: 9 Jesus before the beginning of **t**,
4: 3 For the **t** will come when men will
4: 6 and the **t** has come for my departure.
Tit 1: 2 promised before the beginning of **t**,
3: 3 At one **t** we too were foolish,
3:10 once, and then warn him a second **t**.
Heb 3: 8 the **t** of testing in the desert,
4: 7 when a long **t** later he spoke
4:16 grace to help us in our **t** of need.
5:12 In fact, though by this **t** you ought
8:10 after that **t**, declares the Lord.
9: 9 an illustration for the present **t**,
9:10 until the **t** of the new order.
9:28 and he will appear a second **t**,
10:12 for all **t** one sacrifice for sins,
10:13 Since that **t** he waits for his
10:16 them after that **t**, says the Lord.
11:25 the pleasures of sin for a short **t**.
11:32 I do not have **t** to tell about Gideon,
12:11 seems pleasant at the **t**, but
12:26 At that **t** his voice shook the earth,
1Pe 1: 5 ready to be revealed in the last **t**.
1:11 trying to find out the **t** and
4: 3 For you have spent enough **t** in the
4:17 For it is **t** for judgment to begin
5: 6 that he may lift you up in due **t**.
2Pe 3: 6 of that **t** was deluged and destroyed.
Rev 1: 3 in it, because the **t** is near.
2:21 I have given her **t** to repent of her
3: 3 know at what **t** I will come to you.
11: 6 during the **t** they are prophesying;
11:18 The **t** has come for judging the dead,
12:12 he knows that his **t** is short."
12:14 care of for a **t**, times and half a **t**
14:15 because the **t** to reap has come, for
20: 3 he must be set free for a short **t**.
22:10 of this book, because the **t** is near.

Time is coming

1Sa 2:31 The **t** when I will cut short your
Jer 31:31 "The **t**," declares the LORD, "when I
Lk 17:22 he said to his disciples, "The **t**
Jn 4:21 "Believe me, woman, a **t** when you
4:23 Yet a **t** and has now come when the
5:25 I tell you the truth, a **t** and has
5:28 "Do not be amazed at this, for a **t**
16: 2 a **t** when anyone who kills you will
16:25 a **t** when I will no longer use this
16:32 "But a **t**, and has come, when you
Heb 8: 8 "The **t**, declares the Lord, when I

Times (Time)

Ge 4:15 will suffer vengeance seven **t** over.
4:24 If Cain is avenged seven **t**, then
4:24 then Lamech seventy-seven **t**."
27:36 these two **t**: He took my birthright,
31: 7 me by changing my wages ten **t**.
31:41 and you changed my wages ten **t**.
33: 3 bowed down to the ground seven **t**
43:34 was five **t** as much as anyone else's.
Ex 18:22 as judges for the people at all **t**,
18:26 as judges for the people at all **t**.
23:14 "Three **t** a year you are to celebrate
23:17 "Three **t** a year all the men are to
25:30 this table to be before me at all **t**.
34:23 Three **t** a year all your men are to
34:24 go up three **t** each year to appear
Lev 4: 6 some of it seven **t** before the LORD,
4:17 LORD seven **t** in front of the curtain
8:11 of the oil on the altar seven **t**,
14: 7 Seven **t** he shall sprinkle the one
14:16 some of it before the LORD seven **t**.
14:27 his palm seven **t** before the LORD.
14:51 and sprinkle the house seven **t**.
16:14 seven **t** before the atonement cover.
16:19 his finger seven **t** to cleanse it
23: 4 to proclaim at their appointed **t**:
25: 8 seven **t** seven years—so that the
26:18 you for your sins seven **t** over.
26:21 seven **t** over, as your sins deserve.
26:24 you for your sins seven **t** over.
26:28 you for your sins seven **t** over.
Nu 10:10 Also at your **t** of rejoicing—your
14:22 disobeyed me and tested me ten **t**—
19: 4 sprinkle it seven **t** towards the
22:28 to make you beat me these three **t**?"
22:32 beaten your donkey these three **t**?
22:33 turned away from me these three **t**.
24: 1 not resort to sorcery as at other **t**,
24:10 you have blessed them these three **t**.
Dt 1:11 increase you a thousand **t** and bless
16:16 Three **t** a year all your men must
Jos 6: 4 march around the city seven **t**, with
6:15 the city seven **t** in the same manner,
6:15 day they circled the city seven **t**.
Ru 4: 7 (Now in earlier **t** in Israel, for the
1Sa 3:10 as at the other **t**, "Samuel! Samuel!"
20:41 bowed down before Jonathan three **t**,
27: 8 (From ancient **t** these peoples had
2Sa 12: 6 He must pay for that lamb four **t**
24: 3 the troops a hundred **t** over,
1Ki 9:25 Three **t** a year Solomon sacrificed
17:21 boy three **t** and cried to the LORD,
18:43 Seven **t** Elijah said, "Go back."
22:16 The king said to him, "How many **t**
2Ki 4:35 sneezed seven **t** and opened his eyes.
5:10 "Go, wash yourself seven **t** in the
5:14 himself in the Jordan seven **t**,
13:18 He struck it three **t** and stopped.
13:19 struck the ground five or six **t**;
13:19 you will defeat it only three **t**."
2Ki 13:25 Three **t** Jehoash defeated him, and so
1Ch 4:22 (These records are from ancient **t**.)
9:20 In earlier **t** Phinehas son of Eleazar
12:32 men of Issachar, who understood the **t**
21: 3 his troops a hundred **t** over.
2Ch 18:15 The king said to him, "How many **t**
Ezr 4:15 a place of rebellion from ancient **t**.
Ne 4:12 them came and told us ten **t** over,
6: 4 Four **t** they sent me the same message,
10:34 at set **t** each year a contribution
13:31 wood at designated **t**, and for the
Est 1:13 the wise men who understood the **t**
9:31 days of Purim at their designated **t**,
9:31 their **t** of fasting and lamentation.
Job 19: 3 Ten **t** now you have reproached me;
24: 1 "Why does the Almighty not set **t** for
27:10 Will he call upon God at all **t**?
33:29 to a man—twice, even three **t**—
38:23 which I reserve for **t** of trouble,
Ps 9: 9 a stronghold in **t** of trouble.
10: 1 you hide yourself in **t** of trouble?
12: 6 a furnace of clay, purified seven **t**.
31:15 My **t** are in your hands; deliver me
34: 1 I will extol the LORD at all **t**; his
37:19 In **t** of disaster they will not
41: 1 LORD delivers him in **t** of trouble.
59:16 fortress, my refuge in **t** of trouble.
60: 3 have shown your people desperate **t**;
62: 8 Trust in him at all **t**, O people;
79:12 seven **t** the reproach they have
106:43 Many **t** he delivered them, but they
119:20 with longing for your laws at all **t**.
119:164 Seven **t** a day I praise you for your
Pr 17:17 A friend loves at all **t**, and a
24:10 If you falter in **t** of trouble, how
24:16 a righteous man falls seven **t**,
25:19 on the unfaithful in **t** of trouble.
Ecc 7:14 **t** are good, be happy; but when **t** are
7:22 many **t** you yourself have cursed
9:12 **t** that fall unexpectedly upon them.
Isa 30:26 and the sunlight will be seven **t**
33: 6 be the sure foundation for your **t**,
46:10 ancient **t**, what is still to come.
64: 4 Since ancient **t** no-one has heard, no
Jer 14: 8 O Hope of Israel, its Saviour in **t**
15:11 in **t** of disaster and **t** of distress.
21: 2 perform wonders for us as in **t** past
28: 8 From early **t** the prophets who
46:26 as in **t** past," declares the LORD.
Eze 4:10 to eat each day and eat it at set **t**.
4:11 hin of water and drink it at set **t**.
21:14 sword strike twice, even three **t**.
Da 1:20 he found them ten **t** better than all
2:21 He changes **t** and seasons; he sets up
3:19 be heated seven **t** hotter than
4:16 till seven **t** pass by for him.
4:23 until seven **t** pass by for him.'
4:25 Seven **t** will pass by for you until
4:32 Seven **t** will pass by for you until
6:10 Three **t** a day he got down on his
6:13 He still prays three **t** a day."
7:10 **t** ten thousand stood before him.
7:25 to change the set **t** and the laws.
7:25 him for a time, **t** and half a time.
9:25 and a trench, but in **t** of trouble.
11:14 "In those **t** many will rise against
12: 7 be for a time, **t** and half a time.
Am 4: 9 "Many **t** I struck your gardens and
5:13 quiet in such **t**, for the **t** are evil.
Mic 5: 2 are from of old, from ancient **t**."
Na 1: 7 The LORD is good, a refuge in **t** of
Mt 13: 8 sixty or thirty **t** what was sown.
13:23 sixty or thirty **t** what was sown."
16: 3 cannot interpret the signs of the **t**.
18:21 "Lord, how many **t** shall I forgive my
18:21 he sins against me? Up to seven **t**?"
18:22 not seven **t**, but seventy-seven **t**.
19:29 will receive a hundred **t** as much
26:34 crows, you will disown me three **t**."
26:75 crows, you will disown me three **t**.
Mk 4: 8 thirty, sixty, or even a hundred **t**."
4:20 or even a hundred **t** what was sown."
10:30 will fail to receive a hundred **t** as
14:30 yourself will disown me three **t**."
14:72 twice you will disown me three **t**.
Lk 8: 8 a hundred **t** more than was sown.

Lk 8:29 Many t it had seized him, and though
17: 4 If he sins against you seven t in a
17: 4 and seven t comes back to you and
18:30 will fail to receive many t as much
19: 8 I will pay back four t the amount."
21:24 the t of the Gentiles are fulfilled.
22:34 will deny three t that you know me."
22:61 today, you will disown me three t."
Jn 13:38 crows, you will disown me three t!
Ac 1: 7 "It is not for you to know the t or
3:19 that t of refreshing may come from
10:16 This happened three t, and
11:10 This happened three t, and then it
15:21 in every city from the earliest t
17:26 and he determined the t set for them
Ro 1:10 in my prayers at all t; and I pray
1:13 brothers, that I planned many t to
2Co 9: 8 so that in all things at all t,
11:24 Five t I received from the Jews the
11:25 Three t I was beaten with rods, once
11:25 once I was stoned, three t I was
12: 8 Three t I pleaded with the Lord to
Eph 1:10 to be put into effect when the t
1Th 5: 1 Now, brothers, about t and dates we
2Th 3:16 you peace at all t and in every way.
1Ti 4: 1 later t some will abandon the faith
2Ti 3: 1 mark this: There will be terrible t
Heb 1: 1 at many t and in various ways,
9:26 t since the creation of the world.
10:33 at other t you stood side by side
1Pe 1:20 in these last t for your sake.
Jude :18 They said to you, "In the last t
Rev 5:11 and ten thousand t ten thousand.
12:14 for a time, t and half a time,

Timid (Timidity)
2Co 10: 1 "t" when face to face with you,
1Th 5:14 encourage the t, help the weak, be

Timidity (Timid)
2Ti 1: 7 For God did not give us a spirit of t

Timna
Ge 36:12 named T, who bore him Amalek.
36:22 Hori and Homam. T was Lotan's sister.
36:40 and regions: T, Alvah, Jetheth,
1Ch 1:36 Zepho, Gatam and Kenaz; by T: Amalek.
1:39 Hori and Homam. T was Lotan's sister.
1:51 of Edom were: T, Alvah, Jetheth,

Timnah (Timnite's)
1. Town in hill country of Judah (Jos 15:57) where Judah was going when he was tricked by Tamar (Ge 38:12–18). **2.** Town on border of territory of Judah (Jos 15:10), belonging to Dan (Jos 19:43). Here Samson met and married a Philistine woman (Jdg 14:1–8), who was subsequently killed by her own people (Jdg 15:6). The town was captured and occupied by the Philistines (2Ch 28:18).

Ge 38:12 he went up to T, to the men who were
38:13 on his way to T to shear his sheep,"
38:14 to Enaim, which is on the road to T.
Jos 15:10 to Beth Shemesh and crossed to T.
15:57 Kain, Gibeah and T—ten towns and
19:43 Elon, T, Ekron,
Jdg 14: 1 Samson went down to T and saw there
14: 2 seen a Philistine woman in T;
14: 5 Samson went down to T together with
14: 5 they approached the vineyards of T,
2Ch 28:18 as well as Soco, T and Gimzo, with

Timnath Heres
Jdg 2: 9 at T in the hill country of Ephraim,

Timnath Serah
Jos 19:50 T in the hill country of Ephraim.
24:30 at T in the hill country of Ephraim,

Timnite's (Timnah)
Jdg 15: 6 "Samson, the T son-in-law, because

Timon
Ac 6: 5 Procorus, Nicanor, T, Parmenas, and

Timothy
Disciple from Lystra (Ac 16:1); convert of Paul (1Ti 1:2), probably during first missionary journey (2Ti 3:10–11). Circumcised by Paul and taken with him on second missionary journey (Ac 16:2–18:22; 2Co 1:19). Ministry confirmed by prophetic utterances (1Ti 1:18) and laying on of hands (1Ti 4:14; 2Ti 1:6). Sent by Paul to Thessalonica (1Th 3:2); Macedonia (Ac 19:22); Corinth (1Co 4:17). Accompanied Paul to Jerusalem (Ac 20:4–16). Remained in Ephesus to give leadership to church (1Ti 1:3). Imprisoned and released (Heb 13:23).
Timid (1Co 16:10–11; 2Ti 1:7), needing encouragement (1Ti 4:12; 2Ti 1:8; 2:1); but warmly commended by Paul as co-worker and son in the faith (Ro 16:21; 1Co 4:17; Php 2:19–22; 1Th 3:2; 2Ti 1:1–5). Associated with Paul in the writing of the letters to the Thessalonians (1Th 1:1; 2Th 1:1) and to Philemon (Phm 1).

Ac 16: 1 where a disciple named T lived,
17:14 but Silas and T stayed at Berea.
17:15 T to join him as soon as possible.
18: 5 Silas and T came from Macedonia,
19:22 He sent two of his helpers, T and
20: 4 Gaius from Derbe, T also, and
Ro 16:21 T, my fellow-worker, sends his
1Co 4:17 For this reason I am sending to you T
16:10 If T comes, see to it that he has
2Co 1: 1 and T our brother, To the church of
1:19 by me and Silas and T, was not "Yes"
Php 1: 1 Paul and T, servants of Christ Jesus,
2:19 I hope in the Lord Jesus to send T
2:22 you know that T has proved himself,
Col 1: 1 the will of God, and T our brother,
1Th 1: 1 Paul, Silas and T, To the church of
3: 2 We sent T, who is our brother and
3: 6 T has just now come to us from you
2Th 1: 1 Paul, Silas and T, To the church of
1Ti 1: 2 To T my true son in the faith: Grace,
1:18 T, my son, I give you this
6:20 T, guard what has been entrusted to
2Ti 1: 2 To T, my dear son: Grace, mercy and
Phm : 1 a prisoner of Christ Jesus, and T
Heb 13:23 I want you to know that our brother T

Tin
Nu 31:22 Gold, silver, bronze, iron, t,
Eze 22:18 t, iron and lead left inside a
22:20 copper, iron, lead and t into a
27:12 t and lead for your merchandise.

Tinder
Isa 1:31 The mighty man will become t and his

Tingle
1Sa 3:11 ears of everyone who hears of it t.
2Ki 21:12 of everyone who hears of it will t.
Jer 19: 3 ears of everyone who hears of it t.

Tip
Jdg 6:21 With the t of the staff that was in
1Ki 6:24 cubits from wing t to wing t.
Est 5: 2 and touched the t of the sceptre.
Job 33: 2 my words are on the t of my tongue.
38:37 t over the water jars of the
Lk 16:24 send Lazarus to dip the t of his

Tiphsah
1Ki 4:24 from T to Gaza, and had peace on all
2Ki 15:16 attacked T and everyone in the city
15:16 He sacked T and ripped open all the

Tiras
Ge 10: 2 Madai, Javan, Tubal, Meshech and T.
1Ch 1: 5 Madai, Javan, Tubal, Meshech and T.

Tirathites
1Ch 2:55 the T, Shimeathites and Sucathites.

Tire (Tired)
Jer 2:24 pursue her need not t themselves;
2Th 3:13 never t of doing what is right.

Tired (Tire)
Ex 17:12 Moses' hands grew t, they took a
Jdg 16:16 after day until he was t to death.
2Sa 17:29 and t and thirsty in the desert."
23:10 hand grew t and froze to the sword.
Isa 5:27 Not one of them grows t or stumbles,
40:28 He will not grow t or weary, and his
40:30 Even youths grow t and weary, and
Jn 4: 6 Jacob's well was there, and Jesus, t

Tirhakah
2Ki 19: 9 Sennacherib received a report that T
Isa 37: 9 Sennacherib received a report that T

Tirhanah
1Ch 2:48 was the mother of Sheber and T.

Tiria
1Ch 4:16 Ziph, Ziphah, T and Asarel.

Tirzah
Ancient Canaanite town about 8 miles east of Samaria and 5 miles north-east of Shechem. Captured by the Israelites under Joshua (Jos 12:24). It replaced Shechem as the capital of the northern kingdom, and remained so until Omri moved his capital to Samaria (1Ki 16:23–28). From this base Menahem launched his coup against King Shallum in Samaria (2Ki 15:14). Known for its beauty (SS 6:4).

Nu 26:33 Mahlah, Noah, Hoglah, Milcah and T.
27: 1 Mahlah, Noah, Hoglah, Milcah and T.
36:11 Zelophehad's daughters—Mahlah, T,
Jos 12:24 the king of T one thirty-one kings
17: 3 Mahlah, Noah, Hoglah, Milcah and T.
1Ki 14:17 wife got up and left and went to T.
15:21 building Ramah and withdrew to T.
15:33 became king of all Israel in T,
16: 6 his fathers and was buried in T.
16: 8 and he reigned in T for two years.
16: 9 Elah was in T at the time, getting
16: 9 man in charge of the palace at T.
16:15 Zimri reigned in T for seven days.
16:17 from Gibbethon and laid siege to T.
16:23 for twelve years, six of them in T.
2Ki 15:14 Menahem son of Gadi went from T up
15:16 starting out from T, attacked
SS 6: 4 You are beautiful, my darling, as T,

Tishbe (Tishbite)
1Ki 17: 1 Now Elijah the Tishbite, from T in

Tishbite (Tishbe)
1Ki 17: 1 Now Elijah the T, from Tishbe in
21:17 of the LORD came to Elijah the T:
21:28 of the LORD came to Elijah the T:
2Ki 1: 3 of the LORD said to Elijah the T,
1: 8 king said, "That was Elijah the T.
9:36 through his servant Elijah the T:

Tithe (Ten)
Lev 27:30 "'A t of everything from the land,
27:31 If a man redeems any of his t, he
27:32 The entire t of the herd and
Nu 18:26 t I give you as your inheritance,
18:26 of that t as the LORD's offering.
Dt 12:17 t of your grain and new wine and oil,
14:23 Eat the t of your grain, new wine
14:24 cannot carry your t (because the
14:25 exchange your t for silver, and take
26:12 the year of the t, you shall give it
2Ch 31: 5 a great amount, a t of everything.
31: 6 also brought a t of their herds
31: 6 flocks and a t of the holy things
Ne 10:37 we will bring a t of our crops to
Mal 3:10 Bring the whole t into the

Tithes (Ten)
Nu 18:21 "I give to the Levites all the **t** in
18:24 Levites as their inheritance the **t**
18:28 **t** you receive from the Israelites.
18:28 From these **t** you must give the
Dt 12: 6 your **t** and special gifts, what you
12:11 your **t** and special gifts, and all
14:28 bring all the **t** of that year's
2Ch 31:12 contributions, **t** and dedicated gifts
Ne 10:37 Levites who collect the **t** in all
10:38 the Levites when they receive the **t**,
10:38 of the **t** up to the house of our God,
12:44 contributions, firstfruits and **t**.
13: 5 and also the **t** of grain, new wine
13:12 All Judah brought the **t** of grain,
Am 4: 4 morning, your **t** every three years.
Mal 3: 8 do we rob you?' "In **t** and offerings.

Titius
Ac 18: 7 of **T** Justus, a worshipper of God.

Title
Isa 45: 4 and bestow on you a **t** of honour,
Eph 1:21 power and dominion, and every **t** that
Rev 17: 5 This **t** was written on her forehead:

Titus
Gentile convert and companion of Paul (Tit 1:4; 2Ti 4:10; 2Co 8:23). Accompanied Paul and Barnabas to Jerusalem (Gal 2:1–3). Sent to Corinth to deal with difficulties; brought good news to Paul in Macedonia (2Co 7:6–16). In Corinth again to complete collection (2Co 8:6,16–17). Left by Paul in Crete to consolidate work (Tit 1:5).

2Co 2:13 I did not find my brother **T** there.
7: 6 comforted us by the coming of **T**,
7:13 delighted to see how happy **T** was,
7:14 to **T** has proved to be true as well.
8: 6 we urged **T**, since he had earlier
8:16 **T** the same concern I have for you.
8:17 For **T** not only welcomed our appeal,
8:23 for **T**, he is my partner and
12:18 I urged **T** to go to you and I sent
12:18 **T** did not exploit you, did he? Did
Gal 2: 1 with Barnabas. I took **T** along also.
2: 3 Yet not even **T**, who was with me, was
2Ti 4:10 gone to Galatia, and **T** to Dalmatia.
Tit 1: 4 To **T**, my true son in our common

Tizite
1Ch 11:45 of Shimri, his brother Joha the **T**,

Toah
1Ch 6:34 the son of Eliel, the son of **T**,

Tob
Jdg 11: 3 and settled in the land of **T**,
11: 5 to get Jephthah from the land of **T**.
2Sa 10: 6 and also twelve thousand men from **T**.
10: 8 Rehob and the men of **T** and Maacah

Tob-Adonijah
2Ch 17: 8 Jehonathan, Adonijah, Tobijah and **T**

Tobiah (Tobiah's)
Ezr 2:60 The descendants of Delaiah, **T** and
Ne 2:10 Sanballat the Horonite and **T** the
2:19 when Sanballat the Horonite, **T** the
4: 3 **T** the Ammonite, who was at his side,
4: 7 when Sanballat, **T**, the Arabs, the
6: 1 word came to Sanballat, **T**, Geshem
6:12 **T** and Sanballat had hired him.
6:14 Remember **T** and Sanballat, O my God,
6:17 Judah were sending many letters to **T**
6:17 replies from **T** kept coming to them.
6:19 And **T** sent letters to intimidate me.
7:62 the descendants of Delaiah, **T** and
13: 4 He was closely associated with **T**,
13: 7 providing **T** a room in the courts of

Tobiah's (Tobiah)
Ne 13: 8 **T** household goods out of the room.

Tobijah
2Ch 17: 8 Jehonathan, Adonijah, **T** and
Zec 6:10 from the exiles, Heldai, **T** and
6:14 The crown will be given to Heldai, **T**

Today (Today's)
Ge 4:14 **T** you are driving me from the land,
19:37 is the father of the Moabites of **t**.
19:38 is the father of the Ammonites of **t**.
21:26 me, and I heard about it only **t**."
24:12 give me success **t**, and show
24:42 "When I came to the spring **t**, I said
30:32 Let me go through all your flocks **t**
31:43 Yet what can I do **t** about these
31:48 is a witness between you and me **t**.
40: 7 "Why are your faces so sad **t**?
41: 9 "**T** I am reminded of my shortcomings.
47:23 you and your land **t** for Pharaoh,
47:26 still in force **t**—that a fifth of
Ex 2:18 "Why have you returned so early **t**?
5:14 bricks yesterday or **t**, as before?"
13: 4 **T**, in the month of Abib, you are
14:13 the LORD will bring you **t**.
14:13 you see **t** you will never see again.
16:25 "Eat it **t**," Moses said, "because **t**
16:25 not find any of it on the ground **t**.
19:10 and consecrate them **t** and tomorrow.
32:29 have been set apart to the LORD **t**,
34:11 Obey what I command you **t**. I will
Lev 8:34 What has been done **t** was commanded
9: 4 For **t** the LORD will appear to you.'
10:19 Aaron replied to Moses, "**T** they
10:19 if I had eaten the sin offering **t**?"
Dt 1:10 that **t** you are as many as the stars
2:18 "**T** you are to pass by the region of
4: 4 the LORD your God are still alive **t**.
4: 8 of laws I am setting before you **t**?
4:38 for your inheritance, as it is **t**.
4:40 which I am giving you **t**, so that it
5: 1 laws I declare in your hearing **t**.
5: 3 with all of us who are alive here **t**.
5:24 **T** we have seen that a man can live
6: 6 These commandments that I give you **t**
6:24 and be kept alive, as is the case **t**.
7:11 decrees and laws I give you **t**.
8: 1 every command I am giving you **t**,
8:18 to your forefathers, as it is **t**.
8:19 I testify against you **t** that you
9: 3 be assured **t** that the LORD your God
10: 8 in his name, as they still do **t**.
10:13 I am giving you **t** for your own good?
10:15 above all the nations, as it is **t**.
11: 2 Remember **t** that your children were
11: 8 all the commands I am giving you **t**,
11:13 you **t**—to love the LORD your God
11:26 See, I am setting before you **t** a
11:27 LORD your God that I am giving you **t**
11:28 you **t** by following other gods,
11:32 and laws I am setting before you **t**.
12: 8 You are not to do as we do here **t**,
13:18 his commands that I am giving you **t**
15: 5 these commands I am giving you **t**.
15:15 is why I give you this command **t**.
19: 9 you **t**—to love the LORD your God
20: 3 He shall say: "Hear, O Israel, **t** you
26: 3 "I declare **t** to the LORD your God
27: 1 these commands that I give you **t**.
27: 4 you **t**, and coat them with plaster.
27:10 and decrees that I give you **t**."
28: 1 all his commands that I give you **t**,
28:14 any of the commands I give you **t**,
28:15 and decrees I am giving you **t**,
29:10 All of you are standing **t** in the
29:15 who are standing here with us **t** in
29:15 also with those who are not here **t**.
29:18 clan or tribe among you **t** whose
30: 2 to everything I command you **t**,
30: 8 all his commands I am giving you **t**.
30:11 Now what I am commanding you **t** is
30:15 See, I set before you **t** life and
30:16 For I command you **t** to love the LORD
Jos 3: 7 the LORD said to Joshua, "**T** I will
Jos 5: 9 the LORD said to Joshua, "**T** I have
7:25 The LORD will bring trouble on you **t**.
14:10 here I am **t**, eighty-five years old!
14:11 I am still as strong **t** as the day
22:18 'If you rebel against the LORD **t**,
22:29 turn away from him **t** by building an
22:31 "**T** we know that the LORD is with us,
Jdg 9:18 (but **t** you have revolted against my
9:19 towards Jerub-Baal and his family **t**,
12: 3 why have you come up **t** to fight me?"
21: 3 tribe be missing from Israel **t**?"
21: 6 "**T** one tribe is cut off from Israel,
Ru 2:19 "Where did you glean **t**? Where did
2:19 "The name of the man I worked with **t**
3:18 rest until the matter is settled **t**."
4: 9 "**T** you are witnesses that I have
4:10 town records. **T** you are witnesses!"
1Sa 4: 3 upon us **t** before the Philistines?
9: 9 of **t** used to be called a seer.)
9:12 now; he has just come to our town **t**,
9:19 for **t** you are to eat with me, and in
10: 2 you leave me **t**, you will meet two
11:13 "No-one shall be put to death **t**, for
14:28 'Cursed be any man who eats food **t**!'
14:30 have been if the men had eaten **t**
14:38 out what sin has been committed **t**.
14:45 for he did this **t** with God's help.
15:28 the kingdom of Israel from you **t**
17:46 **T** I will give the carcasses of the
20:27 to the meal, either yesterday or **t**?"
21: 5 How much more so **t**!"
22: 8 lie in wait for me, as he does **t**."
22:13 lies in wait for me, as he does **t**?"
24:19 well for the way you treated me **t**.
25:32 who has sent you **t** to meet me.
26: 8 Abishai said to David, "**T** God has
26:21 **t**, I will not try to harm you again.
26:23 The LORD gave you into my hands **t**,
26:24 surely as I valued your life **t**, so
27:10 "Where did you go raiding **t**?" David
28:18 the LORD has done this to you **t**.
2Sa 3:39 **t**, though I am the anointed king, I
6:20 Israel has distinguished himself **t**,
14:22 Joab said, "**T** your servant knows
15:20 You came only yesterday. And **t** shall
16: 3 '**T** the house of Israel will give me
16:12 for the cursing I am receiving **t**."
18:20 to take the news **t**," Joab told him.
18:20 **t**, because the king's son is dead."
18:31 The LORD has delivered you **t** from
19: 5 "**T** you have humiliated all your men,
19: 6 You have made it clear **t** that the
19: 6 alive **t** and all of us were dead.
19:20 but **t** I have come here as the first
19:22 anyone be put to death in Israel **t**?
19:22 know that **t** I am king over Israel?"
1Ki 1:25 **T** he has gone down and sacrificed
1:30 I will surely carry out **t** what I
1:48 to see a successor on my throne **t**.
1:51 'Let King Solomon swear to me **t** that
2:24 Adonijah shall be put to death **t**!"
5: 7 "Praise be to the LORD **t**, for he has
8: 8 Place; and they are still there **t**.
8:24 you have fulfilled it—as it is **t**.
12: 7 They replied, "If **t** you will be a
18:15 surely present myself to Ahab **t**."
18:36 let it be know **t** that you are God
20:13 I will give it into your hand **t**,
2Ki 2: 3 to take your master from you **t**?"
2: 5 to take your master from you **t**?"
4:23 "Why go to him **t**?" he asked. "It's
6:28 **t**, and tomorrow we'll eat my son.'
6:31 Shaphat remains on his shoulders **t**!"
1Ch 29: 5 to consecrate himself **t** to the LORD
2Ch 5: 9 Place; and they are still there **t**.
6:15 you have fulfilled it—as it is **t**.
Ezr 9: 7 hand of foreign kings, as it is **t**.
Ne 1:11 Give your servant success **t** by
9:32 of the kings of Assyria until **t**.
9:36 "But see, we are slaves **t**, slaves in
Est 5: 4 together with Haman, come **t** to a
Job 23: 2 "Even **t** my complaint is bitter; his
Ps 2: 7 my Son; **t** I have become your Father.
95: 7 **T**, if you hear his voice,
Pr 7:14 at home; **t** I fulfilled my vows.
22:19 the LORD, I teach you **t**, even you.

Isa 38:19 as I am doing **t**; fathers tell their
48: 7 you have not heard of them before **t**.
56:12 will be like **t**, or even far better."
58: 4 You cannot fast as you do **t** and
Jer 1:10 See, **t** I appoint you over nations
1:18 **T** I have made you a fortified city,
11: 5 and honey'—the land you possess **t**.
11: 7 forefathers up from Egypt until **t**,
25:18 scorn and cursing, as they are **t**;
40: 4 **t** I am freeing you from the chains
42:19 Be sure of this: I warn you **t**
42:21 I have told you **t**, but you still
44: 2 **T** they lie deserted and in ruins
44: 6 them the desolate ruins they are **t**.
44:22 without inhabitants, as it is **t**.
Mt 6:11 Give us **t** our daily bread.
6:30 which is here **t** and tomorrow is
16: 3 in the morning, '**T** it will be stormy
21:28 go and work **t** in the vineyard.'
27:19 deal **t** in a dream because of him."
Mk 14:30 "**t**—yes, tonight—before the cock
Lk 2:11 **T** in the town of David a Saviour has
4:21 he began by saying to them, "**T** this
5:26 "We have seen remarkable things **t**.
12:28 which is here **t**, and tomorrow is
13:32 and heal people **t** and tomorrow,
13:33 In any case, I must keep going **t** and
19: 5 I must stay at your house **t**."
19: 9 Jesus said to him, "**T** salvation has
22:34 Peter, before the cock crows **t**, you
22:61 **t**, you will disown me three times."
23:43 **t** you will be with me in paradise."
Ac 4: 9 If we are being called to account **t**
13:33 Son; **t** I have become your Father.',
20:26 Therefore, I declare to you **t** that I
22: 3 zealous for God as any of you are **t**.
24:21 that I am on trial before you **t**.
26: 2 fortunate to stand before you **t** as
26: 6 our fathers that I am on trial **t**.
26:29 to me **t** may become what I am,
Heb 1: 5 "You are my Son; **t** I have become
3: 7 So, as the Holy Spirit says: "**T**, if
3:13 as long as it is called **T**, so that
3:15 has just been said: "**T**, if you hear
4: 7 calling it **T**, when a long time later
4: 7 "**T**, if you hear his voice, do not
5: 5 Son; **t** I have become your Father.",
13: 8 same yesterday and **t** and for ever.
Jas 4:13 Now listen, you who say, "**T** or

Today's (Today)
Ac 19:40 with rioting because of **t** events.

Toe (Toes)
Lev 8:23 and on the big **t** of his right foot.
14:14 and on the big **t** of his right foot.
14:17 and on the big **t** of his right foot,
14:25 and on the big **t** of his right foot.
14:28 and on the big **t** of his right foot.

Toes (Toe)
Ex 29:20 on the big **t** of their right feet.
Lev 8:24 on the big **t** of their right feet.
Jdg 1: 6 and cut off his thumbs and big **t**.
1: 7 big **t** cut off have picked up scraps
2Sa 21:20 six **t** on each foot—twenty-four in
1Ch 20: 6 six **t** on each foot—twenty-four in
Da 2:41 Just as you saw that the feet and **t**
2:42 the **t** were partly iron and partly

Togarmah
Ge 10: 3 of Gomer: Ashkenaz, Riphath and **T**.
1Ch 1: 6 of Gomer: Ashkenaz, Riphath and **T**.

Tohu
1Sa 1: 1 **T**, the son of Zuph, an Ephraimite.

Toil (Toiled, Toiling, Toils, Toilsome)
Ge 3:17 through painful **t** you will eat of it
5:29 painful **t** of our hands caused by the
31:42 my hardship and the **t** of my hands,
Dt 26: 7 saw our misery, **t** and oppression.
Jos 24:13 not **t** and cities you did not build;
Pr 5:10 your **t** enrich another man's house.
Ecc 2:22 What does a man get for all the **t**
3: 9 What does the worker gain from his **t**?
3:13 all his **t**—this is the gift of God.
4: 6 with **t** and chasing after the wind.
4: 8 There was no end to his **t**, yet his
Isa 65:23 They will not **t** in vain or bear
Lam 5:13 Young men **t** at the millstones; boys
1Th 2: 9 Surely you remember, brothers, our **t**

Toiled (Toil)
Job 20:18 What he **t** for he must give back
Ps 105:44 fell heir to what others had **t** for—
Ecc 2:11 done and what I had **t** to achieve,
2:18 I hated all the things I had **t** for
Isa 62: 8 the new wine for which you have **t**;
2Co 11:27 I have laboured and **t** and have often

Toiling (Toil)
Ps 127: 2 **t** for food to eat—for he grants
Ecc 4: 8 "For whom am I **t**," he asked, "and
2Th 3: 8 labouring and **t** so that we would not

Toils (Toil)
Ecc 1: 3 labour at which he **t** under the sun?
5:16 he gain, since he **t** for the wind?

Toilsome (Toil)
Ecc 2:20 over all my **t** labour under the sun.
5:18 find satisfaction in his **t** labour
9: 9 and in your **t** labour under the sun.

Token
1Ch 4:32 Rimmon, **T** and Ashan—five towns—

Tokhath
2Ch 34:22 was the wife of Shallum son of **T**,

Tola (Tolaite)
Ge 46:13 The sons of Issachar: **T**, Puah,
Nu 26:23 by their clans were: through **T**,
Jdg 10: 1 **T** son of Puah, the son of Dodo, rose
1Ch 7: 1 The sons of Issachar: **T**, Puah,
7: 2 The sons of **T**: Uzzi, Rephaiah,
7: 2 the descendants of **T** listed as

Tolad
1Ch 4:29 Bilhah, Ezem, **T**,

Tolaite (Tola)
Nu 26:23 through Tola, the **T** clan; through

Tolerance (Tolerate)
Ro 2: 4 **t** and patience, not realising that

Tolerate (Tolerance, Tolerated)
Est 3: 8 the king's best interest to **t** them.
Hab 1: 3 Why do you **t** wrong? Destruction and
1:13 to look on evil; you cannot **t** wrong.
1:13 Why then do you **t** the treacherous?
Rev 2: 2 I know that you cannot **t** wicked men,
2:20 I have this against you: You **t** that

Tolerated (Tolerate)
Est 3: 4 Mordecai's behaviour would be **t**,

Tomb (Tombs, Tombstone)
Ge 23: 6 you his **t** for burying your dead."
35:20 Over her **t** Jacob set up a pillar,
35:20 day that pillar marks Rachel's **t**.
50: 5 "I am about to die; bury me in the **t**
Jdg 8:32 was buried in the **t** of his father
16:31 in the **t** of Manoah his father.
1Sa 10: 2 will meet two men near Rachel's **t**,
2Sa 2:32 him in his father's **t** at Bethlehem.
3:32 the king wept aloud at Abner's **t**.
4:12 buried it in Abner's **t** at Hebron.
17:23 and was buried in his father's **t**.
19:37 near the **t** of my father and mother.
21:14 in the **t** of Saul's father Kish,
1Ki 13:22 be buried in the **t** of your fathers.
13:30 he laid the body in his own **t**, and
2Ki 9:28 in his **t** in the City of David.
2Ki 13:21 the man's body into Elisha's **t**.
23:17 "It marks the **t** of the man of God
23:30 and buried him in his own **t**.
2Ch 16:14 They buried him in the **t** that he had
Job 21:32 grave, and watch is kept over his **t**.
Isa 14:18 lie in state, each in his own **t**.
14:19 you are cast out of your **t** like a
Mt 27:60 placed it in his own new **t** that he
27:60 the entrance to the **t** and went away.
27:61 were sitting there opposite the **t**.
27:64 give the order for the **t** to be made
27:65 the **t** as secure as you know how."
27:66 they went and made the **t** secure by
28: 1 other Mary went to look at the **t**.
28: 2 going to the **t**, rolled back the
28: 8 the women hurried away from the **t**,
Mk 6:29 took his body and laid it in a **t**.
15:46 placed it in a **t** cut out of rock.
15:46 stone against the entrance of the **t**.
16: 2 they were on their way to the **t**
16: 3 away from the entrance of the **t**?"
16: 5 they entered the **t**, they saw a young
16: 8 women went out and fled from the **t**.
Lk 23:53 placed it in a **t** cut in the rock,
23:55 **t** and how his body was laid in it.
24: 1 they had prepared and went to the **t**.
24: 2 the stone rolled away from the **t**,
24: 9 they came back from the **t**, they told
24:12 however, got up and ran to the **t**.
24:22 They went to the **t** early this
24:24 some of our companions went to the **t**
Jn 11:17 already been in the **t** for four days.
11:31 was going to the **t** to mourn there.
11:38 more deeply moved, came to the **t**.
12:17 when he called Lazarus from the **t**
19:41 and in the garden a new **t**, in which
19:42 **t** was near by, they laid Jesus there
20: 1 Mary Magdalene went to the **t** and saw
20: 2 have taken the Lord out of the **t**,
20: 3 other disciple started for the **t**.
20: 4 Peter and reached the **t** first.
20: 6 him, arrived and went into the **t**.
20: 8 the **t** first, also went inside.
20:11 Mary stood outside the **t** crying. As
20:11 she bent over to look into the **t**
Ac 2:29 and his **t** is here to this day.
7:16 placed in the **t** that Abraham had
13:29 from the tree and laid him in a **t**.

Tombs (Tomb)
Ge 23: 6 your dead in the choicest of our **t**.
2Ki 23:16 and when he saw the **t** that were
2Ch 21:20 David, but not in the **t** of the kings
24:25 David, but not in the **t** of the kings
28:27 in the **t** of the kings of Israel.
32:33 the **t** of David's descendants are.
35:24 He was buried in the **t** of his
Ne 3:16 to a point opposite the **t** of David,
Ps 49:11 Their **t** will remain their houses for
Mt 8:28 men coming from the **t** met him.
23:27 You are like whitewashed **t**,
23:29 you hypocrites! You build **t** for the
27:52 The **t** broke open and the bodies of
27:53 They came out of the **t**, and after
Mk 5: 2 spirit came from the **t** to meet him.
5: 3 This man lived in the **t**, and no-one
5: 5 Night and day among the **t** and in the
Lk 8:27 in a house, but had lived in the **t**.
11:47 "Woe to you, because you build **t** for
11:48 the prophets, and you build their **t**.

Tombstone (Stone, Tomb)
2Ki 23:17 The king asked, "What is that **t** I

Tomorrow
Ex 8:10 "**T**," Pharaoh said. Moses replied,
8:23 This miraculous sign will occur **t**.'
8:29 I will pray to the LORD, and **t** the
9: 5 The LORD set a time and said, "**T** the
9:18 Therefore, at this time **t** I will
10: 4 bring locusts into your country **t**.
16:23 '**T** is to be a day of rest, a holy
17: 9 **T** I will stand on top of the hill
19:10 and consecrate them today and **t**.
32: 5 "**T** there will be a festival to the

Nu 11:18 for **t**, when you will eat meat.
14:25 turn back **t** and set out towards the
16: 7 **t** put fire and incense in them
16:16 the LORD **t**—you and they and Aaron.
Jos 3: 5 "Consecrate yourselves, for **t** the
7:13 in preparation for **t**; for this is
11: 6 because by this time **t** I will hand
22:18 **t** he will be angry with the whole
Jdg 19: 9 Stay and enjoy yourself. Early **t**
20:28 **t** I will give them into your hands."
1Sa 9:16 "About this time **t** I will send you a
11: 9 sun is hot **t**, you will be delivered.
11:10 They said to the Ammonites, "**T** we
19: 2 Be on your guard **t** morning; go into
19:11 life tonight, **t** you'll be killed."
20: 5 David said, "Look, **t** is the New Moon
20: 5 the evening of the day after **t**.
20:12 father by this time the day after **t**!
20:18 Jonathan said to David: "**T** is the
20:19 The day after **t**, towards evening, go
28:19 **t** you and your sons will be with me.
2Sa 11:12 day, and **t** I will send you back.
1Ki 19: 2 if by this time **t** I do not make your
20: 6 about this time **t** I am going to send
2Ki 6:28 him today, and **t** we'll eat my son.'
7: 1 the LORD says: About this time **t**,
7:18 "About this time **t**, a seah of flour
10: 6 to me in Jezreel by this time **t**.
2Ch 20:16 **T** march down against them. They will
20:17 Go out to face them **t**, and the LORD
Est 5: 8 let the king and Haman come **t** to the
5:12 invited me along with the king **t**.
9:13 carry out this day's edict **t** also,
Pr 3:28 I'll give it **t**"—when you now have
27: 1 Do not boast about **t**, for you do not
Isa 22:13 drink," you say, "for **t** we die!"
56:12 of beer! And **t** will be like today,
Mt 6:30 which is here today and **t** is thrown
6:34 do not worry about **t**, for **t** will
Lk 12:28 which is here today, and **t** is thrown
13:32 demons and heal people today and **t**,
13:33 I must keep going today and **t** and
Ac 23:20 bring Paul before the Sanhedrin **t**
25:22 He replied, "**T** you will hear him."
1Co 15:32 "Let us eat and drink, for **t** we die.
Jas 4:13 Now listen, you who say, "Today or **t**
4:14 do not even know what will happen **t**.

Tone

Gal 4:20 change my **t**, because I am perplexed

Tongs

1Ki 7:49 gold floral work and lamps and **t**;
2Ch 4:21 the gold floral work and lamps and **t**
Isa 6: 6 he had taken with **t** from the altar.

Tongue (Tongues)

Ex 4:10 I am slow of speech and **t**."
2Sa 23: 2 through me; his word was on my **t**.
Est 1:22 proclaiming in each people's **t** that
Job 5:21 be protected from the lash of the **t**,
12:11 Does not the ear test words as the **t**
15: 5 you adopt the **t** of the crafty.
20:12 mouth and he hides it under his **t**,
27: 4 and my **t** will utter no deceit.
33: 2 my words are on the tip of my **t**.
34: 3 For the ear tests words as the **t**
41: 1 or tie down his **t** with a rope?
Ps 5: 9 with their **t** they speak deceit.
10: 7 trouble and evil are under his **t**.
12: 3 flattering lips and every boastful **t**
15: 3 has no slander on his **t**, who does
16: 9 my heart is glad and my **t** rejoices
22:15 and my **t** sticks to the roof of my
34:13 keep your **t** from evil and your lips
35:28 My **t** will speak of your
37:30 and his **t** speaks what is just.
39: 1 "I will watch my ways and keep my **t**
39: 3 fire burned; then I spoke with my **t**:
45: 1 my **t** is the pen of a skilful writer.
50:19 evil and harness your **t** to deceit.
51:14 **t** will sing of your righteousness.
52: 2 Your **t** plots destruction; it is like
52: 4 harmful word, O you deceitful **t**!
66:17 my mouth; his praise was on my **t**.
Ps 71:24 My **t** will tell of your righteous
114: 1 of Jacob from a people of foreign **t**,
119:172 May my **t** sing of your word, for all
120: 3 what more besides, O deceitful **t**?
137: 6 May my **t** cling to the roof of my
139: 4 Before a word is on my **t** you know it
Pr 6:17 haughty eyes, a lying **t**, hands that
6:24 the smooth **t** of the wayward wife.
10:19 but he who holds his **t** is wise.
10:20 The **t** of the righteous is choice
10:31 but a perverse **t** will be cut out.
11:12 a man of understanding holds his **t**.
12:18 the **t** of the wise brings healing.
12:19 but a lying **t** lasts only a moment.
15: 2 The **t** of the wise commends knowledge,
15: 4 The **t** that brings healing is a tree
15: 4 a deceitful **t** crushes the spirit.
16: 1 the LORD comes the reply of the **t**.
17: 4 pays attention to a malicious **t**.
17:20 **t** is deceitful falls into trouble.
17:28 and discerning if he holds his **t**.
18:21 The **t** has the power of life and
21: 6 A fortune made by a lying **t** is a
21:23 He who guards his mouth and his **t**
25:15 and a gentle **t** can break a bone.
25:23 a north wind brings rain, so a sly **t**
26:28 A lying **t** hates those it hurts, and
28:23 than he who has a flattering **t**.
31:26 faithful instruction is on her **t**.
SS 4:11 milk and honey are under your **t**.
Isa 30:27 and his **t** is a consuming fire.
32: 4 the stammering **t** will be fluent and
33:19 their strange, incomprehensible **t**.
35: 6 deer, and the mute **t** shout for joy.
45:23 will bow; by me every **t** will swear.
50: 4 LORD has given me an instructed **t**,
54:17 refute every **t** that accuses you.
57: 4 you sneer and stick out your **t**?
59: 3 and your **t** mutters wicked things.
Jer 9: 3 "They make ready their **t** like a bow,
9: 8 Their **t** is a deadly arrow; it speaks
Lam 4: 4 of thirst the infant's **t** sticks to
Eze 3:26 I will make your **t** stick to the roof
Mk 7:33 Then he spat and touched the man's **t**
7:35 the man's ears were opened, his **t**
Lk 1:64 was opened and his **t** was loosed,
16:24 his finger in water and cool my **t**,
Ac 2:26 Therefore my heart is glad and my **t**
Ro 14:11 me; every **t** will confess to God.
1Co 14: 2 For anyone who speaks in a **t** does
14: 4 He who speaks in a **t** edifies himself,
14: 9 intelligible words with your **t**,
14:13 who speaks in a **t** should pray that
14:14 For if I pray in a **t**, my spirit
14:19 than ten thousand words in a **t**.
14:26 a **t** or an interpretation.
14:27 If anyone speaks in a **t**, two—or at
Php 2:11 every **t** confess that Jesus Christ is
Jas 1:26 does not keep a tight rein on his **t**,
3: 5 Likewise the **t** is a small part of
3: 6 The **t** also is a fire, a world of
3: 8 no man can tame the **t**. It is a
3: 9 With the **t** we praise our Lord and
1Pe 3:10 see good days must keep his **t** from
1Jn 3:18 with words or **t** but with actions

Tongues (Tongue)

Jdg 7: 5 who lap the water with their **t**
Job 29:10 **t** stuck to the roof of their mouths.
Ps 12: 4 "We will triumph with our **t**; we own
31:20 you keep them safe from accusing **t**.
57: 4 arrows, whose **t** are sharp swords.
64: 3 They sharpen their **t** like swords and
64: 8 He will turn their own **t** against
68:23 **t** of your dogs have their share."
73: 9 **t** take possession of the earth.
78:36 mouths, lying to him with their **t**;
109: 2 have spoken against me with lying **t**.
120: 2 lying lips and from deceitful **t**.
126: 2 laughter, our **t** with songs of joy.
140: 3 They make their **t** as sharp as a
Isa 5:24 Therefore, as **t** of fire lick up
28:11 **t** God will speak to this people,
41:17 their **t** are parched with thirst.
66:18 come and gather all nations and **t**,
Jer 9: 5 They have taught their **t** to lie;
18:18 So come, let's attack him with our **t**
23:31 who wag their own **t** and yet declare,
Mic 6:12 liars and their **t** speak deceitfully.
Zec 14:12 their **t** will rot in their mouths.
Mk 16:17 demons; they will speak in new **t**;
Ac 2: 3 They saw what seemed to be **t** of fire
2: 4 other **t** as the Spirit enabled them.
2:11 the wonders of God in our own **t**!"
10:46 For they heard them speaking in **t**
19: 6 and they spoke in **t** and prophesied.
Ro 3:13 graves; their **t** practise deceit.
1Co 12:10 speaking in different kinds of **t**,
12:10 another the interpretation of **t**.
12:28 speaking in different kinds of **t**.
12:30 Do all speak in **t**? Do all interpret?
13: 1 If I speak in the **t** of men and of
13: 8 they will cease; where there are **t**,
14: 5 like every one of you to speak in **t**,
14: 5 is greater than one who speaks in **t**,
14: 6 if I come to you and speak in **t**,
14:18 I thank God that I speak in **t** more
14:21 "Through men of strange **t** and
14:22 **T**, then, are a sign, not for
14:23 together and everyone speaks in **t**,
14:39 and do not forbid speaking in **t**.
Rev 16:10 Men gnawed their **t** in agony

Tonight

Ge 19: 5 Where are the men who came to you **t**?
19:34 Let's get him to drink wine again **t**,
30:15 **t** in return for your son's mandrakes.
Nu 22:19 Now stay here **t** as the others did,
Jos 2: 2 come here **t** to spy out the land."
4: 3 down at the place where you stay **t**."
Jdg 19: 6 "Please stay **t** and enjoy yourself.
Ru 1:12 even if I had a husband **t** and then
3: 2 a kinsman of ours? **T** he will be
1Sa 19:11 life **t**, tomorrow you'll be killed."
2Sa 17: 1 and set out **t** in pursuit of David.
Mk 14:30 "today—yes, **t**—before the cock
Ac 23:23 to go to Caesarea at nine **t**.

Tool (Tools)

Ex 20:25 will defile it if you use a **t** on it.
32: 4 of a calf, fashioning it with a **t**.
Dt 27: 5 Do not use any iron **t** upon them.
Jos 8:31 on which no iron **t** had been used.
2Sa 23: 7 Whoever touches thorns uses a **t** of
1Ki 6: 7 chisel or any other iron **t** was heard
Job 19:24 inscribed with an iron **t** on lead,
Isa 44:12 The blacksmith takes a **t** and works
Jer 17: 1 sin is engraved with an iron **t**,

Tools (Tool)

Ge 4:22 kinds of **t** out of bronze and iron.

Tooth (Teeth)

Ex 21:24 eye for eye, **t** for **t**, hand for hand,
21:27 if he knocks out the **t** of a
21:27 go free to compensate for the **t**.
Lev 24:20 for fracture, eye for eye, **t** for **t**.
Dt 19:21 eye for eye, **t** for **t**, hand for hand,
Pr 25:19 Like a bad **t** or a lame foot is
Mt 5:38 said, 'Eye for eye, and **t** for **t**.'

Topaz

Ex 28:17 shall be a ruby, a **t** and a beryl;
39:10 there was a ruby, a **t** and a beryl;
Job 28:19 The **t** of Cush cannot compare with it;
Eze 28:13 **t** and emerald, chrysolite, onyx and
Rev 21:20 the eighth beryl, the ninth **t**, the

Tophel

Dt 1: 1 and **T**, Laban, Hazeroth and Dizahab.

Topheth

2Ki 23:10 He desecrated **T**, which was in the
Isa 30:33 **T** has long been prepared; it has
Jer 7:31 They have built the high places of **T**
7:32 it **T** or the Valley of Ben Hinnom,
7:32 in **T** until there is no more room.
19: 6 place **T** or the Valley of Ben Hinnom,
19:11 in **T** until there is no more room.

Jer 19:12 I will make this city like T.
19:13 T—all the houses where they burned
19:14 Jeremiah then returned from T, where

Topple

Ps 62: 4 They fully intend to t him from his
Isa 40:20 to set up an idol that will not t.
41: 7 down the idol so that it will not t.

Torch (Torches)

Ge 15:17 a smoking brazier with a blazing t
Jdg 15: 4 fastened a t to every pair of tails,
Isa 62: 1 her salvation like a blazing t.
Zec 12: 6 like a flaming t among sheaves.
Rev 8:10 and a great star, blazing like a t,

Torches (Torch)

Jdg 7:16 hands of all of them, with t inside.
7:20 Grasping the t in their left hands
15: 5 lit the t and let the foxes loose in
Isa 50:11 provide yourselves with flaming t,
50:11 and of the t you have set ablaze.
Eze 1:13 burning coals of fire or like t.
Da 10: 6 his eyes like flaming t, his arms
Na 2: 4 They look like flaming t; they dart
Jn 18: 3 carrying t, lanterns and weapons.

Tore (Tear[2])

Ge 37:29 was not there, he t his clothes.
37:34 Jacob t his clothes, put on
44:13 At this, they t their clothes. Then
Nu 14: 6 explored the land, t their clothes
Jos 7: 6 Joshua t his clothes and fell face
Jdg 11:35 he saw her, he t his clothes and
14: 6 t the lion apart with his bare hands
16: 3 and t them loose, bar and all.
1Sa 15:27 of the hem of his robe, and it t.
2Sa 1:11 hold of their clothes and t them.
13:19 Tamar put ashes on her head and t
13:31 The king stood up, t his clothes and
1Ki 11:30 wearing and t it into twelve pieces.
14: 8 I t the kingdom away from the house
19:11 Then a great and powerful wind t
21:27 Ahab heard these words, he t his
2Ki 2:12 of his own clothes and t them apart.
5: 7 he t his robes and said, "Am I God?
6:30 the woman's words, he t his robes.
10:27 Baal and t down the temple of Baal,
11:14 Then Athaliah t her robes and called
11:18 to the temple of Baal and t it down.
17:21 he t Israel away from the house of
19: 1 King Hezekiah heard this, he t his
22:11 the Book of the Law, he t his robes.
22:19 and because you t your robes and
23: 7 He also t down the quarters of the
2Ch 23:13 Then Athaliah t her robes and
23:17 to the temple of Baal and t it down.
34: 7 he t down the altars and the Asherah
34:19 words of the Law, he t his robes.
34:27 t your robes and wept in my presence,
Ezr 9: 3 I heard this, I t my tunic and cloak,
Est 4: 1 he t his clothes, put on sackcloth
Job 1:20 At this, Job got up and t his robe
2:12 and they t their robes and sprinkled
Isa 22:10 t down houses to strengthen the wall.
37: 1 King Hezekiah heard this, he t his
Jer 2:20 yoke and t off your bonds; you said,
Eze 29: 7 you splintered and you t open their
Mt 26:65 the high priest t his clothes and
Mk 5: 4 but he t the chains apart and broke
14:63 The high priest t his clothes. "Why
Ac 14:14 they t their clothes and rushed out

Torment (Tormented, Tormenting, Tormentors)

Job 13:25 Will you t a wind-blown leaf? Will
15:20 his days the wicked man suffers t
19: 2 "How long will you t me and crush me
Isa 50:11 my hand: You will lie down in t.
Lam 1:20 how distressed I am! I am in t
2:11 My eyes fail from weeping, I am in t
Lk 16:23 In hell, where he was in t, he
16:28 not also come to this place of t.'
2Co 12: 7 a messenger of Satan, to t me.
Rev 9:10 power to t people for five months.
14:11 the smoke of their t rises for ever
18:10 Terrified at her t, they will stand
18:15 stand far off, terrified at her t.

Tormented (Torment)

1Sa 16:14 an evil spirit from the LORD t him.
Pr 28:17 A man t by the guilt of murder will
Ac 5:16 bringing their sick and those t by
2Pe 2: 8 was t in his righteous soul by the
Rev 11:10 had t those who live on earth.
14:10 He will be t with burning sulphur in
20:10 t day and night for ever and ever.

Tormenting (Torment)

1Sa 16:15 an evil spirit from God is t you.

Tormentors (Torment)

Ps 137: 3 our t demanded songs of joy; they
Isa 51:23 put it into the hands of your t,

Torn (Tear[2])

Ge 31:39 I did not bring you animals t by
37:33 Joseph has surely been t to pieces."
44:28 "He has surely been t to pieces.
Ex 22:13 If it was t to pieces by a wild
22:13 be required to pay for the t animal.
22:31 meat of an animal t by wild beasts;
Lev 7:24 The fat of an animal found dead or t
13:45 disease must wear t clothes,
14:40 the contaminated stones be t out
14:43 after the stones have been t out
14:45 must be t down—its stones, timbers
17:15 who eats anything found dead or t by
22: 8 found dead or t by wild animals,
22:24 are bruised, crushed, t or cut.
Jdg 14: 6 as he might have t a young goat.
1Sa 4:12 his clothes t and dust on his head.
15:28 Samuel said to him, "The LORD has t
28:17 The LORD has t the kingdom out of
2Sa 1: 2 clothes t and with dust on his head.
13:31 stood by with their clothes t.
15:32 his robe t and dust on his head.
2Ki 5: 8 the king of Israel had t his robes,
5: 8 "Why have you t your robes? Make the
18:37 with their clothes t, and told him
2Ch 34: 4 the altars of the Baals were t down;
Ezr 9: 5 with my tunic and cloak t, and fell
Job 8:18 is t from its spot, that place
18:14 He is t from the security of his
Ps 60: 2 You have shaken the land and t it
124: 6 has not let us be t by their teeth.
Pr 2:22 the unfaithful will be t from it.
Isa 36:22 with their clothes t, and told him
Jer 5: 5 off the yoke and t off the bonds.
13:22 t off and your body ill-treated.
18: 7 be uprooted, t down and destroyed,
33: 4 that have been t down to be used
41: 5 t their clothes and cut themselves
50:15 towers fall, her walls are t down.
Lam 2: 2 in his wrath he has t down the
Eze 4:14 found dead or t by wild animals.
30: 4 away and her foundations t down.
44:31 found dead or t by wild animals.
Da 7: 4 I watched until its wings were t off
Hos 6: 1 He has t us to pieces but he will
Mt 27:51 was t in two from top to bottom.
Mk 1:10 he saw heaven being t open and the
15:38 The curtain of the temple was t in
Lk 5:36 If he does, he will have t the new
23:45 curtain of the temple was t in two.
Jn 21:11 even with so many the net was not t.
Ac 21: 1 After we had t ourselves away from
23:10 Paul would be t to pieces by them.
Ro 11: 3 prophets and t down your altars;
Gal 4:15 t out your eyes and given them to me.
Php 1:23 I am t between the two: I desire to
1Th 2:17 But, brothers, when we were t away

Torrent (Torrents)

Ps 124: 4 us, the t would have swept over us,
Isa 30:28 His breath is like a rushing t,
Jer 47: 2 they will become an overflowing t.
Lk 6:48 When the flood came, the t struck
6:49 The moment the t struck that house,
Rev 12:15 woman and sweep her away with the t.

Torrents (Torrent)

2Sa 22: 5 the t of destruction overwhelmed me.
Job 14:19 water wears away stones and t wash
38:25 Who cuts a channel for the t of rain,
Ps 18: 4 the t of destruction overwhelmed me.
Eze 13:11 Rain will come in t, and I will send
13:13 and in my anger hailstones and t of
38:22 I will pour down t of rain,
Hab 3:10 T of water swept by; the deep

Torture (Tortured)

Mt 8:29 to t us before the appointed time?"
Mk 5: 7 Swear to God that you won't t me!"
Lk 8:28 High God? I beg you, don't t me!"
Rev 9: 5 but only to t them for five months.
18: 7 Give her as much t and grief as the

Tortured (Torture)

Mt 18:34 him over to the jailers to be t,
Heb 11:35 Others were t and refused to be

Toss (Tossed, Tosses, Tossing)

Ex 9: 8 have Moses t it into the air in the
Job 7: 4 night drags on, and I t till dawn.
30:22 wind; you t me about in the storm.
Ps 60: 8 washbasin, upon Edom I t my sandal;
108: 9 washbasin, upon Edom I t my sandal;
Mt 15:26 bread and t it to their dogs."
Mk 7:27 bread and t it to their dogs."

Tossed (Toss)

Ex 9:10 Moses t it into the air, and
Eph 4:14 we will no longer be infants, t back
Jas 1: 6 of the sea, blown and t by the wind.

Tosses (Toss)

2Ki 19:21 of Jerusalem t her head as you flee.
Isa 37:22 of Jerusalem t her head as you flee.

Tossing (Toss)

Isa 57:20 the wicked are like the t sea, which
Lk 21:25 at the roaring and t of the sea.

Totter (Tottering)

Jer 10: 4 and nails so that it will not t.

Tottering (Totter)

Ps 62: 3 this leaning wall, this t fence?

Tou

2Sa 8: 9 T king of Hamath heard that David
8:10 who had been at war with T.
1Ch 18: 9 T king of Hamath heard that David
18:10 who had been at war with T.

Touch (Touched, Touches, Touching)

Ge 3: 3 you must not t it, or you will die.
20: 6 That is why I did not let you t her.
27:21 "Come near so I can t you, my son,
Ex 12:13 will t you when I strike Egypt.
19:12 up the mountain or t the foot of it.
Lev 11: 8 You must not eat their meat or t
12: 4 She must not t anything sacred or go
Nu 4:15 But they must not t the holy things
16:26 Do not t anything belonging to them,
Dt 14: 8 eat their meat or t their carcasses.
28:56 would not venture to t the ground
Jos 9:19 of Israel, and we cannot t them now.
Ru 2: 9 I have told the men not to t you.
1Sa 24:12 to me, but my hand will not t you.
24:13 deeds,' so my hand will not t you.
2Sa 21:10 not let the birds of the air t them
1Ch 16:22 "Do not t my anointed ones; do my
Job 6: 7 I refuse to t it; such food makes me
Ps 105:15 "Do not t my anointed ones; do my
144: 5 t the mountains, so that they smoke.
Isa 28:15 it cannot t us, for we have made a
52:11 out from there! T no unclean thing!
Jer 13: 1 waist, but do not let it t water."

Jer 14:15 sword or famine will t this land.
Lam 4:14 no-one dares to t their garments.
4:15 "Away! Away! Don't t us!" When they
Eze 9: 6 do not t anyone who has the mark.
Mt 9:21 She said to herself, "If I only t
14:36 begged him to let the sick just t
Mk 3:10 were pushing forward to t him.
5:28 she thought, "If I just t his
6:56 They begged him to let them t even
8:22 blind man and begged Jesus to t him.
10:13 to Jesus to have him t them,
Lk 6:19 the people all tried to t him,
18:15 babies to Jesus to have him t them.
24:39 It is I myself! T me and see; a
2Co 6:17 T no unclean thing, and I will
Col 2:21 handle! Do not taste! Do not t!"?
Heb 11:28 would not t the firstborn of Israel.

Touched (Touch)

Ge 27:22 who t him and said, "The voice is
32:25 he t the socket of Jacob's hip so
32:32 Jacob's hip was t near the tendon.
Ex 4:25 foreskin and t Moses' feet with it.
Nu 19:18 sprinkle anyone who has t a human
31:19 who have killed anyone or t anyone
Jos 3:15 and their feet t the water's edge,
16: 7 t Jericho and came out at the Jordan.
19:11 Going west it ran to Maralah, t
19:22 The boundary t Tabor, Shahazumah and
19:26 t Carmel and Shihor Libnath.
19:27 t Zebulun and the Valley of Iphtah
19:34 It t Zebulun on the south, Asher on
Jdg 6:21 t the meat and the unleavened bread.
1Sa 10:26 valiant men whose hearts God had t.
1Ki 6:27 The wing of one cherub t one wall,
6:27 while the wing of the other t the
6:27 and their wings t each other in the
19: 5 All at once an angel t him and said,
19: 7 a second time and t him and said,
2Ki 13:21 When the body t Elisha's bones, the
2Ch 3:11 cubits long and t the temple wall,
3:11 t the wing of the other cherub.
3:12 long and t the other temple wall,
3:12 t the wing of the first cherub.
Est 5: 2 and t the tip of the sceptre.
Isa 6: 7 With it he t my mouth and said, "See,
6: 7 "See, this has t your lips; your
Jer 1: 9 the LORD reached out his hand and t
Eze 1: 9 their wings t one another. Each one
Da 4:11 and strong and its top t the sky;
8:18 he t me and raised me to my feet.
10: 3 no meat or wine t my lips; and I
10:10 A hand t me and set me trembling on
10:16 one who looked like a man t my lips,
10:18 the one who looked like a man t me
Mt 8: 3 Jesus reached out his hand and t the
8:15 He t her hand and the fever left her,
9:20 him and t the edge of his cloak.
9:29 he t their eyes and said, "According
14:36 and all who t him were healed.
17: 7 Jesus came and t them. "Get up," he
20:34 Jesus had compassion on them and t
Mk 1:41 reached out his hand and t the man.
5:27 him in the crowd and t his cloak,
5:30 crowd and asked, "Who t my clothes?
5:31 and yet you can ask, 'Who t me?'
6:56 and all who t him were healed.
7:33 Then he spat and t the man's tongue.
Lk 5:13 Jesus reached out his hand and t the
7:14 he went up and t the coffin, and
8:44 She came up behind him and t the
8:45 "Who t me?" Jesus asked. When they
8:46 Jesus said, "Someone t me; I know
8:47 she told why she had t him and how
22:51 he t the man's ear and healed him.
Ac 19:12 had t him were taken to the sick,
Heb 12:18 be t and that is burning with fire;
1Jn 1: 1 our hands have t—this we proclaim

Touches (Touch)

Ge 27:12 What if my father t me? I would
Ex 19:12 Whoever t the mountain shall surely
29:37 and whatever t it will be holy.
30:29 and whatever t them will be holy.
Lev 5: 2 "'Or if a person t anything
Lev 5: 3 "'Or if he t human uncleanness
6:18 Whatever t it will become holy.'
6:27 Whatever t any of the flesh will
7:19 "'Meat that t anything ceremonially
7:21 If anyone t something unclean
11:24 whoever t their carcasses will be
11:26 whoever t the carcass of any of them
11:27 whoever t their carcasses will be
11:31 Whoever t them when they are dead
11:36 t one of these carcasses is unclean.
11:39 anyone who t the carcass will be
15: 5 Anyone who t his bed must wash his
15: 7 "'Whoever t the man who has a
15:10 whoever t any of the things that
15:11 "'Anyone the man with a discharge t
15:12 "'A clay pot that the man t must be
15:19 t her will be unclean till evening.
15:21 Whoever t her bed must wash his
15:22 Whoever t anything she sits on must
15:23 when anyone t it, he will be unclean
15:24 with her and her monthly flow t him,
15:27 Whoever t them will be unclean; he
22: 4 He will also be unclean if he t
22: 5 or if he t any crawling thing that
22: 6 The one who t any such thing will be
Nu 19:11 "Whoever t the dead body of anyone
19:13 Whoever t the dead body of anyone
19:16 "Anyone out in the open who t
19:16 or anyone who t a human bone or a
19:21 and anyone who t the water of
19:22 Anything that an unclean person t
19:22 t it becomes unclean till evening."
2Sa 23: 7 Whoever t thorns uses a tool of iron
Job 20: 6 heavens and his head t the clouds,
Ps 104:32 who t the mountains, and they smoke.
Pr 6:29 no-one who t her will go unpunished.
Am 9: 5 the LORD Almighty, he who t the earth
Hag 2:12 and that fold t some bread or stew,
2:13 a dead body t one of these things,
Zec 2: 8 t you t the apple of his eye—
Heb 12:20 t the mountain, it must be stoned."

Touching (Touch)

Eze 1:11 one t the wing of another creature
Da 4:20 with its top t the sky, visible to
8: 5 whole earth without t the ground.
Lk 7:39 he would know who is t him and what

Towel

Jn 13: 4 and wrapped a t round his waist.
13: 5 the t that was wrapped round him.

Tower (Towered, Towering, Towers, Watchtower, Watchtowers)

Ge 11: 4 with a t that reaches to the heavens,
11: 5 the t that the men were building.
Jdg 8: 9 triumph, I will tear down this t."
8:17 He also pulled down the t of Peniel
9:46 the citizens in the t of Shechem
9:49 the people in the t of Shechem
9:51 however, was a strong t, to which
9:51 in and climbed up on the t roof.
9:52 Abimelech went to the t and stormed
9:52 entrance to the t to set it on fire,
2Ki 9:17 the lookout standing on the t in
Ne 3: 1 building as far as the T of the
3: 1 and as far as the T of Hananel.
3:11 section and the T of the Ovens.
3:25 the t projecting from the upper
3:26 the east and the projecting t.
3:27 projecting t to the wall of Ophel.
12:38 T of the Ovens to the Broad Wall,
12:39 the T of Hananel and the T of the
Ps 61: 3 refuge, a strong t against the foe.
Pr 18:10 The name of the LORD is a strong t;
SS 4: 4 Your neck is like the t of David,
7: 4 Your neck is like an ivory t. Your
7: 4 Your nose is like the t of Lebanon
Isa 2:15 for every lofty t and every
Jer 31:38 the T of Hananel to the Corner Gate.
Eze 31:14 are ever to t proudly on high,
Zec 14:10 from the T of Hananel to the royal
Lk 13: 4 Or those eighteen who died when the t
14:28 one of you wants to build a t.

Towered (Tower)

Eze 19:11 t high above the thick foliage,
31: 3 the forest; it t on high, its top
31: 5 t higher than all the trees of the
31:10 LORD says: Because it t on high,

Towering (Tower)

Isa 2:14 for all the t mountains and all the

Towers (Tower)

2Ch 14: 7 round them, with t, gates and bars.
26: 9 Uzziah built t in Jerusalem at the
26:10 He also built t in the desert and
26:15 by skilful men for use on the t
27: 4 and forts and t in the wooded areas.
32: 5 of the wall and building t on it.
Ps 48:12 Zion, go round her, count her t,
SS 8: 9 If she is a wall, we will build t of
8:10 a wall, and my breasts are like t.
Isa 23:13 they raised up their siege t,
29: 3 I will encircle you with t and set
30:25 when the t fall, streams of water
33:18 is the officer in charge of the t?"
Jer 50:15 her t fall, her walls are torn down.
Lam 4:17 from our t we watched for a nation
Eze 26: 4 walls of Tyre and pull down her t;
26: 9 demolish your t with his weapons.
27:11 side; men of Gammad were in your t.
Zep 1:16 cities and against the corner t.

Towing

Jn 21: 8 t the net full of fish, for they

Town (Towns, Townsmen, Townspeople)

Ge 19:20 Look, here is a t near enough to run
19:21 not overthrow the t you speak of.
19:22 (That is why the t was called Zoar.)
24:10 and made his way to the t of Nahor.
24:11 the t; it was towards evening,
26:33 name of the t has been Beersheba.
Lev 14:40 into an unclean place outside the t.
14:41 into an unclean place outside the t.
14:45 out of the t to an unclean place.
14:53 in the open fields outside the t.
25:33 a house sold in any t they hold—and
Nu 20:16 a t on the edge of your territory.
22:36 the Moabite t on the Arnon border,
35: 4 hundred feet from the t wall.
35: 5 Outside the t, measure three
35: 5 the north, with the t in the centre.
Dt 2:36 and from the t in the gorge, even as
2:36 not one t was too strong for us.
13:13 led the people of their t astray,
13:15 to the sword all who live in that t.
13:16 Gather all the plunder of the t into
13:16 completely burn the t and all its
16: 5 in any t the LORD your God gives
16:18 t the LORD your God is giving you,
19:12 the elders of his t shall send for
21: 3 the elders of the t nearest the body
21: 6 all the elders of the t nearest the
21:19 to the elders at the gate of his t.
21:21 all the men of his t shall stone him
22:15 virgin to the t elders at the gate.
22:17 cloth before the elders of the t,
22:21 of her t shall stone her to death.
22:23 If a man happens to meet in a t a
22:24 both of them to the gate of that t
22:24 in a t and did not scream for help,
23:16 likes and in whatever t he chooses.
25: 7 go to the elders at the t gate
25: 8 the elders of his t shall summon him
Jos 3:16 at a t called Adam in the vicinity
13: 9 and from the t in the middle of the
13:16 and from the t in the middle of the
18: 9 t by t, in seven parts, and returned
18:14 Jearim), a t of the people of Judah.
19:50 They gave him the t he asked for
19:50 he built up the t and settled there.
20: 6 home in the t from which he fled."
Jdg 6:27 of his family and the men of the t,
6:28 In the morning when the men of the t
6:30 The men of the t demanded of Joash,

Jdg 8:14 of Succoth, the elders of the **t**.
8:16 He took the elders of the **t** and
8:17 Peniel and killed the men of the **t**.
8:27 which he placed in Ophrah, his **t**.
12: 7 and was buried in a **t** in Gilead.
14:18 day the men of the **t** said to him,
17: 8 left that **t** in search of some other
Ru 1:19 the whole **t** was stirred because of
2:18 She carried it back to **t**, and her
3:15 Then he went back to **t**.
4: 1 Meanwhile Boaz went up to the **t** gate
4: 2 Boaz took ten of the elders of the **t**
4:10 his family or from the **t** records.
1Sa 1: 3 man went up from his **t** to worship
4:13 When the man entered the **t** and told
4:13 happened, the whole **t** sent up a cry.
8:22 "Everyone is to go back to his **t**.
9: 6 servant replied, "Look, in this **t**
9:10 for the **t** where the man of God was.
9:11 they were going up the hill to the **t**,
9:12 Hurry now; he has just come to our **t**
9:13 soon as you enter the **t**, you will
9:14 They went up to the **t**, and as they
9:25 down from the high place to the **t**,
9:27 going down to the edge of the **t**,
10: 5 As you approach the **t**, you will meet
16: 4 of the **t** trembled when they met him.
20: 6 his home **t**, because an annual
20:29 is observing a sacrifice in the **t**
20:40 and said, "Go, carry them back to **t**.
20:42 and Jonathan went back to the **t**.
22:19 He also put to the sword Nob, the **t**
23: 7 entering a **t** with gates and bars."
23:10 destroy that **t** on account of me.
28: 3 buried him in his own **t** of Ramah.
2Sa 12: 1 There were two men in a certain **t**,
15: 2 "What **t** are you from?" He would
15:12 to come from Giloh, his home **t**.
17:23 set out for his house in his home **t**.
19:37 that I may die in my own **t** near the
24: 5 south of the **t** in the gorge, and
1Ki 15:27 a Philistine **t**, while Nadab and all
16:15 near Gibbethon, a Philistine **t**.
17:10 When he came to the **t** gate, a widow
22:36 man to his **t**; everyone to his land!"
2Ki 2:19 our lord, this **t** is well situated
2:23 came out of the **t** and jeered at him.
3:19 fortified city and every major **t**.
2Ch 14: 5 incense altars in every **t** in Judah,
20: 4 from every **t** in Judah to seek him.
28:25 In every **t** in Judah he built high
30:10 The couriers went from **t** to **t** in
Ezr 2: 1 and Judah, each to his own **t**,
10:14 the elders and judges of each **t**,
Ne 7: 6 and Judah, each to his own **t**,
Job 39: 7 He laughs at the commotion in the **t**;
Ecc 10:15 him; he does not know the way to **t**.
Isa 22: 2 O **t** full of commotion, O city of
25: 2 of rubble the fortified **t** a ruin,
Jer 3:14 I will choose you—one from a **t** and
4:29 and archers every **t** takes to flight.
48: 8 every **t**, and not a **t** will escape.
49:25 abandoned, the **t** in which I delight?
Eze 39:16 (Also a **t** called Hamonah will be
Am 4: 6 lack of bread in every **t**, yet you
4: 7 I sent rain on one **t**, but withheld
4: 8 People staggered from **t** to **t** for
5: 3 the **t** that marches out a hundred
Mic 1:14 The **t** of Aczib will prove deceptive
Hab 2:12 and establishes a **t** by crime!
Mt 2:23 he went and lived in a **t** called
8:33 went into the **t** and reported all
8:34 the whole **t** went out to meet Jesus.
9: 1 crossed over and came to his own **t**.
10: 5 or enter any **t** of the Samaritans.
10:11 "Whatever **t** or village you enter,
10:14 feet when you leave that home or **t**.
10:15 the day of judgment than for that **t**.
13:54 Coming to his home **t**, he began
13:57 "Only in his home **t** and in his own
23:34 synagogues and pursue from **t** to **t**.
Mk 1:33 The whole **t** gathered at the door,
1:45 Jesus could no longer enter a **t**
5:14 this in the **t** and countryside,
6: 1 left there and went to his home **t**,
6: 4 "Only in his home **t**, among his
Mk 6:10 stay there until you leave that **t**.
Lk 1:26 Gabriel to Nazareth, a **t** in Galilee,
1:39 to a **t** in the hill country of Judea,
2: 3 everyone went to his own **t** to
2: 4 Joseph also went up from the **t** of
2: 4 to Bethlehem the **t** of David, because
2:11 Today in the **t** of David a Saviour
2:39 Galilee to their own **t** of Nazareth.
4:23 Do here in your home **t** what we have
4:24 prophet is accepted in his home **t**.
4:29 They got up, drove him out of the **t**,
4:29 the hill on which the **t** was built,
4:31 to Capernaum, a **t** in Galilee,
7:11 Soon afterwards, Jesus went to a **t**
7:12 he approached the **t** gate, a dead
7:12 large crowd from the **t** was with her.
7:37 had lived a sinful life in that **t**
8: 1 Jesus travelled about from one **t** and
8: 4 **t** after **t**, he told this parable:
8:27 by a demon-possessed man from the **t**.
8:34 this in the **t** and countryside,
8:39 told all over the **t** how much Jesus
9: 4 stay there until you leave that **t**.
9: 5 **t**, as a testimony against them."
9:10 themselves to a **t** called Bethsaida,
10: 1 **t** and place where he was about to go.
10: 8 "When you enter a **t** and are welcomed,
10:10 when you enter a **t** and are not
10:11 'Even the dust of your **t** that sticks
10:12 that day for Sodom than for that **t**.
14:21 of the **t** and bring in the poor,
18: 2 He said: "In a certain **t** there was a
18: 3 there was a widow in that **t** who kept
23:51 from the Judean **t** of Arimathea
Jn 1:44 Peter, was from the **t** of Bethsaida.
4: 5 he came to a **t** in Samaria called
4: 8 (His disciples had gone into the **t**
4:28 to the **t** and said to the people,
4:30 They came out of the **t** and made
4:39 Many of the Samaritans from that **t**
7:42 Bethlehem, the **t** where David lived?"
Ac 16: 4 they travelled from **t** to **t**, they
27: 8 Fair Havens, near the **t** of Lasea.
Tit 1: 5 in every **t**, as I directed you.

Towns (Town)

Ge 35: 5 the terror of God fell upon the **t**
Lev 25:32 the Levitical **t**, which they possess.
25:33 because the houses in the **t** of the
25:34 the pasture-land belonging to their **t**
Nu 13:19 Is it good or bad? What kind of **t** do
21: 3 destroyed them and their **t**;
31:10 They burned all the **t** where the
35: 2 give the Levites **t** to live in from
35: 2 them pasture-lands around the **t**.
35: 3 they will have **t** to live in and
35: 4 "The pasture-lands around the **t** that
35: 5 this area as pasture-land for the **t**.
35: 6 "Six of the **t** you give the Levites
35: 6 give them forty-two other **t**.
35: 7 **t**, together with their pasture-lands.
35: 8 The **t** you give the Levites from the
35: 8 many **t** from a tribe that has many,
35:11 select some **t** to be your cities of
35:13 These six **t** you give will be your
35:15 These six **t** will be a place of
Dt 1:22 to take and the **t** we will come to."
2:34 At that time we took all his **t** and
2:35 the plunder from the **t** we had
2:37 nor that around the **t** in the hills.
3:10 We took all the **t** on the plateau,
3:10 Edrei, **t** of Og's kingdom in Bashan.
3:12 of Gilead, together with its **t**.
3:19 may stay in the **t** I have given you,
12:12 and the Levites from your **t**, who
12:15 your animals in any of your **t**
12:17 You must not eat in your own **t** the
12:18 and the Levites from your **t**—and you
12:21 and in your own **t** you may eat as
13:12 one of the **t** the LORD your God is
14:21 to an alien living in any of your **t**,
14:27 the Levites living in your **t**,
14:28 produce and store it in your **t**,
14:29 the widows who live in your **t** may
15: 7 among your brothers in any of the **t**
Dt 15:22 You are to eat it in your own **t**.
16:11 the Levites in your **t**, and the
16:14 and the widows who live in your **t**.
17: 2 living among you in one of the **t**
18: 6 If a Levite moves from one of your **t**
19: 1 and settled in their **t** and houses,
21: 2 from the body to the neighbouring **t**.
24:14 or an alien living in one of your **t**.
26:12 may eat in your **t** and be satisfied.
31:12 and the aliens living in your **t**—so
Jos 11:21 totally destroyed them and their **t**.
13:10 all the **t** of Sihon king of the
13:17 to Heshbon and all its **t** on the
13:21 —all the **t** on the plateau and the
13:23 These **t** and their villages were the
13:25 The territory of Jazer, all the **t** of
13:28 These **t** and their villages were the
13:30 of Jair in Bashan, sixty **t**,
14: 4 of the land but only **t** to live in,
15: 9 came out at the **t** of Mount Ephron
15:21 The southernmost **t** of the tribe of
15:32 of twenty-nine **t** and their villages.
15:36 —fourteen **t** and their villages.
15:41 —sixteen **t** and their villages.
15:44 Keilah, Aczib and Mareshah—nine **t**
15:51 Goshen, Holon and Giloh—eleven **t**
15:54 and Zior—nine **t** and their villages.
15:57 Kain, Gibeah and Timnah—ten **t** and
15:59 Eltekon—six **t** and their villages.
15:60 Rabbah—two **t** and their villages.
15:62 En Gedi—six **t** and their villages.
16: 9 also included all the **t** and their
17: 9 There were **t** belonging to Ephraim
17: 9 lying among the **t** of Manasseh,
17:12 were not able to occupy these **t**,
18:24 Geba—twelve **t** and their villages.
18:28 —fourteen **t** and their villages.
19: 6 and Sharuhen—thirteen **t** and their
19: 7 Ain, Rimmon, Ether and Ashan—four **t**
19: 8 all the villages around these **t** as
19:15 were twelve **t** and their villages.
19:16 These **t** and their villages were the
19:22 were sixteen **t** and their villages.
19:23 These **t** and their villages were the
19:30 twenty-two **t** and their villages.
19:31 These **t** and their villages were the
19:38 were nineteen **t** and their villages.
19:39 These **t** and their villages were the
19:48 These **t** and their villages were the
21: 2 Moses that you give us **t** to live in,
21: 3 gave the Levites the following **t**
21: 4 thirteen **t** from the tribes of Judah,
21: 5 allotted ten **t** from the clans of
21: 6 allotted thirteen **t** from the clans
21: 7 clan by clan, received twelve **t** from
21: 8 these **t** and their pasture-lands,
21: 9 allotted the following **t** by name
21:10 (these **t** were assigned to the
21:16 —nine **t** from these two tribes.
21:18 with their pasture-lands—four **t**.
21:19 All the **t** for the priests, the
21:20 **t** from the tribe of Ephraim:
21:22 with their pasture-lands—four **t**.
21:24 with their pasture-lands—four **t**.
21:25 with their pasture-lands—two **t**.
21:26 All these ten **t** and their
21:27 with their pasture-lands—two **t**;
21:29 with their pasture-lands—four **t**;
21:31 with their pasture-lands—four **t**;
21:32 with their pasture-lands—three **t**.
21:33 All the **t** of the Gershonite clans
21:35 with their pasture-lands—four **t**;
21:37 with their pasture-lands—four **t**;
21:39 their pasture-lands—four **t** in all.
21:40 All the **t** allotted to the Merarite
21:41 The **t** of the Levites in the
21:42 Each of these **t** had pasture-lands
21:42 it; this was true for all these **t**.
Jdg 10: 4 They controlled thirty **t** in Gilead,
11:26 and all the **t** along the Arnon.
11:33 He devastated twenty **t** from Aroer to
20:14 From their **t** they came together at
20:15 thousand swordsmen from their **t**,
20:42 out of the **t** cut them down there.
20:48 and put all the **t** to the sword,
20:48 **t** they came across they set on fire.

Jdg 21:23 rebuilt the t and settled in them.
1Sa 6:18 t belonging to the five rulers
6:18 t with their country villages.
7:14 The t from Ekron to Gath that the
18: 6 the women came out from all the t of
27: 5 country t, that I may live there.
30:29 Racal; to those in the t of the
31: 7 they abandoned their t and fled.
2Sa 2: 1 "Shall I go up to one of the t of
2: 3 they settled in Hebron and its t.
8: 8 From Tebah and Berothai, t that
12:31 He did this to all the Ammonite t.
24: 7 the t of the Hivites and Canaanites.
1Ki 9:11 King Solomon gave twenty t in
9:12 the t that Solomon had given him,
9:13 "What kind of t are these you have
9:19 the t for his chariots and for his
12:17 who were living in the t of Judah,
13:32 high places in the t of Samaria
15:20 his forces against the t of Israel.
2Ki 3:25 They destroyed the t, and each man
13:25 t he had taken in battle from his
13:25 and so he recovered the Israelite t.
17: 6 River and in the t of the Medes.
17: 9 high places in all their t.
17:24 Sepharvaim and settled them in the t
17:24 over Samaria and lived in its t.
17:26 resettled in the t of Samaria do not
17:29 in the several t where they settled,
18:11 Habor River, and in t of the Medes.
23: 5 the high places of the t of Judah
23: 8 all the priests from the t of Judah
23:19 Israel had built in the t of Samaria
1Ch 2:22 controlled twenty-three t in Gilead.
2:23 surrounding settlements—sixty t.
4:31 their t until the reign of David.
4:32 Rimmon, Token and Ashan—five t—
4:33 all the villages around these t as
6:60 These t, which were distributed
6:61 allotted ten t from the clans of
6:62 were allotted thirteen t from the
6:63 were allotted twelve t from the
6:64 these t and their pasture-lands.
6:65 allotted the previously named t.
6:66 t from the tribe of Ephraim.
7:29 son of Israel lived in these t.
9: 2 in their own t were some Israelites,
10: 7 they abandoned their t and fled.
13: 2 them in their t and pasture-lands,
18: 8 From Tebah and Cun, t that belonged
19: 7 their t and moved out for battle.
20: 3 David did this to all the Ammonite t
27:25 t, the villages and the watchtowers.
2Ch 10:17 who were living in the t of Judah,
11: 5 and built up t for defence in Judah:
13:19 and took from him the t of Bethel,
14: 7 "Let us build up these t," he said
15: 8 Benjamin and from the t he had
16: 4 his forces against the t of Israel.
17: 2 put garrisons in Judah and in the t
17: 7 Micaiah to teach in the t of Judah.
17: 9 t of Judah and taught the people.
17:13 had large supplies in the t of Judah
23: 2 Israelite families from all the t.
24: 5 "Go to the t of Judah and collect
25:13 Judean t from Samaria to Beth Horon.
26: 6 He then rebuilt t near Ashdod and
27: 4 He built t in the Judean hills and
28:18 while the Philistines had raided t
31: 1 there went out to the t of Judah,
31: 1 own t and to their own property.
31: 6 Judah who lived in the t of Judah
31:15 faithfully in the t of the priests,
31:19 around their t or in any other t,
34: 6 In the t of Manasseh, Ephraim and
Ezr 2:59 The following came up from the t of
2:70 servants settled in their own t,
2:70 the Israelites settled in their t.
3: 1 Israelites had settled in their t,
10:14 Then let everyone in our t who has
Ne 7:61 The following came up from the t of
7:73 Israelites, settled in their own t.
7:73 Israelites had settled in their t,
8:15 throughout their t and in Jerusalem:
10:37 who collect the tithes in all the t
11: 1 nine were to stay in their own t.

Ne 11: 3 servants lived in the t of Judah,
11: 3 his own property in the various t,
11:20 were in all the t of Judah, each on
12:44 From the fields around the t they
Job 15:28 he will inhabit ruined t and houses
Isa 40: 9 do not be afraid; say to the t of
42:11 Let the desert and its t raise their
44:26 'It shall be inhabited,' of the t of
Jer 1:15 and against all the t of Judah.
2:15 land; his t are burned and deserted.
2:28 as many gods as you have t, O Judah.
4: 7 Your t will lie in ruins without
4:26 its t lay in ruins before the LORD,
4:29 t are deserted; no-one lives in them.
5: 6 will lie in wait near their t to
7:17 they are doing in the t of Judah
7:34 bridegroom in the t of Judah and the
9:11 and I will lay waste the t of Judah
10:22 It will make the t of Judah desolate,
11: 6 "Proclaim all these words in the t
11:12 The t of Judah and the people of
11:13 You have as many gods as you have t,
17:26 People will come from the t of Judah
20:16 May that man be like the t the LORD
22: 6 like a desert, like t not inhabited.
25:18 Jerusalem and the t of Judah, its
26: 2 speak to all the people of the t of
31:21 O Virgin Israel, return to your t.
31:23 t will once again use these words:
31:24 all its t—farmers and those who
32:44 in the t of Judah and in the t of
33:10 Yet in the t of Judah and the
33:12 without men or animals—in all its t
33:13 In the t of the hill country, of the
33:13 Jerusalem and in the t of Judah,
34: 1 Jerusalem and all its surrounding t,
34:22 And I will lay waste the t of Judah
36: 6 of Judah who come in from their t.
36: 9 who had come from the t of Judah.
40: 5 has appointed over the t of Judah,
40:10 live in the t you have taken over."
44: 2 Jerusalem and on all the t of Judah.
44: 6 it raged against the t of Judah and
44:17 our officials did in the t of Judah
44:21 incense burned in the t of Judah
47: 2 the t and those who live in them.
48: 9 waste; her t will become desolate,
48:15 Moab will be destroyed and her t
48:24 to Kerioth and Bozrah—to all the t
48:28 Abandon your t and dwell among the
49: 1 Why do his people live in its t?
49:13 its t will be in ruins for ever."
49:18 along with their neighbouring t,"
50:32 I will kindle a fire in her t that
50:40 along with their neighbouring t,"
51:43 Her t will be desolate, a dry and
Lam 5:11 Zion, and virgins in the t of Judah.
Eze 6: 6 Wherever you live, the t will be
12:20 The inhabited t will be laid waste
19: 7 strongholds and devastated their t.
25: 9 beginning at its frontier t—Beth
35: 4 I will turn your t into ruins and
35: 9 ever; your t will not be inhabited.
36: 4 the deserted t that have been
36:10 The t will be inhabited and the
36:33 I will resettle your t, and the
39: 9 "'Then those who live in the t of
45: 5 their possession for t to live in.
Hos 8:14 palaces; Judah has fortified many t.
13:10 Where are your rulers in all your t,
Ob :20 will possess the t of the Negev.
Zec 1:12 Jerusalem and from the t of Judah,
1:17 'My t will again overflow with
7: 7 t were at rest and prosperous,
Mt 9:35 Jesus went through all the t and
11: 1 and preach in the t of Galilee.
14:13 followed him on foot from the t.
Mk 6:33 the t and got there ahead of them.
6:56 wherever he went—into villages, t
Lk 4:43 kingdom of God to the other t also,
5:12 While Jesus was in one of the t, a
13:22 Jesus went through the t and
Ac 5:16 Crowds gathered also from the t
8:40 all the t until he reached Caesarea.
15:36 visit the brothers in all the t
Jude : 7 Gomorrah and the surrounding t gave

Townsmen (Town)
Ge 34:20 city to speak to their fellow t.
Ru 3:11 All my fellow t know that you are a

Townspeople (Town)
Ge 24:13 the t are coming out to draw water.

Trace (Traced, Tracing)
Da 2:35 swept them away without leaving a t.
Heb 7: 6 This man, however, did not t his

Traced (Trace)
Ro 9: 5 and from them is t the human

Tracing (Trace)
Ro 11:33 and his paths beyond t out!

Track (Tracked, Tracks)
1Sa 23:23 I will t him down among all the
Job 14:16 my steps but not keep t of my sin.

Tracked (Track)
Ps 17:11 They have t me down, they now

Trackless
Job 12:24 them wandering through a t waste.
Ps 107:40 made them wander in a t waste.

Tracks (Track)
SS 1: 8 follow the t of the sheep and graze

Traconitis
Lk 3: 1 Philip tetrarch of Iturea and T,

Tract (Tracts)
Jos 24:32 buried at Shechem in the t of land

Tracts (Tract)
Jos 17: 5 Manasseh's share consisted of ten t

Trade (Traded, Traders, Trades, Trading)
Ge 34:10 t in it, and acquire property in it.
34:21 "Let them live in our land and t in
42:34 to you, and you can t in the land.
2Ch 20:37 and were not able to set sail to t.
Isa 23:17 will ply her t with all the kingdoms
Eze 27: 9 came alongside to t for your wares.
28:16 Through your widespread t you were
28:18 By your many sins and dishonest t
Zep 1:11 who t with silver will be ruined.
Ac 19:27 There is danger not only that our t
Rev 18:22 No workman of any t will ever be

Traded (Trade)
Eze 27:13 "'Greece, Tubal and Meshech t with
27:15 "'The men of Rhodes t with you, and
27:17 "'Judah and Israel t with you; they
27:20 "'Dedan t in saddle blankets with
27:22 'The merchants of Sheba and Raamah t
27:23 Sheba, Asshur and Kilmad t with you.
27:24 In your market-place they t with you
Joel 3: 3 They cast lots for my people and t

Traders (Trade)
1Ki 10:15 revenues from merchants and t and
2Ch 9:14 brought in by merchants and t.
Job 41: 6 Will t barter for him? Will they
Isa 23: 8 whose t are renowned in the earth?
Eze 17: 4 where he planted it in a city of t.
1Ti 1:10 for slave t and liars and perjurers—

Trades (Trade)
Ac 19:25 along with the workmen in related t,

Trading (Trade)
1Ki 10:22 The king had a fleet of t ships at
22:48 Jehoshaphat built a fleet of t ships
2Ch 9:21 The king had a fleet of t ships
20:36 him to construct a fleet of t ships.
Job 20:18 not enjoy the profit from his t.

Pr 31:18 She sees that her **t** is profitable,
Isa 2:16 for every **t** ship and every stately
Eze 28: 5 By your great skill in **t** you have

Tradition (Traditions)

2Ch 35:25 These became a **t** in Israel and are
Mt 15: 2 "Why do your disciples break the **t**
15: 3 of God for the sake of your **t**?
15: 6 word of God for the sake of your **t**.
Mk 7: 3 holding to the **t** of the elders.
7: 5 according to the **t** of the elders
7:13 by your **t** that you have handed down.
Col 2: 8 which depends on human **t** and the

Traditions (Tradition)

Mic 6:16 and you have followed their **t**.
Mk 7: 4 And they observe many other **t**, such
7: 8 and are holding on to the **t** of men."
7: 9 God in order to observe your own **t**!
Gal 1:14 zealous for the **t** of my fathers.

Trafficked

Isa 47:15 with and **t** with since childhood.

Tragedy

1Ki 17:20 brought **t** also upon this widow

Trail

Job 41:30 **t** in the mud like a threshing-sledge
1Ti 5:24 the sins of others **t** behind them.

Train (Trained, Training, Trains, Well-trained)

Ps 68:18 you led captives in your **t**; you
Pr 22: 6 **T** a child in the way he should go,
Isa 2: 4 nor will they **t** for war any more.
6: 1 the **t** of his robe filled the temple.
Mic 4: 3 nor will they **t** for war any more.
Eph 4: 8 in his **t** and gave gifts to men."
1Ti 4: 7 rather, **t** yourself to be godly.
Tit 2: 4 they can **t** the younger women to love

Trained (Train)

Ge 14:14 he called out the 318 **t** men born in
1Ch 5:18 a bow, and who were **t** for battle.
25: 7 with their relatives—all of them **t**
2Ch 2:14 He is **t** to work in gold and silver,
26:13 an army of 307,500 men **t** for war,
Da 1: 5 They were to be **t** for three years,
Hos 7:15 I **t** them and strengthened them, but
10:11 Ephraim is a **t** heifer that loves to
Lk 6:40 is fully **t** will be like his teacher.
Ac 22: 3 Under Gamaliel I was thoroughly **t** in
2Co 11: 6 I may not be a **t** speaker, but I do
Heb 5:14 by constant use have **t** themselves
12:11 for those who have been **t** by it.

Training (Train)

1Co 9:25 in the games goes into strict **t**.
Eph 6: 4 the **t** and instruction of the Lord.
1Ti 4: 8 For physical **t** is of some value, but
2Ti 3:16 correcting and **t** in righteousness,

Trains (Train)

2Sa 22:35 He **t** my hands for battle; my arms
Ps 18:34 He **t** my hands for battle; my arms
144: 1 my Rock, who **t** my hands for war,

Traitor (Traitors)

2Ki 17: 4 discovered that Hoshea was a **t**,
Isa 21: 2 The **t** betrays, the looter takes loot
33: 1 O **t**, you who have not been betrayed!
Lk 6:16 and Judas Iscariot, who became a **t**.
Jn 18: 5 the **t** was standing there with them.)

Traitors (Traitor)

Ps 59: 5 nations; show no mercy to wicked **t**.
Mic 2: 4 from me! He assigns our fields to **t**.

Trample (Trampled, Trampling)

Dt 33:29 you will **t** down their high places."
Job 39:15 that some wild animal may **t** them.
Ps 7: 5 let him **t** my life to the ground and
44: 5 through your name we **t** our foes.
60:12 and he will **t** down our enemies.
91:13 **t** the great lion and the serpent.
108:13 and he will **t** down our enemies.
Isa 10: 6 **t** them down like mud in the streets.
14:25 on my mountains I will **t** him down.
26: 6 Feet **t** it down—the feet of the
Jer 12:10 my vineyard and **t** down my field;
Eze 26:11 The hoofs of his horses will **t** all
34:18 Must you also **t** the rest of your
Joel 3:13 **t** the grapes, for the winepress
Am 2: 7 They **t** on the heads of the poor as
5:11 You **t** on the poor and force him to
8: 4 Hear this, you who **t** the needy and
Mal 4: 3 you will **t** down the wicked; they
Mt 7: 6 If you do, they may **t** them under
Lk 10:19 I have given you authority to **t** on
Rev 11: 2 **t** on the holy city for 42 months.

Trampled (Trample)

2Sa 22:43 and **t** them like mud in the streets.
2Ki 7:17 and the people **t** him in the gateway,
7:20 **t** him in the gateway, and he died.
9:33 the horses as they **t** her underfoot.
14: 9 along and **t** the thistle underfoot.
2Ch 25:18 along and **t** the thistle underfoot.
Isa 5: 5 down its wall, and it will be **t**.
14:19 Like a corpse **t** underfoot,
16: 8 The rulers of the nations have **t**
25:10 but Moab will be **t** under him as
25:10 as straw is **t** down in the manure.
28: 3 drunkards, will be **t** underfoot.
63: 3 I **t** them in my anger and trod them
63: 6 I **t** the nations in my anger; in my
63:18 enemies have **t** down your sanctuary.
Jer 51:33 threshing-floor at the time it is **t**;
Lam 1:15 has **t** the Virgin Daughter of Judah.
3:16 gravel; he has **t** me in the dust.
Eze 34:19 my flock feed on what you have **t**
Da 7: 7 and **t** underfoot whatever was left.
7:19 and **t** underfoot whatever was left.
8: 7 him to the ground and **t** on him,
8:10 down to the earth and **t** on them.
8:13 the host that will be **t** underfoot?"
Hos 5:11 Ephraim is oppressed, **t** in judgment,
Mic 7:10 **t** underfoot like mire in the streets.
Hab 3:15 You **t** the sea with your horses,
Mt 5:13 to be thrown out and **t** by men.
Lk 8: 5 some fell along the path; it was **t**
21:24 Jerusalem will be **t** on by the
Heb 10:29 who has **t** the Son of God under foot,
Rev 14:20 They were **t** in the winepress outside

Trampling (Trample)

Isa 1:12 this of you, this **t** of my courts?
22: 5 has a day of tumult and **t** and terror
Da 7:23 earth, **t** it down and crushing it.
Zec 10: 5 men **t** the muddy streets in battle.
Lk 12: 1 so that they were **t** on one another,

Trance

Ac 10:10 being prepared, he fell into a **t**.
11: 5 praying, and in a **t** I saw a vision.
22:17 at the temple, I fell into a **t**

Tranquillity

Ecc 4: 6 Better one handful with **t** than two

Transaction (Transactions)

Jer 32:25 silver and have the **t** witnessed.

Transactions (Transaction)

Ru 4: 7 method of legalising **t** in Israel.)

Transcends

Php 4: 7 the peace of God, which **t** all

Trans-Euphrates (Euphrates)

Ezr 4:10 city of Samaria and elsewhere in **T**.
4:11 From your servants, the men of **T**:
4:16 you will be left with nothing in **T**.
4:17 and elsewhere in **T**: Greetings.
4:20 kings ruling over the whole of **T**,
5: 3 At that time Tattenai, governor of **T**
5: 6 governor of **T**, and Shethar-Bozenai
5: 6 officials of **T**, sent to King Darius.
6: 6 Now then, Tattenai, governor of **T**,
6: 8 from the revenues of **T**, so that the
6:13 Tattenai, governor of **T**, and
7:21 order all the treasurers of **T** to
7:25 justice to all the people of **T**—
8:36 to the governors of **T** who then gave
Ne 2: 7 I have letters to the governors of **T**
2: 9 I went to the governors of **T** and
3: 7 the authority of the governor of **T**.

Transfer (Transferred)

Ru 4: 7 for the redemption and **t** of property
2Sa 3:10 **t** the kingdom from the house of Saul

Transferred (Transfer)

Ac 25: 3 as a favour to them, to have Paul **t**

Transfigured

Mt 17: 2 There he was **t** before them. His face
Mk 9: 2 There he was **t** before them.

Transform (Transformed)

Php 3:21 will **t** our lowly bodies so that they

Transformed (Transform)

Job 28: 5 food comes, is **t** below as by fire;
Ro 12: 2 be **t** by the renewing of your mind.
2Co 3:18 are being **t** into his likeness with

Transgressed (Transgression)

Da 9:11 All Israel has **t** your law and turned

Transgression (Transgressed, Transgressions, Transgressors)

Ps 19:13 I be blameless, innocent of great **t**.
Isa 53: 8 the **t** of my people he was stricken.
Da 9:24 and your holy city to finish **t**,
Mic 1: 5 All this is because of Jacob's **t**,
1: 5 What is Jacob's **t**? Is it not Samaria
3: 8 to Jacob his **t**, to Israel his sin.
6: 7 Shall I offer my firstborn for my **t**,
7:18 who pardons sin and forgives the **t**
Ro 4:15 where there is no law there is no **t**.
11:11 because of their **t**, salvation has
11:12 if their **t** means riches for the

Transgressions (Transgression)

Ps 32: 1 Blessed is he whose **t** are forgiven,
32: 5 I said, "I will confess my **t** to the
39: 8 Save me from all my **t**; do not make
51: 1 your great compassion blot out my **t**.
51: 3 For I know my **t**, and my sin is
65: 3 by sins, you forgave our **t**.
103:12 so far has he removed our **t** from us.
Isa 43:25 even I, am he who blots out your **t**,
50: 1 of your **t** your mother was sent away.
53: 5 he was pierced for our **t**, he was
Mic 1:13 the **t** of Israel were found in you.
Ro 4: 7 "Blessed are they whose **t** are
Gal 3:19 It was added because of **t** until the
Eph 2: 1 for you, you were dead in your **t** and
2: 5 Christ even when we were dead in **t**

Transgressors (Transgression)

Ps 51:13 I will teach **t** your ways, and
Isa 53:12 death, and was numbered with the **t**.
53:12 and made intercession for the **t**.
Lk 22:37 'And he was numbered with the **t**';

Translated

Ezr 4:18 has been read and **t** in my presence.
Jn 1:42 Cephas" (which, when **t**, is Peter).
Ac 9:36 Tabitha (which, when **t**, is Dorcas),

Transparent
Rev 21:21 city was of pure gold, like t glass.

Transplanted (Plant)
Eze 17:10 Even if it is t, will it thrive?

Transport
Ge 46: 5 that Pharaoh had sent to t him.

Trap (Trapped, Traps)
1Sa 28: 9 Why have you set a t for my life to
Job 18: 9 A t seizes him by the heel; a snare
18:10 on the ground; a t lies in his path.
40:24 eyes, or t him and pierce his nose?
Ps 31: 4 Free me from the t that is set for
69:22 may it become retribution and a t.
Pr 20:25 It is a t for a man to dedicate
28:10 evil path will fall into his own t,
Ecc 7:26 is a t and whose hands are chains.
Isa 8:14 Jerusalem he will be a t and a snare
Jer 9: 8 in his heart he sets a t for him.
50:24 I set a t for you, O Babylon, and
Am 3: 5 Does a bird fall into a t on the
3: 5 Does a t spring up from the earth
Ob : 7 eat your bread will set a t for you,
Mt 22:15 laid plans to t him in his words.
22:18 why are you trying to t me?
Mk 12:15 "Why are you trying to t me?" he
Lk 20:26 They were unable to t him in what he
21:34 close on you unexpectedly like a t.
Jn 8: 6 They were using this question as a t
Ro 11: 9 their table become a snare and a t,
1Ti 3: 7 disgrace and into the devil's t.
6: 9 a t and into many foolish and
2Ti 2:26 and escape from the t of the devil,

Trapped (Trap)
Pr 6: 2 if you have been t by what you said,
11: 6 unfaithful are t by evil desires.
12:13 An evil man is t by his sinful talk,
Ecc 9:12 so men are t by evil times that fall
Isa 42:22 t in pits or hidden away in prisons.
Jer 8: 9 shame; they will be dismayed and t.
Eze 19: 4 him, and he was t in their pit.
19: 8 for him, and he was t in their pit.

Traps (Trap)
Jos 23:13 they will become snares and t for
Ps 38:12 Those who seek my life set their t,
140: 5 and have set t for me along my path.
141: 9 for me, from the t set by evildoers.
Jer 5:26 like those who set t to catch men.
Lam 4:20 life breath, was caught in their t.

Travel (Travelled, Traveller, Travellers, Travelling, Travels)
Ex 13:21 that they could t by day or night.
Nu 20:17 We will t along the king's highway
21:22 We will t along the king's highway
2Ch 15: 5 In those days it was not safe to t
Job 21:29 you never questioned those who t
Pr 4:15 Avoid it, do not t on it; turn from
Eze 39:11 of those who t east towards the Sea.
Mt 23:15 you hypocrites! You t over land and
Rev 18:17 "Every sea captain, and all who t by

Travelled (Travel)
Ge 12: 6 Abram t through the land as far as
41:46 presence and t throughout Egypt.
Ex 15:22 For three days they t in the desert
Nu 10:12 t from place to place until the
10:33 of the LORD and t for three days.
11:35 From Kibroth Hattaavah the people t
21: 4 They t from Mount Hor along the
22: 1 the Israelites t to the plains of
33: 8 and when they had t for three days
Dt 2: 8 and t along the desert road of Moab.
10: 6 (The Israelites t from the wells of
10: 7 From there they t to Gudgodah and on
Jos 24:17 all the nations through which we t.
Jdg 11:18 "Next they t through the desert,
2Sa 4: 7 t all night by way of the Arabah.
1Ki 19: 8 Strengthened by that food, he t for
2Ki 5:19 After Naaman had t some distance,
Isa 41: 3 a path his feet have not t before.
Mk 1:39 he t throughout Galilee, preaching
Lk 2:44 their company, they t on for a day.
8: 1 After this, Jesus t about from one
10:33 a Samaritan, as he t, came where the
17:11 Now on his way to Jerusalem, Jesus t
Ac 8:36 they t along the road, they came to
8:40 appeared at Azotus and t about
9:32 Peter t about the country, he went
11:19 with Stephen t as far as Phoenicia,
13: 6 They t through the whole island
13:31 t with him from Galilee to Jerusalem.
15: 3 and as they t through Phoenicia and
16: 4 they t from town to town, they
16: 6 Paul and his companions t throughout
16:12 From there we t to Philippi, a Roman
18:23 Paul set out from there and t from
20: 2 He t through that area, speaking
28:15 and they t as far as the Forum of

Traveller (Travel)
Jdg 19:17 he looked and saw the t in the city
2Sa 12: 4 "Now a t came to the rich man, but
12: 4 meal for the t who had come to him.
Job 31:32 my door was always open to the t—
Jer 14: 8 like a t who stays only a night?

Travellers (Travel)
Jdg 5: 6 abandoned; t took to winding paths.
Isa 33: 8 The highways are deserted, no t are
Jer 9: 2 in the desert a lodging place for t,
Eze 39:11 It will block the way of t, because

Travelling (Travel)
Ex 14:19 the angel of God, who had been t in
17: 1 t from place to place as the LORD
1Ki 18:27 is deep in thought, or busy, or t.
Job 6:19 t merchants of Sheba look in hope.
Isa 60:15 with no-one t through, I will make
Lk 14:25 Large crowds were t with Jesus, and
Ac 9: 7 The men t with Saul stood there
19:29 Paul's t companions from Macedonia,

Travels (Travel)
Ex 40:36 In all the t of the Israelites,
40:38 house of Israel during all their t.
Jer 2: 6 where no-one t and no-one lives?'
51:43 lives, through which no man t.

Trays
Ex 25:38 Its wick trimmers and t are to be of
37:23 wick trimmers and t, of pure gold.
Nu 4: 9 its wick trimmers and t, and all its

Treacherous (Treachery)
Ps 25: 3 to shame who are t without excuse.
Isa 24:16 away! Woe to me! The t betray!
24:16 With treachery the t betray!"
48: 8 Well do I know how t you are; you
Hab 1:13 Why then do you tolerate the t? Why
Zep 3: 4 prophets are arrogant; they are t
2Ti 3: 4 t, rash, conceited, lovers of

Treacherously (Treachery)
Jdg 9:23 who acted t against Abimelech.
Ac 7:19 He dealt t with our people and

Treachery (Treacherous, Treacherously)
Lev 26:40 the sins of their fathers—their t
2Ki 9:23 fled, calling out to Ahaziah, "T,
Isa 24:16 With t the treacherous betray!"
59:13 rebellion and t against the LORD,

Tread (Treading, Treads, Trod, Trodden)
Job 24:11 t the winepresses, yet suffer thirst
Ps 91:13 You will t upon the lion and the
Jer 25:30 He will shout like those who t the
Mic 7:19 you will t our sins underfoot and
Na 3:14 t the mortar, repair the brickwork!

Treading (Tread)
Dt 25: 4 Do not muzzle an ox while it is t
Ne 13:15 In those days I saw men in Judah t
Isa 41:25 as if he were a potter t the clay.
63: 2 like those of one t the winepress?
Am 9:13 and the planter by the one t grapes.
1Co 9: 9 an ox while it is t out the grain.
1Ti 5:18 "Do not muzzle the ox while it is t

Treads (Tread)
Job 9: 8 and t on the waves of the sea.
Isa 16:10 no-one t out wine at the presses,
41:25 He t on rulers as if they were
Jer 48:33 no-one t them with shouts of joy.
Am 4:13 and t the high places of the earth—
Mic 1: 3 and t the high places of the earth.
Rev 19:15 He t the winepress of the fury of

Treason
2Ki 11:14 her robes and called out, "T! T!
2Ch 23:13 tore her robes and shouted, "T! T!

Treasure (Treasured, Treasure-house, Treasurer, Treasurers, Treasures)
Ge 43:23 has given you t in your sacks; I
Job 3:21 for it more than for hidden t,
20:20 he cannot save himself by his t.
Pr 2: 4 and search for it as for hidden t,
15: 6 of the righteous contains great t,
Ecc 2: 8 and the t of kings and provinces.
Isa 33: 6 of the LORD is the key to this t.
44: 9 and the things they t are worthless.
Mt 6:21 For where your t is, there your
13:44 "The kingdom of heaven is like t
19:21 poor, and you will have t in heaven.
Mk 10:21 poor, and you will have t in heaven.
Lk 12:33 a t in heaven that will not be
12:34 For where your t is, there your
18:22 poor, and you will have t in heaven.
2Co 4: 7 we have this t in jars of clay to
1Ti 6:19 In this way they will lay up t for

Treasured (Treasure)
Ex 19: 5 nations you will be my t possession.
Dt 7: 6 to be his people, his t possession.
14: 2 chosen you to be his t possession.
26:18 his t possession as he promised, and
Job 23:12 I have t the words of his mouth more
Ps 135: 4 own, Israel to be his t possession.
Isa 64:11 and all that we t lies in ruins.
Eze 7:22 and they will desecrate my t place;
Mal 3:17 day when I make up my t possession.
Lk 2:19 Mary t up all these things and
2:51 t all these things in her heart.

Treasure-house (House, Treasure)
Da 1: 2 and put in the t of his god.

Treasurer (Treasure)
Ezr 1: 8 them brought by Mithredath the t,

Treasurers (Treasure)
2Ki 12: 5 receive the money from one of the t,
12: 7 Take no more money from your t,
Ezr 7:21 King Artaxerxes, order all the t of
Da 3: 2 prefects, governors, advisers, t,
3: 3 prefects, governors, advisers, t,

Treasures (Treasure)
Dt 33:19 seas, on the t hidden in the sand."
1Ki 14:26 He carried off the t of the temple
14:26 LORD and the t of the royal palace.
2Ki 20:13 and everything found among his t.
20:15 my t that I did not show them."
24:13 Nebuchadnezzar removed all the t
1Ch 29: 3 God I now give my personal t of gold
2Ch 12: 9 he carried off the t of the temple
12: 9 LORD and the t of the royal palace.
25:24 together with the palace t and the
36:18 both large and small, and the t of
36:18 the t of the king and his officials.
Job 20:26 darkness lies in wait for his t

Job 28:10 the rock; his eyes see all its **t**.
Pr 10: 2 Ill-gotten **t** are of no value, but
24: 4 filled with rare and beautiful **t**.
Isa 2: 7 gold; there is no end to their **t**.
10:13 I plundered their **t**; like a mighty
30: 6 their **t** on the humps of camels, to
39: 2 and everything found among his **t**.
39: 4 my **t** that I did not show them."
45: 3 I will give you the **t** of darkness,
Jer 15:13 Your wealth and your **t** I will give
17: 3 your **t** I will give away as plunder,
20: 5 and all the **t** of the kings of Judah.
50:37 her **t**! They will be plundered.
51:13 by many waters and are rich in **t**,
Lam 1: 7 the **t** that were hers in days of old.
1:10 The enemy laid hands on all her **t**;
1:11 they barter their **t** for food to
Eze 22:25 take **t** and precious things and make
Da 11:43 He will gain control of the **t** of
Hos 9: 6 Their **t** of silver will be taken over
13:15 will be plundered of all its **t**.
Joel 3: 5 off my finest **t** to your temples.
Ob : 6 be ransacked, his hidden **t** pillaged!
Mic 6:10 O wicked house, your ill-gotten **t**
Na 2: 9 endless, the wealth from all its **t**!
Mt 2:11 Then they opened their **t** and
6:19 "Do not store up for yourselves **t** on
6:20 store up for yourselves **t** in heaven,
13:52 his storeroom new **t** as well as old."
Col 2: 3 in whom are hidden all the **t** of
Heb 11:26 greater value than the **t** of Egypt,

Treasuries (Treasury)

1Ki 7:51 them in the **t** of the LORD's temple.
15:18 gold that was left in the **t** of the
2Ki 12:18 all the gold found in the **t** of the
14:14 and in the **t** of the royal palace.
16: 8 in the **t** of the royal palace and
18:15 and in the **t** of the royal palace.
1Ch 9:26 the rooms and **t** in the house of God.
26:20 charge of the **t** of the house of God
26:20 and the **t** for the dedicated things.
26:22 of the **t** of the temple of the LORD.
26:24 was the officer in charge of the **t**.
26:26 were in charge of all the **t** for the
28:12 for the **t** of the temple of God and
28:12 for the **t** for the dedicated things.
2Ch 5: 1 them in the **t** of God's temple.
8:15 any matter, including that of the **t**.
16: 2 gold out of the **t** of the LORD's
32:27 and he made **t** for his silver and
Pr 8:21 who love me and making their **t** full.
Eze 28: 4 amassed gold and silver in your **t**.

Treasury (Treasuries)

Jos 6:19 to the LORD and must go into his **t**."
6:24 iron into the **t** of the LORD's house.
1Ch 29: 8 gave them to the **t** of the temple of
Ezr 2:69 they gave to the **t** for this work,
6: 1 archives stored in the **t** at Babylon.
6: 4 costs are to be paid by the royal **t**.
6: 8 to be fully paid out of the royal **t**,
7:20 you may provide from the royal **t**.
Ne 7:70 to the **t** 1,000 drachmas of gold
7:71 gave to the **t** for the work 20,000
10:38 our God, to the storerooms of the **t**.
Est 3: 9 silver into the royal **t** for the men
4: 7 promised to pay into the royal **t**
Jer 38:11 to a room under the **t** in the palace.
Mt 27: 6 the **t**, since it is blood money."
Mk 12:41 their money into the temple **t**.
12:43 more into the **t** than all the others.
Lk 21: 1 their gifts into the temple **t**.
Ac 8:27 in charge of all the **t** of Candace,

Treat (Treated, Treating, Treatment, Treatments, Treats)

Ge 19: 9 judge! We'll **t** you worse than them.
30:20 This time my husband will **t** me with
Lev 22: 2 "Tell Aaron and his sons to **t** with
Nu 10:29 Come with us and we will **t** you well,
11:15 If this is how you are going to **t** me
14:11 "How long will these people **t** me
25:17 "**T** the Midianites as enemies and
Dt 20:15 This is how you are to **t** all the
21:14 You must not sell her or **t** her as a
Jos 2:14 we will **t** you kindly and faithfully
2Sa 19:43 So why do you **t** us with contempt?
Job 6:26 and **t** the words of a despairing man
Ps 103:10 he does not **t** us as our sins deserve
Jer 3:19 'How gladly would I **t** you like sons
29:22 'The LORD **t** you like Zedekiah and
34:18 I will **t** like the calf they cut in
Eze 15: 6 I **t** the people living in Jerusalem.
35:11 I will **t** you in accordance with the
35:15 desolate, that is how I will **t** you.
Da 1:13 and **t** your servants in accordance
Hos 11: 8 Israel? How can I **t** you like Admah?
Na 3: 6 I will **t** you with contempt and make
Mt 18:17 **t** him as you would a pagan or a tax
18:35 how my heavenly Father will **t** each
Jn 15:21 They will **t** you this way because of
1Co 12:23 honourable we **t** with special honour.
Gal 4:14 did not **t** me with contempt or scorn.
Eph 6: 9 masters, **t** your slaves in the same
1Th 5:20 do not **t** prophecies with contempt.
1Ti 5: 1 **T** younger men as brothers,
1Pe 3: 7 and **t** them with respect as the

Treated (Treat)

Ge 12:13 so that I will be **t** well for your
12:16 He **t** Abram well for her sake, and
26:29 molest you but always **t** you well
34:31 they replied, "Should he have **t** our
39:19 slave **t** me," he burned with anger.
42:30 **t** us as though we were spying on the
Ex 5:15 have you **t** your servants this way?
18:11 those who had **t** Israel arrogantly."
Lev 19:34 The alien living with you must be **t**
25:40 He is to be **t** as a hired worker or a
25:53 He is to be **t** as a man hired from
Nu 14:23 **t** me with contempt will ever see it.
16:30 men have **t** the LORD with contempt."
25:18 they **t** you as enemies when they
Jdg 1:24 we will see that you are **t** well."
8: 1 "Why have you **t** us like this? Why
9:16 if you have **t** him as he deserves—
1Sa 2:14 This is how they **t** all the Israelites
6: 6 Pharaoh did? When he **t** them harshly,
24:17 **t** me well, but I have **t** you badly.
24:19 you well for the way you **t** me today.
1Ki 1:21 son Solomon will be **t** as criminals."
1Ch 24:31 **t** the same as those of the youngest.
Ne 9:10 how arrogantly the Egyptians **t** them.
Lam 2:20 and consider: Whom have you ever **t**
Eze 22: 7 In you they have **t** father and mother
Mt 21:36 the tenants **t** them in the same way.
Mk 12: 4 on the head and **t** him shamefully.
Lk 2:48 "Son, why have you **t** us like this?
6:23 is how their fathers **t** the prophets.
6:26 their fathers **t** the false prophets.
20:11 but that one also they beat and **t**
1Co 4:11 we are brutally **t**, we are homeless.
12:23 are **t** with special modesty,
Heb 10:29 who has **t** as an unholy thing the
10:33 by side with those who were so **t**.
Rev 18:20 judged her for the way she **t** you.

Treating (Treat)

Ge 18:25 **t** the righteous and the wicked alike
50:17 they committed in **t** you so badly.
Lev 22: 9 and die for **t** them with contempt.
1Sa 2:17 **t** the LORD's offering with contempt.
25:39 Nabal for **t** me with contempt.
Heb 12: 7 as discipline; God is **t** you as sons.

Treatment (Treat)

1Sa 20:34 at his father's shameful **t** of David.
Isa 66: 4 I also will choose harsh **t** for them
1Co 12:24 presentable parts need no special **t**.
Col 2:23 and their harsh **t** of the body,

Treatments (Treat)

Est 2: 3 and let beauty **t** be given to them.
2: 9 with her beauty **t** and special food.
2:12 beauty **t** prescribed for the women,

Treats (Treat)

Dt 24: 7 and **t** him as a slave or sells him,
Job 39:16 She **t** her young harshly, as if they
41:27 Iron he **t** like straw and bronze like
Pr 27:11 anyone who **t** me with contempt.

Treaty

Ge 21:27 Abimelech, and the two men made a **t**.
21:32 After the **t** had been made at
26:28 Let us make a **t** with you
Ex 34:12 Be careful not to make a **t** with
34:15 "Be careful not to make a **t** with
Dt 7: 2 **t** with them, and show them no mercy.
23: 6 Do not seek a **t** of friendship with
Jos 9: 6 distant country; make a **t** with us."
9: 7 How then can we make a **t** with you?"
9:11 are your servants; make a **t** with us.
9:15 Joshua made a **t** of peace with them
9:16 Three days after they made the **t**
10: 1 had made a **t** of peace with Israel
11:19 not one city made a **t** of peace with
1Sa 11: 1 "Make a **t** with us, and we will be
11: 2 "I will make a **t** with you only on
1Ki 5:12 and the two of them made a **t**.
15:19 "Let there be a **t** between me and you,
15:19 Now break your **t** with Baasha king of
20:34 ⌊Ahab said,⌋ "On the basis of a **t**
20:34 made a **t** with him, and let him go.
2Ch 16: 3 "Let there be a **t** between me and you,
16: 3 Now break your **t** with Baasha king of
Ezr 9:12 Do not seek a **t** of friendship with
Isa 33: 8 The **t** is broken, its witnesses are
Eze 17:13 **t** with him, putting him under oath.
17:14 surviving only by keeping his **t**.
17:15 Will he break the **t** and yet escape?
17:16 he despised and whose **t** he broke.
Hos 12: 1 He makes a **t** with Assyria and sends
Am 1: 9 disregarding a **t** of brotherhood,

Tree (Fig-tree, Fig-trees, *Tree of life*, Trees)

Ge 1:29 **t** that has fruit with seed in it.
2: 9 **t** of the knowledge of good and evil.
2:16 to eat from any **t** in the garden;
2:17 you must not eat from the **t** of the
3: 1 not eat from any **t** in the garden'?"
3: 3 'You must not eat fruit from the **t**
3: 6 woman saw that the fruit of the **t**
3:11 Have you eaten from the **t** from which
3:12 fruit from the **t**, and I ate it."
3:17 the **t** about which I commanded you,
12: 6 of the great **t** of Moreh at Shechem.
18: 4 your feet and rest under this **t**.
18: 8 ate, he stood near them under a **t**.
21:33 Abraham planted a tamarisk **t** in
40:19 off your head and hang you on a **t**.
Ex 9:25 in the fields and stripped every **t**.
10: 5 **t** that is growing in your fields.
10:15 **t** or plant in all the land of Egypt.
Lev 19:23 **t**, regard its fruit as forbidden.
Dt 12: 2 under every spreading **t** where the
19: 5 as he swings his axe to fell a **t**,
21:22 death and his body is hung on a **t**,
21:23 you must not leave his body on the **t**
21:23 is hung on a **t** is under God's curse.
22: 6 either in a **t** or on the ground, and
Jos 8:29 He hung the king of Ai on a **t** and
8:29 them to take his body from the **t**
19:33 Heleph and the large **t** in Zaanannim,
Jdg 4:11 great **t** in Zaanannim near Kedesh.
9: 6 great **t** at the pillar in Shechem
9: 8 said to the olive **t**, 'Be our king.'
9: 9 But the olive **t** answered, 'Should I
9:37 direction of the soothsayers' **t**."
1Sa 10: 3 you reach the great **t** of Tabor.
14: 2 under a pomegranate **t** in Migron.
22: 6 was seated under the tamarisk **t** on
31:13 them under a tamarisk **t** at Jabesh,
2Sa 18: 9 Absalom's head got caught in the **t**.
18:10 seen Absalom hanging in an oak **t**."
18:14 Absalom was still alive in the oak **t**
1Ki 13:14 He found him sitting under an oak **t**
14:23 hill and under every spreading **t**.
19: 4 He came to a broom **t**, sat down under
19: 5 he lay down under the **t** and fell

2Ki 3:19 You will cut down every good **t**, stop
3:25 springs and cut down every good **t**.
6: 5 one of them was cutting down a **t**,
16: 4 and under every spreading **t**.
17:10 hill and under every spreading **t**.
1Ch 10:12 bones under the great **t** in Jabesh,
2Ch 3: 5 it with palm **t** and chain designs.
28: 4 and under every spreading **t**.
Ne 10:35 of our crops and of every fruit **t**.
Job 14: 7 "At least there is hope for a **t**: If
15:33 an olive **t** shedding its blossoms.
19:10 gone; he uproots my hope like a **t**.
24:20 remembered but are broken like a **t**.
30: 4 food was the root of the broom **t**.
Ps 1: 3 He is like a **t** planted by streams of
37:35 like a green **t** in its native soil,
52: 8 I am like an olive **t** flourishing in
92:12 will flourish like a palm **t**,
120: 4 with burning coals of the broom **t**.
Ecc 11: 3 Whether a **t** falls to the south or to
12: 5 when the almond **t** blossoms and the
SS 2: 3 Like an apple **t** among the trees of
4:14 with every kind of incense **t**, with
7: 8 I said, "I will climb the palm **t**; I
8: 5 Under the apple **t** I roused you;
Isa 17: 6 as when an olive **t** is beaten,
24:13 as when an olive **t** is beaten, or as
55:13 the thornbush will grow the pine **t**,
56: 3 eunuch complain, "I am only a dry **t**.
57: 5 oaks and under every spreading **t**;
65:22 For as the days of a **t**, so will be
Jer 1:11 branch of an almond **t**," I replied.
2:20 under every spreading **t** you lay
3: 6 **t** and has committed adultery there.
3:13 spreading **t**, and have not obeyed me,
8:13 There will be no figs on the **t**, and
10: 3 they cut a **t** out of the forest,
11:16 **t** with fruit beautiful in form.
11:19 "Let us destroy the **t** and its fruit;
17: 8 He will be like a **t** planted by the
Eze 6:13 under every spreading **t** and every
17:24 tall **t** and make the low **t** grow tall.
17:24 green **t** and make the dry **t** flourish.
20:28 saw any high hill or any leafy **t**,
31: 8 no **t** in the garden of God could
31:13 of the air settled on the fallen **t**,
40:22 portico and its palm **t** decorations
40:26 it had palm **t** decorations on the
41:19 the face of a man towards the palm **t**
41:19 towards the palm **t** on the other.
Da 4:10 stood a **t** in the middle of the land.
4:11 The **t** grew large and strong and its
4:14 'Cut down the **t** and trim off its
4:20 The **t** you saw, which grew large and
4:22 you, O king, are that **t**! You have
4:23 'Cut down the **t** and destroy it, but
4:26 the stump of the **t** with its roots
Hos 14: 6 splendour will be like an olive **t**,
14: 8 I am like a green pine **t**;
Joel 1:12 the palm and the apple **t**—all the
Hag 2:19 the olive **t** have not borne fruit.
Zec 11: 2 Wail, O pine **t**, for the cedar has
Mt 3:10 and every **t** that does not produce
7:17 Likewise every good **t** bears good
7:17 fruit, but a bad **t** bears bad fruit.
7:18 A good **t** cannot bear bad fruit, and
7:18 and a bad **t** cannot bear good fruit.
7:19 Every **t** that does not bear good
12:33 "Make a **t** good and its fruit will be
12:33 or make a **t** bad and its fruit will
12:33 for a **t** is recognised by its fruit.
13:32 of garden plants and becomes a **t**,
21:19 again!" Immediately the **t** withered.
Mk 11:14 he said to the **t**, "May no-one ever
Lk 3: 9 and every **t** that does not produce
6:43 "No good **t** bears bad fruit, nor does
6:43 nor does a bad **t** bear good fruit.
6:44 Each **t** is recognised by its own
13:19 It grew and became a **t**, and the
17: 6 you can say to this mulberry **t**, 'Be
19: 4 climbed a sycamore-fig **t** to see him,
23:31 if men do these things when the **t**
Ac 5:30 had killed by hanging him on a **t**.
10:39 killed him by hanging him on a **t**,
13:29 from the **t** and laid him in a tomb.
Ro 11:24 if you were cut out of an olive **t**
11:24 grafted into a cultivated olive **t**,
11:24 be grafted into their own olive **t**!
Gal 3:13 is everyone who is hung on a **t**."
1Pe 2:24 bore our sins in his body on the **t**,
Rev 7: 1 the land or on the sea or on any **t**.
9: 4 of the earth or any plant or **t**,
22: 2 **t** are for the healing of the nations.

Tree of life

Ge 2: 9 the middle of the garden were the **t**
3:22 the **t** and eat, and live for ever."
3:24 and forth to guard the way to the **t**.
Pr 3:18 She is a **t** to those who embrace her;
11:30 The fruit of the righteous is a **t**,
13:12 but a longing fulfilled is a **t**.
15: 4 tongue that brings healing is a **t**
Rev 2: 7 **t**, which is in the paradise of God.
22: 2 each side of the river stood the **t**,
22:14 they may have the right to the **t**
22:19 share in the **t** and in the holy city,

Trees (Tree)

Ge 1:11 seed-bearing plants and **t** on the
1:12 **t** bearing fruit with seed in it
2: 9 the LORD God made all kinds of **t**
2: 9 **t** that were pleasing to the eye
3: 2 eat fruit from the **t** in the garden,
3: 8 LORD God among the **t** of the garden.
13:18 near the great **t** of Mamre at Hebron,
14:13 the great **t** of Mamre the Amorite,
18: 1 Abraham near the great **t** of Mamre
23:17 and all the **t** within the borders of
30:37 almond and plane **t** and made white
Ex 10:15 the fields and the fruit on the **t**.
15:27 twelve springs and seventy palm **t**,
Lev 23:40 are to take choice fruit from the **t**,
26: 4 and the **t** of the field their fruit.
26:20 the **t** of the land yield their fruit.
27:30 from the soil or fruit from the **t**,
Nu 13:20 Is it fertile or poor? Are there **t**
33: 9 palm **t**, and they camped there.
Dt 11:30 near the great **t** of Moreh, in the
20:19 do not destroy its **t** by putting an
20:19 Do not cut them down. Are the **t** of
20:20 However, you may cut down **t** that you
20:20 **t** that you know are not fruit **t**
24:20 you beat the olives from your **t**, do
28:40 You will have olive **t** throughout
28:42 your **t** and the crops of your land.
Jos 10:26 the kings and hung them on five **t**,
10:26 left hanging on the **t** until evening.
10:27 they took them down from the **t** and
Jdg 9: 8 One day the **t** went out to anoint a
9: 9 honoured, to hold sway over the **t**?'
9:10 "Next, the **t** said to the fig-tree,
9:11 and sweet, to hold sway over the **t**?'
9:12 "Then the **t** said to the vine, 'Come
9:13 and men, to hold sway over the **t**?'
9:14 "Finally all the **t** said to the
9:15 "The thornbush said to the **t**, 'If
2Sa 5:23 them in front of the balsam **t**.
5:24 in the tops of the balsam **t**,
1Ki 6:29 cherubim, palm **t** and open flowers.
6:32 palm **t** and open flowers, and
6:32 and palm **t** with beaten gold.
6:35 He carved cherubim, palm **t** and open
7:36 lions and palm **t** on the surfaces of
10:27 as sycamore-fig **t** in the foothills.
2Ki 6: 4 the Jordan and began to cut down **t**.
18:32 a land of olive **t** and honey.
1Ch 14:14 them in front of the balsam **t**.
14:15 in the tops of the balsam **t**,
16:33 the **t** of the forest will sing, they
27:28 **t** in the western foothills.
2Ch 1:15 as sycamore-fig **t** in the foothills.
9:27 as sycamore-fig **t** in the foothills.
Ne 8:15 from olive and wild olive **t**,
8:15 palms and shade **t**, to make booths"
9:25 groves and fruit **t** in abundance.
10:37 of the fruit of all our **t** and of
Ps 74: 5 axes to cut through a thicket of **t**.
96:12 **t** of the forest will sing for joy;
104:16 The **t** of the LORD are well watered,
104:17 stork has its home in the pine **t**.
105:33 shattered the **t** of their country.
Ps 148: 9 you mountains and all hills, fruit **t**
Ecc 2: 5 all kinds of fruit **t** in them.
2: 6 to water groves of flourishing **t**.
SS 2: 3 Like an apple tree among the **t** of
6:11 I went down to the grove of nut **t** to
Isa 7: 2 as the **t** of the forest are shaken by
10:19 the remaining **t** of his forests will
10:33 The lofty **t** will be felled, the tall
14: 8 Even the pine **t** and the cedars of
44: 4 like poplar **t** by flowing streams.
44:14 He let it grow among the **t** of the
44:23 you forests and all your **t**, for the
55:12 **t** of the field will clap their hands.
Jer 6: 6 "Cut down the **t** and build siege
7:20 on man and beast, on the **t** of the
17: 2 spreading **t** and on the high hills.
46:22 with axes, like men who cut down **t**.
Eze 15: 2 on any of the **t** in the forest?
15: 6 **t** of the forest as fuel for the fire,
17:24 All the **t** of the field will know
20:47 all your **t**, both green and dry.
27: 5 They made all your timbers of pine **t**
31: 4 channels to all the **t** of the field.
31: 5 towered higher than all the **t** of the
31: 8 nor could the pine **t** equal its
31: 8 nor could the plane **t** compare with
31: 9 the **t** of Eden in the garden of God.
31:14 Therefore no other **t** by the waters
31:14 No other **t** so well-watered are ever
31:15 the **t** of the field withered away.
31:16 Then all the **t** of Eden, the choicest
31:16 all the **t** that were well-watered,
31:18 "'Which of the **t** of Eden can be
31:18 will be brought down with the **t** of
34:27 The **t** of the field will yield their
36:30 I will increase the fruit of the **t**
40:16 walls were decorated with palm **t**.
40:31 court; palm **t** decorated its jambs,
40:34 **t** decorated the jambs on either side,
40:37 **t** decorated the jambs on either side,
41:18 were carved cherubim and palm **t**.
41:18 Palm **t** alternated with cherubim.
41:20 cherubim and palm **t** were carved on
41:25 **t** like those carved on the walls,
41:26 with palm **t** carved on each side.
47: 7 of **t** on each side of the river.
47:12 Fruit **t** of all kinds will grow on
Joel 1:12 the **t** of the field—are dried up.
1:19 burned up all the **t** of the field.
2:22 The **t** are bearing their fruit; the
Am 4: 9 devoured your fig and olive **t**, yet
7:14 I also took care of sycamore-fig **t**.
Zec 1: 8 among the myrtle **t** in a ravine.
1:10 the man standing among the myrtle **t**
1:11 who was standing among the myrtle **t**,
4: 3 Also there are two olive **t** by it,
4:11 "What are these two olive **t** on the
11: 2 the stately **t** are ruined! Wail,
Mt 3:10 axe is already at the root of the **t**,
21: 8 cut branches from the **t** and spread
Mk 8:24 they look like **t** walking around."
Lk 3: 9 axe is already at the root of the **t**,
21:29 "Look at the fig-tree and all the **t**.
Jude :12 blown along by the wind; autumn **t**,
Rev 7: 3 harm the land or the sea or the **t**
8: 7 a third of the **t** were burned up, and
11: 4 These are the two olive **t** and the

Tremble (Trembled, Trembles, Trembling)

Ex 15:14 The nations will hear and **t**; anguish
Dt 2:25 **t** and be in anguish because of you."
1Ch 16:30 **T** before him, all the earth! The
Job 9: 6 its place and makes its pillars **t**.
Ps 96: 9 **t** before him, all the earth.
99: 1 The LORD reigns, let the nations **t**;
114: 7 **T**, O earth, at the presence of the
Ecc 12: 3 the keepers of the house **t**, and the
Isa 13:13 Therefore I will make the heavens **t**;
14:16 shook the earth and made kingdoms **t**,
19: 1 The idols of Egypt **t** before him, and
21: 4 My heart falters, fear makes me **t**;
23:11 the sea and made its kingdoms **t**.
32:10 will **t**; the grape harvest will fail,
32:11 **T**, you complacent women; shudder,

Isa 41: 5 and fear; the ends of the earth **t**.
44: 8 Do not **t**, do not be afraid. Did I
64: 1 the mountains would **t** before you!
66: 5 Hear the word of the LORD, you who **t**
Jer 5:22 "Should you not **t** in my presence? I
23: 9 is broken within me; all my bones **t**.
33: 9 and they will be in awe and will **t**
49:21 of their fall the earth will **t**;
50:46 Babylon's capture the earth will **t**;
Eze 7:27 of the people of the land will **t**.
12:18 "Son of man, **t** as you eat your food,
26:10 Your walls will **t** at the noise of
26:15 **t** at the sound of your fall,
26:18 Now the coastlands **t** on the day of
31:16 I made the nations **t** at the sound of
32:10 will **t** every moment for his life.
38:20 of the earth will **t** at my presence.
Joel 2: 1 Let all who live in the land **t**, for
3:16 the earth and the sky will **t**.
Am 3: 6 do not the people **t**? When disaster
8: 8 "Will not the land **t** for this, and
Na 2:10 bodies **t**, every face grows pale.
Hab 2: 7 make you **t**? Then you will become
3: 6 he looked, and made the nations **t**.

Trembled (Tremble)

Ge 27:33 Isaac **t** violently and said, "Who was
Ex 19:16 blast. Everyone in the camp **t**.
19:18 the whole mountain **t** violently,
20:18 mountain in smoke, they **t** with fear.
1Sa 16: 4 of the town **t** when they met him.
21: 1 Ahimelech **t** when he met him, and
2Sa 22: 8 "The earth **t** and quaked, the
22: 8 shook; they **t** because he was angry.
Ezr 9: 4 everyone who **t** at the words of the
Ps 18: 7 The earth **t** and quaked, and the
18: 7 shook; they **t** because he was angry.
77:18 the world; the earth **t** and quaked.
Isa 64: 3 and the mountains **t** before you.
Hos 13: 1 Ephraim spoke, men **t**; he was exalted
Hab 3:16 crept into my bones, and my legs **t**.
Ac 7:32 **t** with fear and did not dare to look.

Trembles (Tremble)

Jdg 7: 3 'Anyone who **t** with fear may turn
Ps 97: 4 up the world; the earth sees and **t**.
104:32 he who looks at the earth, and it **t**,
119:120 My flesh **t** in fear of you; I stand
119:161 cause, but my heart **t** at your word.
Pr 30:21 "Under three things the earth **t**,
Isa 10:29 Ramah **t**; Gibeah of Saul flees.
66: 2 in spirit, and **t** at my word.
Jer 8:16 of their stallions the whole land **t**.
10:10 When he is angry, the earth **t**; the
51:29 The land **t** and writhes, for the
Joel 2:10 the sky **t**, the sun and moon are
Na 1: 5 The earth **t** at his presence, the

Trembling (Tremble)

Ge 42:28 turned to each other **t** and said,
Ex 15:15 of Moab will be seized with **t**,
2Sa 22:46 They all lose heart; they come **t**
Job 4:14 fear and **t** seized me and made all my
21: 6 I am terrified; **t** seizes my body.
Ps 2:11 LORD with fear and rejoice with **t**.
18:45 They all lose heart; they come **t**
48: 6 **T** seized them there, pain like that
55: 5 Fear and **t** have beset me; horror has
Isa 33:14 are terrified; **t** grips the godless.
Eze 26:16 **t** every moment, appalled at you.
Da 10:10 A hand touched me and set me **t** on my
10:11 he said this to me, I stood up **t**.
Hos 3: 5 They will come **t** to the LORD and to
11:10 children will come **t** from the west.
11:11 They will come **t** like birds from
Mic 7:17 They will come **t** out of their dens;
Mk 5:33 came and fell at his feet and, **t**
16: 8 **T** and bewildered, the women went out
Lk 8:47 came **t** and fell at his feet.
Ac 16:29 in and fell **t** before Paul and Silas.
1Co 2: 3 weakness and fear, and with much **t**.
2Co 7:15 receiving him with fear and **t**.
Php 2:12 out your salvation with fear and **t**,
Heb 12:21 that Moses said, "I am **t** with fear.

Tremendous

Rev 16:18 been on earth, so **t** was the quake.

Trench

1Ki 18:32 and he dug a **t** round it large enough
18:35 the altar and even filled the **t**.
18:38 also licked up the water in the **t**.
Da 9:25 be rebuilt with streets and a **t**,

Trespass (Trespasses)

Ro 5:15 the gift is not like the **t**. For if
5:15 For if the many died by the **t** of the
5:17 For if, by the **t** of the one man,
5:18 just as the result of one **t** was
5:20 The law was added so that the **t**

Trespasses (Trespass)

Ro 5:16 many **t** and brought justification.

Tresses

SS 7: 5 the king is held captive by its **t**.

Trial (Trials)

Nu 35:12 he stands **t** before the assembly.
Jos 20: 6 he has stood **t** before the assembly
20: 9 to standing **t** before the assembly.
Ps 37:33 them be condemned when brought to **t**.
Mk 13:11 you are arrested and brought to **t**,
Ac 12: 4 out for public **t** after the Passover.
12: 6 before Herod was to bring him to **t**,
16:37 "They beat us publicly without a **t**,
23: 6 I stand on **t** because of my hope in
24:21 that I am on **t** before you today.
25: 9 **t** before me there on these charges?"
25:20 and stand **t** there on these charges.
26: 6 our fathers that I am on **t** today.
27:24 You must stand **t** before Caesar; and
2Co 8: 2 Out of the most severe **t**, their
Gal 4:14 Even though my illness was a **t** to
Jas 1:12 is the man who perseveres under **t**,
1Pe 4:12 at the painful **t** you are suffering,
Rev 3:10 keep you from the hour of **t** that is

Trials (Trial)

Dt 7:19 saw with your own eyes the great **t**,
29: 3 your own eyes you saw those great **t**,
Lk 22:28 those who have stood by me in my **t**.
1Th 3: 3 would be unsettled by these **t**.
2Th 1: 4 persecutions and **t** you are enduring.
Jas 1: 2 whenever you face **t** of many kinds,
1Pe 1: 6 to suffer grief in all kinds of **t**.
2Pe 2: 9 how to rescue godly men from **t**

Tribal (Tribe)

Ge 25:16 the names of the twelve **t** rulers
Nu 4:18 "See that the Kohathite **t** clans are
7: 2 the **t** leaders in charge of those
25:15 Zur, a **t** chief of a Midianite family.
36: 4 **t** inheritance of our forefathers."
36: 6 within the **t** clan of their father.
36: 7 keep the **t** land inherited from his
36: 8 someone in her father's **t** clan,
Dt 1:15 and of tens and as **t** officials.
Jos 11:23 according to their **t** divisions.
12: 7 according to their **t** divisions—
14: 1 **t** clans of Israel allotted to them.
18:10 according to their **t** divisions.
19:51 the heads of the **t** clans of Israel
21: 1 of the other **t** families of Israel
Eze 45: 7 parallel to one of the **t** portions.
48: 8 will equal one of the **t** portions;
48:21 **t** portions will belong to the prince,

Tribe (Tribal, Tribes)

Ex 31: 2 the son of Hur, of the **t** of Judah,
31: 6 of the **t** of Dan, to help him.
35:30 the son of Hur, of the **t** of Judah,
35:34 of the **t** of Dan, the ability to
38:22 the son of Hur, of the **t** of Judah,
38:23 of the **t** of Dan—a craftsman and
Nu 1: 4 One man from each **t**, each the head
1:21 The number from the **t** of Reuben was
1:23 The number from the **t** of Simeon was
1:25 number from the **t** of Gad was 45,650
1:27 The number from the **t** of Judah was
1:29 The number from the **t** of Issachar
1:31 The number from the **t** of Zebulun was
1:33 The number from the **t** of Ephraim was
1:35 The number from the **t** of Manasseh
1:37 The number from the **t** of Benjamin
1:39 number from the **t** of Dan was 62,700
1:41 The number from the **t** of Asher was
1:43 The number from the **t** of Naphtali
1:47 The families of the **t** of Levi,
1:49 "You must not count the **t** of Levi or
2: 5 The **t** of Issachar will camp next to
2: 7 The **t** of Zebulun will be next. The
2:12 The **t** of Simeon will camp next to
2:14 The **t** of Gad will be next. The
2:20 The **t** of Manasseh will be next to
2:22 The **t** of Benjamin will be next. The
2:27 The **t** of Asher will camp next to
2:29 The **t** of Naphtali will be next. The
3: 6 "Bring the **t** of Levi and present
7:12 son of Amminadab of the **t** of Judah.
10:15 the division of the **t** of Issachar,
10:16 the division of the **t** of Zebulun.
10:19 the division of the **t** of Simeon,
10:20 over the division of the **t** of Gad.
10:23 the division of the **t** of Manasseh,
10:24 the division of the **t** of Benjamin.
10:26 over the division of the **t** of Asher,
10:27 the division of the **t** of Naphtali.
13: 2 From each ancestral **t** send one of
13: 4 their names: from the **t** of Reuben,
13: 5 from the **t** of Simeon, Shaphat son of
13: 6 from the **t** of Judah, Caleb son of
13: 7 from the **t** of Issachar, Igal son of
13: 8 from the **t** of Ephraim, Hoshea son of
13: 9 from the **t** of Benjamin, Palti son of
13:10 from the **t** of Zebulun, Gaddiel son
13:11 the **t** of Manasseh (a **t** of Joseph)
13:12 from the **t** of Dan, Ammiel son of
13:13 from the **t** of Asher, Sethur son of
13:14 from the **t** of Naphtali, Nahbi son of
13:15 from the **t** of Gad, Geuel son of Maki.
17: 3 for the head of each ancestral **t**.
18: 2 from your ancestral **t** to join you
24: 2 out and saw Israel encamped **t** by **t**,
26:55 to the names for its ancestral **t**.
31: 5 a thousand from each **t**, were
31: 6 a thousand from each **t**, along with
34:14 the families of the **t** of Reuben, the
34:14 the **t** of Gad and the half-tribe of
34:18 appoint one leader from each **t** to
34:19 of Jephunneh, from the **t** of Judah;
34:20 Shemuel son of Ammihud, from the **t**
34:21 Elidad son of Kislon, from the **t** of
34:22 Jogli, the leader from the **t** of Dan;
34:23 the **t** of Manasseh son of Joseph;
34:24 from the **t** of Ephraim son of Joseph;
34:25 the leader from the **t** of Zebulun;
34:26 the leader from the **t** of Issachar;
34:27 the leader from the **t** of Asher;
34:28 the leader from the **t** of Naphtali."
35: 8 to the inheritance of each **t**:
35: 8 many towns from a **t** that has many,
36: 3 to that of the **t** they marry into.
36: 4 that of the **t** into which they marry,
36: 5 "What the **t** of the descendants of
36: 7 in Israel is to pass from **t** to **t**,
36: 8 inherits land in any Israelite **t**
36: 9 No inheritance may pass from **t** to **t**,
36: 9 **t** is to keep the land it inherits."
36:12 in their father's clan and **t**.
Dt 1:23 twelve of you, one man from each **t**.
10: 8 the LORD set apart the **t** of Levi to
18: 1 who are Levites—indeed the whole **t**
29:18 clan or **t** among you today whose
Jos 3:12 tribes of Israel, one from each **t**.
4: 2 among the people, one from each **t**,
4: 4 the Israelites, one from each **t**,
7: 1 the **t** of Judah, took some of them.
7:14 morning, present yourselves **t** by **t**.
7:14 The **t** that the LORD takes shall come
7:18 Zerah, of the **t** of Judah, was taken.
13: 7 and half of the **t** of Manasseh."
13:14 But to the **t** of Levi he gave no
13:15 Moses had given to the **t** of Reuben

Jos 13:24 what Moses had given to the t of Gad
13:33 to the t of Levi, Moses had given no
15: 1 The allotment for the t of Judah,
15:20 the inheritance of the t of Judah
15:21 The southernmost towns of the t of
16: 8 t of the Ephraimites, clan by clan.
17: 1 the allotment for the t of Manasseh
17: 6 the daughters of the t of Manasseh
18: 4 Appoint three men from each t. I
18:11 lot came up for the t of Benjamin
18:21 The t of Benjamin, clan by clan, had
19: 1 The second lot came out for the t of
19: 8 t of the Simeonites, clan by clan.
19:23 of the t of Issachar, clan by clan.
19:24 The fifth lot came out for the t of
19:31 of the t of Asher, clan by clan.
19:39 of the t of Naphtali, clan by clan.
19:40 The seventh lot came out for the t
19:48 of the t of Dan, clan by clan.
20: 8 on the plateau in the t of Reuben,
20: 8 Ramoth in Gilead in the t of Gad,
20: 8 Golan in Bashan in the t of Manasseh.
21:17 from the t of Benjamin they gave
21:20 towns from the t of Ephraim:
21:23 Also from the t of Dan they received
21:25 From half the t of Manasseh they
21:28 from the t of Issachar, Kishion,
21:30 from the t of Asher, Mishal, Abdon,
21:32 from the t of Naphtali, Kedesh in
21:34 the t of Zebulun, Jokneam, Kartah,
21:36 from the t of Reuben, Bezer, Jahaz,
21:38 from the t of Gad, Ramoth in Gilead
22: 7 and to the other half of the t
Jdg 18: 1 in those days the t of the Danites
18:19 Isn't it better that you serve a t
18:30 and his sons were priests for the t
20:12 men throughout the t of Benjamin,
21: 3 Why should one t be missing from
21: 6 "Today one t is cut off from Israel,
21:17 a t of Israel will not be wiped out.
1Sa 9:21 from the smallest t of Israel, and
9:21 all the clans of the t of Benjamin?
10:20 near, the t of Benjamin was chosen.
10:21 he brought forward the t of Benjamin
2Sa 4: 2 Beerothite from the t of Benjamin
1Ki 7:14 whose mother was a widow from the t
8:16 I have not chosen a city in any t of
11:13 but will give him one t for the sake
11:32 of Israel, he will have one t.
11:36 I will give one t to his son so that
12:20 Only the t of Judah remained loyal
12:21 the t of Benjamin—a hundred and
2Ki 17:18 Only the t of Judah was left,
1Ch 6:60 from the t of Benjamin they were
6:61 the clans of half the t of Manasseh.
6:62 the t of Manasseh that is in Bashan.
6:66 towns from the t of Ephraim.
6:70 from half the t of Manasseh the
6:72 from the t of Issachar they received
6:74 from the t of Asher they received
6:76 from the t of Naphtali they received
6:77 t of Zebulun they received Jokneam,
6:78 from the t of Reuben across the
6:80 from the t of Gad they received
12: 2 of Saul from the t of Benjamin):
12:31 men of half the t of Manasseh,
23:14 counted as part of the t of Levi.
27:20 t of Manasseh: Joel son of Pedaiah;
2Ch 6: 5 I have not chosen a city in any t of
11:16 Those from every t of Israel who set
19:11 the leader of the t of Judah, will
Est 2: 5 of Susa a Jew of the t of Benjamin,
Job 30:12 On my right the t attacks; they lay
Ps 68:27 There is the little t of Benjamin,
74: 2 the t of your inheritance, whom you
78:67 he did not choose the t of Ephraim;
78:68 he chose the t of Judah, Mount Zion,
Jer 10:16 Israel, the t of his inheritance
51:19 including the t of his inheritance—
Eze 47:23 In whatever t the alien settles,
Lk 2:36 of Phanuel, of the t of Asher.
Ac 13:21 of the t of Benjamin, who ruled for
Ro 11: 1 of Abraham, from the t of Benjamin.
Php 3: 5 of the t of Benjamin, a Hebrew of
Heb 7:13 are said belonged to a different t,
7:13 that t has ever served at the altar.
Heb 7:14 regard to that t Moses said nothing
Rev 5: 5 "Do not weep! See, the Lion of the t
5: 9 t and language and people and nation.
7: 5 the t of Judah 12,000 were sealed
7: 5 from the t of Reuben 12,000,
7: 5 from the t of Gad 12,000,
7: 6 from the t of Asher 12,000,
7: 6 from the t of Naphtali 12,000,
7: 6 from the t of Manasseh 12,000,
7: 7 from the t of Simeon 12,000,
7: 7 from the t of Levi 12,000,
7: 7 from the t of Issachar, 12,000,
7: 8 from the t of Zebulun 12,000,
7: 8 from the t of Joseph 12,000,
7: 8 from the t of Benjamin 12,000.
7: 9 from every nation, t, people and
11: 9 t, language and nation will gaze on
13: 7 t, people, language and nation.
14: 6 nation, t, language and people.

Tribes (Tribe)

Ge 49:16 people as one of the t of Israel.
49:28 All these are the twelve t of Israel
Ex 24: 4 representing the twelve t of Israel.
28:21 the name of one of the twelve t.
39:14 the name of one of the twelve t.
Nu 1:16 the leaders of their ancestral t.
10: 5 a trumpet blast is sounded, the t
17: 2 leader of each of their ancestral t.
17: 6 of each of their ancestral t, and
30: 1 Moses said to the heads of the t of
31: 4 men from each of the t of Israel."
32:28 the family heads of the Israelite t.
33:54 it according to your ancestral t.
34:13 be given to the nine and a half t,
34:15 These two and a half t have received
36: 3 marry men from other Israelite t;
Dt 1:13 respected men from each of your t,
1:15 I took the leading men of your t,
5:23 your t and your elders came to me.
12: 5 choose from among all your t to put
12:14 LORD will choose in one of your t,
16:18 officials for each of your t in
18: 5 their descendants out of all your t
27:12 you have crossed the Jordan, these t
27:13 these t shall stand on Mount Ebal to
29:21 all the t of Israel for disaster,
31:28 of your t and all your officials,
33: 5 along with the t of Israel.
Jos 3:12 t of Israel, one from each tribe.
4: 5 number of the t of the Israelites,
4: 8 according to the number of the t of
7:16 forward by t, and Judah was taken.
12: 7 an inheritance to the t of Israel
13: 7 as an inheritance among the nine t
14: 2 by lot to the nine-and-a-half t,
14: 3 granted the two-and-a-half t their
14: 4 become two t—Manasseh and Ephraim.
18: 2 there were still seven Israelite t
18:11 between the t of Judah and Joseph:
21: 4 the t of Judah, Simeon and Benjamin.
21: 5 from the clans of the t of Ephraim,
21: 6 from the clans of the t of Issachar,
21: 7 the t of Reuben, Gad and Zebulun.
21: 9 From the t of Judah and Simeon they
21:16 —nine towns from these two t.
22:14 one for each of the t of Israel,
23: 4 as an inheritance for your t
24: 1 Joshua assembled all the t of Israel
Jdg 18: 1 inheritance among the t of Israel.
20: 2 leaders of all the people of the t
20:10 hundred from all the t of Israel,
20:12 The t of Israel sent men throughout
21: 5 "Who from all the t of Israel has
21: 8 they asked, "Which one of the t of
21:15 had made a gap in the t of Israel.
21:24 and went home to their t and clans,
1Sa 2:28 I chose your father out of all the t
10:19 before the LORD by your t and clans
10:20 Samuel brought all the t of Israel
15:17 become the head of the t of Israel?
2Sa 5: 1 All the t of Israel came to David at
15: 2 is from one of the t of Israel."
15:10 throughout the t of Israel to say,
19: 9 Throughout the t of Israel, the
2Sa 20:14 Sheba passed through all the t of
24: 2 "Go throughout the t of Israel from
1Ki 8: 1 all the heads of the t and the
11:31 Solomon's hand and give you ten t.
11:32 t of Israel, he will have one tribe.
11:35 his son's hands and give you ten t.
14:21 t of Israel in which to put his Name.
18:31 one for each of the t descended from
2Ki 21: 7 chosen out of all the t of Israel,
1Ch 6:62 towns from the t of Issachar,
6:63 the t of Reuben, Gad and Zebulun.
6:65 From the t of Judah, Simeon and
27:16 The officers over the t of Israel:
27:22 the officers over the t of Israel.
28: 1 Jerusalem: the officers over the t,
29: 6 the officers of the t of Israel, the
2Ch 5: 2 all the heads of the t and the
12:13 t of Israel in which to put his Name.
33: 7 chosen out of all the t of Israel,
Ezr 6:17 one for each of the t of Israel.
Ps 72: 9 The desert t will bow before him and
78:55 the t of Israel in their homes.
105:37 from among their t no-one faltered.
122: 4 That is where the t go up, the t of
Isa 49: 6 servant to restore the t of Jacob
63:17 the t that are your inheritance.
Eze 37:19 the Israelite t associated with him,
45: 8 the land according to their t.
47:13 among the twelve t of Israel,
47:21 according to the t of Israel.
47:22 inheritance among the t of Israel.
48: 1 "These are the t, listed by name: At
48:19 will come from all the t of Israel.
48:23 "As for the rest of the t: Benjamin
48:29 an inheritance to the t of Israel,
48:31 will be named after the t of Israel.
Hos 5: 9 Among the t of Israel I proclaim
Zec 9: 1 eyes of men and all the t of Israel
Mt 19:28 judging the twelve t of Israel.
Lk 22:30 judging the twelve t of Israel.
Ac 26: 7 This is the promise our twelve t are
Jas 1: 1 To the twelve t scattered among the
Rev 7: 4 144,000 from all the t of Israel.
21:12 the names of the twelve t of Israel.

Tribulation

Rev 7:14 who have come out of the great t;

Tribute

Nu 31:28 set apart as t for the LORD one out
31:29 Take this t from their half share
31:37 of which the t for the LORD was 675;
31:38 36,000 cattle, of which the t for
31:39 30,500 donkeys, of which the t for
31:40 16,000 people, of which the t for
31:41 Moses gave the t to Eleazar the
Jdg 3:15 him with t to Eglon king of Moab.
3:17 He presented the t to Eglon king of
3:18 After Ehud had presented the t, he
2Sa 8: 2 subject to David and brought t.
8: 6 became subject to him and brought t.
1Ki 4:21 These countries brought t and were
2Ki 17: 3 vassal and had paid him t.
17: 4 and he no longer paid t to the king
1Ch 18: 2 became subject to him and brought t.
18: 6 became subject to him and brought t.
2Ch 17:11 Jehoshaphat gifts and silver as t,
26: 8 The Ammonites brought t to Uzziah,
Ezr 4:13 no more taxes, t or duty will be
4:20 taxes, t and duty were paid to them.
7:24 t or duty on any of the priests,
Est 10: 1 King Xerxes imposed t throughout the
Ps 72:10 distant shores will bring t to him;
89:22 No enemy will subject him to t; no
Isa 16: 1 Send lambs as t to the ruler of the
Hos 10: 6 will be carried to Assyria as t for

Trick (Trickery, Tricking)

1Th 2: 3 motives, nor are we trying to t you.

Trickery (Trick)

Ac 13:10 full of all kinds of deceit and t.
2Co 12:16 fellow that I am, I caught you by t!

Tricking (Trick)
Ge 27:12 I would appear to be t him and would

Tried (Try)
Ge 37:21 Reuben heard this, he t to rescue
Ex 2:15 Pharaoh heard of this, he t to kill
8:18 when the magicians t to produce
Dt 4:34 Has any god ever t to take for
13: 5 he has t to turn you from the way
13:10 Stone him to death, because he t to
1Sa 17:39 over the tunic and t walking around,
19:10 Saul t to pin him to the wall with
2Sa 4: 8 your enemy, who t to take your life.
21: 2 had t to annihilate them.
1Ki 11:40 Solomon t to kill Jeroboam, but
Ps 73:16 I t to understand all this, it was
95: 9 where your fathers tested and t me,
109: 7 he is t, let him be found guilty,
Ecc 2: 3 I t cheering myself with wine, and
Lam 3:53 They t to end my life in a pit and
Eze 24:13 Because I t to cleanse you but you
Da 6: 4 the satraps t to find grounds for
Mt 3:14 John t to deter him, saying, "I need
Lk 4:42 t to keep him from leaving them.
5:18 t to take him into the house to lay
6:19 the people all t to touch him,
9: 9 things about?" And he t to see him.
9:49 in your name and we t to stop him,
Jn 5:18 For this reason the Jews t all the
7:30 At this they t to seize him, but
10:39 Again they t to seize him, but he
11: 8 "a short while ago the Jews t to
19:12 From then on, Pilate t to set Jesus
Ac 7:26 He t to reconcile them by saying,
9:26 he came to Jerusalem, he t to join
9:29 Grecian Jews, but they t to kill him
13: 8 t to turn the proconsul from the
16: 7 they t to enter Bithynia, but the
19:13 t to invoke the name of the Lord
24: 6 even t to desecrate the temple; so
25:10 court, where I ought to be t.
26:11 and I t to force them to blaspheme.
26:21 the temple courts and t to kill me.
28:23 t to convince them about Jesus from
Gal 1:13 church of God and t to destroy it.
1:23 the faith he once t to destroy."
Heb 3: 9 where your fathers tested and t me
11:29 t to do so, they were drowned.

Tries (Try)
Job 34: 9 nothing when he t to please God.'
Lk 17:33 Whoever t to keep his life will lose
Rev 11: 5 If anyone t to harm them, fire comes

Trifling
Ne 9:32 do not let all this hardship seem t

Trim (Trimmed, Trimmers)
Dt 21:12 her shave her head, t her nails
Da 4:14 'Cut down the tree and t off its

Trimmed (Trim)
2Sa 19:24 or t his moustache or washed his
1Ki 6:36 and one course of t cedar beams.
7: 2 columns supporting t cedar beams.
7: 9 t with a saw on their inner and
7:12 and one course of t cedar beams,
Eze 44:20 to keep the hair of their heads t.
Mt 25: 7 virgins woke up and t their lamps,

Trimmers (Trim)
Ex 25:38 Its wick t and trays are to be of
37:23 its wick t and trays, of pure gold.
Nu 4: 9 together with its lamps, its wick t
1Ki 7:50 the pure gold dishes, wick t,
2Ki 12:13 wick t, sprinkling bowls, trumpets
25:14 shovels, wick t, dishes and all the
2Ch 4:22 the pure gold wick t, sprinkling
Jer 52:18 shovels, wick t, sprinkling bowls,

Trip (Tripping)
Ps 140: 4 of violence who plan to t my feet.

Tripolis
Ezr 4: 9 and officials over the men from T,

Tripping (Trip)
Isa 3:16 flirting with their eyes, t along

Triumph (Triumphal, Triumphant, Triumphed, Triumphing, Triumphs)
Jdg 8: 9 in t, I will tear down this tower."
11:31 to meet me when I return in t from
1Sa 26:25 will do great things and surely t.
Job 17: 4 therefore you will not let them t.
Ps 9:19 Arise, O LORD, let not man t; let
12: 4 says, "We will t with our tongues;
13: 2 How long will my enemy t over me?
25: 2 shame, nor let my enemies t over me.
41:11 me, for my enemy does not t over me.
54: 7 my eyes have looked in t on my foes.
60: 6 "In t I will parcel out Shechem and
60: 8 over Philistia I shout in t."
108: 7 "In t I will parcel out Shechem and
108: 9 over Philistia I shout in t."
112: 8 end he will look in t on his foes.
118: 7 I will look in t on my enemies.
Pr 28:12 the righteous t, there is great
Isa 13: 3 wrath—those who rejoice in my t.
42:13 cry and will t over his enemies.
Jer 9: 3 by truth that they t in the land.
51:14 and they will shout in t over you.
Mic 5: 9 Your hand will be lifted up in t

Triumphal (Triumph)
Isa 60:11 their kings led in t procession.
2Co 2:14 who always leads us in t procession

Triumphant (Triumph)
Da 11:12 thousands, yet he will not remain t.

Triumphed (Triumph)
Dt 32:27 say, 'Our hand has t; the LORD has
1Sa 17:50 David t over the Philistine with a
Lam 1: 9 my affliction, for the enemy has t.
Rev 5: 5 of Judah, the Root of David, has t.

Triumphing (Triumph)
Col 2:15 of them, t over them by the cross.

Triumphs (Triumph)
Jas 2:13 Mercy t over judgment!

Troas
Port on coast of Mysia in north-western Asia Minor. Paul had a vision here and was called to Macedonia (Ac 16:8–11). On his travels he revisited here, the first time hoping to find Titus (2Co 2:12–13), and the second time reviving a man from a fatal accident (Ac 20:5–12). He probably returned on at least one further occasion (2Ti 4:13).

Ac 16: 8 passed by Mysia and went down to T.
16:11 From T we put out to sea and sailed
20: 5 on ahead and waited for us at T.
20: 6 at T, where we stayed seven days.
2Co 2:12 Now when I went to T to preach the
2Ti 4:13 cloak that I left with Carpus at T,

Trod (Tread)
Job 22:15 the old path that evil men have t?
Isa 63: 3 I trampled them in my anger and t

Trodden (Tread)
Jdg 9:27 and gathered the grapes and t them,
Isa 63: 3 "I have t the winepress alone;

Troop (Troops)
2Sa 22:30 your help I can advance against a t
Ps 18:29 your help I can advance against a t

Troops (Troop)
Ex 14: 9 horsemen and t—pursued the
Jos 10: 5 They moved up with all their t and
11: 4 They came out with all their t and a
Jdg 4: 7 with his chariots and his t to the
4:16 All the t of Sisera fell by the
8: 5 "Give my t some bread; they are worn
8: 6 Why should we give bread to your t?"
9:34 Abimelech and all his t set out by
1Sa 13: 7 t with him were quaking with fear.
14:24 So none of the t tasted food.
18:13 David led the t in their campaigns.
2Sa 10: 9 so he selected some of the best t in
10:13 Joab and the t with him advanced to
12:28 Now muster the rest of the t and
16: 6 though all the t and the special
17: 8 will not spend the night with the t.
17: 9 If he should attack your t first,
17: 9 among the t who follow Absalom.'
18: 2 David sent the t out—a third under
18: 2 The king told the t, "I myself will
18: 5 And all the t heard the king giving
18:16 Joab sounded the trumpet, and the t
19: 2 because on that day the t heard it
19:40 All the t of Judah and half the t of
20:12 that all the t came to a halt there.
20:15 the t with Joab came and beseiged
23:10 The t returned to Eleazar, but only
23:11 lentils, Israel's t fled from them.
24: 3 multiply the t a hundred times over,
2Ki 9:17 in Jezreel saw Jehu's t approaching,
9:17 he called out, "I see some t coming.
11:15 who were in charge of the t: "Bring
1Ch 11:13 the t fled from the Philistines.
19: 7 as the king of Maacah with his t,
19:10 so he selected some of the best t in
19:14 Joab and the t with him advanced to
21: 2 to Joab and the commanders of the t,
21: 3 multiply his t a hundred times over.
2Ch 12: 3 and the innumerable t of Libyans,
13: 3 with eight hundred thousand able t.
13:13 Now Jeroboam had sent t round to the
17: 2 He stationed t in all the fortified
23:14 who were in charge of the t, and
25: 7 "O king, these t from Israel must
25: 9 I paid for these Israelite t?"
25:10 Amaziah dismissed the t who had come
25:13 Meanwhile the t that Amaziah had
Job 19:12 His t advance in force; they build a
29:25 I dwelt as a king among his t; I was
Ps 110: 3 Your t will be willing on your day
SS 6: 4 majestic as t with banners.
Eze 12:14 all his t—and I will pursue them
17:21 All his fleeing t will fall by the
38: 6 also Gomer with all its t, and
38: 6 its t—the many nations with you.
38: 9 You and all your t and the many
38:22 on his t and on the many nations
39: 4 all your t and the nations with you.
Da 11:15 even their best t will not have the
Mic 5: 1 Marshal your t, O city of t, for a
Na 2: 5 He summons his picked t, yet they
3:13 Look at your t—they are all women!
Ac 21:31 the commander of the Roman t
23:10 He ordered the t to go down and take
23:27 but I came with my t and rescued him,
Rev 9:16 The number of the mounted t was two

Trophimus
Ac 20: 4 and T from the province of Asia.
21:29 had previously seen T the Ephesian
2Ti 4:20 and I left T sick in Miletus.

Trouble (Troubled, Troublemaker, Troublemakers, Troubler, Troubles, Troublesome, Troubling)
Ge 34:30 "You have brought t on me by making
41:51 God has made me forget all my t
43: 6 "Why did you bring this t on me by
Ex 5:19 they were in t when they were told,
5:22 "O Lord, why have you brought t upon
5:23 he has brought t upon this people,
Nu 11:11 "Why have you brought this t on your
33:55 t in the land where you will live.
Jos 6:18 to destruction and bring t on it.

Jos 7:25 "Why have you brought this **t** on us?
7:25 The LORD will bring **t** on you today.
Jdg 10:14 Let them save you when you are in **t**!
11: 7 come to me now, when you're in **t**?"
1Sa 4: 7 "We're in **t**! Nothing like this has
14:29 Jonathan said, "My father has made **t**
20:19 where you hid when this **t** began,
26:24 my life and deliver me from all **t**."
2Sa 4: 9 who has delivered me out of all **t**,
1Ki 1:29 who has delivered me out of every **t**,
11:25 adding to the **t** caused by Hadad.
18:18 "I have not made **t** for Israel,"
20: 7 "See how this man is looking for **t**!
2Ki 4:13 'You have gone to all this **t** for us.
14:10 but stay at home! Why ask for **t** and
1Ch 2: 7 who brought **t** on Israel by violating
2Ch 25:19 But stay at home! Why ask for **t** and
28:20 him, but gave him **t** instead of help.
28:22 In his time of **t** King Ahaz became
Ne 1: 3 are in great **t** and disgrace.
2:17 I said to them, "You see the **t** we
4: 8 Jerusalem and stir up **t** against it.
Job 2:10 we accept good from God, and not **t**?"
3:10 womb on me to hide **t** from my eyes.
4: 5 now **t** comes to you, and you are
4: 8 evil and those who sow **t** reap it.
5: 6 nor does **t** sprout from the ground.
5: 7 Yet man is born to **t** as surely as
11:16 You will surely forget your **t**,
14: 1 woman is of few days and full of **t**.
15:35 They conceive **t** and give birth to
19:28 the root of the **t** lies in him,'
30:25 Have I not wept for those in **t**? Has
31:29 over the **t** that came to him—
38:23 which I reserve for times of **t**, for
42:11 the **t** the LORD had brought upon him,
Ps 7:14 **t** gives birth to disillusionment.
7:16 The **t** he causes recoils on himself;
9: 9 a stronghold in times of **t**.
10: 1 do you hide yourself in times of **t**?
10: 6 always be happy and never have **t**."
10: 7 **t** and evil are under his tongue.
10:14 you, O God, do see **t** and grief; you
22:11 Do not be far from me, for **t** is near
27: 5 For in the day of **t** he will keep me
32: 7 you will protect me from **t** and
37:39 he is their stronghold in time of **t**.
41: 1 the LORD delivers him in times of **t**.
46: 1 strength, an ever-present help in **t**.
50:15 call upon me in the day of **t**; I will
55: 2 hear me and answer me. My thoughts **t**
59:16 fortress, my refuge in times of **t**.
66:14 and my mouth spoke when I was in **t**.
69:17 answer me quickly, for I am in **t**.
86: 7 In the day of my **t** I will call to
88: 3 For my soul is full of **t** and my life
90:10 yet their span is but **t** and sorrow,
90:15 for as many years as we have seen **t**.
91:15 with him in **t**, I will deliver him
94:13 you grant him relief from days of **t**,
106:32 and **t** came to Moses because of them;
107: 6 cried out to the LORD in their **t**
107:13 they cried to the LORD in their **t**,
107:19 they cried to the LORD in their **t**,
107:28 cried out to the LORD in their **t**
116: 3 me; I was overcome by **t** and sorrow.
119:143 **T** and distress have come upon me,
138: 7 Though I walk in the midst of **t**, you
140: 9 with the **t** their lips have caused.
142: 2 before him; before him I tell my **t**.
143:11 righteousness, bring me out of **t**.
Pr 1:27 when distress and **t** overwhelm you.
10:22 wealth, and he adds no **t** to it.
11: 8 The righteous man is rescued from **t**,
11:17 but a cruel man brings **t** on himself.
11:29 He who brings **t** on his family will
12:13 talk, but a righteous man escapes **t**.
12:21 but the wicked have their fill of **t**.
13:17 A wicked messenger falls into **t**, but
15: 6 income of the wicked brings them **t**.
15:27 A greedy man brings **t** to his family,
17:20 tongue is deceitful falls into **t**.
19:23 one rests content, untouched by **t**.
22: 8 He who sows wickedness reaps **t**, and
24: 2 and their lips talk about making **t**.
24:10 If you falter in times of **t**, how
Pr 25:19 on the unfaithful in times of **t**.
28:14 who hardens his heart falls into **t**.
Ecc 12: 1 before the days of **t** come and the
Isa 59: 4 conceive **t** and give birth to evil.
Jer 2:27 in **t**, they say, 'Come and save us!'
2:28 they can save you when you are in **t**!
20:18 I ever come out of the womb to see **t**
30: 7 It will be a time of **t** for Jacob,
Eze 32: 9 I will **t** the hearts of many peoples
Da 9:25 and a trench, but in times of **t**.
Ob :12 boast so much in the day of their **t**.
:14 survivors in the day of their **t**.
Jnh 1: 8 for making all this **t** for us?
Na 1: 7 LORD is good, a refuge in times of **t**.
1: 9 end; **t** will not come a second time.
Zep 1:15 a day of **t** and ruin, a day of
Zec 10:11 They will pass through the sea of **t**;
Mt 6:34 Each day has enough **t** of its own.
13:21 When **t** or persecution comes because
28:14 satisfy him and keep you out of **t**."
Mk 4:17 When **t** or persecution comes because
Lk 7: 6 "Lord, don't **t** yourself, for I do
Jn 16:33 In this world you will have **t**. But
Ac 17: 6 "These men who have caused **t** all
Ro 2: 9 There will be **t** and distress for
8:35 Shall **t** or hardship or persecution
1Co 7:21 Don't let it **t** you—although if you
2Co 1: 4 can comfort those in any **t** with the
Gal 6:17 Finally, let no-one cause me **t**, for
Php 1:17 up **t** for me while I am in chains.
3: 1 It is no **t** for me to write the same
2Th 1: 6 will pay back **t** to those who **t** you
1Ti 5:10 helping those in **t** and devoting
Heb 12:15 grows up to cause **t** and defile many.
Jas 5:13 Is any one of you in **t**? He should

Troubled (Trouble)

Ge 41: 8 In the morning his mind was **t**, so he
Nu 11:10 exceedingly angry, and Moses was **t**.
1Sa 1:15 "I am a woman who is deeply **t**.
15:11 Samuel was **t**, and he cried out to
Job 20: 2 "My **t** thoughts prompt me to answer
Ps 38:18 I confess my iniquity; I am **t** by my
77: 4 from closing; I was too **t** to speak.
Isa 38:14 I am **t**; O Lord, come to my aid!"
Jer 49:23 **t** like the restless sea.
Da 2: 1 mind was **t** and he could not sleep.
7:15 "I, Daniel, was **t** in spirit, and the
7:28 I, Daniel, was deeply **t** by my
Mt 26:37 and he began to be sorrowful and **t**.
Mk 14:33 began to be deeply distressed and **t**.
Lk 1:29 Mary was greatly **t** at his words and
6:18 Those **t** by evil spirits were cured,
24:38 He said to them, "Why are you **t**, and
Jn 11:33 he was deeply moved in spirit and **t**.
12:27 "Now my heart is **t**, and what shall I
13:21 After he had said this, Jesus was **t**
14: 1 "Do not let your hearts be **t**. Trust
14:27 hearts be **t** and do not be afraid.
Ac 16:18 Finally Paul became so **t** that he
2Th 1: 7 give relief to you who are **t**, and to

Troublemaker (Trouble)

2Sa 20: 1 Now a **t** named Sheba son of Bicri, a
Ac 24: 5 "We have found this man to be a **t**,

Troublemakers (Trouble)

1Sa 10:27 some **t** said, "How can this fellow
30:22 all the evil men and **t** among David's

Troubler (Trouble)

1Ki 18:17 "Is that you, you **t** of Israel?

Troubles (Trouble)

Job 2:11 heard about all the **t** that had come
Ps 25:17 The **t** of my heart have multiplied;
25:22 Israel, O God, from all their **t**!
34: 6 him; he saved him out of all his **t**.
34:17 he delivers them from all their **t**.
34:19 A righteous man may have many **t**, but
40:12 For **t** without number surround me; my
54: 7 he has delivered me from all my **t**
71:20 Though you have made me see **t**, many
Ecc 11:10 and cast off the **t** of your body,
Isa 22: 1 What **t** you now, that you have all
46: 7 it cannot save him from his **t**.
65:16 For the past **t** will be forgotten and
Da 2: 3 "I have had a dream that **t** me and I
Ac 7:10 rescued him from all his **t**. He gave
1Co 7:28 But those who marry will face many **t**
2Co 1: 4 who comforts us in all our **t**, so
4:17 For our light and momentary **t** are
6: 4 in **t**, hardships and distresses;
7: 4 in all our **t** my joy knows no bounds.
Php 4:14 it was good of you to share in my **t**.

Troublesome (Trouble)

Ezr 4:15 **t** to kings and provinces, a place of

Troubling (Trouble)

2Sa 14: 5 The king asked her, "What is **t** you?"
2Ch 15: 6 **t** them with every kind of distress.
Est 4: 5 out what was **t** Mordecai and why.
Ac 15:24 you, **t** your minds by what they said.

Trough (Troughs)

Ge 24:20 quickly emptied her jar into the **t**,
Dt 28: 5 Your basket and your kneading **t** will
28:17 Your basket and your kneading **t** will

Troughs (Trough)

Ge 30:38 branches in all the watering **t**,
30:41 would place the branches in the **t**
Ex 2:16 the **t** to water their father's flock.
8: 3 and into your ovens and kneading **t**.
12:34 in kneading **t** wrapped in clothing.

Trousers

Da 3:21 these men, wearing their robes, **t**,

Trudge

Isa 45:14 be yours; they will **t** behind you,

True (*True God*, Truth)

Nu 11:23 not what I say will come **t** for you."
12: 7 this is not **t** of my servant Moses;
Dt 13:14 And if it is **t** and it has been
17: 4 If it is **t** and it has been proved
18:22 LORD does not take place or come **t**,
22:20 If, however, the charge is **t** and no
Jos 7:20 Achan replied, "It is **t**! I have
21:42 it; this was **t** for all these towns.
23:15 of the LORD your God has come **t**,
Jdg 13:17 honour you when your word comes **t**?"
Ru 3:12 Although it is **t** that I am near of
1Sa 9: 6 and everything he says comes **t**.
1Ki 8:26 your servant David my father come **t**.
10: 6 achievements and your wisdom is **t**.
13:32 of Samaria will certainly come **t**."
2Ki 9:12 That's not **t**!" they said. "Tell us."
19:17 "It is **t**, O LORD, that the Assyrian
2Ch 6:17 promised your servant David come **t**.
9: 5 achievements and your wisdom is **t**.
Ne 6: 6 Geshem says it is **t**—that you
Est 2:23 was investigated and found to be **t**,
Job 5:27 "We have examined this, and it is **t**.
9: 2 "Indeed, I know that this is **t**. But
11: 6 wisdom, for **t** wisdom has two sides.
19: 4 If it is **t** that I have gone astray,
Ps 33: 4 the word of the LORD is right and **t**
105:19 the word of the LORD proved him **t**.
119:142 is everlasting and your law is **t**.
119:151 O LORD, and all your commands are **t**.
119:160 All your words are **t**; all your
144:15 are the people of whom this is **t**;
Pr 8: 7 My mouth speaks what is **t**, for my
22:21 teaching you **t** and reliable words,
Ecc 12:10 and what he wrote was upright and **t**.
Isa 37:18 "It is **t**, O LORD, that the Assyrian
43: 9 others may hear and say, "It is **t**.
Jer 28: 9 LORD only if his prediction comes **t**.
37:14 "That's not **t**!" Jeremiah said. "I am
40:16 are saying about Ishmael is not **t**."
42: 5 "May the LORD be a **t** and faithful
50: 7 their **t** pasture, the LORD, the hope
Eze 16:45 You are a **t** daughter of your mother,
16:45 you are a **t** sister of your sisters,
33:33 "When all this comes **t**—and it

Da 2:45 in the future. The dream is **t** and
3:14 said to them, "Is it **t**, Shadrach,
7:16 asked him the **t** meaning of all this.
7:19 "Then I wanted to know the **t** meaning
8:26 that has been given you is **t**,
10: 1 Its message was **t** and it concerned a
Am 2:11 Is this not **t**, people of Israel?"
7: 7 wall that had been built **t** to plumb,
Mic 7:20 You will be **t** to Jacob, and show
Zec 7: 9 'Administer **t** justice; show mercy
8:16 **t** and sound judgment in your courts;
Mal 2: 6 **T** instruction was in his mouth and
Lk 1:20 will come **t** at their proper time."
16:11 who will trust you with **t** riches?
24:34 saying, "It is **t**! The Lord has risen
Jn 1: 9 The **t** light that gives light to
1:47 "Here is a **t** Israelite, in whom
4:18 What you have just said is quite **t**."
4:23 has now come when the **t** worshippers
4:37 'One sows and another reaps' is **t**.
6:32 gives you the **t** bread from heaven.
7:28 on my own, but he who sent me is **t**.
10:41 John said about this man was **t**."
15: 1 "I am the **t** vine, and my Father is
19:35 testimony, and his testimony is **t**.
21:24 We know that his testimony is **t**.
Ac 7: 1 asked him, "Are these charges **t**?"
10:34 "I now realise how **t** it is that God
11:23 **t** to the Lord with all their hearts.
14:22 them to remain **t** to the faith.
17:11 day to see if what Paul said was **t**.
24: 9 asserting that these things were **t**.
25:11 against me by these Jews are not **t**,
26:25 What I am saying is **t** and reasonable
Ro 3: 4 Let God be **t**, and every man a liar.
1Co 15:54 saying that is written will come **t**:
2Co 7:14 as everything we said to you was **t**,
7:14 to Titus has proved to be **t** as well.
Eph 4:24 God in **t** righteousness and holiness.
Php 1:15 is **t** that some preach Christ out of
1:18 motives or **t**, Christ is preached.
4: 8 Finally, brothers, whatever is **t**,
1Ti 1: 2 To Timothy my **t** son in the faith:
2: 7 of the **t** faith to the Gentiles.
Tit 1: 4 To Titus, my **t** son in our common
1:13 This testimony is **t**. Therefore,
3: 2 to show **t** humility towards all men.
Heb 8: 2 in the sanctuary, the **t** tabernacle
9:24 the **t** one; he entered heaven itself,
12: 8 illegitimate children and not **t** sons
1Pe 5:12 that this is the **t** grace of God.
2Pe 2:10 This is especially **t** of those who
2:22 Of them the proverbs are **t**: "A dog
1Jn 2: 8 and the **t** light is already shining.
5:20 so that we may know him who is **t**.
5:20 And we are in him who is **t**—even in
3Jn :12 you know that our testimony is **t**.
Rev 2:13 Yet you remain **t** to my name. You did
3: 7 and **t**, who holds the key of David.
3:14 the faithful and **t** witness, the
6:10 Sovereign Lord, holy and **t**, until
15: 3 **t** are your ways, King of the ages.
16: 7 **t** and just are your judgments."
19: 2 for **t** and just are his judgments.
19: 9 "These are the **t** words of God.
19:11 rider is called Faithful and **T**.
21: 5 these words are trustworthy and **t**."
22: 6 "These words are trustworthy and **t**.

True God

2Ch 15: 3 long time Israel was without the **t**,
Jer 10:10 the LORD is the **t**; he is the living
Jn 17: 3 the only **t**, and Jesus Christ, whom
1Th 1: 9 idols to serve the living and **t**,
1Jn 5:20 He is the **t** and eternal life.

Truly (Truth)

Ps 116:16 O LORD, **t** I am your servant; I am
Pr 11:19 The **t** righteous man attains life,
Isa 10:20 down but will **t** rely on the LORD,
45:15 **T** you are a God who hides himself,
Jer 28: 9 recognised as one **t** sent by the LORD
Mt 14:33 saying, "**T** you are the Son of God.
Jn 17:19 that they too may be **t** sanctified.
21:15 "Simon son of John, do you **t** love me
Jn 21:16 Simon son of John, do you **t** love me?
1Ti 6:19 hold of the life that is **t** life.
1Jn 2: 5 God's love is **t** made complete in him.

Trumpet (Trumpeters, Trumpets)

Ex 19:16 mountain, and a very loud **t** blast.
19:19 the sound of the **t** grew louder and
20:18 the **t** and saw the mountain in smoke,
Lev 23:24 assembly commemorated with **t** blasts.
25: 9 have the **t** sounded everywhere on the
25: 9 sound the **t** throughout your land.
Nu 10: 5 a **t** blast is sounded, the tribes
Jos 6:16 when the priests sounded the **t** blast
6:20 and at the sound of the **t**, when the
Jdg 3:27 he arrived there, he blew a **t** in the
6:34 and he blew a **t**, summoning the
1Sa 13: 3 Then Saul had the **t** blown throughout
2Sa 2:28 Joab blew the **t**, and all the men
18:16 Joab sounded the **t**, and the troops
20: 1 He sounded the **t** and shouted, "We
20:22 So he sounded the **t**, and his men
1Ki 1:34 Blow the **t** and shout, 'Long live
1:39 Then they sounded the **t** and all the
1:41 On hearing the sound of the **t**, Joab
2Ki 9:13 Then they blew the **t** and shouted,
Ne 4:18 who sounded the **t** stayed with me.
4:20 Wherever you hear the sound of the **t**,
Job 39:24 stand still when the **t** sounds.
39:25 At the blast of the **t** he snorts,
Ps 150: 3 Praise him with the sounding of the **t**
Isa 18: 3 when a **t** sounds, you will hear it.
27:13 in that day a great **t** will sound.
58: 1 Raise your voice like a **t**. Declare
Jer 4: 5 'Sound the **t** throughout the land!'
4:19 the **t**; I have heard the battle cry.
4:21 and hear the sound of the **t**?
6: 1 Flee from Jerusalem! Sound the **t** in
6:17 'Listen to the sound of the **t**!' But
42:14 hear the **t** or be hungry for bread,'
51:27 Blow the **t** among the nations!
Eze 7:14 Though they blow the **t** and get
33: 3 and blows the **t** to warn the people,
33: 4 if anyone hears the **t** but does not
33: 5 Since he heard the sound of the **t**
33: 6 does not blow the **t** to warn the
Hos 5: 8 "Sound the **t** in Gibeah, the horn in
8: 1 "Put the **t** to your lips! An eagle is
Joel 2: 1 Blow the **t** in Zion; sound the alarm
2:15 Blow the **t** in Zion, declare a holy
Am 2: 2 war cries and the blast of the **t**.
3: 6 a **t** sounds in a city, do not the
Zep 1:16 a day of **t** and battle cry against
Zec 9:14 The Sovereign LORD will sound the **t**;
Mt 24:31 will send his angels with a loud **t**
1Co 14: 8 Again, if the **t** does not sound a
15:52 twinkling of an eye, at the last **t**.
15:52 For the **t** will sound, the dead will
1Th 4:16 the **t** call of God, and the dead in
Heb 12:19 to a **t** blast or to such a voice
Rev 1:10 behind me a loud voice like a **t**,
4: 1 heard speaking to me like a **t** said,
8: 7 The first angel sounded his **t**, and
8: 8 The second angel sounded his **t**, and
8:10 The third angel sounded his **t**, and a
8:12 The fourth angel sounded his **t**, and
8:13 because of the **t** blasts about to be
9: 1 The fifth angel sounded his **t**, and I
9:13 The sixth angel sounded his **t**, and I
9:14 to the sixth angel who had the **t**
10: 7 angel is about to sound his **t**,
11:15 The seventh angel sounded his **t**, and

Trumpeters (Trumpet)

2Ki 11:14 The officers and the **t** were beside
2Ch 5:13 The **t** and singers joined in unison,
23:13 The officers and the **t** were beside
29:28 the singers sang and the **t** played.
Rev 18:22 **t**, will never be heard in you again.

Trumpets (Trumpet)

Nu 10: 2 "Make two **t** of hammered silver, and
10: 7 To gather the assembly, blow the **t**,
10: 8 the priests, are to blow the **t**.
10: 9 you, sound a blast on the **t**.
Nu 10:10 the **t** over your burnt offerings
29: 1 It is a day for you to sound the **t**.
31: 6 sanctuary and the **t** for signalling.
Jos 6: 4 Make seven priests carry **t** of rams'
6: 4 with the priests blowing the **t**.
6: 5 them sound a long blast on the **t**,
6: 6 priests carry **t** in front of it."
6: 8 seven priests carrying the seven **t**
6: 8 blowing their **t**, and the ark of the
6: 9 ahead of the priests who blew the **t**,
6: 9 All this time the **t** were sounding.
6:13 carrying the seven **t** went forward,
6:13 ark of the LORD and blowing the **t**.
6:13 the LORD, while the **t** kept sounding.
6:20 the **t** sounded, the people shouted,
Jdg 7: 8 the provisions and **t** of the others.
7:16 he placed **t** and empty jars in the
7:18 I and all who are with me blow our **t**
7:19 They blew their **t** and broke the jars
7:20 The three companies blew the **t** and
7:20 right hands the **t** they were to blow,
7:22 the three hundred **t** sounded, the
2Sa 6:15 LORD with shouts and the sound of **t**.
15:10 soon as you hear the sound of the **t**,
2Ki 11:14 land were rejoicing and blowing **t**.
12:13 wick trimmers, sprinkling bowls, **t**
1Ch 13: 8 lyres, tambourines, cymbals and **t**.
15:24 to blow **t** before the ark of God.
15:28 the sounding of rams' horns and **t**,
16: 6 blow the **t** regularly before the ark
16:42 for the sounding of the **t** and
2Ch 5:12 by 120 priests sounding **t**.
5:13 Accompanied by **t**, cymbals and other
7: 6 the priests blew their **t**, and all
13:12 His priests with their **t** will sound
13:14 The priests blew their **t**
15:14 with shouting and with **t** and horns.
20:28 the LORD with harps and lutes and **t**.
23:13 land were rejoicing and blowing **t**,
29:26 and the priests with their **t**.
29:27 accompanied by **t** and the instruments
Ezr 3:10 in their vestments and with **t**,
Ne 12:35 well as some priests with **t**, and
12:41 Zechariah and Hananiah with their **t**
Ps 47: 5 the LORD amid the sounding of **t**.
98: 6 with **t** and the blast of the ram's
Mt 6: 2 do not announce it with **t**, as the
Rev 8: 2 God, and to them were given seven **t**.
8: 6 the seven angels who had the seven **t**

Trust (Trusted, Trustees, Trustfully, Trusting, Trusts, Trustworthy)

Ex 14:31 **t** in him and in Moses his servant.
19: 9 and will always put their **t** in you.
Nu 20:12 "Because you did not **t** in me enough
Dt 1:32 In spite of this, you did not **t** in
9:23 You did not **t** him or obey him.
28:52 walls in which you **t** fall down.
Jdg 11:20 Sihon, however, did not **t** Israel to
2Ki 17:14 who did not **t** in the LORD their God.
18:30 Do not let Hezekiah persuade you to **t**
1Ch 9:22 to their positions of **t** by David
Job 4:18 If God places no **t** in his servants,
15:15 If God places no **t** in his holy ones,
31:24 "If I have put my **t** in gold or said
39:12 Can you **t** him to bring in your grain
Ps 4: 5 Offer right sacrifices and **t** in the
9:10 Those who know your name will **t** in
13: 5 I **t** in your unfailing love; my heart
20: 7 Some **t** in chariots and some in
20: 7 **t** in the name of the LORD our God.
22: 4 In you our fathers put their **t**; they
22: 9 **t** in you even at my mother's breast.
25: 2 in you I **t**, O my God. Do not let me
31: 6 to worthless idols; I **t** in the LORD.
31:14 I **t** in you, O LORD; I say, "You are
33:21 In him our hearts rejoice, for we **t**
37: 3 **T** in the LORD and do good; dwell in
37: 5 Commit your way to the LORD; **t** in
40: 3 fear and put their **t** in the LORD.
40: 4 is the man who makes the LORD his **t**,
44: 6 I do not **t** in my bow, my sword does
49: 6 those who **t** in their wealth and
49:13 This is the fate of those who **t** in
52: 8 I **t** in God's unfailing love for ever

Ps 55:23 But as for me, I **t** in you.
56: 3 I am afraid, I will **t** in you.
56: 4 in God I **t**; I will not be afraid.
56:11 in God I **t**; I will not be afraid.
62: 8 **T** in him at all times, O people;
62:10 Do not **t** in extortion or take pride
78: 7 they would put their **t** in God and
78:22 for they did not believe in God or **t**
91: 2 my fortress, my God, in whom I **t**."
115: 8 them, and so will all who **t** in them.
115: 9 O house of Israel, **t** in the LORD—
115:10 O house of Aaron, **t** in the LORD—he
115:11 You who fear him, **t** in the LORD—he
118: 8 refuge in the LORD than to **t** in man.
118: 9 in the LORD than to **t** in princes.
119:42 who taunts me, for I **t** in your word.
125: 1 Those who **t** in the LORD are like
135:18 them, and so will all who **t** in them.
143: 8 love, for I have put my **t** in you.
146: 3 Do not put your **t** in princes, in
Pr 3: 5 **T** in the LORD with all your heart
21:22 down the stronghold in which they **t**.
22:19 that your **t** may be in the LORD, I
Isa 8:17 I will put my **t** in him.
12: 2 Surely God is my salvation; I will **t**
26: 4 **T** in the LORD for ever, for the LORD,
30:15 in quietness and **t** is your strength,
31: 1 who rely on horses, who **t** in the
36:15 not let Hezekiah persuade you to **t**
42:17 those who **t** in idols, who say to
50:10 who has no light, **t** in the name of
Jer 2:37 the LORD has rejected those you **t**;
5:17 the fortified cities in which you **t**.
7: 4 Do not **t** in deceptive words and say,
7:14 the temple you **t** in, the place I
9: 4 "Beware of your friends; do not **t**
12: 6 Do not **t** them, though they speak
28:15 persuaded this nation to **t** in lies.
39:18 because you **t** in me, declares the
48: 7 Since you **t** in your deeds and riches,
49: 4 you **t** in your riches and say, 'Who
49:11 Your widows too can **t** in me."
Mic 7: 5 Do not **t** a neighbour; put no
Na 1: 7 He cares for those who **t** in him,
Zep 3: 2 She does not **t** in the LORD, she does
3:12 who **t** in the name of the LORD.
Lk 16:11 who will **t** you with true riches?
Jn 12:36 Put your **t** in the light while you
14: 1 **T** in God; **t** also in me.
Ac 14:23 Lord, in whom they had put their **t**.
Ro 15:13 all joy and peace as you **t** in him,
1Co 4: 2 been given a **t** must prove faithful.
9:17 discharging the **t** committed to me.
2Co 13: 6 I **t** that you will discover that we
Heb 2:13 again, "I will put my **t** in him." And

Trusted (Trust)

1Sa 27:12 Achish **t** David and said to himself,
2Ki 18: 5 Hezekiah **t** in the LORD, the God of
1Ch 5:20 prayers, because they **t** in him.
Job 12:20 He silences the lips of **t** advisers
Ps 5: 9 Not a word from their mouth can be **t**
22: 4 they **t** and you delivered them.
22: 5 they **t** and were not disappointed.
26: 1 have **t** in the LORD without wavering.
41: 9 Even my close friend, whom I **t**, he
52: 7 but **t** in his great wealth and grew
Pr 27: 6 Wounds from a friend can be **t**, but
Isa 20: 5 Those who **t** in Cush and boasted in
25: 9 God; we **t** in him, and he saved us.
25: 9 This is the LORD, we **t** in him; let
47:10 You have **t** in your wickedness and
Jer 13:25 forgotten me and **t** in false gods.
38:22 you—those **t** friends of yours.
48:13 was ashamed when they **t** in Bethel.
Eze 16:15 "'But you **t** in your beauty and used
Da 3:28 They **t** in him and defied the king's
6:23 on him, because he had **t** in his God.
Lk 11:22 the man **t** and divides up the spoils.
16:10 "Whoever can be **t** with very little
16:10 very little can also be **t** with much,
Ac 12:20 a **t** personal servant of the king,
Tit 2:10 to show that they can be fully **t**,
3: 8 so that those who have **t** in God may

Trustees (Trust)

Gal 4: 2 He is subject to guardians and **t**

Trustfully (Trust)

Pr 3:29 neighbour, who lives **t** near you.

Trusting (Trust)

Job 15:31 Let him not deceive himself by **t**
Ps 112: 7 heart is steadfast, **t** in the LORD.
Isa 2:22 Stop **t** in man, who has but a breath
Jer 7: 8 look, you are **t** in deceptive words

Trusts (Trust)

Job 8:14 What he **t** in is fragile; what he
Ps 21: 7 For the king **t** in the LORD; through
22: 8 "He **t** in the LORD; let the LORD
28: 7 my heart **t** in him, and I am helped.
32:10 love surrounds the man who **t** in him.
84:12 blessed is the man who **t** in you.
86: 2 God; save your servant who **t** in you.
Pr 11:28 Whoever **t** in his riches will fall,
16:20 and blessed is he who **t** in the LORD.
28:25 he who **t** in the LORD will prosper.
28:26 He who **t** in himself is a fool, but
29:25 whoever **t** in the LORD is kept safe.
Isa 26: 3 is steadfast, because he **t** in you.
28:16 one who **t** will never be dismayed.
Jer 17: 5 "Cursed is the one who **t** in man, who
17: 7 blessed is the man who **t** in the LORD
Eze 33:13 but then he **t** in his righteousness
Hab 2:18 who makes it **t** in his own creation;
Mt 27:43 He **t** in God. Let God rescue him now
Ro 4: 5 the man who does not work but **t** God
9:33 **t** in him will never be put to shame.
10:11 **t** in him will never be put to shame
1Co 13: 7 always protects, always **t**, always
1Pe 2: 6 **t** in him will never be put to shame.

Trustworthy (Trust)

Ex 18:21 **t** men who hate dishonest gain—and
2Sa 7:28 you are God! Your words are **t**, and
Ne 13:13 because these men were considered **t**.
Ps 19: 7 LORD are **t**, making wise the simple.
111: 7 and just; all his precepts are **t**.
119:86 All your commands are **t**; help me,
119:138 are righteous; they are fully **t**.
Pr 11:13 but a **t** man keeps a secret.
13:17 but a **t** envoy brings healing.
25:13 a **t** messenger to those who send him;
Da 2:45 true and the interpretation is **t**."
6: 4 **t** and neither corrupt nor negligent.
Lk 16:11 if you have not been **t** in handling
16:12 if you have not been **t** with someone
19:17 'Because you have been **t** in a very
1Co 7:25 as one who by the Lord's mercy is **t**.
1Ti 1:15 Here is a **t** saying that deserves
3: 1 Here is a **t** saying: If anyone sets
3:11 but temperate and **t** in everything.
4: 9 This is a **t** saying that deserves
2Ti 2:11 Here is a **t** saying: If we died with
Tit 1: 9 He must hold firmly to the **t** message
3: 8 This is a **t** saying. And I want you
Rev 21: 5 for these words are **t** and true."
22: 6 to me, "These words are **t** and true.

Truth (*I tell you the truth*, Truly, Truthful, Truthfulness, Truths)

Ge 42:16 to see if you are telling the **t**.
1Ki 17:24 the LORD from your mouth is the **t**."
22:16 but the **t** in the name of the LORD
2Ch 18:15 but the **t** in the name of the LORD
Ps 15: 2 who speaks the **t** from his heart
25: 5 guide me in your **t** and teach me, for
26: 3 and I walk continually in your **t**.
31: 5 redeem me, O LORD, the God of **t**.
40:10 and your **t** from the great assembly.
40:11 love and your **t** always protect me.
43: 3 Send forth your light and your **t**,
45: 4 forth victoriously on behalf of **t**,
51: 6 Surely you desire **t** in the inner
52: 3 rather than speaking the **t**.
86:11 O LORD, and I will walk in your **t**;
96:13 and the peoples in his **t**.
119:30 I have chosen the way of **t**; I have
Ps 119:43 Do not snatch the word of **t** from my
145:18 on him, to all who call on him in **t**.
Pr 16:13 they value a man who speaks the **t**.
23:23 Buy the **t** and do not sell it; get
Isa 45:19 I, the LORD, speak the **t**; I declare
48: 1 but not in **t** or righteousness—
59:14 **t** has stumbled in the streets,
59:15 **T** is nowhere to be found, and
65:16 the land will do so by the God of **t**;
65:16 the land will swear by the God of **t**.
Jer 5: 1 who deals honestly and seeks the **t**,
5: 3 O LORD, do not your eyes look for **t**?
7:28 **T** has perished; it has vanished from
9: 3 by **t** that they triumph in the land.
9: 5 friend, and no-one speaks the **t**.
26:15 for in **t** the LORD has sent me to you
Da 8:12 and **t** was thrown to the ground
9:13 sins and giving attention to your **t**.
10:21 what is written in the Book of **T**.
Am 5:10 and despise him who tells the **t**.
Zec 8: 3 will be called the City of **T**,
8:16 to do: Speak the **t** to each other,
8:19 Therefore love **t** and peace."
Mt 22:16 way of God in accordance with the **t**.
Mk 5:33 with fear, told him the whole **t**.
12:14 way of God in accordance with the **t**.
Lk 20:21 way of God in accordance with the **t**.
Jn 1:14 the Father, full of grace and **t**.
1:17 and **t** came through Jesus Christ.
3:21 whoever lives by the **t** comes into
4:23 worship the Father in spirit and **t**,
4:24 must worship in spirit and in **t**."
5:33 John and he has testified to the **t**.
7:18 is a man of **t**; there is nothing
8:32 you will know the **t**, and the **t** will
8:40 you the **t** that I heard from God.
8:44 to the **t**, for there is no **t** in him.
8:45 Yet because I tell the **t**, you do not
8:46 the **t**, why don't you believe me?
14: 6 am the way and the **t** and the life.
14:17 the Spirit of **t**. The world cannot
15:26 the Spirit of **t** who goes out from
16:13 when he, the Spirit of **t**, comes, he
16:13 comes, he will guide you into all **t**.
17:17 them by the **t**; your word is **t**.
18:23 spoke the **t**, why did you strike me?"
18:37 into the world, to testify to the **t**.
18:37 on the side of **t** listens to me."
18:38 "What is **t**?" Pilate asked. With this
19:35 He knows that he tells the **t**, and he
Ac 20:30 distort the **t** in order to draw away
21:24 is no **t** in these reports about you,
21:34 get at the **t** because of the uproar,
24: 8 learn the **t** about all these charges
28:25 "The Holy Spirit spoke the **t** to your
Ro 1:18 suppress the **t** by their wickedness,
1:25 They exchanged the **t** of God for a
2: 2 who do such things is based on **t**.
2: 8 who reject the **t** and follow evil,
2:20 the embodiment of knowledge and **t**—
9: 1 I speak the **t** in Christ—I am not
15: 8 of the Jews on behalf of God's **t**,
1Co 5: 8 yeast, the bread of sincerity and **t**.
13: 6 in evil but rejoices with the **t**.
2Co 4: 2 by setting forth the **t** plainly we
11:10 surely as the **t** of Christ is in me,
12: 6 because I would be speaking the **t**.
13: 8 against the **t**, but only for the **t**.
Gal 2: 5 so that the **t** of the gospel might
2:14 in line with the **t** of the gospel,
4:16 your enemy by telling you the **t**?
5: 7 you and kept you from obeying the **t**?
Eph 1:13 heard the word of **t**, the gospel of
4:15 Instead, speaking the **t** in love, we
4:21 with the **t** that is in Jesus.
5: 9 all goodness, righteousness and **t**)
6:14 Stand firm then, with the belt of **t**
Col 1: 5 about in the word of **t**, the
1: 6 understood God's grace in all its **t**.
2Th 2:10 to love the **t** and so be saved.
2:12 have not believed the **t** but have
2:13 Spirit and through belief in the **t**.
1Ti 2: 4 and to come to a knowledge of the **t**.
2: 7 and an apostle—I am telling the **t**,
3:15 the pillar and foundation of the **t**.
4: 3 who believe and who know the **t**.

1Ti 6: 5 who have been robbed of the **t** and
2Ti 2:15 who correctly handles the word of **t**.
2:18 who have wandered away from the **t**.
2:25 them to a knowledge of the **t**,
3: 7 but never able to acknowledge the **t**.
3: 8 so also these men oppose the **t**—men
4: 4 from the **t** and turn aside to myths.
Tit 1: 1 of the **t** that leads to godliness—
1:14 commands of those who reject the **t**.
Heb 10:26 knowledge of the **t**, no sacrifice
Jas 1:18 give us birth through the word of **t**,
3:14 do not boast about it or deny the **t**.
5:19 wander from the **t** and someone
1Pe 1:22 purified yourselves by obeying the **t**
2Pe 1:12 established in the **t** you now have.
2: 2 bring the way of **t** into disrepute.
1Jn 1: 6 we lie and do not live by the **t**.
1: 8 ourselves and the **t** is not in us.
2: 4 is a liar, and the **t** is not in him.
2: 8 its **t** is seen in him and you,
2:20 Holy One, and all of you know the **t**.
2:21 you because you do not know the **t**,
2:21 and because no lie comes from the **t**.
3:18 or tongue but with actions and in **t**.
3:19 how we know that we belong to the **t**,
4: 6 of **t** and the spirit of falsehood.
5: 6 because the Spirit is the **t**.
2Jn : 1 her children, whom I love in the **t**—
: 1 I only, but also all who know the **t**
: 2 of the **t**, which lives in us and will
: 3 Son, will be with us in **t** and love.
: 4 **t**, just as the Father commanded us.
3Jn : 1 friend Gaius, whom I love in the **t**.
: 3 about your faithfulness to the **t**
: 3 how you continue to walk in the **t**.
: 4 my children are walking in the **t**.
: 8 that we may work together for the **t**.
:12 everyone—and even by the **t** itself.

Truthful (Truth)
Pr 12:17 A **t** witness gives honest testimony,
12:19 **T** lips endure for ever, but a lying
12:22 but he delights in men who are **t**.
14: 5 A **t** witness does not deceive, but a
14:25 A **t** witness saves lives, but a false
Jer 4: 2 if in a **t**, just and righteous way
Jn 3:33 it has certified that God is **t**.
2Co 6: 7 in **t** speech and in the power of God;

Truthfulness (Truth)
Ro 3: 7 "If my falsehood enhances God's **t**

Truths (Truth)
1Co 2:13 spiritual **t** in spiritual words.
1Ti 3: 9 They must keep hold of the deep **t** of
4: 6 brought up in the **t** of the faith and
Heb 5:12 **t** of God's word all over again.

Try (Tried, Tries, Trying)
Nu 20:18 may not pass through here; if you **t**,
Jdg 19:13 He added, "Come, let's **t** to reach
Ru 3: 1 "My daughter, should I not **t** to find
1Sa 26:21 I will not **t** to harm you again.
Job 17:10 "But come on, all of you, **t** again!
Ps 26: 2 Test me, O LORD, and **t** me, examine
Isa 7:13 not enough to **t** the patience of men?
7:13 you **t** the patience of my God also?
22: 4 Do not **t** to console me over the
Eze 7:26 They will **t** to get a vision from the
Da 7:25 oppress his saints and **t** to change
11:26 provisions will **t** to destroy him;
Zec 12: 3 **t** to move it will injure themselves.
Mal 1: 8 is that not wrong? **T** offering them
Lk 12:58 **t** hard to be reconciled to him on
13:24 **t** to enter and will not be able to.
14:19 and I'm on my way to **t** them out.
Ac 15:10 Now then, why do you **t** to test God
1Co 10:33 even as I **t** to please everybody in
14:12 **t** to excel in gifts that build up
2Co 5:11 fear the Lord, we **t** to persuade men.
1Th 5:15 but always **t** to be kind to each
Tit 2: 9 to **t** to please them, not to talk

Trying (Try)
Nu 16:10 you are **t** to get the priesthood too.
Jdg 6:31 Are you **t** to save him? Whoever
1Sa 20: 1 that he is **t** to take my life?"
2Sa 14:16 the man who is **t** to cut off both me
16:11 my own flesh, is **t** to take my life.
20:19 You are **t** to destroy a city that is
1Ki 19:10 and now they are **t** to kill me too."
19:14 and now they are **t** to kill me too."
2Ki 5: 7 he is **t** to pick a quarrel with me!"
Ne 6: 9 They were all **t** to frighten us,
6:14 who have been **t** to intimidate me.
Isa 28: 9 "Who is it he is **t** to teach? To whom
Da 2: 8 "I am certain that you are **t** to gain
8:15 was watching the vision and **t** to
Mt 2:20 **t** to take the child's life are dead.
22:18 why are you **t** to trap me?
23:13 you let those enter who are **t** to.
Mk 12:15 "Why are you **t** to trap me?" he asked
Lk 19:47 among the people were **t** to kill him.
Jn 5: 7 While I am **t** to get in, someone else
7:19 Why are you **t** to kill me?"
7:20 "Who is **t** to kill you?"
7:25 this the man they are **t** to kill?
Ac 17:18 "What is this babbler **t** to say?"
18: 4 **t** to persuade Jews and Greeks.
21:31 While they were **t** to kill him, news
Ro 11: 3 left, and they are **t** to kill me"?
1Co 10:22 Are we **t** to arouse the Lord's
2Co 5:12 We are not **t** to commend ourselves to
10: 9 I do not want to seem to be **t** to
Gal 1: 7 **t** to pervert the gospel of Christ.
1:10 Am I now **t** to win the approval of
1:10 or of God? Or am I **t** to please men?
1:10 If I were still **t** to please men,
3: 3 are you now **t** to attain your goal by
5: 4 You who are **t** to be justified by law
6:12 **t** to compel you to be circumcised.
1Th 2: 3 motives, nor are we **t** to trick you.
2: 4 We are not **t** to please men but God,
1Pe 1:11 **t** to find out the time and
1Jn 2:26 those who are **t** to lead you astray.

Tryphena
Ro 16:12 Greet **T** and Tryphosa, those women

Tryphosa
Ro 16:12 Greet Tryphena and **T**, those women

Tubal
Ge 10: 2 Madai, Javan, **T**, Meshech and Tiras.
1Ch 1: 5 Madai, Javan, **T**, Meshech and Tiras.
Isa 66:19 to **T** and Greece, and to the distant
Eze 27:13 "'Greece, **T** and Meshech traded with
32:26 "Meshech and **T** are there, with all
38: 2 Meshech and **T**; prophesy against
38: 3 O Gog, chief prince of Meshech and **T**
39: 1 O Gog, chief prince of Meshech and **T**

Tubal-Cain (Tubal-Cain's)
Ge 4:22 Zillah also had a son, **T**, who forged

Tubal-Cain's (Tubal-Cain)
Ge 4:22 **T** sister was Naamah.

Tubes
Job 40:18 His bones are **t** of bronze, his limbs

Tuck (Tucked, Tucking)
2Ki 4:29 Elisha said to Gehazi, "**T** your cloak
9: 1 "**T** your cloak into your belt, take
Eze 5: 3 take a few strands of hair and **t**

Tucked (Tuck)
Ex 12:11 with your cloak **t** into your belt,

Tucking (Tuck)
1Ki 18:46 **t** his cloak into his belt, he ran

Tumbles (Tumbling)
Ge 49:17 heels so that its rider **t** backwards.

Tumble-weed (Weed)
Ps 83:13 Make them like **t**, O my God, like
Isa 17:13 on the hills, like **t** before a gale.

Tumbling (Tumbles)
Jdg 7:13 "A round loaf of barley bread came **t**

Tumours
Dt 28:27 with the boils of Egypt and with **t**,
1Sa 5: 6 upon them and afflicted them with **t**.
5: 9 and old, with an outbreak of **t**.
5:12 did not die were afflicted with **t**,
6: 4 "Five gold **t** and five gold rats,
6: 5 Make models of the **t** and of the rats
6:11 gold rats and the models of the **t**.
6:17 These are the gold **t** the Philistines

Tumult
1Sa 14:19 the **t** in the Philistine camp
Isa 22: 2 town full of commotion, O city of **t**
22: 5 the LORD Almighty, has a day of **t**
Jer 25:31 The **t** will resound to the ends of
Eze 1:24 the Almighty, like the **t** of an army.
Am 2: 2 Moab will go down in great **t** amid

Tune (Tuned)
Ps 9: T To ⌊the **t** of⌋ "The Death of the
22: T To ⌊the **t** of⌋ "The Doe of the
45: T To ⌊the **t** of⌋ "Lilies". Of David
56: T To ⌊the **t** of⌋ "A Dove on Distant
57: T ⌊To the **t** of⌋ "Do Not Destroy".
58: T ⌊To the **t** of⌋ "Do Not Destroy".
59: T ⌊To the **t** of⌋ "Do Not Destroy".
60: T To ⌊the **t** of⌋ "The Lily of the
69: T To ⌊the **t** of⌋ "Lilies". Of David
75: T ⌊To the **t** of⌋ "Do Not Destroy".
80: T To ⌊the **t** of⌋ "The Lilies of the
58: 5 will not heed the **t** of the charmer
1Co 14: 7 how will anyone know what **t** is being

Tuned (Tune)
Job 30:31 My harp is **t** to mourning, and my

Tunic (Tunics)
Ex 28: 4 a woven **t**, a turban and a sash.
28:39 "Weave the **t** of fine linen and make
29: 5 garments and dress Aaron with the **t**,
Lev 8: 7 He put the **t** on Aaron, tied the sash
16: 4 He is to put on the sacred linen **t**,
1Sa 17:38 Saul dressed David in his own **t**. He
17:39 over the **t** and tried walking around,
18: 4 along with his **t**, and even his sword,
2Sa 20: 8 Joab was wearing his military **t**, and
Ezr 9: 3 I heard this, I tore my **t** and cloak,
9: 5 with my **t** and cloak torn, and fell
Mt 5:40 take your **t**, let him have your cloak
10:10 or extra **t**, or sandals or a staff;
Mk 6: 9 Wear sandals but not an extra **t**.
Lk 6:29 do not stop him from taking your **t**.
9: 3 bag, no bread, no money, no extra **t**.

Tunics (Tunic)
Ex 28:40 Make **t**, sashes and headbands for
29: 8 Bring his sons and dress them in **t**
39:27 For Aaron and his sons, they made **t**
40:14 Bring his sons and dress them in **t**.
Lev 8:13 put **t** on them, tied sashes around
10: 5 still in their **t**, outside the camp,
Lk 3:11 John answered, "The man with two **t**

Tunnel (Tunnels)
2Ki 20:20 how he made the pool and the **t** by

Tunnels (Tunnel)
Job 28:10 He **t** through the rock; his eyes see

Turban (Turbans)
Ex 28: 4 robe, a woven tunic, a **t** and a sash.
28:37 cord to it to attach it to the **t**;
28:37 it is to be on the front of the **t**
28:39 linen and make the **t** of fine linen.
29: 6 Put the **t** on his head and attach the
29: 6 attach the sacred diadem to the **t**.
39:28 the **t** of fine linen, the linen
39:31 the **t**, as the LORD commanded Moses.
Lev 8: 9 he placed the **t** on Aaron's head and
16: 4 around him and put on the linen **t**.
Job 29:14 justice was my robe and my **t**.
Eze 21:26 Take off the **t**, remove the crown.
24:17 Keep your **t** fastened and your
Zec 3: 5 I said, "Put a clean **t** on his head."
3: 5 So they put a clean **t** on his head

Turbans (Turban)
Eze 23:15 waists and flowing **t** on their heads;
24:23 You will keep your **t** on your heads
44:18 They are to wear linen **t** on their
Da 3:21 wearing their robes, trousers, **t** and

Turbulent
Ge 49: 4 **T** as the waters, you will no longer

Turmoil
2Ch 15: 5 of the lands were in great **t**.
Job 3:17 There the wicked cease from **t**, and
3:26 I have no rest, but only **t**."
Ps 65: 7 waves, and the **t** of the nations.
Pr 15:16 the LORD than great wealth with **t**.
Isa 14: 3 suffering and **t** and cruel bondage,
Eze 22: 5 you, O infamous city, full of **t**.
Ac 17: 8 city officials were thrown into **t**.

Turn (Turned, Turning, Turns)
Ge 19: 2 "My lords," he said, "please **t** aside
24:49 me, so I may know which way to **t**."
37:30 boy isn't there! Where can I **t** now?"
Ex 7:19 they will **t** to blood. Blood will be
14: 2 "Tell the Israelites to **t** back and
23:27 your enemies **t** their backs and run.
32: 8 They have been quick to **t** away from
32:12 earth'? **T** from your fierce anger;
34:22 of Ingathering at the **t** of the year.
Lev 13:16 Should the raw flesh change and **t**
19: 4 "'Do not **t** to idols or make gods of
19:29 or the land will **t** to prostitution
19:31 "'Do not **t** to mediums or seek out
26:31 I will **t** your cities into ruins and
Nu 6:26 the LORD **t** his face towards you and
14:25 **t** back tomorrow and set out towards
20:17 not **t** to the right or to the left
21:22 We will not **t** aside into any field
22:26 place where there was no room to **t**,
25: 4 anger may **t** away from Israel."
32:15 If you **t** away from following him, he
34: 5 where it will **t**, join the Wadi of
Dt 1:40 as for you, **t** round and set out
2: 3 country long enough; now **t** north.
2:27 **t** aside to the right or to the left.
5:32 **t** aside to the right or to the left.
7: 4 for they will **t** your sons away from
11:16 or you will be enticed to **t** away and
11:28 **t** from the way that I command you
13: 5 he has tried to **t** you from the way
13:10 because he tried to **t** you away from
13:17 so that the LORD will **t** from his
17:11 Do not **t** aside from what they tell
17:20 **t** from the law to the right or to
23:14 indecent and **t** away from you.
28:14 Do not **t** aside from any of the
28:24 The LORD will **t** the rain of your
30:10 **t** to the LORD your God with all your
31:20 they will **t** to other gods and
31:29 **t** from the way I have commanded you.
Jos 1: 7 do not **t** from it to the right or to
Jos 7:12 they **t** their backs and run because
22:16 How could you **t** away from the LORD
22:23 own altar to **t** away from the LORD
22:29 **t** away from him today by building an
23:12 "But if you **t** away and ally
24:20 he will **t** and bring disaster on you
Jdg 1: 3 We in **t** will go with you into yours.
7: 3 may **t** back and leave Mount Gilead.
7:22 **t** on each other with their swords.
14:17 She in **t** explained the riddle to her
20:39 the men of Israel would **t** in the
Ru 1:16 to leave you or to **t** back from you.
1Sa 6:12 not **t** to the right or to the left.
12:20 yet do not **t** away from the LORD,
12:21 Do not **t** away after useless idols.
22:17 "**T** and kill the priests of the LORD,
22:18 The king then ordered Doeg, "You **t**
29: 4 **t** against us during the fighting.
29: 7 **T** back and go in peace; do nothing
2Sa 1:22 the bow of Jonathan did not **t** back,
2:21 Abner said to him, "**T** aside to the
14:19 my lord the king, no-one can **t** to
15:31 "O LORD, **t** Ahithophel's counsel
22:37 me, so that my ankles do not **t** over.
22:38 not **t** back till they were destroyed.
22:41 You made my enemies **t** their backs in
1Ki 8:33 and when they **t** back to you and
8:35 confess your name and **t** from their
8:48 if they **t** back to you with all their
8:58 May he **t** our hearts to him, to walk
9: 6 "But if you or your sons **t** away from
11: 2 **t** your hearts after their gods.
12:15 this **t** of events was from the LORD
13:16 The man of God said, "I cannot **t**
17: 3 "Leave here, **t** eastward and hide in
2Ki 3: 3 commit; he did not **t** away from them.
10:29 However, he did not **t** away from the
10:31 He did not **t** away from the sins of
13: 2 and he did not **t** away from them.
13: 6 they did not **t** away from the sins of
13:11 did not **t** away from any of the sins
14:24 did not **t** away from any of the sins
15: 9 He did not **t** away from the sins of
15:18 entire reign he did not **t** away from
15:24 He did not **t** away from the sins of
15:28 He did not **t** away from the sins of
17:13 and seers: "**T** from your evil ways.
17:22 Jeroboam and did not **t** away from
23:26 the LORD did not **t** away from the
1Ch 12:23 to **t** Saul's kingdom over to him,
2Ch 6:24 they **t** back and confess your name,
6:26 confess your name and **t** from their
6:38 if they **t** back to you with all their
7:14 face and **t** from their wicked ways,
7:19 "But if you **t** away and forsake the
10:15 for this **t** of events was from God,
24:23 At the **t** of the year, the army of
29:10 fierce anger will **t** away from us.
30: 8 fierce anger will **t** away from you.
30: 9 He will not **t** his face from you if
35:22 Josiah, however, would not **t** away
36:13 **t** to the LORD, the God of Israel.
Ne 4: 4 **T** their insults back on their own
4:12 Wherever you **t**, they will attack us.
9:26 them in order to **t** them back to you;
9:35 serve you or **t** from their evil ways.
Est 2:12 Before a girl's **t** came to go in to
2:15 the **t** came for Esther (the girl
2:22 who in **t** reported it to the king,
Job 3: 4 That day—may it **t** to darkness; may
5: 1 To which of the holy ones will you **t**
6:18 Caravans **t** aside from their routes;
10: 8 Will you now **t** and destroy me?
10: 9 Will you now **t** me to dust again?
10:20 **T** away from me so that I can have
13: 9 Would it **t** out well if he examined
13:16 this will **t** out for my deliverance
17:12 These men **t** night into day; in the
20:14 yet his food will **t** sour in his
30:21 You **t** on me ruthlessly; with the
33:17 to **t** man from wrongdoing and keep
33:30 to **t** back his soul from the pit,
36:18 not let a large bribe **t** you aside.
Ps 4: 2 How long, O men, will you **t** my glory
6: 4 **T**, O LORD, and deliver me; save me
6:10 they will **t** back in sudden disgrace.
Ps 9: 3 My enemies **t** back; they stumble and
18:36 me, so that my ankles do not **t** over.
18:37 not **t** back till they were destroyed.
18:40 You made my enemies **t** their backs in
21:12 for you will make them **t** their backs
22:27 will remember and **t** to the LORD,
25:16 **T** to me and be gracious to me, for I
27: 9 do not **t** your servant away in anger;
28: 1 my Rock; do not **t** a deaf ear to me.
31: 2 **T** your ear to me, come quickly to my
34:14 **T** from evil and do good; seek peace
37: 8 Refrain from anger and **t** from wrath;
37:27 **T** from evil and do good; then you
40: 4 to those who **t** aside to false gods.
49: 4 I will **t** my ear to a proverb; with
51:13 and sinners will **t** back to you.
56: 9 my enemies will **t** back when I call
64: 8 He will **t** their own tongues against
69:16 love; in your great mercy **t** to me.
70: 3 Aha!" **t** back because of their shame.
71: 2 **t** your ear to me and save me.
73:10 Therefore their people **t** to them and
74: 3 **T** your steps towards these
78: 6 they in **t** would tell their children.
80:18 we will not **t** away from you; revive
81:14 and **t** my hand against their foes!
86:16 **T** to me and have mercy on me; grant
88: 2 before you; **t** your ear to my cry.
90: 3 You **t** men back to dust, saying,
102: 2 **T** your ear to me; when I call,
119:36 **T** my heart towards your statutes and
119:37 **T** my eyes away from worthless things
119:51 but I do not **t** from your law.
119:79 May those who fear you **t** to me,
119:132 **T** to me and have mercy on me, as you
125: 5 those who **t** to crooked ways the LORD
Pr 1:26 I in **t** will laugh at your disaster;
4:15 do not travel on it; **t** from it
5: 7 me; do not **t** aside from what I say.
7:25 Do not let your heart **t** to her ways
22: 6 he is old he will not **t** from it.
24:18 and **t** his wrath away from him.
29: 8 a city, but wise men **t** away anger.
SS 2:17 **t**, my lover, and be like a gazelle
6: 1 Which way did your lover **t**, that we
6: 5 **T** your eyes from me; they overwhelm
Isa 1:25 I will **t** my hand against you; I will
3:12 astray; they **t** you from the path.
6:10 their hearts, and **t** and be healed."
9:21 together they will **t** against Judah.
14:23 "I will **t** her into a place for owls
14:27 out, and who can **t** it back?
17: 7 **t** their eyes to the Holy One of
19:22 They will **t** to the LORD, and he will
22: 4 Therefore I said, "**T** away from me;
28: 6 who **t** back the battle at the gate.
29:16 You **t** things upside down, as if the
30:21 Whether you **t** to the right or to the
41:18 I will **t** the desert into pools of
42:15 I will **t** rivers into islands and dry
42:16 I will **t** the darkness into light
45:22 "**T** to me and be saved, all you ends
49:11 I will **t** all my mountains into roads
50: 2 I **t** rivers into a desert; their fish
55: 7 Let him **t** to the LORD, and he will
56:11 they all **t** to their own way,
58: 7 **t** away from your own flesh and blood
Jer 2:21 How then did you **t** against me into a
3:19 and not **t** away from following me.
4:28 I have decided and will not **t** back."
6: 8 O Jerusalem, or I will **t** away from
8: 5 always **t** away? They cling to deceit;
12:10 they will **t** my pleasant field into a
13:16 You hope for light, but he will **t** it
15:19 **t** to you, but you must not **t** to them.
17:13 Those who **t** away from you will be
18:11 So **t** from your evil ways, each one
18:20 to **t** your wrath away from them.
21: 4 says: I am about to **t** against you
23:20 The anger of the LORD will not **t**
25: 5 They said, "**T** now, each of you, from
26: 3 and each will **t** from his evil way.
30:24 anger of the LORD will not **t** back
31:13 I will **t** their mourning into
31:39 hill of Gareb and then **t** to Goah.
32:40 that they will never **t** away from me.

Jer 35:15 They said, "Each of you must **t** from
36: 3 each of them will **t** from his wicked
36: 7 and each will **t** from his wicked ways,
44: 5 they did not **t** from their wickedness
46:21 They too will **t** and flee together,
47: 3 Fathers will not **t** to help their
49: 8 **T** and flee, hide in deep caves, you
50: 5 They will ask the way to Zion and **t**
Eze 1: 9 ahead; they did not **t** as they moved.
1:17 not **t** about as the creatures went.
3:19 he does not **t** from his wickedness or
4: 3 the city and **t** your face towards it.
4: 7 **T** your face towards the siege of
4: 8 with ropes so that you cannot **t**
7:20 Therefore I will **t** these into an
7:22 I will **t** my face away from them, and
10:11 not **t** about as the cherubim went.
13:22 not to **t** from their evil ways
14: 6 Repent! **T** from your idols and
16:42 jealous anger will **t** away from you;
18:23 they **t** from their ways and live?
18:30 Repent! **T** away from all your
23:24 I will **t** you over to them for
25: 5 I will **t** Rabbah into a pasture for
33: 9 if you do warn the wicked man to **t**
33:11 they **t** from their ways and live.
33:11 **T**! **T** from your evil ways! Why will
35: 4 I will **t** your towns into ruins and
38: 4 I will **t** you around, put hooks in
38:12 I will plunder and loot and **t** my
39: 2 I will **t** you around and drag you
Da 9:16 **t** away your anger and your wrath
11:18 he will **t** his attention to the
11:18 will **t** his insolence back upon him.
11:19 After this, he will **t** back towards
11:30 Then he will **t** back and vent his
Hos 2: 3 **t** her into a parched land, and slay
3: 1 though they **t** to other gods and love
4:13 your daughters **t** to prostitution
4:14 when they **t** to prostitution,
7:14 and new wine but **t** away from me.
7:16 They do not **t** to the Most High; they
9:12 Woe to them when I **t** away from them!
11: 7 My people are determined to **t** from
11: 9 nor will I **t** and devastate Ephraim.
Joel 2:14 Who knows? He may **t** and have pity
Am 1: 3 four, I will not **t** back my wrath.
1: 6 four, I will not **t** back my wrath.
1: 8 I will **t** my hand against Ekron, till
1: 9 four, I will not **t** back my wrath.
1:11 four, I will not **t** back my wrath.
1:13 four, I will not **t** back my wrath.
2: 1 four, I will not **t** back my wrath.
2: 4 four, I will not **t** back my wrath.
2: 6 four, I will not **t** back my wrath.
5: 7 You who **t** justice into bitterness
8: 3 in the temple will **t** to wailing.
8:10 I will **t** your religious feasts into
Jnh 3: 9 with compassion **t** from his fierce
Mic 7:17 they will **t** in fear to the LORD our
Hab 2:16 Now it is your **t**! Drink and be
Zep 1: 6 those who **t** back from following the
Hag 2:17 did not **t** to me,' declares the LORD.
Zec 1: 4 '**T** from your evil ways and your evil
13: 7 **t** my hand against the little ones.
Mal 4: 6 He will **t** the hearts of the fathers
Mt 5:39 cheek, **t** to him the other also.
5:42 and do not **t** away from the one who
7: 6 and then **t** and tear you to pieces.
10:35 I have come to **t** "'a man against
13:15 and **t**, and I would heal them.'
15:36 and they in **t** to the people.
20:19 will **t** him over to the Gentiles to
24:10 At that time many will **t** away from
Mk 4:12 they might **t** and be forgiven!"
Lk 1:17 to **t** the hearts of the fathers to
6:29 one cheek, **t** to him the other also.
12:58 and the judge **t** you over to the
Jn 2:16 **t** my Father's house into a market!"
12:22 Andrew and Philip in **t** told Jesus.
12:40 nor **t**—and I would heal them."
16:20 but your grief will **t** to joy.
Ac 3:19 Repent, then, and **t** to God, so that
6: 3 **t** this responsibility over to them
13: 8 to **t** the proconsul from the faith.
13:46 life, we now **t** to the Gentiles.
Ac 14:15 telling you to **t** from these
20:21 Greeks that they must **t** to God in
21:21 the Gentiles to **t** away from Moses,
26:18 to open their eyes and **t** them from
26:20 **t** to God and prove their repentance
28:27 and **t**, and I would heal them.'
Ro 11:26 will **t** godlessness away from Jacob.
1Co 14:31 For you can all prophesy in **t** so
15:23 each in his own **t**: Christ, the
2Co 7: 5 but we were harassed at every **t**
8:14 so that in **t** their plenty will
Php 1:19 to me will **t** out for my deliverance.
Col 4:16 in **t** read the letter from Laodicea.
1Ti 6:20 **T** away from godless chatter and the
2Ti 2:19 Lord must **t** away from wickedness."
4: 4 They will **t** their ears away from the
4: 4 from the truth and **t** aside to myths.
Heb 12:25 how much less will we, if we **t** away
Jas 3: 3 obey us, we can **t** the whole animal.
1Pe 3:11 He must **t** from evil and do good; he
2Pe 2:21 than to have known it and then to **t**
Rev 10: 9 It will **t** your stomach sour, but in
11: 6 and they have power to **t** the waters

Turned (Turn)

Ge 9:23 Their faces were **t** the other way so
14: 7 they **t** back and went to En Mishpat
18:22 The men **t** away and went towards
41:13 things **t** out exactly as he
42:24 He **t** away from them and began to
42:24 then **t** back and spoke to them again.
42:28 Their hearts sank and they **t** to
Ex 4: 4 it **t** back into a staff in his hand.
7:23 Instead, he **t** and went into his
10: 6 Then Moses **t** and left Pharaoh.
14:21 east wind and **t** it into dry land.
32:15 Moses **t** and went down the mountain
Lev 13: 3 if the hair in the sore has **t** white
13: 4 and the hair in it has not **t** white,
13:10 the skin that has **t** the hair white
13:13 it has all **t** white, he is clean.
13:17 and if the sores have **t** white, the
13:20 deep and the hair in it has **t** white,
13:25 and if the hair in it has **t** white,
Nu 12:10 Aaron **t** towards her and saw that she
14:43 Because you have **t** away from the
16:42 and **t** towards the Tent of Meeting,
20:21 territory, Israel **t** away from them.
21:33 they **t** and went up along the road
22:23 she **t** off the road into a field.
22:33 The donkey saw me and **t** away from me
22:33 If she had not **t** away, I would
24: 1 but **t** his face towards the desert.
25:11 the son of Aaron, the priest, has **t**
33: 7 left Etham, **t** back to Pi Hahiroth
Dt 1:45 weeping and **t** a deaf ear to you.
2: 1 we **t** back and set out towards the
2: 8 We **t** from the Arabah road, which
3: 1 Next we **t** and went up along the road
9:12 They have **t** away quickly from what I
9:15 I **t** and went down from the mountain
9:16 You had **t** aside quickly from the way
23: 5 **t** the curse into a blessing for you,
26:13 I have not **t** aside from your
Jos 7:26 the LORD **t** from his fierce anger.
8:20 had **t** back against their pursuers.
8:21 **t** round and attacked the men of Ai.
10:38 Joshua and all Israel with him **t**
11:10 At that time Joshua **t** back and
15: 7 of Achor and **t** north to Gilgal,
15:11 **t** towards Shikkeron, passed along to
18:14 **t** south along the western side
19:12 **t** east from Sarid towards the
19:13 out at Rimmon and **t** towards Neah.
19:27 then **t** east towards Beth Dagon,
19:29 The boundary then **t** back towards
19:29 **t** towards Hosah and came out at the
Jdg 2:17 Unlike their fathers, they quickly **t**
3:19 he himself **t** back and said, "I have
6:14 The LORD **t** to him and said, "Go in
14: 8 he **t** aside to look at the lion's
18: 3 so they **t** in there and asked him,
18:15 they **t** in there and went to the
18:21 front of them, they **t** away and left.
18:23 the Danites **t** and said to Micah,
Jdg 18:26 for him, **t** round and went back home.
20:40 the Benjamites **t** and saw the smoke
20:41 the men of Israel **t** on them, and the
20:45 they **t** and fled towards the desert
20:47 six hundred men **t** and fled into the
Ru 2: 3 As it **t** out, she found herself
3: 8 and he **t** and discovered a woman
1Sa 8: 3 They **t** aside after dishonest gain
9:20 whom is all the desire of Israel **t**,
10: 9 Saul **t** to leave Samuel, God changed
11: 7 people, and they **t** out as one man.
13:17 One **t** towards Ophrah in the vicinity
14:47 Wherever he **t**, he inflicted
15:11 because he has **t** away from me and
15:12 has **t** and gone on down to Gilgal."
15:27 Samuel **t** to leave, Saul caught hold
17:30 He then **t** away to someone else and
17:35 When it **t** on me, I seized it by its
17:51 their hero was dead, they **t** and ran.
22:18 So Doeg the Edomite **t** and struck
25:12 David's men **t** round and went back.
28:15 me, and God has **t** away from me.
28:16 now that the LORD has **t** away from
2Sa 1: 7 he **t** round and saw me, he called out
19: 2 that day was **t** into mourning,
22:23 I have not **t** away from his decrees.
1Ki 6:34 having two leaves that **t** in sockets.
8:14 the king **t** round and blessed them.
11: 4 Solomon grew old, his wives **t** his
11: 9 his heart had **t** away from the LORD,
22:32 So they **t** to attack him, but when
2Ki 2:24 He **t** round, looked at them and
4:35 Elisha **t** away and walked back and
5:12 So he **t** and went off in a rage.
9:23 Joram **t** about and fled, calling out
12:17 Then he **t** to attack Jerusalem.
19:25 that you have **t** fortified cities
20: 2 Hezekiah **t** his face to the wall and
23:25 him who **t** to the LORD as he did
1Ch 10:14 put him to death and **t** the kingdom
21:20 he **t** and saw the angel; his four
2Ch 6: 3 the king **t** round and blessed them.
11: 4 **t** back from marching against
12:12 the LORD's anger **t** from him, and he
13:14 Judah **t** and saw that they were being
15: 4 in their distress they **t** to the LORD,
18:31 So they **t** to attack him, but
19: 4 Ephraim and **t** them back to the LORD,
20:10 so they **t** away from them and did not
25:27 From the time that Amaziah **t** away
29: 6 They **t** their faces away from the
29: 6 and **t** their backs on him.
Ezr 10:14 in this matter is **t** away from us."
Ne 2:15 Finally, I **t** back and re-entered
9:29 Stubbornly they **t** their backs on you,
13: 2 **t** the curse into a blessing.)
Est 9: 1 but now the tables were **t** and the
9:22 as the month when their sorrow was **t**
Job 16:11 God has **t** me over to evil men and
19:19 me; those I love have **t** against me.
31: 7 if my steps have **t** from the path, if
34:27 they **t** from following him and had no
Ps 14: 3 All have **t** aside, they have together
18:22 I have not **t** away from his decrees.
22:14 My heart has **t** to wax; it has melted
30:11 You **t** my wailing into dancing; you
35: 4 plot my ruin be **t** back in dismay.
40: 1 the LORD; he **t** to me and heard
40:14 my ruin be **t** back in disgrace.
44:18 Our hearts had not **t** back; our feet
53: 3 Everyone has **t** away, they have
66: 6 He **t** the sea into dry land, they
70: 2 my ruin be **t** back in disgrace.
78: 9 bows, **t** back on the day of battle;
78:30 before they **t** from the food they
78:34 him; they eagerly **t** to him again.
78:44 He **t** their rivers to blood; they
85: 3 You set aside all your wrath and **t**
89:43 You have **t** back the edge of his
105:25 whose hearts he **t** to hate his people,
105:29 He **t** their waters into blood,
105:32 He **t** their rain into hail, with
107:33 He **t** rivers into a desert, flowing
107:35 He **t** the desert into pools of water
114: 3 sea looked and fled, the Jordan **t**
114: 5 you fled, O Jordan, that you **t** back,

Ps 114: 8 who t the rock into a pool, the hard
116: 2 he t his ear to me, I will call on
119:59 I have considered my ways and have t
119:157 but I have not t from your statutes.
129: 5 May all who hate Zion be t back in
Ecc 2:12 I t my thoughts to consider wisdom,
7:25 I t my mind to understand, to
Isa 1: 4 of Israel and t their backs on him.
5:25 t away, his hand is still upraised.
7:25 are t loose and where sheep run.
9:12 t away, his hand is still upraised.
9:17 t away, his hand is still upraised.
9:21 t away, his hand is still upraised.
10: 4 t away, his hand is still upraised.
12: 1 t away and you have comforted me.
23:13 bare and t it into a ruin.
29:17 will not Lebanon be t into a fertile
34: 9 Edom's streams will be t into pitch,
37:26 that you have t fortified cities
38: 2 Hezekiah t his face to the wall and
42:17 will be t back in utter shame.
53: 6 have gone astray, each of us has t
59: 8 They have t them into crooked roads;
63:10 So he t and became their enemy and
Jer 2:27 They have t their backs to me and
4: 8 of the LORD has not t away from us.
5:23 they have t aside and gone away.
6:12 Their houses will be t over to
8: 5 Why then have these people t away?
23:22 would have t them from their evil
30: 6 labour, every face t deathly pale?
32:33 They t their backs to me and not
34:16 now you have t round and profaned my
40: 5 However, before Jeremiah t to go,
41:14 had taken captive at Mizpah t and
49:24 has become feeble, she has t to flee
Lam 1:13 He spread a net for my feet and t me
3: 3 indeed, he has t his hand against me
4: 6 moment without a hand t to help her.
5: 2 Our inheritance has been t over to
5:15 our dancing has t to mourning.
Eze 6: 9 which have t away from me, and by
17: 6 Its branches t towards him, but its
21:16 the left, wherever your blade is t.
23:17 she t away from them in disgust.
23:18 I t away from her in disgust, just
23:18 as I had t away from her sister.
23:22 those you t away from in disgust,
23:28 to those you t away from in disgust.
42:19 he t to the west side and measured;
Da 2: 5 your houses t into piles of rubble.
2:29 O king, your mind t to things to
3:29 houses be t into piles of rubble,
5: 6 His face t pale and he was so
7:28 and my face t pale, but I kept the
9: 3 I t to the Lord God and pleaded with
9: 5 t away from your commands and laws.
9:11 and t away, refusing to obey you.
10: 8 t deathly pale and I was helpless.
Hos 5: 3 t to prostitution; Israel is corrupt.
5:13 then Ephraim t to Assyria, and sent
7: 8 Ephraim is a flat cake not t over.
14: 4 for my anger has t away from them.
Joel 2:31 The sun will be t to darkness and
Am 6:12 But you have t justice into poison
Jnh 3:10 God saw what they did and how they t
Zep 3:15 he has t back your enemy. The LORD
Hag 1: 9 expected much, but see, it t out
Zec 7:11 stubbornly they t their backs and
8:10 t every man against his neighbour.
Mal 1: 3 Esau I have hated, and I have t his
2: 6 uprightness, and t many from sin.
2: 8 you have t from the way and by your
3: 7 you have t away from my decrees
Mt 9:22 Jesus t and saw her. "Take heart,
16:23 Jesus t and said to Peter, "Get
18:34 In anger his master t him over to
Mk 5:30 He t around in the crowd and asked,
8:33 Jesus t and looked at his disciples
15: 1 him away and t him over to Pilate.
Lk 7:44 he t towards the woman and said to
9:55 But Jesus t and rebuked them,
10:23 he t to his disciples and said
18:32 He will be t over to the Gentiles.
22:32 t back, strengthen your brothers."
22:61 The Lord t and looked straight at
Lk 23:28 Jesus t and said to them, "Daughters
Jn 2: 9 the water that had been t into wine.
4:46 where he had t the water into wine.
6:66 t back and no longer followed him.
9:17 Finally they t again to the blind
20:14 At this, she t round and saw Jesus
20:16 Jesus said to her, "Mary." She t
21:20 Peter t and saw that the disciple
Ac 2:20 The sun will be t to darkness and
7:39 and in their hearts t back to Egypt.
7:42 God t away and gave them over to the
9:35 Sharon saw him and t to the Lord.
11:21 people believed and t to the Lord.
16:18 he t round and said to the spirit,
18:17 Then they all t on Sosthenes the
Ro 3:12 All have t away, they have together
1Th 1: 9 They tell how you t to God from
3: 4 it t out that way, as you well know.
1Ti 1: 6 these and t to meaningless talk.
5:15 Some have in fact already t away to
Heb 8: 9 t away from them, declares the Lord.
11:34 whose weakness was t to strength;
Rev 1:12 I t round to see the voice that was
1:12 I t I saw seven golden lampstands,
6:12 The sun t black like sackcloth made
6:12 hair, the whole moon t blood red,
8: 8 A third of the sea t into blood,
8:11 A third of the waters t bitter, and
8:12 so that a third of them t dark.
10:10 I had eaten it, my stomach t sour.
16: 3 and it t into blood like that of a

Turning (Turn)

Nu 31:16 were the means of t the Israelites
Dt 31:18 their wickedness in t to other gods.
Jos 22:18 are you now t away from the LORD?
23: 6 t aside to the right or to the left.
Jdg 8:20 T to Jether, his oldest son, he said,
11: 8 "Nevertheless, we are t to you now;
2Sa 2:19 He chased Abner, t neither to the
22:22 have not done evil by t from my God.
1Ki 18:37 you are t their hearts back again."
2Ki 21:13 wiping it and t it upside-down.
22: 2 t aside to the right or to the left.
2Ch 34: 2 t aside to the right or to the left.
Job 23:11 kept to his way without t aside.
36:21 Beware of t to evil, which you seem
Ps 18:21 have not done evil by t from my God.
Pr 2: 2 t your ear to wisdom and applying
13:14 t a man from the snares of death.
13:19 soul, but fools detest t from evil.
14:27 t a man from the snares of death.
Isa 59:13 t our backs on our God, fomenting
Eze 1:12 would go, without t as they went.
10:11 head faced, without t as they went.
29:16 of their sin in t to her for help.
Da 9:13 the LORD our God by t from our sins
Hos 7:11 calling to Egypt, now t to Assyria.
Lk 7: 9 he was amazed at him, and t to the
14:25 with Jesus, and t to them he said:
Jn 1:38 T round, Jesus saw them following
Ac 3:26 t each of you from your wicked ways.
9:40 T towards the dead woman, he said,
15:19 for the Gentiles who are t to God.
Gal 1: 6 and are t to a different gospel—
4: 9 that you are t back to those weak

Turns (Turn)

Lev 20: 6 against the person who t to mediums
Dt 29:18 t away from the LORD our God to go
30:17 if your heart t away and you are not
2Sa 22:29 the LORD t my darkness into light.
2Ki 11: 6 who take t guarding the temple—
Job 1: 4 His sons used to take t holding
23: 9 I do not see him; when he t to the
Ps 18:28 my God t my darkness into light.
Pr 15: 1 A gentle answer t away wrath, but a
17: 8 wherever he t, he succeeds.
26:14 As a door t on its hinges, so a
26:14 hinges, so a sluggard t on his bed.
28: 9 If anyone t a deaf ear to the law,
Ecc 1: 6 The wind blows to the south and t to
7: 7 Extortion t a wise man into a fool,
Isa 24:11 out for wine; all joy t to gloom,
41: 2 He t them to dust with his sword, to
Isa 44:25 of the wise and t it into nonsense,
Jer 8: 4 a man t away, does he not return?
17: 5 whose heart t away from the LORD.
23:14 that no-one t from his wickedness.
48:39 How they wail! How Moab t her back
Lam 1: 8 she herself groans and t away.
Eze 3:20 "Again, when a righteous man t from
18:21 "But if a wicked man t away from all
18:24 "But if a righteous man t from his
18:26 If a righteous man t from his
18:27 if a wicked man t away from the
18:28 has committed and t away from them,
33:12 cause him to fall when he t from it.
33:14 but he then t away from his sin
33:18 If a righteous man t from his
33:19 if a wicked man t away from his
Joel 2: 6 are in anguish; every face t pale.
Am 4:13 he who t dawn to darkness, and
5: 8 who t blackness into dawn and
Na 2: 8 Stop!" they cry, but no-one t back
2Co 3:16 whenever anyone t to the Lord, the
Heb 3:12 that t away from the living God.
Jas 5:20 remember this: Whoever t a sinner

Turquoise

Ex 28:18 in the second row a t, a sapphire
39:11 in the second row a t, a sapphire
1Ch 29: 2 as well as onyx for the settings, t,
Isa 54:11 I will build you with stones of t,
Eze 27:16 they exchanged t, purple fabric,
28:13 and jasper, sapphire, t and beryl.

Tusks

Eze 27:15 paid you with ivory t and ebony.

Twelfth (Twelve)

Nu 7:78 On the t day Ahira son of Enan, the
1Ki 19:19 he himself was driving the t pair.
2Ki 8:25 In the t year of Joram son of Ahab
17: 1 In the t year of Ahaz king of Judah,
25:27 twenty-seventh day of the t month.
1Ch 24:12 the eleventh to Eliashib, the t to
25:19 the t to Hashabiah, his sons and
27:15 The t, for the t month, was Heldai
2Ch 34: 3 In his t year he began to purge
Ezr 8:31 On the t day of the first month we
Est 3: 7 In the t year of King Xerxes, in the
3: 7 on the t month, the month of Adar.
3:13 the thirteenth day of the t month,
8:12 of the t month, the month of Adar.
9: 1 On the thirteenth day of the t month,
Jer 52:31 the twenty-fifth day of the t month.
Eze 29: 1 in the tenth month on the t day, the
32: 1 In the t year, in the t month on the
32:17 In the t year, on the fifteenth day
33:21 In the t year of our exile, in the
Rev 21:20 jacinth, and the t amethyst.

Twelve (Twelfth)

Ge 14: 4 For t years they had been subject to
17:20 He will be the father of t rulers,
25:16 and these are the names of the t
35:22 Jacob had t sons:
42:13 they replied, "Your servants were t
42:32 We were t brothers, sons of one
49:28 All these are the t tribes of Israel,
Ex 15:27 Elim, where there were t springs and
24: 4 set up t stone pillars representing
24: 4 representing the t tribes of Israel.
28:21 There are to be t stones, one for
28:21 the name of one of the t tribes.
39:14 There were t stones, one for each of
39:14 the name of one of the t tribes.
Lev 24: 5 "Take fine flour and bake t loaves
Nu 1:44 Aaron and the t leaders of Israel,
7: 3 t oxen—an ox from each leader and a
7:84 it was anointed: t silver plates,
7:84 t silver sprinkling bowls and t gold
7:86 The t gold dishes filled with
7:87 offering came to t young bulls,
7:87 t rams and t male lambs a year old,
7:87 T male goats were used for the sin
17: 2 to the Israelites and get t staffs
17: 6 and their leaders gave him t staffs,

Nu 29:17 "'On the second day prepare **t** young
31: 5 **t** thousand men armed for battle, a
33: 9 where there were **t** springs and
Dt 1:23 **t** of you, one man from each tribe.
Jos 3:12 Now then, choose **t** men from the
4: 2 "Choose **t** men from among the people,
4: 3 tell them to take up **t** stones from
4: 4 Joshua called together the **t** men he
4: 8 They took **t** stones from the middle
4: 9 Joshua set up the **t** stones that had
4:20 Joshua set up at Gilgal the **t** stones
8:25 **T** thousand men and women fell that
18:24 Ophni and Geba—**t** towns and
19:15 were **t** towns and their villages.
21: 7 clan by clan, received **t** towns from
21:40 the rest of the Levites, were **t**.
Jdg 19:29 limb by limb, into **t** parts and sent
21:10 So the assembly sent **t** thousand
2Sa 2:15 stood up and were counted off—**t** men
2:15 Bosheth son of Saul, and **t** for David.
10: 6 and also **t** thousand men from Tob.
17: 1 "I would choose **t** thousand men and
1Ki 4: 7 Solomon also had **t** district
4:26 horses, and **t** thousand horses.
7:15 high and **t** cubits round, by line.
7:25 The Sea stood on **t** bulls, three
7:44 the Sea and the **t** bulls under it;
10:20 **T** lions stood on the six steps, one
10:26 chariots and **t** thousand horses,
11:30 wearing and tore it into **t** pieces.
16:23 for **t** years, six of them in Tirzah.
18:31 Elijah took **t** stones, one for each
19:19 He was ploughing with **t** yoke of oxen,
2Ki 3: 1 Judah, and he reigned for **t** years.
21: 1 Manasseh was **t** years old when he
1Ch 6:63 clan by clan, were allotted **t** towns
2Ch 1:14 chariots and **t** thousand horses,
4: 4 The Sea stood on **t** bulls, three
4:15 the Sea and the **t** bulls under it;
9:19 **T** lions stood on the six steps, one
9:25 and **t** thousand horses, which he kept
12: 3 With **t** hundred chariots and sixty
33: 1 Manasseh was **t** years old when he
Ezr 6:17 for all Israel, **t** male goats, one
8:24 I set apart **t** of the leading priests,
8:35 of Israel: **t** bulls for all Israel,
8:35 as a sin offering, **t** male goats.
Ne 5:14 his thirty-second year—**t** years
Est 2:12 she had to complete **t** months of
Ps 60: T struck down **t** thousand Edomites in
Jer 52:20 the Sea and the **t** bronze bulls under
52:21 high and **t** cubits in circumference;
Eze 40:49 and **t** cubits from front to back.
43:16 The altar hearth is square, **t** cubits
43:16 **t** cubits long and **t** cubits wide.
47:13 among the **t** tribes of Israel,
Da 4:29 **T** months later, as the king was
Mt 9:20 for **t** years came up behind him
10: 1 He called his **t** disciples to him and
10: 2 These are the names of the **t**
10: 5 These **t** Jesus sent out with the
11: 1 instructing his **t** disciples, he went
14:20 the disciples picked up **t** basketfuls
19:28 me will also sit on **t** thrones,
19:28 judging the **t** tribes of Israel.
20:17 **t** disciples aside and said to them,
26:14 one of the **T**—the one called Judas
26:20 reclining at the table with the **T**.
26:47 Judas, one of the **T**, arrived.
26:53 more than **t** legions of angels?
Mk 3:14 He appointed **t**—designating them
3:16 These are the **t** he appointed: Simon
4:10 he was alone, the **T** and the others
5:25 subject to bleeding for **t** years.
5:42 walked around (she was **t** years old).
6: 7 Calling the **T** to him, he sent them
6:43 the disciples picked up **t** basketfuls
8:19 did you pick up?" "**T**," they replied.
9:35 Sitting down, Jesus called the **T** and
10:32 Again he took the **T** aside and told
11:11 he went out to Bethany with the **T**.
14:10 Judas Iscariot, one of the **T**, went
14:17 came, Jesus arrived with the **T**.
14:20 "It is one of the **T**," he replied,
14:43 Judas, one of the **T**, appeared.
Lk 2:42 he was **t** years old, they went up to
6:13 to him and chose **t** of them, whom he
8: 1 The **T** were with him,
8:42 his only daughter, a girl of about **t**,
8:43 subject to bleeding for **t** years,
9: 1 Jesus had called the **T** together, he
9:12 Late in the afternoon the **T** came to
9:17 the disciples picked up **t** basketfuls
18:31 Jesus took the **T** aside and told them,
22: 3 Judas, called Iscariot, one of the **T**.
22:30 judging the **t** tribes of Israel.
22:47 one of the **T**, was leading them.
Jn 6:13 gathered them and filled **t** baskets
6:67 too, do you?" Jesus asked the **T**.
6:70 the **T**? Yet one of you is a devil!"
6:71 of the **T**, was later to betray him.)
11: 9 "Are there not **t** hours of daylight?
20:24 one of the **T**, was not with the
Ac 6: 2 the **T** gathered all the disciples
7: 8 the father of the **t** patriarchs.
19: 7 There were about **t** men in all.
24:11 verify that no more than **t** days ago
26: 7 This is the promise our **t** tribes are
1Co 15: 5 to Peter, and then to the **T**.
Jas 1: 1 To the **t** tribes scattered among the
Rev 12: 1 and a crown of **t** stars on her head.
21:12 had a great, high wall with **t** gates,
21:12 and with **t** angels at the gates.
21:12 the names of the **t** tribes of Israel.
21:14 wall of the city had **t** foundations
21:14 names of the **t** apostles of the Lamb.
21:21 The **t** gates were **t** pearls, each gate
22: 2 bearing **t** crops of fruit, yielding

Twig (Twigs)
Hos 10: 7 a **t** on the surface of the waters.

Twigs (Twig)
Isa 27:11 its **t** are dry, they are broken off
64: 2 fire sets **t** ablaze and causes water
Mt 24:32 **t** get tender and its leaves come out
Mk 13:28 **t** get tender and its leaves come out

Twilight (Light[1])
Ex 12: 6 of Israel must slaughter them at **t**.
16:12 Tell them, 'At **t** you will eat meat,
29:39 in the morning and the other at **t**.
29:41 Sacrifice the other lamb at **t** with
30: 8 again when he lights the lamps at **t**
Lev 23: 5 The LORD's Passover begins at **t** on
Nu 9: 3 at **t** on the fourteenth day of this
9: 5 did so in the Desert of Sinai at **t**
9:11 day of the second month at **t**.
28: 4 in the morning and the other at **t**,
28: 8 Prepare the second lamb at **t**, along
Pr 7: 9 at **t**, as the day was fading, as the
Isa 21: 4 the **t** I longed for has become a
59:10 At midday we stumble as if it were **t**;

Twin (Twins)
Ge 25:24 there were **t** boys in her womb.
38:27 there were **t** boys in her womb.
SS 4: 2 has its **t**; not one of them is alone.
4: 5 like **t** fawns of a gazelle that
6: 6 has its **t**, not one of them is alone.
Ac 28:11 of the **t** gods Castor and Pollux.

Twinkling
1Co 15:52 in a flash, in the **t** of an eye, at

Twins (Twin)
SS 7: 3 Your breasts are like two fawns, **t**
Ro 9:11 Yet, before the **t** were born or had

Twist (Twisted, Twisting, Twists)
Ps 56: 5 All day long they **t** my words; they

Twisted (Twist)
Ex 26: 1 curtains of finely **t** linen and blue,
26:31 and scarlet yarn and finely **t** linen,
26:36 **t** linen—the work of an embroiderer.
27: 9 to have curtains of finely **t** linen,
27:16 scarlet yarn and finely **t** linen—the
27:18 with curtains of finely **t** linen five
28: 6 and of finely **t** linen—the work of a
28: 8 yarn, and with finely **t** linen.
28:15 scarlet yarn, and of finely **t** linen.
36: 8 curtains of finely **t** linen and blue,
36:35 and scarlet yarn and finely **t** linen,
36:37 **t** linen—the work of an embroiderer;
38: 9 and had curtains of finely **t** linen,
38:16 courtyard were of finely **t** linen.
38:18 **t** linen—the work of an embroiderer.
39: 2 scarlet yarn, and of finely **t** linen.
39: 5 **t** linen, as the LORD commanded Moses.
39: 8 scarlet yarn, and of finely **t** linen.
39:24 **t** linen around the hem of the robe.
39:28 the undergarments of finely **t** linen.
39:29 The sash was of finely **t** linen and
Ecc 1:15 What is **t** cannot be straightened;
Eze 27:24 with cords **t** and tightly knotted.
Mt 27:29 **t** together a crown of thorns and set
Mk 15:17 **t** together a crown of thorns and set
Jn 19: 2 The soldiers **t** together a crown of

Twisting (Twist)
Pr 30:33 and as **t** the nose produces blood, so

Twists (Twist)
Ex 23: 8 and **t** the words of the righteous.
Dt 16:19 and **t** the words of the righteous.
Ps 29: 9 The voice of the LORD **t** the oaks and

Tychicus
Ac 20: 4 Timothy also, and **T** and Trophimus
Eph 6:21 **T**, the dear brother and faithful
Col 4: 7 **T** will tell you all the news about
2Ti 4:12 I sent **T** to Ephesus.
Tit 3:12 soon as I send Artemas or **T** to you,

Tying (Tie)
Pr 26: 8 Like **t** a stone in a sling is the

Type
1Ch 12:33 for battle with every **t** of weapon,
12:37 with every **t** of weapon—120,000.

Tyrannical (Tyranny)
Pr 28:16 A **t** ruler lacks judgment, but he who

Tyrannus
Ac 19: 9 daily in the lecture hall of **T**.

Tyranny (Tyrannical)
Isa 54:14 **T** will be far from you; you will

Tyre (Tyrians)
Important sea port on Mediterranean coast, about 25 miles south of Sidon and 35 miles north of Carmel. A fortress built upon a rock (Eze 26:4, 14) with a commanding position over the sea (Eze 26:17; 27:3). Renowned for its strength and prosperity (Ps 45:12). Good trade relations existed between Tyre and Israel at the time of David and Solomon's building works (2Sa 5:11; 1Ki 5:1; 7:13–14; 9:11–12; 1Ch 14:1; 2Ch 2:3, 11–14), and during Zerubbabel's rebuilding (Ezr 3:7). Its dramatic fall was foretold by the prophets because of its pride and faithlessness (Isa 23; Eze 26–28; Joel 3:4; Am 1:9–10; Zec 9:2–3). Despite its wickedness, Jesus spoke of it more favourably than some of the towns of Galilee (Mt 11:21–22; Lk 10:13–14). While visiting he praised a Canaanite woman's faith and healed her daughter (Mt 15:21–28; Mk 7:24–31). Many of its people went to Galilee to hear Jesus (Mk 3:8; Lk 6:17). Its people sought peace with King Herod (Ac 12:20), and Paul used its port on his third missionary journey (Ac 21:3, 7).

Jos 19:29 and went to the fortified city of **T**,
2Sa 5:11 Now Hiram king of **T** sent messengers
24: 7 they went towards the fortress of **T**
1Ki 5: 1 Hiram king of **T** heard that Solomon
7:13 King Solomon sent to **T** and brought
7:14 man of **T** and a craftsman in bronze.
9:11 towns in Galilee to Hiram king of **T**,
9:12 when Hiram went from **T** to see the
1Ch 14: 1 Now Hiram king of **T** sent messengers

2Ch 2: 3 this message to Hiram king of **T**:
2:11 Hiram king of **T** replied by letter to
2:14 Dan and whose father was from **T**.
Ezr 3: 7 oil to the people of Sidon and **T**,
Ne 13:16 Men from **T** who lived in Jerusalem
Ps 45:12 The Daughter of **T** will come with a
83: 7 Philistia, with the people of **T**.
87: 4 and **T**, along with Cush—and will
Isa 23: 1 An oracle concerning **T**: Wail,
23: 1 For **T** is destroyed and left without
23: 3 of the Nile was the revenue of **T**,
23: 5 be in anguish at the report from **T**.
23: 8 Who planned this against **T**, the
23:15 At that time **T** will be forgotten for
23:15 **T** as in the song of the prostitute:
23:17 years, the LORD will deal with **T**.
Jer 25:22 all the kings of **T** and Sidon; the
27: 3 Moab, Ammon, **T** and Sidon through the
47: 4 who could help **T** and Sidon.
Eze 26: 2 "Son of man, because **T** has said of
26: 3 LORD says: I am against you, O **T**
26: 4 They will destroy the walls of **T** and
26: 7 to bring against **T** Nebuchadnezzar
26:15 what the Sovereign LORD says to **T**:
27: 2 man, take up a lament concerning **T**.
27: 3 Say to **T**, situated at the gateway to
27: 3 say, O **T**, "I am perfect in beauty.
27: 8 O **T**, were aboard as your seamen.
27:32 like **T**, surrounded by the sea?"
28: 2 "Son of man, say to the ruler of **T**,
28:12 the king of **T** and say to him:
29:18 army in a hard campaign against **T**;
29:18 from the campaign he led against **T**.
Hos 9:13 I have seen Ephraim, like **T**, planted
Joel 3: 4 "Now what have you against me, O **T**
Am 1: 9 "For three sins of **T**, even for four,
1:10 I will send fire upon the walls of **T**
Zec 9: 2 which borders on it, and upon **T** and
9: 3 **T** has built herself a stronghold;
Mt 11:21 had been performed in **T** and Sidon,
11:22 it will be more bearable for **T** and
15:21 to the region of **T** and Sidon.
Mk 3: 8 the Jordan and around **T** and Sidon.
7:24 place and went to the vicinity of **T**.
7:31 Jesus left the vicinity of **T** and
Lk 6:17 and from the coast of **T** and Sidon,
10:13 had been performed in **T** and Sidon,
10:14 will be more bearable for **T** and
Ac 12:20 with the people of **T** and Sidon;
21: 3 We landed at **T**, where our ship was
21: 7 We continued our voyage from **T** and

Tyrians (Tyre)
1Ch 22: 4 for the Sidonians and **T** had brought

Ucal
Pr 30: 1 to Ithiel, to Ithiel and to **U**:

Uel
Ezr 10:34 of Bani: Maadai, Amram, **U**,

Ugly
Ge 41: 3 After them, seven other cows, **u** and
41: 4 the cows that were **u** and gaunt ate
41:19 —scrawny and very **u** and lean.
41:19 **u** cows in all the land of Egypt.
41:20 The lean, **u** cows ate up the seven
41:21 they looked just as **u** as before.
41:27 The seven lean, **u** cows that came up
Rev 16: 2 and **u** and painful sores broke out on

Ulai
Da 8: 2 the vision I was beside the **U** Canal.
8:16 I heard a man's voice from the **U**

Ulam
1Ch 7:15 and his sons were **U** and Rakem.
7:17 The son of **U**: Bedan. These were the
8:39 his brother Eshek: **U** his firstborn
8:40 The sons of **U** were brave warriors

Ulla
1Ch 7:39 The sons of **U**: Arah, Hanniel and

Ummah
Jos 19:30 **U**, Aphek and Rehob. There were

Unable
Lev 25:35 is **u** to support himself among you,
Jdg 1:19 but they were **u** to drive the people
Isa 46: 2 **u** to rescue the burden, they
Eze 3:26 will be silent and **u** to rebuke them,
17:14 **u** to rise again, surviving only by
Da 6: 4 affairs, but they were **u** to do so.
Lk 1:22 to them but remained **u** to speak.
20:26 They were **u** to trap him in what he
Jn 8:43 Because you are **u** to hear what I say.
21: 6 they were **u** to haul the net in
Ac 13:11 be **u** to see the light of the sun.
Heb 4:15 **u** to sympathise with our weaknesses

Unafraid
Ps 78:53 guided them safely, so they were **u**

Unanswered
Job 11: 2 "Are all these words to go **u**? Is
Ps 35:13 When my prayers returned to me **u**,

Unapproachable
1Ti 6:16 immortal and who lives in **u** light,

Unashamed
1Jn 2:28 and **u** before him at his coming.

Unauthorised
Lev 10: 1 they offered **u** fire before the LORD,
22:13 No **u** person, however, may eat any of
Nu 3: 4 an offering with **u** fire before him
26:61 before the LORD with **u** fire.)

Unaware
Lev 4:13 the community is **u** of the matter,
5: 2 ground—even though he is **u** of it,
5: 3 unclean—even though he is **u** of it,
5: 4 about—even though he is **u** of it,
Ps 35:15 gathered against me when I was **u**.
Pr 28:22 and is **u** that poverty awaits him.
Lk 2:43 in Jerusalem, but they were **u** of it.
Ro 1:13 I do not want you to be **u**, brothers,
2Co 2:11 For we are not **u** of his schemes.

Unbelief (Unbeliever, Unbelievers, Unbelieving)
Mk 9:24 I do believe; help me overcome my **u**!
Ro 4:20 Yet he did not waver through **u**
11:20 they were broken off because of **u**,
11:23 if they do not persist in **u**, they
1Ti 1:13 because I acted in ignorance and **u**.
Heb 3:19 able to enter, because of their **u**.

Unbeliever (Unbelief)
1Co 7:15 if the **u** leaves, let him do so.
10:27 If some **u** invites you to a meal and
14:24 if an **u** or someone who does not
2Co 6:15 a believer have in common with an **u**?
1Ti 5: 8 the faith and is worse than an **u**.

Unbelievers (Unbelief)
Lk 12:46 and assign him a place with the **u**.
Ro 15:31 that I may be rescued from the **u**
1Co 6: 6 another—and this in front of **u**!
14:22 not for believers but for **u**;
14:22 is for believers, not for **u**.
14:23 do not understand or some **u** come in,
2Co 4: 4 this age has blinded the minds of **u**,
6:14 Do not be yoked together with **u**. For

Unbelieving (Unbelief)
Mt 17:17 "O **u** and perverse generation," Jesus
Mk 9:19 "O **u** generation," Jesus replied,
Lk 9:41 "O **u** and perverse generation," Jesus
1Co 7:14 For the **u** husband has been
7:14 and the **u** wife has been sanctified
Heb 3:12 none of you has a sinful, **u** heart
Rev 21: 8 the cowardly, the **u**, the vile, the

Unblemished
Heb 9:14 Spirit offered himself **u** to God,

Unborn
Ps 22:31 his righteousness to a people yet **u**

Unbound
Da 3:25 in the fire, **u** and unharmed, and

Unceasing (Unceasingly)
Isa 14: 6 struck down peoples with **u** blows,
Ro 9: 2 I have great sorrow and **u** anguish

Unceasingly (Unceasing)
Lam 3:49 My eyes will flow **u**, without relief

Uncertain
1Ti 6:17 hope in wealth, which is so **u**,

Unchangeable (Unchanged)
Heb 6:18 did this so that, by two **u** things

Unchanged (Unchangeable, Unchanging)
Lev 13: 5 and if he sees that the sore is **u**
13:23 if the spot is **u** and has not spread,
13:28 If, however, the spot is **u** and has
13:37 If, however, in his judgment it is **u**
Jer 48:11 as she did, and her aroma is **u**.

Unchanging (Unchanged)
Heb 6:17 to make the **u** nature of his purpose

Unchecked
Am 1:11 continually and his fury flamed **u**,

Uncircumcised (Uncircumcision)
Ge 17:14 Any **u** male, who has not been
Ex 12:48 No **u** male may eat of it.
Lev 26:41 when their **u** hearts are humbled
Jos 5: 7 They were still **u** because they had
Jdg 14: 3 to the **u** Philistines to get a wife?"
15:18 and fall into the hands of the **u**?"
1Sa 14: 6 to the outpost of those **u** fellows.
17:26 Who is this **u** Philistine that he
17:36 this **u** Philistine will be like one
31: 4 or these **u** fellows will come and run
2Sa 1:20 lest the daughters of the **u** rejoice.
1Ch 10: 4 **u** fellows will come and abuse me.
Isa 52: 1 The **u** and defiled will not enter you
Jer 9:26 For all these nations are really **u**,
9:26 house of Israel is **u** in heart."
Eze 28:10 You will die the death of the **u** at
31:18 you will lie among the **u**, with
32:19 Go down and be laid among the **u**.'
32:21 they lie with the **u**, with those
32:24 went down **u** to the earth below.
32:25 All of them are **u**, killed by the
32:26 All of them are **u**, killed by the
32:27 not lie with the other **u** warriors
32:28 will lie among the **u**, with those
32:29 They lie with the **u**, with those
32:30 They lie **u** with those killed by the
32:32 his hordes will be laid among the **u**,
44: 7 you brought foreigners **u** in heart
44: 9 No foreigner **u** in heart and flesh is
Ac 7:51 stiff-necked people, with **u** hearts
11: 3 "You went into the house of **u** men
Ro 3:30 and the **u** through that same faith.
4: 9 circumcised, or also for the **u**?
4:11 had by faith while he was still **u**.
1Co 7:18 was called? He should not become **u**.
7:18 Was a man **u** when he was called? He
Eph 2:11 and called "**u**" by those who call
Col 3:11 circumcised or **u**, barbarian,

Uncircumcision (Uncircumcised)
1Co 7:19 is nothing and **u** is nothing.
Gal 5: 6 circumcision nor **u** has any value.
6:15 circumcision nor **u** means anything
Col 2:13 and in the **u** of your sinful nature,

Uncle (Uncle's)

Lev 10: 4 sons of Aaron's **u** Uzziel, and said
20:20 his aunt, he has dishonoured his **u**.
25:49 An **u** or a cousin or any
1Sa 10:14 Now Saul's **u** asked him and his
10:15 Saul's **u** said, "Tell me what Samuel
10:16 But he did not tell his **u** what
14:50 son of Ner, and Ner was Saul's **u**.
2Ki 24:17 He made Mattaniah, Jehoiachin's **u**,
1Ch 27:32 Jonathan, David's **u**, was a
2Ch 36:10 he made Jehoiachin's **u**, Zedekiah,
Est 2:15 the daughter of his **u** Abihail) to go
Jer 32: 7 Hanamel son of Shallum your **u** is

Uncle's (Uncle)

Ge 29:10 the well and watered his **u** sheep.

Unclean (Uncleanness)

Ge 7: 2 two of every kind of **u** animal, a
7: 8 Pairs of clean and **u** animals, of
Lev 5: 2 touches anything ceremonially **u**
5: 2 the carcasses of **u** wild animals
5: 2 of **u** livestock or of **u** creatures
5: 2 he has become **u** and is guilty.
5: 3 anything that would make him **u**—
7:19 ceremonially **u** must not be eaten;
7:20 if anyone who is **u** eats any meat of
7:21 If anyone touches something **u**—
7:21 or an **u** animal or any unclean,
10:10 common, between the **u** and the clean,
11: 4 hoof; it is ceremonially **u** for you.
11: 5 have a split hoof; it is **u** for you.
11: 6 have a split hoof; it is **u** for you.
11: 7 not chew the cud; it is **u** for you.
11: 8 their carcasses; they are **u** for you.
11:24 You will make yourselves **u** by these
11:24 carcasses will be **u** till evening.
11:25 and he will be **u** till evening.
11:26 does not chew the cud is **u** for you;
11:26 carcass of any of them will be **u**.
11:27 those that walk on their paws are **u**
11:27 carcasses will be **u** till evening.
11:28 **u** till evening. They are **u** for you.
11:29 these are **u** for you: the weasel, the
11:31 the ground, these are **u** for you.
11:31 are dead will be **u** till evening.
11:32 whatever its use, will be **u**, whether
11:32 it will be **u** till evening, and then
11:33 everything in it will be **u**, and you
11:34 water on it from such a pot is **u**,
11:34 that could be drunk from it is **u**.
11:35 their carcasses falls on becomes **u**;
11:35 **u**, and you are to regard them as **u**.
11:36 touches one of these carcasses is **u**.
11:38 falls on it, it is **u** for you.
11:39 the carcass will be **u** till evening.
11:40 and he will be **u** till evening.
11:40 and he will be **u** till evening.
11:43 **u** by means of them or be made **u** by
11:44 Do not make yourselves **u** by any
11:47 You must distinguish between the **u**
12: 2 be ceremonially **u** for seven days,
12: 2 she is **u** during her monthly period.
12: 5 will be **u**, as during her period.
13: 3 shall pronounce him ceremonially **u**.
13: 8 he shall pronounce him **u**; it is an
13:11 the priest shall pronounce him **u**.
13:11 isolation, because he is already **u**.
13:14 flesh appears on him, he will be **u**.
13:15 raw flesh, he shall pronounce him **u**.
13:15 The raw flesh is **u**; he has an
13:20 the priest shall pronounce him **u**.
13:22 pronounce him **u**; it is infectious.
13:25 The priest shall pronounce him **u**;
13:27 the priest shall pronounce him **u**;
13:30 shall pronounce that person **u**;
13:36 for yellow hair; the person is **u**.
13:44 the man is diseased and is **u**. The
13:44 **u** because of the sore on his head.
13:45 of his face and cry out, '**U**! **U**!'
13:46 he has the infection he remains **u**.
13:51 mildew; the article is **u**.
13:55 though it has not spread, it is **u**.
13:59 for pronouncing them clean or **u**.
14:36 in the house will be pronounced **u**.
Lev 14:40 into an **u** place outside the town.
14:41 into an **u** place outside the town.
14:44 destructive mildew; the house is **u**.
14:45 taken out of the town to an **u** place.
14:46 is closed up will be **u** till evening.
14:57 when something is clean or **u**.
15: 2 discharge, the discharge is **u**.
15: 3 or is blocked, it will make him **u**.
15: 4 with a discharge lies on will be **u**,
15: 4 and anything he sits on will be **u**.
15: 5 and he will be **u** till evening.
15: 6 and he will be **u** till evening.
15: 7 and he will be **u** till evening.
15: 8 and he will be **u** till evening.
15: 9 man sits on when riding will be **u**,
15:10 under him will be **u** till evening;
15:10 and he will be **u** till evening.
15:11 and he will be **u** till evening.
15:16 and he will be **u** till evening.
15:17 and it will be **u** till evening.
15:18 and they will be **u** till evening.
15:19 touches her will be **u** till evening.
15:20 lies on during her period will be **u**,
15:20 and anything she sits on will be **u**.
15:21 and he will be **u** till evening.
15:22 and he will be **u** till evening.
15:23 it, he will be **u** till evening.
15:24 him, he will be **u** for seven days;
15:24 days; any bed he lies on will be **u**.
15:25 she will be **u** as long as she has the
15:26 her discharge continues will be **u**,
15:26 anything she sits on will be **u**,
15:27 Whoever touches them will be **u**; he
15:27 and he will be **u** till evening.
15:31 from things that make them **u**,
15:32 made **u** by an emission of semen,
15:33 with a woman who is ceremonially **u**.
17:15 will be ceremonially **u** till evening
20:25 **u** animals and between **u** and clean
20:25 which I have set apart as **u** for you.
21: 1 must not make himself ceremonially **u**
21: 3 her he may make himself **u**.
21: 4 He must not make himself **u** for
21:11 He must not make himself **u**, even
22: 3 your descendants is ceremonially **u**
22: 4 He will also be **u** if he touches
22: 5 any crawling thing that makes him **u**,
22: 5 or any person who makes him **u**,
22: 6 such thing will be **u** till evening.
22: 8 animals, and so become **u** through it.
27:11 he vowed is a ceremonially **u** animal
27:27 If it is one of the **u** animals, he
Nu 5: 2 **u** because of a dead body.
6: 7 ceremonially **u** on account of them,
9: 6 **u** on account of a dead body.
9: 7 said to Moses, "We have become **u**
9:10 **u** because of a dead body or are
18:15 every firstborn male of **u** animals.
19: 7 will be ceremonially **u** till evening.
19: 8 and he too will be **u** till evening.
19:10 and he too will be **u** till evening.
19:11 of anyone will be **u** for seven days.
19:13 he is **u**; his uncleanness remains
19:14 is in it will be **u** for seven days,
19:15 a lid fastened on it will be **u**.
19:16 a grave, will be **u** for seven days.
19:17 "For the **u** person, put some ashes
19:19 sprinkle the **u** person on the third
19:20 if a person who is **u** does not purify
19:20 been sprinkled on him, and he is **u**.
19:21 of cleansing will be **u** till evening.
19:22 that an **u** person touches becomes **u**,
19:22 touches it becomes **u** till evening
Dt 12:15 ceremonially **u** and the clean may eat
12:22 ceremonially **u** and the clean may eat
14: 7 they are ceremonially **u** for you.
14: 8 The pig is also **u**; although it has
14:10 you may not eat; for you it is **u**.
14:19 All flying insects that swarm are **u**
15:22 Both the ceremonially **u** and the
23:10 If one of your men is **u** because of
26:14 I removed any of it while I was **u**,
Jdg 13: 4 and that you do not eat anything **u**,
13: 7 drink and do not eat anything **u**,
13:14 fermented drink nor eat anything **u**.
1Sa 20:26 him ceremonially **u**—surely he is **u**.
2Ch 23:19 who was in any way **u** might enter.
29:16 everything **u** that they found in the
Ezr 2:62 excluded from the priesthood as **u**.
6:21 from the **u** practices of their
Ne 7:64 excluded from the priesthood as **u**.
Ecc 9: 2 the clean and the **u**, those who offer
Isa 6: 5 ruined! For I am a man of **u** lips
6: 5 and I live among a people of **u** lips,
35: 8 The **u** will not journey on it; it
52:11 go out from there! Touch no **u** thing!
64: 6 of us have become like one who is **u**,
65: 4 and whose pots hold broth of **u** meat;
Jer 13:27 Jerusalem! How long will you be **u**?"
Lam 1: 8 sinned greatly and so has become **u**.
1:17 has become an **u** thing among them.
4:15 "Go away! You are **u**!" men cry to
Eze 4:14 No **u** meat has ever entered my mouth.
7:19 and their gold will be an **u** thing.
7:20 turn these into an **u** thing for them.
22:10 when they are ceremonially **u**.
22:26 between the **u** and the clean;
44:23 between the **u** and the clean.
Hos 9: 3 to Egypt and eat **u** food in Assyria.
9: 4 all who eat them will be **u**.
Mt 15:11 does not make him '**u**', but what
15:11 mouth, that is what makes him '**u**'."
15:18 the heart, and these make a man '**u**'.
15:20 These are what make a man '**u**'; but
15:20 hands does not make him '**u**'."
23:27 dead men's bones and everything **u**.
Mk 7: 2 that were "**u**", that is, unwashed.
7: 5 eating their food with '**u**' hands?"
7:15 outside a man can make him '**u**' by
7:15 out of a man that makes him '**u**'."
7:18 from the outside can make him '**u**'?
7:20 out of a man is what makes him '**u**'.
7:23 from inside and make a man '**u**'."
Ac 10:14 never eaten anything impure or **u**."
10:28 should not call any man impure or **u**.
11: 8 or **u** has ever entered my mouth.'
Ro 14:14 that no food is **u** in itself.
14:14 as **u**, then for him it is **u**.
1Co 7:14 your children would be **u**, but as it
2Co 6:17 Touch no **u** thing, and I will receive
Heb 9:13 on those who are ceremonially **u**
Rev 18: 2 for every **u** and detestable bird.

Uncleanness (Unclean)

Lev 5: 3 "'Or if he touches human **u**—
7:21 whether human **u** or an unclean animal
14:19 the one to be cleansed from his **u**.
15: 3 his discharge will bring about **u**:
15:30 the LORD for the **u** of her discharge.
15:31 so they will not die in their **u** for
16:16 **u** and rebellion of the Israelites,
16:16 among them in the midst of their **u**.
16:19 it from the **u** of the Israelites.
18:19 during the **u** of her monthly period.
22: 5 him unclean, whatever the **u** may be.
Nu 19:13 he is unclean; his **u** remains on him.
2Sa 11: 4 She had purified herself from her **u**.
Eze 22:15 and I will put an end to your **u**.
36:17 a woman's monthly **u** in my sight.
36:29 I will save you from all your **u**. I
39:24 to their **u** and their offences,
Jn 18:28 and to avoid ceremonial **u** the Jews

Unclothed

2Co 5: 4 not wish to be **u** but to be clothed

Unconcerned

Eze 16:49 were arrogant, overfed and **u**;

Uncover (Uncovered, Uncovers)

Ru 3: 4 Then go and **u** his feet and lie down.
Jer 49:10 I will **u** his hiding-places, so that

Uncovered (Uncover)

Ge 9:21 drunk and lay **u** inside his tent.
44:16 God has **u** your servants' guilt.
Lev 20:18 of her flow, and she has also **u** it.
Ru 3: 7 quietly, **u** his feet and lay down.
Job 26: 6 before God; Destruction lies **u**.
Isa 47: 3 will be exposed and your shame **u**.

Isa 57: 8 Forsaking me, you **u** your bed, you
Eze 16:57 before your wickedness was **u**. Even
Hab 3: 9 You **u** your bow, you called for many
1Co 11: 5 with her head **u** dishonours her head
11:13 to pray to God with her head **u**?
Heb 4:13 Everything is **u** and laid bare before

Uncovers (Uncover)
Ex 21:33 "If a man **u** a pit or digs one and
Isa 22: 6 and horses; Kir **u** the shield.

Uncut
Jos 8:31 Law of Moses—an altar of **u** stones,
Job 8:12 While still growing and **u**, they

Undeniable
Ac 19:36 Therefore, since these facts are **u**,

Undependable
Job 6:15 my brothers are as **u** as intermittent

Under the sun
Ecc 1:3, 9, 14; 2:11, 17, 18, 19, 20, 22; 3:16; 4:1, 3, 7, 15; 5:13, 18; 6:1, 12; 8:9, 15, 17; 9:3, 6, 9, 11, 13; 10:5

Underfoot (Foot)
2Ki 9:33 the horses as they trampled her **u**.
14: 9 along and trampled the thistle **u**.
2Ch 25:18 along and trampled the thistle **u**.
Isa 14:19 Like a corpse trampled **u**,
28: 3 drunkards, will be trampled **u**.
Lam 3:34 To crush **u** all prisoners in the land
Da 7: 7 and trampled **u** whatever was left.
7:19 and trampled **u** whatever was left.
8:13 the host that will be trampled **u**?"
Mic 7:10 trampled **u** like mire in the streets.
7:19 you will tread our sins **u** and hurl

Undergarment (Garment)
Jn 19:23 each of them, with the **u** remaining.

Undergarments (Garment)
Ex 28:42 "Make linen **u** as a covering for the
39:28 and the **u** of finely twisted linen.
Lev 6:10 with linen **u** next to his body, and
16: 4 with linen **u** next to his body; he is
Eze 44:18 and linen **u** round their waists.

Undergo (Undergoes, Undergoing)
Ge 17:11 You are to **u** circumcision, and it
Lk 12:50 I have a baptism to **u**, and how

Undergoes (Undergo)
Heb 12: 8 (and everyone **u** discipline),

Undergoing (Undergo)
1Pe 5: 9 are **u** the same kind of sufferings.

Undergrowth (Growth)
Job 30: 7 the bushes and huddled in the **u**.
Isa 17: 9 places abandoned to thickets and **u**.

Underlings
2Ki 19: 6 words with which the **u** of the king
Isa 37: 6 words with which the **u** of the king

Undermine
Job 15: 4 you even **u** piety and hinder devotion

Undersides
Job 41:30 His **u** are jagged potsherds, leaving

Understand (Understanding, Understands, Understood)
Ge 11: 7 so they will not **u** each other."
42:23 realise that Joseph could **u** them,
Dt 9: 6 **U**, then, that it is not because of
28:49 whose language you will not **u**,
32:29 If only they were wise and would **u**
1Sa 24:11 Now **u** and recognise that I am not
1Sa 28: 1 Achish said to David, "You must **u**
2Ki 18:26 servants in Aramaic, since we **u** it.
Ne 8: 2 women and all who were able to **u**.
8: 3 men, women and others who could **u**.
8: 8 people could **u** what was being read.
10:28 and daughters who are able to **u**—
Job 26:14 can **u** the thunder of his power?"
32: 9 only the aged who **u** what is right.
36:29 Who can **u** how he spreads out the
38: 4 foundation? Tell me, if you **u**.
42: 3 Surely I spoke of things I did not **u**,
Ps 14: 2 to see if there are any who **u**,
53: 2 to see if there are any who **u**,
73:16 I tried to **u** all this, it was
81: 5 we heard a language we did not **u**.
82: 5 "They know nothing, they **u** nothing.
92: 6 man does not know, fools do not **u**,
119:27 Let me **u** the teaching of your
119:79 to me, those who **u** your statutes.
119:125 that I may **u** your statutes.
Pr 2: 5 you will **u** the fear of the LORD and
2: 9 you will **u** what is right and just
20:24 How then can anyone **u** his own way?
28: 5 Evil men do not **u** justice, but those
28: 5 those who seek the LORD **u** it fully.
30:18 for me, four that I do not **u**:
Ecc 7:25 I turned my mind to **u**, to
7:25 to **u** the stupidity of wickedness
11: 5 so you cannot **u** the work of God, the
Isa 1: 3 does not know, my people do not **u**."
6:10 their ears, **u** with their hearts,
32: 4 The mind of the rash will know and **u**,
36:11 servants in Aramaic, since we **u** it.
41:20 may consider and **u**, that the hand of
42:25 yet they did not **u**; it consumed them
43:10 and believe me and **u** that I am he.
44:18 They know nothing, they **u** nothing;
44:18 minds closed so that they cannot **u**.
52:15 they have not heard, they will **u**.
Jer 5:15 not know, whose speech you do not **u**.
9:12 What man is wise enough to **u** this?
15:15 You **u**, O LORD; remember me and care
17: 9 and beyond cure. Who can **u** it?
23:20 days to come you will **u** it clearly.
30:24 In days to come you will **u** this.
31:19 after I came to **u**, I beat my breast.
Eze 3: 6 language, whose words you cannot **u**.
12: 3 Perhaps they will **u**, though they are
Da 1: 4 well informed, quick to **u**, and
1:17 **u** visions and dreams of all kinds.
2:30 may **u** what went through your mind.
5:23 which cannot see or hear or **u**.
8:15 the vision and trying to **u** it,
8:17 "Son of man," he said to me, "**u** that
9:23 the message and **u** the vision:
9:25 "Know and **u** this: From the issuing
12: 8 I heard, but I did not **u**. So I asked,
12:10 None of the wicked will **u**,
12:10 but those who are wise will **u**.
Hos 14: 9 Who is discerning? He will **u** them.
Mic 4:12 they do not **u** his plan, he who
Mt 13:13 hearing, they do not hear or **u**.
13:15 with their ears, **u** with their hearts
13:19 about the kingdom and does not **u** it,
15:10 to him and said, "Listen and **u**.
16: 9 Do you still not **u**? Don't you
16:11 How is it you don't **u** that I was not
24:15 prophet Daniel—let the reader **u**—
24:43 **u** this: If the owner of the house
Mk 4:13 Jesus said to them, "Don't you **u**
4:13 How then will you **u** any parable?
4:33 to them, as much as they could **u**.
7:14 "Listen to me, everyone, and **u** this.
8:17 Do you still not see or **u**? Are your
8:21 He said to them, "Do you still not **u**?
9:32 they did not **u** what he meant and
13:14 does not belong—let the reader **u**—
14:68 he denied it. "I don't know or **u**
Lk 2:50 they did not **u** what he was saying to
8:10 though hearing, they may not **u**.'
9:45 they did not **u** what this meant. It
12:39 **u** this: If the owner of the house
18:34 The disciples did not **u** any of this.
24:45 he opened their minds so they could **u**
Jn 3:10 "and do you not **u** these things?
8:27 They did not **u** that he was telling
Jn 10: 6 did not **u** what he was telling them.
10:38 that you may know and **u** that the
12:16 his disciples did not **u** all this
12:40 nor **u** with their hearts, nor
13: 7 I am doing, but later you will **u**."
13:12 "Do you **u** what I have done for you?"
16:18 We don't **u** what he is saying."
20: 9 (They still did not **u** from Scripture
Ac 8:30 "Do you **u** what you are reading?"
22: 9 but they did not **u** the voice of him
28:27 with their ears, **u** with their hearts
Ro 7:15 I do not **u** what I do. For what I
10:19 Again I ask: Did Israel not **u**? First,
15:21 those who have not heard will **u**."
1Co 2:12 may **u** what God has freely given us.
2:14 and he cannot **u** them, because they
14:16 among those who do not **u** say "Amen"
14:23 and some who do not **u** or some
14:24 or someone who does not **u** comes in
2Co 1:13 you anything you cannot read or **u**.
1:14 you will come to **u** fully that you
Gal 3: 7 **U**, then, that those who believe are
Eph 3: 4 you will be able to **u** my insight
5:17 Therefore do not be foolish, but **u**
Heb 11: 3 By faith we **u** that the universe was
2Pe 1:20 you must **u** that no prophecy of
2:12 blaspheme in matters they do not **u**.
3: 3 First of all, you must **u** that in the
3: 9 his promise, as some **u** slowness.
3:16 some things that are hard to **u**,
Jude :10 against whatever they do not **u**;
:10 what things they do **u** by instinct,

Understanding (Understand)
Dt 1:13 some wise, **u** and respected men
4: 6 your wisdom and **u** to the nations,
4: 6 nation is a wise and **u** people."
32:21 angry by a nation that has no **u**.
Jdg 13:18 do you ask my name? It is beyond **u**."
1Ki 4:29 and a breadth of **u** as measureless as
1Ch 22:12 the LORD give you discretion and **u**
28:19 he gave me **u** in all the details of
2Ch 30:22 good **u** of the service of the LORD.
Job 8:10 not bring forth words from their **u**?
12:12 aged? Does not long life bring **u**?
12:13 and power; counsel and **u** are his.
17: 4 You have closed their minds to **u**;
20: 3 me, and my **u** inspires me to reply.
28:12 wisdom be found? Where does **u** dwell?
28:20 come from? Where does **u** dwell?
28:28 is wisdom, and to shun evil is **u**.
32: 8 of the Almighty, that gives him **u**.
34:10 "So listen to me, you men of **u**. Far
34:16 "If you have **u**, hear this; listen to
34:34 "Men of **u** declare, wise men who hear
36:26 How great is God—beyond our **u**! The
37: 5 he does great things beyond our **u**.
38:36 with wisdom or gave **u** to the mind?
Ps 32: 9 which have no **u** but must be
49: 3 utterance from my heart will give **u**.
49:20 A man who has riches without **u** is
111:10 who follow his precepts have good **u**.
119:34 Give me **u**, and I will keep your law
119:73 give me **u** to learn your commands.
119:100 I have more **u** than the elders, for
119:104 I gain **u** from your precepts;
119:130 light; it gives **u** to the simple.
119:144 give me **u** that I may live.
119:169 give me **u** according to your word.
136: 5 who by his **u** made the heavens, His
147: 5 mighty in power; his **u** has no limit.
Pr 1: 2 discipline; for **u** words of insight;
1: 6 for **u** proverbs and parables, the
2: 2 wisdom and applying your heart to **u**,
2: 3 out for insight and cry aloud for **u**,
2: 6 from his mouth come knowledge and **u**.
2:11 protect you, and **u** will guard you.
3: 5 heart and lean not on your own **u**;
3:13 finds wisdom, the man who gains **u**,
3:19 by **u** he set the heavens in place;
4: 1 pay attention and gain **u**.
4: 5 Get wisdom, get **u**; do not forget my
4: 7 Though it cost all you have, get **u**.
7: 4 my sister," and call **u** your kinsman;
8: 1 Does not **u** raise her voice?

Pr 8: 5 you who are foolish, gain **u**.
8:14 are mine; I have **u** and power.
9: 6 you will live; walk in the way of **u**.
9:10 and knowledge of the Holy One is **u**.
10:23 but a man of **u** delights in wisdom.
11:12 but a man of **u** holds his tongue.
13:15 Good **u** wins favour, but the way of
14:29 A patient man has great **u**, but a
15:21 a man of **u** keeps a straight course.
15:32 whoever heeds correction gains **u**.
16:16 to choose **u** rather than silver!
16:22 **U** is a fountain of life to those who
17:27 and a man of **u** is even-tempered.
18: 2 A fool finds no pleasure in **u** but
19: 8 he who cherishes **u** prospers.
20: 5 but a man of **u** draws them out.
21:16 A man who strays from the path of **u**
23:23 get wisdom, discipline and **u**.
24: 3 and through **u** it is established;
28: 2 a man of **u** and knowledge maintains
30: 2 of men; I do not have a man's **u**.
Ecc 1:17 I applied myself to the **u** of wisdom,
Isa 5:13 will go into exile for lack of **u**;
6: 9 'Be ever hearing, but never **u**; be
10:13 and by my wisdom, because I have **u**.
11: 2 the Spirit of wisdom and of **u**,
27:11 For this is a people without **u**; so
28:19 The **u** of this message will bring
29:24 are wayward in spirit will gain **u**;
40:14 or showed him the path of **u**?
40:28 weary, and his **u** no-one can fathom.
44:19 no-one has the knowledge or **u** to say,
56:11 They are shepherds who lack **u**; they
Jer 3:15 will lead you with knowledge and **u**.
4:22 senseless children; they have no **u**.
10:12 stretched out the heavens by his **u**.
51:15 stretched out the heavens by his **u**.
Eze 28: 4 By your wisdom and **u** you have gained
Da 1:17 **u** of all kinds of literature and
1:20 In every matter of wisdom and **u**
5:12 a keen mind and knowledge and **u**,
8:27 by the vision; it was beyond **u**.
9:22 now come to give you insight and **u**.
10: 1 The **u** of the message came to him in
10:12 that you set your mind to gain **u**
Hos 4:11 wine and new, which take away the **u**
4:14 people without **u** will come to ruin!
Ob : 8 men of **u** in the mountains of Esau?
Mt 13:14 You will be ever hearing but never **u**
Mk 4:12 and ever hearing but never **u**;
12:33 with all your **u** and with all your
Lk 2:47 was amazed at his **u** and his answers.
Ac 28:26 You will be ever hearing but never **u**
Ro 10:19 angry by a nation that has no **u**."
13:11 And do this, **u** the present time.
2Co 6: 6 in purity, **u**, patience and kindness;
Eph 1: 8 on us with all wisdom and **u**.
4:18 They are darkened in their **u** and
Php 4: 7 which transcends all **u**, will guard
Col 1: 9 through all spiritual wisdom and **u**.
2: 2 have the full riches of complete **u**,
Phm : 6 have a full **u** of every good thing
Jas 3:13 Who is wise and **u** among you? Let him
1Jn 5:20 of God has come and has given us **u**,

Understands (Understand)

Dt 29: 4 a mind that **u** or eyes that see or
1Ch 28: 9 **u** every motive behind the thoughts.
Job 28:23 God **u** the way to it and he alone
Pr 29:19 though he **u**, he will not respond.
Isa 57: 1 and no-one **u** that the righteous are
Jer 9:24 **u** and knows me, that I am the LORD
Mt 13:23 the man who hears the word and **u** it.
Ro 3:11 there is no-one who **u**, no-one who
1Co 14: 2 Indeed, no-one **u** him; he utters
1Ti 6: 4 he is conceited and **u** nothing. He

Understood (Understand)

1Ch 12:32 men of Issachar, who **u** the times and
Ne 8:12 because they now **u** the words that
Est 1:13 with the wise men who **u** the times
Job 13: 1 this, my ears have heard and **u** it.
Ps 73:17 God; then I **u** their final destiny.
Isa 40:13 Who has **u** the mind of the LORD, or
40:21 not **u** since the earth was founded?
Isa 48: 8 You have neither heard nor **u**; from
Da 9: 2 I, Daniel, **u** from the Scriptures,
Mt 13:51 "Have you **u** all these things?" Jesus
16:12 they **u** that he was not telling them
17:13 the disciples **u** that he was talking
Mk 6:52 for they had not **u** about the loaves;
Jn 1: 5 but the darkness has not **u** it.
13:28 no-one at the meal **u** why Jesus said
Ro 1:20 being **u** from what has been made, so
1Co 2: 8 None of the rulers of this age **u** it,
2Co 1:14 you have **u** us in part, you will come
Col 1: 6 and **u** God's grace in all its truth.

Undertaken (Undertook)

1Ki 7:40 Huram finished all the work he had **u**
2Ch 4:11 So Huram finished the work he had **u**
Lk 1: 1 Many have **u** to draw up an account of

Undertakes (Undertook)

Jos 6:26 the man who **u** to rebuild this city,

Undertook (Undertaken, Undertakes)

2Ki 18: 7 he was successful in whatever he **u**.
2Ch 31:21 In everything that he **u** in the
32:30 He succeeded in everything he **u**.
Ecc 2: 4 I **u** great projects: I built houses

Undeserved

Pr 26: 2 an **u** curse does not come to rest.

Undesirable

Jos 24:15 if serving the LORD seems **u** to you,

Undetected

Nu 5:13 her impurity is **u** (since there is no

Undignified

2Sa 6:22 I will become even more **u** than this,

Undisciplined

Pr 9:13 The woman Folly is loud; she is **u**

Undisturbed

Job 12: 6 The tents of marauders are **u**, and
Isa 32:18 secure homes, in **u** places of rest.

Undivided

1Ch 12:33 to help David with **u** loyalty—
Ps 86:11 give me an **u** heart, that I may fear
Eze 11:19 I will give them an **u** heart and put
1Co 7:35 right way in **u** devotion to the Lord.

Undoing (Undone)

2Ch 22: 4 they became his advisers, to his **u**.
Pr 18: 7 A fool's mouth is his **u**, and his

Undone (Undoing)

Jos 11:15 he left nothing **u** of all that the
Lk 11:42 latter without leaving the former **u**

Undying

Eph 6:24 Lord Jesus Christ with an **u** love.

Uneaten

Job 20:18 he toiled for he must give back **u**;

Unending

Jer 15:18 Why is my pain **u** and my wound

Unequalled

Mt 24:21 **u** from the beginning of the world
Mk 13:19 will be days of distress **u** from the

Unexpectedly

Ecc 9:12 by evil times that fall **u** upon them.
Lk 21:34 day will close on you **u** like a trap.

Unfading

1Pe 3: 4 the **u** beauty of a gentle and quiet

Unfailing (*Unfailing love*)

1Sa 20:14 show me **u** kindness like that of the
2Sa 22:51 he shows **u** kindness to his anointed,
Ps 18:50 he shows **u** kindness to his anointed,

Unfailing love

Ex 15:13 "In your **u** you will lead the people
Ps 6: 4 save me because of your **u**.
13: 5 I trust in your **u**; my heart rejoices
21: 7 through the **u** of the Most High he
31:16 on your servant; save me in your **u**.
32:10 but the LORD's **u** surrounds the man
33: 5 justice; the earth is full of his **u**.
33:18 on those whose hope is in his **u**,
33:22 May your **u** rest upon us, O LORD,
36: 7 How priceless is your **u**! Both high
44:26 redeem us because of your **u**.
48: 9 O God, we meditate on your **u**.
51: 1 O God, according to your **u**;
52: 8 I trust in God's **u** for ever and ever.
77: 8 Has his **u** vanished for ever? Has his
85: 7 Show us your **u**, O LORD, and grant us
90:14 with your **u**, that we may sing for
107: 8 give thanks to the LORD for his **u**
107:15 give thanks to the LORD for his **u**
107:21 give thanks to the LORD for his **u**
107:31 give thanks to the LORD for his **u**
119:41 May your **u** come to me, O LORD, your
119:76 May your **u** be my comfort, according
130: 7 with the LORD is **u** and with him is
143: 8 the morning bring me word of your **u**
143:12 In your **u**, silence my enemies;
147:11 him, who put their hope in his **u**.
Pr 19:22 What a man desires is **u**; better to
20: 6 Many a man claims to have **u**, but a
Isa 54:10 yet my **u** for you will not be shaken
Lam 3:32 show compassion, so great is his **u**.
Hos 10:12 reap the fruit of **u**, and break up

Unfair

Mt 20:13 'Friend, I am not being **u** to you.

Unfaithful (Unfaithfully, Unfaithfulness)

Lev 6: 2 "If anyone sins and is **u** to the LORD
Nu 5: 6 **u** to the LORD, that person is guilty
5:12 wife goes astray and is **u** to him
5:27 she has defiled herself and been **u**
Dt 32:20 generation, children who are **u**.
Jdg 19: 2 she was **u** to him. She left him and
1Ch 5:25 they were **u** to the God of their
10:13 Saul died because he was **u** to the
2Ch 12: 2 because they had been **u** to the LORD
26:16 He was **u** to the LORD his God, and
26:18 for you have been **u**; and you will
28:19 and had been most **u** to the LORD.
28:22 Ahaz became even more **u** to the LORD.
29: 6 Our fathers were **u**; they did evil in
30: 7 who were **u** to the LORD, the God of
36:14 the people became more and more **u**,
Ezr 10: 2 "We have been **u** to our God by
10:10 "You have been **u**; you have married
Ne 1: 8 'If you are **u**, I will scatter you
13:27 are being **u** to our God by marrying
Job 31:28 I would have been **u** to God on high.
Ps 73:27 you destroy all who are **u** to you.
Pr 2:22 and the **u** will be torn from it.
11: 3 **u** are destroyed by their duplicity.
11: 6 the **u** are trapped by evil desires.
13: 2 the **u** have a craving for violence.
13:15 but the way of the **u** is hard.
21:18 and the **u** for the upright.
22:12 he frustrates the words of the **u**.
23:28 and multiplies the **u** among men.
25:19 on the **u** in times of trouble.
Jer 3: 7 and her **u** sister Judah saw it.
3: 8 that her **u** sister Judah had no fear
3:10 her **u** sister did not return to me
3:11 is more righteous than **u** Judah.
3:20 like a woman **u** to her husband, so
3:20 been **u** to me, O house of Israel,"
5:11 **u** to me," declares the LORD.
9: 2 all adulterers, a crowd of **u** people.
31:22 long will you wander, O **u** daughter?
49: 4 O **u** daughter, you trust in your

Eze 14:13 country sins against me by being **u**
15: 8 desolate because they have been **u**,
17:20 him there because he was **u** to me.
39:23 sin, because they were **u** to me.
Hos 2: 5 Their mother has been **u** and has
4:12 astray; they are **u** to their God.
5: 7 They are **u** to the LORD; they give
6: 7 covenant—they were **u** to me there.
9: 1 For you have been **u** to your God;

Unfaithfully (Unfaithful)

Jos 7: the Israelites acted **u** in regard to
22:20 Achan son of Zerah acted **u** regarding
22:31 have not acted **u** towards the LORD in

Unfaithfulness (Unfaithful)

Nu 14:33 suffering for your **u**, until the last
1Ch 9: 1 to Babylon because of their **u**.
2Ch 29:19 removed in his **u** while he was king.
33:19 as well as all his sins and **u**, and
Ezr 9: 2 have led the way in this **u**."
9: 4 me because of this **u** of the exiles.
10: 6 to mourn over the **u** of the exiles.
Eze 18:24 Because of the **u** he is guilty of and
39:26 all the **u** they showed towards me
Da 9: 7 us because of our **u** to you.
Hos 1: 2 adulterous wife and children of **u**,
2: 2 and the **u** from between her breasts.
Mt 5:32 except for marital **u**, causes her to
19: 9 except for marital **u**, and marries

Unfamiliar

Isa 42:16 along **u** paths I will guide them;

Unfanned

Job 20:26 A fire **u** will consume him and devour

Unfavourable

Jer 42: 6 Whether it is favourable or **u**, we

Unfeeling

Ps 119:70 Their hearts are callous and **u**, but

Unfilled

Jer 14: 3 They return with their jars **u**;

Unfinished

Tit 1: 5 straighten out what was left **u**

Unfit

Tit 1:16 and **u** for doing anything good.

Unfolding

Ps 119:130 The **u** of your words gives light;

Unforgiving

2Ti 3: 3 without love, **u**, slanderous, without

Unformed

Ps 139:16 your eyes saw my **u** body. All the

Unfriendly

Pr 18: 1 An **u** man pursues selfish ends;

Unfruitful

Mt 13:22 of wealth choke it, making it **u**.
Mk 4:19 in and choke the word, making it **u**.
1Co 14:14 my spirit prays, but my mind is **u**.

Unfulfilled

Eze 19: 5 "'When she saw her hope **u**, her

Unfurled

Ps 60: 4 a banner to be **u** against the bow.

Ungodliness (Ungodly)

Isa 32: 6 He practises **u** and spreads error
Jer 23:15 **u** has spread throughout the land."
Tit 2:12 teaches us to say "No" to **u** and

Ungodly (Ungodliness)

Job 17: 8 innocent are aroused against the **u**.
Ps 35:16 Like the **u** they maliciously mocked;
43: 1 plead my cause against an **u** nation
Pr 11:31 how much more the **u** and the sinner!
Isa 9:17 for everyone is **u** and wicked, every
Ro 5: 6 powerless, Christ died for the **u**.
1Co 6: 1 dare he take it before the **u** for
1Ti 1: 9 the **u** and sinful, the unholy and
2Ti 2:16 in it will become more and more **u**.
1Pe 4:18 what will become of the **u** and the
2Pe 2: 5 brought the flood on its **u** people,
2: 6 what is going to happen to the **u**;
3: 7 judgment and destruction of **u** men.
Jude :15 convict all the **u** of all the **u** acts
:15 they have done in the **u** way,
:18 will follow their own **u** desires."

Ungrateful

Lk 6:35 he is kind to the **u** and wicked.
2Ti 3: 2 to their parents, **u**, unholy,

Unharmed

1Sa 24:19 does he let him get away **u**? May the
2Sa 17: 3 of all; all the people will be **u**."
Ps 55:18 He ransoms me **u** from the battle
Da 3:25 unbound and **u**, and the fourth looks

Unhealthy

1Ti 6: 4 an **u** interest in controversies

Unheard-of

Eze 7: 5 Disaster! An **u** disaster is coming.
Da 11:36 **u** things against the God of gods.

Unholy

1Ti 1: 9 the ungodly and sinful, the **u** and
2Ti 3: 2 to their parents, ungrateful, **u**,
Heb 10:29 who has treated as an **u** thing the

Unimpressive

2Co 10:10 but in person he is **u** and his

Uninformed

2Co 1: 8 We do not want you to be **u**, brothers

Unintentional (Unintentionally)

Nu 15:26 people were involved in the **u** wrong

Unintentionally (Unintentional)

Lev 4: 2 When anyone sins **u** and does what is
4:13 whole Israelite community sins **u**
4:22 "'When a leader sins **u** and does
4:27 If a member of the community sins **u**
5:15 sins **u** in regard to any of the
5:18 for the wrong he has committed **u**,
Nu 15:22 "'Now if you **u** fail to keep any of
15:24 if this is done **u** without the
15:27 "'But if just one person sins **u**, he
15:28 for the one who erred by sinning **u**,
15:29 law applies to everyone who sins **u**,
35:22 another or throws something at him **u**
Dt 4:42 if he had **u** killed his neighbour
19: 4 kills his neighbour **u**, without
Jos 20: 3 kills a person accidentally and **u**
20: 5 because he killed his neighbour **u**
Eze 45:20 who sins **u** or through ignorance;

Union (Unite)

Zec 11: 7 called one Favour and the other **U**,
11:14 I broke my second staff called **U**,
Mt 1:25 he had no **u** with her until she gave

Unique

SS 6: 9 my dove, my perfect one, is **u**, the
Zec 14: 7 will be a **u** day, without daytime or

Unison (Unite)

2Ch 5:13 trumpeters and singers joined in **u**,
Ac 19:34 all shouted in **u** for about two hours

Unit (Units)

Ex 26: 6 so that the tabernacle is a **u**.
26:11 to fasten the tent together as a **u**.
36:13 so that the tabernacle was a **u**.
36:18 to fasten the tent together as a **u**.
1Sa 17:18 cheeses to the commander of their **u**.
1Co 12:12 The body is a **u**, though it is made

Unite (Union, Unison, United, Unites, Unity)

1Ch 12:17 I am ready to have you **u** with me.
Job 16:10 in scorn and **u** together against me.
Isa 14: 1 them and **u** with the house of Jacob.
1Co 6:15 and **u** them with a prostitute? Never!

United (Unite)

Ge 2:24 and mother and be **u** to his wife,
Jdg 20:11 and **u** as one man against the city.
Da 2:43 be a mixture and will not remain **u**,
Mt 19: 5 and mother and be **u** to his wife,
Mk 10: 7 and mother and be **u** to his wife,
Ac 18:12 the Jews made a **u** attack on Paul and
Ro 6: 5 If we have been **u** with him like this
6: 5 be **u** with him in his resurrection.
1Co 1:10 be perfectly **u** in mind and thought.
Eph 5:31 and mother and be **u** to his wife,
Php 2: 1 from being **u** with Christ, if any
Col 2: 2 encouraged in heart and **u** in love,

Unites (Unite)

1Co 6:16 he who **u** himself with a prostitute
6:17 he who **u** himself with the Lord is

Units (Unit)

Nu 10:25 as the rear guard for all the **u**, the
31:48 who were over the **u** of the army—
1Sa 29: 2 their **u** of hundreds and thousands,
2Sa 18: 4 in **u** of hundreds and of thousands.
2Ki 11: 4 the commanders of **u** of a hundred,
11: 9 The commanders of **u** of a hundred did
11:15 the commanders of **u** of a hundred,
1Ch 12:20 of **u** of a thousand in Manasseh.
15:25 the commanders of **u** of a thousand
2Ch 17:14 commanders of **u** of 1,000: Adnah the
23: 1 the commanders of **u** of a hundred:
23: 9 the commanders of **u** of a hundred
23:14 the commanders of **u** of a hundred,

Unity (Unite)

2Ch 30:12 **u** of mind to carry out what the king
Ps 133: 1 is when brothers live together in **u**!
Jn 17:23 May they be brought to complete **u** to
Ro 15: 5 encouragement give you a spirit of **u**
Eph 4: 3 effort to keep the **u** of the Spirit
4:13 until we all reach **u** in the faith
Col 3:14 them all together in perfect **u**.

Universe

1Co 4: 9 been made a spectacle to the whole **u**
Eph 4:10 in order to fill the whole **u**.)
Php 2:15 which you shine like stars in the **u**
Heb 1: 2 and through whom he made the **u**.
11: 3 By faith we understand that the **u**

Unjust

Job 6:29 Relent, do not be **u**; reconsider, for
27: 7 wicked, my adversaries like the **u**!
Ps 82: 2 "How long will you defend the **u** and
Isa 10: 1 Woe to those who make **u** laws, to
Jer 17:11 the man who gains riches by **u** means.
Eze 18:25 **u**? Is it not your ways that are **u**?
18:29 Are my ways **u**, O house of Israel?
18:29 Is it not your ways that are **u**?
22:12 excessive interest and make **u** gain
22:13 at the **u** gain you have made
22:27 and kill people to make **u** gain.
33:31 their hearts are greedy for **u** gain.
Hab 2: 9 him who builds his realm by **u** gain
Lk 18: 6 "Listen to what the **u** judge says.
Ro 3: 5 what shall we say? That God is **u** in
9:14 What then shall we say? Is God **u**?
Heb 6:10 God is not **u**; he will not forget
1Pe 2:19 under the pain of **u** suffering

Unkempt
Lev 10: 6 "Do not let your hair become **u**, and
13:45 let his hair be **u**, cover the lower
21:10 must not let his hair become **u** or

Unknown
Dt 28:36 a nation **u** to you or your fathers.
Isa 48: 6 things, of hidden things **u** to you.
Da 11:38 a god **u** to his fathers he will
Ac 17:23 this inscription: TO AN U GOD.
17:23 what you worship as something **u** I
2Co 6: 9 known, yet regarded as **u**; dying, and
Gal 1:22 I was personally **u** to the churches

Unlawful
Mt 12: 2 are doing what is **u** on the Sabbath."
Mk 2:24 doing what is **u** on the Sabbath?"
Lk 6: 2 you doing what is **u** on the Sabbath?"
Ac 16:21 by advocating customs **u** for us

Unleash (Unleashed, Unleashes)
Job 40:11 **U** the fury of your wrath, look at
Eze 7: 3 and I will **u** my anger against you.
13:13 In my wrath I will **u** a violent wind,

Unleashed (Unleash)
Ex 15: 7 You **u** your burning anger; it
Ps 78:49 He **u** against them his hot anger, his

Unleashes (Unleash)
Job 37: 3 He **u** his lightning beneath the whole

Unleavened (*Feast of Unleavened Bread, Unleavened bread*)
1Ch 23:29 the **u** wafers, the baking and the

Unleavened bread (*Feast of Unleavened Bread*)
Ex 12:20 Wherever you live, you must eat **u**."
12:39 from Egypt, they baked cakes of **u**.
13: 7 Eat **u** during those seven days;
Nu 6:17 He is to present the basket of **u** and
9:11 together with **u** and bitter herbs.
Dt 16: 3 but for seven days eat **u**, the bread
16: 8 For six days eat **u** and on the
Jos 5:11 of the land: **u** and roasted grain.
Jdg 6:20 "Take the meat and the **u**, place them
6:21 the LORD touched the meat and the **u**.
2Ki 23: 9 ate **u** with their fellow priests.
Lk 22: 7 came the day of **U** on which the

Unlimited
1Ti 1:16 might display his **u** patience as

Unload (Unloaded)
Ac 21: 3 where our ship was to **u** its cargo.

Unloaded (Unload)
Ge 24:32 to the house, and the camels were **u**.

Unlocked
Jdg 3:25 room, they took a key and **u** them.

Unloved
Dt 21:17 acknowledge the son of his **u** wife
Pr 30:23 an **u** woman who is married, and a

Unmarked
Lk 11:44 because you are like **u** graves

Unmarried
Lev 21: 3 or an **u** sister who is dependent on
Ru 1:13 remain **u** for them? No, my daughters.
Eze 44:25 **u** sister, then he may defile himself.
Ac 21: 9 He had four **u** daughters who
1Co 7: 8 Now to the **u** and the widows I say:
7: 8 is good for them to stay **u**, as I am.
7:11 if she does, she must remain **u** or
7:27 Are you **u**? Do not look for a wife.
7:32 An **u** man is concerned about the
7:34 An **u** woman or virgin is concerned

Unmindful
Job 39:15 **u** that a foot may crush them, that

Unnatural
Ro 1:26 natural relations for **u** ones.

Unni
1Ch 15:18 Jaaziel, Shemiramoth, Jehiel, **U**,
15:20 Aziel, Shemiramoth, Jehiel, **U**, Eliab
Ne 12: 9 Bakbukiah and **U**, their associates,

Unnoticed
1Sa 24: 4 Then David crept up **u** and cut off
Job 4:20 to pieces; **u**, they perish for ever.
Lk 8:47 seeing that she could not go **u**, came

Unoccupied
Mt 12:44 the house **u**, swept clean and put in

Unploughed
Ex 23:11 year let the land lie **u** and unused.
Jer 4: 3 Break up your **u** ground and do not
Hos 10:12 and break up your **u** ground; for it

Unprepared
2Co 9: 4 come with me and find you **u**,

Unpresentable
1Co 12:23 **u** are treated with special modesty,

Unproductive
2Ki 2:19 the water is bad and the land is **u**."
2:21 it cause death or make the land **u**.
Tit 3:14 necessities and not live **u** lives.
2Pe 1: 8 **u** in your knowledge of our Lord

Unprofitable
Isa 30: 6 humps of camels, to that **u** nation,
Tit 3: 9 because these are **u** and useless.

Unprotected
Ge 42: 9 come to see where our land is **u**."
42:12 come to see where our land is **u**."

Unpunished
Ex 34: 7 Yet he does not leave the guilty **u**;
Nu 14:18 Yet he does not leave the guilty **u**;
Job 10:14 and would not let my offence go **u**.
Pr 6:29 no-one who touches her will go **u**.
11:21 of this: The wicked will not go **u**,
16: 5 Be sure of this: They will not go **u**.
17: 5 gloats over disaster will not go **u**.
19: 5 A false witness will not go **u**, and
19: 9 A false witness will not go **u**, and
28:20 one eager to get rich will not go **u**.
Jer 25:29 you indeed go **u**? You will not go **u**,
30:11 I will not let you go entirely **u**.'
46:28 I will not let you go entirely **u**."
49:12 should you go **u**? You will not go **u**,
Na 1: 3 LORD will not leave the guilty **u**.
Zec 11: 5 Their buyers slaughter them and go **u**.
Ro 3:25 left the sins committed beforehand **u**

Unquenchable (Unquenched)
Jer 17:27 I will kindle an **u** fire in the gates
Mt 3:12 burning up the chaff with **u** fire."
Lk 3:17 will burn up the chaff with **u** fire."

Unquenched (Unquenchable)
Isa 29: 8 he awakens faint, with his thirst **u**.

Unreasonable (Unreasoning)
Ac 25:27 For I think it is **u** to send on a

Unreasoning (Unreasonable)
Jude :10 by instinct like **u** animals—these

Unrelenting
Job 6:10 my joy in **u** pain—that I had not

Unreliable
Ps 78:57 and faithless, as **u** as a faulty bow.

Unrepentant
Ro 2: 5 your stubbornness and your **u** heart,

Unrest
Jer 50:34 but **u** to those who live in Babylon.
Am 3: 9 see the great **u** within her and the

Unrighteous (Unrighteousness)
Zep 3: 5 not fail, yet the **u** know no shame.
Mt 5:45 rain on the righteous and the **u**.
1Pe 3:18 for the **u**, to bring you to God.
2Pe 2: 9 hold the **u** for the day of judgment,

Unrighteousness (Unrighteous)
Jer 22:13 to him who builds his palace by **u**,
Ro 3: 5 if our **u** brings out God's
1Jn 1: 9 our sins and purify us from all **u**.

Unripe
Job 15:33 a vine stripped of its **u** grapes,

Unrolled (Unrolling)
Eze 2:10 which he **u** before me. On both sides

Unrolling (Unrolled)
Lk 4:17 **U** it, he found the place where it is

Unruly
Jer 31:18 You disciplined me like an **u** calf,
Eze 5: 7 have been more **u** than the nations
Hos 11:12 And Judah is **u** against God, even

Unsandalled
Dt 25:10 in Israel as The Family of the **U**.

Unsatisfied
2Sa 1:22 the sword of Saul did not return **u**.

Unscalable
Pr 18:11 they imagine it an **u** wall.

Unscathed
Job 9: 4 Who has resisted him and come out **u**?
Isa 41: 3 He pursues them and moves on **u**, by a
Jer 43:12 himself and depart from there **u**.

Unschooled
Ac 4:13 John and realised that they were **u**,

Unsealed
Ne 6: 5 and in his hand was an **u** letter
Jer 32:11 conditions, as well as the **u** copy—
32:14 both the sealed and **u** copies of the

Unsearchable
Pr 25: 3 deep, so the hearts of kings are **u**.
Jer 33: 3 great and **u** things you do not know.'
Ro 11:33 How **u** his judgments, and his paths
Eph 3: 8 the Gentiles the **u** riches of Christ,

Unseen
Mt 6: 6 and pray to your Father, who is **u**.
6:18 but only to your Father, who is **u**;
2Co 4:18 on what is seen, but on what is **u**.
4:18 temporary, but what is **u** is eternal.

Unsettled
1Th 3: 3 that no-one would be **u** by these
2Th 2: 2 not to become easily **u** or alarmed by

Unsharpened
Ecc 10:10 If the axe is dull and its edge **u**,

Unsheathed
Eze 21: 4 my sword will be **u** against everyone

Unshrunk
Mt 9:16 "No-one sews a patch of **u** cloth on
Mk 2:21 "No-one sews a patch of **u** cloth on

Unspiritual
Ro 7:14 but I am **u**, sold as a slave to sin.
Col 2:18 and his **u** mind puffs him up with
Jas 3:15 but is earthly, **u**, of the devil.

Unstable
Jas 1: 8 double-minded man, **u** in all he does
2Pe 2:14 they seduce the **u**; they are experts
3:16 which ignorant and **u** people distort,

Unstopped
Isa 35: 5 opened and the ears of the deaf **u**.

Unstrung
Job 30:11 Now that God has **u** my bow and

Unsuccessful
Dt 28:29 You will be **u** in everything you do;

Unsuitable (Unsuited)
Ac 27:12 Since the harbour was **u** to winter in,

Unsuited (Unsuitable)
Pr 17: 7 Arrogant lips are **u** to a fool—how

Unsuspecting
Ge 34:25 attacked the **u** city, killing every
Jdg 8:11 Jogbehah and fell upon the **u** army.
18: 7 like the Sidonians, **u** and secure.
18:10 you will find an **u** people and an
18:27 against a peaceful and **u** people.
Eze 38:11 will attack a peaceful and **u** people

Unswerving (Unswervingly)
1Ch 28: 7 he is **u** in carrying out my commands

Unswervingly (Unswerving)
Heb 10:23 Let us hold **u** to the hope we profess

Untended
Lev 25: 5 harvest the grapes of your **u** vines.
25:11 of itself or harvest the **u** vines.

Unthinkable
Job 34:12 It is **u** that God would do wrong,

Untie (Untied, Untying)
Isa 58: 6 and **u** the cords of the yoke,
Mt 21: 2 **U** them and bring them to me.
Mk 1: 7 I am not worthy to stoop down and **u**.
11: 2 **U** it and bring it here.
Lk 3:16 whose sandals I am not worthy to **u**.
13:15 **u** his ox or donkey from the stall
19:30 **U** it and bring it here.
Jn 1:27 whose sandals I am not worthy to **u**."
Ac 13:25 whose sandals I am not worthy to **u**.'

Untied (Untie)
Job 39: 5 donkey go free? Who **u** his ropes?
Mk 11: 4 tied at a doorway. As they **u** it,
Ac 27:40 **u** the ropes that held the rudders.

Untiring
Ps 77: 2 at night I stretched out **u** hands and

Untouched
Pr 19:23 Then one rests content, **u** by trouble.

Untravelled
Jer 9:10 They are desolate and **u**, and the

Untrue
Jos 24:27 you if you are **u** to your God."

Untying (Untie)
Mk 11: 5 "What are you doing, **u** that colt?
Lk 19:31 anyone asks you, 'Why are you **u** it?
19:33 they were **u** the colt, its owners
19:33 "Why are you **u** the colt?

Unused
Ex 23:11 let the land lie unploughed and **u**.

Unusual
Ac 28: 2 The islanders showed us **u** kindness.
28: 6 and seeing nothing **u** happen to him,

Unveiled
2Co 3:18 we, who with **u** faces all reflect the

Unwalled
Nu 13:19 live in? Are they **u** or fortified?
Dt 3: 5 were also a great many **u** villages.
Eze 38:11 "I will invade a land of **u** villages;

Unwashed
Mt 15:20 eating with **u** hands does not make
Mk 7: 2 that were "unclean", that is, **u**.

Unweighed
1Ki 7:47 Solomon left all these things **u**,

Unwholesome
Eph 4:29 Do not let any **u** talk come out of

Unwilling
Ge 24: 5 "What if the woman is **u** to come back
24: 8 If the woman is **u** to come back with
Dt 1:26 you were **u** to go up; you rebelled
Jdg 19:10 But, **u** to stay another night, the
1Sa 15: 9 These they were **u** to destroy
2Ki 13:23 To this day he has been **u** to destroy
Isa 30: 9 children **u** to listen to the LORD's
1Co 16:12 He was quite **u** to go now, but he
Rev 2:21 of her immorality, but she is **u**.

Unwise
Dt 32: 6 O foolish and **u** people? Is he not
Eph 5:15 how you live—not as **u** but as wise,

Unworthy
Ge 32:10 I am **u** of all the kindness and
Job 40: 4 "I am **u**—how can I reply to you?
Lk 17:10 'We are **u** servants; we have only
1Co 11:27 the cup of the Lord in an **u** manner

Unyielding
Ex 7:14 Pharaoh's heart is **u**; he refuses to
9: 7 his heart was **u** and he would not
Pr 18:19 An offended brother is more **u** than a
SS 8: 6 death, its jealousy **u** as the grave.
Eze 3: 8 I will make you as **u** and hardened as

Uphaz
Jer 10: 9 from Tarshish and gold from **U**.

Upheld (Uphold)
1Sa 25:39 who has **u** my cause against Nabal
2Ch 20:20 the LORD your God and you will be **u**;
Ps 9: 4 For you have **u** my right and my cause
Isa 46: 3 you whom I have **u** since you were

Uphold (Upheld, Upholding, Upholds)
Dt 27:26 who does not **u** the words of this law
32:51 **u** my holiness among the Israelites.
1Sa 24:15 May he consider my cause and **u** it;
1Ki 8:45 and their plea, and **u** their cause.
8:49 and their plea, and **u** their cause.
8:59 he may **u** the cause of his servant
2Ch 6:35 and their plea, and **u** their cause.
6:39 and their pleas, and **u** their cause.
9: 8 and his desire to **u** them for ever,
Ps 41:12 In my integrity you **u** me and set me
119:117 **U** me, and I shall be delivered;
Isa 34: 8 of retribution, to **u** Zion's cause.
41:10 **u** you with my righteous right hand.
42: 1 "Here is my servant, whom I **u**, my
Lam 3:59 the wrong done to me. **U** my cause!
Ro 3:31 Not at all! Rather, we **u** the law.

Upholding (Uphold)
Isa 9: 7 establishing and **u** it with justice

Upholds (Uphold)
Ps 37:17 but the LORD **u** the righteous.
37:24 for the LORD **u** him with his hand.
63: 8 clings to you; your right hand **u** me.
140:12 poor and **u** the cause of the needy.
145:14 The LORD **u** all those who fall and
146: 7 He **u** the cause of the oppressed and

Upholstered
SS 3:10 Its seat was **u** with purple, its

Uplifted (Lift)
Ex 6: 8 with **u** hand to give to Abraham,
Nu 14:30 swore with **u** hand to make your home,
Ne 9:15 had sworn with **u** hand to give them.
Ps 106:26 he swore to them with **u** hand that he
Isa 19:16 will shudder with fear at the **u** hand
Eze 20: 5 I swore with **u** hand to the
20: 5 With **u** hand I said to them, "I am
20:15 Also with **u** hand I swore to them in
20:23 Also with **u** hand I swore to them in
20:42 had sworn with **u** hand to give to
36: 7 I swear with **u** hand that the nations
44:12 therefore I have sworn with **u** hand
47:14 Because I swore with **u** hand to give

Upraised (Raise)
Job 38:15 light, and their **u** arm is broken.
Isa 5:25 turned away, his hand is still **u**.
9:12 turned away, his hand is still **u**.
9:17 turned away, his hand is still **u**.
9:21 turned away, his hand is still **u**.
10: 4 turned away, his hand is still **u**.

Upright (Uprightly, Uprightness, Uprights)
Ge 37: 7 suddenly my sheaf rose and stood **u**,
Ex 26:15 "Make **u** frames of acacia wood for
36:20 They made **u** frames of acacia wood
Dt 32: 4 who does no wrong, **u** and just is he.
1Ki 2:32 better men and more **u** than he.
3: 6 to you and righteous and **u** in heart.
Job 1: 1 This man was blameless and **u**;
1: 8 like him; he is blameless and **u**,
2: 3 like him; he is blameless and **u**,
4: 7 Where were the **u** ever destroyed?
8: 6 if you are pure and **u**, even now he
17: 8 **U** men are appalled at this; the
23: 7 There an **u** man could present his
33: 3 My words come from an **u** heart; my
Ps 7:10 Most High, who saves the **u** in heart.
11: 2 from the shadows at the **u** in heart.
11: 7 **u** men will see his face.
25: 8 Good and **u** is the LORD; therefore he
32:11 sing, all you who are **u** in heart!
33: 1 is fitting for the **u** to praise him.
36:10 righteousness to the **u** in heart.
37:14 to slay those whose ways are **u**.
37:37 the blameless, observe the **u**;
49:14 The **u** will rule over them in the
64:10 let all the **u** in heart praise him!
92:15 proclaiming, "The LORD is **u**; he is
94:15 all the **u** in heart will follow it.
97:11 righteous and joy on the **u** in heart.
107:42 The **u** see and rejoice, but all the
111: 1 in the council of the **u** and in the
112: 2 generation of the **u** will be blessed.
112: 4 in darkness light dawns for the **u**,
119: 7 I will praise you with an **u** heart as
125: 4 good, to those who are **u** in heart.
140:13 name and the **u** will live before you.
Pr 2: 7 He holds victory in store for the **u**,
2:21 For the **u** will live in the land, and
3:32 but takes the **u** into his confidence.
11: 3 The integrity of the **u** guides them,

Pr 11: 6 The righteousness of the **u** delivers
11:11 Through the blessing of the **u** a city
12: 6 the speech of the **u** rescues them.
14: 2 He whose walk is **u** fears the LORD,
14: 9 but goodwill is found among the **u**.
14:11 but the tent of the **u** will flourish.
15: 8 but the prayer of the **u** pleases him.
15:19 but the path of the **u** is a highway.
16:17 The highway of the **u** avoids evil;
21: 8 the conduct of the innocent is **u**.
21:18 and the unfaithful for the **u**.
21:29 an **u** man gives thought to his ways.
28:10 He who leads the **u** along an evil
29:10 of integrity and seek to kill the **u**.
29:27 dishonest; the wicked detest the **u**.
Ecc 7:28 I found one **u** man among a thousand,
7:28 but not one **u** woman among them all.
7:29 have I found: God made mankind **u**,
12:10 and what he wrote was **u** and true.
Isa 26: 7 O **u** One, you make the way of the
Mic 2: 7 do good to him whose ways are **u**?
7: 2 the land; not one **u** man remains.
7: 4 the most **u** worse than a thorn hedge.
Hab 2: 4 puffed up; his desires are not **u**
Lk 1: 6 Both of them were **u** in the sight of
23:50 of the Council, a good and **u** man,
Tit 1: 8 **u**, holy and disciplined.
2:12 self-controlled, **u** and godly lives

Uprightly (Upright)
Ps 58: 1 justly? Do you judge **u** among men?
75: 2 appointed time; it is I who judge **u**.
Isa 57: 2 Those who walk **u** enter into peace;

Uprightness (Upright)
1Ki 9: 4 me in integrity of heart and **u**,
Ps 25:21 May integrity and **u** protect me,
111: 8 ever, done in faithfulness and **u**.
Isa 26:10 in a land of **u** they go on doing evil
Mal 2: 6 He walked with me in peace and **u**,

Uprights (Upright)
1Ki 7:28 They had side panels attached to **u**.
7:29 On the panels between the **u** were
7:29 and cherubim—and on the **u** as well.

Uprising
Mk 15: 7 who had committed murder in the **u**.

Uproar
1Sa 4: 6 Hearing the **u**, the Philistines asked,
4:14 "What is the meaning of this **u**?" The
Ps 46: 6 Nations are in **u**, kingdoms fall;
74:23 the **u** of your enemies, which rises
Isa 13: 4 an **u** among the kingdoms, like
17:12 the **u** of the peoples—they roar
25: 5 You silence the **u** of foreigners;
66: 6 Hear that **u** from the city, hear that
Mt 27:24 but that instead an **u** was starting,
Ac 16:20 and are throwing our city into an **u**
19:29 Soon the whole city was in an **u**.
20: 1 the **u** had ended, Paul sent for the
21:31 whole city of Jerusalem was in an **u**.
21:34 get at the truth because of the **u**,
23: 9 There was a great **u**, and some of the

Uproot (Uprooted, Uproots)
1Ki 14:15 He will **u** Israel from this good land
2Ch 7:20 I will **u** Israel from my land, which
Ps 52: 5 **u** you from the land of the living.
Ecc 3: 2 a time to plant and a time to **u**,
Jer 1:10 and kingdoms to **u** and tear down,
12:14 I will **u** them from their lands and I
12:14 **u** the house of Judah from among them.
12:15 after I **u** them, I will again have
12:17 **u** and destroy it," declares the LORD.
24: 6 I will plant them and not **u** them.
31:28 Just as I watched over them to **u** and
42:10 I will plant you and not **u** you,
45: 4 **u** what I have planted, throughout
Mic 5:14 **u** from among you your Asherah poles

Uprooted (Uproot)
Dt 28:63 You will be **u** from the land you are
29:28 in great wrath the LORD **u** them from
Job 31: 8 I have sown, and may my crops be **u**.
31:12 it would have **u** my harvest.
Ps 9: 6 you have **u** their cities; even the
Pr 10:30 The righteous will never be **u**, but
12: 3 but the righteous cannot be **u**.
Jer 18: 7 is to be **u**, torn down and destroyed,
31:40 never again be **u** or demolished."
Eze 17: 9 Will it thrive? Will it not be **u** and
19:12 was **u** in fury and thrown to the
Da 7: 8 of the first horns were **u** before it.
11: 4 will be **u** and given to others.
Am 9:15 **u** from the land I have given them,"
Zep 2: 4 Ashdod will be emptied and Ekron **u**.
Lk 17: 6 'Be **u** and planted in the sea,' and
Jude :12 without fruit and **u**—twice dead.

Uproots (Uproot)
Job 19:10 I am gone; he **u** my hope like a tree.

Upset
2Sa 11:25 'Don't let this **u** you; the sword
Lk 10:41 are worried and **u** about many things,

Upside
Isa 29:16 You turn things **u** down, as if the

Upside-down
2Ki 21:13 a dish, wiping it and turning it **u**.

Upstairs (Stairs)
Da 6:10 he went home to his **u** room where the
Ac 1:13 they arrived, they went **u** to the
9:37 was washed and placed in an **u** room.
9:39 arrived he was taken **u** to the room.
20: 8 There were many lamps in the **u** room
20:11 he went **u** again and broke bread and

Upstream (Stream)
Jos 3:16 the water from **u** stopped flowing.

Ur
City in southern Mesopotamia, home of Abram's family (Ge 11:28–32), from which God brought him to the promised land (Ge 15:7; Ne 9:7).

Ge 11:28 Haran died in **U** of the Chaldeans, in
11:31 set out from **U** of the Chaldeans to
15: 7 out of **U** of the Chaldeans to give
1Ch 11:35 Sacar the Hararite, Eliphal son of **U**,
Ne 9: 7 out of **U** of the Chaldeans and named

Urbanus
Ro 16: 9 Greet **U**, our fellow-worker in Christ

Urge (Urged, Urging)
Ru 1:16 Ruth replied, "Don't **u** me to leave
Est 4: 8 and he told him to **u** her to go into
Ac 27:22 now I **u** you to keep up your courage,
27:34 Now I **u** you to take some food. You
Ro 12: 1 Therefore, I **u** you, brothers, in
15:30 I **u** you, brothers, by our Lord Jesus
16:17 I **u** you, brothers, to watch out for
1Co 4:16 Therefore I **u** you to imitate me.
16:15 I **u** you, brothers,
2Co 2: 8 I **u** you, therefore, to reaffirm your
6: 1 **u** you not to receive God's grace in
9: 5 necessary to **u** the brothers to visit
Eph 4: 1 I **u** you to live a life worthy of
1Th 4: 1 Now we ask you and **u** you in the Lord
4:10 Yet we **u** you, brothers, to do so
5:14 we **u** you, brothers, warn those who
2Th 3:12 Such people we command and **u** in the
1Ti 2: 1 I **u**, then, first of all, that
6: 2 you are to teach and **u** on them.
Heb 13:19 I particularly **u** you to pray so that
13:22 Brothers, I **u** you to bear with my
1Pe 2:11 Dear friends, I **u** you, as aliens and
Jude : 3 I felt I had to write and **u** you to

Urged (Urge)
Ge 19:15 the angels **u** Lot, saying, "Hurry!
Ex 12:33 The Egyptians **u** the people to hurry
Jos 15:18 **u** him to ask her father for a field.
Jdg 1:14 **u** him to ask her father for a field.
1Sa 24:10 Some **u** me to kill you, but I spared
2Sa 3:35 they all came and **u** David to eat
13:25 Although Absalom **u** him, he still
13:27 Absalom **u** him, so he sent with him
1Ki 21:25 the LORD, **u** on by Jezebel his wife.
2Ki 4: 8 there, who **u** him to stay for a meal.
5:16 though Naaman **u** him, he refused.
5:23 He **u** Gehazi to accept them, and then
2Ch 18: 2 and **u** him to attack Ramoth Gilead.
Jer 36:25 Delaiah and Gemariah **u** the king not
Da 2:18 He **u** them to plead for mercy from
Mt 15:23 his disciples came to him and **u** him
Lk 24:29 they **u** him strongly, "Stay with us,
Jn 4:31 Meanwhile his disciples **u** him,
4:40 they **u** him to stay with them, and he
Ac 9:38 they sent two men to him and **u** him,
13:43 who talked with them and **u** them to
21: 4 **u** Paul not to go on to Jerusalem.
27:33 before dawn Paul **u** them all to eat.
1Co 16:12 **u** him to go to you with the brothers.
2Co 8: 6 we **u** Titus, since he had earlier
12:18 I **u** Titus to go to you and I sent
1Ti 1: 3 I **u** you when I went into Macedonia,

Urgent
Nu 22:37 "Did I not send you an **u** summons?
1Sa 21: 8 because the king's business was **u**."
Da 3:22 The king's command was so **u** and the

Urging (Urge)
Ru 1:18 to go with her, she stopped **u** her.
1Sa 28:23 But his men joined the woman in **u**
1Th 2:12 **u** you to live lives worthy of God,

Uri
Ex 31: 2 "See I have chosen Bezalel son of **U**,
35:30 LORD has chosen Bezalel son of **U**,
38:22 (Bezalel son of **U**, the son of Hur,
1Ki 4:19 Geber son of **U**—in Gilead (the
1Ch 2:20 the father of **U**, and **U** the father of
2Ch 1: 5 bronze altar that Bezalel son of **U**,
Ezr 10:24 gatekeepers: Shallum, Telem and **U**.

Uriah (Uriah's)
Hittite. Husband of Bathsheba; killed on David's order (2Sa 11).

2Sa 11: 3 Eliam and the wife of **U** the Hittite?"
11: 6 to Joab: "Send me **U** the Hittite.
11: 7 **U** came to him, David asked him how
11: 8 David said to **U**, "Go down to your
11: 8 So **U** left the palace, and a gift
11: 9 **U** slept at the entrance to the
11:10 David was told, "**U** did not go home,"
11:11 **U** said to David, "The ark and Israel
11:12 So **U** remained in Jerusalem that day
11:13 But in the evening **U** went out to
11:14 a letter to Joab and sent it with **U**.
11:15 In it he wrote, "Put **U** in the front
11:16 he put **U** at a place where he knew
11:17 moreover, **U** the Hittite died.
11:21 your servant **U** the Hittite is dead.
11:24 your servant **U** the Hittite is dead."
12: 9 You struck down **U** the Hittite with
12:10 of **U** the Hittite to be your own.'
23:39 and **U** the Hittite. There were
1Ki 15: 5 in the case of **U** the Hittite.
2Ki 16:10 sent to **U** the priest a sketch of the
16:11 **U** the priest built an altar in
16:15 gave these orders to **U** the priest:
16:16 **U** the priest did just as King Ahaz
1Ch 11:41 **U** the Hittite, Zabad son of Ahlai,
Ezr 8:33 of Meremoth son of **U**, the priest.
Ne 3: 4 Meremoth son of **U**, the son of Hakkoz,
3:21 Next to him, Meremoth son of **U**, the
8: 4 Shema, Anaiah, **U**, Hilkiah and
Isa 8: 2 I will call in **U** the priest and
Jer 26:20 (Now **U** son of Shemaiah from Kiriath
26:21 But **U** heard of it and fled in fear
26:23 They brought **U** out of Egypt and took

Uriah's (Uriah)
2Sa 11:26 **U** wife heard that her husband was
12:15 the child that **U** wife had borne to
Mt 1: 6 whose mother had been **U** wife,

Uriel
1Ch 6:24 Tahath his son, **U** his son, Uzziah
15: 5 From the descendants of Kohath, **U**
15:11 and **U**, Asaiah, Joel, Shemaiah, Eliel
2Ch 13: 2 Maacah, a daughter of **U** of Gibeah.

Urim (*Urim and Thummim*)
Ex 28:30 Also put the **U** and the Thummim in
Nu 27:21 enquiring of the **U** before the LORD.
Dt 33: 8 **U** belong to the man you favoured.
1Sa 28: 6 him by dreams or **U** or prophets.

Urim and Thummim
Lev 8: 8 and put the **U** in the breastpiece.
Ezr 2:63 was a priest ministering with the **U**.
Ne 7:65 be a priest ministering with the **U**.

Urine
2Ki 18:27 own filth and drink their own **u**?"
Isa 36:12 own filth and drink their own **u**?"

Useful
Eze 15: 3 taken from it to make anything **u**?
15: 4 middle, is it then **u** for anything?
15: 5 If it was not **u** for anything when it
15: 5 can it be made into something **u**
Eph 4:28 but must work, doing something **u**
2Ti 2:21 made holy, **u** to the Master and
3:16 God-breathed and is **u** for teaching,
Phm :11 has become **u** both to you and to me.
Heb 6: 7 that produces a crop **u** to those for

Useless
1Sa 12:21 Do not turn away after **u** idols. They
12:21 they rescue you, because they are **u**.
25:21 David had just said, "It's been **u**
Job 15: 3 Would he argue with **u** words, with
Pr 1:17 How **u** to spread a net in full view
Isa 30: 5 shame because of a people **u** to them,
30: 7 to Egypt, whose help is utterly **u**.
59: 6 Their cobwebs are **u** for clothing;
Jer 13: 7 now it was ruined and completely **u**.
13:10 be like this belt—completely **u**!
Mal 1:10 so that you would not light **u** fires
1Co 15:14 preaching is **u** and so is your faith.
1Th 3: 5 and our efforts might have been **u**.
Tit 3: 9 these are unprofitable and **u**.
Phm :11 Formerly he was **u** to you, but now he
Heb 7:18 set aside because it was weak and **u**
Jas 2:20 that faith without deeds is **u**?

Ushers
Pr 18:16 **u** him into the presence of the great

Usury
Ne 5: 7 I told them, "You are exacting **u**
5:10 But let the exacting of **u** stop!
5:11 and also the **u** you are charging them
Ps 15: 5 who lends his money without **u** and
Eze 18: 8 He does not lend at **u** or take
18:13 He lends at **u** and takes excessive
18:17 takes no **u** or excessive interest.
22:12 you take **u** and excessive interest

Utensils
Ex 27: 3 Make all its **u** of bronze—its pots
30:28 its **u**, and the basin with its stand.
31: 9 its **u**, the basin with its stand—
35:16 grating, its poles and all its **u**;
38: 3 They made all its **u** of bronze—its
38:30 its bronze grating and all its **u**,
39:39 grating, its poles and all its **u**;
40:10 of burnt offering and all its **u**;
Lev 8:11 anointing the altar and all its **u**
Nu 4:14 they are to place on it all the **u**
7: 1 consecrated the altar and all its **u**.
2Ch 29:18 of burnt offering with all its **u**,
Eze 40:42 On them were placed the **u** for

Uthai
1Ch 9: 4 **U** son of Ammihud, the son of Omri,
Ezr 8:14 of the descendants of Bigvai, **U** and

Utmost
2Ki 19:23 mountains, the **u** heights of Lebanon.
Job 34:36 that Job might be tested to the **u**
Ps 48: 2 Like the **u** heights of Zaphon is
Isa 14:13 **u** heights of the sacred mountain.
37:24 mountains, the **u** heights of Lebanon.

Utter[1] (Utterance, Uttered, Uttering, Utters)
Nu 30: 6 after her lips **u** a rash promise by
Dt 23:23 Whatever your lips **u** you must be
Jdg 17: 2 about which I heard you **u** a curse—
Job 26: 4 Who has helped you **u** these words?
27: 4 and my tongue will **u** no deceit.
Ps 59:12 For the curses and lies they **u**,
78: 2 **u** hidden things, things from of old
115: 7 they **u** a sound with their throats.
Ecc 5: 2 your heart to **u** anything before God.
Jer 15:19 you **u** worthy, not worthless, words,
Eze 13: 9 visions and **u** lying divinations.
14: 9 prophet is enticed to **u** a prophecy,
Mt 13:35 I will **u** things hidden since the
Rev 13: 5 The beast was given a mouth to **u**

Utter[2]
2Sa 12:14 enemies of the LORD show **u** contempt,
Ps 31:11 enemies, I am the **u** contempt of my
Pr 5:14 I have come to the brink of **u** ruin
Isa 8:22 they will be thrust into **u** darkness.
42:17 will be turned back in **u** shame.

Utterance (Utter[1])
Ps 49: 3 the **u** from my heart will give

Uttered (Utter[1])
Nu 23: 7 Balaam **u** his oracle: "Balak brought
23:18 he **u** his oracle: "Arise, Balak, and
24: 3 he **u** his oracle: "The oracle of
24:15 he **u** his oracle: "The oracle of
24:20 Balaam saw Amalek and **u** his oracle:
24:21 he saw the Kenites and **u** his oracle:
24:23 he **u** his oracle: "Ah, who can live
Jos 10:21 **u** a word against the Israelites.
Ps 89:34 or alter what my lips have **u**.
Isa 45:23 my mouth has **u** in all integrity a
Eze 13: 7 visions and **u** lying divinations

Uttering (Utter[1])
Isa 59:13 **u** lies our hearts have conceived.

Utters (Utter[1])
Ps 37:30 mouth of the righteous man **u** wisdom
1Co 14: 2 he **u** mysteries with his spirit.

Uz
Ge 10:23 The sons of Aram: **U**, Hul, Gether and
22:21 **U** the firstborn, Buz his brother,
36:28 The sons of Dishan: **U** and Aran.
1Ch 1:17 of Aram: **U**, Hul, Gether and Meshech.
1:42 The sons of Dishan: **U** and Aran.
Job 1: 1 In the land of **U** there lived a man
Jer 25:20 all the kings of **U**; all the kings of
Lam 4:21 Edom, you who live in the land of **U**.

Uzai
Ne 3:25 Palal son of **U** worked opposite the

Uzal
Ge 10:27 Hadoram, **U**, Diklah,
1Ch 1:21 Hadoram, **U**, Diklah,
Eze 27:19 "'Danites and Greeks from **U** bought

Uzza
2Ki 21:18 his palace garden, the garden of **U**.
21:26 in his grave in the garden of **U**.
1Ch 8: 7 who was the father of **U** and Ahihud.
Ezr 2:49 **U**, Paseah, Besai,
Ne 7:51 Gazzam, **U**, Paseah,

Uzzah
2Sa 6: 3 **U** and Ahio, sons of Abinadab, were
6: 6 **U** reached out and took hold of the
6: 7 The LORD's anger burned against **U**
6: 8 wrath had broken out against **U**,
1Ch 6:29 his son, Shimei his son, **U** his son,
13: 7 cart, with **U** and Ahio guiding it.
13: 9 **U** reached out his hand to steady the
13:10 The LORD's anger burned against **U**,
13:11 wrath had broken out against **U**,

Uzzen Sheerah
1Ch 7:24 and Upper Beth Horon as well as **U**.

Uzzi
1Ch 6: 5 of Bukki, Bukki the father of **U**,
6: 6 **U** the father of Zerahiah, Zerahiah
6:51 Bukki his son, **U** his son, Zerahiah
7: 2 The sons of Tola: **U**, Rephaiah,
7: 3 The son of **U**: Izrahiah. The sons of
7: 7 The sons of Bela: Ezbon, **U**, Uzziel,
9: 8 Ibneiah son of Jeroham; Elah son of **U**
Ezr 7: 4 the son of Zerahiah, the son of **U**,
Ne 11:22 in Jerusalem was **U** son of Bani,
11:22 **U** was one of Asaph's descendants,
12:19 Joiarib's, Mattenai; of Jedaiah's, **U**;
12:42 also Maaseiah, Shemaiah, Eleazar, **U**,

Uzzia
1Ch 11:44 **U** the Ashterathite, Shama and Jeiel

Uzziah (Azariah, Uzziah's)
Also called Azariah. King of Judah; son of Amaziah (2Ki 14:21–22; 15:1–2; 2Ch 26:1–3). Commended, though failed to remove high places (2Ki 15:3–4; 2Ch 26:4–5). Extended power and prestige; strengthened Jerusalem's defences (2Ch 26:6–15). Pride in assuming priestly authority led to affliction with leprosy and isolation (2Ki 15:5; 2Ch 26:16–21). Death (1Ki 15:7; 2Ch 26:23; Isa 6:1).

2Ki 15:13 year of **U** king of Judah,
15:30 twentieth year of Jotham son of **U**.
15:32 son of **U** king of Judah began to
15:34 LORD, just as his father **U** had done.
1Ch 6:24 his son, Uriel his son, **U** his son
27:25 Jonathan son of **U** was in charge of
2Ch 26: 1 all the people of Judah took **U**, who
26: 3 **U** was sixteen years old when he
26: 8 The Ammonites brought tribute to **U**,
26: 9 **U** built towers in Jerusalem at the
26:11 **U** had a well-trained army, ready to
26:14 **U** provided shields, spears, helmets,
26:16 after **U** became powerful, his pride
26:18 It is not right for you, **U**, to burn
26:19 **U**, who had a censer in his hand
26:21 King **U** had leprosy until the day he
26:23 **U** rested with his fathers and was
27: 2 just as his father **U** had done, but
Ezr 10:21 Elijah, Shemaiah, Jehiel and **U**.
Ne 11: 4 of Judah: Athaiah son of **U**,
Isa 1: 1 of Amoz saw during the reigns of **U**,
6: 1 In the year that King **U** died, I saw
7: 1 Ahaz son of Jotham, the son of **U**,
Hos 1: 1 son of Beeri during the reigns of **U**,
Am 1: 1 when **U** was king of Judah and
Zec 14: 5 in the days of **U** king of Judah.
Mt 1: 8 of Jehoram, Jehoram the father of **U**,
1: 9 **U** the father of Jotham, Jotham the

Uzziah's (Uzziah)
2Ch 26:22 The other events of **U** reign, from

Uzziel (Uzzielites)
Ex 6:18 were Amram, Izhar, Hebron and **U**.
6:22 The sons of **U** were Mishael, Elzaphan
Lev 10: 4 sons of Aaron's uncle **U**, and said to
Nu 3:19 clans: Amram, Izhar, Hebron and **U**.
3:30 clans was Elizaphan son of **U**.
1Ch 4:42 Neariah, Rephaiah and **U**, the sons of
6: 2 Kohath: Amram, Izhar, Hebron and **U**.
6:18 Kohath: Amram, Izhar, Hebron and **U**.
7: 7 The sons of Bela: Ezbon, Uzzi, **U**,
15:10 from the descendants of **U**, Amminadab

1Ch 23:12 Izhar, Hebron and U—four in all.
23:20 The sons of U: Micah the first and
24:24 The son of U: Micah; from the sons
25: 4 Mattaniah, U, Shubael and Jerimoth;
2Ch 29:14 of Jeduthun, Shemaiah and U.
Ne 3: 8 U son of Harhaiah, one of the

Uzzielites (Uzziel)

Nu 3:27 U; these were the Kohathite clans.
1Ch 26:23 Izharites, the Hebronites and the U:

Vain

Lev 26:16 You will plant seed in v, because
26:20 Your strength will be spent in v,
Job 3: 9 may it wait for daylight in v and
9:29 guilty, why should I struggle in v?
24: 1 know him look in v for such days?
39:16 cares not that her labour was in v,
Ps 2: 1 conspire and the peoples plot in v?
33:17 A horse is a v hope for deliverance;
39: 6 He bustles about, but only in v;
73:13 Surely in v have I kept my heart
73:13 in v have I washed my hands in
119:118 for their deceitfulness is in v.
127: 1 the house, its builders labour in v.
127: 1 city, the watchmen stand guard in v.
127: 2 In v you rise early and stay up late,
Isa 45:19 Jacob's descendants, 'Seek me in v.
49: 4 I have spent my strength in v and
65:23 They will not toil in v or bear
Jer 2:30 "In v I punished your people; they
4:30 with paint? You adorn yourself in v.
6:29 the refining goes on in v;
46:11 you multiply remedies in v; there is
Lam 4:17 eyes failed, looking in v for help
Eze 6:10 I did not threaten in v to bring
Zec 10: 2 are false, they give comfort in v.
Mt 15: 9 They worship me in v; their
Mk 7: 7 They worship me in v; their
Ac 4:25 rage and the peoples plot in v?
1Co 15: 2 Otherwise, you have believed in v.
15:58 your labour in the Lord is not in v.
2Co 6: 1 you not to receive God's grace in v.
Gal 2: 2 was running or had run my race in v.
Php 2: 3 of selfish ambition or v conceit,

Vaizatha

Est 9: 9 Parmashta, Arisai, Aridai and V,

Valiant (Valiantly)

Jdg 20:44 fell, all of them v fighters.
20:46 fell, all of them v fighters.
1Sa 10:26 v men whose hearts God had touched.
31:12 all their v men journeyed through
2Sa 23:20 son of Jehoiada was a v fighter
2Ki 5: 1 was a v soldier, but he had leprosy.
1Ch 10:12 all their v men went and took the
11:22 son of Jehoiada was a v fighter
2Ch 17:17 From Benjamin: Eliada, a v soldier,
Ps 76: 5 V men lie plundered, they sleep
Jer 48:14 'We are warriors, men v in battle'?

Valiantly (Valiant)

1Sa 14:48 He fought v and defeated the

Valid

2Sa 15: 3 "Look, your claims are v and proper,
Jn 5:31 about myself, my testimony is not v.
5:32 that his testimony about me is v.
8:13 witness; your testimony is not v."
8:14 my testimony is v, for I know where
8:17 that the testimony of two men is v.

Valley (Valleys)

Ge 14: 3 in the V of Siddim (the Salt Sea).
14: 8 battle lines in the V of Siddim
14:10 Now the V of Siddim was full of tar
14:17 V of Shaveh (that is, the King's V).
26:17 in the V of Gerar and settled there.
26:19 Isaac's servants dug in the v and
37:14 he sent him off from the V of Hebron
Nu 13:23 they reached the V of Eshcol, they
13:24 place was called the V of Eshcol
21:12 moved on and camped in the Zered V.
Nu 21:20 from Bamoth to the v in Moab where
32: 9 they went up to the V of Eshcol
Dt 1:24 to the V of Eshcol and explored it.
2:13 the Zered V. So we crossed the v.
2:14 until we crossed the Zered V.
3:29 we stayed in the v near Beth Peor.
4:46 were in the v near Beth Peor east of
21: 4 lead her down to a v that has not
21: 4 There in the v they are to break the
21: 6 whose neck was broken in the v,
34: 3 whole region from the V of Jericho,
34: 6 in Moab, in the v opposite Beth Peor
Jos 7:24 all that he had, to the V of Achor.
7:26 called the V of Achor ever since.
8:11 the v between them and the city.
8:13 That night Joshua went into the v.
10:12 O moon, over the V of Aijalon."
11: 8 and to the V of Mizpah on the east,
11:17 the V of Lebanon below Mount Hermon.
12: 7 from Baal Gad in the V of Lebanon to
13:19 Zereth Shahar on the hill in the v,
13:27 in the v, Beth Haram, Beth Nimrah,
15: 7 up to Debir from the V of Achor
15: 8 ran up the V of Ben Hinnom along the
15: 8 top of the hill west of the Hinnom V
15: 8 northern end of the V of Rephaim.
17:16 and those in the V of Jezreel."
18:16 the hill facing the V of Ben Hinnom
18:16 Hinnom, north of the V of Rephaim.
18:16 It continued down the Hinnom V along
19:14 and ended at the V of Iphtah El.
19:27 touched Zebulun and the V of Iphtah
Jdg 5:15 Barak, rushing after him into the v.
6:33 and camped in the V of Jezreel.
7: 1 in the v near the hill of Moreh.
7: 8 of Midian lay below him in the v.
7:12 settled in the v, thick as locusts.
16: 4 V of Sorek whose name was Delilah.
18:28 The city was in a v near Beth Rehob.
1Sa 6:13 harvesting their wheat in the v,
13:18 the V of Zeboim facing the desert.
17: 2 camped in the V of Elah and drew up
17: 3 another, with the v between them.
17:19 the men of Israel in the V of Elah,
21: 9 whom you killed in the V of Elah, is
31: 7 the Israelites along the v and those
2Sa 5:18 and spread out in the V of Rephaim;
5:22 and spread out in the V of Rephaim;
8:13 thousand Edomites in the V of Salt.
15:23 The king also crossed the Kidron V,
17:13 and we will drag it down to the v
18:18 King's V as a monument to himself,
23:13 was encamped in the V of Rephaim.
1Ki 2:37 you leave and cross the Kidron V,
15:13 down and burned it in the Kidron V.
18:40 the Kishon V and slaughtered there.
2Ki 2:16 down on some mountain or in some v.
3:16 says: Make this v full of ditches.
3:17 this v will be filled with water,
14: 7 thousand Edomites in the V of Salt
23: 4 in the fields of the Kidron V and
23: 6 to the Kidron V outside Jerusalem
23:10 which was in the V of Ben Hinnom,
23:12 threw the rubble into the Kidron V.
1Ch 4:39 of Gedor to the east of the v
10: 7 all the Israelites in the v saw that
11:15 was encamped in the V of Rephaim.
14: 9 come and raided the V of Rephaim;
14:13 more the Philistines raided the v;
18:12 thousand Edomites in the V of Salt.
2Ch 14:10 in the V of Zephathah near Mareshah.
15:16 it up and burned it in the Kidron V.
20:26 they assembled in the V of Beracah,
20:26 called the V of Beracah to this day.
25:11 and led his army to the V of Salt,
26: 9 at the V Gate and at the angle of
28: 3 sacrifices in the V of Ben Hinnom
29:16 and carried it out to the Kidron V.
30:14 and threw them into the Kidron V.
33: 6 in the fire in the V of Ben Hinnom,
33:14 west of the Gihon spring in the v,
Ne 2:13 I went out through the V Gate
2:15 I went up the v by night, examining
2:15 and re-entered through the V Gate.
3:13 The V Gate was repaired by Hanun and
11:30 from Beersheba to the V of Hinnom.
Ne 11:35 and in the V of the Craftsmen.
Job 21:33 The soil in the v is sweet to him;
Ps 23: 4 the v of the shadow of death,
60: T thousand Edomites in the V of Salt
60: 6 and measure off the V of Succoth.
84: 6 they pass through the V of Baca,
108: 7 and measure off the V of Succoth.
Pr 30:17 pecked out by the ravens of the v,
SS 6:11 to look at the new growth in the v,
Isa 17: 5 ears of corn in the V of Rephaim.
22: 1 oracle concerning the V of Vision:
22: 5 and terror in the V of Vision,
28: 1 set on the head of a fertile v—
28: 4 set on the head of a fertile v, will
28:21 rouse himself as in the V of Gibeon
40: 4 Every v shall be raised up, every
65:10 and the V of Achor a resting place
Jer 2:23 See how you behaved in the v;
7:31 in the V of Ben Hinnom to burn their
7:32 it Topheth or the V of Ben Hinnom,
7:32 but the V of Slaughter, for they
19: 2 go out to the V of Ben Hinnom, near
19: 6 Topheth or the V of Ben Hinnom,
19: 6 Ben Hinnom, but the V of Slaughter.
21:13 you who live above this v on the
31:40 The whole v where dead bodies and
31:40 all the terraces out to the Kidron V
32:35 in the V of Ben Hinnom to sacrifice
48: 8 The v will be ruined and the plateau
Eze 37: 1 set me in the middle of a v; it was
37: 2 on the floor of the v, bones that
39:11 in the v of those who travel east
39:11 will be called the V of Hamon Gog.
39:15 buried it in the V of Hamon Gog.
Hos 1: 5 Israel's bow in the V of Jezreel."
2:15 make the V of Achor a door of hope.
Joel 3: 2 them down to the V of Jehoshaphat.
3:12 advance into the V of Jehoshaphat,
3:14 multitudes in the v of decision!
3:14 LORD is near in the v of decision.
3:18 and will water the v of acacias.
Am 1: 5 the king who is in the V of Aven
6:14 Lebo Hamath to the v of the Arabah.
Mic 1: 6 I will pour her stones into the v
Zec 14: 4 forming a great v, with half of the
14: 5 You will flee by my mountain v, for
Lk 3: 5 Every v shall be filled in, every
Jn 18: 1 disciples and crossed the Kidron V.

Valleys (Valley)

Nu 14:25 and Canaanites are living in the v,
24: 6 "Like v they spread out, like
Dt 8: 7 springs flowing in the v and hills;
11:11 and v that drinks rain from heaven.
2Sa 22:16 The v of the sea were exposed and
1Ki 18: 5 the land to all the springs and v.
20:28 of the hills and not a god of the v,
1Ch 12:15 the v, to the east and to the west.
27:29 was in charge of the herds in the v.
Job 39:10 Will he till the v behind you?
Ps 18:15 The v of the sea were exposed and
65:13 and the v are mantled with corn;
104: 8 they went down into the v, to the
SS 2: 1 a rose of Sharon, a lily of the v.
Isa 22: 7 choicest v are full of chariots,
41:18 heights, and springs within the v.
Jer 49: 4 your v, boast of your v so fruitful
Eze 6: 3 to the ravines and v: I am about to
7:16 moaning like doves of the v, each
31:12 on the mountains and in all the v;
32: 5 and fill the v with your remains.
35: 8 in your v and in all your ravines.
36: 4 to the ravines and v, to the
36: 6 to the ravines and v: 'This is what
Mic 1: 4 beneath him and the v split apart,

Valuable (Value)

2Ch 32:23 v gifts for Hezekiah king of Judah.
Ezr 1: 6 and with v gifts, in addition to all
Pr 1:13 we will get all sorts of v things
Da 11: 8 their v articles of silver and gold
Mt 6:26 Are you not much more v than they?
12:12 How much more v is a man than a
Lk 12:24 how much more v you are than birds!
Jas 5: 7 for the land to yield its v crop

Valuables (Value)
2Ch 32:27 spices, shields and all kinds of v.
Jer 20: 5 all its v and all the treasures of

Value (Valuable, Valuables, Valued, Values)
Lev 5:15 and of the proper v in silver,
5:16 add a fifth of the v to that and
5:18 without defect and of the proper v.
6: 5 add a fifth of the v to it and give
6: 6 without defect and of the proper v.
22:14 and add a fifth of the v to it.
25:27 he is to determine the v for the
27: 3 set the v of a male between the ages
27: 4 if it is a female, set her v at
27: 5 the v of a male at twenty shekels
27: 6 set the v of a male at five shekels
27: 7 the v of a male at fifteen shekels
27: 8 who will set the v for him according
27:12 Whatever v the priest then sets,
27:13 he must add a fifth to its v.
27:14 Whatever v the priest then sets, so
27:15 he must add a fifth to its v, and
27:16 its v is to be set according to the
27:17 the v that has been set remains.
27:18 the priest will determine the v
27:18 and its set v will be reduced.
27:19 he must add a fifth to its v, and
27:23 the priest will determine its v up
27:23 and the man must pay its v on that
27:25 Every v is to be set according to
27:27 set v, adding a fifth of the v to
27:27 it is to be sold at its set v.
27:31 he must add a fifth of the v to it.
1Sa 26:24 so may the LORD v my life and
1Ki 10:21 of little v in Solomon's days.
20: 6 They will seize everything you v and
2Ch 9:20 of little v in Solomon's day.
20:25 and clothing and also articles of v
21: 3 silver and gold and articles of v,
36:10 together with articles of v from the
36:19 and destroyed everything of v there.
Job 15: 3 words, with speeches that have no v?
Pr 10: 2 Ill-gotten treasures are of no v,
10:20 heart of the wicked is of little v.
16:13 they v a man who speaks the truth.
31:11 in her and lacks nothing of v.
Eze 7:11 that crowd—no wealth, nothing of v.
Hab 2:18 "Of what v is an idol, since a man
Mt 13:46 he found one of great v, he went
Ac 19:19 When they calculated the v of the
Ro 2:25 Circumcision has v if you observe
3: 1 or what v is there in circumcision?
4:14 no v and the promise is worthless,
Gal 5: 2 Christ will be of no v to you at all.
5: 6 nor uncircumcision has any v.
Col 2:23 v in restraining sensual indulgence.
1Ti 4: 8 For physical training is of some v,
4: 8 but godliness has v for all things,
2Ti 2:14 it is of no v, and only ruins those
Heb 4: 2 they heard was of no v to them,
11:26 of greater v than the treasures of
13: 9 are of no v to those who eat them.

Valued (Value)
1Sa 26:24 surely as I v your life today, so
Ezr 8:27 20 bowls of gold v at 1,000 darics,
Lk 7: 2 whom his master v highly, was sick
16:15 What is highly v among men is

Values (Value)
Lev 27: 2 to the LORD by giving equivalent v,

Vaniah
Ezr 10:36 V, Meremoth, Eliashib,

Vanish (Vanished, Vanishes)
Job 6:17 in the heat v from their channels.
Ps 37:20 fields, they will v—v like smoke.
58: 7 Let them v like water that flows
102: 3 For my days v like smoke; my bones
104:35 may sinners v from the earth and the
Isa 11:13 Ephraim's jealousy will v, and
16: 4 the aggressor will v from the land.
29:14 of the intelligent will v."
29:20 The ruthless will v, the mockers
34:12 all her princes will v away.
51: 6 the heavens will v like smoke,
Jer 18:14 Does the snow of Lebanon ever v from
31:36 "Only if these decrees v from my

Vanished (Vanish)
Ps 12: 1 the faithful have v from among men.
77: 8 Has his unfailing love v for ever?
Ecc 9: 6 their jealousy have long since v;
Jer 7:28 perished; it has v from their lips.
Rev 18:14 have v, never to be recovered.'

Vanishes (Vanish)
Job 7: 9 a cloud v and is gone, so he who
30:15 the wind, my safety v like a cloud.
Jas 4:14 for a little while and then v.

Vapour
Pr 21: 6 is a fleeting v and a deadly snare.

Vashti
Queen of Persia; wife of Xerxes. Deposed for refusal to appear at banquet (Est 1). Replaced by Esther (Est 2:1–17).

Est 1: 9 Queen V also gave a banquet for the
1:11 to bring before him Queen V, wearing
1:12 command, Queen V refused to come.
1:15 must be done to Queen V?" he asked.
1:16 "Queen V has done wrong, not only
1:17 'King Xerxes commanded Queen V to be
1:19 that V is never again to enter the
2: 1 he remembered V and what she had
2: 4 the king be queen instead of V.
2:17 and made her queen instead of V.

Vassal (Vassals)
2Ki 16: 7 Assyria, "I am your servant and v.
17: 3 who had been Shalmaneser's v and
24: 1 became his v for three years.

Vassals (Vassal)
2Sa 10:19 all the kings who were v of
1Ch 19:19 the v of Hadadezer saw that they had

Vast
Ge 2: 1 were completed in all their v array.
Dt 1:19 all that v and dreadful desert
2: 7 your journey through this v desert.
8:15 through the v and dreadful desert
1Ki 8:65 all Israel with him—a v assembly,
20:13 'Do you see this v army? I will give
20:28 I will deliver this v army into your
2Ch 7: 8 all Israel with him—a v assembly,
13: 8 You are indeed a v army and have
14: 9 a v army and three hundred chariots,
14:11 we have come against this v army.
20: 2 "A v army is coming against you from
20:12 this v army that is attacking us.
20:15 discouraged because of this v army.
20:24 and looked towards the v army,
32: 7 of Assyria and the v army with him,
Est 1: 4 the v wealth of his kingdom
1:20 throughout all his v realm,
5:11 boasted to them about his v wealth
Job 9: 4 wisdom is profound, his power is v.
38:18 Have you comprehended the v expanses
Ps 104:25 There is the sea, v and spacious,
139:17 O God! How v is the sum of them!
Eze 26:19 over you and its v waters cover you,
37:10 stood up on their feet—a v army.

Vat (Vats)
Hag 2:16 When anyone went to a wine v to draw

Vats (Vat)
Ex 22:29 from your granaries or your v.
1Ch 27:27 of the vineyards for the wine v.
Pr 3:10 your v will brim over with new wine.
Joel 2:24 the v will overflow with new wine
3:13 winepress is full and the v overflow

Vaulted (Vaults)
Job 22:14 as he goes about in the v heavens.
Jer 37:16 Jeremiah was put into a v cell in a

Vaults (Vaulted)
Dt 32:34 in reserve and sealed it in my v?

Vaunts
Job 15:25 and v himself against the Almighty,

Vegetable (Vegetables)
Dt 11:10 it by foot as in a v garden.
1Ki 21: 2 your vineyard to use for a v garden,

Vegetables (Vegetable)
Pr 15:17 Better a meal of v where there is
Da 1:12 but v to eat and water to drink.
1:16 to drink and gave them v instead.
Ro 14: 2 whose faith is weak, eats only v.

Vegetation
Ge 1:11 God said, "Let the land produce v:
1:12 The land produced v: plants bearing
19:25 cities—and also the v in the land.
Dt 29:23 sprouting, no v growing on it.
Isa 15: 6 v is gone and nothing green is left.
42:15 and hills and dry up all their v;

Veil (Veiled, Veils)
Ge 24:65 she took her v and covered herself.
38:14 covered herself with a v to disguise
38:19 After she left, she took off her v
Ex 34:33 to them, he put a v over his face.
34:34 he removed the v until he came out.
34:35 Then Moses would put the v back over
Job 22:14 Thick clouds v him, so he does not
SS 4: 1 Your eyes behind your v are doves.
4: 3 Your temples behind your v are like
6: 7 Your temples behind your v are like
Isa 47: 2 and grind flour; take off your v.
Lam 3:65 Put a v over their hearts, and may
2Co 3:13 who would put a v over his face to
3:14 for to this day the same v remains
3:15 is read, a v covers their hearts.
3:16 to the Lord, the v is taken away.

Veiled (Veil)
SS 1: 7 Why should I be like a v woman
2Co 4: 3 even if our gospel is v, it is v to

Veils (Veil)
Isa 3:19 the ear-rings and bracelets and v,
Eze 13:18 make v of various lengths for their
13:21 I will tear off your v and save my

Vengeance (Avenge, Avenged, Avenger, Avenges, Avenging, Revenge)
Ge 4:15 he will suffer v seven times over.
Nu 31: 2 "Take v on the Midianites for the
31: 3 to carry out the LORD's v on them.
Dt 32:41 I will take v on my adversaries and
32:43 he will take v on his enemies and
Ps 149: 7 to inflict v on the nations and
Isa 34: 8 For the LORD has a day of v, a year
35: 4 he will come with v; with divine
47: 3 I will take v; I will spare no-one."
59:17 he put on the garments of v and
61: 2 favour and the day of v of our God,
63: 4 For the day of v was in my heart,
Jer 11:20 let me see your v upon them, for to
20:12 let me see your v upon them, for to
46:10 a day of v, for v on his foes.
50:15 Since this is the v of the LORD,
50:15 take v on her; do to her as she has
50:28 God has taken v, for his temple.
51: 6 It is time for the LORD's v; he will
51:11 LORD will take v, for his temple.
Lam 3:60 You have seen the depth of their v,
Eze 16:38 I will bring upon you the blood v
25:14 I will take v on Edom by the hand of
25:14 they will know my v, declares the
25:15 'Because the Philistines acted in v
25:17 I will carry out great v on them and

Eze 25:17 I am the LORD, when I take v on them.
Mic 5:15 I will take v in anger and wrath
Na 1: 2 takes v and is filled with wrath.
1: 2 The LORD takes v on his foes and

Venom (Venomous)
Dt 32:24 v of vipers that glide in the dust.
32:33 Their wine is the v of serpents, the
Job 20:14 become the v of serpents within him.
Ps 58: 4 Their v is like the v of a snake,

Venomous (Venom)
Nu 21: 6 the LORD sent v snakes among them;
Dt 8:15 with its v snakes and scorpions.
Isa 14:29 fruit will be a darting, v serpent.
Jer 8:17 "See, I will send v snakes among you,

Vent
Job 15:13 that you v your rage against God and
20:23 God will v his burning anger against
Pr 29:11 A fool gives full v to his anger,
Lam 4:11 LORD has given full v to his wrath
Da 11:30 he will turn back and v his fury

Venture (Ventures)
Dt 28:56 gentle that she would not v to touch
Jer 5: 6 to tear to pieces any who v out,
Ac 19:31 him not to v into the theatre.
Ro 15:18 I will not v to speak of anything

Ventures (Venture)
Job 4: 2 "If someone v a word with you, will

Verdant
SS 1:16 Oh, how charming! And our bed is v.

Verdict
Dt 17: 9 them and they will give you the v.
Jdg 20: 7 speak up and give your v."
1Ki 3:28 all Israel heard the v the king had
2Ch 19: 6 is with you whenever you give a v.
Da 4:17 the holy ones declare the v, so that
Jn 3:19 This is the v: Light has come into

Verified (Verify)
Ge 42:20 may be v and that you may not die.

Verify (Verified)
Ac 24:11 You can easily v that no more than

Versed
Ezr 7: 6 He was a teacher well v in the Law

Verses
Ps 45: 1 theme as I recite my v for the king

Vessel (Vessels)
Isa 2:16 trading ship and every stately v.

Vessels (Vessel)
Isa 22:24 all its lesser v, from the bowls to
52:11 you who carry the v of the LORD.
66:20 of the LORD in ceremonially clean v.

Vestments
Ezr 3:10 the priests in their v and with

Veteran
Eze 27: 9 V craftsmen of Gebal were on board

Vexed
Ps 78:41 they v the Holy One of Israel.
112:10 The wicked man will see and be v, he

Vicinity
Dt 11:30 in the Arabah in the v of Gilgal.
Jos 3:16 called Adam in the v of Zarethan
15:46 all that were in the v of Ashdod
Jdg 11:33 v of Minnith, as far as Abel Keramim.
20:43 them in the v of Gibeah on the east.
1Sa 5: 6 upon the people of Ashdod and its v;
1Sa 13:17 towards Ophrah in the v of Shual,
2Ki 15:16 and everyone in the city and its v,
Mt 2:16 in Bethlehem and its v who were two
15:22 A Canaanite woman from that v came
15:39 boat and went to the v of Magadan.
Mk 7:24 place and went to the v of Tyre.
7:31 Jesus left the v of Tyre and went
Lk 24:50 led them out to the v of Bethany

Victim (Victims)
Ps 10:14 The v commits himself to you;
Hab 2: 7 Then you will become their v.

Victims (Victim)
Nu 23:24 prey and drinks the blood of his v."
31: 8 Among their v were Evi, Rekem, Zur,
Job 29:17 and snatched the v from their teeth.
Ps 10: 8 watching in secret for his v.
10:10 His v are crushed, they collapse;
Pr 7:26 Many are the v she has brought down;
Eze 34:29 and they will no longer be v of
Da 7: 7 it crushed and devoured its v and
7:19 devoured its v and trampled
Na 3: 1 full of plunder, never without v!

Victor's (Victory)
2Ti 2: 5 he does not receive the v crown

Victories (Victory)
2Sa 22:51 He gives his king great v; he shows
Ps 18:50 He gives his king great v; he shows
21: 1 great is his joy in the v you give!
21: 5 Through the v you gave, his glory is
44: 4 and my God, who decrees v for Jacob.

Victorious (Victory)
1Ki 22:12 "Attack Ramoth Gilead and be v,"
22:15 "Attack and be v," he answered, "for
2Ch 13:18 and the men of Judah were v because
18:11 "Attack Ramoth Gilead and be v,"
18:14 "Attack and be v," he answered, "for
Ps 20: 5 We will shout for joy when you are v
Da 11: 7 he will fight against them and be v.
Hab 3: 8 your horses and your v chariots?
Rev 15: 2 those who had been v over the beast

Victoriously (Victory)
Ps 45: 4 In your majesty ride forth v on

Victory (Victor's, Victories, Victorious, Victoriously)
Ex 32:18 "It is not the sound of v, it is not
Dt 20: 4 against your enemies to give you v."
Jos 10:10 them in a great v at Gibeon.
Jdg 12: 3 the LORD gave me the v over them.
15:18 given your servant this great v.
1Sa 19: 5 The LORD won a great v for all
2Sa 8: 6 LORD gave David v wherever he went.
8:10 on his v in battle over Hadadezer,
8:14 LORD gave David v wherever he went.
19: 2 for the whole army the v that day
22:36 You give me your shield of v;
23:10 The LORD brought about a great v
23:12 the LORD brought about a great v.
2Ki 5: 1 him the LORD had given v to Aram.
13:17 arrow of v, the arrow of v over Aram
14:10 Glory in your v, but stay at home!
1Ch 11:14 the LORD brought about a great v.
18: 6 LORD gave David v everywhere he went
18:10 on his v in battle over Hadadezer,
18:13 LORD gave David v everywhere he went
Job 12:16 To him belong strength and v; both
Ps 18:35 You give me your shield of v, and
44: 3 nor did their arm bring them v; it
44: 6 bow, my sword does not bring me v;
44: 7 you give us v over our enemies, you
60:12 With God we shall gain the v, and he
108:13 With God we shall gain the v, and he
118:15 Shouts of joy and v resound in the
129: 2 they have not gained the v over me.
144:10 to the One who gives v to kings, who
Pr 2: 7 He holds v in store for the upright,
11:14 but many advisers make v sure.
Pr 21:31 battle, but v rests with the LORD.
24: 6 guidance, and for v many advisers.
Mt 12:20 out, till he leads justice to v.
1Co 15:54 "Death has been swallowed up in v.
15:55 "Where, O death, is your v? Where,
15:57 thanks be to God! He gives us the v
1Jn 5: 4 This is the v that has overcome the

View (Viewed, Viewpoint, Views)
Nu 23: 9 see them, from the heights I v them.
33: 3 in full v of all the Egyptians,
Dt 32:49 across from Jericho, and v Canaan,
Ne 9:38 "In v of all this, we are making a
Ps 48:13 well her ramparts, v her citadels
68:24 Your procession has come into v,
Pr 1:17 a net in full v of all the birds!
5:21 ways are in full v of the LORD,
17:24 A discerning man keeps wisdom in v,
Isa 33:17 and v a land that stretches afar.
Mk 2:12 walked out in full v of them all.
Ro 12: 1 you, brothers, in v of God's mercy,
1Co 9: 8 this merely from a human point of v?
2Co 5:16 no-one from a worldly point of v.
Gal 5:10 Lord that you will take no other v.
Php 3:15 should take such a v of things.
2Ti 4: 1 and in v of his appearing and his
Rev 13:13 heaven to earth in full v of men.

Viewed (View)
Nu 32: 9 the Valley of Eshcol and v the land,
Ps 102:19 on high, from heaven he v the earth,

Viewpoint (View)
1Jn 4: 5 speak from the v of the world,

Views (View)
Job 28:24 for he v the ends of the earth and
Ac 28:22 we want to hear what your v are, for

Vigil
Ex 12:42 the LORD kept v that night to bring
12:42 all the Israelites are to keep v to
Isa 65: 4 spend their nights keeping secret v

Vigorous (Vigour)
Ex 1:19 they are v and give birth before the
Jos 14:11 I'm just as v to go out to battle
Jdg 3:29 Moabites, all v and strong; not a
Ps 38:19 Many are those who are my v enemies;

Vigorously (Vigour)
Pr 31:17 She sets about her work v; her arms
Jer 50:34 He will v defend their cause so that
Ac 18:28 For he v refuted the Jews in public
23: 9 Pharisees stood up and argued v.

Vigour (Vigorous, Vigorously)
Job 5:26 You will come to the grave in full v
18: 7 The v of his step is weakened; his
20:11 The youthful v that fills his bones
21:23 One man dies in full v, completely
30: 2 since their v had gone from them?
Pr 31: 3 your v on those who ruin kings.
Ecc 11:10 for youth and v are meaningless.

Vile (Vileness, Vilest)
Jdg 19:23 "No, my friends, don't be so v.
2Ki 23:13 the v goddess of the Sidonians,
23:13 for Chemosh the v god of Moab, and
Est 7: 6 adversary and enemy is this v Haman.
Job 15:16 how much less man, who is v and
Ps 12: 8 what is v is honoured among men.
14: 1 They are corrupt, their deeds are v
15: 4 who despises a v man but honours
41: 8 "A v disease has beset him; he will
53: 1 are corrupt and their ways are v;
101: 3 I will set before my eyes no v thing
Jer 16:18 lifeless forms of their v images
Eze 5:11 v images and detestable practices,
7:20 their detestable idols and v images
11:18 its v images and detestable idols.
11:21 their v images and detestable idols,
16:52 Because your sins were more v than

Eze 20: 7 get rid of the v images you have
20: 8 they did not get rid of the v images
20:30 did and lust after their v images?
37:23 and v images or with any of their
Hos 9:10 became as v as the thing they loved.
Na 1:14 prepare your grave, for you are v."
Rev 21: 8 the cowardly, the unbelieving, the v
22:11 let him who is v continue to be v;

Vileness (Vile)

Jdg 20:10 for all this v done in Israel."
Isa 9:17 and wicked, every mouth speaks v.

Vilest (Vile)

1Ki 21:26 He behaved in the v manner by going
Hos 1: 2 the land is guilty of the v adultery

Village (Villages)

Jdg 5: 7 V life in Israel ceased, ceased
Mt 10:11 "Whatever town or v you enter,
21: 2 saying to them, "Go to the v ahead
Mk 6: 6 went round teaching from v to v.
8:23 the hand and led him outside the v.
8:26 home, saying, "Don't go into the v.
11: 2 saying to them, "Go to the v ahead
Lk 5:17 who had come from every v of Galilee
8: 1 from one town and v to another,
9: 6 they set out and went from v to v,
9:52 who went into a Samaritan v to get
9:56 and they went to another v.
10:38 he came to a v where a woman named
17:12 he was going into a v, ten men who
19:30 "Go to the v ahead of you, and as
24:13 were going to a v called Emmaus,
24:28 they approached the v to which they
Jn 11: 1 the v of Mary and her sister Martha.
11:30 Now Jesus had not yet entered the v,
11:54 to a v called Ephraim, where he

Villages (Village)

Lev 25:31 houses in v without walls round them
Dt 2:23 for the Avvites who lived in v as
3: 5 were also a great many unwalled v.
Jos 10:37 its king, its v and everyone in it.
10:39 took the city, its king and its v,
13:23 These towns and their v were the
13:28 These towns and their v were the
15:32 of twenty-nine towns and their v.
15:36 —fourteen towns and their v.
15:41 Makkedah—sixteen towns and their v
15:44 Mareshah—nine towns and their v.
15:45 its surrounding settlements and v;
15:46 of Ashdod, together with their v;
15:47 its surrounding settlements and v;
15:47 its settlements and v, as far as the
15:51 and Giloh—eleven towns and their v.
15:54 and Zior—nine towns and their v.
15:57 and Timnah—ten towns and their v.
15:59 and Eltekon—six towns and their v.
15:60 and Rabbah—two towns and their v.
15:62 and En Gedi—six towns and their v.
16: 9 their v that were set aside for the
18:24 and Geba—twelve towns and their v.
18:28 Kiriath—fourteen towns and their v.
19: 6 Sharuhen—thirteen towns and their v
19: 7 and Ashan—four towns and their v—
19: 8 all the v around these towns as far
19:15 There were twelve towns and their v.
19:16 These towns and their v were the
19:22 There were sixteen towns and their v
19:23 These towns and their v were the
19:30 were twenty-two towns and their v.
19:31 These towns and their v were the
19:38 were nineteen towns and their v.
19:39 These towns and their v were the
19:48 These towns and their v were the
21:12 the fields and v around the city
1Sa 6:18 towns with their country v.
1Ch 4:32 Their surrounding v were Etam, Ain,
4:33 all the v around these towns as far
5:16 in Bashan and its outlying v, and on
6:56 the fields and v around the city
7:28 Bethel and its surrounding v,
7:28 Naaran to the east, Gezer and its v
1Ch 7:28 its v all the way to Ayyah and its v
7:29 and Dor, together with their v.
8:12 Ono and Lod with its surrounding v),
9:16 lived in the v of the Netophathites.
9:22 registered by genealogy in their v.
9:25 Their brothers in their v had to
18: 1 he took Gath and its surrounding v
27:25 towns, the v and the watchtowers.
2Ch 8: 2 Solomon rebuilt the v that Hiram had
13:19 Ephron, with their surrounding v.
14:14 They destroyed all the v around
14:14 They plundered all these v, since
28:18 and Gimzo, with their surrounding v.
32:29 He built v and acquired great
Ne 6: 2 in one of the v on the plain of Ono.
11:25 for the v with their fields, some of
11:25 settlements, in Jekabzeel and its v,
11:30 Zanoah, Adullam and their v, in
12:28 the v of the Netophathites,
12:29 singers had built v for themselves
Est 9:19 those living in v—observe the
Ps 10: 8 He lies in wait near the v; from
48:11 rejoices, the v of Judah are glad
97: 8 rejoices and the v of Judah are glad
SS 7:11 let us spend the night in the v.
Jer 17:26 of Judah and the v around Jerusalem,
19:15 the v around it every disaster I
32:44 in the v around Jerusalem, in the
33:13 in the v around Jerusalem and in the
49: 2 surrounding v will be set on fire.
Eze 30:18 and her v will go into captivity.
38:11 I will invade a land of unwalled v;
38:13 and all her v will say to you,
Mt 9:35 went through all the towns and v,
14:15 so that they can go to the v and buy
Mk 1:38 to the nearby v—so that I can
6:36 v and buy themselves something to
6:56 wherever he went—into v, towns or
8:27 to the v around Caesarea Philippi.
Lk 9:12 so they can go to the surrounding v
13:22 Jesus went through the towns and v,
Ac 8:25 the gospel in many Samaritan v.

Villain

Pr 6:12 A scoundrel and v, who goes about

Vindicate (Vindicated, Vindicates, Vindication)

1Sa 24:15 v me by delivering me from your hand
Ps 26: 1 V me, O LORD, for I have led a
35:24 V me in your righteousness, O LORD
43: 1 V me, O God, and plead my cause
54: 1 by your name; v me by your might.
135:14 For the LORD will v his people and

Vindicated (Vindicate)

Ge 20:16 are with you; you are completely v.
30: 6 Rachel said, "God has v me; he has
Job 11: 2 unanswered? Is this talker to be v?
13:18 my case, I know I will be v.
Jer 51:10 "'The LORD has v us; come, let us
1Ti 3:16 was v by the Spirit, was seen by

Vindicates (Vindicate)

Isa 50: 8 He who v me is near. Who then will

Vindication (Vindicate)

Ps 17: 2 May my v come from you; may your
24: 5 the LORD and v from God his Saviour.
35:27 May those who delight in my v shout
Isa 54:17 their v from me," declares the LORD.

Vine (Vines, Vineyard, Vineyards, Vintage)

Ge 40: 9 In my dream I saw a v in front of me,
40:10 on the v were three branches. As
49:11 He will tether his donkey to a v,
49:22 Joseph is a fruitful v, a fruitful v
Dt 32:32 Their v comes from the v of Sodom
Jdg 9:12 "Then the trees said to the v, 'Come
9:13 "But the v answered, 'Should I give
1Ki 4:25 man under his own v and fig-tree.
2Ki 4:39 to gather herbs and found a wild v.
18:31 one of you will eat from his own v
Job 15:33 He will be like a v stripped of its
Ps 80: 8 You brought a v out of Egypt; you
80:14 heaven and see! Watch over this v,
80:16 Your v is cut down, it is burned
128: 3 Your wife will be like a fruitful v
SS 7: 8 be like the clusters of the v,
Isa 24: 7 new wine dries up and the v withers;
34: 4 like withered leaves from the v,
36:16 one of you will eat from his own v
Jer 2:21 I had planted you like a choice v of
2:21 against me into a corrupt, wild v?
6: 9 of Israel as thoroughly as a v;
8:13 There will be no grapes on the v.
Eze 15: 2 Son of man, how is the wood of a v
15: 6 As I have given the wood of the v
17: 6 and became a low, spreading v.
17: 6 So it became a v and produced
17: 7 The v now sent out its roots towards
17: 8 bear fruit and become a splendid v.'
19:10 "'Your mother was like a v in your
Hos 10: 1 Israel was a spreading v; he brought
14: 7 He will blossom like a v, and his
Joel 1:11 you farmers, wail, you v growers;
1:12 The v is dried up and the fig-tree
2:22 and the v yield their riches.
Jnh 4: 6 the LORD God provided a v and made
4: 6 Jonah was very happy about the v.
4: 7 chewed the v so that it withered.
4: 9 a right to be angry about the v?"
4:10 You have been concerned about this v
Mic 4: 4 Every man will sit under his own v
Hag 2:19 the v and the fig-tree, the
Zec 3:10 to sit under his v and fig-tree,
8:12 well, the v will yield its fruit,
Mt 26:29 not drink of this fruit of the v from
Mk 14:25 drink again of the fruit of the v
Lk 22:18 drink again of the fruit of the v
Jn 15: 1 "I am the true v, and my Father is
15: 4 by itself; it must remain in the v.
15: 5 "I am the v; you are the branches.
Rev 14:18 grapes from the earth's v, because

Vinegar

Nu 6: 3 must not drink v made from wine or
Ru 2:14 some bread and dip it in the wine v.
Ps 69:21 my food and gave me v for my thirst.
Pr 10:26 v to the teeth and smoke to the eyes,
25:20 or like v poured on soda, is one who
Mt 27:48 He filled it with wine v, put it on
Mk 15:36 filled a sponge with wine v, put it
Lk 23:36 mocked him. They offered him wine v
Jn 19:29 A jar of wine v was there, so they

Vines (Vine)

Lev 25: 5 the grapes of your untended v.
25:11 of itself or harvest the untended v.
Dt 8: 8 a land with wheat and barley, v and
24:21 do not go over the v again.
Ps 78:47 He destroyed their v with hail and
105:33 he struck down their v and fig-trees
SS 2:13 blossoming v spread their fragrance.
6:11 to see if the v had budded or the
7:12 to see if the v have budded,
Isa 5: 2 and planted it with the choicest v.
7:23 v worth a thousand silver shekels,
16: 8 of Heshbon wither, the v of Sibmah
16: 8 have trampled down the choicest v,
16: 9 as Jazer weeps, for the v of Sibmah
17:10 finest plants and plant imported v,
32:12 pleasant fields, for the fruitful v
Jer 5:17 herds, devour your v and fig-trees.
48:32 as Jazer weeps, O v of Sibmah
Hos 2:12 I will ruin her v and her fig-trees,
Joel 1: 7 has laid waste my v and ruined my
Na 2: 2 them waste and have ruined their v.
Hab 3:17 and there are no grapes on the v,
Mal 3:11 and the v in your fields will not

Vineyard (Vine)

Ge 9:20 of the soil, proceeded to plant a v.
Ex 22: 5 his livestock in a field or v
22: 5 from the best of his own field or v.
23:11 with your v and your olive grove.
Lev 19:10 Do not go over your v a second time
Nu 20:17 will not go through any field or v,

Nu 21:22 not turn aside into any field or **v**,
Dt 20: 6 Has anyone planted a **v** and not begun
22: 9 two kinds of seed in your **v**; if you
22: 9 the fruit of the **v** will be defiled.
23:24 If you enter your neighbour's **v**, you
24:21 you harvest the grapes in your **v**, do
28:30 You will plant a **v**, but you will not
1Ki 21: 1 **v** belonging to Naboth the Jezreelite
21: 1 The **v** was in Jezreel, close to the
21: 2 "Let me have your **v** to use for a
21: 2 I will give you a better **v** or,
21: 6 'Sell me your **v**; or if you prefer,
21: 6 give you another **v** in its place.
21: 6 he said, 'I will not give you my **v**.
21: 7 you the **v** of Naboth the Jezreelite."
21:15 Get up and take possession of the **v**
21:16 to take possession of Naboth's **v**.
21:18 He is now in Naboth's **v**, where he
Pr 24:30 the **v** of the man who lacks judgment;
31:16 out of her earnings she plants a **v**.
SS 1: 6 my own **v** I have neglected.
8:11 Solomon had a **v** in Baal Hamon; he
8:11 he let out his **v** to tenants.
8:12 But my own **v** is mine to give;
Isa 1: 8 Zion is left like a shelter in a **v**,
3:14 "It is you who have ruined my **v**;
5: 1 the one I love a song about his **v**:
5: 1 one had a **v** on a fertile hillside.
5: 3 of Judah, judge between me and my **v**.
5: 4 for my **v** than I have done for it?
5: 5 what I am going to do to my **v**:
5: 7 The **v** of the LORD Almighty is the
5:10 A ten-acre **v** will produce only a
27: 2 "Sing about a fruitful **v**:
Jer 12:10 Many shepherds will ruin my **v** and
Eze 19:10 vine in your **v** planted by the water
Mic 7: 1 fruit at the gleaning of the **v**;
Mt 20: 1 to hire men to work in his **v**.
20: 2 the day and sent them into his **v**.
20: 4 'You also go and work in my **v**, and
20: 7 'You also go and work in my **v**.'
20: 8 the owner of the **v** said to his
21:28 'Son, go and work today in the **v**.'
21:33 was a landowner who planted a **v**.
21:33 Then he rented the **v** to some farmers
21:39 threw him out of the **v** and killed him
21:40 when the owner of the **v** comes,
21:41 "and he will rent the **v** to other
Mk 12: 1 in parables: "A man planted a **v**.
12: 1 Then he rented the **v** to some farmers
12: 2 them some of the fruit of the **v**.
12: 8 him, and threw him out of the **v**.
12: 9 will the owner of the **v** do? He will
12: 9 tenants and give the **v** to others.
Lk 13: 6 planted in his **v**, and he went to
13: 7 to the man who took care of the **v**,
20: 9 "A man planted a **v**, rented it to
20:10 give him some of the fruit of the **v**.
20:13 "Then the owner of the **v** said, 'What
20:15 they threw him out of the **v** and
20:15 will the owner of the **v** do to them?
20:16 tenants and give the **v** to others.
1Co 9: 7 Who plants a **v** and does not eat of

Vineyards (Vine)

Lev 25: 3 prune your **v** and gather their crops.
25: 4 not sow your fields or prune your **v**.
Nu 16:14 us an inheritance of fields and **v**.
22:24 two **v**, with walls on both sides.
Dt 6:11 wells you did not dig, and **v** and
28:39 You will plant **v** and cultivate them
Jos 24:13 and you live in them and eat from **v**
Jdg 14: 5 As they approached the **v** of Timnah,
15: 5 with the **v** and olive groves.
21:20 saying, "Go and hide in the **v**
21:21 then rush from the **v** and each of you
1Sa 8:14 take the best of your fields and **v**
22: 7 Jesse give all of you fields and **v**?
2Ki 5:26 olive groves, **v**, flocks, herds, or
18:32 a land of bread and **v**, a land of
19:29 reap, plant **v** and eat their fruit.
25:12 the land to work the **v** and fields.
1Ch 27:27 Ramathite was in charge of the **v**.
27:27 produce of the **v** for the wine vats.
2Ch 26:10 **v** in the hills and in the fertile
Ne 5: 3 We are mortgaging our fields, our **v**
5: 4 the king's tax on our fields and **v**.
5: 5 fields and our **v** belong to others."
5:11 **v**, olive groves and houses, and also
9:25 wells already dug, **v**, olive groves
Job 24: 6 and glean in the **v** of the wicked.
24:18 so that no-one goes to the **v**.
Ps 107:37 They sowed fields and planted **v** that
Ecc 2: 4 houses for myself and planted **v**.
SS 1: 6 made me take care of the **v**; my own
1:14 blossoms from the **v** of En Gedi.
2:15 ruin the **v**, our **v** that are in bloom.
7:12 Let us go early to the **v** to see if
Isa 16:10 no-one sings or shouts in the **v**;
36:17 and new wine, a land of bread and **v**.
37:30 reap, plant **v** and eat their fruit.
61: 5 will work your fields and **v**.
65:21 will plant **v** and eat their fruit.
Jer 5:10 "Go through her **v** and ravage them,
31: 5 Again you will plant **v** on the hills
32:15 **v** will again be bought in this land.
35: 7 sow seed or plant **v**; you must never
35: 9 or built houses to live in or had **v**,
39:10 that time he gave them **v** and fields.
52:16 the land to work the **v** and fields.
Eze 28:26 and will build houses and plant **v**;
Hos 2:15 There I will give her back her **v**,
Am 4: 9 times I struck your gardens and **v**,
5:11 planted lush **v**, you will not drink
5:17 There will be wailing in all the **v**,
9:14 They will plant **v** and drink their
Mic 1: 6 of rubble, a place for planting **v**.
Zep 1:13 will plant **v** but not drink the wine.

Vintage (Vine)

1Sa 8:15 of your **v** and give it to his

Violate (Violated, Violates, Violating, Violation)

Lev 26:15 my commands and so **v** my covenant,
Jos 23:16 If you **v** the covenant of the LORD
Ps 89:31 if they **v** my decrees and fail to
89:34 I will not **v** my covenant or alter
Eze 22:10 who **v** women during their period,
Ac 23: 3 yet you yourself **v** the law by

Violated (Violate)

Dt 22:24 man because he **v** another man's wife.
22:29 marry the girl, for he has **v** her.
Jos 7:11 they have **v** my covenant, which I
7:15 He has **v** the covenant of the LORD
Jdg 2:20 this nation has **v** the covenant
1Sa 15:24 I **v** the LORD's command and your
2Ki 18:12 but had **v** his covenant—all that
Isa 24: 5 **v** the statutes and broken the
Jer 34:18 The men who have **v** my covenant and
Da 11:32 those who have **v** the covenant,
Mal 2: 8 you have **v** the covenant with Levi,"

Violates (Violate)

Ps 55:20 his friends; he **v** his covenant.
Eze 22:11 and another **v** his sister, his own

Violating (Violate)

1Ch 2: 7 **v** the ban on taking devoted things.

Violation (Violate)

Lev 5:15 "When a person commits a **v** and sins
Dt 17: 2 LORD your God in **v** of his covenant,
Heb 2: 2 and every **v** and disobedience

Violence (Violent)

Ge 6:11 in God's sight and was full of **v**.
6:13 is filled with **v** because of them.
49: 5 their swords are weapons of **v**.
1Ch 12:17 when my hands are free from **v**,
Job 16:17 yet my hands have been free of **v** and
Ps 7: 9 bring to an end the **v** of the wicked
7:16 his **v** comes down on his own head.
11: 5 and those who love **v** his soul hates.
27:12 rise up against me, breathing out **v**.
55: 9 for I see **v** and strife in the city.
58: 2 your hands mete out **v** on the earth.
Ps 72:14 rescue them from oppression and **v**,
73: 6 they clothe themselves with **v**.
74:20 haunts of **v** fill the dark places of
140: 1 evil men; protect me from men of **v**,
140: 4 men of **v** who plan to trip my feet.
140:11 may disaster hunt down men of **v**.
Pr 4:17 wickedness and drink the wine of **v**.
10: 6 **v** overwhelms the mouth of the wicked
10:11 **v** overwhelms the mouth of the wicked
13: 2 the unfaithful have a craving for **v**.
21: 7 **v** of the wicked will drag them away
24: 2 for their hearts plot **v**, and their
26: 6 or drinking **v** is the sending of a
Isa 42:25 his burning anger, the **v** of war.
53: 9 though he had done no **v**, nor was any
59: 6 and acts of **v** are in their hands.
60:18 No longer will **v** be heard in your
Jer 6: 7 **V** and destruction resound in her;
20: 8 out proclaiming **v** and destruction.
22: 3 Do no wrong or **v** to the alien, the
51:35 May the **v** done to our flesh be upon
51:46 rumours of **v** in the land and of
Eze 7:11 **V** has grown into a rod to punish
7:23 bloodshed and the city is full of **v**
8:17 Must they also fill the land with **v**
12:19 of the **v** of all who live there.
22:26 Her priests do **v** to my law and
28:16 you were filled with **v**, and you
45: 9 Give up your **v** and oppression and
Hos 12: 1 all day and multiplies lies and **v**.
Joel 3:19 **v** done to the people of Judah,
Ob :10 of the **v** against your brother Jacob,
Jnh 3: 8 give up their evil ways and their **v**.
Hab 1: 2 Or cry out to you, "**V**!" but
1: 3 Destruction and **v** are before me;
1: 9 they all come bent on **v**. Their
2:17 The **v** you have done to Lebanon will
Zep 1: 9 of their gods with **v** and deceit.
3: 4 the sanctuary and do **v** to the law.
Mal 2:16 with **v** as well as with his garment,"
Ac 21:35 the **v** of the mob was so great that he
Rev 18:21 "With such **v** the great city of

Violent (Violence)

2Sa 22: 3 my saviour—from **v** men you save me.
22:49 my foes; from **v** men you rescued me.
Ps 17: 4 kept myself from the ways of the **v**.
18:48 my foes; from **v** men you rescued me.
Pr 3:31 Do not envy a **v** man or choose any of
16:29 A **v** man entices his neighbour and
Eze 13:11 down, and **v** winds will burst forth.
13:13 In my wrath I will unleash a **v** wind,
18:10 "Suppose he has a **v** son, who sheds
28: 8 a **v** death in the heart of the seas.
Da 11:14 The **v** men among your own people will
Am 1:14 amid **v** winds on a stormy day.
Jnh 1: 4 and such a **v** storm arose that the
Mic 6:12 Her rich men are **v**; her people are
Mt 8:28 were so **v** that no-one could pass
28: 2 There was a **v** earthquake, for an
Ac 2: 2 the blowing of a **v** wind came from
16:26 there was such a **v** earthquake that
23:10 The dispute became so **v** that the
27:18 We took such a **v** battering from the
1Ti 1:13 and a persecutor and a **v** man,
3: 3 not **v** but gentle, not quarrelsome
Tit 1: 7 not **v**, not pursuing dishonest gain.

Viper (Viper's, Vipers)

Ge 49:17 a **v** along the path, that bites the
Pr 23:32 like a snake and poisons like a **v**.
Isa 14:29 of that snake will spring up a **v**,
Ac 28: 3 as he put it on the fire, a **v**,

Viper's (Viper)

Isa 11: 8 child put his hand into the **v** nest.

Vipers (Viper)

Dt 32:24 venom of **v** that glide in the dust.
Ps 140: 3 the poison of **v** is on their lips.
Isa 59: 5 They hatch the eggs of **v** and spin a
Jer 8:17 **v** that cannot be charmed, and they
Mt 3: 7 "You brood of **v**! Who warned you to
12:34 You brood of **v**, how can you who are

Mt 23:33 "You snakes! You brood of v! How
Lk 3: 7 "You brood of v! Who warned you to
Ro 3:13 "The poison of v is on their lips."

Virgin (Virgin's, Virginity, Virgins)
Ge 24:16 The girl was very beautiful, a v;
Ex 22:16 "If a man seduces a v who is not
Lev 21:13 "'The woman he marries must be a v.
21:14 but only a v from his own people,
Dt 22:15 proof she was a v to the town elders
22:17 not find your daughter to be a v.
22:19 has given an Israelite v a bad name.
22:23 in a town a v pledged to be married
22:28 If a man happens to meet a v who is
Jdg 11:39 And she was a v. From this comes the
19:24 Look, here is my v daughter, and his
21:11 and every woman who is not a v."
2Sa 13: 2 for she was a v, and it seemed
13:18 the v daughters of the king wore.
1Ki 1: 2 "Let us look for a young v to attend
2Ki 19:21 'The V Daughter of Zion despises you
Ps 45:14 her v companions follow her and are
Isa 7:14 The v will be with child and will
23:12 O V Daughter of Sidon, now crushed
37:22 "The V Daughter of Zion despises and
47: 1 in the dust, V Daughter of Babylon;
Jer 14:17 for my v daughter—my people—has
18:13 thing has been done by V Israel.
31: 4 and you will be rebuilt, O V Israel.
31:21 O V Israel, return to your towns.
46:11 get balm, O V Daughter of Egypt.
Lam 1:15 trampled the V Daughter of Judah.
2:13 comfort you, O V Daughter of Zion?
Eze 23: 3 fondled and their v bosoms caressed.
23: 8 caressed her v bosom and poured out
Joel 1: 8 Mourn like a v in sackcloth grieving
Am 5: 2 "Fallen is V Israel, never to rise
Mt 1:23 "The v will be with child and will
Lk 1:27 to a v pledged to be married to a
1:34 asked the angel, "since I am a v?"
1Co 7:28 if a v marries, she has not sinned.
7:34 An unmarried woman or v is concerned
7:36 towards the v he is engaged to,
7:37 made up his mind not to marry the v
7:38 he who marries the v does right,
2Co 11: 2 present you as a pure v to him.

Virgin's (Virgin)
Lk 1:27 The v name was Mary.

Virginity (Virgin)
Dt 22:14 I did not find proof of her v,"
22:17 is the proof of my daughter's v.
22:20 proof of the girl's v can be found,

Virgins (Virgin)
Ex 22:17 still pay the bride-price for v.
Est 2: 2 for beautiful young v for the king.
2:17 more than any of the other v.
2:19 the v were assembled a second time,
SS 6: 8 concubines, and v beyond number;
Lam 5:11 Zion, and v in the towns of Judah.
Eze 44:22 marry only v of Israelite descent
Mt 25: 1 be like ten v who took their lamps
25: 7 "Then all the v woke up and trimmed
25:10 The v who were ready went in with
1Co 7:25 Now about v: I have no command from

Virtues
Col 3:14 over all these v put on love, which

Visible
Ge 8: 5 the tops of the mountains became v.
Da 4:11 it was v to the ends of the earth.
4:20 the sky, v to the whole earth,
Mt 24:27 from the east is v even in the west,
Eph 5:13 exposed by the light becomes v,
5:14 it is light that makes everything v.
Col 1:16 v and invisible, whether thrones or
Heb 11: 3 seen was not made out of what was v.

Vision (Visions)
Ge 15: 1 in a v: "Do not be afraid, Abram.
46: 2 God spoke to Israel in a v at night
Nu 24: 4 who sees a v from the Almighty, who
24:16 who sees a v from the Almighty, who
1Sa 3:15 He was afraid to tell Eli the v,
2Ch 32:32 in the v of the prophet Isaiah
Job 20: 8 banished like a v of the night.
33:15 In a dream, in a v of the night,
Ps 89:19 Once you spoke in a v, to your
Isa 1: 1 The v concerning Judah and Jerusalem
21: 2 A dire v has been shown to me: The
22: 1 An oracle concerning the Valley of V
22: 5 and terror in the Valley of V,
29: 7 a dream, with a v in the night—
29:11 For you this whole v is nothing but
Eze 7:13 for the v concerning the whole crowd
7:26 They will try to get a v from the
8: 4 as in the v I had seen in the plain.
11:24 in the v given by the Spirit of God.
11:24 the v I had seen went up from me,
12:22 go by and every v comes to nothing'?
12:23 near when every v will be fulfilled.
12:27 'The v he sees is for many years
43: 3 The v I saw was like the v I had
Da 2:19 was revealed to Daniel in a v.
2:45 is the meaning of the v of the rock
7: 2 Daniel said: "In my v at night I
7: 7 "After that, in my v at night I
7:13 "In my v at night I looked, and
8: 1 I, Daniel, had a v, after the one
8: 2 In my v I saw myself in the citadel
8: 2 the v I was beside the Ulai Canal.
8:13 "How long will it take for the v to
8:13 v concerning the daily sacrifice,
8:15 While I, Daniel, was watching the v
8:16 tell this man the meaning of the v."
8:17 the v concerns the time of the end."
8:19 because the v concerns the appointed
8:26 "The v of the evenings and mornings
8:26 but seal up the v, for it concerns
8:27 I was appalled by the v; it was
9:21 the man I had seen in the earlier v,
9:23 the message and understand the v:
9:24 to seal up v and prophecy and to
10: 1 of the message came to him in a v.
10: 7 was the only one who saw the v;
10: 8 alone, gazing at this great v;
10:14 the v concerns a time yet to come."
10:16 the v, my lord, and I am helpless.
11:14 in fulfilment of the v, but without
Ob : 1 The v of Obadiah. This is what the
Mic 1: 1 the v he saw concerning Samaria
Na 1: 1 of the v of Nahum the Elkoshite.
Zec 1: 8 During the night I had a v—and
13: 4 will be ashamed of his prophetic v.
Lk 1:22 They realised he had seen a v in the
24:23 v of angels, who said he was alive.
Ac 9:10 The Lord called to him in a v,
9:12 In a v he has seen a man named
10: 3 three in the afternoon he had a v.
10:17 about the meaning of the v,
10:19 Peter was still thinking about the v
11: 5 praying, and in a trance I saw a v.
12: 9 he thought he was seeing a v.
16: 9 During the night Paul had a v of a
16:10 After Paul had seen the v, we got
18: 9 night the Lord spoke to Paul in a v:
26:19 disobedient to the v from heaven.
Rev 9:17 The horses and riders I saw in my v

Visions (*See visions*, Vision)
Nu 12: 6 I reveal myself to him in v, I speak
1Sa 3: 1 LORD was rare; there were not many v
2Ch 9:29 in the v of Iddo the seer concerning
Job 7:14 with dreams and terrify me with v,
Isa 28: 7 they stagger when seeing v, they
30:10 say to the seers, "See no more v
30:10 "Give us no more v of what is right!
Jer 14:14 They are prophesying to you false v,
23:16 They speak v from their own minds,
Lam 2: 9 no longer find v from the LORD.
2:14 The v of your prophets were false
Eze 1: 1 were opened and I saw v of God.
8: 3 in v of God he took me to Jerusalem,
12:24 For there will be no more false v or
13: 6 Their v are false and their
13: 7 Have you not seen false v and
13: 8 of your false words and lying v,
13: 9 false v and utter lying divinations.
13:16 saw v of peace for her when there
13:23 see false v or practise divination.
21:29 Despite false v concerning you and
22:28 by false v and lying divinations.
40: 2 In v of God he took me to the land
43: 3 the v I had seen by the Kebar River,
Da 1:17 v and dreams of all kinds.
2:28 Your dream and the v that passed
4: 5 the images and v that passed through
4:10 These are the v I saw while lying in
4:13 "In the v I saw while lying in my
7: 1 v passed through his mind as he was
7:15 the v that passed through my mind
Hos 12:10 gave them many v and told parables
Mic 3: 6 without v, and darkness, without
2Co 12: 1 I will go on to v and revelations

Visit (Visited, Visitor, Visitors, Visits)
Ge 34: 1 went out to v the women of the land.
Jdg 15: 1 a young goat and went to v his wife.
2Ch 18: 2 Some years later he went down to v
22: 7 Through Ahaziah's v to Joram, God
Jnh 3: 3 city—a v required three days.
Mt 25:36 was in prison and you came to v me.'
25:39 sick or in prison and go to v you?'
Jn 11:45 of the Jews who had come to v Mary,
Ac 7:12 sent our fathers on their first v.
7:13 On their second v, Joseph told his
7:23 decided to v his fellow Israelites.
9:32 he went to v the saints in Lydda.
10:28 associate with a Gentile or v him.
15:36 "Let us go back and v the brothers
19:21 he said, "I must v Rome also.
Ro 15:24 I hope to v you while passing
15:28 go to Spain and v you on the way.
1Co 16: 7 you now and make only a passing v;
2Co 1:15 I planned to v you first so that you
1:16 I planned to v you on my way to
2: 1 not make another painful v to you.
9: 5 the brothers to v you in advance
12:14 Now I am ready to v you for the
13: 1 This will be my third v to you.
1Th 2: 1 our v to you was not a failure.
2Jn :12 Instead, I hope to v you and talk

Visited (Visit)
Jn 4:46 Once more he v Cana in Galilee,
19:39 who earlier had v Jesus at night.

Visitor (Visit)
Lk 24:18 "Are you only a v to Jerusalem and

Visitors (Visit)
Ac 2:10 of Libya near Cyrene; v from Rome

Visits (Visit)
Mic 7: 4 has come, the day God v you.
1Pe 2:12 and glorify God on the day he v us.

Voice (*Voice of the LORD*, Voices)
Ge 27:22 "The v is the v of Jacob, but the
Ex 19:19 spoke and the v of God answered him.
24: 3 they responded with one v,
Nu 7:89 he heard the v speaking to him from
Dt 4:12 but saw no form; there was only a v.
4:33 any other people heard the v of God
4:36 From heaven he made you hear his v
5:22 the LORD proclaimed in a loud v to
5:23 you heard the v out of the darkness,
5:24 we have heard his v from the fire.
5:26 ever heard the v of the living God
26: 7 and the LORD heard our v and saw our
27:14 the people of Israel in a loud v:
30:20 to his v, and hold fast to him.
Jdg 5:11 the v of the singers at the watering
18: 3 recognised the v of the young Levite
1Sa 1:13 were moving but her v was not heard.
24:16 "Is that your v, David my son?"
26:17 Saul recognised David's v and said,
26:17 "Is that your v, David my son?"
28:12 she cried out at the top of her v

2Sa 22: 7 heard my v; my cry came to his ears.
22:14 the v of the Most High resounded.
1Ki 8:55 of Israel in a loud v, saying:
19:13 Then a v said to him, "What are you
2Ki 19:22 Against whom have you raised your v
2Ch 5:13 as with one v, to give praise and
20:19 God of Israel, with a very loud v.
Ezr 10:12 assembly responded with a loud v:
Job 4:16 my eyes, and I heard a hushed v:
37: 2 Listen! Listen to the roar of his v,
37: 4 he thunders with his majestic v.
37: 4 v resounds, he holds nothing back.
37: 5 God's v thunders in marvellous ways;
38:34 "Can you raise your v to the clouds
40: 9 and can your v thunder like his?
Ps 5: 3 the morning, O LORD, you hear my v
18: 6 From his temple he heard my v; my
18:13 the v of the Most High resounded.
19: 3 language where their v is not heard.
19: 4 Their v goes out into all the earth,
27: 7 Hear my v when I call, O LORD;
46: 6 he lifts his v, the earth melts.
55: 3 at the v of the enemy, at the stares
55:17 out in distress, and he hears my v.
64: 1 Hear me, O God, as I v my complaint;
66:19 listened and heard my v in prayer.
68:33 above, who thunders with mighty v.
93: 3 the seas have lifted up their v;
95: 7 Today, if you hear his v,
116: 1 I love the LORD, for he heard my v;
119:149 Hear my v in accordance with your
130: 2 O Lord, hear my v. Let your ears be
141: 1 Hear my v when I call to you.
142: 1 I lift up my v to the LORD for mercy.
Pr 1:20 raises her v in the public squares;
8: 1 Does not understanding raise her v?
8: 4 I raise my v to all mankind.
SS 2:14 let me hear your v; for your v is
8:13 in attendance, let me hear your v!
Isa 28:23 Listen and hear my v; pay attention
29: 4 Your v will come ghostlike from the
30:21 your ears will hear a v behind you,
30:30 cause men to hear his majestic v
33: 3 At the thunder of your v, the
37:23 Against whom have you raised your v
40: 3 A v of one calling: "In the desert
40: 6 A v says, "Cry out." And I said,
40: 9 lift up your v with a shout, lift it
42: 2 out, or raise his v in the streets.
58: 1 Raise your v like a trumpet. Declare
58: 4 expect your v to be heard on high.
Jer 4:15 A v is announcing from Dan,
22:20 let your v be heard in Bashan, cry
31:15 LORD says: "A v is heard in Ramah
31:16 "Restrain your v from weeping and
Eze 1:24 like the v of the Almighty, like the
1:25 there came a v from above the
1:28 and I heard the v of one speaking.
9: 1 I heard him call out in a loud v,
10: 5 like the v of God Almighty when he
11:13 face down and cried out in a loud v,
27:30 They will raise their v and cry
33:32 sings love songs with a beautiful v
43: 2 His v was like the roar of rushing
Da 4:14 He called in a loud v: 'Cut down the
4:31 his lips when a v came from heaven,
6:20 called to Daniel in an anguished v,
8:16 I heard a man's v from the Ulai
10: 6 his v like the sound of a multitude.
Mt 2:18 "A v is heard in Ramah, weeping and
3: 3 "A v of one calling in the desert,
3:17 a v from heaven said, "This is my
12:19 will hear his v in the streets.
17: 5 and a v from the cloud said, "This
27:46 hour Jesus cried out in a loud v,
27:50 Jesus had cried out again in a loud v
Mk 1: 3 "a v of one calling in the desert,
1:11 a v came from heaven: "You are my
5: 7 He shouted at the top of his v,
9: 7 and a v came from the cloud: "This
15:34 hour Jesus cried out in a loud v,
Lk 1:42 In a loud v she exclaimed: "Blessed
3: 4 "A v of one calling in the desert,
3:22 And a v came from heaven: "You are
4:33 He cried out at the top of his v,
8:28 shouting at the top of his v, "What
Lk 9:35 A v came from the cloud, saying,
9:36 the v had spoken, they found that
17:13 called out in a loud v, "Jesus,
17:15 came back, praising God in a loud v.
23:18 With one v they cried out, "Away
23:46 Jesus called out with a loud v,
Jn 1:23 "I am the v of one calling in the
3:29 when he hears the bridegroom's v.
5:25 will hear the v of the Son of God
5:28 are in their graves will hear his v
5:37 never heard his v nor seen his form,
7:37 Jesus stood and said in a loud v,
10: 3 him, and the sheep listen to his v.
10: 4 follow him because they know his v.
10: 5 do not recognise a stranger's v."
10:16 They too will listen to my v, and
10:27 My sheep listen to my v; I know them,
11:43 Jesus called in a loud v, "Lazarus,
12:28 Then a v came from heaven, "I have
12:30 Jesus said, "This v was for your
Ac 2:14 raised his v and addressed the crowd:
7:31 more closely, he heard the Lord's v:
9: 4 He fell to the ground and heard a v
10:13 a v told him, "Get up, Peter. Kill
10:15 The v spoke to him a second time,
11: 7 I heard a v telling me, 'Get up,
11: 9 "The v spoke from heaven a second
12:14 she recognised Peter's v, she was so
12:22 shouted, "This is the v of a god,
22: 7 I fell to the ground and heard a v
22: 9 the v of him who was speaking to me.
26:14 and I heard a v saying to me in
Ro 10:18 "Their v has gone out into all the
1Th 4:16 with the v of the archangel and
Heb 3: 7 "Today, if you hear his v,
3:15 "Today, if you hear his v, do not
4: 7 "Today, if you hear his v, do not
12:19 to a trumpet blast or to such a v
12:26 At that time his v shook the earth,
2Pe 1:17 the v came to him from the
1:18 heard this v that came from heaven
2:16 speech—who spoke with a man's v
Rev 1:10 behind me a loud v like a trumpet,
1:12 I turned round to see the v that was
1:15 and his v was like the sound of
3:20 If anyone hears my v and opens the
4: 1 And the v I had first heard speaking
5: 2 angel proclaiming in a loud v,
5:11 I looked and heard the v of many
5:12 In a loud v they sang: "Worthy is
6: 1 creatures say in a v like thunder,
6: 6 I heard what sounded like a v among
6: 7 I heard the v of the fourth living
6:10 They called out in a loud v, "How
7: 2 He called out in a loud v to the
7:10 they cried out in a loud v:
8:13 in mid-air call out in a loud v:
9:13 and I heard a v coming from the
10: 4 but I heard a v from heaven say,
10: 8 the v that I had heard from heaven
11:12 they heard a loud v from heaven
12:10 I heard a loud v in heaven say: "Now
14: 7 He said in a loud v, "Fear God and
14: 9 followed them and said in a loud v:
14:13 I heard a v from heaven say, "Write:
14:15 called in a loud v to him who was
14:18 called in a loud v to him who had
16: 1 I heard a loud v from the temple
16:17 and out of the temple came a loud v
18: 2 With a mighty v he shouted: "Fallen!
18: 4 I heard another v from heaven say:
18:23 The v of bridegroom and bride will
19: 5 a v came from the throne, saying:
19:17 who cried in a loud v to all the
21: 3 I heard a loud v from the throne

Voice of the LORD/Lord
Ex 15:26 "If you listen carefully to the v
Dt 5:25 if we hear the v our God any longer.
18:16 "Let us not hear the v our God nor
1Sa 15:22 as much as in obeying the v? To obey
Ps 29: 3 The v is over the waters; the God of
29: 4 The v is powerful; the v is majestic.
29: 5 The v breaks the cedars; the LORD
29: 7 The v strikes with flashes of
Ps 29: 8 The v shakes the desert; the LORD
29: 9 The v twists the oaks and strips the
Isa 6: 8 I heard the v saying, "Whom shall I
30:31 The v will shatter Assyria; with his
Hag 1:12 the people obeyed the v their God

Voices (Voice)
Nu 14: 1 raised their v and wept aloud.
Jos 6:10 do not raise your v, do not say a
Jdg 21: 2 raising their v and weeping bitterly
2Sa 19:35 Can I still hear the v of men and
2Ch 5:13 they raised their v in praise to the
Ne 9: 4 with loud v to the LORD their God.
Job 29:10 the v of the nobles were hushed, and
Isa 6: 4 At the sound of their v the
15: 4 v are heard all the way to Jahaz.
24:14 They raise their v, they shout for
42:11 desert and its towns raise their v;
52: 8 Listen! Your watchmen lift up their v
Jer 7:34 to the v of bride and bridegroom
16: 9 to the v of bride and bridegroom
25:10 the v of bride and bridegroom, the
33:11 the v of bride and bridegroom
33:11 and the v of those who bring
51:55 the roar of their v will resound.
Da 5:10 The queen, hearing the v of the king
Na 2:13 The v of your messengers will no
Lk 19:37 to praise God in loud v for all the
Ac 4:24 they heard this, they raised their v
7:57 yelling at the top of their v, they
22:22 Then they raised their v and shouted,
Rev 10: 3 the v of the seven thunders spoke.
11:15 and there were loud v in heaven,

Voluntarily (Volunteers)
2Ki 12: 4 the money brought v to the temple.
2Ch 35: 8 His officials also contributed v to
1Co 9:17 preach v, I have a reward; if not v,

Volunteered (Volunteers)
1Ch 12:38 All these were fighting men who v
2Ch 17:16 next, Amasiah son of Zicri, who v
Ne 11: 2 the men who v to live in Jerusalem.

Volunteers (Voluntarily, Volunteered)
Jdg 5: 9 with the willing v among the people.

Vomit (Vomited)
Lev 18:28 defile the land, it will v you out
20:22 you to live may not v you out.
Job 20:15 God will make his stomach v them up.
Pr 23: 8 You will v up the little you have
25:16 too much of it, and you will v.
26:11 a dog returns to its v, so a fool
Isa 19:14 a drunkard staggers around in his v.
28: 8 All the tables are covered with v
Jer 25:27 says: Drink, get drunk and v, and
48:26 Let Moab wallow in her v; let her
2Pe 2:22 "A dog returns to its v," and, "A

Vomited (Vomit)
Lev 18:25 and the land v out its inhabitants.
18:28 it will vomit you out as it v out
Jnh 2:10 commanded the fish, and it v Jonah

Vophsi
Nu 13:14 tribe of Naphtali, Nahbi son of V;

Vote
Ac 26:10 to death, I cast my v against them.

Vouch
Col 4:13 I v for him that he is working hard

Vow (Vowed, Vows)
Ge 28:20 Jacob made a v, saying, "If God will
31:13 pillar and where you made a v to me.
Lev 7:16 his offering is the result of a v or
22:18 a v or as a freewill offering,
22:21 special v or as a freewill offering,
22:23 be accepted in fulfilment of a v.
27: 2 'If anyone makes a special v to

Lev 27: 8 If anyone making the v is too poor
27: 8 the man making the v can afford.
Nu 6: 2 or woman wants to make a special v,
6: 2 a v of separation to the LORD as a
6: 5 "'During the entire period of his v
6:21 He must fulfil the v he has made,
15: 8 or sacrifice, for a special v or a
21: 2 Israel made this v to the LORD: "If
29:39 "'In addition to what you v and
30: 2 a man makes a v to the LORD or takes
30: 3 makes a v to the LORD or binds
30: 4 her father hears about her v or
30: 6 "If she marries after she makes a v
30: 8 he nullifies the v that binds her or
30: 9 "Any v or obligation taken by a
30:10 makes a v or binds herself by a
30:13 confirm or nullify any v she makes
Dt 23:18 of the LORD your God to pay any v,
23:21 If you make a v to the LORD your God,
23:22 if you refrain from making a v, you
23:23 because you made your v freely to
Jdg 11:30 Jephthah made a v to the LORD: "If
11:35 v to the LORD that I cannot break."
1Sa 1:11 she made a v, saying, "O LORD
1:21 to the LORD and to fulfil his v,
2Sa 15: 7 and fulfil a v I made to the LORD.
15: 8 I made this v: 'If the LORD takes me
Ps 132: 2 made a v to the Mighty One of Jacob:
Ecc 5: 4 you make a v to God, do not delay in
5: 4 no pleasure in fools; fulfil your v.
5: 5 is better not to v than to make a v
5: 6 "My v was a mistake." Why should
Ac 18:18 Cenchrea because of a v he had taken.
21:23 four men with us who have made a v.

Vowed (Vow)

Lev 23:38 whatever you have v and all the
27: 9 "'If what he v is an animal that is
27:11 If what he v is a ceremonially
Dt 12: 6 what you have v to give and your
12:11 possessions you have v to the LORD.
12:17 or whatever you have v to give, or
12:26 and whatever you have v to give,
Jdg 11:39 and he did to her as he had v.
Jnh 2: 9 What I have v I will make good.

Vows (Vow)

Nu 6:21 the Nazirite who v his offering to
15: 3 for special v or freewill offerings
30: 4 then all her v and every pledge by
30: 5 none of her v or the pledges by
30: 7 then her v or the pledges by which
30:11 then all her v or the pledges by
30:12 then none of the v or pledges that
30:14 her v or the pledges binding on her.
2Ki 12: 4 the money received from personal v
Job 22:27 you, and you will fulfil your v.
Ps 22:25 who fear you will I fulfil my v.
50:14 God, fulfil your v to the Most High,
56:12 I am under v to you, O God; I will
61: 5 For you have heard my v, O God; you
61: 8 name and fulfil my v day after day.
65: 1 to you our v will be fulfilled.
66:13 offerings and fulfil my v to you—
66:14 v my lips promised and my mouth
76:11 Make v to the LORD your God and
116:14 I will fulfil my v to the LORD in
116:18 I will fulfil my v to the LORD in
Pr 7:14 at home; today I fulfilled my v.
20:25 and only later to consider his v.
31: 2 O son of my womb, O son of my v,
Isa 19:21 make v to the LORD and keep them.
Jer 44:25 'We will certainly carry out the v
44:25 do what you promised! Keep your v!
Jnh 1:16 to the LORD and made v to him.
Na 1:15 O Judah, and fulfil your v.
Mal 1:14 male in his flock and v to give it,

Voyage

Ac 21: 7 We continued our v from Tyre and
27:10 "Men, I can see that our v is going

Vulgar

2Sa 6:20 his servants as any v fellow would.

Vulture (Vultures)

Lev 11:13 the eagle, the v, the black v,
Dt 14:12 eat: the eagle, the v, the black v,
Mic 1:16 make yourselves as bald as the v,
Hab 1: 8 They fly like a v swooping to devour;

Vultures (Vulture)

Job 15:23 He wanders about—food for v;
Pr 30:17 the valley, will be eaten by the v.
Mt 24:28 a carcass, there the v will gather.
Lk 17:37 dead body, there the v will gather."

Wade

Isa 47: 2 legs, and w through the streams.

Wadi

Nu 34: 5 it will turn, join the W of Egypt
Jos 15: 4 the W of Egypt, ending at the sea.
15:47 as far as the W of Egypt and the
1Ki 8:65 from Lebo Hamath to the W of Egypt.
2Ki 24: 7 W of Egypt to the Euphrates River.
2Ch 7: 8 from Lebo Hamath to the W of Egypt.
Isa 27:12 flowing Euphrates to the W of Egypt,
Eze 47:19 the W of Egypt to the Great Sea.
48:28 the W of Egypt to the Great Sea.

Wafer (Wafers)

Ex 29:23 and a cake made with oil, and a w.
Lev 8:26 and one made with oil, and a w; he
Nu 6:19 and a cake and a w from the basket,

Wafers (Wafer)

Ex 16:31 and tasted like w made with honey.
29: 2 with oil, and w spread with oil.
Lev 2: 4 or w made without yeast and spread
7:12 w made without yeast and spread with
Nu 6:15 with oil, and w spread with oil.
1Ch 23:29 the unleavened w, the baking and the

Wag

Jer 23:31 "I am against the prophets who w

Wage (Waged, Wages, Waging)

Jos 11:20 hearts to w war against Israel,
Pr 20:18 if you w war, obtain guidance.
Isa 19:10 the w earners will be sick at heart.
41:12 Those who w war against you will be
Da 11:25 The king of the South will w war
Mic 3: 5 they prepare to w war against him.
2Co 10: 3 we do not w war as the world does.

Waged (Wage)

Jos 11:18 Joshua w war against all these kings
1Ki 5: 3 "You know that because of the wars w
1Ch 5:10 During Saul's reign they w war
5:19 They w war against the Hagrites,
Ps 55:18 from the battle w against me,

Wages (Wage)

Ge 29:15 Tell me what your w should be."
30:28 He added, "Name your w, and I will
30:32 speckled goat. They will be my w.
30:33 you check on the w you have paid me.
31: 7 me by changing my w ten times.
31: 8 'The speckled ones will be your w,'
31: 8 'The streaked ones will be your w,'
31:41 and you changed my w ten times.
Lev 19:13 not hold back the w of a hired man
Nu 18:31 for it is your w for your work at
Dt 24:15 Pay him his w each day before sunset,
1Ki 5: 6 you for your men whatever w you set.
Job 7: 2 hired man waiting eagerly for his w,
Pr 10:16 The w of the righteous bring them
11:18 The wicked man earns deceptive w,
Hos 9: 1 you love the w of a prostitute at
Mic 1: 7 her gifts from the w of prostitutes,
1: 7 as the w of prostitutes they will
Hag 1: 6 You earn w, only to put them in a
Zec 8:10 Before that time there were no w for
Mal 3: 5 who defraud labourers of their w,
Mt 20: 8 the workers and pay them their w,
Mk 6:37 take eight months of a man's w!
14: 5 more than a year's w and the money
Lk 10: 7 you, for the worker deserves his w.
Jn 4:36 Even now the reaper draws his w,
6: 7 Philip answered him, "Eight months' w
12: 5 the poor? It was worth a year's w."
Ro 4: 4 Now when a man works, his w are not
6:23 For the w of sin is death, but the
1Ti 5:18 and "The worker deserves his w.
Jas 5: 4 Look! The w you failed to pay the
2Pe 2:15 Beor, who loved the w of wickedness.
Rev 6: 6 "A quart of wheat for a day's w, and
6: 6 quarts of barley for a day's w,

Waging (Wage)

Jdg 11:27 doing me wrong by w war against me.
Pr 24: 6 for w war you need guidance, and for
Da 7:21 I watched, this horn was w war
Ro 7:23 w war against the law of my mind and

Wagons

Isa 66:20 and w, and on mules and camels,"
Eze 23:24 chariots and w and with a throng of
26:10 w and chariots when he enters your

Waheb

Nu 21:14 W in Suphah and the ravines, the

Wail (Wailed, Wailing, Wails)

Isa 13: 6 W, for the day of the LORD is near;
14:31 W, O gate! Howl, O city! Melt away,
15: 3 they all w, prostrate with weeping.
16: 7 Therefore the Moabites w, they w
22:12 you on that day to weep and to w,
23: 1 An oracle concerning Tyre: W,
23: 6 Cross over to Tarshish; w, you
23:14 W, you ships of Tarshish; your
65:14 heart and w in brokenness of spirit.
Jer 4: 8 put on sackcloth, lament and w, for
9:10 I will weep and w for the mountains
9:18 Let them come quickly and w over us
9:20 to w; teach one another a lament.
14: 2 her cities languish; they w for the
25:34 Weep and w, you shepherds; roll in
47: 2 all who dwell in the land will w
48:20 W and cry out! Announce by the Arnon
48:31 Therefore I w over Moab, for all
48:39 "How shattered she is! How they w!
49: 3 "W, O Heshbon, for Ai is destroyed!
51: 8 W over her! Get balm for her pain;
Eze 21:12 Cry out and w, son of man, for it is
27:32 they w and mourn over you, they will
30: 2 'W and say, "Alas for that day!
32:18 "Son of man, w for the hordes of
Hos 7:14 their hearts but w upon their beds.
Joel 1: 5 Wake up, you drunkards, and weep! W,
1: 5 w because of the new wine, for it
1:11 Despair, you farmers, w, you vine
1:13 w, you who minister before the altar.
Am 5:16 to weep and the mourners to w.
Mic 1: 8 of this I will weep and w; I will go
Zep 1:11 W, you who live in the market
Zec 11: 2 W, O pine tree, for the cedar has
11: 2 W, oaks of Bashan; the dense forest
11: 3 Listen to the w of the shepherds:
Mal 2:13 You weep and w because he no longer
Jas 4: 9 Grieve, mourn and w. Change your
5: 1 you rich people, weep and w because

Wailed (Wail)

Nu 11:18 The LORD heard you when you w, "If
11:20 who is among you, and have w before
Lk 23:27 women who mourned and w for him.

Wailing (Wail)

Ex 11: 6 There will be loud w throughout
12:30 and there was loud w in Egypt, for
Nu 11: 4 and again the Israelites started w
11:10 w, each at the entrance to his tent.
11:13 keep w to me, 'Give us meat to eat!'
2Sa 13:36 the king's sons came in, w loudly.
Est 4: 1 the city, w loudly and bitterly.
4: 3 Jews, with fasting, weeping and w.
Job 30:31 and my flute to the sound of w.
Ps 30:11 You turned my w into dancing; you
Isa 15: 8 their w reaches as far as Eglaim,

Jer 6:26 with bitter w as for an only son,
9:17 "Consider now! Call for the w women
9:19 The sound of w is heard from Zion:
20:16 May he hear w in the morning, a
25:36 Hear the cry of the shepherds, the w
Am 5:16 "There will be w in all the streets
5:17 There will be w in all the vineyards,
8: 3 songs in the temple will turn to w.
Zep 1:10 w from the New Quarter, and a loud
Mk 5:38 with people crying and w loudly.
5:39 "Why all this commotion and w?
Lk 8:52 Meanwhile, all the people were w and
8:52 "Stop w," Jesus said. "She is not

Wails (Wail)
Isa 15: 2 weep; Moab w over Nebo and Medeba.

Waist (Waists)
Ex 28:42 reaching from the w to the thigh.
2Sa 20: 8 and strapped over it at his w was a
1Ki 2: 5 his w and the sandals on his feet.
12:10 is thicker than my father's w.
2Ki 1: 8 and with a leather belt round his w.
2Ch 10:10 is thicker than my father's w.
Job 12:18 and ties a loincloth round their w.
15:27 fat and his w bulges with flesh,
SS 7: 2 Your w is a mound of wheat encircled
Isa 5:27 not a belt is loosened at the w,
11: 5 faithfulness the sash round his w.
Jer 13: 1 linen belt and put it round your w,
13: 2 LORD directed, and put it round my w.
13: 4 bought and are wearing round your w,
13:11 as a belt is bound round a man's w,
48:37 every w is covered with sackcloth.
Eze 1:27 w up he looked like glowing metal,
8: 2 From what appeared to be his w down
47: 4 through water that was up to the w.
Da 10: 5 belt of the finest gold round his w.
Mt 3: 4 he had a leather belt round his w.
Mk 1: 6 a leather belt round his w, and he
Jn 13: 4 and wrapped a towel round his w.
Eph 6:14 belt of truth buckled round your w,

Waistband
Ex 28: 8 Its skilfully woven w is to be like
28:27 seam just above the w of the ephod.
28:28 connecting it to the w, so that the
29: 5 on him by its skilfully woven w.
39: 5 Its skilfully woven w was like
39:20 seam just above the w of the ephod.
39:21 connecting it to the w so that the
Lev 8: 7 woven w; so it was fastened on him.

Waists (Waist)
1Ki 20:31 our w and ropes round our heads.
20:32 Wearing sackcloth round their w and
Isa 32:11 clothes, put sackcloth round your w.
Eze 23:15 with belts round their w and flowing
44:18 linen undergarments round their w.

Wait (Await, Awaits, Waited, Waiting, Waits)
Ex 7:15 W on the bank of the Nile to meet
24:14 He said to the elders, "W here for
Lev 12: 4 the woman must w thirty-three days
12: 5 Then she must w sixty-six days to be
Nu 9: 8 Moses answered them, "W until I find
Dt 19:11 his neighbour and lies in w for him,
Jos 8: 9 and lay in w between Bethel and Ai,
18: 3 "How long will you w before you
Jdg 6:18 And the LORD said, "I will w until
9:32 come and lie in w in the fields.
16: 2 w for him all night at the city gate.
19: 8 W till afternoon!" So the two of
Ru 1:13 would you w until they grew up?
3:18 Naomi said, "W, my daughter, until
1Sa 10: 8 but you must w seven days until I
14: 9 If they say to us, 'W there until we
20:19 began, and w by the stone Ezel.
22: 8 lie in w for me, as he does today."
22:13 lies in w for me, as he does today?"
2Sa 15:28 I will w at the fords in the desert
18:14 Joab said, "I am not going to w like
18:30 The king said, "Stand aside and w
2Ki 6:33 Why should I w for the LORD any
7: 9 If we w until daylight, punishment
Job 3: 9 may it w for daylight in vain and
14:14 I will w for my renewal to come.
20:26 total darkness lies in w for his
32:16 Must I w, now that they are silent,
35:14 before him and you must w for him,
38:40 they crouch in their dens or lie in w
Ps 5: 3 before you and w in expectation.
10: 8 He lies in w near the villages; from
10: 9 He lies in w like a lion in cover;
10: 9 he lies in w to catch the helpless;
27:14 W for the LORD; be strong and take
27:14 and take heart and w for the LORD.
33:20 We w in hope for the LORD; he is our
37: 7 Be still before the LORD and w
37:32 The wicked lie in w for the
37:34 W for the LORD and keep his way. He
38:15 I w for you, O LORD; you will answer,
59: 3 See how they lie in w for me! Fierce
71:10 who w to kill me conspire together.
106:13 done and did not w for his counsel.
119:84 How long must your servant w? When
119:166 I w for your salvation, O LORD, and
130: 5 I w for the LORD, my soul waits, and
130: 6 than watchmen w for the morning,
130: 6 than watchmen w for the morning.
Pr 1:11 "Come along with us; let's lie in w
1:18 These men lie in w for their own
12: 6 The words of the wicked lie in w for
20:22 for this wrong!" W for the LORD,
23:28 Like a bandit she lies in w, and
24:15 Do not lie in w like an outlaw
Isa 8:17 I will w for the LORD, who is hiding
26: 8 we w for you; your name and renown
30:18 Blessed are all who w for him!
51: 5 look to me and w in hope for my arm.
64: 4 on behalf of those who w for him.
Jer 5: 6 a leopard will lie in w near their
5:26 lie in w like men who snare birds
Lam 3:10 Like a bear lying in w, like a lion
3:24 therefore I will w for him."
3:26 is good to w quietly for the
4:19 and lay in w for us in the desert.
Eze 44:26 After he is cleansed, he must w
Hos 12: 6 justice, and w for your God always.
Ob :14 You should not w at the crossroads
Mic 5: 7 not w for man or linger for mankind.
7: 2 All men lie in w to shed blood; each
7: 7 I watch in hope for the LORD, I w
Hab 2: 3 Though it linger, w for it; it will
3:16 Yet I will w patiently for the day
Zep 3: 8 Therefore w for me," declares the
Mt 8:15 she got up and began to w on him.
Mk 1:31 left her and she began to w on them.
Lk 4:39 up at once and began to w on them.
12:37 table and will come and w on them.
17: 8 get yourself ready and w on me while
Jn 18:16 Peter had to w outside at the door.
Ac 1: 4 "Do not leave Jerusalem, but w for
6: 2 word of God in order to w on tables.
Ro 8:23 groan inwardly as we w eagerly for
8:25 not yet have, we w for it patiently.
1Co 1: 7 any spiritual gift as you eagerly w
4: 5 time; w till the Lord comes.
11:33 together to eat, w for each other.
1Th 1:10 to w for his Son from heaven, whom
Tit 2:13 while we w for the blessed hope—the
Jude :21 as you w for the mercy of our Lord
Rev 6:11 and they were told to w a little

Waited (Wait)
Ge 8:10 He w seven more days and again sent
8:12 He w seven more days and sent the
Jdg 3:25 They w to the point of embarrassment,
3:26 While they w, Ehud got away. He
1Sa 13: 8 He w for seven days, the time set by
25: 9 in David's name. Then they w.
1Ki 1: 4 took care of the king and w on him,
Job 29:23 They w for me as for showers and
32: 4 Now Elihu had w before speaking to
32:11 I w while you spoke, I listened to
Ps 40: 1 I w patiently for the LORD; he
Isa 38:13 I w patiently till dawn, but like a
Lam 2:16 This is the day we have w for; we
Jnh 4: 5 sat in its shade and w to see what
Ac 20: 5 These men went on ahead and w for us
1Pe 3:20 who disobeyed long ago when God w

Waiting (Wait)
Ex 5:20 Moses and Aaron w to meet them,
2Sa 16: 1 of Mephibosheth, w to meet him.
1Ki 20:38 stood by the road w for the king.
Job 7: 2 a hired man w eagerly for his wages,
29:21 "Men listened to me expectantly, w
Ps 119:95 The wicked are w to destroy me, but
Pr 8:34 daily at my doors, w at my doorway.
Jer 3: 2 By the roadside you sat w for lovers,
20:10 All my friends are w for me to slip,
Mic 1:12 w for relief, because disaster has
Mk 15:43 who was himself w for the kingdom of
Lk 1:21 the people were w for Zechariah and
2:25 He was w for the consolation of
3:15 The people were w expectantly and
11:54 w to catch him in something he might
12:36 like men w for their master to
23:51 and he was w for the kingdom of God.
Jn 7: 1 Jews there were w to take his life.
Ac 17:16 While Paul was w for them in Athens,
22:16 now what are you w for? Get up, be
23:21 of them are w in ambush for him.
23:21 w for your consent to their request."
28: 6 but after w a long time and seeing
1Co 11:21 ahead without w for anybody else.
Heb 6:15 after w patiently, Abraham received
9:28 to those who are w for him.

Waits (Wait)
Ps 130: 5 I wait for the LORD, my soul w, and
130: 6 My soul w for the Lord more than
Da 12:12 Blessed is the one who w for and
Jn 3:29 bridegroom w and listens for him,
Ro 8:19 The creation w in eager expectation
Heb 10:13 Since that time he w for his enemies
Jas 5: 7 See how the farmer w for the land to

Wake (Awake, Awaken, Awakened, Awakens, Awakes, Awoke, Wakened, Wakens, Wakes, Woke)
Jdg 5:12 'W up, w up, Deborah! w up, w up,
1Sa 26:12 knew about it, nor did anyone w up.
Job 41:32 Behind him he leaves a glistening w;
Ps 3: 5 I lie down and sleep; I w again,
Pr 23:35 I w up so I can find another drink?"
Isa 26:19 You who dwell in the dust, w up and
Joel 1: 5 W up, you drunkards, and weep! Wail,
Hab 2: 7 Will they not w up and make you
2:19 'W up!' Can it give guidance? It is
Jn 11:11 but I am going there to w him up."
Ro 13:11 The hour has come for you to w up
Eph 5:14 why it is said: "W up, O sleeper,
Rev 3: 2 W up! Strengthen what remains and is
3: 3 But if you do not w up, I will come

Wakened (Wake)
Zec 4: 1 w me, as a man is w from his sleep.

Wakens (Wake)
Isa 50: 4 He w me morning by morning, w my ear

Wakes (Wake)
Ps 78:65 as a man w from the stupor of wine.

Walk (Walked, Walking, Walks)
Ge 13:17 Go, w through the length and breadth
17: 1 w before me and be blameless.
Ex 17: 5 The LORD answered Moses, "W on ahead
Lev 11:20 flying insects that w on all fours
11:21 some winged creatures that w on all
11:27 Of all the animals that w on all
11:27 those that w on their paws are
26:12 I will w among you and be your God,
26:13 you to w with heads held high.
Nu 11:31 far as a day's w in any direction.
Dt 5:33 W in all the way that the LORD your
6: 7 home and when you w along the road,
10:12 to w in all his ways, to love him,
11:19 home and when you w along the road,

Dt 11:22 to w in all his ways and to hold
19: 9 to w always in his ways—then you
26:17 God and that you will w in his ways,
28: 9 the LORD your God and w in his ways.
30:16 to w in his ways, and to keep his
Jos 22: 5 to w in all his ways, to obey his
Jdg 2:22 w in it as their forefathers did."
5:10 you who w along the road, consider
1Sa 8: 3 his sons did not w in his ways. They
8: 5 your sons do not w in your ways;
2Sa 3:31 and w in mourning in front of Abner.
1Ki 2: 3 your God requires: W in his ways,
2: 4 and if they w faithfully before me
3:14 if you w in my ways and obey my
8:25 do to w before me as you have done.'
8:58 May he turn our hearts to him, to w
9: 4 "As for you, if you w before me in
11:38 w in my ways and do what is right in
2Ki 21:22 did not w in the way of the LORD.
2Ch 6:16 to w before me according to my law,
6:31 that they will fear you and w in
7:17 "As for you, if you w before me as
Ne 5: 9 Shouldn't you w in the fear of our
Ps 1: 1 Blessed is the man who does not w in
15: 2 He whose w is blameless and who does
23: 4 Even though I w through the valley
26: 3 and I w continually in your truth.
48:12 W about Zion, go round her, count
56:13 w before God in the light of life.
82: 5 They w about in darkness; all the
84:11 from those whose w is blameless.
86:11 O LORD, and I will w in your truth;
89:15 who w in the light of your presence,
101: 2 w in my house with blameless heart.
101: 6 w is blameless will minister to me.
115: 7 feet, but they cannot w; nor can
116: 9 that I may w before the LORD in the
119: 1 w according to the law of the LORD.
119: 3 They do nothing wrong; they w in his
119:45 I will w about in freedom, for I
128: 1 fear the LORD, who w in his ways.
138: 7 Though I w in the midst of trouble,
142: 3 I w men have hidden a snare for me.
Pr 2: 7 to those whose w is blameless,
2:13 who leave the straight paths to w in
2:20 Thus you will w in the ways of good
4:12 When you w, your steps will not be
4:14 wicked or w in the way of evil men.
6:22 you w, they will guide you; when you
6:28 Can a man w on hot coals without his
8:20 I w in the way of righteousness,
9: 6 live; w in the way of understanding.
14: 2 He whose w is upright fears the LORD,
19: 1 Better a poor man whose w is
28: 6 Better a poor man whose w is
28:18 He whose w is blameless is kept safe,
Isa 2: 3 ways, so that we may w in his paths.
2: 5 Come, O house of Jacob, let us w in
23:16 "Take up a harp, w through the city,
30:21 saying, "This is the way; w in it.
35: 8 it will be for those who w in that
35: 9 But only the redeemed will w there,
38:15 I will w humbly all my years because
40:31 weary, they will w and not be faint.
42: 5 and life to those who w on it:
43: 2 When you w through the fire, you
50:11 go, w in the light of your fires and
51:23 prostrate that we may w over you.
57: 2 Those who w uprightly enter into
59: 9 but we w in deep shadows.
65: 2 who w in ways not good, pursuing
Jer 6:16 ask where the good way is, and w in
6:16 But you said, 'We will not w in it.'
6:25 Do not go out to the fields or w on
7:23 W in all the ways I command you,
10: 5 be carried because they cannot w.
18:15 They made them w in bypaths and on
Lam 3: 2 He has driven me away and made me w
4:18 so we could not w in our streets.
Eze 36:12 my people Israel, to w upon you.
Da 4:37 who w in pride he is able to humble.
Hos 11: 3 was I who taught Ephraim to w,
14: 9 are right; the righteous w in them,
Am 3: 3 Do two w together unless they have
Mic 2: 3 You will no longer w proudly, for it
4: 2 ways, so that we may w in his paths.
Mic 4: 5 All the nations may w in the name of
4: 5 we will w in the name of the LORD
6: 8 mercy and to w humbly with your God.
Zep 1:17 and they will w like blind men,
Zec 3: 7 'If you will w in my ways and keep
10:12 they will w," declares the LORD.
Mt 9: 5 or to say, 'Get up and w'?
11: 5 The blind receive sight, the lame w,
Mk 2: 9 say, 'Get up, take your mat and w'?
12:38 They like to w around in flowing
Lk 5:23 or to say, 'Get up and w'?
7:22 the lame w, those who have leprosy
11:44 men w over without knowing it."
20:46 They like to w around in flowing
24:17 discussing together as you w along?"
Jn 5: 8 "Get up! Pick up your mat and w.
5:11 said to me, 'Pick up your mat and w.
5:12 who told you to pick it up and w?"
8:12 Whoever follows me will never w in
12:35 W while you have the light, before
Ac 1:12 a Sabbath day's w from the city.
3: 6 of Jesus Christ of Nazareth, w."
3: 8 He jumped to his feet and began to w.
3:12 or godliness we had made this man w?
14:10 the man jumped up and began to w.
Ro 4:12 w in the footsteps of the faith
2Co 6:16 "I will live with them and w among
Col 3: 7 You used to w in these ways, in the
1Jn 1: 6 with him yet w in the darkness,
1: 7 if we w in the light, as he is in
2: 6 Whoever claims to live in him must w
2Jn : 6 this is love: that we w in obedience
: 6 his command is that you w in love.
3Jn : 3 how you continue to w in the truth.
Rev 3: 4 will w with me, dressed in white
9:20 that cannot see or hear or w.
21:24 The nations will w by its light, and

Walked (Walk)

Ge 5:22 Enoch w with God 300 years and had
5:24 Enoch w with God; then he was no
6: 9 of his time, and he w with God.
9:23 then they w in backwards and covered
18:16 and Abraham w along with them to see
24:40 'The LORD, before whom I have w,
48:15 whom my fathers Abraham and Isaac w,
Ex 15:19 w through the sea on dry ground.
Jos 14: 9 'The land on which your feet have w
Jdg 2:17 way in which their fathers had w,
1Sa 19:23 and he w along prophesying until he
2Sa 3:31 King David himself w behind the bier.
11: 2 w around on the roof of the palace.
1Ki 11:33 and have not w in my ways, nor done
16: 2 but you w in the ways of Jeroboam
16:26 He w in all the ways of Jeroboam son
22:43 In everything he w in the ways of
22:52 because he w in the ways of his
2Ki 2: 6 leave you." So the two of them w on.
4:35 Elisha turned away and w back and
8:18 He w in the ways of the kings of
8:27 He w in the ways of the house of
16: 3 He w in the ways of the kings of
20: 3 "Remember, O LORD, how I have w
21:21 He w in all the ways of his father;
22: 2 w in all the ways of his father
2Ch 17: 3 w in the ways that his father David
20:32 He w in the ways of his father Asa
21: 6 He w in the ways of the kings of
21:12 'You have not w in the ways of your
21:13 you have w in the ways of the kings
22: 3 He too w in the ways of the house of
27: 6 Jotham grew powerful because he w
28: 2 He w in the ways of the kings of
34: 2 w in the ways of his father David,
Est 2:11 Every day he w to and fro near the
Job 29: 3 by his light I w through darkness!
31: 5 "If I have w in falsehood or my foot
38:16 or w in the recesses of the deep?
Ps 55:14 sweet fellowship as we w with the
Ecc 4:15 I saw that all who lived and w under
Isa 38: 3 "Remember, O LORD, how I have w
51:23 ground, like a street to be w over."
Jer 34:18 two and then w between its pieces.
34:19 w between the pieces of the calf,
Eze 16:47 You not only w in their ways and
Eze 28:14 God; you w among the fiery stones.
Mal 2: 6 He w with me in peace and
Mt 14:29 w on the water and came towards
Mk 1:16 Jesus w beside the Sea of Galilee,
2:12 He got up, took his mat and w out in
2:14 he w along, he saw Levi son of
2:23 and as his disciples w along, they
5:42 Immediately the girl stood up and w
Lk 4:30 he w right through the crowd and
24:15 came up and w along with them;
Jn 5: 9 cured; he picked up his mat and w.
Ac 12:10 When they had w the length of one
14: 8 was lame from birth and had never w.
17:23 For as I w around and looked

Walking (Walk)

Ge 3: 8 LORD God as he was w in the garden
Ex 2: 5 were w along the river bank.
Dt 8: 6 God, w in his ways and revering him.
1Sa 17:39 over the tunic and tried w around,
2Sa 6: 4 it, and Ahio was w in front of it.
1Ki 3: 3 w according to the statutes of his
15:26 w in the ways of his father and in
15:34 w in the ways of Jeroboam and in his
16:19 w in the ways of Jeroboam and in the
18: 7 Obadiah was w along, Elijah met him.
2Ki 2:11 they were w along and talking
2:23 As he was w along the road, some
2Ch 11:17 w in the ways of David and Solomon
Pr 7: 8 w along in the direction of her
Isa 3:16 "The women of Zion are haughty, w
9: 2 The people w in darkness have seen a
26: 8 Yes, LORD, w in the way of your laws,
Da 3:25 He said, "Look! I see four men w
4:29 as the king was w on the roof of the
Mt 4:18 Jesus was w beside the Sea of
14:25 went out to them, w on the lake.
14:26 the disciples saw him w on the lake,
15:31 the lame w and the blind seeing.
24: 1 Jesus left the temple and was w away
Mk 6:48 he went out to them, w on the lake.
6:49 when they saw him w on the lake,
8:24 they look like trees w around."
11:27 and while Jesus was w in the temple
16:12 while they were w in the country.
Lk 9:57 they were w along the road, a man
Jn 6:19 w on the water; and they were
10:23 Jesus was in the temple area w in
Ac 3: 8 w and jumping, and praising God.
3: 9 all the people saw him w and
2Jn : 4 of your children w in the truth,
3Jn : 4 that my children are w in the truth.

Walks (Walk)

Ex 21:19 and w around outside with his staff;
Lev 11:42 whether it moves on its belly or w
Pr 10: 9 The man of integrity w securely, but
13:20 He who w with the wise grows wise,
28:26 but he who w in wisdom is kept safe.
Ecc 2:14 while the fool w in the darkness;
10: 3 Even as he w along the road, the
Isa 33:15 He who w righteously and speaks what
50:10 Let him who w in the dark, who has
59: 8 who w in them will know peace.
Jn 11: 9 A man who w by day will not stumble,
11:10 is when he w by night that he
12:35 The man who w in the dark does not
1Jn 2:11 and w around in the darkness;
Rev 2: 1 w among the seven golden lampstands:

Wall (Walled, Walls)

Ge 49:22 whose branches climb over a w.
Ex 14:22 with a w of water on their right and
14:29 with a w of water on their right and
15: 8 surging waters stood firm like a w;
Lev 11:30 the monitor lizard, the w lizard,
14:37 be deeper than the surface of the w,
Nu 22:25 to the w, crushing Balaam's foot
35: 4 hundred feet from the town w.
Jos 2:15 she lived in was part of the city w.
6: 5 then the w of the city will collapse
6:20 the w collapsed; so every man
1Sa 18:11 himself, "I'll pin David to the w.
19:10 Saul tried to pin him to the w with
19:10 as Saul drove the spear into the w.

1Sa 20:25 sat in his customary place by the w,
25:16 Night and day they were a w around
31:10 his body to the w of Beth Shan.
31:12 from the w of Beth Shan and went
2Sa 11:20 they would shoot arrows from the w?
11:21 upper millstone on him from the w,
11:21 Why did you get so close to the w?'
11:24 arrows at your servants from the w,
18:24 to the roof of the gateway by the w.
20:15 battering the w to bring it down,
20:21 will be thrown to you from the w."
22:30 troop; with my God I can scale a w.
1Ki 3: 1 LORD, and the w around Jerusalem.
6:27 The wing of one cherub touched one w,
6:27 of the other touched the other w,
7:12 w of three courses of dressed stone
9:15 the w of Jerusalem, and Hazor,
11:27 w of the city of David his father.
20:30 Aphek, where the w collapsed on
21:23 devour Jezebel by the w of Jezreel.'
2Ki 3:27 him as a sacrifice on the city w.
6:26 of Israel was passing by on the w,
6:30 As he went along the w, the people
9:33 some of her blood spattered the w
14:13 broke down the w of Jerusalem from
18:26 the hearing of the people on the w."
18:27 and not to the men sitting on the w—
20: 2 Hezekiah turned his face to the w
25: 4 the city w was broken through, and
1Ch 11: 8 terraces to the surrounding w,
2Ch 3:11 long and touched the temple w,
3:12 long and touched the other temple w,
25:23 broke down the w of Jerusalem from
26: 9 of the w, and he fortified them.
27: 3 work on the w at the hill of Ophel.
32: 5 of the w and building towers on it.
32: 5 He built another w outside that one
32:18 of Jerusalem who were on the w,
33:14 Afterwards he rebuilt the outer w of
36:19 and broke down the w of Jerusalem;
Ezr 9: 9 he has given us a w of protection
Ne 1: 3 The w of Jerusalem is broken down,
2: 8 for the city w and for the residence
2:15 valley by night, examining the w.
2:17 Come, let us rebuild the w of
3: 8 Jerusalem as far as the Broad W.
3:13 of the w as far as the Dung Gate.
3:15 He also repaired the w of the Pool
3:27 projecting tower to the w of Ophel.
4: 1 heard that we were rebuilding the w,
4: 2 Will they restore their w? Will they
4: 3 would break down their w of stones!"
4: 6 we rebuilt the w till all of it
4:10 that we cannot rebuild the w."
4:13 of the w at the exposed places,
4:15 to the w, each to his own work.
4:17 who were building the w. Those who
4:19 from each other along the w.
5:16 myself to the work on this w.
6: 1 enemies that I had rebuilt the w
6: 6 therefore you are building the w.
6:15 So the w was completed on the
7: 1 After the w had been rebuilt and I
12:27 At the dedication of the w of
12:30 the people, the gates and the w.
12:31 of Judah go up on top of the w.
12:31 One was to proceed on top of the w
12:37 City of David on the ascent to the w
12:38 I followed them on top of the w,
12:38 Tower of the Ovens to the Broad W,
13:21 "Why do you spend the night by the w?
Ps 18:29 troop; with my God I can scale a w.
62: 3 leaning w, this tottering fence?
78:13 made the water stand firm like a w.
Pr 18:11 they imagine it an unscalable w.
24:31 weeds, and the stone w was in ruins.
Ecc 10: 8 whoever breaks through a w may be
SS 2: 9 Look! There he stands behind our w,
8: 9 If she is a w, we will build towers
8:10 I am a w, and my breasts are like
Isa 2:15 lofty tower and every fortified w,
5: 5 down its w, and it will be trampled.
22:10 down houses to strengthen the w.
25: 4 is like a storm driving against a w
30:13 will become for you like a high w,
36:11 the hearing of the people on the w."
Isa 36:12 and not to the men sitting on the w—
38: 2 Hezekiah turned his face to the w
59:10 Like the blind we grope along the w,
Jer 1:18 an iron pillar and a bronze w to
15:20 I will make you a w to this people,
15:20 a fortified w of bronze; they will
21: 4 who are outside the w besieging you.
39: 2 year, the city w was broken through.
51:44 And the w of Babylon will fall.
51:58 "Babylon's thick w will be levelled
52: 7 the city w was broken through, and
Lam 2: 8 the w around the Daughter of Zion.
2:18 O w of the Daughter of Zion, let
Eze 4: 3 place it as an iron w between you
8: 7 I looked, and I saw a hole in the w.
8: 8 me, "Son of man, now dig into the w.
8: 8 into the w and saw a doorway there.
12: 5 While they watch, dig through the w
12: 7 I dug through the w with my hands.
12:12 dug in the w for him to go through.
13: 5 to the breaks in the w to repair it
13:10 when a flimsy w is built, they
13:12 the w collapses, will people not ask
13:14 I will tear down the w you have
13:15 I will spend my wrath against the w
13:15 I will say to you, "The w is gone
22:30 among them who would build up the w
23:14 She saw men portrayed on a w,
38:20 and every w will fall to the ground.
40: 5 I saw a w completely surrounding the
40: 5 He measured the w; it was one
40:12 In front of each alcove was a w one
40:13 the top of the rear w of one alcove
40:40 By the outside w of the portico of
40:43 were attached to the w all around.
41: 5 he measured the w of the temple; it
41: 6 There were ledges all round the w of
41: 6 inserted into the w of the temple.
41: 9 The outer w of the side rooms was
41:12 The w of the building was five
41:16 The floor, the w up to the windows,
41:20 on the w of the outer sanctuary.
42: 1 the outer w on the north side.
42: 7 There was an outer w parallel to the
42:10 length of the w of the outer court,
42:10 and opposite the outer w, were
42:12 corresponding w extending eastward,
42:20 It had a w round it, five hundred
43: 8 with only a w between me and them,
Da 5: 5 and wrote on the plaster of the w,
Hos 2: 6 I will w her in so that she cannot
Joel 2: 9 upon the city; they run along the w.
Am 4: 3 out through breaks in the w, and
5:19 the w only to have a snake bite him.
7: 7 w that had been built true to plumb,
Na 2: 5 They dash to the city w; the
3: 8 was her defence, the waters her w.
Hab 2:11 The stones of the w will cry out,
Zec 2: 5 I myself will be a w of fire around
Mt 21:33 put a w around it, dug a winepress
Mk 12: 1 He put a w around it, dug a pit for
Ac 9:25 basket through an opening in the w.
23: 3 you whitewashed w! You sit there to
2Co 11:33 the w and slipped through his hands.
Eph 2:14 the dividing w of hostility,
Rev 21:12 had a great, high w with twelve
21:14 The w of the city had twelve
21:17 He measured its w and it was 144
21:18 The w was made of jasper, and the

Walled (Wall)

Lev 25:29 If a man sells a house in a w city
25:30 the house in the w city shall belong
1Ki 4:13 w cities with bronze gate bars);
Lam 3: 7 He has w me in so that I cannot

Wallow (Wallowing)

Jer 48:26 Let Moab w in her vomit; let her be

Wallowing (Wallow)

2Sa 20:12 Amasa lay w in his blood in the
2Pe 2:22 goes back to her w in the mud."

Walls (Wall)

Lev 14:37 He is to examine the mildew on the w,
14:39 If the mildew has spread on the w,
14:41 He must have all the inside w of the
25:31 houses in villages without w round
Nu 22:24 two vineyards, with w on both sides.
Dt 1:28 are large, with w up to the sky.
3: 5 with high w and with gates and bars,
9: 1 cities that have w up to the sky.
28:52 w in which you trust fall down.
1Ki 4:33 to the hyssop that grows out of w.
6: 5 Against the w of the main hall and
6: 6 would be inserted into the temple w.
6:15 He lined its interior w with cedar
6:29 On the w all round the temple, in
2Ki 25: 4 the two w near the king's garden,
25:10 broke down the w around Jerusalem.
1Ch 29: 4 of the w of the buildings,
2Ch 3: 7 door-frames, w and doors of the
3: 7 and he carved cherubim on the w.
8: 5 with w and with gates and bars,
14: 7 "and put w round them, with towers,
26: 6 the w of Gath, Jabneh and Ashdod.
Ezr 4:12 the w and repairing the foundations.
4:13 is built and its w are restored,
4:16 is built and its w are restored,
5: 8 and placing the timbers in the w.
Ne 2:13 examining the w of Jerusalem, which
4: 7 to Jerusalem's w had gone ahead
Ps 51:18 build up the w of Jerusalem.
55:10 prowl about on its w; malice and
80:12 Why have you broken down its w so
89:40 You have broken through all his w
122: 7 May there be peace within your w and
144:14 There will be no breaching of w, no
Pr 25:28 Like a city whose w are broken down
SS 5: 7 my cloak, those watchmen of the w!
Isa 22: 5 a day of battering down w and of
22:11 two w for the water of the Old Pool,
25:12 high fortified w and lay them low;
26: 1 makes salvation its w and ramparts.
49:16 my hands; your w are ever before me.
54:12 and all your w of precious stones.
56: 5 its w a memorial and a name better
58:12 will be called Repairer of Broken W,
60:10 "Foreigners will rebuild your w, and
60:18 you will call your w Salvation and
62: 6 I have posted watchmen on your w,
Jer 1:15 against all her surrounding w and
39: 4 through the gate between the two w,
39: 8 and broke down the w of Jerusalem.
49: 3 rush here and there inside the w,
49:27 "I will set fire to the w of
50:15 towers fall, her w are torn down.
51:12 Lift up a banner against the w of
52: 7 the two w near the king's garden,
52:14 down all the w around Jerusalem.
Lam 2: 7 to the enemy the w of her palaces;
2: 8 He made ramparts and w lament;
Eze 5:12 fall by the sword outside your w;
8:10 and I saw portrayed all over the w
26: 4 They will destroy the w of Tyre and
26: 8 build a ramp up to your w and raise
26: 9 his battering-rams against your w
26:10 Your w will tremble at the noise of
26:10 whose w have been broken through.
26:12 they will break down your w and
27:10 on your w, bringing you splendour.
27:11 Men of Arvad and Helech manned your w
27:11 hung their shields around your w;
33:30 by the w and at the doors of the
38:11 living without w and without gates
40: 7 and the projecting w between the
40:10 and the faces of the projecting w on
40:14 along the faces of the projecting w
40:16 The alcoves and the projecting w
40:16 w were decorated with palm trees.
40:21 on each side—its projecting w
40:26 of the projecting w on each side.
40:29 Its alcoves, its projecting w and
40:33 Its alcoves, its projecting w and
40:36 did its alcoves, its projecting w
40:48 its projecting w were three cubits
41: 2 and the projecting w on each side of
41: 3 and the projecting w on each side of

Eze 41:13 w were also a hundred cubits long.
41:17 on the w at regular intervals all
41:25 trees like those carved on the w,
41:26 On the side w of the portico were
Joel 2: 7 they scale w like soldiers. They
Am 1: 7 I will send fire upon the w of Gaza
1:10 I will send fire upon the w of Tyre
1:14 I will set fire to the w of Rabbah
Mic 7:11 The day for building your w will
Na 3:17 that settle in the w on a cold day
Zec 2: 4 'Jerusalem will be a city without w
Lk 19:44 you and the children within your w.
Heb 11:30 By faith the w of Jericho fell,
Rev 21:15 the city, its gates and its w.
21:19 The foundations of the city w were

Wander (Wandered, Wanderer, Wanderers, Wandering, Wanders)

Ge 20:13 God caused me to w from my father's
Nu 32:13 w in the desert for forty years,
2Sa 15:20 And today shall I make you w about
2Ki 21: 8 w from the land I gave their
Job 38:41 to God and w about for lack of food?
Ps 59:11 them w about, and bring them down.
59:15 They w about for food and howl if
107:40 made them w in a trackless waste.
Pr 17:24 eyes w to the ends of the earth.
Isa 63:17 Why, O Lord, do you make us w from
Jer 14:10 They greatly love to w; they do not
31:22 How long will you w, O unfaithful
Lam 4:15 us!" When they flee and w about,
Am 8:12 sea to sea and w from north to east,
Zec 10: 2 Therefore the people w like sheep
Mt 18:13 the ninety-nine that did not w off.
Jas 5:19 My brothers, if one of you should w

Wandered (Wander)

Ge 21:14 and w in the desert of Beersheba.
1Ch 16:20 they w from nation to nation, from
Ps 105:13 they w from nation to nation, from
107: 4 Some w in desert wastelands, finding
Jer 50: 6 They w over mountain and hill and
Eze 34: 6 My sheep w over all the mountains
44:10 who w from me after their idols must
Mt 18:12 go to look for the one that w off?
1Ti 1: 6 Some have w away from these and
6:10 Some people, eager for money, have w
6:21 in so doing have w from the faith.
2Ti 2:18 who have w away from the truth. They
Heb 11:38 They w in deserts and mountains, and
2Pe 2:15 They have left the straight way and w

Wanderer (Wander)

Ge 4:12 will be a restless w on the earth."
4:14 I will be a restless w on the earth,
Isa 58: 7 to provide the poor w with shelter—

Wanderers (Wander)

Hos 9:17 they will be w among the nations.

Wandering (Wander)

Ge 37:15 a man found him w around in the
Ex 14: 3 'The Israelites are w around the
23: 4 your enemy's ox or donkey w off,
Dt 26: 5 "My father was a w Aramean, and he
Job 12:24 them w through a trackless waste.
Ps 109:10 May his children be w beggars; may
Lam 1: 7 In the days of her affliction and w
3:19 I remember my affliction and my w,
Hos 8: 9 Assyria like a wild donkey w alone.
Jude :13 foaming up their shame; w stars, for

Wanders (Wander)

Job 15:23 He w about—food for vultures; he
18: 8 into a net and he w into its mesh.
Mt 18:12 and one of them w away, will he not

Wane

Isa 60:20 and your moon will w no more; the

Want (Wanted, Wanting, Wants)

Ge 24: 3 I w you to swear by the Lord, the
29:21 completed, and I w to lie with her."
42:36 and now you w to take Benjamin.
Ex 16: 8 all the bread you w in the morning,
16:23 So bake what you w to bake and boil
16:23 to bake and boil what you w to boil.
21: 5 children and do not w to go free,'
Lev 26: 5 eat all the food you w and live in
Nu 16:13 now you also w to lord it over us?
20:19 We only w to pass through on
Dt 12:15 eat as much of the meat as you w,
12:20 you may eat as much of it as you w.
12:21 may eat as much of them as you w.
15:16 "I do not w to leave you," because
23:24 eat all the grapes you w, but do
25: 7 if a man does not w to marry his
25: 8 saying, "I do not w to marry her,
Jdg 9:15 'If you really w to anoint me king
1Sa 2:16 and then take whatever you w,"
8:19 "No!" they said. "We w a king over
12:12 'No, we w a king to rule over
20: 4 you w me to do, I'll do for you."
21: 9 If you w it, take it; there is no
2Sa 14:32 Now then, I w to see the king's
18:22 "My son, why do you w to go? You
18:23 He said, "Come what may, I w to run."
20:19 Why do you w to swallow up the
21: 4 "What do you w me to do for you?"
24: 3 lord the king w to do such a thing?"
1Ki 1:16 "What is it you w?" the king asked.
3: 5 for whatever you w me to give you."
5: 8 will do all you w in providing the
11:22 "What have you lacked here that you w
1Ch 21: 3 Why does my lord w to do this? Why
2Ch 1: 7 for whatever you w me to give you."
Ne 2: 4 "What is it you w?" Then I prayed to
Job 24:16 they w nothing to do with the light.
30: 3 Haggard from w and hunger, they
33:32 speak up, for I w you to be cleared.
37:20 Should he be told that I w to speak?
Ps 23: 1 is my shepherd, I shall not be in w.
71:13 may those who w to harm me be
Jer 40: 4 if you do not w to, then don't come.
42:22 place where you w to go to settle."
Eze 20:32 say, "We w to be like the nations
36:32 I w you to know that I am not doing
Da 2: 3 me and I w to know what it means."
3:18 even if he does not, we w you to
Mt 1:19 w to expose her to public disgrace,
8:29 "What do you w with us, Son of God?"
12:38 w to see a miraculous sign from you."
13:28 you w us to go and pull them up?'
15:32 I do not w to send them away hungry,
19:17 If you w to enter life, obey the
19:21 Jesus answered, "If you w to be
20:14 Take your pay and go. I w to give
20:15 Don't I have the right to do what I w
20:21 "What is it you w?" he asked. She
20:32 "What do you w me to do for you?" he
20:33 they answered, "we w our sight."
26:17 "Where do you w us to make
27:17 "Which one do you w me to release to
27:21 "Which of the two do you w me to
Mk 1:24 "What do you w with us, Jesus of
5: 7 "What do you w with me, Jesus, Son
6:22 you w, and I'll give it to you."
6:25 "I w you to give me right now the
6:26 guests, he did not w to refuse her.
7:24 He entered a house and did not w
7:27 let the children eat all they w,"
9:30 w anyone to know where they were,
10:35 w you to do for us whatever we ask."
10:36 "What do you w me to do for you?" he
10:51 "What do you w me to do for you?"
10:51 The blind man said, "Rabbi, I w to
14: 7 you can help them any time you w.
14:12 "Where do you w us to go and make
15: 9 "Do you w me to release to you the
Lk 4: 6 and I can give it to anyone I w to.
4:34 "Ha! What do you w with us, Jesus of
8:28 "What do you w with me, Jesus, Son
9:54 "Lord, do you w us to call fire down
16:26 so that those who w to go from here
18:41 "What do you w me to do for you?"
18:41 "Lord, I w to see," he replied.
19:14 don't w this man to be our king.'
19:27 those enemies of mine who did not w
22: 9 "Where do you w us to prepare for it?
Jn 1:38 asked, "What do you w?" They said,
4:27 But no-one asked, "What do you w?"
5: 6 asked him, "Do you w to get well?
6:67 "You do not w to leave too, do you?"
8:44 w to carry out your father's desire.
9:27 Why do you w to hear it again? Do
9:27 you w to become his disciples, too?"
17:24 "Father, I w those you have given me
18: 4 asked them, "Who is it you w?"
18: 7 Again he asked them, "Who is it you w
18:39 Do you w me to release 'the king of
19:31 Because the Jews did not w the
21:18 lead you where you do not w to go."
21:22 Jesus answered, "If I w him to
21:23 "If I w him to remain alive until I
Ac 7:26 why do you w to hurt each other?'
7:28 Do you w to kill me as you killed
13:22 will do everything I w him to do.'
13:38 my brothers, I w you to know that
16:37 And now do they w to get rid of us
17:20 and we w to know what they mean."
17:32 w to hear you again on this subject."
19:39 If there is anything further you w
23:19 "What is it you w to tell me?
28:22 we w to hear what your views are,
28:28 "Therefore I w you to know that
Ro 1:13 I do not w you to be unaware,
7:15 For what I w to do I do not do, but
7:16 if I do what I do not w to do, I
7:19 For what I do is not the good I w to
7:19 not w to do—this I keep on doing.
7:20 Now if I do what I do not w to do,
7:21 I find this law at work: When I w to
11:25 I do not w you to be ignorant of
13: 3 Do you w to be free from fear of the
16:19 w you to be wise about what is good,
1Co 4: 8 Already you have all you w! Already
7:28 life, and I w to spare you this.
10: 1 For I do not w you to be ignorant of
10:20 w you to be participants with demons.
10:27 you to a meal and you w to go,
11: 3 Now I w you to realise that the head
12: 1 I do not w you to be ignorant.
14:35 If they w to enquire about something,
15: 1 Now, brothers, I w to remind you of
16: 7 I do not w to see you now and make
2Co 1: 8 We do not w you to be uninformed,
8: 1 now, brothers, we w you to know
8: 8 I am not commanding you, but I w to
8:20 We w to avoid any criticism of the
10: 9 I do not w to seem to be trying to
10:16 For we do not w to boast about work
11:12 those who w an opportunity to be
12:14 I w is not your possessions but you.
12:20 I may not find you as I w you to be,
12:20 may not find me as you w me to be.
Gal 1:11 I w you to know, brothers, that the
4:17 What they w is to alienate you from
4:21 Tell me, you who w to be under the
5:17 so that you do not do what you w.
6:12 Those who w to make a good
6:13 yet they w you to be circumcised
Php 1:12 Now I w you to know, brothers, that
3:10 I w to know Christ and the power of
4:12 whether living in plenty or in w.
Col 2: 1 I w you to know how much I am
1Th 4:13 Brothers, we do not w you to be
1Ti 1: 7 They w to be teachers of the law,
2: 8 I w men everywhere to lift up holy
2: 9 I also w women to dress modestly,
5:11 to Christ, they w to marry.
6: 9 People who w to get rich fall into
2Ti 4: 3 what their itching ears w to hear.
Tit 3: 8 I w you to stress these things, so
Phm :14 I did not w to do anything without
Heb 6:11 We w each of you to show this same
6:12 We do not w you to become lazy, but
13:23 I w you to know that our brother
Jas 2:20 You foolish man, do you w evidence
4: 2 You w something but don't get it.
4: 2 but you cannot have what you w.
2Pe 3: 2 I w you to recall the words spoken
2Jn :12 but I do not w to use paper and ink.
3Jn :10 He also stops those who w to do so
:13 I do not w to do so with pen and ink.
Jude : 5 Though you already know all this, I w
Rev 11: 6 kind of plague as often as they w.

Wanted (Want)

Ex 4:19 the men who w to kill you are dead."
16: 3 of meat and ate all the food we w,
Ru 2:14 all she w and had some left over.
2Sa 3:17 you have w to make David your king.
3:19 the whole house of Benjamin w to do.
1Ki 5:10 all the cedar and pine logs he w,
9:11 the cedar and pine and gold he w.
13:33 Anyone who w to become a priest he
Est 2:13 Anything she w was given to her to
Ps 35:25 "Aha, just what we w!" or say, "We
71:24 for those who w to harm me have been
Ecc 2: 3 I w to see what was worth while for
Jer 49: 9 not steal only as much as they w?
Da 5:19 Those the king w to put to death, he
5:19 he put to death; those he w to spare,
5:19 he spared; those he w to promote, he
5:19 those he w to humble, he humbled.
7:19 "Then I w to know the true meaning
7:20 I also w to know about the ten horns
Ob : 5 not steal only as much as they w?
Jnh 4: 8 He w to die, and said, "It would be
Mt 14: 5 Herod w to kill John, but he was
18:23 a king who w to settle accounts
21:31 of the two did what his father w?"
Mk 3:13 those he w, and they came to him.
6:19 against John and w to kill him.
Lk 10:24 kings w to see what you see but did
10:29 he w to justify himself, so he asked
19: 3 He w to see who Jesus was, but being
Jn 6:11 who were seated as much as they w.
7:44 Some w to seize him, but no-one laid
16:19 Jesus saw that they w to ask him
18:28 w to be able to eat the Passover.
21:18 yourself and went where you w;
Ac 5:33 furious and w to put them to death.
10:10 He became hungry and w something to
13: 7 he w to hear the word of God.
14:13 crowd w to offer sacrifices to them.
15:37 Barnabas w to take John, also called
16: 3 Paul w to take him along on the
18:27 Apollos w to go to Achaia, the
19:30 Paul w to appear before the crowd,
22:30 the commander w to find out exactly
23:28 I w to know why they were accusing
24:27 because Felix w to grant a favour
27:13 they had obtained what they w;
27:38 they had eaten as much as they w,
27:43 the centurion w to spare Paul's life
28:18 They examined me and w to release me,
1Co 12:18 of them, just as he w them to be.
1Th 2:18 For we w to come to you—certainly I,
Heb 6:17 God w to make the unchanging nature
12:17 when he w to inherit this blessing,

Wanting (Want)

Da 5:27 weighed on the scales and found w.
Mt 12:46 stood outside, w to speak to him.
12:47 outside, w to speak to you."
Mk 15:15 W to satisfy the crowd, Pilate
Lk 8:20 are standing outside, w to see you."
23: 8 long time he had been w to see him.
23:20 W to release Jesus, Pilate appealed
Ac 23:15 on the pretext of w more accurate
23:20 w more accurate information about him
2Pe 3: 9 He is patient with you, not w anyone

Wanton

Isa 47: 8 "Now then, listen, you w creature,
Na 3: 4 all because of the w lust of a

Wants (Want)

Ge 19: 9 and now he w to play the judge!
43:18 He w to attack us and overpower us
Ex 12:48 "An alien living among you who w to
Nu 6: 2 'If a man or woman w to make a
9:14 "'An alien living among you who w
Ru 3:13 w to redeem, good; let him redeem.
1Sa 18:25 'The king w no other price for the
Jer 22:28 broken pot, an object no-one w? Why
48:38 that no-one w," declares the LORD.
Eze 46: 7 and with the lambs as much as he w
Mt 5:40 if someone w to sue you and take
5:42 the one who w to borrow from you.
16:25 For whoever w to save his life will
20:26 Not so with you. Instead, whoever w
20:27 whoever w to be first must be your
27:43 Let God rescue him now if he w him,
Mk 8:35 For whoever w to save his life will
9:35 "If anyone w to be first, he must be
10:43 Not so with you. Instead, whoever w
10:44 whoever w to be first must be slave
Lk 5:39 no-one after drinking old wine w the
9:24 For whoever w to save his life will
12:47 does not do what his master w will
13:31 somewhere else. Herod w to kill you
14:28 "Suppose one of you w to build a
Jn 7: 4 No-one who w to become a public
Ro 9:18 Therefore God has mercy on whom he w
9:18 and he hardens whom he w to harden.
1Co 7:36 to marry, he should do as he w.
11:16 If anyone w to be contentious about
1Ti 2: 4 who w all men to be saved and to
2Ti 2: 4 w to please his commanding officer.
3:12 everyone who w to live a godly life
Jas 3: 4 rudder wherever the pilot w to go.
1Pe 5: 2 as God w you to be; not greedy for
Rev 11: 5 anyone who w to harm them must die.

War (Warfare, War-horses, Warrior, Warrior's, Warriors, Wars)

Ge 14: 2 went to w against Bera king of Sodom,
31:26 off my daughters like captives in w.
Ex 1:10 if w breaks out, will join our
13:17 For God said, "If they face w, they
17:16 The LORD will be at w against the
32:17 There is the sound of w in the camp."
Nu 31: 3 "Arm some of your men to go to w
32: 6 go to w while you sit here?
Dt 2: 5 Do not provoke them to w, for I will
2: 9 the Moabites or provoke them to w,
2:19 harass them or provoke them to w,
4:34 by w, by a mighty hand and an
20: 1 you go to w against your enemies and
20:20 until the city at w with you falls.
21:10 you go to w against your enemies and
24: 5 married, he must not be sent to w
Jos 4:13 LORD to the plains of Jericho for w.
6:10 "Do not give a w cry, do not raise
9: 2 they came together to make w against
11:18 Joshua waged w against all these
11:20 hearts to wage w against Israel,
11:23 Then the land had rest from w.
14:15 Then the land had rest from w.
22:12 at Shiloh to go to w against them.
22:33 talked no more about going to w
Jdg 3:10 became Israel's judge and went to w.
5: 8 they chose new gods, w came to the
11: 4 when the Ammonites made w on Israel,
11:27 me wrong by waging w against me.
21:22 not get wives for them during the w,
1Sa 8:12 to make weapons of w and equipment
14:52 was bitter w with the Philistines,
15:18 the Amalekites; make w on them until
17: 1 gathered their forces for w and
17:13 sons had followed Saul to the w:
17:20 positions, shouting the w cry.
19: 8 Once more w broke out, and David
2Sa 1:27 The weapons of w have perished!"
3: 1 The w between the house of Saul and
3: 6 During the w between the house of
8:10 who had been at w with Tou.
11: 1 at the time when kings go off to w,
11: 7 were and how the w was going.
1Ki 8:44 "When your people go to w against
12:21 make w against the house of Israel
15: 6 There was w between Rehoboam and
15: 7 was w between Abijah and Jeroboam.
15:16 There was w between Asa and Baasha
15:32 There was w between Asa and Baasha
20:18 come out for w, take them alive."
22: 1 For three years there was no w
22: 6 "Shall I go to w against Ramoth
22:15 "Micaiah, shall we go to w against
2Ki 6: 8 Now the king of Aram was at w with
8:28 to w against Hazael king of Aram
13:12 including his w against Amaziah king
14:15 including his w against Amaziah king
24:16 strong and fit for w, and a thousand
1Ch 5:10 During Saul's reign they waged w
1Ch 5:19 They waged w against the Hagrites,
7:11 fighting men ready to go out to w.
18:10 who had been at w with Tou.
20: 1 at the time when kings go off to w,
20: 4 In the course of time, w broke out
2Ch 6:34 "When your people go to w against
11: 1 men—to make w against Israel
13: 2 was w between Abijah and Jeroboam.
14: 6 No-one was at w with him during
15:19 There was no more w until the
16: 9 and from now on you will be at w."
17:10 did not make w with Jehoshaphat.
18: 3 people; we will join you in the w."
18: 5 "Shall we go to w against Ramoth
18:14 "Micaiah, shall we go to w against
20: 1 came to make w on Jehoshaphat.
22: 5 to w against Hazael king of Aram
25:13 not allowed to take part in the w
26: 6 He went to w against the Philistines
26:13 army of 307,500 men trained for w,
27: 5 Jotham made w on the king of the
28:12 those who were arriving from the w.
32: 2 he intended to make w on Jerusalem,
35:21 but the house with which I am at w.
Job 38:23 trouble, for days of w and battle?
Ps 27: 3 will not fear; though w break out
55:21 His speech is smooth as butter, yet w
68:30 Scatter the nations who delight in w.
76: 3 and the swords, the weapons of w.
120: 7 but when I speak, they are for w.
140: 2 hearts and stir up w every day.
144: 1 hands for w, my fingers for battle.
Pr 20:18 if you wage w, obtain guidance.
24: 6 for waging w you need guidance, and
Ecc 3: 8 a time for w and a time for peace.
8: 8 As no-one is discharged in time of w,
9:18 Wisdom is better than weapons of w,
Isa 2: 4 nor will they train for w any more.
8: 9 Raise the w cry, you nations, and be
13: 4 Almighty is mustering an army for w.
41:12 Those who wage w against you will be
42:25 burning anger, the violence of w.
Jer 4:16 a w cry against the cities of Judah.
21: 4 weapons of w that are in your hands,
28: 8 you and me have prophesied w,
42:14 where we will not see w or hear the
51:20 "You are my w club, my weapon for
Eze 17:17 will be of no help to him in w,
26:10 at the noise of the w horses,
27:14 horses, w horses and mules for your
32:27 the grave with their weapons of w,
38: 8 a land that has recovered from w,
39: 9 and arrows, the w clubs and spears.
Da 7:21 I watched, this horn was waging w
9:26 W will continue until the end,
10: 1 was true and it concerned a great w.
11:10 His sons will prepare for w and
11:25 The king of the South will wage w
Hos 10: 9 Did not w overtake the evildoers in
Joel 3: 9 Prepare for w! Rouse the warriors!
Am 1:14 amid w cries on the day of battle,
2: 2 w cries and the blast of the trumpet.
Mic 3: 5 they prepare to wage w against him.
4: 3 nor will they train for w any more.
Lk 14:31 to go to w against another king.
Ro 7:23 waging w against the law of my mind
2Co 10: 3 we do not wage w as the world does.
1Pe 2:11 desires, which w against your soul.
Rev 12: 7 there was w in heaven. Michael and
12:17 went off to make w against the rest
13: 4 beast? Who can make w against him?"
13: 7 He was given power to make w against
17:14 They will make w against the Lamb,
19:11 With justice he judges and makes w.
19:19 w against the rider on the horse

Ward

2Sa 5: 6 blind and the lame can w you off.
Isa 47:11 that you cannot w off with a ransom;
Lam 2:14 your sin to w off your captivity.

Warder

Ge 39:21 favour in the eyes of the prison w.
39:22 the w put Joseph in charge of all
39:23 The w paid no attention to anything

Wardrobe
2Ki 10:22 Jehu said to the keeper of the w,
22:14 the son of Harhas, keeper of the w.
2Ch 34:22 the son of Hasrah, keeper of the w.

Wares
2Ki 8: 9 of all the finest w of Damascus.
Eze 27: 9 came alongside to trade for your w.
27:13 and articles of bronze for your w.
27:17 honey, oil and balm for your w.
27:19 iron, cassia and calamus for your w.
27:25 serve as carriers for your w.
27:27 Your wealth, merchandise and w, your
27:33 with your great wealth and your w
27:34 your w and all your company have

Warfare (War)
Jdg 3: 2 (he did this only to teach w to the
1Ki 14:30 There was continual w between
2Ch 12:15 w between Rehoboam and Jeroboam.
Isa 27: 8 By w and exile you contend with her—

War-horses (Horse, War)
Hos 14: 3 cannot save us; we will not mount w.
Zec 9:10 Ephraim and the w from Jerusalem,

Warm (Lukewarm, Warmed, Warming, Warms)
Jos 9:12 This bread of ours was w when we
1Ki 1: 1 w even when they put covers over him.
1: 2 that our lord the king may keep w."
2Ki 4:34 out upon him, the boy's body grew w.
Job 39:14 ground and lets them w in the sand,
Ecc 4:11 lie down together, they will keep w.
4:11 But how can one keep w alone?
Isa 44:16 says, "Ah! I am w; I see the fire.
47:14 Here are no coals to w anyone;
Hag 1: 6 You put on clothes, but are not w.
Jn 18:18 a fire they had made to keep w.
Jas 2:16 "Go, I wish you well; keep w and

Warmed (Warm)
Mk 14:54 guards and w himself at the fire.

Warming (Warm)
Job 31:20 his heart did not bless me for w him
Mk 14:67 she saw Peter w himself, she looked
Jn 18:18 was standing with them, w himself.
18:25 Simon Peter stood w himself, he was

Warms (Warm)
Isa 44:15 some of it he takes and w himself,
44:16 He also w himself and says, "Ah! I

Warn (Warned, Warning, Warnings, Warns)
Ex 19:21 the LORD said to him, "Go down and w
Nu 24:14 but come, let me w you of what this
1Sa 8: 9 Now listen to them; but w them
1Ki 2:42 you swear by the LORD and w you,
2Ch 19:10 you are to w them not to sin
Ps 81: 8 "Hear, O my people, and I will w you
Jer 42:19 Be sure of this: I w you today
Eze 3:18 you do not w him or speak out to
3:19 if you do w the wicked man and he
3:20 Since you did not w him, he will die
3:21 if you do w the righteous man not to
33: 3 blows the trumpet to w the people,
33: 6 does not blow the trumpet to w the
33: 9 if you do w the wicked man to turn
Lk 16:28 for I have five brothers. Let him w
Ac 4:17 we must w these men to speak no
1Co 4:14 but to w you, as my dear children.
Gal 5:21 I w you, as I did before, that those
1Th 5:14 we urge you, brothers, w those who
2Th 3:15 as an enemy, but w him as a brother.
2Ti 2:14 W them before God against
Tit 3:10 W a divisive person once, and then w
Rev 22:18 I w everyone who hears the words of

Warned (Warn)
Ge 43: 3 Judah said to him, "The man w us
Ex 19:23 because you yourself w us, 'Put
Ex 21:29 the owner has been w but has not
Nu 16:26 He w the assembly, "Move back from
1Sa 19: 2 w him, "My father Saul is looking
19:11 But Michal, David's wife, w him, "If
2Sa 2:22 Again Abner w Asahel, "Stop chasing
1Ki 13:26 as the word of the LORD had w him."
2Ki 6:10 Time and again Elisha w the king, so
17:13 The LORD w Israel and Judah through
17:23 as he had w through all his servants
Ne 9:29 "You w them to return to your law,
13:15 Therefore I w them against selling
13:21 I w them and said, "Why do you spend
Ps 2:10 Therefore, you kings, be wise; be w,
19:11 By them is your servant w; in
Ecc 12:12 Be w, my son, of anything in
Jer 11: 7 I w them again and again, saying,
18: 8 if that nation I w repents of its
22:21 I w you when you felt secure, but
Mt 2:12 having been w in a dream not to go
2:22 Having been w in a dream, he
3: 7 w you to flee from the coming wrath?
9:30 their sight was restored. Jesus w
16:20 he w his disciples not to tell
Mk 8:15 "Be careful," Jesus w them. "Watch
8:30 Jesus w them not to tell anyone
Lk 3: 7 w you to flee from the coming wrath?
9:21 Jesus strictly w them not to tell
Jn 16: 4 you will remember that I w you.
Ac 2:40 With many other words he w them; and
27: 9 was after the Fast. So Paul w them,
1Th 4: 6 we have already told you and w you.
Heb 8: 5 This is why Moses was w when he was
11: 7 By faith Noah, when w about things
12:25 refused him who w them on earth,

Warning (Warn)
Nu 26:10 And they served as a w sign.
2Ki 10:24 eighty men outside with this w:
Ecc 4:13 who no longer knows how to take w.
Isa 8:11 w me not to follow the way of this
Jer 6: 8 Take w, O Jerusalem, or I will turn
6:10 To whom can I speak and give w? Who
Eze 3:17 I speak and give them w from me.
3:21 will surely live because he took w,
5:15 a w and an object of horror to the
23:48 may take w and not imitate you.
33: 4 the trumpet but does not take w
33: 5 the trumpet but did not take w,
33: 5 If he had taken w, he would have
33: 7 I speak and give them w from me.
Mt 8:24 Without w, a furious storm came up
12:16 w them not to tell who he was.
Mk 1:43 him away at once with a strong w:
Ac 20:31 I never stopped w each of you night
2Co 13: 2 I already gave you a w when I was
1Ti 5:20 so that the others may take w.

Warnings (Warn)
2Ki 17:15 fathers and the w he had given them.
Ne 9:34 commands or the w you gave them.
Job 33:16 their ears and terrify them with w,
1Co 10:11 and were written down as w for us,

Warns (Warn)
Ac 20:23 the Holy Spirit w me that prison
Heb 12:25 away from him who w us from heaven?

Warped
Dt 32: 5 but a w and crooked generation.
Pr 12: 8 but men with w minds are despised.
Tit 3:11 You may be sure that such a man is w

Warranted
2Co 12: 6 of me than is w by what I do or say.

Warrior (War)
Ge 10: 8 grew to be a mighty w on the earth.
Ex 15: 3 The LORD is a w; the LORD is his
Jdg 6:12 "The LORD is with you, mighty w.
11: 1 Jephthah the Gileadite was a mighty w
1Sa 16:18 He is a brave man and a w. He speaks
1Ch 1:10 who grew to be a mighty w on earth.
12:28 Zadok, a brave young w, with 22
28: 3 you are a w and have shed blood.'
2Ch 28: 7 Zicri, an Ephraimite w, killed
Job 16:14 upon me; he rushes at me like a w.
Ps 33:16 no w escapes by his great strength.
89:19 "I have bestowed strength on a w; I
127: 4 Like arrows in the hands of a w are
Pr 16:32 Better a patient man than a w, a man
Isa 3: 2 the hero and w, the judge and
42:13 like a w he will stir up his zeal;
Jer 14: 9 like a w powerless to save? You are
20:11 the LORD is with me like a mighty w;
46:12 One w will stumble over another;
Am 2:14 and the w will not save his life.
Zep 1:14 bitter, the shouting of the w there.

Warrior's (War)
2Sa 18:11 ten shekels of silver and a w belt."
Ps 120: 4 punish you with a w sharp arrows
Isa 9: 5 Every w boot used in battle and
Zec 9:13 Greece, and make you like a w sword.

Warriors (War)
Jdg 5:11 righteous acts of his w in Israel.
18: 2 the Danites sent five w from Zorah
1Sa 2: 4 "The bows of the w are broken, but
2Sa 20: 7 Pelethites and all the mighty w went
1Ch 5:24 They were brave w, famous men, and
7:40 brave w and outstanding leaders.
8:40 The sons of Ulam were brave w who
12: 1 the w who helped him in battle;
12: 8 They were brave w, ready for battle
12:21 for all of them were brave w, and
12:25 men of Simeon, w ready for battle
12:30 men of Ephraim, brave w, famous in
28: 1 the mighty men and all the brave w.
Ps 76: 5 not one of the w can lift his hands.
SS 3: 7 by sixty w, the noblest of Israel,
4: 4 shields, all of them shields of w.
Isa 3:25 fall by the sword, your w in battle.
10:16 a wasting disease upon his sturdy w;
13: 3 I have summoned my w to carry out my
21:17 The survivors of the bowmen, the w
49:24 Can plunder be taken from w, or
49:25 "Yes, captives will be taken from w,
Jer 5:16 grave; all of them are mighty w.
46: 5 retreating, their w are defeated.
46: 9 O charioteers! March on, O w—men
46:15 Why will your w be laid low? They
48:14 "How can you say, 'We are w, men
48:41 In that day the hearts of Moab's w
49:22 In that day the hearts of Edom's w
50: 9 w who do not return empty-handed.
50:36 A sword against her w! They will be
51:30 Babylon's w have stopped fighting;
51:56 Babylon; her w will be captured,
51:57 her governors, officers and w as
Lam 1:15 "The Lord has rejected all the w in
Eze 23: 5 after her lovers, the Assyrians—w
23:12 w in full dress, mounted horsemen,
32:27 uncircumcised w who have fallen,
32:27 though the terror of these w had
Hos 10:13 own strength and on your many w,
Joel 2: 7 They charge like w; they scale walls
3: 9 Prepare for war! Rouse the w! Let
3:11 Bring down your w, O LORD!
Am 2:16 Even the bravest w will flee naked
Ob : 9 Your w, O Teman, will be terrified,
Na 2: 3 are red; the w are clad in scarlet.
Hab 3:14 his w stormed out to scatter us,

Wars (War)
Nu 21:14 That is why the Book of the W of the
Jdg 3: 1 experienced any of the w in Canaan
1Ki 5: 3 "You know that because of the w
14:19 his w and how he ruled, are written
1Ch 22: 8 much blood and have fought many w.
2Ch 27: 7 including all his w and the other
Ps 46: 9 He makes w cease to the ends of the
Mt 24: 6 You will hear of w and rumours of w,
Mk 13: 7 you hear of w and rumours of w, do
Lk 21: 9 you hear of w and revolutions, do

Warts
Lev 22:22 w or festering or running sores.

Wash (Washed, Washerman's, Washing, Washings, Whitewash, Whitewashed)
Ge 18: 4 w your feet and rest under this tree.
19: 2 You can w your feet and spend the
24:32 for him and his men to w their feet.
43:24 gave them water to w their feet and
49:11 he will w his garments in wine,
Ex 19:10 Make them w their clothes
29: 4 of Meeting and w them with water.
29:17 Cut the ram into pieces and w the
30:19 Aaron and his sons are to w their
30:20 they shall w with water so that they
30:21 they shall w their hands and feet so
40:12 of Meeting and w them with water.
40:31 used it to w their hands and feet.
Lev 1: 9 He is to w the inner parts and the
1:13 He is to w the inner parts and the
6:27 you must w it in a holy place.
11:25 their carcasses must w his clothes,
11:28 their carcasses must w his clothes,
11:40 of the carcass must w his clothes,
11:40 up the carcass must w his clothes,
13: 6 w his clothes, and he will be clean.
13:34 w his clothes, and he will be clean.
14: 8 "The person to be cleansed must w
14: 9 He must w his clothes and bathe
14:47 in the house must w his clothes.
15: 5 Anyone who touches his bed must w
15: 6 w his clothes and bathe with water,
15: 7 w his clothes and bathe with water,
15: 8 that person must w his clothes and
15:10 w his clothes and bathe with water,
15:11 w his clothes and bathe with water,
15:13 he must w his clothes and bathe
15:21 Whoever touches her bed must w his
15:22 w his clothes and bathe with water,
15:27 w his clothes and bathe with water,
16:26 as a scapegoat must w his clothes
16:28 The man who burns them must w his
17:15 w his clothes and bathe with water,
17:16 if he does not w his clothes and
Nu 5:23 w them off into the bitter water.
8: 7 whole bodies and w their clothes,
19: 7 After that, the priest must w his
19: 8 The man who burns it must also w his
19:10 the heifer must also w his clothes,
19:19 The person being cleansed must w his
19:21 cleansing must also w his clothes,
31:24 On the seventh day w your clothes
Dt 21: 6 shall w their hands over the heifer
23:11 as evening approaches he is to w
Ru 3: 3 W and perfume yourself, and put on
1Sa 25:41 w the feet of my master's servants."
2Sa 11: 8 down to your house and w your feet.
2Ki 5:10 "Go, w yourself seven times in the
5:12 I w in them and be cleansed?"
5:13 he tells you, 'W and be cleansed'?"
Job 14:19 stones and torrents w away the soil,
Ps 26: 6 I w my hands in innocence, and go
51: 2 W away all my iniquity and cleanse
51: 7 and I shall be clean; w me, and I
SS 8: 7 love; rivers cannot w it away.
Isa 1:16 w and make yourselves clean. Take
4: 4 The Lord will w away the filth of
Jer 2:22 Although you w yourself with soda
4:14 O Jerusalem, w the evil from your
Mt 6:17 oil on your head and w your face,
15: 2 w their hands before they eat!"
Mk 7: 4 they do not eat unless they w.
Lk 11:38 Jesus did not first w before the
Jn 9: 7 told him, "w in the Pool of Siloam"
9:11 He told me to go to Siloam and w. So
13: 5 and began to w his disciples' feet,
13: 6 "Lord, are you going to w my feet?
13: 8 "No," said Peter, "you shall never w
13: 8 I w you, you have no part with me."
13:10 w his feet; his whole body is clean.
13:14 also should w one another's feet.
Ac 22:16 be baptised and w your sins away,
Jas 4: 8 W your hands, you sinners, and
Rev 22:14 "Blessed are those who w their robes,

Washbasin (Basin)
Ps 60: 8 Moab is my w, upon Edom I toss my
108: 9 Moab is my w, upon Edom I toss my

Washed (Wash)
Ge 43:31 After he had w his face, he came out
Ex 19:14 them, and they w their clothes.
40:32 They w whenever they entered the
Lev 8: 6 sons forward and w them with water.
8:21 He w the inner parts and the legs
9:14 He w the inner parts and the legs
13:54 that the contaminated article be w.
13:55 After the affected article has been w
13:56 faded after the article has been w,
13:58 has been w and is rid of the mildew,
13:58 be w again, and it will be clean."
15:17 semen on it must be w with water,
Nu 8:21 The Levites purified themselves and w
Jdg 19:21 After they had w their feet, they
2Sa 12:20 After he had w, put on lotions and
19:24 or w his clothes from the day the
1Ki 22:38 They w the chariot at a pool in
Job 9:30 Even if I w myself with soap and my
22:16 their foundations w away by a flood.
Ps 73:13 vain have I w my hands in innocence.
SS 5: 3 w my feet—must I soil them again?
5:12 w in milk, mounted like jewels.
Eze 16: 4 nor were you w with water to make
16: 9 "'I bathed you with water and w the
40:38 where the burnt offerings were w.
Mt 27:24 w his hands in front of the crowd.
Jn 9: 7 went and w, and came home seeing.
9:11 I went and w, and then I could see."
9:15 replied, "and I w, and now I see.
13:14 your Lord and Teacher, have w your
Ac 9:37 w and placed in an upstairs room.
16:33 jailer took them and w their wounds;
1Co 6:11 But you were w, you were sanctified,
Heb 10:22 having our bodies w with pure water.
2Pe 2:22 "A sow that is w goes back to her
Rev 7:14 they have w their robes and made

Washerman's (Wash)
2Ki 18:17 Pool, on the road to the W Field.
Isa 7: 3 Pool, on the road to the W Field.
36: 2 Pool, on the road to the W Field,

Washing (Wash)
Ex 30:18 basin, with its bronze stand, for w.
40:30 the altar and put water in it for w,
2Ch 4: 6 He then made ten basins for w and
4: 6 was to be used by the priests for w.
Job 9:30 with soap and my hands with w soda,
SS 4: 2 just shorn, coming up from the w.
6: 6 flock of sheep coming up from the w.
Mk 7: 3 give their hands a ceremonial w,
7: 4 w of cups, pitchers and kettles.)
Lk 5: 2 fishermen, who were w their nets.
Jn 2: 6 used by the Jews for ceremonial w,
3:25 Jew over the matter of ceremonial w.
13:12 he had finished w their feet, he put
Eph 5:26 the w with water through the word,
1Ti 5:10 showing hospitality, w the feet of
Tit 3: 5 He saved us through the w of rebirth

Washings (Wash)
Heb 9:10 drink and various ceremonial w—

Waste (Wasted, Wastes, Wasting)
Lev 26:31 ruins and lay w your sanctuaries,
26:32 I will lay w the land, so that your
26:33 Your land will be laid w, and your
26:39 Those of you who are left will w
26:39 fathers' sins they will w away.
Nu 5:21 to w away and your abdomen to swell.
5:27 will swell and her thigh w away,
Dt 29:23 The whole land will be a burning w
32:10 him, in a barren and howling w.
Jdg 16:24 w our land and multiplied our slain."
2Ki 19:17 Assyrian kings have laid w these
22:19 would become accursed and laid w,
1Ch 20: 1 He laid w the land of the Ammonites
Job 12:24 wandering through a trackless w.
Ps 107:34 fruitful land into a salt w, because
Ps 107:40 made them wander in a trackless w.
112:10 he will gnash his teeth and w away;
Isa 1: 7 w as when overthrown by strangers.
6:13 the land, it will again be laid w.
7:16 two kings you dread will be laid w.
17: 4 the fat of his body will w away.
24: 1 See, the LORD is going to lay w the
24: 3 The earth will be completely laid w
24:16 But I said, "I w away, I w away!
37:18 Assyrian kings have laid w all
42:15 I will lay w the mountains and hills
49:17 who laid you w depart from you.
49:19 made desolate and your land laid w,
64: 7 made us w away because of our sins.
Jer 2:15 They have laid w his land; his towns
4: 7 He has left his place to lay w your
9:11 and I will lay w the towns of Judah
9:12 laid w like a desert that no-one can
12:11 w because there is no-one who cares.
18:16 Their land will be laid w, an object
25:37 The peaceful meadows will be laid w
32:43 'It is a desolate w, without men or
33:10 desolate w, without men or animals.
34:22 And I will lay w the towns of Judah
44:22 a desolate w without inhabitants,
46:19 for Memphis will be laid w and lie
48: 9 for she will be laid w; her towns
50: 3 will attack her and lay w her land.
51:29 to lay w the land of Babylon so
Lam 2: 6 He has laid w his dwelling like a
4: 9 they w away for lack of food from
Eze 4:17 will w away because of their sin.
6: 6 the towns will be laid w and the
6: 6 so that your altars will be laid w
6:14 make the land a desolate w from the
12:20 The inhabited towns will be laid w
24:23 will w away because of your sins
25: 3 land of Israel when it was laid w
25:13 I will lay it w, and from Teman to
29:10 a desolate w from Migdol to Aswan,
30:12 lay w the land and everything in it.
30:14 I will lay w Upper Egypt, set fire
33:28 I will make the land a desolate w,
33:29 I have made the land a desolate w
35: 3 you and make you a desolate w.
35: 7 I will make Mount Seir a desolate w
35:12 You said, "They have been laid w and
36:35 "This land that was laid w has
Hos 4: 3 and all who live in it w away; the
5: 9 Ephraim will be laid w on the day of
8:10 They will begin to w away under the
Joel 1: 7 has laid w my vines and ruined my
2: 3 a desert w—nothing escapes them.
3:19 Edom a desert w, because of violence
Na 2: 2 destroyers have laid them w and
Mt 26: 8 "Why this w?" they asked.
Mk 14: 4 "Why this w of perfume?

Wasted (Waste)
Ge 47:13 Canaan w away because of the famine.
Ps 32: 3 I kept silent, my bones w away
106:43 and they w away in their sin.
Pr 23: 8 and will have w your compliments.
Lam 2: 8 walls lament; together they w away.
Jn 6:12 are left over. Let nothing be w."
Gal 4:11 I fear for you, that somehow I have w

Wasteland (Land)
Nu 21:20 the top of Pisgah overlooks the w.
23:28 the top of Peor, overlooking the w.
2Sa 2:24 Giah on the way to the w of Gibeon.
Job 6:18 they go up into the w and perish.
24: 5 w provides food for their children.
38:27 to satisfy a desolate w and make it
39: 6 I gave him the w as his home, the
Ps 68: 7 you marched through the w,
78:40 the desert and grieved him in the w!
106:14 in the w they put God to the test.
Isa 5: 6 I will make it a w, neither pruned
32:14 watchtower will become a w for ever,
41:19 I will set pines in the w, the fir
43:19 in the desert and streams in the w.
43:20 in the desert and streams in the w,
Jer 12:10 my pleasant field into a desolate w.
12:11 will be made a w, parched and

Jer 25:11 country will become a desolate **w**,
Eze 29: 9 Egypt will become a desolate **w**. Then
Zep 2: 9 weeds and salt pits, a **w** for ever.
Mal 1: 3 I have turned his mountains into a **w**

Wastelands (Land)
Job 30: 3 parched land in desolate **w** at night.
Ps 107: 4 Some wandered in desert **w**, finding
Isa 51: 3 her **w** like the garden of the LORD.
Jer 17: 6 He will be like a bush in the **w**; he

Wastes (Waste)
Nu 5:22 swells and your thigh **w** away.
Job 13:28 "So man **w** away like something rotten,
33:21 His flesh **w** away to nothing, and his
Isa 10:18 destroy, as when a sick man **w** away.
33: 9 The land mourns and **w** away, Lebanon

Wasting (Waste)
Lev 26:16 **w** diseases and fever that will
Dt 28:22 LORD will strike you with **w** disease
32:24 I will send **w** famine against them,
Ps 106:15 for, but sent a **w** disease upon them.
Isa 10:16 LORD Almighty, will send a **w** disease
Eze 33:10 and we are **w** away because of them.
Lk 16: 1 was accused of **w** his possessions.
2Co 4:16 Though outwardly we are **w** away, yet

Watch (Watched, Watcher, Watches, Watchful, Watching, Watchman, Watchmen)
Ge 21:16 thought, "I cannot **w** the boy die.
28:15 I am with you and will **w** over you
28:20 "If God will be with me and will **w**
31:49 "May the LORD keep **w** between you and
Ex 14:24 During the last **w** of the night the
Dt 4: 9 Only be careful, and **w** yourselves
4:15 **w** yourselves very carefully,
Jdg 7:17 "**W** me," he told them. "Follow my
7:19 at the beginning of the middle **w**,
21:21 **w**. When the girls of Shiloh come out
Ru 2: 9 **W** the field where the men are
1Sa 11:11 during the last **w** of the night they
17:28 you came down only to **w** the battle."
19:11 Saul sent men to David's house to **w**
2Sa 13: 5 **w** her and then eat it from her hand.
13:34 Now the man standing **w** looked up and
1Ki 2: 4 'If your descendants **w** how they live,
2Ch 23: 4 Sabbath are to keep **w** at the doors,
Ne 11:19 who kept **w** at the gates—172 men.
Job 13:27 you keep close **w** on all my paths by
21:32 grave, and **w** is kept over his tomb.
33:11 he keeps close **w** on all my paths.'
39: 1 Do you **w** when the doe bears her fawn?
Ps 32: 8 I will counsel you and **w** over you.
39: 1 I said, "I will **w** my ways and keep
56: 6 They conspire, they lurk, they **w** my
59: T Saul had sent men to **w** David's house
59: 9 O my Strength, I **w** for you; you,
66: 7 his eyes **w** the nations—let not the
80:14 heaven and see! **W** over this vine,
90: 4 gone by, or like a **w** in the night.
121: 7 all harm—he will **w** over your life;
121: 8 the LORD will **w** over your coming and
141: 3 keep **w** over the door of my lips.
Pr 4: 6 love her, and she will **w** over you.
6:22 they will **w** over you; when you awake,
15: 3 keeping **w** on the wicked and the
22:12 The eyes of the LORD keep **w** over
Isa 27: 3 I, the LORD, **w** over it; I water it
Jer 24: 6 My eyes will **w** over them for their
31:10 **w** over his flock like a shepherd.'
31:28 **w** over them to build and to plant,"
48:19 Stand by the road and **w**, you who
Eze 12: 3 as they **w**, set out and go from where
12: 4 During the daytime, while they **w**,
12: 5 While they **w**, dig through the wall
Da 7:11 "Then I continued to **w** because of
Mic 7: 7 for me, I **w** in hope for the LORD, I
Na 2: 1 Guard the fortress, **w** the road,
Hab 1: 5 "Look at the nations and **w**—and be
2: 1 I will stand at my **w** and station
Zec 9: 8 my people, for now I am keeping **w**.
Mt 7:15 "**W** out for false prophets. They come
14:25 During the fourth **w** of the night
24: 4 Jesus answered: "**W** out that no-one
24:42 "Therefore keep **w**, because you do
24:43 he would have kept **w** and would not
25:13 "Therefore keep **w**, because you do
26:38 Stay here and keep **w** with me."
26:40 "Could you men not keep **w** with me
26:41 "**W** and pray so that you will not
27:36 sitting down, they kept **w** over him
Mk 6:48 About the fourth **w** of the night he
8:15 "**W** out for the yeast of the
12:38 Jesus said, "**W** out for the teachers
13: 5 Jesus said to them: "**W** out that
13:34 tells the one at the door to keep **w**.
13:35 "Therefore keep **w** because you do not
13:37 to you, I say to everyone: '**W**!'
14:34 to them. "Stay here and keep **w**."
14:37 Could you not keep **w** for one hour?
14:38 **W** and pray so that you will not fall
Lk 2: 8 **w** over their flocks at night.
12:15 he said to them, "**W** out! Be on your
12:38 the second or third **w** of the night.
17: 3 **w** yourselves. "If your brother sins,
20:20 Keeping a close **w** on him, they sent
21: 8 He replied: "**W** out that you are not
21:36 Be always on the **w**, and pray that
Ac 9:24 Day and night they kept close **w** on
20:28 Keep **w** over yourselves and all the
Ro 16:17 I urge you, brothers, to **w** out for
Gal 5:15 **w** out or you will be destroyed by
6: 1 But **w** yourself, or you also may be
Php 3: 2 **W** out for those dogs, those men who
1Ti 4:16 **W** your life and doctrine closely.
Heb 13:17 They keep **w** over you as men who must
2Jn : 8 **W** out that you do not lose what you

Watched (Watch)
Ge 24:21 Without saying a word, the man **w** her
Ex 2:11 and **w** them at their hard labour.
3:16 I have **w** over you and have seen what
Dt 2: 7 He has **w** over your journey through
33: 9 but he **w** over your word and guarded
Jos 4:11 the other side while the people **w**.
Jdg 13:19 thing while Manoah and his wife **w**:
1Sa 17:55 Saul **w** David going out to meet the
2Sa 6:16 daughter of Saul **w** from a window.
1Ch 15:29 daughter of Saul **w** from a window.
Job 10:12 in your providence **w** over my spirit.
29: 2 by, for the days when God **w** over me,
Jer 31:28 Just as I **w** over them to uproot and
Lam 4:17 from our towers we **w** for a nation
Eze 10: 2 And as I **w**, he went in.
10:19 While I **w**, the cherubim spread their
12: 7 them on my shoulders while they **w**.
Da 5: 5 The king **w** the hand as it wrote.
7: 4 I **w** until its wings were torn off
7:21 I **w**, this horn was waging war
8: 4 I **w** the ram as he charged towards
Mt 26:16 then on Judas **w** for an opportunity
Mk 3: 2 so they **w** him closely to see if he
12:41 **w** the crowd putting their money into
14:11 So he **w** for an opportunity to hand
Lk 6: 7 so they **w** him closely to see if he
14: 1 Pharisee, he was being carefully **w**.
22: 6 He consented, and **w** for an
Rev 6: 1 I **w** as the Lamb opened the first of
6:12 I **w** as he opened the sixth seal.
8:13 I **w**, I heard an eagle that was

Watcher (Watch)
Job 7:20 what have I done to you, O **w** of men?

Watches (Watch)
Nu 19: 5 While he **w**, the heifer is to be
Job 24:15 The eye of the adulterer **w** for dusk;
Ps 1: 6 For the LORD **w** over the way of the
33:14 from his dwelling-place he **w** all who
63: 6 of you through the **w** of the night.
119:148 My eyes stay open through the **w** of
121: 3 he who **w** over you will not slumber;
121: 4 indeed, he who **w** over Israel will
121: 5 The LORD **w** over you—the LORD is
127: 1 Unless the LORD **w** over the city, the
145:20 The LORD **w** over all who love him,
146: 9 The LORD **w** over the alien and
Pr 31:27 She **w** over the affairs of her
Ecc 11: 4 Whoever **w** the wind will not plant;
Lam 2:19 Arise, cry out in the night, as the **w**
4:16 them; he no longer **w** over them.

Watchful (Watch)
Zec 12: 4 "I will keep a **w** eye over the house
Col 4: 2 Devote yourselves to prayer, being **w**

Watching (Watch)
Ge 30:31 tending your flocks and **w** over them:
Ex 33: 8 **w** Moses until he entered the tent.
Dt 28:32 and you will wear out your eyes **w**
Jdg 16:27 men and women **w** Samson perform.
1Sa 4:13 **w**, because his heart feared for the
6: 9 keep **w** it. If it goes up to its own
25:21 "It's been useless—all my **w** over
2Ki 2:15 who were **w**, said, "The spirit of
Ezr 5: 5 the eye of their God was **w** over the
Job 10:14 If I sinned, you would be **w** me and
Ps 10: 8 **w** in secret for his victims.
Pr 8:34 **w** daily at my doors, waiting at my
Jer 1:12 **w** to see that my word is fulfilled."
7:11 But I have been **w**! declares the LORD.
19:10 while those who go with you are **w**,
43: 9 "While the Jews are **w**, take some
44:27 For I am **w** over them for harm, not
Eze 12: 4 while they are **w**, go out like those
12: 6 are **w** and carry them out at dusk.
28:18 in the sight of all who were **w**.
Da 2:34 While you were **w**, a rock was cut out,
8:15 While I, Daniel, was **w** the vision
Zec 11:11 the flock who were **w** me knew it was
Mt 27:55 Many women were there, **w** from a
Mk 15:40 Some women were **w** from a distance.
Lk 12:37 master finds them **w** when he comes.
23:35 The people stood **w**, and the rulers
23:49 stood at a distance, **w** these things.
Jn 7:11 Now at the Feast the Jews were **w** for

Watchman (Watch)
2Sa 13:34 The **w** went and told the king, "I see
18:24 the **w** went up to the roof of the
18:25 The **w** called out to the king and
18:26 the **w** saw another man running, and
18:27 The **w** said, "It seems to me that the
Job 27:18 cocoon, like a hut made by a **w**.
Isa 21:11 "**W**, what is left of the night? **W**,
21:12 The **w** replies, "Morning is coming,
Eze 3:17 "Son of man, I have made you a **w** for
33: 2 of their men and make him their **w**,
33: 6 if the **w** sees the sword coming and
33: 6 the **w** accountable for his blood.'
33: 7 "Son of man, I have made you a **w** for
Hos 9: 8 along with my God, is the **w** over
Jn 10: 3 The **w** opens the gate for him, and

Watchmen (Watch)
Ps 127: 1 the city, the **w** stand guard in vain.
130: 6 more than **w** wait for the morning,
130: 6 more than **w** wait for the morning.
SS 3: 3 The **w** found me as they made their
5: 7 The **w** found me as they made their
5: 7 away my cloak, those **w** of the walls!
Isa 52: 8 Listen! Your **w** lift up their voices;
56:10 Israel's **w** are blind, they all lack
62: 6 I have posted **w** on your walls,
Jer 6:17 I appointed **w** over you and said,
31: 6 There will be a day when **w** cry out
51:12 station the **w**, prepare an ambush!
Mic 7: 4 The day of your **w** has come, the day

Watchtower (Tower)
2Ki 17: 9 From **w** to fortified city they built
18: 8 From **w** to fortified city, he
Isa 5: 2 He built a **w** in it and cut out a
21: 8 I stand on the **w**; every night I stay
32:14 citadel and **w** will become a wasteland
Mic 4: 8 As for you, O **w** of the flock,
Mt 21:33 dug a winepress in it and built a **w**.
Mk 12: 1 pit for the winepress and built a **w**.

Watchtowers (Tower)
1Ch 27:25 the towns, the villages and the **w**.

Water (*Living water*, Water's, Water-carriers, Watercourse, Watered, Waterfalls, Watering, Waters, Watery, Well-watered)

Ge 1: 6 the waters to separate **w** from **w**."
1: 7 separated the **w** under the expanse
1: 7 the expanse from the **w** above it.
1: 9 God said, "Let the **w** under the sky
1:20 God said, "Let the **w** teem with
1:21 moving thing with which the **w** teems,
1:22 number and fill the **w** in the seas,
7:18 ark floated on the surface of the **w**.
8: 3 The **w** receded steadily from the
8: 3 and fifty days the **w** had gone down,
8: 7 the **w** had dried up from the earth.
8: 8 he sent out a dove to see if the **w**
8: 9 **w** over all the surface of the earth;
8:11 the **w** had receded from the earth.
8:13 the **w** had dried up from the earth.
18: 4 Let a little **w** be brought, and then
21:14 a skin of **w** and gave them to Hagar.
21:15 the **w** in the skin was gone, she put
21:19 her eyes and she saw a well of **w**.
21:19 with **w** and gave the boy a drink.
21:25 well of **w** that Abimelech's servants
24:11 the time the women go out to draw **w**.
24:13 are coming out to draw **w**.
24:14 'Drink, and I'll **w** your camels too'—
24:17 give me a little **w** from your jar."
24:19 "I'll draw **w** for your camels too,
24:20 ran back to the well to draw more **w**,
24:32 and **w** for him and his men to wash
24:43 out to draw **w** and I say to her,
24:43 me drink a little **w** from your jar,"
24:44 "Drink, and I'll draw **w** for your
24:45 went down to the spring and drew **w**,
24:46 'Drink, and I'll **w** your camels too.
26:19 discovered a well of fresh **w** there.
26:20 "The **w** is ours!" So he named the
26:32 They said, "We've found **w**!"
29: 3 the well's mouth and **w** the sheep.
29: 7 **W** the sheep and take them back to
29: 8 Then we will **w** the sheep."
37:24 was empty; there was no **w** in it.
43:24 gave them **w** to wash their feet and
Ex 2:10 saying, "I drew him out of the **w**.
2:16 and they came to draw **w** and fill the
2:16 troughs to **w** their father's flock.
2:19 **w** for us and watered the flock."
4: 9 take some **w** from the Nile and pour
4: 9 The **w** you take from the river will
7:15 the morning as he goes out to the **w**.
7:17 I will strike the **w** of the Nile,
7:18 will not be able to drink its **w**.
7:20 and struck the **w** of the Nile,
7:20 all the **w** was changed into blood.
7:21 the Egyptians could not drink its **w**.
7:24 along the Nile to get drinking **w**,
7:24 could not drink the **w** of the river.
8:20 as he goes to the **w** and say to him,
12: 9 not eat the meat raw or cooked in **w**,
14:16 divide the **w** so that the Israelites
14:22 **w** on their right and on their left.
14:28 The **w** flowed back and covered the
14:29 **w** on their right and on their left.
15:22 in the desert without finding **w**.
15:23 drink its **w** because it was bitter.
15:25 He threw it into the **w**, and the **w**
15:27 and they camped there near the **w**.
17: 1 was no **w** for the people to drink.
17: 2 Moses and said, "Give us **w** to drink.
17: 3 the people were thirsty for **w** there,
17: 6 Strike the rock, and **w** will come out
23:25 blessing will be on your food and **w**.
29: 4 Tent of Meeting and wash them with **w**.
30:18 and the altar, and put **w** in it.
30:19 their hands and feet with **w** from it.
30:20 with **w** so that they will not die.
32:20 **w** and made the Israelites drink it.
34:28 without eating bread or drinking **w**.
40: 7 and the altar and put **w** in it.
40:12 Tent of Meeting and wash them with **w**.
40:30 altar and put **w** in it for washing,
Lev 1: 9 the inner parts and the legs with **w**,
1:13 the inner parts and the legs with **w**,
Lev 6:28 is to be scoured and rinsed with **w**.
8: 6 sons forward and washed them with **w**.
8:21 the legs with **w** and burned the whole
11: 9 the **w** of the seas and the streams,
11:10 in the **w**—you are to detest.
11:12 Anything living in the **w** that does
11:32 Put it in **w**; it will be unclean till
11:34 **w** on it from such a pot is unclean,
11:36 or a cistern for collecting **w**
11:38 if **w** has been put on the seed and a
11:46 living thing that moves in the **w**
14: 5 killed over fresh **w** in a clay pot.
14: 6 that was killed over the fresh **w**.
14: 8 off all his hair and bathe with **w**;
14: 9 with **w**, and he will be clean.
14:50 birds over fresh **w** in a clay pot.
14:51 of the dead bird and the fresh **w**,
14:52 the fresh **w**, the live bird, the
15: 5 wash his clothes and bathe with **w**,
15: 6 wash his clothes and bathe with **w**,
15: 7 wash his clothes and bathe with **w**,
15: 8 wash his clothes and bathe with **w**,
15:10 wash his clothes and bathe with **w**,
15:11 hands with **w** must wash his clothes
15:11 wash his clothes and bathe with **w**,
15:12 article is to be rinsed with **w**.
15:13 with fresh **w**, and he will be clean.
15:16 he must bathe his whole body with **w**,
15:17 semen on it must be washed with **w**,
15:18 both must bathe with **w**, and they
15:21 wash his clothes and bathe with **w**,
15:22 wash his clothes and bathe with **w**,
15:27 wash his clothes and bathe with **w**,
16: 4 with **w** before he puts them on.
16:24 He shall bathe himself with **w** in a
16:26 clothes and bathe himself with **w**;
16:28 clothes and bathe himself with **w**;
17:15 wash his clothes and bathe with **w**,
22: 6 unless he has bathed himself with **w**.
Nu 5:17 he shall take some holy **w** in a clay
5:17 the tabernacle floor into the **w**.
5:18 the bitter **w** that brings a curse.
5:19 **w** that brings a curse not harm you.
5:22 May this **w** that brings a curse enter
5:23 wash them off into the bitter **w**.
5:24 the bitter **w** that brings a curse,
5:24 and this **w** will enter her and cause
5:26 he is to make the woman drink the **w**.
5:27 to drink the **w** that brings a curse,
8: 7 do this: Sprinkle the **w** of cleansing
19: 7 clothes and bathe himself with **w**.
19: 8 wash his clothes and bathe with **w**,
19: 9 for use in the **w** of cleansing;
19:12 He must purify himself with the **w** on
19:13 Because the **w** of cleansing has not
19:17 a jar and pour fresh **w** over them.
19:18 dip it in the **w** and sprinkle the
19:19 bathe with **w**, and that evening he
19:20 The **w** of cleansing has not been
19:21 "The man who sprinkles the **w** of
19:21 and anyone who touches the **w** of
20: 2 Now there was no **w** for the community,
20: 5 And there is no **w** to drink!"
20: 8 eyes and it will pour out its **w**.
20: 8 You will bring **w** out of the rock for
20:10 we bring you **w** out of this rock?"
20:11 **W** gushed out, and the community and
20:17 vineyard, or drink **w** from any well.
20:19 any of your **w**, we will pay for it.
21: 5 There is no bread! There is no **w**!
21:16 together and I will give them **w**."
21:22 vineyard, or drink **w** from any well.
24: 7 **W** will flow from their buckets;
24: 7 their seed will have abundant **w**.
31:23 be purified with the **w** of cleansing.
31:23 fire must be put through that **w**.
33:14 was no **w** for the people to drink.
Dt 2: 6 food you eat and the **w** you drink.
2:28 Sell us food to eat and **w** to drink
8: 7 land with streams and pools of **w**,
8:15 He brought you **w** out of hard rock.
9: 9 I ate no bread and drank no **w**.
9:18 I ate no bread and drank no **w**,
10: 7 Jotbathah, a land with streams of **w**.
12:16 pour it out on the ground like **w**.
12:24 pour it out on the ground like **w**.
Dt 14: 9 Of all the creatures living in the **w**,
15:23 pour it out on the ground like **w**.
23: 4 meet you with bread and **w** on your
29:11 who chop your wood and carry your **w**.
Jos 2:10 LORD dried up the **w** of the Red Sea
3:16 the **w** from upstream stopped flowing.
3:16 while the **w** flowing down to the Sea
7: 5 the people melted and became like **w**.
15:19 Negev, give me also springs of **w**.
Jdg 1:15 Negev, give me also springs of **w**.
4:19 "Please give me some **w**." She opened
5: 4 poured, the clouds poured down **w**.
5:25 He asked for **w**, and she gave him
6:38 wrung out the dew—a bowlful of **w**.
7: 4 Take them down to the **w**, and I will
7: 5 Gideon took the men down to the **w**.
7: 5 "Separate those who lap the **w** with
15:19 place in Lehi, and **w** came out of it.
Ru 2: 9 the **w** jars the men have filled."
1Sa 7: 6 **w** and poured it out before the LORD.
9:11 met some girls coming out to draw **w**,
25:11 Why should I take my bread and **w**,
26:11 Now get the spear and **w** jug that are
26:12 David took the spear and **w** jug near
26:16 and **w** jug that were near his head?"
30:11 him **w** to drink and food to eat—
30:12 or drunk any **w** for three days
2Sa 5: 8 the **w** shaft to reach those 'lame
12:27 Rabbah and taken its **w** supply.
14:14 Like **w** spilled on the ground, which
23:15 David longed for **w** and said, "Oh,
23:15 someone would get me a drink of **w**
23:16 drew **w** from the well near the gate
1Ki 13: 8 would I eat bread or drink **w** here.
13: 9 or drink **w** or return by the way
13:16 or drink **w** with you in this place.
13:17 'You must not eat bread or drink **w**
13:18 that he may eat bread and drink **w**.
13:22 ate bread and drank **w** in the place
14:15 be like a reed swaying in the **w**.
17:10 **w** in a jar so I may have a drink?"
18: 4 had supplied them with food and **w**.
18:13 and supplied them with food and **w**.
18:33 "Fill four large jars with **w** and
18:35 The **w** ran down around the altar and
18:38 also licked up the **w** in the trench.
19: 6 over hot coals, and a jar of **w**.
22:27 bread and **w** until I return safely.
2Ki 2: 8 it up and struck the **w** with it.
2: 8 The **w** divided to the right and to
2:14 from him and struck the **w** with it.
2:14 When he struck the **w**, it divided to
2:19 as you can see, but the **w** is bad and
2:21 LORD says: 'I have healed this **w**.
2:22 the **w** has remained wholesome to this
3: 9 seven days, the army had no more **w**
3:11 to pour **w** on the hands of Elijah."
3:17 this valley will be filled with **w**,
3:20 there it was—**w** flowing from the
3:20 Edom! And the land was filled with **w**.
3:22 the sun was shining on the **w**.
3:22 way, the **w** looked red—like blood.
6: 5 the iron axe-head fell into the **w**.
6:22 Set food and **w** before them so that
8:15 soaked it in **w** and spread it over
18:31 and drink **w** from his own cistern,
19:24 foreign lands and drunk the **w** there.
20:20 by which he brought **w** into the city,
1Ch 11:17 David longed for **w** and said, "Oh,
11:17 someone would get me a drink of **w**
11:18 drew **w** from the well near the gate
2Ch 18:26 bread and **w** until I return safely.
32: 3 **w** from the springs outside the city,
32: 4 and find plenty of **w**?" they said.
32:30 channelled the **w** down to the west
Ezr 10: 6 he ate no food and drank no **w**,
Ne 3:26 the **W** Gate towards the east and the
4:23 his weapon, even when he went for **w**.
8: 1 man in the square before the **W** Gate.
8: 3 **W** Gate in the presence of the men,
8:16 in the square by the **W** Gate and the
9:15 you brought them **w** from the rock;
9:20 you gave them **w** for their thirst.
12:37 of David to the **W** Gate on the east.
13: 2 food and **w** but had hired Balaam to
Job 3:24 of food; my groans pour out like **w**.

Job 5:10 he sends w upon the countryside.
6:19 The caravans of Tema look for w, the
8:11 marsh? Can reeds thrive without w?
14: 9 yet at the scent of w it will bud
14:11 w disappears from the sea or a river
14:19 w wears away stones and torrents
15:16 corrupt, who drinks up evil like w!
22: 7 You gave no w to the weary and you
22:11 and why a flood of w covers you.
24:18 are foam on the surface of the w;
29:19 My roots will reach to the w, and
34: 7 like Job, who drinks scorn like w?
36:27 "He draws up the drops of w, which
37:13 or to w his earth and show his love.
38:26 to w a land where no man lives, a
38:34 cover yourself with a flood of w?
38:37 tip over the w jars of the heavens
Ps 1: 3 like a tree planted by streams of w,
22:14 I am poured out like w, and all my
42: 1 the deer pants for streams of w, so
58: 7 Let them vanish like w that flows
63: 1 and weary land where there is no w.
65: 9 You care for the land and w it; you
65: 9 The streams of God are filled with w
66:12 heads; we went through fire and w,
77:17 The clouds poured down w, the skies
78:13 made the w stand firm like a wall.
78:15 gave them w as abundant as the seas;
78:16 and made w flow down like rivers.
78:20 he struck the rock, w gushed out,
79: 3 They have poured out blood like w
104:10 He makes springs pour w into the
104:11 They give w to all the beasts of the
105:41 He opened the rock, and w gushed out;
107:35 He turned the desert into pools of w
109:18 like w, into his bones like oil.
114: 8 the hard rock into springs of w.
Pr 5:15 Drink w from your own cistern,
5:15 running w from your own well.
5:16 streams of w in the public squares?
8:24 were no springs abounding with w;
9:17 "Stolen w is sweet; food eaten in
25:21 he is thirsty, give him w to drink.
25:25 Like cold w to a weary soul is good
27:19 w reflects a face, so a man's heart
30:16 which is never satisfied with w, and
Ecc 2: 6 I made reservoirs to w groves of
11: 3 If clouds are full of w, they pour
SS 4:15 w streaming down from Lebanon.
5:12 His eyes are like doves by the w
Isa 1:22 your choice wine is diluted with w.
1:30 leaves, like a garden without w.
3: 1 of food and all supplies of w,
7:19 thornbushes and at all the w holes.
12: 3 With joy you will draw w from the
18: 2 by sea in papyrus boats over the w.
19: 8 throw nets on the w will pine away.
21:14 bring w for the thirsty; you who
22: 9 you stored up w in the Lower Pool.
22:11 two walls for the w of the Old Pool,
27: 3 I, the LORD, watch over it; I w it
28:17 w will overflow your hiding-place.
30:14 or scooping w out of a cistern."
30:20 adversity and the w of affliction,
30:25 when the towers fall, streams of w
32: 2 like streams of w in the desert and
32: 6 and from the thirsty he withholds w.
33:16 supplied, and w will not fail him.
35: 6 W will gush forth in the wilderness
36:16 and drink w from his own cistern,
37:25 foreign lands and drunk the w there.
41:17 "The poor and needy search for w,
41:18 turn the desert into pools of w,
43:20 because I provide w in the desert
44: 3 I will pour w on the thirsty land
44:12 he drinks no w and grows faint.
48:21 he made w flow for them from the
48:21 he split the rock and w gushed out.
49:10 and lead them beside springs of w.
50: 2 rot for lack of w and die of thirst.
64: 2 fire sets twigs ablaze and causes w
Jer 2:13 broken cisterns that cannot hold w.
2:18 Now why go to Egypt to drink w from
2:18 Assyria to drink w from the River?
6: 7 a well pours out its w, so she pours
8:14 and given us poisoned w to drink,
Jer 9: 1 Oh, that my head were a spring of w
9:15 bitter food and drink poisoned w.
9:18 and w streams from our eyelids.
13: 1 waist, but do not let it touch w."
14: 3 The nobles send their servants for w;
14: 3 go to the cisterns but find no w.
17: 8 be like a tree planted by the w
17:13 the LORD, the spring of living w.
23:15 bitter food and drink poisoned w,
31: 9 I will lead them beside streams of w
38: 6 into the cistern; it had no w in it,
Lam 2:19 like w in the presence of the Lord.
5: 4 We must buy the w we drink; our wood
Eze 4:11 hin of w and drink it at set times.
4:16 and drink rationed w in despair,
4:17 for food and w will be scarce. They
7:17 every knee will become as weak as w.
12:18 shudder in fear as you drink your w.
12:19 and drink their w in despair, for
16: 4 nor were you washed with w to make
16: 9 "'I bathed you with w and washed
17: 5 it like a willow by abundant w,
17: 7 out its branches to him for w.
17: 8 w so that it would produce branches,
19:10 in your vineyard planted by the w;
19:10 of branches because of abundant w.
21: 7 and every knee become as weak as w.
24: 3 pot; put it on and pour w into it.
32: 2 churning the w with your feet and
34:18 not enough for you to drink clear w?
36:25 I will sprinkle clean w on you, and
47: 1 and I saw w coming out from under
47: 1 The w was coming down from under the
47: 2 w was flowing from the south side.
47: 3 me through w that was ankle-deep.
47: 4 led me through w that was knee-deep.
47: 4 through w that was up to the waist.
47: 5 because the w had risen and was deep
47: 8 He said to me, "This w flows towards
47: 8 the Sea, the w there becomes fresh.
47: 9 because this w flows there and makes
47: 9 there and makes the salt w fresh;
47:12 w from the sanctuary flows to them.
Da 1:12 vegetables to eat and w to drink.
Hos 2: 5 who give me my food and my w, my
5:10 my wrath on them like a flood of w.
6: 3 the spring rains that w the earth."
Joel 1:20 the streams of w have dried up and
3:18 ravines of Judah will run with w.
3:18 and will w the valley of acacias.
Am 4: 8 for w but did not get enough to
8:11 a famine of food or a thirst for w,
Mic 1: 4 fire, like w rushing down a slope.
Na 2: 8 Nineveh is like a pool, and its w is
3: 8 situated on the Nile, with w around
3:14 Draw w for the siege, strengthen
Hab 3:10 Torrents of w swept by; the deep
Mt 3:11 "I baptise you with w for repentance.
3:16 baptised, he went up out of the w.
8:32 into the lake and died in the w.
10:42 if anyone gives even a cup of cold w
14:28 "tell me to come to you on the w.
14:29 on the w and came towards Jesus.
17:15 falls into the fire or into the w.
27:24 he took w and washed his hands in
Mk 1: 8 I baptise you with w, but he will
1:10 Jesus was coming up out of the w, he
9:22 him into fire or w to kill him.
9:41 anyone who gives you a cup of w in
14:13 carrying a jar of w will meet you.
Lk 3:16 them all, "I baptise you with w.
5: 4 into deep w, and let down the nets
7:44 You did not give me any w for my
8:25 winds and the w, and they obey him."
13:15 stall and lead it out to give it w?
16:24 his finger in w and cool my tongue,
22:10 carrying a jar of w will meet you.
Jn 1:26 "I baptise with w," John replied,
1:31 the reason I came baptising with w
1:33 sent me to baptise with w told me,
2: 6 Nearby stood six stone w jars, the
2: 7 "Fill the jars with w"; so they
2: 9 w that had been turned into wine.
2: 9 servants who had drawn the w knew.
3: 5 he is born of w and the Spirit.
3:23 because there was plenty of w, and
Jn 4: 7 a Samaritan woman came to draw w,
4:13 drinks this w will be thirsty again,
4:14 whoever drinks the w I give him will
4:14 Indeed, the w I give him will become
4:14 of w welling up to eternal life."
4:15 "Sir, give me this w so that I won't
4:15 have to keep coming here to draw w."
4:28 Then, leaving her w jar, the woman
4:46 where he had turned the w into wine.
5: 7 into the pool when the w is stirred.
6:19 on the w; and they were terrified.
13: 5 After that, he poured w into a basin
19:34 a sudden flow of blood and w.
21: 7 taken it off) and jumped into the w.
Ac 1: 5 For John baptised with w, but in a
8:36 they came to some w and the eunuch
8:36 the eunuch said, "Look, here is w.
8:38 into the w and Philip baptised him.
8:39 they came up out of the w, the
10:47 people from being baptised with w?
11:16 'John baptised with w, but you will
27:28 found that the w was one hundred and
Eph 5:26 the washing with w through the word,
1Ti 5:23 Stop drinking only w, and use a
Heb 9:19 together with w, scarlet wool and
10:22 our bodies washed with pure w.
Jas 3:11 Can both fresh w and salt w flow
3:12 can a salt spring produce fresh w.
1Pe 3:20 eight in all, were saved through w,
3:21 this w symbolises baptism that now
2Pe 2:17 These men are springs without w and
3: 5 earth was formed out of w and by w.
1Jn 5: 6 This is the one who came by w and
5: 6 He did not come by w only, but by w
5: 8 the Spirit, the w and the blood; and
Rev 8:10 the rivers and on the springs of w—
12:15 from his mouth the serpent spewed w
14: 7 the sea and the springs of w."
16: 4 springs of w, and they became blood.
16:12 and its w was dried up to prepare
21: 6 from the spring of the w of life.
22: 1 me the river of the w of life,
22:17 take the free gift of the w of life.

Water's (Water)

Jos 3:15 and their feet touched the w edge,
Mk 4: 1 were along the shore at the w edge.
Lk 5: 2 he saw at the w edge two boats, left

Water-carriers (Water)

Jos 9:21 and w for the entire community.
9:23 and w for the house of my God."
9:27 w for the community and for the

Watercourse (Water)

Pr 21: 1 it like a w wherever he pleases.

Watered (Water)

Ge 2: 6 streams came up from the earth and w
13:10 plain of the Jordan was well w,
24:46 I drank, and she w the camels also.
29: 2 the flocks were w from that well.
29:10 of the well and w his uncle's sheep.
Ex 2:17 to their rescue and w their flock.
2:19 drew water for us and w the flock."
Dt 29:19 on the w land as well as the dry.
Ps 104:16 The trees of the LORD are well w,
1Co 3: 6 I planted the seed, Apollos w it,

Waterfalls (Water)

Ps 42: 7 calls to deep in the roar of your w;

Watering (Water)

Ge 2:10 A river w the garden flowed from
30:38 branches in all the w troughs,
Jdg 5:11 of the singers at the w places
Ps 72: 6 field, like showers w the earth.
Isa 55:10 and do not return to it without w

Waterless

Dt 8:15 that thirsty and w land, with its
Zec 9:11 free your prisoners from the w pit.

Waters (Water)

Ge 1: 2 of God was hovering over the w.
1: 6 the w to separate water from water."
1:10 and the gathered w he called "seas".
7: 7 ark to escape the w of the flood.
7:17 and as the w increased they lifted
7:18 The w rose and increased greatly on
7:20 The w rose and covered the mountains
7:24 The w flooded the earth for a
8: 1 over the earth, and the w receded.
8: 5 The w continued to recede until the
9:11 life be cut off by the w of a flood;
9:15 w become a flood to destroy all life.
49: 4 Turbulent as the w, you will no
Ex 7:19 stretch out your hand over the w of
8: 6 out his hand over the w of Egypt,
14:21 into dry land. The w were divided,
14:26 w may flow back over the Egyptians
15: 5 The deep w have covered them; they
15: 8 By the blast of your nostrils the w
15: 8 The surging w stood firm like a wall;
15: 8 w congealed in the heart of the sea.
15:10 They sank like lead in the mighty w.
15:19 the LORD brought the w of the sea
20: 4 the earth beneath or in the w below.
Nu 20:13 These were the w of Meribah, where
20:24 my command at the w of Meribah.
24: 6 the LORD, like cedars beside the w.
27:14 at the w in the Desert of Zin,
27:14 (These were the w of Meribah Kadesh,
Dt 4:18 ground or any fish in the w below.
5: 8 the earth beneath or in the w below.
11: 4 how he overwhelmed them with the w
32:51 at the w of Meribah Kadesh in the
33: 8 with him at the w of Meribah.
33:13 and with the deep w that lie below;
Jos 3: 8 the edge of the Jordan's w, go and
3:13 its w flowing downstream will be cut
4: 7 the w of the Jordan were cut off.
4:18 the w of the Jordan returned to their
11: 5 W of Merom, to fight against Israel.
11: 7 at the W of Merom and attacked them,
15: 7 It continued along to the w of En
15: 9 the spring of the w of Nephtoah,
16: 1 east of the w of Jericho, and went
18:15 at the spring of the w of Nephtoah.
Jdg 5:19 at Taanach by the w of Megiddo,
7:24 seize the w of the Jordan ahead of
7:24 w of the Jordan as far as Beth Barah.
2Sa 5:20 He said, "As w break out, the LORD
22:17 of me; he drew me out of deep w.
2Ki 5:12 better than any of the w of Israel?
1Ch 14:11 He said, "As w break out, God has
Ne 9:11 depths, like a stone into mighty w.
Job 11:16 recalling it only as w gone by.
12:15 If he holds back the w, there is
20:28 rushing w on the day of God's wrath.
26: 5 the w and all that live in them.
26: 8 He wraps up the w in his clouds, yet
26:10 the w for a boundary between light
28:25 of the wind and measured out the w,
37:10 ice, and the broad w become frozen.
38:30 the w become hard as stone, when the
Ps 18:16 of me; he drew me out of deep w.
23: 2 he leads me beside quiet w,
24: 2 seas and established it upon the w.
29: 3 The voice of the LORD is over the w;
29: 3 the LORD thunders over the mighty w.
32: 6 w rise, they will not reach him.
33: 7 He gathers the w of the sea into
46: 3 though its w roar and foam and the
66: 6 they passed through the w on foot—
69: 1 Save me, O God, for the w have come
69: 2 the deep w; the floods engulf me.
69:14 those who hate me, from the deep w.
73:10 to them and drink up w in abundance.
74:13 the heads of the monster in the w.
77:16 The w saw you, O God, the w saw you
77:19 your way through the mighty w,
81: 7 I tested you at the w of Meribah.
93: 4 than the thunder of the great w,
104: 3 of his upper chambers on their w.
104: 6 the w stood above the mountains.
104: 7 at your rebuke the w fled, at the
104:12 The birds of the air nest by the w;
Ps 104:13 He w the mountains from his upper
105:29 He turned their w into blood,
106:11 The w covered their adversaries; not
106:32 By the w of Meribah they angered the
107:23 they were merchants on the mighty w.
124: 5 the raging w would have swept us
136: 6 who spread out the earth upon the w,
144: 7 rescue me from the mighty w, from
147:18 up his breezes, and the w flow.
148: 4 heavens and you w above the skies.
Pr 8:29 w would not overstep his command,
18: 4 The words of a man's mouth are deep w
20: 5 of a man's heart are deep w,
30: 4 Who has wrapped up the w in his
Ecc 11: 1 Cast your bread upon the w, for
SS 8: 7 Many w cannot quench love; rivers
Isa 8: 6 the gently flowing w of Shiloah
10:26 over the w, as he did in Egypt.
11: 9 of the LORD as the w cover the sea.
15: 6 The w of Nimrim are dried up and the
15: 9 Dimon's w are full of blood, but I
17:12 roar like the roaring of great w!
17:13 roar like the roar of surging w,
19: 5 The w of the river will dry up, and
23: 3 On the great w came the grain of the
40:12 Who has measured the w in the hollow
43: 2 you pass through the w, I will be
43:16 sea, a path through the mighty w,
51:10 the w of the great deep, who made a
54: 9 when I swore that the w of Noah
55: 1 come to the w; and you who have no
58:11 like a spring whose w never fail.
63:12 who divided the w before them, to
Jer 10:13 he thunders, the w in the heavens
18:14 Do its cool w from distant sources
46: 7 the Nile, like rivers of surging w?
46: 8 the Nile, like rivers of surging w.
47: 2 "See how the w are rising in the
48:34 even the w of Nimrim are dried up.
50:38 A drought on her w! They will dry up.
51:13 You who live by many w and are rich
51:16 he thunders, the w in the heavens
51:55 of enemies will rage like great w;
Lam 3:54 the w closed over my head, and I
Eze 1:24 like the roar of rushing w, like the
26:19 over you and its vast w cover you,
27:34 by the sea in the depths of the w;
31: 4 The w nourished it, deep springs
31: 5 spreading because of abundant w.
31: 7 its roots went down to abundant w.
31:14 Therefore no other trees by the w
31:15 and its abundant w were restrained.
32:13 her cattle from beside abundant w
32:14 I will let her w settle and make her
43: 2 was like the roar of rushing w,
47:19 as far as the w of Meribah Kadesh,
48:28 Tamar to the w of Meribah Kadesh,
Da 12: 6 who was above the w of the river,
12: 7 who was above the w of the river,
Hos 10: 7 like a twig on the surface of the w.
Am 5: 8 who calls for the w of the sea and
9: 6 who calls for the w of the sea and
Jnh 2: 5 The engulfing w threatened me, the
Na 3: 8 was her defence, the w her wall.
Hab 2:14 of the LORD, as the w cover the sea.
3:15 your horses, churning the great w.
Lk 8:24 the raging w; the storm subsided,
Jn 6:18 A strong wind was blowing and the w
1Co 3: 7 neither he who plants nor he who w
3: 8 The man who plants and the man who w
2Pe 3: 6 By these w also the world of that
Rev 1:15 was like the sound of rushing w.
8:11 A third of the w turned bitter, and
8:11 from the w that had become bitter.
11: 6 and they have power to turn the w
14: 2 like the roar of rushing w and like
16: 5 I heard the angel in charge of the w
17: 1 prostitute, who sits on many w.
17:15 the angel said to me, "The w you saw,
19: 6 like the roar of rushing w and like

Watery (Water)

Isa 44:27 who says to the w deep, 'Be dry, and

Wave (*Wave offering*, Wave offerings, Waved, Waves, Wavy)

Ex 29:24 his sons and w them before the LORD
29:26 ordination, w it before the LORD as a
Lev 7:30 together with the breast, and w the
14:12 he shall w them before the LORD as a
14:24 with the log of oil, and w them
23:11 He is to w the sheaf before the LORD
23:11 w it on the day after the Sabbath.
23:12 On the day you w the sheaf, you must
23:20 The priest is to w the two lambs
Nu 5:25 w it before the LORD and bring it to
6:20 The priest shall then w them before
2Ki 5:11 w his hand over the spot and cure me
Job 10:17 forces come against me w upon w.
Jas 1: 6 he who doubts is like a w of the sea

Wave offering

Ex 29:24 wave them before the LORD as a w.
29:26 as a w, and it will be your share.
35:22 their gold as a w to the LORD.
38:24 total amount of the gold from the w
38:29 The bronze from the w was 70 talents
Lev 7:30 the breast before the LORD as a w.
8:27 waved them before the LORD as a w.
8:29 as a w, as the LORD commanded Moses.
9:21 the LORD as a w, as Moses commanded.
10:15 to be waved before the LORD as a w.
14:12 wave them before the LORD as a w.
14:24 wave them before the LORD as a w.
23:15 the w, count off seven full weeks.
23:17 as a w of firstfruits to the LORD.
23:20 two lambs before the LORD as a w,
Nu 6:20 wave them before the LORD as a w;
8:11 the LORD as a w from the Israelites,
8:13 present them as a w to the LORD.
8:15 Levites and presented them as a w,
8:21 Then Aaron presented them as a w
18:18 the w and the right thigh are yours.

Wave offerings

Nu 18:11 from the gifts of all the w of the

Waved (Wave)

Ex 29:27 w and the thigh that was presented.
Lev 7:34 I have taken the breast that is w
8:27 his sons and w them before the LORD
8:29 w it before the LORD as a wave
9:21 Aaron w the breasts and the right
10:14 may eat the breast that was w
10:15 the breast that was w must be
10:15 w before the LORD as a wave offering.
14:21 to be w to make atonement for him,
Nu 6:20 together with the breast that was w

Waver (Wavering)

1Ki 18:21 "How long will you w between two
Ro 4:20 Yet he did not w through unbelief

Wavering (Waver)

Ps 26: 1 I have trusted in the LORD without w.

Waves (Wave)

2Sa 22: 5 "The w of death swirled about me;
Job 9: 8 and treads on the w of the sea.
38:11 here is where your proud w halt'?
Ps 42: 7 w and breakers have swept over me.
65: 7 the roaring of their w, and the
88: 7 have overwhelmed me with all your w.
89: 9 when its w mount up, you still them.
93: 3 have lifted up their pounding w.
107:25 up a tempest that lifted high the w.
107:29 the w of the sea were hushed.
Isa 48:18 righteousness like the w of the sea.
51:15 who churns up the sea so that its w
57:20 rest, whose w cast up mire and mud.
Jer 5:22 The w may roll, but they cannot
31:35 who stirs up the sea so that its w
51:42 its roaring w will cover her.
51:55 W of enemies will rage like great
Eze 26: 3 like the sea casting up its w.
Jnh 2: 3 your w and breakers swept over me.
Hab 3:10 roared and lifted its w on high.
Mt 8:24 so that the w swept over the boat.

Mt 8:26 the w, and it was completely calm.
8:27 Even the winds and the w obey him!"
14:24 w because the wind was against it.
Mk 4:37 A furious squall came up, and the w
4:39 said to the w, "Quiet! Be still!"
4:41 Even the wind and the w obey him!"
Eph 4:14 tossed back and forth by the w, and
Jude :13 They are wild w of the sea, foaming

Wavy (Wave)
SS 5:11 his hair is w and black as a raven.

Wax
Ps 22:14 to w; it has melted away within me.
68: 2 may you blow them away; as w melts
97: 5 The mountains melt like w before the
Mic 1: 4 like w before the fire, like water

Way (Doorway, Doorways, *Way of the Lord*, *Way of the Lord*, Ways)
Ge 3:24 to guard the w to the tree of life.
9:23 Their faces were turned the other w
12:20 and they sent him on his w, with his
18: 5 then go on your w—now that you have
18:16 with them to see them on their w.
19: 2 go on your w early in the morning.
19: 9 "Get out of our w," they replied.
21:14 She went on her w and wandered in
24: 1 the LORD had blessed him in every w.
24:10 and made his w to the town of Nahor.
24:49 me, so I may know which w to turn."
24:50 nothing to you one w or the other.
24:54 said, "Send me on my w to my master.
24:56 on my w so I may go to my master."
24:59 sent their sister Rebekah on her w,
26:31 their w, and they left him in peace.
27: 9 your father, just the w he likes it.
27:14 just the w his father liked it.
28: 5 Isaac sent Jacob on his w, and he
30:25 "Send me on my w so that I can go
30:26 served you, and I will be on my w.
30:43 In this w the man grew exceedingly
32: 1 Jacob also went on his w, and the
33:12 Esau said, "Let us be on our w; I'll
33:16 that day Esau started on his w back
35:19 Rachel died and was buried on the w
37:25 their w to take them down to Egypt.
38:13 his w to Timnah to shear his sheep,"
41:43 "Make w!" Thus he put him in charge
44: 3 sent on their w with their donkeys.
45:24 to them, "Don't quarrel on the w!"
48: 7 while we were still on the w, a
Ex 2:12 Glancing this w and that and seeing
3: 9 w the Egyptians are oppressing them.
4:14 He is already on his w to meet you,
4:24 At a lodging place on the w, the
5:15 you treated your servants this w?
13:21 of cloud to guide them on their w
16: 4 In this w I will test them and see
18: 8 hardships they had met along the w
18:20 and show them the w to live and the
18:27 Moses sent his father-in-law on his w
19:21 their w through to see the LORD
19:24 w through to come up to the LORD,
23:20 of you to guard you along the w
23:28 and Hittites out of your w.
26:17 frames of the tabernacle in this w.
26:24 the bottom all the w to the top,
28:11 the w a gem cutter engraves a seal.
29: 9 In this w you shall ordain Aaron and
33: 3 and I might destroy you on the w."
36:22 frames of the tabernacle in this w.
36:29 the bottom all the w to the top
Lev 4:20 In this w the priest will make
4:26 In this w the priest will make
4:31 In this w the priest will make
4:35 In this w the priest will make
5: 5 must confess in what w he has
5:10 burnt offering in the prescribed w
5:13 In this w the priest will make
5:18 In this w the priest will make
6: 7 In this w the priest will make
9:16 and offered it in the prescribed w.
12: 8 In this w the priest will make
14:31 In this w the priest will make
Lev 14:53 In this w he will make atonement for
15:15 In this w he will make atonement
15:30 In this w he will make atonement for
16:16 In this w he will make atonement for
19: 5 sacrifice it in such a w that it
19:25 In this w your harvest will be
22:29 sacrifice it in such a w that it
Nu 2:34 that is the w they encamped under
2:34 and that is the w they set out, each
5: 6 wrongs another in any w and so is
8:14 In this w you are to set the Levites
14:45 beat them down all the w to Hormah.
15:13 this w when he brings an offering
18:28 In this w you also will present an
21: 4 the people grew impatient on the w;
21:30 is destroyed all the w to Dibon.
24:25 home and Balak went his own w.
28:24 In this w prepare the food for the
Dt 1:31 all the w you went until you reached
1:33 and to show you the w you should go.
1:44 down from Seir all the w to Hormah.
2: 1 w around the hill country of Seir.
2: 3 "You have made your w around this
4: 7 the w the LORD our God is near us
5:33 Walk in all the w that the LORD your
8: 2 w in the desert these forty years,
9:16 w that the LORD had commanded you.
10:11 "and lead the people on their w, so
11:28 turn from the w that I command you
12: 4 the LORD your God in their w.
12:31 the LORD your God in their w,
13: 5 he has tried to turn you from the w
16:17 w the LORD your God has blessed you.
17:16 You are not to go back that w again."
20: 3 or give w to panic before them.
23: 4 your w when you came out of Egypt,
24: 9 the w after you came out of Egypt.
25:17 the w when you came out of Egypt.
29:16 through the countries on the w here.
29:19 though I persist in going my own w.
31:29 from the w I have commanded you.
32: 6 Is this the w you repay the LORD,
Jos 2: 5 I don't know which w they went. Go
2:16 they return, and then go on your w."
3: 4 you will know which w to go, since
3: 4 you have never been this w before.
5: 4 desert on the w after leaving Egypt.
5: 7 had not been circumcised on the w.
9:22 'We live a long w from you,' while
10:10 all the w to Azekah and Makkedah.
11: 8 them all the w to Greater Sidon,
18: 8 the men started on their w to map
23: 5 will drive them out of your w.
23:14 "Now I am about to go the w of all
Jdg 2:17 they quickly turned from the w in
2:17 the w of obedience to the LORD's
3:18 their w the men who had carried it.
4: 6 and lead the w to Mount Tabor.
4: 9 But because of the w you are going
6: 4 ruined the crops all the w to Gaza
9:40 the w to the entrance to the gate.
11:13 the Jabbok, all the w to the Jordan.
17: 8 On his w he came to Micah's house in
18: 7 Also, they lived a long w from the
18:12 On their w they set up camp near
18:26 the Danites went their w, and Micah,
18:28 they lived a long w from Sidon
19: 9 can get up and be on your w home."
19:18 He answered, "We are on our w from
19:27 stepped out to continue on his w,
20:36 Now the men of Israel had given w
1Sa 1:18 Then she went her w and ate
6: 6 so that they could go on their w?
6: 8 a guilt offering. Send it on its w,
6:12 on the road and lowing all the w;
7:11 the w to a point below Beth Car.
9: 6 he will tell us what w to take."
9: 8 he will tell us what w to take."
9:14 them on his w up to the high place.
9:26 and I will send you on your w."
12:23 you the w that is good and right.
15: 7 all the w from Havilah to Shur,
16: 1 your horn with oil and be on your w;
19:24 He lay that w all that day and night.
24: 3 He came to the sheep pens along the w
24: 7 Saul left the cave and went his w.
1Sa 24:19 well for the w you treated me today.
26:25 on his w, and Saul returned home.
28:22 have the strength to go on your w."
30: 2 them off as they went on their w.
2Sa 2:24 on the w to the wasteland of Gibeon.
3:16 behind her all the w to Bahurim.
4: 7 all night by w of the Arabah.
5:25 all the w from Gibeon to Gezer.
7:19 Is this your usual w of dealing with
12:21 "Why are you acting in this w? While
13:30 While they were on their w, the
15: 6 Absalom behaved in this w towards
18:23 "Run!" Then Ahimaaz ran by w of the
19:31 and to send him on his w from there.
19:36 should the king reward me in this w?
20: 2 the w from the Jordan to Jerusalem.
22:31 "As for God, his w is perfect; the
22:33 strength and makes my w perfect.
1Ki 2: 2 "I am about to go the w of all the
5:10 In this w Hiram kept Solomon
6:33 In the same w he made four-sided
7:37 This is the w he made the ten stands.
8:23 continue wholeheartedly in your w.
8:36 Teach them the right w to live, and
11:29 him on the w, wearing a new cloak.
13: 9 water or return by the w you came.
13:10 by the w he had come to Bethel.
13:12 Their father asked them, "Which w
13:17 there or return by the w you came.
13:24 he went on his w, a lion met him on
18:46 ahead of Ahab all the w to Jezreel.
19:15 The LORD said to him, "Go back the w
22:24 "Which w did the spirit from the
2Ki 2: 1 Elisha were on their w from Gilgal.
3:22 To the Moabites across the w, the
4: 9 comes our w is a holy man of God.
8: 7 of God has come all the w up here,"
9:15 Jehu said, "If this is the w you
9:27 on the w up to Gur near Ibleam,
10:15 Recab, who was on his w to meet him.
11:19 by w of the gate of the guards.
19:28 make you return by the w you came.'
19:33 By the w that he came he will return;
1Ch 7:28 all the w to Ayyah and its villages.
14:16 all the w from Gibeon to Gezer.
15:13 how to do it in the prescribed w."
23:31 and in the w prescribed for them.
2Ch 6:14 continue wholeheartedly in your w.
6:27 Teach them the right w to live, and
18:23 "Which w did the spirit from the
23:19 was in any w unclean might enter.
29:25 harps and lyres in the w prescribed
Ezr 7:27 of the LORD in Jerusalem in this w
8:31 enemies and bandits along the w.
9: 2 led the w in this unfaithfulness."
Ne 5:13 "In this w may God shake out of his
9:12 light on the w they were to take.
9:19 to shine on the w they were to take.
11:30 So they were living all the w from
Est 1: 8 was allowed to drink in his own w,
1:18 all the king's nobles in the same w.
3: 6 Instead Haman looked for a w to
9:27 in the w prescribed and at the time
Job 3:23 Why is life given to a man whose w
8:15 He leans on his web, but it gives w;
19: 8 He has blocked my w so that I cannot
22:21 this w prosperity will come to you.
23:10 he knows the w that I take; when he
23:11 kept to his w without turning aside.
28:23 God understands the w to it and he
29:25 I chose the w for them and sat as
32: 3 because they had found no w to
33:14 For God does speak—now one w, now
36:31 This is the w he governs the nations
38:19 "What is the w to the abode of light?
38:24 What is the w to the place where the
38:35 on their w? Do they report to you,
Ps 1: 1 wicked or stand in the w of sinners
1: 6 For the LORD watches over the w of
1: 6 but the w of the wicked will perish.
2:12 and you be destroyed in your w,
5: 8 make straight your w before me.
18:30 for God, his w is perfect; the word
18:32 strength and makes my w perfect.
25: 9 is right and teaches them his w.
25:12 him in the w chosen for him.

Ps 27:11 Teach me your w, O LORD; lead me in
32: 8 teach you in the w you should go;
37: 5 Commit your w to the LORD; trust in
37:23 If the LORD delights in a man's w,
37:34 Wait for the LORD and keep his w. He
46: 2 though the earth give w and the
50:23 and he prepares the w so that I may
77:19 Your path led through the sea, your w
85:13 and prepares the w for his steps.
86:11 Teach me your w, O LORD, and I will
107: 4 w to a city where they could settle.
107: 7 He led them by a straight w to a
109:24 My knees give w from fasting; my
110: 7 drink from a brook beside the w;
119: 9 How can a young man keep his w pure?
119:30 I have chosen the w of truth; I have
139:24 See if there is any offensive w in
139:24 and lead me in the w everlasting.
142: 3 within me, it is you who know my w.
143: 8 Show me the w I should go, for to
Pr 2: 8 protects the w of his faithful ones.
3:23 you will go on your w in safety, and
4:11 I guide you in the w of wisdom and
4:14 wicked or walk in the w of evil men.
4:15 it; turn from it and go on your w.
4:19 the w of the wicked is like deep
5: 6 She gives no thought to the w of
6:23 of discipline are the w to life,
8: 2 On the heights along the w, where
8:20 I walk in the w of righteousness,
9: 6 walk in the w of understanding.
9:15 pass by, who go straight on their w.
10:17 He who heeds discipline shows the w
11: 5 makes a straight w for them,
12:15 The w of a fool seems right to him,
12:26 w of the wicked leads them astray.
12:28 In the w of righteousness there is
13:15 but the w of the unfaithful is hard.
14:12 There is a w that seems right to a
15: 9 The LORD detests the w of the wicked
15:19 The w of the sluggard is blocked
16:17 he who guards his w guards his life.
16:25 There is a w that seems right to a
18:16 A gift opens the w for the giver and
19: 2 nor to be hasty and miss the w.
20:24 can anyone understand his own w?
21: 8 The w of the guilty is devious, but
22: 6 Train a child in the w he should go,
25:26 man who gives w to the wicked.
30:19 the w of an eagle in the sky, the
30:19 the w of a snake on a rock, the w of
30:19 and the w of a man with a maiden.
30:20 "This is the w of an adulteress: She
Ecc 10:15 him; he does not know the w to town.
SS 6: 1 most beautiful of women? Which w did
Isa 8:11 not to follow the w of this people.
9: 1 the w of the sea, along the Jordan—
15: 4 voices are heard all the w to Jahaz.
15: 5 They go up the w to Luhith, weeping
22:25 into the firm place will give w;
26: 7 make the w of the righteous smooth.
26: 8 Yes, LORD, walking in the w of your
28:26 him and teaches him the right w.
30:11 Leave this w, get off this path, and
30:21 saying, "This is the w; walk in it.
35: 3 hands, steady the knees that give w;
35: 8 be for those who walk in that W;
35: 8 will be called the W of Holiness.
37:29 make you return by the w you came.
37:34 By the w that he came he will return;
40: 3 "In the desert prepare the w for the
40:14 and who taught him the right w? Who
40:27 "My w is hidden from the LORD; my
43:16 he who made a w through the sea,
43:19 I am making a w in the desert and
48:17 directs you in the w you should go.
51: 5 my salvation is on the w, and my arm
53: 6 each of us has turned to his own w;
55: 7 Let the wicked forsake his w and the
56:11 own w, each seeks his own gain.
57:14 out of the w of my people."
58:13 honour it by not going your own w
59: 8 The w of peace they do not know;
59:10 feeling our w like men without eyes.
62:10 gates! Prepare the w for the people.
Jer 2:17 your God when he led you in the w?
Jer 4: 2 just and righteous w you swear, 'As
5:31 and my people love it this w.
6:16 ask where the good w is, and walk in
12: 1 Why does the w of the wicked prosper?
13: 9 'In the same w I will ruin the pride
21: 8 the w of life and the w of death.
22:21 This has been your w from your youth;
26: 3 and each will turn from his evil w.
28:11 'In the same w will I break the yoke
28:11 the prophet Jeremiah went on his w.
36: 3 of them will turn from his wicked w;
39: 4 at night by w of the king's garden,
41:17 near Bethlehem on their w to Egypt
48: 5 They go up the w to Luhith, weeping
50: 5 They will ask the w to Zion and turn
Lam 2:15 All who pass your w clap their hands
3: 9 He has barred my w with blocks of
Eze 4:13 The LORD said, "In this w the people
18:25 Hear, O house of Israel: Is my w
20:30 Will you defile yourselves the w
23:13 both of them went the same w.
23:31 You have gone the w of your sister;
32: 6 blood all the w to the mountains,
33:17 But it is their w that is not just.
39:11 It will block the w of travellers,
44: 3 He is to enter by w of the portico
44: 3 the gateway and go out the same w."
44: 4 the man brought me by w of the north
46: 8 and he is to come out the same w.
Da 1: 8 not to defile himself in this w.
3:29 no other god can save in this w."
5: 6 together and his legs gave w.
12: 9 He replied, "Go your w, Daniel,
12:13 "As for you, go your w till the end.
Hos 2: 6 in so that she cannot find her w.
Am 6:14 that will oppress you all the w from
Mic 2:13 One who breaks open the w will go up
Na 1: 3 His w is in the whirlwind and the
2: 5 troops, yet they stumble on their w.
2:10 stripped! Hearts melt, knees give w,
Mal 2: 8 you have turned from the w and by
3: 1 who will prepare the w before me.
Mt 2: 9 they went on their w, and the star
3: 3 'Prepare the w for the Lord, make
4:15 the w to the sea, along the Jordan,
5:12 for in the same w they persecuted
5:16 In the same w, let your light shine
5:25 you are still with him on the w,
7: 2 For in the same w as you judge
8:28 that no-one could pass that w.
11:10 who will prepare your w before you.'
15:32 or they may collapse on the w."
17:12 In the same w the Son of Man is
18:14 In the same w your Father in heaven
19: 8 was not this w from the beginning.
19:12 because they were born that w;
19:12 others were made that w by men; and
21:18 w back to the city, he was hungry.
21:32 to show you the w of righteousness,
21:36 tenants treated them in the same w.
21:46 They looked for a w to arrest him,
22:16 that you teach the w of God in
23:28 In the same w, on the outside you
25:10 "But while they were on their w to
26: 4 Jesus in some sly w and kill him.
26:54 that say it must happen in this w?"
27:41 In the same w the chief priests, the
27:44 In the same w the robbers who were
28:11 While the women were on their w,
Mk 1: 2 of you, who will prepare your w"—
1: 3 'Prepare the w for the Lord, make
7: 9 he said to them: "You have a fine w
8: 3 they will collapse on the w, because
8:27 On the w he asked them, "Who do
9:34 they kept quiet because on the w
10:17 Jesus started on his w, a man ran up
10:32 They were on their w up to Jerusalem,
10:32 with Jesus leading the w, and the
11:18 began looking for a w to kill him,
12:12 they looked for a w to arrest him
12:14 but you teach the w of God in
14: 1 sly w to arrest Jesus and kill him.
15:21 was passing by on his w in from the
15:31 In the same w the chief priests and
16: 2 they were on their w to the tomb
Lk 1:76 the Lord to prepare the w for him,
Lk 3: 4 'Prepare the w for the Lord, make
4:30 through the crowd and went on his w.
5:19 they could not find a w to do this
7:27 who will prepare your w before you.'
7:29 acknowledged that God's w was right,
8:14 but as they go on their w they are
8:42 As Jesus was on his w, the crowds
10:38 and his disciples were on their w,
12:58 to be reconciled to him on the w,
13: 2 because they suffered this w?
13:22 as he made his w to Jerusalem.
14:19 and I'm on my w to try them out.
14:32 the other is still a long w off
14:33 In the same w, any of you who does
15: 7 I tell you that in the same w there
15:10 In the same w, I tell you, there is
15:20 "But while he was still a long w off,
16:16 everyone is forcing his w into it.
17:11 Now on his w to Jerusalem, Jesus
18:39 Those who led the w rebuked him and
19: 4 him, since Jesus was coming that w.
19:48 Yet they could not find any w to do
20:19 for a w to arrest him immediately,
20:21 teach the w of God in accordance
20:31 and in the same w the seven died,
22: 2 for some w to get rid of Jesus,
22:20 In the same w, after the supper he
23: 5 Galilee and has come all the w here."
23:26 who was on his w in from the country,
24:35 two told what had happened on the w,
Jn 1:23 'Make straight the w for the Lord.
4:30 town and made their w towards him.
4:51 While he was still on the w, his
7:46 "No-one ever spoke the w this man
10: 1 other w, is a thief and a robber.
12:12 Jesus was on his w to Jerusalem.
14: 4 You know the w to the place where I
14: 5 going, so how can we know the w?"
14: 6 Jesus answered, "I am the w and the
15:21 They will treat you this w because
18:22 "Is this the w you answer the high
21: 1 Sea of Tiberias. It happened this w
Ac 1:11 w you have seen him go into heaven."
7: 6 God spoke to him in this w: 'Your
8:27 he started out, and on his w he met
8:28 on his w home was sitting in his
8:39 again, but went on his w rejoicing.
9: 2 any there who belonged to the W,
13: 4 The two of them, sent on their w by
14:16 he let all nations go their own w.
15: 3 The church sent them on their w, and
16:17 are telling you the w to be saved."
17:22 in every w you are very religious.
18:26 to him the w of God more adequately.
19: 9 believe and publicly maligned the W.
19:20 In this w the word of the Lord
19:23 a great disturbance about the W.
21: 5 up, we left and continued on our w.
21:11 'In this w the Jews of Jerusalem
22: 4 I persecuted the followers of this W
24: 3 Everywhere and in every w, most
24:14 of the W, which they call a sect.
24:22 who was well acquainted with the W,
25: 3 an ambush to kill him along the w.
26: 4 "The Jews all know the w I have
27:15 gave w to it and were driven along.
27:44 w everyone reached land in safety.
Ro 1:10 the w may be opened for me to come
1:27 In the same w the men also abandoned
3: 2 Much in every w! First of all, they
3:17 the w of peace they do not know."
5:12 and in this w death came to all men,
6:11 In the same w, count yourselves dead
7: 6 we serve in the new w of the Spirit,
7: 6 in the old w of the written code.
8:26 In the same w, the Spirit helps us
10: 5 Moses describes in this w the
14:13 or obstacle in your brother's w.
14:18 anyone who serves Christ in this w
15:19 So from Jerusalem all the w round to
15:25 however, I am on my w to Jerusalem
15:28 go to Spain and visit you on the w.
16: 2 Lord in a w worthy of the saints
16:17 put obstacles in your w that are
1Co 1: 5 in every w—in all your speaking
2:11 In the same w no-one knows the

1Co 4:17 He will remind you of my w of life
7: 4 In the same w, the husband's body
7:35 in a right w in undivided devotion
8:12 sin against your brothers in this w
9:14 In the same w, the Lord has
9:24 Run in such a w as to get the prize.
10:13 he will also provide a w out so that
10:33 I try to please everybody in every w.
11:25 In the same w, after supper he took
12:31 I will show you the most excellent w.
14: 1 Follow the w of love and eagerly
14:40 be done in a fitting and orderly w.
16:11 Send him on his w in peace so that
2Co 1:16 I planned to visit you on my w to
1:16 have you send me on my w to Judea.
5:16 Christ in this w, we do so no longer.
6: 4 we commend ourselves in every w: in
7: 9 so were not harmed in any w by us.
8:20 w we administer this liberal gift.
9:11 You will be made rich in every w so
11: 6 perfectly clear to you in every w.
11: 9 any w, and will continue to do so.
11:18 Since many are boasting in the w the
Gal 1:13 For you have heard of my previous w
4:23 woman was born in the ordinary w;
4:29 the son born in the ordinary w
5:12 whole w and emasculate themselves!
6: 2 w you will fulfil the law of Christ.
Eph 1:23 him who fills everything in every w.
4:20 did not come to know Christ that w.
4:22 with regard to your former w of life,
5:28 In this same w, husbands ought to
6: 9 treat your slaves in the same w.
Php 1: 7 is right for me to feel this w about
1:18 important thing is that in every w,
1:20 hope that I will in no w be ashamed,
1:28 without being frightened in any w by
Col 1:10 may please him in every w: bearing
4: 5 Be wise in the w you act towards
1Th 2:16 In this w they always heap up their
3: 4 turned out that w, as you well know.
3: 5 I was afraid that in some w the
3:11 clear the w for us to come to you.
4: 4 in a w that is holy and honourable,
2Th 2: 3 Don't let anyone deceive you in any w
2: 7 do so till he is taken out of the w.
3:16 peace at all times and in every w.
1Ti 3:11 In the same w, their wives are to be
5:25 In the same w, good deeds are
6:19 In this w they will lay up treasure
2Ti 3: 6 They are the kind who worm their w
3:10 know all about my teaching, my w of
Tit 2: 3 to be reverent in the w they live,
2:10 so that in every w they will make
3:13 Apollos on their w and see that they
Heb 2:17 made like his brothers in every w,
4:15 one who has been tempted in every w,
9: 8 that the w into the Most Holy Place
9:21 In the same w, he sprinkled with the
9:25 the w the high priest enters the
10:20 by a new and living w opened for us
13: 7 w of life and imitate their faith.
13:18 to live honourably in every w.
Jas 1:11 In the same w, the rich man will
2:17 In the same w, faith by itself, if
2:25 In the same w, was not even Rahab
5:20 of his w will save him from death
1Pe 1:18 redeemed from the empty w of life
3: 1 Wives, in the same w be submissive
3: 5 For this is the w the holy women of
3: 6 is right and do not give w to fear.
3: 7 Husbands, in the same w be
5: 5 Young men, in the same w be
2Pe 2: 2 bring the w of truth into disrepute.
2:15 They have left the straight w and
2:15 follow the w of Balaam son of Beor,
2:21 have known the w of righteousness,
3:11 will be destroyed in this w,
3:16 He writes the same w in all his
1Jn 4:17 In this w, love is made complete
3Jn : 6 their w in a manner worthy of God.
Jude : 7 In a similar w, Sodom and Gomorrah
: 8 In the very same w, these dreamers
:11 They have taken the w of Cain;
:15 they have done in the ungodly w,
Rev 16:12 the w for the kings from the East.
18:20 her for the w she treated you.

Way of the LORD

Ge 18:19 w by doing what is right and just,
Jdg 2:22 see whether they will keep the w and
2Ki 21:22 fathers, and did not walk in the w.
Pr 10:29 The w is a refuge for the righteous,
Jer 5: 4 w, the requirements of their God.
5: 5 w, the requirements of their God.

Way of the Lord

Eze 18:25 "Yet you say, 'The w is not just.'
18:29 Yet the house of Israel says, 'The w
33:17 "Yet your countrymen say, 'The w is
33:20 Israel, you say, 'The w is not just.
Ac 18:25 He had been instructed in the w, and

Waylaid (Waylay)

1Sa 15: 2 w them as they came up from Egypt.

Waylay (Waylaid)

Pr 1:11 blood, let's w some harmless soul;
1:18 own blood; they w only themselves!

Ways (*Evil ways*, Way)

Ge 6:12 on earth had corrupted their w.
Ex 33:13 teach me your w so I may know you
Lev 5: 5 anyone is guilty in any of these w,
18:24 defile yourselves in any of these w,
25:54 is not redeemed in any of these w,
Dt 8: 6 walking in his w and revering him.
10:12 to walk in all his w, to love him,
11:22 all his w and to hold fast to him—
18: 9 detestable w of the nations there.
19: 9 to walk always in his w—then you
26:17 God and that you will walk in his w,
28: 9 the LORD your God and walk in his w.
30:16 to walk in his w, and to keep his
32: 4 are perfect, and all his w are just.
Jos 22: 5 to walk in all his w, to obey his
Jdg 2:19 the people returned to w even more
2:19 their evil practices and stubborn w.
1Sa 8: 3 his sons did not walk in his w. They
8: 5 and your sons do not walk in your w;
2Sa 14:14 he devises w so that a banished
22:22 For I have kept the w of the LORD; I
1Ki 2: 3 your God requires: Walk in his w,
3:14 if you walk in my w and obey my
8:58 to walk in all his w and to keep the
11:33 and have not walked in my w, nor
11:38 walk in my w and do what is right in
15:26 walking in the w of his father and
15:34 walking in the w of Jeroboam and in
16: 2 but you walked in the w of Jeroboam
16:19 walking in the w of Jeroboam and in
16:26 He walked in all the w of Jeroboam
22:43 In everything he walked in the w of
22:52 because he walked in the w of his
22:52 in the w of Jeroboam son of Nebat,
2Ki 8:18 He walked in the w of the kings of
8:27 He walked in the w of the house of
16: 3 He walked in the w of the kings of
16: 3 following the detestable w of the
21:21 He walked in all the w of his father;
22: 2 in all the w of his father David,
2Ch 6:31 walk in your w all the time they
7:14 face and turn from their wicked w,
11:17 walking in the w of David and
17: 3 w that his father David had followed.
17: 6 His heart was devoted to the w of
20:32 He walked in the w of his father Asa
21: 6 He walked in the w of the kings of
21:12 'You have not walked in the w of
21:13 you have walked in the w of the
22: 3 He too walked in the w of the house
28: 2 He walked in the w of the kings of
28: 3 following the detestable w of the
28:26 events of his reign and all his w,
34: 2 walked in the w of his father David,
Est 5:11 the w the king had honoured him
Job 4: 6 and your blameless w your hope?
13:15 will surely defend my w to his face.
17: 9 the righteous will hold to their w,
Job 21:14 We have no desire to know your w.
22: 3 he gain if your w were blameless?
22:28 and light will shine on your w.
24:13 not know its w or stay in its paths.
24:23 but his eyes are on their w.
27:11 w of the Almighty I will not conceal.
31: 4 Does he not see my w and count my
34:21 "His eyes are on the w of men; he
34:27 and had no regard for any of his w.
36:23 Who has prescribed his w for him, or
37: 5 God's voice thunders in marvellous w;
Ps 10: 5 His w are always prosperous; he is
17: 4 myself from the w of the violent.
18:21 For I have kept the w of the LORD; I
25: 4 Show me your w, O LORD, teach me
25: 7 of my youth and my rebellious w;
25: 8 he instructs sinners in his w.
25:10 All the w of the LORD are loving and
37: 7 fret when men succeed in their w,
37:14 to slay those whose w are upright.
39: 1 I said, "I will watch my w and keep
51:13 I will teach transgressors your w,
53: 1 are corrupt, and their w are vile;
55:19 their w and have no fear of God.
67: 2 that your w may be known on earth,
77:13 Your w, O God, are holy. What god is
81:13 to me, if Israel would follow my w,
91:11 you to guard you in all your w;
95:10 and they have not known my w."
103: 7 He made known his w to Moses, his
107:17 fools through their rebellious w
119: 1 Blessed are they whose w are
119: 3 nothing wrong; they walk in his w.
119: 5 Oh, that my w were steadfast in
119:15 your precepts and consider your w.
119:26 I recounted my w and you answered me;
119:29 Keep me from deceitful w; be
119:59 I have considered my w and have
119:168 for all my w are known to you.
125: 5 those who turn to crooked w the LORD
128: 1 fear the LORD, who walk in his w.
138: 5 May they sing of the w of the LORD,
139: 3 you are familiar with all my w.
145:17 The LORD is righteous in all his w
146: 9 he frustrates the w of the wicked.
Pr 1:22 you simple ones love your simple w?
1:31 they will eat the fruit of their w
2:12 Wisdom will save you from the w of
2:13 straight paths to walk in dark w,
2:15 and who are devious in their w.
2:20 Thus you will walk in the w of good
3: 6 in all your w acknowledge him, and
3:17 Her w are pleasant w, and all her
3:31 violent man or choose any of his w,
4:26 feet and take only w that are firm.
5:21 For a man's w are in full view of
6: 6 consider its w and be wise!
7:25 Do not let your heart turn to her w
8:32 me; blessed are those who keep my w.
9: 6 Leave your simple w and you will
11:20 in those whose w are blameless.
14: 2 he whose w are devious despises him.
14: 8 is to give thought to their w,
14:14 will be fully repaid for their w,
16: 2 All a man's w seem innocent to him,
16: 7 a man's w are pleasing to the LORD,
19:16 is contemptuous of his w will die.
21: 2 All a man's w seem right to him, but
21:29 upright man gives thought to his w.
22:25 or you may learn his w and get
23:26 and let your eyes keep to my w,
28: 6 a rich man whose w are perverse.
28:18 w are perverse will suddenly fall.
Ecc 11: 9 Follow the w of your heart and
Isa 2: 3 He will teach us his w, so that we
42:16 I will lead the blind by w they have
42:24 his w; they did not obey his law.
45:13 I will make all his w straight.
55: 8 are your w my w," declares the LORD.
55: 9 so are my w higher than your w and
57:10 You were wearied by all your w, but
57:17 yet he kept on in his wilful w.
57:18 I have seen his w, but I will heal
58: 2 out; they seem eager to know my w,
59: 7 ruin and destruction mark their w.
63:17 do you make us wander from your w

Isa 64: 5 do right, who remember your w.
65: 2 who walk in w not good, pursuing
66: 3 They have chosen their own w, and
Jer 2:33 of women can learn from your w.
2:36 changing your w? You will be
3:21 because they have perverted their w
6:27 you may observe and test their w.
7: 3 says: Reform your w and your actions,
7: 5 If you really change your w and your
7:23 Walk in all the w I command you,
10: 2 "Do not learn the w of the nations
12:16 if they learn well the w of my
15: 7 for they have not changed their w.
16:17 My eyes are on all their w; they are
18:11 and reform your w and your actions.'
18:15 in their w and in the ancient paths.
26:13 Now reform your w and your actions
32:19 Your eyes are open to all the w of
35:15 wicked w and reform your actions;
36: 7 each will turn from his wicked w,
Lam 3:40 Let us examine our w and test them,
Eze 16:47 You not only walked in their w and
16:47 but in all your w you soon became
16:61 you will remember your w and be
18:23 they turn from their w and live?
18:25 Is it not your w that are unjust?
18:29 Are my w unjust, O house of Israel?
18:29 Is it not your w that are unjust?
18:30 each one according to his w,
28:15 You were blameless in your w from
33: 8 out to dissuade him from his w,
33: 9 from his w and he does not do so,
33:11 they turn from their w and live.
33:20 each of you according to his own w."
Da 4:37 is right and all his w are just.
5:23 his hand your life and all your w.
Hos 4: 9 punish both of them for their w
4:18 their rulers dearly love shameful w.
12: 2 punish Jacob according to his w
14: 9 The w of the LORD are right; the
Mic 2: 7 do good to him whose w are upright?
4: 2 He will teach us his w, so that we
Hab 3: 6 hills collapsed. His w are eternal.
Hag 1: 5 "Give careful thought to your w.
1: 7 "Give careful thought to your w.
Zec 1: 6 us what our w and practices deserve,
3: 7 'If you will walk in my w and keep
Mal 2: 9 because you have not followed my w
Lk 3: 5 become straight, the rough w smooth.
Ac 3:26 each of you from your wicked w."
13:10 perverting the right w of the Lord?
18:13 God in w contrary to the law."
28:10 They honoured us in many w and when
Ro 1:30 they invent w of doing evil; they
3:16 ruin and misery mark their w,
1Co 13:11 a man, I put childish w behind me.
2Co 4: 2 shameful w; we do not use deception,
8:22 to us in many w that he is zealous,
Eph 2: 2 you followed the w of this world
Col 3: 7 You used to walk in these w, in the
2Ti 1:18 how many w he helped me in Ephesus.
Heb 1: 1 at many times and in various w,
3:10 and they have not known my w.'
Jas 3: 2 We all stumble in many w. If anyone
2Pe 2: 2 Many will follow their shameful w
Rev 2:22 unless they repent of her w.
15: 3 true are your w, King of the ages.

Wayward (Waywardness)

Ps 58: 3 the womb they are w and speak lies.
Pr 2:16 the w wife with her seductive words,
6:24 the smooth tongue of the w wife.
7: 5 the w wife with her seductive words.
20:16 pledge if he does it for a w woman.
23:27 pit and a w wife is a narrow well.
27:13 pledge if he does it for a w woman.
Isa 29:24 Those who are w in spirit will gain

Waywardness (Wayward)

Pr 1:32 For the w of the simple will kill
Hos 14: 4 "I will heal their w and love them

Weak (Weakened, Weakening, Weaker, Weakest, Weakling, Weakness, Weaknesses, Weak-willed)

Ge 27: 1 Isaac was old and his eyes were so w
29:17 Leah had w eyes, but Rachel was
30:42 if the animals were w, he would not
30:42 So the w animals went to Laban and
Nu 13:18 there are strong or w, few or many.
Dt 34: 7 were not w nor his strength gone.
Jdg 16: 7 I'll become as w as any other man."
16:11 I'll become as w as any other man."
16:13 I'll become as w as any other man."
16:17 would become as w as any other man."
1Sa 3: 2 whose eyes were becoming so w that
15: 9 and w they totally destroyed.
2Sa 3:39 I am w, and these sons of Zeruiah
17: 2 attack him while he is weary and w.
2Ch 28:15 All those who were w they put on
Ne 6: 9 "Their hands will get too w for the
Ps 6: 7 My eyes grow w with sorrow; they
10: 2 the wicked man hunts down the w,
12: 5 "Because of the oppression of the w
31: 9 my eyes grow w with sorrow, my soul
31:10 my affliction, and my bones grow w.
34:10 The lions may grow w and hungry, but
41: 1 is he who has regard for the w;
72:13 He will take pity on the w and the
82: 3 Defend the cause of the w and
82: 4 Rescue the w and needy; deliver them
Isa 14:10 "You also have become w, as we are;
38:14 My eyes grew w as I looked to the
40:29 and increases the power of the w.
Eze 7:17 knee will become as w as water.
21: 7 and every knee become as w as water.
29:15 I will make it so w that it will
34: 4 You have not strengthened the w or
34:16 up the injured and strengthen the w,
34:21 butting all the w sheep with your
Mt 26:41 is willing, but the body is w."
Mk 14:38 is willing, but the body is w."
Ac 20:35 of hard work we must help the w,
Ro 6:19 you are w in your natural selves.
14: 1 Accept him whose faith is w, without
14: 2 faith is w, eats only vegetables.
15: 1 the w and not to please ourselves.
1Co 1:27 God chose the w things of the world
4:10 you are so wise in Christ! We are w,
8: 7 conscience is w, it is defiled.
8: 9 become a stumbling-block to the w.
8:10 For if anyone with a w conscience
8:11 this w brother, for whom Christ died,
8:12 w conscience, you sin against Christ.
9:22 To the w I became w, to win the w. I
11:30 That is why many among you are w and
2Co 11:21 I admit that we were too w for that!
11:29 Who is w, and I do not feel w? Who
12:10 For when I am w, then I am strong.
13: 3 He is not w in dealing with you, but
13: 4 Likewise, we are w in him, yet by
13: 9 We are glad whenever we are w but
Gal 4: 9 to those w and miserable principles?
1Th 5:14 help the w, be patient with
Heb 7:18 aside because it was w and useless
7:28 priests men who are w; but the oath,
12:12 your feeble arms and w knees!

Weakened (Weak)

Job 18: 7 The vigour of his step is w; his own
Ro 8: 3 that it was w by the sinful nature,

Weakening (Weak)

Ro 4:19 Without w in his faith, he faced the

Weaker (Weak)

2Sa 3: 1 the house of Saul grew w and w.
1Co 12:22 that seem to be w are indispensable,
1Pe 3: 7 treat them with respect as the w

Weakest (Weak)

Jdg 6:15 Israel? My clan is the w in Manasseh,

Weakling (Weak)

Joel 3:10 Let the w say, "I am strong!"

Weakness (Weak)

Lam 1: 6 in w they have fled before the
Ro 8:26 way, the Spirit helps us in our w.
1Co 1:25 and the w of God is stronger than
2: 3 I came to you in w and fear, and
15:43 is sown in w, it is raised in power;
2Co 11:30 boast of the things that show my w.
12: 9 for my power is made perfect in w.
13: 4 For to be sure, he was crucified in w
Heb 5: 2 since he himself is subject to w.
11:34 whose w was turned to strength; and

Weaknesses (Weak)

2Co 12: 5 about myself, except about my w.
12: 9 all the more gladly about my w,
12:10 for Christ's sake, I delight in w,
Heb 4:15 is unable to sympathise with our w,

Weak-willed (Weak, Will)

Eze 16:30 "'How w you are, declares the
2Ti 3: 6 homes and gain control over w women,

Wealth (Wealthy)

Ge 26:13 The man became rich, and his w
31: 1 w from what belonged to our father."
31:16 Surely all the w that God took away
34:29 They carried off all their w and all
Dt 8:17 hands have produced this w for me."
8:18 gives you the ability to produce w,
Jos 22: 8 with your great w—with large herds
1Sa 2: 7 The LORD sends poverty and w; he
17:25 The king will give great w to the
1Ki 3:11 not for long life or w for yourself,
10: 7 in wisdom and w you have far
1Ch 29:12 W and honour come from you; you are
29:28 enjoyed long life, w and honour.
2Ch 1:11 desire and you have not asked for w,
1:12 And I will also give you w, riches
17: 5 so that he had great w and honour.
18: 1 Now Jehoshaphat had great w and
Est 1: 4 displayed the vast w of his kingdom
5:11 boasted to them about his vast w,
Job 5: 5 and the thirsty pant after his w.
6:22 pay a ransom for me from your w,
15:29 be rich and his w will not endure,
20:10 his own hands must give back his w.
22:20 and fire devours their w.'
31:25 if I have rejoiced over my great w,
36:19 Would your w or even all your mighty
Ps 17:14 they store up w for their children.
37:16 have than the w of many wicked;
39: 6 up w, not knowing who will get it.
39:11 you consume their w like a moth—
45:12 men of w will seek your favour.
49: 6 those who trust in their w and boast
49:10 perish and leave their w to others.
52: 7 but trusted in his great w and grew
73:12 always carefree, they increase in w.
112: 3 W and riches are in his house, and
Pr 3: 9 Honour the LORD with your w, with
5:10 lest strangers feast on your w and
6:31 it costs him all the w of his house.
8:18 honour, enduring w and prosperity.
8:21 bestowing w on those who love me and
10: 4 poor, but diligent hands bring w.
10:15 The w of the rich is their fortified
10:22 The blessing of the LORD brings w,
11: 4 W is worthless in the day of wrath,
11:16 but ruthless men gain only w.
13: 7 to be poor, yet has great w.
13:22 w is stored up for the righteous.
14:24 The w of the wise is their crown,
15:16 the LORD than great w with turmoil.
18:11 The w of the rich is their fortified
19: 4 W brings many friends, but a poor
19:14 Houses and w are inherited from
22: 4 LORD bring w and honour and life.
22:16 the poor to increase his w
28: 8 He who increases his w by exorbitant
29: 3 of prostitutes squanders his w.
Ecc 2:26 storing up w to hand it over to the
4: 8 eyes were not content with his w.
5:10 whoever loves w is never satisfied
5:13 w hoarded to the harm of its owner,
5:14 or w lost through some misfortune,

Ecc 5:19 Moreover, when God gives any man **w**
6: 2 God gives a man **w**, possessions and
9:11 to the wise or **w** to the brilliant
SS 8: 7 If one were to give all the **w** of his
Isa 8: 4 the **w** of Damascus and the plunder
10:14 so my hand reached for the **w** of the
15: 7 the **w** they have acquired and stored
60: 5 **w** on the seas will be brought to you,
60:11 so that men may bring you the **w** of
61: 6 You will feed on the **w** of nations,
66:12 and the **w** of nations like a flooding
Jer 15:13 Your **w** and your treasures I will
17: 3 My mountain in the land and your **w**
20: 5 **w** of this city—all its products,
48:36 The **w** they acquired is gone.
Eze 7:11 that crowd—no **w**, nothing of value.
16:36 Because you poured out your **w** and
26:12 They will plunder your **w** and loot
27:12 **w** of goods; they exchanged silver,
27:18 many products and great **w** of goods,
27:27 Your **w**, merchandise and wares, your
27:33 with your great **w** and your wares you
28: 4 understanding you have gained **w** for
28: 5 trading you have increased your **w**,
28: 5 your **w** your heart has grown proud.
29:19 Babylon, and he will carry off its **w**.
30: 4 When the slain fall in Egypt, her **w**
Da 11: 2 When he has gained power by his **w**,
11:24 loot and **w** among his followers.
11:28 to his own country with great **w**,
Hos 12: 8 With all my **w** they will not find in
Ob :11 while strangers carried off his **w**
:13 **w** in the day of their disaster.
Mic 4:13 **w** to the Lord of all the earth.
Na 2: 9 the **w** from all its treasures!
Zep 1:13 Their **w** will be plundered, their
Zec 14:14 The **w** of all the surrounding nations
Mt 13:22 the deceitfulness of **w** choke it,
19:22 away sad, because he had great **w**.
Mk 4:19 the deceitfulness of **w** and the
10:22 away sad, because he had great **w**.
12:44 They all gave out of their **w**; but
Lk 15:13 squandered his **w** in wild living.
16: 9 use worldly **w** to gain friends
16:11 trustworthy in handling worldly **w**,
18:23 because he was a man of great **w**.
21: 4 gave their gifts out of their **w**;
1Ti 6:17 arrogant nor to put their hope in **w**,
Jas 5: 2 Your **w** has rotted, and moths have
5: 3 You have hoarded **w** in the last days.
Rev 3:17 acquired **w** and do not need a thing.
5:12 to receive power and **w** and wisdom
18:15 their **w** from her will stand far off,
18:17 In one hour such great **w** has been
18:19 the sea became rich through her **w**!

Wealthy (Wealth)

Ge 13: 2 Abram had become very **w** in livestock
24:35 abundantly, and he has become **w**.
26:13 to grow until he became very **w**.
1Sa 25: 2 there at Carmel, was very **w**.
2Sa 19:32 Mahanaim, for he was a very **w** man.
2Ki 15:20 Every **w** man had to contribute fifty
Job 27:19 He lies down **w**, but will do so no
Hos 12: 8 "I am very rich; I have become **w**.
Hab 2: 6 and makes himself **w** by extortion!
Lk 19: 2 was a chief tax collector and was **w**.

Weaned

Ge 21: 8 The child grew and was **w**, and on the
21: 8 was **w** Abraham held a great feast.
1Sa 1:22 "After the boy is **w**, I will take him
1:23 "Stay here until you have **w** him;
1:23 nursed her son until she had **w** him.
1:24 After he was **w**, she took the boy
Ps 131: 2 like a **w** child with its mother,
131: 2 like a **w** child is my soul within me.
Isa 28: 9 To children **w** from their milk,
Hos 1: 8 After she had **w** Lo-Ruhamah, Gomer

Weapon (Weapons)

1Sa 21: 8 brought my sword or any other **w**,
1Ki 20:35 with your **w**," but the man refused.
2Ki 11: 8 each man with his **w** in his hand.
11:11 The guards, each with his **w** in his
1Ch 12:33 for battle with every type of **w**,
12:37 armed with every type of **w**—120,000.
2Ch 23:10 each with his **w** in his hand, round
Ne 4:17 one hand and held a **w** in the other,
4:23 his **w**, even when he went for water.
Job 20:24 Though he flees from an iron **w**, a
Isa 54:16 and forges a **w** fit for its work.
54:17 no **w** forged against you will prevail,
Jer 51:20 "You are my war club, my **w** for
Eze 9: 1 here, each with a **w** in his hand."
9: 2 each with a deadly **w** in his hand.

Weapons (Weapon)

Ge 27: 3 Now then, get your **w**—your quiver
49: 5 their swords are **w** of violence.
Dt 1:41 So every one of you put on his **w**,
1Sa 8:12 and still others to make **w** of war
17:54 the Philistine's **w** in his own tent.
20:40 Jonathan gave his **w** to the boy and
2Sa 1:27 mighty have fallen! The **w** of war
2:21 young men and strip him of his **w**.
1Ki 10:25 **w** and spices, and horses and mules.
2Ki 10: 2 and horses, a fortified city and **w**,
2Ch 9:24 **w** and spices, and horses and mules.
23: 7 each man with his **w** in his hand.
32: 5 made large numbers of **w** and shields.
Ps 7:13 He has prepared his deadly **w**; he
76: 3 and the swords, the **w** of war.
Ecc 9:18 Wisdom is better than **w** of war, but
Isa 13: 5 the **w** of his wrath—to destroy the
22: 8 the **w** in the Palace of the Forest;
Jer 21: 4 the **w** of war that are in your hands,
22: 7 each man with his **w**, and they will
50:25 and brought out the **w** of his wrath,
Eze 23:24 They will come against you with **w**,
26: 9 and demolish your towers with his **w**.
32:27 to the grave with their **w** of war,
39: 9 use the **w** for fuel and burn them up—
39:10 they will use the **w** for fuel.
Jn 18: 3 carrying torches, lanterns and **w**.
2Co 6: 7 with **w** of righteousness in the right
10: 4 The **w** we fight with are not the **w** of

Wear (Wearing, Wears, Wore, Worn, Worn-out)

Ge 28:20 give me food to eat and clothes to **w**
Ex 18:18 to you will only **w** yourselves out.
28:35 Aaron must **w** it when he ministers.
28:43 Aaron and his sons must **w** them
29:30 Holy Place is to **w** them seven days.
Lev 13:45 disease must **w** torn clothes,
19:19 "'Do not **w** clothing woven of two
21:10 ordained to **w** the priestly garments,
Dt 8: 4 Your clothes did not **w** out and your
22: 5 A woman must not **w** men's clothing,
22: 5 nor a man **w** women's clothing, for
22:11 Do not **w** clothes of wool and linen
22:12 the four corners of the cloak you **w**.
28:32 and you will **w** out your eyes
29: 5 your clothes did not **w** out, nor did
Jdg 8:24 Ishmaelites to **w** gold ear-rings.)
1Sa 2:28 and to **w** an ephod in my presence.
1Ki 22:30 but you **w** your royal robes.
2Ch 18:29 but you **w** your royal robes.
Ne 9:21 their clothes did not **w** out nor did
Job 27:17 what he lays up the righteous will **w**,
31:36 Surely I would **w** it on my shoulder,
Ps 102:26 they will all **w** out like a garment.
Pr 23: 4 Do not **w** yourself out to get rich;
Isa 15: 3 In the streets they **w** sackcloth; on
49:18 "you will **w** them all as ornaments;
50: 9 They will all **w** out like a garment;
51: 6 the earth will **w** out like a garment
Jer 12:13 **w** themselves out but gain nothing.
Eze 44:17 they are to **w** linen clothes; they
44:17 they must not **w** any woollen garment
44:18 They are to **w** linen turbans on their
44:18 **w** anything that makes them perspire.
Am 8:10 I will make all of you **w** sackcloth
Mt 6:25 or about your body, what you will **w**.
6:31 we drink?' or 'What shall we **w**?'
11: 8 **w** fine clothes are in kings' palaces.
Mk 6: 9 **W** sandals but not an extra tunic.
Lk 7:25 those who **w** expensive clothes and
12:22 or about your body, what you will **w**.
12:33 for yourselves that will not **w** out,
18: 5 **w** me out with her coming!'
Heb 1:11 they will all **w** out like a garment.
Rev 3:18 become rich; and white clothes to **w**,
19: 8 and clean, was given her to **w**.

Wearied (Weary)

Isa 43:22 not **w** yourselves for me, O Israel.
43:23 nor **w** you with demands for incense.
43:24 sins and **w** me with your offences.
57:10 You were **w** by all your ways, but you
Mal 2:17 You have **w** the LORD with your words.
2:17 "How have we **w** him?" you ask. By

Wearies (Weary)

Ecc 10:15 A fool's work **w** him; he does not
12:12 no end, and much study **w** the body.

Wearing (Wear)

Ge 37:23 richly ornamented robe he was **w**—
Ex 32: 2 are **w**, and bring them to me."
Dt 21:13 put aside the clothes she was **w** when
Ru 3:15 the shawl you are **w** and hold it out.
1Sa 2:18 the LORD—a boy **w** a linen ephod.
14: 3 was Ahijah, who was **w** an ephod.
18: 4 Jonathan took off the robe he was **w**
28:14 "An old man **w** a robe is coming up,"
2Sa 6:14 David, **w** a linen ephod, danced
13:18 She was **w** a richly ornamented robe,
13:19 tore the ornamented robe she was **w**.
20: 8 Joab was **w** his military tunic, and
1Ki 11:29 met him on the way, **w** a new cloak.
11:30 he was **w** and tore it into twelve
20:32 **W** sackcloth round their waists and
2Ki 19: 2 all **w** sackcloth, to the prophet
Ne 9: 1 fasting and **w** sackcloth and having
Est 1:11 him Queen Vashti, **w** her royal crown
8:15 king's presence **w** royal garments
SS 3: 8 all of them **w** the sword, all
3:11 and look at King Solomon **w** the crown,
Isa 37: 2 leading priests, all **w** sackcloth,
Jer 13: 4 "Take the belt you bought and are **w**
Da 3:21 these men, **w** their robes, trousers,
Mt 22:11 there who was not **w** wedding clothes.
Mk 14:51 A young man, **w** nothing but a linen
Jn 19: 5 Jesus came out **w** the crown of thorns
Ac 12:21 Herod, **w** his royal robes, sat on
Jas 2: 2 **w** a gold ring and fine clothes,
2: 3 to the man **w** fine clothes and say,
1Pe 3: 3 **w** of gold jewellery and fine clothes.
Rev 7: 9 They were **w** white robes and were

Wearisome (Weary)

Ecc 1: 8 All things are **w**, more than one can

Wears (Wear)

Job 14:19 water **w** away stones and torrents
Ps 119:139 My zeal **w** me out, for my enemies
Isa 16:12 she only **w** herself out; when she

Weary (Wearied, Wearies, Wearisome)

Dt 25:18 you were **w** and worn out, they met
28:65 anxious mind, eyes **w** with longing,
Jos 7: 3 take it and do not **w** all the people,
2Sa 17: 2 I would attack him while he is **w** and
Job 3:17 and there the **w** are at rest.
22: 7 You gave no water to the **w** and you
31:16 or let the eyes of the widow grow **w**,
Ps 63: 1 and **w** land where there is no water.
68: 9 you refreshed your **w** inheritance.
119:28 My soul is **w** with sorrow; strengthen
Pr 25:25 Like cold water to a **w** soul is good
Isa 1:14 to me; I am **w** of bearing them.
28:12 the resting-place, let the **w** rest";
40:28 He will not grow tired or **w**, and his
40:29 He gives strength to the **w** and
40:30 Even youths grow tired and **w**, and
40:31 will run and not grow **w**, they will
46: 1 are burdensome, a burden for the **w**.
50: 4 know the word that sustains the **w**.
Jer 9: 5 lie; they **w** themselves with sinning.
20: 9 **w** of holding it in; indeed, I cannot.
31:25 I will refresh the **w** and satisfy the

Lam 5: 5 heels; we are w and find no rest.
Zec 11: 8 detested me, and I grew w of them
Mt 11:28 "Come to me, all you who are w and
Ac 24: 4 in order not to w you further, I
Gal 6: 9 Let us not become w in doing good,
Heb 12: 3 you will not grow w and lose heart.
Rev 2: 3 for my name, and have not grown w.

Weasel
Lev 11:29 w, the rat, any kind of great lizard,

Weather
Mt 16: 2 will be fair w, for the sky is red,'

Weave (Interwoven, Weaver, Weaver's, Weavers, Weaving, Wove, Woven)
Ex 28:39 "W the tunic of fine linen and make
Jdg 16:13 He replied, "If you w the seven

Weaver (Weave)
Ex 39:22 of blue cloth—the work of a w—
39:27 of fine linen—the work of a w—
Isa 38:12 Like a w I have rolled up my life,

Weaver's (Weave)
1Sa 17: 7 His spear shaft was like a w rod,
2Sa 21:19 a spear with a shaft like a w rod.
1Ch 11:23 a spear like a w rod in his hand,
20: 5 a spear with a shaft like a w rod.
Job 7: 6 days are swifter than a w shuttle

Weavers (Weave)
Ex 35:35 and w—all of them master craftsmen
Isa 19: 9 the w of fine linen will lose hope.

Weaving (Weave)
2Ki 23: 7 and where women did w for Asherah.

Web (Cobwebs)
Job 8:14 what he relies on is a spider's w.
8:15 He leans on his w, but it gives way;
Isa 59: 5 of vipers and spin a spider's w.

Wedding
Jdg 14:20 who had attended him at his w.
1Ki 9:16 gave it as a w gift to his daughter,
Ps 45: T Sons of Korah. A maskil. A w song.
78:63 and their maidens had no w songs;
SS 3:11 his w, the day his heart rejoiced.
Jer 2:32 a bride her w ornaments? Yet my
Mt 22: 2 prepared a w banquet for his son.
22: 4 is ready. Come to the w banquet.'
22: 8 said to his servants, 'The w banquet
22:10 the w hall was filled with guests.
22:11 there who was not wearing w clothes.
22:12 w clothes?' The man was speechless.
25:10 went in with him to the w banquet.
Lk 12:36 master to return from a w banquet,
14: 8 "When someone invites you to a w
Jn 2: 1 On the third day a w took place at
2: 2 had also been invited to the w.
Rev 19: 7 For the w of the Lamb has come,
19: 9 invited to the w supper of the Lamb!'

Wedge
Jos 7:21 a w of gold weighing fifty shekels,
7:24 the silver, the robe, the gold w,

Weed (Seaweed, Tumble-weed, Weeds)
Mt 13:41 and they will w out of his kingdom

Weeds (Weed)
Job 31:40 of wheat and w instead of barley.
Pr 24:31 the ground was covered with w, and
Hos 10: 4 poisonous w in a ploughed field.
Zep 2: 9 a place of w and salt pits,
Mt 13:25 came and sowed w among the wheat,
13:26 ears, then the w also appeared.
13:27 Where then did the w come from?'
13:29 'because while you are pulling the w,
Mt 13:30 First collect the w and tie them in
13:36 the parable of the w in the field."
13:38 The w are the sons of the evil one,
13:40 "As the w are pulled up and burned

Week (Weeks)
Ge 29:27 Finish this daughter's bridal w;
29:28 Jacob did so. He finished the w with
Mt 28: 1 at dawn on the first day of the w,
Mk 16: 2 Very early on the first day of the w,
16: 9 early on the first day of the w,
Lk 18:12 I fast twice a w and give a tenth of
24: 1 On the first day of the w, very
Jn 19:14 of Passover W, about the sixth hour.
20: 1 Early on the first day of the w,
20:19 evening of that first day of the w,
20:26 A w later his disciples were in the
Ac 20: 7 On the first day of the w we came
28:14 invited us to spend a w with them.
1Co 16: 2 On the first day of every w, each

Weeks (*Feast of weeks*, Week)
Lev 12: 5 for two w the woman will be unclean,
23:15 offering, count off seven full w.
Dt 16: 9 Count off seven w from the time you
Jer 5:24 us of the regular w of harvest.'
Da 10: 2 time I, Daniel, mourned for three w.
10: 3 at all until the three w were over.

Weep (Weeping, Weeps, Wept)
Ge 23: 2 mourn for Sarah and to w over her.
29:11 Jacob kissed Rachel and began to w
42:24 away from them and began to w,
43:30 out and looked for a place to w.
Jdg 11:37 the hills and w with my friends,
1Sa 30: 4 they had no strength left to w.
2Sa 1:24 "O daughters of Israel, w for Saul,
2Ki 8:11 Then the man of God began to w.
Ne 8: 9 Do not mourn or w." For all the
Job 2:12 him; they began to w aloud,
27:15 their widows will not w for them.
Ps 69:10 I w and fast, I must endure scorn;
78:64 sword, and their widows could not w.
Ecc 3: 4 a time to w and a time to laugh, a
Isa 15: 2 to its high places to w; Moab wails
16: 9 I w, as Jazer weeps, for the vines
22: 4 Turn away from me; let me w bitterly.
22:12 called you on that day to w and to
30:19 in Jerusalem, you will w no more.
33: 7 the envoys of peace w bitterly.
Jer 9: 1 I would w day and night for the
9:10 I will w and wail for the mountains
13:17 if you do not listen, I will w in
13:17 your pride; my eyes will w bitterly,
22:10 Do not w for the dead king or mourn
22:10 w bitterly for him who is exiled,
25:34 W and wail, you shepherds; roll in
48:32 I w for you, as Jazer weeps, O vines
Lam 1:16 "This is why I w and my eyes
Eze 24:16 not lament or w or shed any tears.
24:23 You will not mourn or w but will
27:31 They will w over you with anguish of
Joel 1: 5 Wake up, you drunkards, and w! Wail,
2:17 who minister before the LORD, w
Am 5:16 to w and the mourners to wail.
Mic 1: 8 of this I will w and wail; I will go
1:10 Tell it not in Gath; w not at all.
Mal 2:13 You w and wail because he no longer
Lk 6:21 you who w now, for you will laugh.
6:25 laugh now, for you will mourn and w.
23:28 do not w for me; w for yourselves
Jn 16:20 I tell you the truth, you will w and
Jas 5: 1 Now listen, you rich people, w and
Rev 5: 5 "Do not w! See, the Lion of the
18: 9 they will w and mourn over her.
18:11 "The merchants of the earth will w
18:15 her torment. They will w and mourn

Weeping (Weep, *Weeping and gnashing of teeth*)
Ge 45:14 wept, and Benjamin embraced him, w.
Nu 25: 6 were w at the entrance to the Tent
Dt 1:45 your w and turned a deaf ear to you.
34: 8 the time of w and mourning was over.
Jdg 20:26 there they sat w before the LORD.
21: 2 raising their voices and w bitterly.
1Sa 1: 8 "Hannah, why are you w? Why don't
11: 5 with the people? Why are they w?"
2Sa 3:16 w behind her all the way to Bahurim.
13:19 and went away, w aloud as she went.
15:30 w as he went; his head was covered
15:30 too and were w as they went up.
19: 1 Joab was told, "The king is w and
2Ki 8:12 "Why is my lord w?" asked Hazael.
Ezr 3:13 shouts of joy from the sound of w,
10: 1 w and throwing himself down before
Ne 8: 9 For all the people had been w as
Est 4: 3 Jews, with fasting, w and wailing.
8: 3 the king, falling at his feet and w.
Job 16:16 My face is red with w, deep shadows
Ps 6: 6 I flood my bed with w and drench
6: 8 evil, for the LORD has heard my w.
30: 5 w may remain for a night, but
35:14 in grief as though w for my mother.
39:12 cry for help; be not deaf to my w.
126: 6 He who goes out w, carrying seed to
Isa 15: 3 they all wail, prostrate with w.
15: 5 They go up the way to Luhith, w as
65:19 the sound of w and of crying will be
Jer 3:21 the w and pleading of the people of
31: 9 They will come with w; they will
31:15 great w, Rachel w for her children
31:16 "Restrain your voice from w and your
41: 6 Mizpah to meet them, w as he went.
48: 5 They go up the way to Luhith, w
Lam 2:11 My eyes fail from w, I am in torment
Joel 2:12 with fasting and w and mourning."
Am 8:10 and all your singing into w.
Zec 12:11 On that day the w in Jerusalem will
12:11 like the w of Hadad Rimmon in the
Mt 2:18 w and great mourning, Rachel w for
Mk 16:10 him and who were mourning and w.
Lk 7:38 she stood behind him at his feet w,
13:28 "There will be w there, and gnashing
Jn 11:33 Jesus saw her w, and the Jews who
11:33 who had come along with her also w,
Ac 21:13 Paul answered, "Why are you w and
Rev 18:19 and with w and mourning cry out:

Weeping and gnashing of teeth
Mt 8:12 darkness, where there will be w."
13:42 furnace, where there will be w.
13:50 furnace, where there will be w.
22:13 darkness, where there will be w.'
24:51 hypocrites, where there will be w.
25:30 darkness, where there will be w.'

Weeps (Weep)
Isa 16: 9 I weep, as Jazer w, for the vines of
Jer 48:32 I weep for you, as Jazer w, O vines
Lam 1: 2 Bitterly she w at night, tears are

Weigh (Outweigh, Outweighs, Weighed, Weighing, Weighs, Weight, Weightier, Weights, Weighty)
2Sa 14:26 too heavy for him—he would w it,
Ezr 8:29 carefully until you w them out in
Job 31: 6 let God w me in honest scales and he
Isa 46: 6 bags and w out silver on the scales;
Eze 4:10 W out twenty shekels of food to eat
33:10 "Our offences and sins w us down,
1Co 14:29 should w carefully what is said.

Weighed (Weigh)
Ge 23:16 w out for him the price he had named
Nu 7:85 Each silver plate w a hundred and
7:85 Altogether, the silver dishes w two
7:86 with incense w ten shekels each,
7:86 w a hundred and twenty shekels.
31:52 a gift to the LORD w 16,750 shekels.
1Sa 2: 3 who knows, and by him deeds are w.
17: 7 iron point w six hundred shekels.
2Sa 18:12 "Even if a thousand shekels were w
21:16 whose bronze spearhead w three
2Ki 25:16 the LORD, was more than could be w.
1Ch 22: 3 and more bronze than could be w.
22:14 great to be w, and wood and stone.
2Ch 3: 9 The gold nails w fifty shekels. He

Ezr 8:25 I w out to them the offering of
8:26 I w out to them 650 talents of
8:30 sacred articles that had been w out
8:33 in the house of our God, we w out
Job 6: 2 "If only my anguish could be w and
28:15 nor can its price be w in silver.
Ps 62: 9 the highborn are but a lie; if w on
Pr 16: 2 him, but motives are w by the LORD.
Isa 40:12 or w the mountains on the scales and
Jer 6:11 the old, those w down with years.
32: 9 w out for him seventeen shekels of
32:10 and w out the silver on the scales.
52:20 the LORD, was more than could be w.
Lam 3: 7 he has w me down with chains.
Da 5:27 You have been w on the scales and
Lk 21:34 "Be careful, or your hearts will be w
Ac 27:13 so they w anchor and sailed along

Weighing (Weigh)

Ge 24:22 took out a gold nose ring w a beka
24:22 two gold bracelets w ten shekels.
Nu 7:13 one silver plate w a hundred and
7:13 sprinkling bowl w seventy shekels,
7:14 one gold dish w ten shekels, filled
7:19 w a hundred and thirty shekels,
7:19 sprinkling bowl w seventy shekels,
7:20 one gold dish w ten shekels, filled
7:25 one silver plate w a hundred and
7:25 sprinkling bowl w seventy shekels,
7:26 one gold dish w ten shekels, filled
7:31 one silver plate w a hundred and
7:31 sprinkling bowl w seventy shekels,
7:32 one gold dish w ten shekels, filled
7:37 one silver plate w a hundred and
7:37 sprinkling bowl w seventy shekels,
7:38 one gold dish w ten shekels, filled
7:43 one silver plate w a hundred and
7:43 sprinkling bowl w seventy shekels
7:44 one gold dish w ten shekels, filled
7:49 one silver plate w a hundred and
7:49 sprinkling bowl w seventy shekels
7:50 one gold dish w ten shekels, filled
7:55 one silver plate w a hundred and
7:55 sprinkling bowl w seventy shekels
7:56 one gold dish w ten shekels, filled
7:61 one silver plate w a hundred and
7:61 sprinkling bowl w seventy shekels
7:62 one gold dish w ten shekels, filled
7:67 one silver plate w a hundred and
7:67 sprinkling bowl w seventy shekels
7:68 one gold dish w ten shekels, filled
7:73 one silver plate w a hundred and
7:73 sprinkling bowl w seventy shekels
7:74 one gold dish w ten shekels, filled
7:79 one silver plate w a hundred and
7:79 sprinkling bowl w seventy shekels
7:80 one gold dish w ten shekels, filled
Jos 7:21 and a wedge of gold w fifty shekels,
1Sa 17: 5 of bronze w five thousand shekels;
Ezr 8:26 w 100 talents, 100 talents of gold,

Weighs (Weigh)

Ex 30:13 shekel, which w twenty gerahs.
Nu 3:47 shekel, which w twenty gerahs.
18:16 shekel, which w twenty gerahs.
Pr 12:25 An anxious heart w a man down, but a
15:28 The heart of the righteous w its
21: 2 to him, but the LORD w the heart.
24:12 not he who w the heart perceive it?
Ecc 6: 1 the sun, and it w heavily on men:
8: 6 a man's misery w heavily upon him.
Isa 40:15 he w the islands as though they were

Weight (Weigh)

Ge 23:16 the w current among the merchants.
43:21 exact w—in the mouth of his sack.
Lev 19:35 measuring length, w or quantity.
26:26 they will dole out the bread by w.
Jdg 8:26 The w of the gold rings he asked for
2Sa 12:30 king—its w was a talent of gold,
14:26 and its w was two hundred shekels by
1Ki 7:47 w of the bronze was not determined.
10:14 The w of the gold that Solomon
1Ch 20: 2 w was found to be a talent of gold,
28:14 He designated the w of gold for all
1Ch 28:14 and the w of silver for all the
28:15 the w of gold for the gold
28:15 with the w for each lampstand and
28:15 and the w of silver for each silver
28:16 the w of gold for each table for
28:16 w of silver for the silver tables;
28:17 the w of pure gold for the forks,
28:17 the w of gold for each gold dish;
28:17 w of silver for each silver dish;
28:18 the w of the refined gold for the
2Ch 4:18 w of the bronze was not determined.
9:13 The w of the gold that Solomon
Ezr 8:34 was accounted for by number and w,
8:34 entire w was recorded at that time.
Job 26: 8 clouds do not burst under their w.
Lam 4: 2 once worth their w in gold, are now

Weightier (Weigh)

Jn 5:36 "I have testimony w than that of

Weights (Weigh)

Lev 19:36 Use honest scales and honest w, an
Dt 25:13 Do not have two differing w in your
25:15 You must have accurate and honest w
Pr 11: 1 but accurate w are his delight.
16:11 the w in the bag are of his making.
20:10 Differing w and differing measures—
20:23 The LORD detests differing w, and
Mic 6:11 scales, with a bag of false w?

Weighty (Weigh)

2Co 10:10 For some say, "His letters are w and

Welcome (Welcomed, Welcomes)

Jdg 19:20 "You are w at my house," the old man
Mt 10:14 If anyone will not w you or listen
Mk 6:11 if any place will not w you or
9:37 not w me but the one who sent me."
Lk 9: 5 If people do not w you, shake the
9:53 the people there did not w him,
16: 4 people will w me into their houses.'
Ac 18:27 to the disciples there to w him.
Php 2:29 W him in the Lord with great joy,
Col 4:10 him; if he comes to you, w him.)
Phm :17 if you consider me a partner, w him
:17 a partner, w him as you would w me.
2Pe 1:11 you will receive a rich w into the
2Jn :10 take him into your house or w him.
3Jn :10 that, he refuses to w the brothers.

Welcomed (Welcome)

Jdg 19: 3 her father saw him, he gladly w him.
Ps 21: 3 You w him with rich blessings and
Lk 8:40 when Jesus returned, a crowd w him
9:11 He w them and spoke to them about
10: 8 "When you enter a town and are w,
10:10 when you enter a town and are not w,
16: 9 will be w into eternal dwellings.
19: 6 he came down at once and w him
Jn 4:45 in Galilee, the Galileans w him.
Ac 15: 4 they came to Jerusalem, they were w
17: 7 Jason has w them into his house.
28: 2 They built a fire and w us all
28: 7 He w us to his home and for three
28:30 house and w all who came to see him.
2Co 8:17 For Titus not only w our appeal, but
Gal 4:14 you w me as if I were an angel of
1Th 1: 6 you w the message with the joy given
Heb 11:13 saw them and w them from a distance.
11:31 because she w the spies, was not

Welcomes (Welcome)

Mt 18: 5 "And whoever w a little child like
18: 5 child like this in my name w me.
Mk 9:37 "Whoever w one of these little
9:37 little children in my name w me;
9:37 and whoever w me does not welcome me
Lk 9:48 w this little child in my name w me;
9:48 whoever w me w the one who sent me.
15: 2 man w sinners, and eats with them."
2Jn :11 Anyone who w him shares in his

Welding

Isa 41: 7 He says of the w, "It is good." He

Welfare

Ne 2:10 to promote the w of the Israelites.
Est 10: 3 spoke up for the w of all the Jews.
Php 2:20 takes a genuine interest in your w.

Well (Well's, Welled, Welling, Wells)

Ge 16:14 That is why the w was called Beer
21:19 God opened her eyes and she saw a w
21:25 complained to Abimelech about a w
21:30 as a witness that I dug this w."
24:11 down near the w outside the town;
24:20 ran back to the w to draw more water,
26:19 discovered a w of fresh water there.
26:20 is ours!" So he named the w Esek,
26:21 they dug another w, but they
26:22 and dug another w, and no-one
26:25 and there his servants dug a w.
26:32 told him about the w they had dug.
29: 2 There he saw a w in the field, with
29: 2 the flocks were watered from that w.
29: 2 over the mouth of the w was large.
29: 3 its place over the mouth of the w.
29: 8 rolled away from the mouth of the w.
29:10 the w and watered his uncle's sheep.
Ex 2:15 in Midian, where he sat down by a w.
Nu 20:17 vineyard, or drink water from any w.
21:16 the w where the LORD said to Moses,
21:17 "Spring up, O w! Sing about it,
21:18 about the w that the princes dug,
21:22 vineyard, or drink water from any w.
2Sa 3:26 him back from the w of Sirah.
17:18 He had a w in his courtyard, and
17:19 the w and scattered grain over it.
17:21 the two climbed out of the w and
23:15 the w near the gate of Bethlehem!"
23:16 drew water from the w near the gate
2Ki 10:14 the w of Beth Eked—forty-two men.
1Ch 11:17 the w near the gate of Bethlehem!"
11:18 drew water from the w near the gate
Ne 2:13 the Jackal W and the Dung Gate,
Pr 5:15 running water from your own w.
23:27 and a wayward wife is a narrow w.
25:26 Like a muddied spring or a polluted w
Ecc 12: 6 or the wheel broken at the w,
SS 4:15 You are a garden fountain, a w of
Jer 6: 7 a w pours out its water, so she
Hos 13:15 spring will fail and his w dry up.
Lk 14: 5 falls into a w on the Sabbath day,
Jn 4: 6 Jacob's w was there, and Jesus,
4: 6 from the journey, sat down by the w.
4:11 to draw with and the w is deep.
4:12 who gave us the w and drank from it

Well's (Well)

Ge 29: 3 the stone away from the w mouth

Well-being

Ezr 6:10 for the w of the king and his sons.
Ps 35:27 delights in the w of his servant."
119:122 Ensure your servant's w; let not the
Jer 14:11 Do not pray for the w of this people.

Well-built (Build)

Ge 39: 6 Now Joseph was w and handsome,

Well-dressed (Dress)

Isa 3:24 a rope; instead of w hair, baldness;

Welled (Well)

2Co 8: 2 poverty w up in rich generosity.

Well-fed (Feed)

Jer 5: 8 They are w, lusty stallions, each

Welling (Well)

Jn 4:14 of water w up to eternal life."

Well-kneaded (Knead)

Lev 7:12 of fine flour w and mixed with oil.

Well-known (Know)

Nu 16: 2 Israelite men, w community leaders

Well-mixed (Mix)
Lev 6:21 bring it w and present the grain

Well-nourished (Nourish)
Ne 9:25 They ate to the full and were w;

Well-nurtured (Nurtured)
Ps 144:12 their youth will be like w plants,

Wells (Well)
Ge 26:15 all the w that his father's servants
26:18 Isaac reopened the w that had been
Dt 6:11 w you did not dig, and vineyards and
10: 6 from the w of the Jaakanites to
2Ki 19:24 I have dug w in foreign lands and
Ne 9:25 w already dug, vineyards, olive
Isa 12: 3 draw water from the w of salvation.
37:25 I have dug w in foreign lands and

Wellspring (Spring[2])
Pr 4:23 your heart, for it is the w of life.

Well-to-do
2Ki 4: 8 And a w woman was there, who urged

Well-trained (Train)
2Ch 26:11 Uzziah had a w army, ready to go out

Well-watered (Water)
Job 8:16 He is like a w plant in the sunshine,
Isa 58:11 You will be like a w garden, like a
Jer 31:12 They will be like a w garden, and
Eze 31:14 No other trees so w are ever to
31:16 all the trees that were w, were
45:15 from the w pastures of Israel.

Wept (Weep)
Ge 27:38 too, my father!" Then Esau w aloud.
33: 4 his neck and kissed him. And they w.
37:35 So his father w for him.
43:30 into his private room and w there.
45: 2 he w so loudly that the Egyptians
45:14 around his brother Benjamin and w,
45:15 he kissed all his brothers and w
46:29 his father and w for a long time.
50: 1 and w over him and kissed him.
50:17 their message came to him, Joseph w.
Nu 14: 1 raised their voices and w aloud.
Dt 1:45 You came back and w before the LORD,
Jdg 2: 4 the Israelites, the people w aloud,
11:38 and w because she would never marry.
20:23 The Israelites went up and w before
Ru 1: 9 Then she kissed them and they w
1:14 At this they w again. Then Orpah
1Sa 1: 7 her till she w and would not eat.
1:10 In bitterness of soul Hannah w much
11: 4 to the people, they all w aloud.
20:41 w together—but David w the most.
24:16 David my son?" And he w aloud.
30: 4 David and his men w aloud until they
2Sa 1:12 They mourned and w and fasted till
3:32 the king w aloud at Abner's tomb.
3:32 All the people w also.
3:34 And all the people w over him again.
12:21 you fasted and w, but now that the
12:22 was still alive, I fasted and w.
13:36 all his servants w very bitterly.
15:23 The whole countryside w aloud as all
18:33 to the room over the gateway and w.
2Ki 13:14 went down to see him and w over him.
20: 3 And Hekeziah w bitterly.
22:19 your robes and w in my presence,
2Ch 34:27 your robes and w in my presence,
Ezr 3:12 who had seen the former temple, w
10: 1 They too w bitterly.
Ne 1: 4 these things, I sat down and w.
Job 30:25 Have I not w for those in trouble?
Ps 137: 1 By the rivers of Babylon we sat and w
Isa 38: 3 And Hekeziah w bitterly.
Hos 12: 4 him; he w and begged for his favour.
Mt 26:75 And he went outside and w bitterly.
Mk 14:72 And he broke down and w.
Lk 19:41 and saw the city, he w over it
Lk 22:62 he went outside and w bitterly.
Jn 11:35 Jesus w.
20:11 As she w, she bent over to look into
Ac 20:37 They all w as they embraced him and
Rev 5: 4 I w and w because no-one was found

West (North-west, South-west, Western, Westward)
Ge 12: 8 Bethel on the w and Ai on the east.
13:14 look north and south, east and w.
28:14 and you will spread out to the w and
Ex 10:19 the wind to a very strong w wind,
26:22 is, the w end of the tabernacle,
26:27 frames on the w, at the far end of
27:12 "The w end of the courtyard shall be
36:27 is, the w end of the tabernacle,
36:32 frames on the w, at the far end of
38:12 The w end was fifty cubits wide and
Nu 2:18 On the w will be the divisions of
3:23 on the w, behind the tabernacle.
34: 6 This will be your boundary on the w.
35: 5 three thousand on the w and three
Dt 3:27 Go up to the top of Pisgah and look w
11:30 w of the road, towards the setting
Jos 1: 4 country—to the Great Sea on the w.
5: 1 Now when all the Amorite kings w of
8: 9 to the w of Ai—but Joshua spent
8:12 Bethel and Ai, to the w of the city.
8:13 city and the ambush to the w of it.
9: 1 Now when all the kings w of the
11: 2 and in Naphoth Dor on the w;
11: 3 to the Canaanites in the east and w;
12: 7 on the w side of the Jordan, from
15: 8 of the hill w of the Hinnom Valley
15:46 w of Ekron, all that were in the
16: 8 From Tappuah the border went w to
18:12 and headed w into the hill country,
18:15 of Kiriath Jearim on the w,
19:11 Going w it ran to Maralah, touched
19:26 On the w the boundary touched Carmel
19:34 The boundary ran w through Aznoth
19:34 on the w and the Jordan on the east.
22: 7 land on the w side of the Jordan
23: 4 Jordan and the Great Sea in the w.
Jdg 18:12 This is why the place w of Kiriath
20:33 out of its place on the w of Gibeah.
2Sa 13:34 many people on the road w of him,
1Ki 4:24 For he ruled over all the kingdoms w
7:25 three facing north, three facing w,
1Ch 7:28 Gezer and its villages to the w, and
9:24 sides: east, w, north and south.
12:15 valleys, to the east and to the w.
26:16 The lots for the W Gate and the
26:18 for the court to the w, there were
26:30 were responsible in Israel w of the
2Ch 4: 4 three facing north, three facing w,
32:30 to the w side of the City of David.
33:14 w of the Gihon spring in the valley,
Job 18:20 Men of the w are appalled at his
23: 8 if I go to the w, I do not find him.
Ps 75: 6 No-one from the east or the w or
103:12 far as the east is from the w, so
107: 3 east and w, from north and south.
Isa 9:12 Philistines from the w have devoured
11:14 on the slopes of Philistia to the w;
24:14 from the w they acclaim the LORD's
43: 5 the east and gather you from the w.
49:12 some from the w, some from the
59:19 From the w, men will fear the name
Eze 41:12 the w side was seventy cubits wide.
42:19 he turned to the w side and measured;
45: 7 It will extend westward from the w
47:20 "On the w side, the Great Sea will
47:20 This will be the w boundary.
48: 1 from the east side to the w side.
48: 2 the territory of Dan from east to w.
48: 3 territory of Asher from east to w.
48: 4 of Naphtali from east to w.
48: 5 of Manasseh from east to w.
48: 6 territory of Ephraim from east to w.
48: 7 territory of Reuben from east to w.
48: 8 territory of Judah from east to w
48: 8 and its length from east to w will
48:10 10,000 cubits wide on the w side,
48:16 and the w side 4,500 cubits.
Eze 48:17 the east, and 250 cubits on the w.
48:18 and 10,000 cubits on the w side.
48:23 from the east side to the w side.
48:24 of Benjamin from east to w.
48:25 territory of Simeon from east to w.
48:26 of Issachar from east to w.
48:27 territory of Zebulun from east to w.
48:34 the w side, which is 4,500 cubits
Da 8: 4 the w and the north and the south.
8: 5 between his eyes came from the w,
Hos 11:10 will come trembling from the w.
Zec 6: 6 with the white horses towards the w,
8: 7 the countries of the east and the w.
14: 4 will be split in two from east to w,
Mt 8:11 will come from the east and the w,
24:27 the east is visible even in the w,
Lk 12:54 When you see a cloud rising in the w,
13:29 People will come from east and w and
Rev 21:13 on the south and three on the w.

Western (West)
Nu 34: 6 "'Your w boundary will be the coast
Dt 1: 7 in the mountains, in the w foothills,
3:17 Its w border was the Jordan in the
11:24 the Euphrates River to the w sea.
34: 2 land of Judah as far as the w sea,
Jos 9: 1 in the w foothills, and along the
10:40 the Negev, the w foothills and the
11: 2 in the w foothills and in Naphoth
11:16 region of Goshen, the w foothills
12: 8 the hill country, the w foothills,
15:12 The w boundary is the coastline of
15:33 In the w foothills: Eshtaol, Zorah,
18:14 turned south along the w side
18:14 This was the w side.
Jdg 1: 9 the Negev and the w foothills.
1Ch 27:28 trees in the w foothills.
Jer 17:26 of Benjamin and the w foothills,
32:44 of the w foothills and of the Negev,
33:13 of the w foothills and of the Negev,
Eze 45: 7 running lengthwise from the w to the
46:19 and showed me a place at the w end.
48:21 the 25,000 cubits to the w border.
Da 11:30 Ships of the w coastlands will
Joel 2:20 those in the rear into the w sea.
Zec 7: 7 and the w foothills were settled?'
14: 8 the w sea, in summer and in winter.

Westward (West)
Jos 15:10 curved w from Baalah to Mount Seir,
16: 3 descended w to the territory of the
Eze 45: 7 It will extend w from the west side
48:21 and w from the 25,000 cubits to the

Wet
Job 31:38 all its furrows are w with tears,
Lk 7:38 began to w his feet with her tears.
7:44 but she w my feet with her tears and

Wheat
Ge 30:14 During w harvest, Reuben went out
Ex 9:32 The w and spelt, however, were not
29: 2 from fine w flour, without yeast,
34:22 the firstfruits of the w harvest,
Dt 8: 8 a land with w and barley, vines and
32:14 Bashan and the finest grains of w.
Jdg 6:11 Gideon was threshing w in a
15: 1 Later on, at the time of w harvest,
Ru 2:23 barley and w harvests were finished.
1Sa 6:13 harvesting their w in the valley,
12:17 Is it not w harvest now? I will call
2Sa 4: 6 of the house as if to get some w,
17:28 They also brought w and barley,
1Ki 5:11 cors of w as food for his household,
1Ch 21:20 While Araunah was threshing w, he
21:23 and the w for the grain offering.
2Ch 2:10 twenty thousand cors of ground w,
2:15 let my lord send his servants the w
27: 5 w and ten thousand cors of barley.
Ezr 6: 9 and w, salt, wine and oil, as
7:22 a hundred cors of w, a hundred baths
Job 31:40 let briers come up instead of w and
Ps 81:16 you would be fed with the finest of w
147:14 satisfies you with the finest of w.

SS 7: 2 is a mound of w encircled by lilies.
Isa 28:25 Does he not plant w in its place,
Jer 12:13 They will sow w but reap thorns;
41: 8 "Don't kill us! We have w and barley,
Eze 4: 9 "Take w and barley, beans and
27:17 w from Minnith and confections,
45:13 of an ephah from each homer of w
Joel 1:11 you vine growers; grieve for the w
Am 8: 5 market w?"—skimping the measure,
8: 6 even the sweepings with the w.
Mt 3:12 gathering his w into the barn and
13:25 weeds among the w, and went away.
13:26 the w sprouted and formed ears, then
13:29 you may root up the w with them.
13:30 the w and bring it into my barn.
Lk 3:17 and to gather the w into his barn,
16: 7 A thousand bushels of w,' he replied.
22:31 Satan has asked to sift you as w.
Jn 12:24 unless a grain of w falls to the
1Co 15:37 perhaps of w or of something else.
Rev 6: 6 "A quart of w for a day's wages, and
18:13 of fine flour and w; cattle and

Wheel (Wheels)
1Ki 7:32 of each w was a cubit and a half.
22:34 told his chariot driver, "W round
2Ch 18:33 told the chariot driver, "W around
Pr 20:26 he drives the threshing w over them.
Ecc 12: 6 spring, or the w broken at the well,
Jer 18: 3 and I saw him working at the w.
Eze 1:15 I saw a w on the ground beside each
1:16 be made like a w intersecting a w.
10: 6 man went in and stood beside a w.
10:10 each was like a w intersecting a w.

Wheels (Wheel)
Ex 14:25 He made the w of their chariots come
1Ki 7:30 Each stand had four bronze w with
7:32 The four w were under the panels,
7:32 of the w were attached to the stand.
7:33 The w were made like chariot w; the
Isa 5:28 their chariot w like a whirlwind.
28:28 Though he drives the w of his
Jer 47: 3 chariots and the rumble of their w.
Eze 1:16 w: They sparkled like chrysolite,
1:17 the w did not turn about as the
1:19 the living creatures moved, the w
1:19 from the ground, the w also rose.
1:20 they would go, and the w would rise
1:20 the living creatures was in the w.
1:21 the w rose along with them, because
1:21 the living creatures was in the w.
3:13 w beside them, a loud rumbling sound.
10: 2 in among the w beneath the cherubim.
10: 6 "Take fire from among the w, from
10: 9 I saw beside the cherubim four w,
10: 9 the w sparkled like chrysolite.
10:11 the w did not turn about as the
10:12 full of eyes, as were their four w.
10:13 the w being called "the whirling w".
10:16 the cherubim moved, the w beside
10:16 the w did not leave their side.
10:19 as they went, the w went with them.
11:22 the cherubim, with the w beside them,
Da 7: 9 fire, and its w were all ablaze.
Na 3: 2 The crack of whips, the clatter of w,

Whip (Whips)
Pr 26: 3 A w for the horse, a halter for the
Isa 10:26 Almighty will lash them with a w,
Jn 2:15 he made a w out of cords, and drove
1Co 4:21 Shall I come to you with a w,

Whips (Whip)
Jos 23:13 w on your backs and thorns in your
1Ki 12:11 My father scourged you with w; I
12:14 My father scourged you with w; I
2Ch 10:11 My father scourged you with w; I
10:14 My father scourged you with w; I
Na 3: 2 The crack of w, the clatter of

Whirling
Eze 10:13 wheels being called "the w wheels".

Whirlwind (Wind)
2Ki 2: 1 to take Elijah up to heaven in a w,
2:11 and Elijah went up to heaven in a w.
Ps 77:18 Your thunder was heard in the w,
Pr 1:27 disaster sweeps over you like a w,
Isa 5:28 their chariot wheels like a w.
40:24 and a w sweeps them away like chaff.
66:15 and his chariots are like a w; he
Jer 4:13 his chariots come like a w, his
23:19 a w swirling down on the heads of
Hos 4:19 A w will sweep them away, and their
8: 7 "They sow the wind and reap the w.
Na 1: 3 His way is in the w and the storm,
Zec 7:14 'I scattered them with a w among all

Whirlwinds (Wind)
Isa 21: 1 w sweeping through the southland,

Whirring
Isa 18: 1 Woe to the land of w wings along the

Whisper (Whispered, Whispering)
1Ki 19:12 And after the fire came a gentle w.
Job 4:12 to me, my ears caught a w of it.
26:14 how faint the w we hear of him! Who
Ps 41: 7 All my enemies w together against me;
107:29 He stilled the storm to a w; the
Isa 8:19 who w and mutter, should not a
26:16 them, they could barely w a prayer.
29: 4 out of the dust your speech will w.
Lam 3:62 what my enemies w and mutter against

Whispered (Whisper)
Mt 10:27 speak in the daylight; what is w in
Lk 12: 3 and what you have w in the ear in

Whispering (Whisper)
2Sa 12:19 servants were w among themselves
Jer 20:10 I hear many w, "Terror on every side!
Jn 7:12 there was widespread w about him.
7:32 The Pharisees heard the crowd w such

Whistle (Whistles, Whistling)
Isa 7:18 In that day the LORD will w for

Whistles (Whistle)
Isa 5:26 w for those at the ends of the earth.

Whistling (Whistle)
Jdg 5:16 to hear the w for the flocks?

White (Reddish-white, Whiter)
Ge 30:35 goats (all that had w on them)
30:37 plane trees and made w stripes
30:37 the w inner wood of the branches.
Ex 16:31 It was w like coriander seed and
Lev 11:18 the w owl, the desert owl, the
13: 3 if the hair in the sore has turned w
13: 4 If the spot on his skin is w but
13: 4 and the hair in it has not turned w,
13:10 and if there is a w swelling in the
13:10 the skin that has turned the hair w
13:13 it has all turned w, he is clean.
13:16 turn w, he must go to the priest.
13:17 and if the sores have turned w, the
13:19 where the boil was, a w swelling
13:20 and the hair in it has turned w,
13:21 there is no w hair in it and it is
13:24 a reddish-white or w spot appears in
13:25 and if the hair in it has turned w,
13:26 there is no w hair in the spot and
13:38 "When a man or woman has w spots on
13:39 and if the spots are dull w, it is a
Dt 14:16 little owl, the great owl, the w owl
Jdg 5:10 "You who ride on w donkeys, sitting
2Ki 5:27 and he was leprous, as w as snow.
Est 1: 6 The garden had hangings of w and
1: 6 fastened with cords of w linen and
8:15 royal garments of blue and w,
Job 6: 6 is there flavour in the w of an egg?
41:32 one would think the deep had w hair.
Ecc 9: 8 Always be clothed in w, and always
Isa 1:18 they shall be as w as snow; though
Da 7: 9 His clothing was as w as snow; the
7: 9 hair of his head was w like wool.
Joel 1: 7 it away, leaving their branches w.
Zec 1: 8 him were red, brown and w horses.
6: 3 the third w, and the fourth dappled—
6: 6 the one with the w horses towards
Mt 5:36 make even one hair w or black.
17: 2 clothes became as w as the light.
28: 3 and his clothes were w as snow.
Mk 9: 3 His clothes became dazzling w,
16: 5 saw a young man dressed in a w robe
Jn 20:12 saw two angels in w, seated where
Ac 1:10 men dressed in w stood beside them.
Rev 1:14 His head and hair were w like wool,
1:14 as w as snow, and his eyes were like
2:17 I will also give him a w stone with
3: 4 dressed in w, for they are worthy.
3: 5 will, like them, be dressed in w.
3:18 become rich; and w clothes to wear
4: 4 They were dressed in w and had
6: 2 and there before me was a w horse!
6:11 each of them was given a w robe, and
7: 9 They were wearing w robes and were
7:13 "These in w robes—who are they, and
7:14 them w in the blood of the Lamb.
14:14 and there before me was a w cloud,
19:11 and there before me was a w horse,
19:14 riding on w horses and dressed in
19:14 dressed in fine linen, w and clean.
20:11 I saw a great w throne and him who

Whiter (White)
Ge 49:12 than wine, his teeth w than milk.
Ps 51: 7 wash me, and I shall be w than snow.
Lam 4: 7 brighter than snow and w than milk,
Mk 9: 3 His clothes became dazzling white, w

Whitewash (Wash)
Eze 13:10 wall is built, they cover it with w,
13:11 tell those who cover it with w that
13:12 "Where is the w you covered it with?
13:14 the wall you have covered with w
13:15 against those who covered it with w.
22:28 Her prophets w these deeds for them

Whitewashed (Wash)
Eze 13:15 is gone and so are those who w it,
Mt 23:27 you hypocrites! You are like w tombs,
Ac 23: 3 "God will strike you, you w wall!

Whole (*Whole body*, *Whole earth*, *Whole nation*, Wholehearted, Wholeheartedly, Wholly)
Ge 2: 6 the w surface of the ground—
7: 1 into the ark, you and your w family
11: 1 Now the w world had one language and
11: 9 the language of the w world.
13: 9 Is not the w land before you? Let's
13:10 looked up and saw that the w plain
13:11 Lot chose for himself the w plain of
14: 7 and they conquered the w territory
17: 8 The w land of Canaan, where you are
18:26 spare the w place for their sake."
18:28 the w city because of five people?"
29:14 had stayed with him for a w month,
41:41 in charge of the w land of Egypt."
41:43 in charge of the w land of Egypt.
41:54 the w land of Egypt there was food.
41:56 the famine had spread over the w
47:13 no food, however, in the w region
Ex 8: 2 plague your w country with frogs.
9: 9 become fine dust over the w land
12: 3 Tell the w community of Israel that
12: 4 household is too small for a w lamb
12:47 The w community of Israel must
16: 1 The w Israelite community set out
16: 2 In the desert the w community
16:10 While Aaron was speaking to the w
17: 1 The w Israelite community set out
19:18 the w mountain trembled violently,
22: 6 or standing corn or the w field,
35: 1 Moses assembled the w Israelite
35: 4 Moses said to the w Israelite
35:20 the w Israelite community withdrew

Lev 4:13 "'If the w Israelite community sins
8:21 with water and burned the w ram on
10: 6 will be angry with the w community.
16:17 and the w community of Israel.
Nu 1: 2 "Take a census of the w Israelite
1:18 they called the w community together
3: 7 for the w community at the Tent of
8: 7 shave their w bodies and wash their
8: 9 assemble the w Israelite community.
8:20 Moses, Aaron and the w Israelite
10: 3 both are sounded, the w community is
11:20 for a w month—until it comes out of
11:21 them meat to eat for a w month!'
13:26 Aaron and the w Israelite community
13:26 to the w assembly and showed them
14: 2 and the w assembly said to them, "If
14: 5 w Israelite assembly gathered there.
14:10 the w assembly talked about stoning
14:35 things to this w wicked community,
14:36 and made the w community grumble
15:24 then the w community is to offer a
15:25 for the w Israelite community,
15:26 The w Israelite community and the
15:33 Moses and Aaron and the w assembly,
15:35 The w assembly must stone him
16: 3 The w community is holy, every one
16:41 The next day the w Israelite
20: 1 In the first month the w Israelite
20:22 The w Israelite community set out
20:27 Hor in the sight of the w community.
20:29 the w community learned that Aaron
21:33 and Og king of Bashan and his w army
21:34 you, with his w army and his land.
21:35 w army, leaving them no survivors.
25: 6 the w assembly of Israel while they
26: 2 "Take a census of the w Israelite
27: 2 and the w assembly, and said,
27:20 w Israelite community will obey him.
27:22 the priest and the w assembly.
32:13 until the w generation of those who
32:33 Bashan—the w land with its cities
Dt 2:33 with his sons and his w army.
3: 1 Og king of Bashan with his w army
3: 2 to you with his w army and his land.
3: 4 from them—the w region of Argob,
3:13 (The w region of Argob in Bashan
3:14 took the w region of Argob as far as
5:22 in a loud voice to your w assembly
6:22 and Pharaoh and his w household.
11: 3 king of Egypt and to his w country;
11:25 you on the w land, wherever you go.
13:16 its plunder as a w burnt offering
18: 1 who are Levites—indeed the w tribe
19: 8 you the w land he promised them,
29:23 The w land will be a burning waste
31:30 hearing of the w assembly of Israel:
33:10 and w burnt offerings on your altar.
34: 1 him the w land—from Gilead to Dan,
34: 3 the Negev and the w region from the
34:11 all his officials and to his w land.
Jos 2: 3 have come to spy out the w land."
2:24 LORD has surely given the w land
6:24 they burned the w city and
8: 1 Take the w army with you, and go up
8: 3 Joshua and the w army moved out to
8:35 read to the w assembly of Israel,
9:18 The w assembly grumbled against the
9:24 Moses to give you the w land
10:21 The w army then returned safely to
10:40 Joshua subdued the w region,
10:41 the w region of Goshen to Gibeon.
11: 7 Joshua and his w army came against
11:16 all the Negev, the w region of
13: 9 w plateau of Medeba as far as Dibon,
13:12 that is, the w kingdom of Og in
13:16 gorge, and the w plateau past
18: 1 The w assembly of the Israelites
22:12 the w assembly of Israel gathered at
22:16 "The w assembly of the LORD says:
22:18 with the w community of Israel.
22:20 wrath come upon the w community
Jdg 1:25 but spared the man and his w family.
2:10 After that w generation had been
7:14 and the w camp into his hands."
9:29 Abimelech, 'Call out your w army!'
14:17 She cried the w seven days of the
Jdg 16:31 brothers and his father's w family
20:37 out and put the w city to the sword.
20:40 of the w city going up into the sky.
21:13 the w assembly sent an offer of
Ru 1:19 the w town was stirred because of
1Sa 1:28 give him to the LORD. For his w life
4:13 happened, the w town sent up a cry.
7: 3 Samuel said to the w house of Israel,
7: 9 as a w burnt offering to the LORD.
13:19 be found in the w land of Israel,
14:15 panic struck the w army—those in
17:46 and the w world will know that there
19: 7 and told him the w conversation.
20: 6 is being made there for his w clan.'
22:11 of Ahitub and his father's w family,
22:15 nothing at all about this w affair."
22:16 you and your father's w family."
22:22 the death of your father's w family.
25: 7 and the w time they were at Carmel
25:15 did not ill-treat us, and the w time
25:17 over our master and his w household.
2Sa 2:29 the w Bithron and came to Mahanaim.
3:19 w house of Benjamin wanted to do.
6: 5 David and the w house of Israel were
6:19 person in the w crowd of Israelites,
11: 1 king's men and the w Israelite army.
14: 7 Now the w clan has risen up against
15:23 The w countryside wept aloud as all
18: 8 The battle spread out over the w
19: 2 for the w army the victory that day
19:20 the w house of Joseph to come down
1Ki 6:22 he overlaid the w interior with gold.
8:14 While the w assembly of Israel was
8:22 front of the w assembly of Israel,
8:55 He stood and blessed the w assembly
10:24 The w world sought audience with
11:13 Yet I will not tear the w kingdom
11:28 he put him in charge of the w labour
11:34 "'But I will not take the w kingdom
12: 3 and he and the w assembly of Israel
12:21 he mustered the w house of Judah and
12:23 to the w house of Judah and Benjamin,
15:29 he killed Jeroboam's w family.
16:11 he killed off Baasha's w family.
16:12 Zimri destroyed the w family of
2Ki 7:15 and they found the w road strewn
9: 8 The w house of Ahab will perish. I
11: 1 to destroy the w royal family.
21: 8 will keep the w Law that my servant
25: 1 against Jerusalem with his w army.
25: 4 and the w army fled at night through
25:10 The w Babylonian army, under the
1Ch 11:10 w land, as the LORD had promised—
13: 2 He then said to the w assembly of
13: 4 The w assembly agreed to do this,
28: 4 chose me from my w family to be king
29: 1 King David said to the w assembly:
29:10 in the presence of the w assembly,
29:20 David said to the w assembly,
2Ch 1: 3 Solomon and the w assembly went to
6: 3 While the w assembly of Israel was
6:12 front of the w assembly of Israel
6:13 knelt down before the w assembly
15: 8 idols from the w land of Judah
22:10 w royal family of the house of Judah.
23: 3 the w assembly made a covenant with
29:28 The w assembly bowed in worship,
30: 2 his officials and the w assembly
30: 4 to the king and to the w assembly.
30:23 The w assembly then agreed to
31:18 and daughters of the w community
Ezr 2:64 The w company numbered 42,360,
4:20 over the w of Trans-Euphrates,
10:12 The w assembly responded with a loud
10:14 Let our officials act for the w
Ne 5:13 At this the w assembly said, "Amen,"
7:66 The w company numbered 42,360,
8:17 The w company that had returned from
Est 3: 6 throughout the w kingdom of Xerxes.
Job 17: 7 grief; my w frame is but a shadow.
34:13 Who put him in charge of the w world?
37: 3 his lightning beneath the w heaven
Ps 35:10 My w being will exclaim, "Who is
51:19 sacrifices, w burnt offerings to
Pr 1:12 w, like those who go down to the pit;
5:14 in the midst of the w assembly."
Pr 8:31 rejoicing in his w world and
Ecc 12:13 for this is the w duty of man.
Isa 1: 5 rebellion? Your w head is injured,
1: 5 is injured, your w heart afflicted.
10:23 destruction decreed upon the w land.
13: 5 wrath—to destroy the w country.
14:26 the plan determined for the w world
28:22 decreed against the w land.
29:11 For you this w vision is nothing but
31: 4 though a w band of shepherds is
Jer 1:18 w land—against the kings of Judah,
4:20 disaster; the w land lies in ruins
4:27 the LORD says: "The w land will be
8:16 their stallions the w land trembles.
9:26 and even the w house of Israel is
12:11 the w land will be laid waste
13:11 so I bound the w house of Israel and
13:11 and the w house of Judah to me,'
15:10 a man with whom the w land strives
25:11 This w country will become a
31:40 The w valley where dead bodies and
35: 3 sons—the w family of the Recabites.
39: 1 his w army and laid siege to it.
40: 4 Look, the w country lies before you;
44:28 Then the w remnant of Judah who came
51:47 her w land will be disgraced and her
52: 4 against Jerusalem with his w army.
52: 7 broken through, and the w army fled.
52:14 The w Babylonian army under the
Eze 3: 7 the w house of Israel is hardened
5: 4 from there to the w house of Israel.
7:12 for wrath is upon the w crowd.
7:13 the w crowd will not be reversed.
7:14 for my wrath is upon the w crowd.
11:15 the w house of Israel—are those of
12:10 w house of Israel who are there.'
15: 5 useful for anything when it was w,
32:22 "Assyria is there with her w army;
36:10 you, even the w house of Israel.
37:11 bones are the w house of Israel.
38: 4 out with your w army—your horses,
41:19 were carved all round the w temple.
43:11 exits and entrances—its w design
45: 6 belong to the w house of Israel.
Da 1:20 and enchanters in his w kingdom.
6: 3 to set him over the w kingdom.
7:27 of the kingdoms under the w heaven
9:12 Under the w heaven nothing has ever
Am 1: 6 w communities and sold them to Edom,
1: 9 Because she sold w communities of
3: 1 w family I brought up out of Egypt:
8: 8 The w land will rise like the Nile;
9: 5 the w land rises like the Nile,
Zep 1:18 the w world will be consumed, for
3: 8 The w world will be consumed by the
Hag 1:12 the high priest, and the w remnant
1:14 of the w remnant of the people.
Zec 1:11 the w world at rest and in peace."
5: 3 that is going out over the w land;
6: 5 presence of the Lord of the w world.
13: 8 In the w land," declares the LORD,
14:10 The w land, from Geba to Rimmon,
Mal 3:10 Bring the w tithe into the
Mt 3: 5 Judea and the w region of the Jordan.
8:32 and the w herd rushed down the steep
8:34 the w town went out to meet Jesus.
16:26 for a man if he gains the w world,
21:10 Jesus entered Jerusalem, the w city
24:14 will be preached in the w world
26:59 chief priests and the w Sanhedrin
27:27 the w company of soldiers round him.
Mk 1: 5 The w Judean countryside and all the
1:28 over the w region of Galilee.
1:33 The w town gathered at the door,
5:33 with fear, told him the w truth.
6:55 They ran throughout that w region
8:36 the w world, yet forfeit his soul?
11:18 w crowd was amazed at his teaching.
14:55 chief priests and the w Sanhedrin
15: 1 the w Sanhedrin, reached a decision.
15:16 together the w company of soldiers.
15:33 the w land until the ninth hour.
Lk 4:14 spread through the w countryside.
9:25 is it for a man to gain the w world,
15:14 a severe famine in that w country
19:37 the w crowd of disciples began

Lk 23: 1 the w assembly rose and led him off
23:44 the w land until the ninth hour,
Jn 7:23 healing the w man on the Sabbath?
12:19 how the w world has gone after him!"
21:25 I suppose that even the w world
Ac 1:21 the w time the Lord Jesus went in
2: 2 the w house where they were sitting.
5:11 Great fear seized the w church and
6: 5 This proposal pleased the w group.
7:14 his w family, seventy-five in all.
11:26 So for a w year Barnabas and Saul
13: 6 They travelled through the w island
13:44 the next Sabbath almost the w city
13:49 Lord spread through the w region.
15:12 The w assembly became silent as they
15:22 and elders, with the w church,
16:34 believe in God—he and his w family.
19:26 practically the w province of Asia.
19:29 Soon the w city was in an uproar.
20:18 "You know how I lived the w time I
20:27 proclaim to you the w will of God.
21:27 up the w crowd and seized him,
21:30 The w city was aroused, and the
21:31 w city of Jerusalem was in an uproar.
25:24 you see this man! The w Jewish
28:30 For two w years Paul stayed there in
Ro 1: 9 God, whom I serve with my w heart in
3:19 the w world held accountable to God.
8:22 We know that the w creation has been
11:16 then the w batch is holy; if the
16:23 whose hospitality I and the w church
1Co 4: 9 made a spectacle to the w universe,
5: 6 works through the w batch of dough?
14:23 if the w church comes together and
Gal 3:22 the w world is a prisoner of sin,
4: 1 although he owns the w estate.
5: 3 he is required to obey the w law.
5: 9 "A little yeast works through the w
5:12 the w way and emasculate themselves!
Eph 2:21 In him the w building is joined
3:15 from whom his w family in heaven and
4:10 in order to fill the w universe.)
4:13 w measure of the fulness of Christ.
Php 1:13 clear throughout the w palace guard
1Th 5:23 May your w spirit, soul and body be
Tit 1:11 they are ruining w households by
Jas 2:10 For whoever keeps the w law and yet
3: 3 obey us, we can turn the w animal.
3: 6 It corrupts the w person, sets the w
1Jn 2: 2 also for the sins of the w world.
5:19 and that the w world is under the
Rev 3:10 is going to come upon the w world
6:12 hair, the w moon turned blood red,
12: 9 Satan, who leads the w world astray.
13: 3 The w world was astonished and
16:14 go out to the kings of the w world,

Whole body

Ge 25:25 and his w was like a hairy garment;
Lev 13:13 if the disease has covered his w,
15:16 he must bathe his w with water, and
Pr 4:22 find them and health to a man's w.
Mt 5:29 for your w to be thrown into hell.
5:30 than for your w to go into hell.
6:22 good, your w will be full of light.
6:23 if your eyes are bad, your w will be
Lk 11:34 When your eyes are good, your w also
11:36 if your w is full of light, and no
Jn 13:10 to wash his feet; his w is clean.
1Co 12:17 If the w were an eye, where would
12:17 of hearing be? If the w were an ear,
Eph 4:16 From him the w, joined and held
Col 2:19 from whom the w, supported and held
Jas 3: 2 man, able to keep his w in check.

Whole earth

Ge 1:29 plant on the face of the w
11: 4 scattered over the face of the w."
11: 9 them over the face of the w.
Ex 19: 5 Although the w is mine,
Nu 14:21 the glory of the LORD fills the w,
Job 37:12 w to do whatever he commands them.
Ps 48: 2 in its loftiness, the joy of the w.
72:19 may the w be filled with his glory.
110: 6 and crushing the rulers of the w.
Isa 6: 3 the w is full of his glory."
Jer 50:23 shattered is the hammer of the w!
51: 7 LORD's hand; she made the w drunk.
51:25 destroy the w," declares the LORD.
51:41 the boast of the w seized! What a
Lam 2:15 of beauty, the joy of the w?"
Eze 34: 6 They were scattered over the w, and
35:14 w rejoices, I will make you desolate.
Da 2:35 a huge mountain and filled the w.
2:39 one of bronze, will rule over the w.
4:20 touching the sky, visible to the w,
7:23 will devour the w, trampling it down
8: 5 the w without touching the ground.
Hab 1: 6 who sweep across the w to seize
Zec 14: 9 The LORD will be king over the w. On
Lk 21:35 those who live on the face of the w.
Ac 17:26 that they should inhabit the w; and

Whole nation

Jos 3:17 the w had completed the crossing
4: 1 the w had finished crossing the
5: 8 after the w had been circumcised,
Mal 3: 9 You are under a curse—the w of you—
Jn 11:50 the people than that the w perish."

Wholehearted (Whole)

2Ki 20: 3 faithfully and with w devotion
1Ch 28: 9 and serve him with w devotion and
29:19 give my son Solomon the w devotion
Isa 38: 3 faithfully and with w devotion

Wholeheartedly (Whole)

Nu 14:24 a different spirit and follows me w,
32:11 'Because they have not followed me w,
32:12 Nun, for they followed the LORD w.'
Dt 1:36 on, because he followed the LORD w."
Jos 14: 8 however, followed the LORD my God w.
14: 9 have followed the LORD my God w.'
14:14 the LORD, the God of Israel, w.
1Ki 8:23 servants who continue w in your way.
1Ch 29: 9 had given freely and w to the LORD.
2Ch 6:14 servants who continue w in your way.
15:15 oath because they had sworn it w.
19: 9 and w in the fear of the LORD.
25: 2 in the eyes of the LORD, but not w.
31:21 he sought his God and worked w.
Ro 6:17 you w obeyed the form of teaching to
Eph 6: 7 Serve w, as if you were serving the

Wholesome

2Ki 2:22 the water has remained w to this day,
2Pe 3: 1 to stimulate you to w thinking.

Wholly (Whole)

Nu 3: 9 who are to be given w to him.
8:16 who are to be given w to me.
1Ti 4:15 matters; give yourself w to them,

Wick

Ex 25:38 Its w trimmers and trays are to be
37:23 w trimmers and trays, of pure gold.
Nu 4: 9 with its lamps, its w trimmers
1Ki 7:50 the pure gold dishes, w trimmers,
2Ki 12:13 w trimmers, sprinkling bowls,
25:14 shovels, w trimmers, dishes and all
2Ch 4:22 the pure gold w trimmers, sprinkling
Isa 42: 3 smouldering w he will not snuff out.
43:17 extinguished, snuffed out like a w:
Jer 52:18 shovels, w trimmers, sprinkling
Mt 12:20 and a smouldering w he will not

Wicked (Overwicked, Wickedly, Wickedness)

Ge 13:13 Now the men of Sodom were w and were
18:23 sweep away the righteous with the w?
18:25 kill the righteous with the w,
18:25 the righteous and the w alike.
19: 7 my friends. Don't do this w thing.
38: 7 Er, Judah's firstborn, was w in the
38:10 What he did was w in the LORD's
39: 9 such a w thing and sin against God?"
44: 5 This is a w thing you have done.
Ex 23: 1 w man by being a malicious witness.
Lev 20:14 a woman and her mother, it is w.
Nu 14:27 "How long will this w community
14:35 things to this whole w community,
16:26 back from the tents of these w men!
Dt 13:13 that w men have arisen among you and
15: 9 not to harbour this w thought:
Jdg 19:22 some of the w men of the city
20:13 Now surrender those w men of Gibeah
1Sa 1:16 take your servant for a w woman
2: 9 the w will be silenced in darkness.
2:12 Eli's sons were w men; they had no
2:23 people about these w deeds of yours.
15:18 completely destroy those w people
17:28 you are and how w your heart is;
25:17 w man that no-one can talk to him."
25:25 no attention to that w man Nabal.
2Sa 3:34 You fell as one falls before w men."
4:11 How much more—when w men have
7:10 W people shall not oppress them any
13:12 in Israel! Don't do this w thing.
13:13 like one of the w fools in Israel.
2Ki 17:11 They did w things that provoked the
1Ch 2: 3 Er, Judah's firstborn, was w in the
17: 9 W people will not oppress them any
2Ch 7:14 my face and turn from their w ways,
19: 2 "Should you help the w and love
24: 7 the sons of that w woman Athaliah
Ezr 4:12 that rebellious and w city.
Ne 13:17 "What is this w thing you are doing—
Job 3:17 There the w cease from turmoil, and
8:22 the tents of the w will be no more."
9:22 both the blameless and the w.'
9:24 a land falls into the hands of the w,
10: 3 you smile on the schemes of the w?
11:20 the eyes of the w will fail, and
15:20 All his days the w man suffers
16:11 me into the clutches of the w.
18: 5 "The lamp of the w is snuffed out;
20: 5 that the mirth of the w is brief,
20:29 Such is the fate God allots the w,
21: 7 Why do the w live on, growing old
21:16 aloof from the counsel of the w.
21:17 "Yet how often is the lamp of the w
21:28 house, the tents where w men lived?'
22:18 aloof from the counsel of the w.
24: 6 and glean in the vineyards of the w.
27: 7 "May my enemies be like the w, my
27:13 "Here is the fate God allots to the w
29:17 I broke the fangs of the w and
31: 3 Is it not ruin for the w, disaster
34: 8 evildoers; he associates with w men.
34:18 and to nobles, 'You are w,'
34:36 utmost for answering like a w man!
35:12 because of the arrogance of the w.
36: 6 He does not keep the w alive but
36:17 with the judgment due to the w;
38:13 the edges and shake the w out of it?
38:15 The w are denied their light, and
40:12 him, crush the w where they stand.
Ps 1: 1 not walk in the counsel of the w
1: 4 Not so the w! They are like chaff
1: 5 Therefore the w will not stand in
1: 6 but the way of the w will perish.
3: 7 the jaw; break the teeth of the w.
5: 4 evil; with you the w cannot dwell.
7: 9 the w and make the righteous secure.
9: 5 the nations and destroyed the w;
9:16 the w are ensnared by the work of
9:17 The w return to the grave, all the
10: 2 In his arrogance the w man hunts
10: 4 In his pride the w does not seek him;
10:13 Why does the w man revile God? Why
10:15 Break the arm of the w and evil man;
11: 2 For look, the w bend their bows;
11: 5 the w and those who love violence
11: 6 On the w he will rain fiery coals
12: 8 The w freely strut about when what
17: 9 from the w who assail me, from my
17:13 rescue me from the w by your sword.
21:11 w schemes, they cannot succeed;
26: 5 and refuse to sit with the w.
26:10 in whose hands are w schemes, whose
28: 3 Do not drag me away with the w, with
31:17 but let the w be put to shame and
32:10 Many are the woes of the w, but the
34:21 Evil will slay the w; the foes of

Ps 36: 1 concerning the sinfulness of the w:
36: 3 The words of his mouth are w and
36:11 nor the hand of the w drive me away.
37: 7 when they carry out their w schemes.
37:10 A little while, and the w will be no
37:12 The w plot against the righteous and
37:13 the Lord laughs at the w, for he
37:14 The w draw the sword and bend the
37:16 have than the wealth of many w;
37:17 the power of the w will be broken,
37:20 the w will perish: The LORD's
37:21 The w borrow and do not repay, but
37:28 offspring of the w will be cut off;
37:32 The w lie in wait for the righteous,
37:34 the w are cut off, you will see it.
37:35 I have seen a w and ruthless man
37:38 the future of the w will be cut off.
37:40 them from the w and saves them,
39: 1 long as the w are in my presence."
43: 1 rescue me from deceitful and w men.
49: 5 come, when w deceivers surround me—
50:16 to the w, God says: "What right have
55: 3 at the stares of the w; for they
55: 9 Confuse the w, O Lord, confound
55:23 you, O God, will bring down the w
58: 3 Even from birth the w go astray;
58: 9 or dry—the w will be swept away.
58:10 their feet in the blood of the w.
59: 5 show no mercy to w traitors.
64: 2 Hide me from the conspiracy of the w,
68: 2 fire, may the w perish before God.
71: 4 O my God, from the hand of the w,
73: 3 when I saw the prosperity of the w.
73:12 This is what the w are like—always
75: 4 and to the w, 'Do not lift up your
75: 8 and all the w of the earth drink it
75:10 I will cut off the horns of all the w
82: 2 and show partiality to the w?
82: 4 deliver them from the hand of the w.
84:10 God than dwell in the tents of the w.
89:22 tribute; no w man will oppress him.
91: 8 and see the punishment of the w.
92: 7 though the w spring up like grass
92:11 have heard the rout of my w foes.
94: 3 How long will the w, O LORD, how
94: 3 how long will the w be jubilant?
94:13 till a pit is dug for the w.
94:16 Who will rise up for me against the w
97:10 them from the hand of the w.
101: 8 to silence all the w in the land;
104:35 from the earth and the w be no more.
106:18 followers; a flame consumed the w.
106:29 the LORD to anger by their w deeds,
107:42 but all the w shut their mouths.
109: 2 for w and deceitful men have opened
112:10 The w man will see and be vexed, he
112:10 of the w will come to nothing.
119:53 Indignation grips me because of the w
119:61 Though the w bind me with ropes, I
119:95 The w are waiting to destroy me, but
119:110 The w have set a snare for me, but I
119:119 All the w of the earth you discard
119:150 Those who devise w schemes are near,
119:155 Salvation is far from the w, for
125: 3 The sceptre of the w will not remain
129: 4 cut me free from the cords of the w.
139:19 If only you would slay the w, O God!
140: 4 O LORD, from the hands of the w;
140: 8 do not grant the w their desires,
141: 4 to take part in w deeds with men who
141: 6 and the w will learn that my words
141:10 Let the w fall into their own nets,
145:20 him, but all the w he will destroy.
146: 9 but he frustrates the ways of the w.
147: 6 but casts the w to the ground.
Pr 2:12 save you from the ways of w men,
2:22 the w will be cut off from the land,
3:25 or of the ruin that overtakes the w,
3:33 curse is on the house of the w,
4:14 Do not set foot on the path of the w
4:19 way of the w is like deep darkness
5:22 The evil deeds of a w man ensnare
6:18 a heart that devises w schemes, feet
9: 7 rebukes a w man incurs abuse.
10: 3 but he thwarts the craving of the w.
10: 6 overwhelms the mouth of the w.
Pr 10: 7 but the name of the w will rot.
10:11 overwhelms the mouth of the w.
10:16 of the w brings them punishment.
10:20 heart of the w is of little value.
10:24 What the w dreads will overtake him;
10:25 storm has swept by, the w are gone
10:27 the years of the w are cut short.
10:28 the hopes of the w come to nothing.
10:30 the w will not remain in the land.
10:32 of the w only what is perverse.
11: 5 but the w are brought down by their
11: 7 a w man dies, his hope perishes; all
11: 8 and it comes on the w instead.
11:10 w perish, there are shouts of joy.
11:11 the mouth of the w it is destroyed.
11:18 The w man earns deceptive wages, but
11:21 Be sure of this: The w will not go
11:23 but the hope of the w only in wrath.
12: 5 the advice of the w is deceitful.
12: 6 The words of the w lie in wait for
12: 7 W men are overthrown and are no more,
12:10 the kindest acts of the w are cruel.
12:12 The w desire the plunder of evil men,
12:21 the w have their fill of trouble.
12:26 the way of the w leads them astray.
13: 5 but the w bring shame and disgrace.
13: 9 the lamp of the w is snuffed out.
13:17 A w messenger falls into trouble,
13:25 the stomach of the w goes hungry.
14:11 The house of the w will be destroyed,
14:19 the w at the gates of the righteous.
14:32 calamity comes, the w are brought
15: 3 keeping watch on the w and the good.
15: 6 income of the w brings them trouble.
15: 8 LORD detests the sacrifice of the w,
15: 9 The LORD detests the way of the w
15:26 LORD detests the thoughts of the w,
15:28 but the mouth of the w gushes evil.
15:29 The LORD is far from the w but he
16: 4 even the w for a day of disaster.
17: 4 A w man listens to evil lips; a liar
17:23 A w man accepts a bribe in secret to
18: 5 is not good to be partial to the w
19:28 the mouth of the w gulps down evil.
20:26 A wise king winnows out the w; he
21: 4 heart, the lamp of the w, are sin!
21: 7 The violence of the w will drag them
21:10 The w man craves evil; his neighbour
21:12 of the w and brings the w to ruin.
21:18 The w become a ransom for the
21:27 The sacrifice of the w is detestable
21:29 A w man puts up a bold front, but an
22: 5 In the paths of the w lie thorns and
24: 1 Do not envy w men, do not desire
24:16 the w are brought down by calamity.
24:19 of evil men or be envious of the w,
24:20 lamp of the w will be snuffed out.
25: 5 remove the w from the king's
25:26 man who gives way to the w.
28: 1 The w man flees though no-one
28: 4 who forsake the law praise the w,
28:12 w rise to power, men go into hiding.
28:15 w man ruling over a helpless people.
28:28 the w rise to power, people go into
28:28 the w perish, the righteous thrive.
29: 2 when the w rule, the people groan.
29: 7 but the w have no such concern.
29:12 to lies, all his officials become w.
29:16 the w thrive, so does sin, but the
29:27 dishonest; the w detest the upright.
Ecc 3:17 both the righteous and the w,
7:15 w man living long in his wickedness.
8:10 too, I saw the w buried—those who
8:12 Although a w man commits a hundred
8:13 Yet because the w do not fear God,
8:14 men who get what the w deserve,
8:14 and w men who get what the righteous
9: 2 destiny—the righteous and the w,
10:13 at the end they are w madness—
Isa 3:11 Woe to the w! Disaster is upon them!
9:17 and w, every mouth speaks vileness.
11: 4 of his lips he will slay the w.
13:11 for its evil, the w for their sins.
14: 5 The LORD has broken the rod of the w,
14:20 the w will never be mentioned again.
26:10 Though grace is shown to the w, they
Isa 31: 2 against the house of the w, against
32: 7 The scoundrel's methods are w, he
35: 8 Way; w fools will not go about on it.
48:22 no peace," says the LORD, "for the w
53: 9 He was assigned a grave with the w,
55: 7 Let the w forsake his way and the
57:20 the w are like the tossing sea,
57:21 no peace," says my God, "for the w.
58: 4 in striking each other with w fists.
59: 3 and your tongue mutters w things.
Jer 4:14 How long will you harbour w thoughts?
5:26 "Among my people are w men who lie
6:29 in vain; the w are not purged out.
12: 1 Why does the way of the w prosper?
12: 4 Because those who live in it are w,
12:14 "As for all my w neighbours who
13:10 These w people, who refuse to listen
15:21 save you from the hands of the w
20:13 the needy from the hands of the w.
23:19 swirling down on the heads of the w.
25:31 mankind and put the w to the sword,
30:23 swirling down on the heads of the w.
35:15 you must turn from your w ways
36: 3 turn from his w way; then I will
36: 7 and each will turn from his w ways,
44:22 no longer endure your w actions
Eze 3:18 I say to a w man, 'You will surely
3:18 that w man will die for his sin, and
3:19 if you do warn the w man and he does
6:11 "Alas!" because of all the w and
7:21 and as loot to the w of the earth,
7:24 I will bring the most w of the
8: 9 he said to me, "Go in and see the w
11: 2 and giving w advice in this city.
13:22 and because you encouraged the w not
14: 3 put w stumbling-blocks before their
14: 4 puts a w stumbling-block before his
14: 7 puts a w stumbling-block before his
18:20 the w will be charged against him.
18:21 "But if a w man turns away from all
18:23 pleasure in the death of the w?
18:24 detestable things the w man does,
18:27 if a w man turns away from the
21: 3 you both the righteous and the w.
21: 4 to cut off the righteous and the w,
21:25 "'O profane and w prince of Israel,
21:29 necks of the w who are to be slain,
33: 8 I say to the w, 'O w man, you will
33: 8 that w man will die for his sin, and
33: 9 if you do warn the w man to turn
33:11 no pleasure in the death of the w,
33:12 and the wickedness of the w man will
33:14 if I say to the w man, 'You will
33:19 if a w man turns away from his
36:31 remember your evil ways and w deeds,
Da 2: 9 to tell me misleading and w things,
8:23 rebels have become completely w,
9: 5 We have been w and have rebelled; we
12:10 but the w will continue to be w.
12:10 None of the w will understand, but
Hos 6: 8 Gilead is a city of w men, stained
12:11 Is Gilead w? Its people are
Mic 6:10 Am I still to forget, O w house,
Na 1:15 No more will the w invade you; they
Hab 1: 4 The w hem in the righteous, so that
1:13 Why are you silent while the w
1:15 The w foe pulls all of them up with
Zep 1: 3 The w will have only heaps of rubble
Mal 1: 4 They will be called the W Land, a
3:18 between the righteous and the w,
4: 3 you will trample down the w; they
Mt 12:39 He answered, "A w and adulterous
12:45 other spirits more w than itself,
12:45 it will be with this w generation."
13:49 separate the w from the righteous
16: 4 A w and adulterous generation looks
18:32 'You w servant,' he said, 'I
24:48 suppose that servant is w and says
25:26 "His master replied, 'You w, lazy
Lk 6:35 he is kind to the ungrateful and w.
11:26 other spirits more w than itself,
11:29 Jesus said, "This is a w generation.
19:22 you w servant! You knew, did you,
Ac 2:23 with the help of w men, put him to
3:26 each of you from your w ways."
24:15 of both the righteous and the w.

Ro 4: 5 but trusts God who justifies the w,
1Co 5:13 "Expel the w man from among you."
6: 9 Do you not know that the w will not
2Th 3: 2 pray that we may be delivered from w
2Jn :11 welcomes him shares in his w work.
Rev 2: 2 know that you cannot tolerate w men

Wickedly (Wicked)

1Ki 8:47 have done wrong, we have acted w';
2Ch 6:37 we have done wrong and acted w';
Ne 1: 7 We have acted very w towards you. We
Job 13: 7 Will you speak w on God's behalf?
Ps 106: 6 did; we have done wrong and acted w.
Jer 16:12 you have behaved more w than your
38: 9 these men have acted w in all they

Wickedness (Wicked)

Ge 6: 5 The LORD saw how great man's w on
Ex 34: 7 and forgiving w, rebellion and sin.
34: 9 forgive our w and our sin, and take
Lev 16:21 confess over it all the w and
18:17 That is w.
19:29 prostitution and be filled with w.
20:14 so that no w will be among you.
Dt 9: 4 No, it is on account of the w of
9: 5 account of the w of these nations,
9:27 this people, their w and their sin.
31:18 their w in turning to other gods.
Jdg 9:56 Thus God repaid the w that Abimelech
9:57 men of Shechem pay for all their w.
2Ch 20:35 king of Israel, who was guilty of w.
28:19 for he had promoted w in Judah and
Ne 9: 2 sins and the w of their fathers.
13:27 too are doing all this terrible w
Job 6:30 Is there any w on my lips? Can my
22: 5 Is not your w great? Are not your
22:23 If you remove w far from your
27: 4 my lips will not speak w, and my
34:26 He punishes them for their w where
35: 8 Your w affects only a man like
35:15 does not take the least notice of w.
Ps 10:15 his w that would not be found out.
45: 7 You love righteousness and hate w;
92:15 my Rock, and there is no w in him."
94:23 sins and destroy them for their w;
107:34 of the w of those who lived there.
Pr 4:17 They eat the bread of w and drink
8: 7 what is true, for my lips detest w.
11: 5 are brought down by their own w.
12: 3 A man cannot be established through w
13: 6 but w overthrows the sinner.
18: 3 w comes, so does contempt, and with
22: 8 He who sows w reaps trouble, and the
26:26 w will be exposed in the assembly.
Ecc 3:16 the place of judgment—w was there,
3:16 the place of justice—w was there.
7:15 a wicked man living long in his w.
7:25 of w and the madness of folly.
8: 8 so w will not release those who
Isa 5:18 of deceit, and w as with cart ropes,
9:18 Surely w burns like a fire; it
47:10 You have trusted in your w and have
Jer 1:16 because of their w in forsaking me,
2:19 Your w will punish you; your
3: 2 land with your prostitution and w.
6: 7 its water, so she pours out her w.
7:12 of the w of my people Israel.
8: 6 No-one repents of his w, saying,
11:15 engage in your w, then you rejoice."
14:10 remember their w and punish them for
14:20 O LORD, we acknowledge our w and the
16:18 I will repay them double for their w
22:22 and disgraced because of all your w.
23:11 I find their w," declares the LORD.
23:14 so that no-one turns from his w.
31:34 "For I will forgive their w and will
33: 5 from this city because of all its w.
36: 3 will forgive their w and their sin."
36:31 and his attendants for their w;
44: 5 they did not turn from their w or
44: 9 Have you forgotten the w committed
44: 9 queens of Judah and the w committed
Lam 1:22 "Let all their w come before you;
4:22 punish your sin and expose your w.
Eze 3:19 from his w or from his evil ways,
5: 6 Yet in her w she has rebelled
7:11 into a rod to punish w; none of the
16:23 In addition to all your other w,
16:57 before your w was uncovered. Even so,
18:20 and the w of the wicked will be
18:27 if a wicked man turns away from the w
28:15 created till w was found in you.
31:11 him to deal with according to its w.
33:12 and the w of the wicked man will not
33:19 if a wicked man turns away from his w
Da 4:27 is right and your w by being kind
9:24 an end to sin, to atone for w,
Hos 4: 8 of my people and relish their w.
7: 3 "They delight the king with their w,
8:13 Now he will remember their w and
9: 9 God will remember their w and
9:15 "Because of all their w in Gilgal, I
10: 8 The high places of w will be
10:13 you have planted w, you have reaped
10:15 O Bethel, because your w is great.
Joel 3:13 overflow—so great is their w!"
Jnh 1: 2 its w has come up before me."
Mic 3:10 bloodshed, and Jerusalem with w.
Na 1:11 against the LORD and counsels w.
Hab 3:13 crushed the leader of the land of w,
Zec 5: 8 He said, "This is w," and he pushed
Mt 23:28 you are full of hypocrisy and w.
24:12 of the increase of w, the love of
Lk 11:39 inside you are full of greed and w.
Ac 1:18 (With the reward he got for his w,
8:22 Repent of this w and pray to the
Ro 1:18 w of men who suppress the truth by
1:18 who suppress the truth by their w,
1:29 of w, evil, greed and depravity.
6:13 as instruments of w, but rather
6:19 impurity and to ever-increasing w,
1Co 5: 8 the yeast of malice and w, but with
2Co 6:14 For what do righteousness and w have
2Th 2:12 the truth but have delighted in w.
2Ti 2:19 of the Lord must turn away from w."
Tit 2:14 for us to redeem us from all w
Heb 1: 9 loved righteousness and hated w;
8:12 For I will forgive their w and will
2Pe 2:15 of Beor, who loved the wages of w.

Wide (Widened, Wider, Width)

Ge 6:15 long, 75 feet w and 45 feet high.
Ex 25:10 a cubit and a half w, and a cubit
25:17 long and a cubit and a half w.
25:23 cubit w and a cubit and a half high.
25:25 a rim a handbreadth w and put a
26: 2 cubits long and four cubits w.
26: 8 cubits long and four cubits w.
26:16 long and a cubit and a half w,
27: 1 five cubits long and five cubits w.
27:12 be fifty cubits w and have curtains,
27:13 shall also be fifty cubits w.
27:18 cubits long and fifty cubits w,
28:16 and a span w—and folded double.
30: 2 a cubit long and a cubit w, and two
36: 9 cubits long and four cubits w.
36:15 cubits long and four cubits w.
36:21 long and a cubit and a half w,
37: 1 a cubit and a half w, and a cubit
37: 6 long and a cubit and a half w.
37:10 a cubit w, and a cubit and a half
37:12 a rim a handbreadth w and put a
37:25 a cubit long and a cubit w, and two
38: 1 five cubits long and five cubits w.
38:12 The west end was fifty cubits w and
38:13 sunrise, was also fifty cubits w.
39: 9 was square—a span long and a span w
Dt 3:11 thirteen feet long and six feet w.
1Sa 26:13 there was a w space between them.
1Ki 6: 2 long, twenty w and thirty high.
6: 6 The lowest floor was five cubits w,
6:20 long, twenty w and twenty high.
7: 2 fifty w and thirty high, with four
7: 6 fifty cubits long and thirty w.
7:27 cubits long, four w and three high.
1Ch 13: 2 let us send word far and w to the
2Ch 3: 3 twenty cubits w (using the cubit of
3: 8 cubits long and twenty cubits w.
4: 1 twenty cubits w and ten cubits high.
6:13 five cubits long, five cubits w and
2Ch 26:15 His fame spread far and w, for he
Ezr 6: 3 ninety feet high and ninety feet w,
Ps 22:13 prey open their mouths w against me.
81:10 Open w your mouth and I will fill it.
Isa 18: 2 to a people feared far and w, an
18: 7 from a people feared far and w, an
30:33 fire pit has been made deep and w,
45: 8 Let the earth open w, let salvation
54: 2 stretch your tent curtains w, do not
57: 8 you climbed into it and opened it w;
Lam 2:16 All your enemies open their mouths w
3:46 opened their mouths w against us.
Eze 40: 7 were one rod long and one rod w,
40:18 and was as w as they were long;
40:21 long and twenty-five cubits w.
40:25 long and twenty-five cubits w.
40:29 long and twenty-five cubits w.
40:30 cubits w and five cubits deep.)
40:33 long and twenty-five cubits w.
40:36 long and twenty-five cubits w.
40:42 cubit and a half w and a cubit high.
40:47 cubits long and a hundred cubits w.
40:48 were five cubits w on either side.
40:48 were three cubits w on either side.
40:49 The portico was twenty cubits w, and
41: 2 The entrance was ten cubits w, and
41: 2 each side of it were five cubits w.
41: 2 cubits long and twenty cubits w.
41: 3 the entrance; each was two cubits w.
41: 3 The entrance was six cubits w, and
41: 3 each side of it were seven cubits w.
41: 5 round the temple was four cubits w.
41:10 priests' rooms was twenty cubits w
41:11 area was five cubits w all round.
41:12 the west side was seventy cubits w.
42: 2 cubits long and fifty cubits w.
42: 4 an inner passageway ten cubits w
42:20 long and five hundred cubits w,
43:13 is a cubit deep and a cubit w,
43:14 it is two cubits high and a cubit w,
43:14 is four cubits high and a cubit w.
43:16 cubits long and twelve cubits w.
43:17 cubits long and fourteen cubits w,
45: 1 20,000 cubits w; the entire area
45: 3 cubits long and 10,000 cubits w.
45: 5 cubits w will belong to the Levites,
45: 6 an area 5,000 cubits w and 25,000
46:22 cubits long and thirty cubits w;
48: 8 It will be 25,000 cubits w, and its
48: 9 cubits long and 10,000 cubits w.
48:10 10,000 cubits w on the west side,
48:10 10,000 cubits w on the east side and
48:13 cubits long and 10,000 cubits w.
48:15 "The remaining area, 5,000 cubits w
Da 3: 1 ninety feet high and nine feet w,
Mic 4: 3 for strong nations far and w.
Na 3:13 land are w open to your enemies;
Zec 2: 2 find out how w and how long it is."
5: 2 feet long and fifteen feet w."
Mt 7:13 w is the gate and broad is the road
23: 5 They make their phylacteries w and
2Co 6:11 and opened w our hearts to you.
6:13 children—open w your hearts also.
Eph 3:18 to grasp how w and long and high and
Rev 21:16 like a square, as long as it was w.
21:16 and as w and high as it is long.

Widened (Wide)

Eze 41: 7 that the rooms w as one went upward.

Wider (Wide)

Job 11: 9 than the earth and w than the sea.
Eze 41: 7 were w at each successive level.

Widespread (Spread)

Eze 28:16 Through your w trade you were filled
Jn 7:12 there was w whispering about him.

Widow (Widow's, Widowhood, Widows, Widows')

Ge 38:11 "Live as a w in your father's house
Ex 22:22 "Do not take advantage of a w or an
Lev 21:14 He must not marry a w, a divorced
22:13 if a priest's daughter becomes a w

Nu 30: 9 "Any vow or obligation taken by a w
Dt 10:18 cause of the fatherless and the w,
24:17 take the cloak of the w as a pledge.
24:19 the fatherless and the w, so that
24:20 the alien, the fatherless and the w.
24:21 the alien, the fatherless and the w.
25: 5 w must not marry outside the family.
25: 9 his brother's w shall go up to him
26:12 the alien, the fatherless and the w,
26:13 the alien, the fatherless and the w
27:19 the alien, the fatherless or the w.
Ru 4: 5 you acquire the dead man's w, in
4:10 Mahlon's w, as my wife, in order to
1Sa 27: 3 Abigail of Carmel, the w of Nabal.
30: 5 Abigail, the w of Nabal of Carmel.
2Sa 2: 2 Abigail, the w of Nabal of Carmel.
3: 3 Kileab the son of Abigail the w of
14: 5 am indeed a w; my husband is dead.
1Ki 7:14 whose mother was a w from the tribe
11:26 and his mother was a w named Zeruah.
17: 9 I have commanded a w in that place
17:10 a w was their gathering sticks.
17:20 brought tragedy also upon this w
Job 24:21 and to the w show no kindness.
31:16 or let the eyes of the w grow weary,
31:18 and from my birth I guided the w—
Ps 94: 6 They slay the w and the alien; they
109: 9 be fatherless and his wife a w.
146: 9 sustains the fatherless and the w,
Isa 1:17 fatherless, plead the case of the w.
47: 8 I will never be a w or suffer the
Jer 7: 6 the fatherless or the w and do not
22: 3 the fatherless or the w, and do not
Lam 1: 1 full of people! How like a w is she,
Eze 22: 7 the fatherless and the w.
Zec 7:10 Do not oppress the w or the
Mt 22:24 the w and have children for him.
Mk 12:19 must marry the w and have children
12:21 The second one married the w, but he
12:42 a poor w came and put in two very
12:43 "I tell you the truth, this poor w
Lk 2:37 was a w until she was eighty-four.
4:26 but to a w in Zarephath in the
7:12 son of his mother, and she was a w.
18: 3 there was a w in that town who kept
18: 5 yet because this w keeps bothering
20:28 the man must marry the w and have
21: 2 He also saw a poor w put in two very
21: 3 "this poor w has put in more than
1Ti 5: 4 if a w has children or grandchildren,
5: 5 The w who is really in need and left
5: 6 the w who lives for pleasure is dead
5: 9 No w may be put on the list of
Rev 18: 7 am not a w, and I will never mourn.'

Widow's (Widow)

Ge 38:14 she took off her w clothes, covered
38:19 veil and put on her w clothes again.
Job 24: 3 donkey and take the w ox in pledge.
29:13 blessed me; I made the w heart sing.
Pr 15:25 he keeps the w boundaries intact.
Isa 1:23 w case does not come before them.

Widowhood (Widow)

Isa 47: 9 single day: loss of children and w.
54: 4 no more the reproach of your w.

Widows (Widow)

Ex 22:24 your wives will become w and your
Dt 14:29 the fatherless and the w who live in
16:11 and the w living among you.
16:14 and the w who live in your towns.
2Sa 20: 3 the day of their death, living as w.
Job 22: 9 you sent w away empty-handed and
27:15 and their w will not weep for them.
Ps 68: 5 a defender of w, is God in his holy
78:64 sword, and their w could not weep.
Isa 9:17 will he pity the fatherless and w,
10: 2 making w their prey and robbing the
Jer 15: 8 I will make their w more numerous
18:21 wives be made childless and w;
49:11 Your w too can trust in me."
Lam 5: 3 and fatherless, our mothers like w.
Eze 22:25 things and make many w within her.
44:22 They must not marry w or divorced
Eze 44:22 Israelite descent or w of priests.
Mal 3: 5 who oppress the w and the fatherless,
Lk 4:25 I assure you that there were many w
Ac 6: 1 their w were being overlooked in
9:39 All the w stood around him, crying
9:41 w and presented her to them alive.
1Co 7: 8 Now to the unmarried and the w I say:
1Ti 5: 3 Give proper recognition to those w
5: 9 No widow may be put on the list of w
5:11 for younger w, do not put them on
5:14 I counsel younger w to marry, to
5:16 If any woman who is a believer has w
5:16 help those w who are really in need.
Jas 1:27 to look after orphans and w in their

Widows' (Widow)

Mk 12:40 They devour w houses and for a show
Lk 20:47 They devour w houses and for a show

Width (Wide)

1Ki 6: 3 temple extended the w of the temple,
2Ch 3: 4 long across the w of the building
3: 8 its length corresponding to the w of
Eze 40:11 he measured the w of the entrance to
40:20 he measured the length and w of the
40:48 The w of the entrance was fourteen
41: 1 the w of the jambs was six cubits on
41: 4 and its w was twenty cubits across
41:14 The w of the temple courtyard on the
42:11 had the same length and w, with
48:13 cubits and its w 10,000 cubits.

Wield (Wielding)

Isa 10:15 a rod were to w him who lifts it up,

Wielding (Wield)

Ps 74: 5 They behaved like men w axes to cut

Wife (Wife's, Wives, Wives')

Ge 2:24 be united to his w, and they will
2:25 The man and his w were both naked,
3: 8 the man and his w heard the sound of
3:17 "Because you listened to your w and
3:20 Adam named his w Eve, because she
3:21 for Adam and his w and clothed them.
4: 1 Adam lay with his w Eve, and she
4:17 Cain lay with his w, and she became
4:25 Adam lay with his w again, and she
6:18 your w and your sons' wives with
7: 7 Noah and his sons and his w and his
7:13 together with his w and the wives of
8:16 "Come out of the ark, you and your w
8:18 sons and his w and his sons' wives.
11:29 The name of Abram's w was Sarai, and
11:29 and the name of Nahor's w was Milcah;
11:31 Sarai, the w of his son Abram, and
12: 5 He took his w Sarai, his nephew Lot,
12:11 he said to his w Sarai, "I know what
12:12 you, they will say, 'This is his w.
12:17 because of Abram's w Sarai.
12:18 didn't you tell me she was your w?
12:19 be my w? Now then, here is your w.
12:20 with his w and everything he had.
13: 1 with his w and everything he had,
16: 1 Now Sarai, Abram's w, had borne him
16: 3 Sarai his w took her Egyptian
16: 3 gave her to her husband to be his w.
17:15 "As for Sarai your w, you are no
17:19 God said, "Yes, but your w Sarah
18: 9 "Where is your w Sarah?" they asked
18:10 and Sarah your w will have a son.
19:15 "Hurry! Take your w and your two
19:16 the hands of his w and of his two
19:26 Lot's w looked back, and she became
20: 2 there Abraham said of his w Sarah,
20: 7 Now return the man's w, for he is a
20:11 they will kill me because of my w.'
20:12 of my mother; and she became my w.
20:14 and he returned Sarah his w to him.
20:17 and God healed Abimelech, his w and
20:18 because of Abraham's w Sarah.
21:21 mother got a w for him from Egypt.
23: 3 Abraham rose from beside his dead w
23:19 Afterwards Abraham buried his w
Ge 24: 3 that you will not get a w for my son
24: 4 and get a w for my son Isaac."
24: 7 can get a w for my son from there.
24:15 the w of Abraham's brother Nahor.
24:36 My master's w Sarah has borne him a
24:37 'You must not get a w for my son
24:38 own clan, and get a w for my son.'
24:40 so that you can get a w for my son
24:51 and let her become the w of your
24:67 So she became his w, and he loved
25: 1 Abraham took another w, whose name
25:10 Abraham was buried with his w Sarah.
25:21 of his w, because she was barren.
25:21 and his w Rebekah became pregnant.
26: 7 his w, he said, "She is my sister,"
26: 7 he was afraid to say, "She is my w.
26: 8 saw Isaac caressing his w Rebekah.
26: 9 "She is really your w! Why did you
26:10 might well have slept with your w,
26:11 his w shall surely be put to death."
27:46 If Jacob takes a w from among the
28: 2 Take a w for yourself there, from
28: 6 Paddan Aram to take a w from there,
29:21 Jacob said to Laban, "Give me my w.
29:28 him his daughter Rachel to be his w.
30: 4 gave him her servant Bilhah as a w.
30: 9 Zilpah and gave her to Jacob as a w.
34: 4 Hamor, "Get me this girl as my w.
34: 8 Please give her to him as his w.
34:12 Only give me the girl as my w."
36:10 the son of Esau's w Adah, and Reuel,
36:10 Reuel, the son of Esau's w Basemath.
36:12 were grandsons of Esau's w Adah.
36:13 were grandsons of Esau's w Basemath.
36:14 The sons of Esau's w Oholibamah
36:17 were grandsons of Esau's w Basemath.
36:18 The sons of Esau's w Oholibamah:
36:18 Esau's w Oholibamah daughter of Anah.
38: 6 Judah got a w for Er, his firstborn,
38: 8 "Lie with your brother's w and
38: 9 he lay with his brother's w,
38:12 After a long time Judah's w, the
38:14 had not been given to him as his w.
39: 7 after a while his master's w took
39: 9 except you, because you are his w.
39:19 his master heard the story his w
41:45 Potiphera, priest of On, to be his w.
44:27 know that my w bore me two sons.
46:19 The sons of Jacob's w Rachel: Joseph
49:31 There Abraham and his w Sarah were
49:31 there Isaac and his w Rebekah were
Ex 4:20 Moses took his w and sons, put them
18: 2 After Moses had sent away his w
18: 5 together with Moses' sons and w,
18: 6 you with your w and her two sons."
20:17 shall not covet your neighbour's w,
21: 3 but if he has a w when he comes,
21: 4 If his master gives him a w and she
21: 5 'I love my master and my w and
22:16 bride-price, and she shall be his w.
Lev 18: 8 relations with your father's w;
18:11 the daughter of your father's w,
18:14 his w to have sexual relations;
18:15 your son's w; do not have relations
18:16 relations with your brother's w;
18:18 your wife's sister as a rival w
18:18 with her while your w is living.
18:20 neighbour's w and defile yourself
20:10 adultery with another man's w—
20:10 with the w of his neighbour—both
20:11 If a man sleeps with his father's w
20:21 "'If a man marries his brother's w,
Nu 5:12 'If a man's w goes astray and is
5:14 he suspects his w and she is impure—
5:15 he is to take his w to the priest.
5:30 a man because he suspects his w.
12: 1 Moses because of his Cushite w,
26:59 the name of Amram's w was Jochebed,
30:16 between a man and his w,
Dt 5:21 shall not covet your neighbour's w.
13: 6 son or daughter, or the w you love
21:11 to her, you may take her as your w.
21:13 her husband and she shall be your w.
21:15 the son of the w he does not love,
21:16 to the son of the w he loves
21:16 the son of the w he does not love.

Dt 21:17 the son of his unloved w as the
22:13 If a man takes a w and, after lying
22:19 She shall continue to be his w; he
22:22 found sleeping with another man's w,
22:24 because he violated another man's w.
22:30 A man is not to marry his father's w;
24: 2 she becomes the w of another man,
24: 5 happiness to the w he has married.
25: 7 not want to marry his brother's w,
25:11 If two men are fighting and the w of
27:20 man who sleeps with his father's w,
28:54 w he loves or his surviving children,
Jdg 4: 4 Deborah, a prophetess, the w of
4:17 the w of Heber the Kenite, because
4:21 Jael, Heber's w, picked up a tent
5:24 "Most blessed of women be Jael, the w
11: 2 Gilead's w also bore him sons, and
13: 2 had a w who was sterile and remained
13:11 Manoah got up and followed his w.
13:11 talked to my w?" "I am," he said.
13:13 w must do all that I have told her.
13:19 while Manoah and his w watched:
13:20 Seeing this, Manoah and his w fell
13:21 himself again to Manoah and his w,
13:22 doomed to die!" he said to his w.
13:23 his w answered, "If the LORD had
14: 2 Timnah; now get her for me as my w."
14: 3 Philistines to get a w?" But Samson
14:15 they said to Samson's w, "Coax your
14:16 Samson's w threw herself on him,
14:20 Samson's w was given to the friend
15: 1 young goat and went to visit his w.
15: 6 his w was given to his friend.
21:18 who gives a w to a Benjamite.'
21:21 each of you seize a w from the girls
21:23 one and carried her off to be his w.
Ru 1: 1 together with his w and two sons,
4:10 Mahlon's widow, as my w, in order to
4:13 Boaz took Ruth and she became his w.
1Sa 1: 4 of the meat to his w Peninnah
1:19 his w, and the LORD remembered her.
2:20 Eli would bless Elkanah and his w,
4:19 daughter-in-law, the w of Phinehas
19:11 But Michal, David's w, warned him,
25:14 One of the servants told Nabal's w
25:37 when Nabal was sober, his w told him
25:39 Abigail, asking her to become his w.
25:40 to you to take you to become his w."
25:42 David's messengers and became his w.
25:44 David's w, to Paltiel son of Laish,
30:22 may take his w and children and go."
2Sa 3: 5 Ithream the son of David's w Eglah.
3:14 "Give me my w Michal, whom I
11: 3 and the w of Uriah the Hittite?"
11:11 with my w? As surely as you live,
11:26 Uriah's w heard that her husband was
11:27 she became his w and bore him a son.
12: 9 sword and took his w to be your own.
12:10 took the w of Uriah the Hittite to
12:15 that Uriah's w had borne to David,
12:24 David comforted his w Bathsheba, and
17:19 His w took a covering and spread it
1Ki 2:17 me Abishag the Shunammite as my w."
9:16 gift to his daughter, Solomon's w.
11:19 own w, Queen Tahpenes, in marriage.
14: 2 Jeroboam said to his w, "Go,
14: 2 be recognised as the w of Jeroboam.
14: 4 Jeroboam's w did what he said and
14: 5 "Jeroboam's w is coming to ask you
14: 6 he said, "Come in, w of Jeroboam.
14:17 Jeroboam's w got up and left and
21: 5 His w Jezebel came in and asked him,
21: 7 Jezebel his w said, "Is this how you
21:25 the LORD, urged on by Jezebel his w.
2Ki 4: 1 The w of a man from the company of
5: 2 Israel, and she served Naaman's w.
22:14 who was the w of Shallum son of
1Ch 2:18 by his w Azubah (and by Jerioth).
2:24 Abijah the w of Hezron bore him
2:26 Jerahmeel had another w, whose name
2:29 Abishur's w was named Abihail, who
3: 3 the sixth, Ithream, by his w Eglah.
4:18 (His Judean w gave birth to Jered
4:19 The sons of Hodiah's w, the sister
7:15 Makir took a w from among the
7:16 Makir's w Maacah gave birth to a
1Ch 7:23 he lay with his w again, and she
8: 9 By his w Hodesh he had Jobab, Zibia,
2Ch 8:11 "My w must not live in the palace of
22:11 the daughter of King Jehoram and w
34:22 who was the w of Shallum son of
Est 5:10 his friends and Zeresh, his w,
5:14 His w Zeresh and all his friends
6:13 told Zeresh his w and all his
6:13 His advisers and his w Zeresh said
Job 2: 9 His w said to him, "Are you still
19:17 My breath is offensive to my w; I am
31:10 may my w grind another man's grain,
Ps 109: 9 be fatherless and his w a widow.
128: 3 Your w will be like a fruitful vine
Pr 2:16 wayward w with her seductive words,
5:18 you rejoice in the w of your youth.
5:20 the bosom of another man's w?
6:24 the smooth tongue of the wayward w.
6:29 is he who sleeps with another man's w
7: 5 wayward w with her seductive words.
12: 4 A w of noble character is her
12: 4 a disgraceful w is like decay in
18:22 He who finds a w finds what is good
19:13 a quarrelsome w is like a constant
19:14 but a prudent w is from the LORD.
21: 9 share a house with a quarrelsome w.
21:19 a quarrelsome and ill-tempered w.
23:27 and a wayward w is a narrow well.
25:24 share a house with a quarrelsome w.
27:15 A quarrelsome w is like a constant
31:10 A w of noble character who can find?
Ecc 9: 9 Enjoy life with your w, whom you
Isa 54: 6 back as if you were a w deserted
54: 6 in spirit—a w who married young,
Jer 3: 1 "If a man divorces his w and she
5: 8 each neighing for another man's w.
6:11 husband and w will be caught in it,
Eze 16:32 "'You adulterous w! You prefer
18: 6 He does not defile his neighbour's w
18:11 He defiles his neighbour's w.
18:15 He does not defile his neighbour's w.
22:11 offence with his neighbour's w,
24:18 and in the evening my w died.
33:26 of you defiles his neighbour's w.
Hos 1: 2 take to yourself an adulterous w and
2: 2 not my w, and I am not her husband.
3: 1 "Go, show your love to your w again,
12:12 of Aram; Israel served to get a w,
Am 7:17 'Your w will become a prostitute in
Mal 2:14 between you and the w of your youth,
2:14 the w of your marriage covenant.
2:15 faith with the w of your youth.
Mt 1: 6 whose mother had been Uriah's w,
1:20 afraid to take Mary home as your w,
1:24 him and took Mary home as his w.
5:31 'Anyone who divorces his w must give
5:32 you that anyone who divorces his w,
14: 3 of Herodias, his brother Philip's w,
18:25 his w and his children and all that
19: 3 his w for any and every reason?"
19: 5 and mother and be united to his w,
19: 7 give his w a certificate of divorce
19: 9 you that anyone who divorces his w,
19:10 and w, it is better not to marry."
22:25 he left his w to his brother.
22:28 at the resurrection, whose w will
27:19 his w sent him this message: "Don't
Mk 6:17 Philip's w, whom he had married.
6:18 for you to have your brother's w."
10: 2 lawful for a man to divorce his w?"
10: 7 and mother and be united to his w,
10:11 "Anyone who divorces his w and
12:19 dies and leaves a w but no children,
12:23 At the resurrection whose w will she
Lk 1: 5 his w Elizabeth was also a
1:13 Your w Elizabeth will bear you a son,
1:18 man and my w is well on in years."
1:24 After this his w Elizabeth became
3:19 his brother's w, and all the other
8: 3 Joanna the w of Chuza, the manager
14:26 his w and children, his brothers and
16:18 "Anyone who divorces his w and
17:32 Remember Lot's w!
18:29 "no-one who has left home or w or
20:28 dies and leaves a w but no children,
20:33 at the resurrection whose w will she
Jn 19:25 the w of Clopas, and Mary Magdalene.
Ac 5: 1 together with his w Sapphira, also
5: 7 About three hours later his w came
18: 2 from Italy with his w Priscilla,
24:24 his w Drusilla, who was a Jewess.
1Co 5: 1 pagans: A man has his father's w.
7: 2 each man should have his own w, and
7: 3 duty to his w, and likewise the w
7: 4 to him alone but also to his w.
7:10 w must not separate from her husband.
7:11 And a husband must not divorce his w.
7:12 If any brother has a w who is not a
7:14 has been sanctified through his w,
7:14 and the unbelieving w has been
7:16 How do you know, w, whether you will
7:16 whether you will save your w?
7:27 you unmarried? Do not look for a w.
7:33 world—how he can please his w—
9: 5 to take a believing w along with us,
Eph 5:23 For the husband is the head of the w
5:28 He who loves his w loves himself.
5:31 be united to his w, and the two
5:33 must love his w as he loves himself,
5:33 and the w must respect her husband.
1Ti 3: 2 the husband of but one w, temperate,
3:12 must be the husband of but one w
Tit 1: 6 the husband of but one w, a man
Rev 21: 9 you the bride, the w of the Lamb."

Wife's (Wife)

Ge 36:39 his w name was Mehetabel daughter
Lev 18:18 "'Do not take your w sister as a
Jdg 15: 1 He said, "I'm going to my w room."
Ru 1: 2 was Elimelech, his w name Naomi,
1Sa 14:50 His w name was Ahinoam daughter of
25: 3 His name was Nabal and his w name
1Ch 1:50 his w name was Mehetabel daughter
8:29 His w name was Maacah,
9:35 His w name was Maacah,
Ac 5: 2 With his w full knowledge he kept
1Co 7: 4 The w body does not belong to her

Wild (Wilder, Wilderness, Wilds)

Ge 1:24 and w animals, each according to its
1:25 God made the w animals according to
3: 1 the w animals the LORD God had made.
3:14 the livestock and all the w animals!
7:14 They had with them every w animal
7:21 livestock, w animals, all the
8: 1 God remembered Noah and all the w
9:10 the livestock and all the w animals,
16:12 He will be a w donkey of a man; his
25:28 Isaac, who had a taste for w game,
27: 3 country to hunt some w game for me.
31:39 bring you animals torn by w beasts
Ex 22:13 was torn to pieces by a w animal
22:31 by w beasts; throw it to the dogs.
23:11 w animals may eat what they leave.
23:29 the w animals too numerous for you.
32:25 saw that the people were running w
Lev 5: 2 the carcasses of unclean w animals
7:24 found dead or torn by w animals
17:15 by w animals must wash his clothes
22: 8 found dead or torn by w animals,
25: 7 for your livestock and the w animals
26:22 I will send w animals against you,
Nu 23:22 they have the strength of a w ox.
24: 8 they have the strength of a w ox.
Dt 7:22 w animals will multiply around you.
14: 5 gazelle, the roe deer, the w goat
32:24 against them the fangs of w beasts,
33:17 his horns are the horns of a w ox.
1Sa 24: 2 men near the Crags of the W Goats.
2Sa 2:18 was as fleet-footed as a w gazelle.
17: 8 as a w bear robbed of her cubs.
21:10 by day or the w animals by night.
2Ki 4:39 to gather herbs and found a w vine.
14: 9 Then a w beast in Lebanon came
2Ch 25:18 Then a w beast in Lebanon came
Ne 8:15 from olive and w olive trees,
Job 5:23 w animals will be at peace with you.
6: 5 Does a w donkey bray when it has
11:12 a w donkey's colt can be born a man.
24: 5 Like w donkeys in the desert, the
39: 5 "Who let the w donkey go free? Who

Job 39: 9 "Will the **w** ox consent to serve you?
39:15 that some **w** animal may trample them.
40:20 and all the **w** animals play nearby.
Ps 22:21 me from the horns of the **w** oxen.
29: 6 a calf, Sirion like a young **w** ox.
74:19 the life of your dove to **w** beasts;
92:10 exalted my horn like that of a **w** ox;
104:11 the **w** donkeys quench their thirst.
104:18 mountains belong to the **w** goats;
148:10 **w** animals and all cattle, small
Isa 13:21 there the **w** goats will leap about.
18: 6 birds of prey and to the **w** animals;
18: 6 summer, the **w** animals all winter.
34: 7 the **w** oxen will fall with them, the
34:14 and **w** goats will bleat to each other;
43:20 The **w** animals honour me, the jackals
Jer 2:21 against me into a corrupt, **w** vine?
2:24 a **w** donkey accustomed to the desert,
12: 9 the **w** beasts; bring them to devour.
14: 6 **W** donkeys stand on the barren
27: 6 even the **w** animals subject to him.
28:14 give him control over the **w** animals.
Eze 4:14 found dead or torn by **w** animals.
5:17 I will send famine and **w** beasts
14:15 "Or if I send **w** beasts through that
14:21 famine and **w** beasts and plague—to
33:27 to the **w** animals to be devoured,
34: 5 became food for all the **w** animals.
34: 8 become food for all the **w** animals,
34:25 rid the land of **w** beasts so that
34:28 nor will **w** animals devour them.
39: 4 carrion birds and to the **w** animals.
39:17 kind of bird and all the **w** animals:
44:31 found dead or torn by **w** animals.
Da 4:23 let him live like the **w** animals,
4:25 and will live with the **w** animals;
4:32 and will live with the **w** animals;
5:21 he lived with the **w** donkeys and ate
Hos 2:12 and **w** animals will devour them.
8: 9 like a **w** donkey wandering alone.
13: 8 a **w** animal will tear them apart.
Joel 1:20 Even the **w** animals pant for you; the
2:22 Be not afraid, O **w** animals, for the
Zep 2:15 a lair for **w** beasts! All who pass by
Mt 3: 4 His food was locusts and **w** honey.
Mk 1: 6 and he ate locusts and **w** honey.
1:13 He was with the **w** animals, and
Lk 15:13 squandered his wealth in **w** living.
Ac 11: 6 **w** beasts, reptiles, and birds of the
Ro 11:17 and you, though a **w** olive shoot,
11:24 an olive tree that is **w** by nature,
1Co 15:32 If I fought **w** beasts in Ephesus for
Tit 1: 6 charge of being **w** and disobedient.
Jas 1:10 he will pass away like a **w** flower.
Jude :13 They are **w** waves of the sea, foaming
Rev 6: 8 and by the **w** beasts of the earth.

Wilder (Wild)

Jnh 1:13 for the sea grew even **w** than before.

Wilderness (Wild)

Isa 35: 1 the **w** will rejoice and blossom.
35: 6 in the **w** and streams in the desert.
40: 3 in the **w** a highway for our God.
Jer 2: 6 and led us through the barren **w**,
50:12 nations—a **w**, a dry land, a desert.

Wilds (Wild)

Job 39: 4 thrive and grow strong in the **w**;

Wilful (Will)

Ps 19:13 Keep your servant also from **w** sins;
Isa 10:12 Assyria for the **w** pride of his heart
57:17 anger, yet he kept on in his **w** ways.

Wilfully (Will)

Ps 78:18 They **w** put God to the test by

Will (Freewill, Weak-willed, Wilful, Wilfully, *Will of God*, Willing, Willingly, Willingness, Wills)

Ex 18:15 the people come to me to seek God's **w**
Lev 24:12 until the **w** of the LORD should be
25:46 You can **w** them to your children as
Dt 10:10 It was not his **w** to destroy you.
15: 9 ill **w** towards your needy brother and
33:21 he carried out the LORD's righteous **w**
1Sa 2:25 it was the LORD's **w** to put them
2Sa 7:21 your word and according to your **w**,
1Ch 13: 2 if it is the **w** of the LORD our God,
17:19 your servant and according to your **w**,
Ezr 7:18 in accordance with the **w** of your God.
10:11 God of your fathers, and do his **w**.
Ps 40: 8 I desire to do your **w**, O my God;
103:21 you his servants who do his **w**.
143:10 Teach me to do your **w**, for you are my
Isa 53:10 the LORD's **w** to crush him and cause
53:10 the **w** of the LORD will prosper in his
Mt 6:10 your **w** be done on earth as it is in
7:21 the **w** of my Father who is in heaven.
10:29 apart from the **w** of your Father.
12:50 the **w** of my Father in heaven is my
26:42 I drink it, may your **w** be done
Mk 3:35 Whoever does God's **w** is my brother
Lk 12:47 That servant who knows his master's **w**
22:42 yet not my **w**, but yours be done."
23:25 and surrendered Jesus to their **w**.
Jn 1:13 of human decision or a husband's **w**
4:34 "is to do the **w** of him who sent me
6:38 not to do my **w** but to do the **w** of him
6:39 this is the **w** of him who sent me,
6:40 my Father's **w** is that everyone who
7:17 If anyone chooses to do God's **w**, he
9:31 to the godly man who does his **w**.
Ac 4:28 did what your power and **w** had decided
18:21 "I will come back if it is God's **w**."
21:14 "The Lord's **w** be done."
22:14 fathers has chosen you to know his **w**
Ro 1:10 by God's **w** the way may be opened for
2:18 if you know his **w** and approve of what
8:20 by the **w** of the one who subjected it
9:19 For who resists his **w**?
12: 2 test and approve what God's **w** is—
12: 2 his good, pleasing and perfect **w**.
15:32 by God's **w** I may come to you with joy
1Co 7:37 but has control over his own **w**.
2Co 8: 5 then to us in keeping with God's **w**.
Gal 1: 4 according to the **w** of our God and
Eph 1: 5 in accordance with his pleasure and **w**
1: 9 his **w** according to his good pleasure,
1:11 conformity with the purpose of his **w**,
5:17 but understand what the Lord's **w** is.
Col 1: 9 fill you with the knowledge of his **w**
1Th 4: 3 God's **w** that you should be sanctified:
5:18 is God's **w** for you in Christ Jesus.
2Ti 2:26 has taken them captive to do his **w**.
Heb 2: 4 distributed according to his **w**.
9:16 In the case of a **w**, it is necessary
9:17 a **w** is in force only when somebody
10:10 by that **w**, we have been made holy
10: 7 I have come to do your **w**, O God.'"
10: 9 Here I am, I have come to do your **w**.
13:21 with everything good for doing his **w**,
Jas 4:15 ought to say, "If it is the Lord's **w**,
1Pe 2:15 it is God's **w** that by doing good you
3:17 if it is God's **w**, to suffer for doing
4:19 those who suffer according to God's **w**
2Pe 1:21 prophecy never had its origin in the **w**
1Jn 5:14 if we ask anything according to his **w**
Rev 2:26 To him who overcomes and does my **w** to
4:11 by your **w** they were created and have

Will of God

Ac 20:27 to proclaim to you the whole **w**.
1Co 1: 1 by the **w**, and our brother Sosthenes,
2Co 1: 1 an apostle of Christ Jesus by the **w**,
Eph 1: 1 an apostle of Christ Jesus by the **w**,
6: 6 Christ, doing the **w** from your heart.
Col 1: 1 by the **w**, and Timothy our brother,
4:12 all the **w**, mature and fully assured.
2Ti 1: 1 an apostle of Christ Jesus by the **w**,
Heb 10:36 so that when you have done the **w**,
1Pe 4: 2 human desires, but rather for the **w**.
1Jn 2:17 man who does the **w** lives for ever.

Willing (Will)

Ge 23: 8 He said to them, "If you are **w** to
Ex 10:27 and he was not **w** to let them go.
35: 5 Everyone who is **w** is to bring to the
Ex 35:21 everyone who was **w** and whose heart
35:22 All who were **w**, men and women alike,
35:26 all the women who were **w** and had the
35:29 women who were **w** brought to the LORD
36: 2 who was **w** to come and do the work.
Dt 29:20 The LORD will never be **w** to forgive
Jdg 5: 9 the **w** volunteers among the people.
Ru 3:13 But if he is not **w**, as surely as the
1Sa 22:17 But the king's officials were not **w**
2Sa 6:10 He was not **w** to take the ark of the
2Ki 8:19 the LORD was not **w** to destroy Judah.
24: 4 and the LORD was not **w** to forgive.
1Ch 19:19 were not **w** to help the Ammonites
28: 9 devotion and with a **w** mind,
28:21 and every **w** man skilled in any craft
29: 5 Now, who is **w** to consecrate himself
29: 9 people rejoiced at the **w** response
2Ch 21: 7 not **w** to destroy the house of David.
29:31 were **w** brought burnt offerings.
Job 6: 9 that God would be **w** to crush me, to
Ps 51:12 grant me a **w** spirit, to sustain me.
110: 3 Your troops will be **w** on your day of
119:108 Accept, O LORD, the **w** praise of my
Pr 11:26 crowns him who is **w** to sell.
19:18 do not be a **w** party to his death.
Isa 1:19 If you are **w** and obedient, you will
Eze 3: 7 the house of Israel is not **w** to
3: 7 they are not **w** to listen to me,
Da 3:28 and were **w** to give up their lives
Mt 8: 2 you are **w**, you can make me clean."
8: 3 "I am **w**," he said. "Be clean!"
11:14 if you are **w** to accept it, he is the
18:14 not **w** that any of these little ones
23: 4 not **w** to lift a finger to move them.
23:37 under her wings, but you were not **w**.
26:15 asked, "What are you **w** to give me if
26:41 spirit is **w**, but the body is weak."
Mk 1:40 If you are **w**, you can make me clean."
1:41 "I am **w**," he said. "Be clean!"
14:38 spirit is **w**, but the body is weak."
Lk 5:12 you are **w**, you can make me clean."
5:13 "I am **w**," he said. "Be clean!" And
13:34 under her wings, but you were not **w**!
22:42 "Father, if you are **w**, take this cup
Jn 6:21 they were **w** to take him into the
Ac 25: 9 "Are you **w** to go up to Jerusalem and
25:20 so I asked if he would be **w** to go to
26: 5 if they are **w**, that according to the
Ro 12:16 Do not be proud, but be **w** to
1Co 4:19 if the Lord is **w**, and then I will
7:12 and she is **w** to live with him,
7:13 and he is **w** to live with her,
1Ti 6:18 and to be generous and **w** to share.
1Pe 5: 2 but because you are **w**, as God wants

Willingly (Will)

Jdg 5: 2 **w** offer themselves—praise the LORD!
1Ch 29: 6 in charge of the king's work gave **w**.
29:17 All these things have I given **w** and
29:17 And now I have seen with joy how **w**
Lam 3:33 For he does not **w** bring affliction

Willingness (Will)

2Co 8:11 so that your eager **w** to do it may be
8:12 For if the **w** is there, the gift is

Willow

Eze 17: 5 it like a **w** by abundant water,

Wills (Will)

Dt 21:16 he **w** his property to his sons, he

Wily

Job 5:13 the schemes of the **w** are swept away.

Win (Winning, Wins, Won)

Pr 3: 4 you will **w** favour and a good name in
Jer 5:28 the case of the fatherless to **w** it,
Mt 23:15 land and sea to **w** a single convert,
1Co 9:19 everyone, to **w** as many as possible.
9:20 I became like a Jew, to **w** the Jews.
9:20 so as to **w** those under the law.
9:21 so as to **w** those not having the law.
9:22 To the weak I became weak, to **w** the

Gal 1:10 Am I now trying to w the approval of
4:17 Those people are zealous to w you
Eph 6: 6 Obey them not only to w their favour
Php 3:14 I press on towards the goal to w the
Col 3:22 eye is on you and to w their favour,
1Th 4:12 your daily life may w the respect

Wind (*Chasing after the wind*, Whirlwind, Whirlwinds, Wind-blown, Winds[1], Windstorm)

Ge 8: 1 and he sent a w over the earth, and
41: 6 and scorched by the east w.
41:23 and thin and scorched by the east w.
41:27 scorched by the east w: They are
Ex 10:13 and the LORD made an east w blow
10:13 the w had brought the locusts;
10:19 the w to a very strong west w,
14:21 east w and turned it into dry land.
Nu 11:31 Now a w went out from the LORD and
2Sa 22:11 he soared on the wings of the w.
1Ki 18:45 the w rose, a heavy rain came on and
19:11 Then a great and powerful w tore
19:11 LORD, but the LORD was not in the w.
19:11 After the w there was an earthquake,
2Ki 3:17 You will see neither w nor rain,
Job 1:19 suddenly a mighty w swept in from
6:26 the words of a despairing man as w?
8: 2 Your words are a blustering w.
15: 2 fill his belly with the hot east w?
21:18 like straw before the w, like chaff
27:21 The east w carries him off, and he
28:25 he established the force of the w
30:15 as by the w, my safety vanishes
30:22 drive me before the w; you toss me
37:17 land lies hushed under the south w,
37:21 after the w has swept them clean.
Ps 1: 4 like chaff that the w blows away.
11: 6 a scorching w will be their lot.
18:10 he soared on the wings of the w.
18:42 them as fine as dust borne on the w;
35: 5 May they be like chaff before the w,
48: 7 of Tarshish shattered by an east w.
68: 2 smoke is blown away by the w, may
78:26 He let loose the east w from the
78:26 led forth the south w by his power.
83:13 O my God, like chaff before the w.
103:16 the w blows over it and it is gone,
104: 3 and rides on the wings of the w.
135: 7 out the w from his storehouses.
Pr 11:29 on his family will inherit only w,
25:14 Like clouds and w without rain is a
25:23 a north w brings rain, so a sly
27:16 like restraining the w or grasping
30: 4 Who has gathered up the w in the
Ecc 1: 6 The w blows to the south and turns
5:16 he gain, since he toils for the w?
8: 8 No man has power over the w to
11: 4 Whoever watches the w will not plant;
11: 5 you do not know the path of the w,
SS 4:16 Awake, north w, and come, south w!
Isa 7: 2 of the forest are shaken by the w.
11:15 with a scorching w he will sweep his
17:13 driven before the w like chaff on
24:20 it sways like a hut in the w; so
26:18 in pain, but we gave birth to w.
27: 8 out, as on a day the east w blows.
28: 2 Like a hailstorm and a destructive w,
32: 2 a shelter from the w and a refuge
41:16 You will winnow them, the w will
41:29 images are but w and confusion.
57:13 The w will carry all of them off,
64: 6 like the w our sins sweep us away.
Jer 2:24 sniffing the w in her craving—in
4:11 "A scorching w from the barren
4:12 a w too strong for that comes from
5:13 The prophets are but w and the word
10:13 out the w from his storehouses.
13:24 like chaff driven by the desert w.
18:17 Like a w from the east, I will
22:22 The w will drive all your shepherds
30:23 a driving w swirling down on the
51:16 out the w from his storehouses.
Eze 5: 2 And scatter a third to the w. For I
13:13 my wrath I will unleash a violent w,
17:10 when the east w strikes it—wither
Eze 19:12 The east w made it shrivel, it was
27:26 But the east w will break you to
Da 2:35 The w swept them away without
Hos 8: 7 "They sow the w and reap the
12: 1 Ephraim feeds on the w; he pursues
12: 1 he pursues the east w all day and
13:15 An east w from the LORD will come,
Am 4:13 creates the w, and reveals his
Jnh 1: 4 the LORD sent a great w on the sea,
4: 8 God provided a scorching east w, and
Hab 1: 9 hordes advance like a desert w and
1:11 they sweep past like the w and go on
Zec 5: 9 with the w in their wings! They had
Mt 11: 7 to see? A reed swayed by the w?
14:24 waves because the w was against it.
14:30 when he saw the w, he was afraid and,
14:32 into the boat, the w died down.
Mk 4:39 He got up, rebuked the w and said to
4:39 Be still!" Then the w died down
4:41 Even the w and the waves obey him!"
6:48 because the w was against them.
6:51 boat with them, and the w died down.
Lk 7:24 to see? A reed swayed by the w?
8:24 rebuked the w and the raging waters;
12:55 the south w blows, you say, 'It's
Jn 3: 8 The w blows wherever it pleases. You
6:18 A strong w was blowing and the
Ac 2: 2 of a violent w came from heaven
27: 7 When the w did not allow us to hold
27:13 a gentle south w began to blow, they
27:14 Before very long, a w of hurricane
27:15 storm and could not head into the w;
27:40 to the w and made for the beach.
28:13 The next day the south w came up,
Eph 4:14 and blown here and there by every w
Jas 1: 6 the sea, blown and tossed by the w.
Jude :12 blown along by the w; autumn trees,
Rev 6:13 fig-tree when shaken by a strong w.
7: 1 to prevent any w from blowing on the

Wind-blown (Blow, Wind)

Lev 26:36 of a w leaf will put them to flight.
Job 13:25 Will you torment a w leaf? Will you
Isa 41: 2 his sword, to w chaff with his bow.

Winding (Winds[2])

Jdg 5: 6 travellers took to w paths.

Window (Windows)

Ge 8: 6 After forty days Noah opened the w
26: 8 Philistines looked down from a w
Jos 2:15 them down by a rope through the w,
2:18 the w through which you let us down,
2:21 she tied the scarlet cord in the w.
Jdg 5:28 "Through the w peered Sisera's
1Sa 19:12 Michal let David down through a w,
2Sa 6:16 daughter of Saul watched from a w.
2Ki 9:30 her hair and looked out of a w.
9:32 He looked up at the w and called out,
13:17 "Open the east w," he said, and he
1Ch 15:29 daughter of Saul watched from a w.
Pr 7: 6 At the w of my house I looked out
Hos 13: 3 like smoke escaping through a w.
Ac 20: 9 Seated in a w was a young man named
2Co 11:33 I was lowered in a basket from a w

Windows (Window)

1Ki 6: 4 He made narrow clerestory w in the
7: 4 Its w were placed high in sets of
Ecc 12: 3 looking through the w grow dim;
SS 2: 9 the w, peering through the lattice.
Jer 9:21 Death has climbed in through our w
22:14 So he makes large w in it, panels
Eze 41:16 the narrow w and galleries round the
41:16 up to the w, and the w were covered.
41:26 narrow w with palm trees carved on
Da 6:10 the w opened towards Jerusalem.
Joel 2: 9 thieves they enter through the w.
Zep 2:14 Their calls will echo through the w,

Winds[1] (Wind)

Job 37: 9 the cold from the driving w.
38:24 east w are scattered over the earth?
Ps 104: 4 He makes w his messengers, flames of
Ps 148: 8 stormy w that do his bidding,
Jer 49:32 I will scatter to the w those who
49:36 I will bring against Elam the four w
49:36 I will scatter them to the four w,
Eze 5:10 scatter all your survivors to the w.
5:12 will scatter to the w and pursue
12:14 I will scatter to the w all those
13:11 and violent w will burst forth.
17:21 will be scattered to the w.
37: 9 LORD says: Come from the four w,
Da 7: 2 and there before me were the four w
8: 8 up towards the four w of heaven.
11: 4 out towards the four w of heaven.
Am 1:14 amid violent w on a stormy day.
Zec 2: 6 w of heaven," declares the LORD.
Mt 7:25 the streams rose, and the w blew and
7:27 the streams rose, and the w blew and
8:26 up and rebuked the w and the waves,
8:27 Even the w and the waves obey him!"
24:31 gather his elect from the four w,
Mk 13:27 gather his elect from the four w,
Lk 8:25 w and the water, and they obey him."
Ac 27: 4 Cyprus because the w were against us.
Heb 1: 7 makes his angels w, his servants
Jas 3: 4 so large and are driven by strong w,
Rev 7: 1 holding back the four w of the earth

Winds[2] (Winding)

Ge 2:11 w through the entire land of Havilah,
2:13 w through the entire land of Cush.

Windstorm (Storm, Wind)

Isa 29: 6 with w and tempest and flames of a
Eze 1: 4 I looked, and I saw a w coming out

Wine (*New wine*, Wines)

Ge 9:21 he drank some of its w, he became
9:24 Noah awoke from his w and found out
14:18 of Salem brought out bread and w.
19:32 Let's get our father to drink w and
19:33 they got their father to drink w,
19:34 Let's get him to drink w again
19:35 they got their father to drink w
27:25 and he brought some w and he drank.
49:11 he will wash his garments in w,
49:12 His eyes will be darker than w, his
Ex 29:40 of a hin of w as a drink offering.
Lev 10: 9 "You and your sons are not to drink w
23:13 offering of a quarter of a hin of w.
Nu 6: 3 he must abstain from w and other
6: 3 w or from other fermented drink.
6:20 After that, the Nazirite may drink w.
15: 5 of a hin of w as a drink offering.
15: 7 a third of a hin of w as a drink
15:10 Also bring half a hin of w as a
28:14 of half a hin of w; with the ram,
Dt 14:26 sheep, w or other fermented drink,
28:39 drink the w or gather the grapes,
29: 6 You ate no bread and drank no w or
32:33 Their w is the venom of serpents,
32:38 the w of their drink offerings?
Jdg 9:13 'Should I give up my w, which cheers
13: 4 Now see to it that you drink no w or
13: 7 Now then, drink no w or other
13:14 nor drink any w or other fermented
19:19 w for ourselves your servants—me,
Ru 2:14 Have some bread and dip it in the w
1Sa 1:14 getting drunk? Get rid of your w."
1:15 I have not been drinking w or beer;
1:24 an ephah of flour and a skin of w,
10: 3 of bread, and another a skin of w.
16:20 a skin of w and a young goat and
25:18 two skins of w, five dressed sheep,
2Sa 13:28 from drinking w and I say to you,
16: 1 cakes of figs and a skin of w.
16: 2 and the w is to refresh those who
1Ch 9:29 w, and the oil, incense and spices.
12:40 fig cakes, raisin cakes, w, oil,
27:27 of the vineyards for the w vats.
2Ch 2:10 twenty thousand baths of w and
2:15 and the olive oil and w he promised,
11:11 supplies of food, olive oil and w.
Ezr 6: 9 and wheat, salt, w and oil, as
7:22 a hundred baths of w, a hundred
Ne 2: 1 when w was brought for him, I took

Ne 2: 1 I took the **w** and gave it to the king.
5:15 from them in addition to food and **w**.
5:18 abundant supply of **w** of all kinds.
13:15 together with **w**, grapes, figs and
Est 1: 7 **W** was served in goblets of gold,
1: 7 and the royal **w** was abundant, in
1: 8 for the king instructed all the **w**
1:10 Xerxes was in high spirits from **w**,
5: 6 they were drinking **w**, the king again
7: 2 they were drinking **w** on that second
7: 7 The king got up in a rage, left his **w**
Job 1:13 **w** at the oldest brother's house,
1:18 **w** at the oldest brother's house,
32:19 inside I am like bottled-up **w**, like
Ps 60: 3 given us **w** that makes us stagger.
75: 8 **w** mixed with spices; he pours it out,
78:65 as a man wakes from the stupor of **w**.
104:15 **w** that gladdens the heart of man,
Pr 4:17 and drink the **w** of violence.
9: 2 her **w**; she has also set her table.
9: 5 "Come, eat my food and drink the **w** I
20: 1 **W** is a mocker and beer a brawler;
21:17 loves **w** and oil will never be rich.
23:20 much **w** or gorge themselves on meat,
23:30 **w**, who go to sample bowls of mixed **w**.
23:31 Do not gaze at **w** when it is red,
31: 4 not for kings to drink **w**, not for
31: 6 **w** to those who are in anguish;
Ecc 2: 3 I tried cheering myself with **w**, and
9: 7 and drink your **w** with a joyful heart,
10:19 laughter, and **w** makes life merry,
SS 1: 2 your love is more delightful than **w**.
1: 4 will praise your love more than **w**.
4:10 more pleasing is your love than **w**,
5: 1 I have drunk my **w** and my milk.
7: 2 goblet that never lacks blended **w**.
7: 9 your mouth like the best **w**. May the **w**
8: 2 I would give you spiced **w** to drink,
Isa 1:22 your choice **w** is diluted with water.
5:10 will produce only a bath of **w**,
5:11 night till they are inflamed with **w**.
5:12 tambourines and flutes and **w**, but
5:22 heroes at drinking **w** and champions
16:10 no-one treads out **w** at the presses,
22:13 of **w**! "Let us eat and drink,"
24: 9 No longer do they drink **w** with a
24:11 In the streets they cry out for **w**;
25: 6 a banquet of aged **w**—the best of
28: 1 the pride of those laid low by **w**!
28: 7 these also stagger from **w** and reel
28: 7 with **w**; they reel from beer,
29: 9 from **w**, stagger, but not from beer.
49:26 drunk on their own blood, as with **w**.
51:21 one, made drunk, but not with **w**.
55: 1 come, buy and eat! Come, buy **w** and
56:12 "Come," each one cries, "let me get **w**
65:11 fill bowls of mixed **w** for Destiny,
Jer 13:12 wineskin should be filled with **w**.
13:12 wineskin should be filled with **w**?'
23: 9 like a man overcome by **w**, because of
25:15 cup filled with the **w** of my wrath
35: 2 the LORD and give them **w** to drink."
35: 5 I set bowls full of **w** and some cups
35: 5 and said to them, "Drink some **w**.
35: 6 they replied, "We do not drink **w**,
35: 6 your descendants must ever drink **w**.
35: 8 sons and daughters have ever drunk **w**
35:14 ordered his sons not to drink **w**
35:14 To this day they do not drink **w**,
40:10 but you are to harvest the **w**, summer
40:12 an abundance of **w** and summer fruit.
48:11 like **w** left on its dregs, not poured
48:33 I have stopped the flow of **w** from
51: 7 The nations drank her **w**; therefore
Lam 2:12 "Where is bread and **w**?" as they
Eze 27:18 **w** from Helbon and wool from Zahar.
44:21 No priest is to drink **w** when he
Da 1: 5 of food and **w** from the king's table.
1: 8 himself with the royal food and **w**,
1:16 the **w** they were to drink and gave
5: 1 of his nobles and drank **w** with them.
5: 2 While Belshazzar was drinking his **w**,
5: 4 they drank the **w**, they praised the
5:23 your concubines drank **w** from them.
10: 3 I ate no choice food; no meat or **w**
Hos 4:11 to prostitution, to old **w** and new,
Hos 7: 5 the princes become inflamed with **w**,
9: 4 They will not pour out **w** offerings
14: 7 will be like the **w** from Lebanon.
Joel 1: 5 all you drinkers of **w**; wail because
3: 3 girls for **w** that they might drink.
Am 2: 8 god they drink **w** taken as fines.
2:12 "But you made the Nazirites drink **w**
5:11 you will not drink their **w**.
6: 6 You drink **w** by the bowlful and use
9:14 plant vineyards and drink their **w**;
Mic 2:11 'I will prophesy for you plenty of **w**
6:15 crush grapes but not drink the **w**.
Na 1:10 among thorns and drunk from their **w**;
Hab 2: 5 indeed, **w** betrays him; he is
Zep 1:12 who are like **w** left on its dregs,
1:13 plant vineyards but not drink the **w**.
Hag 2:12 some **w**, oil or other food, does it
2:16 When anyone went to a **w** vat to draw
Zec 9:15 They will drink and roar as with **w**;
10: 7 their hearts will be glad as with **w**.
Mt 9:17 the skins will burst, the **w** will run
27:34 There they offered Jesus **w** to drink,
27:48 He filled it with **w** vinegar, put it
Mk 2:22 If he does, the **w** will burst the
2:22 **w** and the wineskins will be ruined.
15:23 they offered him **w** mixed with myrrh,
15:36 One man ran, filled a sponge with **w**
Lk 1:15 He is never to take **w** or other
5:37 the **w** will run out and the wineskins
5:39 no-one after drinking old **w** wants
7:33 nor drinking **w**, and you say, 'He
10:34 his wounds, pouring on oil and **w**.
23:36 They offered him **w** vinegar
Jn 2: 3 the **w** was gone, Jesus' mother said
2: 3 said to him, "They have no more **w**.
2: 9 water that had been turned into **w**.
2:10 "Everyone brings out the choice **w**
2:10 then the cheaper **w** after the guests
4:46 he had turned the water into **w**.
19:29 A jar of **w** vinegar was there, so
Ac 2:13 and said, "They have had too much **w**.
Ro 14:21 is better not to eat meat or drink **w**
Eph 5:18 Do not get drunk on **w**, which leads
1Ti 3: 8 not indulging in much **w**, and not
5:23 and use a little **w** because of your
Tit 2: 3 much **w**, but to teach what is good.
Rev 6: 6 do not damage the oil and the **w**!"
14: 8 the maddening **w** of her adulteries."
14:10 he, too, will drink of the **w** of
16:19 with the **w** of the fury of his wrath.
17: 2 with the **w** of her adulteries."
18: 3 the maddening **w** of her adulteries.
18:13 myrrh and frankincense, of **w** and

Winepress (Winepresses)

Nu 18:27 threshing-floor or juice from the **w**.
18:30 of the threshing-floor or the **w**.
Dt 15:14 your threshing-floor and your **w**.
16:13 of your threshing-floor and your **w**.
Jdg 6:11 a **w** to keep it from the Midianites.
7:25 of Oreb, and Zeeb at the **w** of Zeeb.
2Ki 6:27 the threshing-floor? From the **w**?"
Isa 5: 2 in it and cut out a **w** as well.
63: 2 like those of one treading the **w**?
63: 3 "I have trodden the **w** alone; from
Lam 1:15 In his **w** the Lord has trampled the
Joel 3:13 Come, trample the grapes, for the **w**
Mt 21:33 He put a wall around it, dug a **w** in
Mk 12: 1 for the **w** and built a watchtower.
Rev 14:19 into the great **w** of God's wrath.
14:20 They were trampled in the **w** outside
19:15 He treads the **w** of the fury of the

Winepresses (Winepress)

Ne 13:15 in Judah treading **w** on the Sabbath
Job 24:11 they tread the **w**, yet suffer thirst.
Hos 9: 2 Threshing-floors and **w** will not feed
Zec 14:10 the Tower of Hananel to the royal **w**.

Wines (Wine)

Isa 25: 6 best of meats and the finest of **w**.

Wineskin (Wineskins)

Ps 119:83 Though I am like a **w** in the smoke, I
Jer 13:12 Every **w** should be filled with wine.
13:12 every **w** should be filled with wine?'
Hab 2:15 pouring it from the **w** till they are

Wineskins (Wineskin)

Jos 9: 4 sacks and old **w**, cracked and mended.
9:13 these **w** that we filled were new, but
Job 32:19 wine, like new **w** ready to burst.
Mt 9:17 do men pour new wine into old **w**.
9:17 run out and the **w** will be ruined.
9:17 into new **w**, and both are preserved."
Mk 2:22 no-one pours new wine into old **w**. If
2:22 the wine and the **w** will be ruined.
2:22 No, he pours new wine into new **w**."
Lk 5:37 no-one pours new wine into old **w**. If
5:37 run out and the **w** will be ruined.
5:38 new wine must be poured into new **w**.

Wing (Winged, Wings, Wing-span)

1Ki 6:24 One **w** of the first cherub was five
6:24 and the other **w** five cubits—ten
6:24 cubits from **w** tip to **w** tip.
6:27 The **w** of one cherub touched one wall,
6:27 while the **w** of the other touched the
2Ch 3:11 One **w** of the first cherub was five
3:11 while its other **w**, also five cubits
3:11 touched the **w** of the other cherub.
3:12 Similarly one **w** of the second cherub
3:12 and its other **w**, also five cubits
3:12 touched the **w** of the first cherub.
Ecc 10:20 on the **w** may report what you say.
Isa 10:14 not one flapped a **w**, or opened its
Eze 1:11 one touching the **w** of another
Da 9:27 And on a **w** of the temple he will set

Winged (Wing)

Ge 1:21 every **w** bird according to its kind.
Lev 11:21 There are, however, some **w** creatures
11:23 all other **w** creatures that have four
Dt 14:20 any **w** creature that is clean you may

Wings (Wing)

Ge 7:14 to its kind, everything with **w**.
Ex 19: 4 eagles' **w** and brought you to myself.
25:20 cherubim are to have their **w** spread
37: 9 The cherubim had their **w** spread
Lev 1:17 He shall tear it open by the **w**, not
Dt 32:11 that spreads its **w** to catch them and
Ru 2:12 God of Israel, under whose **w** you
2Sa 22:11 he soared on the **w** of the wind.
1Ki 6:27 the temple, with their **w** spread out.
6:27 and their **w** touched each other in
8: 6 it beneath the **w** of the cherubim.
8: 7 The cherubim spread their **w** over the
1Ch 28:18 of gold that spread their **w**
2Ch 3:13 The **w** of these cherubim extended
5: 7 it beneath the **w** of the cherubim.
5: 8 The cherubim spread their **w** over the
Job 39:13 "The **w** of the ostrich flap joyfully,
39:26 and spread his **w** towards the south?
Ps 17: 8 eye; hide me in the shadow of your **w**
18:10 he soared on the **w** of the wind.
36: 7 find refuge in the shadow of your **w**.
55: 6 "Oh, that I had the **w** of a dove!
57: 1 take refuge in the shadow of your **w**
61: 4 refuge in the shelter of your **w**.
63: 7 I sing in the shadow of your **w**.
68:13 the **w** of my dove are sheathed with
91: 4 and under his **w** you will find refuge;
104: 3 and rides on the **w** of the wind.
139: 9 If I rise on the **w** of the dawn, if I
Pr 23: 5 for they will surely sprout **w** and
Isa 6: 2 each with six **w**: With two **w** they
8: 8 Its outspread **w** will cover the
18: 1 Woe to the land of whirring **w** along
34:15 her young under the shadow of her **w**;
40:31 They will soar on **w** like eagles;
Jer 48:40 down, spreading its **w** over Moab.
49:22 down, spreading its **w** over Bozrah.
Eze 1: 6 of them had four faces and four **w**.
1: 8 Under their **w** on their four sides
1: 8 All four of them had faces and **w**,

Eze 1: 9 their w touched one another. Each
1:11 Such were their faces. Their w were
1:11 spread out upwards; each had two w,
1:11 side, and two w covering its body.
1:23 Under the expanse their w were
1:23 each had two w covering its body.
1:24 I heard the sound of their w, like
1:24 stood still, they lowered their w.
1:25 heads as they stood with lowered w.
3:13 the sound of the w of the living
10: 5 The sound of the w of the cherubim
10: 8 (Under the w of the cherubim could
10:12 their hands and their w, were
10:16 their w to rise from the ground,
10:19 the cherubim spread their w and rose
10:21 Each had four faces and four w, and
10:21 and under their w was what looked
11:22 spread their w, and the glory of the
17: 3 says: A great eagle with powerful w,
17: 7 with powerful w and full plumage.
Da 7: 4 lion, and it had the w of an eagle.
7: 4 I watched until its w were torn off
7: 6 And on its back it had four w like
Zec 5: 9 with the wind in their w! They had w
Mal 4: 2 will rise with healing in its w.
Mt 23:37 hen gathers her chicks under her w,
Lk 13:34 hen gathers her chicks under her w,
Rev 4: 8 the four living creatures had six w
4: 8 eyes all around, even under his w.
9: 9 and the sound of their w was like
12:14 The woman was given the two w of a

Wing-span (Wing)
2Ch 3:11 The total w of the cherubim was

Wink (Winks)
Ps 35:19 reason maliciously w the eye.

Winks (Wink)
Pr 6:13 who w with his eye, signals with his
10:10 He who w maliciously causes grief,
16:30 He who w with his eye is plotting

Winning (Win)
Ex 17:11 the Israelites were w, but whenever
17:11 his hands, the Amalekites were w.

Winnow (Winnowing, Winnows)
Isa 41:16 You will w them, the wind will pick
Jer 4:11 my people, but not to w or cleanse;
15: 7 I will w them with a winnowing fork
51: 2 to w her and to devastate her land;

Winnowing (Winnow)
Ru 3: 2 be w barley on the threshing-floor.
Jer 15: 7 I will winnow them with a w fork at
Mt 3:12 His w fork is in his hand, and he
Lk 3:17 His w fork is in his hand to clear

Winnows (Winnow)
Pr 20: 8 he w out all evil with his eyes.
20:26 A wise king w out the wicked; he

Wins (Win)
Pr 11:30 of life, and he who w souls is wise.
13:15 Good understanding w favour, but the

Winter (Wintered)
Ge 8:22 w, day and night will never cease."
Ps 74:17 earth; you made both summer and w.
SS 2:11 See! The w is past; the rains are
Isa 18: 6 all summer, the wild animals all w.
Jer 36:22 king was sitting in the w apartment,
Hos 6: 3 he will come to us like the w rains,
Am 3:15 I will tear down the w house along
Zec 14: 8 the western sea, in summer and in w.
Mt 24:20 take place in w or on the Sabbath.
Mk 13:18 that this will not take place in w,
Jn 10:22 Dedication at Jerusalem. It was w,
Ac 27:12 the harbour was unsuitable to w in,
27:12 hoping to reach Phoenix and w there.
1Co 16: 6 or even spend the w, so that you can
2Ti 4:21 Do your best to get here before w.
Tit 3:12 because I have decided to w there.

Wintered (Winter)
Ac 28:11 in a ship that had w in the island.

Wipe (Wiped, Wipes, Wiping)
Ge 6: 7 the LORD said, "I will w mankind,
7: 4 and I will w from the face of the
Ex 23:23 Jebusites, and I will w them out.
32:12 w them off the face of the earth'?
Dt 7:24 w out their names from under heaven.
12: 3 w out their names from those places.
Jos 7: 9 and w out our name from the earth.
9:24 to w out all its inhabitants from
1Sa 24:21 w out my name from my father's family
2Ki 21:13 I will w out Jerusalem as one wipes
Isa 25: 8 The Sovereign LORD will w away the
Lk 10:11 to our feet we w off against you.
Rev 7:17 w away every tear from their eyes."
21: 4 He will w every tear from their eyes.

Wiped (Wipe)
Ge 7:23 on the face of the earth was w out;
7:23 of the air were w from the earth.
Ex 9:15 that would have w you off the earth.
Jdg 21:17 a tribe of Israel will not be w out.
1Sa 15:18 on them until you have w them out.'
Ps 119:87 They almost w me from the earth, but
Pr 6:33 and his shame will never be w away;
Isa 26:14 ruin; you w out all memory of them.
Eze 6: 6 down, and what you have made w out.
Zep 1:11 all your merchants will be w out,
Lk 7:38 Then she w them with her hair,
7:44 her tears and w them with her hair.
Jn 11: 2 Lord and w his feet with her hair.
12: 3 feet and w his feet with her hair.
Ac 3:19 so that your sins may be w out, that

Wipes (Wipe)
2Ki 21:13 wipe out Jerusalem as one w out a
Pr 30:20 She eats and w her mouth and says,

Wiping (Wipe)
2Ki 21:13 w it and turning it upside-down.

Wisdom
Ge 3: 6 gaining w, she took some and ate it.
Ex 28: 3 skilled men to whom I have given w
Dt 4: 6 for this will show your w and
34: 9 was filled with the spirit of w
2Sa 14:20 My lord has w like that of an angel
1Ki 2: 6 Deal with him according to your w,
2: 9 You are a man of w; you will know
3:28 w from God to administer justice.
4:29 God gave Solomon w and very great
4:30 Solomon's w was greater than the w
4:30 and greater than all the w of Egypt.
4:34 came to listen to Solomon's w,
4:34 the world, who had heard of his w.
5:12 The LORD gave Solomon w, just as he
10: 4 the queen of Sheba saw all the w of
10: 6 achievements and your w is true.
10: 7 not even half was told me; in w and
10: 8 stand before you and hear your w!
10:23 w than all the other kings of the
10:24 hear the w God had put in his heart.
11:41 the w he displayed—are they not
2Ch 1:10 Give me w and knowledge, that I may
1:11 not asked for a long life but for w
1:12 therefore w and knowledge will be
9: 3 the queen of Sheba saw the w of
9: 5 achievements and your w is true.
9: 6 the greatness of your w was told me;
9: 7 stand before you and hear your w!
9:22 w than all the other kings of the
9:23 hear the w God had put in his heart.
Ezr 7:25 you, Ezra, in accordance with the w
Job 4:21 up, so that they die without w?'
9: 4 His w is profound, his power is vast.
11: 6 disclose to you the secrets of w,
11: 6 of w, for true w has two sides.
12: 2 people, and w will die with you!
12:12 Is not w found among the aged? Does
Job 12:13 "To God belong w and power; counsel
13: 5 silent! For you, that would be w.
15: 8 council? Do you limit w to yourself?
26: 3 you have offered to one without w!
26:12 by his w he cut Rahab to pieces.
28:12 "But where can w be found? Where
28:18 the price of w is beyond rubies.
28:20 "Where then does w come from? Where
28:27 he looked at w and appraised it; he
28:28 The fear of the Lord—that is w,
32: 7 advanced years should teach w.'
32:13 Do not say, 'We have found w; let
33:33 be silent, and I will teach you w."
38:36 Who endowed the heart with w or gave
38:37 Who has the w to count the clouds?
39:17 for God did not endow her with w or
39:26 "Does the hawk take flight by your w
Ps 37:30 mouth of the righteous man utters w,
49: 3 My mouth will speak words of w; the
51: 6 you teach me w in the inmost place.
90:12 that we may gain a heart of w.
104:24 your works, O LORD! In w you made
105:22 he pleased and teach his elders w.
111:10 of the LORD is the beginning of w;
Pr 1: 2 for attaining w and discipline; for
1: 7 but fools despise w and discipline.
1:20 W calls aloud in the street, she
2: 2 turning your ear to w and applying
2: 6 For the LORD gives w, and from his
2:10 For w will enter your heart, and
2:12 W will save you from the ways of
3:13 Blessed is the man who finds w, the
3:19 By w the LORD laid the earth's
4: 5 Get w, get understanding; do not
4: 6 Do not forsake w, and she will
4: 7 W is supreme; therefore get w.
4:11 I guide you in the way of w and lead
5: 1 My son, pay attention to my w,
7: 4 Say to w, "You are my sister," and
8: 1 Does not w call out? Does not
8:11 for w is more precious than rubies,
8:12 "I, w, dwell together with prudence;
9: 1 W has built her house; she has hewn
9:10 of the LORD is the beginning of w,
9:12 If you are wise, your w will reward
10:13 W is found on the lips of the
10:23 man of understanding delights in w.
10:31 of the righteous brings forth w,
11: 2 disgrace, but with humility comes w.
12: 8 A man is praised according to his w,
13:10 Pride only breeds quarrels, but w is
14: 6 The mocker seeks w and finds none,
14: 8 The w of the prudent is to give
14:33 W reposes in the heart of the
15:33 The fear of the LORD teaches a man w,
16:16 How much better to get w than gold,
17:16 since he has no desire to get w?
17:24 A discerning man keeps w in view,
18: 4 fountain of w is a bubbling brook.
19: 8 He who gets w loves his own soul; he
19:11 A man's w gives him patience; it is
21:11 the simple gain w; when a wise man
21:30 There is no w, no insight, no plan
23: 4 rich; have the w to show restraint.
23: 9 he will scorn the w of your words.
23:23 get w, discipline and understanding.
24: 3 By w a house is built, and through
24: 7 W is too high for a fool; in the
24:14 Know also that w is sweet to your
28:26 but he who walks in w is kept safe.
29: 3 A man who loves w brings joy to his
29:15 The rod of correction imparts w, but
30: 3 I have not learned w, nor have I
31:26 She speaks with w, and faithful
Ecc 1:13 by w all that is done under heaven.
1:16 I have grown and increased in w more
1:16 experienced much of w and knowledge
1:17 myself to the understanding of w,
1:18 For with much w comes much sorrow;
2: 3 mind still guiding me with w.
2: 9 In all this my w stayed with me.
2:12 I turned my thoughts to consider w,
2:13 I saw that w is better than folly,
2:21 For a man may do his work with w,
2:26 God gives w, knowledge and happiness,
7:11 W, like an inheritance, is a good

Ecc 7:12 W is a shelter as money is a shelter,
7:12 that w preserves the life of its
7:19 W makes one wise man more powerful
7:23 All this I tested by w and I said,
7:24 Whatever w may be, it is far off and
7:25 to investigate and to search out w
8: 1 W brightens a man's face and changes
8:16 I applied my mind to know w and to
9:10 nor planning nor knowledge nor w.
9:13 of w that greatly impressed me:
9:15 and he saved the city by his w.
9:16 I said, "W is better than strength."
9:16 But the poor man's w is despised,
9:18 W is better than weapons of war, but
10: 1 little folly outweighs w and honour.
Isa 10:13 my w, because I have understanding.
11: 2 Spirit of w and of understanding,
28:29 in counsel and magnificent in w.
29:14 the w of the wise will perish,
33: 6 a rich store of salvation and w and
47:10 Your w and knowledge mislead you
Jer 8: 9 LORD, what kind of w do they have?
9:23 "Let not the wise man boast of his w
10:12 he founded the world by his w and
49: 7 "Is there no longer w in Teman? Has
49: 7 the prudent? Has their w decayed?
51:15 he founded the world by his w and
Eze 28: 4 By your w and understanding you have
28: 7 swords against your beauty and w
28:12 full of w and perfect in beauty.
28:17 your w because of your splendour.
Da 1:20 In every matter of w and
2:14 Daniel spoke to him with w and tact.
2:20 ever and ever; w and power are his.
2:21 He gives w to the wise and knowledge
2:23 You have given me w and power,
2:30 not because I have greater w than
5:11 and w like that of the gods.
5:14 intelligence and outstanding w.
Hos 13:13 but he is a child without w; when
Mic 6: 9 to fear your name is w—"Heed the
Mt 11:19 w is proved right by her actions."
12:42 the earth to listen to Solomon's w,
13:54 "Where did this man get this w and
Mk 6: 2 "What's this w that has been given
Lk 1:17 the disobedient to the w of the
2:40 he was filled with w, and the grace
2:52 Jesus grew in w and stature, and in
7:35 w is proved right by all her
11:31 the earth to listen to Solomon's w,
11:49 of this, God in his w said, 'I will
21:15 For I will give you words and w that
Ac 6: 3 to be full of the Spirit and w.
6:10 they could not stand up against his w
7:10 He gave Joseph w and enabled him to
7:22 Moses was educated in all the w of
Ro 11:33 Oh, the depth of the riches of the w
1Co 1:17 gospel—not with words of human w,
1:19 "I will destroy the w of the wise;
1:20 God made foolish the w of the world?
1:21 For since in the w of God the world
1:21 through its w did not know him,
1:22 signs and Greeks look for w,
1:24 the power of God and the w of God.
1:25 of God is wiser than man's w,
1:30 who has become for us w from God
2: 1 come with eloquence or superior w
2: 5 rest on men's w, but on God's power.
2: 6 We do, however, speak a message of w
2: 6 but not the w of this age or of the
2: 7 No, we speak of God's secret w, a w
2:13 not in words taught us by human w
3:19 For the w of this world is
12: 8 through the Spirit the message of w,
2Co 1:12 not according to worldly w but
Eph 1: 8 that he lavished on us with all w
1:17 may give you the Spirit of w and
3:10 through the church, the manifold w
Col 1: 9 all spiritual w and understanding.
1:28 and teaching everyone with all w,
2: 3 the treasures of w and knowledge.
2:23 indeed have an appearance of w,
3:16 and admonish one another with all w,
Jas 1: 5 If any of you lacks w, he should ask
3:13 in the humility that comes from w.
3:15 Such "w" does not come down from
Jas 3:17 the w that comes from heaven is
2Pe 3:15 to you with the w that God gave him.
Rev 5:12 to receive power and wealth and w
7:12 saying: "Amen! Praise and glory and w
13:18 This calls for w. If anyone has
17: 9 "This calls for a mind with w. The

Wise (Overwise, *Wise men*, Wisely, Wiser, Wisest)

Ge 41:33 w man and put him in charge of the
41:39 no-one so discerning and w as you.
Dt 1:13 Choose some w, understanding and
1:15 w and respected men, and appointed
4: 6 is a w and understanding people."
16:19 a bribe blinds the eyes of the w
32:29 If only they were w and would
2Sa 14: 2 had a w woman brought from there.
20:16 a w woman called from the city,
20:22 to all the people with her w advice,
1Ki 3:12 I will give you a w and discerning
5: 7 w son to rule over this great nation.
1Ch 26:14 a w counsellor, and the lot for the
2Ch 2:12 He has given King David a w son,
Job 5:13 He catches the w in their craftiness,
11:12 a witless man can no more become w
15: 2 "Would a w man answer with empty
17:10 I will not find a w man among you.
22: 2 God? Can even a w man benefit him?
32: 9 is not only the old who are w, not
37:24 have regard for all the w in heart?"
Ps 2:10 Therefore, you kings, be w; be
19: 7 trustworthy, making w the simple.
36: 3 has ceased to be w and to do good.
94: 8 you fools, when will you become w?
107:43 Whoever is w, let him heed these
Pr 1: 5 let the w listen and add to their
1: 6 the sayings and riddles of the w.
3: 7 Do not be w in your own eyes; fear
3:35 The w inherit honour, but fools he
6: 6 consider its ways and be w!
8:33 Listen to my instruction and be w;
9: 8 rebuke a w man and he will love you.
9: 9 Instruct a w man and he will be
9:12 If you are w, your wisdom will
10: 1 The proverbs of Solomon: A w son
10: 5 gathers crops in summer is a w son
10: 8 The w in heart accept commands, but
10:19 but he who holds his tongue is w.
11:29 the fool will be servant to the w.
11:30 of life, and he who wins souls is w.
12:15 him, but a w man listens to advice.
12:18 the tongue of the w brings healing.
13: 1 A w son heeds his father's
13:14 The teaching of the w is a fountain
13:20 He who walks with the w grows w, but
14: 1 The w woman builds her house, but
14: 3 but the lips of the w protect them.
14:16 A w man fears the LORD and shuns
14:24 The wealth of the w is their crown,
14:35 A king delights in a w servant, but
15: 2 The tongue of the w commends
15: 7 The lips of the w spread knowledge;
15:12 he will not consult the w.
15:20 A w son brings joy to his father,
15:24 path of life leads upward for the w
15:31 rebuke will be at home among the w.
16:14 death, but a w man will appease it.
16:21 The w in heart are called discerning,
16:23 A w man's heart guides his mouth,
17: 2 A w servant will rule over a
17:28 Even a fool is thought w if he keeps
18:15 the ears of the w seek it out.
19:20 and in the end you will be w.
20: 1 is led astray by them is not w.
20:26 A w king winnows out the wicked; he
21:11 the simple gain wisdom; when a w man
21:20 In the house of the w are stores of
21:22 A w man attacks the city of the
22:17 listen to the sayings of the w;
23:15 My son, if your heart is w, then my
23:19 Listen, my son, and be w, and keep
23:24 he who has a w son delights in him.
24: 5 A w man has great power, and a man
24:23 These also are sayings of the w: To
25:12 a w man's rebuke to a listening ear.
Pr 26: 5 or he will be w in his own eyes.
26:12 Do you see a man w in his own eyes?
27:11 Be w, my son, and bring joy to my
28:11 A rich man may be w in his own eyes,
29: 9 If a w man goes to court with a fool,
29:11 a w man keeps himself under control.
30:24 are small, yet they are extremely w:
Ecc 2:14 The w man has eyes in his head,
2:15 What then do I gain by being w?" I
2:16 For the w man, like the fool, will
2:16 the fool, the w man too must die!
2:19 who knows whether he will be a w man
4:13 Better a poor but w youth than an
6: 8 What advantage has a w man over a
7: 4 The heart of the w is in the house
7: 5 is better to heed a w man's rebuke
7: 7 Extortion turns a w man into a fool,
7:10 it is not w to ask such questions.
7:19 Wisdom makes one w man more powerful
7:23 to be w"—but this was beyond me.
8: 1 Who is like the w man? Who knows the
8: 5 and the w heart will know the proper
8:17 Even if a w man claims he knows, he
9: 1 the w and what they do are in God's
9:11 nor does food come to the w or
9:15 lived in that city a man poor but w,
9:17 The quiet words of the w are more to
10: 2 The heart of the w inclines to the
10:12 Words from a w man's mouth are
12: 9 Not only was the Teacher w, but also
12:11 The words of the w are like goads,
Isa 5:21 Woe to those who are w in their own
19:11 the w counsellors of Pharaoh give
29:14 the wisdom of the w will perish,
31: 2 Yet he too is w and can bring
44:25 of the w and turns it into nonsense,
Jer 8: 8 "'How can you say, "We are w, for
8: 9 The w will be put to shame; they
9:12 What man is w enough to understand
9:23 "Let not the w man boast of his
18:18 counsel from the w, nor the word
Eze 28: 2 you think you are as w as a god.
28: 6 you think you are w, as w as a god,
Da 2:21 He gives wisdom to the w and
2:27 Daniel replied, "No w man, enchanter,
11:33 "Those who are w will instruct many,
11:35 Some of the w will stumble, so that
12: 3 Those who are w will shine like the
12:10 but those who are w will understand.
Hos 14: 9 Who is w? He will realise these
Mt 7:24 them into practice is like a w man
11:25 these things from the w and learned,
24:45 "Who then is the faithful and w
25: 2 them were foolish and five were w.
25: 4 The w, however, took oil in jars
25: 8 The foolish ones said to the w,
Lk 10:21 these things from the w and learned,
12:42 "Who then is the faithful and w
Ac 15:38 Paul did not think it w to take him,
Ro 1:14 both to the w and the foolish.
1:22 Although they claimed to be w, they
16:19 want you to be w about what is good,
16:27 to the only w God be glory for ever
1Co 1:19 "I will destroy the wisdom of the w;
1:20 Where is the w man? Where is the
1:26 Not many of you were w by human
1:27 things of the world to shame the w;
2: 4 not with w and persuasive words,
3:18 If any one of you thinks he is w by
3:18 a "fool" so that he may become w.
3:19 catches the w in their craftiness";
3:20 the thoughts of the w are futile."
4:10 but you are so w in Christ! We are
6: 5 nobody among you w enough to judge
2Co 10:12 with themselves, they are not w.
11:19 up with fools since you are so w!
Eph 5:15 you live—not as unwise but as w,
Col 4: 5 Be w in the way you act towards
2Ti 3:15 able to make you w for salvation
Jas 3:13 Who is w and understanding among you?

Wise men

Ge 41: 8 all the magicians and w of Egypt.
Ex 7:11 Pharaoh then summoned the w and
Est 1:13 with the w who understood the

Job 15:18 what w have declared, hiding nothing
34: 2 "Hear my words, you w; listen to me,
34:34 "Men of understanding declare, w who
Ps 49:10 For all can see that w die; the
Pr 10:14 W store up knowledge, but the mouth
29: 8 Mockers stir up a city, but w turn
Isa 19:11 say to Pharaoh, "I am one of the w,
19:12 Where are your w now? Let them show
Jer 10: 7 Among all the w of the nations and
50:35 and against her officials and w!
51:57 I will make her officials and w
Da 2:12 execution of all the w of Babylon.
2:13 the decree was issued to put the w
2:14 had gone out to put to death the w
2:18 with the rest of the w of Babylon.
2:24 to execute the w of Babylon,
2:24 "Do not execute the w of Babylon.
2:48 placed him in charge of all its w.
4: 6 I commanded that all the w of
4:18 for none of the w in my kingdom can
5: 7 and said to these w of Babylon,
5: 8 all the king's w came in, but they
5:15 The w and enchanters were brought
Ob :8 "will I not destroy the w of Edom,
Mt 23:34 you prophets and w and teachers.

Wisely (Wise)

2Ch 11:23 He acted w, dispersing some of his
Isa 52:13 See, my servant will act w; he will
Jer 23: 5 a King who will reign w and do what
Mk 12:34 Jesus saw that he had answered w, he

Wiser (Wise)

1Ki 4:31 He was w than any other man,
4:31 including Ethan the Ezrahite—w than
Job 35:11 us w than the birds of the air?'
Ps 119:98 Your commands make me w than my
Pr 9: 9 Instruct a wise man and he will be w
26:16 The sluggard is w in his own eyes
Eze 28: 3 Are you w than Daniel? Is no secret
1Co 1:25 For the foolishness of God is w than

Wisest (Wise)

Jdg 5:29 The w of her ladies answer her;

Wish (Wished, Wishes, Wishing)

Ex 4:18 Jethro said, "Go, and I w you well."
Nu 11:29 I w that all the LORD's people were
Dt 14:26 fermented drink, or anything you w.
Jdg 19:24 them and do to them whatever you w.
1Sa 24: 4 hands for you to deal with as you w.
1Ki 5: 9 And you are to grant my w by
Ezr 7:13 who w to go to Jerusalem with you,
Job 10:18 I w I had died before any eye saw me.
11: 5 Oh, how I w that God would speak,
Mt 17: 4 If you w, I will put up three
Lk 12:49 and how I w it were already kindled!
Jn 15: 7 you w, and it will be given you.
Ro 9: 3 For I could w that I myself were
1Co 4: 8 How I w that you really had become
7: 7 I w that all men were as I am. But
2Co 5: 4 because we do not w to be unclothed
Gal 4: 9 Do you w to be enslaved by them all
4:20 how I w I could be with you now and
5:12 for those agitators, I w they would
Phm :20 I do w, brother, that I may have
Jas 2:16 says to him, "Go, I w you well;
Rev 3:15 I w you were either one or the other!

Wished (Wish)

2Sa 19:18 over and to do whatever he w.
Est 1: 8 to serve each man what he w.
Job 9: 3 Though one w to dispute with him, he
Jer 34:16 you had set free to go where they w.
Mt 17:12 have done to him everything they w.
Mk 9:13 done to him everything they w, just

Wishes (Wish)

Lev 27:13 If the owner w to redeem the animal,
27:19 If the man who dedicates the field w
Dt 21:14 with her, let her go wherever she w.
Da 4:17 gives them to anyone he w and sets
4:25 men and gives them to anyone he w.
4:32 men and gives them to anyone he w."
Da 5:21 men and sets over them anyone he w.
1Co 7:39 free to marry anyone she w, but he
Rev 22:17 let him come; and whoever w, let him

Wishing (Wish)

Ac 25: 9 Festus, w to do the Jews a favour,

Witchcraft (Bewitched)

Dt 18:10 interprets omens, engages in w,
2Ki 9:22 w of your mother Jezebel abound?"
2Ch 33: 6 practised sorcery, divination and w,
Mic 5:12 I will destroy your w and you will
Na 3: 4 prostitution and peoples by her w.
Gal 5:20 idolatry and w; hatred, discord,

Withdraw (Withdrawn, Withdraws, Withdrew)

Lev 26:25 When you w into your cities, I will
1Sa 14:19 So Saul said to the priest, "W your
2Sa 11:15 Then w from him so that he will be
20:21 Hand over this one man, and I'll w
24:16 the people, "Enough! W your hand.
1Ki 15:19 Israel so that he will w from me."
2Ki 18:14 W from me, and I will pay whatever
1Ch 21:15 the people, "Enough! W your hand.
2Ch 16: 3 Israel so that he will w from me."
Job 13:21 W your hand far from me, and stop
Jer 21: 2 past so that he will w from us."
Eze 5:11 I myself will w my favour; I will
Ac 4:15 they ordered them to w from the

Withdrawn (Withdraw)

Jer 16: 5 because I have w my blessing, my
34:21 of Babylon, which has w from you.
37:11 After the Babylonian army had w from
Lam 2: 3 He has w his right hand at the
Hos 5: 6 him; he has w himself from them.

Withdraws (Withdraw)

2Sa 17:13 If he w into a city, then all Israel

Withdrew (Withdraw)

Ex 14:19 army, w and went behind them.
35:20 the whole Israelite community w from
1Sa 14:46 and they w to their own land.
1Ki 8:10 the priests w from the Holy Place,
15:21 building Ramah and w to Tirzah.
16:17 all the Israelites with him w from
2Ki 3:27 w and returned to their own land.
12:18 of Aram, who then w from Jerusalem.
15:20 w and stayed in the land no longer.
19: 8 he w and found the king fighting
19:36 king of Assyria broke camp and w.
2Ch 5:11 The priests then w from the Holy
24:25 the Arameans w, they left Joash
32:21 So he w to his own land in disgrace.
Ezr 10: 6 Ezra w from before the house of God
Job 34:14 If it were his intention and he w
Isa 37: 8 he w and found the king fighting
37:37 king of Assyria broke camp and w.
Jer 37: 5 about them, they w from Jerusalem.
Mt 2:22 he w to the district of Galilee,
12:15 Aware of this, Jesus w from that
14:13 Jesus heard what had happened, he w
15:21 Leaving that place, Jesus w to the
Mk 3: 7 Jesus w with his disciples to the
Lk 5:16 Jesus often w to lonely places and
9:10 they w by themselves to a town
22:41 He w about a stone's throw beyond
Jn 6:15 w again to a mountain by himself.
11:54 Instead he w to a region near the
Ac 22:29 about to question him w immediately.

Wither (Withered, Withers)

Job 8:12 While still growing and uncut, they w
15:30 darkness; a flame will w his shoots,
18:16 up below and his branches w above.
Ps 1: 3 in season and whose leaf does not w.
37: 2 for like the grass they will soon w,
37:19 In times of disaster they will not w;
102:11 evening shadow; I w away like grass.
Isa 16: 8 The fields of Heshbon w, the vines
19: 6 The reeds and rushes will w,
Isa 40:24 than he blows on them and they w,
Jer 8:13 the tree, and their leaves will w.
Eze 17: 9 withers? All its new growth will w.
17:10 will it thrive? Will it not w
17:10 w away in the plot where it grew?'
47:12 Their leaves will not w, nor will
Na 1: 4 w and the blossoms of Lebanon fade.
Zec 9: 5 and Ekron too, for her hope will w.
Mt 21:20 "How did the fig-tree w so quickly?"

Withered (Wither)

Ge 41:23 seven other ears sprouted—w and
Ps 90: 6 up new, by evening it is dry and w.
102: 4 My heart is blighted and w like
Isa 15: 6 are dried up and the grass is w;
34: 4 fall like w leaves from the vine,
Jer 12: 4 and the grass in every field be w?
23:10 the pastures in the desert are w.
Eze 19:12 branches w and fire consumed them.
31:15 all the trees of the field w away.
Hos 9:16 Ephraim is blighted, their root is w,
Joel 1:12 the fig-tree is w; the pomegranate,
1:12 Surely the joy of mankind is w away.
Jnh 4: 7 which chewed the vine so that it w.
Zec 11:17 May his arm be completely w, his
Mt 13: 6 and they w because they had no root.
21:19 again!" Immediately the tree w.
Mk 4: 6 and they w because they had no root.
11:20 saw the fig-tree w from the roots.
11:21 The fig-tree you cursed has w!"
Lk 8: 6 w because they had no moisture.

Withers (Wither)

Job 8:19 Surely its life w away, and from the
14: 2 He springs up like a flower and w
Ps 129: 6 roof, which w before it can grow;
Isa 24: 4 The earth dries up and w, the world
24: 4 The earth dries up and w, the
24: 7 The new wine dries up and the vine w;
33: 9 Lebanon is ashamed and w; Sharon is
40: 7 The grass w and the flowers fall,
40: 8 The grass w and the flowers fall,
Eze 17: 9 stripped of its fruit so that it w?
Am 1: 2 dry up, and the top of Carmel w."
Jn 15: 6 and w; such branches are picked up,
Jas 1:11 with scorching heat and w the plant;
1Pe 1:24 the grass w and the flowers fall,

Withheld (Withhold)

Ge 22:12 w from me your son, your only son."
22:16 have not w your son, your only son,
39: 9 My master has w nothing from me
Job 22: 7 and you w food from the hungry,
Ps 21: 2 have not w the request of his lips.
66:20 my prayer or w his love from me!
77: 9 Has he in anger w his compassion?"
Isa 63:15 and compassion are w from us.
Jer 3: 3 Therefore the showers have been w,
Eze 20:22 I w my hand, and for the sake of my
Joel 1:13 are w from the house of your God.
Am 4: 7 "I also w rain from you when the
4: 7 I sent rain on one town, but w it
Hag 1:10 the heavens have w their dew and

Withhold (Withheld, Withholding, Withholds)

Ne 9:20 You did not w your manna from their
Ps 40:11 Do not w your mercy from me, O LORD;
84:11 no good thing does he w from those
Pr 3:27 Do not w good from those who deserve
23:13 Do not w discipline from a child; if
Isa 10: 2 w justice from the oppressed of my
Lam 2: 8 did not w his hand from destroying.
Zec 1:12 Almighty, how long will you w mercy

Withholding (Withhold)

2Co 6:12 We are not w our affection from you,
6:12 you, but you are w yours from us.

Withholds (Withhold)

Dt 27:19 "Cursed is the man who w justice
Pr 11:24 w unduly, but comes to poverty.
Isa 32: 6 and from the thirsty he w water.

Eze 18: 8 He w his hand from doing wrong and
18:17 He w his hand from sin and takes no

Withstand (Withstood)

Nu 31:23 anything else that can w fire must
31:23 And whatever cannot w fire must be
Jos 10: 8 one of them will be able to w you."
23: 9 day no-one has been able to w you.
2Ch 20: 6 in your hand, and no-one can w you.
Ps 147:17 Who can w his icy blast?
Lam 1:14 handed me over to those I cannot w.
Na 1: 6 Who can w his indignation? Who can

Withstood (Withstand)

Jos 21:44 Not one of their enemies w them; the

Witless

Job 11:12 a w man can no more become wise than

Witness (Eye-witnesses, *Faithful witness*, *False witness*, Witnessed, Witnesses)

Ge 21:30 hand as a w that I dug this well."
31:44 and let it serve as a w between us."
31:48 Laban said, "This heap is a w
31:50 that God is a w between you and me."
31:52 This heap is a w, and this pillar is
31:52 and this pillar is a w, that I will
Ex 23: 1 a wicked man by being a malicious w.
Nu 5:13 (since there is no w against her
35:30 on the testimony of only one w.
Dt 17: 6 on the testimony of only one w.
19:15 One w is not enough to convict a man
19:16 If a malicious w takes the stand to
19:18 and if the w proves to be a liar,
31:19 it may be a w for me against them.
31:26 it will remain as a w against you.
Jos 22:27 On the contrary, it is to be a w
22:28 but as a w between us and you.'
22:34 A W Between Us that the LORD is God.
24:27 "This stone will be a w against us.
24:27 It will be a w against you if you
Jdg 11:10 "The LORD is our w; we will
1Sa 6:18 is a w to this day in the field of
12: 5 Samuel said to them, "The LORD is w
12: 5 and also his anointed is w this day,
12: 5 "He is w," they said.
20:23 is w between you and me for ever."
20:42 'The LORD is w between you and me,
Job 16: 8 bound me—and it has become a w;
16:19 Even now my w is in heaven; my
Pr 12:17 A truthful w gives honest testimony,
14: 5 A truthful w does not deceive, but a
14:25 A truthful w saves lives, but a
19:28 A corrupt w mocks at justice, and
Isa 19:20 will be a sign and w to the LORD
30: 8 to come it may be an everlasting w.
55: 4 See, I have made him a w to the
Jer 29:23 I know it and am a w to it,"
Mic 1: 2 that the Sovereign LORD may w
Mal 2:14 LORD is acting as the w between you
Lk 23:48 all the people who had gathered to w
Jn 1: 7 He came as a w to testify concerning
1: 8 he came only as a w to the light.
8:13 own w; your testimony is not valid."
8:18 other w is the Father, who sent me."
Ac 1:22 a w with us of his resurrection."
22:15 You will be his w to all men of what
26:16 as a w of what you have seen of me
Ro 1: 9 my w how constantly I remember
2:15 their consciences also bearing w,
2Co 1:23 I call God as my w that it was in
1Th 2: 5 to cover up greed—God is our w.
1Pe 5: 1 I appeal as a fellow-elder, a w of
Rev 3:14 true w, the ruler of God's creation.

Witnessed (Witness)

Jer 32:10 had it w, and weighed out the silver
32:25 silver and have the transaction w.
32:44 sealed and w in the territory of

Witnesses (Witness)

Nu 35:30 murderer only on the testimony of w.
Dt 4:26 I call heaven and earth as w against
17: 6 On the testimony of two or three w a
17: 7 The hands of the w must be the first
19:15 by the testimony of two or three w.
30:19 This day I call heaven and earth as w
Jos 24:22 Joshua said, "You are w against
24:22 "Yes, we are w," they replied.
Ru 4: 9 "Today you are w that I have bought
4:10 the town records. Today you are w!"
4:11 those at the gate said, "We are w.
Job 10:17 You bring new w against me and
Ps 27:12 for false w rise up against me,
35:11 Ruthless w come forward; they
Isa 8: 2 of Jeberekiah as reliable w for me."
33: 8 w are despised, no-one is respected.
43: 9 in their w to prove they were right,
43:10 "You are my w," declares the LORD,
43:12 You are my w," declares the LORD,
44: 8 foretell it long ago? You are my w.
Jer 6:18 O w, what will happen to them.
32:12 of the w who had signed the deed and
Mt 10:18 as w to them and to the Gentiles.
18:16 by the testimony of two or three w.'
26:60 though many false w came forward.
26:65 Why do we need any more w? Look,
Mk 13: 9 governors and kings as w to them.
14:63 "Why do we need any more w?" he
Lk 21:13 This will result in your being w to
24:48 You are w of these things.
Ac 1: 8 and you will be my w in Jerusalem,
2:32 life, and we are all w of the fact.
3:15 from the dead. We are w of this.
5:32 We are w of these things, and so is
6:13 They produced false w, who testified,
7:58 Meanwhile, the w laid their clothes
10:39 "We are w of everything he did in
10:41 but by w whom God had already chosen
13:31 They are now his w to our people.
1Co 15:15 we are then found to be false w
2Co 13: 1 by the testimony of two or three w."
1Th 2:10 You are w, and so is God, of how
1Ti 5:19 it is brought by two or three w.
6:12 in the presence of many w.
2Ti 2: 2 me say in the presence of many w
Heb 10:28 on the testimony of two or three w.
12: 1 by such a great cloud of w,
Rev 11: 3 I will give power to my two w, and

Wits'

Ps 107:27 men; they were at their w end.

Wives (Wife)

Ge 4:23 Lamech said to his w, "Adah and
4:23 to me; w of Lamech, hear my words.
6:18 your wife and your sons' w with you.
7: 7 his wife and his sons' w entered the
7:13 w of his three sons, entered the ark.
8:16 your wife and your sons and their w.
8:18 sons and his wife and his sons' w.
28: 9 in addition to the w he already had.
30:26 Give me my w and children, for whom
31:17 Jacob put his children and his w on
31:50 you take any w besides my daughters,
32:22 Jacob got up and took his two w,
36: 2 Esau took his w from the women of
36: 6 Esau took his w and sons and
37: 2 his father's w, and he brought their
45:19 w, and get your father and come.
46: 5 their children and their w in the
46:26 sons' w—numbered sixty-six persons.
Ex 22:24 your w will become widows and your
32: 2 off the gold ear-rings that your w,
34:16 their daughters as w for your sons
Nu 14: 3 Our w and children will be taken as
16:27 out and were standing with their w,
32:26 Our children and w, our flocks and
Dt 3:19 However, your w, your children and
17:17 He must not take many w, or his
21:15 If a man has two w, and he loves one
29:11 with your children and your w,
Jos 1:14 Your w, your children and your
Jdg 8:30 sons of his own, for he had many w.
12: 9 women as w from outside his clan.
21: 7 "How can we provide w for those who
21:16 provide w for the men who are left?
21:18 We can't give them our daughters as w
Jdg 21:22 because we did not get w for them
1Sa 1: 2 He had two w; one was called Hannah
25:43 Jezreel, and they both were his w.
27: 3 and David had his two w: Ahinoam of
30: 3 their w and sons and daughters taken
30: 5 David's two w had been captured—
30:18 had taken, including his two w.
2Sa 2: 2 David went up there with his two w,
5:13 David took more concubines and w in
12: 8 and your master's w into your arms.
12:11 your very eyes I will take your w
12:11 lie with your w in broad daylight.
19: 5 the lives of your w and concubines.
1Ki 11: 3 He had seven hundred w of royal
11: 3 and his w led him astray.
11: 4 Solomon grew old, his w turned his
11: 8 He did the same for all his foreign w
20: 3 of your w and children are mine.
20: 5 and gold, your w and your children.
20: 7 he sent for my w and my children,
2Ki 24:15 his w, his officials and the leading
1Ch 4: 5 Ashhur the father of Tekoa had two w,
4:17 One of Mered's w gave birth to
7: 4 for they had many w and children.
8: 8 had divorced his w Hushim and Baara.
14: 3 In Jerusalem David took more w and
2Ch 11:21 any of his other w and concubines.
11:21 In all he had eighteen w and sixty
11:23 provisions and took many w for them.
13:21 He married fourteen w and had
20:13 All the men of Judah, with their w
21:14 your sons, your w and everything
21:17 together with his sons and w.
24: 3 Jehoiada chose two w for him, and he
28: 8 thousand w, sons and daughters.
29: 9 and our w are in captivity.
31:18 the w, and the sons and daughters of
Ezr 9: 2 as w for themselves and their sons,
10:11 around you and from your foreign w."
10:19 hands in pledge to put away their w,
10:44 of them had children by these w.
Ne 4:14 daughters, your w and your homes."
5: 1 Now the men and their w raised a
10:28 together with their w and all their
Isa 13:16 will be looted and their w ravished.
Jer 6:12 with their fields and their w,
8:10 Therefore I will give their w to
14:16 w, their sons or their daughters.
18:21 Let their w be made childless and
29: 6 find w for your sons and give your
29:23 adultery with their neighbours' w
35: 8 Neither we nor our w nor our sons
38:23 "All your w and children will be
44: 9 your w in the land of Judah and the
44:15 all the men who knew that their w
44:25 says: You and your w have shown by
Da 5: 2 his w and his concubines might drink
5: 3 w and his concubines drank from them.
5:23 and you and your nobles, your w and
6:24 along with their w and children.
Zec 12:12 each clan by itself, with their w by
12:12 of the house of David and their w,
12:12 of the house of Nathan and their w,
12:13 w, the clan of Shimei and their w,
12:14 all the rest of the clans and their w
Mt 19: 8 divorce your w because your hearts
Ac 21: 5 All the disciples and their w and
1Co 7:29 those who have w should live as if
Eph 5:22 W, submit to your husbands as to the
5:24 so also w should submit to their
5:25 Husbands, love your w, just as
5:28 to love their w as their own bodies.
Col 3:18 W, submit to your husbands, as is
3:19 Husbands, love your w and do not be
1Ti 3:11 In the same way, their w are to be
1Pe 3: 1 W, in the same way be submissive to
3: 1 words by the behaviour of their w,
3: 7 considerate as you live with your w,

Wives' (Wife)

1Ti 4: 7 myths and old w tales; rather,

Woe (Woes)

Nu 21:29 W to you, O Moab! You are destroyed,
1Sa 4: 8 W to us! Who will deliver us from

Job 10:15 If I am guilty—w to me! Even if I
Ps 120: 5 W to me that I dwell in Meshech,
Pr 23:29 Who has w? Who has sorrow? Who has
Ecc 10:16 W to you, O land whose king was a
Isa 3: 9 W to them! They have brought
3:11 W to the wicked! Disaster is upon
5: 8 W to you who add house to house and
5:11 W to those who rise early in the
5:18 W to those who draw sin along with
5:20 W to those who call evil good and
5:21 W to those who are wise in their own
5:22 W to those who are heroes at
6: 5 "W to me!" I cried. "I am ruined!
10: 1 W to those who make unjust laws, to
10: 5 "W to the Assyrian, the rod of my
18: 1 W to the land of whirring wings
24:16 "I waste away, I waste away! W to me!
28: 1 W to that wreath, the pride of
29: 1 W to you, Ariel, Ariel, the city
29:15 W to those who go to great depths to
30: 1 "W to the obstinate children,"
31: 1 W to those who go down to Egypt for
33: 1 W to you, O destroyer, you who have
33: 1 W to you, O traitor, you who have
45: 9 "W to him who quarrels with his
45:10 W to him who says to his father,
Jer 4:13 W to us! We are ruined!
10:19 W to me because of my injury! My
13:27 W to you, O Jerusalem! How long will
22:13 "W to him who builds his palace by
23: 1 "W to the shepherds who are
45: 3 You said, 'W to me! The LORD has
48: 1 "W to Nebo, for it will be ruined.
48:46 W to you, O Moab! The people of
50:27 W to them! For their day has come,
Lam 5:16 W to us, for we have sinned!
Eze 2:10 words of lament and mourning and w.
13: 3 W to the foolish prophets who follow
13:18 W to the women who sew magic charms
16:23 "'W! W to you, declares the
24: 6 'W to the city of bloodshed, to the
24: 9 'W to the city of bloodshed! I, too,
34: 2 W to the shepherds of Israel who
Hos 7:13 W to them, because they have strayed
9:12 W to them when I turn away from them!
Am 5:18 W to you who long for the day of the
6: 1 W to you who are complacent in Zion,
Mic 2: 1 W to those who plan iniquity, to
Na 3: 1 W to the city of blood, full of lies,
Hab 2: 6 'W to him who piles up stolen goods
2: 9 "W to him who builds his realm by
2:12 "W to him who builds a city with
2:15 "W to him who gives drink to his
2:19 W to him who says to wood, 'Come to
Zep 2: 5 W to you who live by the sea,
3: 1 W to the city of oppressors,
Zec 11:17 "W to the worthless shepherd, who
Mt 11:21 "W to you, Korazin! W to you,
18: 7 "W to the world because of the
18: 7 w to the man through whom they come!
23:13 "W to you, teachers of the law and
23:15 "W to you, teachers of the law and
23:16 "W to you, blind guides! You say,
23:23 "W to you, teachers of the law and
23:25 "W to you, teachers of the law and
23:27 "W to you, teachers of the law and
23:29 "W to you, teachers of the law and
26:24 But w to that man who betrays the
Mk 14:21 But w to that man who betrays the
Lk 6:24 "But w to you who are rich, for you
6:25 W to you who are well fed now, for
6:25 W to you who laugh now, for you will
6:26 W to you when all men speak well of
10:13 "W to you, Korazin! W to you,
11:42 "W to you Pharisees, because you
11:43 "W to you Pharisees, because you
11:44 "W to you, because you are like
11:46 you experts in the law, w to you,
11:47 "W to you, because you build tombs
11:52 "W to you experts in the law,
17: 1 but w to that person through whom
22:22 but w to that man who betrays him."
1Co 9:16 W to me if I do not preach the
Jude :11 W to them! They have taken the way
Rev 8:13 "W! W! W to the inhabitants of the
9:12 The first w is past; two other woes
11:14 The second w has passed; the third w
12:12 But w to the earth and the sea,
18:10 'W! W, O great city, O Babylon, city
18:16 cry out: "'W! W, O great city,
18:19 'W! W, O great city, where all who

Woes (Woe)
Ps 32:10 Many are the w of the wicked, but
Rev 9:12 The first woe is past; two other w

Woke (Wake)
Ge 41: 4 sleek, fat cows. Then Pharaoh w up.
41: 7 Pharaoh w up; it had been a dream.
41:21 as ugly as before. Then I w up.
Mt 1:24 Joseph w up, he did what the angel
8:25 The disciples went and w him, saying,
25: 7 "Then all the virgins w up and
Mk 4:38 The disciples w him and said to him,
Lk 8:24 The disciples went and w him, saying,
Ac 12: 7 struck Peter on the side and w him
16:27 The jailer w up, and when he saw the

Wolf (Wolves)
Ge 49:27 "Benjamin is a ravenous w; in the
Isa 11: 6 The w will live with the lamb, the
65:25 The w and the lamb will feed
Jer 5: 6 a w from the desert will ravage them,
Jn 10:12 So when he sees the w coming, he
10:12 w attacks the flock and scatters it.

Wolves (Wolf)
Eze 22:27 Her officials within her are like w
Hab 1: 8 leopards, fiercer than w at dusk.
Zep 3: 3 w, who leave nothing for the morning.
Mt 7:15 but inwardly they are ferocious w.
10:16 sending you out like sheep among w.
Lk 10: 3 sending you out like lambs among w.
Ac 20:29 I know that after I leave, savage w

Woman (Woman's, Women, Women's)
Ge 2:22 the LORD God made a w from the rib
2:23 'w', for she was taken out of man."
3: 1 He said to the w, "Did God really
3: 2 The w said to the serpent, "We may
3: 4 die," the serpent said to the w.
3: 6 the w saw that the fruit of the tree
3:12 The man said, "The w you put here
3:13 the LORD God said to the w, "What is
3:13 The w said, "The serpent deceived
3:15 put enmity between you and the w,
3:16 To the w he said, "I will greatly
12:11 "I know what a beautiful w you are.
12:14 saw that she was a very beautiful w.
20: 3 w you have taken; she is a married w.
21:10 "Get rid of that slave w and her son,
24: 5 The servant asked him, "What if the w
24: 8 If the w is unwilling to come back
24:39 the w will not come back with me?'
28: 1 him: "Do not marry a Canaanite w.
28: 6 "Do not marry a Canaanite w,"
38:20 from the w, but he did not find her.
46:10 and Shaul the son of a Canaanite w.
Ex 2: 1 house of Levi married a Levite w,
2: 9 the w took the baby and nursed him.
3:22 Every w is to ask her neighbour and
3:22 any w living in her house for
6:15 and Shaul the son of a Canaanite w.
21: 4 the w and her children shall belong
21:10 If he marries another w, he must not
21:22 who are fighting hit a pregnant w
21:28 "If a bull gores a man or a w to
21:29 penned up and it kills a man or w,
35:25 Every skilled w spun with her hands
36: 6 "No man or w is to make anything
Lev 12: 2 'A w who becomes pregnant and gives
12: 4 the w must wait thirty-three days to
12: 5 for two weeks the w will be unclean,
12: 7 w who gives birth to a boy or a girl.
13:29 "If a man or w has a sore on the
13:38 "When a man or w has white spots on
15:18 a man lies with a w and there is an
15:19 "'When a w has her regular flow of
15:25 "'When a w has a discharge of blood
15:33 for a w in her monthly period, for a
15:33 for a man or a w with a discharge,
15:33 a w who is ceremonially unclean.
18:17 with both a w and her daughter.
18:19 "'Do not approach a w to have
18:22 lies with a w; that is detestable.
18:23 A w must not present herself to an
19:20 "'If a man sleeps with a w who is a
20:11 Both the man and the w must be put
20:13 with a man as one lies with a w,
20:14 "'If a man marries both a w and her
20:16 "'If a w approaches an animal to
20:16 it, kill both the w and the animal.
20:18 "'If a man lies with a w during her
20:27 "'A man or w who is a medium or
21:13 "'The w he marries must be a virgin.
21:14 a divorced w, or a w defiled by
24:11 The son of the Israelite w
Nu 3:12 male offspring of every Israelite w.
5: 6 'When a man or w wrongs another in
5:18 After the priest has made the w
5:19 the priest shall put the w under
5:21 here the priest is to put the w
5:22 "'Then the w is to say, "Amen. So
5:24 He shall make the w drink the bitter
5:26 he is to make the w drink the water.
5:28 If, however, the w has not defiled
5:29 is the law of jealousy when a w goes
5:31 but the w will bear the consequences
6: 2 'If a man or w wants to make a
8:16 offspring from every Israelite w.
25: 6 brought to his family a Midianite w
25:14 Midianite w was Zimri son of Salu,
25:15 the name of the Midianite w who was
25:18 the w who was killed when the plague
30: 3 "When a young w still living in her
30: 9 divorced w will be binding on her.
30:10 "If a w living with her husband
31:17 every w who has slept with a man,
Dt 4:16 whether formed like a man or a w,
15:12 If a fellow Hebrew, a man or w,
17: 2 If a man or w living among you in
17: 5 take the man or w who has done this
20: 7 Has anyone become pledged to a w and
21:11 a beautiful w and are attracted to
22: 5 A w must not wear men's clothing,
22:14 "I married this w, but when I
22:22 slept with her and the w must die.
23:17 No Israelite man or w is to become a
24: 1 If a man marries a w who becomes
28:30 be pledged to be married to a w,
28:56 The most gentle and sensitive w
29:18 Make sure there is no man or w, clan
Jos 2: 4 the w had taken the two men and
Jdg 4: 9 LORD will hand Sisera over to a w.
9:53 a w dropped an upper millstone on
9:54 they can't say, 'A w killed him.'
11: 2 you are the son of another w."
13: 6 the w went to her husband and told
13: 9 angel of God came again to the w
13:10 The w hurried to tell her husband,
13:24 The w gave birth to a boy and named
14: 1 and saw there a young Philistine w.
14: 2 "I have seen a Philistine w in
14: 3 "Isn't there an acceptable w among
14: 7 he went down and talked with the w,
14:10 Now his father went down to see the w
16: 4 he fell in love with a w in the
19:26 At daybreak the w went back to the
20: 4 the husband of the murdered w, said,
21:11 and every w who is not a virgin."
Ru 2: 5 "Whose young w is that?
3: 8 discovered a w lying at his feet.
3:11 that you are a w of noble character.
3:14 a w came to the threshing-floor."
4:11 May the LORD make the w who is
4:12 the LORD gives you by this young w,
1Sa 1:15 "I am a w who is deeply troubled.
1:16 take your servant for a wicked w;
1:23 So the w stayed at home and nursed
1:26 my lord, I am the w who stood here
2:20 LORD give you children by this w
20:30 son of a perverse and rebellious w!
25: 3 was an intelligent and beautiful w,
27: 9 he did not leave a man or w alive,
27:11 He did not leave a man or w alive to

1Sa 28: 7 "Find me a w who is a medium, so
28: 8 night he and two men went to the w.
28: 9 the w said to him, "Surely you know
28:11 the w asked, "Whom shall I bring up
28:12 the w saw Samuel, she cried out at
28:13 What do you see?" The w said, "I see
28:21 the w came to Saul and saw that he
28:23 But his men joined the w in urging
28:24 The w had a fattened calf at the
2Sa 3: 8 me of an offence involving this w!
11: 2 From the roof he saw a w bathing.
11: 2 The w was very beautiful,
11: 5 The w conceived and sent word to
11:21 Didn't a w throw an upper millstone
13:17 "Get this w out of here and bolt the
13:20 Absalom's house, a desolate w.
14: 2 and had a wise w brought from there.
14: 2 Act like a w who has spent many days
14: 4 the w from Tekoa went to the king,
14: 8 The king said to the w, "Go home,
14: 9 the w from Tekoa said to him, "My
14:12 the w said, "Let your servant speak
14:13 The w said, "Why then have you
14:18 the king said to the w, "Do not keep
14:18 my lord the king speak," the w said
14:19 The w answered, "As surely as you
14:27 Tamar, and she became a beautiful w.
17:20 Absalom's men came to the w at the
17:20 The w answered them, "They crossed
20:16 a wise w called from the city,
20:21 The w said to Joab, "His head will
20:22 the w went to all the people with
1Ki 3:17 One of them said, "My lord, this w
3:18 was born, this w also had a baby.
3:22 The other w said, "No! The living
3:26 The w whose son was alive was filled
3:27 the living baby to the first w.
17:15 Elijah and for the w and her family.
17:17 Some time later the son of the w who
17:24 the w said to Elijah, "Now I know
2Ki 4: 8 And a well-to-do w was there, who
4:17 the w became pregnant, and the next
6:26 a w cried to him, "Help me, my lord
6:28 "This w said to me, 'Give up your
8: 1 Now Elisha had said to the w whose
8: 2 The w proceeded to do as the man of
8: 5 the w whose son Elisha had brought
8: 5 Gehazi said, "This is the w, my lord
8: 6 The king asked the w about it, and
9:34 "Take care of that cursed w," he
1Ch 2: 3 a Canaanite w, the daughter of Shua.
16: 3 raisins to each Israelite man and w.
2Ch 15:13 whether small or great, man or w.
24: 7 Now the sons of that wicked w
24:26 son of Shimeath an Ammonite w, and
24:26 son of Shimrith a Moabite w.
36:17 man nor young w, old man or aged.
Ezr 10:14 a foreign w come at a set time,
Est 4:11 man or w who approaches the king
Job 2:10 "You are talking like a foolish w.
14: 1 "Man born of w is of few days and
15:14 or one born of w, that he could be
24:21 prey on the barren and childless w,
25: 4 God? How can one born of w be pure?
31: 9 "If my heart has been enticed by a w,
Ps 48: 6 pain like that of a w in labour.
113: 9 He settles the barren w in her home
Pr 6:24 keeping you from the immoral w, from
7:10 out came a w to meet him, dressed
9:13 The w Folly is loud; she is
11:16 A kind-hearted w gains respect, but
11:22 beautiful w who shows no discretion.
14: 1 The wise w builds her house, but
20:16 if he does it for a wayward w.
27:13 if he does it for a wayward w.
30:23 an unloved w who is married, and a
31:30 and beauty is fleeting; but a w who
Ecc 7:26 I find more bitter than death the w
7:28 not one ⌊upright⌋ w among them all.
SS 1: 7 like a veiled w beside the flocks
Isa 13: 8 they will writhe like a w in labour.
21: 3 pangs seize me, like those of a w in
26:17 a w with child and about to give
42:14 But now, like a w in childbirth, I
54: 1 "Sing, O barren w, you who never
54: 1 are the children of the desolate w
Jer 3:20 like a w unfaithful to her husband,
4:31 I hear a cry as of a w in labour, a
6:24 us, pain like that of a w in labour.
13:21 grip you like that of a w in labour?
22:23 pain like that of a w in labour!
30: 6 on his stomach like a w in labour,
31:22 on earth—a w will surround a man."
48:19 and the w escaping, ask them,
48:41 be like the heart of a w in labour.
49:22 be like the heart of a w in labour.
49:24 pain like that of a w in labour.
50:43 pain like that of a w in labour.
51:22 with you I shatter man and w, with
Eze 18: 6 or lie with a w during her period.
23:42 put bracelets on the arms of the w
Hos 13:13 Pains as of a w in childbirth come
Mic 4: 9 you like that of a w in labour?
4:10 O Daughter of Zion, like a w in
Zec 5: 7 and there in the basket sat a w!
Mt 5:28 anyone who looks at a w lustfully
5:32 the divorced w commits adultery.
9:20 Just then a w who had been subject
9:22 the w was healed from that moment.
13:33 heaven is like yeast that a w took
15:22 A Canaanite w from that vicinity
15:25 The w came and knelt before him.
15:28 Jesus answered, "W, you have great
19: 9 marries another w commits adultery."
22:27 Finally, the w died.
26: 7 a w came to him with an alabaster
26:10 "Why are you bothering this w? She
Mk 5:25 a w was there who had been subject
5:33 the w, knowing what had happened to
7:25 as soon as she heard about him, a w
7:26 The w was a Greek, born in Syrian
10:11 marries another w commits adultery
12:22 Last of all, the w died too.
14: 3 a w came with an alabaster jar of
Lk 7:37 a w who had lived a sinful life in
7:39 of w she is—that she is a sinner."
7:44 he turned towards the w and said to
7:44 see this w? I came into your house.
7:45 but this w, from the time I entered,
7:50 Jesus said to the w, "Your faith has
8:43 a w was there who had been subject
8:47 the w, seeing that she could not go
10:38 he came to a village where a w named
11:27 Jesus was saying these things, a w
13:11 a w was there who had been crippled
13:12 "W, you are set free from your
13:16 should not this w, a daughter of
13:21 is like yeast that a w took and
15: 8 "Or suppose a w has ten silver coins
16:18 marries another w commits adultery,
16:18 a divorced w commits adultery.
20:29 one married a w and died childless.
20:32 Finally, the w died too.
22:57 he denied it. "W, I don't know him,"
Jn 2: 4 "Dear w, why do you involve me?"
4: 7 a Samaritan w came to draw water,
4: 9 The Samaritan w said to him, "You
4: 9 You are a Jew and I am a Samaritan w.
4:11 "Sir," the w said, "you have nothing
4:15 The w said to him, "Sir, give me
4:19 "Sir," the w said, "I can see that
4:21 Jesus declared, "Believe me, w, a
4:25 The w said, "I know that Messiah"
4:27 to find him talking with a w.
4:28 Then, leaving her water jar, the w
4:42 They said to the w, "We no longer
8: 3 brought in a w caught in adultery.
8: 4 said to Jesus, "Teacher, this w was
8: 9 with the w still standing there.
8:10 "W, where are they? Has no-one
16:21 A w giving birth to a child has pain
19:26 "Dear w, here is your son,
20:13 They asked her, "W, why are you
20:15 "W," he said, "why are you crying?
Ac 9:40 Turning towards the dead w, he said,
16:14 those listening was a w named Lydia
17:34 also a w named Damaris, and a
Ro 7: 2 For example, by law a married w is
16:12 another w who has worked very hard
1Co 7: 2 wife, and each w her own husband.
7:13 if a w has a husband who is not a
7:15 A believing man or w is not bound in
1Co 7:34 An unmarried w or virgin is
7:34 But a married w is concerned about
7:39 A w is bound to her husband as long
11: 3 and the head of the w is man, and
11: 5 every w who prays or prophesies with
11: 6 If a w does not cover her head, she
11: 6 for a w to have her hair cut or
11: 7 God; but the w is the glory of man.
11: 8 For man did not come from w, but w
11: 9 neither was man created for w, but w
11:10 because of the angels, the w ought
11:11 In the Lord, however, w is not
11:11 of man, nor is man independent of w.
11:12 For as w came from man, so also man
11:12 from man, so also man is born of w.
11:13 Is it proper for a w to pray to God
11:15 that if a w has long hair, it is her
14:35 for a w to speak in the church.
Gal 4: 4 Son, born of a w, born under law,
4:22 slave w and the other by the free w.
4:23 His son by the slave w was born in
4:23 but his son by the free w was born
4:27 "Be glad, O barren w, who bears no
4:27 are the children of the w than of
4:30 "Get rid of the slave w and her son,
4:31 of the slave w, but of the free w.
1Th 5: 3 as labour pains on a pregnant w,
1Ti 2:11 A w should learn in quietness and
2:12 I do not permit a w to teach or to
2:14 it was the w who was deceived and
5:16 If any w who is a believer has
Rev 2:20 you: You tolerate that w Jezebel,
12: 1 in heaven: a w clothed with the sun,
12: 4 The dragon stood in front of the w
12: 6 The w fled into the desert to a
12:13 he pursued the w who had given birth
12:14 The w was given the two wings of a
12:15 to overtake the w and sweep her away
12:16 the earth helped the w by opening
12:17 the dragon was enraged at the w and
17: 3 There I saw a w sitting on a scarlet
17: 4 The w was dressed in purple and
17: 6 I saw that the w was drunk with the
17: 7 of the w and of the beast she rides,
17: 9 are seven hills on which the w sits.
17:18 The w you saw is the great city that

Woman's (Woman)

Ge 21:10 for that slave w son will never
Ex 21:22 whatever the w husband demands
Nu 25: 8 the Israelite and into the w body.
1Ki 3:19 "During the night this w son died
2Ki 6:30 the king heard the w words, he tore
Eze 36:17 a w monthly uncleanness in my sight.
Jn 4:39 in him because of the w testimony,
Gal 4:30 for the slave w son will never share
4:30 inheritance with the free w son."

Womb (Wombs)

Ge 20:18 for the LORD had closed up every w
25:23 "Two nations are in your w, and two
25:24 there were twin boys in her w.
29:31 opened her w, but Rachel was barren.
30:22 he listened to her and opened her w.
38:27 there were twin boys in her w.
49:25 blessings of the breast and w.
Ex 13: 2 The first offspring of every w among
13:12 LORD the first offspring of every w.
13:15 the first male offspring of every w
34:19 "The first offspring of every w
Nu 12:12 w with its flesh half eaten away."
18:15 The first offspring of every w, both
Dt 7:13 He will bless the fruit of your w,
28: 4 The fruit of your w will be blessed,
28:11 prosperity—in the fruit of your w,
28:18 The fruit of your w will be cursed,
28:53 you will eat the fruit of the w, the
28:57 the afterbirth from her w and the
30: 9 hands and in the fruit of your w,
1Sa 1: 5 her, and the LORD had closed her w.
1: 6 the LORD had closed her w, her rival
Job 1:21 Naked I came from my mother's w,
3:10 shut the doors of the w on me to
3:11 birth, and die as I came from the w?
10:18 then did you bring me out of the w?

Job 10:19 straight from the w to the grave!
15:35 to evil; their w fashions deceit."
24:20 The w forgets them, the worm feasts
31:15 Did not he who made me in the w make
38: 8 when it burst forth from the w,
38:29 From whose w comes the ice? Who
Ps 22: 9 Yet you brought me out of the w; you
22:10 my mother's w you have been my God.
58: 3 from the w they are wayward and
71: 6 brought me forth from my mother's w.
110: 3 from the w of the dawn you will
139:13 knit me together in my mother's w.
Pr 30:16 the grave, the barren w, land, which
31: 2 "O my son, O son of my w, O son of
Ecc 5:15 Naked a man comes from his mother's w
11: 5 the body is formed in a mother's w,
Isa 44: 2 who formed you in the w, and who
44:24 who formed you in the w: I am the
49: 5 he who formed me in the w to be his
66: 9 "Do I close up the w when I bring to
Jer 1: 5 "Before I formed you in the w I knew
20:17 For he did not kill me in the w,
20:17 my grave, her w enlarged for ever.
20:18 Why did I ever come out of the w to
Hos 12: 3 In the w he grasped his brother's
13:13 not come to the opening of the w.
Lk 1:41 the baby leaped in her w, and
1:44 the baby in my w leaped for joy.
Jn 3: 4 into his mother's w to be born!"
Ro 4:19 that Sarah's w was also dead.

Wombs (Womb)

Hos 9:14 Give them w that miscarry and
Lk 23:29 barren women, the w that never bore

Women (Woman)

Ge 4:19 Lamech married two w, one named Adah
14:16 with the w and the other people.
24:11 the time the w go out to draw water.
27:46 living because of these Hittite w.
27:46 wife from among the w of this land,
27:46 from Hittite w like these, my life
28: 8 Canaanite w were to his father Isaac;
30:13 Leah said, "How happy I am! The w
31:43 Laban answered Jacob, "The w are my
33: 5 Esau looked up and saw the w and
34: 1 went out to visit the w of the land.
34:29 wealth and all their w and children,
36: 2 Esau took his wives from the w of
Ex 1:16 "When you help the Hebrew w in
1:19 "Hebrew w are not like Egyptian w;
2: 7 Hebrew w to nurse the baby for you?"
10:10 along with your w and children!
10:24 Even your w and children may go with
11: 2 Tell the people that men and w alike
12:37 men on foot, besides w and children.
15:20 and all the w followed her, with
35:22 All who were willing, men and w
35:26 all the w who were willing and had
35:29 All the Israelite men and w who were
38: 8 from the mirrors of the w who
Lev 21: 7 "'They must not marry w defiled by
26:26 I cut off your supply of bread, ten w
Nu 25: 1 in sexual immorality with Moabite w,
31: 9 Israelites captured the Midianite w
31:15 "Have you allowed all the w to live?"
31:35 32,000 w who had never slept with a
32:16 and cities for our w and children.
32:17 Meanwhile our w and children will
32:24 Build cities for your w and children,
Dt 2:34 destroyed them—men, w and children.
3: 6 every city—men, w and children.
7:14 of your men or w will be childless,
20:14 for the w, the children, the
31:12 Assemble the people—men, w and
32:25 Young men and young w will perish,
Jos 6:21 every living thing in it—men and w,
8:25 Twelve thousand men and w fell that
8:35 including the w and children, and
Jdg 5:24 "Most blessed of w be Jael, the wife
5:24 most blessed of tent-dwelling w.
9:49 a thousand men and w, also died.
9:51 w—all the people of the city—fled.
11:40 that each year the young w of Israel
12: 9 w as wives from outside his clan.
Jdg 16:27 temple was crowded with men and w;
16:27 men and w watching Samson perform.
21:10 there, including the w and children.
21:12 w who had never slept with a man,
21:14 were given the w of Jabesh Gilead
21:16 "With the w of Benjamin destroyed,
Ru 1: 4 They married Moabite w, one named
1:19 the two w went on until they came to
1:19 and the w exclaimed, "Can this be
4:14 The w said to Naomi: "Praise be to
4:17 The w living there said, "Naomi has
1Sa 2:22 how they slept with the w who served
4:20 she was dying, the w attending her
15: 3 spare them; put to death men and w,
15:33 "As your sword has made w childless,
15:33 your mother be childless among w.
18: 6 the w came out from all the towns of
21: 4 men have kept themselves from w."
21: 5 David replied, "Indeed w have been
22:19 with its men and w, its children and
30: 2 had taken captive the w and all who
2Sa 1:26 more wonderful than that of w.
6:19 crowd of Israelites, both men and w.
19:35 the voices of men and w singers?
1Ki 11: 1 however, loved many foreign w
2Ki 8:12 and rip open their pregnant w."
15:16 and ripped open all the pregnant w.
23: 7 and where w did weaving for Asherah.
2Ch 28:10 now you intend to make the men and w
35:25 and to this day all the men and w
Ezr 2:65 they also had 200 men and w singers.
10: 1 w and children—gathered round him.
10: 2 w from the peoples around us.
10: 3 away all these w and their children,
10:10 foreign w, adding to Israel's guilt.
10:17 the men who had married foreign w.
10:18 the following had married foreign w:
10:44 All these had married foreign w, and
Ne 7:67 they also had 245 men and w singers.
8: 2 which was made up of men and w and
8: 3 w and others who could understand.
12:43 The w and children also rejoiced.
13:23 w from Ashdod, Ammon and Moab.
13:26 he was led into sin by foreign w.
13:27 to our God by marrying foreign w?"
Est 1: 9 w in the royal palace of King Xerxes.
1:17 will become known to all the w,
1:18 Median w of the nobility who have
1:20 all the w will respect their
2: 3 who is in charge of the w; and let
2:12 treatments prescribed for the w,
2:17 more than to any of the other w,
3:13 w and little children—on a single
8:11 them and their w and children;
Job 42:15 w as beautiful as Job's daughters,
Ps 45: 9 of kings are among your honoured w;
Pr 31: 3 do not spend your strength on w,
31:29 "Many w do noble things, but you
Ecc 2: 8 I acquired men and w singers, and a
SS 1: 8 most beautiful of w, follow the
5: 9 most beautiful of w? How is your
6: 1 most beautiful of w? Which way did
Isa 3:12 Youths oppress my people, w rule
3:16 The LORD says, "The w of Zion are
3:17 sores on the heads of the w of Zion;
4: 1 In that day seven w will take hold
4: 4 away the filth of the w of Zion;
16: 2 w of Moab at the fords of the Arnon.
19:16 day the Egyptians will be like w.
27:11 and w come and make fires with them.
32: 9 You w who are so complacent, rise up
32:11 Tremble, you complacent w; shudder,
Jer 2:33 worst of w can learn from your ways.
7:18 and the w knead the dough and make
9:17 now! Call for the wailing w to come;
9:20 Now, O w, hear the word of the LORD;
16: 3 about the w who are their mothers
31: 8 expectant mothers and w in labour; a
38:22 All the w left in the palace of the
38:22 Those w will say to you: "'They
40: 7 w and children who were the poorest
41:16 w, children and court officials he
43: 6 They also led away all the men, w
44: 7 off from Judah the men and w,
44:15 along with all the w who were
44:19 The w added, "When we burned incense
Jer 44:20 men and w, who were answering him,
44:24 including the w, "Hear the word of
50:37 in her ranks! They will become w.
51:30 exhausted; they have become like w.
Lam 2:10 The young w of Jerusalem have bowed
2:20 this? Should w eat their offspring,
3:51 because of all the w of my city.
4:10 With their own hands compassionate w
5:11 W have been ravished in Zion, and
Eze 8:14 w sitting there, mourning for Tammuz.
9: 6 young men and maidens, w and
13:18 Woe to the w who sew magic charms on
16:38 punishment of w who commit adultery
16:41 on you in the sight of many w.
22:10 who violate w during their period,
23: 2 "Son of man, there were two w,
23:10 She became a byword among w, and
23:44 those lewd w, Oholah and Oholibah.
23:45 w who commit adultery and shed blood,
23:48 that all w may take warning and not
44:22 must not marry widows or divorced w;
Da 11:37 fathers or for the one desired by w,
Hos 13:16 their pregnant w ripped open."
Joel 2:29 Even on my servants, both men and w,
Am 1:13 he ripped open the pregnant w of
4: 1 you w who oppress the poor and crush
8:13 "In that day "the lovely young w and
Mic 2: 9 You drive the w of my people from
Na 3:13 Look at your troops—they are all w!
Zec 5: 9 up—and there before me were two w,
8: 4 "Once again men and w of ripe old
9:17 thrive, and new wine the young w.
14: 2 houses ransacked, and the w raped.
Mt 11:11 Among those born of w there has not
14:21 men, besides w and children.
15:38 thousand, besides w and children.
24:19 for pregnant w and nursing mothers!
24:41 Two w will be grinding with a hand
27:55 Many w were there, watching from a
28: 5 The angel said to the w, "Do not be
28: 8 the w hurried away from the tomb,
28:11 While the w were on their way, some
Mk 13:17 for pregnant w and nursing mothers!
15:40 Some w were watching from a distance.
15:41 In Galilee these w had followed him
15:41 Many other w who had come up with
16: 8 Trembling and bewildered, the w went
Lk 1:42 "Blessed are you among w, and
7:28 I tell you, among those born of w
8: 2 also some w who had been cured of
8: 3 These w were helping to support them
17:35 Two w will be grinding grain
21:23 for pregnant w and nursing mothers!
23:27 w who mourned and wailed for him.
23:29 'Blessed are the barren w, the wombs
23:49 including the w who had followed him
23:55 The w who had come with Jesus from
24: 1 very early in the morning, the w
24: 5 In their fright the w bowed down
24:11 they did not believe the w, because
24:22 In addition, some of our w amazed us.
24:24 found it just as the w had said,
Jn 8: 5 Moses commanded us to stone such w.
Ac 1:14 along with the w and Mary the mother
2:18 Even on my servants, both men and w,
5:14 Nevertheless, more and more men and w
8: 3 men and w and put them in prison.
8:12 they were baptised, both men and w.
9: 2 whether men or w, he might take them
13:50 the Jews incited the God-fearing w
16:13 to the w who had gathered there.
17: 4 Greeks and not a few prominent w.
17:12 Greek w and many Greek men.
22: 4 and w and throwing them into prison,
Ro 1:26 Even their w exchanged natural
1:27 abandoned natural relations with w
16:12 Greet Tryphena and Tryphosa, those w
1Co 14:34 w should remain silent in the
Gal 4:24 for the w represent two covenants.
Php 4: 3 loyal yokefellow, help these w who
1Ti 2: 9 I also want w to dress modestly,
2:10 with good deeds, appropriate for w
2:15 w will be saved through childbearing
3:11 their wives are to be w worthy of
5: 2 older w as mothers, and younger w as
2Ti 3: 6 and gain control over weak-willed w,

Tit 2: 3 Likewise, teach the older w to be
2: 4 they can train the younger w to love
Heb 11:35 W received back their dead, raised
1Pe 3: 5 For this is the way the holy w of
Rev 14: 4 did not defile themselves with w,

Women's (Woman)

Dt 22: 5 nor a man wear w clothing, for the
Rev 9: 8 Their hair was like w hair, and

Won (Win)

Ge 30: 8 with my sister, and I have w.
1Sa 19: 5 The LORD w a great victory for all
2Sa 19:14 He w over the hearts of all the men
Est 2: 9 The girl pleased him and w his
2:15 w the favour of everyone who saw her.
2:17 and she w his favour and approval
Ps 44: 3 was not by their sword that they w
Mt 18:15 you, you have w your brother over.
Ac 14:19 and Iconium and w the crowd over.
14:21 and w a large number of disciples.
1Pe 3: 1 they may be w over without words by

Wonder (Wondered, Wondering, Wonders, Wondrous)

Dt 13: 1 to you a miraculous sign or w,
13: 2 if the sign or w of which he has
28:46 They will be a sign and a w to you
Job 6: 3 no w my words have been impetuous.
Ps 17: 7 Show the w of your great love, you
SS 1: 3 No w the maidens love you!
Isa 29:14 astound these people with w upon w;
Mk 9:15 with w and ran to greet him.
Ac 3:10 and they were filled with w and
13:41 "'Look, you scoffers, w and perish,
2Co 11:14 no w, for Satan himself masquerades

Wondered (Wonder)

Lk 1:29 w what kind of greeting this might
1:66 Everyone who heard this w about it,

Wonderful (Wonderfully)

2Sa 1:26 me was w, more w than that of women.
1Ch 16: 9 to him; tell of all his w acts.
Job 42: 3 things too w for me to know.
Ps 26: 7 and telling of all your w deeds.
31:21 for he showed his w love to me when
75: 1 is near; men tell of your w deeds.
105: 2 to him; tell of all his w acts.
107: 8 love and his w deeds for men,
107:15 love and his w deeds for men,
107:21 love and his w deeds for men.
107:24 the works of the LORD, his w deeds
107:31 love and his w deeds for men.
119:18 Open my eyes that I may see w things
119:129 Your statutes are w; therefore I
131: 1 matters or things too w for me.
139: 6 Such knowledge is too w for me, too
139:14 works are w, I know that full well.
145: 5 and I will meditate on your w works.
Isa 9: 6 And he will be called W Counsellor,
28:29 w in counsel and magnificent in
Mt 21:15 of the law saw the w things he did
Lk 13:17 with all the w things he was doing.
1Pe 2: 9 out of darkness into his w light.

Wonderfully (Wonderful)

Ps 139:14 I am fearfully and w made;

Wondering (Wonder)

Lk 1:21 w why he stayed so long in the
3:15 were all w in their hearts if John
24: 4 While they were w about this,
24:12 w to himself what had happened.
Ac 5:24 puzzled, w what would come of this.
10:17 While Peter was w about the meaning

Wonders (Wonder, *Miraculous signs and wonders, Signs and wonders*)

Ex 3:20 w that I will perform among them.
4:21 w I have given you the power to do.
11: 9 my w may be multiplied in Egypt."
11:10 Moses and Aaron performed all these w
15:11 awesome in glory, working w?
34:10 Before all your people I will do w
Dt 10:21 w you saw with your own eyes.
29: 3 those miraculous signs and great w.
Jdg 6:13 Where are all his w that our fathers
2Sa 7:23 and to perform great and awesome w
1Ch 16:12 Remember the w he has done, his
17:21 and to perform great and awesome w
Job 5: 9 He performs w that cannot be
9:10 He performs w that cannot be
37:14 Job; stop and consider God's w.
37:16 w of him who is perfect in knowledge?
Ps 9: 1 my heart; I will tell of all your w.
40: 5 Many, O LORD my God, are the w you
65: 8 Those living far away fear your w;
78: 4 his power, and the w he has done.
78:11 They forgot what he had done, the w
78:32 of his w, they did not believe.
78:43 Egypt, his w in the region of Zoan.
88:10 Do you show your w to the dead? Do
88:12 Are your w known in the place of
89: 5 The heavens praise your w, O LORD,
105: 5 Remember the w he has done, his
105:27 them, his w in the land of Ham.
111: 4 He has caused his w to be remembered;
119:27 then I will meditate on your w.
136: 4 to him who alone does great w, His
Jer 21: 2 Perhaps the LORD will perform w for
Da 4: 3 how mighty his w! His kingdom is an
Joel 2:26 who has worked w for you; never
2:30 I will show w in the heavens and on
Mic 7:15 of Egypt, I will show them my w."
Ac 2:11 the w of God in our own tongues!"
2:19 I will show w in the heaven above
2:22 w and signs, which God did among you
2:43 and many w and miraculous signs were
6: 8 did great w and miraculous signs
7:36 He led them out of Egypt and did w
2Co 12:12 w and miracles—were done among you
Heb 2: 4 God also testified to it by signs, w

Wondrous (Wonder)

Rev 12: 1 A great and w sign appeared in

Wood (Brushwood, Woodcutters, Wooded, Wooden, Woodpile, Woods, Woodsman, Woodsmen, Woodwork)

Ge 6:14 make yourself an ark of cypress w;
22: 3 When he had cut enough w for the
22: 6 Abraham took the w for the burnt
22: 7 "The fire and w are here," Isaac
22: 9 there and arranged the w on it.
22: 9 him on the altar, on top of the w.
30:37 the white inner w of the branches.
Ex 15:25 the LORD showed him a piece of w.
25: 5 red and hides of sea cows; acacia w;
25:10 "Have them make a chest of acacia w—
25:13 make poles of acacia w and overlay
25:23 "Make a table of acacia w—two
25:28 Make the poles of acacia w, overlay
26:15 "Make upright frames of acacia w for
26:26 "Also make crossbars of acacia w:
26:32 of acacia w overlaid with gold
26:37 of acacia w overlaid with gold.
27: 1 "Build an altar of acacia w, three
27: 6 Make poles of acacia w for the altar
30: 1 "Make an altar of acacia w for
30: 5 Make the poles of acacia w and
31: 5 to cut and set stones, to work in w,
35: 7 red and hides of sea cows; acacia w;
35:24 and everyone who had acacia w for
35:33 to cut and set stones, to work in w
36:20 They made upright frames of acacia w
36:31 They also made crossbars of acacia w:
36:36 They made four posts of acacia w for
37: 1 Bezalel made the ark of acacia w
37: 4 he made poles of acacia w and
37:10 They made the table of acacia w—two
37:15 made of acacia w and were overlaid
37:25 altar of incense out of acacia w.
37:28 They made the poles of acacia w and
Ex 38: 1 altar of burnt offering of acacia w,
38: 6 They made the poles of acacia w and
Lev 1: 7 the altar and arrange w on the fire.
1: 8 the burning w that is on the altar.
1:12 the burning w that is on the altar.
1:17 w that is on the fire on the altar.
3: 5 offering that is on the burning w,
4:12 burn it in a w fire on the ash heap.
11:32 made of w, cloth, hide or sackcloth.
14: 4 live clean birds and some cedar w,
14: 6 together with the cedar w, the
14:49 cedar w, scarlet yarn and hyssop.
14:51 he is to take the cedar w, the
14:52 cedar w, the hyssop and the scarlet
Nu 15:32 gathering w on the Sabbath day.
15:33 Those who found him gathering w
19: 6 The priest is to take some cedar w,
31:20 made of leather, goat hair or w."
Dt 4:28 man-made gods of w and stone,
10: 3 I made the ark out of acacia w and
19: 5 forest with his neighbour to cut w,
28:36 other gods, gods of w and stone.
28:64 other gods—gods of w and stone,
29:11 chop your w and carry your water.
29:17 of w and stone, of silver and gold.
Jdg 6:26 Using the w of the Asherah pole that
1Sa 6:14 The people chopped up the w of the
2Sa 24:22 and ox yokes for the w.
1Ki 6:23 of olive w, each ten cubits high.
6:31 of olive w with five-sided jambs.
6:32 on the two olive w doors he carved
6:33 jambs of olive w for the entrance
18:23 it on the w but not set fire to it.
18:23 it on the w but not set fire to it.
18:33 He arranged the w, cut the bull into
18:33 into pieces and laid it on the w.
18:33 it on the offering and on the w."
18:38 the w, the stones and the soil, and
2Ki 19:18 for they were not gods but only w
1Ch 21:23 the threshing-sledges for the w, and
22:14 to be weighed, and w and stone.
29: 2 iron for the iron and w for the w,
2Ch 2:14 bronze and iron, stone and w, and
Ne 10:34 times each year a contribution of w
13:31 of w at designated times, and for
Job 41:27 like straw and bronze like rotten w.
Pr 26:20 Without w a fire goes out; without
26:21 charcoal to embers and as w to fire,
SS 3: 9 he made it of w from Lebanon.
Isa 10:15 or a club brandish him who is not w!
30:33 with an abundance of fire and w; the
37:19 for they were not gods but only w
40:20 selects w that will not rot.
44:16 Half of the w he burns in the fire;
44:19 Shall I bow down to a block of w?"
45:20 idols of w, who pray to gods that
60:17 Instead of w I will bring you bronze,
Jer 2:27 They say to w, 'You are my father,'
3: 9 committed adultery with stone and w.
5:14 and these people the w it consumes.
7:18 The children gather w, the fathers
Lam 5: 4 our w can be had only at a price.
5:13 boys stagger under loads of w.
Eze 15: 2 "Son of man, how is the w of a vine
15: 3 Is w ever taken from it to make
15: 6 As I have given the w of the vine
20:32 of the world, who serve w and stone.
24: 5 take the pick of the flock. Pile w
24: 9 I, too, will pile the w high.
24:10 heap on the w and kindle the fire.
27: 6 of cypress w from the coasts of
37:16 "Son of man, take a stick of w and
37:16 Then take another stick of w, and
37:19 making them a single stick of w, and
39:10 They will not need to gather w from
41:16 the threshold was covered with w.
41:22 its base and its sides were of w.
Da 5: 4 of bronze, iron, w and stone.
5:23 of bronze, iron, w and stone, which
Hos 4:12 and are answered by a stick of w.
Hab 2:19 Woe to him who says to w, 'Come to
1Co 3:12 costly stones, w, hay or straw,
2Ti 2:20 but also of w and clay; some are for
Rev 9:20 silver, bronze, stone and w—idols
18:12 cloth; every sort of citron w,
18:12 costly w, bronze, iron and marble;

Woodcutters (Wood)
Jos 9:21 "Let them live, but let them be w
9:23 You will never cease to serve as w
9:27 That day he made the Gibeonites w

Wooded (Wood)
2Ch 27: 4 and forts and towers in the w areas.

Wooden (Wood)
Ex 7:19 in the w buckets and stone jars."
Lev 15:12 w article is to be rinsed with water.
Nu 35:18 Or if anyone has a w object in his
Dt 10: 1 the mountain. Also make a w chest.
16:21 Do not set up any w Asherah pole
Ne 8: 4 scribe stood on a high w platform
Isa 48: 5 w image and metal god ordained them.'
Jer 10: 8 are taught by worthless w idols.
28:13 LORD says: You have broken a w yoke,
Eze 41:22 There was a w altar three cubits
41:25 and there was a w overhang on the
Hos 4:12 of my people. They consult a w idol
10: 6 will be ashamed of its w idols.

Woodpile (Wood)
Zec 12: 6 of Judah like a brazier in a w,

Woods (Wood)
1Sa 14:25 The entire army entered the w, and
14:26 they went into the w, they saw the
2Ki 2:24 two bears came out of the w and

Woodsman (Wood, Man)
Isa 14: 8 low, no w comes to cut us down."

Woodsmen (Wood, Man)
2Ch 2:10 I will give your servants, the w who

Woodwork (Wood)
Hab 2:11 and the beams of the w will echo it.

Wooing
Job 36:16 "He is w you from the jaws of

Wool (Woollen)
Lev 13:48 or knitted material of linen or w,
13:52 or knitted material of w or linen,
Nu 19: 6 hyssop and scarlet w and throw them
Dt 18: 4 w from the shearing of your sheep,
22:11 Do not wear clothes of w and linen
Jdg 6:37 look, I will place a w fleece on the
2Ki 3: 4 the w of a hundred thousand rams.
Ps 147:16 He spreads the snow like w and
Pr 31:13 She selects w and flax and works
Isa 1:18 as crimson, they shall be like w.
51: 8 the worm will devour them like w.
Eze 27:18 wine from Helbon and w from Zahar.
34: 3 clothe yourselves with the w and
Da 7: 9 hair of his head was white like w.
Hos 2: 5 w and my linen, my oil and my drink.'
2: 9 I will take back my w and my linen,
Heb 9:19 together with water, scarlet w and
Rev 1:14 His head and hair were white like w,

Woollen (Wool)
Lev 13:47 mildew—any w or linen clothing,
13:59 by mildew in w or linen clothing,
Eze 44:17 they must not wear any w garment

Word (Byword, *Word of God, Word of the LORD, Word of the Lord*, Words)
Ge 24:21 Without saying a w, the man watched
27:45 I'll send w for you to come back
31: 4 Jacob sent w to Rachel and Leah to
37: 4 and could not speak a kind w to him.
37:14 the flocks, and bring w back to me.
41:44 "I am Pharaoh, but without your w
44:18 your servant speak a w to my lord.
50:16 they sent w to Joseph, saying, "Your
Ex 18: 6 Jethro had sent w to him, "I, your
36: 6 sent this w throughout the camp:
Nu 15:31 he has despised the LORD's w and
30: 2 he must not break his w but must do
Dt 8: 3 live on bread alone but on every w
30:14 No, the w is very near you; it is in
33: 9 watched over your w and guarded
Jos 1:18 Whoever rebels against your w and
6:10 do not say a w until the day I tell
8:35 There was not a w of all that Moses
10: 6 The Gibeonites then sent w to Joshua
10:21 uttered a w against the Israelites.
11: 1 he sent w to Jobab king of Madon, to
Jdg 11:36 "you have given your w to the LORD.
12: 6 could not pronounce the w correctly,
13:17 honour you when your w comes true?"
16:18 she sent w to the rulers of the
18:19 him, "Be quiet! Don't say a w.
1Sa 1:23 only may the LORD make good his w.
3:21 himself to Samuel through his w.
4: 1 Samuel's w came to all Israel. Now
14:39 But not one of the men said a w.
16:22 Saul sent w to Jesse, saying, "Allow
19:19 W came to Saul: "David is in Naioth
20:12 I not send you w and let you know?
25:12 they arrived, they reported every w.
25:39 Then David sent w to Abigail,
2Sa 3:11 not dare to say another w to Abner,
7:21 For the sake of your w and according
11: 5 The woman conceived and sent w to
11: 6 David sent this w to Joab: "Send me
12:25 sent w through Nathan the prophet
13: 7 David sent w to Tamar at the palace:
13:22 Absalom never said a w to Amnon,
14:12 speak a w to my lord the king.
14:17 'May the w of my lord the king bring
14:32 Absalom said to Joab, "Look, I sent w
15:28 w comes from you to inform me."
19:14 They sent w to the king, "Return,
23: 2 through me; his w was on my tongue.
24: 4 The king's w, however, overruled
1Ki 2:27 fulfilling the w the LORD had spoken
5: 8 Hiram sent w to Solomon: "I have
8:26 now, O God of Israel, let your w
8:56 Not one w has failed of all the good
12:15 to fulfil the w the LORD had spoken
17: 1 the next few years except at my w."
18:20 Ahab sent w throughout all Israel
20:33 and were quick to pick up his w.
21:14 they sent w to Jezebel: "Naboth has
22:13 Let your w agree with theirs, and
2Ki 2:22 to the w Elisha had spoken.
6: 9 The man of God sent w to the king of
10:10 Know then, that not a w the LORD has
10:21 he sent w throughout Israel, and all
18:25 this place without w from the LORD?
18:28 "Hear the w of the great king, the
19: 9 messengers to Hezekiah with this w:
19:21 This is the w that the LORD has
1Ch 13: 2 let us send w far and wide to the
16:15 the w he commanded, for a thousand
21: 4 The king's w, however, overruled
21:19 David went up in obedience to the w
2Ch 6:17 O LORD, God of Israel, let your w
10:15 to fulfil the w that the LORD had
18:12 Let your w agree with theirs, and
30: 1 Hezekiah sent w to all Israel and
36:15 the God of their fathers, sent w to
Ne 6: 1 w came to Sanballat, Tobiah, Geshem
8:15 that they should proclaim this w and
Est 7: 8 soon as the w left the king's mouth,
9:26 were called Purim, from the w pur.
Job 2:13 No-one said a w to him, because they
4: 2 "If someone ventures a w with you,
4:12 "A w was secretly brought to me, my
Ps 5: 9 Not a w from their mouth can be
17: 4 by the w of your lips I have kept
52: 4 You love every harmful w, O you
56: 4 In God, whose w I praise, in God I
56:10 In God, whose w I praise, in the
56:10 in the LORD, whose w I praise—
68:11 The Lord announced the w, and great
103:20 who do his bidding, who obey his w.
105: 8 the w he commanded, for a thousand
107:20 He sent forth his w and healed them;
119: 9 pure? By living according to your w.
119:11 I have hidden your w in my heart
119:16 decrees; I will not neglect your w.
119:17 and I will live; I will obey your w.
119:25 my life according to your w.
Ps 119:28 strengthen me according to your w.
119:37 my life according to your w.
119:42 taunts me, for I trust in your w.
119:43 Do not snatch the w of truth from my
119:49 Remember your w to your servant, for
119:65 servant according to your w, O LORD.
119:67 I went astray, but now I obey your w.
119:74 for I have put my hope in your w.
119:81 but I have put my hope in your w.
119:89 Your w, O LORD, is eternal; it
119:101 path so that I might obey your w.
119:105 Your w is a lamp to my feet and a
119:107 life, O LORD, according to your w.
119:114 I have put my hope in your w.
119:133 my footsteps according to your w;
119:147 help; I have put my hope in your w.
119:158 for they do not obey your w.
119:161 but my heart trembles at your w.
119:169 understanding according to your w.
119:172 May my tongue sing of your w, for
130: 5 waits, and in his w I put my hope.
138: 2 all things your name and your w.
139: 4 Before a w is on my tongue you know
143: 8 Let the morning bring me w of your
147:15 to the earth; his w runs swiftly.
147:18 He sends his w and melts them; he
147:19 He has revealed his w to Jacob, his
Pr 12:25 down, but a kind w cheers him up.
15: 1 wrath, but a harsh w stirs up anger.
15:23 reply—and how good is a timely w!
25:11 A w aptly spoken is like apples of
Ecc 7:21 Do not pay attention to every w
8: 4 Since a king's w is supreme, who can
Isa 5:24 the w of the Holy One of Israel.
8:20 this w, they have no light of dawn.
16:13 This is the w the LORD has already
23: 1 land of Cyprus w has come to them.
23: 5 w comes to Egypt, they will be in
24: 3 The LORD has spoken this w.
29:21 those who with a w make a man out to
37: 9 messengers to Hezekiah with this w:
37:22 this is the w the LORD has spoken
40: 8 the w of our God stands for ever."
45:23 a w that will not be revoked:
50: 4 know the w that sustains the weary.
50:10 LORD and obeys the w of his servant?
55:11 is my w that goes out from my mouth:
66: 2 in spirit, and trembles at my w.
66: 5 you who tremble at his w; "Your
Jer 1:12 to see that my w is fulfilled."
5:13 but wind and the w is not in them;
7: 1 This is the w that came to Jeremiah
11: 1 This is the w that came to Jeremiah
14:17 "Speak this w to them: "'Let my
18: 1 This is the w that came to Jeremiah
18:18 wise, nor the w from the prophets.
20: 9 his w is in my heart like a fire,
21: 1 The w came to Jeremiah from the LORD
23:18 w? Who has listened and heard his w?
23:28 who has my w speak it faithfully.
23:29 "Is not my w like fire," declares
23:36 because every man's own w becomes
25: 1 The w came to Jeremiah concerning
26: 1 of Judah, this w came from the LORD:
26: 2 I command you; do not omit a w.
27: 1 w came to Jeremiah from the LORD:
27: 3 send w to the kings of Edom, Moab,
30: 1 This is the w that came to Jeremiah
32: 1 This is the w that came to Jeremiah
34: 1 w came to Jeremiah from the LORD:
34: 8 The w came to Jeremiah from the LORD
35: 1 This is the w that came to Jeremiah
36: 1 w came to Jeremiah from the LORD:
37:17 "Is there any w from the LORD?"
40: 1 The w came to Jeremiah from the LORD
44: 1 This w came to Jeremiah concerning
44:28 whose w will stand—mine or theirs.
50: 1 This is the w the LORD spoke through
Lam 2:17 his w, which he decreed long ago.
Eze 3:17 so hear the w I speak and give them
6: 3 hear the w of the Sovereign LORD.
9:11 kit at his side brought back w,
25: 3 Say to them, 'Hear the w of the
33: 7 so hear the w I speak and give them
36: 4 O mountains of Israel, hear the w of
Am 3: 1 Hear this w the LORD has spoken

Am 4: 1 Hear this w, you cows of Bashan on
5: 1 Hear this w, O house of Israel, this
Zec 1:14 "Proclaim this w: This is what the
Mt 4: 4 every w that comes from the mouth
8: 8 hears the w, and my servant will be
8:16 with a w and healed all the sick.
12:32 Anyone who speaks a w against the
12:36 every careless w they have spoken.
13:20 hears the w and at once receives it
13:21 of the w, he quickly falls away.
13:22 thorns is the man who hears the w,
13:23 who hears the w and understands it.
14:35 w to all the surrounding country.
15:23 Jesus did not answer a w. So his
19:11 "Not everyone can accept this w, but
22:46 No-one could say a w in reply, and
26:75 Peter remembered the w Jesus had
Mk 2: 2 door, and he preached the w to them.
4:14 The farmer sows the w.
4:15 along the path, where the w is sown.
4:15 away the w that was sown in them.
4:16 hear the w and at once receive it
4:17 of the w, they quickly fall away.
4:18 seed sown among thorns, hear the w;
4:19 choke the w, making it unfruitful.
4:20 hear the w, accept it, and produce a
4:33 parables Jesus spoke the w to them,
14:72 Then Peter remembered the w Jesus
16:20 confirmed his w by the signs that
Lk 1: 2 eye-witnesses and servants of the w.
2:17 they had seen him, they spread the w
7: 7 say the w, and my servant will be
8:12 takes away the w from their hearts,
8:13 the w with joy when they hear it,
8:15 who hear the w, retain it, and by
8:21 God's w and put it into practice."
12:10 everyone who speaks a w against the
22:61 Then Peter remembered the w the Lord
24:19 "He was a prophet, powerful in w and
Jn 1: 1 In the beginning was the W, and the
1: 1 W was with God, and the W was God.
1:14 The W became flesh and made his
4:50 took Jesus at his w and departed.
5:24 whoever hears my w and believes him
5:38 nor does his w dwell in you, for you
7:26 and they are not saying a w to him.
8:37 because you have no room for my w.
8:51 keeps my w, he will never see death
8:52 your w, he will never taste death.
8:55 but I do know him and keep his w.
9: 7 Pool of Siloam" (this w means Sent).
11: 3 the sisters sent w to Jesus, "Lord,
12:17 the dead continued to spread the w.
12:38 This was to fulfil the w of Isaiah
12:48 that very w which I spoke will
15: 3 of the w I have spoken to you.
17: 6 to me and they have obeyed your w.
17:14 I have given them your w and the
17:17 them by the truth; your w is truth.
Ac 4:29 to speak your w with great boldness.
6: 4 prayer and the ministry of the w."
8: 4 preached the w wherever they went.
13:15 the synagogue rulers sent w to them,
14:25 they had preached the w in Perga,
15:27 by w of mouth what we are writing.
16: 6 the w in the province of Asia.
20:32 "Now I commit you to God and to the w
Ro 9: 6 is not as though God's w had failed.
10: 8 what does it say? "The w is near you;
10: 8 the w of faith we are proclaiming:
10:17 is heard through the w of Christ.
1Co 14: 6 or prophecy or w of instruction?
14:26 everyone has a hymn, or a w of
15: 2 firmly to the w I preached to you.
Gal 6: 6 who receives instruction in the w
Eph 1:13 Christ when you heard the w of truth,
5:26 washing with water through the w,
Php 2:16 you hold out the w of life—in order
Col 1: 5 about in the w of truth, the gospel
3:16 Let the w of Christ dwell in you
3:17 whatever you do, whether in w or
1Th 2:13 you accepted it not as the w of men,
4:15 According to the Lord's own w, we
2Th 2:15 whether by w of mouth or by letter.
2:17 you in every good deed and w.
2Ti 2: 9 But God's w is not chained.
2Ti 2:15 correctly handles the w of truth.
4: 2 Preach the W; be prepared in season
Tit 1: 3 brought his w to light through the
Heb 1: 3 all things by his powerful w.
5:12 truths of God's w all over again.
12: 5 you have forgotten that w of
12:19 that no further w be spoken to them,
12:24 a better w than the blood of Abel.
13:22 bear with my w of exhortation,
Jas 1:18 us birth through the w of truth,
1:21 w planted in you, which can save you.
1:22 Do not merely listen to the w, and
1:23 Anyone who listens to the w but does
1Pe 1:25 is the w that was preached to you.
3: 1 if any of them do not believe the w,
2Pe 1:19 we have the w of the prophets made
3: 5 ago by God's w the heavens existed
3: 7 By the same w the present heavens
1Jn 1: 1 proclaim concerning the W of life.
1:10 and his w has no place in our lives.
2: 5 if anyone obeys his w, God's love is
Rev 3: 8 kept my w and have not denied my
12:11 Lamb and by the w of their testimony;

Word of God

1Ki 12:22 this w came to Shemaiah the man of
1Ch 17: 3 That night the w came to Nathan,
Pr 30: 5 "Every w is flawless; he is a shield
Mt 15: 6 w for the sake of your tradition.
Mk 7:13 Thus you nullify the w by your
Lk 3: 2 the w came to John son of Zechariah
5: 1 round him and listening to the w,
8:11 of the parable: The seed is the w.
11:28 those who hear the w and obey it."
Jn 10:35 'gods', to whom the w came—and the
Ac 4:31 Holy Spirit and spoke the w boldly.
6: 2 of the w in order to wait on tables.
6: 7 the w spread. The number of
8:14 Samaria had accepted the w, they
11: 1 Gentiles also had received the w.
12:24 the w continued to increase and
13: 5 the w in the Jewish synagogues.
13: 7 Saul because he wanted to hear the w.
13:46 "We had to speak the w to you first.
17:13 Paul was preaching the w at Berea,
18:11 and a half, teaching them the w.
1Co 14:36 Did the w originate with you? Or are
2Co 2:17 we do not peddle the w for profit.
4: 2 deception, nor do we distort the w.
Eph 6:17 sword of the Spirit, which is the w.
Php 1:14 to speak the w more courageously
Col 1:25 to you the w in its fulness—
1Th 2:13 when you received the w, which you
2:13 but as it actually is, the w, which
1Ti 4: 5 it is consecrated by the w and
Tit 2: 5 so that no-one will malign the w.
Heb 4:12 For the w is living and active.
6: 5 who have tasted the goodness of the w
13: 7 leaders, who spoke the w to you.
1Pe 1:23 through the living and enduring w.
1Jn 2:14 are strong, and the w lives in you
Rev 1: 2 w and the testimony of Jesus Christ.
1: 9 of the w and the testimony of Jesus.
6: 9 who had been slain because of the w
19:13 in blood, and his name is the W.
20: 4 for Jesus and because of the w.

Word of the LORD

Ge 15: 1 After this, the w came to Abram in a
15: 4 the w came to him: "This man will
Ex 9:20 of Pharaoh who feared the w hurried
9:21 those who ignored the w left their
Nu 3:16 them, as he was commanded by the w.
3:51 sons, as he was commanded by the w.
Dt 5: 5 LORD and you to declare to you the w,
1Sa 3: 1 In those days the w was rare; there
3: 7 w had not yet been revealed to him.
15:10 Then the w came to Samuel:
15:23 the w, he has rejected you as king."
15:26 You have rejected the w, and the
2Sa 7: 4 That night the w came to Nathan,
12: 9 Why did you despise the w by doing
22:31 way is perfect; the w is flawless.
24:11 the w had come to Gad the prophet,
1Ki 6:11 The w came to Solomon:
1Ki 12:24 So they obeyed the w and went home
13: 1 By the w a man of God came from
13: 2 the altar by the w: "O altar,
13: 5 given by the man of God by the w.
13: 9 For I was commanded by the w: 'You
13:17 I have been told by the w: 'You must
13:18 And an angel said to me by the w:
13:20 the w came to the old prophet who
13:21 'You have defied the w and have not
13:26 is the man of God who defied the w.
13:26 him, as the w had warned him."
13:32 For the message he declared by the w
15:29 according to the w given through his
16: 1 the w came to Jehu son of Hanani
16: 7 Moreover, the w came through the
16:12 in accordance with the w spoken
16:34 the w spoken by Joshua son of Nun.
17: 2 Then the w came to Elijah:
17: 8 Then the w came to him:
17:16 keeping with the w spoken by Elijah.
17:24 the w from your mouth is the truth."
18: 1 in the third year, the w came to
18:31 to whom the w had come, saying,
19: 9 And the w came to him: "What are you
20:35 By the w one of the sons of the
21:17 the w came to Elijah the Tishbite:
21:28 the w came to Elijah the Tishbite:
22:19 "Therefore hear the w: I saw the
22:38 up his blood, as the w had declared.
2Ki 1:17 he died, according to the w that
3:12 Jehoshaphat said, "The w is with him.
4:44 some left over, according to the w.
7: 1 Elisha said, "Hear the w. This is
9:26 plot, in accordance with the w."
9:36 "This is the w that he spoke through
10:17 according to the w spoken to Elijah.
14:25 in accordance with the w, the God of
15:12 the w spoken to Jehu was fulfilled:
20: 4 the middle court, the w came to him:
20:16 Isaiah said to Hezekiah, "Hear the w:
20:19 "The w you have spoken is good,"
23:16 in accordance with the w proclaimed
24: 2 in accordance with the w proclaimed
1Ch 10:13 to the LORD; he did not keep the w,
15:15 commanded in accordance with the w.
22: 8 this w came to me: 'You have shed
2Ch 11: 2 this w came to Shemaiah the man of
12: 7 this w came to Shemaiah: "Since they
18:18 "Therefore hear the w: I saw the
29:15 king had ordered, following the w.
30:12 had ordered, following the w.
34:21 our fathers have not kept the w;
36:12 the prophet, who spoke the w.
36:21 of the w spoken by Jeremiah.
36:22 in order to fulfil the w spoken by
Ezr 1: 1 in order to fulfil the w spoken by
Ps 18:30 way is perfect; the w is flawless.
33: 4 For the w is right and true; he is
33: 6 By the w were the heavens made,
105:19 to pass, till the w proved him true.
Isa 1:10 Hear the w, you rulers of Sodom;
2: 3 out from Zion, the w from Jerusalem.
28:13 then, the w to them will become: Do
28:14 Therefore hear the w, you scoffers
38: 4 Then the w came to Isaiah:
39: 5 Isaiah said to Hezekiah, "Hear the w
39: 8 "The w you have spoken is good,"
66: 5 Hear the w, you who tremble at his
Jer 1: 2 The w came to him in the thirteenth
1: 4 The w came to me, saying,
1:11 The w came to me: "What do you see,
1:13 The w came to me again: "What do you
2: 1 The w came to me:
2: 4 Hear the w, O house of Jacob, all
2:31 consider the w: "Have I been a
6:10 The w is offensive to them; they
7: 2 'Hear the w, all you people of Judah
8: 9 Since they have rejected the w,
9:20 Now, O women, hear the w; open your
13: 3 the w came to me a second time:
13: 8 Then the w came to me:
14: 1 This is the w to Jeremiah concerning
16: 1 Then the w came to me:
17:15 is the w? Let it now be fulfilled!"
17:20 Say to them, 'Hear the w, O kings of
18: 5 Then the w came to me:

Jer 19: 3 say, ‘Hear the w, O kings of Judah
20: 8 So the w has brought me insult and
21:11 royal house of Judah, ‘Hear the w;
22: 2 ‘Hear the w, O king of Judah, you
22:29 O land, land, land, hear the w!
24: 4 Then the w came to me:
25: 3 this very day—the w has come to me
27:18 If they are prophets and have the w,
28:12 Jeremiah, the w came to Jeremiah:
29:20 Therefore, hear the w, all you
29:30 Then the w came to Jeremiah:
31:10 “Hear the w, O nations; proclaim it
32: 6 Jeremiah said, “The w came to me:
32: 8 “I knew that this was the w;
32:26 Then the w came to Jeremiah:
33: 1 the w came to him a second time:
33:19 The w came to Jeremiah:
33:23 The w came to Jeremiah:
34:12 Then the w came to Jeremiah:
35:12 the w came to Jeremiah, saying:
36:27 dictation, the w came to Jeremiah:
37: 6 the w came to Jeremiah the prophet:
39:15 of the guard, the w came to him:
42: 7 Ten days later the w came to
42:15 hear the w, O remnant of Judah. This
43: 8 In Tahpanhes the w came to Jeremiah:
44:24 “Hear the w, all you people of Judah
44:26 hear the w, all Jews living in Egypt:
46: 1 This is the w that came to Jeremiah
47: 1 This is the w that came to Jeremiah
49:34 This is the w that came to Jeremiah
Eze 1: 3 the w came to Ezekiel the priest,
3:16 At the end of seven days the w came
6: 1 The w came to me:
7: 1 The w came to me:
11:14 The w came to me:
12: 1 The w came to me:
12: 8 In the morning the w came to me:
12:17 The w came to me:
12:21 The w came to me:
12:26 The w came to me:
13: 1 The w came to me:
13: 2 their own imagination: ‘Hear the w!
14: 2 Then the w came to me:
14:12 The w came to me:
15: 1 The w came to me:
16: 1 The w came to me:
16:35 you prostitute, hear the w!
17: 1 The w came to me:
17:11 Then the w came to me:
18: 1 The w came to me:
20: 2 Then the w came to me:
20:45 The w came to me:
20:47 to the southern forest: ‘Hear the w.
21: 1 The w came to me:
21: 8 The w came to me:
21:18 The w came to me:
22: 1 The w came to me:
22:17 Then the w came to me:
22:23 Again the w came to me:
23: 1 The w came to me:
24: 1 on the tenth day, the w came to me:
24:15 The w came to me:
24:20 I said to them, “The w came to me:
25: 1 The w came to me:
26: 1 day of the month, the w came to me:
27: 1 The w came to me:
28: 1 The w came to me:
28:11 The w came to me:
28:20 The w came to me:
29: 1 the twelfth day, the w came to me:
29:17 on the first day, the w came to me:
30: 1 The w came to me:
30:20 the seventh day, the w came to me:
31: 1 on the first day, the w came to me:
32: 1 on the first day, the w came to me:
32:17 day of the month, the w came to me:
33: 1 The w came to me:
33:23 Then the w came to me:
34: 1 The w came to me:
34: 7 Therefore, you shepherds, hear the w:
34: 9 therefore, O shepherds, hear the w:
35: 1 The w came to me:
36: 1 ‘O mountains of Israel, hear the w.
36:16 Again the w came to me:
37: 4 say to them, ‘Dry bones, hear the w!
Eze 37:15 The w came to me:
38: 1 The w came to me:
Da 9: 2 according to the w given to Jeremiah
Hos 1: 1 The w that came to Hosea son of
4: 1 Hear the w, you Israelites, because
Joel 1: 1 The w that came to Joel son of
Am 7:16 Now then, hear the w. You say, “‘Do
8:12 the w, but they will not find it.
Jnh 1: 1 The w came to Jonah son of Amittai:
3: 1 the w came to Jonah a second time:
3: 3 Jonah obeyed the w and went to
Mic 1: 1 The w that came to Micah of
4: 2 out from Zion, the w from Jerusalem.
Zep 1: 1 The w that came to Zephaniah son of
2: 5 O Kerethite people; the w is against
Hag 1: 1 the w came through the prophet
1: 3 the w came through the prophet
2: 1 w came through the prophet Haggai:
2:10 the w came to the prophet Haggai:
2:20 The w came to Haggai a second time
Zec 1: 1 the w came to the prophet Zechariah
1: 7 in the second year of Darius, the w
4: 6 he said to me, “This is the w to
4: 8 Then the w came to me:
6: 9 The w came to me:
7: 1 the w came to Zechariah on the
7: 4 Then the w Almighty came to me:
7: 8 the w came again to Zechariah:
8: 1 Again the w Almighty came to me.
8:18 Again the w Almighty came to me.
9: 1 The w is against the land of Hadrach
11:11 were watching me knew it was the w.
12: 1 This is the w concerning Israel. The
Mal 1: 1 An oracle: The w to Israel through

Word of the Lord

Ac 8:25 had testified and proclaimed the w,
13:44 whole city gathered to hear the w.
13:48 they were glad and honoured the w;
13:49 The w spread through the whole
15:35 others taught and preached the w.
15:36 the w and see how they are doing.”
16:32 they spoke the w to him and to all
19:10 in the province of Asia heard the w.
19:20 In this way the w spread widely and
1Pe 1:25 the w stands for ever.” And this is

Words (Word)

Ge 4:23 to me; wives of Lamech, hear my w.
27:34 Esau heard his father’s w, he burst
42:16 so that your w may be tested to see
42:20 so that your w may be verified and
44: 6 them, he repeated these w to them.
Ex 4:15 You shall speak to him and put w in
19: 6 These are the w you are to speak to
19: 7 set before them all the w the Lord
20: 1 And God spoke all these w:
23: 8 and twists the w of the righteous.
24: 3 people all the Lord’s w and laws,
24: 8 you in accordance with all these w.”
33: 4 the people heard these distressing w,
34: 1 and I will write on them the w that
34:27 said to Moses, “Write down these w,
34:27 for in accordance with these w I
34:28 And he wrote on the tablets the w of
Nu 12: 6 he said, “Listen to my w: “When a
24: 4 the oracle of one who hears the w of
24:16 the oracle of one who hears the w of
Dt 1: 1 These are the w Moses spoke to all
4:10 to hear my w so that they may learn
4:12 You heard the sound of w but saw no
4:36 heard his w from out of the fire.
10: 2 I will write on the tablets the w
11:18 Fix these w of mine in your hearts
13: 3 you must not listen to the w of that
16:19 and twists the w of the righteous.
17:19 the w of this law and these decrees
18:18 I will put my w in his mouth,
18:19 If anyone does not listen to my w
27: 3 Write on them all the w of this law
27: 8 shall write very clearly all the w
27:26 w of this law by carrying them out.
28:58 follow all the w of this law,
29:19 such a person hears the w of this
29:29 we may follow all the w of this law.
Dt 31: 1 Moses went out and spoke these w to
31:12 carefully all the w of this law.
31:24 w of this law from beginning to end,
31:28 so that I can speak these w in their
31:30 Moses recited the w of this song
32: 1 hear, O earth, the w of my mouth.
32: 2 like rain and my w descend like dew,
32:44 spoke all the w of this song in the
32:45 Moses finished reciting all these w
32:46 “Take to heart all the w I have
32:46 carefully all the w of this law.
32:47 They are not just idle w for you—
Jos 1:18 your word and does not obey your w,
3: 9 to the w of the Lord your God.
8:34 Afterwards, Joshua read all the w of
24:27 It has heard all the w the Lord has
Jdg 11:11 all his w before the Lord in Mizpah.
13:12 Manoah asked him, “When your w are
1Sa 3:19 none of his w fall to the ground.
8:10 Samuel told all the w of the Lord to
11: 6 Saul heard their w, the Spirit of
17:11 On hearing the Philistine’s w, Saul
18:23 They repeated these w to David. But
21:12 David took these w to heart and was
24: 7 With these w David rebuked his men
25:35 your w and granted your request.”
26:19 the king listen to his servant’s w.
28:20 with fear because of Samuel’s w.
2Sa 7:17 Nathan reported to David all the w
7:28 you are God! Your w are trustworthy
14: 3 go to the king and speak these w to
14: 3 And Joab put the w in her mouth.
14:19 w into the mouth of your servant.
22: 1 David sang to the Lord the w of this
23: 1 These are the last w of David: “The
1Ki 8:59 may these w of mine, which I have
21:27 Ahab heard these w, he tore his
22:28 Then he added, “Mark my w, all you
2Ki 6:12 very w you speak in your bedroom.”
6:30 the king heard the woman’s w, he
18:20 but you speak only empty w.
19: 4 all the w of the field commander,
19: 4 the w the Lord your God has heard.
19: 6 those w with which the underlings of
19:16 listen to the w Sennacherib has
22:11 the king heard the w of the Book of
22:13 have not obeyed the w of this book;
22:18 says concerning the w you heard:
23: 2 He read in their hearing all the w
23: 3 thus confirming the w of the
1Ch 17:15 Nathan reported to David all the w
2Ch 11: 4 So they obeyed the w of the Lord
15: 8 Asa heard these w and the prophecy
18:27 Then he added, “Mark my w, all you
29:30 w of David and of Asaph the seer.
32: 6 and encouraged them with these w:
33:18 the w the seers spoke to him in the
34:19 the king heard the w of the Law, he
34:26 says concerning the w you heard:
34:30 He read in their hearing all the w
34:31 and to obey the w of the covenant
36:16 despised his w and scoffed at his
Ezr 9: 4 everyone who trembled at the w of
Ne 1: 1 The w of Nehemiah son of Hacaliah:
8: 9 they listened to the w of the Law.
8:12 w that had been made known to them.
8:13 give attention to the w of the Law.
Est 4:12 Esther’s w were reported to Mordecai,
9:30 Xerxes—w of goodwill and assurance—
Job 4: 4 Your w have supported those who
6: 3 no wonder my w have been impetuous.
6:10 not denied the w of the Holy One.
6:25 How painful are honest w! But what
6:26 the w of a despairing man as wind?
8: 2 Your w are a blustering wind.
8:10 forth w from their understanding?
9:14 How can I find w to argue with him?
11: 2 “Are all these w to go unanswered?
12:11 Does not the ear test w as the
13:17 Listen carefully to my w; let your
15: 3 Would he argue with useless w, with
15:11 for you, w spoken gently to you?
15:13 and pour out such w from your mouth?
19: 2 you torment me and crush me with w?
19:23 “Oh, that my w were recorded, that
21: 2 “Listen carefully to my w; let this

Job 22:22 and lay up his w in your heart.
23:12 I have treasured the w of his mouth
24:25 false and reduce my w to nothing?"
26: 4 Who has helped you utter these w?
29:22 my w fell gently on their ears.
29:23 drank in my w as the spring rain.
31:40 The w of Job are ended.
32:11 while you were searching for w,
32:14 Job has not marshalled his w against
32:15 no more to say; w have failed them.
32:18 For I am full of w, and the spirit
33: 1 "But now, Job, listen to my w; pay
33: 2 my w are on the tip of my tongue.
33: 3 My w come from an upright heart; my
33: 8 in my hearing—I heard the very w—
33:13 him that he answers none of man's w?
34: 2 "Hear my w, you wise men; listen to
34: 3 For the ear tests w as the tongue
34:35 'Job speaks without knowledge; his w
34:37 and multiplies his w against God."
35:16 without knowledge he multiplies w."
36: 4 Be assured that my w are not false;
38: 2 my counsel with w without knowledge?
41: 3 Will he speak to you with gentle w?
Ps 5: 1 Give ear to my w, O LORD, consider
12: 6 the w of the LORD are flawless, like
18: T sang to the LORD the w of this song
19: 4 their w to the ends of the world.
19:14 May the w of my mouth and the
22: 1 so far from the w of my groaning?
36: 3 The w of his mouth are wicked and
49: 3 My mouth will speak w of wisdom; the
50:17 You hate my instruction and cast my w
54: 2 O God; listen to the w of my mouth.
55:21 his w are more soothing than oil,
56: 5 All day long they twist my w; they
59:12 for the w of their lips, let them be
64: 3 and aim their w like deadly arrows.
78: 1 listen to the w of my mouth.
94: 4 They pour out arrogant w; all the
105:28 had they not rebelled against his w?
106:33 and rash w came from Moses' lips.
107:11 for they had rebelled against the w
109: 3 With w of hatred they surround me;
119:57 LORD; I have promised to obey your w.
119:103 How sweet are your w to my taste,
119:130 The unfolding of your w gives light;
119:139 out, for my enemies ignore your w.
119:160 All your w are true; all your
138: 4 when they hear the w of your mouth.
141: 6 learn that my w were well spoken.
Pr 1: 2 for understanding w of insight;
2: 1 My son, if you accept my w and store
2:12 men, from men whose w are perverse,
2:16 wayward wife with her seductive w,
4: 4 "Lay hold of my w with all your
4: 5 not forget my w or swerve from them.
4:20 what I say; listen closely to my w.
5: 1 listen well to my w of insight,
6: 2 ensnared by the w of your mouth,
7: 1 My son, keep my w and store up my
7: 5 wayward wife with her seductive w.
7:21 With persuasive w she led him astray;
8: 8 All the w of my mouth are just; none
10:19 When w are many, sin is not absent,
12: 6 The w of the wicked lie in wait for
12:18 Reckless w pierce like a sword, but
16:21 and pleasant w promote instruction.
16:24 Pleasant w are a honeycomb, sweet to
17:27 A man of knowledge uses w with
18: 4 The w of a man's mouth are deep
18: 8 The w of a gossip are like choice
19:27 will stray from the w of knowledge.
22:12 frustrates the w of the unfaithful.
22:21 teaching you true and reliable w, so
23: 9 he will scorn the wisdom of your w.
23:12 and your ears to w of knowledge.
26:22 The w of a gossip are like choice
29:19 cannot be corrected by mere w;
30: 6 Do not add to his w, or he will
Ecc 1: 1 The w of the Teacher, son of David,
5: 2 are on earth, so let your w be few.
5: 3 of a fool when there are many w.
5: 7 Much dreaming and many w are
6:11 The more the w, the less the meaning,
9:16 and his w are no longer heeded.
Ecc 9:17 The quiet w of the wise are more to
10:12 W from a wise man's mouth are
10:13 At the beginning his w are folly; at
10:14 the fool multiplies w. No-one knows
10:20 a bird of the air may carry your w,
12:10 searched to find just the right w,
12:11 The w of the wise are like goads,
Isa 3: 8 Judah is falling; their w and deeds
29:11 is nothing but w sealed in a scroll.
29:18 In that day the deaf will hear the w
31: 2 he does not take back his w.
36: 5 but you speak only empty w.
36:13 "Hear the w of the great king, the
37: 4 hear the w of the field commander,
37: 4 the w the LORD your God has heard.
37: 6 those w with which the underlings of
37:17 listen to all the w Sennacherib has
41:26 it, no-one heard any w from you.
44:26 who carries out the w of his
51:16 I have put my w in your mouth and
58:13 as you please or speaking idle w,
59:21 "My Spirit, who is on you, and my w
Jer 1: 1 The w of Jeremiah son of Hilkiah,
1: 9 "Now, I have put my w in your mouth.
5:14 the people have spoken these w,
5:14 I will make my w in your mouth a
6:19 to my w and have rejected my law.
7: 4 Do not trust in deceptive w and say,
7: 8 look, you are trusting in deceptive w
9:20 your ears to the w of his mouth.
11: 6 "Proclaim all these w in the towns
11:10 who refused to listen to my w.
13:10 who refuse to listen to my w, who
15:16 your w came, I ate them; they were
15:19 you utter worthy, not worthless, w
19: 2 There proclaim the w I tell you,
19:15 and would not listen to my w.
23: 9 because of the LORD and his holy w.
23:22 they would have proclaimed my w to
23:30 one another w supposedly from me.
23:36 you distort the w of the living God,
23:38 You used the w, 'This is the oracle
25: 8 you have not listened to my w,
25:30 "Now prophesy all these w against
26: 5 if you do not listen to the w of my
26: 7 these w in the house of the LORD.
26:15 speak all these w in your hearing."
26:21 officers and officials heard his w,
27:14 Do not listen to the w of the
28: 6 May the LORD fulfil the w you have
29:19 For they have not listened to my w,"
29:19 "w that I sent to them again and
30: 2 book all the w I have spoken to you.
30: 4 These are the w the LORD spoke
31:23 use these w: 'The LORD bless you,
35:13 and obey my w?' declares the LORD.
36: 2 write on it all the w I have spoken
36: 4 the w the LORD had spoken to him,
36: 6 from the scroll the w of the LORD
36: 8 the w of the LORD from the scroll.
36:10 the w of Jeremiah from the scroll.
36:11 the w of the LORD from the scroll,
36:16 they heard all these w, they looked
36:16 report all these w to the king."
36:18 "he dictated all these w to me, and
36:24 heard all these w showed no fear,
36:27 burned the scroll containing the w
36:28 the w that were on the first scroll,
36:32 Baruch wrote on it all the w of the
36:32 many similar w were added to them.
37: 2 paid any attention to the w the
39:16 says: I am about to fulfil my w
43: 1 all the w of the LORD their God
45: 1 the w Jeremiah was then dictating:
51:61 see that you read all these w aloud.
51:64 The w of Jeremiah end here.
Eze 2: 6 do not be afraid of them or their w.
2: 7 You must speak my w to them, whether
2:10 w of lament and mourning and woe.
3: 4 of Israel and speak my w to them.
3: 6 whose w you cannot understand.
3:10 to heart all the w I speak to you.
12:28 None of my w will be delayed any
13: 6 they expect their w to be fulfilled.
13: 8 of your false w and lying visions,
33:31 sit before you to listen to your w,
Eze 33:32 w but do not put them into practice.
Da 4:31 The w were still on his lips when a
5:26 "This is what these w mean: Mene:
7:11 boastful w the horn was speaking.
9:12 You have fulfilled the w spoken
10:11 consider carefully the w I am about
10:12 your w were heard, and I have come
12: 4 you, Daniel, close up and seal the w
12: 9 "Go your way, Daniel, because the w
Hos 6: 5 I killed you with the w of my mouth;
7:16 sword because of their insolent w.
14: 2 Take w with you and return to the
Am 1: 1 The w of Amos, one of the shepherds
7:10 The land cannot bear all his w.
8:11 famine of hearing the w of the LORD.
Mic 2: 7 "Do not my w do good to him whose
7: 5 your embrace be careful of your w.
Zec 1: 6 did not my w and my decrees, which I
1:13 the LORD spoke kind and comforting w
7: 7 Are these not the w the LORD
7:12 not listen to the law or to the w
8: 9 "You who now hear these w spoken by
Mal 2:17 You have wearied the LORD with your w
Mt 6: 7 be heard because of their many w.
7:24 "Therefore everyone who hears these w
7:26 everyone who hears these w of mine
10:14 not welcome you or listen to your w,
12: 7 If you had known what these w mean,
12:37 For by your w you will be acquitted,
12:37 by your w you will be condemned."
22:15 and laid plans to trap him in his w.
24:35 away, but my w will never pass away.
Mk 8:38 If anyone is ashamed of me and my w
10:24 The disciples were amazed at his w.
12:13 to Jesus to catch him in his w.
13:31 away, but my w will never pass away.
Lk 1:20 because you did not believe my w,
1:29 Mary was greatly troubled at his w
3: 4 is written in the book of the w of
3:18 with many other w John exhorted the
4:22 gracious w that came from his lips.
6:47 my w and puts them into practice.
6:49 the one who hears my w and does not
7:29 when they heard Jesus' w,
9:26 If anyone is ashamed of me and my w,
19:22 'I will judge you by your own w, you
19:48 all the people hung on his w.
21:15 For I will give you w and wisdom
21:33 away, but my w will never pass away.
24: 8 Then they remembered his w.
24:11 w seemed to them like nonsense.
Jn 1:23 John replied in the w of Isaiah
2:22 and the w that Jesus had spoken.
3:34 God has sent speaks the w of God,
4:41 of his w many more became believers.
6:63 The w I have spoken to you are
6:68 go? You have the w of eternal life.
7:40 On hearing his w, some of the people
8:20 He spoke these w while teaching in
10:19 At these w the Jews were again
12:47 "As for the person who hears my w
12:48 rejects me and does not accept my w;
14:10 w I say to you are not just my own.
14:24 These w you hear are not my own;
15: 7 If you remain in me and my w remain
15:20 Remember the w I spoke to you: 'No
17: 8 For I gave them the w you gave me
18: 9 This happened so that the w he had
18:32 This happened so that the w Jesus
Ac 2:40 With many other w he warned them;
6:11 "We have heard Stephen speak w of
7:35 the w, 'Who made you ruler and judge?
7:38 received living w to pass on to us.
10:44 Peter was still speaking these w,
13:27 they fulfilled the w of the prophets
13:34 to decay, is stated in these w:
14:18 Even with these w, they had
15:15 The w of the prophets are in
18:15 since it involves questions about w
20: 2 speaking many w of encouragement to
20:35 remembering the w the Lord Jesus
22:14 One and to hear w from his mouth.
Ro 3: 2 entrusted with the very w of God.
4:23 The w "it was credited to him" were
8:26 with groans that w cannot express.
9: 8 In other w, it is not the natural

Ro 10:18 their w to the ends of the world."
1Co 1:17 gospel—not with w of human wisdom,
2: 4 were not with wise and persuasive w,
2:13 This is what we speak, not in w
2:13 but in w taught by the Spirit,
2:13 spiritual truths in spiritual w.
14: 9 Unless you speak intelligible w with
14:19 intelligible w to instruct others
14:19 than ten thousand w in a tongue.
Gal 5: 2 Mark my w! I, Paul, tell you that if
Eph 5: 6 Let no-one deceive you with empty w,
6:19 that whenever I open my mouth, w may
1Th 1: 5 came to you not simply with w,
4:18 encourage each other with these w.
1Ti 6: 4 quarrels about w that result in
2Ti 2:14 about w; it is of no value,
Heb 4: 4 about the seventh day in these w:
12:19 speaking w that those who heard it
12:27 The w "once more" indicate the
1Pe 3: 1 won over without w by the behaviour
4:11 as one speaking the very w of God.
2Pe 2:18 For they mouth empty, boastful w and,
3: 2 I want you to recall the w spoken in
1Jn 3:18 Dear children, let us not love with w
Jude :15 and of all the harsh w ungodly
Rev 1: 3 Blessed is the one who reads the w
2: 1 These are the w of him who holds the
2: 8 These are the w of him who is the
2:12 are the w of him who has the sharp,
2:18 These are the w of the Son of God,
3: 1 These are the w of him who holds the
3: 7 the w of him who is holy and true,
3:14 write: These are the w of the Amen,
13: 5 was given a mouth to utter proud w
17:17 rule, until God's w are fulfilled.
19: 9 added, "These are the true w of God.
21: 5 these w are trustworthy and true."
22: 6 The angel said to me, "These w are
22: 7 the w of the prophecy in this book."
22: 9 of all who keep the w of this book.
22:10 he told me, "Do not seal up the w of
22:18 I warn everyone who hears the w of
22:19 if anyone takes w away from this

Wore (Wear)

Jos 9: 5 on their feet and w old clothes.
1Sa 17: 5 w a coat of scale armour of bronze
17: 6 on his legs he w bronze greaves, and
22:18 men who w the linen ephod.
2Sa 13:18 the virgin daughters of the king w.
1Ch 15:27 David also w a linen ephod.
Ne 4:18 each of the builders w his sword at
Ps 109:18 He w cursing as his garment; it
Mk 1: 6 John w clothing made of camel's hair,
Rev 9: 7 On their heads they w something like
15: 6 w golden sashes round their chests.

Work (*Good work*, Hardworking, Metalworker, *Work of God*, Worked, Worker, Workers, Working, Workman, Workman's, Workmanship, Workmen, Works)

Ge 2: 2 finished the w he had been doing;
2: 2 day he rested from all his w.
2: 3 the w of creating that he had done.
2: 5 there was no man to w the ground,
2:15 of Eden to w it and take care of it.
3:23 to w the ground from which he had
4:12 you w the ground, it will no longer
29:15 should you w for me for nothing?
29:18 "I'll w for you seven years in
29:27 for another seven years of w."
30:26 know how much w I've done for you."
Ex 1:14 with all kinds of w in the fields;
5: 4 their labour? Get back to your w!"
5: 9 Make the w harder for the men so
5:11 your w will not be reduced at all.
5:13 "Complete the w required of you for
5:18 Now get to w. You will not be given
12:16 Do no w at all on these days, except
18:18 The w is too heavy for you; you
20: 9 you shall labour and do all your w,
20:10 On it you shall not do any w,
23:12 "Six days do your w, but on the
23:12 but on the seventh day do not w, so
Ex 26:36 linen—the w of an embroiderer.
27:16 finely twisted linen—the w of an
28: 6 linen—the w of a skilled craftsman.
28:15 the w of a skilled craftsman.
28:39 is to be the w of an embroiderer.
30:25 fragrant blend, the w of a perfumer.
30:35 of incense, the w of a perfumer.
31: 4 to make artistic designs for w in
31: 5 to cut and set stones, to w in wood,
31:14 whoever does any w on that day must
31:15 For six days, w is to be done, but
31:15 Whoever does any w on the Sabbath
31:17 day he abstained from w and rested.
34:10 w that I, the LORD, will do for you.
35: 2 For six days, w is to be done, but
35: 2 any w on it must be put to death.
35:21 for the w on the Tent of Meeting,
35:24 for any part of the w brought it.
35:29 freewill offerings for all the w
35:32 to make artistic designs for w in
35:33 to cut and set stones, to w in wood
35:35 to do all kinds of w as craftsmen,
36: 1 the w of constructing the sanctuary
36: 1 w just as the LORD has commanded."
36: 2 was willing to come and do the w.
36: 3 the w of constructing the sanctuary.
36: 4 the w on the sanctuary left their w
36: 5 w the LORD commanded to be done."
36: 7 more than enough to do all the w.
36:37 linen—the w of an embroiderer;
37:29 incense—the w of a perfumer.
38:18 linen—the w of an embroiderer.
38:24 w on the sanctuary was 29 talents
39: 3 linen—the w of a skilled craftsman.
39: 8 the breastpiece—the w of a skilled
39:22 of blue cloth—the w of a weaver—
39:27 of fine linen—the w of a weaver—
39:29 purple and scarlet yarn—the w of an
39:32 all the w on the tabernacle, the
39:42 The Israelites had done all the w
39:43 Moses inspected the w and saw that
40:33 And so Moses finished the w.
Lev 16:29 not do any w—whether native-born or
23: 3 "'There are six days when you may w,
23: 3 You are not to do any w; wherever
23: 7 sacred assembly and do no regular w.
23: 8 sacred assembly and do no regular w.
23:21 sacred assembly and do no regular w.
23:25 Do no regular w, but present an
23:28 Do no w on that day, because it is
23:30 anyone who does any w on that day.
23:31 You shall do no w at all. This is to
23:35 a sacred assembly; do no regular w.
23:36 closing assembly; do no regular w.
25:39 you, do not make him w as a slave.
25:40 w for you until the Year of Jubilee.
Nu 3: 7 by doing the w of the tabernacle.
3: 8 by doing the w of the tabernacle.
4: 3 in the w in the Tent of Meeting.
4: 4 "This is the w of the Kohathites in
4:19 man his w and what he is to carry.
4:23 in the w at the Tent of Meeting.
4:24 clans as they w and carry burdens:
4:27 whether carrying or doing other w,
4:30 in the w at the Tent of Meeting.
4:33 Merarite clans as they w at the
4:35 in the w in the Tent of Meeting,
4:39 in the w at the Tent of Meeting,
4:43 in the w at the Tent of Meeting,
4:47 age who came to do the w of serving
4:49 his w and told what to carry.
7: 5 in the w at the Tent of Meeting.
7: 5 Levites as each man's w requires."
7: 7 Gershonites, as their w required,
7: 8 the Merarites, as their w required.
8:11 be ready to do the w of the LORD.
8:15 do their w at the Tent of Meeting.
8:19 his sons to do the w at the Tent of
8:22 the Levites came to do their w at
8:24 in the w at the Tent of Meeting,
8:25 regular service and w no longer.
8:26 they themselves must not do the w.
16: 9 brought you near himself to do the w
18: 4 of Meeting—all the w at the Tent
18: 6 to do the w at the Tent of Meeting.
18:21 in return for the w they do while
Nu 18:23 is the Levites who are to do the w
18:31 for your w at the Tent of Meeting.
28:18 sacred assembly and do no regular w.
28:25 sacred assembly and do no regular w.
28:26 sacred assembly and do no regular w.
29: 1 sacred assembly and do no regular w.
29: 7 You must deny yourselves and do no w.
29:12 sacred assembly and do no regular w.
29:35 an assembly and do no regular w.
Dt 2: 7 you in all the w of your hands.
5:13 you shall labour and do all your w,
5:14 On it you shall not do any w,
14:29 you in all the w of your hands.
15:10 God will bless you in all your w
15:19 put the firstborn of your oxen to w,
16: 8 to the LORD your God and do no w.
16:15 and in all the w of your hands,
20:11 forced labour and shall w for you.
24:19 you in all the w of your hands.
27:15 the w of the craftsman's hands—and
28:12 to bless all the w of your hands.
30: 9 in all the w of your hands and in
33:11 be pleased with the w of his hands.
Jdg 13:12 the rule for the boy's life and w?"
19:16 came in from his w in the fields.
Ru 2:19 Where did you w? Blessed be the man
2Sa 12:31 and he made them w at brickmaking.
1Ki 5: 6 My men will w with yours, and I will
7:14 in all kinds of bronze w.
7:14 and did all the w assigned to him.
7:22 the w on the pillars was completed.
7:29 bulls were wreaths of hammered w.
7:40 So Huram finished all the w he had
7:49 gold floral w and lamps and tongs;
7:51 all the w King Solomon had done for
9:23 supervising the men who did the w.
11:28 how well the young man did his w,
2Ki 12:11 to supervise the w on the temple.
22: 5 to supervise the w on the temple.
25:12 land to w the vineyards and fields.
1Ch 9:33 responsible for the w day and night.
22:15 as men skilled in every kind of w
22:16 begin the w, and the LORD be with
23: 4 the w of the temple of the LORD
26: 8 do the w—descendants of Obed-Edom,
26:30 Jordan for all the w of the LORD
28:10 Be strong and do the w."
28:13 and for all the w of serving in the
28:20 strong and courageous, and do the w.
28:20 or forsake you until all the w for
28:21 for all the w on the temple of God,
28:21 craft will help you in all the w.
29: 2 of my God—gold for the gold w,
29: 5 for the gold w and the silver w, and
29: 5 the w to be done by the craftsmen.
29: 6 of the king's w gave willingly.
29: 7 They gave towards the w on the
2Ch 2: 7 therefore, a man skilled to w in
2: 7 to w in Judah and Jerusalem with my
2: 8 My men shall w with yours
2:14 He is trained to w in gold and
2:14 He will w with your craftsmen and
4:11 So Huram finished the w he had
4:21 the gold floral w and lamps and
5: 1 all the w Solomon had done for the
8: 9 the Israelites for his w; they were
8:16 All Solomon's w was carried out,
15: 7 up, for your w will be rewarded."
16: 5 building Ramah and abandoned his w.
24:12 the w required for the temple of the
24:13 The men in charge of the w were
27: 3 w on the wall at the hill of Ophel.
29:12 these Levites set to w: from the
32:19 of the world—the w of men's hands.
34:10 the w on the LORD's temple.
34:12 The men did the w faithfully. Over
Ezr 2:69 gave to the treasury for this w
4: 5 They hired counsellors to w against
4:21 an order to these men to stop w,
4:24 Thus the w on the house of God in
5: 2 Jeshua son of Jozadak set to w to
5: 8 The w is being carried on with
6: 7 Do not interfere with the w on this
6: 8 so that the w will not stop.
6:22 so that he assisted them in the w on
Ne 2:16 any others who would be doing the w.

Ne 3: 1 to **w** and rebuilt the Sheep Gate.
3: 5 to the **w** under their supervisors.
4:11 kill them and put an end to the **w**."
4:15 to the wall, each to his own **w**.
4:16 half of my men did the **w**, while the
4:17 materials did their **w** with one hand
4:19 "The **w** is extensive and spread out,
4:21 we continued the **w** with half the men
5:16 Instead, I devoted myself to the **w**
5:16 assembled there for the **w**; we did
6: 3 Why should the **w** stop while I leave
6: 9 the **w**, and it will not be completed.
6:16 because they realised that this **w**
7:70 the families contributed to the **w**.
7:71 gave to the treasury for the **w**
10:37 tithes in all the towns where we **w**.
11:12 their associates, who carried on **w**
11:16 the outside **w** of the house of God;
Job 1:10 You have blessed the **w** of his hands,
10: 3 to spurn the **w** of your hands, while
23: 9 he is at **w** in the north, I do not
34:19 for they are all the **w** of his hands?
36:24 Remember to extol his **w**, which men
37: 7 all men he has made may know his **w**,
39:11 Will you leave your heavy **w** to him?
Ps 8: 3 your heavens, the **w** of your fingers
9:16 ensnared by the **w** of their hands.
19: 1 skies proclaim the **w** of his hands.
28: 4 their deeds and for their evil **w**;
55:11 Destructive forces are at **w** in the
90:17 the **w** of our hands for us—yes,
90:17 yes, establish the **w** of our hands.
92: 4 sing for joy at the **w** of your hands.
102:25 the heavens are the **w** of your hands.
104:13 is satisfied by the fruit of his **w**.
104:23 man goes out to his **w**, to his labour
Pr 12:14 as the **w** of his hands rewards him.
14:23 All hard **w** brings a profit, but mere
18: 9 One who is slack in his **w** is brother
21:25 him, because his hands refuse to **w**.
22:29 Do you see a man skilled in his **w**?
24:27 Finish your outdoor **w** and get your
31:17 She sets about her **w** vigorously; her
Ecc 2:10 My heart took delight in all my **w**,
2:17 I hated life, because the **w** that is
2:19 **w** into which I have poured my effort
2:21 For a man may do his **w** with wisdom,
2:23 All his days his **w** is pain and grief;
2:24 and find satisfaction in his **w**.
3:22 his **w**, because that is his lot.
4: 9 they have a good return for their **w**:
5: 6 and destroy the **w** of your hands?
5:19 in his **w**—this is a gift of God.
8:15 Then joy will accompany him in his **w**
10:15 A fool's **w** wearies him; he does not
SS 7: 1 the **w** of a craftsman's hands.
Isa 1:31 become tinder and his **w** a spark;
2: 8 bow down to the **w** of their hands,
5:12 no respect for the **w** of his hands.
5:19 hasten his **w** so that we may see it.
10:12 the Lord has finished all his **w**
17: 8 the **w** of their hands, and they will
19: 9 Those who **w** with combed flax will
28:21 the Valley of Gibeon—to do his **w**,
28:21 his strange **w**, and perform his task,
29:15 who do their **w** in darkness and think,
29:23 the **w** of my hands, they will keep my
30:24 The oxen and donkeys that **w** the soil
45: 9 Does your **w** say, 'He has no hands'?
45:11 me orders about the **w** of my hands?
54:16 and forges a weapon fit for its **w**.
54:16 created the destroyer to **w** havoc;
60:21 the **w** of my hands, for the display
61: 5 will **w** your fields and vineyards.
64: 8 we are all the **w** of your hand.
Jer 17:22 houses or do any **w** on the Sabbath,
17:24 day holy by not doing any **w** on it,
22:13 making his countrymen **w** for nothing,
25:14 deeds and the **w** of their hands."
31:16 tears, for your **w** will be rewarded,"
48:10 who is lax in doing the LORD's **w**!
50:25 Almighty has **w** to do in the land of
52:16 land to **w** the vineyards and fields.
Lam 4: 2 of clay, the **w** of a potter's hands!
Eze 27:14 "'Men of Beth Togarmah exchanged **w**
27:16 purple fabric, embroidered **w**, fine
Eze 27:24 blue fabric, embroidered **w** and
44:14 all the **w** that is to be done in it.
Hos 13: 2 all of them the **w** of craftsmen.
Mic 5:13 bow down to the **w** of your hands.
Na 3:14 strengthen your defences! **W** the clay,
Hag 1:14 They came and began **w** on the house
2: 4 land,' declares the LORD, 'and **w**.
2:17 I struck all the **w** of your hands
Mt 14: 2 miraculous powers are at **w** in him."
20: 1 to hire men to **w** in his vineyard.
20: 4 He told them, 'You also go and **w** in
20: 7 'You also go and **w** in my vineyard.'
20:12 of the **w** and the heat of the day.'
20:13 Didn't you agree to **w** for a denarius?
21:28 Son, go and **w** today in the vineyard.'
25:16 his money to **w** and gained five more.
Mk 6:14 miraculous powers are at **w** in him."
Lk 10:40 **w** by myself? Tell her to help me!"
13:14 people, "There are six days for **w**.
19:13 'Put this money to **w**,' he said,
Jn 4:34 him who sent me and to finish his **w**.
4:38 Others have done the hard **w**, and you
5:17 "My Father is always at his **w** to
5:36 For the very **w** that the Father has
6:27 Do not **w** for food that spoils, but
9: 4 long as it is day, we must do the **w**
9: 4 Night is coming, when no-one can **w**.
14:10 living in me, who is doing his **w**.
17: 4 completing the **w** you gave me to do.
Ac 13: 2 the **w** to which I have called them."
13:25 John was completing his **w**, he said:
14:26 God for the **w** they had now completed.
15:38 not continued with them in the **w**.
20:35 of hard **w** we must help the weak,
Ro 4: 5 However, to the man who does not **w**
7: 5 by the law were at **w** in our bodies,
7:21 I find this law at **w**: When I want to
7:23 I see another law at **w** in the
7:23 law of sin at **w** within my members.
15:23 place for me to **w** in these regions,
16:12 those women who **w** hard in the Lord.
1Co 3:13 his **w** will be shown for what it is,
3:13 test the quality of each man's **w**.
4:12 We **w** hard with our own hands. When
9: 1 not the result of my **w** in the Lord?
9: 6 Barnabas who must **w** for a living?
9:13 Don't you know that those who **w** in
12:11 All these are the **w** of one and the
12:29 Are all teachers? Do all **w** miracles?
15:58 fully to the **w** of the Lord,
16: 9 a great door for effective **w** has
16:10 on the **w** of the Lord, just as I am.
16:16 joins in the **w**, and labours at it.
2Co 1:24 but we **w** with you for your joy,
4:12 at **w** in us, but life is at **w** in you.
6: 5 hard **w**, sleepless nights and hunger;
8:11 Now finish the **w**, so that your eager
10:15 by boasting of **w** done by others.
10:16 For we do not want to boast about **w**
Gal 2: 8 For God, who was at **w** in the
2: 8 was also at **w** in my ministry as an
3: 5 Does God give you his Spirit and **w**
Eph 2: 2 at **w** in those who are disobedient.
3:20 to his power that is at **w** within us,
4:16 up in love, as each part does its **w**.
4:28 but must **w**, doing something useful
Php 2:12 to **w** out your salvation with fear
2:22 with me in the **w** of the gospel.
2:30 he almost died for the **w** of Christ,
Col 3:23 Whatever you do, **w** at it with all
4:17 **w** you have received in the Lord."
1Th 1: 3 and Father your **w** produced by faith,
2:13 which is at **w** in you who believe.
4:11 to mind your own business and to **w**
5:12 brothers, to respect those who **w**
5:13 regard in love because of their **w**.
2Th 2: 7 of lawlessness is already at **w**;
2: 9 the **w** of Satan displayed in all
2:13 the sanctifying **w** of the Spirit
3:10 a man will not **w**, he shall not eat."
1Ti 1: 4 than God's **w**—which is by faith.
5:17 whose **w** is preaching and teaching.
2Ti 4: 5 do the **w** of an evangelist,
Tit 1: 7 overseer is entrusted with God's **w**,
Heb 1:10 the heavens are the **w** of your hands.
4: 3 And yet his **w** has been finished
Heb 4: 4 day God rested from all his **w**."
4:10 his own **w**, just as God did from his.
6:10 he will not forget your **w** and the
13:17 Obey them so that their **w** will be a
13:21 and may he **w** in us what is pleasing
Jas 1: 4 Perseverance must finish its **w** so
1Pe 1: 2 through the sanctifying **w** of the
1:17 who judges each man's **w** impartially,
1Jn 3: 8 was to destroy the devil's **w**.
2Jn :11 welcomes him shares in his wicked **w**.
3Jn : 8 we may **w** together for the truth.
Rev 2: 2 I know your deeds, your hard **w** and
9:20 not repent of the **w** of their hands;

Work of God

Ex 32:16 The tablets were the **w**; the writing
Ecc 11: 5 the **w**, the Maker of all things.
Jn 6:29 Jesus answered, "The **w** is this: to
9: 3 **w** might be displayed in his life.
Ro 14:20 Do not destroy the **w** for the sake of

Worked (Work)

Ge 4: 2 kept flocks, and Cain **w** the soil.
29:30 he **w** for Laban another seven years.
30:29 "You know how I have **w** for you and
31: 6 You know that I've **w** for your father
31:41 I **w** for you fourteen years for your
Ex 1:13 and **w** them ruthlessly.
26: 1 **w** into them by a skilled craftsman.
26:31 **w** into it by a skilled craftsman.
36: 8 **w** into them by a skilled craftsman.
36:35 **w** into it by a skilled craftsman.
39: 3 cut strands to be **w** into the blue,
Dt 21: 3 been **w** and has never worn a yoke
Ru 2: 7 She went into the field and has **w**
2:19 "The name of the man I **w** with today
2Ki 12:11 With it they paid those who **w** on the
1Ch 4:23 stayed there and **w** for the king.
2Ch 3:14 fine linen, with cherubim **w** into it.
25:20 would not listen, for God so **w** that
31:21 sought his God and **w** wholeheartedly.
32: 5 he **w** hard repairing all the broken
Ne 3:25 Palal son of Uzai **w** opposite the
4: 6 the people **w** with all their heart.
4:18 wore his sword at his side as he **w**.
Est 10: 3 because he **w** for the good of his
Ps 98: 1 holy arm have **w** salvation for him.
Ecc 2:21 to someone who has not **w** for it.
Isa 59:16 so his own arm **w** salvation for him,
63: 5 so my own arm **w** salvation for me,
Eze 23:29 take away everything you have **w** for.
Joel 2:26 who has **w** wonders for you; never
Mt 13:33 until it **w** all through the dough."
20:12 'These men who were hired last **w**
Mk 16:20 and the Lord **w** with them and
Lk 5: 5 Simon answered, "Master, we've **w**
13:21 until it **w** all through the dough."
Jn 4:38 you to reap what you have not **w** for.
Ac 18: 3 were, he stayed and **w** with them.
Ro 16: 6 Greet Mary, who **w** very hard for you.
16:12 who has **w** very hard in the Lord.
1Co 15:10 No, I **w** harder than all of them—yet
2Co 11:23 I am more. I have **w** much harder,
1Th 2: 9 our toil and hardship; we **w** night
2Th 3: 8 On the contrary, we **w** night and day,
2Jn : 8 you do not lose what you have **w** for,

Worker (Fellow-worker, Fellow-workers, Work)

Ex 12:45 a temporary resident and a hired **w**
Lev 22:10 of a priest or his hired **w** eat it.
25: 6 and the hired **w** and temporary
25:40 He is to be treated as a hired **w** or
Ecc 3: 9 What does the **w** gain from his toil?
Mt 10:10 staff; for the **w** is worth his keep.
Lk 10: 7 you, for the **w** deserves his wages.
1Ti 5:18 and "The **w** deserves his wages.

Workers (Work)

Ru 2:21 'Stay with my **w** until they finish
2Ki 12:15 they gave the money to pay the **w**,
22: 5 **w** who repair the temple of the LORD—
22: 9 **w** and supervisors at the temple."
1Ch 4:21 clans of the linen **w** at Beth Ashbea,

1Ch 23:24 that is, the w twenty years old or
27:26 of the field w who farmed the land.
2Ch 24:12 and also w in iron and bronze to
34:10 These men paid the w who repaired
34:13 supervised all the w from job to
34:17 it to the supervisors and w."
Ezr 7:24 or other w at this house of God.
Isa 19:10 The w in cloth will be dejected, and
58: 3 you please and exploit all your w.
Jer 10: 9 and purple—all made by skilled w.
Eze 48:18 supply food for the w of the city.
48:19 The w from the city who farm it will
Mt 9:37 is plentiful but the w are few.
9:38 send out w into his harvest field."
20: 8 'Call the w and pay them their wages,
20: 9 "The w who were hired about the
Lk 10: 2 is plentiful, but the w are few.
10: 2 send out w into his harvest field.
1Co 12:28 third teachers, then w of miracles,

Working (Work)

Ex 5: 5 and you are stopping them from w."
5: 9 w and pay no attention to lies."
15:11 awesome in glory, w wonders?
Ru 2: 3 she found herself w in a field
2:19 one at whose place she had been w.
2Ch 2:18 over them to keep the people w.
26:10 He had people w his fields and
Ezr 3: 9 those w on the house of God.
Ne 10:31 w the land and will cancel all debts.
Ecc 9:10 there is neither w nor planning nor
Jer 18: 3 house, and I saw him w at the wheel.
Eze 46: 1 is to be shut on the six w days,
Jn 5:17 to this very day, and I, too, am w."
1Co 12: 6 There are different kinds of w, but
Eph 1:19 like the w of his mighty strength,
3: 7 given me through the w of his power.
Col 3:23 as w for the Lord, not for men,
4:13 I vouch for him that he is w hard
Jas 2:22 and his actions were w together,

Workman (Work, Man)

2Ti 2:15 a w who does not need to be ashamed
Rev 18:22 No w of any trade will ever be found

Workman's (Work, Man)

Jdg 5:26 her right hand for the w hammer.

Workmanship (Work)

Eph 2:10 For we are God's w, created in

Workmen (Work, Man)

Ex 36: 8 All the skilled men among the w made
1Ki 5:16 the project and directed the w.
2Ki 12:14 was paid to the w, who used it to
1Ch 22:15 You have many w: stonecutters,
Ne 4:22 us as guards by night and w by day."
Ac 19:25 along with the w in related trades,
2Co 11:13 deceitful w, masquerading as
Jas 5: 4 The wages you failed to pay the w

Works (Work)

Dt 3:24 do the deeds and mighty w you do?
20:20 use them to build siege w until the
32: 4 He is the Rock, his w are perfect,
2Ki 25: 1 and built siege w all around it.
Job 26:14 are but the outer fringe of his w;
40:19 He ranks first among the w of God,
Ps 8: 6 You made him ruler over the w of
28: 5 Since they show no regard for the w
46: 8 Come and see the w of the LORD, the
64: 9 proclaim the w of God and ponder
66: 5 how awesome his w on man's behalf!
77:12 I will meditate on all your w and
92: 5 How great are your w, O LORD, how
103: 6 The LORD w righteousness and justice
103:22 Praise the LORD, all his w
104:24 How many are your w, O LORD! In
104:31 may the LORD rejoice in his w—
107:22 and tell of his w with songs of joy.
107:24 They saw the w of the LORD, his
111: 2 Great are the w of the LORD; they
111: 6 shown his people the power of his w,
111: 7 The w of his hands are faithful and
Ps 138: 8 do not abandon the w of your hands.
139:14 your w are wonderful, I know that
143: 5 I meditate on all your w and
145: 4 One generation will commend your w
145: 5 I will meditate on your wonderful w.
145: 6 tell of the power of your awesome w,
Pr 8:22 me forth as the first of his w
12:11 He who w his land will have abundant
16: 4 The LORD w out everything for his
16:26 The labourer's appetite w for him;
26:28 and a flattering mouth w ruin.
28:19 He who w his land will have abundant
31:13 She selects wool and flax and w with
31:31 w bring her praise at the city gate.
Isa 29: 3 and set up my siege w against you.
41:24 and your w are utterly worthless;
44:12 The blacksmith takes a tool and w
57:12 expose your righteousness and your w
65:22 long enjoy the w of their hands.
Jer 11:15 w out her evil schemes with many?
52: 4 and built siege w all around it.
Eze 4: 2 lay siege to it: Erect siege w
17:17 seige w erected to destroy many
21:22 build a ramp and to erect siege w.
26: 8 he will set up siege w against you,
Jn 6:28 we do to do the w God requires?"
7:18 but he who w for the honour of the
Ro 4: 2 in fact, Abraham was justified by w,
4: 4 Now when a man w, his wages are not
4: 6 credits righteousness apart from w:
8:28 we know that in all things God w for
9:12 not by w but by him who calls—she
9:32 not by faith but as if it were by w.
11: 6 then it is no longer by w; if it
16:23 is the city's director of public w,
1Co 5: 6 w through the whole batch of dough?
12: 6 same God w all of them in all men.
Gal 5: 9 "A little yeast w through the whole
Eph 1:11 plan of him who w out everything
2: 9 not by w, so that no-one can boast.
2:10 in Christ Jesus to do good w,
4:12 to prepare God's people for w of
Php 2:13 for it is God who w in you to will
Col 1:29 energy, which so powerfully w in me.

World (*Prince of this world*, World's, Worldly)

Ge 11: 1 Now the whole w had one language and
11: 9 the language of the whole w.
41:57 the famine was severe in all the w.
Ex 34:10 done in any nation in all the w.
1Sa 2: 8 LORD's; upon them he has set the w.
17:46 and the whole w will know that there
1Ki 4:34 the w, who had heard of his wisdom.
8:53 of the w to be your own inheritance,
10:24 The whole w sought audience with
2Ki 5:15 God in all the w except in Israel.
1Ch 16:30 The w is firmly established; it
2Ch 32:19 of the w—the work of men's hands.
Job 18:18 darkness and is banished from the w.
34:13 Who put him in charge of the whole w?
Ps 9: 8 He will judge the w in righteousness;
17:14 this w whose reward is in this life.
19: 4 their words to the ends of the w.
24: 1 it, the w, and all who live in it;
33: 8 all the people of the w revere him.
49: 1 listen, all who live in this w,
50:12 w is mine, and all that is in it.
77:18 your lightning lit up the w;
89:11 founded the w and all that is in it.
90: 2 brought forth the earth and the w,
93: 1 The w is firmly established; it
96:10 The w is firmly established, it
96:13 He will judge the w in righteousness
97: 4 His lightning lights up the w; the
98: 7 it, the w, and all who live in it.
98: 9 He will judge the w in righteousness
Pr 8:23 the beginning, before the w began.
8:26 fields or any of the dust of the w.
8:31 rejoicing in his whole w and
Isa 12: 5 let this be known to all the w.
13:11 I will punish the w for its evil,
14: 9 all those who were leaders in the w;
14:17 the man who made the w a desert, who
14:26 the plan determined for the whole w;
Isa 18: 3 All you people of the w, you who
24: 4 The earth dries up and withers, the w
26: 9 people of the w learn righteousness.
26:18 not given birth to people of the w.
27: 6 and fill all the w with fruit.
34: 1 the w, and all that comes out of it!
38:11 with those who now dwell in this w.
40:23 the rulers of this w to nothing.
Jer 10:12 he founded the w by his wisdom and
51:15 he founded the w by his wisdom and
Eze 20:32 of the w, who serve wood and stone.
Da 4: 1 all the w: May you prosper greatly!
Na 1: 5 the w and all who live in it.
Zep 1:18 the whole w will be consumed, for
3: 8 The whole w will be consumed by the
Zec 1:11 the whole w at rest and in peace."
6: 5 presence of the Lord of the whole w.
Mt 4: 8 of the w and their splendour.
5:14 "You are the light of the w. A city
13:35 hidden since the creation of the w."
13:38 The field is the w, and the good
16:26 for a man if he gains the whole w,
18: 7 "Woe to the w because of the things
24:14 in the whole w as a testimony to
24:21 the beginning of the w until now
25:34 for you since the creation of the w.
26:13 gospel is preached throughout the w,
Mk 8:36 the whole w, yet forfeit his soul?
9: 3 anyone in the w could bleach them.
13:19 when God created the w, until
14: 9 gospel is preached throughout the w,
16:15 He said to them, "Go into all the w
Lk 2: 1 be taken of the entire Roman w.
4: 5 instant all the kingdoms of the w.
9:25 is it for a man to gain the whole w,
11:50 shed since the beginning of the w,
12:30 For the pagan w runs after all such
16: 8 For the people of this w are more
21:26 of what is coming on the w, for the
Jn 1: 9 to every man was coming into the w.
1:10 He was in the w, and though the w
1:10 him, the w did not recognise him.
1:29 God, who takes away the sin of the w!
3:16 "For God so loved the w that he gave
3:17 God did not send his Son into the w
3:17 to condemn the w, but to save the w
3:19 verdict: Light has come into the w,
4:42 man really is the Saviour of the w."
6:14 Prophet who is to come into the w."
6:33 heaven and gives life to the w."
6:51 I will give for the life of the w."
7: 4 things, show yourself to the w."
7: 7 The w cannot hate you, but it hates
8:12 he said, "I am the light of the w.
8:23 are of this w; I am not of this w.
8:26 I have heard from him I tell the w."
9: 5 in the w, I am the light of the w."
9:39 For judgment I have come into this w,
10:36 as his very own and sent into the w?
11:27 of God, who was to come into the w."
12:19 how the whole w has gone after him!"
12:25 hates his life in this w will keep
12:31 is the time for judgment on this w;
12:46 I have come into the w as a light,
12:47 come to judge the w, but to save it.
13: 1 leave this w and go to the Father.
13: 1 loved his own who were in the w,
14:17 the Spirit of truth. The w cannot
14:19 Before long, the w will not see me
14:22 yourself to us and not to the w?"
14:27 I do not give to you as the w gives.
14:31 the w must learn that I love the
15:18 "If the w hates you, keep in mind
15:19 If you belonged to the w, it would
15:19 As it is, you do not belong to the w,
15:19 but I have chosen you out of the w.
15:19 That is why the w hates you.
16: 8 he comes, he will convict the w of
16:20 weep and mourn while the w rejoices.
16:21 joy that a child is born into the w.
16:28 from the Father and entered the w;
16:28 the w and going back to the Father."
16:33 In this w you will have trouble. But
16:33 take heart! I have overcome the w."
17: 5 I had with you before the w began.
17: 6 those whom you gave me out of the w.

Jn 17: 9 I am not praying for the w, but for
17:11 I will remain in the w no longer,
17:11 in the w, and I am coming to you.
17:13 things while I am still in the w,
17:14 I have given them your word and the w
17:14 the w any more than I am of the w.
17:15 not that you take them out of the w
17:16 They are not of the w, even as I am
17:18 the w, I have sent them into the w.
17:21 w may believe that you have sent me.
17:23 to let the w know that you sent me
17:24 me before the creation of the w.
17:25 "Righteous Father, though the w does
18:20 "I have spoken openly to the w,"
18:36 said, "My kingdom is not of this w.
18:37 into the w, to testify to the truth.
21:25 I suppose that even the whole w
Ac 11:28 spread over the entire Roman w.
17: 6 all over the w have now come here,
17:24 "The God who made the w and
17:31 set a day when he will judge the w
19:27 the province of Asia and the w,
19:35 "Men of Ephesus, doesn't all the w
24: 5 riots among the Jews all over the w.
Ro 1: 8 is being reported all over the w.
1:20 For since the creation of the w
3: 6 were so, how could God judge the w?
3:19 the whole w held accountable to God.
4:13 that he would be heir of the w,
5:12 Therefore, just as sin entered the w
5:13 the law was given, sin was in the w.
10:18 their words to the ends of the w."
11:12 means riches for the w, and their
11:15 is the reconciliation of the w,
12: 2 any longer to the pattern of this w,
1Co 1:20 God made foolish the wisdom of the w?
1:21 For since in the wisdom of God the w
1:27 God chose the foolish things of the w
1:27 things of the w to shame the strong.
1:28 He chose the lowly things of this w
2:12 not received the spirit of the w but
3:19 the wisdom of this w is foolishness
3:22 Paul or Apollos or Cephas or the w or
4:13 of the earth, the refuse of the w.
5:10 people of this w who are immoral,
5:10 case you would have to leave this w.
6: 2 w? And if you are to judge the w,
7:31 those who use the things of the w,
7:31 For this w in its present form is
7:33 this w—how he can please his wife—
7:34 about the affairs of this w—how
8: 4 an idol is nothing at all in the w
11:32 we will not be condemned with the w.
14:10 are all sorts of languages in the w,
2Co 1:12 have conducted ourselves in the w,
5:19 that God was reconciling the w to
10: 2 we live by the standards of this w.
10: 3 For though we live in the w, we do
10: 3 we do not wage war as the w does.
10: 4 with are not the weapons of the w.
11:18 way the w does, I too will boast.
Gal 3:22 the whole w is a prisoner of sin,
4: 3 under the basic principles of the w.
6:14 through which the w has been
6:14 crucified to me, and I to the w.
Eph 1: 4 the creation of the w to be holy
2: 2 you followed the ways of this w
2:12 hope and without God in the w.
6:12 against the powers of this dark w
Col 1: 6 All over the w this gospel is
2: 8 of this w rather than on Christ.
2:20 to the basic principles of this w,
1Ti 1:15 Christ Jesus came into the w to save
3:16 on in the w, was taken up in glory.
6: 7 For we brought nothing into the w,
6:17 who are rich in this present w
2Ti 4:10 for Demas, because he loved this w,
Heb 1: 6 God brings his firstborn into the w,
2: 5 that he has subjected the w to come,
4: 3 since the creation of the w.
9:26 times since the creation of the w.
10: 5 when Christ came into the w, he said:
11: 7 By his faith he condemned the w and
11:38 the w was not worthy of them. They
Jas 1:27 from being polluted by the w.
2: 5 eyes of the w to be rich in faith
Jas 3: 6 The tongue also is a fire, a w of
4: 4 with the w is hatred towards God?
4: 4 of the w becomes an enemy of God.
1Pe 1: 1 To God's elect, strangers in the w,
1:20 chosen before the creation of the w,
2:11 as aliens and strangers in the w, to
5: 9 your brothers throughout the w are
2Pe 1: 4 in the w caused by evil desires.
2: 5 if he did not spare the ancient w
2:20 of the w by knowing our Lord
3: 6 By these waters also the w of that
1Jn 2: 2 also for the sins of the whole w.
2:15 not love the w or anything in the w.
2:16 For everything in the w—the
2:16 not from the Father but from the w.
2:17 The w and its desires pass away, but
3: 1 The reason the w does not know us is
3:13 my brothers, if the w hates you.
4: 1 prophets have gone out into the w.
4: 3 and even now is already in the w.
4: 4 than the one who is in the w.
4: 5 They are from the w and therefore
4: 5 of the w, and the w listens to them.
4: 9 his one and only Son into the w
4:14 his Son to be the Saviour of the w.
4:17 because in this w we are like him.
5: 4 born of God overcomes the w.
5: 4 has overcome the w, even our faith.
5: 5 Who is it that overcomes the w? Only
5:19 and that the whole w is under the
2Jn : 7 the flesh, have gone out into the w.
Rev 3:10 is going to come upon the whole w
11:15 "The kingdom of the w has become the
12: 9 Satan, who leads the whole w astray.
13: 3 The whole w was astonished and
13: 8 slain from the creation of the w.
16:14 go out to the kings of the whole w,
17: 8 of life from the creation of the w

World's (World)

Lam 4:12 nor did any of the w people, that
Jn 11: 9 for he sees by this w light.
Rev 18:23 Your merchants were the w great men.

Worldly (World)

Lk 16: 9 I tell you, use w wealth to gain
16:11 trustworthy in handling w wealth,
1Co 3: 1 but as w—mere infants in Christ.
3: 3 You are still w. For since there is
3: 3 are you not w? Are you not acting
2Co 1:12 done so not according to w wisdom
1:17 Or do I make my plans in a w manner
5:16 regard no-one from a w point of
7:10 regret, but w sorrow brings death.
Tit 2:12 "No" to ungodliness and w passions,

Worm (Worms)

Job 17:14 to the w, 'My mother' or 'My sister
24:20 The womb forgets them, the w feasts
25: 6 a son of man, who is only a w!"
Ps 22: 6 I am a w and not a man, scorned by
Isa 41:14 Do not be afraid, O w Jacob,
51: 8 the w will devour them like wool.
66:24 against me; their w will not die,
Jnh 4: 7 at dawn the next day God provided a w
Mk 9:48 where "'their w does not die, and
2Ti 3: 6 They are the kind who w their way

Worms (Worm)

Dt 28:39 the grapes, because w will eat them.
Job 7: 5 My body is clothed with w and scabs,
21:26 in the dust, and w cover them both.
Isa 14:11 out beneath you and w cover you.
Ac 12:23 and he was eaten by w and died.

Wormwood

Rev 8:11 the name of the star is W. A third

Worn (Wear)

Ge 18:12 "After I am w out and my master is
Ex 35:19 the woven garments w for ministering
39:26 of the robe to be w for ministering,
39:41 the woven garments w for ministering
Dt 21: 3 been worked and has never w a yoke
Dt 25:18 you were weary and w out, they met
Jos 9: 5 The men put w and patched sandals on
9:13 are w out by the very long journey."
Jdg 8: 5 troops some bread; they are w out,
8:26 the purple garments w by the kings
Est 6: 8 robe the king has w and a horse the
Job 16: 7 Surely, O God, you have w me out;
Ps 6: 6 I am w out from groaning; all night
69: 3 I am w out calling for help; my
Isa 47:13 have received has only w you out!
Jer 12: 5 men on foot and they have w you out,
45: 3 w out with groaning and find no rest.
Eze 23:43 about the one w out by adultery
Lk 8:27 long time this man had not w clothes

Worn-out (Wear)

Jos 9: 4 with w sacks and old wineskins,
Jer 38:11 He took some old rags and w clothes
38:12 "Put these old rags and w clothes

Worried (Worry)

1Sa 10: 2 about them and is w about you.
Lk 10:41 are w and upset about many things,

Worries (Worry)

Jer 17: 8 It has no w in a year of drought and
Mt 13:22 but the w of this life and the
Mk 4:19 w of this life, the deceitfulness
Lk 8:14 way they are choked by life's w,

Worry (Worried, Worries, Worrying)

1Sa 9:20 w about them; they have been found.
Mt 6:25 "Therefore I tell you, do not w
6:28 "And why do you w about clothes? See
6:31 do not w, saying, 'What shall we eat?
6:34 Therefore do not w about tomorrow,
6:34 for tomorrow will w about itself.
10:19 when they arrest you, do not w about
Mk 13:11 not w beforehand about what to say.
Lk 12:11 rulers and authorities, do not w
12:22 "Therefore I tell you, do not w
12:26 thing, why do you w about the rest?
12:29 eat or drink; do not w about it.
21:14 But make up your mind not to w

Worrying (Worry)

1Sa 9: 5 the donkeys and start w about us."
Mt 6:27 Who of you by w can add a single
Lk 12:25 Who of you by w can add a single

Worse (Bad)

Ge 19: 9 judge! We'll treat you w than them.
Ex 11: 6 w than there has ever been or ever
2Sa 19: 7 This will be w for you than all the
1Ki 17:17 He grew w and w, and finally stopped
Pr 17: 7 how much w lying lips to a ruler!
19:10 w for a slave to rule over princes!
Eze 14:21 How much w will it be when I send
Da 1:10 Why should he see you looking w than
Mic 7: 4 most upright w than a thorn hedge.
Mt 9:16 from the garment, making the tear w.
12:45 of that man is w than the first.
27:64 deception will be w than the first."
Mk 2:21 from the old, making the tear w.
5:26 of getting better she grew w.
Lk 11:26 of that man is w than the first."
13: 2 that these Galileans were w sinners
Jn 5:14 or something w may happen to you."
1Co 8: 8 God; we are no w if we do not eat,
1Ti 5: 8 faith and is w than an unbeliever.
2Ti 3:13 to w, deceiving and being deceived.
2Pe 2:20 they are w off at the end than they

Worship (Worshipped, Worshipper, Worshippers, Worshipping, Worships)

Ge 22: 5 w and then we will come back to you."
Ex 3:12 you will w God on this mountain."
4:23 "Let my son go, so that he may w me.
7:16 so that they may w me in the desert.
8: 1 my people go, so that they may w me.
8:20 my people go, so that they may w me.
9: 1 people go, so that they may w me."
9:13 my people go, so that they may w me,

Ex 10: 3 my people go, so that they may **w** me.
10: 7 that they may **w** the LORD their God.
10: 8 "Go, **w** the LORD your God," he said.
10:11 No! Let only the men go; and **w** the
10:24 Moses and said, "Go, **w** the LORD.
10:26 what we are to use to **w** the LORD."
12:31 Go, **w** the LORD as you have requested.
20: 5 You shall not bow down to them or **w**
23:24 or **w** them or follow their practices.
23:25 **W** the LORD your God, and his
23:33 because the **w** of their gods will
24: 1 You are to **w** at a distance,
34:14 Do not **w** any other god, for the LORD,
Dt 4:28 There you will **w** man-made gods of
5: 9 You shall not bow down to them or **w**
8:19 gods and **w** and bow down to them,
11:16 **w** other gods and bow down to them.
12: 2 you are dispossessing **w** their gods.
12: 4 You must not **w** the LORD your God in
12:31 You must not **w** the LORD your God in
13: 2 have not known) "and let us **w** them,
13: 6 "Let us go and **w** other gods" (gods
13:13 "Let us go and **w** other gods" (gods
28:36 **w** other gods, gods of wood and stone.
28:64 There you will **w** other gods—gods of
29:18 go and **w** the gods of those nations;
30:17 bow down to other gods and **w** them,
31:20 they will turn to other gods and **w**
Jos 22:27 that we will **w** the LORD at his
Jdg 6:10 'I am the LORD your God; do not **w**
1Sa 1: 3 this man went up from his town to **w**
15:25 with me, so that I may **w** the LORD."
15:30 so that I may **w** the LORD your God."
2Sa 15: 8 I will **w** the LORD in Hebron.
15:32 where people used to **w** God, Hushai
1Ki 1:47 And the king bowed in **w** on his
9: 6 off to serve other gods and **w** them,
12:30 as far as Dan to **w** the one there.
16:31 and began to serve Baal and **w** him.
2Ki 10:28 Jehu destroyed Baal **w** in Israel.
10:29 **w** of the golden calves at Bethel
17:25 they did not **w** the LORD; so he sent
17:28 and taught them how to **w** the LORD.
17:34 They neither **w** the LORD nor adhere
17:35 "Do not **w** any other gods or bow down
17:36 is the one you must **w**. To him you
17:37 wrote for you. Do not **w** other gods.
17:38 with you, and do not **w** other gods.
17:39 Rather, **w** the LORD your God; it is
18:22 **w** before this altar in Jerusalem"?
1Ch 16:29 **w** the LORD in the splendour of his
2Ch 7:19 off to serve other gods and **w** them,
20:18 fell down in **w** before the LORD.
29:28 The whole assembly bowed in **w**, while
32:12 'You must **w** before one altar and
Ezr 7:19 you for **w** in the temple of your God.
Ne 9: 6 and the multitudes of heaven **w** you.
Job 1:20 Then he fell to the ground in **w**
Ps 22:29 rich of the earth will feast and **w**;
29: 2 **w** the LORD in the splendour of his
86: 9 made will come and **w** before you,
95: 6 Come, let us bow down in **w**, let us
96: 9 **W** the LORD in the splendour of his
97: 7 All who **w** images are put to shame,
97: 7 in idols—**w** him, all you gods!
99: 5 Exalt the LORD our God and **w** at his
99: 9 Exalt the LORD our God and **w** at his
100: 2 **W** the LORD with gladness; come
102:22 the kingdoms assemble to **w** the LORD.
132: 7 let us **w** at his footstool—
Isa 2:20 idols of gold, which they made to **w**.
19:21 They will **w** with sacrifices and
19:23 and Assyrians will **w** together.
27:13 **w** the LORD on the holy mountain in
29:13 Their **w** of me is made up only of
36: 7 "You must **w** before this altar"
46: 6 a god, and they bow down and **w** it.
56: 6 and to **w** him, all who keep the
Jer 7: 2 through these gates to **w** the LORD.
13:10 other gods to serve and **w** them,
23:27 forgot my name through Baal **w**.
25: 6 other gods to serve and **w** them;
26: 2 come to **w** in the house of the LORD.
Eze 46: 2 He is to **w** at the threshold of the
46: 3 **w** in the presence of the LORD at the
46: 9 to **w** is to go out by the south gate;
Da 3: 5 you must fall down and **w** the image
3: 6 Whoever does not fall down and **w**
3:10 fall down and **w** the image of gold,
3:11 that whoever does not fall down and **w**
3:12 **w** the image of gold you have set up."
3:14 **w** the image of gold I have set up?
3:15 and **w** the image I made, very good.
3:15 But if you do not **w** it, you will be
3:18 **w** the image of gold you have set up."
3:28 or **w** any god except their own God.
7:27 and all rulers will **w** and obey him.'
Hos 13: 1 he became guilty of Baal **w** and died.
Jnh 1: 9 He answered, "I am a Hebrew and I **w**
Zep 1: 5 those who bow down on the roofs to **w**
2:11 nations on every shore will **w** him,
Zec 14:16 go up year after year to **w** the King,
14:17 go up to Jerusalem to **w** the King,
Mt 2: 2 in the east and have come to **w** him."
2: 8 me, so that I too may go and **w** him."
4: 9 "if you will bow down and **w** me.
4:10 '**W** the Lord your God, and serve him
15: 9 They **w** me in vain; their teachings
Mk 7: 7 They **w** me in vain; their teachings
Lk 4: 7 if you **w** me, it will all be yours."
4: 8 is written: '**W** the Lord your God
Jn 4:20 where we must **w** is in Jerusalem."
4:21 a time is coming when you will **w** the
4:22 You Samaritans **w** what you do not
4:22 do not know; we **w** what we do know,
4:23 **w** the Father in spirit and truth,
4:24 must **w** in spirit and in truth."
12:20 those who went up to **w** at the Feast.
Ac 7: 7 country and **w** me in this place.'
7:42 to the **w** of the heavenly bodies.
7:43 god Rephan, the idols you made to **w**.
8:27 This man had gone to Jerusalem to **w**,
13:16 Gentiles who **w** God, listen to me!
17:23 carefully at your objects of **w**,
17:23 Now what you **w** as something unknown
18:13 **w** God in ways contrary to the law."
24:11 ago I went up to Jerusalem to **w**.
24:14 However, I admit that I **w** the God of
Ro 9: 4 law, the temple **w** and the promises.
12: 1 God—this is your spiritual act of **w**.
1Co 14:25 So he will fall down and **w** God,
Php 3: 3 we who **w** by the Spirit of God, who
Col 2:18 the **w** of angels disqualify you for
2:23 with their self-imposed **w**, their
1Ti 2:10 for women who profess to **w** God.
Heb 1: 6 says, "Let all God's angels **w** him.
9: 1 covenant had regulations for **w**
10: 1 perfect those who draw near to **w**.
12:28 let us be thankful, and so **w** God
Rev 4:10 **w** him who lives for ever and ever.
13: 8 All inhabitants of the earth will **w**
13:12 its inhabitants **w** the first beast,
13:15 refused to **w** the image to be killed.
14: 7 **W** him who made the heavens, the
14:11 those who **w** the beast and his image,
15: 4 All nations will come and **w** before
19:10 At this I fell at his feet to **w** him.
19:10 **W** God! For the testimony of Jesus is
22: 8 I fell down to **w** at the feet of the
22: 9 keep the words of this book. **W** God!

Worshipped (Worship)

Ge 24:26 the man bowed down and **w** the LORD,
24:48 I bowed down and **w** the LORD. I
47:31 and Israel **w** as he leaned on the top
Ex 4:31 their misery, they bowed down and **w**.
12:27 Then the people bowed down and **w**.
33:10 **w**, each at the entrance to his tent.
34: 8 bowed to the ground at once and **w**.
Dt 17: 3 contrary to my command has **w** other
29:26 They went off and **w** other gods and
Jos 24: 2 beyond the River and **w** other gods.
24:14 **w** beyond the River and in Egypt,
Jdg 2:12 They followed and **w** various gods of
2:17 themselves to other gods and **w** them.
7:15 and its interpretation, he **w** God.
1Sa 1:19 **w** before the LORD and then went back
1:28 And he **w** the LORD there.
15:31 back with Saul, and Saul **w** the LORD.
2Sa 12:20 into the house of the LORD and **w**.
1Ki 11:33 **w** Ashtoreth the goddess of the
1Ki 18:12 have **w** the LORD since my youth.
22:53 He served and **w** Baal and provoked
2Ki 17: 7 They **w** other gods
17:12 They **w** idols, though the LORD had
17:16 the starry hosts, and they **w** Baal.
17:32 They **w** the LORD, but they also
17:33 They **w** the LORD, but they also
21: 3 to all the starry hosts and **w** them.
21:21 he **w** the idols his father had **w**,
2Ch 7: 3 and they **w** and gave thanks to the
24:18 and **w** Asherah poles and idols.
29:29 present with him knelt down and **w**.
29:30 and bowed their heads and **w**.
33: 3 to all the starry hosts and **w** them.
33:22 Amon **w** and offered sacrifices to all
Ne 8: 6 Amen!" Then they bowed down and **w**
Ps 74: 8 place where God was **w** in the land.
106:19 At Horeb they made a calf and **w** an
106:36 They **w** their idols, which became a
Jer 8: 2 have followed and consulted and **w**.
16:11 other gods and served and **w** them.
22: 9 God and have **w** and served other gods.
Da 3: 7 **w** the image of gold that King
7:14 and men of every language **w** him.
Mt 2:11 Mary, and they bowed down and **w** him.
14:33 those who were in the boat **w** him,
28: 9 to him, clasped his feet and **w** him.
28:17 they saw him, they **w** him; but some
Lk 2:37 **w** night and day, fasting and praying.
24:52 they **w** him and returned to Jerusalem
Jn 4:20 Our fathers **w** on this mountain, but
9:38 "Lord, I believe," and he **w** him.
Ac 19:27 and the goddess herself, who is **w**
Ro 1:25 and **w** and served created things
2Th 2: 4 that is called God or is **w**,
Heb 11:21 and **w** as he leaned on the top of his
Rev 5:14 and the elders fell down and **w**.
7:11 faces before the throne and **w** God,
11:16 God, fell on their faces and **w** God,
13: 4 Men **w** the dragon because he had
13: 4 and they also **w** the beast and asked,
16: 2 mark of the beast and **w** his image.
19: 4 **w** God, who was seated on the throne.
19:20 mark of the beast and **w** his image.
20: 4 They had not **w** the beast or his

Worshipper (Worship)

Ac 16:14 of Thyatira, who was a **w** of God.
18: 7 house of Titius Justus, a **w** of God.
Heb 9: 9 to clear the conscience of the **w**.

Worshippers (Worship)

Zep 3:10 From beyond the rivers of Cush my **w**,
Lk 1:10 assembled **w** were praying outside.
Jn 4:23 has now come when the true **w** will
4:23 are the kind of **w** the Father seeks.
4:24 God is spirit, and his **w** must
Heb 10: 2 For the **w** would have been cleansed
Rev 11: 1 the altar, and count the **w** there.

Worshipping (Worship)

Ex 10:26 We have to use some of them in **w** the
Nu 25: 3 Israel joined in **w** the Baal of Peor.
25: 5 have joined in **w** the Baal of Peor."
Dt 4:19 **w** things the LORD your God has
12:31 because in **w** their gods, they do all
20:18 things they do in **w** their gods,
Jdg 2:19 other gods and serving and **w** them.
8:27 prostituted themselves by **w** it
1Ki 9: 9 and have embraced other gods, **w** and
2Ki 17:41 Even while these people were **w** the
19:37 One day, while he was **w** in the
2Ch 7:22 and have embraced other gods, **w** and
28: 2 made cast idols for **w** the Baals.
Ne 9: 3 and in **w** the LORD their God.
Isa 37:38 One day, while he was **w** in the
Jer 1:16 and in **w** what their hands have made.
44: 3 by **w** other gods that neither they
Ac 13: 2 While they were **w** the Lord and
Rev 9:20 hands; they did not stop **w** demons,

Worships (Worship)

Isa 44:15 But he also fashions a god and **w** it;
44:17 his idol; he bows down to it and **w**.

Isa 66: 3 incense, like one who w an idol.
Rev 14: 9 "If anyone w the beast and his image

Worst (Bad)

Ex 9:18 w hailstorm that has ever fallen
9:24 It was the w storm in all the land
Ps 41: 7 they imagine the w for me, saying,
Jer 2:33 w of women can learn from your ways.
1Ti 1:15 to save sinners—of whom I am the w.
1:16 the w of sinners, Christ Jesus might

Worth (Worthy)

Ge 23:15 the land is w four hundred shekels
27:46 my life will not be w living."
Dt 15:18 these six years has been w twice as
2Sa 18: 3 but you are w ten thousand of us.
1Ki 21: 2 I will pay you whatever it is w."
Job 28:13 Man does not comprehend its w; it
Pr 31:10 find? She is w far more than rubies.
Ecc 2: 3 I wanted to see what was w while for
Isa 7:23 vines w a thousand silver shekels,
Lam 4: 2 Zion, once w their weight in gold
Mt 10:10 staff; for the worker is w his keep.
10:31 don't be afraid; you are w more than
Mk 12:42 coins, w only a fraction of a penny.
Lk 12: 7 you are w more than many sparrows.
Jn 12: 5 the poor? It was w a year's wages."
Ac 20:24 I consider my life w nothing to me,
Ro 1:28 since they did not think it w while
8:18 sufferings are not w comparing with
1Pe 1: 7 your faith—of greater w than gold,
3: 4 which is of great w in God's sight.

Worthless

Ge 41:27 and so are the seven w ears of corn
Dt 32:21 and angered me with their w idols.
1Ki 16:13 Israel, to anger by their w idols.
16:26 Israel, to anger by their w idols.
2Ki 17:15 w idols and themselves became w.
2Ch 13: 7 Some w scoundrels gathered around
Job 13: 4 you are w physicians, all of you!
15:31 trusting what is w, for he will get
34:18 says to kings, 'You are w,' and to
Ps 31: 6 I hate those who cling to w idols; I
60:11 the enemy, for the help of man is w.
108:12 the enemy, for the help of man is w.
119:37 Turn my eyes away from w things;
Pr 11: 4 Wealth is w in the day of wrath, but
Isa 40:17 by him as w and less than nothing.
41:24 your works are utterly w; he who
44: 9 and the things they treasure are w.
Jer 2: 5 w idols and became w themselves.
2: 8 by Baal, following w idols.
2:11 exchanged their Glory for w idols.
7: 8 in deceptive words that are w.
8:19 images, with their w foreign idols?"
10: 3 For the customs of the peoples are w;
10: 8 they are taught by w wooden idols.
10:15 They are w, the objects of mockery;
14:22 Do any of the w idols of the nations
15:19 if you utter worthy, not w, words,
16:19 gods, w idols that did them no good.
18:15 me; they burn incense to w idols,
51:18 They are w, the objects of mockery;
Lam 2:14 of your prophets were false and w;
Hos 8: 8 is among the nations like a w thing.
12:11 Is Gilead wicked? Its people are w!
Jnh 2: 8 "Those who cling to w idols forfeit
Zec 11:17 "Woe to the w shepherd, who deserts
Mt 25:30 throw that w servant outside, into
Ac 14:15 you to turn from these w things
Ro 3:12 they have together become w; there
4:14 has no value and the promise is w,
Heb 6: 8 produces thorns and thistles is w
Jas 1:26 himself and his religion is w.

Worthy (Worth)

2Sa 22: 4 to the LORD, who is w of praise
1Ki 1:42 Adonijah said, "Come in. A w man
1:52 "If he shows himself to be a w man,
2Ki 10: 3 choose the best and most w of your
1Ch 16:25 For great is the LORD and most w of
Job 28:18 and jasper are not w of mention
Ps 18: 3 to the LORD, who is w of praise
48: 1 Great is the LORD, and most w of
96: 4 For great is the LORD and most w of
145: 3 Great is the LORD and most w of
Pr 8: 6 Listen, for I have w things to say;
Jer 15:19 you may serve me; if you utter w,
Mt 10:11 search for some w person there and
10:37 mother more than me is not w of me;
10:37 more than me is not w of me;
10:38 cross and follow me is not w of me.
26:66 do you think?" "He is w of death
Mk 1: 7 I am not w to stoop down and untie.
14:64 They all condemned him as w of death.
Lk 3:16 whose sandals I am not w to untie.
7: 7 consider myself w to come to you.
15:19 I am no longer w to be called your
15:21 no longer w to be called your son.'
20:35 those who are considered w of taking
Jn 1:27 whose sandals I am not w to untie."
Ac 5:41 w of suffering disgrace for the Name.
13:25 whose sandals I am not w to untie.'
13:46 yourselves w of eternal life,
Ro 16: 2 the Lord in a way w of the saints
Eph 4: 1 w of the calling you have received.
Php 1:27 a manner w of the gospel of Christ.
Col 1:10 you may live a life w of the Lord
1Th 2:12 urging you to live lives w of God,
2Th 1: 5 be counted w of the kingdom of God,
1:11 that our God may count you w of his
1Ti 3: 8 Deacons, likewise, are to be men w
3:11 their wives are to be women w of
5:17 church well are w of double honour,
6: 1 their masters w of full respect,
Tit 2: 2 w of respect, self-controlled, and
Heb 3: 3 Jesus has been found w of greater
11:38 the world was not w of them. They
3Jn : 6 on their way in a manner w of God.
Rev 3: 4 dressed in white, for they are w.
4:11 "You are w, our Lord and God, to
5: 2 "Who is w to break the seals and
5: 4 w to open the scroll or look inside.
5: 9 they sang a new song: "You are w to
5:12 sang: "W is the Lamb, who was slain

Wound (Wounded, Wounding, Wounds)

Ex 21:25 burn for burn, w for w, bruise for
1Ki 22:35 The blood from his w ran onto the
Job 34: 6 his arrow inflicts an incurable w.'
Ps 69:26 For they persecute those you w and
Jer 6:14 They dress the w of my people as
8:11 They dress the w of my people as
8:22 no healing for the w of my people?
10:19 of my injury! My w is incurable!
14:17 a grievous w, a crushing blow.
15:18 my pain unending and my w grievous
30:12 'Your w is incurable, your injury
30:15 Why do you cry out over your w, your
Lam 2:13 Zion? Your w is as deep as the sea.
Da 6:23 no w was found on him, because he
Mic 1: 9 For her w is incurable; it has come
Na 3:19 Nothing can heal your w; your injury
1Co 8:12 way and w their weak conscience,
Rev 13: 3 w, but the fatal w had been healed.
13:12 whose fatal w had been healed.

Wounded (Wound)

Dt 32:39 I have w and I will heal, and no-one
Jdg 9:40 Abimelech chased him, and many fell w
1Sa 31: 3 overtook him, they w him critically.
1Ki 20:37 So the man struck him and w him.
22:34 out of the fighting. I've been w."
2Ki 8:28 Ramoth Gilead. The Arameans w Joram
8:29 son of Ahab, because he had been w.
9:27 "Kill him too!" They w him in his
1Ch 10: 3 archers overtook him, they w him.
2Ch 18:33 out of the fighting. I've been w."
22: 5 Ramoth Gilead. The Arameans w Joram
22: 6 son of Ahab because he had been w.
24:25 they left Joash severely w.
35:23 "Take me away; I am badly w.
Job 24:12 the souls of the w cry out for help.
Ps 109:22 needy, and my heart is w within me.
Jer 37:10 only w men were left in their tents,
51: 4 Babylon, fatally w in her streets.
51:52 her land the w will groan.
Lam 2:12 w men in the streets of the city,
Eze 26:15 when the w groan and the slaughter
30:24 before him like a mortally w man.
Lk 20:12 sent still a third, and they w him
Rev 13:14 was w by the sword and yet lived.

Wounding (Wound)

Ge 4:23 I have killed a man for w me,

Wounds (Wound)

2Ki 8:29 to recover from the w the Arameans
9:15 to recover from the w the Arameans
18:21 which pierces a man's hand and w him
2Ch 22: 6 to Jezreel to recover from the w
Job 5:18 For he w, but he also binds up; he
9:17 and multiply my w for no reason.
Ps 38: 5 My w fester and are loathsome
38:11 avoid me because of my w; my
147: 3 broken-hearted and binds up their w.
Pr 20:30 Blows and w cleanse away evil, and
26:10 Like an archer who w at random is he
27: 6 W from a friend can be trusted, but
Isa 1: 6 only w and bruises and open sores,
30:26 people and heals the w he inflicted.
36: 6 which pierces a man's hand and w him
53: 5 him, and by his w we are healed.
Jer 6: 7 sickness and w are ever before me.
19: 8 and will scoff because of all its w.
30:17 store you to health and heal your w,'
49:17 and will scoff because of all its w.
50:13 and scoff because of all her w.
Hos 6: 1 us but he will bind up our w.
Zec 13: 6 'What are these w on your body?' he
13: 6 'The w I was given at the house of
Lk 10:34 He went to him and bandaged his w,
Ac 16:33 jailer took them and washed their w;
1Pe 2:24 by his w you have been healed.

Wove (Weave)

Jdg 16:13 seven braids of his head, w them

Woven (Weave)

Ex 28: 4 a w tunic, a turban and a sash.
28: 8 Its skilfully w waistband is to be
28:32 There shall be a w edge like a
29: 5 on him by its skilfully w waistband.
31:10 also the w garments, both the sacred
35:19 the w garments worn for ministering
39: 1 scarlet yarn they made w garments
39: 5 Its skilfully w waistband was like
39:41 the w garments worn for ministering
Lev 8: 7 to him by its skilfully w waistband;
13:48 any w or knitted material of linen
13:49 or leather, or w or knitted material,
13:51 or the w or knitted material, or the
13:52 or the w or knitted material of wool
13:53 or the w or knitted material, or the
13:56 or the w or knitted material.
13:57 or in the w or knitted material, or
13:58 The clothing, or the w or knitted
13:59 clothing, w or knitted material, or
19:19 clothing w of two kinds of material.
Dt 22:11 of wool and linen w together.
Ps 139:15 When I was w together in the depths
Lam 1:14 by his hands they were w together.
Jn 19:23 w in one piece from top to bottom.

Wrap (Wrapped, Wraps)

Nu 4:10 Then they are to w it and all its
4:12 w them in a blue cloth, cover that
Isa 28:20 blanket too narrow to w around you.
Jer 43:12 so will he w Egypt round himself and
Ac 12: 8 And Peter did so. "W your cloak

Wrapped (Wrap)

Ex 12:34 in kneading troughs w in clothing.
1Sa 21: 9 it is w in a cloth behind the ephod.
Job 38: 9 I made the clouds its garment and w
Ps 109:19 May it be like a cloak w about him,
109:29 and w in shame as in a cloak.
Pr 30: 4 Who has w up the waters in his cloak?
Isa 59:17 and w himself in zeal as in a cloak.
Eze 16: 4 you rubbed with salt or w in cloths.
Jnh 2: 5 me; seaweed was w around my head.

Mt 27:59 Joseph took the body, w it in a
Mk 15:46 took down the body, w it in the
Lk 2: 7 She w him in cloths and placed him
2:12 w in cloths and lying in a manger."
23:53 he took it down, w it in linen cloth
Jn 11:44 his hands and feet w with strips of
13: 4 and w a towel round his waist.
13: 5 with the towel that was w round him.
19:40 Taking Jesus' body, the two of them w
21: 7 "It is the Lord," he w his outer
Ac 5: 6 young men came forward, w up his body

Wraps (Wrap)

Job 26: 8 He w up the waters in his clouds,
Ps 104: 2 He w himself in light as with a
Jer 43:12 As a shepherd w his garment round

Wrath (*Day of wrath, God's wrath, Wrath of God*)

Nu 1:53 w will not fall on the Israelite
16:46 W has come out from the LORD; the
18: 5 so that w will not fall on the
Dt 9: 8 At Horeb you aroused the LORD's w so
9:19 I feared the anger and w of the LORD,
29:20 his w and zeal will burn against
29:28 In furious anger and in great w the
32:22 For a fire has been kindled by my w,
Jos 9:20 so that w will not fall on us for
22:20 did not w come upon the whole
1Sa 28:18 his fierce w against the Amalekites,
2Sa 6: 8 David was angry because the LORD's w
1Ch 13:11 David was angry because the LORD's w
27:24 W came on Israel on account of this
2Ch 12: 7 My w will not be poured out on
19: 2 this, the w of the LORD is upon you.
19:10 w will come on you and your brothers.
32:25 therefore the LORD's w was on him
32:26 therefore the LORD's w did not come
36:16 scoffed at his prophets until the w
Ezr 7:23 Why should there be w against the
Ne 13:18 Now you are stirring up more w
Job 19:29 w will bring punishment by the sword,
21:20 him drink of the w of the Almighty.
40:11 Unleash the fury of your w, look at
Ps 2: 5 and terrifies them in his w, saying,
2:12 for his w can flare up in a moment.
6: 1 anger or discipline me in your w.
7:11 a God who expresses his w every day.
21: 9 In his w the LORD will swallow them
37: 8 Refrain from anger and turn from w;
38: 1 anger or discipline me in your w.
38: 3 of your w there is no health in my
59:13 consume them in w, consume them till
69:24 Pour out your w on them; let your
76:10 Surely your w against men brings you
76:10 survivors of your w are restrained.
78:21 Jacob, and his w rose against Israel,
78:38 and did not stir up his full w.
78:49 his w, indignation and hostility—a
79: 6 Pour out your w on the nations that
85: 3 You set aside all your w and turned
88: 7 Your w lies heavily upon me; you
88:16 Your w has swept over me; your
89:46 How long will your w burn like fire?
90: 9 All our days pass away under your w;
90:11 For your w is as great as the fear
102:10 of your great w, for you have taken
106:23 to keep his w from destroying them.
110: 5 crush kings on the day of his w.
Pr 11:23 the hope of the wicked only in w.
14:35 but a shameful servant incurs his w.
15: 1 A gentle answer turns away w, but a
16:14 A king's w is a messenger of death,
20: 2 A king's w is like the roar of a
21:14 in the cloak pacifies great w.
22:14 the LORD's w will fall into it.
24:18 and turn his w away from him.
Isa 9:19 By the w of the LORD Almighty the
10: 5 in whose hand is the club of my w!
10:25 my w will be directed to their
13: 3 my warriors to carry out my w—
13: 5 the LORD and the weapons of his w
13: 9 with w and fierce anger—to make
13:13 place at the w of the LORD Almighty,
26:20 while until his w has passed by.
Isa 30:27 of smoke; his lips are full of w,
34: 2 his w is upon all their armies.
48: 9 For my own name's sake I delay my w;
51:13 because of the w of the oppressor,
51:13 For where is the w of the oppressor?
51:17 hand of the LORD the cup of his w,
51:20 They are filled with the w of the
51:22 of my w, you will never drink again.
59:18 so will he repay w to his enemies
63: 3 trod them down in my w; their blood
63: 5 for me, and my own w sustained me.
63: 6 in my w I made them drunk and poured
Jer 3: 5 will you always be angry? Will your w
4: 4 or my w will break out and burn like
6:11 I am full of the w of the LORD, and
7:20 w will be poured out on this place,
7:29 this generation that is under his w.
10:10 the nations cannot endure his w.
10:25 Pour out your w on the nations that
18:20 to turn your w away from them.
21: 5 arm in anger and fury and great w.
21:12 or my w will break out and burn like
23:19 of the LORD will burst out in w,
25:15 cup filled with the wine of my w
30:23 of the LORD will burst out in w,
32:31 city has so aroused my anger and w
32:37 in my furious anger and great w;
33: 5 men I will slay in my anger and w.
36: 7 for the anger and w pronounced
42:18 'As my anger and w have been poured
42:18 so will my w be poured out on you
50:25 brought out the weapons of his w,
Lam 2: 2 in his w he has torn down the
2: 4 he has poured out his w like fire on
3: 1 seen affliction by the rod of his w.
4:11 The LORD has given full vent to his w
Eze 5:13 "Then my anger will cease and my w
5:13 And when I have spent my w upon them,
5:15 and in w and with stinging rebuke.
6:12 So will I spend my w upon them.
7: 8 I am about to pour out my w on you
7:12 for w is upon the whole crowd.
7:14 for my w is upon the whole crowd.
7:19 them in the day of the LORD's w.
9: 8 outpouring of your w on Jerusalem?"
13:13 my w I will unleash a violent wind,
13:15 I will spend my w against the wall
14:19 out my w upon it through bloodshed,
16:38 vengeance of my w and jealous anger.
16:42 my w against you will subside and my
20: 8 So I said I would pour out my w on
20:13 So I said I would pour out my w on
20:21 So I said I would pour out my w on
20:33 arm and with outpoured w.
20:34 arm and with outpoured w.
21:17 together, and my w will subside.
21:31 I will pour out my w upon you and
22:20 gather you in my anger and my w and
22:21 blow on you with my fiery w, and
22:22 LORD have poured out my w upon you.
22:31 I will pour out my w on them and
24: 8 To stir up w and take revenge I put
24:13 until my w against you has subsided.
25:14 with my anger and my w; they will
25:17 on them and punish them in my w.
30:15 I will pour out my w on Pelusium,
36: 6 I speak in my jealous w because you
36:18 I poured out my w on them because
38:19 In my zeal and fiery w I declare
Da 8:19 will happen later in the time of w,
9:16 turn away your anger and your w from
11:36 until the time of w is completed,
Hos 5:10 my w on them like a flood of water.
11: 9 among you. I will not come in w.
13:11 a king, and in my w I took him away.
Am 1: 3 for four, I will not turn back my w.
1: 6 for four, I will not turn back my w.
1: 9 for four, I will not turn back my w.
1:11 for four, I will not turn back my w.
1:13 for four, I will not turn back my w.
2: 1 for four, I will not turn back my w.
2: 4 for four, I will not turn back my w.
2: 6 for four, I will not turn back my w.
Mic 5:15 I will take vengeance in anger and w
7: 9 I will bear the LORD's w, until he
Na 1: 2 vengeance and is filled with w.
Na 1: 2 maintains his w against his enemies.
1: 6 His w is poured out like fire;
Hab 3: 2 them known; in w remember mercy.
3: 8 Was your w against the streams?
3:12 In w you strode through the earth
Zep 1:18 them on the day of the LORD's w.
2: 2 day of the LORD's w comes upon you.
3: 8 my w on them—all my fierce anger.
Mal 1: 4 always under the w of the LORD.
Mt 3: 7 you to flee from the coming w?
Lk 3: 7 you to flee from the coming w?
21:23 the land and w against this people.
Ro 2: 5 you are storing up w against
2: 8 evil, there will be w and anger.
3: 5 is unjust in bringing his w on us?
4:15 law brings w. And where there is no
9:22 What if God, choosing to show his w
9:22 of his w—prepared for destruction?
13: 4 He is God's servant, an agent of w
Eph 2: 3 we were by nature objects of w.
1Th 1:10 who rescues us from the coming w.
5: 9 God did not appoint us to suffer w
Rev 6:16 throne and from the w of the Lamb!
6:17 For the great day of their w has
11:18 The nations were angry; and your w
14:10 full strength into the cup of his w.
16:19 with the wine of the fury of his w.

Wrath of God

Ro 1:18 The w is being revealed from heaven
Col 3: 6 Because of these, the w is coming.
1Th 2:16 The w has come upon them at last.
Rev 15: 7 golden bowls filled with the w,
19:15 of the fury of the w Almighty.

Wreath (Wreaths)

Isa 28: 1 Woe to that w, the pride of
28: 3 That w, the pride of Ephraim's
28: 5 a beautiful w for the remnant of

Wreaths (Wreath)

1Ki 7:29 and bulls were w of hammered work.
7:30 supports, cast with w on each side.
7:36 available space, with w all around.
Ac 14:13 brought bulls and w to the city

Wrecked (Shipwreck, Shipwrecked)

1Ki 22:48 sail—they were w at Ezion Geber.
2Ch 20:37 The ships were w and were not able

Wrenched

Ge 32:25 was w as he wrestled with the man.
Eze 29: 7 you broke and their backs were w.

Wrestle (Wrestled, Wrestling)

Ps 13: 2 How long must I w with my thoughts

Wrestled (Wrestle)

Ge 32:24 Jacob was left alone, and a man w
32:25 was wrenched as he w with the man.

Wrestling (Wrestle)

Col 4:12 He is always w in prayer for you,

Wretched (Wretches)

Jdg 11:35 You have made me miserable and w,
Pr 15:15 All the days of the oppressed are w,
Hab 3:14 to devour the w who were in hiding.
Mt 21:41 will bring those wretches to a w end
Ro 7:24 What a w man I am! Who will rescue
Rev 3:17 w, pitiful, poor, blind and naked.

Wretches (Wretched)

Mt 21:41 "He will bring those w to a wretched

Wring

Lev 1:15 w off the head and burn it on the
5: 8 He is to w its head from its neck,

Wrinkle

Eph 5:27 without stain or w or any other

Wrist (Wrists)

Ge 38:28 tied it on his w and said, "This
38:30 who had the scarlet thread on his w,

Wrists (Wrist)

Jer 40: 4 you from the chains on your w.
Eze 13:18 who sew magic charms on all their w
Ac 12: 7 and the chains fell off Peter's w.

Write (Writer, Writes, Writing, Writings, Written, Wrote)

Ex 17:14 the LORD said to Moses, "W this on a
34: 1 and I will w on them the words that
34:27 the LORD said to Moses, "W down
Nu 5:23 "'The priest is to w these curses
17: 2 W the name of each man on his staff.
17: 3 On the staff of Levi w Aaron's name,
Dt 6: 9 W them on the door-frames of your
10: 2 I will w on the tablets the words
11:20 W them on the door-frames of your
17:18 he is to w for himself on a scroll a
27: 3 W on them all the words of this law
27: 8 you shall w very clearly all the
31:19 "Now w down for yourselves this song
Jos 18: 4 land and to w a description of it,
18: 8 the land and w a description of it.
Ezr 5:10 so that we could w down the names of
Est 8: 8 Now w another decree in the king's
Job 13:26 For you w down bitter things against
Ps 87: 6 The LORD will w in the register of
Pr 3: 3 w them on the tablet of your heart.
7: 3 Bind them on your fingers; w them on
Isa 8: 1 "Take a large scroll and w on it
10:19 few that a child could w them down.
30: 8 Go now, w it on a tablet for them,
44: 5 still another will w on his hand,
Jer 30: 2 'W in a book all the words I have
31:33 minds and w it on their hearts.
36: 2 "Take a scroll and w on it all the
36:17 w all this? Did Jeremiah dictate it?"
36:28 "Take another scroll and w on it all
36:29 "Why did you w on it that the king
Eze 37:16 take a stick of wood and w on it,
37:16 and w on it, 'Ephraim's stick,
43:11 W these down before them so that
Hab 2: 2 the LORD replied: "W down the
Mk 10: 4 "Moses permitted a man to w a
Lk 1: 3 it seemed good also to me to w an
Jn 8: 6 to w on the ground with his finger.
19:21 "Do not w 'The King of the Jews',
Ac 15:20 Instead we should w to them, telling
25:26 I have nothing definite to w to His
25:26 I may have something to w.
1Co 16:21 I, Paul, w this greeting in my own
2Co 1:13 For we do not w to you anything you
9: 1 There is no need for me to w to you
13:10 This is why I w these things when I
Gal 6:11 See what large letters I use as I w
Php 3: 1 to w the same things to you again,
Col 4:18 I, Paul, w this greeting in my own
1Th 4: 9 love we do not need to w to you,
5: 1 dates we do not need to w to you,
2Th 3:17 I, Paul, w this greeting in my own
3:17 in all my letters. This is how I w.
Phm :21 Confident of your obedience, I w to
Heb 8:10 minds and w them on their hearts.
10:16 and I will w them on their minds."
1Jn 1: 4 We w this to make our joy complete.
2: 1 My dear children, I w this to you so
2:12 I w to you, dear children, because
2:13 I w to you, fathers, because you
2:13 I w to you, young men, because you
2:13 I w to you, dear children, because
2:14 I w to you, fathers, because you
2:14 I w to you, young men, because you
2:21 I do not w to you because you do not
5:13 I w these things to you who believe
2Jn :12 I have much to w to you, but I do
3Jn :13 I have much to w to you, but I do
Jude : 3 although I was very eager to w to
: 3 I felt I had to w and urge you to
Rev 1:11 which said: "W on a scroll what you
1:19 "W, therefore, what you have seen,
2: 1 angel of the church in Ephesus w:
2: 8 the angel of the church in Smyrna w:
Rev 2:12 angel of the church in Pergamum w:
2:18 angel of the church in Thyatira w:
3: 1 the angel of the church in Sardis w:
3: 7 of the church in Philadelphia w:
3:12 I will w on him the name of my God
3:12 I will also w on him my new name.
3:14 w: These are the words of the Amen,
10: 4 I was about to w; but I heard a
10: 4 have said and do not w it down."
14:13 I heard a voice from heaven say, "W:
19: 9 the angel said to me, "W: 'Blessed
21: 5 "W this down, for these words are

Writer (Write)

Ps 45: 1 my tongue is the pen of a skilful w.

Writes (Write)

Dt 24: 1 he w her a certificate of divorce,
24: 3 her second husband dislikes her and w
2Pe 3:16 He w the same way in all his letters,

Writhe (Writhed, Writhes)

Isa 13: 8 they will w like a woman in labour.
Jer 4:19 anguish, my anguish! I w in pain
Eze 30:16 to Egypt; Pelusium will w in agony.
Mic 1:12 Those who live in Maroth w in pain,
4:10 W in agony, O Daughter of Zion, like
Zec 9: 5 it and fear; Gaza will w in agony,

Writhed (Writhe)

Ps 77:16 O God, the waters saw you and w;
Isa 26:18 We were with child, we w in pain,
Hab 3:10 the mountains saw you and w.

Writhes (Writhe)

Isa 26:17 birth w and cries out in her pain,
Jer 51:29 The land trembles and w, for the

Writing (Write)

Ex 32:16 work of God; the w was the w of God,
Dt 31:24 After Moses finished w in a book the
1Ch 28:19 "All this," David said, "I have in w
2Ch 36:22 his realm and to put it in w:
Ezr 1: 1 his realm and to put it in w:
Ne 9:38 putting it in w, and our leaders,
Job 31:35 my accuser put his indictment in w.
Isa 38: 9 A w of Hezekiah king of Judah after
Eze 9: 2 linen who had a w kit at his side.
9: 3 linen who had the w kit at his side
9:11 the man in linen with the w kit at
Da 5: 7 "Whoever reads this w and tells me
5: 8 they could not read the w or tell
5:12 he will tell you what the w means."
5:15 this w and tell me what it means,
5:16 If you can read this w and tell me
5:17 Nevertheless, I will read the w for
6: 8 issue the decree and put it in w so
6: 9 King Darius put the decree in w.
6:13 king, or to the decree you put in w.
Lk 1:63 He asked for a w tablet, and to
Ac 15:27 by word of mouth what we are w.
1Co 4:14 I am not w this to shame you, but to
5:11 now I am w to you that you must not
9:15 And I am not w this in the hope that
14:37 I am w to you is the Lord's command.
Gal 1:20 that what I am w to you is no lie.
1Ti 3:14 am w you these instructions so that,
Phm :19 I, Paul, am w this with my own hand.
1Jn 2: 7 Dear friends, I am not w you a new
2: 8 Yet I am w you a new command; its
2:26 I am w these things to you about
2Jn : 5 now, dear lady, I am not w you a new
Rev 5: 1 a scroll with w on both sides

Writings (Write)

Mt 26:56 that the w of the prophets might be
Ro 16:26 w by the command of the eternal God,

Written (*It is Written*, Write)

Ge 5: 1 This is the w account of Adam's line.
Ex 24:12 I have w for their instruction."
32:32 blot me out of the book you have w."
Dt 10: 4 these tablets what he had w before,
Dt 28:58 which are w in this book, and do not
29:20 All the curses w in this book will
29:21 covenant w in this Book of the Law.
29:27 on it all the curses w in this book.
30:10 decrees that are w in this Book of
Jos 1: 8 be careful to do everything w in it.
8:31 He built it according to what is w
8:32 the law of Moses, which he had w.
18: 6 After you have w descriptions of the
23: 6 w in the Book of the Law of Moses,
1Ki 2: 3 his laws and requirements, as w in
11:41 are they not w in the book of the
14:19 his wars and how he ruled, are w in
14:29 and all he did, are they not w in
15: 7 and all he did, are they not w in
15:23 are they not w in the book of the
15:31 and all he did, are they not w in
16: 5 are they not w in the book of the
16:14 and all he did, are they not w in
16:20 are they not w in the book of the
16:27 are they not w in the book of the
21:11 in the letters she had w to them.
22:39 are they not w in the book of the
22:45 are they not w in the book of the
2Ki 1:18 and what he did, are they not w in
8:23 and all he did, are they not w in
10:34 are they not w in the book of the
12:19 and all he did, are they not w in
13: 8 are they not w in the book of the
13:12 are they not w in the book of the
14: 6 in accordance with what is w in the
14:15 are they not w in the book of the
14:18 are they not w in the book of the
14:28 are they not w in the book of the
15: 6 and all he did, are they not w in
15:11 w in the book of the annals of the
15:15 and the conspiracy he led, are w in
15:21 and all he did, are they not w in
15:26 and all he did, are w in the book of
15:31 and all he did, are they not w in
15:36 and what he did, are they not w in
16:19 and what he did, are they not w in
20:20 are they not w in the book of the
21:17 are they not w in the book of the
21:25 and what he did, are they not w in
22:13 w in this book that has been found.
22:13 all that is w there concerning us."
22:16 according to everything w in the
23: 3 of the covenant w in this book.
23:24 the requirements of the law w in
23:28 and all he did, are they not w in
24: 5 and all he did, are they not w in
1Ch 16:40 in accordance with everything w in
29:29 from beginning to end, they are w in
2Ch 9:29 are they not w in the records of
12:15 are they not w in the records of
13:22 what he did and what he said, are w
16:11 from beginning to end, are w in the
20:34 from beginning to end, are w in the
23:18 the LORD as w in the Law of Moses,
24:27 w in the annotations on the book of
25: 4 with what is w in the Law,
25:26 are they not w in the book of the
27: 7 are w in the book of the kings of
28:26 from beginning to end, are w in the
30: 5 numbers according to what was w.
30:18 Passover, contrary to what was w.
31: 3 feasts as w in the Law of the LORD.
32:32 his acts of devotion are w in the
33:18 the God of Israel, are w in the
33:19 are w in the records of the seers.
34:21 w in this book that has been found.
34:21 with all that is w in this book."
34:24 its people—all the curses w in the
34:31 of the covenant w in this book.
35: 4 according to the directions w by
35:12 LORD, as is w in the Book of Moses.
35:25 in Israel and are w in the Laments.
35:26 what is w in the Law of the LORD—
35:27 from beginning to end, are w in the
36: 8 are w in the book of the kings of
Ezr 3: 2 w in the Law of Moses the man of God.
3: 4 in accordance with what is w, they
4: 7 The letter was w in Aramaic script
5: 5 Darius and his w reply be received.
6: 2 and this was w on it: Memorandum:

Ezr 6:18 to what is **w** in the Book of Moses.
Ne 6: 6 in which was **w**: "It is reported
7: 5 This is what I found **w** there:
8:14 They found **w** in the Law, which the
10:36 "As it is also **w** in the Law, we will
13: 1 there it was found **w** that no
Est 1:19 **w** in the laws of Persia and Media,
3:12 These were **w** in the name of King
8: 5 let an order be **w** overruling the
8: 8 no document **w** in the king's name
8: 9 These orders were **w** in the script of
9:23 doing what Mordecai had **w** to them.
9:25 he issued **w** orders that the evil
9:26 Because of everything **w** in this
9:32 and it was **w** down in the records.
10: 2 are they not **w** in the book of the
Job 19:23 that they were **w** on a scroll,
Ps 102:18 Let this be **w** for a future
139:16 All the days ordained for me were **w**
149: 9 to carry out the sentence **w** against
Pr 22:20 Have I not **w** thirty sayings for you,
Isa 65: 6 "See, it stands **w** before me; I will
Jer 17:13 away from you will be **w** in the dust
25:13 all that are **w** in this book and
36:27 Baruch had **w** at Jeremiah's dictation,
45: 1 after Baruch had **w** on a scroll the
51:60 Jeremiah had **w** on a scroll about all
Eze 2:10 On both sides of it were **w** words of
37:20 their eyes the sticks you have **w**
Da 5:25 "This is the inscription that was **w**:
9:11 judgments **w** in the Law of Moses,
10:21 first I will tell you what is **w** in
12: 1 **w** in the book—will be delivered.
Mal 3:16 A scroll of remembrance was **w** in his
Mt 2: 5 "for this is what the prophet has **w**
4: 7 Jesus answered him, "It is also **w**:
27:37 Above his head they placed the **w**
Mk 1: 2 is **w** in Isaiah the prophet: "I will
9:12 Why then is it **w** that the Son of Man
11:17 he taught them, he said, "Is it not **w**
15:26 The **w** notice of the charge against
Lk 3: 4 is **w** in the book of the words of
10:20 that your names are **w** in heaven."
10:26 "What is **w** in the Law?" he replied.
18:31 and everything that is **w** by the
20:17 is the meaning of that which is **w**:
21:22 fulfilment of all that has been **w**.
22:37 is **w**: 'And he was numbered with the
22:37 Yes, what is **w** about me is reaching
23:38 There was a **w** notice above him,
24:44 is **w** about me in the Law of Moses,
24:46 He told them, "This is what is **w**:
Jn 6:45 is **w** in the Prophets: 'They will all
10:34 Jesus answered them, "Is it not **w** in
12:16 these things had been **w** about him
15:25 this is to fulfil what is **w** in their
19:20 was **w** in Aramaic, Latin and Greek.
19:22 answered, "What I have **w**, I have **w**.
20:31 these are **w** that you may believe
21:25 If every one of them were **w** down, I
21:25 room for the books that would be **w**.
Ac 7:42 This agrees with what is **w** in the
13:29 they had carried out all that was **w**
21:25 for the Gentile believers, we have **w**
24:14 Law and that is **w** in the Prophets,
Ro 2:15 of the law are **w** on their hearts,
2:24 is **w**: "God's name is blasphemed
2:27 even though you have the **w** code and
2:29 by the Spirit, not by the **w** code.
3:10 is **w**: "There is no-one righteous,
4:17 is **w**: "I have made you a father of
4:23 "it was credited to him" were **w** not
7: 6 not in the old way of the **w** code.
8:36 is **w**: "For your sake we face death
9:33 is **w**: "See, I lay in Zion a stone
11: 8 is **w**: "God gave them a spirit of
14:11 is **w**: "'As surely as I live,' says
15: 4 was **w** in the past was **w** to teach us,
15:15 I have **w** to you quite boldly on some
1Co 4: 6 saying, "Do not go beyond what is **w**.
5: 9 I have **w** to you in my letter not to
9:10 doesn't he? Yes, this was **w** for us,
10:11 and were **w** down as warnings for us,
15:45 is **w**: "The first man Adam became a
15:54 then the saying that is **w** will come
2Co 3: 2 You yourselves are our letter, **w** on
2Co 3: 3 the result of our ministry, **w** not
4:13 is **w**: "I believed; therefore I have
8:15 is **w**: "He who gathered much did not
9: 9 is **w**: "He has scattered abroad his
Gal 3:10 **w** in the Book of the Law."
Eph 3: 3 as I have already **w** briefly.
Col 2:14 having cancelled the **w** code, with
Heb 12:23 whose names are **w** in heaven.
13:22 I have **w** you only a short letter.
1Pe 5:12 I have **w** to you briefly, encouraging
2Pe 3: 1 I have **w** both of them as reminders
Jude : 4 men whose condemnation was **w** about
Rev 1: 3 **w** in it, because the time is near.
2:17 white stone with a new name **w** on it,
13: 8 all whose names have not been **w** in
14: 1 Father's name **w** on their foreheads.
17: 5 This title was **w** on her forehead:
17: 8 whose names have not been **w** in the
19:12 He has a name **w** on him that no-one
19:16 and on his thigh he has this name **w**:
20:15 If anyone's name was not found **w** in
21:12 On the gates were **w** the names of the
21:27 are **w** in the Lamb's book of life.

Wrong (Wrongdoer, Wrongdoing, Wrongdoings, Wronged, Wronging, Wrongs)

Ge 16: 5 for the **w** I am suffering.
Ex 2:13 He asked the one in the **w**, "Why are
9:27 and I and my people are in the **w**.
23: 2 "Do not follow the crowd in doing **w**.
Lev 5:18 **w** he has committed unintentionally,
Nu 5: 7 make full restitution for his **w**,
5: 8 restitution can be made for the **w**,
15:25 their **w** an offering made by fire
15:26 involved in the unintentional **w**.
Dt 32: 4 does no **w**, upright and just is he.
Jdg 11:27 doing me **w** by waging war against me.
1Sa 11: 5 "What is **w** with the people? Why are
19: 4 "Let not the king do **w** to his
19: 5 Why then would you do **w** to an
25:39 He has kept his servant from doing **w**
26:18 I done, and what **w** am I guilty of?
2Sa 7:14 When he does **w**, I will punish him
13:16 would be a greater **w** than what you
19:19 how your servant did **w** on the day
24:17 the one who has sinned and done **w**.
1Ki 2:44 the **w** you did to my father David.
3: 9 to distinguish between right and **w**.
8:47 done **w**, we have acted wickedly';
18: 9 "What have I done **w**," asked Obadiah,
2Ki 18:14 Assyria at Lachish: "I have done **w**.
1Ch 21:17 the one who has sinned and done **w**.
2Ch 6:37 we have done **w** and acted wickedly';
22: 3 mother encouraged him in doing **w**.
Ne 9:33 acted faithfully, while we did **w**.
Est 1:16 "Queen Vashti has done **w**, not only
Job 6:24 quiet; show me where I have been **w**.
21:27 the schemes by which you would **w** me.
31: 3 wicked, disaster for those who do **w**?
32:12 But not one of you has proved Job **w**;
34:10 do evil, from the Almighty to do **w**.
34:12 is unthinkable that God would do **w**,
34:32 done **w**, I will not do so again.'
36:23 or said to him, 'You have done **w**'?
Ps 5: 5 presence; you hate all who do **w**.
15: 3 who does his neighbour no **w** and
36: 4 and does not reject what is **w**.
37: 1 men or be envious of those who do **w**;
59: 4 I have done no **w**, yet they are ready
106: 6 we have done **w** and acted wickedly.
119: 3 They do nothing **w**; they walk in his
119:104 therefore I hate every **w** path.
119:128 precepts right, I hate every **w** path.
Pr 2:14 who delight in doing **w** and rejoice
20:22 "I'll pay you back for this **w**!" Wait
28:21 man will do **w** for a piece of bread.
28:24 "It's not **w**"—he is partner to him
30:20 and says, 'I've done nothing **w**.'
Ecc 5: 1 who do not know that they do **w**.
8:11 are filled with schemes to do **w**.
Isa 1:16 deeds out of my sight! Stop doing **w**,
7:15 reject the **w** and choose the right.
7:16 reject the **w** and choose the right,
Jer 16:10 What **w** have we done? What sin have
Jer 22: 3 Do no **w** or violence to the alien,
51:24 all the **w** they have done in Zion,"
Lam 3:59 You have seen, O LORD, the **w** done to
Eze 18: 8 He withholds his hand from doing **w**
18:18 and did what was **w** among his people.
Da 6:22 ever done any **w** before you, O king."
9: 5 we have sinned and done **w**. We have
9:15 day, we have sinned, we have done **w**.
Hab 1: 3 Why do you tolerate **w**? Destruction
1:13 look on evil; you cannot tolerate **w**.
Zep 3: 5 her is righteous; he does no **w**.
3:13 The remnant of Israel will do no **w**;
Mal 1: 8 is that not **w**? When you sacrifice
1: 8 is that not **w**? Try offering them to
Lk 23:41 But this man has done nothing **w**."
Jn 18:23 "If I said something **w**," Jesus
18:23 replied, "testify as to what is **w**.
Ac 23: 9 "We find nothing **w** with this man,"
25: 5 there, if he has done anything **w**."
25: 8 "I have done nothing **w** against the
25:10 I have not done any **w** to the Jews,
Ro 13: 3 do right, but for those who do **w**.
13: 4 But if you do **w**, be afraid, for he
14:20 All food is clean, but it is **w** for a
1Co 6: 8 cheat and do **w**, and you do this
2Co 7:12 did the **w** or of the injured party,
12:13 a burden to you? Forgive me this **w**!
13: 7 God that you will not do anything **w**.
Gal 2:11 because he was clearly in the **w**.
4:12 You have done me no **w**.
Col 3:25 who does **w** will be repaid for his **w**,
1Th 4: 6 that in this matter no-one should **w**
5:15 sure that nobody pays back **w** for **w**,
Phm :18 If he has done you any **w** or owes you
Heb 8: 7 For if there had been nothing **w** with
Jas 4: 3 because you ask with **w** motives, that
1Pe 2:12 though they accuse you of doing **w**,
2:14 to punish those who do **w** and to
2:20 a beating for doing **w** and endure it?
Rev 22:11 Let him who does **w** continue to do **w**;

Wrongdoer (Wrong)

Ro 13: 4 wrath to bring punishment on the **w**.

Wrongdoing (Wrong)

Lev 5:19 been guilty of **w** against the LORD."
Nu 5:31 The husband will be innocent of any **w**
1Sa 24:11 I am not guilty of **w** or rebellion.
25:28 Let no **w** be found in you as long as
25:39 Nabal's **w** down on his own head.
1Ki 2:44 the LORD will repay you for your **w**.
Job 1:22 did not sin by charging God with **w**.
24:12 But God charges no-one with **w**.
33:17 to turn man from **w** and keep him from
Pr 16:12 Kings detest **w**, for a throne is
2Pe 2:16 he was rebuked for his **w** by a donkey
1Jn 5:17 All **w** is sin, and there is sin that

Wrongdoings (Wrong)

Jer 5:25 Your **w** have kept these away; your

Wronged (Wrong)

Ge 20: 9 How have I **w** you that you have
Nu 5: 7 give it all to the person he has **w**.
16:15 them, nor have I **w** any of them."
Jdg 11:27 I have not **w** you, but you are doing
1Sa 19: 4 his servant David; he has not **w** you,
20: 1 my crime? How have I **w** your father,
24:11 I have not **w** you, but you are
Job 19: 6 know that God has **w** me and drawn his
19: 7 "Though I cry, 'I've been **w**!' I get
1Co 6: 7 Why not rather be **w**? Why not rather
2Co 7: 2 We have **w** no-one, we have corrupted

Wronging (Wrong)

Ps 119:78 put to shame for **w** me without cause;

Wrongs (Wrong)

Ge 50:15 back for all the **w** we did to him?"
50:17 the **w** they committed in treating you
Nu 5: 6 'When a man or woman **w** another in
1Sa 24:12 And may the LORD avenge the **w** you
1Ki 8:31 "When a man **w** his neighbour and is
2Ch 6:22 "When a man **w** his neighbour and is

Job 13:23 How many w and sins have I committed?
Pr 10:12 but love covers over all w.
Zep 3:11 for all the w you have done to me,
1Co 13: 5 angered, it keeps no record of w.

Wrote (Write)

Ex 24: 4 Moses then w down everything the
34:28 And he w on the tablets the words of
Dt 4:13 then w them on two stone tablets.
5:22 Then he w them on two stone tablets
10: 4 The LORD w on these tablets what he
31: 9 Moses w down this law and gave it to
31:22 Moses w down this song that day and
Jos 18: 9 They w its description on a scroll,
Jdg 8:14 and the young man w down for him the
1Sa 10:25 He w them down on a scroll and
2Sa 11:14 In the morning David w a letter to
11:15 In it he w, "Put Uriah in the front
1Ki 21: 8 she w letters in Ahab's name, placed
21: 9 In those letters she w: "Proclaim a
2Ki 10: 1 So Jehu w letters and sent them to
10: 6 Jehu w them a second letter, saying,
17:37 the laws and commands he w for you.
2Ch 30: 1 w letters to Ephraim and Manasseh,
32:17 The king also w letters insulting
Ezr 4: 7 associates w a letter to Artaxerxes.
4: 8 Shimshai the secretary w a letter
Est 3:12 They w out in the script of each
8: 5 the Agagite, devised and w to
8: 9 They w out all Mordecai's orders to
8:10 Mordecai w in the name of King
9:22 He w to them to observe the days as
9:29 along with Mordecai the Jew, w with
Ecc 12:10 and what he w was upright and true.
Jer 36: 4 to him, Baruch w them on the scroll.
36: 6 the LORD that you w as I dictated.
36:18 and I w them in ink on the scroll."
36:32 and as Jeremiah dictated, Baruch w
Da 5: 5 and w on the plaster of the wall,
5: 5 The king watched the hand as it w.
5:24 Therefore he sent the hand that w
6:25 King Darius w to all the peoples,
7: 1 He w down the substance of his dream.
Hos 8:12 I w for them the many things of my
Mk 10: 5 Moses w you this law," Jesus replied.
12:19 "Teacher," they said, "Moses w for
Lk 1:63 he w, "His name is John.
20:28 "Teacher," they said, "Moses w for
Jn 1:45 "We have found the one Moses w about
1:45 and about whom the prophets also w
5:46 would believe me, for he w about me.
5:47 since you do not believe what he w,
8: 8 Again he stooped down and w on the
21:24 to these things and who w them down.
Ac 1: 1 In my former book, Theophilus, I w
18:27 the brothers encouraged him and w to
23:25 He w a letter as follows:
Ro 16:22 I, Tertius, who w down this letter,
1Co 7: 1 Now for the matters you w about: It
2Co 2: 3 I w as I did so that when I came I
2: 4 For I w to you out of great distress
2: 9 The reason I w to you was to see if
7:12 even though I w to you, it was not
2Pe 3:15 our dear brother Paul also w to you
3Jn : 9 I w to the church, but Diotrephes,

Wrought

Eze 27:19 merchandise; they exchanged w iron,

Wrung

Jdg 6:38 w out the dew—a bowlful of water.

Xerxes

King of Persia (Ezr 4:6; Est 1:1–2); father of Darius (Da 9:1). Deposed Vashti; married Esther (Est 1–2). Assassination attempt uncovered by Mordecai (Est 2:21–23). Gave assent to Haman's edict to kill Jews (Est 3); allowed Esther to see him without being called (Est 5:1–8); hanged Haman (Est 7). Exalted Mordecai (Est 8:1–2; 9:4; 10); allowed Jews to defend themselves (Est 8–9).

Ezr 4: 6 At the beginning of the reign of X,
Est 1: 1 during the time of X, the X who
1: 2 At that time King X reigned from his
Est 1: 9 women in the royal palace of King X.
1:10 On the seventh day, when King X was
1:15 not obeyed the command of King X
1:16 of all the provinces of King X.
1:17 King X commanded Queen Vashti to be
1:19 to enter the presence of King X.
2: 1 Later when the anger of King X had
2:12 girl's turn came to go in to King X,
2:16 She was taken to King X in the royal
2:21 and conspired to assassinate King X.
3: 1 King X honoured Haman son of
3: 6 throughout the whole kingdom of X.
3: 7 In the twelfth year of King X, in
3: 8 Haman said to King X, "There is a
3:12 in the name of King X himself
6: 2 had conspired to assassinate King X.
7: 5 King X asked Queen Esther, "Who is
8: 1 That same day King X gave Queen
8: 7 King X replied to Queen Esther and
8:10 Mordecai wrote in the name of King X
8:12 in all the provinces of King X was
9: 2 in all the provinces of King X to
9:20 provinces of King X, near and far,
9:30 127 provinces of the kingdom of X
10: 1 King X imposed tribute throughout
10: 3 Jew was second in rank to King X,
Da 9: 1 the first year of Darius son of X

Yards

Jos 3: 4 thousand y between you and the ark;
Ne 3:13 repaired five hundred y of the wall
Jn 21: 8 far from shore, about a hundred y.

Yarn

Ex 25: 4 blue, purple and scarlet y and fine
26: 1 purple and scarlet y, with cherubim
26:31 purple and scarlet y and finely
26:36 purple and scarlet y and finely
27:16 of blue, purple and scarlet y and
28: 5 and scarlet y, and fine linen.
28: 6 and of blue, purple and scarlet y,
28: 8 with blue, purple and scarlet y,
28:15 of blue, purple and scarlet y,
28:33 purple and scarlet y around the hem
35: 6 blue, purple and scarlet y and fine
35:23 purple or scarlet y or fine linen,
35:25 purple or scarlet y or fine linen.
35:35 purple and scarlet y and fine linen,
36: 8 purple and scarlet y, with cherubim
36:35 purple and scarlet y and finely
36:37 purple and scarlet y and finely
38:18 purple and scarlet y and finely
38:23 and scarlet y and fine linen.)
39: 1 From the blue, purple and scarlet y
39: 2 of blue, purple and scarlet y,
39: 3 purple and scarlet y and fine linen—
39: 5 and with blue, purple and scarlet y,
39: 8 of blue, purple and scarlet y,
39:24 purple and scarlet y and finely
39:29 purple and scarlet y—the work of an
Lev 14: 4 scarlet y and hyssop be brought for
14: 6 the scarlet y and the hyssop, into
14:49 cedar wood, scarlet y and hyssop.
14:51 the hyssop, the scarlet y and the
14:52 wood, the hyssop and the scarlet y.
2Ch 2: 7 and in purple, crimson and blue y,
2:14 blue and crimson y and fine linen.
3:14 purple and crimson y and fine linen,

Yaudi

2Ki 14:28 which had belonged to Y, are they

Year (Year's, *Year of Jubilee*, Yearling, Yearly, Year-old, Years)

Ge 7:11 In the six hundredth y of Noah's
8:13 of Noah's six hundred and first y,
14: 4 in the thirteenth y they rebelled.
14: 5 In the fourteenth y, Kedorlaomer and
17:21 bear to you by this time next y."
18:10 to you about this time next y,
18:14 next y and Sarah will have a son."
26:12 and the same y reaped a hundredfold,
47:17 And he brought them through that y
47:18 that y was over, they came to him
Ge 47:18 they came to him the following y and
Ex 12: 2 month, the first month of your y.
13:10 at the appointed time y after y.
21: 2 But in the seventh y, he shall go
23:11 during the seventh y let the land
23:14 "Three times a y you are to
23:16 of Ingathering at the end of the y,
23:17 "Three times a y all the men are to
23:29 not drive them out in a single y,
29:38 each day: two lambs a y old.
30:10 Once a y Aaron shall make atonement
34:22 of Ingathering at the turn of the y.
34:23 Three times a y all your men are to
34:24 you go up three times each y to
40:17 of the first month in the second y.
Lev 9: 3 a calf and a lamb—both a y old and
14:10 male lambs and one ewe lamb a y old,
16:34 Atonement is to be made once a y
19:24 In the fourth y all its fruit will
19:25 in the fifth y you may eat its fruit
23:12 LORD a lamb a y old without defect,
23:18 each a y old and without defect, one
23:19 a y old, for a fellowship offering.
23:41 to the LORD for seven days each y.
25: 4 in the seventh y the land is to have
25: 5 The land is to have a y of rest.
25: 6 land yields during the sabbath y
25:10 Consecrate the fiftieth y and
25:11 The fiftieth y shall be a jubilee
25:20 "What will we eat in the seventh y
25:21 such a blessing in the sixth y that
25:22 While you plant during the eighth y,
25:22 the harvest of the ninth y comes in.
25:29 redemption a full y after its sale.
25:30 it is not redeemed before a full y
25:50 the time from the y he sold himself
25:53 treated as a man hired from y to y;
Nu 1: 1 of the second month of the second y
7:15 lamb a y old, for a burnt offering;
7:17 goats and five male lambs a y old,
7:21 lamb a y old, for a burnt offering;
7:23 goats and five male lambs a y old,
7:27 lamb a y old, for a burnt offering;
7:29 goats and five male lambs a y old,
7:33 lamb a y old, for a burnt offering;
7:35 goats and five male lambs a y old,
7:39 lamb a y old, for a burnt offering;
7:41 goats and five male lambs a y old,
7:45 lamb a y old, for a burnt offering;
7:47 goats and five male lambs a y old,
7:51 lamb a y old, for a burnt offering;
7:53 goats and five male lambs a y old,
7:57 lamb a y old, for a burnt offering;
7:59 goats and five male lambs a y old,
7:63 lamb a y old, for a burnt offering;
7:65 goats and five male lambs a y old,
7:69 lamb a y old, for a burnt offering;
7:71 goats and five male lambs a y old,
7:75 lamb a y old, for a burnt offering;
7:77 goats and five male lambs a y old,
7:81 lamb a y old, for a burnt offering;
7:83 goats and five male lambs a y old,
7:87 rams and twelve male lambs a y old,
7:88 goats and sixty male lambs a y old.
9: 1 in the first month of the second y
9:22 for two days or a month or a y,
10:11 of the second month of the second y,
14:34 For forty years—one y for each of
28: 3 two lambs a y old without defect,
28: 9 make an offering of two lambs a y
28:11 lambs a y old, all without defect.
28:14 made at each new moon during the y.
28:19 lambs a y old, all without defect.
28:27 one ram and seven male lambs a y old
29: 2 lambs a y old, all without defect.
29: 8 lambs a y old, all without defect.
29:13 lambs a y old, all without defect.
29:17 lambs a y old, all without defect.
29:20 lambs a y old, all without defect.
29:23 lambs a y old, all without defect.
29:26 lambs a y old, all without defect.
29:29 lambs a y old, all without defect.
29:32 lambs a y old, all without defect.
29:36 lambs a y old, all without defect.
33:38 the fifth month of the fortieth y
Dt 1: 3 In the fortieth y, on the first day

Dt 11:12 the beginning of the y to its end.
14:22 all that your fields produce each y.
15: 9 "The seventh y, the y for cancelling
15:12 seventh y you must let him go free.
15:20 Each y you and your family are to
16:16 Three times a y all your men must
24: 5 For one y he is to be free to stay
26:12 of all your produce in the third y,
26:12 the y of the tithe, you shall give
31:10 in the y for cancelling debts,
Jos 5:12 that y they ate of the produce of
Jdg 10: 8 who that y shattered and crushed
11:40 that each y the young women of
17:10 ten shekels of silver a y, your
1Sa 1: 3 Y after y this man went up from his
1: 7 This went on y after y. Whenever
2:19 Each y his mother made him a little
7:16 From y to y he went on a circuit
27: 7 territory for a y and four months.
29: 3 already been with me for over a y,
1Ki 4: 7 supplies for one month in the y.
5:11 to do this for Hiram y after y.
6: 1 In the four hundred and eightieth y
6: 1 in the fourth y of Solomon's reign
6:37 the fourth y, in the month of Ziv.
6:38 In the eleventh y in the month of
9:25 Three times a y Solomon sacrificed
10:25 Y after y, everyone who came brought
14:25 In the fifth y of King Rehoboam,
15: 1 In the eighteenth y of the reign of
15: 9 In the twentieth y of Jeroboam king
15:25 the second y of Asa king of Judah,
15:28 Baasha killed Nadab in the third y
15:33 In the third y of Asa king of Judah,
16: 8 In the twenty-sixth y of Asa king of
16:10 in the twenty-seventh y of Asa king
16:15 In the twenty-seventh y of Asa king
16:23 In the thirty-first y of Asa king of
16:29 In the thirty-eighth y of Asa king
18: 1 After a long time, in the third y,
22: 2 in the third y Jehoshaphat king of
22:41 the fourth y of Ahab king of Israel.
22:51 seventeenth y of Jehoshaphat king
2Ki 1:17 in the second y of Jehoram son of
3: 1 in the eighteenth y of Jehoshaphat
4:16 "About this time next y," Elisha
4:17 and the next y about that same time
8:16 In the fifth y of Joram son of Ahab
8:25 In the twelfth y of Joram son of
8:26 he reigned in Jerusalem for one y.
9:29 (In the eleventh y of Joram son of
11: 4 In the seventh y Jehoiada sent for
12: 1 In the seventh y of Jehu, Joash
12: 6 by the twenty-third y of King Joash
13: 1 In the twenty-third y of Joash son
13:10 In the thirty-seventh y of Joash
14: 1 In the second y of Jehoash son of
14:23 In the fifteenth y of Amaziah son of
15: 1 In the twenty-seventh y of Jeroboam
15: 8 In the thirty-eighth y of Azariah
15:13 in the thirty-ninth y of Uzziah
15:17 In the thirty-ninth y of Azariah
15:23 In the fiftieth y of Azariah king of
15:27 In the fifty-second y of Azariah
15:30 twentieth y of Jotham son of Uzziah.
15:32 In the second y of Pekah son of
16: 1 In the seventeenth y of Pekah son of
17: 1 In the twelfth y of Ahaz king of
17: 4 of Assyria, as he had done y by y.
17: 6 In the ninth y of Hoshea, the king
18: 1 In the third y of Hoshea son of Elah
18: 9 In King Hezekiah's fourth y, which
18: 9 which was the seventh y of Hoshea
18:10 was captured in Hezekiah's sixth y,
18:10 ninth y of Hoshea king of Israel.
18:13 the fourteenth y of King Hezekiah's
19:29 O Hezekiah: This y you will eat what
19:29 the second y what springs from that.
19:29 But in the third y sow and reap,
22: 3 In the eighteenth y of his reign,
23:23 in the eighteenth y of King Josiah,
24:12 In the eighth y of the reign of the
25: 1 in the ninth y of Zedekiah's reign,
25: 2 the eleventh y of King Zedekiah.
25: 8 the nineteenth y of Nebuchadnezzar
25:27 In the thirty-seventh y of the exile
2Ki 25:27 in the y Evil-Merodach became king
1Ch 26:31 In the fortieth y of David's reign
27: 1 month by month throughout the y.
2Ch 3: 2 month in the fourth y of his reign.
9:24 Y after y, everyone who came brought
12: 2 in the fifth y of King Rehoboam.
13: 1 In the eighteenth y of the reign of
15:10 of the fifteenth y of Asa's reign.
15:19 the thirty-fifth y of Asa's reign.
16: 1 In the thirty-sixth y of Asa's reign
16:12 In the thirty-ninth y of his reign
16:13 in the forty-first y of his reign
17: 7 In the third y of his reign he sent
21:19 at the end of the second y, his
22: 2 he reigned in Jerusalem for one y.
23: 1 In the seventh y Jehoiada showed his
24:23 At the turn of the y, the army of
27: 5 That y the Ammonites paid him a
29: 3 In the first month of the first y of
34: 3 In the eighth y of his reign, while
34: 3 In his twelfth y he began to purge
34: 8 In the eighteenth y of Josiah's
35:19 the eighteenth y of Josiah's reign.
36:22 In the first y of Cyrus king of
Ezr 1: 1 In the first y of Cyrus king of
3: 8 In the second month of the second y
4:24 until the second y of the reign of
5:13 "However, in the first y of Cyrus
6: 3 In the first y of King Cyrus, the
6:15 sixth y of the reign of King Darius.
7: 7 in the seventh y of King Artaxerxes.
7: 8 month of the seventh y of the king.
Ne 1: 1 month of Kislev in the twentieth y,
2: 1 the twentieth y of King Artaxerxes,
5:14 the twentieth y of King Artaxerxes
5:14 until his thirty-second y—twelve
10:31 Every seventh y we will forgo
10:32 to give a third of a shekel each y
10:34 at set times each y a contribution
10:35 each y the firstfruits of our crops
13: 6 for in the thirty-second y of
Est 1: 3 in the third y of his reign he gave
2:16 in the seventh y of his reign.
3: 7 In the twelfth y of King Xerxes, in
9:27 observe these two days every y,
Job 3: 6 among the days of the y nor be
Ps 65:11 You crown the y with your bounty,
Isa 6: 1 In the y that King Uzziah died, I
14:28 This oracle came in the y King Ahaz
20: 1 In the y that the supreme commander,
21:16 "Within one y, as a servant bound by
29: 1 Add y to y and let your cycle of
32:10 In little more than a y you who feel
34: 8 a y of retribution, to uphold Zion's
36: 1 the fourteenth y of King Hezekiah's
37:30 "This y you will eat what grows by
37:30 the second y what springs from that.
37:30 But in the third y sow and reap,
61: 2 proclaim the y of the LORD's favour
63: 4 and the y of my redemption has come.
Jer 1: 2 thirteenth y of the reign of Josiah
1: 3 fifth month of the eleventh y of
11:23 in the y of their punishment.
17: 8 It has no worries in a y of drought
23:12 on them in the y they are punished,"
25: 1 in the fourth y of Jehoiakim son of
25: 1 first y of Nebuchadnezzar king of
25: 3 from the thirteenth y of Josiah son
28: 1 In the fifth month of that same y,
28: 1 the fourth y, early in the reign of
28:16 This very y you are going to die,
28:17 In the seventh month of that same y,
32: 1 tenth y of Zedekiah king of Judah,
32: 1 the eighteenth y of Nebuchadnezzar.
34:14 'Every seventh y each of you must
36: 1 In the fourth y of Jehoiakim son of
36: 9 month of the fifth y of Jehoiakim
39: 1 In the ninth y of Zedekiah king of
39: 2 month of Zedekiah's eleventh y,
45: 1 in the fourth y of Jehoiakim son of
46: 2 in the fourth y of Jehoiakim son of
48:44 upon Moab the y of her punishment,"
51:46 the land; one rumour comes this y,
51:59 Judah in the fourth y of his reign.
52: 4 in the ninth y of Zedekiah's reign,
52: 5 the eleventh y of King Zedekiah.
Jer 52:12 the nineteenth y of Nebuchadnezzar
52:28 exile: in the seventh y, 3,023 Jews;
52:29 in Nebuchadnezzar's eighteenth y, 832
52:30 in his twenty-third y, 745 Jews
52:31 In the thirty-seventh y of the exile
52:31 in the y Evil-Merodach became king
Eze 1: 1 In the thirtieth y, in the fourth
1: 2 the fifth y of the exile of King
4: 6 you 40 days, a day for each y.
8: 1 In the sixth y, in the sixth month
20: 1 In the seventh y, in the fifth month
24: 1 In the ninth y, in the tenth month
26: 1 In the eleventh y, on the first day
29: 1 In the tenth y, in the tenth month
29:17 In the twenty-seventh y, in the
30:20 In the eleventh y, in the first
31: 1 In the eleventh y, in the third
32: 1 In the twelfth y, in the twelfth
32:17 In the twelfth y, on the fifteenth
33:21 In the twelfth y of our exile, in
40: 1 In the twenty-fifth y of our exile,
40: 1 at the beginning of the y, on the
40: 1 in the fourteenth y after the fall
46:17 may keep it until the y of freedom
Da 1: 1 In the third y of the reign of
1:21 until the first y of King Cyrus.
2: 1 In the second y of his reign,
7: 1 In the first y of Belshazzar king of
8: 1 In the third y of King Belshazzar's
9: 1 In the first y of Darius son of
9: 2 in the first y of his reign, I,
10: 1 In the third y of Cyrus king of
11: 1 in the first y of Darius the Mede,
Mic 6: 6 offerings, with calves a y old?
Hag 1: 1 In the second y of King Darius, on
1:15 in the second y of King Darius.
2:10 in the second y of Darius, the word
Zec 1: 1 In the eighth month of the second y
1: 7 in the second y of Darius, the word
7: 1 In the fourth y of King Darius, the
14:16 go up y after y to worship the King,
Lk 2:41 Every y his parents went to
3: 1 In the fifteenth y of the reign of
4:19 proclaim the y of the Lord's favour
13: 8 'leave it alone for one more y, and
13: 9 If it bears fruit next y, fine! If
Jn 11:49 who was high priest that y, spoke up
11:51 but as high priest that y he
18:13 of Caiaphas, the high priest that y
Ac 11:26 So for a whole y Barnabas and Saul
18:11 Paul stayed for a y and a half,
2Co 8:10 Last y you were the first not only
9: 2 telling them that since last y you
Heb 9: 7 and that only once a y, and never
9:25 enters the Most Holy Place every y
10: 1 repeated endlessly y after y,
Jas 4:13 spend a y there, carry on business
Rev 9:15 day and month and y were released to

Year's (Year)

Lev 26:10 will still be eating last y harvest
Dt 14:28 y produce and store it in your towns,
Mk 14: 5 been sold for more than a y wages
Jn 12: 5 the poor? It was worth a y wages."

Year of Jubilee

Lev 25:13 In this Y everyone is everyone is
25:28 of the buyer until the Y.
25:40 he is to work for you until the Y.
25:50 the year he sold himself up to the Y
25:52 only a few years remain until the Y
25:54 are to be released in the Y,
27:17 he dedicates his field during the Y,
27:18 years that remain until the next Y,
27:23 determine its value up to the Y,
27:24 In the Y the field will revert to
Nu 36: 4 the Y for the Israelites comes,

Yearling (Year)

Isa 11: 6 the calf and the lion and the y

Yearly (Year)
1Ki 10:14 Solomon received y was 666 talents,
2Ch 9:13 Solomon received y was 666 talents,
Hos 2:11 her celebrations: her y festivals,

Yearns
Job 19:27 How my heart y within me!
Ps 84: 2 My soul y, even faints, for the
Isa 26: 9 My soul y for you in the night; in
Jer 31:20 Therefore my heart y for him; I have

Year-old (Year)
Ex 12: 5 animals you choose must be y males
Lev 12: 6 a y lamb for a burnt offering
Nu 6:12 a y male lamb as a guilt offering.
6:14 a y male lamb without defect for a
6:14 a y ewe lamb without defect for a
15:27 a y female goat for a sin offering.
Eze 46:13 you are to provide a y lamb without

Years (*Forty years*, Years)
Ge 1:14 to mark seasons and days and y,
5: 3 Adam had lived 130 y, he had a son
5: 4 Seth was born, Adam lived 800 y
5: 5 Altogether, Adam lived 930 y, and
5: 6 Seth had lived 105 y, he became the
5: 7 Seth lived 807 y and had other sons
5: 8 Altogether, Seth lived 912 y, and
5: 9 Enosh had lived 90 y, he became the
5:10 Enosh lived 815 y and had other sons
5:11 Altogether, Enosh lived 905 y, and
5:12 Kenan had lived 70 y, he became the
5:13 Kenan lived 840 y and had other sons
5:14 Altogether, Kenan lived 910 y, and
5:15 Mahalalel had lived 65 y, he became
5:16 Mahalalel lived 830 y and had other
5:17 Altogether, Mahalalel lived 895 y,
5:18 Jared had lived 162 y, he became the
5:19 Jared lived 800 y and had other sons
5:20 Altogether, Jared lived 962 y, and
5:21 Enoch had lived 65 y, he became the
5:22 Enoch walked with God 300 y and had
5:23 Altogether, Enoch lived 365 y.
5:25 Methuselah had lived 187 y, he
5:26 Methuselah lived 782 y and had other
5:27 Altogether, Methuselah lived 969 y,
5:28 Lamech had lived 182 y, he had a son
5:30 Lamech lived 595 y and had other
5:31 Altogether, Lamech lived 777 y, and
5:32 After Noah was 500 y old, he became
6: 3 will be a hundred and twenty y."
7: 6 Noah was six hundred y old when the
9:28 After the flood Noah lived 350 y.
9:29 Altogether, Noah lived 950 y, and
11:10 Two y after the flood, when
11:10 when Shem was 100 y old, he became
11:11 Shem lived 500 y and had other sons
11:12 Arphaxad had lived 35 y, he became
11:13 Arphaxad lived 403 y and had other
11:14 Shelah had lived 30 y, he became the
11:15 Shelah lived 403 y and had other
11:16 Eber had lived 34 y, he became the
11:17 Eber lived 430 y and had other sons
11:18 Peleg had lived 30 y, he became the
11:19 Peleg lived 209 y and had other
11:20 Reu had lived 32 y, he became the
11:21 Reu lived 207 y and had other sons
11:22 Serug had lived 30 y, he became the
11:23 Serug lived 200 y and had other
11:24 Nahor had lived 29 y, he became the
11:25 Nahor lived 119 y and had other sons
11:26 After Terah had lived 70 y, he
11:32 Terah lived 205 y, and he died in
12: 4 Abram was seventy-five y old when he
14: 4 For twelve y they had been subject
15: 9 a goat and a ram, each three y old,
15:13 and ill-treated four hundred y.
16: 3 had been living in Canaan ten y,
16:16 Abram was eighty-six y old when
17: 1 Abram was ninety-nine y old, the
17:17 be born to a man a hundred y old?
17:24 Abraham was ninety-nine y old when
18:11 already old and well advanced in y,
21: 5 Abraham was a hundred y old when his
23: 1 be a hundred and twenty-seven y old.
Ge 24: 1 was now old and well advanced in y,
25: 7 lived a hundred and seventy-five y.
25: 8 old age, an old man and full of y;
25:17 lived a hundred and thirty-seven y.
25:26 Isaac was sixty y old when Rebekah
29:18 I'll work for you seven y in return
29:20 Jacob served seven y to get Rachel,
29:27 return for another seven y of work."
29:30 he worked for Laban another seven y.
31:38 "I have been with you for twenty y
31:41 was like this for the twenty y I was
31:41 I worked for you fourteen y for your
31:41 daughters and six y for your flocks,
35:28 Isaac lived a hundred and eighty y.
35:29 to his people, old and full of y.
41: 1 two full y had passed, Pharaoh had a
41:26 The seven good cows are seven y, and
41:26 seven good ears of corn are seven y
41:27 that came up afterwards are seven y,
41:27 wind: They are seven y of famine.
41:29 Seven y of great abundance are
41:30 seven y of famine will follow them.
41:34 during the seven y of abundance.
41:35 of these good y that are coming
41:36 used during the seven y of famine
41:46 Joseph was thirty y old when he
41:47 During the seven y of abundance the
41:48 those seven y of abundance in Egypt
41:50 Before the y of famine came, two
41:53 The seven y of abundance in Egypt
41:54 the seven y of famine began, just as
45: 6 For two y now there has been famine
45: 6 and for the next five y there will
45:11 five y of famine are still to come.
47: 9 The y of my pilgrimage are a hundred
47: 9 My y have been few and difficult,
47: 9 do not equal the y of the pilgrimage
47:28 Jacob lived in Egypt seventeen y,
47:28 the y of his life were a hundred and
50:22 He lived a hundred and ten y
Ex 6:16 Levi lived 137 y.
6:18 Kohath lived 133 y.
6:20 Amram lived 137 y.
7: 7 Moses was eighty y old and Aaron
12:40 people lived in Egypt was 430 y.
12:41 At the end of the 430 y, to the very
21: 2 he is to serve you for six y.
23:10 For six y you are to sow your fields
30:14 those twenty y old or more, are to
38:26 twenty y old or more, a total of 603,
Lev 19:23 For three y you are to consider it
25: 3 six y sow your fields, and for six y
25: 8 "'Count off seven sabbaths of
25: 8 seven times seven y—so that the
25: 8 so that the seven sabbaths of y
25: 8 amount to a period of forty-nine y.
25:15 the number of y since the Jubilee.
25:15 number of y left for harvesting
25:16 the y are many, you are to increase
25:16 and when the y are few, you are to
25:21 land will yield enough for three y.
25:27 value for the y since he sold it
25:50 to a hired man for that number of y.
25:51 If many y remain, he must pay for
25:52 If only a few y remain until the
26:34 the land will enjoy its sabbath y
27: 6 person between one month and five y
27: 7 If it is a person sixty y old or
27:18 the number of y that remain until
Nu 1: 3 the men in Israel twenty y old or
1:18 and the men twenty y old or more
1:20 All the men twenty y old or more who
1:22 All the men twenty y old or more who
1:24 All the men twenty y old or more who
1:26 All the men twenty y old or more who
1:28 All the men twenty y old or more who
1:30 All the men twenty y old or more who
1:32 All the men twenty y old or more who
1:34 All the men twenty y old or more who
1:36 All the men twenty y old or more who
1:38 All the men twenty y old or more who
1:40 All the men twenty y old or more who
1:42 All the men twenty y old or more who
1:45 All the Israelites twenty y old or
4: 3 men from thirty to fifty y of age
4:23 men from thirty to fifty y of age
Nu 4:30 men from thirty to fifty y of age
4:35 men from thirty to fifty y of age
4:39 men from thirty to fifty y of age
4:43 men from thirty to fifty y of age
4:47 men from thirty to fifty y of age
8:24 Men twenty-five y old or more shall
13:22 built seven y before Zoan in Egypt.)
14:29 every one of you twenty y old or
20:15 Egypt, and we lived there many y.
26: 2 all those twenty y old or more who
26: 4 "Take a census of men twenty y old
32:11 not one of the men twenty y old or
33:39 a hundred and twenty-three y old
Dt 2:14 Thirty-eight y passed from the time
14:28 At the end of every three y, bring
15: 1 At the end of every seven y you must
15:12 himself to you and serves you six y,
15:18 his service to you these six y has
30:20 he will give you many y in the land
31: 2 "I am now a hundred and twenty y old
31:10 "At the end of every seven y, in the
34: 7 Moses was a hundred and twenty y old
Jos 13: 1 Joshua was old and well advanced in y
14:10 has kept me alive for forty-five y
14:10 here I am today, eighty-five y old!
23: 1 by then old and well advanced in y,
23: 2 "I am old and well advanced in y.
Jdg 3: 8 Israelites were subject for eight y.
3:14 Eglon king of Moab for eighteen y.
3:30 and the land had peace for eighty y.
4: 3 the Israelites for twenty y, they
6: 1 and for seven y he gave them into
6:25 father's herd, the one seven y old.
9:22 had governed Israel for three y,
10: 2 He led Israel for twenty-three y;
10: 3 who led Israel for twenty-two y.
10: 8 For eighteen y they oppressed all
11:26 For three hundred y Israel occupied
12: 7 Jephthah led Israel for six y. Then
12: 9 Ibzan led Israel for seven y.
12:11 the Zebulunite led Israel for ten y.
12:14 He led Israel for eight y.
15:20 Samson led Israel for twenty y in
16:31 He had led Israel for twenty y.
Ru 1: 4 they had lived there about ten y,
1Sa 4:15 who was ninety-eight y old and whose
7: 2 was a long time, twenty y in all,
13: 1 over Israel for ⌊forty-⌋ two y.
13: 1 Saul was thirty years old when he
17:12 he was old and well advanced in y.
2Sa 2:10 over Israel, and he reigned two y.
2:11 of Judah was seven y and six months.
4: 4 He was five y old when the news
5: 4 David was thirty y old when he
5: 5 Judah for seven y and six months,
5: 5 Israel and Judah for thirty-three y.
13:23 Two y later, when Absalom's
13:38 Geshur, he stayed there for three y.
14:28 Absalom lived for two y in Jerusalem
15: 7 At the end of four y, Absalom said
19:32 was a very old man, eighty y of age.
19:34 "How many more y shall I live, that
19:35 I am now eighty y old. Can I tell
21: 1 was a famine for three successive y;
24:13 "Shall there come upon you three y
1Ki 1: 1 David was old and well advanced in y,
2:11 seven y in Hebron and thirty-three
2:39 three y later, two of Shimei's
6:38 He had spent seven y building it.
7: 1 took Solomon thirteen y, however, to
9:10 At the end of twenty y, during which
10:22 Once every three y it returned
14:20 He reigned for twenty-two y and then
14:21 He was forty-one y old when he
14:21 and he reigned for seventeen y in
15: 2 he reigned in Jerusalem for three y.
15:10 in Jerusalem for forty-one y.
15:25 he reigned over Israel for two y.
15:33 and he reigned for twenty-four y.
16: 8 and he reigned in Tirzah for two y.
16:23 for twelve y, six of them in Tirzah.
16:29 Samaria over Israel for twenty-two y
17: 1 dew nor rain in the next few y
22: 1 For three y there was no war between
22:42 Jehoshaphat was thirty-five y old
22:42 in Jerusalem for twenty-five y.

1Ki 22:51 he reigned over Israel for two y.
2Ki 3: 1 Judah, and he reigned for twelve y.
8: 1 in the land that will last seven y."
8: 2 land of the Philistines for seven y.
8: 3 At the end of the seven y she came
8:17 He was thirty-two y old when he
8:17 he reigned in Jerusalem for eight y.
8:26 Ahaziah was twenty-two y old when he
10:36 Israel in Samaria was twenty-eight y.
11: 3 six y while Athaliah ruled the land.
11:21 Joash was seven y old when he began
12: 2 all the y Jehoiada the priest
13: 1 and he reigned for seventeen y.
13:10 and he reigned for sixteen y.
14: 2 He was twenty-five y old when he
14: 2 in Jerusalem for twenty-nine y.
14:17 lived for fifteen y after the death
14:21 Azariah who was sixteen y old, and
14:23 and he reigned for forty-one y.
15: 2 He was sixteen y old when he became
15: 2 in Jerusalem for fifty-two y.
15:17 and he reigned in Samaria for ten y.
15:23 Samaria, and he reigned for two y.
15:27 Samaria, and he reigned for twenty y
15:33 He was twenty-five y old when he
15:33 reigned in Jerusalem for sixteen y.
16: 2 Ahaz was twenty y old when he became
16: 2 reigned in Jerusalem for sixteen y.
17: 1 Samaria, and he reigned for nine y.
17: 5 and laid siege to it for three y.
18: 2 He was twenty-five y old when he
18: 2 in Jerusalem for twenty-nine y.
18:10 At the end of three y the Assyrians
20: 6 I will add fifteen y to your life.
21: 1 Manasseh was twelve y old when he
21: 1 in Jerusalem for fifty-five y.
21:19 Amon was twenty-two y old when he
21:19 he reigned in Jerusalem for two y.
22: 1 Josiah was eight y old when he
22: 1 in Jerusalem for thirty-one y.
23:31 Jehoahaz was twenty-three y old when
23:36 Jehoiakim was twenty-five y old when
23:36 reigned in Jerusalem for eleven y.
24: 1 became his vassal for three y.
24: 8 Jehoiachin was eighteen y old when
24:18 Zedekiah was twenty-one y old when
24:18 reigned in Jerusalem for eleven y.
1Ch 2:21 married her when he was sixty y old
3: 4 reigned for seven y and six months.
3: 4 in Jerusalem for thirty-three y,
21:12 three y of famine, three months of
23: 1 David was old and full of y, he made
23: 3 The Levites thirty y old or more
23:24 that is, the workers twenty y old or
23:27 from those twenty y old or more.
27:23 of the men twenty y old or less,
2Ch 8: 1 At the end of twenty y, during which
9:21 Once every three y it returned,
11:17 Rehoboam son of Solomon for three y,
12:13 He was forty-one y old when he
12:13 and he reigned for seventeen y in
13: 2 he reigned in Jerusalem for three y.
14: 1 the country was at peace for ten y.
14: 6 was at war with him during those y,
17: 3 in his early y he walked in the ways
18: 2 Some y later he went down to visit
20:31 He was thirty-five y old when he
20:31 in Jerusalem for twenty-five y.
21: 5 Jehoram was thirty-two y old when he
21: 5 he reigned in Jerusalem for eight y.
21:20 Jehoram was thirty-two y old when he
21:20 he reigned in Jerusalem for eight y.
22: 2 Ahaziah was twenty-two y old when he
22:12 for six y while Athaliah ruled the
24: 1 Joash was seven y old when he became
24: 2 all the y of Jehoiada the priest.
24:15 Now Jehoiada was old and full of y,
25: 1 Amaziah was twenty-five y old when
25: 1 in Jerusalem for twenty-nine y.
25: 5 He then mustered those twenty y old
25:25 lived for fifteen y after the death
26: 1 took Uzziah, who was sixteen y old,
26: 3 Uzziah was sixteen y old when he
26: 3 in Jerusalem for fifty-two y.
27: 1 Jotham was twenty-five y old when he
27: 1 reigned in Jerusalem for sixteen y.
2Ch 27: 5 also in the second and third y.
27: 8 He was twenty-five y old when he
27: 8 reigned in Jerusalem for sixteen y.
28: 1 Ahaz was twenty y old when he became
28: 1 reigned in Jerusalem for sixteen y.
29: 1 Hezekiah was twenty-five y old when
29: 1 in Jerusalem for twenty-nine y.
31:16 distributed to the males three y old
31:17 to the Levites twenty y old or more,
33: 1 Manasseh was twelve y old when he
33: 1 in Jerusalem for fifty-five y.
33:21 Amon was twenty-two y old when he
33:21 he reigned in Jerusalem for two y.
34: 1 Josiah was eight y old when he
34: 1 in Jerusalem for thirty-one y.
36: 2 Jehoahaz was twenty-three y old when
36: 5 Jehoiakim was twenty-five y old when
36: 5 reigned in Jerusalem for eleven y.
36: 9 Jehoiachin was eighteen y old when
36:11 Zedekiah was twenty-one y old when
36:11 reigned in Jerusalem for eleven y.
36:21 until the seventy y were completed
Ezr 3: 8 appointing Levites twenty y of age
5:11 temple that was built many y ago,
Ne 5:14 his thirty-second year—twelve y
9:30 For many y you were patient with
Job 10: 5 or your y like those of a man,
15:20 through all the y stored up for him.
16:22 "Only a few y will pass before I go
21:13 They spend their y in prosperity and
32: 6 "I am young in y, and you are old;
32: 7 advanced y should teach wisdom.'
36:11 and their y in contentment.
36:26 number of his y is past finding out.
38:21 born! You have lived so many y!
42:17 he died, old and full of y.
Ps 31:10 by anguish and my y by groaning;
39: 5 the span of my y is as nothing before
61: 6 life, his y for many generations.
77: 5 the former days, the y of long ago;
77:10 y of the right hand of the Most High
78:33 in futility and their y in terror.
90: 4 For a thousand y in your sight are
90: 9 we finish our y with a moan.
90:10 The length of our days is seventy y
90:15 as many y as we have seen trouble.
102:24 y go on through all generations.
102:27 the same, and your y will never end.
Pr 3: 2 they will prolong your life many y
4:10 and the y of your life will be many
5: 9 and your y to one who is cruel,
9:11 and y will be added to your life.
10:27 the y of the wicked are cut short.
Ecc 6: 3 a hundred children and live many y;
6: 6 even if he lives a thousand y twice
11: 8 However many y a man may live, let
12: 1 the y approach when you will say,
Isa 7: 8 Within sixty-five y Ephraim will be
16:14 now the LORD says: "Within three y,
20: 3 stripped and barefoot for three y,
23:15 Tyre will be forgotten for seventy y
23:15 But at the end of these seventy y,
23:17 At the end of seventy y, the LORD
38: 5 I will add fifteen y to your life.
38:10 and be robbed of the rest of my y?"
38:15 I will walk humbly all my y because
65:20 old man who does not live out his y;
Jer 6:11 the old, those weighed down with y.
25: 3 For twenty-three y—from the
25:11 the king of Babylon for seventy y.
25:12 when the seventy y are fulfilled
28: 3 Within two y I will bring back to
28:11 of all the nations within two y.
29:10 "When seventy y are completed for
34:14 After he has served you for six y,
52: 1 Zedekiah was twenty-one y old when
52: 1 reigned in Jerusalem for eleven y.
Eze 4: 5 of days as the y of their sin.
12:27 'The vision he sees is for many y
22: 4 and the end of your y has come.
38: 8 In future y you will invade a land
38:17 At that time they prophesied for y
39: 9 seven y they will use them for fuel.
Da 1: 5 They were to be trained for three y,
9: 2 of Jerusalem would last seventy y.
11: 6 After some y, they will become
Da 11: 8 For some y he will leave the king of
11:13 after several y, he will advance
11:20 In a few y, however, he will be
Joel 2:25 "I will repay you for the y the
Am 1: 1 Israel two y before the earthquake,
4: 4 morning, your tithes every three y.
Zec 1:12 been angry with these seventy y?"
7: 3 as I have done for so many y?"
7: 5 months for the past seventy y,
Mal 3: 4 as in days gone by, as in former y.
Mt 2:16 who were two y old and under,
9:20 subject to bleeding for twelve y
Mk 5:25 subject to bleeding for twelve y.
5:42 around (she was twelve y old).
Lk 1: 7 and they were both well on in y.
1:18 man and my wife is well on in y."
2:36 husband seven y after her marriage,
2:42 he was twelve y old, they went up to
3:23 Jesus himself was about thirty y old
4:25 sky was shut for three and a half y
8:43 subject to bleeding for twelve y,
12:19 of good things laid up for many y.
13: 7 For three y now I've been coming to
13:11 crippled by a spirit for eighteen y.
13:16 has kept bound for eighteen long y,
15:29 'Look! All these y I've been slaving
Jn 2:20 "It has taken forty-six y to build
5: 5 been an invalid for thirty-eight y.
8:57 "You are not yet fifty y old," the
Ac 7: 6 and ill-treated for four hundred y.
9:33 who had been bedridden for eight y.
13:20 All this took about 450 y. "After
19:10 This went on for two y, so that all
20:31 Remember that for three y I never
24:10 "I know that for a number of y you
24:17 "After an absence of several y, I
24:27 two y had passed, Felix was
28:30 For two whole y Paul stayed there in
Ro 4:19 since he was about a hundred y old
15:23 been longing for many y to see you,
1Co 7:36 and if she is getting on in y and he
2Co 12: 2 a man in Christ who fourteen y ago
Gal 1:18 after three y, I went up to
2: 1 Fourteen y later I went up again to
3:17 The law, introduced 430 y later,
4:10 days and months and seasons and y!
Heb 1:12 same, and your y will never end."
Jas 5:17 on the land for three and a half y.
2Pe 3: 8 the Lord a day is like a thousand y
3: 8 and a thousand y are like a day.
Rev 20: 2 and bound him for a thousand y.
20: 3 until the thousand y were ended.
20: 4 with Christ for a thousand y.
20: 5 until the thousand y were ended.
20: 6 reign with him for a thousand y.
20: 7 the thousand y are over, Satan will

Yeast

Ge 19: 3 bread without y, and they ate.
Ex 12: 8 herbs, and bread made without y.
12:15 you are to eat bread made without y.
12:15 remove the y from your houses, for
12:15 whoever eats anything with y in
12:18 you are to eat bread made without y,
12:19 For seven days no y is to be found
12:19 And whoever eats anything with y in
12:20 Eat nothing made with y. Wherever
12:34 their dough before the y was added,
12:39 The dough was without y because they
13: 3 Eat nothing containing y.
13: 6 seven days eat bread made without y
13: 7 nothing with y in it is to be seen
13: 7 nor shall any y be seen anywhere
23:15 seven days eat bread made without y
23:18 along with anything containing y.
29: 2 from fine wheat flour, without y,
29:23 the basket of bread made without y,
34:18 seven days eat bread made without y
34:25 along with anything containing y,
Lev 2: 4 cakes made without y and mixed with
2: 4 wafers made without y and spread
2: 5 flour mixed with oil, and without y.
2:11 to the LORD must be made without y,
2:11 for you are not to burn any y or
6:16 it is to be eaten without y in a

Lev 6:17 must not be baked with y; I have
7:12 cakes of bread made without y and
7:12 wafers made without y and spread
7:13 with cakes of bread made with y.
8: 2 containing bread made without y,
8:26 the basket of bread made without y,
10:12 prepared without y beside the altar,
23: 6 you must eat bread made without y.
23:17 baked with y, as a wave offering of
Nu 6:15 a basket of bread made without y
6:19 the basket, both made without y.
28:17 seven days eat bread made without y.
Dt 16: 3 Do not eat it with bread made with y
16: 4 Let no y be found in your possession
Jdg 6:19 of flour he made bread without y.
1Sa 28:24 it and baked bread without y.
Eze 45:21 you shall eat bread made without y.
Mt 13:33 "The kingdom of heaven is like y
16: 6 against the y of the Pharisees and
16:11 against the y of the Pharisees and
16:12 guard against the y used in bread,
Mk 8:15 "Watch out for the y of the
Lk 12: 1 "Be on your guard against the y of
13:21 is like y that a woman took and
1Co 5: 6 Don't you know that a little y works
5: 7 Get rid of the old y that you may be
5: 7 you may be a new batch without y
5: 8 not with the old y, the y of malice
5: 8 with bread without y, the bread of
Gal 5: 9 "A little y works through the whole

Yelling

Ac 7:57 y at the top of their voices, they

Yellow

Lev 13:30 and the hair in it is y and thin,
13:32 there is no y hair in it and it does
13:36 does not need to look for y hair;
Rev 9:17 red, dark blue, and y as sulphur.

Yesterday

Ex 5:14 of bricks y or today, as before?"
1Sa 20:27 to the meal, either y or today?"
2Sa 15:20 You came only y. And today shall I
2Ki 9:26 'Y I saw the blood of Naboth and the
Job 8: 9 for we were born only y and know
Jn 4:52 left him y at the seventh hour."
Ac 7:28 me as you killed the Egyptian y?'
Heb 13: 8 Jesus Christ is the same y and today

Yield (Yielded, Yielding, Yields)

Ge 4:12 will no longer y its crops for you.
Lev 25:19 the land will y its fruit, and you
25:21 land will y enough for three years.
26: 4 and the ground will y its crops and
26:20 your soil will not y its crops,
26:20 the trees of the land y their fruit.
Dt 11:17 and the ground will y no produce,
13: 8 do not y to him or listen to him.
33:14 forth and the finest the moon can y;
Jos 24:23 you and y your hearts to the LORD,
2Sa 1:21 fields that y offerings of grain.
Job 31:39 devoured its y without payment
Ps 67: 6 the land will y its harvest, and God
85:12 and our land will y its harvest.
Pr 8:19 what I y surpasses choice silver.
Isa 5: 4 good grapes, why did it y only bad?
48:11 I will not y my glory to another.
Eze 34:27 The trees of the field will y their
34:27 and the ground will y its crops;
36:37 Once again I will y to the plea of
Hos 8: 7 Were it to y grain, foreigners
9:16 root is withered, they y no fruit.
Joel 2:22 and the vine y their riches.
Zec 8:12 the vine will y its fruit, the
Jas 5: 7 for the land to y its valuable crop

Yielded (Yield)

Ps 107:37 vineyards that y a fruitful harvest;
Isa 5: 2 grapes, but it y only bad fruit.
Lk 8: 8 It came up and y a crop, a hundred

Yielding (Yield)

SS 5:13 are like beds of spice y perfume.
Mt 13:23 He produces a crop, y a hundred,
Rev 22: 2 of fruit, y its fruit every month.

Yields (Yield)

Lev 25: 6 Whatever the land y during the
Ps 1: 3 which y its fruit in season and
Pr 3:14 and y better returns than gold.
14:24 but the folly of fools y folly.
Isa 55:10 so that it y seed for the sower and

Yoke (Yoked, Yokefellow, Yokes)

Ge 27:40 throw his y from off your neck."
Ex 6: 6 from under the y of the Egyptians.
6: 7 from under the y of the Egyptians.
Lev 26:13 I broke the bars of your y and
Nu 19: 2 and that has never been under a y.
Dt 21: 3 been worked and has never worn a y
28:48 He will put an iron y on your neck
1Ki 12: 4 "Your father put a heavy y on us,
12: 4 labour and the heavy y he put on us,
12: 9 the y your father put on us'?"
12:10 'Your father put a heavy y on us,
12:10 but make our y lighter'—tell them,
12:11 My father laid on you a heavy y;
12:14 My father made your y heavy; I will
19:19 was ploughing with twelve y of oxen
19:21 He took his y of oxen and
2Ch 10: 4 "Your father put a heavy y on us,
10: 4 labour and the heavy y he put on us,
10: 9 the y your father put on us'?"
10:10 'Your father put a heavy y on us,
10:10 but make our y lighter'—tell them,
10:11 My father laid on you a heavy y;
10:14 My father made your y heavy; I will
Job 1: 3 five hundred y of oxen and five
42:12 a thousand y of oxen and a thousand
Isa 9: 4 shattered the y that burdens them,
10:27 their y from your neck; the y will
14:25 His y will be taken from my people,
47: 6 on the aged you laid a very heavy y.
58: 6 and untie the cords of the y,
58: 6 oppressed free and break every y?
58: 9 you do away with the y of oppression
Jer 2:20 "Long ago you broke off your y and
5: 5 they too had broken off the y and
27: 2 "Make a y out of straps and
27: 8 Babylon or bow its neck under his y,
27:11 under the y of the king of Babylon
27:12 I said, "Bow your neck under the y
28: 2 break the y of the king of Babylon.
28: 4 break the y of the king of Babylon.
28:10 the prophet Hananiah took the y off
28:11 'In the same way will I break the y
28:12 broken the y off the neck of the
28:13 says: You have broken a wooden y,
28:13 its place you will get a y of iron.
28:14 I will put an iron y on the necks
30: 8 'I will break the y off their necks
Lam 1:14 "My sins have been bound into a y;
3:27 is good for a man to bear the y
Eze 30:18 when I break the y of Egypt;
34:27 when I break the bars of their y and
Hos 10:11 so I will put a y on her fair neck.
11: 4 I lifted the y from their neck and
Na 1:13 will break their y from your neck
Mt 11:29 Take my y upon you and learn from me,
11:30 For my y is easy and my burden is
Lk 14:19 'I have just bought five y of oxen,
Ac 15:10 on the necks of the disciples a y
Gal 5: 1 be burdened again by a y of slavery
1Ti 6: 1 All who are under the y of slavery

Yoked (Yoke)

Dt 22:10 with an ox and a donkey y together.
1Sa 6: 7 have calved and have never been y.
Ps 106:28 y themselves to the Baal of Peor
2Co 6:14 Do not be y together with

Yokefellow (Yoke)

Php 4: 3 Yes, and I ask you, loyal y, help

Yokes (Yoke)

2Sa 24:22 and ox y for the wood.

Young (Younger, Youngest, Youth, Youthful, Youths)

Ge 4:23 me, a y man for injuring me.
15: 9 along with a dove and a y pigeon."
19: 4 y and old—surrounded the house.
19:11 y and old, with blindness so that
27: 9 and bring me two choice y goats,
30:39 And they bore y that were streaked
30:40 Jacob set apart the y of the flock
31: 8 flocks gave birth to speckled y;
31: 8 then all the flocks bore streaked y.
32:15 thirty female camels with their y,
33:13 and cows that are nursing their y.
34:19 The y man, who was the most honoured
37: 2 Joseph, a y man of seventeen, was
38:17 "I'll send you a y goat from my
38:20 Meanwhile Judah sent the y goat by
38:23 I did send her this y goat, but you
41:12 Now a y Hebrew was there with us, a
44:20 a y son born to him in his old age.
Ex 10: 9 "We will go with our y and old, with
23:19 cook a y goat in its mother's milk.
24: 5 he sent y Israelite men, and they
24: 5 sacrificed y bulls as fellowship
29: 1 a y bull and two rams without defect
33:11 but his y assistant Joshua son of Nun
34:26 cook a y goat in its mother's milk."
Lev 1: 5 He is to slaughter the y bull before
1:14 he is to offer a dove or a y pigeon.
4: 3 he must bring to the LORD a y bull
4:14 the assembly must bring a y bull as
5: 7 to bring two doves or two y pigeons
5:11 afford two doves or two y pigeons
12: 6 a y pigeon or a dove for a sin
12: 8 to bring two doves or two y pigeons
14:22 two doves or two y pigeons, which he
14:30 sacrifice the doves or the y pigeons
15:14 take two doves or two y pigeons
15:29 take two doves or two y pigeons
16: 3 with a y bull for a sin offering and
22:28 a sheep and its y on the same day.
23:18 defect, one y bull and two rams.
Nu 6:10 bring two doves or two y pigeons to
7:15 one y bull, one ram and one male
7:21 one y bull, one ram and one male
7:27 one y bull, one ram and one male
7:33 one y bull, one ram and one male
7:39 one y bull, one ram and one male
7:45 one y bull, one ram and one male
7:51 one y bull, one ram and one male
7:57 one y bull, one ram and one male
7:63 one y bull, one ram and one male
7:69 one y bull, one ram and one male
7:75 one y bull, one ram and one male
7:81 one y bull, one ram and one male
7:87 offering came to twelve y bulls,
8: 8 Make them take a y bull with its
8: 8 a second y bull for a sin offering.
11:27 A y man ran and told Moses, "Eldad
15: 8 "'When you prepare a y bull as a
15:11 bull or ram, each lamb or y goat
15:24 whole community is to offer a y bull
28:11 LORD a burnt offering of two y bulls,
28:19 a burnt offering of two y bulls, one
28:27 a burnt offering of two y bulls
29: 2 a burnt offering of one y bull
29: 8 LORD a burnt offering of one y bull,
29:13 a burnt offering of thirteen y bulls,
29:17 second day prepare twelve y bulls
30: 3 "When a y woman still living in her
30:16 y daughter still living in his house.
Dt 7:14 nor any of your livestock without y.
14:21 cook a y goat in its mother's milk.
22: 6 and the mother is sitting on the y
22: 6 do not take the mother with the y.
22: 7 You may take the y, but be sure to
28: 4 and the y of your livestock—
28:11 the y of your livestock and the
28:50 for the old or pity for the y.
28:51 will devour the y of your livestock
30: 9 the y of your livestock and the
32:11 up its nest and hovers over its y,

Dt 32:25 Y men and y women will perish,
Jos 6:21 y and old, cattle, sheep and donkeys
6:23 the y men who had done the spying
Jdg 6:19 Gideon went in, prepared a y goat,
8:14 He caught a y man of Succoth and
8:14 and the y man wrote down for him the
11:40 that each year the y women of Israel
12: 9 brought in thirty y women as wives
13:15 until we prepare a y goat for you."
13:19 Manoah took a y goat, together with
14: 1 and saw there a y Philistine woman.
14: 5 a y lion came roaring towards him.
14: 6 as he might have torn a y goat.
15: 1 Samson took a y goat and went to
17: 7 A y Levite from Bethlehem in Judah,
17:11 and the y man was to him like one of
17:12 the y man became his priest and
18: 3 recognised the voice of the y Levite
18:15 went to the house of the y Levite at
19:19 maidservant, and the y man with us.
21:12 four hundred y women who had never
Ru 2: 5 "Whose y woman is that?
4:12 the LORD gives you by this y woman,
1Sa 1:24 took the boy with her, y as he was
2:17 This sin of the y men was very great
5: 9 both y and old, with an outbreak of
9: 2 an impressive y man without equal
10: 3 One will be carrying three y goats,
14: 1 to the y man bearing his armour,
14: 6 Jonathan said to his y armour-bearer
16:20 a skin of wine and a y goat and sent
17:55 "Abner, whose son is that y man?"
17:56 "Find out whose son this y man is.
17:58 "Whose son are you, y man?" Saul
25: 5 he sent ten y men and said to them,
25: 8 be favourable towards my y men,
26:22 of your y men come over and get it.
30: 2 all who were in it, both y and old.
30:17 except four hundred y men who rode
30:19 Nothing was missing: y or old, boy
2Sa 1: 5 David said to the y man who brought
1: 6 be on Mount Gilboa," the y man said,
1:13 David said to the y man who brought
2:14 "Let's have some of the y men get up
2:21 take on one of the y men and strip
9:12 Mephibosheth had a y son named Mica,
14:21 Go, bring back the y man Absalom."
17:18 a y man saw them and told Absalom.
18: 5 with the y man Absalom for my sake.
18:12 the y man Absalom for my sake.'
18:29 The king asked, "Is the y man
18:32 "Is the y man Absalom safe?"
18:32 up to harm you be like that y man."
1Ki 1: 2 "Let us look for a y virgin to
11:28 when Solomon saw how well the y man
12: 8 consulted the y men who had grown up
12:10 The y men who had grown up with him
12:14 he followed the advice of the y men
20:14 'The y officers of the provincial
20:15 Ahab summoned the y officers of the
20:17 The y officers of the provincial
20:19 The y officers of the provincial
2Ki 3:21 y and old, who could bear arms was
5: 2 taken captive a y girl from Israel,
5:14 became clean like that of a y boy.
5:22 master sent me to say, 'Two y men
8:12 kill their y men with the sword,
9: 4 the y man, the prophet, went to
1Ch 12:28 Zadok, a brave y warrior, with 22
22: 5 David said, "My son Solomon is y and
25: 8 Y and old alike, teacher as well as
26:13 to their families, y and old alike.
29: 1 has chosen, is y and inexperienced.
2Ch 10: 8 consulted the y men who had grown up
10:10 The y men who had grown up with him
10:14 he followed the advice of the y men
13: 7 son of Solomon when he was y and
13: 9 to consecrate himself with a y bull
31:15 to their divisions, old and y alike.
34: 3 while he was still y, he began to
36:17 who killed their y men with the
36:17 y man nor y woman, old man or aged.
Ezr 6: 9 Whatever is needed—y bulls, rams,
Est 2: 2 beautiful y virgins for the king.
3:13 y and old, women and little children
Job 29: 8 the y men saw me and stepped aside
Job 32: 6 "I am y in years, and you are old;
38:41 the raven when its y cry out to God
39: 3 crouch down and bring forth their y
39: 4 Their y thrive and grow strong in
39:16 She treats her y harshly, as if they
39:30 His y ones feast on blood, and where
Ps 29: 6 a calf, Sirion like a y wild ox.
37:25 I was y and now I am old, yet I have
78:31 cutting down the y men of Israel.
78:63 Fire consumed their y men, and their
84: 3 where she may have her y—a place
89:19 a y man from among the people.
119: 9 How can a y man keep his way pure?
147: 9 and for the y ravens when they call.
148:12 y men and maidens, old men and
Pr 1: 4 knowledge and discretion to the y—
7: 7 y men, a youth who lacked judgment.
20:29 The glory of y men is their strength,
Ecc 11: 9 Be happy, y man, while you are y,
SS 1: 8 graze your y goats by the tents of
2: 3 forest is my lover among the y men.
2: 9 lover is like a gazelle or a y stag
2:17 like a y stag on the rugged hills.
8: 8 We have a y sister, and her breasts
8:14 y stag on the spice-laden mountains.
Isa 3: 5 The y will rise up against the old,
5:29 they roar like y lions; they growl
7:21 keep alive a y cow and two goats.
9:17 will take no pleasure in the y men,
11: 7 their y will lie down together, and
11: 8 and the y child put his hand into
13:18 bows will strike down the y men;
20: 4 y and old, with buttocks bared—to
31: 8 y men will be put to forced labour.
33: 4 is harvested as by y locusts;
34:15 and care for her y under the shadow
40:11 he gently leads those that have y.
40:30 weary, and y men stumble and fall;
54: 6 who married y, only to be rejected,"
60: 6 land, y camels of Midian and Ephah.
61:11 For as the soil makes the y plant
62: 5 a y man marries a maiden, so will
Jer 6:11 and on the y men gathered together;
9:21 the y men from the public squares.
11:22 Their y men will die by the sword,
15: 8 against the mothers of their y men;
18:21 y men slain by the sword in battle.
31:12 oil, the y of the flocks and herds.
31:13 dance and be glad, y men and old
48:15 y men will go down in the slaughter,"
49:20 The y of the flock will be dragged
49:26 Surely, her y men will fall in the
50:27 Kill all her y bulls; let them go
50:30 Therefore, her y men will fall in
50:45 The y of the flock will be dragged
51: 3 Do not spare her y men; completely
51:22 with you I shatter y man and maiden,
51:38 Her people all roar like y lions,
Lam 1:15 army against me to crush my y men.
1:18 My y men and maidens have gone into
2:10 The y women of Jerusalem have bowed
2:21 "Y and old lie together in the dust
2:21 my y men and maidens have fallen by
3:27 man to bear the yoke while he is y.
4: 3 their breasts to nurse their y,
5:13 Y men toil at the millstones; boys
5:14 the y men have stopped their music.
Eze 9: 6 Slaughter old men, y men and maidens
19: 2 the y lions and reared her cubs.
23: 6 y men, and mounted horsemen.
23:12 horsemen, all handsome y men.
23:21 caressed and your y breasts fondled.
23:23 handsome y men, all of them
30:17 The y men of Heliopolis and Bubastis
43:19 You are to give a y bull as a sin
43:23 you are to offer a y bull and a ram
43:25 a y bull and a ram from the flock,
45:18 are to take a y bull without defect
46: 6 New Moon he is to offer a y bull,
Da 1: 4 y men without any physical defect,
1:10 than the other y men of your age?
1:13 of the y men who eat the royal food,
1:15 of the y men who ate the royal food.
1:17 To these four y men God gave
Hos 14: 6 his y shoots will grow. His
Joel 1: 4 have left the y locusts have eaten;
Joel 1: 4 what the y locusts have left other
2:25 the great locust and the y locust,
2:28 dreams, your y men will see visions.
Am 2:11 and Nazirites from among your y men.
4:10 I killed your y men with the sword,
8:13 the lovely y women and strong y men
Mic 5: 8 like a y lion among flocks of sheep,
Na 2:11 the place where they fed their y,
2:13 the sword will devour your y lions.
Zec 2: 4 said to him: "Run, tell that y man,
9:17 Grain will make the y men thrive,
9:17 thrive, and new wine the y women.
11:16 or seek the y, or heal the injured,
Mt 19:20 these I have kept," the y man said
19:22 the y man heard this, he went away
Mk 14:51 A y man, wearing nothing but a linen
16: 5 entered the tomb, they saw a y man
Lk 2:24 "a pair of doves or two y pigeons".
7:14 He said, "Y man, I say to you, get
15:29 Yet you never gave me even a y goat
Jn 12:14 Jesus found a y donkey and sat upon
Ac 2:17 your y men will see visions, your
5: 6 the y men came forward, wrapped up
5:10 Then the y men came in and, finding
7:58 at the feet of a y man named Saul.
20: 9 Seated in a window was a y man named
20:10 y man and put his arms around him.
20:12 The people took the y man home alive
23:17 "Take this y man to the commander;
23:18 asked me to bring this y man to you
23:19 The commander took the y man by the
23:22 The commander dismissed the y man
1Ti 4:12 look down on you because you are y,
Tit 2: 6 Similarly, encourage the y men to be
1Pe 5: 5 Y men, in the same way be submissive
1Jn 2:13 I write to you, y men, because you
2:14 I write to you, y men, because you

Younger (Young)

Ge 19:31 the older daughter said to the y,
19:34 the older daughter said to the y,
19:35 y daughter went and lay with him.
19:38 The y daughter also had a son, and
25:23 and the older will serve the y."
27:15 and put them on her y son Jacob.
27:42 she sent for her y son Jacob and
29:16 and the name of the y was Rachel.
29:18 return for your y daughter Rachel."
29:26 to give the y daughter in marriage
29:27 we will give you the y one also,
48:14 though he was the y, and crossing
48:19 Nevertheless, his y brother will be
Jdg 1:13 son of Kenaz, Caleb's y brother,
3: 9 Caleb's y brother, who saved them.
15: 2 Isn't her y sister more attractive?
Ru 3:10 the y men, whether rich or poor.
1Sa 14:49 Merab, and that of the y was Michal.
Job 30: 1 "But now they mock me, men y than I,
Eze 16:46 her daughters; and your y sister,
16:61 older than you and those who are y.
Mk 15:40 James the y and of Joses, and Salome.
Lk 15:12 The y one said to his father,
15:13 "Not long after that, the y son got
Jn 21:18 I tell you the truth, when you were y
Ro 9:12 told, "The older will serve the y.
1Ti 5: 1 Treat y men as brothers,
5: 2 older women as mothers, and y women
5:11 for y widows, do not put them on
5:14 I counsel y widows to marry, to have
Tit 2: 4 they can train the y women to love

Youngest (Young)

Ge 9:24 out what his y son had done to him,
42:13 The y is now with our father, and
42:15 unless your y brother comes here.
42:20 you must bring your y brother to me,
42:32 y is now with our father in Canaan.'
42:34 bring your y brother to me so I will
43:29 "Is this your y brother, the one you
43:33 from the firstborn to the y; and
44: 2 in the mouth of the y one's sack,
44:12 the oldest and ending with the y.
44:23 'Unless your y brother comes down
44:26 Only if our y brother is with us
44:26 unless our y brother is with us.'

Jos 6:26 of his y will he set up its gates."
Jdg 9: 5 But Jotham, the y son of Jerub-Baal,
1Sa 16:11 "There is still the y," Jesse
17:14 David was the y. The three oldest
1Ki 16:34 at the cost of his y son Segub,
1Ch 24:31 treated the same as those of the y.
2Ch 21:17 left to him except Ahaziah, the y.
22: 1 Jehoram's y son, king in his place,
Lk 22:26 among you should be like the y,

Youth (Young)

Lev 22:13 in her father's house as in her y,
Nu 11:28 had been Moses' assistant since y,
1Sa 12: 2 leader from my y until this day.
17:33 has been a fighting man from his y."
2Sa 19: 7 come upon you from your y till now."
1Ki 18:12 have worshipped the LORD since my y.
Job 13:26 make me inherit the sins of my y.
31:18 from my y I reared him as would a
33:25 is restored as in the days of his y.
36:14 They die in their y, among male
Ps 25: 7 Remember not the sins of my y and my
71: 5 LORD, my confidence since my y.
71:17 Since my y, O God, you have taught
88:15 From my y I have been afflicted and
89:45 You have cut short the days of his y;
103: 5 your y is renewed like the eagle's.
110: 3 you will receive the dew of your y.
127: 4 a warrior are sons born in one's y.
129: 1 have greatly oppressed me from my y
129: 2 have greatly oppressed me from my y,
144:12 our sons in their y will be like
Pr 2:17 who has left the partner of her y
5:18 you rejoice in the wife of your y.
7: 7 young men, a y who lacked judgment.
29:21 If a man pampers his servant from y,
Ecc 4:13 Better a poor but wise y than an old
4:14 The y may have come from prison to
4:15 the y, the king's successor.
11: 9 give you joy in the days of your y.
11:10 for y and vigour are meaningless.
12: 1 your Creator in the days of your y,
Isa 54: 4 You will forget the shame of your y
65:20 a hundred will be thought a mere y;
Jer 2: 2 'I remember the devotion of your y,
3: 4 'My Father, my friend from my y,
3:24 From our y shameful gods have
3:25 from our y till this day we have
22:21 This has been your way from your y;
31:19 I bore the disgrace of my y.'
32:30 but evil in my sight from their y;
48:11 "Moab has been at rest from y, like
51:22 with you I shatter old man and y,
Eze 4:14 From my y until now I have never
16:22 did not remember the days of your y,
16:43 did not remember the days of your y
16:60 made with you in the days of your y,
23: 3 in prostitution from their y.
23: 8 when during her y men slept with her
23:19 as she recalled the days of her y,
23:21 longed for the lewdness of your y
Hos 2:15 will sing as in the days of her y,
Joel 1: 8 grieving for the husband of her y.
Zec 13: 5 has been my livelihood since my y.'
Mal 2:14 between you and the wife of your y,
2:15 break faith with the wife of your y
2Ti 2:22 Flee the evil desires of y, and

Youthful (Young)

Job 20:11 The y vigour that fills his bones

Youths (Young)

2Ki 2:23 some y came out of the town and
2:24 woods and mauled forty-two of the y.
Isa 3:12 Y oppress my people, women rule over
40:30 Even y grow tired and weary, and

Zaanan

Mic 1:11 Those who live in Z will not come

Zaanannim

Jos 19:33 from Heleph and the large tree in Z,
Jdg 4:11 by the great tree in Z near Kedesh.

Zaavan

Ge 36:27 The sons of Ezer: Bilhan, Z and Akan
1Ch 1:42 The sons of Ezer: Bilhan, Z and Akan

Zabad

1Ch 2:36 of Nathan, Nathan the father of Z,
2:37 Z the father of Ephlal, Ephlal the
7:21 Z his son and Shuthelah his son.
11:41 Uriah the Hittite, Z son of Ahlai,
2Ch 24:26 who conspired against him were Z,
Ezr 10:27 Mattaniah, Jeremoth, Z and Aziza.
10:33 Mattattah, Z, Eliphelet, Jeremai,
10:43 Z, Zebina, Jaddai, Joel and Benaiah.

Zabbai

Ezr 10:28 Jehohanan, Hananiah, Z and Athlai.
Ne 3:20 Next to him, Baruch son of Z

Zabdi

1Ch 8:19 Jakim, Zicri, Z,
27:27 Z the Shiphmite was in charge of the
Ne 11:17 Mattaniah son of Mica, the son of Z,

Zabdiel

1Ch 27: 2 first month, was Jashobeam son of Z.
Ne 11:14 officer was Z son of Haggedolim.

Zabud

1Ki 4: 5 Z son of Nathan—a priest and

Zaccai

Ezr 2: 9 of Z 760
Ne 7:14 of Z 760

Zacchaeus

Tax collector; climbed tree to see Jesus (Lk 19:2-10).

Lk 19: 2 A man was there by the name of Z;
19: 5 to him, "Z, come down immediately.
19: 8 Z stood up and said to the Lord,

Zaccur

Nu 13: 4 tribe of Reuben, Shammua son of Z;
1Ch 4:26 son, Z his son and Shimei his son.
24:27 Jaaziah: Beno, Shoham, Z and Ibri.
25: 2 From the sons of Asaph: Z, Joseph,
25:10 the third to Z, his sons and
Ezr 8:14 Uthai and Z, and with them 70 men.
Ne 3: 2 Z son of Imri built next to them.
10:12 Z, Sherebiah, Shebaniah,
12:35 the son of Z, the son of Asaph,
13:13 storerooms and made Hanan son of Z,

Zadok (Zadokites)

Priest; descendant of Aaron (1Ch 6:3–8). With Abiathar, served David (2Sa 8:17; 1Ch 15:11; 16:39–40); in charge of ark (2Sa 15:24–29). Anointed Solomon as David's successor when Abiathar supported Adonijah (1Ki 1:8,32–48). Descendants served as chief priests (2Ch 31:10; Eze 40:46; 43:19; 44:15).

2Sa 8:17 Z son of Ahitub and Ahimelech son of
15:24 Z was there, too, and all the
15:25 the king said to Z, "Take the ark of
15:27 The king also said to Z the priest,
15:29 Z and Abiathar took the ark of God
15:35 Won't the priests Z and Abiathar be
15:36 Their two sons, Ahimaaz son of Z and
17:15 Hushai told Z and Abiathar, the
18:19 Now Ahimaaz son of Z said, "Let me
18:22 Ahimaaz son of Z again said to Joab,
18:27 one runs like Ahimaaz son of Z.
19:11 King David sent this message to Z
20:25 Sheva was secretary; Z and Abiathar
1Ki 1: 8 Z the priest, Benaiah son of
1:26 me your servant, and Z the priest,
1:32 David said, "Call in Z the priest
1:34 There shall Z the priest and Nathan
1:38 Z the priest, Nathan the prophet,
1:39 Z the priest took the horn of oil
1:44 king has sent with him Z the priest
1:45 Z the priest and Nathan the prophet
2:35 replaced Abiathar with Z the priest.
1Ki 4: 2 Azariah son of Z—the priest;
4: 4 Z and Abiathar—priests;
2Ki 15:33 name was Jerusha daughter of Z.
1Ch 6: 8 Ahitub the father of Z, Z the father
6:12 Ahitub the father of Z, Z the father
6:53 Z his son and Ahimaaz his son.
9:11 the son of Meshullam, the son of Z,
12:28 Z, a brave young warrior, with 22
15:11 David summoned Z and Abiathar the
16:39 David left Z the priest and his
18:16 Z son of Ahitub and Ahimelech son of
24: 3 With the help of Z a descendant of
24: 6 and of the officials: Z the priest,
24:31 the presence of King David and of Z,
27:17 son of Kemuel; over Aaron: Z;
29:22 LORD to be ruler and Z to be priest.
2Ch 27: 1 name was Jerusha daughter of Z.
31:10 from the family of Z, answered,
Ezr 7: 2 the son of Shallum, the son of Z,
Ne 3: 4 Z son of Baana also made repairs.
3:29 Next to them, Z son of Immer made
10:21 Meshezabel, Z, Jaddua,
11:11 the son of Meshullam, the son of Z,
13:13 Shelemiah the priest, Z the scribe
Eze 40:46 These are the sons of Z, who are the
43:19 who are Levites, of the family of Z,
44:15 descendants of Z and who faithfully
Mt 1:14 Azor the father of Z, Z the father

Zadokites (Zadok)

Eze 48:11 the Z, who were faithful in serving

Zaham

2Ch 11:19 him sons: Jeush, Shemariah and Z.

Zahar

Eze 27:18 in wine from Helbon and wool from Z.

Zair

2Ki 8:21 Jehoram went to Z with all his

Zalaph

Ne 3:30 son of Z, repaired another section.

Zalmon

Jdg 9:48 he and all his men went up Mount Z.
2Sa 23:28 Z the Ahohite, Maharai the
Ps 68:14 land, it was like snow fallen on Z.

Zalmonah

Nu 33:41 They left Mount Hor and camped at Z.
33:42 They left Z and camped at Punon.

Zalmunna

Jdg 8: 5 Zebah and Z, the kings of Midian."
8: 6 of Zebah and Z in your possession?
8: 7 when the LORD has given Zebah and Z
8:10 Now Zebah and Z were in Karkor with
8:12 Zebah and Z, the two kings of Midian,
8:15 "Here are Zebah and Z, about whom
8:15 of Zebah and Z in your possession?
8:18 he asked Zebah and Z, "What kind of
8:21 Zebah and Z said, "Come, do it
Ps 83:11 all their princes like Zebah and Z,

Zamzummites

Dt 2:20 but the Ammonites called them Z.

Zanoah

Jos 15:34 Z, En Gannim, Tappuah, Enam,
15:56 Jezreel, Jokdeam, Z,
1Ch 4:18 Soco, and Jekuthiel the father of Z.
Ne 3:13 by Hanun and the residents of Z.
11:30 Z, Adullam and their villages, in

Zaphenath-Paneah

Ge 41:45 Pharaoh gave Joseph the name Z and

Zaphon

Jos 13:27 Beth Nimrah, Succoth and Z with the
Jdg 12: 1 crossed over to Z and said to
Ps 48: 2 Like the utmost heights of Z is

Zarephath
City on Mediterranean coast, between Tyre and Sidon. Here Elijah was given hospitality by a widow whose son he restored from death (1Ki 17:9–24). Jesus praised this widow's faith, and contrasted it with the faith of those from his home town (Lk 4:26).

1Ki 17: 9 "Go at once to **Z** of Sidon and stay
17:10 he went to **Z**. When he came to the
Ob :20 will possess the land as far as **Z**;
Lk 4:26 a widow in **Z** in the region of Sidon.

Zarethan
Jos 3:16 called Adam in the vicinity of **Z**,
1Ki 4:12 and in all of Beth Shan next to **Z**
7:46 of the Jordan between Succoth and **Z**.
2Ch 4:17 of the Jordan between Succoth and **Z**.

Zattu
Ezr 2: 8 of **Z** 945
8: 5 of the descendants of **Z**, Shecaniah
10:27 From the descendants of **Z**: Elioenai,
Ne 7:13 of **Z** 845
10:14 Parosh, Pahath-Moab, Elam, **Z**, Bani,

Zaza
1Ch 2:33 The sons of Jonathan: Peleth and **Z**.

Zeal (*Zeal of the LORD Almighty*, Zealous)
Nu 25:11 in my **z** I did not put an end to them
Dt 29:20 and **z** will burn against that man.
2Sa 21: 2 Saul in his **z** for Israel and Judah
2Ki 10:16 said, "Come with me and see my **z**
Ps 69: 9 for **z** for your house consumes me,
119:139 My **z** wears me out, for my enemies
Pr 19: 2 is not good to have **z** without
Isa 26:11 Let them see your **z** for your people
42:13 a warrior he will stir up his **z**;
59:17 wrapped himself in **z** as in a cloak.
63:15 Where are your **z** and your might?
Eze 5:13 that I the LORD have spoken in my **z**.
36: 5 In my burning **z** I have spoken
38:19 In my **z** and fiery wrath I declare
Jn 2:17 "**Z** for your house will consume me.
Ro 10: 2 their **z** is not based on knowledge.
12:11 Never be lacking in **z**, but keep your
Php 3: 6 as for **z**, persecuting the church;

Zeal of the LORD Almighty
2Ki 19:31 The **z** will accomplish this.
Isa 9: 7 The **z** will accomplish this.
37:32 The **z** will accomplish this.

Zealot
Mt 10: 4 Simon the **Z** and Judas Iscariot, who
Mk 3:18 of Alphaeus, Thaddaeus, Simon the **Z**
Lk 6:15 Alphaeus, Simon who was called the **Z**,
Ac 1:13 Simon the **Z**, and Judas son of James.

Zealous (Zeal)
Nu 25:11 **z** as I am for my honour among them,
25:13 because he was **z** for the honour of
1Ki 19:10 He replied, "I have been very **z** for
19:14 He replied, "I have been very **z** for
Pr 23:17 be **z** for the fear of the LORD.
Eze 39:25 and I will be **z** for my holy name.
Ac 21:20 and all of them are **z** for the law.
22: 3 **z** for God as any of you are today.
Ro 10: 2 about them that they are **z** for God,
2Co 8:22 to us in many ways that he is **z**,
Gal 1:14 **z** for the traditions of my fathers.
4:17 Those people are **z** to win you over,
4:17 us, so that you may be **z** for them.
4:18 is fine to be **z**, provided the

Zebadiah
1Ch 8:15 **Z**, Arad, Eder,
8:17 **Z**, Meshullam, Hizki, Heber,
12: 7 Joelah and **Z** the sons of Jeroham
26: 2 **Z** the third, Jathniel the fourth,
27: 7 Joab; his son **Z** was his successor.
2Ch 17: 8 Nethaniah, **Z**, Asahel, Shemiramoth,
19:11 and **Z** son of Ishmael, the leader of
Ezr 8: 8 of the descendants of Shephatiah, **Z**
10:20 descendants of Immer: Hanani and **Z**.

Zebah
Jdg 8: 5 **Z** and Zalmunna, the kings of Midian.
8: 6 "Do you already have the hands of **Z**
8: 7 when the LORD has given **Z** and
8:10 Now **Z** and Zalmunna were in Karkor
8:12 **Z** and Zalmunna, the two kings of
8:15 "Here are **Z** and Zalmunna, about whom
8:15 'Do you already have the hands of **Z**
8:18 he asked **Z** and Zalmunna, "What kind
8:21 **Z** and Zalmunna said, "Come, do it
Ps 83:11 their princes like **Z** and Zalmunna,

Zebedee (Zebedee's)
Mt 4:21 James son of **Z** and his brother John.
4:21 father **Z**, preparing their nets.
10: 2 James son of **Z**, and his brother John
26:37 He took Peter and the two sons of **Z**
Mk 1:19 he saw James son of **Z** and his
1:20 and they left their father **Z** in the
3:17 James son of **Z** and his brother John
10:35 James and John, the sons of **Z**, came
Lk 5:10 were James and John, the sons of **Z**,
Jn 21: 2 the sons of **Z**, and two other

Zebedee's (Zebedee)
Mt 20:20 the mother of **Z** sons came to Jesus
27:56 and Joses, and the mother of **Z** sons.

Zebidah
2Ki 23:36 His mother's name was **Z** daughter of

Zebina
Ezr 10:43 Zabad, **Z**, Jaddai, Joel and Benaiah.

Zeboiim
Ge 10:19 Admah and **Z**, as far as Lasha.
14: 2 Shemeber king of **Z**, and the king of
14: 8 the king of Admah, the king of **Z** and
Dt 29:23 Admah and **Z**, which the LORD
Hos 11: 8 How can I make you like **Z**? My heart

Zeboim
1Sa 13:18 the Valley of **Z** facing the desert.
Ne 11:34 in Hadid, **Z** and Neballat,

Zebul
Jdg 9:28 and isn't **Z** his deputy? Serve the
9:30 **Z** the governor of the city heard
9:36 Gaal saw them, he said to **Z**, "Look,
9:36 tops of the mountains!" **Z** replied,
9:38 **Z** said to him, "Where is your big
9:41 **Z** drove Gaal and his brothers out of

Zebulun (Zebulunite)
1. Son of Jacob by Leah (Ge 30:20; 35:23; 1Ch 2:1). Blessed by Jacob (Ge 49:13). **2.** Tribe descended from Zebulun. Blessed by Moses (Dt 33:18–19). Included in census (Nu 1:30–31; 26:26–27). **3.** Mountainous territory at northern end of Palestine, between Asher and Naphtali. Allotted to the descendants of Jacob's tenth son, its towns and borders were clearly listed (Jos 19:10–16). Its former Canaanite inhabitants were not driven out but enslaved (Jdg 1:30). Isaiah predicted a time of great honour for this land (Isa 9:1). This was fulfilled in the coming of Christ (Mt 4:13–16).

Ge 30:20 six sons." So she named him **Z**.
35:23 Simeon, Levi, Judah, Issachar and **Z**.
46:14 The sons of **Z**: Sered, Elon and
49:13 "**Z** will live by the seashore and
Ex 1: 3 Issachar, **Z** and Benjamin;
Nu 1: 9 from **Z**, Eliab son of Helon;
1:30 From the descendants of **Z**: All the
1:31 The number from the tribe of **Z** was
2: 7 The tribe of **Z** will be next. The
2: 7 people of **Z** is Eliab son of Helon.
7:24 people of **Z**, brought his offering.
10:16 over the division of the tribe of **Z**.
13:10 from the tribe of **Z**, Gaddiel son of
26:26 The descendants of **Z** by their clans
Nu 26:27 These were the clans of **Z**; those
34:25 the leader from the tribe of **Z**;
Dt 27:13 Gad, Asher, **Z**, Dan and Naphtali.
33:18 About **Z** he said: "Rejoice, **Z**, in
Jos 19:10 The third lot came up for **Z**, clan by
19:16 the inheritance of **Z**, clan by clan.
19:27 touched **Z** and the Valley of Iphtah
19:34 It touched **Z** on the south, Asher on
21: 7 the tribes of Reuben, Gad and **Z**.
21:34 the tribe of **Z**, Jokneam, Kartah,
Jdg 1:30 Neither did **Z** drive out the
4: 6 ten thousand men of Naphtali and **Z**
4:10 where he summoned **Z** and Naphtali.
5:14 from **Z** those who bear a commander's
5:18 The people of **Z** risked their very
6:35 and also into Asher, **Z** and Naphtali,
12:12 buried in Aijalon in the land of **Z**.
1Ch 2: 1 Simeon, Levi, Judah, Issachar, **Z**,
6:63 the tribes of Reuben, Gad and **Z**.
6:77 tribe of **Z** they received Jokneam,
12:33 men of **Z**, experienced soldiers
12:40 **Z** and Naphtali came bringing food on
27:19 over **Z**: Ishmaiah son of Obadiah;
2Ch 30:10 as far as **Z**, but the people scorned
30:11 some men of Asher, Manasseh and **Z**
30:18 Manasseh, Issachar and **Z** had not
Ps 68:27 the princes of **Z** and of Naphtali.
Isa 9: 1 In the past he humbled the land of **Z**
Eze 48:26 "**Z** will have one portion; it will
48:27 territory of **Z** from east to west.
48:33 gate of Issachar and the gate of **Z**.
Mt 4:13 lake in the area of **Z** and Naphtali—
4:15 "Land of **Z** and land of Naphtali, the
Rev 7: 8 from the tribe of **Z** 12,000, from the

Zebulunite (Zebulun)
Jdg 12:11 After him, Elon the **Z** led Israel for

Zechariah (Zechariah's)
1. King of Israel; son of Jeroboam II; assassinated (2Ki 14:29; 15:8–12). **2.** Prophet who, with Haggai, encouraged rebuilding of temple (Ezr 5:1; 6:14; Zec 1:1). **3.** Priest; father of John the Baptist; struck dumb because of unbelief at the angel Gabriel's announcement of the birth of a son (Lk 1:5–22,59–79).

2Ki 14:29 And **Z** his son succeeded him as king.
15: 8 **Z** son of Jeroboam became king of
15:10 son of Jabesh conspired against **Z**.
18: 2 name was Abijah daughter of **Z**.
1Ch 5: 7 records: Jeiel the chief, **Z**,
9:21 **Z** son of Meshelemiah was the
9:37 Gedor, Ahio, **Z** and Mikloth.
15:18 them their brothers next in rank: **Z**,
15:20 **Z**, Aziel, Shemiramoth, Jehiel, Unni,
15:24 Joshaphat, Nethanel, Amasai, **Z**,
16: 5 Asaph was the chief, **Z** second, then
24:25 Isshiah; from the sons of Isshiah: **Z**.
26: 2 had sons: **Z** the firstborn, Jediael
26:11 Tabaliah the third and **Z** the fourth.
26:14 Then lots were cast for his son **Z**, a
27:21 Iddo son of **Z**; over Benjamin:
2Ch 17: 7 Obadiah, **Z**, Nethanel and Micaiah to
20:14 LORD came upon Jahaziel son of **Z**,
21: 2 **Z**, Azariahu, Michael and Shephatiah.
24:20 upon **Z** son of Jehoida the priest.
26: 5 He sought God during the days of **Z**,
29: 1 name was Abijah daughter of **Z**.
29:13 of Asaph, **Z** and Mattaniah;
34:12 and **Z** and Meshullam, descended from
35: 8 Hilkiah, **Z** and Jehiel, the
Ezr 5: 1 Haggai the prophet and **Z** the prophet
6:14 prophet and **Z**, a descendant of Iddo.
8: 3 **Z**, and with him were registered
8:11 descendants of Bebai, **Z** son of Bebai
8:16 Jarib, Elnathan, Nathan, **Z** and
10:26 **Z**, Jehiel, Abdi, Jeremoth and Elijah
Ne 8: 4 Hashbaddanah, **Z** and Meshullam.
11: 4 the son of **Z**, the son of Amariah,
11: 5 son of **Z**, a descendant of Shelah.
11:12 the son of Amzi, the son of **Z**, the
12:16 of Iddo's, **Z**; of Ginnethon's,
12:35 and also **Z** son of Jonathan, the son
12:41 **Z** and Hananiah with their trumpets—
Isa 8: 2 the priest and **Z** son of Jeberekiah

Zec 1: 1 **Z** son of Berekiah, the son of Iddo:
1: 7 **Z** son of Berekiah, the son of Iddo.
7: 1 the word of the LORD came to **Z** on
7: 8 the word of the LORD came again to **Z**:
Mt 23:35 to the blood of **Z** son of Barakiah,
Lk 1: 5 of Judea there was a priest named **Z**,
1:12 **Z** saw him, he was startled and was
1:13 Do not be afraid, **Z**; your prayer has
1:18 **Z** asked the angel, "How can I be
1:21 the people were waiting for **Z** and
1:59 to name him after his father **Z**,
1:67 His father **Z** was filled with the
3: 2 came to John son of **Z** in the desert.
11:51 the blood of Abel to the blood of **Z**,

Zechariah's (Zechariah)

2Ki 15:11 The other events of **Z** reign are
2Ch 24:22 kindness **Z** father Jehoiada had shown
Lk 1: 8 Once when **Z** division was on duty and
1:40 where she entered **Z** home and greeted

Zedad

Nu 34: 8 Then the boundary will go to **Z**,
Eze 47:15 Hethlon road past Lebo Hamath to **Z**,

Zedekiah (Zedekiah's)

1. Last king of Judah. Son of Josiah, formerly Mattaniah. Installed by Nebuchadnezzar (2Ki 24:17–18). Evil denounced (Jer 24:8–10; Eze 21:25); dealings with Jeremiah (2Ch 36:12; Jer 37; 38:14–28). Rebellion and broken oath led to fall of Jerusalem (2Ki 24:20–25:7; 2Ch 36:13–21; Jer 39; Eze 17:12–15).
2. Leader of false prophets at Ahab's court (1Ki 22:11–24; 2Ch 18:10–23).

1Ki 22:11 Now **Z** son of Kenaanah had made iron
22:24 **Z** son of Kenaanah went up and
2Ki 24:17 his place and changed his name to **Z**.
24:18 **Z** was twenty-one years old when he
24:20 Now **Z** rebelled against the king of
25: 2 until the eleventh year of King **Z**.
25: 7 They killed the sons of **Z** before his
1Ch 3:15 **Z** the third, Shallum the fourth.
3:16 Jehoiakim: Jehoiachin his son, and **Z**
2Ch 18:10 Now **Z** son of Kenaanah had made iron
18:23 **Z** son of Kenaanah went up and
36:10 **Z**, king over Judah and Jerusalem.
36:11 **Z** was twenty-one years old when he
Ne 10: 1 governor, the son of Hacaliah. **Z**,
Jer 1: 3 of **Z** son of Josiah king of Judah,
21: 1 King **Z** sent to him Pashhur son of
21: 3 Jeremiah answered them, "Tell **Z**,
21: 7 I will hand over **Z** king of Judah,
24: 8 so will I deal with **Z** king of Judah,
27: 1 in the reign of **Z** son of Josiah
27: 3 to Jerusalem to **Z** king of Judah.
27:12 the same message to **Z** king of Judah
28: 1 in the reign of **Z** king of Judah,
29: 3 whom **Z** king of Judah sent to King
29:21 of Kolaiah and **Z** son of Maaseiah,
29:22 'The LORD treat you like **Z** and Ahab,
32: 1 the tenth year of **Z** king of Judah,
32: 3 Now **Z** king of Judah had imprisoned
32: 4 **Z** king of Judah will not escape out
32: 5 He will take **Z** to Babylon, where he
34: 2 the God of Israel, says: Go to **Z**
34: 4 of the LORD, O **Z** king of Judah.
34: 6 to **Z** king of Judah, in Jerusalem,
34: 8 after King **Z** had made a covenant
34:21 "I will hand **Z** king of Judah and his
36:12 son of Shaphan, **Z** son of Hananiah,
37: 1 **Z** son of Josiah was made king of
37: 3 King **Z**, however, sent Jehucal son of
37:17 King **Z** sent for him and had him
37:18 Jeremiah said to King **Z**, "What crime
37:21 King **Z** then gave orders for Jeremiah
38: 5 is in your hands," King **Z** answered
38:14 King **Z** sent for Jeremiah the prophet
38:15 Jeremiah said to **Z**, "If I give you
38:16 King **Z** swore this oath secretly to
38:17 Jeremiah said to **Z**, "This is what
38:19 King **Z** said to Jeremiah, "I am
38:24 **Z** said to Jeremiah, "Do not let
39: 1 the ninth year of **Z** king of Judah,
39: 4 **Z** king of Judah and all the soldiers
Jer 39: 5 overtook **Z** in the plains of Jericho.
39: 6 the sons of **Z** before his eyes
44:30 just as I handed **Z** king of Judah
49:34 in the reign of **Z** king of Judah:
51:59 went to Babylon with **Z** king of Judah
52: 1 **Z** was twenty-one years old when he
52: 3 Now **Z** rebelled against the king of
52: 5 until the eleventh year of King **Z**.
52: 8 the Babylonian army pursued King **Z**
52:10 the sons of **Z** before his eyes;

Zedekiah's (Zedekiah)

2Ki 25: 1 in the ninth year of **Z** reign, on the
Jer 39: 2 the fourth month of **Z** eleventh year,
39: 7 he put out **Z** eyes and bound him with
52: 4 in the ninth year of **Z** reign, on the
52:11 he put out **Z** eyes, bound him with

Zeeb

Jdg 7:25 the Midianite leaders, Oreb and **Z**.
7:25 Oreb, and **Z** at the winepress of **Z**.
7:25 heads of Oreb and **Z** to Gideon,
8: 3 God gave Oreb and **Z**, the Midianite
Ps 83:11 Make their nobles like Oreb and **Z**,

Zeker

1Ch 8:31 Gedor, Ahio, **Z**

Zela

2Sa 21:14 at **Z** in Benjamin, and did everything

Zelah

Jos 18:28 **Z**, Haeleph, the Jebusite city (that

Zelek

2Sa 23:37 **Z** the Ammonite, Naharai the
1Ch 11:39 **Z** the Ammonite, Naharai the

Zelophehad (Zelophehad's)

Nu 26:33 (**Z** son of Hepher had no sons; he had
27: 1 The daughters of **Z** son of Hepher,
36: 2 of our brother **Z** to his daughters.
Jos 17: 3 Now **Z** son of Hepher, the son of
1Ch 7:15 Another descendant was named **Z**, who

Zelophehad's (Zelophehad)

Nu 27: 7 "What **Z** daughters are saying is
36: 6 This is what the LORD commands for **Z**
36:10 **Z** daughters did as the LORD
36:11 **Z** daughters—Mahlah, Tirzah, Hoglah,

Zelzah

1Sa 10: 2 at **Z** on the border of Benjamin.

Zemaraim

Jos 18:22 Beth Arabah, **Z**, Bethel,
2Ch 13: 4 Abijah stood on Mount **Z**, in the hill

Zemarites

Ge 10:18 Arvadites, **Z** and Hamathites. Later
1Ch 1:16 Arvadites, **Z** and Hamathites.

Zemirah

1Ch 7: 8 The sons of Beker: **Z**, Joash, Eliezer,

Zenan

Jos 15:37 **Z**, Hadashah, Migdal Gad,

Zenas

Tit 3:13 you can to help **Z** the lawyer and

Zephaniah

Prophet during reign of Josiah; descended from Hezekiah (Zep 1:1).

2Ki 25:18 **Z** the priest next in rank and the
1Ch 6:36 the son of Azariah, the son of **Z**,
Jer 21: 1 and the priest **Z** son of Maaseiah.
29:25 to **Z** son of Maaseiah the priest, and
29:25 You said to **Z**,
29:29 **Z** the priest, however, read the
37: 3 with the priest **Z** son of Maaseiah
Jer 52:24 **Z** the priest next in rank and the
Zep 1: 1 The word of the LORD that came to **Z**
Zec 6:10 to the house of Josiah son of **Z**.
6:14 Tobijah, Jedaiah and Hen son of **Z**

Zephath

Jdg 1:17 attacked the Canaanites living in **Z**,

Zephathah

2Ch 14:10 in the Valley of **Z** near Mareshah.

Zepho

Ge 36:11 The sons of Eliphaz: Teman, Omar, **Z**,
36:15 Esau: Chiefs Teman, Omar, **Z**, Kenaz,
1Ch 1:36 The sons of Eliphaz: Teman, Omar, **Z**,

Zephon (Zephonite)

Ge 46:16 The sons of Gad: **Z**, Haggi, Shuni,
Nu 26:15 Gad by their clans were: through **Z**,

Zephonite (Zephon)

Nu 26:15 the **Z** clan; through Haggi, the

Zer

Jos 19:35 The fortified cities were Ziddim, **Z**,

Zerah (Zerahite, Zerahites)

Ge 36:13 The sons of Reuel: Nahath, **Z**,
36:17 Chiefs Nahath, **Z**, Shammah and Mizzah
36:33 Jobab son of **Z** from Bozrah succeeded
38:30 out and he was given the name **Z**.
46:12 Onan, Shelah, Perez and **Z** (but Er
Nu 26:13 through **Z**, the Zerahite clan;
26:20 clan; through **Z**, the Zerahite clan.
Jos 7: 1 the son of Zimri, the son of **Z**, of
7:18 **Z**, of the tribe of Judah, was taken.
7:24 took Achan son of **Z**, the silver, the
22:20 Achan son of **Z** acted unfaithfully
1Ch 1:37 The sons of Reuel: Nahath, **Z**,
1:44 Jobab son of **Z** from Bozrah succeeded
2: 4 bore him Perez and **Z**.
2: 6 The sons of **Z**: Zimri, Ethan, Heman,
4:24 Nemuel, Jamin, Jarib, **Z** and Shaul;
6:21 his son, Iddo his son, **Z** his son
6:41 the son of Ethni, the son of **Z**, the
2Ch 14: 9 **Z** the Cushite marched out against
Ne 11:24 of the descendants of **Z** son of Judah
Mt 1: 3 Judah the father of Perez and **Z**,

Zerahiah

1Ch 6: 6 Uzzi the father of **Z**, **Z** the father
6:51 his son, Uzzi his son, **Z** his son,
Ezr 7: 4 the son of **Z**, the son of Uzzi, the
8: 4 son of **Z**, and with him 200 men;

Zerahite (Zerah)

Nu 26:13 through Zerah, the **Z** clan; through
26:20 clan; through Zerah, the **Z** clan.
1Ch 27:11 was Sibbecai the Hushathite, a **Z**.
27:13 was Maharai the Netophathite, a **Z**.

Zerahites (Zerah)

Jos 7:17 came forward, and he took the **Z**.
7:17 He had the clan of the **Z** come
1Ch 9: 6 Of the **Z**: Jeuel. The people from

Zered Valley

Nu 21:12 they moved on and camped in the **Z**.
Dt 2:13 "Now get up and cross the **Z**.
2:14 Kadesh Barnea until we crossed the **Z**

Zeredah

1Ki 11:26 an Ephraimite from **Z**, and his mother

Zererah

Jdg 7:22 army fled to Beth Shittah towards **Z**

Zeresh

Est 5:10 his friends and **Z**, his wife,
5:14 His wife **Z** and all his friends said
6:13 told **Z** his wife and all his friends
6:13 His advisers and his wife **Z** said to

Zereth
1Ch 4: 7 The sons of Helah: **Z**, Zohar, Ethnan,

Zereth Shahar
Jos 13:19 Sibmah, **Z** on the hill in the valley

Zeri
1Ch 25: 3 from his sons: Gedaliah, **Z**, Jeshaiah,

Zeror
1Sa 9: 1 the son of **Z**, the son of Becorath,

Zeruah
1Ki 11:26 and his mother was a widow named **Z**.

Zerubbabel
Leader of returning exiles (Ne 12:1; Hag 1:1; 2:2); began work on temple (Ezr 3); after delay, encouraged to continue by Haggai (Ezr 5:1–2; Hag 1:2–15; 2) and Zechariah (Zec 4:6–10).

1Ch 3:19 The sons of Pedaiah: **Z** and Shimei.
3:19 The sons of **Z**: Meshullam and
Ezr 2: 2 in company with **Z**, Jeshua, Nehemiah,
3: 2 and **Z** son of Shealtiel and his
3: 8 **Z** son of Shealtiel, Jeshua son of
4: 2 they came to **Z** and to the heads of
4: 3 **Z**, Jeshua and the rest of the heads
5: 2 **Z** son of Shealtiel and Jeshua son of
Ne 7: 7 in company with **Z**, Jeshua, Nehemiah,
12: 1 **Z** son of Shealtiel and with Jeshua:
12:47 in the days of **Z** and of Nehemiah,
Hag 1: 1 Haggai to **Z** son of Shealtiel,
1:12 **Z** son of Shealtiel, Joshua son of
1:14 the LORD stirred up the spirit of **Z**
2: 2 "Speak to **Z** son of Shealtiel,
2: 4 now be strong, O **Z**,' declares the
2:21 "Tell **Z** governor of Judah that I
2:23 my servant **Z** son of Shealtiel,'
Zec 4: 6 "This is the word of the LORD to **Z**: '
4: 7 Before **Z** you will become level
4: 9 "The hands of **Z** have laid the
4:10 see the plumb-line in the hand of **Z**.
Mt 1:12 Shealtiel, Shealtiel the father of **Z**
1:13 **Z** the father of Abiud, Abiud the
Lk 3:27 the son of Rhesa, the son of **Z**, the

Zeruiah (Zeruiah's)
1Sa 26: 6 the Hittite and Abishai son of **Z**,
2Sa 2:13 Joab son of **Z** and David's men went
2:18 The three sons of **Z** were there:
3:39 sons of **Z** are too strong for me.
8:16 Joab son of **Z** was over the army;
14: 1 Joab son of **Z** knew that the king's
16: 9 Abishai son of **Z** said to the king,
16:10 I have in common, you sons of **Z**?
17:25 and sister of **Z** the mother of Joab.
18: 2 Joab's brother Abishai son of **Z**,
19:21 Abishai son of **Z** said, "Shouldn't
19:22 I have in common, you sons of **Z**?
21:17 Abishai son of **Z** came to David's
23:18 Abishai the brother of Joab son of **Z**
23:37 the armour-bearer of Joab son of **Z**,
1Ki 1: 7 conferred with Joab son of **Z** and
2: 5 know what Joab son of **Z** did to me—
2:22 the priest and Joab son of **Z**!"
1Ch 2:16 Their sisters were **Z** and Abigail.
11: 6 Joab son of **Z** went up first, and so
11:39 the armour-bearer of Joab son of **Z**,
18:12 Abishai son of **Z** struck down
18:15 Joab son of **Z** was over the army;
26:28 Abner son of Ner and Joab son of **Z**,
27:24 Joab son of **Z** began to count the men

Zeruiah's (Zeruiah)
1Ch 2:16 **Z** three sons were Abishai, Joab and

Zetham
1Ch 23: 8 the first, **Z** and Joel—three in all.
26:22 **Z** and his brother Joel. They were in

Zethan
1Ch 7:10 Kenaanah, **Z**, Tarshish and Ahishahar

Zethar
Est 1:10 Bigtha, Abagtha, **Z** and Carcas—

Zeus
Ac 14:12 Barnabas they called **Z**, and Paul
14:13 The priest of **Z**, whose temple was

Zia
1Ch 5:13 Jacan, **Z** and Eber—seven in all.

Ziba (Ziba's)
2Sa 9: 2 servant of Saul's household named **Z**
9: 2 the king said to him, "Are you **Z**?"
9: 3 **Z** answered the king, "There is still
9: 4 **Z** answered, "He is at the house of
9: 9 the king summoned **Z**, Saul's servant,
9:10 (Now **Z** had fifteen sons and twenty
9:11 **Z** said to the king, "Your servant
16: 1 there was **Z**, the steward of
16: 2 The king asked **Z**, "Why have you
16: 2 **Z** answered, "The donkeys are for the
16: 3 **Z** said to him, "He is staying in
16: 4 the king said to **Z**, "All that
16: 4 "I humbly bow," **Z** said. "May I find
19:17 along with **Z**, the steward of Saul's
19:26 But **Z** my servant betrayed me.
19:29 you and **Z** to divide the fields."

Ziba's (Ziba)
2Sa 9:12 and all the members of **Z** household

Zibeon
Ge 36: 2 and granddaughter of **Z** the Hivite—
36:14 of Anah and granddaughter of **Z**,
36:20 the region: Lotan, Shobal, **Z**, Anah,
36:24 The sons of **Z**: Aiah and Anah. This
36:24 grazing the donkeys of his father **Z**.
36:29 chiefs: Lotan, Shobal, **Z**, Anah,
1Ch 1:38 The sons of Seir: Lotan, Shobal, **Z**,
1:40 The sons of **Z**: Aiah and Anah.

Zibia
1Ch 8: 9 By his wife Hodesh he had Jobab, **Z**,

Zibiah
2Ki 12: 1 His mother's name was **Z**; she was
2Ch 24: 1 His mother's name was **Z**; she was

Zicri
Ex 6:21 of Izhar were Korah, Nepheg and **Z**.
1Ch 8:19 Jakim, **Z**, Zabdi,
8:23 Abdon, **Z**, Hanan,
8:27 Jaareshiah, Elijah and **Z** were the
9:15 Mica, the son of **Z**, the son of Asaph;
26:25 **Z** his son and Shelomith his son.
27:16 Eliezer son of **Z**; over the
2Ch 17:16 next, Amasiah son of **Z**, who
23: 1 of Adaiah, and Elishaphat son of **Z**.
28: 7 **Z**, an Ephraimite warrior, killed
Ne 11: 9 Joel son of **Z** was their chief
12:17 of Abijah's, **Z**; of Miniamin's and of

Ziddim
Jos 19:35 The fortified cities were **Z**, Zer,

Ziha
Ezr 2:43 descendants of **Z**, Hasupha, Tabbaoth,
Ne 7:46 descendants of **Z**, Hasupha, Tabbaoth,
11:21 **Z** and Gishpa were in charge of them.

Ziklag
Town in the Negev, about 10 miles north of Beersheba. Allotted by Joshua to the tribe of Judah (Jos 15:31), but later assigned to Simeon (Jos 19:5; 1Ch 4:30). Achish gave it to David as a refuge from Saul (1Sa 27:6; 1Ch 12:1, 20). Here the Amalekites took captive Israelite wives and children (1Sa 30). After Saul's death David stayed here for 2 days (2Sa 1:1) executing the man who claimed he had killed Saul (2Sa 1:8–15). After the exile it was occupied by Judeans (Ne 11:28).

Jos 15:31 **Z**, Madmannah, Sansannah,
19: 5 **Z**, Beth Marcaboth, Hazar Susah,
1Sa 27: 6 on that day Achish gave him **Z**, and
30: 1 David and his men reached **Z** on the
30: 1 had raided the Negev and **Z**.
30: 1 They had attacked **Z** and burned it,
30: 3 David and his men came to **Z**, they
30:14 Negev of Caleb. And we burned **Z**."
30:26 David arrived in **Z**, he sent some of
2Sa 1: 1 Amalekites and stayed in **Z** two days.
4:10 him and put him to death in **Z**.
1Ch 4:30 Bethuel, Hormah, **Z**,
12: 1 were the men who came to David at **Z**,
12:20 David went to **Z**, these were the men
Ne 11:28 in **Z**, in Meconah and its settlements,

Zillah
Ge 4:19 one named Adah and the other **Z**.
4:22 **Z** also had a son, Tubal-Cain, who
4:23 said to his wives, "Adah and **Z**,

Zillethai
1Ch 8:20 Elienai, **Z**, Eliel,
12:20 Michael, Jozabad, Elihu and **Z**,

Zilpah
Ge 29:24 Laban gave his servant girl **Z** to his
30: 9 she took her maidservant **Z** and gave
30:10 Leah's servant **Z** bore Jacob a son.
30:12 Leah's servant **Z** bore Jacob a second
35:26 The sons of Leah's maidservant **Z**:
37: 2 sons of Bilhah and the sons of **Z**,
46:18 the children born to Jacob by **Z**,

Zimmah
1Ch 6:20 his son, Jehath his son, **Z** his son,
6:42 the son of Ethan, the son of **Z**, the
2Ch 29:12 Joah son of **Z** and Eden son of Joah;

Zimran
Ge 25: 2 She bore him **Z**, Jokshan, Medan,
1Ch 1:32 Abraham's concubine: **Z**, Jokshan,

Zimri (Zimri's)
Nu 25:14 Midianite woman was **Z** son of Salu,
Jos 7: 1 the son of **Z**, the son of Zerah, of
7:17 by families, and **Z** was taken.
7:18 the son of **Z**, the son of Zerah, of
1Ki 16: 9 **Z**, one of his officials, who had
16:10 **Z** came in, struck him down and
16:12 **Z** destroyed the whole family of
16:15 **Z** reigned in Tirzah for seven days.
16:16 that **Z** had plotted against the king
16:18 **Z** saw that the city was taken, he
2Ki 9:31 "Have you come in peace, **Z**, you
1Ch 2: 6 The sons of Zerah: **Z**, Ethan, Heman,
8:36 and **Z**, and **Z** was the father of Moza.
9:42 and **Z**, and **Z** was the father of Moza.
Jer 25:25 all the kings of **Z**, Elam and Media;

Zimri's (Zimri)
1Ki 16:20 for the other events of **Z** reign, and

Zin, Desert of
Desert region south of the Negev, through which the Israelites wandered on their way from Egypt to the promised land (Nu 13:21; 33:36). Here Miriam died and was buried (Nu 20:1), and Moses and Aaron disobeyed God's instructions (Nu 27:14; Dt 32:51). Part of it was included in the promised land (Nu 34:3–4), and was eventually allotted to the tribe of Judah (Jos 15:1, 3).

Nu 13:21 the Desert of **Z** as far as Rehob,
20: 1 arrived at the Desert of **Z**, and they
27:14 at the waters in the Desert of **Z**,
27:14 Meribah Kadesh, in the Desert of **Z**.)
33:36 at Kadesh, in the Desert of **Z**.
34: 3 Desert of **Z** along the border of Edom.
34: 4 to **Z** and go south of Kadesh Barnea.
Dt 32:51 Meribah Kadesh in the Desert of **Z**
Jos 15: 1 Desert of **Z** in the extreme south.
15: 3 continued on to **Z** and went over to

Zion See Jerusalem (*Daughter of Zion, Mount Zion*, Zion's)

2Sa 5: 7 fortress of **Z**, the City of David.
1Ki 8: 1 covenant from **Z**, the City of David.
2Ki 19:21 Virgin Daughter of **Z** despises you
1Ch 11: 5 fortress of **Z**, the City of David.
2Ch 5: 2 covenant from **Z**, the City of David.
Ps 2: 6 "I have installed my King on **Z**, my
9:11 praises to the LORD, enthroned in **Z**
14: 7 for Israel would come out of **Z**!
20: 2 and grant you support from **Z**.
48:12 Walk about **Z**, go round her, count
50: 2 From **Z**, perfect in beauty, God
51:18 In your good pleasure make **Z** prosper
53: 6 for Israel would come out of **Z**!
65: 1 Praise awaits you, O God, in **Z**;
69:35 for God will save **Z** and rebuild the
76: 2 in Salem, his dwelling-place in **Z**.
84: 7 till each appears before God in **Z**.
87: 2 the LORD loves the gates of **Z** more
87: 4 will say, 'This one was born in **Z**.
87: 5 Indeed, of **Z** it will be said, "This
87: 6 peoples: "This one was born in **Z**.
97: 8 **Z** hears and rejoices and the
99: 2 Great is the LORD in **Z**; he is
102:13 will arise and have compassion on **Z**,
102:16 For the LORD will rebuild **Z** and
102:21 of the LORD will be declared in **Z**
110: 2 extend your mighty sceptre from **Z**;
126: 1 LORD brought back the captives to **Z**
128: 5 May the LORD bless you from **Z** all
129: 5 May all who hate **Z** be turned back in
132:13 For the LORD has chosen **Z**, he has
134: 3 heaven and earth, bless you from **Z**.
135:21 Praise be to the LORD from **Z**, to him
137: 1 sat and wept when we remembered **Z**.
137: 3 "Sing us one of the songs of **Z**!
146:10 your God, O **Z**, for all generations.
147:12 O Jerusalem; praise your God, O **Z**,
149: 2 people of **Z** be glad in their King.
SS 3:11 Come out, you daughters of **Z**, and
Isa 1:27 **Z** will be redeemed with justice, her
2: 3 The law will go out from **Z**, the
3:16 The LORD says, "The women of **Z** are
3:17 on the heads of the women of **Z**;
3:26 The gates of **Z** will lament and mourn;
4: 3 Those who are left in **Z**, who remain
4: 4 away the filth of the women of **Z**;
10:24 "O my people who live in **Z**, do not
12: 6 people of **Z**, for great is the Holy
14:32 "The LORD has established **Z**, and in
28:16 "See, I lay a stone in **Z**, a tested
30:19 O people of **Z**, who live in Jerusalem,
31: 9 whose fire is in **Z**, whose furnace
33: 5 he will fill **Z** with justice and
33:14 The sinners in **Z** are terrified;
33:20 Look upon **Z**, the city of our
33:24 No-one living in **Z** will say, "I am
35:10 They will enter **Z** with singing;
40: 9 You who bring good tidings to **Z**, go
41:27 I was the first to tell **Z**, 'Look,
46:13 I will grant salvation to **Z**, my
49:14 **Z** said, "The LORD has forsaken me,
51: 3 The LORD will surely comfort **Z** and
51:11 They will enter **Z** with singing;
51:16 who say to **Z**, 'You are my people.
52: 1 Awake, awake, O **Z**, clothe yourself
52: 7 who say to **Z**, "Your God reigns!"
52: 8 When the LORD returns to **Z**, they
59:20 "The Redeemer will come to **Z**, to
60:14 LORD, **Z** of the Holy One of Israel.
61: 3 provide for those who grieve in **Z**—
64:10 even **Z** is a desert, Jerusalem a
66: 8 Yet no sooner is **Z** in labour than
Jer 3:14 two from a clan—and bring you to **Z**.
4: 6 Raise the signal to go to **Z**! Flee
8:19 "Is the LORD not in **Z**? Is her King
9:19 The sound of wailing is heard from **Z**:
14:19 Do you despise **Z**? Why have you
26:18 '**Z** will be ploughed like a field,
30:17 outcast, **Z** for whom no-one cares.'
31: 6 us go up to **Z**, to the LORD our God.
31:12 shout for joy on the heights of **Z**;
50: 5 They will ask the way to **Z** and turn
50:28 refugees from Babylon declaring in **Z**
Jer 51:10 let us tell in **Z** what the LORD our
51:24 all the wrong they have done in **Z**,"
51:35 Babylon," say the inhabitants of **Z**.
Lam 1: 4 The roads to **Z** mourn, for no-one
1:17 **Z** stretches out her hands, but there
2: 6 The LORD has made **Z** forget her
4: 2 How the precious sons of **Z**, once
4:11 He kindled a fire in **Z** that consumed
5:11 Women have been ravished in **Z**, and
Joel 2: 1 Blow the trumpet in **Z**; sound the
2:15 Blow the trumpet in **Z**, declare a
2:23 Be glad, O people of **Z**, rejoice in
3:16 The LORD will roar from **Z** and
3:17 your God, dwell in **Z**, my holy hill.
3:21 The LORD dwells in **Z**!
Am 1: 2 He said: "The LORD roars from **Z** and
6: 1 Woe to you who are complacent in **Z**,
Mic 3:10 who build **Z** with bloodshed, and
3:12 **Z** will be ploughed like a field,
4: 2 The law will go out from **Z**, the
4:11 defiled, let our eyes gloat over **Z**!"
Zep 3:16 "Do not fear, O **Z**; do not let your
Zec 1:14 am very jealous for Jerusalem and **Z**,
1:17 comfort **Z** and choose Jerusalem.
2: 7 "Come, O **Z**! Escape, you who live in
8: 2 "I am very jealous for **Z**; I am
8: 3 return to **Z** and dwell in Jerusalem.
9:13 I will rouse your sons, O **Z**, against
Ro 9:33 is written: "See, I lay in **Z** a stone
11:26 "The deliverer will come from **Z**; he
1Pe 2: 6 "See, I lay a stone in **Z**, a chosen

Zion's (Zion)

Isa 34: 8 of retribution, to uphold **Z** cause.
62: 1 For **Z** sake I will not keep silent,

Zior

Jos 15:54 (that is, Hebron) and **Z**—nine towns

Ziph (Ziphites)

1. Town in southernmost corner of Judah, on the border with Edom (Jos 15:21, 24). **2.** Town in hill country of Judah, about 4 miles south-east of Hebron. Probably named after Caleb's grandson (1Ch 2:42), and later fortified by Rehoboam (2Ch 11:8). Saul searched for David here, after a tip-off from some of its inhabitants, but he did not find him (1Sa 23:19, 24). **3.** Desert region surrounding 2 above, where David hid to escape Saul's pursuit (1Sa 26:1–2), and where Jonathan brought him encouragement (1Sa 23:14–15).

Jos 15:24 **Z**, Telem, Bealoth,
15:55 Maon, Carmel, **Z**, Juttah,
1Sa 23:14 and in the hills of the Desert of **Z**.
23:15 was at Horesh in the Desert of **Z**,
23:24 they set out and went to **Z** ahead of
26: 2 Saul went down to the Desert of **Z**,
1Ch 2:42 who was the father of **Z**, and his son
4:16 The sons of Jehallelel: **Z**, Ziphah,
2Ch 11: 8 Gath, Mareshah, **Z**,

Ziphah

1Ch 4:16 The sons of Jehallelel: Ziph, **Z**,

Ziphites (Ziph)

1Sa 23:19 The **Z** went up to Saul at Gibeah and
26: 1 The **Z** went to Saul at Gibeah and
Ps 54: T the **Z** has gone to Saul and said,

Ziphron

Nu 34: 9 continue to **Z** and end at Hazar Enan.

Zippor

Nu 22: 2 Now Balak son of **Z** saw all that
22: 4 **Z**, who was king of Moab at that time,
22:10 Balaam said to God, "Balak son of **Z**,
22:16 "This is what Balak son of **Z** says:
23:18 Balak, and listen; hear me, son of **Z**.
Jos 24: 9 Balak son of **Z**, the king of Moab,
Jdg 11:25 Are you better than Balak son of **Z**,

Zipporah

Daughter of Jethro; wife of Moses (Ex 2:21–22; 18:2); circumcised son to save Moses' life (Ex 4:20–26).

Ex 2:21 his daughter **Z** to Moses in marriage.
2:22 **Z** gave birth to a son, and Moses
4:25 **Z** took a flint knife, cut off her
18: 2 After Moses had sent away his wife **Z**,

Zither

Da 3: 5 flute, **z**, lyre, harp, pipes and all
3: 7 flute, **z**, lyre, harp and all kinds
3:10 flute, **z**, lyre, harp, pipes and all
3:15 flute, **z**, lyre, harp, pipes and all

Ziv

1Ki 6: 1 in the month of **Z**, the second month,
6:37 the fourth year, in the month of **Z**.

Ziz

2Ch 20:16 be climbing up by the Pass of **Z**,

Ziza

1Ch 4:37 **Z** son of Shiphi, the son of Allon,
23:10 the sons of Shimei: Jahath, **Z**, Jeush
23:11 was the first and **Z** the second,
2Ch 11:20 him Abijah, Attai, **Z** and Shelomith.

Zoan

Ancient city in Egypt, on the north-east side of the Nile Delta. Its people witnessed the miracles of God at the exodus (Ps 78:12, 43), and its wise men were counsellors to Pharaoh (Isa 19:11, 13). However, God's power and wisdom surpasses any found within Egypt (Isa 30:1–5; Eze 30:14).

Nu 13:22 seven years before **Z** in Egypt.)
Ps 78:12 land of Egypt, in the region of **Z**.
78:43 his wonders in the region of **Z**.
Isa 19:11 The officials of **Z** are nothing but
19:13 The officials of **Z** have become fools,
30: 4 Though they have officials in **Z** and
Eze 30:14 set fire to **Z** and inflict punishment

Zoar

City in Jordan Valley, south of the Dead Sea, near Sodom and Gomorrah (Ge 13:10). Originally known as Bela (Ge 14:2, 14), God refrained from destroying it along with Sodom and Gomorrah, so that Lot could find refuge there (Ge 19:22–23). Lot did not stay long, however, preferring the safety of the mountains (Ge 19:30). A landmark at the southernmost point of the promised land (Dt 34:3), on the border with Moab (Isa 15:5; Jer 48:34).

Ge 13:10 like the land of Egypt, towards **Z**.
14: 2 and the king of Bela (that is, **Z**).
14: 8 the king of Bela (that is, **Z**)
19:22 (That is why the town was called **Z**.)
19:23 By the time Lot reached **Z**, the sun
19:30 Lot and his two daughters left **Z** and
19:30 for he was afraid to stay in **Z**.
Dt 34: 3 the City of Palms, as far as **Z**.
Isa 15: 5 her fugitives flee as far as **Z**, as
Jer 48:34 from **Z** as far as Horonaim and Eglath

Zobah

1Sa 14:47 the kings of **Z**, and the Philistines.
2Sa 8: 3 king of **Z**, when he went to restore
8: 5 came to help Hadadezer king of **Z**,
8:12 Hadadezer son of Rehob, king of **Z**.
10: 6 foot soldiers from Beth Rehob and **Z**,
10: 8 while the Arameans of **Z** and Rehob
23:36 Igal son of Nathan from **Z**, the son
1Ki 11:23 his master, Hadadezer king of **Z**.
11:24 David destroyed the forces ⌊of **Z**⌋;
1Ch 18: 3 David fought Hadadezer king of **Z**, as
18: 5 came to help Hadadezer king of **Z**,
18: 9 entire army of Hadadezer king of **Z**,
19: 6 Aram Naharaim, Aram Maacah and **Z**.
2Ch 8: 3 Solomon then went to Hamath **Z** and

Zohar

Ge 23: 8 with Ephron son of **Z** on my
25: 9 of Ephron son of **Z** the Hittite,
46:10 Jamin, Ohad, Jakin, **Z** and Shaul the
Ex 6:15 Jamin, Ohad, Jakin, **Z** and Shaul the
1Ch 4: 7 The sons of Helah: Zereth, **Z**, Ethnan,

Zoheleth
1Ki 1: 9 at the Stone of **Z** near En Rogel.

Zoheth
1Ch 4:20 of Ishi: **Z** and Ben-Zoheth.

Zophah
1Ch 7:35 The sons of his brother Helem: **Z**,
7:36 The sons of **Z**: Suah, Harnepher,

Zophai
1Ch 6:26 Elkanah his son, **Z** his son, Nahath

Zophar See Job[1]2.
Job 2:11 and **Z** the Naamathite, heard about
11: 1 **Z** the Naamathite replied:
20: 1 **Z** the Naamathite replied:
42: 9 and **Z** the Naamathite did what the

Zophim
Nu 23:14 he took him to the field of **Z** on the

Zorah
City in the lowlands of Judah near Eshtaol (Jos 15:33), in territory of Dan (Jos 19:41). Home of Manoah and his son Samson (Jdg 13:2–3, 24), who were both buried between here and Eshtaol (Jdg 16:31). Its warriors were sent to spy out Laish for the Danites (Jdg 18:2, 8, 11). Later Rehoboam strengthened its fortifications (2Ch 11:10).

Jos 15:33 In the western foothills: Eshtaol, **Z**,
19:41 included: **Z**, Eshtaol, Ir Shemesh,
Jdg 13: 2 A certain man of **Z**, named Manoah,
13:25 Mahaneh Dan, between **Z** and Eshtaol.
16:31 buried him between **Z** and Eshtaol in
18: 2 the Danites sent five warriors from **Z**
18: 8 they returned to **Z** and Eshtaol,
18:11 battle, set out from **Z** and Eshtaol.
2Ch 11:10 **Z**, Aijalon and Hebron. These were
Ne 11:29 in En Rimmon, in **Z**, in Jarmuth,

Zorathites
1Ch 2:53 descended the **Z** and Eshtaolites.
4: 2 These were the clans of the **Z**.

Zorites
1Ch 2:54 Joab, half the Manahathites, the **Z**,

Zuar
Nu 1: 8 from Issachar, Nethanel son of **Z**;
2: 5 of Issachar is Nethanel son of **Z**.
7:18 On the second day Nethanel son of **Z**,
7:23 the offering of Nethanel son of **Z**.
10:15 Nethanel son of **Z** was over the

Zuph (Zuphite)
1Sa 1: 1 Tohu, the son of **Z**, an Ephraimite.
9: 5 they reached the district of **Z**, Saul
1Ch 6:35 the son of **Z**, the son of Elkanah,

Zuphite (Zuph)
1Sa 1: 1 a **Z** from the hill country of Ephraim,

Zur
Nu 25:15 to death was Cozbi daughter of **Z**,
31: 8 Rekem, **Z**, Hur and Reba—the five
Jos 13:21 Evi, Rekem, **Z**, Hur and Reba—princes
15:58 Halhul, Beth **Z**, Gedor,
1Ch 8:30 followed by **Z**, Kish, Baal, Ner,
9:36 followed by **Z**, Kish, Baal, Ner,

Zuriel
Nu 3:35 Merarite clans was **Z** son of Abihail

Zurishaddai
Nu 1: 6 from Simeon, Shelumiel son of **Z**;
2:12 of Simeon is Shelumiel son of **Z**.
7:36 the fifth day Shelumiel son of **Z**,
7:41 the offering of Shelumiel son of **Z**.
10:19 Shelumiel son of **Z** was over the

Zuzites
Ge 14: 5 the **Z** in Ham, the Emites in Shaveh

Words Omitted from the NIV Comprehensive Concordance

a
abomination
about
above
absolutely
acceptably
according
accordingly
across
actual
actually
adjoining
afar
aforethought
after
afterwards
again
against
ago
ah
aha
ahead
alike
all
almost
along
alongside
already
also
although
altogether
am
amid
among
amply
an
and
another
another's
answer
answered
answering
answers
any
anybody
anyone
anyone's
anything
anywhere
apart
are
aren't
around
article
articles
as
aside
ask
asked
asking
asks
assuredly
at
away
awhile

back
backs
backward
backwards
barely
be
became
because
become
becomes
becoming
been
before
beforehand
began
begin
begins
begun
behind
being
beings
below
beneath
beside
besides
between

beyond
both
bottom
break
breaking
breaks
brightly
bring
bringing
brings
broke
broken
brought
burnt
but
by

came
can
cannot
can't
come
comes
coming
completely
concerning
contemptuously
could
couldn't
critically

deceptively
definitely
despite
did
didn't
discreetly
distinctly
do
does
doesn't
doing
done
don't
doubly
doubtless
down
duly
during

each
earlier
earliest
early
effectively
eight
eighteen
eighteenth
eighth
eightieth
eighty
eighty-five
eighty-four
eighty-six
eighty-three
either
eleven
eleventh
else
else's
elsewhere
emphatically
encouragingly
endlessly
enough
entirely
especially
even
evenly
eventually
every
everybody
everybody's
everyday
everyone
everyone's
everything
everywhere
except
extremely

far
faraway
far-off
farther
farthest
fatally
few
fewest
fifteen
fifteenth
fifth
fifties
fiftieth
fifty
fifty-five

fifty-second
fifty-two
finally
finely
five
five-sided
for
foremost
former
formerly
forth
forty-eight
forty-first
forty-five
forty-nine
forty-one
forty-seven
forty-six
forty-two
forward
four
four-drachma
four-fifths
four-footed
fours
four-sided
fourteen
fourteenth
fourth
frankly
freewill
frequent
frequently
freshly
fro
from
front
frontal
further
furthermore

get
gets
getting
go
goes
going
gone
got
grudgingly

ha
had
half
half-district
half-tribe
halfway
halves
hardly
harshly
has
hasn't
have
haven't
having
he
he's
her
here
here's
hereby
hers
herself
highly
him
himself
his
hotly
how
however
hurriedly

I
I'll
I'm
if
improperly
in
inasmuch
include
included
includes
including
incomparably
indeed
indignantly
individually
indoors
innocently
inside
insistently
instead
into
is
isn't
it

Words Omitted from the NIV Comprehensive Concordance (*continued*)

its
it's
itself
I've

large
larger
largest
lately
later
latest
latter
least
less
lesser
lest
lets
let's
letting
liberally
lightly
like
liked
likely
liken
likes
likewise
little
longer
louder
loudly
lovingly

made
make
makes
making
manifold
many
material
materials
matter
mattered
matters
may
maybe
me
meanwhile
meekly
mercilessly
mere
merely
middle
midst
minus
more
moreover
most
much
must
my
myself

namely
naught
near
nearby
neared
nearer
nearest
nearly
neither
nevertheless
newly
next
nine
nine-and-a-half
nineteen
nineteenth
ninety
ninety-eight
ninety-nine
ninety-six
ninth
no
nobody
none
no-one
no-one's
nor
normally
not
nothing
now
nowhere

O
of
off
often
oh
on
once
one
one's
ones

oneself
one-tenth
one-third
only
onto
open
opened
opening
openings
openly
opens
opposite
or
other
other's
others
otherwise
ought
our
ours
ourselves
out
outdoor
outside
over
own

particularly
partly
per
perfectly
perhaps
personal
personally
persuasively
pertaining
place
places
plus
possibly
practically
precisely
prior
purposely
put
puts
putting
quarter
quite

rapidly
rarely
rather
reach
reached
reaches
reaching
readily
rear
reared
rearing
recent
recently
regarding
regardless
relating
reluctantly
reopened
repeatedly
replied
replies
reply
resolutely
richly
rightfully
rightly
round
roundabout

said
same
saw
say
saying
sayings
says
scarcely
second
see
seeing
seem
seemed
seems
seen
sees
seldom
selves
set
sets
setting
settings
seventeen
seventeenth
seventy
seventy-five
seventy-seven

seventy-two
several
shall
shamelessly
sharply
she
she's
shorter
shortly
should
shouldn't
sighting
similar
similarly
simply
since
sincerely
sir
sirs
six
sixteen
sixteenth
sixth
sixty
sixty-eight
sixty-five
sixty-six
sixty-two
slowly
smaller
smoother
smoothly
smooths
so
solemnly
some
somebody
somehow
someone
someone's
something
sometimes
somewhat
somewhere
soon
sooner
speak
speaking
speaks
speedily
spite
spoke
spoken

spokes
stead
steadily
strongly
successfully
such
supposedly
surely
surpassingly
swiftly

tabernacles
take
taken
takes
taking
talk
talked
talker
talkers
talking
talks
tell
telling
tells
ten-acre
terms
terribly
than
that
that's
the
their
theirs
them
themselves
then
there
there's
therefore
these
they
thicker
thickness
thing
things
third
thirds
thirteen
thirteenth
thirtieth
thirty
thirty-eight

Words Omitted from the NIV Comprehensive Concordance (*continued*)

thirty-eighth
thirty-fifth
thirty-first
thirty-five
thirty-ninth
thirty-one
thirty-second
thirty-seven
thirty-seventh
thirty-six
thirty-sixth
thirty-three
thirty-two
this
thorough
thoroughly
those
though
thoughtlessly
three-pronged
three-tenths
three-year-old
through
throughout
thus
tightly
till
timely
to
together
told
too
took
top
topmost
tops
total
totalled
totally
towards
trivial
truthfully
twentieth
twenty
twenty-eight
twenty-fifth
twenty-first
twenty-five
twenty-four
twenty-fourth
twenty-nine
twenty-one
twenty-second
twenty-seven
twenty-seventh
twenty-six
twenty-sixth
twenty-third
twenty-three
twenty-two
twice
two
two-and-a-half
two-drachma
two-horned
two-tenths
two-thirds

under
underneath
undoubtedly
unduly
unjustly
unless
unlike
until
unto
up
upon
upper
upward
upwards
urgently
us
use
used
uses
using
usual
usually
utterly

varied
various
vehemently
very
viciously
violently

warmly
was
wasn't
we
we'll
went
were

we're
weren't
we've
what
what's
whatever
when
whenever
where
wherever
whether
which
while
who
whoever
whom
whose
why
widely
will
with
within
without
won't
would
wouldn't

yes
yet
you
you'll
your
you're
yours
yourself
yourselves
you've

zealously

Spelling Differences Between the North American and Anglicised Editions

North American	*Anglicised*
afterward	afterwards
aging	ageing
algumwood	algum-wood
almugwood	almug-wood
anymore	any more
armor-bearer	armour-bearer
armor-bearers	armour-bearers
armor	armour
armory	armoury
authorization	authorisation
authorized	authorised
ax	axe
axhead	axe-head
backward	backwards
baptize	baptise
baptizing	baptising
battering rams	battering-rams
battle bow	battle-bow
behavior	behaviour
birth pains	birth-pains
blood relative	blood-relative
blood relatives	blood-relatives
bowshot	bow-shot
brokenhearted	broken-hearted
burned-out	burnt-out
caldron	cauldron
caldrons	cauldrons
canceled	cancelled
canceling	cancelling
center	centre
centers	centres
channeled	channelled
chiseled	chiselled
chiseling	chiselling
clamor	clamour
colored	coloured
colorful	colourful
colors	colours
commander in chief	commander-in-chief
coneys	conies
counseled	counselled
counselor	counsellor

Spelling Differences Between the North American and Anglicised Editions (*continued*)

counselors	counsellors
criticized	criticised
Cuza	Chuza
dark-colored	dark-coloured
defense	defence
defenses	defences
dishonor	dishonour
dishonored	dishonoured
dishonors	dishonours
distill	distil
doorframe	door-frame
doorframes	door-frames
doorkeeper	door-keeper
doorpost	door-post
dragnet	drag-net
dwelling place	dwelling-place
dwelling places	dwelling-places
earnngs	ear-rings
inquire	enquire
inquired	enquired
inquires	enquires
inquiring	enquiring
inquiry	enquiry
enroll	enrol
enrollment	enrolment
equaled	equalled
ever flowing	ever-flowing
eyewitnesses	eye-witnesses
facedown	face down
fainthearted	faint-hearted
faultfinders	fault-finders
favor	favour
favorable	favourable
favorably	favourably
favored	favoured
favorite	favourite
favoritism	favouritism
favors	favours
fellow citizens	fellow-citizens
fellow elder	fellow-elder
fellowman	fellow-man
fellow men	fellow-men
fellow prisoner	fellow-prisoner
fellow prisoners	fellow-prisoners
fellow servant	fellow-servant
fellow servants	fellow-servants
fellow soldier	fellow-soldier
fellow worker	fellow-worker
fellow workers	fellow-workers
fertilize	fertilise
fervor	fervour
fig tree	fig-tree
fig trees	fig-trees

Spelling Differences Between the North American and Anglicised Editions (*continued*)

fishhooks	fish-hooks
flavor	flavour
forever	for ever
forevermore	for evermore
fulfill	fulfil
fulfillment	fulfilment
fulfills	fulfils
fullness	fulness
good-by	good-bye
grape pickers	grape-pickers
gray	grey
gray-haired	grey-haired
half dead	half-dead
half tribe	half-tribe
handmill	hand mill
harbor	harbour
harbored	harboured
harbors	harbours
Hazazon Tamar	Hazezon Tamar
hardhearted	hard-hearted
headdresses	head-dresses
heavenward	heavenwards
hiding place	hiding-place
hiding places	hiding-places
hometown	home town
honor	honour
honorable	honourable
honorably	honourably
honored	honoured
honoring	honouring
honors	honours
jawbone	jaw-bone
Jehoash	Joash
jewelry	jewellery
kindhearted	kind-hearted
labor	labour
labored	laboured
laborer	labourer
laborer's	labourer's
laborers	labourers
laboring	labouring
labors	labours
laughing-stock	laughing-stock
lawbreaker	law-breaker
lawbreakers	law-breakers
legalizing	legalising
leveled	levelled
license	licence
lifetime	life-time
luster	lustre
marketplace	market-place
marketplaces	market-places
marshaled	marshalled

Spelling Differences Between the North American and Anglicised Editions (*continued*)

marveled	marvelled
marveling	marvelling
marvelous	marvellous
Micmash	Michmash
midair	mid-air
misdemeanor	misdemeanour
mobilized	mobilised
molded	moulded
molding	moulding
molds	moulds
moldy	mouldy
moneylender	money-lender
multicolored	multicoloured
mustache	moustache
naive	naïve
nearby	near by
nearsighted	near-sighted
neighbor	neighbour
neighbor's	neighbour's
neighboring	neighbouring
neighbors	neighbours
neighbors'	neighbours
newly built	newly-built
nighttime	night-time
no one	no-one
no one's	no-one's
northeaster	north-easter
northwest	north-west
odor	odour
offense	offence
offenses	offences
openhanded	open-handed
overrighteous	over-righteous
paneled	panelled
paneling	panelling
paralyzed	paralysed
parceled	parcelled
pastureland	pasture-land
pasturelands	pasture-lands
plow	plough
plowed	ploughed
plowing	ploughing
plowman	ploughman
plowmen	ploughmen
plows	ploughs
plowshares	ploughshares
plumb line	plumb-line
practice	practise
practiced	practised
practices	practises
preeminent	pre-eminent
pretense	pretence
quarreled	quarrelled

Spelling Differences Between the North American and Anglicised Editions *(continued)*

quarreling	quarrelling
realize	realise
realized	realised
realizing	realising
recognize	recognise
recognized	recognised
recognizes	recognises
recognizing	recognising
reentered	re-entered
reestablished	re-established
resting place	resting-place
reveled	revelled
revelers	revellers
reveling	revelling
riverbed	river bed
rumor	rumour
rumors	rumours
sandaled	sandalled
sandbar	sand-bar
sandbars	sand-bars
Savior	Saviours
sawed	sawn
scepter	sceptre
scepters	sceptres
sheepshearers	sheep-shearers
shield bearer	shield-bearer
shrine prostitute	shrine-prostitute
shrine prostitutes	shrine-prostitutes
shriveled	shrivelled
sickbed	sick-bed
sidewalls	side-walls
signaled	signalled
signaling	signalling
simplehearted	simple-hearted
skillful	skilful
skillfillly	skilfully
smolder	smoulder
smoldering	smouldering
smolders	smoulders
somber	sombre
southeast	south-east
southwest	south-west
splendor	splendour
story	storey
stouthearted	stout-hearted
stumbling block	stumbling-block
stumbling blocks	stumbling-blocks
stumbling stone	stumbling-stone
subdivision	sub-division
subdivisions	sub-divisions
sulfur	sulphur
symoblizes	symbolises
sympathize	sympathise

Spelling Differences Between the North American and Anglicised Editions (*continued*)

sympathized	sympathised
thank offering	thank-offering
thank offerings	thank-offerings
theater	theatre
threshing cart	threshing-cart
threshing floor	threshing-floor
threshing floors	threshing-floors
threshing sledge	threshing-sledge
threshing sledges	threshing-sledges
tightfisted	tight-fisted
totaled	totalled
toward	towards
traveled	travelled
traveler	traveller
travelers	travellers
traveling	travelling
treasure house	treasure-house
tumbleweed	tumble-weed
tumors	tumours
unauthorized	unauthorised
unequaled	unequalled
unfavorable	unfavourable
unplowed	unploughed
unsandaled	unsandalled
untraveled	untravelled
upside down	upside-down
upward	upwards
vapor	vapour
vigor	vigour
water carrier	water-carrier
water carriers	water-carriers
willful	wilfill
willfully	wilfully
windblown	wind-blown
wingspan	wing-span
woolen	woollen
worshiped	worshipped
worshiper	worshipper
worshipers	worshippers
worshiping	worshipping
worthwhile	worth while
yokefellow	yoke-fellow

Word Differences Between the North American and Anglicised Editions

North American	*Anglicised*	*Verse Reference*
afire	on fire	Dt 32:22
aide	assistant	Ex 24:13
aide	assistant	Ex 33:11
aide	assistant	Nu 11:28
aide	assistant	Jos 1:1
aide	assistant	Ne 6:5
ankles do not turn	ankles do not turn over	2Sa 22:37
ankles do not turn	ankles do not turn over	Ps 18:36
anyone	a man	Jn 7:51
around	round	Ge 37:7
around	round	Lev 25:31
around	round	Eph 6:14
at flood stage	in flood	Jos 3:15
at flood stage	in flood	Jos 4:18
back and forth	to and fro	Est 2:11
back and forth	to and fro	Job 1:7
back and forth	to and fro	Job 2:2
back and forth	to and fro	Eze 37:2
basins	dishes	1Ki 7:50
be	become	1Ki 1:17
burned-out	burnt-out	Jer 51:25
butchered	slaughtered	1Sa 28:24
butchered	slaughtered	Mt 22:4
crafted	handcrafted	Nu 31:51
Cuza	Chuza	Lk 8:3
deeded	legally made over	Ge 23:17
deeded	legally made over	Ge 23:20
delivered	gave	1Sa 24:10
delivered	gave	1Sa 24:18
delivered	gave	1Sa 26:23
delivered	given	1Sa 26:8
encamp	camp	Ex 14:2 [twice]
entryway	entrance	2Ki 16:18
entryway	entrance	Mk 14:68
farther	further	Lk 24:28
fieldstones	stones from the field	Dt 27:6
firepot	brazier	Ge 15:17
firepot	brazier	Jer 36:22
firepot	brazier	Jer 36:23
firepot	brazier	Zec 12:6
fishnets	fishing nets	Eze 26:5

Word Differences Between the North American and Anglicised Editions (*continued*)

fishnets	fishing nets	Eze 26:14
get	call	Nu 20:25
get away	go	1Sa 20:29
gets	receives	2Sa 15:4
grain	corn	Ge 37:7
grain	corn	Jdg 15:5 [twice]
grain	corn	Ps 65:9
grain	corn	Ps 65:13
grain	corn	Ps 72:16
grain	corn	Isa 17:5
grain	corn	Isa 36:17
grain	corn	Jer 9:22
grain	corn	Jer 50:11
grain	corn	Eze 36:29
grain	corn	Hos 14:7
grain	corn	Mk 4:28
grainfield	cornfield	Dt 23:25
grainfields	cornfields	Mt 12:1
grainfields	cornfields	Mk 2:23
grainfields	cornfields	Lk 6:1
had	made	Ge 24:11
had	made	Lev 23:43
had	made	Nu 5:18
had	made	Nu 11:24
had	made	Nu 27:22
had	made	1Sa 16:8
had	made	1Sa 16:9
had	made	1Sa 16:10
had	made	1Sa 20:17
had	made	2Ch 34:32
had	made	2Ch 34:33
handed him over	turned him over	Mk 15:1
handed over	turned over	Lk 18:32
have	let	Ex 10:11
have	make	Ge 45:1
have	make	Ex 19:10
have	make	Ex 28:5
have	make	Nu 5:16
have	make	Nu 5:24
have	make	Nu 5:26
have	make	Nu 5:30
have	make	Nu 8:7
have	make	Nu 8:8
have	make	Nu 8:13
have	make	Nu 9:2
have	make	Nu 11:16
have	make	Nu 27:19
have	make	Dt 21:12
have	make	Dt 31:19
have	make	Jos 6:4
have	make	Jos 6:5
have	make	Jos 6:6

Word Differences Between the North American and Anglicised Editions (*continued*)

have	make	2Ki 7:13
have	make	2Ki 17:27
have	make	2Ki 22:4
have	make	2Ki 22:5
have	make	2Ki 22:6
have	make	Ne 7:3
have	make	Lk 9:14
have	make	Jn 6:10
have	make	2Ki 5:8
Hazazon Tamar	Hazezon Tamar	2Ch 20:2
headed	was in the ear	Ex 9:31
heads	ears	Mt 13:26
heads of grain	ears of corn	Ge 41:5 [three times]
heads of grain	ears of corn	Ge 41:6 [twice]
heads of grain	ears of corn	Ge 41:7
heads of grain	ears of corn	Ge 41:22
heads of grain	ears of corn	Ge 41:24
heads of grain	ears of corn	Ge 41:26
heads of grain	ears of corn	Ge 41:27
heads of grain	ears of com	Job 24:24
heads of grain	ears of corn	Isa 17:5
heads of grain	ears of corn	Mt 12:1
heads of grain	ears of corn	Mk 2:23
heads of grain	ears of corn	Lk 6:1
I'm	I am	2Sa 18:14
in back	behind	Rev 4:6
just saw	have just seen	2Sa 18:10
kernel	grain	Jn 12:24
kernel in the head	grain in the ear	Mk 4:28
kernels	ears	Dt 23:25
kernels	grain	Lk 6:1
kernels	grains	Dt 32:14
light to the other side	light to the other	Ex 14:20
limber	supple	Ge 49:24
lumber	timber	2Ch 2:9
made . . . post bond	put . . .on bail	Ac 17:9
melt with fear	sink	Jos 14:8
melted	sank	Jos 2:11
mistreat	ill-treat	Ge 31:50
mistreat	ill-treat	Ex 22:21
mistreat	ill-treat	Lev 19:33
mistreat	ill-treat	1Sa 25:7
mistreat	ill-treat	1Sa 25:15
mistreat	ill-treat	Jer 38:19
mistreat	ill-treat	Eze 22:29
mistreat	ill-treat	Lk 6:28
mistreat	ill-treat	Ac 14:5
mistreated	ill-treated	Eze 22:7
mistreated	ill-treated	Ge 15:13
mistreated	ill-treated	Ge 16:6
mistreated	ill-treated	Nu 20:15

mistreated	ill-treated	Dt 26:6
mistreated	ill-treated	Jer 13:22
mistreated	ill-treated	Mt 22:6
mistreated	ill-treated	Ac 7:6
mistreated	ill-treated	Ac 7:24
mistreated	ill-treated	Heb 11:25
mistreated	ill-treated	Heb 11:37
mistreated	ill-treated	Heb 13:3
mistreating	ill-treating	Ac 7:27
nearsighted	short-sighted	2Pe 1:9
no place	nowhere	Mt 8:20
no place	nowhere	Lk 9:58
obligates	binds	Nu 30:10
obligate	bind	Nu 30:2
obligated	bound	Nu 30:4
obligated	bound	Nu 30:5
obligated	bound	Nu 30:7
obligated	bound	Nu 30:11
obligated	bound	Ro 1:14
obligated	required	Gal 5:3
obligates	binds	Nu 30:3
obligates	binds	Nu 30:6
obligates	binds	Nu 30:8 [twice]
on	onto	2Ki 4:35
on hand	to hand	1Sa 21:3
on hand	to hand	1Sa 21:4
pile	heap	Lk 14:35
pretended to be insane	feigned insanity	1Sa 21:13
quieted	quietened	Ps 131:2
quieted	quietened	Ac 19:35
raised	caused	Ac 9:21
rawboned	scrawny	Ge 49:14
rear	bring up	Hos 9:12
reared	brought up	Isa 51:18
rearing them	bringing them up	2Ki 10:6
rooster	cock	Pr 30:31
rooster	cock	Mt 26:34
rooster	cock	Mt 26:74
rooster	cock	Mt 26:75
rooster	cock	Mk 13:35
rooster	cock	Mk 14:30
rooster	cock	Mk 14:72
rooster	cock	Lk 22:34
rooster	cock	Lk 22:60
rooster	cock	Lk 22:61
rooster	cock	Jn 13:38
rooster	cock	Jn 18:27
sawed	sawn	Heb 11:37
shoves	pushes	Nu 35:20
shoves	pushes	Nu 35:22
spend	expend	Dt 32:23
spit	spat	Nu 12:14

Word Differences Between the North American and Anglicised Editions (*continued*)

spit	spat	Mt 26:67
spit	spat	Mt 27:30
spit	spat	Mk 7:33
spit	spat	Mk 15:19
spit	spat	Jn 9:6
sprout	young plant	Isa 61:11
standing grain	standing corn	Ex 22:6
standing grain	standing corn	Dt 16:9
standing grain	standing corn	Dt 23 :25
standing grain	standing corn	Jdg 15:5 [twice]
standing grain	standing corn	Isa 17:5
stench	offence	1Sa 13:4
stench	offence	2Sa 10:6
stench	offence	2Sa 16:21
stench	offence	1Ch 19:6
take care of	tidy up	Ac 9:34
tar	bitumen	Ge 11:3
three hundred and sixty	360	2Sa 2:31
through	until	Ex 12:15
took	brought	Lk 10:34
turn	give	Nu 27:7
turn	give	Nu 27:8
turn	hand	Ps 27:12
turned	handed	Jer 39:14
twenty-seven hundred	two thousand seven hundred	Ch 26:32
twenty-six hundred	two thousand six hundred	2Ch 35:8
violated	raped	Ge 34:2
warden	warder	Ge 39:21
warden	warder	Ge 39:22
warden	warder	Ge 39:23
welts	bruises	Isa 1:6
will	shall	Nu 17:12